AUBREYs

in association with

InterContinental Hotels Group

ALIO OPTIMUS

THE OFFICIAL REGISTER OF LONDON MARATHON RUNNERS 2001–2010

LONDON MARATHON

Foreword by David Bedford
Introductions by John Bryant

Aubrey Books

Published in the UK in 2010 by
Aubrey Books Ltd, Omnibus Business Centre,
39–41 North Road, London N7 9DP
email: info@aubreybooks.com
www.aubreybooks.com

ISBN: 978-0-9566715-0-9

Typeset in New Baskerville by Marie Doherty

Printed in the UK by
CPI William Clowes Beccles NR34 7TL

STAY IMPRESSED.

Prepare for a few double takes. Enter our stylish lobbies and you'll experience an even warmer welcome from our friendly teams. And in every refreshed room, a choice of soft and firm pillows and a more invigorating shower experience. So when you stay, you can stay totally impressed.

Holiday Inn are the proud sponsors of the Virgin London Marathon helping competitors get their day off to a great start and a medal winning finish.

Our warmest welcome ever.

STAY YOU.™

I'm running for Ruby – who are **you** running for?

Run for Shelter and help people, like Ruby and her family, who are living in bad housing or facing homelessness.

Got your own place? Join our team and you will get a fantastic support package:

- free adidas/Shelter running vest
- training plan, ongoing advice and a team training session
- post-race reception with showers, food and a massage!

Call our events team **NOW** on **0844 515 1190**, email **marathon@shelter.org.uk** or visit **shelter.org.uk/marathon**

Until there's a home for everyone

Supported by:

adidas

Thanks to:

FRSB
FundRaising
Standards Board

Shelter

Registered charity in England and Wales (263710) and in Scotland (SC002327)
Photo: Anita Steindstad. Illustration: The Boy Fitz Hammond RH2754

Contents

Sponsor's Message

Successful training and ultimately great performance, particularly for endurance sport, is a balance between mental attitude, physical graft and recovery. It has been said that winning athletes are not those that train the hardest, but those who recover the most effectively.

Scientific studies have backed this up and have shown that a poor night's sleep can lead to increased levels of cortisol (a stress hormone), decreased activity of human growth hormone (which is active during tissue repair), and a decreased glucose metabolism.

Whether you are a first-timer or a veteran, running the London Marathon is not the same as any other sporting event – months of dedication are required to build up strength and stamina. Over the last 5 years, IHG (InterContinental Hotels Group) have been delighted to help runners on their big day by providing a great night's sleep.

Pasta meals, early breakfasts with plenty of bananas, and a coach transfer to the start of the race have kept the race-day stress to a minimum, preparing runners for the day ahead. With physiotherapists and masseurs awaiting guests' return, our hotels have played their part in making a truly memorable day for runners.

IHG, through our London Holiday Inn, Crowne Plaza and InterContinental Hotels, are delighted to continue as Official Hotel partner of the Virgin London Marathon, and help runners get a great night's sleep.

Adrian White, IHG Partnership Director

Foreword

It doesn't matter whether you are Sammy Wanjiru gliding around the London Marathon in a little over two hours, or whether you are dressed as a chicken and desperately focusing on your watch as you try to break five hours. There's something every marathon runner will remember when they cross the line: their finishing time. Ask anyone who's been there what their time was and they will tell you to the second. It's something to be very proud of.

This book gives you the opportunity to fix that memory forever, to remember how it felt when you crossed the line and believed that you could take on the world.

As London Marathon Race Director for many years, I am very proud of my team who lay on this great event, and the many hundreds of thousands – champions and also-rans alike – who have tackled the distance over the decades.

April 2010 saw the first London Marathon sponsored by Virgin, with record finisher figures of 36,550 and it continues to be the largest annual fundraising event in the world with more than £50m raised in 2010 and more than £500m since the race started! A total of 783,185 runners have now completed the London Marathon since it began.

It wasn't always like that. I remember the first one, way back in 1981. It was not my finest hour athletically, and I realised how tough a marathon could be. It was a fine occasion, but many wondered how long this marathon craze could last. But thanks to the vision and determination of Chris Brasher and John Disley, plus the thousands of volunteers, the race took off. And it's now reckoned to be the greatest marathon race in the world.

One aspect makes the London experience so special: its approach to charity.

London was the first marathon to understand the benefits of integrating runners of all abilities. It's produced not just elite fields that can match anything seen at the Olympic Games, but a great carnival of colour and sound that delights the runners, the crowds and the millions who catch it on TV. Rival organizers come to London and are amazed by the atmosphere, the charity support teams, the costumes, the joy and the emotion generated by thousands who run for charitable causes.

Naturally, I am very proud of the London. But also of the thousands who've completed the 26 miles and 385 yards. Your name and your time have made the London Marathon what it is. So share this record with pride.

David Bedford, Race Director

The 2001 London Marathon

Twenty years on from the first London Marathon the 2001 race seemed a giant by comparison. When Joyce Smith finished as the women's winner in the infant London Marathon of 1981 she was rewarded with her modest medal, and a trophy – a watch – valued at less than £100. 'Had Joyce been running now,' said Dave Bedford, the race director in 2001, 'and been a British winner in a world record time, she would be receiving more than $500,000 – and a lot more applause.'

The London Marathon's first-year budget was £75,000, which wouldn't have gone far in putting men from Kenya, Morocco and Portugal – favourites for this race – on the start line. Morocco's Abdelkader El Mouaziz clinched his second success in three years winning the 2001 race in his fastest ever time of 2:07:11. Paul Tergat of Kenya, running his first Marathon, was second and defending champion Antonio Pinto from Portugal came third. The first Briton home was Mark Steinle in sixth place.

El Mouaziz, second in 2000, went one better while Tegla Loroupe provided early drama in the women's race. Loroupe, the world record holder, came to an abrupt halt during the second mile and seemed in two minds about whether she could continue. Dramatically, she stopped to stretch and to loosen her pelvis and for the best part of a minute it seemed her race was over. But once she got going again it seemed the longer she ran the more the injury eased up. She eventually finished eighth in 2:26:10.

At 24 miles, five runners were still together in the women's race – Svetlana Zakharova, Lidia Simon, Joyce Chepchumba, Nuta Olaru and track runner Derartu Tulu who to that point

had never once showed in the lead but who was running confidently and relaxed. Tulu at last made a positive surge after crossing Parliament Square and quickly established a lead over Zakharova.

Dramatically, two men leapt across the barrier within yards of the finishing tape, but swift action by Dave Bedford and others soon bundled them out of the way. Dodging them, Tulu came home to set a personal best. Zakharova improved her time by 3 minutes. Chepchumba raised her pace down the straight for her fifth sub-2:25:00 clocking in six races.

In the men's race, many were impressed by Paul Tergat's marathon debut. There are very few who can come in and win on their first outing, so to get as close as Tergat did to an on-form Abdelkader El Mouaziz and run 2:08:15 was a fantastic performance. The first significant move appeared to come as a large group approached Tower Bridge. Here the 1999 winner El Mouaziz sprinted up to the pacemakers. Tergat couldn't hold him, and the race from then was between El Mouaziz and the clock. Still looking strong, El Mouaziz celebrated down the final straight, crossed the tape in a personal best of 2:07:11, and kissed the ground beyond the finish line.

Mark Steinle delighted British fans with his sixth place in 2:10:46, though Britain's leading marathon runner, Jon Brown, was forced to pull out soon after half way. Brown had been struggling with a bronchial complaint in the build-up to the race, plus his training had been hampered by a hip injury. He came adrift and he eventually retired.

Tanni Grey-Thompson claimed a fifth women's title in the wheelchair marathon, despite the problem of a puncture which slowed her

progress. The eight-time Olympic gold medallist showed why she is one of the greatest British athletes of all time.

Frenchman Denis Lemeunier won the men's wheelchair marathon by 2 minutes from defending champion Kevin Papworth in 1:42:37. The two took the lead from the start and opened a gap of more than a minute on the chasers by the 10km mark. At half way the Frenchman, contesting his first London Marathon, led Papworth by more than 40 seconds and was almost 4 minutes ahead of Britons David Weir and Tushar Patel.

But for many other runners, it's the taking part that matters as they struggle to make it around the course. Instantly recognisable former world heavyweight champion Frank Bruno got tremendous support from his home London crowd. And Britain's greatest Olympian, the rower Sir Steve Redgrave, was the official starter and in his first marathon completed the course in less than five hours – not bad for a man who's 6 foot 6 inches and 16 stone.

Explanation of placing system

Each London Marathon year in this register is divided up into four categories: first, a summary of the **Elite Athletes**, containing names (last, first) and times (hours : minutes : seconds) of the top 50 male runners, top 50 female runners, top 3 male and top 2 female wheelchair entrants; then **Male Runners**, **Female Runners** and **Wheelchair Entrants**. These last three sections display the individual names and times of *every* entrant, including elite athletes, alphabetically and with their overall finishing position in that year's Marathon displayed in brackets alongside.

Some entrants have chosen to enhance past London Marathon entries with photos and recollections online at **www.aubreybooks.com**. Please visit the website to find out more about appearing in future editions.

ELITE ATHLETES

Top 50 male runners

El Mouaziz, Abdelkader	2:07:11
Tergat, Paul	2:08:15
Pinto, Antonio	2:09:36
Jifar, Tesfaye	2:09:45
Kosgei, Japhet	2:10:45
Steinle, Mark	2:10:46
Inubushi, Takayuki	2:11:42
Anton, Abel	2:11:57
Ramaala, Hendrick	2:12:02
Thys, Gert	2:12:11
Hudspith, Mark	2:13:12
Mereng, Joseph	2:13:26
El Hattab, Mohammed	2:14:26
Shemweta, Alfred	2:15:34
Wainana, Eric	2:15:43
Kirkwood, Craig	2:16:25
Pride, Simon	2:16:27
Makori, David	2:17:09
Burns, Billy	2:18:29
Holladay, Rob	2:19:26
Jones, Rodri	2:19:27
Royden, Barry	2:19:31
Francis, Nick	2:20:00
Alahyan, Mohamed	2:20:23
Dwyer, Julian	2:20:29
Coleman, Michael	2:21:47
Fisher, Ian	2:21:52
Mason, Richard	2:22:32
Zwicky, Christian	2:22:48
Mason, Duncan	2:23:08
Proudlove, Michael	2:23:17
Kagwe, John	2:23:28
Vensdasalam, Nathan	2:23:46
Fernandez Atienza, José Maria	2:23:48
Fitzsimmons, James	2:24:24
Butler, Kenneth	2:24:45

Raymer, Bruce	2:25:56
Utting, Oliver	2:26:51
Malone, Ian	2:27:23
Loader, Joe	2:27:37
Heap, John	2:27:41
Speake, William	2:27:51
Ellis, Ieuan	2:27:53
Mezgebu, Ayele	2:27:57
Masumpa, Makaya	2:28:09
Bilton, Darran	2:28:10
Maros, Elvin	2:28:18
Macdonald, Stewart	2:28:24
Duffy, Tony	2:28:52
Williams, Gareth	2:29:02

Top 50 female runners

Tulu, Derartu	2:23:57
Zakharova, Svetlana	2:24:03
Chepchumba, Joyce	2:24:12
Simon, Lidia	2:24:15
Alemu, Elfenesh	2:24:29
Olaru, Nuta	2:25:18
Ivanova, Alina	2:25:34
Loroupe, Tegla	2:26:10
Fernandez, Adriana	2:26:21
Biktagirova, Madina	2:27:14
Renders, Marleen	2:28:31
Hiroyama, Harumi	2:29:01
Vassilevskaja, Ledya	2:31:36
Bogacheva, Irina	2:32:28
Duffy, Theresa	2:35:27
MacDougall, Lynne	2:37:20
Hartigan, Bev	2:37:45
Cedillo, Sara	2:38:53
Jones, Tania	2:39:10
Adachi, Mika	2:41:35
Moon, Melissa	2:41:58

Robinson, Debra	2:42:19
Watson, Louise	2:43:49
Joseph, Restituta	2:43:52
Pincombe, Vicky	2:43:52
Pauzers, Clare	2:44:35
Pickvance, Ruth	2:46:14
Dixon, Sharon	2:46:32
Clark, Megan	2:47:24
Wood, Kerrie	2:49:12
Fletcher, Alison	2:49:18
Spink, Mandy	2:50:58
Oakley, Judy	2:51:29
Knights, Lisa	2:51:43
Massey, Sarah	2:52:06
Latto, Emma	2:52:18
Clark, Juiette	2:54:27
Kirtley, Anne	2:54:39
Wilson, Beverley	2:55:58
Dering, Jo	2:56:08
Morrall, Zelah	2:56:27
Angell, Margaret	2:56:58
Selby, Jane	2:56:59
Gray, Jenny	2:57:06
Parker, Barbara	2:58:17
Massey, Jaqueline	2:58:29
Perry, Victoria	2:59:00
Dennison, Andrea	2:59:15
Whiley, Lesley	2:59:31
Elmore, Lisa	2:59:38

Top 3 male and top 2 female wheelchair entrants

Lemeunier, Denis	1:42:37
Papworth, Kevin	1:44:54
Weir, David	1:50:55
Grey-Thompson, Tanni	2:13:55
Brennan, Deborah	2:36:50

MALE RUNNERS

Aaker, Thomas 2:57:51 (802)
Aaron, Peter 6:29:39 (29,402)
Aarons, Brett 4:41:19 (19,031)
Aass, Lars 4:22:18 (14,886)
Abbey, Jonathan 4:55:10 (21,772)
Abbey, Richard 4:44:24 (19,656)
Abbot, Brian 5:58:17 (28,337)
Abbott, Ben 4:29:40 (16,591)
Abbott, Christopher 3:06:04 (1,429)
Abbott, David 3:28:43 (3,939)
Abbott, David 4:37:05 (18,142)
Abbott, Gyles 3:46:57 (7,026)
Abbott, Ian 4:11:21 (12,472)
Abbott, Paul 3:53:42 (8,425)
Abbott, Philip 3:51:43 (8,011)
Abdellaoui, Nordine 2:53:05 (546)
Abderrakib, Aziz 5:44:36 (27,536)
Abe, Yasuo 4:47:06 (20,184)
Abel, Eamon 4:19:35 (14,276)
Abel, Lawrence 2:58:51 (919)
Abley, Bev 5:02:55 (22,994)
Abraham, Adetokunbo 5:33:56 (26,684)
Abraham, Philip 3:39:22 (5,641)
Abraham, William 5:36:44 (26,926)
Abrahams, Ian 3:20:24 (2,806)
Abram, Barry 3:09:31 (1,715)
Abram, Grahame 5:07:10 (23,645)
Abram, Ron 4:22:52 (15,024)
Abrams, Reuben 3:53:20 (8,344)
Abruzzo, Vito 3:14:45 (2,189)
Absolon, Christopher 3:43:05 (6,323)
Accleton, Robert 3:34:30 (4,838)
Achard, Michel 5:21:58 (25,580)
Acheson, Austin 3:45:18 (6,718)
Acheson, David 7:27:55 (30,123)
Acid, Rab 4:12:17 (12,687)
Acker, Edward 4:18:14 (13,926)
Ackers, Allan 5:05:55 (23,451)
Ackroyd, Andrew 3:13:26 (2,055)
A'Court, Andy 3:45:58 (6,851)
Adair, David 5:22:40 (25,665)
Adair, John 3:44:56 (6,670)
Adair, Philip 3:27:32 (3,714)
Adamiw, Greg 4:49:14 (20,569)
Adams, Andrew 4:04:02 (10,889)
Adams, Brian 6:15:49 (29,054)
Adams, Christopher 3:42:40 (6,247)
Adams, Christopher 4:13:21 (12,889)
Adams, Christopher 5:19:20 (25,295)
Adams, David 5:38:02 (27,023)
Adams, Douglas 3:54:05 (8,490)
Adams, Gary 7:00:36 (29,947)
Adams, Gerald 5:33:42 (26,664)
Adams, Gerard 4:12:28 (12,730)
Adams, Graham 3:50:36 (7,790)
Adams, Ian 3:27:45 (3,756)
Adams, James 3:01:27 (1,108)
Adams, Jamie 4:53:57 (21,499)
Adams, John 4:15:12 (13,308)
Adams, John 4:33:46 (17,492)
Adams, John 4:33:50 (17,507)
Adams, Kevin 3:58:32 (9,616)
Adams, Mark 4:43:45 (19,553)
Adams, Mark 5:28:21 (26,217)
Adams, Michael 5:02:58 (23,000)
Adams, Neill 4:13:39 (12,971)
Adams, Paul 3:34:00 (4,754)
Adams, Paul 4:37:36 (18,280)
Adams, Paul 4:44:31 (19,680)
Adams, Paul 4:53:38 (21,444)
Adams, Paul 5:49:10 (27,856)
Adams, Peter 4:25:02 (15,520)
Adams, Peter 4:41:16 (19,025)
Adams, Richard 3:29:16 (4,042)
Adams, Robert 3:35:11 (4,929)
Adams, Robert 3:39:01 (5,575)
Adams, Russell 4:59:58 (22,616)
Adams, Scott 5:14:33 (24,713)
Adams, Steve 3:11:11 (1,855)
Adams, Steven 4:26:38 (15,878)
Adams, Steven 4:35:05 (17,731)
Adams, Terence 4:00:40 (10,199)
Adams, William 3:50:46 (7,820)
Adams, William 3:51:55 (8,054)
Adams Murphy, John 6:04:32 (28,622)
Adamson, Robert 4:24:25 (15,374)
Adamson, Simon 4:07:41 (11,692)
Adby, Geoff 4:29:01 (16,425)
Adby, Terry 5:31:37 (26,498)
Adcock, Norman 4:15:37 (13,390)
Addis, Matthew 4:25:34 (15,632)
Addis, Patrick 3:50:07 (7,709)
Addis, Peter 4:22:33 (14,938)
Addis, William 3:43:32 (6,403)
Addison, Blair 4:51:56 (21,081)
Addison, Peter 5:27:33 (26,130)
Addy, Oliver 4:35:30 (17,813)
Adetoro, David 4:18:17 (13,946)
Adiseshiah, Mohan 5:25:28 (25,938)
Adkins, David 3:15:30 (2,271)
Adkins, John 3:18:56 (2,649)
Adkins, Paul 4:23:56 (15,279)
Adlam, Nicholas 4:48:44 (20,475)
Adlard, Simon 3:19:52 (2,749)
Adler, Michael 4:55:15 (21,798)
Adler, Philip 4:55:00 (21,732)
Admani, Suleman 6:40:51 (29,660)
Adolph, Adolf 4:01:27 (10,383)
Adoult, Alain 3:24:59 (3,375)
Adow, Andy 4:46:30 (20,054)
Adriaensen, Mil 3:22:40 (3,068)
Affleck, Michael 3:32:34 (4,545)
Afonso, Donny 3:20:18 (2,795)
Afshar, Dan 3:19:48 (2,739)
Aftab, Mudassar 7:29:08 (30,133)
Agar, Matthew 4:31:24 (16,961)
Agassis, Jean-Luc 4:08:27 (11,862)
Agbamu, Alexander 4:01:22 (10,365)
Ageros, James 4:48:02 (20,354)
Aguh, Melvin 4:54:49 (21,682)
Aguilar, Rafael 4:05:13 (11,156)
Ahearn, Rob 4:36:55 (18,110)
Ahearne, Brian 4:26:56 (15,945)
Ahearne, Gareth 3:20:36 (2,835)
Ahearne, Matthew 4:06:24 (11,433)
Ahearnee, Brian 5:08:57 (23,930)
Aherne, Brendan 5:51:19 (27,971)
Aherne, Daniel 4:33:45 (17,489)
Ahlberg, Staffan 3:31:49 (4,442)
Ahlfeldt, Derrick 5:04:57 (23,290)
Ahmed, Jabar 4:26:13 (15,780)
Ahmed, Suhail 5:38:46 (27,074)
Ahmet, Ahmet 4:41:09 (19,004)
Ahnien, Mario 3:32:50 (4,577)
Ahrend, Norbert 4:09:01 (11,990)
Aimable, Michael 5:29:52 (26,359)
Aindow, Colin 4:03:39 (10,812)
Ainley, Simon 3:58:56 (9,732)
Ainsley, David 5:24:14 (25,810)
Ainslie, Paul 3:15:48 (2,295)
Ainsworth, Clark 4:17:00 (13,668)
Ainsworth, Paul 5:01:27 (22,796)
Ainsworth, Robert 5:52:13 (28,030)
Aironi, Maurice 4:21:07 (14,613)
Airs, Mark 4:00:49 (10,245)
Aitchison, Craig 3:46:08 (6,885)
Aitchison, Mark 4:04:32 (11,001)
Aitelhadj, Ali 2:55:28 (649)
Aitken, Darryn 4:58:50 (22,432)
Aitken, Douglas 4:30:49 (16,809)
Aitken, Lawrence 3:09:43 (1,732)
Aitken, Lyle 4:39:25 (18,670)
Aitken, Peter 5:16:40 (25,008)
Aitken, William 5:08:31 (23,849)
Aizlewood, Stephen 6:30:12 (29,414)
Akahara, Hisashi 5:08:14 (23,806)
Akehurst, David 5:15:50 (24,914)
Akenhead, David 5:47:28 (27,724)
Akrigg, Stanley 3:22:14 (3,029)
Akuta, Yasuo 3:54:10 (8,504)
Alabaster, Rupert 6:14:10 (28,994)
Alabaster, Terence 3:32:09 (4,489)
Alahyan, Mohamed 2:20:23 (24)
Alaka, Aderemi 5:16:01 (24,928)
Albert, Jacques 3:43:26 (6,385)
Albertinelli, Roberto 5:20:50 (25,449)
Albiston, Nigel 4:56:15 (22,032)
Albone, Paul 4:21:09 (14,616)
Alcantara, Luis 2:56:13 (703)
Alcock, George 5:08:38 (23,876)
Alcock, Meirion 5:30:40 (26,424)
Alden, James 6:25:48 (29,301)
Alden, Kevin 6:18:27 (29,125)
Alden, Lawrence 4:45:37 (19,877)
Aldenhoven, Simon 4:24:53 (15,474)
Alderman, Nicholas 4:51:22 (20,963)
Alderson, Mark 4:31:57 (17,105)
Alderson, Steven 4:24:54 (15,479)
Al-Dhaen, Othman Yacoob 4:29:47 (16,619)
Aldis, Gary 4:15:17 (13,330)
Aldorino, Julio 3:38:43 (5,525)
Aldous, Colin 3:02:55 (1,208)
Aldred, Alexander 4:01:03 (10,292)
Aldred, Toby 4:00:42 (10,211)
Aldridge, Andrew 4:19:36 (14,279)
Aldridge, David 4:28:30 (16,314)
Aldridge, Gary 2:53:55 (577)
Aldridge, Keith 3:30:38 (4,267)
Aldridge, Lee 4:27:39 (16,105)
Aldridge, Nigel 3:23:40 (3,194)
Aldrighi, Mario 4:00:43 (10,217)
Alessandri, Salvatore 4:00:04 (10,067)
Alexander, Barry 4:27:46 (16,140)
Alexander, Colin 3:31:00 (4,327)
Alexander, David 3:30:54 (4,314)
Alexander, David 3:34:29 (4,835)
Alexander, Dean 3:09:32 (1,719)
Alexander, Dean 4:17:19 (13,738)
Alexander, Eddie 4:15:17 (13,330)
Alexander, James 4:03:35 (10,797)
Alexander, Joseph 4:53:17 (21,368)
Alexander, Nigel 3:37:29 (5,333)
Alexander, Paul 4:55:37 (21,928)
Alexander, Roderick 5:55:10 (28,161)
Alexander, Rohan 4:12:55 (12,815)
Alexander, Scott 4:06:33 (11,459)
Alexander, Simon 3:07:55 (1,584)
Alexander, Stanley 4:42:34 (19,284)
Al-Falaki, Layth 4:14:59 (13,260)
Alford, Mark 4:29:36 (16,577)
Algacs, Julian 8:48:13 (30,266)
Algierski, Jaroslaw 4:21:05 (14,608)
Alhaeuser, Jochen 2:58:14 (826)
Ali, Ajmol 5:21:42 (25,548)
Ali, Yeor 5:28:45 (26,260)
Alibocus, Del 5:13:08 (24,522)
Allain, Bruno 3:00:54 (1,076)
Allan, Charles 4:51:51 (21,062)
Allan, David 4:32:41 (17,243)
Allan, Douglas 4:10:47 (12,332)
Allan, Douglas 5:05:29 (23,381)
Allan, John 3:59:37 (9,953)
Allan, Mark 4:41:02 (18,981)
Allan, Nathan 4:29:14 (16,482)
Allan, Stephen 3:57:57 (9,478)
Allanson, Tobby 4:43:09 (19,416)
Allard, Charles 3:05:08 (1,360)
Allard, Paul 5:08:10 (23,792)
Allard, Ralph James 4:57:58 (22,288)
Allard, Rod 3:09:36 (1,726)
Allaway, David 2:51:09 (472)
Allband, Tony 6:17:09 (29,090)
Allcard, Neil 3:45:06 (6,699)
Allday, Graham 3:43:23 (6,374)
Allen, Alex 3:36:24 (5,140)
Allen, Andrew 3:28:14 (3,851)
Allen, Andrew 5:20:22 (25,390)
Allen, Anthony 4:07:41 (11,692)
Allen, Antony 3:09:19 (1,697)
Allen, Cedric 3:29:49 (4,138)
Allen, Charlie 4:11:20 (12,466)
Allen, Chris 3:45:20 (6,721)
Allen, Christian 4:13:55 (13,022)
Allen, Christopher 3:57:28 (9,318)
Allen, Christopher 4:33:58 (17,531)
Allen, Christopher 4:36:17 (17,973)
Allen, David 2:50:41 (453)
Allen, David 3:40:35 (5,883)

Allen, David	3:50:05 (7,704)
Allen, David	4:04:54 (11,096)
Allen, David	5:00:05 (22,632)
Allen, Doug	4:18:04 (13,880)
Allen, Gavin	3:26:09 (3,518)
Allen, Graham	2:59:53 (1,015)
Allen, Ian	4:22:45 (14,993)
Allen, James	5:09:31 (24,017)
Allen, Jeremy	4:02:38 (10,597)
Allen, Jeremy	4:09:52 (12,136)
Allen, Jim	3:38:24 (5,466)
Allen, John	4:39:27 (18,678)
Allen, John	4:44:30 (19,674)
Allen, John	4:50:26 (20,793)
Allen, Jon	5:36:47 (26,931)
Allen, Jonathan	4:22:52 (15,024)
Allen, Keiran	3:44:11 (6,522)
Allen, Lee	5:56:43 (28,254)
Allen, Luke	4:47:10 (20,194)
Allen, Marcus	3:57:33 (9,347)
Allen, Mark	3:49:58 (7,680)
Allen, Mark Ian	3:34:52 (4,886)
Allen, Michael	3:27:24 (3,689)
Allen, Michael	5:56:43 (28,254)
Allen, Mike	4:32:50 (17,282)
Allen, Nicholas	5:17:18 (25,084)
Allen, Nick	4:45:55 (19,921)
Allen, Paul	3:51:57 (8,064)
Allen, Paul	4:38:18 (18,452)
Allen, Peter	3:32:12 (4,493)
Allen, Raymond	3:32:37 (4,551)
Allen, Richard	4:20:27 (14,464)
Allen, Samuel	4:36:50 (18,091)
Allen, Sean	3:49:07 (7,484)
Allen, Steve	2:57:23 (777)
Allen, Stuart	3:49:15 (7,509)
Allen, Tim	4:07:10 (11,582)
Allen, Tony	5:35:39 (26,856)
Allen, Trace	3:23:48 (3,210)
Allender, Karl	4:37:38 (18,287)
Alley, Nicholas	5:32:22 (26,557)
Allison, Arthur	6:35:24 (29,531)
Allison, Chris	4:41:14 (19,018)
Allison, Mark	4:05:56 (11,333)
Allison, Patrick	5:38:41 (27,064)
Allison, Steven	4:33:40 (17,470)
Allport, Trevor	3:56:24 (9,025)
Allsop, Alan	4:48:45 (20,480)
Allsop, Andrew	3:53:31 (8,380)
Allsop, Timothy	3:09:41 (1,729)
Allsopp, Brian	6:23:19 (29,237)
Allsopp, Craig	3:04:59 (1,348)
Allsopp, Roger	5:19:54 (25,356)
Alon, Shlomo	4:30:59 (16,847)
Alonso Bienzobas, Javier	2:58:34 (864)
Alsharif, Mohsin	3:39:23 (5,645)
Alsop, Neil	4:05:55 (11,327)
Alston, David	3:43:25 (6,382)
Alston, David	4:55:17 (21,810)
Alty, Gareth	4:36:46 (18,072)
Alty, Richard	4:41:02 (18,981)
Alvarez Meijide, José Luis	3:52:01 (8,079)
Amadio, Giorgio	4:46:19 (20,010)
Amagat, Pierre	4:31:34 (16,996)
Amarandos, Peter	6:04:37 (28,626)
Amaya, Edwin	4:26:45 (15,898)
Ames, Chris	4:07:51 (11,730)
Amies, Peter	4:26:11 (15,774)
Amirahmadi, Ash	4:14:59 (13,260)
Ammon, Donald	3:56:41 (9,101)
Amor, Philip	3:01:55 (1,143)
Amos, Andrew	4:21:44 (14,741)
Amos, Christian	3:44:50 (6,647)
Amos, James	4:19:54 (14,341)
Amos, John	3:18:43 (2,621)
Amos, John	5:02:10 (22,904)
Amos, Nigel	4:13:58 (13,035)
Amos, Peter	3:14:51 (2,200)
Amos, Peter	5:26:50 (26,070)
Amps, Philip	5:34:47 (26,779)
Anahory, David	6:04:05 (28,597)
Anderegg, Guido	4:34:29 (17,623)
Andersen, Lee	4:05:28 (11,202)
Andersen, Niels	3:36:23 (5,134)
Anderson, Adrian	3:36:56 (5,232)
Anderson, Alan	4:13:39 (12,971)
Anderson, Brian	3:20:48 (2,865)
Anderson, David	3:22:56 (3,099)
Anderson, David	4:06:22 (11,422)
Anderson, Dean	5:54:28 (28,136)
Anderson, Fraser	4:32:30 (17,215)
Anderson, Frazer	5:38:00 (27,019)
Anderson, Garth	4:09:25 (12,066)
Anderson, Ian	2:39:15 (161)
Anderson, Ian	4:36:47 (18,078)
Anderson, James	3:34:58 (4,901)
Anderson, John	4:53:17 (21,368)
Anderson, Leroy	5:33:45 (26,667)
Anderson, Michael	3:22:10 (3,023)
Anderson, Michael	4:07:45 (11,717)
Anderson, Neil	3:24:10 (3,268)
Anderson, Neil	4:40:40 (18,915)
Anderson, Peter	4:12:56 (12,817)
Anderson, Richard	3:12:20 (1,944)
Anderson, Rob	5:26:26 (26,039)
Anderson, Sean	3:27:54 (3,789)
Anderson, Stephen	4:14:51 (13,222)
Anderson, Steve	2:59:15 (953)
Anderson, Stig	4:29:55 (16,665)
Anderson, Warwick	3:53:41 (8,422)
Andrea, Grant	3:33:00 (4,601)
Andrea, Massa	2:56:02 (686)
Andreis, Alex	4:26:52 (15,926)
Andreotti, Danielle	5:12:52 (24,477)
Andrew, Antony	5:59:37 (28,398)
Andrew, Edward	5:28:35 (26,236)
Andrew, Martin	4:30:45 (16,794)
Andrews, Barry	3:41:46 (6,085)
Andrews, Colin	5:20:17 (25,384)
Andrews, Edward	4:38:53 (18,585)
Andrews, Gregory	3:51:56 (8,060)
Andrews, Ian	2:42:17 (223)
Andrews, Jonathan	3:52:45 (8,220)
Andrews, Julian	4:08:51 (11,947)
Andrews, Lee	5:07:23 (23,676)
Andrews, Mark	3:23:51 (3,222)
Andrews, Mark	4:09:13 (12,026)
Andrews, Mark	5:09:43 (24,045)
Andrews, Matthew	6:37:59 (29,589)
Andrews, Michael	4:05:49 (11,305)
Andrews, Nick	4:21:38 (14,720)
Andrews, Paul	3:30:47 (4,291)
Andrews, Paul	3:42:52 (6,278)
Andrews, Philip	5:08:12 (23,797)
Andrews, Rob	5:06:18 (23,520)
Andrews, Robert	3:35:01 (4,905)
Andrews, Tom	4:16:53 (13,644)
Anello, Massimiliano	3:24:36 (3,328)
Ang, Richard	5:33:04 (26,616)
Angell, Barry	3:12:21 (1,947)
Angell, Christopher	4:19:56 (14,348)
Angell, Dean	3:09:22 (1,702)
Angell, Stephen	4:27:31 (16,063)
Anghileri, Giuseppe	3:08:13 (1,608)
Angier, John	4:18:23 (13,982)
Angus, David	4:54:33 (21,604)
Angus Felton, Ian	4:38:14 (18,437)
Ankers, Karl	3:45:39 (6,779)
Anley, Brian	5:39:16 (27,111)
Anley, Marc	3:06:27 (1,456)
Annals, Marc	3:46:42 (6,990)
Annear, Matthew	4:33:57 (17,526)
Ansell, Anthony	4:29:12 (16,472)
Ansell, Mark	3:46:08 (6,885)
Ansell, Richard	2:59:48 (1,007)
Anselm, Alain	4:31:00 (16,850)
Anson, Alexander	3:48:27 (7,349)
Anstee, Nicholas	4:17:42 (13,814)
Ansteeg, Lars	3:38:14 (5,437)
Antcliffe, Mark	3:53:18 (8,333)
Antell, Morgan	4:56:23 (22,048)
Anteyi, Alex	6:19:48 (29,153)
Anthony, Anthony	4:24:36 (15,422)
Anthony, Eric	5:45:37 (27,602)
Anthony, Paul	3:39:24 (5,652)
Antiga, Leopoldo	4:05:43 (11,273)
Anton, Abel	2:11:57 (8)
Anton, Carmelo	2:29:05 (63)
Antonelli, Nik	4:23:04 (15,080)
Antony, Mark	4:00:56 (10,270)
Anzalone, Leon	4:49:45 (20,661)
Aoki, Takery	5:43:52 (27,462)
Aperghis, Michael	3:29:49 (4,138)
Appell, Nick	4:32:42 (17,247)
Appleby, Glenn	5:16:27 (24,979)
Appleby, James	4:50:10 (20,747)
Appleby, Jason	4:01:25 (10,373)
Appleby, Keith	5:47:40 (27,736)
Appleby, Paul	3:05:35 (1,396)
Appleby, Paul	4:50:53 (20,859)
Appleby, Richard	4:37:12 (18,172)
Appleby, Stewart	4:37:33 (18,264)
Applegate, Christopher	2:53:28 (556)
Appleton, Brian	4:05:40 (11,256)
Appleton, Paul	4:04:22 (10,959)
Appleton, Russ	3:24:23 (3,295)
Appleyard, Andrew	5:39:18 (27,115)
Aquilina, Ricky	4:36:39 (18,053)
Aram, Jim	5:52:11 (28,029)
Araujo Afonso, Antonio	2:45:15 (297)
Arber, Ben	4:32:45 (17,263)
Arbery, Nigel	5:34:00 (26,692)
Archer, Andrew	3:22:21 (3,041)
Archer, Mark	3:40:15 (5,821)
Archer, Mark	5:25:21 (25,924)
Archer, Michael	3:16:40 (2,386)
Archer, Michael	4:53:22 (21,393)
Archer, Paul	3:18:20 (2,581)
Archer, Paul	3:52:47 (8,227)
Archer, Rob	3:53:47 (8,439)
Ardern, David	2:39:11 (160)
Ardern, Geoffrey	2:58:33 (862)
Ardin, James	2:50:18 (441)
Ardron, Philip	4:12:08 (12,653)
Aregger, Arthur	2:41:22 (199)
Arena, Leo	5:05:52 (23,444)
Arentsen, Henning	3:55:44 (8,854)
Argent, Alan	5:14:14 (24,663)
Argent, Dean	4:06:29 (11,445)
Argent, Simon	4:35:58 (17,925)
Argyle, Neil	3:43:43 (6,442)
Arif, Mohammed	5:33:00 (26,613)
Aristotelous, Panos	3:50:41 (7,802)
Ark, Bahadar	4:33:32 (17,428)
Arkell, Charles	5:13:54 (24,616)
Arli, Tayfun	5:09:23 (23,995)
Armer, Chris	3:00:06 (1,033)
Armer, Michael	3:39:18 (5,625)
Armistead, Charles	4:04:20 (10,953)
Armitage, Christopher	5:20:42 (25,431)
Armitage, Mark	3:59:16 (9,836)
Armitage, Robert	4:11:41 (12,546)
Armitage, Stuart	4:35:09 (17,739)
Armitage, Timothy	5:04:07 (23,148)
Armour, William	3:25:57 (3,498)
Armriding, Tony	5:36:17 (26,897)
Armsden, Richard	5:23:58 (25,790)
Armstron, John	5:28:59 (26,287)
Armstrong, Alan	3:39:40 (5,703)
Armstrong, Aleks	4:26:40 (15,885)
Armstrong, Antony	4:38:12 (18,427)
Armstrong, Colm	5:24:36 (25,845)
Armstrong, Darren	4:57:06 (22,155)
Armstrong, David	3:00:05 (1,032)
Armstrong, David	4:06:07 (11,364)
Armstrong, David	4:18:24 (13,990)
Armstrong, Don	6:41:37 (29,681)
Armstrong, Gerry	3:48:33 (7,371)
Armstrong, Graeme	3:38:48 (5,537)
Armstrong, Graham	2:57:43 (792)
Armstrong, James	5:09:37 (24,032)
Armstrong, John	5:14:31 (24,708)
Armstrong, Kevin	4:05:08 (11,145)
Armstrong, Michael	3:30:15 (4,205)
Armstrong, Nigel	4:23:39 (15,218)
Armstrong, Paul	4:53:43 (21,457)
Armstrong, Peter	3:27:38 (3,727)
Armstrong, Robert	5:45:35 (27,599)
Armstrong, Stephen	2:51:32 (491)

Armstrong, Stuart 4:43:32 (19,504)
Armstrong, Thomas 4:33:07 (17,329)
Armstrong, Thomas 8:15:13 (30,237)
Arnel, Chris 4:38:03 (18,382)
Arnel, Richard 4:38:03 (18,382)
Arnell, Robert 4:54:35 (21,616)
Arnold, Alan 4:06:29 (11,445)
Arnold, Colin 2:50:44 (455)
Arnold, Darren 5:22:49 (25,686)
Arnold, Dave 2:53:10 (550)
Arnold, James 2:34:38 (90)
Arnold, James 4:36:39 (18,053)
Arnold, John 3:59:54 (10,026)
Arnold, Jonathan 4:10:20 (12,237)
Arnold, Paul 4:39:40 (18,729)
Arnold, Stephen 4:19:01 (14,123)
Arnold, Stuart 4:23:33 (15,189)
Arnold, Stuart 4:25:56 (15,712)
Arnot, David 4:26:50 (15,916)
Arnott, Francis 4:05:00 (11,118)
Aronberg, Alex 3:35:43 (5,019)
Arragon, Michael 5:03:52 (23,111)
Arranz, José 4:31:26 (16,967)
Arrindell, Rolando 4:10:12 (12,208)
Arrizabalo Montoro, Xabier 3:18:13 (2,564)
Arruda, José 6:53:23 (29,854)
Arshar, Dan 3:11:14 (1,857)
Arthey, Christopher 2:58:38 (875)
Arthur, Bernard 3:34:48 (4,878)
Arthur, Nigel 3:57:52 (9,453)
Arthur, Peter 4:51:04 (20,904)
Arthur, Richard 4:39:44 (18,740)
Arthur, Robert 4:29:08 (16,458)
Arthur, Steve 6:50:09 (29,806)
Asbury, Andrew 4:33:00 (17,309)
Ash, James 5:10:11 (24,100)
Ash, Kevin 3:19:13 (2,676)
Ash, Nicholas 5:12:58 (24,493)
Ash, Paul 5:17:34 (25,113)
Ashby, Gerald 3:52:23 (8,148)
Ashby, Mike 3:31:22 (4,382)
Ashby, Nick 3:51:59 (8,068)
Ashby, Quentin 3:31:17 (4,370)
Ashcroft, Derek 2:59:05 (941)
Ashcroft, Neil 3:00:57 (1,080)
Ashdown, David 4:28:15 (16,249)
Asher, Dainne 5:35:34 (26,852)
Ashford, Richard 3:48:57 (7,451)
Ashforth, Alan 3:42:10 (6,155)
Ashida, Kazuyoshi 5:14:28 (24,699)
Ashill, Nick 4:33:38 (17,464)
Ashley, Brian 5:38:39 (27,059)
Ashley, John 3:28:03 (3,808)
Ashley, Philip 3:55:50 (8,879)
Ashman, Andrew 4:32:26 (17,201)
Ashman, Roderick 4:44:10 (19,613)
Ashman-Lee, Tom 4:45:19 (19,826)
Ashmore, Stephen 4:43:23 (19,462)
Ashton, Craig 4:24:33 (15,408)
Ashton, John 3:17:00 (2,429)
Ashton, Paul 5:55:51 (28,206)
Ashton, Timothy 4:07:06 (11,571)
Ashwell, Mark 3:53:59 (8,475)
Ashwood, Keith 3:39:48 (5,739)
Ashworth, Chris 3:09:51 (1,737)
Ashworth, Howard 4:22:39 (14,968)
Ashworth, Jeremy 3:39:01 (5,575)
Ashworth, Michael 5:30:58 (26,449)
Ashworth, Mike 4:09:41 (12,105)
Ashworth, Paul 3:52:36 (8,190)
Ashworth, Stephen 4:58:36 (22,394)
Asiedu, Eric 4:25:10 (15,550)
Asigno, Daniel 6:18:34 (29,129)
Asileppi, Virgilio 5:44:13 (27,493)
Askew, Duncan 3:36:39 (5,181)
Askew, Mark 3:13:36 (2,067)
Askew, Phil 4:21:45 (14,746)
Askew, Robert 3:13:47 (2,087)
Askew, Simeon 3:31:19 (4,373)
Askland, Tor Jan 3:50:51 (7,837)
Aslett, Noel 4:52:54 (21,292)
Asmerom, Bram 3:56:18 (8,994)
Asnong, Kris 5:25:41 (25,956)
Aspden, Douglas 3:15:13 (2,245)
Aspess, Brad 4:51:34 (20,999)
Aspin, David 3:39:00 (5,573)
Aspin, John 4:04:11 (10,926)
Asplen, David 4:11:44 (12,556)
Astbury, Nick 4:26:32 (15,851)
Astbury, Peter 4:43:35 (19,516)
Astell, Nigel 4:04:09 (10,910)
Astell, Trevor 4:00:22 (10,123)
Astins, David 3:33:36 (4,695)
Astle, Stephen 4:31:13 (16,908)
Astley, Shaun 5:13:14 (24,543)
Aston, Andrew 3:06:20 (1,444)
Aston, Andrew 4:19:53 (14,333)
Aston, Anthony 5:23:44 (25,763)
Aston, David 4:29:36 (16,577)
Aston, Jeffrey 3:11:43 (1,888)
Astrow, Kjell 4:46:35 (20,074)
Atchinson, Robert 4:47:56 (20,333)
Athawes, Jon 4:10:14 (12,216)
Atherton, Miles 4:05:50 (11,311)
Atherton, Paul 4:20:17 (14,427)
Athorne, Richard 5:12:54 (24,483)
Atkins, Darren 4:01:23 (10,371)
Atkins, Ian 4:54:27 (21,578)
Atkins, Ted 4:01:09 (10,311)
Atkins, Terry 3:51:45 (8,015)
Atkinson, Andrew 4:06:17 (11,404)
Atkinson, Christopher 4:52:20 (21,169)
Atkinson, David 3:05:17 (1,371)
Atkinson, Francis 3:23:33 (3,181)
Atkinson, Frederick 4:34:46 (17,669)
Atkinson, Gary 3:19:45 (2,734)
Atkinson, Jason 4:11:39 (12,535)
Atkinson, Michael 4:04:55 (11,100)
Atkinson, Michael 5:12:07 (24,365)
Atkinson, Nick 4:11:13 (12,448)
Atkinson, Paul 5:56:53 (28,265)
Atkinson, Peter 3:35:26 (4,977)
Atkinson, Stuart 3:56:48 (9,133)
Atkinson, Terry 4:11:35 (12,521)
Atkinson, Timothy 4:50:44 (20,830)
Atkiss, Richard 4:53:19 (21,378)
Atlan, Gerard 3:59:01 (9,761)
Atley, Toby 4:44:41 (19,712)
Atraghji, David 4:27:05 (15,994)
Attewell, Martin 5:16:30 (24,989)
Attfield, Brian 4:29:47 (16,619)
Attle, David 4:41:30 (19,061)
Atton, Craig 4:49:06 (20,544)
Attree, Kevin 4:55:17 (21,810)
Attwell, Charles 4:47:37 (20,284)
Attwood, Anthony 4:22:41 (14,978)
Attwood, Mark 5:03:00 (23,004)
Attwood, Paul 4:31:23 (16,954)
Attwood, Simon 4:28:32 (16,321)
Attwood, Stephen 3:30:51 (4,302)
Atwell, Royston 4:44:37 (19,698)
Atwell, Victor 7:19:21 (30,075)
Auberix, Remi 4:18:54 (14,098)
Aubert, Denis 3:53:12 (8,309)
Aubrey, Kevin 3:48:51 (7,431)
Aubrey-Fletcher, Thomas 4:20:52 (14,564)
Auchettl, Benjamin 4:30:53 (16,823)
Auci, Mauro 3:15:04 (2,230)
Audenshaw, Anthony 3:33:02 (4,608)
Audifferen, John 4:18:00 (13,870)
Audretsch, Werner 4:46:06 (19,960)
Audsley, Anthony 3:34:45 (4,869)
Aughterlony, Mark 5:27:39 (26,143)
Aughton, Tim 4:32:36 (17,227)
Auld, Gary 4:29:41 (16,594)
Aulsford, Liz 5:14:21 (24,679)
Austin, Alan 3:04:31 (1,314)
Austin, Barry 5:02:25 (22,929)
Austin, Brian 3:34:34 (4,843)
Austin, Christopher 3:23:17 (3,146)
Austin, Clive 5:12:34 (24,436)
Austin, David 3:41:04 (5,970)
Austin, David 5:58:25 (28,344)
Austin, John 2:52:20 (526)
Austin, Leslie 4:01:26 (10,379)
Austin, Patrick 4:17:35 (13,789)
Austin, Peter 3:49:33 (7,596)
Austin, Richard 4:19:04 (14,136)
Austin, Robert 4:30:40 (16,780)
Austin, Shaun 4:46:51 (20,132)
Austin, Tommy 5:24:39 (25,849)
Avery, Joe 5:55:35 (28,197)
Avery, Marc 3:53:22 (8,349)
Avery, Philip 4:32:36 (17,227)
Aves, Clayton 3:16:40 (2,386)
Aveta, Domenico 3:11:39 (1,879)
Aviles, Angelo 5:23:20 (25,726)
Avis, Charles 4:29:29 (16,544)
Avis, Craig 4:35:52 (17,899)
Avis, Michael 5:29:06 (26,295)
Avrahampour, Eli 6:51:57 (29,832)
Awbery, Nicholas 4:55:37 (21,928)
Axe, Alan 3:00:52 (1,074)
Axe, Edward 4:51:48 (21,056)
Axelsen, Andrew 5:29:02 (26,291)
Axelson, Richard 4:44:58 (19,770)
Axford, Colin 4:14:02 (13,046)
Axon, Michael 4:58:53 (22,438)
Axsel, Frederich 4:39:39 (18,727)
Axten, Bruce 3:39:20 (5,635)
Ayari, Mehdi 3:56:15 (8,980)
Aycliffe, Dave 4:53:20 (21,384)
Ayers, David 6:15:49 (29,054)
Ayers, Duncan 4:49:50 (20,682)
Ayers, Robert 6:49:17 (29,792)
Ayles, Duncan 3:56:00 (8,919)
Aylett, Graham 5:08:04 (23,778)
Aylett, John 4:46:58 (20,160)
Ayling, Dean 4:05:54 (11,320)
Aylmer, Kerry 4:37:31 (18,252)
Aylott, Jason 3:46:11 (6,895)
Aylott, Wayne 3:51:31 (7,972)
Aylward, Colin 4:36:02 (17,936)
Aylward, Robin 3:59:58 (10,047)
Aynge, Gareth 4:49:59 (20,715)
Ayoub, Jack 4:39:57 (18,777)
Ayre, Gareth 4:07:57 (11,750)
Ayre, Gareth 4:28:54 (16,397)
Ayres, Arthur 4:09:02 (11,995)
Ayres, John 3:15:45 (2,293)
Ayres, Lee 4:50:45 (20,835)
Ayres, Richard 4:31:58 (17,109)
Ayres, Robin 2:54:01 (580)
Ayson, Richard 3:35:38 (5,009)
Aziz, Damian 4:06:48 (11,502)
Azouri, Jamil 5:21:20 (25,510)
Babaahmady, Esmail 3:33:50 (4,732)
Babalola, Kolawole 3:44:57 (6,678)
Babbit, Harold 4:27:33 (16,075)
Babcock, Nobby 4:42:01 (19,163)
Babicki, Joseph 3:46:14 (6,902)
Bacchetta, Massimo 4:15:58 (13,457)
Bacher, Heimo 4:22:41 (14,978)
Bachmann, Judith 4:10:19 (12,231)
Bachmann, Kurt 4:49:45 (20,661)
Bachmann, Mathis 2:56:50 (734)
Back, Nicholas 5:20:02 (25,364)
Backhurst, Ian 5:48:08 (27,784)
Bacon, Jason 4:29:05 (16,445)
Bacon, John 5:28:18 (26,208)
Bacon, Jonathan 5:08:08 (23,788)
Bacon, Peter 6:22:22 (29,221)
Bacon, Steven 4:14:42 (13,173)
Bacon, Walter 5:38:36 (27,056)
Baddeley, Stephen 4:30:45 (16,794)
Bader, Brett 6:22:39 (29,225)
Bader, Reiner 4:36:48 (18,085)
Badesha, Harjit 4:23:49 (15,254)
Badgery, Stephen 3:02:41 (1,195)
Badii, Claudio 3:09:29 (1,710)
Badillo, José 3:41:02 (5,963)
Badyra, Peter 3:50:00 (7,690)
Baerwald, Oliver 4:00:06 (10,073)
Bagenal, John 5:32:25 (26,567)
Baggaley, Clive 3:35:01 (4,905)
Baggott, David 3:24:13 (3,272)
Bagnall, Christopher 3:28:26 (3,895)
Bagnall, David 5:54:36 (28,143)
Bagnall, Garry 4:24:27 (15,386)

Bagnall, Stewart	4:58:34	(22,390)
Bagshaw, Ian	4:12:19	(12,698)
Baharloo, Abdol Reza	7:02:35	(29,966)
Baiker, Ralf	3:52:44	(8,215)
Bailes, Richard	4:26:00	(15,730)
Bailes, Steve	4:09:02	(11,995)
Bailey, Andrew	3:47:59	(7,262)
Bailey, Ashman	4:22:51	(15,021)
Bailey, Brian	3:28:48	(3,963)
Bailey, Carl	4:10:42	(12,311)
Bailey, Christopher	3:24:46	(3,351)
Bailey, David	5:04:37	(23,235)
Bailey, David	5:24:51	(25,862)
Bailey, Duncan	3:35:15	(4,942)
Bailey, Gareth	4:43:23	(19,462)
Bailey, Gareth	4:46:48	(20,114)
Bailey, Ian	4:07:41	(11,692)
Bailey, Jason	4:50:48	(20,843)
Bailey, Jeremy	3:45:31	(6,751)
Bailey, Jez	4:19:48	(14,315)
Bailey, Kevin	3:41:42	(6,074)
Bailey, Kevin	3:46:40	(6,985)
Bailey, Malcolm	3:24:35	(3,326)
Bailey, Mark	3:37:41	(5,363)
Bailey, Mark	4:06:21	(11,418)
Bailey, Mark	4:23:02	(15,071)
Bailey, Mark	4:28:44	(16,367)
Bailey, Martin	2:59:16	(958)
Bailey, Neal	3:35:15	(4,942)
Bailey, Nicholas	3:47:46	(7,203)
Bailey, Nicholas	6:28:44	(29,378)
Bailey, Nick	3:53:24	(8,357)
Bailey, Paul	3:10:29	(1,794)
Bailey, Paul	3:53:36	(8,404)
Bailey, Paul	4:38:02	(18,378)
Bailey, Paul	4:47:37	(20,284)
Bailey, Ralph	5:48:26	(27,812)
Bailey, Richard	4:26:52	(15,926)
Bailey, Richard	4:51:08	(20,912)
Bailey, Sean	6:36:15	(29,551)
Bailey, Steve	4:26:46	(15,902)
Bailey, Stuart	4:52:48	(21,271)
Bailey, Tom	5:19:26	(25,301)
Bailie, Iain	4:46:21	(20,020)
Baillee, Michael	5:22:08	(25,604)
Baillie, Darren	3:31:31	(4,393)
Baillie, Michael	2:49:25	(408)
Bain, Alasdair	4:01:27	(10,383)
Bain, Thomas	5:08:11	(23,796)
Bainbridge, Peter	4:54:53	(21,699)
Baines, Jeremy	4:20:52	(14,564)
Baines, Lee	5:35:13	(26,820)
Baines, Steven	3:58:42	(9,674)
Bainger, Graham	3:18:14	(2,567)
Bains, Narinder	3:58:09	(9,528)
Baio, Antonio	5:41:27	(27,294)
Baird, Gordon	3:07:05	(1,509)
Baird, Ian	5:10:23	(24,127)
Baird, James	4:34:18	(17,595)
Baird, John	4:20:38	(14,507)
Baird, John	4:27:51	(16,163)
Baixauli Santaya, José	4:33:21	(17,387)
Baker, Adrain	4:45:23	(19,841)
Baker, Andrew	5:40:04	(27,194)
Baker, Barry	5:08:33	(23,855)
Baker, Brian	3:25:18	(3,418)
Baker, Carl	2:56:20	(710)
Baker, Chris	3:21:56	(2,988)
Baker, Christopher	4:11:17	(12,460)
Baker, Clifford	4:01:49	(10,446)
Baker, Clifford	5:21:06	(25,480)
Baker, Clive	3:22:58	(3,107)
Baker, Clive	3:25:32	(3,447)
Baker, Colin	2:49:36	(411)
Baker, Colin	6:16:27	(29,069)
Baker, Dave	5:07:16	(23,658)
Baker, David	5:06:39	(23,569)
Baker, Derek	3:45:32	(6,755)
Baker, Gary	4:26:25	(15,824)
Baker, Gary	5:33:16	(26,631)
Baker, George	4:45:59	(19,934)
Baker, Graham	3:13:33	(2,064)
Baker, Guy	4:05:35	(11,235)
Baker, James	4:59:00	(22,462)
Baker, John	3:37:54	(5,393)
Baker, John	4:00:44	(10,227)
Baker, John	4:48:07	(20,371)
Baker, Jonathan	3:41:50	(6,097)
Baker, Kevin	3:45:05	(6,698)
Baker, Kim	3:20:13	(2,785)
Baker, Lal	6:26:39	(29,323)
Baker, Lee	5:23:38	(25,759)
Baker, Martin	5:09:49	(24,061)
Baker, Martin	5:27:51	(26,164)
Baker, Murray	4:40:40	(18,915)
Baker, Nick	3:03:58	(1,280)
Baker, Nigel	4:58:57	(22,451)
Baker, Nigel	5:24:25	(25,824)
Baker, Paul	3:43:44	(6,446)
Baker, Paul	4:28:04	(16,201)
Baker, Philip	4:47:20	(20,225)
Baker, Richard	4:13:45	(12,988)
Baker, Robert	5:29:28	(26,333)
Baker, Russell	4:01:16	(10,330)
Baker, Simon	4:28:23	(16,283)
Baker, Stephen	4:01:14	(10,323)
Baker, Tim	3:49:30	(7,584)
Baker, William	4:54:59	(21,728)
Bakker, John	4:15:41	(13,402)
Balasubramaniam, Ravivarma	3:59:39	(9,964)
Balasubraramaniam, Krishnakumar	7:28:14	(30,128)
Balch, Oliver	3:47:33	(7,154)
Balchin, Ivan	2:58:40	(885)
Balchin, Nick	4:33:33	(17,438)
Balderson, Paul	3:22:12	(3,027)
Baldi, Antonio	2:37:02	(115)
Balding, Nicholas	3:16:41	(2,390)
Baldock, Michael	3:23:36	(3,185)
Baldock, Robert	3:51:08	(7,901)
Baldoni, Roberto	3:29:31	(4,082)
Baldwin, Alistair	3:16:16	(2,338)
Baldwin, David	3:53:23	(8,351)
Baldwin, Marcus	3:35:53	(5,050)
Baldwin, Mark	3:26:57	(3,616)
Baldwin, Matthew	4:05:19	(11,168)
Baldwin, Richard	3:46:30	(6,948)
Baldwin, Robert	4:24:07	(15,314)
Baldwin, Steven	3:39:13	(5,612)
Baldwin, Stuart	3:39:26	(5,660)
Bale, Adam	6:22:48	(29,227)
Bale, Ian	4:49:26	(20,605)
Bale, Keith	4:29:44	(16,607)
Bale, Stephen	4:15:22	(13,338)
Balfour, Ian	6:18:25	(29,124)
Balfour, Scott	2:57:32	(783)
Bali, Vik	4:14:41	(13,166)
Ball, Brian	4:23:57	(15,281)
Ball, David	3:28:20	(3,878)
Ball, David	5:59:49	(28,411)
Ball, Derek	3:17:46	(2,507)
Ball, Ian	3:22:56	(3,099)
Ball, James	4:27:16	(16,022)
Ball, James	5:01:14	(22,774)
Ball, Kevin	4:44:40	(19,707)
Ball, Mark	3:22:20	(3,040)
Ball, Martin	4:28:09	(16,221)
Ball, Matthew	5:02:21	(22,924)
Ball, Michael	5:22:52	(25,693)
Ball, Philip	4:42:35	(19,290)
Ball, Philip	4:55:24	(21,849)
Ball, Richard	4:44:40	(19,707)
Ball, Roy	4:31:50	(17,069)
Ball, Simon	4:33:25	(17,398)
Ball, Stephen	3:36:29	(5,156)
Ball, Stephen	4:04:02	(10,889)
Ball, William	3:47:10	(7,059)
Balladon, Oscar	5:26:46	(26,067)
Balland, Lionel	4:51:17	(20,943)
Ballantine, Robert	4:29:31	(16,549)
Ballantyne, Henry	3:33:24	(4,674)
Ballantyne, Malcolm	4:13:09	(12,850)
Ballard, John	3:24:59	(3,375)
Ballarini, Sergio	5:41:19	(27,278)
Balleny, Giles	4:46:48	(20,114)
Ballinger, William	6:04:14	(28,604)
Balls, Alex	4:17:16	(13,730)
Baltaian, Armel	3:27:44	(3,751)
Balzarini, Guiseppe	4:23:34	(15,200)
Bamberger, Nicholas	3:41:36	(6,054)
Bamert, Urs	3:54:20	(8,542)
Bamford, Colin	4:24:13	(15,334)
Bamford, Karl	4:21:40	(14,727)
Bamforth, Charles	3:59:23	(9,876)
Bampton, Paul	3:20:03	(2,770)
Bamsey, Jonathan	3:41:59	(6,121)
Bamsey, Philip	3:00:00	(1,031)
Bamsey, Robert	2:47:05	(343)
Banawich, Brian	3:53:16	(8,322)
Bance, Elliott	3:57:32	(9,338)
Bance, Nick	2:58:11	(819)
Bancroft, Ian	4:29:11	(16,467)
Bandandala, Remy	4:45:05	(19,785)
Bandurak, Stefan	5:56:21	(28,229)
Banerji, Udai	6:09:58	(28,858)
Banfi, Jim	4:37:22	(18,215)
Banfield, Simon	4:07:22	(11,629)
Banks, George	5:40:19	(27,211)
Banks, Jonathan	4:10:43	(12,315)
Banks, Kenneth	4:32:04	(17,133)
Banks, Mathew	5:03:22	(23,049)
Banks, Peter	5:13:05	(24,515)
Banks, Philip	5:06:54	(23,601)
Banks, Stephen	3:48:26	(7,346)
Banks, Stuart	4:15:53	(13,444)
Banks, Thomas	3:32:43	(4,561)
Banks, Thomas	4:59:38	(22,544)
Banks, William	3:44:17	(6,540)
Banner, John	4:06:47	(11,498)
Bannerman, Keith	3:04:50	(1,337)
Bannister, Michael	3:02:13	(1,169)
Bannister, Philip	4:58:41	(22,412)
Bannister, Richard	4:41:32	(19,067)
Bannister, Stuart	2:51:44	(504)
Bannon, Alan	5:09:30	(24,015)
Bansal, Sandeep	3:24:26	(3,304)
Bantoft, Charles	5:42:23	(27,364)
Banton, Lewis	2:53:30	(560)
Banwell, Chris	5:01:38	(22,820)
Banwell, Kevin	4:03:34	(10,793)
Banwell, Tom	4:24:54	(15,479)
Banyard, Danny	4:55:01	(21,739)
Baranowski, Marcel	3:27:16	(3,667)
Barbacoui, Renzo	4:58:52	(22,437)
Barbe, Yvan	4:06:41	(11,481)
Barber, Andrew	4:24:30	(15,398)
Barber, Benjamin	4:54:43	(21,648)
Barber, David	4:16:58	(13,658)
Barber, Ian	3:00:37	(1,061)
Barber, Martin	4:39:01	(18,611)
Barber, Nigel	3:38:47	(5,536)
Barber, Owen	6:37:28	(29,577)
Barber, Peter	3:40:19	(5,832)
Barber, Steven	3:34:22	(4,810)
Barber, Wayne	6:48:16	(29,781)
Barbero, Massimo	4:15:18	(13,332)
Barbour, Walter	4:25:45	(15,662)
Barclay, James	5:28:49	(26,272)
Barclay, Jeffrey	3:25:56	(3,496)
Barclay, Raymond	3:34:33	(4,842)
Barclay, Simon	3:58:28	(9,596)
Barclay, William	2:49:59	(428)
Bard, Daniel	5:34:50	(26,789)
Bardell, Graham	3:38:34	(5,491)
Barden, Roy	3:24:19	(3,284)
Bardock, Matthew	4:09:36	(12,093)
Bardosse, Emmanuel	4:32:19	(17,175)
Bardoux, Thierry	3:41:15	(5,999)
Bardwell, Julian	3:48:13	(7,307)
Bareham, Iain	3:27:10	(3,652)
Barfoot, David	4:16:58	(13,658)
Barford, Nicholas	4:17:10	(13,708)
Bargery, Paul	4:03:53	(10,859)
Barguach, Noureddine	7:24:51	(30,105)
Barham, Andrew	4:10:45	(12,321)
Barham, Jeffrey	5:05:56	(23,456)
Barham, Malcolm	3:48:34	(7,374)
Barham, Steve	4:49:35	(20,631)
Barison, Stefano	3:46:13	(6,900)
Baritel, Pascal	5:04:24	(23,200)

Barkas, Mike 4:09:28 (12,073)
Barke, Norman 5:44:12 (27,492)
Barker, Andrew 4:33:54 (17,519)
Barker, Andrew 4:40:22 (18,850)
Barker, Aran 4:27:47 (16,147)
Barker, Charles 3:43:36 (6,415)
Barker, David 3:56:11 (8,963)
Barker, Edward 4:14:10 (13,070)
Barker, John 2:54:05 (583)
Barker, John 3:33:10 (4,636)
Barker, John 3:55:43 (8,848)
Barker, John-Paul 3:47:03 (7,042)
Barker, Kit 3:48:17 (7,320)
Barker, Lee 5:05:58 (23,465)
Barker, Leslie 5:06:49 (23,593)
Barker, Michael 3:10:09 (1,752)
Barker, Michael 3:53:30 (8,375)
Barker, Nigel 3:51:27 (7,952)
Barker, Peter 3:47:35 (7,161)
Barker, Philip 5:05:52 (23,444)
Barker, Richard 4:14:45 (13,194)
Barker, Robert 3:58:07 (9,519)
Barker, Ryan 2:54:37 (615)
Barker, Stephen 3:52:29 (8,167)
Barker, Tim 4:56:25 (22,054)
Barkes, Tom 4:04:17 (10,947)
Barkman, Charles 3:15:18 (2,255)
Barkwith, Duncan 4:04:37 (11,023)
Barkworth, Peter 3:34:05 (4,770)
Barley, Allan 5:15:09 (24,813)
Barley, Kenneth 3:49:06 (7,482)
Barley, Steve 4:09:12 (12,022)
Barlow, Antony 4:31:11 (16,898)
Barlow, Chris 3:58:38 (9,649)
Barlow, Howard 3:31:07 (4,343)
Barlow, James 4:16:11 (13,506)
Barlow, Lawrence 6:22:34 (29,224)
Barlow, Mike 3:57:00 (9,178)
Barlow, Philip 4:26:31 (15,849)
Barlow, Richard 5:11:18 (24,255)
Barlow, Roger 4:08:39 (11,906)
Barlow, Stephen 3:16:45 (2,400)
Barltrop, Paul 3:47:43 (7,196)
Barnaby, Matthew 4:51:02 (20,891)
Barnard, Adrian 5:15:43 (24,894)
Barnard, John 4:37:20 (18,206)
Barnard, Robert 4:16:02 (13,474)
Barnaville, Michael 5:54:30 (28,137)
Barnes, Alan 3:29:01 (4,001)
Barnes, Allan 4:13:35 (12,952)
Barnes, Andrew 4:00:15 (10,099)
Barnes, Andrew 4:34:33 (17,636)
Barnes, Anthony 4:04:37 (11,023)
Barnes, Anthony 4:12:21 (12,703)
Barnes, Antony 4:41:35 (19,081)
Barnes, Antony 5:35:27 (26,838)
Barnes, David 3:25:19 (3,421)
Barnes, Gary 3:14:11 (2,135)
Barnes, Gary 4:13:06 (12,836)
Barnes, Gavin 4:25:23 (15,590)
Barnes, Ian 4:09:03 (11,997)
Barnes, Jeremy 4:07:57 (11,750)
Barnes, John 4:10:14 (12,216)
Barnes, John 5:21:11 (25,487)
Barnes, Julian 4:18:09 (13,903)
Barnes, Kevin 5:44:34 (27,532)
Barnes, Michael 4:10:20 (12,237)
Barnes, Nigel 4:08:06 (11,785)
Barnes, Paul 2:51:21 (481)
Barnes, Peter 3:51:30 (7,966)
Barnes, Richard 5:20:33 (25,415)
Barnes, Robert 5:07:32 (23,700)
Barnes, Robert 5:21:37 (25,538)
Barnes, Roy 3:29:35 (4,095)
Barnes, Simon 5:02:15 (22,909)
Barnes, Steven 3:55:13 (8,738)
Barnes, Terry 5:25:37 (25,953)
Barnes, Trevor 4:51:54 (21,069)
Barnes Yallowley, William 4:12:41 (12,768)
Barnett, David 4:48:57 (20,518)
Barnett, David 5:08:53 (23,920)
Barnett, Duncan 4:19:21 (14,209)
Barnett, Graham 3:51:25 (7,947)
Barnett, Jonathan 4:28:36 (16,339)
Barnett, Michael 3:31:10 (4,351)
Barnett, Paul 4:59:56 (22,608)
Barnett, Robert 3:39:43 (5,715)
Barningham, Richard 4:18:56 (14,107)
Barns, John 3:45:20 (6,721)
Baron, Cliff 5:17:17 (25,082)
Barot, Krishna 5:29:12 (26,310)
Barr, Alistair 4:59:55 (22,603)
Barr, Andrew 4:37:08 (18,152)
Barr, David 3:24:01 (3,248)
Barr, James 4:16:23 (13,547)
Barr, Roger 2:57:03 (747)
Barraclough, Roger 4:30:33 (16,761)
Barrance, Tony 4:21:35 (14,708)
Barrass, Anthony 3:27:38 (3,727)
Barratt, Steven 4:48:18 (20,407)
Barratt, Steven 4:48:19 (20,410)
Barret, Vincent 5:08:46 (23,899)
Barrett, Charles 4:44:26 (19,662)
Barrett, Christopher 3:46:25 (6,935)
Barrett, Daren 4:21:02 (14,599)
Barrett, David 3:10:50 (1,822)
Barrett, David 6:06:38 (28,707)
Barrett, Edward 4:54:29 (21,587)
Barrett, Gerard 3:57:45 (9,412)
Barrett, Ian 3:59:55 (10,033)
Barrett, John 4:51:39 (21,019)
Barrett, Jonathan 5:26:31 (26,045)
Barrett, Matthew 3:55:45 (8,861)
Barrett, Paul 3:46:46 (6,999)
Barrett, Peter James 3:38:58 (5,568)
Barrett, Philip 4:23:12 (15,108)
Barrett, Steve 3:09:14 (1,688)
Barrett-Lennard, Dacre 3:56:00 (8,919)
Barribal, Scott 4:00:40 (10,199)
Barrie, Michael 4:16:15 (13,516)
Barrier, Ernest 4:49:52 (20,687)
Barrieux, Laurent 4:24:17 (15,345)
Barrington, Dale 3:00:56 (1,079)
Barrington-Evans, Robert 4:01:28 (10,386)
Barrois, Bernard 4:02:27 (10,561)
Barron, Anthony 3:45:22 (6,726)
Barron, John 4:57:44 (22,253)
Barron, Jon 5:39:50 (27,169)
Barron, Shaun 2:57:30 (780)
Barrow, Christopher 4:31:07 (16,876)
Barrow, Michael 4:05:38 (11,248)
Barrow, Steve 4:11:12 (12,440)
Barrowman, Michael 4:02:07 (10,507)
Barrows, Darren 4:48:50 (20,493)
Barrs, Gary 4:54:06 (21,533)
Barr-Sim, Andrew 3:43:11 (6,341)
Barry, Andrew 3:01:20 (1,097)
Barry, John 3:26:47 (3,595)
Barry, Lee 5:28:56 (26,285)
Barry, Paul 3:36:26 (5,147)
Barry, Paul 3:49:39 (7,614)
Barry, Richard 4:26:58 (15,955)
Barstow, John 4:00:23 (10,127)
Barstow, Michael 4:21:26 (14,679)
Barter, Nigel 3:39:50 (5,745)
Bartholomew, David 6:01:36 (28,483)
Barthorpe, Carl 4:06:19 (11,411)
Bartlett, Anthony 3:57:17 (9,250)
Bartlett, Christopher 3:42:14 (6,169)
Bartlett, David 4:03:52 (10,855)
Bartlett, Edwin 3:55:00 (8,702)
Bartlett, John 3:42:23 (6,199)
Bartlett, John 4:40:12 (18,811)
Bartlett, John 5:35:22 (26,834)
Bartlett, Keith Brian 4:31:07 (16,876)
Bartlett, Mike 4:21:48 (14,761)
Bartlett, Nicholas 4:06:54 (11,527)
Bartlett, Robin 4:32:07 (17,138)
Bartlett, Simon 5:51:53 (28,011)
Bartlett, Stephen 4:53:02 (21,322)
Bartmeier, Frederick 4:38:22 (18,473)
Barton, Alan 5:32:24 (26,564)
Barton, Ashley 5:41:33 (27,302)
Barton, Graham 4:58:18 (22,341)
Barton, Ian 4:51:00 (20,881)
Barton, James 4:53:26 (21,403)
Barton, Ken 3:42:07 (6,141)
Barton, Michael 4:02:59 (10,657)
Barton, Neal 4:15:27 (13,358)
Barton, Nigel 4:58:25 (22,362)
Barton, Paul 4:52:37 (21,241)
Barton, Russell John 4:12:02 (12,620)
Bartosik, James 4:28:53 (16,392)
Bartram, Dwayne 3:38:50 (5,544)
Bartram, Mark 3:29:22 (4,061)
Bartram, Matt 3:31:58 (4,463)
Bartram, Simon 5:19:19 (25,294)
Baruah, Dean 5:20:45 (25,438)
Barwick, Alan 6:10:15 (28,868)
Barwick, Darren 3:06:47 (1,487)
Barwick, Lloyd 3:57:14 (9,236)
Baseggio, John 3:39:45 (5,725)
Basford, Pete 3:49:02 (7,471)
Basham, Brian 6:38:55 (29,605)
Basham, Chris 4:50:15 (20,758)
Basham, David 3:49:00 (7,465)
Basham, Lawrence 4:09:37 (12,096)
Basham, Richard 4:05:05 (11,133)
Bashford, Bryan 4:38:26 (18,488)
Bashford, Graham 5:39:14 (27,106)
Bashford, Guy 4:26:14 (15,789)
Basler, René 3:28:52 (3,975)
Basnett, Roy 6:03:21 (28,557)
Bason, Stephen 3:16:29 (2,364)
Bass, Clive 3:49:20 (7,533)
Bass, Richard 2:51:58 (514)
Bassett, Cliff 4:55:28 (21,878)
Bassett, David 3:40:26 (5,854)
Bassett, Edward 4:53:01 (21,318)
Bassett, Robert 5:21:04 (25,475)
Bassingthwaighte, Thomas 4:35:46 (17,877)
Bastawrous, Andrew 3:58:55 (9,726)
Bastible, Eoin 4:34:04 (17,547)
Bastick, Mark 4:31:39 (17,023)
Bastin, Colin 5:21:22 (25,516)
Bastin, Simon 5:26:00 (25,987)
Basu, Subhashis 4:20:28 (14,468)
Bataille, Jean Pierre 3:53:12 (8,309)
Bataille, Jean-François 5:31:24 (26,483)
Batchelor, Gary 4:20:27 (14,464)
Batchelor, Keith 5:17:03 (25,056)
Batchelor, Mark 4:47:13 (20,207)
Batchelor, Nick 3:27:50 (3,771)
Batchelor, William 5:13:21 (24,558)
Bately, Theo 2:47:11 (345)
Bateman, David 3:23:56 (3,235)
Bateman, Del 3:25:25 (3,435)
Bateman, Edward 3:56:17 (8,989)
Bateman, Jeremy 2:45:35 (311)
Bater, Bernie 3:51:32 (7,974)
Bater, Michael 4:17:42 (13,814)
Bates, Christopher 4:41:45 (19,112)
Bates, Glenn 5:04:45 (23,252)
Bates, Ian 3:36:06 (5,091)
Bates, Jonathan 3:35:38 (5,009)
Bates, Kevin 3:09:22 (1,702)
Bates, Mike 5:06:01 (23,472)
Bates, Paul 3:28:13 (3,848)
Bates, Paul 3:55:02 (8,705)
Bates, Paul 6:01:55 (28,502)
Bates, Philip 3:49:51 (7,657)
Bates, Roger 6:03:11 (28,550)
Bates, Simon 6:11:03 (28,890)
Bates, Stephen 3:56:46 (9,128)
Bates, Stephen 4:01:09 (10,311)
Bates, Stephen 4:33:37 (17,459)
Bates, Steven 6:03:11 (28,550)
Bates, Tim 4:16:12 (13,509)
Bateson, Nicholas 2:43:08 (240)
Bateson Hill, John 3:49:10 (7,489)
Bathurst, Geoffrey 5:44:50 (27,552)
Bathurst, Kevin 6:55:04 (29,880)
Batizovszey, Wayne 4:42:21 (19,239)
Batsford, Mark 3:59:27 (9,903)
Batstone, David 2:50:49 (456)
Battaglion, Giorgio 5:42:14 (27,348)
Batten, Colin 4:15:21 (13,335)
Batten, Samuel 4:17:17 (13,732)
Batterbury, Clive 3:41:08 (5,976)

Battersby, Gordon	6:27:57 (29,353)	
Battersby, Michael	5:15:09 (24,813)	
Battersby, Stephen	4:46:53 (20,140)	
Battiston, Patrice	3:51:24 (7,944)	
Battle, Andrew	3:52:51 (8,238)	
Battle, Matt	4:27:19 (16,027)	
Battle, Richard	3:39:38 (5,699)	
Battle, William	3:55:12 (8,734)	
Batty, Darren	4:01:43 (10,432)	
Batty, Phillip	6:40:10 (29,644)	
Batty, Richard	3:55:06 (8,713)	
Batty, Richard	4:30:57 (16,839)	
Battye, Mark	4:32:15 (17,165)	
Battye, Michael	4:38:02 (18,378)	
Baty, Adrian	3:55:52 (8,887)	
Baucutt, Neil	4:28:16 (16,256)	
Baulch, James	3:26:05 (3,510)	
Baulch, Stuart	3:38:14 (5,437)	
Baum, Herbert	4:05:26 (11,191)	
Baumann, Andreas	4:59:56 (22,608)	
Baumann, Heinz	3:40:16 (5,825)	
Baumann, Jochen	3:51:42 (8,006)	
Baumann, Stephen	3:40:47 (5,908)	
Baumann, Uwe	4:37:57 (18,357)	
Baumgarten, Karl	3:54:14 (8,519)	
Baussant, Trene	4:20:51 (14,560)	
Baverstock, Ian	4:56:25 (22,054)	
Bavin, Nigel	5:41:45 (27,310)	
Bawden, Glynn	3:56:33 (9,066)	
Bawden, Phillip	3:56:33 (9,066)	
Bawden, Simon	4:36:27 (18,007)	
Bax, Robert	5:54:30 (28,137)	
Baxendale, Peter	5:18:44 (25,237)	
Baxendale, Samuel	3:56:47 (9,129)	
Baxter, Adam	4:40:46 (18,934)	
Baxter, André	4:49:00 (20,528)	
Baxter, Andrew	4:40:13 (18,816)	
Baxter, Billy	5:55:24 (28,178)	
Baxter, Brian	6:55:47 (29,898)	
Baxter, Charlie	3:25:35 (3,455)	
Baxter, David	3:51:04 (7,884)	
Baxter, Eric	3:28:21 (3,881)	
Baxter, Gordon	3:12:42 (1,979)	
Baxter, Gordon	4:27:37 (16,096)	
Baxter, Lee	3:20:59 (2,889)	
Baxter, Paul	4:47:48 (20,308)	
Baxter, Robert	3:59:15 (9,832)	
Baxter, Simon	4:02:49 (10,626)	
Baxter, Trevor	6:51:19 (29,823)	
Baybour, Rob	3:46:58 (7,028)	
Bayer, Malcolm	2:47:33 (354)	
Bayes, Graham	3:49:44 (7,629)	
Bayes, Peter	4:45:42 (19,882)	
Bayford, Paul	5:24:55 (25,874)	
Bayley, Christopher	4:15:39 (13,396)	
Bayley-Dainton, Stuart	3:27:54 (3,789)	
Bayliss, Michael	5:07:54 (23,758)	
Bayliss, Rob	4:33:52 (17,513)	
Baynes, Charles	3:41:02 (5,963)	
Baynes, Chris	3:57:27 (9,311)	
Baynes, Edwin	2:46:57 (340)	
Baynes, Ron	5:21:16 (25,498)	
Baynham, Anthony	4:52:26 (21,191)	
Bays, Richard	4:03:26 (10,756)	
Bazso, Peter	2:59:14 (952)	
Beacall, Reg	3:21:55 (2,984)	
Beaconsfield, Garry	4:24:53 (15,474)	
Beadell, Warren	3:08:16 (1,612)	
Beadle, Bob	3:04:46 (1,331)	
Beadle, Darren	4:45:02 (19,779)	
Beadle, Dennis	3:45:19 (6,719)	
Beagley, Alistair	3:58:12 (9,537)	
Beagley, Mark	3:08:27 (1,627)	
Beal, Peter	3:33:44 (4,719)	
Beale, David	5:14:30 (24,706)	
Beale, Douglas	4:35:03 (17,723)	
Beale, James	3:21:48 (2,974)	
Beale, Nicholas	4:28:02 (16,197)	
Beale, Rupert	3:38:34 (5,491)	
Beales, James	3:01:03 (1,087)	
Bealing, Steven	3:38:38 (5,507)	
Beaman, Andrew	3:24:19 (3,284)	
Bean, Anthony	4:16:59 (13,661)	
Bean, John	4:00:08 (10,077)	
Beange, Peter	4:29:32 (16,553)	
Beanland, Anthony	3:44:29 (6,572)	
Beard, Elliott	5:13:12 (24,530)	
Beard, Mick	3:56:01 (8,930)	
Beard, Neil	3:50:30 (7,772)	
Beardmore, Adrian	4:55:26 (21,863)	
Beardmore, Roger	3:09:05 (1,678)	
Beardshall, Martin	4:23:09 (15,098)	
Beardsley, Dick	3:09:45 (1,734)	
Beardsmore, Keith	2:58:44 (900)	
Beare, Julian	4:27:57 (16,181)	
Beasley, Andrew	5:08:30 (23,847)	
Beasley, Glen	4:00:28 (10,142)	
Beasley, Mervyn	5:10:21 (24,122)	
Beasley, Thomas	4:48:35 (20,451)	
Beaton, Michael	2:56:17 (707)	
Beaton, Robert	4:21:50 (14,772)	
Beattie, David	2:57:51 (802)	
Beattie, David	4:09:42 (12,108)	
Beattie, David	4:25:16 (15,568)	
Beattie, Keith	3:35:25 (4,975)	
Beattie, Mark	3:52:44 (8,215)	
Beattle, Ian	3:07:53 (1,580)	
Beaufrere, Philippe	3:57:38 (9,379)	
Beaumont, Andrew	4:04:09 (10,910)	
Beaumont, David	5:14:18 (24,673)	
Beaumont, Richard	3:06:20 (1,444)	
Beaumont, Roy	4:58:20 (22,347)	
Beaumont, Simon	4:41:56 (19,149)	
Beaux, Jean François	3:56:45 (9,121)	
Beaven, Steven	4:16:12 (13,509)	
Beaver, Alan	5:21:48 (25,566)	
Beaver, Dennis	3:53:10 (8,302)	
Beavis, Paul	4:17:01 (13,672)	
Beazer, Derek	5:28:20 (26,212)	
Beazer, Hadyn	4:55:02 (21,744)	
Beazer, John	5:28:21 (26,217)	
Beccani, Alessandro	4:43:01 (19,389)	
Bech, Einar	4:26:19 (15,810)	
Bech, Stein	3:37:04 (5,256)	
Bechart, Bernard	2:56:31 (718)	
Bechu, Domitille	4:14:56 (13,248)	
Beck, Anthony	4:48:33 (20,446)	
Beck, Garford	5:21:25 (25,520)	
Beck, Graham	5:12:41 (24,453)	
Beck, Jeff	2:54:19 (594)	
Beck, Patrick	3:27:50 (3,771)	
Beck, Paul	3:36:56 (5,232)	
Beck, Peter	3:53:06 (8,292)	
Beck, Peter	4:31:45 (17,048)	
Beckett, Adrian	4:38:07 (18,408)	
Beckett, Anthony	5:04:12 (23,162)	
Beckett, David	4:01:00 (10,280)	
Beckett, Kevin	6:16:39 (28,708)	
Beckett, Paul	6:12:39 (28,948)	
Beckford, Martin	4:28:06 (16,210)	
Becks, Andrew	6:08:58 (28,815)	
Becks, Ryan	4:00:52 (10,254)	
Becquhart, Denis	2:56:18 (709)	
Bedding, Duncan	4:22:58 (15,055)	
Beddis, Graham	4:07:35 (11,675)	
Beddoes, Tom	5:12:43 (24,461)	
Bedell, Nigel	3:27:16 (3,667)	
Bedford, Graham	4:58:04 (22,308)	
Bedford, Matthew	4:12:28 (12,730)	
Bedford, Michael	4:48:53 (20,500)	
Bedford, Trevor	4:57:37 (22,232)	
Bedin, Robert	3:34:15 (4,792)	
Bedingfield, Jonathan	4:16:53 (13,644)	
Bedingfield, Simon	4:44:53 (19,754)	
Bedington, Terence	3:55:13 (8,738)	
Bednall, Michael	4:09:00 (11,978)	
Bednarek, Richard	4:51:20 (20,954)	
Bedwell, John-Paul	6:00:51 (28,450)	
Bedwell, Paul	4:41:28 (19,057)	
Bedwell, Peter	4:27:30 (16,058)	
Bee, David	3:19:51 (2,745)	
Bee, Graham	4:50:41 (20,825)	
Beebee, Michael	6:18:48 (29,133)	
Beech, Gary	3:34:37 (4,853)	
Beech, Jonathan	4:49:25 (20,602)	
Beech, Timothy	4:51:26 (20,975)	
Beecham, George	5:41:57 (27,330)	
Beecher, Michael	3:01:24 (1,103)	
Beechey, Stephen	5:51:50 (28,007)	
Beer, Byron	5:15:29 (24,867)	
Beer, Leon	4:13:38 (12,968)	
Beer, Martin	3:22:19 (3,038)	
Beer, Michael	3:52:21 (8,142)	
Beer, Peter	3:05:57 (1,416)	
Beesley, Ian	3:50:18 (7,734)	
Beeson, Graham	5:44:48 (27,546)	
Beeson, Spencer	4:43:44 (19,548)	
Beeton, Andrew	5:44:07 (27,484)	
Beever, Rob	3:39:09 (5,599)	
Begard, Ralph	3:31:59 (4,468)	
Begley, Kenneth	2:44:24 (272)	
Begley, Patrick	3:27:46 (3,760)	
Behan, David	4:08:50 (11,943)	
Behar, Daniele	2:58:21 (840)	
Behar, Isaac	4:54:15 (21,555)	
Behrems, Guenther	4:15:55 (13,447)	
Beighton, Stephen	4:17:00 (13,668)	
Beijen, Jan	5:21:54 (25,573)	
Bejsovec, Karel	3:02:51 (1,204)	
Belcher, Ben	3:14:33 (2,172)	
Belcher, Carl	3:32:36 (4,549)	
Belcher, Daniel	4:00:32 (10,166)	
Belcher, David	4:13:09 (12,850)	
Belcher, Mark	2:56:40 (724)	
Belcher, Paul	3:16:57 (2,418)	
Belcher, Paul	3:59:27 (9,903)	
Belcher, Peter	2:45:49 (315)	
Beldon, Steve	3:55:28 (8,794)	
Belfrage, Rupert	3:33:26 (4,680)	
Bell, Adrian	4:45:52 (19,914)	
Bell, Anthony	3:13:43 (2,077)	
Bell, Dave	4:24:42 (15,437)	
Bell, David	7:10:21 (30,023)	
Bell, Edward	3:30:12 (4,200)	
Bell, Giles	4:39:57 (18,777)	
Bell, Graeme	3:32:17 (4,504)	
Bell, Graeme	4:06:39 (11,476)	
Bell, Ian	3:21:32 (2,953)	
Bell, Ian	4:02:24 (10,553)	
Bell, Ian	4:34:08 (17,564)	
Bell, John	3:39:45 (5,725)	
Bell, John	4:05:23 (11,182)	
Bell, John	4:43:07 (19,407)	
Bell, John	4:52:54 (21,292)	
Bell, John	6:17:02 (29,087)	
Bell, Jonathan	3:41:52 (6,104)	
Bell, Kevin	3:34:26 (4,824)	
Bell, Mark	4:17:07 (13,692)	
Bell, Martin	3:20:44 (2,853)	
Bell, Martin	3:52:41 (8,207)	
Bell, Martin	4:35:09 (17,739)	
Bell, Michael	3:35:58 (5,068)	
Bell, Michael	4:19:47 (14,312)	
Bell, Oliver	4:31:05 (16,866)	
Bell, Richard	4:55:34 (21,907)	
Bell, Richard	7:07:22 (30,000)	
Bell, Robert	3:55:11 (8,728)	
Bell, Roderick	4:31:54 (17,090)	
Bell, Ronald	5:27:33 (26,130)	
Bell, Royce	4:03:31 (10,776)	
Bell, Simon	2:35:25 (95)	
Bell, Stephen	4:36:02 (17,936)	
Bell, Wayne	3:47:06 (7,051)	
Bellamy, Guy	3:16:33 (2,376)	
Bellamy, Simon	3:23:49 (3,213)	
Bellinger, James	5:29:11 (26,307)	
Bellingham, Dave	3:17:17 (2,459)	
Bellis, Thomas	2:56:25 (712)	
Bellis, Thomas	3:06:30 (1,461)	
Bellotti, Valter	4:31:21 (16,944)	
Belmont, Tony	4:24:57 (15,491)	
Belringer, Richard	5:16:31 (24,991)	
Belson, Nigel	4:44:16 (19,633)	
Belt, Keith	3:32:01 (4,473)	
Belton, Adrian	3:29:34 (4,092)	
Belton, Chris	3:03:39 (1,260)	
Belton, David	6:05:32 (28,669)	
Belza, Augustin	3:57:56 (9,472)	
Benato, Giuliano	4:04:05 (10,901)	

Benbow, Alastair 3:14:40 (2,178)
Benbow, James 5:39:35 (27,142)
Benbow, Mark 3:48:59 (7,462)
Bendel, Colin 4:18:29 (14,009)
Bendle, Stephen 4:17:41 (13,808)
Bendon, Charles 4:13:20 (12,884)
Bendon, Jamie 4:07:50 (11,727)
Benedetti, Duncan 5:26:41 (26,059)
Benedict, Daniel 3:50:40 (7,800)
Benest, Peter 4:27:57 (16,181)
Benford, Nigel 6:04:46 (28,633)
Ben-Halim, Amr 5:44:38 (27,537)
Benigni, Michel 3:19:58 (2,764)
Benincasa, Francesco 4:09:50 (12,131)
Benjamin, Chimal 4:29:03 (16,431)
Benmore, Mark 4:19:32 (14,264)
Benn, Andrew 3:13:02 (2,007)
Ben-Nathan, Marc 3:24:24 (3,298)
Bennell, Kevin 4:22:12 (14,861)
Bennet, James 4:30:54 (16,826)
Bennett, Adam 4:00:57 (10,276)
Bennett, Adam 4:02:32 (10,580)
Bennett, Alan 5:15:09 (24,813)
Bennett, Alan 5:15:48 (24,906)
Bennett, Andrew 3:52:16 (8,129)
Bennett, Angus 3:50:21 (7,747)
Bennett, Anthony 3:42:32 (6,223)
Bennett, Brian 4:13:26 (12,917)
Bennett, Christopher 3:50:37 (7,792)
Bennett, David 3:07:14 (1,521)
Bennett, David 5:07:13 (23,652)
Bennett, Delme 4:33:11 (17,346)
Bennett, Jason 6:03:10 (28,549)
Bennett, Jonathan 3:50:54 (7,847)
Bennett, Jonathan 5:20:41 (25,428)
Bennett, Kevin 5:27:52 (26,168)
Bennett, Kevin 6:40:15 (29,649)
Bennett, Lee 4:22:26 (14,913)
Bennett, Mark 3:46:58 (7,028)
Bennett, Matt 5:32:36 (26,585)
Bennett, Maurice 5:57:43 (28,311)
Bennett, Michael 4:21:54 (14,786)
Bennett, Nicholas 3:24:57 (3,370)
Bennett, Paul 3:39:23 (5,645)
Bennett, Peter 3:59:20 (9,856)
Bennett, Peter 5:46:56 (27,695)
Bennett, Philip 3:54:13 (8,512)
Bennett, Richard 4:21:39 (14,724)
Bennett, Ronald 5:36:21 (26,905)
Bennett, Ross 3:48:26 (7,346)
Bennett, Tim 3:04:19 (1,303)
Bennetts, Philip 4:18:19 (13,959)
Bennewith, Mark 3:41:13 (5,987)
Bennington, Glenn 3:48:17 (7,320)
Bennion, Chris 3:43:32 (6,403)
Bennion, David 3:29:41 (4,119)
Benson, David 5:52:07 (28,023)
Benson, James 3:35:34 (4,999)
Benson, Keith 4:16:17 (13,521)
Benson, Kenneth 4:38:24 (18,480)
Benson, Mark 4:07:25 (11,647)
Benson, Stephen 3:12:02 (1,917)
Benstead, Matthew 4:26:36 (15,871)
Bent, Christopher 5:12:18 (24,392)
Bent, Daniel 3:18:19 (2,577)
Bentall, Steven 5:27:36 (26,138)
Bentall, William 4:21:28 (14,685)
Bentham, Warren 4:36:57 (18,118)
Bentley, Alex 3:33:07 (4,630)
Bentley, Clive 3:54:13 (8,512)
Bentley, David 4:26:22 (15,819)
Bentley, Gary 4:00:27 (10,136)
Bentley, Mark 3:12:04 (1,919)
Bentley, Robin 2:35:58 (104)
Benton, Mark 4:11:16 (12,456)
Benton, Mark 5:22:31 (25,651)
Benton, Trevor 3:58:05 (9,509)
Benton, Warren 3:57:30 (9,326)
Benveniste, David 4:38:57 (18,594)
Benvenuti, Alessandro 3:54:42 (8,634)
Benz, Jochen 4:05:33 (11,228)
Beresford, Alastair 3:52:30 (8,169)
Beresford, Jeff 4:02:42 (10,608)
Berezicki, Mark 4:50:19 (20,774)
Berg, Ty 2:37:06 (118)
Bergan, Arild 4:51:11 (20,922)
Bergen, Rien 3:21:07 (2,897)
Berger, David 5:59:57 (28,416)
Berger, Hakon 6:01:16 (28,466)
Berghorst, Hans 3:38:40 (5,514)
Bergin, Ian 4:29:48 (16,625)
Bergin, Liam 3:41:35 (6,048)
Bergvall, Karl Gustav 6:21:43 (29,210)
Berini, Brian 3:56:26 (9,034)
Berini, Mark 4:42:08 (19,188)
Berisford, Andrew 3:29:28 (4,075)
Berkhold, Patrick 3:17:19 (2,463)
Berkley, James 4:51:33 (20,995)
Berkompas, Derrek 6:05:04 (28,643)
Berks, Daniel 3:28:41 (3,935)
Berkvens, Jan 3:31:01 (4,331)
Berland, Dominique 3:30:03 (4,181)
Berlivet, Jean Yves 3:27:21 (3,682)
Berman, Darren 4:26:39 (15,882)
Bernard, Noel 4:00:24 (10,130)
Bernard, Nysten 3:06:32 (1,463)
Bernardini, Michel 3:13:12 (2,026)
Bernberg, Brian 3:30:28 (4,241)
Berndes, Christopher 5:27:16 (26,109)
Bernstein, Richard 3:45:59 (6,853)
Berridge, Roger 4:51:39 (21,019)
Berrill, Darren 4:46:02 (19,945)
Berriman, Lyn 5:06:12 (23,501)
Berry, Christopher 5:13:51 (24,612)
Berry, Daniel 4:26:06 (15,758)
Berry, Derek 3:58:11 (9,533)
Berry, Gavin 3:14:00 (2,121)
Berry, James 3:54:13 (8,512)
Berry, John 3:38:13 (5,433)
Berry, Jonathan 5:12:48 (24,470)
Berry, Malcolm 4:09:38 (12,101)
Berry, Michael 5:12:36 (24,443)
Berry, Robert 4:29:41 (16,594)
Berry, Stephen 4:15:28 (13,361)
Berryman, Steve 5:04:45 (23,252)
Bertocchi, Samuele 3:54:24 (8,562)
Bertolone, Enzo 5:21:14 (25,493)
Bertram, Stephen 7:06:12 (29,986)
Bertwistle, Gary 3:41:03 (5,967)
Berwick, Michael 4:18:47 (14,078)
Bessant, Stephen 3:34:21 (4,808)
Bessey, Matthew 4:42:05 (19,174)
Besson, Serge 3:35:13 (4,935)
Best, Barry 4:37:37 (18,282)
Best, Dickon 4:28:56 (16,410)
Best, Richard 3:00:27 (1,051)
Beszant, Robert 3:44:29 (6,572)
Bethell, Mark 3:39:31 (5,679)
Betsworth, Glyn 4:07:36 (11,678)
Bett, Tim 4:12:27 (12,725)
Bettcher, Roy 2:58:34 (864)
Bettini, Paul 4:36:09 (17,947)
Bettis, Stephen 6:04:01 (28,593)
Bettles, David 5:57:13 (28,277)
Betts, Dean 3:38:23 (5,462)
Betts, Jonathan 4:08:10 (11,795)
Betts, Mark 3:40:17 (5,827)
Betts, Noel 3:44:22 (6,557)
Beueridge, William 4:32:56 (17,298)
Beuzeval, David 5:38:44 (27,070)
Bevan, Andy 3:22:49 (3,089)
Bevan, Daniel 4:32:40 (17,239)
Bevan, Graham 5:33:34 (26,655)
Bevan, Joseph 4:23:00 (15,063)
Bevan, Mark 5:11:59 (24,351)
Bevan, Michael 4:27:15 (16,017)
Bevan, Richard 5:33:33 (26,653)
Bevan, Steve 3:35:22 (4,964)
Beveridge, David 3:32:13 (4,495)
Beveridge, Stephen 3:58:05 (9,509)
Beverley, Thor 4:31:03 (16,862)
Beverly, Michael 4:23:04 (15,080)
Bevers, Gary 3:41:35 (6,048)
Bevington, Dale 3:38:58 (5,568)
Bewers, Paul 5:09:55 (24,072)
Bexon, Brian 3:55:24 (8,781)
Bey, Deen 4:41:32 (19,067)
Beynon, Mark 4:31:13 (16,908)
Beynon, Robert 5:10:24 (24,129)
Beytout, Jean 3:34:26 (4,824)
Bezuidenhout, Glen 3:09:31 (1,715)
Bhalla, Mark 4:40:28 (18,868)
Bhana, Sunil 5:23:29 (25,741)
Bhangal, Jasbinder 4:07:19 (11,617)
Bhasin, Sumit 4:50:17 (20,767)
Bhatiani, Wirin 5:17:03 (25,056)
Bhudia, Suresh 6:29:55 (29,407)
Bhudia, Sushil 6:44:53 (29,734)
Bhukhureea, Virsingh 5:58:36 (28,349)
Bhumber, Satbindersingh 5:44:07 (27,484)
Bialkowski, Darren 5:37:16 (26,962)
Bialogroozki, Steve 3:38:29 (5,478)
Bianchi, Dario 5:56:06 (28,218)
Bianchina, Marco 4:41:44 (19,108)
Biasi, Carlo 5:03:27 (23,059)
Biau, Patrick 3:36:20 (5,129)
Bibby, Neil 5:02:22 (22,925)
Bickel, Ronald 3:33:06 (4,622)
Bickerdike, Leigh 4:09:30 (12,076)
Bickley, Alan 5:24:46 (25,854)
Bickley, Paul 3:59:51 (10,010)
Bickley, Steve 4:28:02 (16,197)
Bickmore, Paul 5:55:32 (28,194)
Bicknell, Andrew 5:14:35 (24,720)
Bicknell, Graham 3:21:22 (2,928)
Biddick, Dominic 2:52:32 (531)
Biddiscombe, Martyn 4:15:45 (13,414)
Biddlecombe, Brian 4:34:06 (17,557)
Biddulph, David 2:51:23 (483)
Biddulph, Simon 4:34:29 (17,623)
Bidduph, Christopher 2:49:24 (407)
Bidman, Ian 5:17:16 (25,077)
Bidnell, David 4:41:55 (19,144)
Bidston, Mark 3:55:11 (8,728)
Bidwell, Jonathan 4:47:35 (20,280)
Bieris, Stan 3:54:42 (8,634)
Biggart, Graham 5:04:01 (23,133)
Biggs, Clive 5:31:07 (26,464)
Biggs, Gavin 3:53:05 (8,288)
Biggs, Gerard 4:10:04 (12,173)
Biggs, Michael 5:04:20 (23,185)
Biggs, Richard 4:11:11 (12,436)
Biggs, Roger 3:59:13 (9,823)
Bighi, Moris 4:32:21 (17,183)
Bigland, Phil 4:37:33 (18,264)
Bigmore, Jonathan 3:10:09 (1,752)
Bignell, Melvyn 5:16:35 (24,997)
Billimore, Trevor 4:50:35 (20,811)
Billingham, Stuart 4:32:52 (17,289)
Billings, Peter 4:30:42 (16,786)
Billington, Gary 3:42:57 (6,294)
Bills, David 4:25:27 (15,602)
Bills, Robert 4:41:05 (18,992)
Billups, Darren 4:08:04 (11,781)
Bilsborough, Brian 3:11:41 (1,886)
Bilton, Darran 2:28:10 (56)
Bindert, Darren 3:46:15 (6,905)
Bindon, Mark 5:40:39 (27,243)
Binesh, Shervin 4:17:23 (13,745)
Bing, Steven 4:16:20 (13,529)
Bingham, Charles 4:47:29 (20,255)
Bingham, Graham 4:03:53 (10,859)
Bingham, Hugh 2:58:28 (848)
Bingham, John 5:42:20 (27,360)
Bingham, Nicholas 3:00:35 (1,055)
Bingham, Roger 5:11:16 (24,250)
Bingham, Stuart 3:28:06 (3,826)
Bingley, Kenneth 3:47:50 (7,218)
Binkhorst, Paul 2:56:04 (687)
Binks, Richard 4:27:23 (16,036)
Binmore, Nigel 4:21:44 (14,741)
Binnendijk, Andrew 3:55:57 (8,906)
Binney, Keith 4:20:28 (14,468)
Binney, Mark 4:20:11 (14,405)
Binning, Robert 5:35:05 (26,812)
Binns, Charles 4:58:05 (22,312)
Binns, Mark 5:08:27 (23,840)
Birch, Alexander 4:07:09 (11,579)
Birch, Brendan 5:32:20 (26,552)

Birch, Chris 5:24:02 (25,793)
Birch, David 2:58:20 (838)
Birch, Gary 5:16:36 (25,003)
Birch, John 3:11:28 (1,864)
Birch, Keith 4:19:27 (14,241)
Birch, Simon 3:28:22 (3,885)
Birch, Thomas 4:36:33 (18,032)
Birchall, Martin 3:35:52 (5,047)
Birchall, Michael 4:59:23 (22,508)
Birchall, Steven 4:49:34 (20,629)
Bircham, Robin 4:26:50 (15,916)
Bird, Alan 4:19:07 (14,150)
Bird, Andrew 3:23:02 (3,118)
Bird, Chris 4:18:43 (14,056)
Bird, Colin 6:59:57 (29,942)
Bird, Danny 2:56:05 (689)
Bird, Dave 3:49:29 (7,574)
Bird, James 6:05:41 (28,673)
Bird, John 4:41:13 (19,015)
Bird, Jonathan 3:55:24 (8,781)
Bird, Mark 3:15:15 (2,249)
Bird, Nicholas 4:44:51 (19,743)
Bird, Philip 3:53:20 (8,344)
Bird, Richard 3:47:33 (7,154)
Bird, Robert 5:14:12 (24,655)
Bird, Stephen 3:20:56 (2,881)
Birditt, Julian 5:16:56 (25,040)
Birds, Steven 5:14:36 (24,727)
Birka, Hans 3:19:43 (2,730)
Birkett, Stephen 4:08:17 (11,820)
Birkin, Adrian 5:56:32 (28,245)
Birkman, Peter 5:17:02 (25,054)
Birks, Alan 4:39:54 (18,769)
Birks, Peter 4:00:32 (10,166)
Birocco, Alberto 4:14:44 (13,185)
Birrell, Stuart 3:33:21 (4,667)
Birt, Dean 3:47:39 (7,179)
Birtchnell, Peter 5:43:28 (27,437)
Bisatt, Alistair 3:57:59 (9,486)
Biscomb, Geoffrey 3:06:25 (1,453)
Bishop, Anthony 3:05:43 (1,403)
Bishop, Darren 3:23:47 (3,208)
Bishop, David 4:11:09 (12,428)
Bishop, David 4:20:09 (14,397)
Bishop, Geoff 4:27:25 (16,040)
Bishop, Grant 5:06:22 (23,529)
Bishop, Jonathan 3:33:41 (4,713)
Bishop, Keith 5:10:21 (24,122)
Bishop, Mark 4:12:54 (12,809)
Bishop, Mark 5:42:23 (27,364)
Bishop, Martin 3:27:06 (3,638)
Bishop, Murray 4:03:37 (10,805)
Bishop, Nicholas 3:12:13 (1,934)
Bishop, Richard 3:44:12 (6,525)
Bishop, Stephen 4:31:17 (16,927)
Bishop, Steve 4:26:47 (15,906)
Bishop, Steve 4:47:03 (20,173)
Bishop, Timothy 3:05:10 (1,364)
Bisley, William 5:01:07 (22,752)
Biss, Andrew 2:43:21 (246)
Bissell, Peter 3:21:31 (2,951)
Bisset, Robert 6:07:54 (28,757)
Bissett, Leigh 3:51:52 (8,043)
Bissett, Richard 4:56:57 (22,137)
Bittles, Kevin 5:30:58 (26,449)
Bizby, Alun 5:23:27 (25,737)
Bizby, David 5:06:21 (23,526)
Bizio, Marcello 3:32:27 (4,527)
Bjelland, Paal 3:37:09 (5,275)
Bjoersvik, Roald Jan 3:47:19 (7,090)
Black, Alistair 2:49:57 (425)
Black, Alistair 4:04:35 (11,017)
Black, Ben 3:10:11 (1,757)
Black, Daniel 4:45:46 (19,896)
Black, Ian 4:04:04 (10,897)
Black, Richard 5:06:20 (23,525)
Black, Stephen 4:42:47 (19,326)
Black, William 3:21:03 (2,894)
Blackburn, David 5:16:07 (24,940)
Blackburn, Jon 4:54:21 (21,568)
Blackburn, William 5:03:33 (23,066)
Blacker, Anthony 4:58:57 (22,451)
Blackford, Colin 3:26:56 (3,615)
Blackford, Mel 4:31:10 (16,893)
Blackford, Robert 4:52:17 (21,153)
Blackledge, John 2:57:20 (768)
Blackledge, Simon 3:27:49 (3,767)
Blackman, Clive 3:20:53 (2,875)
Blackman, David 4:43:42 (19,539)
Blackman, Matt 3:04:38 (1,325)
Blackmoor, Stuart 4:02:27 (10,561)
Blackmore, Darren 4:31:35 (17,003)
Blackmore, Michael 3:50:02 (7,694)
Blackmore, Simon 3:52:23 (8,148)
Blackmore, Steven 4:29:53 (16,654)
Blackshaw, Phillip 3:56:50 (9,142)
Blackwell, Graham 4:10:31 (12,278)
Blackwell, John 3:51:34 (7,983)
Blackwell, Neil 4:59:54 (22,600)
Blackwell, Nicholas 3:39:35 (5,690)
Blackwell, Robert 5:22:27 (25,644)
Blacoe, Mathew 2:58:12 (820)
Blades, Richard 3:39:44 (5,719)
Blaikley, Alex 4:37:59 (18,365)
Blainey, Laurence 4:21:48 (14,761)
Blair, Bradley 6:13:30 (28,973)
Blair, Jim 4:45:48 (19,902)
Blair, John 3:56:35 (9,074)
Blair, Murray 3:49:03 (7,475)
Blais, Donald 4:42:32 (19,280)
Blake, Alan 4:10:06 (12,179)
Blake, Jem 5:35:58 (26,875)
Blake, John 5:56:26 (28,238)
Blake, Justin 4:05:47 (11,293)
Blake, Kevin 4:25:51 (15,688)
Blake, Philip 4:52:56 (21,299)
Blake, Viv 6:08:47 (28,802)
Blakeburn, Colin 4:11:59 (12,606)
Blakemore, Simon 5:03:01 (23,008)
Blakeney Edwards, Julian 4:10:46 (12,327)
Blakesbrough, Ian 4:10:44 (12,318)
Blakey, Brian 4:12:30 (12,740)
Blakey, Damon 4:41:09 (19,004)
Blakey, Dominic 4:40:45 (18,931)
Blamires, Robert 3:28:05 (3,816)
Blanc, Gilles 4:15:02 (13,277)
Blanchard, Anthony 3:44:31 (6,580)
Blanchfield, Phillip 2:50:04 (430)
Bland, Alan 4:22:02 (14,822)
Bland, Andrew 5:02:05 (22,887)
Bland, Graham 6:07:30 (28,745)
Bland, Philip 5:01:12 (22,768)
Bland, Steven 5:38:25 (27,046)
Blandford, Andrew 4:25:01 (15,514)
Blaney, Geoffrey 3:13:12 (2,026)
Blaney, Stephen 6:00:38 (28,436)
Blank, Tony 4:47:49 (20,310)
Blann, Andrew 5:48:09 (27,787)
Blanshard, Roger 5:06:14 (23,508)
Blantz, Andrew 4:54:58 (21,721)
Blas, Navarrete 2:52:17 (524)
Blatchford, Tony 4:48:03 (20,359)
Blaylock, Stuart 5:36:28 (26,914)
Blazier, Darren 2:56:08 (695)
Bleakney, David 5:25:06 (25,895)
Bleckwehl, Foachim 3:37:07 (5,268)
Blencowe, Rupert 5:05:20 (23,348)
Blenkowski, Steve 3:39:36 (5,693)
Blewett, Piers 4:51:13 (20,926)
Bligh, Jerry 5:32:19 (26,550)
Blignaut, J Renier 3:57:24 (9,289)
Bliss, Alastair 3:23:25 (3,162)
Blissett, Paul 5:10:16 (24,115)
Blissett, Stephen 4:53:01 (21,318)
Bloch, Graeme 4:13:08 (12,845)
Bloch, Norbert 3:57:54 (9,462)
Blocher, Gerhard 4:11:46 (12,562)
Bloess, Ulrich 5:58:14 (28,336)
Blofield, David 4:31:55 (17,095)
Blok, Jem 4:23:58 (15,286)
Blomfield, Alex 3:48:57 (7,451)
Blondel, Graham 3:36:23 (5,134)
Blondiaux, André 4:40:29 (18,872)
Bloomfield, Clive 6:41:15 (29,666)
Bloomfield, Colin 3:44:20 (6,551)
Bloomfield, Ian 4:21:58 (14,802)
Bloomfield, Martin 4:16:52 (13,642)
Bloomfield, Stephen 3:59:50 (10,005)
Bloor, Kenneth 3:25:00 (3,380)
Blower, Damien 4:10:46 (12,327)
Blower, David 4:30:48 (16,806)
Blowers, Peter 4:52:57 (21,306)
Blowing, Michael 4:25:05 (15,528)
Blundell, Rodger 3:28:27 (3,898)
Blunden, Keith 4:23:00 (15,063)
Blunden, Martin 4:07:27 (11,655)
Blunt, Lee 4:52:15 (21,142)
Blyth, Andrew 2:38:00 (136)
Blyth, Anthony 5:53:36 (28,097)
Blythe, Terence 3:40:59 (5,952)
Boa, Phil 5:43:45 (27,454)
Board, Andrew 4:50:54 (20,861)
Board, Kevin 4:51:06 (20,908)
Boardley, Ian 3:10:51 (1,823)
Boardman, Keith 2:58:12 (820)
Boardman, Mark 4:55:21 (21,831)
Boardman, Stephen 5:30:32 (26,415)
Bobbin, Anthony 3:37:27 (5,327)
Bober, Richard 3:07:17 (1,527)
Bocchi, Fabrizio 3:55:35 (8,814)
Bocres, Abib 5:31:33 (26,491)
Bodard, George 3:21:29 (2,944)
Boddy, Clifford 3:33:50 (4,732)
Boddy, Clifford 5:28:55 (26,284)
Boden, Daniel 3:44:46 (6,632)
Boden, David 3:56:28 (9,046)
Boden, Kevin 4:04:31 (10,996)
Boden, Marc 4:53:54 (21,495)
Boden, Tony 4:41:44 (19,108)
Bodenmuller, Frank 3:58:07 (9,519)
Bodini, Guido 4:35:03 (17,723)
Bodnar, Zygmunt 4:22:09 (14,845)
Boehm, Stephan 4:48:56 (20,512)
Boehnue, Frank 4:24:43 (15,443)
Boen, Ges 4:56:26 (22,057)
Bogdanovski, Alex 5:44:08 (27,487)
Boggan, Ian 4:41:13 (19,015)
Boggeri, Andreino 3:41:58 (6,118)
Bogle, Martin 4:37:13 (18,175)
Boisset, Christophe 3:42:16 (6,174)
Boissiere, Bruce 4:52:09 (21,124)
Bojanczyk, Tadeusz 6:11:56 (28,923)
Bol, Michael 4:10:05 (12,177)
Bolam, Jeremy 3:03:04 (1,217)
Bolbery, Chris 5:17:02 (25,054)
Boldick, Steve 5:12:08 (24,368)
Bole, Robert 2:58:37 (873)
Bolland, Michael 4:44:08 (19,605)
Bolland, Terry 3:02:10 (1,167)
Bolliger, Adolf 6:01:37 (28,484)
Bolster, Eric 5:28:37 (26,243)
Bolster, John 4:55:37 (21,928)
Bolt, Nigel 3:18:33 (2,602)
Bolton, Anthony 3:28:49 (3,965)
Bolton, Daniel 4:19:04 (14,136)
Bolton, David 5:13:00 (24,500)
Bolton, Ian 4:43:32 (19,504)
Bolton, James 5:31:11 (26,469)
Bolton, Mark 6:01:28 (28,477)
Bolton, Matthew 6:01:28 (28,477)
Bolton, Peter 3:51:22 (7,940)
Bolton, Wayne 3:40:47 (5,908)
Bom, Lars 3:20:50 (2,868)
Bonaccolta, Carmelo 5:12:10 (24,372)
Bonard, Mark 3:57:50 (9,440)
Bonato, Marco 4:28:43 (16,362)
Bonaventura, Giorgio 4:14:59 (13,260)
Bonaventura, Roberto 4:22:48 (15,008)
Bond, Andy 3:31:21 (4,378)
Bond, Darren 3:23:43 (3,202)
Bond, Frank 3:45:02 (6,693)
Bond, Graham 4:02:22 (10,544)
Bond, Jason 3:39:23 (5,645)
Bond, John 3:48:49 (7,426)
Bond, Michael 3:41:19 (6,013)
Bond, Peter 4:45:07 (19,789)
Bondergaard, Mads 3:15:57 (2,317)
Bondy, Michael 4:55:03 (21,749)
Bone, Andrew 3:51:50 (8,035)

Bone, Douglas 3:55:57 (8,906)
Bone, Garry 4:48:58 (20,521)
Bone, Peter 5:09:01 (23,944)
Bonet, Patrick 4:55:42 (21,947)
Bonetti, Benjamin 4:24:59 (15,501)
Bonfield, Nick 3:06:39 (1,474)
Bonfield, Richard 5:20:56 (25,458)
Bonmati-Molina, Rafael 3:02:16 (1,171)
Bonner, Andrew 4:13:16 (12,866)
Bonner, David 5:24:04 (25,798)
Bonner, Gary 3:08:07 (1,598)
Bonner, Jason 4:05:08 (11,145)
Bonner, Peter 4:16:31 (13,577)
Bonnet, Serge 3:52:34 (8,184)
Bonnett, Glenn 3:32:17 (4,504)
Bonney, Keith 5:02:54 (22,993)
Bonnici, Timothy 3:56:29 (9,050)
Bonthron, Barney 4:14:51 (13,222)
Bonthron, Marc 3:55:19 (8,763)
Bonthrone, Steven 3:53:46 (8,436)
Bontoft, Alan 2:53:33 (562)
Bonye, Matthew 4:17:33 (13,783)
Booker, Colin 7:56:01 (30,200)
Boole, Barry 3:07:42 (1,566)
Boomer, Andrew 4:46:01 (19,941)
Boon, Gary 3:04:14 (1,297)
Boon, Jeremy 4:40:43 (18,927)
Boon, Richard 3:15:25 (2,262)
Boon, Robert 2:54:59 (628)
Boorkman, Lars 5:59:28 (28,392)
Boorman, William 5:58:05 (28,324)
Boosey, Trevor 4:38:18 (18,452)
Boot, David 2:48:54 (388)
Booter, Joel 5:46:22 (27,651)
Booth, Adrian 4:28:58 (16,414)
Booth, Adrian 4:53:15 (21,361)
Booth, Andrew 3:49:12 (7,498)
Booth, David 4:09:06 (12,004)
Booth, Douglas 4:35:34 (17,829)
Booth, Gary 3:41:00 (5,956)
Booth, Gordon 4:28:55 (16,404)
Booth, Graham 3:54:19 (8,538)
Booth, Graham 5:03:33 (23,066)
Booth, James 4:08:01 (11,768)
Booth, John 3:33:19 (4,664)
Booth, John 4:15:57 (13,453)
Booth, Joseph 4:24:29 (15,393)
Booth, Michael 4:33:40 (17,470)
Booth, Nicholas 3:55:15 (8,751)
Booth, Paul 3:44:35 (6,594)
Booth, Roger 2:54:41 (619)
Booth, Rupert 5:48:42 (27,828)
Booth, Simon 3:29:45 (4,129)
Booth, Stephen 4:34:42 (17,658)
Booth, Terence 4:17:23 (13,745)
Booth, Vincent 2:48:57 (391)
Booth, William 3:57:11 (9,219)
Boothman, David 4:25:34 (15,632)
Boothroyd, Nigel 5:32:25 (26,567)
Bootle, Richard 5:09:15 (23,977)
Booton, Gary 3:38:31 (5,484)
Booty, Martin 3:40:54 (5,926)
Borch, Michael 4:29:07 (16,453)
Boren, Laurent 4:19:44 (14,302)
Borer, Stephen 4:53:03 (21,325)
Borgman, Paul 4:26:13 (15,780)
Borgund, Ole Jan 4:24:35 (15,416)
Borie, Didier 3:12:02 (1,917)
Borland, John 4:01:21 (10,357)
Borland, Kelvin 3:01:36 (1,122)
Borland, Mark 4:20:07 (14,390)
Borley, David 4:04:10 (10,918)
Borley, David 4:33:36 (17,455)
Bornemissza, Zoltan 3:54:35 (8,610)
Borrell, David 3:45:37 (6,769)
Borst, Pieter 3:54:24 (8,562)
Borstelmann, Jens 4:09:32 (12,080)
Borthwick, Robert 3:51:55 (8,054)
Bory, George 4:37:35 (18,276)
Bos, Fabrice 3:17:48 (2,512)
Bos, Henk 5:35:17 (26,826)
Bosac, Creana 4:19:13 (14,165)
Bosc, Alain 3:57:32 (9,338)
Bosc, Arnaud 3:54:40 (8,624)
Bosc, Roger 3:10:39 (1,805)
Bosch, Ulf 2:55:57 (677)
Bosco, Alessandro 4:05:31 (11,220)
Boshoff, Kevin 4:08:52 (11,949)
Bosker, Maarten 5:01:54 (22,854)
Bossant, Daniel 3:22:45 (3,078)
Bosson, Paul 2:48:46 (384)
Bosson, Peter 3:31:43 (4,425)
Bostock, Colin 3:40:34 (5,878)
Boswall, Ian 4:12:02 (12,620)
Boswell, Guy 4:07:03 (11,564)
Boswell, Stuart 3:13:44 (2,080)
Bosworth, Jim 3:55:53 (8,889)
Bosworth, Mark 3:31:48 (4,438)
Botes, Riaan 4:34:47 (17,672)
Botfield, Glyn 4:17:43 (13,818)
Botha, Dieter 4:23:59 (15,291)
Botha, Guy 5:10:17 (24,117)
Botha, Theunis 3:21:47 (2,971)
Botham, Andrew 3:57:15 (9,241)
Bothe, Joerg 4:00:47 (10,238)
Bott, Charles 3:43:02 (6,312)
Bott, Simon 4:05:28 (11,202)
Botterill, Adrian 4:09:44 (12,112)
Bottle, Simon 3:18:05 (2,544)
Bottomley, Alan 3:12:50 (1,989)
Bottoms, Dave 4:20:30 (14,478)
Bottoms, Edward 4:51:46 (21,048)
Boucard, Cervais 3:39:37 (5,696)
Bouche, Jean Marc 3:58:25 (9,588)
Boudon, Thierry 3:52:08 (8,104)
Boudry, Rik 4:02:29 (10,570)
Boughen, Kevin 4:49:40 (20,645)
Boughton, Brian 5:09:04 (23,951)
Boughton, Nick 4:14:06 (13,056)
Boughton, Stephen 4:01:09 (10,311)
Bould, Paul 4:15:51 (13,434)
Bould, Philip 3:31:40 (4,418)
Boulding, Simon 4:43:18 (19,451)
Bouloing, Paul 3:43:58 (6,483)
Boulter, Adam 4:08:46 (11,928)
Boulter, Geoffrey 4:20:45 (14,533)
Boulter, Kevin 3:19:38 (2,722)
Boulton, Christopher 4:46:22 (20,028)
Boulton, Jude 3:38:29 (5,478)
Boulton, Simon 5:26:41 (26,059)
Bouman, Raymond 3:09:43 (1,732)
Boundy, Geoffrey 4:12:09 (12,658)
Bourez, Jean Marc 3:37:49 (5,383)
Bourgeais, Denis 3:20:34 (2,830)
Bourgeais, Loic 3:12:30 (1,959)
Bourgeois, Mark 3:11:08 (1,847)
Bourgogne, Pascal 3:50:42 (7,808)
Bourgoin, Sebastien 3:32:42 (4,560)
Bourhill, Joseph 3:39:47 (5,735)
Bourne, Laurence 5:56:33 (28,247)
Bourne, William 4:37:34 (18,270)
Bourne Lange, Robert 5:31:01 (26,455)
Bournes, Graham 4:59:23 (22,508)
Bournes, Philip 4:59:23 (22,508)
Bourquin, Marc 3:11:55 (1,908)
Boury, Thierry 4:52:16 (21,148)
Boutcher, Kelly 5:05:26 (23,369)
Boutin, Thierry 4:33:30 (17,419)
Bouziat, Jean François 3:44:14 (6,529)
Bowater, Andrew 3:44:49 (6,643)
Bowd, Ryan 2:59:07 (943)
Bowden, Bernard 4:15:26 (13,356)
Bowden, Keir 5:15:10 (24,823)
Bowden, Michael 3:41:40 (6,069)
Bowden, Rodney 3:39:56 (5,768)
Bowden, Trevor 3:56:04 (8,943)
Bowden, William 4:17:52 (13,846)
Bowder, Jonathan 4:19:45 (14,305)
Bowdery, Roy 3:27:43 (3,748)
Bowe, Anthony 3:34:55 (4,892)
Bowe, Michael 4:06:00 (11,351)
Bowen, Colin 3:19:25 (2,696)
Bowen, David 3:13:07 (2,013)
Bowen, Jeremy 5:15:46 (24,901)
Bowen, Nicholas 4:37:00 (18,131)
Bowen, Richard 4:31:39 (17,023)
Bowen, Simon 3:27:35 (3,721)
Bowen, Spencer 3:52:05 (8,095)
Bower, Andrew 4:00:53 (10,259)
Bower, Brian 3:24:31 (3,312)
Bower, Kevin 4:55:05 (21,757)
Bower, Matthew 3:39:41 (5,709)
Bower, Robert 4:03:01 (10,667)
Bowerman, Andy 3:58:57 (9,738)
Bowers, Andrew 4:24:10 (15,324)
Bowers, John 5:25:31 (25,941)
Bowers, Mark 4:24:56 (15,487)
Bowers, Xavier 3:39:53 (5,754)
Bowgen, Leslie 3:33:03 (4,611)
Bowie, Bill 4:52:22 (21,175)
Bowker, Peter 3:37:48 (5,378)
Bowler, Jonathan 3:36:52 (5,220)
Bowler, Robin 4:37:26 (18,233)
Bowler, William 3:51:49 (8,031)
Bowles, Daniel 4:20:25 (14,453)
Bowles, Guy 3:53:30 (8,375)
Bowles, John 4:01:40 (10,426)
Bowles, Richard 6:37:25 (29,576)
Bowling, Christopher 3:43:20 (6,369)
Bowlzer, Nicholas 3:47:49 (7,213)
Bowman, Andrew 3:48:31 (7,365)
Bowman, David 3:52:55 (8,252)
Bowman, Henry 4:57:05 (22,152)
Bowman, Scott 5:26:55 (26,079)
Bowman, Stuart 4:48:13 (20,388)
Bowyer, Darren 5:39:34 (27,137)
Bowyer, Gary 3:59:44 (9,984)
Bowyer, Jeff 5:03:40 (23,077)
Bowyer, Malcolm 3:12:36 (1,967)
Bowyer, Peter 5:42:54 (27,403)
Bowyer, Richard 3:33:55 (4,742)
Box, James 3:29:51 (4,142)
Box, Matthew 3:16:26 (2,355)
Box, Michael 4:30:55 (16,832)
Box, Nicholas 4:41:41 (19,101)
Boxall, Dennis 3:30:16 (4,209)
Boxall, Gordon 3:49:25 (7,555)
Boxall, John 5:17:28 (25,103)
Boyce, Daniel 4:26:51 (15,920)
Boyce, David 2:53:29 (558)
Boyce, Martin 3:32:58 (4,595)
Boyd, Anthony 4:15:00 (13,268)
Boyd, David 4:19:04 (14,136)
Boyd, Eric 5:17:19 (25,086)
Boyd, Matthew 5:01:49 (22,842)
Boyd, Peter 4:00:31 (10,158)
Boyd, Reuther 3:31:11 (4,354)
Boyd Phillips, James 4:38:57 (18,594)
Boyden, Michael 4:01:54 (10,463)
Boyer, John 6:47:53 (29,776)
Boyle, Alistair 3:59:34 (9,940)
Boyle, Andrew 4:44:43 (19,720)
Boyle, Colin 3:53:27 (8,366)
Boyle, Jim 5:16:35 (24,997)
Boyle, John 5:33:39 (26,659)
Boyles, Tom 3:50:54 (7,847)
Bozzato, Mirko 3:44:49 (6,643)
Brace, Gareth 3:55:32 (8,805)
Bracey, James 3:28:08 (3,830)
Bracher, Anthony 5:55:50 (28,204)
Bracher, Mark 4:55:11 (21,778)
Brackburn, Robert 7:31:21 (30,142)
Bracken, Peter 3:34:31 (4,839)
Brackenbury, Robert 4:46:43 (20,095)
Bradburn, Edward 4:27:49 (16,154)
Bradbury, David 5:26:37 (26,052)
Bradbury, Richard 3:07:17 (1,527)
Bradbury, Richard 5:47:16 (27,716)
Bradbury, Rod 4:54:30 (21,594)
Bradbury, Simon 4:11:06 (12,416)
Bradbury, Thomas 4:34:51 (17,685)
Bradford, Alec 6:35:05 (29,523)
Bradford, Antony 2:41:14 (197)
Bradford, James 5:05:47 (23,429)
Bradford, Jon 4:55:10 (21,772)
Bradford, Leigh 4:05:42 (11,268)
Bradford, Paul 4:09:17 (12,039)
Bradish, Christopher 3:38:03 (5,406)
Bradley, Barrington 3:56:11 (8,963)

Bradley, David	5:01:36 (22,816)	
Bradley, Eamon	3:44:05 (6,505)	
Bradley, Garry	4:55:23 (21,842)	
Bradley, Graham	3:26:39 (3,578)	
Bradley, Harvey	3:33:19 (4,664)	
Bradley, Lawrence	7:29:02 (30,132)	
Bradley, Mike	5:11:21 (24,262)	
Bradley, Nigel	6:55:18 (29,885)	
Bradley, Paul	5:10:51 (24,191)	
Bradley, Simon	3:21:03 (2,894)	
Bradley Goad, Simon	5:19:51 (25,349)	
Bradley-Jones, Luke	5:08:22 (23,824)	
Bradnam, Colin	4:07:43 (11,703)	
Bradnam, Stephen	4:20:42 (14,519)	
Bradshaw, Eric	3:45:37 (6,769)	
Bradshaw, James	4:50:06 (20,737)	
Bradshaw, Matthew	4:11:26 (12,491)	
Bradshaw, Neil	3:56:43 (9,109)	
Bradshaw, Nicholas	4:36:27 (18,007)	
Brady, Peter	4:19:32 (14,264)	
Brady, Peter	4:25:29 (15,613)	
Brady, Stephen	5:27:12 (26,102)	
Bragg, Thomas	4:03:46 (10,836)	
Braggins, Nigel	8:30:46 (30,245)	
Bragoli, Mark	4:43:41 (19,535)	
Braham, Rollo	3:06:55 (1,497)	
Braidwood, Billy	3:50:08 (7,712)	
Braidwood, Peter	4:21:13 (14,631)	
Brailsford, Dale	3:02:21 (1,178)	
Brain, David	4:01:10 (10,314)	
Brain, John	3:42:53 (6,283)	
Brainerd, Derrick	5:34:17 (26,732)	
Braithwaite, Alistair	4:21:38 (14,720)	
Braithwaite, Philip	5:18:25 (25,200)	
Braker, Robert	4:17:32 (13,780)	
Brakewell, Harry	5:07:09 (23,641)	
Braley, Mark	3:55:39 (8,832)	
Bramall, Cameron	3:20:38 (2,840)	
Bramley, Iain	5:46:55 (27,693)	
Bramley, Ian	4:14:54 (13,236)	
Bramley, James	5:09:42 (24,043)	
Bramley, Nigel	4:59:26 (22,519)	
Bramtjes, Ahore	5:15:51 (24,917)	
Bramwell, Peter	4:04:55 (11,100)	
Branch, Andrew	4:18:11 (13,914)	
Brand, Edward	4:10:42 (12,311)	
Brand, Neal	4:22:54 (15,035)	
Brand, Nicholas	4:33:04 (17,322)	
Brand, Philip	4:39:05 (18,619)	
Brandon, Steven	3:53:19 (8,338)	
Brandt, David	4:27:00 (15,964)	
Brannan, Bernard	3:19:12 (2,673)	
Brannan, Damian	3:34:03 (4,763)	
Brannan, John	3:16:18 (2,341)	
Brannelly, John	3:27:53 (3,785)	
Brannigan, Malachy	4:22:14 (14,870)	
Brannigan, Paul	2:50:24 (443)	
Brannigan, William	3:36:39 (5,181)	
Brannon, Guy	4:28:25 (16,289)	
Branscombe, Richard	3:25:43 (3,470)	
Bransford, Michael	4:19:21 (14,209)	
Brant, Barry	4:48:56 (20,512)	
Brassington, John	4:22:54 (15,035)	
Bratt, Michael	4:40:51 (18,946)	
Bratteli, Einar	4:25:09 (15,543)	
Braund, Michael	5:51:41 (27,995)	
Bravery, Andrew	4:13:32 (12,939)	
Bray, Francis	3:14:28 (2,164)	
Bray, Keith	4:02:55 (10,649)	
Bray, Kevin	2:58:07 (817)	
Bray, Simon	4:47:51 (20,316)	
Bray, Stephen	6:02:40 (28,526)	
Braybrook, Richard	4:12:17 (12,687)	
Brayford, Brian	4:26:33 (15,856)	
Brayshaw, Nicholas	4:39:06 (18,622)	
Brazendale, David	4:34:13 (17,573)	
Breaa, Michael	3:37:00 (5,246)	
Breaden, Andrew	4:29:51 (16,642)	
Bream, Clive	5:55:22 (28,174)	
Bream, James	4:53:58 (21,505)	
Brean, Vaughan	5:21:08 (25,482)	
Brearley-Smith, Justin	4:48:28 (20,435)	
Brech, Zachary	4:20:40 (14,513)	
Breckell, Barrie	4:14:30 (13,127)	
Breda, Errol	4:54:47 (21,672)	
Breen, Francis	3:57:46 (9,416)	
Breen, Graham	2:43:36 (248)	
Breen, Martin	4:03:14 (10,707)	
Breese, Allan	3:18:59 (2,654)	
Breitsprecher, Hermy	4:18:43 (14,056)	
Bremner, Andrew	4:12:15 (12,679)	
Bremner, David	5:57:00 (28,271)	
Bremner, Sean	3:35:31 (4,988)	
Brenchley, Michael	4:32:55 (17,295)	
Brennan, David	4:31:14 (16,913)	
Brennan, Joseph	4:35:58 (17,925)	
Brennan, Kevin	2:53:44 (572)	
Brennan, Mark	4:53:51 (21,489)	
Brennan, Paul	4:49:16 (20,575)	
Brennan, Peter	4:14:11 (13,072)	
Brennan, Peter	4:43:09 (19,416)	
Brennan, Richard	5:09:20 (23,986)	
Brennand, Robin	5:33:04 (26,616)	
Brennard, Martin	5:34:37 (26,765)	
Brent, Peter	4:38:05 (18,398)	
Brent, Robert	5:44:24 (27,500)	
Breown, Terry	3:13:05 (2,009)	
Bressington, Darrell	4:11:30 (12,501)	
Bretherton, Edward	4:07:16 (11,604)	
Bretherton, Michael	4:12:09 (12,658)	
Breton, Edward	3:19:13 (2,676)	
Brett, Christopher	4:23:52 (15,266)	
Brett, Dennis	4:40:12 (18,811)	
Brett, Eric	3:53:35 (8,399)	
Brett, Jeremy	4:11:43 (12,552)	
Brett, Matthew	4:54:09 (21,542)	
Brett, Stephen	3:09:13 (1,687)	
Brettell, Mike	4:55:26 (21,863)	
Brettkelly, Damian	4:41:47 (19,120)	
Brewer, Charles	4:14:47 (13,205)	
Brewer, Derrick	6:53:29 (29,857)	
Brewer, Gavin	5:49:01 (27,843)	
Brewer, Graham	4:37:55 (18,350)	
Brewer, Jeremy	3:55:47 (8,867)	
Brewer, John	4:32:35 (17,224)	
Brewis, Jacques	4:22:28 (14,919)	
Brewster, Graham	5:34:05 (26,710)	
Brewster, Matthew	5:16:09 (24,943)	
Brewster, Nicholas	3:58:03 (9,501)	
Brewster, Terry	6:00:38 (28,436)	
Breytenbach, Johann	4:05:30 (11,213)	
Briant, Pierre	3:54:58 (8,696)	
Briars, Michael	4:53:45 (21,463)	
Bribben, Michael	4:09:59 (12,163)	
Bric, Muiris	3:32:27 (4,527)	
Bricart, Laurent	3:50:50 (7,831)	
Brickwood, James	5:45:48 (27,617)	
Brickwood, Stephen	4:08:40 (11,908)	
Bridge, Adrian	3:44:51 (6,650)	
Bridge, Kevin	3:09:52 (1,739)	
Bridge, Simon	3:59:23 (9,876)	
Bridge, Stephen	3:16:13 (2,333)	
Bridgeman, Matt	4:27:08 (16,000)	
Bridger, Terry	4:11:28 (12,495)	
Bridges, Alex	5:04:50 (23,272)	
Bridges, Anthony	3:17:20 (2,465)	
Bridges, Bob	4:51:59 (21,088)	
Bridges, George	5:37:02 (26,949)	
Bridges, Keith	5:15:43 (24,894)	
Bridges, Mark	5:50:43 (27,937)	
Bridges, Russell	2:50:10 (435)	
Bridges, Terry	3:40:41 (5,894)	
Bridgestock, Bruce	2:58:43 (894)	
Bridgwagter, Christopher	4:53:53 (21,492)	
Bridle, Trevor	4:06:05 (11,361)	
Briens, Jean Marc	4:22:34 (14,943)	
Briens, Peter	4:03:16 (10,713)	
Brier, Anthony	4:41:52 (19,131)	
Brier, Christopher	4:05:57 (11,339)	
Briere, Thierry	3:58:22 (9,580)	
Brierley, Andrew	3:34:26 (4,824)	
Brierley, Matthew	4:36:24 (17,998)	
Brierley, Peter	4:07:27 (11,655)	
Brierley, Trevor	4:36:26 (18,003)	
Brierly, William	5:43:01 (27,410)	
Briffa, John	3:57:40 (9,387)	
Briffett, Philip	4:57:25 (22,205)	
Brigdale, Sherman	5:38:54 (27,080)	
Briggs, Chris	4:46:46 (20,109)	
Briggs, Danny	5:46:06 (27,635)	
Briggs, Edward	3:49:08 (7,485)	
Briggs, Eric	5:56:44 (28,256)	
Briggs, Francis	7:28:09 (30,126)	
Briggs, Michael	4:42:34 (19,284)	
Brigham, Peter	5:00:05 (22,632)	
Brighetti, Claudio	3:59:58 (10,047)	
Brighouse, John	4:27:42 (16,119)	
Brighouse, Robert	3:53:13 (8,313)	
Bright, Clive	3:24:40 (3,337)	
Bright, Matthew	6:07:07 (28,724)	
Bright, Richard	3:33:40 (4,708)	
Bright, Robert	3:54:32 (8,594)	
Brightley, Leo	3:24:55 (3,366)	
Brightwell, Terry	3:02:45 (1,199)	
Brimble, David	5:38:21 (27,038)	
Brindley, Simon	4:06:03 (11,360)	
Brine, Martin	3:13:17 (2,034)	
Brinkerhoff, Thomas	3:51:41 (8,003)	
Brinkhurst, George	3:36:24 (5,140)	
Brinklow, David	4:38:12 (18,427)	
Briscoe, James	3:24:29 (3,307)	
Briscoe, Mark	4:14:58 (13,254)	
Bristaut, Patrick	3:01:45 (1,134)	
Bristol, Allister	2:39:21 (163)	
Bristow, Donald	4:59:32 (22,530)	
Bristow, Ian	4:22:26 (14,913)	
Bristow, Nicholas	3:09:28 (1,709)	
Bristow, Richard	4:14:09 (13,065)	
Britcher, Daniel	4:01:58 (10,479)	
Britchford, Langley	4:48:48 (20,486)	
Britnell, Darren	3:42:45 (6,262)	
Britt, Andi	3:37:08 (5,272)	
Brittain, David	6:35:01 (29,520)	
Brittain, Lawrence	5:57:18 (28,283)	
Brittain, Scott	2:57:39 (788)	
Britten, Andrew	5:21:19 (25,506)	
Britten, Tony	3:11:33 (1,868)	
Brittleton, Peter	3:20:32 (2,828)	
Britton, Alistair	5:22:25 (25,638)	
Britton, Glen	5:31:40 (26,504)	
Britton, Harold	6:20:53 (29,189)	
Britton, Jonathan	5:30:25 (26,404)	
Britton, Mark	6:20:52 (29,188)	
Britton, Toby	3:44:29 (6,572)	
Broad, Nick	3:58:07 (9,519)	
Broadbent, Paul	5:30:24 (26,401)	
Broadbent, Steven	3:21:30 (2,949)	
Broadfield, Andrew	4:07:48 (11,721)	
Broadfoot, David	3:22:01 (3,003)	
Broadfoot, Keith	3:18:42 (2,619)	
Broadhead, Richard	4:21:36 (14,714)	
Broadhurst, Carl	3:19:51 (2,745)	
Broadhurst, Keith	3:06:28 (1,457)	
Broadhurst, Steven	3:17:36 (2,491)	
Broadway, Andrew	4:16:42 (13,609)	
Broadway, Jeremy	4:22:38 (14,962)	
Broadway, Kevin	4:06:25 (11,435)	
Brocanelli, Giuseppe	4:34:02 (17,541)	
Brock, Daniel	4:54:04 (21,527)	
Brock, David	3:29:25 (4,066)	
Brock, Kevin	4:12:05 (12,640)	
Brockbank, Carl	5:48:37 (27,823)	
Brockbank, Christopher	5:33:54 (26,681)	
Brocken, Alan	4:02:22 (10,544)	
Brocklehurst, Aaron	4:04:54 (11,096)	
Brockway, Andrew	3:11:40 (1,882)	
Brodie, Alexander	3:48:06 (7,287)	
Brodie, James	4:42:14 (19,211)	
Broekhuizen, Richard	5:00:22 (22,652)	
Brogden, Chris	5:04:56 (23,287)	
Brogden, Dale	4:07:20 (11,622)	
Brogden, John	5:28:48 (26,269)	
Brogden, Paul	4:38:32 (18,511)	
Brogden, Richard	5:28:47 (26,267)	
Brokenshire, Terry	5:03:39 (23,075)	
Bromage, Mark	4:46:50 (20,126)	
Bromfield, Tim	4:47:00 (20,163)	
Bromley, Michael	4:30:56 (16,836)	
Bromley, Michael	4:36:34 (18,035)	

Bromley, Nigel 4:00:11 (10,087)
Bromwell, Richard 4:19:51 (14,325)
Bronckaerts, Patrick 3:06:15 (1,438)
Brook, Giles 3:43:54 (6,472)
Brook, Ian 4:40:12 (18,811)
Brook, John 3:54:56 (8,690)
Brook, Matt 5:03:54 (23,114)
Brook, Michael 3:59:13 (9,823)
Brook, Nick 3:53:05 (8,288)
Brook, William 4:42:57 (19,376)
Brooke, Charles 3:13:00 (2,003)
Brooke, Craig 3:17:19 (2,463)
Brooke, David 4:06:54 (11,527)
Brooke, James 5:23:53 (25,779)
Brooker, John 3:17:27 (2,482)
Brooker, Keith 4:40:52 (18,951)
Brooker, Peter 3:57:41 (9,391)
Brooker, Philip 4:12:35 (12,752)
Brookes, Brian 3:41:18 (6,007)
Brookes, David 3:39:59 (5,782)
Brookes, Jonathan 4:01:35 (10,406)
Brookes, Karl 4:58:53 (22,438)
Brookes, Nicholas 3:57:21 (9,273)
Brookes, Nigel 3:17:28 (2,484)
Brookes, Stuart 5:15:47 (24,905)
Brooklyn, David 4:41:22 (19,040)
Brooks, Bryan 5:31:37 (26,498)
Brooks, Chris 5:21:35 (25,532)
Brooks, Duncan 4:50:44 (20,830)
Brooks, Gary 3:50:39 (7,796)
Brooks, Graham 4:22:39 (14,968)
Brooks, Guy 4:39:06 (18,622)
Brooks, Henry 4:29:27 (16,534)
Brooks, John 5:11:16 (24,250)
Brooks, Mark 5:08:41 (23,883)
Brooks, Michael 3:22:34 (3,059)
Brooks, Nigel 4:43:18 (19,451)
Brooks, Paul 4:03:56 (10,871)
Brooks, Paul 4:19:20 (14,202)
Brooks, Paul 4:55:20 (21,824)
Brooks, Peter 3:57:19 (9,262)
Brooks, Phillip 3:37:41 (5,363)
Brooks, Roger 3:53:18 (8,333)
Brooks, Simon 3:55:12 (8,734)
Brooks, Stephen 3:59:05 (9,781)
Brooks, Timothy 4:57:11 (22,171)
Brooksbank, Dale 3:58:33 (9,625)
Broom, Jack 3:35:01 (4,905)
Broom, Michael 4:31:22 (16,947)
Broom, Neil 4:04:40 (11,036)
Broom, Nigel 5:06:22 (23,529)
Broom, Richard 4:05:32 (11,223)
Broom, Shaun 3:47:38 (7,175)
Brooman, David 4:37:23 (18,219)
Broome, George 5:14:06 (24,639)
Broome, Tyrone 4:10:18 (12,226)
Broomfield, Timothy 3:20:42 (2,847)
Brophy, John 3:48:47 (7,420)
Brosnan, Michael 5:10:42 (24,176)
Broster, Carl 4:29:23 (16,516)
Brough, Bob 3:54:07 (8,495)
Brough, Brian 5:44:02 (27,478)
Brough, Christopher 3:31:53 (4,452)
Broughton, Philip 5:15:39 (24,884)
Broughton, Richard 4:39:32 (18,700)
Broughton, Robert 3:57:30 (9,326)
Brouwers, Louis 3:40:27 (5,859)
Brouze, Frederic 3:06:56 (1,499)
Brown, Adrian 4:06:22 (11,422)
Brown, Alan 3:39:21 (5,638)
Brown, Alan 4:03:17 (10,718)
Brown, Alan 4:22:59 (15,059)
Brown, Alan 4:33:20 (17,378)
Brown, Alastair 3:48:55 (7,442)
Brown, Albert 7:16:01 (30,051)
Brown, André 4:33:30 (17,419)
Brown, Andrew 2:43:51 (256)
Brown, Andy 4:08:57 (11,965)
Brown, Anthony 4:32:43 (17,252)
Brown, Arthur 3:37:26 (5,325)
Brown, Bryan 5:35:49 (26,868)
Brown, Carl 3:34:13 (4,791)
Brown, Chris 3:17:47 (2,508)
Brown, Chris 5:09:06 (23,953)
Brown, Christopher 4:25:52 (15,694)
Brown, Christopher 4:39:06 (18,622)
Brown, Colin 4:03:22 (10,740)
Brown, Colin 4:33:37 (17,459)
Brown, Craig 4:26:16 (15,798)
Brown, Daniel 5:05:21 (23,349)
Brown, David 3:52:10 (8,111)
Brown, David 4:47:55 (20,330)
Brown, David 5:00:30 (22,663)
Brown, David 5:55:56 (28,211)
Brown, Dean 4:05:08 (11,145)
Brown, Dennis 3:29:40 (4,115)
Brown, Derek 2:36:47 (113)
Brown, Douglas 3:43:36 (6,415)
Brown, Duncan 4:45:46 (19,896)
Brown, Francis 4:26:04 (15,748)
Brown, Gary 4:11:24 (12,481)
Brown, Gordon 3:41:34 (6,044)
Brown, Gordon 4:46:17 (20,006)
Brown, Graeme 4:35:55 (17,910)
Brown, Graham 3:44:13 (6,527)
Brown, Graham 4:52:54 (21,292)
Brown, Gregor 4:33:27 (17,405)
Brown, Harry 4:52:08 (21,122)
Brown, Hayden 5:41:50 (27,318)
Brown, Henry 2:49:13 (400)
Brown, Howard 4:13:47 (12,995)
Brown, Ian 2:59:17 (961)
Brown, Ian 4:16:07 (13,490)
Brown, James 3:07:13 (1,518)
Brown, James 3:50:52 (7,841)
Brown, James 4:22:34 (14,943)
Brown, James 4:43:41 (19,535)
Brown, James 4:55:24 (21,849)
Brown, James 5:25:53 (25,975)
Brown, Jeffrey 4:16:47 (13,632)
Brown, Jim 4:15:25 (13,350)
Brown, John 3:09:51 (1,737)
Brown, John 3:24:59 (3,375)
Brown, John 4:30:17 (16,728)
Brown, John 4:55:29 (21,885)
Brown, Keith 3:22:02 (3,005)
Brown, Ken 5:22:11 (25,612)
Brown, Kevin 4:03:37 (10,805)
Brown, Mark 3:35:41 (5,016)
Brown, Mark 3:59:37 (9,953)
Brown, Martin 4:14:56 (13,248)
Brown, Matthew 3:28:03 (3,808)
Brown, Maurice 4:53:31 (21,427)
Brown, Michael 3:14:17 (2,144)
Brown, Michael 3:46:10 (6,893)
Brown, Neale 3:29:40 (4,115)
Brown, Neville 3:39:48 (5,739)
Brown, Neville 4:20:40 (14,513)
Brown, Nigel 4:33:32 (17,428)
Brown, Oliver 5:56:23 (28,235)
Brown, Patrick 4:35:23 (17,795)
Brown, Paul 3:44:54 (6,661)
Brown, Paul 4:28:32 (16,321)
Brown, Peter 4:00:43 (10,217)
Brown, Peter 5:07:16 (23,658)
Brown, Peter 5:36:52 (26,936)
Brown, Phil 3:18:43 (2,621)
Brown, Philip 4:31:24 (16,961)
Brown, Ray 4:41:34 (19,077)
Brown, Raymond 5:08:58 (23,935)
Brown, Raymond 3:33:51 (4,735)
Brown, Raymond 5:05:51 (23,439)
Brown, Richard 5:01:45 (22,832)
Brown, Robert 4:38:01 (18,375)
Brown, Robin 3:46:32 (6,956)
Brown, Rod 4:37:45 (18,313)
Brown, Roger 4:22:46 (14,996)
Brown, Sean 3:35:14 (4,939)
Brown, Simon 3:27:25 (3,692)
Brown, Simon 4:05:30 (11,213)
Brown, Stephen 3:42:27 (6,208)
Brown, Stephen 3:52:39 (8,202)
Brown, Stephen 3:55:31 (8,800)
Brown, Stephen 4:13:04 (12,832)
Brown, Stephen 4:53:36 (21,441)
Brown, Stephen 5:07:16 (23,658)
Brown, Stephen 6:03:38 (28,572)
Brown, Steve 4:00:19 (10,109)
Brown, Stuart 3:43:50 (6,460)
Brown, Stuart 4:05:05 (11,133)
Brown, Stuart 4:43:49 (19,561)
Brown, Thomas 4:36:38 (18,048)
Brown, Thomas 4:50:26 (20,793)
Brown, Timothy 3:18:22 (2,585)
Brown, Timothy 4:09:35 (12,088)
Brown, Tom 3:34:29 (4,835)
Brown, Wayne 4:42:50 (19,343)
Brown, William 3:59:00 (9,754)
Brown, William 6:27:46 (29,345)
Browne, Anthony 4:29:20 (16,504)
Browne, Christopher 3:43:40 (6,428)
Browne, Christopher 4:03:49 (10,843)
Browne, James 2:53:31 (561)
Browne, Jeremy 4:55:17 (21,810)
Browne, Mike 4:03:49 (10,843)
Browne, Peter 5:46:02 (27,633)
Browne, Richard 2:39:05 (158)
Browne, Roger 4:52:56 (21,299)
Browne, Steve 4:44:42 (19,718)
Brownhill, Robert 4:19:27 (14,241)
Browning, Colin 3:51:56 (8,060)
Browning, David 5:14:37 (24,730)
Browning, Nick 3:10:47 (1,816)
Browning, Robert 5:28:16 (26,204)
Browning, Roger 4:12:18 (12,693)
Brownjohn, Ian 5:49:23 (27,864)
Brownlie, John 3:49:29 (7,574)
Brownlow, Marcus 4:08:30 (11,871)
Brownstone, Hugh 6:41:58 (29,691)
Broxton, Keith 3:06:49 (1,489)
Bruce, Alasdair 2:54:21 (597)
Bruce, Alex 4:09:08 (12,007)
Bruce, Duncan 4:31:34 (16,996)
Bruce, Nigel 4:03:03 (10,671)
Bruce, Peter 4:29:00 (16,420)
Bruce, Rodney 3:31:00 (4,327)
Brueck, Klaus 4:22:47 (15,000)
Bruetsch, Stefan 3:33:18 (4,660)
Brufladt, Harald 3:21:38 (2,961)
Bruhin, Joseph 4:26:49 (15,913)
Brumby, Richard 3:35:49 (5,035)
Bruna, Margal 3:47:38 (7,175)
Brundle, Paul 3:32:43 (4,561)
Brungies, Colin 5:25:33 (25,943)
Bruni, Sandro 4:46:42 (20,092)
Brunner, Hermann 2:57:22 (774)
Brunning, James 4:12:29 (12,738)
Brunning, Peter 3:55:36 (8,819)
Brunnmeier, Wolfram 3:34:51 (4,884)
Bruno, Frank 4:16:32 (13,581)
Bruno, Yernaux 3:28:04 (3,812)
Brunskill, Michael 2:49:52 (422)
Brunskill, Nicholas 3:20:19 (2,797)
Brunt, David 4:28:14 (16,246)
Brunt, John 3:57:20 (9,267)
Brunt, Steve 2:40:21 (177)
Brunton, Kevin 4:25:51 (15,688)
Bruschi, Massimo 4:02:09 (10,514)
Brustow, Clive 4:35:22 (17,791)
Bruusgaard, Thomas 3:27:55 (3,794)
Bruxner, George 4:17:17 (13,732)
Bryan, Anthony 5:15:09 (24,813)
Bryan, Barry 5:14:49 (24,751)
Bryan, Glenn 5:03:29 (23,062)
Bryan, James 3:33:37 (4,699)
Bryan, John 6:07:18 (28,738)
Bryan, Peter 4:43:35 (19,516)
Bryant, Ben 3:24:40 (3,337)
Bryant, David 4:30:23 (16,741)
Bryant, Dudley 4:22:50 (15,016)
Bryant, Graham 4:47:57 (20,337)
Bryant, Lee 3:08:14 (1,611)
Bryant, Mark 5:34:01 (26,696)
Bryant, Richard 5:17:06 (25,062)
Bryant, Wayne 3:36:27 (5,151)
Bryatn, Michael 4:26:26 (15,828)
Bryce, Greg 3:05:17 (1,371)
Bryer, Daniel 4:09:11 (12,018)
Brynie, Jens Harald 3:55:48 (8,870)

Bryon, David....4:12:44 (12,778)
Bryson, Christopher....4:47:32 (20,273)
Bryson, Martin....4:13:39 (12,971)
Brzeskwinski, Simon....3:59:24 (9,885)
Bucci, Giuseppe....3:36:34 (5,167)
Buchan, Robert....3:26:25 (3,546)
Buchan, Stuart....2:41:31 (205)
Buchan Hepburn, Christopher...4:23:35 (15,201)
Buchanan, Bob....5:49:54 (27,894)
Buchanan, Ian....4:24:32 (15,404)
Buchanan, Ian....4:27:43 (16,125)
Buchanan, Jason....3:56:24 (9,025)
Buchanan, Neil....2:45:28 (308)
Bucher, Roger....5:05:14 (23,327)
Buck, Russell....5:29:08 (26,300)
Bucke, David....4:14:46 (13,202)
Bucke, John....3:44:01 (6,496)
Buckingham, Donald....4:41:23 (19,045)
Buckingham, Ian....3:03:35 (1,252)
Buckingham, James....3:37:21 (5,314)
Buckingham, Pete....4:04:10 (10,918)
Buckingham, Simon....4:44:39 (19,704)
Buckland, Charles....4:26:41 (15,887)
Buckle, Jonathan....5:02:02 (22,880)
Buckler, David....3:07:56 (1,587)
Buckley, Allan....4:08:16 (11,816)
Buckley, Colin....3:23:58 (3,241)
Buckley, Daniel....4:18:14 (13,926)
Buckley, Derek....2:56:07 (692)
Buckley, James....4:36:35 (18,037)
Buckley, Lee....4:18:14 (13,926)
Buckley, Paul....4:18:14 (13,926)
Buckley, Robert....5:22:30 (25,647)
Buckley, Stephen....4:03:51 (10,850)
Buckley, Stephen....4:15:27 (13,358)
Buckley, William....6:02:04 (28,509)
Bucks, Simon....5:11:53 (24,341)
Budano, Carlo....4:37:40 (18,294)
Budd, Graeme....4:59:34 (22,537)
Budd, Ian....4:15:33 (13,377)
Budd, Kevin....4:18:23 (13,982)
Budd, Stephen....5:05:47 (23,429)
Buddin, Timothy....5:39:25 (27,123)
Buehler, Paul Marie....5:23:33 (25,752)
Buender, Marcel....3:59:37 (9,953)
Buergler, Michael....4:26:42 (15,890)
Buessow, Juergen....5:10:53 (24,194)
Bufe, Michael....2:59:56 (1,024)
Buffrey, Gareth....3:52:09 (8,110)
Bufton, Richard....3:28:09 (3,834)
Bugby, Antony....5:22:30 (25,647)
Buick, Craig....3:25:05 (3,387)
Buick, Gary....3:58:56 (9,732)
Buick, James....2:57:45 (794)
Buick, Jason....4:44:09 (19,609)
Bujok, Jan Paul....3:27:29 (3,704)
Buky, Rob....3:53:52 (8,453)
Bulger, David....4:21:52 (14,779)
Bulger, Martin....3:38:35 (5,498)
Bulgin, Duncan....4:39:46 (18,749)
Bull, Andrew....4:41:46 (19,117)
Bull, Colin....5:42:35 (27,387)
Bull, Ian....4:49:29 (20,616)
Bull, John....4:25:41 (15,650)
Bull, John....4:29:30 (16,545)
Bull, Kevin....4:31:27 (16,969)
Bull, Martyn....6:25:15 (29,289)
Bull, Michael....3:53:34 (8,394)
Bull, Nicholas....5:39:54 (27,177)
Bull, Paul....5:29:57 (26,374)
Bull, Roger....4:10:33 (12,284)
Bull, Ross....6:33:01 (29,481)
Bull, Steve....3:29:06 (4,015)
Bull, Timothy....4:37:52 (18,341)
Bullen, Nigel....3:47:23 (7,112)
Bullen, Philip....5:55:25 (28,181)
Bullen, Richard....5:20:25 (25,400)
Bulley, Brian....3:28:48 (3,963)
Bulley, James....3:42:04 (6,131)
Bulley, Simon....4:42:48 (19,331)
Bullingham, Simon....4:19:58 (14,355)
Bullivant, Guy....3:30:01 (4,172)
Bullivant, Mark....4:03:55 (10,866)
Bullivant, Paul....3:30:02 (4,176)
Bullman, Timothy....4:20:59 (14,589)
Bullock, Derek Allan....6:00:29 (28,430)
Bullock, Kevin....3:50:07 (7,709)
Bullock, Peter....4:14:22 (13,110)
Bullus, Gerald....5:11:32 (24,292)
Bulmer, Kelvin....3:05:01 (1,351)
Bulpett, Iain....5:39:51 (27,171)
Bulteel, Kelvin....4:08:46 (11,928)
Bumpsteed, Jame....4:55:02 (21,744)
Bunbury, Anthony....4:38:45 (18,559)
Bunce, Philip....4:52:19 (21,164)
Bungay, Alan....4:56:02 (21,990)
Bunn, Daniel....5:16:07 (24,940)
Bunn, Julian....3:58:44 (9,682)
Bunniss, Christopher....4:21:56 (14,793)
Bunting, Alistair....3:29:29 (4,076)
Bunting, Anthony....4:33:26 (17,402)
Bunting, Colin....3:10:28 (1,792)
Bunting, Richard....3:52:12 (8,117)
Bunting, Simon....4:36:55 (18,110)
Bunting, Timothy....5:04:00 (23,131)
Bunting, William....4:22:18 (14,886)
Bunyan, Peter....4:17:23 (13,745)
Burbela, Igor....5:20:54 (25,453)
Burbidge, Reginald....5:18:13 (25,178)
Burbridge, Duncan....6:18:02 (29,115)
Burbridge, Steven....4:51:55 (21,073)
Burchell, Barry....5:15:24 (24,855)
Burchett, Rainer....3:27:36 (3,723)
Burdett, Daniel....3:56:11 (8,963)
Burdett, George....4:35:51 (17,891)
Burdett, Jeremy....4:34:58 (17,707)
Burdett, Kevin....4:56:18 (22,036)
Burditt, Gary....3:15:39 (2,283)
Burdon, Antony....4:02:28 (10,566)
Burdon, Michael....3:51:41 (8,003)
Burdsall, Bjorn....4:58:48 (22,426)
Burfoot, Ambrose....3:59:30 (9,921)
Burfoot, Gary....4:07:22 (11,629)
Burford, Bruce....4:03:04 (10,677)
Burford, Graeme....4:49:51 (20,684)
Burford, Lawrence....4:47:14 (20,212)
Burford, Peter....3:47:08 (7,058)
Burge, Alan....5:01:16 (22,780)
Burgess, Andrew....4:08:17 (11,820)
Burgess, Daniel....4:02:52 (10,635)
Burgess, Mark....3:54:39 (8,623)
Burgess, Matthew....3:52:25 (8,158)
Burgess, Rae....3:54:23 (8,559)
Burgess, Roy....4:19:13 (14,165)
Burgess, Steven Peter....5:21:47 (25,562)
Burgess, Tom....3:24:19 (3,284)
Burgin, Len....5:06:56 (23,605)
Burgoyne, Jack....5:18:00 (25,166)
Burin, Nigel....3:57:20 (9,267)
Burke, Darren....5:27:03 (26,085)
Burke, Geoff....4:54:00 (21,511)
Burke, Harry....6:30:20 (29,420)
Burke, Iain....3:09:07 (1,681)
Burke, Martin....4:12:46 (12,784)
Burke, Martin....6:30:20 (29,420)
Burke, Neil....3:48:05 (7,283)
Burke, Nicky....6:36:05 (29,544)
Burke, Peter....4:10:12 (12,208)
Burke, Richard....4:59:58 (22,616)
Burke, Shaun....4:54:28 (21,585)
Burkhill, John....6:38:55 (29,605)
Burleton, Ryan....5:23:50 (25,772)
Burman, Colin....4:25:48 (15,672)
Burmester, Frank....4:14:36 (13,148)
Burnand, Henry....3:47:15 (7,072)
Burnard, Steven....4:37:31 (18,252)
Burne, Richard....4:33:18 (17,368)
Burnell, Henry....5:31:34 (26,493)
Burness, Keith....5:16:27 (24,979)
Burness, Kevin....4:20:07 (14,390)
Burness, Tim....4:15:11 (13,299)
Burnett, Allan....3:54:49 (8,664)
Burnett, Christopher....4:36:32 (18,026)
Burnett, David....5:09:01 (23,944)
Burnett, Gavin....6:26:44 (29,325)
Burnett, Iain....3:52:56 (8,255)
Burnett, Michael....4:22:30 (14,930)
Burnett, Robert....4:54:58 (21,721)
Burnett, Steven....7:12:29 (30,036)
Burnham, Derek....4:58:58 (22,456)
Burnham, Kevin....3:13:47 (2,087)
Burnham, Robert....3:09:07 (1,681)
Burnie, Peter....6:12:12 (28,930)
Burnie, Stuart....3:41:52 (6,104)
Burningham, Leo....2:53:21 (554)
Burnip, Garry....3:08:50 (1,657)
Burns, Adrian....4:06:19 (11,411)
Burns, Anthony....6:23:14 (29,236)
Burns, Billy....2:18:29 (19)
Burns, Dean....4:29:57 (16,675)
Burns, Denis....3:05:50 (1,409)
Burns, Duncan....3:07:34 (1,552)
Burns, Francis....4:24:48 (15,459)
Burns, Gary....3:44:45 (6,625)
Burns, John....3:57:16 (9,245)
Burns, Oliver....6:33:07 (29,484)
Burns, Paul....3:30:54 (4,314)
Burns, Peter....3:59:56 (10,037)
Burns, Robert....3:14:25 (2,162)
Burr, Stuart....3:29:06 (4,015)
Burrell, David....4:54:06 (21,533)
Burrell, Fitz....3:22:16 (3,031)
Burrell, Steven....5:55:55 (28,210)
Burrells, Robert....4:04:31 (10,996)
Burren, Ian....3:51:11 (7,909)
Burrett, Laurie....4:30:38 (16,775)
Burridge, Peter....4:16:54 (13,647)
Burrows, Andrew....4:50:20 (20,778)
Burrows, Daniel....3:53:57 (8,470)
Burrows, Geoff....5:21:34 (25,530)
Burrows, James....5:07:37 (23,717)
Burrows, Jon....4:52:28 (21,197)
Burrows, Paul....4:41:17 (19,027)
Burrows, Robert....4:05:39 (11,252)
Burrows, Robert....4:31:02 (16,858)
Burrows, Stephen....3:43:45 (6,449)
Burry, Karl....3:56:02 (8,934)
Bursnall, Paul....4:38:39 (18,537)
Burt, Cameron....3:17:04 (2,434)
Burt, Nicholas....3:43:50 (6,460)
Burt, Peter....4:50:44 (20,830)
Burt, Richard....4:27:40 (16,107)
Burteaux, Gerard....3:25:50 (3,484)
Burthem, Stephen....2:43:20 (245)
Burton, Alan....3:18:23 (2,587)
Burton, Carl....3:20:54 (2,877)
Burton, Frank....5:11:29 (24,284)
Burton, Jim....4:53:03 (21,325)
Burton, John....3:29:35 (4,095)
Burton, Martyn....5:35:31 (26,844)
Burton, Michael....3:41:13 (5,987)
Burton, Neil....5:09:40 (24,041)
Burton, Neville....5:25:02 (25,890)
Burton, Nicholas....3:39:29 (5,669)
Burton, Paul....3:14:03 (2,127)
Burton, Paul....5:50:05 (27,907)
Burton, Rob....4:47:09 (20,193)
Burton, Shaun....3:46:00 (6,856)
Burton, Simon....4:59:48 (22,575)
Burton, Terence....3:56:23 (9,018)
Burton, Warren....4:05:07 (11,141)
Burwood, Christopher....3:41:57 (6,116)
Busby, John....4:02:04 (10,498)
Busby, Patrick....4:48:22 (20,420)
Busch, Graham....3:07:44 (1,568)
Bush, Adam....3:08:13 (1,608)
Bush, Damien....4:21:47 (14,754)
Bush, Edward....3:10:09 (1,752)
Bush, Gary....4:25:28 (15,609)
Bush, Kevin....3:06:01 (1,424)
Bush, Richard....3:26:38 (3,576)
Bushby, Pat....5:32:28 (26,576)
Bushby, Ray....3:04:05 (1,288)
Bushby, Rob....3:19:27 (2,700)
Bushell, Gavin....5:18:52 (25,256)
Bushnell-Wye, Graham....4:13:55 (13,022)
Bushrod, Derek....5:27:06 (26,089)
Bussmann, Marc....4:26:35 (15,868)
Busto, Jarrett....5:31:29 (26,488)

Butcher, Alan	3:42:21	(6,191)
Butcher, Christopher	6:12:24	(28,937)
Butcher, Gavin	4:27:49	(16,154)
Butcher, Harry	5:08:57	(23,930)
Butcher, John	3:58:54	(9,723)
Butcher, Joseph	4:25:49	(15,679)
Butcher, Nicholas	3:38:37	(5,502)
Butcher, Robert	4:38:08	(18,415)
Butcher, William	5:00:08	(22,636)
Butet, Guy	4:36:14	(17,961)
Butler, Andrew	3:39:47	(5,735)
Butler, Anthony	2:56:00	(683)
Butler, Bryan	4:06:50	(11,512)
Butler, Cavan	3:51:16	(7,925)
Butler, Colin	4:45:25	(19,852)
Butler, David	2:58:39	(881)
Butler, David	3:29:05	(4,011)
Butler, David	4:33:40	(17,470)
Butler, Frank	4:33:13	(17,351)
Butler, Graham	3:17:23	(2,473)
Butler, Graham	4:21:52	(14,779)
Butler, James	4:53:13	(21,357)
Butler, Kenneth	2:24:45	(41)
Butler, Lyle	3:19:40	(2,725)
Butler, Martin	4:04:08	(10,908)
Butler, Matthew	3:39:29	(5,669)
Butler, Paul	5:18:33	(25,219)
Butler, Peter	3:24:00	(3,245)
Butler, Peter	3:34:46	(4,874)
Butler, Peter	4:28:45	(16,371)
Butler, Richard	3:36:03	(5,084)
Butler, Robert	3:40:57	(5,946)
Butler, Stephen	5:22:40	(25,665)
Butt, Philip	3:04:12	(1,295)
Butt, Stuart	4:36:12	(17,954)
Butterworth, Graham	4:17:43	(13,818)
Butterworth, James	3:54:43	(8,641)
Butterworth, Peter	4:57:45	(22,260)
Butterworth, Philip	3:28:39	(3,930)
Butterworth, Stephen	5:36:24	(26,911)
Butterworth, Timothy	4:43:59	(19,583)
Button, Christopher	4:22:48	(15,008)
Button, Christopher	4:34:04	(17,547)
Buxey, Marc	4:42:30	(19,273)
Buxton, David	5:07:44	(23,737)
Buxton, Lynton	4:57:17	(22,187)
Buxton, Paul	5:14:35	(24,720)
Byam, Phillip	3:54:05	(8,490)
Byansi, Malachi	2:36:35	(110)
Byard, Paul	5:19:14	(25,287)
Byatt, Andrew	4:54:40	(21,628)
Byatt, James	3:54:07	(8,495)
Bye, Martin	4:56:04	(21,997)
Byers, Anthony	4:39:57	(18,777)
Byford, Nigel	5:23:46	(25,768)
Bynarowicz, Michael	4:23:25	(15,153)
Byrne, Anthony	6:07:59	(28,760)
Byrne, Connor	3:58:45	(9,685)
Byrne, David	2:47:46	(361)
Byrne, David	4:55:35	(21,913)
Byrne, David	5:08:56	(23,926)
Byrne, Duncan	3:55:11	(8,728)
Byrne, Gerald	3:43:41	(6,432)
Byrne, John	4:44:13	(19,625)
Byrne, Matt	3:51:48	(8,027)
Byrne, Patrick	4:04:14	(10,936)
Byrne, Richard	4:50:51	(20,854)
Byrnes, David	4:52:59	(21,312)
Byrom, Andrew	3:51:51	(8,040)
Ca Rota, Carl John	5:20:58	(25,462)
Cadby, John	5:14:41	(24,738)
Cadden, Paul	4:43:30	(19,497)
Cadden, Paul	5:11:14	(24,247)
Caddy, David	3:19:53	(2,752)
Caddy, Ian	4:22:56	(15,048)
Cadeddu, Achille	3:13:37	(2,068)
Cadman, Milton	4:05:52	(11,313)
Cadogan, John	4:44:00	(19,586)
Cadogan, Richard	4:11:41	(12,546)
Cadwell, Steven	3:55:02	(8,705)
Caffyn, Timothy	3:59:24	(9,885)
Caflisch, Felix	3:54:16	(8,527)
Cahalane, Kevin	4:03:11	(10,699)
Cahill, Barry	3:37:48	(5,378)
Cahill, Bernard	5:50:09	(27,912)
Cahill, Declan	3:31:40	(4,418)
Cahill, Graham	3:05:58	(1,419)
Cahill, Neil	4:03:14	(10,707)
Cahill, Thomas	4:05:43	(11,273)
Cahill, Tim	3:54:26	(8,575)
Cahn, Jarrod	5:20:13	(25,377)
Cain, Alex	4:10:47	(12,332)
Cain, John	5:11:28	(24,279)
Cain, Scott	4:16:00	(13,463)
Cairns, Grant	4:01:22	(10,365)
Cairns, Guy	4:23:38	(15,215)
Cairns, Thomas	4:16:59	(13,661)
Caisley, Alastair	4:25:31	(15,622)
Cakebread, John	3:10:14	(1,762)
Calaminus, Simon	4:11:32	(12,508)
Calaz, Neal	4:07:15	(11,600)
Calder, Alan	5:22:37	(25,661)
Calder, Charles	4:03:03	(10,671)
Calder, George	6:12:41	(28,949)
Calder, Hamish	5:23:25	(25,733)
Calder, Stuart	4:11:59	(12,606)
Caldwell, Andrew	4:19:31	(14,260)
Caldwell, Bryan	2:57:21	(771)
Caldwell, Ronald	5:31:56	(26,528)
Caleb, Larner	5:41:23	(27,286)
Califano, Salvatore	3:04:54	(1,342)
Calise, Francesco	2:48:21	(371)
Callaghan, Mark	3:43:52	(6,464)
Callaghan, Richard	4:32:22	(17,186)
Callaghan, Robert	3:32:12	(4,493)
Callaghan, Simon	5:21:19	(25,506)
Callaghan, Thomas	5:15:08	(24,802)
Callaghan, Toby	4:17:32	(13,780)
Callander, Ian	4:14:59	(13,260)
Callen, Simon	4:47:34	(20,278)
Callender, Daren	5:42:50	(27,400)
Callender, Richard	4:08:06	(11,785)
Caller, Mark	4:26:09	(15,769)
Callister, Robert	2:48:33	(379)
Callow, Ian	3:21:28	(2,942)
Callow, Leo	3:59:02	(9,765)
Calloway, Tony	5:31:02	(26,456)
Calosi, Alberto	3:43:12	(6,345)
Calver, Vincent	3:57:27	(9,311)
Calvert, Glenn	3:02:57	(1,209)
Calvert, Ian	6:01:39	(28,491)
Calvert, Jonathan	3:20:54	(2,877)
Calvey, John	4:01:57	(10,475)
Cambell, Andrew	3:30:43	(4,282)
Cambiago, Umberto	2:52:04	(516)
Cambiano, Dario	3:45:36	(6,764)
Cambiano, Giorgio	3:45:36	(6,764)
Cambre, Danny	3:15:43	(2,291)
Cambridge, Andrew	3:50:21	(7,747)
Cambridge, Gary	4:26:38	(15,878)
Cameron, Alastair	4:21:40	(14,727)
Cameron, Alexander	7:31:17	(30,141)
Cameron, Colin	4:34:14	(17,580)
Cameron, David	2:44:09	(265)
Cameron, David	4:54:33	(21,604)
Cameron, Ewan	3:08:51	(1,659)
Cameron, Ewen	3:34:45	(4,869)
Cameron, Ian	5:15:09	(24,813)
Cameron, James	3:22:02	(3,005)
Cameron, John	3:14:18	(2,149)
Cameron, Michael	4:12:16	(12,683)
Cameron, Neil	4:27:25	(16,040)
Cameron, Paul	3:24:04	(3,255)
Cameron, Paul	3:26:55	(3,613)
Cameron, Paul	4:09:34	(12,084)
Cameron, William	3:17:22	(2,472)
Camidge, Jonathan	4:48:18	(20,407)
Camiller, Andrew	4:54:51	(21,691)
Camillo, Marco	5:54:36	(28,143)
Cammarata, Mario Claudio	4:42:54	(19,363)
Cammell, Brian	3:36:58	(5,239)
Cammish, Christopher	3:52:59	(8,263)
Campanelli, Leo	2:51:46	(505)
Company, Tim	3:32:56	(4,591)
Campbell, Adam	3:11:55	(1,908)
Campbell, Alexander	5:03:11	(23,029)
Campbell, Alistair	4:19:26	(14,236)
Campbell, Alistair	5:43:55	(27,466)
Campbell, Angus	4:19:12	(14,164)
Campbell, Brian	4:15:29	(13,364)
Campbell, Cassius	5:06:10	(23,493)
Campbell, David	4:27:03	(15,981)
Campbell, David	5:09:34	(24,024)
Campbell, Don	4:05:27	(11,197)
Campbell, Donald	3:28:24	(3,890)
Campbell, Douglas	3:59:14	(9,828)
Campbell, Eric	3:43:10	(6,336)
Campbell, Eric	3:51:07	(7,900)
Campbell, Ewan	4:49:39	(20,642)
Campbell, Gordon	4:21:37	(14,718)
Campbell, Graham	3:13:49	(2,093)
Campbell, Hew	4:34:45	(17,668)
Campbell, Iain	3:40:08	(5,806)
Campbell, Iain	4:32:09	(17,145)
Campbell, Ian	3:55:33	(8,808)
Campbell, James	4:00:40	(10,199)
Campbell, Kenneth	3:55:41	(8,839)
Campbell, Lee	3:12:07	(1,924)
Campbell, Lewis	4:39:28	(18,683)
Campbell, Lindsay	5:08:26	(23,835)
Campbell, Mark	4:29:00	(16,420)
Campbell, Michael	4:29:43	(16,603)
Campbell, Neill	4:14:39	(13,158)
Campbell, Paul	4:01:27	(10,383)
Campbell, Paul	4:44:41	(19,712)
Campbell, Paul	4:49:44	(20,659)
Campbell, Richard	3:28:59	(3,996)
Campbell, Richard	3:48:53	(7,436)
Campbell, Robert	4:07:18	(11,612)
Campbell, Ruairidh	2:39:34	(165)
Campbell, Stuart	4:37:50	(18,326)
Campbell Barnard, Will	3:45:28	(6,739)
Campbell-Barnard, James	4:30:42	(16,786)
Campen, James	4:20:19	(14,432)
Campion, Charles	4:56:35	(22,086)
Campobasso, Romanino	6:04:19	(28,606)
Campos, Joao	3:18:46	(2,629)
Camps, Werner	3:35:10	(4,927)
Camwell, Derek	4:50:19	(20,774)
Candey, Robert	4:04:56	(11,103)
Candlin, Ben	4:14:52	(13,228)
Candlin, David	3:29:36	(4,098)
Candlish, Alistair	4:19:56	(14,348)
Caney, Simon	3:13:26	(2,055)
Cannatella, Howard	3:38:42	(5,520)
Cannell, David	4:33:33	(17,438)
Cannell, Paul	3:36:19	(5,125)
Cannell, Tom	5:34:45	(26,777)
Canniffe, Mike	5:11:51	(24,337)
Canning, George	3:20:57	(2,885)
Canning, Justin	3:50:39	(7,796)
Canning, Paul	4:00:13	(10,092)
Canning, Stephen	3:53:28	(8,367)
Canning-Matthews, Simon	5:16:23	(24,970)
Cannon, Jim	4:24:45	(15,450)
Cannon, John	3:00:31	(1,053)
Cannon, Nick	3:30:19	(4,217)
Cannon, Sandy	4:00:13	(10,092)
Cant, Christopher	5:45:57	(27,631)
Cant, Christopher	6:01:14	(28,465)
Cant, Cliff	3:53:45	(8,433)
Cantelow, Andrew	4:04:29	(10,983)
Canterbury, Daniel	3:35:48	(5,033)
Cantle, Steven	4:17:11	(13,716)
Capel, Dominic	4:32:44	(17,257)
Capelin, Michael	5:07:23	(23,676)
Capelli, Bruno	5:56:46	(28,257)
Capewell, Nicholas	5:11:04	(24,218)
Capey, Paul	3:32:37	(4,551)
Capezio, Francesco	5:43:31	(27,441)
Capirossi, Pierre	4:13:33	(12,943)
Caplan, Nicholas	4:17:26	(13,756)
Capon, Alain	4:31:51	(17,074)
Capon, Ian	4:23:30	(15,172)
Capp, Peter	5:16:57	(25,042)
Capra, Sergio	4:04:45	(11,057)
Capstick, Neil	4:20:09	(14,397)
Card, Carl	6:41:36	(29,680)
Cardell, Michael	4:56:02	(21,990)

Carden, Peter 4:17:42 (13,814)
Cardon, Clive 3:59:36 (9,948)
Cardon, Trevor 4:40:55 (18,959)
Cardoso, James 4:11:23 (12,478)
Cardwell, Mark 4:00:27 (10,136)
Cardy, Ian 2:40:34 (185)
Carette, Bruno 3:41:55 (6,112)
Carey, Christopher 3:15:25 (2,262)
Carey, Kenneth 4:16:03 (13,478)
Carey, Tony 6:35:01 (29,520)
Cargill, Jamie 4:02:19 (10,533)
Caria, Domenico 3:15:08 (2,236)
Carimalo, Daniel 3:04:59 (1,348)
Carlile, Wayne 4:14:53 (13,231)
Carlill, Angus 3:34:26 (4,824)
Carlin, Christopher 4:10:47 (12,332)
Carlisle, Richard 4:18:44 (14,063)
Carlsson, Bert 5:11:58 (24,350)
Carmichael, Jeremy 3:11:10 (1,852)
Carmichael, Paul 3:31:07 (4,343)
Carn, Simon 4:07:13 (11,590)
Carneiro, Joao 4:45:42 (19,882)
Carneiro, Rui 4:55:16 (21,802)
Carnet, Jean Paul 4:08:44 (11,920)
Carnie, Robert 4:51:32 (20,991)
Carnody, Paul 4:00:35 (10,181)
Caro, Danny 6:51:57 (29,832)
Caron, Dominique 3:34:27 (4,831)
Carpenter, John 5:44:44 (27,542)
Carpenter, Kevin 3:08:11 (1,604)
Carpenter, Neil 3:54:40 (8,624)
Carpenter, Paul 4:38:04 (18,389)
Carpenter, Peter 5:10:23 (24,127)
Carpenter, Richard 4:29:03 (16,431)
Carpentier, Sylvan 4:02:07 (10,507)
Carpin, Rhys 5:22:54 (25,694)
Carr, Antony 5:33:59 (26,689)
Carr, David 3:26:06 (3,512)
Carr, Geoffrey 4:11:38 (12,531)
Carr, James 4:26:43 (15,893)
Carr, John 4:26:43 (15,893)
Carr, Mike 4:19:33 (14,270)
Carr, Paul 4:40:32 (18,878)
Carr, Philip 4:18:40 (14,044)
Carr, Tom 3:58:34 (9,633)
Carre, Christopher 3:00:11 (1,040)
Carrell, Edward 4:05:24 (11,187)
Carrington, James 5:09:30 (24,015)
Carroll, Anthony 3:25:42 (3,467)
Carroll, Christopher 4:33:12 (17,347)
Carroll, Gerard 3:45:45 (6,810)
Carroll, Ivor 4:13:20 (12,884)
Carroll, Mark 4:31:05 (16,866)
Carroll, Mick 4:02:52 (10,635)
Carroll, Paj 4:37:18 (18,197)
Carroll, Paul 2:59:15 (953)
Carroll, Paul 3:50:20 (7,741)
Carroll, Paul 3:55:05 (8,710)
Carroll, Paul 4:16:32 (13,581)
Carroll, Rob 3:15:33 (2,276)
Carroll, Stephen 4:06:25 (11,435)
Carroll Junior, Anthony 4:48:21 (20,416)
Carruthers, Lee 5:01:25 (22,792)
Carruthers, Nigel 5:53:37 (28,098)
Carruthers, Roland 2:56:56 (739)
Carson, Derek 4:56:46 (22,101)
Carson, Ian 2:56:26 (713)
Carson, Leon 3:57:56 (9,472)
Carson, Robert 3:38:23 (5,462)
Carter, Alex 5:19:39 (25,323)
Carter, Andrew 3:37:04 (5,256)
Carter, Chris 5:54:31 (28,140)
Carter, Christopher 4:32:36 (17,227)
Carter, Craig 4:19:08 (14,155)
Carter, Dave 3:35:35 (5,000)
Carter, David 2:52:39 (533)
Carter, Dominic 5:18:07 (25,175)
Carter, Eric 4:03:44 (10,825)
Carter, Gordon 4:47:06 (20,184)
Carter, James 4:01:18 (10,340)
Carter, Kevin 3:08:50 (1,657)
Carter, Kevin 3:14:51 (2,200)
Carter, Leslie 4:00:28 (10,142)
Carter, Mark 4:17:17 (13,732)
Carter, Martin 4:31:46 (17,054)
Carter, Nicholas 4:51:18 (20,946)
Carter, Nicholas 5:19:07 (25,277)
Carter, Owen 4:01:32 (10,401)
Carter, Paul 5:34:38 (26,768)
Carter, Richard 4:00:32 (10,166)
Carter, Richard 4:51:31 (20,985)
Carter, Robert 4:10:46 (12,327)
Carter, Roy 3:30:11 (4,198)
Carter, Stephen 3:14:00 (2,121)
Carter, Stephen 3:17:25 (2,476)
Carter, Stephen 4:43:43 (19,543)
Carter, Steven 4:14:43 (13,177)
Carter, Timothy 4:01:28 (10,386)
Carter, Toby 3:16:49 (2,405)
Carter Shaw, Nicholas 4:06:08 (11,366)
Cartier, Philippe 3:07:40 (1,563)
Cartledge, Brian 4:46:38 (20,080)
Cartmale, Tom 5:01:42 (22,824)
Carton, Kenneth 3:59:30 (9,921)
Cartwright, Barry 4:22:35 (14,948)
Cartwright, David 2:59:20 (968)
Cartwright, Matthew 3:53:35 (8,399)
Cartwright, Paul 4:32:19 (17,175)
Cartwright, Richard 3:49:36 (7,608)
Carty, Nicholas 4:09:14 (12,031)
Caruth, Brian 6:55:48 (29,899)
Carvalho, Adelino 4:06:49 (11,505)
Carvalho, Antonio 4:02:42 (10,608)
Carvalho, Brendon 3:24:00 (3,245)
Carvell, Andrew 4:21:14 (14,635)
Cary, Clive 4:07:07 (11,572)
Casallas, Hugo 3:59:26 (9,896)
Caselton, Kevin 4:53:45 (21,463)
Casey, David 3:51:55 (8,054)
Casey, Paul 4:53:45 (21,463)
Cash, Jamie 4:53:30 (21,419)
Cash, Max 3:47:50 (7,218)
Cashman, Gerard 4:34:40 (17,652)
Cashman, Philip 3:57:21 (9,273)
Casper, Craig 4:22:19 (14,891)
Casper, Nigel 4:22:19 (14,891)
Cass, David 3:57:45 (9,412)
Casserley, Rob 3:31:36 (4,411)
Cassetta, Christian 4:02:31 (10,576)
Cassidy, Mark 3:29:31 (4,082)
Cassidy, Michael 5:03:36 (23,070)
Cassidy, Terry 4:07:34 (11,672)
Cassini, Augusto 4:37:43 (18,303)
Casson, Neil 6:21:16 (29,200)
Casson, Randal 5:35:14 (26,821)
Castaldo, Paul 3:41:21 (6,020)
Castell, Martin 3:45:31 (6,751)
Castle, David 4:37:28 (18,243)
Castle, John 2:34:48 (92)
Castle, Lorne 3:35:37 (5,005)
Castle, Robert 3:57:08 (9,207)
Castle, Simon 4:13:25 (12,912)
Castledine, Ian 4:33:45 (17,489)
Castro, Fernando 5:25:57 (25,982)
Casturo, Don 3:39:59 (5,782)
Caswell, Gary 5:31:14 (26,471)
Catalfamo, Salvatore 4:53:27 (21,407)
Catalini, Emannelito 2:59:47 (1,006)
Catanzaro, Vincenzo 4:50:01 (20,723)
Catchpole, Charles 4:04:21 (10,955)
Catchpole, Phil 3:54:47 (8,655)
Cater, Nicholas 3:22:17 (3,035)
Cates, Michael 2:51:37 (497)
Catherall, Michael 5:02:58 (23,000)
Cathrow, Stuart 4:55:00 (21,732)
Catlin, Michael 5:03:45 (23,091)
Catling, Howard 3:59:34 (9,940)
Catling, Justin 4:19:16 (14,183)
Catling, Michael 3:44:18 (6,544)
Catmull, Jeremy 3:15:01 (2,224)
Catmur, John 3:33:54 (4,741)
Catt, Timothy 3:55:43 (8,848)
Cattai, Mauro 3:59:01 (9,761)
Cattaneo, Luigi Guglielmo 3:47:26 (7,125)
Cattaneo, Marco Dino 4:07:34 (11,672)
Cattell, Michael 5:39:13 (27,105)
Catterfeld, Paul 5:19:02 (25,268)
Cattermole, David 3:00:59 (1,083)
Cattley, Adrian 4:26:05 (15,752)
Catto, John 3:21:38 (2,961)
Catton, Pete 3:56:12 (8,967)
Cauchi, Donald 4:57:30 (22,217)
Cauey, Simon 3:57:56 (9,472)
Caulder, Graham 3:22:45 (3,078)
Cauley, Patrick 5:02:01 (22,874)
Caulfield, Martin 3:56:32 (9,062)
Caulkett, Daniel 4:18:48 (14,081)
Caulkett, Justin 3:52:51 (8,238)
Caulton, Stephen 4:59:49 (22,578)
Caunter, Timothy 3:49:53 (7,664)
Causbysmith, Ian 5:42:00 (27,334)
Causon, Benjamin 4:03:32 (10,783)
Causon, Roger 3:58:32 (9,616)
Cava, Juan 4:50:58 (20,874)
Cavaco, Nelson 4:36:19 (17,978)
Cavanagh, Daniel 3:32:15 (4,500)
Cavanagh, Mark 4:35:56 (17,913)
Cavanagh, Russell 4:09:22 (12,054)
Cavanagh, Sean 4:13:28 (12,925)
Cave, Phillip 4:29:22 (16,511)
Cave, Richard 4:42:55 (19,366)
Cave, Ronald 3:55:28 (8,794)
Cave, Stephen 4:05:15 (11,162)
Cave, Terence 4:13:54 (13,019)
Caveney, Terence 2:57:52 (805)
Cawley, Emmett 5:01:45 (22,832)
Cawte, Graham 3:15:51 (2,302)
Cazares, Javier 3:55:51 (8,883)
Cazeaux, James 4:22:52 (15,024)
Cecchetto, Graziano 4:04:44 (11,050)
Cech, Francis 4:33:25 (17,398)
Cehuk, Stephen 5:47:51 (27,759)
Celeghin, Andrea 3:56:16 (8,986)
Cerely, Francis 3:50:55 (7,853)
Cespeoes, Marcelo 4:48:04 (20,362)
Chackal, Michael 5:56:20 (28,228)
Chacksfield, Gary 5:29:31 (26,336)
Chadeyras, Bernard 3:26:06 (3,512)
Chadha, Gad 4:59:25 (22,515)
Chadwick, Andrew 3:39:14 (5,617)
Chadwick, David 4:43:50 (19,564)
Chadwick, Gary 3:41:13 (5,987)
Chadwick, Nicholas 3:58:55 (9,726)
Chadwick, Nick 3:49:26 (7,559)
Chadwick, Paul 4:28:00 (16,195)
Chadwick, Peter 4:31:47 (17,056)
Chadwick, Philip 4:39:36 (18,718)
Chadwick, Shaun 3:56:38 (9,085)
Chadwick, Simon 4:55:38 (21,939)
Chadwick, Steven 4:54:57 (21,718)
Chaffe, Bruce 3:51:00 (7,875)
Chaffe, Richard 3:17:20 (2,465)
Chaffer, Paul 3:41:33 (6,042)
Chaffey, Daniel 4:33:59 (17,532)
Chaffin, John 5:10:08 (24,093)
Chairon, Laurent 2:37:25 (126)
Chakravarty Agbo, Celestine 4:42:53 (19,359)
Chalavatzis, Marin 3:23:21 (3,155)
Chalcraft, Jonathan 5:35:20 (26,832)
Chalfen, David 2:59:40 (992)
Chalke, Stephen 3:59:07 (9,791)
Chalker, William 4:10:51 (12,359)
Chalkie, Joshua 4:11:59 (12,606)
Challis, Jason 4:21:03 (14,603)
Challis, Peter 3:36:15 (5,114)
Challoner, Michael 4:57:36 (22,228)
Chalmers, Henry 4:54:55 (21,709)
Chalmers, Iain 5:10:14 (24,110)
Chalmers, Paul 3:14:54 (2,208)
Chalmers, Vince 4:03:21 (10,735)
Chalmers, Warrick 5:24:46 (25,854)
Chamberlain, Frank 5:39:36 (27,144)
Chamberlain, Gary 3:41:40 (6,069)
Chamberlain, George 5:07:38 (23,719)
Chamberlain, John 4:53:50 (21,483)
Chamberlain, Mark 5:05:57 (23,461)
Chamberlain, Paul 3:31:16 (4,367)
Chamberlain, Stephen 3:42:54 (6,288)
Chamberlin, David 3:56:49 (9,137)

Chambers, Bryan.............4:39:14 (18,642)
Chambers, Colin 4:54:42 (21,640)
Chambers, Jamie.............3:52:21 (8,142)
Chambers, Peter.............4:24:15 (15,341)
Chambers, Shannon.............4:58:20 (22,347)
Chambers, Thomas.............4:20:48 (14,547)
Chambon, Thierry.............3:11:07 (1,845)
Champion, Ian.............5:47:03 (27,710)
Champion, Ross.............3:50:19 (7,738)
Champion, Stuart.............4:05:49 (11,305)
Chan, Aaron.............4:59:46 (22,565)
Chan, Chong.............3:19:29 (2,705)
Chan, Danny.............3:46:46 (6,999)
Chan, David.............4:10:18 (12,226)
Chana, Amardeep.............4:38:04 (18,389)
Chana, Jaswant.............3:39:14 (5,617)
Chana, Mandeep.............3:42:58 (6,298)
Chana, Ravinder.............4:57:18 (22,190)
Chance, William.............2:57:16 (764)
Chandler, Barrie.............3:27:53 (3,785)
Chandler, David.............4:26:13 (15,780)
Chandler, David.............4:46:30 (20,054)
Chandler, Gary.............3:28:39 (3,930)
Chandler, Howard.............5:25:13 (25,911)
Chandler, Matthew.............4:59:33 (22,535)
Chandler, Michael.............3:03:19 (1,235)
Chandler, Paul.............5:25:51 (25,973)
Chandler, Peter.............3:53:08 (8,296)
Chandler, Stephen.............3:52:32 (8,179)
Chandley, Paul.............4:13:13 (12,858)
Chandor, Benjamin.............3:52:18 (8,134)
Chandramohan, Vayrmuthu.....7:07:45 (30,004)
Channing, Adrian.............3:44:53 (6,658)
Channings, George.............3:23:00 (3,113)
Channon, David.............5:24:10 (25,805)
Channon, Simon.............4:52:28 (21,197)
Chanona, Alfonso.............4:24:18 (15,349)
Chant, Ian.............3:25:16 (3,411)
Chantler, Adrian.............4:28:24 (16,288)
Chantler, John.............5:14:18 (24,673)
Chant-Sempill, Ian.............4:38:35 (18,528)
Chapat, Bernard.............4:44:45 (19,726)
Chapillon, Matthew.............4:33:23 (17,394)
Chaplin, David.............2:48:07 (365)
Chaplin, Ian.............2:59:19 (964)
Chaplin, Neil.............3:29:08 (4,023)
Chaplin, Peter.............4:01:02 (10,288)
Chaplin, Rowan.............5:12:21 (24,403)
Chaplin, Stephen.............3:40:52 (5,920)
Chaplin, Tony.............3:51:10 (7,906)
Chapman, Andrew.............4:03:44 (10,825)
Chapman, Andrew.............4:41:36 (19,083)
Chapman, Barry.............5:02:26 (22,931)
Chapman, Clive.............5:16:57 (25,042)
Chapman, Colin.............4:05:04 (11,129)
Chapman, Colin.............4:58:20 (22,347)
Chapman, Craig.............3:28:17 (3,863)
Chapman, David.............3:40:06 (5,800)
Chapman, Dean.............5:05:56 (23,456)
Chapman, Derek.............5:31:58 (26,533)
Chapman, Graham.............5:13:56 (24,622)
Chapman, Ian.............4:31:17 (16,927)
Chapman, John.............3:45:41 (6,791)
Chapman, Kenny.............3:45:59 (6,853)
Chapman, Laurence.............6:28:59 (29,386)
Chapman, Leslie.............6:01:18 (28,469)
Chapman, Mark.............3:28:19 (3,872)
Chapman, Matthew.............3:59:47 (9,992)
Chapman, Michael.............3:46:34 (6,963)
Chapman, Michael.............3:54:11 (8,506)
Chapman, Nigel.............3:36:19 (5,125)
Chapman, Nigel.............4:46:05 (19,954)
Chapman, Paul.............4:35:08 (17,736)
Chapman, Peter.............3:36:43 (5,195)
Chapman, Richard.............3:35:04 (4,912)
Chapman, Richard.............3:49:29 (7,574)
Chapman, Richard.............4:34:13 (17,573)
Chapman, Simon.............4:22:39 (14,968)
Chapman, Stewart.............3:24:32 (3,316)
Chapman, Tim.............5:01:24 (22,791)
Chapman, Tim.............5:13:03 (24,508)
Chappell, Aaron.............4:00:43 (10,217)
Chappell, Paul.............3:38:50 (5,544)

Chapple, Stephen.............3:01:59 (1,147)
Chaptal, Gerard.............3:43:30 (6,398)
Chard, Brian.............3:18:54 (2,645)
Chard, Daniel.............3:56:35 (9,074)
Charles, Danny.............4:23:40 (15,221)
Charles, Gordon.............4:33:10 (17,341)
Charles, Gregory.............3:37:50 (5,386)
Charles, Paul.............3:02:52 (1,205)
Charlesworth, Arthur.............6:34:28 (29,511)
Charlesworth, Mike.............4:54:18 (21,562)
Charlesworth, Paul.............3:43:03 (6,316)
Charlet, Andrew.............4:26:38 (15,878)
Charlton, David.............4:33:06 (17,328)
Charlton, Ian.............3:40:10 (5,810)
Charlton, John.............4:38:38 (18,534)
Charlton, Paul.............4:58:25 (22,362)
Charlton, Stuart.............4:21:41 (14,731)
Charlton, Trevor.............3:58:03 (9,501)
Charluteau, Nicolas.............3:40:42 (5,899)
Charman, Bernard.............5:13:14 (24,543)
Charman, Derek.............3:42:33 (6,226)
Chart, Robert.............3:29:29 (4,076)
Charter, Nicholas.............4:56:11 (22,021)
Chase, Rodney.............4:07:03 (11,564)
Chatelard, Philippe.............2:30:29 (68)
Chatenet, Pascal.............4:11:06 (12,416)
Chater, Nicholas.............3:40:28 (5,863)
Chattaway, Nick.............2:57:12 (759)
Chatterton, Christopher.............4:41:31 (19,066)
Chauhan, Arun.............4:42:27 (19,264)
Chauncy, Charlie.............4:06:11 (11,379)
Chauveau, Bernard.............3:28:03 (3,808)
Chaveroux, Patrick.............3:39:12 (5,610)
Chavira, Jorge.............3:33:01 (4,606)
Cheal, Benjamin.............4:35:18 (17,775)
Cheek, Nicholas.............3:30:57 (4,322)
Cheema, Irfan.............4:18:41 (14,049)
Cheeseman, Robin.............2:46:55 (339)
Cheesman, Charles.............6:01:20 (28,470)
Cheesman, Clifford.............3:53:19 (8,338)
Cheesman, Darren.............4:16:02 (13,474)
Cheesman, David.............5:06:57 (23,608)
Cheetham, David.............5:21:44 (25,552)
Chehowah, Jacques.............5:16:18 (24,958)
Chell, Philip.............4:42:26 (19,260)
Chelton, Lee.............4:54:51 (21,691)
Chemstie, Douglas.............3:21:31 (2,951)
Chen, Theodore.............3:08:46 (1,653)
Chenery, Duncan.............4:07:22 (11,629)
Cheney, Vincent.............3:49:23 (7,548)
Cheng, Stanley.............4:58:19 (22,343)
Cheong, Kirk.............5:26:20 (26,022)
Cherrington, Jay.............4:25:36 (15,637)
Cherrington, Keith.............8:10:29 (30,232)
Cherry, James.............8:14:59 (30,235)
Cherry, Nicholas.............3:44:26 (6,565)
Cherry, Phillip.............3:14:00 (2,121)
Chesi, Rino.............4:00:05 (10,070)
Chessa, Gianfranco.............3:13:48 (2,091)
Chester, John.............5:23:28 (25,739)
Chester, Kevin.............6:03:28 (28,563)
Chester, Martin.............3:27:26 (3,693)
Chester, Richard.............5:28:05 (26,187)
Chesterman, Christopher.............4:55:19 (21,819)
Chesters, Paul.............5:05:27 (23,372)
Chestnutt, Francis.............4:17:13 (13,722)
Chetwynd Talbot, Nicholas.............3:58:38 (9,649)
Cheung, Vincent.............4:55:35 (21,913)
Chevaleyre, Laurent.............4:04:26 (10,973)
Chevalier, Jean Luc.............4:02:07 (10,507)
Chevrier, Jean Pierre.............4:15:36 (13,387)
Cheyne, Brian.............4:37:15 (18,182)
Chezeaud, Jacques.............4:39:13 (18,639)
Chick, Ian.............4:01:25 (10,373)
Chilcott, Nicholas.............4:08:55 (11,959)
Child, Dominic.............3:54:59 (8,698)
Child, Timothy.............4:17:15 (13,727)
Childe, Michael.............3:42:32 (6,223)
Childerhosue, Erik.............5:01:47 (22,837)
Childs, Andrew.............4:04:32 (11,001)
Childs, Chris.............6:39:42 (29,622)
Childs, Gary.............4:07:28 (11,658)
Childs, Gordon.............4:45:08 (19,791)

Childs, Graham.............3:24:57 (3,370)
Childs, Peter.............3:15:01 (2,224)
Childs, Peter.............3:42:36 (6,235)
Childs, Phillip.............3:12:01 (1,915)
Childs, Roger.............4:09:42 (12,108)
Chilleystone, Neil.............5:33:52 (26,676)
Chilton, Stephen.............4:22:11 (14,856)
Chilvers, Graeme.............5:05:17 (23,337)
Chima, Santokh Singh.............6:00:35 (28,434)
Chin, Yao.............6:33:29 (29,494)
Chin Asang, Raymond.............4:37:41 (18,297)
Chiodini, Daniele.............3:07:42 (1,566)
Chiplin, Terry.............3:48:55 (7,442)
Chippendale, Neil.............2:50:42 (454)
Chisholm, Barry.............3:00:51 (1,072)
Chittell, Hayden.............4:19:36 (14,279)
Chivers, John.............5:10:08 (24,093)
Chivers, Peter.............3:17:36 (2,491)
Choblet, Frank.............3:56:56 (9,163)
Chong, Heong.............3:42:13 (6,166)
Choong, Andrew.............6:12:24 (28,937)
Chorley, Stephen.............4:00:23 (10,127)
Chorlton, Gordon.............4:39:41 (18,731)
Chow, Richard.............5:22:12 (25,615)
Chowdhri, Sanjeen.............4:26:08 (15,762)
Chowdhury, Minto.............3:56:56 (9,163)
Chowdhury, Naziullah.............5:30:51 (26,442)
Christen, Roger.............5:32:39 (26,588)
Christensen, Knudage.............4:38:13 (18,431)
Christensen, Tormod.............3:42:03 (6,129)
Christian, David.............4:42:48 (19,331)
Christian, Robin.............4:10:23 (12,252)
Christian, Tris.............4:16:21 (13,536)
Christiansen, Kennet.............3:51:17 (7,929)
Christianson, Steve.............4:56:48 (22,108)
Christie, Alistair.............3:54:14 (8,519)
Christie, Campbell.............3:41:08 (5,976)
Christie, Paul.............4:43:00 (19,385)
Christol, Pierre.............3:50:20 (7,741)
Christopher, Leonard.............2:49:03 (395)
Christopher, Marcus.............3:57:09 (9,210)
Christopher, Mark.............3:54:36 (8,614)
Christopher, Robert.............4:14:39 (13,158)
Christopherson, Macleay.............3:53:17 (8,327)
Christou, Cos.............4:55:14 (21,791)
Chubb, Christopher.............4:15:21 (13,335)
Chubb, Damian.............4:04:00 (10,881)
Chubb, Karl.............4:22:02 (14,822)
Chubb, Nicholas.............5:10:34 (24,159)
Chubb, Paul.............5:20:56 (25,458)
Chubb, Richard.............4:20:58 (14,584)
Chubb, William.............5:41:19 (27,278)
Chudley, John.............5:51:07 (27,959)
Chugg, Mark.............4:32:24 (17,194)
Chumber, Vinod.............5:56:05 (28,217)
Chung, Alex.............4:33:51 (17,510)
Chung, Kam.............3:37:19 (5,305)
Church, Anthony.............3:56:31 (9,058)
Church, Christopher.............3:57:32 (9,338)
Church, Martin.............4:19:07 (14,150)
Church, Michael.............5:10:53 (24,194)
Church, Nicholas.............4:57:20 (22,195)
Church, Stewart.............5:20:46 (25,441)
Church, Timothy.............5:04:47 (23,259)
Churchill, Alexander.............3:25:51 (3,486)
Churchill, Nigel.............3:15:39 (2,283)
Chuter, Matthew.............5:19:31 (25,308)
Cianciabella, Marcello.............5:04:11 (23,159)
Ciappi, Darren.............4:53:44 (21,461)
Ciccaglione, Alessandro.............3:03:13 (1,227)
Cichero, Paolo.............4:27:23 (16,036)
Cicu, Stefano.............4:21:34 (14,704)
Cieciel, Jaroslaw.............3:26:32 (3,561)
Cielak, Andrés.............3:39:50 (5,745)
Cierocki, David.............3:33:26 (4,680)
Cifuentes, José.............4:46:14 (19,993)
Cilliers, Derek.............4:32:15 (17,165)
Cimino, Carmelo.............3:59:19 (9,849)
Cimmati, Serge.............4:23:53 (15,269)
Cinque, Giuseppe.............4:18:31 (14,017)
Ciurleo, Roberto.............3:25:54 (3,493)
Clachers, Liam.............4:12:34 (12,750)
Clackston, Michael.............3:55:24 (8,781)

Clacy, Philip 4:01:06 (10,300)
Claesson, Tom 4:18:30 (14,012)
Clanchy, Derek 5:34:02 (26,700)
Clancy, Danny 6:06:11 (28,691)
Clapham, Jeremy 3:16:29 (2,364)
Clapham, Nicholas 3:05:23 (1,380)
Clapp, Franchot 4:47:49 (20,310)
Clapp, John 3:38:48 (5,537)
Clapp, Michael 5:00:37 (22,680)
Clapp, William 3:27:05 (3,633)
Clapson, Barrie 4:21:52 (14,779)
Clare, Daniel 5:20:44 (25,436)
Clare, Jason 5:13:15 (24,546)
Clare, Jonathan 3:06:43 (1,480)
Clare, Keith 5:33:23 (26,639)
Clare, Nick 4:29:32 (16,553)
Clarehugh, Mark 2:45:27 (307)
Claridge, Robert 3:14:58 (2,218)
Clark, Andrew 3:48:27 (7,349)
Clark, Andrew 4:08:23 (11,846)
Clark, Andrew 4:20:41 (14,516)
Clark, Andrew 4:31:50 (17,069)
Clark, Antony 3:42:52 (6,278)
Clark, Colin 4:44:34 (19,690)
Clark, Darrin 4:59:50 (22,581)
Clark, David 3:45:43 (6,802)
Clark, David 3:55:47 (8,867)
Clark, David 4:04:19 (10,952)
Clark, David 4:47:11 (20,198)
Clark, David 5:24:03 (25,797)
Clark, David 6:17:58 (29,112)
Clark, Geoff 4:28:23 (16,283)
Clark, Geoffrey 6:40:01 (29,633)
Clark, Graham 4:39:59 (18,787)
Clark, Hamish 3:37:17 (5,298)
Clark, Hamish 4:46:43 (20,095)
Clark, Ian 3:39:30 (5,673)
Clark, Ian 4:39:25 (18,670)
Clark, Jeff 4:55:34 (21,907)
Clark, John 4:18:24 (13,990)
Clark, John 5:42:30 (27,375)
Clark, Jonathon 5:21:55 (25,576)
Clark, Julian 4:11:15 (12,453)
Clark, Kenneth 4:06:42 (11,485)
Clark, Lee 3:57:45 (9,412)
Clark, Leslie 3:59:07 (9,791)
Clark, Malcolm 5:11:08 (24,232)
Clark, Martin 3:49:22 (7,543)
Clark, Matthew 4:04:53 (11,088)
Clark, Michael 3:29:39 (4,111)
Clark, Michael 3:55:45 (8,861)
Clark, Nicholas 4:32:12 (17,155)
Clark, Nigel 5:40:41 (27,246)
Clark, Paul 4:07:08 (11,576)
Clark, Peter 4:08:21 (11,837)
Clark, Peter 5:27:25 (26,120)
Clark, Richard 2:58:30 (856)
Clark, Richard 5:36:09 (26,889)
Clark, Robert 4:26:45 (15,898)
Clark, Robert 5:04:29 (23,214)
Clark, Roger 4:58:10 (22,324)
Clark, Scott 3:27:20 (3,680)
Clark, Simon 3:27:11 (3,657)
Clark, Stephen 4:20:19 (14,432)
Clark, Steven 7:47:46 (30,185)
Clark, Stuart 4:19:49 (14,318)
Clarke, Andrew 3:01:31 (1,112)
Clarke, Andrew 3:12:44 (1,981)
Clarke, Andrew 3:23:45 (3,205)
Clarke, Andrew 3:54:26 (8,575)
Clarke, Andrew 5:14:24 (24,688)
Clarke, Anthony 3:48:26 (7,346)
Clarke, Anthony 5:25:56 (25,980)
Clarke, Barry 4:48:52 (20,496)
Clarke, Brian 5:37:18 (26,965)
Clarke, Cedric 3:38:01 (5,401)
Clarke, Christopher 3:50:58 (7,861)
Clarke, Christopher 3:56:59 (9,174)
Clarke, Christopher 4:13:58 (13,035)
Clarke, Dale 4:20:52 (14,564)
Clarke, Daniel 5:14:12 (24,655)
Clarke, Gordon 4:22:55 (15,039)
Clarke, Graham 3:28:14 (3,851)
Clarke, Graham 4:20:52 (14,564)
Clarke, Graham 5:53:44 (28,106)
Clarke, Guy 4:43:00 (19,385)
Clarke, Ian 3:23:50 (3,219)
Clarke, James 4:00:53 (10,259)
Clarke, James 4:21:31 (14,695)
Clarke, James 5:45:56 (27,630)
Clarke, Jeremy 5:11:41 (24,310)
Clarke, John 3:06:44 (1,482)
Clarke, John 3:53:56 (8,466)
Clarke, John 4:02:30 (10,571)
Clarke, John 4:51:19 (20,950)
Clarke, John 4:59:33 (22,535)
Clarke, Jonathon 3:41:58 (6,118)
Clarke, Karteek 3:39:04 (5,584)
Clarke, Kenneth 3:57:52 (9,453)
Clarke, Kenneth 5:23:12 (25,720)
Clarke, Kenneth 5:59:27 (28,391)
Clarke, Lee 4:16:04 (13,480)
Clarke, Malcolm 4:16:32 (13,581)
Clarke, Martin 3:05:07 (1,356)
Clarke, Martin 4:06:50 (11,512)
Clarke, Martin 4:46:12 (19,988)
Clarke, Michael 3:24:02 (3,250)
Clarke, Michael 3:54:24 (8,562)
Clarke, Michael 5:34:47 (26,779)
Clarke, Nicholas 3:01:54 (1,141)
Clarke, Nicholas 4:31:53 (17,085)
Clarke, Nicholas 4:35:16 (17,767)
Clarke, Nigel 3:10:10 (1,755)
Clarke, Paul 3:04:08 (1,291)
Clarke, Paul 4:31:54 (17,090)
Clarke, Paul 4:32:03 (17,130)
Clarke, Paul 4:43:29 (19,490)
Clarke, Peter 3:33:29 (4,688)
Clarke, Peter 4:16:26 (13,561)
Clarke, Phil 3:57:53 (9,460)
Clarke, Philip 4:19:56 (14,348)
Clarke, Richard 5:36:50 (26,932)
Clarke, Robert 3:59:09 (9,800)
Clarke, Roger 3:20:45 (2,857)
Clarke, Stephen 4:22:37 (14,958)
Clarke, Steven 4:00:00 (10,054)
Clarke, Trevor 5:12:20 (24,400)
Clarke, Wayne 4:34:02 (17,541)
Clarke Geeson, Paul 3:28:15 (3,855)
Clarke Jones, Lynne 5:01:36 (22,816)
Clarkson, Dean 6:09:48 (28,855)
Clarkson, Edward 3:32:49 (4,574)
Clarkson, Frank 5:07:06 (23,630)
Clarkson, Graham 3:18:19 (2,577)
Clarkson, Nigel 5:07:09 (23,641)
Clarkson, Thomas 3:53:53 (8,457)
Clasby, Patrick 4:59:47 (22,571)
Claud, Laurent 3:44:56 (6,670)
Clavey, John 3:58:59 (9,749)
Claxton, Jules 6:12:29 (28,946)
Claxton, Nigel 5:05:34 (23,391)
Clay, Adrian 4:12:17 (12,687)
Clay, Toby 3:13:38 (2,070)
Claydon, Christopher 4:47:30 (20,260)
Clayton, Andy 4:33:52 (17,513)
Clayton, David 4:01:14 (10,323)
Clayton, David 5:44:33 (27,526)
Clayton, Edward 3:44:10 (6,521)
Clayton, Graham 4:48:54 (20,503)
Clayton, Ian 2:45:44 (313)
Clayton, James 5:07:24 (23,682)
Clayton, Jonathan 3:59:33 (9,936)
Clayton, Jonathan 4:04:41 (11,038)
Clayton, Matthew 5:22:40 (25,665)
Clayton, Rory 4:54:08 (21,539)
Clayton, Stephen 2:59:16 (958)
Clayton Jones, Giles 5:39:04 (27,090)
Clazey, Graeme 4:04:04 (10,897)
Cleary, Andrew 3:07:14 (1,521)
Cleary, Michael 3:00:36 (1,058)
Cleary, Ryan 3:09:19 (1,697)
Cleaver, James 3:55:41 (8,839)
Clegg, Andrew 3:32:05 (4,478)
Clegg, David 5:15:49 (24,910)
Clegg, Malcolm 5:43:47 (27,457)
Clemente, Peter 4:41:43 (19,104)
Clements, Andrew 2:34:44 (91)
Clements, Jonathan 4:49:59 (20,715)
Clements, Martin 3:01:14 (1,093)
Clements, Martin 4:20:29 (14,471)
Clements, Martin 5:15:24 (24,855)
Clements, Martyn 3:45:33 (6,757)
Clements, Richard 6:24:42 (29,277)
Clements, Toby 4:06:22 (11,422)
Clements, Trevor 3:28:20 (3,878)
Clemmensen, Poul 2:59:04 (939)
Clenaghan, Stuart 4:45:44 (19,891)
Cleverley, David 2:55:46 (668)
Cleverly, Daron 4:58:19 (22,343)
Cleverly, James 5:30:09 (26,383)
Cleverly, Joseph 4:12:59 (12,825)
Cleworth, Paul 4:36:47 (18,078)
Clews, Stephen 2:53:08 (549)
Cliff, Simon 5:13:40 (24,592)
Cliffe, Christopher 4:21:29 (14,689)
Cliffe, Shane 5:56:29 (28,241)
Cliffe, Tom 4:31:40 (17,028)
Clifford, Callum 4:40:39 (18,911)
Clifford, Glen 6:14:47 (29,015)
Clifford, Marcus 5:12:36 (24,443)
Clifford, Tim 5:16:31 (24,991)
Clift, Andrew 4:10:08 (12,189)
Clifton, Mick 2:57:11 (758)
Clinton, Brian 4:19:01 (14,123)
Clitherow, Paul 5:35:26 (26,837)
Clochez, Olivier 3:29:33 (4,088)
Clohessy, Stephen 3:47:55 (7,248)
Cloke, Simon 4:38:42 (18,548)
Close, Ian 3:24:54 (3,364)
Close, Rob 4:11:30 (12,501)
Close Brooks, William 3:23:41 (3,195)
Clough, Paul 4:24:12 (15,330)
Clough, Stephen 4:24:12 (15,330)
Cloughley, John 4:47:04 (20,177)
Clouston, David 2:59:18 (963)
Clover, Dominic 3:51:09 (7,904)
Clowes, Nigel 5:47:51 (27,759)
Clucas, Merle 4:54:54 (21,702)
Clulee, John 5:21:44 (25,552)
Clune, David 5:01:13 (22,772)
Clyne, James 3:31:32 (4,396)
Clyne, Michael 5:05:55 (23,451)
Clynes, Declan 2:58:34 (864)
Coade, David 3:45:55 (6,839)
Coadou, Bernard 3:18:29 (2,596)
Coady, Mark 4:32:52 (17,289)
Coate, Clive 4:28:14 (16,246)
Coates, Alistair 5:39:40 (27,154)
Coates, Andrew 3:54:56 (8,690)
Coates, Andrew 4:10:10 (12,200)
Coates, Bob 3:17:10 (2,442)
Coates, Christopher 3:58:36 (9,642)
Coates, Ian 3:50:55 (7,853)
Coates, Ian 3:51:02 (7,880)
Coates, Michael 4:51:16 (20,935)
Coates, Mike 4:56:13 (22,028)
Coates, Phil 3:42:36 (6,235)
Coates, Phillip 3:35:12 (4,933)
Coates, Robert 4:24:05 (15,307)
Coates, Robert 5:23:01 (25,708)
Coates, Tom 4:42:07 (19,182)
Cobb, David 4:29:52 (16,648)
Cobb, Nigel 2:50:29 (446)
Cobb, Norman 4:10:45 (12,321)
Cobb, Parrish 4:46:55 (20,151)
Cobbett, Giles 3:54:50 (8,668)
Cobbett, Richard 4:24:05 (15,307)
Coburn, Martin 3:44:35 (6,594)
Cocchi, Massimiliano 4:10:55 (12,378)
Cochard, Philippe 3:32:35 (4,548)
Cochran, Gary 4:04:38 (11,028)
Cochrane, Ian 4:13:18 (12,874)
Cochrane, Jason 6:54:29 (29,868)
Cochrane, William 4:22:07 (14,838)
Cock, Mark 4:53:08 (21,343)
Cockayne, John 5:09:57 (24,076)
Cockbill, David 3:43:12 (6,345)
Cockbill, David 4:05:28 (11,202)
Cockburn, Howard 4:51:41 (21,029)

Cocker, Daniel	5:09:34 (24,024)	
Cocker, James	4:52:19 (21,164)	
Cocker, John	3:52:14 (8,122)	
Cockerell, Barney	3:47:53 (7,237)	
Cockerell, Justin	3:25:11 (3,400)	
Cockerell, William	2:32:27 (73)	
Cocking, George	5:10:14 (24,110)	
Coddington, Russell	4:21:39 (14,724)	
Codrington, Charles	3:18:13 (2,564)	
Coe, Steven	3:20:56 (2,881)	
Coeck, Danny	4:00:31 (10,158)	
Coetzee, Etienne	4:35:06 (17,733)	
Coffey, Andrew	3:57:43 (9,399)	
Coffey, Dan	7:30:48 (30,138)	
Coffey, Keith	3:10:21 (1,780)	
Coffill, Anthony	6:13:33 (28,979)	
Coffin, Benjamin	4:19:58 (14,355)	
Coffin, Rodney	6:19:32 (29,145)	
Coffin, Tim	4:10:33 (12,284)	
Coggins, Andrew	3:22:21 (3,041)	
Coghlan, Anthony	3:34:28 (4,832)	
Coghlan, Greg	5:09:43 (24,045)	
Coghlan, Guy	4:02:03 (10,495)	
Cogswell, Nicholas	4:18:22 (13,976)	
Cohen, Adam	4:55:55 (21,971)	
Cohen, Elliott	5:07:42 (23,729)	
Cohen, Erez	3:52:00 (8,075)	
Cohen, Gary	4:16:13 (13,511)	
Cohen, Howard	3:38:49 (5,540)	
Cohen, Kfir	4:32:48 (17,276)	
Cohen, Leon	3:57:38 (9,379)	
Cohen, Ronald	5:12:47 (24,465)	
Coinu, Giuseppe	4:02:07 (10,507)	
Coke, Rupert	4:44:06 (19,597)	
Coker, Ben	4:51:34 (20,999)	
Colavitti, Marco	2:59:56 (1,024)	
Colbourne, Jonathan	4:08:02 (11,774)	
Colbridge, Ian	4:59:57 (22,613)	
Colby, John	4:21:35 (14,708)	
Cole, Anthony	4:28:07 (16,217)	
Cole, Anthony	4:54:30 (21,594)	
Cole, Blue	4:55:37 (21,928)	
Cole, Brendan	3:38:46 (5,532)	
Cole, Brian	2:32:44 (78)	
Cole, Brian	4:37:13 (18,175)	
Cole, Edward	4:10:22 (12,244)	
Cole, George	4:20:18 (14,429)	
Cole, Jonathan	4:23:45 (15,236)	
Cole, Martin	6:23:49 (29,255)	
Cole, Matthew	6:23:25 (29,240)	
Cole, Michael	5:56:14 (28,222)	
Cole, Paul	4:34:21 (17,606)	
Cole, Ray	3:17:27 (2,482)	
Cole, Rob	3:07:49 (1,574)	
Cole, Roger	3:38:37 (5,502)	
Cole, Spencer	4:29:39 (16,585)	
Cole, Stephen	3:53:26 (8,364)	
Cole, Stuart	4:57:26 (22,208)	
Cole, Terence	3:30:52 (4,305)	
Colein, Amaury	3:53:38 (8,409)	
Coleman, Adam	4:32:26 (17,201)	
Coleman, Jason	4:51:51 (21,062)	
Coleman, John	4:32:02 (17,124)	
Coleman, John	6:38:32 (29,599)	
Coleman, Mark	4:40:53 (18,953)	
Coleman, Michael	2:21:47 (26)	
Coleman, Paul	4:06:56 (11,535)	
Coleman, Paul	4:55:04 (21,754)	
Coleman, Philip	3:49:11 (7,493)	
Coleman, Rory	5:00:48 (22,703)	
Coleman, Stanley	4:58:23 (22,357)	
Coleman, Tony	5:41:38 (27,305)	
Colenso, David	4:05:43 (11,273)	
Coles, Andy	6:45:25 (29,743)	
Coles, Daniel	5:16:23 (24,970)	
Coles, Roger	4:10:44 (12,318)	
Coles, Tim	3:26:24 (3,544)	
Coles, Vernon	5:48:59 (27,840)	
Coley, David	3:38:51 (5,548)	
Coley, Philip	4:49:01 (20,530)	
Collavini, Sergio	2:49:58 (427)	
Colledge, Simon	3:56:23 (9,018)	
Collenberg, Norbert	3:28:34 (3,920)	

Collett, Ray	6:10:45 (28,882)	
Collett, Ryan	3:28:36 (3,924)	
Collette, Gilles	3:48:45 (7,412)	
Colley, Frank	7:17:56 (30,067)	
Colley, John	4:03:19 (10,728)	
Colley, John	5:35:46 (26,864)	
Colley, Jonathan	3:00:44 (1,067)	
Colley, Mark	4:26:28 (15,836)	
Colley, Richard	3:58:07 (9,519)	
Colley, Stan	4:06:17 (11,404)	
Collie, John	3:13:37 (2,068)	
Collier, Adam	4:39:50 (18,758)	
Collier, Darren	6:21:20 (29,202)	
Collier, David	2:46:10 (321)	
Collier, Edward	3:15:23 (2,259)	
Collier, Jeffrey	3:31:05 (4,338)	
Collier, John	4:48:24 (20,426)	
Collier, Mark	4:39:18 (18,646)	
Collier, Matthew	4:35:36 (17,843)	
Collier, Michael	3:59:18 (9,841)	
Collier, Paul	3:51:30 (7,966)	
Collier, Paul	4:16:32 (13,581)	
Collier, Ronald	4:46:05 (19,954)	
Collier Brown, Bradley	4:24:37 (15,424)	
Collin, Anthony	4:30:49 (16,809)	
Collin, Peter	5:59:46 (28,407)	
Colling, Mark	3:24:21 (3,291)	
Collingbourne, Robert	4:03:42 (10,821)	
Collins, Adrian	4:04:10 (10,918)	
Collins, Andrew	4:27:43 (16,125)	
Collins, Andrew	5:02:02 (22,880)	
Collins, Andy	3:12:49 (1,988)	
Collins, Barnaby	4:28:44 (16,367)	
Collins, Barrie	3:58:38 (9,649)	
Collins, David	3:43:42 (6,437)	
Collins, Eric	6:07:21 (28,739)	
Collins, Gary	3:06:49 (1,489)	
Collins, Gary	3:59:46 (9,989)	
Collins, Gavin	3:58:03 (9,501)	
Collins, Gerard	3:30:02 (4,176)	
Collins, Gerard	5:04:02 (23,138)	
Collins, Graham	3:00:33 (1,054)	
Collins, Ian	4:16:59 (13,661)	
Collins, James	3:56:33 (9,066)	
Collins, James	4:23:33 (15,189)	
Collins, John	4:59:46 (22,565)	
Collins, John	5:18:47 (25,249)	
Collins, John	5:26:05 (25,994)	
Collins, Joseph	5:12:03 (24,361)	
Collins, Lyndon	3:08:57 (1,667)	
Collins, Mark	3:27:12 (3,660)	
Collins, Maurice	2:41:30 (203)	
Collins, Michael	3:47:18 (7,085)	
Collins, Michael	5:39:18 (27,115)	
Collins, Neil	5:24:51 (25,862)	
Collins, Nicholas	3:37:23 (5,320)	
Collins, Nigel	3:26:03 (3,507)	
Collins, Nigel	3:59:47 (9,992)	
Collins, Patrick	3:15:41 (2,287)	
Collins, Patrick	3:58:19 (9,565)	
Collins, Peter	4:06:27 (11,440)	
Collins, Peter	4:32:07 (17,138)	
Collins, Richard	4:40:59 (18,974)	
Collins, Rob	5:24:27 (25,829)	
Collins, Russell	4:19:37 (14,284)	
Collins, Sean	4:00:29 (10,148)	
Collins, Stephen	3:12:33 (1,964)	
Collins, Steve	3:54:51 (8,672)	
Collins, Terry	5:10:59 (24,209)	
Collins, Trevor	5:31:47 (26,515)	
Collinson, Andrew	2:51:25 (485)	
Collinson, Andrew	5:48:09 (27,787)	
Collinson, David	3:35:27 (4,978)	
Collinson, Francis	4:01:38 (10,418)	
Collinson, Jonathan	3:37:00 (5,246)	
Collis, Brian	3:40:34 (5,878)	
Collis, James	3:12:18 (1,941)	
Collis, James	3:29:06 (4,015)	
Collis, Martin	5:28:28 (26,227)	
Collis, Michael	5:01:02 (22,738)	
Collison, Daniel	5:09:07 (23,955)	
Collison, Nigel	4:04:30 (10,988)	
Collman, Stephen	4:33:18 (17,368)	

Collom, Robert	3:50:43 (7,812)	
Collyer, Michael	3:24:47 (3,352)	
Colman, Paul	3:39:59 (5,782)	
Colmer, Douglas	4:17:55 (13,856)	
Colmer, Geoffrey	4:30:46 (16,801)	
Colnaghi, Piercarlo	3:51:54 (8,049)	
Coloigner, Gilbert	3:49:17 (7,518)	
Colquhoun, Alasdair	3:53:35 (8,399)	
Colquhoun, Gavin	4:27:27 (16,050)	
Colson, William	3:51:28 (7,956)	
Colston, Adrian	5:19:04 (25,271)	
Colston, Stuart	5:22:36 (25,660)	
Colston, Tim	4:57:36 (22,228)	
Coltelli, Tyrone	4:05:42 (11,268)	
Coltham, Andrew	3:33:50 (4,732)	
Colton, John	3:37:28 (5,329)	
Colvin, Paul	4:38:00 (18,371)	
Colwell, James	4:21:51 (14,774)	
Colyer, Adam	4:04:24 (10,969)	
Colyer, Duncan	4:13:24 (12,907)	
Comanducci, Gianfranco	3:47:38 (7,175)	
Combe, Charlie	4:38:45 (18,559)	
Combellack, Ian	4:08:16 (11,816)	
Comber, Barrie	5:32:21 (26,554)	
Comber, Steven	3:38:24 (5,466)	
Comerford, Jeremy	3:53:56 (8,466)	
Comette, Allan	5:08:34 (23,859)	
Comiskey, John	4:19:23 (14,220)	
Comonte, Crispin	3:18:01 (2,535)	
Comonte, Dominic	3:41:58 (6,118)	
Compton, David	4:48:08 (20,375)	
Compton, James	4:09:41 (12,105)	
Compton, Nicholas	4:34:53 (17,690)	
Conaghan, Peter	3:46:11 (6,895)	
Concannon, Kenneth	5:37:58 (27,016)	
Concannon, Peter	3:34:02 (4,759)	
Condliffe, James	5:03:46 (23,094)	
Condon, Peter	5:32:02 (26,535)	
Coney, Wiliam	3:49:28 (7,567)	
Coningham, Matt	3:23:50 (3,219)	
Coningham-Rolls, John	4:51:32 (20,991)	
Conlan, Sean	4:02:21 (10,539)	
Conlin, S	3:47:11 (7,062)	
Conlon, Ian	4:16:21 (13,536)	
Conlon, Michael	3:09:08 (1,685)	
Conlon, Niall	5:34:32 (26,760)	
Conmy, James	5:26:31 (26,045)	
Conneally, George	4:39:44 (18,740)	
Conneely, Ruairi	4:09:15 (12,034)	
Connell, Anthony	4:28:53 (16,392)	
Connell, John	3:33:42 (4,714)	
Connell, Phillip	4:07:27 (11,655)	
Connell, Richard	3:50:16 (7,732)	
Connelly, Martin	2:39:53 (170)	
Conner, Andrew	3:54:21 (8,549)	
Conners, Kevin	3:30:57 (4,322)	
Connet, David	5:48:09 (27,787)	
Connett, David	4:27:11 (16,004)	
Connock, Adrian	5:11:10 (24,238)	
Connolly, Brendan	4:49:05 (20,540)	
Connolly, Christopher	4:59:25 (22,515)	
Connolly, David	3:57:14 (9,236)	
Connolly, James	5:40:32 (27,227)	
Connolly, Matthew	5:39:25 (27,123)	
Connolly, Ray	4:10:25 (12,260)	
Connolly, Sean	3:28:13 (3,848)	
Connolly, Shane	2:59:54 (1,018)	
Connolly, Terry	4:52:35 (21,233)	
Connolly, Wayne	3:05:57 (1,416)	
Connop, David	3:53:48 (8,442)	
Connor, David	4:53:50 (21,483)	
Connor, Hadley	5:28:41 (26,252)	
Connor, Hugh	4:05:42 (11,268)	
Connor, Justin	4:50:37 (20,814)	
Connor, Paul	3:14:14 (2,137)	
Connor, Peter	3:01:34 (1,118)	
Connor-Stead, Philip	4:05:42 (11,268)	
Conquest, Johnny	3:11:07 (1,845)	
Conrads, Peter	3:43:37 (6,418)	
Conroy, Kieron	3:33:22 (4,668)	
Constable, Eric	5:45:00 (27,561)	
Constant, Robert	3:17:03 (2,432)	
Constantino, Conceicao	3:53:36 (8,404)	

Constantino, James 4:46:19 (20,010)
Conway, Donal 3:59:25 (9,891)
Conway, Gerard 3:42:17 (6,179)
Conway, Huw 4:26:39 (15,882)
Conway, Jerome 4:25:13 (15,560)
Conway, John 3:47:54 (7,241)
Conway, Neil 4:23:52 (15,266)
Conway, Nic 4:18:55 (14,103)
Conway, Paul 3:39:19 (5,631)
Conway, Richard 3:42:24 (6,201)
Conway, Shane 5:27:53 (26,170)
Conway, Steven 4:17:35 (13,789)
Conway, Terry 6:18:50 (29,134)
Coode, Matthew 3:55:42 (8,843)
Coode, Richard 5:41:45 (27,310)
Coogan, Andy 4:56:10 (22,015)
Cook, Alan 2:49:48 (418)
Cook, Albert 4:23:12 (15,108)
Cook, Alistair 4:59:20 (22,503)
Cook, Andrew 3:09:56 (1,744)
Cook, Chris 3:48:46 (7,415)
Cook, Christopher 3:16:09 (2,331)
Cook, Christopher 3:45:45 (6,810)
Cook, David 3:01:58 (1,145)
Cook, David 5:02:38 (22,952)
Cook, Derek 4:22:46 (14,996)
Cook, George 3:52:37 (8,195)
Cook, George 3:56:59 (9,174)
Cook, Glen 4:59:00 (22,462)
Cook, Hugh 3:41:13 (5,987)
Cook, John 3:26:06 (3,512)
Cook, John 5:00:29 (22,659)
Cook, John 5:06:58 (23,611)
Cook, Keith 3:27:33 (3,718)
Cook, Len 4:19:25 (14,231)
Cook, Leonard 5:33:41 (26,662)
Cook, Mark 3:47:59 (7,262)
Cook, Martin 6:00:48 (28,446)
Cook, Michael 3:44:54 (6,661)
Cook, Michael 4:23:36 (15,205)
Cook, Neil 4:22:57 (15,052)
Cook, Paul 3:18:34 (2,605)
Cook, Paul 4:51:10 (20,920)
Cook, Peter 4:24:33 (15,408)
Cook, Phil 2:37:05 (117)
Cook, Philip 4:20:13 (14,411)
Cook, Philip 5:05:08 (23,310)
Cook, Raymond 6:17:28 (29,098)
Cook, Robert 3:52:37 (8,195)
Cook, Robert 4:07:34 (11,672)
Cook, Stephen 4:37:06 (18,144)
Cook, Stuart 4:27:11 (16,004)
Cook, Terry 5:23:37 (25,758)
Cook, Timothy 3:58:59 (9,749)
Cook, Timothy 4:34:01 (17,538)
Cook, Tony 4:50:39 (20,818)
Cook, Trevor 2:45:26 (306)
Cook, William 4:31:18 (16,934)
Cook, William 4:32:30 (17,215)
Cooke, Alan 4:26:33 (15,856)
Cooke, Andrew 3:58:16 (9,557)
Cooke, Andy 4:35:42 (17,865)
Cooke, Bradley 5:57:25 (28,292)
Cooke, Bruce 3:14:48 (2,196)
Cooke, Howard 3:30:13 (4,203)
Cooke, Ian 4:32:49 (17,278)
Cooke, Jason 2:50:34 (449)
Cooke, Jeremy 5:17:51 (25,147)
Cooke, Kevin 3:52:44 (8,215)
Cooke, Paul 3:48:55 (7,442)
Cooke, Paul 3:57:51 (9,446)
Cooke, Simon 4:19:32 (14,264)
Cooke, Stuart 4:42:25 (19,255)
Cookman, Graham 3:54:56 (8,690)
Cooksey, Andrew 4:23:22 (15,146)
Cookson, Colin 4:12:47 (12,788)
Cookson, Ian 3:43:58 (6,483)
Coole, Timothy 4:14:29 (13,123)
Cooley, David 5:15:25 (24,858)
Coolican, David 3:48:47 (7,420)
Cooling, Mark 5:13:13 (24,535)
Coombe, Joshua 3:57:22 (9,279)
Coomber, Mark 5:09:22 (23,992)
Coombes, David 5:02:01 (22,874)
Coombes, Eric 3:54:49 (8,664)
Coombes, Ian 5:19:36 (25,318)
Coombes, Lee 5:12:58 (24,493)
Coombes, Michael 4:16:37 (13,591)
Coombs, Michael 4:49:23 (20,592)
Coombs, Peter 5:11:52 (24,339)
Coombs, Stephen 6:13:27 (28,967)
Cooney, Alvin 3:24:58 (3,372)
Cooney, Andrew 3:15:05 (2,232)
Coop, Richard 5:01:28 (22,799)
Coope, Bernie 4:46:31 (20,059)
Coope, David 3:24:42 (3,342)
Coope, Philip 4:35:42 (17,865)
Cooper, Allan 3:56:55 (9,159)
Cooper, Andrew 2:44:13 (268)
Cooper, Arjen 5:33:44 (26,665)
Cooper, Ashley 5:22:01 (25,588)
Cooper, Ben 5:09:05 (23,952)
Cooper, Benjamin 4:11:58 (12,600)
Cooper, Benjamin 5:15:04 (24,794)
Cooper, Bryan 4:39:42 (18,734)
Cooper, Carl 3:14:33 (2,172)
Cooper, Chris 3:52:41 (8,207)
Cooper, Christopher 4:01:41 (10,428)
Cooper, Craig 3:58:02 (9,497)
Cooper, Dave 4:00:27 (10,136)
Cooper, David 3:18:47 (2,631)
Cooper, David 3:34:45 (4,869)
Cooper, David 4:35:17 (17,771)
Cooper, Douglas 3:13:41 (2,072)
Cooper, Edwin 4:06:30 (11,450)
Cooper, Elliott 5:13:16 (24,548)
Cooper, Gary 4:29:58 (16,684)
Cooper, Gary 5:39:06 (27,095)
Cooper, Glen 5:41:12 (27,271)
Cooper, Grant 5:55:24 (28,178)
Cooper, Huw 4:08:42 (11,914)
Cooper, Ian 2:59:55 (1,020)
Cooper, Ian 3:29:17 (4,045)
Cooper, Ian 4:07:42 (11,699)
Cooper, John 3:27:17 (3,672)
Cooper, John 3:39:20 (5,635)
Cooper, John 3:59:24 (9,885)
Cooper, John 4:02:45 (10,617)
Cooper, John 4:17:38 (13,799)
Cooper, Ken 4:14:45 (13,194)
Cooper, Leonard 4:42:05 (19,174)
Cooper, Mark 4:01:35 (10,406)
Cooper, Mark 5:08:29 (23,844)
Cooper, Michael 4:26:58 (15,955)
Cooper, Micholas 4:56:17 (22,035)
Cooper, Mike 6:03:23 (28,560)
Cooper, Nicholas 3:14:14 (2,137)
Cooper, Paul 3:52:06 (8,097)
Cooper, Paul 3:57:56 (9,472)
Cooper, Peter 3:10:37 (1,803)
Cooper, Peter 5:08:20 (23,822)
Cooper, Philip 4:25:54 (15,702)
Cooper, Ralph 5:04:51 (23,276)
Cooper, Richard 4:12:21 (12,703)
Cooper, Richard 4:25:40 (15,646)
Cooper, Richard 4:59:52 (22,594)
Cooper, Robert 3:57:26 (9,304)
Cooper, Robert 4:35:39 (17,855)
Cooper, Rowan 5:44:34 (27,532)
Cooper, Seamus 3:55:19 (8,763)
Cooper, Stephen 4:07:09 (11,579)
Cooper, Terry 4:44:23 (19,652)
Cooper, Tom 6:02:34 (28,523)
Cooper, Vincent 5:39:15 (27,110)
Cooperman, first name unknown 3:43:07 (6,328)
Coote, Ian 4:16:37 (13,591)
Cope, Christopher 4:55:12 (21,783)
Cope, David 4:10:57 (12,389)
Cope, Trevor 3:36:18 (5,123)
Copeland, Robert 4:43:51 (19,565)
Copestick, Robin 2:40:25 (181)
Copithorne, Joe 3:15:50 (2,298)
Copland, David 4:18:53 (14,095)
Copland, Terence 5:41:54 (27,327)
Copleston, Edward 3:35:56 (5,060)
Copley, Andrew 4:48:29 (20,437)
Copley, Brian 2:57:05 (750)
Copley, John 4:44:53 (19,754)
Copp, Alan 4:47:30 (20,260)
Copp, Austin 3:52:27 (8,162)
Coppier, Alain 3:50:04 (7,697)
Copsey, Richard 4:15:37 (13,390)
Copsey, Simon 3:52:51 (8,238)
Copus, Christopher 3:00:20 (1,048)
Corbae, Gerald 4:55:29 (21,885)
Corban, Ian 5:43:58 (27,473)
Corbett, Clive 4:31:44 (17,043)
Corbett, David 3:57:12 (9,226)
Corbett, David 4:43:57 (19,581)
Corbett, Oliver 3:58:24 (9,585)
Corbett, Richard 4:37:34 (18,270)
Corbett, Robert 4:51:43 (21,036)
Corbin, David 3:25:51 (3,486)
Corbin, Matthew 4:22:16 (14,877)
Corbould, Stephen 3:49:28 (7,567)
Cordall, Michael 3:23:00 (3,113)
Corden, Adrian 5:08:34 (23,859)
Corden, James 3:15:55 (2,312)
Corden-Lloyd, James 4:14:06 (13,056)
Cording, John 3:45:15 (6,713)
Cording, Stephen 3:59:24 (9,885)
Cordwell, Jeff 4:15:25 (13,350)
Cordwell, Julian 4:20:48 (14,547)
Corfe, Andrew 3:33:59 (4,752)
Corfield, Patrick 3:48:03 (7,276)
Corjeon, Jacques 5:02:28 (22,933)
Cork, Adrian 4:22:04 (14,833)
Corke, Adrian 4:25:22 (15,587)
Corke, Frank 4:59:47 (22,571)
Corke, Simon 4:22:38 (14,962)
Corlett, Daniel 3:37:17 (5,298)
Corlett, Michael 4:48:30 (20,439)
Corlett, Neil 3:31:03 (4,336)
Cornally, James 4:59:48 (22,575)
Corneille, Dean 5:37:32 (26,981)
Cornelius, Gary 3:53:40 (8,416)
Cornelius, Ian 4:11:08 (12,423)
Cornelius, Karl Heinz 5:46:29 (27,658)
Cornelius, Nigel 3:44:45 (6,625)
Cornes, Nicholas 4:06:10 (11,372)
Corney, Paul 4:04:45 (11,057)
Cornforth, Stephen 3:43:45 (6,449)
Cornick, Andrew 4:01:01 (10,285)
Cornish, Alan 3:16:02 (2,324)
Cornish, Benjamin 5:33:20 (26,636)
Cornish, Jeff 3:45:49 (6,827)
Cornter, Danny 3:44:16 (6,535)
Cornwall, Dale 3:51:42 (8,006)
Cornwall, Michael 3:16:58 (2,420)
Cornwell, Michael 3:52:43 (8,213)
Corpe, Jonathan 3:39:54 (5,759)
Corper, Simon 3:51:39 (7,997)
Corr, Eugene 4:55:31 (21,901)
Corrie, Justin 3:17:06 (2,435)
Corriette, Michael 4:37:00 (18,131)
Corrigan, John 4:53:03 (21,325)
Corvin, Dara 4:52:22 (21,175)
Cory, Timothy 3:22:57 (3,104)
Cosby, John 4:43:10 (19,422)
Cosby, Scott 4:35:34 (17,829)
Cosford, Tim 4:21:05 (14,608)
Cosh, Adrian 4:20:27 (14,464)
Cosh, Ian 3:23:31 (3,178)
Cosh, William 5:02:31 (22,939)
Cosi, Fabrizio 3:28:27 (3,898)
Cosi, Vanni 3:42:59 (6,299)
Cossar, Ants 4:01:46 (10,442)
Cossar, Martin 4:06:47 (11,498)
Cosson, Thierry 4:26:38 (15,878)
Costa, José 7:52:59 (30,195)
Costa, Pedro 4:08:25 (11,853)
Costa, Tony 4:05:32 (11,223)
Costa Fernandes, Casimiro 3:12:56 (1,998)
Costain, Nigel 3:45:42 (6,796)
Costaras, Chris 3:43:07 (6,328)
Costello, Andrew 4:18:34 (14,027)
Costello, Brendan 4:37:47 (18,316)
Costello, John 6:05:34 (28,672)
Costello, Mark 4:49:50 (20,682)

Costello, Patrick 4:44:23 (19,652)
Costello, Paul 3:30:02 (4,176)
Costello, Paul 5:30:03 (26,379)
Costellow, Robert 3:57:34 (9,352)
Costi, Chris 4:17:39 (13,802)
Costidell, Peter 3:53:30 (8,375)
Costin, Jonathan 5:42:53 (27,402)
Costley, Simon 4:32:41 (17,243)
Cosway, David 3:43:11 (6,341)
Cottam, Christopher 4:07:33 (11,666)
Cotter, Trevor 4:07:14 (11,595)
Cotterell, Alan 3:36:08 (5,095)
Cotterill, Mark 3:18:33 (2,602)
Cotterill, Phillip 3:10:32 (1,796)
Cotterill, Robert 6:14:56 (29,020)
Cottingham, Bernard 6:05:13 (28,648)
Cottingham, Paul 4:02:30 (10,571)
Cottis, John 2:58:32 (860)
Cottis, Roy 3:49:50 (7,651)
Cotton, Anthony 3:27:30 (3,707)
Cotton, Mark 5:24:32 (25,841)
Cotton, Roger 5:50:49 (27,946)
Cottrell, Brendan 3:20:24 (2,806)
Cottrell, Michael 4:14:53 (13,231)
Cottrill, Brian 4:15:34 (13,381)
Couch, David 4:19:27 (14,241)
Couch, Jon 3:19:34 (2,713)
Couch, Nigel 4:12:25 (12,719)
Couchman, James 5:40:24 (27,217)
Coudrey, Joric 3:51:33 (7,978)
Coughlan, Edward 5:10:54 (24,197)
Coughlan, Robert 4:41:45 (19,112)
Couldrey, Bill 7:20:45 (30,081)
Couldridge, Simon 4:38:22 (18,473)
Coulson, Andrew 6:23:44 (29,253)
Coulson, Robert 3:23:58 (3,241)
Coulson, Stephen 3:56:36 (9,077)
Coulson, Stephen 4:25:00 (15,509)
Coulson, Wayne 3:04:29 (1,313)
Coult, Graham 4:22:00 (14,813)
Coulter, Barry 2:57:45 (794)
Coulter, Finn 4:53:51 (21,489)
Coulthard, William 4:34:36 (17,643)
Coulthurst, Andrew 3:28:05 (3,816)
Coulton, Robert 5:20:28 (25,407)
Counsell, Mathew 3:58:06 (9,515)
Counsell, Richard 7:13:27 (30,042)
Counsell, Steve 4:08:36 (11,892)
Coupar, Carl 4:03:34 (10,793)
Courivaud, Jacques 3:49:04 (7,480)
Court, Alan 3:37:18 (5,301)
Court, Andrew 5:42:28 (27,367)
Court, Daniel 3:30:50 (4,298)
Court, David 3:44:37 (6,598)
Court, Richard 3:52:17 (8,133)
Court, Robert 2:54:51 (624)
Courtier, Robert 4:55:35 (21,913)
Courtiour, Michael 4:12:11 (12,669)
Courtney, John 5:51:41 (27,995)
Courtney, Kevin 2:51:09 (472)
Cousens, Charles 4:25:59 (15,727)
Cousins, Jon 4:14:03 (13,050)
Cousins, Nicholas 3:51:46 (8,021)
Cousins, Patrick 3:01:39 (1,129)
Coussens, Stephen 4:06:21 (11,418)
Coutts, David 4:36:36 (18,040)
Coutts, Eric 4:14:55 (13,239)
Couvreur, Pierre 2:51:31 (490)
Covey, Sean 3:05:41 (1,400)
Covey, Wayne 4:29:07 (16,453)
Covington, Richard 4:25:01 (15,514)
Covus, Steve 5:34:17 (26,732)
Cowan, Christopher 4:41:03 (18,987)
Cowan, Jamie 4:47:24 (20,238)
Coward, Edgar 4:04:49 (11,070)
Coward, Jeremy 3:05:01 (1,351)
Cowdry, Roland 4:06:52 (11,522)
Cowell, Iain 4:03:31 (10,776)
Cowell, Mark 3:57:57 (9,478)
Cowell, Robert 2:40:03 (173)
Cowell, William 5:25:06 (25,895)
Cowham, Terry 5:00:36 (22,678)
Cowie, Duncan 3:30:41 (4,275)
Cowie, Graeme 7:27:54 (30,121)
Cowie, Michael 3:29:56 (4,159)
Cowin, Malcolm 3:46:21 (6,922)
Cowley, Nicholas 4:57:47 (22,264)
Cowley, Roger 4:38:06 (18,401)
Cowling, Antony 4:48:15 (20,395)
Cowling, Steven 4:31:06 (16,872)
Cowpe, Chris 5:13:54 (24,616)
Cowpe, Matthew 5:42:17 (27,354)
Cox, Alan 3:28:31 (3,911)
Cox, Andrew 4:04:03 (10,894)
Cox, Andrew 4:35:51 (17,891)
Cox, Anthony 4:03:54 (10,863)
Cox, Brian 4:19:07 (14,150)
Cox, Brian 5:02:05 (22,887)
Cox, Christopher 4:12:25 (12,719)
Cox, Christopher 5:54:02 (28,114)
Cox, Darren 4:33:08 (17,334)
Cox, David 3:16:08 (2,328)
Cox, Don 3:35:05 (4,914)
Cox, Elwyn 4:56:43 (22,093)
Cox, Glen 2:41:24 (200)
Cox, Grahame 5:16:57 (25,042)
Cox, Ian 4:58:05 (22,312)
Cox, John 2:44:27 (274)
Cox, John 4:54:38 (21,622)
Cox, John 6:08:08 (28,771)
Cox, Leslie 3:52:00 (8,075)
Cox, Martin 5:15:20 (24,846)
Cox, Marty 6:56:55 (29,910)
Cox, Mathew 3:40:52 (5,920)
Cox, Matthew 3:49:21 (7,538)
Cox, Matthew 4:57:35 (22,225)
Cox, Michael 3:39:39 (5,702)
Cox, Michael 4:18:01 (13,872)
Cox, Nigel 3:06:55 (1,497)
Cox, Nigel 5:12:27 (24,421)
Cox, Paul 4:14:13 (13,078)
Cox, Paul 4:25:57 (15,718)
Cox, Paul 5:06:48 (23,591)
Cox, Peter 4:38:16 (18,445)
Cox, Peter 4:55:19 (21,819)
Cox, Richard 5:39:37 (27,148)
Cox, Rob 4:28:23 (16,283)
Cox, Roland 4:25:04 (15,525)
Cox, Stephen 4:58:05 (22,312)
Cox, Steve 3:35:52 (5,047)
Cox, Trevor 4:02:52 (10,635)
Coxall, Paul 4:31:53 (17,085)
Coxhead, Ian 3:15:23 (2,259)
Coxhead, Mark 3:30:15 (4,205)
Coxon, Ben 4:55:37 (21,928)
Coxon, Peter 3:59:52 (10,016)
Coy, Gerard 3:06:01 (1,424)
Coyle, Jeff 3:33:15 (4,652)
Coyle, Maurice 3:28:22 (3,885)
Coyne, Michael 4:38:25 (18,485)
Cozens, Christopher 5:08:52 (23,915)
Crabb, David 4:14:56 (13,248)
Crabtree, Mark 2:58:56 (927)
Crabtree, Peter 3:57:32 (9,338)
Crack, Alastair 4:17:39 (13,802)
Cracknell, David 3:15:59 (2,321)
Cradden, Brendan 3:13:18 (2,037)
Craddock, Stephen 4:36:53 (18,101)
Crader, Michael 4:20:45 (14,533)
Crafford, Pieter 3:47:06 (7,051)
Cragg, Stephen 3:46:43 (6,994)
Craggs, Graham 3:50:31 (7,775)
Craig, George 4:58:16 (22,338)
Craig, Mark 3:45:50 (6,832)
Craig, Michael 4:51:19 (20,950)
Craig, Robert 3:19:04 (2,661)
Craig, Robert 4:42:03 (19,171)
Craig, William 2:46:59 (341)
Craigie, Kenneth 4:34:52 (17,689)
Cramp, Philip 4:23:12 (15,108)
Cramphorn, John 3:25:26 (3,438)
Crampton, Gary 3:32:46 (4,568)
Crampton, Ian 2:34:20 (87)
Crane, Alastair 5:03:22 (23,049)
Crane, Carl 3:09:02 (1,675)
Crane, Howard 3:35:56 (5,060)
Crane, Melvin 4:56:25 (22,054)
Crane, Michael 4:06:37 (11,471)
Crane, Neil 4:41:21 (19,038)
Crane, Peter 3:23:09 (3,132)
Crane, Robert 3:52:08 (8,104)
Crane, William 3:08:54 (1,664)
Cranham, Nicholas 3:46:16 (6,910)
Crankshaw, David 5:11:09 (24,237)
Cranshaw, Ian 4:53:17 (21,368)
Cranshaw, Julius 4:42:59 (19,383)
Craplet, Thierry 3:38:29 (5,478)
Craplet, Xavier 4:47:54 (20,325)
Craske, Anthony 3:50:58 (7,861)
Crate, Malcolm 4:07:33 (11,666)
Craven, Ashley 4:17:56 (13,861)
Craven, Christopher 4:04:09 (10,910)
Craven, James 4:34:16 (17,588)
Craven, Paul 4:21:22 (14,660)
Crawford, Anthony 5:36:58 (26,943)
Crawford, David 4:19:28 (14,249)
Crawford, Ian 3:08:31 (1,634)
Crawford, Joseph 3:53:46 (8,436)
Crawford, Kenneth 4:33:44 (17,485)
Crawford, Mark 5:04:25 (23,204)
Crawford, Matthew 3:32:51 (4,580)
Crawford, Philip 4:24:55 (15,482)
Crawford, Richard 4:08:49 (11,938)
Crawley, John 5:13:35 (24,576)
Cray, Matthew 4:33:22 (17,392)
Creamer, Mark 4:59:48 (22,575)
Creaney Birch, Neil 4:00:39 (10,193)
Cree, Neil 5:06:17 (23,517)
Creech, Anthony 4:40:35 (18,895)
Creed, Gareth 4:13:26 (12,917)
Creed, Jeremy 3:11:35 (1,869)
Creed, Paul 5:16:57 (25,042)
Creer, Colin 3:35:08 (4,924)
Creffield, Mark 4:47:43 (20,296)
Crellin, Kevin 4:52:10 (21,130)
Cresswell, James 5:20:24 (25,397)
Cresswell, Jamie 3:56:54 (9,154)
Cresswell, Robert 3:58:47 (9,694)
Cresswell, Simon 3:34:58 (4,901)
Cretney, David 5:38:17 (27,034)
Crew, Danny 3:45:03 (6,695)
Cribb, Paul 4:30:54 (16,826)
Crichton, Robin 3:07:50 (1,577)
Crichton, Simon 5:41:29 (27,298)
Crick, Steve 4:21:48 (14,761)
Crimes, Russell 3:31:21 (4,378)
Crimmen, Daniel 3:03:00 (1,212)
Crimmins, Perry 3:16:53 (2,410)
Cripps, Jason 3:56:50 (9,142)
Cripps, Matthew 4:18:29 (14,009)
Crisinel, Jeremie 3:10:08 (1,750)
Criso, John 3:57:21 (9,273)
Crisp, Gordon 5:03:59 (23,125)
Crisp, Graham 3:38:12 (5,431)
Crisp, Robert 3:37:46 (5,374)
Crisp, Toby 4:39:31 (18,697)
Critchley, Brian 4:12:43 (12,775)
Critchley, David 3:58:49 (9,703)
Critchley, David 5:19:11 (25,281)
Critchlow, Martin 2:56:11 (700)
Critoph, Neville 3:30:30 (4,245)
Crocker, Adam 4:03:45 (10,832)
Crocker, Timothy 4:23:17 (15,127)
Crockett, Mark 4:02:12 (10,523)
Crockford, John 2:56:30 (717)
Crockford, Thomas 4:00:10 (10,081)
Croffey, Lee 4:33:14 (17,355)
Croft, Anthony 2:55:10 (635)
Croft, Christopher 3:53:01 (8,269)
Croft, Clive 4:13:17 (12,871)
Croft, Michael 4:31:12 (16,905)
Crofts, Joe 4:28:25 (16,289)
Crofty, Joe 5:15:25 (24,858)
Croiset, Dominique 2:43:16 (244)
Croll, Stewart 3:24:45 (3,349)
Crombie, Andrew 3:26:30 (3,559)
Crombie, John 4:02:39 (10,599)
Crompton, Carl 3:34:15 (4,792)
Crompton, Duncan 3:31:39 (4,416)

Crompton, Neil 2:48:54 (388)
Cron, Jean Luc 5:19:37 (25,319)
Crone, Mark 3:43:41 (6,432)
Crone, William 5:04:23 (23,197)
Cronin, Damian 4:00:35 (10,181)
Cronin, Michael 2:48:23 (373)
Crook, Keith 4:55:04 (21,754)
Crook, Neil 4:21:36 (14,714)
Crook, Simon 4:08:01 (11,768)
Crook, Stephen 4:38:19 (18,456)
Crook, Stephen 4:46:47 (20,111)
Crook, Steven 4:29:17 (16,493)
Crook, Warren 2:50:33 (448)
Crookes, Danny 3:16:28 (2,361)
Crooks, Alistair 4:49:43 (20,657)
Crooks, Bill 4:57:37 (22,232)
Crooks, John 3:58:47 (9,694)
Crooks, Melvyn 4:59:05 (22,473)
Crooks, Neil 3:21:41 (2,966)
Crooks, Robert 5:51:18 (27,969)
Croome, Jonathan 3:17:16 (2,455)
Cropper, Mark 4:46:20 (20,016)
Crosbie, Raymond 4:31:08 (16,883)
Crosby, Angus 3:32:59 (4,598)
Crosby, Paul 3:35:11 (4,929)
Crosby, Peter 3:46:44 (6,995)
Crosby, Richard 3:59:03 (9,773)
Crosby, Richard 5:12:22 (24,408)
Crosland, Ian 3:24:23 (3,295)
Cross, Andrew 5:13:11 (24,527)
Cross, Andrew 6:33:06 (29,483)
Cross, Arthur 4:28:29 (16,310)
Cross, Gary 5:14:54 (24,766)
Cross, Howard 4:52:31 (21,210)
Cross, James 3:58:29 (9,601)
Cross, Kevin 6:36:07 (29,545)
Cross, Martin 3:43:03 (6,316)
Cross, Matthew 5:04:50 (23,272)
Cross, Paul 4:12:34 (12,750)
Cross, Peter 3:15:10 (2,243)
Cross, Peter 4:30:45 (16,794)
Cross, Peter 5:11:47 (24,326)
Cross, Roger 4:31:51 (17,074)
Cross, Stephen 4:06:05 (11,361)
Cross, Thomas 4:59:23 (22,508)
Crossland, John 3:56:58 (9,169)
Crossland, Mark 3:50:59 (7,867)
Crossland, Paul 4:53:31 (21,427)
Crossland-Page, Keith 4:08:00 (11,764)
Crossley, Errol 3:31:14 (4,360)
Crossley, John 7:25:36 (30,110)
Crossley, Peter 5:22:02 (25,590)
Crossley, Richard 4:34:36 (17,643)
Crossman, Peter 3:52:31 (8,173)
Crosswell, Christopher 3:33:06 (4,622)
Crothers, David 4:19:37 (14,284)
Crotti, Enzo 3:26:37 (3,573)
Crouch, Daniel 4:58:36 (22,394)
Crouch, Garry 4:34:18 (17,595)
Crouch, Michael 4:44:57 (19,765)
Crouch, Robert 3:24:39 (3,336)
Croucher, Michael 3:57:35 (9,359)
Crow, Graham 3:41:15 (5,999)
Crow, Mike 6:45:10 (29,739)
Crow, Peter 3:38:42 (5,520)
Crowder, David 5:15:31 (24,871)
Crowder, John 4:28:09 (16,221)
Crowe, Darren 4:46:14 (19,993)
Crowe, David 5:24:42 (25,852)
Crowell, Peter 4:40:02 (18,793)
Crowle, Mark 4:28:01 (16,196)
Crowley, David 3:51:47 (8,023)
Crowley, Jonathan 5:12:36 (24,443)
Crowley, Vincent 3:05:55 (1,414)
Crown, James 4:54:31 (21,599)
Crowney, Paul 5:45:54 (27,626)
Crowson, Paul 3:55:22 (8,775)
Crowther, Bill 2:37:14 (121)
Crowther, Denis 5:56:36 (28,249)
Crowther, Mark 4:05:31 (11,220)
Crowther, Nicholas 3:58:57 (9,738)
Croxford, Ricky 3:00:51 (1,072)
Croxford, Trent 4:51:40 (21,025)

Crudgington, James 4:20:33 (14,489)
Cruickshank, Angus 3:49:41 (7,620)
Cruickshank, Haitham 4:26:05 (15,752)
Cruikshanks, Neville 4:59:22 (22,506)
Crumley, Euan 4:14:49 (13,213)
Crummett, George 4:15:13 (13,312)
Crummett, Stephen 4:28:33 (16,326)
Crunp, Wayne 3:32:59 (4,598)
Crust, Adam 4:34:32 (17,633)
Crutch, Nicholas 3:15:24 (2,261)
Crutcher, Eric 4:41:02 (18,981)
Cruttenden, Mark 6:55:23 (29,890)
Cruttwell, Greg 3:35:59 (5,071)
Cruz, Carlos 3:49:55 (7,669)
Csapo, Adam 3:03:36 (1,253)
Cubbon, Thomas 3:25:17 (3,413)
Cubitt, Jonathan 4:50:31 (20,804)
Cuby, Joe 8:07:30 (30,222)
Cudd, Albert 3:17:00 (2,429)
Cudd, Bernard 4:09:37 (12,096)
Cuddimy, Marc 4:02:38 (10,597)
Cudlipp, Ashley 3:57:15 (9,241)
Cudlipp, Martin 4:08:19 (11,827)
Cudworth, David 5:15:12 (24,832)
Cue, Philip 4:55:23 (21,842)
Cuell, Hugh 3:57:06 (9,196)
Cuer, Martyn 5:15:02 (24,786)
Cuffe, John 5:40:32 (27,227)
Cuffie, Nicholas 4:55:04 (21,754)
Culbert, Sean 3:54:40 (8,624)
Culbert, William 4:06:10 (11,372)
Culkin, John 4:49:54 (20,696)
Cullen, Eddie 2:45:54 (316)
Cullen, Eric 4:56:51 (22,116)
Cullen, Martin 4:02:53 (10,641)
Cullen, Richard 3:26:09 (3,518)
Cullen, Robbie 7:03:20 (29,971)
Cullen, Simon 4:18:09 (13,903)
Cullern, Doug 4:35:55 (17,910)
Culley, Edward 4:53:47 (21,470)
Cullimore, Philip 4:13:25 (12,912)
Cullinan, Liam 4:33:31 (17,423)
Culling, David 4:38:46 (18,568)
Culling, Timothy 4:56:35 (22,086)
Cullington, Mark 4:23:51 (15,261)
Cullingworth, Ian 3:46:59 (7,033)
Cullwick, Michael 3:58:20 (9,569)
Culmer, Mark 4:00:36 (10,186)
Cumber, Geoffrey 3:03:27 (1,243)
Cumberland, Roy 6:00:12 (28,424)
Cumbers, Leonard 4:32:08 (17,141)
Cumiskey, Michael 3:37:24 (5,321)
Cummings, Denzal 3:58:39 (9,658)
Cummings, John 4:20:09 (14,397)
Cummings, Tony 2:59:40 (992)
Cummins, Eugene 3:42:49 (17,278)
Cummins, John 3:32:50 (4,577)
Cummins, Mark 3:45:08 (6,700)
Cummins, Tim 4:35:42 (17,865)
Cummins, Vernon 5:52:37 (28,043)
Cuninngham, Michael 4:38:56 (18,591)
Cunliffe, Ian 4:11:08 (12,423)
Cunliffe, Luke 5:15:28 (24,864)
Cunniam, Richard 4:56:31 (22,069)
Cunniff, Gordon 3:33:03 (4,611)
Cunningham, Darren 5:55:13 (28,165)
Cunningham, Dean 4:10:20 (12,237)
Cunningham, Ian 4:54:37 (21,620)
Cunningham, John 2:48:11 (369)
Cunningham, John 3:15:54 (2,310)
Cunningham, John 4:14:45 (13,194)
Cunningham, John 4:17:36 (13,793)
Cunningham, Martin 3:49:40 (7,618)
Cunningham, Michael 4:10:07 (12,185)
Cunningham, Paul 4:59:01 (22,465)
Cunningham, Philip 3:44:40 (6,605)
Cunningham, Simon 5:08:37 (23,874)
Cunningham, Steven 3:03:50 (1,270)
Cunningham, Tom 4:03:45 (10,832)
Cunnington, Kelvin 4:42:35 (19,290)
Cunnington, Stephen 3:51:16 (7,925)
Curiger, Andreas 2:44:38 (281)
Curless, Brent 4:11:00 (12,400)

Curley, John 4:04:38 (11,028)
Curphey, Paul 2:46:54 (338)
Curran, David 4:55:29 (21,885)
Curran, Kevin 5:27:07 (26,091)
Curran, Noel 5:14:37 (24,730)
Curran, Patrick 4:39:49 (18,754)
Curran, Philip 3:24:41 (3,340)
Curran, Shaun 4:32:45 (17,263)
Currant, Steven 3:37:24 (5,321)
Currie, John 3:39:49 (5,743)
Currie, John 3:53:19 (8,338)
Currie, Lachlan 4:27:30 (16,058)
Currie, Lyndon 3:38:51 (5,548)
Currie, Michael 4:03:58 (10,876)
Currie, Thomas 3:46:50 (7,007)
Curry, Andrew 4:39:12 (18,638)
Curry, Declan 5:20:11 (25,374)
Curry, John 3:51:59 (8,068)
Curtin, Anthony 5:22:03 (25,595)
Curtis, Daniel 3:41:01 (5,960)
Curtis, Derrick 6:31:39 (29,446)
Curtis, James 4:14:59 (13,260)
Curtis, Keith 4:39:28 (18,683)
Curtis, Matthew 3:44:56 (6,670)
Curtis, Michael 5:43:23 (27,432)
Curtis, Nicholas 3:58:43 (9,679)
Curtis, Robert 3:34:09 (4,779)
Curtis, Robert 5:19:44 (25,339)
Curtis, Sean 4:11:43 (12,552)
Curtis, Timothy 4:52:53 (21,287)
Curtis, Tony 3:48:57 (7,451)
Curwood, Keith 3:56:33 (9,066)
Curzon, Mark 4:27:59 (16,192)
Cusack, Dermot 3:51:45 (8,015)
Cushing, Ian 5:22:44 (25,679)
Cushion, Michael 3:42:21 (6,191)
Cushion, Michael 4:06:52 (11,522)
Cusk, Dominic 5:47:53 (27,766)
Cust, Nigel 6:30:15 (29,419)
Cuthbert, Jim 4:47:04 (20,177)
Cuthbert, Martin 4:23:51 (15,261)
Cuthbert, Philip 3:08:39 (1,644)
Cuthbertson, Alistair 4:16:42 (13,609)
Cutler, Michael 4:05:59 (11,350)
Cutler, Peitr 4:13:28 (12,925)
Cutts, Michael 4:06:27 (11,440)
Cuzzolin, Giancarlo 4:23:36 (15,205)
Cxon, Sean 4:12:47 (12,788)
Cybyk, Beau 3:48:12 (7,303)
Czajkowski, Marek 4:46:32 (20,063)
Da Silva, Diogo 4:28:51 (16,388)
Da Silva, Jaime 3:38:37 (5,502)
Dabinett, John 4:33:54 (17,519)
Dable, Thomas 3:04:51 (1,339)
Daborn, David 4:16:28 (13,566)
Dackombe, Richard 4:28:12 (16,238)
Dade, Mike 3:51:06 (7,896)
Daden, Richard 8:05:12 (30,211)
Dadswell, Jonathan 4:33:41 (17,476)
Dady, Stephen 3:25:12 (3,401)
Daems, Patrick 4:14:38 (13,155)
Daggianti, Tony 5:17:26 (25,098)
Dagnell, Adam 4:19:59 (14,361)
Daguati, Pietro 3:57:51 (9,446)
Dahabiyeh, Hassan 3:29:54 (4,150)
Dahill, Brendan 4:45:43 (19,887)
Dahme, Dirk 4:10:00 (12,168)
Dainty, Andrew 4:03:41 (10,816)
Dainty, Leonard 4:33:48 (17,501)
Dajlid, James 3:29:43 (4,122)
Dakin, Anthony 5:29:25 (26,331)
D'Albertanson, Russell 5:15:37 (24,879)
D'Albertanson, Stephen 5:15:38 (24,882)
Dalby, Andrew 4:28:42 (16,359)
Dalby, Kevin 4:10:23 (12,252)
Daldry, Simon 4:41:11 (19,009)
Dale, Adrian 3:03:32 (1,249)
Dale, Colin 3:52:47 (8,227)
Dale, Francis 4:21:12 (14,628)
Dale, Ian 6:58:12 (29,919)
Dale, Jack 4:03:48 (10,841)
Dale, Jeffrey 3:29:43 (4,122)
Dale, John 4:40:49 (18,942)

Dale, Kevin	4:24:12 (15,330)	
Daley, James	4:06:49 (11,505)	
Daley, John	3:50:50 (7,831)	
Daley, Neil	3:48:47 (7,420)	
Dalgarno, Lawrence	4:16:51 (13,641)	
Dalgleish, Charles	5:10:22 (24,125)	
Dalgliesh, Alex	4:59:54 (22,600)	
D'All, Gordon	3:34:26 (4,824)	
Dalla Rovere, Francesco	4:20:25 (14,453)	
Dallas, Gordon	3:35:16 (4,946)	
Dalley, Peter	4:52:41 (21,248)	
Dallow, Alan	4:05:55 (11,327)	
Dally, James	4:20:48 (14,547)	
Dally, Paul	3:29:00 (3,997)	
Dalrymple Smith, James	3:41:44 (6,079)	
Dalton, Carl	4:25:47 (15,669)	
Dalton, Mark	2:55:32 (654)	
Dalton, Nicholas	3:12:39 (1,974)	
Dalton, Sean	3:50:11 (7,721)	
Daly, Andrew	4:52:03 (21,102)	
Daly, Anthony	4:28:59 (16,417)	
Daly, James	4:26:21 (15,815)	
Daly, John	3:52:02 (8,082)	
Daly, John	3:55:09 (8,722)	
Daly, John	4:47:03 (20,173)	
Daly, Joseph	3:41:47 (6,088)	
Daly, Kevin	4:37:06 (18,144)	
Daly, Neil	4:09:21 (12,051)	
Daly, Peter	3:36:01 (5,077)	
Daly Gourdialsing, Adam	5:48:05 (27,781)	
Dalzell, Mark	4:43:20 (19,458)	
Dalziel, Hugh	3:23:16 (3,143)	
Dam, Mogens	4:52:57 (21,306)	
D'Ambrosio, Gino	5:09:08 (23,959)	
Damgaard, Erik	4:37:47 (18,316)	
Damm, Christian	3:08:00 (1,593)	
Dampier, James	4:14:15 (13,087)	
Dams, Tim	4:38:19 (18,456)	
Danby, James	4:41:27 (19,054)	
Dangerfield, Roland	4:04:09 (10,910)	
Daniel, Jean	3:47:50 (7,218)	
Daniel, Jeremy	5:29:06 (26,295)	
Daniel, Peter	3:27:13 (3,662)	
Daniel, Richard	3:21:51 (2,980)	
Daniels, Andrew	3:54:43 (8,641)	
Daniels, Christopher	4:59:32 (22,530)	
Daniels, Clive	4:00:49 (10,245)	
Daniels, John	3:57:49 (9,437)	
Daniels, Kevin	5:15:08 (24,802)	
Daniels, Lee	3:42:03 (6,129)	
Daniels, Mark	5:05:34 (23,391)	
Daniels, Matthew	5:32:53 (26,605)	
Daniels, Michael	3:23:13 (3,137)	
Daniels, Michael	4:04:45 (11,057)	
Daniels, Nigel	3:50:45 (7,818)	
Daniels, Paul	3:59:47 (9,992)	
Daniels, Peter	4:21:10 (14,621)	
Daniels, Terence	5:32:52 (26,603)	
Danielsen, Per Olan	3:29:38 (4,106)	
Danks, James	4:00:36 (10,186)	
Danks, Rick	3:46:54 (7,020)	
Danks, Simon	3:49:50 (7,651)	
Dann, George	5:00:29 (22,659)	
Danne, Ivan	4:58:22 (22,354)	
Danne, Philippe	5:40:37 (27,240)	
Danoe, Claus	3:07:34 (1,552)	
Danon, Ronnie	5:16:19 (24,962)	
Darbishire, Owen	4:16:26 (13,561)	
Darby, John	4:47:08 (20,191)	
Darch, Frank	3:52:23 (8,148)	
Darcy, Keith	6:47:32 (29,769)	
Dardelet, Jean Claude	3:27:28 (3,700)	
Dare, Martin	3:42:38 (6,243)	
Dargue, Robert	3:58:46 (9,690)	
Dariol, Roberto	4:20:37 (14,503)	
Darke, Lawrence	5:06:05 (23,484)	
Darke, Tony	4:36:31 (18,024)	
Darling, Michael	3:10:43 (1,810)	
Darling, Stephen	4:31:07 (16,876)	
Darlison, Martin	3:12:01 (1,915)	
Darmawan, Rudy	3:37:08 (5,272)	
Darne, Gaetan	4:46:24 (20,034)	
Darnell, Bob	4:15:19 (13,333)	

Darnell, Derek	3:19:31 (2,707)	
Darnley, Murray	5:09:51 (24,063)	
Darrell, Peter	4:06:43 (11,488)	
Darroch, Robert	4:06:20 (11,414)	
Dartois, Eric	5:12:00 (24,356)	
Darvell, Jack	4:42:17 (19,224)	
Dash, Satya	5:17:33 (25,112)	
Dathan, David	4:27:57 (16,181)	
Dattani, Romin	4:55:16 (21,802)	
Daubannes, Jean Jacques	3:17:26 (2,479)	
Daubord, Daniel	3:21:55 (2,984)	
Daugherty, Brian	4:08:00 (11,764)	
Daulton, Richard	3:23:51 (3,222)	
Dauncey, Chris	3:11:43 (1,888)	
Dauris, Kenneth	5:37:33 (26,983)	
Dauwens, Alain	4:15:28 (13,361)	
Davenport, Daniel	4:28:29 (16,310)	
Davenport, Dominic	3:14:51 (2,200)	
Davenport, Graham	4:27:25 (16,040)	
Davenport, Robert	4:39:22 (18,659)	
Davey, Alan	4:24:47 (15,456)	
Davey, Ben	4:31:22 (16,947)	
Davey, Geoff	4:16:21 (13,536)	
Davey, Ian	4:54:47 (21,672)	
Davey, Kevin	2:56:13 (703)	
Davey, Paul	5:19:05 (25,274)	
Davey, Richard	4:43:25 (19,469)	
David, Dominique	3:28:12 (3,844)	
David, Orson	5:10:26 (24,134)	
David, Reto	4:06:51 (11,518)	
David John, Chedalavada	5:28:22 (26,220)	
Davidescu, John	3:48:03 (7,276)	
Davidson, Alan	3:37:05 (5,262)	
Davidson, Alan	4:11:35 (12,521)	
Davidson, Bruc	3:10:51 (1,823)	
Davidson, Chris	5:04:10 (23,153)	
Davidson, Colin	4:56:20 (22,041)	
Davidson, Crawford	4:37:17 (18,194)	
Davidson, Doug	3:53:38 (8,409)	
Davidson, Eric	4:38:49 (18,578)	
Davidson, Frederick	4:04:29 (10,983)	
Davidson, Garry	3:56:55 (9,159)	
Davidson, George	3:48:19 (7,324)	
Davidson, Gregory	3:46:21 (6,922)	
Davidson, Ian	3:58:14 (9,551)	
Davidson, Ian	4:18:47 (14,078)	
Davidson, James	3:24:53 (3,362)	
Davidson, James	5:34:08 (26,713)	
Davidson, Jan Ake	4:34:12 (17,570)	
Davidson, Mark	4:15:43 (13,406)	
Davidson, Neil	3:47:22 (7,104)	
Davidson, Nigel	3:03:00 (1,212)	
Davidson, Robin	3:32:17 (4,504)	
Davidson, Sean	5:27:07 (26,091)	
Davidson, Stuart	2:59:43 (999)	
Davie, John	3:59:25 (9,891)	
Davie, Jonathan	3:38:41 (5,515)	
Davie, Robert	3:39:53 (5,754)	
Davie, Tim	3:32:46 (4,568)	
Davies, Adam	4:30:02 (16,699)	
Davies, Adrian	3:47:22 (7,104)	
Davies, Alan	4:21:16 (14,642)	
Davies, Alexander	3:44:38 (6,601)	
Davies, Alexander	4:54:42 (21,640)	
Davies, Alun	4:31:36 (17,011)	
Davies, Andrew	3:14:47 (2,195)	
Davies, Andrew	3:20:18 (2,795)	
Davies, Andrew	4:22:10 (14,847)	
Davies, Brian	4:26:26 (15,828)	
Davies, Brian	4:38:47 (18,574)	
Davies, Chris	4:51:46 (21,048)	
Davies, Colin	4:14:58 (13,254)	
Davies, Colin	5:42:40 (27,392)	
Davies, Damian	3:55:38 (8,829)	
Davies, Dave	4:15:22 (13,338)	
Davies, David	4:51:07 (20,909)	
Davies, Derek	4:42:12 (19,205)	
Davies, Edward	4:18:42 (14,051)	
Davies, Elwyn	5:22:56 (25,699)	
Davies, Gareth	2:59:51 (1,011)	
Davies, Gareth	3:08:37 (1,640)	
Davies, Gareth	3:30:35 (4,260)	
Davies, Gareth	3:34:28 (4,832)	

Davies, Gareth	3:55:25 (8,786)	
Davies, Gareth	3:59:19 (9,849)	
Davies, Gareth	5:09:09 (23,965)	
Davies, Gareth	5:12:15 (24,388)	
Davies, Gary	8:06:58 (30,219)	
Davies, Graham	2:54:31 (609)	
Davies, Graham	5:48:50 (27,833)	
Davies, Gregory	4:34:51 (17,685)	
Davies, Gwilym	3:34:12 (4,787)	
Davies, Hadyn	4:33:33 (17,438)	
Davies, Ian	4:18:55 (14,103)	
Davies, Ian	4:42:43 (19,315)	
Davies, James	3:20:29 (2,822)	
Davies, James	3:27:07 (3,640)	
Davies, James	4:45:24 (19,846)	
Davies, Jason	5:37:04 (26,950)	
Davies, Jeremy	3:13:18 (2,037)	
Davies, John	3:07:00 (1,505)	
Davies, John	4:56:29 (22,064)	
Davies, John	5:07:26 (23,688)	
Davies, Jonathan	3:56:26 (9,034)	
Davies, Keith	3:03:07 (1,220)	
Davies, Keith	4:10:12 (12,208)	
Davies, Keith	4:50:48 (20,843)	
Davies, Kenneth	4:26:30 (15,846)	
Davies, Kevin	4:06:30 (11,450)	
Davies, Kurt	2:56:31 (718)	
Davies, Lawrence	4:22:14 (14,870)	
Davies, Leighton	3:03:36 (1,253)	
Davies, Len	4:52:09 (21,124)	
Davies, Leslie	4:26:08 (15,762)	
Davies, Malcolm	4:37:26 (18,233)	
Davies, Mark	3:18:37 (2,610)	
Davies, Mark	3:45:30 (6,744)	
Davies, Mark	3:45:41 (6,791)	
Davies, Mark	5:03:16 (23,036)	
Davies, Martin	4:42:09 (19,192)	
Davies, Michael	3:23:27 (3,168)	
Davies, Michael	4:55:01 (21,739)	
Davies, Michael	5:05:15 (23,332)	
Davies, Neil	3:34:01 (4,757)	
Davies, Nicholas	3:06:19 (1,443)	
Davies, Nigel	3:53:28 (8,367)	
Davies, Nigel	5:00:51 (22,715)	
Davies, Paul	2:58:34 (864)	
Davies, Paul	3:26:55 (3,613)	
Davies, Paul	3:43:42 (6,437)	
Davies, Paul	3:55:40 (8,834)	
Davies, Peter	4:11:25 (12,486)	
Davies, Philip	3:47:17 (7,079)	
Davies, Rhys	4:54:50 (21,687)	
Davies, Richard	3:29:15 (4,036)	
Davies, Richard	3:35:29 (4,985)	
Davies, Rob	5:01:26 (22,794)	
Davies, Robert	4:14:05 (13,053)	
Davies, Rodger	4:57:09 (22,165)	
Davies, Roger	3:55:40 (8,834)	
Davies, Roland	4:06:41 (11,481)	
Davies, Roy	4:28:28 (16,306)	
Davies, Rupert	4:02:48 (10,625)	
Davies, Stephen	2:36:14 (107)	
Davies, Stephen	4:33:19 (17,374)	
Davies, Stuart	5:20:32 (25,412)	
Davies, Stuart	5:34:58 (26,804)	
Davies, Thomas	4:03:25 (10,752)	
Davies, Thomas	5:32:23 (26,558)	
Davies, Timothy	3:01:26 (1,105)	
Davies, Tom	3:41:38 (6,064)	
Davies, Tom	4:44:30 (19,674)	
Davies, Trevor	3:37:33 (5,342)	
Davies, Vernon	4:58:15 (22,336)	
Davies, William	3:17:58 (2,531)	
Davies, Yvonne	3:51:29 (7,960)	
D'Avila, Donald	4:22:39 (14,968)	
Davis, Adrian	2:38:31 (148)	
Davis, Ben	5:51:56 (28,014)	
Davis, Chris	4:52:58 (21,309)	
Davis, Christopher	4:02:32 (10,580)	
Davis, Clive	2:51:35 (494)	
Davis, Danny	3:39:54 (5,759)	
Davis, Frank	4:57:41 (22,246)	
Davis, Geoffrey	3:19:34 (2,713)	
Davis, Hugh	3:27:24 (3,689)	

Davis, Ian 3:52:02 (8,082)
Davis, Ian 6:46:17 (29,752)
Davis, Jim 4:20:22 (14,443)
Davis, Joseph 4:15:48 (13,423)
Davis, Laurence 4:10:52 (12,363)
Davis, Lee 5:21:36 (25,533)
Davis, Mark 3:37:20 (5,313)
Davis, Mark 4:17:54 (13,851)
Davis, Mark 5:14:14 (24,663)
Davis, Martin 2:41:06 (195)
Davis, Matthew 4:42:51 (19,347)
Davis, Michael 5:34:18 (26,736)
Davis, Nicholas 4:16:45 (13,629)
Davis, Patrick 4:48:16 (20,400)
Davis, Paul 3:49:46 (7,639)
Davis, Paul 4:36:13 (17,959)
Davis, Paul 4:44:25 (19,659)
Davis, Peter 5:08:10 (23,792)
Davis, Richard 3:30:42 (4,278)
Davis, Richard 3:41:12 (5,983)
Davis, Richard 4:35:33 (17,822)
Davis, Robert 3:02:10 (1,167)
Davis, Robert 5:07:44 (23,737)
Davis, Shane 4:24:38 (15,427)
Davis, Simon 3:40:06 (5,800)
Davis, Stephen 3:50:41 (7,802)
Davis, Steve 2:42:10 (221)
Davis, Terry 3:38:08 (5,419)
Davis, Timothy 5:13:19 (24,553)
Davis, Tony 6:34:13 (29,507)
Davison, Adam 4:18:22 (13,976)
Davison, Paul 5:19:52 (25,350)
Davison, Robert 3:10:08 (1,750)
Davison, Robin 3:43:42 (6,437)
Davison, Robin 5:13:38 (24,588)
Davison, Sean 4:31:13 (16,908)
Davison, Stephen 4:46:32 (20,063)
Davison, William 4:43:29 (19,490)
Davitt, Patrick 3:22:54 (3,097)
D'Avolio, John 3:39:56 (5,768)
Davren, Paul 3:07:39 (1,561)
Davy, Jason 4:55:09 (21,769)
Davy, Jonathan 3:13:05 (2,009)
Davy, Paul 3:26:54 (3,610)
Davy, Tayo 3:57:23 (9,283)
Dawber, Nigel 3:17:42 (2,501)
Dawe, Quentin 4:49:08 (20,548)
Dawes, Duncan 3:01:06 (1,090)
Dawes, Jason 4:09:15 (12,034)
Dawes, Jonathan 4:07:12 (11,588)
Dawes, Phil 4:28:40 (16,355)
Dawkins, Colin 3:31:41 (4,422)
Dawnay, Christopher 4:03:32 (10,783)
Daws, Peter 2:50:56 (464)
Dawson, Benjamin 3:45:45 (6,810)
Dawson, Christopher 3:15:38 (2,282)
Dawson, Ian 4:11:36 (12,525)
Dawson, James 3:33:06 (4,622)
Dawson, John 4:37:59 (18,365)
Dawson, Kevin 4:42:23 (19,244)
Dawson, Mark 5:12:28 (24,424)
Dawson, Mark 5:48:36 (27,822)
Dawson, Peter 4:47:08 (20,191)
Dawson, Peter 4:48:29 (20,437)
Dawson, Richard 3:37:12 (5,282)
Dawson, Richard 3:47:04 (7,046)
Dawson, Simon 3:53:30 (8,375)
Dawson, Simon 6:01:34 (28,482)
Dawson, Tony 4:10:48 (12,341)
Day, Andrew 6:58:46 (29,927)
Day, David 3:26:34 (3,568)
Day, David 4:15:48 (13,423)
Day, Geoffrey 2:40:23 (180)
Day, Gerald 4:49:35 (20,631)
Day, Ian 6:09:46 (28,850)
Day, Javan 4:30:56 (16,836)
Day, John 3:43:34 (6,408)
Day, Jonathan 3:56:00 (8,919)
Day, Matthew 5:03:59 (23,125)
Day, Russell 4:43:03 (19,397)
Day, Thomas 4:14:29 (13,123)
Day, Thomas 4:49:32 (20,620)
Day, Tim 4:22:16 (14,877)
Dayer, Mark 5:09:52 (24,065)
Daykin, Laurie 4:50:14 (20,757)
Dayman, Graham 6:50:23 (29,811)
De Beer, Zac 4:30:25 (16,745)
De Belder, Toby 4:33:34 (17,443)
De Bell, Gerard 4:49:23 (20,592)
De Bellis, Giovanni 3:32:36 (4,549)
De Boer, Johan 3:10:10 (1,755)
De Boer, Luitzen 4:31:17 (16,927)
De Borchgrave, Simon 3:34:04 (4,766)
De Bruin, Marc 4:48:05 (20,365)
De Chezelles, Christophe 3:29:53 (4,145)
De Courcy-Grylls, Christopher 4:13:12 (12,857)
De Frateschi, Michael 3:23:10 (3,134)
De Freitas, Marco 2:40:29 (182)
De Friend, Mike 4:32:58 (17,303)
De Gennard, Fabio 3:49:19 (7,528)
De Guzman, Rafael 3:42:53 (6,283)
De Haes, Chris 3:15:31 (2,274)
De Jong, Frank 4:51:59 (21,088)
De Jong, Jacobus 4:16:23 (13,547)
De Jong, Robert 3:20:25 (2,809)
De Klerk, Ben 2:44:36 (280)
De Kok, René 3:50:59 (7,867)
De Lange, Leyton 4:00:32 (10,166)
De Lima, Braz 3:42:46 (6,265)
De Lorenzi, Fausto 4:35:59 (17,930)
De Luca, Paolo 3:14:52 (2,206)
De Marchi, Emanuele 4:31:30 (16,981)
De Maurois, Adrien 4:13:48 (13,003)
De Mendoza, Consalvo 5:26:08 (26,001)
De Nardi, Maurizio 4:13:49 (13,007)
De Oliveira, José 2:57:20 (768)
De Regt, Laurie 4:54:39 (21,623)
De Rome, Paul 4:41:54 (19,140)
De Sa, Eugenio 2:51:47 (506)
De Ste Croix, Danny 5:12:01 (24,359)
De Ste Croix, Robert 6:05:13 (28,648)
De Trenquelleon, Marc De Batz 3:08:52 (1,662)
De Vaal, Sarita 5:26:20 (26,022)
De Vette, Johannes 4:50:36 (20,813)
De Villiers, Phil 3:19:19 (2,689)
De Vos, Jan 4:20:25 (14,453)
De Wilton, Nick 3:18:04 (2,541)
De Wyche, Duncan 4:47:31 (20,267)
Deacon, Alan 3:51:29 (7,960)
Deacon, Anthony 3:27:23 (3,686)
Deacon, Rodney 4:46:01 (19,941)
Deakin, Nicholas 4:54:49 (21,682)
Deakin, Russell 4:19:55 (14,343)
Deakins, Archie 3:22:05 (3,011)
Deal, Gary 5:14:27 (24,694)
Dean, Anthony 5:43:55 (27,466)
Dean, Fraser 2:56:09 (697)
Dean, Gary 4:55:03 (21,749)
Dean, Graham 3:47:56 (7,252)
Dean, Ken 4:10:09 (12,194)
Dean, Marc 5:23:00 (25,706)
Dean, Michael 3:35:05 (4,914)
Dean, Michael 4:55:36 (21,922)
Dean, Paul 3:08:49 (1,656)
Dean, Paul 3:49:16 (7,515)
Dean, Peter 3:55:37 (8,821)
Dean, Russell 4:54:55 (21,709)
Dean, Trevor 3:25:29 (3,444)
Dean, William 4:08:20 (11,833)
Deane, Alan 5:04:27 (23,211)
Deane, Christopher 5:24:26 (25,825)
Deane, Steve 4:52:40 (21,246)
Deans, Graham 5:34:51 (26,791)
Deans, Jamie 4:35:43 (17,869)
Deans, Martin 3:42:20 (6,188)
Dear, Richard 3:45:01 (6,691)
Dear, Stephen 4:24:01 (15,298)
Deardon, Raymond 5:53:19 (28,085)
Dearing, Anthony 3:06:42 (1,478)
Dearle, Brent 5:06:57 (23,608)
Dearman, Alan 4:15:11 (13,299)
Dearnaley, David 5:12:47 (24,465)
Dearson, Michael 6:06:55 (28,716)
Deasy, Colin 2:50:06 (433)
De'ath, Paul 4:00:09 (10,079)
Deathridge, Gary 4:11:36 (12,525)
Deaton, Christopher 4:58:41 (22,412)
Deavin, Alistair 4:43:26 (19,473)
Debbi, Adriano 2:37:34 (127)
Debney, Andrew 5:02:25 (22,929)
Debowicz, Carlos 4:44:38 (19,701)
Decarne, Emanuele 3:11:58 (1,911)
Decent, Michael 3:35:56 (5,060)
Dechantsreiter, Franz 3:43:12 (6,345)
Decker, Christoph 4:20:01 (14,374)
Decker, Roy 5:54:47 (28,154)
Decourcy, Graham 3:14:06 (2,130)
Dedaieb, Moncef 4:03:36 (10,801)
Dedman, Jonathan 5:00:36 (22,678)
Dedoncker, Michael 5:12:49 (24,475)
Deeprose, William 3:22:51 (3,091)
Deer, William 4:30:37 (16,769)
Deery, Mark 3:55:15 (8,751)
Defer, Gerard 4:02:50 (10,628)
Deffains, Peter 4:55:20 (21,824)
De-Flaviis, Gianni 4:05:46 (11,292)
Dehan, Chris 3:28:41 (3,935)
Deighton, Matthew 3:07:03 (1,508)
Deist, Stephen 3:56:56 (9,163)
De-Kerpel, Stephane 5:20:14 (25,380)
Dekker, Erik 5:20:00 (25,362)
Del Bianco, Stefano 7:18:37 (30,071)
Del Miglio, Luciano 4:13:37 (12,961)
Del Valle-Garrido, Manuel 3:02:16 (1,171)
De'laet, Jimmy 3:55:37 (8,821)
Delahunty, Phil 4:34:41 (17,655)
Delamare, Paul 4:57:44 (22,253)
Delaney, James 3:19:10 (2,667)
Delannoy, Michel 4:43:49 (19,561)
Delatouche, David 4:36:54 (18,104)
Delaval, Dominique 3:11:30 (1,865)
Delderfield, Keith 3:39:17 (5,622)
Delfaud, Sebastien 4:41:52 (19,131)
Delhoy, Mark 4:43:05 (19,400)
Delisser, Scott 5:40:48 (27,253)
Dell, Andrew 2:59:21 (971)
Dell, Graeme 4:19:09 (14,157)
Dell, Richard 4:04:28 (10,981)
Dellar, Russell 3:48:43 (7,406)
Dellor, Tim 3:40:55 (5,931)
Delobel, David 4:35:14 (17,758)
Deloffre, Jean-Pierre 3:44:48 (6,640)
Delooze, Andrew 4:54:54 (21,702)
Delport, Stephen 5:26:19 (26,021)
Delporte, Jacques 3:44:46 (6,632)
Delsahut, Gerard 4:00:27 (10,136)
Delsasso, Eddy 4:46:52 (20,136)
Delteil, Christian 6:02:08 (28,510)
Delucchi, Carlo 4:09:20 (12,049)
Deluoa, Stefano 4:38:19 (18,456)
Delves, Frederick 5:33:53 (26,678)
Demaret, Eric 3:53:18 (8,333)
Dembrey, Rob 3:25:54 (3,493)
Demczak, Bogdan 3:32:30 (4,536)
Demetridu, Nicholas 6:50:27 (29,812)
Demetriou, Mario 4:56:46 (22,101)
Dempsey, Edward 5:18:49 (25,251)
Dempsey, Robert 3:08:23 (1,623)
Dempster, Iain 7:00:58 (29,952)
Demyan, Glenn 3:52:30 (8,169)
Den Reijer, Paul 4:24:27 (15,386)
Denbigh, Mike 4:02:46 (10,622)
Dench, Gary 2:56:01 (684)
Denham, Lee 4:50:09 (20,743)
Denicolo, Piero 3:14:49 (2,197)
Deninson, Jon 3:13:21 (2,046)
Denison, Colin 5:39:42 (27,156)
Denison-Pender, Peter 3:58:13 (9,542)
Denman, John 4:31:40 (17,028)
Denner, Michael 4:02:05 (10,501)
Denness, Jack 4:51:36 (21,010)
Dennett, Paul 4:57:44 (22,253)
Dennett, Peter 3:24:50 (3,358)
Denning, Christopher 5:14:29 (24,701)
Denning, Mark 4:20:51 (14,560)
Dennis, Brian 5:09:20 (23,986)
Dennis, Geoffrey 5:47:30 (27,728)
Dennis, Mark 4:29:54 (16,660)
Dennis, Paul 5:40:34 (27,236)

Dennis, Philip....3:50:15 (7,728)
Dennis, Tony....4:31:52 (17,081)
Denny, Ian....5:08:31 (23,849)
Denny, Paul....3:53:35 (8,399)
Denny, Paul....4:03:49 (10,843)
Denny, Reginald....4:27:04 (15,988)
Densham, Stephen....4:50:44 (20,830)
Densham, Stephen....4:58:29 (22,374)
Dent, Adrian....4:50:27 (20,795)
Dent, David....3:49:56 (7,671)
Dent, Geoff....4:48:17 (20,403)
Dent, Malcolm....4:14:27 (13,116)
Dent, Simon....4:13:57 (13,033)
Denton, Michael....3:48:05 (7,283)
Denton, Zane....3:43:26 (6,385)
Denyer, John....3:06:45 (1,485)
Denyer, Mark....7:04:11 (29,975)
Deol, Akwala....5:33:40 (26,661)
Deolercq, Philippe....4:22:27 (14,915)
Deoorde, Herve....3:09:36 (1,726)
Depas, Marcel....3:11:54 (1,905)
Depla, Stephen....4:27:38 (16,103)
Depourcq, Eric....4:29:12 (16,472)
Depper, Geoff....3:19:02 (2,658)
Derbyshire, Anthony....3:19:13 (2,676)
Derbyshire, Ken....4:48:59 (20,525)
Derbyshire, Stephen....4:49:47 (20,669)
Derissy, Zakaria....5:32:41 (26,591)
Derkson, Norm....4:12:18 (12,693)
Dermody, John....3:22:28 (3,052)
Derovet, Eric....4:39:43 (18,736)
Derrett, Keith....4:13:33 (12,943)
Des Forges, Tim....3:45:47 (6,820)
Desai, Chintu....4:09:54 (12,140)
Desai, Jeremy....4:27:48 (16,152)
Desai, Julian....4:25:05 (15,528)
Desai, Mukesh....3:30:44 (4,284)
Desbaux, Carole....5:46:26 (27,653)
Descheemacker, Vianney....3:53:12 (8,309)
Desgrandchamps, François....3:57:59 (9,486)
Deshmukh, Andy....3:47:30 (7,139)
Desmond, Jason....5:03:49 (23,103)
Desmond, Jim....3:20:35 (2,831)
De-Souza, Desmond....4:38:22 (18,473)
Despres, Stephen....3:44:34 (6,592)
Dessup, Daniel....4:17:57 (13,863)
Detivaud, Dominique....3:20:58 (2,888)
Detrieux, Erick....3:52:07 (8,102)
Detruit, Joel....2:56:01 (684)
Dettmar, Michael....5:57:22 (28,287)
Devall, John....3:37:34 (5,344)
Devani, Ameet....5:06:34 (23,554)
Devany, Alan....2:57:19 (767)
Deveen, Wim....4:25:58 (15,723)
Deveney, John....4:04:49 (11,070)
Devenish, Alistair....6:38:35 (29,600)
Devenish, Malcolm....4:02:30 (10,571)
Devenish, Peter....6:33:37 (29,499)
Devenish, William....3:59:30 (9,921)
Deverell, James....4:52:14 (21,138)
Deverell Jones, David....5:04:22 (23,193)
Devereux, Michael....2:56:37 (723)
Deverill, Paul....4:30:15 (16,724)
Devey, Dennis....4:25:25 (15,597)
Devey, Richard....3:50:53 (7,844)
Devial, Jonathan....3:57:54 (9,462)
Devine, James....6:05:20 (28,656)
Devine, William....4:52:29 (21,200)
Devlic, Robert....3:58:38 (9,649)
Devlin, Alex....4:57:38 (22,235)
Devlin, Arthur....5:50:40 (27,935)
Devlin, Colin....4:09:45 (12,117)
Devlin, John....4:34:21 (17,606)
Devonport, Andrew....4:35:37 (17,846)
Devonport, Karl....4:22:47 (15,000)
Devonshire, Stephen....5:13:21 (24,558)
Devoy, Neil....4:41:44 (19,108)
Devries, Foppe....3:30:05 (4,185)
D'Evry, Gilles....4:44:20 (19,643)
Devulder, Jean Pierre....2:44:35 (278)
Dewar, Paul....3:23:45 (3,205)
Dewar, Paul....5:32:21 (26,554)
Dewhurst, Brian....3:33:43 (4,716)
Dewhurst, Clive....4:30:15 (16,724)
Dewick, first name unknown....4:00:40 (10,199)
Dewine, Anthony....3:03:00 (1,212)
Dewis, Mark....3:54:25 (8,570)
Dexter, Brett....6:37:24 (29,575)
Dexter, Colin....6:00:16 (28,426)
Dexter, Richard....5:14:22 (24,684)
Dey, Partha....4:48:58 (20,521)
Deyes, E....4:54:39 (21,623)
Dezulier, Daniel....3:49:17 (7,518)
Di Vita, Antonio....4:33:19 (17,374)
Diable, Mark....5:26:12 (26,005)
Diakowsky, Michael....4:11:12 (12,440)
Diamond, Samuel....3:19:27 (2,700)
Dias, Richard....4:54:42 (21,640)
Dibaba, Siraj....3:28:22 (3,885)
Dibble, Kevin....5:15:39 (24,884)
Dibbs, Stephen....6:29:38 (29,400)
Dibley, Allan....5:20:34 (25,417)
Dicerbo, Francis....3:35:53 (5,050)
Dick, John....3:43:38 (6,421)
Dick, Les....4:41:59 (19,159)
Dick, Michael....3:42:08 (6,145)
Dickens, Ivan....4:50:45 (20,835)
Dickens, Stephen....3:08:55 (1,665)
Dickenson, Andrew....2:48:18 (370)
Dickenson, Michael....6:25:33 (29,296)
Dicker, Mick....2:58:17 (831)
Dickerson, Joseph....3:54:20 (8,542)
Dickey, Martin....3:13:11 (2,023)
Dickinson, Benjamin....5:48:07 (27,782)
Dickinson, Christopher....3:48:30 (7,361)
Dickinson, John....4:04:41 (11,038)
Dickinson, Matthew....5:14:17 (24,671)
Dickinson, Stephen....4:29:44 (16,607)
Dickinson, Stephen....5:27:15 (26,108)
Dickson, Andrew....3:43:18 (6,360)
Dickson, Andrew....3:52:49 (8,234)
Dickson, Colin....3:29:56 (4,159)
Dickson, Howard....4:43:18 (19,451)
Dickson, Jim....5:09:25 (24,003)
Dickson, Robert....3:33:00 (4,601)
Didlock, Anthony....3:31:31 (4,393)
Diebel, Gerry....3:29:32 (4,086)
Diebel, Michael....3:41:41 (6,072)
Dietrich, Eckhard....3:57:21 (9,273)
Dietrich, Henning....3:24:48 (3,354)
Dietrich, Martin....4:19:31 (14,260)
Dietterle, Michael....3:42:39 (6,244)
Differding, Christian....3:58:41 (9,669)
Digby Baker, Hugh....5:36:22 (26,908)
Diggelmann, Heini....4:40:54 (18,956)
Diggens, Nigel....5:42:58 (27,407)
Diggins, Jess....5:05:10 (23,313)
Digiacomo, Thomas....4:04:42 (11,042)
Dignam, Alan....5:02:04 (22,886)
Digpal, Amur Paul....6:40:45 (29,658)
Dijkstra, Dieter....3:20:51 (2,871)
Dill, Wayne....3:37:29 (5,333)
Dillard, Dean....3:42:22 (6,197)
Dilley, David....3:53:34 (8,394)
Dilley, Maurice....3:56:27 (9,040)
Dilley, Nicholas....4:42:35 (19,290)
Dilley, Paul....4:12:23 (12,710)
Dillon, Donal....3:48:43 (7,406)
Dillon, Kevin....4:46:29 (20,048)
Dillow, Gavin....4:02:22 (10,544)
Dillow, Peter....3:28:41 (3,935)
Dills, Robert....4:25:23 (15,590)
Dilworth, Arthur....5:07:27 (23,692)
Dimbleby, Peter....2:54:03 (582)
Dimech, Phil....4:04:58 (11,111)
Dimmel, Wolfgang....5:35:06 (26,816)
Dimmick, Roy....4:38:36 (18,529)
Dimmock, Greame....7:16:20 (30,055)
Dimmock, Matthew....3:28:05 (3,816)
Dimmock, Matthew....5:22:41 (25,671)
Dimmock, Paul....3:06:06 (1,431)
Dimmock, Stuart....4:31:02 (16,858)
Dindsa, Fauja Singh....6:54:55 (29,877)
Dingley, Fraser....4:37:53 (18,344)
Dingwall, Gregory....3:22:39 (3,067)
Dingwall, James....2:56:26 (713)
Dingwall, Stuart....4:19:59 (14,361)
Dinsey, Eric....4:56:52 (22,121)
Dinsmore, Brian....4:15:21 (13,335)
Dionisio, Tiago....2:43:04 (239)
Dipre, Stephen....3:12:53 (1,992)
Diprose, Brian....4:10:41 (12,308)
Diquet, Michel....4:13:11 (12,856)
Dirkes, Martin....2:56:43 (726)
Disken, Bernard....3:29:45 (4,129)
Disley, Brian....3:37:45 (5,370)
Disney, Paul....4:09:30 (12,076)
Disu, Olukayode....5:32:34 (26,584)
Ditch, Neil....4:51:55 (21,073)
Ditcher, Mark....4:45:20 (19,829)
Dite, Christopher....5:42:30 (27,375)
Diventura, Angelo....4:20:49 (14,552)
Diver, John....5:04:51 (23,276)
Dix, Barry....5:13:44 (24,599)
Dix, Chris....3:47:53 (7,237)
Dix, Kevin....3:42:31 (6,222)
Dixon, Brad....3:15:34 (2,278)
Dixon, Charles....4:00:34 (10,178)
Dixon, David....3:35:31 (4,988)
Dixon, David....4:37:56 (18,353)
Dixon, Geoff....3:58:34 (9,633)
Dixon, Giles....5:05:40 (23,409)
Dixon, Gordon....2:37:38 (129)
Dixon, Guy....4:27:57 (16,181)
Dixon, Ian....4:37:21 (18,212)
Dixon, Jim....4:11:47 (12,566)
Dixon, Keith....4:26:39 (15,882)
Dixon, Kevin....4:03:52 (10,855)
Dixon, Mark....3:49:24 (7,553)
Dixon, Matt....3:35:57 (5,066)
Dixon, Nigel....3:55:36 (8,819)
Dixon, Ross....4:14:37 (13,152)
Dixon, Thomas....3:43:35 (6,413)
Dixon, Thomas....3:49:05 (7,481)
Dixon Gough, Richard....3:46:24 (6,931)
Djebbari, Fathi....4:02:01 (10,489)
Dlander, Harry....4:42:37 (19,298)
Dllon, Terence....4:54:45 (21,660)
Doak, Ian....4:15:57 (13,453)
Doar, Barrie....6:45:12 (29,740)
Dobbs, Andrew....4:25:06 (15,531)
Dobbs, Patrick....2:59:30 (979)
Dobbs, Paul....4:54:49 (21,682)
Dobbs, Simon....2:48:08 (366)
Dobie, Daniel....4:05:49 (11,305)
Dobler, Thomas....3:57:20 (9,267)
Dobson, Andrew....3:57:36 (9,363)
Dobson, David....4:30:02 (16,699)
Dobson, Graham....3:04:55 (1,345)
Dobson, Jonathan....3:43:10 (6,336)
Dobson, Nigel....4:07:58 (11,755)
Dobson, Peter....4:27:42 (16,119)
Dobson, Rupert....3:36:05 (5,086)
Docherty, Craig....3:53:35 (8,399)
Docherty, Craig....4:04:14 (10,936)
Docherty, David....4:28:19 (16,264)
Docherty, Douglas....5:20:57 (25,461)
Docherty, John....4:02:46 (10,622)
Docherty, John....5:37:05 (26,953)
Docherty, Joseph....3:01:23 (1,099)
Docherty, Martin....4:36:36 (18,040)
Dock, Steven....3:50:52 (7,841)
Dockerill, David....3:49:34 (7,599)
Docksey, Robin....4:51:04 (20,904)
Dodanis, Christos....3:00:11 (1,040)
Dodd, Alan....4:22:11 (14,856)
Dodd, Alexander....5:10:25 (24,132)
Dodd, David....3:42:59 (6,299)
Dodd, Richard....4:43:25 (19,469)
Dodd, Simon....4:34:53 (17,690)
Dodd, Toby....4:26:32 (15,851)
Dodd, Tom....4:22:55 (15,039)
Dodds, George....3:00:18 (1,044)
Dodds, Rupert....2:59:48 (1,007)
Dodge, Richard....4:21:50 (14,772)
Dodgson, David....4:02:07 (10,507)
Dodkins, Alan....3:47:48 (7,210)
Dodoo, Eddie....3:14:20 (2,152)
Dodson, Adrian....3:57:16 (9,245)

Dodson, Jason 5:24:47 (25,857)
Dodson, Martin 3:53:23 (8,351)
Dodsworth, Nathan 4:19:22 (14,215)
Doe, Adrian 4:51:21 (20,959)
Doe, David 5:14:17 (24,671)
Doe, Don 3:11:48 (1,897)
Doe, Matthew 4:03:57 (10,873)
Doerr, Albert 4:56:44 (22,096)
Doggett, Nigel 3:55:19 (8,763)
Doherty, Brian 6:20:45 (29,184)
Doherty, Christopher 4:00:47 (10,238)
Doherty, Danny 4:51:20 (20,954)
Doherty, Frank 4:36:03 (17,940)
Doherty, James 3:56:34 (9,072)
Doherty, James 4:16:04 (13,480)
Doherty, Jason 5:24:41 (25,851)
Doherty, John 3:22:57 (3,104)
Doherty, Mark 3:45:39 (6,779)
Doherty, Martin 3:50:06 (7,707)
Doherty, Michael 3:04:56 (1,346)
Doherty, Paul 3:21:18 (2,919)
Doherty, Stuart 5:54:03 (28,116)
Doherty, Terry 4:02:01 (10,489)
Dokter, Walter 3:30:45 (4,286)
Dolan, Aidan 3:51:50 (8,035)
Dolan, Carl 4:35:05 (17,731)
Dolan, Robert 2:55:26 (648)
Dolan, Stanley 3:46:21 (6,922)
Dolbey, Alex 4:51:59 (21,088)
Dolby, Graham 3:57:42 (9,396)
Dolder, Ross 4:09:20 (12,049)
Dolling, Adam 3:35:19 (4,957)
Dollman, Michael 4:24:21 (15,359)
Dolman, Antony 4:20:54 (14,573)
Dolmatch, Bart 5:04:13 (23,166)
Dolphin, Christopher 4:41:51 (19,130)
Dolphin, Huw 3:45:03 (6,695)
Dolton, Alan 3:40:24 (5,849)
Domenget, Jean-Pierre 5:20:17 (25,384)
Domican, Mark 4:27:44 (16,128)
Dominey, Alwyn 3:24:14 (3,274)
Dominice, Jean 4:35:10 (17,746)
Dominique, Gerard 3:30:18 (4,213)
Dommett, Robert 6:30:38 (29,428)
Don, Ian 5:06:57 (23,608)
Donagh, Jason 4:21:18 (14,647)
Donagh, Jerome 4:08:58 (11,971)
Donaghey, Alistair 6:04:11 (28,603)
Donaghy, Steve 4:00:44 (10,227)
Donald, Andrew 4:35:12 (17,751)
Donald, Chris 3:10:11 (1,757)
Donaldson, Andrew 3:25:52 (3,490)
Donaldson, David 4:42:49 (19,336)
Donaldson, Gavin 4:51:55 (21,073)
Donaldson, Grant 2:58:57 (929)
Donaldson, John 5:53:16 (28,081)
Donaldson, Nick 3:29:04 (4,008)
Donaldson, Nick 3:57:30 (9,326)
Donaldson, Oliver 4:43:01 (19,389)
Donaldson, Richard 4:37:52 (18,341)
Done, Fred 3:08:45 (1,650)
Donegan, Paul 4:42:01 (19,163)
Donkin, Neil 3:41:15 (5,999)
Donkin, Raymond 3:07:38 (1,559)
Donn, Ivan 4:20:39 (14,510)
Donnan, Patrick 6:50:48 (29,820)
Donnellan, Austen 4:23:05 (15,083)
Donnellan, Barney 4:43:16 (19,442)
Donnelly, Dave 5:31:35 (26,496)
Donnelly, John 6:31:53 (29,449)
Donnelly, Mark 4:08:33 (11,880)
Donnelly, Shane 3:06:51 (1,494)
Donnelly, Terry 4:01:54 (10,463)
D'Onofrio, Americo 3:53:33 (8,391)
Donoghue, John 3:22:11 (3,024)
Donoghue, Paul 4:20:55 (14,575)
Donohoe, Molua 3:45:40 (6,785)
Donovan, Martin 5:21:47 (25,562)
Donovan, Ray 3:41:54 (6,110)
Donovan, Roy Jnr 5:27:10 (26,097)
Doody, Raymond 3:54:14 (8,519)
Dooey, John 2:50:06 (433)
Doogan, John 4:03:55 (10,866)
Doole, Tim 4:53:19 (21,378)
Dooms, Pascal 3:04:31 (1,314)
Doore, Steven 3:47:22 (7,104)
Dooris, William 6:30:50 (29,434)
Doornkaat, Fritz 4:38:14 (18,437)
Doran, Kevin 3:37:31 (5,339)
Doran, Nicholas 3:27:04 (3,630)
Doran, Patrick 7:11:11 (30,029)
Doran, Stanley 4:36:27 (18,007)
Dorber, Matthew 3:31:20 (4,376)
Dorey, Nick 2:46:12 (322)
Dorey, Stephen 3:49:37 (7,611)
Dorian, Douglas 4:44:15 (19,628)
Dorlanne, Jean-Michel 3:35:40 (5,014)
Dorlencourt, Luc 3:17:21 (2,469)
Dorn, Heinz 5:33:25 (26,641)
Dornan, Michael 5:07:55 (23,762)
Dorne, Didier 3:11:56 (1,910)
Dorrian, Brendan 5:51:41 (27,995)
Dorrian, John 4:51:02 (20,891)
Dorrian, Matthew 3:00:23 (1,049)
Dosanjh, Tony 4:06:32 (11,456)
Dosanjh, Virinder 5:15:02 (24,786)
Dotinga, Harmen 4:16:21 (13,536)
Double, Michael 5:15:12 (24,832)
Doubleday, James 4:47:01 (20,167)
Doubleday, John 4:47:00 (20,163)
Dougherty, David 4:27:42 (16,119)
Doughty, John 4:23:29 (15,169)
Doughty, Martin 3:21:22 (2,928)
Douglas, Dick 6:02:12 (28,512)
Douglas, Garrath 4:03:04 (10,677)
Douglas, John 4:28:48 (16,380)
Douglas, Jon 3:47:04 (7,046)
Douglas, Paul 2:54:56 (626)
Douglas, Paul 5:36:41 (26,923)
Douglas, Rowley 3:50:56 (7,857)
Douglas, Stuart 3:01:36 (1,122)
Douglas, Tony 2:56:36 (722)
Douglas-Hamilton, Andrew 4:16:32 (13,581)
Douglass, Paul 4:12:05 (12,640)
Dourado, Vaughn 4:29:55 (16,665)
Doust, James 4:16:04 (13,480)
Dove, Graham 4:14:50 (13,218)
Dove, Howard 4:31:08 (16,883)
Dove, John 4:31:44 (17,043)
Dove, Kenneth 3:20:37 (2,837)
Dovedi, Stephen 3:37:14 (5,288)
Dover, Gary 3:30:23 (4,228)
Dover, Terry 3:19:26 (2,698)
Dowd, Charlie 4:15:00 (13,268)
Dowd, Christopher 4:57:38 (22,235)
Dowden, Andrew 5:41:05 (27,265)
Dowdeswell, Robert 3:25:58 (3,499)
Dowdy, Michael 4:02:10 (10,518)
Dowell, Paul 4:12:48 (12,794)
Dowle, Peter 3:39:46 (5,731)
Dowling, Jonathan 3:06:00 (1,420)
Dowling, Paul 4:47:29 (20,255)
Down, James 4:18:08 (13,895)
Downer, Dave 5:07:41 (23,726)
Downer, Hugh 5:13:02 (24,505)
Downer, Matthew 4:05:57 (11,339)
Downer, Michael 4:17:04 (13,680)
Downes, Graeme 3:54:48 (8,659)
Downes, Kevin 3:25:15 (3,409)
Downes, Shane 3:38:00 (5,400)
Downes, Simon 3:36:32 (5,163)
Downes, Steven 4:44:55 (19,762)
Downey, Brandan 4:35:13 (17,754)
Downey, Desmond 4:20:53 (14,572)
Downey, Kevin 5:37:01 (26,948)
Downie, Alan 5:17:13 (25,072)
Downie, Colin 4:14:43 (13,177)
Downie, David 5:54:41 (28,147)
Downing, David 3:59:22 (9,869)
Downing, Kavan 5:15:08 (24,802)
Downing, Lee 3:42:24 (6,201)
Downing, Oliver 3:14:23 (2,156)
Dowse, Peter 5:05:19 (23,340)
Dowsett, Frederick 3:45:55 (6,839)
Dowsett, Kevin 3:57:12 (9,226)
Dowsett, Matthew 4:13:37 (12,961)
Dowsett, Peter 3:12:11 (1,929)
Dowton, Alan 3:52:48 (8,230)
Doyle, Brendan 4:47:15 (20,213)
Doyle, Craig 3:39:56 (5,768)
Doyle, Ian 3:26:18 (3,536)
Doyle, Ian 4:15:20 (13,334)
Doyle, James 3:37:37 (5,352)
Doyle, John 4:10:48 (12,341)
Doyle, John 4:29:41 (16,594)
Doyle, John 4:32:27 (17,208)
Doyle, John 5:14:43 (24,741)
Doyle, Mark 3:13:14 (2,031)
Doyle, Michael 3:27:19 (3,677)
Doyle, Orville 3:25:06 (3,390)
Doyle, Pat Jnr 3:36:43 (5,195)
Doyle, Patrick 3:27:55 (3,794)
Doyle, Peter 4:54:32 (21,602)
Doyle, Richard 4:22:25 (14,908)
Doyle, Robert 3:06:06 (1,431)
Doyle, Simon 3:02:00 (1,150)
Doyle, Simon 4:44:52 (19,750)
Doyle, Stuart 4:51:53 (21,067)
Doyle, Tim 2:58:29 (852)
Drabwell, Lee 4:36:51 (18,094)
Dradey, Thomas 5:20:34 (25,417)
Drake, Christopher 4:00:00 (10,054)
Drake, Gary 4:38:33 (18,515)
Drake, Oliver 4:07:14 (11,595)
Draper, Dennis 4:44:08 (19,605)
Draper, Gary 3:47:26 (7,125)
Draper, Robert 4:05:56 (11,333)
Dray, Roger 7:15:04 (30,049)
Draycott, Andrew 4:34:51 (17,685)
Drechsler, Rolf 4:48:53 (20,500)
Dreelan, Ian 4:03:18 (10,725)
Drew, David 4:14:35 (13,145)
Drew, Dorian 4:36:25 (18,000)
Drew, Liam 3:44:48 (6,640)
Drew, Philip 4:59:02 (22,468)
Drew, Robert 4:31:27 (16,969)
Drew, Stephen 4:05:01 (11,121)
Drew, Stephen 5:15:01 (24,781)
Drew, Steven 4:15:16 (13,327)
Drew, Warren 4:27:34 (16,081)
Drewery, Colin 5:11:20 (24,259)
Drewett, Peter 4:55:26 (21,863)
Driemeyer, Frank 3:28:11 (3,840)
Drinkwater, Anthony 3:36:50 (5,213)
Drinkwater, Paul 3:51:32 (7,974)
Drinnan, Michael 4:57:42 (22,249)
Driscoll, Bernard 7:27:27 (30,117)
Driscoll, Michael 4:22:07 (14,838)
Driscoll, Michael 5:54:46 (28,153)
Driscoll, Patrick 5:20:54 (25,453)
Driver, Christopher 4:11:20 (12,466)
Driver, Gary 3:36:13 (5,107)
Driver, Mark 4:19:03 (14,130)
Drley, Daniel 3:15:49 (2,297)
Drohan, William 4:35:38 (17,849)
Dror, Yuval 4:42:00 (19,162)
Drown, William 4:12:01 (12,619)
Druce, Nicholas 3:26:26 (3,547)
Drumm, Paul 4:35:31 (17,815)
Drury, David 4:42:02 (19,169)
Drury, Eric 6:14:57 (29,022)
Drury, Jason 5:04:37 (23,235)
Drury, Robert 4:54:29 (21,587)
Dry, Peter 3:52:22 (8,146)
Dryburgh, George 8:36:33 (30,255)
Dryden, John 2:47:25 (348)
Dryden, Peter 3:48:55 (7,442)
Dryland, Keith 3:44:52 (6,653)
Drysdale, Tim 3:49:58 (7,680)
Drzazga, Edward 3:45:31 (6,751)
D'Santos, Paul 3:42:16 (6,174)
Du Feu, John 3:08:57 (1,667)
Du Plessis, Barend 6:47:43 (29,772)
Dubery, Mark 6:23:56 (29,257)
Dubery, Robert 5:19:20 (25,295)
Dubost, Alain 2:40:43 (188)
Dubrow, Ethan 3:23:09 (3,132)
Ducaat, Arie 5:26:53 (26,076)
Duck, Terrence 4:29:03 (16,431)

Duckett, Ewan	4:55:07 (21,761)
Duckfield, Michael	5:14:43 (24,741)
Duckworth, Kevin	3:13:05 (2,009)
Ducorney, Lucien	3:25:03 (3,384)
Dudack, Lee	5:14:07 (24,641)
Dudley, Dennis	4:11:17 (12,460)
Dudley, John	4:19:59 (14,361)
Dudley, Maurice	4:03:44 (10,825)
Dudley, Peter	4:23:00 (15,063)
Dudman, Niall	4:25:15 (15,565)
Dudman, Nicholas	5:07:54 (23,758)
Dudman, Richard	4:03:33 (10,789)
Dudney, Alan	5:01:44 (22,828)
Duffey, Christopher	4:01:11 (10,317)
Duffey, Matthew	4:04:22 (10,959)
Duffield, Geoff	5:45:47 (27,615)
Duffield, Michael	5:13:13 (24,535)
Duffill, Graham	3:59:13 (9,823)
Duffy, Andrew	3:35:37 (5,005)
Duffy, Clive	3:41:02 (5,963)
Duffy, Eugene	6:16:10 (29,063)
Duffy, Michael	3:17:23 (2,473)
Duffy, Patrick	4:24:26 (15,381)
Duffy, Paul	3:34:02 (4,759)
Duffy, Philip	3:37:43 (5,367)
Duffy, Tony	2:28:52 (60)
Dufour, Marc	4:10:55 (12,378)
Dufour, Pascal	3:42:43 (6,256)
Dufour, Yves	4:06:50 (11,512)
Dufty, Wayne	4:10:32 (12,279)
Dugdale, Martin	3:51:17 (7,929)
Dugdale-Moore, Nicholas	4:56:57 (22,137)
Duggal, Hans	3:27:14 (3,664)
Duggan, Andrew	4:19:17 (14,189)
Duggan, Anthony	3:58:45 (9,685)
Duggan, James	5:59:48 (28,410)
Duggan, Martin	4:39:09 (18,628)
Duggua, Rodney	5:55:39 (28,199)
Dugontier, Dominique	4:16:15 (13,516)
Dujardin, Jean-Jacques	3:28:57 (3,987)
Duke, Trevor	7:02:35 (29,966)
Dukes, David	3:42:19 (6,183)
Dulai, Gurinderjit	4:16:54 (13,647)
Dulieu, Leigh	5:12:20 (24,400)
Dulong, Philippe	4:40:45 (18,931)
Dumbleton, Neil	4:59:07 (22,479)
Dumbreck, Alan	3:49:02 (7,471)
Dumper, Alan	3:07:49 (1,574)
Dun, Craig	4:28:36 (16,339)
Dunbabin, Richard	3:25:55 (3,495)
Duncalf, Christopher	3:36:45 (5,204)
Duncan, Alan	5:26:08 (26,001)
Duncan, Andrew	4:45:12 (19,808)
Duncan, Andrew	5:38:03 (27,025)
Duncan, Brian	4:36:53 (18,101)
Duncan, Edward	3:12:37 (1,969)
Duncan, Eric	3:11:09 (1,849)
Duncan, Geoff	4:25:29 (15,613)
Duncan, Mark	3:49:56 (7,671)
Duncan, Paul	3:52:21 (8,142)
Duncan, Paul	4:33:42 (17,479)
Duncan, Peter	4:00:31 (10,158)
Duncanson, Malcolm	3:48:19 (7,324)
Duncton, Matthew	4:56:54 (22,128)
Dunford, John	3:58:17 (9,560)
Dunford, Rodney	2:57:59 (812)
Dungey, Kevin	4:38:54 (18,586)
Dunkin, Stephen	5:45:49 (27,621)
Dunkley, Ian	5:01:54 (22,854)
Dunkley, Jon	5:08:46 (23,899)
Dunkley, Simon	3:57:11 (9,219)
Dunlea, Brian	4:07:55 (11,745)
Dunleavy, David	4:00:48 (10,242)
Dunleavy, Mark	4:31:38 (17,019)
Dunlop, Andy	4:47:42 (20,293)
Dunlop, Cameron	5:12:13 (24,381)
Dunlop, Mark	3:57:37 (9,369)
Dunn, Alan	3:57:24 (9,289)
Dunn, Barrie	3:31:41 (4,422)
Dunn, Bryon	4:35:40 (17,859)
Dunn, Chris	4:48:40 (20,463)
Dunn, Darren	2:45:48 (314)
Dunn, David	3:02:02 (1,154)

Dunn, Derek	3:23:22 (3,157)
Dunn, Edward	4:29:39 (16,585)
Dunn, Gary	4:19:16 (14,183)
Dunn, Gordon	4:49:57 (20,708)
Dunn, Malcolm	4:14:55 (13,239)
Dunn, Mark	3:45:42 (6,796)
Dunn, Nicholas	4:58:01 (22,296)
Dunn, Robert	4:17:10 (13,708)
Dunn, Roger	3:31:35 (4,408)
Dunn, Simon	4:16:40 (13,601)
Dunn, Steve	3:39:02 (5,579)
Dunn, William	2:59:55 (1,020)
Dunnaker, Ian	4:36:32 (18,026)
Dunne, Eric	4:28:06 (16,210)
Dunnell, Nick	4:52:17 (21,153)
Dunning, David	4:30:28 (16,750)
Dunning, Nicholas	3:58:56 (9,732)
Dunning, Peter	5:05:27 (23,372)
Dunnington, Gary	5:37:35 (26,992)
Dunphy, Brian	5:11:43 (24,317)
Dunscombe, Mark	3:16:13 (2,333)
Dunstan, Paul	3:59:41 (9,969)
Dunstan, Richard	4:27:58 (16,188)
Dunstone, Philip	3:07:15 (1,525)
Dunton, Ian	4:38:30 (18,506)
Duperray, Gilbert	3:43:57 (6,480)
Dupont, Eric	3:17:15 (2,450)
Dupoux, Bernard	4:21:38 (14,720)
Dupuy, Barry	4:35:32 (17,819)
Dupuy, Michel	3:21:14 (2,909)
Durand, Lucien	3:13:42 (2,074)
Durat, Alain	3:51:59 (8,068)
Durbin, James	4:29:24 (16,519)
Durden, Gary	3:55:32 (8,805)
Durell, Philip	5:24:36 (25,845)
Durham, Edward	3:18:45 (2,627)
Durlatti, Laurent	4:02:09 (10,514)
Durmier, Jean-Pierre	3:16:39 (2,383)
Durnall, Paul	3:38:53 (5,555)
Durrani, Amer	5:29:10 (26,304)
Durrant, David	6:20:06 (29,161)
Durrant, Geoffrey	4:13:21 (12,889)
Durrant, Jon	3:51:48 (8,027)
Durrant, Keith	7:19:21 (30,075)
Durrant, Kevin	4:21:10 (14,621)
Durrant, Robert	3:44:48 (6,640)
Durst, Michael	3:54:38 (8,620)
Dussard, Philip	4:55:49 (21,955)
Dutch, David	4:53:15 (21,361)
Dutch, James	4:42:54 (19,363)
Dutheil, Jacky	3:42:08 (6,145)
Duthie, Ian	4:43:25 (19,469)
Dutnall, Barry	4:36:27 (18,007)
Dutton, Timothy	5:03:49 (23,103)
Duyck, Xavier	3:41:27 (6,035)
Dwane, Michael	5:32:07 (26,542)
Dweh, Garry	4:31:58 (17,109)
Dwyer, Graham	3:33:47 (4,726)
Dwyer, Jason	3:25:06 (3,390)
Dwyer, John	3:15:58 (2,319)
Dwyer, Julian	2:20:29 (25)
Dwyer, Mark	4:23:17 (15,127)
Dwyer, Terence	5:09:33 (24,021)
Dyce, Craig	3:32:26 (4,525)
Dyckes, John	3:24:48 (3,354)
Dyckhoff, Glenn	3:20:28 (2,820)
Dyde, Martin	2:50:57 (466)
Dye, Jonathan	4:35:49 (17,882)
Dye, Richard	3:35:42 (5,018)
Dyer, Bryan	4:10:24 (12,255)
Dyer, Charles	4:07:00 (11,551)
Dyer, Matthew	3:07:12 (1,517)
Dyer, Paul	3:48:08 (7,291)
Dyer, Richard	4:23:20 (15,141)
Dyke, Brian	6:26:38 (29,322)
Dykes, Robert	4:04:05 (10,901)
Dysart, Dave	4:54:54 (21,702)
Dyson, Andrew	3:46:35 (6,968)
Dyson, Ian	4:18:18 (13,953)
Dziubak, Stefan	4:31:05 (16,866)
Eade, Darren	4:15:43 (13,406)
Eadsforth, James	4:16:20 (13,529)
Eady, Andrew	3:25:45 (3,474)

Eagle, Paul	4:42:30 (19,273)
Eagles, Graham	3:54:01 (8,483)
Ealand, Nigel	3:25:36 (3,456)
Eames, David	4:29:46 (16,614)
Eames, John	4:47:02 (20,169)
Eames, Joseph	6:20:34 (29,176)
Eames, Paul	3:35:51 (5,042)
Eames, Richard	4:52:20 (21,169)
Earey, Richard	5:29:51 (26,355)
Earl, Andrew	5:31:56 (26,528)
Earl, Charles	3:21:37 (2,960)
Earl, David	4:05:37 (11,244)
Earl, Dennis	3:23:17 (3,146)
Earl, Derek	3:50:18 (7,734)
Earl, Jared	3:54:06 (8,492)
Earl, Martin	3:17:20 (2,465)
Earlam, Charles	3:52:03 (8,085)
Earle, James	5:39:04 (27,090)
Earle, Kenneth	3:54:22 (8,555)
Earle, Matthew	4:49:14 (20,569)
Earle, Philip	4:56:28 (22,060)
Earles, Ian	4:15:03 (13,278)
Earley, David	4:00:20 (10,113)
Early, David	5:15:13 (24,834)
Earnshaw, Adam	3:46:41 (7,002)
Earnshaw, Elliott	4:37:55 (18,350)
Earnshaw, Marcus	3:54:58 (8,696)
Earp, Blieu	4:37:40 (18,294)
Eason, Adam	3:46:20 (6,921)
Eason, Andy	3:08:31 (1,634)
Eason, Scott	4:00:30 (10,154)
Eason, Simon	4:46:31 (20,059)
Eassom, Simon	4:28:49 (16,385)
East, David	3:58:40 (9,661)
East, Edward	3:36:28 (5,153)
East, John	4:35:44 (17,872)
East, Julian	3:39:57 (5,775)
East, Trevor	3:42:37 (6,238)
Eastaugh-Waring, Stephen	3:13:28 (2,058)
Easthope, John	4:33:07 (17,329)
Eastick, John	4:13:55 (13,022)
Eastlake, Simon	3:08:07 (1,598)
Eastman, Daniel	4:06:20 (11,414)
Eastman, Dave	5:41:15 (27,274)
Eastman, William	5:10:24 (24,129)
Easto, Simon	3:19:14 (2,684)
Easton, Carl	3:16:26 (2,355)
Easton, Mark	5:07:25 (23,684)
Eastwood, Adrian	3:57:29 (9,323)
Eastwood, Kevin	3:44:13 (6,527)
Easy, Jason	3:29:24 (4,064)
Eaton, Albert	7:10:34 (30,024)
Eaton, Andrew	4:56:08 (22,009)
Eaton, Christopher	3:09:17 (1,692)
Eaton, Duncan	5:11:59 (24,351)
Eaton, Ken	5:17:32 (25,111)
Eaton, Michael	4:18:15 (13,935)
Eaton, Peter	3:58:45 (9,685)
Eavers, Christopher	3:43:08 (6,332)
Ebbesen, Gunnar	5:36:27 (26,913)
Ebden, Paddy	5:18:57 (25,262)
Ebert, David	4:18:29 (14,009)
Eccles, Dvid	3:28:56 (3,982)
Eccles, Paul	2:45:11 (294)
Eccles, Richard	4:19:53 (14,333)
Eccleshare, William	3:56:26 (9,034)
Eccleston, Alan	3:57:39 (9,384)
Eccleston, Christopher	3:01:08 (1,091)
Eckersley, Richard	4:58:28 (22,371)
Eckl, Hans Peter	4:55:39 (21,940)
Eckleben, Wolfgang	3:40:47 (5,908)
Economou, Jon	5:00:44 (22,697)
Eddes, Remro	4:36:58 (18,120)
Eddleston, Michael	3:40:23 (5,845)
Ede, David	5:10:46 (24,180)
Edelmann, Anton	4:41:40 (19,097)
Eden, John	4:56:12 (22,024)
Edensor, Ray	5:04:58 (23,291)
Edgar, Ian	4:19:19 (14,198)
Edgar, Jim	5:39:24 (27,122)
Edgar, Stephen	3:25:24 (3,431)
Edge, Andrew	4:41:19 (19,031)
Edge, Ian	3:04:09 (1,292)

Edge, Shane 3:16:22 (2,348)
Edge, Trevor 3:26:33 (3,565)
Edgecombe, Mervyn 4:41:30 (19,061)
Edgecombe, Nigel 4:26:28 (15,836)
Edgington, Adrian 3:27:22 (3,683)
Edgson, Stephen 6:14:36 (29,009)
Edmond, Kenneth 4:49:53 (20,691)
Edmonds, John 5:18:05 (25,173)
Edmonds, John 6:00:45 (28,444)
Edmonds, Mark 2:46:49 (335)
Edmonds, Richard 5:08:13 (23,800)
Edmonds, Stephen 4:17:18 (13,735)
Edmonds, Steven 4:46:23 (20,031)
Edmondson, David 4:35:33 (17,822)
Edmondson, Ian 3:45:27 (6,736)
Edmondson, William 3:32:37 (4,551)
Edney, Roger 4:08:32 (11,877)
Edridge, Norman 3:52:58 (8,260)
Edser, Jonathan 4:37:59 (18,365)
Edwards, Alan 2:59:19 (964)
Edwards, Alan 4:20:08 (14,393)
Edwards, Allan 4:34:33 (17,636)
Edwards, Andrew 5:50:44 (27,939)
Edwards, Anthony 5:22:22 (25,633)
Edwards, Benjamin 4:19:49 (14,318)
Edwards, Benjamin 7:43:50 (30,178)
Edwards, Charles 3:47:31 (7,143)
Edwards, Charles 4:07:17 (11,606)
Edwards, Christopher 4:11:34 (12,515)
Edwards, Christopher 4:20:12 (14,409)
Edwards, Christopher 4:45:11 (19,804)
Edwards, Christopher 4:52:29 (21,200)
Edwards, Christopher 5:29:01 (26,290)
Edwards, Clive 4:16:50 (13,639)
Edwards, Dave 4:02:55 (10,649)
Edwards, David 3:06:37 (1,471)
Edwards, Dominic 5:14:49 (24,751)
Edwards, Duncan 4:38:42 (18,548)
Edwards, Gary 5:25:57 (25,982)
Edwards, George 5:30:58 (26,449)
Edwards, Ian 2:50:54 (461)
Edwards, James 3:09:35 (1,724)
Edwards, Jeremy 4:03:00 (10,661)
Edwards, John 4:18:14 (13,926)
Edwards, Jon 4:55:55 (21,971)
Edwards, Keith 3:30:53 (4,310)
Edwards, Keith 3:49:10 (7,489)
Edwards, Lee 5:14:46 (24,746)
Edwards, Mark 3:10:38 (1,804)
Edwards, Mark 3:49:40 (7,618)
Edwards, Mark 4:13:04 (12,832)
Edwards, Mark 4:27:37 (16,096)
Edwards, Mark 4:53:26 (21,403)
Edwards, Matt 5:08:13 (23,800)
Edwards, Michael 3:13:44 (2,080)
Edwards, Michael 3:39:18 (5,625)
Edwards, Michael 5:01:18 (22,783)
Edwards, Neil 4:28:30 (16,314)
Edwards, Neil 5:05:12 (23,318)
Edwards, Owen 3:59:23 (9,876)
Edwards, Paul 3:16:13 (2,333)
Edwards, Paul 4:56:11 (22,021)
Edwards, Peter 3:29:43 (4,122)
Edwards, Peter 4:00:43 (10,217)
Edwards, Phillip 4:13:56 (13,028)
Edwards, Richard 3:36:26 (5,147)
Edwards, Richard 4:09:18 (12,042)
Edwards, Richard 4:25:29 (15,613)
Edwards, Robert 2:45:00 (287)
Edwards, Robert 4:46:53 (20,140)
Edwards, Robert 5:56:42 (28,252)
Edwards, Robin 4:12:30 (12,740)
Edwards, Simon 3:48:54 (7,440)
Edwards, Simon 3:56:57 (9,166)
Edwards, Stephen 3:58:38 (9,649)
Edwards, Stephen 4:01:56 (10,473)
Edwards, Stuart 4:55:17 (21,810)
Edwards, Tim 3:59:54 (10,026)
Edwards, Tony 3:17:52 (2,517)
Edwards, William 4:04:33 (11,007)
Edwards, William 6:27:08 (29,335)
Edwards-Moss, Jonathan 4:44:51 (19,743)
Edye, Simon 2:57:40 (790)

Egan, Anthony 3:58:13 (9,542)
Egan, James 4:41:17 (19,027)
Egan, Lee 3:19:37 (2,720)
Egan, Liam 4:46:54 (20,144)
Egan, Marcus 4:10:19 (12,231)
Egan, Simon 4:04:32 (11,001)
Egan, Tim 3:59:48 (9,998)
Egdell, Roger 3:06:00 (1,420)
Egerton, Charles 6:12:24 (28,937)
Egerton, Philip 5:19:56 (25,358)
Eggeling, Ronald 4:25:45 (15,662)
Eggett, Tim 4:16:09 (13,496)
Eggins, Greg 4:14:38 (13,155)
Eggleston, Andrew 6:55:29 (29,892)
Eggleston, David 3:22:48 (3,086)
Eglen, Roger 3:14:46 (2,192)
Ehrhart, Andrew 3:33:40 (4,708)
Ehrler, Rolf 5:00:59 (22,732)
Ehrlich, Michael 3:56:54 (9,154)
Eichert, Paul 3:09:31 (1,715)
Eisele, Steve 4:12:46 (12,784)
Eisenhut, Axel 3:08:19 (1,617)
Eisert, Hans 4:18:17 (13,946)
Ek, Gustav 4:42:19 (19,231)
Ekfeldt, Magnus 3:51:27 (7,952)
Ekins, Stephen 4:49:28 (20,613)
El Habbal, Magdi 4:36:56 (18,116)
El Hattab, Mohammed 2:14:26 (13)

El Mouaziz, Abdelkader 2:07:11 (1)

Abdelkader El Mouaziz (born 1 January 1969) is a Moroccan long-distance runner, a two-time winner of the London Marathon: 1999, 2001; and was runner-up in 2000. He also won the 1994 Madrid Marathon and the New York City Marathon in 2000. He was fifth at the 2002 Chicago Marathon and seventh in the 2000 Sydney Olympics marathon. But for a gusting wind coming in off the River Thames, El Mouaziz might have improved Antonio Pinto's London course record of 2:06:36 set in 2000, but he nevertheless produced one of the race's biggest winning margins of 1 minute 4 seconds. He also became the first man to hold the titles in both London and New York after winning there in November 2000. El Mouaziz became only the third man to win in London and New York, joining Briton Steve Jones and Kenyan Douglas Wakihuri. The 32-year-old Moroccan clocked 2:07:11, a personal best and the quickest time of the year.

Elana, Erick Kali 5:17:05 (25,060)
Elbert, Carsten 4:45:44 (19,891)
Elborn, Ian 3:59:55 (10,033)
Elbourn, Tim 4:44:54 (19,759)
Elbourne, Lawrence 4:36:52 (18,097)
Elcock, Sherwood 5:28:02 (26,185)
Elder, David 3:56:48 (9,133)
Elder, Roderick 4:31:10 (16,893)
Elderfield, Colin 4:24:35 (15,416)
Elderkin, William 3:38:25 (5,469)
Elders, Stephen 4:16:01 (13,468)
Elding, Robert 3:48:50 (7,429)

Eldred, Keith 3:58:41 (9,669)
Eldred, Norman 3:44:06 (6,509)
Eldridge, David 5:39:16 (27,111)
Eldridge, Reginald 6:18:28 (29,128)
Eleftheriou, Chris 3:59:17 (9,837)
Eley, Steve 4:49:48 (20,675)
Elgar, Jamie 4:55:27 (21,872)
Elgood, William 4:54:48 (21,678)
Ell, Anthony 4:57:27 (22,210)
Ellaway, Ian 4:17:24 (13,750)
Elleman, Peter 5:29:23 (26,329)
Ellemann, Tom 4:31:52 (17,081)
Ellen, John 4:56:06 (22,003)
Ellerby, Vincent 3:08:37 (1,640)
Ellerton, Steven 3:56:38 (9,085)
Ellice, Peter 4:49:08 (20,548)
Ellicott, Neil 4:46:24 (20,034)
Ellingford, Raymond 4:13:16 (12,866)
Ellingham, Mark 3:40:54 (5,926)
Elliot, Martin 3:40:21 (5,841)
Elliot, Ross 2:59:09 (947)
Elliott, Andrew 4:00:42 (10,211)
Elliott, Andrew 4:28:22 (16,277)
Elliott, Andrew 4:44:50 (19,738)
Elliott, Barry 6:15:38 (29,048)
Elliott, David 3:48:35 (7,376)
Elliott, David 4:15:32 (13,373)
Elliott, Gavin 3:20:28 (2,820)
Elliott, Hugh 4:52:52 (21,280)
Elliott, James 5:02:41 (22,961)
Elliott, Jamie 4:37:10 (18,162)
Elliott, Keith 3:42:28 (6,211)
Elliott, Kevin 6:13:17 (28,963)
Elliott, Malcolm 3:15:28 (2,269)
Elliott, Mark 3:06:26 (1,454)
Elliott, Martin 3:48:28 (7,353)
Elliott, Matthew 3:09:35 (1,724)
Elliott, Mike 4:58:30 (22,376)
Elliott, Neill 3:28:44 (3,944)
Elliott, Peter 4:31:54 (17,090)
Elliott, Simon 3:22:46 (3,084)
Elliott, Simon 4:16:37 (13,591)
Elliott, Stephen 4:00:07 (10,075)
Ellis, Benjamin 5:30:28 (26,409)
Ellis, Colin 4:41:46 (19,117)
Ellis, Darren 3:13:42 (2,074)
Ellis, David 3:07:38 (1,559)
Ellis, Gwyn 4:01:22 (10,365)
Ellis, Hubert 4:37:25 (18,229)
Ellis, Ieuan 2:27:53 (53)
Ellis, Jeremy 4:04:59 (11,115)
Ellis, John 3:44:17 (6,540)
Ellis, John 4:34:12 (17,570)
Ellis, John 5:47:00 (27,703)
Ellis, Jonathan 5:00:32 (22,667)
Ellis, Keith 4:46:00 (19,938)
Ellis, Kevan 3:30:41 (4,275)
Ellis, Laurence 3:26:05 (3,510)
Ellis, Martin 4:46:43 (20,095)
Ellis, Michael 3:59:19 (9,849)
Ellis, Nathan 5:01:08 (22,754)
Ellis, Peter 3:34:56 (4,897)
Ellis, Robert 5:02:51 (22,984)
Ellis, Stephen 4:07:39 (11,687)
Ellis, Steve 5:44:30 (27,514)
Ellis, Timothy 4:11:58 (12,600)
Ellison, David 3:18:26 (2,592)
Ellison, Mark 2:59:43 (999)
Ellison, Wayne 4:22:42 (14,985)
Elliston, Barry 4:31:07 (16,876)
Elliston, David 5:01:58 (22,866)
Ellithorn, Mark 3:08:44 (1,649)
Ellwood, Michael 4:44:29 (19,668)
Elmer, Paul 5:49:47 (27,888)
Elmer, Philip 4:35:57 (17,920)
Elms, Haydn 4:14:44 (13,185)
Elms, Robert 4:43:10 (19,422)
Elphick, Charles 4:21:34 (14,704)
Elphick, Peter 4:07:49 (11,724)
Elrick, James 3:20:38 (2,840)
Elrick, Peter 5:49:04 (27,844)
Else, Bernard 4:20:52 (14,564)
Else, Simon 4:05:35 (11,235)

Elsey, John ... 5:45:19 (27,578)
Elsmore, Ian ... 3:49:49 (7,648)
Elson, Benjamin ... 3:53:38 (8,409)
Elson, Donald ... 4:07:24 (11,639)
Elston, Francis ... 4:24:18 (15,349)
Elston, Paul ... 3:09:17 (1,692)
Elstub, Michael ... 4:24:06 (15,312)
Eltham, Richard ... 5:13:12 (24,530)
Elton, Mark ... 3:56:24 (9,025)
Elvidge, Marc ... 5:11:23 (24,271)
Elwell, Adam ... 4:21:54 (14,786)
Elwood, John ... 3:42:45 (6,262)
Ely, Jason ... 3:37:59 (5,398)
Emanuel, Andrew ... 4:55:35 (21,913)
Emanuel, Christopher ... 4:55:35 (21,913)
Ember, Matthew ... 3:42:01 (6,125)
Emberson, John ... 3:40:45 (5,906)
Emberson, Peter ... 6:08:00 (28,762)
Embley, Tim ... 4:53:40 (21,448)
Emblin, Brett ... 5:21:12 (25,489)
Emeny, Mark ... 4:15:38 (13,393)
Emerson, Andrew ... 4:42:03 (19,171)
Emerton, Mark ... 3:58:32 (9,616)
Emery, Christopher ... 5:21:16 (25,498)
Emery, Neil ... 4:48:15 (20,395)
Emery, Nigel ... 3:44:06 (6,509)
Emery, Peter ... 3:13:43 (2,077)
Emery, Peter ... 4:35:11 (17,749)
Emmerson, Bob ... 3:17:16 (2,455)
Emmerson, Duncan ... 4:16:24 (13,552)
Emmerson, Jeffrey ... 4:00:00 (10,054)
Emmet, Adrian ... 3:47:51 (7,224)
Emmines, Jim ... 3:02:48 (1,200)
Emmings, Chris ... 4:35:10 (17,746)
Emmitt, Colin ... 6:33:28 (29,492)
Emus, William ... 4:03:34 (10,793)
Endemano, Mark ... 3:17:55 (2,522)
Endres, Foachim ... 3:56:27 (9,040)
Enfield, David ... 4:31:34 (16,996)
Engel, Bib ... 4:25:50 (15,685)
England, Clive ... 4:49:56 (20,706)
England, Lee ... 4:40:30 (18,874)
England, Martin ... 3:05:25 (1,384)
England, Paul ... 4:53:04 (21,330)
England, Philip ... 3:29:54 (4,150)
England, Richard ... 3:53:16 (8,322)
England, Russell ... 4:46:35 (20,074)
England, Steven ... 5:45:07 (27,566)
Engle, James ... 4:11:33 (12,513)
English, Denis ... 4:44:32 (19,684)
English, Robert ... 3:25:00 (3,380)
Enion, David ... 3:49:49 (7,648)
Ennebeck, Thierry ... 2:44:10 (267)
Ennis, John ... 4:39:00 (18,603)
Ennis, Patrick ... 3:38:21 (5,456)
Ennis, Rob ... 4:00:25 (10,133)
Ennis, Stephen ... 5:11:22 (24,266)
Enright, Edward ... 4:02:52 (10,635)
Enright, Michael ... 4:17:06 (13,685)
Enright, Michael ... 4:18:03 (13,877)
Ensink, Jos ... 3:48:03 (7,276)
Entwistle, Michael ... 3:17:15 (2,450)
Entwistle, Michael ... 5:44:28 (27,509)
Entwistle, Peter ... 2:54:21 (597)
Entwistle, William ... 4:30:25 (16,745)
Entzian, Tobias ... 3:45:16 (6,715)
Eplett, Liam ... 3:56:59 (9,174)
Epsom, Joseph ... 3:53:19 (8,338)
Erasmus, James ... 4:02:22 (10,544)
Erasmus, Luther ... 4:10:14 (12,216)
Erasmus, Nickey ... 4:49:41 (20,648)
Eraud, Philippe ... 3:21:24 (2,935)
Erculisse, Laurent ... 3:30:24 (4,233)
Ericksen, John ... 3:08:22 (1,620)
Eriksson, Bo ... 3:59:17 (9,837)
Erith, Mike ... 3:01:42 (1,131)
Ernest, Jan ... 5:00:07 (22,634)
Errington, Vic ... 4:54:34 (21,613)
Erry, John ... 5:07:45 (23,740)
Esam, John ... 4:08:58 (11,971)
Escalona, Antonio ... 4:21:51 (14,774)
Espagnet, Philippe ... 3:56:44 (9,115)
Essam, Keith ... 4:36:12 (17,954)
Esser, Nicholas ... 3:41:40 (6,069)
Essery Gilpin, James ... 3:19:30 (2,706)
Estall, Jim ... 3:35:43 (5,019)
Estall, Mark ... 5:15:09 (24,813)
Eswaranathan, Selvarajah ... 5:25:26 (25,935)
Eterovic, Adrian ... 3:33:19 (4,664)
Etheridge, Ian ... 4:21:24 (14,668)
Etherington, John ... 3:40:14 (5,819)
Etherington, Philip ... 4:39:50 (18,758)
Etherton, Neil ... 3:39:49 (5,743)
Etridge, Malcolm ... 4:59:59 (22,619)
Ettinger, Roy ... 5:20:13 (25,377)
Ettlinger, Anthony ... 4:07:56 (11,747)
Eustace, David ... 5:30:52 (26,443)
Evamy, James ... 3:55:16 (8,756)
Evans, Alexander ... 3:49:39 (7,614)
Evans, Alexander ... 6:01:59 (28,505)
Evans, Andrew ... 3:01:24 (1,103)
Evans, Andrew ... 4:15:47 (13,421)
Evans, Andrew John ... 5:11:47 (24,326)
Evans, Antony ... 5:01:22 (22,788)
Evans, Barrie ... 3:43:39 (6,427)
Evans, Ben ... 5:08:22 (23,824)
Evans, Benedict ... 3:25:58 (3,499)
Evans, Bryan ... 3:26:14 (3,526)
Evans, Carl ... 5:06:30 (23,544)
Evans, Christopher ... 4:32:35 (17,224)
Evans, Clive ... 3:21:18 (2,919)
Evans, Colin ... 3:33:15 (4,652)
Evans, Colin ... 4:37:26 (18,233)
Evans, Daniel ... 4:19:59 (14,361)
Evans, Daniel ... 5:21:30 (25,525)
Evans, David ... 3:52:50 (8,235)
Evans, David ... 3:57:41 (9,391)
Evans, David ... 4:22:14 (14,870)
Evans, David ... 4:28:33 (16,326)
Evans, David ... 4:35:47 (17,879)
Evans, David ... 5:28:10 (26,189)
Evans, Des ... 4:01:37 (10,414)
Evans, Duncan ... 4:06:35 (11,467)
Evans, Ewan ... 4:25:43 (15,657)
Evans, Francis ... 3:51:06 (7,896)
Evans, Gareth ... 4:53:59 (21,509)
Evans, George ... 3:44:59 (6,684)
Evans, Glenn ... 5:33:46 (26,670)
Evans, Glyn ... 2:58:33 (862)
Evans, Graeme ... 5:35:55 (26,872)
Evans, Graham ... 4:04:10 (10,918)
Evans, Heddwyn ... 4:58:41 (22,412)
Evans, Hywel ... 3:46:07 (6,881)
Evans, James ... 5:55:46 (28,202)
Evans, Jason ... 4:08:10 (11,795)
Evans, John ... 3:49:35 (7,604)
Evans, John ... 4:11:56 (12,591)
Evans, John ... 4:32:56 (17,298)
Evans, Julian ... 3:58:14 (9,551)
Evans, Julian ... 4:22:07 (14,838)
Evans, Marc ... 5:08:39 (23,879)
Evans, Mark ... 3:48:18 (7,322)
Evans, Mervyn ... 2:59:46 (1,004)
Evans, Michael ... 2:37:37 (128)
Evans, Michael ... 3:06:57 (1,500)
Evans, Michael ... 3:22:35 (3,062)
Evans, Michael ... 3:57:44 (9,403)
Evans, Michael ... 4:03:08 (10,692)
Evans, Michael ... 4:50:25 (20,789)
Evans, Mike ... 4:07:03 (11,564)
Evans, Mike ... 4:17:27 (13,761)
Evans, Neil ... 4:54:53 (21,699)
Evans, Neil ... 4:55:29 (21,885)
Evans, Nicholas ... 4:03:39 (10,812)
Evans, Nicholas ... 4:20:25 (14,453)
Evans, Paul ... 4:46:55 (20,151)
Evans, Peter ... 5:22:28 (25,645)
Evans, Peter ... 5:55:57 (28,213)
Evans, Philip ... 3:44:03 (6,499)
Evans, Philip ... 3:46:18 (6,917)
Evans, Ray ... 3:48:57 (7,451)
Evans, Richard ... 4:25:06 (15,531)
Evans, Robert ... 4:03:58 (10,876)
Evans, Robert ... 4:20:55 (14,575)
Evans, Robert ... 4:43:09 (19,416)
Evans, Roy ... 3:49:29 (7,574)
Evans, Russell ... 3:27:15 (3,665)
Evans, Scott ... 5:15:51 (24,917)
Evans, Simon ... 3:36:16 (5,117)
Evans, Simon ... 4:13:45 (12,988)
Evans, Stefan ... 5:39:52 (27,173)
Evans, Stephen ... 3:48:41 (7,398)
Evans, Stephen ... 4:36:58 (18,120)
Evans, Stephen ... 4:43:35 (19,516)
Evans, Stephen ... 4:47:10 (20,194)
Evans, Stephen ... 4:55:19 (21,819)
Evans, Stewart ... 3:52:51 (8,238)
Evans, Stuart ... 4:07:01 (11,557)
Evans, Stuart ... 5:30:29 (26,411)
Evans, Timothy ... 4:31:13 (16,908)
Evans, Tom ... 3:24:05 (3,257)
Evans, Tony ... 3:59:31 (9,925)
Evanson, Leslie ... 5:23:20 (25,726)
Eve, Kevin ... 7:16:21 (30,056)
Eve, Michael ... 3:22:59 (3,111)
Evelyn, Roch ... 4:44:24 (19,656)
Evenett, Glyn ... 3:49:58 (7,680)
Everard, Alan ... 4:14:17 (13,094)
Everard, Jim ... 3:38:19 (5,451)
Everard, Roger ... 2:58:51 (919)
Everett, Barry ... 3:43:41 (6,432)
Everett, David ... 4:31:45 (17,048)
Everett, James ... 6:13:29 (28,970)
Everett, Jerry ... 4:28:46 (16,374)
Everett, Jerry ... 5:31:44 (26,510)
Everett, Leigh ... 5:51:45 (28,005)
Everett, Michael ... 6:13:29 (28,970)
Everett, Paul ... 4:08:18 (11,825)
Everett, Wayne ... 4:04:42 (11,042)
Everitt, Matthew ... 6:42:26 (29,698)
Everitt, Michael ... 4:38:20 (18,462)
Everson, James ... 2:58:36 (870)
Everson, Peter ... 4:02:53 (10,641)
Eves, Peter ... 3:43:03 (6,316)
Eves, Trevor ... 5:34:03 (26,703)
Eveson, Norman ... 4:18:20 (13,964)
Eveson, Peter ... 4:51:19 (20,950)
Evison, Mark ... 3:44:44 (6,622)
Ewan, James ... 5:33:47 (26,671)
Ewen, Mark ... 4:04:23 (10,965)
Ewing, Alan ... 4:37:50 (18,326)
Exell, Richard ... 4:23:38 (15,215)
Exley, Jonathan ... 3:19:35 (2,716)
Exley, Malcolm ... 4:50:22 (20,786)
Eydmann, Garry ... 4:42:58 (19,379)
Eyer, Willen ... 4:44:17 (19,635)
Eymard, Philippe ... 2:42:53 (234)
Eyre, Douglas ... 3:17:34 (2,490)
Eyre, Gary ... 3:36:05 (5,086)
Eyres, Anthony ... 4:07:33 (11,666)
Fabbri, Antonio ... 4:18:00 (13,870)
Fabes, Jez ... 3:47:27 (7,130)
Fabrizi, Anthony ... 4:16:31 (13,577)
Faccini, Victor ... 3:38:10 (5,421)
Facey, Mark ... 4:26:17 (15,800)
Facknell, Steven ... 4:05:52 (11,313)
Facq, Frederic ... 5:20:47 (25,445)
Faerbinger, Peter ... 3:41:30 (6,037)
Faes, Daniel ... 3:33:56 (4,745)
Fagan, Christopher ... 4:12:03 (12,630)
Fagan, Gary ... 4:40:34 (18,889)
Fagerlund, Cas-Erik ... 3:33:06 (4,622)
Faggionato, Lamberto ... 5:31:20 (26,478)
Fahy, Edward ... 3:21:59 (2,994)
Faint, David ... 4:40:52 (18,951)
Fair, Peter ... 4:07:39 (11,687)
Fairbairn, David ... 4:28:17 (16,261)
Fairbras, Stewart ... 4:31:56 (17,102)
Fairbrother, Anthony ... 4:54:47 (21,672)
Fairclough, Rob ... 3:39:18 (5,625)
Faires, Gareth ... 4:13:58 (13,035)
Fairfield, William ... 5:14:01 (24,631)
Fairfoull, Andrew ... 3:45:36 (6,764)
Fairhead, Adrian ... 6:50:03 (29,804)
Fairhead, Allan ... 6:50:03 (29,804)
Fairhurst, Gerald ... 4:19:13 (14,165)
Fairie, Andrew ... 5:32:23 (26,558)
Fairley, Jon ... 3:05:46 (1,405)
Fais, Pierclaudio ... 3:59:06 (9,786)

Fake, David 5:07:38 (23,719)
Falck-Therkelsen, Erik 3:35:03 (4,909)
Falconer, James 4:20:32 (14,483)
Falconi, David 4:54:43 (21,648)
Falk, Joshua 5:58:55 (28,363)
Falkiner, Max 5:32:48 (26,601)
Falkingham, Jason 5:05:16 (23,334)
Falkner, David 3:20:42 (2,847)
Fallen, Paul 4:41:23 (19,045)
Fallon, Chris 4:32:32 (17,217)
Fallon, Dan 4:58:49 (22,430)
Fallon, Gary 3:16:44 (2,398)
Fallon, Geoffrey 3:51:15 (7,921)
Fallon, Thomas 4:58:26 (22,366)
Fallon, Tom 3:07:09 (1,515)
Fallows, Jeremy 6:01:39 (28,491)
Fallows, Kelvin 4:58:43 (22,418)
Falquero, Edward 3:36:01 (5,077)
Fanning, Jerome 3:26:39 (3,578)
Fanti, Maurizio 3:33:23 (4,672)
Fareham, Peter 4:55:12 (21,783)
Farey, Christopher 5:09:53 (24,068)
Farinasso, Alberto 2:55:30 (651)
Farley, Michael 3:07:10 (1,516)
Farley-Moore, Peter 5:04:48 (23,264)
Farmer, Anthony 4:07:01 (11,557)
Farmer, Anthony 5:59:02 (28,368)
Farmer, Graham 3:59:21 (9,863)
Farmer, Marc 4:16:23 (13,547)
Farmer, Mark 4:25:21 (15,583)
Farmer, Michael 4:21:43 (14,737)
Farmer, Michael 5:13:50 (24,611)
Farmer, Sean 5:46:15 (27,644)
Farmer, Stephen 4:20:02 (14,378)
Farmer, Stirling 3:35:04 (4,912)
Farnan, Stephen 4:39:35 (18,712)
Farnell, Mark 2:43:13 (242)
Farnham, Malcolm 3:49:18 (7,525)
Farnham, Robert 4:27:19 (16,027)
Farnish, Keith 4:30:37 (16,769)
Farnsworth, Benjamin 3:58:47 (9,694)
Farnworth, Eric 3:32:50 (4,577)
Farquhar, Andrew 5:33:44 (26,665)
Farquharson, Stuart 4:54:43 (21,648)
Farr, Damiane 5:54:52 (28,155)
Farr, James 4:43:05 (19,400)
Farrant, Lee 5:35:41 (26,859)
Farrant, Paul 4:06:54 (11,527)
Farrar, Alasdair 5:22:20 (25,630)
Farrar, Jamie 6:07:21 (28,739)
Farrar, Steven 3:28:21 (3,881)
Farrell, Bernard 4:01:48 (10,444)
Farrell, Brian 4:29:34 (16,564)
Farrell, David 3:59:04 (9,777)
Farrell, Edward 3:48:40 (7,393)
Farrell, John 5:52:43 (28,051)
Farrell, Nyall 3:56:29 (9,050)
Farrell, Patrick 3:20:41 (2,844)
Farrimond, John 5:01:23 (22,789)
Farrimond, Stuart 4:04:42 (11,042)
Farrin, Dennis 5:06:51 (23,595)
Farrington, Derek 3:22:44 (3,077)
Farrington, Stephen 3:55:39 (8,832)
Farrow, John 4:27:54 (16,178)
Farrow, Michael 4:31:00 (16,850)
Farthing, David 3:49:43 (7,625)
Farwell, Geoffrey 3:55:06 (8,713)
Faturoti, Remi 5:21:18 (25,504)
Faughnan, Mark 3:05:30 (1,392)
Faulds, David 5:27:34 (26,134)
Faulkner, Donald 3:53:13 (8,313)
Faulkner, James 4:24:30 (15,398)
Faulkner, John 3:25:13 (3,403)
Faulkner, Jon 4:22:52 (15,024)
Faulkner, Jonathan 4:41:52 (19,131)
Faulkner, Kevin 3:55:37 (8,821)
Faulkner, Nigel 4:03:06 (10,685)
Faulkner, Robert 4:23:45 (15,236)
Faulkner, Roger 3:58:33 (9,625)
Faulkner, Stephen 3:20:20 (2,800)
Faulkner, Steven 4:54:55 (21,709)
Faure, Wynton 3:14:56 (2,213)
Faure Walker, Edward 4:43:32 (19,504)
Faure Walker, Nicholas 5:10:48 (24,186)
Favaro, Giusto 3:48:37 (7,382)
Fawcett, Malcolm 3:54:00 (8,479)
Fawke, Mark 3:54:16 (8,527)
Fawkes, John 5:23:06 (25,715)
Fay, Gerard 5:59:36 (28,397)
Fazackerley, Antony Mark 5:47:51 (27,759)
Feacey, David 5:05:39 (23,406)
Fearn, Matthew 4:10:27 (12,266)
Fearn, Neil 4:42:42 (19,310)
Fearn, Stuart 6:01:38 (28,487)
Fearnhead, Alan 4:11:51 (12,580)
Fearnley, Adrian 3:08:56 (1,666)
Fearon, Alexander 4:13:38 (12,968)
Fearon, Graeme 4:06:12 (11,385)
Feasey, Barry 6:40:14 (29,647)
Featherstone, Jeffrey 4:56:22 (22,044)
Featherstone, Paul 3:53:16 (8,322)
Fedi, Daniele 3:57:29 (9,323)
Feeney, Sean 5:08:44 (23,894)
Fehsenfeld, Burkhard 3:08:47 (1,654)
Feinblum, Deon 3:07:13 (1,518)
Feintuck, David 3:50:04 (7,697)
Feitknecht, Andy 2:42:52 (233)
Feld, David 3:38:49 (5,540)
Felder, Claus 4:12:21 (12,703)
Feldman, Brian 3:46:50 (7,007)
Feldman, Vincent 3:56:40 (9,095)
Fell, Adrian 4:08:45 (11,923)
Fell, Samuel 3:43:24 (6,377)
Fell, Simon 4:29:00 (16,420)
Fellingham, Richard 4:10:40 (12,306)
Fellows, Keith 3:43:16 (6,355)
Fellows, Lee 5:06:06 (23,487)
Fellows, Mark 3:55:26 (8,792)
Fellows, Simon 5:14:43 (24,741)
Felstead, Graham 5:06:05 (23,484)
Felstead, Iain 3:32:44 (4,565)
Felstead, Paul 4:59:17 (22,495)
Feltham, Barry 4:42:12 (19,205)
Felton, Christopher 3:34:00 (4,754)
Fenelon, Liam 4:24:57 (15,491)
Fenioux, Denis 3:42:41 (6,251)
Fenlon, Graham 4:06:42 (11,485)
Fenlon, Mark 3:26:48 (3,598)
Fenn, James 4:02:31 (10,576)
Fennell, Brett 4:58:04 (22,308)
Fennelly, Brian 3:56:26 (9,034)
Fennelly, Peter 3:36:17 (5,121)
Fenson, Graham 3:28:58 (3,991)
Fenton, Andrew 4:07:04 (11,567)
Fenton, Leslie 3:42:34 (6,229)
Fenton, Sean 5:22:10 (25,606)
Fenwick, Euan 3:59:11 (9,810)
Fenwick, Oliver 3:38:42 (5,520)
Fenwick, Roger 4:21:51 (14,774)
Ferdinando, Andrew 5:26:20 (26,022)
Fereday, David 3:49:53 (7,664)
Ferguson, Andrew 4:52:59 (21,312)
Ferguson, Carl 3:58:53 (9,722)
Ferguson, David 6:39:26 (29,616)
Ferguson, Douglas 4:57:10 (22,167)
Ferguson, James 4:25:59 (15,727)
Ferguson, Mark 4:06:21 (11,418)
Ferguson, Mark 5:22:16 (25,624)
Ferguson, Martin 2:32:40 (77)
Ferguson, Michael 3:37:08 (5,272)
Ferguson, Neil 4:58:28 (22,371)
Ferguson, Paul 4:20:11 (14,405)
Ferguson, Simon 4:13:50 (13,009)
Ferguson, William 4:44:30 (19,674)
Ferguson, William 4:58:45 (22,421)
Fergusson, Duncan 5:10:47 (24,181)
Ferlie, Peter 3:14:31 (2,169)
Fernandes, Alan 3:58:20 (9,569)
Fernandes, Brian 5:23:45 (25,766)
Fernandes Marques, Joad 4:10:39 (12,302)
Fernandez, Franklin 4:12:14 (12,677)
Fernandez Atienza, José Maria 2:23:48 (34)
Fernando, Lawrence 4:33:59 (17,532)
Fernando Henriques, José 3:21:17 (2,917)
Fernee, Ronald 3:41:22 (6,023)
Fernez, José 4:28:27 (16,301)
Fernez, Pascal 2:58:48 (910)
Ferns, Douglas 5:08:25 (23,831)
Ferns, Gerard 3:56:44 (9,115)
Ferraboli, Vittorio 3:28:44 (3,944)
Ferragamo, James 6:27:41 (29,343)
Ferrar, Balvatore 3:54:51 (8,672)
Ferrar, Ian 4:51:18 (20,946)
Ferrar, Mark 5:01:15 (22,777)
Ferrar, Phillip 4:44:15 (19,628)
Ferrar, Simon 4:26:27 (15,832)
Ferrari, Angelo 4:27:32 (16,069)
Ferre, Anthony 3:18:17 (2,574)
Ferreira, Ignatius 3:21:55 (2,984)
Ferrier, Andrew 3:55:42 (8,843)
Ferrington, Andrew 5:52:07 (28,023)
Ferris, Jonathan 3:57:07 (9,200)
Ferro, Daniel 3:53:03 (8,277)
Ferry, Gaston 4:02:26 (10,556)
Fesche, Frank 4:08:20 (11,833)
Fessey, David 4:57:18 (22,190)
Fethers, Andrew 3:45:36 (6,764)
Fettah, Allan 3:30:23 (4,228)
Fevre, Eric 5:05:27 (23,372)
Fewings, Alan 3:23:33 (3,181)
Fewings, Auther 3:20:17 (2,791)
Fickert, Gregory 4:05:23 (11,182)
Fiddes, Christopher 6:07:07 (28,724)
Fiddes, David 4:09:19 (12,045)
Fiddes, Gary 3:59:53 (10,024)
Field, Alan 4:22:18 (14,886)
Field, Alfred 4:13:23 (12,899)
Field, Andrew 2:54:12 (587)
Field, Chris 3:41:22 (6,023)
Field, Geoffrey 3:40:30 (5,869)
Field, Graham 5:04:55 (23,286)
Field, Jeremy 4:22:30 (14,930)
Field, John 5:02:01 (22,874)
Field, Martin 4:24:54 (15,479)
Field, Roy 4:04:03 (10,894)
Field, Stephen 3:01:26 (1,105)
Field, Stuart 4:25:02 (15,520)
Field, Terry 3:46:34 (6,963)
Fielder, Paul 5:30:20 (26,399)
Fielding, Gideon 4:25:04 (15,525)
Fielding, Kevin 4:40:15 (18,826)
Fielding, Paul 2:59:54 (1,018)
Fielding, Paul 5:09:20 (23,986)
Fields, Steven 4:00:53 (10,259)
Fieldsend, Mark 3:28:50 (3,970)
Fiennes, Ranulph 3:39:07 (5,592)
Fievez, Marcus 6:06:16 (28,694)
Fifield, John 4:03:26 (10,756)
Fildes, Jonathan 4:33:31 (17,423)
Filer, Andrew 5:19:46 (25,343)
Filley, Mark 3:50:04 (7,697)
Fillingham, Joseph 3:27:49 (3,767)
Finch, David 4:07:24 (11,639)
Finch, Matt 5:26:52 (26,074)
Finch, Michael 4:14:19 (13,098)
Finch, Michael 5:22:26 (25,640)
Finch, Philip 3:57:40 (9,387)
Finch, Robert 4:08:37 (11,896)
Fincham, Andrew 3:58:34 (9,633)
Fincher, Mark 3:19:53 (2,752)
Findel-Hawkins, David 2:57:46 (797)
Finder, Tom 4:30:50 (16,813)
Findlay, Alistair 5:05:25 (23,363)
Findlay, Ewen 3:59:33 (9,936)
Fine, Greg 3:14:58 (2,218)
Fine, Martin 3:52:18 (8,134)
Finegan, Timothy 4:54:43 (21,648)
Finestone, Philip 2:59:08 (946)
Finill, Chris 2:41:27 (201)
Finn, Andrew 3:36:54 (5,228)
Finn, Anthony 4:33:57 (17,526)
Finn, Conor 5:07:07 (23,632)
Finn, David 2:49:23 (406)
Finn, Geoffrey 4:35:20 (17,781)
Finn, Jonathan 4:09:32 (12,080)
Finn, Julian 4:48:19 (20,410)
Finnegan, Stephen 3:47:33 (7,154)
Finnegan, Thomas 3:52:39 (8,202)
Finnemore, Bernard 4:46:31 (20,059)

Finnerty, Andrew 4:20:46 (14,539)
Finney, David 3:46:29 (6,944)
Finney, Mark 3:54:56 (8,690)
Fiocco, Gilberto 3:52:59 (8,263)
Fiorenzo, Bodini 4:03:13 (10,706)
Firminger, Michael 3:42:29 (6,215)
Firth, Andrew 4:47:22 (20,232)
Firth, Clive 5:12:30 (24,431)
Firth, Colin 3:42:29 (6,215)
Firth, John 2:59:43 (999)
Firth, John 4:29:11 (16,467)
Firth, Michael 5:38:28 (27,050)
Fischer, Georg 3:33:43 (4,716)
Fischer, Ralf 4:40:47 (18,938)
Fish, Andrew 4:09:37 (12,096)
Fish, Grayhame 4:40:21 (18,847)
Fisher, Alan 2:45:05 (289)
Fisher, Andrew 4:24:56 (15,487)
Fisher, Ben 3:08:28 (1,629)
Fisher, Brian 4:20:39 (14,510)
Fisher, Dan 5:18:43 (25,236)
Fisher, David 3:45:55 (6,839)
Fisher, Derek 4:45:32 (19,867)
Fisher, Ian 2:21:52 (27)
Fisher, John 3:32:37 (4,551)
Fisher, John 5:04:29 (23,214)
Fisher, Kevin 5:07:39 (23,723)
Fisher, Marcus 5:46:07 (27,636)
Fisher, Mark 4:07:33 (11,666)
Fisher, Matthew 4:28:34 (16,331)
Fisher, Matthew 5:44:59 (27,560)
Fisher, Neil 3:31:17 (4,370)
Fisher, Nigel 4:31:56 (17,102)
Fisher, Patrick 3:37:02 (5,251)
Fisher, Peter 4:33:29 (17,414)
Fisher, Peter 4:43:16 (19,442)
Fisher, Philip 4:07:21 (11,627)
Fisher, Robert 3:53:42 (8,425)
Fisher, Roderick 3:36:10 (5,099)
Fisher, Roger 3:51:31 (7,972)
Fisher, Rupert 5:08:58 (23,935)
Fisher, Simon 3:25:53 (3,491)
Fisher, Stephen 3:59:20 (9,856)
Fisher, Steven 4:00:20 (10,113)
Fisher, Warren 3:56:21 (9,007)
Fishpool, Sean 3:28:19 (3,872)
Fishwick, Kevin 6:15:13 (29,031)
Fitch, Gavin 4:52:43 (21,257)
Fitchet, Charles 4:46:29 (20,048)
Fitt, James 3:52:32 (8,179)
Fitt, Steven 5:47:48 (27,752)
Fitter, Carl 3:18:05 (2,544)
Fitzgerald, Jack 5:57:36 (28,302)
Fitzgerald, Mark 3:36:50 (5,213)
Fitzgerald, Michael 3:40:28 (5,863)
Fitzgerald, Michael 3:40:44 (5,903)
Fitzgerald, Stephen 3:30:42 (4,278)
Fitzharris, David 5:19:41 (25,332)
Fitzhugh, Martin 3:26:47 (3,595)
Fitzmaurice, James 4:39:11 (18,634)
Fitzpatrick, Anthony 4:06:16 (11,400)
Fitzpatrick, John 4:22:35 (14,948)
Fitzpatrick, John 4:30:21 (16,736)
Fitzpatrick, Mark 5:50:43 (27,937)
Fitzsimmonds, Andrew 4:35:49 (17,882)
Fitzsimmons, James 2:24:24 (39)
Fitzsimmons, Sean 4:09:03 (11,997)
Fitzsimmons, Thomas 5:41:41 (27,309)
Fitzwilliams, Ben 3:56:04 (8,943)
Fivey, Dan 4:54:27 (21,578)
Flack, Karl 3:46:51 (7,012)
Flack, Richard 3:13:29 (2,059)
Flagg, Duncan 3:05:47 (1,406)
Flanagan, Christopher 4:36:11 (17,953)
Flanagan, Graham 3:21:27 (2,940)
Flanagan, Michael 4:03:41 (10,816)
Flanagan, Sean 4:49:02 (20,534)
Flanaghan, John 4:58:02 (22,301)
Flannagan, Michael 6:58:47 (29,928)
Flannery, Raymond 5:22:38 (25,664)
Flashman, Martin 5:05:39 (23,406)
Flatley, Mick 3:03:53 (1,276)
Flatley, Patrick 4:02:01 (10,489)
Flatnitzer, Karl-Heinz 4:03:55 (10,866)
Flaxman, Jonathan 5:42:06 (27,343)
Fleck, Michael 3:20:15 (2,788)
Fleet, Mark 5:05:57 (23,461)
Fleischer, Michael 4:31:47 (17,056)
Flello, Steve 5:35:17 (26,826)
Fleming, Ian 4:44:07 (19,601)
Fleming, Jackson 5:52:51 (28,054)
Fleming, Liam 3:09:34 (1,723)
Fleming, Mark 3:19:18 (2,688)
Fleming, Mark 3:56:27 (9,040)
Fleming, Paul 3:18:03 (2,540)
Fleming, Peter 3:42:02 (6,126)
Fleming, Simon 4:51:24 (20,970)
Fleming, Timothy 4:03:52 (10,855)
Fleming, Victor 5:48:29 (27,816)
Flemming, Gregory 5:17:35 (25,114)
Flemming, Ian 4:41:10 (19,007)
Fletcher, Alan 4:10:35 (12,293)
Fletcher, Andrew 6:16:07 (29,060)
Fletcher, Barry 4:56:53 (22,125)
Fletcher, David 4:23:36 (15,205)
Fletcher, Gordon 3:56:52 (9,147)
Fletcher, Jeremy 4:46:13 (19,990)
Fletcher, Jeremy 6:02:41 (28,528)
Fletcher, Jonathan 3:55:35 (8,814)
Fletcher, Julian 5:14:12 (24,655)
Fletcher, Michael 5:17:58 (25,159)
Fletcher, Neil 4:09:44 (12,112)
Fletcher, Nicholas 4:19:24 (14,227)
Fletcher, Robert 9:19:40 (30,281)
Fletcher, Robin 4:13:16 (12,866)
Fletcher, Stephen 3:43:24 (6,377)
Fletcher, William 4:07:24 (11,639)
Flett, Gordon 4:24:42 (15,437)
Fletton, Robert 5:36:20 (26,903)
Fleurence, Daniel 4:00:44 (10,227)
Fleury, Jean-Jacques 3:59:41 (9,969)
Flint, Andrew 3:57:24 (9,289)
Flint, Howard 4:25:19 (15,578)
Flint, Robert 5:01:10 (22,760)
Flint, Tim 3:57:19 (9,262)
Flintoff, Andrew 5:24:52 (25,868)
Flood, David 4:58:15 (22,336)
Floodpage, Jonathan 3:55:15 (8,751)
Flook, Brett 2:51:40 (500)
Flordh, Mats 3:21:15 (2,911)
Florence, Tristan 6:13:57 (28,990)
Flores, Enrique 4:37:21 (18,212)
Flottard, Eric 4:29:03 (16,431)
Flower, Mark 5:00:01 (22,625)
Flower, Steven 3:53:21 (8,347)
Flowerdew, David 4:09:34 (12,084)
Flowers, Geoffrey 5:15:48 (24,906)
Floyd, Giles 4:52:55 (21,296)
Fluckiger, Hans 3:28:16 (3,859)
Flynn, Darren 5:42:18 (27,356)
Flynn, John 3:30:31 (4,249)
Flynn, John 3:34:12 (4,787)
Flynn, Jonathan 4:35:41 (17,863)
Flynn, Matthew 4:09:59 (12,163)
Flynn, Peter 4:18:06 (13,887)
Flynn, Tommy 3:19:21 (2,691)
Foale, Peter 4:30:38 (16,775)
Foddering, Simon 6:09:51 (28,857)
Fogarty, Gerry 4:40:01 (18,790)
Fogden, Terry 4:53:48 (21,474)
Foglio, Anthony 5:47:54 (27,769)
Fok, Marian 5:33:22 (26,638)
Foldesi, Tom 3:28:55 (3,981)
Foley, Benjamin 3:57:15 (9,241)
Foley, Brendan 5:11:05 (24,222)
Foley, Dominic 3:54:49 (8,664)
Foley, Gerry 4:17:53 (13,848)
Foley, John 4:09:07 (12,006)
Foley, John 4:43:40 (19,530)
Foley, Sean 5:47:51 (27,759)
Foley, Steven 3:07:37 (1,557)
Folkerd, David 5:15:08 (24,802)
Folland, Mike 3:58:36 (9,642)
Follen, Mark 3:59:28 (9,909)
Folley, Duncan 3:29:30 (4,079)
Fonseca, Pedro 6:25:14 (29,288)
Fontenoy, Dominique 3:34:43 (4,866)
Foord, Daniel 3:45:12 (6,707)
Foord, James 4:11:12 (12,440)
Foord, Jeremy 4:50:59 (20,879)
Foord, Roger 3:51:05 (7,889)
Foot, Gary 4:56:12 (22,024)
Foot, Paul 4:56:12 (22,024)
Forbes, Michael 4:20:49 (14,552)
Ford, André 4:55:23 (21,842)
Ford, Christopher 3:54:12 (8,509)
Ford, David 3:57:32 (9,338)
Ford, David 5:50:14 (27,915)
Ford, Don 4:19:21 (14,209)
Ford, Gary 3:37:51 (5,389)
Ford, Ian 4:24:37 (15,424)
Ford, Martin 2:54:42 (620)
Ford, Martin 4:25:34 (15,632)
Ford, Martin 4:33:57 (17,526)
Ford, Melvyn 4:30:54 (16,826)
Ford, Paul 3:51:49 (8,031)
Ford, Peter 3:28:43 (3,939)
Ford, Stephen 4:15:40 (13,398)
Ford, Steven 3:55:06 (8,713)
Ford, Timothy 4:18:33 (14,023)
Ford, Tom 4:37:34 (18,270)
Ford Hunt, Lee 4:24:52 (15,473)
Forder, Gary 5:50:23 (27,919)
Fordham, Darryl 4:15:11 (13,299)
Fordham, John 3:51:43 (8,011)
Fordham, Stuart 3:57:48 (9,431)
Fordyce, Bruce 3:57:38 (9,379)
Foreman, Colin 3:23:49 (3,213)
Foreman, Eddie 5:06:00 (23,469)
Foreman, James 5:59:50 (28,413)
Foreman, Paul 4:31:49 (17,062)
Forey, Simon 3:38:34 (5,491)
Forge, Martin 5:18:23 (25,197)
Forino, Darren 3:47:35 (7,161)
Forkin, Harry 4:46:40 (20,087)
Forman, Geoffrey 3:49:43 (7,625)
Formby, Charles 4:41:14 (19,018)
Foroughi, Kamran 4:51:16 (20,935)
Forrest, Duncan 4:01:25 (10,373)
Forrest, John 3:04:47 (1,334)
Forrester, David 4:18:18 (13,953)
Forrester, Gary 3:17:14 (2,447)
Forrester, Graham 4:55:23 (21,842)
Forrester, Keith 4:22:27 (14,915)
Forrester, Keith 4:30:29 (16,753)
Forrester, Neil 4:11:30 (12,501)
Forsey, Gary 4:46:21 (20,020)
Forsman, Jouni 3:48:55 (7,442)
Forster, Adrian 4:30:21 (16,736)
Forster, David 4:03:22 (10,740)
Forster, Ian 3:20:41 (2,844)
Forster, James 5:03:23 (23,055)
Forster, Paul 4:22:12 (14,861)
Forster, Paul 8:36:33 (30,255)
Forster Jones, Paul 3:39:09 (5,599)
Forsyth, Alan 4:36:21 (17,985)
Forsyth, Andrew 2:54:15 (591)
Forsyth, Andrew 3:54:54 (8,687)
Forsyth, Ian 5:22:13 (25,619)
Fort, Joel 3:10:17 (1,772)
Forte, Philip 2:58:36 (870)
Fortescue, Michael 5:02:09 (22,901)
Forteza, Pablo 4:11:46 (12,562)
Forth, Michael 3:54:12 (8,509)
Fortino, Giovanni 3:23:37 (3,187)
Fortune, David 3:57:02 (9,184)
Fortune, Kieran 3:48:32 (7,367)
Fortune, Martin 3:31:55 (4,457)
Foskett, Geoffrey 4:04:07 (10,905)
Foskett, Kevin 4:54:00 (21,511)
Foster, Alan 4:42:11 (19,202)
Foster, Andrew 4:55:22 (21,837)
Foster, Ben 4:08:34 (11,885)
Foster, Bob 6:08:47 (28,802)
Foster, Charles 5:24:59 (25,884)
Foster, Charles 5:43:15 (27,423)
Foster, Christopher 4:52:04 (21,108)
Foster, David 3:42:53 (6,283)
Foster, David 4:06:29 (11,445)

Foster, David..............4:31:21 (16,944)	Frampton, Brian..............3:23:27 (3,168)	Freestone, Bruce..............5:50:37 (27,930)
Foster, David..............5:35:28 (26,840)	France, Gary..............5:46:13 (27,640)	Freier, John..............5:22:26 (25,640)
Foster, Dominic..............5:17:26 (25,098)	France, Matthew..............6:09:15 (28,822)	Fremantle, Thomas..............4:52:42 (21,251)
Foster, Grant..............5:39:44 (27,159)	Francey, Alan..............4:19:26 (14,236)	Fremeaux, Christian..............3:29:55 (4,163)
Foster, Jamie..............3:04:39 (1,327)	Franchi, Mark..............5:42:31 (27,382)	French, Adam..............5:49:55 (27,895)
Foster, Jonathan..............2:50:56 (464)	Francis, Anthony..............5:52:09 (28,027)	French, Alexander..............4:06:07 (11,364)
Foster, Lawrence..............3:44:27 (6,567)	Francis, Glyn..............3:55:31 (8,800)	French, Andrew..............6:40:00 (29,630)
Foster, Mark..............5:12:31 (24,433)	Francis, Jason..............4:46:33 (20,067)	French, Anthony..............3:50:34 (7,786)
Foster, Mark..............6:00:07 (28,422)	Francis, Keith..............4:52:17 (21,153)	French, Barry..............5:11:04 (24,218)
Foster, Martin..............4:15:23 (13,342)	Francis, Lee..............3:09:07 (1,681)	French, Craig..............5:04:22 (23,193)
Foster, Michael..............3:57:49 (9,437)	Francis, Nick..............2:20:00 (23)	French, David..............5:23:13 (25,723)
Foster, Michael..............4:36:51 (18,094)	Francis, Paul..............4:36:07 (17,945)	French, Gerald..............4:54:44 (21,656)
Foster, Neil..............3:37:46 (5,374)	Francis, Raymond..............2:58:46 (904)	French, Hugh..............4:35:34 (17,829)
Foster, Paul..............5:20:35 (25,420)	Francis, Richard..............3:11:40 (1,882)	French, Jason..............3:11:42 (1,887)
Foster, Richard..............3:25:09 (3,393)	Francis, Richard..............3:25:32 (3,447)	French, John..............3:26:30 (3,559)
Foster, Robert..............4:05:07 (11,141)	Francis, Roger..............4:31:12 (16,905)	French, John..............3:57:11 (9,219)
Foster, Stephen..............3:33:49 (4,731)	Francis, Stephen..............4:39:23 (18,664)	French, Paul..............3:50:41 (7,802)
Foster, Stephen..............3:54:32 (8,594)	Francisco, Manuel..............5:08:49 (23,910)	French, Paul..............4:31:27 (16,969)
Foster, Stephen..............4:11:59 (12,606)	Francisco, Velasco Espejo..............3:54:35 (8,610)	French, Peter..............3:53:46 (8,436)
Foster, Stuart..............4:56:05 (22,001)	Francksen, John..............4:59:26 (22,519)	French, Peter..............5:04:09 (23,151)
Foster, Terence..............3:39:10 (5,602)	Franco, Cantelli..............3:34:34 (4,843)	French, Richard..............2:54:01 (580)
Foster, Timothy..............3:52:29 (8,167)	François, Christian..............4:05:43 (11,273)	French, Tim..............4:11:01 (12,402)
Foster, Will..............3:55:58 (8,911)	Francome, Colin..............6:03:22 (28,559)	Frere Cook, David..............5:14:16 (24,669)
Fostervold, Thomas..............5:02:45 (22,967)	Francquembergue, Guy..............6:08:18 (28,777)	Fresco, Robert..............5:12:14 (24,385)
Fotherby, Andrew..............4:40:58 (18,971)	Frankel, Andrew..............5:08:26 (23,835)	Frescura, Alessandro..............3:02:00 (1,150)
Fotherby, Kenneth..............2:42:51 (232)	Frankinet, Albert..............3:22:53 (3,095)	Fretwell, Andrew..............4:41:20 (19,033)
Fotheringham, Bill..............3:39:32 (5,680)	Frankish, Mark..............4:00:11 (10,087)	Frew, Marcus..............4:31:06 (16,872)
Foucard, Franck..............3:23:56 (3,235)	Frankland, Andrew..............4:28:25 (16,289)	Frew, Robert..............4:37:16 (18,190)
Fouche, Christophe..............4:10:22 (12,244)	Frankland, Barrie..............3:59:00 (9,754)	Frew, Stewart..............4:24:41 (15,435)
Fouche, Dominique..............4:26:21 (15,815)	Frankland, John..............4:38:32 (18,511)	Frewin, Gerard..............4:07:20 (11,622)
Fougere, Bruno..............3:59:43 (9,979)	Frankland, Mark..............5:18:26 (25,206)	Frey, Daniel..............4:42:04 (19,173)
Foulds, Allan..............5:03:03 (23,012)	Franklin, Andrew..............4:10:28 (12,268)	Fribence, Terry..............4:10:33 (12,284)
Foulds, Frank..............4:33:13 (17,351)	Franklin, Neil..............3:29:53 (4,145)	Fricker, Colin..............3:17:21 (2,469)
Foulds, John..............3:46:49 (7,004)	Franklin-Adams, Jonathan..............4:26:59 (15,959)	Fricker, Michael..............4:11:11 (12,436)
Foulkes, Bartley..............3:33:24 (4,674)	Franks, Paul..............3:38:59 (5,571)	Friday, Antony..............3:34:41 (4,861)
Foulkes, Mark..............6:23:55 (29,256)	Frankum, Martin..............4:19:06 (14,148)	Friedenreich, Gregor..............4:46:54 (20,144)
Foulkes, Stephen..............3:14:50 (2,199)	Fraser, Anthony..............5:02:47 (22,973)	Friel, Desmond..............4:14:40 (13,163)
Fountain, David..............5:11:27 (24,276)	Fraser, Daniel..............4:20:10 (14,403)	Frisby, Andrew..............4:35:20 (17,781)
Fournier, Patrice..............4:24:29 (15,393)	Fraser, Jeremy..............5:41:23 (27,286)	Frith, Jonathon..............4:34:31 (17,631)
Fowden, Sean..............6:10:26 (28,874)	Fraser, Keith..............3:23:49 (3,213)	Fritsch, Bernhard..............3:16:22 (2,348)
Fowell, Mark..............4:44:30 (19,674)	Fraser, Neil..............3:28:18 (3,866)	Fritsch, Sylvain..............3:31:58 (4,463)
Fowkes, Cyril..............3:54:37 (8,618)	Fraser, Paul..............3:56:11 (8,963)	Fritz, Pieper..............4:19:25 (14,231)
Fowkes, Gary..............5:15:41 (24,887)	Fraser, Robert..............4:34:58 (17,707)	Froc, Olivier..............4:11:51 (12,580)
Fowle, Mark..............4:18:12 (13,921)	Fraser, Stewart..............4:14:19 (13,098)	Frodsham, Leonard..............4:52:36 (21,238)
Fowle, Michael..............4:12:53 (12,806)	Fraser, William..............3:35:12 (4,933)	Froggatt, Mark..............4:47:53 (20,322)
Fowler, Andrew..............3:49:42 (7,624)	Fraser, William..............3:39:22 (5,641)	Froggatt, Stephen..............4:42:12 (19,205)
Fowler, David..............5:22:17 (25,626)	Fraser-Mackenzie, John..............5:14:04 (24,634)	Frohlich, David..............5:17:48 (25,138)
Fowler, Dennis..............4:05:54 (11,320)	Frater, Graham..............4:25:55 (15,707)	Fromage, Stephen..............5:20:40 (25,426)
Fowler, Jim..............5:49:06 (27,848)	Frauenknecht, René..............4:25:08 (15,541)	Fromaget, Didier..............3:33:22 (4,668)
Fowler, Keith..............4:14:48 (13,209)	Frawley, Mike..............4:27:26 (16,046)	Froment, Roger..............4:50:11 (20,751)
Fowler, Nick..............3:44:06 (6,509)	Fray, Clive..............4:18:57 (14,109)	Frontiere, Dominique..............5:04:18 (23,180)
Fowler, Richard..............3:04:00 (1,282)	Frazer, Michael..............3:45:43 (6,802)	Frost, Andy..............5:24:28 (25,833)
Fowles, John..............5:21:46 (25,559)	Frean, Pattrick..............3:40:31 (5,871)	Frost, Charles..............3:54:20 (8,542)
Fox, Andrew..............5:17:30 (25,108)	Freaney, Alan..............4:39:41 (18,731)	Frost, Gary..............5:02:29 (22,934)
Fox, Brian..............3:29:51 (4,142)	Frearson, Paul..............4:03:47 (10,838)	Frost, Grant..............3:57:41 (9,391)
Fox, David..............5:24:38 (25,848)	Fred, Van Ostaeyeh..............5:42:01 (27,337)	Frost, John..............5:24:27 (25,829)
Fox, Edward..............3:29:53 (4,145)	Fredriksson, Stefan..............4:48:36 (20,453)	Frost, Justin..............4:18:05 (13,884)
Fox, Geoff..............4:34:05 (17,553)	Free, Charles..............4:16:43 (13,617)	Frost, Keith..............3:29:25 (4,066)
Fox, Gerald..............3:58:12 (9,537)	Free, Trevor..............3:17:39 (2,496)	Frost, Kevin..............4:46:35 (20,074)
Fox, Grant..............4:55:23 (21,842)	Freeburn, David..............4:26:01 (15,736)	Frost, Mike..............7:53:50 (30,197)
Fox, John..............4:37:39 (18,291)	Freed, David..............5:24:40 (25,850)	Frost, Simon..............4:55:54 (21,968)
Fox, Malcolm..............5:10:43 (24,178)	Freedman, Paul..............4:52:03 (21,102)	Frost, Simon..............5:01:28 (22,799)
Fox, Mark..............5:28:59 (26,287)	Freedman, Ross..............4:54:06 (21,533)	Frost, Spencer..............3:48:40 (7,393)
Fox, Martin..............3:15:08 (2,236)	Freel, Derek..............4:01:29 (10,392)	Froud, Michael..............4:18:03 (13,877)
Fox, Michael..............4:19:03 (14,130)	Freelove, Nigel..............5:15:46 (24,901)	Fructuoso, Flores-Bernal..............2:52:16 (522)
Fox, Michael..............4:37:14 (18,179)	Freeman, Anthony..............4:37:04 (18,138)	Fry, Aynsley..............4:59:16 (22,493)
Fox, Neil..............4:18:35 (14,031)	Freeman, Brian..............4:50:15 (20,758)	Fry, Clifford..............3:54:07 (8,495)
Fox, Patrick..............3:50:42 (7,808)	Freeman, Charles..............5:24:31 (25,838)	Fry, Henry..............3:20:29 (2,822)
Fox, Paul..............3:45:38 (6,776)	Freeman, Darren..............4:38:45 (18,559)	Fry, Malcolm..............4:45:22 (19,835)
Fox, Richard..............4:37:33 (18,264)	Freeman, David..............4:27:30 (16,058)	Fry, Nigel..............6:51:29 (29,825)
Fox, Simon..............3:42:52 (6,278)	Freeman, David..............5:32:40 (26,590)	Fryer, Andrew..............3:27:05 (3,633)
Fox, Stephen..............4:12:09 (12,658)	Freeman, Graham..............5:50:09 (27,912)	Fryer, Conan..............3:28:46 (3,953)
Fox, Steven..............3:56:10 (8,960)	Freeman, Jethro..............3:44:45 (6,625)	Fryer, Howard..............4:31:09 (16,888)
Fox, Thomas..............4:13:53 (13,017)	Freeman, Julian..............4:12:18 (12,693)	Fryer, John..............4:51:34 (20,999)
Fox, Thomas..............5:35:22 (26,834)	Freeman, Mark..............5:33:41 (26,662)	Fryer, Mark..............3:51:16 (7,925)
Fox Miyashima, Alberto..............3:54:21 (8,549)	Freeman, Matthew..............3:16:29 (2,364)	Fryer, Paul..............5:04:10 (23,153)
Foxhall, John..............5:27:21 (26,115)	Freeman, Michael..............5:31:06 (26,462)	Fryer, Richard..............5:05:10 (23,313)
Foxton, George..............4:14:37 (13,152)	Freeman, Nigel..............4:12:28 (12,730)	Fryer, Robert..............5:28:34 (26,235)
Foxwell, Matthew..............3:39:15 (5,619)	Freeman, Robert..............4:36:40 (18,057)	Fryer, Robin..............3:29:39 (4,111)
Foy, Michael..............4:07:58 (11,755)	Freeman, Stephen..............4:41:35 (19,081)	Fryer, Terry..............3:55:21 (8,772)
Foyle, Stephen..............4:49:24 (20,598)	Freeman, Thomas..............5:10:58 (24,208)	Fuchs, Aimé..............4:14:34 (13,141)
Fraga, Vincent..............3:26:24 (3,544)	Freer, Art..............3:10:44 (1,811)	Fuge, Stephen..............4:40:53 (18,953)
Frame, Stewart..............4:35:16 (17,767)	Freeston, Paul..............4:24:11 (15,327)	Fulcher, Ian..............4:58:40 (22,407)

Fulcher, John.................3:53:02 (8,272)
Fulcher, John.................5:34:09 (26,716)
Fulford, Matthew..............3:53:23 (8,351)
Fulford, Paul.................5:19:33 (25,312)
Full, Philip..................3:18:29 (2,596)
Fullaondo, Emilio.............4:05:31 (11,220)
Fuller, Adrian................3:18:16 (2,570)
Fuller, Bill..................4:05:49 (11,305)
Fuller, Dylan.................3:20:36 (2,835)
Fuller, John..................3:10:12 (1,760)
Fuller, John..................4:55:48 (21,954)
Fuller, Kevin.................4:58:53 (22,438)
Fuller, Mick..................4:09:56 (12,147)
Fuller, Robert................3:54:04 (8,489)
Fuller, Roger.................2:58:42 (891)
Fuller, Russell...............4:58:27 (22,369)
Fuller, Simon.................4:30:49 (16,809)
Fullerbrook, Richard..........3:53:04 (8,284)
Fulthorpe, Michael............3:49:46 (7,639)
Fulton, Alan..................4:14:20 (13,103)
Fulton, Gary..................5:49:55 (27,895)
Fulton, Ken...................4:50:54 (20,861)
Fulton, Peter.................4:43:53 (19,572)
Fulton, Roger.................5:28:08 (26,188)
Fumagalli, Sergio.............3:33:22 (4,668)
Funk, Mark....................3:51:42 (8,006)
Funnell, Simon................3:45:25 (6,732)
Funnell, Simon................4:31:49 (17,062)
Furbank, Peter................5:53:05 (28,069)
Furber, Garry.................5:12:34 (24,436)
Furber, Jeremy................4:25:26 (15,599)
Furlone, Antonio..............4:07:35 (11,675)
Furlong, Ian..................4:44:49 (19,736)
Furlong, Patrick..............5:01:06 (22,748)
Furlonger, Ian................4:33:49 (17,503)
Furmston, Nicholas............4:06:25 (11,435)
Furness, Scott................3:24:33 (3,320)
Furness, T....................4:04:53 (11,088)
Furniss, Andrew...............4:22:37 (14,958)
Fursey, Robert................3:23:24 (3,159)
Furze, Jim....................3:36:50 (5,213)
Fusi, Mauro...................3:24:56 (3,369)
Fussell, David................3:30:47 (4,291)
Fussell, Ian..................3:39:45 (5,725)
Fussell, Sean.................4:54:48 (21,678)
Futrell, Rodney...............3:21:29 (2,944)
Futter, Clive.................4:52:25 (21,189)
Futter, Nigel.................3:49:01 (7,467)
Fyfe, Andrew..................5:14:34 (24,717)
Fyfe, Scott...................4:17:23 (13,745)
Fysh, Andrew..................3:54:20 (8,542)
Fyson, Alan...................5:16:55 (25,038)
Gaade, John...................3:42:16 (6,174)
Gable, Jeff...................3:57:30 (9,326)
Gabriel, Christophe...........5:11:30 (24,285)
Gabriel, Michael..............6:07:11 (28,729)
Gabriel, Pierre...............4:01:29 (10,392)
Gabriel, Simon................4:48:17 (20,403)
Gabriel, Steven...............4:01:36 (10,412)
Gabriel, Thomas...............3:57:36 (9,363)
Gabrielle, Silvano............4:05:28 (11,202)
Gaches, Anton.................4:24:33 (15,408)
Gadeke, Chris.................5:02:39 (22,956)
Gadgil, Devendra..............6:31:19 (29,440)
Gadrat, Emmanuel..............4:18:05 (13,884)
Gadsden, Ian..................5:16:29 (24,986)
Gaffuri, Giovanni.............3:04:01 (1,284)
Gage, Matthew.................4:01:52 (10,455)
Gage, Trevor..................3:05:15 (1,370)
Gailhard, Thierry.............3:44:37 (6,598)
Gaillard, Steeve..............4:05:38 (11,248)
Gainey, Stewart...............4:50:05 (20,733)
Gair, Martyn..................5:12:59 (24,497)
Gaitely, Christopher..........4:13:16 (12,866)
Gajbutowicz, Andrzej..........5:08:53 (23,920)
Gal, Robert...................3:46:02 (6,863)
Galcazar, Guillermo...........3:55:07 (8,719)
Gale, Clifford................3:41:20 (6,017)
Gale, Marcus..................4:54:09 (21,542)
Gales, Wayne..................4:25:54 (15,702)
Gall, Alan....................4:56:48 (22,108)
Gallacher, Jim................4:53:30 (21,419)
Gallagher, Anthony............4:14:06 (13,056)

Gallagher, Darren.............4:06:15 (11,397)
Gallagher, Eoghan.............4:42:08 (19,188)
Gallagher, Francis............3:47:56 (7,252)
Gallagher, Francis............4:40:50 (18,945)
Gallagher, Gerard.............5:30:56 (26,448)
Gallagher, John...............3:38:43 (5,525)
Gallagher, Joseph.............4:45:42 (19,882)
Gallagher, Michael............3:47:47 (7,206)
Gallagher, Neil...............4:29:55 (16,665)
Gallagher, Paul...............3:57:56 (9,472)
Gallagher, Paul...............4:23:00 (15,063)
Gallagher, Sean...............4:00:44 (10,227)
Gallagher, Shaun..............5:47:40 (27,736)
Gallazzi, Giulio..............3:55:59 (8,915)
Galle, Nick...................4:47:06 (20,184)
Gallen SJ, Gerard.............4:05:39 (11,252)
Gallet, Paul..................4:09:56 (12,147)
Galletta, Alessandra..........6:20:32 (29,174)
Galley, André.................3:16:59 (2,424)
Gallichan, Jonathan...........6:27:53 (29,349)
Gallimore, Adam...............3:57:26 (9,304)
Gallimore, Colin..............4:04:34 (11,013)
Gallivan, John................7:02:17 (29,963)
Gallo, Matthew................5:24:02 (25,793)
Gallo, Simon..................5:24:02 (25,793)
Galloway, George..............6:10:27 (28,875)
Galloway, John................5:04:49 (23,268)
Galt, Timothy.................4:08:44 (11,920)
Galtier, Jean-Luc.............3:51:29 (7,960)
Galvin, Bob...................4:01:49 (10,446)
Galvin, Michael...............5:08:31 (23,849)
Galy, Patrick.................6:04:32 (28,622)
Gamberini, Adler..............3:27:58 (3,802)
Gambino, Daniel...............3:07:25 (1,536)
Gamble, Colin.................5:05:13 (23,323)
Gamble, Craig.................5:04:05 (23,146)
Gamble, Nick..................4:28:59 (16,417)
Gambrill, Michael.............4:33:19 (17,374)
Game, Stephen John............3:15:52 (2,305)
Game, Steven..................5:06:36 (23,559)
Gaminde, Txomin...............3:28:27 (3,898)
Gammage, Richard..............3:27:56 (3,797)
Gammelin, Gert................3:11:08 (1,847)
Gammon, Andrew................3:35:25 (4,975)
Gammond, Bob..................3:48:33 (7,371)
Gamper, Nicholas..............4:29:58 (16,684)
Gamsby, Paul..................4:01:45 (10,436)
Gan, Andrew...................3:13:09 (2,020)
Gan, Yona.....................4:04:33 (11,007)
Gander, Frank.................3:39:35 (5,690)
Ganderton, Wayne..............4:35:47 (17,879)
Gandhi, Eric..................5:06:02 (23,473)
Ganesi, Gilberto..............4:32:17 (17,171)
Ganeson, Ponnusamy............5:10:12 (24,103)
Gann, Terry...................3:37:48 (5,378)
Gannon, Brian.................4:49:47 (20,669)
Gannon, John..................3:29:13 (4,029)
Gannon, Martin................3:12:37 (1,969)
Gant, James...................3:59:32 (9,931)
Gant, Matthew.................4:13:48 (13,003)
Gant, Simon...................4:33:10 (17,341)
Garaway, David................3:59:57 (10,042)
Garbett, Nigel................4:05:27 (11,197)
Garbutt, Frank................4:10:21 (12,241)
Garcha, Parvinder.............4:28:43 (16,362)
Garcia, Antonio...............3:58:20 (9,569)
Garcia, Derek.................3:42:51 (6,276)
Garcia, Jai...................4:49:05 (20,540)
Garcia, Ricardo...............4:24:37 (15,424)
Garciapina, Carlos............3:22:08 (3,017)
Garcia-Woods, Julian..........3:33:00 (4,601)
Gardener, James...............5:42:28 (27,367)
Gardener, Nigel...............3:47:58 (7,260)
Gardener, Richard.............4:12:47 (12,788)
Gardfalo, Giorgio.............3:23:37 (3,187)
Gardin, Albino................3:49:01 (7,467)
Gardiner, Albert..............5:23:21 (25,728)
Gardiner, Craig...............4:25:40 (15,646)
Gardiner, Frank...............4:25:41 (15,650)
Gardiner, Gary................4:07:20 (11,622)
Gardiner, James...............3:41:34 (6,044)
Gardiner, John................3:12:38 (1,972)
Gardiner, Kieron..............4:18:05 (13,884)

Gardiner, Matthew.............3:26:52 (3,605)
Gardiner, Peter...............4:23:06 (15,085)
Gardiner, Trevor..............4:47:15 (20,213)
Gardner, Adrian...............3:37:21 (5,314)
Gardner, Andrew...............3:42:10 (6,155)
Gardner, Andrew...............3:58:21 (9,576)
Gardner, Dave.................3:13:53 (2,101)
Gardner, David................4:22:25 (14,908)
Gardner, David................4:37:28 (18,243)
Gardner, David................5:05:23 (23,356)
Gardner, Graham...............4:18:26 (13,998)
Gardner, John.................4:25:48 (15,672)
Gardner, Malcolm..............4:32:10 (17,150)
Gardner, Martin...............4:37:06 (18,144)
Gardner, Nicholas.............4:20:02 (14,378)
Gardner, Paul.................5:13:06 (24,518)
Gardner, Peter................4:22:22 (14,899)
Gardner, Philip...............4:40:36 (18,898)
Gargialo, Biagio James........3:27:48 (3,762)
Garius, Mark..................6:01:47 (28,496)
Garland, Christopher..........3:24:24 (3,298)
Garland, David................5:17:45 (25,130)
Garland, Ian..................3:25:25 (3,435)
Garlick, Nicholas.............4:21:49 (14,766)
Garman, David.................4:27:19 (16,027)
Garner, Alan..................4:23:31 (15,179)
Garner, Mark..................5:28:37 (26,243)
Garner, Michael...............4:47:34 (20,278)
Garner, Paul..................3:47:59 (7,262)
Garner, Richard...............4:05:30 (11,213)
Garner, Richard...............4:31:05 (16,866)
Garner, Terence...............4:31:19 (16,938)
Garnero, Alfred...............4:07:41 (11,692)
Garnett, Terry................4:33:00 (17,309)
Garnish, Jeffrey..............4:19:02 (14,127)
Garrard, Boyd.................3:30:18 (4,213)
Garrard, William..............4:54:00 (21,511)
Garraway, Christopher.........5:05:06 (23,305)
Garrett, Charles..............4:43:34 (19,512)
Garrett, David................5:21:01 (25,471)
Garrett, James................5:20:04 (25,367)
Garrett, Jeremy...............3:44:58 (6,681)
Garrett, Martin...............3:58:32 (9,616)
Garrett, Richard..............4:11:06 (12,416)
Garrett, Richard..............5:48:14 (27,795)
Garretty, Damian..............4:18:33 (14,023)
Garrick, Davy.................3:27:09 (3,647)
Garrity, Roger................3:56:12 (8,967)
Garrity, Stewart..............5:40:32 (27,227)
Garrod, Leslie................3:31:34 (4,405)
Garrod, Mark..................3:32:56 (4,591)
Garry, David..................4:45:46 (19,896)
Garry, Michael................3:44:36 (6,596)
Garstang, Richard.............4:52:16 (21,148)
Garthwaite, Keith.............3:53:38 (8,409)
Garvey, Rory..................4:56:07 (22,006)
Garvey, Stephen...............3:31:24 (4,385)
Garvin, John..................5:32:52 (26,603)
Garwood, Lee..................5:02:46 (22,971)
Gaschler, André...............4:37:05 (18,142)
Gascoigne-Pees, Edward........5:09:56 (24,073)
Gashe, Terence................3:37:35 (5,346)
Gaskell, Philip...............4:40:17 (18,836)
Gaskill, Eddy.................4:52:45 (21,264)
Gaslain, Yann.................3:20:10 (2,782)
Gaspart, Jean.................4:17:54 (13,851)
Gasper, Matthew...............4:24:44 (15,448)
Gasson, William...............5:24:52 (25,868)
Gastaldo, Laurent.............6:04:37 (28,626)
Gaston, James.................6:21:38 (29,200)
Gaston, Reginald..............4:06:01 (11,354)
Gater, Marcus.................3:58:52 (9,718)
Gatfield, David...............4:56:52 (22,121)
Gathercole, Andrew............4:26:15 (15,795)
Gatiss, Ian...................5:50:59 (27,954)
Gatt, Joseph..................4:14:03 (13,050)
Gattrell, Anthony.............5:03:39 (23,075)
Gatward, William..............4:17:31 (13,776)
Gaubert, André................4:02:11 (10,522)
Gaudat, Gerard................3:20:07 (2,775)
Gaudreau, Robert..............3:59:22 (9,869)
Gaughan, Martin...............3:27:08 (3,645)
Gaukrodger, Darren............3:43:13 (6,348)

Gauld, Sid	3:28:49 (3,965)	
Gaulder, Nicholas	3:37:01 (5,249)	
Gault, Justin	4:18:48 (14,081)	
Gaultney, Steven	4:51:44 (21,038)	
Gaunt, Colin	5:29:55 (26,370)	
Gaunt, Jonathan	3:26:09 (3,518)	
Gaunt, Keith	6:31:17 (29,439)	
Gaunt, Mike	4:01:08 (10,307)	
Gautier, Marc	4:13:10 (12,853)	
Gavagan, Michael	4:45:28 (19,860)	
Gavelle, Daniel	3:18:08 (2,553)	
Gavelle, Joseph	2:56:46 (731)	
Gavigan, James	4:32:38 (17,235)	
Gavin, Matthew	4:51:08 (20,912)	
Gavins, David	5:34:16 (26,729)	
Gawen, Peter	5:13:39 (24,590)	
Gay, Daniel	4:34:03 (17,544)	
Gay, Richard	3:28:24 (3,890)	
Gaydon, Daniel	4:29:57 (16,675)	
Gaygan, Robert	3:42:52 (6,278)	
Gaylard, Michael	3:21:52 (2,982)	
Gayle, Richard	5:13:05 (24,515)	
Gayler, Ryan	4:03:20 (10,732)	
Gaynor, Colin	4:01:54 (10,463)	
Gayter, William	3:24:29 (3,307)	
Gaze, Stevie	4:21:47 (14,754)	
Gazzi, Alessandro	4:11:56 (12,591)	
Gazzoni, Tommaso	3:56:13 (8,971)	
Gear, Ian	4:10:32 (12,279)	
Gearing, Daniel	3:35:13 (4,935)	
Gearing, Peter	4:42:23 (19,244)	
Gebbie, Martyn	4:26:34 (15,865)	
Gebhard, Bertrand	3:34:52 (4,886)	
Gedeon, Beca	4:20:14 (14,415)	
Gedir, Jarett	3:15:36 (2,280)	
Gee, Chris	5:07:58 (23,767)	
Gee, David	4:20:03 (14,381)	
Gee, David	4:31:11 (16,898)	
Gee, Gary	4:46:53 (20,140)	
Gee, Geoffrey	3:11:45 (1,892)	
Gee, Ian	4:47:00 (20,163)	
Gee, Jason	5:07:36 (23,712)	
Gee, Simon	5:35:40 (26,857)	
Geear, Derek	3:37:12 (5,282)	
Geen, Peter	4:17:50 (13,840)	
Geenen, Giles	4:14:28 (13,120)	
Geerah, John	4:45:51 (19,912)	
Geeson, Andrew	3:57:11 (9,219)	
Geffrotin, Guy	4:51:35 (21,007)	
Geggie, Stuart	2:54:31 (609)	
Geh Asongned, Eddie	5:46:36 (27,673)	
Geldart, Jon	4:49:39 (20,642)	
Geldart, Richard	4:11:21 (12,472)	
Geldeart, Paul	3:47:23 (7,112)	
Gelderblom, Robert	4:53:48 (21,474)	
Gellard, Ian	5:08:41 (23,883)	
Gelmi, Luciano	4:18:22 (13,976)	
Gemmell, John	4:08:40 (11,908)	
Gemmell, Mathew	4:32:33 (17,219)	
Genders, Richard	4:17:01 (13,672)	
Generalis, Sotos	4:55:46 (21,951)	
Genes, Christopher	4:20:22 (14,443)	
Gengembre, Jean-Marc	3:38:43 (5,525)	
Genot, Bernard	4:17:40 (13,806)	
Genoud, Patrick	3:01:18 (1,094)	
Genovese, Paolo	5:00:49 (22,705)	
Genower, Peter	5:11:31 (24,288)	
Gent, John	4:18:45 (14,067)	
Gentieu, Herve	5:20:09 (25,372)	
Gentle, Henry	3:37:54 (5,393)	
Geoghegan, Patrick	3:43:44 (6,446)	
Geoghegan, Peter	3:11:39 (1,879)	
George, Ben	3:10:36 (1,800)	
George, Christopher	4:57:51 (22,275)	
George, David	3:46:16 (6,910)	
George, David	4:57:02 (22,142)	
George, Derek	4:00:00 (10,054)	
George, Errol	3:58:37 (9,648)	
George, Glen	4:16:08 (13,492)	
George, Michael	4:25:21 (15,583)	
George, Michael	4:25:59 (15,727)	
George, Nick	3:57:05 (9,194)	
George, Ralph	3:20:55 (2,880)	

George, Roberto	5:05:48 (23,432)	
Georgeson, Ian	4:33:27 (17,405)	
Georghiou, Marc	6:15:43 (29,051)	
Georgi, Bernd	4:12:28 (12,730)	
Georgiadis, Nick	4:01:51 (10,454)	
Georgieff, Fabien	4:49:11 (20,556)	
Georgiou, Yiannis	3:59:01 (9,761)	
Geraghty, Roger	2:48:58 (392)	
Gerard, Pierrot	4:41:05 (18,992)	
Gerard, Richard	4:46:57 (20,158)	
Gerassi, José Eduardo	2:57:13 (762)	
Gerbeau, Vincent	4:13:22 (12,897)	
Gerlack, Matthew	3:55:25 (8,786)	
Germain, Bernard	3:25:36 (3,456)	
German, Mark	4:13:46 (12,992)	
German, Piers	6:25:19 (29,293)	
Gerrard, Colin	3:37:02 (5,251)	
Gerrard, David	3:46:32 (6,956)	
Gerreira Raposo, Antonio Rui	5:19:40 (25,326)	
Gerstenhauer, Thomas	3:47:21 (7,100)	
Gerundini, Anthony	5:14:56 (24,767)	
Gethin, Reginald	5:07:07 (23,632)	
Gettings, Andy	5:04:35 (23,232)	
Gettins, Mark	4:39:29 (18,690)	
Ghigo, Emmanuel	4:55:10 (21,772)	
Ghislain, Gotfroi	4:46:39 (20,082)	
Ghosh, Boyd	4:38:52 (18,582)	
Ghuloom, Ebrahim	3:38:17 (5,445)	
Gibb, Andrew	3:44:51 (6,650)	
Gibb, Anthony	3:21:19 (2,922)	
Gibb, David	5:47:48 (27,752)	
Gibb, Ewan	6:32:40 (29,469)	
Gibbon, Roland	4:36:03 (17,940)	
Gibbons, Alastair	3:13:23 (2,049)	
Gibbons, David	5:39:07 (27,097)	
Gibbons, Gerard	4:50:01 (20,723)	
Gibbons, Jeremy	3:58:45 (9,685)	
Gibbons, John	4:27:49 (16,154)	
Gibbons, Martyn	3:25:13 (3,403)	
Gibbons, Nigel	4:13:18 (12,874)	
Gibbons, Peter	3:39:55 (5,762)	
Gibbons, Robert	4:32:16 (17,168)	
Gibbs, Christopher	4:52:06 (21,113)	
Gibbs, Glyn	3:25:32 (3,447)	
Gibbs, Ian	3:48:58 (7,458)	
Gibbs, James	5:04:16 (23,175)	
Gibbs, John	3:07:54 (1,583)	
Gibbs, Keith	4:44:44 (19,724)	
Gibbs, Michael	4:48:12 (20,384)	
Gibbs, Paul	5:05:36 (23,402)	
Gibney, Kenneth	4:19:15 (14,178)	
Gibson, Alastair	4:41:36 (19,083)	
Gibson, Barry	4:13:20 (12,884)	
Gibson, Chris	3:30:19 (4,217)	
Gibson, Christopher	4:59:51 (22,588)	
Gibson, David	5:10:59 (24,209)	
Gibson, Graham	4:48:48 (20,486)	
Gibson, Ivor	4:25:39 (15,643)	
Gibson, John	3:50:34 (7,786)	
Gibson, Mark	4:11:14 (12,450)	
Gibson, Mark	5:14:26 (24,692)	
Gibson, Paul	4:31:59 (17,117)	
Gibson, Paul	4:32:24 (17,194)	
Gibson, Paul	5:20:16 (25,383)	
Gibson, Peter	3:16:50 (2,406)	
Gibson, Philip	4:59:09 (22,483)	
Gibson, Robert	3:59:37 (9,953)	
Gibson, Steve	5:13:53 (24,614)	
Gichengo, Geoffrey	4:37:21 (18,212)	
Gicquiaux, Eric	3:51:01 (7,877)	
Gidden, Anthony	4:08:04 (11,781)	
Gie, Paul	4:23:51 (15,261)	
Giebuen, Walter	3:42:55 (6,290)	
Giertsen, Bjoern	4:00:34 (10,178)	
Gifford, Andrew	4:43:16 (19,442)	
Gifford, Robert	5:44:03 (27,480)	
Giger, Marcel	4:48:49 (20,490)	
Giger, Oscar	4:25:07 (15,536)	
Gigg, Gerard	4:49:47 (20,669)	
Gilardi, Antony	3:59:23 (9,876)	
Gilbert, Alan	3:50:22 (7,751)	
Gilbert, Barry	4:35:54 (17,908)	
Gilbert, Brendon	4:05:13 (11,156)	

Gilbert, Christopher	3:46:58 (7,028)	
Gilbert, Colin	4:53:28 (21,411)	
Gilbert, David	6:51:57 (29,832)	
Gilbert, Geoffrey	3:37:07 (5,268)	
Gilbert, Jonathan	3:18:17 (2,574)	
Gilbert, Julian	4:48:40 (20,463)	
Gilbert, Michael	4:26:54 (15,936)	
Gilbert, Michael	5:38:01 (27,022)	
Gilbert, Peter	3:41:25 (6,030)	
Gilbert, Ralph	3:56:22 (9,013)	
Gilbert, Reg	4:22:40 (14,976)	
Gilbert, Timothy	4:00:40 (10,199)	
Gilbert, Trevor	4:25:54 (15,702)	
Gilbertson, John	3:57:16 (9,245)	
Gilby, Paul	5:36:23 (26,909)	
Gilby, Pete	3:36:29 (5,156)	
Gilchrist, Francis	3:24:55 (3,366)	
Gilchrist, John	4:11:05 (12,412)	
Gilchrist, Robin	4:21:54 (14,786)	
Gilchrist, Tyrone	4:39:35 (18,712)	
Giles, Adrian	4:09:46 (12,122)	
Giles, Christopher	3:30:43 (4,282)	
Giles, Geraint	4:17:21 (13,742)	
Giles, John	5:17:46 (25,133)	
Giles, Mark	4:13:23 (12,899)	
Giles, Martin	2:38:17 (141)	
Giles, Paul	3:44:31 (6,580)	
Giles, Paul	4:30:55 (16,832)	
Giles, Stuart	3:46:24 (6,931)	
Giles, Stuart	5:09:35 (24,030)	
Gilfillan, Geoffrey	4:29:11 (16,467)	
Gilkes, Norman	4:39:53 (18,767)	
Gill, Adrian	3:35:35 (5,000)	
Gill, Amarjit	5:45:52 (27,624)	
Gill, Colin	5:06:37 (23,564)	
Gill, Daniel	4:37:00 (18,131)	
Gill, Dave	3:53:23 (8,351)	
Gill, Emmanuel	4:53:43 (21,457)	
Gill, Gavin	4:20:40 (14,513)	
Gill, Jason	5:39:12 (27,103)	
Gill, Lyndon	4:02:59 (10,657)	
Gill, Paul	3:39:01 (5,575)	
Gill, Shami	5:02:07 (22,893)	
Gill, Thomas	3:28:19 (3,872)	
Gillam, Andrew	4:27:33 (16,075)	
Gillard, Martin	5:46:15 (27,644)	
Gillen, Timothy	3:43:26 (6,385)	
Gillespie, John	4:04:23 (10,965)	
Gillespie, John	4:54:18 (21,562)	
Gillespie, Michael	3:07:05 (1,509)	
Gillett, Richard	3:48:29 (7,357)	
Gillies, Michael	6:07:08 (28,727)	
Gillies, Robert	3:54:20 (8,542)	
Gillies, Roderick	3:15:00 (2,223)	
Gilligan, Barry	4:14:36 (13,148)	
Gilligan, David	3:55:53 (8,889)	
Gilligan, Martin	4:00:29 (10,148)	
Gilliland, Crawford	5:49:56 (27,898)	
Gilling, Ian	4:27:32 (16,069)	
Gillingham, Henry	3:55:20 (8,767)	
Gillion, Stephen	4:03:18 (10,725)	
Gillison, Matthew	4:41:37 (19,085)	
Gillman, Clive	3:17:33 (2,489)	
Gill-Martin, Simon	3:16:51 (2,407)	
Gillon, Thomas	3:15:56 (2,314)	
Gillott, Martin	4:05:34 (11,232)	
Gillott, Tim	4:09:13 (12,026)	
Gillson, Richard	4:48:06 (20,367)	
Gillson, Stephen	3:06:26 (1,454)	
Gilman, Colin	4:46:49 (20,119)	
Gilmartin, John	3:34:16 (4,795)	
Gilmartin, Noel	4:32:23 (17,189)	
Gilmour, Rory	4:01:00 (10,280)	
Gilroy, Stephen	4:05:20 (11,172)	
Gimblett, Wayne	3:25:30 (3,445)	
Gimmel, Tobias	4:20:01 (14,374)	
Gingell, David	4:19:19 (14,198)	
Ginger, David	4:53:47 (21,470)	
Ginn, Christopher	4:53:48 (21,474)	
Ginn, Richard	3:18:49 (2,635)	
Ginsberg, Clive	4:00:04 (10,067)	
Ginty, Mark	4:18:28 (14,005)	
Gioppo, Simone	3:59:01 (9,761)	

Giordani, Michel	3:22:58 (3,107)	
Giovenali, Anthony	3:53:12 (8,309)	
Giraudeau, Chris	5:57:57 (28,321)	
Giraudon, Michel	3:24:18 (3,281)	
Gird, Michael	3:36:54 (5,228)	
Girling, Simon	4:01:20 (10,348)	
Girling, Stephen	4:37:42 (18,299)	
Girnary, Nazim	5:24:55 (25,874)	
Girvan, Martin	4:25:03 (15,524)	
Girvan, Raymond	4:05:53 (11,317)	
Gisborne, James	4:01:43 (10,432)	
Gisby, Alan	3:50:25 (7,760)	
Gislason, Gudmundur	3:16:39 (2,383)	
Gittens, Nicola	6:52:59 (29,844)	
Gjelsvik, Einar	3:26:08 (3,516)	
Gjelvik, Eric	4:07:51 (11,730)	
Glackin, Brian	3:23:59 (3,244)	
Gladikowski, Jens	4:20:14 (14,415)	
Gladman, Alan	4:20:13 (14,411)	
Gladman, Alan	4:50:25 (20,789)	
Glasgow, Oliver	3:08:30 (1,631)	
Glasgow, Paul	4:09:08 (12,007)	
Glass, Garry	3:28:16 (3,859)	
Glass, Graham	4:29:45 (16,610)	
Glass, John	3:57:08 (9,207)	
Glasspole, Julian	6:02:15 (28,515)	
Glasspool, Alan	5:12:35 (24,441)	
Glasspool, Gary	3:52:39 (8,202)	
Glaves, Guy	3:59:37 (9,953)	
Glaze, Paul	3:59:14 (9,828)	
Glazebrook, Martin	4:46:51 (20,132)	
Glazer, Anthony	4:25:53 (15,698)	
Glazier, Daiel	4:42:29 (19,270)	
Glazier, David	4:14:58 (13,254)	
Gleadall, Owen	4:18:08 (13,895)	
Glebke, Stefan	4:19:23 (14,220)	
Glebke, Suergen	4:19:23 (14,220)	
Gledhill, Andrew	4:45:32 (19,867)	
Gleeson, Andrew	3:02:44 (1,198)	
Gleeson, Declan	5:43:01 (27,410)	
Gleeson, James	4:22:48 (15,008)	
Gleeson, John	5:58:50 (28,358)	
Glen, David	4:50:49 (20,849)	
Glen, Roy	4:11:24 (12,481)	
Glencross, Philip	3:33:44 (4,719)	
Glendinning, Paul	3:07:31 (1,545)	
Glenn, Stephen	3:31:25 (4,386)	
Glenn, Steven	4:53:20 (21,384)	
Glenville, David	4:33:29 (17,414)	
Glerum, Jonathan	3:44:27 (6,567)	
Glesti, Rudolf	3:05:29 (1,389)	
Glister, Ronald	5:26:24 (26,034)	
Glock, Mark	4:23:17 (15,127)	
Glockshuber, Rudolf	3:23:39 (3,192)	
Gloeckler, Kai Kuuo	3:32:34 (4,545)	
Gloor, Peter	3:19:02 (2,658)	
Glover, Adrian	4:58:31 (22,381)	
Glover, Anthony	3:48:38 (7,385)	
Glover, Barry	4:13:26 (12,917)	
Glover, David	6:16:16 (29,065)	
Glover, Graham	3:42:11 (6,159)	
Glover, Ian	4:29:28 (16,537)	
Glover, James	4:51:44 (21,038)	
Glover, John	4:05:54 (11,320)	
Glover, Steven	5:22:17 (25,626)	
Glover, Toby	3:52:08 (8,104)	
Gloyne, Peter	4:27:33 (16,075)	
Gluyas, Jon	3:59:54 (10,026)	
Glyn Jones, Sion	4:14:13 (13,078)	
Glyn Owen, Julian	4:23:28 (15,165)	
Go, Hyunk-Sik	3:34:04 (4,766)	
Goad, Hallam	4:09:27 (12,071)	
Goad, Harry	5:10:31 (24,146)	
Goad, Oli	5:10:31 (24,146)	
Goad, Richard	3:32:18 (4,508)	
Gocalves Paulo, Antonio	3:28:10 (3,838)	
Godbee, Peter	3:52:36 (8,190)	
Goddard, Andy	3:51:04 (7,884)	
Goddard, Barry	4:19:11 (14,161)	
Goddard, Christopher	4:29:59 (16,689)	
Goddard, Mark	4:23:49 (15,254)	
Goddard, Matthew	4:29:10 (16,464)	
Goddard, Phil	3:30:58 (4,325)	
Goddard, Trevor	3:09:27 (1,707)	
Godden, Ian	2:55:15 (640)	
Godden, Mike	6:08:20 (28,779)	
Godfrey, Chris	3:41:05 (5,973)	
Godfrey, Christopher	4:46:25 (20,036)	
Godfrey, David	3:48:38 (7,385)	
Godfrey, James	4:08:14 (11,813)	
Godfrey, John	4:08:13 (11,808)	
Godfrey, Keith	4:55:33 (21,905)	
Godfrey, Keith	5:25:06 (25,895)	
Godfrey, Nick	5:04:39 (23,240)	
Godfrey, Richard	3:58:02 (9,497)	
Godfrey, Roger	4:55:13 (21,789)	
Godfrey, Tommy	4:06:23 (11,427)	
Godley, William	4:50:04 (20,731)	
Godman, Michael	3:35:59 (5,071)	
Godsal, Tom	3:23:52 (3,225)	
Godwin, David	4:23:56 (15,279)	
Godwin, Glenn	4:53:30 (21,419)	
Godwyn, Bryan	4:33:44 (17,485)	
Goederes, René	4:26:57 (15,950)	
Goeggel, Reto	3:40:56 (5,939)	
Goggin, David	5:13:13 (24,535)	
Goggs, Dominic	3:46:33 (6,960)	
Goggs, Robert	3:22:36 (3,063)	
Gohil, Bhavesh	5:52:17 (28,032)	
Gohil, Sunil	3:06:39 (1,474)	
Goisque, Pierre	2:57:43 (792)	
Gold, Alan	3:56:58 (9,169)	
Gold, David	4:37:15 (18,182)	
Gold, James	4:23:58 (15,286)	
Gold, Jonathan	4:45:36 (19,875)	
Gold, Lawrence	5:02:45 (22,967)	
Gold, Paul	3:41:03 (5,967)	
Goldberger, Danny	6:06:00 (28,686)	
Golder, Terence	4:38:46 (18,568)	
Goldie Scott, Duncan	3:39:52 (5,750)	
Golding, Alastair	3:21:47 (2,971)	
Golding, Graham	4:32:08 (17,141)	
Golding, Peter	4:27:44 (16,128)	
Golding, Shaun	4:25:16 (15,568)	
Goldman, David	4:24:25 (15,374)	
Goldman, Paul	4:10:11 (12,203)	
Goldring, Mark	4:39:44 (18,740)	
Goldsmith, Andrew	4:40:19 (18,841)	
Goldsmith, Paul	3:21:41 (2,966)	
Goldsmith, Stuart	3:15:26 (2,264)	
Goldspink, Colin	3:20:31 (2,826)	
Goldspink, Len	5:15:08 (24,802)	
Goldstone, Barry	4:23:26 (15,155)	
Golightly, Michael	3:08:11 (1,604)	
Golland, Clive	3:44:19 (6,546)	
Gollins, Simon	3:57:06 (9,196)	
Gomery, Simon	3:56:01 (8,930)	
Gomes, Jaime	3:59:56 (10,037)	
Gomez, Francisco	3:57:44 (9,403)	
Gomez, Luis	3:17:26 (2,479)	
Gomez-Duran, Dan	3:57:44 (9,403)	
Gomez-Sanchez, David	3:49:52 (7,662)	
Gonde, Chris	3:36:26 (5,147)	
Gonsalves, Victor	3:56:21 (9,007)	
Gooch, James	3:53:08 (8,296)	
Gooch, Roger	3:49:20 (7,533)	
Good, Christopher	3:30:53 (4,310)	
Goodall, Adrian	4:14:35 (13,145)	
Goodall, Benedict	3:17:54 (2,520)	
Goodall, Graham	4:05:48 (11,298)	
Goodall, Malcolm	5:51:41 (27,995)	
Goodall, Martin	3:50:49 (7,825)	
Goodard, Giles	3:51:30 (7,966)	
Goodard, Peter	3:12:30 (1,959)	
Goodban, Andrew	4:59:42 (22,553)	
Goodband, Stephen	3:52:20 (8,140)	
Goodburn, Steve	4:23:33 (15,189)	
Goodchild, Keith	5:08:02 (23,773)	
Goodchild, Ricky	6:18:34 (29,129)	
Goode, James	3:50:40 (7,800)	
Goode, Nicholas	4:49:19 (20,584)	
Goode, Philip	3:05:18 (1,374)	
Goode, Simon	5:04:09 (23,151)	
Goode, Tom	5:22:10 (25,606)	
Gooden, Steven	5:10:54 (24,197)	
Goodenough, Patrick	3:12:23 (1,951)	
Goodenough, Paul	4:31:37 (17,016)	
Goodey, David	5:47:00 (27,703)	
Goodey, Paul	4:20:34 (14,494)	
Goodfellow, Jeremy	4:24:35 (15,416)	
Goodger, Ken	4:28:12 (16,238)	
Goodhand, Jonathan	3:05:42 (1,402)	
Goodhen, Mike	3:57:37 (9,369)	
Goodie, Christopher	4:07:19 (11,617)	
Gooding, Jonathan	5:19:58 (25,360)	
Gooding, Richard	4:21:24 (14,668)	
Goodley, Paul	4:38:36 (18,529)	
Goodliff, David	5:23:35 (25,754)	
Goodman, Kevin	4:57:31 (22,219)	
Goodman, Patrick	4:15:53 (13,444)	
Goodman, Paul	4:54:43 (21,648)	
Goodrich, Barney	3:49:33 (7,596)	
Goodrich, Steven	5:30:31 (26,413)	
Goodrich, Tom	4:22:03 (14,829)	
Goodship, Mark	4:10:29 (12,272)	
Goodson, Andrew	3:54:59 (8,698)	
Goodson, Keith	5:44:06 (27,483)	
Goodwin, Bruce	3:17:57 (2,526)	
Goodwin, David	3:59:54 (10,026)	
Goodwin, Ian	3:58:42 (9,674)	
Goodwin, Kevin	3:07:33 (1,549)	
Goodwin, Leon	3:39:51 (5,749)	
Goodwin, Malcolm	4:16:25 (13,557)	
Goodwin, Michael	4:19:14 (14,174)	
Goodwin, Paul	5:06:58 (23,611)	
Goodwin, Peter	4:26:10 (15,772)	
Goodwin, Peter	4:34:32 (17,633)	
Goodwin, Robert	3:09:04 (1,677)	
Goodwin, Simon	4:43:34 (19,512)	
Goodwin, Stephen	3:44:50 (6,647)	
Goodwyn, James	3:49:21 (7,538)	
Goodyer, Stephen	5:05:43 (23,418)	
Goold, Andrew	5:44:27 (27,506)	
Goosman, Kevin	4:25:43 (15,657)	
Gopsill, Stuart	4:47:10 (20,194)	
Gordon, Anthony	4:05:47 (11,293)	
Gordon, Bob	4:06:21 (11,418)	
Gordon, Christopher	3:57:01 (9,182)	
Gordon, Christopher	4:05:44 (11,283)	
Gordon, David	4:10:08 (12,189)	
Gordon, Frank	2:58:44 (900)	
Gordon, Jay	3:28:56 (3,982)	
Gordon, Jeffrey	3:43:22 (6,373)	
Gordon, Julian	3:50:21 (7,747)	
Gordon, Murray	4:10:28 (12,268)	
Gordon, Patrick	3:57:02 (9,184)	
Gordon, Peter	3:25:38 (3,460)	
Gordon, Richard	5:24:53 (25,871)	
Gordon, Thomas	3:56:08 (8,956)	
Gore, Amos	2:58:38 (875)	
Gore, David	6:12:05 (28,928)	
Gore, Jason	4:37:16 (18,190)	
Gore, Martin	3:42:14 (6,169)	
Gore, Mick	4:05:37 (11,244)	
Goreham, Peter	3:03:59 (1,281)	
Goreham, Ray	5:44:23 (27,499)	
Gorham, Stephen	5:02:50 (22,982)	
Goringe, Philip	4:29:37 (16,580)	
Gorji, Imran	8:58:44 (30,272)	
Gorman, David	3:50:00 (7,690)	
Gorman, Noel	3:25:40 (3,462)	
Gormer, Frederick	3:16:55 (2,414)	
Gormley, Gerard	3:34:31 (4,839)	
Gormley, Matthew	4:38:21 (18,466)	
Gorrod, James	4:18:47 (14,078)	
Gorton, Ian	4:33:15 (17,356)	
Gosbee, Norman	3:57:51 (9,446)	
Gosbee, Robert	5:42:59 (27,408)	
Gosden, Chris	4:12:38 (12,760)	
Goslett, David	4:22:23 (14,901)	
Gosling, David	3:45:41 (6,791)	
Gosling, Peter	3:06:20 (1,444)	
Goss, Kenneth	4:33:47 (17,496)	
Goss, Malcolm	3:47:39 (7,179)	
Gotke, Peter	4:10:52 (12,363)	
Gottelier, Patrick	4:41:08 (19,001)	
Gottlieb, Craig	5:16:00 (24,927)	
Gottlieb, Kim	5:24:46 (25,854)	
Gotts, Mark	3:37:05 (5,262)	

Gotts, Nigel	3:31:48 (4,438)	
Gotts, Terry	3:31:47 (4,435)	
Gouache, Guy	4:06:36 (11,468)	
Goudeau, Bernard	5:23:58 (25,790)	
Gough, Andrew	4:45:53 (19,919)	
Gough, James	5:54:26 (28,131)	
Gough, Kevin	3:52:47 (8,227)	
Gough, Mark	3:55:43 (8,848)	
Gough, Michael	3:46:16 (6,910)	
Gough, Nicholas	4:06:53 (11,525)	
Gough, William	4:27:37 (16,096)	
Goulandris, Alexander	5:10:42 (24,176)	
Gould, Daniel	4:37:20 (18,206)	
Gould, Kevin	3:58:57 (9,738)	
Gould, Martin	2:50:13 (438)	
Gould, Norman	4:25:12 (15,559)	
Gould, Norman	8:58:44 (30,272)	
Gould, Richard	3:52:45 (8,220)	
Goulden, Graham	4:31:51 (17,074)	
Gouldime, Michael	4:21:47 (14,754)	
Goulding, John	4:42:41 (19,309)	
Gouldstone, Timothy	5:08:15 (23,807)	
Gourlay, Mark	4:19:27 (14,241)	
Gournay, Kevin	3:54:52 (8,680)	
Goury, Karim	3:14:54 (2,208)	
Govaert, Bart	5:43:24 (27,433)	
Govaert, Eddy	3:51:25 (7,947)	
Gover, Paul	5:04:24 (23,200)	
Gow, Elliot	3:32:29 (4,532)	
Gow, William	4:08:33 (11,880)	
Gowans, Robert	4:22:46 (14,996)	
Gowe, Neil	4:32:44 (17,257)	
Gowen, Brian	4:18:27 (14,002)	
Gower, Keith	4:22:27 (14,915)	
Gower, Kevin	4:37:57 (18,357)	
Gower, Matthew	4:04:44 (11,050)	
Gower, Simon	5:07:11 (23,649)	
Gowers, Richard	3:36:14 (5,112)	
Gowing, Luke	3:53:29 (8,370)	
Gowland, Graham	4:32:55 (17,295)	
Goymer, Carl	3:54:31 (8,590)	
Goymer, Michael	8:07:00 (30,221)	
Goyvaerts, Bruno	3:14:24 (2,158)	
Grace, Kevin	6:21:13 (29,199)	
Grace, Simon	3:38:10 (5,421)	
Gracey, John	3:54:35 (8,610)	
Gracie, Nick	3:34:18 (4,801)	
Grady, Angus	5:33:20 (26,636)	
Grady, John	3:28:25 (3,894)	
Graff, Paul	5:22:14 (25,621)	
Graham, Alistair	3:59:42 (9,974)	
Graham, Charles	4:01:35 (10,406)	
Graham, Chris	3:34:15 (4,792)	
Graham, Douglas	4:07:49 (11,724)	
Graham, Duncan	3:53:03 (8,277)	
Graham, Geoff	5:18:05 (25,173)	
Graham, Greg	4:43:55 (19,575)	
Graham, Herol	3:53:29 (8,370)	
Graham, Ian	5:09:43 (24,045)	
Graham, James	6:00:39 (28,439)	
Graham, Jeremy	4:22:21 (14,897)	
Graham, John	4:10:54 (12,374)	
Graham, Kenneth	6:06:49 (28,711)	
Graham, Martin	3:59:39 (9,964)	
Graham, Martin	4:55:29 (21,885)	
Graham, Martin	5:39:25 (27,123)	
Graham, Matthew	3:58:20 (9,569)	
Graham, Neil	4:28:26 (16,297)	
Graham, Peter	3:14:04 (2,129)	
Graham, Peter	4:12:58 (12,823)	
Graham, Peter	4:22:05 (14,834)	
Graham, Peter	6:20:29 (29,170)	
Graham, Robert	5:13:00 (24,500)	
Graham, Ronald	3:56:32 (9,062)	
Graham, Rowland	5:21:12 (25,489)	
Graham, Simon	3:58:47 (9,694)	
Graham, Stuart	3:03:37 (1,256)	
Graham, Stuart	3:50:20 (7,741)	
Graham, Warren	4:06:31 (11,454)	
Grainger, David	3:34:34 (4,843)	
Grainger, Gary	4:00:01 (10,058)	
Grainger, Mark	5:07:00 (23,615)	
Grainger, Matt	4:49:39 (20,642)	

Grainger, Nick	5:10:41 (24,174)	
Grammati Kopoulos, Theodoros	4:54:03 (21,523)	
Granata, Cesare	3:00:18 (1,044)	
Granfield, Keith	3:51:25 (7,947)	
Granger, Robert	4:51:40 (21,025)	
Granito, Salvatore	4:22:55 (15,039)	
Grannell, Andy	4:10:48 (12,341)	
Grant, Alistair	3:54:26 (8,575)	
Grant, Andrew	3:15:45 (2,293)	
Grant, Andrew	4:55:39 (21,940)	
Grant, Andrew	5:22:59 (25,704)	
Grant, Ben	3:27:36 (3,723)	
Grant, Duncan	4:04:30 (10,988)	
Grant, Frank	4:15:13 (13,312)	
Grant, Hamish	4:09:39 (12,103)	
Grant, Ian	3:58:20 (9,569)	
Grant, Ian	5:39:11 (27,102)	
Grant, Kenneth	4:24:26 (15,381)	
Grant, Mark	5:11:36 (24,301)	
Grant, Matthew	3:40:48 (5,912)	
Grant, Stuart	4:51:45 (21,043)	
Grant, Thomas	4:04:31 (10,996)	
Grant, Thomas	5:43:25 (27,434)	
Grant, William	2:45:14 (296)	
Grantham, Simon	3:27:20 (3,680)	
Grassmann, Heinz	4:17:10 (13,708)	
Grasso, Remo	5:30:49 (26,441)	
Gratton, Kenneth	4:09:37 (12,096)	
Gravatt, Christopher	4:08:17 (11,820)	
Grave, Friedrich	4:00:14 (10,095)	
Gravell, Darren	4:51:44 (21,038)	
Gravell, Oliver	5:12:13 (24,381)	
Gravells, John	3:48:03 (7,276)	
Gravelsons, Brian	4:33:18 (17,368)	
Graversen, Henriik	3:22:34 (3,059)	
Graves, Adrian	4:51:42 (21,034)	
Graves, Alex	5:39:36 (27,144)	
Graves, Dan	4:21:24 (14,668)	
Graves, Derek	3:26:32 (3,561)	
Graves, Howard	3:48:46 (7,415)	
Graves, Joseph	3:22:25 (3,047)	
Graves, Michael	3:41:00 (5,956)	
Gray, Alan	4:09:59 (12,163)	
Gray, Andrew	3:42:09 (6,151)	
Gray, Anthony	2:55:43 (663)	
Gray, Brian	4:13:37 (12,961)	
Gray, Charles	4:54:31 (21,599)	
Gray, Dave	4:42:22 (19,241)	
Gray, David	3:24:55 (3,366)	
Gray, Don	3:49:32 (7,591)	
Gray, Ian	5:30:43 (26,430)	
Gray, Jim	4:18:20 (13,964)	
Gray, John	3:51:00 (7,875)	
Gray, Malcolm	6:01:51 (28,500)	
Gray, Mark	4:33:56 (17,525)	
Gray, Matthew	4:10:35 (12,293)	
Gray, Michael	3:45:51 (6,833)	
Gray, Mitchell	5:29:39 (26,342)	
Gray, Neil	3:52:28 (8,163)	
Gray, Paul	4:17:13 (13,722)	
Gray, Paul	5:33:16 (26,631)	
Gray, Peter	5:47:53 (27,766)	
Gray, Philip	3:07:45 (1,570)	
Gray, Richard	4:59:25 (22,515)	
Gray, Rory	4:55:34 (21,907)	
Gray, Shaun	4:58:40 (22,407)	
Gray, Simon	3:30:46 (4,289)	
Gray, Simon	4:11:59 (12,606)	
Gray, William	3:15:30 (2,271)	
Graydon, Simon	3:29:38 (4,106)	
Grealy, Vince	3:44:02 (6,498)	
Greaney, James	3:59:43 (9,979)	
Greasby, Colin	5:27:41 (26,148)	
Greasby, Dennis	4:08:19 (11,827)	
Greatholder, Jacko	3:18:42 (2,619)	
Greaves, Alvin	4:43:16 (19,442)	
Greaves, Mark	3:07:02 (1,507)	
Greaves, Matt	4:32:04 (17,133)	
Greaves, Nick	4:19:52 (14,330)	
Greaves, Sean	3:33:45 (4,723)	
Greedy, Philip	3:42:02 (6,126)	
Greeff, Mike	5:16:46 (25,023)	
Green, Alan	3:34:25 (4,820)	

Green, Alan	4:38:07 (18,408)	
Green, Andrew	2:54:10 (586)	
Green, Andrew	4:01:54 (10,463)	
Green, Andy	3:59:04 (9,777)	
Green, Aron	4:12:27 (12,725)	
Green, Ashley	5:19:43 (25,337)	
Green, Ben	4:21:55 (14,791)	
Green, Brian	4:22:39 (14,968)	
Green, Clive	5:15:22 (24,848)	
Green, Colin	5:30:26 (26,406)	
Green, Daniel	4:15:14 (13,319)	
Green, Darrin	5:15:22 (24,848)	
Green, Daryl	3:51:09 (7,904)	
Green, David	3:09:15 (1,690)	
Green, David	3:28:08 (3,830)	
Green, David	3:30:12 (4,200)	
Green, Duncan	4:10:24 (12,255)	
Green, Edward	3:25:44 (3,472)	
Green, Graham	4:04:36 (11,022)	
Green, John	3:43:02 (6,312)	
Green, Justin	5:02:11 (22,906)	
Green, Lloyd	3:42:24 (6,201)	
Green, Mark	2:38:40 (151)	
Green, Martin	4:08:16 (11,816)	
Green, Matthew	4:02:40 (10,602)	
Green, Michael	4:46:15 (19,998)	
Green, Mick	2:51:25 (485)	
Green, Nicholas	5:38:17 (27,034)	
Green, Paul	3:15:53 (2,309)	
Green, Paul	4:37:15 (18,182)	
Green, Paul	5:12:13 (24,381)	
Green, Peter	4:03:32 (10,783)	
Green, Phillip	2:37:19 (123)	
Green, Richard	4:46:03 (19,949)	
Green, Rodney	7:24:58 (30,106)	
Green, Roger	3:34:40 (4,858)	
Green, Simon	3:05:23 (1,380)	
Green, Stephen	5:22:07 (25,600)	
Green, Steven	3:39:02 (5,579)	
Green, Thomas	6:18:07 (29,118)	
Green, Tim	3:29:00 (3,997)	
Green, Tony	3:22:38 (3,066)	
Greenall, John	3:29:38 (4,106)	
Greenaway, Andy	3:38:36 (5,501)	
Greenaway, Martyn	3:45:24 (6,729)	
Greenbank, Martin	4:50:09 (20,743)	
Greene, Shaun	3:35:30 (4,986)	
Greener, John	3:42:11 (6,159)	
Greener, John	3:50:24 (7,757)	
Greenhalgh, Andrew	3:49:09 (7,486)	
Greenhalgh, Ian	3:16:32 (2,374)	
Greenhalgh, Mark	5:06:03 (23,476)	
Greenhalgh, Paul	3:43:04 (6,319)	
Greenhalgh, Paul	4:41:38 (19,090)	
Greenham, David	3:47:55 (7,248)	
Greenhill, David	5:17:43 (25,126)	
Greenhow, Paul	3:35:27 (4,978)	
Greenland, Edward	3:45:41 (6,791)	
Greenleaf, Daniel	3:53:22 (8,349)	
Greenslade, Heath	4:37:53 (18,344)	
Greenspan, Steve	2:50:52 (459)	
Greenstein, David	3:42:21 (6,191)	
Greenstreet, David	3:49:09 (7,486)	
Greenwood, Adrian	5:38:21 (27,038)	
Greenwood, Andrew	4:51:42 (21,034)	
Greenwood, David	4:20:50 (14,556)	
Greenwood, Doug	5:55:48 (28,203)	
Greenwood, Peter	3:59:39 (9,964)	
Greenwood, Peter	4:46:55 (27,693)	
Greer, Mervyn	5:34:27 (26,751)	
Greer, Richard	3:28:12 (3,844)	
Greet, Adrian	5:10:30 (24,142)	
Greet, Mark	4:00:42 (10,211)	
Greeves, Jerry	2:38:04 (138)	
Greffiths, Michael	4:37:43 (18,303)	
Gregg, William	3:43:01 (6,310)	
Gregg, William	5:21:36 (25,533)	
Gregoire, Peter	3:08:40 (1,646)	
Gregor, Zdenek	3:51:49 (8,031)	
Gregory, Andrew	3:58:52 (9,718)	
Gregory, Andrew	4:00:19 (10,109)	
Gregory, Anthony	3:50:54 (7,847)	
Gregory, Christopher	3:33:24 (4,674)	

Gregory, David 4:53:15 (21,361)
Gregory, John 4:26:52 (15,926)
Gregory, John 4:48:20 (20,413)
Gregory, John 5:07:36 (23,712)
Gregory, Jonathan 4:18:06 (13,887)
Gregory, Jonathan 5:08:03 (23,774)
Gregory, Kevin 4:52:18 (21,158)
Gregory, Mark 4:12:28 (12,730)
Gregory, Paul 4:46:06 (19,960)
Gregory, Trevor 3:11:50 (1,899)
Greiner, Hermann 3:07:55 (1,584)
Gremmelmaier, Bernd 5:08:35 (23,863)
Gremo, Stuart 4:57:28 (22,211)
Gretton, Stephen 5:23:55 (25,786)
Grew, Roy 3:19:53 (2,752)
Grewal, Bobby 5:29:22 (26,326)
Grewal, Hardeep 4:04:09 (10,910)
Grewal, Varinder 5:38:27 (27,049)
Grey, Gordon 5:03:58 (23,123)
Grey, Richard 4:10:21 (12,241)
Grey, Robert 4:59:50 (22,581)
Gribbin, Adrian 4:40:16 (18,830)
Gribble, Antony 5:49:53 (27,893)
Grice, David 4:01:21 (10,357)
Grief, Barry 4:55:05 (21,757)
Grieshaber, Jeremy 3:53:24 (8,357)
Grieve, James 3:51:53 (8,045)
Griffen, Richard 4:18:04 (13,880)
Griffies, Miles 4:51:02 (20,891)
Griffin, Andrew 4:19:15 (14,178)
Griffin, Barry 3:51:42 (8,006)
Griffin, Brian 3:40:12 (5,816)
Griffin, Buddy 4:12:15 (12,679)
Griffin, David 5:08:43 (23,892)
Griffin, Gareth 4:54:11 (21,548)
Griffin, John 5:26:28 (26,042)
Griffin, Mark 2:59:49 (1,010)
Griffin, Martin 5:18:22 (25,196)
Griffin, Philip 4:45:56 (19,926)
Griffin, Raymond 7:56:07 (30,202)
Griffin, Richard 4:17:14 (13,725)
Griffin, Richard 5:42:15 (27,351)
Griffin, Robert 4:38:34 (18,519)
Griffin, Thomas 3:40:41 (5,894)
Griffin, Tim 3:59:49 (10,002)
Griffith, Chris 4:10:32 (12,279)
Griffith, Paul 3:59:03 (9,773)
Griffith, Tom 3:46:05 (6,873)
Griffiths, Andrew 4:43:06 (19,404)
Griffiths, Anthony 4:50:06 (20,737)
Griffiths, Bryn 3:26:02 (3,503)
Griffiths, Dean 3:30:55 (4,317)
Griffiths, Geoff 5:03:11 (23,029)
Griffiths, Graeme 3:18:21 (2,583)
Griffiths, Hugh 2:58:51 (919)
Griffiths, Ian 3:52:28 (8,163)
Griffiths, Jason 3:58:40 (9,661)
Griffiths, John 3:24:25 (3,302)
Griffiths, John 4:52:55 (21,296)
Griffiths, Mark 4:23:39 (15,218)
Griffiths, Michael 4:16:38 (13,598)
Griffiths, Paul 4:12:11 (12,669)
Griffiths, Paul 4:29:50 (16,634)
Griffiths, Peter 3:40:31 (5,871)
Griffiths, Peter 4:33:32 (17,428)
Griffiths, Rob 5:02:05 (22,887)
Griffiths, Robert 3:57:57 (9,478)
Griffiths, Roy 3:53:38 (8,409)
Griffiths, Simon 3:47:19 (7,090)
Griffiths, Simon 4:52:56 (21,299)
Griffiths, Vaughan 3:41:37 (6,059)
Griggs, David 5:28:37 (26,243)
Griggs, Gavin 3:51:05 (7,889)
Griggs, Kevin 4:02:45 (10,617)
Griggs, Martyn 3:52:23 (8,148)
Grigoleit, Peter 4:16:19 (13,527)
Grillas, Pascal 3:52:39 (8,202)
Grimditch, Mark 4:07:15 (11,600)
Grime, Nick 4:21:56 (14,793)
Grimes, Kevin 5:32:54 (26,607)
Grimes, Mark 4:58:01 (22,296)
Grimes, Norman 4:52:29 (21,200)
Grimley, Stephen 4:17:09 (13,703)
Grimm, Manfred 4:08:03 (11,779)
Grimme, Andrew 5:35:34 (26,852)
Grimmer, Harold 6:02:34 (28,523)
Grimsdale, Martin 3:22:46 (3,084)
Grimshaw, Paul 6:07:13 (28,731)
Grimstead, Calvin 4:41:32 (19,067)
Grimwood, Kevin 4:16:52 (13,642)
Grinberg, Simon 3:45:33 (6,757)
Grindley, Jamie 4:51:07 (20,909)
Grindon, Jason 4:27:27 (16,050)
Grindu, Louis 3:38:12 (5,431)
Grinham, Colin 3:59:56 (10,037)
Gripton, George 3:37:06 (5,265)
Grisdale, Simon 3:19:13 (2,676)
Grisdale, Timothy 3:43:40 (6,428)
Grisley, Jeffrey 4:29:37 (16,580)
Grixti, Peter 3:54:16 (8,527)
Grobelaar, Adrian 3:48:55 (7,442)
Grobler, Thorsten 3:32:58 (4,595)
Grocott, Ian 3:58:30 (9,604)
Groenhardt, Ioerg 3:57:55 (9,469)
Groenli, Sture 2:38:59 (156)
Groombridge, Jeremy 4:06:45 (11,493)
Groombridge, Stephen 2:44:49 (284)
Grose, Ian 3:54:08 (8,501)
Gross, Gary 4:56:03 (21,993)
Gross, Michael 5:07:28 (23,693)
Gross, Sam 4:10:27 (12,266)
Gross, Toomas 3:33:53 (4,737)
Grosvenor, Michael 4:28:39 (16,350)
Grounds, Freddie 3:43:24 (6,377)
Grout, Andrew 5:14:13 (24,660)
Grout, Jonathan 3:25:04 (3,385)
Grove, Rob 4:37:23 (18,219)
Grover, Frederick 5:08:17 (23,813)
Groves, Andrew 4:09:42 (12,108)
Groves, Ian 4:07:43 (11,703)
Groves, Nick 3:06:16 (1,441)
Groves-Burke, Andy 3:22:09 (3,019)
Grubb, Andrew 3:20:42 (2,847)
Grubb, Stephen 4:49:22 (20,590)
Gruber, Norbert 4:49:12 (20,562)
Gruening, Christoph 5:09:20 (23,986)
Grundmann, Joachim 5:09:19 (23,983)
Grundy, David 3:59:07 (9,791)
Grundy, David 4:54:18 (21,562)
Grundy, James 4:52:01 (21,094)
Grundy, Trevor 4:15:25 (13,350)
Grunstaudl, Gerhard 4:02:30 (10,571)
Grylls, Edward 5:12:28 (24,424)
Gryparis, Viannis 5:44:24 (27,500)
Guarino, Carmine 2:59:15 (953)
Guarino, Tony 4:22:10 (14,847)
Gubb, Jonathan 4:13:54 (13,019)
Gudgin, Terence 6:32:44 (29,471)
Gudka, Chandrakant 5:23:02 (25,709)
Gudka, Piyush 4:15:03 (13,278)
Guesdon, Alain 3:29:20 (4,053)
Guest, David 6:14:19 (29,001)
Guest, Martin 4:53:48 (21,474)
Guest, Paul 4:46:09 (19,972)
Guest, Stuart 2:40:21 (177)
Guichard, Mark 2:42:14 (222)
Guiden, Noel 3:15:50 (2,298)
Guilbeault, Scott 3:59:31 (9,925)
Guinard, Patrick 3:42:11 (6,159)
Guinemand, Claude 4:55:19 (21,819)
Guithou, Claude 3:42:33 (6,226)
Gule, Trygue 4:05:22 (11,179)
Gulland, Matt 4:37:32 (18,257)
Gullis, Michael 3:40:43 (5,900)
Gullis, Peter 3:39:44 (5,719)
Gulliver, Keith 5:45:06 (27,565)
Gulliver, Martin 4:59:45 (22,562)
Gumbs, Randolph 4:23:28 (15,165)
Gummery, Keith 4:20:52 (14,564)
Gummery, Richard 3:25:41 (3,463)
Gundabolu, Samba Siva 6:09:46 (28,850)
Gundersen, Kjell 5:34:05 (26,710)
Gunn, Graham 4:23:02 (15,071)
Gunn, James 3:59:12 (9,815)
Gunn, Paul 3:07:53 (1,580)
Gunner, Ian 3:32:15 (4,500)
Gunner, John 3:30:21 (4,221)
Gunnsteinssom, Sigurdur 3:47:29 (7,135)
Gunston, Andrew 4:21:37 (14,718)
Gunston, Ian 3:03:55 (1,278)
Gupta, Anil 5:54:12 (28,125)
Gurd, Richard 3:14:15 (2,140)
Gurdon, Tim 4:12:43 (12,775)
Gurney, Henry 3:55:26 (8,792)
Gustafsson, Bernt 5:09:39 (24,039)
Gustafsson, Kenny 4:18:37 (14,035)
Gustavsson, Glenn 3:23:05 (3,124)
Gustavsson, Ingemar 4:05:44 (11,283)
Gutch, Tim 5:40:34 (27,236)
Guthrie, Adrian 3:29:13 (4,029)
Guthrie, Andy 3:29:13 (4,029)
Gutierrez, Raul 3:06:44 (1,482)
Gutteridge, Adam 5:07:50 (23,751)
Guttridge, David 3:37:36 (5,350)
Guttridge, Kevin 4:05:36 (11,241)
Guy, Colin 4:34:23 (17,612)
Guy, Dave 3:38:51 (5,548)
Guy, David 5:08:54 (23,922)
Guy, Len 4:48:56 (20,512)
Guyon, Sylvain 3:50:41 (7,802)
Gwalchmai, Mark 4:59:27 (22,522)
Gwillam, Andrew 2:55:59 (681)
Gwillim, Craig 4:01:45 (10,436)
Gwynne, Serge 3:53:03 (8,277)
Gyles, Paul 4:31:23 (16,954)
Gynn, Trevor 2:44:08 (264)
Gyss, Nicholas 4:19:41 (14,299)
Gyte, Barr 3:02:48 (1,200)
Haake, Rainer 2:41:00 (192)
Haan, Ruurd 3:28:30 (3,907)
Habershon, Stephen 4:02:10 (10,518)
Habibi, Hamid 4:44:09 (19,609)
Hackenberg, Dirk 3:58:20 (9,569)
Hacker, Terry 3:24:25 (3,302)
Hackett, Alan 5:37:50 (27,010)
Hackett, Christopher 4:40:02 (18,793)
Hacking, John 5:24:51 (25,862)
Hackney, Roger 2:57:57 (809)
Hadaway, David 3:25:08 (3,392)
Hadden, Nicolas 3:39:16 (5,620)
Hadden-Wight, Paul 4:24:38 (15,427)
Haddon, Michael 3:38:04 (5,412)
Haddow, David 3:40:48 (5,912)
Haddrell, Rodney 4:06:14 (11,393)
Haden, Arthur 6:17:42 (29,104)
Hadfield, Frank 3:53:03 (8,277)
Hadfield, Jeremy 3:59:09 (9,800)
Hadfield, Warren 3:06:39 (1,474)
Hadgraft, Peter 5:15:05 (24,796)
Hadingham, Timothy 4:03:36 (10,801)
Hadjidakis, Dimitri 4:46:17 (20,006)
Hadley, Kent 3:40:55 (5,931)
Hadley, Peter 3:53:37 (8,407)
Hadley, William 3:53:03 (8,277)
Haeffner, Henry 4:33:35 (17,450)
Haegel, Thierry 3:00:37 (1,061)
Haertel, Rainer 5:26:23 (26,031)
Haesener, Sven 3:29:48 (4,134)
Haetta, Nils 2:58:04 (816)
Haetzman, Andrew 3:53:31 (8,380)
Hagan, Brian 4:09:01 (11,990)
Hagell, Ron 3:59:00 (9,754)
Hagenbach, Pascal 2:58:40 (885)
Haggart, Robin 3:54:17 (8,533)
Haggarthy, Kevin 5:21:47 (25,562)
Haggas, Neil 2:58:28 (848)
Haggett, John 5:10:25 (24,132)
Hague, Joseph 5:10:27 (24,136)
Hague Holmes, Gerard 3:34:42 (4,862)
Hagyard, Andrew 3:56:22 (9,013)
Haig, Derek 3:35:43 (5,019)
Haigh, John 3:52:44 (8,215)
Haigh, Martin 3:36:05 (5,086)
Haigh, Robert 4:04:15 (10,939)
Haigh, Stewart 4:22:34 (14,943)
Hailwood, Ernie 4:36:47 (18,078)
Haines, Derek 4:08:19 (11,827)
Haines, Mark 4:43:26 (19,473)
Haines, Matthew 4:44:48 (19,733)

Haines, Stephen 3:36:50 (5,213)
Haines, Stephen 4:35:20 (17,781)
Hains, Kevin 3:40:27 (5,859)
Hainsworth, David 3:38:20 (5,453)
Hainsworth, Paul 3:11:13 (1,856)
Haire, Geoffrey 4:14:14 (13,082)
Haire, Kenneth 3:47:59 (7,262)
Haith, Kenneth 3:28:57 (3,987)
Hajducki, Andrw 5:32:47 (26,599)
Hajioff, Gideon 4:51:37 (21,012)
Hake, Paul 4:26:40 (15,885)
Haldeman, David 3:43:59 (6,491)
Halderthay, Richard 4:31:15 (16,918)
Hale, Christopher 4:38:34 (18,519)
Hale, Jason 6:29:48 (29,403)
Hale, Leigh 3:40:48 (5,912)
Hale, Michael 5:14:53 (24,762)
Hale, Robert 3:32:29 (4,532)
Haleem, Malik 4:23:10 (15,101)
Hales, Roger 3:23:13 (3,137)
Hales, Vernon 4:28:33 (16,326)
Haley, Brian 5:28:12 (26,196)
Haley, Colin 3:42:52 (6,278)
Haley, Glen 3:57:21 (9,273)
Halford, Philip 3:23:20 (3,154)
Halkett, David 4:18:42 (14,051)
Hall, Alan 3:38:22 (5,458)
Hall, Andrew 3:28:17 (3,863)
Hall, Andy 4:11:35 (12,521)
Hall, Ben 4:05:56 (11,333)
Hall, Chris 3:26:02 (3,503)
Hall, Christopher 3:46:31 (6,951)
Hall, Christopher 3:46:37 (6,979)
Hall, Christopher 4:26:51 (15,920)
Hall, David 3:59:05 (9,781)
Hall, David 4:07:14 (11,595)
Hall, David 5:42:22 (27,363)
Hall, Dennis 5:03:10 (23,027)
Hall, Derek 4:44:39 (19,704)
Hall, Edward 4:41:11 (19,009)
Hall, Frederick 4:39:32 (18,700)
Hall, Gareth 3:27:05 (3,633)
Hall, Gary 4:25:10 (15,550)
Hall, Gary 4:32:53 (17,293)
Hall, Gavin 3:16:58 (2,420)
Hall, George 3:18:40 (2,616)
Hall, George 4:08:49 (11,938)
Hall, Gerrard 5:46:19 (27,648)
Hall, Giles 3:57:52 (9,453)
Hall, Giles 4:29:04 (16,438)
Hall, Ian 4:26:31 (15,849)
Hall, Ian 4:35:17 (17,771)
Hall, Ian 5:08:13 (23,800)
Hall, James 4:11:10 (12,431)
Hall, Jamie 4:39:20 (18,650)
Hall, Jeremy 3:49:26 (7,559)
Hall, John 3:34:24 (4,817)
Hall, John 3:56:06 (8,951)
Hall, John 3:59:27 (9,903)
Hall, John 4:24:59 (15,501)
Hall, John 4:51:25 (20,974)
Hall, John 5:20:58 (25,462)
Hall, Jonathan 3:30:51 (4,302)
Hall, Leslie 4:37:56 (18,353)
Hall, Mark 3:57:54 (9,462)
Hall, Martin 3:28:45 (3,949)
Hall, Matthew 3:13:44 (2,080)
Hall, Matthew 4:03:45 (10,832)
Hall, Matthew 6:36:22 (29,552)
Hall, Michael 3:42:40 (6,247)
Hall, Michael 3:54:14 (8,519)
Hall, Mike 4:22:36 (14,955)
Hall, Nicholas 3:45:45 (6,810)
Hall, Nicholas 3:55:22 (8,775)
Hall, Nicholas 4:03:44 (10,825)
Hall, Nicholas 6:03:03 (28,544)
Hall, Nigel 3:39:33 (5,684)
Hall, Patrick 2:58:38 (875)
Hall, Patrick 4:33:38 (17,464)
Hall, Peter 4:28:07 (16,217)
Hall, Peter 5:01:00 (22,734)
Hall, Richard 4:24:25 (15,374)
Hall, Richard 4:40:28 (18,868)
Hall, Rob 2:48:31 (378)
Hall, Robert 3:04:17 (1,301)
Hall, Robert 3:57:50 (9,440)
Hall, Simon 3:35:30 (4,986)
Hall, Stephen 4:55:12 (21,783)
Hall, Steven 3:47:41 (7,189)
Hall, Steven 6:23:30 (29,243)
Hall, William 4:04:49 (11,070)
Hallam, Andrew 4:02:33 (10,584)
Hallatt, Richard 3:46:27 (6,940)
Hallett, James 4:20:38 (14,507)
Hallett, Martin 5:05:41 (23,410)
Halley, Stuart 4:59:42 (22,553)
Halliday, Alasdair 4:30:40 (16,780)
Halliday, Kelvin 3:16:40 (2,386)
Hallinan, Christopher 4:07:07 (11,572)
Hallinan, Neil 3:39:00 (5,573)
Halliwell, Roger 4:25:09 (15,543)
Hallmark, Robert 4:27:36 (16,090)
Hallson, David 3:22:00 (3,000)
Hallsworth, David 5:44:20 (27,497)
Halsall, Dean 6:04:25 (28,615)
Halse, Tarquin 5:55:28 (28,187)
Halsey, Michael 5:21:20 (25,510)
Halsey, Neil 4:54:51 (21,691)
Halstead, Robert 4:23:33 (15,189)
Halton, Andrew 5:14:56 (24,767)
Halton, Raymond 4:10:32 (12,279)
Halvatzis, Nicos 3:29:25 (4,066)
Halvorsen, Konrad 5:13:35 (24,576)
Ham, Clive 3:30:11 (4,198)
Hama, Kensuke 5:31:47 (26,515)
Hamalainen, Markku 4:39:05 (18,619)
Hambelton, Matthew 5:23:51 (25,774)
Hambleton, Steven 4:38:16 (18,445)
Hamblin, Alasdair 3:49:59 (7,686)
Hambury, Roger 5:18:13 (25,178)
Hamer, Colin 4:55:16 (21,802)
Hamer, David 3:13:56 (2,106)
Hamer, Gabriel 2:56:04 (687)
Hamer, Ian 3:42:16 (6,174)
Hamer, Paul 3:55:37 (8,821)
Hamers, Gert 3:49:11 (7,493)
Hamerstehl, Bruno 3:07:36 (1,556)
Hames, Philip 4:12:10 (12,667)
Hamid, Abdul 5:35:06 (26,816)
Hamid, Terry 3:47:07 (7,054)
Hamill, Gary 4:11:57 (12,596)
Hamill, Richard 3:20:17 (2,791)
Hamilton, Angus 6:15:31 (29,045)
Hamilton, Anthony 3:50:31 (7,775)
Hamilton, Dave 4:58:14 (22,332)
Hamilton, Duncan 4:43:48 (19,557)
Hamilton, Edward 3:09:46 (1,736)
Hamilton, Ian 4:35:56 (17,913)
Hamilton, Ian 5:03:20 (23,046)
Hamilton, Jamie 4:05:12 (11,154)
Hamilton, Keith 3:51:06 (7,896)
Hamilton, Kil 5:18:56 (25,261)
Hamilton, Michael 5:26:01 (25,989)
Hamilton, Robert 3:54:31 (8,590)
Hamilton, Robert 4:43:48 (19,557)
Hamilton, Robert 5:12:26 (24,419)
Hamilton, Stephen 5:21:14 (25,493)
Hamilton, Stuart 4:55:28 (21,878)
Hamilton Brown, Robert 6:14:36 (29,009)
Hamilton-Davies, Colin 4:10:22 (12,244)
Hamlet, Colin 3:46:12 (6,899)
Hammer, Christoph 5:55:19 (28,170)
Hammer, Matthias 5:10:32 (24,152)
Hammerman, Eddie 6:37:46 (29,585)
Hammersley, Christopher 4:12:35 (12,752)
Hammerton, Robbie 5:35:20 (26,832)
Hammond, Garry 4:15:04 (13,282)
Hammond, Guy 3:20:27 (2,815)
Hammond, John 3:41:31 (6,039)
Hammond, Justin 3:11:37 (1,874)
Hammond, Mark 2:54:50 (623)
Hammond, Mark 4:38:36 (18,529)
Hammond, Michael 3:50:35 (7,789)
Hammond, Michael 6:50:44 (29,818)
Hammond, Nigel 6:44:10 (29,723)
Hammond, Peter 6:05:31 (28,666)
Hammond, Steve 3:39:58 (5,778)
Hammond, Tony 4:33:05 (17,324)
Hamon, Jean-Marc 4:13:21 (12,889)
Hamon, Olivier 3:24:02 (3,250)
Hamon, Patrick 3:12:33 (1,964)
Hamp, William 5:33:55 (26,682)
Hampshaw, Chris 3:24:27 (3,306)
Hampshire, John 4:40:53 (18,953)
Hampson, Andrew 3:53:51 (8,451)
Hampson, Brian 5:12:32 (24,434)
Hampson, Christopher 3:25:09 (3,393)
Hampson, Graham 3:33:03 (4,611)
Hampson, Richard 3:59:05 (9,781)
Hampton, Anthony 3:27:22 (3,683)
Hampton, Ray 3:23:30 (3,176)
Hampton, Vincent 4:48:14 (20,391)
Hampton, William 5:22:24 (25,635)
Hamsher, Mark 4:12:49 (12,795)
Hamud, Hector 4:18:16 (13,943)
Hanbury, Daniel 3:40:39 (5,890)
Hanby, John 4:37:30 (18,250)
Hancock, Anthony 3:10:59 (1,834)
Hancock, Clifford 4:27:43 (16,125)
Hancock, Dave 3:51:18 (7,932)
Hancock, Hartley 3:35:05 (4,914)
Hancock, John 5:45:46 (27,613)
Hancock, Jonathan 3:46:30 (6,948)
Hancock, Keith 4:56:54 (22,128)
Hancock, Martin 3:36:40 (5,184)
Hancock, Simon 4:05:33 (11,228)
Hancock, Timothy 3:54:42 (8,634)
Hand, Gordon 4:19:07 (14,150)
Hand, Michael 3:16:30 (2,367)
Hand, Michael 6:25:34 (29,297)
Hand, Terence 4:06:41 (11,481)
Hand, Warren 7:22:23 (30,093)
Handel, Paul 5:11:43 (24,317)
Handley, John 3:57:06 (9,196)
Handley, Mark 4:44:04 (19,593)
Handley, Michael 4:09:54 (12,140)
Handslip, Nicholas 3:04:24 (1,306)
Hankin, Anthony 6:17:30 (29,101)
Hanley, Alan 3:23:24 (3,159)
Hanley, Anthony 4:03:27 (10,760)
Hanley, Michael 5:07:13 (23,652)
Hanlon, Francis 4:21:02 (14,599)
Hanlon, John 4:45:11 (19,804)
Hanlon, John 5:40:57 (27,259)
Hanna, Steven 3:26:35 (3,570)
Hanna, William 3:49:46 (7,639)
Hannah, Craig 4:26:52 (15,926)
Hannah, David 3:55:35 (8,814)
Hannah, Giles 3:58:46 (9,690)
Hannah, Howard 4:10:04 (12,173)
Hannah, Tom 3:27:48 (3,762)
Hannam, Philip 5:05:42 (23,416)
Hannan, Sean 4:14:41 (13,166)
Hannaway, Liam 4:17:34 (13,784)
Hannell, Guy 4:02:55 (10,649)
Hanney, Mark 5:47:44 (27,745)
Hannibal, Stephen 4:39:44 (18,740)
Hannington, Dorian 4:53:29 (21,416)
Hannon, Philip 3:53:38 (8,409)
Hannum, John 3:27:42 (3,741)
Hanover, Phillip 5:17:07 (25,064)
Hanratty, Daniel 4:26:01 (15,736)
Hanreck, Michael 3:51:44 (8,013)
Hans, Paramjit 5:11:47 (24,326)
Hanscomb, John 3:50:59 (7,867)
Hansel, Jac 4:33:43 (17,482)
Hansen, Aage 3:53:11 (8,305)
Hansen, Dougls 3:22:51 (3,091)
Hansen, Morten 3:13:54 (2,105)
Hansen, Paul 3:29:56 (4,159)
Hansford, William 8:08:52 (30,229)
Hanslip, Mark 4:42:56 (19,373)
Hanson, David 4:59:19 (22,500)
Hanson, Gareth 3:02:54 (1,207)
Hanson, Kenny 4:27:34 (16,081)
Hanson, Mark 4:33:20 (17,378)
Hanson, Mark 4:40:02 (18,793)
Hanson, Mark 4:42:49 (19,336)
Hanson, Paul 3:05:07 (1,356)

Hanson, Stephen	3:57:00 (9,178)	
Hanson, Stephen	4:23:14 (15,114)	
Haragan, Scott	4:30:57 (16,839)	
Haralampiev, Michail	4:30:13 (16,720)	
Haraldstad, Gunnar	3:48:07 (7,289)	
Harber, David	4:29:13 (16,478)	
Harber, Mark	3:56:07 (8,952)	
Harbor, Barry	5:44:49 (27,550)	
Harborow, Adam	4:34:15 (17,585)	
Harbottle, Julian	4:53:34 (21,436)	
Harbour, Jason	2:41:59 (219)	
Harbron, Christopher	3:24:09 (3,266)	
Harby, Alan	4:53:57 (21,499)	
Harby, Glynn	3:22:00 (3,000)	
Harcombe, Ian	4:26:03 (15,743)	
Harcourt, David	4:53:07 (21,339)	
Harcus, Charles	4:11:43 (12,552)	
Hard, David	4:14:48 (13,209)	
Hardcastle, Dominic	4:48:54 (20,503)	
Hardcastle, Kenneth	4:06:40 (11,480)	
Hardcastle, Robert	3:44:59 (6,684)	
Hardgrave, Jamie	5:14:48 (24,749)	
Hardie, John	4:17:13 (13,722)	
Hardie, John	4:35:38 (17,849)	
Hardie, Peter	4:18:43 (14,056)	
Harding, Andrew	4:10:48 (12,341)	
Harding, Anthony	5:17:49 (25,142)	
Harding, Brian	3:42:06 (6,137)	
Harding, Brian	4:41:15 (19,024)	
Harding, Colin	4:48:31 (20,441)	
Harding, David	4:30:34 (16,762)	
Harding, Fred	3:23:55 (3,231)	
Harding, James	3:19:08 (2,664)	
Harding, Jeffrey	4:38:41 (18,544)	
Harding, John	5:08:54 (23,922)	
Harding, John	6:03:03 (28,544)	
Harding, Nicolas	3:12:16 (1,938)	
Harding, Peter	4:18:54 (14,098)	
Harding, Robert	4:08:42 (11,914)	
Harding, Sacha	4:07:20 (11,622)	
Harding, Simon	4:01:37 (10,414)	
Harding, Thomas	3:15:40 (2,286)	
Hardinges, John	5:55:32 (28,194)	
Hardisty, Michael	4:04:33 (11,007)	
Hardisty, Paul	5:03:18 (23,042)	
Hardman, Bob	3:08:29 (1,630)	
Hardman, Gareth	3:44:31 (6,580)	
Hardman, Gordon	4:44:26 (19,662)	
Hardman, Neil	3:02:20 (1,177)	
Hardstone, Roger	3:44:06 (6,509)	
Hardwell, Keith	4:01:42 (10,430)	
Hardwick, John	3:51:39 (7,997)	
Hardwick, Timothy	3:50:49 (7,825)	
Hardwicke, Edward	3:54:12 (8,509)	
Hardy, Anthony	4:29:32 (16,553)	
Hardy, David	3:08:58 (1,669)	
Hardy, Helmut	3:36:54 (5,228)	
Hardy, John	2:55:51 (671)	
Hardy, Martin	4:19:04 (14,136)	
Hardy, Matthew	4:08:34 (11,885)	
Hardy, Paul	5:20:42 (25,431)	
Hardy, Peter	4:22:39 (14,968)	
Hardy, Richard	3:56:05 (8,946)	
Hardy, Richard	3:57:50 (9,440)	
Hardy, Richard	4:35:48 (17,881)	
Hardy, Robert	3:52:04 (8,091)	
Hardy, Ruari	3:32:47 (4,570)	
Hardy, Russell	4:24:36 (15,422)	
Hardy, Stephen	3:46:36 (6,973)	
Hare, Johan	5:51:53 (28,011)	
Hare, Paul	3:52:41 (8,207)	
Harefors, Melker	4:29:49 (16,630)	
Hares, Colin	3:47:46 (7,203)	
Hares, Richard	5:41:51 (27,321)	
Harfield, Patrick	6:42:58 (29,707)	
Harfield, Simon	3:51:17 (7,929)	
Harfield, Stephen	6:42:58 (29,707)	
Hargrave, Paul	3:47:51 (7,224)	
Hargrave, Paul	4:40:36 (18,898)	
Hargreaves, Daniel	4:18:06 (13,887)	
Hargreaves, David	4:19:58 (14,355)	
Hargreaves, John	3:11:24 (1,861)	
Hargreaves, Mark	3:06:48 (1,488)	
Hargreaves, Michael	4:54:57 (21,718)	
Hargreaves, Stephen	4:54:33 (21,604)	
Harizi, Dominique	3:07:48 (1,572)	
Harju, Pekka	3:55:25 (8,786)	
Harker, Andrew	3:10:16 (1,771)	
Harker, Anthony	4:25:39 (15,643)	
Harker, Peter	5:41:51 (27,321)	
Harkins, Brian	3:46:42 (6,990)	
Harkins, Dominic	3:39:28 (5,667)	
Harkins, Michael	4:35:28 (17,806)	
Harkness, Lee	3:32:04 (4,475)	
Harkus, Gavin	2:44:58 (286)	
Harland, Colin	4:35:57 (17,920)	
Harland, Paul	3:10:42 (1,808)	
Harler, Andrew	4:18:06 (13,887)	
Harley, James	4:36:22 (17,988)	
Harley, Michael	4:51:52 (21,066)	
Harling, Joseph	4:41:39 (19,093)	
Harling, Malcolm	4:28:06 (16,210)	
Harlingten, Croft	4:27:53 (16,172)	
Harlow, Dominic	4:42:45 (19,320)	
Harlow, Thomas	3:30:35 (4,260)	
Harman, Gary	3:39:56 (5,768)	
Harman, Keir	4:37:49 (18,320)	
Harman, Martin	4:31:23 (16,954)	
Harman, Peter	4:58:14 (22,332)	
Harman, Peter	6:15:35 (29,047)	
Harman, Richard	3:46:52 (7,014)	
Harmer, Wayne	5:51:26 (27,978)	
Harnden, Shaun	3:51:05 (7,889)	
Harnett, Dennis	5:27:36 (26,138)	
Harney, Brian	3:04:37 (1,324)	
Harney, Mark	3:44:05 (6,505)	
Harper, Alfred	4:31:37 (17,016)	
Harper, Andrew	3:40:56 (5,939)	
Harper, Brian	4:39:21 (18,654)	
Harper, Charles	3:09:55 (1,743)	
Harper, Chris	4:29:13 (16,478)	
Harper, Ian	4:26:00 (15,730)	
Harper, Ian	4:48:07 (20,371)	
Harper, John	4:33:54 (17,519)	
Harper, Kevin	4:50:10 (20,747)	
Harper, Mark	3:42:04 (6,131)	
Harper, Peter	5:01:36 (22,816)	
Harper, Stephen	4:19:26 (14,236)	
Harper, Stephen	4:32:09 (17,145)	
Harper Tee, Adrian	4:46:15 (19,998)	
Harrap, Chris	3:56:00 (8,919)	
Harrap, John	3:10:17 (1,772)	
Harrild, Benjamin	3:45:40 (6,785)	
Harrill, George	4:50:55 (20,865)	
Harrington, Patrick	4:44:25 (19,659)	
Harrington, Stephen	4:38:23 (18,477)	
Harris, Alan	3:23:13 (3,137)	
Harris, Alan	3:41:17 (6,005)	
Harris, Alan	4:27:39 (16,105)	
Harris, Bryan	4:05:37 (11,244)	
Harris, Clive	6:01:38 (28,487)	
Harris, Colin	5:05:59 (23,466)	
Harris, Dave	6:28:38 (29,376)	
Harris, David	3:22:14 (3,029)	
Harris, David	3:36:59 (5,241)	
Harris, David	3:47:59 (7,262)	
Harris, Ewan	3:51:08 (7,901)	
Harris, Fred	6:41:21 (29,675)	
Harris, Glen	4:36:10 (17,950)	
Harris, Iestyn	3:44:39 (6,604)	
Harris, Jason	4:33:16 (17,360)	
Harris, John	4:25:20 (15,580)	
Harris, John	5:12:24 (24,416)	
Harris, Jonathan	4:49:47 (20,669)	
Harris, Julian	3:58:30 (9,604)	
Harris, Keith	7:10:20 (30,022)	
Harris, Kelvyn	3:20:44 (2,853)	
Harris, Kenneth	4:46:11 (19,983)	
Harris, Kevin	4:02:22 (10,544)	
Harris, Lee	4:37:51 (18,333)	
Harris, Michael	3:59:18 (9,841)	
Harris, Owen	4:42:29 (19,270)	
Harris, Paul	4:18:17 (13,946)	
Harris, Paul	4:21:33 (14,701)	
Harris, Paul	5:59:57 (28,416)	
Harris, Peter	4:02:12 (10,523)	
Harris, Peter	4:19:05 (14,143)	
Harris, Peter	5:59:57 (28,416)	
Harris, Phillip	4:24:51 (15,466)	
Harris, Ralph	4:11:32 (12,508)	
Harris, Raymond	3:58:50 (9,709)	
Harris, Raymond	4:57:04 (22,149)	
Harris, Richard	2:57:18 (766)	
Harris, Richard	3:23:55 (3,231)	
Harris, Richard	3:24:53 (3,362)	
Harris, Robert	3:57:24 (9,289)	
Harris, Robert	4:14:52 (13,228)	
Harris, Robert	6:04:04 (28,596)	
Harris, Ross	3:10:05 (1,748)	
Harris, Roy	5:58:50 (28,358)	
Harris, Simon	3:18:41 (2,618)	
Harris, Simon	3:31:35 (4,408)	
Harris, Stephen	3:11:43 (1,888)	
Harris, Steve	3:42:08 (6,145)	
Harris, Thomas	6:04:47 (28,634)	
Harris, Vaughan	7:12:10 (30,034)	
Harrison, Christopher	3:37:49 (5,383)	
Harrison, Christopher	4:48:27 (20,433)	
Harrison, Clive	3:33:36 (4,695)	
Harrison, Craig	5:02:47 (22,973)	
Harrison, Darren	4:41:02 (18,981)	
Harrison, David	4:12:35 (12,752)	
Harrison, Dion	5:17:27 (25,100)	
Harrison, Donald	5:14:21 (24,679)	
Harrison, Edward	3:13:48 (2,091)	
Harrison, Graeme	4:21:10 (14,621)	
Harrison, Graham	5:00:56 (22,722)	
Harrison, Harry	4:02:28 (10,566)	
Harrison, John	2:56:51 (735)	
Harrison, Keith	4:57:03 (22,146)	
Harrison, Mark	3:30:00 (4,170)	
Harrison, Matthew	2:50:49 (456)	
Harrison, Michael	4:12:20 (12,620)	
Harrison, Michael	4:12:25 (12,719)	
Harrison, Neale	5:46:17 (27,647)	
Harrison, Nick	4:04:51 (11,077)	
Harrison, Paul	4:05:05 (11,133)	
Harrison, Paul	4:19:28 (14,249)	
Harrison, Paul	4:55:16 (21,802)	
Harrison, Phil	4:46:11 (19,983)	
Harrison, Philip	4:14:14 (13,082)	
Harrison, Richard	3:38:22 (5,458)	
Harrison, Richard	3:45:13 (6,710)	
Harrison, Richard	5:01:21 (22,787)	
Harrison, Scott	4:13:50 (13,009)	
Harrison, Simon	5:17:45 (25,130)	
Harrison, Stephen	4:13:40 (12,975)	
Harrison, Thomas	3:18:51 (2,637)	
Harrison, Tim	4:15:13 (13,312)	
Harrison, Timothy	3:48:07 (7,289)	
Harrison, Trevor	3:46:00 (6,856)	
Harris-Rowe, Colin	4:58:12 (22,328)	
Harrod, Mark	4:21:41 (14,731)	
Harron, Gareth	3:53:53 (8,457)	
Harrop, Mark	5:08:26 (23,835)	
Harry, Ian	3:35:18 (4,952)	
Harry, Richard	4:03:48 (10,841)	
Harryman, Michael	4:23:02 (15,071)	
Harsant, Andrew	5:05:53 (23,446)	
Hart, Alan	5:12:47 (24,465)	
Hart, Andrew	4:05:57 (11,339)	
Hart, Andrew	4:35:57 (17,920)	
Hart, Christopher	4:21:49 (14,766)	
Hart, Colin	3:22:18 (3,037)	
Hart, David	3:51:22 (7,940)	
Hart, Edward	5:31:06 (26,462)	
Hart, Gareth	4:46:19 (20,010)	
Hart, George	2:53:46 (573)	
Hart, Matthew	3:48:00 (7,269)	
Hart, Matthew	4:29:34 (16,564)	
Hart, Paul	3:12:04 (1,919)	
Hart, Paul	3:30:49 (4,295)	
Hart, Peter	2:57:04 (748)	
Hart, Richard	3:43:43 (6,442)	
Hart, Robert	3:18:07 (2,550)	
Hart, Stephen	4:47:57 (20,337)	
Hart, Stephen	4:50:55 (20,865)	
Hart, Terry	3:28:28 (3,903)	
Harte, David	3:26:34 (3,568)	

Harte, John	3:55:38 (8,829)	
Hartigan, John	3:56:02 (8,934)	
Hartigan, Paul	4:21:14 (14,635)	
Hartland, Christopher	3:57:39 (9,384)	
Hartley, Alex	3:32:08 (4,486)	
Hartley, Ian	5:43:04 (27,418)	
Hartley, Jalaal	3:59:48 (9,998)	
Hartley, John	2:41:48 (212)	
Hartley, Neil	4:02:55 (10,649)	
Hartley, Roger	4:44:05 (19,596)	
Hartley, Simon	4:36:20 (17,982)	
Hartop, James	3:49:31 (7,588)	
Harvatt, Neil	4:04:33 (11,007)	
Harvey, Andrew	4:44:37 (19,698)	
Harvey, Andrew	6:49:16 (29,791)	
Harvey, Ben	4:55:16 (21,802)	
Harvey, David	3:58:28 (9,596)	
Harvey, David	4:33:37 (17,459)	
Harvey, Edward	4:52:32 (21,216)	
Harvey, Gary	4:10:53 (12,368)	
Harvey, Glen	3:45:22 (6,726)	
Harvey, Ian	3:07:06 (1,512)	
Harvey, James	3:50:42 (7,808)	
Harvey, Jonathan	5:35:58 (26,875)	
Harvey, Kenneth	4:18:10 (13,910)	
Harvey, Kevin	3:24:42 (3,342)	
Harvey, Nick	3:57:26 (9,304)	
Harvey, Paul	3:57:08 (9,207)	
Harvey, Paul	4:10:54 (12,374)	
Harvey, Simon	2:58:42 (891)	
Harvey, Simon	4:51:40 (21,025)	
Harvey, Stephen	4:28:25 (16,289)	
Harvey, Steven	3:44:41 (6,610)	
Harvey, Timothy	4:39:51 (18,762)	
Harvey, Trevor	4:00:22 (10,123)	
Harward, Andrew	4:53:12 (21,353)	
Harwood, Clive	2:56:12 (701)	
Harwood, Jeff	4:26:37 (15,875)	
Harwood, Paul	2:30:45 (71)	
Harwood, Peter	6:30:14 (29,418)	
Harwood, Richard	4:41:54 (19,140)	
Harwood, Tim	6:29:08 (29,392)	
Hasan, Salam	7:33:07 (30,148)	
Haseley, Harry	3:22:56 (3,099)	
Haselwood, Timothy	4:18:16 (13,943)	
Hasenbohler, Patrick	3:07:30 (1,543)	
Hasenstab, Gerhard	3:47:54 (7,241)	
Haslam, Neil	4:16:08 (13,492)	
Haslam, Peter	3:51:51 (8,040)	
Haslan, Alexander	3:13:20 (2,044)	
Hasler, Ralph	4:41:08 (19,001)	
Haslett, Francis	5:51:34 (27,988)	
Hasoon, Andrew	5:56:53 (28,265)	
Hassall, Glyn	5:03:46 (23,094)	
Hassan, Isik	5:01:28 (22,799)	
Hassan, Osman	5:34:55 (26,799)	
Hassan, Sami	5:01:09 (22,758)	
Hassbecker, Tim	4:06:27 (11,440)	
Hasselby, Kevin	4:04:01 (10,886)	
Hassell, Andrew	3:42:49 (6,272)	
Hassell, Desmond	3:33:44 (4,719)	
Hasson, Stephen	5:44:32 (27,523)	
Hastie, David	3:40:00 (5,788)	
Hastings, Adrian	5:34:41 (26,773)	
Hastings, Brian	6:18:39 (29,131)	
Hastings, Derek	4:05:49 (11,305)	
Hastings, Giles	3:48:41 (7,398)	
Hastings, Steven	4:00:20 (10,113)	
Hatch, Gregory	5:26:24 (26,034)	
Hatch, James	4:13:30 (12,932)	
Hatch, Mark	5:59:39 (28,401)	
Hatch, Peter	5:18:17 (25,189)	
Hatfield, Chris	5:34:22 (26,742)	
Hatfield, Edward	4:05:06 (11,138)	
Hatfield, Rupert	4:58:04 (22,308)	
Hathaway, David	3:27:17 (3,672)	
Hathaway, Edward	5:07:00 (23,615)	
Hathway, Kevin	3:35:24 (4,971)	
Hattan, Simon	3:47:30 (7,139)	
Hatten, Kurt	3:01:50 (1,139)	
Hatter, Anthony	4:06:06 (11,363)	
Hatter, Wayne	5:29:10 (26,304)	
Hattersley, David	3:39:58 (5,778)	
Hatton, David	3:47:16 (7,077)	
Hatton, Matthew	3:23:01 (3,115)	
Hatwell, Paul	4:55:11 (21,778)	
Hatwood, Christopher	4:28:31 (16,319)	
Haufe, André	4:32:19 (17,175)	
Haughey, James	6:39:15 (29,610)	
Haughey, Ted	3:58:04 (9,508)	
Haughton, Colin	3:55:10 (8,726)	
Haughton, James	5:48:32 (27,820)	
Havard, Andrew	4:26:12 (15,778)	
Havard, Christopher	4:59:02 (22,468)	
Havard, Frederick	6:10:27 (28,875)	
Havelin, Fintan	3:57:12 (9,226)	
Havelock, John	4:08:38 (11,903)	
Havers, Brian	4:59:35 (22,538)	
Havis, Stephen	4:21:12 (14,628)	
Haw, Steven	5:35:58 (26,875)	
Haward, David	4:01:19 (10,342)	
Hawes, Andrew	4:47:50 (20,312)	
Hawes, Joseph	4:46:27 (20,040)	
Hawes, Mark	5:17:57 (25,155)	
Hawes, Steven	4:54:50 (21,687)	
Hawes, Steven	7:20:57 (30,086)	
Hawes, William	3:00:44 (1,067)	
Hawke, Aubrey	4:49:26 (20,605)	
Hawke, David	3:55:54 (8,894)	
Hawken, Michael	4:02:35 (10,590)	
Hawker, Paul	4:20:32 (14,483)	
Hawker, Simon	2:54:27 (603)	
Hawkes, Giles	4:55:52 (21,964)	
Hawkes, Kevin	4:13:47 (12,995)	
Hawkes, Peter	3:11:02 (1,838)	
Hawkins, Andrew	2:50:04 (430)	
Hawkins, Ben	5:11:54 (24,344)	
Hawkins, David	4:43:14 (19,436)	
Hawkins, John	4:40:41 (18,917)	
Hawkins, Michael	4:56:21 (22,043)	
Hawkins, Nigel	4:25:09 (15,543)	
Hawkins, Paul	3:08:36 (1,637)	
Hawkins, Paul	6:09:46 (28,850)	
Hawkins, Peter	3:11:10 (1,852)	
Hawkins, Richard	3:53:33 (8,391)	
Hawkins, Robert	3:01:26 (1,105)	
Hawkins, Simon	4:19:20 (14,202)	
Hawkins, Stephen	3:13:19 (2,040)	
Hawliczek, Edward	3:32:24 (4,520)	
Haworth, Jeremy	4:43:27 (19,481)	
Haworth, Kentigern	4:43:28 (19,484)	
Haworth, Nick	4:08:23 (11,846)	
Haworth, Richard	3:55:44 (8,854)	
Hawthorn, Michael	4:58:06 (22,316)	
Hawtree, Stephen	3:16:42 (2,393)	
Hay, Charles	4:09:08 (12,007)	
Hay, Douglas	5:33:15 (26,629)	
Hay, Gordon	3:43:46 (6,453)	
Hay, Paul	3:34:42 (4,862)	
Hay, Trevor	4:42:18 (19,226)	
Hay, William	4:01:57 (10,475)	
Haycraft, Daniel	3:49:29 (7,574)	
Hayday, Marcus	3:59:18 (9,841)	
Hayden, Mark	4:08:52 (11,949)	
Hayden, Peter	4:42:42 (19,310)	
Hayes, Billy	4:39:57 (18,777)	
Hayes, Christopher	4:24:19 (15,352)	
Hayes, Conor	3:47:17 (7,079)	
Hayes, James	5:14:25 (24,690)	
Hayes, Neil	4:11:01 (12,402)	
Hayes, Nick	3:54:33 (8,601)	
Hayes, Paul	2:46:52 (336)	
Hayes, Paul	4:55:26 (21,863)	
Hayes, Russell	4:31:49 (17,062)	
Hayes, Shaun	5:18:51 (25,254)	
Hayes, Simon	3:56:41 (9,101)	
Hayes, Simon	4:53:38 (21,444)	
Hayes, Stephen	3:27:10 (3,652)	
Hayes, Stephen	3:31:05 (4,338)	
Hayhow, Christopher	3:26:26 (3,547)	
Hayhurst, Andrew	3:57:42 (9,396)	
Hayhurst, Stephen	5:19:02 (25,268)	
Haylor, David	5:45:25 (27,585)	
Hayman, Edward	5:05:55 (23,451)	
Hayman, Mark	2:38:58 (155)	
Haymes, Anthony	4:56:56 (22,135)	
Haymes, Chris	3:49:11 (7,493)	
Haynes, Daniel	5:41:09 (27,269)	
Haynes, Darren	4:12:41 (12,768)	
Haynes, Frank	4:54:48 (21,678)	
Haynes, Kevin	3:14:14 (2,137)	
Haynes, Kevin	3:57:10 (9,215)	
Haynes, Lee	4:26:29 (15,842)	
Haynes, Paul	4:00:50 (10,248)	
Hayson, Stephen	4:26:03 (15,743)	
Hayter, Brian	6:12:44 (28,951)	
Hayter, Steven	4:17:41 (13,808)	
Hayton, David	3:19:26 (2,698)	
Hayward, Adrian	3:36:24 (5,140)	
Hayward, Alastair	4:48:22 (20,420)	
Hayward, Andrew	3:02:02 (1,154)	
Hayward, Anthony	4:23:07 (15,088)	
Hayward, Daniel	4:19:13 (14,165)	
Hayward, David	4:12:11 (12,669)	
Hayward, Jim	4:11:01 (12,402)	
Hayward, Martin	4:54:46 (21,665)	
Hayward, Neil	3:59:38 (9,960)	
Hayward, Neil	4:09:58 (12,156)	
Hayward, Peter	4:19:23 (14,220)	
Hayward, Philip	4:09:55 (12,143)	
Haywood, Anthony	5:01:57 (22,864)	
Haywood, Cliff	3:59:52 (10,016)	
Haywood, Dean	5:21:04 (25,475)	
Haywood, Jerry	3:47:17 (7,079)	
Haywood, Kevin	4:02:31 (10,576)	
Haywood, Nicholas	5:06:41 (23,575)	
Haywood, Richard	4:11:12 (12,440)	
Haza, Philippe	3:58:05 (9,509)	
Hazel, Anthony	3:21:48 (2,974)	
Hazell, Damon	5:32:37 (26,586)	
Hazell, Gary	5:12:11 (24,375)	
Hazell, Stephen	4:59:11 (22,486)	
Hazelton, David	4:01:14 (10,323)	
Hazlehurst, Mark	4:04:13 (10,933)	
Hazlett, Peter	4:39:07 (18,626)	
Head, George	6:52:10 (29,836)	
Head, Peter	5:12:36 (24,443)	
Head, Reece	4:20:05 (14,385)	
Head, Robert	3:54:42 (8,634)	
Heading, Jeremy	3:49:50 (7,651)	
Headly, Nick	6:12:55 (28,955)	
Headon, David	2:47:26 (349)	
Heal, Christopher	3:36:27 (5,151)	
Heal, David	4:46:39 (20,082)	
Heald, Andrew	4:37:30 (18,250)	
Heald, David	4:03:35 (10,797)	
Heale, Simon	3:32:22 (4,516)	
Heale, Stanley	4:01:28 (10,386)	
Healey, Philip	4:01:25 (10,373)	
Healy, Ken	6:26:17 (29,310)	
Healy, Lee	4:05:53 (11,317)	
Healy, Mark	2:33:31 (81)	
Heap, Carl	2:59:41 (996)	
Heap, John	2:27:41 (51)	
Heap, Simon	3:31:15 (4,365)	
Heaphy, Andrew	5:00:35 (22,675)	
Heapy, Christopher	3:50:31 (7,775)	
Hearle, Adrian	3:39:27 (5,665)	
Hearn, Andrew	5:03:16 (23,036)	
Hearn, Geoffrey	5:39:37 (27,148)	
Hearn, James	4:53:09 (21,346)	
Hearn, John	4:29:17 (16,493)	
Hearn, Martin	5:35:05 (26,812)	
Hearne, Clive	4:39:00 (18,603)	
Hearne, David	4:27:47 (16,147)	
Hearne, Keith	5:36:07 (26,888)	
Hearne, Stephen	6:15:04 (29,025)	
Heasman, Paul	3:20:59 (2,889)	
Heasman, Robert	3:23:57 (3,238)	
Heath, Charles	5:11:30 (24,285)	
Heath, David	3:39:21 (5,638)	
Heath, David	3:49:21 (7,538)	
Heath, David	4:05:45 (11,287)	
Heath, Frederick	4:03:28 (10,764)	
Heath, James	3:30:17 (4,211)	
Heath, Oliver	3:42:46 (6,265)	
Heath, Richard	4:35:29 (17,810)	
Heath, Roger	4:48:00 (20,345)	
Heath, Tony	3:43:57 (6,480)	

Heath, Tristan	3:28:06 (3,826)
Heathcote, Michael	3:21:33 (2,956)
Heather, David	6:03:55 (28,587)
Heathwood, Michael	3:16:56 (2,417)
Heaton, Andrew	3:18:06 (2,548)
Heaton, Andrew	4:51:20 (20,954)
Heaton, Ian	4:02:54 (10,645)
Heaton, Peter	4:06:28 (11,443)
Heaver, Michael	3:54:51 (8,672)
Heavey, Michael	4:32:42 (17,247)
Hebblewhite, Keith	5:22:03 (25,595)
Hebborn, Ian	4:31:42 (17,038)
Hebden, Matthew	4:29:24 (16,519)
Hebson, Simon	4:29:14 (16,482)
Heckert, Mark	4:22:53 (15,032)
Heckford, John	3:37:48 (5,378)
Heckford, Richard	3:29:31 (4,082)
Hector, Bryan	5:12:28 (24,424)
Hector, Ed	4:27:40 (16,107)
Hector, Lee	5:57:03 (28,272)
Heddon, Robin	5:46:23 (27,652)
Hedge, Peter	5:19:39 (25,323)
Hedgecock, Mark	3:49:37 (7,611)
Hedges, Andrew	3:28:18 (3,866)
Hedges, Clive	3:32:29 (4,532)
Hedges, Darren	4:40:05 (18,801)
Hedges, David	5:24:29 (25,834)
Hedges, Keith	3:39:44 (5,719)
Hedges, Michael	4:15:51 (13,434)
Hedigan, Philip	4:25:33 (15,629)
Hedley, Brian	3:18:16 (2,570)
Hedley, Don	5:00:23 (22,655)
Hedley, Mark	5:05:46 (23,427)
Hedley, Stephen	4:19:38 (14,291)
Hedmann, Lindsay	3:20:47 (2,862)
Heeks, Steve	3:24:16 (3,278)
Heffer, Vincent	4:51:02 (20,891)
Hefferman, Terry	3:40:29 (5,867)
Heffey, John	3:02:49 (1,202)
Heffron, Ian	9:06:12 (30,276)
Hegarty, Darren	3:59:08 (9,795)
Hegarty, Jack	3:33:38 (4,702)
Hegarty, Simon	5:08:12 (23,797)
Heggen, Leif	4:15:38 (13,393)
Hehir, Christopher	4:52:26 (21,191)
Hehir, Gerry	3:24:59 (3,375)
Heidler, K	4:31:20 (16,940)
Heighes, Alex	4:24:46 (15,452)
Heim, Ruediger	6:39:39 (29,620)
Heinrich, Anton	4:15:05 (13,287)
Heinrich, Nigel	6:01:28 (28,477)
Heinritz, Holger	4:13:24 (12,907)
Heiriss, Siegfried	4:35:01 (17,714)
Helbig, Wolfgang	3:11:31 (1,866)
Helcmanocki, Nicolas	4:36:23 (17,991)
Heley, Tobias	4:45:11 (19,804)
Helland, Jan Petter	4:13:09 (12,850)
Hellawell, Richard	4:51:33 (20,995)
Hellen, David	3:52:32 (8,179)
Hellesund, Dag	3:23:18 (3,149)
Hellings, Terry	3:05:39 (1,398)
Helliwell, Ian	4:12:28 (12,730)
Helliwell, Nick	4:52:01 (21,094)
Helliwell, Peter	3:54:47 (8,655)
Helly, Neal	4:07:00 (11,551)
Helm, Careth	6:40:09 (29,642)
Helm, David	6:40:08 (29,640)
Helm, Ian	5:16:18 (24,958)
Helm, Roger	3:42:16 (6,174)
Helme, Gerry	2:53:43 (570)
Helme, James	4:20:26 (14,460)
Helme, Tom	5:05:25 (23,363)
Helsby, Philip	4:13:06 (12,836)
Hemaz, Rachid	3:47:11 (7,062)
Hember, Simon	5:25:18 (25,920)
Hemingway, Graham	4:54:15 (21,555)
Hemingway, James	4:53:08 (21,343)
Hemingway, Steven	4:54:15 (21,555)
Hemming, Lance	2:49:50 (421)
Hemming, Norman	3:40:22 (5,843)
Hemmings, Andrew	2:42:53 (234)
Hemmings, Kenneth	3:11:00 (1,836)
Hemmings, Nicholas	5:55:27 (28,185)

Hems, Simon	5:02:55 (22,994)
Hender, Nick	3:16:16 (2,338)
Henderson, Bryan	4:37:17 (18,194)
Henderson, David	3:53:58 (8,471)
Henderson, Ian	4:48:17 (20,403)
Henderson, Jonathan	5:20:32 (25,412)
Henderson, Keith	5:49:38 (27,878)
Henderson, Marcus	4:39:21 (18,654)
Henderson, Mark	4:38:59 (18,600)
Henderson, Michael	3:45:30 (6,744)
Henderson, Stuart	2:58:18 (834)
Henderson, Stuart	3:21:58 (2,991)
Henderson, Stuart	4:37:17 (18,194)
Henderson, Tim	3:40:53 (5,924)
Henderson, Tony	4:11:34 (12,515)
Henderson, Vincent	4:48:19 (20,410)
Henderson, Wesley	4:49:56 (20,706)
Henderson, William	2:59:40 (992)
Henderson, William	5:30:13 (26,387)
Hendley, Darren	4:05:36 (11,241)
Hendrick, Peter	4:20:38 (14,507)
Hendry, Mark	4:18:12 (13,921)
Hendry, William	3:40:19 (5,832)
Hendry, William	5:53:10 (28,076)
Hendy, Malcolm	4:20:36 (14,500)
Heneghan, Dominic	5:30:06 (26,380)
Henke, Daniel	4:38:14 (18,437)
Hennebery, John	5:34:18 (26,736)
Hennegan, Peter	6:03:26 (28,561)
Hennes, Peter	3:57:38 (9,379)
Hennessey, Brian	2:43:40 (249)
Hennessey, Justin	3:34:28 (4,832)
Hennessy, Darren	4:12:09 (12,658)
Hennessy, Tony	6:44:28 (29,728)
Hennessy, William	5:01:20 (22,785)
Hennings, Peter	4:49:24 (20,598)
Hennis, Richard	5:37:33 (26,983)
Henriques, Roberto	4:39:01 (18,611)
Henry, Errol	5:06:33 (23,552)
Henry, Nigel	5:20:26 (25,402)
Henry, Paul	3:59:03 (9,773)
Henry, Simon	3:31:33 (4,402)
Hensey, Michael	4:10:08 (12,189)
Henshaw, Robert	3:13:58 (2,114)
Henson, David	4:35:33 (17,822)
Henson, Simon	3:39:46 (5,731)
Henson, Stuart	5:14:19 (24,676)
Henwood, Gary	3:08:06 (1,597)
Heppell, Andrew	4:52:32 (21,216)
Heppenstall, Peter	5:03:14 (23,034)
Heppenstall, Robert	3:34:26 (4,824)
Hepper, Alan	3:42:12 (6,164)
Hepworth, Ian	3:30:15 (4,205)
Herbert, Adam	3:47:52 (7,231)
Herbert, Alan	4:01:52 (10,455)
Herbert, Carl	4:07:44 (11,709)
Herbert, James	5:01:04 (22,741)
Herbert, John	4:34:11 (17,568)
Herbert, Neil	3:07:33 (1,549)
Herbert, Raymond	4:54:50 (21,687)
Herbert, Russell	4:57:37 (22,232)
Herbert, Spencer	4:26:46 (15,902)
Herbert, Stephen	3:41:45 (6,083)
Herbert, Stephen	3:52:16 (8,129)
Hercus, Mitchell	7:37:43 (30,156)
Herdman, Ian	4:29:22 (16,511)
Heritage, Robert	4:24:48 (15,459)
Herman, Christopher	3:40:55 (5,931)
Herman, David	5:19:40 (25,326)
Hermant, Olivier	2:56:43 (726)
Hern, John	4:35:33 (17,822)
Hernandez-Leon, Juan	3:29:13 (4,029)
Heron, Alex	3:21:10 (2,904)
Heron, Clinton	3:43:58 (6,483)
Herrero, Manuel	3:26:12 (3,523)
Herridge, Mark	3:53:28 (8,367)
Herriman, Ewen	4:08:13 (11,808)
Herring, Ray	3:19:11 (2,669)
Herring, Richard	4:22:14 (14,870)
Hersee, Peter	4:18:26 (13,998)
Herve, Patrice	4:47:11 (20,198)
Herzmark, Adrian	4:30:38 (16,775)
Hesketh, Alan	4:52:49 (21,273)

Hesketh, Benjamin	5:15:35 (24,876)
Hesketh, Peter	6:27:29 (29,341)
Hesling, Peter	4:52:47 (21,268)
Heslip, Charles	4:25:17 (15,572)
Heslop, David	3:01:32 (1,114)
Hesp, Robert	2:59:19 (964)
Hesse, Mark	5:07:16 (23,658)
Hester, Liam	3:19:27 (2,700)
Hester, Richard	4:14:15 (13,087)
Hetherington, Allan	2:57:00 (744)
Hetherington, Lee	3:58:16 (9,557)
Hetherington, Mark	5:40:31 (27,226)
Hetherington, Martin	4:53:03 (21,325)
Hewat, Nick	4:38:57 (18,594)
Heweler, Sanne	4:23:13 (15,112)
Hewer, Michael	4:54:52 (21,697)
Hewett, Simon	3:35:47 (5,029)
Hewison, Matt	4:49:14 (20,569)
Hewison, Mike	4:17:48 (13,832)
Hewitt, Christopher	4:11:31 (12,505)
Hewitt, Christopher	4:34:27 (17,618)
Hewitt, David	4:23:53 (15,269)
Hewitt, Dennis	6:04:27 (28,616)
Hewitt, Graham	4:00:33 (10,173)
Hewitt, Graham	4:43:52 (19,569)
Hewitt, Michael	4:00:32 (10,166)
Hewitt, Myles	5:37:25 (26,973)
Hewitt, Roger	3:55:38 (8,829)
Hewitt, Simon	3:36:15 (5,114)
Hewitt, Simon	4:04:04 (10,897)
Hewitt, Stephen	4:26:20 (15,812)
Hewitt, Steven	4:42:22 (19,241)
Hewlitt, Rob	3:46:50 (7,007)
Hext, Roger	5:39:38 (27,152)
Heyden, Andrew	2:59:06 (942)
Heyes, Andrew	4:42:39 (19,303)
Heyes, Keith	4:24:28 (15,388)
Heyhoe Flint, Ben	4:11:02 (12,407)
Heyler, Christopher	3:39:32 (5,680)
Heylings, Simon	5:04:21 (23,189)
Heyman, Lee	5:12:38 (24,450)
Heynes, Andrew	4:43:23 (19,462)
Heys, Geoffrey	5:17:49 (25,142)
Heyward, Daniel	3:25:17 (3,413)
Heyworth, Paul	3:52:37 (8,195)
Hibberd, Barry	3:53:59 (8,475)
Hibberd, Duncan	4:45:01 (19,777)
Hibberd, Roy	4:13:03 (12,830)
Hibbert, Adam	5:18:39 (25,229)
Hibbert, Adam	6:02:54 (28,534)
Hibbert, Grant	3:45:30 (6,744)
Hibbert, Malcolm	4:12:31 (12,743)
Hibbert, Paul	4:49:21 (20,588)
Hibbert, Paul	5:36:46 (26,930)
Hibbs, Richard	5:47:34 (27,730)
Hible, Raymond	3:41:30 (6,037)
Hible, Stephen	3:29:20 (4,053)
Hichens, Robert	4:50:46 (20,838)
Hick, Jonathan	5:50:06 (27,909)
Hick, Martin	5:14:32 (24,711)
Hickey, Barry	3:53:47 (8,439)
Hickey, David	3:51:47 (8,023)
Hickey, Patrick	3:28:57 (3,987)
Hickish, Angus	3:36:25 (5,144)
Hickish, Joseph	3:06:49 (1,489)
Hickish, Tamas	2:54:12 (587)
Hickles, Peter	3:38:27 (5,473)
Hickling, Gavin	4:23:26 (15,155)
Hickling, Graham	3:41:10 (5,979)
Hickling, Jeffrey	4:33:34 (17,443)
Hickling, Julian	4:19:21 (14,209)
Hicks, Alan	3:34:11 (4,784)
Hicks, Anthony	2:55:09 (634)
Hicks, Chris	3:51:53 (8,045)
Hicks, Jamie	5:02:40 (22,958)
Hicks, John	6:15:55 (29,056)
Hicks, Kevin	4:31:07 (16,876)
Hicks, Malcolm	5:42:31 (27,382)
Hicks, Michael	3:07:40 (1,563)
Hicks, Robert	4:02:26 (10,556)
Hicks, Stephen	3:01:23 (1,099)
Hicks, Thomas	4:02:44 (10,616)
Hicks, Timothy	3:06:35 (1,468)

Hickson, Paul 5:21:39 (25,541)
Hickson, Thomas 5:51:29 (27,982)
Hide, Philip 3:31:14 (4,360)
Hide, William 5:43:22 (27,430)
Hides, Nick 3:19:59 (2,767)
Hieber, Benedikt 2:49:37 (412)
Hier, Darrel 3:56:16 (8,986)
Hieri, Stergio 4:24:55 (15,482)
Hiesler, Rohan 5:06:45 (23,579)
Higashi, Sellchi 5:16:24 (24,973)
Higginbotham, John 5:03:44 (23,087)
Higgins, Bernard 3:38:46 (5,532)
Higgins, Christopher 3:59:21 (9,863)
Higgins, Darren 3:02:19 (1,176)
Higgins, Ian 4:20:46 (14,539)
Higgins, Richard 5:50:16 (27,917)
Higgins, Shaun 3:51:36 (7,990)
Higgins, Simon 5:16:09 (24,943)
Higgins, Thomas 4:46:16 (20,002)
Higgins, William 5:11:34 (24,298)
Higginson, Guy 5:12:59 (24,497)
Higginson, Jeremy 4:01:00 (10,280)
Higgitt, Martin 4:20:20 (14,437)
Higgs, Bobbi 4:23:35 (15,201)
Higgs, David 3:23:27 (3,168)
Higgs, Mark 3:20:07 (2,775)
Higgs, Simon 5:27:10 (26,097)
Higham, Duncan 4:09:08 (12,007)
Higham, Richard 4:50:00 (20,720)
Higham, Roland 5:07:08 (23,638)
Highton, Mark 4:04:46 (11,062)
Higley, Steven 4:02:01 (10,489)
Higson, Rennie 3:36:40 (5,184)
Higson, Toby 4:41:13 (19,015)
Hilary, David 3:51:38 (7,993)
Hilborne, Mike 3:59:17 (9,837)
Hildesley, Simon 3:48:58 (7,458)
Hilditch, Jonathan 4:06:44 (11,492)
Hilditch, Steven 2:55:34 (658)
Hildyard, Michael 3:41:36 (6,054)
Hiles, Colin 4:42:49 (19,336)
Hill, Alistair 4:15:51 (13,434)
Hill, Andrew 3:50:26 (7,761)
Hill, Anthony 3:50:22 (7,751)
Hill, Antony 3:01:38 (1,127)
Hill, Brian 5:46:34 (27,667)
Hill, Christopher 3:33:16 (4,656)
Hill, Christopher 4:38:55 (18,589)
Hill, Christopher 4:46:05 (19,954)
Hill, Christopher 4:46:07 (19,964)
Hill, Daniel 3:28:05 (3,816)
Hill, Doug 4:01:20 (10,348)
Hill, Duncan 3:44:52 (6,653)
Hill, Edward 3:26:46 (3,592)
Hill, Fraser 3:24:29 (3,307)
Hill, Gareth 4:04:57 (11,106)
Hill, Gavin 3:18:16 (2,570)
Hill, Ian 3:18:06 (2,548)
Hill, James 3:39:41 (5,709)
Hill, Jason 3:23:42 (3,197)
Hill, Jason 3:42:53 (6,283)
Hill, John 4:16:30 (13,573)
Hill, John 5:40:32 (27,227)
Hill, Justin 3:33:53 (4,737)
Hill, Leslie 2:51:05 (470)
Hill, Leslie 3:26:18 (3,536)
Hill, Malcolm 6:37:16 (29,567)
Hill, Mark 3:44:30 (6,576)
Hill, Mark 4:01:19 (10,342)
Hill, Martin 4:12:12 (12,672)
Hill, Martin 4:38:10 (18,421)
Hill, Michael 3:35:06 (4,919)
Hill, Michael 3:43:34 (6,408)
Hill, Peter 2:56:09 (697)
Hill, Peter 5:15:02 (24,786)
Hill, Raymond 2:50:25 (445)
Hill, Raymond 3:53:18 (8,333)
Hill, Richard 4:17:54 (13,851)
Hill, Richard 5:08:49 (23,910)
Hill, Robert 4:05:01 (11,121)
Hill, Robert 5:16:41 (25,011)
Hill, Roger 3:27:39 (3,732)
Hill, Roger 3:31:36 (4,411)
Hill, Simon 3:46:07 (6,881)
Hill, Simon 5:12:16 (24,391)
Hill, Stephen 5:56:22 (28,231)
Hill, Steven 4:59:51 (22,588)
Hill, Tim 4:11:39 (12,535)
Hill, Tim 4:18:18 (13,953)
Hill, Timothy 4:35:33 (17,822)
Hill, Tony 4:57:44 (22,253)
Hill, Walter 2:44:04 (262)
Hillary, Andrew 4:33:31 (17,423)
Hillary, Ian 5:36:05 (26,886)
Hillebrandt, Rodney 3:15:52 (2,305)
Hiller, Christoph 3:41:37 (6,059)
Hillestad, Kjetil 2:41:19 (198)
Hilliar, Darryl 2:55:43 (663)
Hilliard, David 4:42:25 (19,255)
Hillier, Jeffery 5:45:41 (27,607)
Hillier, Joe 3:46:33 (6,960)
Hillman, John 4:51:35 (21,007)
Hillman, Mark 5:01:06 (22,748)
Hills, Chris 4:27:03 (15,981)
Hills, David 4:48:54 (20,503)
Hills, David 5:09:12 (23,970)
Hills, Gerald 3:56:41 (9,101)
Hills, Mike 5:34:54 (26,798)
Hills, Paul 3:52:03 (8,085)
Hillsley, Glen 3:49:10 (7,489)
Hilmi, Mahmut 4:12:09 (12,658)
Hilton, Chris 3:46:00 (6,856)
Hilton, Clifford 4:19:00 (14,115)
Hilton, Michael 5:45:22 (27,581)
Hilton, Peter 6:01:04 (28,458)
Hilton, Stephen 2:51:06 (471)
Hilton, Stephen 2:56:48 (733)
Himmelbauer, Manfred 4:17:47 (13,829)
Hinchelwood, Richard 6:04:57 (28,641)
Hinchliffe, Robert 3:48:24 (7,338)
Hinckson, Stephon 4:59:50 (22,581)
Hinde, Martin 4:38:13 (18,431)
Hindell, James 3:58:51 (9,713)
Hinderling, Georg 3:31:01 (4,331)
Hindle, Adrian 4:31:09 (16,888)
Hindlet, Alan 4:55:22 (21,837)
Hindmarch, Arthur 4:58:25 (22,362)
Hindmarch, Stuart 3:24:20 (3,288)
Hindmarsh, Carl 5:20:59 (25,466)
Hine, Christopher 3:33:10 (4,636)
Hine, David 3:16:58 (2,420)
Hine, Gregory 5:24:15 (25,812)
Hine, John 2:56:17 (707)
Hines, Kevin 3:34:17 (4,798)
Hinton, Alexander 4:10:09 (12,194)
Hinton, Geofrey 3:52:10 (8,111)
Hinton, Lee 4:13:08 (12,845)
Hintzen, Lodewyk 4:19:31 (14,260)
Hinz, Harald 3:55:06 (8,713)
Hipkin, Laurence 4:57:13 (22,173)
Hipkin, Richard 3:53:59 (8,475)
Hipsley, Stephen 4:39:38 (18,724)
Hirani, Surendra 5:35:38 (26,855)
Hirano, Yukio 3:52:08 (8,104)
Hird, Frank 2:58:42 (891)
Hird, Ian 3:47:52 (7,231)
Hirn, Joseph 5:06:38 (23,567)
Hiron, Michael 5:12:11 (24,375)
Hirota, Naoto 4:15:36 (13,387)
Hirsch, Glyn 3:25:05 (3,387)
Hirsig, Bernhard 3:59:47 (9,992)
Hirst, Chris 3:49:53 (7,664)
Hirst, Clayton 4:49:23 (20,592)
Hirst, David 3:59:00 (9,754)
Hirst, John 4:59:53 (22,597)
Hirst, John 5:14:15 (24,668)
Hirst, Matthew 4:26:57 (15,950)
Hirst, Mervyn 3:28:22 (3,885)
Hirst, Philip 4:08:54 (11,956)
Hirst, Robert 2:45:19 (301)
Hirst, Robert 3:42:06 (6,137)
Hirst, Stephen 4:09:00 (11,978)
Hiscock, Martin 4:15:14 (13,319)
Hiscock, Ron 5:03:42 (23,081)
Hiscocks, Tom 4:44:06 (19,597)
Hiscox, John 3:20:26 (2,811)
Hisirlioglu, Ertugrul 3:40:35 (5,883)
Hislop, Alexander 5:13:56 (24,622)
Hislop, Tim 4:30:14 (16,721)
Hita-Hita, Luis 3:15:09 (2,239)
Hitchcroft, Nicholas 5:14:56 (24,767)
Hitchens, Christopher 4:04:52 (11,081)
Hoare, Andrew 4:36:32 (18,026)
Hoare, Chris 6:34:24 (29,510)
Hoare, Ian 3:50:28 (7,767)
Hoare, Jerry 4:52:42 (21,251)
Hoare, Peter 4:17:07 (13,692)
Hoare, Ronald 4:16:39 (13,599)
Hoare, Steven 4:25:31 (15,622)
Hoate, Simon 4:10:34 (12,289)
Hoban, Martin 3:36:36 (5,169)
Hoban, Michael 5:53:58 (28,112)
Hobbs, Antony 4:04:40 (11,036)
Hobbs, Bernard 3:21:13 (2,906)
Hobbs, Graham 3:23:15 (3,142)
Hobbs, Ian 4:18:40 (14,044)
Hobbs, John 3:23:36 (3,185)
Hobbs, Robert 3:18:22 (2,585)
Hobbs, Roland 3:26:02 (3,503)
Hobbs, Stephen 3:39:48 (5,739)
Hobby, Stephen 5:55:31 (28,192)
Hobday, Michael 3:22:32 (3,056)
Hobden, David 4:08:06 (11,785)
Hobden, Greg 3:29:55 (4,155)
Hobden, Tim 4:28:33 (16,326)
Hobley, Andrew 5:03:16 (23,036)
Hochman, Jeffrey 3:13:25 (2,054)
Hockett, Michael 5:08:36 (23,869)
Hockey, Jason 4:43:12 (19,427)
Hocking, Martin 4:58:12 (22,328)
Hocking, Robert 4:37:45 (18,313)
Hocking, Zack 4:02:57 (10,656)
Hockley, Ryan 4:21:19 (14,651)
Hoda, Feroz 3:32:04 (4,475)
Hoddell, David 2:58:43 (894)
Hodder, Mark 4:04:15 (10,939)
Hodell, Phillip 3:07:13 (1,518)
Hodge, Anthony 3:56:36 (9,077)
Hodge, Ian 3:38:23 (5,462)
Hodge, Johnathan 3:55:47 (8,867)
Hodge, Paul 4:24:50 (15,464)
Hodge, Paul 4:28:29 (16,310)
Hodge, Steven 4:33:49 (17,503)
Hodge, Tony 3:15:05 (2,232)
Hodges, Anthony 4:11:24 (12,481)
Hodges, Darren 4:10:47 (12,332)
Hodges, Frederick 4:14:16 (13,092)
Hodges, Michael 4:26:00 (15,730)
Hodges, Nicholas 2:49:48 (418)
Hodges, Paul 5:32:59 (26,611)
Hodges, Peter 4:15:35 (13,385)
Hodgetts, Peter 3:48:21 (7,331)
Hodgetts, Stephen 3:18:53 (2,641)
Hodgins, Steven 4:04:29 (10,983)
Hodgkin, Christopher 3:16:02 (2,324)
Hodgkin, Neil 4:30:24 (16,743)
Hodgkins, Richard 4:59:45 (22,562)
Hodgkinson, Mark 3:29:01 (4,001)
Hodgkinson, Michael 5:27:08 (26,094)
Hodgkinson, Simon 3:59:38 (9,960)
Hodgkinson, Stephen 5:26:15 (26,013)
Hodgson, Alton 5:06:04 (23,480)
Hodgson, Andrew 3:35:37 (5,005)
Hodgson, David 3:40:11 (5,814)
Hodgson, David 4:09:26 (12,070)
Hodgson, Keith 5:42:40 (27,392)
Hodgson, Kevin 4:35:36 (17,843)
Hodgson, Michael 3:49:32 (7,591)
Hodgson, Paul 4:19:30 (14,255)
Hodgson, Paul 4:27:31 (16,063)
Hodgson, Paul 4:32:12 (17,155)
Hodgson, Richard 4:21:09 (14,616)
Hodgson, Timothy 4:30:42 (16,786)
Hodgson, Tony 3:23:11 (3,135)
Hodsdon, Trevor 4:02:20 (10,535)
Hodsoll, Mark 3:45:52 (6,836)
Hodson, Alan 6:23:19 (29,237)
Hodson, Richard 3:58:03 (9,501)
Hodson, Thomas 5:11:22 (24,266)

Hodson, Tony	7:17:40 (30,064)	
Hoefle, Wolfgang	4:21:07 (14,613)	
Hoffman, Nicholas	4:58:51 (22,434)	
Hoffmann, Bernard	2:53:11 (551)	
Hoffmann, Jonathan	6:10:32 (28,879)	
Hofmeyr, Philip	3:39:45 (5,725)	
Hofwolt, Daryl	4:33:44 (17,485)	
Hogan, David	6:00:38 (28,436)	
Hogan, Gary	5:56:51 (28,263)	
Hogan, James	5:22:25 (25,638)	
Hogan, James	6:33:35 (29,497)	
Hogan, Noel	2:58:39 (881)	
Hogben, Simon	5:18:29 (25,212)	
Hogbin, Darren	4:12:03 (12,630)	
Hogg, Graham	4:20:23 (14,447)	
Hogg, Jonathan	4:20:58 (14,584)	
Hogg, Matthew	5:22:35 (25,657)	
Hogg, Robert	3:38:11 (5,425)	
Hoggard, Mark	5:06:45 (23,579)	
Hoggett, Paul	4:38:26 (18,488)	
Hoglund, Greger	5:16:09 (24,943)	
Hogman, Timothy	4:22:56 (15,048)	
Hogwood, Roger	3:46:19 (6,919)	
Hoier, Kim	3:57:26 (9,304)	
Hoiman, Lee	4:19:55 (14,343)	
Hoker, Michael	3:53:40 (8,416)	
Holbeche, Neil	4:02:06 (10,503)	
Holbrook, Ben	4:59:57 (22,613)	
Holbrook, Graham	5:40:17 (27,206)	
Holbrook, Gregory	3:47:52 (7,231)	
Holbrook, John	3:33:39 (4,705)	
Holbrook, Philip	3:57:47 (9,425)	
Holcher, Jean	3:59:08 (9,795)	
Holcroft, Allan	4:19:13 (14,165)	
Holdaway, Keith	4:06:31 (11,454)	
Holden, David	4:21:52 (14,779)	
Holden, Frank	5:41:39 (27,306)	
Holden, Kevin	5:43:57 (27,471)	
Holden, Maurice	4:33:59 (17,532)	
Holden, Michael	3:38:32 (5,487)	
Holden, Peter	4:00:29 (10,148)	
Holden, Philip	4:08:08 (11,790)	
Holden, Richard	5:19:05 (25,274)	
Holden, Simon	3:29:40 (4,115)	
Holden, Stephen	3:31:45 (4,428)	
Holden, Tim	3:46:16 (6,910)	
Holder, Allen	4:55:15 (21,798)	
Holder, Andrew	4:22:13 (14,865)	
Holder, Graham	3:37:22 (5,317)	
Holder, John	3:42:43 (6,256)	
Holder, Philip	3:55:44 (8,854)	
Holder, Sam	3:59:12 (9,815)	
Holdich, Brian	7:32:22 (30,143)	
Holding, Neil	2:57:20 (768)	
Holding, Simon	3:58:30 (9,604)	
Holdsworth, John	5:03:55 (23,119)	
Holdsworth, Mark	5:26:06 (25,996)	
Holdway, John	3:38:52 (5,552)	
Hole, Laurie	5:22:07 (25,600)	
Holgate, James	4:12:24 (12,714)	
Holgate, John	4:12:25 (12,719)	
Holgate, Paul	3:47:12 (7,064)	
Holgate, Robin	4:22:57 (15,052)	
Holguin, Henry	4:13:02 (12,829)	
Holl, James	3:49:56 (7,671)	
Holladay, Rob	2:19:26 (20)	
Holland, Ashley	4:31:19 (16,938)	
Holland, Craig	3:42:15 (6,171)	
Holland, Ian	3:39:33 (5,684)	
Holland, Ian	3:54:09 (8,502)	
Holland, James	5:01:33 (22,811)	
Holland, John	4:49:53 (20,691)	
Holland, Jonathan	5:14:32 (24,711)	
Holland, Michael	4:18:27 (14,002)	
Holland, Morton	3:56:29 (9,050)	
Holland, Neil	4:17:25 (13,753)	
Holland, Peter	4:07:15 (11,600)	
Holland, Robert	4:35:44 (17,872)	
Holland, Simon	4:31:16 (16,922)	
Holland, Steven	4:00:47 (10,238)	
Holland, William	4:18:07 (13,892)	
Holle, Wilhelm	4:07:00 (11,551)	
Hollenstein, Roger	5:29:19 (26,322)	
Holleron, Dominic	4:26:49 (15,913)	
Holliday, Brian	4:52:39 (21,243)	
Holliday, Neil	4:01:30 (10,396)	
Holliday, Simon	5:44:43 (27,540)	
Hollingsworth, David	5:58:25 (28,344)	
Hollinshead, Steven	3:29:59 (4,168)	
Hollis, Ashley	2:54:14 (589)	
Hollis, Iain	4:39:09 (18,628)	
Hollis, James	3:50:20 (7,741)	
Hollis, Paul	5:29:54 (26,368)	
Hollister, Mark	3:47:20 (7,097)	
Hollodick, George	3:28:52 (3,975)	
Holloway, Jason	4:15:03 (13,278)	
Holloway, John	6:32:51 (29,474)	
Holloway, Richard	3:20:45 (2,857)	
Holloway, Stephen	4:49:40 (20,645)	
Holloway, Vernon	4:50:12 (20,754)	
Hollyoak, Michael	5:02:22 (22,925)	
Hollyoak, William	4:24:19 (15,352)	
Holman, Bob	4:11:28 (12,495)	
Holman, Michael	3:38:34 (5,491)	
Holman, Timothy	5:06:02 (23,473)	
Holmans, Michael	3:50:22 (7,751)	
Holmes, Adrian	4:59:19 (22,500)	
Holmes, Andrew	5:31:23 (26,482)	
Holmes, Barry	5:04:49 (23,268)	
Holmes, Bernard	4:19:40 (14,297)	
Holmes, Darren	4:31:16 (16,922)	
Holmes, David	3:22:40 (3,068)	
Holmes, David	4:24:05 (15,307)	
Holmes, Francis	2:58:47 (906)	
Holmes, Graham	3:30:56 (4,320)	
Holmes, John	3:38:18 (5,449)	
Holmes, John	4:21:04 (14,606)	
Holmes, John	5:24:59 (25,884)	
Holmes, John Andrew	4:37:33 (18,264)	
Holmes, Kenneth	3:41:23 (6,026)	
Holmes, Lawrie	4:27:02 (15,975)	
Holmes, Mark	4:16:13 (13,511)	
Holmes, Melvyn	3:40:05 (5,797)	
Holmes, Michael	4:11:34 (12,515)	
Holmes, Mike	2:35:44 (101)	
Holmes, Neil	4:30:06 (16,708)	
Holmes, Peter	4:53:49 (21,480)	
Holmes, Philip	4:25:17 (15,572)	
Holmes, Richard	3:14:24 (2,158)	
Holmes, Richard	4:27:36 (16,090)	
Holmes, Robert	4:04:49 (11,070)	
Holmes, Stanley	5:17:55 (25,150)	
Holmes, Stephen	4:21:28 (14,685)	
Holmes, Thomas	3:38:06 (5,414)	
Holmquist, Edwin	3:34:19 (4,804)	
Holohan, James	4:04:30 (10,988)	
Holohan, Ruairl	4:11:12 (12,440)	
Holroyd, Alan	4:15:15 (13,324)	
Holroyd, Thomas	5:18:58 (25,264)	
Holsgrove, Paul	4:42:06 (19,178)	
Holt, Alan	3:40:20 (5,836)	
Holt, Christopher	5:41:32 (27,301)	
Holt, Darrel	4:29:09 (16,463)	
Holt, Graham	3:16:30 (2,367)	
Holt, Keith	2:49:22 (405)	
Holt, Neil	4:16:28 (13,566)	
Holt, Nicholas	4:33:39 (17,469)	
Holt, Paul	3:52:57 (8,257)	
Holt, Roy	4:27:00 (15,964)	
Holt, Simon	3:44:25 (6,563)	
Holt, Tim	4:57:44 (22,253)	
Holt, Tony	3:27:59 (3,803)	
Holtaway, Benjamin	4:00:33 (10,173)	
Holton, Frank	4:26:47 (15,906)	
Holton, Kevin	3:46:07 (6,881)	
Holtzhausen, Stuart	3:45:38 (6,776)	
Holyhead, Kevin	4:57:23 (22,202)	
Holyneaux, Ryan	4:23:13 (15,112)	
Holzinger, Erik	3:59:22 (9,869)	
Homa, Peter	4:35:33 (17,822)	
Homden, Damien	5:12:21 (24,403)	
Homer, Anthony	3:26:51 (3,602)	
Homes, Andrew	5:12:27 (24,421)	
Homewood, Stephen	4:46:23 (20,031)	
Homfray, Russell	4:15:11 (13,299)	
Homouda, Mohammad	4:22:49 (15,012)	
Hone, Andrew	4:44:42 (19,718)	
Honeywood, Lee	4:22:13 (14,865)	
Honor, Chris	4:22:00 (14,813)	
Honore, Antoine	4:19:57 (14,353)	
Honorio, François	3:05:00 (1,350)	
Honour, Mark	4:31:43 (17,041)	
Hood, Andrew	3:50:49 (7,825)	
Hood, Christopher	4:33:32 (17,428)	
Hood, Gordon	4:47:26 (20,248)	
Hood, James	5:01:58 (22,866)	
Hood, Mike	3:15:43 (2,291)	
Hood, Robin	7:29:57 (30,137)	
Hood, Scott	4:43:05 (19,400)	
Hoogervorst, Piet	4:47:19 (20,223)	
Hoogeveen, Johannes	3:35:23 (4,967)	
Hook, Adrian	5:04:39 (23,240)	
Hook, David	3:23:58 (3,241)	
Hook, James	4:54:56 (21,713)	
Hook, Steven	4:33:34 (17,443)	
Hook, Trevor	2:57:39 (788)	
Hooke, Andrew	3:37:03 (5,254)	
Hooker, Bob	3:49:23 (7,548)	
Hooker, Gary	4:37:09 (18,158)	
Hooker, Kevin	3:52:06 (8,097)	
Hoole, John	3:59:45 (9,988)	
Hoole, Peter	6:16:38 (29,076)	
Hooper, Barry	5:39:56 (27,185)	
Hooper, Graham	4:12:04 (12,633)	
Hooper, Martin	4:07:00 (11,551)	
Hooper, Patrick	4:25:26 (15,599)	
Hooper, Peter	3:45:40 (6,785)	
Hooper, Philip	3:07:32 (1,548)	
Hooper, Simon	3:14:37 (2,175)	
Hooton, Chris	5:16:01 (24,928)	
Hooton, Michael	4:23:33 (15,189)	
Hoover, Roderick	4:01:48 (10,444)	
Hopcraft, Andrew	4:25:49 (15,679)	
Hope, David	4:10:49 (12,350)	
Hope, Gary	4:58:00 (22,295)	
Hope, Geoffrey	4:58:29 (22,374)	
Hope, Lee	3:18:53 (2,641)	
Hope, Lee	6:14:18 (29,000)	
Hope, Mark	3:24:42 (3,342)	
Hope, Richard	4:46:02 (19,945)	
Hope, Robert	4:19:28 (14,249)	
Hopegood, James	4:31:32 (16,985)	
Hope-Hawkins, Rupert	4:59:38 (22,544)	
Hopes, John	4:06:28 (11,443)	
Hopgood, Martin	4:17:48 (13,832)	
Hopgood, Peter	5:05:49 (23,433)	
Hopkins, Andrew	4:54:33 (21,604)	
Hopkins, David	4:56:32 (22,074)	
Hopkins, Karl	3:30:55 (4,317)	
Hopkins, Mick	4:28:10 (16,228)	
Hopkins, Nigel	5:21:57 (25,579)	
Hopkins, Paul	4:01:44 (10,434)	
Hopkins, Rodney	4:48:25 (20,429)	
Hopkins, Simon	4:16:00 (13,463)	
Hopkinson, Matthew	3:48:29 (7,357)	
Hopley, Peter	3:13:11 (2,023)	
Hopper, Andrew	4:54:33 (21,604)	
Hopperton, Edward	3:29:22 (4,061)	
Hopperton, James	4:15:45 (13,414)	
Hopson, Bernard	4:47:05 (20,183)	
Hopwood, Duncan	3:24:19 (3,284)	
Horan, Tim	4:37:18 (18,197)	
Horbury, Julian	3:39:56 (5,768)	
Hore, Morgan	3:43:37 (6,418)	
Horgan, James	4:27:46 (16,140)	
Horgan, Michael	4:27:12 (16,011)	
Hori, Eijior	4:13:14 (12,861)	
Horler, David	4:35:02 (17,717)	
Horn, Gavin	5:30:26 (26,406)	
Horn, Maurice	5:56:30 (28,242)	
Horn, Roger	3:23:31 (3,178)	
Horn, Steven	4:27:31 (16,063)	
Hornbrook, Charles	4:12:46 (12,784)	
Hornby, Keith	4:45:03 (19,780)	
Hornby, Philip	4:17:50 (13,840)	
Horne, Christopher	4:35:38 (17,849)	
Horne, David	3:18:38 (2,614)	
Horne, Matthew	3:27:05 (3,633)	
Horne, Tom	4:11:07 (12,421)	

Horner, Ben 3:58:38 (9,649)
Horner, David 4:20:43 (14,524)
Horner, Ian 4:33:46 (17,492)
Horner, Michael 3:11:47 (1,896)
Horner, Victor 7:24:00 (30,101)
Hornsby, Richard 5:59:45 (28,406)
Hornsey, Richard 5:49:41 (27,881)
Hornsey, Robert 3:05:51 (1,411)
Horreau, Nick 5:24:21 (25,820)
Horrell, Tom 5:28:13 (26,199)
Horrocks, David 3:19:44 (2,733)
Horrocks, Paul 5:01:11 (22,763)
Horsell, Edwin 4:09:09 (12,012)
Horsfall, Brian 3:24:20 (3,288)
Horsfall, Mark 3:59:06 (9,786)
Horsfall, Mark 4:10:30 (12,275)
Horsfall, Michael 4:48:37 (20,456)
Horsfield, Christopher 4:18:11 (13,914)
Horsley, Simon 3:23:42 (3,197)
Horsman, Joseph 3:50:37 (7,792)
Horsman, Neil 3:30:22 (4,226)
Horsman, Stephen 4:49:02 (20,534)
Horsnell, Richard 5:22:49 (25,686)
Horst, Robert 4:18:18 (13,953)
Horsthuis, Peter 3:59:53 (10,024)
Horswell, Stuart 4:46:10 (19,977)
Horton, Andrew 4:21:27 (14,682)
Horton, David 4:16:09 (13,496)
Horton, John 3:21:23 (2,932)
Horton, Martyn 3:59:28 (9,909)
Horton, Peter 3:03:30 (1,245)
Horton, Richard 3:40:54 (5,926)
Horton, Robert 3:46:04 (6,869)
Horton, Robert 4:55:45 (21,950)
Horwick, Pius 3:02:40 (1,194)
Horwood, James 4:06:08 (11,366)
Horwood, Mike 3:19:55 (2,761)
Hosein, Colin 5:01:00 (22,734)
Hosemann, Paul 3:55:57 (8,906)
Hoskin, Paul 6:01:08 (28,462)
Hoskins, Ian 4:13:08 (12,845)
Hoskins, Jean-Paul 3:29:05 (4,011)
Hoskins, Mark 3:57:18 (9,258)
Hoskins, Stephen 4:25:33 (15,629)
Hoskyn, John 4:56:18 (22,036)
Hossack, Robert 5:28:46 (26,264)
Hossain, Saad 3:04:35 (1,321)
Hostetler, Thomas 3:29:38 (4,106)
Hostler, Thomas 4:34:17 (17,591)
Hothersall, Christopher 4:11:37 (12,528)
Hough, Anthony 3:32:55 (4,588)
Hough, Barry 4:36:26 (18,003)
Hough, Derek 4:42:34 (19,284)
Hough, Keith 3:57:11 (9,219)
Hough, Richard 3:48:02 (7,271)
Hough, Stpehen 5:56:19 (28,227)
Hougham, Gary 4:13:30 (12,932)
Houghton, David 4:23:48 (15,250)
Houghton, Greg 4:45:59 (19,934)
Houghton, James 4:34:12 (17,570)
Houghton, Malcolm 4:49:57 (20,708)
Houghton, Michael 3:36:38 (5,177)
Houghton, Michael 4:39:06 (18,622)
Houghton, Philip 4:25:32 (15,625)
Houghton, Toby 3:23:54 (3,230)
Houlder, Peter 4:38:48 (18,576)
Houlot, Geoffrey 3:51:01 (7,877)
Hoult, Kevin 3:35:05 (4,914)
Hoult, Robert 4:24:24 (15,370)
Houlton, David 3:43:45 (6,449)
Hourigan, Keith 5:08:07 (23,787)
Houriham, Mark 4:33:38 (17,464)
Housden, Stephen 3:50:31 (7,775)
House, Paul 4:32:57 (17,301)
Houseman, Christopher 4:06:23 (11,427)
Housley, Philip 3:45:00 (6,688)
Houston, Edward 4:23:51 (15,261)
How, David 4:01:00 (10,280)
How, Ned 3:11:16 (1,859)
Howard, Andrew 4:58:24 (22,361)
Howard, Chris 6:51:46 (29,827)
Howard, Clive 4:22:18 (14,886)
Howard, Colin 4:06:33 (11,459)
Howard, David 4:35:01 (17,714)
Howard, David 4:40:51 (18,946)
Howard, Gavin 4:52:42 (21,251)
Howard, Glenn 4:25:51 (15,688)
Howard, Ivor 2:59:04 (939)
Howard, Jeremy 3:28:28 (3,903)
Howard, Jonathan 4:08:23 (11,846)
Howard, Kevin 4:28:58 (16,414)
Howard, Mark 4:47:44 (20,300)
Howard, Neil 6:43:09 (29,710)
Howard, Paul 4:15:33 (13,377)
Howard, Paul 5:06:17 (23,517)
Howard, Philip 3:20:03 (2,770)
Howard, Philip 3:56:29 (9,050)
Howard, Richard 4:03:25 (10,752)
Howard, Robert 4:39:07 (18,626)
Howard, Robin 4:24:28 (15,388)
Howard, Stephen 3:23:42 (3,197)
Howard, Stuart 4:20:39 (14,510)
Howard, Stuart 4:54:32 (21,602)
Howard, William 4:47:51 (20,316)
Howarth, Ben 3:49:36 (7,608)
Howarth, Ian 6:01:53 (28,501)
Howarth, Lance 3:12:32 (1,962)
Howarth, Lee 4:18:18 (13,953)
Howarth, Martin 4:31:18 (16,934)
Howarth, Peter 3:48:09 (7,294)
Howarth, Philip 3:34:25 (4,820)
Howarth, Philip 4:13:24 (12,907)
Howarth, Raymond 3:13:58 (2,114)
Howe, Andrew 3:22:43 (3,073)
Howe, Andrew 3:33:44 (4,719)
Howe, Gary 2:58:53 (923)
Howe, Jacob 3:03:56 (1,279)
Howe, Mark 4:26:33 (15,856)
Howe, Philip 6:25:16 (29,291)
Howe, Robert 3:24:31 (3,312)
Howe, Robert 4:13:37 (12,961)
Howe, Steven 5:23:52 (25,777)
Howell, Adam 4:47:25 (20,246)
Howell, Barrie 3:18:16 (2,570)
Howell, Christopher 5:53:02 (28,064)
Howell, James 3:46:41 (6,987)
Howell, Richard 3:37:03 (5,254)
Howell, Richard 6:33:36 (29,498)
Howell, Scott 3:10:39 (1,805)
Howell, Tom 4:26:51 (15,920)
Howells, Adrian 5:27:46 (26,154)
Howells, Christopher 4:29:20 (16,504)
Howells, David 4:03:57 (10,873)
Howells, Denis 4:24:08 (15,316)
Howells, Donald 4:42:49 (19,336)
Howells, Gareth 4:47:04 (20,177)
Howells, Malcolm 3:10:19 (1,777)
Howells, Michael 6:10:00 (28,860)
Howells, Trevor 3:36:42 (5,191)
Howes, Greg 3:30:57 (4,322)
Howes, Robert 4:28:50 (16,386)
Howes, Stuart 4:38:49 (18,578)
Howes, Toby 4:11:58 (12,600)
Howes, William 3:07:29 (1,541)
Howett, Ian 3:36:17 (5,121)
Howett, Tim 4:21:54 (14,786)
Howgego, Chris 5:22:01 (25,588)
Howick, Laurence 4:00:53 (10,259)
Howkins, Alex 5:11:08 (24,232)
Howland, Anthony 5:04:51 (23,276)
Howles, Damon 4:44:50 (19,738)
Howlett, James 6:03:50 (28,584)
Howlett, John 4:49:49 (20,678)
Howlett, Timothy 3:45:10 (6,705)
Howley, David 4:31:08 (16,883)
Howling, Steve 3:35:23 (4,967)
Howse, Ian 4:28:16 (16,256)
Howse, Jimmy 3:06:36 (1,470)
Hoy, David 3:17:16 (2,455)
Hoy, David 5:17:21 (25,088)
Hoy, Paul 5:06:11 (23,497)
Hoyet, Christian 4:37:11 (18,167)
Hoyle, Raymond 5:08:29 (23,844)
Hoyle, Sean 4:58:46 (22,423)
Hpkins, Peter 4:47:26 (20,248)
Hrynczak, Stephen 4:26:53 (15,932)
Huband, David 3:11:59 (1,913)
Hubbard, John 3:44:14 (6,529)
Hubbard, Philip 3:36:59 (5,241)
Hubbard, Tony 4:10:48 (12,341)
Hubber, Eric 3:50:10 (7,717)
Hubber, Steve 5:55:25 (28,181)
Hubble, David 6:17:29 (29,100)
Huber, Rudolf 3:28:12 (3,844)
Huchon, Chris 7:13:50 (30,044)
Huchon, Patrick 3:42:28 (6,211)
Huck, Dave 2:57:21 (771)
Huck, Ernest 3:19:55 (2,761)
Huckell, Nicolas 5:27:59 (26,178)
Hucker, Kevin 3:13:45 (2,084)
Hucker, Martin 4:28:09 (16,221)
Hucker, Peter 5:55:13 (28,165)
Huckerby, Darren 5:21:48 (25,566)
Huddart, Andrew 3:59:34 (9,940)
Huddlestone, Paul 3:22:05 (3,011)
Hudson, Alan 2:58:49 (912)
Hudson, Andrew 3:22:26 (3,048)
Hudson, Andrew 4:29:52 (16,648)
Hudson, Ben 3:26:29 (3,557)
Hudson, David 4:10:24 (12,255)
Hudson, David 4:11:08 (12,423)
Hudson, Dean 3:52:11 (8,114)
Hudson, Ernest 4:02:24 (10,553)
Hudson, Gary 3:34:35 (4,847)
Hudson, Graham 3:43:06 (6,326)
Hudson, Jason 3:50:05 (7,704)
Hudson, Jeremy 5:06:46 (23,582)
Hudson, Jonathan 4:15:04 (13,282)
Hudson, Jonathan 4:34:49 (17,681)
Hudson, Mark 3:35:32 (4,994)
Hudson, Michael 4:10:34 (12,289)
Hudson, Nicholas 5:35:14 (26,821)
Hudson, Nick 3:38:53 (5,555)
Hudson, Paul 6:12:22 (28,935)
Hudson, Philip 5:29:22 (26,326)
Hudson, Raymond 7:26:03 (30,112)
Hudson, Richard 5:10:10 (24,098)
Hudson, Ronald 5:36:20 (26,903)
Hudson, Shaun 4:05:48 (11,298)
Hudson, Tony 3:01:59 (1,147)
Hudspith, John 2:56:59 (742)
Hudspith, Mark 2:13:12 (11)
Huechting, Joerg 3:48:10 (7,297)
Hueger, Bernhard 3:09:07 (1,681)
Huett, Colin 5:00:41 (22,688)
Huff, Timothy 5:52:37 (28,043)
Huggett, David 5:19:25 (25,300)
Huggins, Mervyn 3:39:07 (5,592)
Hughes, Bleddyn 3:41:46 (6,085)
Hughes, Brian 5:41:39 (27,306)
Hughes, Carl 5:30:55 (26,447)
Hughes, Carwyn 3:36:37 (5,174)
Hughes, Christopher 4:10:53 (12,368)
Hughes, Clifford 3:41:12 (5,983)
Hughes, Colin 3:55:34 (8,812)
Hughes, David 4:08:03 (11,779)
Hughes, Evan Richard 3:37:50 (5,386)
Hughes, Frank 3:04:50 (1,337)
Hughes, Gareth 5:43:28 (27,437)
Hughes, Gary 3:46:57 (7,026)
Hughes, Geraint 4:10:53 (12,368)
Hughes, Gerraint 2:59:35 (984)
Hughes, Glyn 4:01:17 (10,333)
Hughes, Grant 4:26:29 (15,842)
Hughes, Ian 4:05:23 (11,182)
Hughes, James 5:51:41 (27,995)
Hughes, John 5:43:46 (27,456)
Hughes, John 5:47:38 (27,732)
Hughes, Keith 3:58:12 (9,537)
Hughes, Kenny 3:47:18 (7,085)
Hughes, Mark 3:09:31 (1,715)
Hughes, Mark 5:28:11 (26,194)
Hughes, Martyn 4:30:22 (16,738)
Hughes, Michael 3:50:23 (7,754)
Hughes, Nigel 4:33:19 (17,374)
Hughes, Peter 4:18:45 (14,067)
Hughes, Richard 4:41:54 (19,140)
Hughes, Robert 3:57:35 (9,359)
Hughes, Robert 5:06:39 (23,569)

Hughes, Ron	6:03:50 (28,584)
Hughes, Sean	5:11:04 (24,218)
Hughes, Simon	3:11:44 (1,891)
Hughes, Stephen	4:26:12 (15,778)
Hughes, Steven	3:35:37 (5,005)
Hughes, Wayne	4:44:59 (19,773)
Hughes, Wyn	5:42:59 (27,408)
Hughes-Jones, Geoffrey	3:40:58 (5,948)
Hughes-Roberts, John	3:39:37 (5,696)
Hughson, David	4:23:16 (15,122)
Hugill, Gary	3:14:00 (2,121)
Hugo, Jeremy	3:33:47 (4,726)
Huguelet, Eugene	5:46:28 (27,654)
Huguerre, Daniel	3:50:04 (7,697)
Huitinga, Ronaldus	3:56:02 (8,934)
Hulatt, Laurence	2:58:41 (888)
Hulburd, Jack	4:39:38 (18,724)
Hulcoop, Stephen	4:28:23 (16,283)
Hull, Jeffrey	5:45:38 (27,604)
Hull, Keith	3:18:43 (2,621)
Hull, Richard	5:47:45 (27,747)
Human, Laurence	4:29:46 (16,614)
Humbert, Larry	3:56:44 (9,115)
Humble, Brian	3:23:42 (3,197)
Hume, Chris	3:34:12 (4,787)
Hume, Iain	6:16:38 (29,076)
Hume, Robin	4:40:55 (18,959)
Hummel, Konrao	3:23:17 (3,146)
Hummel, Martin	3:48:45 (7,412)
Hummelmose, Martins	3:43:58 (6,483)
Humphreys, Alastair	5:03:50 (23,107)
Humphreys, David	3:53:09 (8,300)
Humphreys, Paul	4:21:11 (14,626)
Humphreys, Peter	2:57:58 (810)
Humphries, Bruce	3:48:48 (7,423)
Humphries, John	3:44:42 (6,613)
Humphries, Keith	4:37:35 (18,276)
Humphries, Kevin	3:33:34 (4,691)
Humphries, Lynton	3:11:36 (1,871)
Humphries, Stephen	3:28:13 (3,848)
Humphries, Stephen	3:54:26 (8,575)
Humphries, Stephen	4:00:33 (10,173)
Humphryes, Mick	4:40:32 (18,878)
Humpries, John	4:53:41 (21,450)
Humpries, John	5:39:37 (27,148)
Hundsnes, Staale	2:56:34 (721)
Hunt, Adrian	5:48:07 (27,782)
Hunt, Alan	4:02:33 (10,584)
Hunt, Andrew	3:47:54 (7,241)
Hunt, Andrew	4:33:20 (17,378)
Hunt, Anthony	5:23:44 (25,763)
Hunt, Bruce	4:13:29 (12,930)
Hunt, Christopher	3:10:14 (1,762)
Hunt, Colin	3:55:24 (8,781)
Hunt, David	3:59:06 (9,786)
Hunt, David	5:17:40 (25,122)
Hunt, Denzil	3:13:19 (2,040)
Hunt, George	4:24:15 (15,341)
Hunt, James	5:22:42 (25,674)
Hunt, John	3:27:09 (3,647)
Hunt, John	4:08:00 (11,764)
Hunt, John	4:14:15 (13,087)
Hunt, John	4:32:24 (17,194)
Hunt, John	4:36:05 (17,944)
Hunt, Jonathan	5:03:02 (23,009)
Hunt, Karl	5:53:02 (28,064)
Hunt, Matthew	4:54:53 (21,699)
Hunt, Matthew	5:13:20 (24,556)
Hunt, Michael	6:09:02 (28,816)
Hunt, Paul	3:41:00 (5,956)
Hunt, Ross	3:44:41 (6,610)
Hunt, Russell	4:50:10 (20,747)
Hunt, Simon	3:58:12 (9,537)
Hunt, Simon	4:04:21 (10,955)
Hunt, Thomas	3:48:46 (7,415)
Hunt, Timothy	4:42:48 (19,331)
Hunt, William	3:36:26 (5,147)
Hunt-Davis, Ben	4:01:19 (10,342)
Hunt-Davis, Peter	3:19:11 (2,669)
Hunter, Alex	4:27:44 (16,128)
Hunter, Alistair	3:46:49 (7,004)
Hunter, Colin	4:07:23 (11,636)
Hunter, Graeme	5:21:40 (25,543)

Hunter, Joe	4:02:20 (10,535)
Hunter, Kevin	3:47:50 (7,218)
Hunter, Mark	3:44:57 (6,678)
Hunter, Mark	4:40:42 (18,921)
Hunter, Paul	4:40:46 (18,934)
Hunter, Seth	4:33:17 (17,363)
Hunter, Simon	3:41:01 (5,960)
Hunter, Stephen	3:19:55 (2,761)
Hunter, Stephen	3:46:31 (6,951)
Hunter, Stephen	5:07:19 (23,665)
Hunter, William	4:06:20 (11,414)
Huntington, Philip	4:47:59 (20,343)
Huntley, Noah	3:16:41 (2,390)
Huntley, Richard	5:08:03 (23,774)
Hunton, Allan	5:09:40 (24,041)
Hunton, Chris	6:40:15 (29,649)
Hupin, Jean-Pierre	3:16:44 (2,398)
Hurcombe, Nigel	4:52:44 (21,260)
Hurd, Philip	2:57:30 (780)
Hurkett, Clive	6:30:06 (29,411)
Hurley, Andrew	4:56:24 (22,052)
Hurley, David	3:30:21 (4,221)
Hurley, Richard	3:29:44 (4,126)
Hurley, Steve	4:10:49 (12,350)
Hurley, Steve	4:12:13 (12,674)
Hurlstone, Nigel	4:31:58 (17,109)
Hurn, Anthony	2:57:22 (774)
Hurrell, Richard	4:13:23 (12,899)
Hurren, John	5:09:56 (24,073)
Hursey, David	4:12:22 (12,707)
Hurst, David	3:52:52 (8,248)
Hurst, Jerry	4:55:10 (21,772)
Hurst, Stephen	3:36:44 (5,200)
Hurst, Stephen	4:48:25 (20,429)
Hurstfield, Christopher	3:39:41 (5,709)
Hursthouse, Simon	3:49:43 (7,625)
Hursti, Jani	3:30:08 (4,194)
Hurth, Alexander	5:04:08 (23,150)
Hurtley, Duncan	4:48:01 (20,349)
Hurwitz, Stuart	4:40:42 (18,921)
Hurworth, Mark	5:12:53 (24,479)
Husband, Anthony	3:54:14 (8,519)
Husband, Edward	3:32:20 (4,512)
Husband, Glyndwe	3:26:11 (3,522)
Huson, David	5:01:32 (22,808)
Hussain, Kamal	6:29:38 (29,400)
Hussain, Moz	5:30:53 (26,444)
Hussein, Palash Shamim	4:34:21 (17,606)
Hussey, Bill	4:00:49 (10,245)
Hussey, Lascelles	5:07:46 (23,743)
Hussey, Nicholas	6:01:28 (28,477)
Hussey, Paul	4:27:22 (16,033)
Huston, Christopher	5:17:23 (25,091)
Hutcheson, Adam	3:35:50 (5,039)
Hutcheson, Adam	3:43:18 (6,360)
Hutcheson, Christopher	3:53:42 (8,425)
Hutchings, Ashley	5:01:11 (22,763)
Hutchings, Gerard	4:55:57 (21,979)
Hutchings, Paul	3:59:02 (9,765)
Hutchings, Terry	4:27:05 (15,994)
Hutchings, William	3:59:35 (9,944)
Hutchins, David	5:05:29 (23,381)
Hutchins, Derek	5:04:21 (23,189)
Hutchins, Steven	5:05:06 (23,305)
Hutchinson, Deryck	4:37:29 (18,247)
Hutchinson, Garry	3:30:20 (4,219)
Hutchinson, Ian	4:23:01 (15,069)
Hutchinson, Malcolm	3:18:24 (2,590)
Hutchinson, Nicholas	5:02:56 (22,996)
Hutchinson, Phillip	5:18:11 (25,177)
Hutchinson, Stephen	3:41:24 (6,028)
Hutchinson, Stuart	3:31:06 (4,342)
Hutchinson, Tim	4:35:56 (17,913)
Hutchison, Kyle	4:57:03 (22,146)
Hutchison, Michael	3:46:39 (6,983)
Hutchison, Robert	4:09:22 (12,054)
Hutchison, Ross	4:29:59 (16,689)
Huthwaite, Laurence	5:06:40 (23,572)
Hutt, Ian	4:41:02 (18,981)
Hutt, Michael	4:14:29 (13,123)
Hutton, Adrian	9:00:36 (30,274)
Hutton, Craig	3:56:49 (9,137)
Hutton, Danny	3:30:32 (4,255)

Hutton, Keith	4:58:01 (22,296)
Hutton, Kevin	5:17:00 (25,052)
Hutton, Mark	4:48:22 (20,420)
Hutton, Maxwell	3:57:05 (9,194)
Hutton, Peter	3:28:58 (3,991)
Huws, Lfion Dwyrd	4:01:17 (10,333)
Huxtable, Julian	4:36:59 (18,124)
Huyton, Stephen	3:39:26 (5,660)
Hyams, David	3:55:59 (8,915)
Hyatt, David	5:28:58 (26,286)
Hyatt, Gary	3:27:54 (3,789)
Hyde, Christopher	4:15:14 (13,319)
Hyde, Gordon	7:44:50 (30,181)
Hyde, Mark	4:32:09 (17,145)
Hyde, Steven	3:54:31 (8,590)
Hyder, Jonathan	4:45:52 (19,914)
Hydon, David	3:01:20 (1,097)
Hyland, Edward	4:32:44 (17,257)
Hyland, Nicholas	3:39:23 (5,645)
Hyland, Ray	4:43:36 (19,521)
Hylton, Ken	4:28:27 (16,301)
Hyman, Lawrence	4:44:31 (19,680)
Hyner, Derek	4:27:36 (16,090)
Iafrate, Fernando	3:22:11 (3,024)
Ibberson, Alan	3:33:36 (4,695)
Ibberson, Mark	4:18:15 (13,935)
Ibbetson, Colin	4:39:19 (18,648)
Ibbott, Christopher	5:05:12 (23,318)
Ibbott, Paul	5:05:11 (23,317)
Ibbs, James	2:59:40 (992)
Ibrahim, Huseyin	2:36:41 (112)
Ibrahim, Salih	5:25:22 (25,925)
Ibrahim, Sufiyanu	4:25:07 (15,536)
Ibrahim, Suleyman	4:39:10 (18,630)
Icely, Dominic	5:07:33 (23,701)
Icely, Nick Icely	5:07:33 (23,701)
Iceton, Andy	3:58:00 (9,490)
Iddon, Colin	4:19:37 (14,284)
Ide, Philip	3:01:33 (1,116)
Idle, Jonathan	3:25:30 (3,445)
Igoe, James Jnr	2:51:54 (511)
Ihlow, Werner	4:22:20 (14,894)
Ikoli, Tandy	4:37:31 (18,252)
Ilankovan, Nimalan	4:29:47 (16,619)
Ilchyshyn, Andrew	4:10:42 (12,311)
Iles, Andrew	3:53:40 (8,416)
Iles, Stephen	3:55:37 (8,821)
Iley, Paul	4:06:18 (11,408)
Iley, Stuart	5:17:59 (25,164)
Illingworth, Colin	4:57:16 (22,181)
Illingworth, Simon	3:57:49 (9,437)
Illingworth, Stuart	3:54:26 (8,575)
Illsley, Shaun	5:10:12 (24,103)
Ilott, Martin	3:13:19 (2,040)
Imburghia, Gerald	4:52:20 (21,169)
Imeri, Fadil	3:55:15 (8,751)
Imray, Malcolm	3:16:18 (2,341)
Ince, Philip	4:53:44 (21,461)
Inch, Gary	4:25:11 (15,554)
Inchbald, Alex	3:40:03 (5,794)
Ing, John	5:13:47 (24,605)
Ingham, Richard	5:25:34 (25,944)
Ingham, Stephen	2:40:42 (187)
Ingle, Nicholas	5:19:31 (25,308)
Ingleby, Geoffrey	3:30:07 (4,191)
Inglis, Patrick	5:38:34 (27,055)
Ingoe, Phil	2:59:26 (973)
Ingpen, Andrew	5:20:05 (25,368)
Ingpen, Paul	4:34:00 (17,536)
Ingram, Anthony	4:25:21 (15,583)
Ingram, Charles	3:37:16 (5,296)
Ingram, David	4:30:50 (16,813)
Ingram, Kevin	5:03:28 (23,060)
Ingram, Michael	3:50:04 (7,697)
Ingram, Philip	4:02:53 (10,641)
Ingram, Richard	5:18:50 (25,253)
Ingram, Stewart	4:19:39 (14,294)
Ingroville, Paul	2:38:28 (146)
Inker, Gareth	4:03:29 (10,772)
Inman, Ian	4:37:54 (18,347)
Inman, Tom	4:33:15 (17,356)
Innes, Janice	6:24:06 (29,264)
Innes, Justin	3:32:39 (4,556)

Inns, Neil 3:30:50 (4,298)
Instance, Kevin 3:31:13 (4,357)
Instone, Stephen 3:14:58 (2,218)
Inubushi, Takayuki 2:11:42 (7)
Inwards, Clive 4:53:28 (21,411)
Ioannou, John 4:47:20 (20,225)
Iqbal, Aurangzeb 5:59:03 (28,369)
Iraggi, Gandolfo 4:23:06 (15,085)
Ireland, Ian 4:07:09 (11,579)
Ireland, Kevin 5:09:33 (24,021)
Ireland, Richard 5:54:08 (28,121)
Ireland, Stephen 4:25:36 (15,637)
Irish, Jonathan 4:22:24 (14,903)
Irons, Matthew 4:56:33 (22,079)
Irvine, David 4:32:13 (17,158)
Irvine, Philip 5:06:44 (23,577)
Irvine, Stuart 3:15:09 (2,239)
Irving, Andrew 3:47:18 (7,085)
Irving, David 5:38:18 (27,036)
Irwin, David 5:44:27 (27,506)
Irwin, Paul 4:05:48 (11,298)
Isaac, Wayne 5:24:37 (25,847)
Isaacs, David 3:54:17 (8,533)
Isaacs, David 5:31:33 (26,491)
Isaacs, David 6:30:13 (29,417)
Isaacs, Graham 4:52:15 (21,142)
Isaacs, John 4:52:15 (21,142)
Isaacs, Tony 3:43:29 (6,396)
Isbill, Robert 3:29:20 (4,053)
Isherwood, Damien 4:34:55 (17,697)
Islam, Mohammed 4:55:16 (21,802)
Isman Eqal, Nasser 4:58:45 (22,421)
Issatt, Howard 3:23:52 (3,225)
Issroff, David 3:52:23 (8,148)
Isted, Stephen 4:51:00 (20,881)
Ito, Hideki 3:58:51 (9,713)
Ito, Tomoaki 6:02:56 (28,537)
Ivanoff, Plamen 4:51:16 (20,935)
Ivansson, Richard 4:25:57 (15,718)
Ives, Denis 4:04:45 (11,057)
Ives, Roger 4:25:34 (15,632)
Ives, Stephen 4:34:03 (17,544)
Iveson, Robert 4:00:39 (10,193)
Ivey, Nick 4:46:36 (20,077)
Ivimy, Derick 4:19:58 (14,355)
Izouaouen, Younes 4:33:25 (17,398)
Izzard, Stephen 3:03:20 (1,236)
Jabbour, Ramsey 4:42:30 (19,273)
Jack, Cameron 3:08:12 (1,606)
Jack, Christopher 4:05:26 (11,191)
Jack, Robert 4:37:42 (18,299)
Jackett, Mark 2:54:18 (593)
Jackson, Alison 4:44:55 (19,762)
Jackson, Ashley 9:00:36 (30,274)
Jackson, Christopher 3:01:48 (1,137)
Jackson, Christopher 3:38:54 (5,560)
Jackson, Christopher 4:33:52 (17,513)
Jackson, David 2:49:41 (415)
Jackson, David 4:12:39 (12,763)
Jackson, David 4:25:10 (15,550)
Jackson, Dean 4:13:42 (12,981)
Jackson, Edward 4:17:27 (13,761)
Jackson, Howard 3:58:32 (9,616)
Jackson, Iain 4:26:18 (15,807)
Jackson, John 4:54:29 (21,587)
Jackson, John 5:11:57 (24,347)
Jackson, Karl 4:39:11 (18,634)
Jackson, Mark 4:21:09 (14,616)
Jackson, Mark 6:38:58 (29,608)
Jackson, Mark Andrew 4:39:11 (18,634)
Jackson, Martin 4:09:13 (12,026)
Jackson, Martyn 4:12:59 (12,825)
Jackson, Michael 6:59:28 (29,935)
Jackson, Mowbray 4:54:58 (21,721)
Jackson, Nick 4:23:45 (15,236)
Jackson, Paul 3:48:01 (7,270)
Jackson, Peter 3:53:13 (8,313)
Jackson, Peter 4:40:24 (18,857)
Jackson, Philip 3:22:08 (3,017)
Jackson, Philip 4:48:10 (20,380)
Jackson, Randall 3:58:31 (9,611)
Jackson, Richard 3:46:41 (6,987)
Jackson, Robert 2:41:30 (203)
Jackson, Samuel 3:37:28 (5,329)
Jackson, Simon 3:44:16 (6,535)
Jackson, Stephen 3:08:45 (1,650)
Jackson, Stephen 3:57:50 (9,440)
Jackson, Stephen 4:36:59 (18,124)
Jackson, Steve 3:11:02 (1,838)
Jackson, Steven 4:07:54 (11,740)
Jackson, Tim 4:04:45 (11,057)
Jackson, Trevor 3:59:22 (9,869)
Jacob, Andrew 2:59:55 (1,020)
Jacobs, Alan 4:21:20 (14,653)
Jacobs, Blair 5:07:38 (23,719)
Jacobs, Philip 3:41:36 (6,054)
Jacobs, Robert 2:42:48 (230)
Jacobs, Rupert 4:05:33 (11,228)
Jacobs, Stephen 4:43:07 (19,407)
Jacobsen, Finn 3:40:41 (5,894)
Jacobson, David 3:17:15 (2,450)
Jacques, David 3:51:55 (8,054)
Jacques, Ian 3:56:17 (8,989)
Jacques, Richard 5:34:49 (26,786)
Jacques, Stephen 4:11:59 (12,606)
Jaeger, Andreas 5:15:55 (24,923)
Jaeger, Thomas 4:55:18 (21,817)
Jaegler, Raymond 3:19:11 (2,669)
Jaffier, Martin 6:02:54 (28,534)
Jaffier, Tim 5:36:26 (26,912)
Jager, Peer 4:46:38 (20,080)
Jaggard, Russell 3:53:55 (8,464)
Jagles, Garth 5:50:27 (27,922)
Jagpal, Rajvinder 4:38:21 (18,466)
Jaijee, Anoop 5:12:55 (24,485)
Jain, Rajnish 5:32:29 (26,578)
Jaines, John 4:26:04 (15,748)
Jakeman, Michael 5:04:30 (23,217)
Jakeman, Simon 3:32:13 (4,495)
Jakob, Friedel 5:07:57 (23,766)
Jakobi, Donovan 4:59:50 (22,581)
Jakobsen, Stevan 5:18:41 (25,232)
Jakubovic, David 3:46:38 (6,981)
Jalloh, Ibrahim 3:13:46 (2,086)
James, Alan 3:14:49 (2,197)
James, André 3:50:26 (7,761)
James, Andrew 2:38:38 (150)
James, Andrew 4:12:36 (12,755)
James, Anthony 4:50:21 (20,782)
James, Chris 5:24:56 (25,878)
James, Christian 4:32:08 (17,141)
James, Christopher 4:14:13 (13,078)
James, Cliff 5:07:20 (23,669)
James, Darren 5:00:43 (22,695)
James, David 3:09:16 (1,691)
James, David 3:35:27 (4,978)
James, David 3:39:57 (5,775)
James, David 3:54:31 (8,590)
James, David 4:19:17 (14,189)
James, Jerome 5:38:05 (27,026)
James, Julian 2:57:12 (759)
James, Justin 3:45:19 (6,719)
James, Kaare 4:09:12 (12,022)
James, Keith 5:06:36 (23,559)
James, Kenneth 3:57:17 (9,250)
James, Kevin 3:34:36 (4,850)
James, Malcolm 5:10:35 (24,163)
James, Mark 4:25:56 (15,712)
James, Matt 5:13:29 (24,572)
James, Matthew 4:42:09 (19,192)
James, Melvyn 3:44:04 (6,503)
James, Michael 4:21:45 (14,746)
James, Nicholas 3:25:38 (3,460)
James, Nico 4:22:23 (14,901)
James, Paul 4:07:24 (11,639)
James, Paul 5:15:07 (24,800)
James, Peter 3:05:04 (1,354)
James, Philip 4:10:57 (12,389)
James, Richard 3:37:19 (5,305)
James, Robert 3:09:18 (1,694)
James, Roy 3:24:26 (3,304)
James, Russell 4:12:43 (12,775)
James, Ryan 3:18:37 (2,610)
James, Stepehn 4:02:33 (10,584)
James, Stephen 5:08:40 (23,881)
James, Steve 3:31:32 (4,396)
James, William 3:35:53 (5,050)
James, William 5:35:16 (26,825)
James, William 5:52:42 (28,048)
James, William 5:58:06 (28,326)
James Bowen, Rod 4:16:44 (13,621)
Jameson, Andrew 4:27:44 (16,128)
Jameson, Andrew 4:39:49 (18,754)
Jameson, Brendan 5:12:48 (24,470)
Jameson, David 3:18:04 (2,541)
Jameson, John 4:11:48 (12,570)
Jamieson, Alexander 3:45:00 (6,688)
Jamieson, Christopher 3:43:17 (6,357)
Jamieson, Craig 3:56:21 (9,007)
Jamieson, Gordon 4:34:54 (17,694)
Jamieson, Hunter 4:22:51 (15,021)
Jamieson, Stuart 5:05:16 (23,334)
Jandu, Dhanwant 5:43:33 (27,442)
Jandu, Randeep 5:43:33 (27,442)
Janeczko, Jared 3:12:15 (1,937)
Janes, Jeremy 3:17:40 (2,497)
Janes, Mark 4:03:47 (10,838)
Janes, Murray 3:29:50 (4,141)
Janes, Phil 4:46:36 (20,077)
Janisch, Adam 3:13:17 (2,034)
Janouin, Didier 3:01:23 (1,099)
Jans, Ruud 4:04:02 (10,889)
Janse Van Vuuren, Andrew 4:37:00 (18,131)
Janssen, Carl 3:06:22 (1,448)
Januschkowetz, Johann 3:03:31 (1,246)
Janvier, Nicolas 2:29:54 (66)
Jaquelin, Christophe 3:43:36 (6,415)
Jaques, Michael 4:54:02 (21,521)
Jardaneh, Kamal 4:37:54 (18,347)
Jardin, Howie 3:12:16 (1,938)
Jardine, Michael 5:55:57 (28,213)
Jarman, Gary 4:10:39 (12,302)
Jarman, Les 4:05:15 (11,162)
Jarred, Robert 4:36:31 (18,024)
Jarrett, Michael 4:23:33 (15,189)
Jarrett, Neale 3:27:28 (3,700)
Jarrold, Darren 3:11:36 (1,871)
Jarvie, James 3:52:23 (8,148)
Jarvis, Andrew 6:00:57 (28,454)
Jarvis, Benjamin 4:22:27 (14,915)
Jarvis, Derry 3:54:37 (8,618)
Jarvis, Ian 4:28:59 (16,417)
Jarvis, James 2:53:41 (567)
Jarvis, John 3:21:59 (2,994)
Jarvis, John 3:24:16 (3,278)
Jarvis, Keith 6:28:26 (29,367)
Jarvis, Nicholas 4:06:45 (11,493)
Jarvis, Simon 4:13:47 (12,995)
Jarvis, Steven 4:54:04 (21,527)
Jasnoch, Paul 3:10:34 (1,797)
Jason, Jonathan 7:49:53 (30,189)
Jason, Trevor 3:19:31 (2,707)
Jaswal, Kulbir Singh 3:36:38 (5,177)
Jat, Parmjit 3:41:25 (6,030)
Jaukkari, Mauno 7:20:50 (30,083)
Jay, Nicolas 5:40:58 (27,260)
Jay, Stephen 3:51:04 (7,884)
Jayaram, Hari 3:36:47 (5,208)
Jeacock, Simon 4:25:51 (15,688)
Jeal, Nick 5:02:50 (22,982)
Jeal, Stephen 3:44:45 (6,625)
Jean, Goffaux 4:43:29 (19,490)
Jean François, Rigau 3:16:08 (2,328)
Jean Paul, Desmond 4:38:03 (18,382)
Jean-Charles, Pierre 3:56:45 (9,121)
Jeanes, Chris 2:51:11 (474)
Jeans, Nicholas 3:57:59 (9,486)
Jebb, Christopher 3:17:07 (2,437)
Jedry, Victor 3:17:59 (2,532)
Jee, Jeremy 4:00:19 (10,109)
Jeeves, Karl 4:01:05 (10,296)
Jefferies, Graham 5:24:05 (25,799)
Jefferies, Ian 4:49:23 (20,592)
Jefferies, Mark 3:37:04 (5,256)
Jefferies, Richard 4:48:02 (20,354)
Jefferies, Tim 4:00:31 (10,158)
Jefferis, Christopher 4:39:55 (18,771)
Jeffers, Kenneth 4:42:24 (19,250)
Jefferson, Alan 4:14:32 (13,137)

Jefferson, Simon	4:36:12 (17,954)	
Jeffery, John	4:36:22 (17,988)	
Jeffery, Phillip	3:16:35 (2,379)	
Jeffery, Timothy	3:19:54 (2,756)	
Jefford, Alan	3:52:05 (8,095)	
Jeffrey, David	6:38:08 (29,591)	
Jeffrey, Iain	3:42:06 (6,137)	
Jeffrey, Ian	6:04:05 (28,597)	
Jeffrey, Peter	3:31:17 (4,370)	
Jeffrey, Rupert	3:06:15 (1,438)	
Jeffreys, Karl	4:00:43 (10,217)	
Jeffreys, Paul	4:51:20 (20,954)	
Jeffries, Alan	4:35:49 (17,882)	
Jeffries, Richard	4:36:10 (17,950)	
Jeffries, Robert	4:47:04 (20,177)	
Jeffs, Richard	3:38:54 (5,560)	
Jehannin, Gerard	3:28:07 (3,828)	
Jelley, David	2:59:19 (964)	
Jellicoe, George	4:12:04 (12,633)	
Jellis, David	4:52:50 (21,274)	
Jenkin, Daniel	3:26:44 (3,589)	
Jenkin, James	2:58:50 (918)	
Jenkin, Peter	4:42:13 (19,209)	
Jenkins, Alan	3:45:35 (6,761)	
Jenkins, Allan	4:50:52 (20,856)	
Jenkins, Alun	3:49:34 (7,599)	
Jenkins, Anthony	3:58:56 (9,732)	
Jenkins, Barry	5:37:34 (26,989)	
Jenkins, Brian	3:34:07 (4,774)	
Jenkins, Charles	3:25:46 (3,479)	
Jenkins, Chris	4:55:35 (21,913)	
Jenkins, Christopher	3:27:41 (3,738)	
Jenkins, Christopher	3:56:43 (9,109)	
Jenkins, David	4:11:17 (12,460)	
Jenkins, David	6:57:49 (29,917)	
Jenkins, Gareth	3:46:06 (6,877)	
Jenkins, Howard	4:53:00 (21,316)	
Jenkins, Huw	3:02:21 (1,178)	
Jenkins, Jamie	3:42:21 (6,191)	
Jenkins, Jonathan	4:33:02 (17,316)	
Jenkins, Lee	3:43:09 (6,334)	
Jenkins, Michael	5:15:16 (24,839)	
Jenkins, Nigel	3:57:54 (9,462)	
Jenkins, Nigel	4:35:51 (17,891)	
Jenkins, Paul	2:59:56 (1,024)	
Jenkins, Paul	4:52:06 (21,113)	
Jenkins, Paul	6:40:16 (29,651)	
Jenkins, Phillip	3:31:44 (4,427)	
Jenkins, Phillip	4:43:42 (19,539)	
Jenkins, Robert	4:52:59 (21,312)	
Jenkins, Scott	3:49:35 (7,604)	
Jenkins, Sean	3:57:31 (9,334)	
Jenkins, Steven	4:32:07 (17,138)	
Jenkins, Thomas	4:07:17 (11,606)	
Jenkins, Timothy	5:17:21 (25,088)	
Jenkins, Tom	4:45:37 (19,877)	
Jenkins, William	5:19:27 (25,302)	
Jenkinson, Paul	4:16:05 (13,485)	
Jenkinson, Stephen	4:49:28 (20,613)	
Jenner, Jason	3:16:37 (2,381)	
Jenner, Marc	4:26:21 (15,815)	
Jenner, Mark	4:05:58 (11,347)	
Jenner, Simon	4:21:45 (14,746)	
Jennings, Andy	3:12:21 (1,947)	
Jennings, Cliff	5:44:01 (27,477)	
Jennings, Colin	3:28:58 (3,991)	
Jennings, David	4:10:24 (12,255)	
Jennings, Jason	4:03:59 (10,879)	
Jennings, Joseph	5:14:12 (24,655)	
Jennings, Mark	4:49:02 (20,534)	
Jennings, Matthew	3:48:44 (7,410)	
Jennings, Odran	4:07:53 (11,737)	
Jennings, Paul	3:47:07 (7,054)	
Jennings, Paul	4:40:23 (18,853)	
Jennings, Peter	2:58:29 (852)	
Jennings, Richard	4:36:36 (18,040)	
Jennings, Robert	3:14:43 (2,185)	
Jennings, Terry	4:29:02 (16,428)	
Jenny, Kurt	2:50:24 (443)	
Jensen, Leif	3:49:17 (7,518)	
Jensen, Vidar	3:24:12 (3,270)	
Jensen, Winter	3:02:02 (1,154)	
Jeong, Dong	4:06:59 (11,547)	

Jepp, Bryan	3:59:18 (9,841)	
Jepson, Ben	4:29:25 (16,526)	
Jepson, Giles	4:31:38 (17,019)	
Jerome, Darren	2:41:53 (215)	
Jerram, Alan	6:17:10 (29,091)	
Jervis, Geoff	3:24:18 (3,281)	
Jervis, Mark	4:36:38 (18,048)	
Jervis, Michael	4:56:44 (22,096)	
Jessep, Craig	3:43:26 (6,385)	
Jessep, Ian	3:32:24 (4,520)	
Jessop, Julian	2:59:30 (979)	
Jessop, Mark	5:00:58 (22,729)	
Jesty, Ben	5:54:12 (28,125)	
Jewitt, Justin	4:50:40 (20,821)	
Jeyapaul, Premkumar	4:17:35 (13,789)	
Jeyes, Philip	4:12:24 (12,714)	
Jifar, Tesfaye	2:09:45 (4)	
Jiggins, Mark	4:22:11 (14,856)	
Jimenez-Saez, Dionisio	3:07:22 (1,533)	
Jno-Lewis, Spencer	4:03:03 (10,671)	
Job, Barry	4:37:15 (18,182)	
Job, Michael	3:45:39 (6,779)	
Jobling, Alan	3:25:32 (3,447)	
Jobling, David	3:46:38 (6,981)	
Jobling, Thomas	5:20:43 (25,435)	
Jocelyn, Steven	4:29:07 (16,453)	
Jocys, John	4:38:29 (18,504)	
Joffe, Michael	4:14:48 (13,209)	
Jogi, Manesh	4:31:22 (16,947)	
Johansson, Boris	4:49:53 (20,691)	
John, Christopher	8:31:00 (30,246)	
John, Colin	6:44:04 (29,718)	
John, David	4:44:30 (19,674)	
John, Gilbert	3:33:39 (4,705)	
John, Peter	3:47:22 (7,104)	
John, Tim	4:18:23 (13,982)	
Johnes, John	5:41:17 (27,275)	
Johnes, Mark	3:24:24 (3,298)	
John-Lewis, Johnson	3:39:23 (5,645)	
Johns, Alun	3:22:07 (3,014)	
Johns, Christopher	3:19:38 (2,722)	
Johns, Daniel	3:30:37 (4,265)	
Johns, Marcus	4:30:48 (16,806)	
Johns, Matthew	5:35:01 (26,806)	
Johns, Michael	4:45:35 (19,874)	
Johns, Stephen	3:20:32 (2,828)	
Johns, Warren	3:45:48 (6,825)	
Johnson, Adam	4:42:10 (19,198)	
Johnson, Alan	3:32:05 (4,478)	
Johnson, Andrew	3:09:01 (1,673)	
Johnson, Andrew	3:45:49 (6,827)	
Johnson, Anthony	4:34:20 (17,602)	
Johnson, Ben	4:47:35 (20,280)	
Johnson, Bernard	3:17:40 (2,497)	
Johnson, Christopher	4:49:22 (20,590)	
Johnson, Christopher	5:37:35 (26,992)	
Johnson, David	3:19:54 (2,756)	
Johnson, David	4:23:42 (15,228)	
Johnson, Dean	3:40:22 (5,843)	
Johnson, Dvid	3:47:22 (7,104)	
Johnson, Gary	4:03:31 (10,776)	
Johnson, Geoff	4:40:32 (18,878)	
Johnson, Glen	3:10:49 (1,819)	
Johnson, Glenn	4:14:00 (13,042)	
Johnson, Graham	3:49:49 (7,648)	
Johnson, Grahm	3:30:25 (4,236)	
Johnson, Guy	3:47:35 (7,161)	
Johnson, Ian	3:39:34 (5,688)	
Johnson, James	3:50:58 (7,861)	
Johnson, John	4:11:30 (12,501)	
Johnson, Jon-Paul	3:57:56 (9,472)	
Johnson, Keith	4:18:40 (14,044)	
Johnson, Ken	3:28:05 (3,816)	
Johnson, Lawrence	5:59:14 (28,377)	
Johnson, Lee	3:00:58 (1,081)	
Johnson, Leslie	5:10:04 (24,088)	
Johnson, Mark	3:56:20 (9,004)	
Johnson, Mark	4:22:35 (14,948)	
Johnson, Mark	4:43:42 (19,539)	
Johnson, Mark	5:06:25 (23,538)	
Johnson, Martin	3:43:59 (6,491)	
Johnson, Maxwell	4:40:54 (18,956)	
Johnson, Michael	3:57:03 (9,189)	

Johnson, Michael	4:37:54 (18,347)	
Johnson, Nicholas	3:54:50 (8,668)	
Johnson, Nigel	4:22:48 (15,008)	
Johnson, Paul	3:14:57 (2,216)	
Johnson, Paul	3:57:13 (9,232)	
Johnson, Paul	4:23:21 (15,143)	
Johnson, Paul	5:28:35 (26,236)	
Johnson, Paul	5:31:08 (26,465)	
Johnson, Peter	2:34:23 (88)	
Johnson, Peter	4:06:23 (11,427)	
Johnson, Peter	4:21:11 (14,626)	
Johnson, Ray	3:49:51 (7,657)	
Johnson, Raymond	4:09:09 (12,012)	
Johnson, Rex	4:31:48 (17,060)	
Johnson, Richard	3:45:01 (6,691)	
Johnson, Richard	4:46:55 (20,151)	
Johnson, Robert	3:16:45 (2,400)	
Johnson, Robin	5:02:19 (22,918)	
Johnson, Russell	3:42:08 (6,145)	
Johnson, Seain	4:16:47 (13,632)	
Johnson, Simon	4:09:22 (12,054)	
Johnson, Stephen	4:19:45 (14,305)	
Johnson, Stephen	4:52:47 (21,268)	
Johnson, Stephen	6:09:15 (28,822)	
Johnson, Steve	4:56:32 (22,074)	
Johnson, Thomas	4:27:42 (16,119)	
Johnson, Timothy	5:08:06 (23,783)	
Johnson, William	5:23:13 (25,723)	
Johnston, Adam	3:43:28 (6,392)	
Johnston, Alastair	3:05:34 (1,395)	
Johnston, Barry	2:42:28 (226)	
Johnston, David	3:55:52 (8,887)	
Johnston, David	3:56:23 (9,018)	
Johnston, Graeme	2:57:24 (778)	
Johnston, James	4:27:28 (16,055)	
Johnston, John	5:01:31 (22,807)	
Johnston, Michael	3:22:16 (3,031)	
Johnston, Paul	3:43:15 (6,353)	
Johnston, Paul	4:40:22 (18,850)	
Johnston, Robert	2:55:32 (654)	
Johnston, Sandy	2:49:17 (401)	
Johnston, Stephen	5:02:48 (22,977)	
Johnstone, John	4:41:58 (19,155)	
Johnstone, Martin	5:06:38 (23,567)	
Jokipii, Kim	5:03:53 (23,113)	
Jokstad, Asbjoern	3:05:29 (1,389)	
Jolliffe, Gary	3:35:46 (5,027)	
Jolly, Robert	3:57:17 (9,250)	
Jolly, Simon	4:17:50 (13,840)	
Jolly, Stephen	4:46:01 (19,941)	
Jonas, Gary	3:56:40 (9,095)	
Jonas, Harry	3:55:37 (8,821)	
Jonassen, Suend	3:58:59 (9,749)	
Jones, Alan	3:03:15 (1,230)	
Jones, Alan	4:14:50 (13,218)	
Jones, Alan	5:20:17 (25,384)	
Jones, Allen	2:47:39 (356)	
Jones, Allen	5:45:42 (27,609)	
Jones, Alun	4:32:25 (17,199)	
Jones, Alun	5:40:45 (27,249)	
Jones, Andrew	3:00:17 (1,043)	
Jones, Andrew	3:16:55 (2,414)	
Jones, Andrew	4:05:25 (11,188)	
Jones, Andrew	4:09:48 (12,125)	
Jones, Andrew	4:36:26 (18,003)	
Jones, Andy	2:58:38 (875)	
Jones, Austin	4:15:30 (13,366)	
Jones, Aydn	3:58:14 (9,551)	
Jones, Barry	3:54:51 (8,672)	
Jones, Ben	4:03:19 (10,728)	
Jones, Bernard	3:39:30 (5,673)	
Jones, Bernard	6:25:51 (29,302)	
Jones, Brian	3:37:22 (5,317)	
Jones, Brian	4:12:47 (12,788)	
Jones, Brian	4:50:48 (20,843)	
Jones, Carl	4:23:29 (15,169)	
Jones, Cerith	4:05:26 (11,191)	
Jones, Chris	5:22:43 (25,676)	
Jones, Christian	4:29:33 (16,561)	
Jones, Christopher	3:22:16 (3,031)	
Jones, Christopher	3:52:46 (8,225)	
Jones, Christopher	4:39:44 (18,740)	
Jones, Clyndwr	4:52:31 (21,210)	

Jones, Colin ... 3:23:47 (3,208)
Jones, Colin ... 3:45:44 (6,808)
Jones, Colin ... 4:26:10 (15,772)
Jones, Craig ... 3:44:01 (6,496)
Jones, Damian ... 3:07:17 (1,527)
Jones, Daniel ... 3:49:33 (7,596)
Jones, Daniel ... 4:23:10 (15,101)
Jones, Daniel ... 4:33:18 (17,368)
Jones, Daniel ... 5:45:43 (27,610)
Jones, Darren ... 4:29:26 (16,528)
Jones, Darren ... 5:39:25 (27,123)
Jones, Daryl ... 4:34:05 (17,553)
Jones, David ... 2:52:57 (540)
Jones, David ... 3:01:45 (1,134)
Jones, David ... 3:33:31 (4,689)
Jones, David ... 3:55:12 (8,734)
Jones, David ... 4:00:47 (10,238)
Jones, David ... 4:18:56 (14,107)
Jones, David ... 4:30:39 (16,779)
Jones, David ... 4:43:35 (19,516)
Jones, David ... 4:52:22 (21,175)
Jones, David ... 4:52:23 (21,180)
Jones, David ... 4:57:05 (22,152)
Jones, David ... 5:02:07 (22,893)
Jones, David ... 5:23:41 (25,762)
Jones, David Alan ... 3:35:19 (4,957)
Jones, Dennis ... 4:52:58 (21,309)
Jones, Derek ... 3:17:51 (2,516)
Jones, Derek ... 3:58:47 (9,694)
Jones, Derwyn ... 4:02:41 (10,604)
Jones, Dewi ... 3:01:40 (1,130)
Jones, Donald ... 4:21:24 (14,668)
Jones, Dylan ... 5:01:08 (22,754)
Jones, Frederick ... 6:43:12 (29,712)
Jones, Gareth ... 3:25:09 (3,393)
Jones, Gareth ... 3:33:23 (4,672)
Jones, Gareth ... 4:03:11 (10,699)
Jones, Gareth ... 4:50:48 (20,843)
Jones, Gareth ... 4:50:51 (20,854)
Jones, Gareth ... 5:06:22 (23,529)
Jones, Garry ... 3:39:06 (5,589)
Jones, Gary ... 5:08:25 (23,831)
Jones, George ... 5:39:49 (27,164)
Jones, Glyn ... 6:29:15 (29,394)
Jones, Glynn ... 4:54:47 (21,672)
Jones, Glynne ... 4:15:14 (13,319)
Jones, Graham ... 4:55:50 (21,959)
Jones, Gwilym ... 3:22:03 (3,007)
Jones, Gwyn ... 4:31:03 (16,862)
Jones, Haydn ... 3:03:21 (1,237)
Jones, Herbert ... 4:40:01 (18,790)
Jones, Howard ... 4:01:06 (10,300)
Jones, Huw ... 3:59:20 (9,856)
Jones, Huw ... 4:12:00 (12,616)
Jones, Hywel ... 5:37:13 (26,958)
Jones, Ian ... 4:34:01 (17,538)
Jones, Ian ... 5:47:46 (27,748)
Jones, Ifor ... 6:34:54 (29,518)
Jones, Iwan ... 4:25:01 (15,514)
Jones, Jamie ... 2:32:31 (75)
Jones, Jason ... 4:09:14 (12,031)
Jones, Jeffrey ... 4:57:15 (22,178)
Jones, Jeremy ... 4:46:14 (19,993)
Jones, John ... 4:06:02 (11,355)
Jones, John ... 4:30:50 (16,813)
Jones, John ... 5:32:23 (26,558)
Jones, Keith ... 3:12:46 (1,984)
Jones, Keith ... 4:31:30 (16,981)
Jones, Keith ... 5:20:59 (25,466)
Jones, Kelvin ... 4:59:14 (22,490)
Jones, Kenneth ... 3:59:09 (9,800)
Jones, Kevin ... 3:04:05 (1,288)
Jones, Kevin ... 4:11:16 (12,456)
Jones, Kieran ... 5:19:40 (25,326)
Jones, Leon ... 3:30:06 (4,190)
Jones, Leslie ... 6:37:08 (29,564)
Jones, Malcolm ... 4:28:37 (16,344)
Jones, Marc ... 3:56:24 (9,025)
Jones, Mark ... 3:51:54 (8,049)
Jones, Mark ... 4:23:33 (15,189)
Jones, Mark ... 4:28:35 (16,334)
Jones, Mark ... 4:36:57 (18,118)
Jones, Mark ... 4:49:27 (20,609)
Jones, Mark ... 5:13:23 (24,564)
Jones, Martyn ... 5:36:50 (26,932)
Jones, Matthew ... 3:23:29 (3,174)
Jones, Matthew ... 4:13:54 (13,019)
Jones, Matthew ... 4:37:32 (18,257)
Jones, Matthew ... 5:40:48 (27,253)
Jones, Maurice ... 4:14:07 (13,061)
Jones, Max ... 4:54:10 (21,545)
Jones, Michael ... 2:52:25 (528)
Jones, Michael ... 3:11:10 (1,852)
Jones, Michael ... 3:37:35 (5,346)
Jones, Michael ... 3:52:13 (8,119)
Jones, Michael ... 3:59:12 (9,815)
Jones, Michael ... 4:10:46 (12,327)
Jones, Michael ... 4:29:05 (16,445)
Jones, Michael ... 4:35:25 (17,800)
Jones, Michael ... 4:51:58 (21,085)
Jones, Michael ... 4:54:43 (21,648)
Jones, Michael ... 5:24:30 (25,836)
Jones, Mike ... 4:57:29 (22,214)
Jones, Mike ... 5:01:34 (22,813)
Jones, Neil ... 4:17:40 (13,806)
Jones, Nigel ... 2:43:40 (249)
Jones, Nigel ... 3:51:32 (7,974)
Jones, Nigel ... 4:18:49 (14,086)
Jones, Nigel ... 4:42:40 (19,307)
Jones, Nigel ... 4:57:07 (22,158)
Jones, Oliver ... 3:52:31 (8,173)
Jones, Paul ... 4:05:30 (11,213)
Jones, Paul ... 4:09:25 (12,066)
Jones, Paul ... 4:32:03 (17,130)
Jones, Paul ... 4:59:40 (22,550)
Jones, Peter ... 3:48:25 (7,341)
Jones, Peter ... 3:55:06 (8,713)
Jones, Peter ... 4:03:07 (10,690)
Jones, Peter ... 4:30:35 (16,764)
Jones, Peter ... 4:34:43 (17,662)
Jones, Peter ... 4:36:42 (18,062)
Jones, Peter ... 4:38:27 (18,494)
Jones, Peter ... 4:55:20 (21,824)
Jones, Peter ... 5:27:32 (26,129)
Jones, Peter ... 5:56:48 (28,261)
Jones, Philip ... 2:36:36 (111)
Jones, Philip ... 4:22:55 (15,039)
Jones, Philip ... 4:31:34 (16,996)
Jones, Philip ... 4:38:14 (18,437)
Jones, Philip ... 5:37:14 (26,959)
Jones, Philip ... 5:57:38 (28,305)
Jones, Piers ... 5:04:11 (23,159)
Jones, Raymond ... 3:39:02 (5,579)
Jones, Reginald ... 5:43:59 (27,474)
Jones, Rex ... 4:08:12 (11,802)
Jones, Rhodri ... 4:27:58 (16,188)
Jones, Richard ... 3:52:34 (8,184)
Jones, Richard ... 4:09:15 (12,034)
Jones, Richard ... 4:18:12 (13,921)
Jones, Richard ... 4:25:28 (15,609)
Jones, Rob ... 4:28:43 (16,362)
Jones, Robert ... 3:31:55 (4,457)
Jones, Robert ... 3:57:25 (9,300)
Jones, Robert ... 4:08:51 (11,947)
Jones, Robert ... 5:27:30 (26,127)
Jones, Robert ... 6:37:17 (29,568)
Jones, Rodri ... 2:19:27 (21)
Jones, Roger ... 5:42:30 (27,375)
Jones, Ronnie ... 4:14:22 (13,110)
Jones, Roy ... 2:55:44 (665)
Jones, Russell ... 4:19:37 (14,284)
Jones, Sam ... 4:41:53 (19,139)
Jones, Sean ... 5:11:10 (24,238)
Jones, Simon ... 3:43:10 (6,336)
Jones, Simon ... 4:12:04 (12,633)
Jones, Simon ... 4:23:43 (15,230)
Jones, Stephen ... 2:56:07 (692)
Jones, Stephen ... 3:31:46 (4,430)
Jones, Stephen ... 3:50:45 (7,818)
Jones, Stephen ... 3:54:30 (8,587)
Jones, Stephen ... 4:23:55 (15,277)
Jones, Steven ... 3:16:30 (2,367)
Jones, Steven ... 4:07:19 (11,617)
Jones, Steven ... 4:37:32 (18,257)
Jones, Tim ... 3:32:31 (4,538)
Jones, Timothy ... 2:59:56 (1,024)
Jones, Tony ... 5:39:00 (27,085)
Jones, Vincent ... 2:57:34 (784)
Jones, Walter ... 4:24:48 (15,459)
Jones, Wayne ... 5:56:57 (28,268)
Jones, William ... 4:05:19 (11,168)
Jonkergouw, Mark ... 3:55:55 (8,897)
Jordan, Andrew ... 3:36:41 (5,186)
Jordan, Andy ... 4:29:41 (16,594)
Jordan, David ... 4:17:45 (13,825)
Jordan, John ... 4:07:32 (11,665)
Jordan, Miles ... 4:27:05 (15,994)
Jordan, Peter ... 4:21:59 (14,808)
Jordan, Richard ... 4:12:39 (12,763)
Jordan, Stephen ... 3:47:56 (7,252)
Jordan, Steven ... 4:06:23 (11,427)
Jordan, Thomas ... 3:19:41 (2,727)
Jordan, William ... 3:54:21 (8,549)
Jorgensen, Christian ... 4:35:34 (17,829)
Jorgensen, Henrik ... 2:48:36 (382)
Jorgensen, Torben ... 4:52:42 (21,251)
Joseph, David ... 4:32:33 (17,219)
Joseph, Lloyd ... 4:55:52 (21,964)
Josey, Gary ... 3:36:19 (5,125)
Joshi, Kamaleshkumar ... 5:54:30 (28,137)
Joslin, Alan ... 4:27:36 (16,090)
Joslin, Brian ... 5:39:54 (27,177)
Jost, Robert ... 2:58:20 (838)
Joules, Robert ... 3:35:39 (5,011)
Jourdan, Daniel ... 4:32:08 (17,141)
Jouveneau, Philippe ... 4:52:18 (21,158)
Joux, Philippe ... 3:33:39 (4,705)
Jowes, Nigel ... 4:34:47 (17,672)
Jowett, Kenneth ... 5:27:59 (26,178)
Joy, Tom ... 3:38:42 (5,520)
Joyce, David ... 4:49:44 (20,659)
Joyce, David ... 4:58:57 (22,451)
Joyce, Ian ... 4:40:16 (18,830)
Joyce, John ... 4:49:18 (20,581)
Joyce, Matthew ... 3:19:39 (2,724)
Joyce, Michael ... 5:11:30 (24,285)
Joyce, Simon ... 4:54:36 (21,619)
Joynes, Nicholas ... 4:42:50 (19,343)
Juan Ramon, Pastor ... 4:17:43 (13,818)
Jubb, Chris ... 3:33:40 (4,708)
Judd, Andrew ... 4:13:35 (12,952)
Judd, Garry ... 2:38:31 (148)
Judd, Keith ... 5:24:57 (25,879)
Judd, Paul ... 4:58:55 (22,443)
Judd, Philip ... 4:13:35 (12,952)
Judd, Simon ... 4:07:14 (11,595)
Judd, Simon ... 5:37:35 (26,992)
Jude, Stephen ... 5:54:31 (28,140)
Judge, Bruce ... 2:42:38 (228)
Juett, Michael ... 6:47:06 (29,758)
Jugg, Andrew ... 5:20:48 (25,446)
Jugnarain, Pravin ... 5:56:47 (28,258)
Juhl Nielsen, Bernt ... 4:28:22 (16,277)
Jukes, Frank ... 3:40:09 (5,809)
Julian, John ... 4:33:05 (17,324)
Jun, Myung ... 2:54:14 (589)
Jungblut, Jean ... 3:07:14 (1,521)
Jungers, Jean Michel ... 3:46:03 (6,865)
Junkere, Jerry ... 5:06:32 (23,548)
Jupp, Matthew ... 5:05:00 (23,294)
Jurgens, Rainer ... 3:43:43 (6,442)
Justesen, Leo ... 3:04:54 (1,342)
Kacher, Michael ... 4:09:01 (11,990)
Kadinopoulos, Ben ... 3:59:27 (9,903)
Kaelin, Roger ... 4:01:45 (10,436)
Kaewsakun, Phongsak ... 6:08:38 (28,793)
Kagwe, John ... 2:23:28 (32)
Kahlow, Edward ... 3:44:19 (6,546)
Kaiser, Herbert ... 3:25:24 (3,431)
Kaiser, Joerg ... 3:28:46 (3,953)
Kaiser, Rudolf ... 4:30:48 (16,806)
Kajan, Velautham ... 3:30:49 (4,295)
Kajzar, Anthony ... 5:08:19 (23,819)
Kajzer Hughes, Gareth ... 4:09:46 (12,122)
Kakoullis, Panos ... 4:14:55 (13,239)
Kalaker, Raymond ... 4:17:50 (13,840)
Kalbhenn, Karl-Heinz ... 3:56:40 (9,095)
Kalenik, Zbigniew ... 3:54:41 (8,628)
Kalinsky, Sydney ... 6:58:33 (29,923)

Kalli, Paul	4:29:42 (16,599)	
Kalogeras, Viannis	4:03:41 (10,816)	
Kalogeropoulos, Angelos	5:21:12 (25,489)	
Kalsi, Pratipal	6:31:11 (29,436)	
Kameen, Christopher	4:38:13 (18,431)	
Kameya, Takeo	3:35:35 (5,000)	
Kamis, David	3:11:03 (1,840)	
Kamli, Gamel	3:50:04 (7,697)	
Kampstra, John	3:49:20 (7,533)	
Kampstra, Rein	3:43:20 (6,369)	
Kan, Yuk Man	4:22:31 (14,933)	
Kan, Yuk Mo	4:22:31 (14,933)	
Kang, Dalbir	5:46:16 (27,646)	
Kanselaar, Johan	4:16:22 (13,543)	
Kantaria, Jiten	4:36:55 (18,110)	
Kanth, Rasan	5:30:54 (26,445)	
Kaplan, Arnie	5:56:56 (28,267)	
Kaponig Dipl Ing, Franz	3:28:17 (3,863)	
Kapoor, Neil	3:38:08 (5,419)	
Karageorghis, Panos	5:21:47 (25,562)	
Karathanasis, Dimitris	4:47:33 (20,277)	
Karczewski, Guy	4:31:22 (16,947)	
Karge, Horst Dieter	3:09:42 (1,731)	
Karlcut, Harpal	5:05:25 (23,363)	
Karlsson, Henrik	3:19:32 (2,709)	
Karlsson, Kent	4:50:34 (20,808)	
Karlsson, Patrik	2:59:17 (961)	
Karnfalt, Anders	2:55:37 (660)	
Karrer, Raphael	4:02:54 (10,645)	
Kasprzak, Mark	4:55:37 (21,928)	
Kassapian, Paul	3:06:00 (1,420)	
Kat, Gregory	3:27:52 (3,779)	
Katechia, Bhagesh	3:19:41 (2,727)	
Katkov, Gennady	3:49:32 (7,591)	
Kato, Seiji	4:15:51 (13,434)	
Katz, Gregory	3:28:09 (3,834)	
Katzler, Ron	6:47:59 (29,777)	
Kaudze, Albert	5:15:25 (24,858)	
Kaufman, Patrick	5:59:05 (28,371)	
Kavanagh, John	4:38:54 (18,586)	
Kavanagh, Mike	4:24:39 (15,431)	
Kavanagh, Terence	6:05:32 (28,669)	
Kavanagh, Thomas	3:49:26 (7,559)	
Kavita, Erling	4:45:24 (19,846)	
Kay, Barney	4:14:25 (13,115)	
Kay, David	3:31:16 (4,367)	
Kay, Robert	3:46:52 (7,014)	
Kay, Tom	2:51:49 (508)	
Kaya, Taner	4:42:39 (19,303)	
Kaye, Michael	4:29:35 (16,570)	
Kazimierski, Michael	2:37:48 (133)	
Keal, Ian	3:48:41 (7,398)	
Kean, Alasdair	2:35:23 (94)	
Kean, David	6:55:59 (29,900)	
Keane, Glenn	5:28:45 (26,260)	
Keane, Glenn	6:47:10 (29,761)	
Keane, Neil	3:36:36 (5,169)	
Keane, Simon	4:16:17 (13,521)	
Keane, Simon	4:19:29 (14,253)	
Kear, Dave	4:06:59 (11,547)	
Kearey, Stuart	5:55:10 (28,161)	
Kearney, Gerard	3:54:32 (8,594)	
Kearns, Brian	3:44:12 (6,525)	
Kearns, Joe	4:01:01 (10,285)	
Kearns, Michael	5:34:11 (26,723)	
Kearsey, Martin	4:51:55 (21,073)	
Keating, Steven	4:31:37 (17,016)	
Keddie, Anthony	4:13:23 (12,899)	
Keeble, Ford	4:00:50 (10,248)	
Keeble, John	4:04:52 (11,081)	
Keeble, Paul	5:58:56 (28,364)	
Keeble, Simon	4:04:52 (11,081)	
Keech, Steven	4:37:51 (18,333)	
Keech, Tony	3:20:22 (2,803)	
Keefe, Daniel	4:33:21 (17,387)	
Keel, Anthony	4:12:03 (12,630)	
Keel, Stuart	3:50:12 (7,724)	
Keeler, James	3:45:46 (6,816)	
Keeling, Trevor	4:55:14 (21,791)	
Keen, Allen	4:56:16 (22,034)	
Keen, Bob	4:51:34 (20,999)	
Keen, Howard	4:35:35 (17,839)	
Keen, Peter	5:40:34 (27,236)	
Keen, Tim	5:00:34 (22,672)	
Keenaghan, Shaun	3:45:39 (6,779)	
Keenan, John	5:06:59 (23,613)	
Keenan, Lloyd	3:01:19 (1,095)	
Keene, Graham	4:09:56 (12,147)	
Keene, Stephen	5:20:55 (25,456)	
Keenleyside, Piers	3:50:01 (7,693)	
Keers, Alexander	5:18:17 (25,189)	
Keeves, Colin	4:19:05 (14,143)	
Keevil, Christopher	5:11:52 (24,339)	
Kehlenbach, Rolf	5:40:29 (27,221)	
Keighley, Stuart	3:19:47 (2,737)	
Keir, Howard	3:25:05 (3,387)	
Kekewich, Colin	3:12:06 (1,922)	
Kelford, Colin	4:45:18 (19,823)	
Kellaway, Andrew	2:51:55 (512)	
Kellaway, Roy	3:07:00 (1,505)	
Kelleher, Con	2:59:21 (971)	
Kelleher, Stephen	3:06:52 (1,495)	
Keller, Gale	5:36:36 (26,918)	
Keller, Hansruedi	4:15:12 (13,308)	
Keller, Volker	3:47:49 (7,213)	
Kellett, Gary	3:12:42 (1,979)	
Kellett, Neil	3:17:24 (2,475)	
Kellett, Ronald	4:18:40 (14,044)	
Kelley, Kevin	3:59:12 (9,815)	
Kellow, James	4:10:28 (12,268)	
Kells, Paul	3:23:41 (3,195)	
Kelly, Andrew	4:27:26 (16,046)	
Kelly, Brendan	6:08:48 (28,807)	
Kelly, Christopher	3:50:29 (7,771)	
Kelly, Christopher	3:51:59 (8,068)	
Kelly, David	3:33:28 (4,685)	
Kelly, David	4:02:32 (10,580)	
Kelly, David	4:29:21 (16,508)	
Kelly, David	4:49:23 (20,592)	
Kelly, Dean	4:22:59 (15,059)	
Kelly, Edward	3:36:21 (5,131)	
Kelly, Hugh	3:31:14 (4,360)	
Kelly, James	3:59:54 (10,026)	
Kelly, John	3:56:33 (9,066)	
Kelly, John	4:15:39 (13,396)	
Kelly, John	5:19:07 (25,277)	
Kelly, Joseph	4:51:34 (20,999)	
Kelly, Kevin	3:31:12 (4,355)	
Kelly, Lee	4:06:47 (11,498)	
Kelly, Leon	5:03:54 (23,114)	
Kelly, Liam	4:38:28 (18,500)	
Kelly, Malcolm	4:07:51 (11,730)	
Kelly, Martin	3:35:58 (5,068)	
Kelly, Michael	5:25:17 (25,918)	
Kelly, Michael	7:20:46 (30,082)	
Kelly, Neil	4:00:21 (10,120)	
Kelly, Paul	4:16:55 (13,651)	
Kelly, Peter	3:27:37 (3,725)	
Kelly, Peter	3:53:45 (8,433)	
Kelly, Phillip	5:17:30 (25,108)	
Kelly, Raymond	3:55:32 (8,805)	
Kelly, Richard	3:27:52 (3,779)	
Kelly, Richard	4:45:30 (19,864)	
Kelly, Robert	4:21:41 (14,731)	
Kelly, Robin	4:36:47 (18,078)	
Kelly, Sean	4:36:32 (18,026)	
Kelly, Stephen	3:10:55 (1,829)	
Kelly, Stephen	4:05:32 (11,223)	
Kelly, Stephen	5:16:22 (24,966)	
Kelly, Tarla	3:44:43 (6,618)	
Kelly, Terence	3:40:34 (5,878)	
Kelly, Thomas	4:03:44 (10,825)	
Kelly, Thomas	5:04:52 (23,280)	
Kelly, Thomas	5:19:41 (25,332)	
Kelly, Thomas	5:32:59 (26,611)	
Kelly, Timothy	5:27:39 (26,143)	
Kelsall, Mike	5:46:29 (27,658)	
Kelting, John	3:26:51 (3,602)	
Kelz, Bert	5:03:43 (23,084)	
Kemmett, Gavin	3:30:07 (4,191)	
Kemmis, Oliver	4:32:21 (17,183)	
Kemmitt, David	5:33:04 (26,616)	
Kemp, Adrian	3:48:49 (7,426)	
Kemp, Albert	3:35:44 (5,024)	
Kemp, Bob	6:10:50 (28,885)	
Kemp, Christopher	5:04:32 (23,219)	
Kemp, Jon	2:58:34 (864)	
Kemp, Jonathan	4:46:08 (19,967)	
Kemp, Malcolm	5:00:49 (22,705)	
Kemp, Mark	3:42:42 (6,252)	
Kemp, Martyn	4:21:35 (14,708)	
Kemp, Michael	4:40:16 (18,830)	
Kemp, Nicholas	5:36:11 (26,892)	
Kemp, Richard	4:13:20 (12,884)	
Kemp, Richard	4:31:36 (17,011)	
Kemp, Simon	3:24:36 (3,328)	
Kempe, Michael	4:05:52 (11,313)	
Kemplay, Miles	3:29:04 (4,008)	
Kempsell, Robert	4:10:55 (12,378)	
Kempson, Graeme	5:31:00 (26,452)	
Kemp-Symonds, Jeremy	3:39:04 (5,584)	
Kempton, Douglas	4:09:24 (12,063)	
Kenchington, Christopher	3:08:36 (1,637)	
Kenchington, Nicholas	2:41:41 (208)	
Kendall, John	2:45:15 (297)	
Kendall, Jonathan	4:00:56 (10,270)	
Kendell, Lee	3:51:45 (8,015)	
Kenderdine, Robert	3:25:33 (3,451)	
Kendle, Matthew	3:29:25 (4,066)	
Kendrick, Chris	4:44:47 (19,729)	
Kendrick, Neil	4:38:08 (18,415)	
Kennard, Andrew	5:12:14 (24,385)	
Kennard, Stephen	5:07:25 (23,684)	
Kennaway, Anthony	3:34:02 (4,759)	
Kennedy, Andrew	5:22:50 (25,688)	
Kennedy, Antony	3:32:20 (4,512)	
Kennedy, Christopher	4:23:07 (15,088)	
Kennedy, Christopher	5:27:59 (26,178)	
Kennedy, Chuck	7:40:49 (30,166)	
Kennedy, David	5:49:33 (27,875)	
Kennedy, Donald	2:58:55 (925)	
Kennedy, George	3:49:26 (7,559)	
Kennedy, Ian	3:04:00 (1,282)	
Kennedy, James	4:10:52 (12,363)	
Kennedy, Joseph	4:41:21 (19,038)	
Kennedy, Juilian	4:14:43 (13,177)	
Kennedy, Martin	5:01:30 (22,805)	
Kennedy, Peter	4:40:56 (18,963)	
Kennedy, Richard	3:42:44 (6,258)	
Kennedy, Richard	4:10:47 (12,332)	
Kennedy, Robin	3:46:59 (7,033)	
Kennedy, William	3:48:10 (7,297)	
Kennedy Martin, Matthew	5:33:58 (26,686)	
Kennerdale, Simon	3:57:51 (9,446)	
Kennett, David	3:55:19 (8,763)	
Kennett, Steffan	3:35:17 (4,949)	
Kenny, Andrew	4:03:00 (10,661)	
Kenny, Bernard	4:27:41 (16,114)	
Kenny, Chris	3:46:09 (6,888)	
Kenny, Cormac	5:27:46 (26,154)	
Kenny, Jack	4:01:22 (10,365)	
Kenny, John	4:29:26 (16,528)	
Kenny, Laurie	9:33:15 (30,283)	
Kenny, Neil	3:06:33 (1,464)	
Kenny, Ronald	3:46:09 (6,888)	
Kenny, Thomas	4:04:22 (10,959)	
Kensington, Nick	3:40:14 (5,819)	
Kent, Clark	6:20:45 (29,184)	
Kent, David	4:50:42 (20,826)	
Kent, Emerson	4:18:19 (13,959)	
Kent, Geoffrey	4:57:50 (22,270)	
Kent, Jeremy	4:48:56 (20,512)	
Kent, John	5:45:34 (27,597)	
Kent, Paul	3:02:06 (1,161)	
Kent, Richard	5:01:43 (22,826)	
Kenton, Peter	3:24:52 (3,360)	
Kenward, Graham	3:50:50 (7,831)	
Kenyon, Stephen	3:27:13 (3,662)	
Keogh, James	6:03:30 (28,566)	
Keohane, Paul	4:37:23 (18,219)	
Kepper, Sascha	3:44:40 (6,605)	
Kerfers, Alain	4:22:44 (14,991)	
Kerley, William	4:11:20 (12,466)	

Kern, Horst...................4:17:55 (13,856)
Kern, Reinhard 3:39:53 (5,754)
Kerr, Ben......................5:25:41 (25,956)
Kerr, Gordon.................3:46:22 (6,927)
Kerr, Richard 6:18:06 (29,117)
Kerr, Will......................3:05:26 (1,385)
Kerridge, Donald..........3:20:08 (2,778)
Kerry, Mark...................5:28:40 (26,249)
Kershaw, Craig..............3:31:31 (4,393)
Kershaw, John...............3:15:26 (2,264)
Kershaw, Richard..........5:21:16 (25,498)
Kershaw, Steven...........5:45:37 (27,602)
Kershaw, Stuart.............3:44:27 (6,567)
Kesby, William 4:30:19 (16,730)
Keska, John...................3:14:19 (2,151)
Kester, Blair..................5:05:12 (23,318)
Kestle, Michael 3:04:36 (1,323)
Kestle, Ryan..................3:18:52 (2,639)
Ketab, Daniel 4:38:34 (18,519)
Ketchell, Robert............3:36:18 (5,123)
Kett, Brian 4:56:40 (22,091)
Ketterick, Edward..........5:01:49 (22,842)
Kettering, Ian................3:58:55 (9,726)
Kettle, Stephen 5:46:40 (27,677)
Keuchel, Joachim 3:22:45 (3,078)
Keun, Andries................6:13:15 (28,960)
Kevan, Stuart 3:34:50 (4,882)
Kevill, Russell................4:08:36 (11,892)
Kew, Graeme..................5:13:36 (24,581)
Kew, John 4:51:13 (20,926)
Key, David 5:22:09 (25,605)
Keyes, Jason 5:19:49 (25,348)
Keynes, Jonathan...........4:37:24 (18,225)
Keys, Andy 4:46:48 (20,114)
Keys, Duncan.................5:15:50 (24,914)
Keys, Stephen 3:13:32 (2,063)
Keywood, Glen 4:29:33 (16,561)
Keywood, Stephen..........2:34:03 (83)
Khaihra, Harvey.............3:19:03 (2,660)
Khan, Ahmed Ali............7:08:46 (30,011)
Khan, Sajid 5:50:44 (27,939)
Khan, Saleem................5:13:19 (24,553)
Khan, Shakeel 5:05:13 (23,323)
Khan, Sid 3:51:19 (7,935)
Khandoker, Fazle 4:20:15 (14,418)
Khanzada, Mohammed....4:35:18 (17,775)
Khonsaraki, Behrooz 4:42:52 (19,352)
Khosa, Kartar Singh 5:54:06 (28,117)
Khurana, Rohit...............4:41:56 (19,149)
Kibble, Michael 4:06:55 (11,531)
Kiberd, Peter 5:51:44 (28,004)
Kiberd, Stephen 3:33:38 (4,702)
Kibrya, Richard 3:30:28 (4,241)
Kidd, Alex......................3:58:52 (9,718)
Kidd, Douglas.................6:26:48 (29,326)
Kidd, Jason 4:35:09 (17,739)
Kiddle, Rick...................2:46:22 (325)
Kidney, Edward 4:24:26 (15,381)
Kidwell, Peter 2:57:07 (755)
Kidwell, Steven..............2:59:27 (978)
Kiefer, Roland 4:26:01 (15,736)
Kierman, Samuel............4:34:55 (17,697)
Kiesel, Berna 4:22:38 (14,962)
Kiff, Alan 5:07:06 (23,630)
Kiffin, David 4:44:54 (19,759)
Kikuchi, Tatsuji..............4:13:31 (12,935)
Kilbane, James..............5:21:36 (25,533)
Kilby, Andrew 3:47:21 (7,100)
Kile, Reynold 4:50:54 (20,861)
Kilkenny, Kevin..............3:35:59 (5,071)
Kilmartin, Kieran............4:14:05 (13,053)
Kilpatrick, Declan 4:53:18 (21,373)
Kiltie, David 3:53:20 (8,344)
Kilvert, Philip 3:18:24 (2,590)
Kim, Jong 4:07:38 (11,684)
Kim, Sahng 3:57:46 (9,416)
Kimber, Gary 3:33:11 (4,642)
Kimber, Philip 3:36:56 (5,232)
Kimber, Thomas.............3:16:28 (2,361)
Kimberley, Darren...........3:57:07 (9,200)
Kimberley, Simon 3:49:18 (7,525)
Kimpton, John................3:15:17 (2,253)
Kinber, John 5:23:34 (25,753)

Kincaid, Colm.................4:17:39 (13,802)
Kincaid, Michael 6:44:42 (29,731)
Kincaid, Sam..................2:49:42 (416)
Kinchington, David..........3:46:29 (6,944)
Kind, Matthew 3:42:25 (6,206)
King, Adrian 4:40:20 (18,845)
King, Andrew 2:46:31 (329)
King, Andrew 3:29:45 (4,129)
King, Andrew 3:57:44 (9,403)
King, Andrew 4:37:43 (18,303)
King, Christopher 3:08:26 (1,625)
King, Christopher 3:17:08 (2,440)
King, Christopher 4:49:58 (20,711)
King, Dave 4:56:46 (22,101)
King, David 3:16:45 (2,400)
King, David 4:11:40 (12,544)
King, David 4:12:58 (12,823)
King, David 5:25:01 (25,887)
King, David 5:34:52 (26,794)
King, Dominic 3:49:39 (7,614)
King, Donald 4:22:03 (14,829)
King, Gary 5:31:05 (26,459)
King, Gerard 4:27:10 (16,003)
King, Gerry 3:32:40 (4,557)
King, Graeme 4:06:59 (11,547)
King, Graham 4:18:26 (13,998)
King, Ian 3:14:41 (2,183)
King, Ian 3:44:43 (6,618)
King, Jason 6:45:57 (29,749)
King, Job 2:37:07 (119)
King, John 5:24:12 (25,808)
King, John 5:40:05 (27,197)
King, Jonathan 4:29:55 (16,665)
King, Leslie 4:38:18 (18,452)
King, Leslie 5:28:51 (26,277)
King, Malcolm 3:55:20 (8,767)
King, Patrick 5:57:33 (28,300)
King, Paul 4:21:22 (14,660)
King, Paul 4:25:43 (15,657)
King, Paul 4:46:14 (19,993)
King, Richard 4:22:29 (14,924)
King, Richard 4:30:40 (16,780)
King, Richard 5:33:29 (26,647)
King, Robert 3:55:11 (8,728)
King, Robin 4:07:05 (11,568)
King, Stefan 3:48:42 (7,402)
King, Stephen 4:15:43 (13,406)
King, Steven 3:52:33 (8,182)
King, Terry 5:36:37 (26,919)
King, Walter 4:51:38 (21,016)
Kingdon, Adam 4:11:35 (12,521)
Kingdon, Charles 4:44:26 (19,662)
Kingdon, David 4:01:39 (10,424)
Kingsleigh-Smith, Diarmuid........3:53:19 (8,338)
Kingsley Williams, Jonathan 4:28:55 (16,404)
Kingstad, Richard...........2:50:37 (451)
Kingston, Andrew 5:02:49 (22,980)
Kingston, Bernard...........5:22:15 (25,622)
Kingston, Leo 4:54:39 (21,623)
Kingston, Neil 4:51:41 (21,029)
Kingston, Robert 4:12:49 (12,795)
Kingston, Sam 3:36:06 (5,091)
Kininmonth, Alex 4:55:21 (21,831)
Kinnest, Christopher 4:51:18 (20,946)
Kinney, Andrew 5:16:34 (24,996)
Kinnill, Philip 3:50:10 (7,717)
Kinsell, Paul..................5:14:07 (24,641)
Kinsella, Gary 5:43:20 (27,428)
Kinsella, Simon 3:59:59 (10,052)
Kinsey, Nicholas 2:36:03 (106)
Kinson, Phil 5:00:48 (22,703)
Kinugawa, Yoshiaki.........4:13:29 (12,930)
Kinzler, Harald 3:37:19 (5,305)
Kiraz, Serkan 4:23:17 (15,127)
Kirby, Alan 5:23:52 (25,777)
Kirby, Alex 4:50:15 (20,758)
Kirby, Andrew 3:59:42 (9,974)
Kirby, Andrew 4:03:50 (10,848)
Kirby, Andrew 5:02:37 (22,949)
Kirby, David 4:03:09 (10,696)
Kirby, Edward 4:13:40 (12,975)
Kirby, Graham 3:32:37 (4,551)
Kirby, Ian 4:33:47 (17,496)

Kirby, Jeff 5:31:52 (26,521)
Kirby, Jeremy 4:00:14 (10,095)
Kirby, Michael 3:42:57 (6,294)
Kirby, Richard 4:20:00 (14,368)
Kirby, Richard 5:18:44 (25,237)
Kirby, Roger 4:18:28 (14,005)
Kirby, Stephen 3:47:26 (7,125)
Kirby, Steve 3:02:08 (1,164)
Kirby, Studney 4:28:41 (16,357)
Kirchin, Stephen 3:12:45 (1,983)
Kiritharanathan, Kailayanathan ..5:45:27 (27,588)
Kirk, Andrew 4:53:21 (21,388)
Kirk, Andrew 5:16:29 (24,986)
Kirk, Clive 4:06:38 (11,473)
Kirk, Colin 3:41:52 (6,104)
Kirk, David 4:15:58 (13,457)
Kirk, David 4:51:31 (20,985)
Kirk, Elliott 3:39:55 (5,762)
Kirk, Jonathan 4:24:34 (15,413)
Kirk, Michael 4:38:46 (18,568)
Kirk, Neil 3:04:10 (1,293)
Kirk, Richard 4:42:48 (19,331)
Kirk, Richard 6:42:02 (29,692)
Kirkbride, Nigel 4:06:48 (11,502)
Kirkbright, Nigel 3:28:26 (3,895)
Kirkby, Kevin 3:45:57 (6,847)
Kirkdale, M 4:26:13 (15,780)
Kirkham, David 3:50:20 (7,741)
Kirkham, John 4:00:51 (10,251)
Kirkham, Stan 4:36:54 (18,104)
Kirkland, Daniel 3:49:41 (7,620)
Kirkland, James 3:25:34 (3,452)
Kirkpatrick, Andrew........5:08:05 (23,780)
Kirkpatrick, Ivor 5:43:35 (27,444)
Kirkpatrick, Stephen 3:29:25 (4,066)
Kirkpatrick, William 4:31:11 (16,898)
Kirkup, John 5:17:05 (25,060)
Kirkwood, Craig 2:16:25 (16)
Kirsten, Jens 3:31:30 (4,392)
Kirwan, Stephen 5:13:12 (24,530)
Kirwin, Peter..................3:17:32 (2,488)
Kisenyi, Jonathan 5:11:07 (24,228)
Kisielewicz, Justin 8:31:58 (30,247)
Kissane, John 4:51:39 (21,019)
Kitcat, David 4:56:22 (22,044)
Kitchen, Neil 3:28:19 (3,872)
Kitchener, Alan 4:16:30 (13,573)
Kitchener, Steven 3:17:42 (2,501)
Kitchener, Tristan 3:50:54 (7,847)
Kitchenside, Philip 5:25:03 (25,892)
Kitcher, Stephen.............5:04:14 (23,170)
Kitchin, Paul 5:47:38 (27,732)
Kitching, Andrew 4:21:30 (14,693)
Kitching, Barrie 3:25:20 (3,422)
Kitching, Ian 2:50:00 (429)
Kitching, Leslie 4:51:37 (21,012)
Kitney, Stephen 5:11:05 (24,222)
Kitteridge, Steven 3:59:57 (10,042)
Kitton, Daniel 5:53:30 (28,090)
Kittrell, Charles 4:25:55 (15,707)
Kivlehan, David 4:33:22 (17,392)
Kjaer, Mogens 3:58:10 (9,530)
Klaber, Robert 5:25:35 (25,948)
Klamminger, Hans 5:00:00 (22,622)
Klein, Alexander 3:22:42 (3,072)
Kleinrock, Michael 5:19:16 (25,289)
Klimmer, Josef 4:42:25 (19,255)
Klinger, Robert 5:11:47 (24,326)
Klitz, Peter 4:35:54 (17,908)
Klug, Bryan 3:49:59 (7,686)
Knapman, Barrie 4:09:48 (12,125)
Knapp, Adrian 3:46:31 (6,951)
Knapp, Neil 3:18:08 (2,553)
Knapp, Robert 3:37:30 (5,336)
Knapton, Peter 4:05:44 (11,283)
Knattress, Stephen 4:12:24 (12,714)
Knaut, Wolf 4:57:15 (22,178)
Kneale, Stewart 3:42:00 (6,124)
Kneale, William 4:34:48 (17,677)
Kneiding, Dieter 3:45:43 (6,802)
Knibbs, Alec 6:09:33 (28,837)
Knibbs, Ian 5:30:46 (26,437)
Knibbs, Tim 4:31:35 (17,003)

Knight, Adam 3:51:49 (8,031)
Knight, Adrian 3:44:42 (6,613)
Knight, Alan 4:00:43 (10,217)
Knight, Alan 4:52:44 (21,260)
Knight, Andrew 4:00:01 (10,058)
Knight, Andrew 4:36:33 (18,032)
Knight, Andrew 4:49:49 (20,678)
Knight, Andy 4:58:08 (22,319)
Knight, Brian 4:24:11 (15,327)
Knight, Brian 6:40:19 (29,652)
Knight, Christopher 4:21:47 (14,754)
Knight, Daren 5:19:38 (25,321)
Knight, Dave 4:27:46 (16,140)
Knight, David 2:45:22 (304)
Knight, David 3:58:36 (9,642)
Knight, Duncan 3:56:35 (9,074)
Knight, John 3:56:43 (9,109)
Knight, Jonathan 4:21:48 (14,761)
Knight, Kevin 3:44:34 (6,592)
Knight, Kevin 4:11:21 (12,472)
Knight, Malcolm 3:31:38 (4,415)
Knight, Mark 3:53:17 (8,327)
Knight, Michael 5:20:24 (25,397)
Knight, Nick 4:19:34 (14,273)
Knight, Peter 4:25:53 (15,698)
Knight, Robert 4:12:23 (12,710)
Knight, Roger 5:01:48 (22,838)
Knight, Ronald 4:22:53 (15,032)
Knight, Roy 3:47:19 (7,090)
Knight, Roy 5:43:56 (27,468)
Knight, Simon 5:02:42 (22,964)
Knight, Stephen 4:29:21 (16,508)
Knight, Terry 5:11:45 (24,321)
Knight, Timothy 4:25:29 (15,613)
Knight, Tony 4:31:18 (16,934)
Knight, Vincent 3:49:16 (7,515)
Knight, William 5:08:52 (23,915)
Knightley, John 5:31:57 (26,531)
Knights, Christopher 4:55:17 (21,810)
Knights, Colin 4:09:00 (11,978)
Knights, Henry 4:35:44 (17,872)
Knights, Jim 5:12:12 (24,380)
Knights, Karl 3:56:32 (9,062)
Knoll, Gottfried 2:58:49 (912)
Knolle, Eike 4:54:44 (21,656)
Knop, Werner 4:55:39 (21,940)
Knott, Gregory 3:34:07 (4,774)
Knott, Jonathan 4:26:17 (15,800)
Knott, Peter 4:43:08 (19,413)
Knott, Stephen 4:35:38 (17,849)
Knott, Trevor 3:38:16 (5,444)
Knowles, Maxwell 4:14:21 (13,107)
Knowles, Paul 4:37:32 (18,257)
Knowles, Roy 4:39:23 (18,664)
Knox, Barry 3:22:48 (3,086)
Knox, Frederick 3:53:02 (8,272)
Knox, Mark 4:11:58 (12,600)
Knox, Roger 3:23:34 (3,183)
Knuchel, Jean Rodolphe 3:55:29 (8,797)
Knuckey, Alan 6:20:29 (29,170)
Knudgaard, Ole 4:23:39 (15,218)
Knust, Achim 4:50:57 (20,870)
Ko, Kenneth 4:38:26 (18,488)
Kobr, Michael 3:40:59 (5,952)
Koch De Gooreynd, Alex 6:01:39 (28,491)
Koda, Genjiro 5:00:56 (22,722)
Koe, Digby 4:42:16 (19,218)
Koe, Simon 4:42:15 (19,215)
Koemans, Clemens 4:10:55 (12,378)
Koeppel, Paul 3:50:44 (7,814)
Koffman, Andrew 4:58:59 (22,460)
Kogler, Christian 5:39:59 (27,188)
Kohara, Nobuharu 4:21:26 (14,679)
Kohl, Russell 4:09:08 (12,007)
Kohn, Alan 4:55:42 (21,947)
Kollnberger, Adrian 3:55:35 (8,814)
Kolodziej, Jerzy 7:41:33 (30,167)
Kolthof, Thomas 3:25:46 (3,479)
Komischke, Uwe 3:58:38 (9,649)
Kong, Cheuk 4:22:10 (14,847)
Konigsberger, Martin 3:49:32 (7,591)
Konishi, Yoshiharu 4:06:14 (11,393)
Konrath, Gerhard 5:47:40 (27,736)
Koorts, Kobus 3:52:03 (8,085)
Koozehkanani, Ala 6:16:52 (29,084)
Kophamel, Andrew 4:34:39 (17,651)
Kor, Michael 4:36:48 (18,085)
Korayem, Adam 5:00:04 (22,631)
Korba, David 4:16:25 (13,557)
Korsak-Koulagenko, Youri 5:22:23 (25,634)
Kosgei, Japhet 2:10:45 (5)
Kositzky, David 3:49:43 (7,625)
Koster, Niek 3:53:41 (8,422)
Kotarski, Dominic 4:38:37 (18,532)
Kovacs, Gabriel 5:01:46 (22,835)
Kovacs, Ian 4:31:27 (16,969)
Kpedekpo, Malcolm 4:06:33 (11,459)
Krahn, Mike 3:41:38 (6,064)
Krause, John 4:08:47 (11,934)
Krause, Ludwig 3:29:15 (4,036)
Krause, Philip 4:12:51 (12,799)
Kreckeler, Kevin 4:29:00 (16,420)
Kreeger, Stephen 4:12:05 (12,640)
Kreisef, Hernz 5:57:18 (28,283)
Kreitzberg, Martin 5:04:59 (23,293)
Kremer, Dominik 4:31:13 (16,908)
Kremer, Johannes 5:26:15 (26,013)
Kretzschmar, Geoffrey 5:32:01 (26,534)
Kretzschmar, Gerd 4:03:17 (10,718)
Kreuter, Eric 4:33:46 (17,492)
Kreutner, Walter 4:13:32 (12,939)
Kriek, Jan 4:30:36 (16,765)
Krievs, Frank 4:51:41 (21,029)
Kriscovich, Scott 3:12:11 (1,929)
Krishnamoorthy, Appadurai 4:27:28 (16,055)
Kristensen, Kaj 3:30:24 (4,233)
Kristiansen, Koell 3:39:59 (5,782)
Kristof, Joseph 3:41:26 (6,034)
Krois, Peter 3:30:35 (4,260)
Krook, Rudy 5:38:41 (27,064)
Kropf, Peter 3:16:51 (2,407)
Krosnar-Clarke, Steven 4:23:57 (15,281)
Kruk, Nigel 3:55:44 (8,854)
Krummenacher, Reto 4:43:26 (19,473)
Krupka, James 4:41:55 (19,144)
Kruppa, Peter 4:10:26 (12,262)
Kruppa, Robert 4:34:08 (17,564)
Kuah, En 3:52:15 (8,124)
Kubo, Hiroki 4:28:05 (16,205)
Kuch, Frank 4:32:45 (17,263)
Kuipers, John 3:56:05 (8,946)
Kuka, Selman 3:35:49 (5,035)
Kulartz, Peter 3:15:55 (2,312)
Kulina, Andy 5:29:52 (26,359)
Kumar, Mahesh 3:15:42 (2,289)
Kunerth, Bernard 4:43:11 (19,425)
Kunin, Seth 4:43:35 (19,516)
Kuningas, Richard 5:04:24 (23,200)
Kuosmanen, Pasi 4:23:07 (15,088)
Kupse, John 5:51:18 (27,969)
Kurkjian, Christopher 3:54:25 (8,570)
Kurvers, Willem 4:09:05 (12,003)
Kusel, John 5:47:11 (27,713)
Kuster, Jochen 3:30:47 (4,291)
Kutner, Christian 4:54:33 (21,604)
Kutner, Daryn 4:54:33 (21,604)
Kuypers, Paul 3:58:17 (9,560)
Kvalvaag, Robert 4:10:49 (12,350)
Kvernes, Peter 4:04:39 (11,033)
Kwiatkowski, Richard 4:47:13 (20,207)
Kyd, Laurence 4:17:54 (13,851)
Kyle, Richard 3:41:16 (6,003)
Kynoch, Graham 3:52:35 (8,188)
Kynoch, Michael 4:10:44 (12,318)
Kyprianou, Ermis 4:56:45 (22,098)
Kyriakides, Lakis 5:17:13 (25,072)
Kyritsis, Nick 4:26:54 (15,936)
La Plante, Charles 5:37:04 (26,950)
Labuschagne, Timothy 3:25:09 (3,393)
Lace, Ryan 6:35:14 (29,529)
Lacey, Adam 7:18:37 (30,071)
Lacey, Mark 3:01:58 (1,145)
Lachaud, Robert 3:31:58 (4,463)
Lacheteau, Jean Jaques 3:56:37 (9,081)
Lack, Andy 3:06:24 (1,452)
Lacreuse, Eric 3:30:40 (4,272)
Lacreuse, Lionel 3:30:40 (4,272)
Lacy, Dave 3:04:38 (1,325)
Lacy, David 4:43:02 (19,395)
Lacy-Smith, Paul 4:08:43 (11,916)
Ladanowski, John 3:52:34 (8,184)
Laden, Ron 4:46:30 (20,054)
Ladkin, Christopher 4:04:41 (11,038)
Ladner, Kevin 3:55:33 (8,808)
Ladocha, David 3:18:12 (2,563)
Ladoue, Didier 3:01:19 (1,095)
Ladwa, Daylal 3:57:30 (9,326)
Laedrach, Hansjuerg 3:22:48 (3,086)
Lafranchi, Bruno 2:35:34 (98)
Laganga, Marco 3:41:38 (6,064)
Lagarde, Noel 3:19:42 (2,729)
Laghi, Franco 3:37:55 (5,395)
Lahdelma, Sami 4:43:40 (19,530)
Lahutte, Pierre 3:28:45 (3,949)
Laidlaw, Graham 6:47:20 (29,763)
Laidlaw, Ross 4:59:43 (22,556)
Laing, Andrew 4:03:24 (10,747)
Laing, James 3:55:43 (8,848)
Laing, Michael 4:42:54 (19,363)
Lainson, Colin 4:37:47 (18,316)
Laird, Gordon 4:50:05 (20,733)
Laird, John 5:00:00 (22,622)
Laird, Martin 5:05:31 (23,387)
Laity, Alan 4:41:25 (19,050)
Lake, Earl 4:17:09 (13,703)
Lake, Ewan 4:35:34 (17,829)
Lake, Matthew 4:12:45 (12,781)
Lake, Stewart 3:26:27 (3,552)
Lakeland, Peter 3:24:32 (3,316)
Laker, Andrew 3:19:53 (2,752)
Lakey, Daniel 4:03:12 (10,702)
Lakha, Gulamabbas 5:35:33 (26,850)
Lakhani, Sunil 5:58:36 (28,349)
Lakner, James 3:22:50 (3,090)
Lally, Patrick 4:03:03 (10,671)
Lam, David 4:52:23 (21,180)
Lam, Wayne 4:15:09 (13,293)
Lamb, Adrian 4:21:40 (14,727)
Lamb, Andy 2:39:00 (157)
Lamb, George 4:20:04 (14,384)
Lamb, Ian 3:28:05 (3,816)
Lamb, John 4:18:03 (13,877)
Lamb, Michael 3:46:44 (6,995)
Lamb, Russell 4:51:09 (20,918)
Lambden, Murray 2:43:47 (254)
Lambden, Richard 4:29:43 (16,603)
Lambert, Allan 6:35:13 (29,527)
Lambert, Andrew 3:33:27 (4,683)
Lambert, Brian 3:59:52 (10,016)
Lambert, David 3:52:51 (8,238)
Lambert, Ian 3:29:25 (4,066)
Lambert, John 4:54:03 (21,523)
Lambert, Jonathan 5:00:57 (22,725)
Lambert, Matthew 4:54:23 (21,572)
Lambert, Nicholas 4:02:49 (10,626)
Lambert, Nigel 3:48:59 (7,462)
Lambertucci, Ulderico 5:32:31 (26,582)
Lambeth, David 4:19:01 (14,123)
Lambropoulos, Alexi 5:28:00 (26,182)
Lamey, Timothy 4:00:39 (10,193)
Laming, Paul 3:49:15 (7,509)
Lammali, Aziouz 2:40:09 (174)
Lammas, Edward 5:21:56 (25,577)
Lammas, John 3:20:52 (2,873)
Lamont, Christopher 2:51:41 (501)
Lamont, Christopher 4:08:23 (11,846)
Lamprecht, Markus 4:00:16 (10,103)
Lamprell, Ian 5:43:01 (27,410)
Lancashire, James 5:24:26 (25,825)
Lancaster, Dave 3:10:21 (1,780)
Lancaster, David 5:56:10 (28,219)
Lancaster, Kenneth 5:13:10 (24,526)
Lancaster, Paul 3:28:47 (3,957)
Lancelle, Didier 3:35:35 (5,000)
Lancucki, Tadeusz 4:25:16 (15,568)
Land, Adrian 3:43:08 (6,332)
Land, Martin 5:48:41 (27,827)
Landau, Andrew 4:43:26 (19,473)
Landells, Stephen 3:31:48 (4,438)

Lander, Christopher 3:54:22 (8,555)
Lander, Graham 4:43:40 (19,530)
Landers, Dene 4:39:02 (18,615)
Landier, Yannick 3:49:30 (7,584)
Landolt, Alfred 3:56:31 (9,058)
Lane, Adam 3:50:04 (7,697)
Lane, Alan 4:21:58 (14,802)
Lane, Andrew 3:17:41 (2,500)
Lane, Barnard 4:37:51 (18,333)
Lane, Brian 3:33:34 (4,691)
Lane, Christopher 4:02:54 (10,645)
Lane, John 3:18:30 (2,599)
Lane, Justin 3:00:37 (1,061)
Lane, Kevin 5:16:45 (25,019)
Lane, Kevin 5:48:42 (27,828)
Lane, Lewis 4:10:07 (12,185)
Lane, Mark 4:23:59 (15,291)
Lane, Matthew 3:58:13 (9,542)
Lane, Paul 5:39:54 (27,177)
Lane, Peter 4:54:41 (21,634)
Lane, Philip 4:15:57 (13,453)
Lane, Raymond 5:07:33 (23,701)
Lane, Ronald 3:06:33 (1,464)
Lanet, Maurice 3:29:41 (4,119)
Lang, Thomas 4:37:04 (18,138)
Langan, Francis 4:48:47 (20,483)
Langan, Paul 3:46:50 (7,007)
Langdale, Alfred 8:02:53 (30,210)
Langdon, Benjamin 4:11:04 (12,409)
Langdon, Jeremy 4:34:17 (17,591)
Langdon, Robert 6:08:00 (28,762)
Langer, Mark 4:18:39 (14,041)
Langevin, Karl 2:45:09 (292)
Langford, Don 3:57:30 (9,326)
Langford, Keith 2:50:53 (460)
Langford, Michael 7:23:35 (30,095)
Langford, Paul 3:36:08 (5,095)
Langham, Brian 3:21:25 (2,937)
Langley, Colin 3:17:43 (2,503)
Langley, Julian 4:24:05 (15,307)
Langley, Lawrence 3:10:42 (1,808)
Langley, Manfred 5:19:04 (25,271)
Langridge, Adam 3:54:10 (8,504)
Langridge, John 4:15:57 (13,453)
Langridge, Simon 3:13:49 (2,093)
Langston, Brian 4:27:15 (16,017)
Langston, Paul 4:11:28 (12,495)
Langton, Andrew 4:23:36 (15,205)
Lani, Alain 3:19:16 (2,685)
Lankshear, Ian 5:57:27 (28,294)
Lannigan, Gerry 6:11:47 (28,922)
Lansell, Mark 3:39:58 (5,778)
Lantsbery, David 3:27:37 (3,725)
Lapinskis, Jeffrey 5:09:50 (24,062)
Lappin, Richard 4:31:03 (16,862)
Larby, Cyril 5:15:14 (24,837)
Larcombe, Peter 4:04:08 (10,908)
Lardner, Andrew 4:04:39 (11,033)
Large, Neil 3:55:13 (8,738)
Large, Steven 3:01:54 (1,141)
Larkin, Kevin 4:51:49 (21,058)
Larkin, Matthew 3:30:50 (4,298)
Larkin, Robert 3:34:47 (4,875)
Larkins, Simon 3:14:00 (2,121)
Larmer, Richard 5:30:23 (26,400)
Larnard, Richard 4:52:34 (21,228)
Larsen, Arne 3:56:19 (8,998)
Larsen, Jan 3:12:20 (1,944)
Larsen, Ulf 4:56:32 (22,074)
Larsson, Charles 4:28:57 (16,411)
Larthe, Russell 4:10:45 (12,321)
Lartigue, Didier 3:07:37 (1,557)
Lascelles, Paul 5:51:52 (28,009)
Lashmar, Anthony Paul 2:59:58 (1,029)
Laslett, Jason 4:24:01 (15,298)
Lassave, Herve 2:50:59 (468)
Lassmann, Werner 4:00:35 (10,181)
Last, Fraser 4:49:54 (20,696)
Last, Philip 5:05:24 (23,361)
Lataste, Gerard 3:18:28 (2,594)
Latham, Andrew 4:02:51 (10,632)
Latham, Anthony 4:01:35 (10,406)
Latham, Martin 3:50:47 (7,823)
Latham, Paul 3:33:18 (4,660)
Latham, Philip 4:56:55 (22,131)
Lathwell, Stuart 6:18:07 (29,118)
Latto, Brian 3:38:30 (5,481)
Latus, James 4:53:11 (21,350)
Lauesen, Preben 3:45:57 (6,847)
Lauga, Philippe 3:14:56 (2,213)
Laughton, Philip 3:47:03 (7,042)
Launder, Kevin 4:01:30 (10,396)
Laurence, Garry 4:07:24 (11,639)
Laurence, Peter 3:27:43 (3,748)
Laurenson, Anthony 4:36:52 (18,097)
Laurent, Dominique 3:55:09 (8,722)
Laurent, Thierry 5:24:10 (25,805)
Laustsen, Niels 3:02:58 (1,210)
Lautenschlager, Nicky 4:06:50 (11,512)
Lavault, Patrick 4:13:59 (13,038)
Lavelle, Andrew 5:30:25 (26,404)
Lavelle, Jon 3:54:47 (8,655)
Lavender, Christopher 4:32:28 (17,210)
Lavender, Fred 4:28:12 (16,238)
Lavender, Jack 4:37:44 (18,308)
Laver, Toby 3:12:29 (1,958)
Laverick, John 3:52:36 (8,190)
Lavery, Adrian 3:10:49 (1,819)
Lavery, Gregory 5:13:59 (24,628)
Lavery, Malcolm 3:52:20 (8,140)
Lavery, Richard 3:24:15 (3,277)
Lavin, Stephen 5:32:44 (26,597)
Lavy, Jeremy 4:07:44 (11,709)
Law, Alan 4:03:51 (10,850)
Law, Albert 4:07:25 (11,647)
Law, Andrew 4:57:09 (22,165)
Law, Andrew 4:57:39 (22,239)
Law, Dale 4:14:01 (13,043)
Law, David 4:49:58 (20,711)
Lawes, Leslie 5:47:29 (27,727)
Lawes, Richard 2:49:45 (417)
Lawford, Andrew 4:06:34 (11,464)
Lawler, Christopher 4:45:08 (19,791)
Lawler, Kieron 5:31:57 (26,531)
Lawler, Tim 5:09:00 (23,941)
Lawley, Tom 3:20:42 (2,847)
Lawlor, John 4:43:54 (19,574)
Lawlor, Kevin 4:36:20 (17,982)
Lawrance, Terry 4:36:29 (18,017)
Lawrence, Andrew 3:04:40 (1,328)
Lawrence, Anthony 4:07:36 (11,678)
Lawrence, Frank 5:27:50 (26,161)
Lawrence, Gary 5:05:10 (23,313)
Lawrence, Gavin 3:58:02 (9,497)
Lawrence, John 5:37:00 (26,947)
Lawrence, Keith 4:42:57 (19,376)
Lawrence, Lee 5:03:03 (23,012)
Lawrence, Malcolm 6:31:28 (29,442)
Lawrence, Matthew 4:16:31 (13,577)
Lawrence, Nick 4:09:52 (12,136)
Lawrence, Peter 5:28:25 (26,225)
Lawrence, Raymond 5:02:32 (22,940)
Lawrence, Richard 4:35:51 (17,891)
Lawrence, Rodney 4:44:36 (19,697)
Lawrence, Scott 3:08:30 (1,631)
Lawrence, Simon 4:40:56 (18,963)
Lawrence, Simon 5:01:17 (22,781)
Lawrence, Stephen 5:11:28 (24,279)
Lawrence, Steven 4:49:12 (20,562)
Lawrence, Wayne 6:01:37 (28,484)
Lawrie, Mark 4:46:49 (20,119)
Lawrie, Neil 4:15:00 (13,268)
Lawrie, Neil 4:54:11 (21,548)
Lawrinson-Chettoe, Philip 3:58:05 (9,509)
Laws, Allan 3:21:32 (2,953)
Laws, Andrew 4:52:17 (21,153)
Laws, Graeme 4:00:28 (10,142)
Laws, Michael 5:56:31 (28,244)
Lawson, Adam 3:45:51 (6,833)
Lawson, Craig 5:54:09 (28,122)
Lawson, David 4:05:43 (11,273)
Lawson, David 5:11:47 (24,326)
Lawson, Ian 5:52:33 (28,040)
Lawson, Matthew 3:35:06 (4,919)
Lawson-Cruttenden, Timothy 5:57:24 (28,291)
Lawther, Dennis 3:57:24 (9,289)
Lawton, Alan 4:23:37 (15,211)
Lawton, Bruce 3:18:38 (2,614)
Lawton, David 3:15:09 (2,239)
Lawton, Jeffrey 2:50:12 (437)
Lawton, Peter 3:36:25 (5,144)
Lawton, Richard 5:16:27 (24,979)
Lawton, Sydney 3:49:19 (7,528)
Lay, Donald 3:40:17 (5,827)
Laycock, Nic 5:17:12 (25,071)
Laycock, Peter 4:53:34 (21,436)
Layland, John 5:21:41 (25,545)
Layton, Simon 4:19:32 (14,264)
Lazarus, Robert 4:58:44 (22,419)
Lazenby, Simon 3:58:58 (9,744)
Lazos, Antonios 4:39:24 (18,669)
Lazou, Peter 3:47:28 (7,133)
L'Azou, Daniel 3:46:22 (6,927)
Lazzari, Bernard 4:26:58 (15,955)
Lazzeri, Mario 4:40:43 (18,927)
Le Blanc Smith, Paul 4:24:00 (15,296)
Le Cocq, Nicholas 4:22:12 (14,861)
Le Cornu, Jean 3:40:56 (5,939)
Le Douaron, Nicolas 3:08:24 (1,624)
Le Feuvre MBE, John 3:36:11 (5,103)
Le Fevre, Stuart 4:16:23 (13,547)
Le Goueff, Bernard 4:14:54 (13,236)
Le Paih, Jean-François 4:13:33 (12,943)
Le Rasle, Timothy 4:27:46 (16,140)
Le Seach, Christian 2:53:53 (576)
Lea, Chris 3:20:20 (2,800)
Lea, Jeff 3:33:02 (4,608)
Leach, Anthony 4:26:59 (15,959)
Leach, David 4:01:10 (10,314)
Leach, David 4:18:45 (14,067)
Leach, Edward 4:34:18 (17,595)
Leach, Graham 4:44:52 (19,750)
Leach, Timothy 4:31:00 (16,850)
Leadbetter, Martin 5:01:13 (22,772)
Leader, David 3:07:27 (1,540)
Leader, Mark 3:44:30 (6,576)
Leads, Andrew 4:37:49 (18,320)
Leaf, John 3:20:08 (2,778)
Leagard, Ian 3:38:35 (5,498)
Leahy, Aidan 3:25:17 (3,413)
Leahy, Christopher 3:18:40 (2,616)
Leahy, John 4:41:38 (19,090)
Leake, Martin 3:17:53 (2,518)
Leake, Steven 4:05:36 (11,241)
Leaker, Iain 4:25:01 (15,514)
Leaks, Clinton 3:45:36 (6,764)
Leaman, Michael 3:24:00 (3,245)
Leane, Patrick 3:57:25 (9,300)
Leaning, Sean 4:04:28 (10,981)
Lear, David 5:22:30 (25,647)
Lear, Mark 6:48:27 (29,786)
Learad, Dennis 3:22:17 (3,035)
Leat, Ashley 3:42:42 (6,252)
Leather, Giles 6:14:21 (29,004)
Leathwood, Matthew 3:30:52 (4,305)
Leaver, David 3:54:25 (8,570)
Lebeaupin, Philippe 3:01:59 (1,147)
Lebeter, Robert 5:22:19 (25,629)
Leboutillier, Phil Jnr 4:46:09 (19,972)
Lebouvier, Eric 2:47:42 (359)
Lecendreux, Christophe 3:37:06 (5,265)
Lecerf, Marc 3:32:08 (4,486)
Leck, Andrew 2:59:12 (951)
Leck, Michael 4:24:51 (15,466)
Leclercq, Philippe 4:41:11 (19,009)
Lecoeur, Pascal 4:30:59 (16,847)
Lecomte, Michael 3:24:07 (3,263)
Lecornu, Christophe 4:17:08 (13,699)
Leddin, Anthony 3:40:51 (5,919)
Leddy, Timothy 4:19:00 (14,115)
Ledger, Mark 4:48:47 (20,483)
Ledwidge, Alan 3:47:59 (7,262)
Lee, Adrian 3:54:40 (8,624)
Lee, Alex 5:10:33 (24,154)
Lee, Andrew 3:15:01 (2,224)
Lee, Andy 5:44:26 (27,503)
Lee, Aylmer 6:58:05 (29,918)
Lee, Chris 4:39:26 (18,673)
Lee, Dan 5:04:19 (23,182)

Lee, David	3:36:23 (5,134)	
Lee, David	3:57:11 (9,219)	
Lee, David	4:13:33 (12,943)	
Lee, Francis	4:47:50 (20,312)	
Lee, Harry	5:56:33 (28,247)	
Lee, Ivan	6:54:36 (29,872)	
Lee, James	3:59:26 (9,896)	
Lee, Johnson	4:10:55 (12,378)	
Lee, Jonathan	4:05:29 (11,209)	
Lee, Ken	3:02:42 (1,197)	
Lee, Kwang	3:44:50 (6,647)	
Lee, Laurence	4:12:18 (12,693)	
Lee, Marcus	4:12:07 (12,650)	
Lee, Martin	2:44:55 (285)	
Lee, Martin	3:54:34 (8,605)	
Lee, Michael	4:39:35 (18,712)	
Lee, Michael	5:09:45 (24,051)	
Lee, Nigel	3:26:26 (3,547)	
Lee, Reuben	4:06:09 (11,369)	
Lee, Robert	4:40:02 (18,793)	
Lee, Stephen	5:45:59 (27,632)	
Lee, Steven	4:39:37 (18,721)	
Lee, William	4:06:51 (11,518)	
Lee, William	4:14:43 (13,177)	
Lee, Yoon	3:23:01 (3,115)	
Lee, Yoon-Hee	3:49:45 (7,634)	
Leech, Brian	5:40:43 (27,247)	
Leech, Richard	6:33:08 (29,485)	
Leech, Terry	3:04:04 (1,287)	
Leedham, David	4:31:31 (16,983)	
Leedham, Neil	3:41:12 (5,983)	
Leefe, Tim	3:34:49 (4,881)	
Leeming, John	4:42:31 (19,277)	
Leen, David	4:16:29 (13,571)	
Lees, Andrew	3:39:26 (5,660)	
Lees, Jamie	5:21:45 (25,557)	
Lees, Robin	4:29:53 (16,654)	
Leesing, Glynn	3:48:38 (7,385)	
Leeson, Michael	4:33:52 (17,513)	
Leet, Jeremy	4:14:57 (13,252)	
Leger, Stephane	2:54:44 (621)	
Legerton, Mark	4:37:49 (18,320)	
Leggate, Rees	4:16:49 (13,637)	
Legge, Timothy	3:03:41 (1,261)	
Leggett, Alan	4:29:13 (16,478)	
Leggett, Christopher	5:03:22 (23,049)	
Leggett, James	4:11:06 (12,416)	
Legister, Gerry	4:05:12 (11,154)	
Legland, John	5:05:24 (23,361)	
Legrand, Stanislas	3:25:36 (3,456)	
Lehmann, Martin	4:53:50 (21,483)	
Lehmann, Walter	3:56:09 (8,958)	
Lehrbaum, Wolfgang	4:29:04 (16,438)	
Leigh, Graham	5:10:47 (24,181)	
Leigh, Les	5:42:28 (27,367)	
Leigh, Michael	4:40:24 (18,857)	
Leigh, Rob	5:28:37 (26,243)	
Leigh, Robert	3:42:35 (6,234)	
Leighfield, Stephen	3:21:30 (2,949)	
Leighton, Paul	3:25:18 (3,418)	
Leinster, Robert	3:59:28 (9,909)	
Leishman, Benjamin	3:17:17 (2,459)	
Leishman, Craig	3:17:15 (2,450)	
Leitch, David	3:31:04 (4,337)	
Leitchman, Thomas	4:34:19 (17,599)	
Leith, Craig	3:21:59 (2,994)	
Leivers, David	4:39:41 (18,731)	
Lejart, Loic	3:30:27 (4,239)	
Lelant, John	5:24:22 (25,822)	
Lemaire, Dominique	3:43:37 (6,418)	
Leman, Jeffrey	4:31:52 (17,081)	
Lemasson, Christophe	2:50:54 (461)	
Lemasson, Pierre	3:05:29 (1,389)	
Lemke, Grant	3:16:21 (2,345)	
Lemmon, Paul	2:46:38 (332)	
Lenaghan, Christopher	4:52:40 (21,246)	
Lenaghen, Stephen	3:31:35 (4,408)	
Lenehan, Raymond	2:58:29 (852)	
Lenihan, John	5:37:06 (26,954)	
Lennard, Matthew	4:00:40 (10,199)	
Lennon, Clifford	5:28:15 (26,201)	
Lentell, Ross	3:45:09 (6,702)	
Lentschner, Gary	4:50:18 (20,771)	

Lentz, Jean	3:59:55 (10,033)	
Leo, James	4:02:42 (10,608)	
Leon, Clement	4:20:48 (14,547)	
Leonard, Chris	3:56:58 (9,169)	
Leonard, Christopher	4:03:39 (10,812)	
Leonard, Eamonn	4:29:05 (16,445)	
Leonard, Gary	6:47:04 (29,757)	
Leonard, Graham	4:08:53 (11,952)	
Leonard, Guy	3:45:34 (6,759)	
Leonard, Mark	4:56:24 (22,052)	
Leonard, Paul	2:58:30 (856)	
Leonard, Stephen	5:08:26 (23,835)	
Leonard, Steven	3:55:28 (8,794)	
Lepinoy, Bernard	3:45:42 (6,796)	
Lepore, Tonio	4:35:03 (17,723)	
Leppard, Ciaran	4:24:46 (15,452)	
Leppard, Phil	5:56:42 (28,252)	
Leprince, Didier	4:29:04 (16,438)	
Lerchl, Wolfgang	3:58:28 (9,596)	
Lerman, Antony	3:54:52 (8,680)	
Leroyer, Patrice	4:31:51 (17,074)	
Lesaffre, Damien	4:07:13 (11,590)	
Lescott, Rupert	3:52:00 (8,075)	
Lesko, Michael	5:33:08 (26,621)	
Leslie, Allan	4:20:21 (14,440)	
Leslie, Andrew	5:08:00 (23,770)	
Leslie, David	4:23:09 (15,098)	
Leslie, Glen	4:18:24 (13,990)	
Leslie, Stephen	5:00:50 (22,707)	
Lester, James	4:38:27 (18,494)	
Lester, Matthew	4:38:27 (18,494)	
Lester, Simon	4:23:24 (15,150)	
Leston, John	3:50:54 (7,847)	
Lethaby, Dean	5:08:44 (23,894)	
Lethaby, John	3:57:26 (9,304)	
Lett, Tony	5:01:11 (22,763)	
Lettington, Paul	4:13:01 (12,827)	
Letts, Dudley	4:13:49 (13,007)	
Leveghi, Franco	3:21:22 (2,928)	
Lever, Alexander	4:19:11 (14,161)	
Lever, Ian	4:27:27 (16,050)	
Levert, Bruno	4:41:09 (19,004)	
Leverton, Jacob	3:28:34 (3,920)	
Levet, Sylvain	3:30:51 (4,302)	
Levett, Peter	4:32:52 (17,289)	
Levey, Paul	4:55:25 (21,857)	
Levin, Joseph	4:47:59 (20,343)	
Levison, John	3:07:44 (1,568)	
Levitt, Paul	3:44:11 (6,522)	
Levrault, Christian	3:53:40 (8,416)	
Levrino, Gianfranco	3:03:05 (1,219)	
Levy, David	4:23:46 (15,245)	
Levy, Douglas	5:55:21 (28,173)	
Levy, Gavin	5:37:44 (27,004)	
Levy, Jason	5:11:06 (24,226)	
Levy, Richard	4:37:24 (18,225)	
Lewars, Dwayne	4:00:01 (10,058)	
Lewin, Bernard	5:26:24 (26,034)	
Lewin, Peter	4:50:21 (20,782)	
Lewin, Roger	4:23:38 (15,215)	
Lewington, Steven	5:02:34 (22,942)	
Lewis, Adam	2:51:33 (492)	
Lewis, Alan	3:17:57 (2,526)	
Lewis, Barry	4:25:46 (15,667)	
Lewis, Bryan	3:35:24 (4,971)	
Lewis, Bryn	4:12:31 (12,743)	
Lewis, Christopher	3:20:52 (2,873)	
Lewis, Christopher	4:07:54 (11,740)	
Lewis, Christopher	5:05:19 (23,340)	
Lewis, Clive	3:44:38 (6,601)	
Lewis, Dai	4:13:42 (12,981)	
Lewis, David	3:10:36 (1,800)	
Lewis, David	3:47:53 (7,237)	
Lewis, David	4:02:36 (10,593)	
Lewis, David	4:12:05 (12,640)	
Lewis, David	5:14:11 (24,652)	
Lewis, David	5:24:52 (25,868)	
Lewis, David	5:42:49 (27,399)	
Lewis, Ewart	4:44:29 (19,668)	
Lewis, Gareth	5:05:25 (23,363)	
Lewis, Gary	5:13:09 (24,525)	
Lewis, Geoffrey	3:43:56 (6,477)	
Lewis, Geoffrey	4:37:18 (18,197)	

Lewis, Gerald	4:39:33 (18,704)	
Lewis, Glynn	5:24:57 (25,879)	
Lewis, Guy	4:24:17 (15,345)	
Lewis, James	3:57:46 (9,416)	
Lewis, James	5:47:41 (27,742)	
Lewis, Joe	7:10:37 (30,028)	
Lewis, John	3:13:22 (2,048)	
Lewis, John	3:29:31 (4,082)	
Lewis, John	4:12:33 (12,746)	
Lewis, Kenny	4:08:56 (11,964)	
Lewis, Kevin	2:41:46 (209)	
Lewis, Martin	3:04:42 (1,329)	
Lewis, Martin	4:54:07 (21,537)	
Lewis, Martin	5:22:51 (25,692)	
Lewis, Michael	4:38:21 (18,466)	
Lewis, Neil	4:32:24 (17,194)	
Lewis, Nicholas	4:19:26 (14,236)	
Lewis, Patrick	3:47:16 (7,077)	
Lewis, Paul	3:14:43 (2,185)	
Lewis, Paul	4:37:34 (18,270)	
Lewis, Peter	3:17:07 (2,437)	
Lewis, Ralph	5:14:10 (24,650)	
Lewis, Rhodri	4:19:18 (14,194)	
Lewis, Richard	6:54:11 (29,862)	
Lewis, Robert	3:25:41 (3,463)	
Lewis, Roger	3:59:31 (9,925)	
Lewis, Ronald	4:10:09 (12,194)	
Lewis, Roy	4:12:41 (12,768)	
Lewis, Roy	6:32:55 (29,477)	
Lewis, Simon	2:44:21 (270)	
Lewis, Simon	4:03:00 (10,661)	
Lewis, Simon	4:09:25 (12,066)	
Lewis, Simon	4:45:26 (19,856)	
Lewis, Simon	4:51:24 (20,970)	
Lewis, Stephen	3:23:35 (3,184)	
Lewis, Steve	4:44:23 (19,652)	
Lewis, Steven	4:51:24 (20,970)	
Lewis, Stuart	6:28:09 (29,360)	
Lewis, Timothy	4:41:01 (18,979)	
Lewis, Tony	3:36:30 (5,160)	
Lewis, Trevor	4:34:31 (17,631)	
Lewis, Tristan	5:29:39 (26,342)	
Lewis, Vernon	5:33:27 (26,644)	
Lewis Jones, Jonathan	4:27:00 (15,964)	
Lewton, Anthony	3:43:46 (6,453)	
Lewzey, Clive	4:56:03 (21,993)	
Ley, Glyn	4:41:26 (19,052)	
Leyden, James	3:54:32 (8,594)	
Leyenda, Manuel	3:30:31 (4,249)	
Leyland, Colin	4:44:41 (19,712)	
Leyne, Jon	4:01:20 (10,348)	
Lhommeau, Pascal	3:32:49 (4,574)	
Li, Robert	3:48:13 (7,307)	
Li, Sammy	4:20:21 (14,440)	
Liddel, Ian	3:15:14 (2,246)	
Liddell, Kevin	3:59:11 (9,810)	
Liddle, Alex	3:36:43 (5,195)	
Liddle, Alexander	3:10:26 (1,789)	
Liddle, George	3:31:21 (4,378)	
Liddle, George	3:47:02 (7,040)	
Liddle, Mike	5:28:22 (26,220)	
Liebling, Simon	3:47:25 (7,122)	
Light, Tim	4:06:57 (11,541)	
Lightbody, Craig	2:57:50 (801)	
Lightburn, Darren	4:00:42 (10,211)	
Lightburn, Steve	4:41:58 (19,155)	
Lightfoot, Alan	3:30:04 (4,183)	
Lightfoot, Mark	4:17:19 (13,738)	
Lightley, Thomas	4:01:10 (10,314)	
Lightowler, Phillip	3:29:29 (4,076)	
Lightwood, Barry	5:33:47 (26,671)	
Liles Taylor, Philip	4:55:03 (21,749)	
Lilley, Jeffrey	4:06:51 (11,518)	
Lilley, Stephen	4:24:00 (15,296)	
Lillie, John	4:52:32 (21,216)	
Lillie, Roger	4:48:57 (20,518)	
Lilly, John	4:46:21 (20,020)	
Lilwall, Robert	3:17:49 (2,513)	
Lim, Eng	4:29:04 (16,438)	
Lima, Martin	4:20:24 (14,449)	
Limb, David	6:14:19 (29,001)	
Limberopoulos, Peter	4:33:28 (17,410)	
Limbert, Stephen	5:16:58 (25,047)	

Limbu, Kumar	3:13:21 (2,046)
Lin, Roland	5:40:47 (27,252)
Linares, Charles	4:54:46 (21,665)
Linbourne, Matt	2:51:18 (478)
Lincoln, Alan	4:58:55 (22,443)
Lincoln, Gary	3:57:24 (9,289)
Lincoln, Tim	3:57:26 (9,304)
Lind, Geoff	4:30:28 (16,750)
Linden, Gerry	5:58:07 (28,329)
Lindford, Maurice	3:03:41 (1,261)
Lindo, Denis	5:01:56 (22,861)
Lindo, Joseph	4:53:14 (21,360)
Lindsay, Alastair	4:04:25 (10,970)
Lindsay, Brendan	5:20:44 (25,436)
Lindsay, Brian	4:15:00 (13,268)
Lindsay, Donald	3:25:45 (3,474)
Lindsay, Fraser	4:16:43 (13,617)
Lindsay, Patrick	4:17:05 (13,684)
Lindsley, Charles	4:51:54 (21,069)
Lindstrom, Roger	4:46:30 (20,054)
Line, David	7:28:34 (30,130)
Line, Geoffrey	6:01:50 (28,498)
Line, Graham	4:13:23 (12,899)
Linehan, Conor	3:27:38 (3,727)
Lines, Jim	4:21:59 (14,808)
Linfield, John	4:37:39 (18,291)
Ling, Mark	3:13:56 (2,106)
Ling, Robin	4:45:14 (19,812)
Ling, Trevor	5:04:54 (23,283)
Lingard, John	3:02:18 (1,175)
Linkstead, Andrew	5:15:46 (24,901)
Linstead, Michael	5:09:38 (24,035)
Linter, Johann	4:39:27 (18,678)
Lintott, Richard	5:50:33 (27,927)
Lintott, Wayne	3:53:47 (8,439)
Lione, Mark	5:36:13 (26,896)
Lipin, Daniel	4:40:11 (18,809)
Lipman, Frank	8:58:10 (30,271)
Lipp, Eric	5:39:49 (27,164)
Lippiatt, Huw	3:57:34 (9,352)
Lipscomb, J Blake	4:43:30 (19,497)
Lisamore, Philip	5:09:45 (24,051)
Lischinsky, Sven	4:16:25 (13,557)
Lisiewicz, John	2:38:17 (141)
Lissauer, David	3:38:13 (5,433)
List, Hans	4:33:42 (17,479)
List, Peter	3:06:54 (1,496)
Lister, Andrew	4:29:52 (16,648)
Lister, Ewart	5:08:03 (23,774)
Lister, John	4:40:07 (18,804)
Lister, Robert	3:34:22 (4,810)
Liston, Gerard	4:11:50 (12,577)
Liston, James	2:58:55 (925)
Liszka, Levente	3:28:38 (3,928)
Litchfield, David	4:05:04 (11,129)
Litchfield, Edward	6:14:31 (29,007)
Litherland, Peter	5:11:01 (24,216)
Little, David	4:41:30 (19,061)
Little, Ian	3:04:14 (1,297)
Little, Jonathan	4:22:52 (15,024)
Little, Robert	4:46:09 (19,972)
Little, Stewart	3:10:14 (1,762)
Little, Thomas	4:18:27 (14,002)
Little, Tony	4:26:54 (15,936)
Little, William	5:10:28 (24,138)
Littledale, Andrew	4:10:52 (12,363)
Littlefield, Glen	4:35:52 (17,899)
Littlefield, Ian	4:23:17 (15,127)
Littler, Darren	5:34:44 (26,776)
Littler, Steve	2:32:38 (76)
Littleton, James	5:46:35 (27,669)
Littlewood, Paul Alan	6:01:24 (28,475)
Livermore, Ben	3:28:50 (3,970)
Liversidge, Will	3:18:47 (2,631)
Livesey, Antony	4:37:38 (18,287)
Livesey, Richard	3:28:50 (3,970)
Livett, Stephen	3:26:41 (3,584)
Livings, Simon	4:57:16 (22,181)
Livingston, George	5:12:21 (24,403)
Livingstone, Iain	4:19:26 (14,236)
Livingstone, Thomas	4:30:02 (16,699)
Livingstone, Tomos	5:12:57 (24,490)
Livingston-Learmonth, Max	4:13:24 (12,907)
Llanos-Madrigal, José	4:04:57 (11,106)
Llewelly Jones, Ivor	3:42:42 (6,252)
Llewellyn, John	5:57:18 (28,283)
Llewellyn, Richard	5:49:27 (27,868)
Lloyd, Alan	4:25:49 (15,679)
Lloyd, Alexander	4:51:35 (21,007)
Lloyd, Daniel	4:28:39 (16,350)
Lloyd, Daniel	4:49:35 (20,631)
Lloyd, David	3:58:27 (9,595)
Lloyd, Edward	4:41:25 (19,050)
Lloyd, Gareth	4:16:11 (13,506)
Lloyd, Gareth	4:57:10 (22,167)
Lloyd, Gary	5:53:25 (28,088)
Lloyd, Graham	4:09:53 (12,139)
Lloyd, Gregory	7:02:20 (29,964)
Lloyd, Ian	3:10:18 (1,775)
Lloyd, Ian	3:56:12 (8,967)
Lloyd, Jonathan	5:08:53 (23,935)
Lloyd, Mark	3:41:05 (5,973)
Lloyd, Nigel	4:05:40 (11,256)
Lloyd, Peter	4:20:07 (14,390)
Lloyd, Simon	3:44:03 (6,499)
Lloyd, Simon	4:28:35 (16,334)
Lloyd, Steve	4:38:56 (18,591)
Lloyd, Stewart	3:37:19 (5,305)
Lloyd, Tim	3:46:36 (6,973)
Lloyd, William	4:20:15 (14,418)
Lloyd Mostyn, James	4:36:23 (17,991)
Llywelyn, Owain	5:12:07 (24,365)
Lo, Lamne	4:20:06 (14,389)
Loader, Joe	2:27:37 (50)
Lobascio, Giovanni	3:48:58 (7,458)
Lobo, Keith	4:37:08 (18,152)
Lobo, Patrick	3:54:06 (8,492)
Locatelli, Edgardo	3:22:04 (3,009)
Locher, Peter	4:00:46 (10,235)
Lochtie, David	4:15:49 (13,428)
Lock, Anthony	2:56:52 (736)
Lock, David	4:12:52 (12,804)
Lock, David	6:09:15 (28,822)
Lock, Gary	4:26:49 (15,913)
Lock, Ian	4:42:11 (19,202)
Lock, John	4:51:00 (20,881)
Lock, Martin	3:43:58 (6,483)
Locke, Barrie	3:36:19 (5,125)
Locke, Dean	7:07:15 (29,996)
Lockett, Allan	6:16:46 (29,080)
Lockett, Patrick	2:52:29 (530)
Lockie, David	4:24:28 (15,388)
Locking, Tom	5:00:32 (22,667)
Lockley, Nigel	5:01:27 (22,796)
Lockwood, Alexander	4:20:22 (14,443)
Lockwood, Alistair	3:52:54 (8,250)
Lockwood, Andrew	4:34:50 (17,683)
Lockwood, Michael	2:49:38 (414)
Lockwood, Nimrod	3:17:14 (2,447)
Lockwood, Robert	3:50:52 (7,841)
Lockwood, Stephen	3:25:00 (3,380)
Lockyear, Kevin	2:58:07 (817)
Lockyer, Jeremy	3:12:06 (1,922)
Lockyer, Mervyn	4:14:44 (13,185)
Lodberg Jensen, Christian	3:31:27 (4,389)
Loder, Adam	4:34:13 (17,573)
Lodge, Alain	4:10:19 (12,231)
Lodge, John	3:59:38 (9,960)
Lodo, Franco	4:00:20 (10,113)
Loew, Daniel	4:00:58 (10,278)
Loffler, Dieter	3:24:45 (3,349)
Loftus, Kevin	2:58:49 (912)
Lofty, John	6:23:43 (29,251)
Logan, Graham	3:56:18 (8,994)
Logan, Matt	4:06:02 (11,355)
Loganathan, Gananathan	4:29:47 (16,619)
Logie, Sylvain	4:44:47 (19,729)
Lohmann, Ken	4:09:22 (12,054)
Lohmann, Rudolf	3:48:18 (7,322)
Loiseau, Alain	5:02:35 (22,946)
Loiseau, Patrice	3:18:59 (2,654)
Loizou, Christopher	2:50:16 (440)
Lomas, David	4:00:11 (10,087)
Lomas, Garry	3:38:30 (5,481)
Lomas, Terry	3:58:30 (9,604)
Lomax, Christopher	5:06:34 (23,554)
Lombroso, Eytan	4:35:53 (17,903)
Lonas, Gary	5:26:43 (26,063)
Lond, Jeremy	3:21:48 (2,974)
London, Christopher	5:02:40 (22,958)
London, Michael	4:06:49 (11,505)
Londra, Thomas	4:44:28 (19,667)
Lonergan, John	2:57:00 (744)
Lonfat, Jean Luc	5:21:37 (25,538)
Lonfat, Pierre-Marie	2:52:35 (532)
Long, Christopher	3:40:17 (5,827)
Long, Christopher	4:27:13 (16,014)
Long, Christopher	5:15:42 (24,891)
Long, David	3:13:31 (2,062)
Long, Ian	5:08:27 (23,840)
Long, Jeremy	3:38:14 (5,437)
Long, Keith	2:54:29 (607)
Long, Kent	3:49:20 (7,533)
Long, Martin	3:35:53 (5,050)
Long, Matt	2:49:53 (423)
Long, Richard	4:48:12 (20,384)
Long, Rupert	4:36:10 (17,950)
Long, Tim	4:29:16 (16,487)
Longbottom, Andy	3:55:20 (8,767)
Longbottom, James	3:56:10 (8,960)
Longbottom, James	4:25:42 (15,655)
Longbottom, Matthew	3:41:44 (6,079)
Longbottom, Simon	3:49:50 (7,651)
Longden, Julian	4:19:46 (14,309)
Longden, Paul	4:35:35 (17,839)
Longden, Ralph	4:12:44 (12,778)
Longhi, Martino	3:49:19 (7,528)
Longhurst, Christopher	5:29:43 (26,348)
Longhurst, Guy	5:08:25 (23,831)
Longhurst, Paul	4:08:37 (11,896)
Longhurst, Raymond	4:29:57 (16,675)
Longley, Malcolm	5:32:23 (26,558)
Longley, Paul	4:15:48 (13,423)
Longman, Paul	3:34:19 (4,804)
Longmore, Huw	4:06:48 (11,502)
Longstaff, Martyn	3:58:57 (9,738)
Longthorn, Andrew	3:51:59 (8,068)
Longthorne, Keith	3:40:20 (5,836)
Lonie, Robbie	7:39:09 (30,162)
Loom, Jason	5:48:53 (27,837)
Looms, Andrew	4:47:12 (20,204)
Looney, Walter	4:03:26 (10,756)
Loong, Hing Tong	6:50:30 (29,814)
Looper, Toby	4:58:49 (22,430)
Loots, Willem	4:49:11 (20,556)
Lopeman, Kevan	3:22:27 (3,051)
Lopez, Ciro	4:16:37 (13,591)
Lopez, Gerard	5:29:59 (26,377)
Lopez, Jerome	4:51:45 (21,043)
Lopez, Paulo	4:51:45 (21,043)
Lopez, Robert	4:30:57 (16,839)
Lord, Alistair	4:24:43 (15,443)
Lord, Andrew	3:16:30 (2,367)
Lord, James	3:35:48 (5,033)
Lord, Ken	4:43:28 (19,484)
Lord, Nick	6:40:08 (29,640)
Lord, Paul	4:20:21 (14,440)
Lord, Stephen	5:42:16 (27,352)
Lord, William	3:33:18 (4,660)
Lorenisson, David	5:06:52 (23,598)
Lorenz, Michael	3:32:09 (4,489)
Lorkin, David	4:04:39 (11,033)
Lormang, Eric	3:22:41 (3,070)
Loryman, Keith	5:18:16 (25,188)
Losekoot, Erwin	3:16:39 (2,383)
Lothian, Paul	4:33:09 (17,337)
Lott, Gary	4:21:57 (14,796)
Lotze, Michael	4:00:56 (10,270)
Louden, Ian	5:30:46 (26,437)
Lougher, Gareth	5:16:43 (25,014)
Loughlan, Joseph	3:59:22 (9,869)
Loughlin, Kevin	5:08:42 (23,888)
Loughlin, Paul	4:12:53 (12,806)
Loughnane, Martin	3:34:18 (4,801)
Loughran, Raymond	3:30:24 (4,214)
Louis, Tiri	3:35:47 (5,029)
Lounguidy, Claude	3:25:36 (3,456)
Lourengo, Carlos	3:40:08 (5,806)
Lourie, Robert	5:06:13 (23,504)

Louth, Alexander..........5:40:29 (27,221)
Loutrage, Jean Yves..........4:14:24 (13,112)
Louw, Mark..........4:09:57 (12,153)
Lovage, Paul..........5:07:35 (23,710)
Lovatt, John..........4:41:38 (19,090)
Love, Rob..........4:57:40 (22,243)
Lovelace, Philip..........3:38:30 (5,481)
Lovell, David..........3:32:19 (4,509)
Lovell, Joseph..........4:18:04 (13,880)
Lovell, Paul..........3:01:32 (1,114)
Lovell, Peter..........3:25:48 (3,483)
Lovell, Simon..........4:18:04 (13,880)
Lovell, Steve..........5:19:40 (25,326)
Lovelock, Robert..........5:29:07 (26,298)
Loveridge, Pete..........4:25:05 (15,528)
Loveridge, Robert..........5:45:41 (27,607)
Lovesey, Daniel..........4:50:32 (20,805)
Lovesey, Robert..........3:28:29 (3,905)
Lovesy, Ralph..........4:34:28 (17,620)
Lovett, Jamie..........4:58:57 (22,451)
Lovewell, Peter..........5:26:54 (26,077)
Lovewell, Roger..........3:11:50 (1,899)
Low, Daniel..........4:17:48 (13,832)
Low, Daren..........4:09:58 (12,156)
Low, John..........4:17:27 (13,761)
Low, Nicholas..........3:56:02 (8,934)
Low, Roger..........3:32:24 (4,520)
Lowe, Christopher..........4:33:27 (17,405)
Lowe, David..........4:05:35 (11,235)
Lowe, Duncan..........5:57:51 (28,319)
Lowe, Jeremy..........4:06:55 (11,531)
Lowe, Jonathan..........5:06:30 (23,544)
Lowe, Matthew..........3:22:22 (3,043)
Lowe, Paul..........4:11:32 (12,508)
Lowe, Peter..........5:02:30 (22,936)
Lowe, Richard..........2:43:58 (260)
Lower, Robert..........3:05:37 (1,397)
Lowery, John..........3:47:49 (7,213)
Lowing, Paul..........6:28:22 (29,365)
Lown, Brian..........5:22:48 (25,683)
Lowndes, Charly..........5:14:08 (24,645)
Lowndes, Nigel..........5:21:50 (25,570)
Lowrie, James..........3:06:57 (1,500)
Lowrie, Martyn..........3:19:24 (2,693)
Lowry, Barry..........3:39:36 (5,693)
Lowry, Ian..........5:24:06 (25,800)
Lowry, Paul..........3:48:36 (7,379)
Lowry, William..........5:24:06 (25,800)
Lowson, Richard..........3:54:46 (8,650)
Lowthian, Keith..........4:52:34 (21,228)
Lowton, Mark..........4:07:21 (11,627)
Loxton, Nicholas..........4:33:00 (17,309)
Lozano, Jorge..........3:47:40 (7,185)
Loze, Didier..........5:07:42 (23,729)
Luard, David..........4:20:45 (14,533)
Luby, Michael..........6:14:45 (29,014)
Lucas, Gary..........4:57:10 (22,167)
Lucas, Gerry..........4:37:26 (18,233)
Lucas, John..........3:32:21 (4,514)
Lucas, Paul..........4:51:05 (20,906)
Lucas, Victor..........4:45:22 (19,835)
Lucas, William..........4:53:29 (21,416)
Lucey, Michael..........4:47:52 (20,318)
Lucini, Paolo..........3:27:28 (3,700)
Luck, Jamie..........3:20:04 (2,772)
Luck, Ronald..........4:30:20 (16,732)
Luckett, David..........3:45:26 (6,734)
Luckman, Andrew..........5:05:41 (23,410)
Ludbrook, Scott..........4:21:13 (14,631)
Ludden, Padhraik..........2:58:49 (912)
Ludlow, Nick..........4:52:14 (21,138)
Ludt, Gordon..........4:28:37 (16,344)
Ludwig, Andreas..........3:23:18 (3,149)
Luedemann, Juergen..........5:16:36 (25,003)
Luff, Edward..........4:40:18 (18,838)
Luff, John..........4:40:59 (18,974)
Luff, Michael..........4:30:54 (16,826)
Luff, Michael..........4:30:55 (16,832)
Luffman, Christopher..........4:40:33 (18,885)
Lugmair, Rudolf..........3:12:53 (1,992)
Luisi, Vito..........4:07:17 (11,606)
Luiten, Anthony..........4:33:26 (17,402)
Luke, Christopher..........4:52:20 (21,169)
Luke, Godfrey..........3:47:39 (7,179)
Luke, Simon..........3:38:43 (5,525)
Lumb, Alistair..........5:25:35 (25,948)
Lumber, Ralph..........5:04:46 (23,256)
Lund, David..........6:08:23 (28,781)
Lund, Simon..........2:40:22 (179)
Lund, Tom..........4:39:28 (18,683)
Lundall, Alex..........3:53:11 (8,305)
Lunn, Martin..........4:39:14 (18,642)
Lunn, Richard..........3:58:03 (9,501)
Lunn, Robert..........5:29:11 (26,307)
Lunn, Simon..........3:44:20 (6,551)
Lunnon, Greg..........4:48:06 (20,367)
Lunt, Brian..........5:04:01 (23,133)
Lunt, David..........5:15:41 (24,887)
Lunt, Thomas..........4:26:07 (15,760)
Luond, Thomas..........3:55:17 (8,759)
Lupton, David..........3:22:07 (3,014)
Lupton, John..........3:48:08 (7,291)
Lusardi, Julian..........3:00:46 (1,071)
Luther, James..........5:08:06 (23,783)
Luton, Paul..........5:19:31 (25,308)
Luty, Clive..........4:24:46 (15,452)
Luzurer, Bernard..........4:16:30 (13,573)
Ly, Albert..........4:28:05 (16,205)
Lyall, Graham..........3:10:02 (1,745)
Lyden, John..........3:27:45 (3,756)
Lye, Jonathan..........4:13:35 (12,952)
Lyle, Alex..........3:19:48 (2,739)
Lyle, Robert..........4:31:24 (16,961)
Lynam, Robert..........3:54:36 (8,614)
Lynas, Andrew..........4:14:01 (13,043)
Lynas, Stewart..........2:47:29 (353)
Lynch, Barry..........7:12:01 (30,032)
Lynch, Cornelius..........5:32:24 (26,564)
Lynch, David..........3:46:30 (6,948)
Lynch, Jamie..........4:45:58 (19,932)
Lynch, Joseph..........3:34:38 (4,854)
Lynch, Kelvin..........3:29:07 (4,019)
Lynch, Kevin..........4:46:50 (20,126)
Lynch, Matthew..........5:37:19 (26,966)
Lynch, Richard..........4:54:27 (21,578)
Lynch, Stuart..........4:34:40 (17,652)
Lynch, Tony..........4:04:44 (11,050)
Lynch, Warren..........2:45:02 (288)
Lynch Warden, John..........4:53:42 (21,454)
Lyne, Eliot..........3:13:09 (2,020)
Lynn, Chris..........4:53:13 (21,357)
Lynn, Christopher..........4:16:26 (13,561)
Lynn, Michael..........3:44:05 (6,505)
Lynn, Raymond..........3:40:27 (5,859)
Lynn, Wayne..........4:03:42 (10,821)
Lyon, Andrew..........3:29:36 (4,098)
Lyon, David..........4:10:11 (12,203)
Lyon, Fred..........4:55:42 (21,947)
Lyon, James..........3:55:21 (8,772)
Lyon, Kerry..........5:46:45 (27,683)
Lyon, Malcolm..........4:08:12 (11,802)
Lyon, Mark..........4:52:00 (21,091)
Lyon, Robert..........4:54:29 (21,587)
Lyons, Alan..........3:52:00 (8,075)
Lyons, Andrew..........3:33:07 (4,630)
Lyons, Anthony..........3:14:46 (2,192)
Lyons, Dale..........4:08:06 (11,785)
Lyons, Edward..........4:24:33 (15,408)
Lyons, Ivan..........3:40:15 (5,821)
Lyons, James..........4:18:20 (13,964)
Lyons, John..........4:02:50 (10,628)
Lyons, Peter..........4:00:55 (10,267)
Lyons, Stephen..........5:20:36 (25,421)
Lyons, Tony..........4:42:36 (19,295)
Lysak, Anthony..........3:28:47 (3,957)
Lysons, Mark..........4:56:47 (22,107)
Lyster-Binns, Richard..........6:06:11 (28,691)
Lythe, Arthur..........4:18:53 (14,095)
Mabb, Philip..........4:54:59 (21,728)
Mabbott, Wayne..........3:32:06 (4,481)
Mabbutt, Paul..........3:48:59 (7,462)
Mabey, Peter..........3:11:39 (1,879)
Macaffer, Menzies..........2:55:36 (659)
Macanna, Kenneth..........3:53:48 (8,442)
Macapugay, Martin..........4:22:58 (15,055)
Macaree, Nick..........3:19:33 (2,712)
MacArthur, Allan..........4:14:08 (13,063)
Macartney, Andrew..........5:02:45 (22,967)
Macaskill, Andy..........3:27:27 (3,698)
Macaulay, John..........3:47:23 (7,112)
Macaulay, Ludwig..........5:05:21 (23,349)
Macbeth, Ian..........3:26:53 (3,608)
Macbride-Stewart, Sean..........3:59:37 (9,953)
MacCrimmon, Stuart..........3:43:50 (6,460)
Macdonald, Alexander..........3:34:08 (4,777)
Macdonald, Alexander..........4:50:46 (20,838)
Macdonald, Darren..........5:04:19 (23,182)
Macdonald, Gary..........4:23:07 (15,088)
Macdonald, Hamish..........4:27:46 (16,140)
Macdonald, James..........3:52:58 (8,260)
Macdonald, James..........4:41:27 (19,054)
Macdonald, Joe..........4:55:30 (21,893)
Macdonald, Malcolm..........5:02:07 (22,893)
Macdonald, Mark..........5:34:01 (26,696)
Macdonald, Neil..........4:58:30 (22,376)
Macdonald, Paul..........4:30:53 (16,823)
Macdonald, Paul..........4:47:18 (20,220)
Macdonald, Robin..........4:27:31 (16,063)
Macdonald, Roddy..........3:36:59 (5,241)
Macdonald, Stephen..........5:14:20 (24,678)
Macdonald, Stewart..........2:28:24 (58)
Macdonald, Thomas..........3:35:31 (4,988)
Macdonald-Jones, Glenn..........3:01:37 (1,125)
Mace, Nicholas..........3:27:49 (3,767)
Macenhill, Damian..........3:57:37 (9,369)
Macey, Andy..........4:31:25 (16,966)
Macey, Mark..........4:31:33 (16,988)
Macey, Terence..........3:55:33 (8,808)
Macfarlane, Bruce..........4:37:29 (18,247)
Macfarlane, Fraser..........4:35:52 (17,899)
Macfarlane, Keith..........3:41:34 (6,044)
Macfarlane, Sandy..........4:01:05 (10,296)
MacGarvey, Andrew..........5:21:41 (25,545)
MacGillivray, Kevin..........4:42:18 (19,226)
MacGowan, Tom..........4:42:52 (19,352)
MacGregor, Christopher..........4:15:51 (13,434)
MacGregor, David..........5:40:21 (27,214)
MacGregor, John..........3:20:57 (2,885)
MacGregor, Calum..........3:12:10 (1,928)
MacGruer, Gavin..........4:52:46 (21,267)
Machado, Americo..........2:46:28 (327)
Machell, Simon..........5:48:44 (27,831)
Machin, Alan..........4:51:34 (20,999)
Machin, Hugo..........4:53:49 (21,480)
Machin, Richard..........4:26:27 (15,832)
Machray, Simon..........3:45:55 (6,839)
MacInnes, John..........3:36:54 (5,228)
Macintyre, Ivan..........5:47:52 (27,763)
MacIver, Oliver..........3:47:48 (7,210)
Mack, Colin..........5:44:31 (27,516)
Mack, Michael..........4:25:53 (15,698)
Mack, Timothy..........4:23:43 (15,230)
Mackaness, Oliver..........5:04:44 (23,251)
Mackay, Brian..........4:20:29 (14,471)
Mackay, Bruce..........3:55:13 (8,738)
Mackay, David..........3:56:57 (9,166)
Mackay, David..........4:08:27 (11,862)
Mackay, Gordon..........5:16:40 (25,008)
Mackay, James..........3:55:13 (8,738)
Mackay, James..........5:13:01 (24,504)
Mackay, John..........6:31:25 (29,441)
Mackay, Kenneth..........6:35:06 (29,525)
Mackay, Michael..........4:30:15 (16,724)
Mackay, Ross..........4:13:23 (12,899)
Mackay, Steve..........5:02:01 (22,874)
Mackenzie, Colin..........4:50:19 (20,774)
Mackenzie, Jamie..........6:04:30 (28,618)
Mackenzie, Jonathan..........4:29:24 (16,519)
Mackenzie, Morris..........4:31:23 (16,954)
Mackenzie, Norman..........4:52:14 (21,138)
Mackenzie, Paul..........3:28:56 (3,982)
Mackenzie, Stuart..........6:14:23 (29,006)
MacKeown, Jeremy..........3:57:53 (9,460)
MacKeown, Piers..........4:09:19 (12,045)
Mackey, George..........5:47:57 (27,772)
Mackie, Alan..........3:46:36 (6,973)
Mackinlay, Murray..........4:13:21 (12,889)
Mackintosh, Alastair..........4:01:53 (10,461)
Macklin, Harry..........3:52:26 (8,160)

Mackmurdie, Richard	3:58:51 (9,713)	
Mackrell, William	4:32:00 (17,120)	
Mackrell-Hey, Langley	3:47:51 (7,224)	
MacLaren, Daniel	5:13:21 (24,558)	
Maclean, Anthony	3:53:02 (8,272)	
Maclean, Mark	5:39:48 (27,163)	
Maclean, Paul	3:45:40 (6,785)	
Maclean, Robert	3:41:11 (5,980)	
Maclean, Rod	3:29:17 (4,045)	
Maclean, Stewart	5:01:15 (22,777)	
MacLellan, Craig	3:41:19 (6,013)	
MacLennan, Graeme	4:40:18 (18,838)	
MacLennan, Gregor	4:51:51 (21,062)	
Macleod, Allan	4:26:16 (15,798)	
Macleod, Andrew	4:18:21 (13,972)	
Macleod, Charles	3:35:03 (4,909)	
Macleod, Don	4:45:59 (19,934)	
Macleod, Donald	3:58:31 (9,611)	
Macleod, Duncan	3:54:17 (8,533)	
Macleod, Johnnie	4:19:34 (14,273)	
Macleod, Kevan	4:28:32 (16,321)	
Macleod, Malcolm	3:38:50 (5,544)	
Macleod, Rory	3:24:17 (3,280)	
Macmillan, Graham	4:48:09 (20,377)	
Macmillan, Hamish	4:13:19 (12,878)	
Macmillan, John	5:43:29 (27,439)	
Macmillan, Mark	5:58:40 (28,352)	
MacNaughtan, Malcolm	3:20:44 (2,853)	
MacNaughton, Grant	4:52:52 (21,280)	
MacNeill, Stewart	4:59:25 (22,515)	
Macpherson, Alan	3:21:51 (2,980)	
Macpherson, Anthony	3:57:33 (9,347)	
MacQueen, Ian	3:58:00 (9,490)	
Macquet, Roger	5:15:10 (24,823)	
Macrae, Robert	4:49:31 (20,619)	
Macro, Richard	4:31:51 (17,074)	
Madden, Hywell	4:03:57 (10,873)	
Madden, Joseph	3:59:21 (9,863)	
Madden, Michael	4:20:42 (14,519)	
Madden, Rick	5:51:03 (27,958)	
Maddison, Robert	6:19:38 (29,150)	
Maddison, Simon	4:48:38 (20,457)	
Maddock, Lloyd	2:53:59 (579)	
Maddock, William	4:22:58 (15,055)	
Maddocks, Andrew	4:44:32 (19,684)	
Maddocks, Terence	3:54:48 (8,659)	
Maddox, Keith	3:59:29 (9,919)	
Maddrewll, Geoffrey	4:15:49 (13,428)	
Madeley, Sean	4:29:59 (16,689)	
Madin, Andrew	4:08:15 (11,814)	
Madin, Jonathan	4:21:31 (14,695)	
Madsen, Jason	3:42:54 (6,288)	
Madson, Victor	4:00:28 (10,142)	
Madura, Percy	4:32:51 (17,285)	
Magagnoli, Claudio	5:06:14 (23,508)	
Magalhaes, Lineu	4:33:30 (17,419)	
Magee, Dominic	4:38:26 (18,488)	
Magee, Ken	4:04:44 (11,050)	
Magee, Liam	4:56:26 (22,057)	
Magee, Richard	2:57:08 (756)	
Magee, Terry	3:39:40 (5,703)	
Maggs, Adrian	3:13:12 (2,026)	
Maggs, Geoffrey	4:57:58 (22,288)	
Magill, Brian	4:44:51 (19,743)	
Magnarini, Giancarlo	3:43:29 (6,396)	
Magnier, Paul	4:12:09 (12,658)	
Magnus, Daniel	4:09:49 (12,129)	
Magor, Matt	5:28:33 (26,233)	
Maguer, Jereme	3:37:14 (5,288)	
Maguire, Conor	4:27:23 (16,036)	
Maguire, Fergus	3:45:34 (6,759)	
Maguire, Graham	4:22:13 (14,865)	
Maguire, Joseph	4:57:06 (22,155)	
Maguire, Kevin	5:08:40 (23,881)	
Maguire, Matthew	4:44:08 (19,605)	
Maguire, Paul	3:16:30 (2,367)	
Maguire, Terence	5:50:45 (27,943)	
Mahay, Dharminder	5:21:22 (25,516)	
Maher, Adam	5:38:23 (27,043)	
Maher, Craig	5:27:00 (26,083)	
Maher, Derek	4:12:33 (12,746)	
Maher, John	5:13:45 (24,600)	
Maher, Patrick	3:33:45 (4,723)	

Maheswaran, Shanmuga	5:49:05 (27,846)	
Mahmood, Mazhar	4:01:28 (10,386)	
Mahmout, Turkel	4:31:10 (16,893)	
Mahon, Christopher	3:15:30 (2,271)	
Mahon, Michael	3:56:00 (8,919)	
Mahon, Sean	5:16:35 (24,997)	
Mahoney, Andy	3:01:27 (1,108)	
Mahoney, Mark	4:57:21 (22,198)	
Maia Da Silva, Manuel	3:34:22 (4,810)	
Maides, Greg	4:03:29 (10,772)	
Maidment, Paul	3:52:50 (8,235)	
Maier, Johann	5:25:02 (25,890)	
Maier, Robert	4:09:52 (12,136)	
Maigne, Michel	4:54:27 (21,578)	
Maije, Wolfgang	4:22:10 (14,847)	
Mail, Markham	5:01:58 (22,866)	
Maile, Chris	2:56:43 (726)	
Main, David	5:37:43 (27,002)	
Main, Iain	4:38:15 (18,442)	
Main, Iain	5:37:31 (26,978)	
Mainprice, Peter	5:52:07 (28,023)	
Mainstone, Keith	3:57:48 (9,431)	
Mainwood, Christopher	5:18:35 (25,222)	
Mainwood, Richard	4:32:55 (17,295)	
Mair, Gary	4:29:53 (16,654)	
Maitland-Carew, Edward	3:58:40 (9,661)	
Majer, Raymond	4:35:12 (17,751)	
Major, Alan	2:57:45 (794)	
Major, Andy	3:07:06 (1,512)	
Major, Andy	5:28:20 (26,212)	
Major, Paul	2:51:22 (482)	
Mak, Yun Fat	4:23:21 (15,143)	
Makant, Paul	4:06:37 (11,471)	
Makepeace, Adam	4:26:57 (15,950)	
Makepeace, Neil	4:29:05 (16,445)	
Makin, Frank	3:36:59 (5,241)	
Makin, Paul	4:28:26 (16,297)	
Makin, Stephen	4:20:54 (14,573)	
Makori, David	2:17:09 (18)	
Makwana, Milan	3:37:38 (5,355)	
Mal, Firouz	2:59:31 (981)	
Malattia, Roberto	4:05:39 (11,252)	
Malby, Anthony	3:06:49 (1,489)	
Malcolm, Andrew	3:53:11 (8,305)	
Malcolm, Andrew	5:53:53 (28,110)	
Malcolm, Peter	4:35:15 (17,761)	
Malcolm, Solomon	4:32:03 (17,130)	
Malcolm Smith, Michael	3:33:05 (4,619)	
Maldar, Alec	4:15:08 (13,292)	
Malde, Rahul	4:08:11 (11,799)	
Malden, Nicholas	5:31:47 (26,515)	
Male, Anthony	4:33:35 (17,450)	
Male, Dominick	5:05:02 (23,297)	
Malet, Charles	3:38:46 (5,532)	
Malherbe, Martin	4:14:12 (13,076)	
Malik, Abdul	4:29:59 (16,689)	
Malik, Adnan	4:03:00 (10,661)	
Malik, Karam	4:06:33 (11,459)	
Maliney, Keith	3:38:11 (5,425)	
Malinowski, Andy	3:45:24 (6,729)	
Maliwat, Chris	6:08:14 (28,776)	
Malkin, Roger	3:40:34 (5,878)	
Mallen, David	4:29:01 (16,425)	
Mallen, John	4:28:12 (16,238)	
Mallery, Phillip	3:27:42 (3,741)	
Mallett, George	6:34:28 (29,511)	
Mallinder, Stephen	5:23:54 (25,782)	
Mallinson, Ian	4:36:34 (18,035)	
Malloch, Timothy	3:58:55 (9,726)	
Mallon, Con	4:25:45 (15,662)	
Malloy, William	5:09:31 (24,017)	
Malone, Ian	2:27:23 (49)	
Malone, James	6:53:21 (29,852)	
Malone, Lawrence	3:03:41 (1,261)	
Maloney, Liam	3:19:45 (2,734)	
Malpas, Richard	4:14:21 (13,107)	
Maltby, Benjamin	5:19:52 (25,350)	
Maltby, Christopher	4:25:06 (15,531)	
Maltby, Jonathan	6:11:21 (28,900)	
Malvern, Neil	3:48:50 (7,429)	
Malynn, Nicholas	3:13:18 (2,037)	
Malyon, Gary	6:04:36 (28,625)	
Man, Kwok	4:40:51 (18,946)	

Manabe, Hiromitsu	4:52:24 (21,185)	
Mancel, Guy	3:44:47 (6,636)	
Manchester, Ian	4:23:36 (15,205)	
Manda, Michel	2:54:17 (592)	
Mandall, William	3:56:23 (9,018)	
Mander, Richard	3:59:12 (9,815)	
Mander, William	4:32:13 (17,158)	
Manderioli, Vittorio	4:12:15 (12,679)	
Manderson, Craig	3:59:09 (9,800)	
Mandeville, Tim	3:13:59 (2,120)	
Mangelshot, Lawrence	2:55:52 (672)	
Manger, Garth	3:40:00 (5,788)	
Mangion, Ted	3:33:22 (4,668)	
Mangold, Charles	5:25:15 (25,915)	
Mankee, Grant	3:40:25 (5,853)	
Manley, David	4:22:25 (14,908)	
Manley, Martin	4:44:22 (19,647)	
Mann, Alan	3:17:45 (2,505)	
Mann, Colin	4:05:28 (11,202)	
Mann, Dave	2:48:08 (366)	
Mann, Dennis	4:29:45 (16,610)	
Mann, James	3:27:00 (3,623)	
Mann, Lionel	5:11:38 (24,303)	
Mann, Martin	4:02:06 (10,503)	
Mann, Paul	3:10:47 (1,816)	
Mann, Phil	3:23:25 (3,162)	
Mann, Stephen	5:11:12 (24,244)	
Mann, Stuart	2:57:21 (771)	
Manning, Brian	5:31:26 (26,486)	
Manning, Gary	4:28:32 (16,321)	
Manning, Jason	3:13:14 (2,031)	
Manning, Julian	3:04:03 (1,286)	
Manning, Norman	3:55:48 (8,870)	
Manning, Paul	4:01:15 (10,326)	
Manning, Phillip	4:08:50 (11,943)	
Manning, Richard	3:29:14 (4,034)	
Manojlovic, Rade	4:40:07 (18,804)	
Manota, Ashok	6:53:37 (29,859)	
Mansbridge, Christopher	5:36:01 (26,882)	
Mansbridge, David	2:35:31 (97)	
Mansbridge, Stuart	4:48:40 (20,463)	
Mansell, Kevin	3:59:09 (9,800)	
Manser, Darren	3:35:41 (5,016)	
Mansfield, Andrew	4:23:47 (15,248)	
Mansfield, David	3:03:44 (1,265)	
Mansfield, David	3:38:55 (5,565)	
Mansfield, David	3:48:37 (7,382)	
Mansfield, Derek	3:40:58 (5,948)	
Mansfield, Jonathan	3:41:14 (5,993)	
Mansfield, Stephen	3:52:28 (8,163)	
Mansfield, William	4:05:23 (11,182)	
Mansfield, William	4:31:27 (16,969)	
Mansi, Andrew	2:59:24 (975)	
Mansifled, John	4:50:56 (20,868)	
Mansilla, Mario	4:10:05 (12,177)	
Mansley, Justin	3:44:58 (6,681)	
Mansley, Mark	5:36:44 (26,926)	
Mansley, Nick	4:01:07 (10,303)	
Mansley, Stephen	4:45:48 (19,902)	
Manson, David	4:55:55 (21,971)	
Manson, Leon	5:53:23 (28,087)	
Manson, Tom	5:13:54 (24,616)	
Manston, Shaun	4:21:03 (14,603)	
Mant, Richard	5:14:53 (24,762)	
Mantel, John	3:57:47 (9,425)	
Mantell, Nick	4:04:46 (11,062)	
Mantle, Zak	3:36:39 (5,181)	
Manzoni, Marco	4:01:29 (10,392)	
Maranta, Michael	4:11:11 (12,436)	
Marasca, Giouanni	4:41:46 (19,117)	
Marchand, Patrick	3:35:28 (4,984)	
Marchant, Andrew	5:15:16 (24,839)	
Marchant, Roy	4:38:23 (18,477)	
Marchese, Peter	4:17:28 (13,766)	
Marchmont, Richard	4:58:55 (22,443)	
Marcus, Ian	4:37:33 (18,264)	
Margelisch, David	4:40:17 (18,836)	
Margrett, Giles	4:51:38 (21,016)	
Margretts, Simon	4:19:09 (14,157)	
Marie, Antonio	5:46:51 (27,689)	
Marien, Richard John	3:41:23 (6,026)	
Mariette, Bernard	5:18:04 (25,172)	
Marivin, Gerard	4:22:16 (14,877)	

Markham, David	4:39:18 (18,646)
Markham, Jonathan	4:27:41 (16,114)
Marks, Bill	4:07:37 (11,681)
Marks, Daniel	5:29:50 (26,353)
Marks, Michael	4:32:26 (17,201)
Marks, Owen	3:49:30 (7,584)
Marks, Philip	3:02:01 (1,153)
Markwell, Robin	3:24:11 (3,269)
Marland, Simon	2:55:17 (642)
Marley, Mark	3:47:37 (7,167)
Marlow, Graham	3:58:01 (9,495)
Marlow, Richard	5:14:07 (24,641)
Marney, Craig	5:38:51 (27,076)
Marns, Jason	4:04:53 (11,088)
Maros, Elvin	2:28:18 (57)
Marotti, Germano	4:21:54 (14,786)
Marquant, Philippe	3:18:00 (2,534)
Marques, Albert	3:17:15 (2,450)
Marques, Sandy	4:32:46 (17,270)
Marques E Marques, Arsenio	3:32:21 (4,514)
Marr, Alan	3:35:50 (5,039)
Marr, Nick	5:39:28 (27,132)
Marrale, Jonathan	3:37:42 (5,366)
Marras, Giovanni	3:17:37 (2,494)
Marriage, Paul	4:24:53 (15,474)
Marriage, Tom	3:57:36 (9,363)
Marriott, Colin	4:12:24 (12,714)
Marriott, Dean	4:23:02 (15,071)
Marriott, Ivor	3:48:10 (7,297)
Marriott, Neil	3:38:25 (5,469)
Marriott, Steven	3:24:44 (3,348)
Marrow, Stephen	4:32:19 (17,175)
Marschall, Uwe	3:43:13 (6,348)
Marsden, Andrew	4:11:51 (12,580)
Marsden, Andrew	4:12:39 (12,763)
Marsden, Chris	5:39:45 (27,161)
Marsden, John	4:22:22 (14,899)
Marsden, Paul	3:38:33 (5,489)
Marsden, Peter	5:11:05 (24,222)
Marsden, Philip	4:31:44 (17,043)
Marsh, Adrian	3:40:20 (5,836)
Marsh, Alan	3:11:36 (1,871)
Marsh, Andrew	5:08:48 (23,907)
Marsh, Andrew	5:34:04 (26,707)
Marsh, Christopher	5:28:24 (26,223)
Marsh, Gary	4:12:40 (12,767)
Marsh, Ian	5:00:02 (22,627)
Marsh, Ken	4:02:37 (10,594)
Marsh, Oliver	3:36:44 (5,200)
Marsh, Pete	2:58:47 (906)
Marsh, Philip	4:11:56 (12,591)
Marsh, Richard	4:10:26 (12,262)
Marsh, Richard	4:57:26 (22,208)
Marsh, Richard	5:11:22 (24,266)
Marsh, Simon	4:19:52 (14,330)
Marshall, Alan	3:18:50 (2,636)
Marshall, Alastair	4:47:54 (20,325)
Marshall, Andrew	3:42:57 (6,294)
Marshall, Andrew	3:56:52 (9,147)
Marshall, Anthony	3:39:24 (5,652)
Marshall, Cameron	4:12:04 (12,633)
Marshall, David	4:19:44 (14,302)
Marshall, David	4:38:27 (18,494)
Marshall, Gary	4:54:08 (21,539)
Marshall, Giles	2:56:12 (701)
Marshall, Howard	4:46:03 (19,949)
Marshall, Ian	3:03:38 (1,258)
Marshall, Ivan	4:37:29 (18,247)
Marshall, John	3:39:24 (5,652)
Marshall, Kevin	3:46:11 (6,895)
Marshall, Lee	4:10:19 (12,231)
Marshall, Lee	5:50:05 (27,907)
Marshall, Nigel	5:40:23 (27,216)
Marshall, Norman	4:23:41 (15,224)
Marshall, Peter	3:28:05 (3,816)
Marshall, Peter	4:06:51 (11,518)
Marshall, Simon	4:21:19 (14,651)
Marshall, Stuart	3:16:28 (2,361)
Marshall, Timothy	3:37:11 (5,279)
Marshall, William	4:53:48 (21,474)
Marshall, Wilson	4:33:47 (17,496)
Marsland, Alan	5:15:23 (24,851)
Marsland, James	5:15:23 (24,851)
Marson, John	4:43:40 (19,530)
Marson, Stuart	4:36:36 (18,040)
Marston, Carl	2:52:52 (538)
Marston, Daniel	4:51:21 (20,959)
Marston, Glyn	3:16:55 (2,414)
Marston, Justin	6:28:26 (29,367)
Marston, Robert	4:21:59 (14,808)
Martell, Paul	3:40:11 (5,814)
Martell, Robert	4:04:49 (11,070)
Martin, Andrew	4:35:49 (17,882)
Martin, Barry	5:22:59 (25,704)
Martin, Brett	5:46:33 (27,666)
Martin, Bruce	4:11:56 (12,591)
Martin, Christopher	2:58:28 (848)
Martin, Ciaran	4:29:50 (16,634)
Martin, Daniel	5:17:48 (25,138)
Martin, David	4:28:04 (16,201)
Martin, Don	6:15:11 (29,029)
Martin, Edward	5:39:53 (27,176)
Martin, Gareth	4:07:10 (11,582)
Martin, Graeme	4:07:05 (11,568)
Martin, Guy	6:05:19 (28,655)
Martin, Hugh	3:47:39 (7,179)
Martin, Ian	4:46:11 (19,983)
Martin, Ivan	4:13:15 (12,865)
Martin, James	4:56:55 (22,131)
Martin, James	5:04:41 (23,243)
Martin, Jean	3:42:02 (6,126)
Martin, Jim	4:51:55 (21,073)
Martin, John	4:36:17 (17,973)
Martin, Justin	5:05:37 (23,404)
Martin, Kenneth	4:42:53 (19,359)
Martin, Mark	4:34:26 (17,617)
Martin, Michael	3:14:39 (2,177)
Martin, Michael	3:48:40 (7,393)
Martin, Michael	5:59:56 (28,415)
Martin, Nicholas	3:43:57 (6,480)
Martin, Nicholas	3:57:09 (9,210)
Martin, Paul	3:28:26 (3,895)
Martin, Pete	6:17:42 (29,104)
Martin, Peter	4:12:02 (12,620)
Martin, Peter	4:31:38 (17,019)
Martin, Philip	4:13:18 (12,874)
Martin, Richard	3:53:24 (8,357)
Martin, Ricky	4:35:22 (17,791)
Martin, Robert	5:53:41 (28,101)
Martin, Robin	4:25:32 (15,625)
Martin, Ron	4:52:34 (21,228)
Martin, Sean	4:10:09 (12,194)
Martin, Steve	5:48:10 (27,791)
Martin, Terry	4:18:48 (14,081)
Martin, Thomas	4:45:30 (19,864)
Martin-Baez, David	4:32:38 (17,235)
Martindale, Sean	4:30:14 (16,721)
Martindill, Clifford	4:07:23 (11,636)
Martinez, Laurent	3:30:42 (4,278)
Martinez, Pascal	3:37:21 (5,314)
Martins, Ricardo	4:34:13 (17,573)
Martiradonna, Marcello	3:28:33 (3,918)
Martire, Jean Michel	5:06:46 (23,582)
Martson, Andrés	4:08:22 (11,843)
Martyn, Matthew	4:36:15 (17,964)
Martyn, Nicholas	2:37:40 (130)
Martzloff, Michel	3:48:03 (7,276)
Maru, Tony	3:04:18 (1,302)
Marudkar, Mangesh	4:03:28 (10,764)
Maruzzi, Lino	5:25:38 (25,954)
Marval, Jonathan	4:03:41 (10,816)
Marwick, Grant	5:28:22 (26,220)
Marx, Stephan	5:08:44 (23,894)
Maryan, Alan	4:10:19 (12,231)
Marzocchi, Marco	5:00:15 (22,643)
Masanovic, Branislav	4:56:46 (22,101)
Mascarenhas, Nigel	4:05:11 (11,151)
Mascold, Anthony	5:46:13 (27,640)
Masetti, Pietro	4:03:23 (10,744)
Mash, Raymond	5:29:16 (26,316)
Masi, Franco	4:15:52 (13,442)
Masi, Massimiliano	3:13:57 (2,110)
Masini, Martino	5:26:39 (26,055)
Maskell, John	5:02:35 (22,946)
Maskell, Paul	4:41:08 (19,001)
Maskell, Robert	4:45:29 (19,863)
Maskens, David	5:05:50 (23,435)
Maslakovic, Marko	4:35:16 (17,767)
Maslen, Benjamin	4:12:09 (12,658)
Maslen, Paul	3:57:24 (9,289)
Maslinski, Julian	3:11:38 (1,877)
Mason, Alan	4:14:41 (13,166)
Mason, Anthony	5:38:40 (27,062)
Mason, Craig	4:29:28 (16,537)
Mason, David	5:11:21 (24,262)
Mason, Derk	3:37:14 (5,288)
Mason, Duncan	2:23:08 (30)
Mason, Eamon	3:31:10 (4,351)
Mason, Graham	4:47:11 (20,198)
Mason, Iain	4:36:02 (17,936)
Mason, Jack	3:47:22 (7,104)
Mason, James	4:18:54 (14,098)
Mason, James	4:20:48 (14,547)
Mason, John	4:00:20 (10,113)
Mason, John	4:21:38 (14,720)
Mason, John	4:25:00 (15,509)
Mason, Jonathan	6:06:24 (28,697)
Mason, Keith	3:28:00 (3,804)
Mason, Lance	3:18:19 (2,577)
Mason, Leslie	3:35:27 (4,978)
Mason, Mike	4:44:07 (19,601)
Mason, Nicholas	4:04:27 (10,977)
Mason, Nicholas	5:18:27 (25,209)
Mason, Oli	4:46:54 (20,144)
Mason, Peter	3:44:55 (6,666)
Mason, Peter	4:08:43 (11,916)
Mason, Richard	2:22:32 (28)
Mason, Richard	4:51:00 (20,881)
Mason, Shaun	4:17:55 (13,856)
Mason, Terry	4:49:45 (20,661)
Mason, William	3:54:13 (8,512)
Massa, Carlo	3:21:59 (2,994)
Massey, Jim	4:38:11 (18,424)
Massey, John	4:35:27 (17,804)
Massey, Julian	5:12:37 (24,448)
Massey, Kevin	5:11:22 (24,266)
Massey, Paul	5:36:11 (26,892)
Massingham, Paul	3:13:23 (2,049)
Master, Moosa	4:01:11 (10,317)
Masterman, Daren	5:48:52 (27,835)
Masters, Adam	3:15:52 (2,305)
Masters, Christopher	4:25:10 (15,550)
Masters, James	4:29:50 (16,634)
Masters, Mathew	4:04:07 (10,905)
Masters, Michael	4:28:19 (16,264)
Masters, Richard	3:04:05 (1,288)
Mastino, Francesco	4:28:31 (16,319)
Mastrorilli, Giovanni	4:08:49 (11,938)
Masumpa, Makaya	2:28:09 (55)
Masutier-Macabich, Antonio	3:34:25 (4,820)
Matcham, Garry	5:50:27 (27,922)
Mathe, James	4:03:26 (10,756)
Mather, Colin	5:20:22 (25,390)
Mather, Harold	3:52:54 (8,250)
Mather, Paul	3:29:59 (4,168)
Mathers, George	3:59:50 (10,005)
Matheson, James	4:08:46 (11,928)
Mathew, Mark	4:14:49 (13,213)
Mathews, Denis	5:08:42 (23,888)
Mathews, Stuart	3:53:39 (8,415)
Mathewson, Peter	4:22:37 (14,958)
Mathias, Kieron	4:16:01 (13,468)
Mathie, Paul	4:10:02 (12,170)
Mathieson, Steven	3:06:29 (1,460)
Mathieson Cheater, Andrew	3:57:54 (9,462)
Mathurin, Mark Anthony	4:07:54 (11,740)
Matre, Reidar	2:55:42 (662)
Matson, Alistair	3:16:09 (2,331)
Matsumoto, Manabu	4:08:29 (11,868)
Matsumura, Kazuhiro	6:12:45 (28,953)
Matsunaga, Tomio	2:58:03 (815)
Matthew, David	3:29:00 (3,997)
Matthews, Allan	3:54:53 (8,683)
Matthews, Andrew	3:40:26 (5,854)
Matthews, Andrew	4:38:52 (18,582)
Matthews, Barry	3:27:55 (3,794)
Matthews, Christopher	3:52:18 (8,134)
Matthews, Daniel	4:14:19 (13,098)
Matthews, Gary	2:37:50 (135)

Matthews, Gerry 5:05:56 (23,456)
Matthews, Greg 5:23:14 (25,725)
Matthews, Hamilton 3:30:39 (4,270)
Matthews, John 3:42:34 (6,229)
Matthews, John 4:52:31 (21,210)
Matthews, Joseph 4:28:21 (16,271)
Matthews, Mark 3:12:53 (1,992)
Matthews, Mark 4:40:39 (18,911)
Matthews, Michael 3:30:31 (4,249)
Matthews, Neal 4:30:32 (16,757)
Matthews, Neil 4:12:27 (12,725)
Matthews, Nick 5:32:25 (26,567)
Matthews, Paul 3:24:22 (3,293)
Matthews, Peter 4:38:31 (18,509)
Matthews, Ricky 5:08:05 (23,780)
Matthews, Shaun 4:48:31 (20,441)
Matthews, Stuart 4:19:45 (14,305)
Matthias, Ian 4:13:19 (12,878)
Matthiasson, Pall 5:13:36 (24,581)
Matthys, Kris 3:28:51 (3,973)
Mattiko, Gregory 4:01:58 (10,479)
Mattin, Andrew 4:16:37 (13,591)
Mattingly, Roger 4:43:55 (19,575)
Mattock, Robert 3:47:31 (7,143)
Mattocks, Craig 3:00:07 (1,035)
Mattocks, Darryl 5:38:23 (27,043)
Matulewicz, Michael 4:32:06 (17,137)
Matuszax, Graham 5:21:42 (25,548)
Matyska, Tomas 3:54:02 (8,486)
Maublant, Pierre 3:46:37 (6,979)
Maucorps, Jacques 4:08:04 (11,781)
Maud, Greg 5:04:22 (23,193)
Maude, Christopher 4:29:26 (16,528)
Maude, Stephen 3:47:56 (7,252)
Maudslay, Chester 4:43:48 (19,557)
Mauger, Nicholas 4:59:56 (22,608)
Maughan, Christopher 4:19:35 (14,276)
Maughan, Gary 3:42:45 (6,262)
Maughan, Martin 5:13:49 (24,608)
Maughan, Simon 4:20:24 (14,449)
Mauldon, Kenneth 3:51:12 (7,912)
Mauleverer, Barnaby 5:10:48 (24,186)
Maun, Adam 5:07:10 (23,645)
Maund, Nigel 5:15:03 (24,790)
Maunder, John 4:30:51 (16,816)
Maunder, Kingsley 4:52:18 (21,158)
Maunders, David 5:38:25 (27,046)
Maurer, Josef 5:07:40 (23,725)
Mauri, Carlo 4:00:17 (10,106)
Maurice Jones, Mark 4:18:22 (13,976)
Mawer, Craig 4:13:24 (12,907)
Mawer, Roger 3:49:10 (7,489)
Max, David 3:55:30 (8,798)
Maxted, Simon 3:55:48 (8,870)
Maxwell, Benjamin 4:26:17 (15,800)
Maxwell, Ian 4:04:04 (10,897)
Maxwell, Marcus 4:21:01 (14,595)
Maxwell, Patrick 4:36:00 (17,932)
Maxwell, Paul 4:57:04 (22,149)
Maxwell, Peter 4:03:51 (10,850)
May, Adam 4:43:30 (19,497)
May, Anthony 5:30:41 (26,428)
May, Colin 4:44:22 (19,647)
May, Darran 4:10:51 (12,359)
May, Francis 4:05:02 (11,123)
May, Howard 3:57:20 (9,267)
May, Kieron 4:59:29 (22,524)
May, Lindy 4:55:56 (21,976)
May, Peter 4:55:15 (21,798)
May, Stuart 4:38:08 (18,415)
May, Tom 2:53:42 (568)
Maydon, Marcus 3:59:46 (9,989)
Mayers, Nick 2:40:17 (176)
Mayers, Tim 4:14:30 (13,127)
Mayes, Andrew 3:49:34 (7,599)
Mayes, Henry 5:08:47 (23,904)
Mayes, Simon 3:20:30 (2,825)
Mayfield, Mark 4:15:09 (13,293)
Mayger, David 3:36:38 (5,177)
Mayhew, David 4:32:20 (17,179)
Mayhew, Gavin 3:53:40 (8,416)
Mayhew, John 4:41:18 (19,029)
Mayhook, Mark 3:49:48 (7,646)
Maynard, Andrew 3:24:40 (3,337)
Maynard, Graham 3:26:02 (3,503)
Maynard, Mark 4:14:49 (13,213)
Mayo, Peter 5:11:01 (24,216)
Mayo, Robert 4:04:18 (10,949)
Mayo, Simon 3:20:17 (2,791)
Mayo, Thomas 5:42:33 (27,384)
Maywood, Bryan 4:51:30 (20,982)
Mazet, Laurent 3:06:50 (1,493)
Mazur, Philip 3:35:54 (5,055)
Mazza, Christopher 3:10:12 (1,760)
Mazzon, Claudio 3:44:42 (6,613)
Mazzone, Pierino 5:17:28 (25,103)
Mazzoni-Dacton, Jim 3:53:05 (8,288)
Mazzucco, Mario 3:57:37 (9,369)
Mbulawa, Archie 4:01:29 (10,392)
McAllen, Brian 3:16:58 (2,420)
McAllister, Christopher 3:11:53 (1,903)
McAllister, Francis 3:27:26 (3,693)
McAllister, Jonathan 3:57:43 (9,399)
McAlorum, Frank 3:45:56 (6,843)
McAlpine, Colin 3:38:06 (5,414)
McAndie, Gordon 4:57:18 (22,190)
McAndrew, Eamon 3:58:51 (9,713)
McAnespie, Colin 2:54:34 (612)
McAnulty, Simon 5:34:55 (26,799)
McAsures, Keith 4:12:39 (12,763)
McAulay, Tom 4:09:21 (12,051)
McAuley, Mark 3:48:57 (7,451)
McAuliffe, Nick 3:29:01 (4,001)
McAuliffe, Paul 3:26:41 (3,584)
McAuliffe, Peter 4:20:50 (14,556)
McAuliffe, Vincent 3:35:46 (5,027)
McAuliffe, William 3:50:50 (7,831)
McAuliffe, William 4:38:03 (18,382)
McAvoy, George 5:24:27 (25,829)
McAvoy, Stephen 5:01:25 (22,792)
McBain, Richard 4:37:43 (18,303)
McBride, David 5:07:43 (23,732)
McBride, Geoff 4:48:41 (20,466)
McBride, Michael 4:00:15 (10,099)
McBride, William 4:10:58 (12,396)
McCabe, Andrew 4:30:30 (16,754)
McCabe, Anthony 4:41:20 (19,033)
McCabe, Antony 3:59:28 (9,909)
McCabe, David 3:41:45 (6,083)
McCabe, Gary 4:30:30 (16,754)
McCabe, Matthew 4:47:11 (20,198)
McCafferty, Michael 3:55:25 (8,786)
McCaffrey, Charles 4:44:15 (19,628)
McCaig, David 4:45:42 (19,882)
McCall, Steve 3:40:50 (5,917)
McCallion, Seamus 3:04:11 (1,294)
McCallum, Charlie 3:30:00 (4,170)
McCallum, Hamish 4:34:48 (17,677)
McCann, Gerard 2:57:37 (786)
McCann, John 3:33:40 (4,708)
McCann, John 3:46:33 (6,960)
McCann, Noel 4:29:39 (16,585)
McCann, Paul 4:27:11 (16,004)
McCann, Paul 5:03:45 (23,091)
McCann, Philip 3:36:11 (5,103)
McCann, Stephen 5:35:54 (26,871)
McCann, Thomas 4:02:22 (10,544)
McCanny, Claire 5:04:10 (23,153)
McCarrick, Derek 6:19:39 (29,151)
McCarten, Stephen 3:27:18 (3,676)
McCarthy, Andrew 4:24:09 (15,318)
McCarthy, Brendan 6:53:21 (29,852)
McCarthy, Brian 3:44:28 (6,570)
McCarthy, Colin 4:35:57 (17,920)
McCarthy, Colin 5:38:23 (27,043)
McCarthy, Daniel 3:29:49 (4,138)
McCarthy, David 4:16:36 (13,589)
McCarthy, David 5:46:13 (27,640)
McCarthy, Gary 3:58:34 (9,633)
McCarthy, Gary 4:26:05 (15,752)
McCarthy, Gregory 6:11:42 (28,916)
McCarthy, Ian 5:16:26 (24,975)
McCarthy, John 4:03:23 (10,744)
McCarthy, Keith 4:09:58 (12,156)
McCarthy, Martin 3:16:42 (2,393)
McCarthy, Martin 3:54:00 (8,479)
McCarthy, Michael 4:19:20 (14,202)
McCarthy, Michael 4:40:49 (18,942)
McCarthy, Michael 5:34:16 (26,729)
McCarthy, Mike 3:57:00 (9,178)
McCarthy, Nigel 3:33:14 (4,649)
McCarthy, Robert 3:17:20 (2,465)
McCarthy, Stephen 4:17:43 (13,818)
McCarthy, Stephen 4:31:14 (16,913)
McCartney, John 4:22:41 (14,978)
McCartney, Mark 5:12:00 (24,356)
McCartney, Sean 3:02:52 (1,205)
McCarty, Paul 4:39:52 (18,765)
McCaul, Christian 3:45:41 (6,791)
McCaul, Craig 4:15:46 (13,419)
McCaul, Sean 4:49:34 (20,629)
McCheyne, Ian 5:44:08 (27,487)
McClean, Paul 3:43:10 (6,336)
McClean, Paul 4:02:52 (10,635)
McClean, Philip 4:07:53 (11,737)
McCleery, Sean 4:31:32 (16,985)
McClelland, John 3:35:15 (4,942)
McClements, Alexander 4:24:25 (15,374)
McClennon, Steve 3:55:53 (8,889)
McCloskey, Brian 5:44:31 (27,516)
McCloskey, Michael 3:58:41 (9,669)
McCloskey, Peter 5:01:38 (22,820)
McCloud, Stephen 3:43:28 (6,392)
McCloy, Alexander 4:29:27 (16,534)
McClure, John 5:54:39 (28,145)
McClurg, Jill 4:39:27 (18,678)
McCluskey, Kevin 3:22:26 (3,048)
McColgan, Martin 3:24:42 (3,342)
McConaghie, Keith 5:11:40 (24,307)
McConalogue, Ian 6:26:15 (29,306)
McCondichie, Mark 5:34:05 (26,710)
McCondochie, Mark 4:03:21 (10,735)
McConnachy, Justin 4:57:05 (22,152)
McConnell, Steve 3:28:43 (3,939)
McConville, John 3:07:40 (1,563)
McCool, Anthony 5:04:26 (23,206)
McCool, Peter 4:54:52 (21,697)
McCord, Richard 3:27:23 (3,686)
McCord, William 4:43:14 (19,436)
McCorkell, Wayne 3:10:51 (1,823)
McCormack, Kyle 4:01:57 (10,475)
McCormack, Patrick 4:18:28 (14,005)
McCormack, Thomas 4:16:04 (13,480)
McCormick, Andrew 3:29:19 (4,051)
McCormick, Andrew 4:18:20 (13,964)
McCormick, James 6:01:40 (28,495)
McCormick, Paul 4:44:50 (19,738)
McCourt, Alan 3:56:37 (9,081)
McCourt, William 5:29:52 (26,359)
McCoy, Maxwell 4:46:15 (19,998)
McCoy, Paul 3:32:51 (4,580)
McCoy, Trevor 3:42:50 (6,275)
McCreadie, Brian 4:45:19 (19,826)
McCready, Ian 4:28:25 (16,289)
McCrory, Finn 3:04:32 (1,317)
McCrossan, Dermot 2:39:51 (168)
McCuaig, Ian 3:03:17 (1,233)
McCullie, John 4:29:13 (16,478)
McCulloch, Jonathan 3:20:13 (2,785)
McCullough, John 3:36:25 (5,144)
McCully, Kenneth 4:38:03 (18,382)
McCusker, Eamonn 3:31:02 (4,335)
McCutheon, Loarn 3:57:19 (9,262)
McDaid, Gerard 3:50:26 (7,761)
McDaid, Steve 4:31:35 (17,003)
McDavid, Nigel 4:35:29 (17,810)
McDermott, Ben 5:23:06 (25,715)
McDermott, Christopher 4:01:57 (10,475)
McDermott, Dominic 3:09:26 (1,706)
McDermott, Ian 4:53:24 (21,398)
McDermott, Michael 4:34:18 (17,595)
McDermott, Stuart 5:11:59 (24,351)
McDonagh, Barry 3:59:00 (9,754)
McDonagh, Gerry 3:37:39 (5,360)
McDonagh, Patrick 5:10:07 (24,092)
McDonagh, Terence 4:36:27 (18,007)
McDonald, Alan 3:08:17 (1,613)
McDonald, Andrew 3:45:12 (6,707)
McDonald, Ben 4:47:20 (20,225)

McDonald, Darryl	2:42:27 (225)	
McDonald, Frank	4:42:49 (19,336)	
McDonald, Geoffrey	3:37:13 (5,285)	
McDonald, Jonathan	5:13:00 (24,500)	
McDonald, Liam	3:53:52 (8,453)	
McDonald, Peter	3:23:18 (3,149)	
McDonald, Phillip	4:43:28 (19,484)	
McDonald, Randall	4:39:45 (18,746)	
McDonald, Richard	3:16:53 (2,410)	
McDonald, Robert	3:05:57 (1,416)	
McDonald, Rod	3:48:19 (7,324)	
McDonald-Liggins, Tony	3:31:36 (4,411)	
McDonnell, James	2:56:33 (720)	
McDonnell, Peter	4:15:25 (13,350)	
McDougal, George	3:04:13 (1,296)	
McDough, William	4:59:53 (22,597)	
McDowell, Alastair	4:21:57 (14,796)	
McDowell, Gregory	3:12:55 (1,997)	
McDowell, James	4:00:41 (10,208)	
McDowell, Lee	7:05:28 (29,979)	
McDowell, Michael	4:18:36 (14,033)	
McElheron, Michael	5:13:40 (24,592)	
McElwee, Graham	4:21:34 (14,704)	
McEnery, Richard	4:11:34 (12,515)	
McEntee, Colin	4:33:05 (17,324)	
McEntee, Kevin	3:54:11 (8,506)	
McEntee, Scott	4:33:05 (17,324)	
McEuen, James	4:54:43 (21,648)	
McEvoy, Barry	4:47:00 (20,163)	
McEvoy, Gerry	5:10:20 (24,120)	
McEwan, Neil	6:04:31 (28,621)	
McEwen, Kelsall	5:07:52 (23,756)	
McFadden, Roger	3:41:25 (6,030)	
McFadden, Thomas	4:48:36 (20,453)	
McFarlane, Colin	4:33:09 (17,337)	
McFarlane, James	3:22:22 (3,043)	
McFarlane, John	2:30:14 (67)	
McFarlane, Leonard	4:38:10 (18,421)	
McFarlane, Scott	4:47:12 (20,204)	
McFerran, George	4:14:44 (13,185)	
McGachen, Roger	3:52:31 (8,173)	
McGahey, Timothy	3:27:52 (3,779)	
McGarry, David	5:53:58 (28,112)	
McGarry, Francis	3:49:59 (7,686)	
McGarry, James	5:02:19 (22,918)	
McGarry, John	3:41:36 (6,054)	
McGarry, Kevin	3:36:51 (5,217)	
McGarty, William	5:26:18 (26,020)	
McGaughey, James	3:06:28 (1,457)	
McGavran, David	4:25:51 (15,688)	
McGechie, Noel	4:00:46 (10,235)	
McGee, Cathal	6:10:08 (28,865)	
McGee, David	5:27:12 (26,102)	
McGee, Gareth	2:43:45 (252)	
McGee, John	6:10:08 (28,865)	
McGee, Matthew	3:18:23 (2,587)	
McGeever, Keith	5:46:31 (27,664)	
McGeever, Mike	7:17:12 (30,062)	
McGeoch, Mick	2:37:20 (124)	
McGeown, James	5:43:37 (27,446)	
McGeown, Patsy	5:33:39 (26,659)	
McGhee, Douglas	3:24:08 (3,264)	
McGhee, James	4:31:05 (16,866)	
McGhee, John	4:14:43 (13,177)	
McGibbon, Andrew	4:44:17 (19,635)	
McGibney, Garrett	3:18:27 (2,593)	
McGillan, David	4:03:04 (10,677)	
McGinty, Gary	5:34:03 (26,703)	
McGlade, David	3:48:27 (7,349)	
McGlashan, Sandy	5:23:50 (25,772)	
McGlasson, Craig	3:29:51 (4,142)	
McGlennon, David	2:51:39 (499)	
McGloin, Kevin	4:59:08 (22,482)	
McGlynn, Jim	3:44:17 (6,540)	
McGlynn, Joe	3:23:50 (3,219)	
McGlynn, John	4:21:00 (14,592)	
McGlynn, Robert	5:30:45 (26,434)	
McGlynn, Stephen	3:11:45 (1,892)	
McGonigle, Dermot	2:35:51 (102)	
McGouran, Lee	5:42:03 (27,341)	
McGovern, Brian	6:55:02 (29,878)	
McGovern, Tony	3:59:26 (9,896)	
McGowan, John	5:40:09 (27,203)	
McGowan, Kevin	4:04:15 (10,939)	
McGowan, Stuart	3:52:06 (8,097)	
McGrady, Ray	6:00:57 (28,454)	
McGranaghan, John	3:34:06 (4,773)	
McGranaghan, Sean	3:47:06 (7,051)	
McGrath, Eddie	2:40:32 (184)	
McGrath, Ian	5:55:24 (28,178)	
McGrath, Kenneth	5:26:36 (26,051)	
McGrath, Martin	4:57:50 (22,270)	
McGrath, Martin	4:58:26 (22,366)	
McGrath, Michael	3:13:35 (2,066)	
McGrath, Paul	4:10:38 (12,300)	
McGrath, Stephen	4:58:09 (22,320)	
McGregor, Andrew	3:43:19 (6,365)	
McGregor, Campbell	4:05:54 (11,320)	
McGregor, Ian	3:41:12 (5,983)	
McGregor, James	3:43:00 (6,305)	
McGrenera, Richard	4:53:06 (21,336)	
McGroarty, Patrick	3:26:10 (3,521)	
McGroarty, Thomas	7:10:18 (30,021)	
McGuigan, Daniel	3:23:16 (3,143)	
McGuinness, James	4:43:22 (19,461)	
McGuinness, Martin	3:54:28 (8,584)	
McGuire, Daniel	5:09:44 (24,049)	
McHugh, Bryan	4:26:17 (15,800)	
McHugh, Steve	3:52:38 (8,199)	
McIachen, Allan	3:45:14 (6,712)	
McInekney, John	7:20:36 (30,080)	
McInerney, David	4:01:08 (10,307)	
McInerney, Ian	4:43:25 (19,469)	
McInerney, John	5:11:07 (24,228)	
McInnes, Duncan	4:29:35 (16,570)	
McInnes, Ewan	3:59:10 (9,807)	
McIntosh, Arthur	4:44:38 (19,701)	
McIntosh, Billy	4:16:44 (13,621)	
McIntosh, Christopher	3:17:44 (2,504)	
McIntosh, Christopher	4:55:16 (21,802)	
McIntosh, David	6:20:36 (29,178)	
McIntosh, Euan	2:56:21 (711)	
McIntosh, Graeme	4:04:30 (10,988)	
McIntosh, James	5:06:03 (23,476)	
McIntosh, Mark	3:28:37 (3,926)	
McIntosh, Nairn	3:32:00 (4,470)	
McIntyre, Angus	3:32:53 (4,585)	
McIntyre, Eddie	4:08:02 (11,774)	
McIntyre, Robert	4:23:44 (15,234)	
McIntyre, Russell	3:33:15 (4,652)	
McIntyre, Timothy	4:32:05 (17,135)	
McInulty, Brian	4:59:51 (22,588)	
McIver, Christopher	3:46:02 (6,863)	
McKane, Christopher	4:46:50 (20,126)	
McKay, Andrew	4:19:53 (14,333)	
McKay, Duncan	6:35:33 (29,534)	
McKay, Kevin	4:58:38 (22,401)	
McKay, Peter	4:54:07 (21,537)	
McKeating, Simon	4:17:24 (13,750)	
McKechnie, James	4:50:34 (20,808)	
McKechnie Sharma, Hamish	4:44:32 (19,684)	
McKee, Robert	3:34:42 (4,862)	
McKee, Tom	3:54:21 (8,549)	
McKeever, Stephen	3:12:09 (1,926)	
McKellar, Archie	4:03:28 (10,764)	
McKellar, James	4:01:20 (10,348)	
McKendrick, Gerard	4:19:36 (14,279)	
McKenna, Eugene	3:42:22 (6,197)	
McKenna, Jason	4:57:15 (22,178)	
McKenna, Michael	5:52:57 (28,060)	
McKenna, Shane	3:18:09 (2,557)	
McKenzie, Charles	4:18:32 (14,020)	
McKenzie, Craig	4:48:07 (20,371)	
McKenzie, Lindsay	5:04:10 (23,153)	
McKenzie, Michael	4:00:52 (10,254)	
McKenzie, Neil	4:28:09 (16,221)	
McKenzie, Peter	4:03:55 (10,866)	
McKenzie, Simon	4:35:24 (17,797)	
McKeown, Jimmy	4:36:01 (17,935)	
McKeown, Thomas	3:54:43 (8,641)	
McKessar, Ron	4:12:41 (12,768)	
McKie, Richard	4:32:37 (17,232)	
McKillop, Christopher	4:25:20 (15,580)	
McKinley, Paul	4:38:09 (18,419)	
McKinley, Paul	5:12:41 (24,453)	
McKinnel, Ian	4:03:31 (10,776)	
McKinnell, Nigel	5:07:26 (23,688)	
McKinney, Steve	4:46:14 (19,993)	
McKinnon, Eric	6:33:45 (29,500)	
McKinstray, Richard	4:53:37 (21,442)	
McLachlan, Robert	4:59:50 (22,581)	
McLaren, James	4:41:39 (19,093)	
McLaren, Rory	6:11:45 (28,920)	
McLatchie, Matthew	3:46:59 (7,033)	
McLaughlin, Barrie	4:18:38 (14,036)	
McLaughlin, Declan	4:01:17 (10,333)	
McLaughlin, Philip	5:22:24 (25,635)	
McLaughlin, Simon	3:43:50 (6,460)	
McLean, Alan	5:24:07 (25,803)	
McLean, Charles	4:01:58 (10,479)	
McLean, Craig	3:39:08 (5,596)	
McLean, Craig	3:52:48 (8,230)	
McLean, Donald	4:43:17 (19,447)	
McLean, Ian	3:53:15 (8,318)	
McLean, James	3:39:34 (5,688)	
McLean, Peter	4:19:51 (14,325)	
McLeish, Norman	3:12:36 (1,967)	
McLelland, Steve	3:39:43 (5,715)	
McLeod, Christopher	3:46:28 (6,942)	
McLeod, Ian	5:06:02 (23,473)	
McLeod, Roderick	3:50:49 (7,825)	
McLeod, Sandy	4:04:26 (10,973)	
McLure, Charles	3:48:20 (7,328)	
McMahon, Allan	4:52:39 (21,243)	
McMahon, Neal	5:24:49 (25,860)	
McMahon, Paul	5:08:32 (23,853)	
McMahon, Simon	3:27:50 (3,771)	
McManmon, Pascal	4:24:24 (15,370)	
McManus, Aidan	4:47:03 (20,173)	
McManus, Andrew	5:20:37 (25,423)	
McManus, Brian	4:07:52 (11,734)	
McManus, David	3:35:21 (4,962)	
McManus, John	4:37:31 (18,252)	
McManus, Kevin	2:58:57 (929)	
McMenamin, Andrew	5:47:28 (27,724)	
McMenamin, John	4:24:09 (15,318)	
McMenamin, Ray	3:57:32 (9,338)	
McMillan, David	4:46:54 (20,144)	
McMillan, David	4:54:34 (21,613)	
McMillan, Iain	4:16:50 (13,639)	
McMillan, Ian	4:32:40 (17,239)	
McMillan, Kevin	3:18:18 (2,576)	
McMillan, Neil	4:04:44 (11,050)	
McMonagle, Jamie	2:56:58 (740)	
McMorrow, Patrick	4:18:39 (14,041)	
McMullan, Edward	4:34:41 (17,655)	
McMurray, Robert	4:35:33 (17,822)	
McMurray, Tony	6:11:21 (28,900)	
McNabb, Robert	3:49:24 (7,553)	
McNally, John	2:55:47 (669)	
McNally, John	3:57:10 (9,215)	
McNamara, Duncan	4:46:02 (19,945)	
McNamara, Mark	3:52:23 (8,148)	
McNamara, Michael	5:15:57 (24,924)	
McNamee, Stephen	5:10:37 (24,167)	
McNaught, Brian	5:13:06 (24,518)	
McNaught, Iain	4:02:54 (10,645)	
McNaughton, Gavin	4:15:41 (13,402)	
McNaull, Allisdhair	3:36:41 (5,186)	
McNealy, Steve	3:36:53 (5,223)	
McNeil, Ian	4:23:09 (15,098)	
McNeill, Alan	4:18:09 (13,903)	
McNeill, David	4:18:25 (13,995)	
McNeill, Ian	3:18:19 (2,577)	
McNeilly, Tom	4:35:53 (17,903)	
McNelis, Robin	3:36:23 (5,134)	
McNicholas, Paul	3:40:53 (5,924)	
McNicholas, Vincent	5:29:07 (26,298)	
McNicholl, Michael	2:55:06 (633)	
McNicoll, Craig	5:22:43 (25,676)	
McNinch, Rob	3:05:13 (1,369)	
McNulty, David	4:07:56 (11,747)	
McNulty, James	3:22:41 (3,070)	
McNulty, Michael	3:45:58 (6,851)	
McNulty, Michael	4:50:08 (20,742)	
McNulty, Peter	4:58:10 (22,324)	
McParlan, Gary	4:26:29 (15,842)	
McParlin, Peter	4:53:35 (21,439)	
McPaul, Robert	4:24:21 (15,359)	

McPhail, Paul 4:52:12 (21,134)
McPhail, Thomas 3:43:19 (6,365)
McPherson, Derek 6:04:03 (28,595)
McPherson, Judah 4:06:55 (11,531)
McQuade, Gary 4:55:30 (21,893)
McQuade, Steve 2:56:07 (692)
McQuaid, Patrick 4:54:00 (21,511)
McQueen, Simon 4:23:15 (15,118)
McQuhae, Benjamin 4:48:11 (20,382)
McQuillan, John 4:37:57 (18,357)
McQuillan, Paul 3:44:21 (6,555)
McQuin, Andrew 3:53:42 (8,425)
McQuin, Steven 3:37:28 (5,329)
McRitchie, Andrew 4:25:47 (15,669)
McRoy, Luke 5:24:31 (25,838)
McShane, Desmond 3:27:19 (3,677)
McSherry, Timothy 5:04:18 (23,180)
McSweeney, Gordon 4:53:10 (21,348)
McSweeney, Rodney 6:57:27 (29,913)
McTague, James 4:52:03 (21,102)
McVeigh, Alistair 4:20:50 (14,556)
McVey, Fergus 5:37:11 (26,956)
McWall, Paul 4:50:12 (20,754)
McWhinnie, Alex 5:07:20 (23,669)
McWhir, Andrew 4:29:48 (16,625)
McWilliams, Alan 3:39:08 (5,596)
Mea, Philippe 4:11:17 (12,460)
Meacher, Barrington 4:05:28 (11,202)
Mead, Adrian 2:57:04 (748)
Mead, Marc 4:45:25 (19,852)
Mead, Steve 2:48:00 (362)
Meade, Ben 4:42:27 (19,264)
Meaden, Andrew 4:38:43 (18,551)
Meadows, David 4:03:01 (10,667)
Meadows, Thomas 4:00:54 (10,265)
Meads, Steven 3:57:02 (9,184)
Meagor, Lucas 4:32:40 (17,239)
Meakin, Alan 5:38:52 (27,077)
Meaking, Billy 3:27:33 (3,718)
Meakins, Christopher 4:35:24 (17,797)
Mealor, Paul 4:06:43 (11,488)
Meaning, Jason 4:45:13 (19,810)
Mearns, Trevor 4:32:13 (17,158)
Measures, Peter 4:16:20 (13,529)
Meates, John 5:16:22 (24,966)
Mechri, Nacer 5:03:17 (23,040)
Medcraft, David 5:21:25 (25,520)
Meddeman, Clint 5:06:26 (23,541)
Medeiro, Joao 3:31:59 (4,468)
Medlam, Dave 3:47:20 (7,097)
Medley, Malcolm 4:07:17 (11,606)
Medlock, Anthony 4:13:14 (12,861)
Medlock, Nathan 3:29:54 (4,150)
Medokpo, Victor 4:49:58 (20,711)
Meech, Robert 4:35:09 (17,739)
Meehan, Thomas 4:15:38 (13,393)
Meeking, Christopher 4:52:42 (21,251)
Meering, Richard 4:14:06 (13,056)
Megali, Basile 3:56:44 (9,115)
Meghezzi, Rachid 4:55:47 (21,952)
Mehmed, Deniz 3:41:35 (6,048)
Mehmet, John 4:34:17 (17,591)
Mehra, Ramji 3:40:05 (5,797)
Mehta, Ajay 4:45:40 (19,880)
Meiek, Antoine 4:16:01 (13,468)
Meier, Michael 3:48:33 (7,371)
Meier, Roland 3:40:40 (5,891)
Meier, Roland 4:40:32 (18,878)
Meijer, Nick 3:53:19 (8,338)
Mein, William 4:21:07 (14,613)
Meintjes, Thomas 5:21:16 (25,498)
Meisel, James 4:47:24 (20,238)
Meister, Peter 3:15:08 (2,236)
Meixner, Helmut 2:49:33 (410)
Mel, Edwin 3:36:58 (5,239)
Melbourne, John 3:19:12 (2,673)
Melbourne, William 4:11:21 (12,472)
Meldrum, Julian 3:17:55 (2,522)
Melhuish, Steve 4:18:10 (13,910)
Melin, Laurent 3:58:42 (9,674)
Melis, David 4:13:35 (12,952)
Mell, David 5:41:31 (27,300)
Mellen, Philip 5:14:12 (24,655)
Meller, David 2:51:36 (495)
Meller, Peter 4:53:37 (21,442)
Melling, Anthony 4:24:34 (15,413)
Melling, Phillip 3:29:37 (4,102)
Mellon, James 4:49:02 (20,534)
Mellor, Adrian 3:28:16 (3,859)
Mellor, James 4:42:35 (19,290)
Mellor, John 4:52:56 (21,299)
Mellor, Keith 3:12:05 (1,921)
Mellor, Neil 4:57:56 (22,284)
Mellor, Paul 5:10:03 (24,087)
Mellor, Rex 4:00:41 (10,208)
Mellor, Thomas 3:49:20 (7,533)
Mellors, Nigel 3:39:40 (5,703)
Mellows, Steve 4:57:52 (22,277)
Melloy, Peter 3:31:56 (4,459)
Melrose, Graham 3:10:21 (1,780)
Melven, Derek 3:57:12 (9,226)
Melville, Darin 4:06:12 (11,385)
Melville, Toby 4:03:56 (10,871)
Melville-Brown, Martin 4:27:32 (16,069)
Melvin, Richard 4:28:28 (16,306)
Membre, Eric 3:48:44 (7,410)
Menday, Robert 4:57:14 (22,175)
Mendelssohn, Christopher 5:34:43 (26,775)
Mendham, Gavin 3:13:41 (2,072)
Mendoza, Daniel 6:32:55 (29,477)
Menin, Andrew 4:17:26 (13,756)
Menmuir, Christopher 4:23:26 (15,155)
Mensa-Annan, Richard 3:28:44 (3,944)
Mentiply, Iain 6:24:46 (29,278)
Menzies Conacher, Simon 3:53:37 (8,407)
Mepham, Derek 4:14:41 (13,166)
Mercer, Darren 3:51:48 (8,027)
Mercer, Ian 4:28:52 (16,391)
Mercer, Jonathan 3:19:09 (2,666)
Mercer, Philip 4:46:29 (20,048)
Meredew, Paul 4:02:33 (10,584)
Meredith, Nigel 5:15:29 (24,867)
Mereng, Joseph 2:13:26 (12)
Merenius, Thomas 4:44:13 (19,625)
Merfield, Gordon 3:28:19 (3,872)
Merfield, Graham 3:08:22 (1,620)
Merialdo, Enrico 4:11:44 (12,556)
Merifield, Graeme 5:33:58 (26,686)
Merlaud, Philippe 3:56:05 (8,946)
Merle, Bernard 3:14:53 (2,207)
Merrell, Gary 4:01:20 (10,348)
Merrell, Lee 3:29:07 (4,019)
Merrell, Stephen 4:14:43 (13,177)
Merrett, Anthony 3:17:59 (2,532)
Merrett, Jonathan 4:29:59 (16,689)
Merrett, Trevor 6:14:32 (29,008)
Merrey, James 3:27:34 (3,720)
Merrick, Andrew 3:50:07 (7,709)
Merrick, Andrew 4:46:45 (20,105)
Merriman, Christopher 4:14:31 (13,131)
Merriman, David 4:11:13 (12,448)
Merriman, John 3:39:07 (5,592)
Merritt, Barrie 6:15:20 (29,039)
Merritt, Simon 3:21:36 (2,957)
Merritt, Terry 4:08:57 (11,965)
Merry, Andy 4:14:17 (13,094)
Merry, Richard 4:49:48 (20,675)
Mesa, Mario 2:56:46 (731)
Messenger, Iain 4:39:21 (18,654)
Messenger, Peter 2:52:57 (540)
Messer, Ben 3:18:08 (2,553)
Messer, Laurence 4:14:59 (13,260)
Messervy Whiting, Charles 3:15:19 (2,256)
Messuti, Renato 5:47:20 (27,718)
Meston, James 4:41:48 (19,123)
Meston, Thomas 3:57:17 (9,250)
Mesure, Derek 6:32:32 (29,464)
Metaye, Jean François 4:08:31 (11,875)
Metcalf, Richard 4:45:28 (19,860)
Metcalfe, Anthony 2:55:14 (639)
Metcalfe, Charles 5:26:02 (25,990)
Metcalfe, Leonard 4:06:12 (11,385)
Metcalfe, Sam 4:38:46 (18,568)
Metcalfe, Stephen 3:47:12 (7,064)
Metcalfe, Tom 2:55:40 (661)
Metcalfe, Trevor 4:16:54 (13,647)
Metherell, Mark 4:12:51 (12,799)
Metraux, Claude 4:50:53 (20,859)
Metters, Mark 4:38:25 (18,485)
Meunier, Jean Paul 3:36:57 (5,237)
Meurice, Nicholas 4:55:00 (21,732)
Mew, Ian 3:27:06 (3,638)
Mew, Jonathan 5:18:13 (25,178)
Mewton, Craig 3:52:30 (8,169)
Mewton, Derek 4:56:13 (22,028)
Meyer, Brett 7:06:00 (29,984)
Meyer, Karsten 3:49:06 (7,482)
Meyer, Manfred 4:20:45 (14,533)
Meyler, Jason 3:52:11 (8,114)
Mezgebu, Ayele 2:27:57 (54)
Miah, Matin 5:47:14 (27,714)
Michael, Dave 5:30:45 (26,434)
Michael, Garry 3:52:56 (8,255)
Michael, Girmay 3:13:07 (2,013)
Michael, Nicholas 4:11:39 (12,535)
Michaelis, John 5:14:27 (24,694)
Michaels, Joe 3:40:33 (5,875)
Michalski, Antony 4:39:34 (18,708)
Michatowski, Witold 4:23:15 (15,118)
Michel, James 3:52:46 (8,225)
Michel, Jean Pierre 3:45:11 (6,706)
Michell, Hugh 4:56:04 (21,997)
Michell, Nick 4:42:51 (19,347)
Michenot, Jean Jacques 2:59:25 (976)
Michie, James 3:03:51 (1,274)
Michiels, Rudv 3:46:36 (6,973)
Micho, Jim 4:31:45 (17,048)
Mickleborough, Tim 2:48:24 (374)
Mickleburgh, Benjamin 4:44:52 (19,750)
Mickleburgh, Trevor 3:43:48 (6,456)
Middlehurst, Philip 4:50:52 (20,856)
Middlemas, Bruce 3:29:30 (4,079)
Middler, Tim 4:37:11 (18,167)
Middleton, Craig 4:27:53 (16,172)
Middleton, Ewan 3:29:46 (4,132)
Middleton, Guy 2:58:49 (912)
Middleton, John 4:05:56 (11,333)
Middleton, Kevan 4:21:14 (14,635)
Middleton, Martin 5:09:08 (23,959)
Middleton, Nicholas 3:58:03 (9,501)
Middleton, Peter 3:40:34 (5,878)
Middleton, Ranulf 5:59:20 (28,387)
Middleton, Simon 2:59:53 (1,015)
Middleton, Simon 4:25:04 (15,525)
Middleton Cassini, Stephen 4:11:25 (12,486)
Middlewick, Andrew 3:54:24 (8,562)
Midgley, Martin 3:08:08 (1,601)
Midgley, Michael 4:03:24 (10,747)
Midgley, Richard 3:43:10 (6,336)
Mignaud, Justin 4:41:03 (18,987)
Mikami, Akihiro 4:25:38 (15,641)
Miki, Raita 4:56:49 (22,111)
Mikulski, Richard 4:48:52 (20,496)
Milazzo, Giuseppe 6:09:17 (28,826)
Milbank, Terry 3:54:14 (8,519)
Milbourne, Bill 4:00:32 (10,166)
Milburn, Ian 3:30:01 (4,172)
Milburn, Martin 3:30:37 (4,265)
Milburn, Michael 3:28:31 (3,911)
Mildon, John 4:27:32 (16,069)
Mildon, Paul 4:18:46 (14,074)
Milenski, Emerson 3:38:59 (5,571)
Miles, Brian 4:28:06 (16,210)
Miles, Christopher 4:11:49 (12,574)
Miles, Christopher 4:20:31 (14,479)
Miles, David 2:57:17 (765)
Miles, Dell 4:12:38 (12,760)
Miles, Dominic 3:32:22 (4,516)
Miles, Graham 3:59:27 (9,903)
Miles, John 3:12:26 (1,955)
Miles, Mark 4:19:20 (14,202)
Miles, Paul 3:07:20 (1,532)
Miles, Phillip 3:03:08 (1,222)
Miles, Robert 4:05:18 (11,165)
Miles, Robin 4:06:43 (11,488)
Miles, Roger 4:33:44 (17,485)
Miles, Stanley 6:00:20 (28,427)
Miles, Steve 5:45:03 (27,564)
Milito, Eduardo 3:07:30 (1,543)

Millanase, James 4:04:53 (11,088)
Millar, Alan 5:01:05 (22,745)
Millar, Clive 3:37:12 (5,282)
Millar, David 5:00:01 (22,625)
Millar, Gordon 4:13:27 (12,921)
Millar, Iain 4:24:43 (15,443)
Millar, James 4:27:50 (16,160)
Millar, John 3:42:44 (6,258)
Millar, Stephen 4:28:21 (16,271)
Millar, Stuart 4:50:47 (20,842)
Millard, Adrian 4:18:52 (14,090)
Millard, Duncan 3:34:08 (4,777)
Millard, Iain 6:08:18 (28,777)
Millard, Jonathan 3:39:41 (5,709)
Millard, Mark 4:59:53 (22,597)
Millbank, Steve 4:03:42 (10,821)
Miller, Adam 3:35:18 (4,952)
Miller, Adrian 3:37:06 (5,265)
Miller, Andrew 3:53:17 (8,327)
Miller, Charles 3:49:55 (7,669)
Miller, Clifton 5:52:22 (28,033)
Miller, Craig 5:15:15 (24,838)
Miller, Dave 5:29:58 (26,376)
Miller, David 3:56:25 (9,032)
Miller, Edward 3:23:02 (3,118)
Miller, Frank 3:29:35 (4,095)
Miller, Graeme 3:29:39 (4,111)
Miller, Grant 4:25:47 (15,669)
Miller, Jim 3:40:48 (5,912)
Miller, Joe 6:26:03 (29,303)
Miller, John 3:40:15 (5,821)
Miller, John 4:40:06 (18,803)
Miller, Joseph 4:32:50 (17,282)
Miller, Les 5:10:54 (24,197)
Miller, Leslie 4:12:09 (12,658)
Miller, Mark 5:47:42 (27,743)
Miller, Martin 3:43:07 (6,328)
Miller, Matthew 5:44:04 (27,481)
Miller, Patrick 4:24:09 (15,318)
Miller, Paul 3:00:44 (1,067)
Miller, Paul 3:06:00 (1,420)
Miller, Paul 4:39:20 (18,650)
Miller, Paul 4:42:01 (19,163)
Miller, Peter 2:58:13 (824)
Miller, Philip 5:24:27 (25,829)
Miller, Phillip 4:52:05 (21,110)
Miller, Raymond 3:08:36 (1,637)
Miller, Richard 4:50:40 (20,821)
Miller, Roger 5:20:05 (25,368)
Miller, Stephen 4:01:38 (10,418)
Miller, Stephen 4:49:20 (20,587)
Miller, Steve 4:41:59 (19,159)
Miller, Stuart 4:33:03 (17,320)
Miller, Stuart 5:05:22 (23,353)
Miller, Thomas 5:48:13 (27,794)
Miller, Thomas 5:48:24 (27,808)
Miller, Timothy 3:28:57 (3,987)
Millers, Paul 4:31:51 (17,074)
Millership, Tony 3:13:47 (2,087)
Millican, Keith 3:45:56 (6,843)
Millichap, Simon 3:30:03 (4,181)
Millichean, Philip 3:43:15 (6,353)
Millington, John 3:48:16 (7,316)
Millington, Nigel 4:48:16 (20,400)
Millman, Geoffrey 4:58:14 (22,332)
Milloy, Mathew 3:57:19 (9,262)
Mills, Alan 5:24:58 (25,882)
Mills, Cliff 6:14:58 (29,023)
Mills, Darren 3:40:40 (5,891)
Mills, Darren 4:03:17 (10,718)
Mills, David 3:21:06 (2,896)
Mills, David 3:28:53 (3,978)
Mills, David 4:07:20 (11,622)
Mills, Fabian 3:39:37 (5,696)
Mills, Gary 4:18:11 (13,914)
Mills, Gerald 3:46:00 (6,856)
Mills, Glyn 5:20:36 (25,421)
Mills, Ian 4:41:48 (19,123)
Mills, Jonathan 3:39:10 (5,602)
Mills, Matthew 5:09:45 (24,051)
Mills, Nathan 4:56:30 (22,065)
Mills, Nick 4:46:13 (19,990)
Mills, Peter 5:38:50 (27,075)

In the beginning

The first London Marathon was held on a rainy day on 29 March 1981. More than 20,000 people applied to run; 6,747 were accepted and 6,255 finished. The Marathon provided a bright moment in what was a grim time for Britain: Margaret Thatcher had won her first election less than two years before the event and was shaping up for a showdown with the miners; IRA bombs were going off in the streets of London; there were race riots and looting in Brixton and Britain's major cities. Yet 1981 was a great time for runners. The British team had defied a Thatcher-led boycott of the 1980 Moscow Olympic Games. Seb Coe and Steve Ovett had produced the greatest duel of those Games over 1500m and 800m, and in 1981 cinemas were packed out for the Oscar-winning *Chariots of Fire*. Runners flocked to this infant marathon and since then the total number of people who have completed the London Marathon to date is 783,185. The London Marathon has become one of the hottest tickets in town and recognised as one of the greatest races on Earth.

Mills, Robert 4:44:09 (19,609)
Mills, Simon 5:16:30 (24,989)
Mills, Stuart 3:32:31 (4,538)
Mills, Stuart 3:44:23 (6,559)
Mills, Titus 4:29:10 (16,464)
Mills, Vincent 2:56:43 (726)
Mills-Baker, Peter 4:47:24 (20,238)
Millward, Alex 3:57:52 (9,453)
Millward, Brett 3:22:06 (3,013)
Millward, Piers 3:21:46 (2,970)
Milne, Alan 3:35:56 (5,060)
Milne, Alex 3:00:29 (1,052)
Milne, Andrew 4:11:04 (12,409)
Milne, Andrew 5:07:22 (23,675)
Milne, David 5:08:38 (23,876)
Milne, Graham 4:59:51 (22,588)
Milne, John 2:52:41 (534)
Milne, Jonathan 4:31:40 (17,028)
Milne, Leslie 5:51:35 (27,989)
Milne, Mick 4:17:03 (13,677)
Milne, Robert 4:36:07 (17,945)
Milne, Vincent 5:33:26 (26,643)
Milner, Andrew 5:34:09 (26,716)
Milner, Charles 3:33:06 (4,622)
Milner, David 3:11:32 (1,867)
Milner, James 3:47:59 (7,262)
Milner, Kenneth 5:52:57 (28,060)
Milner, Nicholas 4:14:09 (13,065)
Milnes, Gary 3:02:25 (1,184)
Milton, Andrew 3:09:18 (1,694)
Milton, Mark 4:28:15 (16,249)
Milton, Michael 4:28:15 (16,249)
Milton, Steven 6:30:12 (29,414)
Milward, David 5:05:50 (23,435)
Minagawa, Tatsuya 2:55:32 (654)
Mineau, Didier 3:03:07 (1,220)
Minister, David 3:06:03 (1,428)

Minnett, Nigel 4:58:21 (22,351)
Minty, Kevin 2:45:15 (297)
Miotto, Tommaso 5:31:20 (26,478)
Mirkhani, Seyed 5:41:45 (27,310)
Mirza, Rozib 4:16:01 (13,468)
Misselbrook, Richard 3:35:24 (4,971)
Missions, David 5:16:54 (25,034)
Mistry, Alpesh 4:32:50 (17,282)
Mistry, Hitesh 3:48:38 (7,385)
Mistry, Jayanti 4:16:59 (13,661)
Mistry, Nimesh 4:46:45 (20,105)
Mistry, Umesh 5:49:48 (27,889)
Miszkowski, Henry 4:09:35 (12,088)
Mitchell, Adam 6:14:04 (28,993)
Mitchell, Alex 2:45:42 (312)
Mitchell, Andrew 3:50:10 (7,717)
Mitchell, Andrew 5:08:44 (23,894)
Mitchell, Barry 5:54:07 (28,119)
Mitchell, Bernard 3:49:35 (7,604)
Mitchell, Carl 4:16:25 (13,557)
Mitchell, Colin 3:06:23 (1,450)
Mitchell, David 3:28:15 (3,855)
Mitchell, Derek 5:07:02 (23,621)
Mitchell, Ewan 3:04:26 (1,308)
Mitchell, George 4:01:21 (10,357)
Mitchell, Graeme 3:48:25 (7,341)
Mitchell, Gregory 4:55:14 (21,791)
Mitchell, James 3:59:29 (9,919)
Mitchell, James 4:29:04 (16,438)
Mitchell, Jen 4:41:40 (19,097)
Mitchell, Jerry 3:59:04 (9,777)
Mitchell, John 3:55:56 (8,901)
Mitchell, Julian 4:13:48 (13,003)
Mitchell, Kevin 4:54:41 (21,634)
Mitchell, Matthew 4:04:00 (10,881)
Mitchell, Michael 3:04:31 (1,314)
Mitchell, Michael 6:29:33 (29,399)
Mitchell, Neil 3:48:41 (7,398)
Mitchell, Patrick 3:51:15 (7,921)
Mitchell, Paul 6:50:48 (29,820)
Mitchell, Richard 3:21:23 (2,932)
Mitchell, Robert 4:02:35 (10,590)
Mitchell, Rodney 4:59:29 (22,524)
Mitchell, Stephen 4:04:57 (11,106)
Mitchell, Stephen 4:30:08 (16,714)
Mitchell, Stephen 4:38:21 (18,466)
Mitchell, Tim 3:57:47 (9,425)
Mitford, Barry 4:53:05 (21,335)
Mitford, Tomothy 4:29:21 (16,508)
Mitterhuber, Paul 4:14:55 (13,239)
Mittman, Scott 4:08:29 (11,868)
Mitton, Simeon 3:41:00 (5,956)
Mo, Tai 4:24:14 (15,338)
Moat, Colin 4:40:57 (18,967)
Modaher, Jasvir 5:21:22 (25,516)
Modinger, Walter 4:05:14 (11,159)
Moffat, Alexander 4:45:33 (19,869)
Moffat, Mark 4:15:25 (13,350)
Moffat, Paul 4:19:24 (14,227)
Moffat, Stephen 2:53:36 (565)
Moffett, David 3:03:29 (1,244)
Moffett, James 5:31:08 (26,465)
Moffett, Paul 3:36:53 (5,223)
Moffett, Russell 4:16:10 (13,500)
Mogford, Brian 3:52:55 (8,252)
Moglia, Alessandro 3:41:41 (6,072)
Mogridge, Chris 4:36:51 (18,094)
Mohamed, Mohamed 7:28:05 (30,125)
Mohamed, Tarek 5:14:34 (24,717)
Mohammad, Naeem 3:36:04 (5,085)
Mohammed, Wahab 4:50:37 (20,814)
Moldon, Nicholas 2:54:38 (616)
Mole, Denis 3:49:31 (7,588)
Molesworth, Tony 4:13:16 (12,866)
Molesworth, William 3:33:12 (4,646)
Mollaret, Brno 3:00:09 (1,039)
Moller, Allan 4:11:08 (12,423)
Molloy, Adrian 3:03:14 (1,228)
Molloy, Christopher 4:42:07 (19,182)
Molloy, James 4:32:58 (17,303)
Molloy, Peter 3:39:59 (5,782)
Molony, Weldon 4:08:46 (11,928)
Molotoala, Sylvain 4:19:41 (14,299)

Molyneux, Graham 3:21:40 (2,965)
Molyneux, Pierre 3:49:15 (7,509)
Momilovic, George 4:36:29 (18,017)
Monaghan, Keith 4:40:58 (18,971)
Monaghan, Thomas 5:25:34 (25,944)
Moncrieff, Paul 4:38:08 (18,415)
Moncur, Lloyd 3:46:06 (6,877)
Mondor, Thierry 3:44:56 (6,670)
Mondrup, Jens 3:55:58 (8,911)
Moniatis, Jonathan 5:53:42 (28,104)
Monk, Chris 2:37:03 (116)
Monk, Gary 3:18:23 (2,587)
Monk, John 2:58:49 (912)
Monk, Jonathan 5:13:13 (24,535)
Monk, Paul 3:53:32 (8,387)
Monk, Phillip 4:08:34 (11,885)
Monk, Richard 5:02:12 (22,907)
Monk, Roy 4:53:43 (21,457)
Monkman, Ian 2:56:05 (689)
Monks, Andrew 4:03:28 (10,764)
Monks, Daniel 3:47:07 (7,054)
Monks, Lewis 3:53:26 (8,364)
Monks, Paul 3:20:37 (2,837)
Monnier, Jean François 3:50:46 (7,820)
Montague, Ian 3:38:35 (5,498)
Montague, Joe 3:36:41 (5,186)
Montague, John 2:52:25 (528)
Montague, Peter 6:26:15 (29,306)
Montanari, Jacky 4:10:10 (12,200)
Montaque, Peter 4:27:02 (15,975)
Monteil, Richard 3:29:37 (4,102)
Monteiro, Rui 3:36:38 (5,177)
Montgomery, Nicholas 4:53:50 (21,483)
Montgomery, Richard 4:53:07 (21,339)
Montgomery, Simon 3:35:23 (4,967)
Monticelli, Robert 4:27:35 (16,084)
Moodie, Dane 4:22:20 (14,894)
Moody, Adrian 4:30:03 (16,702)
Moody, Alf 5:00:32 (22,667)
Moody, Anthony 5:57:09 (28,276)
Moody, Colin 2:58:56 (927)
Moody, Jerome 4:05:34 (11,232)
Moody, Simon 4:34:54 (17,694)
Moody, Stephen 4:25:07 (15,536)
Moody, Steve 3:14:59 (2,221)
Moon, Chris 4:21:45 (14,746)
Moon, Gerard 5:20:33 (25,415)
Moon, John 4:36:45 (18,070)
Moon, Jung 3:27:07 (3,640)
Moon, Paul 4:16:18 (13,525)
Moonen, Roger 4:42:19 (19,231)
Mooney, Jason 3:47:31 (7,143)
Mooney, Jeremy 5:03:08 (23,023)
Mooney, Patrick 4:16:00 (13,463)
Mooney, Sean 4:23:33 (15,189)
Moont, Joshua 7:27:38 (30,119)
Moor, Michael 5:03:48 (23,098)
Moorby, Richard 4:08:12 (11,802)
Moorby, Richard 4:51:53 (21,067)
Moore, Alistair 5:58:13 (28,333)
Moore, Andrew 3:54:21 (8,549)
Moore, Andrew 3:57:47 (9,425)
Moore, Andrew 4:15:14 (13,319)
Moore, Brendan 4:49:17 (20,579)
Moore, Brian 3:57:18 (9,258)
Moore, Brian 5:14:28 (24,699)
Moore, Brian 5:25:17 (25,918)
Moore, Charles 6:41:19 (29,672)
Moore, Chris 4:06:26 (11,439)
Moore, Colin 3:45:47 (6,820)
Moore, Darren 5:07:23 (23,676)
Moore, David 3:15:41 (2,287)
Moore, David 4:12:54 (12,809)
Moore, Duncan 4:02:39 (10,599)
Moore, Edwin 4:18:17 (13,946)
Moore, Gareth 4:27:58 (16,188)
Moore, Gerry 3:19:32 (2,709)
Moore, Graeme 3:44:09 (6,518)
Moore, Graham 3:20:50 (2,868)
Moore, Ian 3:32:47 (4,570)
Moore, Ian 3:37:13 (5,285)
Moore, Ian 3:49:56 (7,671)
Moore, Ian 5:17:47 (25,137)
Moore, Ian 6:06:52 (28,714)
Moore, James 4:10:59 (12,397)
Moore, John 3:34:31 (4,839)
Moore, John 3:42:33 (6,226)
Moore, John 4:21:25 (14,673)
Moore, John 5:04:33 (23,223)
Moore, Keith 5:06:24 (23,536)
Moore, Mark 4:09:47 (12,124)
Moore, Mark 4:21:21 (14,656)
Moore, Martin 5:31:00 (26,452)
Moore, Matthew 5:11:08 (24,232)
Moore, Melwyn 4:06:39 (11,476)
Moore, Michael 2:41:47 (210)
Moore, Michael 3:49:15 (7,509)
Moore, Michael 4:18:17 (13,946)
Moore, Mick 3:05:28 (1,388)
Moore, Mike 4:20:45 (14,533)
Moore, Neil 3:10:35 (1,798)
Moore, Neil 5:05:59 (23,466)
Moore, Nigel 5:34:15 (26,727)
Moore, Patrick 4:29:04 (16,438)
Moore, Patrick 7:05:31 (29,980)
Moore, Paul 3:30:05 (4,185)
Moore, Paul 4:14:50 (13,218)
Moore, Paul 4:34:37 (17,646)
Moore, Paul 5:03:44 (23,087)
Moore, Paul 5:17:48 (25,138)
Moore, Peter 4:04:10 (10,918)
Moore, Peter 4:21:42 (14,736)
Moore, Ralph 3:17:18 (2,462)
Moore, Ralph 3:27:40 (3,735)
Moore, Richard 4:27:32 (16,069)
Moore, Richard 4:30:52 (16,818)
Moore, Robert 3:44:17 (6,540)
Moore, Robert 4:00:52 (10,254)
Moore, Simon 3:41:59 (6,121)
Moore, Simon 4:21:20 (14,653)
Moore, Simon 5:15:41 (24,887)
Moore, Stephen 5:58:13 (28,333)
Moore, Stuart 3:49:03 (7,475)
Moore, Timothy 4:06:58 (11,545)
Moore, Wayne 4:45:19 (19,826)
Moores, Gary 4:46:19 (20,010)
Moorey, Paul 5:38:00 (27,019)
Moorhead, Andrew 3:39:20 (5,635)
Moorhead, Thomas 4:56:31 (22,069)
Moorhouse, Graham 3:00:08 (1,037)
Moosa, Adam 4:26:51 (15,920)
Moppett, Benjamin 3:43:52 (6,464)
Mora, Patrick 3:43:54 (6,472)
Morales, Stephen 3:38:11 (5,425)
Morales Rodolfo, Hernandez 3:35:22 (4,964)
Moran, Anthony 3:26:41 (3,584)
Moran, Brendan 4:10:22 (12,244)
Moran, John 4:18:35 (14,031)
Moran, John 4:52:34 (21,228)
Moran, Mark 3:25:25 (3,435)
Moran, Mark 3:28:31 (3,911)
Moran, Michael 3:29:53 (4,145)
Moran, Paschal 3:18:47 (2,631)
Moran, Paul 4:51:21 (20,959)
Moran, Roger 4:10:22 (12,244)
Morant, William 4:26:13 (15,780)
Morcombe, Andy 3:31:32 (4,396)
Morcombe, Gary 3:34:05 (4,770)
Mordue, Stefan 4:49:58 (20,711)
Morel, Franck 4:06:29 (11,445)
Moreland, Michael 5:14:35 (24,720)
Morely, Ian 4:27:03 (15,981)
More-Molyneux, Michael 5:29:49 (26,352)
Morentin Latasa, Alberto 3:41:50 (6,097)
Moreton, Adrian 2:58:13 (824)
Moreton, Lloyd 5:25:06 (25,895)
Moreton, Matthew 4:42:28 (19,267)
Morewood, Richard 3:46:27 (6,940)
Morgan, Andrew 5:00:22 (22,652)
Morgan, Anthony 5:06:04 (23,480)
Morgan, Christopher 4:30:09 (16,715)
Morgan, Dafydd 4:37:32 (18,257)
Morgan, David 3:58:55 (9,726)
Morgan, David 4:24:11 (15,327)
Morgan, Derek 3:44:57 (6,678)
Morgan, Derrick 3:05:49 (1,408)
Morgan, Gareth 3:58:28 (9,596)
Morgan, Gareth 5:47:46 (27,748)
Morgan, Geoffrey 5:17:24 (25,093)
Morgan, Glyn 4:55:07 (21,761)
Morgan, Jack 4:01:50 (10,452)
Morgan, John 4:20:42 (14,519)
Morgan, Matthew 4:09:17 (12,039)
Morgan, Maurice 5:18:29 (25,212)
Morgan, Peter 3:07:31 (1,545)
Morgan, Phillip 4:26:13 (15,780)
Morgan, Robert 3:28:04 (3,812)
Morgan, Robert 5:03:54 (23,114)
Morgan, Robert 6:13:03 (28,957)
Morgan, Roger 3:14:31 (2,169)
Morgan, Roger 5:12:09 (24,369)
Morgan, Sam 6:12:34 (28,947)
Morgan, Simon 3:03:04 (1,217)
Morgan, Stephen 3:35:51 (5,042)
Morgan, Stewart 3:58:08 (9,525)
Morgan, Stuart 5:06:13 (23,504)
Morgan, Terry 4:43:24 (19,465)
Morgan, Thomas 5:12:19 (24,396)
Morgan, Tim 5:11:31 (24,288)
Morgan, Vivian 4:31:36 (17,011)
Morgan, Wesley 3:48:56 (7,448)
Morgans, Dewi 4:07:13 (11,590)
Moriarty, Alexander 2:53:00 (543)
Morisset, Eric 5:05:45 (23,422)
Moritko, Christian 3:20:43 (2,852)
Morley, Alex 4:22:10 (14,847)
Morley, Angus 4:05:38 (11,248)
Morley, Charles 4:45:09 (19,796)
Morley, Christopher 6:08:45 (28,799)
Morley, Christopher 6:20:37 (29,180)
Morley, Eric 6:09:42 (28,845)
Morley, Oliver 3:43:52 (6,464)
Morley, Richard 4:46:43 (20,095)
Morley, Roger 3:32:49 (4,574)
Moroney, James 5:25:48 (25,967)
Morpurgo, James 5:05:49 (23,433)
Morpuss, Guy 3:55:02 (8,705)
Morran, Stephen 5:05:09 (23,312)
Morrell, Ashley 4:24:58 (15,497)
Morrell, Piers 4:32:52 (17,289)
Morrell, Stephen 4:45:06 (19,788)
Morrice, Richard 4:04:16 (10,943)
Morris, Alan 5:14:46 (24,746)
Morris, Andrew 3:56:00 (8,919)
Morris, Andrew 4:04:44 (11,050)
Morris, Andrew 4:54:04 (21,527)
Morris, Barry 4:21:45 (14,746)
Morris, Brian 3:37:24 (5,321)
Morris, Colin 3:26:59 (3,621)
Morris, Colin 4:12:55 (12,815)
Morris, Daniel 3:34:12 (4,787)
Morris, Gail 4:14:32 (13,137)
Morris, Gerard 4:54:56 (21,713)
Morris, Howard 4:53:35 (21,439)
Morris, Joe 5:49:29 (27,871)
Morris, John 4:37:40 (18,294)
Morris, Joshua 4:23:11 (15,105)
Morris, Keith 4:01:21 (10,357)
Morris, Kevin 3:50:58 (7,861)
Morris, Mark 4:13:14 (12,861)
Morris, Max 5:29:30 (26,335)
Morris, Nick 7:06:24 (29,990)
Morris, Nigel 3:52:38 (8,199)
Morris, Paul 3:03:41 (1,261)
Morris, Paul 3:21:13 (2,906)
Morris, Paul 4:58:12 (22,328)
Morris, Peter 4:51:57 (21,084)
Morris, Philip 4:11:46 (12,562)
Morris, Phill 3:16:59 (2,424)
Morris, Phillip 3:24:04 (3,255)
Morris, Richard 3:11:49 (1,898)
Morris, Robert 3:26:15 (3,528)
Morris, Robert 4:22:49 (15,012)
Morris, Robin 3:46:44 (6,995)
Morris, Russell 4:30:43 (16,790)
Morris, Ryan 4:41:45 (19,112)
Morris, Shaun 3:28:18 (3,866)
Morris, Stephen 4:32:43 (17,252)
Morris, Stephen 4:34:43 (17,662)

Morris, Tim	6:04:44 (28,631)	
Morris, Timothy	5:03:09 (23,026)	
Morris, Trevor	4:13:04 (12,832)	
Morris, William	4:51:09 (20,918)	
Morrison, Barry	3:05:21 (1,378)	
Morrison, Blake	3:25:20 (3,422)	
Morrison, Brian	3:37:33 (5,342)	
Morrison, Craig	3:52:16 (8,129)	
Morrison, George	3:40:38 (5,887)	
Morrison, James	3:26:57 (3,616)	
Morrison, James	3:55:53 (8,889)	
Morrison, James	4:11:44 (12,556)	
Morrison, Kevin	4:20:55 (14,575)	
Morrison, Neil	3:54:00 (8,479)	
Morrison, Sid	3:16:31 (2,373)	
Morrison, Stuart	5:07:56 (23,764)	
Morrissey, Brian	6:13:50 (28,988)	
Morrissey, Michael	4:28:18 (16,262)	
Morrissy, Paul	4:44:12 (19,619)	
Morrow, John	3:34:36 (4,850)	
Morrow, Michael	3:51:30 (7,966)	
Morrow, Michael	4:51:01 (20,889)	
Morse, Martin	4:55:20 (21,824)	
Morsley, John	4:19:10 (14,160)	
Mort, Allan	4:21:26 (14,679)	
Mort, Gary	3:06:42 (1,478)	
Mort, Kenneth	4:07:46 (11,719)	
Mort, Nick	3:36:53 (5,223)	
Mortazavi, Mahmood	4:19:25 (14,231)	
Mortensen, Karl	4:33:07 (17,329)	
Mortimer, Daniel	4:23:58 (15,286)	
Mortimer, Ian	4:19:51 (14,325)	
Mortimer, Richard	4:27:02 (15,975)	
Mortimer, Timothy	3:56:44 (9,115)	
Mortin, John	4:14:43 (13,177)	
Morton, Alan	4:03:52 (10,855)	
Morton, Andrew	4:22:15 (14,875)	
Morton, Brian	3:39:38 (5,699)	
Morton, Chris	3:27:10 (3,652)	
Morton, Christopher	3:56:29 (9,050)	
Morton, Clive	3:48:09 (7,294)	
Morton, Colin	4:35:22 (17,791)	
Morton, Derek	4:55:08 (21,765)	
Morton, George	5:48:54 (27,838)	
Morton, Jonathan	4:47:52 (20,318)	
Morton, Mark	3:33:06 (4,622)	
Morton, Paul	5:19:18 (25,292)	
Morton, Rex	5:08:09 (23,789)	
Morton, William	4:13:39 (12,971)	
Morum, Greg	3:29:40 (4,115)	
Morvan, Oliver	5:55:22 (28,174)	
Mosaid, Sarwat	4:43:26 (19,473)	
Mosalaesi, Adolf	4:47:21 (20,229)	
Moscato, Antonio	4:29:15 (16,485)	
Moschos, Vassilis	4:56:07 (22,006)	
Moseby, Gavin	4:26:50 (15,916)	
Moseley, Andrew	3:15:56 (2,314)	
Moseley, Daniel	3:10:21 (1,780)	
Moseley, David	3:46:22 (6,927)	
Moseley, John	4:37:51 (18,333)	
Moseley, Paul	4:49:55 (20,703)	
Moseley, Peter	6:08:10 (28,774)	
Moseling, Christopher	4:03:59 (10,879)	
Moser, Felix	3:49:29 (7,574)	
Moser, Francesco	4:05:34 (11,232)	
Moser, Jeroen	4:22:29 (14,924)	
Moses, Ephraim	5:40:22 (27,215)	
Moses, Moddy	3:46:55 (7,022)	
Mosforth, Jeffrey	4:38:30 (18,506)	
Mosiane, Kgomonare	3:56:16 (8,986)	
Mosiane, Nthamane	4:28:55 (16,404)	
Mosley, Lachlan	2:58:36 (870)	
Mosley, Paul	5:44:14 (27,494)	
Mosley, Stuart	5:39:20 (27,119)	
Moss, Alan	3:45:15 (6,713)	
Moss, Andrew	4:03:28 (10,764)	
Moss, Andrew	4:20:41 (14,516)	
Moss, Andrew	4:52:17 (21,153)	
Moss, Andrew	5:05:19 (23,340)	
Moss, Barry	3:56:55 (9,159)	
Moss, Graham	3:59:43 (9,979)	
Moss, James	3:01:05 (1,088)	
Moss, Oliver	4:21:23 (14,666)	

Moss, Peter	4:03:04 (10,677)	
Moss, Roger	6:03:19 (28,556)	
Moss, Tony	4:08:30 (11,871)	
Moss, Trevor	3:51:46 (8,021)	
Mossop, Andrew	4:23:45 (15,236)	
Mote, Alex	3:54:09 (8,502)	
Mote, Nathan	4:17:06 (13,685)	
Mote, Thomas	5:17:45 (25,130)	
Mothersdale, David	4:42:38 (19,301)	
Motley, Michael	3:34:51 (4,884)	
Mottershead, Gary	3:39:29 (5,669)	
Moufarrige, Patrick	4:17:36 (13,793)	
Mould, John	4:23:01 (15,069)	
Mould, Keith	4:30:37 (16,769)	
Moulds, Stephen	4:44:30 (19,674)	
Moule, John	5:19:28 (25,303)	
Moultrie, Paul	5:13:18 (24,552)	
Moum, Sverre	3:58:20 (9,569)	
Mount, Mike	3:38:52 (5,552)	
Mountain, Andrew	3:23:14 (3,141)	
Mountain, Julian	3:41:47 (6,088)	
Mounter, Sean	5:14:05 (24,637)	
Mountford, Andrew	5:18:59 (25,265)	
Mountford, David	4:24:55 (15,482)	
Mountford, Edward	4:48:05 (20,365)	
Mountford, Ian	4:13:28 (12,925)	
Mournian, David	4:04:16 (10,943)	
Moussi, Mo	4:15:09 (13,293)	
Mousson, Pierre	4:55:56 (21,976)	
Moustakim, Mohamed	6:36:47 (29,559)	
Mouton, Jacques	3:56:14 (8,975)	
Mowbray, Ian	4:18:17 (13,946)	
Mower, Derek	4:04:34 (11,013)	
Mowle, Lee	3:02:21 (1,178)	
Moxham, Graham	3:42:27 (6,208)	
Moxon, David	3:59:51 (10,010)	
Moxon, David	4:49:10 (20,553)	
Moy, Dax	4:47:50 (20,312)	
Moy, Dean	3:10:25 (1,787)	
Moy, Peter	3:48:42 (7,402)	
Moyes, Leslie	4:33:24 (17,396)	
Moyes, Paul	3:38:53 (5,555)	
Moylan, John	6:26:48 (29,326)	
Moyle, Geoffrey	3:39:18 (5,625)	
Moyle, Geoffrey	4:38:13 (18,431)	
Moyse, Graham	2:57:55 (808)	
Muckle, Martin	5:54:52 (28,155)	
Muckleston, Liam	5:33:30 (26,650)	
Muddimer, Dave	4:22:40 (14,976)	
Muehlbauer, Michael	3:47:57 (7,258)	
Mueller, Detlev	4:17:11 (13,716)	
Mueller, Frite	3:55:04 (8,709)	
Mueller, Herbert	3:59:35 (9,944)	
Mueller, Jens Dominik	3:23:27 (3,168)	
Muellner, Wolfgang	3:37:19 (5,305)	
Mugglestone, John	5:43:29 (27,439)	
Mughal, Shahid	4:27:57 (16,181)	
Muhmood, Tareq	3:49:31 (7,588)	
Muir, Graham	4:15:13 (13,312)	
Muir, Jonathan	3:47:15 (7,072)	
Muir, Richard	4:33:51 (17,510)	
Muir, Ronald	4:44:09 (19,609)	
Muirhead, Cameron	3:49:32 (7,591)	
Muirhead, Graham	3:59:32 (9,931)	
Muirhead, James	4:54:55 (21,709)	
Mukadam, Hussain	4:30:58 (16,844)	
Mulgrew, Gerry	4:48:47 (20,483)	
Mulholland, David	4:04:52 (11,081)	
Mulholland, Patrick	5:28:21 (26,217)	
Mulkerrins, Colm	3:31:46 (4,430)	
Mullally, Martin	4:09:24 (12,063)	
Mullan, John	5:00:25 (22,658)	
Mullan, Liam	5:08:23 (23,829)	
Mullane, Danny	3:57:16 (9,245)	
Mullaney, David	3:35:14 (4,939)	
Mullarkey, Brian	5:39:42 (27,156)	
Mullarkey, Peter	3:09:33 (1,721)	
Mullen, Brian	4:08:29 (11,868)	
Mullen, Kenneth	3:57:21 (9,273)	
Mullens, Stephen	4:42:38 (19,301)	
Muller, Anton	3:36:37 (5,174)	
Muller, François	4:23:08 (15,093)	
Muller, Gregory	4:21:00 (14,592)	

Muller, Wayne	2:48:56 (390)	
Mullery, Peter	3:12:21 (1,947)	
Mulley, Ian	3:21:00 (2,893)	
Mulley, John	4:21:27 (14,682)	
Mulligan, John	4:58:59 (22,460)	
Mullins, Andrew	4:16:30 (13,573)	
Mullins, Geoffrey	4:00:43 (10,217)	
Mullins, Nick	5:08:06 (23,783)	
Mulot, Jacques	3:35:17 (4,949)	
Mulqueen, Mark	4:34:04 (17,547)	
Multhaupt, Stephan	4:18:38 (14,036)	
Multon, Richard	3:57:24 (9,289)	
Mulvihill, Nicholas	3:26:06 (3,512)	
Mulvihill, Peter	4:30:43 (16,790)	
Mumberson, Robert	5:31:22 (26,481)	
Mumby, Nicholas	4:37:46 (18,315)	
Mumford, Alex	4:53:17 (21,368)	
Mumford, Darren	4:27:15 (16,017)	
Mumford, Kenneth	4:00:32 (10,166)	
Mumford, Michael	6:09:28 (28,832)	
Mumford, Richard	4:47:15 (20,213)	
Muncie, Gordon	5:47:28 (27,724)	
Muncie, Keith	5:04:21 (23,189)	
Munday, Bob	4:18:02 (13,874)	
Mundie, Philip	3:58:35 (9,639)	
Mundle, Chris	4:50:55 (20,865)	
Mundy, James	3:28:39 (3,930)	
Mundy, Robert	4:31:42 (17,038)	
Mundy, Stuart	5:02:07 (22,893)	
Mungin-Jenkins II, Escye	4:32:23 (17,189)	
Munim, Abdul	5:54:16 (28,127)	
Munk, David	4:38:33 (18,515)	
Munn, John	5:08:36 (23,869)	
Munn, Wayne	4:55:36 (21,922)	
Munnings, Andy	5:31:05 (26,459)	
Munns, Brian	3:34:35 (4,847)	
Munro, David	3:08:18 (1,615)	
Munro, Neil	4:12:19 (12,698)	
Munro, Robert	7:28:21 (30,129)	
Munro, William	3:40:24 (5,849)	
Munroe, Andrew	3:58:10 (9,530)	
Munslow, Graham	3:56:52 (9,147)	
Munson, William	4:41:22 (19,040)	
Munt, Tom	5:25:28 (25,938)	
Muntus, Michael	4:45:31 (19,866)	
Muratsubaki, Ryuta	3:30:01 (4,172)	
Murden, Terence	4:52:56 (21,299)	
Murdey, Ian	2:48:30 (377)	
Murdey, Lawrence	4:42:58 (19,379)	
Murdoch, Cambell	3:59:39 (9,964)	
Murdoch, Graeme	3:08:07 (1,598)	
Murfin, Mark	4:20:03 (14,381)	
Murfin, Michael	4:36:48 (18,085)	
Murfitt, Darren	3:07:29 (1,541)	
Murgatroyd, Steve	4:28:05 (16,205)	
Murgatroyd, Timothy	6:05:29 (28,663)	
Murie, Kirk	3:13:30 (2,060)	
Murley, Allan	3:59:32 (9,931)	
Murphy, Alan	5:44:54 (27,556)	
Murphy, Antony	3:58:46 (9,690)	
Murphy, Brendan	4:22:33 (14,938)	
Murphy, Colin	4:15:06 (13,289)	
Murphy, Dale	4:25:41 (15,650)	
Murphy, Damian	5:14:30 (24,706)	
Murphy, David	4:37:31 (18,252)	
Murphy, Eddie	5:43:05 (27,419)	
Murphy, James	3:59:51 (10,010)	
Murphy, John	3:57:02 (9,184)	
Murphy, John	4:30:37 (16,769)	
Murphy, John	5:58:39 (28,351)	
Murphy, Kevin	5:13:43 (24,597)	
Murphy, Leo	4:15:58 (13,457)	
Murphy, Mark	3:47:42 (7,195)	
Murphy, Martin	4:25:49 (15,679)	
Murphy, Michael	4:38:40 (18,541)	
Murphy, Paul	4:30:32 (16,757)	
Murphy, Paul	4:31:51 (17,074)	
Murphy, Simon	4:50:30 (20,802)	
Murphy, Stephen	3:14:51 (2,200)	
Murphy, Stephen	4:31:08 (16,883)	
Murphy, Thomas	6:15:33 (29,046)	
Murphy, Trevor	4:28:07 (16,217)	
Murray, Alan	5:57:04 (28,273)	

Murray, Alexander ... 4:42:24 (19,250)
Murray, Andrew ... 3:14:11 (2,135)
Murray, Anthony ... 6:44:04 (29,718)
Murray, Barry ... 4:24:58 (15,497)
Murray, Brian ... 3:29:58 (4,165)
Murray, Chris ... 8:21:02 (30,239)
Murray, Daniel ... 5:41:46 (27,313)
Murray, David ... 3:12:46 (1,984)
Murray, David ... 3:56:48 (9,133)
Murray, David ... 5:35:32 (26,846)
Murray, Francis ... 3:41:37 (6,059)
Murray, Gary ... 4:53:40 (21,448)
Murray, Graeme ... 4:27:48 (16,152)
Murray, Iain ... 3:56:20 (9,004)
Murray, Ian ... 4:49:16 (20,575)
Murray, James ... 3:25:14 (3,406)
Murray, James ... 5:16:59 (25,050)
Murray, Jeff ... 4:22:33 (14,938)
Murray, Jim ... 4:13:17 (12,871)
Murray, John ... 4:53:57 (21,499)
Murray, John ... 5:41:00 (27,261)
Murray, John ... 7:43:44 (30,177)
Murray, Keith ... 2:51:16 (477)
Murray, Kenneth ... 4:22:01 (14,818)
Murray, Kirk ... 4:37:44 (18,308)
Murray, Luke ... 4:57:49 (22,269)
Murray, Nel ... 4:36:46 (18,072)
Murray, Phillip ... 3:48:19 (7,324)
Murray, Ray ... 3:44:16 (6,535)
Murray, Robin ... 3:20:59 (2,889)
Murray, Stephen ... 2:59:07 (943)
Murray, Stephen ... 3:16:19 (2,343)
Murray, Stephen ... 3:34:29 (4,835)
Murray, Stephen ... 4:12:13 (12,674)
Murray, Stuart ... 4:37:35 (18,276)
Murray-Jones, William ... 3:43:24 (6,377)
Mursell, John ... 3:31:00 (4,327)
Murtagh, John ... 3:27:23 (3,686)
Murtagh, Tim ... 4:33:28 (17,410)
Muscroft, Chris ... 4:04:47 (11,065)
Musgrave, Paul ... 4:24:17 (15,345)
Musgrove, John ... 3:19:36 (2,718)
Muskett, Alan ... 3:40:23 (5,845)
Musruck, Daas ... 3:29:11 (4,025)
Musselle, Shirl ... 4:01:03 (10,292)
Mussenbrock, Elmar ... 3:38:52 (5,552)
Mussett, Steve ... 4:20:26 (14,460)
Musson, Adrian ... 3:31:32 (4,396)
Mustafa, Mustafa ... 6:23:12 (29,234)
Mustafa, Yusuf ... 5:57:15 (28,278)
Musty, Jason ... 4:06:43 (11,488)
Muth, Cornelius ... 3:17:21 (2,469)
Mutter, Dave ... 3:31:14 (4,360)
Muzzell, James ... 5:23:22 (25,730)
Myanger, Deepak ... 5:36:03 (26,885)
Myatt, James ... 4:00:01 (10,058)
Myers, John ... 4:06:30 (11,450)
Myers, Keiran ... 4:49:59 (20,715)
Myers, Nicholas ... 4:47:31 (20,267)
Myers, Roy ... 3:29:22 (4,061)
Myers, Terry ... 4:13:48 (13,003)
Myhill, Ben ... 4:29:30 (16,545)
Myhill, Douglas ... 3:55:51 (8,883)
Myhill, Ian ... 4:31:14 (16,913)
Mynard, Andrew ... 3:18:44 (2,625)
Mynett, Michael ... 3:47:36 (7,165)
Naftalin, Alan ... 4:13:37 (12,961)
Nagahara, Tadao ... 3:47:51 (7,224)
Nagel, Stefan ... 3:12:50 (1,989)
Nagy, Robin ... 3:57:27 (9,311)
Nagy, Timothy ... 4:31:10 (16,893)
Naidoo, Ralph ... 5:49:41 (27,881)
Naik, Rajnikant ... 6:52:53 (29,842)
Nailor, Philip ... 3:27:00 (3,623)
Namba, Shinobu ... 4:59:43 (22,556)
Nanalal, Manish ... 6:44:56 (29,737)
Nanji, Amin ... 5:34:36 (26,764)
Nanthan, Sivasothilingam ... 5:30:54 (26,445)
Napier, Alwyn ... 4:00:30 (10,154)
Napier, Charlie ... 4:21:01 (14,595)
Napthine, Adam ... 5:25:22 (25,925)
Narsi, Jason ... 4:22:12 (14,861)
Naseem, Muhammad ... 4:13:07 (12,843)

Nash, Colin ... 6:35:44 (29,541)
Nash, Damian ... 4:29:32 (16,553)
Nash, David ... 2:48:05 (363)
Nash, David ... 7:20:55 (30,085)
Nash, David ... 8:14:03 (30,234)
Nash, Liam ... 4:49:47 (20,669)
Nash, Philip ... 3:33:48 (4,729)
Nash, Robin ... 4:23:33 (15,189)
Nash, Steven ... 4:38:24 (18,480)
Nash, Steven ... 4:57:59 (22,292)
Nash, Trevor ... 3:27:29 (3,704)
Nashir, Tooran ... 5:47:40 (27,736)
Nastri, Philip ... 5:58:02 (28,323)
Nathan, Anthony ... 3:56:59 (9,174)
Nathan, Hugo ... 4:13:21 (12,889)
Natho, Uwe ... 4:53:53 (21,492)
Nathwani, Hitesh ... 3:55:18 (8,760)
Naughtohn, Kevan ... 2:53:07 (548)
Navasse, Dominique ... 3:52:59 (8,263)
Navin, Michael ... 4:14:44 (13,185)
Navrady, Jeremy ... 3:38:58 (5,568)
Nayee, Kiran ... 3:41:17 (6,005)
Nayler, Ian ... 3:20:01 (2,768)
Nayler, Mark ... 3:20:01 (2,768)
Naylor, Dave ... 3:06:58 (1,503)
Naylor, John ... 4:33:15 (17,356)
Naylor, Roger ... 4:49:12 (20,562)
Nazarin, Jeremy ... 3:34:23 (4,814)
Ne, Michael ... 4:49:04 (20,539)
Neagus, Russell ... 4:30:46 (16,801)
Neal, Gregory ... 4:15:24 (13,347)
Neal, Ian ... 4:27:08 (16,000)
Neal, Jack ... 5:26:00 (25,987)
Neal, Trevor ... 4:50:22 (20,786)
Neale, Brian ... 4:19:13 (14,165)
Neale, Colin ... 4:25:57 (15,718)
Neale, John ... 3:12:19 (1,943)
Neale, Nick ... 3:47:03 (7,042)
Neale, Paul ... 3:19:49 (2,743)
Neale, Rayment ... 5:37:50 (27,010)
Nealon, Nick ... 3:18:11 (2,559)
Neary, Michael ... 5:02:01 (22,874)
Neary, Stephen ... 5:24:29 (25,834)
Neave, David ... 4:05:19 (11,168)
Neaves, Grant ... 5:01:04 (22,741)
Neaves, Rodney ... 5:16:28 (24,984)
Nectoux, François ... 4:37:06 (18,144)
Needham, David ... 3:09:54 (1,741)
Needham, Kevin ... 5:07:48 (23,747)
Needle, Paul ... 5:35:17 (26,826)
Neher, Fergus-John ... 3:28:53 (3,978)
Neiland, Thomas ... 5:11:11 (24,241)
Neill, David ... 2:34:18 (86)
Neill, John ... 4:31:23 (16,954)
Neill, Lawrence ... 3:27:45 (3,756)
Neill, Peter ... 4:01:25 (10,373)
Neillis, John ... 3:51:28 (7,956)
Neimes, Steven ... 5:12:23 (24,413)
Nel, Morne ... 3:59:19 (9,849)
Nel, Spencer ... 4:44:11 (19,616)
Nelhams, Michael ... 2:53:11 (551)
Nellins, Christopher ... 3:03:15 (1,230)
Nelmes, John ... 3:34:16 (4,795)
Nelson, Anthony ... 6:15:13 (29,031)
Nelson, Blair ... 5:04:33 (23,223)
Nelson, Carl ... 4:06:22 (11,422)
Nelson, David ... 5:11:32 (24,292)
Nelson, Geoffrey ... 4:36:00 (17,932)
Nelson, Ian ... 4:26:26 (15,828)
Nelson, James ... 4:12:29 (12,738)
Nelson, Marc ... 7:27:54 (30,121)
Nemeti, Olivier ... 3:48:53 (7,436)
Nendick, Stephen ... 4:03:31 (10,776)
Nendy, David ... 4:54:51 (21,691)
Neo, Meng Kong ... 2:58:58 (931)
Nesbit, Douglas ... 2:58:16 (830)
Nesbit, Simon ... 4:32:33 (17,219)
Nesbitt, Joe ... 5:04:56 (23,287)
Nester, Michael ... 2:51:55 (512)
Neumann, Mark ... 3:45:28 (6,739)
Neve, John ... 3:50:49 (7,825)
Nevill, Alex ... 3:59:59 (10,052)
Nevill, David ... 4:29:55 (16,665)

Neville, Paul ... 4:11:42 (12,549)
Neville, Stephen ... 4:42:58 (19,379)
New, Andrew ... 5:05:51 (23,439)
New, Edward ... 4:06:33 (11,459)
New, Peter ... 5:19:04 (25,271)
New, Stephen ... 6:09:38 (28,841)
Newberry, Ben ... 5:11:19 (24,258)
Newberry, Brian ... 4:03:53 (10,859)
Newbold, Phillip ... 4:45:27 (19,858)
Newbould, Paul ... 4:43:51 (19,565)
Newbury, Andrew ... 3:26:35 (3,570)
Newby, Christopher ... 2:49:57 (425)
Newby, Ray ... 4:20:44 (14,529)
Newcombe, Martin ... 4:30:44 (16,793)
Newell, Mark ... 3:46:15 (6,905)
Newell, Mark ... 5:39:49 (27,164)
Newell, Paul ... 5:54:27 (28,134)
Newell, Peter ... 4:14:19 (13,098)
Newell, Terence ... 5:13:11 (24,527)
Newitt, Joseph ... 4:02:23 (10,552)
Newland, William ... 3:13:40 (2,071)
Newlands, Alistair ... 3:33:28 (4,685)
Newman, Anthony ... 3:26:15 (3,528)
Newman, Brian ... 3:48:23 (7,335)
Newman, Chris ... 4:44:18 (19,640)
Newman, David ... 4:23:59 (15,291)
Newman, David ... 4:27:01 (15,971)
Newman, David ... 4:51:39 (21,019)
Newman, David ... 4:55:30 (21,893)
Newman, Dominic ... 4:16:17 (13,521)
Newman, James ... 4:16:42 (13,609)
Newman, John ... 4:03:36 (10,801)
Newman, Jonathan ... 5:28:41 (26,252)
Newman, Martin ... 3:28:58 (3,991)
Newman, Maurice ... 3:54:57 (8,695)
Newman, Michael ... 3:38:14 (5,437)
Newman, Michael ... 4:44:21 (19,644)
Newman, Paul ... 3:18:02 (2,538)
Newman, Paul ... 4:02:43 (10,614)
Newman, Paul ... 4:27:56 (16,180)
Newman, Paul ... 6:45:17 (29,741)
Newman, Ralph ... 3:27:03 (3,628)
Newmarch, Mark ... 4:20:19 (14,432)
Newnham, Andrew ... 4:39:23 (18,664)
Newport, John ... 4:31:12 (16,905)
Newrick, Paul ... 3:16:24 (2,352)
Newsam, Michael ... 3:55:05 (8,710)
Newsham, Jim ... 4:16:44 (13,621)
Newsome, Christopher ... 4:20:29 (14,471)
Newsome, Richard ... 4:32:21 (17,183)
Newson, Paul ... 4:28:51 (16,388)
Newstead, Mark ... 3:43:18 (6,360)
Newth, Tom ... 4:19:30 (14,255)
Newton, Andrew ... 3:27:42 (3,741)
Newton, Brian ... 3:39:06 (5,589)
Newton, Christopher ... 4:17:29 (13,769)
Newton, Ickford ... 3:39:19 (5,631)
Newton, Kevin Glynn ... 3:39:44 (5,719)
Newton, Mark ... 4:43:32 (19,504)
Newton, Martin ... 2:59:57 (1,028)
Newton, Mike ... 4:30:51 (16,816)
Newton, Nicholas ... 2:59:38 (987)
Newton, Paul ... 3:58:32 (9,616)
Newton, Peter ... 3:44:21 (6,555)
Newton, Philip ... 3:44:40 (6,605)
Newton, Ray ... 4:58:02 (22,301)
Newton, Warrick ... 3:17:55 (2,522)
Ng, Jeffrey ... 4:06:36 (11,468)
Ng, Kee ... 5:47:23 (27,721)
Ngo, Chan ... 4:42:44 (19,318)
Ngo, Thomas ... 3:10:14 (1,762)
Nibaudeau, Jean Pierre ... 3:18:59 (2,654)
Niblett, Stephen ... 3:23:18 (3,149)
Nice, Gordon ... 3:54:30 (8,587)
Nichol, Ian ... 3:54:44 (8,646)
Nicholas, Gary ... 4:12:56 (12,817)
Nicholas, Phillip ... 5:01:59 (22,871)
Nicholas, Ronny ... 4:57:06 (22,155)
Nicholl, Andrew ... 3:43:34 (6,408)
Nicholl, James ... 5:22:47 (25,682)
Nicholls, Andrew ... 3:14:26 (2,163)
Nicholls, Andrew ... 4:32:28 (17,210)
Nicholls, Clive ... 4:27:53 (16,172)

Nicholls, David 5:07:28 (23,693)
Nicholls, David 5:18:19 (25,194)
Nicholls, Jonathan 4:39:13 (18,639)
Nicholls, Keith 4:28:10 (16,228)
Nicholls, Marshall 3:59:31 (9,925)
Nicholls, Michael 3:43:47 (6,455)
Nicholls, Michael 5:06:34 (23,554)
Nicholls, Mike 5:43:03 (27,415)
Nicholls, Paul 4:01:21 (10,357)
Nicholls, Tim 3:45:39 (6,779)
Nicholls-Lee, Alex 6:26:19 (29,312)
Nichols, Andrew 3:55:24 (8,781)
Nichols, Carl 4:09:19 (12,045)
Nichols, Dave 3:49:03 (7,475)
Nichols, David 4:59:24 (22,513)
Nichols, Kevin 5:24:18 (25,817)
Nichols, Martin 4:31:23 (16,954)
Nichols, Michael 3:07:23 (1,534)
Nichols, Michael 4:13:31 (12,935)
Nichols, Robert 4:07:26 (11,651)
Nichols, Stephen 3:43:00 (6,305)
Nichols, Stephen 4:11:48 (12,570)
Nichols, Stewart 3:34:52 (4,886)
Nicholson, David 5:54:26 (28,131)
Nicholson, Gary 4:17:49 (13,839)
Nicholson, Ian 4:01:16 (10,330)
Nicholson, Jonathan 4:33:13 (17,351)
Nicholson, Mark 3:33:57 (4,748)
Nicholson, Peter 6:20:31 (29,173)
Nicholson, Robert 4:15:51 (13,434)
Nicholson, Roy 3:56:40 (9,095)
Nicholson, Steven 5:34:25 (26,746)
Nickau, Hanno 2:51:48 (507)
Nickells, Paul 3:24:22 (3,293)
Nickels, Marc 3:28:47 (3,957)
Nickless, Andrew 4:22:44 (14,991)
Nicklin, Brian 4:15:00 (13,268)
Nicklin, Mick 4:49:37 (20,637)
Nicolas, Denis 2:46:42 (333)
Nicolle, Serge 4:35:12 (17,751)
Niedojadlo, Mietek 3:58:40 (9,661)
Niedojadlo, Stephen 4:54:41 (21,634)
Nield, John 3:50:53 (7,844)
Nielsen, Henrik 3:27:02 (3,627)
Nielsen, Kai 4:34:28 (17,620)
Niewenhuis, Hans 4:54:46 (21,665)
Nigg, Thomas 3:03:31 (1,246)
Nightingale, Peter 4:28:41 (16,357)
Nightingale, Steven 3:39:41 (5,709)
Nightingale, Tim 2:58:46 (904)
Nilsson, Karl 2:51:43 (502)
Nilsson, Stanley 4:29:16 (16,487)
Nimmo, Howard 4:01:40 (10,426)
Nimmo, Thomas 7:06:12 (29,986)
Nini, Nanilo 3:49:27 (7,566)
Nisbet, Derren 4:21:15 (14,639)
Nisbet, Jack 3:57:34 (9,352)
Nisbett, Mark 4:51:08 (20,912)
Nishaharan, Siva 4:55:01 (21,739)
Nishikawa, Yoichiro 5:05:47 (23,429)
Nitsch, Bob 4:02:12 (10,523)
Nix, Michael 4:06:32 (11,456)
Nixon, Alan 3:46:46 (6,999)
Nixon, Craig 4:38:11 (18,424)
Nixon, David 3:54:17 (8,533)
Nixon, James 4:52:38 (21,242)
Njotea, Patrick 3:41:21 (6,020)
Noad, Peter 3:22:23 (3,045)
Noakes, Gary 3:55:40 (8,834)
Nobbs, Dean 3:26:08 (3,516)
Nobbs, Martin 3:03:14 (1,228)
Noble, Angus 4:22:33 (14,938)
Noble, Geoffrey 5:13:26 (24,567)
Noble, John 5:41:25 (27,293)
Noble, Mark 5:40:18 (27,209)
Noble, Michael 4:22:38 (14,962)
Noble, Ray 3:07:39 (1,561)
Noble, Richard 4:16:49 (13,637)
Noble, Robert 4:00:40 (10,199)
Noble, Samuel 3:55:50 (8,879)
Noblet, Alan 3:47:37 (7,167)
Noblett, Antony 3:59:31 (9,925)
Nock, Graham 3:47:19 (7,090)
Noel, Selwyn 4:58:35 (22,391)
Noel, Thomas 5:12:28 (24,424)
Noke, Ray 3:19:37 (2,720)
Nolan, Bill 4:54:05 (21,530)
Nolan, Dermot 4:29:57 (16,675)
Nolan, James 3:09:24 (1,704)
Nolan, Michael 4:28:50 (16,386)
Nolan, Rich 2:48:45 (383)
Noll, Stefan 3:46:34 (6,963)
Nombreuse, Georges 5:15:23 (24,851)
Nonomura, Shinkichi 3:29:14 (4,034)
Noon, Stephen 4:40:47 (18,938)
Noon, Wayne 3:51:34 (7,983)
Noone, Jim 3:57:31 (9,334)
Norbury, Antony 3:53:49 (8,448)
Norbury, Michael 3:28:05 (3,816)
Norcott, William 4:21:21 (14,656)
Nordell, John 5:31:38 (26,502)
Norman, Alan 3:54:34 (8,605)
Norman, Barry 4:03:31 (10,776)
Norman, Christopher 4:26:59 (15,959)
Norman, David 4:04:29 (10,983)
Norman, John 4:15:40 (13,398)
Norman, Nigel 3:52:16 (8,129)
Norman, Phillip 4:36:50 (18,091)
Norman, Tim 4:48:48 (20,486)
Norman Butler, Philip 3:55:44 (8,854)
Norman-Walker, Arthur 4:40:42 (18,921)
Normington, Peter 3:56:24 (9,025)
Norridge, Christopher 4:14:42 (13,173)
Norris, Andrew 2:53:47 (574)
Norris, Anthony 5:10:16 (24,115)
Norris, Charles 5:32:42 (26,594)
Norris, Colin 5:33:51 (26,675)
Norris, John 3:50:12 (7,724)
Norris, Keith 5:12:35 (24,441)
Norris, Kevin 4:58:11 (22,326)
Norris, Mathew 3:55:22 (8,775)
Norris, Raymond 3:37:29 (5,333)
Norris, Richard 5:17:49 (25,142)
Norris, Tim 4:15:55 (13,447)
Norris Jones, James 4:17:00 (13,668)
Norrish, Roger 5:03:34 (23,068)
North, Cedrick 3:49:14 (7,502)
North, David 4:03:04 (10,677)
North, David 5:12:52 (24,477)
North, Ernest 4:21:18 (14,647)
North, Glenn 3:24:31 (3,312)
North, Matthew 3:08:13 (1,608)
North, Ryan 5:05:27 (23,372)
North, Shaun 2:37:16 (122)
North, Thomas 4:42:09 (19,192)
Northcott, Adrian 3:49:23 (7,548)
Northey, Michael 3:04:28 (1,310)
North-Lewis, David 3:55:48 (8,870)
Northover, Anthony 6:20:29 (29,170)
Norton, Bradley 4:31:22 (16,947)
Norton, Brent 4:14:21 (13,107)
Norton, David 4:28:11 (16,231)
Norton, Francis 5:00:14 (22,642)
Norton, Jim 2:59:39 (990)
Norton, Mark 3:32:33 (4,544)
Norton, Paul 4:36:44 (18,067)
Norton, Peter 4:37:59 (18,365)
Norville, Philip 5:11:54 (24,344)
Noschese, Giuseppe 4:52:16 (21,148)
Nossek, Arnold 4:25:11 (15,554)
Nothard, John 4:22:11 (14,856)
Notley, Andrew 3:41:52 (6,104)
Notley, Glenn 4:15:33 (13,377)
Notley, Marc 4:59:00 (22,462)
Nott, James 4:34:22 (17,610)
Nott, Simon 3:50:31 (7,775)
Nottroth, Martin 4:23:45 (15,236)
Nouillan, Bill 4:20:02 (14,378)
Novelli, Gennaro 4:18:38 (14,036)
Novik, Guy 6:00:32 (28,431)
Novis, Bob 2:45:18 (300)
Nudd, Grant 4:32:11 (17,152)
Nugent, Andrew 4:07:42 (11,699)
Nugent, Patrick 3:55:22 (8,775)
Nullmeyer, Oeivind 4:28:53 (16,392)
Nunan, Daniel 5:22:02 (25,590)
Nundy, Simon 5:20:41 (25,428)
Nunes, Antonio 5:19:40 (25,326)
Nunn, David 5:17:09 (25,067)
Nunn, John 4:08:12 (11,802)
Nunn, John 5:10:26 (24,134)
Nunn, Nicholas 3:48:12 (7,303)
Nunney, Ray 5:32:51 (26,602)
Nunt, U. 4:08:08 (11,790)
Nurse, Roger 4:13:18 (12,874)
Nusser, Winfried 4:48:59 (20,525)
Nute, Benjamin 4:47:57 (20,337)
Nutley, Kevin 5:40:38 (27,242)
Nutley, Philip 4:36:22 (17,988)
Nutt, Matthew 3:24:05 (3,257)
Nuttall, Antony 3:20:09 (2,781)
Nuttall, Ray 3:34:20 (4,807)
Nutter, Keith 4:55:51 (21,961)
Nuttie, Gavin 5:42:18 (27,356)
Nutton, David 3:59:09 (9,800)
Nwagwe, Chrishopher 4:14:47 (13,205)
Nye, Dennis 4:05:41 (11,263)
Nye, John 4:52:02 (21,098)
Nyfeler, Hans 3:57:51 (9,446)
Nykolyszyn, Roman 3:45:48 (6,825)
Oak, David 4:08:55 (11,959)
Oakes, Mark 2:38:03 (137)
Oakes, Tony 4:42:56 (19,373)
Oakes, Wally 5:06:37 (23,564)
Oakes, Wayne 2:58:19 (836)
Oakley, Andrew 3:50:13 (7,726)
Oakley, Mark 4:48:30 (20,439)
Oakley, Robert 4:19:00 (14,115)
Oakley, Timothy 4:25:56 (15,712)
Oakley, William 3:49:17 (7,518)
Oakton, Neil 4:35:53 (17,903)
Oakton, Robin 5:08:19 (23,819)
Oastler, Richard 6:26:21 (29,313)
Oaten, Mark 5:57:40 (28,309)
Oates, John 4:53:53 (21,492)
O'Beirne, Andrew 2:58:32 (860)
O'Berg, Ben 3:59:55 (10,033)
Oberheide, Juergen 4:08:57 (11,965)
Obertuter, Markus 3:24:13 (3,272)
Obileye, Olumuyiwa 4:42:07 (19,182)
O'Brien, Andrew 4:26:56 (15,945)
O'Brien, Anthony 3:30:35 (4,260)
O'Brien, Christophe 4:42:01 (19,163)
O'Brien, Christopher 3:43:25 (6,382)
O'Brien, Christopher 4:59:44 (22,559)
O'Brien, David 6:12:02 (28,926)
O'Brien, Frank 4:38:20 (18,462)
O'Brien, John 3:33:10 (4,636)
O'Brien, John 4:19:33 (14,270)
O'Brien, Jonathan 6:46:14 (29,751)
O'Brien, Justin 4:37:08 (18,152)
O'Brien, Mark 4:55:22 (21,837)
O'Brien, Michael 3:26:49 (3,600)
O'Brien, Michael 5:04:17 (23,178)
O'Brien, Neil 3:25:45 (3,474)
O'Brien, Neil 5:33:48 (26,673)
O'Brien, Patrick 4:56:15 (22,032)
O'Brien, Paul 5:11:51 (24,337)
O'Brien, Peter 3:13:52 (2,097)
O'Brien, Robin 4:10:07 (12,185)
O'Brien, Sean 4:08:26 (11,859)
O'Brien, Simon 4:48:59 (20,525)
O'Brien, Stephen 5:29:25 (26,331)
O'Brien, Stuart 5:34:03 (26,703)
O'Brien Brackenburey, Brendan 5:16:53 (25,032)
O'Byrnes, Stephen 4:17:07 (13,692)
Ocakli, Hasan 3:55:50 (8,879)
Ocknell, Timothy 3:21:55 (2,984)
O'Connell, Charles 4:23:59 (15,291)
O'Connell, Desmond 4:37:32 (18,257)
O'Connell, James 3:50:59 (7,867)
O'Connell, Kevin 6:43:37 (29,713)
O'Connell, Martin 3:01:05 (1,088)
O'Connell, Paul 4:41:14 (19,018)
O'Connor, Andrew 3:10:11 (1,757)
O'Connor, Brendan 3:58:13 (9,542)
O'Connor, Brett 4:41:42 (19,102)
O'Connor, Chris 5:18:40 (25,231)
O'Connor, John 5:57:36 (28,302)

O'Connor, Judd 6:08:46 (28,800)
O'Connor, Kevin 4:13:59 (13,038)
O'Connor, Leonard 3:59:11 (9,810)
O'Connor, Liam 4:28:15 (16,249)
O'Connor, Martin 5:01:53 (22,849)
O'Connor, Michael 2:52:42 (535)
O'Connor, Pat 3:37:07 (5,268)
O'Connor, Patrick 4:53:02 (21,322)
O'Connor, Ray 5:10:12 (24,103)
O'Connor, Rory 4:00:52 (10,254)
O'Connor, Steven 3:56:58 (9,169)
O'Connor, Thomas 6:24:22 (29,270)
O'Connor, William 5:31:55 (26,525)
O'Conor, Edward 3:04:28 (1,310)
Octave, Michael 4:11:47 (12,566)
Oddy, James 4:33:42 (17,479)
Oddy, Jonathan 3:57:33 (9,347)
O'Dell, Simon 5:46:28 (27,654)
Odens, Ode 3:59:42 (9,974)
O'Doherty, Kieran 3:29:48 (4,134)
O'Donahue, Paul 4:32:49 (17,278)
O'Donnell, Gerry 4:59:49 (22,578)
O'Donnell, John 3:23:43 (3,202)
O'Donnell, John 3:59:21 (9,863)
O'Donnell, Kieron 4:23:53 (15,269)
O'Donnell, Timothy 4:22:50 (15,016)
O'Donoghue, Daniel 2:55:10 (635)
O'Donoghue, Thomas 3:13:03 (2,008)
O'Donovan, Paul 5:49:31 (27,873)
O'Donovan, Timothy 3:36:05 (5,086)
O'Dowd, John 5:07:14 (23,656)
O'Dowd, Robert 4:54:44 (21,656)
O'Dowd, Robin 3:33:37 (4,699)
O'Dwyer, David 4:57:48 (22,266)
O'Dwyer, Marc 3:41:48 (6,091)
O'Dwyer, Michael 4:38:32 (18,511)
O'Dwyer, Noel 3:01:33 (1,116)
Oestreicher, Martin 4:20:16 (14,425)
Offiah, Christian 6:41:30 (29,679)
Offord, Paul 6:11:40 (28,914)
O'Gara, Kevin 3:57:46 (9,416)
Ogawa, Yutaka 3:10:47 (1,816)
Ogden, Ian 4:43:55 (19,575)
Ogden, Mark 4:03:38 (10,810)
Ogden, Peter 4:18:42 (14,051)
Ogden, Simon 4:53:26 (21,403)
Ogg, David 3:07:57 (1,589)
Ogilvie, Martin 5:45:00 (27,561)
Ogilvy, Peter 5:03:54 (23,114)
Ogle, Christopher 3:58:43 (9,679)
Ogle, Michael 4:41:20 (19,033)
Oglesby, Mark 2:53:42 (568)
O'Grady, Paul 4:20:37 (14,503)
O'Grady, Vincent 3:17:40 (2,497)
Ogusu, Kazuo 4:10:52 (12,363)
Oh, Joo 3:46:53 (7,017)
O'Hagan, Bernard 3:51:33 (7,978)
O'Hanlon, Patrick 4:14:40 (13,163)
O'Hara, Caven 5:05:28 (23,378)
O'Hara, Michael 3:54:13 (8,512)
O'Hara, Phil 4:22:05 (14,834)
O'Hare, Brian 4:30:18 (16,729)
Ohene-Djan, Kingsley 4:43:37 (19,523)
O'Higgins, Thomas 5:21:32 (25,528)
Ohler, Fritz 4:02:08 (10,513)
Ohlson, Gary 4:36:15 (17,964)
Ohrner, Thomas 5:16:59 (25,050)
Ohta, Makiya 3:09:05 (1,678)
Oi, Nobuo 4:51:10 (20,920)
O'Kane, Brian 2:43:41 (251)
O'Keefe, Paul 6:49:52 (29,802)
O'Keefe, Timothy 4:43:57 (19,581)
O'Keeffe, David 3:39:43 (5,715)
O'Keeffe, Paul 3:38:26 (5,472)
O'Keeffe, Terence 3:49:51 (7,657)
O'Keeffe, William 4:02:06 (10,503)
Okuda, Mitsunori 4:46:41 (20,091)
Olaus, Rainer 4:17:10 (13,708)
Oldacres, John 4:03:27 (10,760)
Oldaker, David 5:05:19 (23,340)
Olden, Mark 3:12:48 (1,986)
Older, Paul 4:43:27 (19,481)
Older, Tim 3:08:37 (1,640)
Oldfield, Dave 3:53:10 (8,302)
Oldfield, David 3:14:59 (2,221)
Oldfield, Raymond 4:06:02 (11,355)
Oldfield, Richard 4:35:17 (17,771)
Oldham, David 4:18:24 (13,990)
Oldham, Justin 3:48:09 (7,294)
Oldham, Peter 4:53:49 (21,480)
Olding, Jonathan 3:39:10 (5,602)
Olding, Keith 3:47:31 (7,143)
O'Leary, Anthony 5:11:16 (24,250)
O'Leary, Brian 3:56:31 (9,058)
O'Leary, Donal 4:00:14 (10,095)
O'Leary, James 4:05:45 (11,287)
O'Leary, Jim 4:17:44 (13,822)
Olivant, Vernon 2:58:45 (902)
Oliveira, Christopher 4:21:25 (14,673)
Oliveira Mota, Vitor Manuel 3:48:52 (7,433)
Oliver, Albert 5:06:09 (23,490)
Oliver, Alison 7:16:18 (30,053)
Oliver, Allan 4:44:40 (19,707)
Oliver, Charles 3:38:34 (5,491)
Oliver, Gary 4:35:28 (17,806)
Oliver, Ian 4:27:42 (16,119)
Oliver, James 3:54:48 (8,659)
Oliver, Martin 4:46:10 (19,977)
Oliver, Martin 5:11:42 (24,315)
Oliver, Michael 4:33:51 (17,510)
Oliver, Rob 3:39:04 (5,584)
Oliver, Robert 4:07:28 (11,658)
Oliver, Tony 5:11:46 (24,323)
Olivo, Franco 3:38:01 (5,401)
Ollerenshaw, Robert 3:50:41 (7,802)
Ollila, Vilho 4:25:13 (15,560)
Ollivent, Michael 4:29:42 (16,599)
Olliver, Andrew 4:41:57 (19,153)
Ollivere, John 4:31:27 (16,969)
Ologhlen, Niall 4:04:43 (11,046)
Olorenshaw, Andrew 4:22:55 (15,039)
Olsen, David 3:34:02 (4,759)
Olsen, Mark 5:02:18 (22,915)
Olubodun, Andrew 4:50:57 (20,870)
Oluborode, Anthony 4:08:48 (11,937)
O'Mahoney, Kevin 4:22:39 (14,968)
O'Mahoney, Patrick 5:14:53 (24,762)
O'Mahony, John 3:20:23 (2,805)
O'Malley, Thomas 5:40:48 (27,253)
O'Mara, Philip 5:33:57 (26,685)
O'Mara, Robert 3:51:10 (7,906)
O'Meara, Pat 4:10:50 (12,355)
Omotajo, Jyde 3:45:42 (6,796)
O'Neale, Gary 5:02:16 (22,911)
O'Neil, Anthony 2:47:28 (352)
O'Neill, Aidan 3:03:23 (1,239)
O'Neill, Andrew 4:04:55 (11,100)
O'Neill, Charles 4:42:16 (19,218)
O'Neill, David 5:01:56 (22,861)
O'Neill, John 5:26:48 (26,069)
O'Neill, Martin 6:08:47 (28,802)
O'Neill, Paul 4:26:14 (15,789)
O'Neill, Robert 3:22:34 (3,059)
O'Neill, Sean 3:51:34 (7,983)
O'Neill, Stephen 6:06:14 (28,693)
O'Neill, Shane 3:31:40 (4,418)
O'Neill, Stephen 4:24:31 (15,402)
O'Neill, Stephen 4:58:58 (22,456)
O'Neill, Stuart 4:00:05 (10,070)
O'Neill, Terry 4:35:14 (17,758)
O'Neill, William 5:01:46 (22,835)
O'Neill-Egan, John 2:55:18 (643)
Ongcharit, Pat 5:13:07 (24,520)
Ono, Takao 5:24:21 (25,820)
Onojobi, Peter 4:38:44 (18,557)
Onslow, Chris 6:37:36 (29,580)
Onslow-Dewey, Ian 5:06:30 (23,544)
Oo, Tun 5:55:28 (28,187)
Ooso, Didier 4:16:14 (13,513)
Openshaw, Neil 3:57:19 (9,262)
Ophuis, Ton 4:17:42 (13,814)
Opie, Shaun 3:43:16 (6,355)
Opoku, Samuel 5:13:36 (24,581)
Oppermann, Herbert 2:47:17 (346)
O'Rathille, Conn 4:37:06 (18,144)
Orchard, Gerald 3:27:08 (3,645)
Orchard, Mark 4:47:15 (20,213)
Orde, Hugh 3:55:11 (8,728)
Orde, Sam 3:21:59 (2,994)
Ordeus, Daniel 3:51:56 (8,060)
Ordeus, Ulf 3:53:41 (8,422)
Ore, Andrew 4:58:42 (22,416)
O'Regan, Ken 3:47:25 (7,122)
O'Reilly, Donovan 3:54:59 (8,698)
O'Reilly, Eamonn 4:13:30 (12,932)
O'Reilly, Edward 3:02:28 (1,187)
O'Reilly, Garrett 4:49:17 (20,579)
O'Reilly, John 4:10:14 (12,216)
O'Reilly, Martin 3:59:05 (9,781)
O'Reilly, Terence 3:35:27 (4,978)
Organ, James 3:55:25 (8,786)
Orial, Daniel 4:50:03 (20,728)
Orkamfat, Patrick 4:30:04 (16,704)
Ormandy, Paul 4:24:50 (15,464)
Orme, Richard 3:32:19 (4,509)
Orme Smith, James 3:44:49 (6,643)
Ormerod, George 5:22:10 (25,606)
Ormond, Paul 4:15:50 (13,432)
Orosz, Nicholas 4:43:30 (19,497)
O'Rourke, Declan 4:23:03 (15,077)
Orr, Billy 2:37:49 (134)
Orr, David 3:13:56 (2,106)
Orr, Jim 3:06:15 (1,438)
Orr, John 3:46:18 (6,917)
Orr, Michael 3:31:46 (4,430)
Orr, Richard 6:03:06 (28,546)
Orrell, Stewart 4:28:43 (16,362)
Orrells, Stephen 4:08:38 (11,903)
Orriss, Mike 6:36:13 (29,547)
Orsini, Angelo 3:42:10 (6,155)
Ortalli, Carlo 3:51:54 (8,049)
Ortega Erazo, Ivan 4:24:21 (15,359)
Ortega-Ramos, José 3:49:53 (7,664)
Orth, Dieter 5:03:32 (23,065)
Orth, Lars 4:57:13 (22,173)
Ortiz, Jorge 3:39:04 (5,584)
Orton, Ian 6:06:31 (28,701)
Orton, Wilfred 3:41:06 (5,975)
Osaye, Stevan 4:40:34 (18,889)
Osbone, Douglas 4:09:58 (12,156)
Osborn, David 5:47:47 (27,751)
Osborn, Mark 3:32:27 (4,527)
Osborn, Mark 3:53:15 (8,318)
Osborn, Peter 2:59:10 (948)
Osborn, Thomas 4:58:22 (22,354)
Osborne, Andrew 3:33:08 (4,633)
Osborne, Ashley 4:26:59 (15,959)
Osborne, Dale 3:33:55 (4,742)
Osborne, Lee 4:39:56 (18,772)
Osborne, Matthew 3:30:44 (4,284)
Osborne, Matthew 5:13:17 (24,550)
Osborne, Nicolas 4:49:35 (20,631)
Osborne, Peter 4:45:27 (19,858)
Osborne, Richard 4:29:59 (16,689)
Osborne, Steven 4:21:30 (14,693)
Osburn, Barry 4:00:29 (10,148)
O'Shea, James 6:40:14 (29,647)
O'Shea, Michael 4:11:00 (12,400)
Osher, Mark 4:19:53 (14,333)
Osinowo, Remi 3:36:16 (5,117)
Osman, Rick 4:35:38 (17,849)
Oster, Merrill 3:17:47 (2,508)
Ostermann, Wolfgang 3:40:52 (5,920)
Ostermeyer, Marcel 3:02:16 (1,171)
Ostheide, Claus 3:40:38 (5,887)
Ostrowski, Francis 4:33:31 (17,423)
O'Sullivan, Daniel 4:35:36 (17,843)
O'Sullivan, James 4:35:08 (17,736)
O'Sullivan, John 3:14:08 (2,131)
O'Sullivan, Joseph 2:52:22 (527)
O'Sullivan, Martin 4:41:52 (19,131)
O'Sullivan, Michael 3:28:47 (3,957)
O'Sullivan, Paul 4:13:06 (12,836)
O'Sullivan, Sean 3:48:10 (7,297)
O'Sullivan, Tim 3:48:15 (7,312)
Oswald, James 3:19:23 (2,692)
Oswald, James 4:20:25 (14,453)
O'Toole, John 5:30:40 (26,424)
O'Toole, Martin 4:39:10 (18,630)

O'Toole, Michael	3:27:16 (3,667)	
Ottaviami, Paolo	2:51:26 (487)	
Ottaway, Ronald	4:26:18 (15,807)	
Ottaway, William	4:48:16 (20,400)	
Ottey, Martin	4:11:16 (12,456)	
Ottfnelli, Lorenzo	2:51:29 (488)	
Ottoy, Marcel	3:34:43 (4,866)	
Ousby, Gary	3:38:11 (5,425)	
Outhwaite, Jeffrey	3:46:06 (6,877)	
Ouvry, Tom	4:54:43 (21,648)	
Ovenden, Timothy	3:36:33 (5,165)	
Ovens, James	3:31:05 (4,338)	
Overson, Brian	5:59:07 (28,372)	
Overton, Andrew	4:36:42 (18,062)	
Overton, Michael	4:19:38 (14,291)	
Overvoorde, Peter	3:52:48 (8,230)	
Ovington, Neil	2:55:52 (672)	
Owen, Andrew	3:01:42 (1,131)	
Owen, Andrew	4:14:38 (13,155)	
Owen, Bryan	4:23:30 (15,172)	
Owen, Chris	3:57:09 (9,210)	
Owen, Christopher	5:34:12 (26,724)	
Owen, Christopher	6:41:46 (29,684)	
Owen, Crispin	3:38:46 (5,532)	
Owen, Daniel	3:46:04 (6,869)	
Owen, Douglas	3:45:31 (6,751)	
Owen, Duncan	4:10:15 (12,220)	
Owen, Dylan	3:08:22 (1,620)	
Owen, Dylan	5:36:18 (26,899)	
Owen, Eugene	3:42:57 (6,294)	
Owen, Gareth	3:56:45 (9,121)	
Owen, Gareth	4:16:27 (13,564)	
Owen, Gareth	4:19:56 (14,348)	
Owen, Glyn	6:11:57 (28,924)	
Owen, Harry	4:09:54 (12,140)	
Owen, Huw	3:41:11 (5,980)	
Owen, Ian	3:41:32 (6,041)	
Owen, Ian	3:48:03 (7,276)	
Owen, James	5:34:13 (26,725)	
Owen, John	4:31:33 (16,988)	
Owen, John	6:44:44 (29,732)	
Owen, Julian	2:53:34 (564)	
Owen, Kevin	2:44:41 (282)	
Owen, Matthew	3:21:27 (2,940)	
Owen, Patrick	4:53:19 (21,378)	
Owen, Paul	3:45:46 (6,816)	
Owen, Paul	4:24:26 (15,381)	
Owen, Paul	4:35:09 (17,739)	
Owen, Peter	5:24:13 (25,809)	
Owen, Richard	5:46:35 (27,669)	
Owen, Robert	5:51:25 (27,976)	
Owen, Roger	4:19:55 (14,343)	
Owen, Shaun	4:05:44 (11,283)	
Owen, Stanley	3:53:30 (8,375)	
Owen, Stephen	3:28:14 (3,851)	
Owen, Stephen	4:28:47 (16,378)	
Owen, Steven	3:27:16 (3,667)	
Owen, Steven	3:44:56 (6,670)	
Owen, Steven	3:45:12 (6,707)	
Owen, Tristram	4:42:25 (19,255)	
Owen, William	3:24:32 (3,316)	
Owens, David	5:51:25 (27,976)	
Owens, Ivor	8:07:36 (30,223)	
Owens, Melfyn	4:57:14 (22,175)	
Owens, Padraig	4:07:40 (11,690)	
Owens, Robert	4:25:24 (15,593)	
Owers, Ian	4:54:40 (21,628)	
Owsnett, Neil	4:20:12 (14,409)	
Oxborough, Craig	4:05:41 (11,263)	
Oxlade, Colin	3:18:34 (2,605)	
Oxton, Alan	4:36:28 (18,013)	
Ozenda, Jacques	3:29:33 (4,088)	
Paccafelo, Enrico	5:14:11 (24,652)	
Pace, Adam	4:54:00 (21,511)	
Pace, Lee	3:56:09 (8,958)	
Pach, Miso	5:34:59 (26,805)	
Pack, James	4:36:59 (18,124)	
Packard, Oliver	4:24:35 (15,416)	
Packer, Malcolm	2:43:14 (243)	
Packer, Richard	4:39:53 (18,767)	
Packer, Scott	4:43:43 (19,543)	
Packer, Simon	4:45:05 (19,785)	
Packham, Andrew	5:40:17 (27,206)	

Packham, David	5:19:13 (25,284)	
Padington, Mark	4:35:13 (17,754)	
Padley, Michael	3:50:19 (7,738)	
Pafitis, Demosthenis	5:26:54 (26,077)	
Paganessi, Andrea	3:01:02 (1,085)	
Page, Aaron	3:51:05 (7,889)	
Page, Allan	6:01:24 (28,475)	
Page, Andy	3:37:09 (5,275)	
Page, Bob	5:24:35 (25,843)	
Page, Carl	3:26:27 (3,552)	
Page, Colin	3:28:30 (3,907)	
Page, Colin	4:28:10 (16,228)	
Page, Daniel	5:02:09 (22,901)	
Page, Darren	4:18:34 (14,027)	
Page, Darryl	5:30:37 (26,421)	
Page, David	3:28:11 (3,840)	
Page, Gary	4:03:03 (10,671)	
Page, Gary	4:32:43 (17,252)	
Page, Graham	4:42:55 (19,366)	
Page, Ian	6:44:47 (29,733)	
Page, James	5:02:10 (22,904)	
Page, Jamie	4:51:41 (21,029)	
Page, Jeffrey	4:18:09 (13,903)	
Page, Jeremy	3:45:30 (6,744)	
Page, Martin	3:31:28 (4,391)	
Page, Michael	4:30:52 (16,818)	
Page, Mick	2:46:24 (326)	
Page, Richard	3:42:37 (6,238)	
Page, Richard	4:44:48 (19,733)	
Page, Robert	5:11:32 (24,292)	
Page, Tony	5:35:02 (26,808)	
Page, Trevor	5:07:26 (23,688)	
Page Croft, Jamie	5:10:48 (24,186)	
Paget, David	7:19:04 (30,073)	
Pagliaro, Paul	2:58:23 (845)	
Paillet, Guillaume	3:21:16 (2,912)	
Pailor, Robert	4:28:21 (16,271)	
Pain, Matthew	3:37:10 (5,278)	
Paine, Clive	4:10:09 (12,194)	
Paine, David	3:38:18 (5,449)	
Painter, James	4:18:33 (14,023)	
Painting, John	5:08:43 (23,892)	
Paisley, Nicholas	3:58:18 (9,563)	
Paix, Guillaume	3:26:49 (3,600)	
Pakenham, Dermot	5:27:50 (26,161)	
Pakenham, Frank	4:40:14 (18,819)	
Pakenham Walsh, Simon	3:55:58 (8,911)	
Paley, Sean	5:33:28 (26,645)	
Palfrey, Daryl	3:10:05 (1,748)	
Palladini, Massimo	3:07:19 (1,531)	
Pallant, Robert	4:01:19 (10,342)	
Pallaruello, Gilles	3:21:36 (2,957)	
Pallavoini, Stephane	3:49:17 (7,518)	
Pallister, Andrew	4:53:47 (21,470)	
Palmer, Adam	4:22:24 (14,903)	
Palmer, Alan	4:32:42 (17,247)	
Palmer, Alan	4:58:41 (22,412)	
Palmer, Ambrose	4:48:01 (20,349)	
Palmer, Andy	5:52:24 (28,034)	
Palmer, Ben	3:56:48 (9,133)	
Palmer, Carl	4:52:20 (21,169)	
Palmer, David	3:25:24 (3,431)	
Palmer, Ed	4:21:13 (14,631)	
Palmer, Edward	3:43:04 (6,319)	
Palmer, Eric	3:02:23 (1,183)	
Palmer, Ian	4:56:56 (22,135)	
Palmer, Ian	6:01:04 (28,458)	
Palmer, James	3:43:59 (6,491)	
Palmer, Jason	5:41:22 (27,283)	
Palmer, John	5:14:40 (24,737)	
Palmer, John	6:28:45 (29,379)	
Palmer, Kenneth	3:12:24 (1,954)	
Palmer, Mark	3:07:52 (1,579)	
Palmer, Mark	5:08:10 (23,792)	
Palmer, Mark	5:14:10 (24,650)	
Palmer, Matthew	4:15:16 (13,327)	
Palmer, Michael	3:48:36 (7,379)	
Palmer, Neil	4:20:15 (14,418)	
Palmer, Nicholas	4:27:16 (16,022)	
Palmer, Paul	4:26:29 (15,842)	
Palmer, Paul	5:58:05 (28,324)	
Palmer, Philip	4:28:43 (16,362)	
Palmer, Robert	5:06:47 (23,586)	

Palmer, Rod	3:26:38 (3,576)	
Palmer, Roy	2:42:05 (220)	
Palmer, Stuart	4:21:46 (14,752)	
Palmer, Timothy	3:56:53 (9,151)	
Palmer, Warren	4:26:14 (15,789)	
Palmer Bawn, Peter	5:10:00 (24,081)	
Palmer-Malt, Graham	3:56:51 (9,146)	
Palmigiano, Vincenzo	3:25:23 (3,429)	
Palombo, Alastair	3:56:38 (9,085)	
Pan, Moncho	4:55:49 (21,955)	
Panayiotou, Sotiris	3:15:03 (2,229)	
Panditaratne, Heshan	6:06:00 (28,686)	
Panesar, Harpal	4:25:44 (15,661)	
Pank, Anthony	5:48:23 (27,805)	
Pankhania, Mahendra	6:35:20 (29,530)	
Pankhurst, David	5:17:25 (25,096)	
Pankhurst, Shaun	3:18:01 (2,535)	
Pannett, Simon	5:49:34 (27,876)	
Panozzo, Enzo	4:28:35 (16,334)	
Pant, Muktesh	4:45:51 (19,912)	
Panter, Matthew	4:05:27 (11,197)	
Papay, Barna	4:34:01 (17,538)	
Pape, Andrew	4:55:24 (21,849)	
Pape, Christopher	4:12:27 (12,725)	
Pape, John-Paul	4:00:44 (10,227)	
Papworth, Matthew	3:47:23 (7,112)	
Paramore, Ian	2:51:20 (479)	
Parbhu, Nathaniel	3:32:15 (4,500)	
Parcell, Geoff	4:12:23 (12,710)	
Parchment, Anthony	6:52:53 (29,842)	
Pardon, Andrew	4:35:58 (17,925)	
Parekh, Bhupesh	6:30:12 (29,414)	
Paren, Martin	3:19:49 (2,743)	
Parfitt, Kenneth	5:47:05 (27,711)	
Parfitt, Stephen	4:42:26 (19,260)	
Parfitt, William	5:18:15 (25,185)	
Paridon, Hans Van	3:15:04 (2,230)	
Parikh, Krishna	5:35:05 (26,812)	
Parikm, Pranav	5:35:05 (26,812)	
Parisek, Theodore	3:29:06 (4,015)	
Parish, Brian	4:18:19 (13,959)	
Parish, Duncan	4:17:20 (13,741)	
Parish, Stephen	4:12:06 (12,648)	
Parisi Presicce, Alberto	4:13:46 (12,992)	
Park, Bruce	5:43:26 (27,435)	
Park, Gregor	3:22:19 (3,038)	
Park, John	3:41:18 (6,007)	
Park, Nicholas	3:38:56 (5,566)	
Park, Thomas	4:57:40 (22,243)	
Parker, Adam	4:23:16 (15,122)	
Parker, Adam	4:33:17 (17,363)	
Parker, Alexander	4:44:14 (19,627)	
Parker, Barry	6:30:31 (29,427)	
Parker, Charly	4:26:28 (15,836)	
Parker, Gary	3:59:22 (9,869)	
Parker, Giles	4:42:01 (19,163)	
Parker, Gregory	3:39:44 (5,719)	
Parker, Ian	3:12:39 (1,974)	
Parker, James	4:58:56 (22,448)	
Parker, Nigel	4:22:55 (15,039)	
Parker, Philip	3:09:41 (1,729)	
Parker, Philip	3:43:11 (6,341)	
Parker, Richard	3:30:22 (4,226)	
Parker, Robert	5:33:15 (26,629)	
Parker, Simon	4:22:41 (14,978)	
Parker, Stephen	3:42:19 (6,183)	
Parker, Stephen	4:58:37 (22,399)	
Parker, Stephen	5:05:50 (23,435)	
Parker, Terence	5:05:53 (23,446)	
Parker, Timothy	3:28:20 (3,878)	
Parker-Mead, Gary	4:36:54 (18,104)	
Parkes, Alan	5:02:15 (22,909)	
Parkes, Caelim	3:46:36 (6,973)	
Parkes, Ralph	4:16:34 (13,586)	
Parkes, Timothy	3:58:33 (9,625)	
Parkin, Barry	4:47:52 (20,318)	
Parkington, David	2:59:42 (997)	
Parkinson, James	3:50:41 (7,802)	
Parkinson, Mark	3:31:27 (4,389)	
Parkinson, Nigel	4:50:17 (20,767)	
Parkinson, Peter	3:48:06 (7,287)	
Parkinson, Roy	3:27:26 (3,693)	
Parkman, Trevor	4:05:42 (11,268)	

Parmley, Andrew 5:00:42 (22,692)
Parncutt, Andrew 4:28:30 (16,314)
Parnell, Lee 2:50:05 (432)
Parnell, Robert 4:06:12 (11,385)
Parr, Bryan 4:37:11 (18,167)
Parr, Nicholas 4:43:29 (19,490)
Parr, Richard 4:56:18 (22,036)
Parris, George 4:11:44 (12,556)
Parris, James 4:17:37 (13,796)
Parrish, James 4:24:51 (15,466)
Parrish, Paul 4:23:00 (15,063)
Parrott, Nick 4:54:51 (21,691)
Parry, Alister 5:29:55 (26,370)
Parry, Antony 3:04:48 (1,335)
Parry, Guy 4:08:41 (11,910)
Parry, Jason 5:25:46 (25,964)
Parry, John 3:03:01 (1,215)
Parry, Karl 4:05:09 (11,149)
Parry, Martyn 4:13:40 (12,975)
Parry, Sion 4:47:58 (20,342)
Parry, Stephen 3:43:38 (6,421)
Parry, Stephen 4:41:52 (19,131)
Parry, Stephen 5:43:37 (27,446)
Parry, Walter 4:43:51 (19,565)
Parsley, Elvis 2:43:46 (253)
Parslow, David 5:23:47 (25,769)
Parsons, Adam 4:08:02 (11,774)
Parsons, Alec 6:55:13 (29,883)
Parsons, Andrew 3:27:32 (3,714)
Parsons, Andrew 3:37:00 (5,246)
Parsons, Andrew 4:08:11 (11,799)
Parsons, Ean 4:02:56 (10,654)
Parsons, Harry 5:22:10 (25,606)
Parsons, John 4:18:46 (14,074)
Parsons, Philip 3:23:16 (3,143)
Parsons, Richard 2:58:17 (831)
Parsons, Richard 4:17:37 (13,796)
Parsons, Terry 3:29:33 (4,088)
Parthoens, Alain 3:33:28 (4,685)
Partington, Shaun Leslie 4:16:02 (13,474)
Partington, Stephen 4:11:10 (12,431)
Partner, Nicholas 4:16:57 (13,655)
Parton, Anthony 4:12:57 (12,820)
Parton, Terence 3:03:46 (1,268)
Partridge, Bill 4:19:56 (14,348)
Partridge, Francis 4:32:02 (17,124)
Partridge, Geoffrey 4:08:25 (11,853)
Partridge, Keith 3:02:07 (1,162)
Partridge, Robert 5:19:53 (25,352)
Partridge, Simon 2:55:21 (644)
Partridge, Simon 4:14:47 (13,205)
Partridge, Stephen 3:27:52 (3,779)
Partridge, Tom 3:36:51 (5,217)
Pasa, Riccardo 3:43:27 (6,390)
Pascoe, Barry 3:58:34 (9,633)
Pasini, Claudio 2:45:29 (309)
Pasini, Roberto 4:40:34 (18,889)
Pasola, Richard 4:52:58 (21,309)
Pasquet, Michel 4:07:48 (11,721)
Passe, Neil 6:36:14 (29,549)
Passeri, Daniele 4:20:08 (14,393)
Passi, Pradeep 4:49:12 (20,562)
Passmore, Rory 4:59:43 (22,556)
Passway, Norman 3:05:04 (1,354)
Pastena, Lucio 6:03:29 (28,565)
Paszkiewicz, Maurycy 5:49:24 (27,867)
Patch, Michael 3:52:31 (8,173)
Patchett, Edward 5:34:52 (26,794)
Patel, Anant 5:09:47 (24,056)
Patel, Anish 4:40:12 (18,811)
Patel, Bhupendra 4:31:20 (16,940)
Patel, Dee 2:55:45 (666)
Patel, Hinal 5:04:03 (23,141)
Patel, Jatin 4:05:25 (11,188)
Patel, Kamlesh 3:19:11 (2,669)
Patel, Keyur 3:57:23 (9,283)
Patel, Nalin 4:24:28 (15,388)
Patel, Nilesh 5:03:02 (23,009)
Patel, Omar 5:05:26 (23,369)
Patel, Rajesh 4:28:48 (16,380)
Patel, Ramesh 5:38:57 (27,083)
Patel, Ravin 5:23:36 (25,756)
Patel, Sandeep 6:43:55 (29,717)
Patel, Yogesh 3:34:26 (4,824)
Pateman, Simon 5:03:30 (23,063)
Patenall, Simon 3:58:05 (9,509)
Paterson, Alastair 4:29:11 (16,467)
Paterson, Andrew 3:39:32 (5,680)
Paterson, Gordon 5:28:36 (26,240)
Paterson, Malcolm 4:38:39 (18,537)
Paterson, Marshall 4:36:23 (17,991)
Paterson, Martin 5:33:32 (26,652)
Paterson, Michael 3:49:41 (7,620)
Paterson, Rowan 4:07:30 (11,660)
Paterson, Stephen 6:25:10 (29,286)
Paterson, Stewart 3:46:25 (6,935)
Pathak, Nakul 3:44:05 (6,505)
Pathmanathan, Kangesu 5:45:13 (27,574)
Pathy, Damian 3:22:30 (3,054)
Patience, Nigel 3:59:46 (9,989)
Patient, Peter 3:21:16 (2,912)
Patlewicz, Aleks 6:27:49 (29,348)
Paton, Colin 2:41:39 (207)
Paton, John 4:05:35 (11,235)
Paton, Malcolm 3:36:43 (5,195)
Paton, Richard 4:22:02 (14,822)
Paton, Stuart 3:25:01 (3,383)
Paton, Stuart 5:04:11 (23,159)
Patrick, Paul 3:33:17 (4,658)
Patten, Kevin 3:54:27 (8,583)
Patterson, Christopher 3:42:29 (6,215)
Patterson, Eric 4:58:36 (22,394)
Patterson, Paul 5:09:24 (23,999)
Patterson, Richard 4:16:21 (13,536)
Pattimore, Mark 4:10:53 (12,368)
Pattinson, Danny 5:31:52 (26,521)
Pattison, Guy 4:25:52 (15,694)
Pattison, Mark 3:35:44 (5,024)
Pattison, Michael 4:02:41 (10,604)
Pattison, Raymond 4:45:20 (19,829)
Patton, Felix 4:19:48 (14,315)
Patton, Michael 4:07:47 (11,720)
Patton, Neil 3:40:15 (5,821)
Paul, Duncan 4:25:07 (15,536)
Paul, Ken 4:49:52 (20,687)
Paul, Nicholas 5:13:49 (24,608)
Paul, Richard 4:35:26 (17,802)
Paul, Rupert 3:41:14 (5,993)
Paull, Stephen 3:27:30 (3,707)
Pavett, Steven 4:32:14 (17,163)
Pavey, David 4:18:51 (14,089)
Pawlicki, Andrzej 3:26:16 (3,532)
Pawlowski, Christopher 3:34:10 (4,782)
Pawlowski, Francis 5:06:21 (23,526)
Pawson, Rob 3:35:57 (5,066)
Paxton, Paul 4:05:54 (11,320)
Payn, David 4:03:42 (10,821)
Payn, William 4:25:40 (15,646)
Payne, Andrew 4:55:18 (21,817)
Payne, Anthony 3:01:35 (1,120)
Payne, Anthony 3:39:47 (5,735)
Payne, David 3:20:56 (2,881)
Payne, David 4:44:38 (19,701)
Payne, Donald 3:25:27 (3,440)
Payne, Gary 4:31:33 (16,988)
Payne, Gary 5:04:50 (23,272)
Payne, Ian 4:39:20 (18,650)
Payne, Ian 4:46:10 (19,977)
Payne, Nigel 2:36:30 (109)
Payne, Oscar 5:06:46 (23,582)
Payne, Richard 5:46:38 (27,676)
Payne, Robin 3:56:13 (8,971)
Payne, Roger 4:09:40 (12,104)
Payne, Simon 3:50:08 (7,712)
Payne, Steven 4:04:30 (10,988)
Payne, Timothy 4:39:33 (18,704)
Payne, Trevor 5:08:22 (23,824)
Peace, Michael 2:46:00 (318)
Peach, Antony 4:14:55 (13,239)
Peach, Matthew 4:38:30 (18,506)
Peach, Timothy 4:40:12 (18,811)
Peacher, Ricky 3:33:04 (4,616)
Peachey, Kenneth 5:07:05 (23,628)
Peacock, David 4:42:47 (19,326)
Peacock, John 4:35:18 (17,775)
Peacock, Jonathan 4:14:14 (13,082)
Peacock, Lewis 5:02:38 (22,952)
Peacock, Robert 4:13:06 (12,836)
Peacock, Roger 4:48:46 (20,481)
Peacock, Stephen 2:39:31 (164)
Peacock, Stephen 4:24:59 (15,501)
Peaks, Stephen 3:19:34 (2,713)
Peaple, Derek 4:09:10 (12,017)
Pearce, Andrew 4:10:39 (12,302)
Pearce, Colin 4:37:27 (18,238)
Pearce, David 2:53:29 (558)
Pearce, David 4:07:13 (11,590)
Pearce, David 4:33:34 (17,443)
Pearce, David 4:57:31 (22,219)
Pearce, Gareth 5:35:41 (26,859)
Pearce, James 4:38:05 (18,398)
Pearce, Jonathan 3:36:16 (5,117)
Pearce, Mark 4:12:26 (12,723)
Pearce, Michael 3:28:21 (3,881)
Pearce, Michael 4:59:32 (22,530)
Pearce, Michael 5:15:45 (24,898)
Pearce, Nicholas 2:55:53 (674)
Pearce, Nicholas 3:59:56 (10,037)
Pearce, Paul 6:17:02 (29,087)
Pearce, Peter 3:44:49 (6,643)
Pearce, Raymond 2:52:04 (516)
Pearce, Robert 2:59:11 (949)
Pearce, Robert 3:05:32 (1,393)
Pearce, Robert 4:08:22 (11,843)
Pearce, Roy 5:27:51 (26,164)
Pearce, Sean 5:48:23 (27,805)
Pearce, Steve 4:24:31 (15,402)
Pearcey, David 3:58:25 (9,588)
Pearch, Sam 3:31:36 (4,411)
Pearey, Michael 4:51:55 (21,073)
Pearl, Andrew 3:14:03 (2,127)
Pearman, Clive 5:05:43 (23,418)
Pearman, Thomas 4:20:09 (14,397)
Pearn, Toby 4:08:50 (11,943)
Pears, Bryan 3:55:55 (8,897)
Pears, Darron 5:21:41 (25,545)
Pearson, Anthony 3:40:56 (5,939)
Pearson, Charles 5:06:09 (23,490)
Pearson, Charlie 3:18:04 (2,541)
Pearson, Christopher 3:40:12 (5,816)
Pearson, David 3:15:09 (2,239)
Pearson, Ian 3:36:37 (5,174)
Pearson, Jamie 6:49:19 (29,793)
Pearson, John 4:53:12 (21,353)
Pearson, Kevin 3:36:02 (5,080)
Pearson, Lindsey 3:35:31 (4,988)
Pearson, Mark 3:10:51 (1,823)
Pearson, Martin 3:59:36 (9,948)
Pearson, Michael 4:09:41 (12,105)
Pearson, Richard 3:09:27 (1,707)
Pearson, Robert 4:20:33 (14,489)
Pearson, Toby 5:00:41 (22,688)
Pease, Michael 4:37:32 (18,257)
Pease Watkin, David 3:20:37 (2,837)
Peasland, Alex 4:25:02 (15,520)
Peasnell, John 3:39:44 (5,719)
Peat, Dan 4:47:53 (20,322)
Peatman, Barry 4:10:09 (12,194)
Pech, Daniel 4:04:59 (11,115)
Peck, Graham 4:27:04 (15,988)
Peck, Iain 4:43:52 (19,569)
Peck, Ian 5:06:18 (23,520)
Peck, Martin 4:05:40 (11,256)
Peckett, Mark 4:14:02 (13,046)
Pecoraro, Antonio 2:47:41 (357)
Pedder, Chris 3:00:58 (1,081)
Peddie, Alan 4:13:37 (12,961)
Peddie, Alexander 2:57:58 (810)
Pedeches, Jean Claude 4:17:32 (13,780)
Pedersen, Anderg 4:13:47 (12,995)
Pedersen, Johnny 4:17:44 (13,822)
Pedersen, Jonas 4:23:35 (15,201)
Pedersen, Jorgen 3:36:57 (5,237)
Pedersen, Lars 3:20:25 (2,809)
Pedersen, Poul Erik 3:22:43 (3,073)
Pedlow, Martin 3:17:17 (2,459)
Pedrick, Matthew 6:26:39 (29,323)
Pedroni, Mario 4:31:39 (17,023)
Peed, Mike 4:01:15 (10,326)

Peek, Andrew	3:13:58 (2,114)	
Peel, Edward	4:44:07 (19,601)	
Peel, Ian	3:38:54 (5,560)	
Peel, John	4:26:48 (15,910)	
Peel, Mike	3:47:02 (7,040)	
Peepall, Jonathan	3:48:22 (7,332)	
Peers, Alan	3:20:49 (2,867)	
Peers, Stephen	4:22:50 (15,016)	
Peet, Andrew	3:53:55 (8,464)	
Peet, Bruce	3:32:22 (4,516)	
Peet, Robert	3:43:30 (6,398)	
Pegg, Barry	4:01:21 (10,357)	
Pegg, Roland	4:47:40 (20,292)	
Pegler, Wayne	4:22:05 (14,834)	
Peguri, Vittorio	5:31:20 (26,478)	
Peill, David	3:38:53 (5,555)	
Peirce, Robert	3:58:05 (9,509)	
Peiris, Anthony	6:20:39 (29,183)	
Pelham, David	7:00:16 (29,946)	
Pelham, Mark	4:59:37 (22,541)	
Pelidis, John	4:28:44 (16,367)	
Pelizza, Stefano	4:21:44 (14,741)	
Pellaton, Olivier	4:47:30 (20,260)	
Pellaton, Steven	4:30:14 (16,721)	
Pellecchia, Pasquale	3:10:55 (1,829)	
Pellegrini, Valerio	3:55:55 (8,897)	
Pellettier, Giovanni	4:00:14 (10,095)	
Pelley, Mark	4:36:58 (18,120)	
Pellicioli, Lorenzo	4:01:35 (10,406)	
Pellier Samakian, Christian	4:16:59 (13,661)	
Pelling, Sean	4:45:23 (19,841)	
Pellow, Jeremy	5:02:49 (22,980)	
Pellow, Matthew	3:30:52 (4,305)	
Pelly, Stephen	5:32:29 (26,578)	
Pelois, Alexandre	5:18:24 (25,198)	
Peltier, Jean-Jacques	4:59:07 (22,479)	
Pelzer, Horst	3:23:19 (3,153)	
Pema, Natuarlal	5:23:28 (25,739)	
Pemble, Doug	4:15:32 (13,373)	
Pembroke, George	4:19:17 (14,189)	
Pender, Paul	3:44:47 (6,636)	
Pender, Stephen	5:21:36 (25,533)	
Pendlebury, Gary	2:48:06 (364)	
Pendleton, Alan	5:37:33 (26,983)	
Pendleton, David	3:59:33 (9,936)	
Penfold, Nigel	4:51:00 (20,881)	
Pengelly, Nigel	3:54:41 (8,628)	
Pengelly, Stephen	4:18:09 (13,903)	
Pengilly, Keith	3:53:29 (8,370)	
Penhallow, Russell	2:56:06 (691)	
Penlington, Simon	4:21:33 (14,701)	
Penman, Michael	3:01:09 (1,092)	
Penn, Roger	4:10:59 (12,397)	
Penn Barwell, Jowan	3:28:08 (3,830)	
Pennec, Thierry	3:20:27 (2,815)	
Penney, Simon	2:57:13 (762)	
Penniall, Simon	4:33:47 (17,496)	
Pennington, Jon	5:04:45 (23,252)	
Pennington, Miles	6:08:04 (28,767)	
Pennington, Timothy	3:42:09 (6,151)	
Penniston, Chris	5:27:40 (26,145)	
Pennock, Martin	3:19:06 (2,662)	
Penny, Chris	4:01:28 (10,386)	
Penny, Kenton	4:10:41 (12,308)	
Penny, Mark	3:10:20 (1,779)	
Penny, Michael	3:48:23 (7,335)	
Penny, Richard	3:42:26 (6,207)	
Pennycook, Dave	5:06:40 (23,572)	
Penrose, Noel	4:29:39 (16,585)	
Pentin, Richard	3:15:52 (2,305)	
Pentney, Mark	5:58:06 (28,326)	
Penwarden, Peter	4:39:26 (18,673)	
Peplow, Neil	5:25:48 (25,967)	
Pepper, Darren	3:30:26 (4,237)	
Pepper, Eric	4:41:14 (19,018)	
Pepper, Gary Robert	5:31:28 (26,487)	
Pepper, James	4:31:41 (17,036)	
Pepper, Tony	6:11:19 (28,899)	
Peppiatt, Malcolm	4:28:53 (16,392)	
Percival, Paul	4:53:07 (21,339)	
Percival, Simon	4:45:56 (19,926)	
Percivall, David	4:58:09 (22,320)	
Perego, Gianpaolo	2:55:47 (669)	

Peregrine, Michael	3:37:15 (5,294)	
Pereira, Joaquim	5:39:22 (27,121)	
Pereira, Norman	4:50:21 (20,782)	
Pereira Magalhaes, Manuel	3:34:22 (4,810)	
Perella, Nicholas	4:21:33 (14,701)	
Perez, Allen	6:04:00 (28,590)	
Perfect, Fred	5:40:01 (27,189)	
Perkins, Alistair	3:36:02 (5,080)	
Perkins, John	6:36:14 (29,549)	
Perkins, Martyn	3:55:40 (8,834)	
Perkins, Michael	4:21:46 (14,752)	
Perks, Julian	3:34:40 (4,858)	
Perks, Tim	3:14:16 (2,142)	
Perlmutter, Jonathan	4:38:21 (18,466)	
Pernigo, Leonello	4:02:37 (10,594)	
Perregaard, Peter	3:43:19 (6,365)	
Perren, Antony	5:20:55 (25,456)	
Perren, Peter	5:22:26 (25,640)	
Perrett, John	3:20:20 (2,800)	
Perrin, David	3:34:42 (4,862)	
Perrin, Geoffrey	5:27:42 (26,151)	
Perrin, Ian	4:53:27 (21,407)	
Perrin, Robert	6:11:15 (28,898)	
Perrinjaquet, Philippe	3:42:12 (6,164)	
Perris, Edward	3:27:56 (3,797)	
Perrott, Graham	4:49:32 (20,620)	
Perrott, Mike	2:54:39 (617)	
Perrott, Philip	5:54:59 (28,157)	
Perruchon, Etienne	3:47:31 (7,143)	
Perry, Andrew	3:59:07 (9,791)	
Perry, Christopher	4:17:07 (13,692)	
Perry, John	3:47:43 (7,196)	
Perry, Kirk	5:32:27 (26,575)	
Perry, Michael	4:11:39 (12,535)	
Perry, Robert	3:15:37 (2,281)	
Perry, Roger	5:02:33 (22,941)	
Perry, Scott	4:01:20 (10,348)	
Perry, Simon	5:42:02 (27,338)	
Perry, Stephen	4:40:35 (18,895)	
Persegona, Emanuele	3:27:44 (3,751)	
Persson, Eric	4:01:19 (10,342)	
Persson, Per	3:28:35 (3,923)	
Pertusini, Miro	3:30:54 (4,314)	
Perzylo, Kurt	4:44:29 (19,668)	
Petagna, Daniele	3:50:14 (7,727)	
Petch, Christopher	3:31:01 (4,331)	
Peter, Stephen	3:44:09 (6,518)	
Peters, John	5:16:42 (25,013)	
Peters, Paul	4:15:00 (13,268)	
Peters, Robin	3:31:21 (4,378)	
Peters, Stewart	3:56:21 (9,007)	
Peters, Stuart	3:47:14 (7,069)	
Peters, Warren	3:47:30 (7,139)	
Peters, William	3:35:17 (4,949)	
Petersen, Leif	3:49:17 (7,518)	
Petersen, Mogens	3:21:09 (2,901)	
Petersen, Toni	4:00:52 (10,254)	
Peterson, Andrew	3:59:48 (9,998)	
Peterson, Timothy	4:29:39 (16,585)	
Pether, Douglas	3:27:07 (3,640)	
Petitclerc, Alain	4:15:43 (13,406)	
Petrowski, Peter	3:59:26 (9,896)	
Petruso, Salvatore	3:43:18 (6,360)	
Pettersson, Tommy	4:23:10 (15,101)	
Pettie, Barrie	4:38:04 (18,389)	
Pettit, Nicholas	4:42:49 (19,336)	
Pettit, Simon	3:31:15 (4,365)	
Pettitt, Glenn	4:07:42 (11,699)	
Pettman, Simon	3:42:23 (6,199)	
Petts, Jonathan	4:51:45 (21,043)	
Peverley, James	3:38:15 (5,442)	
Peyton, Ben	4:44:37 (19,698)	
Pezzopane, Pasquale	5:08:29 (23,844)	
Pfadenhawer, Peter	4:43:01 (19,389)	
Pfaller, Franco	4:24:32 (15,404)	
Phasey, Andrew	4:57:44 (22,253)	
Phelan, James	4:59:41 (22,552)	
Phelps, Stephen	4:53:22 (21,393)	
Philbert, Pierre	3:34:55 (4,892)	
Philbrick, Ashley	4:25:28 (15,609)	
Philbrick, Mark	4:06:16 (11,400)	
Philip, Cameron	4:25:18 (15,576)	
Philipps, Martin	4:10:51 (12,359)	

Philipson, John	4:18:17 (13,946)	
Phillips, Alan	4:13:23 (12,899)	
Phillips, Bradley	5:24:11 (25,807)	
Phillips, Brian	4:40:01 (18,790)	
Phillips, Christopher	3:23:38 (3,189)	
Phillips, Craig	5:06:15 (23,511)	
Phillips, Daiel	5:02:45 (22,967)	
Phillips, David	4:08:13 (11,808)	
Phillips, David	4:36:29 (18,017)	
Phillips, David	4:51:54 (21,069)	
Phillips, Eric	5:45:00 (27,561)	
Phillips, Gareth	4:44:27 (19,665)	
Phillips, Gary	3:02:07 (1,162)	
Phillips, Gerald	3:57:17 (9,250)	
Phillips, Graeme	5:08:56 (23,926)	
Phillips, Gregg	3:56:22 (9,013)	
Phillips, Ian	3:51:39 (7,997)	
Phillips, James	4:15:43 (13,406)	
Phillips, Jamie	5:34:48 (26,783)	
Phillips, Jeremy	3:40:29 (5,867)	
Phillips, Jonathan	3:28:43 (3,939)	
Phillips, Kevin	5:51:00 (27,955)	
Phillips, Malcolm	3:13:01 (2,005)	
Phillips, Marcus	4:46:52 (20,136)	
Phillips, Mark	3:44:46 (6,632)	
Phillips, Mark	4:22:33 (14,938)	
Phillips, Mark	4:33:17 (17,363)	
Phillips, Martin	3:56:47 (9,129)	
Phillips, Mervyn	3:57:00 (9,178)	
Phillips, Michael	4:51:16 (20,935)	
Phillips, Neil	3:42:19 (6,183)	
Phillips, Nicholas	5:34:40 (26,770)	
Phillips, Paul	2:40:54 (189)	
Phillips, Peter	5:27:18 (26,110)	
Phillips, Rex	5:06:14 (23,508)	
Phillips, Richard	4:03:24 (10,747)	
Phillips, Robert	5:31:55 (26,525)	
Phillips, Sean	5:34:51 (26,791)	
Phillips, Simon	3:54:47 (8,655)	
Phillips, Stephen	5:06:04 (23,480)	
Phillips, Steven Neil	4:12:27 (12,725)	
Phillips, Tony	4:10:43 (12,315)	
Phillips, Wilfred	4:51:16 (20,935)	
Phillipson, Neil	4:05:38 (11,248)	
Phillipson, Peter	3:56:03 (8,940)	
Phillipson, Peter	4:58:04 (22,308)	
Phillis, Ben	3:52:15 (8,124)	
Phillis, Timothy	3:50:38 (7,795)	
Philo, Mark	3:29:44 (4,126)	
Philpin, Simon	4:42:55 (19,366)	
Philpot, Ceri	4:53:28 (21,411)	
Philpot, Garry	4:17:16 (13,730)	
Philpot, Howard	3:57:13 (9,232)	
Philpot, Michael	3:20:35 (2,831)	
Philpott, Trevor	3:56:26 (9,034)	
Phimister, Neil	5:15:10 (24,823)	
Phipps, Bryan	4:23:55 (15,277)	
Phoenix, Mike	4:07:49 (11,724)	
Piacentini, Arnaldo	2:48:47 (385)	
Piachaud, James	3:47:51 (7,224)	
Piasecki, Radoslaw	2:35:09 (93)	
Piau, Bernard	4:02:00 (10,486)	
Picard, Michel	3:25:51 (3,486)	
Pick, Robert	3:20:35 (2,831)	
Pickering, Dean	4:20:10 (14,403)	
Pickering, Derrick	4:08:57 (11,965)	
Pickering, Richard	3:16:59 (2,424)	
Pickering, Roger	3:33:52 (4,736)	
Pickering, Steven	3:54:35 (8,610)	
Pickett, Gary	5:55:50 (28,204)	
Pickett, Stephen	4:06:10 (11,372)	
Pickin, Lee	4:47:37 (20,284)	
Pickles, Robert	3:41:48 (6,091)	
Pickles, Robert	4:04:09 (10,910)	
Pickton, Barry	4:48:35 (20,451)	
Pickup, Graham	3:31:05 (4,338)	
Pidgeon, Nicholas	4:32:13 (17,158)	
Pieloor, Ronald	3:28:45 (3,949)	
Piemontese, Ezio	4:06:46 (11,495)	
Pierce, Jonathan	4:34:50 (17,683)	
Pierce, Mark	4:08:59 (11,974)	
Pierce, Stewart	3:56:47 (9,129)	
Piercey, Gordon	4:45:26 (19,856)	

Powell, Adrian	4:23:32	(15,184)
Powell, Andrew	3:14:57	(2,216)
Powell, Andrew	3:49:51	(7,657)
Powell, Anthony	3:26:32	(3,561)
Powell, Ashley	5:03:40	(23,077)
Powell, Christopher	3:37:09	(5,275)
Powell, David	2:58:47	(906)
Powell, David	3:52:44	(8,215)
Powell, David	4:01:38	(10,418)
Powell, Dean	5:06:51	(23,595)
Powell, Gareth	4:31:09	(16,888)
Powell, Jason	5:16:08	(24,942)
Powell, John	4:32:46	(17,270)
Powell, John	4:36:32	(18,026)
Powell, John	4:57:02	(22,142)
Powell, John	5:07:10	(23,645)
Powell, Jonathan	4:27:15	(16,017)
Powell, Kevin	4:14:27	(13,116)
Powell, Marcus	4:25:50	(15,685)
Powell, Matthew	2:55:04	(632)
Powell, Michael	4:05:07	(11,141)
Powell, Michael	5:07:03	(23,625)
Powell, Michael	5:18:25	(25,200)
Powell, Nathan	4:07:25	(11,647)
Powell, Richard	3:48:58	(7,458)
Powell, Robert	5:13:48	(24,606)
Powell, Sam	4:12:00	(12,616)
Powell, Steven	4:31:43	(17,041)
Powell, Tarquin	4:11:12	(12,440)
Powell, Terence	4:29:38	(16,584)
Powell, Tim	3:59:54	(10,026)
Powell, Tim	5:13:35	(24,576)
Powell, Virginia	4:35:39	(17,855)
Power, Andrew	2:59:15	(953)
Power, Brian	3:41:18	(6,007)
Power, Brian	4:15:58	(13,457)
Power, David	5:43:44	(27,452)
Power, Samuel	5:25:34	(25,944)
Powles, James	5:04:14	(23,170)
Pownall, Lee	4:06:47	(11,498)
Powney, Steven	4:35:30	(17,813)
Powrie, Duncan	4:52:34	(21,228)
Powter, Charlie	3:58:30	(9,604)
Poynter, Colin	3:42:29	(6,215)
Poynton, Malcolm	3:52:03	(8,085)
Poyton, John	4:18:23	(13,982)
Prabakaran, Perampalam	4:46:28	(20,045)
Prangley, Michael	4:19:28	(14,249)
Pratheepan, Thavaraja	5:03:46	(23,094)
Prato, Eduardo	3:52:37	(8,195)
Pratt, Alan	3:17:02	(2,431)
Pratt, Brian	4:10:06	(12,179)
Pratt, David	3:35:13	(4,935)
Pratt, Derek	4:29:51	(16,642)
Pratt, Dominic	2:40:39	(186)
Pratt, Ian	3:16:59	(2,424)
Pratt, James	3:39:32	(5,680)
Pratt, Steven	3:34:57	(4,899)
Pready, Nick	5:03:08	(23,023)
Preece, Michael	5:05:06	(23,305)
Preidl, Gerald	4:35:58	(17,925)
Prendergast, Christopher	4:46:27	(20,040)
Prentice, Ian	3:37:37	(5,352)
Prescott, Kevin	3:25:34	(3,452)
Prescott, Rhys	5:10:11	(24,100)
Prescott, Richard	4:04:12	(10,927)
Presence, Neil	5:04:43	(23,247)
Presland, Andy	5:29:15	(26,314)
Presland, Geoff	4:06:29	(11,445)
Presland, Paul	4:35:35	(17,839)
Press, Dietmar	3:52:51	(8,238)
Press, James	3:51:27	(7,952)
Prest, Michael	5:17:28	(25,103)
Prest, Simon	3:50:11	(7,721)
Preston, Andrew	4:44:48	(19,733)
Preston, Chris	5:34:08	(26,713)
Preston, John	5:59:21	(28,388)
Preston, Paul	4:09:35	(12,088)
Preston, Stephen	3:14:40	(2,178)
Preston, Stuart	3:28:11	(3,840)
Preston, Terry	3:43:04	(6,319)
Prestridge, Jeff	3:53:08	(8,296)
Prestwood, Mark	2:41:04	(194)

Pretorius, Errol	3:30:39	(4,270)
Pretty, Stephen	4:06:15	(11,397)
Prevett, Mark	4:38:06	(18,401)
Previte, Matthew	4:29:24	(16,519)
Previti, Stefano	4:09:44	(12,112)
Prevost, Ivan	4:56:33	(22,079)
Prewer, Carl	2:42:50	(231)
Prewett, Joseph	3:56:32	(9,062)
Price, Andrew	3:20:27	(2,815)
Price, Bryn	5:35:58	(26,875)
Price, Carl	2:54:22	(600)
Price, Carl	6:55:37	(29,896)
Price, Christopher	4:20:01	(14,374)
Price, Christopher	4:52:44	(21,260)
Price, Colin	3:51:08	(7,901)
Price, Darrin	5:19:17	(25,291)
Price, Dave	3:07:14	(1,521)
Price, David	4:44:04	(19,593)
Price, David	4:58:02	(22,301)
Price, Frank	4:46:00	(19,938)
Price, Gareth	4:18:52	(14,090)
Price, Herbert	3:49:14	(7,502)
Price, Howard	2:58:52	(922)
Price, Ian	3:00:42	(1,065)
Price, Ian	4:29:31	(16,549)
Price, James	2:48:59	(394)
Price, Jason	4:25:24	(15,593)
Price, Jeremy	4:12:20	(12,701)
Price, John	4:09:35	(12,088)
Price, Jonathan	4:10:07	(12,185)
Price, Julian	3:46:13	(6,900)
Price, Lynn	4:40:43	(18,927)
Price, Malcolm	4:11:14	(12,450)
Price, Marcus	3:26:53	(3,608)
Price, Martin	4:10:47	(12,332)
Price, Michael	3:27:53	(3,785)
Price, Michael	4:05:26	(11,191)
Price, Neil	5:43:01	(27,410)
Price, Nigel	3:36:29	(5,156)
Price, Paul	3:26:54	(3,610)
Price, Richard	4:14:19	(13,098)
Price, Robert	3:13:08	(2,017)
Price, Robin	3:55:46	(8,864)
Price, Rupert	3:39:48	(5,739)
Price, Stan	3:44:45	(6,625)
Price, Stewart	4:33:02	(17,316)
Price, Stuart	3:24:37	(3,332)
Price, Tim	4:19:30	(14,255)
Prickett, Colin	5:28:53	(26,282)
Prickett, Peter	4:46:26	(20,039)
Priddy, Emmanuel	3:51:15	(7,921)
Pride, Simon	2:16:27	(17)
Priest, Andrew	4:28:20	(16,267)
Priest, Darren	2:45:13	(295)
Priest, Park	5:16:53	(25,032)
Priestley, Ian	4:55:34	(21,907)
Priestley, Paul	4:15:23	(13,342)
Priestman, Adrian	5:45:53	(27,625)
Priezkalns, Eric	5:47:59	(27,775)
Prime, David	4:47:54	(20,325)
Primrose, Steven	4:26:14	(15,789)
Prince, Dave	4:10:40	(12,306)
Prince, Guy	4:28:26	(16,297)
Pring, Philip	5:23:53	(25,779)
Pring, Robert	5:23:54	(25,782)
Pringle, Alan	4:16:16	(13,519)
Pringle, Stuart	5:25:58	(25,984)
Prins, Diether	4:52:18	(21,158)
Print, Antony	3:39:12	(5,610)
Prinzivalli, Ernest	3:08:58	(1,669)
Prior, David	4:29:57	(16,675)
Prior, David	5:03:40	(23,077)
Prior, Robert	4:43:33	(19,508)
Prior, Stephen	4:28:39	(16,350)
Prior, Thomas	4:40:34	(18,889)
Prior, Tony	5:18:39	(25,229)
Pritchad, Roger	3:43:41	(6,432)
Pritchard, Chris	5:20:14	(25,380)
Pritchard, Colin	3:42:44	(6,258)
Pritchard, Ed	3:48:12	(7,303)
Pritchard, Keith	5:44:27	(27,506)
Pritchard, Nigel	3:23:56	(3,235)
Pritchard, Simon	2:35:38	(100)

Pritchard, Terry	4:34:07	(17,562)
Pritchard, Timothy	3:58:40	(9,661)
Pritchard, William	4:10:10	(12,200)
Pritchett, William	4:09:00	(11,978)
Procope, Harry	4:13:50	(13,009)
Procter, Andrew	5:03:08	(23,023)
Procter, John	3:10:44	(1,811)
Procter, Scott	3:43:14	(6,351)
Proctor, Andrew	5:05:51	(23,439)
Proctor, Charles	4:12:47	(12,788)
Prodromou, Luke	3:17:47	(2,508)
Proffitt-White, John	3:58:51	(9,713)
Pronk, Martin	2:58:43	(894)
Prosser, John	7:05:13	(29,977)
Prothero, Bob	2:46:06	(320)
Proto, Vince	4:35:01	(17,714)
Protopapa, Peter	5:24:06	(25,800)
Proud, William	5:04:35	(23,232)
Proudfoot, Cameron	4:14:59	(13,260)
Proudfoot, Trevor	4:32:18	(17,172)
Proudlove, Michael	2:23:17	(31)
Proudlove, Shaun	4:03:16	(10,713)
Prouse, Paul	3:54:38	(8,620)
Provedel, Maurizio	3:51:03	(7,881)
Prudham, Joseph	3:31:32	(4,396)
Prud'homme, Philippe	2:55:00	(629)
Prugh, Gregory	3:44:36	(6,596)
Pryor, David	3:59:52	(10,016)
Pryor, John	4:54:46	(21,665)
Pryor, Martin	4:05:05	(11,133)
Prytherch, David	5:00:57	(22,725)
Przybyl, Wladyslaw	2:50:40	(452)
Pucci, Geoffrey	3:21:13	(2,906)
Pucelle, Bruno	3:27:38	(3,727)
Pugh, Anthony	4:50:20	(20,778)
Pugh, Christopher	4:48:20	(20,413)
Pugh, Cliff	3:42:13	(6,166)
Pugh, Nick	4:21:17	(14,645)
Pugh, Patrick	3:32:29	(4,532)
Pugh, Richard	4:38:41	(18,544)
Pugh, Simon	3:36:23	(5,134)
Pugh, Stephen	4:30:36	(16,765)
Pugliese, Maurizio	4:22:01	(14,818)
Pulford, Andy	4:22:45	(14,993)
Pullan, Nicholas	5:49:05	(27,846)
Pullar, Neil	3:52:36	(8,190)
Pullen, Gregory	3:51:05	(7,889)
Pullen, Leslie	4:17:41	(13,808)
Pullen, Timothy	3:30:48	(4,294)
Pullin, Roger	5:21:38	(25,540)
Pullinger, Jack	4:04:50	(11,076)
Pullman, David	3:39:07	(5,592)
Pumfleet, Stephen	5:19:58	(25,360)
Punkka, Veikko	3:47:57	(7,258)
Punter, Nicholas	3:44:23	(6,559)
Puntis, Anthony	3:43:23	(6,374)
Purcell, Edward	5:02:29	(22,934)
Purcell, Jim	7:52:31	(30,194)
Purchas, Simon	4:40:36	(18,898)
Purchase, Alan	3:16:57	(2,418)
Puri, Chander	4:53:34	(21,436)
Purnell, Brian	4:53:31	(21,427)
Purnell, Raymond	3:31:50	(4,444)
Purro, Michel	3:09:00	(1,672)
Pursall, Martin	4:17:55	(13,856)
Purser, David	3:31:46	(4,430)
Purser, John	4:01:25	(10,373)
Purser, Kevin	4:49:40	(20,645)
Pursglove, Mark	3:52:15	(8,124)
Purves, David	4:11:27	(12,493)
Pussard, Marc	4:30:34	(16,762)
Puttock, Simon	3:29:07	(4,019)
Puttock, Simon	3:32:09	(4,489)
Pybus, Andrew	4:58:23	(22,357)
Pye, Alan	3:31:39	(4,416)
Pye, David	4:58:46	(22,423)
Pye, Steven	3:35:32	(4,994)
Quaife, Nicholas	3:49:14	(7,502)
Quant, Daniel	4:00:17	(10,106)
Quantrill, Derek	3:52:51	(8,238)
Quartermain, Julian	4:38:02	(18,378)
Quartermaine, Andrew	5:01:00	(22,734)
Quartermaine, Richard	4:07:10	(11,582)

Quarterman, Bill 5:18:57 (25,262)
Quartino, Marco 2:58:31 (859)
Quartly, Leonard 4:13:25 (12,912)
Quattrocchi, Federico 4:55:35 (21,913)
Quaye, Humphrey 5:51:38 (27,990)
Quayle, Andrew 4:07:02 (11,560)
Quayle, Malcolm 3:23:49 (3,213)
Queenan, John 3:24:42 (3,342)
Quemard, Peter 3:51:52 (8,043)
Quennell, Richard 2:49:37 (412)
Querss, Detlef 3:22:26 (3,048)
Queyrou, Yannick 4:52:23 (21,180)
Quibell, Richard 4:37:58 (18,363)
Quick, Andrew 4:56:43 (22,093)
Quick, Jonathan 4:20:24 (14,449)
Quick, Paul 3:07:59 (1,591)
Quick, Paul 6:47:14 (29,762)
Quickfall, Gerard 5:25:34 (25,944)
Quigley, Peter 5:29:53 (26,362)
Quince, Roger 4:01:34 (10,403)
Quincy, Jean Claude 5:37:42 (27,000)
Quinlan, Bernard 5:49:41 (27,881)
Quinlivan, David 3:28:56 (3,982)
Quinlivan, Michael 4:08:46 (11,928)
Quinn, Bob 4:42:20 (19,236)
Quinn, Colm 4:50:09 (20,743)
Quinn, David 3:16:59 (2,424)
Quinn, Greg 3:22:32 (3,056)
Quinn, Hilton 4:02:13 (10,527)
Quinn, James 4:28:45 (16,371)
Quinn, Joe 3:43:30 (6,398)
Quinn, John 4:17:31 (13,776)
Quinn, Malcolm 4:23:47 (15,248)
Quinn, Martin 3:07:24 (1,535)
Quinn, Martin 3:59:57 (10,042)
Quinn, Michael 4:19:37 (14,284)
Quinn, Mike 3:06:33 (1,464)
Quinn, Nigel 4:20:00 (14,368)
Quinn, Patrick 4:52:01 (21,094)
Quinn, Robert 2:50:35 (450)
Quinn, Sean 3:38:48 (5,537)
Quinn, Thomas 3:41:50 (6,097)
Quinnell, Stephen 4:13:28 (12,925)
Quinton, Colin 5:49:50 (27,891)
Quintos, Carlos 4:26:52 (15,926)
Quirk, Dixon 5:27:03 (26,085)
Quirk, Peter 6:14:01 (28,991)
Quist, Ole 4:16:53 (13,644)
Raaphorst, Joop 3:41:15 (5,999)
Rabey, Derrick 3:21:36 (2,957)
Rabey, Shaun 5:02:41 (22,961)
Rabinowitz, Gideon 4:14:41 (13,166)
Race, Stuart 5:11:39 (24,304)
Racher, Graham 4:29:05 (16,445)
Rack, Iain 4:20:58 (14,584)
Rackham, Michael 5:48:12 (27,792)
Rackham, Robert 5:39:29 (27,134)
Racle, Simon 4:11:47 (12,566)
Radcliffe, Richard 3:20:15 (2,788)
Radcliffe, Toby 3:18:36 (2,608)
Radford, Mark 5:35:43 (26,861)
Radford, Philip 3:22:45 (3,078)
Radford, Philip 6:37:41 (29,583)
Radhakrishnan, Nerukav 5:26:08 (26,001)
Radley, Alan 5:20:10 (25,373)
Radziwon, Czeslaw 3:36:00 (5,075)
Rae, Angus 4:03:53 (10,859)
Rae, Ian 3:56:14 (8,975)
Rae, Neil 2:55:29 (650)
Rae, Phillip 4:28:11 (16,231)
Raeber, Walter 3:41:11 (5,980)
Raffa, Giovanni 3:40:18 (5,830)
Rafferty, Michael 4:23:04 (15,080)
Raffill, Jason 4:06:23 (11,427)
Raffington, John 3:06:40 (1,477)
Rafiq-Craske, Matthew 4:05:51 (11,312)
Ragab, Mostafa 5:04:38 (23,238)
Ragan, Christopher 3:41:14 (5,993)
Ragg, Peter 5:08:51 (23,913)
Raghlani, Rajendra 5:45:38 (27,604)
Ragnarsson, Gisli 3:42:48 (6,271)
Rahaman, Kalim 3:52:06 (8,097)
Rahsbrook, Gary 5:26:46 (26,067)
Rai, Tesh 6:31:55 (29,450)
Railton, Peter 6:59:00 (29,930)
Rainbow, Mark 3:51:51 (8,040)
Rainsby, Ian 4:16:10 (13,500)
Raishbrook, Ian 3:58:21 (9,576)
Raistrick, Nicolas 4:22:16 (14,877)
Raithby, Christopher 3:35:51 (5,042)
Raithhatha, Nickyl 4:27:13 (16,014)
Raja, Hamid 5:24:26 (25,825)
Rake, Matt 4:19:52 (14,330)
Raker, Peter 4:33:38 (17,464)
Rakusen, Lloyd 3:58:54 (9,723)
Ralph, Andrew 4:30:53 (16,823)
Ralph, David 5:29:46 (26,350)
Ralph Davies, John 4:26:01 (15,736)
Ralphs, Paul 4:54:54 (21,702)
Ramaala, Hendrick 2:12:02 (9)
Ramakrishna, Sushmith 4:28:42 (16,359)
Ramamurthy, Srinath 4:40:58 (18,971)
Ramelot, Frederic 3:09:09 (1,686)
Ramiz, Ersin 4:04:42 (11,042)
Rampling, Jeremy 3:42:10 (6,155)
Rampling, Laurence 5:15:08 (24,802)
Ramsay, Craig 4:21:55 (14,791)
Ramsay, Douglas 3:39:30 (5,673)
Ramsay, Gordon 3:56:39 (9,091)
Ramsay, Grant 3:05:11 (1,365)
Ramsay, Peter 3:45:49 (6,827)
Ramsbottom, Roger 3:43:32 (6,403)
Ramsden, Adrian 6:14:10 (28,994)
Ramsden, Alex 3:33:11 (4,642)
Ramsden, John 3:45:30 (6,744)
Ramsden, Nigel 4:36:55 (18,110)
Ramsden, Paul 4:30:32 (16,757)
Ramsell, Christopher 3:03:50 (1,270)
Ramsey, John 3:23:03 (3,122)
Ramsey, Mark 4:29:57 (16,675)
Ranadive, Rahul 4:33:32 (17,428)
Rance, Keith 3:45:32 (6,755)
Rance, Mark 3:41:56 (6,113)
Rance, Matt 4:43:44 (19,548)
Rancon, Pierre 4:02:55 (10,649)
Randall, André 3:22:57 (3,104)
Randall, Barry 4:24:13 (15,334)
Randall, Gary 4:03:05 (10,683)
Randall, Jonathan 4:01:26 (10,379)
Randall, Michael 4:00:45 (10,234)
Randall, Michael 4:26:35 (15,868)
Randell, Timothy 4:53:18 (21,373)
Randem, Amund 3:37:14 (5,288)
Randle, Richard 3:13:45 (2,084)
Randles, Stephen 3:54:32 (8,594)
Rands, Steven 4:26:25 (15,824)
Rang, David 4:04:53 (11,088)
Rangalam, Stewart 5:16:11 (24,948)
Ranger, Jamie 3:32:41 (4,558)
Ranger, Terry 5:14:52 (24,760)
Rankin, Charles 5:06:55 (23,603)
Rankin, Geoffrey 3:32:10 (4,492)
Rankin, Gordon 4:21:14 (14,635)
Rankine, Stuart 3:34:47 (4,875)
Ransome, Craig 5:11:56 (24,346)
Ransome, David 2:48:25 (375)
Ransome, David 3:51:14 (7,917)
Ransome, Dorian 4:26:48 (15,910)
Ranson, Charles 4:59:13 (22,488)
Ranson, Lee 4:11:37 (12,528)
Ranson, Robert 4:26:22 (15,819)
Ranson, Scott 4:05:06 (11,138)
Rant, Keith 4:11:39 (12,535)
Rapley, Greig 4:35:52 (17,899)
Rapley, Nicholas 4:31:00 (16,850)
Rappini, David 4:50:48 (20,843)
Rapson, Ian 4:57:45 (22,260)
Rasell, Stephen 4:24:25 (15,374)
Rashid, Tahir 5:20:46 (25,441)
Rashidian, Reza 4:00:31 (10,158)
Rason, Keir 3:49:23 (7,548)
Rassau, Andreas 5:37:29 (26,976)
Rassinger, Johann 3:39:25 (5,657)
Rata, Colin 4:28:12 (16,238)
Ratcliff, Steve 3:03:34 (1,251)
Ratcliffe, Barney 4:43:44 (19,548)
Ratcliffe, Christopher 3:52:45 (8,220)
Ratcliffe, David 3:27:41 (3,738)
Ratcliffe, Guy 3:42:40 (6,247)
Ratcliffe, Jonathan 3:34:09 (4,779)
Ratcliffe, Jonathan 3:45:00 (6,688)
Ratcliffe, Paul 6:00:37 (28,435)
Ratcliffe, Sam 4:10:11 (12,203)
Rathbone, Colin 3:01:46 (1,136)
Rathbone, David 4:59:39 (22,548)
Ratley, David 4:25:18 (15,576)
Rauf, Andy 6:07:32 (28,747)
Rault, Bernard 4:07:58 (11,755)
Raurich, Ferran 4:08:32 (11,877)
Ravalia, Divyesh 5:07:51 (23,754)
Raven, Hugh 4:16:42 (13,609)
Raven, Kris 4:11:49 (12,574)
Ravine, James 5:12:48 (24,470)
Ravn Hagen, Oeivind 4:47:56 (20,333)
Raw, Andrew 4:47:22 (20,232)
Rawat, Mehender 4:29:12 (16,472)
Rawcliffe, Paul 4:55:26 (21,863)
Rawding, Andrew 3:10:15 (1,768)
Rawle, Adam 4:04:16 (10,943)
Rawlings, Edward 4:29:45 (16,610)
Rawlings, Jonathan 4:28:16 (16,256)
Rawlings, Peter 4:38:58 (18,598)
Rawlins, Craig 5:04:15 (23,173)
Rawlins, James 3:59:28 (9,909)
Rawlins, John 3:35:39 (5,011)
Rawlins, William 6:16:35 (29,071)
Rawlinson, David 3:53:24 (8,357)
Rawlinson, John 2:59:11 (949)
Rawlinson, Nigel 5:33:53 (26,678)
Rawlinson, Roger 4:32:36 (17,227)
Rawson, David 3:49:21 (7,538)
Ray, Geoffrey 3:29:21 (4,058)
Ray, Paul 5:31:44 (26,510)
Ray, Paul 5:40:39 (27,243)
Ray, Sanjit 4:55:36 (21,922)
Rayatt, Devinder 3:16:22 (2,348)
Raybould, Gordon 5:10:37 (24,167)
Rayfield, David 3:05:54 (1,413)
Rayment, Lee 4:56:49 (22,111)
Raymer, Bruce 2:25:56 (44)
Raymond, Andrew 5:38:11 (27,029)
Raymond, Byron 2:54:30 (608)
Raymonde Parker, Ian 5:05:56 (23,456)
Rayner, Glenn 4:52:32 (21,216)
Rayner, Kenneth 4:48:41 (20,466)
Rayner, Michael 3:00:16 (1,042)
Rayner, Ralph 5:27:31 (26,128)
Rayner, Trevor 2:55:12 (637)
Raynor, Andrew 5:28:00 (26,182)
Raynor, David 3:58:24 (9,585)
Raynor, Leonard 3:32:25 (4,523)
Raza, Ashraf 5:45:48 (27,617)
Razaq, Mohammed 3:19:24 (2,693)
Rea, James 4:19:15 (14,178)
Rea, Lawerence 3:36:02 (5,080)
Rea, Paul 3:21:47 (2,971)
Read, Alfred 4:11:11 (12,436)
Read, Antony 4:01:55 (10,469)
Read, Brian 3:25:41 (3,463)
Read, Graham 5:57:15 (28,278)
Read, John 3:41:28 (6,036)
Read, John 4:53:46 (21,467)
Read, Jonathan 3:28:29 (3,905)
Read, Keith 3:06:08 (1,433)
Read, Malcolm 3:36:53 (5,223)
Read, Ronald 3:47:23 (7,112)
Read, Steven 3:32:55 (4,588)
Reade, Timothy 3:57:25 (9,300)
Reader, Andrew 5:17:39 (25,118)
Reading, Richard 5:15:17 (24,841)
Readman, Benjamin 3:14:34 (2,174)
Ready, Charles 4:41:05 (18,992)
Realini, Pietro 3:41:25 (6,030)
Reape, Anthony 4:10:13 (12,213)
Rear, Ian 3:28:44 (3,944)
Reardon, James 4:23:12 (15,108)
Reardon, Paul 4:03:19 (10,728)
Reatchlous, James 6:37:23 (29,574)
Reavey, Simon 4:03:21 (10,735)

Reay, Gordon 3:47:21 (7,100)
Reay, Kenneth 5:31:05 (26,459)
Reay, Tom 4:31:26 (16,967)
Rebair Brown, Gavin 4:01:08 (10,307)
Rebellato, Mario 6:40:03 (29,636)
Reber, Ueli 4:11:39 (12,535)
Reboa, Sergio 4:23:21 (15,143)
Rebstock, Dieter 3:35:54 (5,055)
Recardo, Winston 4:58:11 (22,326)
Redden, Phil 5:44:28 (27,509)
Redden, William 4:34:19 (17,599)
Reddy, Bruno 4:33:50 (17,507)
Reddy, Peter 3:55:37 (8,821)
Redfearn, Peter 4:01:08 (10,307)
Redfern, David 5:11:17 (24,254)
Redfern, Ian 4:04:52 (11,081)
Redfern, John 4:17:37 (13,796)
Redford, Bryce 5:39:06 (27,095)
Redford, Roy 6:26:28 (29,316)

Redgrave, Steven 4:55:36 (21,922)

Redgrove, Nicholas 3:35:03 (4,909)
Redhead, Darryl 4:13:41 (12,978)
Redhead, Robbie 5:37:47 (27,006)
Redman, Christopher 3:59:02 (9,765)
Redman, Christopher 4:42:06 (19,178)
Redmill, Michael 5:08:41 (23,883)
Redmond, Alasdair 4:37:56 (18,353)
Redmond, Andrew 4:11:38 (12,531)
Redmond, Ben 4:21:25 (14,673)
Redmond, Ian 5:21:49 (25,568)
Redmond, John 2:29:49 (65)
Redpath, Alan 4:45:14 (19,812)
Redshaw, Peter 3:59:18 (9,841)
Reece, Jarrod 4:31:03 (16,862)
Reed, Alan 3:03:31 (1,246)
Reed, Chris 4:51:02 (20,891)
Reed, Christopher 3:23:02 (3,118)
Reed, Christopher 5:10:29 (24,140)
Reed, David 2:45:05 (289)
Reed, David 4:28:14 (16,246)
Reed, David 4:32:15 (17,165)
Reed, Ian 4:50:20 (20,778)
Reed, James 4:07:42 (11,699)
Reed, Michael 3:31:50 (4,444)
Reed, Michael 4:08:27 (11,862)
Reed, Peter 4:08:12 (11,802)
Reed, Peter 4:44:35 (19,692)
Reed, Philip 3:31:56 (4,459)
Reed, Philip 3:49:09 (7,486)
Reed, Stuart 4:33:47 (17,496)
Reed, William 3:18:30 (2,599)
Reeman, David 4:46:39 (20,082)
Reep, Michael 3:02:05 (1,159)
Rees, Adrian 4:45:49 (19,905)
Rees, Alistair 3:05:50 (1,409)
Rees, Andrew 2:30:41 (70)
Rees, Christopher 4:43:39 (19,527)
Rees, Colin 3:10:59 (1,834)
Rees, David 4:32:20 (17,179)
Rees, Dorian 4:51:03 (20,898)
Rees, Gareth 4:13:59 (13,038)
Rees, Gary 3:34:39 (4,856)
Rees, Gavin 3:38:01 (5,401)
Rees, James 5:00:40 (22,686)
Rees, Jeff 3:08:09 (1,603)
Rees, Jim 4:16:28 (13,566)
Rees, John 3:58:58 (9,744)
Rees, John 4:11:55 (12,589)
Rees, John 4:50:12 (20,754)
Rees, Lyn 3:05:17 (1,371)
Rees, Martin 8:11:33 (30,233)
Rees, Martyn 4:49:24 (20,598)
Rees, Michael 3:27:05 (3,633)
Rees, Michael 3:52:24 (8,156)
Rees, Michael 5:41:20 (27,280)
Rees, Nigel 4:02:26 (10,556)
Rees, Simon 4:07:43 (11,703)
Rees, Stephen 4:38:40 (18,541)
Rees, Thomas 4:46:19 (20,010)
Rees, William 5:05:19 (23,340)
Reeve, Andy 5:00:10 (22,639)
Reeve, Michael 4:45:11 (19,804)
Reeve, Nicholas 4:14:40 (13,163)
Reeve, Robin 3:56:25 (9,032)
Reeve, Simon 5:37:20 (26,967)
Reeve, Thomas 7:49:52 (30,188)
Reeve-Johnson, Lloyd 3:06:01 (1,424)
Reeves, Alan 5:32:26 (26,572)
Reeves, Andrew 3:33:10 (4,636)
Reeves, Gavin 4:48:33 (20,446)
Reeves, Stephen 3:56:14 (8,975)
Reeves, Steve 3:24:31 (3,312)
Reeves, Stuart 2:57:02 (746)
Regan, John 5:15:06 (24,797)
Regan, Kevin 5:27:26 (26,123)
Regan, Peter 4:39:10 (18,630)
Regelous, Paul 3:42:20 (6,188)
Regent, Jonathan 4:04:35 (11,017)
Regnier, Jean Paul 4:40:46 (18,934)
Reid, Brian 4:05:00 (11,118)
Reid, Clive 3:04:53 (1,340)
Reid, Dale 4:21:02 (14,599)
Reid, David 3:39:21 (5,638)
Reid, David 4:01:13 (10,321)
Reid, Douglas 3:21:19 (2,922)
Reid, Ean 3:32:32 (4,542)
Reid, Graeme 3:37:31 (5,339)
Reid, Graham 4:00:18 (10,108)
Reid, John 4:14:51 (13,222)
Reid, Karl 4:45:21 (19,832)
Reid, Nel 3:20:26 (2,811)
Reid, Peter 3:19:24 (2,693)
Reid, Scott 3:22:13 (3,028)
Reid, Thomas 3:50:36 (7,790)
Reidy, John Joe 5:23:40 (25,761)
Reiertsen, Arvid 3:03:12 (1,226)
Reilly, John Joe 4:19:01 (14,123)
Reilly, Richard 4:48:43 (20,473)
Reinert, Brad 6:54:51 (29,874)
Reinert, Richard 3:56:05 (8,946)
Reis, Francis 4:35:21 (17,786)
Reitz, Richard 3:53:43 (8,429)
Relph, James 3:58:59 (9,749)
Relton, Richard 3:43:14 (6,351)
Remaud, Alain 5:28:10 (26,189)
Renals, Paul 3:15:27 (2,268)
Renaudeau, Serge 4:05:43 (11,273)
Renette, André 4:22:10 (14,847)
Renie, John 4:44:57 (19,765)
Rennie, Ian 4:28:36 (16,339)
Rennie, Les 3:58:56 (9,732)
Rennie, Michael 3:38:21 (5,456)
Rennie, Nicholas 5:42:14 (27,348)
Rennie, Robert 6:29:53 (29,405)
Rennie, Stephen 2:40:16 (175)
Rennison, Mark 3:25:16 (3,411)
Rennison, Mark 4:21:41 (14,731)
Renny, Christopher 5:01:43 (22,826)
Renny, Stephen 5:35:08 (26,818)
Renoux, Bruno 4:24:26 (15,381)
Renoux, Tristan 3:56:31 (9,058)
Renshaw, David 5:12:53 (24,479)
Renshaw, Gareth 3:48:46 (7,415)
Renton, Alan 5:10:39 (24,170)
Renton, Alex 4:16:40 (13,601)
Renton, Fred 4:33:29 (17,414)
Renton, Neil 4:01:07 (10,303)
Renyard, Malcolm 3:09:20 (1,700)
Reps, Paul 5:16:10 (24,947)
Resnick, Brian 4:55:24 (21,849)
Resnick, Julian 4:04:53 (11,088)
Retalic, Ronald 3:48:54 (7,440)
Rettinger, Gerhard 4:04:31 (10,996)
Reucroft, Peter 4:08:34 (11,885)
Reunbrouck, Frank 6:34:40 (29,516)
Revell, David 4:22:32 (14,936)
Revell, Kevin 2:49:48 (418)
Revington, Mike 5:59:09 (28,374)
Reyes, Abel 6:03:33 (28,568)
Reyl, François 3:47:37 (7,167)
Reynolds, Brett 2:58:28 (848)
Reynolds, Christopher 3:39:36 (5,693)
Reynolds, Dave 3:46:35 (6,968)
Reynolds, David 5:27:27 (26,124)
Reynolds, Edward 3:36:11 (5,103)
Reynolds, first name unknown 4:22:52 (15,024)
Reynolds, Glen 3:45:28 (6,739)
Reynolds, Gordon 4:43:12 (19,427)
Reynolds, Graham 3:46:55 (7,022)
Reynolds, Jonathan 4:52:03 (21,102)
Reynolds, Martin 4:19:18 (14,194)
Reynolds, Michael 3:26:26 (3,547)
Reynolds, Neil 3:50:28 (7,767)
Reynolds, Nick 6:10:47 (28,883)
Reynolds, Paul 3:00:08 (1,037)
Reynolds, Peter 3:37:24 (5,321)
Reynolds, Rhon 4:42:16 (19,218)
Reynolds, Robert 3:58:00 (9,490)
Reynolds, Robert 4:14:02 (13,046)
Reynolds, Shaun 4:52:02 (21,098)
Reynolds, Sidney 3:45:02 (6,693)
Reynolds, Simon 5:08:56 (23,926)
Reynolds, Simon 5:34:33 (26,761)
Reynolds, Stephen 4:26:18 (15,807)
Reynolds, Steven 5:55:41 (28,201)
Reynolds, Stuart 3:20:50 (2,868)
Reynolds, Stuart 3:29:18 (4,050)
Rhbhsse, Pierre 3:17:47 (2,508)
Rhimes, Godfrey 2:38:17 (141)
Rhind, Stuart 5:02:47 (22,973)
Rhoades, Andy 4:00:43 (10,217)
Rhodes, Bernie 4:20:15 (14,418)
Rhodes, Christopher 5:58:06 (28,326)
Rhodes, Daniel 4:15:04 (13,282)
Rhodes, David 3:15:33 (2,276)
Rhodes, David 3:54:53 (8,683)
Rhodes, Ian 5:13:14 (24,543)
Rhodes, Michael 4:08:33 (11,880)
Rhodes, Nick 3:56:26 (9,034)
Rhys-Dillon, Brian 4:31:41 (17,036)
Riach, Kenneth 3:29:54 (4,150)
Ribault, Philippe 5:21:30 (25,525)
Riccio, Gennaro 3:54:06 (8,492)
Rice, Brian 4:54:02 (21,521)
Rice, Darren 4:54:17 (21,559)
Rice, Michael 4:06:11 (11,379)
Rice-Tucker, Andrew 5:35:17 (26,826)
Rich, Al 2:47:35 (355)
Rich, Andrew 3:14:01 (2,126)
Rich, Andrew 4:13:21 (12,889)
Rich, Stephen 3:58:59 (9,749)
Rich, Tony 5:25:18 (25,920)
Richard, Nugent 4:12:08 (12,653)
Richards, Andrew 4:38:31 (18,509)
Richards, Anthony 5:37:09 (26,955)
Richards, Daniel 4:34:47 (17,672)

Richards, David	4:47:27 (20,250)	
Richards, Edward	4:09:45 (12,117)	
Richards, Gavin	3:49:57 (7,676)	
Richards, John	5:27:41 (26,148)	
Richards, Ken	4:04:54 (11,096)	
Richards, Mark	3:59:13 (9,823)	
Richards, Nathaniel	3:51:39 (7,997)	
Richards, Paul	2:30:34 (69)	
Richards, Paul	3:33:58 (4,750)	
Richards, Paul	4:39:22 (18,659)	
Richards, Paul	5:10:27 (24,136)	
Richards, Robert	3:26:44 (3,589)	
Richards, Robert	3:54:21 (8,549)	
Richards, Simon	4:19:19 (14,198)	
Richards, Stephen	4:22:07 (14,838)	
Richards, Trevor	5:06:15 (23,511)	
Richardson, Alan	4:11:24 (12,481)	
Richardson, Alan	5:10:59 (24,209)	
Richardson, Anthony	3:45:37 (6,769)	
Richardson, Carl	3:58:19 (9,565)	
Richardson, Christopher	5:28:35 (26,236)	
Richardson, Clive	3:27:01 (3,626)	
Richardson, Derek	3:44:56 (6,670)	
Richardson, Doug	5:38:56 (27,082)	
Richardson, Eamonn	3:38:06 (5,414)	
Richardson, Gary	3:28:42 (3,938)	
Richardson, Geoffrey	5:49:00 (27,842)	
Richardson, Henry	3:58:30 (9,604)	
Richardson, Ian	5:37:31 (26,978)	
Richardson, Jack	3:26:26 (3,547)	
Richardson, John	3:29:17 (4,045)	
Richardson, John	6:44:30 (29,730)	
Richardson, Lance	3:21:26 (2,938)	
Richardson, Lawrence	4:27:02 (15,975)	
Richardson, Michael	4:19:39 (14,294)	
Richardson, Neil	3:21:28 (2,942)	
Richardson, Oisin	3:05:41 (1,400)	
Richardson, Paul	5:15:24 (24,855)	
Richardson, Peter	3:47:10 (7,059)	
Richardson, Peter	4:26:08 (15,762)	
Richardson, Peter	4:51:05 (20,906)	
Richardson, Peter	5:38:36 (27,056)	
Richardson, Phil	4:19:46 (14,309)	
Richardson, Robert	4:29:11 (16,467)	
Richardson, Robin	4:52:53 (21,287)	
Richardson, Roger	3:14:45 (2,189)	
Richardson, Simon	2:40:58 (191)	
Richardson, Stephen	3:23:48 (3,210)	
Richardson, Steven	3:40:01 (5,791)	
Richardson, Tim	4:14:05 (13,053)	
Riche, Luke	4:49:15 (20,574)	
Riches, Edward	4:35:40 (17,859)	
Riches, John	4:42:33 (19,281)	
Riches, Matthew	4:47:23 (20,236)	
Riches, Neil	5:00:44 (22,697)	
Richman, Andrew	5:50:29 (27,925)	
Richmond, David	3:53:52 (8,453)	
Richmond, James	4:53:57 (21,499)	
Richmond, Jonathan	4:37:50 (18,326)	
Richmond, Nolan	4:46:09 (19,972)	
Richmond, William	4:50:42 (20,826)	
Rickard, Marcus	5:42:38 (27,390)	
Rickards, Neil	4:51:28 (20,981)	
Rickett, Dave	4:41:47 (19,120)	
Rickett, Peter	5:02:08 (22,897)	
Ricou, Patrice	3:59:19 (9,849)	
Riddaway, Bobby	2:58:41 (888)	
Riddell, Ken	3:32:13 (4,495)	
Riddick, Matthew	4:38:41 (18,544)	
Riddle, Andrew	5:05:05 (23,303)	
Riddle, Thomas	5:38:22 (27,040)	
Riddoch, Allan	5:35:37 (26,854)	
Rider, Jerry	5:15:13 (24,834)	
Rider, Michael	5:17:11 (25,069)	
Rider, Nicholas	4:23:33 (15,189)	
Rider, Steve	5:51:30 (27,983)	
Rider, Tim	3:53:10 (8,302)	
Ridge, Tim	4:12:00 (12,616)	
Ridgeon, Duncan	4:50:19 (20,774)	
Ridgeway, Christopher	3:41:51 (6,101)	
Ridgewell, Stanley	4:16:16 (13,519)	
Ridgwell, Lloyd	3:28:27 (3,898)	
Ridler, Adam	4:19:27 (14,241)	
Ridler, Mark	4:23:14 (15,114)	
Ridley, Andrew	5:35:31 (26,844)	
Ridley, Bill	3:55:48 (8,870)	
Ridley, Neil	3:24:37 (3,332)	
Ridout, Alexander	4:24:22 (15,362)	
Ridout, John	3:23:43 (3,202)	
Ridout, Nick	4:52:19 (21,164)	
Ridsdale, Neil	3:10:26 (1,789)	
Ridsdill Smith, Mark	4:38:12 (18,427)	
Rief, Michael	3:33:56 (4,745)	
Rieger, Matthias	3:47:26 (7,125)	
Riehm, Rainer	3:30:53 (4,310)	
Rielly, James	3:08:51 (1,659)	
Rigby, Carl	4:15:49 (13,428)	
Rigby, Geoffrey	3:36:34 (5,167)	
Rigby, Mark	3:56:49 (9,137)	
Rigby, Reginald	5:23:23 (25,732)	
Rigby, Roy	4:04:34 (11,013)	
Rigg, Nigel	3:34:23 (4,814)	
Rigg, Richard	4:41:02 (18,981)	
Riggs, Darren	3:19:12 (2,673)	
Rigler, Adam	4:58:39 (22,403)	
Rigler, Melvin	5:11:28 (24,279)	
Rigolli, Gianfranco	4:27:31 (16,063)	
Rigo-Rigo, Jaume	3:31:47 (4,435)	
Rigot, Jacques	4:30:22 (16,738)	
Rijpstra, Eelke	4:14:34 (13,141)	
Riley, Barrie	3:38:54 (5,560)	
Riley, Carl	3:06:31 (1,462)	
Riley, David	4:49:52 (20,687)	
Riley, David	6:28:27 (29,369)	
Riley, John	4:59:32 (22,530)	
Riley, Martin	2:34:32 (89)	
Riley, Melvyn	4:31:22 (16,947)	
Riley, Peter	3:26:21 (3,540)	
Riley, Peter	4:43:13 (19,431)	
Riley, Peter	4:43:29 (19,490)	
Riley, Steve	4:04:20 (10,953)	
Riley Jordan, Peter	5:43:22 (27,430)	
Rimmer, Scott	5:25:28 (25,938)	
Rimmington, Stephen	3:51:19 (7,935)	
Rinchey, Alan	3:13:12 (2,026)	
Rindlisbacher, Daniel	3:13:24 (2,053)	
Ring, Charlie	4:51:03 (20,898)	
Ringressi, Dominique	4:25:17 (15,572)	
Ringrose, David	3:58:47 (9,694)	
Ringrose, Philip	4:34:23 (17,612)	
Ringrose, Simon	5:32:30 (26,581)	
Riniker, Urs	3:10:17 (1,772)	
Rintoul, Archie	4:15:41 (13,402)	
Riordan, Tony	4:31:35 (17,003)	
Ripley, Simon	4:23:51 (15,261)	
Ripley Jones, Scott	3:44:56 (6,670)	
Risby, Floyd	3:48:28 (7,353)	
Risby, Mark	5:13:36 (24,581)	
Riseley, Mark	3:05:27 (1,386)	
Risley, Michael	5:46:48 (27,687)	
Risse, Eberhard	4:52:07 (21,117)	
Rist, Peter	4:37:12 (18,172)	
Ritchie, Alan	4:49:21 (20,588)	
Ritchie, Alexander	3:56:15 (8,980)	
Ritchie, Graeme	4:01:49 (10,446)	
Ritchie, Graham	3:19:10 (2,667)	
Ritchie, Graham	5:44:26 (27,503)	
Ritchie, Keith	5:44:33 (27,526)	
Ritchie, Martin	4:48:36 (20,453)	
Ritchie, Terence	3:55:59 (8,915)	
Ritson, Martin	4:33:01 (17,313)	
Ritter, Daniel	3:47:56 (7,252)	
Rivenson, Gary	4:36:59 (18,124)	
Rivera-Gaxiola, Alonso	3:58:25 (9,588)	
Riverol, Kevin	4:00:08 (10,077)	
Rivers, Brian	3:18:56 (2,649)	
Rivers, Roderick	4:29:25 (16,610)	
Rivers, Sydney	4:29:26 (16,528)	
Rivers, Thomas	6:42:22 (29,697)	
Rivett, Andrew	4:52:56 (21,299)	
Rivett, Colin	4:29:49 (16,630)	
Rivett, Paul	4:57:56 (22,284)	
Rivlin, Richard	5:29:43 (26,348)	
Rivoire, Sylvan	4:07:26 (11,651)	
Rivola, Roberto	3:42:49 (6,272)	
Rix, Jonathan	2:55:16 (641)	
Rix, Russell	3:33:02 (4,608)	
Rixon, George	5:07:29 (23,695)	
Rixon, Paul	4:19:13 (14,165)	
Rixson, Michael	4:34:08 (17,564)	
Roach, John	4:09:24 (12,063)	
Roach, Michael	4:25:26 (15,599)	
Roach, Stephen	3:22:29 (3,053)	
Roach, Timothy	4:45:18 (19,823)	
Roach, William	3:55:02 (8,705)	
Roadley, Nicholas	4:07:44 (11,709)	
Robb, Andrew	3:44:19 (6,546)	
Robb, Ian	3:03:33 (1,250)	
Robbens, Tom	3:48:52 (7,433)	
Robbie, Simon	4:32:26 (17,201)	
Robbins, Jason	3:18:31 (2,601)	
Robbins, Jon	3:53:33 (8,391)	
Robbins, Keith	4:17:11 (13,716)	
Robbins, Mike	2:53:43 (570)	
Robe, Alec	4:42:40 (19,307)	
Roberson, Andrew	5:05:06 (23,305)	
Roberson, Nigel	3:40:26 (5,854)	
Robert, Franck	4:25:46 (15,667)	
Robert, Jean	3:20:26 (2,811)	
Roberts, Alan	3:27:19 (3,677)	
Roberts, Alan	4:22:07 (14,838)	
Roberts, Alan	4:35:55 (17,910)	
Roberts, Alan	4:59:32 (22,530)	
Roberts, Alfred	4:17:44 (13,822)	
Roberts, Alun	5:08:05 (23,780)	
Roberts, Andrew	4:58:55 (22,443)	
Roberts, Andrew	4:59:24 (22,513)	
Roberts, Anthony	3:57:35 (9,359)	
Roberts, Bernard	4:04:32 (11,001)	
Roberts, Brian	4:29:28 (16,537)	
Roberts, Charles	5:29:59 (26,377)	
Roberts, Chris	4:23:17 (15,127)	
Roberts, Colin	3:36:08 (5,095)	
Roberts, Craig	4:03:24 (10,747)	
Roberts, Dan	5:37:33 (26,983)	
Roberts, David	3:55:56 (8,901)	
Roberts, David	5:07:01 (23,618)	
Roberts, Duncan	4:56:36 (22,088)	
Roberts, Gerald	4:06:38 (11,473)	
Roberts, Ian Wynne	3:29:39 (4,111)	
Roberts, Ifor	3:53:54 (8,460)	
Roberts, James	5:07:13 (23,652)	
Roberts, Jamie	3:27:31 (3,713)	
Roberts, Jason	4:40:39 (18,911)	
Roberts, John	3:44:24 (6,562)	
Roberts, John	4:15:48 (13,423)	
Roberts, John	5:13:42 (24,596)	
Roberts, John	6:47:20 (29,763)	
Roberts, Kelvin	5:07:24 (23,682)	
Roberts, Lee	3:35:14 (4,939)	
Roberts, Lee	4:52:27 (21,194)	
Roberts, Malcolm	6:55:26 (29,891)	
Roberts, Mark	3:19:32 (2,709)	
Roberts, Mark	3:37:30 (5,336)	
Roberts, Mark	4:25:57 (15,718)	
Roberts, Mark	4:26:15 (15,795)	
Roberts, Matthew	4:46:22 (20,028)	
Roberts, Matthew	6:09:45 (28,849)	
Roberts, Michael	3:40:16 (5,825)	
Roberts, Michael	4:22:29 (14,924)	
Roberts, Mike	5:08:39 (23,879)	
Roberts, Nyn	4:24:09 (15,318)	
Roberts, Peter	3:21:41 (2,966)	
Roberts, Peter	3:57:44 (9,403)	
Roberts, Peter	4:40:41 (18,917)	
Roberts, Phillip	3:39:08 (5,596)	
Roberts, Raymond	3:50:34 (7,786)	
Roberts, Richard	3:29:34 (4,092)	
Roberts, Richard	3:34:36 (4,850)	
Roberts, Richard	4:27:31 (16,063)	
Roberts, Richard	5:34:37 (26,765)	
Roberts, Roy	4:52:15 (21,142)	
Roberts, Simon	3:14:29 (2,165)	
Roberts, Simon	4:03:11 (10,699)	
Roberts, Simon	4:22:43 (14,987)	
Roberts, Stephen	2:59:33 (983)	
Roberts, Stephen	3:03:03 (1,216)	
Roberts, Stephen	3:46:39 (6,983)	
Roberts, Stephen	3:54:34 (8,605)	

Roberts, Steve 3:34:04 (4,766)
Roberts, Tony 3:28:31 (3,911)
Roberts, Vincent 3:55:53 (8,889)
Roberts, William 3:51:03 (7,881)
Roberts, William 4:37:49 (18,320)
Roberts, William 5:52:48 (28,053)
Robertshaw, Andrew 2:40:57 (190)
Robertshaw, Iain 4:31:50 (17,069)
Robertshaw, Jason 3:43:28 (6,392)
Robertshaw, John 5:26:59 (26,082)
Robertson, David 4:12:02 (12,620)
Robertson, David 5:30:32 (26,415)
Robertson, Derek 4:16:02 (13,474)
Robertson, Giles 3:56:22 (9,013)
Robertson, Iain 3:02:31 (1,190)
Robertson, John 3:47:54 (7,241)
Robertson, Jon 4:31:06 (16,872)
Robertson, Lex 3:51:01 (7,877)
Robertson, Mark 4:59:04 (22,472)
Robertson, Mike 5:15:52 (24,920)
Robertson, Neil 5:40:48 (27,253)
Robertson, Peter 5:39:19 (27,117)
Robertson, Stephen 3:40:38 (5,887)
Robertson, William 4:35:06 (17,733)
Robie, Colin 4:24:42 (15,437)
Robinette, Christopher 5:03:38 (23,073)
Robins, Mark 5:46:45 (27,683)
Robins, Steven 3:24:18 (3,281)
Robinson, Andrew 4:29:16 (16,487)
Robinson, Anthony 3:48:24 (7,338)
Robinson, Anthony 4:14:17 (13,094)
Robinson, Ben 5:12:36 (24,443)
Robinson, Bjorn 3:31:00 (4,327)
Robinson, Brian 5:15:57 (24,924)
Robinson, Cecil 4:27:17 (16,025)
Robinson, Charles 4:04:30 (10,988)
Robinson, Clive 3:57:44 (9,403)
Robinson, Dale 3:58:13 (9,542)
Robinson, Dale 5:07:25 (23,684)
Robinson, Daniel 4:51:49 (21,058)
Robinson, Dave 5:04:26 (23,206)
Robinson, David 3:21:58 (2,991)
Robinson, David 4:07:33 (11,666)
Robinson, David 4:43:06 (19,404)
Robinson, Frank 6:26:18 (29,311)
Robinson, Geoff 3:56:07 (8,952)
Robinson, Geoffrey 2:41:52 (214)
Robinson, Geoffrey 4:38:59 (18,600)
Robinson, Gerald 4:33:37 (17,459)
Robinson, Giles 4:05:54 (11,320)
Robinson, Glenn 3:10:35 (1,798)
Robinson, Ian 4:15:30 (13,366)
Robinson, Jeff 5:01:09 (22,758)
Robinson, John 3:27:15 (3,665)
Robinson, John 6:10:29 (28,877)
Robinson, Jonathan 3:38:20 (5,453)
Robinson, Kelvin 4:37:27 (18,238)
Robinson, Kevin 3:52:15 (8,124)
Robinson, Lewis 5:18:01 (25,170)
Robinson, Mark 3:28:58 (3,991)
Robinson, Mark 4:40:56 (18,963)
Robinson, Mark 4:48:22 (20,420)
Robinson, Matthew 4:29:18 (16,500)
Robinson, Matthew 5:19:45 (25,341)
Robinson, Michael 3:19:54 (2,756)
Robinson, Michael 4:39:28 (18,683)
Robinson, Michael 5:52:51 (28,054)
Robinson, Nick 4:08:20 (11,833)
Robinson, Nigel 3:47:49 (7,213)
Robinson, Patrick 4:52:30 (21,206)
Robinson, Peter 3:19:13 (2,676)
Robinson, Peter 3:43:45 (6,449)
Robinson, Peter 4:28:11 (16,231)
Robinson, Peter 5:10:35 (24,163)
Robinson, Peter 5:50:42 (27,936)
Robinson, Phil 4:09:36 (12,093)
Robinson, Philip 3:53:08 (8,296)
Robinson, Roy 4:18:10 (13,910)
Robinson, Simon 3:38:14 (5,437)
Robinson, Simon 4:00:22 (10,123)
Robinson, Simon 4:37:51 (18,333)
Robinson, Simon 4:38:55 (18,589)
Robinson, Stephen 5:47:00 (27,703)
Robinson, Terry 5:07:36 (23,712)
Robinson, Thomas 5:07:31 (23,698)
Robinson, Thomas 5:26:13 (26,010)
Robinson, Timothy 4:14:45 (13,194)
Robinson, Toby 3:33:04 (4,616)
Robinson, Tom 4:50:09 (20,743)
Robinson, Trevor 5:14:27 (24,694)
Robson, Brian 4:04:21 (10,955)
Robson, Dave 4:24:51 (15,466)
Robson, Fred 5:00:03 (22,629)
Robson, George 3:47:52 (7,231)
Robson, Jonathan 4:30:41 (16,783)
Robson, Mark 3:42:15 (6,171)
Robson, Mark 4:25:49 (15,679)
Robson, Paul 4:48:10 (20,380)
Robson, Terrence 3:36:49 (5,211)
Roby, John 5:37:57 (27,015)
Rocco, Claudio 3:41:44 (6,079)
Roche, Desmond 3:30:28 (4,241)
Roche, Francis 4:49:47 (20,669)
Roche, James 4:15:13 (13,312)
Roche, Paul 3:57:32 (9,338)
Rochford, David 4:29:27 (16,534)
Rock, Daniel 5:45:50 (27,622)
Rock, Nigel 3:46:55 (7,022)
Rockliffe, Albert 3:19:51 (2,745)
Rockliffe, Graham 5:14:29 (24,701)
Rockliffe, Richard 4:20:45 (14,533)
Rockman, Jamie 5:20:53 (25,451)
Rocle, Domenico 4:17:54 (13,851)
Rocolle, Jean 4:36:55 (18,110)
Rodbert, Mark 5:59:40 (28,405)
Rodda, Philip 4:08:21 (11,837)
Roddie, Richard 4:43:29 (19,490)
Roddy, Royston 4:27:36 (16,090)
Rode, Paul 4:07:44 (11,709)
Rodenas, Fructuoso 3:34:25 (4,820)
Rodenas, Juan 2:39:41 (167)
Roderick, Mark 3:42:37 (6,238)
Roderick, Stephen 4:05:06 (11,138)
Rodger, Alan 5:04:32 (23,219)
Rodger, Edward 3:39:26 (5,660)
Rodger, Peter 3:08:08 (1,601)
Rodgers, James 2:44:09 (265)
Rodgers, John 3:38:11 (5,425)
Rodgers, John 3:55:57 (8,906)
Rodgers, Nigel 5:18:46 (25,246)
Rodgers, Sean 5:11:15 (24,248)
Rodi, Carlo 2:42:58 (238)
Rodrigues, Malcolm 6:31:49 (29,447)
Rodrigues, Pedro 3:33:37 (4,699)
Rodriguez, Marcio 4:20:20 (14,437)
Rodriguez, Marcos 5:02:24 (22,928)
Roduner, Daniel 3:48:28 (7,353)
Rodway, Anthony 4:12:47 (12,788)
Rodway, Fraser 4:28:25 (16,289)
Rodwell, Gordon 6:13:49 (28,987)
Rodwell, Patrik 3:26:13 (3,525)
Rodwell, Peter 3:43:00 (6,305)
Roe, David 3:30:18 (4,213)
Roe, John 4:17:23 (13,745)
Roe, Karl 5:05:44 (23,421)
Roedel, Bernd 4:53:18 (21,373)
Roedl, Christian 3:56:45 (9,121)
Roff, Keith 3:48:48 (7,423)
Roff, Neil 3:46:07 (6,881)
Roffey, David 4:01:35 (10,406)
Roger, Marcel 2:55:58 (679)
Roger, Simon 4:39:11 (18,634)
Roger, Verhulst 3:58:02 (9,497)
Rogers, Andrew 2:57:47 (798)
Rogers, Andrew 3:51:23 (7,942)
Rogers, Callan 4:38:14 (18,437)
Rogers, Christopher 4:18:53 (14,095)
Rogers, Colin 4:19:49 (14,318)
Rogers, David 4:18:20 (13,964)
Rogers, David 5:20:13 (25,377)
Rogers, Derek 3:00:18 (1,044)
Rogers, Edward 6:09:34 (28,838)
Rogers, Geoffrey 4:07:12 (11,588)
Rogers, Graham 5:39:38 (27,152)
Rogers, James 5:03:44 (23,087)
Rogers, Jeremy 3:14:46 (2,192)
Rogers, John 3:48:02 (7,271)
Rogers, John 4:42:55 (19,366)
Rogers, Matthew 5:44:53 (27,554)
Rogers, Patrick 4:40:25 (18,860)
Rogers, Paul 4:42:53 (19,359)
Rogers, Peter 3:50:55 (7,853)
Rogers, Phillip 2:58:27 (847)
Rogers, Scott 4:03:33 (10,789)
Rogers, Scott 4:05:21 (11,175)
Rogers, Stephen 3:22:23 (3,045)
Rogers, Stuart 4:11:15 (12,453)
Rogers, Stuart 5:16:35 (24,997)
Rogers, Terence 3:20:47 (2,862)
Rogers, Tim 5:12:23 (24,413)
Rogerson, Alan 3:35:43 (5,019)
Rogerson, Philip 4:09:03 (11,997)
Rogez, Jacques 4:06:10 (11,372)
Rohleder, Michael 3:49:45 (7,634)
Rohloff, Gray 4:01:17 (10,333)
Rohrlach, Greg 4:07:38 (11,684)
Rojas, Norberto 4:54:45 (21,660)
Roland, Lionel 3:27:42 (3,741)
Rolandi, Ivano 4:35:23 (17,795)
Rolfe, Alan 5:06:30 (23,544)
Rolfe, Michael 3:06:13 (1,436)
Rolfe, Michael 3:58:42 (9,674)
Rollett, Andy 5:30:13 (26,387)
Rollings, Adrian 2:51:36 (495)
Rollinson, Jason 4:48:04 (20,362)
Rollinson, Paul 4:40:37 (18,905)
Rollinson, Philip 3:13:27 (2,057)
Rollison, David 2:53:40 (566)
Rolls, Terence 4:27:41 (16,114)
Rolph, Trevor 4:56:45 (22,098)
Rolstone, Bill 5:45:48 (27,617)
Romain, Graeme 4:45:57 (19,929)
Romaneschi, Alberto 4:29:44 (16,607)
Romann, Christian 4:29:12 (16,472)
Romeo, Thomas 5:26:12 (26,005)
Romero, Antonio 3:36:06 (5,091)
Ronaldson, James 3:56:41 (9,101)
Ronayne, Patrick 4:28:54 (16,397)
Ronchini, Stefano 3:35:20 (4,961)
Rondet, Patrick 4:02:21 (10,539)
Rondi, Luigi 3:37:38 (5,355)
Ronga, Sergio 6:06:33 (28,703)
Ronnan, Andrew 5:13:20 (24,556)
Rook, John 3:55:42 (8,843)
Rooke, Anthony 5:18:13 (25,178)
Rooke, Mark 5:03:11 (23,029)
Rooney, John 3:43:07 (6,328)
Rooney, Tom 4:19:21 (14,209)
Root, Richard 5:09:00 (23,941)
Rootes, Bryan 4:37:38 (18,287)
Roots, Clive 3:23:27 (3,168)
Roper, Bevan 4:30:04 (16,704)
Roper, Ian 4:19:59 (14,361)
Roper, Pete 2:33:56 (82)
Roper Medhurst, Charles 5:39:34 (27,137)
Ropner, Robert 4:06:34 (11,464)
Roquebert, Laurent 3:38:28 (5,477)
Rorison, Philip 4:14:36 (13,148)
Rosall, Jeremy 3:51:54 (8,049)
Rosati, Davide 3:47:27 (7,130)
Rosbrook, Simon 4:03:54 (10,863)
Roscoe, Gregory 3:46:34 (6,963)
Rose, Adam 3:23:12 (3,136)
Rose, Alan 4:31:08 (16,883)
Rose, Alan 4:51:13 (20,926)
Rose, Darren 4:08:27 (11,862)
Rose, David 3:16:52 (2,409)
Rose, David 3:27:44 (3,751)
Rose, David 5:45:23 (27,582)
Rose, Dean 6:49:37 (29,799)
Rose, Kevin 4:09:11 (12,018)
Rose, Leslie 4:22:16 (14,877)
Rose, Martin 4:01:03 (10,292)
Rose, Nick 3:42:51 (6,276)
Rose, Nigel 4:38:06 (18,401)
Rose, Philip 4:15:15 (13,324)
Rose, Robert 6:05:22 (28,660)
Rose, Simon 3:36:22 (5,132)
Roseblade, John 4:27:52 (16,167)

Roseburgh, Laistair 4:18:43 (14,056)
Rosemeier, Frank 5:49:28 (27,869)
Rosen, Harold 5:27:54 (26,171)
Rosenbach, Jonathan 3:45:37 (6,769)
Rosenthal, Anthony 4:35:31 (17,815)
Rosenthal, Eric 3:49:47 (7,643)
Rosewell, David 4:53:31 (21,427)
Rosher, Paul 3:05:20 (1,377)
Rosier, Lee 4:16:39 (13,599)
Rosier, Serge 3:02:58 (1,210)
Rosier, Steven 3:24:12 (3,270)
Rosler, Michael 3:36:13 (5,107)
Rosman, Hans 3:53:00 (8,267)
Ross, Alexander 3:45:38 (6,776)
Ross, Andrew 4:20:31 (14,479)
Ross, Brian 4:06:11 (11,379)
Ross, Chris 3:26:03 (3,507)
Ross, David 4:15:24 (13,347)
Ross, David 5:14:33 (24,713)
Ross, Douglas 3:13:15 (2,033)
Ross, Innes 3:32:06 (4,481)
Ross, Jonathan 4:34:04 (17,547)
Ross, Paul 3:04:28 (1,310)
Ross, Peter 3:37:04 (5,256)
Ross, Richard 3:24:50 (3,358)
Ross, Richard 4:52:19 (21,164)
Ross, Stephen 2:34:15 (85)
Ross, Stephen 5:13:19 (24,553)
Ross McNairn, Jonathon 5:00:38 (22,681)
Rossborough, Keith 4:13:07 (12,843)
Rossborough, Paul Anthony 4:33:18 (17,368)
Rosser, David 4:39:48 (18,753)
Rossetti, Giuseppe 3:47:39 (7,179)
Rossi, Daniele 3:35:07 (4,922)
Rossi, Guiseppe 7:08:00 (30,007)
Rossiter, Christopher 4:23:26 (15,155)
Rossiter, John 3:46:05 (6,873)
Rossiter, John 4:47:31 (20,267)
Rossiter, Philippe 4:27:45 (16,135)
Rossiter, Scott 4:22:35 (14,948)
Rossmann, Markus 3:14:08 (2,131)
Rossor, Martin 4:48:31 (20,441)
Rossor, Thomas 4:48:31 (20,441)
Rossouw, François 3:59:51 (10,010)
Rostaine, Alexandre 3:48:36 (7,379)
Rostern, Paul 3:01:02 (1,085)
Rota, Fabrizio 3:56:23 (9,018)
Rota, Yvon 3:24:14 (3,274)
Roth, Christian 4:23:41 (15,224)
Roth, Jakob 2:58:43 (894)
Rothery, Mark 3:46:35 (6,968)
Rothwell, Alan 3:33:47 (4,726)
Rottenburg, Alexander 5:23:48 (25,770)
Rottgen, Raphael 4:05:57 (11,339)
Roughan, Barry 5:08:59 (23,940)
Roughsedge, Peter 5:10:30 (24,142)
Roulstone, John 4:11:51 (12,580)
Roumelian, Olivier 3:31:09 (4,349)
Rounce, Phillip 4:46:05 (19,954)
Round, Anton 5:02:51 (22,984)
Round, Simon 3:51:14 (7,917)
Rouse, Adam 2:59:55 (1,020)
Rouse, Andrew 4:19:00 (14,115)
Rouse, Anthony 4:20:50 (14,556)
Rouse, Christopher 3:45:57 (6,847)
Rouse, Stephen 3:34:17 (4,798)
Rousell, Michael 3:55:49 (8,877)
Rousewell, Dean 4:37:09 (18,158)
Rout, Russell 3:10:28 (1,792)
Routh, Alan 4:53:21 (21,388)
Routier, Philippe 3:13:00 (2,003)
Routledge, Calvin 2:53:06 (547)
Routledge, George 5:56:22 (28,231)
Routley, Nathan 3:55:20 (8,767)
Routurou, Herve 3:47:37 (7,167)
Roux, Michel 3:13:52 (2,097)
Roux, Michel 5:52:26 (28,036)
Rouxel, Philippe 3:05:12 (1,367)
Row, Paul 3:57:09 (9,210)
Rowbotham, Mark 3:31:45 (4,428)
Rowe, Alex 2:34:08 (84)
Rowe, Christopher 3:35:00 (4,904)
Rowe, Christopher 7:10:17 (30,020)
Rowe, Clive 6:09:26 (28,831)
Rowe, Colin 4:53:19 (21,378)
Rowe, David 4:58:38 (22,401)
Rowe, James 5:27:03 (26,085)
Rowe, John 3:41:22 (6,023)
Rowe, John 6:00:44 (28,443)
Rowe, Martin 3:46:15 (6,905)
Rowe, Paul 3:51:45 (8,015)
Rowe, Simon 4:45:12 (19,808)
Rowe, Stephen 4:24:13 (15,334)
Rowell, Alan 3:13:23 (2,049)
Rowell, Barry 4:24:43 (15,443)
Rowell, Chris 5:01:29 (22,803)
Rowell, Steve 5:28:37 (26,243)
Roweth, Stephen 3:26:28 (3,555)
Rowland, Andrew 2:42:36 (227)
Rowland, Andrew 3:44:38 (6,601)
Rowland, Gareth 5:28:02 (26,185)
Rowland, Gary 4:36:00 (17,932)
Rowland, John 5:26:44 (26,065)
Rowland, Mark 4:30:22 (16,738)
Rowland, Michael 4:28:32 (16,321)
Rowland, Michael 5:29:22 (26,326)
Rowland, Nicholas 3:47:35 (7,161)
Rowland, Paul 4:41:07 (18,998)
Rowland, Robert 3:37:19 (5,305)
Rowland, Stewart 5:46:58 (27,702)
Rowlands, Anthony 3:35:47 (5,029)
Rowlands, Clive 3:27:40 (3,735)
Rowlands, Colin 5:32:47 (26,599)
Rowlands, Gwyndaf 3:48:16 (7,316)
Rowlands, Peter 4:10:56 (12,387)
Rowlands, Peter 5:03:22 (23,049)
Rowles, Raymond 4:07:44 (11,709)
Rowley, Alex 5:48:19 (27,801)
Rowley, Alistair 4:05:58 (11,347)
Rowley, Christopher 4:25:27 (15,602)
Rowley, Martin 3:38:17 (5,445)
Rowley, Nicholas 4:36:16 (17,967)
Rowley, Ronan 3:57:38 (9,379)
Rowntree, Matt 4:32:51 (17,285)
Rowsell, David 4:27:01 (15,971)
Rowson, Andrew 3:51:38 (7,993)
Roy, Robin 3:56:30 (9,057)
Roy, Steve 4:50:48 (20,843)
Royall, Paul 3:28:15 (3,855)
Royan, Mark 4:03:17 (10,718)
Royde, Matthew 3:59:44 (9,984)
Royden, Barry 2:19:31 (22)
Royle, Simon 4:23:41 (15,224)
Royston, Josh 3:51:14 (7,917)
Rozental, Steven 5:34:53 (26,796)
Ruane, Anthony 4:49:07 (20,547)
Ruarc, Gianni 4:10:33 (12,284)
Rubenstein, Brian 4:41:34 (19,077)
Rubini, Adriano 3:57:37 (9,369)
Rubino, Jack 4:48:00 (20,345)
Rubins, Joe 4:54:29 (21,587)
Rucinski, Andrzej 3:14:44 (2,187)
Rucker, Edward 3:46:42 (6,990)
Rudd, Andrew 4:08:37 (11,896)
Rudd, Bevna 5:16:01 (24,928)
Rudd, Michael 3:55:40 (8,834)
Ruddick, Jules 5:01:02 (22,738)
Ruddick, Matthew 4:26:26 (15,828)
Ruddick, Michael 3:26:32 (3,561)
Rudge, Adrian 4:34:03 (17,544)
Rudge, Andrew 4:21:36 (14,714)
Rudge, Laurence 2:55:59 (681)
Rudman, Phil 3:42:08 (6,145)
Rudrof, Thomas 3:16:27 (2,359)
Rudrum, Martyn 5:43:17 (27,424)
Ruef, Reinhold 3:01:36 (1,122)
Ruell, Christopher 3:49:58 (7,680)
Ruff, Keith 3:35:40 (5,014)
Ruffell, Richard 3:21:09 (2,901)
Rufus, Renato 5:41:17 (27,275)
Rugg, John 5:05:36 (23,402)
Rugg, Richard 3:57:46 (9,416)
Rugg, Tom 4:05:27 (11,197)
Rugg-Easey, Paul 4:41:16 (19,025)
Ruggles, Bruce 4:33:29 (17,414)
Ruia, Alok 3:45:51 (6,833)
Ruia, Sunil 5:01:04 (22,741)
Ruisinger, Helmut 3:41:03 (5,967)
Ruiz De Sa, Daniel 3:04:53 (1,340)
Rule, Matthew 3:14:21 (2,153)
Rulten, Brian 5:36:55 (26,938)
Rumble, John 3:30:33 (4,256)
Rumbles, Charles 4:12:50 (12,797)
Rumblow, John 4:52:27 (21,194)
Rumbold, Keith 3:50:24 (7,757)
Rumsey, James 3:58:16 (9,557)
Runacres, Mark 4:08:37 (11,896)
Rundin, Ake 4:24:59 (15,501)
Rundle, Michael 3:48:15 (7,312)
Rundle, Richard 4:52:14 (21,138)
Rundle, Simon 3:41:51 (6,101)
Ruocco, Christian 6:19:50 (29,155)
Ruocco, Christopher 5:38:08 (27,028)
Ruparelia, Milan 5:34:21 (26,739)
Rupp, Wayne 6:35:43 (29,540)
Ruprecht, Hans 4:09:17 (12,039)
Rusci, Sergio 4:00:07 (10,075)
Ruscoe, Matthew 4:48:53 (20,500)
Ruscoe Icke, Andrew 4:38:38 (18,534)
Rushton, Paul 4:24:20 (15,356)
Rushworth, Hamish 5:14:22 (24,684)
Rushworth, Paul 3:20:12 (2,784)
Rusling, Guy 5:00:59 (22,732)
Russell, Andrew 3:54:23 (8,559)
Russell, Brian 3:07:55 (1,584)
Russell, Brian 4:50:57 (20,870)
Russell, Charles 5:59:39 (28,401)
Russell, Darren 4:06:39 (11,476)
Russell, David 3:50:03 (7,695)
Russell, David 3:51:11 (7,909)
Russell, David 4:58:44 (22,419)
Russell, Gerard 3:27:35 (3,721)
Russell, Graham 4:20:37 (14,503)
Russell, Guy 4:24:57 (15,491)
Russell, Ian 2:44:31 (276)
Russell, Ian 4:27:33 (16,075)
Russell, John 3:29:11 (4,025)
Russell, John 4:41:34 (19,077)
Russell, Jonathan 3:51:30 (7,966)
Russell, Kelvin 3:02:02 (1,154)
Russell, Malcolm 4:52:53 (21,287)
Russell, Mark 3:31:58 (4,463)
Russell, Michael 3:59:05 (9,781)
Russell, Mike 3:07:50 (1,577)
Russell, Mike 3:42:09 (6,151)
Russell, Niall 4:39:49 (18,754)
Russell, Nic 2:39:51 (168)
Russell, Nigel 2:48:28 (376)
Russell, Paul 6:04:19 (28,606)
Russell, Peter 4:13:47 (12,995)
Russell, Philip 3:45:57 (6,847)
Russell, Philip 4:57:57 (22,286)
Russell, Phillip 4:14:45 (13,194)
Russell, Shaune 2:58:37 (873)
Russell, Stephen 3:26:16 (3,532)
Russell, Tony 4:07:41 (11,692)
Russell Rickards, Tony 7:32:28 (30,145)
Rust, James 2:57:05 (750)
Ruston, Chad 5:09:02 (23,948)
Ruston, Christopher 4:34:17 (17,591)
Ruston, Howard 4:51:46 (21,048)
Ruston, Michael 6:13:31 (28,977)
Rustrick, Sean 4:05:26 (11,191)
Rutherford, David 4:03:35 (10,797)
Rutherford, Peter 4:58:30 (22,376)
Rutherford, Stewart 4:02:09 (10,514)
Rutland, Ashley 5:23:32 (25,749)
Rutledge, Alan 3:33:01 (4,606)
Rutter, Bill 4:55:28 (21,878)
Rutter, John 2:58:35 (869)
Rutter, Mark 5:12:32 (24,434)
Rutter, Neil 5:40:04 (27,194)
Rutter, Nick 4:08:13 (11,808)
Ruwiel, Bastien 3:24:33 (3,320)
Ruxton, David 4:23:32 (15,184)
Ruzewicz, Raymond 4:14:39 (13,158)
Ryall, Jeremy 3:41:39 (6,067)
Ryall, John 3:56:42 (9,108)
Ryan, Alan 5:59:08 (28,373)

Ryan, Angus.................4:48:44 (20,475)
Ryan, Anthony.................3:12:13 (1,934)
Ryan, Christopher.................4:19:27 (14,241)
Ryan, Ciaran.................5:10:40 (24,172)
Ryan, Graham.................3:04:15 (1,299)
Ryan, James.................5:16:01 (24,928)
Ryan, Joe.................3:50:59 (7,867)
Ryan, John.................4:15:40 (13,398)
Ryan, John Joseph.................2:42:56 (236)
Ryan, Kendall.................3:59:15 (9,832)
Ryan, Lee.................4:36:35 (18,037)
Ryan, Michael.................3:51:13 (7,914)
Ryan, Michael.................4:34:04 (17,547)
Ryan, Michael.................4:36:52 (18,097)
Ryan, Paul.................4:29:28 (16,537)
Ryan, Richard.................4:00:24 (10,130)
Ryan, Sean.................5:24:16 (25,814)
Ryczanowski, David.................4:14:53 (13,231)
Ryder, David.................3:39:11 (5,607)
Ryder, Dele.................4:11:07 (12,421)
Rylance, Tom.................4:28:30 (16,314)
Ryles, David.................4:36:17 (17,973)
Rymes, Leslie.................4:53:58 (21,505)
Ryvell, James.................7:18:03 (30,070)
Sabah, Ahmet.................5:49:17 (27,859)
Sabatino, Anthony.................5:05:15 (23,332)
Sabiston, Andrew.................5:12:38 (24,450)
Saby Kuchler, Nicolas.................4:00:13 (10,092)
Sacarello, Craig.................4:54:46 (21,665)
Sacares, Peter.................3:27:29 (3,704)
Saccoh, Teddy.................3:55:43 (8,848)
Sacher, Gregory.................5:30:44 (26,431)
Sachs, Fred.................4:55:03 (21,749)
Sacks, Daniel.................4:01:16 (10,330)
Sacmons, Johnny.................5:25:27 (25,936)
Sadler, Benjamin.................5:26:40 (26,057)
Sadler, Dexter.................4:13:34 (12,949)
Sadler, Kevin.................2:51:53 (510)
Sadler, Matthew.................6:05:24 (28,661)
Sadler, Philip.................3:45:28 (6,739)
Sadler, Phillip.................4:28:11 (16,231)
Sadler, Richard.................4:23:40 (15,221)
Sadoun, Bertrand.................3:15:50 (2,298)
Sadrian, Luke.................3:32:16 (4,503)
Saebdal, Sverre.................2:58:00 (813)
Saebi, Payman.................4:01:44 (10,434)
Sagal, David.................5:50:39 (27,931)
Sager, Richard.................3:28:12 (3,844)
Sagis, Joe.................5:47:38 (27,732)
Sahota, Kalbir.................4:48:09 (20,377)
Sahwcroft, Graham.................3:40:26 (5,854)
Said, Gidon.................3:36:12 (5,106)
Sainsbury, Derek.................4:14:55 (13,239)
Saint, Steven.................3:45:43 (6,802)
Saint, Tim.................5:40:01 (27,189)
Sairlao, Boonhark.................3:43:56 (6,477)
Saito, Takao.................3:34:23 (4,814)
Saker, Matthew.................3:31:01 (4,331)
Sakho, David.................6:10:15 (28,868)
Sakurada, Seiji.................4:37:37 (18,282)
Salaets, Marc.................3:12:23 (1,951)
Saldarini, Matteo.................3:15:07 (2,235)
Sale, Andrew.................4:26:33 (15,856)
Sale, Graham.................4:34:16 (17,588)
Sale, Stewart.................4:21:49 (14,766)
Salem, Paul.................4:23:28 (15,165)
Salih, Mustafa.................3:13:33 (2,064)
Salih, Salih.................4:37:59 (18,365)
Salisbury, Carl.................3:52:51 (8,238)
Salisbury, Martin.................3:30:50 (4,298)
Salisbury, Martin.................4:06:19 (11,411)
Salisbury, Martin.................4:15:12 (13,308)
Sallespupo, Carlos Alberto.................3:29:34 (4,092)
Sallis, Roger.................3:33:25 (4,677)
Salman, Bilal.................5:35:04 (26,811)
Salmon, Allen.................4:36:58 (18,120)
Salmon, Andrew.................3:54:30 (8,587)
Salmon, Geoffrey.................3:26:35 (3,570)
Salmon, Ian.................5:40:43 (27,247)
Salmon, Philip.................4:40:54 (18,956)
Salmon, Spencer.................4:20:09 (14,397)
Salmon, Terence.................4:56:12 (22,024)
Salsbury, Brendan.................4:08:25 (11,853)

Salt, Bruce.................4:19:23 (14,220)
Salt, Philip.................4:00:10 (10,081)
Salter, Christopher.................4:23:27 (15,163)
Salter, Dennis.................3:43:42 (6,437)
Salter, Neil.................4:58:14 (22,332)
Salter, Peter.................4:11:12 (12,440)
Saltrick, Chris.................3:45:35 (6,761)
Salvadori, Renzo.................3:25:20 (3,422)
Salvage, Ross.................4:21:48 (14,761)
Salway, Eric.................4:49:30 (20,618)
Sambrook, Stuart.................3:23:48 (3,210)
Sammut, Emanuel.................4:42:25 (19,255)
Sampson, Alan.................4:20:47 (14,543)
Sampson, Richard.................7:49:15 (30,186)
Samra, Parminderjit.................5:10:13 (24,108)
Samuel, Mark.................4:02:35 (10,590)
Samuel, Nicolas.................4:16:42 (13,609)
Samuels, Emlyn.................4:35:50 (17,887)
Samuels, Gavin.................5:02:02 (22,880)
Sanassy, Shane.................4:11:10 (12,431)
Sanchez, Daniel.................4:08:33 (11,880)
Sanchez, Francisco.................3:10:22 (1,786)
Sanchez, José.................4:52:11 (21,133)
Sanchez Carrasco, Omar.................3:08:18 (1,615)
Sanchez Carrasco, Richard.................3:17:26 (2,479)
Sancto, David.................3:39:55 (5,762)
Sandall, Michael.................5:01:32 (22,808)
Sanday, John.................3:56:58 (9,169)
Sandercombe, Robert.................3:47:34 (7,159)
Sanders, Adrian.................4:05:32 (11,223)
Sanders, Andrew.................3:44:00 (6,494)
Sanders, Brian.................4:57:47 (22,264)
Sanders, Charles.................3:20:17 (2,791)
Sanders, David.................3:41:49 (6,096)
Sanders, David.................3:50:06 (7,707)
Sanders, Eddie.................3:20:04 (2,772)
Sanders, Johan.................3:49:39 (7,614)
Sanders, Kevin.................3:26:59 (3,621)
Sanders, Neil.................4:01:17 (10,333)
Sanders, Stephen.................5:52:06 (28,022)
Sanders, Steve.................3:55:13 (8,738)
Sanderson, Andrew.................4:19:58 (14,355)
Sanderson, Brian.................3:49:00 (7,465)
Sanderson, Daniel.................3:28:32 (3,916)
Sanderson, David.................4:30:00 (16,696)
Sanderson, Dennis.................4:11:45 (12,561)
Sanderson, Gavin.................4:40:57 (18,967)
Sanderson, Laurie.................3:10:56 (1,831)
Sanderson, Neil.................4:34:29 (17,623)
Sanderson, Paul.................2:51:23 (483)
Sandford, Noel.................4:19:32 (14,264)
Sandford, Peter.................2:57:52 (805)
Sandhu, John.................5:11:20 (24,259)
Sandhu, Kanwarjit.................4:42:47 (19,326)
Sandmann, Hans.................4:11:53 (12,587)
Sandre, Stefano.................3:15:17 (2,253)
Sands, David.................3:25:51 (3,486)
Sands, Leslie.................4:53:30 (21,419)
Sands, Peter.................3:23:46 (3,207)
Sanghera, Jas.................4:20:17 (14,427)
Sanghera, Kirn.................3:55:50 (8,879)
Sangster, Lee.................5:04:58 (23,291)
Sanham, Robert.................4:25:14 (15,563)
Sanna, Julio.................3:10:36 (1,800)
Sanna, Ruggero.................4:40:08 (18,808)
Sansom, Howard.................4:06:09 (11,369)
Sansom, Matthew.................4:41:57 (19,153)
Santesson, Kjell.................4:19:45 (14,305)
Santos Rodrigues, Armindo G.....3:58:39 (9,658)
Saouli, Mohammed Mood.........4:34:13 (17,573)
Sapjenza, David.................3:13:53 (2,101)
Sapsard, Paul.................2:58:59 (933)
Sarad, Peter.................3:54:03 (8,487)
Saratain, John.................4:01:59 (10,482)
Sardat, Gianni.................3:29:54 (4,150)
Sarell, Will.................4:12:13 (12,674)
Sargeant, David.................4:32:14 (17,163)
Sargeant, Robert.................2:58:25 (846)
Sargeant, Scott.................5:26:56 (26,080)
Sargeant, Stephen.................3:30:56 (4,320)
Sargent, Peter.................2:58:45 (902)
Sargent, Steve.................4:02:43 (10,614)
Sarney, Andrew.................3:44:51 (6,650)

Sarosi, Adrian.................4:03:22 (10,740)
Sarson, Peter.................2:59:43 (999)
Sarvari, Daniel.................3:54:16 (8,527)
Sassone, Joseph.................4:07:07 (11,572)
Satchell, Peter.................4:00:02 (10,064)
Sauer, Ulrich.................3:57:32 (9,338)
Saund, Pritpal.................4:56:51 (22,116)
Saunders, Andrew.................4:58:23 (22,357)
Saunders, Dennis.................4:11:43 (12,552)
Saunders, Gavin.................4:14:11 (13,072)
Saunders, Gavin.................5:35:27 (26,838)
Saunders, Graham.................3:57:25 (9,300)
Saunders, Jeffrey.................5:22:44 (25,679)
Saunders, Jody.................4:43:33 (19,508)
Saunders, John.................3:16:25 (2,354)
Saunders, John.................4:22:55 (15,039)
Saunders, Linda.................6:15:57 (29,058)
Saunders, Martin.................4:42:18 (19,226)
Saunders, Peter.................3:33:45 (4,723)
Saunders, Stephen.................3:54:33 (8,601)
Saunders, Stephen.................4:27:41 (16,114)
Saunders, Stephen.................5:31:15 (26,473)
Saunders, Steven.................4:09:51 (12,134)
Sautereau, Laurent.................4:00:53 (10,259)
Sauvary, Kelvyn.................4:55:17 (21,810)
Saux, Christophe.................3:49:01 (7,467)
Savage, Damien.................4:43:49 (19,561)
Savage, Harry.................6:04:49 (28,636)
Savage, Kevin.................4:58:17 (22,340)
Savage, Michael.................4:02:20 (10,535)
Savage, Richard.................4:25:52 (15,694)
Savage, Tom.................3:44:08 (6,517)
Savariaux, Martial.................3:49:29 (7,574)
Savary, Daniel.................4:16:24 (13,552)
Savell-Boss, Ashley.................4:52:23 (21,180)
Savidge, Paul.................4:12:45 (12,781)
Savill, Peter.................5:15:11 (24,831)
Saville, Kevin.................3:58:26 (9,592)
Saville, Philip.................4:06:15 (11,397)
Savin, David.................3:57:57 (9,478)
Savvides, Andreas.................4:39:29 (18,690)
Sawer, Martin.................3:12:28 (1,957)
Sawyer, David.................4:30:01 (16,697)
Sawyer, John.................3:46:25 (6,935)
Sawyer, Jonathan.................4:01:12 (10,319)
Sawyer, Keith.................3:16:32 (2,374)
Sawyer, Michael.................4:02:51 (10,632)
Sawyer, Perry.................3:33:00 (4,601)
Sawyer, Robert.................3:30:20 (4,219)
Sawyer, Steve.................4:26:44 (15,895)
Saxelby, Jai.................3:11:23 (1,860)
Saxton, Gary.................5:11:12 (24,244)
Sayer, Daniel.................5:21:46 (25,559)
Sayer, John.................4:00:20 (10,113)
Sayer, Malcolm.................4:07:24 (11,639)
Sayer, Timothy.................5:11:53 (24,341)
Sayers, Brian.................5:45:12 (27,573)
Sayers, Paul.................3:25:41 (3,463)
Sayers, Robert.................3:52:48 (8,230)
Sayers, Roderick.................4:29:05 (16,445)
Sayers, Victor.................3:07:31 (1,545)
Sayle, Alan.................5:32:05 (26,539)
Sayle, Mark.................5:32:05 (26,539)
Scadding, John.................3:47:18 (7,085)
Scaglianti, Marco.................4:31:55 (17,095)
Scaglioni, Francesco.................4:16:20 (13,529)
Scaife, Paul.................5:55:18 (28,169)
Scaini, Pietro.................4:57:54 (22,281)
Scales, Robin.................3:48:43 (7,406)
Scally, Mark.................4:27:05 (15,994)
Scamell, Colin.................4:24:01 (15,298)
Scammell, Neil.................4:25:22 (15,587)
Scanlon, Bernard.................4:52:15 (21,142)
Scanlon, Christopher.................5:14:09 (24,648)
Scanlon, Paul.................4:20:32 (14,483)
Scarlett, Iain.................5:29:14 (26,313)
Scarrott, Martin.................4:50:29 (20,800)
Scase, Douglas.................4:36:52 (18,097)
Schaag, Stuart.................3:21:24 (2,935)
Schab, Karl.................5:06:00 (23,469)
Schaebernack, Klaus.................4:13:41 (12,978)
Schaldenbrandt, Jean-Jacques.....4:09:23 (12,061)
Schauber, René.................3:45:47 (6,820)

Schaufelberger, Werner	4:07:26 (11,651)	
Schaufler, Alfred	3:40:02 (5,793)	
Scheer, Michael	4:15:28 (13,361)	
Scheiber, Stefan	4:24:10 (15,324)	
Schembri, Mark	4:04:51 (11,077)	
Schemkes, Frank	3:39:46 (5,731)	
Schenk, Guido	5:11:40 (24,307)	
Schertzer, Bernard	3:17:25 (2,476)	
Scheunemann, Andreas	4:56:48 (22,108)	
Schifand, Fabrizio	4:56:55 (22,131)	
Schillinger, Alois	4:37:07 (18,150)	
Schindlegger, Harald	5:47:40 (27,736)	
Schirmar, Jobst Christoph	4:09:00 (11,978)	
Schlaefice, Dieter	4:17:10 (13,708)	
Schlecht, Johann	4:23:11 (15,105)	
Schlorholtz, Mike	3:13:08 (2,017)	
Schmaler, Andreas	3:58:30 (9,604)	
Schmetzer, Paulo	4:43:53 (19,572)	
Schmid, Andreas	4:23:30 (15,172)	
Schmid, Paul	5:10:00 (24,081)	
Schmider, Patrick	5:06:55 (23,603)	
Schmidt, Andrew	4:09:56 (12,147)	
Schmidt, Frank	4:37:19 (18,200)	
Schmidt, Ingo	4:36:19 (17,978)	
Schmidt, Udo	4:15:12 (13,308)	
Schmied, Walter	3:33:17 (4,658)	
Schmitt, Bruno	3:58:55 (9,726)	
Schmitz, Herbert	4:05:00 (11,118)	
Schmitz, Johannes	5:10:32 (24,152)	
Schmitz, Thomas	4:15:51 (13,434)	
Schneider, Daniel	3:47:40 (7,185)	
Schneider, Karl	5:27:41 (26,148)	
Schneider, Nick	5:39:05 (27,092)	
Schnetzer, Markus	3:46:09 (6,888)	
Schnkel, Alan	3:59:15 (9,832)	
Schnuriger, Murray	3:18:56 (2,649)	
Schoass, Helmut	5:32:21 (26,554)	
Schoenle, Michael	3:32:00 (4,470)	
Schoenmakers, Ronald	3:09:29 (1,710)	
Schofield, Adam	4:24:13 (15,334)	
Schofield, Alan	3:40:46 (5,907)	
Schofield, Darren	4:52:15 (21,142)	
Schofield, David	4:23:28 (15,165)	
Schofield, Graham	3:33:18 (4,660)	
Schofield, Mark	3:14:45 (2,189)	
Schofield, Mark	5:11:50 (24,333)	
Schofield, Michael	4:40:31 (18,877)	
Schofield, Paul	3:27:17 (3,672)	
Schofield, Robert	5:05:02 (23,297)	
Schogger, Stephen	5:26:23 (26,031)	
Schokman, Tony	5:09:23 (23,995)	
Scholes, David	4:13:27 (12,921)	
Scholes, George	4:12:18 (12,693)	
Scholes, Graham	4:33:40 (17,470)	
Scholey, Nigel	4:39:43 (18,736)	
Scholz, Jurgen	3:18:55 (2,646)	
Schorr, Stefan	4:10:33 (12,284)	
Schott, Patrick	3:34:38 (4,854)	
Schoumacker, Marcel	4:16:20 (13,529)	
Schoy, Rolf	3:05:44 (1,404)	
Schrade, Kurt	3:48:16 (7,316)	
Schray, Joseph	3:53:44 (8,430)	
Schroder, David	5:16:43 (25,014)	
Schroder, Robert	4:33:28 (17,410)	
Schroer, Thorsten	3:53:58 (8,471)	
Schuchter, David	4:49:05 (20,540)	
Schuett, Walter	4:25:54 (15,702)	
Schulz Meentzen, Markus	3:33:31 (4,689)	
Schumacher, Michael	4:51:32 (20,991)	
Schwalm, Daniel	3:54:36 (8,614)	
Schwalm, Mark	4:53:22 (21,393)	
Schwartz, Larry	4:31:49 (17,062)	
Schwartz, Serge	4:37:19 (18,200)	
Schwarz, David	5:45:29 (27,589)	
Schwarz, Ernst	6:40:19 (29,652)	
Sclater, James	4:42:27 (19,264)	
Scogings, Andrew	3:01:00 (1,084)	
Scollick, Craig	3:47:43 (7,196)	
Scoones, Eric	3:29:15 (4,036)	
Scorer, Mark	4:28:25 (16,289)	
Scotcher, David	3:44:26 (6,565)	
Scotchmer, Daniel	6:08:27 (28,786)	
Scott, Alan	4:53:25 (21,402)	

Scott, Alan	5:23:30 (25,747)
Scott, Andrew	3:33:06 (4,622)
Scott, Andrew	3:47:13 (7,068)
Scott, Angus	4:29:51 (16,642)
Scott, Brian	5:22:30 (25,647)
Scott, Brough	3:59:32 (9,931)
Scott, Crispin	3:09:30 (1,713)
Scott, Danny	2:53:58 (578)
Scott, David	3:02:50 (1,203)
Scott, Douglas	3:13:57 (2,110)
Scott, Finlay	5:13:13 (24,535)
Scott, Gary	5:14:45 (24,745)
Scott, Ian	3:56:20 (9,004)
Scott, James	5:45:46 (27,613)
Scott, Jason	4:31:17 (16,927)
Scott, John	4:00:06 (10,073)
Scott, Jonathan	5:49:56 (27,898)
Scott, Kenneth	3:58:48 (9,700)
Scott, Malcolm	3:54:24 (8,562)
Scott, Martin	4:29:46 (16,614)
Scott, Martyn	4:39:57 (18,777)
Scott, Matthew	4:36:29 (18,017)
Scott, Michael	4:57:07 (22,158)
Scott, Mike	2:39:54 (171)
Scott, Mike	5:04:49 (23,268)
Scott, Paul	4:19:13 (14,165)
Scott, Paul	4:26:25 (15,824)
Scott, Richard	4:23:17 (15,127)
Scott, Richard	4:28:09 (16,221)
Scott, Robert	3:59:49 (10,002)
Scott, Robert	4:38:41 (18,544)
Scott, Robin	2:59:52 (1,012)
Scott, Ryan	4:02:12 (10,523)
Scott, Simon	4:19:05 (14,143)
Scott, Simon	4:22:35 (14,948)
Scott, Tim	4:38:04 (18,389)
Scott, William	3:43:17 (6,357)
Scott, William	3:47:12 (7,064)
Scott-Kennedy, Andrew	4:03:30 (10,774)
Scragg, Mark	3:12:38 (1,972)
Scragg, Terence	5:05:22 (23,353)
Scrini, Alex	3:55:48 (8,870)
Scriven, Marcos	3:12:08 (1,925)
Scrivener, Paul	3:29:57 (4,163)
Scrivener, Peter	5:08:36 (23,869)
Scroggins, Jay	4:19:07 (14,150)
Scruton, Neil	2:49:20 (404)
Scrutton, Mark	4:40:23 (18,853)
Scudds, Paul	4:10:06 (12,179)
Scully, Steve	5:12:44 (24,462)
Scully, Wayne	4:33:07 (17,329)
Scutt, Alan	4:53:01 (21,318)
Scutt, Frank	4:33:20 (17,378)
Scutt, Nigel	5:31:36 (26,497)
Seabrook, James	4:44:22 (19,647)
Seabrook, Joe	3:59:02 (9,765)
Seabrook, Mark	3:29:32 (4,086)
Seaden Jones, Peter	4:21:28 (14,685)
Seager, Andrew	4:08:19 (11,827)
Seager, Neil	5:12:44 (24,462)
Seager, Neil	4:14:42 (13,173)
Seager, Timothy	5:52:33 (28,040)
Seagrove, Stephen	3:46:05 (6,873)
Seal, Michael	6:49:21 (29,794)
Seale, Gavin	4:55:00 (21,765)
Sealey, Jon	4:52:53 (21,287)
Sealey, Robert	5:01:00 (22,734)
Seaman, Stuart	5:02:46 (22,971)
Seamark, Jamie	3:38:38 (5,507)
Seamons, Peter	5:55:34 (28,196)
Searight, James	4:35:57 (17,920)
Searle, Alan	4:55:15 (21,798)
Searle, Alastair	4:51:27 (20,979)
Searle, Peter	3:30:31 (4,249)
Seaton, Steven	4:00:31 (10,158)
Sechi, Salvatore	3:22:36 (3,063)
Secker, Jamie	3:03:45 (1,267)
Secker, Russell	3:29:37 (4,102)
Secli, Stefano	3:30:17 (4,211)
Seddon, Alfred	5:00:21 (22,651)
Seddon, Kirk	4:39:00 (18,603)
Seddon, Mike	4:27:33 (16,075)
Sedgley, Trevor	4:31:02 (16,858)

Sedgwick, Keith	4:27:12 (16,011)
Sedgwick, Stephen	3:44:07 (6,514)
Sedgwick, Stephen	4:12:37 (12,757)
Sedman, Lindon	4:46:55 (20,151)
Sedman, Nigel	3:35:10 (4,927)
Seed, Jeremy	3:56:15 (8,980)
Seel, Olaf	4:10:45 (12,321)
Seelandt, Frank	3:24:14 (3,274)
Sefton, Paul	3:41:34 (6,044)
Segal, Eliezer	4:44:23 (19,652)
Segall, Michael	7:47:36 (30,183)
Segebart, Dieter	3:32:56 (4,591)
Seheult, Allan	4:08:58 (11,971)
Seifert, Guenther	5:11:40 (24,307)
Seilo, James	5:05:55 (23,451)
Sein, Edward	5:20:21 (25,389)
Seini, Ian	3:23:55 (3,231)
Sejourne, Serge	4:03:14 (10,707)
Seki, Masao	5:15:00 (24,779)
Sekiguchi, Shizuo	4:12:37 (12,757)
Selby, David	3:56:28 (9,046)
Selby, Ian	3:37:39 (5,360)
Selby, Paul	5:05:21 (23,349)
Sell, Alexander	3:27:51 (3,777)
Sellars, Neil	4:31:15 (16,918)
Sellers, Scott	4:30:03 (16,702)
Sellwood, Darren	4:05:02 (11,123)
Selves, Stephen	4:03:12 (10,702)
Selwyn, Raymond	3:09:03 (1,676)
Semegran, Evan	4:04:34 (11,013)
Semeraro, John	5:04:28 (23,213)
Semple, Ian	4:42:52 (19,352)
Semple, Jason	4:41:03 (18,987)
Senaillet, Eric	3:43:30 (6,398)
Senatore, Nunzio	3:29:19 (4,051)
Senft, Jonathan	4:34:33 (17,636)
Senior, Mark	5:52:52 (28,056)
Senior, Richard	5:31:52 (26,521)
Senneck, Oliver	4:22:41 (14,978)
Seon, Joo	3:47:38 (7,175)
Sephton, Christopher	4:52:51 (21,277)
Sephton, David	4:43:26 (19,473)
Serale, Michel	4:00:03 (10,065)
Sercombe, Stephen	4:21:43 (14,737)
Sergeant, Graeme	3:11:46 (1,894)
Sermons, Neale	4:43:48 (19,557)
Sessions, John	4:37:04 (18,138)
Setford, Christopher	4:47:13 (20,207)
Setford, John	4:06:02 (11,355)
Sethi, Javed	4:06:25 (11,435)
Sethna, Jonathan	5:48:51 (27,834)
Seton, Richard	4:32:18 (17,172)
Setzer, Michael	4:55:25 (21,857)
Seve, André	3:59:13 (9,823)
Sevetier, André	4:19:24 (14,227)
Sew Kwan Kan, Nigel	3:42:11 (6,159)
Sewell, Andrew	3:12:30 (1,959)
Sewell, Ben	5:37:42 (27,000)
Sewell, Colin	3:27:41 (3,738)
Sewell, Mike	4:59:38 (22,544)
Sewell, Nicholas	4:22:49 (15,012)
Sewell, Nigel	3:20:16 (2,790)
Sexton, John	4:58:26 (22,366)
Sexton, Patrick	5:17:22 (25,090)
Sexton, Steve	4:07:44 (11,709)
Sextone, John	5:26:24 (26,034)
Seymour, Jonathan	4:55:00 (21,732)
Seymour, Kevin	4:08:57 (11,965)
Seymour, Richard	4:05:49 (11,305)
Shabbir, Antonio	5:16:09 (24,943)
Shackell, Christopher	3:14:09 (2,133)
Shackleton, David	4:39:31 (18,697)
Shackleton, Harvey	4:32:37 (17,232)
Shadbolt, Geoff	5:14:38 (24,732)
Shadbolt, Oliver	3:17:54 (2,520)
Shaddock, Robert	5:22:00 (25,585)
Shafie, Abdul Riza	3:36:51 (5,217)
Shah, Hiten	5:08:42 (23,888)
Shah, Sunil	5:23:22 (25,730)
Shaikh, Nadeem	3:19:48 (2,739)
Shakeshaft, Andrew	3:12:26 (1,955)
Shambayati, Behdad	4:12:54 (12,809)
Shambrook, Paul	4:03:28 (10,764)

Shanahan, Michael 4:28:04 (16,201)
Shand, Michael 3:57:35 (9,359)
Shand, Wayne 5:38:53 (27,078)
Shand, Will 2:45:19 (301)
Shankar, Sambasivan 4:36:19 (17,978)
Shanley, Paul 4:53:30 (21,419)
Shannon, Anthony 4:01:54 (10,463)
Shannon, David 4:12:05 (12,640)
Shanta, Sam 5:32:17 (26,547)
Shapka, Richard 3:28:31 (3,911)
Shapland, John 2:54:47 (622)
Sharkey, Jonathan 3:20:27 (2,815)
Sharkey, Thomas 3:52:07 (8,102)
Sharland, Roger 4:15:23 (13,342)
Sharma, Neel 5:04:26 (23,206)
Sharma, Robin 5:22:11 (25,612)
Sharma, Sridhar 4:12:23 (12,710)
Sharman, Mark 5:03:13 (23,033)
Sharp, David 3:40:10 (5,810)
Sharp, Jeremy 3:44:53 (6,658)
Sharp, Jeremy 4:07:30 (11,660)
Sharp, Kenneth 3:54:42 (8,634)
Sharp, Melvyn 4:36:23 (17,991)
Sharp, Michael 3:39:25 (5,657)
Sharp, Peter 3:33:25 (4,677)
Sharp, Timothy 4:29:43 (16,603)
Sharpe, Christopher 3:29:20 (4,053)
Sharpe, Jack 5:08:41 (23,883)
Sharpe, Justin 4:18:30 (14,012)
Sharples, Ian 2:41:58 (217)
Sharples, Richard 4:28:11 (16,231)
Sharples, Stephen 5:18:51 (25,254)
Shattock, Gerry 4:40:26 (18,864)
Shattock, Ronnie 5:34:56 (26,802)
Shaw, Adam 5:41:23 (27,286)
Shaw, Andrew 3:47:41 (7,189)
Shaw, Andrew 4:52:22 (21,175)
Shaw, Anthony 3:12:57 (1,999)
Shaw, Craig 4:02:00 (10,486)
Shaw, Darren 7:19:22 (30,077)
Shaw, Dave 4:13:36 (12,958)
Shaw, David 2:55:13 (638)
Shaw, Derry 4:55:01 (21,739)
Shaw, Gary 3:02:30 (1,188)
Shaw, Gerry 3:10:46 (1,815)
Shaw, Howard 6:34:37 (29,515)
Shaw, James 3:40:32 (5,873)
Shaw, Michael 4:13:38 (12,968)
Shaw, Mike 3:58:00 (9,490)
Shaw, Nicholas 4:31:27 (16,969)
Shaw, Peter 3:51:34 (7,983)
Shaw, Philip 4:43:00 (19,385)
Shaw, Richard 4:16:54 (13,647)
Shaw, Stephen 4:04:14 (10,936)
Shaw, Steven 3:57:44 (9,403)
Shaw, Stuart 2:44:28 (275)
Shaw, Tobias 4:00:54 (10,265)
Shaw, William 3:43:19 (6,365)
Shaw-Taylor, Stewart 3:28:40 (3,933)
Shea, Martin 4:54:58 (21,721)
Shea, Ronald 4:07:56 (11,747)
Shean, John 3:30:33 (4,256)
Shear, Errol 4:23:53 (15,269)
Shearer, Malcolm 4:39:26 (18,673)
Shearman, Clifford 4:09:36 (12,093)
Shearn, Mark 4:15:56 (13,450)
Shears, Russell 5:07:43 (23,732)
Sheath, Peter 3:56:13 (8,971)
Shebson, Jeremy 4:00:34 (10,178)
Sheckleford, Ashley 2:59:20 (968)
Sheehan, Andrew 4:40:36 (18,898)
Sheehan, Jonathan 3:49:14 (7,502)
Sheehan, Nicholas 5:49:21 (27,863)
Sheekey, Adam 6:04:09 (28,599)
Sheen, Darren 3:52:45 (8,220)
Sheen, Spencer 4:37:23 (18,219)
Sheeran, David 4:35:53 (17,903)
Sheffield, Anthony 3:42:07 (6,141)
Sheffield, John 4:07:10 (11,582)
Sheibani, Askar 4:12:20 (12,701)
Sheil, Peter 6:56:59 (29,911)
Sheils, Liam 4:43:09 (19,416)
Shelbourne, Stephen 4:02:21 (10,539)
Sheldon, Anthony 3:39:30 (5,673)
Sheldon, Anthony 3:45:16 (6,715)
Sheldon, Jeremy 3:30:42 (4,278)
Sheldon, John 4:36:28 (18,013)
Sheldon, Leonard 4:01:42 (10,430)
Shellard, Michael 3:55:44 (8,854)
Shelley, Paul 3:45:09 (6,702)
Shelly, Kevin 3:03:36 (1,253)
Shelly, Richard 4:18:34 (14,027)
Shelton, Michael 3:04:19 (1,303)
Shelton, Nick 6:09:46 (28,850)
Shelton, Scott 4:04:10 (10,918)
Shemmings, Carl 5:45:30 (27,591)
Shemweta, Alfred 2:15:34 (14)
Shenoy, Anil 4:46:40 (20,087)
Shepard, Steve 3:12:09 (1,926)
Shepheard, Peter 5:10:37 (24,167)
Shepherd, Alan 3:59:34 (9,940)
Shepherd, Alan 4:24:58 (15,497)
Shepherd, Ben 3:49:15 (7,509)
Shepherd, Brian 4:13:56 (13,028)
Shepherd, Christopher 3:37:35 (5,346)
Shepherd, Darran 4:10:45 (12,321)
Shepherd, David 3:43:53 (6,467)
Shepherd, Duncan 5:33:28 (26,645)
Shepherd, Gary 5:22:34 (25,656)
Shepherd, Lee 4:12:41 (12,768)
Shepherd, Mark 3:27:39 (3,732)
Shepherd, Mark 5:25:18 (25,920)
Shepherd, Neil 4:26:05 (15,752)
Shepherd, Peter 5:11:00 (24,212)
Shepherd, Philip 3:53:31 (8,380)
Shepherd, Stephen 4:26:13 (15,780)
Shepherd, Timothy 4:47:10 (20,194)
Shepherd, Tom 4:30:38 (16,775)
Sheppard, Andrew 3:32:28 (4,531)
Sheppard, Andy 5:13:56 (24,622)
Sheppard, Antony 2:55:03 (631)
Sheppard, Ben 4:09:19 (12,045)
Sheppard, Bill 3:52:15 (8,124)
Sheppard, Christopher 4:34:46 (17,669)
Sheppard, David 5:22:12 (25,615)
Sheppard, Guy 3:39:09 (5,599)
Sheppard, John William 3:41:46 (6,085)
Sheppard, Roy 4:24:35 (15,416)
Sheren, Michael 3:40:13 (5,818)
Sheridan, Michael 4:24:12 (15,330)
Sheridan, Robert 7:10:35 (30,025)
Sheridan, Thomas 3:14:29 (2,165)
Sheriff, Antony 6:33:11 (29,486)
Sherlock, Keith 3:43:35 (6,413)
Sherman, Julian 3:27:32 (3,714)
Sherman, Mike 4:23:40 (15,221)
Sherpa, Mukhiya 4:03:34 (10,793)
Sherrell, Paul 4:41:14 (19,018)
Sherry, Stevan 3:54:13 (8,512)
Sherwen, Peter 4:54:13 (21,553)
Sherwin, Robert 4:45:09 (19,796)
Sherwood, Bryan 3:36:44 (5,200)
Sherwood, Colin 4:05:53 (11,317)
Sherwood, Marcus 3:27:07 (3,640)
Sherwood, Oliver 4:07:08 (11,576)
Shettle, Gary 4:23:02 (15,071)
Shettle, Mark 5:28:24 (26,223)
Shevels, Keith 3:54:46 (8,650)
Shewan, Brian 5:04:25 (23,204)
Shiel, Adrian 6:05:13 (28,648)
Shield, Jeffrey 4:38:48 (18,576)
Shield, Jerry 3:21:16 (2,912)
Shields, Damian 4:38:03 (18,382)
Shields, Peter 5:00:52 (22,717)
Shilabeer, Michael 5:04:31 (23,218)
Shilling, Andrew 4:20:05 (14,385)
Shilling, David 3:46:10 (6,893)
Shilling, Michael 3:05:18 (1,374)
Shimizu, Hajime 3:41:14 (5,993)
Shimmen, Andy 4:14:45 (13,194)
Shimmen, Russell 3:23:38 (3,189)
Shimmin, Greg 3:49:45 (7,634)
Shimomise, Yuji 3:29:55 (4,155)
Shiner, Francis 4:03:25 (10,752)
Shinohara, Hiroaki 5:40:17 (27,206)
Shipley, David 4:53:31 (21,427)
Shipman, John 6:13:26 (28,966)
Shipp, Geoffrey 3:57:48 (9,431)
Shippam, Mark 3:28:33 (3,918)
Shipperley, David 4:24:38 (15,427)
Shipton, Brian 5:14:31 (24,708)
Shipway, Richard 4:37:25 (18,229)
Shires, Neil 3:54:25 (8,570)
Shirley, Christopher 6:05:27 (28,662)
Shirley, David 3:23:25 (3,162)
Shirley, Robert 4:03:21 (10,735)
Shirley, Simon 3:59:37 (9,953)
Shoebridge, Matthew 3:50:44 (7,814)
Shoebridge, Roy 4:10:49 (12,350)
Shoesmith, Edward 3:04:32 (1,317)
Shohara, Ryo 4:31:21 (16,944)
Shonola, Oladapo 3:48:29 (7,357)
Shopper, Matthew 5:27:46 (26,154)
Shore, Ian 4:34:07 (17,562)
Shore, Martin 2:39:19 (162)
Shore, Richard 4:05:22 (11,179)
Shore, Terence 4:14:10 (13,070)
Shorey, Stephen 4:23:50 (15,257)
Shorney, Stephen 5:14:04 (24,634)
Short, Alan 4:13:43 (12,985)
Short, Arthur 3:03:47 (1,269)
Short, Colin 4:36:47 (18,078)
Short, Duncan 3:53:09 (8,300)
Short, Garry 3:00:26 (1,050)
Short, Mark 3:48:23 (7,335)
Short, Michael 4:39:45 (18,746)
Short, Nicholas 5:26:12 (26,005)
Shortill, Michael 3:43:11 (6,341)
Shotbolt, Adrian 4:21:15 (14,639)
Shotton, Joel 4:02:21 (10,539)
Shoubridge, Daniel 5:17:17 (25,082)
Shoults, Will 3:55:15 (8,751)
Shrestha, Bijaya 5:08:23 (23,829)
Shrigley, John 4:29:20 (16,504)
Shrubsole, Clive 4:01:38 (10,418)
Shtaingos, Raviv 4:46:51 (20,132)
Shukla, Nitin 5:41:08 (27,268)
Shuter, Donald 4:09:51 (12,134)
Shuttle, David 5:05:16 (23,334)
Shuttleworth, Richard 3:57:07 (9,200)
Sibson, Andrew 4:38:20 (18,462)
Sibun, Andrew 3:59:23 (9,876)
Siddall, Stuart 3:59:47 (9,992)
Siddle, Matthew 3:53:03 (8,277)
Sidebotham, John 2:53:24 (555)
Sidgwick, Benjamin 3:28:47 (3,957)
Sidher, Sunil 4:01:22 (10,365)
Sidhu, Balvinder 4:03:25 (10,752)
Sidimoussa, Abdelkader 3:14:18 (2,149)
Siebert, Stefan 3:48:39 (7,391)
Sieel, Richard 8:31:58 (30,247)
Sieger, Robin 5:12:39 (24,452)
Sierewicz, Wieslaw 3:44:55 (6,666)
Siers, Stephen 6:19:15 (29,139)
Sigrist, Joerg 3:21:58 (2,991)
Sijbrands, Chris 5:37:33 (26,983)
Silberschmidl, Peter 3:35:05 (4,914)
Silcock, Dave 4:18:30 (14,012)
Silk, Dominic 4:02:51 (10,632)
Sillett, Jonathan 5:23:26 (25,735)
Sillett, Stephen 4:07:33 (11,666)
Sillett, Steven 4:40:14 (18,819)
Sillince, Ian 4:51:47 (21,053)
Sillitoe, Chris 5:03:48 (23,098)
Sillitoe, Mike 3:57:13 (9,232)
Sills, Andrew 4:01:56 (10,473)
Silva, Alfredo 4:08:25 (11,853)
Silva, José 4:27:47 (16,147)
Silva, Steven 5:39:51 (27,171)
Silva Calgada, Darcilio 3:50:59 (7,867)
Silva Mota, Antonio 3:02:26 (1,186)
Silver, Marc 4:58:25 (22,362)
Silverman, Noel 4:07:59 (11,762)
Silversides, Nicholas 4:27:35 (16,084)
Silverton, Ross 3:42:34 (6,229)
Silvester, Michael 4:36:37 (18,045)
Silvester, Richard 4:42:42 (19,310)
Silvester, Robin 3:25:17 (3,413)
Silvey, M 3:02:33 (1,192)

Sim, Paul 5:22:10 (25,606)
Simcock, Andrew 4:33:35 (17,450)
Simcock, Anthony 4:18:38 (14,036)
Sime, Andrew 4:20:18 (14,429)
Simenton, Robert 5:03:54 (23,114)
Simes, Peter 4:42:14 (19,211)
Simkin, Sar 3:52:19 (8,138)
Simkins, Grenville 4:36:19 (17,978)
Simkins, Paul 3:48:43 (7,406)
Simmonds, Gareth 5:22:42 (25,674)
Simmonds, Lee 5:01:59 (22,871)
Simmonds, Martin 3:23:52 (3,225)
Simmonds, Matthew 4:22:34 (14,943)
Simmonds, Richard 3:00:36 (1,058)
Simmonds, Robert 4:53:16 (21,366)
Simmonds, Roger 3:36:53 (5,223)
Simmonds, Steve 3:45:39 (6,779)
Simmonite, Stephen 6:18:09 (29,121)
Simmons, Barry 3:47:40 (7,185)
Simmons, Cyril 6:17:14 (29,095)
Simmons, James 4:42:16 (19,218)
Simmons, James 5:07:13 (23,652)
Simmons, Malcolm 5:14:42 (24,740)
Simmons, Michael 3:49:25 (7,555)
Simmons, Michael 6:18:24 (29,123)
Simmons, Peter 4:12:08 (12,653)
Simmons, Steven 3:41:04 (5,970)
Simmons, Trevor 2:58:53 (923)
Simms, Malcolm 3:24:34 (3,324)
Simms, Michael 4:29:54 (16,660)
Simms, Rupert 3:18:43 (2,621)
Simms, William 5:43:11 (27,421)
Simner, Kevin 4:39:36 (18,718)
Simnett, John 4:27:53 (16,172)
Simon, Andrew 3:38:44 (5,530)
Simon, Carsten 3:12:41 (1,978)
Simon, Heinz 3:39:40 (5,703)
Simon, Jaques 4:15:13 (13,312)
Simon, Jonathan 5:56:02 (28,216)
Simon, Lothar 3:23:57 (3,238)
Simon, Matthias 3:20:39 (2,842)
Simon, Thierry 3:58:03 (9,501)
Simonds, Guy 4:34:10 (17,567)
Simone, Mario 4:54:54 (21,702)
Simonite, Roger 4:22:47 (15,000)
Simpkin, Ian 3:54:24 (8,562)
Simpkins, Michael 4:47:50 (20,312)
Simpkins, Peter 4:09:34 (12,084)
Simpkins, Ryan 4:17:41 (13,808)
Simpson, Adrian 3:41:51 (6,101)
Simpson, Alan 4:44:40 (19,707)
Simpson, Andrew 3:47:34 (7,159)
Simpson, Andrew 4:39:29 (18,690)
Simpson, Benjamin 4:27:23 (16,036)
Simpson, Brian 4:41:56 (19,149)
Simpson, Brian 4:55:24 (21,849)
Simpson, Chad 5:36:02 (26,884)
Simpson, Colin 4:49:18 (20,581)
Simpson, Craig 5:39:25 (27,123)
Simpson, David 3:45:35 (6,761)
Simpson, David 4:36:35 (18,037)
Simpson, Douglas 4:48:34 (20,449)
Simpson, Gary 5:42:57 (27,406)
Simpson, Guy 3:35:19 (4,957)
Simpson, Helen 5:32:02 (26,535)
Simpson, Henry 4:07:58 (11,755)
Simpson, Iain 4:14:31 (13,131)
Simpson, John 4:44:25 (19,659)
Simpson, Keith 4:45:09 (19,796)
Simpson, Kevin 4:24:45 (15,450)
Simpson, Kieran 3:54:16 (8,527)
Simpson, Mark 3:42:15 (6,171)
Simpson, Mark 4:30:45 (16,794)
Simpson, Matthew 4:01:59 (10,482)
Simpson, Peter 3:12:11 (1,929)
Simpson, Peter 5:04:16 (23,175)
Simpson, Philip 6:10:05 (28,863)
Simpson, Richard 3:44:00 (6,494)
Simpson, Robert 3:37:04 (5,256)
Simpson, Steven 4:31:06 (16,872)
Simpson, Stuart 4:40:59 (18,974)
Simpson, Timothy 4:40:36 (18,898)
Simpson-Gee, Will 5:55:57 (28,213)
Sims, Anthony 2:57:09 (757)
Sims, Paul 4:03:08 (10,692)
Sims, Paul 4:40:45 (18,931)
Sims, Ray 4:38:33 (18,515)
Sims, Steven 5:18:34 (25,220)
Sinar, Barry 3:56:45 (9,121)
Sinclair, Adrian 5:13:58 (24,625)
Sinclair, Alastair 3:28:40 (3,933)
Sinclair, Arthur 4:36:12 (17,954)
Sinclair, Colin 4:05:02 (11,123)
Sinclair, Kevin 3:39:56 (5,768)
Sinclair, Malcolm 3:46:01 (6,861)
Sinclair, Mark 3:47:47 (7,206)
Sinclair, Martin 3:57:42 (9,396)
Sinclair, Nigel 3:10:25 (1,787)
Sinclair, Paul 4:45:22 (19,835)
Sinclair, Simon 4:45:08 (19,791)
Sinclair, Thomas 4:01:30 (10,396)
Sinclair, Thomas 4:59:06 (22,475)
Sinden, Philip 5:03:48 (23,098)
Sindhar, Amritpal 6:32:00 (29,451)
Singer, Robin 4:56:23 (22,048)
Singh, Ajit 5:17:08 (25,065)
Singh, Alok 5:04:47 (23,259)
Singh, Amrik 5:30:42 (26,429)
Singh, Anil 4:03:04 (10,677)
Singh, Baljit 5:09:15 (23,977)
Singh, Gurch 6:12:16 (28,932)
Singh, Harbhag 3:40:06 (5,800)
Singh, Harmander 8:32:11 (30,249)
Singh, Jagjit 5:10:12 (24,103)
Singh, Rajinder 5:12:11 (24,375)
Singh Flora, Singh Dip 4:37:33 (18,264)
Single, Peter 3:15:10 (2,243)
Singleton, David 3:59:50 (10,005)
Singleton, James 4:43:42 (19,539)
Singleton, Jonathan 4:23:25 (15,153)
Singleton, Peter 3:33:53 (4,737)
Sini, Giovanni 4:19:55 (14,343)
Sinnott, Philip 4:15:30 (13,366)
Sinton, James 4:31:34 (16,996)
Sippel, Ludwig 4:23:30 (15,172)
Sireau, Michel 3:39:55 (5,762)
Sirett, Michael 3:28:16 (3,859)
Sirha, Satvinder 5:27:54 (26,171)
Sirrell, Brett 3:54:50 (8,668)
Sirs, Nicholas 2:38:23 (145)
Sisson, Gary 3:47:05 (7,048)
Sissons, Robert 7:05:32 (29,981)
Siswick, Dave 5:08:54 (23,922)
Sitch, Mark 3:52:33 (8,182)
Sitt, Benjamin 3:39:50 (5,745)
Siviero, Luigi 4:17:15 (13,727)
Sivyer, Stephen 4:46:07 (19,964)
Sizeland, Sam 4:54:40 (21,628)
Skaarup, Nils 4:21:32 (14,698)
Skaarup, Steen 3:14:51 (2,200)
Skea, Christopher 4:36:14 (17,961)
Skeels, John 3:56:00 (8,919)
Skeet, John 3:22:01 (3,003)
Skegg, Stephen 3:38:04 (5,412)
Skeggs, Simon 4:13:51 (13,013)
Skeggs, Steven 3:53:40 (8,416)
Skelton, Philip 4:39:26 (18,673)
Skelton, Robert 4:12:10 (12,667)
Skelton, Stephen 5:53:18 (28,083)
Skelton, Terry 3:11:35 (1,869)
Skentelbery, Neil 3:59:19 (9,849)
Skerry, Philip 4:31:49 (17,062)
Skidmore, Paul 3:17:57 (2,526)
Skilton, Colin 3:56:23 (9,018)
Skilton, Stuart 4:21:39 (14,724)
Skinner, Andrew 4:23:14 (15,114)
Skinner, Chris 5:13:58 (24,625)
Skinner, Christian 4:35:16 (17,767)
Skinner, Gary 4:32:23 (17,189)
Skinner, James 4:52:35 (21,233)
Skinner, Jeff 4:42:12 (19,205)
Skinner, John 3:57:37 (9,369)
Skinner, Jonathan 5:01:20 (22,785)
Skinner, Martin 4:34:14 (17,580)
Skinner, Matthew 4:05:57 (11,339)
Skinner, Peter 5:12:10 (24,372)
Skinner, Stephen 4:57:54 (22,281)
Skipp, Asa 5:06:48 (23,591)
Skipp, Keith 4:00:10 (10,081)
Skipp, Paul 2:54:57 (627)
Skipper, Edward 4:17:18 (13,735)
Skivington, Ian 4:53:46 (21,467)
Skivington, Peter 5:40:20 (27,212)
Skoett, Soeren 4:44:59 (19,773)
Skovron, Gary 4:00:38 (10,192)
Skuse, Clive 4:47:48 (20,308)
Slack, Gordon 3:37:26 (5,325)
Slack, Jonathan 4:12:50 (12,797)
Slade, Darren 3:03:38 (1,258)
Slade, David 5:29:53 (26,362)
Slade, Nick 3:42:08 (6,145)
Slade, Nigel 4:54:49 (21,682)
Slaiding, Ian 3:30:09 (4,196)
Slaney, Mark 3:21:26 (2,938)
Slater, Alfred 4:27:26 (16,046)
Slater, Andrew 4:30:19 (16,730)
Slater, George 4:37:34 (18,270)
Slater, Matthew 3:52:42 (8,211)
Slater, Paul 3:29:02 (4,004)
Slater, Paul 3:36:52 (5,220)
Slater, Paul 5:15:09 (24,813)
Slater, Peter 6:17:32 (29,102)
Slater, Phil 4:02:47 (10,624)
Slator, Clive 3:36:45 (5,204)
Slattery, David 5:37:39 (26,998)
Slattery, Paul 2:53:28 (556)
Slattery, Stephen 4:31:20 (16,940)
Slavin, Neil 3:58:23 (9,582)
Slayford, Laurie 6:38:16 (29,594)
Slazak, Andrzej 3:05:08 (1,360)
Sleap, Jason 4:49:28 (20,613)
Sleath, David 5:28:48 (26,269)
Slegg, Christopher 4:41:11 (19,009)
Sleigh, Vincent 4:27:03 (15,981)
Slessor, John 4:53:50 (21,483)
Sloan, Ian 5:42:13 (27,347)
Sloan, Ronald 3:29:17 (4,045)
Sloper, Christopher 5:27:50 (26,161)
Slot, Peter 4:01:52 (10,455)
Slotte, Clas Eirik 3:34:55 (4,892)
Slow, Gareth 4:30:28 (16,750)
Sluman, John 3:56:24 (9,025)
Sluman, Mark 4:03:17 (10,718)
Slydel, Royston 6:32:41 (29,470)
Slyfield, Morgan 2:50:30 (447)
Smailes, Brian 4:33:20 (17,378)
Small, Brian 3:17:12 (2,445)
Small, Christopher 3:58:06 (9,515)
Small, Edward 4:51:14 (20,929)
Small, Jason 5:10:39 (24,170)
Small, Kevin 3:44:30 (6,576)
Small, Nathaniel 4:25:00 (15,509)
Smalldridge, Danny 5:04:52 (23,280)
Smalley, John 5:06:18 (23,520)
Smallman, Christopher 2:59:52 (1,012)
Smalls, Allen 2:51:13 (475)
Smart, Alan 4:14:47 (13,205)
Smart, Andy 6:40:09 (29,642)
Smart, Christopher 3:27:30 (3,707)
Smart, Colin 4:53:03 (21,325)
Smart, Darren 4:35:07 (17,735)
Smart, Geoffrey 4:11:40 (12,544)
Smart, Ian 4:40:26 (18,864)
Smart, Kevin 3:13:01 (2,005)
Smart, Matthew 4:44:27 (19,665)
Smart, Michael 5:20:49 (25,447)
Smart, Nicholas 6:03:42 (28,574)
Smart, Oliver 3:42:21 (6,191)
Smart, Robert 3:44:25 (6,563)
Smart, Roy 3:56:49 (9,137)
Smeal, Gary 3:36:42 (5,191)
Smeddle, Jeremy 4:31:09 (16,888)
Smedley, Stephen 4:43:52 (19,569)
Smeeth, Jeremy 3:59:36 (9,948)
Smethurst, Andrew 4:47:39 (20,291)
Smieja, Frank 4:24:32 (15,404)
Smiles, Paul 4:26:46 (15,902)
Smith, Adrian 4:39:37 (18,721)
Smith, Adrian 4:41:01 (18,979)

Smith, Alan	3:27:38 (3,727)	
Smith, Alan	3:30:09 (4,196)	
Smith, Alan	3:32:13 (4,495)	
Smith, Alan	3:36:10 (5,099)	
Smith, Alan	3:50:51 (7,837)	
Smith, Alan	4:23:50 (15,257)	
Smith, Alan	4:25:00 (15,509)	
Smith, Andrew	2:52:55 (539)	
Smith, Andrew	3:07:26 (1,539)	
Smith, Andrew	3:41:13 (5,987)	
Smith, Andrew	3:42:39 (6,244)	
Smith, Andrew	3:42:42 (6,252)	
Smith, Andrew	4:16:43 (13,617)	
Smith, Andrew	4:22:35 (14,948)	
Smith, Andrew	4:48:02 (20,354)	
Smith, Andrew	6:41:44 (29,683)	
Smith, Andy	4:22:25 (14,908)	
Smith, Andy	5:02:40 (22,958)	
Smith, Anthony	3:21:38 (2,961)	
Smith, Anthony	3:53:15 (8,318)	
Smith, Anthony	4:10:06 (12,179)	
Smith, Anthony	4:46:21 (20,020)	
Smith, Anthony	4:55:34 (21,907)	
Smith, Barry	4:59:46 (22,565)	
Smith, Ben	4:04:48 (11,067)	
Smith, Benjamin	4:49:32 (20,620)	
Smith, Brian	3:29:12 (4,027)	
Smith, Brian	4:15:00 (13,268)	
Smith, Brian	4:19:50 (14,323)	
Smith, Brian	4:54:17 (21,559)	
Smith, Carl	4:03:54 (10,863)	
Smith, Charles	3:33:57 (4,748)	
Smith, Chris	3:02:41 (1,195)	
Smith, Chris	4:00:36 (10,186)	
Smith, Christian	4:53:19 (21,378)	
Smith, Christopher	3:01:34 (1,118)	
Smith, Christopher	4:52:21 (21,174)	
Smith, Christopher	4:53:54 (21,495)	
Smith, Cliff	3:27:07 (3,640)	
Smith, Clifford	3:51:20 (7,938)	
Smith, Clive	3:59:28 (9,909)	
Smith, Clive	4:19:35 (14,276)	
Smith, Clive	4:43:15 (19,438)	
Smith, Colin	4:42:06 (19,178)	
Smith, Colin	6:08:34 (28,788)	
Smith, Colin	6:16:36 (29,074)	
Smith, Craig	5:12:23 (24,413)	
Smith, Daniel	4:13:47 (12,995)	
Smith, David	3:20:59 (2,889)	
Smith, David	3:31:22 (4,382)	
Smith, David	3:37:22 (5,317)	
Smith, David	3:39:30 (5,673)	
Smith, David	3:40:10 (5,810)	
Smith, David	3:41:36 (6,054)	
Smith, David	4:11:48 (12,570)	
Smith, David	4:29:59 (16,689)	
Smith, David	4:57:29 (22,214)	
Smith, David	5:29:16 (26,316)	
Smith, David	7:25:45 (30,111)	
Smith, Derek	4:30:58 (16,844)	
Smith, Derek	6:14:37 (29,012)	
Smith, Derrick	4:56:10 (22,015)	
Smith, Edward	4:17:47 (13,829)	
Smith, Eric	5:20:34 (25,417)	
Smith, Erik	2:52:46 (537)	
Smith, Garfield	4:38:04 (18,389)	
Smith, Garry	6:48:29 (29,787)	
Smith, Gary	6:21:57 (29,215)	
Smith, Geoff	4:50:37 (20,814)	
Smith, George	3:56:01 (8,930)	
Smith, George	6:04:24 (28,613)	
Smith, Gerry	2:44:42 (283)	
Smith, Giles	3:43:40 (6,428)	
Smith, Graeme	4:39:47 (18,751)	
Smith, Graham	3:37:45 (5,370)	
Smith, Graham	3:58:15 (9,556)	
Smith, Graham	4:16:14 (13,513)	
Smith, Graham	4:21:32 (14,698)	
Smith, Grant	3:20:29 (2,822)	
Smith, Guy	4:14:14 (13,082)	
Smith, Harvey	4:54:01 (21,519)	
Smith, Ian	2:57:31 (782)	
Smith, Ian	3:49:53 (7,664)	
Smith, Ian	4:04:13 (10,933)	
Smith, Ian	4:07:35 (11,675)	
Smith, Ian	4:37:19 (18,200)	
Smith, Ian	4:55:25 (21,857)	
Smith, Jack	3:40:28 (5,863)	
Smith, James	3:49:28 (7,567)	
Smith, James	4:15:11 (13,299)	
Smith, James	4:33:21 (17,387)	
Smith, James	4:52:52 (21,280)	
Smith, Jamie	4:18:09 (13,903)	
Smith, Jason	5:30:14 (26,390)	
Smith, Jeff	3:56:00 (8,919)	
Smith, Jeffrey	5:39:42 (27,156)	
Smith, Jeremy	3:34:17 (4,798)	
Smith, Jeremy	5:12:41 (24,453)	
Smith, John	3:47:17 (7,079)	
Smith, John	4:26:05 (15,752)	
Smith, John	4:43:24 (19,465)	
Smith, John	5:32:11 (26,543)	
Smith, John	7:00:58 (29,952)	
Smith, Jonathan	3:59:10 (9,807)	
Smith, Jonathan	4:05:02 (11,123)	
Smith, Jonathan	4:27:50 (16,160)	
Smith, Jonathan	5:21:21 (25,514)	
Smith, Julian	3:11:38 (1,877)	
Smith, Julian	3:24:06 (3,259)	
Smith, Karl	3:54:07 (8,495)	
Smith, Keith	3:02:22 (1,181)	
Smith, Keith	3:57:37 (9,369)	
Smith, Keith	4:20:13 (14,411)	
Smith, Keith	4:20:55 (14,575)	
Smith, Ken	3:25:50 (3,484)	
Smith, Kevin	3:00:52 (1,074)	
Smith, Kevin	3:05:12 (1,367)	
Smith, Kevin	4:04:56 (11,103)	
Smith, Kevin	5:45:33 (27,596)	
Smith, Kit	4:04:37 (11,023)	
Smith, Kit	6:45:30 (29,746)	
Smith, Larry	5:18:25 (25,200)	
Smith, Les	4:10:12 (12,208)	
Smith, Leslie	4:38:45 (18,559)	
Smith, Leslie	6:55:38 (29,897)	
Smith, Malcolm	3:27:42 (3,741)	
Smith, Malcolm	4:00:01 (10,058)	
Smith, Mark	3:35:11 (4,929)	
Smith, Mark	3:43:42 (6,437)	
Smith, Mark	3:56:36 (9,077)	
Smith, Mark	4:27:13 (16,014)	
Smith, Martin	3:51:26 (7,951)	
Smith, Martin	4:25:48 (15,672)	
Smith, Martin	4:37:28 (18,243)	
Smith, Martin	4:43:38 (19,524)	
Smith, Martin	4:49:57 (20,708)	
Smith, Martin	5:08:31 (23,849)	
Smith, Martyn	4:46:21 (20,020)	
Smith, Matt	5:05:00 (23,294)	
Smith, Matthew	3:08:39 (1,644)	
Smith, Matthew	3:24:06 (3,259)	
Smith, Matthew James	4:38:47 (18,574)	
Smith, Michael	3:33:36 (4,695)	
Smith, Michael	3:46:36 (6,973)	
Smith, Michael	3:53:06 (8,292)	
Smith, Michael	3:54:26 (8,575)	
Smith, Michael	5:06:23 (23,533)	
Smith, Michael	6:09:07 (28,820)	
Smith, Mike	4:49:19 (20,584)	
Smith, Nathan	4:19:24 (14,227)	
Smith, Neil	4:47:32 (20,273)	
Smith, Nicholas	3:15:39 (2,283)	
Smith, Nicholas	3:31:40 (4,418)	
Smith, Nicholas	3:46:05 (6,873)	
Smith, Nicholas	4:42:02 (19,169)	
Smith, Nicholas	5:11:33 (24,296)	
Smith, Nicholas	5:14:59 (24,777)	
Smith, Nigel	3:19:52 (2,749)	
Smith, Nigel	5:47:00 (27,703)	
Smith, Paul	3:23:01 (3,115)	
Smith, Paul	3:51:32 (7,974)	
Smith, Paul	4:00:33 (10,173)	
Smith, Paul	4:04:13 (10,933)	
Smith, Paul	4:44:12 (19,619)	
Smith, Paul	4:54:51 (21,691)	
Smith, Paul	5:58:22 (28,343)	
Smith, Peter	2:41:53 (215)	
Smith, Peter	4:05:14 (11,159)	
Smith, Peter	4:11:26 (12,491)	
Smith, Peter	4:33:12 (17,347)	
Smith, Peter	5:02:09 (22,901)	
Smith, Peter	5:13:25 (24,565)	
Smith, Peter	5:20:27 (25,405)	
Smith, Peter	5:25:36 (25,952)	
Smith, Peter	6:48:29 (29,787)	
Smith, Phil	4:08:35 (11,890)	
Smith, Philip	3:55:18 (8,760)	
Smith, Philip	4:28:02 (16,197)	
Smith, Philip	4:42:57 (19,376)	
Smith, Phillip	4:45:50 (19,908)	
Smith, Phillip	6:02:45 (28,532)	
Smith, Ray	4:09:55 (12,143)	
Smith, Richard	3:04:54 (1,342)	
Smith, Richard	4:04:48 (11,067)	
Smith, Richard	4:42:51 (19,347)	
Smith, Richard	4:54:24 (21,573)	
Smith, Robert	3:28:14 (3,851)	
Smith, Robert	4:01:05 (10,296)	
Smith, Robert	4:09:06 (12,004)	
Smith, Robert	4:40:20 (18,845)	
Smith, Robert	5:00:10 (22,639)	
Smith, Robert	5:05:51 (23,439)	
Smith, Robert	5:26:56 (26,080)	
Smith, Roger	3:45:25 (6,732)	
Smith, Roger	4:29:19 (16,502)	
Smith, Ron	3:39:24 (5,652)	
Smith, Roy	3:01:29 (1,110)	
Smith, Royston	3:10:53 (1,827)	
Smith, Scott	6:30:08 (29,413)	
Smith, Shaun	4:21:24 (14,668)	
Smith, Shaun	4:48:03 (20,359)	
Smith, Simon	3:14:16 (2,142)	
Smith, Simon	3:16:43 (2,396)	
Smith, Simon	4:10:35 (12,293)	
Smith, Simon	4:23:37 (15,211)	
Smith, Simon	5:17:57 (25,155)	
Smith, Simon	5:42:52 (27,401)	
Smith, Stanley	3:46:03 (6,865)	
Smith, Stephen	3:23:02 (3,118)	
Smith, Stephen	3:42:30 (6,219)	
Smith, Stephen	4:08:25 (11,853)	
Smith, Stephen	4:44:12 (19,619)	
Smith, Stephen	4:53:38 (21,444)	
Smith, Stephen	5:00:16 (22,644)	
Smith, Steve	2:46:53 (337)	
Smith, Steve	3:30:52 (4,305)	
Smith, Steven	4:56:50 (22,114)	
Smith, Steven	5:16:44 (25,017)	
Smith, Steven	5:18:17 (25,189)	
Smith, Stuart	3:17:16 (2,455)	
Smith, Stuart	4:47:38 (20,287)	
Smith, Terrance	3:40:20 (5,836)	
Smith, Terry	4:40:21 (18,847)	
Smith, Thomas	3:18:55 (2,646)	
Smith, Thomas	4:11:19 (12,465)	
Smith, Tim	4:12:54 (12,809)	
Smith, Victor	4:09:50 (12,131)	
Smith, Wayne	3:16:05 (2,327)	
Smith, William	3:11:05 (1,842)	
Smith, William	3:23:24 (3,159)	
Smith, Willie	4:01:34 (10,403)	
Smith, Xavier	5:01:12 (22,768)	
Smithson, David	4:33:35 (17,450)	
Smithson, James	5:49:07 (27,849)	
Smithson, Martin	5:09:48 (24,058)	
Smithson, Russell	2:51:20 (479)	
Smithson, Will	4:08:22 (11,843)	
Smity, Neil	4:38:32 (18,511)	
Smoult, Robin	3:17:08 (2,440)	
Smowton, Dave	3:56:27 (9,040)	
Smyth, Paul	3:22:52 (3,093)	
Smyth, Peter	4:19:11 (14,161)	
Smyth, Raymond	5:06:10 (23,493)	
Smyth, Trevor	5:34:04 (26,707)	
Smythe, Steve	2:58:47 (906)	
Smythe, Steve	3:14:17 (2,144)	
Snaith, Roger	4:53:59 (21,509)	
Snapcott, Terry	5:14:48 (24,749)	
Snape, Geoffrey	4:31:15 (16,918)	

Snape, Nicholas.....5:16:41 (25,011)
Snary, Paul.....3:52:13 (8,119)
Snead, Thomas.....4:18:34 (14,027)
Snead, William.....6:01:16 (28,466)
Snelgrove, John.....4:29:50 (16,634)
Snelgrove, William.....2:41:47 (210)
Snell, Mark.....3:45:40 (6,785)
Snoad, Alan.....4:35:28 (17,806)
Snoek, Nicholas.....3:55:30 (8,798)
Snook, Peter.....4:32:54 (17,294)
Snowdon, Peter.....3:35:19 (4,957)
Snyder, Stephen.....4:39:26 (18,673)
Soaglianti, Roberto.....4:31:55 (17,095)
Soames, Brian.....6:03:41 (28,573)
Soares Silva Seabra, Antonio.....3:33:04 (4,616)
Sobey, Richard.....3:15:14 (2,246)
Sobkowiak, Eric.....3:28:05 (3,816)
Soddin, James.....3:37:58 (5,397)
Soderman, Robert.....2:36:28 (108)
Soejima, Kazwya.....4:56:28 (22,060)
Soguel, Claude Alain.....2:39:55 (172)
Sohail, Nick.....3:40:59 (5,952)
Sohigian, James.....2:59:39 (990)
Sola, Jacques.....3:44:46 (6,632)
Sola, Markus.....4:26:42 (15,890)
Solberg, John.....3:26:04 (3,509)
Sole, Joe.....6:09:17 (28,826)
Solesbury, Tom.....4:15:32 (13,373)
Soliot, Bernard.....3:00:43 (1,066)
Solly, M.....4:56:05 (22,001)
Solomon, Martin.....4:21:58 (14,802)
Solomon, Trevor.....5:58:32 (28,347)
Solomons, Alan.....3:43:13 (6,348)
Somes Charlton, Chris.....4:25:11 (15,554)
Sommeling, Erwin.....3:57:28 (9,318)
Sommerlad, Brian.....3:38:01 (5,401)
Sommers, Rupert.....3:59:06 (9,786)
Sonenfield, Nicholas.....5:50:39 (27,931)
Sones, Marvin.....4:01:34 (10,403)
Soni, Karan.....5:23:29 (25,741)
Sonnex, Tim.....3:44:20 (6,551)
Soper, John.....6:27:04 (29,334)
Sorensen, Brian.....4:57:21 (22,198)
Sorger, Karl.....3:05:24 (1,383)
Sotheran, Gavin.....3:58:52 (9,718)
Soto, John.....4:06:53 (11,525)
Souchon, Thierry.....4:11:20 (12,466)
Soulsby, Paul.....5:13:43 (24,597)
Soupene, Jacques.....3:34:58 (4,901)
South, Ian.....6:09:43 (28,847)
South, Michael.....4:27:22 (16,033)
Southall, Peter.....3:13:43 (2,077)
Southerton, Michael.....4:10:28 (12,268)
Southwell, Chris.....3:50:08 (7,712)
Southwell, Craig.....4:10:57 (12,389)
Southwell, Matthew.....4:24:40 (15,433)
Southwell, Michael.....5:02:01 (22,874)
Southwell, Nathan.....4:12:44 (12,778)
Southwell, Philip.....4:08:13 (11,808)
Southworth, Henry.....4:05:23 (11,182)
Sovegjarto, Pete.....3:42:18 (6,180)
Sowin, Raymond.....4:11:25 (12,486)
Soyer, Patrice.....3:49:17 (7,518)
Spackman, David.....3:48:11 (7,302)
Spagna, Michele.....3:47:47 (7,206)
Spain, David.....3:36:01 (5,077)
Spanier, Dominik.....3:59:47 (9,992)
Spare, Kevin.....2:41:28 (202)
Spare, Tracey.....4:19:58 (14,355)
Sparey, Kevin.....3:04:16 (1,300)
Sparey, Russell.....5:12:11 (24,375)
Sparkes, Matthew.....4:28:48 (16,380)
Sparks, Paul.....3:40:23 (5,845)
Sparks, Steve.....3:46:16 (6,910)
Sparks, Tony.....5:01:11 (22,763)
Sparrow, Clive.....3:56:54 (9,154)
Sparrow, Matthew.....3:11:40 (1,882)
Sparrow, Roger.....4:25:58 (15,723)
Sparrowhawk, Terry.....5:15:08 (24,802)
Speake, Andrew.....4:54:54 (21,702)
Speake, Malcolm.....4:43:12 (19,427)
Speake, William.....2:27:51 (52)
Spear, Derek.....4:00:43 (10,217)
Spear, Philip.....5:34:01 (26,696)
Spearing, Matthew.....4:41:37 (19,085)
Spearpoint, Paul.....4:37:57 (18,357)
Specker, Axel.....4:59:16 (22,493)
Speed, David.....4:05:03 (11,128)
Speed, Kim.....5:45:23 (27,582)
Speed, Morley.....3:30:34 (4,259)
Speers, Gary.....5:10:13 (24,108)
Speir, Robert.....5:28:17 (26,205)
Speirs, Archie.....4:14:55 (13,239)
Speirs, Owen.....3:49:21 (7,538)
Speissegger, Sven.....3:30:12 (4,200)
Spence, Alan.....4:26:37 (15,875)
Spence, Bryan.....4:03:49 (10,843)
Spence, Colin.....4:37:58 (18,363)
Spence, Darren.....4:53:13 (21,357)
Spence, David.....3:07:05 (1,509)
Spence, Gary.....5:03:04 (23,016)
Spence, Peter.....4:23:16 (15,122)
Spence, Stephen.....3:06:13 (1,436)
Spenceley, Matt.....4:08:23 (11,846)
Spencer, Adrian.....6:05:50 (28,679)
Spencer, Anthony.....4:14:06 (13,056)
Spencer, Chris.....4:26:00 (15,730)
Spencer, Colin.....3:57:16 (9,245)
Spencer, David.....3:22:03 (3,007)
Spencer, David.....4:18:57 (14,109)
Spencer, Dennis.....4:38:27 (18,494)
Spencer, Herbert.....5:11:04 (24,218)
Spencer, Ian.....3:10:15 (1,768)
Spencer, Ian.....3:32:59 (4,598)
Spencer, Jez.....4:35:20 (17,781)
Spencer, Joe.....5:10:08 (24,093)
Spencer, John.....4:26:19 (15,810)
Spencer, John.....5:32:16 (26,546)
Spencer, John.....5:40:45 (27,249)
Spencer, Keith.....3:18:36 (2,608)
Spencer, Kevin.....2:58:39 (881)
Spencer, Martin.....4:34:16 (17,588)
Spencer, Matt.....2:59:20 (968)
Spencer, Melvyn.....3:40:57 (5,946)
Spencer, Oliver.....4:40:43 (18,927)
Spencer, Robert.....4:19:23 (14,220)
Spencer, Robert.....5:56:47 (28,258)
Spencer, Stuart.....3:37:53 (5,392)
Spencer, William.....3:18:51 (2,637)
Spencer Smith, Jason.....4:55:39 (21,940)
Spendlove, Terence.....3:30:04 (4,183)
Spensley, Robert.....5:24:47 (25,857)
Sperring, Danny.....4:31:17 (16,927)
Spiceley, Paul.....3:27:48 (3,762)
Spicer, Michael.....4:32:57 (17,301)
Spicer, Paul.....6:11:41 (28,915)
Spicer, Philip.....4:48:17 (20,403)
Spicer, Steven.....4:14:50 (13,218)
Spieler, Peter.....2:54:28 (605)
Spiller, Gerry.....4:37:50 (18,326)
Spilsbury, Ian.....2:52:14 (520)
Spina, Marco.....2:40:29 (182)
Spink, Paddy.....3:57:02 (9,184)
Spinneker, Helmut.....4:06:57 (11,541)
Spiro, Mark.....4:42:34 (19,284)
Spiteri, Thomas.....3:58:39 (9,658)
Spokes, Graham.....4:05:55 (11,327)
Spooner, Carl.....4:27:49 (16,154)
Spooner, John.....3:51:36 (7,990)
Spooner, Paul.....4:27:49 (16,154)
Spotswood, Robert.....3:59:57 (10,042)
Spradbury, Matthew.....3:46:17 (6,916)
Spragg, Martin.....4:34:53 (17,690)
Spraggett, Simon.....4:09:18 (12,042)
Spreadborough, David.....6:28:45 (29,379)
Spriggs, Andrew.....4:31:42 (17,038)
Springer, Marcellus.....3:13:23 (2,049)
Sproston, Clive.....4:52:48 (21,271)
Sproston, Garry.....3:40:43 (5,900)
Sprott, Yodi.....3:54:19 (8,538)
Sprules, Christopher.....3:17:53 (2,518)
Spurling, Scott.....3:44:03 (6,499)
Squance, Charles.....4:17:19 (13,738)
Squibb, Roderick.....5:03:48 (23,098)
Squire, Craig.....4:42:23 (19,244)
Squire, Mark.....4:20:43 (14,524)
Squire, Simon.....5:05:34 (23,391)
Squires, David.....5:41:22 (27,283)
Squires, Gary.....3:27:48 (3,762)
Squires, James.....6:23:41 (29,250)
Squires, Paul.....4:00:40 (10,199)
Srinivasan, Rahul.....3:42:19 (6,183)
St Charles, Aragon.....4:34:38 (17,650)
St Croix, Dennis.....3:30:31 (4,249)
St Louis, Brian.....4:37:15 (18,182)
St Pierre, James.....4:39:56 (18,772)
St Quintin, Daniel.....3:57:22 (9,279)
St Quinton, Nicholas.....4:38:11 (18,424)
Staab, Alexander.....5:01:05 (22,745)
Staal, Martin.....3:36:32 (5,163)
Stables, Craig.....4:15:37 (13,390)
Stables, David.....3:52:51 (8,238)
Stables, Kenneth.....3:26:37 (3,573)
Stacey, Ian.....3:54:42 (8,634)
Stacey, Jonathan.....3:56:01 (8,930)
Stacey, Michael.....4:44:03 (19,592)
Stacey, Simon.....4:06:52 (11,522)
Stachowiak, Leszek.....3:28:04 (3,812)
Stack, Dave.....4:58:05 (22,312)
Stack, Raymond.....5:01:58 (22,866)
Staddon, Craig.....5:09:08 (23,959)
Staddon, Ian.....4:45:08 (19,791)
Staderini, Pietro.....3:43:27 (6,390)
Staff, Gary Colin.....4:30:54 (16,826)
Stafford, Andrew.....5:17:08 (25,065)
Stafford, John.....3:49:58 (7,680)
Stafford, Thomas.....4:32:10 (17,150)
Staggs, Robert.....4:04:12 (10,927)
Stahlke, Reinhard.....4:10:30 (12,275)
Stainer, Peter.....2:50:49 (456)
Staines, Michael.....3:51:28 (7,956)
Staines, Paul.....6:44:54 (29,735)
Stainton, Joel.....3:37:14 (5,288)
Staite, Richard.....3:10:21 (1,780)
Stallard, Guy.....4:16:09 (13,496)
Stalley, Andrew.....3:23:05 (3,124)
Stamatescu, Petre.....4:23:06 (15,085)
Stammers, Michael.....4:10:53 (12,368)
Stamp, Richard.....3:51:41 (8,003)
Stanaway, Anthony.....5:23:49 (25,771)
Stanbridge, Philip.....4:37:56 (18,353)
Standen, Mark.....4:37:50 (18,326)
Standen, Melvin.....3:50:24 (7,757)
Standing, Peter.....3:05:21 (1,378)
Standing, Robert.....4:53:15 (21,361)
Standley, Mark.....4:20:51 (14,560)
Stanford, Guy.....4:22:20 (14,894)
Stanford, Patrick.....3:35:15 (4,942)
Stanier, Lawrence.....4:28:54 (16,397)
Staniford, Andrew.....3:55:48 (8,870)
Stanley, Anthony.....4:35:02 (17,717)
Stanley, David.....4:29:32 (16,553)
Stanley, Grahame.....4:29:22 (16,511)
Stanley, John.....3:16:14 (2,336)
Stanley, Kevin.....4:38:43 (18,551)
Stanley, Roger.....4:17:01 (13,672)
Stanley, Shaun.....4:13:55 (13,022)
Stanley-Smith, Christopher.....3:31:20 (4,376)
Stanmore, Carl.....4:30:12 (16,718)
Stannard, Jonathan.....5:31:37 (26,498)
Stanner, Philip.....5:13:27 (24,568)
Stannett, Charlie.....5:16:44 (25,017)
Stansfield, Roger.....5:09:34 (24,024)
Stanton, Jonathan.....4:23:18 (15,134)
Stanton, Richard.....4:45:21 (19,832)
Stanton, Richard.....5:22:41 (25,671)
Stanton Hughes, Michael.....3:53:54 (8,460)
Stanzler, Daniel.....4:51:17 (20,943)
Staples, Paul.....6:04:14 (28,604)
Staples, Sheldon.....6:10:08 (28,865)
Stapleton, Alan.....5:18:25 (25,200)
Stapleton, John.....5:49:46 (27,886)
Stapleton, Philip.....3:57:30 (9,326)
Stapleton, Phillip.....5:18:26 (25,206)
Stapley, Richard.....3:50:33 (7,782)
Starbrook, Samuel.....5:08:22 (23,824)
Stares, David.....4:57:45 (22,260)
Stark, Ian.....3:43:06 (6,326)
Stark, Ian.....5:04:02 (23,138)

Stark, Roger	4:52:33 (21,224)
Starke, Klaus	4:50:11 (20,751)
Starkey, Tom	4:48:12 (20,384)
Starling, Michael	4:34:13 (17,573)
Starnoni, Mauro	3:50:00 (7,690)
Starr, Michael	3:26:46 (3,592)
Starr, Nigel	3:35:33 (4,997)
Starr, Paul	3:47:15 (7,072)
Starti, Richard	5:10:00 (24,081)
Startup, John	4:18:42 (14,051)
Starz, Peter	4:23:35 (15,201)
Stasiczek, Jan	3:30:02 (4,176)
Statham, Jeremy	3:44:42 (6,613)
Statham, Malcolm	3:37:35 (5,346)
Staton, James	4:45:44 (19,891)
Staton, Mark	3:12:40 (1,977)
Statter, Graham	4:41:07 (18,998)
Statter, Ian	4:23:19 (15,138)
Statter, Paul	4:29:37 (16,580)
Stayt, David	3:49:59 (7,686)
Stead, David	5:25:08 (25,901)
Stead, Jonathan	3:35:58 (5,068)
Steadman, Karl	3:56:50 (9,142)
Steadman, Terry	3:33:13 (4,648)
Steans, Nicholas	4:52:33 (21,224)
Stearn, Desmond	5:25:59 (25,985)
Stearn, Nicholas	3:24:23 (3,295)
Stearne, Giles	3:51:59 (8,068)
Steckline, Michael	3:17:06 (2,435)
Steed, Kevin	4:49:54 (20,696)
Steel, Andrew	3:30:52 (4,305)
Steel, Andrew	4:47:46 (20,303)
Steel, Colin	4:05:57 (11,339)
Steel, Grant	3:54:51 (8,672)
Steele, Anthony	3:21:56 (2,988)
Steele, Nicholas	4:36:13 (17,959)
Steele, Nigel	5:17:48 (25,138)
Steele, Roy	2:55:33 (657)
Steele, William	4:00:30 (10,154)
Steen, Mark	5:15:03 (24,790)
Steenekamp, Nico	3:25:58 (3,499)
Steenson, Dean	5:49:19 (27,862)
Steer, Graham	3:46:53 (7,017)
Steer, Mark	3:54:51 (8,672)
Stefanopoli, Pierppolo	3:05:27 (1,386)
Steffensen, Jonny	4:39:45 (18,746)
Steibelt, Chris	3:59:51 (10,010)
Stein, Peter	2:55:30 (651)
Steiner, Christian	4:20:31 (14,479)
Steiner, Und	4:24:28 (15,388)
Steinle, Mark	2:10:46 (6)
Steinpress, Laurence	4:05:18 (11,165)
Stelfox, Andrew	4:06:00 (11,351)
Stell, Patrick	4:51:39 (21,019)
Steller, Larry	4:21:43 (14,737)
Stemp, Iain	3:20:39 (2,842)
Stennett, Stewart	4:27:51 (16,163)
Stent, Nigel	4:55:53 (21,967)
Stenton, Christopher	4:11:57 (12,596)
Stephane, Claude	3:40:04 (5,795)
Stephen, Harry	5:12:15 (24,388)
Stephen, John	4:07:58 (11,755)
Stephen, Jonathan	5:09:01 (23,944)
Stephen, Paul	5:09:01 (23,944)
Stephen, Stuart	5:03:18 (23,042)
Stephens, Alan	4:58:18 (22,341)
Stephens, Chris	6:24:03 (29,260)
Stephens, Christopher	4:12:30 (12,740)
Stephens, Craig	5:09:48 (24,058)
Stephens, David	3:44:45 (6,625)
Stephens, George	2:45:22 (304)
Stephens, Giles	4:05:45 (11,287)
Stephens, John	5:08:35 (23,863)
Stephens, Malcolm	6:05:45 (28,676)
Stephens, Mark	4:08:54 (11,956)
Stephens, Michael	4:05:26 (11,191)
Stephens, Neale	3:04:58 (1,347)
Stephens, Nicholas	2:58:15 (828)
Stephens, Nigel	4:23:19 (15,138)
Stephensen, Jon	3:35:21 (4,962)
Stephenson, Andrew	2:58:22 (842)
Stephenson, Duncan	4:05:55 (11,327)
Stephenson, Guy	4:14:28 (13,120)
Stephenson, John	3:23:05 (3,124)
Stephenson, John	8:45:09 (30,264)
Stephenson, Mark	4:19:03 (14,130)
Stephenson, Martin	5:51:17 (27,966)
Stephenson, Michael	4:34:56 (17,700)
Sterland, Paul	3:40:33 (5,875)
Sterling, David	4:12:51 (12,799)
Sterling, Lloyston	4:51:58 (21,085)
Stern, Franklin	5:34:23 (26,745)
Stern, Joseph	4:32:43 (17,252)
Sternkopf, Stefan	2:59:01 (936)
Steuart Fothringham, Ian	4:51:15 (20,930)
Steven, Clinton	3:43:24 (6,337)
Steven, Roy	3:03:44 (1,265)
Stevens, Alan	3:27:10 (3,652)
Stevens, Alan	4:07:22 (11,629)
Stevens, Anthony	3:41:53 (6,109)
Stevens, Anthony	5:06:26 (23,541)
Stevens, Chris	4:48:09 (20,377)
Stevens, Clifford	4:26:54 (15,936)
Stevens, Daniel	4:09:09 (12,012)
Stevens, Frank	2:47:07 (344)
Stevens, Gareth	5:19:42 (25,335)
Stevens, Graham	3:06:37 (1,471)
Stevens, Graham	3:50:32 (7,780)
Stevens, Greg	2:37:09 (120)
Stevens, Ian	6:04:33 (28,624)
Stevens, John	4:40:46 (18,934)
Stevens, Jonathan	4:59:39 (22,548)
Stevens, Lloyd	4:29:30 (16,545)
Stevens, Mark	4:41:49 (19,126)
Stevens, Paul	3:00:45 (1,070)
Stevens, Paul	4:06:24 (11,433)
Stevens, Peter	3:42:20 (6,188)
Stevens, Philip	4:25:56 (15,712)
Stevens, Roger	4:01:07 (10,303)
Stevens, Roy	3:38:39 (5,510)
Stevens, Simon	2:38:51 (152)
Stevens, Sydney	4:43:09 (19,416)
Stevens, Thomas	4:53:09 (21,346)
Stevens, Will	4:11:15 (12,453)
Stevenson, Andrew	5:25:47 (25,965)
Stevenson, Bert	3:15:21 (2,258)
Stevenson, Clive	3:22:45 (3,078)
Stevenson, David	4:31:00 (16,850)
Stevenson, Gary	4:21:58 (14,802)
Stevenson, George	5:44:14 (27,494)
Stevenson, Graham	5:09:25 (24,003)
Stevenson, Mark	3:38:34 (5,491)
Stevenson, Mark	4:53:57 (21,499)
Stevenson, Nigel	4:21:05 (14,608)
Stevenson, Paul	3:07:18 (1,530)
Stevenson, Paul	3:16:27 (2,359)
Stevenson, Peter	3:59:23 (9,876)
Stevenson, Peter	4:28:23 (16,283)
Stevenson, Robert	4:27:22 (16,033)
Stevenson, Trevor	5:18:44 (25,237)
Stevenson, Warren	5:20:12 (25,375)
Stevinson, David	4:20:08 (14,393)
Stewardson, Stephen	3:59:44 (9,984)
Stewart, Alan	3:39:19 (5,631)
Stewart, Alexander	4:57:59 (22,292)
Stewart, Bill	3:55:35 (8,814)
Stewart, Brian	5:15:03 (24,790)
Stewart, Derek	4:57:50 (22,270)
Stewart, Fergus	4:32:02 (17,124)
Stewart, Gary	3:20:07 (2,775)
Stewart, Graham	2:52:12 (519)
Stewart, Iain	3:28:11 (3,840)
Stewart, Irwin	4:43:07 (19,407)
Stewart, Jackie	2:51:50 (509)
Stewart, Jacob	5:05:12 (23,318)
Stewart, James	3:51:55 (8,054)
Stewart, James	4:59:50 (22,581)
Stewart, James	5:28:42 (26,256)
Stewart, Jimmy	4:34:27 (17,618)
Stewart, Kenneth	4:39:56 (18,772)
Stewart, Michael	3:02:16 (1,171)
Stewart, Nick	4:24:46 (15,452)
Stewart, Richard	4:08:37 (11,896)
Stewart, Steven	4:54:24 (21,573)
Stewart, William	4:09:16 (12,038)
Stewart-Mole, Edmund	5:15:32 (24,874)
Steyn, Deon	4:38:09 (18,419)
Steyn, Rory	3:57:37 (9,369)
Stickland, Andrew	4:26:46 (15,902)
Stickley, Marc	5:48:19 (27,801)
Stiefel, Eric	4:58:30 (22,376)
Stiff, Kevin	5:07:15 (23,657)
Stiffin, Robert	4:50:44 (20,830)
Stileman, Mark	2:56:09 (697)
Stiles, Andrew	3:28:24 (3,890)
Stiles, Andrew	4:24:29 (15,393)
Still, Christopher	4:20:05 (14,385)
Still, Michael	5:22:24 (25,635)
Stillwell, Graeme	4:09:57 (12,153)
Stilwell, Stephen	5:13:48 (24,606)
Stimpson, Barry	5:00:43 (22,695)
Stimpson, Craig	3:50:11 (7,721)
Stimson, Gary	4:46:21 (20,020)
Stinner, Juergen	4:29:40 (16,591)
Stinton, Howard	3:36:10 (5,099)
Stirling, Andrew	3:49:02 (7,471)
Stirling, Michael	5:23:03 (25,711)
Stirling, Scott	4:55:31 (21,901)
Stirnemann, Andreas	3:14:17 (2,144)
Stirrup, John	4:18:15 (13,935)
Stoakes, Paul	5:39:02 (27,088)
Stoat, Tony	3:44:14 (6,529)
Stobbart, Darren	4:24:34 (15,413)
Stobbs, Craig	5:30:31 (26,413)
Stock, Jonathan	3:07:49 (1,574)
Stock, Leonard	3:12:59 (2,002)
Stock, Mark	3:09:21 (1,701)
Stockbridge, Matt	5:19:47 (25,345)
Stockdale, Andrew	5:28:40 (26,249)
Stockdale, Desmond Henry	4:31:58 (17,109)
Stockholm, Raymond	4:38:43 (18,551)
Stocks, Martin	3:11:01 (1,837)
Stocks, Paul	4:55:34 (21,907)
Stoddart, Keith	4:28:15 (16,249)
Stoddart, Neil	4:20:15 (14,418)
Stojanavic, Marce	4:06:49 (11,505)
Stoker, David	3:55:21 (8,772)
Stoker, Robert	4:17:57 (13,863)
Stokes, Clifford	4:29:51 (16,642)
Stokes, David	5:14:49 (24,751)
Stokes, John	6:26:14 (29,305)
Stokes, Kit	2:43:32 (247)
Stokes, Paul	4:15:31 (13,371)
Stokes, Rob	5:34:00 (26,692)
Stokes, Wayne	3:52:26 (8,160)
Stokoe, David	4:04:30 (10,988)
Stokvis, Carsten	3:42:34 (6,229)
Stoller, Tim	3:43:53 (6,467)
Stollery, Michael	4:36:16 (17,967)
Stolwisk, Aad	3:59:21 (9,863)
Stone, Alexander	5:31:39 (26,503)
Stone, Barry	3:20:26 (2,811)
Stone, Chris	5:18:21 (25,195)
Stone, Colin	5:03:20 (23,046)
Stone, David	2:36:54 (114)
Stone, Gaby	4:34:47 (17,672)
Stone, Ian	5:15:01 (24,781)
Stone, John	3:14:44 (2,187)
Stone, Jonathan	3:50:37 (7,792)
Stone, Jonathan	4:09:09 (12,012)
Stone, Leon	6:05:08 (28,645)
Stone, Matthew	6:07:00 (28,720)
Stone, Paul	6:32:35 (29,467)
Stone, Richard	3:38:03 (5,406)
Stone, Roger	3:11:53 (1,903)
Stone, Stefan	6:41:50 (29,687)
Stone, Stephen	3:38:03 (5,406)
Stone, Steven	4:07:57 (11,750)
Stone, Timothy	4:01:59 (10,482)
Stonefield, Richard	5:12:59 (24,497)
Stoneham, Adrian	3:36:43 (5,195)
Stoneley, Andrew	4:18:32 (14,020)
Stoneley, Jonathan	3:11:14 (1,857)
Stoneman, Brian	6:11:21 (28,900)
Stones, Raymond	4:25:20 (15,580)
Stonham, Albert	4:34:34 (17,640)
Stonier, Christopher	3:12:34 (1,966)
Stoodley, Stephen	4:03:28 (10,764)
Stopford, Pete	5:58:18 (28,338)

Stopher, Louis	3:29:38 (4,106)	
Storer, Alan	3:27:09 (3,647)	
Storer, Graham	3:58:13 (9,542)	
Storey, David	3:56:18 (8,994)	
Storey, John	5:03:22 (23,049)	
Storey, John	5:44:34 (27,532)	
Storey, Kenneth	3:47:33 (7,154)	
Storey, Miles	4:09:30 (12,076)	
Storey, Philip	4:01:01 (10,285)	
Storey, Robert	3:33:05 (4,619)	
Storie, Christopher	3:52:08 (8,104)	
Stork, Robert	4:20:25 (14,453)	
Storr, Martin	5:01:06 (22,748)	
Storrie, Martin	4:05:02 (11,123)	
Stoten, Paul	3:39:40 (5,703)	
Stott, Darren	4:31:58 (17,109)	
Stott, Derek	3:48:03 (7,276)	
Stott, Peter	4:32:05 (17,135)	
Stouffer, Craig	5:11:41 (24,310)	
Stoute, Colin	4:23:32 (15,184)	
Strachan, Darren	3:50:15 (7,728)	
Strachan, Ewan	3:57:57 (9,478)	
Strachan, Iain	3:44:31 (6,580)	
Strack, William	4:20:55 (14,575)	
Strain, David	4:45:18 (19,823)	
Stratford, Matthew	3:13:42 (2,074)	
Strathie, Gavin	4:41:32 (19,067)	
Stratton, Gary	4:20:18 (14,429)	
Stratton, Iain	5:12:53 (24,479)	
Stratton, John	4:53:27 (21,407)	
Stratulis, Steven	5:38:11 (27,029)	
Strauss, Hendrik	4:28:42 (16,359)	
Stravers, Robert	4:36:27 (18,007)	
Straw, Jonathan	3:31:32 (4,396)	
Straw, Kevin	3:13:57 (2,110)	
Streather, Peter	5:08:04 (23,778)	
Street, Andrew	4:41:06 (18,996)	
Street, Christopher	4:06:00 (11,351)	
Street, David	4:21:06 (14,611)	
Street, Mark	5:11:50 (24,333)	
Street, Paul	4:45:34 (19,872)	
Streeter, Alan	3:15:50 (2,298)	
Streeter, Duncan	4:31:35 (17,003)	
Streeton, Patrick	4:00:35 (10,181)	
Streit, Ulrich	4:47:29 (20,255)	
Streng, Chris	4:54:22 (21,570)	
Stressler, Christoph	4:19:51 (14,325)	
Stretch, Keith	4:40:14 (18,819)	
Strevens, Paul	4:43:02 (19,395)	
Stricker, Ronald	5:01:34 (22,813)	
Strickland, Andrew	4:30:27 (16,749)	
Strickland, Stephen	4:59:46 (22,565)	
Stringer, David	3:56:00 (8,919)	
Stringer, Mark	4:15:50 (13,432)	
Stringer, Neal	5:26:12 (26,005)	
Stringer, Roy	5:38:30 (27,051)	
Stringer, Thoams	3:31:57 (4,462)	
Stringhini, Angelo	5:24:23 (25,823)	
Strobel, Markus	5:06:15 (23,511)	
Strong, Adam	4:45:55 (19,921)	
Strong, Clifford	3:16:53 (2,410)	
Strong, Darryl	4:54:13 (21,553)	
Strong, Stuart	5:38:40 (27,062)	
Stroud, Andrew	4:49:32 (20,620)	
Stroud, Martin	6:33:55 (29,503)	
Stroud, Mike	4:52:35 (21,233)	
Stroud, Robert	3:53:00 (8,267)	
Stroud, Steven	4:15:09 (13,293)	
Strowbridge, Andrew	4:04:41 (11,038)	
Strubi, Jean Charles	4:10:54 (12,374)	
Strutton, Mark	4:37:42 (18,299)	
Strydom, Hendrik	3:47:12 (7,064)	
Strydom, Peter	4:53:41 (21,450)	
Stuart, James	3:29:24 (4,064)	
Stuart, Paul	3:37:17 (5,298)	
Stuart, Steven	3:02:13 (1,169)	
Stuart, Tony	5:06:17 (23,517)	
Stuart-Smith, Innes	4:33:34 (17,443)	
Stuart-Smith, Paul	3:45:47 (6,820)	
Stubbles, David	4:54:49 (21,682)	
Stubbs, Bernard	4:18:43 (14,056)	
Stubbs, Colin	3:02:00 (1,150)	
Stubbs, Gareth	3:31:33 (4,402)	
Stubbs, Nigel	4:48:50 (20,493)	
Stubbs, Tim	4:11:20 (12,466)	
Stucki, Christoph	3:31:52 (4,449)	
Studd, Paul	3:36:05 (5,086)	
Studd, Philip	4:42:18 (19,226)	
Studds, Gerard	3:21:14 (2,909)	
Studds, Philip	3:11:54 (1,905)	
Studley, Alan	4:19:37 (14,284)	
Studwick, Antony	3:48:14 (7,309)	
Sturdy, Philip	4:13:43 (12,985)	
Sturges, Robert	4:54:44 (21,656)	
Sturgess, Keith	5:12:47 (24,465)	
Sturla, James	4:38:26 (18,488)	
Sturley, John	5:01:53 (22,849)	
Sturrock, Stewart	5:17:25 (25,096)	
Sturton Davies, Stephen	4:31:40 (17,028)	
Stutz, Benjamin	4:08:17 (11,820)	
Styles, Mark	4:25:52 (15,694)	
Styles, Simon	5:07:04 (23,627)	
Stylianou, Andrew	3:06:17 (1,442)	
Styling, Andrew	4:42:52 (19,352)	
Styling, Jonathan	4:34:44 (17,667)	
Subramanian, Harriharan	6:28:24 (29,366)	
Suddury, Brian	4:51:39 (21,019)	
Sudell, Philip	4:39:33 (18,704)	
Sudo, Seiji	5:10:15 (24,113)	
Sugarhood, Paul	3:37:38 (5,355)	
Sugden, Brian	4:33:38 (17,464)	
Sugden, Gavin	3:49:50 (7,651)	
Sugden, George	4:33:29 (17,414)	
Sugden, Michael	4:58:09 (22,320)	
Suller, Jason	3:51:03 (7,881)	
Sullivan, Anthony	5:10:47 (24,181)	
Sullivan, Dieter	6:13:35 (28,982)	
Sullivan, Liam	5:00:50 (22,707)	
Sullivan, Raymond	4:29:17 (16,493)	
Sullivan, Richard	5:03:02 (23,009)	
Sullivan, Stuart	6:36:09 (29,546)	
Sullivan, Timothy	4:30:57 (16,839)	
Sullivan, Toby	3:20:46 (2,860)	
Sullivan, Thomas Jnr	4:14:30 (13,127)	
Sulmon, Christan	4:41:07 (18,998)	
Sulyok, Louis	4:55:29 (21,885)	
Sum, Stephen	4:26:11 (15,774)	
Summerfield, Richard	3:26:43 (3,588)	
Summerfield, Richard	4:34:57 (17,704)	
Summers, David	5:17:57 (25,155)	
Summers, David	5:53:33 (28,094)	
Summers, Derek	3:35:08 (4,924)	
Summers, Jonty	3:48:38 (7,385)	
Summers, Norman	5:23:30 (25,747)	
Summers, Shaun	3:43:17 (6,357)	
Summers, Shaun	6:17:12 (29,094)	
Summers, Thomas	6:02:20 (28,517)	
Summerton, John	4:33:08 (17,334)	
Sumner, Andrew	5:01:29 (22,803)	
Sumner, Edward	4:27:37 (16,096)	
Sumption, Bernard	4:38:45 (18,559)	
Sunderland, Oliver	3:07:53 (1,580)	
Sundvik, Harri	4:04:47 (11,065)	
Sunley, Nigel	5:35:49 (26,868)	
Sunley, Richard	3:27:22 (3,683)	
Surendran, Joel	4:45:25 (19,852)	
Surgay, Clive	4:11:05 (12,412)	
Surman, Giles	4:00:27 (10,136)	
Surrage, Ralph	4:51:46 (21,048)	
Surridge, Mark	3:44:56 (6,670)	
Sury, Michael	4:17:21 (13,742)	
Sussens, John	5:20:42 (25,431)	
Suswain, Andrew	3:29:03 (4,006)	
Sutaria, Yatish	6:35:28 (29,532)	
Sutcliffe, Andrew	3:45:43 (6,802)	
Sutcliffe, Mark	7:02:14 (29,961)	
Suter, John	4:42:24 (19,250)	
Suter, Tony	3:29:37 (4,102)	
Sutherland, Ben	5:18:49 (25,251)	
Sutherland, Graham	4:19:16 (14,183)	
Sutherland, Graham	4:43:36 (19,521)	
Sutherland, John	4:21:12 (14,628)	
Sutherland, Martin	4:48:06 (20,367)	
Sutherland, Paul	3:16:34 (2,378)	
Sutherland, Scott	5:58:48 (28,356)	
Sutherland, William	2:49:17 (401)	
Sutherland, William	4:59:10 (22,485)	
Sutherns, Robin	4:41:05 (18,992)	
Sutterby, Philip	4:13:06 (12,836)	
Suttle, Stephen	3:03:50 (1,270)	
Sutton, Darren	3:42:59 (6,299)	
Sutton, David	4:04:09 (10,910)	
Sutton, Harold	4:20:44 (14,529)	
Sutton, Michael	4:37:59 (18,365)	
Sutton, Nathan	5:24:31 (25,838)	
Sutton, Richard	4:10:22 (12,244)	
Sutton, Richard	4:21:35 (14,708)	
Sutton, Richard	4:32:16 (17,168)	
Sutton, Ron	5:41:48 (27,316)	
Sutton-Gibbs, Peter	4:10:22 (12,244)	
Suzuki, Nobuhide	3:35:50 (5,039)	
Svennilson, Peter	4:00:31 (10,158)	
Svenningsen, Jon	3:58:57 (9,738)	
Svensson, Tom	3:13:57 (2,110)	
Swadling, Andrew	5:08:58 (23,935)	
Swai, Jonathan	4:54:45 (21,660)	
Swailes, Cliff	3:59:14 (9,828)	
Swain, Bradley	4:02:25 (10,555)	
Swaine, Kevin	5:09:09 (23,965)	
Swainson, Christopher	3:56:15 (8,980)	
Swainson, Patrick	3:39:23 (5,645)	
Swaleheen, Azee	3:47:54 (7,241)	
Swales, Philip	4:51:22 (20,963)	
Swan, Alan	3:30:23 (4,228)	
Swan, Martin	4:23:32 (15,184)	
Swan, Paul	4:06:32 (11,456)	
Swan, Toby	4:17:04 (13,680)	
Swann, Andrew	4:54:00 (21,511)	
Swann, Graham	4:11:44 (12,556)	
Swanson, Thomas	4:09:59 (12,163)	
Swarbrick, Alexander	4:16:36 (13,589)	
Swart, Charles	3:50:39 (7,796)	
Swart, Pieter	5:26:07 (25,999)	
Swartz, Elton	4:48:00 (20,345)	
Swash, Kevin	5:02:57 (22,999)	
Swatton, Greg	4:14:20 (13,103)	
Swatton, Neville	3:03:37 (1,256)	
Swayne, Julian	4:07:59 (11,762)	
Sweeney, Anthony	5:00:03 (22,629)	
Sweeney, Christopher	3:43:18 (6,360)	
Sweeney, Christopher	7:17:41 (30,066)	
Sweeney, John	4:48:22 (20,420)	
Sweeney, Neil	3:39:24 (5,652)	
Sweeney-Fenton, Alistair	6:10:41 (28,881)	
Sweet, David	3:44:22 (6,557)	
Sweet, Michael	4:06:39 (11,476)	
Sweeting, John	3:26:57 (3,616)	
Swensen, Brett	4:16:41 (13,607)	
Swensson, Martin	3:40:55 (5,931)	
Sweny, John	3:51:05 (7,889)	
Swift, Derrick	3:05:07 (1,356)	
Swift, Ian	3:41:52 (6,104)	
Swift, John	4:43:34 (19,512)	
Swift, Simon	4:06:14 (11,393)	
Swift, William Emrys	3:07:35 (1,555)	
Swindells, Graham	3:59:28 (9,909)	
Swinden, Jeremy	3:55:57 (8,906)	
Swinden, Mark	3:34:10 (4,782)	
Swindle, Kevin	4:40:25 (18,860)	
Swingle, Steven	4:04:58 (11,111)	
Swingler, David	3:48:42 (7,402)	
Swinnerton, Joseph	5:59:35 (28,396)	
Swinton, Clive	3:54:53 (8,683)	
Swiss, Andrew	4:29:26 (16,528)	
Switzman, John	7:44:15 (30,180)	
Swycher, Stuart	5:01:30 (22,805)	
Sydenham, Michael	5:45:34 (27,597)	
Sykes, Adrian	3:59:20 (9,856)	
Sykes, Alexander	5:45:35 (27,599)	
Sykes, Andrew	4:26:44 (15,895)	
Sykes, Mark	3:48:30 (7,361)	
Sykes, Matthew	5:00:40 (22,686)	
Sykes, Peter John	3:54:26 (8,575)	
Sykes, Richard	4:54:25 (21,576)	
Sylge, Oliver	4:55:31 (21,901)	
Sylvester, Klaus Dieter	3:33:34 (4,691)	
Symns, Paul	3:47:45 (7,200)	
Symonds, Andrew	4:17:04 (13,680)	
Symonds, Christopher	3:10:58 (1,832)	

Symonds, Lee	4:40:57 (18,967)	
Symons, David	2:29:33 (64)	
Symons, Gareth	6:42:03 (29,693)	
Symons, Kevin	4:15:22 (13,338)	
Synnott, David	4:09:22 (12,054)	
Syrett, Stephen	3:35:56 (5,060)	
Sysum, Reginald	2:57:38 (787)	
Szafarczyk, Jerzy	3:33:15 (4,652)	
Szenker, Ber	4:23:43 (15,230)	
Szlamka, Julian	7:00:56 (29,951)	
Szynkaruk, Anthony	4:27:44 (16,128)	
Tabb, Chris	4:20:27 (14,464)	
Tabenor, Peter	3:10:15 (1,768)	
Tabor, Frank	5:29:39 (26,342)	
Tack, Ian	2:54:28 (605)	
Tadman, Mike	8:36:33 (30,255)	
Taft, Kevin	5:07:35 (23,710)	
Taggart, James	4:16:11 (13,506)	
Taggart, William	4:18:26 (13,998)	
Taheri, Peyman	3:49:28 (7,567)	
Tai, Nigel	4:00:29 (10,148)	
Tai, Wai-Land	4:10:29 (12,272)	
Tailor, Navnit	4:36:03 (17,940)	
Tainon, Jacky	3:31:58 (4,463)	
Tait, Christopher	4:48:08 (20,375)	
Tait, David	5:31:45 (26,513)	
Tait, James	3:20:24 (2,806)	
Tait, Robin	4:03:16 (10,713)	
Taitz, Jonny	4:06:57 (11,541)	
Takano, Satoshi	3:43:23 (6,374)	
Talamonti, Mauro	3:14:29 (2,165)	
Talbert, Stuart	4:38:29 (18,504)	
Talbot, Christopher	4:14:24 (13,112)	
Talbot, Ian	4:15:11 (13,299)	
Talbot, Luke	4:37:19 (18,200)	
Talbot, Michael	3:23:25 (3,162)	
Talbot, Simon	3:18:57 (2,653)	
Talbot, Stephen	4:17:48 (13,832)	
Talbot, Wilf	4:44:58 (19,770)	
Tall, Richard	4:18:15 (13,935)	
Tallan, William	4:24:55 (15,482)	
Talman, Christopher	5:07:26 (23,688)	
Tam, Patrick	3:48:32 (7,367)	
Tamburro, Anthony	4:22:51 (15,021)	
Tambuyser, Kurt	3:41:20 (6,017)	
Tame, Alex	4:01:50 (10,452)	
Tame, Kevin	3:49:01 (7,467)	
Tampin, Steven	4:28:21 (16,271)	
Tamplin, Phillip	4:27:11 (16,004)	
Tamplin, Simon	4:50:25 (20,789)	
Tan, Usaly	4:54:16 (21,558)	
Tanaka, Hiro	4:39:13 (18,639)	
Tanaka, Kiyoshi	3:18:08 (2,553)	
Tancock, Stephen	2:53:00 (543)	
Tanguy, Eric	2:54:19 (594)	
Tannassee, Thomas	4:31:17 (16,927)	
Tanner, Adrian	2:46:15 (324)	
Tanner, Anthony	4:37:13 (18,175)	
Tanner, Graham	4:27:28 (16,055)	
Tanos, Paul	4:33:31 (17,423)	
Tansey, Mark	5:20:58 (25,462)	
Tansey, Michael	3:51:04 (7,884)	
Tantam, Robert	4:07:36 (11,678)	
Taplin, Alan	3:46:48 (7,003)	
Taplin, Derek	5:36:10 (26,890)	
Taplin, Richard	3:38:10 (5,421)	
Tapp, Raymond	5:44:11 (27,491)	
Tapper, Andrew	4:33:43 (17,482)	
Tarantino, Giovanni	4:14:24 (13,112)	
Targett, David	4:38:19 (18,456)	
Tarling, Stephen	3:47:49 (7,213)	
Tarpey, Paul	3:00:55 (1,078)	
Tarran, Paul	4:56:23 (22,048)	
Tarsey, David	3:59:54 (10,026)	
Tasker, David	3:31:26 (4,387)	
Tasker, David	4:19:14 (14,174)	
Tasker, John	3:08:51 (1,659)	
Tasquier, Nick	3:48:57 (7,451)	
Tate, Chris	3:19:43 (2,730)	
Tate, Douglas	5:05:23 (23,356)	
Tate, John	4:21:32 (14,698)	
Tatham, Ben	4:25:56 (15,712)	
Tatham, Christopher	4:08:19 (11,827)	

Tatham, David	4:42:18 (19,226)	
Tattersall, Alan	3:57:40 (9,387)	
Tattersall, Rex	3:27:28 (3,700)	
Tattum, Paul	3:26:47 (3,595)	
Taupin, Emmanuel	3:24:03 (3,252)	
Tavares, Miguel	2:54:23 (601)	
Tavendale, Stephen	3:44:31 (6,580)	
Tavner, Charles	3:01:52 (1,140)	
Tawn, Michael	3:43:28 (6,392)	
Tawn, Robin	4:46:20 (20,016)	
Taylor, Adam	3:57:10 (9,215)	
Taylor, Adrian	5:30:36 (26,419)	
Taylor, Alasdair	3:30:46 (4,289)	
Taylor, Andrew	2:50:55 (463)	
Taylor, Andrew	5:22:20 (25,630)	
Taylor, Andrew	5:55:31 (28,192)	
Taylor, Anthony	5:08:03 (23,774)	
Taylor, Argie	3:39:18 (5,625)	
Taylor, Barrie	6:55:29 (29,892)	
Taylor, Barry	4:25:42 (15,655)	
Taylor, Brian	3:50:51 (7,837)	
Taylor, Brian	3:57:23 (9,283)	
Taylor, Brian	4:24:51 (15,466)	
Taylor, Brian	4:59:18 (22,497)	
Taylor, Bruce	4:25:09 (15,543)	
Taylor, Bryon	4:56:34 (22,083)	
Taylor, Byron	6:14:56 (29,020)	
Taylor, Carl	4:18:08 (13,895)	
Taylor, Charles	3:39:11 (5,607)	
Taylor, Chris	4:49:16 (20,575)	
Taylor, Christopher	4:00:37 (10,190)	
Taylor, Christopher	4:10:04 (12,173)	
Taylor, Colin	3:55:13 (8,738)	
Taylor, Craig	4:21:29 (14,689)	
Taylor, Craig	5:59:19 (28,383)	
Taylor, Daniel	3:48:15 (7,312)	
Taylor, Darren	3:35:01 (4,905)	
Taylor, Darren	3:59:28 (9,909)	
Taylor, David	3:51:34 (7,983)	
Taylor, David	3:56:22 (9,013)	
Taylor, David	4:05:43 (11,273)	
Taylor, David	4:08:41 (11,910)	
Taylor, David	5:12:07 (24,365)	
Taylor, David	6:24:28 (29,273)	
Taylor, Desmond	3:30:21 (4,221)	
Taylor, Dominic	4:39:23 (18,664)	
Taylor, Edward	4:20:11 (14,405)	
Taylor, Eric	3:18:07 (2,550)	
Taylor, Gary	2:59:58 (1,029)	
Taylor, Gary	5:09:36 (24,031)	
Taylor, George	2:44:04 (262)	
Taylor, Gordon	3:41:48 (6,091)	
Taylor, Graham	2:55:53 (674)	
Taylor, Graham	5:39:56 (27,185)	
Taylor, Harry	3:58:33 (9,625)	
Taylor, Ian	3:50:30 (7,772)	
Taylor, Ian	4:32:37 (17,232)	
Taylor, Ian	4:50:16 (20,763)	
Taylor, Ian	4:54:35 (21,616)	
Taylor, Ian	4:55:21 (21,831)	
Taylor, James	4:20:33 (14,489)	
Taylor, Jeffrey	3:47:19 (7,090)	
Taylor, Jeffrey	4:34:59 (17,709)	
Taylor, Jeremy	3:59:28 (9,909)	
Taylor, Jim	4:26:55 (15,943)	
Taylor, Jim	4:37:15 (18,182)	
Taylor, John	4:37:20 (18,206)	
Taylor, John	4:43:47 (19,554)	
Taylor, Keith	3:47:03 (7,042)	
Taylor, Ken	6:48:12 (29,780)	
Taylor, Kevan	4:55:11 (21,778)	
Taylor, Kevin	4:54:00 (21,511)	
Taylor, Laurence	4:01:15 (10,326)	
Taylor, Laurence	5:21:44 (25,552)	
Taylor, Luke	4:00:28 (10,142)	
Taylor, Mark	3:06:43 (1,480)	
Taylor, Mark	3:51:13 (7,914)	
Taylor, Mark	4:30:16 (16,727)	
Taylor, Mark	4:36:16 (17,967)	
Taylor, Martin	4:46:43 (20,095)	
Taylor, Michael	3:25:28 (3,441)	
Taylor, Michael	3:28:52 (3,975)	
Taylor, Michael	3:36:41 (5,186)	

Taylor, Miles	3:51:50 (8,035)	
Taylor, Nathan	4:35:41 (17,863)	
Taylor, Neil	3:43:49 (6,458)	
Taylor, Neil	3:57:47 (9,425)	
Taylor, Neil	4:21:44 (14,741)	
Taylor, Neville	4:24:29 (15,393)	
Taylor, Nicholas	3:28:23 (3,889)	
Taylor, Nicholas	3:39:03 (5,582)	
Taylor, Nicholas	4:31:47 (17,056)	
Taylor, Nick	4:27:04 (15,988)	
Taylor, Paul	3:58:41 (9,669)	
Taylor, Paul	4:03:38 (10,810)	
Taylor, Paul	4:23:31 (15,179)	
Taylor, Paul	5:41:50 (27,318)	
Taylor, Peter	3:11:37 (1,874)	
Taylor, Peter	4:01:55 (10,469)	
Taylor, Peter	4:44:35 (19,692)	
Taylor, Peter	5:47:50 (27,757)	
Taylor, Phil	4:37:52 (18,341)	
Taylor, Philip	2:42:56 (236)	
Taylor, Phillip	2:57:51 (802)	
Taylor, Ray	3:48:30 (7,361)	
Taylor, Raymond	4:13:19 (12,878)	
Taylor, Richard	3:19:47 (2,737)	
Taylor, Richard	5:16:52 (25,029)	
Taylor, Richard	5:18:25 (25,200)	
Taylor, Richie	4:57:52 (22,277)	
Taylor, Robert	2:48:35 (381)	
Taylor, Robert	4:33:04 (17,322)	
Taylor, Robert	5:31:44 (26,510)	
Taylor, Robert	5:35:29 (26,841)	
Taylor, Robin	3:54:50 (8,668)	
Taylor, Robin	4:11:31 (12,505)	
Taylor, Ron	4:18:58 (14,112)	
Taylor, Simon	4:17:07 (13,692)	
Taylor, Simon	4:46:19 (20,010)	
Taylor, Stephen	4:02:50 (10,628)	
Taylor, Stephen	4:09:56 (12,147)	
Taylor, Stephen	4:54:42 (21,640)	
Taylor, Steven	5:05:54 (23,448)	
Taylor, Stuart	3:19:46 (2,736)	
Taylor, Stuart	3:52:38 (8,199)	
Taylor, Thomas	4:25:50 (15,685)	
Taylor, Timothy	3:57:34 (9,352)	
Taylor, Timothy	4:19:34 (14,273)	
Taylor, Tony	5:28:42 (26,256)	
Taylor, Warwick John	3:49:44 (7,629)	
Taylor, Wayne	3:06:22 (1,448)	
Taylorson, Stan	4:08:46 (11,928)	
Teare, Jonathan	3:56:47 (9,129)	
Tearle, Charles	3:46:04 (6,869)	
Tearle, Ewart	3:43:58 (6,483)	
Teasdale, David	5:17:56 (25,151)	
Teasdale, Martin	5:24:35 (25,843)	
Tebb, Ron	6:15:21 (29,042)	
Tebbutt, Andrew	4:29:43 (16,603)	
Tebbutt, David	3:54:24 (8,562)	
Tedder, Colin	4:35:51 (17,891)	
Tedoldi, Alessandro	4:04:35 (11,017)	
Tee, Julian	3:57:54 (9,462)	
Tee, Paul	2:48:47 (385)	
Telfer, Charles	4:42:26 (19,260)	
Telfer, Richard	4:29:39 (16,585)	
Telfer, Robert	4:01:53 (10,461)	
Tellem, Geraint	3:18:07 (2,550)	
Temby, Lester	4:34:14 (17,580)	
Tempelman, Jaap	4:29:15 (16,485)	
Tempest, Stephen	3:56:44 (9,115)	
Temple, Paul	5:28:50 (26,273)	
Templeman, Paul	4:36:41 (18,059)	
Temple-Smith, Matthew	6:46:43 (29,754)	
Tennant, Jim	4:42:07 (19,182)	
Tergat, Paul	2:08:15 (2)	
Terrill, Chris	3:32:45 (4,567)	
Terrill, Graham	4:26:42 (15,890)	
Terry, Andrew	3:21:20 (2,925)	
Terry, Christopher	5:50:58 (27,953)	
Terry, Colin	3:56:45 (9,121)	
Terry, Dave	8:29:04 (30,243)	
Terry, Kenneth	4:25:13 (15,560)	
Terry, Michael	4:27:57 (16,181)	
Terry, William	5:59:03 (28,369)	
Tessanne, Laurent	3:34:07 (4,774)	

Tessier, Pascal 3:16:04 (2,326)
Testar, Stuart 4:07:05 (11,568)
Tester, Jeremy 4:52:04 (21,108)
Tetley, Phil 5:34:53 (26,796)
Tetsill, Ian 5:03:00 (23,004)
Tetstall, Peter 3:51:59 (8,068)
Tevenaw, John 4:08:33 (11,880)
Teverson, Ross 4:37:26 (18,233)
Tew, Nicholas 4:18:50 (14,087)
Tew, Stephen 4:07:08 (11,576)
Thacker, David 4:03:58 (10,876)
Thacker, Jonathan 5:41:09 (27,269)
Thacker, Michael 5:52:09 (28,027)
Thacker, Simon 3:31:19 (4,373)
Thackeray, Brian 4:29:57 (16,675)
Thackstone, Mark 4:31:09 (16,888)
Thackwell, Colin 4:54:05 (21,530)
Thadchanamoorthy, James 3:33:40 (4,708)
Tham, Lawrence 4:43:43 (19,543)
Thatcher, Gary 5:17:06 (25,062)
Thatcher, Michael 3:54:41 (8,628)
Thatcher, Steve 3:48:40 (7,393)
Thavapalasundaram, Sundar 5:20:53 (25,451)
Thaw, George 5:42:30 (27,375)
Theaker, Edward 4:31:36 (17,011)
Theakston, Edward 4:07:18 (11,612)
Theakston, Timothy 4:02:16 (10,530)
Thedenat, Bruno 3:39:53 (5,754)
Theo, Richard 4:38:13 (18,431)
Theobald, Stephen 5:11:21 (24,262)
Theodoulou, Orthodoxos 6:09:31 (28,835)
Theodoulou, Tony 5:47:49 (27,755)
Theret, Bernard 4:23:20 (15,141)
Thexton, Kent 3:08:38 (1,643)
Thibeau, Arnaud 4:17:58 (13,866)
Thick, Rod 4:27:15 (16,017)
Thiery, Michel 3:22:11 (3,024)
Thilwell, Graeme 5:58:58 (28,366)
Thinsa, Jasbir 5:52:39 (28,045)
Thirkettle, Peter 3:59:41 (9,969)
Thirunesan, Thambiah 5:37:15 (26,960)
Thiry, Gilles 3:52:03 (8,085)
Thistlethwaite, Anthony 3:27:12 (3,660)
Thoday, Corin 3:56:40 (9,095)
Thomann, Alastair 3:45:23 (6,728)
Thomas, Adrian 5:25:16 (25,917)
Thomas, Alan 4:45:04 (19,783)
Thomas, Alan 5:15:28 (24,864)
Thomas, Alex 4:37:44 (18,308)
Thomas, Andrew 3:21:39 (2,964)
Thomas, Andrew 4:19:06 (14,148)
Thomas, Andrew 4:22:31 (14,933)
Thomas, Benjamin 4:00:12 (10,091)
Thomas, Bevan 4:25:40 (15,646)
Thomas, Bobby 4:12:16 (12,683)
Thomas, Brian 3:43:04 (6,319)
Thomas, Calvin 2:54:34 (612)
Thomas, Dale 5:05:28 (23,378)
Thomas, Daniel 7:13:56 (30,045)
Thomas, Darren 3:13:19 (2,040)
Thomas, Darren 4:39:28 (18,683)
Thomas, Dave 3:38:19 (5,451)
Thomas, David 2:58:48 (910)
Thomas, David 3:54:14 (8,519)
Thomas, David 4:11:20 (12,466)
Thomas, David 4:11:59 (12,606)
Thomas, David 4:13:22 (12,897)
Thomas, David 4:17:09 (13,703)
Thomas, David 4:17:29 (13,769)
Thomas, David 4:19:20 (14,202)
Thomas, David 4:29:35 (16,570)
Thomas, Derek 3:35:49 (5,035)
Thomas, Dewi 5:46:57 (27,700)
Thomas, Dominic 5:08:10 (23,792)
Thomas, Dylan 4:45:55 (19,921)
Thomas, Edward 4:10:50 (12,355)
Thomas, Evan 3:53:36 (8,404)
Thomas, Evan 4:40:26 (18,864)
Thomas, Frank 3:05:09 (1,362)
Thomas, Frank 3:55:59 (8,915)
Thomas, Gareth 4:35:32 (17,819)
Thomas, Gareth 5:56:47 (28,258)
Thomas, Gary 4:02:59 (10,657)

LONDON MARATHON

Thomas, George 4:01:20 (10,348)
Thomas, Geriant 3:41:13 (5,987)
Thomas, Graham 3:29:55 (4,155)
Thomas, Graham 3:51:19 (7,935)
Thomas, Howard 4:50:50 (20,851)
Thomas, Iain 4:12:54 (12,809)
Thomas, Ian 3:47:30 (7,139)
Thomas, Ivor 3:51:23 (7,942)
Thomas, Iwan 5:08:27 (23,840)
Thomas, Jeremy 4:35:40 (17,859)
Thomas, John 3:27:57 (3,799)
Thomas, John 3:37:37 (5,352)
Thomas, Julian 3:42:24 (6,201)
Thomas, Justin 3:24:59 (3,375)
Thomas, Justin 3:59:28 (9,909)
Thomas, Kevin 3:07:34 (1,552)
Thomas, Kevin 4:09:55 (12,143)
Thomas, Kevin 4:16:10 (13,500)
Thomas, Kevin 4:44:50 (19,738)
Thomas, Leighton 3:14:54 (2,208)
Thomas, Michael 5:26:38 (26,054)
Thomas, Michael 5:50:53 (27,950)
Thomas, N 4:40:16 (18,830)
Thomas, Neil 4:20:29 (14,471)
Thomas, Neil 5:28:25 (26,225)
Thomas, Nick 3:59:58 (10,047)
Thomas, Nick 4:14:07 (13,061)
Thomas, Nick 4:58:20 (22,347)
Thomas, Owen 3:15:32 (2,275)
Thomas, Paul 3:29:15 (4,036)
Thomas, Paul 3:35:22 (4,964)
Thomas, Paul 4:04:15 (10,939)
Thomas, Paul 5:29:54 (26,368)
Thomas, Peter 3:50:20 (7,741)
Thomas, Philip 4:26:17 (15,800)
Thomas, Philip 4:47:03 (20,173)
Thomas, Richard 2:56:16 (705)
Thomas, Robert 3:38:32 (5,487)
Thomas, Robert 4:41:04 (18,990)
Thomas, Rodney 4:57:29 (22,214)
Thomas, Ron 4:44:47 (19,729)
Thomas, Roy 3:06:38 (1,473)
Thomas, Russell 2:58:19 (836)
Thomas, Simon 3:48:49 (7,426)
Thomas, Simon 3:54:49 (8,664)
Thomas, Simon 4:42:15 (19,215)
Thomas, Simon 4:57:14 (22,175)
Thomas, Spencer 3:40:54 (5,926)
Thomas, Stephen 4:45:17 (19,821)
Thomas, Stephen 4:58:42 (22,416)
Thomas, Steve 4:56:30 (22,065)
Thomas, Wayne 3:21:07 (2,897)
Thomas, William 3:26:15 (3,528)
Thomason, Francis 3:09:29 (1,710)
Thomassen, Jorgen 3:48:30 (7,361)
Thompson, Alan 4:22:06 (14,837)
Thompson, Alastair 3:38:27 (5,473)
Thompson, Andrew 2:51:59 (515)
Thompson, Barry 3:01:37 (1,125)
Thompson, Brian 4:46:49 (20,119)
Thompson, Charlie 3:58:21 (9,576)
Thompson, Daniel 3:38:13 (5,433)
Thompson, Daniel 5:37:58 (27,016)
Thompson, Dave 4:03:40 (10,815)
Thompson, David 2:58:14 (826)
Thompson, David 3:21:09 (2,901)
Thompson, David 3:47:39 (7,179)
Thompson, David 4:19:16 (14,183)
Thompson, David 4:57:58 (22,288)
Thompson, Dennis 3:56:14 (8,975)
Thompson, Edward 3:47:31 (7,143)
Thompson, Gary 4:21:15 (14,639)
Thompson, Gary 5:48:59 (27,840)
Thompson, Gerard 4:02:45 (10,617)
Thompson, Glenn 3:40:18 (5,830)

Thompson, Glyn 4:09:35 (12,088)
Thompson, Graham 4:37:39 (18,291)
Thompson, Gregory 3:14:23 (2,156)
Thompson, John 2:57:47 (798)
Thompson, John 3:22:56 (3,099)
Thompson, John 4:14:35 (13,145)
Thompson, Jolyon 4:35:18 (17,775)
Thompson, Jonathan 4:35:13 (17,754)
Thompson, Joseph 4:20:23 (14,447)
Thompson, Larry 5:41:22 (27,283)
Thompson, Mark 2:56:41 (725)
Thompson, Mark 3:34:24 (4,817)
Thompson, Mark 3:36:48 (5,209)
Thompson, Mark 4:36:33 (18,032)
Thompson, Martyn 5:24:51 (25,862)
Thompson, Michael 3:16:38 (2,382)
Thompson, Michael 4:49:25 (20,602)
Thompson, Michael 5:10:41 (24,174)
Thompson, Mike 3:46:35 (6,968)
Thompson, Noel 6:51:51 (29,831)
Thompson, Oliver 4:57:53 (22,279)
Thompson, Paul 3:44:52 (6,653)
Thompson, Peter 3:28:49 (3,965)
Thompson, Peter 4:04:09 (10,910)
Thompson, Phlip 4:58:16 (22,338)
Thompson, Ray 4:37:16 (18,190)
Thompson, Richard 3:20:06 (2,774)
Thompson, Robert 4:13:08 (12,845)
Thompson, Robert 4:28:21 (16,271)
Thompson, Ron 4:27:35 (16,084)
Thompson, Simon 4:17:34 (13,784)
Thompson, Stephen 2:59:42 (997)
Thompson, Stephen 3:33:42 (4,714)
Thompson, Stephen 4:36:40 (18,057)
Thompson, Terence 4:07:30 (11,660)
Thompson, Tony 5:44:31 (27,516)
Thompstone, Rodger 3:34:47 (4,875)
Thomsett, Roger 4:18:20 (13,964)
Thomson, Alan 4:19:14 (14,174)
Thomson, Alec 4:16:45 (13,629)
Thomson, Alistair 4:43:47 (19,554)
Thomson, Clifford 4:45:10 (19,801)
Thomson, Colin 5:34:49 (26,786)
Thomson, Dave 3:45:56 (6,843)
Thomson, David 5:30:44 (26,431)
Thomson, Euan 4:04:38 (11,028)
Thomson, James 4:37:36 (18,280)
Thomson, John 4:16:00 (13,463)
Thomson, Michael 2:58:58 (931)
Thomson, Paul 3:32:43 (4,561)
Thomson, Paul 4:44:51 (19,743)
Thomson, Robert 4:59:31 (22,529)
Thomson, Rod 3:41:20 (6,017)
Thomson, Simon 3:52:25 (8,158)
Thomson, Stephen 3:15:05 (2,232)
Thorburn, Peter 3:48:32 (7,367)
Thorburn, William 5:10:50 (24,189)
Thorn, Mike 4:19:19 (14,198)
Thorn, Richard 3:16:41 (2,390)
Thorn, Tony 6:08:26 (28,784)
Thorne, Colin 4:58:27 (22,369)
Thorne, Nathan 4:26:30 (15,846)
Thorne Jones, Russell 5:12:20 (24,400)
Thorne Jones, Stuart 5:27:25 (26,120)
Thornhill, Ernest 3:21:50 (2,978)
Thornhill, Kevin 5:57:46 (28,315)
Thornley, Andrew 4:19:50 (14,323)
Thornton, David 2:57:05 (750)
Thornton, David 5:37:26 (26,974)
Thornton, Dean 2:54:33 (611)
Thornton, Joe 4:41:30 (19,061)
Thornton, Kevin 3:14:17 (2,144)
Thornton, Mark 4:25:27 (15,602)
Thornton, Stanley 4:16:24 (13,552)
Thornton, Stuart 5:57:43 (28,311)
Thornton, William 8:55:23 (30,270)
Thornton Clarke, Jeremy 4:08:53 (11,952)
Thorogood, Keith 4:44:18 (19,640)
Thorogood, Matthew 3:20:47 (2,862)
Thorold, Marcus 4:03:31 (10,776)
Thorpe, Anthony 5:17:43 (25,126)
Thorpe, Benjamin 5:55:28 (28,187)
Thorpe, Gary 4:29:34 (16,564)

Thorpe, James	4:59:17 (22,495)	
Thorpe, Philip	4:52:06 (21,113)	
Thorpe, Steven	4:54:28 (21,585)	
Thorpe, Terry	4:34:05 (17,553)	
Thorpe, Walter	4:19:16 (14,183)	
Thraves, Peter	3:58:24 (9,585)	
Threlfall, Mark	3:57:27 (9,311)	
Thripp, Michael	4:36:38 (18,048)	
Thrower, Gary	4:29:01 (16,425)	
Thrower, Neil	3:52:36 (8,190)	
Thrussell, Neil	4:22:38 (14,962)	
Thurgood, Gary	4:33:32 (17,428)	
Thurgood, Peter	5:49:11 (27,857)	
Thurlow, Ivan	4:35:53 (17,903)	
Thurman, Mitchell	4:29:34 (16,564)	
Thurstance, Anthony	4:49:00 (20,528)	
Thurston, Colin	3:19:27 (2,700)	
Thurston, Will	4:14:44 (13,185)	
Thys, Gert	2:12:11 (10)	
Tibbs, Stephen	2:44:02 (261)	
Tice, Andrew	4:54:21 (21,568)	
Tickle, Andrew	6:08:10 (28,774)	
Tickner, Alan	3:28:02 (3,807)	
Tickner, David	4:25:58 (15,723)	
Tidey, Paul	4:12:02 (12,620)	
Tierney, Kevin	4:10:06 (12,179)	
Tierney, Robin	4:04:23 (10,965)	
Tierney, Trevor	3:53:15 (8,318)	
Tietz, Karl	3:29:41 (4,119)	
Tiezzi, Moreno	3:22:30 (3,054)	
Tiffin, Ian	4:50:18 (20,771)	
Tilby, Stephen	4:48:15 (20,395)	
Till, Ian Charles	4:32:48 (17,276)	
Tillbrooke, Tony	4:16:44 (13,621)	
Tiller, Nicholas	3:51:18 (7,932)	
Tillery, Andrew	2:59:00 (934)	
Tillett, Ian	3:24:58 (3,372)	
Tilley, Andrew	4:10:16 (12,222)	
Tilley, Glen	5:16:54 (25,034)	
Tilley, Ian	4:10:24 (12,255)	
Tilley, Jonathan	4:44:12 (19,619)	
Tilley, Kevin	2:35:36 (99)	
Tilley, Stephen	4:38:38 (18,534)	
Tilsley, Andrew	3:03:23 (1,239)	
Timbrell, Leonard	4:50:18 (20,771)	
Timbs, Adrian	4:04:10 (10,918)	
Timm, John	5:51:13 (27,962)	
Timmins, James	4:44:31 (19,680)	
Timmins, Simon	4:26:45 (15,898)	
Timmis, William	3:51:47 (8,023)	
Timmiss, Derek	6:40:12 (29,645)	
Timms, Mitchell	4:07:43 (11,703)	
Timms, Paul	3:46:42 (6,990)	
Timotheou, Andrew	4:45:24 (19,846)	
Timson, Andrew	3:39:52 (5,750)	
Tinco, Daniel	4:07:53 (11,737)	
Tindal, Peter	4:15:04 (13,282)	
Tindall, Mark	4:48:38 (20,457)	
Tindle, Vincent	2:46:47 (334)	
Tinegate, Geoffrey	4:58:19 (22,343)	
Ting, Vincent	3:41:33 (6,042)	
Tingle, Christopher	4:34:56 (17,700)	
Tingle, Nicholas	4:40:30 (18,874)	
Tingle, Philip	5:41:28 (27,295)	
Tinker, Darren	3:47:19 (7,090)	
Tinker, Kenneth	4:45:24 (19,846)	
Tinsey, Jason	5:43:01 (27,410)	
Tinsley, David	2:58:22 (842)	
Tinsley, Peter	3:53:54 (8,460)	
Tipper, David	4:29:36 (16,577)	
Tipper, Jeremy	4:20:58 (14,584)	
Tippie, Matt	4:01:17 (10,333)	
Tipping, John	4:08:28 (11,867)	
Tiptaft, Simon	3:59:58 (10,047)	
Tirrell, James	4:43:28 (19,484)	
Titarenko, Taras	4:16:44 (13,621)	
Titchener, Frank	3:16:33 (2,376)	
Titchener, Michael	4:49:53 (20,691)	
Titheridge, Alex	3:57:20 (9,267)	
Titterton, Daniel	3:59:49 (10,002)	
Tittle, Nicholas	3:50:51 (7,837)	
Tivnen, Mike	4:15:26 (13,356)	
Tjarnehav, Lars	4:21:58 (14,802)	
Tmms, Christopher	5:54:22 (28,129)	
Tnat, Eric	2:59:48 (1,007)	
Tobin, John	3:57:37 (9,369)	
Tobin, Leonard	4:15:46 (13,419)	
Tobin, Raymond	4:39:28 (18,683)	
Tock, Chris	4:32:58 (17,303)	
Tod, Andrew	4:22:56 (15,048)	
Todd, Alan	3:58:33 (9,625)	
Todd, Alastair	3:47:01 (7,039)	
Todd, Andrew	4:11:55 (12,589)	
Todd, David	3:41:18 (6,007)	
Todd, David	4:32:09 (17,145)	
Todd, Michael	5:37:33 (26,983)	
Todd, Paul	2:59:38 (987)	
Todd, Philip	4:26:28 (15,836)	
Todd, Richard	4:57:25 (22,205)	
Todd, Stephen	3:29:12 (4,027)	
Todd, William	3:29:46 (4,132)	
Todhunter, Nigel	4:20:15 (14,418)	
Toersen, Henk	4:51:20 (20,954)	
Tofield, Phillip	3:41:04 (5,970)	
Toft, Kevin	5:04:15 (23,173)	
Tofte, Matt	5:48:19 (27,801)	
Togher, William	5:21:36 (25,533)	
Tokairin, Tsugio	5:17:39 (25,118)	
Tolley, David	5:06:36 (23,559)	
Tolley, Vivian	2:45:08 (291)	
Tollner, Eric	4:08:37 (11,896)	
Tollner, Kenneth	4:08:37 (11,896)	
Tomany, Declan	4:34:43 (17,662)	
Tomblin, David	4:55:57 (21,979)	
Tombs, Jonathan	3:50:05 (7,704)	
Tomkins, David	4:38:34 (18,519)	
Tomkins, James	3:58:13 (9,542)	
Tomkinson, Aaron	4:26:53 (15,932)	
Tomkinson, Carl	4:42:28 (19,267)	
Tomkinson, Richard	3:19:08 (2,664)	
Tomlin, Alan	3:30:38 (4,267)	
Tomlin, Peter	4:04:51 (11,077)	
Tomlinson, Adam	3:27:53 (3,785)	
Tomlinson, Andrew	2:55:24 (647)	
Tomlinson, Andrew	3:17:56 (2,525)	
Tomlinson, Bill	3:50:18 (7,734)	
Tomlinson, David	3:23:42 (3,197)	
Tomlinson, Dean	4:00:55 (10,267)	
Tomlinson, Frederick	7:21:26 (30,088)	
Tomlinson, Ian	3:27:57 (3,799)	
Tomlinson, James	4:29:31 (16,549)	
Tomlinson, James	6:08:08 (28,771)	
Tomlinson, Joseph	4:32:20 (17,179)	
Tomlinson, Mark	5:26:15 (26,013)	
Tomlinson, Neil	3:27:54 (3,789)	
Tomlinson, Richard	3:53:14 (8,316)	
Tomlinson, Richard	5:48:20 (27,804)	
Tomlinson, Warren	3:32:00 (4,470)	
Tompkins, Kevin	4:57:34 (22,221)	
Tompkins, Simon	4:54:42 (21,640)	
Toms, David	4:22:32 (14,936)	
Toms, Neil	4:46:04 (19,951)	
Tomson, Paul	4:53:30 (21,419)	
Tonge, Philip	3:38:17 (5,445)	
Tongue, Steven	4:28:05 (16,205)	
Tonkin, Andrew	5:02:20 (22,921)	
Tood, Robert	4:18:21 (13,972)	
Toohey, Jonathan	4:39:44 (18,740)	
Tooke, Brian	5:46:54 (27,692)	
Toolan, John	3:38:39 (5,510)	
Toole, Anthony	4:06:08 (11,366)	
Toon, Keith	3:56:00 (8,919)	
Toon, Ken	5:33:59 (26,689)	
Toon, Mark	5:09:38 (24,035)	
Toone, Richard	3:22:58 (3,107)	
Tooth, Douglas	5:16:47 (25,025)	
Torbet, Alex	4:12:54 (12,809)	
Torchio, Pietro	5:05:33 (23,389)	
Torfree, James	5:06:13 (23,504)	
Torigoe, Fukuo	4:26:20 (15,812)	
Torr, Anthony	4:13:03 (12,830)	
Torre, Peter	4:47:38 (20,287)	
Torres, Hector	4:01:49 (10,446)	
Torry, Nicholas	2:58:21 (840)	
Torsiello, Antonino	4:31:33 (16,988)	
Toseland, Simon	4:15:44 (13,411)	
Tosic, Severino	4:01:17 (10,333)	
Tostain, Norbert	5:18:28 (25,210)	
Totman, Christopher	3:21:07 (2,897)	
Totterdell, Graham	4:34:37 (17,646)	
Tottman, Philip	6:04:56 (28,640)	
Touchais, René	3:39:55 (5,762)	
Tournadour, Bernard	4:04:06 (10,903)	
Tout, Andrew	4:40:13 (18,816)	
Tout, Richard	3:27:26 (3,693)	
Tovey, John	4:55:37 (21,928)	
Tow, Kelvyn	5:03:23 (23,055)	
Towe, Andrew	4:44:29 (19,668)	
Towers, Geoffrey	3:37:47 (5,376)	
Towers, Jim	4:29:54 (16,660)	
Towler, Kelvin	4:06:11 (11,379)	
Towler, Paul	5:08:19 (23,819)	
Town, Trevor	8:10:20 (30,230)	
Townend, Dene	3:28:45 (3,949)	
Towner, John	3:51:36 (7,990)	
Towns, Neil	5:10:06 (24,090)	
Townsend, Andrew	4:26:17 (15,800)	
Townsend, Graham	3:24:33 (3,320)	
Townsend, John	4:18:19 (13,959)	
Townsend, Kevin	4:18:50 (14,087)	
Townsend, Mark	5:06:18 (23,520)	
Townsend, Philip	3:01:29 (1,110)	
Townsend, Steven	6:41:17 (29,669)	
Townsend, Ted	3:57:40 (9,387)	
Townsend, Terence	3:15:48 (2,295)	
Townsend, Victor	5:40:32 (27,227)	
Townson, John	3:51:12 (7,912)	
Townson, Matthew	4:06:09 (11,369)	
Toye, David	5:57:30 (28,299)	
Toye, Francis	4:26:14 (15,789)	
Toyne, Christopher	3:26:16 (3,532)	
Tozer, Don	4:27:16 (16,022)	
Tozer, Ross	2:52:16 (522)	
Tozzi, Alexandre	2:36:00 (105)	
Tracey, Mark	3:46:15 (6,905)	
Tracey, Shaun	4:40:02 (18,793)	
Trafford, Trevor	7:42:41 (30,172)	
Trainor, Timothy	4:28:40 (16,355)	
Tran Dang, Eric	3:13:51 (2,096)	
Tranmer, John	5:20:58 (25,462)	
Tranter, Mark	3:36:28 (5,153)	
Tranter, Paul	2:59:52 (1,012)	
Trapp, Bart	4:39:31 (18,697)	
Travers, Matthew	4:46:54 (20,144)	
Travers, Will	5:26:28 (26,042)	
Travis, Quintus	2:59:16 (958)	
Travis, Stephen	5:56:12 (28,220)	
Traynor, Mark	2:47:41 (357)	
Traynor, Patrick	6:19:10 (29,138)	
Treacher, David	4:00:35 (10,181)	
Treacy, Matthew	5:45:21 (27,580)	
Treadwell, Gregory	4:27:59 (16,192)	
Treadwell, Paul	3:44:31 (6,580)	
Treadwell, Robert	3:40:55 (5,931)	
Treagus, Justin	3:36:52 (5,220)	
Treasure, Guy	3:33:14 (4,649)	
Trebilcock, Norman	4:26:48 (15,910)	
Tredinnick, Terence	4:18:23 (13,982)	
Tredwell, Mark	4:20:05 (14,385)	
Tredwell, Martin	6:00:13 (28,425)	
Tregoning, Harry	5:19:55 (25,357)	
Trehard, Joel	3:35:43 (5,019)	
Treharne, Keith	3:40:52 (5,920)	
Treherne, Jonathan	4:41:56 (19,149)	
Tremain, Andrew	4:38:06 (18,401)	
Tremain, Dax	4:41:22 (19,040)	
Trembirth, Anthony	3:17:30 (2,485)	
Trenbath, Egnest	4:51:08 (20,912)	
Trench, Steven	4:01:24 (10,372)	
Trenchard, Martin	3:54:29 (8,585)	
Trenkel, Christian	3:16:43 (2,396)	
Trennery, David	4:31:55 (17,095)	
Tresias, Andrew	4:48:26 (20,431)	
Tresidder, Charles	4:03:21 (10,735)	
Tresidder, Rob	4:27:25 (16,040)	
Trevarthen, Alan	4:20:42 (14,519)	
Treves, Michael	5:11:37 (24,302)	
Treves, William	4:27:11 (16,004)	
Trevett, Gordon	4:20:36 (14,500)	

Underhill, Kevan	3:10:19 (1,777)
Underwood, Barrie	6:32:21 (29,458)
Underwood, Neil	3:50:56 (7,857)
Underwood, Simon	3:54:03 (8,487)
Underwood, Stuart	2:54:20 (596)
Underwood, Victor	4:11:52 (12,585)
Undhjen, Kjetil	3:28:34 (3,920)
Unfried, Andreas	3:18:44 (2,625)
Unger, Karl	5:55:35 (28,197)
Unitt, Peter	4:30:37 (16,769)
Unsworth, John	3:38:27 (5,473)
Unsworth, Leslie	3:21:18 (2,919)
Unterwaditzer, Peter	4:55:27 (21,872)
Unwin, Andy	4:52:09 (21,124)
Unwin, David	2:58:12 (820)
Unwin, David	3:53:48 (8,442)
Unwin, William	4:22:02 (14,822)
Upsall, Trevor	4:41:24 (19,048)
Upshall, Trevor	4:00:37 (10,190)
Upton, Brian	3:16:54 (2,413)
Upton, David	3:54:07 (8,495)
Upton, Martin	4:17:21 (13,742)
Upton, Roderick	4:37:25 (18,229)
Urand, Kevin	6:03:49 (28,583)
Urbano, Antonio	5:14:35 (24,720)
Urmston, Michael	3:38:31 (5,484)
Urquhart, Craig	3:58:44 (9,682)
Urron, Geoffrey	3:37:34 (5,344)
Urry, Simon	3:35:23 (4,967)
Urvik, Gisle	5:52:34 (28,042)
Urwin, Corey	3:26:21 (3,540)
Urwin, Kenneth	4:51:17 (20,943)
Useldnger, Pascal	3:41:16 (6,003)
Usher, John	5:55:30 (28,191)
Usher, Keith	3:28:36 (3,924)
Usher, Richard	2:57:41 (791)
Usher, Wayne	4:33:34 (17,443)
Ushida, Matsunori	3:54:32 (8,594)
Utting, Oliver	2:26:51 (47)
Uttley, Paul	4:43:01 (19,389)
Uzzell, David	4:24:59 (15,501)
Uzzell, Kevin	2:50:15 (439)
Vadaine, Philippe	3:44:47 (6,636)
Vadapolas, Einius	2:47:26 (349)
Vaidyanathan, Raju	6:19:02 (29,137)
Valansot, Pascal	5:25:01 (25,887)
Vale, David	4:29:31 (16,549)
Vale, Peter	3:12:57 (1,999)
Valek, Paul	2:49:55 (424)
Valentin, Michel	3:37:32 (5,341)
Valentine, Carl	4:03:36 (10,801)
Valentine, Ian	3:57:52 (9,453)
Valentini, Bruno	4:11:59 (12,606)
Valetine, Lerdy	3:52:35 (8,188)
Valetti, Yves	3:20:45 (2,857)
Vallabh, Bharat	5:23:29 (25,741)
Vallabh, Bhupandra	5:23:29 (25,741)
Valle Jones, Chris	5:35:18 (26,830)
Vallejo, Carlos	4:39:40 (18,729)
Valler, Daniel	5:04:32 (23,219)
Vallett, Lee	4:05:11 (11,151)
Valley, David	4:40:32 (18,878)
Vallorani, Francesco	3:45:46 (6,816)
Vamplew, Peter	4:46:01 (19,941)
Van Bergen, Theo	3:47:41 (7,189)
Van Breukelen, Robert	4:26:11 (15,774)
Van Caeneghem, Johan	5:17:27 (25,100)
Van De Brumhuijzen, Frans	5:01:54 (22,854)
Van De Giessen, Hans	4:58:03 (22,307)
Van Den Bergh, Wayne	3:54:24 (8,562)
Van Der Does, David	4:28:27 (16,301)
Van Der Eycken, Rudy	5:10:56 (24,204)
Van Der Helstraete, Marcel	4:47:04 (20,177)
Van Der Hoorn, Han	3:44:55 (6,666)
Van Der Horst, Richard	3:08:59 (1,671)
Van Der Horst, Rupert	3:49:34 (7,599)
Van Der Meer, JR	3:29:56 (4,159)
Van Der Spoel, Arend	3:10:14 (1,762)
Van Der Vliet, Bart	3:58:36 (9,642)
Van Der Wel, Karl	3:44:18 (6,544)
Van Der Werff, Ivo-Jan	3:26:46 (3,592)
Van Der Weyden, Cornelius	4:48:41 (20,466)
Van Derwal, Dominic	3:45:46 (6,816)

Van Dijk, Robert	3:26:40 (3,582)
Van Dyk, Eugene	2:55:57 (677)
Van Dyk, Johannes	5:19:44 (25,339)
Van Emst, Rob	4:18:25 (13,995)
Van Gent, Rob	4:09:44 (12,112)
Van Hal, Erik	3:25:53 (3,491)
Van Hoeserlande, Yves	3:31:16 (4,367)
Van Kempen, Wilfried	4:11:01 (12,402)
Van Kessel, Frans	4:28:54 (16,397)
Van Koert, Robin	4:04:29 (10,983)
Van Leest, Joop	3:57:07 (9,200)
Van Meerten, Hendrik	3:49:50 (7,651)
Van Niekerk, Etienne	3:19:51 (2,745)
Van Nispen, Cor	4:04:48 (11,067)
Van Noordt, Rob	2:53:01 (545)
Van Onselen, David	4:14:13 (13,078)
Van Oranje, Pieter Christiaan	4:35:56 (17,913)
Van Os, Alexander	4:44:41 (19,712)
Van Oss, David	4:12:37 (12,757)
Van Peelen, John	4:50:59 (20,879)
Van Riemsdyk, Paul	4:26:35 (15,868)
Van Rooyen, Innis	5:25:41 (25,956)
Van Rooyen, Jeffrey	4:11:08 (12,423)
Van Rooyen, Rynhardt	3:33:53 (4,737)
Van Staalduine, Jacob	3:53:48 (8,442)
Van Toren, Iwan	4:12:42 (12,774)
Van Wauwe, Walter	4:41:55 (19,144)
Van Weert, Martin	5:28:52 (26,280)
Van Wieringen, Ton	5:31:37 (26,498)
Van Wijk, Nigel	3:41:18 (6,007)
Van Winden, Oskar	3:43:56 (6,477)
Van Wonderen, Jan	3:12:22 (1,950)
Van Wyk, Willem	3:58:10 (9,530)
Van Zetten, David	4:33:32 (17,428)
Van Zijl, Hans	6:15:16 (29,033)
Van Zon, Frans	4:28:46 (16,374)
Van Zuuk, Hans	3:44:14 (6,529)
Van Zyl, Oloff	2:59:01 (936)
Vancappel, Oliver	6:34:20 (29,508)
Vancoillie, Dominique	3:36:48 (5,209)
Vandale, Michael	4:44:35 (19,692)
Vandenabeele, Pablo	3:57:22 (9,279)
Vandereyken, Jean	3:53:24 (8,357)
Vandermolen, Jonathan	4:37:34 (18,270)
Vandewiel, Mark	3:47:40 (7,185)
Vane, Andrew	5:09:21 (23,991)
Vanhulsel, Peter	2:53:50 (575)
Vanicatte, Gerard	3:59:11 (9,810)
Vanmeensel, François	3:49:29 (7,574)
Vanner, Terry	2:58:01 (814)
Vanneufville, Bertrand	4:25:09 (15,543)
Vanoppen, Guy	3:08:00 (1,593)
Van-Orden, Simon	3:00:35 (1,055)
Vanson, Neil	4:29:23 (16,516)
Vaquier, Claude	3:34:04 (4,766)
Varah, Paul	4:07:13 (11,590)
Varcoe, Robert	4:16:27 (13,564)
Vardon, Ian	5:11:11 (24,241)
Vardy, Andrew	5:01:27 (22,796)
Varga, Ferenc	2:55:23 (646)
Varney, Adrian	3:37:45 (5,370)
Varney, Steven	2:54:09 (584)
Vartan, Alexander	3:34:53 (4,889)
Varty, David	4:27:45 (16,135)
Vasak, Christian	4:14:36 (13,148)
Vassie, Christopher	3:53:51 (8,451)
Vasuthevan, Loganathan	5:31:55 (26,525)
Vaughan, Bernard	4:00:22 (10,123)
Vaughan, Bryan	4:17:51 (13,844)
Vaughan, Danny	2:44:32 (277)
Vaughan, David	3:58:12 (9,537)
Vaughan, Mark	3:51:58 (8,066)
Vaughan, Philip	5:25:25 (25,932)
Vaughan, Richard	5:22:16 (25,624)
Vaughan, Stephen	3:25:26 (3,438)
Vautier, Neal	3:29:21 (4,058)
Vaz, Danny	4:26:52 (15,926)
Vazquez, Nicolas	4:32:26 (17,201)
Vear, Peter	4:10:30 (12,275)
Veebel, Ronald	6:03:14 (28,552)
Veitch, Paul	3:49:28 (7,567)
Vejdani, Kio	3:51:53 (8,045)
Venables, Edward	4:18:24 (13,990)

Vensdasalam, Nathan	2:23:46 (33)
Venton, Graham	3:56:02 (8,934)
Ventour, Brian	6:20:02 (29,159)
Veraghtert, Paul	3:11:09 (1,849)
Veraza, Carlos	4:29:35 (16,570)
Verde, Nick	3:47:22 (7,104)
Verdie, Antony	3:35:59 (5,071)
Vere, Derek	4:27:30 (16,058)
Vereecken, Hubert	3:30:33 (4,256)
Verga, Mark	3:49:28 (7,567)
Verheijdt, Peter	3:38:41 (5,515)
Verhulst, Georges	3:28:49 (3,965)
Verma, Deepak	5:05:03 (23,302)
Vermeere, Daniel	3:26:22 (3,543)
Vermeulen, Ben	5:14:23 (24,687)
Vernon, Mike	4:22:00 (14,813)
Vernon, Simon	4:15:06 (13,289)
Vero, Richard	3:21:16 (2,912)
Verrall, Charles	3:01:35 (1,120)
Verrecchia, Steven	4:11:21 (12,472)
Verspoor, Jan	3:17:37 (2,494)
Verster, Johan	4:14:09 (13,065)
Veschi, Jean Michel	3:34:11 (4,784)
Vesely, Ondrej	4:02:30 (10,571)
Vesin, Armand	4:01:28 (10,386)
Vestergaard, Ole	4:32:18 (17,172)
Vesty, Robert	4:29:35 (16,570)
Veyre, Patrick	3:44:32 (6,587)
Vezzu, Loris	2:57:26 (779)
Vialette, Vincent	4:46:27 (20,040)
Vials, Simon	4:34:13 (17,573)
Vian, Andrew	3:16:26 (2,355)
Vian, Robert	4:18:18 (13,953)
Vicedo, Herve	3:28:10 (3,838)
Vickers, Andrew	4:40:28 (18,868)
Vickers, Geoffrey	4:48:54 (20,503)
Vickers, Keith	3:37:11 (5,279)
Vickers, Keith	4:00:19 (10,109)
Vickers, Kevan	3:54:53 (8,683)
Vickers, Peter	6:19:00 (29,136)
Vickers, Rob	5:52:04 (28,020)
Vickerstaff, Stephen	4:43:13 (19,431)
Vickery, James	5:23:54 (25,782)
Vickery, Mark	5:14:36 (24,727)
Vidgen, Danny	4:29:46 (16,614)
Vidler, Lee	5:05:33 (23,389)
Viegas, Paulo	4:47:42 (20,293)
Viegas Assungao, Joaquim	3:40:56 (5,939)
Vieira, Constantino	3:15:57 (2,317)
Vigano, Jamie	5:07:08 (23,638)
Vigne, James	3:29:27 (4,073)
Vilk, Andy	4:04:46 (11,062)
Villa, Marcello	3:22:53 (3,095)
Villa-Clarke, David	4:16:21 (13,536)
Villar, Richard	3:03:10 (1,225)
Vimpari, Janne	3:27:09 (3,647)
Vin Meister, Alexander	4:01:37 (10,414)
Vinall, Chris	4:10:04 (12,173)
Vince, Marcus	4:05:32 (11,223)
Vincent, Charles	4:56:01 (21,987)
Vincent, Danny	3:34:48 (4,878)
Vincent, Dean	3:47:55 (7,248)
Vincent, Ian	3:38:37 (5,502)
Vincent, John	3:49:48 (7,646)
Vincent, Mark	5:16:56 (25,040)
Vincent, Paul	4:23:24 (15,150)
Vincent, Philippe	4:03:44 (10,825)
Vincent, Wayne	3:04:35 (1,321)
Vine, Jeremy	6:12:13 (28,931)
Vine, Terry	3:29:48 (4,134)
Viney, Guy	4:04:35 (11,017)
Violette, Roger	6:25:06 (29,284)
Virdee, Sital	4:23:03 (15,077)
Virgo, Robert	3:25:21 (3,428)
Vischer, Erik	4:57:38 (22,235)
Visser, Frederike	5:15:10 (24,823)
Vitale, Michael	3:47:17 (7,079)
Vito Piero, Ancora	3:54:01 (8,483)
Viton, Gilles	4:36:50 (18,093)
Vitse, Eric	3:53:23 (8,351)
Vittoni, Maurizio	3:08:47 (1,654)
Vivian, Lee	4:13:55 (13,022)
Vlasseman, Patrick	3:10:58 (1,832)

Name	Time (Position)
Vloemans, Frans	5:13:04 (24,509)
Vo Phuoc, Alain	4:52:30 (21,206)
Vogel, Stephen	4:40:00 (18,788)
Vogel, William	3:37:19 (5,305)
Vogler, Jonathan	3:44:44 (6,622)
Vogt, Heinz	4:11:32 (12,508)
Vogt, Jim	4:07:58 (11,755)
Voisey, Keith	4:31:16 (16,922)
Vokes, Geoffrey	4:08:12 (11,802)
Vola, Marco	3:20:27 (2,815)
Volkon, Alexander	4:16:06 (13,487)
Vollmer, Justin	4:05:41 (11,263)
Volpin, Alessandro	5:04:34 (23,228)
Volponi, Carlo	4:33:33 (17,438)
Von Doetinchem De, Joachim	3:36:41 (5,186)
Von Habsburg, Maximilian	3:35:27 (4,978)
Von Huelsen, Johann	3:47:29 (7,135)
Von Peter, Lutz	4:40:05 (18,801)
Von Toggenburg, Christoph.	4:22:21 (14,897)
Vorley, Brett	5:19:12 (25,283)
Vos, Jacob	2:38:06 (140)
Vosloc, Chris	3:23:49 (3,213)
Voss, Stacey	3:24:08 (3,264)
Vout, Tony	2:58:38 (875)
Vowles, Alexander	5:15:10 (24,823)
Voyce, Ian Robert	5:15:29 (24,867)
Voyer, Stephane	4:15:10 (13,297)
Vrvsas, George	4:54:47 (21,672)
Vuagniaux, Nigel	3:25:09 (3,393)
Vuorinen, Jorma	3:11:52 (1,902)
Waage, Soeren	4:27:52 (16,167)
Wacogne, Matthew	5:42:28 (27,367)
Waddams, Alan	4:08:59 (11,974)
Waddell, Alan	3:53:44 (8,430)
Waddell, Bruce	4:18:20 (13,964)
Waddell, Douglas	3:15:16 (2,251)
Waddington, David	3:23:05 (3,124)
Waddington, Simon	3:41:18 (6,007)
Wade, Daniel	4:06:12 (11,385)
Wade, Ian	3:59:17 (9,837)
Wade, James	3:53:17 (8,327)
Wade, Spencer	5:10:34 (24,159)
Wadeley, Roger	3:34:01 (4,757)
Wadham, Simon	4:05:21 (11,175)
Wadie, Abu	4:21:22 (14,660)
Wadley, Robert	4:31:40 (17,028)
Wadman, Richard	3:57:28 (9,318)
Wadrup, Richard	5:12:22 (24,408)
Wadsley, Nick	3:34:54 (4,891)
Wadsworth, Adrian	3:40:05 (5,797)
Wadsworth, Christopher	4:23:19 (15,138)
Wadsworth, David	3:56:33 (9,066)
Wadsworth, Robert	2:55:31 (653)
Wafer, Aidan	4:10:02 (12,170)
Wafer, John	3:55:09 (8,722)
Wagenheim, Mark	3:57:36 (9,363)
Waghorn, Arthur	3:38:02 (5,405)
Waghorn, Hayden	3:28:56 (3,982)
Wagland, Elliot	5:18:26 (25,206)
Wagland, Gareth	3:11:26 (1,862)
Wagner, Fiorian	2:47:04 (342)
Wagner, Juergen	3:08:27 (1,627)
Wagner, Rich	4:49:45 (20,661)
Wagstaff, Alan	5:22:12 (25,615)
Wagstaff, Michael	4:52:06 (21,113)
Wagstaff, Richard	4:37:57 (18,357)
Wahed, Lloyd	3:48:45 (7,412)
Wahlstrom, Curth	9:07:48 (30,278)
Wain, Gary	3:42:21 (6,191)
Wain, Jim	5:34:40 (26,770)
Wainana, Eric	2:15:43 (15)
Waine, Michael	2:32:51 (79)
Wainman, Paul	5:30:16 (26,394)
Wainwright, Philip	4:05:30 (11,213)
Waisman, Shai	3:58:57 (9,738)
Waite, Colin	4:36:41 (18,059)
Waite, Mark	4:16:42 (13,609)
Waite, Mark	4:29:52 (16,648)
Waite, Stephen	5:21:25 (25,520)
Waite, Tony	4:42:50 (19,343)
Wakayama, Toshiyasu	4:49:32 (20,620)
Wake, Adam	3:42:24 (6,201)
Wakefield, Clifford	4:19:30 (14,255)
Wakefield, Jonathan	3:59:11 (9,810)
Wakefield, Stuart	5:31:09 (26,467)
Wakefield, Timothy	4:02:27 (10,561)
Wakeford, Geoffrey	4:36:49 (18,089)
Wakeford, Martin	3:26:57 (3,616)
Wakeford, Stephen	3:16:36 (2,380)
Wakeham, Glenn	4:19:05 (14,143)
Wakeham, Lee	4:43:56 (19,579)
Wakelin, James	5:16:35 (24,997)
Wakeling, Mark	4:46:16 (20,002)
Wakenshaw, Trevor	3:43:54 (6,472)
Wakering, Mark	3:20:14 (2,787)
Walburn, Kenneth	5:35:53 (26,870)
Walchester, Ian	4:46:49 (20,119)
Waldeland, Oddvar	4:03:19 (10,728)
Walder, Christopher	4:27:00 (15,964)
Waldner, Wolfgang	4:00:28 (10,142)
Waldon, Chris	4:03:10 (10,697)
Waldram, Timothy	3:33:14 (4,649)
Waldron, David	3:01:44 (1,133)
Waldron, Graham	3:39:46 (5,731)
Waldron, Michael	5:39:56 (27,185)
Walewski, Przemyslaw	2:48:33 (379)
Walford, Alastair	3:00:36 (1,058)
Walford, Kevin	4:47:19 (20,223)
Walford, Michael	3:30:05 (4,185)
Walia, Sanmeet	6:26:52 (29,330)
Walker, Alan	4:34:20 (17,602)
Walker, Allan	6:40:07 (29,639)
Walker, Andrew	5:05:10 (23,313)
Walker, Andrew Kenneth	4:01:33 (10,402)
Walker, Andy	5:07:16 (23,658)
Walker, Anthony	5:20:30 (25,408)
Walker, Bob	4:37:27 (18,238)
Walker, Carl	3:27:03 (3,628)
Walker, Christopher	5:49:09 (27,854)
Walker, Colin	3:32:34 (4,545)
Walker, Darren	4:01:26 (10,379)
Walker, David	3:27:52 (3,779)
Walker, David	3:30:40 (4,272)
Walker, David	3:47:07 (7,054)
Walker, David	3:58:13 (9,542)
Walker, David	4:16:28 (13,566)
Walker, David	5:10:11 (24,100)
Walker, David	6:27:58 (29,355)
Walker, Gary	3:47:24 (7,117)
Walker, George	6:21:55 (29,214)
Walker, Gerald	3:11:27 (1,863)
Walker, Gerard	3:26:48 (3,598)
Walker, Graham	4:12:02 (12,620)
Walker, Henry	4:37:53 (18,344)
Walker, Ian	3:11:37 (1,874)
Walker, James	3:28:18 (3,866)
Walker, James	4:58:46 (22,423)
Walker, Jim	4:45:15 (19,815)
Walker, Keith	5:06:09 (23,490)
Walker, Kevin	3:12:32 (1,962)
Walker, Marc	3:38:31 (5,484)
Walker, Martin	3:15:26 (2,264)
Walker, Michael	3:06:44 (1,482)
Walker, Michael	4:18:07 (13,892)
Walker, Michael	5:44:31 (27,516)
Walker, Mike	2:54:52 (625)
Walker, Nicholas	4:26:54 (15,936)
Walker, Oliver	4:33:18 (17,368)
Walker, Peter	4:55:36 (21,922)
Walker, Richard	3:41:57 (6,116)
Walker, Richard	4:38:04 (18,389)
Walker, Robert	3:46:03 (6,865)
Walker, Roger	3:33:25 (4,677)
Walker, Simon	4:40:30 (18,874)
Walker, Steven	5:15:01 (24,781)
Walker, Stuart	5:44:28 (27,509)
Walker, Tim	2:52:45 (536)
Walker, Tony	3:56:52 (9,147)
Walker, William	5:19:21 (25,298)
Walkerdine, Martin	4:02:01 (10,489)
Walkley, Anthony	5:01:45 (22,832)
Walkley, Anthony	5:05:18 (23,338)
Walkley, Darrell	5:06:32 (23,548)
Wall, Alex	4:50:49 (20,849)
Wall, Christopher	3:46:35 (6,968)
Wall, John	4:14:11 (13,072)
Wall, Jonathan	4:58:56 (22,448)
Wall, Richard	3:41:35 (6,048)
Wall, Simon	4:36:09 (17,947)
Wall, Terry	2:33:30 (80)
Wallace, Andrew	3:34:39 (4,856)
Wallace, Brian	4:25:33 (15,629)
Wallace, Clark	3:59:08 (9,795)
Wallace, Eric	4:32:01 (17,122)
Wallace, Joe	4:42:37 (19,298)
Wallace, Malcolm	4:40:21 (18,847)
Wallace, Mark	4:17:12 (13,720)
Wallace, Mark	4:43:21 (19,459)
Wallace, Martin	3:33:06 (4,622)
Wallace, Richard	5:17:19 (25,086)
Wallace, Robert	3:13:44 (2,080)
Wallace, Sandy	4:27:00 (15,964)
Wallace, Steven	3:47:05 (7,048)
Wallace, Steven	4:01:49 (10,446)
Wallace, Tom	3:58:35 (9,639)
Wallace, Victor	5:15:10 (24,823)
Walland, John	4:57:58 (22,288)
Walland, Kevin	4:16:03 (13,478)
Wallbank, John	4:37:11 (18,167)
Waller, Adrian	4:40:51 (18,946)
Waller, Andrew	6:25:08 (29,285)
Waller, Graham	4:39:51 (18,762)
Waller, Ian	4:34:14 (17,580)
Waller, Paul	5:20:37 (25,423)
Waller, Richard	4:21:18 (14,647)
Waller, Stuart	3:53:01 (8,269)
Wallhead, Ian	4:00:21 (10,120)
Wallis, Gary	3:44:47 (6,636)
Wallis, Gordon	4:41:55 (19,144)
Wallis, Gregory	4:57:20 (22,195)
Wallis, Paul	4:17:56 (13,861)
Wallis, Philip	3:37:15 (5,294)
Wallman, Marcus	3:19:17 (2,687)
Wallman, Richard	3:53:21 (8,347)
Walls, William	4:42:56 (19,373)
Wallwork, Daniel	4:17:28 (13,766)
Walmsley, Brian	4:04:18 (10,949)
Walne, Toby	5:03:10 (23,027)
Walpole, Stuart	2:49:07 (397)
Walsgrove, John	3:28:27 (3,898)
Walsh, Andrew	4:00:21 (10,120)
Walsh, Antony	3:16:08 (2,328)
Walsh, Ben	4:25:58 (15,723)
Walsh, David	4:01:55 (10,469)
Walsh, Gerry	4:08:34 (11,885)
Walsh, Greg	4:48:38 (20,457)
Walsh, Jimmy	5:38:18 (27,036)
Walsh, John	6:35:28 (29,532)
Walsh, Kevin	4:10:18 (12,226)
Walsh, Laurence	5:29:04 (26,294)
Walsh, Lee	4:57:19 (22,194)
Walsh, Michael	4:09:15 (12,034)
Walsh, Michael	5:47:21 (27,719)
Walsh, Owen	3:42:37 (6,238)
Walsh, Paul	3:41:19 (6,013)
Walsh, Peter	4:13:04 (12,832)
Walsh, Peter	4:43:38 (19,524)
Walsh, Peter	4:54:33 (21,604)
Walsh, Raymond	3:37:43 (5,367)
Walsh, Simon	5:02:08 (22,897)
Walsh, Terrence	4:52:55 (21,296)
Walsh, William	4:08:26 (11,859)
Walshaw, John	4:00:46 (10,235)
Walter, Philip	4:11:46 (12,562)
Walter, Richard	3:57:14 (9,236)
Walters, David	4:49:13 (20,568)
Walters, Keith	5:54:43 (28,152)
Walters, Kenneth	5:15:07 (24,800)
Walters, Morgan	2:45:32 (310)
Walters, Paul	3:57:45 (9,412)
Walters, Paul	6:16:09 (29,062)
Walters, Peter	4:39:04 (18,617)
Walters, Scott	5:05:06 (23,305)
Walters, Spencer	3:55:18 (8,760)
Walters, Tudor	3:35:36 (5,004)
Walthall, Barry	5:38:22 (27,040)
Walton, Aaron	3:00:19 (1,047)
Walton, Andrew	4:10:36 (12,297)
Walton, Anthony	2:59:53 (1,015)

Walton, Bradley	3:02:05 (1,159)	
Walton, Christopher	4:40:57 (18,967)	
Walton, Colin	4:26:56 (15,945)	
Walton, Danny	4:57:50 (22,270)	
Walton, David	3:43:38 (6,421)	
Walton, David	4:08:02 (11,774)	
Walton, David	4:47:42 (20,293)	
Walton, David	5:01:10 (22,760)	
Walton, Godfrey	4:01:21 (10,357)	
Walton, James	4:12:26 (12,723)	
Walton, Jim	3:38:42 (5,520)	
Walton, John	3:24:03 (3,252)	
Walton, Kevin	4:27:03 (15,981)	
Walton, Roger	4:59:59 (22,619)	
Walton, Stephen	4:34:15 (17,585)	
Wand, Dominic	6:56:48 (29,905)	
Wand, Martyn	5:46:10 (27,637)	
Wangemann, Eicke	3:47:15 (7,072)	
Wansbone, Paul	5:05:54 (23,448)	
Wapnick, Jeffrey	4:23:54 (15,275)	
Warburton, John	6:01:16 (28,466)	
Warburton, Lance	4:23:03 (15,077)	
Warburton, Paul	3:07:33 (1,549)	
Warburton, Peter	3:21:11 (2,905)	
Ward, Alan	3:51:50 (8,035)	
Ward, Alan	4:07:25 (11,647)	
Ward, Andrew	3:39:42 (5,714)	
Ward, Andrew	4:55:07 (21,761)	
Ward, Andy	3:24:24 (3,298)	
Ward, Anthony	4:05:29 (11,209)	
Ward, Bill	5:53:09 (28,074)	
Ward, Brian	5:14:02 (24,632)	
Ward, Christopher	4:48:24 (20,426)	
Ward, Colin	3:31:41 (4,422)	
Ward, Darren	4:49:36 (20,635)	
Ward, David	3:42:18 (6,180)	
Ward, Desmond	3:58:29 (9,601)	
Ward, Gary	4:59:50 (22,581)	
Ward, Hamish	5:26:22 (26,027)	
Ward, Ian	4:35:51 (17,891)	
Ward, James	4:38:51 (18,580)	
Ward, James	5:19:42 (25,335)	
Ward, John	3:20:53 (2,875)	
Ward, John	4:29:46 (16,614)	
Ward, John	6:35:47 (29,542)	
Ward, Julian	3:44:07 (6,514)	
Ward, Layton	3:53:48 (8,442)	
Ward, Malcolm	4:08:50 (11,943)	
Ward, Mark	3:33:55 (4,742)	
Ward, Mark	4:39:22 (18,659)	
Ward, Mathew	4:57:23 (22,202)	
Ward, Matthew	3:50:23 (7,754)	
Ward, Michael	3:52:13 (8,119)	
Ward, Michael	4:38:06 (18,401)	
Ward, Neil	4:07:22 (11,629)	
Ward, Neil	4:32:26 (17,201)	
Ward, Nigel	5:47:53 (27,766)	
Ward, Paul	4:02:53 (10,641)	
Ward, Paul	4:20:59 (14,589)	
Ward, Peter	4:29:18 (16,500)	
Ward, Peter	4:33:24 (17,396)	
Ward, Richard	4:43:39 (19,527)	
Ward, Rodger	3:09:01 (1,673)	
Ward, Simon	3:43:58 (6,483)	
Ward, Simon	4:44:53 (19,754)	
Ward, Stephen	3:58:58 (9,744)	
Ward, Steve	3:56:54 (9,154)	
Ward, Steve	4:44:32 (19,684)	
Ward, Timothy	3:25:23 (3,429)	
Ward Smith, Wayland	4:22:24 (14,903)	
Wardale, Robert	3:39:35 (5,690)	
Ward-Brown, Jonathan	4:23:36 (15,205)	
Wardell, Chris	3:31:19 (4,373)	
Warden, Martin	6:09:02 (28,816)	
Warden, Robert	5:44:09 (27,489)	
Wardlaw, Steve	3:54:16 (8,527)	
Wardle, Daniel	4:45:34 (19,872)	
Wardle, Kim	4:02:27 (10,561)	
Wardner, Matthew	4:13:32 (12,939)	
Wardrope, David	3:53:31 (8,380)	
Ware, Darren	4:54:30 (21,594)	
Ware, George	4:08:25 (11,853)	
Ware, Thomas	3:41:50 (6,097)	
Wareham, Sean	4:18:11 (13,914)	
Wareing, Brian	3:08:33 (1,636)	
Wareing, Brian	4:57:36 (22,228)	
Wareing, Nathan	4:10:11 (12,203)	
Warenghem, Roger	3:25:47 (3,482)	
Warham, Roger	4:04:38 (11,028)	
Warhurst, Ian	3:29:00 (3,997)	
Warlow, Geraint	4:50:29 (20,800)	
Warmsley, Stuart	4:58:02 (22,301)	
Warn, Timothy	3:21:29 (2,944)	
Warne, Andrew	3:59:26 (9,896)	
Warne, Mark	4:56:27 (22,059)	
Warne, Reginald	3:26:39 (3,578)	
Warne, Richard	5:04:17 (23,178)	
Warne, Stephen	3:25:14 (3,406)	
Warner, Anthony	4:29:26 (16,528)	
Warner, David	4:49:43 (20,657)	
Warner, Duncan	4:06:38 (11,473)	
Warner, Geoffrey	3:59:35 (9,944)	
Warner, Giles	4:32:36 (17,227)	
Warner, John	4:19:15 (14,178)	
Warner, Kevin	4:08:10 (11,795)	
Warner, Kim	3:37:52 (5,390)	
Warner, Lance	4:58:31 (22,381)	
Warner, Mark	4:19:03 (14,130)	
Warner, Michael	3:12:18 (1,941)	
Warner, Michael	4:16:22 (13,543)	
Warner, Neil	4:14:39 (13,158)	
Warner, Stephen	3:30:21 (4,221)	
Warner, Tim	3:47:10 (7,059)	
Warner, Tony	3:19:20 (2,690)	
Warnes, Dennis	4:09:01 (11,990)	
Warnock, Dennis	5:59:19 (28,383)	
Warnock, James	4:06:57 (11,541)	
Warran, Richard	5:04:56 (23,287)	
Warren, Andrew	4:10:08 (12,189)	
Warren, Huw	3:51:28 (7,956)	
Warren, Ian	3:55:54 (8,894)	
Warren, Matthew	3:52:24 (8,156)	
Warren, Peter	4:26:54 (15,936)	
Warren, Peter	5:32:23 (26,558)	
Warren, Rob	5:38:43 (27,069)	
Warren, Stephen	4:50:27 (20,795)	
Warrilow, Stewart	3:51:56 (8,060)	
Warriner, Ian	4:41:12 (19,013)	
Warrington, Dafydd	5:15:50 (24,914)	
Warton, Paul	3:06:28 (1,457)	
Warwick, Gary	3:50:10 (7,717)	
Warwick, John	3:58:18 (9,563)	
Warwick, Lee	5:03:42 (23,081)	
Warzecha, Reinhard	4:09:45 (12,117)	
Wasdell, Andrew	2:57:06 (753)	
Washer, Rolf	3:48:12 (7,303)	
Washington, John	4:19:59 (14,361)	
Wass, David	4:16:55 (13,651)	
Watanuki, Koichiro	4:03:15 (10,711)	
Waterfield, Mark	4:37:00 (18,131)	
Waterfield, Mark	6:05:29 (28,663)	
Waterhouse, John	4:05:48 (11,298)	
Waterhouse, Paul	4:05:11 (11,151)	
Waterhouse, Robin	4:54:35 (21,616)	
Wateridge, Steven	2:51:34 (493)	
Waterman, David	3:31:22 (4,382)	
Waterman, David	3:48:02 (7,271)	
Waters, Darren	4:38:58 (18,598)	
Waters, David	5:53:53 (28,110)	
Waters, John	4:11:51 (12,580)	
Waters, Kelvin	4:37:49 (18,320)	
Waters, Matthew	5:15:51 (24,871)	
Waterson, David	5:23:26 (25,735)	
Waterston, Kevin	3:53:32 (8,387)	
Waterston, Tony	4:09:30 (12,076)	
Wates, William	4:04:56 (11,103)	
Wathen, Anthony	3:44:55 (6,666)	
Watkins, Bryan	4:23:27 (15,163)	
Watkins, David	5:07:08 (23,638)	
Watkins, James	3:40:19 (5,832)	
Watkins, John	4:55:11 (21,778)	
Watkins, Lawrence	4:04:32 (11,001)	
Watkins, Mark	4:08:55 (11,959)	
Watkins, Robert	4:59:44 (22,559)	
Watkins, Toby	6:11:23 (28,903)	
Watkinson, Barry	4:40:39 (18,911)	
Watkinson, Chris	5:12:37 (24,448)	
Watkinson, Peter	3:17:57 (2,526)	
Watkiss, Colin David	4:53:52 (21,491)	
Watling, Richard	4:06:18 (11,408)	
Watmore, Bruce	3:24:21 (3,291)	
Watson, Alastair	2:50:11 (436)	
Watson, Andrew	2:57:12 (759)	
Watson, Andrew	3:55:14 (8,747)	
Watson, Andrew	5:43:56 (27,468)	
Watson, Andy	4:27:35 (16,084)	
Watson, Angus	4:21:16 (14,642)	
Watson, Ben	4:18:02 (13,874)	
Watson, Craig	4:27:59 (16,192)	
Watson, David	3:07:25 (1,536)	
Watson, David	4:34:54 (17,694)	
Watson, David	5:04:32 (23,219)	
Watson, Dudley	4:40:55 (18,959)	
Watson, Euan	6:16:50 (29,082)	
Watson, Frederick	4:55:07 (21,761)	
Watson, Ian	3:08:01 (1,595)	
Watson, Ian	3:53:59 (8,475)	
Watson, James	4:03:20 (10,732)	
Watson, James	4:34:53 (17,690)	
Watson, James	4:36:23 (17,991)	
Watson, Jeff	5:15:49 (24,910)	
Watson, Jeremy	4:13:28 (12,925)	
Watson, John	5:13:13 (24,535)	
Watson, Lewis	5:48:29 (27,816)	
Watson, Matthew	4:59:20 (22,503)	
Watson, Michael	3:10:04 (1,747)	
Watson, Michael	4:15:48 (13,423)	
Watson, Paul	3:18:13 (2,564)	
Watson, Peter	3:37:18 (5,301)	
Watson, Peter	4:23:45 (15,236)	
Watson, Richard	6:32:56 (29,479)	
Watson, Robert	3:31:48 (4,438)	
Watson, Robert	6:02:37 (28,525)	
Watson, Simon	4:19:29 (14,253)	
Watson, Stephen	4:57:07 (22,158)	
Watson, Stuart	2:50:20 (442)	
Watson, Timothy	3:43:02 (6,312)	
Watt, Alexander	4:10:43 (12,315)	
Watt, Brian	4:12:02 (12,620)	
Watt, David	4:31:50 (17,069)	
Watt, David	4:37:51 (18,333)	
Watt, John	3:46:58 (7,028)	
Watt, Peter	4:03:32 (10,783)	
Watt, Ritchie	5:52:08 (28,026)	
Watt, Robert	4:49:48 (20,675)	
Wattis, Jimmy	3:29:09 (4,024)	
Wattley, Travis	3:59:22 (9,869)	
Watton, Brett	4:57:39 (22,187)	
Watton, Desmond	3:49:22 (7,543)	
Watts, Adam	4:17:07 (13,692)	
Watts, Allen	4:53:30 (21,419)	
Watts, Andrew	3:04:20 (1,305)	
Watts, Andrew	4:09:13 (12,026)	
Watts, Andrew	4:45:43 (19,887)	
Watts, Barry	4:18:46 (14,074)	
Watts, Bill	4:46:10 (19,977)	
Watts, Chris	4:39:30 (18,694)	
Watts, Christopher	4:28:47 (16,378)	
Watts, David	4:14:18 (13,097)	
Watts, David	5:28:51 (26,277)	
Watts, Matthew	4:21:18 (14,647)	
Watts, Neal	4:22:43 (14,987)	
Watts, Neil	4:59:37 (22,541)	
Watts, Nicholas	5:21:46 (25,559)	
Watts, Nigel	3:58:34 (9,633)	
Watts, Paul	5:08:13 (23,800)	
Watts, Richard	4:15:00 (13,268)	
Watts, Robert	3:42:05 (6,134)	
Watts, Roy	4:39:15 (18,644)	
Watts, Simon	3:46:28 (6,942)	
Watts, Stephen	3:26:39 (3,578)	
Waughman, Gary	5:26:42 (26,062)	
Waving, Steven	3:53:29 (8,370)	
Wavrant, Marc	3:06:11 (1,435)	
Wawman, Peter	4:14:46 (13,202)	
Way, Charles	3:26:40 (3,582)	
Way, Lawrence	4:25:15 (15,565)	
Way, Martin	4:01:38 (10,418)	
Way, Stephen	5:37:52 (27,012)	

Way, Steven	6:19:57 (29,156)	Weeden, Mark	5:28:42 (26,256)	Wermuth, Jean Pierre	4:01:49 (10,446)
Wayne, Carl	3:58:23 (9,582)	Weedon, Warren	4:11:38 (12,531)	Werner, Denis	4:50:30 (20,802)
Wayne, Robert	5:29:56 (26,373)	Weekes, James	6:16:22 (29,067)	Wescomb, Christopher	3:39:10 (5,602)
Weafer Cok, Colin	4:34:14 (17,580)	Weekes, Jason	4:19:31 (14,260)	Wesener, Rainer	3:17:25 (2,476)
Weait, James	5:18:53 (25,258)	Weekes, Roderick	4:16:40 (13,601)	Wesley, Paul	4:55:16 (21,802)
Weale, Adrian	4:53:32 (21,434)	Weeks, Chris	4:23:57 (15,281)	Wesley, Stephen	4:06:02 (11,355)
Weall, Jonathan	6:13:30 (28,973)	Weeks, David	3:58:49 (9,703)	Wesselink, Paul	5:05:41 (23,410)
Weatherby, Johnny	6:12:25 (28,941)	Weeks, Jeremy	4:40:27 (18,867)	Wesson, Dave	5:56:22 (28,231)
Weatherhead, Guy	4:30:52 (16,818)	Weeks, Stuart	5:51:14 (27,963)	Wesson, Steven	4:44:51 (19,743)
Weatherhead, James	5:47:26 (27,723)	Wegg, Terry	3:54:59 (8,698)	West, Alexander	5:10:31 (24,146)
Weatherhead, Thomas	3:58:41 (9,669)	Wehrle, Stephen	3:54:11 (8,506)	West, Andrew	3:08:45 (1,650)
Weatherill, Alex	4:26:53 (15,932)	Weibel, Gusty	3:46:31 (6,951)	West, Andrew	3:51:15 (7,921)
Weaver, Darryl	5:48:08 (27,784)	Weighill, Robert	4:04:37 (11,023)	West, Gary	5:37:35 (26,992)
Weaver, Derek	2:59:37 (985)	Weintraub, Abraham	7:37:41 (30,153)	West, Geoff	6:35:10 (29,526)
Weaver, Ian	4:16:20 (13,529)	Weir, Andrew	3:59:12 (9,815)	West, Graham	3:38:27 (5,473)
Weaver, Jay	3:25:10 (3,398)	Weir, Ben	4:47:13 (20,207)	West, Julian	4:22:29 (14,924)
Weaver, Mark	3:35:39 (5,011)	Weir, Glenn	3:44:40 (6,605)	West, Mark	4:07:45 (11,717)
Weaver, Mark	3:42:19 (6,183)	Weir, Mike	3:27:43 (3,748)	West, Mark	4:21:22 (14,660)
Weavers, Terry	3:21:21 (2,927)	Weisfeld, Benjamin	4:20:35 (14,496)	West, Martyn	4:17:26 (13,756)
Weaving, Peter	3:01:55 (1,143)	Weiss, Martin	5:16:27 (24,979)	West, Peter	5:05:21 (23,349)
Weavis, Andrew	4:51:03 (20,898)	Welbourn, Richard	3:25:45 (3,474)	West, Philip	4:02:04 (10,498)
Webb, Alan	4:04:30 (10,988)	Welch, Alan	2:44:16 (269)	West, Stephen	4:08:41 (11,910)
Webb, Alex	3:15:29 (2,270)	Welch, Andrew	3:56:36 (9,077)	West, Stephen	4:21:25 (14,673)
Webb, Alexander	4:37:51 (18,333)	Welch, Christopher	4:28:46 (16,374)	West, Stephen	4:55:09 (21,769)
Webb, Andrew	2:59:37 (985)	Welch, Dick	4:55:27 (21,872)	West, Steve	4:52:16 (21,148)
Webb, Anthony	2:35:52 (103)	Welch, Neil	3:47:20 (7,097)	Westall, Mark	5:14:13 (24,660)
Webb, Bruce	6:01:11 (28,464)	Welch, Stephen	3:22:58 (3,107)	Westbrook, Ernest	4:28:03 (16,200)
Webb, Christopher	4:35:56 (17,913)	Welch, Timothy	4:38:15 (18,442)	Westbrooke, Mark	5:12:42 (24,457)
Webb, Christopher	4:55:00 (21,732)	Weldon, Anthony	5:54:42 (28,150)	Westcott, Richard	4:07:41 (11,692)
Webb, Colin	4:04:01 (10,886)	Weldon, Martin	3:33:10 (4,636)	Wester, Jos	3:37:13 (5,285)
Webb, Colin	4:27:40 (16,107)	Welham, Lee	5:44:33 (27,526)	Westerman, Jeremy	4:05:55 (11,327)
Webb, David	4:11:06 (12,416)	Welham, Robert	4:15:59 (13,461)	Westerman, Mick	3:44:29 (6,572)
Webb, Gary	3:17:03 (2,432)	Welham, Robert	5:07:01 (23,618)	Westgarth, Steven	5:53:31 (28,093)
Webb, Ian	5:02:37 (22,949)	Well, Harald	3:14:56 (2,213)	Westgate, Stuart	3:52:42 (8,211)
Webb, John	4:55:51 (21,961)	Wellbelove, Luke	3:52:45 (8,220)	Westhead, Nick	4:14:48 (13,209)
Webb, Jonathan	3:36:31 (5,161)	Wellburn, Richard	4:47:06 (20,184)	Westlake, Andrew	5:00:57 (22,725)
Webb, Lewis	3:42:06 (6,137)	Weller, Colin	4:01:36 (10,412)	Westlake, Graham	3:45:27 (6,736)
Webb, Nick	4:12:12 (12,672)	Weller, Darren	4:24:43 (15,443)	Westley, Ian	4:15:47 (13,421)
Webb, Nigel	3:57:46 (9,416)	Weller, Geoffrey	3:43:02 (6,312)	Westoby, Guy	5:34:22 (26,742)
Webb, Paul	7:06:10 (29,985)	Weller, Martin	4:25:15 (15,565)	Weston, Benjamin	4:29:19 (16,502)
Webb, Peter	4:05:20 (11,172)	Weller, Peter	3:22:43 (3,073)	Weston, David	4:23:05 (15,083)
Webb, Peter	4:55:21 (21,831)	Weller-Poley, Guy	3:50:21 (7,747)	Weston, Mark	3:54:51 (8,672)
Webb, Roy	3:12:44 (1,981)	Wellings, Daniel	5:37:36 (26,996)	Weston, Nick	4:03:17 (10,718)
Webb, Simon	4:07:55 (11,745)	Wellings, Ian	4:35:20 (17,781)	Weston, Paul	4:19:37 (14,284)
Webb, Stuart	3:36:31 (5,161)	Wellings, Robert	3:10:45 (1,814)	Westphall, Mark	3:24:36 (3,328)
Webb, Tim	5:05:02 (23,297)	Wellington, Philip	4:21:58 (14,802)	Westrop, Glenn	5:32:56 (26,610)
Webbe, Kevin	5:04:52 (23,280)	Wellington, Stephen	5:06:10 (23,493)	Westwood, Jamie	3:31:46 (4,430)
Webber, Anthony	3:41:08 (5,976)	Wells, Anthony	5:50:52 (27,948)	Westwood, Mark	4:55:35 (21,913)
Webber, Colin	5:09:08 (23,959)	Wells, Bob	2:58:43 (894)	Westwood, Nigel	5:00:42 (22,692)
Webber, Donald	4:15:29 (13,364)	Wells, Christian	5:10:09 (24,096)	Westwood, Paul	2:59:21 (971)
Webber, Ian	3:40:08 (5,806)	Wells, Colin	5:31:10 (26,468)	Westwood, Paul	3:49:35 (7,604)
Webber, James	4:14:53 (13,231)	Wells, David	3:18:10 (2,558)	Westwood, Tom	5:06:40 (23,572)
Webber, Matthew	4:16:10 (13,500)	Wells, David	4:34:24 (17,616)	Wetherill, Andrew	2:37:40 (130)
Webber, Nathan	3:54:36 (8,614)	Wells, David	4:35:15 (17,761)	Wetli, Alexander	2:47:44 (360)
Webber, Paul	4:18:40 (14,044)	Wells, David	4:55:22 (21,837)	Whale, David	3:58:25 (9,588)
Weber, Matthias	4:34:51 (17,685)	Wells, Dennis	5:26:14 (26,011)	Whale, Matthew	3:13:06 (2,012)
Weber, Peter	5:43:53 (27,463)	Wells, John	5:07:47 (23,746)	Whale, Richard	5:07:21 (23,671)
Weber, Warrick	3:56:55 (9,159)	Wells, Leigh	5:40:29 (27,221)	Whalen, Dean	4:25:07 (15,536)
Websdale, Lee	4:17:00 (13,668)	Wells, Mark	3:45:49 (6,827)	Whalley, Adrian	3:15:01 (2,224)
Webster, Andrew	3:28:03 (3,808)	Wells, Martin	5:04:26 (23,206)	Whalley, Gareth	4:07:02 (11,560)
Webster, Andrew	4:00:15 (10,099)	Wells, Neil	4:06:10 (11,372)	Wharmby, Nicholas	4:52:23 (21,180)
Webster, Andrew	4:15:42 (13,405)	Wells, Peter	3:36:56 (5,232)	Wharton, Andrew	3:58:19 (9,565)
Webster, Andrew	4:28:36 (16,339)	Wells, Philip	4:17:09 (13,703)	Wharton, Brian	3:59:52 (10,016)
Webster, Bryan	5:00:35 (22,675)	Wells, Rob	3:54:00 (8,479)	Wharton, David	5:27:24 (26,119)
Webster, Christopher	4:37:22 (18,215)	Wells, Robert	6:45:57 (29,749)	Wharton, Paul	7:42:21 (30,171)
Webster, Christopher	7:07:17 (29,997)	Wells, Trevor	4:09:27 (12,071)	Whatford, Howard	4:24:51 (15,466)
Webster, Colin	4:09:00 (11,978)	Welsby, Gary	4:10:16 (12,222)	Whealan, David	6:55:36 (29,895)
Webster, Gilbert	5:12:42 (24,457)	Welsh, Angus	3:50:26 (7,761)	Wheatley, Adrian	3:27:52 (3,779)
Webster, Jof	3:41:44 (6,079)	Welsh, Darryn	4:23:08 (15,093)	Wheatley, Craig	5:08:17 (23,813)
Webster, Karl	3:01:23 (1,099)	Welsh, Irvine	5:14:51 (24,756)	Wheatley, Dennis	3:39:33 (5,684)
Webster, Mark	3:20:19 (2,797)	Welsh, Peter	4:02:34 (10,588)	Wheatley, Stephen	4:45:52 (19,914)
Webster, Michael	3:56:28 (9,046)	Welsh, William	2:56:53 (737)	Wheddon, Paul	3:55:25 (8,786)
Webster, Peter	4:25:48 (15,672)	Wenborn, Michael	6:08:05 (28,769)	Wheeldon, Brian	3:58:31 (9,611)
Webster, Sean	3:32:44 (4,565)	Wendenburg, Gerd	3:49:14 (7,502)	Wheeler, Alan	3:53:02 (8,272)
Webster, Shaun	4:40:38 (18,906)	Wendling, Emil	5:44:30 (27,514)	Wheeler, Allan	5:00:58 (22,729)
Webster, Stephen	3:30:23 (4,228)	Wenlock, Tony	3:51:25 (7,947)	Wheeler, Andy	3:47:15 (7,072)
Webster, Stephen	5:46:19 (27,648)	Wentworth, Alfred	4:04:53 (11,088)	Wheeler, Benjamin	6:48:25 (29,784)
Webster, Terry	3:51:10 (7,906)	Wentworth, Daniel	3:46:09 (6,888)	Wheeler, Bradley	4:45:28 (19,860)
Weck, Charles	4:23:18 (15,134)	Wentzel, Allen	4:03:28 (10,764)	Wheeler, Christopher	4:07:37 (11,681)
Wedderburn, James	5:44:43 (27,540)	Wentzel, Ignatius	2:58:38 (875)	Wheeler, John	4:39:29 (18,690)
Wedge, Iain	2:56:16 (705)	Wentzell, David	4:58:21 (22,351)	Wheeler, Mark	2:57:22 (774)
Wedge, Marcus	3:52:52 (8,248)	Wenzel, Matthias	3:18:52 (2,639)	Wheeler, Michael	4:04:18 (10,949)
Wedlake, Peter	4:59:55 (22,603)	Wenzel, Simon	4:38:00 (18,371)	Wheeler, Miles	3:05:56 (1,415)

Wheeler, Nicholas 5:28:50 (26,273)
Wheeler, Paul 3:27:48 (3,762)
Wheeler, Paul 3:53:17 (8,327)
Wheeler, Peter 3:46:40 (6,985)
Wheeler, Ralph 3:30:36 (4,264)
Wheeler, Simon 3:56:07 (8,952)
Wheeler, Simon 4:54:46 (21,665)
Wheeler, Stephen 5:42:16 (27,352)
Wheeler, Steven 3:39:17 (5,622)
Wheeler, Sydney 5:08:13 (23,800)
Wheelwright, Charles 4:36:48 (18,085)
Whelan, Andrew 4:29:42 (16,599)
Whelan, Michael 4:14:58 (13,254)
Whelan, Ryan 4:09:29 (12,075)
Whetter, Richard 4:31:33 (16,988)
Whewell, Tom 3:51:47 (8,023)
Whickman, David 3:24:32 (3,316)
Whiley, Neil 4:50:50 (20,851)
Whillans, David 4:59:06 (22,475)
Whinney, Charlie 3:43:40 (6,428)
Whitaker, Gary 4:12:02 (12,620)
Whitaker, Keith 3:56:19 (8,998)
Whitby, Mark 5:05:19 (23,340)
Whitcomb, Garth 6:23:38 (29,248)
Whitcomb, Matthew 3:30:45 (4,286)
Whitcomb, Richard 5:14:39 (24,735)
White, Alex 4:12:07 (12,650)
White, Andrew 2:57:34 (784)
White, Andrew 3:32:55 (4,588)
White, Andrew 4:23:11 (15,105)
White, Andrew 4:37:01 (18,136)
White, Andrew 5:16:31 (24,991)
White, Andrew 6:36:54 (29,562)
White, Anthony 2:59:02 (938)
White, Anthony 4:21:35 (14,708)
White, Anthony 4:22:36 (14,955)
White, Barry 3:07:59 (1,591)
White, Brian 2:39:35 (166)
White, Brian 5:31:03 (26,458)
White, Christopher 3:41:59 (6,121)
White, Colin 4:55:30 (21,893)
White, Craig 5:04:12 (23,162)
White, Daniel 4:27:11 (16,004)
White, David 2:45:10 (293)
White, David 4:10:47 (12,332)
White, David 4:24:41 (15,435)
White, David 4:28:19 (16,264)
White, David 4:29:07 (16,453)
White, David 6:05:48 (28,678)
White, Douglas 5:25:50 (25,971)
White, Edward 6:10:56 (28,889)
White, Gareth 4:28:26 (16,297)
White, Gary 4:19:04 (14,136)
White, Graham 2:58:22 (842)
White, Graham 5:14:19 (24,676)
White, Graham 5:44:50 (27,552)
White, Grahame 4:28:54 (16,397)
White, Grenvile 4:04:43 (11,046)
White, Haydn 4:22:59 (15,059)
White, Ian 2:45:21 (303)
White, James 4:32:23 (17,189)
White, James 4:35:51 (17,891)
White, James 4:47:46 (20,303)
White, James 4:58:22 (22,354)
White, John 3:30:38 (4,267)
White, John 3:45:56 (6,843)
White, John 4:12:08 (12,653)
White, John 5:54:41 (28,147)
White, Kevin 5:36:52 (26,936)
White, Len 3:12:54 (1,996)
White, Mark 4:16:58 (13,658)
White, Mark 4:28:33 (16,326)
White, Martin 3:19:58 (2,764)
White, Martin 4:49:46 (20,665)
White, Martin 7:12:34 (30,039)
White, Martyn 3:51:42 (8,006)
White, Nicholas 4:41:39 (19,093)
White, Nick 4:31:07 (16,876)
White, Paul 3:23:23 (3,158)
White, Paul 5:12:21 (24,403)
White, Peter 3:14:38 (2,176)
White, Peter 4:58:33 (22,386)
White, Philip 3:49:58 (7,680)
White, Raymond 6:06:16 (28,694)
White, Rex 4:10:16 (12,222)
White, Robert 4:03:15 (10,711)
White, Robert 5:23:53 (25,779)
White, Roy 4:14:41 (13,166)
White, Russell 3:41:01 (5,960)
White, Simon 4:30:55 (16,832)
White, Stephen 5:12:53 (24,479)
White, Stephen 5:18:32 (25,216)
White, Steven 4:38:10 (18,421)
White, Stewart 3:16:21 (2,345)
White, Stuart 3:51:55 (8,054)
White, Stuart 3:52:01 (8,079)
Whiteaker, James 4:40:34 (18,889)
Whitefield, Christopher 4:21:04 (14,606)
Whitehall, Mark 4:54:29 (21,587)
Whitehead, Christopher 4:08:19 (11,827)
Whitehead, David 3:28:18 (3,866)
Whitehead, Gary 6:38:53 (29,603)
Whitehead, Harvey 5:15:13 (24,834)
Whitehead, Ian 3:21:49 (2,977)
Whitehead, Malcolm 4:26:57 (15,950)
Whitehead, Peter 3:30:16 (4,209)
Whitehead, Peter 4:49:10 (20,553)
Whitehead, Peter 5:04:20 (23,185)
Whitehead, William 3:24:09 (3,266)
Whitehead Cochrane, Robert 3:27:44 (3,751)
Whitehouse, Darren 4:09:58 (12,156)
Whitehouse, David 4:31:32 (16,985)
Whitehouse, Jacob 5:14:58 (24,772)
Whitehouse, Neil 3:47:05 (7,048)
Whitehurst, Stephen 5:36:58 (26,943)
Whitelaw, Mark 2:43:09 (241)
Whitelaw, Patrick 4:07:52 (11,734)
Whitelegg, Peter 6:19:59 (29,157)
Whitelegg, Richard 2:38:28 (146)
Whiteley, Andy 4:51:43 (21,036)
Whiteley, David 3:30:15 (4,205)
Whitelock, Mark 3:27:50 (3,771)
Whitelock, Tom 4:22:59 (15,059)
Whiteman, Creighton 4:54:20 (21,567)
Whiteman, Daniel 6:20:34 (29,176)
Whiteman, Matthew 4:40:35 (18,895)
Whiten, Mark 4:48:18 (20,407)
White-Thomson, Charles 4:49:49 (20,678)
Whiteway, Tony 3:14:22 (2,155)
Whitfield, David 5:11:18 (24,255)
Whitfield, Dean 4:13:46 (12,992)
Whitfield, Matthew 3:14:42 (2,184)
Whitfield, Nicholas 4:28:22 (16,277)
Whitford, Frank 3:10:30 (1,795)
Whiting, Glen 4:16:22 (13,543)
Whiting, Richard 4:09:18 (12,042)
Whitington, Stephen 3:25:17 (3,413)
Whitley, Anthony 5:58:44 (28,354)
Whitley, William 3:30:30 (4,245)
Whitlock, Michael 4:40:34 (18,889)
Whitlock, Paul 2:56:54 (738)
Whitlock, Russell 3:24:20 (3,288)
Whitman, Aaron 4:27:49 (16,154)
Whitman, Anthony 3:30:23 (4,228)
Whitman, Stuart 5:05:02 (23,297)
Whitman, Tony 3:27:11 (3,657)
Whitmarsh, Jim 3:44:42 (6,613)
Whitmore, Ivon 2:59:46 (1,004)
Whitmore, Philip 3:36:24 (5,140)
Whitney, Mark 4:30:32 (16,757)
Whitney, Simon 4:09:22 (12,054)
Whittaker, Steven 5:24:51 (25,862)
Whittaker, Stuart 5:15:48 (24,906)
Whittall, Robert 4:15:52 (13,442)
Whittell, Stuart 3:39:52 (5,750)
Whitten, Robert 4:53:31 (21,427)
Whittingham, Matthew 4:29:17 (16,493)
Whittingham, Paul 4:45:13 (19,810)
Whittle, Andrew 3:44:14 (6,529)
Whittle, David 3:56:17 (8,989)
Whittle, Stephen 3:39:10 (5,602)
Whittle, Stephen 3:43:38 (6,421)
Whittleton, Raymond 4:24:57 (15,491)
Whitton, Mark 5:42:30 (27,375)
Whitty, Iain 3:39:18 (5,625)
Whitwell, Neil 4:09:48 (12,125)
Whitwood, Steven 3:35:49 (5,035)
Whitworth, Bill 3:50:59 (7,867)
Whitworth, Jonathan 3:56:53 (9,151)
Whorlow, Derek 3:54:41 (8,628)
Whybrow, Christopher 3:50:53 (7,844)
Whyman, Mark 5:07:31 (23,698)
Whyndham, Matthew 4:05:39 (11,252)
Whyte, Alistair 4:19:53 (14,333)
Whyte, Ian 3:17:31 (2,487)
Whyte, Mark 3:20:46 (2,860)
Whyte, Stuart 4:11:16 (12,456)
Wichman, Carl 3:47:55 (7,248)
Wickens, Nicholas 4:26:27 (15,832)
Wickens, Paul 4:27:26 (16,046)
Wickham, Mark 4:48:04 (20,362)
Wickham, Peter 3:06:02 (1,427)
Wickham, Stephen 3:13:30 (2,060)
Wickham, Webster 5:12:09 (24,369)
Wickman, Stuart 4:02:10 (10,518)
Wicks, Benjamin 3:44:45 (6,625)
Wicks, Edward 5:02:58 (23,000)
Wicks, Peter 3:27:30 (3,707)
Wictome, Matthew 4:33:49 (17,503)
Widegren, Stefan 4:35:27 (17,804)
Widuch, Christian 3:51:04 (7,884)
Wiegandt, Ronald 3:16:42 (2,393)
Wieland, Mark 3:39:01 (5,575)
Wiener, Adolf 3:52:43 (8,213)
Wierenga, Michael 5:32:29 (26,578)
Wigemyr, Gunstein 3:18:55 (2,646)
Wiggans, Andrew 4:03:51 (10,850)
Wiggins, Norman 3:02:09 (1,165)
Wigginton, Richard 4:18:25 (13,995)
Wiggs, Richard 3:41:35 (6,048)
Wigham, Kelvin 6:48:37 (29,790)
Wightman, Gregor 5:07:23 (23,676)
Wigley, Gavin 3:14:32 (2,171)
Wigley, Timothy 2:58:39 (881)
Wigmore, Andy 5:28:42 (26,256)
Wigram, Nick 4:55:37 (21,928)
Wikenheiser, Dean 3:39:38 (5,699)
Wilbraham, James 3:55:14 (8,747)
Wilbraham, Stephen 3:29:44 (4,126)
Wilby, Stephen 3:31:54 (4,454)
Wilby Manning, Michael 4:24:59 (15,501)
Wilce, Stephen 5:03:58 (23,123)
Wilcock, Ian 4:06:50 (11,512)
Wilcock, Paul 3:23:38 (3,189)
Wilcock, Peter 5:06:56 (23,605)
Wilcock, Robert 6:06:27 (28,698)
Wilcox, Robert 5:36:40 (26,922)
Wild, David 4:45:46 (19,896)
Wild, Gregg 3:51:11 (7,909)
Wild, Ron 5:02:34 (22,942)
Wildbore, David 3:49:03 (7,475)
Wilde, Anthony 4:04:59 (11,115)
Wilde, Christopher 6:32:06 (29,453)
Wilde, Dale 3:58:11 (9,533)
Wilde, Denis 4:22:15 (14,875)
Wilde, Russell 5:15:01 (24,781)
Wilder, Jack 4:23:46 (15,245)
Wildfire, Adrian 3:53:31 (8,380)
Wilding, Keith 4:41:04 (18,990)
Wilding, Kenneth 4:38:44 (18,557)
Wildman, Nick 3:54:45 (8,648)
Wildman, Roy 3:44:11 (6,522)
Wildman, Steve 4:43:24 (19,465)
Wilensky, Larry 3:54:22 (8,555)
Wiles, Andrew 4:02:06 (10,503)
Wiles, Gerry 4:38:24 (18,480)
Wiles, Richard 3:49:26 (7,559)
Wiles, Simon 3:06:35 (1,468)
Wilgoss, Christopher 4:36:28 (18,013)
Wilhelm, Eric 4:38:43 (18,551)
Wilikinson, Nigel 3:13:50 (2,095)
Wilkes, David 3:42:53 (6,283)
Wilkes, Michael 5:09:51 (24,063)
Wilkes, Roger 3:30:49 (4,295)
Wilkes, Stephen 4:53:55 (21,498)
Wilkey, Ian 6:10:31 (28,878)
Wilkie, Colin 4:11:41 (12,546)
Wilkie, Graeme 4:47:30 (20,260)
Wilkie, Thomas 5:00:13 (22,641)

Name	Time	(Position)
Wilkin, Paul	5:14:44	(24,744)
Wilkin, Paul	5:20:19	(25,387)
Wilkins, Blake	3:35:52	(5,047)
Wilkins, Glen	4:14:34	(13,141)
Wilkins, Glenn	3:37:18	(5,301)
Wilkins, Jeremy	4:14:31	(13,131)
Wilkins, John	4:30:46	(16,801)
Wilkins, Peter	4:56:14	(22,030)
Wilkins, Philip	4:07:15	(11,600)
Wilkins, Robin	3:42:55	(6,290)
Wilkins, Ronald	6:04:20	(28,609)
Wilkinson, Christopher	3:30:45	(4,286)
Wilkinson, Christopher	3:46:53	(7,017)
Wilkinson, Dale	3:52:02	(8,082)
Wilkinson, David	3:46:50	(7,007)
Wilkinson, David	4:18:22	(13,976)
Wilkinson, David	4:40:23	(18,853)
Wilkinson, Derek	5:05:35	(23,397)
Wilkinson, Dirk	4:09:13	(12,026)
Wilkinson, Garth	4:57:34	(22,221)
Wilkinson, Geoffrey	4:41:54	(19,140)
Wilkinson, George	4:58:54	(22,441)
Wilkinson, Graham	2:48:08	(366)
Wilkinson, Ian	4:02:39	(10,599)
Wilkinson, Ian	4:09:37	(12,096)
Wilkinson, James	5:42:12	(27,346)
Wilkinson, Jeff	6:05:02	(28,642)
Wilkinson, Jeffrey	4:10:51	(12,359)
Wilkinson, John	3:45:49	(6,827)
Wilkinson, John	4:27:53	(16,172)
Wilkinson, John	4:46:57	(20,158)
Wilkinson, Keith	4:13:25	(12,912)
Wilkinson, Mark	4:14:15	(13,087)
Wilkinson, Matt	3:51:33	(7,978)
Wilkinson, Michael	5:11:31	(24,288)
Wilkinson, Mike	4:48:50	(20,493)
Wilkinson, Nicholas	3:54:20	(8,542)
Wilkinson, Nicholas	5:04:43	(23,247)
Wilkinson, Paul	3:28:38	(3,928)
Wilkinson, Paul	4:46:59	(20,161)
Wilkinson, Philip	4:34:55	(17,697)
Wilkinson, Richard	5:22:07	(25,600)
Wilkinson, Richard	5:53:18	(28,083)
Wilkinson, Stephen	3:28:04	(3,812)
Wilkinson, Stephen	3:49:41	(7,620)
Wilkinson, Stephen	3:50:03	(7,695)
Wilkinson, Stephen	5:36:00	(26,880)
Wilkinson, Stuart	3:57:17	(9,250)
Wilkinson, Thomas	2:59:45	(1,003)
Wilkinson, Tom	4:14:27	(13,116)
Wilkinson, Wayne	3:42:44	(6,258)
Willans, Michael	4:19:47	(14,312)
Willcocks, Matt	5:00:58	(22,729)
Willcox, Michael	2:54:21	(597)
Willdridge, Daniel	3:57:27	(9,311)
Willems, Jo	3:33:48	(4,729)
Willerton, Andrew	3:57:14	(9,236)
Willett, Lee	4:13:35	(12,952)
Willett, Sam	4:37:24	(18,225)
Willett, Stephen	4:40:15	(18,826)
Willetts, Alan	4:55:02	(21,744)
Willetts, John	4:31:38	(17,019)
Willetts, Martin	3:51:48	(8,027)
Willetts, Paul	3:16:45	(2,400)
Willetts, Stephen	3:30:26	(4,237)
Willey, Brian	3:32:13	(4,495)
Williams, Adam	5:30:27	(26,408)
Williams, Adrian	3:58:17	(9,560)
Williams, Alan	3:44:54	(6,661)
Williams, Alan	4:05:35	(11,235)
Williams, Alan	4:15:34	(13,381)
Williams, Aled	4:26:24	(15,823)
Williams, Aled	4:57:21	(22,198)
Williams, Ambrose	3:51:50	(8,035)
Williams, Andrew	3:48:25	(7,341)
Williams, Andrew	5:08:34	(23,859)
Williams, Andrew	5:29:50	(26,353)
Williams, Andy	4:54:56	(21,713)
Williams, Angus	4:17:03	(13,677)
Williams, Anthony	4:57:23	(22,202)
Williams, Arwyn	4:19:00	(14,115)
Williams, Ashley	4:09:28	(12,073)
Williams, Barrie	3:45:59	(6,853)
Williams, Ben	4:21:09	(14,616)
Williams, Benjamin	3:39:52	(5,750)
Williams, Bill	4:52:45	(21,264)
Williams, Brian	4:25:24	(15,593)
Williams, Charlie	4:47:22	(20,232)
Williams, Christopher	4:17:30	(13,773)
Williams, Christopher	4:28:54	(16,397)
Williams, Christopher	4:47:17	(20,218)
Williams, Christopher	4:55:02	(21,744)
Williams, Christopher	5:15:29	(24,867)
Williams, Colin	3:35:31	(4,988)
Williams, Colin	3:57:59	(9,486)
Williams, Craig	4:25:31	(15,622)
Williams, Daniel	4:26:17	(15,800)
Williams, Danny	3:30:55	(4,317)
Williams, Darren	4:18:42	(14,051)
Williams, Darren	4:46:10	(19,977)
Williams, David	3:16:01	(2,323)
Williams, David	3:35:54	(5,055)
Williams, David	3:45:30	(6,744)
Williams, David	4:19:22	(14,215)
Williams, David	4:23:16	(15,122)
Williams, David	4:41:50	(19,128)
Williams, David	4:56:06	(22,003)
Williams, David	5:02:37	(22,949)
Williams, David	5:12:18	(24,392)
Williams, David	5:12:18	(24,392)
Williams, David	5:21:20	(25,510)
Williams, Denis	2:41:08	(196)
Williams, Dennis	3:17:11	(2,444)
Williams, Ellis	3:46:21	(6,922)
Williams, Frank	3:15:01	(2,224)
Williams, Gareth	2:29:02	(62)
Williams, Gareth	4:55:20	(21,824)
Williams, Garth	3:57:23	(9,283)
Williams, Gary	3:31:08	(4,347)
Williams, Gary	5:30:34	(26,418)
Williams, Gary	5:51:02	(27,956)
Williams, Gavin	3:01:31	(1,112)
Williams, Geoffrey	5:04:45	(23,252)
Williams, Gideon	5:01:57	(22,864)
Williams, Gregory	4:35:34	(17,829)
Williams, Haydn	4:01:22	(10,365)
Williams, Huw	3:29:55	(4,155)
Williams, Huw	3:53:06	(8,292)
Williams, James	3:31:54	(4,454)
Williams, James	4:08:45	(11,923)
Williams, James	4:47:13	(20,207)
Williams, Jamie	3:55:46	(8,864)
Williams, Jamie	5:08:35	(23,863)
Williams, Jason	4:25:41	(15,650)
Williams, Jeffrey	5:36:10	(26,890)
Williams, Jim	3:47:32	(7,150)
Williams, Joel	4:15:45	(13,414)
Williams, John	3:16:15	(2,337)
Williams, John	4:06:36	(11,468)
Williams, John	5:03:43	(23,084)
Williams, John Gerard	3:47:41	(7,189)
Williams, Joseph	5:13:04	(24,509)
Williams, Julian	3:59:02	(9,765)
Williams, Kevin	2:45:59	(317)
Williams, Kevin	3:37:39	(5,360)
Williams, Les	4:21:51	(14,774)
Williams, Marcus	3:44:16	(6,535)
Williams, Mark	3:20:41	(2,844)
Williams, Mark	3:29:48	(4,134)
Williams, Mark	4:04:51	(11,077)
Williams, Mark	4:07:24	(11,639)
Williams, Mark	4:16:05	(13,485)
Williams, Mark	4:29:53	(16,654)
Williams, Mark	4:31:01	(16,855)
Williams, Mark	4:53:08	(21,343)
Williams, Mark	4:57:42	(22,249)
Williams, Mark	5:10:57	(24,206)
Williams, Mark	5:28:37	(26,243)
Williams, Martin	4:19:25	(14,231)
Williams, Matthew	3:40:04	(5,795)
Williams, Matthew	5:30:45	(26,434)
Williams, Meirion	4:17:25	(13,753)
Williams, Michael	2:47:27	(351)
Williams, Michael	3:21:23	(2,932)
Williams, Michael	3:50:26	(7,761)
Williams, Michael	4:36:37	(18,045)
Williams, Michael	6:21:05	(29,195)
Williams, Neal	3:37:30	(5,336)
Williams, Neal	3:39:19	(5,631)
Williams, Nefyn	3:49:44	(7,629)
Williams, Nefyn	4:00:51	(10,251)
Williams, Neil	4:32:58	(17,303)
Williams, Nick	3:24:52	(3,360)
Williams, Nigel	6:02:55	(28,536)
Williams, Paul	3:53:25	(8,362)
Williams, Paul	3:56:28	(9,046)
Williams, Paul	4:09:32	(12,080)
Williams, Paul	4:24:42	(15,437)
Williams, Peter	3:09:05	(1,678)
Williams, Peter	3:20:22	(2,803)
Williams, Peter	4:33:28	(17,410)
Williams, Philip	4:31:57	(17,105)
Williams, Phillip	3:47:27	(7,130)
Williams, Ray	3:30:41	(4,275)
Williams, Raymond	4:53:11	(21,350)
Williams, Rhys	4:39:19	(18,648)
Williams, Richard	3:45:27	(6,736)
Williams, Richard	4:35:42	(17,865)
Williams, Richard	5:08:09	(23,789)
Williams, Robert	3:40:10	(5,810)
Williams, Rodney	4:05:29	(11,209)
Williams, Ronald	3:04:49	(1,336)
Williams, Royston	4:35:04	(17,728)
Williams, Rupert	3:47:41	(7,189)
Williams, Ryan	5:00:38	(22,681)
Williams, Shane	4:27:04	(15,988)
Williams, Simon	3:13:07	(2,013)
Williams, Simon	4:09:12	(12,022)
Williams, Simon	5:03:00	(23,004)
Williams, Stephen	3:29:03	(4,006)
Williams, Stephen	4:31:33	(16,988)
Williams, Steve	3:45:21	(6,724)
Williams, Steven	4:47:54	(20,325)
Williams, Stuart	4:33:01	(17,313)
Williams, Tim	3:25:46	(3,479)
Williams, Tim	4:24:35	(15,416)
Williams, Tim	5:07:45	(23,740)
Williams, Timothy	4:06:42	(11,485)
Williams, Timothy	5:04:20	(23,185)
Williams, Tony	3:49:26	(7,559)
Williams, Tucker	3:10:18	(1,775)
Williams, Vaughan	5:13:21	(24,558)
Williams, William	5:32:45	(26,598)
Williams Lucas, Garry	3:30:07	(4,191)
Williamsa, John	3:57:51	(9,446)
Williams-Denton, Neil	4:42:45	(19,320)
Williamson, Alan	6:08:40	(28,794)
Williamson, Alistair	3:42:34	(6,229)
Williamson, Anthony	4:54:10	(21,545)
Williamson, Bruce	4:40:18	(18,838)
Williamson, Colin	7:17:31	(30,063)
Williamson, Dave	4:17:59	(13,867)
Williamson, David	3:26:27	(3,552)
Williamson, David	4:51:00	(20,881)
Williamson, Dennis	5:27:09	(26,095)
Williamson, Gary	4:51:33	(20,995)
Williamson, Lee	4:38:28	(18,500)
Williamson, Mark	3:28:44	(3,944)
Williamson, Nick	3:50:27	(7,766)
Williamson, Paul	5:04:48	(23,264)
Williamson, Simon	3:08:21	(1,619)
Willingham, George	4:57:39	(22,239)
Willis, David	4:19:03	(14,130)
Willis, James	5:00:39	(22,685)
Willis, John	3:57:53	(9,347)
Willis, John	4:42:48	(19,331)
Willis, Kevin	3:39:23	(5,645)
Willis, Martin	3:57:46	(9,416)
Willis, Michael	3:18:21	(2,583)
Willis, Norman	3:36:36	(5,169)
Willis, Paul	3:45:52	(6,836)
Willis, Richard	4:50:25	(20,789)
Willis, Robert	3:18:14	(2,567)
Willis, Stephen	3:12:37	(1,969)
Willis, Stephen	3:16:26	(2,355)
Willmitt, William	3:19:25	(2,696)
Willmott, Ian	3:52:58	(8,260)
Willoughby, Gary	3:37:38	(5,355)
Willoughby, John	3:02:25	(1,184)

Willoughby, Mark....5:13:41 (24,594)
Willoughby, Rae....4:19:55 (14,343)
Willoughby, Rex....5:08:47 (23,904)
Willows, Duncan....3:49:56 (7,671)
Wills, Brian....3:36:42 (5,191)
Wills, David....3:59:41 (9,969)
Wills, Gordon....4:07:54 (11,740)
Wills, Harry....6:11:45 (28,920)
Wills, Iain....4:57:48 (22,266)
Wills, Oliver....4:01:02 (10,288)
Wills, Robert....3:57:06 (9,196)
Wills, Timothy....4:10:54 (12,374)
Willson, Anthony....5:16:06 (24,939)
Willson, Jonathon....5:21:56 (25,577)
Willson, Robert....6:11:06 (28,894)
Willy, Williquet....3:50:18 (7,734)
Wilmot, Alfred....4:39:33 (18,704)
Wilmot, Andrew....3:09:53 (1,740)
Wilmot, Christian....6:02:12 (28,512)
Wilmot, Terence....4:23:23 (15,148)
Wilmot, Thomas....4:35:45 (17,875)
Wilmshurst, Peter....5:13:29 (24,572)
Wilshaw, John....6:33:32 (29,495)
Wilson, Alan....2:57:52 (805)
Wilson, Alastair....3:41:14 (5,993)
Wilson, Alex....4:15:00 (13,268)
Wilson, Allen....3:56:38 (9,085)
Wilson, Andrew....2:56:45 (730)
Wilson, Andrew....3:38:15 (5,442)
Wilson, Andrew....3:48:20 (7,328)
Wilson, Andrew....3:56:37 (9,081)
Wilson, Andrew....4:29:17 (16,493)
Wilson, Andy....3:30:28 (4,241)
Wilson, Anthony....4:26:04 (15,748)
Wilson, Anthony....5:46:29 (27,658)
Wilson, Barry....2:49:09 (398)
Wilson, Brian....3:57:43 (9,399)
Wilson, Brian....4:26:32 (15,851)
Wilson, Brian....5:27:06 (26,089)
Wilson, Bruce....5:33:07 (26,620)
Wilson, Bryce....4:50:20 (20,778)
Wilson, Charles....4:09:09 (12,012)
Wilson, Chris....4:54:42 (21,640)
Wilson, Christopher....3:47:56 (7,252)
Wilson, Daniel....3:37:28 (5,329)
Wilson, Darren....4:14:15 (13,087)
Wilson, David....3:25:15 (3,409)
Wilson, David....4:17:09 (13,703)
Wilson, David....4:53:24 (21,398)
Wilson, Derek....3:34:43 (4,866)
Wilson, Derek....4:49:12 (20,562)
Wilson, Donough....7:21:05 (30,087)
Wilson, Douglas....5:57:15 (28,278)
Wilson, Duncan....3:48:53 (7,436)
Wilson, Eric....2:38:05 (139)
Wilson, Fitzroy....5:13:37 (24,587)
Wilson, James....3:28:32 (3,916)
Wilson, James....4:05:48 (11,298)
Wilson, Jason....3:58:19 (9,565)
Wilson, John....5:20:31 (25,411)
Wilson, Jonathan....5:01:56 (22,861)
Wilson, Keith....3:55:20 (8,767)
Wilson, Keith....4:16:01 (13,468)
Wilson, Kevin....5:07:36 (23,712)
Wilson, Lee....5:03:03 (23,012)
Wilson, Leigh....3:35:55 (5,059)
Wilson, Marc....3:21:22 (2,928)
Wilson, Mark....3:35:16 (4,946)
Wilson, Mark....3:48:40 (7,393)
Wilson, Mathew....3:18:37 (2,610)
Wilson, Matthew....3:48:31 (7,365)
Wilson, Michael....3:19:40 (2,725)
Wilson, Michael....3:21:16 (2,912)
Wilson, Michael....4:12:33 (12,746)
Wilson, Nicholas....4:14:52 (13,228)
Wilson, Oliver....3:38:41 (5,515)
Wilson, Paul....3:08:40 (1,646)
Wilson, Paul....3:38:41 (5,515)
Wilson, Paul....3:40:59 (5,952)
Wilson, Paul....4:44:52 (19,750)
Wilson, Peter....3:59:43 (9,979)
Wilson, Ray....7:19:55 (30,078)
Wilson, Richard....2:48:58 (392)

Wilson, Robert....2:44:24 (272)
Wilson, Robert....3:04:01 (1,284)
Wilson, Robert....4:25:23 (15,590)
Wilson, Robert....4:31:45 (17,048)
Wilson, Robert....4:57:50 (22,270)
Wilson, Robert....5:39:28 (27,132)
Wilson, Robin....4:15:30 (13,366)
Wilson, Robin....4:23:08 (15,093)
Wilson, Robin....5:10:24 (24,129)
Wilson, Scott....3:36:00 (5,075)
Wilson, Sean....5:13:25 (24,565)
Wilson, Stephen....3:51:05 (7,889)
Wilson, Stephen....4:11:25 (12,486)
Wilson, Stephen....5:04:23 (23,197)
Wilson, Steven....3:44:53 (6,658)
Wilson, Steven....4:08:21 (11,837)
Wilson, Stuart....3:39:50 (5,745)
Wilson, Stuart....3:56:43 (9,109)
Wilson, Stuart....3:59:36 (9,948)
Wilson, Terence....5:27:25 (26,120)
Wilson, Thomas....5:22:07 (25,600)
Wilson, Toby....4:25:19 (15,578)
Wilson, Victor....3:17:14 (2,447)
Wilson Young, Ian....3:44:19 (6,546)
Wilson-Hooper, Mark....6:31:36 (29,443)
Wilton, Robert....3:30:27 (4,239)
Wilton, Steve....5:10:56 (24,204)
Wiltshire, Dean....4:49:06 (20,544)
Wiltshire, John....3:47:54 (7,241)
Wimble, Christopher....3:51:14 (7,917)
Windebank, Mark....3:24:29 (3,307)
Windebank, William....5:15:10 (24,823)
Winder, Bill....5:43:53 (27,463)
Windisch, Johann....4:07:30 (11,660)
Windle, Andrew....4:53:23 (21,396)
Windmill, Stephen....3:53:16 (8,322)
Windover, Jonathan....4:36:23 (17,991)
Windows, James....4:04:43 (11,046)
Windsor Richards, Matthew....3:47:45 (7,200)
Winfield, Andrew....2:58:40 (885)
Winfield, Darren....3:54:41 (8,628)
Wingate, Carl....4:54:39 (21,623)
Wingerning, Mike....5:09:22 (23,992)
Wingfield, Mike....3:43:05 (6,323)
Wingrave, Michael....4:41:42 (19,102)
Wingrove, Philip....5:05:45 (23,422)
Winkelmayer, Herbert....3:54:38 (8,620)
Winman, Philip....4:24:01 (15,298)
Winnepenninckx, Paul....2:46:05 (319)
Winser, Julian....5:14:50 (24,755)
Winship, Stewart....6:01:55 (28,502)
Winslow, Michael....3:44:33 (6,588)
Winslow, Nick....4:37:55 (18,350)
Winsor, James....4:21:21 (14,656)
Winstanley, Stephen....3:40:07 (5,803)
Winston, David....5:11:34 (24,298)
Winston, Stephen....4:06:56 (11,535)
Wint, Andrew....4:00:16 (10,103)
Winter, Andrew....6:09:43 (28,847)
Winter, John....3:38:50 (5,544)
Winter, John....3:46:15 (6,905)
Winter, Keith....4:13:19 (12,878)
Winter, Rudolf....6:15:44 (29,052)
Winter, Timothy....4:14:08 (13,063)
Winterberger, Andreas....3:53:18 (8,333)
Winterbottom, Ian....4:57:35 (22,225)
Winterbottom, Mark....4:22:00 (14,813)
Winterflood, Ian....2:43:57 (259)
Wintersgill, Graham....4:32:32 (17,217)
Wintour, David....4:33:08 (17,334)
Wintrip, Tim....4:09:22 (12,054)
Winward, John....4:32:59 (17,308)
Wipfli, Franz....5:01:42 (22,824)
Wirght, Ivan....3:42:49 (6,272)
Wirth, Helmut....3:20:51 (2,871)
Wisdom, John....5:55:25 (28,181)
Wisdom, Martin....3:32:53 (4,585)
Wise, Carl....4:05:40 (11,256)
Wise, David....4:00:57 (10,276)
Wiseman, Benedict....4:49:37 (20,637)
Wiseman, James....4:19:33 (14,270)
Wiseman, Neil....3:51:33 (7,978)
Wishart, Keith....3:48:51 (7,431)

Wishart, Robbie....4:28:37 (16,344)
Wisner, Phil....4:14:51 (13,222)
Wisniewski, Adam....3:55:01 (8,704)
Wistow, Richard....4:02:07 (10,507)
Witcher, Paul....3:18:11 (2,559)
Witherall, John....4:55:12 (21,783)
Witherick, Roger....3:05:01 (1,351)
Withers, David....4:07:00 (11,551)
Withers, David....4:38:02 (18,378)
Withers, Julian....4:14:28 (13,120)
Withers, Neil....6:28:59 (29,386)
Withers, Robert....3:59:52 (10,016)
Withers, Stephen....3:30:02 (4,176)
Withers, Stuart....5:00:45 (22,700)
Withers, Thomas....4:03:12 (10,702)
Witherspoon, Murray....3:42:28 (6,211)
Withey, Gavin....5:09:48 (24,058)
Withey, Jonathan....3:36:36 (5,169)
Withey, Nigel....5:35:56 (26,873)
Witt, Knut....3:52:41 (8,207)
Wittemann, Rolf....5:16:43 (25,014)
Witthop, Peter....2:58:43 (894)
Wittmershaus, Dietrich....3:19:06 (2,662)
Witts, Neil....4:36:18 (17,977)
Wivell, Michael....4:43:15 (19,438)
Wlson, Andrew....4:11:56 (12,591)
Wod, Robert....3:46:03 (6,865)
Wodhouse, Toby....4:49:14 (20,569)
Wognall, Derek....3:57:04 (9,191)
Wohlert, Lamb....4:21:17 (14,645)
Wohrle, Achim....4:19:51 (14,325)
Wojciechowski, Peter....5:10:55 (24,201)
Wolf, Alistair....4:22:45 (14,993)
Wolf, Spencer....4:04:22 (10,959)
Wolf, Stuart....4:28:16 (16,256)
Wolfarth, Colin....3:49:44 (7,629)
Wolfenden, Michael....3:29:53 (4,145)
Wolff, David....3:57:32 (9,338)
Wolles, Herman....4:24:23 (15,365)
Wolmarans, Leigh....6:17:10 (29,091)
Woltering, Heinz....3:32:27 (4,527)
Wolton, Sam....3:57:47 (9,425)
Wolverson, Guy....3:59:23 (9,876)
Wonfor, Noel....3:27:24 (3,689)
Wong, Chi....4:33:36 (17,455)
Wong, Jimmy....4:41:43 (19,104)
Wong, Kian....5:59:10 (28,375)
Wong, Sai....4:27:01 (15,971)
Wong, Will....4:59:54 (22,600)
Wood, Alan....3:03:24 (1,241)
Wood, Alan....3:54:56 (8,690)
Wood, Alan....5:40:32 (27,227)
Wood, Andrew....4:58:02 (22,301)
Wood, Anthony....4:19:36 (14,279)
Wood, Brian....4:25:01 (15,514)
Wood, Carl....3:57:07 (9,200)
Wood, Charles....3:48:56 (7,448)
Wood, Chris....4:29:12 (16,472)
Wood, Christopher....4:07:18 (11,612)
Wood, Daniel....4:29:22 (16,511)
Wood, Daniel....4:55:26 (21,863)
Wood, David....3:30:31 (4,249)
Wood, David....3:56:50 (9,142)
Wood, David....4:00:33 (10,173)
Wood, David....5:40:32 (27,227)
Wood, Derek....4:33:30 (17,419)
Wood, Douglas....4:16:43 (13,617)
Wood, Fraser....4:05:56 (11,333)
Wood, Graham....3:47:24 (7,117)
Wood, Ian....3:24:48 (3,354)
Wood, Ian....3:38:49 (5,540)
Wood, Ian....5:01:35 (22,815)
Wood, James....3:30:21 (4,221)
Wood, Jason....5:51:50 (28,007)
Wood, Jeremy....5:11:00 (24,212)
Wood, Keith....3:38:22 (5,458)
Wood, Kevin....4:04:44 (11,050)
Wood, Kevin....4:22:30 (14,930)
Wood, Kevin....5:53:30 (28,090)
Wood, Matthew....4:22:24 (14,903)
Wood, Michael....3:33:07 (4,630)
Wood, Michael....3:49:02 (7,471)
Wood, Michael....4:25:37 (15,640)

Wood, Michael 5:06:59 (23,613)
Wood, Mike 2:58:41 (888)
Wood, Oliver 3:42:27 (6,208)
Wood, Paul 3:29:04 (4,008)
Wood, Peter 4:40:38 (18,906)
Wood, Peter 4:55:14 (21,791)
Wood, Philip 3:07:45 (1,570)
Wood, Ray 5:07:12 (23,650)
Wood, Richard 3:24:37 (3,332)
Wood, Robert 3:42:40 (6,247)
Wood, Robert 3:45:37 (6,769)
Wood, Robert 4:05:57 (11,339)
Wood, Robert 4:22:10 (14,847)
Wood, Robert 4:42:23 (19,244)
Wood, Simon 2:59:07 (943)
Wood, Simon 3:54:46 (8,650)
Wood, Stanley 4:14:58 (13,254)
Wood, Stephen 3:28:46 (3,953)
Wood, Steve 3:25:18 (3,418)
Wood, Steven 4:10:42 (12,311)
Wood, Steven 4:26:07 (15,760)
Woodage, Phil 3:32:52 (4,582)
Woodall, Eric 3:53:05 (8,288)
Woodall, Paul 3:19:28 (2,704)
Woodbridge, James 4:47:21 (20,229)
Woodburn, Kevin 4:12:17 (12,687)
Woodburn, Robin 5:10:30 (24,142)
Woodcock, Alan 4:26:02 (15,742)
Woodcock, Brian 4:29:24 (16,519)
Woodcock, Clive 3:27:54 (3,789)
Woodcock, Marc 3:17:07 (2,437)
Woodcock, Timothy 4:05:41 (11,263)
Woodd, Benjamin 2:58:18 (834)
Wooders, Andrew 5:15:26 (24,861)
Woodeson, James 4:12:46 (12,784)
Woodfine, William 4:46:21 (20,020)
Woodford, Colin 3:58:14 (9,551)
Woodford, John 5:09:20 (23,986)
Woodgate, Bradley 4:23:02 (15,071)
Woodhall, Richard 4:10:53 (12,368)
Woodham, Derrick 3:42:07 (6,141)
Woodhead, Richard 3:50:50 (7,831)
Woodhead, Simon 4:11:38 (12,531)
Woodhouse, Christopher 4:16:18 (13,525)
Woodhouse, Mark 4:13:43 (12,985)
Woodhouse, Paul 4:21:52 (14,779)
Woodhouse, Richard 3:44:41 (6,610)
Wooding, Nigel 4:32:58 (17,303)
Wooding, Peter 5:32:05 (26,539)
Wooding, Ross 5:07:33 (23,701)
Woodley, Ben 4:33:20 (17,378)
Woodley, Dave 3:57:51 (9,446)
Woodley, David 4:31:50 (17,069)
Woodley, Lawrence 4:42:16 (19,218)
Woodman, Mark 2:44:21 (270)
Woodman, Tom 3:13:17 (2,034)
Woodmansey, David 4:56:10 (22,015)
Woodridge, David 4:43:01 (19,389)
Woodroffe, Ian 4:38:04 (18,389)
Woodroof, Alan 5:10:35 (24,163)
Woodrow, Alan 5:27:47 (26,157)
Woodrow, Jonathan 6:02:12 (28,512)
Woodruff, Raymond 3:49:22 (7,543)
Woodrup, Roger 4:20:36 (14,500)
Woods, Andrew 3:27:45 (3,756)
Woods, Ben 4:27:35 (16,084)
Woods, Christopher 4:46:52 (20,136)
Woods, Colin 3:40:33 (5,875)
Woods, Damon 3:53:04 (8,284)
Woods, Dennis 4:24:55 (15,482)
Woods, Duncan 4:20:56 (14,581)
Woods, George 3:58:08 (9,525)
Woods, George 4:50:35 (20,811)
Woods, Joe 4:03:51 (10,850)
Woods, Joshua 4:39:01 (18,611)
Woods, Michael 4:00:58 (10,278)
Woods, Michael 4:15:40 (13,398)
Woods, Peter 3:47:37 (7,167)
Woods, Richard 5:46:57 (27,700)
Woods, Scott 3:59:57 (10,042)
Woods, Simon 4:39:30 (18,694)
Woods, Thomas 4:22:01 (14,818)
Woods, William 4:01:02 (10,288)
Woodsford, Kyne 4:26:33 (15,856)
Woodthorpe, Peter 4:58:40 (22,407)
Woodward, Andrew 4:24:25 (15,374)
Woodward, Aston 3:24:41 (3,340)
Woodward, Brian 3:55:16 (8,756)
Woodward, Christopher 4:50:05 (20,733)
Woodward, David 4:45:03 (19,780)
Woodward, David 5:44:33 (27,526)
Woodward, Kevin 4:54:12 (21,552)
Woodward, Michael 4:35:50 (17,887)
Woodward, Nick 2:58:12 (820)
Woodward, Paul 5:25:45 (25,963)
Woodward, Peter 5:23:11 (25,718)
Woodward, Robert 4:07:14 (11,595)
Woodward, Simon 3:54:46 (8,650)
Woodward, William 3:28:09 (3,834)
Wookey, David 4:37:09 (18,158)
Woolard, Martin 5:33:19 (26,634)
Woolard, Stephen 5:33:19 (26,634)
Wooldridge, Simon 2:53:33 (562)
Wooley, Ricky 3:42:30 (6,219)
Woolf, Milton 4:46:21 (20,020)
Woolgar, Richard 5:06:52 (23,598)
Woolland, Dominic 4:50:15 (20,758)
Woollard, John Geoffrey 5:47:50 (27,757)
Wooller, Tristan 3:58:01 (9,495)
Woollett, Stephen 4:09:34 (12,084)
Woolley, Alan 3:36:45 (5,204)
Woolley, David 4:52:13 (21,136)
Woolley, David 4:55:33 (21,905)
Woolley, Keith 4:38:04 (18,389)
Woolley, Simon 4:12:16 (12,683)
Woolley, Stephen 4:36:21 (17,985)
Woolliams, Stephen 3:40:24 (5,849)
Woolmer, Tim 3:40:07 (5,803)
Wooloughan, John 5:11:42 (24,315)
Woon, Jayson 3:57:12 (9,226)
Wootton, Alfred 5:01:44 (22,828)
Wootton, Anthony 3:55:45 (8,861)
Wootton, Neil 3:43:38 (6,421)
Wootton, Nicholas 4:14:49 (13,213)
Wootton, Paul 3:26:45 (3,591)
Wootton, Robin 4:34:19 (17,599)
Wootton, Terence 3:55:56 (8,901)
Wordley, Philip 4:13:13 (12,858)
Wormald, Carl 2:49:26 (409)
Worn, Steven 3:55:22 (8,775)
Worrall, David 6:04:24 (28,613)
Worrall, Keith 2:42:45 (229)
Worrall, Michael 4:03:01 (10,667)
Worrall, Simon 4:00:53 (10,259)
Worsey, Peter 4:12:04 (12,633)
Worsley, Dominic 3:39:06 (5,589)
Worsley, Martin 4:13:50 (13,009)
Worsley, Paul 4:19:46 (14,309)
Worsley, Steven 2:58:30 (856)
Worssam, Richard 5:28:15 (26,201)
Worswick, Neil 2:48:50 (387)
Wort, Steven 3:14:24 (2,158)
Worth, Daniel 3:55:34 (8,812)
Worthington, Barrie 4:05:21 (11,175)
Worthy, Ian 5:16:45 (25,019)
Wragg, Anthony 4:22:03 (14,829)
Wragg, Peter 6:17:27 (29,097)
Wraight, Simon 3:59:43 (9,979)
Wrangles, Paul 3:48:32 (7,367)
Wrathall, Paul 4:32:35 (17,224)
Wray, Lionel 3:46:44 (6,995)
Wray, Michael 3:35:11 (4,929)
Wray, Paul 4:32:23 (17,189)
Wray, Peter 5:28:13 (26,199)
Wreghitt, Guy 4:34:28 (17,620)
Wren, Danny 4:48:13 (20,388)
Wren, Graham 5:02:03 (22,884)
Wren, Steven 6:08:26 (28,784)
Wrench, Benjamin 3:25:56 (3,496)
Wrench, Clive 5:33:24 (26,640)
Wrest, William 5:14:25 (24,690)
Wretham, Graham 4:46:49 (20,119)
Wright, Adam 4:32:49 (17,278)
Wright, Adam 4:43:18 (19,451)
Wright, Alan 4:47:18 (20,220)
Wright, Bernard 3:35:33 (4,997)
Wright, Chris 4:21:52 (14,779)
Wright, Christopher 3:51:24 (7,944)
Wright, Christopher 4:41:37 (19,085)
Wright, Christopher 4:50:40 (20,821)
Wright, Christopher 5:07:52 (23,756)
Wright, Christopher 5:28:45 (26,260)
Wright, Colin 3:38:39 (5,510)
Wright, Darren 4:13:31 (12,935)
Wright, David 2:54:09 (584)
Wright, David 3:21:20 (2,925)
Wright, David 5:11:28 (24,279)
Wright, David 6:37:52 (29,588)
Wright, Dennis 5:35:24 (26,836)
Wright, Edwin 4:18:01 (13,872)
Wright, Eric 4:23:26 (15,155)
Wright, Gary 4:17:06 (13,685)
Wright, Gary 4:38:45 (18,559)
Wright, Graham 4:12:17 (12,687)
Wright, Harry 5:03:36 (23,070)
Wright, Ian 4:24:44 (15,448)
Wright, James 4:18:23 (13,982)
Wright, John 3:46:29 (6,944)
Wright, John 4:22:09 (14,845)
Wright, John 5:59:52 (28,414)
Wright, John 6:28:43 (29,377)
Wright, Ken 4:05:43 (11,273)
Wright, Kenneth 4:22:17 (14,883)
Wright, Kevin 3:35:13 (4,935)
Wright, Mark 2:41:48 (212)
Wright, Martin 4:11:25 (12,486)
Wright, Matthew 4:04:37 (11,023)
Wright, Michael 3:57:52 (9,453)
Wright, Michael 4:20:09 (14,397)
Wright, Nicholas 4:28:48 (16,380)
Wright, Noel 4:23:30 (15,172)
Wright, Paul 3:19:13 (2,676)
Wright, Paul 4:27:53 (16,172)
Wright, Peter 4:55:55 (21,971)
Wright, Peter 5:14:02 (24,632)
Wright, Phillip 4:16:40 (13,601)
Wright, Robert 5:57:40 (28,309)
Wright, Robert 6:01:56 (28,504)
Wright, Ross 3:26:52 (3,605)
Wright, Simon 3:39:30 (5,673)
Wright, Stephen 2:57:47 (798)
Wright, Steven 3:42:05 (6,134)
Wright, Steven 4:39:56 (18,772)
Wright, Steven 4:48:52 (20,496)
Wright, Stuart 4:18:21 (13,972)
Wright, Terence 5:06:12 (23,501)
Wright, Tim 5:12:24 (24,416)
Wright, Tim 5:26:43 (26,063)
Wright, Tony 2:38:57 (154)
Wright, William 3:47:50 (7,218)
Wrigley, Alexander 3:36:36 (5,169)
Wrigley, Justin 4:24:10 (15,324)
Wroblewski, Mark 4:53:46 (21,467)
Wrottesley, Mike 3:57:34 (9,352)
Wulf, Lars 4:21:53 (14,785)
Wulvik, Gunnar 3:38:23 (5,462)
Wunderlich, Stefan 4:17:10 (13,708)
Wyatt, Andrew 3:00:07 (1,035)
Wyatt, Dominic 4:27:45 (16,135)
Wyeth, Simon 3:24:29 (3,307)
Wylde, Sean 5:42:28 (27,367)
Wylie, Ian 3:47:24 (7,117)
Wyman, Anthony 5:58:09 (28,332)
Wynn, Ludo 4:51:22 (20,963)
Wynn, Martin 3:49:29 (7,574)
Wynne, Anthony 4:43:28 (19,484)
Wynne, Jeremy 3:03:08 (1,222)
Wynne, Kieran 3:47:25 (7,122)
Wynne, Michael 4:55:55 (21,971)
Wynne-Williams, Harry 3:27:51 (3,777)
Wyse, Malcolm 4:12:21 (12,703)
Wyss, Laurent 4:05:47 (11,293)
Wyss, Werner 3:40:23 (5,845)
Wythe, Dickie 3:00:54 (1,076)
Xavier, Botifoll 3:48:53 (7,436)
Xifaras, Michael 4:26:20 (15,812)
Yadave, Rush 4:47:35 (20,280)
Yallop, Tony 4:18:58 (14,112)
Yamada, Shigeo 3:18:29 (2,596)

Yan, Henry....4:48:38 (20,457)
Yandell, John....3:40:55 (5,931)
Yandell, Lawrence....3:50:44 (7,814)
Yapp, Ian....3:26:19 (3,538)
Yarde-Buller, Benjamin....4:04:22 (10,959)
Yardley, Nicholas....5:02:44 (22,966)
Yarker, Christopher....4:40:47 (18,938)
Yarker, John....5:02:47 (22,973)
Yarnold, Stuart....3:52:04 (8,091)
Yassi, Hocine....4:44:57 (19,765)
Yasunobu, Shigenori....5:13:15 (24,546)
Yates, Anthony....3:18:11 (2,559)
Yates, Chris....4:18:52 (14,090)
Yates, Damien....6:08:47 (28,802)
Yates, Eric....4:32:42 (17,247)
Yates, Gary....2:55:01 (630)
Yates, Ian....3:51:57 (8,064)
Yates, Ian....5:03:59 (23,125)
Yates, Joseph....3:07:16 (1,526)
Yates, Matthew....3:00:06 (1,033)
Yates, Neville....3:39:56 (5,768)
Yates, Robert....4:00:15 (10,099)
Yau, Kinwo....3:50:28 (7,767)
Yderberk, Patrik....3:32:04 (4,475)
Yearsley, Fred....3:23:25 (3,162)
Yeates, Kevin....4:15:27 (13,358)
Yeats, Gavin....4:10:34 (12,289)
Yelding, Steven....4:38:06 (18,401)
Yeldon, Peter....6:35:03 (29,522)
Yelland, David....3:44:28 (6,570)
Yeo, John....3:29:13 (4,029)
Yeomans, Arnold....3:43:49 (6,458)
Yeomans, Martin....3:10:44 (1,811)
Yeomans, Stephen....3:41:48 (6,091)
Yetts, Trevor....6:18:27 (29,125)
Yeung, Hoi....5:25:27 (25,936)
Yin, Peter....4:31:11 (16,898)
Yong, Derek....5:17:03 (25,056)
Yoo, Byung....3:53:02 (8,272)
York, Martin....5:03:06 (23,019)
York, Philip....3:32:41 (4,558)
York, Richard....4:49:55 (20,703)
York, Stephen....4:27:30 (16,058)
Yoshida, Tamotsu....4:37:37 (18,282)
Youds, Francis....4:23:22 (15,146)
Youle, Richard....4:33:49 (17,503)
Young, Alastair....3:15:26 (2,264)
Young, Alastair....4:28:16 (16,256)
Young, Barry....3:54:25 (8,570)
Young, Bryn....4:46:11 (19,983)
Young, Charles....4:11:09 (12,428)
Young, Charles....4:24:23 (15,365)
Young, Chris....3:49:52 (7,662)
Young, David....3:21:32 (2,953)
Young, George....5:04:29 (23,214)
Young, Jerry....4:42:10 (19,198)
Young, John....3:41:56 (6,113)
Young, John....4:51:15 (20,930)
Young, Kevin....4:06:34 (11,464)
Young, Leon....3:59:00 (9,754)
Young, Lester....3:00:40 (1,064)
Young, Mark....3:49:30 (7,584)
Young, Mark....4:37:50 (18,326)
Young, Mark....4:40:13 (18,816)
Young, Mark....5:28:11 (26,194)
Young, Matthew....3:32:05 (4,478)
Young, Michael....3:06:34 (1,467)
Young, Mickey....5:15:36 (24,878)
Young, Nigel....3:47:44 (7,199)
Young, Patrick....3:17:36 (2,491)
Young, Paul....3:13:58 (2,114)
Young, Paul....5:15:39 (24,884)
Young, Robin....4:13:19 (12,878)
Young, Roger....4:06:12 (11,385)
Young, Roger....4:48:24 (20,426)
Young, Roy....4:16:45 (13,629)
Young, Simon....3:34:11 (4,784)
Young, Stephen....4:01:13 (10,321)
Young, Stephen....4:33:50 (17,507)
Young, Terry....4:22:54 (15,035)
Young, Tim....5:21:00 (25,470)
Young, William....6:13:07 (28,958)
Young Wootton, Alex....5:21:49 (25,568)
Yoxall, Philip....4:50:00 (20,720)
Ytterland, Asbjoern....3:39:27 (5,665)
Yu, Kenny....3:59:14 (9,828)
Yudkin, John....3:49:47 (7,643)
Yuestal, Ove....5:33:33 (26,653)
Yuill, Chick....5:35:01 (26,806)
Yuill, Ian....2:52:15 (521)
Yuill, Paul....4:44:11 (19,616)
Yule, Lee....5:09:43 (24,045)
Yutar, Darryl....3:58:11 (9,533)
Yvon, Jean Marc....5:32:15 (26,544)
Zaczek, Karl....5:18:36 (25,224)
Zaghi, Giancarlo....2:46:34 (331)
Zago, Stefano....7:43:23 (30,174)
Zahra, Frans....3:36:56 (5,232)
Zandona, Mauro....4:19:47 (14,312)
Zaniboni, Giancarlo....5:05:13 (23,323)
Zanirato, Walter....5:16:58 (25,047)
Zanni, Paolo....4:43:00 (19,385)
Zanolla, Angelo....4:08:49 (11,938)
Zanon, Albino....4:13:26 (12,917)
Zanoni, Massimo....4:52:27 (21,194)
Zanotti, Cesare....5:05:23 (23,356)
Zenasni, Miloud....5:26:27 (26,041)
Zepernick, Richard....3:46:51 (7,012)
Zeraschi, Michael....5:30:48 (26,440)
Zink, James....4:39:52 (18,765)
Zink, Timothy....3:52:19 (8,138)
Zipperlen, Peder....4:22:47 (15,000)
Zlattinger, André....3:52:03 (8,085)
Zollinser-Read, Paul....4:45:50 (19,908)
Zomer, Konrad....3:43:00 (6,305)
Zotzer, August....3:39:43 (5,715)
Zugic, Richard....3:47:52 (7,231)
Zugriegel, Walter....5:02:53 (22,991)
Zulehner, Christian....3:27:44 (3,751)
Zuleia, Ingo....4:32:02 (17,124)
Zuluaga, Gustavo....3:50:19 (7,738)
Zwicky, Christian....2:22:48 (29)
Zwinkels, Peter....4:13:17 (12,871)

FEMALE RUNNERS

Abbey, Gail....4:27:11 (16,004)
Abbot, Lorraine....5:58:18 (28,338)
Abbott, Lisa....4:42:31 (19,277)
Abbott, Sarah....5:29:38 (26,341)
Able, Lisa....5:42:08 (27,344)
Abomeli, Obianagha....4:07:52 (11,734)
Abrahams, Nicola....3:58:40 (9,661)
Abrahams, Susan....4:47:57 (20,337)
Abrams, Christine....5:29:42 (26,346)
Abramson, Madeleine....5:41:00 (27,261)
Ackers, Margaret....4:00:42 (10,211)
Ackroyd, Jacqueline....3:30:01 (4,172)
Adachi, Mika....2:41:35 (206)
Adams, Amanda....4:50:39 (20,818)
Adams, Ann....4:40:38 (18,906)
Adams, Anne....6:15:18 (29,037)
Adams, Eve....5:06:23 (23,533)
Adams, Heather....5:17:36 (25,115)
Adams, Jane....6:48:02 (29,778)
Adams, Jessica....4:00:41 (10,208)
Adams, Melanie....4:49:41 (20,648)
Adams, Rebecca....3:13:58 (2,114)
Adams, Susan....4:38:37 (18,532)
Adamson, Alison....4:52:19 (21,164)
Adaway, Maria....6:05:31 (28,666)
Addington, Diane....5:45:26 (27,586)
Addrison, Anne....4:17:30 (13,773)
Addy, Patricia....5:00:31 (22,666)
Adebanjo, Susan....5:15:35 (24,876)
Adragna, Marie....4:33:17 (17,363)
Afrough, Ariane....4:39:34 (18,708)
Ahern, Henrietta....3:45:09 (6,702)
Aherne, Christine....3:49:45 (7,634)
Ahmed, Nabeela....6:33:46 (29,502)
Aiken, Jennifer....6:30:49 (29,432)
Aimon, Marie....4:30:59 (16,847)
Ainsworth, Adrienne....5:27:21 (26,115)
Ainsworth, Pat....4:55:57 (21,979)
Airey, Delores....6:55:03 (29,879)
Aitken, Janet....4:33:12 (17,347)
Aitken, Maryanne....5:51:48 (28,006)
Akeroyd, Suzanne....3:21:17 (2,917)
Al Zoubi, Julie....4:20:59 (14,589)
Alam, Saima....6:50:12 (29,807)
Albutt, Kate....6:32:34 (29,466)
Alden, Tracey....3:49:57 (7,676)
Aldridge, Carolyn....4:53:42 (21,454)
Aldridge, Helen....4:31:14 (16,913)
Aldridge, Julie....4:47:02 (20,169)
Aldridge, Sarah....5:04:39 (23,240)
Alemu, Elfenesh....2:24:29 (40)
Alexander, Karen....5:58:48 (28,356)
Alexandrou, Tracey....3:38:07 (5,418)
Alga, Melise....4:32:02 (17,124)
Alger, Anne....6:35:36 (29,537)
Alison, Margaret....5:22:10 (25,606)
Allaire, Noella....4:18:31 (14,017)
Allan, Sharon....6:27:16 (29,336)
Allaston, Alison....5:18:00 (25,166)
Allday, Gill....6:15:42 (29,049)
Allday, Suki....4:53:21 (21,388)
Allen, Edna....4:58:35 (22,391)
Allen, Heather....3:42:32 (6,223)
Allen, Margaret....6:56:43 (29,902)
Allen, Sandra....3:47:53 (7,237)
Alley, Erin....5:01:55 (22,859)
Allibone, Rosalind....3:21:53 (2,983)
Allison, Susan....5:08:17 (23,813)
Allison, Wendy....5:13:49 (24,608)
Almoayed, Alia....5:39:05 (27,092)
Alrayes, Haneen....5:36:33 (26,917)
Alvarez, Idalis....5:26:12 (26,005)
Amayo, Mary....6:28:32 (29,375)
Ambiavagar, Nalini....4:59:46 (22,565)
Ammar, Thoraya....5:59:14 (28,377)
Amos, Lesley....5:04:10 (23,153)
Andersen, Anna....4:36:49 (18,089)
Andersen, Inger....4:07:50 (11,727)
Anderson, Beth....5:36:18 (26,899)
Anderson, Birgit....5:04:36 (23,234)
Anderson, Fiona....5:07:07 (23,632)
Anderson, Hilary....5:27:12 (26,102)
Anderson, Jennifer....4:36:02 (17,936)
Anderson, Mary....4:15:30 (13,366)
Anderson, Nina....3:48:24 (7,338)
Anderson, Rachel....5:10:12 (24,103)
Anderson, Rachel....5:14:51 (24,756)
Andi Yapan, Katherine....5:12:55 (24,485)
Andrew, Jane....4:12:36 (12,755)
Andrew, Lisa....3:27:30 (3,707)
Andrew, Sarah....4:13:33 (12,943)
Andrew, Sharon....3:27:30 (3,707)
Andrew, Vera....4:45:09 (19,796)
Andrews, Jane Elizabeth....4:07:44 (11,709)
Andrews, Valerie....5:29:53 (26,362)
Angel, Andrea....6:35:37 (29,538)
Angel, Heidi....4:14:46 (13,202)
Angel, Melanie....4:43:21 (19,459)
Angell, Margaret....2:56:58 (740)
Anker, Lucy....4:16:37 (13,591)
Annals, Jacqueline....4:51:38 (21,016)
Annan, Lucy....4:24:57 (15,491)
Anne, Kerie....5:58:01 (28,322)
Annetts, Elizabeth....5:27:56 (26,175)
Ansell, Christina....4:11:50 (12,577)
Ansell, Debbie....6:07:21 (28,739)
Ansell, Lizbeth....4:08:11 (11,799)
Ansell, Tracy....5:29:55 (26,370)
Anstiss, Sue....5:22:44 (25,679)
Antell, Helen....5:13:55 (24,620)
Anthony, Claire....5:33:45 (26,667)
Anwyll, Catarina....4:41:18 (19,029)
Apaloo, Caroline....6:47:46 (29,774)
Apostolico, Eileen....4:20:43 (14,524)
Apperley, Mavis....4:25:55 (15,707)
Appleby, Bonny....3:28:37 (3,926)
Arch, Helen....5:45:16 (27,575)
Archbold, Kathryn....5:40:07 (27,198)
Archer, Eliza....5:37:20 (26,967)
Archer, Hilary....4:04:00 (10,881)
Archer, Skye....4:37:27 (18,238)
Ardigo, Mariarosa....4:32:47 (17,274)
Ardron, Susie....4:12:09 (12,658)
Argent, Patricia....5:14:14 (24,663)

Armitage, Cheryl 4:19:22 (14,215)
Armitage, Jacqui 6:02:02 (28,507)
Armitage, Katherine 3:11:09 (1,849)
Armstrong, Alyssa 4:18:55 (14,103)
Armstrong, Carole 4:37:06 (18,144)
Armstrong, Christine 3:59:36 (9,948)
Armstrong, Christine 4:19:53 (14,333)
Armstrong, Elizabeth 5:10:02 (24,085)
Armstrong, Melanie 3:52:39 (8,202)
Armstrong, Susan 6:02:33 (28,522)
Armytage, Gee 3:34:48 (4,878)
Arnett, Karen 4:54:42 (21,640)
Arnold, Marion 3:30:05 (4,185)
Arnold, Patricia 4:54:56 (21,713)
Arscott, Sally 4:07:02 (11,560)
Arter, Elina 3:12:39 (1,974)
Arthur, Helen 3:58:33 (9,625)
Arwas, Louise 5:05:45 (23,422)
Ash, Carole 5:56:48 (28,261)
Ashcroft, Joanne 4:19:40 (14,297)
Asher, Carolyn 5:41:14 (27,273)
Ashford, Deborah 6:34:12 (29,506)
Ashford-Smith, Paulette...........4:28:46 (16,374)
Ashlee, Michele 4:34:48 (17,677)
Ashley, Emma 3:24:01 (3,248)
Ashley, Justine 5:51:33 (27,987)
Ashley, Lisa 5:17:18 (25,084)
Ashley, Susan 3:23:03 (3,122)
Ashley Jones, Debbie...............4:33:12 (17,347)
Ashmore, Justine 5:03:56 (23,121)
Ashmore, Susan 3:47:37 (7,167)
Ashton, Helen 3:58:06 (9,515)
Ashton, Jane 5:20:23 (25,395)
Ashton, Karen 4:41:30 (19,061)
Ashton, Susan 3:53:34 (8,394)
Askwith, Celia 6:27:16 (29,336)
Asplin, Sharon 5:02:52 (22,988)
Astley, Jacqueline 4:32:51 (17,285)
Aston, Glenys 5:41:07 (27,266)
Athol, Jenny 4:03:32 (10,783)
Atkins, Carmel 4:48:20 (20,413)
Atkins, Daphne 4:47:45 (20,301)
Atkins, Lisa 5:12:22 (24,408)
Atkins, Michelle 5:34:29 (26,754)
Atkins, Sharon 4:57:46 (22,263)
Atkinson, Corinna 4:02:03 (10,495)
Atkinson, Jan 4:53:32 (21,434)
Atkinson, Rachel 5:15:49 (24,910)
Atkinson, Sam 3:56:17 (8,989)
Attal, Rivka 3:53:31 (8,380)
Attfield, Diane 6:30:25 (29,424)
Attwell, Christine 4:20:51 (14,560)
Atwell, Sandy 6:41:21 (29,675)
Auer, Elizabeth 4:48:49 (20,490)
August, Dianne 3:49:22 (7,543)
Austin, Tracey 6:39:37 (29,619)
Auton, Rachael 4:29:37 (16,580)
Avent, Jane 4:18:55 (14,103)
Averill, Torill 4:07:57 (11,750)
Avery, Heidi 6:04:39 (28,628)
Aves, Susan 3:50:33 (7,782)
Awoderu, Funke 6:01:39 (28,491)
Axten, Sam 5:10:34 (24,159)
Axton, Christine 5:11:15 (24,248)
Ayling, Angela 4:50:58 (20,874)
Ayling, Katharyn 5:32:55 (26,608)
Aylott, Sarah 4:24:53 (15,474)
Baali, Louise 5:59:14 (28,377)
Babb, Kim 5:14:06 (24,639)
Back, Lucy 3:27:17 (3,672)
Backley, Julie 3:35:51 (5,042)
Bacon, Michelle 5:38:36 (27,056)
Badcock, Janine 4:24:42 (15,437)
Badenoch, Emma 4:28:20 (16,267)
Bader, Inge 5:48:40 (27,824)
Badham, Jennifer 5:32:18 (26,548)
Badman, Dawn 4:22:36 (14,955)
Bae, Jennifer 7:05:32 (29,981)
Baerselman, Tessa 4:22:13 (14,865)
Bagley, Emma 5:03:51 (23,108)
Bagnall, Bridget 4:19:13 (14,165)
Bagshaw, Allison 6:28:28 (29,371)
Bailey, Alison 4:57:57 (22,286)

LONDON MARATHON

Bailey, Andrea 5:16:23 (24,970)
Bailey, Dawn 5:43:21 (27,429)
Bailey, Estina 4:54:59 (21,728)
Bailey, Jacqueline 5:45:50 (27,622)
Bailey, Jacqueline 6:07:05 (28,722)
Bailey, Jayne 5:38:16 (27,033)
Bailey, Jennifer 5:00:22 (22,652)
Bailey, Joanne 4:22:03 (14,829)
Bailey, Lisa 4:39:39 (18,727)
Bailey, Louise 4:09:50 (12,131)
Bailey, Marianne 4:40:23 (18,853)
Bailey, Rachel 3:40:36 (5,885)
Bailey, Rebecca 5:36:38 (26,920)
Bailey, Sheila 3:38:17 (5,445)
Bailey, Veronica 5:56:26 (28,238)
Baillie, Louise 4:34:20 (17,602)
Bain, Ellen 4:01:45 (10,436)
Bain, Karen 4:03:37 (10,805)
Bainbridge, Angela 6:08:41 (28,795)
Bainbridge, Natalie 5:21:32 (25,528)
Bainbridge, Wendy 5:15:00 (24,779)
Baines, Samantha 3:18:05 (2,544)
Baines, Shelagh 5:39:25 (27,123)
Baird, Lorraine 4:30:45 (16,794)
Baird, Sonya 5:55:11 (28,163)
Baitup, Christine 4:07:54 (11,740)
Baker, Gemma 4:53:12 (21,353)
Baker, Jacqueline 5:06:11 (23,497)
Baker, Jennifer 3:50:57 (7,859)
Baker, Mouse 3:47:45 (7,200)
Baker, Patricia 5:16:14 (24,950)
Baker, Paula 4:40:19 (18,841)
Baker, Paula 5:42:00 (27,334)
Baker, Rhona 5:11:05 (24,222)
Baker, Sandra 4:53:18 (21,373)
Balac, Charmaine 5:27:12 (26,102)
Baldino, Maria 5:26:17 (26,019)
Baldock, Karen 3:57:39 (9,384)
Baldrey, Charlotte 3:25:58 (3,499)
Baldwin, Carol 5:51:39 (27,991)
Balfour, Anne Marie 4:11:49 (12,574)
Balfour, Fay 4:55:12 (21,783)
Balfour, Margaret 5:15:09 (24,813)
Balisciano, Marcia 5:02:19 (22,918)
Ball, Deborah 3:40:58 (5,948)
Ball, Elizabeth 4:25:45 (15,662)
Ball, Tanya 5:00:19 (22,647)
Ballantine, Jeri 6:45:29 (29,744)
Ballantyne, Margaret 8:06:05 (30,213)
Ballard, Alison 4:49:10 (20,553)
Ballard, Diane 3:22:07 (3,014)
Ballentine, Julie 4:47:07 (20,189)
Ballm, Clare 4:21:47 (14,754)
Balment, Julia 6:54:52 (29,875)
Baltazar, Lisa 6:05:21 (28,657)
Baltzer, Martina 4:33:45 (17,489)
Bamfield, Melanie 4:47:31 (20,267)
Bamford, Janet 5:12:22 (24,408)
Bamford, Lindsay 4:59:26 (22,519)
Banford, Nichola 3:42:18 (6,180)
Banks, Audra 4:26:28 (15,836)
Banks, Christine 4:33:15 (17,356)
Bannatyne, Lucy 4:11:50 (12,577)
Bannenberg, Susan 5:00:55 (22,721)
Banner, Andrea 3:13:52 (2,097)
Banstead, Janene 4:15:23 (13,342)
Banville, Elaine 3:55:05 (8,710)
Banyard, Gillian 5:04:41 (23,243)
Barber, Kenwynne 5:29:37 (26,339)
Barber, Sue 4:16:00 (13,463)
Barbero, Genevieve 3:57:26 (9,304)
Barclay, Rebecca 5:51:57 (28,015)
Bardner, Lucy 4:05:29 (11,209)
Bareham, Jill 6:06:58 (28,718)
Barfield, Abigail 5:11:26 (24,274)
Bargh, Janet 5:31:16 (26,474)

Barker, Ann 3:13:58 (2,114)
Barker, Della 4:12:28 (12,730)
Barker, Emma 5:15:09 (24,813)
Barker, Jackie 3:33:03 (4,611)
Barker, Jane 4:48:14 (20,391)
Barker, Kathryn 4:22:17 (14,883)
Barker, Pauline 5:23:54 (25,782)
Barker, Ros 3:13:52 (2,097)
Barklem, Lydia 4:11:05 (12,412)
Barley, Julie 3:30:30 (4,245)
Barlier, Anne Catherine............3:25:20 (3,422)
Barlow, Helen 5:11:18 (24,255)
Barlow, Julie 4:59:55 (22,603)
Barlow, Line 4:26:30 (15,846)
Barnes, Christina 5:01:17 (22,781)
Barnes, Elaine 4:10:46 (12,327)
Barnes, Julie 3:59:52 (10,016)
Barnett, Caroline 4:48:44 (20,475)
Barnett, Christina 5:41:47 (27,314)
Barnett, Marion 7:51:09 (30,191)
Barnett, Susan 4:10:48 (12,341)
Barr, Janice 5:27:18 (26,110)
Barratt, Philippa 4:46:47 (20,111)
Barret, Helene 5:08:46 (23,899)
Barrett, Anita 4:23:08 (15,093)
Barrett, Gillian 4:04:33 (11,007)
Barrett, Teresa 4:12:28 (12,730)
Bartell, Claire 5:49:50 (27,891)
Barter, Patricia 5:07:34 (23,708)
Barter, Pauline 4:44:57 (19,765)
Bartlett, Florence 6:17:28 (29,098)
Bartlett, Lisle 4:20:44 (14,529)
Bartlett, Natalie 3:40:43 (5,900)
Bartlett, Rosamund 4:11:59 (12,606)
Bartley, Deirdre 4:17:36 (13,793)
Barton, Catherine 4:53:27 (21,407)
Barton, Jillian 4:52:52 (21,280)
Barton, Linda 4:05:04 (11,129)
Barton, Rebella 6:30:48 (29,431)
Bartrum, Dawn 4:27:27 (16,050)
Barvaux, Claudine 3:39:53 (5,754)
Baseley, Denise 5:39:36 (27,144)
Bass, Irenie 3:40:55 (5,931)
Bassett, Michelle 5:37:53 (27,013)
Bastien, Brigitte 4:27:04 (15,988)
Bastow, Sally 4:34:06 (17,557)
Batch, Catherine 4:02:31 (10,576)
Bate, Sharon 5:29:11 (26,307)
Bateman, Emma 5:40:30 (27,224)
Bateman, Joanna 3:43:26 (6,385)
Bateman, Judith 3:09:30 (1,713)
Bateman, Lyn 8:37:48 (30,261)
Bates, Angela 3:35:18 (4,952)
Bates, Caron 4:15:35 (13,385)
Bates, Maurita 6:59:12 (29,932)
Bates, Samantha 3:58:50 (9,709)
Batey, Deborah 4:27:25 (16,040)
Bath, Doreen 3:48:34 (7,374)
Batterbee, Deborah 5:44:46 (27,545)
Battersby, Alice 4:38:19 (18,456)
Battersby, Barbara 5:17:56 (25,151)
Battista, Connie 5:21:14 (25,493)
Batty, Jane 3:28:49 (3,965)
Bauchop, Sheila 3:31:52 (4,449)
Bayliss, Hannah 4:03:18 (10,725)
Baynard, Luiza 6:32:39 (29,468)
Beach, Carolyn 5:08:17 (23,813)
Beach, Rosemary 6:11:23 (28,903)
Beacham, Margaret 5:22:56 (25,699)
Beale, Sharon 4:39:22 (18,659)
Bear, Angie 3:39:29 (5,669)
Beasley, Ewa 5:39:34 (27,137)
Beaton, Janette 3:13:56 (2,106)
Beaumont, Amanda 3:45:21 (6,724)
Beaumont, Rosalind 6:09:15 (28,822)
Beaumont, Sylvia 4:12:32 (12,745)
Beavis, Andrea 4:50:03 (20,728)
Beckett, Sandra 6:38:00 (29,590)
Beckett, Suzanne 6:33:12 (29,487)
Beckley, Alice 4:00:44 (10,227)
Beddis, Gail 5:19:45 (25,341)
Bedford, Susan 6:24:54 (29,281)
Bedwell, Maggie 3:57:54 (9,462)

Bee, Alix 5:27:34 (26,134)
Bee, Peta 3:39:45 (5,725)
Beeby, Linda Caryl 5:21:34 (25,530)
Beechinor-Carter, Susan 5:11:16 (24,250)
Beecroft, Janet 4:08:55 (11,959)
Beeden, Jayne 6:08:47 (28,802)
Beedham, Sue 4:15:24 (13,347)
Beedles, Jillian 5:31:41 (26,506)
Beeke, Vikki 4:56:33 (22,079)
Beesley, Marlene 5:19:53 (25,352)
Beeston, Charlotte 4:03:49 (10,843)
Begent, Adrienne 5:05:41 (23,410)
Beggs, Etain 6:27:54 (29,350)
Belbin, Ruth 4:09:59 (12,163)
Belk, Elizabeth 4:18:45 (14,067)
Belk, Rachel 4:18:45 (14,067)
Belk, Wendy 4:18:45 (14,067)
Bell, Alexandra 6:06:39 (28,708)
Bell, Annette 3:17:45 (2,505)
Bell, Charlotte 4:45:55 (19,921)
Bell, Fiona 5:30:29 (26,411)
Bell, Gaynor 3:34:55 (4,892)
Bell, Jane 4:17:51 (13,844)
Bell, Jean 5:38:55 (27,081)
Bell, Karen 4:55:10 (21,772)
Bell, Maura 4:58:37 (22,399)
Bell, Rachel 5:59:32 (28,393)
Bell, Sandie 5:17:59 (25,164)
Bell, Terry 6:07:56 (28,758)
Bell, Tracey 5:48:48 (27,832)
Bellinger, Jasmine 5:29:10 (26,304)
Bellingham, Susan 6:27:59 (29,356)
Bellini, Liliana 4:27:25 (16,040)
Bellini, Marina 4:00:26 (10,135)
Belo, Vanda 4:53:24 (21,398)
Benacchio, Catherine 4:10:18 (12,226)
Bending, Karen 5:20:41 (25,428)
Bendon, Tania 5:39:14 (27,106)
Benjamin, Floella 5:34:57 (26,803)
Benn, Sandra 3:47:52 (7,231)
Bennett, Camilla 5:21:10 (25,483)
Bennett, Catherine 4:49:23 (20,592)
Bennett, Dinah 9:08:03 (30,279)
Bennett, Joanna 5:21:14 (25,493)
Bennett, Lesley 8:14:59 (30,235)
Bennett, Lisa 3:53:53 (8,457)
Bennett, Nicola 5:01:04 (22,741)
Bennett, Sally 6:09:32 (28,836)
Bennett, Senga 4:33:55 (17,523)
Bennett, Susan 3:50:50 (7,831)
Bennett, Susan 5:25:10 (25,902)
Bennett, Suzanne 7:59:22 (30,207)
Bennett, Virginia 5:34:38 (26,768)
Bennett, Yvonne 5:33:50 (26,674)
Bennett Hornsey, Lindsay 4:05:07 (11,141)
Bennetts, Sarah 3:43:38 (6,421)
Bennettt, Karen 4:45:24 (19,846)
Bennion, Joan 6:45:08 (29,738)
Benrahmoun, Hadda 3:53:04 (8,284)
Bensley, Lesley 4:35:02 (17,717)
Benstead, Amanda 3:58:38 (9,649)
Bensted, Christine 4:14:43 (13,177)
Bensusan, Iona 6:09:49 (28,856)
Bentley, Carolyn 5:39:34 (27,137)
Bentley, Catherine 4:11:22 (12,477)
Bentley, Elizabeth 6:04:50 (28,637)
Bentley, Julie 6:08:05 (28,769)
Bentley, Sarah 4:11:04 (12,409)
Bentley, Sarah 6:09:35 (28,840)
Benton, Karen 6:23:56 (29,257)
Bentz, Caroline 3:46:04 (6,869)
Beresford, Deborah 4:58:35 (22,391)
Bergesen, Ingun 4:18:13 (13,924)
Bernard, Bettina 5:33:30 (26,650)
Berridge, Catheryn 4:59:05 (22,473)
Berridge, Diahann 4:40:14 (18,819)
Berridge, Marilyn 5:26:02 (25,990)
Berrill, Anna 3:14:21 (2,153)
Berriman, Heather 5:06:12 (23,501)
Berry, Angela 4:24:16 (15,344)
Berry, Catherine 4:04:53 (11,088)
Berry, Janet 6:42:48 (29,702)
Berry, Pamela 4:54:19 (21,566)
Bertani, Emanuela 4:03:46 (10,836)
Besag, Nicola 6:02:24 (28,518)
Best, Rachael 5:07:19 (23,665)
Best, Sarah 3:58:31 (9,611)
Bethune, Deirdre 4:07:43 (11,703)
Bettis, Nancy 6:04:00 (28,590)
Betts, Karen 4:43:10 (19,422)
Betts, Sally Ann 4:51:47 (21,053)
Bevan, Helen 5:30:12 (26,386)
Bevan, Jean 4:58:54 (22,441)
Bevan, Julie 4:00:25 (10,133)
Bevan, Lorraine 4:41:47 (19,120)
Bevan, Theresa 4:50:46 (20,838)
Bevington, Deborah 5:13:11 (24,527)
Bevington, Kathleen 7:52:24 (30,192)
Bewley, Jennifer 4:23:53 (15,269)
Beyer, Deanna 5:16:21 (24,963)
Beynon, Rachel 4:18:52 (14,090)
Bhamra, Billy 4:57:08 (22,162)
Bhogal, Harjit 4:36:54 (18,104)
Bickley, Susan 5:06:56 (23,605)
Bickley, Tracy 5:23:51 (25,774)
Biddle, Kylie 4:49:18 (20,581)
Bide, Donna 4:51:00 (20,881)
Bidmead, Jane 4:18:15 (13,935)
Bielby, Patricia 3:34:45 (4,869)
Bielecka, Polly 4:37:28 (18,243)
Bien, Melanie 4:49:51 (20,684)
Bierton, Pauline 5:24:18 (25,817)
Bifield, Jenny 7:14:17 (30,046)
Biggs, Moira 4:30:11 (16,717)
Biktagirova, Madina 2:27:14 (48)
Bille, Marie-Thérèse 5:40:33 (27,234)
Billiar, Sharon 3:50:49 (7,825)
Billington, Lisa 6:41:18 (29,671)
Billington, Shirley 3:37:59 (5,398)
Bilsborrow, Sherida 5:32:23 (26,558)
Bilton, Janet 4:21:41 (14,731)
Binet, Aline 6:50:12 (29,807)
Binks, Yvonne 4:13:36 (12,958)
Binns, Clare 5:05:39 (23,406)
Birch, Abigail 5:08:25 (23,831)
Birch, Annie 4:14:20 (13,103)
Birch, Victoria 5:03:11 (23,029)
Bird, Annie 4:31:55 (17,095)
Bird, Elisabeth 4:31:56 (17,102)
Bird, Norma 3:26:51 (3,602)
Birdthistle, Tanya 5:57:37 (28,304)
Birkenhead, Kate 3:37:02 (5,251)
Birkett, Christine 5:16:14 (24,950)
Birkwood, Ann 5:27:13 (26,106)
Birnie, Lucy 4:06:14 (11,393)
Birrane, Rosaria 8:32:30 (30,251)
Birtwhistle, Angela 4:15:10 (13,297)
Bishop, Anna 4:38:59 (18,600)
Bishop, Clare 4:30:37 (16,769)
Bishop, Fiona 4:05:37 (11,244)
Bishop, Jane 3:20:57 (2,885)
Bishop, Liz 5:40:08 (27,200)
Bissett, Liz 5:14:27 (24,694)
Bissland, Nicola 4:53:41 (21,450)
Bister, Anna 4:45:04 (19,783)
Bithell, Victoria 4:10:03 (12,172)
Bitten, Elly 9:06:32 (30,277)
Bjerke, Marianne 5:05:56 (23,456)
Black, Catherine 3:27:39 (3,732)
Black, Claire 4:26:03 (15,743)
Black, Kathryn 3:39:11 (5,607)
Black, Louise 5:47:16 (27,716)
Black, Maggie 5:30:15 (26,391)
Black, Minnie 3:59:25 (9,891)
Black, Pauline 4:14:30 (13,127)
Black, Rebecca 4:28:20 (16,267)
Black, Sophie 4:27:57 (16,181)
Blackburn, Colette 5:18:44 (25,237)
Blackburn, Helen 5:15:18 (24,842)
Blackburn, Marie 3:49:47 (7,643)
Blackburne, Gill 6:01:38 (28,487)
Blackford, Stacey 4:36:54 (18,104)
Blackledge, Vanessa 5:10:31 (24,146)
Blackman, Salena 6:37:22 (29,572)
Blackshaw, Gail 4:06:17 (11,404)
Blackwell, Rebecca 4:17:34 (13,784)
Bladt, Inger 5:25:23 (25,928)
Blagdon, Sarah 5:39:37 (27,148)
Blain, Moya 5:42:36 (27,389)
Blair, Jacqueline 4:10:11 (12,203)
Blais, Françoise 4:24:56 (15,487)
Blake, Ann Maree 5:02:34 (22,942)
Blake, Sarah 4:45:15 (19,815)
Blake, Sheila 5:02:48 (22,977)
Blakeley, Pamela 5:17:16 (25,077)
Blanchard, Sarah 5:23:21 (25,728)
Blaney, Pamela 4:16:22 (13,543)
Blankertz, Julia 4:21:25 (14,673)
Blasdale, Rebecca 4:35:39 (17,855)
Blenkin, Harriet 4:20:28 (14,468)
Blenkinsop, Mandy 4:42:58 (19,379)
Blight, Rachael 3:29:36 (4,098)
Blinko, Lyn 3:28:30 (3,907)
Bliss, Belinda 4:42:31 (19,277)
Bliss, Sandra 6:40:04 (29,638)
Bloodworth, Karen 3:41:19 (6,013)
Blount, Emma 4:40:49 (18,942)
Blunt, Susan 4:22:25 (14,908)
Blyth, Christine 4:34:57 (17,704)
Blyth, Sally 4:06:16 (11,400)
Blyth, Sarah 5:25:18 (25,920)
Boast, Rebecca 4:26:41 (15,887)
Boby, Fay 5:25:50 (25,971)
Bocchi, Grazia 4:56:03 (21,993)
Boddice, Janet 5:41:07 (27,266)
Boehm, Monika 5:12:57 (24,490)
Bogacheva, Irina 2:32:28 (74)
Bogard, Heidi 4:46:33 (20,067)
Boggon, Caroline 4:46:56 (20,156)
Bohea, Fay 6:37:19 (29,571)
Bolam, Anita 5:37:15 (26,960)
Bolam, Caroline 3:31:56 (4,459)
Boland, Helen 4:44:08 (19,605)
Bolcoa, Jen 5:05:02 (23,297)
Bollyky, Andrea 6:27:41 (29,343)
Bolster, Denise 5:28:35 (26,236)
Bolton, Danielle 4:07:26 (11,651)
Bolton, Janet 5:24:26 (25,825)
Bolton, Victoria 3:38:33 (5,489)
Bolton Carter, Henrietta 3:49:25 (7,555)
Bolwell, Julie 3:32:47 (4,570)
Bonavero, Claire 5:13:04 (24,509)
Bond, Elly 5:48:12 (27,792)
Bond, Lesley 4:55:49 (21,955)
Bond, Monique 5:25:12 (25,906)
Bond, Susan 4:14:49 (13,213)
Bonfield, Lisa 5:20:56 (25,458)
Bonfield, Wendy 5:25:35 (25,948)
Bongard, Denny 5:03:07 (23,021)
Bongers, Paula 3:22:16 (3,031)
Boniface, Sheila 4:45:25 (19,852)
Bonner, Elizabeth 4:48:31 (20,441)
Bonner, Laura 4:59:18 (22,497)
Bonner-Murphy, Dawn 4:08:20 (11,833)
Bonser, Kim 5:10:33 (24,154)
Bonthrone, Mandy 4:29:32 (16,553)
Booker, Helen 4:17:45 (13,825)
Booth, Anita 4:51:08 (20,912)
Booth, Fiona 5:48:24 (27,808)
Booth, Janet 5:39:07 (27,097)
Booth, Juliet 5:22:11 (25,612)
Booth, Nicole 4:11:42 (12,549)
Booth, Theresa 3:39:17 (5,622)
Booth, Tracey 5:11:20 (24,259)
Borden, Cindy 6:01:03 (28,456)
Bordini, Alice 5:57:39 (28,307)
Borley, Elaine 4:37:25 (18,229)
Bosch, Estelle 5:10:09 (24,096)
Bosley, Helen 5:03:57 (23,122)
Bostick, Melanie 5:04:34 (23,228)
Boston, Angela 4:49:59 (20,715)
Boston, Jaki 5:33:10 (26,623)
Boswall, Sarah 4:40:00 (18,788)
Botting, Paula 5:51:52 (28,009)
Bottomer, Claire 7:28:03 (30,124)
Botton, Anita 3:55:06 (8,713)
Bottrill, Helena 5:27:23 (26,118)
Boughton, Sarah 4:02:22 (10,544)
Bouillon, Solange 4:19:04 (14,136)

Boulton, Jane 3:03:18 (1,234)
Bourne, Helen 5:38:45 (27,072)
Bourne, Janet 4:37:43 (18,303)
Bourne, Joanna 3:27:40 (3,735)
Bourne, Kathryn 4:50:28 (20,798)
Bourne, Sussannah 4:56:00 (21,984)
Bourne, Wendy 5:20:42 (25,431)
Bourne Lange, Lesley Ann 6:07:31 (28,746)
Bovill, Oriel 4:33:43 (17,482)
Bowater, Helene 4:45:42 (19,882)
Bowden, Josephine 5:41:40 (27,308)
Bowden, Tracy 5:22:54 (25,694)
Bowen, Claire 4:39:43 (18,736)
Bowen, Joanna 4:31:39 (17,023)
Bowen, Lowri 5:12:54 (24,483)
Bowen, Rachel 3:59:25 (9,891)
Bowen, Retta 4:29:04 (16,438)
Bowen, Samantha 6:13:33 (28,979)
Bowen, Sian 5:28:50 (26,273)
Bowler, Stephanie 4:22:28 (14,919)
Bowles, Ann 3:40:27 (5,859)
Bowles, Victoria 3:40:47 (5,908)
Bowman, Jude 3:43:00 (6,305)
Bowman, Natalie 3:18:56 (2,649)
Box, Carol 4:44:31 (19,680)
Boxall, Martine 4:11:24 (12,481)
Boxall, Sarah 5:52:40 (28,046)
Boyd, Catherine 4:12:07 (12,650)
Boyd, Christine 5:27:48 (26,159)
Boyd, Felicity 3:41:31 (6,039)
Boyd, Lina 6:05:12 (28,647)
Boyd, Nicola 4:23:57 (15,281)
Boyd, Valerie 5:03:14 (23,034)
Boydell, Tammy 5:00:53 (22,718)
Boyden, Michelle 4:43:13 (19,431)
Boyle, Brenda 4:38:13 (18,431)
Boyle, Vicki 3:19:13 (2,676)
Boyne, Joyce 4:35:49 (17,882)
Boynton, Patricia 7:49:32 (30,187)
Bracken, Clare 4:29:34 (16,564)
Brackley, Sharon 4:52:00 (21,091)
Bradford, Kate 5:22:15 (25,622)
Bradford, Susanne 5:37:31 (26,978)
Bradley, Ann 5:06:35 (23,557)
Bradley, Margaret 4:53:26 (21,403)
Bradley Grant, Georgia 4:34:37 (17,646)
Brady, Maria 4:39:32 (18,700)
Bragg, Emma 4:21:02 (14,599)
Braham, Alice 3:00:35 (1,055)
Braham, Julie 4:29:54 (16,660)
Braid, Josephine 4:09:48 (12,125)
Braig, Monika 4:34:42 (17,658)
Braker, Julie 4:38:07 (18,408)
Brand, Allison 4:42:06 (19,178)
Branigan, Patricia 5:22:37 (25,661)
Brannan, Gail 4:05:30 (11,213)
Brannon, Kathy 4:08:36 (11,892)
Bransford, Gretchen 4:19:21 (14,209)
Brant, Claire 4:52:41 (21,248)
Branton, Allison 3:43:25 (6,382)
Brar, first name unknown 4:35:04 (17,728)
Brassington, Donna 4:12:45 (12,781)
Braun, Babette 5:18:15 (25,185)
Braun, Ines 4:09:00 (11,978)
Bray, Helen 6:02:40 (28,526)
Bray, Kim 4:07:57 (11,750)
Braznell, Kimberley 3:39:59 (5,782)
Breaa, Benedicte 3:40:58 (5,948)
Breach, Nicola 4:09:04 (12,001)
Breakel, Melanie 4:29:41 (16,594)
Breen, Marie 4:36:25 (18,000)
Brees, Joanna 5:01:07 (22,752)
Bremner, Brigitte 4:53:04 (21,330)
Bremner, Jane 3:34:16 (4,795)
Bremner, Ruth 4:46:02 (19,945)
Brennan, Anne 3:47:26 (7,125)
Brennan, Bernadette 6:55:19 (29,886)
Brennan, Catherine 4:01:39 (10,424)
Brennan, Theresa 4:33:01 (17,313)
Brennan Green, Julie 3:49:44 (7,629)
Brennand, Alison 6:37:17 (29,568)
Brent, Lesley 4:07:39 (11,687)
Breslin, Christine 5:46:34 (27,667)
Breslin, Elizabeth 4:32:16 (17,168)
Brewer, Karen 4:26:32 (15,851)
Brewer, Katherine 5:50:07 (27,910)
Brewer, Linda 4:39:30 (18,694)
Brewer, Marian 6:55:35 (29,894)
Brewer, Vicky 4:52:26 (21,191)
Brewin, Sonia 6:28:07 (29,359)
Brewster, Emma 4:37:11 (18,167)
Brewster, Vanessa 4:31:23 (16,954)
Brice, Joanna 4:14:11 (13,072)
Brickell, Lucy 4:42:23 (19,244)
Brickwood, Elli 3:34:03 (4,763)
Bridge, Gillian 5:30:15 (26,391)
Bridges, Anna 4:33:36 (17,455)
Brier, Tina 5:37:43 (27,002)
Brierley, Judith 5:06:50 (23,594)
Briggs, Helen 4:51:32 (20,991)
Briggs, Kathryn 5:34:26 (26,749)
Briggs, Nicola 4:29:57 (16,675)
Briggs, Susan 4:58:57 (22,451)
Brigham, Vicki 6:30:45 (29,429)
Bright, Meg 5:29:13 (26,312)
Brightman, Pat 5:39:07 (27,097)
Brighton, Jennie 7:05:13 (29,977)
Brighton, Susan 4:06:18 (11,408)
Brightwell, Natalie 3:57:20 (9,267)
Brignall, Kirsty 4:55:09 (21,769)
Brill, Geraldine 4:12:04 (12,633)
Brimeyer, Dianne 4:33:59 (17,532)
Brink, Mary Katherine 4:48:26 (20,431)
Brink De Jong, Henriette 5:05:41 (23,410)
Brinkley, Elizabeth 4:48:23 (20,425)
Bristow, Mary 4:44:51 (19,743)
Britten, Caroline 4:52:33 (21,224)
Broad, Joanne 5:21:10 (25,483)
Broad, Katharine 4:23:59 (15,291)
Broad, Lisa 5:14:58 (24,772)
Broadhurst, Maria 4:29:56 (16,672)
Brocanelli, Renata 4:19:57 (14,353)
Brock, Zelda 6:08:42 (28,796)
Brockett, Gill 6:13:25 (28,965)
Brocklesby, Edwina 3:57:27 (9,311)
Brockwell, Alison 9:19:40 (30,281)
Broda, Krysia 4:08:15 (11,814)
Broderick, Anna 4:16:37 (13,591)
Broderstad, Helen 4:20:19 (14,432)
Brodie, Jennifer 4:25:29 (15,613)
Brogan, Joanne 4:35:21 (17,786)
Brogan, Pauline 5:19:13 (25,284)
Brokenshire, Ethel 3:57:46 (9,416)
Bromby, Jo 4:16:04 (13,480)
Bromham, Judith 3:58:07 (9,519)
Brook, Tracy 5:41:24 (27,290)
Brooke, Hannah 4:50:00 (20,720)
Brooker, Claire 4:08:18 (11,825)
Brooker, Teresa 3:38:20 (5,453)
Brookes, Victoria 5:16:12 (24,949)
Brooks, Emma 5:08:22 (23,824)
Brooks, Lucy 3:22:56 (3,099)
Brooks, Rachel 5:42:19 (27,358)
Brooks, Susan 5:14:38 (24,732)
Broom, Philippa 5:06:22 (23,529)
Brosnan, Julie 4:10:55 (12,378)
Brougham, Jean 5:18:45 (25,242)
Broughton, Ellen 4:29:58 (16,684)
Brown, Alison 5:15:09 (24,813)
Brown, Angela 4:59:40 (22,550)
Brown, Barbara 4:02:19 (10,533)
Brown, Carly 6:42:28 (29,699)
Brown, Carol 3:35:31 (4,988)
Brown, Carrie 6:21:45 (29,211)
Brown, Christine 4:47:29 (20,255)
Brown, Elma 4:17:11 (13,716)
Brown, Gillian 4:53:30 (21,419)
Brown, Holly 5:56:22 (28,231)
Brown, Jill 3:52:04 (8,091)
Brown, Joanne 5:08:37 (23,874)
Brown, Judy 3:03:22 (1,238)
Brown, Juliet 4:27:03 (15,981)
Brown, Lesley 4:43:11 (19,425)
Brown, Lynne 5:44:54 (27,556)
Brown, Mandy 4:43:17 (19,447)
Brown, Marilyn 4:45:57 (19,929)
Brown, Natalie 5:59:39 (28,401)
Brown, Rebecca 5:15:51 (24,917)
Brown, Rhona 4:33:27 (17,405)
Brown, Sarah 4:25:06 (15,531)
Brown, Susan 5:19:13 (25,284)
Brown, Suzanne 5:07:49 (23,750)
Brown, Victoria 5:07:00 (23,615)
Brown, Victoria 6:49:49 (29,801)
Browne, Denise 4:49:27 (20,609)
Browne, Gabrielle 3:38:43 (5,525)
Browne, Helen 5:53:48 (28,108)
Browne, Marion 6:20:36 (29,178)
Browne, Susan 4:56:14 (22,030)
Browne Swinburne, Alice 6:22:10 (29,217)
Browning, Jackie 5:39:29 (27,134)
Browrout, Melanie 4:45:41 (19,881)
Bruce, Barbara 3:13:53 (2,101)
Bruce, Rhoda 5:19:29 (25,304)
Bruce, Sarah 3:13:07 (2,013)
Bruce, Susan 3:29:02 (4,004)
Bruggemans, Dominique 4:36:37 (18,045)
Bruhn, Anna 4:58:50 (22,432)
Brumwell, Tracey 5:03:23 (23,055)
Brunnmeier, Marita 4:23:45 (15,236)
Brunsdon, Barbara 5:44:25 (27,502)
Brunton, Deborah 6:47:25 (29,766)
Brunton, Suzanna 3:38:11 (5,425)
Bryan, Delyth 3:39:03 (5,582)
Bryan, Lisa 4:40:36 (18,898)
Bryan Brown, Petra 4:38:43 (18,551)
Bryant, Janice 3:34:00 (4,754)
Bryant, Patricia 5:13:46 (24,602)
Buchanan, Charlotte 5:03:55 (23,119)
Buchanan, Helen 5:53:41 (28,101)
Buchanan, Samantha 5:02:06 (22,892)
Bucher, Sarah 5:31:46 (26,514)
Buck, Grete 4:17:45 (13,825)
Buckingham, Patricia 6:32:00 (29,451)
Buckle, Jennifer 5:28:48 (26,269)
Buckley, Joan 5:14:56 (24,767)
Buckley, Victoria 4:33:26 (17,402)
Budd, Luisa 5:25:15 (25,915)
Budd, Vivien 5:40:30 (27,224)
Buddin, Wendy 6:07:25 (28,743)
Buettell, Delanie 6:28:54 (29,383)
Buffin, Shirani 6:59:57 (29,942)
Buhlmann, Eleanor 6:39:48 (29,623)
Buick, Penelope 6:53:43 (29,860)
Buley, Rona 4:32:22 (17,186)
Bulgin, Amanda 4:36:16 (17,967)
Bull, Helen 5:39:54 (27,177)
Bullen, Nicola 5:23:32 (25,749)
Bullimore, Jane 5:29:29 (26,334)
Bullingham, Maria 6:53:09 (29,848)
Bullivant, Jayne 5:01:15 (22,777)
Bullock, Kimberley 6:01:28 (28,477)
Bunch, Diane 4:30:52 (16,818)
Bunten, Susan 3:39:13 (5,612)
Bunyan, Glennis 5:20:12 (25,375)
Burdon, Caroline 6:21:20 (29,202)
Burfitt, Laura 4:56:28 (22,060)
Burfoot, Jennifer 4:17:26 (13,756)
Burford, Louisa 5:42:02 (27,338)
Burgess, Anne 5:05:18 (23,338)
Burgess, Joanna 5:32:15 (26,544)
Burgess, Maxine 3:47:51 (7,224)
Burgess, Pippa 4:22:52 (15,024)
Burgess, Verna 4:50:38 (20,817)
Burgmair, Margit 3:52:59 (8,263)
Burke, Janet 5:47:15 (27,715)
Burke, Mandy 5:02:41 (22,961)
Burkin, Julie 4:01:02 (10,288)
Burnett, Suzanne 4:54:58 (21,721)
Burnette, Tiffany 4:12:57 (12,820)
Burnham, Christina 6:52:19 (29,838)
Burnham, Susan 5:05:23 (23,356)
Burns, Caroline 5:50:25 (27,920)
Burns, Judith 5:06:46 (23,582)
Burns, Kirsty 4:52:16 (21,148)
Burns, Sheila 4:57:02 (22,142)
Burns, Tracy 5:20:59 (25,466)
Burrells, Jillian 4:31:57 (17,105)
Burrows, Shelly 4:13:27 (12,921)

Burrows, Susan	5:16:26	(24,975)
Burse, Debbie	5:17:01	(25,053)
Bursnall, Deirdre	4:19:20	(14,202)
Burston, Elaine	6:02:41	(28,528)
Burt, Caroline	4:52:01	(21,094)
Burt, Karen	4:46:29	(20,048)
Burtles, Sally	5:02:05	(22,887)
Burton, Abigail	4:42:07	(19,182)
Burton, Alex	4:29:07	(16,453)
Burton, Eleanor	6:23:25	(29,240)
Burton, Sadie	3:56:03	(8,940)
Burton, Sally	4:57:02	(22,142)
Burton, Teresa	3:38:22	(5,458)
Burton Brown, Julia	5:46:03	(27,634)
Bury, Alison	5:22:56	(25,699)
Bush, Harriet	4:01:15	(10,326)
Bush, Jain	4:27:32	(16,069)
Bush, Josephine	4:21:47	(14,754)
Bushell, Claire	4:17:55	(13,856)
Butcher, Alison	5:28:12	(26,196)
Butcher, Amanda	5:34:10	(26,720)
Butcher, Lisa	5:28:54	(26,283)
Butet, Patricia	4:36:14	(17,961)
Butler, Allisson	4:11:59	(12,606)
Butler, Bridget	3:33:26	(4,680)
Butler, Deborah	4:00:56	(10,270)
Butler, Georgina	5:22:56	(25,699)
Butler, Helen	5:08:16	(23,809)
Butler, Jeni	3:50:58	(7,861)
Butler, Kathryn	4:21:59	(14,808)
Butler, Marie	4:20:43	(14,524)
Butler, Patricia	6:09:05	(28,819)
Butler, Sandra	5:00:41	(22,688)
Butters, Nicola	4:45:43	(19,887)
Button, Jennifer	4:55:25	(21,857)
Button, Linda	5:15:45	(24,898)
Buxton, Louise	4:35:17	(17,771)
Bye, Amanda	5:00:17	(22,646)
Bye, Louise	4:04:58	(11,111)
Byrne, Karen	7:47:37	(30,184)
Byrne, Sheila	6:16:35	(29,071)
Bytheway, Helen	4:07:02	(11,560)
Caddell, Bianca	4:41:58	(19,155)
Cadden, Angela	6:24:14	(29,266)
Cadzon, Emma	4:26:55	(15,943)
Cagna-Harding, Yvonne	8:06:52	(30,218)
Cain, Maureen	5:51:20	(27,972)
Cairns, Claire	5:10:05	(24,089)
Calame, Jo	4:05:19	(11,168)
Caldecott, Cynthia	3:43:58	(6,483)
Calder, Helen	3:43:09	(6,334)
Calder, Selena	4:22:43	(14,987)
Calderbank, Ruth	3:53:25	(8,362)
Calderwood, Sharon	3:43:33	(6,407)
Caldwell, Gillian	4:50:16	(20,763)
Callander, Louise	5:45:07	(27,566)
Callandine, Andrea	4:43:07	(19,407)
Callaway, Angela	3:27:49	(3,767)
Callender, Debbie	5:14:22	(24,684)
Callow, Theresa	6:12:58	(28,956)
Calton, Patsy	5:59:47	(28,409)
Calver, Jennifer	4:35:00	(17,713)
Calvert, Ann	4:51:31	(20,985)
Calvert, Jane	4:14:37	(13,152)
Calvert, Lesley-Ann	4:26:36	(15,871)
Calvert, Sue	3:47:24	(7,117)
Camecho, Charlotte	6:24:37	(29,276)
Cameron, Joan	7:56:11	(30,204)
Cameron, Michelle	3:50:43	(7,812)
Camier, Martine	4:23:33	(15,189)
Campbell, Gail	4:27:40	(16,107)
Campbell, Ilidia	4:03:00	(10,661)
Campbell, Lisa	3:50:32	(7,780)
Campbell, Rebecca	6:21:28	(29,204)
Campbell, Sara	4:20:37	(14,503)
Campbell Smith, Terry	3:38:24	(5,466)
Camsey, Rosalind	4:20:19	(14,432)
Candy, Susan	3:13:10	(2,022)
Canning, Angela	4:58:36	(22,394)
Cant, Angela	4:35:24	(17,797)
Cant, Claire	6:03:53	(28,586)
Canton, Janet	4:46:30	(20,054)
Capel, Lara	5:06:03	(23,476)
Capezzali, Concetta	4:05:48	(11,298)
Cappaert, Susan	4:22:11	(14,856)
Capper, Lucy	4:38:00	(18,371)
Carboni, Anna	4:25:27	(15,602)
Cardell, Margaret	4:25:28	(15,609)
Cargill, Katherine	4:02:45	(10,617)
Cargill, Kay	5:18:32	(25,216)
Cariss, Sue	3:28:30	(3,907)
Carleton, Clair	3:41:43	(6,076)
Carlin, Julie	4:36:36	(18,040)
Carlsson, Kerstin	4:35:39	(17,855)
Carmichael, Linda	4:59:45	(22,562)
Carmichael, Lorraine	4:30:26	(16,747)
Carmona, Emily	3:50:08	(7,712)
Carnevale, Adele	6:03:42	(28,574)
Carpenter, Beverley	5:11:57	(24,347)
Carpenter, Christine	5:20:52	(25,450)
Carpenter, Christine	5:48:03	(27,779)
Carpenter, Susan	4:54:11	(21,548)
Carr, Emma	4:40:32	(18,878)
Carr, Karen	4:33:20	(17,378)
Carr, Louise	4:08:01	(11,768)
Carragar, Nicoletta	4:18:20	(13,964)
Carrett, Philippa	5:21:14	(25,493)
Carroli, Lisa	3:44:20	(6,551)
Carroll, Cecilia	4:50:42	(20,826)
Carroll, Dawn	4:49:11	(20,556)
Carroll, Lucy	5:47:44	(27,745)
Carslake, Tina	5:10:19	(24,119)
Carson, Susan	4:56:46	(22,101)
Carson, Suzanne	3:05:33	(1,394)
Carswell, Julia	4:01:31	(10,399)
Carter, Anne	4:49:41	(20,648)
Carter, Gillian	4:23:18	(15,134)
Carter, Helen	4:15:25	(13,350)
Carter, Janet	3:42:11	(6,159)
Carter, Janet	5:02:36	(22,948)
Carter, Julie	5:58:54	(28,362)
Carter, June	6:37:22	(29,572)
Carter, Lois	4:49:42	(20,654)
Carter, Lucy	4:51:03	(20,898)
Carter, Michelle	4:42:14	(19,211)
Carter, Patricia	4:27:44	(16,128)
Carter, Paula	5:25:00	(25,886)
Carter, Sally	4:11:33	(12,513)
Carter, Sandra	5:31:54	(26,524)
Cartledge, Margaret	5:18:45	(25,242)
Cartwright, Elizabeth	4:46:45	(20,105)
Caruana, Wendy	4:46:31	(20,059)
Cash, Caroline	5:07:25	(23,684)
Cassar, Florence	6:03:59	(28,588)
Cassar, Ilona	3:56:15	(8,980)
Cassidy, Jane	5:48:27	(27,813)
Castle, Emma	3:32:26	(4,525)
Castle, Fiona	6:00:49	(28,448)
Castles, Dawn	4:24:19	(15,352)
Castro, Sandra	5:25:55	(25,977)
Cater, Sharon Dawn	6:44:12	(29,726)
Caton, Helen	4:59:03	(22,471)
Cattanach, Jane	5:15:23	(24,851)
Cattell, Catherine	6:06:51	(28,712)
Catterall, Solange	6:11:59	(28,925)
Caulton, Kathryn	4:33:40	(17,470)
Cavanagh, Laura	5:04:37	(23,235)
Cavanagh, Susan	4:15:03	(13,278)
Cave, Rachel	4:19:00	(14,115)
Cavell, Anita	3:28:54	(3,980)
Caven, Hannah	5:04:14	(23,170)
Caverhill, Alison	3:57:29	(9,323)
Cawkwell, Becky	5:58:20	(28,340)
Cazalet, Catherine	5:43:44	(27,452)
Cech, Patricia	4:43:30	(19,497)
Cedillo, Sara	2:38:53	(153)
Celmer, Tracey	8:08:38	(30,228)
Cerutti, Christina	5:39:44	(27,159)
Chabassier, Mireille	4:17:46	(13,828)
Chadd, Gabrielle	5:12:15	(24,388)
Chadwick, Jackie	4:28:53	(16,392)
Chadwick, Joanne	4:36:25	(18,000)
Chaffe, Ann	7:28:52	(30,131)
Chaffey, Heather	5:10:30	(24,142)
Chakravorty, Amita	5:26:07	(25,999)
Chale, Christina	6:14:51	(29,018)
Chalk, Elizabeth	5:15:08	(24,802)
Challis, Janet	4:25:48	(15,672)
Chamberlain, Anne	6:09:38	(28,841)
Chamberlain, Margot	5:39:36	(27,144)
Chambers, Leona	4:17:34	(13,784)
Chambers, Norah	4:51:00	(20,881)
Chambers, Verity	4:38:57	(18,594)
Champion, Pamela	5:59:17	(28,381)
Chan, Frances	4:45:16	(19,818)
Chandler, Julia	4:31:17	(16,927)
Chandler, Kay	4:48:42	(20,471)
Chaplain, Véronique	3:22:09	(3,019)
Chaplin, Ann	5:31:30	(26,489)
Chaplin, Julie	5:21:05	(25,477)
Chaplin, Lucy	4:55:52	(21,964)
Chapman, Alison	4:50:58	(20,874)
Chapman, Brigid	4:10:37	(12,299)
Chapman, Claire	3:52:50	(8,235)
Chapman, Jacqueline	4:46:40	(20,087)
Chapman, Jayne	4:01:21	(10,357)
Chapman, Jeni	4:43:33	(19,508)
Chapman, Linda	5:26:40	(26,057)
Chapman, Mary	3:36:23	(5,134)
Chapman, Nicole	5:25:31	(25,941)
Chapman, Rebecca	5:46:10	(27,637)
Chapman, Sally	3:31:12	(4,355)
Chapple, Janet	4:04:16	(10,943)
Chapple, Kate	3:46:19	(6,919)
Chapple, Kay	5:42:00	(27,334)
Charalambous, Rebecca	5:06:25	(23,538)
Chard, Tracy	5:34:30	(26,756)
Charkiewicz, Angela	6:26:15	(29,306)
Charles, Cynthia	5:40:01	(27,189)
Charles, Marvelyn	4:46:44	(20,102)
Charlesworth, Debra	3:32:03	(4,474)
Charlesworth, Glenys	5:34:10	(26,720)
Charlton, Lisa	4:39:35	(18,712)
Charlton, Rachel	4:26:45	(15,898)
Charnock, Kath	3:03:09	(1,224)
Charnock, Miranda	6:28:55	(29,384)
Chatoo, Ayn	5:53:15	(28,080)
Chatterton, Vanessa	6:20:19	(29,166)
Chatwin, Sophie	3:59:03	(9,773)
Chavda, Asha	7:15:45	(30,050)
Chegwidden, Françoise Chantal	3:52:10	(8,111)
Chen, Wendy	4:30:07	(16,712)
Chepchumba, Joyce	2:24:12	(37)
Chessum, Deborah	4:52:32	(21,216)
Chesworeth, Caroline	4:28:11	(16,231)
Chetwood, Janet	5:38:15	(27,032)
Cheung, Lynn	5:05:46	(23,427)
Chew, Margaret	3:42:46	(6,265)
Chezem, Heather	5:55:20	(28,172)
Chiarella, Juliet	5:01:39	(22,822)
Chidaushe, Dorothy	5:26:50	(26,070)
Chilton, Michelle	5:26:25	(26,038)
Chilvers, Emma	6:29:22	(29,397)
Ching, Tessa	3:30:13	(4,203)
Chinnery, Fay	4:41:40	(19,097)
Chinwala, Yasmine	7:26:23	(30,115)
Chippendale, Joanne	4:11:48	(12,570)
Chippendale, Melanie	4:59:01	(22,465)
Chipperfield, Christine	5:27:52	(26,168)
Chisholm, Helen	4:06:46	(11,495)
Chittenden, Sarah	5:22:35	(25,657)
Chiu Wan, Fock	6:53:23	(29,854)
Chivers, Margot	5:28:36	(26,240)
Christie, Erica	3:07:48	(1,572)
Christie, Nathalie	3:28:07	(3,828)
Christopher, Sophie	5:26:11	(26,004)
Chubb, Fiona	4:45:54	(19,920)
Chudley, Katie	5:51:07	(27,959)
Chupak, Cindy	4:55:14	(21,791)
Church, Rachael	5:49:17	(27,859)
Churchill, Harriet	4:42:39	(19,303)
Churchward, Natalia	5:40:39	(27,243)
Cilliers, Maritsa	4:39:50	(18,758)
Clack, Deborah	5:14:41	(24,738)
Clague, Louise	4:56:50	(22,114)
Claisse, Caroline	5:22:57	(25,703)
Clapham, Jennifer	5:47:46	(27,748)
Clarey, Cynthia	4:24:09	(15,318)
Claridge, Patricia	6:53:15	(29,850)

Clark, Alison	5:17:27 (25,100)
Clark, Fiona	6:23:48 (29,254)
Clark, Georgina	5:22:40 (25,665)
Clark, Gillian	7:00:15 (29,945)
Clark, Heather	5:01:53 (22,849)
Clark, Jenny	5:54:42 (28,150)
Clark, Joanna	4:14:45 (13,194)
Clark, Juiette	2:54:27 (603)
Clark, Liz	4:51:21 (20,959)
Clark, Megan	2:47:24 (347)
Clark, Nicola	4:37:09 (18,158)
Clark, Sharon	4:59:56 (22,608)
Clark, Susan	5:26:22 (26,027)
Clarke, Alison	5:09:24 (23,999)
Clarke, Amanda	3:08:17 (1,613)
Clarke, Andrea	4:25:29 (15,613)
Clarke, Irene	6:00:40 (28,441)
Clarke, Janet	5:11:08 (24,232)
Clarke, Joyce	5:23:29 (25,741)
Clarke, Joyce	5:42:48 (27,398)
Clarke, Judith	5:39:16 (27,111)
Clarke, Kerry	5:28:32 (26,232)
Clarke, Krisztina	5:11:28 (24,279)
Clarke, Linda	5:10:22 (24,125)
Clarke, Lucy	5:04:02 (23,138)
Clarke, Natalie	4:26:03 (15,743)
Clarke, Rebecca	5:47:38 (27,732)
Clarke, Sonia	4:43:43 (19,543)
Clarke, Susan	4:51:22 (20,963)
Clarkson, Penelope	5:36:12 (26,895)
Clausen, Birthe	5:21:29 (25,524)
Clausen, Helle	3:35:51 (5,042)
Clay, Allyson	5:59:57 (28,416)
Clayton, Deborah	4:46:08 (19,967)
Clayton, Denise	4:15:49 (13,428)
Clayton, Patricia	6:20:16 (29,165)
Cleaver, Lisa	4:20:25 (14,453)
Cleaver, Margaret	4:21:00 (14,592)
Clemens, Petra	6:27:57 (29,353)
Clements, Angela	7:34:42 (30,151)
Clements, Paula	5:13:55 (24,620)
Cliff, Anna	4:21:29 (14,689)
Clifford, Emma	5:00:38 (22,681)
Clinton, Jane	3:57:48 (9,431)
Clinton, Margaret Rose	3:48:42 (7,402)
Clitherow, Barbara	4:21:47 (14,754)
Cloke, Yvonne	4:56:30 (22,065)
Clouder, Julie	4:45:24 (19,846)
Clowes, Janine	5:47:52 (27,763)
Clowes, Sophie	3:52:01 (8,079)
Clucas, Barb	5:51:17 (27,966)
Clutterbuck, June	4:04:12 (10,927)
Coates, Linda	4:51:16 (20,935)
Coates, Sophie	5:34:34 (26,763)
Cobb, Olivia	6:42:04 (29,694)
Cobby, Janet	3:44:40 (6,605)
Cobley, Nicky	4:42:05 (19,174)
Cochrane, Clare	4:26:21 (15,815)
Cochrane, Linda	6:55:14 (29,884)
Cockburn, Sally	6:08:44 (28,797)
Cockroft, Karen	4:23:16 (15,122)
Code, Joanne	3:41:02 (5,963)
Coe, Jenny	4:22:53 (15,032)
Coffey, Katherine	4:38:07 (18,408)
Cohen, Linda	5:13:36 (24,581)
Coldrick, Ginastein	4:58:01 (22,296)
Cole, Rachel	4:27:00 (15,964)
Cole, Rosemary	5:36:21 (26,905)
Coleman, Carolyn	4:13:21 (12,889)
Coles, Helen	5:44:48 (27,546)
Coles, Isabel	6:34:04 (29,504)
Coles, Melissa	5:39:00 (27,085)
Collett, Clare	4:44:01 (19,588)
Collett, Lisa	4:54:31 (21,599)
Colley, Bethan	5:35:46 (26,864)
Collier, Laurel	4:34:33 (17,636)
Collinge, Maddy	3:28:51 (3,973)
Collings, Clare	5:52:53 (28,057)
Collington, Joanna	4:15:06 (13,289)
Collins, Ali	5:03:51 (23,108)
Collins, Alicia	4:39:23 (18,664)
Collins, Christine	4:46:56 (20,156)
Collins, Hilary	3:47:33 (7,154)
Collins, Jackie	5:15:45 (24,898)
Collins, Jill	6:07:17 (28,736)
Collins, Linda	6:11:28 (28,907)
Collins, Mary	6:06:33 (28,703)
Collins, Maxine	6:19:29 (29,144)
Collins, Niamh	5:25:59 (25,985)
Collinson, Audrey	5:48:01 (27,776)
Collins-Powell, Lesley-Anne	5:33:08 (26,621)
Collyer, Alison	5:29:02 (26,291)
Colman, Paulette	4:37:57 (18,357)
Colsey, Kathleen	7:24:04 (30,103)
Colzi, Mariapaola	3:04:25 (1,307)
Comer, Debbie	5:18:42 (25,234)
Comerford, Anna	4:41:32 (19,067)
Comiskey, Carmel	3:48:10 (7,297)
Commbs, Marilyn	5:22:02 (25,590)
Company, Daphne	6:20:20 (29,168)
Conaghan, Linda	3:46:11 (6,895)
Coneally, Florence	4:31:01 (16,855)
Coney, Sharon	3:05:39 (1,398)
Connell, Emma	4:53:15 (21,361)
Connelly, Alison	5:09:07 (23,955)
Connelly, Beverley	5:20:27 (25,405)
Connelly, Helen	3:49:51 (7,657)
Connelly, Laura	5:09:07 (23,955)
Connelly, Lesley	4:27:02 (15,975)
Connelly, Tracey	6:15:18 (29,037)
Connett, Emma	4:35:34 (17,829)
Connolly, Bernadette	3:48:15 (7,312)
Connolly, Mary	3:57:55 (9,469)
Connolly, Sally	5:33:25 (26,641)
Connor, Eleri	4:45:52 (19,914)
Connor, Gisele	4:19:32 (14,264)
Connor, Nadine	6:36:48 (29,561)
Conroy, Annie	4:30:23 (16,741)
Constantino, Janet	4:46:16 (20,002)
Convery, Emma	4:37:24 (18,225)
Cooch, Joanna	5:00:50 (22,707)
Cook, Gayle	7:41:55 (30,169)
Cook, Lesley	6:11:04 (28,893)
Cook, Lissa	4:38:42 (18,548)
Cook, Loretta	3:51:34 (7,983)
Cook, Rachel	3:11:58 (1,911)
Cook, Sharon	7:41:55 (30,169)
Cook, Shirley	4:46:42 (20,092)
Cook, Susan	3:24:58 (3,372)
Cooke, Helen	5:27:47 (26,157)
Cooke, Tracey	5:34:17 (26,732)
Cooke-Simmons, Julia	4:27:17 (16,025)
Cooksey, Gigliola	5:21:50 (25,570)
Cooley, Rachel	4:04:17 (10,947)
Cooling, Susanna	5:09:27 (24,010)
Coombs, Ruth	4:51:22 (20,963)
Cooney, Siobhan	5:23:45 (25,766)
Coope, Margaret	5:09:17 (23,980)
Cooper, Adelle	4:35:34 (17,829)
Cooper, Alexandra	5:07:10 (23,645)
Cooper, Allison	5:22:50 (25,688)
Cooper, Antonia	3:55:07 (8,719)
Cooper, Carol	5:07:12 (23,650)
Cooper, Louise	3:12:23 (1,951)
Cooper, Nicky	4:57:51 (22,275)
Cooper, Sally Ann	5:05:34 (23,391)
Cooper, Samantha	4:08:45 (11,923)
Cooper, Theresa	4:29:25 (16,526)
Cope, Gail	5:03:51 (23,108)
Copeman, Helen	4:27:37 (16,096)
Copland, Jacqueline	5:25:12 (25,906)
Copland, Lita	5:25:12 (25,906)
Copley, Emma	5:42:14 (27,348)
Copley, Kathryn	5:22:48 (25,683)
Copsey, Kate	5:43:42 (27,449)
Corbett, Tara-Jane	5:26:22 (26,027)
Cordalis, Jean	4:20:08 (14,393)
Cordeaux, Linda	5:01:14 (22,774)
Cornell, Ranee	6:20:07 (29,162)
Cornwall, Ceri	6:19:37 (29,148)
Cornwell, Naomi	6:08:35 (28,790)
Corriette, Jane	6:28:03 (29,358)
Cosgrove, Sarah	5:08:01 (23,771)
Cossali-Francis, Moira	3:54:33 (8,601)
Cossey, Jenny	4:02:41 (10,604)
Coster, Debbie	4:17:28 (13,766)
Cotham, Shirley	7:07:19 (29,998)
Cottam Wynes, Christen	5:10:17 (24,117)
Cotterell, Srar	4:09:11 (12,018)
Cotterill, Carole	5:00:09 (22,638)
Cotterill, Caroline	4:11:14 (12,450)
Cottis, Tracy	3:18:11 (2,559)
Cotton, Emma	5:05:05 (23,303)
Cotton, Rachel	5:51:28 (27,980)
Coubert, Leigh	4:20:31 (14,479)
Couldrey, Debbie	5:47:54 (27,769)
Couldridge, Caragh	3:59:26 (9,896)
Coulson, Caroline	6:32:52 (29,475)
Coulson, Julie	5:30:24 (26,401)
Coult, Susan	5:11:10 (24,238)
Coulthard, Philippa	7:17:56 (30,067)
Counsell, Joy	5:25:23 (25,928)
Court, Anne	4:10:45 (12,321)
Courtnell, Deborah	4:54:40 (21,628)
Courtney Mumby, Jane	5:35:45 (26,863)
Cousins, Amanda	5:21:31 (25,527)
Coutinho, Loretta	5:39:52 (27,173)
Coverley, Gail	3:49:14 (7,502)
Covi, Donna	6:37:45 (29,584)
Cowan, Barbara	3:52:08 (8,104)
Cowan, Victoria	5:04:41 (23,243)
Cowdrey, Nadia	5:47:40 (27,736)
Cowell, Sasha	5:50:00 (27,903)
Cowen, Samantha	4:18:39 (14,041)
Cowley, Annie	3:37:52 (5,390)
Cowley, Clare	5:16:39 (25,007)
Cowley, Gaye	5:12:26 (24,419)
Cowley Antelo, Maria	5:27:54 (26,171)
Cowling, Gwenda	4:38:24 (18,480)
Cowling, Mary	4:47:06 (20,184)
Cowlishaw, Helen	5:41:23 (27,286)
Cowsill, Elaine	3:59:02 (9,765)
Cox, Christine	4:22:18 (14,886)
Cox, Deborah	5:56:30 (28,242)
Cox, Deborah	6:08:08 (28,771)
Cox, Jean	3:55:56 (8,901)
Cox, Jennai	5:16:03 (24,933)
Cox, Julia	4:55:06 (21,759)
Cox, Maureen	5:13:28 (24,570)
Cox, Michelle	4:33:40 (17,470)
Cox, Sharon	5:34:14 (26,726)
Cox-Nicholls, Tina	4:48:07 (20,371)
Coxwell, Kathryn	5:17:46 (25,133)
Crabtree, Emma	4:35:32 (17,819)
Crabtree, Megs	4:04:52 (11,081)
Craddock, Carole	5:05:35 (23,397)
Cragg, Sandra	4:31:07 (16,876)
Craggs, Anne	5:03:28 (23,060)
Craine, Helen	5:11:31 (24,288)
Crampin, Lucy	3:53:34 (8,394)
Crane, Jacqueline	3:38:03 (5,406)
Crane, Jeanette	5:49:40 (27,880)
Craske, Gill	3:49:22 (7,543)
Craven, Gemma	3:48:25 (7,341)
Crawford, Antoinette	4:21:28 (14,685)
Crawford, Kate	4:44:33 (19,688)
Crawley, Carol	4:23:26 (15,155)
Crawley, Patricia	4:15:11 (13,299)
Cray, Samantha	4:48:43 (20,473)
Crebo, Sally	4:16:20 (13,529)
Credito, Candace	4:33:21 (17,387)
Creech, Kathryn	4:40:36 (18,898)
Creed, Jacqueline	5:05:26 (23,369)
Creegan, Lindsey	4:52:28 (21,197)
Cregan, Alison	4:28:38 (16,348)
Creglia, Juliette	4:47:46 (20,303)
Cremen, Sandra	5:21:40 (25,543)
Crerar-Gilbert, Agnieszka	4:25:14 (15,563)
Crespo, Joana	5:47:52 (27,763)
Cresswell, Claire	5:19:11 (25,281)
Cresswell, Rosamund	4:35:22 (17,791)
Crimes, Yasmin	4:23:15 (15,118)
Crisinel, Sylvie	5:03:30 (23,063)
Criso, Rachael	4:38:16 (18,445)
Crisp, Denise	5:03:59 (23,125)
Crisp, Louisa	5:30:37 (26,421)
Crocker, Marilyn	4:02:02 (10,494)
Crockett, Anna	3:09:18 (1,694)
Crofton, Susan	6:44:06 (29,720)

Cronin Jones, Susan....5:56:59 (28,269)
Cronk, Nicola....4:43:34 (19,512)
Crook, Amanda....5:50:46 (27,944)
Crook, Danielle....4:25:51 (15,688)
Crook, Hazel....6:48:02 (29,778)
Crook, Jill....5:25:24 (25,931)
Crook, Sally....4:46:47 (20,111)
Crooks, Clare....4:18:14 (13,926)
Crooks, Eleanor....5:04:20 (23,185)
Crookshank, Lucy....6:00:45 (28,444)
Croome, Lorraine....4:31:40 (17,028)
Cropper, Lesley....4:50:15 (20,758)
Crosby, Helen....4:30:31 (16,756)
Cross, Anne....5:15:49 (24,910)
Cross, Nicola....4:56:43 (22,093)
Cross, Rita....5:37:49 (27,009)
Cross, Valerie....6:41:46 (29,684)
Crossan, Andrea....5:28:47 (26,267)
Crossland, Ann....4:40:24 (18,857)
Crossley, Julia....7:25:35 (30,109)
Crosswell, Margaret....4:11:47 (12,566)
Crouchman, Susan....4:33:16 (17,360)
Crowe, Patricia....5:25:55 (25,977)
Crowhurst, Maureen....5:27:51 (26,164)
Crowle, Revis....3:09:19 (1,697)
Crowther, Lorraine....6:38:27 (29,597)
Croxford, Tracie....3:55:11 (8,728)
Cruickshank, Moira....4:45:59 (19,934)
Cruise, Helen....4:27:52 (16,167)
Cruse, Susan....7:21:38 (30,090)
Crutchfield, Helen....4:35:09 (17,739)
Cryer, Jackie....4:19:03 (14,130)
Cubberley, Rachael....3:36:02 (5,080)
Cubbon, Frances....5:36:01 (26,882)
Cubitt, Maria....6:09:18 (28,828)
Cuby, Brenda....6:26:28 (29,316)
Cuddon, Sarah....4:24:47 (15,456)
Cudlipp, Sarah....3:57:15 (9,241)
Cuffie, Shirley....3:48:02 (7,271)
Cullen, Anne....4:51:31 (20,985)
Cullen, Jaqueline....7:03:21 (29,972)
Cullen, Katie....4:31:54 (17,090)
Cullen, Linda....4:06:10 (11,372)
Cullin Moir, Linda....4:49:01 (20,530)
Cullum, Sue....4:18:44 (14,063)
Culshaw, Alison....5:05:29 (23,381)
Cummings, Fiona....4:25:11 (15,554)
Cummings, Sarah....3:57:23 (9,283)
Cummins, Kelly....3:26:20 (3,539)
Cunningham, Corinne....4:27:41 (16,114)
Cuoghi, Rachel....3:50:54 (7,847)
Cupido, Gerry....3:56:08 (8,956)
Cure, Janet....4:18:16 (13,943)
Curnow, Anne....4:17:25 (13,753)
Curran, Emma....4:19:20 (14,202)
Currie, Sharon....5:46:35 (27,669)
Currington, Debra....4:29:55 (16,665)
Curry, Julia....4:39:21 (18,654)
Curtis, Eleanor....6:06:51 (28,712)
Curtis, Lisa....5:11:07 (24,228)
Curtis, Louise....3:04:46 (1,331)
Curtis, Naomi....4:46:39 (20,082)
Cushen, Jane....5:34:29 (26,754)
Cutting, Zoe....5:11:13 (24,246)
Cutts, Rita....4:33:02 (17,316)
Da Silva, Selina....5:43:56 (27,468)
Daddy, Sue....5:08:48 (23,907)
Dade, Terri....6:08:34 (28,788)
Dadlani, Emma....4:00:48 (10,242)
Dadoun, Christine....3:57:58 (9,484)
Dahill, Lucy....5:28:51 (26,277)
Dainty, Julia....3:44:23 (6,559)
Dainty, Margery....4:16:08 (13,492)
Dainty, Wendy....4:11:42 (12,549)
Dale, Jacqueline....9:08:03 (30,279)
Dale, Joanna....4:12:24 (12,714)
Dale, Nicola....4:19:17 (14,189)
Dale, Susan....3:49:57 (7,676)
Dale, Susan....5:38:00 (27,019)
Daley, Susan....4:54:54 (21,702)
Daley, Susan....6:22:12 (29,218)
Dallimore, Caroline....4:18:36 (14,033)
Dallyn, Jessica....6:50:52 (29,822)

Dalton, Marjory....6:47:26 (29,768)
Daly, Caragh....6:27:54 (29,350)
Daly, Heather....5:05:08 (23,310)
Dalzell, Julie....3:54:20 (8,542)
Dalziel, Tina....5:00:19 (22,647)
Danch, Julie....4:17:29 (13,769)
Danforth, Sally....6:50:02 (29,803)
Daniel, Elizabeth....4:52:31 (21,210)
Daniel, Julie....4:16:44 (13,621)
Daniels, Naomi....5:05:34 (23,391)
D'Arcy, Lucy....4:12:04 (12,633)
Dare, Janet....5:17:36 (25,115)
Dareve, Sara....4:24:32 (15,404)
Dargie, Mary....4:33:02 (17,316)
Dargo, Joanne....6:41:25 (29,678)
Darke, Robina....5:06:05 (23,484)
Darkes, Debra....4:18:11 (13,914)
Darroch, Liza....4:04:27 (10,977)
Darsley, Anne....4:46:33 (20,067)
Dasey, Elizabeth....4:15:23 (13,342)
Daulton, Julie....4:34:32 (17,633)
Daurat, Simone....3:57:22 (9,279)
Dausch, Karl Heinz....3:54:01 (8,483)
Dauverchain, Andrée Blanche....4:12:53 (12,806)
Davey, Julie....3:59:40 (9,968)
David, Helene....4:49:37 (20,637)
David, Toni....5:50:49 (27,946)
Davidoff, Vanessa....4:15:45 (13,414)
Davidson, Anne....4:28:55 (16,404)
Davidson, Carol....5:30:19 (26,397)
Davidson, Elizabeth....4:31:29 (16,977)
Davidson, Samantha....7:16:18 (30,053)
Davidson, Susanne....5:39:10 (27,101)
Davidson, Violet....5:12:56 (24,489)
Davie, Emma....4:25:30 (15,620)
Davies, Anna....5:40:46 (27,251)
Davies, Bethan....6:15:23 (29,043)
Davies, Carla....5:42:28 (27,367)
Davies, Catriona....5:23:04 (25,712)
Davies, Christine....5:20:03 (25,366)
Davies, Dawn....5:11:48 (24,331)
Davies, Debra....4:49:14 (20,569)
Davies, Elizabeth....6:49:48 (29,800)
Davies, Frances....4:52:09 (21,124)
Davies, Georgina....4:49:26 (20,605)
Davies, Georgina....5:36:51 (26,934)
Davies, Gillian....4:34:05 (17,553)
Davies, Julie....4:45:58 (19,932)
Davies, Karen....3:51:38 (7,993)
Davies, Linda....4:19:09 (14,157)
Davies, Linda....6:23:00 (29,232)
Davies, Lona....5:21:11 (25,487)
Davies, Lorna....5:16:40 (25,008)
Davies, Maria....4:13:47 (12,995)
Davies, Michele....3:40:01 (5,791)
Davies, Paula....4:24:18 (15,349)
Davies, Rachel....6:32:14 (29,456)
Davies, Rita....4:16:35 (13,588)
Davies, Samantha....6:39:55 (29,625)
Davies, Sarah....4:32:41 (17,243)
Davies, Sarah Jane....6:12:19 (28,933)
Davies, Sharon....4:23:45 (15,236)
Davies, Sian....4:42:46 (19,323)
Davies, Sian....5:34:27 (26,751)
Davies, Susan....4:42:22 (19,241)
Davies, Susan....5:04:04 (23,144)
Davies, Wendy....3:05:52 (1,412)
Davi-John, Jean....6:04:44 (28,631)
Davis, Ann....5:09:34 (24,024)
Davis, Hazel....4:22:58 (15,055)
Davis, Helen....4:39:36 (18,718)
Davis, Janet....6:33:03 (29,482)
Davis, Karen....4:17:59 (13,867)
Davis, Kelly....5:29:16 (26,316)
Davis, Mara....5:06:25 (23,538)
Davis, Mary....4:19:02 (14,127)
Davis, Melissa....5:06:28 (23,543)
Davis, Nicola....4:02:40 (10,602)
Davis, Peter....3:22:43 (3,073)
Davis, Sandy....4:47:11 (20,198)
Davis, Victoria....4:02:32 (10,580)
Davter, Sophie....6:32:49 (29,473)
Dawes, Beverley....4:31:24 (16,961)

Dawes, Claire....4:42:05 (19,174)
Dawes, Lucy....4:47:30 (20,260)
Dawkins, Pauline....5:06:07 (23,488)
Dawson, Catherine....6:08:29 (28,787)
Dawson, Clare....4:49:27 (20,609)
Dawson, Katie....6:28:45 (29,379)
Dawson, Sally....3:18:33 (2,602)
Dawson, Susan....4:29:22 (16,511)
Day, Caroline....4:52:03 (21,102)
Day, Carolyn....5:34:04 (26,707)
Day, Gillian....5:58:21 (28,341)
Day, Morag....4:29:49 (16,630)
Day, Nicola....4:26:56 (15,945)
Day Lewis, Tamasin....4:55:06 (21,759)
Daynes, Hayley....5:49:31 (27,873)
De Carvfel, Anouk....5:15:42 (24,891)
De Clouet, Susan....3:55:14 (8,747)
De Jong, Ariena....5:14:24 (24,688)
De Koning, Victoria....6:33:22 (29,490)
De Labouchere, Beatrice....5:16:27 (24,979)
De Machen, Charlotte Ann....3:49:34 (7,599)
De Max, Caroline....4:09:38 (12,101)
De Oliveira Evans, Wanderlea....6:00:55 (28,452)
De Roeper, Sophie....5:07:46 (23,743)
De Vial, Michaela....3:59:04 (9,777)
Deakin, Lindsay....4:41:52 (19,131)
Deal, Jayne....4:59:14 (22,490)
Dean, Elizabeth....5:45:35 (27,599)
Dean, Gillian....4:28:35 (16,334)
Dean, Julia....4:30:49 (16,809)
Dean, Lucy....4:40:14 (18,819)
Dean, Suzanne....4:54:41 (21,634)
Deane, Rebecca....6:45:31 (29,747)
Dearing, Annabel....4:42:08 (19,188)
Dearness, Susan....4:44:51 (19,743)
Debnam, Madelaine....4:25:54 (15,702)
Dechantsreiter, Elizabeth....4:58:19 (22,343)
Dedoncker, Sharon....5:27:36 (26,138)
Deeble, Yvonne....5:39:49 (27,164)
Defis, Catrin....4:48:15 (20,395)
Defoe, Deedrea....4:49:37 (20,637)
Dekker, Janny....3:30:08 (4,194)
Dekker, Sharon....5:19:37 (25,319)
Delahunty, Maria....4:13:31 (12,935)
Delannoy Souchon, Bernadette....4:32:27 (17,208)
Delany, Margaret....5:02:20 (22,921)
Dell, Sally....3:59:52 (10,016)
Deller, Hannah....4:53:43 (21,457)
Delrosa, Anne-Marie....4:39:58 (18,783)
Dely, Janet....4:44:53 (19,754)
Dench, Katherine....4:30:01 (16,697)
Denley, Loretto....3:25:44 (3,472)
Dennard, Rebecca....4:39:00 (18,603)
Denney, Sarah....5:07:41 (23,726)
Denning, Jacqui....4:31:15 (16,918)
Dennis, Beth....4:56:03 (21,993)
Dennis, Demelza....5:01:55 (22,859)
Dennis, Elizabeth....5:36:42 (26,924)
Dennis, Juliana....4:16:06 (13,487)
Dennison, Andrea....2:59:15 (953)
Denny, Anne....5:24:54 (25,873)
Dent, Michelle....4:02:21 (10,539)
Dent, Verity....4:52:07 (21,117)
Denton, Julia....4:26:08 (15,762)
Denwood, Kirsty....4:29:58 (16,684)
Derbyshire, Susan....4:47:46 (20,303)
Dering, Jo....2:56:08 (695)
Derrick, Sarah....3:49:28 (7,567)
Desmaris, Sharon....5:22:05 (25,598)
Desorbay, Thérèse....4:55:29 (21,885)
Detruit, Marie France....4:08:21 (11,837)
Devaney, Tina....3:58:31 (9,611)
Devile, Hannie....5:36:00 (26,880)
Devine, Andrea....3:28:24 (3,890)
Devine, Mary....4:58:23 (22,357)
Devis, Tracy....4:52:36 (21,238)
Devoy, Julie....5:00:42 (22,692)
Dewberry, Julie....4:08:57 (11,965)
Dexter, Michelle....6:33:45 (29,500)
Dey, Julie....4:48:34 (20,449)
Dhadwal, Kuljit....5:44:18 (27,496)
Di Mambro, Hannah....5:18:37 (25,226)
Dibble, Deborah....4:19:48 (14,315)

Emery, Julie 6:23:22 (29,239)
Emery, Leanne 4:55:28 (21,878)
Emery, Tara 4:57:16 (22,181)
Emmanuel, Debbie 4:32:46 (17,270)
Emmett, Maureen 3:34:53 (4,889)
Endres, Christine 5:31:48 (26,518)
Engdahl, Elin 3:05:23 (1,380)
Englhardt, Annette 4:10:19 (12,231)
English, Lucinda 4:34:06 (17,557)
Engseth, Magni Hals 4:27:35 (16,084)
Epifanio, Gail 5:00:41 (22,688)
Erculisse, Maryse 4:35:29 (17,810)
Erdursun, Christine 5:11:24 (24,273)
Ericson, Melissa 4:55:39 (21,940)
Errington, Sandra 7:39:47 (30,164)
Errington-Moers, Kimberley 5:58:57 (28,365)
Erskine, Brenda 4:06:10 (11,372)
Escolme, Kate 3:59:09 (9,800)
Esdaile, Victoria 5:54:02 (28,114)
Espin, Tracy 3:51:40 (8,002)
Espinoza, Paula 5:58:08 (28,331)
Esson, Maria 4:50:34 (20,808)
Estcourt, Lucy 4:28:20 (16,267)
Etheridge, Julia 5:32:55 (26,608)
Eustace, Frances 5:18:24 (25,198)
Evans, Amanda 5:17:15 (25,074)
Evans, Donna-Marie 6:58:50 (29,929)
Evans, Gale 4:47:38 (20,287)
Evans, Gillian 3:59:51 (10,010)
Evans, Heather 6:41:19 (29,672)
Evans, Ingrid 5:10:20 (24,120)
Evans, Katherine 4:59:49 (22,578)
Evans, Kim 5:22:21 (25,632)
Evans, Linda 4:23:30 (15,172)
Evans, Lisa 4:49:27 (20,609)
Evans, Lorraine 4:33:17 (17,363)
Evans, Maggie 5:17:46 (25,133)
Evans, Mandy 6:09:13 (28,821)
Evans, Maria 5:48:17 (27,798)
Evans, Maureen 5:10:33 (24,154)
Evans, Philippa 6:39:21 (29,614)
Evans, Rachel 5:03:42 (23,081)
Evans, Rhian 5:21:16 (25,498)
Evans, Shirley 7:23:35 (30,095)
Evans, Siobhan 3:23:30 (3,176)
Evans, Susan 4:29:16 (16,487)
Evans, Susan 4:29:33 (16,561)
Evans, Trudy 6:18:44 (29,132)
Evans, Vivienne 4:19:02 (14,127)
Evans, Yvonne 6:42:49 (29,703)
Evason, Cheryl 5:26:06 (25,996)
Eve, Susan 3:58:32 (9,616)
Eveleigh, Amanda 6:16:36 (29,074)
Evelyn, Christine 5:28:00 (26,182)
Everett, Penny 5:04:47 (23,259)
Evers, Sally 4:28:34 (16,331)
Everson, Sue 6:05:41 (28,673)
Evetts, Alison 4:17:53 (13,848)
Ewart, Barbara 4:57:59 (22,292)
Ewers, Julie 4:21:25 (14,673)
Ewing, Marsie 4:08:21 (11,837)
Ewing, Suzi 4:55:20 (21,824)
Exton, Alison 4:46:05 (19,954)
Eydes, Claire 3:57:14 (9,236)
Eyer Van Luypen, Henny 4:44:17 (19,635)
Eyre, Annabelle 5:08:09 (23,789)
Fabienne, Garitte 3:46:26 (6,939)
Fagerlund, Linnea 4:14:20 (13,103)
Fairclough, Jane 5:57:06 (28,275)
Fairhead, Alison 3:51:45 (8,015)
Fairs, Bridget 4:31:11 (16,898)
Fakhouri, Dimah 4:09:42 (12,108)
Fallon, Marie 6:17:42 (29,104)
Fallon, Patricia 6:37:32 (29,578)
Famiglietti, Wendy 4:47:01 (20,167)
Fane, Suzanne 3:39:45 (5,725)
Fangl, Ingrid 4:53:12 (21,353)
Farey, Joan 5:34:55 (26,799)
Farley, Susan 6:17:23 (29,096)
Farmer, Janet 3:53:01 (8,269)
Farmer, Jenny 4:07:01 (11,557)
Farmer, Melissa 4:56:00 (21,984)
Farnik, Claudia 4:04:57 (11,106)

The Marathon medal

The medal in the inaugural London Marathon in 1981 was tiny by today's standards (just bigger that a 50p piece). Silver coloured, round, on a blue ribbon, it had a drawing of Tower Bridge on one side and a 'map' of the course on the other. These days (since 1998) the medals are bigger, often square and the ribbons are multi-coloured. But it's still one of the most sought after souvenirs in the world of distance running.

Farrall, Ali 4:35:59 (17,930)
Farrant, Jennifer 6:03:18 (28,555)
Farrier, Jane 3:55:49 (8,877)
Farrington, Debby 3:43:53 (6,467)
Farrow, Anthea 3:33:08 (4,633)
Farrow, Pam 4:57:34 (22,221)
Farthing, Kathryn 4:21:27 (14,682)
Faruqui, Sarwat 5:22:26 (25,640)
Faucherand, Sophie 4:56:04 (21,997)
Faulds-Glover, Shona 4:07:51 (11,730)
Faulkner, Dayle 4:28:15 (16,249)
Fay, Helen 4:46:13 (19,990)
Federici, Paula 6:20:32 (29,174)
Feickert, Deborah 4:28:51 (16,388)
Feldman, Angela 4:49:29 (20,616)
Feldman, Robyn 6:06:59 (28,719)
Feldman, Sue 3:36:07 (5,094)
Feldmann, Teri 4:11:23 (12,478)
Fell, Carol 6:00:33 (28,432)
Fellers, Julienne 5:18:28 (25,210)
Fellows, Deborah 3:49:19 (7,528)
Fellows, Joanne 4:32:34 (17,223)
Felton, Michelle 7:02:20 (29,964)
Fenables, Kay 4:55:11 (21,778)
Fenelon, Patsy 3:33:56 (4,745)
Fenioux, Marie 3:33:11 (4,642)
Fenlon, Mickailah 6:23:04 (29,233)
Fenn, Fiona 3:44:44 (6,622)
Fenwick, Alison 4:41:28 (19,057)
Fenwick, Fay 3:38:03 (5,406)
Ferguson, Ailsa 4:36:47 (18,078)
Ferguson, Emily 3:56:19 (8,998)
Fernandes, Alison 5:06:41 (23,575)
Fernandes, Penny 7:19:56 (30,079)
Fernandes, Rosada 4:46:44 (20,102)
Fernandez, Adriana 2:26:21 (46)
Fernandez, Colette 4:45:33 (19,869)
Fernandez, Françoise 5:21:24 (25,519)
Fernandez, Michelle 4:46:06 (19,960)
Fernie, Sarah 5:53:09 (28,074)
Ferragamo, Vivia 5:29:15 (26,314)
Ferreira, Elizka 3:05:07 (1,356)
Ferreira, Gracinda 4:33:09 (17,337)
Ferrelly, Katherine 4:24:08 (15,316)
Ferrier, Patricia 4:43:38 (19,524)
Ferriter, Josephine 5:21:19 (25,506)
Ferry, Jeanne 4:27:05 (15,994)
Fever, Susanne 5:09:28 (24,012)
Ficken, Pamela 5:45:16 (27,575)
Fickling, Katherine 4:14:34 (13,141)
Fiddes, Tanya 6:07:07 (28,724)
Fidler, Alison 5:13:39 (24,590)
Field, Bente 3:58:14 (9,551)
Field, Christine 6:08:25 (28,783)
Field, Clare 4:59:46 (22,565)
Field, Madeleine 4:55:41 (21,946)
Fielder, Jodie 3:35:06 (4,919)
Filli, Lucrizia 4:35:34 (17,829)
Finch, Clare 5:16:32 (24,995)
Finch, Janet 4:35:43 (17,869)
Findlay, Vanessa 5:29:23 (26,329)
Findlay-Bada, Celia 3:38:37 (5,502)
Fines, Helen 4:52:24 (21,185)
Finnemore, Helen 3:39:05 (5,588)
Finnerty, Susan 4:23:58 (15,286)
Finney, Ruth 3:38:39 (5,510)
Fiot, Florence 4:17:41 (13,808)
Firth, Caroline 4:29:24 (16,519)
Fischer, Christina 5:37:41 (26,999)
Fisher, Charlotte 7:26:19 (30,114)
Fisher, Lisa 4:39:54 (18,769)
Fisher, Michele 4:29:50 (16,634)
Fisher, Monica 6:53:27 (29,856)
Fisher, Naomi 5:10:31 (24,146)
Fisher, Pamela 4:31:49 (17,062)
Fisher, Patricia 7:31:00 (30,139)
Fisher, Tracey 4:08:26 (11,859)
Fishwick, Jillian 5:22:02 (25,590)
Fitches, Nicola 4:31:29 (16,977)
Fitchett, Eve 5:51:39 (27,991)
Fitzgerald, Sarah 5:26:26 (26,039)
Fitzwilliam, Carol 7:38:08 (30,158)
Flacke, Yvette 4:07:10 (11,582)
Flanagan, Paula 4:07:18 (11,612)
Flannery, Patricia 3:53:45 (8,433)
Flannigan, Teresa 4:40:33 (18,885)
Flatters, Sarah 4:43:28 (19,484)
Flaxman, Christine 5:15:41 (24,887)
Flaxton, Michelle 3:21:19 (2,922)
Fleet, Melanie 4:22:02 (14,822)
Fleming, Bridget 4:27:00 (15,964)
Fleming, Fiona 6:44:06 (29,720)
Fleming, Melissa 3:53:04 (8,284)
Fleming, Naomi 5:28:12 (26,196)
Fleming, Sharon 7:06:12 (29,986)
Fletcher, Alison 2:49:18 (403)
Fletcher, Ann-Marie 6:02:18 (28,516)
Fletcher, Caroline 4:07:24 (11,639)
Fletcher, Dawn 3:37:45 (5,370)
Fletcher, Elisabeth 6:32:22 (29,459)
Fletcher, Johanna 3:47:41 (7,189)
Fletcher, Kathryn 5:04:27 (23,211)
Fletcher, Sarah 4:50:58 (20,874)
Fletcher, Zoe 3:49:57 (7,676)
Flint, Helen 5:20:06 (25,370)
Flood, Elizabeth 3:49:15 (7,509)
Floodgate, Elizabeth 5:12:51 (24,476)
Flores, Patricia 4:57:20 (22,195)
Floyd, Zanna 4:52:56 (21,299)
Flynn, Monica 6:27:46 (29,345)
Fogg, Julie 4:26:47 (15,906)
Fogliacco, Eugenia 5:23:08 (25,717)
Foley, Niamh 4:55:25 (21,857)
Folks, Sarah 4:31:18 (16,934)
Fontaine, Dominique 3:56:04 (8,943)
Fontaine, Marie 5:45:32 (27,595)
Fookes, Anita 4:44:01 (19,588)
Foord, Karen 4:06:49 (11,505)
Foot, Susan 4:23:41 (15,224)
Forbes, Valery 3:57:33 (9,347)
Ford, Janet 6:22:24 (29,222)
Ford, Jenny 4:36:30 (18,021)
Ford, Karen 4:01:05 (10,296)
Ford, Katrina 3:42:09 (6,151)
Ford, Liz 5:45:55 (27,629)
Ford, Nina 4:48:01 (20,349)
Fordham, Chloe 4:41:33 (19,074)
Fordyce, Susan 4:18:10 (13,910)
Formby, Louise 4:14:09 (13,065)
Forrest, Debra 6:03:47 (28,579)
Forrest, Maureen 4:52:43 (21,257)
Forst, Janicke 4:08:10 (11,795)
Forster, Nicola 3:51:53 (8,045)
Forsyth, Mirjana 5:22:13 (25,619)
Fortess Mayer, Gail 3:07:56 (1,587)
Fortune, Carole 3:50:16 (7,732)
Fosker, Denise 4:52:24 (21,185)
Foster, Andrea 6:38:37 (29,601)
Foster, Debra 5:12:30 (24,431)
Foster, Eleanor 4:55:21 (21,831)
Foster, Emily 5:42:28 (27,367)
Foster, Jane 5:08:51 (23,913)
Foster, Kate 5:01:28 (22,799)
Foster, Kim 5:51:12 (27,961)

Foster, Rebecca	4:55:23 (21,842)
Foster, Shirley	5:14:38 (24,732)
Foster, Susan	6:39:17 (29,611)
Foster, Timothy	4:37:49 (18,320)
Foster, Tracy	4:29:47 (16,619)
Fouche, Christine	4:38:22 (18,473)
Fouche, Dominique	4:38:21 (18,466)
Fountain, Janine	4:44:12 (19,619)
Fountain, Michelle	5:25:51 (25,973)
Fouweather, Lisa	4:51:19 (20,950)
Fowkes, Gill	3:42:36 (6,235)
Fowler, Angela	4:38:26 (18,488)
Fowler, Anne	5:34:51 (26,791)
Fowler, Claire	4:36:43 (18,065)
Fowler, Jackie	4:10:34 (12,289)
Fowler, Lucy	4:49:46 (20,665)
Fowler, Mouveta	3:51:38 (7,993)
Fox, Amanda	5:13:08 (24,522)
Fox, Denise	3:45:37 (6,769)
Fox, Diana	3:45:45 (6,810)
Fox, Janine	4:55:23 (21,842)
Fox, Lisa	3:40:00 (5,788)
Fox, Sue	3:56:49 (9,137)
Fozzard, Lorraine	4:04:22 (10,959)
Fracas, Lyell	4:09:45 (12,117)
Fradley, Sharon	5:53:39 (28,099)
Fragoso, Belinda	4:52:33 (21,224)
Fraiser, Maureen	6:24:23 (29,271)
Frame, Melissa	4:41:58 (19,155)
France, Jacqueline	3:25:04 (3,385)
Francis, Alexandra	5:00:50 (22,707)
Francis, Annie	5:36:44 (26,926)
Francis, Linda	4:43:18 (19,451)
Francke, Bronwen	4:07:19 (11,617)
Frank, Flora	5:53:30 (28,090)
Frankard, Brigitte	4:46:39 (20,082)
Franke, Bergith	3:44:59 (6,684)
Franklin, Kay	4:07:50 (11,727)
Franklin, Marie	5:04:23 (23,197)
Franks, June	3:36:16 (5,117)
Franks, Susan	4:29:58 (16,684)
Fraser, Elinor	5:18:45 (25,242)
Fredman, Elizabeth	5:15:19 (24,843)
Freeborn, Kym	6:25:42 (29,299)
Freedman, Natasha	4:20:24 (14,449)
Freeman, Debra	6:08:44 (28,797)
Freeman, Jacqueline	6:17:01 (29,086)
Freeman, Kelly	5:41:50 (27,318)
Freeman, Poppy	4:44:15 (19,628)
Freeman, Susan	4:59:02 (22,468)
Freeman, Victoria	3:31:09 (4,349)
Freer, Katherine	6:39:30 (29,617)
French, Dawn	4:19:16 (14,183)
French, Karen	4:16:10 (13,500)
French, Margaret	4:54:29 (21,587)
Frend, Sue	4:50:27 (20,795)
Freriks, Marjan	6:40:12 (29,645)
Freshwater, Dawn	4:42:09 (19,192)
Freston, Claire	5:33:35 (26,657)
Frewin, Elaine	4:03:22 (10,740)
Frick, Anne	4:59:13 (22,488)
Friedel, Jacqueline	5:09:14 (23,973)
Friedman, Beth	4:01:04 (10,295)
Friel, Dympna	4:38:39 (18,537)
Frisby, Amanda	5:58:34 (28,348)
Frisby, Denise	4:52:13 (21,136)
Frisby, Julia	5:51:20 (27,972)
Frith, June	4:23:43 (15,230)
Frogley, Jane	3:21:42 (2,969)
Frommer, Beth	4:24:03 (15,305)
Frost, Lindsay	5:53:11 (28,078)
Fryer, Anna	5:12:34 (24,436)
Fuentes, Teresa	4:14:31 (13,131)
Fugler, Dannie	4:32:45 (17,263)
Fukuda, Kayoko	4:02:13 (10,527)
Fulk, Julie	5:51:17 (27,966)
Fullard, Brenda	3:54:43 (8,641)
Fuller, Lizzie	5:28:15 (26,201)
Furbank, Valerie	4:08:45 (11,923)
Fursey, Susan	6:00:43 (28,442)
Furze, Caroline	4:01:59 (10,482)
Fusger, Carole	6:13:15 (28,960)
Fussell, Valerie	3:59:02 (9,765)

Fyfe, Lesley	8:36:20 (30,253)
Gabbert, Leslie	4:27:45 (16,135)
Gaborit, Murielle	4:15:36 (13,387)
Gabriel, Annie Chantal	4:37:19 (18,200)
Galang, Marialuisa	6:34:21 (29,509)
Galbraith, Deirdre	4:49:37 (20,637)
Gale, Karin	5:08:17 (23,813)
Gallagher, Tess	5:16:57 (25,042)
Gallagher, Vicky	4:25:16 (15,568)
Gallichan, Sharon	7:09:18 (30,013)
Gamble, Claire	6:14:40 (29,013)
Gamblin, Judith	4:20:29 (14,471)
Gambrill, Barbara	4:52:02 (21,098)
Ganney, Gail	4:35:46 (17,877)
Gansheimer, Andrea	5:44:22 (27,498)
Gant, Jane	4:15:16 (13,327)
Gard, Caroline	4:52:32 (21,216)
Gardiner, Emma	5:51:57 (28,015)
Gardiner, Jill	5:13:04 (24,509)
Gardiner, Susan	4:36:46 (18,072)
Gardner, Kelly	5:14:26 (24,692)
Gardner, Sarah	4:52:42 (21,251)
Gardner-Hutchison, Tanya	5:23:02 (25,709)
Garland, Claire-Julia	4:50:16 (20,763)
Garlicki, Natasha	3:44:06 (6,509)
Garner, Susan	3:50:15 (7,728)
Garner-Jones, Annetta	4:22:41 (14,978)
Garnett, Kathleen	4:19:18 (14,194)
Garnier, Anna	4:42:10 (19,198)
Garnish, Nicola	6:59:04 (29,931)
Garrad, Shirley	5:41:02 (27,264)
Garrard, Natalie	5:04:34 (23,228)
Garred, Kerri	4:44:35 (19,692)
Garrett Lund, Rosalind	5:35:48 (26,867)
Garrod, Lorna	3:41:35 (6,048)
Garside, Sally	4:53:38 (21,444)
Garthwaite, Lucinda	4:55:35 (21,913)
Gartland, Alice	4:45:21 (19,832)
Garton, Elaine	5:13:59 (24,628)
Garvin, Sylvia	4:35:19 (17,779)
Garwood, Joanna	3:46:52 (7,014)
Gary, Amy	7:01:47 (29,958)
Gaskell, Kate	4:27:40 (16,107)
Gaskins, Claire	5:24:51 (25,862)
Gaston, Norma	6:21:38 (29,208)
Gates, Kimberly	5:13:12 (24,530)
Gatherer, Caron	6:40:01 (29,633)
Gatzert Snyder, Susan	4:03:37 (10,805)
Gaubert, Patricia	6:14:16 (28,999)
Gauclain, Patricia	4:30:47 (16,804)
Gaudrin, Christiane	3:56:21 (9,007)
Gaughan, Sandra	4:20:32 (14,483)
Gaunt, Nicola	3:32:17 (4,504)
Gautier, Charlyne	3:56:43 (9,109)
Gawne, Maria	5:08:01 (23,771)
Gay, Alison	4:13:36 (12,958)
Gay, Nicola	5:06:47 (23,586)
Gaynor, Claire	4:44:22 (19,647)
Gayter, Sharon	3:34:18 (4,801)
Gaze, Janet	4:22:13 (14,865)
Gazzani, Lena	4:01:52 (10,455)
Gbadamosi, Dayo	6:15:06 (29,027)
Geddes, Alison	3:44:19 (6,546)
Geddes, Trina	5:21:27 (25,523)
Gee, Elaine	4:31:11 (16,898)
Geiser, Françoise	3:59:02 (9,765)
Gellman, Carol	4:09:00 (11,978)
Gent, Sarah	4:13:47 (12,995)
George, Annie	5:00:29 (22,659)
George, Carey	5:46:37 (27,675)
Georghiou, Dorothy	3:12:14 (1,936)
Georgiou, Georgina	5:31:24 (26,483)
Gerassi, Luciana	4:32:56 (17,298)
Gerrard, Mandy	6:16:50 (29,082)
Gerrish, Iona	4:28:11 (16,231)
Gestetner, Sarah	3:45:42 (6,796)
Ghale Soltani, Vanessa	7:37:25 (30,152)
Gibbs, Dawn	3:19:16 (2,685)
Gibbs, Esther	6:02:27 (28,519)
Gibert, Julia	5:03:49 (23,103)
Giblett, Janet	4:23:18 (15,134)
Giboney, Lynda	6:53:02 (29,845)
Gibson, Beverley	3:39:16 (5,620)

Gibson, Clare	7:22:22 (30,092)
Gibson, Colleen	5:42:17 (27,354)
Gibson, Debbie	5:29:53 (26,362)
Gibson, Kirsty	4:38:34 (18,519)
Gibson, Lee-Ann	5:07:01 (23,618)
Gibson, Lesley	6:12:27 (28,945)
Gibson, Margaret	4:37:23 (18,219)
Gielen, Heidi	3:22:00 (3,000)
Gifford, Becky	5:09:38 (24,035)
Gilbert, Beverley	4:16:10 (13,500)
Gilbert, Lynn	4:46:08 (19,967)
Gilbertson, Karen	5:10:57 (24,206)
Gilbertson, Katherine	6:25:15 (29,289)
Giles, Liza	4:56:06 (22,003)
Gilham, Wendy	5:06:35 (23,557)
Gilhooley, Allan	3:48:37 (7,382)
Gilkes, Julia	3:49:26 (7,559)
Gill, Gillian	4:35:43 (17,869)
Gill, Laura	5:41:28 (27,295)
Gill, Lisa	3:52:31 (8,173)
Gill, Michaela	4:48:41 (20,466)
Gillespie, Alyse	6:28:31 (29,374)
Gillespie, Geraldine	4:04:27 (10,977)
Gillespie, Janet	4:35:15 (17,761)
Gillett, Christy	6:13:30 (28,973)
Gillett, Sonja	4:09:04 (12,001)
Gillingham, Rachel	4:01:38 (10,418)
Gillison, Fiona	5:13:02 (24,505)
Gilliver, Melissa	6:38:39 (29,602)
Gillmore, Roopinder	4:40:04 (18,799)
Gilman, Catherine	4:46:49 (20,119)
Gilmer, Natalie	5:02:18 (22,915)
Gilmmer, Wendy	5:05:12 (23,018)
Gilmour, Kerry	4:20:29 (14,471)
Gilroy, Anne	3:47:00 (7,038)
Gisborne, Sally	3:57:48 (9,431)
Gittins, Joanne	3:59:12 (9,815)
Gittins, Sylvia	5:25:54 (25,976)
Glass, Rachel	4:57:43 (22,251)
Glazebrook, Jacqueline	5:33:29 (26,647)
Gleadall, Victoria	4:18:08 (13,895)
Glencross, Amy	4:29:08 (16,458)
Glendinning, Michael	4:17:26 (13,756)
Glover, Beryl	4:22:57 (15,052)
Gluck, Gillian	5:34:31 (26,759)
Goddard, Claire	6:34:58 (29,519)
Goddard, Lesley	5:30:39 (26,423)
Goddard, Lexie	5:33:17 (26,633)
Godding Feltham, Lisa	3:02:30 (1,188)
Godfrey, Lisa	4:16:47 (13,632)
Goeggel, Daniela	3:39:54 (5,759)
Goggin, Patricia	4:30:41 (16,783)
Golding, Samantha	4:37:14 (18,179)
Goldring, Kirstin	5:17:16 (25,077)
Goldsack, Sandra	3:48:22 (7,332)
Goldsmith, Gail	3:54:42 (8,634)
Gomez, Romila	4:06:55 (11,531)
Gomez-Liss, Christine	6:10:16 (28,870)
Good, Juliet	3:53:58 (8,471)
Goodall, Greta	4:28:09 (16,221)
Goodall, Patricia	4:17:14 (13,725)
Goodchild, Sarah	5:55:05 (28,159)
Goode, Stephanie	4:30:36 (16,765)
Goodhead, Emma	3:59:50 (10,005)
Goodier, Joann	8:54:30 (30,269)
Gooding, Melanie	5:15:19 (24,843)
Goodings, Karen	5:17:29 (25,107)
Goodsall, Sarah	6:04:52 (28,638)
Goodwin, Fiona	4:47:28 (20,252)
Goodwin, Helen	4:40:16 (18,830)
Goodwin, Jean	4:16:07 (13,490)
Goodwin, Rhona	4:05:25 (11,188)
Goody, Samantha	5:04:42 (23,246)
Goorno, Sarah	4:51:56 (21,081)
Goosey, Suzanne	4:40:16 (18,830)
Gordon, Hayley	6:53:03 (29,846)
Gordon, Tanya	4:39:58 (18,783)
Gorman, Barbara	5:06:32 (23,548)
Gormill, Sharon	5:19:33 (25,312)
Gormley, Teresa	4:39:32 (18,700)
Gosbee, Karen	4:01:12 (10,319)
Gosden, Charlotte	5:12:48 (24,470)
Gosling, Samantha	5:20:49 (25,447)

Goss, Elizabeth 5:40:28 (27,220)
Goth, Asa 4:30:10 (16,716)
Gothard, Helen 4:03:35 (10,797)
Goudie, Angela 5:47:01 (27,707)
Gough, Anna 3:51:45 (8,015)
Gough, Jean 5:09:17 (23,980)
Gough, Patricia 6:18:02 (29,115)
Gough, Suzanne 5:15:27 (24,862)
Gough, Terri 5:08:16 (23,809)
Goujart, Marielle 6:47:35 (29,770)
Gould, Louise 6:59:14 (29,933)
Gourlay, Moira 4:35:56 (17,913)
Gourlay, Susan 4:35:50 (17,887)
Gowan, Nicki 4:04:33 (11,007)
Grace, Alison 3:31:07 (4,343)
Grace, Lisa 4:35:37 (17,846)
Grace, Tina 6:51:46 (29,827)
Graham, Audrey 4:03:06 (10,685)
Graham, Hermine 4:26:53 (15,932)
Graham, Jane 5:20:22 (25,390)
Graham, Jane 6:06:03 (28,689)
Graham, Jean 5:21:12 (25,489)
Graham, Kate 4:38:45 (18,559)
Graham, Krista 4:48:13 (20,388)
Graham, Teresa 6:06:00 (28,686)
Grahame, Victoria 6:05:10 (28,646)
Grahamslaw, Margaret 4:56:58 (22,139)
Grainger, Louise 4:28:12 (16,238)
Gramlick, Kim 5:51:32 (27,986)
Grammer, Charlotte 4:37:08 (18,152)
Granados, Veronica 3:36:42 (5,191)
Grandy, Sarah 3:29:25 (4,066)
Grange, Larrisa 5:45:30 (27,591)
Grant, Jessica 5:42:19 (27,358)
Grassmann, Eva 5:05:31 (23,387)
Gravell, Rhiannon 4:20:22 (14,443)
Graves, Sharon 4:54:30 (21,594)
Gray, Aerian 5:05:35 (23,397)
Gray, Belinda 4:19:00 (14,115)
Gray, Bernadette 6:13:07 (28,958)
Gray, Jenny 2:57:06 (753)
Gray, Kate 7:27:53 (30,120)
Gray, Melanie 4:29:53 (16,654)
Gray, Miriam 3:41:56 (6,113)
Gray, Rose 5:59:49 (28,411)
Graysmark, Suzanne 3:33:03 (4,611)
Greaves, Deborah 4:54:58 (21,721)
Greaves, Hilary 3:41:48 (6,091)
Greaves, Susan 5:21:52 (25,572)
Green, Ana-Maria 4:03:27 (10,760)
Green, Anne 4:42:26 (19,260)
Green, Anne 5:27:33 (26,130)
Green, Denise 3:33:34 (4,691)
Green, Denise 4:24:24 (15,370)
Green, Heather 4:15:32 (13,373)
Green, Helen 4:41:40 (19,097)
Green, Jan 4:34:42 (17,658)
Green, Jillian 5:45:31 (27,594)
Green, Katharine 4:54:05 (21,530)
Green, Katherine 5:32:19 (26,550)
Green, Kathryn 5:07:45 (23,740)
Green, Mary 5:24:15 (25,812)
Green, Nicola 5:02:22 (22,925)
Green, Rachael 6:02:09 (28,511)
Greene, Karen 4:25:48 (15,672)
Greene, Louise 4:41:32 (19,067)
Greenfield, Corey 6:16:42 (29,078)
Greenfield, Jane 4:58:55 (22,443)
Greenhill, Cheryl 5:26:33 (26,048)
Greenland, Felicity 3:57:31 (9,334)
Greenwood, Celia 3:52:06 (8,097)
Greenwood, Karen 4:58:40 (22,407)
Greenwood, Katherine 5:28:20 (26,212)
Greenwood, Valerie 4:38:00 (18,371)
Greewal, Barbara 4:40:14 (18,819)
Gregory, Joanna 4:30:24 (16,743)
Gregory, Lisa 4:18:46 (14,074)
Gregory, Lisa 4:26:51 (15,920)
Gregson, Anne 6:41:05 (29,663)
Greig, Kirsty 4:08:47 (11,934)
Greswell, Lucy 4:45:23 (19,841)
Grey, Eleanor 3:48:14 (7,309)
Grice, Henrietta 4:48:00 (20,345)
Grice-Jackson, Nichole 4:51:33 (20,995)
Grieveson, Kate 5:10:40 (24,172)
Griffin, Barbara 4:12:15 (12,679)
Griffin, Elizabeth 3:48:56 (7,448)
Griffin, Emma 4:43:12 (19,427)
Griffin, Suzannah 3:31:13 (4,357)
Griffith, Jane 4:16:40 (13,601)
Griffith, Joan 4:34:37 (17,646)
Griffiths, Bethan 5:45:44 (27,611)
Griffiths, Cordelia 4:37:03 (18,137)
Griffiths, Deborah 5:25:12 (25,906)
Griffiths, Donna 4:46:29 (20,048)
Griffiths, Fay 5:34:25 (26,746)
Griffiths, Karrie 3:43:21 (6,371)
Griffiths, Leah 5:14:14 (24,663)
Grill, Mireille 4:24:48 (15,459)
Grilleres, Sandrine 6:02:59 (28,540)
Grimditch, Sandra 6:17:38 (29,103)
Grimshaw, Rachel 4:31:10 (16,893)
Grimwood, Anne 3:12:17 (1,940)
Grindu, Christiane 4:02:34 (10,588)
Grisdale, Caroline 5:19:35 (25,317)
Gristwood, Shelley 4:52:25 (21,189)
Grobler, Gina 4:55:36 (21,922)
Groeneveld, Jolande 5:53:51 (28,109)
Groenningen, Gry-Hege 5:33:12 (26,627)
Groff, Sonja 5:50:52 (27,948)
Grose, Katherine 3:37:38 (5,355)
Grouse, Mandy 4:43:08 (19,413)
Grout, Carol 4:51:37 (21,012)
Grove, Madeleine 4:38:25 (18,485)
Grove, Natalie 6:49:30 (29,796)
Grover, Sonia 5:03:38 (23,073)
Groves, Jamila 5:31:17 (26,476)
Groves, Katheleen 6:09:04 (28,818)
Gruening, Elisabeth 4:56:38 (22,090)
Gruffydd, Mari 5:01:10 (22,760)
Grundy, Karen 5:09:13 (23,972)
Guard, Maureen 4:11:36 (12,525)
Gudka, Punam 6:21:01 (29,193)
Guenard, Susan 5:09:23 (23,995)
Guest, Lynn 4:03:55 (10,866)
Guest, Sarah 3:08:53 (1,663)
Guhl, Bonnie 4:36:38 (18,048)
Guildford, Alison 4:45:49 (19,905)
Guite, Elizabeth 6:30:47 (29,430)
Gulickx, Laura 5:11:35 (24,300)
Gullick, Susan 5:37:34 (26,989)
Gundry, Jacqueline 4:10:25 (12,260)
Gunn, Jane 5:05:38 (23,405)
Gunn, Sandra 4:48:39 (20,461)
Gunn, Simone 4:43:04 (19,399)
Gunter, Fiona 3:42:56 (6,293)
Gurner, Lyn 5:12:22 (24,408)
Gurry, Gaye 4:44:41 (19,712)
Gurtner, Pina 5:05:14 (23,327)
Gurung, Dina 4:55:17 (21,810)
Gustafson, Gerrie 6:32:44 (29,471)
Gustavsson, Margareta 4:42:20 (19,236)
Guttridge, Celia 6:30:25 (29,424)
Guttridge, Kirsty 3:42:55 (6,290)
Guy, Annette 4:08:39 (11,906)
Guy, Rosie 4:28:34 (16,331)
Gwaderi, Razia 6:23:33 (29,246)
Haddleton, Samantha 3:14:54 (2,208)
Hadingham, Jacqueline 4:30:36 (16,765)
Hadingham, Rachel 6:08:37 (28,791)
Hadley, Glynis 4:43:18 (19,451)
Haegel Arpin, Helene 3:36:44 (5,200)
Hagan, Gillian 4:26:34 (15,865)
Hagan, Grace 7:23:48 (30,098)
Haggar, Rachel 4:13:08 (12,845)
Hagger, Wolleen 6:34:32 (29,513)
Haigh, Amanda 3:22:54 (3,097)
Hailey, Dee 3:55:16 (8,756)
Haines, Lindsay 3:51:44 (8,013)
Haines, Sarah 4:10:50 (12,355)
Haining, Leanne 3:23:07 (3,129)
Hainy, Petra 5:15:08 (24,802)
Hakem, Yamini 4:40:41 (18,917)
Hakin, Nazeema 6:05:59 (28,685)
Halbert, Dinah 7:01:17 (29,955)
Hale, Deborah 5:01:44 (22,828)
Hale, Gemma 5:05:51 (23,439)
Hales, Pippa 4:45:36 (19,875)
Hales, Rachel 3:45:03 (6,695)
Hales, Victoria 5:00:53 (22,718)
Halim, Ayesha 6:30:00 (29,409)
Hall, Alison 4:43:15 (19,438)
Hall, Amanda 4:44:43 (19,720)
Hall, Anita 4:44:43 (19,720)
Hall, Beverley 4:28:07 (16,217)
Hall, Carol 4:33:21 (17,387)
Hall, Catriona 5:09:08 (23,959)
Hall, Debi 5:16:22 (24,966)
Hall, Elaine 4:33:25 (17,398)
Hall, Emma 6:04:53 (28,639)
Hall, Gail 3:54:45 (8,648)
Hall, Gillian 4:08:55 (11,959)
Hall, Jennifer 5:34:00 (26,692)
Hall, Jill 5:26:52 (26,074)
Hall, Julia 4:44:39 (19,704)
Hall, Kathryn 6:01:22 (28,473)
Hall, Louise 4:42:33 (19,281)
Hall, Maureen 4:53:41 (21,450)
Hall, Michelle 4:42:17 (19,224)
Hall, Nichola 6:28:17 (29,362)
Hall, Pauline 3:45:43 (6,802)
Hall, Sandra 5:05:27 (23,372)
Hall, Sarah 4:23:00 (15,063)
Hall, Susannah 3:54:34 (8,605)
Hall, Suzanne 4:02:05 (10,501)
Hall, Suzie 6:03:42 (28,574)
Hall, Thérèse 4:31:16 (16,922)
Hall, Victoria 6:07:35 (28,748)
Hallacy, Allison 4:45:16 (19,818)
Hallam, Kathryn 4:13:19 (12,878)
Hallam, Rosemary 4:41:06 (18,996)
Hallett, Helga 5:31:14 (26,471)
Halley, Linda 5:18:37 (25,226)
Halliday, Freja 3:55:31 (8,800)
Halliwell, Tina 4:52:29 (21,200)
Halse, Katy 5:55:29 (28,190)
Halton, Janette 5:06:54 (23,601)
Hambly, Caroline 5:26:34 (26,050)
Hames, Victoria 4:14:29 (13,123)
Hamill, Terri 5:38:39 (27,059)
Hamilton Smith, Joanna 5:51:41 (27,995)
Hamling, Karen 6:47:08 (29,760)
Hammatt, Julie 5:44:44 (27,542)
Hammond, Janet 6:44:11 (29,724)
Hammond, Lesley 4:35:38 (17,849)
Hammond, Paula 4:32:42 (17,247)
Hampshire, Susan 4:34:02 (17,541)
Han, Hannah 5:18:13 (25,178)
Hanby, Rowena 5:22:32 (25,653)
Handford, Polly 4:29:34 (16,564)
Handforth, Deborah 5:24:02 (25,793)
Handley, Patricia 5:12:58 (24,493)
Handscomb, Joanne 4:45:45 (19,894)
Hanley, Patricia 3:43:34 (6,408)
Hanley, Susan 4:34:40 (17,652)
Hanlon, Kate 5:42:39 (27,391)
Hannah, Linda 6:03:47 (28,579)
Hannah, Sally 3:12:12 (1,932)
Hanney, Heather 4:54:27 (21,578)
Hannum, Emily 3:27:42 (3,741)
Hansen, Molly 4:14:53 (13,231)
Hansen, Birthe 3:40:40 (5,891)
Hansen, Gyda 4:25:35 (15,636)
Hanson, Clare 5:07:09 (23,641)
Harding, Clare 4:17:53 (13,848)
Harding, Giselle 4:47:31 (20,267)
Harding, Jonquil 3:59:31 (9,925)
Harding, Tracy 4:48:33 (20,446)
Hardisty, Anne 5:25:47 (25,965)
Hardisty, Jayne Lesley 4:19:59 (14,361)
Hardman, Gina 3:44:33 (6,588)
Hardman, Victoria 4:19:53 (14,333)
Hardwick, Jeanette 3:09:45 (1,734)
Hardwick-Burrow, Anne-Marie 6:11:44 (28,918)
Hardy, Clare 5:34:33 (26,761)
Hardy, Dawn 3:19:13 (2,676)
Hardy, Debbie 4:54:09 (21,542)
Hardy, Karen 5:46:56 (27,695)
Hardy, Lorraine 3:19:36 (2,718)

Hardy, Pauline	5:43:17 (27,424)	
Hardy, Victoria	3:52:18 (8,134)	
Hardyman, Christine	4:05:57 (11,339)	
Hare Duke, Hilary	3:36:10 (5,099)	
Hargie, Patricia	4:54:45 (21,660)	
Hargreaves, Carol	3:12:48 (1,986)	
Hargreaves, Caroline	4:50:43 (20,829)	
Hargy, Helen	4:37:14 (18,179)	
Harland, Rachel	4:15:34 (13,381)	
Harley, Lillie	4:50:33 (20,806)	
Harling, Jane	4:41:39 (19,093)	
Harman, Maria	5:09:54 (24,069)	
Harman, Vanessa	5:12:01 (24,359)	
Harms, Carole	7:06:20 (29,989)	
Harmsworth, Anne	3:57:37 (9,369)	
Harne, Vicky	4:01:19 (10,342)	
Harper, Louise	4:23:23 (15,148)	
Harper, Soumi	4:01:54 (10,463)	
Harries, Barbara	3:09:32 (1,719)	
Harrington, Teresa	4:29:24 (16,519)	
Harris, Clare	4:35:58 (17,925)	
Harris, Clare	6:46:43 (29,754)	
Harris, Deborah	5:17:56 (25,151)	
Harris, Deborah	5:56:25 (28,237)	
Harris, Gillian	6:15:11 (29,029)	
Harris, Hilary	5:01:32 (22,808)	
Harris, Jane	4:40:33 (18,885)	
Harris, Jennifer	4:48:55 (20,509)	
Harris, Julie	5:45:07 (27,566)	
Harris, Margaret	5:49:41 (27,881)	
Harris, Melanie	6:57:28 (29,914)	
Harris, Nikki	4:44:43 (19,720)	
Harris, Rachel	5:06:47 (23,586)	
Harris, Sandra	5:25:25 (25,932)	
Harris, Sue	5:49:59 (27,901)	
Harris, Virginia	5:58:51 (28,360)	
Harris Jones, Rebecca	4:20:32 (14,483)	
Harrison, Angela	5:50:28 (27,924)	
Harrison, Claire	3:59:23 (9,876)	
Harrison, Emma	5:00:50 (22,707)	
Harrison, Fay	5:38:39 (27,059)	
Harrison, Jane	6:54:28 (29,867)	
Harrison, Judith	5:29:51 (26,355)	
Harrison, Julia	5:09:19 (23,983)	
Harrison, Julie	5:11:00 (24,212)	
Harrison, Karen	5:11:41 (24,310)	
Harrison, Lynsey	4:14:31 (13,131)	
Harrison, Sarah	3:49:46 (7,639)	
Harrison, Susanna	3:02:22 (1,181)	
Harrison, Tricia	4:12:17 (12,687)	
Harrop, June	4:34:43 (17,662)	
Hart, Gail	5:03:43 (23,084)	
Hart, Karen	5:10:29 (24,140)	
Hart, Katherine	6:02:58 (28,539)	
Hartas, Angela	4:33:20 (17,378)	
Hartigan, Bev	2:37:45 (132)	
Hartley, Thomas	4:12:02 (12,620)	
Harton-Carter, Elizabeth	6:01:07 (28,461)	
Hartong, Mary	5:02:18 (22,915)	
Hartshorn, Deborah	5:05:25 (23,363)	
Hartsilver, Emma	4:22:35 (14,948)	
Harvey, Diana	3:42:59 (6,299)	
Harvey, Hazel	5:08:30 (23,847)	
Harvey, Joanne	5:09:37 (24,032)	
Harvey, Katherine	3:10:02 (1,745)	
Harvey, Louise	4:47:54 (20,325)	
Harvey, Michelle	4:51:40 (21,025)	
Haselhurst, Sally	4:32:24 (17,194)	
Haselwood, Julie	4:17:07 (13,692)	
Haste, Carol	5:29:37 (26,339)	
Hastings, Karie	3:47:14 (7,069)	
Hastings, Linda	5:50:01 (27,906)	
Hasuda, Junko	5:55:04 (28,158)	
Hatch, Alison	3:26:33 (3,565)	
Hathaway, Daphne	4:42:46 (19,323)	
Hathway, Kelly	5:56:59 (28,269)	
Hathway, Miranda	3:35:24 (4,971)	
Haukeland, Gunhild	4:42:39 (19,303)	
Havard, Linda	6:33:12 (29,487)	
Hawes, Dawn	3:40:28 (5,863)	
Hawes, Sally	4:44:00 (19,586)	
Hawken, Valerie	5:15:06 (24,797)	
Hawker, Pippa	5:30:17 (26,395)	
Hawkes, Pauline	3:44:09 (6,518)	
Hawkins, Natalie	4:17:59 (13,867)	
Hawkins, Patricia	4:42:21 (19,239)	
Hawkins, Sally	6:11:03 (28,890)	
Hawkridge, Julie	6:04:30 (28,618)	
Hay, Anna	4:21:23 (14,666)	
Hay, Collette	7:06:28 (29,991)	
Hay, Helen	5:42:45 (27,394)	
Hay, Laura	4:58:21 (22,351)	
Hay, Melanie	3:57:34 (9,352)	
Hayes, Carol	4:20:33 (14,489)	
Hayes, Kate	5:19:33 (25,312)	
Hayes, Kathy	4:26:33 (15,856)	
Hayes, Virginia	4:37:37 (18,282)	
Hayhow, Prunella	3:19:54 (2,756)	
Hayhow-Khan, Toni	5:18:07 (25,175)	
Hayman, Dawn	3:51:16 (7,925)	
Hayman Hart, Deborah	6:56:53 (29,907)	
Haymes, Joanne Lee	5:27:34 (26,134)	
Hayter, Susan	5:05:45 (23,422)	
Hayton, Diane	4:28:22 (16,277)	
Hayward, Emily	4:17:27 (13,761)	
Hayward, Jan	5:42:56 (27,404)	
Hayward, Keeley	5:07:18 (23,664)	
Hayward, Nikki	3:39:28 (5,667)	
Hayward, Sarah	3:39:13 (5,612)	
Hayward, Tim	3:40:26 (5,854)	
Hayward, Victoria	5:42:56 (27,404)	
Hazle, Kate	4:34:29 (17,623)	
Hazlitt, Fru	4:17:39 (13,802)	
Head, Justine	3:41:37 (6,059)	
Head, Kristen	5:40:33 (27,234)	
Heal, Caroline	3:43:53 (6,467)	
Healey, Jeanne Lilian	5:56:15 (28,224)	
Healy, Susan	5:01:03 (22,740)	
Heaps, Rachael	5:44:05 (27,482)	
Heath, Karen	4:46:32 (20,063)	
Heath, Rachel	4:24:20 (15,356)	
Heath, Renée	3:54:44 (8,646)	
Heather, Julie	4:42:19 (19,231)	
Heather-Hayes, Alice	4:11:29 (12,499)	
Heathfield-Eliott, Lynette	3:38:54 (5,560)	
Heathwood, Tina	4:22:47 (15,000)	
Heaton, Catherine	5:59:59 (28,420)	
Heaton, Maria	6:00:02 (28,421)	
Heaton, Mathilde	3:49:03 (7,475)	
Heaver, Darrell	5:48:28 (27,815)	
Heaver, Eileen	5:16:29 (24,986)	
Heavey, Judith	4:49:09 (20,552)	
Heaviside, Karen	3:12:52 (1,991)	
Heble, Geeta	7:32:55 (30,146)	
Heck, Miranda	4:33:55 (17,523)	
Heckel, Sally-Ann	4:31:47 (17,056)	
Hecks, Mary	4:30:06 (16,708)	
Hector, Sarah	4:14:14 (13,082)	
Hedberg, Maj	4:35:45 (17,875)	
Heffernan Smith, Sue	6:18:16 (29,122)	
Heggs, Donna	6:07:11 (28,729)	
Heilbron, Jane	6:24:51 (29,279)	
Heinze, Angela	4:08:44 (11,920)	
Heiriss, Carole	6:24:04 (29,262)	
Heitman, Anna	6:05:21 (28,657)	
Hellenburgh, Alice	5:56:13 (28,221)	
Heller, Annette	7:55:48 (30,199)	
Hellerman, Molly	4:19:17 (14,189)	
Helliwell, Brenda	4:46:45 (20,105)	
Helmsley, Julia	5:08:52 (23,915)	
Heming, Jenny	4:13:06 (12,836)	
Hemmings, Lisa	5:55:27 (28,185)	
Hemmings, Rachel	4:40:07 (18,804)	
Hemsworth, Caroline	3:09:39 (1,728)	
Hemsworth, Marion	4:05:47 (11,293)	
Henderson, Jane	5:26:33 (26,048)	
Henderson, Kim	5:15:02 (24,786)	
Henderson, Manya	5:09:28 (24,012)	
Heneage, Phoebe	4:56:09 (22,011)	
Henes, Pamela	4:57:43 (22,251)	
Hennessy, Annabel	5:20:19 (25,387)	
Henry, Kathryn	3:39:57 (5,775)	
Henry, Rachel	6:31:10 (29,435)	
Henson, Lorraine	6:09:34 (28,838)	
Hentschke, Rosslyn	3:46:21 (6,922)	
Henwood, Denise	5:28:46 (26,264)	
Hepher, Lesley	4:51:36 (21,010)	
Hepner, Louise	4:21:10 (14,621)	
Heppner, Jane	4:21:10 (14,621)	
Heracleous, Kate	3:50:33 (7,782)	
Hermann, Elizabeth	4:36:17 (17,973)	
Herstritt, Paula	5:06:39 (23,569)	
Hesketh, Brenda	3:48:14 (7,309)	
Heslop, Angela	5:00:30 (22,663)	
Heslop, Christine	4:28:18 (16,262)	
Heslop, Kirstie	5:39:49 (27,164)	
Heslop, Rosalind	7:08:02 (30,008)	
Hesse, Deborah	7:16:36 (30,060)	
Hetland, Grete	4:45:50 (19,908)	
Heuer, Jacqueline	6:00:49 (28,448)	
Heusschen, Brigitte	4:22:01 (14,818)	
Hewitt, Anna	4:16:48 (13,635)	
Hewitt, Elizabeth	5:05:23 (23,356)	
Hewitt, Sally	5:20:30 (25,408)	
Hewlett, Patricia	5:15:33 (24,875)	
Hexwood, Jane	5:07:02 (23,621)	
Hey, Susie	4:21:59 (14,808)	
Heyen, Anita	5:08:48 (23,907)	
Heyer, Kimberly	5:36:51 (26,934)	
Heyes, Jill	4:25:55 (15,707)	
Heys, Susan	5:17:49 (25,142)	
Hibberd, Pam	5:17:23 (25,091)	
Hickey, Audrey	7:08:25 (30,010)	
Hickey, Karen	5:43:51 (27,461)	
Hickling, Tania	4:26:01 (15,736)	
Hickman, Clare	5:34:17 (26,732)	
Hicks, Beverley	6:10:40 (28,880)	
Hicks, India	4:46:20 (20,016)	
Hicks, Janice	4:40:42 (18,921)	
Hicks, Monique	4:40:15 (18,826)	
Hier, Diane	3:40:20 (5,836)	
Higgin, Jilly	4:31:35 (17,003)	
Higgins, Marion	5:55:12 (28,164)	
Higgins, Nicky	4:28:13 (16,244)	
Higgs, Deborah	5:27:10 (26,097)	
Higgs, Sarah	5:14:52 (24,760)	
Higson, Deborah	3:56:00 (8,919)	
Hilder, Lorraine	4:51:22 (20,963)	
Hill, Andrea	3:22:59 (3,111)	
Hill, Angela	5:03:18 (23,042)	
Hill, Beverley	5:34:47 (26,779)	
Hill, Catherine	4:57:22 (22,201)	
Hill, Charlotte	5:35:33 (26,850)	
Hill, Christine	5:22:29 (25,646)	
Hill, Claire	4:38:04 (18,389)	
Hill, Claire	6:28:27 (29,369)	
Hill, Diane	4:12:22 (12,707)	
Hill, Janet	5:39:05 (27,092)	
Hill, Jillian	3:52:22 (8,146)	
Hill, Joanne	5:32:25 (26,567)	
Hill, Judy	5:53:47 (28,107)	
Hill, Julie	3:28:47 (3,957)	
Hill, Lorraine	4:48:02 (20,354)	
Hill, Louisa	4:46:28 (20,045)	
Hill, Naomi	4:21:51 (14,774)	
Hill, Pamela	6:45:23 (29,742)	
Hill, Paula	3:22:04 (3,009)	
Hill, Rachel	4:27:09 (16,002)	
Hill, Sarah	3:59:50 (10,005)	
Hill, Sarah	4:03:17 (10,718)	
Hill, Sarah	5:32:41 (26,591)	
Hill, Sophie	6:50:39 (29,815)	
Hill, Teresa	4:16:34 (13,586)	
Hillary, Judith	5:36:05 (26,886)	
Hiller, Alison	5:50:14 (27,915)	
Hiller, Sandra	5:39:02 (27,088)	
Hill-Firth, Carol	5:46:21 (27,650)	
Hilliard, Marie	6:19:19 (29,140)	
Hills, Amelia	4:15:51 (13,434)	
Hills, Jill	3:16:22 (2,348)	
Hills, Julie	4:53:42 (21,454)	
Hills, Lisa	5:16:03 (24,933)	
Hills, Nicola	3:07:57 (1,589)	
Hiltbrunner, Doris	5:43:54 (27,465)	
Hilton, Clare	5:57:22 (28,287)	
Hilton, Sally	5:25:38 (25,954)	
Hinchelwood, Carol	8:07:36 (30,223)	
Hinchliffe, Sara	4:14:54 (13,236)	
Hinder, Heidi	4:20:33 (14,489)	

LONDON MARATHON

Hindle, Caroline	3:30:59 (4,326)
Hines, Barbara	5:37:29 (26,976)
Hinge, Caroline	4:45:47 (19,900)
Hinne, Stephanie	3:57:24 (9,289)
Hinshelwood, Linda	5:00:57 (22,725)
Hipwell, Carol	4:53:04 (21,330)
Hirn, Catherine	5:06:24 (23,536)
Hiroyama, Harumi	2:29:01 (61)
Hirth, Yvette	7:07:35 (30,002)
Hiscoke, Sarah	5:29:06 (26,295)
Hitch, Helen	3:33:27 (4,683)
Hitchman, Lisa-Jane	7:09:22 (30,014)
Ho, Sandra	7:12:33 (30,037)
Hoard, Carol	4:23:29 (15,169)
Hoare, Elizabeth	5:57:45 (28,314)
Hoare, Nicola	4:05:40 (11,256)
Hobbs, Joanna	4:51:30 (20,982)
Hobbs, Rachel	4:24:02 (15,302)
Hobday, Jackie	4:25:27 (15,602)
Hobson, Dorte	4:08:08 (11,790)
Hodby, Eleanor	3:41:14 (5,993)
Hodges, Claire	4:11:57 (12,596)
Hodges, Laura	4:31:57 (17,105)
Hodgkins, Wendy	4:56:33 (22,079)
Hodgkinson, Hero	3:57:23 (9,283)
Hodgkiss, Nikki	4:00:39 (10,193)
Hodgman, Karen	4:38:17 (18,450)
Hodgson, Charlotte	5:28:18 (26,208)
Hodgson, Kirsten	3:50:33 (7,782)
Hodgson, Lesley Anne	5:19:33 (25,312)
Hodkin, Janet	4:04:57 (11,106)
Hodkinson, Julia	6:16:10 (29,063)
Hodkinson, Sally	5:24:58 (25,882)
Hodsdon, Laura	6:47:45 (29,773)
Hodson, Catherine	5:09:39 (24,039)
Hoffman, Tali	6:39:06 (29,609)
Hofmeijer, Karin	4:19:49 (14,318)
Hogan, Fiona	4:37:51 (18,333)
Hogan, Susan	3:37:36 (5,350)
Hogan, Tracey	5:48:17 (27,798)
Hogg, Heather	5:38:22 (27,040)
Hohl, Jacqueline	4:55:00 (21,732)
Holden, Atie	5:57:39 (28,307)
Holden, Avis	4:41:45 (19,112)
Holden, Denise	4:29:50 (16,634)
Holden, Dorothy	4:58:51 (22,434)
Holden, Janet	5:41:29 (27,298)
Holden, Marissa	3:57:44 (9,403)
Holden, Meriel	4:05:04 (11,129)
Holden, Mo Elizabeth	7:14:37 (30,047)
Holden, Rachael	4:10:57 (12,389)
Holdsworth, Lynn	5:42:29 (27,374)
Holdway, Belinda	3:58:45 (9,685)
Holgate, Catherine	5:30:33 (26,417)
Holgate, Julie	5:23:25 (25,733)
Holguin, Terry	3:42:46 (6,265)
Holland, Claire	4:48:58 (20,521)
Holland, Davina	4:53:47 (21,470)
Holland, Jane	4:14:27 (13,116)
Holland, Justine	4:18:21 (13,972)
Holland, Tamsin	6:02:51 (28,533)
Hollingdale, Mary	8:44:56 (30,263)
Hollinger, Ruth	4:11:32 (12,508)
Hollingsworth, Kelly	4:09:00 (11,978)
Hollis, Bridget	5:42:46 (27,395)
Holloway, Catherine	3:15:58 (2,319)
Holmes, Deborah	4:51:55 (21,073)
Holmes, Elizabeth	4:36:30 (18,021)
Holmes, Emily	5:03:16 (23,036)
Holmes, Gillian	4:15:13 (13,312)
Holmes, Jane	5:10:01 (24,084)
Holmes, Sas	6:39:30 (29,617)
Holmstrom, Katie	3:48:57 (7,451)
Holroyd, Catherine	6:24:19 (29,269)
Holt, Genevieve	5:34:09 (26,716)
Holt, Gillian	5:34:08 (26,713)
Holt, Midge	5:31:41 (26,506)
Holt, Rachel	5:41:33 (27,302)
Homer, Britta	3:11:54 (1,905)
Hone, Rebecca	5:39:47 (27,162)
Honerlagen, Ulrike	5:44:31 (27,516)
Honeybell, Lorraine	5:09:45 (24,051)
Honeybunn, Ellen	6:44:23 (29,727)

Hooftman, Ria	5:03:37 (23,072)
Hooker, Georgina	4:10:48 (12,341)
Hooley, Maureen	4:46:27 (20,040)
Hooper, Janet	4:00:24 (10,130)
Hooper, Tracy	6:03:28 (28,563)
Hope, Alison	4:12:05 (12,640)
Hope, Katharine	4:36:46 (18,072)
Hopkins, Jennifer	3:29:15 (4,036)
Hopkins, Lyn	5:21:05 (25,477)
Hopkins, Sara	4:35:21 (17,786)
Hopkinson, Nicola	3:44:37 (6,598)
Hopper, Alix	4:36:53 (18,101)
Hornby, Carol	6:12:24 (28,937)
Horne, Rebecca	4:40:07 (18,804)
Horner, Elizabeth	4:42:49 (19,336)
Horner, Valerie	5:15:04 (24,794)
Hornsby, Mulenga	6:03:14 (28,552)
Horsey, Gay	4:26:13 (15,780)
Horsfall, Françoise	5:06:00 (23,469)
Horsman, Kathleen	4:02:03 (10,495)
Horton, Lindsay	4:25:41 (15,650)
Horton, Lindsey	3:55:12 (8,734)
Horvath, Katalin	4:37:10 (18,162)
Hosie, Monica	4:47:53 (20,322)
Hosking, Mary	5:38:45 (27,072)
Hougen, Amelia	4:45:01 (19,777)
Hough, Lindsay	6:18:27 (29,125)
Houghton, Susan	5:20:46 (25,441)
Houghton Wallace, Janice	5:18:55 (25,260)
Housden, Sharon	5:44:31 (27,516)
House, Victoria	4:31:58 (17,109)
Houston, Donna	4:42:36 (19,295)
Houtteman, Mieke	4:48:21 (20,416)
Howard, Jacqueline	5:16:22 (24,966)
Howard, Jane	6:42:11 (29,696)
Howard, Jessica	4:07:37 (11,681)
Howard, Joyce	6:10:53 (28,887)
Howard, Lorna	8:07:56 (30,226)
Howard, Rebecca	4:56:34 (22,083)
Howard, Suzette	3:59:56 (10,037)
Howard, Yvonne	5:03:59 (23,125)
Howarth, Barbara	5:34:15 (26,727)
Howarth, Hazel	5:13:21 (24,558)
Howarth, Mary	3:34:57 (4,899)
Howat, Michelle	4:07:30 (11,660)
Howe, Carol	5:05:29 (23,381)
Howe, Kim	4:39:43 (18,736)
Howe, Meriel	3:53:58 (8,471)
Howell, Katrina	5:33:11 (26,624)
Howells, Ruth	5:49:46 (27,886)
Howes, Pauline	4:34:47 (17,672)
Howie, Anne	4:41:37 (19,085)
Howie, Laura	3:37:18 (5,301)
Howie, Lynda	3:51:33 (7,978)
Howland, Rebecca	8:06:05 (30,213)
Howlett, Jacqueline	3:04:46 (1,331)
Howlett, Sarah	4:05:21 (11,175)
Howley, Maria	5:22:00 (25,585)
Hoyland, Sharon	4:44:11 (19,616)
Huang, Jin-Ya	6:15:06 (29,027)
Huber, Isabelle	3:55:13 (8,738)
Huber, Lisa	3:39:13 (5,612)
Hubner, Sarah	3:35:07 (4,922)
Huck, Susan	5:00:02 (22,627)
Huckle, Susan	5:05:25 (23,363)
Hucklesby, Louise	3:57:36 (9,363)
Huddleston, Geraldine	4:52:12 (21,134)
Hudson, Emma	6:12:22 (28,935)
Hudson, Helena	5:34:10 (26,720)
Hudson, Jane	6:22:16 (29,219)
Hudson, Jean	4:10:36 (12,297)
Hudson, Karima	3:35:45 (5,026)
Hudson, Lindsay	3:28:19 (3,872)
Hudson, Naomi	4:42:55 (19,366)
Hudson, Rebecca	4:54:41 (21,634)

Hudson, Sarah	4:23:49 (15,254)
Hudson, Sonia	4:32:45 (17,263)
Huggett, Bridget	5:36:44 (26,926)
Hugh, Deborah	4:39:58 (18,783)
Hugh Jones, Pia	4:57:04 (22,149)
Hughes, Alison	4:12:51 (12,799)
Hughes, Almaira	6:08:50 (28,808)
Hughes, Ann	4:57:41 (22,246)
Hughes, Clare	4:55:22 (21,837)
Hughes, Delyth	5:15:44 (24,896)
Hughes, Dorothy	5:05:41 (23,410)
Hughes, Dyanne	4:46:27 (20,040)
Hughes, Fay	4:08:01 (11,768)
Hughes, Gillian	5:22:32 (25,653)
Hughes, Helen	4:24:30 (15,398)
Hughes, Jessie	4:56:34 (22,083)
Hughes, Maggie	3:04:32 (1,317)
Hughes, Rebecca	4:42:42 (19,310)
Hughes, Rebecca	7:13:49 (30,043)
Hughes, Rebekah	5:13:02 (24,505)
Hughes, Sian	6:14:13 (28,997)
Hughes, Suki	4:08:35 (11,890)
Hughes, Tina	5:25:13 (25,911)
Huguelet, Joyce	5:46:36 (27,673)
Hulance, Lisa	4:11:27 (12,493)
Hulland, Gaynor	4:20:47 (14,543)
Humbert, Alison	4:52:24 (21,185)
Hume, Ann	3:42:59 (6,299)
Hume, Shirley	3:48:27 (7,349)
Humphrey, Karinya	4:46:00 (19,938)
Humphreys, Hazel	5:48:17 (27,798)
Humphreys, Linda	6:41:20 (29,674)
Humphreys, Susan	5:11:48 (24,331)
Humphries, Kirsty	4:32:45 (17,263)
Humphries, Mary	5:06:21 (23,526)
Humphries, Rosemary	6:23:33 (29,246)
Humphries, Sharon	5:16:26 (24,975)
Hunt, Danni	4:20:52 (14,564)
Hunt, Jenni	6:07:05 (28,722)
Hunt, Kimberley	6:32:11 (29,454)
Hunt, Linda	5:48:27 (27,813)
Hunt, Sarah	5:19:18 (25,292)
Hunter, Catherine	7:03:44 (29,973)
Hunter, Felicity	4:26:15 (15,795)
Hunter, Victoria	5:19:29 (25,304)
Hunter-Blair, Camilla	5:12:13 (24,381)
Hurkett, Julie	7:23:35 (30,095)
Hurley, Eilis	6:29:00 (29,389)
Hurran, Rebecca	6:19:25 (29,141)
Hurrell, Karen	4:31:29 (16,977)
Hurst, Yvonne	6:07:15 (28,734)
Hurt, Betsy	4:23:30 (15,172)
Hurwitz Bremner, Marjorie	4:45:08 (19,791)
Huse, Lisa	6:05:15 (28,653)
Huson, Gillian	4:36:55 (18,110)
Hussain, Sally Ann	5:04:01 (23,133)
Hussein, Suzanne	6:32:29 (29,462)
Husted, Carole	6:03:00 (28,541)
Hutchinson, Catherine	5:07:46 (23,743)
Hutchinson, Karen	3:25:14 (3,406)
Hutchinson, Linda	3:52:11 (8,114)
Hutchinson, Sandra	4:31:39 (17,023)
Hutchison, Heidi	4:35:04 (17,724)
Hutley, Charlotte	4:36:16 (17,967)
Hutsby, Kerrie	4:10:20 (12,237)
Hutton, Ceri	5:04:00 (23,131)
Huxley, Kate	5:02:08 (22,897)
Huxley, Linda	3:59:18 (9,841)
Huxley, Tracey	5:36:21 (26,905)
Hyde, Joanne	4:07:07 (11,572)
Hyland, Carol	5:08:35 (23,863)
Hyland, Shirley	6:28:17 (29,362)
Hymers, Chrissie	4:45:50 (19,908)
Hynes, Joanne	5:06:51 (23,595)
Hyppolte, Annick	4:20:34 (14,494)
Ibell, Emma	3:57:07 (9,200)
Ibrahim, Deborah	4:51:15 (20,930)
Icely, Clare	5:07:33 (23,701)
Icely, Linda Icely	4:44:19 (19,642)
Iles, Patricia	5:26:41 (26,059)
Ilott, Karen	4:52:35 (21,233)
Imong, Stella	4:41:34 (19,077)
Impey, Cindy	6:01:50 (28,498)

Impleton, Lisa	5:45:54 (27,626)	
Ingham, Jacqeline	5:09:03 (23,949)	
Inglott, Sasha	6:27:02 (29,332)	
Ingram, Barbara	4:21:06 (14,611)	
Ingram, Margaret	5:06:44 (23,577)	
Inwards, Angela	6:52:50 (29,839)	
I'Ons, Anne	5:36:11 (26,892)	
Iorio, Lisa	3:40:56 (5,939)	
Ireland, Tracey	6:17:06 (29,089)	
Iremonger, Victoria	4:54:30 (21,594)	
Irons, Felicity	4:36:39 (18,053)	
Irvin, Jennifer	4:28:36 (16,339)	
Irving, Vinette	4:50:46 (20,838)	
Ishibashi, Naoko	4:27:06 (15,999)	
Islas Perez, Rosa Maria	4:22:14 (14,870)	
Isle, Veronica	4:02:16 (10,530)	
Ivanciu, Jennifer	5:53:06 (28,072)	
Ivanova, Alina	2:25:34 (43)	
Ivaska, Mari	4:24:17 (15,345)	
Ives, Lesley	4:01:45 (10,436)	
Ivison, Anne	4:33:07 (17,329)	
Ivory, Caitlin	3:57:52 (9,453)	
Jackson, Amanda	5:06:03 (23,476)	
Jackson, Angela	3:23:13 (3,137)	
Jackson, Elizabeth	5:07:21 (23,671)	
Jackson, Judith	4:41:33 (19,074)	
Jackson, Laura	3:45:45 (6,810)	
Jackson, Linda	3:50:42 (7,808)	
Jackson, Lisa	6:11:23 (28,903)	
Jackson, Lucy	3:45:29 (6,743)	
Jackson, Lucy	5:15:31 (24,871)	
Jackson, Lyndi	5:30:44 (26,431)	
Jackson, Pamela	5:14:13 (24,660)	
Jacobson, Rayanne	4:19:14 (14,174)	
Jacques, Elaine	4:42:52 (19,352)	
Jaffe, Susan	4:53:02 (21,322)	
Jaheriss, Kristen	5:46:40 (27,677)	
James, Antonia	5:27:21 (26,115)	
James, Catherine	5:39:16 (27,111)	
James, Hannah	5:56:14 (28,222)	
James, Joanne	5:17:15 (25,074)	
James, Louise	5:25:11 (25,904)	
James, Lucy	4:35:25 (17,800)	
James, Lysbeth	4:54:48 (21,678)	
James, Marlene	4:28:15 (16,249)	
James, Melanie	5:56:27 (28,240)	
James, Susan	6:24:53 (29,280)	
James, Wendy	6:28:30 (29,373)	
Jamieson, Hilary	5:15:53 (24,922)	
Jamieson, Joanna	4:42:42 (19,310)	
Jan, Isabelle	5:08:33 (23,855)	
Janicot, Odile	3:19:58 (2,764)	
Jans, Chris	4:55:14 (21,791)	
Jaques, Dot	3:56:43 (9,109)	
Jaques, Hilary	4:52:52 (21,280)	
Jarvis, Jacqueline	4:55:10 (21,772)	
Jarvis, Manda	5:02:38 (22,952)	
Jarvis, Myra	6:59:16 (29,934)	
Jarvis, Penny	4:04:27 (10,977)	
Jarvis, Rachel	4:52:52 (21,280)	
Jassin-Pages, Martine	5:52:26 (28,036)	
Jay, Carinne	4:03:14 (10,707)	
Jay, Sue	3:56:17 (8,989)	
Jeannette, Christine	3:21:50 (2,978)	
Jeeves, Elizabeth	6:50:19 (29,810)	
Jeeves, Susan	4:26:09 (15,769)	
Jeffery, Della	4:19:15 (14,178)	
Jefford, Caroline	4:24:14 (15,338)	
Jeffreys, Zara	4:32:25 (17,199)	
Jelly, Maureen	5:11:39 (24,304)	
Jenkin, Isobel	5:20:02 (25,364)	
Jenkins, Deborah	3:38:56 (5,566)	
Jenkins, Helena	4:17:38 (13,799)	
Jenkins, Nadine	5:43:48 (27,459)	
Jenkins, Nicola	4:38:19 (18,456)	
Jenkins, Pauline	4:59:09 (22,483)	
Jenkinson, Annie	4:25:43 (15,657)	
Jenkinson, Lauren	4:29:16 (16,487)	
Jenkins-Williams, Lisa	5:35:29 (26,841)	
Jenner, Caroline	3:29:17 (4,045)	
Jenner, Linda	5:14:08 (24,645)	
Jennings, Anne	4:38:17 (18,450)	
Jennings, Claire	4:35:03 (17,723)	
Jennings, Jane	5:57:35 (28,301)	
Jennings, Sally	6:40:03 (29,636)	
Jennings, Val	3:32:48 (4,573)	
Jensen, Birthe Eckmann	4:33:10 (17,341)	
Jensen, Karin Agerbo	4:20:43 (14,524)	
Jensen, Lise	4:32:09 (17,145)	
Jeong, Jum	3:38:06 (5,414)	
Jeremicz, Anna Natalia	6:26:30 (29,318)	
Jessemey, Joanna	6:04:30 (28,618)	
Jessop, Kathryn	4:17:31 (13,776)	
Jewell, Louise	4:39:49 (18,754)	
Jewitt, Cathy	5:34:22 (26,742)	
Jewsbury, Susan	4:24:14 (15,338)	
Jikiemi-Roberts, Carolyn	5:53:03 (28,067)	
Jin, Hong	3:21:56 (2,988)	
Jivraj, Tahera	4:40:29 (18,872)	
Joannou, Maria	6:24:36 (29,275)	
Jobling, Julie	5:11:53 (24,341)	
John, Zoe	4:04:12 (10,927)	
Johns, Lynne	3:25:24 (3,431)	
Johns, Sarah	4:42:53 (19,359)	
Johnson, Amanda	4:38:15 (18,442)	
Johnson, Anne Marie	4:10:47 (12,332)	
Johnson, Bryony	5:08:57 (23,930)	
Johnson, Caroline	6:17:51 (29,110)	
Johnson, Christine	5:04:26 (23,206)	
Johnson, Claire	4:02:04 (10,498)	
Johnson, Dawn	5:04:47 (23,259)	
Johnson, Diane	5:08:58 (23,935)	
Johnson, Erin	5:04:46 (23,256)	
Johnson, Gaynor	4:36:47 (18,078)	
Johnson, Jane	4:42:08 (19,188)	
Johnson, Johanna	4:27:04 (15,988)	
Johnson, Julie	4:49:12 (20,562)	
Johnson, Karen	4:27:42 (16,119)	
Johnson, Katrina	4:35:15 (17,761)	
Johnson, Lena	6:37:17 (29,568)	
Johnson, Louise	4:38:16 (18,445)	
Johnson, Maxine	6:49:35 (29,797)	
Johnson, Nina	4:02:42 (10,608)	
Johnson, Pippa	5:57:23 (28,289)	
Johnson, Sandra	4:47:30 (20,260)	
Johnson, Sandra	5:06:32 (23,548)	
Johnson, Sara	4:27:02 (15,975)	
Johnson, Sue	3:29:05 (4,011)	
Johnson Newell, Suzanne	4:48:11 (20,382)	
Johnston, Alison	4:31:59 (17,117)	
Johnston, Amanda	5:34:03 (26,703)	
Johnston, Helen	5:36:38 (26,920)	
Johnston, Maryanne	5:08:54 (23,922)	
Johnston, Sandra	5:18:25 (25,200)	
Johnston, Terriann	4:43:51 (19,565)	
Johnston, White	3:30:53 (4,310)	
Johnstone, Anita	6:53:04 (29,847)	
Johnstone, Liezel	4:56:46 (22,101)	
Johnstone, Lynne	4:57:41 (22,246)	
Jolliffe, Susan	4:14:55 (13,239)	
Jolliffe, Susanne	4:50:52 (20,856)	
Jonas, Annabel	4:22:28 (14,919)	
Jonas, Heidi	4:25:27 (15,602)	
Jones, Alexandra	4:10:47 (12,332)	
Jones, Amanda	3:58:49 (9,703)	
Jones, Amanda	4:59:56 (22,608)	
Jones, Andrea	5:26:06 (25,996)	
Jones, Ann	6:35:59 (29,543)	
Jones, Ann	7:11:39 (30,030)	
Jones, Anna	4:25:00 (15,509)	
Jones, Barbara	4:44:17 (19,635)	
Jones, Bronwyn	6:04:39 (28,628)	
Jones, Carol	3:54:46 (8,650)	
Jones, Debbie	3:53:31 (8,380)	
Jones, Elaine	7:11:56 (30,031)	
Jones, Elizabeth	4:03:47 (10,838)	
Jones, Elizabeth	4:29:10 (16,464)	
Jones, Elizabeth	5:37:47 (27,006)	
Jones, Emily	5:11:50 (24,333)	
Jones, Hazel	4:03:37 (10,805)	
Jones, Heather	4:32:44 (17,257)	
Jones, Helen	5:04:50 (23,272)	
Jones, Jackie	5:02:00 (22,873)	
Jones, Jean	5:27:33 (26,130)	
Jones, Joan	3:45:13 (6,710)	
Jones, Judith	4:09:01 (11,990)	
Jones, Karen	5:17:57 (25,155)	
Jones, Katherine	6:24:13 (29,265)	
Jones, Kim	6:24:14 (29,266)	
Jones, Leontine	4:48:55 (20,509)	
Jones, Lesley	5:24:55 (25,874)	
Jones, Linda	5:20:59 (25,466)	
Jones, Lindsay	5:57:16 (28,281)	
Jones, Liz	5:00:50 (22,707)	
Jones, Louise	4:01:47 (10,443)	
Jones, Lucy Ann	4:25:36 (15,637)	
Jones, Lynda	4:23:14 (15,114)	
Jones, Margaret	5:52:42 (28,048)	
Jones, Nicola	8:06:05 (30,213)	
Jones, Rebecca	3:41:24 (6,028)	
Jones, Rosemary	5:49:58 (27,900)	
Jones, Sally	4:45:03 (19,780)	
Jones, Shan	3:25:43 (3,470)	
Jones, Sharon	3:54:48 (8,659)	
Jones, Susan	6:54:20 (29,866)	
Jones, Tania	2:39:10 (159)	
Jones, Yvonne	5:55:56 (28,211)	
Jordan, Tracey	4:59:55 (22,603)	
Jordan-Owers, Lorna	5:43:59 (27,474)	
Joseph, Lynda Maxine	6:01:22 (28,473)	
Joseph, Restituta	2:43:52 (257)	
Josey, Louisa	4:48:44 (20,475)	
Joyce, Nicola	4:17:57 (13,863)	
Joyce, Rachel	3:02:02 (1,154)	
Joynson, Britt	4:38:03 (18,382)	
Judge, Jeanette	3:53:23 (8,351)	
Judge, Linda	5:17:24 (25,093)	
Judson, Jill	5:12:41 (24,453)	
Jukes, Rosalba	7:26:40 (30,116)	
Jumansen, Dorthe	3:46:31 (6,951)	
Juneja, Anita	6:07:15 (28,734)	
Kadera, Geraldine	4:31:59 (17,117)	
Kafer, Moe	5:35:40 (26,857)	
Kail, Nancy	4:49:36 (20,635)	
Kaiser, Margit	5:01:11 (22,763)	
Kalberer, Marlies	5:52:55 (28,058)	
Kam, Amy	4:54:45 (21,660)	
Kane, Annie	3:38:41 (5,515)	
Kaneko, Setsuko	4:58:36 (22,394)	
Kannangara, Savanthi	5:27:07 (26,091)	
Karnik, Vijaya	7:32:56 (30,147)	
Katsiara, Martha	4:47:32 (20,273)	
Kaur, Jugjit	5:05:54 (23,448)	
Kavanagh, Alison	4:24:47 (15,456)	
Kavanagh, Frances	5:44:48 (27,546)	
Kavannagh, Anne	4:55:29 (21,885)	
Kawanami, Rena	6:00:55 (28,452)	
Kay, Catherine	5:34:02 (26,700)	
Kaye, Sarah	4:24:59 (15,501)	
Kayum, Elene	4:08:38 (11,903)	
Keane, Sarah	3:52:34 (8,184)	
Kearney, Amanda	6:26:30 (29,318)	
Keating, Zoe	4:35:15 (17,761)	
Keating Drayson, Frances	6:31:11 (29,436)	
Keats, Susan	4:32:44 (17,257)	
Keavey, Anne	3:54:34 (8,605)	
Keech, Jennie	4:49:59 (20,715)	
Keeler, Zoe	4:29:42 (16,599)	
Keeling, Pam	4:11:53 (12,587)	
Keen, Emma	4:18:30 (14,012)	
Keen, Tricia	5:13:35 (24,576)	
Keenleyside, Kathryn	5:10:52 (24,192)	
Keens, Alison	6:42:10 (29,695)	
Kehoe, Donna	5:16:52 (25,029)	
Keilty, Veronica	5:08:35 (23,863)	
Keith, Louise	4:05:10 (11,150)	
Kelleher, Julie Margaux	4:26:37 (15,875)	
Kelleher, Lorna	5:30:09 (26,383)	
Keller, Gabrielle	5:55:54 (28,208)	
Kellerman, Rachel	4:34:23 (17,612)	
Kelley, Rachel	3:58:56 (9,732)	
Kelly, Diane	3:11:40 (1,882)	
Kelly, Doreen	7:39:48 (30,165)	
Kelly, Helen	5:39:35 (27,142)	
Kelly, Jan	5:31:40 (26,504)	
Kelly, Katie	3:55:58 (8,911)	
Kelly, Maureen	5:12:29 (24,429)	
Kelly, Nicola	4:19:49 (14,318)	
Kelly, Patricia	5:21:58 (25,580)	

Kelly, Sarah....4:49:25 (20,602)
Kelly, Stephanie....5:40:24 (27,217)
Kelly, Susan....5:20:45 (25,438)
Kelsey, Verity....4:44:59 (19,773)
Kemp, Alice....4:46:52 (20,136)
Kemp, Alison....5:07:48 (23,747)
Kemp, Elisita....5:19:53 (25,352)
Kemp, Linda....4:54:50 (21,687)
Kemp, Nicola....4:05:27 (11,197)
Kempenaar, Joop....5:02:03 (22,884)
Kempson, Ann....4:57:17 (22,187)
Kendal, Claire....5:14:14 (24,663)
Kenee, Paula....6:41:48 (29,686)
Kennedy, Jane....4:11:39 (12,535)
Kennedy, Marie....5:28:10 (26,189)
Kennedy, Thérèse....4:46:16 (20,002)
Kenning, Julia....4:26:00 (15,730)
Kent, Deborah....5:18:17 (25,189)
Kent, Martina....4:42:07 (19,182)
Kent, Nicola....4:36:43 (18,065)
Kent, Phillipa....6:04:20 (28,609)
Kenworthy, Karen....5:16:18 (24,958)
Kenwright, Dawn....3:09:33 (1,721)
Kernaghan, Lesley....3:58:08 (9,525)
Kerr, Felicity....5:21:59 (25,582)
Kerray, Charlotte....4:01:20 (10,348)
Kershaw, Tracey....5:37:22 (26,970)
Kettlewell, Charlotte....4:55:24 (21,849)
Kettlewell, Julianna....5:31:00 (26,452)
Keun, Rothea....6:13:15 (28,960)
Key, Dawn....4:16:41 (13,607)
Keyes Pearce, Susan....4:25:48 (15,672)
Keynes, Helen....5:40:16 (27,205)
Keyworth, Helen....3:52:55 (8,252)
Khadem, Annoushka....4:14:02 (13,046)
Khaihra, Mary....6:06:55 (28,716)
Kibble, Sally....4:35:34 (17,829)
Kidgell, Nicola....4:55:50 (21,959)
Kight, Kim....4:28:55 (16,404)
Kikoski, Nicole....4:33:32 (17,428)
Kilburn, Catherine....4:42:51 (19,347)
Kilby, Sharon....5:26:22 (26,027)
Kile, Loren....4:50:54 (20,861)
Kiley, Jane....4:04:31 (10,996)
Kilgour, Vivien....3:36:13 (5,107)
Kilkenny, Sian....6:44:11 (29,724)
Killough, Bridget....6:13:30 (28,973)
Kilner, Andrea....5:37:20 (26,967)
Kilner, Claire....5:47:42 (27,743)
Kilshaw, Lynda....4:22:39 (14,968)
Kim, Christine....5:32:20 (26,552)
Kimber, Julie....4:06:56 (11,535)
Kimber, Taryn....5:45:45 (27,612)
Kinchela, Nancy....4:02:28 (10,566)
Kinder, Elizabeth....4:39:35 (18,712)
King, Anne....3:45:40 (6,785)
King, Caroline....4:57:38 (22,235)
King, Jaci....7:56:01 (30,200)
King, Jacqueline....4:25:30 (15,620)
King, Janice....5:33:11 (26,624)
King, Leigh....5:03:59 (23,125)
King, Liz....5:07:50 (23,751)
King, Nadine....3:34:55 (4,892)
King, Paula....4:56:07 (22,006)
King, Shirley....6:08:02 (28,765)
King, Sue....5:43:47 (27,457)
King, Susan....5:44:54 (27,556)
King, Susan....5:51:39 (27,991)
King, Tracey....5:44:32 (27,523)
King, Virginia....4:54:33 (21,604)
Kingdon, Sarah....4:53:29 (21,416)
Kingham, Sharne....5:53:02 (28,064)
Kingsley, Audrey....3:16:00 (2,322)
Kinsella, Barbara....4:56:04 (21,997)
Kippax, Elizabeth....3:58:33 (9,625)
Kirby, Claire....5:43:48 (27,459)
Kirby, Maureen....4:07:16 (11,604)
Kirchmann, Brigitta....3:57:48 (9,431)
Kirk, Elizabeth....4:22:16 (14,877)
Kirk, Jill....5:45:47 (27,615)
Kirkby, Tracey....5:22:02 (25,590)
Kirkman, Dominique....5:03:41 (23,080)
Kirkman, Hannah....4:44:15 (19,628)
Kirkpatrick, Tina....6:58:43 (29,926)
Kirtley, Anne....2:54:39 (617)
Kitchen, Amanda....5:10:52 (24,192)
Kitching, Janette....4:26:33 (15,856)
Kite, Julie....4:50:21 (20,782)
Kitson, Melanie....4:40:28 (18,868)
Kitson, Phyllis....4:17:08 (13,699)
Kjaer, Lene....4:27:45 (16,135)
Kjellerup, Niels....5:40:08 (27,200)
Klempel, Pamela....4:31:45 (17,048)
Klinger, Sylvia....5:16:36 (25,003)
Knight, Clare....5:08:52 (23,915)
Knight, Ellen....4:19:30 (14,255)
Knight, Helen....5:09:08 (23,959)
Knight, Joanne....5:19:38 (25,321)
Knight, Julie....5:56:24 (28,236)
Knight, Kim....4:47:43 (20,296)
Knight, Lynne....4:37:12 (18,172)
Knight, Viola....4:45:05 (19,785)
Knights, Anne....6:28:58 (29,385)
Knights, Diane....4:13:23 (12,899)
Knights, Julia....4:55:27 (21,872)
Knights, Lisa....2:51:43 (502)
Knights, Lisa....5:07:51 (23,754)
Knoll, Paula....3:09:14 (1,688)
Knollman, Gemma....5:40:08 (27,200)
Knopoff, Kathleen....5:38:25 (27,046)
Knopp, Rosalind....4:14:59 (13,260)
Knott, Elspeth....3:56:41 (9,101)
Knott, Kath....4:43:07 (19,407)
Knott, Sarah....4:39:20 (18,650)
Knowles, Alyson....4:30:12 (16,718)
Knowles, Julie....5:11:41 (24,310)
Knowles, Julie....6:16:35 (29,071)
Knowles, Laura....6:07:46 (28,752)
Knowles, Petra....3:27:10 (3,652)
Knox, Joanna....4:58:48 (22,426)
Knuth, Helen....4:56:01 (21,987)
Kok, Adri....6:41:23 (29,677)
Kopelson, Heidi....3:53:52 (8,453)
Kornum, Mette....4:08:09 (11,794)
Korro, Helen....4:37:42 (18,299)
Kortman, Cynthia....6:11:13 (28,896)
Koutsoudis, Marina....4:53:50 (21,483)
Koutsoukos, Demetra....3:56:41 (9,101)
Krala, Anna....5:26:16 (26,017)
Kreuz, Yvonne....5:19:32 (25,311)
Kribben, Kathrin....4:24:53 (15,474)
Krigel, Beth....4:46:48 (20,114)
Kristensen, Kitty....3:29:43 (4,122)
Kronqvist, Gerd....3:34:56 (4,897)
Kruse, Jennifer....4:11:34 (12,515)
Kudo, Ayako....5:57:46 (28,315)
Kudo, Ritsuko....5:57:46 (28,315)
Kullar, Richenda....4:25:49 (15,679)
Kurn, Lesley....4:15:56 (13,450)
Kusel, Heidi....4:42:34 (19,284)
Kwasniewski, Carrie....4:32:28 (17,210)
Kyriacou, Maria....4:52:47 (21,268)
Labram, Fiona....4:28:39 (16,350)
Laceby, Maxine....4:20:47 (14,543)
Lachs, Lynn....4:46:43 (20,095)
Lackey, Deborah....6:17:48 (29,108)
Lackey, Jan....5:02:42 (22,964)
Lacy, Jessie....4:38:34 (18,519)
Lade, Bernice....6:13:39 (28,983)
Lafford, Sarah....6:10:53 (28,887)
Lahdelma, Tanya....4:43:39 (19,527)
Lainchbury, Sarah....5:09:15 (23,977)
Laing, Janet....3:24:35 (3,326)
Laird, Elspeth....3:28:08 (3,830)
Lait, Joanne....3:57:13 (9,232)
Lake, Geraldine....5:16:49 (25,027)
Lalor, Michelle....5:34:21 (26,739)
Lamalle, Sabelle....4:27:46 (16,140)
Lamb, Carol....5:17:39 (25,118)
Lamb, Corinne....6:21:02 (29,194)
Lamb, Emma....4:52:10 (21,130)
Lamb, Jacqueline....3:42:39 (6,244)
Lamb, Katherine....6:05:55 (28,682)
Lamb, Michelle....5:01:12 (22,768)
Lamb, Robyn....5:17:39 (25,118)
Lambert, Lee-Ann....5:56:36 (28,249)
Lambert, Sue....3:39:25 (5,657)
Lambert, Vicky....4:24:57 (15,491)
Lamming, Heather....5:12:05 (24,362)
Lamper, Gillian....5:07:30 (23,697)
Lancaster, Andrea....3:57:01 (9,182)
Lancaster, Jennifer....6:41:53 (29,690)
Lancauchez, Muriel....3:56:45 (9,121)
Land, Elaine....5:46:35 (27,669)
Lane, Frances....4:29:48 (16,625)
Lane, Joanne....4:23:44 (15,234)
Lane, Judy....4:18:48 (14,081)
Lane, Kay....4:10:12 (12,208)
Lane, Nyree....5:47:49 (27,755)
Lane, Ross....3:45:08 (6,700)
Lang, Caroline....5:16:48 (25,026)
Lang, Rosemary....3:53:56 (8,466)
Langager, Yrsa....3:25:45 (3,474)
Langevin, Catherine....5:02:02 (22,880)
Langfield, Jacqueline....4:18:23 (13,982)
Langfield, Katherine....5:53:11 (28,078)
Langford, Lyn....5:04:33 (23,223)
Langlands, Charlotte....6:10:21 (28,871)
Langstaff, Emma....3:58:32 (9,616)
Langston, Denise....3:54:54 (8,687)
Lanigan, Sue....4:17:01 (13,672)
Lanser, Shelley....4:31:34 (16,996)
Laporte, Roberta....5:26:20 (26,022)
Laraman, Catherine....5:07:29 (23,695)
Lardner, Wendy....5:33:04 (26,616)
Larkin, Michelle....5:53:05 (28,069)
Larkin-Bramley, Kathryn....5:36:18 (26,899)
Lartigue, Patricia....4:20:57 (14,583)
Lashbrook, Emma....5:05:01 (23,296)
Laskey, Lory....4:14:42 (13,173)
Lasko, Jill....4:24:23 (15,365)
Last, Sue....6:27:35 (29,342)
Latham, Lyn-Marie....4:49:41 (20,648)
Lathe, Caroline....4:28:09 (16,221)
Latto, Emma....2:52:18 (525)
Latto, Sheila....5:05:13 (23,323)
Laud, Carolyn....4:30:05 (16,706)
Laughlin, Alison....4:00:10 (10,081)
Laughlin, Deirdre....4:00:10 (10,081)
Laurent, Helene....6:03:07 (28,548)
Lavender, Harriet....4:32:29 (17,214)
Lavender, Sally....5:23:56 (25,787)
Laver, Beverley....4:54:18 (21,562)
Laverick, Helen....6:29:05 (29,390)
Lawes, Vivienne....3:53:32 (8,387)
Lawlor, Kim....8:32:27 (30,250)
Lawrence, Alexandra....4:23:58 (15,286)
Lawrence, Barbara....4:15:05 (13,287)
Lawrence, Christa....4:05:18 (11,165)
Lawrence, Elizabeth....3:48:08 (7,291)
Lawrence, Emma....6:11:44 (28,918)
Lawrence, Joanna....5:54:40 (28,146)
Lawrence, Marie....3:59:06 (9,786)
Lawrence, Patricia....6:01:37 (28,484)
Lawrenson-Reid, June....4:16:23 (13,547)
Lawson, Nicola....4:09:55 (12,143)
Lawson, Valerie....4:33:20 (17,378)
Lawson, Vanessa....4:31:53 (17,085)
Lawton, Linda....6:27:03 (29,333)
Laycock, Susan....5:58:41 (28,353)
Layton, Roz....3:29:07 (4,019)
Lazenby, Natasha....4:59:42 (22,553)
Lazenby, Sarah....5:22:35 (25,657)
Le Brasse, Yvette....4:29:56 (16,672)
Le Dily, Catherine....3:48:05 (7,283)
Le Good, Vivien....4:57:55 (22,283)
Le Riche, Nina....4:13:56 (13,028)
Le Ruez, Sue....3:26:57 (3,616)
Leach, Lisa....4:13:52 (13,015)
Leach, Michelle....3:49:29 (7,574)
Leafe, Kathryn....6:00:24 (28,428)
Leaman, Louisa....4:44:07 (19,601)
Leamon, Susan....4:42:52 (19,352)
Leandri, Pauline....4:56:19 (22,039)
Leaver, Claire....4:38:54 (18,586)
Leavesley, Helen....5:00:50 (22,707)
Lebaigue, Angela....4:15:04 (13,282)
Leck, Melissa....4:56:00 (21,984)
Leckie, Norma....5:44:33 (27,526)

Lee, Charlotte 5:56:32 (28,245)
Lee, Emma 4:34:15 (17,585)
Lee, Frances 5:04:19 (23,182)
Lee, Immy 5:48:09 (27,787)
Lee, Jane 3:42:05 (6,134)
Lee, Julie 4:08:47 (11,934)
Lee, Margaret 4:59:37 (22,541)
Lee, Michelle 3:16:20 (2,344)
Lee, Sarah 4:39:34 (18,708)
Lee, Yvonne 4:23:26 (15,155)
Leech, Jennifer 4:48:41 (20,466)
Leech, Rachel 5:14:18 (24,673)
Leedham, Christine 5:37:47 (27,006)
Leeming, Charlotte 5:03:07 (23,021)
Leeming, Tracy 6:03:47 (28,579)
Leeming-Latham, Zoe 4:03:45 (10,832)
Lees, Susan 4:48:49 (20,490)
Leeson, Yvonne 3:57:17 (9,250)
Leete, Jenny 4:25:38 (15,641)
Leigh, Anne 5:22:43 (25,676)
Leigh, Jeanette 4:47:20 (20,225)
Leigh, Kay 3:08:26 (1,625)
Leisegang, Christine 4:48:54 (20,503)
Leishman, Kirsty 3:26:33 (3,565)
Leitch, Jessica 3:41:54 (6,110)
Leitch, Rona 7:03:06 (29,968)
Leith, Sheena 5:18:47 (25,249)
Leleu, Roselyne 3:51:54 (8,049)
Lemmon, Victoria 5:58:26 (28,346)
Lenaghan, Moira 3:46:49 (7,004)
Lentern, Mandy 5:16:15 (24,952)
Leonard, Katy 5:07:23 (23,676)
Leonard, Vanessa 4:06:56 (11,535)
Leonardo, Justine 5:18:15 (25,185)
Leppers, Geraldine 4:22:29 (14,924)
Lequesne, Julie 6:13:52 (28,989)
Leslie, Julie 5:59:24 (28,389)
Leslie, Wendy 4:22:42 (14,985)
Lester, Melanie 4:34:06 (17,557)
Letchford, Angela 4:19:08 (14,155)
Letts, Diana 4:52:22 (21,175)
Lever, Kathryn 5:08:16 (23,809)
Leverett, Ann 4:34:20 (17,602)
Levett, Denize 6:36:39 (29,556)
Levy, Patricia 4:53:06 (21,336)
Lewin, Jennifer 6:13:41 (28,985)
Lewin, Marianne 4:43:13 (19,431)
Lewin, Tracy 5:43:03 (27,415)
Lewis, Ann 5:28:33 (26,233)
Lewis, Georgia 6:48:26 (29,785)
Lewis, Hazel 4:35:02 (17,717)
Lewis, Julie 3:46:29 (6,944)
Lewis, Karen 4:54:25 (21,576)
Lewis, Kathryn 6:20:38 (29,182)
Lewis, Leone 4:50:04 (20,731)
Lewis, Rachel 5:27:27 (26,124)
Lewis, Rebecca 4:54:11 (21,548)
Lewis, Ruth 5:17:03 (25,056)
Lewis, Sarah 6:59:45 (29,941)
Lewis Basson, Judy 3:54:51 (8,672)
Lewtas, Susanne 4:58:02 (22,301)
Libby, Jessica 5:39:12 (27,103)
Liberty, Christine 7:07:54 (30,006)
Lichtarowicz, Paula 4:38:16 (18,445)
Licudi, Julia 3:58:49 (9,703)
Lie, Annette 4:42:55 (19,366)
Lietz, Johanna 4:44:02 (19,590)
Liew, Heather 5:50:31 (27,926)
Ligon, Lisa 5:20:15 (25,382)
Likimani, Sopiato 6:15:42 (29,049)
Lilley, Claire 5:10:33 (24,154)
Lilley, Frances 3:36:13 (5,107)
Lim, Mei 4:22:47 (15,000)
Limacher, Hilda 6:31:36 (29,443)
Lin, Shirley 6:40:54 (29,661)
Lincoln, Deborah 5:15:08 (24,802)
Lindley, Caron 7:29:43 (30,134)
Lindop, Trina 3:30:30 (4,245)
Lindsey, Valerie 4:18:08 (13,895)
Lines, Teresa 4:22:47 (15,000)
Linkson, Naomi 8:22:18 (30,240)
Linley, Elizabeth 4:13:25 (12,912)
Linter, Belinda 4:39:27 (18,678)
Linzmeyer, Colette 4:51:16 (20,935)
Lipede, Kehinde 3:53:56 (8,466)
Lipley, Joanne 5:46:50 (27,688)
Lipman, Michelle 5:01:33 (22,811)
Lipscomb, Ashley 4:43:30 (19,497)
Lipsett, Anthea 5:03:04 (23,016)
Lister, Fiona 4:25:29 (15,613)
Litovsky, Constance 5:16:18 (24,958)
Little, Deborah 4:19:38 (14,291)
Little, Denise 4:41:50 (19,128)
Little, Gina 4:06:30 (11,450)
Little, Janis 6:31:13 (29,438)
Little, Louise 3:40:41 (5,894)
Little, Susan 4:47:45 (20,301)
Littlewood, Serena 6:22:53 (29,229)
Livesey, Sarah 5:00:07 (22,634)
Livings, Ann 4:14:51 (13,222)
Livingston, Linda 4:31:58 (17,109)
Livingstone, Denise 7:03:11 (29,970)
Lizamore, Heather 4:58:06 (22,316)
Llewellyn-Stirling, Jacqueline 4:02:27 (10,561)
Llewelyn, Karen 4:55:25 (21,857)
Lloyd, Carol 5:35:03 (26,810)
Lloyd, Catherine 4:56:19 (22,039)
Lloyd, Elaine 5:25:41 (25,956)
Lloyd, Janet 4:52:52 (21,280)
Lloyd, Philippa 5:24:50 (25,861)
Lloyd Kristensen, Justine 3:58:50 (9,709)
Lloyd Smith, Rebecca 4:56:22 (22,044)
Lloyd-Jones, Johanne 4:21:57 (14,796)
Loader, Carole 4:33:33 (17,438)
Loades, Carol 4:52:02 (21,098)
Lock, Suzanne 5:12:47 (24,465)
Lofting, Diane 6:55:07 (29,881)
Loftus, Claire 4:34:49 (17,681)
Logan, Jane 4:55:14 (21,791)
Login, Susan 3:46:34 (6,963)
Logsdail, Caroline 7:50:02 (30,190)
Lonergan, Kylie 6:08:51 (28,810)
Long, Deborah 5:50:36 (27,929)
Long, Fiona 5:51:57 (28,015)
Long, Janet 5:12:42 (24,457)
Long, Joanne 6:27:56 (29,352)
Long, Kim 5:22:54 (25,694)
Long, Sara 4:39:00 (18,603)
Long, Sheila 4:46:48 (20,114)
Longbone, Sandra 3:43:01 (6,310)
Longhurst, Deanne 5:57:43 (28,311)
Longman, Janet 4:29:14 (16,482)
Lonie, Margot 7:39:08 (30,161)
Lonsdale, Rachel 4:55:54 (21,968)
Loomes, Lynda 5:51:41 (27,995)
Loosley, Claire 4:48:48 (20,486)
Lor, Caroline 4:57:28 (22,211)
Lord, Sharon 5:26:51 (26,072)
Loroupe, Tegla 2:26:10 (45)
Lourens, Natascha 4:42:35 (19,290)
Love, Christine 4:58:30 (22,376)
Loveday, Emma 4:47:07 (20,189)
Loveday, Melanie 5:23:00 (25,706)
Lovegrove, Anna 4:55:49 (21,955)
Lovell, Sally 3:48:38 (7,385)
Lovergrove, Amanda 3:56:19 (8,998)
Low, Patricia 5:18:18 (25,193)
Lowe, Freda 4:46:25 (20,036)
Lowe, Helen 4:51:58 (21,085)
Lowe, Kim 3:41:43 (6,076)
Lowe, Teresa 4:10:17 (12,225)
Lower, Mandy 6:42:53 (29,705)
Lower, Tracey 3:32:53 (4,585)
Lowrey, Carol 4:50:24 (20,788)
Lowson, Maureen 4:03:41 (10,816)
Lowthorpe, Michal 4:58:39 (22,403)
Loxam, Lizz 6:37:36 (29,580)
Loze, Josiane 5:12:24 (24,416)
Lua, Suet 4:43:33 (19,508)
Lucas, Dorothy 4:15:22 (13,338)
Ludwig, Anna 6:18:01 (29,114)
Luedemann, Gisela 5:08:15 (23,807)
Luger, Sibylle 6:47:49 (29,775)
Luis, Angela 5:54:26 (28,131)
Luji-Ross, Latifah 4:06:49 (11,505)
Luke, Jane 5:32:53 (26,605)
Luke, Marie 5:50:39 (27,931)
Lumber, Elizabeth 3:10:49 (1,819)
Lunn, Rebecca 5:49:09 (27,854)
Lurie Luke, Elena 6:11:11 (28,895)
Luscombe, Margo 6:32:19 (29,457)
Luthe, Andrea 4:09:58 (12,156)
Lyall, Caroline 5:39:27 (27,131)
Lyall, Victoria 5:40:54 (27,258)
Lye, Charlotte 4:53:21 (21,388)
Lyle, Christine 3:44:59 (6,684)
Lyman, Ella 4:33:10 (17,341)
Lynch, Kathleen 4:22:10 (14,847)
Lyon, Lynn 4:27:40 (16,107)
Lyon, Lynn 7:16:33 (30,059)
Lyselle, Skye 4:30:54 (16,826)
Maarek, Martine 5:01:18 (22,783)
Maas, Rianne 6:02:56 (28,537)
Maby, Julie 7:17:56 (30,067)
Maca, Viktoria 4:54:58 (21,721)
Macaulay, Sheila 4:35:40 (17,859)
Macauley, Siobhan 4:48:02 (20,354)
MacCabe, Gillian 4:42:11 (19,202)
Maccariello, Bettina 3:48:52 (7,433)
Macdiarmid, Mary 5:17:53 (25,148)
Macdonald, Anne Marie 5:19:08 (25,279)
Macdonald, Hannah 6:12:26 (28,944)
Macdonald, Lucy 4:28:58 (16,414)
Macdonald, Nicky 4:02:50 (10,628)
MacDougall, Lynne 2:37:20 (124)
MacDougall, Pippa 4:56:32 (22,074)
Machin, Betty 4:08:43 (11,916)
Machin, Claire 5:06:19 (23,524)
MacInnes, Christine 5:09:00 (23,941)
MacIver, Mandy 4:16:28 (13,566)
Mack, Elfriede 4:20:58 (14,584)
Mack, Elizabeth 4:44:44 (19,724)
Mackay, Lucy 5:13:59 (24,628)
Mackay, Sharon 4:49:54 (20,696)
Mackay, Suze 3:55:13 (8,738)
Mackenzie, Alison 4:34:41 (17,655)
Mackenzie, Donna 6:07:44 (28,750)
Mackenzie, Henrietta 3:56:38 (9,085)
Mackenzie, Kaeti 4:31:35 (17,003)
MacKeown, Stephanie 3:52:28 (8,163)
Mackie, Helen 3:37:16 (5,296)
Mackie, Jennifer 4:38:27 (18,494)
Mackin, Anne 6:52:51 (29,840)
Mackin, Mary 3:46:16 (6,910)
Mackintosh, Megan 3:31:07 (4,343)
MacLaran, Phillippa 4:44:53 (19,754)
Maclean, Lynda 5:24:09 (25,804)
Maclean, Nicola 4:47:18 (20,220)
MacLellan, Jennifer 4:17:03 (13,677)
Macleod, Juanita 5:36:23 (26,909)
Macleod, Rebecca 4:59:58 (22,616)
Macleod, Susanne 5:14:36 (24,727)
Macleod, Wendy 5:52:15 (28,031)
Macmillan, Tamara 4:29:02 (16,428)
Macpherson, Cam 4:40:51 (18,946)
Macpherson, Kimberley 5:44:56 (27,559)
Madden, Helen 5:06:11 (23,497)
Maddison, Heidi 5:13:51 (24,612)
Maddison, Louise 6:07:56 (28,758)
Maddock, Carole 6:04:09 (28,599)
Maddock, Maureen 5:29:08 (26,300)
Maddock, Natalie 4:45:23 (19,841)
Maddocks, Jennifer 4:00:40 (10,199)
Maddox, Angela 4:12:06 (12,648)
Magee, Louise 5:44:49 (27,550)
Mager, Kathrin 4:29:23 (16,516)
Maghribi, Aby 5:21:20 (25,510)
Maguire, Marie 5:20:25 (25,400)
Mahal, Amarjit 7:06:47 (29,994)
Maher, Jane 3:37:50 (5,386)
Mahn, Derilynn 3:05:11 (1,365)
Mahon, Iola 4:52:09 (21,124)
Mahoney, Margaret 5:41:36 (27,304)
Maier, Elfriede 5:02:53 (22,991)
Mail, Catharina 4:34:06 (17,557)
Maile, Louise 4:38:21 (18,466)
Maillard, Joan 5:18:41 (25,232)
Main, Sally 6:38:22 (29,595)
Main, Zoe 5:21:02 (25,473)

Maitland, Jill	5:04:12 (23,162)	
Maitland, Mary	6:51:20 (29,824)	
Major, Pippa	3:01:48 (1,137)	
Makin, Rachel	5:24:33 (25,842)	
Male, Suzanne	5:43:42 (27,449)	
Maley, Jane	4:58:01 (22,296)	
Malhotra, Surbhi	4:19:44 (14,302)	
Malicka, Danka	5:55:52 (28,207)	
Malim, Sophia	4:43:01 (19,389)	
Mallery, Lynne	5:30:19 (26,397)	
Mallin, Katie	5:06:53 (23,600)	
Malone, Julie	4:26:41 (15,887)	
Maltby, Diana	4:18:41 (14,049)	
Man, Sharon	4:48:39 (20,461)	
Manfield, Nicola	4:48:06 (20,367)	
Mangan, Geraldine	4:22:02 (14,822)	
Manley, Angela	4:23:48 (15,250)	
Manley, Joanne	8:37:30 (30,259)	
Manley, Sarah	4:33:54 (17,519)	
Manly, Rita	3:35:18 (4,952)	
Mann, Elies	4:19:18 (14,194)	
Mann, Fiona	8:50:08 (30,267)	
Mann, Olivia	3:57:43 (9,399)	
Mann, Robin	6:15:56 (29,057)	
Mann, Sarah	5:05:55 (23,451)	
Mannerings, Joanne	4:33:34 (17,443)	
Manners, Deborah	4:08:30 (11,871)	
Manning, Jane	3:47:50 (7,218)	
Mansbridge, Christine	5:59:38 (28,400)	
Mansell, Ann	4:51:47 (21,053)	
Mansell, Leslie	3:47:48 (7,210)	
Manser, Rebecca	5:59:14 (28,377)	
Mansfield, Kay	4:56:53 (22,125)	
Mansfield, Lynn	4:08:45 (11,923)	
Manson, Morna	5:44:09 (27,489)	
Manson, Nicola	4:19:53 (14,333)	
Mantel, Gail	3:24:34 (3,324)	
Manthorpe, Jane	3:44:14 (6,529)	
Manton, Maria	5:52:04 (28,020)	
Manville, Karen	4:49:53 (20,691)	
Maplethorpe, Claire	4:36:21 (17,985)	
March, Trudy	4:55:13 (21,789)	
Marchant, Jane	4:54:56 (21,713)	
Marchant, Norma	7:24:24 (30,104)	
Marchant, Zina	3:10:21 (1,780)	
Margaret, Emma	6:05:31 (28,666)	
Margetts, Sian	4:30:57 (16,839)	
Marien, Margaret	3:37:41 (5,363)	
Mark, Laura	5:44:02 (27,478)	
Markey, Catherine	6:21:29 (29,206)	
Marks, Angela	5:47:58 (27,774)	
Marks, Jemima	4:37:15 (18,182)	
Marks, Sherryl	4:21:22 (14,660)	
Markwick, Louise	4:17:04 (13,680)	
Marlow, Jennifer	5:46:30 (27,661)	
Marnane, Bridget	6:38:09 (29,592)	
Marolf, Rosemarie	5:04:24 (23,200)	
Marot, Véronique	3:11:50 (1,899)	
Marr, Jayne	5:22:32 (25,653)	
Marriott, Catherine	4:33:37 (17,459)	
Marriott, Lucy	5:13:04 (24,509)	
Marriott, Sharon	5:31:19 (26,477)	
Marrison-Astbury, Lisa	5:13:54 (24,616)	
Marsden, Jane	4:44:06 (19,597)	
Marsden, Lynn	7:41:54 (30,168)	
Marsden, Rachel	5:10:53 (24,194)	
Marsden, Winnie	6:09:20 (28,830)	
Marsh, Sara	3:48:29 (7,357)	
Marshall, Christine	5:26:37 (26,052)	
Marshall, Dawn	3:56:27 (9,040)	
Marshall, Julie	4:59:38 (22,544)	
Marshall, Kathryn	6:36:13 (29,547)	
Marshall, Linda	4:17:06 (13,685)	
Marshman, Catherine	5:20:22 (25,390)	
Martell, Corrie	5:29:16 (26,316)	
Martin, Ali	3:57:36 (9,363)	
Martin, Anne	3:58:26 (9,592)	
Martin, Carole	4:10:35 (12,293)	
Martin, Claire	4:52:05 (21,110)	
Martin, Elizabeth	5:31:24 (26,483)	
Martin, Isabel	4:00:23 (10,127)	
Martin, Pauline	3:54:33 (8,601)	
Martin, Rebecca	4:17:38 (13,799)	
Martin, Tamsin	4:49:16 (20,575)	
Martin, Terri	6:47:38 (29,771)	
Martin, Vivien	4:40:04 (18,799)	
Martin-Clarke, Susan	3:07:25 (1,536)	
Martinez, Laura	5:03:03 (23,012)	
Martin-Jenkins, Lucy	4:56:08 (22,009)	
Martyn, Angela	5:33:00 (26,613)	
Martyn, Josephine	5:24:20 (25,819)	
Martyn-Smith, Patricia	5:21:10 (25,483)	
Marzaioli, Sarah	4:40:33 (18,885)	
Mascitti, Rita	3:15:42 (2,289)	
Mason, Elizabeth	6:15:23 (29,043)	
Mason, Joanna	5:12:27 (24,421)	
Mason, Kate	4:36:44 (18,067)	
Mason, Katherine	6:16:17 (29,066)	
Mason, Kelly	5:42:08 (27,344)	
Mason, Laila	5:39:55 (27,181)	
Mason, Madelaine	6:47:22 (29,765)	
Mason, Maxine	3:27:50 (3,771)	
Mason, Susan	5:01:48 (22,838)	
Mason-Perez, Sarah	5:09:14 (23,973)	
Massaro, Mary Anne	4:47:29 (20,255)	
Massey, Jaqueline	2:58:29 (852)	
Massey, Michelle	5:37:32 (26,981)	
Massey, Rachel	6:10:00 (28,860)	
Massey, Sarah	2:52:06 (518)	
Masson, Kim	3:13:08 (2,017)	
Masters, Niamh	4:55:12 (21,783)	
Masters, Wendy	5:09:54 (24,069)	
Masterton, Kathryn	4:42:19 (19,231)	
Masterton, Lorna	4:31:36 (17,011)	
Mather, Carla	5:20:22 (25,390)	
Mather, Caroline	6:13:31 (28,977)	
Mather, Tracey	4:05:52 (11,313)	
Matheson, Patricia	3:06:05 (1,430)	
Mathew, Catherine	4:59:30 (22,527)	
Mathieu, Michelle	4:57:08 (22,162)	
Matin, Tahamina	3:38:49 (5,540)	
Matkovich, Michelle	5:41:59 (27,333)	
Matre, Kristin	3:47:29 (7,135)	
Matsumura, Kyoko	5:18:35 (25,222)	
Matthaei, Irene	4:31:34 (16,996)	
Matthew, Alison	4:47:55 (20,330)	
Matthews, Alison	5:32:25 (26,567)	
Matthews, Sarah	5:21:01 (25,471)	
Matthews, Shirley	5:50:44 (27,939)	
Matthews, Sophie	4:49:05 (20,540)	
Maud, Sarah	5:04:22 (23,193)	
Maude, Dea	5:09:29 (24,014)	
Maudsley, Jane	4:42:34 (19,284)	
Mauland, Kristin	3:12:20 (1,944)	
Mauleverer, Hattie	4:46:18 (20,008)	
Maunder, Claire	5:12:48 (24,470)	
Mauneau, Véronique	3:58:49 (9,703)	
Mauquoi-Tijskens, Ria	3:53:32 (8,387)	
Mawer, Claire	5:29:09 (26,302)	
Mawle, Elizabeth	4:45:49 (19,905)	
Maxfield, Kate	4:46:34 (20,071)	
Maxwell, Claire	3:14:40 (2,178)	
Maxwell, Sarah	6:34:46 (29,517)	
May, Claire	6:41:42 (29,682)	
May, Nicola	6:32:11 (29,454)	
Mayall, Karen	6:06:09 (28,690)	
Mayhew, Annette	3:56:34 (9,072)	
Mayle, Lucy	4:43:15 (19,438)	
Maynard, Charlotte	4:57:25 (22,205)	
Maynard, Colette	3:13:47 (2,087)	
Mayne, Louise	5:19:20 (25,295)	
Mayo, Kristy Anne	5:09:33 (24,021)	
Mayrinck, Christiane	3:36:15 (5,114)	
McAllister-Brown, Emily	5:28:30 (26,229)	
McAlonan, Claire	6:05:14 (28,652)	
McAlpine, Caroline	6:22:02 (29,216)	
McAulay, Frances	4:37:20 (18,206)	
McAuley, Bronach	4:29:17 (16,493)	
McAuliffe, Sharon	5:06:11 (23,497)	
McAvock, Gabrielle	3:59:32 (9,931)	
McBath, Jennifer	5:43:10 (27,420)	
McBean, Emily	6:10:07 (28,864)	
McCabe, Ann	4:57:16 (22,181)	
McCabe, Jennifer	4:41:20 (19,033)	
McCann, Alex	5:29:42 (26,346)	
McCann, Gill	4:18:43 (14,056)	
McCarthy, Claire	4:59:20 (22,503)	
McCarthy, Donna	5:15:42 (24,891)	
McCarthy, Jacqueline	5:59:37 (28,398)	
McCarthy, Laura	5:03:22 (23,049)	
McCarthy, Lisa	6:08:46 (28,800)	
McCartney, Clare	4:40:25 (18,860)	
McCartney, Paula	4:40:25 (18,860)	
McChesney, Angela	4:45:55 (19,921)	
McClellan, Brenda	4:42:52 (19,352)	
McClelland, Tracy	4:34:35 (17,641)	
McClure, Angela	6:02:02 (28,507)	
McCorkell, Lauren	6:28:59 (29,386)	
McCormac, Sherilee	4:29:08 (16,458)	
McCormack, Marie	7:33:10 (30,149)	
McCormick, Samantha	4:29:17 (16,493)	
McCrea, Sarah	5:43:12 (27,422)	
McCreary, Debbie	3:57:30 (9,326)	
McCulloch, Jane	5:12:55 (24,485)	
McCurdie, Susan	4:29:55 (16,665)	
McDade, Brenda	6:29:58 (29,408)	
McDermott, Melita	5:03:52 (23,111)	
McDermott, Sarah	6:18:00 (29,113)	
McDoanld, Linda	4:19:27 (14,241)	
McDonagh, Linda	4:03:30 (10,774)	
McDonald, Ann	4:28:06 (16,210)	
McDonald, Haley	4:18:08 (13,895)	
McDonald, Isabella	6:08:51 (28,810)	
McDonald, Jacqui	4:43:26 (19,473)	
McDonald, Janet	4:34:30 (17,628)	
McDonald, Jennie	5:02:51 (22,984)	
McDonald, Kathryn	5:27:51 (26,164)	
McDonald, Mairi	4:34:30 (17,628)	
McDonald, Ruth	4:25:32 (15,625)	
McDonald, Sarah	5:24:30 (25,836)	
McDonnell, Claire	4:22:46 (14,996)	
McDougal, Patricia	3:47:24 (7,117)	
McDougall, Martha	4:35:03 (17,723)	
McDougall, Susan	4:53:17 (21,368)	
McDowall, Linda	4:40:38 (18,906)	
McDowell, Jennifer	4:21:57 (14,796)	
McElhinney, Rose	4:57:16 (22,181)	
McEnery, Maria	4:32:45 (17,263)	
McEvoy, Lynn	4:31:49 (17,062)	
McEwan, Leena	5:33:45 (26,667)	
McFarland, Kerry	3:22:09 (3,019)	
McFeeney, Siobhan	3:56:53 (9,151)	
McGarry, Elena	6:54:29 (29,868)	
McGarry, Janet	4:25:21 (15,583)	
McGarry, Yvonne	3:36:14 (5,112)	
McGee, Melanie	4:27:01 (15,971)	
McGibbon, Jean	4:44:17 (19,635)	
McGilly, Claire	7:23:52 (30,099)	
McGilvray, Kate	4:25:53 (15,698)	
McGinley, Rebecca	4:44:47 (19,729)	
McGivern, Ruth	4:33:23 (17,394)	
McGlashan, Sheenagh	5:13:41 (24,594)	
McGloin, Fiona	4:56:31 (22,069)	
McGlynn, Claire	4:53:07 (21,339)	
McGonigal, Christine	5:38:42 (27,066)	
McGovern, Carole	4:52:29 (21,200)	
McGovern, Lee	4:18:31 (14,017)	
McGrath, Jacki	5:17:58 (25,159)	
McGrath, Louise	5:57:27 (28,294)	
McGrath, Mary	3:59:21 (9,863)	
McGrath, Rose	5:10:47 (24,181)	
McGuiness, Yvonne	6:39:52 (29,624)	
McGuire, Brenda	5:52:41 (28,047)	
McGuire, Jill	4:19:36 (14,279)	
McGurgan, Julie	5:49:08 (27,851)	
McHarry-Holt, Helen	4:48:14 (20,391)	
McIntosh, Joyce	6:11:30 (28,909)	
McIntosh, Marie	5:01:52 (22,846)	
McIntosh, Sian	3:58:36 (9,642)	
McIntyre, Jill	6:43:51 (29,716)	
McKay, Angela	4:26:23 (15,821)	
McKay, Deborah	4:44:45 (19,726)	
McKay, Glenda	3:29:21 (4,058)	
McKee, Pamela	3:48:35 (7,376)	
McKellar, Lizzi	6:18:58 (29,135)	
McKendrick, Ashley	5:56:40 (28,251)	
McKenna, Natasha	3:42:47 (6,269)	
McKenzie, Fiona	4:57:30 (22,217)	
McKinnon, Robin	6:18:07 (29,118)	

McKnight, Lesley 5:25:04 (25,893)
McLachlan, Helen 3:47:14 (7,069)
McLaren, Julie 4:24:02 (15,302)
McLaughlin, Frances 3:40:24 (5,849)
McLean, Christine 3:24:33 (3,320)
McLean, Dawn 7:16:01 (30,051)
McLean, Penny 5:55:39 (28,199)
McLellam, Amy 3:51:27 (7,952)
McLoughlin, Sarah 3:13:13 (2,030)
McMahon, Patricia 5:16:26 (24,975)
McManus, Christine 5:56:16 (28,226)
McMaster, Ali 4:32:46 (17,270)
McMenamin, Myra 4:16:06 (13,487)
McMillan, Heather 4:28:30 (16,314)
McMillan, Helen 6:38:26 (29,596)
McMillan, Kay 4:20:55 (14,575)
McMullan, Pauline 7:03:06 (29,968)
McMullan, Philippa 4:45:39 (19,879)
McMullen, Sarah 5:45:10 (27,569)
McMurray, Lindsey 3:33:59 (4,752)
McNally, Nicola 3:15:56 (2,314)
McNamara, Angela 6:03:46 (28,577)
McNaughton, Nicola 5:15:20 (24,846)
McNee, Joanna 4:10:57 (12,389)
McNelis, Mary 6:08:23 (28,781)
McNicholl, June 6:35:35 (29,536)
McPherson Kelly, Katrine 4:22:37 (14,958)
McQueen, Toni 4:09:23 (12,061)
McSheary, Caroline 4:51:37 (21,012)
McSherry, Jennifer 4:14:33 (13,140)
McSweeney, Donna 5:21:44 (25,552)
McTigue, Jill 6:14:48 (29,016)
McTigue, Veronica 6:14:48 (29,016)
McWhirter, Emily 5:55:06 (28,160)
Mead, Carolyn 4:41:28 (19,057)
Mead, Sammy 5:46:14 (27,643)
Meadows, Anne 5:10:28 (24,138)
Meads, Johanne 4:34:04 (17,547)
Meakin, Nicola 5:27:01 (26,084)
Meara, Hannah 4:57:01 (22,141)
Meardon, Lita 6:15:16 (29,033)
Mearns, Melanie 4:18:44 (14,063)
Medland, Katherine 6:11:30 (28,909)
Meehan, Annemarie 5:59:17 (28,381)
Meehan, Katie 5:46:32 (27,665)
Meek, Becky 5:12:55 (24,485)
Meffert, Gisela 4:28:27 (16,301)
Meghezzi, Elaine 4:55:47 (21,952)
Meijer, Michelle 4:07:41 (11,692)
Meiners, Susan 5:55:13 (28,165)
Meldrum, Judy 4:36:45 (18,070)
Melhuish, Emily 6:04:21 (28,611)
Melican, Elizabeth 4:49:54 (20,696)
Mellis, Susan 4:59:14 (22,490)
Mellor, Nikki 4:04:58 (11,111)
Melton, Mary Dubbie 6:26:50 (29,329)
Melville, Karen 5:04:13 (23,166)
Melville-James, Anna 5:21:39 (25,541)
Melville-Walker, Samantha 3:18:59 (2,654)
Mendelssohn, Jane 4:45:09 (19,796)
Mendham, Janet 6:06:53 (28,715)
Mendham, Lorraine 4:51:01 (20,889)
Mendoza, Maria 4:37:15 (18,182)
Menzies Gow, Sarah 3:53:03 (8,277)
Mercer, Kate 4:41:43 (19,104)
Mercer, Steph 4:43:17 (19,447)
Merrell, Karen 5:41:55 (27,328)
Merrill, Carol 4:24:09 (15,318)
Merrills, Sharon 4:10:49 (12,350)
Merritt, Marie 6:01:59 (28,505)
Merry, Lianne 5:04:51 (23,276)
Mersey, Annie 5:15:38 (24,882)
Messent, Catherine 6:27:17 (29,338)
Metcalfe, Margaret 5:11:00 (24,212)
Metclafe, Amy 6:12:25 (28,941)
Metivier, Dominique 4:55:57 (21,979)
Metz, Cara 4:58:39 (22,403)
Meyer, Claire 5:23:27 (25,737)
Meyer, Greta 6:04:00 (28,590)
Michez, Lisa 3:59:00 (9,754)
Micklewright, Joanne 3:57:50 (9,440)
Middlehurst, Susan 4:09:58 (12,156)
Middleton, Angela 4:48:42 (20,471)
Middleton, Christine 4:21:01 (14,595)
Middleton, Hope 5:59:19 (28,383)
Middleton, Jo 5:36:56 (26,940)
Middleton, Kay 5:09:59 (24,079)
Middleton, Sally 5:21:44 (25,552)
Middleton, Sarah 5:53:34 (28,096)
Midleton, Julia 3:28:01 (3,805)
Mihill, Karen 5:23:51 (25,774)
Miles, Beverly 5:27:40 (26,145)
Miles, Claire 4:36:32 (18,026)
Miles, Helen 4:42:13 (19,209)
Miles, Julie 5:00:45 (22,700)
Miles, Karen 3:58:40 (9,661)
Miles, Maria 6:08:52 (28,812)
Mill, Martha 4:16:24 (13,552)
Millar, Caroline 4:41:29 (19,060)
Millard, Lisa 4:50:45 (20,835)
Miller, Abigail 4:30:05 (16,706)
Miller, Caroline 4:12:05 (12,640)
Miller, Diana 4:00:42 (10,211)
Miller, Elena 4:39:00 (18,603)
Miller, Elizabeth 4:24:24 (15,370)
Miller, Jacqueline 6:05:13 (28,648)
Miller, Karen 5:03:20 (23,046)
Miller, Linda 4:30:26 (16,747)
Miller, Linda 6:24:34 (29,274)
Miller, Rachel 4:42:10 (19,198)
Miller, Samantha 5:51:41 (27,995)
Miller, Tracy 5:49:04 (27,844)
Miller, Wendy Jane 5:25:10 (25,902)
Millers, Angela 4:56:54 (22,128)
Millington, Eleanor 3:33:10 (4,636)
Millner, Patricia 6:46:54 (29,756)
Mills, Ali 5:26:16 (26,017)
Mills, Hayley 6:50:39 (29,815)
Mills, Jacqueline 4:08:23 (11,846)
Mills, Janette 4:41:52 (19,131)
Mills, Maria 5:15:37 (24,879)
Mills, Nicola 4:33:57 (17,526)
Mills, Sara 6:39:41 (29,621)
Millward, Deborah 3:28:43 (3,939)
Millward, Lisa 4:55:37 (21,928)
Millward, Nicola 4:48:27 (20,433)
Miln, Judy 4:52:07 (21,117)
Milne, Ali 6:08:54 (28,814)
Milne, Sandra 3:42:07 (6,141)
Milner, Linda 5:34:09 (26,716)
Minchella, Natasha 5:28:10 (26,189)
Mindenhall, Lucinda 4:21:40 (14,727)
Minford, Louise 4:16:24 (13,552)
Minter, Briony 5:45:48 (27,617)
Minter-Frier, Tracey 5:30:28 (26,409)
Minty, Joan 3:55:43 (8,848)
Minze-Sparno, Maryellen 4:10:18 (12,226)
Mischler, Beatrix 3:23:25 (3,162)
Missen, Elspeth 4:08:31 (11,875)
Mistry, Claire 5:56:51 (28,263)
Mitchell, Angela 6:19:39 (29,151)
Mitchell, Avril 4:37:37 (18,282)
Mitchell, Carole 5:45:26 (27,586)
Mitchell, Claire 5:28:20 (26,212)
Mitchell, Clare 3:50:09 (7,716)
Mitchell, Elaine 4:08:59 (11,974)
Mitchell, Heather 3:49:11 (7,493)
Mitchell, Jacqueline 5:08:57 (23,930)
Mitchell, Jayne 5:28:36 (26,240)
Mitchell, Kay 5:59:46 (28,407)
Mitchell, Kerry 3:38:10 (5,421)
Mitchell, Vivienne 4:56:36 (22,088)
Mitra, Jane 5:17:36 (25,115)
Mizen, Angela 4:26:23 (15,821)
Mobley, Kate 3:58:11 (9,533)
Moffat, Jane 4:35:15 (17,761)
Moffat, Sharon 6:15:45 (29,053)
Moffatt, Petra 3:48:22 (7,332)
Moffett, Bronwyn 4:30:20 (16,732)
Mollaret, Arielle 4:18:54 (14,098)
Molloy, Sharron 6:30:20 (29,420)
Monaghan, Dottie 5:24:14 (25,810)
Moncada, Anne 4:47:36 (20,283)
Mongia, Saloni 6:56:52 (29,906)
Monk, Emma 4:45:23 (19,841)
Monnier, Bellay 3:50:46 (7,820)
Montgomery, Geraldine 4:44:12 (19,619)
Moody, Alison 6:50:27 (29,812)
Moody, Karen 7:56:50 (30,205)
Moon, Clare 4:57:10 (22,167)
Moon, Melissa 2:41:58 (217)
Mooney, Carole 3:40:56 (5,939)
Moore, Alison 4:27:27 (16,050)
Moore, Elizabeth 4:38:28 (18,500)
Moore, Helen 5:10:44 (24,179)
Moore, Inge 4:36:46 (18,072)
Moore, Jennifer 4:53:04 (21,330)
Moore, Joanne 4:16:21 (13,536)
Moore, Karen 5:27:42 (26,151)
Moore, Rachael 3:44:07 (6,514)
Moore, Rachael 5:37:34 (26,989)
Moore, Rebecca 4:57:12 (22,172)
Moore, Sally 4:27:37 (16,096)
Moore, Tracie 4:51:12 (20,923)
Moorhouse, Shona 4:52:32 (21,216)
Moran, Carol 4:48:21 (20,416)
Moran, Joanne 3:38:51 (5,548)
Moran, Judith 6:08:04 (28,767)
Moran, Sarah 5:16:03 (24,933)
Moranz, Julia 4:00:27 (10,136)
Moreau, Irene 3:17:30 (2,485)
Moreau, Linda 3:15:16 (2,251)
Morel, Susanna 6:42:38 (29,701)
Moreton, Penny 4:05:45 (11,287)
Moreton, Sally 4:46:50 (20,126)
Morgan, Carole 4:33:10 (17,341)
Morgan, Cathy 5:11:21 (24,262)
Morgan, Debra 5:38:33 (27,053)
Morgan, Denise 4:34:56 (17,700)
Morgan, Grainne 4:13:10 (12,853)
Morgan, Helen 5:49:45 (27,885)
Morgan, Joanne 3:23:49 (3,213)
Morgan, June 7:01:28 (29,957)
Morgan, Karen 5:07:43 (23,732)
Morgan, Katherine 5:12:09 (24,369)
Morgan, Kathy 5:33:53 (26,678)
Morgan, Lisa 5:25:07 (25,900)
Morgan, Lowri 3:33:38 (4,702)
Morgan, Lucy 5:00:23 (22,655)
Morgan, Michelle 4:33:36 (17,455)
Morgan, Nicola 3:25:28 (3,441)
Morgan-Wilson, Tracey 5:38:42 (27,066)
Moriarty, Louise 3:55:10 (8,726)
Moric, Natalie 4:47:47 (20,307)
Morley, Clare 4:02:42 (10,608)
Morley, Emma 5:01:54 (22,854)
Morley, Jane 4:02:42 (10,608)
Morley, Sarah 5:07:33 (23,701)
Moroz, Catherine 4:35:08 (17,736)
Morrall, Zelah 2:56:27 (715)
Morrell-Glenister, Diana 6:33:20 (29,489)
Morris, Beryl 6:54:34 (29,870)
Morris, Cassandra 5:08:46 (23,899)
Morris, Charlotte 4:41:22 (19,040)
Morris, Colette 5:11:27 (24,276)
Morris, Dora 6:13:39 (28,983)
Morris, Elizabeth 5:41:24 (27,290)
Morris, Emily 4:27:12 (16,011)
Morris, Erica 4:26:33 (15,856)
Morris, Gina 3:40:32 (5,873)
Morris, Helen 3:42:04 (6,131)
Morris, Hilary 5:08:12 (23,797)
Morris, Jacqui 5:22:00 (25,585)
Morris, Julie 4:18:15 (13,935)
Morris, Karen 4:14:44 (13,185)
Morris, Karen 5:09:24 (23,999)
Morris, Kylie 6:37:48 (29,587)
Morris, Lesley 6:04:42 (28,630)
Morris, Linda 3:34:09 (4,779)
Morris, Lois 5:49:18 (27,861)
Morris, Nikki 4:06:11 (11,379)
Morris, Norma 6:49:29 (29,795)
Morris, Patricia 5:39:50 (27,169)
Morris, Philippa 5:28:31 (26,231)
Morris, Sarah 4:47:31 (20,267)
Morrison, Danethea 3:59:35 (9,944)
Morrison, Zoe 4:00:29 (10,148)
Morrissey, Carole 4:04:32 (11,001)
Morrissey, Helen 6:21:09 (29,197)

Morrissey, Michelle	4:27:33 (16,075)
Morrow, Emma	4:52:51 (21,277)
Morrow, Karen	4:58:28 (22,371)
Morshed, Sima	4:44:10 (19,613)
Mortimer, Alison	4:08:54 (11,956)
Mortimer, Claire	4:46:33 (20,067)
Mortimer, Jacqueline	5:28:46 (26,264)
Mortimore, Hester	4:51:45 (21,043)
Mortlock, Lisa	5:02:39 (22,956)
Morton, Meryl	4:57:35 (22,225)
Morton, Sonia	6:15:00 (29,024)
Morton, Susan	3:14:40 (2,178)
Moshe, Donna	5:38:58 (27,084)
Mosley, Michelle	4:44:49 (19,736)
Moss, Kim	3:51:29 (7,960)
Mostue, Trude	4:50:50 (20,851)
Mott-Brown, Karen	5:14:53 (24,762)
Mottershead, Sally	6:20:56 (29,191)
Mottram, Rachel	5:31:32 (26,490)
Moullin, Alison	7:29:43 (30,134)
Mountain, Christina	8:43:24 (30,262)
Mountney, Alison	4:55:39 (21,940)
Mounty, Maureen	4:20:35 (14,496)
Mourier, Anette	4:24:42 (15,437)
Moylan, Ann	6:26:48 (29,326)
Moyle, Camilla	3:38:25 (5,469)
Muchenje, Juliet	5:41:48 (27,316)
Mugglestone, Sophie	4:01:52 (10,455)
Mukerjee, Rita	4:37:20 (18,206)
Mulholland, Karen	4:18:22 (13,976)
Mullaney, Ann	5:30:40 (26,424)
Mullard, Amanda	4:39:58 (18,783)
Mulligan, Choo-Liang	5:20:26 (25,402)
Mullin, Jacqueline	3:58:49 (9,703)
Mulvey, Margaret	3:17:10 (2,442)
Mundei, Joanne	4:15:11 (13,299)
Mundy, Hannah	6:02:41 (28,528)
Munnings, Linda	5:41:21 (27,282)
Munro, Gail	5:36:57 (26,942)
Munro, Sarah	5:49:49 (27,890)
Munt, Linda	4:24:39 (15,431)
Murati, Murielle	4:07:40 (11,690)
Murchison, Emma	4:30:42 (16,786)
Murdin, Margaret	4:45:56 (19,926)
Murfith, Lorraine	5:28:40 (26,249)
Muris, Nicole	5:10:55 (24,201)
Murkison, Jennifer	5:40:35 (27,239)
Murphy, Bridget	5:27:57 (26,176)
Murphy, Chris	5:33:58 (26,686)
Murphy, Jayne	3:49:13 (7,500)
Murphy, Joanne	4:23:31 (15,179)
Murphy, Karen	3:44:33 (6,588)
Murphy, Kate	3:49:12 (7,498)
Murphy, Lisa	4:01:45 (10,436)
Murphy, Louise	4:26:08 (15,762)
Murphy, Maria	6:51:47 (29,829)
Murphy, Patricia	5:49:08 (27,851)
Murray, Andrea	3:48:39 (7,391)
Murray, Carol	3:29:16 (4,042)
Murray, Catherine	5:44:48 (27,546)
Murray, Lelsey	5:41:00 (27,261)
Murray, Lindsay	4:33:32 (17,428)
Murray, Maeve	4:46:05 (19,954)
Murray, Sue	7:10:36 (30,027)
Murray, Valerie	5:57:04 (28,273)
Murton, Gillian	6:55:19 (29,886)
Mussi, Clare	4:36:30 (18,021)
Muston, Rosemary	3:32:32 (4,542)
Muxworthy, Anja	3:56:13 (8,971)
Myatt, Julia	3:01:38 (1,127)
Mycock, Maria	4:35:21 (17,786)
Mydin, Nooraini	7:38:02 (30,157)
Myers, Catherine	5:20:24 (25,397)
Myerscough, Deborah	3:19:52 (2,749)
Mylne, Sophie	5:12:18 (24,392)
Nafpactitou, Dimitra	5:53:03 (28,067)
Nagahara, Kazuko	5:00:23 (22,655)
Nagai, Tomoko	4:59:59 (22,619)
Naidu, Beverley	4:31:55 (17,095)
Nairn, Janet	5:37:17 (26,963)
Najurally, Narisa	3:50:48 (7,824)
Nandra, Kirat	4:15:44 (13,411)
Nandrup, Michelle	4:51:41 (21,029)

Nandy, Tilottama	5:07:54 (23,758)
Napton, Jane	4:49:11 (20,556)
Narques, Silvia	4:08:27 (11,862)
Nasey, Charlotte	5:09:52 (24,065)
Nash, Claire	4:44:50 (19,738)
Nash, Lesley	5:13:53 (24,614)
Nash, Louise	4:55:24 (21,849)
Nasrallah, Etoile	5:46:28 (27,654)
Neail, Paula	5:04:13 (23,166)
Neal, Alison	5:02:05 (22,887)
Neal, Angela	4:20:56 (14,581)
Neal, Katy	4:57:39 (22,239)
Nealon, Colleen	4:44:55 (19,762)
Neary, Helen	4:34:59 (17,709)
Neath, Prue	5:04:21 (23,189)
Neaves, Kelly	5:16:28 (24,984)
Nedergaard, Hanne	4:26:36 (15,871)
Nelson, Chloe	3:45:20 (6,721)
Nelson, Elizabeth	5:44:29 (27,513)
Nelson, Martine	4:17:30 (13,773)
Nelson, Michelle	3:32:31 (4,538)
Neocleous, Anna	5:10:15 (24,113)
Nequest, Anne	3:52:57 (8,257)
Nesbitt, Allyson	6:13:28 (28,968)
Nesbitt, Sarah	6:23:31 (29,244)
Neve, Michele	6:20:56 (29,191)
Neville, Elizabeth	3:18:53 (2,641)
Nevitt, Katy	5:19:43 (25,337)
Newberry, Helen	5:57:38 (28,305)
Newell, Georgina	4:46:23 (20,031)
Newman, Kate	5:29:12 (26,310)
Newman, Mandy	3:51:29 (7,960)
Newns, Elizabeth	4:37:10 (18,162)
Newport, Melanie	4:09:00 (11,978)
Newsholme, Pauline	5:15:44 (24,896)
Newstead, Johanne	3:40:19 (5,832)
Newton, Amy	7:07:52 (30,005)
Newton, Sarah	3:15:35 (2,279)
Nice, Lorraine	6:04:10 (28,601)
Nicholas, Anna	4:15:33 (13,377)
Nicholls, Alison	3:33:05 (4,619)
Nicholls, Frances	5:09:54 (24,069)
Nicholls, Janet	3:27:50 (3,771)
Nicholls, Sarah	3:21:08 (2,900)
Nichols, Evelyn	5:34:41 (26,773)
Nichols, Karen	5:07:05 (23,628)
Nichols, Louise	4:46:04 (19,951)
Nichols, Olivia	4:45:22 (19,835)
Nicholson, Jenny	5:01:12 (22,768)
Nicholson, Patricia	5:10:14 (24,110)
Nicol, Anne	5:55:23 (28,176)
Nicol, Jacqueline	3:53:54 (8,460)
Nicoll, Gail	5:30:11 (26,385)
Nicolle, Sophie	4:21:31 (14,695)
Nicolle, Susan	4:36:44 (18,067)
Nielsen, Wendy	5:11:08 (24,232)
Nieuwendyk, Cornelia	5:20:26 (25,402)
Nightingale, Roxanne	4:13:52 (13,015)
Nisbet, Sheila	5:45:54 (27,626)
Niven, Clare	4:55:21 (21,831)
Nixon, Sarah	5:25:01 (25,887)
Nkongho, Nnena	6:09:42 (28,845)
Noakes, Fabienne	4:58:32 (22,383)
Noble, Eileen	4:56:09 (22,011)
Noble, Shelley	5:40:18 (27,209)
Noble, Susan	5:01:44 (22,828)
Noble, Yvonne	5:02:38 (22,952)
Nobles, Margaret	4:43:31 (19,503)
Nockles, Dionne	4:46:54 (20,144)
Noon, Andrea	5:19:21 (25,298)
Noon, Lynn	8:07:36 (30,223)
Norbury, Jacqueline	6:30:25 (29,424)
Nordin, Breege	3:30:05 (4,185)
Norlund, Anne	4:03:32 (10,783)
Norman, Rosemary	5:25:22 (25,925)
Norrie, Clare	5:28:30 (26,229)
Norris, Christine	5:00:08 (22,636)
Norris, Cresta	5:37:44 (27,004)
Norris, Maureen	4:38:05 (18,398)
Norris, Natasha	5:40:04 (27,194)
Norris, Rebecca	5:22:06 (25,599)
North, Lisa	4:05:30 (11,213)
North, Lisa	4:49:24 (20,598)

North, Sonia	6:06:36 (28,705)
North, Sonya	5:28:52 (26,280)
Northwood, Jackie	7:23:52 (30,099)
Nortoin, Kirsty	5:01:58 (22,866)
Norton, Anne Lucie	5:12:19 (24,396)
Norton, Deborah	4:16:19 (13,527)
Norton, Fiona	5:16:46 (25,023)
Norton, Georgie	5:11:59 (24,351)
Norton, Kim	6:36:22 (29,552)
Norton, Sara	4:29:06 (16,452)
Norville, Maria	4:55:26 (21,863)
Nouvel, Anne	4:10:32 (12,279)
Nowicka, Helen	4:29:48 (16,625)
Nugent, Natasha	5:39:55 (27,181)
Nuilbercq, Amelie	6:16:23 (29,068)
Nunn, Anne	3:46:09 (6,888)
Nunnerley Hood, Lorena	6:17:55 (29,111)
Nurden, Robert	5:08:50 (23,912)
Nussli, Daniela	3:25:28 (3,441)
Nutley, Claire	7:24:02 (30,102)
Nutt, Victoria	6:16:07 (29,060)
Nuttall, Cynthia	5:37:59 (27,018)
Nyamah, Charity	6:41:13 (29,664)
Nygaard Kristensen, Vinni	6:25:29 (29,295)
Nyker, Jasandra	5:11:11 (24,241)
Nystroem, Lisbeth	4:56:20 (22,041)
Oakes, Anne	4:13:53 (13,017)
Oakes, Kathleen	6:05:17 (28,654)
Oakes, Teresa	4:42:33 (19,281)
Oakley, Judy	2:51:29 (488)
Oates, Caitlin	5:57:28 (28,297)
Oatts, Elizabeth	4:08:05 (11,784)
Oberman, Lucy	4:21:49 (14,766)
Obrastsoff-Rutinsky, Joanna	5:00:16 (22,644)
O'Brien, Bernadette	3:39:22 (5,641)
O'Brien, Johanna	4:13:42 (12,981)
O'Brien, Kamaljit	5:51:14 (27,963)
O'Brien, Mary	3:59:19 (9,849)
O'Brien, Meghan	4:46:12 (19,988)
O'Callaghan, Sarah	5:00:00 (22,622)
O'Connell, Celia	7:56:51 (30,206)
O'Connor, Margaret	3:27:11 (3,657)
O'Connor, Sarah	6:53:29 (29,857)
Odams, Suzanne	5:11:46 (24,323)
Oddie, Elaine	4:32:41 (17,243)
Oddy, Katrina	3:28:15 (3,865)
Odey, Katy	4:09:44 (12,112)
Odgers, Nicky	5:16:25 (24,974)
O'Donnell, Amanda	6:25:05 (29,283)
O'Donnell, Kathleen	5:05:57 (23,461)
O'Dowd, Joanne	3:26:52 (3,605)
Offer, Caroline	4:26:32 (15,851)
Offer, Judith	3:49:13 (7,500)
Offord, Lesley	6:11:39 (28,913)
Offord, Rachel	4:27:51 (16,163)
Offord, Stephanie	6:20:45 (29,184)
Ogawa, Yukiko	4:27:52 (16,167)
Ogden, Jane	4:21:21 (14,656)
Ogilvy-Stuart, Amanda	4:17:48 (13,832)
Ogle, Susan	4:41:44 (19,108)
O'Gorman, Sinead	4:51:34 (20,999)
Oguntoyinbo, Lande	4:33:27 (17,405)
O'Hagan, Collette	4:57:48 (22,266)
Ohayon, Rebecca	4:02:09 (10,514)
O'Heney, Josie	6:08:01 (28,764)
O'Keefe, Collette	4:49:42 (20,654)
Okwu, Antonia	4:17:35 (13,789)
Olaru, Nuta	2:25:18 (42)
Oldacre, Melanie	5:09:57 (24,076)
Oldershaw, Tina	3:22:45 (3,078)
Oldfield, Julie	5:18:59 (25,265)
Oldham, Pauline	4:16:56 (13,653)
Oldman, Zoe	4:48:15 (20,395)
Oldroyd, Susan	4:18:28 (14,005)
O'Leary, Claire	4:31:45 (17,048)
Olesen, Ella	3:44:30 (6,576)
Oliver, Barbara	4:28:39 (16,350)
Oliver, Deborah	3:57:55 (9,469)
Oliver, Donna	5:25:42 (25,960)
Oller-Morris, Eva	4:20:00 (14,368)
Ollis, Helen	5:03:25 (23,058)
Olney, Dita	4:22:43 (14,987)
Omstead, Helen	5:20:07 (25,371)

Onaran, Melia 4:51:34 (20,999)
O'Neill, Anita 6:41:14 (29,665)
O'Neill, Janet......................3:58:33 (9,625)
O'Neill, Julie 6:05:42 (28,675)
O'Neill, Katherine 4:28:21 (16,271)
O'Neill, Monika 4:57:17 (22,187)
O'Neill, Patricia...................3:55:42 (8,843)
O'Neill, Susan 5:39:19 (27,117)
Oneta, Sonia 3:50:55 (7,853)
Onslow, Jaqueline 6:37:36 (29,580)
Openshaw, Elizabeth............4:55:30 (21,893)
Orban, Mary 4:04:54 (11,096)
Ord, Louise 5:49:38 (27,878)
Oregan, Catherine 4:05:22 (11,179)
O'Reilly, May 6:21:51 (29,213)
O'Reilly, Sarah Jane 6:03:46 (28,577)
O'Riordan, Tracy..................5:17:58 (25,159)
Orr, Pearl 4:16:09 (13,496)
Orrells, Caroline 5:09:34 (24,024)
Orth, Barbara 3:49:11 (7,493)
Orth, Jackie 5:02:52 (22,988)
Orton, Lorraine 3:59:58 (10,047)
Osborn, Hayley....................5:37:24 (26,971)
Osborne, Janette 3:56:27 (9,040)
Osborne, Susan 7:43:50 (30,178)
Osborne, Susannah...............3:49:16 (7,515)
Oscroft, Jennifer 4:33:53 (17,518)
Osman, Lucie 4:38:28 (18,500)
Ostojic, Vera 3:59:18 (9,841)
Ostoya, Kasia 5:47:01 (27,707)
O'Sullivan, Marie 4:05:55 (11,327)
O'Sullivan, Theresa..............5:02:13 (22,908)
Otley, Deborah 4:00:20 (10,113)
O'Toole, Anne Marie.............7:28:12 (30,127)
O'Toole, Marie 6:20:01 (29,158)
Ott, Elsbeth 4:20:00 (14,368)
Ottaway, Julia 6:28:46 (29,382)
Otterburn, Phoebe................5:41:28 (27,295)
Otto, Petra 4:51:26 (20,975)
Otton, Carrie 4:24:07 (15,314)
Ovens, Jan 3:37:48 (5,378)
Ovens, Michelle...................5:08:57 (23,930)
Oversby, Ann 5:40:01 (27,189)
Overson, Sally.....................5:14:58 (24,772)
Overy, Nicolette 4:14:57 (13,252)
Owen, Dianne 5:19:48 (25,347)
Owen, Lucy 5:26:39 (26,055)
Owen, Lynne 5:12:05 (24,362)
Owen, Mary 3:46:32 (6,956)
Owen, Rhian 4:47:25 (20,246)
Owens, Jo 5:05:27 (23,372)
Owens, Sheila 4:07:17 (11,606)
Ozdemir, Ayla 5:26:30 (26,044)
Ozminskyj, Annie 5:06:33 (23,552)
Packham, Adele....................4:27:58 (16,188)
Paddon, Lucy.......................4:38:20 (18,462)
Padghan, Melanie 4:40:59 (18,974)
Padilla, Josephine................4:26:13 (15,780)
Pagan, Deborah 3:36:45 (5,204)
Page, Andrea 5:04:43 (23,247)
Page, Clare..........................3:57:09 (9,210)
Page, Sue 4:46:49 (20,119)
Page, Susan 4:28:27 (16,301)
Page, Susannah 4:13:37 (12,961)
Pagett, Charlotte 5:13:17 (24,550)
Paice, Melanie 4:48:55 (20,509)
Pain, Annette.......................4:51:50 (21,060)
Paine, Doreen 4:07:38 (11,684)
Painter, Penelope 4:47:04 (20,177)
Pakenham, Johanna...............5:44:07 (27,484)
Paley, Barbara......................5:51:24 (27,974)
Paling, Judith.......................4:20:13 (14,411)
Palmer, Barbara 3:55:54 (8,894)
Palmer, Brenda 5:16:21 (24,963)
Palmer, Helen 6:11:03 (28,890)
Palmer, Jean 4:32:00 (17,120)
Palmer, Jennifer 3:56:02 (8,934)
Palmer, Jennifer 3:59:25 (9,891)
Palmer, Julia 4:02:45 (10,617)
Palmer, Julie 5:13:38 (24,588)
Palmer, Karen 5:00:29 (22,659)
Palmer, Lucyna.....................5:40:03 (27,193)
Palmer, Lyn 3:57:44 (9,403)

Palmer, Sally 6:32:32 (29,464)
Palmer, Susan 5:33:11 (26,624)
Panayiotodes, Katy 4:59:22 (22,506)
Pang, Yinsan 5:53:01 (28,063)
Pank, Carolyn 5:48:23 (27,805)
Panzera, Diane 5:34:26 (26,749)
Parbhu, Sonal 4:55:27 (21,872)
Pardo, Claire 4:40:55 (18,959)
Pares, Sarah 4:46:08 (19,967)
Parford, Karen 3:53:06 (8,292)
Park, Andrea 6:41:15 (29,666)
Park, Avril 5:24:43 (25,853)
Park, Janice 4:08:00 (11,764)
Parken, Emily 4:25:24 (15,593)
Parken, Helen 5:10:47 (24,181)
Parker, Annette 4:32:22 (17,186)
Parker, Barbara....................2:58:17 (831)
Parker, Deborah 3:16:30 (2,367)
Parker, Gillian 4:56:23 (22,048)
Parker, Helen 4:21:13 (14,631)
Parker, Lesley 5:55:14 (28,168)
Parker, Michaela 3:31:08 (4,347)
Parker, Patricia....................3:16:24 (2,352)
Parker, Patsy 5:01:08 (22,754)
Parker, Yvonne 3:18:46 (2,629)
Parker Armitage, Merilyn 5:41:12 (27,271)
Parker-Leehane, Freda 4:52:32 (21,216)
Parkes, Emma 4:23:15 (15,118)
Parkes, Jennifer 3:58:42 (9,674)
Parkinson, Annie..................4:51:30 (20,982)
Parkinson, Leesa 6:57:24 (29,912)
Parkinson, Maudie 4:46:29 (20,048)
Parkinson, Miranda 5:01:37 (22,819)
Parnell, Helen 6:14:36 (29,009)
Parr, Caroline 5:09:07 (23,955)
Parr, Katherine 7:12:02 (30,033)
Parrish, Elizabeth 5:07:17 (23,663)
Parrott, Moira 5:08:52 (23,915)
Parry, Clare 4:08:41 (11,910)
Parry, Isabel 5:17:58 (25,159)
Parry, Sarah 5:48:02 (27,778)
Parry, Sioned 4:58:48 (22,426)
Parsons, Connie 5:14:16 (24,669)
Parsons, Jennie 6:01:08 (28,462)
Parsons, Kelly 4:57:40 (22,243)
Parsons, Rebecca 5:01:52 (22,846)
Parsons, Sarah 4:47:24 (20,238)
Parsons Perez, Maria.............5:13:12 (24,530)
Parton, Lynne 5:18:36 (25,224)
Partridge, Joan 7:12:20 (30,035)
Partridge, Mary-Anne 3:59:15 (9,832)
Parvin, Rosemary 5:23:35 (25,754)
Paselleri, Mila 6:40:32 (29,654)
Pash, Susan 7:32:24 (30,144)
Pasian, Alessandra................4:23:08 (15,093)
Passway, Tracey 3:36:49 (5,211)
Pastorino, Jodi 6:13:28 (28,968)
Patel, Anita 5:54:07 (28,119)
Patel, Jayshree 6:03:47 (28,579)
Patel, Leena 6:58:41 (29,924)
Patel, Manisha 5:48:16 (27,797)
Patel, Nina 6:08:03 (28,766)
Paterson, Coleen 6:10:52 (28,886)
Paterson, Gail 4:21:22 (14,660)
Paterson, Sharman 5:10:10 (24,098)
Paterson, Susan 5:41:53 (27,325)
Paton, Sarah 7:38:32 (30,160)
Patoureau, Josette 3:16:17 (2,340)
Patrick, Alice 3:51:34 (7,983)
Patrick, Julie 4:20:35 (14,496)
Patten, Victoria....................4:28:38 (16,348)
Pattern, Sonia 4:37:10 (18,162)
Patterson, Kristina 4:51:44 (21,038)
Patterson, Nicole..................4:01:55 (10,469)

Patterson, Shona 3:56:54 (9,154)
Pattison, Alison....................4:13:33 (12,943)
Pattison, Emma 5:48:24 (27,808)
Pattison, Helen 5:16:55 (25,038)
Patton, Angela 4:49:52 (20,687)
Patton, Anne 5:07:39 (23,723)
Paul, Andrea 4:32:02 (17,124)
Paul, Carol 3:57:58 (9,484)
Pautard, Marlene 3:08:20 (1,618)
Pauzers, Clare 2:44:35 (278)
Paxman, Keith......................6:04:10 (28,601)
Paxton, Emily 3:58:44 (9,682)
Pay, Jeanie 4:45:10 (19,801)
Payling, Kilmeny 6:19:32 (29,145)
Payne, Daphne 4:31:05 (16,866)
Payne, Elizabeth 5:35:08 (26,818)
Payne, Nina 4:14:31 (13,131)
Peace, Heather 3:58:38 (9,649)
Peacey, Sandra.....................5:16:54 (25,034)
Peachey, Martine 5:16:52 (25,029)
Peacock, Jemma 5:36:55 (26,938)
Pearce, Annette 6:51:47 (29,829)
Pearce, Debbie 4:18:33 (14,023)
Pearce, Rachel 6:41:50 (29,687)
Pearce, Sally 5:48:33 (27,821)
Pearce, Sue 4:19:25 (14,231)
Pearman, Katharine 5:05:43 (23,418)
Pearson, Sharon 6:11:43 (28,917)
Peart, Rebecca 4:49:51 (20,684)
Peartree, Gillian 4:24:29 (15,393)
Peck, Jane 3:56:37 (9,081)
Peck, Suling 4:39:05 (18,619)
Pedder, Ann 6:33:28 (29,492)
Pedder, Jennifer 6:33:00 (29,480)
Pedersen, Lene 4:45:52 (19,914)
Pedler, Margaret...................4:36:41 (18,059)
Pedro, Nusi 4:28:45 (16,371)
Peel, Lorraine 5:25:14 (25,913)
Pegrari, Madeline 4:26:09 (15,769)
Pei, Vivian 6:02:41 (28,528)
Peiser, Leanne 5:16:45 (25,019)
Pellett, Helen 3:48:05 (7,283)
Pemberton, Deborah 5:06:15 (23,511)
Penfold, Emma 4:29:28 (16,537)
Pengelly, Patricia 7:33:36 (30,150)
Penman, Sarah 5:28:17 (26,205)
Pennanen, Mia 3:54:41 (8,628)
Pennell, Katy 5:24:57 (25,879)
Pennington, Désirée 5:42:46 (27,395)
Penny, Susan 5:14:09 (24,648)
Pennycook, Lynn 5:57:50 (28,318)
Penny-Wagstaff, Lesley.........6:29:51 (29,404)
Pentland, Debbie 4:54:57 (21,718)
Pepper, Karen 3:32:31 (4,538)
Peppiatt, Jenny 3:42:47 (6,269)
Pequigney, Ann 5:18:00 (25,166)
Percival, Mo 4:27:20 (16,030)
Percy, Sharon 3:57:50 (9,440)
Pereira Dos Santos, Palmira 4:52:30 (21,206)
Perham, Elizabeth 5:33:34 (26,655)
Perkins, Elizabeth 5:13:13 (24,535)
Perkins, Julie 6:34:10 (29,505)
Perkins, Laura 5:25:12 (25,906)
Perkins, Peta 4:03:06 (10,685)
Perkins, Shanti 5:13:05 (24,515)
Perks, Wendy 5:47:02 (27,709)
Perrett, Joy 4:47:22 (20,232)
Perrin, Chrissie 4:36:23 (17,991)
Perrin, Joanna 4:42:01 (19,163)
Perrin, Julia 5:20:23 (25,395)
Perrott, Valerie 5:23:29 (25,741)
Perry, Christine 4:23:32 (15,184)
Perry, Jo 6:14:21 (29,004)
Perry, Meghan 5:05:34 (23,391)
Perry, Rosie 5:22:31 (25,651)
Perry, Ruth 4:56:53 (22,125)
Perry, Victoria......................2:59:00 (934)
Persaud, Marcia 5:27:20 (26,114)
Persico, Giovanna 6:20:14 (29,164)
Peschel, Gudrun...................4:28:22 (16,277)
Peschel, Tanja 4:28:22 (16,277)
Peters, Carol 6:04:47 (28,634)
Peters, Clare 4:42:28 (19,267)

LONDON MARATHON

Peters, Nicky 3:29:27 (4,073)	Pond, Lucy 4:31:54 (17,090)	Pruden, Michaela 4:53:18 (21,373)
Peters, Paula 4:47:30 (20,260)	Ponticelli, Martine 4:24:56 (15,487)	Pryce, Joanna 4:15:55 (13,447)
Petersen, Paloma 5:12:28 (24,424)	Pook, Ellisiah 4:41:10 (19,007)	Pryke, Gail 3:09:54 (1,741)
Petre Mears, Katie 5:53:16 (28,081)	Poole, Denise 4:39:15 (18,644)	Pryme, Sandra 5:00:33 (22,670)
Petrie, Sarah 4:55:27 (21,872)	Poole, Lesley 7:01:55 (29,959)	Pucan, Dijana 4:51:03 (20,898)
Petropoulos, Julia 4:18:11 (13,914)	Poole, Lucy 3:54:14 (8,519)	Pucan, Sanja 4:51:03 (20,898)
Petrova, Maria 6:20:19 (29,166)	Poole, Margaret 5:20:54 (25,453)	Puddefoot, Karen 5:04:16 (23,175)
Petrovic, Natasha 4:46:04 (19,951)	Poole, Nicola 4:21:20 (14,653)	Puesche, Johanna 4:55:30 (21,893)
Petry, Petra 3:35:56 (5,060)	Poole, Sue 5:47:37 (27,731)	Pugh, Gillian 3:29:20 (4,053)
Pettitt, Caroline 5:55:54 (28,208)	Poole, Valerie 3:43:48 (6,456)	Pugh, Jane 3:59:24 (9,885)
Pfister, Patricia 3:33:43 (4,716)	Pooley, Heather 5:51:24 (27,974)	Pugh, Michelle 5:06:10 (23,493)
Phelan, Naina 5:02:17 (22,913)	Pope, Brenda 4:17:06 (13,685)	Puplett, Lesley 4:39:27 (18,678)
Phelan, Nicola 4:33:35 (17,450)	Pope, Margaret 4:30:20 (16,732)	Purcell, Helene 4:50:02 (20,725)
Phillimore, Louise 6:40:00 (29,630)	Pope, Nicola 4:53:11 (21,350)	Purchase, Karen 4:20:29 (14,471)
Phillips, Beverley 5:06:15 (23,511)	Pople, Susan 5:18:46 (25,246)	Purkiss, Lisa 3:24:36 (3,328)
Phillips, Christine 5:10:50 (24,189)	Popple, Christine 3:45:47 (6,820)	Purro, Françoise 4:31:31 (16,983)
Phillips, Clare 3:31:53 (4,452)	Popple, Sarah 4:37:16 (18,190)	Purvis, Harriet 4:11:57 (12,596)
Phillips, Lindsay 6:29:28 (29,398)	Port, Louise 4:45:10 (19,801)	Puzey, Tabby 6:13:33 (28,979)
Phillips, Samantha 5:57:29 (28,298)	Porter, Celia 6:19:37 (29,148)	Pyatt, Caroline 4:39:00 (18,603)
Phillips, Siobhan 5:34:50 (26,789)	Porter, Lucy 4:48:56 (20,512)	Pye, Deborah 4:52:09 (21,124)
Phillips, Sonia 3:25:20 (3,422)	Porter, Lynn 4:54:03 (21,523)	Pye, Deborah 5:17:16 (25,077)
Phillips, Sonia 4:20:00 (14,368)	Portman, Carrie 5:46:56 (27,695)	Pyefinch, Suzanne 4:18:08 (13,895)
Phipps, Elaine 3:27:42 (3,741)	Potter, Christine 4:05:40 (11,256)	Qualtrough, Kath 4:10:15 (12,220)
Phipps, Lynda 8:29:03 (30,242)	Potter, Janet 3:26:12 (3,523)	Quarmby, Shirley 4:04:12 (10,927)
Phipps, Sharon 7:01:27 (29,956)	Potter, Kate 3:24:06 (3,259)	Quigley, Anita 6:17:11 (29,093)
Physick, Angela 3:54:54 (8,687)	Potts, Harmony 5:14:11 (24,652)	Quilter, Wendy 5:32:02 (26,535)
Piaut, Nathalie 4:11:09 (12,428)	Potts, Karmel 7:53:44 (30,196)	Quin, Olwen 6:54:35 (29,871)
Pickard, Emma 4:18:45 (14,067)	Poulastides, Frances 5:54:27 (28,134)	Quincy, Sylviane 5:00:20 (22,649)
Pickavant, Helen 6:26:03 (29,303)	Poulton, Mandy 8:22:18 (30,240)	Quinn, Brigid 3:55:51 (8,883)
Pickering, Denise 4:09:12 (12,022)	Poulton, Susan 4:22:34 (14,943)	Quinn, Maria 5:19:47 (25,345)
Pickering, Jane 4:10:26 (12,262)	Powell, Adele 5:19:29 (25,304)	Rabbitte, Aileen 6:03:00 (28,541)
Pickering, Lee 5:54:35 (28,142)	Powell, Alison 3:40:44 (5,903)	Rackman, Amanda 4:47:23 (20,236)
Pickett, Jill 4:25:09 (15,543)	Powell, Fern 6:07:52 (28,754)	Radcliffe, Emma 4:54:06 (21,533)
Pickford, Amy 4:37:08 (18,152)	Powell, Lynne 5:14:47 (24,748)	Radin, Cristina 4:18:43 (14,056)
Pickford, Marilyn 5:31:56 (26,528)	Power, Elizabeth 4:59:18 (22,497)	Radley, Hannah 5:27:38 (26,142)
Pickvance, Ruth 2:46:14 (323)	Power, Janet 4:25:39 (15,643)	Raffault, Elisabeth 4:13:41 (12,978)
Picton, Pauline 4:47:15 (20,213)	Power, Niamh 5:06:37 (23,564)	Raffel, Susana 4:16:57 (13,655)
Piddington, Sally 6:20:02 (29,159)	Powis, Alison 4:56:41 (22,092)	Ragg, Gemma 5:08:36 (23,869)
Pierce, Courtney 3:37:14 (5,288)	Powley, Alisa 4:55:28 (21,878)	Rahman, Sarah 5:34:21 (26,739)
Pierce, Stacy 3:44:43 (6,618)	Pownall, Nicola 4:28:06 (16,210)	Rainbird, Katy 5:23:05 (25,714)
Piercy, Stephanie 5:50:44 (27,939)	Poyner, Alice 4:45:17 (19,821)	Rainbow, Elaine 7:14:37 (30,047)
Pierson, Salma 5:26:03 (25,993)	Pratley, Jennifer 4:22:55 (15,039)	Raines, Helen 4:04:23 (10,965)
Pigott, Kathryn 4:10:55 (12,378)	Pratt, Claire 5:57:16 (28,281)	Rajska, Wendy 5:29:46 (26,350)
Pihl, Karin 4:45:47 (19,900)	Pratt, Laura 5:07:55 (23,762)	Ralph, A 4:43:24 (19,465)
Pike, Trudi 3:58:23 (9,582)	Pratt, Samantha 5:09:37 (24,032)	Ralph, Barbara 3:22:37 (3,065)
Pike, Zoe 3:32:52 (4,582)	Preater, Laura 5:58:47 (28,355)	Ralph, Barbara 5:34:16 (26,729)
Pilgrim Morris, Lindsay 4:08:36 (11,892)	Prendergast, Lesley 4:54:40 (21,628)	Ramsden, Denise 4:49:46 (20,665)
Pim, Deborah 4:55:26 (21,863)	Prentice, Jacqueline 6:16:02 (29,059)	Ramsey, Jane 4:51:46 (21,048)
Pinches, Jane 4:22:08 (14,844)	Prescott, Carol 4:35:51 (17,891)	Ramsey, Paula 4:29:57 (16,675)
Pincombe, Vicky 2:43:52 (257)	Prescott, Eleanor 5:07:07 (23,632)	Rana, Naheed 4:52:18 (21,158)
Pini, Daniela 6:00:11 (28,423)	Presho, Lyn 4:42:43 (19,315)	Rance, Emma 4:43:43 (19,543)
Pinion, Alice 5:09:18 (23,982)	Preslier, Susan 3:25:34 (3,452)	Randall, Anne 6:25:37 (29,298)
Pinkney, Emma 6:21:19 (29,201)	Pressegh, Emma 4:18:52 (14,090)	Randall, Justine 5:01:48 (22,838)
Pinnaduwa, Pri 5:01:05 (22,745)	Prestegar, Lynne 4:01:20 (10,348)	Randle, Natalie 4:38:34 (18,519)
Pipe, Hayley 4:19:00 (14,115)	Prestidge, Karen 6:20:21 (29,169)	Rangarajan, Rosie 5:48:57 (27,839)
Piper, Deborah 4:17:48 (13,832)	Preston, Elizabeth 5:47:56 (27,771)	Ranson, Emma 5:45:29 (27,589)
Piper, Paula 4:46:50 (20,126)	Preston, Jennifer 3:29:58 (4,165)	Rapley, Vivienne 4:59:51 (22,588)
Piper, Rebecca 4:38:07 (18,408)	Preston, Susan 4:00:56 (10,270)	Ratcliffe, Allison 3:53:17 (8,327)
Pirie, Karen 4:15:56 (13,450)	Preston, Susan 4:57:44 (22,253)	Ratcliffe, Megan 3:59:18 (9,841)
Pitkin, Wendy 3:40:07 (5,803)	Preux, Véronique 5:05:22 (23,353)	Ratnarajah, Anne 4:34:59 (17,709)
Pitman, Janice 6:47:25 (29,766)	Prewer, Tracy 4:01:26 (10,379)	Rattan, Anita 6:23:43 (29,251)
Pitts, Sally 3:06:21 (1,447)	Price, Jacqui 4:18:14 (13,926)	Raty, Pia 4:20:49 (14,552)
Pitts, Sonia 5:52:42 (28,048)	Price, Marilyn 4:22:29 (14,924)	Rausch, Manuela 4:34:21 (17,606)
Pitt-Stewart, Pauline 6:49:36 (29,798)	Price, Rosemary 8:05:16 (30,212)	Ravenscroft, Sarah 4:46:54 (20,144)
Plact, Christine 4:37:44 (18,308)	Price, Sarah Jane 5:09:12 (23,970)	Rawlinson, Geraldine 7:19:05 (30,074)
Planner, Sarah 5:21:17 (25,503)	Prickett, Andrea 4:46:25 (20,036)	Rawson, Amanda 3:18:14 (2,567)
Plate, Karin 4:10:39 (12,302)	Prideaux, Lesley 3:55:42 (8,843)	Ray, Rowena 4:14:16 (13,092)
Platt, Jayne 3:34:03 (4,763)	Prideaux, Sally 5:14:31 (24,708)	Ray, Wendy 3:27:04 (3,630)
Plumb, Caroline 4:13:10 (12,853)	Prigmore, Samantha 6:22:29 (29,223)	Rayman, Alison 5:29:51 (26,355)
Plumbley, Joanne 4:46:09 (19,972)	Prince, Julie 3:55:41 (8,839)	Rayman, Linda 5:29:51 (26,355)
Plact, Christine 4:16:17 (13,521)	Pringle, Suzanne 4:36:39 (18,053)	Rayner, Clare 4:52:51 (21,277)
Pocock, Jane 4:16:17 (13,521)	Prior, Marie 4:39:56 (18,772)	Rayner, Samantha 4:28:57 (16,411)
Poelman, Lucia 4:44:16 (19,633)	Pritchard, Louisa 3:36:29 (5,156)	Raynes, Julie 5:37:04 (26,950)
Polalrd, Carol 4:11:58 (12,600)	Pritchett, Jennifer 5:08:32 (23,853)	Razak, Zeenab 5:13:04 (24,509)
Poles, Anne 4:28:04 (16,201)	Probert, Hollie 4:43:27 (19,481)	Read, Kathrine 5:04:04 (23,144)
Poll, Jill 6:12:25 (28,941)	Proctor, Amanda 3:04:27 (1,309)	Reader, Carole 5:01:49 (22,842)
Pollard, Donna 4:31:48 (17,060)	Promnitz, Gudrun 4:21:44 (14,741)	Reading, Jennifer 5:17:49 (25,142)
Pollard, Sonja 4:46:50 (20,126)	Prosser, Carley 6:01:48 (28,497)	Real, Caroline 4:29:48 (16,625)
Pollock, Nicola 3:23:08 (3,131)	Prosser, Carolyn 4:00:39 (10,193)	Reapman, Tamzin 4:58:06 (22,316)
Pollock, Nina 4:34:56 (17,700)	Prosser, Louise 5:22:40 (25,665)	Reardon, Toni 4:37:38 (18,287)
Pollydore, Joan 6:12:20 (28,934)	Provan, Nicole 4:57:00 (22,140)	Reddin, Anne 6:55:21 (29,889)
Poluck, Dedra 4:51:07 (20,909)	Providence, Marsha 6:58:25 (29,922)	Reddyhoff, Susan 4:34:00 (17,536)
Pomeroy, Linda 5:33:14 (26,628)	Prudames, Caroline 5:26:23 (26,031)	Redfearn, Nicola 5:44:33 (27,526)
Pomroy, Carol 5:36:56 (26,940)		

Redfern, Anna	5:34:30 (26,756)	
Redfern, Diane	6:37:33 (29,579)	
Redgrave, Ann	4:55:37 (21,928)	
Redman, Beverley	5:53:06 (28,072)	
Redmond, Caroline	4:47:02 (20,169)	
Redmond, Rosemary	5:40:37 (27,240)	
Redonnett, Christine	4:05:43 (11,273)	
Redpath, Elizabeth	4:08:01 (11,768)	
Reece, Ester	4:17:08 (13,699)	
Reed, Eira	4:02:14 (10,529)	
Reed-De'laet, Doris	5:46:56 (27,695)	
Rees, Bridget	4:01:37 (10,414)	
Rees, Joanna	5:31:34 (26,493)	
Rees, Johanna	4:44:35 (19,692)	
Rees, Rebecca	4:40:42 (18,921)	
Rees, Ruth	5:03:45 (23,091)	
Rees, Sandra	5:10:35 (24,163)	
Rees, Susan	5:34:25 (26,746)	
Reeve, Samantha	4:28:13 (16,244)	
Reeves, Kate	4:31:40 (17,028)	
Regan, Joanne	6:27:01 (29,331)	
Regan, Paulette	5:39:34 (27,137)	
Rehman, Abda	8:01:38 (30,209)	
Rehn, Gudrun	6:43:07 (29,709)	
Rehund, Franziska	4:20:35 (14,496)	
Reid, Carol	3:25:13 (3,403)	
Reid, Jacqueline	4:43:05 (19,400)	
Reid, Judy	4:56:09 (22,011)	
Reid, Kendra	4:31:16 (16,922)	
Reid, Marie	5:14:29 (24,701)	
Reid, Mary	6:40:48 (29,659)	
Reid, Riona	5:40:11 (27,204)	
Reid, Trina	4:34:46 (17,669)	
Reidy, Dee	4:20:42 (14,519)	
Reilly, Tina	4:07:48 (11,721)	
Reinhardt, Susan	4:29:28 (16,537)	
Reinke, Sharon	3:40:37 (5,886)	
Renaudin, Maryline	5:06:45 (23,579)	
Renders, Marleen	2:28:31 (59)	
Rendle, Sarah	4:17:41 (13,808)	
Renew, Anne	5:08:56 (23,926)	
Renie, Anita	4:44:57 (19,765)	
Renoux, Dominique	5:37:28 (26,975)	
Renson, Jill	3:55:09 (8,722)	
Repetto, Orietta	4:31:22 (16,947)	
Resley, Susan	5:23:38 (25,759)	
Ressel, Ellen	4:20:03 (14,381)	
Rest, Elinor	3:25:42 (3,467)	
Retz, Denise	5:44:32 (27,523)	
Reuby, Kirsty	5:07:41 (23,726)	
Revans, Lauren	4:46:07 (19,964)	
Revill, Julia	4:54:39 (21,623)	
Revill, Lillian	4:51:54 (21,069)	
Revis, Debbie	5:12:19 (24,396)	
Reyes, Pauline	6:03:33 (28,568)	
Reynolds, Loretta	8:08:34 (30,227)	
Reynolds, Melanie	4:36:16 (17,967)	
Reynolds, Sarah	4:38:23 (18,477)	
Reynolds, Teresa	4:52:03 (21,102)	
Rezzano, Alessandra	4:18:14 (13,926)	
Rhodes, Amanda	4:54:08 (21,539)	
Rhodes, Anna	5:05:59 (23,466)	
Rhodes, Dusty	3:47:22 (7,104)	
Rhodes, Virginia	4:53:57 (21,499)	
Rhole, Suzanne	4:43:44 (19,548)	
Rhys-Dillon, Ceril	4:24:38 (15,427)	
Riaz, Arifa	4:32:13 (17,158)	
Rice, Amanda	3:37:07 (5,268)	
Rice, Lyndsey	5:32:24 (26,564)	
Rich, Marian	4:26:14 (15,789)	
Rich, Sue	4:27:20 (16,030)	
Richard, Kim	3:51:29 (7,960)	
Richards, Donna Marva	5:54:10 (28,124)	
Richards, Emma	5:04:10 (23,153)	
Richards, Jackie	3:17:12 (2,445)	
Richards, Joanne	4:20:47 (14,543)	
Richards, Lise	4:29:35 (16,570)	
Richards, Romana	5:39:01 (27,087)	
Richards, Sarah	4:59:36 (22,539)	
Richards, Victoria	5:27:44 (26,153)	
Richardson, Bethan	6:38:56 (29,607)	
Richardson, Denise	5:32:26 (26,572)	
Richardson, Jill	4:23:26 (15,155)	
Richardson, Paige	4:10:50 (12,355)	
Richardson, Penny	6:01:03 (28,456)	
Richardson, Peta	5:16:04 (24,936)	
Richardson, Rebecca	6:58:16 (29,921)	
Richardson, Sarah	5:22:55 (25,697)	
Richardson, Wendy	5:46:51 (27,689)	
Richardson-Aitken, Rosie	4:37:07 (18,150)	
Riches, Julie	4:05:28 (11,202)	
Riches, Victoria	4:45:48 (19,902)	
Richmond, Denise	4:47:24 (20,238)	
Richmond, Jane	4:41:33 (19,074)	
Ricketts, Shirley May	4:42:24 (19,250)	
Rickhuss, Joanne	4:59:57 (22,613)	
Riddle, Margaret	7:46:48 (30,182)	
Rideout, Lesley	4:38:45 (18,559)	
Rider, Arlene	5:17:11 (25,069)	
Ridge, Sheila	5:34:19 (26,738)	
Ridger, Christine	5:38:53 (27,078)	
Ridgley, Julie	4:01:31 (10,399)	
Ridgway, Hayley	4:29:50 (16,634)	
Ridley, Stephanie	4:02:59 (10,657)	
Ridout, Anne	3:37:49 (5,383)	
Ridout, Linda	5:08:42 (23,888)	
Rieger, Gabrielle	3:55:23 (8,780)	
Rigby, Holly	5:42:34 (27,386)	
Rigby, Jenny	5:29:20 (26,324)	
Rigg, Louise	4:37:13 (18,175)	
Riggott, Emma	4:02:20 (10,535)	
Riley, Catherine	5:17:10 (25,068)	
Riley, Emma	4:28:29 (16,310)	
Riley, Kate	4:28:06 (16,210)	
Rimmer, Dawn	4:36:56 (18,116)	
Rimmer, Patsy	3:39:26 (5,660)	
Rimmer, Tina	6:26:24 (29,314)	
Rimmington, Carole	4:21:16 (14,642)	
Rinando, Paola	3:32:06 (4,481)	
Ripley Jones, Sarah	4:05:05 (11,133)	
Rippon, Louise	5:11:33 (24,296)	
Risby, Kay	3:55:44 (8,854)	
Risse, Dorothee	4:52:07 (21,117)	
Ritchie, Alison	4:45:33 (19,869)	
Ritchie, Amanda	3:58:58 (9,744)	
Ritchie, Christine	4:26:04 (15,748)	
Ritchie, Deborah	5:00:20 (22,649)	
Ritchie, Jane	4:59:52 (22,594)	
Ritchie, Libby	5:28:19 (26,210)	
Ritchie, Nicola	4:12:05 (12,640)	
Ritchie, Sarah	5:44:26 (27,503)	
Ritz, Dorothee	4:42:55 (19,366)	
Rivers, Charmaine	4:17:24 (13,750)	
Rivers, Helen	4:23:37 (15,211)	
Rivers, Jo	3:59:20 (9,856)	
Rivers-Bulkley, Lucy	6:59:29 (29,936)	
Robarts, Anne	7:22:39 (30,094)	
Robbins, Anita	4:38:39 (18,537)	
Robbins, Sarah	4:41:48 (19,123)	
Robe, Liliane	4:52:53 (21,287)	
Robershaw, Theresa	5:08:35 (23,863)	
Roberts, Alison	4:14:56 (13,248)	
Roberts, Anna	4:22:28 (14,919)	
Roberts, Barbara	5:26:05 (25,994)	
Roberts, Christina	4:21:56 (14,793)	
Roberts, Christine	4:25:22 (15,587)	
Roberts, Christine	6:54:19 (29,863)	
Roberts, Elaine	6:56:53 (29,907)	
Roberts, Gwennan	5:03:44 (23,087)	
Roberts, Helen	4:42:29 (19,270)	
Roberts, Helen	5:46:45 (27,683)	
Roberts, Jan	5:51:57 (28,015)	
Roberts, Jennie	6:15:16 (29,033)	
Roberts, Katherine	3:27:26 (3,693)	
Roberts, Kathryn	4:24:19 (15,352)	
Roberts, Kathryn	6:59:35 (29,940)	
Roberts, Katie	4:50:16 (20,763)	
Roberts, Lara	5:13:00 (24,500)	
Roberts, Sandra	4:23:57 (15,281)	
Roberts, Sarah	4:14:44 (13,185)	
Robertson, Alexandra	7:02:03 (29,960)	
Robertson, Claire	4:21:57 (14,796)	
Robertson, Julia	4:41:20 (19,033)	
Robertson, Kate	4:47:57 (20,337)	
Robertson, Morwenna	5:09:31 (24,017)	
Robertson, Sarah Jane	5:13:46 (24,602)	
Robins, Andrea	3:58:26 (9,592)	
Robinson, Beverly	6:07:04 (28,721)	
Robinson, Caron	5:38:42 (27,066)	
Robinson, Debra	2:42:19 (224)	
Robinson, Emily	4:49:11 (20,556)	
Robinson, Fiona	5:12:19 (24,396)	
Robinson, Heather	3:11:46 (1,894)	
Robinson, Jill	4:29:51 (16,642)	
Robinson, Julie Anne	4:53:20 (21,384)	
Robinson, Kelly	6:35:39 (29,539)	
Robinson, Margaret	5:05:57 (23,461)	
Robinson, Melanie	5:28:19 (26,210)	
Robinson, Melinda	5:43:35 (27,444)	
Robinson, Sally	5:11:07 (24,228)	
Robinson, Sarah	4:53:01 (21,318)	
Robinson, Tracey	3:11:59 (1,913)	
Robson, Dany	3:46:24 (6,931)	
Robson, Emma	6:55:19 (29,886)	
Robson, Jayne	7:09:22 (30,014)	
Robson, Natalia	4:00:16 (10,103)	
Roche-Kelly, Lelia	4:29:50 (16,634)	
Rochford, Denise	6:21:30 (29,207)	
Rockcliffe, Kim	5:14:29 (24,701)	
Rockett, Lisa	6:06:30 (28,699)	
Rockliff, Dawn	3:56:12 (8,967)	
Rockliffe, Kim	5:18:29 (25,212)	
Roderick, Anna	3:54:19 (8,538)	
Rodger, Lindsay	5:04:33 (23,223)	
Rodgers, Leyna	6:27:46 (29,345)	
Rodinsky, Katie	6:12:47 (28,954)	
Rodriguez, Annabelle	5:41:55 (27,328)	
Roe, Karen	5:38:02 (27,023)	
Roebuck, Wendy	4:31:24 (16,961)	
Roethenbaugh, Wendy	3:06:57 (1,500)	
Roffey, Susan	4:04:00 (10,881)	
Rogan, Katy	3:42:59 (6,299)	
Rogan, Louise	5:09:26 (24,007)	
Rogan, Marion	5:09:26 (24,007)	
Rogers, Catherine	3:36:08 (5,095)	
Rogers, Chrissy	6:15:17 (29,036)	
Rogers, Claire	4:49:32 (20,620)	
Rogers, Elaine	4:40:42 (18,921)	
Rogers, Emily	4:39:00 (18,603)	
Rogers, Janet	5:46:56 (27,695)	
Rogers, Maureen	7:13:26 (30,041)	
Rogers, Michelle	5:32:18 (26,548)	
Rogers, Vanessa	6:42:49 (29,703)	
Rogerson, Donna	3:35:53 (5,050)	
Roggenstein, Eva	3:40:54 (5,926)	
Rolfe, Wendy	6:12:44 (28,951)	
Rollings, Ann	3:33:16 (4,656)	
Rollinson, Tessa	5:16:58 (25,047)	
Rolls-King, Ros	4:14:01 (13,043)	
Romano, Kate	4:44:34 (19,690)	
Romans, Chloe	4:21:09 (14,616)	
Rome, Jane	4:36:28 (18,013)	
Roodhouse, Eve	4:31:44 (17,043)	
Roodt, Deborah	5:09:47 (24,056)	
Rookes, Julie	4:56:51 (22,116)	
Roots, Wendy	4:52:50 (21,274)	
Roper, Linda	5:05:19 (23,404)	
Roper, Lucy	4:24:20 (15,356)	
Rose, Andrea	5:46:30 (27,661)	
Rose, Anna Louise	4:54:59 (21,728)	
Rose, Joanne	5:45:11 (27,572)	
Rose, Sally	5:15:01 (24,781)	
Rose, Sherry	6:30:49 (29,432)	
Roseblade, Eleanor	4:08:17 (11,820)	
Rosenbaum, Michele	3:47:51 (7,224)	
Rosen-Nash, Ilkay	4:28:28 (16,306)	
Rosignuolo, Elke	4:32:38 (17,235)	
Rosner, Rebecca	5:29:36 (26,337)	
Ross, Angela	4:56:11 (22,021)	
Ross, Annabel	4:46:20 (20,016)	
Ross, Cathy	4:39:03 (18,616)	
Ross, Jenny	4:26:01 (15,736)	
Ross, Miranda	4:48:12 (20,384)	
Ross, Miranda	5:14:33 (24,713)	
Ross, Rachel	5:42:30 (27,375)	
Ross, Samantha	6:16:59 (29,085)	
Ross, Sarah	5:42:30 (27,375)	
Rossi, Jane	5:23:44 (25,763)	
Rossiter, Carolyn	4:48:28 (20,435)	

Rosswurm, Barbara 7:42:45 (30,173)
Rostron, Alison 3:35:54 (5,055)
Rostron, Isobel 4:52:10 (21,130)
Rouncefield, Sue 4:01:07 (10,303)
Round-Ball, Catherine 4:42:51 (19,347)
Rouse, Amanda 4:03:10 (10,697)
Rouse, Janice 5:04:43 (23,247)
Rouse, Simone 3:59:42 (9,974)
Roussel, Kay 7:03:56 (29,974)
Routier, Fabienne 4:13:34 (12,949)
Routledge, Angela 3:16:40 (2,386)
Routley, Elizabeth 3:40:30 (5,869)
Roux, Lauren 6:54:52 (29,875)
Roux, Sandrine 5:52:27 (28,038)
Rowark, Julie 4:00:04 (10,067)
Rowarth, Janet 6:39:59 (29,629)
Rowbotham, Emma 4:27:38 (16,103)
Rowbotham, Sophie 5:07:38 (23,719)
Rowbottom, Claire 4:38:01 (18,375)
Rowe, Catherine 6:59:32 (29,937)
Rowe, Hilary 4:30:45 (16,794)
Rowe, Juliet 3:48:35 (7,376)
Rowe, Margaret 3:21:59 (2,994)
Rowe, Peggy 6:57:48 (29,915)
Rowe, Shirley 4:15:54 (13,446)
Rowell, Victoria 4:23:50 (15,257)
Rowland, Jennifer 5:24:48 (25,859)
Rowlands, Clare 4:13:45 (12,988)
Rowles, Philippa 3:23:27 (3,168)
Rowles, Valerie 5:14:08 (24,645)
Rowlinson, Maria 6:17:48 (29,108)
Rowntree, Karen 4:28:44 (16,367)
Rox, Jan 4:20:16 (14,425)
Royle, Eileen 3:55:31 (8,800)
Rozental, Patricia 5:19:30 (25,307)
Rubinstein, Madelyn 6:11:13 (28,896)
Rudd, Belinda 4:19:23 (14,220)
Rudrum, Stephanie 5:43:18 (27,426)
Rugg, Brenda 7:16:22 (30,057)
Rule, Lorraine 5:51:30 (27,983)
Runacres, Lorette 6:44:28 (29,728)
Ruprecht, Marjo 3:36:33 (5,165)
Ruscillo, Ann 6:11:27 (28,906)
Rush, Dyana 4:44:21 (19,644)
Rush, Elizabeth 4:59:11 (22,486)
Rushworth, Karen 5:49:36 (27,877)
Rushworth, Melanie 4:25:32 (15,625)
Russell, Bridget 7:10:04 (30,016)
Russell, Cheryl 5:20:32 (25,412)
Russell, Judith 4:49:33 (20,626)
Russell, Margaret 4:06:49 (11,505)
Russell, Sally 6:14:11 (28,996)
Russell, Sarah 4:47:55 (20,330)
Russell, Victoria 4:51:51 (21,062)
Russell, Wendy 5:00:46 (22,702)
Rust, Vivienne 5:26:51 (26,072)
Rutherford, Fearn 4:13:34 (12,949)
Rutterford-Adams, Angela 4:51:26 (20,975)
Ryan, Amy 5:27:09 (26,095)
Ryan, Clare 4:35:31 (17,815)
Ryan, Frances 5:49:23 (27,864)
Ryan, Phyllis 4:03:27 (10,760)
Ryan, Rebecca 4:41:23 (19,045)
Ryan, Victoria 3:24:48 (3,354)
Ryatt, Manjeet 4:08:07 (11,789)
Sabroe-Fussing, Ingrid 4:00:50 (10,248)
Sabrosa, Etelvina 6:07:59 (28,760)
Saddler, Jane 4:15:31 (13,371)
Sadler, Angie 3:12:53 (1,992)
Sadler, Jacqueline 8:45:43 (30,265)
Sadler, Kate 4:18:58 (14,112)
Sadler, Ruth 6:06:48 (28,710)
Saffron, Janet 6:14:01 (28,991)
Sage, Sally 4:07:44 (11,709)
Saggu, Arvinder 4:42:50 (19,343)
Saharig, Elizabeth 6:32:22 (29,459)
Saiman, Nathalie 4:29:05 (16,445)
Salaam, Saira 5:48:52 (27,835)
Salito, Dea 4:30:56 (16,836)
Salkeld, Lynda 3:19:43 (2,730)
Salmon, Claire 4:57:07 (22,158)
Salmon, Gigi 6:37:46 (29,585)
Salt, Adela 3:31:43 (4,425)
Salthouse, Sharon 5:38:33 (27,053)
Saltmarsh, Samantha 4:46:42 (20,092)
Salvatori, Perrine 5:12:34 (24,436)
Salvin, Martina 5:09:38 (24,035)
Sammut, Angela 3:14:55 (2,212)
Sampson, Kathy 3:57:41 (9,391)
Samuel, Margaret 5:27:59 (26,178)
Samuels, Dawn 4:35:50 (17,887)
San, Abigael 6:43:09 (29,710)
San Miguel, Genevieve 6:10:49 (28,884)
Sanders, Christine 5:31:34 (26,493)
Sanders, Kate 4:18:15 (13,935)
Sanders, Tracey 4:50:39 (20,818)
Sanderson, Charlotte 5:07:59 (23,768)
Sanderson, Susan 5:07:59 (23,768)
Sandy, Elisabeth 4:56:52 (22,121)
Santacroce, Maria 5:28:17 (26,205)
Sanwell, Shelly 5:09:09 (23,965)
Sardari Zadeh, Sara 5:04:54 (23,283)
Sargant, Jacqueline 3:57:04 (9,191)
Sargeant, Jennifer 3:27:09 (3,647)
Sargeant, Wendy 4:54:47 (21,672)
Sargent, Joanna 4:44:04 (19,593)
Saroken, Lee 4:19:39 (14,294)
Sarosi, Mia 5:08:34 (23,859)
Sasaki, Izumi 4:22:54 (15,035)
Sassower, Tracy 3:22:52 (3,093)
Saulbrey, Robyn 4:29:03 (16,431)
Saunders, Angela 4:30:45 (16,794)
Saunders, Bonnie 5:10:31 (24,146)
Saunders, Donna 4:29:16 (16,487)
Saunders, Jane 4:34:42 (17,658)
Saunders, Katharine 4:44:02 (19,590)
Saunders, Lorraine 5:49:15 (27,858)
Saunders, Rachel 5:22:55 (25,697)
Saunders, Sally 4:15:45 (13,414)
Saunders, Sharon 6:06:32 (28,702)
Sauzier, Jane 5:45:10 (27,569)
Savill, Anna 3:23:07 (3,129)
Sawan, Nancy 5:20:40 (25,426)
Sawyer, Julia 3:33:00 (4,601)
Sawyer, Stephanie 4:40:48 (18,941)
Sayer, Nicholette 4:22:19 (14,891)
Scadden, Louisa 5:16:31 (24,991)
Scahill, Rachael 4:59:47 (22,571)
Scaife, Helen 3:34:24 (4,817)
Scales, Susan 3:56:23 (9,018)
Scarratt, Rebecca 5:30:36 (26,419)
Scarrott, Yvonne 3:55:31 (8,800)
Schaufelberger, Tekla 4:47:28 (20,252)
Scheuer, Ina 3:57:03 (9,189)
Schirmer, Dagmar 5:35:15 (26,824)
Schischa, Rebecca 4:58:51 (22,434)
Schluter, Jane 4:25:06 (15,531)
Schofield, Christine 4:31:33 (16,988)
Schofield, Emma Jane 5:11:50 (24,333)
Schooling, Tessa 4:03:33 (10,789)
Schooling, Tessa 4:09:25 (12,066)
Schooling-Smith, Tracey 3:48:46 (7,415)
Schramm, Paula 5:06:15 (23,511)
Schreiber, Cheryl 4:33:57 (17,526)
Schreiber, Lauren 3:49:37 (7,611)
Schuaderer, Melissa 5:21:45 (25,557)
Schubert, Christine 4:38:52 (18,582)
Schuberth, Gemma 4:36:12 (17,954)
Schuchter, Samantha 4:49:06 (20,544)
Schuricht, Christine 4:45:45 (19,894)
Sciluna, Kim 5:10:55 (24,201)
Scofield, Kerrie 5:18:14 (25,183)
Scoggins, Sally 4:22:49 (15,012)
Scotford, Laura 4:44:21 (19,644)
Scott, Andrea 5:01:48 (22,838)
Scott, Beverley 5:35:47 (26,866)
Scott, Dianne 4:56:55 (22,131)
Scott, Esther 5:07:33 (23,701)
Scott, Frances 4:38:33 (18,515)
Scott, Gayleen 3:28:46 (3,953)
Scott, Geraldine 6:40:42 (29,657)
Scott, Hannah 3:56:15 (8,980)
Scott, Helen 4:32:43 (17,252)
Scott, Katie-Jane 5:17:41 (25,123)
Scott, Kerry 5:04:03 (23,141)
Scott, Linda 4:54:27 (21,578)
Scott, Natasha 5:43:45 (27,454)
Scott, Phillipa 4:09:00 (11,978)
Scott, Sarah 4:29:51 (16,642)
Scott, Shannon 5:59:32 (28,393)
Scott, Sheila 6:19:48 (29,153)
Scott, Sophie 3:59:33 (9,936)
Scott Gall, Henrietta 5:00:50 (22,707)
Scott-Green, Susan 5:49:30 (27,872)
Scrase, Linda 4:26:44 (15,895)
Scrivener, Sarah 3:31:10 (4,351)
Scroggins, Janella 3:31:52 (4,449)
Scudder, Clare 4:18:14 (13,926)
Scully, Teresa 3:02:31 (1,190)
Seabrook, Patricia 4:22:50 (15,016)
Searing, Mary 4:35:11 (17,749)
Searle, Lisa 4:07:11 (11,587)
Sears, Teresa 5:57:27 (28,294)
Sears, Wendy 7:16:44 (30,061)
Seas, Jane 5:07:36 (23,712)
Seckler, Helen 6:08:50 (28,808)
Sedgwick, Thérèse 3:56:57 (9,166)
Sedman, Alison 3:14:17 (2,144)
Seed, Sandra 6:28:21 (29,364)
Seers, Sally 5:47:31 (27,729)
Segrt, Marija 5:51:40 (27,994)
Seigneurie, Jacqueline 4:16:15 (13,516)
Selby, Jane 2:56:59 (742)
Selby, Jane 4:23:45 (15,236)
Selby, Jenny 4:59:06 (22,475)
Self, Julia 6:43:39 (29,715)
Sellar, Julia 3:58:07 (9,519)
Sellek, Yoko 4:59:47 (22,571)
Selmer-Langaker, Marit 4:55:56 (21,976)
Semple, Mary 3:55:51 (8,883)
Senechal, Catherine 5:04:01 (23,133)
Sengers, Sonja 4:37:22 (18,215)
Senior, Suzi 4:41:32 (19,067)
Seoane, Julio 4:54:34 (21,613)
Sephton, Pamela 4:43:26 (19,473)
Serkovich, Edith 4:40:15 (18,826)
Seth-Smith, Caroline 4:16:44 (13,621)
Settle, Jan 3:53:49 (8,448)
Seward, Hannah 5:32:38 (26,587)
Sexton, Mandy 5:07:21 (23,671)
Seymor, Steffie 3:55:55 (8,897)
Seymour, Ellen 5:49:08 (27,851)
Seymour, Rebecca 4:39:51 (18,762)
Shackman, Deborah 4:16:01 (13,468)
Shadbolt, Janet 6:07:22 (28,742)
Shadrach, Lindsay 5:03:47 (23,097)
Shakespeare, Tanya 5:59:39 (28,401)
Shanley, Nicola 4:11:01 (12,402)
Shannon, Ruth 3:55:46 (8,864)
Sharland, Nicola 6:24:15 (29,268)
Sharman, Suzanne 6:08:22 (28,780)
Sharp, Claire 4:12:57 (12,820)
Sharp, Gemma 4:53:48 (21,474)
Sharp, Justine 5:27:04 (26,088)
Sharp, Naomi 6:22:42 (29,226)
Sharp, Natalie 4:08:23 (11,846)
Sharp, Susan 3:44:04 (6,503)
Sharpe, Amanda 3:27:32 (3,714)
Sharpe, Claire 6:50:44 (29,818)
Sharpe, Fay 4:47:43 (20,296)
Sharron, Hazel 6:10:21 (28,871)
Shaw, Caroline 5:04:48 (23,264)
Shaw, Elizabeth 6:39:20 (29,612)
Shaw, Karen 5:04:47 (23,259)
Shaw, Mary 4:48:54 (20,503)
Shaw, Michelle 4:40:19 (18,841)
Shaw, Rebecka 4:42:15 (19,215)
Shaw, Sarah 5:08:38 (23,876)
Shaw, Sheena 3:49:18 (7,525)
Shaw, Suzanne 3:56:29 (9,050)
Shawcroft, Kathleen Anne 5:16:16 (24,956)
Sheahan, Clodagh 5:11:59 (24,351)
Shekhdar, Anna 4:33:41 (17,476)
Shelley, Victoria 3:59:27 (9,903)
Shelton, Kelly 5:47:08 (27,712)
Shelvey, Gaynor 5:28:29 (26,228)
Shen, Andrea 5:11:45 (24,321)
Shepard, Barbara 5:52:00 (28,019)
Shephard, Jennifer 4:13:59 (13,038)

Shephard, Sally	6:55:07 (29,881)	
Shepherd, Bethan	5:01:06 (22,748)	
Shepherd, Jayne	3:21:29 (2,944)	
Shepherd, Kate	4:37:20 (18,206)	
Shepherd, Katharine	4:57:28 (22,211)	
Sheppard, Jennifer	4:43:13 (19,431)	
Sheppard, Kerry	5:14:21 (24,679)	
Sheridan, Alison	5:36:32 (26,916)	
Sheridan Jones, Carolyn	5:46:28 (27,654)	
Sherman, Elizabeth	7:10:35 (30,025)	
Shibata, Yuko	3:59:12 (9,815)	
Shieldhouse, Loredana	4:34:59 (17,709)	
Shields, Catriona	5:03:35 (23,069)	
Shields, Jenny	4:39:37 (18,721)	
Shiell, Lisa	5:19:15 (25,288)	
Shiell, Susan	4:42:09 (19,192)	
Shiels, Hannah	3:20:54 (2,877)	
Shiels, Kathy	4:31:29 (16,977)	
Shine, Noelle	4:24:02 (15,302)	
Shinner, Clare	4:55:03 (21,749)	
Shinner, Joan	6:23:39 (29,249)	
Shiraishi, Theresa	6:01:21 (28,472)	
Shivers, Marie	4:02:52 (10,635)	
Shorrock, Iris	4:20:15 (14,418)	
Short, Colette	3:54:17 (8,533)	
Short, Karen	5:09:14 (23,973)	
Short, Pat	4:59:23 (22,508)	
Short, Sarah	5:04:54 (23,283)	
Shotton, Terri	6:26:36 (29,321)	
Sidey, Louise	4:55:00 (21,732)	
Sidhu, Ranjit	6:52:03 (29,835)	
Sidney, Abigail	5:22:18 (25,628)	
Siedler, Tami	7:12:33 (30,037)	
Sieloff, Cheryl	5:25:55 (25,977)	
Signate, Odile	4:16:42 (13,609)	
Signy, Helen	5:21:10 (25,483)	
Silva Junior, Dominique	3:45:44 (6,808)	
Silva-Fletcher, Ayona	5:23:11 (25,718)	
Simettinger, Helena	4:48:46 (20,481)	
Simkins, Elizabeth	5:15:27 (24,862)	
Simmonds, Ellen	4:34:22 (17,610)	
Simmonds, Jane	5:25:35 (25,948)	
Simmonite, Jennifer	4:29:30 (16,545)	
Simmons, Julie	3:54:13 (8,512)	
Simmons, Lyn	4:18:08 (13,895)	
Simms, Maxine	3:58:28 (9,596)	
Simnett, Sylvia	5:05:29 (23,381)	
Simon, Genevieve	4:25:17 (15,572)	
Simon, Lidia	2:24:15 (38)	
Simons, Natasha	5:29:53 (26,362)	
Simons, Susan	4:02:26 (10,556)	
Simpkins, Emma	5:04:38 (23,238)	
Simpson, Deborah	6:15:20 (29,039)	
Simpson, Elizabeth	4:17:31 (13,776)	
Simpson, Fiona	4:29:52 (16,648)	
Simpson, Julia	6:04:01 (28,593)	
Simpson, Karen	5:39:20 (27,119)	
Simpson, Maggie	4:50:40 (20,821)	
Simpson, Nicola	6:24:04 (29,262)	
Simpson, Sandy	5:17:30 (25,108)	
Simpson-Eyre, Irene	4:43:17 (19,447)	
Sims, Jennifer	4:55:54 (21,968)	
Sims, Patricia	5:41:58 (27,332)	
Sinclair, Nina	4:25:56 (15,712)	
Sinden, Esme	7:16:22 (30,057)	
Singleton, Phillip	4:05:43 (11,273)	
Singleton, Veronica	3:34:35 (4,847)	
Sinibaldi, Mariagrazia	4:00:11 (10,087)	
Sirkett, Sabina	5:39:14 (27,106)	
Siverd, Lynn	5:31:49 (26,519)	
Siwy, Marty	4:41:37 (19,085)	
Sizer, Jane	6:04:29 (28,617)	
Sjoo, Solweig	4:38:51 (18,580)	
Skelton, Joanne	4:46:28 (20,045)	
Skelton, Vicky	3:11:05 (1,842)	
Skidmore, Flora	3:39:33 (5,684)	
Skilton, Helen	4:25:09 (15,543)	
Skinner, Charlotte	5:01:14 (22,774)	
Skinner, Claire	4:12:22 (12,707)	
Skinner, Jenny	5:13:58 (24,625)	
Skinner, Rachel	4:23:37 (15,211)	
Skinner, Sally	5:14:51 (24,756)	
Skitt, Jean	5:08:26 (23,835)	

Slade, Debra	5:21:21 (25,514)	
Slade, Helen	6:45:34 (29,748)	
Slade, Marjorie	5:14:35 (24,720)	
Slamon, Lynne	4:31:52 (17,081)	
Slane, Victoria	4:26:59 (15,959)	
Slater, Hazel	5:05:14 (23,327)	
Slater, Karen	4:37:35 (18,276)	
Slater, Lesley	3:35:32 (4,994)	
Slater, Victoria	3:51:58 (8,066)	
Slaven, Angela	5:07:09 (23,641)	
Sleath, Susan	3:17:57 (2,526)	
Slevin, Michele	4:16:59 (13,661)	
Slevin, Sally	4:42:46 (19,323)	
Sloan, Nicola	7:06:47 (29,994)	
Slotte, Elisabeth	5:09:26 (24,007)	
Sluggett, Julie-Anne	7:00:37 (29,948)	
Sluggett, Susan	7:00:37 (29,948)	
Sly, Sharon	5:14:58 (24,772)	
Smale, Dee	3:03:50 (1,270)	
Smale, Susan	7:56:07 (30,202)	
Small, Christine	6:23:13 (29,235)	
Small, Laura	5:38:44 (27,070)	
Smart, Tracy	5:34:45 (26,777)	
Smit, Nerida	5:04:03 (23,141)	
Smith, Amanda	5:22:50 (25,688)	
Smith, Amanda	7:21:37 (30,089)	
Smith, Angela	4:38:34 (18,519)	
Smith, Anna	4:18:13 (13,924)	
Smith, Cath	4:38:46 (18,568)	
Smith, Charlotte	4:22:17 (14,883)	
Smith, Christina	4:33:13 (17,351)	
Smith, Christine	5:50:33 (27,927)	
Smith, Davina	4:17:08 (13,699)	
Smith, Diane	4:22:56 (15,048)	
Smith, Elaine	4:52:57 (21,306)	
Smith, Fiona	5:22:50 (25,688)	
Smith, Fiona	5:41:20 (27,280)	
Smith, Glenys	6:07:17 (28,736)	
Smith, Hazel	4:25:57 (15,718)	
Smith, Heather	5:00:38 (22,681)	
Smith, Helen	4:57:36 (22,228)	
Smith, Helene	5:11:27 (24,276)	
Smith, Jennie	5:00:34 (22,672)	
Smith, Jennifer	4:53:20 (21,384)	
Smith, Jennifer	5:49:28 (27,869)	
Smith, Jill	5:33:03 (26,615)	
Smith, Joy	5:28:41 (26,252)	
Smith, Julia	4:24:59 (15,501)	
Smith, Karen	4:24:22 (15,362)	
Smith, Karin	6:54:37 (29,873)	
Smith, Katharine	3:15:51 (2,302)	
Smith, Kathleen	6:16:31 (29,070)	
Smith, Laura	3:23:21 (3,155)	
Smith, Layla	4:10:41 (12,308)	
Smith, Linda	4:03:05 (10,683)	
Smith, Lorraine	3:56:19 (8,998)	
Smith, Lynda	4:26:25 (15,824)	
Smith, Maddy	4:11:39 (12,535)	
Smith, Naomi	3:43:44 (6,446)	
Smith, Nicola	5:32:39 (26,588)	
Smith, Nicola	6:22:21 (29,220)	
Smith, Norma	4:03:06 (10,685)	
Smith, Olwen	7:00:58 (29,952)	
Smith, Pamela	5:59:34 (28,395)	
Smith, Pauline	5:18:42 (25,234)	
Smith, Penelope	4:31:20 (16,940)	
Smith, Rachel	4:50:58 (20,874)	
Smith, Rachel	6:07:45 (28,751)	
Smith, Sarah	4:18:11 (13,914)	
Smith, Sarah	4:38:40 (18,541)	
Smith, Sharon	4:10:48 (12,341)	
Smith, Sheila	6:39:20 (29,612)	
Smith, Susan	4:52:07 (21,117)	
Smith, Susan	5:29:00 (26,289)	
Smith, Vanessa	5:16:15 (24,952)	
Smith, Wendy	4:32:28 (17,210)	
Smithers, Min	4:41:45 (19,112)	
Smithson, Lucie	6:05:51 (28,681)	
Smithson, Sonia	5:49:07 (27,849)	
Smithstone, Karen	4:53:58 (21,505)	
Smyth, Anne	4:12:41 (12,768)	
Smyth, Helena	6:38:09 (29,592)	
Smyth, Nicole	6:07:14 (28,733)	

Smyth, Yvonne	4:00:01 (10,058)	
Snelling, Jean	5:06:08 (23,489)	
Snook, Michelle	4:53:54 (21,495)	
Snook, Sarah	4:56:51 (22,116)	
Snowden, Kate	5:58:21 (28,341)	
Soar, Susan	4:04:12 (10,927)	
Sodha, Reena	6:22:51 (29,228)	
Sodha, Sheena	7:07:21 (29,999)	
Sohlen, Maria	5:46:41 (27,679)	
Sollars, Julia	4:52:31 (21,210)	
Sollas, Samantha	6:29:13 (29,393)	
Somaiya, Alpa	6:05:55 (28,682)	
Somers, Sarah	4:21:01 (14,595)	
Sonenfield, Renée	5:50:39 (27,931)	
Soochak, Sona	5:33:59 (26,689)	
Sorensen, Karen	6:56:43 (29,902)	
Sorger, Sabine	3:50:58 (7,861)	
Soule, Nayelli	6:45:29 (29,744)	
South, Carole	4:39:42 (18,734)	
Sowerbutts, Lucinda	4:09:03 (11,997)	
Sowerby, Henrietta	4:49:46 (20,665)	
Sowerby, Jeanie	6:59:33 (29,939)	
Spalla, Karen	4:37:04 (18,138)	
Sparks, Heidi	3:47:37 (7,167)	
Sparks, Kim	5:19:09 (25,280)	
Sparrow, Julie	5:13:35 (24,576)	
Spaus, Lou	4:09:45 (12,117)	
Speake, Rachel	5:32:42 (26,594)	
Speed, Carolyn	4:31:44 (17,043)	
Speight, Karen	5:04:06 (23,147)	
Speller, Vicki	4:55:30 (21,893)	
Spelling, Joanne	5:42:35 (27,387)	
Spence, Jemma	5:33:29 (26,647)	
Spence, Sally	4:19:54 (14,341)	
Spence, Wendy	3:56:40 (9,095)	
Spencer, Joanne	3:32:58 (4,595)	
Spencer, Julie	4:19:04 (14,136)	
Spencer, Lucy	4:58:58 (22,456)	
Spencer, Sue	4:33:09 (17,337)	
Sperring, Susan	5:15:19 (24,843)	
Spikes, Sarah	3:54:48 (8,659)	
Spiller, Alison	4:02:26 (10,556)	
Spink, Mandy	2:50:58 (467)	
Spinks, Karen	5:24:17 (25,816)	
Spinks, Rachel	6:14:55 (29,019)	
Spokes, Leigh	5:44:39 (27,538)	
Spong, Patricia	4:40:56 (18,963)	
Spong, Sue	3:24:03 (3,252)	
Spratling, Kate	5:29:36 (26,337)	
Sprenger, Nicole	4:02:41 (10,604)	
Sprigg, Nikola	5:03:18 (23,042)	
Spriggs, Helen	6:39:57 (29,628)	
Spriggs, Lisa	5:02:56 (22,996)	
Springings, Dorothy	3:52:23 (8,148)	
Spring, Emma	4:32:47 (17,274)	
Springford, Elizabeth	4:56:10 (22,015)	
Spruit, Phillipa	3:17:50 (2,515)	
Spruyt, Karen	4:47:38 (20,287)	
Squance, Carolyn	4:17:18 (13,735)	
Squirrell, Camilla	4:30:20 (16,732)	
St Hilaire, Marilyn	4:27:03 (15,981)	
St Louis, Nicola	5:45:10 (27,569)	
Stabile, Donna	4:36:59 (18,124)	
Stacey, Delia	7:39:27 (30,163)	
Stacey, Sally	6:09:18 (28,828)	
Stach Kevitz, Adele	3:49:36 (7,608)	
Stalker, Sherry	4:09:57 (12,153)	
Stallwood, Bethan	5:51:28 (27,980)	
Standley, Tina	5:48:03 (27,779)	
Stanford Bennett, Bridie	5:19:39 (25,323)	
Stanger, Alexandra	4:52:18 (21,158)	
Staniforth, Jane	4:58:39 (22,403)	
Stanley, Claire	4:41:43 (19,104)	
Stanley, Lesley	4:31:53 (17,085)	
Stanley, Susan	5:07:02 (23,621)	
Stannard, Caroline	4:17:48 (13,832)	
Stannett, Judith	6:37:09 (29,565)	
Stannett, Kate	5:16:45 (25,019)	
Stanslas, Barbara	6:39:24 (29,615)	
Stanton, Jill	4:36:24 (17,998)	
Stanworth Hall, Shirley	6:54:19 (29,863)	
Stapleton, Julie	4:26:33 (15,856)	
Stapleton, Linda	4:20:46 (14,539)	

Starck Johann, Birgitta 4:00:55 (10,267)
Stares, Diane....3:56:29 (9,050)
State, Marie....5:25:42 (25,960)
Staves, Lisa....3:55:33 (8,808)
Staves, Rosemary....5:46:30 (27,661)
Stayt, Iona....4:26:56 (15,945)
Stead, Deborah....5:58:13 (28,333)
Stead, Helen....3:37:19 (5,305)
Stead, Julie....4:17:12 (13,720)
Steadman, Jacqueline....4:58:12 (22,328)
Steck, Kristen....5:09:10 (23,969)
Stedman, Samantha....4:41:52 (19,131)
Stedman, Susi....5:13:07 (24,520)
Stedman, Tracy....5:45:23 (27,582)
Steel, Charlotte....5:27:54 (26,171)
Steel, Emma....5:39:40 (27,154)
Steel, Nicky....4:18:02 (13,874)
Steel, Philippa....6:35:05 (29,523)
Steele, Julia....4:03:08 (10,692)
Steele, Shona....5:46:10 (27,637)
Steenkamp, Bronwyn....3:45:16 (6,715)
Steenkiste, Christine....5:21:43 (25,551)
Steer, Alison....6:12:02 (28,926)
Steer, Bronwen....3:45:30 (6,744)
Steer, Deborah....3:44:54 (6,661)
Steggell, Heidi....5:05:19 (23,340)
Stein, Victoria....3:57:24 (9,289)
Stenger, Melanie....7:26:08 (30,113)
Stepanowich, Martha....5:13:29 (24,572)
Stephens, Carolyn....5:43:43 (27,451)
Stephens, Emily....5:09:03 (23,949)
Stephens, Heidi....4:51:02 (20,891)
Stephenson, Jane....4:42:43 (19,315)
Stephenson, Kim....3:18:02 (2,538)
Stephenson, Tessa....3:34:34 (4,843)
Stephenson, Trisha....5:14:35 (24,720)
Stevens, Carolne....3:12:12 (1,932)
Stevens, Christine....5:29:53 (26,362)
Stevens, Mary....4:21:35 (14,708)
Stevens, Patricia....4:23:31 (15,179)
Stevenson, Anna....6:05:06 (28,644)
Stevenson, Gillian....3:36:59 (5,241)
Stevenson, Jane....3:58:43 (9,679)
Stevenson, Pauline....5:18:37 (25,226)
Stevenson, Rachel....5:36:19 (26,902)
Stevenson, Victoria....4:13:56 (13,028)
Steward, Ruth....4:49:08 (20,548)
Stewart, Ada....3:34:19 (4,804)
Stewart, Alison....5:02:58 (23,000)
Stewart, Catherine....5:19:16 (25,289)
Stewart, Christina....5:13:08 (24,522)
Stewart, Helen....5:29:16 (26,316)
Stewart, Pamela....5:26:44 (26,065)
Stewart, Rosie....5:07:54 (23,758)
Stewart, Sue....3:52:57 (8,257)
Stiff, Tracy....5:31:12 (26,470)
Stimpson, Lucy....4:39:47 (18,751)
Stimpson, Lucy....6:00:51 (28,450)
Stimson, Donna....5:05:42 (23,416)
Stirling, Jane....4:54:00 (21,511)
Stirling, Sonia....5:02:27 (22,932)
Stirling Whyte, Barbara....3:58:21 (9,576)
Stirton Smith, Catriona....5:24:55 (25,874)
Stobbart, Gloria....4:31:01 (16,855)
Stock, Michelle....5:17:58 (25,159)
Stockton, Paula....3:31:50 (4,444)
Stokes, Reana....6:26:15 (29,306)
Stoll, Sarah....4:51:08 (20,912)
Stonard, Sarah....4:49:41 (20,648)
Stone, Claire....6:41:50 (29,687)
Stone, Gina....3:47:32 (7,150)
Stone, Karen....5:14:27 (24,694)
Stone, Katharina....4:33:52 (17,513)
Stone, Susan....4:40:32 (18,878)
Stone, Veronica....4:31:02 (16,858)
Stonebank, Jenny....4:22:00 (14,813)
Stoneham, Karen....4:11:58 (12,600)
Storey, Ann....5:44:28 (27,509)
Storey, Julia....3:58:40 (9,661)
Storey, Sarah....5:02:16 (22,911)
Storz, Martina....4:47:28 (20,252)
Stothard, Helen....3:49:14 (7,502)
Stott, Bernadine....5:51:26 (27,978)
Stott, Nichola....6:52:18 (29,837)
Stowe, Sara....5:11:46 (24,323)
Strang, Louise....4:33:16 (17,360)
Strang, Veronica....6:53:16 (29,851)
Stratford, Angela....4:34:48 (17,677)
Stratton, Emily....5:16:16 (24,956)
Strazzeri, Rita....4:43:40 (19,530)
Streere, Paula....4:56:10 (22,015)
Streets, Janice....3:44:43 (6,618)
Strettle, Lyn....5:27:19 (26,112)
Stribling, Julie....4:18:19 (13,959)
Stringer, Lynda....6:53:09 (29,848)
Stringer, Nicola....5:01:53 (22,849)
Strnao, Iveta....5:57:23 (28,289)
Strods, Patricia....5:18:45 (25,242)
Stroud, Joanne....5:56:15 (28,224)
Struthers, Sarah....3:58:48 (9,700)
Stuart, Diane....3:58:29 (9,601)
Stuart William, Annette....6:21:28 (29,204)
Stubbings, Jane....4:41:55 (19,144)
Stubbs, Rachel....4:53:21 (21,388)
Stubbs, Sally....3:56:14 (8,975)
Sturman, Susan....4:29:47 (16,619)
Sublette, Theresa....4:50:02 (20,725)
Suffield, Charlotte....4:18:15 (13,935)
Suffling, Hannah....5:27:57 (26,176)
Sugden, Ingrid....5:11:44 (24,320)
Sullivan, Ellen....3:27:46 (3,760)
Summerhayes, Catherine....5:03:04 (23,016)
Summers, Debbie....3:56:39 (9,091)
Summers, Lucinda....4:55:24 (21,849)
Summersall, Nicola....4:37:19 (18,200)
Summerville, Karen Mary....4:59:07 (22,479)
Sumner-Djie, Brigitte....4:17:29 (13,769)
Sumpter, Sue....6:09:58 (28,858)
Sunderland, Linda....4:27:52 (16,167)
Sunderland, Sue....4:02:22 (10,544)
Suquet, Nathalie....3:15:19 (2,256)
Surguy, Eugenie....4:02:00 (10,486)
Surman, Jessica....4:06:20 (11,414)
Susskind, Juliet....7:08:08 (30,009)
Sutcliffe, Denise....4:43:59 (19,583)
Sutcliffe, Justine....4:42:19 (19,231)
Suter, Christa....5:44:41 (27,539)
Suter, Faith....3:44:31 (6,580)
Suter, Mirjam....4:24:15 (15,341)
Sutherland, Leslie....4:49:54 (20,696)
Suthers, Karen....5:35:44 (26,862)
Suttle, Caroline....4:44:24 (19,656)
Suttle, Haley....3:28:21 (3,881)
Sutton, Liza....4:13:14 (12,861)
Sutton, Natasha....5:41:47 (27,314)
Sutton, Nina....6:05:50 (28,679)
Sutton, Tracie....5:17:16 (25,077)
Sutton-Gibbs, Deborah....8:29:04 (30,243)
Swabey, Deborah....6:03:34 (28,570)
Swaby, Jennifer....4:30:58 (16,844)
Swain, Jane....4:55:08 (21,765)
Swaine, June....5:09:09 (23,965)
Swaine, Tessa....4:45:15 (19,815)
Swales, Charlotte....5:03:17 (23,040)
Swan, Rachel....4:12:51 (12,799)
Swann, Lynn....5:35:30 (26,843)
Swanson, Natasha....4:31:11 (16,898)
Swanston, Sarah....5:48:01 (27,776)
Swash, Samantha....4:43:41 (19,535)
Swayne, Philippa....4:02:16 (10,530)
Sweatman, Emma....7:29:43 (30,134)
Swedlund, Brenda....4:56:09 (22,011)
Swensen, Michelle....4:16:42 (13,609)
Swerling, Jo....6:42:29 (29,700)
Swettenham, Katharine....4:11:39 (12,535)
Swift, Pamela....4:55:20 (21,824)
Swingler, Lynsey....4:26:27 (15,832)
Swinnerton, Shelagh....4:49:01 (20,530)
Swire, Nicola....5:53:39 (28,099)
Swithenby, Margaret....3:18:53 (2,641)
Syed, Marium....8:50:08 (30,267)
Syed, Nelofer....4:52:59 (21,312)
Symmonds, Diane....6:13:17 (28,963)
Symonds, Elizabeth....5:12:58 (24,493)
Symonds, Evelyne....4:29:00 (16,420)
Symonds, Samantha....3:43:55 (6,476)
Symons, Emma....6:05:47 (28,677)
Synan, Cathy....5:22:12 (25,615)
Szostak, Teresa....5:03:06 (23,019)
Taberer, Vivienne....4:05:14 (11,159)
Tadier, Vanessa....4:27:37 (16,096)
Taft, Joanna....4:58:33 (22,386)
Tait, Elizabeth....4:39:10 (18,630)
Takao, Hidemi....4:34:23 (17,612)
Takaramoto, Yoko....5:02:34 (22,942)
Talbot, Lesley....6:56:36 (29,901)
Talkington, Jennifer....6:30:00 (29,409)
Tall, Joanna....5:36:59 (26,945)
Tam, Emily....4:18:54 (14,098)
Tamblyn, Ros....5:07:37 (23,717)
Tamplin, Teresa....3:55:08 (8,721)
Tan, Karina....5:34:48 (26,783)
Tanner, Anita....6:53:44 (29,861)
Tanner, Clare....4:07:18 (11,612)
Tanser, Rose....5:24:53 (25,871)
Taplin, Christina....6:23:31 (29,244)
Tapper, Rosemary....4:26:50 (15,916)
Tappin, Bridge....4:56:32 (22,074)
Tarran, Emma....6:29:05 (29,390)
Taylor, Anita....6:03:34 (28,570)
Taylor, Bridgeen....5:06:47 (23,586)
Taylor, Bridget....4:08:53 (11,952)
Taylor, Carol....5:30:15 (26,391)
Taylor, Caroline....4:47:02 (20,169)
Taylor, Charlotte....4:46:06 (19,960)
Taylor, Deborah....3:46:32 (6,956)
Taylor, Dorothy....5:16:15 (24,952)
Taylor, Elaine....5:19:56 (25,358)
Taylor, Emma....4:55:01 (21,739)
Taylor, Gillian....4:46:34 (20,071)
Taylor, Guilaine....6:13:47 (28,986)
Taylor, Helen....5:50:20 (27,918)
Taylor, Jacqueline....4:18:07 (13,892)
Taylor, Jacqueline....6:25:27 (29,294)
Taylor, Joan....5:43:03 (27,415)
Taylor, Joanne....3:50:30 (7,772)
Taylor, Joanne....5:46:43 (27,681)
Taylor, Karen....3:29:05 (4,011)
Taylor, Karen....4:53:31 (21,427)
Taylor, Karen....5:48:08 (27,784)
Taylor, Kelly....4:54:10 (21,545)
Taylor, Leila....4:22:47 (15,000)
Taylor, Lorna....3:41:37 (6,059)
Taylor, Margaret....4:43:47 (19,554)
Taylor, Martine....5:01:49 (22,842)
Taylor, Mary....5:18:44 (25,237)
Taylor, Nichola....3:47:37 (7,167)
Taylor, Samantha....6:36:24 (29,554)
Taylor, Sarah....7:38:31 (30,159)
Taylor, Sharon....5:08:27 (23,840)
Taylor, Sheila....4:37:44 (18,308)
Taylor, Susan....4:23:48 (15,250)
Taylor, Suzanne....5:00:54 (22,720)
Taylor, Tara....3:37:27 (5,327)
Taylor, Tracey....3:53:50 (8,450)
Taylor, Tracey....6:24:02 (29,259)
Taylor, Victoria....5:08:44 (23,894)
Taylor Brooke, Alexandra....6:33:23 (29,491)
Teague, Fiona....4:37:41 (18,297)
Teasdale, Jennifer....5:08:13 (23,800)
Teasdel, Diane....5:48:40 (27,824)
Teebay, Maxine....5:13:16 (24,548)
Teichler, Tanya....3:49:19 (7,528)
Telford, Christine....4:42:47 (19,326)
Telford, Clare....4:05:40 (11,256)
Tempest, Linda....4:37:50 (18,326)
Tempini, Urska....3:33:08 (4,633)
Temple, Lorraine....5:21:59 (25,582)
Temple Smith, Elizabeth....6:46:42 (29,753)
Templeton, Louise....5:23:57 (25,789)
Tennant, Frances....4:22:02 (14,822)
Tennant, Margaret....4:57:16 (22,181)
Tenniswood, Karen....4:27:47 (16,147)
Terkelsen, Gilly....3:41:47 (6,088)
Terris, Catherine....4:50:03 (20,728)
Terris, Jane....4:41:59 (19,159)
Terris, Sally....8:06:05 (30,213)
Terry, Amanda....4:11:23 (12,478)
Terry, Frances....4:52:35 (21,233)

Terry, Gail 5:47:48 (27,752)
Tetley, Julia 5:13:27 (24,568)
Tetlow, Chloe....................4:28:54 (16,397)
Thackeray, Cheri 6:11:33 (28,911)
Thelen, Jennifer....................4:53:28 (21,411)
Thevenet-Smith, Ramona 3:31:14 (4,360)
Thevenot, Virginie 3:32:30 (4,536)
Thiele, Margaret 5:19:02 (25,268)
Thiele, Sharlene....................6:12:05 (28,928)
Thiru, Yamuna 3:57:57 (9,478)
Thistleton, Heather 4:26:34 (15,865)
Thomas, Andrea....................3:39:58 (5,778)
Thomas, Andrea....................5:22:40 (25,665)
Thomas, Ann-Marie 4:12:16 (12,683)
Thomas, Antoinette 3:58:48 (9,700)
Thomas, Caroline 4:56:30 (22,065)
Thomas, Clare 3:58:50 (9,709)
Thomas, Eleanor....................4:42:09 (19,192)
Thomas, Jeannette 3:29:58 (4,165)
Thomas, Joshy 4:51:24 (20,970)
Thomas, Judith....................4:29:28 (16,537)
Thomas, Kate 4:20:49 (14,552)
Thomas, Kerry....................5:26:15 (26,013)
Thomas, Kerry....................6:32:22 (29,459)
Thomas, Louise....................4:21:45 (14,746)
Thomas, Marian 5:39:52 (27,173)
Thomas, Paula....................4:13:51 (13,013)
Thomas, Rachel....................4:59:36 (22,539)
Thomas, Rosemary....................4:49:11 (20,556)
Thomas, Samantha 3:48:20 (7,328)
Thomas, Shannon....................5:36:17 (26,897)
Thomas-Luisi, Michelle 4:13:20 (12,884)
Thomason, Helen 6:11:28 (28,907)
Thompson, Angela 4:34:43 (17,662)
Thompson, Barbara....................4:10:13 (12,213)
Thompson, Candace....................4:14:32 (13,137)
Thompson, Catie 3:57:27 (9,311)
Thompson, Catriona....................5:35:57 (26,874)
Thompson, Clare 4:43:06 (19,404)
Thompson, Emma 5:10:54 (24,197)
Thompson, Gail 5:39:08 (27,100)
Thompson, Jane....................3:24:47 (3,352)
Thompson, Linda 5:56:21 (28,229)
Thompson, Marie 5:41:57 (27,330)
Thompson, Natasha....................4:56:51 (22,116)
Thompson, Nicola 3:06:23 (1,450)
Thompson, Nikki 5:09:42 (24,043)
Thompson, Rebecca 5:53:42 (28,104)
Thompson, Ruth....................5:07:21 (23,671)
Thompson, Sharon 3:50:28 (7,767)
Thompson, Sharon 3:59:24 (9,885)
Thompson, Vanda....................4:54:22 (21,570)
Thompson, Wendy....................5:34:40 (26,770)
Thomson, Jacqueline....................4:16:08 (13,492)
Thomson, Sandra....................4:32:26 (17,201)
Thone, Monique 5:09:25 (24,003)
Thorn, Pauline 5:17:24 (25,093)
Thornber, Nicola....................7:02:14 (29,961)
Thorne, Deborah 4:39:01 (18,611)
Thorne, Felicity....................5:05:14 (23,327)
Thorne, Margaret 6:19:28 (29,143)
Thornton, Jackie 4:59:55 (22,603)
Thornton, Jayne....................6:09:41 (28,843)
Thornton, Rona 4:53:24 (21,398)
Thornton-Paget, Nora 4:07:58 (11,755)
Thorogood, Ann 5:45:39 (27,606)
Thorogood, Wendy....................4:50:02 (20,725)
Thorpe, Gaye....................4:47:24 (20,238)
Thorpe, Leona 6:37:09 (29,565)
Thorpe, Rosemary 5:09:34 (24,024)
Thorpe, Sandra 4:37:23 (18,219)
Throner, Hanna 3:31:26 (4,387)
Thrower, Julie....................4:00:03 (10,065)
Thulborn, Jacky....................6:32:53 (29,476)
Thurlow, Llowes 4:02:56 (10,654)
Thurnell-Read, Jane....................5:48:40 (27,824)
Tibbott, Catherine 5:04:48 (23,264)
Tice, Sandra 4:18:38 (14,036)
Tickner, Caroline 5:35:32 (26,846)
Tidbury, Susanne 4:47:32 (20,273)
Tidey, Paula 4:39:22 (18,659)
Tilbrook, Patricia 5:31:42 (26,508)
Till, Beverley....................5:31:49 (26,519)
Tilt, Carole 4:55:28 (21,878)
Timmins, Sabine 3:43:41 (6,432)
Timothy, Kate 5:50:25 (27,920)
Timpson, Liza....................4:11:10 (12,431)
Tingle, Gladys....................6:00:27 (28,429)
Tinnirello, Gabriella 5:03:00 (23,004)
Tinsley, Judith....................3:43:54 (6,472)
Titterington, Alison 3:53:34 (8,394)
Tllman, Fi 5:09:59 (24,079)
Tobin, Catherine....................4:56:01 (21,987)
Tobin, Vannessa 4:48:57 (20,518)
Todd, Lisa 6:21:06 (29,196)
Todd, Sharon....................5:31:02 (26,456)
Todd, Victoria....................4:55:19 (21,819)
Toft, Christine 3:32:52 (4,582)
Toland, Patricia 4:10:55 (12,378)
Tolliday, Kate 5:43:59 (27,474)
Tomasi, Nathalie 4:14:04 (13,052)
Tombs, Gail....................3:52:04 (8,091)
Tomkinson, Linda....................7:06:39 (29,993)
Tomlinson, Lee 3:55:37 (8,821)
Tomlinson, Samantha....................4:44:58 (19,770)
Tomlinson, Suzan....................5:54:41 (28,147)
Tompkins, Claire....................5:09:22 (23,992)
Tompsett, Anna....................4:36:03 (17,940)
Toms, Nicole....................4:50:17 (20,767)
Toms, Wendy 3:53:48 (8,442)
Tonkin, Claire 5:02:20 (22,921)
Tookey, Elaine 4:15:11 (13,299)
Tooley, Josephine 6:01:20 (28,470)
Toomey, Charlotte....................5:15:28 (24,864)
Tooze, Jacqueline....................4:08:59 (11,974)
Topping, Mary....................7:37:42 (30,154)
Tori, Tiziana 5:16:04 (24,936)
Toste, Guenevere 5:02:56 (22,996)
Toulson, Bonnie....................4:23:07 (15,088)
Toussaint, Candy 6:06:30 (28,699)
Tovell, Anita....................6:22:53 (29,229)
Tovell, Lisa....................6:22:53 (29,229)
Townend, Mandy....................5:50:55 (27,951)
Townend, Samantha 4:06:17 (11,404)
Townsend, Georgina....................5:06:04 (23,480)
Townsend, Laura....................5:11:39 (24,304)
Townsend, Lucy....................3:12:57 (1,999)
Townson, Ann 6:02:31 (28,521)
Tracey, Nicola 5:52:25 (28,035)
Tran Dang, Djima....................4:04:25 (10,970)
Treacher, Tracy....................5:48:24 (27,808)
Treagus, Sarah 5:14:29 (24,701)
Treanor, Jayne 4:20:44 (14,529)
Tree, Clare 4:54:17 (21,559)
Tregaskis, Julia....................4:46:22 (20,028)
Tregunna, Kim 4:24:40 (15,433)
Treharne Jones, Kathryn 6:26:25 (29,315)
Treherne, Elizabeth 4:49:33 (20,626)
Tremaine, Sandra....................4:44:29 (19,668)
Tremlett, Caroline....................4:27:20 (16,030)
Trepy, Germane....................4:02:37 (10,594)
Trevena, Niki 4:23:31 (15,179)
Trevorrow, Philippa....................4:46:10 (19,977)
Tribe, Maxine 5:18:00 (25,166)
Tricker, Janice....................4:51:02 (20,891)
Trimble, Natalie 6:01:04 (28,458)
Trimble, Samantha....................4:57:18 (22,190)
Trinca, Marianne....................4:56:10 (22,015)
Troy, Carlen 7:10:05 (30,017)
Trubridge, Leila 4:33:46 (17,492)
Trubshaw, Susan....................4:54:03 (21,523)
Trump, Amanda....................4:39:57 (18,777)
Trumper, Jane....................4:20:52 (14,564)
Truswell, Sandra....................4:28:48 (16,380)
Tse, Hau Ming....................5:21:42 (25,548)
Tse, Mabel....................6:03:27 (28,562)
Tsigeou, Anastasia 5:34:48 (26,783)
Tuck, Natasha....................4:16:44 (13,621)
Tucker, Sue 3:54:43 (8,641)
Tucker, Terry 5:12:00 (24,356)
Tucker, Tina 4:21:43 (14,737)
Tudball, Sarah 4:10:55 (12,378)
Tuerena, Sue 3:43:43 (6,442)
Tuite, Helen....................4:27:47 (16,147)
Tull, Jane....................5:00:35 (22,675)
Tulloch, Donna 6:09:29 (28,834)
Tully, Anne....................4:47:17 (20,218)

Tulu, Derartu....................2:23:57 (35)

Derartu Tulu was born in 1972 in the village of Bokoji, in the Arsi region of central Ethiopia. She was the seventh child in a family of ten children. Derartu's first significant win came in a 400m race in her school where she outran the school's star male athlete. When she was 17, Derartu was hired by the Ethiopian Police Force. In 1989, she competed in her first international cross-country race of 6km in Norway and finished a modest 23rd. But in 1990 she ran and won the same race. Thereafter, her international progress was rapid. Derartu's win in the 10,000m race in the 1992 Barcelona Olympics was the first gold-medal win ever by a black African woman. After that victory she draped herself with the Ethiopian national flag and did a victory lap with the white South African silver medallist, Elana Meyer, establishing herself as an Ethiopian icon alongside Abebe Bikila, Mamo Wolde and Miruts Yifter. Tulu was not an instant success at the marathon but her victory in London 2001 confirmed her status as one of the world's most accomplished distance runners. In the Sydney Olympics of 2000 it was Tulu who beat Britain's Paula Radcliffe into fourth place with her fast finish to win the 10,000m.

Tunley, Jennie....................4:46:53 (20,140)
Tunley, Johanna 5:49:23 (27,864)
Tunnell, Mary....................6:16:43 (29,079)
Turley, Susan 5:17:54 (25,149)
Turnbull, Anna....................6:35:13 (29,527)
Turnbull, Moira....................4:51:50 (21,060)
Turner, Alison....................3:39:13 (5,612)
Turner, Elke....................5:05:29 (23,381)
Turner, Janet....................4:56:31 (22,069)
Turner, Jennifer....................5:43:18 (27,426)
Turner, Joanne 4:35:13 (17,754)
Turner, Louise....................3:56:38 (9,085)
Turner, Michelle....................4:40:14 (18,819)
Turner, Rebecca 4:00:10 (10,081)
Turner, Sarah....................4:14:44 (13,185)
Turner, Tracy 5:38:07 (27,027)
Turner, Valerie....................6:40:00 (29,630)
Turnstill, Tracey....................6:59:32 (29,937)
Turpin, Clare 4:12:38 (12,760)

Turton, Liz 3:48:48 (7,423)
Tustin, Emma 5:27:34 (26,134)
Tvedt, Anneli 3:47:28 (7,133)
Tweed, Irene 3:14:09 (2,133)
Tweed, Janice 4:51:26 (20,975)
Tweed, Katherine 4:37:22 (18,215)
Twelvetree, Yvonne 4:04:00 (10,881)
Twiss, William 5:16:02 (24,932)
Twmkenycz, Cecilia 5:14:34 (24,717)
Twomey, Caroline 6:07:13 (28,731)
Twomey, Joy 4:11:34 (12,515)
Twomey, Stella 5:13:46 (24,602)
Twyman, Lucy 5:21:02 (25,473)
Tyler, Deborah 4:54:42 (21,640)
Tyler, Imogen 5:13:28 (24,570)
Tyler, Jacky 3:14:29 (2,165)
Tynan, Allison 4:51:48 (21,056)
Tyson, Veronica Sue 4:29:03 (16,431)
Uchiyama, Kuniko 4:48:21 (20,416)
Uhler, Maureen 5:14:21 (24,679)
Ujvari, Lesley 3:46:06 (6,877)
Underwood, Gillian 4:08:53 (11,952)
Underwood, Joanne 5:37:24 (26,971)
Unsworth, Linda 4:03:02 (10,670)
Unsworth, Louise 5:48:29 (27,816)
Unwin, Joanna 6:52:52 (29,841)
Upton, Ann 5:22:41 (25,671)
Upton, Rebecca 4:42:59 (19,383)
Upton, Sasha 4:11:31 (12,505)
Upward, Clare 4:38:46 (18,568)
Urban, Wendy 3:11:05 (1,842)
Ursell, Aldyth 5:15:46 (24,901)
Usher, Clare 4:35:02 (17,717)
Usher, Margaret 4:05:56 (11,333)
Usher, Shenley 5:39:25 (27,123)
Utasi, Lisa 4:05:58 (11,347)
Utteridge, Sharon 4:05:41 (11,263)
Vadhesha, Rupi 6:20:55 (29,190)
Valapinee, Anick 4:22:50 (15,016)
Valdettaro, Sharon 4:52:31 (21,210)
Valender, Rebekah 5:29:03 (26,293)
Vallance, Rachel 5:13:22 (24,563)
Vallely, Karen 5:08:21 (23,823)
Vallerfield, Nicky 4:10:06 (12,179)
Vammeemsel, Tjarda 4:09:11 (12,018)
Van De Zande, Janice 5:51:30 (27,983)
Van Doorn, Carin 4:38:24 (18,480)
Van Geijn Van Veen, Moira 4:26:06 (15,758)
Van Niel, Brigitta 5:02:52 (22,988)
Van Ouwerkerk, Monique 3:55:14 (8,747)
Van Piershill, Karin 5:23:12 (25,720)
Van Wyk, Liesbeth 4:01:06 (10,300)
Vande Velde, Maria Celine 4:06:58 (11,545)
Vanderpump, Katharine 4:35:56 (17,913)
Vandyk, Johanna 7:07:39 (30,003)
Vanes, Rita 4:35:02 (17,717)
Van-Orden, Elaine 3:51:06 (7,896)
Vartanian, Tracey 6:28:29 (29,372)
Vasani, Deepa 4:52:36 (21,238)
Vassilevskaja, Ledya 2:31:36 (72)
Vaughan, Diane 4:43:44 (19,548)
Vaughan, Lucy 4:17:27 (13,761)
Vaughan, Nicky 5:16:04 (24,936)
Vaughan, Rebecca 5:25:04 (25,893)
Vaughan, Siobhan 7:55:24 (30,198)
Vaughan, Susan 4:10:29 (12,272)
V'Chong, Idy 5:37:53 (27,013)
Vegezzi-Boskov, Aleksandra 6:41:03 (29,662)
Veitch, Linda 4:06:56 (11,535)
Venn, Kerry 4:08:02 (11,774)
Venter, Vicky 6:27:23 (29,339)
Verbeij, Betty 4:51:15 (20,930)
Verlander, Sarah 4:55:26 (21,863)
Vernal, Nicola 5:06:36 (23,559)
Vernazza, Patricia 3:57:17 (9,250)
Vernon, Alicia 3:26:17 (3,535)
Veron, Christiane 3:40:44 (5,903)
Versey, Lisa 5:21:18 (25,504)
Vestey, Joanna 4:31:14 (16,913)
Vickers, Christine 5:18:46 (25,246)
Victor, Christina 4:35:14 (17,758)
Viedge, Gerda 7:07:34 (30,001)
Vignolo, Caroline 3:59:08 (9,795)
Viljoen, Estle 3:08:12 (1,606)
Villegas, Paz 4:59:06 (22,475)
Vimsom-Fischer, Heidi 4:57:34 (22,221)
Vincent, Marianne 5:00:30 (22,663)
Vincent, Sarah 3:57:46 (9,416)
Vincent, Sarah 4:23:24 (15,150)
Vine-Jones, Sophie 3:44:03 (6,499)
Vines, Lisa 4:32:12 (17,155)
Vintcent, Barbara 4:19:41 (14,299)
Vinton, Linda 5:14:51 (24,756)
Virdee Dhanjal, Jaspal 5:25:56 (25,980)
Vohmann, Sally 5:41:24 (27,290)
Vohra, Belinda 5:14:56 (24,767)
Voitin, Clare 3:07:07 (1,514)
Von Beokonyi, Ilona 5:12:42 (24,457)
Von Lewinski, Franziska 3:43:05 (6,323)
Vonbylandt, Heike 3:40:55 (5,931)
Vottre, Orianna 5:20:01 (25,363)
Vranic, Dragica 4:17:02 (13,676)
Vuagniaux, Alison 3:05:09 (1,362)
Vyas, Seema 4:51:55 (21,073)
Wade-Thomas, Charlotte 4:38:01 (18,375)
Wadforth, Catherine 3:20:19 (2,797)
Wadhams, Emma 4:27:34 (16,081)
Wadsworth, Jacqueline 3:37:01 (5,249)
Wadsworth, Nichola 6:44:09 (29,722)
Wadsworth, Rachel 5:34:30 (26,756)
Wadsworth, Victoria 4:43:16 (19,442)
Wahab, Aliya 3:54:52 (8,680)
Wahab, Salima 5:05:45 (23,422)
Wailes, Alison 4:42:37 (19,298)
Waite, Jane 6:35:33 (29,534)
Wajima, Noriko 4:32:11 (17,152)
Wakefield, Margery 5:35:14 (26,821)
Wakeling, Maureen 4:00:44 (10,227)
Walden, Emma 4:42:23 (19,244)
Walden, Wendy 4:59:28 (22,523)
Waldner, Elena 5:36:42 (26,924)
Wales, Paula 3:10:53 (1,827)
Wales, Sarah 4:28:05 (16,205)
Walker, Claire 3:41:43 (6,076)
Walker, Debbie 4:41:26 (19,052)
Walker, Elizabeth 4:25:11 (15,554)
Walker, Emma 5:14:07 (24,641)
Walker, Evelyn 6:21:12 (29,198)
Walker, Hayley 5:14:04 (24,634)
Walker, Hilary 3:26:21 (3,540)
Walker, Jennifer 4:35:10 (17,746)
Walker, Jo 4:03:23 (10,744)
Walker, Judy 4:39:28 (18,683)
Walker, Julie 5:11:57 (24,347)
Walker, Julie 6:27:59 (29,356)
Walker, June 4:06:41 (11,481)
Walker, Marion 4:51:31 (20,985)
Walker, Patricia 4:14:09 (13,065)
Walker, Pauline 3:39:47 (5,735)
Walker, Rachel 6:24:56 (29,282)
Walker, Sarah-Ann 4:25:45 (15,662)
Walker, Stephanie 5:43:37 (27,446)
Walker, Susan 5:13:13 (24,535)
Walker, Susanna 6:08:52 (28,812)
Wall, Amanda 5:11:41 (24,310)
Wall, Wendy 4:17:06 (13,685)
Wallace, Alana 6:13:29 (28,970)
Wallace, Dawn 4:09:14 (12,031)
Wallace, Deborah 6:41:17 (29,669)
Wallace, Fiona 5:08:33 (23,855)
Wallace, Louise 5:45:17 (27,577)
Wallace, Susan 4:06:22 (11,422)
Wallen, Debbie 3:57:11 (9,219)
Waller, Anne 4:48:52 (20,496)
Wallis, Elaine 6:57:48 (29,915)
Wallis, Elizabeth 4:18:44 (14,063)
Wallis, Emma 6:24:03 (29,260)
Walmsley, Rachel 5:25:14 (25,913)
Walmsley, Suzie 5:10:02 (24,085)
Walsh, Bernie 4:03:16 (10,713)
Walsh, Beverley 3:57:34 (9,352)
Walsh, Bridget Anne 4:21:34 (14,704)
Walsh, Celia 5:02:30 (22,936)
Walsh, Jennifer 3:31:50 (4,444)
Walsh, Lisa 5:47:21 (27,719)
Walsh, Liz 6:28:12 (29,361)
Walsh, Sheenagh 4:55:51 (21,961)
Walters, Jacqueline 6:09:41 (28,843)
Walters, Sara 4:49:03 (20,538)
Walton, Caroline 4:40:59 (18,974)
Walton, Dawn 6:29:53 (29,405)
Walton, Kathryn 5:07:03 (23,625)
Walton, Sarah 4:55:28 (21,878)
Walton, Valerie 3:35:47 (5,029)
Walwyn, Rosamund 5:07:34 (23,708)
Waple, Karen 4:54:46 (21,665)
Ward, Amanda 4:50:06 (20,737)
Ward, Amanda 5:15:08 (24,802)
Ward, Annette 3:16:47 (2,404)
Ward, Carol 5:30:18 (26,396)
Ward, Caroline 6:47:07 (29,759)
Ward, Davina 4:22:07 (14,838)
Ward, Elizabeth 3:38:03 (5,406)
Ward, Felicity 5:33:55 (26,682)
Ward, Jane 3:33:12 (4,646)
Ward, Jennifer 5:19:34 (25,316)
Ward, Joanne 6:36:45 (29,558)
Ward, Julie 4:50:57 (20,870)
Ward, Louise 4:28:55 (16,404)
Ward, Nita 4:49:33 (20,626)
Ward, Susan 3:53:11 (8,305)
Warde, Abbie 4:45:16 (19,818)
Wardner, Mhairi 4:13:32 (12,939)
Wareing, Hazel 4:38:06 (18,401)
Warhurst, Kathleen 3:26:14 (3,526)
Waring, Gabrielle 3:19:35 (2,716)
Waring, Kate 4:10:38 (12,300)
Warland, Ann 4:24:58 (15,497)
Warn, Claire 5:07:44 (23,737)
Warne, Sarah 4:20:11 (14,405)
Warne, Sharon 4:33:00 (17,309)
Warner, Anne 5:11:26 (24,274)
Warner, Claire 3:20:11 (2,783)
Warner, Pauline 3:59:20 (9,856)
Warner, Stephanie 4:26:08 (15,762)
Warnes, Francis 3:54:07 (8,495)
Warnes, Wendy 4:31:35 (17,003)
Warren, Alison 5:18:52 (25,256)
Warren, Gillian 4:32:01 (17,122)
Warren, Tracey 5:50:10 (27,914)
Waschko, Christina 4:32:51 (17,285)
Wastnage, Rachel 4:17:10 (13,708)
Waters, Eirian 5:27:14 (26,107)
Watkinson, Lynne 3:51:39 (7,997)
Watsham, Rebecca 6:36:41 (29,557)
Watson, Alicia 3:32:43 (4,561)
Watson, Andrea 3:16:21 (2,345)
Watson, Ann 6:06:16 (28,694)
Watson, Denise 5:22:48 (25,683)
Watson, Gill 4:06:46 (11,495)
Watson, Janet 3:44:54 (6,661)
Watson, Janet 5:28:50 (26,273)
Watson, Jennifer 4:11:10 (12,431)
Watson, Lorna 4:27:54 (16,178)
Watson, Louise 2:43:49 (255)
Watson, Rachael 3:28:09 (3,834)
Watson, Sue 4:11:12 (12,440)
Watson, Suzanne 4:58:32 (22,383)
Watson, Tracey 4:54:41 (21,634)
Watt, Marian 6:00:33 (28,432)
Watts, Jean 5:21:19 (25,506)
Watts, Katie 4:43:29 (19,490)
Watts, Patricia 3:57:41 (9,391)
Waugh, Melanie 5:06:23 (23,533)
Waywell, Kathleen 4:24:25 (15,374)
Weald, Caroline 4:26:11 (15,774)
Weatherburn, Nicola 4:27:51 (16,163)
Webb, Amy 3:55:00 (8,702)
Webb, Julie 5:37:37 (26,997)
Webb, Louise 4:04:38 (11,028)
Webb, Melanie 5:59:00 (28,367)
Webb, Mo 5:14:33 (24,713)
Webb, Sarah 4:04:21 (10,955)
Webber, Caroline 4:44:54 (19,759)
Webber, Joanne 5:27:19 (26,112)
Webster, Helen 5:30:13 (26,387)
Webster, Rachel 4:09:00 (11,978)
Webster, Sally 4:13:06 (12,836)
Wedd, Rosaline 5:06:47 (23,586)

Weekes, Lisa 4:17:47 (13,829)
Weeks, Angela 5:52:56 (28,059)
Weeks, Caron....4:01:41 (10,428)
Weeks, Karen 8:06:05 (30,213)
Weeks, Kerrie....4:26:00 (15,730)
Weidemanis, Emma 4:13:27 (12,921)
Weight, Gillian 6:43:38 (29,714)
Weill, Wendy....5:44:53 (27,554)
Weinreich, Amanda 5:07:07 (23,632)
Weir, Moira 5:53:41 (28,101)
Weir, Paulette 6:05:29 (28,663)
Weiss, Lin....6:15:05 (29,026)
Welch, Alexandra....5:34:37 (26,765)
Welch, Claire 5:21:06 (25,480)
Welch, Deborah 5:19:40 (25,326)
Welch, Emma 5:27:40 (26,145)
Welch, Margaret....4:05:47 (11,293)
Welfare, Clare....3:59:10 (9,807)
Welfare, Jean 4:56:52 (22,121)
Welham, Wendy....5:09:06 (23,953)
Wellbelove, Dawn....5:39:33 (27,136)
Weller, Liz 6:25:10 (29,286)
Weller, Susan 5:17:15 (25,074)
Wellman, Amanda....4:30:06 (16,708)
Wells, Diane....4:53:10 (21,348)
Wells, Heather....4:46:46 (20,109)
Wells, Jackie 4:29:08 (16,458)
Wells, Jill 4:46:59 (20,161)
Wells, Lorraine 4:51:16 (20,935)
Wells, Melissa....4:53:04 (21,330)
Wells, Soraya....3:58:06 (9,515)
Welsh, Veronica....5:29:09 (26,302)
Welstead, Barbara 6:07:53 (28,755)
Welstead, Samantha....4:59:01 (22,465)
Wemyss, Sarah 4:29:02 (16,428)
Wenborn, Kerry....4:16:29 (13,571)
Wenman, Debbie....3:46:59 (7,033)
Wentzel, Tiffany 4:14:45 (13,194)
Wenzel, Hazel....4:44:40 (19,707)
Werth, Mandy....5:20:30 (25,408)
Wesselink, Karen 5:09:25 (24,003)
Wessely, Susannah....4:04:01 (10,886)
West, Freddy 4:09:33 (12,083)
West, Jayne....5:37:11 (26,956)
West, Lara 5:53:27 (28,089)
West, Marion 3:41:21 (6,020)
West, Tracey....3:06:59 (1,504)
Westhorp, Carol 5:09:56 (24,073)
Weston, Denise 4:10:48 (12,341)
Weston, Judith....4:06:56 (11,535)
Weston, Kath 4:46:08 (19,967)
Weston, Lynne....3:46:59 (7,033)
Westwood, Sarah 3:54:26 (8,575)
Wetherell, Fiona....4:49:01 (20,530)
Wetherill, Nikki 4:19:27 (14,241)
Wetton, Susan....3:52:12 (8,117)
Whaley, Tiffiney....3:32:06 (4,481)
Whalley, Susie....4:26:57 (15,950)
Wharam, Hilary....4:08:52 (11,949)
Wharton, Emma....3:31:33 (4,402)
Wharton, Millicent....5:12:10 (24,372)
Wheadon, Gail 5:55:19 (28,170)
Wheatley, Andrée....4:06:54 (11,527)
Wheatley, Angela....4:39:38 (18,724)
Wheeldon, Joanne 6:30:20 (29,420)
Wheeler, Adelle 5:08:33 (23,855)
Wheeler, Judith 4:30:41 (16,783)
Wheeler, Rosalind 6:50:14 (29,809)
Wheeler, Sharon....5:30:24 (26,401)
Whelan, Julie 4:50:11 (20,751)
Whiley, Lesley 2:59:31 (981)
Whitbourn, Rachel....4:12:33 (12,746)
Whitby, Julie 4:43:03 (19,397)
White, Berry 5:26:14 (26,011)
White, Caroline 3:35:16 (4,946)
White, Christine 5:18:32 (25,216)
White, Clare....7:12:34 (30,039)
White, Corinne....5:17:56 (25,151)
White, Debbie 7:43:30 (30,176)
White, Elaine 5:48:31 (27,819)
White, Elspeth 5:19:46 (25,343)
White, Helen 5:23:32 (25,749)
White, Jean 5:07:43 (23,732)
White, Jeanette....3:53:44 (8,430)
White, Jenny 4:47:56 (20,333)
White, Jessica....4:20:14 (14,415)
White, Karen 4:26:28 (15,836)
White, Kate 4:36:26 (18,003)
White, Katie 4:47:56 (20,333)
White, Lisa....4:16:48 (13,635)
White, Margaret 4:52:45 (21,264)
White, Margaret 5:38:13 (27,031)
White, Pauline....3:37:11 (5,279)
White, Rachel 4:06:12 (11,385)
White, Rita....6:36:47 (29,559)
White, Rosemary 4:10:57 (12,389)
White, Ruth 4:03:08 (10,692)
White, Samantha....5:07:07 (23,632)
White, Sarah 4:42:47 (19,326)
White, Sonia 4:28:25 (16,289)
White, Suzanne 4:49:55 (20,703)
Whitehead, Gillian 6:38:53 (29,603)
Whitehead, Marjorie....7:09:17 (30,012)
Whitehead, Michelle....4:14:55 (13,239)
Whitehouse, Harriet 5:10:34 (24,159)
Whiteley, Gillian....7:00:10 (29,944)
Whiteley, Jill....3:51:30 (7,966)
Whiteley, Melanie....5:20:45 (25,438)
Whiteside, Elizabeth 4:44:22 (19,647)
Whitfield, Lesley....5:01:54 (22,854)
Whitfield, Sharon....6:07:27 (28,744)
Whitfield, Vivienne 5:55:25 (28,181)
Whitfield, Wendy....6:10:00 (28,860)
Whitham, Susan 6:03:17 (28,554)
Whitmaore, Lindsay....5:07:56 (23,764)
Whitmore, Helena 4:03:16 (10,713)
Whitney, Julie 5:25:42 (25,960)
Whitney, Linda 5:38:30 (27,051)
Whitson Turner, Jane....4:23:52 (15,266)
Whittaker, Maureen 5:21:54 (25,573)
Whittaker, Rachel....5:15:48 (24,906)
Whitters, Caralea....5:46:51 (27,689)
Whittington, Belinda 6:07:46 (28,752)
Whittington, Susan 5:57:21 (28,286)
Whittle, Claire 4:31:33 (16,988)
Whittle, Serena Ann....5:04:34 (23,228)
Whittley, Janette 3:50:57 (7,859)
Whitworth, Claire....6:09:47 (28,854)
Whybourn, Lynne 5:09:44 (24,049)
Whyte, Kathryn....4:50:17 (20,767)
Wickes, Anne....4:53:16 (21,366)
Wickham, Zoe 6:32:30 (29,463)
Wickson, Johanna 5:21:54 (25,573)
Wigemyr, Beate Boe....3:57:18 (9,258)
Wigham, Elizabeth....6:48:36 (29,789)
Wilcox, Janette 3:38:13 (5,433)
Wild, Clare....5:09:52 (24,065)
Wild, Marie....5:22:04 (25,597)
Wild, Rebecca....4:12:08 (12,653)
Wilden, Katherine....5:10:33 (24,154)
Wilensky, Denleigh....3:54:22 (8,555)
Wilkes, Cheryl 4:23:48 (15,250)
Wilkes, Cindy....4:06:11 (11,379)
Wilkes, Elizabeth 5:23:04 (25,712)
Wilkes, Jean 3:58:32 (9,616)
Wilkes, Susan....8:36:20 (30,253)
Wilkins, Christine....4:09:21 (12,051)
Wilkins, Denise....5:09:24 (23,999)
Wilkins, Wendy....3:43:32 (6,403)
Wilkinson, Catherine....4:29:08 (16,458)
Wilkinson, Dawn 5:16:35 (24,997)
Wilkinson, Dorothy....3:40:41 (5,894)
Wilkinson, Joy....3:32:22 (4,516)
Wilkinson, Kirsty 5:12:06 (24,364)
Wilkinson, Lorraine....4:15:59 (13,461)
Wilkinson, Mary 6:42:53 (29,705)
Wilkinson, Pat 6:38:29 (29,598)
Wilkinson, Sally....4:39:04 (18,617)
Willcock, Helen....4:24:49 (15,463)
Willey, Michelle 5:44:34 (27,532)
Willfratt, Louise....5:17:28 (25,103)
Williams, Alison....5:19:41 (25,332)
Williams, Anna 4:30:47 (16,804)
Williams, Barbara 5:04:49 (23,268)
Williams, Bethan 4:24:03 (15,305)
Williams, Carol....6:00:48 (28,446)
Williams, Carole....5:27:36 (26,138)
Williams, Catherine 3:47:32 (7,150)
Williams, Christina....4:00:48 (10,242)
Williams, Claire 4:45:22 (19,835)
Williams, Donna....4:40:02 (18,793)
Williams, Donna....5:43:57 (27,471)
Williams, Esther 4:58:32 (22,383)
Williams, Frances 3:46:24 (6,931)
Williams, Frances 5:19:05 (25,274)
Williams, Gen 3:31:51 (4,448)
Williams, Helen....5:50:00 (27,903)
Williams, Jacqueline....4:51:44 (21,038)
Williams, James 3:52:21 (8,142)
Williams, Joan....7:10:05 (30,017)
Williams, Julie....4:52:30 (21,206)
Williams, Juliet 4:11:29 (12,499)
Williams, Juliet 8:37:30 (30,259)
Williams, Katey....5:45:30 (27,591)
Williams, Kim 4:26:05 (15,752)
Williams, Lynnette 5:51:02 (27,956)
Williams, Margaret....4:00:51 (10,251)
Williams, Margaret....4:48:03 (20,359)
Williams, Nina....4:49:26 (20,605)
Williams, Nina 5:17:41 (25,123)
Williams, Olivia 4:56:45 (22,098)
Williams, Pamela....4:47:11 (20,198)
Williams, Pauline....5:54:06 (28,117)
Williams, Rachael....4:44:41 (19,712)
Williams, Rebecca 4:29:52 (16,648)
Williams, Rebecca 5:46:43 (27,681)
Williams, Rosalind....3:23:52 (3,225)
Williams, Rosemary....4:08:16 (11,816)
Williams, Sarah....6:04:22 (28,612)
Williams, Sarah....6:05:21 (28,657)
Williams, Simone 4:50:28 (20,798)
Williams, Susan 3:46:01 (6,861)
Williams, Susan 4:29:53 (16,654)
Williams, Teresa 4:01:00 (10,280)
Williams, Tracy....6:40:02 (29,635)
Williams, Valerie....5:12:34 (24,436)
Williams Wynne, Chloe....5:39:26 (27,130)
Williamson, Clare....5:04:12 (23,162)
Williamson, Lorraine....6:31:51 (29,448)
Williamson, Tanya....4:43:19 (19,457)
Willingson, Marisol 5:32:32 (26,583)
Willis, Charlotte 3:37:44 (5,369)
Willis, Elizabeth....7:52:25 (30,193)
Willis, Lisa....5:15:06 (24,797)
Willmott, Nikki....5:28:45 (26,260)
Wills, Pamela 6:56:54 (29,909)
Wills, Rosalind....4:36:59 (18,124)
Wills, Sabrina....5:46:41 (27,679)
Wills, Sandra....4:52:29 (21,200)
Wills, Terry....4:03:33 (10,789)
Willson, Caroline 4:20:26 (14,460)
Wilshaw, Lynda....6:33:32 (29,495)
Wilson, Alison....5:09:57 (24,076)
Wilson, Anita 4:50:33 (20,806)
Wilson, Anne....3:31:47 (4,435)
Wilson, Barbara....8:37:08 (30,258)
Wilson, Beverley....2:55:58 (679)
Wilson, Beverley....5:14:39 (24,735)
Wilson, Christel....5:25:23 (25,928)
Wilson, Clare 4:53:28 (21,411)
Wilson, Elaine 4:01:52 (10,455)
Wilson, Emily....5:14:58 (24,772)
Wilson, Freda 6:07:39 (28,749)
Wilson, Janice....4:24:33 (15,408)
Wilson, Joanne 4:22:41 (14,978)
Wilson, Judy....4:26:58 (15,955)
Wilson, Katherine 4:04:03 (10,894)
Wilson, Kathryn....6:19:32 (29,145)
Wilson, Lynne....5:16:54 (25,034)
Wilson, Mandy....4:41:27 (19,054)
Wilson, Michelle....4:56:28 (22,060)
Wilson, Miranda....5:10:21 (24,122)
Wilson, Pamela....5:25:25 (25,932)
Wilson, Rachel....4:03:03 (10,671)
Wilson, Rachele....5:53:10 (28,076)
Wilson, Sally 4:26:36 (15,871)
Wilson, Sara....7:27:27 (30,117)
Wilson, Susan 4:23:10 (15,101)
Wilson, Susan 5:42:24 (27,366)

Wilson, Vanessa.....6:15:20 (29,039)
Wilson, Veronica.....6:29:20 (29,395)
Wilson-Clarke, Georgia.....4:41:12 (19,013)
Wiltshire, Julie.....3:47:31 (7,143)
Wimble, Tanya.....5:41:51 (27,321)
Wimbleton, Tanya.....4:44:46 (19,728)
Winchester, Fiona.....4:54:24 (21,573)
Winchester, Sue.....5:09:46 (24,055)
Winder, Claire.....5:32:03 (26,538)
Winfield, Sian.....4:57:53 (22,279)
Wing, Julia.....5:31:16 (26,474)
Wingate, Katherine.....6:24:23 (29,271)
Wingrove, Jackie.....5:49:59 (27,901)
Winrow, Katherine.....4:43:07 (19,407)
Winslow, Marilyn.....4:35:31 (17,815)
Winstanley, Chantelle.....3:45:54 (6,838)
Winter, Dagmar.....4:51:18 (20,946)
Winter, Margaret.....4:24:30 (15,398)
Winter, Maureen.....5:02:48 (22,977)
Winterhalder, Fiona.....4:29:35 (16,570)
Winwood, Carly.....6:41:16 (29,668)
Wise, Helen.....5:54:22 (28,129)
Wise, Michelle.....5:20:46 (25,441)
Wise, Paula.....5:00:51 (22,715)
Wiseman, Katy.....5:36:59 (26,945)
Wiseman, Zoe.....4:57:08 (22,162)
Wiskin, Claire.....4:53:45 (21,463)
Wisner, Robin.....5:47:57 (27,772)
Wisniewski, Petrina.....5:43:26 (27,435)
Witham, Helen.....3:53:29 (8,370)
Withers, Patricia.....4:42:44 (19,318)
Wivell, Sandra.....4:44:06 (19,597)
Wobben, Natasha.....5:00:34 (22,672)
Wolf, Judith.....3:50:23 (7,754)
Wolfson, Anne.....5:59:19 (28,383)
Woltering, Stefanie.....3:47:19 (7,090)
Wood, Diana.....4:32:33 (17,219)
Wood, Julia.....3:46:08 (6,885)
Wood, Kerrie.....2:49:12 (399)
Wood, Marlene.....4:52:39 (21,243)
Wood, Michelle.....5:27:49 (26,160)
Wood, Penny.....6:19:25 (29,141)
Wood, Rachel.....4:15:34 (13,381)
Wood, Rebecca.....4:36:54 (18,104)
Wood, Susan.....7:06:35 (29,992)
Wood, Trudie.....3:56:05 (8,946)
Wood, Vanessa.....5:54:09 (28,122)
Woodbridge, Wendy.....5:17:44 (25,129)
Woodcock, Elizabeth.....4:38:45 (18,559)
Woodcock, Lynnette.....4:40:19 (18,841)
Woodcock, Pamela.....3:59:26 (9,896)
Woodhead, Tracie.....6:21:45 (29,211)
Woodley, Christine.....5:18:02 (25,171)
Woodley, Helen.....3:14:51 (2,200)
Woodley, Kathryn.....4:42:16 (19,218)
Woodman, Pauline.....5:07:42 (23,729)
Woods, Catherine.....4:46:34 (20,071)
Woods, Jacqueline.....4:04:07 (10,905)
Woodward, Amanda.....4:04:49 (11,070)
Woodward, Barbara.....4:55:08 (21,765)
Woodward, Julie.....3:33:11 (4,642)
Woolcott, Celia.....4:36:38 (18,048)
Woolcott, Sarah.....5:53:05 (28,069)
Wooler, Jo.....5:27:11 (26,100)
Woolgar, Nicola.....6:10:21 (28,871)
Wooller, Diane.....4:08:21 (11,837)
Woolley, Kimberley.....4:41:49 (19,126)
Woolston, Helen.....4:55:32 (21,904)
Woosey, Deborah.....5:13:36 (24,581)
Wooster, Stella.....3:56:39 (9,091)
Worsley, Elizabeth.....4:43:55 (19,575)
Worthington, Victoria.....5:16:15 (24,952)
Woulfe, Joanne.....3:57:24 (9,289)
Wray, Dawn.....5:12:57 (24,490)
Wray, Nicola.....6:39:55 (29,625)
Wren, Hannah.....6:39:55 (29,625)
Wren, Sally.....5:14:35 (24,720)
Wrenfer, Fionuala.....4:00:39 (10,193)
Wrenn, Nick.....3:40:48 (5,912)
Wrennall, Gail.....4:40:22 (18,850)
Wright, Dani.....5:25:49 (25,969)
Wright, Dawn.....5:15:22 (24,848)
Wright, Eileen.....5:16:21 (24,963)
Wright, Frances.....4:42:45 (19,320)
Wright, Gail.....4:31:40 (17,028)
Wright, Karen.....6:05:32 (28,669)
Wright, Nicola.....5:42:20 (27,360)
Wright, Petra.....4:17:34 (13,784)
Wright, Ruth.....4:52:54 (21,292)
Wright, Sandra.....5:08:36 (23,869)
Wright, Sarah.....5:28:10 (26,189)
Wright, Sharon.....4:39:34 (18,708)
Wright, Sharon.....5:34:00 (26,692)
Wright, Yvonne.....7:00:39 (29,950)
Wright-Norris, Marie.....4:18:23 (13,982)
Wu, Grace.....3:08:30 (1,631)
Wu, Liana.....4:43:56 (19,579)
Wyatt, Alison.....4:29:32 (16,553)
Wyatt, Bonnie.....5:19:53 (25,352)
Wyatt, Rachael.....4:52:05 (21,110)
Wyatt, Rachel.....4:35:21 (17,786)
Wykes, Lorraine.....6:20:37 (29,180)
Wyld, Christine.....6:23:29 (29,242)
Wylie, Hannah.....5:18:14 (25,183)
Wylie, Jackie.....4:42:20 (19,236)
Wyman, Louise.....5:40:07 (27,198)
Wynne-Williams, Sarah.....4:37:27 (18,238)
Yate, Tara.....4:40:11 (18,809)
Yates, Lois.....3:45:42 (6,796)
Yearley, Lesley.....4:25:02 (15,520)
Yeates, Julie.....3:18:01 (2,535)
Yelling, Jackie.....7:25:25 (30,107)
Yendley, Susan.....4:46:51 (20,132)
Yeomans, Debra.....4:22:10 (14,847)
York, Elaine.....4:05:15 (11,162)
Youd, Gail.....5:25:06 (25,895)
Youdle, Lorraine.....4:59:30 (22,527)
Young, Carole.....5:29:19 (26,322)
Young, Christine.....4:21:29 (14,689)
Young, Christine.....6:27:27 (29,340)
Young, Joanne.....4:06:13 (11,392)
Young, Katherine.....6:03:06 (28,546)
Young, Linda.....6:40:41 (29,656)
Young, Marie.....4:52:50 (21,274)
Young, Nathalie.....5:30:07 (26,381)
Young, Sarah.....4:10:13 (12,213)
Young, Yvonne.....5:26:31 (26,045)
Younge, Joan.....4:55:30 (21,893)
Younger, Janet.....4:25:55 (15,707)
Yu, Arlene.....5:33:52 (26,676)
Yuill, Margaret.....5:35:02 (26,808)
Yule, Helen.....3:04:32 (1,317)
Zago, Roberta.....7:43:23 (30,174)
Zakharova, Svetlana.....2:24:03 (36)
Zelinsky, Barbara.....4:20:26 (14,460)
Zenati, Sarah.....8:06:58 (30,219)
Zerilli, Emma.....4:44:33 (19,688)
Zeytin, Simone.....4:32:38 (17,235)
Zhang, Helen.....7:25:25 (30,107)
Ziegert, Josephine.....4:43:08 (19,413)
Zimmerman, Gina.....5:34:47 (26,779)
Zink, Carol.....5:23:12 (25,720)
Zino, Francesca.....4:00:30 (10,154)
Zissell, Catherine.....5:13:45 (24,600)
Zuiderwijk-Van Hal, Marion.....5:05:14 (23,327)

WHEELCHAIR ENTRANTS

Alcock, Dave.....3:36:12 (32)
Allen, Geoff.....2:25:52 (17)
Andrews, Steven.....3:04:58 (29)
Armstrong, Martin.....2:50:24 (23)
Binney, Keith.....4:20:28 (33)
Brennan, Deborah.....2:36:50 (21)
Cheek, Andrew.....2:09:55 (11)
Diatchenko, Nicholas.....2:37:09 (22)
Downing, Peter.....3:00:08 (27)
Ford, Darren.....2:51:09 (24)
Fox, Mark.....2:58:23 (26)
Grazier, Edward.....2:08:01 (8)

Grey-Thompson, Tanni.....2:13:55 (13)

Dame Tanni Grey-Thompson (born 26 July 1969 in Cardiff, Wales) was, until her retirement from competitive athletics, a London regular and holder of 11 gold Paralympic medals and 30 world records. She won six London Marathons (1992, 1994, 1996, 1998, 2001, 2002) and is probably the best known and most recognised disabled athlete to take part in the London. Dame Tanni, more than anyone, has raised the status of disability sport to the level where there is huge public enthusiasm and support. She now sits in the House of Lords. She is an established media celebrity, regularly appearing on television and radio. Tanni has a daughter, Carys, and she won her sixth London Marathon just nine weeks after giving birth. Tanni was a presentation member of the team that won the bid to host the 2012 Olympics and Paralympics in London.

Hanks, John.....2:09:52 (10)
Hunt, Paul.....2:13:56 (14)
Hussain, Iftakhar.....2:33:05 (19)
Krol, Bogdan.....2:06:47 (7)

Lemeunier, Denis.....1:42:37 (1)

Denis Lemeunier (born 12 February 1965) is a French wheelchair racer perhaps best known for defeating defending champion, Britain's Kevin Papworth, in the 2001 London Marathon wheelchair race – a feat quite remarkable since his racing wheelchair, that would normally take twelve months to break in was only a matter of weeks old. Lemeunier was formerly a racing cyclist for 12 years until that career was ended by an accident. Today, this veteran athlete is in charge of Paralympic athletics in Brittany. As well as being a stalwart of the London Marathon, Lemeunier earned bronze medals in the marathon and 10,000m at the 2003 Athens Paralympics and a bronze medal in the 4 × 400m relay in the 2008 Beijing Paralympics.

Madden, Chris.....1:53:23 (5)
Marten, Michael.....3:04:38 (28)
Marx, Hartwig.....2:56:31 (25)
Moryc, Rysard.....2:35:10 (20)
Papworth, Kevin.....1:44:54 (2)
Patel, Tushar.....1:50:56 (4)
Pierre, François.....2:10:19 (12)
Powell, Richie.....2:02:31 (6)
Rappe, Guy.....2:20:57 (15)
Rice, Mary.....3:14:37 (30)
Riggs, Stuart.....2:21:20 (16)
Suttie, Kenneth.....2:27:18 (18)
Telford, Mark.....2:08:08 (9)
Watson, Wally.....3:22:01 (31)
Weir, David.....1:50:55 (3)

Denis Lemeunier and Dame Tanni Grey-Thompson

The 2002 London Marathon

This was a year of superlatives as the 2002 London Marathon was one of the fastest ever, with world bests in both races.

Khalid Khannouchi, Moroccan-born but by now a US citizen, ran away from probably the finest men's marathon field ever assembled to beat his own world record in a time of 2:05:38, shaving his previous world best by 4 seconds. But for true marathon fans, and particularly the home crowd, the day belonged to Paula Radcliffe.

The race started in ideal conditions, cool but sunny, a day made for marathon running, and the world's finest soon took advantage. Radcliffe dominated from the start and wiped out every women's marathon record on the books (except Catherine Ndereba's world mark of 2:18:47 – which was set in a mixed race in Chicago and thus not recognised by London).

Paula was always at the front of a leading pack but she broke away at the nine-mile mark, going through mile 10 in 54:26. After that she increased the pace. As the long-legged Radcliffe devoured the miles, many observers shook their heads, believing that it was madness to run this fast in a debut marathon. But she was running strongly, and with the result no longer in doubt, she accelerated still further to knock off miles 24 and 25 in 5:09 and 5:06, to cross the line in 2:18:56.

The next four runners, though over three and a half minutes behind, all recorded personal best times. Zakharova took second place in 2:22:31, a Russian record, beating her countrywoman Petrova by two seconds. Tosa achieved her aim of beating 2:23:00 with her 2:22:46, and Chepkemei overcame sickness to edge inside her previous best by 4 seconds with 2:23:18.

A measure of Radcliffe's time is that it beat the English qualifying standard for the men's marathon in the 2002 Commonwealth Games.

The men's winner, Khalid Khannouchi, made his 26-mile debut at the Chicago Marathon in 1997, where he served notice of his amazing ability by winning in a time of 2:07:10. The following year, he successfully defended his Chicago title before prevailing again in 1999 in a world-record time of 2:05.42. He started running in Morocco, but did not have a global impact until he immigrated to the USA in 1993. Seven years later he was made a US citizen. Having been refused financial assistance by the Moroccan track federation, Khannouchi moved to Brooklyn, where he washed dishes to support his training.

Haile Gebrselassie, running his first marathon, had been seen in this 2002 race as Khannouchi's most serious rival. Haile didn't win, but his amazing debut of 2:06:35 must have delighted him. Meanwhile, Kenya's Paul Tergat beat Gebrselassie for second place, and ran to within 6 seconds of the old world record. Defending champion, Abdelkader El Mouaziz, slipped over after 20 miles but he recovered enough to reduce his best time to 2:06:50 and finish in fourth place.

Tanni Grey-Thompson put on another fine performance to take her sixth title in the women's wheelchair race. Despite giving birth just two months previously, the eight-time gold medallist took it easy by her standards and crossed the line in 2:22:51, well clear of her nearest rivals, fellow Britons Michelle Lewis and Paula Craig.

Briton Dave Weir clinched the men's wheelchair race in 1:39:44 after Frenchman Pierre Fairbank lost ground when he smashed into a traffic island. Tushar Patel came in second after a closely fought sprint finish with France's Denis Lemeunier. The first seven athletes all finished under two hours.

Some five days after the London Marathon had officially finished, Lloyd Scott, a forty-year-old former firefighter from Rainham, Essex lumbered across the finish line in his deep-sea diver's suit. As he crossed the finish line after 5 days, 8 hours, 29 minutes and 46 seconds, he was welcomed by Paula Radcliffe. His run, wearing a rubberised canvas 1940s suit, copper helmet and lead-lined boots, had been every bit as tough as he had expected. 'My boots weigh a ton and I am very top-heavy,' he said.

Explanation of placing system

Each London Marathon year in this register is divided up into four categories: first, a summary of the **Elite Athletes**, containing names (last, first) and times (hours : minutes : seconds) of the top 50 male runners, top 50 female runners, top 3 male and top 2 female wheelchair entrants; then **Male Runners, Female Runners** and **Wheelchair Entrants**. These last three sections display the individual names and times of *every* entrant, including elite athletes, alphabetically and with their overall finishing position in that year's Marathon displayed in brackets alongside.

Some entrants have chosen to enhance past London Marathon entries with photos and recollections online at **www.aubreybooks.com**. Please visit the website to find out more about appearing in future editions.

ELITE ATHLETES

Top 50 male runners

Khannouchi, Khalid	2:05:38
Tergat, Paul	2:05:48
Gebrselassie, Haile	2:06:35
El Mouaziz, Abdelkader	2:06:50
Syster, Ian	2:07:04
Baldini, Stefano	2:07:28
Pinto, Antonio	2:09:09
Steinle, Mark	2:09:16
Jifar, Tesfaye	2:09:49
El Hattab, Mohammed	2:11:49
Buchleitner, Michael	2:14:10
Ghanmouni, Rachid	2:15:27
Kiplagat, William	2:15:58
Burns, Billy	2:17:34
Robinson, Dan	2:17:50
Kimtai, Julius	2:18:13
Wetheridge, Nicholas	2:19:40
Hoiom, Runar	2:20:34
Harris, Damon	2:20:42
Cariss, Christopher	2:20:45
Hilton, Martin	2:20:53
Norman, David	2:21:00
Croasdale, Mark	2:21:09
Lobb, Huw	2:21:15
Bilton, Darran	2:21:23
Fisher, Ian	2:22:07
Francis, Nick	2:22:26
Jones, Rodri	2:22:54
Plant, Ray	2:23:14
Gardiner, Richard	2:23:18
Dickenson, Tim	2:23:35
Taniguchi, Koji	2:23:44
Williams, Gareth	2:24:38
Ogata, Tsuyoshi	2:25:02
Malone, Ian	2:25:09
Badel, Denis	2:25:13

Loader, Joe	2:25:20
Poli, Graziano	2:26:07
Speake, Williams	2:26:47
Janvier, Nicolas	2:27:08
Robertson, David	2:27:10
Jubb, Mike	2:28:08
Shepley, Sebastian	2:28:30
Bentley, Robin	2:28:47
Cavers, Dave	2:28:51
Kubota, Tetsuya	2:28:56
Brown, Derek	2:28:59
Smith, Michael	2:29:02
Alvarado-Camara, Fernando	2:29:11
Hockin, Peter	2:29:14

Top 50 female runners

Radcliffe, Paula	2:18:56
Zakharova, Svetlana	2:22:31
Petrova, Lyudmila	2:22:32
Tosa, Reiko	2:22:46
Chepkemei, Susan	2:23:18
Chepchumba, Joyce	2:26:52
Skvortsova, Silvia	2:27:06
Semenova, Zinaida	2:27:43
Tulu, Derartu	2:28:35
Gemechu, Shitaye	2:28:56
Safarova, Irina	2:29:18
Lodge, Jo	2:38:24
Willix, Helene	2:40:23
Jenkins, Bev	2:44:30
Fletcher, Alison	2:44:41
Dixon, Sharon	2:45:03
Pickvance, Ruth	2:45:33
Wolfrom, Annette	2:46:56
Pauzers, Clare	2:49:24
Cawthorne, Helen	2:49:36
Mycroft, Elizabeth	2:49:36

Hotta, Makiko	2:49:56
Bretherick, Samantha	2:50:33
Benjaminsson, Camilla	2:50:37
Campbell, Sarah	2:51:24
Clark, Juliette	2:52:11
Lee, Michelle	2:53:03
Massey, Jacqueline	2:53:04
McCutcheon, Anna	2:54:31
Messerli-Gerhards, Daniela	2:55:20
Dering, Jo	2:55:33
Allen, Angela	2:55:36
Whiley, Lesley	2:55:58
Brown, Judy	2:56:06
Dolan, Susan	2:56:33
Mellodew, Anita	2:56:43
Alexander, Rosalyn	2:56:56
Vuagniaux, Alison	2:58:24
Spencer-Cusick, Susan	2:58:32
Affleck, Patricia	2:58:38
Iturbe, Veronica	2:58:52
Power, Anne	2:58:54
Bringlow, Véronique	2:59:37
Wilson, Beverley	2:59:42
Edwards, Beverley	2:59:46
Perry, Victoria	3:00:20
Godding-Feltham, Lisa	3:00:21
O'Connor, Gill	3:00:24
Carson, Suzanne	3:01:16
Carney, Treena	3:01:19

Top 3 male and top 2 female wheelchair entrants

Weir, David	1:39:44
Patel, Tushar	1:41:17
Lemeunier, Denis	1:41:17
Grey-Thompson, Tanni	2:22:51
Lewis, Michelle	2:37:07

MALE RUNNERS

Abate, Paolo 3:02:17 (1,324)
Abbadini, Alfredo 5:18:38 (28,735)
Abbas, Omran 4:26:11 (18,569)
Abbate, Giovanni 3:40:51 (6,929)
Abbey, Nick 4:10:27 (14,497)
Abbey, Simon 4:53:34 (25,081)
Abbitt, Philip 5:01:13 (26,487)
Abbott, Ben 4:02:28 (12,648)
Abbott, Colin 7:02:54 (32,659)
Abbott, David 4:33:03 (20,368)
Abbott, Ian 3:36:34 (6,034)
Abbott, Jason 4:16:36 (16,010)
Abbott, John 4:39:54 (22,080)
Abbott, John 4:43:25 (22,938)
Abbott, Jonathan 4:32:24 (20,188)
Abbott, Lee 5:29:55 (29,772)
Abbott, Michael 4:20:24 (16,964)
Abbott, Patrick 3:23:13 (3,680)
Abbott, Peter 3:48:02 (8,634)
Abbott, Peter 4:35:30 (20,946)
Abbott, Stephen 4:58:58 (26,127)
Abbott, Steven 3:55:40 (10,798)
Abbott, Trevor 4:34:36 (20,726)
Abbotts, Dennis 4:16:15 (15,899)
Abdulraheem, Adeyemi 5:12:16 (27,989)
Abecasis, Tiago 3:27:27 (4,408)
Abed, Emile 5:21:44 (29,074)
Abel, James 2:47:11 (366)
Abel, Jeremy 3:58:16 (11,584)
Abela, Alfred 5:46:10 (30,942)
Abeledo, Martin 3:10:45 (2,127)
Ab-Elwyn, Rhys 2:47:39 (388)
Abraham, Brian 4:57:30 (25,856)
Abraham, Philip 3:19:01 (3,135)
Abrahams, Brynly 4:54:33 (25,292)
Abrahams, Gary 4:12:54 (15,062)
Abrahams, Ian 3:37:39 (6,253)
Abrahams, Paul 5:41:01 (30,619)
Abrahamsson, Lennart 3:31:18 (5,077)
Abram, Andy 3:23:31 (3,729)
Abram, Anthony 5:14:30 (28,248)
Abram, Barry 2:57:55 (999)
Abram, Ron 4:10:53 (14,601)
Abrami, Paul 3:58:25 (11,625)
Abrams, Ian 5:08:38 (27,512)
Abrey, Giles 3:58:59 (11,796)
Abruzzo, Craig 3:47:47 (8,584)
Abruzzo, Vito 3:10:06 (2,050)
Absolon, Christopher 4:19:01 (16,597)
Acconcia, Claudio 2:50:20 (503)
Acheson, Timothy 3:35:18 (5,764)
Achilleos, Stelios 6:30:18 (32,286)
Achondo, Javier 2:56:24 (865)
Acid, Rab 3:47:00 (8,381)
Acker, Edward 3:46:56 (8,368)
Ackerman, Keith 3:53:46 (10,228)
Ackerman Martin, Jonathan 3:03:01 (1,370)
Ackland, Peter 3:59:19 (11,887)
Acland, Harry 3:56:12 (10,964)
Adair, John 3:21:24 (3,420)
Adam, Derek 3:49:17 (8,965)
Adam, Douglas 4:53:55 (25,160)
Adam, Gabriel 3:27:43 (4,459)
Adams, Alastair 3:40:02 (6,739)
Adams, Andrew 3:21:47 (3,481)
Adams, Christopher 3:29:03 (4,703)
Adams, Christopher 3:34:21 (5,594)
Adams, David 3:29:02 (4,698)
Adams, Dean 3:54:44 (10,529)
Adams, Dennis 4:09:03 (14,146)
Adams, Douglas 4:01:21 (12,407)
Adams, Gary 2:59:24 (1,121)
Adams, Giles 3:50:12 (9,215)
Adams, Graeme 4:02:18 (12,616)
Adams, Greig 5:35:05 (30,190)
Adams, Hugo 3:48:51 (8,853)
Adams, Ian 3:15:50 (2,772)
Adams, James 3:31:36 (5,124)
Adams, James 3:39:17 (6,586)
Adams, Jason 4:35:27 (20,935)
Adams, Jay 3:23:46 (3,767)
Adams, John 3:31:01 (5,031)
Adams, John 4:03:09 (12,804)
Adams, Leonard 5:03:22 (26,807)
Adams, Mark 3:22:11 (3,548)
Adams, Mark 4:58:49 (26,100)
Adams, Mark 5:35:12 (30,200)
Adams, Martin 4:01:11 (12,361)
Adams, Martin 5:10:21 (27,731)
Adams, Neil 3:16:12 (2,807)
Adams, Nicholas 3:14:04 (2,562)
Adams, Paul 4:49:30 (24,323)
Adams, Paul 5:12:32 (28,027)
Adams, Peter 4:33:43 (20,519)
Adams, Robert 3:19:55 (3,247)
Adams, Robert 3:42:59 (7,385)
Adams, Robin 5:11:45 (27,915)
Adams, Russell 5:19:17 (28,805)
Adams, Stephen 5:27:33 (29,580)
Adams, Steve 3:03:15 (1,396)
Adams, Steven 4:17:19 (16,209)
Adams, Tony 5:07:31 (27,379)
Adams, William 3:40:03 (6,744)
Adamson, Daniel 3:04:54 (1,535)
Adamson, David 3:46:57 (8,373)
Adamson, David 6:07:37 (31,776)
Adamson, Harry 4:13:37 (15,209)
Adamson, Mark 4:30:00 (19,592)
Adamson, Philip 4:38:38 (21,749)
Adamson, Shane 3:46:06 (8,182)
Adcock, Gary 5:27:21 (29,563)
Adcock, Harry 3:55:46 (10,832)
Adcock, Matthew 2:33:31 (84)
Addaway, David 6:02:13 (31,619)
Adderley, Philip 4:05:46 (13,386)
Addis, Peter 4:29:54 (19,575)
Addison, Guy 4:35:42 (21,014)
Addison, Michael 4:51:27 (24,692)
Addison, Neil 4:05:48 (13,393)
Ade Onojobi, Peter 4:24:21 (18,080)
Adelizzi, Stephano 4:35:00 (20,833)
Adewale, Oyeniyi 4:35:31 (20,951)
Adkins, David 3:01:22 (1,253)
Adkins, Peter 3:04:09 (1,481)
Adlard, Simon 3:14:55 (2,662)
Adolphus, Anthony 3:59:49 (12,028)
Adu, Stephen 5:32:09 (29,965)
Ady, Steven 4:19:15 (16,653)
Aeberhard, Rolf 4:29:50 (19,551)
Affleck, Michael 3:25:16 (4,026)
Afforselles, Ben 3:54:54 (10,570)
Afonso, Joao 3:56:07 (10,937)
Agbo, Celestine 3:49:17 (8,965)
Agent, Mark 5:36:05 (30,282)
Agius, Alexander 4:46:18 (23,638)
Agon, Philippe 3:54:33 (10,472)
Agostini, Marco 3:38:27 (6,414)
Aguda, Adeyemi 3:59:33 (11,951)
Aguilar, Gerardo 3:58:54 (11,764)
Agustsson, Kristjan 3:56:13 (10,972)
Ahearne, Brian 4:00:41 (12,220)
Ahearne, Robert 3:21:28 (3,430)
Ahmad, Rafat 3:53:26 (10,116)
Ahmed, Farid 5:35:59 (30,269)
Ahmed, Ishtuiaq 2:52:51 (622)
Ahmed, Ismael 4:19:43 (16,781)
Ahmed, Min 6:39:47 (32,437)
Ahmed, Raza 5:14:05 (28,203)
Ahmed, Syed 5:53:11 (31,285)
Ahmed-Ali, Khaled 4:32:02 (20,096)
Ahmet, Ahmet 4:07:24 (13,777)
Ahnlund, Mats 5:15:11 (28,322)
Ahnlund, Pelle 6:35:35 (32,369)
Ahsunollah, Paul 4:18:18 (16,439)
Aichele, Hermann 6:25:27 (32,191)
Aidroos, Fred 3:39:50 (6,693)
Aimable, Michael 5:37:24 (30,375)
Aimar, Alain 3:28:50 (4,667)
Aindow, Colin 3:50:08 (9,196)
Ainley, Robert 5:23:48 (29,261)
Ainscough, Ian 3:34:15 (5,571)
Ainsworth, David 5:07:29 (27,372)
Ainsworth, John 6:30:12 (32,285)
Ainsworth, Mark 4:05:23 (13,293)
Ainsworth, Rod 3:14:21 (2,596)
Ainz, Robert 3:05:29 (1,589)
Airey, Michael 4:48:01 (24,037)
Airey, Peter 4:36:12 (21,130)
Airlie, Brian 4:06:21 (13,529)
Aisthorpe, Bruce 4:23:10 (17,742)
Ait-Braham, Aziz 3:16:27 (2,837)
Aitken, Brian 3:45:57 (8,148)
Aitken, Edward 4:21:09 (17,156)
Aitken, Lawrence 3:17:18 (2,933)
Aitken, Peter 4:11:56 (14,841)
Aitken, Peter 5:03:46 (26,852)
Aiyyasamy, Kunaseelan 3:24:21 (3,893)
Aizlewood, Stephen 6:17:21 (32,013)
Aked, Peter 2:46:38 (346)
Akenhead, David 5:50:20 (31,155)
Al Halabi, Aboudi 4:59:26 (26,206)
Al Kahlout, Bassim 3:47:57 (8,617)
Alagna, Alessandro 4:10:49 (14,586)
Alaka, Aderemi 4:55:06 (25,391)
Alanen, Tauno 4:11:02 (14,639)
Alasa-Roure, Enric 4:03:59 (12,985)
Alback, James 3:16:25 (2,833)
Albers, Hartmut 4:22:47 (17,631)
Alberti, Silvio 4:58:36 (26,055)
Albes, Jean 3:12:48 (2,404)
Albrighton, Matthew 4:20:14 (16,922)
Albrow, Paul 4:35:23 (20,921)
Alby, Jean 4:40:10 (22,150)
Alcantara, Julian 5:52:33 (31,257)
Alcober, Miguel 3:15:10 (2,684)
Alcock, Meirion 4:41:29 (22,472)
Aldenhoven, Toby 4:41:30 (22,476)
Alder, Jonathan 6:18:43 (32,057)
Aldernan, David 4:15:03 (15,585)
Alderson, Richard 3:41:20 (7,036)
Alderson, Steven 4:05:39 (13,358)
Alderton, Colin 5:13:01 (28,083)
Aldous, Colin 2:58:41 (1,068)
Aldred, Colin 6:10:41 (31,850)
Aldred, Danny 4:22:55 (17,677)
Aldridge, Agnes 5:07:52 (27,419)
Aldridge, Andrew 4:47:00 (23,811)
Aldridge, Graham 4:41:18 (22,425)
Aldridge, Ian 3:32:53 (5,335)
Aldridge, Nigel 3:29:59 (4,870)
Aldridge, Richard 4:57:30 (25,856)
Aldridge, Stephen 4:31:26 (19,940)
Alen, Timothy 5:07:21 (27,349)
Alessandra, Jean 2:43:34 (256)
Alexander, Anthony 3:44:48 (7,889)
Alexander, Barry 4:02:27 (12,642)
Alexander, Eddie 4:02:53 (12,751)
Alexander, Leith 5:22:53 (29,165)
Alexander, Mark 3:03:35 (1,428)
Alexander, Miles 4:36:08 (21,115)
Alexander, Nicholas 4:38:37 (21,748)
Alexander, Rikki 4:25:31 (18,393)
Alexander, Scott 3:36:22 (5,996)
Alexander, Wayne 3:46:09 (8,192)
Alexandrou, John 6:06:19 (31,739)
Alfar, Paulo 3:39:05 (6,544)
Alford, Bryce 3:12:27 (2,353)
Alford, Mark 4:26:41 (18,714)
Alford, Neil 4:01:32 (12,452)
Alfthan, Kristoffer 4:53:07 (25,000)
Ali, Nazim 4:50:52 (24,586)
Ali, Nazim 5:18:59 (28,776)
Ali, Syed 4:24:56 (18,234)
Aliane, Haussine 3:26:08 (4,171)
Alkhlaifaoui, Mahmoud 3:47:09 (8,423)
Allan, Charles 3:46:14 (8,209)
Allan, David 4:52:23 (24,858)
Allan, Jason 4:49:59 (24,419)
Allan, John 3:49:28 (9,033)
Allan, Peter 3:33:49 (5,482)
Allan, Ranald 4:52:21 (24,851)
Allard Austin, Jason 3:13:36 (2,516)
Allard, Charles Jnr 3:04:51 (1,528)
Allardice, Stephen 4:59:55 (26,294)
Allarie, Randy 4:30:14 (19,658)
Allart, Bernard 3:30:37 (4,966)
Allaway, Jeffrey 3:56:01 (10,902)
Allbrook, William 4:03:31 (12,885)

Allcard, Neil 3:59:16 (11,873)
Allcock, Michael 5:17:05 (28,575)
Allely, Simon 4:09:05 (14,151)
Allemby, Dave 3:21:32 (3,446)
Allen, Andrew 2:47:09 (365)
Allen, Andrew 3:37:09 (6,140)
Allen, Andrew 3:48:15 (8,685)
Allen, Andrew 3:59:33 (11,951)
Allen, Andrew 4:29:52 (19,560)
Allen, Antony 3:05:27 (1,584)
Allen, Cedric 3:04:00 (1,467)
Allen, Charlie 4:15:37 (15,728)
Allen, Chris 3:40:54 (6,940)
Allen, Chris 3:42:21 (7,248)
Allen, Christopher 4:33:46 (20,528)
Allen, Christopher 7:02:43 (32,656)
Allen, Crispin 3:22:11 (3,548)
Allen, David 2:51:46 (570)
Allen, David 3:18:36 (3,083)
Allen, David 3:42:15 (7,220)
Allen, David 4:18:44 (16,530)
Allen, David 4:29:46 (19,527)
Allen, Douglas 2:58:29 (1,046)
Allen, Douglas 3:33:26 (5,422)
Allen, Gavin 3:46:08 (8,189)
Allen, Greg 4:20:51 (17,075)
Allen, Greg 5:07:38 (27,390)
Allen, Hugh 3:40:38 (6,878)
Allen, Iain 4:24:05 (18,005)
Allen, Jame 5:13:18 (28,114)
Allen, James 3:09:57 (2,036)
Allen, Jeffrey 4:00:57 (12,295)
Allen, Jez 3:52:50 (9,933)
Allen, Joe 4:13:47 (15,258)
Allen, John 3:19:59 (3,253)
Allen, John 3:49:47 (9,125)
Allen, John 4:11:17 (14,690)
Allen, John 4:28:24 (19,139)
Allen, John 4:39:31 (21,973)
Allen, Jon 5:41:29 (30,653)
Allen, Kevin 3:31:35 (5,121)
Allen, Kevin 3:45:20 (8,006)
Allen, Kevin 4:15:11 (15,614)
Allen, Lee 5:50:53 (31,179)
Allen, Leigh 4:42:46 (22,784)
Allen, Malcolm 3:38:34 (6,443)
Allen, Mark 3:39:09 (6,557)
Allen, Mark 3:55:37 (10,789)
Allen, Martin 4:11:51 (14,825)
Allen, Matthew 5:14:34 (28,255)
Allen, Michael 3:40:53 (6,937)
Allen, Michael 4:24:05 (18,005)
Allen, Michael 5:50:51 (31,177)
Allen, Neil 4:57:03 (25,779)
Allen, Nick 4:23:17 (17,772)
Allen, Paul 4:25:47 (18,459)
Allen, Peter 3:30:18 (4,915)
Allen, Richard 4:23:26 (17,811)
Allen, Richard 4:56:11 (25,628)
Allen, Richard 5:30:49 (29,849)
Allen, Rob 3:24:09 (3,848)
Allen, Robert 4:52:45 (24,926)
Allen, Rodger 4:29:13 (19,384)
Allen, Rodger 4:54:33 (25,292)
Allen, Rodney 3:37:56 (6,300)
Allen, Sean 3:32:05 (5,204)
Allen, Simon 3:42:16 (7,226)
Allen, Simon 3:53:15 (10,061)
Allen, Spencer 4:32:51 (20,320)
Allen, Steve 3:12:27 (2,353)
Allen, Tom 4:26:53 (18,757)
Allerton, Stephen 3:51:26 (9,528)
Alleyne, Victor 4:40:14 (22,168)
Allford, Simon 4:02:34 (12,669)
Allibone, Mark 4:16:58 (16,108)
Alliott, Christopher 3:40:35 (6,872)
Allison, Anthony 5:00:49 (26,430)
Allison, Christopher 4:07:22 (13,767)
Allison, Christopher 5:14:04 (28,202)
Allison, Clive 3:02:39 (1,344)
Allison, Colin 5:00:37 (26,390)
Allison, Jesse 6:43:07 (32,459)
Allison, Mark 3:58:41 (11,701)
Allison, Robert 3:53:39 (10,197)
Allison, Sam 4:32:26 (20,200)
Alliston, John 4:58:45 (26,091)
Allitt, Justin 4:45:41 (23,488)
Allman, Andrew 5:13:05 (28,090)
Allman, Brent 4:11:14 (14,680)
Allman, Philip 4:10:56 (14,621)
Allouah, Abdelatif 3:14:59 (2,666)
Allport, Trevor 3:56:11 (10,957)
Allsop, David 2:53:25 (652)
Allsop, Timothy 2:57:06 (923)
Allsopp, Mark 4:53:02 (24,983)
Allton, Kevin 5:09:35 (27,644)
Allum, William 5:09:48 (27,671)
Almaghrbi, Yaser 7:35:48 (32,808)
Almeida, Antonio 4:04:07 (13,012)
Almond, Steve 2:54:46 (726)
Aloof, Brian 5:51:10 (31,194)
Alsop, Paul 4:23:29 (17,821)
Alsop, Robert 5:26:32 (29,495)
Alston, David 3:44:45 (7,874)
Altbach, Nick 4:44:15 (23,115)
Alteriet, Eric 3:44:06 (7,681)
Altlay, Frank 3:14:34 (2,615)
Alvarado-Camara, Fernando 2:29:11 (59)
Alvarez Meijide, José 3:43:07 (7,418)
Always, Lorne 5:29:15 (29,718)
Amann, Oliver 3:00:34 (1,204)
Ambler, David 3:24:21 (3,893)
Ambrose, David 3:22:30 (3,581)
Ambrose, Jason 3:36:46 (6,069)
Ames, Ashley 4:26:06 (18,549)
Ames, David 3:42:17 (7,231)
Ames, Robert 4:35:23 (20,921)
Amin, Viral 4:58:10 (25,979)
Ammann, Urs 3:39:14 (6,579)
Amoroso, Giuseppe 4:18:19 (16,444)
Amoroso, Guy 4:40:19 (22,187)
Amoroso, Peter 5:12:01 (27,955)
Amos, Anthony 4:39:19 (21,925)
Amos, James 4:45:20 (23,389)
Amos, Jonathan 4:47:40 (23,945)
Amos, Peter 3:43:10 (7,434)
Amris, Patrick 3:46:48 (8,343)
Amsden, Christopher 5:20:04 (28,888)
Amsden, Stephen 5:24:51 (29,349)
Amtenbrink, Fabian 3:32:58 (5,348)
Anahory, David 4:07:00 (13,678)
Anani, Vincent 3:50:41 (9,343)
Anastasi, Anastasis 5:13:36 (28,153)
Anatolitis, Costas 5:12:12 (27,972)
Ancelin, Michel 4:48:42 (24,168)
Andall, Stephen 5:18:19 (28,704)
Anders, Daniel 3:34:27 (5,610)
Andersen, Conrad 4:48:47 (24,190)
Andersen, Mikael 2:41:51 (225)
Andersen, Morten 4:45:15 (23,371)
Andersen, Stig 4:47:45 (23,961)
Anderson, Adrian 3:19:32 (3,206)
Anderson, Alan 4:22:49 (17,648)
Anderson, Anthony 2:38:23 (153)
Anderson, Brian 4:15:13 (15,629)
Anderson, Bruce 5:14:17 (28,228)
Anderson, Christopher 3:37:19 (6,167)
Anderson, Dean 4:26:17 (18,597)
Anderson, Evan 5:02:34 (26,681)
Anderson, Gordon 5:05:38 (27,101)
Anderson, Ian 2:40:44 (198)
Anderson, Ian 4:19:26 (16,700)
Anderson, Ian 4:22:23 (17,512)
Anderson, Ian 4:45:06 (23,333)
Anderson, Ian 4:49:56 (24,412)
Anderson, Jeremy 4:49:38 (24,347)
Anderson, Joe 6:09:46 (31,831)
Anderson, John 4:55:53 (25,554)
Anderson, John 4:57:36 (25,879)
Anderson, Keith 3:29:09 (4,720)
Anderson, Murray 3:20:05 (3,263)
Anderson, Myles 4:37:56 (21,558)
Anderson, Neale 3:08:03 (1,810)
Anderson, Richard 4:08:31 (14,027)
Anderson, Richard 4:20:08 (16,896)
Anderson, Robert 4:33:02 (20,360)
Anderson, Roger 6:17:05 (32,005)
Anderson, Ross 4:40:26 (22,221)
Anderson, Sean 3:05:19 (1,569)
Anderson, Stephen 3:59:46 (12,013)
Anderson, Stephen 4:29:30 (19,458)
Andersson, Roland 4:24:18 (18,067)
Andrade, Peter 4:14:37 (15,473)
Andreis, Alex 4:21:23 (17,218)
Andreu-Suarez, Manuel 4:04:21 (13,057)
Andrew, Ian 3:33:26 (5,422)
Andrew, Jamie 5:56:46 (31,435)
Andrew, Mark 4:18:55 (16,571)
Andrew, Stuart 3:58:19 (11,593)
Andrewartha, David 2:55:48 (809)
Andrews, Allan 4:49:59 (24,419)
Andrews, Barry 3:36:44 (6,061)
Andrews, Daniel 4:11:35 (14,763)
Andrews, David 5:43:56 (30,813)
Andrews, Gary 3:53:19 (10,086)
Andrews, Gary 4:10:19 (14,464)
Andrews, Gordon 4:30:48 (19,785)
Andrews, John 4:49:43 (24,364)
Andrews, Kevin 5:20:43 (28,963)
Andrews, Mark 3:11:44 (2,234)
Andrews, Mark 4:18:54 (16,569)
Andrews, Michael 4:20:24 (16,964)
Andrews, Neil 3:20:44 (3,338)
Andrews, Nick 3:56:30 (11,053)
Andrews, Nigel 4:59:40 (26,259)
Andrews, Paul 3:16:05 (2,796)
Andrews, Paul 4:28:08 (19,065)
Andrews, Robert 3:29:18 (4,752)
Andrews, Timothy 4:47:05 (23,830)
Aneca, Raphael 4:37:56 (21,558)
Angebrand, Josef 3:09:10 (1,948)
Angel, Martin 4:49:28 (24,316)
Angelini, Michele 3:36:31 (6,028)
Angell, Dean 4:47:38 (23,935)
Angell, Keith 5:50:50 (31,176)
Angell, Philip 3:54:40 (10,506)
Angell, Stephen 4:22:01 (17,401)
Anghileri, Alessandro 5:39:56 (30,544)
Anghileri, Giuseppe 3:23:55 (3,803)
Angove, Barry 4:30:01 (19,597)
Angus, Darryl 4:39:07 (21,877)
Angus, Martin 5:15:47 (28,409)
Anichkin, Alexander 4:09:28 (14,264)
Anicliffe, Mark 3:39:38 (6,654)
Anjum, Ashraf 6:28:04 (32,240)
Ankcorn, Peter 3:59:38 (11,977)
Ankers, Daniel 4:24:41 (18,167)
Anley, Brian 4:55:10 (25,416)
Anley, Marc 3:58:21 (11,601)
Annetts, David 5:03:19 (26,800)
Annic, Stephane 3:21:58 (3,516)
Annis, Mark 3:46:43 (8,332)
Anrude, Edward 4:21:41 (17,309)
Anscombe, Vaughan 5:33:09 (30,041)
Ansell, Martin 4:06:24 (13,546)
Ansell, Paul 4:21:06 (17,140)
Ansell, Richard 2:48:14 (417)
Ansorge, Hans 3:28:19 (4,571)
Anstee, Nicholas 3:45:16 (7,992)
Anstey, Mark 3:08:27 (1,860)
Antcliff, Andrew 3:42:19 (7,236)
Antcliff, Paul 4:00:29 (12,184)
Anthony, Ian 3:29:56 (4,862)
Anthony, James 3:54:38 (10,494)
Antonelli, Gianfelice 3:07:00 (1,735)
Antrobus, John 4:42:41 (22,763)
Aplas, Nicholas 4:26:04 (18,539)
Appavoo, Soondra 4:31:25 (19,935)
Appleby, Glenn 5:07:23 (27,354)
Appleby, Nigel 6:32:08 (32,309)
Appleby, Paul 3:12:59 (2,429)
Appleby, Paul 3:37:50 (6,285)
Appleby, Paul 4:31:56 (20,066)
Applegarth, Piers 5:27:42 (29,596)
Applegate, Christopher 2:50:00 (492)
Appleton, Andrew 3:48:49 (8,845)
Appleton, Craig 4:02:49 (12,733)
Appleton, Jamie 4:36:16 (21,142)
Appleton, Paul 4:47:56 (24,018)

Applewhaite, Paul	5:12:16 (27,989)
Apps, Tim	4:23:08 (17,734)
Aquilina, Jonathan	5:19:24 (28,810)
Aquina, Ed	4:41:43 (22,536)
Arbuckle, Simon	4:43:03 (22,849)
Arch, Martin	4:26:52 (18,753)
Archer, Andrew	3:33:36 (5,442)
Archer, Anthony	3:22:18 (3,563)
Archer, Jeff	4:08:38 (14,065)
Archer, Marcus	3:35:21 (5,769)
Archer, Michael	3:58:36 (11,678)
Archer, Paul	3:21:34 (3,450)
Archer, Paul	3:52:37 (9,873)
Archer, Raymond	5:17:06 (28,577)
Archer, Vincent	3:06:19 (1,665)
Archer-Cox, Sebastian	4:14:01 (15,316)
Ardern, David	2:37:28 (134)
Ardern, John	5:08:53 (27,551)
Ardron, Philip	3:51:00 (9,425)
Aregger, Arthur	2:32:39 (78)
Arens, Kristian	3:34:24 (5,598)
Ares-Cernadas, Jesus	3:43:15 (7,459)
Argent, Dean	3:56:43 (11,113)
Argue, Ron	6:03:11 (31,645)
Argyle, Gerald	4:48:55 (24,218)
Ariza, Leonardo	5:16:18 (28,482)
Ark, Bahadar	3:58:05 (11,536)
Arkwright, David	3:49:30 (9,041)
Arkwright, Paul	4:09:07 (14,158)
Arli, Tayfun	4:43:33 (22,971)
Armistead, Brent	4:41:11 (22,398)
Armit, Tim	4:35:25 (20,927)
Armriding, Tony	6:08:19 (31,792)
Armstrong, Don	7:27:00 (32,778)
Armstrong, Frank	4:46:12 (23,623)
Armstrong, James	4:56:12 (25,636)
Armstrong, John	5:26:05 (29,453)
Armstrong, Mark	2:38:47 (162)
Armstrong, Matthew	4:19:24 (16,688)
Armstrong, Peter	3:20:41 (3,335)
Armstrong, Russell	3:52:14 (9,762)
Armytage, Marcus	4:11:10 (14,668)
Arnalds, Ari	4:32:08 (20,122)
Arndt, Andreas	3:37:21 (6,176)
Arndt, Nestor	4:05:56 (13,420)
Arneil, Andrew	4:46:21 (23,652)
Arnel, Christopher	4:45:19 (23,384)
Arnel, Philip	4:11:49 (14,822)
Arnell, Robert	4:21:23 (17,218)
Arnell, Stephen	3:54:57 (10,580)
Arney, Stuart	5:20:10 (28,898)
Arnold, Andrew	4:24:11 (18,029)
Arnold, Christopher	4:35:07 (20,857)
Arnold, Dave	2:57:27 (954)
Arnold, David	5:24:54 (29,354)
Arnold, James	4:29:50 (19,551)
Arnold, James	4:30:33 (19,721)
Arnold, Jonathan	6:14:05 (31,932)
Arnold, Martin	3:00:06 (1,176)
Arnold, Philip	5:22:29 (29,132)
Arnold, Robert	6:27:21 (32,233)
Arnold, Stephen	3:23:53 (3,795)
Arnott, Robert	5:08:12 (27,454)
Arnott, Stuart	5:35:59 (30,269)
Arnsby, Brian	3:24:41 (3,942)
Aron, James	6:58:41 (32,613)
Aronio, Christian	5:47:17 (31,003)
Arora, Roy	5:40:01 (30,549)
Arosanyin, Chrales	4:06:50 (13,636)
Arrowsmith, Lee	3:33:42 (5,457)
Arrowsmith, Leslie	4:06:21 (13,529)
Arrowsmith, Neil	4:20:51 (17,075)
Arskov, Allan	4:24:19 (18,073)
Artajo Rueda, Javier	4:20:29 (16,988)
Arteaga-Martin, Felix	4:54:00 (25,184)
Arthey, Olly	4:43:26 (22,940)
Arthur, David	3:43:17 (7,467)
Arthur, David	3:43:37 (7,555)
Arthur, Gary	4:31:35 (19,993)
Arthur, James	3:56:04 (10,918)
Arthur, Robert	3:53:23 (10,103)
Arthur, William	4:13:43 (15,242)
Artigues-Cabrer, Jordi	3:19:05 (3,148)

Artkinson, Dennis	4:23:12 (17,753)
Arvonio, Pasquola	4:22:54 (17,671)
Asblan, Max	2:58:59 (1,092)
Ash, John	5:05:17 (27,058)
Ash, Kevin	3:38:18 (6,370)
Ash, Matthew	5:01:25 (26,517)
Ashby, Gerald	3:57:50 (11,461)
Ashby, Mark	2:55:08 (753)
Ashby, Nick	3:43:59 (7,655)
Ashby, Paul	2:58:37 (1,058)
Ashby, Paul	4:36:08 (21,115)
Ashcroft, Anthony	4:18:15 (16,427)
Ashe, Daniel	4:05:24 (13,298)
Ashey, Jonathan	4:37:09 (21,348)
Ashford, George	3:55:36 (10,783)
Ashford, Mark	5:14:44 (28,276)
Ashforth, Alan	3:14:11 (2,572)
Ashill, Nicholas	3:44:08 (7,691)
Ashley, David	4:29:21 (19,422)
Ashley, John	3:22:46 (3,627)
Ashman, Gordon	3:48:52 (8,881)
Ashman, Norman	4:18:25 (16,469)
Ashman, Richard	4:17:05 (16,139)
Ashman, Rod	3:47:01 (8,384)
Ashmead, Gareth	4:21:28 (17,238)
Ashmead, Jason	5:11:56 (27,943)
Ashmore, Steve	4:28:35 (19,187)
Ashpole, David	4:32:19 (20,165)
Ashton, Benjamin	5:16:50 (28,533)
Ashton, Jeffrey	3:59:32 (11,947)
Ashton, Sean	4:00:49 (12,258)
Ashton, Timothy	3:52:53 (9,945)
Ashwanden, Jamie	3:56:09 (10,942)
Ashwell, Mark	3:39:58 (6,725)
Ashwell, Mark	4:45:40 (23,484)
Ashwood, Keith	3:41:26 (7,051)
Ashworth, Michael	5:06:51 (27,275)
Ashworth, Stephen	4:50:24 (24,479)
Asiedu, Eric	3:53:14 (10,055)
Asiedu, Kenneth	3:43:06 (7,410)
Aske-Haley, Charles	4:14:17 (15,385)
Askew, Neville	4:48:23 (24,097)
Askew, Philip	3:52:16 (9,771)
Askew, Trevor	4:43:23 (22,929)
Askin, Ben	6:28:46 (32,249)
Askwith, Richard	3:15:02 (2,668)
Aslam, Khayyam	5:55:26 (31,375)
Aspden, Antony	3:33:59 (5,517)
Aspin, Jamie	4:35:01 (20,839)
Aspin, John	3:50:17 (9,248)
Aspin, Kevin	5:10:07 (27,703)
Aspinall, Michael	2:49:43 (472)
Asplen, David	3:42:00 (7,155)
Asser, Gregory	3:40:35 (6,872)
Asser, Jeffrey	2:58:29 (1,046)
Assi, Tariq	4:25:35 (18,410)
Astley, Shaun	4:40:59 (22,350)
Aston, Andrew	3:00:40 (1,207)
Aston, David	3:54:43 (10,519)
Aston, Jeffrey	3:20:12 (3,277)
Aston, Luke	4:35:54 (21,049)
Aston, Stuart	4:34:35 (20,719)
Athawes, Jon	4:30:52 (19,798)
Atherton, Myles	3:52:31 (9,842)
Atherton, Steve	4:13:45 (15,251)
Athorne, Richard	5:02:16 (26,637)
Atkin, Christian	3:03:36 (1,430)
Atkin, Frederick	3:32:59 (5,351)
Atkin, John	4:25:00 (18,266)
Atkin, Paul	4:33:28 (20,455)
Atkin, Richard	4:35:05 (20,851)
Atkin, Rob	3:55:15 (10,679)
Atkin, Robert	4:52:32 (24,882)
Atkin, Tim	3:23:06 (3,668)
Atkin, Tim	3:54:16 (10,392)
Atkins, Ashley	4:27:04 (18,810)
Atkins, Christopher	4:13:54 (15,286)
Atkins, Christopher	4:28:09 (19,071)
Atkins, Gary	4:15:40 (15,747)
Atkins, Kevin	4:11:07 (14,661)
Atkins, Samuel	5:23:35 (29,233)
Atkins, Sherwyn	3:51:48 (9,624)
Atkins, Stephen	5:05:21 (27,071)

Atkinson, Carl	3:47:33 (8,523)
Atkinson, Derek	3:35:14 (5,751)
Atkinson, John	2:44:58 (298)
Atkinson, John	4:43:22 (22,927)
Atkinson, John	5:15:42 (28,394)
Atkinson, Mark	4:47:51 (23,990)
Atkinson, Paul	4:17:20 (16,213)
Atkinson, William	3:26:14 (4,193)
Atlan, Gerard	4:54:15 (25,233)
Attewell, Clifford	4:23:26 (17,811)
Attia, Gerald	3:23:25 (3,710)
Attridge, Gareth	4:32:53 (20,329)
Attwell, John	3:51:28 (9,535)
Attwood, Anthony	4:49:09 (24,272)
Attwood, Mark	4:34:29 (20,688)
Attwood, Tom	3:58:33 (11,660)
Atwell, Daniel	4:07:07 (13,700)
Atwell, Rhys	5:01:38 (26,555)
Atwell, Royston	6:18:42 (32,056)
Aubry, Nicolas	4:01:02 (12,319)
Auburn, Peter	3:59:12 (11,859)
Aubury, Simon	4:30:19 (19,676)
Aucott, Michael	3:03:29 (1,419)
Audas, Allen	3:47:59 (8,625)
Auditore, Chris	2:46:43 (351)
Audley, James	3:50:59 (9,423)
Aughton, Timothy	5:30:10 (29,796)
Aujla, Jaswant	4:55:42 (25,520)
Aust, Jonathan	4:05:57 (13,425)
Austen, Michael	5:29:21 (29,726)
Austin, Adam	5:08:23 (27,480)
Austin, Alan	3:13:21 (2,485)
Austin, Anthony	3:21:22 (3,414)
Austin, Barry	5:04:59 (27,017)
Austin, Barry	5:42:05 (30,700)
Austin, Chris	6:08:28 (31,797)
Austin, Christopher	3:23:19 (3,698)
Austin, Christopher	5:08:24 (27,487)
Austin, Derek	3:59:45 (12,007)
Austin, Fenner	3:40:44 (6,900)
Austin, Gary	4:19:09 (16,634)
Austin, Leslie	4:00:58 (12,301)
Austin, Mark	3:18:48 (3,112)
Austin, Michael	5:08:23 (27,480)
Austin, Miles	4:00:10 (12,125)
Austin, Robert	4:17:49 (16,329)
Austin, Robert	4:34:56 (20,814)
Austin, Stewart	3:57:44 (11,434)
Avery, David	4:22:18 (17,476)
Avery, Greig	4:16:46 (16,056)
Avery, Joe	3:56:52 (11,165)
Avery, Nick	4:15:36 (15,722)
Avery, Paul	4:00:50 (12,262)
Avery, Philip	5:27:04 (29,529)
Aves, Clayton	3:18:28 (3,067)
Avey, Terry	3:46:43 (8,332)
Avigdori, Adam	5:06:43 (27,261)
Avolio, Pier	3:24:17 (3,873)
Axelsen, Richard	4:29:42 (19,506)
Axsel, Fred	3:54:37 (10,491)
Ayers, Christopher	4:30:11 (19,648)
Ayinbode, Augustine	5:35:27 (30,220)
Aylett, Paul	5:04:19 (26,938)
Ayliffe, Ben	4:00:31 (12,190)
Ayling, Colin	3:15:11 (2,686)
Ayling, Dean	4:14:52 (15,542)
Ayling Smith, David	3:54:35 (10,484)
Aylott, Stuart	3:45:29 (8,039)
Aylward, Colin	5:26:06 (29,456)
Aymonnier, Remy	4:15:53 (15,804)
Ayres, Andrew	4:57:48 (25,915)
Ayres, Graham	4:53:56 (25,168)
Ayres, John	3:24:12 (3,861)
Ayres, Roger	4:51:51 (24,753)
Ayriss, Michael	3:48:13 (8,677)
Ayton, Stuart	3:51:06 (9,458)
Azakil, Matthew	4:29:36 (19,482)
Aziz, Yasin	4:26:06 (18,549)
B Ale, Ian	5:30:34 (29,830)
Babbs, Antony	3:55:58 (10,889)
Babcock, Glen	3:48:54 (8,871)
Babecki, Julio	3:12:49 (2,406)
Babey, Mike	4:27:26 (18,896)

Bachellor, William 4:21:17 (17,186)
Bachmann, Richard 4:38:17 (21,651)
Baci, Arber 3:02:01 (1,301)
Back, Leon 4:47:48 (23,978)
Back, Nicholas 4:46:07 (23,594)
Back, Ray 4:16:57 (16,103)
Backhouse, Ian 4:47:00 (23,811)
Backhouse, Paul 4:01:10 (12,356)
Backlin, Christer 4:57:24 (25,845)
Bacon, Gareth 5:50:09 (31,147)
Bacon, John 4:59:27 (26,207)
Bacon, Kenneth 4:12:25 (14,950)
Bacon, Martin 3:51:24 (9,521)
Bacon, Michael 3:59:42 (11,996)
Bacon, Richard 4:24:18 (18,067)
Bacon, Steve 3:18:33 (3,079)
Bacon, Steven 3:51:06 (9,458)
Baddeley, Christopher 3:48:48 (8,842)
Baddeley, John 3:30:38 (4,969)
Badel, Denis 2:25:13 (41)
Bader, Felix 3:36:55 (6,099)
Badger, Lew 3:16:19 (2,821)
Badgery, Stephen 2:47:51 (395)
Badhan, Parminder 3:42:48 (7,342)
Badillo, José 3:36:08 (5,942)
Badman, John 4:49:42 (24,361)
Badr, Ishmail 3:20:27 (3,307)
Baga, Steve 4:41:52 (22,574)
Bagermeister, Gdo 3:54:32 (10,467)
Baggaley, Geoffrey 3:35:55 (5,886)
Baggaley, Michael 3:07:46 (1,792)
Baggott, Jeremy 3:31:07 (5,054)
Baggs, Alistair 3:46:49 (8,349)
Bagley, Graham 5:16:35 (28,509)
Bagley, Grham 4:40:31 (22,234)
Bagnall, Garry 4:21:25 (17,224)
Bagnall, Graham 4:06:16 (13,509)
Bagshaw, Adrian 4:24:47 (18,193)
Bagshaw, John 3:28:31 (4,606)
Bahia, Davinder 5:48:17 (31,048)
Baigent, Derek 3:15:59 (2,785)
Bailey, Adrian 3:40:09 (6,772)
Bailey, Alan 4:49:32 (24,327)
Bailey, Alex 3:31:06 (5,049)
Bailey, Andrew 4:05:08 (13,238)
Bailey, Andrew 4:30:35 (19,729)
Bailey, Andrew 6:12:00 (31,881)
Bailey, Ashman 4:14:05 (15,336)
Bailey, Bart 4:25:29 (18,381)
Bailey, David 4:41:04 (22,367)
Bailey, David 5:34:01 (30,109)
Bailey, Duncan 3:34:08 (5,553)
Bailey, Edmund 3:29:52 (4,852)
Bailey, Gareth 4:17:49 (16,329)
Bailey, Gary 3:42:04 (7,170)
Bailey, Greg 3:49:25 (9,014)
Bailey, Ian 3:37:58 (6,307)
Bailey, Ian 4:09:15 (14,201)
Bailey, Ian 4:10:30 (14,510)
Bailey, John 5:20:30 (28,940)
Bailey, John 5:31:50 (29,937)
Bailey, Julian 4:31:27 (19,951)
Bailey, Julian 5:41:27 (30,649)
Bailey, Kevin 4:55:51 (25,550)
Bailey, Laurence 3:41:06 (6,988)
Bailey, Mark 3:37:23 (6,185)
Bailey, Mark 4:10:13 (14,440)
Bailey, Mark 4:24:00 (17,984)
Bailey, Martin 2:57:25 (950)
Bailey, Martin 4:23:30 (17,825)
Bailey, Maurice 4:42:01 (22,610)
Bailey, Mitch 4:39:34 (21,989)
Bailey, Nicholas 3:32:03 (5,198)
Bailey, Nick 3:49:47 (9,125)
Bailey, Nick 4:52:25 (24,861)
Bailey, Paul 4:37:55 (21,553)
Bailey, Peter 4:22:39 (17,588)
Bailey, Peter 4:45:38 (23,481)
Bailey, Steve 4:29:35 (19,478)
Bailey, Stuart 4:12:55 (15,066)
Bailey, Thomas 5:13:18 (28,114)
Bailey, Thomas 5:41:28 (30,651)
Bailey, Tom 6:14:51 (31,955)
Bailey, William 3:50:58 (9,418)
Bailey-Hague, Charles 4:34:37 (20,731)
Bailie, Derrick 3:51:01 (9,433)
Bailie, Iain 3:42:14 (7,214)
Baillie, Doug 4:56:23 (25,675)
Baillie, Michael 2:47:53 (399)
Baily, Richard 4:36:51 (21,290)
Bain, Alan 4:29:04 (19,341)
Bain, Andy 3:54:10 (10,366)
Bain, Daibhdh 5:15:29 (28,360)
Bainbridge, Michael 2:46:18 (335)
Bainbridge, Paul 3:53:37 (10,182)
Baines, Chris 5:06:52 (27,277)
Baines, Jeremy 3:44:32 (7,804)
Baines, Lee 5:08:17 (27,469)
Baines, Mark 6:30:53 (32,295)
Baines, Matthew 3:36:22 (5,996)
Baines, Ray 3:51:36 (9,573)
Baines, Steven 3:44:36 (7,820)
Bainger, Graham 3:17:12 (2,920)
Bains, Narinder 3:43:02 (7,396)
Baird, Alastair 6:19:09 (32,062)
Baird, Euan 5:13:06 (28,092)
Baird, Ewan 3:43:57 (7,643)
Baird, James 3:04:03 (1,470)
Baird, Robert 4:26:30 (18,653)
Baird Murray, Knill 3:04:33 (1,506)
Bairsto, Nigel 4:02:32 (12,663)
Bairstow, Raymond 4:04:50 (13,167)
Baixauli, Benito 4:58:47 (26,094)
Bajor, Oliver 4:30:04 (19,615)
Bakehouse, Jamie 4:58:23 (26,012)
Baker, Andrew 3:00:55 (1,221)
Baker, Anthony 3:45:04 (7,946)
Baker, Antony 5:15:10 (28,317)
Baker, Carl 2:48:39 (433)
Baker, Chris 3:42:26 (7,269)
Baker, Christopher 4:11:35 (14,763)
Baker, Christopher 4:29:54 (19,575)
Baker, Colin 2:56:43 (889)
Baker, Darron 3:58:48 (11,737)
Baker, David 3:56:15 (10,978)
Baker, David 3:59:31 (11,942)
Baker, David 4:21:43 (17,315)
Baker, David 4:59:32 (26,227)
Baker, David 5:26:54 (29,515)
Baker, Dean 5:07:39 (27,392)
Baker, Graham 2:59:59 (1,167)
Baker, Howard 4:32:37 (20,251)
Baker, Ian 3:52:40 (9,887)
Baker, Kevin 5:05:00 (27,021)
Baker, Kim 3:11:21 (2,189)
Baker, Mark 3:05:20 (1,572)
Baker, Mark 3:57:23 (11,317)
Baker, Mark 4:05:24 (13,298)
Baker, Martin 4:29:05 (19,344)
Baker, Nick 2:57:30 (956)
Baker, Nigel 3:18:53 (3,123)
Baker, Paul 5:52:01 (31,237)
Baker, Philip 3:44:05 (7,675)
Baker, Richard 3:33:51 (5,486)
Baker, Richard 4:17:56 (16,358)
Baker, Richard 4:45:16 (23,374)
Baker, Richard 5:16:28 (28,497)
Baker, Russell 3:43:45 (7,589)
Baker, Stephen 3:27:09 (4,352)
Baker, Stephen 3:53:43 (10,212)
Baker, Stephen 4:08:56 (14,119)
Baker, William 5:23:37 (29,236)
Baker-Smith, Hugh 4:04:14 (13,037)
Bakewell, Anthony 4:14:55 (15,554)
Bakker, John 4:34:24 (20,673)
Balcazar, Guillermo 5:02:52 (26,723)
Balch, Charles 4:32:25 (20,194)
Balchin, Stephen 4:32:11 (20,136)
Balcombe, Gary 3:42:13 (7,204)
Balde, Mansour 3:59:59 (12,080)
Balderson, Paul 3:19:27 (3,196)
Baldessari, Silvio 3:34:02 (5,524)
Baldini, Stefano 2:07:28 (6)
Baldock, David 3:58:43 (11,712)
Baldock, Michael 3:12:58 (2,428)
Baldock, Phil 4:25:59 (18,513)
Baldoni, Roberto 3:50:03 (9,178)
Baldry, Peter 4:27:55 (19,011)
Baldwin, David 4:55:23 (25,461)
Baldwin, Jamie 4:35:30 (20,946)
Baldwin, Leslie 4:44:30 (23,172)
Baldwin, Malcolm 5:07:00 (27,295)
Baldwin, Michael 4:20:45 (17,059)
Baldwin, Richard 4:37:10 (21,355)
Baldwin, Stephen 4:35:29 (20,942)
Baldwin, Steven 3:38:10 (6,335)
Baldwin, Stuart 3:54:04 (10,334)
Baldwin, Stuart 4:25:32 (18,396)
Baldwin, Tristan 4:35:29 (20,942)
Bale, Gareth 4:46:01 (23,569)
Bale, Matthew 4:59:57 (26,300)
Bale, Robert 4:11:46 (14,813)
Balejho, Rysiard 4:32:36 (20,243)
Balfour, Scott 3:00:42 (1,210)
Balfour-Lynn, Ian 5:05:46 (27,121)
Bali, Navneet 4:42:21 (22,687)
Ball, Andrew 3:08:08 (1,818)
Ball, Anthony 4:13:19 (15,149)
Ball, Anthony 4:41:59 (22,603)
Ball, David 3:38:50 (6,491)
Ball, David 4:48:23 (24,097)
Ball, Deryck 4:10:37 (14,539)
Ball, Garreth 4:41:27 (22,463)
Ball, James 4:07:41 (13,836)
Ball, James 4:50:49 (24,572)
Ball, Malcolm 3:44:40 (7,839)
Ball, Peter 4:00:55 (12,281)
Ball, Philip 3:58:32 (11,657)
Ball, Simon 3:44:41 (7,848)
Ball, Stephen 3:41:10 (7,003)
Ball, Stephen 4:25:13 (18,312)
Ballam, Paul 3:30:47 (4,990)
Ballam, Paul 4:12:24 (14,943)
Ballantine, Gordon 4:40:41 (22,270)
Ballantyne, David 3:23:08 (3,670)
Ballantyne, Ian 4:36:49 (21,280)
Ballard, Alan 5:28:15 (29,633)
Ballard, Geoff 4:21:22 (17,210)
Ballesio, Romano 3:07:19 (1,755)
Bally, Norbert 3:55:44 (10,823)
Balsdon, Jon 5:29:58 (29,778)
Balsom, Andrew 4:45:55 (23,545)
Balzan, Trever 4:00:43 (12,233)
Balzano, Gianfranco 3:53:34 (10,171)
Bamber, Jamie 2:58:24 (1,038)
Bamber, Nicholas 6:32:48 (32,321)
Bamberger, Nicholas 3:32:55 (5,341)
Bamford, Allan 3:29:46 (4,838)
Bamford, Tony 4:59:34 (26,236)
Bampton, James 5:49:17 (31,113)
Bampton, Paul 3:08:43 (1,891)
Bamsey, Simon 5:49:45 (31,133)
Banbury, John 5:36:50 (30,337)
Banbury, Peregrine 6:21:50 (32,117)
Bance, Elliott 3:54:49 (10,547)
Bance, Nick 5:07:00 (27,295)
Bancroft, Andrew 4:35:17 (20,898)
Bancroft, Graham 4:51:35 (24,715)
Bancroft, John 5:37:09 (30,357)
Bancroft, Tom 3:53:38 (10,190)
Banett, Michael 3:25:36 (4,081)
Banfi, Jim 5:01:28 (26,523)
Banfi, Michael 3:09:25 (1,983)
Banga, Godfrey 4:36:36 (21,243)
Banks, Allistair 3:40:16 (6,803)
Banks, David 4:19:22 (16,684)
Banks, Ian 3:58:16 (11,584)
Banks, Johnny 3:07:39 (1,779)
Banks, Jonathan 4:41:19 (22,433)
Banks, Peter 4:47:55 (24,010)
Banks, Stuart 4:16:17 (15,909)
Banks, Terence 4:55:14 (25,427)
Banks, Thomas 3:35:35 (5,822)
Banks, Tim 4:08:14 (13,957)
Banner, John 4:07:50 (13,879)
Banner, Tyr 3:49:37 (9,074)
Bannerman, Keith 3:42:43 (7,319)
Bannerman, Ross 4:05:14 (13,260)
Banning, Frederick 4:15:38 (15,733)

Banning, Graham....4:31:32 (19,978)
Banniste, Philip....4:43:24 (22,932)
Bannister, Jonathan....4:44:21 (23,146)
Bannister, Philip....3:57:22 (11,307)
Bannister, Richard....4:31:33 (19,988)
Bannon, Alan....4:33:35 (20,486)
Bantin, Laurie....3:44:49 (7,892)
Bantock, Christopher....4:22:41 (17,603)
Banton, Jonathan....4:10:54 (14,605)
Banton, Lewis....2:51:54 (573)
Banus, Abel....4:09:38 (14,300)
Barber, Andrew....2:31:27 (71)
Barber, Bradley....4:36:26 (21,196)
Barber, David....4:08:48 (14,092)
Barber, Ian....3:07:48 (1,793)
Barber, Ian....4:23:47 (17,913)
Barber, Kyle....3:59:23 (11,914)
Barber, Martin....4:30:03 (19,608)
Barber, Terry....5:35:00 (30,189)
Barbier, Martin....3:53:13 (10,048)
Barbier, Yves....3:31:08 (5,057)
Barbosa, Joaquim....3:07:22 (1,758)
Barclay, Ian....4:06:26 (13,550)
Barclay, Jeffrey....3:13:21 (2,485)
Barclay, Nicholas....3:44:07 (7,683)
Barclay, Paul....4:39:43 (22,030)
Bard, Daniel....5:38:29 (30,448)
Bardll, Graham....3:33:40 (5,450)
Bardon, Richard....3:17:21 (2,941)
Bardouille, Francis....5:52:25 (31,247)
Bardsley, David....4:05:07 (13,235)
Bargh, Donald....3:40:14 (6,794)
Barham, Andrew....4:36:42 (21,261)
Barham, David....6:18:15 (32,041)
Barham, Malcolm....3:56:06 (10,929)
Baring, Edward....3:43:07 (7,418)
Baring, Julian....4:08:25 (13,997)
Barke, Norman....5:05:37 (27,100)
Barker, Christopher....5:09:18 (27,605)
Barker, David....3:36:48 (6,078)
Barker, Gerard....3:23:54 (3,799)
Barker, Graham....5:29:29 (29,735)
Barker, Henry....5:35:49 (30,257)
Barker, Ian....4:34:38 (20,736)
Barker, James....4:15:28 (15,684)
Barker, John....2:52:50 (621)
Barker, John....3:46:25 (8,258)
Barker, John....4:12:22 (14,932)
Barker, John....4:16:54 (16,093)
Barker, Jon....3:26:53 (4,309)
Barker, Joseph....3:33:16 (5,392)
Barker, Karl....4:58:33 (26,041)
Barker, Mark....4:47:10 (23,849)
Barker, Nigel....3:40:17 (6,809)
Barker, Paul....4:13:53 (15,281)
Barker, Paul....4:38:16 (21,645)
Barker, Philip....6:27:10 (32,222)
Barker, Simon....4:45:10 (23,348)
Barker, Stephen....3:53:46 (10,228)
Barker, Victor....4:42:11 (22,646)
Barkers, Charles....3:31:36 (5,124)
Barkley, Ian....6:01:59 (31,607)
Barkley, Simon....4:50:26 (24,491)
Barley, Allan....5:17:01 (28,565)
Barley, David....5:36:21 (30,299)
Barley, Laurence....3:54:27 (10,443)
Barlow, Andrew....4:21:58 (17,382)
Barlow, Antony....4:44:03 (23,074)
Barlow, Chris....3:45:58 (8,153)
Barlow, David....3:50:15 (9,235)
Barlow, Howard....3:44:11 (7,707)
Barlow, Jason....2:49:49 (477)
Barlow, Jonathan....3:28:32 (4,613)
Barlow, Julian....5:14:55 (28,297)
Barlow, Lee....3:26:13 (4,190)
Barlow, Mark....3:48:59 (8,891)
Barlow, Mark....4:59:31 (26,221)
Barlow, Michael....3:43:53 (7,630)
Barlow, Robin....4:01:27 (12,425)
Barlow, William....3:48:03 (8,639)
Barltrop, Paul....3:42:37 (7,307)
Barnard, David....5:19:56 (28,867)
Barnard, Michael....3:42:23 (7,259)
Barnard, Stephen....5:08:41 (27,520)
Barnby, David....4:18:08 (16,394)
Barnes, Andrew....3:24:30 (3,918)
Barnes, Antony....4:42:33 (22,737)
Barnes, Barry....6:09:45 (31,830)
Barnes, Christopher....3:57:57 (11,491)
Barnes, Christopher....6:54:30 (32,586)
Barnes, Clinton....3:54:03 (10,326)
Barnes, Colin....4:24:21 (18,080)
Barnes, Darrell....4:19:50 (16,810)
Barnes, David....3:14:15 (2,587)
Barnes, David....4:10:36 (14,538)
Barnes, David....4:24:26 (18,100)
Barnes, Gary....3:11:47 (2,242)
Barnes, Gary....5:11:21 (27,860)
Barnes, Graham....3:38:54 (6,501)
Barnes, Howard....4:34:27 (20,682)
Barnes, John....4:45:34 (23,461)
Barnes, John....4:56:08 (25,618)
Barnes, Michael....2:58:29 (1,046)
Barnes, Mick....3:13:16 (2,469)
Barnes, Paul....2:54:08 (686)
Barnes, Richard....5:38:00 (30,415)
Barnes, Roy....3:25:37 (4,085)
Barnes, Russell....4:09:50 (14,348)
Barnes, Sean....4:26:56 (18,771)
Barnes, Simon....3:38:19 (6,378)
Barnes, Stephen....3:15:28 (2,720)
Barnes, Trevor....3:25:07 (4,004)
Barnes, William....4:15:52 (15,798)
Barness, Martin....4:20:59 (17,107)
Barnett, Andrew....3:56:39 (11,097)
Barnett, David....4:12:22 (14,932)
Barnett, Ian....3:54:51 (10,557)
Barnett, Jeff....3:28:24 (4,588)
Barnett, Jonathan....4:55:11 (25,417)
Barnett, Robert....3:46:45 (8,336)
Barnett, Sam....3:37:41 (6,259)
Barnett, Simon....3:33:43 (5,462)
Barningham, Richard....3:59:45 (12,007)
Barns, Justin....4:45:11 (23,353)
Barnwell, David....5:38:46 (30,462)
Baron, Ashworth....4:48:12 (24,072)
Baron, Benoit....3:48:43 (8,816)
Baron, Damien....3:23:09 (3,673)
Baron, Ingo....3:38:25 (6,404)
Baron, James....3:19:22 (3,181)
Baron, Steven....4:50:00 (24,423)
Barot, Krishna....5:06:21 (27,204)
Barou, François....3:09:46 (2,014)
Barozzi, Massimo....3:22:46 (3,627)
Barr, David....3:24:30 (3,918)
Barr, Hesham....4:09:57 (14,373)
Barr, Patrick....4:37:19 (21,404)
Barr, Richard....4:09:33 (14,281)
Barra, Guiseppe....3:47:31 (8,515)
Barraclough, Kevan....3:31:29 (5,105)
Barrance, Tony....4:51:38 (24,723)
Barras, Thierry....2:55:00 (741)
Barras, Thierry....3:29:08 (4,716)
Barratt, Ashley....5:16:08 (28,459)
Barratt, Colin....4:17:19 (16,209)
Barratt, Mark....3:48:57 (8,881)
Barratt, Martin....4:57:51 (25,922)
Barratt, Nicholas....4:57:39 (25,887)
Barratt, Raymond....4:05:09 (13,240)
Barrett, Barrie....3:23:34 (3,736)
Barrett, Craig....3:21:52 (3,497)
Barrett, Daniel....4:53:54 (25,147)
Barrett, Darren....5:17:30 (28,628)
Barrett, Gerard....3:57:01 (11,214)
Barrett, Gordon....3:05:21 (1,573)
Barrett, Ian....3:51:03 (9,442)
Barrett, Jonathan....5:18:46 (28,754)
Barrett, Mark....3:53:38 (10,190)
Barrett, Mark....5:19:46 (28,847)
Barrett, Martin....4:54:12 (25,225)
Barrett, Neil....4:35:33 (20,960)
Barrett, Norman....5:47:22 (31,006)
Barrett, Paul....3:17:25 (2,951)
Barrett, Peter....3:54:22 (10,417)
Barrett, Philip....3:33:01 (5,354)
Barrett, Philip....3:51:06 (9,458)
Barrett, Richard....3:01:04 (1,231)
Barrett, Sean....4:28:36 (19,197)
Barrett, Simon....2:54:11 (689)
Barrett, Steven....4:36:19 (21,164)
Barrett, Thomas....3:56:20 (11,001)
Barrett-Evans, Dominic....5:21:34 (29,048)
Barrier, Ernest....4:55:54 (25,561)
Barrier, Mark....4:55:54 (25,561)
Barringer, David....4:41:11 (22,398)
Barritt, Robert....4:39:28 (21,963)
Barron, Karl....3:40:39 (6,885)
Barron, Michael....4:24:11 (18,029)
Barron, Peter....3:33:52 (5,490)
Barron, Robert....4:37:53 (21,542)
Barron, Shaun....3:01:45 (1,277)
Barrow, Bruce....6:51:07 (32,553)
Barrow, Christopher....4:18:14 (16,422)
Barrow, Christopher....4:21:49 (17,342)
Barrow, Clive....3:13:18 (2,473)
Barrow, Julian....3:48:36 (8,782)
Barrow, Martin....4:29:07 (19,354)
Barrow, Paul....5:18:56 (28,769)
Barrow, Peter....5:23:45 (29,259)
Barrowclough, Mark....3:08:54 (1,922)
Barrowman, Michael....3:52:21 (9,797)
Barrows, Gareth....5:45:13 (30,898)
Barrs, Gary....4:33:02 (20,360)
Barry, David....5:47:58 (31,037)
Barry, John....3:37:09 (6,140)
Barry, John....3:49:43 (9,103)
Barry, Michael....4:33:51 (20,548)
Barsanti, Stephen....4:13:20 (15,151)
Barstad, John....3:30:28 (4,938)
Bartell, Matthew....4:42:22 (22,689)
Bartels, Ashley....5:35:28 (30,224)
Barteluk, Steve....4:17:52 (16,341)
Barter, Nigel....3:33:04 (5,362)
Bartholomew, Alister....3:51:56 (9,657)
Bartholomew, David....4:07:35 (13,813)
Bartholomew, Mark....3:56:29 (11,044)
Bartholomew, Michael....3:51:36 (9,573)
Barthorpe, Michael....5:13:04 (28,088)
Bartie, Garry....4:44:20 (23,138)
Bartlett, Bill....3:53:36 (10,178)
Bartlett, David....4:02:46 (12,719)
Bartlett, Edwin....4:00:47 (12,255)
Bartlett, Gareth....4:19:02 (16,602)
Bartlett, Iain....3:38:52 (6,498)
Bartlett, John....3:33:24 (5,417)
Bartlett, John....4:54:27 (25,275)
Bartlett, Justin....4:09:21 (14,232)
Bartlett, Michael....5:15:10 (28,317)
Bartlett, Peter....4:01:47 (12,514)
Bartlett, Robin....4:56:22 (25,673)
Bartmeier, Frederick....4:34:00 (20,579)
Barton, Alan....4:39:24 (21,953)
Barton, Christopher....4:05:23 (13,293)
Barton, David....3:14:58 (2,665)
Barton, David....4:20:31 (16,994)
Barton, Desmond....3:56:42 (11,109)
Barton, Frances....4:03:04 (12,793)
Barton, George....4:26:11 (18,569)
Barton, Glenn....4:36:01 (21,084)
Barton, Michael....4:58:48 (26,096)
Barton, Simon....3:19:29 (3,201)
Bartram, Dwayne....3:27:39 (4,447)
Bartram, Mark....3:21:44 (3,469)
Bartrip, Lee....4:58:57 (26,121)
Barwick, Richard....4:27:38 (18,947)
Barwise, Russell....4:53:20 (25,034)
Baschangel, Helmut....4:04:32 (13,099)
Basford, Darren....4:19:26 (16,700)
Basham, David....3:34:53 (5,693)
Basham, Leslie....4:26:29 (18,649)
Bashford, Bryan....4:23:11 (17,747)
Bashford, Kevin....3:42:44 (7,323)
Bashir, Jamshed....4:31:22 (19,921)
Basini Gazzi, Paolo....3:14:15 (2,587)
Bason, Stephen....3:07:45 (1,790)
Bass, Alex....4:44:44 (23,230)
Bass, Clive....3:31:39 (5,139)
Bass, Peter....4:11:52 (14,828)
Bass, Thomas....3:18:22 (3,053)

Bassett, David 3:58:22 (11,607)
Bassett, Steven 4:38:31 (21,707)
Bastin, Colin 5:18:21 (28,709)
Bataille, Jean 5:31:27 (29,908)
Batchelor, Nick 3:15:20 (2,707)
Batchelor, Robert 2:52:18 (588)
Batchelor, William 4:08:54 (14,112)
Bate, Michael 5:53:30 (31,298)
Bateman, Daniel 4:23:22 (17,791)
Bateman, David 4:11:08 (14,664)
Bateman, Duncan 3:16:51 (2,887)
Bateman, Jeremy 2:54:47 (728)
Bateman, Sam 4:29:06 (19,348)
Bateman, Tom 3:35:06 (5,732)
Bater, Andrew 4:37:54 (21,547)
Bater, Mark 4:32:12 (20,141)
Bater, Philip 3:45:20 (8,006)
Bates, David 3:44:32 (7,804)
Bates, Glenn 4:40:42 (22,277)
Bates, Ian 3:52:35 (9,865)
Bates, Paul 3:19:07 (3,152)
Bates, Philip 3:36:51 (6,086)
Bates, Stephen 3:33:36 (5,442)
Bates, Stephen 3:58:59 (11,796)
Bates, Stuart 5:13:26 (28,131)
Bates, Terry 3:15:19 (2,704)
Bath, Christopher 4:37:17 (21,399)
Bath, Rachhpal 5:14:51 (28,289)
Bath, Tony 5:13:11 (28,099)
Bathgate, Richard 4:22:17 (17,472)
Batho, James 5:20:29 (28,937)
Batley, Lloyd 4:40:41 (22,270)
Batsford, Alan 4:26:27 (18,637)
Batsford, Nick 5:01:18 (26,503)
Batstone, Timothy 3:48:52 (8,859)
Battaglia, Alberto 3:59:08 (11,840)
Battavoine, Robert 3:39:18 (6,589)
Batterbury, Clive 3:45:05 (7,950)
Batterbury, Mark 3:36:26 (6,012)
Batterbury, Paul 3:24:41 (3,942)
Batterham, Richard 2:53:41 (664)
Battersby, James 3:51:56 (9,657)
Battersby, Michael 4:14:43 (15,500)
Battersby, Stephen 4:34:17 (20,645)
Batty, David 4:22:19 (17,486)
Batty, Neil 4:32:23 (20,184)
Batty, Richard 4:54:13 (25,229)
Battye, Hamish 4:04:28 (13,081)
Battye, Michael 4:37:55 (21,553)
Baty, Adrian 3:57:40 (11,416)
Batye, Michael 3:31:53 (5,173)
Baudains, Keith 4:22:15 (17,462)
Baudains, Martin 4:12:30 (14,974)
Baudet, Bernard 3:37:47 (6,277)
Baudoux, François 4:28:01 (19,038)
Bauer, Matthew 4:21:17 (17,186)
Bauer, Rolf 4:45:06 (23,333)
Bauer, Wolfgang 4:09:54 (14,363)
Baujon, Alain 3:25:14 (4,021)
Baulch, Dave 5:02:05 (26,614)
Bauler, Daniel 3:57:58 (11,496)
Baulk, Geoff 5:13:03 (28,086)
Baumann, Michael 3:25:07 (4,004)
Baumbach, Andreas 3:55:24 (10,721)
Baumgartner, Marc 5:26:29 (29,488)
Bausor, Daniel 4:01:42 (12,493)
Baux, Pierre 3:44:04 (7,669)
Baverstam, Dan 3:45:48 (8,120)
Bavin, Scott 5:01:31 (26,527)
Bavington, Michael 3:25:16 (4,026)
Bavister, Giles 3:33:46 (5,469)
Bawden, Glynn 3:37:59 (6,310)
Bawden, Simon 4:14:43 (15,500)
Baxendale, Sam 4:21:05 (17,136)
Baxendale, Steven 3:36:03 (5,915)
Baxendale, Steven 3:45:31 (8,048)
Baxter, Andrew 4:22:46 (17,628)
Baxter, Charlie 3:28:37 (4,628)
Baxter, Dave 4:34:01 (20,582)
Baxter, Eric 3:22:30 (3,581)
Baxter, George 4:13:45 (15,251)
Baxter, Gordon 4:03:23 (12,855)
Baxter, Justin 5:13:38 (28,155)
Baxter, Philip 4:04:50 (13,167)
Baxter, Robert 3:43:48 (7,606)
Baxter, Timothy 3:52:50 (9,933)
Bayer, Malcolm 2:45:26 (308)
Bayes, John 4:35:50 (21,036)
Bayes, Michael 4:41:32 (22,481)
Bayess, Graham 3:47:38 (8,544)
Bayfield, Stewart 4:34:46 (20,766)
Bayley, Andrew 3:18:17 (3,042)
Bayley, Colin 4:29:48 (19,534)
Bayley, Derrick 4:47:03 (23,827)
Bayley, Mark 4:05:24 (13,298)
Baylis, Michael 4:04:24 (13,069)
Baylis, Peter 4:32:39 (20,261)
Bayliss, Justin 3:28:54 (4,679)
Bayliss, Michael 5:04:42 (26,979)
Bayliss, Rob 4:03:56 (12,971)
Bayliss-Strover, Richard 3:51:57 (9,671)
Bayman, Robert 3:13:58 (2,554)
Bayne, Oliver 4:19:48 (16,804)
Baynes, Charles 3:20:58 (3,359)
Baynes, Chris 3:38:46 (6,481)
Baynes, Edwin 2:48:31 (427)
Baynes, Paul 6:19:32 (32,072)
Baynes, Ron 5:26:04 (29,450)
Baynham, Anthony 4:56:15 (25,648)
Bayon, Tony 4:59:39 (26,253)
Bayston, Alan 3:12:31 (2,364)
Bazeley, Michael 5:33:42 (30,085)
Bazeley, Tom 4:44:40 (23,209)
Bazley, Martin 4:01:08 (12,345)
Bazzard, Andrew 4:10:25 (14,490)
Beadle, David 4:43:05 (22,863)
Beadle, Michael 3:40:11 (6,779)
Beadsmoore, Jonathan 4:14:05 (15,336)
Beagles, Tim 3:43:13 (7,450)
Beagley, David 5:14:57 (28,300)
Beagley, Mark 3:13:08 (2,453)
Beake, Jonathan 4:53:47 (25,118)
Beal, Martin 3:56:46 (11,131)
Beale, Marcus 4:39:14 (21,908)
Beales, Matthew 5:20:10 (28,898)
Beaman, Andrew 3:31:32 (5,114)
Beament, Jeremy 4:19:26 (16,700)
Beames, Derek 4:38:44 (21,774)
Beames, Garry 3:31:26 (5,098)
Beamiss, Graham 4:55:40 (25,511)
Beamont, Michael 4:23:17 (17,772)
Bean, Martin 4:20:39 (17,032)
Beard, Ian 3:33:59 (5,517)
Beard, John 3:24:38 (3,934)
Beard, Mike 3:24:42 (3,949)
Beard, Tom 4:01:20 (12,399)
Beard, Zac 4:30:08 (19,635)
Beardmore, Mark 3:35:20 (5,767)
Beardsell, William 3:58:35 (11,671)
Beardsmore, Keith 3:01:38 (1,266)
Beardwell, James 5:07:40 (27,396)
Bearman, Stephen 4:48:02 (24,041)
Bearwish, Darren 3:31:40 (5,145)
Bearwish, Kevin 4:32:08 (20,122)
Bearwish, Neil 3:32:30 (5,269)
Beasley, Andrew 4:39:23 (21,946)
Beasley, Christopher 3:41:06 (6,988)
Beasley, Darrell 4:58:09 (25,973)
Beasley, Mark 4:23:59 (17,976)
Beasor, Robert 3:50:36 (9,322)
Beasty, John 2:50:36 (517)
Beattie, Brian 3:15:12 (2,687)
Beattie, Ian 3:09:11 (1,951)
Beattie, Ian 3:13:58 (2,554)
Beattie, Michael 3:03:12 (1,390)
Beattie, Paul 4:57:06 (25,793)
Beattie-Wilson, Kevin 4:12:01 (14,867)
Beauchamp, Keith 3:56:05 (10,923)
Beaufils, Denis 3:34:38 (5,645)
Beaumont, Alex 4:06:21 (13,529)
Beaumont, Mark 3:53:54 (10,278)
Beaumont, Richard 3:43:24 (7,496)
Beaver, Paul 3:30:05 (4,885)
Beavers, Paul 4:47:17 (23,874)
Beazer, Anthony 4:13:58 (15,301)
Bebb, David 3:29:13 (4,731)
Bebbington, Adrian 4:29:24 (19,436)
Bebbington, Ian 3:55:42 (10,812)
Bebbington, John 3:23:10 (3,674)
Bech, Claus 4:26:58 (18,779)
Bech, Jean 4:16:58 (16,108)
Bechtold, Joerg 3:37:24 (6,189)
Beck, Graham 5:06:55 (27,283)
Beck, Graham 5:48:00 (31,039)
Beck, Hubert 2:53:54 (675)
Beck, Patrick 4:33:01 (20,357)
Beck, Paul 4:15:21 (15,653)
Becker, Martin 3:22:43 (3,615)
Beckers, Stan 4:34:39 (20,739)
Beckert, Udo 4:00:58 (12,301)
Beckett, Nigel 4:51:03 (24,616)
Beckett, Tony 4:28:14 (19,095)
Beckly, Alan 3:42:21 (7,248)
Beddard, Richard 4:54:24 (25,265)
Bedekar, Ajit 5:07:29 (27,372)
Bedell, Nigel 3:10:29 (2,100)
Bedford, Graham 4:31:56 (20,066)
Bedford, Gregory 4:29:41 (19,502)
Bedford, Mark 4:34:03 (20,595)
Bedford, Paul 3:57:32 (11,372)
Bedford, Tim 3:40:11 (6,779)
Bedin, Mario 5:06:36 (27,244)
Bednall, Michael 5:03:35 (26,833)
Bednash, Graham 4:27:09 (18,832)
Bedson, Duncan 6:05:11 (31,700)
Bedwell, Kenneth 4:21:57 (17,376)
Bedwell, Marcus 5:06:13 (27,188)
Bedwell, Mick 3:27:20 (4,383)
Bedwell, Peter 3:57:02 (11,220)
Bedwell, Tim 4:38:43 (21,768)
Bee, David 3:21:08 (3,391)
Bee, Graham 4:35:29 (20,942)
Bee, Nicholas 4:30:07 (19,630)
Beech, Greg 5:17:17 (28,601)
Beech, John 3:09:32 (1,993)
Beech, Keith 4:59:50 (26,279)
Beech, Ken 4:43:45 (23,004)
Beecham, George 5:54:04 (31,315)
Beeche, George 3:13:20 (2,480)
Beecher, Michael 2:57:24 (947)
Beechey, James 4:23:04 (17,723)
Beeching, David 4:05:09 (13,240)
Beeching, Mark 5:01:13 (26,487)
Beecroft, David 3:28:36 (4,626)
Beedles, Andrew 4:16:15 (15,899)
Beeley, Will 3:10:52 (2,140)
Beels, Richard 3:26:33 (4,241)
Beer, Carl 5:55:36 (31,385)
Beer, Ian 5:00:17 (26,344)
Beers, Darren 3:24:12 (3,861)
Beesley, Christopher 3:17:41 (2,972)
Beesley, Ian 3:31:24 (5,092)
Beesley, Paul 5:48:27 (31,059)
Beeson, Paul 3:46:32 (8,294)
Beeston, Adrian 3:35:03 (5,719)
Beeston, Mark 4:06:33 (13,577)
Beeston, Tim 4:34:34 (20,714)
Beet, Simon 4:51:10 (24,643)
Beete, Jon 4:49:29 (24,318)
Beeton, Andrew 4:16:53 (16,086)
Beevers, Alexander 4:03:33 (12,890)
Beevers, Graham 3:08:28 (1,866)
Beevers, James 4:29:44 (19,520)
Beevers, Stephen 3:59:28 (11,935)
Begg, Chris 5:10:23 (27,735)
Begg, Graham 4:13:26 (15,173)
Begley, Kenneth 2:49:56 (487)
Begue, Jean-François 3:04:22 (1,493)
Behrens, Jacky 2:53:36 (659)
Behrmann, Tilo 4:11:01 (14,633)
Behzadi, Shervin 5:10:49 (27,789)
Beketov, Andrei 3:21:51 (3,493)
Bekir, Osman 4:28:28 (19,159)
Belcher, John 5:17:23 (28,615)
Belcher, Mark 2:57:30 (956)
Belcher, Peter 2:41:16 (212)
Belfrage, Rupert 3:43:46 (7,591)
Belgeonne, Christian 3:23:40 (3,755)
Belgrave, Jerome 4:49:08 (24,266)

Belin, Patrick 3:52:59 (9,972)
Belindir, Yahya 3:31:43 (5,154)
Bell, Aaron 4:52:34 (24,895)
Bell, Adrian 3:32:03 (5,198)
Bell, Alasdair 4:00:18 (12,153)
Bell, Andrew 4:54:27 (25,275)
Bell, Anthony 3:31:06 (5,049)
Bell, Anthony 4:01:17 (12,384)
Bell, Barry 3:36:20 (5,985)
Bell, Brian 3:34:35 (5,633)
Bell, Brian 3:42:09 (7,191)
Bell, Damian 4:16:23 (15,945)
Bell, David 3:14:14 (2,585)
Bell, David 3:29:30 (4,795)
Bell, David 3:52:07 (9,726)
Bell, Douglas 3:30:34 (4,957)
Bell, Duncan 2:48:04 (404)
Bell, Eddie 2:52:30 (596)
Bell, Graeme 3:30:53 (5,006)
Bell, Graham 3:03:39 (1,436)
Bell, Graham 4:36:37 (21,244)
Bell, Harold 2:59:06 (1,103)
Bell, James 3:47:59 (8,625)
Bell, John 2:57:11 (928)
Bell, John 4:51:45 (24,735)
Bell, Jonathan 3:04:53 (1,533)
Bell, Joseph 4:12:51 (15,050)
Bell, Kevin 3:28:45 (4,646)
Bell, Mark 3:35:05 (5,725)
Bell, Martin 4:51:25 (24,682)
Bell, Matthew 4:14:04 (15,333)
Bell, Michael 5:39:51 (30,539)
Bell, Neil 4:58:45 (26,091)
Bell, Nicholas 3:40:58 (6,958)
Bell, Nicholas 4:02:06 (12,575)
Bell, Nick 3:24:21 (3,893)
Bell, Nick 5:43:53 (30,810)
Bell, Richard 4:40:15 (22,170)
Bell, Robert 3:28:31 (4,606)
Bell, Robert 3:44:56 (7,915)
Bell, Roderick 4:36:13 (21,134)
Bell, Simon 2:32:15 (76)
Bell, Stephen 4:34:16 (20,643)
Bell, Stephen 4:38:33 (21,720)
Bell, Stuart 4:16:45 (16,052)
Bell, Wayne 3:18:12 (3,033)
Bell, William 4:29:34 (19,473)
Bellamy, Chris 3:32:13 (5,218)
Bellamy, Edward 3:28:19 (4,571)
Bellamy, John 4:33:26 (20,448)
Bellars, Tim 3:27:39 (4,447)
Bellas, Michael 4:03:49 (12,947)
Belledent, Claude 4:42:53 (22,811)
Bellemo, Luca 2:46:42 (349)
Bellemo, Moreno 3:40:06 (6,762)
Bellerby, Steven 4:29:15 (19,398)
Bellicaud, Thierry 3:27:21 (4,385)
Bellis, James 3:42:02 (7,164)
Bellis, John 4:20:58 (17,102)
Bellis, Leonard 4:34:38 (20,736)
Bellis, Stephen 2:58:37 (1,058)
Bellis, Thomas 3:29:36 (4,813)
Bellock, Guy 5:17:01 (28,565)
Belson, Joe 4:00:04 (12,097)
Belton, Chris 2:57:00 (914)
Belton, Frederick 5:36:16 (30,293)
Belton, Robert 3:16:48 (2,881)
Ben Nathan, Marc 3:41:04 (6,980)
Benamri, Abderrezak 2:49:45 (474)
Benat, Bryce 3:59:51 (12,041)
Benbow, Alastair 3:23:37 (3,745)
Benbow, David 4:38:35 (21,730)
Benbow, Mark 3:27:03 (4,339)
Benbow, Piers 3:49:53 (9,148)
Bence Trower, Nicholas 4:59:12 (26,163)
Bench, Geoffrey 4:12:46 (15,034)
Bendall, Jeffrey 4:55:06 (25,391)
Bendicto, Pierre 4:21:36 (17,283)
Bending, Matthew 3:50:44 (9,356)
Bending, Richard 5:20:28 (28,934)
Bendle, Stephen 3:48:13 (8,677)
Benedict, Jerome 7:10:26 (32,706)
Benes, Robert 3:49:50 (9,137)
Benfredj, Sacha 4:01:08 (12,345)
Benge, Stephen 5:09:32 (27,636)
Benham, Kevin 4:29:44 (19,520)
Benham, Matthew 5:26:53 (29,513)
Benham-Crosswell, Patrick 5:36:33 (30,313)
Benigni, Michel 3:10:19 (2,079)
Benigni, Raul 4:41:03 (22,362)
Benmore, Michael 4:12:09 (14,891)
Bennett, Alexander 5:07:51 (27,414)
Bennett, Andrew 3:18:49 (3,114)
Bennett, Barry 3:26:57 (4,321)
Bennett, Brian 5:02:55 (26,729)
Bennett, Clive 4:01:03 (12,328)
Bennett, Colin 3:58:27 (11,635)
Bennett, Conrad 4:10:11 (14,435)
Bennett, Daniel 4:29:23 (19,432)
Bennett, David 3:46:30 (8,285)
Bennett, David 4:33:43 (20,519)
Bennett, Gordon 4:38:08 (21,609)
Bennett, Hamish 4:44:43 (23,226)
Bennett, Hugh 4:47:12 (23,856)
Bennett, Ian 3:38:18 (6,370)
Bennett, Jason 5:52:41 (31,263)
Bennett, Jeremy 3:34:49 (5,679)
Bennett, Jonathan 4:26:45 (18,731)
Bennett, Jonathan 4:34:42 (20,750)
Bennett, Keith 4:46:19 (23,639)
Bennett, Kevin 2:54:49 (729)
Bennett, Kevin 5:10:10 (27,714)
Bennett, Mark 4:21:02 (17,123)
Bennett, Mark 5:04:46 (26,994)
Bennett, Martin 4:48:25 (24,108)
Bennett, Matt 4:29:22 (19,424)
Bennett, Nikki 4:45:13 (23,361)
Bennett, Paul 4:02:31 (12,659)
Bennett, Paul 4:29:02 (19,330)
Bennett, Peter 3:49:24 (9,005)
Bennett, Peter 4:23:46 (17,907)
Bennett, Peter 4:37:06 (21,337)
Bennett, Richard 3:43:25 (7,502)
Bennett, Richard 4:04:43 (13,143)
Bennett, Richard 4:23:39 (17,859)
Bennett, Robin 4:59:46 (26,271)
Bennett, Roger 2:57:13 (931)
Bennett, Seton 4:30:17 (19,669)
Bennett, Simon 5:18:40 (28,740)
Bennett, Steve 2:55:27 (777)
Bennett, Steve 4:19:51 (16,821)
Bennett, Steven 3:38:18 (6,370)
Bennett, Stuart 3:54:34 (10,478)
Bennetts, Thomas 3:21:59 (3,520)
Bennion, Chris 3:26:03 (4,157)
Bennison, Mark 5:58:43 (31,505)
Benoist, Gilles 3:31:49 (5,167)
Benschneider, Robert 3:38:14 (6,351)
Benschneider, Ron 4:48:48 (24,197)
Benskin, Ian 2:58:01 (1,009)
Benson, Ian 2:54:39 (721)
Benson, Kenneth 4:21:59 (17,389)
Benson, Mark 3:52:29 (9,831)
Benson, Rodney 5:49:59 (31,142)
Benson, Stephen 3:11:01 (2,156)
Bent, Alan 3:24:13 (3,866)
Bent, Graham 3:41:06 (6,988)
Bentata, Robert 4:43:10 (22,885)
Bentley, Alex 3:35:06 (5,732)
Bentley, Andrew 4:06:22 (13,536)
Bentley, Anthony 2:48:23 (422)
Bentley, Gary 4:47:59 (24,024)
Bentley, Glenn 4:08:35 (14,051)
Bentley, Kenny 6:21:58 (32,122)
Bentley, Lee 4:25:53 (18,482)
Bentley, Mark 3:04:30 (1,504)
Bentley, Peter 6:19:50 (32,078)
Bentley, Robin 2:28:47 (53)
Bentley, Stephen 6:19:50 (32,078)
Bentley, Stuart 3:28:27 (4,597)
Benton, Brian 3:59:52 (12,046)
Benton, Mark 4:49:13 (24,278)
Benton, Perry 5:29:47 (29,761)
Benton, Phil 4:26:59 (18,782)
Benyon, Mark 4:31:01 (19,831)
Ben-Zui, Nizan 3:29:45 (4,837)
Beran, David 3:45:48 (8,120)
Berben, Jack 4:14:01 (15,316)
Beresford, Jeff 3:55:58 (10,889)
Beresford, Nick 4:58:11 (25,982)
Berezicki, Mark 5:20:40 (28,957)
Bergant, Sigibert 3:43:42 (7,574)
Berger, Florian 4:55:44 (25,527)
Berger, Joerg 3:33:50 (5,484)
Berger, Steve 3:38:56 (6,510)
Bergin, John 3:54:14 (10,379)
Bergin, Patrick 3:54:05 (10,341)
Bergin, Steve 4:35:58 (21,071)
Beringer, Richard 4:07:16 (13,737)
Berkius, Dennis 5:12:44 (28,050)
Berks, Lloyd 4:19:48 (16,804)
Berland, Dominique 3:13:37 (2,517)
Berleen, Abdi Karim 4:03:56 (12,971)
Berman, Daniel 5:36:39 (30,323)
Bernadotte, Edward 5:51:25 (31,210)
Bernaert, Bart 3:34:34 (5,630)
Bernard, Ralph 5:07:53 (27,422)
Bernardini, Oliviero 3:08:49 (1,910)
Berney, Mark 5:03:51 (26,865)
Bernhardt, Mark 3:13:01 (2,434)
Bernini, Sergio 5:31:51 (29,940)
Berridge, James 4:15:59 (15,833)
Berridge, Vincent 4:30:04 (19,615)
Berrill, Nick 2:33:54 (88)
Berrios, Benjamin 3:05:21 (1,573)
Berry, Adam 3:56:36 (11,086)
Berry, Andrew 4:12:34 (14,984)
Berry, Andrew 4:17:05 (16,139)
Berry, David 4:32:42 (20,277)
Berry, David 4:35:28 (20,936)
Berry, Derek 3:46:28 (8,269)
Berry, Ian 4:05:07 (13,235)
Berry, Jason 4:33:56 (20,564)
Berry, Leslie 3:57:37 (11,400)
Berry, Malcolm 4:19:21 (16,677)
Berry, Paul 5:10:51 (27,797)
Berry, Richard 3:37:54 (6,298)
Berry, Roger 3:17:43 (2,979)
Berry, Stephen 4:29:15 (19,398)
Bertelsen, Michael 3:55:07 (10,637)
Bertenshaw, James 4:05:50 (13,398)
Bertram, James 6:06:49 (31,753)
Bertram, Neil 3:52:40 (9,887)
Bertrand, Herve 4:08:12 (13,950)
Berwick, Peter 4:45:40 (23,484)
Besarani, Oler 5:26:47 (29,508)
Besford, Robert 4:28:26 (19,152)
Besley, Adrian 4:56:46 (25,726)
Best, Andrew 4:32:46 (20,294)
Best, Barry 5:07:07 (27,317)
Best, Dvid 3:55:55 (10,877)
Best, Richard 3:57:48 (11,449)
Best, Steven 5:36:22 (30,301)
Bestel, Brian 4:20:06 (16,888)
Bester, Burger 2:53:56 (681)
Bester, Hendrik 3:45:38 (8,077)
Bett, Tim 4:10:49 (14,586)
Betteridge, Lee 3:40:45 (6,909)
Betteridge, Timothy 4:12:39 (15,012)
Bettis, Perry 4:14:02 (15,324)
Bettoni, Aldo 3:25:12 (4,015)
Bettridge, Edgar 5:08:55 (27,559)
Betts, Brian 4:34:25 (20,676)
Betts, Chris 4:39:22 (21,939)
Betts, Jonathan 3:51:05 (9,453)
Betts, Mark 3:30:42 (4,979)
Betts, Michael 4:25:08 (18,295)
Betts, Philip 4:21:28 (17,238)
Betts, Roland 3:36:16 (5,969)
Betts, Russell 3:53:08 (10,025)
Betty, Mark 3:23:30 (3,727)
Betzmeier, Andreas 3:14:00 (2,558)
Bevan, Andrew 3:33:07 (5,368)
Bevan, Andy 3:13:27 (2,498)
Bevan, Jonathan 4:00:15 (12,143)
Bevan, Neil 3:34:05 (5,537)
Bevan, Nigel 4:37:28 (21,439)
Bevan, Paul 4:19:26 (16,700)
Bevan, Philip 3:59:24 (11,919)

Bevan, Richard....5:23:34 (29,229)
Bevan, Robert....6:21:10 (32,110)
Bevan, Steve....3:37:21 (6,176)
Beveridge, Alisdair....4:26:14 (18,586)
Beveridge, Alister....3:21:42 (3,463)
Beveridge, Andrew....5:54:48 (31,343)
Beveridge, David....3:43:12 (7,442)
Beveridge, Dominic....4:38:18 (21,655)
Beveridge, Gavin....5:44:32 (30,859)
Bevington, Victor....3:48:45 (8,829)
Beyer, Michael....5:29:37 (29,752)
Beyer, Stefan....4:27:49 (18,987)
Beyer, Trevelyan....3:47:10 (8,426)
Beylerian, Vincent....2:56:47 (900)
Beynon, Robert....5:03:40 (26,839)
Bhairam, Robin....4:31:46 (20,026)
Bhalla, Vikas....5:29:04 (29,699)
Bhamra, Bhupinder....5:57:56 (31,473)
Bharath, Gurmail....5:45:12 (30,897)
Bhatti, Pardeep....5:10:43 (27,777)
Bhojani, Yogesh....5:33:36 (30,077)
Bhumber, Satbinder....6:04:47 (31,687)
Bhysan, Lokman....5:36:52 (30,340)
Biancardi, Ettore....5:31:50 (29,937)
Bianconi, Giulio....4:40:45 (22,295)
Bibbey, George....4:15:29 (15,689)
Bibby, Christopher....4:04:58 (13,202)
Bibby, Jay....5:43:57 (30,815)
Bibby, Jonathan....3:54:45 (10,537)
Bibby, Keith....3:53:37 (10,182)
Bibby, Paul....4:42:48 (22,791)
Bibby, Paul....4:45:47 (23,512)
Bibby, Trevor....3:13:16 (2,469)
Bickerdike, Leigh....3:38:00 (6,313)
Bickerstaff, Ross....3:34:20 (5,587)
Bickerstaffe, Philip....4:54:33 (25,292)
Bickerton, Michael....5:12:07 (27,966)
Bickle, Andrew....3:49:19 (8,977)
Bickley, Arthur....4:51:10 (24,643)
Bickley, Simon....4:05:48 (13,393)
Bicknell, Andrew....4:40:25 (22,218)
Bicknell, Colin....4:33:26 (20,448)
Bicknell, Martin....4:03:47 (12,936)
Bicknell, Richard....4:03:10 (12,808)
Biddle, Chris....4:24:55 (18,230)
Biddle, David....3:55:37 (10,789)
Biddlecombe, Andrew....5:33:45 (30,087)
Biddlecombe, Brian....4:25:55 (18,493)
Bidgood, Harry....3:46:59 (8,378)
Bidston, Mark....3:36:57 (6,107)
Bidwell, Tobias....4:14:48 (15,526)
Bieris, Stan....3:53:13 (10,048)
Bierton, Andrew....3:20:30 (3,312)
Bierton, Philip....3:47:10 (8,426)
Biggart, Douglas....4:48:48 (24,197)
Biggin, Charles....5:19:57 (28,871)
Biggs, Geoff....3:51:01 (9,433)
Biggs, Gerard....4:02:30 (12,654)
Biggs, Jeffrey....3:54:41 (10,511)
Biggs, Richard....3:53:04 (10,003)
Biggs, Roger....3:55:55 (10,877)
Biggs, Tony....3:51:49 (9,628)
Bigland, Philip....4:40:19 (22,187)
Bigley, Andrew....5:40:10 (30,560)
Bignell, Philip....3:46:53 (8,364)
Bihr, Laurent....3:20:41 (3,335)
Bildosola-San Martin, Pedro....4:14:25 (15,429)
Biles, Dominic....4:05:32 (13,335)
Biles, Gavin....2:48:11 (411)
Bill, Gary....5:20:18 (28,915)
Bill, Rolf....3:38:53 (6,499)
Billa, Bernard....4:14:58 (15,565)
Billesdon, Robert....3:58:55 (11,767)
Billing, David....3:55:05 (10,619)
Billing, Mark....4:14:52 (15,542)
Billing, Shaun....3:02:50 (1,358)
Billings, Michael....5:08:16 (27,467)
Billingsley, Andrew....4:38:07 (21,605)
Billois, Henri-François....3:53:02 (9,994)
Bills, David....4:20:35 (17,019)
Billson, Simon....3:25:53 (4,133)
Bilsborough, Brian....2:54:38 (718)
Bilton, Darran....2:21:23 (26)

Bimson, Kevin....4:05:11 (13,248)
Binder, Simon....4:27:04 (18,810)
Bindseil, Jimmy....4:09:53 (14,360)
Binfield, Paul....4:07:15 (13,734)
Bingham, Hugh....2:51:06 (537)
Bingham, John....5:11:39 (27,901)
Bingham, John....5:36:36 (30,320)
Bingham, Julian....4:29:59 (19,591)
Bingham, Kit....3:37:03 (6,131)
Bingham, Stuart....3:25:49 (4,114)
Bingley, Kenneth....3:42:11 (7,196)
Binks, David....3:55:41 (10,803)
Binnie, Colin....4:34:14 (20,636)
Binnie, David....4:32:33 (20,228)
Binnie, Graeme....5:02:04 (26,613)
Binning, Peter....3:47:38 (8,544)
Binns, Charles....4:44:10 (23,099)
Birch, Alexander....4:14:49 (15,529)
Birch, Andrew....3:57:48 (11,449)
Birch, Brendan....5:21:14 (29,022)
Birch, Craig....4:59:30 (26,216)
Birch, David....2:57:19 (939)
Birch, John....3:22:41 (3,606)
Birch, Malcolm....4:06:03 (13,445)
Birch, Nigel....4:29:26 (19,444)
Birch, Richard....3:30:15 (4,901)
Birch, Robert....5:44:16 (30,837)
Birch, Simon....3:38:36 (6,450)
Birch, Steve....3:11:40 (2,224)
Birch, Stuart....5:52:28 (31,254)
Birch, Tom....3:36:01 (5,907)
Birchall, Grahame....4:42:52 (22,807)
Bircham, Philip....3:02:22 (1,331)
Bircher, Martin....4:26:36 (18,680)
Bird, Bryn....5:12:15 (27,984)
Bird, Danny....2:54:23 (699)
Bird, David....3:45:02 (7,933)
Bird, Geoff....3:41:10 (7,003)
Bird, Jonathan....3:36:30 (6,026)
Bird, Mark....3:06:53 (1,722)
Bird, Martin....4:22:23 (17,512)
Bird, Matthew....5:05:51 (27,135)
Bird, Michael....4:32:34 (20,234)
Bird, Niall....3:33:19 (5,403)
Bird, Robert....4:52:40 (24,908)
Bird, Shaun....2:55:54 (819)
Bird, Thomas....3:53:50 (10,261)
Birditt, Julian....5:26:12 (29,463)
Birds, David....3:25:59 (4,153)
Birdsall, Peter....5:20:43 (28,963)
Birkby, David....4:08:57 (14,121)
Birkett, Fred....4:27:07 (18,822)
Birkett, Stephen....3:53:32 (10,157)
Birkhead, Guy....3:52:32 (9,849)
Birks, David....3:23:28 (3,719)
Birmingham, Tim....4:02:30 (12,654)
Birney, Christopher....4:10:48 (14,576)
Birnie, Derek....3:56:48 (11,144)
Birts, Charles....4:43:55 (23,048)
Birtwell, Stuart....3:38:33 (6,440)
Bisatt, Alistair....3:29:20 (4,761)
Bischoff, Marcus....4:05:45 (13,380)
Biscomb, Geoffrey....3:08:04 (1,812)
Bishop, Alan....5:44:08 (30,829)
Bishop, Benjamin....5:21:00 (28,989)
Bishop, Christopher....5:10:33 (27,756)
Bishop, David....3:34:43 (5,662)
Bishop, David....4:48:29 (24,123)
Bishop, Jeremy....4:43:39 (22,986)
Bishop, Jonathan....3:16:43 (2,866)
Bishop, Murray....3:49:14 (8,950)
Bishop, Nigel....4:27:16 (18,856)
Bishop, Robert....5:27:18 (29,558)
Bishop, Ronald....6:50:13 (32,544)
Bishop, Stephen....3:26:26 (4,217)
Bishop, Timothy....2:58:37 (1,058)
Bisley, William....4:16:10 (15,881)
Bissell, Matthew....4:34:53 (20,798)
Bissell, Peter....3:43:38 (7,559)
Bisset, Gordon....3:40:33 (6,863)
Bissett, Mark....3:49:26 (9,021)
Bissett, Trevor....3:44:31 (7,797)
Bisson, Christopher....4:53:49 (25,124)

Bithell, David....4:05:12 (13,254)
Bithell, Mark....4:29:56 (19,581)
Bittianda, Kal....3:38:29 (6,418)
Bittles, Kevin....5:05:00 (27,021)
Bizio, Marcello....3:45:33 (8,062)
Bizjak, Joseph....4:59:42 (26,265)
Bjarnason, Stefan....4:55:38 (25,499)
Bjork, Stephen....3:00:07 (1,178)
Bjorkman, Anders....6:04:27 (31,671)
Bjornemark, Thomas....3:59:11 (11,849)
Black, Alan....4:39:44 (22,037)
Black, Alistair....3:53:47 (10,237)
Black, Ben....5:17:15 (28,594)
Black, Darren....4:29:37 (19,490)
Black, Douglas....3:25:11 (4,012)
Black, Ewan....6:01:04 (31,579)
Black, Gary....3:59:47 (12,019)
Black, Ian....4:36:38 (21,249)
Black, Ian....4:43:45 (23,004)
Black, John....3:46:23 (8,246)
Blackbourn, Maurice....5:28:52 (29,684)
Blackburn, David....4:50:51 (24,580)
Blackburn, Ian....3:24:31 (3,923)
Blackburn, John....4:31:10 (19,874)
Blackburn, Jonathan....5:19:36 (28,829)
Blackburn, Martin....4:23:47 (17,913)
Blackburn, Paul....3:48:07 (8,656)
Blackburn, Peter....3:09:05 (1,941)
Blackburn, Richard....3:31:06 (5,049)
Blackburn, Robert....6:12:39 (31,896)
Blackburn, Simon....3:58:57 (11,779)
Blackledge, John....2:52:53 (624)
Blackley, David....4:01:13 (12,370)
Blackman, Clive....3:18:41 (3,095)
Blackman, Gary....3:54:43 (10,519)
Blackman, Matt....2:56:22 (863)
Blackman, Roger....4:19:54 (16,836)
Blackman, Roger....4:28:53 (19,284)
Blackmore, Edward....4:43:09 (22,881)
Blackmore, Peter....4:31:40 (20,003)
Blackmore, Peter....4:43:26 (22,940)
Blackshaw, James....4:02:47 (12,725)
Blackshaw, Trevor....4:29:49 (19,543)
Blackwell, Nicholas....3:13:21 (2,485)
Blacoe, Matthew....2:52:51 (622)
Blades, Richard....3:14:44 (2,632)
Blagg, Matthew....2:57:58 (1,003)
Blaine, John....3:05:55 (1,635)
Blair, Graeme....3:25:52 (4,128)
Blair, John....4:57:32 (25,868)
Blair, Paul....3:18:02 (3,013)
Blake, Cole....4:08:59 (14,127)
Blake, James....5:10:48 (27,784)
Blake, Kevin....4:03:53 (12,961)
Blake, Mark....4:22:28 (17,538)
Blake, Paul....4:19:08 (16,627)
Blakeley, David....2:53:03 (630)
Blakeley, Eric....3:56:42 (11,109)
Blakeman, Richard....4:35:05 (20,851)
Blakemore, John....4:59:04 (26,143)
Blakey, Brian....4:07:08 (13,701)
Bland, David....5:00:38 (26,393)
Bland, Martin....3:14:50 (2,646)
Bland, Richard....5:34:18 (30,132)
Bland, Roger....3:55:32 (10,758)
Blank, Jeremy....6:06:50 (31,754)
Blanks, Gary....4:28:13 (19,088)
Blard, Jean....3:11:43 (2,229)
Blascyk, Thomas....4:09:26 (14,261)
Blatchford, Chris....5:17:20 (28,608)
Blatchford, Ian....4:20:09 (16,905)
Blatchford, Tony....5:17:20 (28,608)
Blaxill, Keith....4:35:33 (20,960)
Blaylock, Leslie....3:32:09 (5,215)
Blaylock, Stuart....4:48:28 (24,118)
Blazey, Nigel....5:01:56 (26,594)
Blazier, Darren....2:54:10 (687)
Blazquez, Diego....3:28:58 (4,693)
Bleasdale, Craig....4:08:33 (14,041)
Bleich, Guenter....3:49:26 (9,021)
Blencowe, Rupert....4:45:58 (23,555)
Blenkhorn, John....3:50:02 (9,175)
Blenkinsopp, John....4:22:08 (17,431)

Blenkinsopp, Kevin....4:23:05 (17,726)
Blessett, Matthew....4:07:08 (13,701)
Bletso, St John of....4:15:00 (15,576)
Blewitt, Dan....2:51:12 (543)
Bliss, Owen....4:40:21 (22,199)
Bliss, Robert....5:07:04 (27,306)
Blissett, Stephen....4:25:06 (18,286)
Blizzard, Sean....4:31:58 (20,075)
Bloch, Graeme....4:35:47 (21,025)
Block, Jens....2:52:34 (601)
Block, Robert....3:37:58 (6,307)
Bloemendaal, Gerrit....5:38:33 (30,452)
Blomley, Martin....4:40:15 (22,170)
Bloomfield, Clive....5:47:06 (30,993)
Bloomfield, Colin....3:28:22 (4,583)
Bloomfield, Phil....5:22:05 (29,098)
Bloomfield, Scott....5:05:43 (27,115)
Bloomfields, Thomas....3:22:36 (3,594)
Bloor, Kenneth....2:55:10 (757)
Blors, Richard....5:35:15 (30,204)
Blow, Peter....4:07:31 (13,802)
Blower, Richard....4:26:59 (18,782)
Blower, Simon....3:52:25 (9,815)
Bloye, Graham....5:22:57 (29,172)
Bluck, Trevor....4:33:10 (20,394)
Blum, Edgar....3:44:37 (7,827)
Blundell, Guy....3:09:53 (2,025)
Blundell, Mark....4:16:38 (16,019)
Blundell, Michael....5:21:29 (29,042)
Blundell, Rodger....3:11:51 (2,252)
Blunden, Lee....3:37:55 (6,299)
Blunden, Martin....3:29:49 (4,843)
Blunden, William....5:50:47 (31,173)
Blunden, William....5:50:47 (31,173)
Blundll, Ian....5:07:58 (27,433)
Blunt, David....4:41:48 (22,556)
Blurton, Richard....3:50:57 (9,411)
Blyth, Andrew....3:20:22 (3,298)
Blyth, Ben....4:34:50 (20,788)
Blythman, Mark....4:32:32 (20,225)
Boa, Philip....5:35:36 (30,239)
Boakye, Christopher....4:58:43 (26,082)
Boar, Chris....5:12:47 (28,054)
Board, Anthony....3:33:56 (5,504)
Board, Nigel....3:19:09 (3,156)
Board, Phillip....4:32:40 (20,269)
Boarder, Timothy....5:12:02 (27,959)
Boardley, Ian....3:13:59 (2,557)
Boardley, Neal....3:17:29 (2,956)
Boardman, Allan....4:18:47 (16,541)
Boardman, Keith....2:53:51 (670)
Boardman, Mark....3:54:03 (10,326)
Boardman, Mark....4:12:08 (14,887)
Boardman, Martin....4:18:24 (16,467)
Bober, Richard....3:09:45 (2,012)
Bobia, Philip....4:46:33 (23,702)
Bocchetti, Katio....4:14:21 (15,409)
Bock, Clive....3:37:42 (6,260)
Bockenheim, Zygmunt....3:40:03 (6,744)
Bocock, Barnaby....3:52:41 (9,893)
Boddy, Clifford....5:01:08 (26,473)
Boddy, James....5:21:38 (29,061)
Boddy, Michael....3:19:35 (3,212)
Bode, Hans....3:34:24 (5,598)
Boden, Marc....4:16:24 (15,952)
Boden, Mark....4:26:44 (18,726)
Bodenhausen, Johannes....5:04:39 (26,971)
Body, James....3:59:18 (11,885)
Boeckl, Gottfried....3:36:13 (5,960)
Boer, Stefan....3:08:03 (1,810)
Boerresen, Oeyvind....4:31:31 (19,972)
Boers, Gerthan....4:10:52 (14,597)
Boffin, Charles....3:20:10 (3,274)
Bogner, Joachim....3:05:05 (1,554)
Bogue, James....3:36:16 (5,969)
Bohr, Gerard....3:55:42 (10,812)
Boice, Matthew....3:42:13 (7,204)
Boileau, Remi....3:14:59 (2,666)
Boisseau, Matthew....5:33:51 (30,096)
Boitier, Jean....3:15:33 (2,729)
Boittier, Richard....3:59:11 (11,849)
Bolam, George....2:58:15 (1,028)
Bolam, John....3:54:33 (10,472)
Bolas, Jason....4:41:45 (22,543)
Bolch, Richard....4:01:19 (12,396)
Bolden, David....3:55:15 (10,679)
Bolding, Paul....4:15:03 (15,585)
Boldry, Roger....4:41:48 (22,556)
Bole, Robert....2:55:33 (784)
Boley, Stephen....4:21:28 (17,238)
Bolger, Carl....4:10:45 (14,562)
Bolger, P....3:14:28 (2,610)
Bolger, Sean....4:11:15 (14,682)
Bollen, Mark....4:20:08 (16,896)
Bolley, Ian....5:35:13 (30,202)
Bolliger, Adolf....6:12:28 (31,894)
Bolos, José Angel....3:22:42 (3,610)
Bolster, Eric....3:45:24 (8,021)
Bolt, Jeremy....4:20:32 (17,000)
Bolt, Nigel....3:06:42 (1,706)
Bolt, Richard....4:06:59 (13,674)
Bolton, Andrew....3:21:15 (3,399)
Bolton, Andrew....4:39:47 (22,051)
Bolton, Andrew....4:48:51 (24,206)
Bolton, Christopher....4:03:13 (12,819)
Bolton, David....4:50:41 (24,540)
Bolton, Karl....4:49:01 (24,237)
Bolton, Peter....4:04:55 (13,189)
Bolton, Sean....3:58:35 (11,671)
Bolton, Simon....3:17:53 (2,998)
Bolton, Stephen....3:16:14 (2,812)
Bolton, Stuart....4:21:11 (17,162)
Bolton, Wayne....3:28:38 (4,631)
Bonassi, Luciano....3:28:47 (4,658)
Bond, Allan....4:34:51 (20,791)
Bond, Andrew....4:18:29 (16,482)
Bond, Derek....4:24:39 (18,159)
Bond, Edward....3:45:32 (8,054)
Bond, Gary....4:34:01 (20,582)
Bond, Graham....3:42:46 (7,335)
Bond, Ian....3:46:18 (8,225)
Bond, Ian....4:19:44 (16,785)
Bond, Jamie....3:31:24 (5,092)
Bond, Kevin....4:34:27 (20,682)
Bond, Michael....3:41:33 (7,074)
Bond, Paul....3:22:11 (3,548)
Bond, Rick....3:28:00 (4,516)
Bond, Robert....4:18:56 (16,578)
Bond Gunning, Heyrick....3:17:56 (3,002)
Bondy, Michael....4:46:51 (23,772)
Bone, John....4:37:11 (21,365)
Bone, Kenneth....4:30:59 (19,826)
Bone, Peter....4:56:59 (25,763)
Bonecchi, Adalberto....7:11:22 (32,715)
Boner, Dennis....4:36:24 (21,190)
Bonfield, Richard....3:10:55 (2,144)
Bongiovanni, Claudio....3:55:10 (10,653)
Bonham, Neil....5:52:27 (31,251)
Boniface, David....4:22:39 (17,588)
Bonifazi, Gerhard....3:59:38 (11,977)
Bonmati-Molina, Rafael....3:47:34 (8,530)
Bonnard, Louis....3:44:32 (7,804)
Bonnema, Elsje....4:40:32 (22,239)
Bonner, Clive....3:34:07 (5,546)
Bonner, Clive....4:57:02 (25,774)
Bonner, Dannie....3:56:03 (10,913)
Bonner, Neal....3:28:06 (4,532)
Bonner, Philip....4:41:17 (22,423)
Bonner, Richard....4:13:23 (15,162)
Bonnichon, Pascal....5:11:15 (27,845)
Bonoldi, Achille....4:42:15 (22,659)
Bontoft, Alan....2:56:13 (847)
Bonzi, Franco....4:45:12 (23,356)
Boobyer, Richard....5:07:57 (27,430)
Booker, Alex....3:54:48 (10,541)
Booker, John....3:30:35 (4,958)
Booker, Philip....4:44:38 (23,202)
Boole, Barry....3:29:38 (4,818)
Booley, Matthew....3:52:00 (9,683)
Boon, Clive....5:28:17 (29,635)
Boon, Richard....3:08:21 (1,846)
Boon, Robert....3:11:01 (2,156)
Boonstra, Thomas....4:39:49 (22,062)
Boorer, Bryan....3:50:52 (9,396)
Boot, David....2:50:45 (523)
Booter, Joel....6:15:24 (31,966)
Booth, Andrew....4:28:44 (19,236)
Booth, Anthony....3:38:58 (6,515)
Booth, David....3:44:37 (7,827)
Booth, Gordon....4:29:39 (19,495)
Booth, Graham....3:36:57 (6,107)
Booth, James....3:54:07 (10,351)
Booth, John....4:14:56 (15,558)
Booth, Mark....5:13:07 (28,095)
Booth, Michael....4:42:03 (22,622)
Booth, Peter....3:56:34 (11,075)
Booth, Richard....3:56:20 (11,001)
Booth, Roger....2:51:18 (550)
Booth, Simon....4:12:44 (15,029)
Booth, Vincent....2:48:11 (411)
Booth, William....3:43:41 (7,568)
Boothryd, Richard....3:13:37 (2,517)
Booty, Graham....3:28:32 (4,613)
Bording, Keld....3:15:18 (2,701)
Borella, Mauro....4:36:07 (21,106)
Borer, Matthew....4:31:23 (19,926)
Borg, Alan....4:33:22 (20,432)
Borg, Gunnar....4:57:30 (25,856)
Borges, Jean....3:40:03 (6,744)
Borgund, Ole....4:36:02 (21,088)
Borland, John....4:14:34 (15,460)
Borrero Gomez, José....3:12:08 (2,301)
Borri, Alessandro....4:10:29 (14,507)
Borrington, Richard....4:36:52 (21,292)
Bortolin, Vittorino....3:42:24 (7,262)
Bortoluzzi, Piertro....4:41:54 (22,585)
Bos, Kees....3:44:03 (7,668)
Bos, Michael....4:38:12 (21,626)
Bosch, Ulf....2:47:37 (385)
Boscher, José....4:09:22 (14,242)
Bose, Anil....5:04:16 (26,930)
Boserup, Sored....4:00:50 (12,262)
Bosley, Philip....4:16:03 (15,851)
Bosley, Stuart....3:56:51 (11,159)
Bossar, Albert....3:32:33 (5,278)
Bossard, Sebastien....3:39:37 (6,649)
Bossetti, Martino....3:24:02 (3,830)
Bosshard, Bruno....4:46:33 (23,702)
Bosson, Paul....3:01:28 (1,257)
Bosson, Peter....4:55:39 (25,504)
Bostelmann, David....3:52:31 (9,842)
Bostock, Colin....3:21:31 (3,438)
Boston, David....4:02:19 (12,619)
Boswell, Guy....3:47:19 (8,464)
Boswell, Scott....4:25:19 (18,341)
Boswell, Stuart....3:01:02 (1,227)
Botfield, Andrew....3:56:57 (11,192)
Botfield, Glyn....4:01:51 (12,535)
Botfield, Howard....6:07:09 (31,765)
Botham, Andrew....3:36:03 (5,915)
Bothwell, Ashley....4:03:14 (12,822)
Botschen, Siegfried....3:25:49 (4,114)
Bottle, Simon....3:20:46 (3,341)
Bottomley, Edward....5:26:57 (29,518)
Bottomley, Philip....4:06:16 (13,509)
Boucher, Ian....4:05:15 (13,262)
Boucher, Pascal....4:34:22 (20,664)
Boucherie, Fabrice....3:20:17 (3,290)
Bouchet, Alain....3:42:56 (7,366)
Bouchez, Christophe....4:36:07 (21,106)
Bouday, Luc....3:12:34 (2,370)
Boudeau, Nicolas....3:32:04 (5,202)
Boudry, Rik....3:24:06 (3,837)
Bougara, Robert....4:09:59 (14,380)
Boughton, Brian....5:53:11 (31,285)
Boughton, Stephen....4:35:14 (20,893)
Bougourd, Bruce....4:03:03 (12,792)
Bould, Daniel....4:08:42 (14,079)
Bouldstridge, David....3:41:32 (7,070)
Bouldstridge, Peter....3:33:58 (5,513)
Boullard, Jerome....3:48:15 (8,685)
Boult, John....4:42:53 (22,811)
Boulter, Adam....3:58:59 (11,796)
Boulter, Jonathan....5:11:42 (27,906)
Boulter, Kevin....3:13:02 (2,437)
Boulton, Chris....4:10:55 (14,612)
Boulton, Christopher....3:29:35 (4,811)
Boulton, Richard....3:29:19 (4,757)
Boulton, Richard....5:20:35 (28,948)

Name	Time	(Position)
Bound, John	5:28:19	(29,640)
Bourdon, Didier	5:03:01	(26,746)
Bourgeois, Mark	3:56:14	(10,975)
Bourges, Didier	3:41:19	(7,034)
Bourges, Didier	4:43:04	(22,856)
Bouri, Chan	6:17:49	(32,027)
Bourne, Adrian	4:53:55	(25,160)
Bourne, Gareth	4:06:35	(13,583)
Bourne, Geoffrey	3:23:20	(3,700)
Bourne, James	2:57:11	(928)
Bourne, Martin	4:50:46	(24,553)
Bourne, Patrick	4:48:18	(24,084)
Bourne, Richard	5:45:52	(30,927)
Bourne, Ronnie	6:23:52	(32,164)
Bourne, Simon	3:46:00	(8,161)
Bourne-Lange, Robert	5:09:33	(27,638)
Bousfield, Mark	4:02:55	(12,758)
Boutcher, Jonathan	4:32:41	(20,272)
Bouttell, Christopher	3:03:29	(1,419)
Bouveng, Stuart	2:49:34	(466)
Bouvier, Guy	4:58:16	(25,992)
Bowd, Ryan	3:04:05	(1,473)
Bowden, Gary	3:11:25	(2,193)
Bowden, Jeremy	5:30:07	(29,789)
Bowden, Keir	4:39:47	(22,051)
Bowden, Michael	4:40:46	(22,300)
Bowden, Peter	4:10:14	(14,446)
Bowden, William	4:14:35	(15,467)
Bowdenb, Shaun	4:27:03	(18,805)
Bowder, Jonathan	3:49:49	(9,135)
Bowdrey, Russell	3:25:49	(4,114)
Bowen, Adam	3:54:29	(10,453)
Bowen, Anthony	3:57:12	(11,263)
Bowen, David	3:18:38	(3,089)
Bowen, Eugene	4:44:52	(23,263)
Bowen, Keith	3:31:55	(5,176)
Bowen, Leslie	4:40:25	(22,218)
Bowen, Paul	3:38:40	(6,468)
Bowen, Sean	3:04:59	(1,542)
Bowen, Simon	3:39:22	(6,600)
Bowen, Spencer	3:53:15	(10,061)
Bowen, Stephen	4:02:38	(12,688)
Bower, Robert	3:54:15	(10,386)
Bowerman, John	4:20:15	(16,926)
Bowers, Joe	4:32:57	(20,345)
Bowes, Christopher	3:17:38	(2,967)
Bowes, Damian	4:06:02	(13,442)
Bowes, Stephen	3:04:40	(1,515)
Bowker, Andrew	3:55:35	(10,778)
Bowker, David	4:08:52	(14,107)
Bowker, Robert	4:12:44	(15,029)
Bowler, Dean	4:27:13	(18,847)
Bowles, John	3:48:11	(8,670)
Bowles, Keith	3:47:29	(8,505)
Bowles, Philip	4:47:37	(23,930)
Bowles, Steve	4:07:27	(13,788)
Bowles, Steven	3:35:14	(5,751)
Bowley, Philip	5:04:49	(27,004)
Bowley, Steven	3:33:45	(5,465)
Bowlzer, Nicholas	3:50:50	(9,382)
Bowman, Graham	3:39:47	(6,682)
Bowman, Scott	5:47:50	(31,030)
Bown, Nicholas	4:48:39	(24,156)
Bownes, Kevin	3:38:16	(6,362)
Bowron, Ian	4:15:15	(15,633)
Bowsher, Simon	4:22:15	(17,462)
Bowyer, Andrew	4:01:42	(12,493)
Bowyer, Malcolm	3:05:28	(1,586)
Box, Martin	5:07:13	(27,335)
Box, Matthew	3:03:07	(1,382)
Box, Nicholas	4:49:41	(24,357)
Boxall, Dennis	3:23:39	(3,753)
Boxall, Gordon	3:54:08	(10,358)
Boxall, John	3:57:18	(11,293)
Boxford, James	3:51:32	(9,555)
Boy, Peter	4:37:47	(21,517)
Boyce, Daniel	6:35:09	(32,355)
Boyce, David	2:44:31	(283)
Boyce, Edward	4:06:17	(13,516)
Boyce, James	6:15:51	(31,976)
Boyce, Jamie	5:46:00	(30,934)
Boyce, Michael	4:23:20	(17,785)
Boyce, Raymond	3:37:49	(6,282)
Boyd, Allan	4:35:51	(21,042)
Boyd, David	3:58:35	(11,671)
Boyd, James	3:28:35	(4,622)
Boyd, John	5:04:05	(26,895)
Boyd, Robin	4:10:21	(14,471)
Boyd, William	5:21:07	(29,010)
Boyer, Marc	3:25:29	(4,062)
Boyes, John	2:52:47	(618)
Boylan, Stephen	4:56:19	(25,658)
Boyle, Colin	3:38:17	(6,369)
Boyle, Darren	6:08:00	(31,784)
Boyle, Gerard	4:19:39	(16,763)
Boyle, Patrick	3:50:12	(9,215)
Boyle, Simon	5:51:19	(31,205)
Boyle, Stephen	4:01:39	(12,482)
Boyot, Franck	2:57:38	(973)
Boys, John	5:24:18	(29,307)
Bozza, John	5:02:06	(26,617)
Bozzoli, Andrea	3:56:55	(11,181)
Brabin, Frank	4:48:52	(24,212)
Bracey, Paul	3:56:55	(11,181)
Bracken, Andrew	3:32:20	(5,237)
Bracken, Andy	4:16:08	(15,873)
Bracken, Malcolm	4:48:55	(24,218)
Brackenbury, Robert	4:14:55	(15,554)
Brackpool, Phillip	4:45:46	(23,508)
Brackston, Andy	4:00:29	(12,184)
Brackstone, Mark	4:50:47	(24,556)
Bradbrook, David	3:24:17	(3,873)
Bradbury, Alan	3:11:04	(2,164)
Bradbury, Colin	5:07:06	(27,314)
Bradbury, Craig	3:38:01	(6,316)
Bradbury, Karl	3:36:59	(6,114)
Bradbury, Michael	3:41:06	(6,988)
Bradbury, Richard	4:05:02	(13,216)
Braddick, Hugo	3:58:06	(11,544)
Brader, Michael	3:41:59	(7,149)
Bradford, Antony	2:49:05	(449)
Bradford, Darren	4:01:55	(12,548)
Bradford, Malcolm	6:37:11	(32,402)
Bradford, Paul	3:57:24	(11,325)
Brading, Peter	4:38:19	(21,663)
Bradley, Anthony	5:05:47	(27,124)
Bradley, Colin	4:13:54	(15,286)
Bradley, Dean	3:46:34	(8,303)
Bradley, Gordon	3:29:19	(4,757)
Bradley, Jonathan	2:49:50	(480)
Bradley, Michael	3:51:34	(9,564)
Bradley, Mike	5:14:27	(28,239)
Bradley, Mikk	2:46:38	(346)
Bradley, Patrick	3:58:41	(11,701)
Bradley, Paul	3:21:43	(3,466)
Bradley, Paul	3:37:22	(6,181)
Bradley, Paul	5:15:39	(28,388)
Bradley, Peter	4:33:31	(20,468)
Bradley, Phillip	3:45:26	(8,027)
Bradley, Robert	3:17:11	(2,917)
Bradshaw, Allan	4:08:14	(13,957)
Bradshaw, Allan	4:29:51	(19,557)
Bradshaw, Brian	4:42:42	(22,768)
Bradshaw, Eric	3:35:24	(5,781)
Bradshaw, Gary	4:04:06	(13,008)
Bradshaw, Gavin	3:56:22	(11,009)
Bradshaw, Mark	3:59:27	(11,930)
Bradshaw, Tom	4:35:00	(20,833)
Bradwell, Andrew	5:02:46	(26,704)
Brady, Anthony	3:53:00	(9,976)
Brady, Brian	4:00:12	(12,132)
Brady, Brian	4:17:38	(16,277)
Brady, Eddie	3:45:20	(8,006)
Brady, George	4:59:23	(26,197)
Brady, Joseph	3:48:34	(8,766)
Brady, Paul	4:42:23	(22,691)
Braegger, Heinz	3:42:04	(7,170)
Braeunig, Bert	4:47:23	(23,894)
Bragg, Jeremy	3:17:19	(2,935)
Bragg, Martin	5:23:52	(29,268)
Bragg, Stephen	3:46:48	(8,343)
Bragg, Thomas	3:40:12	(6,786)
Brahams, Nigel	4:26:19	(18,601)
Brain, John	3:48:58	(8,886)
Brain, John	5:17:24	(28,617)
Brain, Paul	4:39:29	(21,965)
Brain, Robert	3:32:34	(5,282)
Braithwaite, Joe	3:47:25	(8,492)
Braithwaite, Martin	4:46:39	(23,724)
Braithwaite, Philip	4:04:34	(13,104)
Braker, Robert	4:13:38	(15,213)
Braley, Nicholas	4:09:20	(14,228)
Bramley, Mark	4:15:48	(15,780)
Bramley, Richard	4:47:44	(23,959)
Brampton, Gary	5:04:57	(27,013)
Brampton, Stuart	3:35:24	(5,781)
Branch, Malcolm	4:38:52	(21,812)
Branch, Paul	3:05:01	(1,546)
Brand, Anthony	3:38:03	(6,322)
Brand, Joop	4:06:51	(13,638)
Brand, Julian	3:03:55	(1,458)
Brand, Neil	4:58:25	(26,021)
Brand, Philip	4:30:02	(19,603)
Brand, Roger	3:37:53	(6,295)
Brandl, Stephen	4:36:24	(21,190)
Brandon, Mark	4:29:36	(19,482)
Brandon, Richard	3:12:30	(2,360)
Brandon, Steven	5:03:36	(26,835)
Brandon, Tony	8:24:09	(32,872)
Brandt, Dan	4:43:09	(22,881)
Brandtner, Gerd	4:31:27	(19,951)
Brandtner, Horst	4:31:28	(19,953)
Brandwood, Timothy	4:19:09	(16,634)
Braniff, Anthony	4:28:25	(19,142)
Brankston, Nigel	4:49:48	(24,380)
Brannac, Andrew	3:40:21	(6,824)
Brannick, Patrick	4:34:58	(20,823)
Brannigan, Malachy	4:19:00	(16,589)
Brannigan, Niall	4:22:58	(17,696)
Bransfield, Robert	5:37:01	(30,350)
Branson, Michael	3:44:24	(7,773)
Branston, Simon	3:56:47	(11,138)
Brantjes, Willem	5:39:13	(30,483)
Brash, Ian	4:18:31	(16,489)
Brash, Paul	3:53:56	(10,287)
Braude, Bruce	5:06:01	(27,160)
Braude, Jonathan	5:06:01	(27,160)
Braun, Nigel	3:50:27	(9,290)
Braund, Steve	2:57:59	(1,005)
Brauss, Michael	3:51:03	(9,442)
Brauton, David	4:55:40	(25,511)
Bravo, Eduardo	4:15:18	(15,638)
Bray, Alan	3:38:10	(6,335)
Bray, Andrew	3:37:36	(6,244)
Bray, Francis	3:11:40	(2,224)
Bray, Kevin	2:57:10	(926)
Bray, Kevin	4:18:52	(16,563)
Bray, Michael	3:59:22	(11,906)
Bray, Robert	4:32:45	(20,289)
Bray, Timothy	4:19:40	(16,765)
Braybrook, Andrew	4:53:21	(25,037)
Braybrooke, Tony	4:23:24	(17,802)
Braycotton, Terence	4:11:33	(14,756)
Brayford, Brian	4:53:56	(25,168)
Brazier, Simon	4:33:02	(20,360)
Brazier, Tony	3:40:31	(6,856)
Brazil, Simon	2:57:40	(977)
Breaa, Michael	3:23:36	(3,743)
Breach, Paul	3:50:28	(9,294)
Breading, Jamie	4:08:12	(13,950)
Breadner, Neil	5:07:51	(27,414)
Breakspear, Chris	4:42:02	(22,617)
Brealey, Ian	5:14:12	(28,215)
Bream, Malcolm	4:02:35	(12,675)
Brearley, Michael	3:05:10	(1,558)
Breen, Graham	2:38:24	(154)
Breen, Martin	3:43:09	(7,431)
Bremm, Simon	4:03:34	(12,895)
Bremner, John	4:50:02	(24,429)
Bremner, Richard	3:28:11	(4,548)
Brenchley, Bob	4:50:22	(24,473)
Brencio, Roberto	3:32:59	(5,351)
Brendel, Jakob	4:41:11	(22,398)
Brennan, Anthony	4:11:15	(14,682)
Brennan, Benedict	4:10:38	(14,541)
Brennan, Brian	5:32:38	(30,002)
Brennan, David	4:36:52	(21,292)
Brennan, Kevin	3:04:55	(1,536)
Brennan, Lawrence	3:33:30	(5,427)

Brennan, Neil 3:01:27 (1,256)
Brennan, Patrick 4:19:50 (16,810)
Brennan, Paul 4:15:00 (15,576)
Brennan, Peter 4:30:29 (19,707)
Brennan, Simon 4:10:17 (14,456)
Brent, Alan 5:02:49 (26,713)
Brereton, Carl 4:36:06 (21,102)
Bresjanac, Michel 4:07:31 (13,802)
Bresnahan, Daniel 4:13:15 (15,134)
Bressington, Darrell 3:57:34 (11,386)
Bretherick, Andrew 3:24:21 (3,893)
Brett, Reginald 3:07:27 (1,764)
Brett, Richard 3:42:27 (7,276)
Brewer, Damian 3:16:58 (2,899)
Brewer, David 4:14:21 (15,409)
Brewer, Geoffrey 4:00:38 (12,212)
Brewer, John 3:43:07 (7,418)
Brewer, John 5:06:43 (27,261)
Brewer, Jonathan 3:45:44 (8,096)
Brewer, Paul 4:38:49 (21,796)
Brewer, Richard 3:21:52 (3,497)
Brewis, Matthew 3:39:55 (6,714)
Brewster, Matthew 4:26:26 (18,631)
Brewster, Michael 3:55:09 (10,650)
Brewster, Philip 3:55:07 (10,637)
Brewster, Richard 5:25:51 (29,432)
Brewster, Trevor 4:40:19 (22,187)
Brey-Avalo, Luis 3:50:44 (9,356)
Briand, Stephane 3:25:35 (4,075)
Bricker, Paul 4:46:07 (23,594)
Briddon, Andrew 4:04:00 (12,989)
Bridge, Kevin 3:28:03 (4,523)
Bridge, Matthew 3:32:16 (5,229)
Bridge, Simon 3:55:04 (10,614)
Bridger, Matt 3:59:01 (11,810)
Bridger, Steve 6:08:58 (31,811)
Bridges, Andrew 5:07:54 (27,423)
Bridges, Anthony 3:32:29 (5,267)
Bridges, Christopher 5:30:32 (29,824)
Bridges, Edward 4:06:37 (13,592)
Bridges, Richard 5:57:11 (31,449)
Bridges, Russell 3:09:20 (1,973)
Bridges, Simon 4:02:57 (12,766)
Brierley, Andrew 3:40:19 (6,817)
Brierley, Andrew 3:58:50 (11,745)
Brierley, David 4:53:58 (25,179)
Brierley, Julian 4:16:16 (15,904)
Brierley, Peter 3:54:29 (10,453)
Brierley, Richard 4:34:37 (20,731)
Brierley, Trevor 4:42:20 (22,683)
Brierly, Christopher 4:41:44 (22,540)
Briffa, John 3:53:01 (9,985)
Brigginshaw, Alex 4:43:07 (22,871)
Briggs, Christopher 4:02:16 (12,609)
Briggs, David 3:09:56 (2,032)
Briggs, David 4:25:22 (18,355)
Briggs, Kevin 4:45:42 (23,494)
Briggs, Lawrence 4:15:42 (15,755)
Briggs, Michael 3:49:46 (9,121)
Briggs, Michael 4:29:28 (19,452)
Briggs, Michael 4:43:47 (23,011)
Briggs, Nicholas 4:14:31 (15,449)
Briggs, Tony 4:47:46 (23,965)
Brighetti, Claudio 3:56:56 (11,187)
Bright, Barry 3:53:31 (10,150)
Bright, David 3:27:46 (4,471)
Bright, Garry 2:49:00 (446)
Bright, Kenny 3:34:55 (5,700)
Bright, Kevin 3:26:53 (4,309)
Bright, Kevin 4:56:23 (25,675)
Bright, Neil 4:34:36 (20,726)
Bright, Nicholas 2:59:43 (1,153)
Bright, Robert 3:46:20 (8,233)
Brightley, Leo 3:21:24 (3,420)
Brightman, Adam 4:42:30 (22,725)
Brightmore, William 6:10:55 (31,856)
Brightwell, Terry 3:03:14 (1,394)
Brignall, David 3:29:56 (4,862)
Brignon, Denis 3:47:40 (8,551)
Brigstocke, Gavin 3:31:39 (5,139)
Brimble, Kevin 3:57:13 (11,269)
Brimmell, Robert 4:14:38 (15,481)
Brindley, Paul 3:33:33 (5,436)
Brine, Martin 3:11:57 (2,267)
Brine, Phil 3:44:21 (7,757)
Brinklow, David 5:27:24 (29,568)
Brinkmann, Joerg 4:28:09 (19,071)
Brinkschulte, Holger 3:54:28 (10,450)
Briones, Eduardo 3:44:20 (7,753)
Brisco, Douglas 2:49:30 (464)
Briscoe, Mark 5:24:54 (29,354)
Brisland, Ian 3:46:18 (8,225)
Bristow, David 4:22:00 (17,393)
Bristow, James 3:45:39 (8,082)
Bristow, Jamie 4:18:39 (16,521)
Bristow, John 2:58:01 (1,009)
Bristowe, Michael 4:26:05 (18,544)
Brito, Matthew 3:41:48 (7,115)
Britt, Paul 3:59:05 (11,827)
Brittain, Mark 4:52:19 (24,846)
Brittain, Scott 2:35:18 (100)
Brittain-Morby, Paul 4:47:18 (23,877)
Britten, David 4:52:05 (24,796)
Britten, Jim 5:39:29 (30,514)
Britten, Tony 3:02:26 (1,335)
Brittleton, Peter 3:12:40 (2,381)
Britton, Alan 5:15:37 (28,385)
Britton, Brian 5:16:15 (28,475)
Britton, Cai 3:13:51 (2,546)
Britton, Charles 4:33:34 (20,477)
Britton, Duncan 3:58:58 (11,787)
Britton, Lee 3:34:26 (5,607)
Britton, Richard 4:21:58 (17,382)
Britton, Robert 3:43:17 (7,467)
Britton, Russell 4:51:58 (24,778)
Brkinshaw, David 4:26:35 (18,675)
Broad, Andy 3:57:37 (11,400)
Broad, Jonathan 5:12:13 (27,975)
Broad, Mark 4:15:55 (15,816)
Broadbent, James 3:41:53 (7,129)
Broadbent, Peter 4:40:33 (22,244)
Broadbent, Richard 4:49:26 (24,309)
Broadbent, Steve 6:14:25 (31,939)
Broadhurst, Carl 3:24:39 (3,936)
Broadhurst, Christopher 4:44:37 (23,199)
Broadhurst, Keith 5:31:07 (29,874)
Broadhurst, Mark 4:21:39 (17,297)
Broadway, Andrew 4:06:38 (13,596)
Broadway, Matthew 4:44:04 (23,080)
Broadwell, Daniel 4:22:57 (17,689)
Brobin, James 4:44:41 (23,214)
Brochier, Stanislas 4:17:22 (16,218)
Brock, Andrew 4:32:19 (20,165)
Brock, Daniel 4:38:38 (21,749)
Brock, Tim 4:45:22 (23,398)
Brockbank, Ross 4:05:31 (13,329)
Brocken, Alan 3:56:05 (10,923)
Brockett, James 3:37:03 (6,131)
Brocklebank, Jason 3:47:29 (8,505)
Brocklesby, David 3:25:29 (4,062)
Brocklesby, Keith 4:01:27 (12,425)
Brockway, Andrew 3:02:01 (1,301)
Brockway, Mark 4:37:09 (21,348)
Broder, Kevin 4:22:20 (17,493)
Brodie, Alexander 4:58:21 (26,005)
Brodie, James 4:45:23 (23,404)
Brodie, Neil 4:42:12 (22,649)
Brogan, David 5:21:04 (29,006)
Brogden, Jason 4:17:00 (16,116)
Brogden, Richard 4:07:37 (13,824)
Brokenshire, Terry 4:41:18 (22,425)
Bromage, Mark 4:39:32 (21,978)
Bromfield, Michael 6:13:51 (31,925)
Bromley, Alec 4:27:31 (18,922)
Bromley, David 3:38:01 (6,316)
Bromley, Hugh 5:04:13 (26,919)
Bromley, Michael 4:17:23 (16,220)
Bromley, Nigel 4:07:47 (13,866)
Brompton, Michael 3:25:49 (4,114)
Bromwich, Lee 4:33:46 (20,528)
Bromwich, Thomas 3:36:22 (5,996)
Brook, Anthony 4:45:24 (23,413)
Brook, Giles 3:37:57 (6,303)
Brook, Graham 4:33:50 (20,541)
Brooke, Craig 3:15:14 (2,692)
Brooke, David 3:22:12 (3,553)
Brooke, David 5:28:08 (29,625)
Brooke, James 4:52:20 (24,850)
Brooke, Ronald 4:12:23 (14,937)
Brooker, Christopher 4:14:40 (15,487)
Brooker, John 3:13:19 (2,476)
Brooker, Matthew 3:54:01 (10,314)
Brooker, Simon 4:10:48 (14,576)
Brookes, Antony 4:39:19 (21,925)
Brookes, Barrie 4:06:09 (13,478)
Brookes, David 5:30:31 (29,822)
Brookes, Gareth 4:20:31 (16,994)
Brookes, Nigel 3:13:30 (2,508)
Brookes, Steven 2:53:51 (670)
Brooking, Paul 3:28:06 (4,532)
Brooks, Adrian 4:45:16 (23,374)
Brooks, Aidan 3:58:02 (11,522)
Brooks, Alan 4:16:38 (16,019)
Brooks, Antony 3:54:29 (10,453)
Brooks, Colin 3:46:29 (8,272)
Brooks, Derek 4:44:17 (23,128)
Brooks, Ian 4:25:57 (18,502)
Brooks, Ivan 4:05:12 (13,254)
Brooks, James 4:05:20 (13,283)
Brooks, Jonathan 4:28:12 (19,081)
Brooks, Mark 3:43:56 (7,638)
Brooks, Matthew 4:09:17 (14,209)
Brooks, Matthew 4:23:51 (17,928)
Brooks, Michael 3:20:36 (3,325)
Brooks, Patrick 4:39:19 (21,925)
Brooks, Paul 3:53:25 (10,113)
Brooks, Paul 4:11:26 (14,727)
Brooks, Richard 3:58:05 (11,536)
Brooks, Roger 4:42:42 (22,768)
Brooks, Russell 3:35:59 (5,901)
Brooks, Stephen 3:31:05 (5,043)
Brooks, Steven 5:50:18 (31,152)
Brooksbank, Quentin 4:26:16 (18,594)
Brooks-Johnson, Alex 4:36:18 (21,153)
Broom, Andrew 3:48:20 (8,705)
Broom, Jonathan 4:34:53 (20,798)
Broom, Neil 3:58:35 (11,671)
Broom, Richard 4:04:04 (13,001)
Brooman, James 4:04:34 (13,104)
Broome, George 5:23:40 (29,246)
Broome, Kevin 5:39:53 (30,540)
Broome, Marcus 3:37:53 (6,295)
Broome, Ricky 5:40:29 (30,582)
Broomfield, Jamie 3:51:46 (9,616)
Broomhall, Neil 4:38:44 (21,774)
Broomhead, Peter 3:47:08 (8,414)
Broomhead, Robert 3:18:39 (3,092)
Brophy, John 4:04:01 (12,993)
Brosi, Henry 4:15:06 (15,597)
Broster, Carl 4:10:35 (14,532)
Broster, Gary 3:34:06 (5,543)
Brotherston, Chris 3:54:02 (10,320)
Brough, Ben 3:10:55 (2,144)
Brough, Paul 3:24:49 (3,959)
Broughton, Christian 4:31:30 (19,968)
Broughton, Daniel 4:37:39 (21,477)
Broughton, Francis 4:59:43 (26,268)
Broughton, Richard 4:54:14 (25,231)
Broughton, Stephen 3:53:47 (10,237)
Broughton, Tim 5:11:51 (27,930)
Browett, Jon 4:26:03 (18,529)
Brown, Alan 3:35:40 (5,837)
Brown, Allan 5:11:14 (27,842)
Brown, Andrew 3:28:54 (4,679)
Brown, Andrew 3:59:38 (11,977)
Brown, Andrew 4:30:50 (19,793)
Brown, Andrew 5:12:36 (28,037)
Brown, Andrew 7:00:45 (32,635)
Brown, Anthony 3:31:22 (5,086)
Brown, Anthony 3:50:42 (9,347)
Brown, Anthony 4:07:05 (13,692)
Brown, Anthony 4:17:45 (16,310)
Brown, Aron 5:12:00 (27,950)
Brown, Chris 3:22:27 (3,577)
Brown, Chris 4:40:06 (22,137)
Brown, Chris 4:41:18 (22,425)
Brown, Christian 4:50:16 (24,462)
Brown, Christopher 3:12:51 (2,412)
Brown, Christopher 3:39:01 (6,532)

Brown, Christopher 3:43:29 (7,517)
Brown, Christopher 4:38:59 (21,841)
Brown, Christopher 4:49:01 (24,237)
Brown, Daniel 3:25:16 (4,026)
Brown, Daniel 3:46:50 (8,351)
Brown, Daniel 4:22:04 (17,415)
Brown, Darren 3:12:51 (2,412)
Brown, David 3:41:44 (7,102)
Brown, David 3:48:37 (8,789)
Brown, David 4:32:42 (20,277)
Brown, David 4:53:31 (25,075)
Brown, David 5:06:20 (27,201)
Brown, David 5:56:17 (31,411)
Brown, David 6:05:06 (31,696)
Brown, Dean 4:37:02 (21,323)
Brown, Derek 2:28:59 (57)
Brown, Derek 4:37:20 (21,408)
Brown, Derek 4:41:26 (22,455)
Brown, Domenic 3:58:22 (11,607)
Brown, Douglas 3:32:51 (5,330)
Brown, Douglas 4:09:35 (14,287)
Brown, Gordon 3:25:56 (4,142)
Brown, Graeme 3:11:01 (2,156)
Brown, Graeme 4:01:43 (12,500)
Brown, Graham 4:02:45 (12,713)
Brown, Harper 5:12:05 (27,963)
Brown, Iain 4:55:30 (25,481)
Brown, Ian 2:59:41 (1,148)
Brown, Ian 4:13:15 (15,134)
Brown, James 3:03:38 (1,435)
Brown, James 3:08:37 (1,884)
Brown, Jem 3:48:15 (8,685)
Brown, John 3:19:52 (3,238)
Brown, John 5:05:06 (27,034)
Brown, Jon 5:30:07 (29,789)
Brown, Jonathan 3:13:53 (2,548)
Brown, Kenneth 4:56:20 (25,667)
Brown, Kevin 3:17:42 (2,978)
Brown, Leon 5:14:20 (28,232)
Brown, Malcolm 4:47:30 (23,912)
Brown, Malcolm 5:27:02 (29,526)
Brown, Marc 3:53:14 (10,055)
Brown, Mark 3:29:17 (4,744)
Brown, Mark 4:45:06 (23,333)
Brown, Martin 4:37:23 (21,418)
Brown, Matthew 3:23:52 (3,789)
Brown, Matthew 4:36:27 (21,200)
Brown, Michael 3:24:12 (3,861)
Brown, Michael 3:56:44 (11,117)
Brown, Michael 4:16:45 (16,052)
Brown, Michael 4:52:54 (24,960)
Brown, Mike 3:42:33 (7,298)
Brown, Neil 4:05:37 (13,352)
Brown, Nicholas 4:16:30 (15,980)
Brown, Nick 5:27:22 (29,565)
Brown, Oliver 5:28:37 (29,666)
Brown, Owen 3:14:16 (2,591)
Brown, Patrick 4:34:40 (20,742)
Brown, Paul 3:47:39 (8,546)
Brown, Paul 4:11:26 (14,727)
Brown, Paul 5:05:02 (27,027)
Brown, Paul 5:28:54 (29,686)
Brown, Peter 3:41:13 (7,019)
Brown, Peter 4:52:54 (24,960)
Brown, Peter 5:15:28 (28,357)
Brown, Phil 3:53:05 (10,013)
Brown, Philip 4:34:29 (20,688)
Brown, Philip 4:42:48 (22,791)
Brown, Phillip 3:53:21 (10,094)
Brown, Ray 5:23:18 (29,202)
Brown, Raymond 4:12:20 (14,927)
Brown, Richard 3:41:44 (7,102)
Brown, Richard 4:30:05 (19,620)
Brown, Richard 5:08:48 (27,539)
Brown, Robert 3:56:24 (11,017)
Brown, Robert 4:12:06 (14,880)
Brown, Robert 4:41:14 (22,408)
Brown, Robert 4:50:48 (24,564)
Brown, Robin 4:05:21 (13,287)
Brown, Rod 4:29:46 (19,527)
Brown, Roger 4:12:11 (14,897)
Brown, Roger 4:50:39 (24,531)
Brown, Rory 3:09:30 (1,989)
Brown, Rupert 4:48:03 (24,047)
Brown, Shane 3:20:47 (3,343)
Brown, Simon 3:58:13 (11,571)
Brown, Simon 4:29:37 (19,490)
Brown, Simon 4:55:38 (25,499)
Brown, Stephen 3:46:34 (8,303)
Brown, Stephen 4:06:31 (13,571)
Brown, Steven 4:49:49 (24,383)
Brown, Steven 5:03:00 (26,738)
Brown, Stuart 3:20:25 (3,303)
Brown, Stuart 5:01:37 (26,548)
Brown, Stuart 5:43:47 (30,801)
Brown, Terence 5:03:58 (26,884)
Brown, Terry 5:31:06 (29,872)
Brown, Timothy 4:38:31 (21,707)
Brown, Tom 4:40:17 (22,176)
Brown, Tony 3:47:33 (8,523)
Brown, Trevor 3:18:05 (3,018)
Brown, Trevor 3:57:33 (11,381)
Brown, Wayne 4:24:18 (18,067)
Brown, Will 4:47:08 (23,840)
Brown, William 5:17:55 (28,663)
Brownbill, Roger 4:51:21 (24,672)
Browne, Christopher 3:38:27 (6,414)
Browne, David 4:04:31 (13,090)
Browne, Kevin 4:45:07 (23,339)
Browne, Mathew 2:58:05 (1,012)
Browne, Richard 3:15:16 (2,696)
Browne, Roger 5:57:47 (31,468)
Browne, Steve 3:50:03 (9,178)
Browne, Tony 4:28:00 (19,032)
Browning, Alan 6:33:36 (32,333)
Browning, Colin 3:45:47 (8,110)
Browning, Geoff 4:29:17 (19,410)
Browning, Jeremy 4:22:23 (17,512)
Browning, Nick 3:01:08 (1,238)
Browning, Paul 3:30:09 (4,891)
Browning, Tim 3:59:41 (11,989)
Brownjohn, Gary 4:42:18 (22,671)
Brownjohn, Ian 4:42:18 (22,671)
Brownlie, Colin 4:54:10 (25,220)
Brownlie, Iain 5:07:56 (27,428)
Brownlow, Marcus 3:51:17 (9,498)
Brownlow, Patrick 5:24:15 (29,301)
Brownsdon, Michael 5:05:06 (27,034)
Brownstein, Leo 5:13:48 (28,169)
Broxholme, Edward 4:56:05 (25,601)
Broxton, Keith 3:15:16 (2,696)
Bruce, Andrew 3:39:53 (6,707)
Bruce, David 3:45:32 (8,054)
Bruce, David 4:20:04 (16,882)
Bruce, Douglas 3:45:27 (8,029)
Bruce, Nigel 3:53:30 (10,145)
Bruce, Nigel 4:13:51 (15,272)
Bruce, Richard 4:10:25 (14,490)
Bruguier, Jean 3:42:25 (7,265)
Brulin, Jacky 3:45:54 (8,134)
Brun, Christian 3:05:38 (1,604)
Brun, Theodore 3:13:19 (2,476)
Bruner, Paul 3:59:26 (11,926)
Brunet, Martin 4:22:26 (17,531)
Bruniges, Colin 4:32:54 (20,335)
Brunner, Peter 3:40:06 (6,762)
Brunner, René 3:40:20 (6,819)
Brunning, James 3:29:16 (4,742)
Brunning, Nigel 5:10:35 (27,761)
Bruno, Frank 4:47:16 (23,871)
Brunold, Andrea 3:26:08 (4,171)
Brunskill, Michael 2:56:36 (882)
Brunt, Jeff 4:27:29 (18,915)
Bruyns, François 3:32:24 (5,252)
Bryan, Andrew 4:41:52 (22,574)
Bryan, Anthony 5:17:01 (28,565)
Bryan, Barry 4:29:53 (19,569)
Bryan, David 3:53:23 (10,103)
Bryan, David 4:45:13 (23,361)
Bryan, James 3:32:14 (5,220)
Bryan, James 3:54:13 (10,376)
Bryan, Jerry 3:37:02 (6,126)
Bryan, John 6:45:21 (32,489)
Bryan, Peter 3:54:08 (10,358)
Bryant, Anthony 4:24:57 (18,242)
Bryant, Gary 3:31:36 (5,124)
Bryant, John 4:43:13 (22,890)
Bryant, Julius 4:42:09 (22,641)
Bryant, Karl 5:15:50 (28,418)
Bryant, Mark 3:32:39 (5,297)
Bryant, Mark 3:44:09 (7,695)
Bryant, Niall 4:15:29 (15,689)
Bryant, Owen 3:46:52 (8,358)
Bryant, Paul 3:56:54 (11,174)
Bryant, Paul 4:39:50 (22,067)
Bryant, Philip 3:58:28 (11,643)
Bryant, Wayne 3:45:05 (7,950)
Bryce, Edward 4:12:11 (14,897)
Bryce, James 4:31:04 (19,844)
Bryce, Stephen 4:53:01 (24,978)
Bryett, Philip 4:28:42 (19,224)
Bryett, Tim 4:38:44 (21,774)
Bryon, Richard 4:58:55 (26,115)
Bubloz, David 4:38:45 (21,782)
Buccellato, Nicolo 4:11:05 (14,654)
Buchan, Stephen 3:14:32 (2,613)
Buchan, Stuart 2:41:41 (223)
Buchanan, Andrew 3:52:20 (9,790)
Buchanan, Iain 3:54:34 (10,478)
Buchanan, Ian 4:05:19 (13,277)
Buchanan, Ian 4:51:50 (24,750)
Buchanan, Jonathan 4:06:30 (13,568)
Buchanan, Stephen 5:45:11 (30,894)
Buchett, Gary 3:35:53 (5,880)
Buchleitner, Michael 2:14:10 (11)
Buckby, Mark 4:16:36 (16,010)
Buckby, Richard 3:47:30 (8,510)
Buckemeyer, Holger 4:06:35 (13,583)
Buckerfield, Lee 4:16:20 (15,924)
Buckingham, David 4:23:08 (17,734)
Buckingham, Donald 4:53:26 (25,055)
Buckingham, Ian 2:55:14 (760)
Buckingham, Ian 3:31:59 (5,186)
Buckingham, Philip 4:28:40 (19,213)
Buckland, Nigel 3:53:21 (10,094)
Buckle, Nicholas 3:25:35 (4,075)
Buckler, Dave 3:56:32 (11,067)
Buckley, Aiden 3:28:20 (4,579)
Buckley, Brian 2:56:13 (847)
Buckley, Colin 4:20:59 (17,107)
Buckley, Derek 3:09:55 (2,029)
Buckley, James 3:47:18 (8,461)
Buckley, Liam 4:41:14 (22,408)
Buckley, Mark 4:43:12 (22,889)
Buckley, Paul 4:53:30 (25,068)
Buckley, Stephen 4:29:15 (19,398)
Buckley, Thomas 4:07:40 (13,831)
Buckley, William 6:22:34 (32,135)
Bucknall, Alan 4:31:28 (19,953)
Bucknall, Thomas 4:10:40 (14,550)
Budai, Aaron 4:58:25 (26,021)
Budd, Anthony 4:22:07 (17,430)
Budd, Ian 4:09:43 (14,321)
Budd, Julian 4:30:12 (19,652)
Budd, Stephen 5:04:47 (26,997)
Budden, Neil 8:51:51 (32,888)
Budden, Patrick 4:45:54 (23,541)
Budden, Patrick 5:56:48 (31,440)
Budge, Kevin 4:36:19 (21,164)
Budge, Nick 4:23:31 (17,830)
Budgen, Jason 3:41:44 (7,102)
Budgen, Mark 3:50:14 (9,232)
Budnik, Pablo 2:51:38 (567)
Buechel, Hilmar 5:46:33 (30,967)
Buehjlmann, Walter 4:11:18 (14,695)
Buergis, Albert 4:01:12 (12,365)
Bugaj, George 4:28:40 (19,213)
Bugby, Antony 4:56:57 (25,756)
Bugiardini, Antonio 4:27:01 (18,792)
Bugiardini, Gelso 4:22:13 (17,449)
Bugler, Andrew 4:38:46 (21,787)
Bugler, John 3:51:44 (9,603)
Bugler, Paul 3:33:12 (5,382)
Buijsman, Nicolas 3:18:16 (3,040)
Buiron, Gerard 5:11:17 (27,853)
Buiron, Nicolas 4:49:45 (24,369)
Buley, Mark 3:49:47 (9,125)
Bull, David 5:26:33 (29,497)
Bull, Geoffrey 4:38:21 (21,672)

Bull, John	4:23:59 (17,976)	
Bull, John	5:49:01 (31,101)	
Bull, Jonathan	4:37:42 (21,491)	
Bull, Martyn	6:53:56 (32,581)	
Bull, Michael	5:37:00 (30,346)	
Bull, Michael-John	6:25:53 (32,198)	
Bull, Nicholas	4:42:48 (22,791)	
Bull, Peter	3:37:57 (6,303)	
Bull, Stephen	5:05:08 (27,038)	
Bull, Steve	4:00:51 (12,267)	
Bullard, Hugh	4:14:33 (15,457)	
Bullen, Gary	3:08:29 (1,869)	
Bullen, John	4:09:31 (14,273)	
Bullen, Nigel	3:49:36 (9,069)	
Bullen, Paul	3:42:45 (7,326)	
Bullen, Peter	4:31:53 (20,053)	
Bullen, Richard	3:56:12 (10,964)	
Bullen, Roger	2:56:58 (912)	
Bulley, David	3:34:51 (5,682)	
Bulley, Simon	4:26:34 (18,670)	
Bullivant, Paul	4:01:20 (12,399)	
Bullivant, Peter	4:07:55 (13,895)	
Bullock, Alastair	3:44:05 (7,675)	
Bullock, Bernard	4:15:39 (15,739)	
Bullock, Derek	4:38:51 (21,808)	
Bullock, Paul	2:56:12 (845)	
Bullock, Terry	2:56:12 (845)	
Bulmer-Jones, Michael	3:20:39 (3,332)	
Bunbury, Anthony	4:29:50 (19,551)	
Bunce, James	4:59:21 (26,186)	
Bunch, Danny	3:54:17 (10,396)	
Bunch, Trevor	4:22:22 (17,507)	
Bunclark, Nick	3:17:37 (2,964)	
Bundock, Richard	4:51:05 (24,625)	
Bundy, William Jnr	3:52:38 (9,877)	
Bungay, Alan	5:24:29 (29,322)	
Bunk, Bradley	3:52:01 (9,693)	
Bunker, Russell	4:48:00 (24,029)	
Bunn, Roder	4:37:02 (21,323)	
Bunney, Christopher	4:36:55 (21,300)	
Bunning, Alex	4:46:30 (23,692)	
Bunning, Paul	4:17:01 (16,121)	
Bunt, Andrew	3:18:52 (3,119)	
Bunting, Alistair	3:34:01 (5,522)	
Bunting, Colin	3:58:32 (11,657)	
Bunting, Simon	4:55:06 (25,391)	
Bunting, William	4:22:56 (17,682)	
Bunton, Paul	3:57:10 (11,252)	
Bunyan, Robert	3:11:57 (2,267)	
Buoncuore, Francesco	6:29:52 (32,273)	
Burbedge, Ian	4:26:01 (18,525)	
Burbidge, Duncan	2:45:42 (319)	
Burbidge, Reginald	5:36:22 (30,301)	
Burch, Graham	4:50:49 (24,572)	
Burchell, Simon	4:34:09 (20,618)	
Burchett, Rainer	3:31:17 (5,075)	
Burdeau, Ishmael	2:50:10 (496)	
Burden, Andrew	4:25:12 (18,309)	
Burden, Keith	6:10:36 (31,848)	
Burden, Malcolm	3:21:43 (3,466)	
Burdett, Daniel	3:52:17 (9,779)	
Burdett, Matthew	4:15:17 (15,637)	
Burdon, David	5:00:38 (26,393)	
Burdon, Paul	4:32:09 (20,129)	
Burfield, Kevin	4:15:38 (15,733)	
Burford, Colin	3:51:04 (9,447)	
Burford, Graeme	4:22:18 (17,476)	
Burford, Lawrence	3:57:07 (11,238)	
Burford, Peter	3:26:41 (4,269)	
Burge, Ben	4:00:40 (12,216)	
Burger, Carl	5:21:40 (29,066)	
Burger, Evert	4:06:49 (13,632)	
Burger, Raymond	4:31:09 (19,870)	
Burgess, Andrew	4:15:52 (15,798)	
Burgess, Craig	4:16:24 (15,952)	
Burgess, Craig	4:41:54 (22,585)	
Burgess, Danny	4:04:19 (13,049)	
Burgess, John	4:30:07 (19,630)	
Burgess, Mark	3:52:16 (9,771)	
Burgess, Mark	5:42:52 (30,743)	
Burgess, Matt	3:07:34 (1,772)	
Burgess, Owen	4:43:54 (23,044)	
Burgess, Roger	4:58:55 (26,115)	
Burgess, Tom	3:52:00 (9,683)	
Burghall, Anthony	3:27:54 (4,501)	
Burgin, Matt	3:12:06 (2,293)	
Burgoyne, Robert	4:13:20 (15,151)	
Burhenne, Raymond	4:14:13 (15,368)	
Burke, Andrew	5:07:40 (27,396)	
Burke, Andy	3:50:03 (9,178)	
Burke, Christopher	3:29:30 (4,795)	
Burke, Christopher	3:49:13 (8,946)	
Burke, Darren	4:03:54 (12,963)	
Burke, Desmond	3:58:16 (11,584)	
Burke, Donal	3:08:17 (1,836)	
Burke, Iain	3:11:58 (2,272)	
Burke, John	6:02:49 (31,634)	
Burke, Marc	4:29:15 (19,398)	
Burke, Michael	4:59:34 (26,236)	
Burke, Peter	5:21:12 (29,018)	
Burke, Robert	4:06:10 (13,480)	
Burke, Shaun	5:03:01 (26,746)	
Burke, Terence	4:43:10 (22,885)	
Burke, Thomas	7:17:40 (32,750)	
Burke-Murphy, Timothy	3:40:09 (6,772)	
Burkhill, John	6:09:53 (31,833)	
Burkinshaw, Jason	3:38:21 (6,386)	
Burkitt, Anthony	4:44:20 (23,138)	
Burleigh, Philip	3:35:32 (5,809)	
Burley, Dennis	4:03:57 (12,976)	
Burlingham, Barry	3:07:03 (1,740)	
Burman, Julian	3:56:44 (11,117)	
Burn, James	4:12:14 (14,909)	
Burn, John	4:16:04 (15,855)	
Burnaby-Davies, Mark	3:55:19 (10,701)	
Burnage, Steven	4:28:07 (19,058)	
Burnand, George	3:53:47 (10,237)	
Burnell, Jonathan	3:46:24 (8,254)	
Burness, Kevin	4:25:49 (18,465)	
Burnett, Christopher	4:00:30 (12,188)	
Burnett, David	3:55:02 (10,603)	
Burnett, Desmond	4:48:14 (24,076)	
Burnett, Michael	4:45:19 (23,384)	
Burnett, Nigel	3:29:48 (4,842)	
Burnett, Philip	4:51:17 (24,665)	
Burnett, Simon	3:53:21 (10,094)	
Burnett-Armstrong, Benedict	4:41:36 (22,498)	
Burnham, Daniel	4:18:17 (16,431)	
Burnham, Derek	4:12:51 (15,050)	
Burnham, James	5:41:42 (30,665)	
Burnham, Richard	3:26:02 (4,154)	
Burnham, Robert	3:05:12 (1,559)	
Burnham, Stephen	4:28:36 (19,197)	
Burningham, Leo	2:51:56 (575)	
Burns, Andrew	5:34:55 (30,177)	
Burns, Billy	2:17:34 (14)	
Burns, Denis	3:10:36 (2,115)	
Burns, Duncan	2:59:42 (1,151)	
Burns, Francis	4:20:08 (16,896)	
Burns, George	3:44:38 (7,831)	
Burns, Graham	3:50:01 (9,171)	
Burns, James	4:29:03 (19,335)	
Burns, John	3:40:55 (6,944)	
Burns, Lawrence	4:13:39 (15,216)	
Burns, Peter	3:55:54 (10,872)	
Burns, Peter	4:15:51 (15,791)	
Burns, Robert	3:08:12 (1,824)	
Burns, Robert	5:05:50 (27,131)	
Burns, Stephen	3:48:50 (8,849)	
Burns, Stephen	5:01:08 (26,473)	
Burnside, Scott	3:57:10 (11,252)	
Burr, David	5:20:37 (28,950)	
Burr, William	3:48:52 (8,859)	
Burrage, Matt	5:20:12 (28,905)	
Burrell, Garry	5:07:05 (27,310)	
Burrell, Jonathan	3:53:45 (10,225)	
Burrell, Simon	4:47:18 (23,877)	
Burridge, Mark	3:16:44 (2,868)	
Burridge, Stephen	6:13:57 (31,926)	
Burrill, Kristian	5:11:23 (27,866)	
Burrow, Gareth	3:49:47 (9,125)	
Burrow, John	4:13:05 (15,100)	
Burrows, Adam	5:20:02 (28,883)	
Burrows, Andrew	4:12:39 (15,012)	
Burrows, Chris	4:50:00 (24,423)	
Burrows, Edward	4:39:02 (21,854)	
Burrows, Geoff	5:31:21 (29,897)	
Burrows, Geoffrey	3:57:35 (11,389)	
Burrows, Ian	3:30:22 (4,924)	
Burrows, Lee	4:40:13 (22,162)	
Burrows, Mark	4:38:30 (21,703)	
Burrows, Paul	4:06:45 (13,621)	
Burrows, Robert	4:01:09 (12,352)	
Bursey, Peter	3:36:04 (5,919)	
Burston, Andrew	4:07:47 (13,866)	
Burstow, Clive	4:08:51 (14,102)	
Burstow, James	3:57:44 (11,434)	
Burt, Adrian	4:17:43 (16,299)	
Burt, Nathan	4:05:55 (13,417)	
Burt, Peter	3:58:30 (11,651)	
Burt, Stephen	5:40:25 (30,579)	
Burthem, Stephen	2:47:47 (393)	
Burton, Alan	3:08:42 (1,889)	
Burton, Carl	3:08:18 (1,840)	
Burton, Charles	5:01:37 (26,548)	
Burton, Denys	4:17:55 (16,349)	
Burton, Gareth	3:18:46 (3,108)	
Burton, Gareth	4:27:08 (18,826)	
Burton, James	4:14:58 (15,565)	
Burton, Jeremy	4:08:10 (13,943)	
Burton, Jeremy	4:33:20 (20,426)	
Burton, Julian	3:44:19 (7,747)	
Burton, Mark	2:55:56 (822)	
Burton, Martyn	5:26:20 (29,468)	
Burton, Neal	5:06:34 (27,239)	
Burton, Nicholas	3:36:04 (5,919)	
Burton, Philip	4:05:29 (13,324)	
Burton, Robert	3:35:34 (5,817)	
Burton, Roderick	3:03:01 (1,370)	
Burton, Shaun	3:49:27 (9,027)	
Burton, Stephen	4:48:47 (24,190)	
Burton, Stephen	5:18:05 (28,680)	
Burton, Tony	2:55:56 (822)	
Burwood, Neil	4:21:54 (17,368)	
Bury, Robert	3:42:20 (7,246)	
Bus, Dirk	3:33:46 (5,469)	
Busby, Harry	4:56:08 (25,618)	
Busby, Nicholas	4:41:14 (22,408)	
Busch, Graham	3:08:47 (1,906)	
Busfield, George	4:32:37 (20,251)	
Bush, Adam	2:57:25 (950)	
Bush, Edward	3:11:39 (2,222)	
Bush, Jason	3:32:30 (5,269)	
Bush, Kevin	3:05:49 (1,620)	
Bush, Kevin	3:48:02 (8,634)	
Bush, Martin	4:31:23 (19,926)	
Bush, Michael	4:25:14 (18,317)	
Bush, Nigel	3:28:17 (4,565)	
Bush, Richard	3:20:28 (3,308)	
Bushby, Ray	2:55:04 (749)	
Bushby, Rob	3:17:06 (2,913)	
Bushell, David	4:02:46 (12,719)	
Bushell, Philip	4:16:18 (15,913)	
Bushell, Stuart	4:19:04 (16,610)	
Bushill, Adrian	5:02:16 (26,637)	
Bushnell, Andrew	4:39:41 (22,016)	
Bushrod, Eddie	3:43:24 (7,496)	
Buskell, Paul	5:12:26 (28,017)	
Buskwood, Mark	3:17:47 (2,988)	
Buss, Michael	4:52:21 (24,851)	
Bussey, Steven	4:33:14 (20,412)	
Bustnes, Trond	3:56:02 (10,906)	
Buswell, James	4:21:08 (17,151)	
Butcher, Alexander	5:48:46 (31,077)	
Butcher, Gary	2:51:06 (537)	
Butcher, James	4:38:02 (21,578)	
Butcher, Jem	4:31:29 (19,962)	
Butcher, Lindsay	3:59:35 (11,962)	
Butcher, Martin	4:18:44 (16,530)	
Butland, Jonathan	4:15:52 (15,798)	
Butler, Aidan	5:34:54 (30,175)	
Butler, Anthony	3:17:11 (2,917)	
Butler, Brian	3:24:53 (3,970)	
Butler, Bruce	3:51:30 (9,543)	
Butler, Bryan	3:50:11 (9,210)	
Butler, Cavan	3:24:26 (3,906)	
Butler, Christopher	4:01:00 (12,308)	
Butler, David	3:21:17 (3,405)	
Butler, David	3:40:16 (6,803)	

Butler, Derek 3:55:25 (10,727)
Butler, Graham 3:15:38 (2,742)
Butler, Jack 4:25:21 (18,348)
Butler, Jeffrey 3:01:02 (1,227)
Butler, Kenneth 4:46:08 (23,602)
Butler, Malcolm 3:33:38 (5,446)
Butler, Mark 3:51:42 (9,593)
Butler, Mark 4:18:49 (16,551)
Butler, Matthew 3:28:55 (4,684)
Butler, Michael 4:41:00 (22,355)
Butler, Paul 4:44:02 (23,071)
Butler, Philip 3:33:16 (5,392)
Butler, Richard 3:37:32 (6,229)
Butler, Robert 4:12:22 (14,932)
Butler, Ross 3:18:24 (3,058)
Butler, Sam 3:52:08 (9,736)
Butler, Shaun 3:45:03 (7,940)
Butler, Stephen 3:39:02 (6,535)
Butler, Steven 5:01:42 (26,560)
Butler-Clack, Iain 4:41:03 (22,362)
Butler-Creagh, Richard 3:38:39 (6,465)
Butt, David 3:58:47 (11,729)
Butt, Nadeem 5:13:31 (28,142)
Buttenmueller, Martin 4:45:50 (23,523)
Butterfield, Karl 5:09:29 (27,630)
Butters, Colin 4:01:11 (12,361)
Butterworth, Jim 4:00:35 (12,203)
Butterworth, Martin 4:32:02 (20,096)
Butterworth, Peter 2:48:23 (422)
Butterworth, Roy 3:15:43 (2,758)
Buttliger, Peter 4:37:47 (21,517)
Button, Phil 3:40:38 (6,878)
Button, Richard 4:21:26 (17,228)
Button, Thomas 4:15:19 (15,644)
Butts, Steve 4:19:38 (16,759)
Butwell, Noel 5:12:50 (28,059)
Buxton, Clifford 3:19:35 (3,212)
Buxton, Darren 3:51:08 (9,466)
Buxton, David 5:04:44 (26,986)
Buys, Ronny 4:29:40 (19,499)
Buzzolini, Caio 3:24:17 (3,873)
Byansi, Malachi 2:40:52 (201)
Byars, Warren 5:13:45 (28,162)
Byatt, Vincenzo 4:18:55 (16,571)
Bye, Alan 3:11:57 (2,267)
Bye, Benjamin 4:08:47 (14,089)
Bye, Roger 4:34:07 (20,611)
Byers, Jonathan 4:10:16 (14,452)
Byford, Giles 3:28:07 (4,535)
Byram, Wayne 3:56:51 (11,159)
Byrd, Michael 3:52:40 (9,887)
Byrne, Anthony 7:05:19 (32,674)
Byrne, Benjamin 3:50:32 (9,306)
Byrne, Connor 3:54:29 (10,453)
Byrne, David 2:46:28 (341)
Byrne, David 4:54:43 (25,328)
Byrne, Dominic 4:33:36 (20,494)
Byrne, Duncan 3:37:37 (6,246)
Byrne, Gary 3:32:58 (5,348)
Byrne, James 3:52:39 (9,881)
Byrne, John 3:32:46 (5,313)
Byrne, John 4:38:47 (21,790)
Byrne, Matthew 5:13:46 (28,167)
Byrne, Michael 4:20:23 (16,962)
Byrne, Paul 3:38:38 (6,459)
Byrne, Paul 4:36:30 (21,221)
Byrne, Steven 4:54:09 (25,215)
Byron, Chris 4:02:49 (12,733)
Bytheway, Mark 3:52:14 (9,762)
Byworth, Matthew 3:01:47 (1,283)
Caballero, Franck 4:44:46 (23,240)
Caballero, Jimmy 4:46:34 (23,706)
Cabassut, Christophe 2:37:45 (139)
Cabello, Felipe 2:51:10 (542)
Cable, Michael 4:26:50 (18,748)
Cable, Stephen 2:52:25 (594)
Cabras, Antonio 4:47:21 (23,885)
Caburn, Richard 3:12:05 (2,289)
Cadavid, Walter 4:41:52 (22,574)
Cadden, John 4:14:02 (15,324)
Cadden, Paul 4:51:04 (24,619)
Caddick, Matthew 4:29:01 (19,325)
Caddy, David 2:53:46 (666)

Cade, Andrew 4:33:46 (20,528)
Cade, Matt 4:28:56 (19,297)
Cade, Nigel 4:23:42 (17,883)
Cadman, Karl 4:00:05 (12,104)
Caffyn, Timothy 3:49:38 (9,078)
Cage, Robert 3:28:50 (4,667)
Cahill, Anthony 3:45:14 (7,983)
Cahill, Michael 4:54:16 (25,236)
Cahill, Michael 5:27:51 (29,604)
Caillot, Charles 3:08:50 (1,913)
Cain, Mark 3:11:24 (2,192)
Cain, Nigel 4:12:25 (14,950)
Cain, Peter 4:12:26 (14,955)
Cain, Scott 4:03:19 (12,838)
Cain, Terence 5:58:30 (31,497)
Caine, Alan 3:32:45 (5,311)
Caird, Gordon 3:31:43 (5,154)
Cairns, David 2:43:03 (245)
Cairns, Mick 3:20:08 (3,270)
Cairns, Peter 3:46:16 (8,215)
Cakebread, John 3:08:16 (1,833)
Calaz, Neal 4:09:55 (14,367)
Calcott, Keith 3:36:53 (6,090)
Calcraft, Robert 3:50:06 (9,190)
Calder, Stuart 3:57:28 (11,350)
Calderhead, William 3:24:18 (3,877)
Caldicott, Stuart 4:34:46 (20,766)
Caldwell, Bryan 2:57:17 (934)
Caldwell, Elliot 4:48:23 (24,097)
Caldwell, Ian 4:55:09 (25,411)
Caldwell, Robert 3:44:56 (7,915)
Caldwell, Ronald 5:15:56 (28,434)
Caldwell, Toby 4:08:46 (14,087)
Caley, David 4:55:25 (25,469)
Califano, Salvatore 2:56:39 (885)
Calisto, Julio 2:59:30 (1,135)
Calkin, Richard 4:48:25 (24,108)
Callachan, David 3:30:29 (4,941)
Callaghan, Bede 3:43:03 (7,400)
Callaghan, James 2:50:51 (528)
Callaghan, Michael 5:19:18 (28,806)
Callaghan, Peter 3:59:50 (12,036)
Callagher, Martin 3:13:04 (2,442)
Callaly, Thomas 3:40:15 (6,799)
Callan, Mark 3:55:00 (10,596)
Callanan, Sean 4:23:55 (17,953)
Callany, Lawrence 4:08:34 (14,045)
Callard, Andrew 4:16:33 (15,991)
Callard, Jonathan 4:02:59 (12,771)
Callay, Yves 4:15:12 (15,621)
Calleja-Martin, Miguel 4:04:54 (13,183)
Callejon, Francis 4:34:11 (20,625)
Caller, Mark 4:18:33 (16,497)
Callis, Sam 4:39:22 (21,939)
Callister, Matthew 4:38:45 (21,782)
Callow, James 3:38:16 (6,362)
Callow, Leo 3:56:10 (10,948)
Callow, Phil 5:53:39 (31,300)
Calnan, Neville 3:50:22 (9,268)
Calthorpe, Euan 4:24:24 (18,091)
Calverley, James 6:12:13 (31,889)
Calvert, Gerald 3:33:14 (5,386)
Calvert, Glenn 3:10:41 (2,121)
Calvert, Jonathan 3:28:10 (4,544)
Calvert, Michael 3:26:36 (4,247)
Cambiano, Dario 3:23:54 (3,799)
Cameron, Colin 4:49:33 (24,332)
Cameron, David 2:41:13 (209)
Cameron, Don 5:05:45 (27,116)
Cameron, Ewan 3:06:04 (1,647)
Cameron, Ewen 3:45:20 (8,006)
Cameron, Jamie 4:29:53 (19,569)
Cameron, Kevin 3:55:46 (10,832)
Cameron, Michael 4:03:51 (12,954)
Cameron, Paul 3:13:05 (2,444)

Cameron, Stuart 3:15:53 (2,777)
Cameron, Stuart 3:56:12 (10,964)
Camillo, Marco 5:34:14 (30,127)
Campany, Tim 3:46:05 (8,178)
Campbell, Adrian 4:35:04 (20,846)
Campbell, Allan 4:10:51 (14,592)
Campbell, Anthony 5:22:01 (29,094)
Campbell, Cameron 4:42:40 (22,760)
Campbell, Charles 4:43:13 (22,890)
Campbell, Christopher 3:40:25 (6,839)
Campbell, David 4:26:32 (18,664)
Campbell, David 5:05:41 (27,112)
Campbell, Gary 3:42:42 (7,316)
Campbell, Gordon 3:28:17 (4,565)
Campbell, Iain 3:56:33 (11,070)
Campbell, Iain 4:12:02 (14,871)
Campbell, James 5:03:43 (26,845)
Campbell, John 3:32:18 (5,232)
Campbell, John 3:37:42 (6,260)
Campbell, John 4:06:14 (13,498)
Campbell, Kevin 4:19:08 (16,627)
Campbell, Lee 2:55:42 (798)
Campbell, Lee 4:10:54 (14,605)
Campbell, Leroy 3:13:01 (2,434)
Campbell, Martin 3:51:54 (9,650)
Campbell, Niall 3:19:18 (3,172)
Campbell, Patrick 4:48:00 (24,029)
Campbell, Paul 4:22:35 (17,568)
Campbell, Paul 4:33:35 (20,486)
Campbell, Ray 3:19:17 (3,169)
Campbell, Richard 5:32:55 (30,017)
Campbell, Ronnie 6:29:39 (32,267)
Campbell, Scott 4:11:25 (14,715)
Campbell, Stephen 4:34:43 (20,754)
Campbell, Wayne 4:08:37 (14,062)
Campbell-Barnard, James 3:09:35 (1,998)
Campbell-Barnard, William 3:44:12 (7,715)
Campion, Brian 6:03:51 (31,659)
Campion, Stephen 3:24:53 (3,970)
Candlish, Alistair 3:41:59 (7,149)
Candy, Robin 3:04:41 (1,516)
Cane, Marc 3:52:07 (9,726)
Canepa, Mario 3:28:47 (4,658)
Canessa, Patrick 4:28:43 (19,231)
Canlorbe, Didier 3:58:05 (11,536)
Cannam, Michael 3:13:00 (2,431)
Cannan, Lee 4:29:00 (19,322)
Cannell, Mark 4:33:05 (20,373)
Canner, Barrie 6:35:44 (32,371)
Canning, Cerne 4:10:46 (14,566)
Canning, Christopher 5:14:18 (28,231)
Canning, Jason 5:41:55 (30,692)
Canning, Stephen 3:49:33 (9,053)
Canning, Stephen 4:02:06 (12,575)
Cannon, John 3:06:49 (1,715)
Cannon, John 4:12:00 (14,862)
Cannon, Mark 3:56:11 (10,957)
Cannon, Mark 4:38:14 (21,636)
Cannon, Russell 4:24:56 (18,234)
Cannon, Sandy 3:41:28 (7,059)
Cant, Christopher 6:07:49 (31,778)
Cant, Cliff 3:50:47 (9,373)
Cantanessi, Giorgio 3:44:42 (7,852)
Cantle, Colin 4:23:10 (17,742)
Cantwell, Matthew 3:53:47 (10,237)
Capel, David 3:47:32 (8,519)
Capel, Dominic 4:07:22 (13,767)
Capetti, Giancomino 3:17:24 (2,949)
Caplan, Gregory 6:17:53 (32,030)
Caplan, Nicholas 3:36:53 (6,090)
Caplin, Terence 3:51:12 (9,482)
Capon, Ian 4:31:22 (19,921)
Capper, Graham 3:00:43 (1,213)
Capper, Paul 3:53:47 (10,237)
Carboni, Gianni 3:43:20 (7,483)
Carbonnel, Herve 4:04:53 (13,179)
Carbowell-Arnau, Salvador 4:38:31 (21,707)
Card, Neil 4:02:01 (12,563)
Carden, Steven 4:40:55 (22,336)
Cardon, Clive 3:51:08 (9,466)
Carduner, Olivier 3:13:28 (2,501)
Carevic, Ross 4:28:51 (19,278)
Carew-Jones, Samuel 3:57:51 (11,464)

Carey, Allan	4:24:57 (18,242)	
Carey, Barry	3:57:17 (11,288)	
Carey, Ben	4:24:59 (18,258)	
Carey, Mark	3:33:13 (5,385)	
Carey, Moray	4:17:58 (16,365)	
Carey, Neil	5:30:00 (29,781)	
Carey, Will	4:08:22 (13,982)	
Cargill, Jamie	3:33:40 (5,450)	
Cariss, Christopher	2:20:45 (21)	
Carley, Martin	4:11:39 (14,782)	
Carli, Giampeitro	4:56:31 (25,692)	
Carlier, Raymond	4:53:30 (25,068)	
Carlin, Brian	2:41:23 (214)	
Carlisle, John	3:32:24 (5,252)	
Carlisle, Paul	4:37:24 (21,422)	
Carlisle, Stephen	3:18:06 (3,020)	
Carlsile, Robert	4:28:46 (19,248)	
Carlson, Alan	8:38:11 (32,880)	
Carlson, Burt	5:20:11 (28,903)	
Carlyle, Peter	4:37:43 (21,493)	
Carmichael, Jeremy	3:18:56 (3,128)	
Carmichael, Stuart	3:50:50 (9,382)	
Carmody, Patrick	4:31:25 (19,935)	
Carne, Malcolm	3:08:27 (1,860)	
Carnell, Michael	6:50:24 (32,546)	
Carnell, Nicholas	4:15:29 (15,689)	
Carneros-Mateo, Antonio	3:49:45 (9,112)	
Carney, Robert	4:32:26 (20,200)	
Carniegie, Malcolm	3:42:26 (7,269)	
Carnoy, Stephane	4:00:54 (12,278)	
Carnwath, Wiliam	4:08:36 (14,059)	
Carpenter, Colin	4:35:44 (21,015)	
Carpenter, Grant	3:49:23 (8,998)	
Carpenter, Ian	5:11:57 (27,945)	
Carpenter, James	4:16:13 (15,895)	
Carpenter, Kevin	3:02:50 (1,358)	
Carpenter, Michael	4:41:52 (22,574)	
Carpenter, Neil	3:53:11 (10,040)	
Carpenter, Tim	4:00:00 (12,085)	
Carpin, Rhys	4:39:04 (21,862)	
Carr, Alan	5:50:08 (31,146)	
Carr, Andy	4:09:51 (14,353)	
Carr, Brian	2:58:16 (1,030)	
Carr, David	2:52:44 (616)	
Carr, David	4:01:50 (12,531)	
Carr, Gordon	5:35:55 (30,262)	
Carr, Graham	4:50:39 (24,531)	
Carr, Ian	3:58:16 (11,584)	
Carr, James	3:44:10 (7,698)	
Carr, Jeremy	4:50:17 (24,463)	
Carr, Kenneth	5:22:33 (29,138)	
Carr, Michael	5:33:14 (30,048)	
Carr, Mike	4:09:02 (14,140)	
Carr, Nathan	4:36:43 (21,264)	
Carr, Peter	5:16:22 (28,489)	
Carr, Philip	3:49:33 (9,053)	
Carre, Christopher	2:52:41 (609)	
Carrette, Bertrand	3:45:39 (8,082)	
Carrier, Dan	5:17:27 (28,621)	
Carrivick, Daniel	2:59:47 (1,156)	
Carrivick, Sean	3:53:00 (9,976)	
Carroll, Graham	4:37:40 (21,484)	
Carroll, Iain	4:41:41 (22,526)	
Carroll, James	4:38:46 (21,787)	
Carroll, John	4:28:55 (19,294)	
Carroll, Martin	4:26:30 (18,653)	
Carroll, Michael	4:17:59 (16,368)	
Carroll, Mick	4:12:52 (15,054)	
Carroll, Patrick	4:16:05 (15,863)	
Carroll, Patrick	4:52:32 (24,882)	
Carroll, Paul	3:19:30 (3,203)	
Carroll, Paul	3:42:59 (7,385)	
Carroll, Paul	4:05:18 (13,273)	
Carroll, Raymond	4:27:54 (19,009)	
Carroll, Rob	3:09:54 (2,027)	
Carroll, Steven	3:47:47 (8,584)	
Carroll, Will	4:12:34 (14,984)	
Carruthers, Graeme	4:46:20 (23,649)	
Carruthers, James	3:43:25 (7,502)	
Carruthers, Roland	2:54:59 (740)	
Carson, Duncan	3:18:36 (3,083)	
Carson, Graham	4:16:40 (16,032)	
Carson, Ian	2:52:42 (611)	
Carson, James	4:12:16 (14,918)	
Carson, Peter	4:14:27 (15,441)	
Carson, Robert	3:32:40 (5,299)	
Carson, Timothy	4:10:34 (14,527)	
Carstairs, Tim	5:08:14 (27,465)	
Carta, Ottavio	3:14:18 (2,592)	
Cartawick, Paul	4:57:15 (25,820)	
Carter, Adam	4:40:51 (22,322)	
Carter, Adrian	3:45:12 (7,975)	
Carter, Andrew	6:21:55 (32,120)	
Carter, Bruce	3:10:56 (2,147)	
Carter, Daniel	4:36:17 (21,147)	
Carter, Darryl	3:14:51 (2,648)	
Carter, Dave	3:40:18 (6,811)	
Carter, David	2:54:49 (729)	
Carter, David	4:00:52 (12,273)	
Carter, David	4:44:38 (23,202)	
Carter, David	5:07:02 (27,301)	
Carter, David	5:21:03 (28,999)	
Carter, Dominic	4:51:12 (24,654)	
Carter, Dylan	3:24:37 (3,932)	
Carter, Hillary	6:44:26 (32,480)	
Carter, Jason	4:23:17 (17,772)	
Carter, Jody	4:24:33 (18,131)	
Carter, John	3:53:04 (10,003)	
Carter, Julian	3:59:22 (11,906)	
Carter, Kevin	5:15:46 (28,406)	
Carter, Lee	5:21:03 (28,999)	
Carter, Les	3:41:34 (7,076)	
Carter, Martin	5:48:13 (31,046)	
Carter, Matthew	3:58:05 (11,536)	
Carter, Michael	4:31:35 (19,993)	
Carter, Paul	2:55:16 (763)	
Carter, Paul	3:40:15 (6,799)	
Carter, Paul	4:16:15 (15,899)	
Carter, Paul	4:21:34 (17,270)	
Carter, Richard	3:39:19 (6,592)	
Carter, Richard	4:53:44 (25,110)	
Carter, Rob	5:05:31 (27,086)	
Carter, Robert	3:50:04 (9,184)	
Carter, Robert	5:23:46 (29,260)	
Carter, Stephen	3:09:11 (1,951)	
Carter, Stephen	3:19:10 (3,157)	
Carter, Stephen	3:25:38 (4,090)	
Carter, Steven	5:33:47 (30,090)	
Carter, Stewart	4:33:54 (20,558)	
Carter, Toby	2:56:22 (863)	
Cartledge, Brian	5:02:19 (26,643)	
Cartlidge, Iain	4:26:51 (18,751)	
Carton, Kenneth	3:51:47 (9,621)	
Carton, Philip	4:08:52 (14,107)	
Cartwright, Adrian	4:35:11 (20,875)	
Cartwright, Andrew	4:40:20 (22,195)	
Cartwright, Paul	3:55:18 (10,696)	
Cartwright, Paul	4:54:01 (25,186)	
Cartwright, Steven	4:07:12 (13,723)	
Carty, Nick	3:51:10 (9,476)	
Caruana, Paul	5:08:58 (27,568)	
Carvajal, Luis Fernando Mazo	2:33:34 (85)	
Carvalho, Manuel	3:36:02 (5,911)	
Carvalho, Miguel	6:53:25 (32,575)	
Carvell, Andrew	4:42:26 (22,706)	
Carver, Peter	4:25:04 (18,277)	
Carveth, Antony	3:37:52 (6,292)	
Carwardine, Peter	3:36:50 (6,081)	
Cary, Clive	3:45:42 (8,090)	
Casali, Emanuele	6:17:05 (32,005)	
Casallas, Hugo	3:34:40 (5,655)	
Casati, Marco	5:55:32 (31,379)	
Case, Barry	4:35:22 (20,914)	
Case, Graham	4:27:22 (18,881)	
Case, Philip	4:09:01 (14,135)	
Case, Stephen	4:09:32 (14,275)	
Casely, Gordon	3:50:15 (9,235)	
Casement, William	4:00:18 (12,153)	
Casey, Jonathan	4:24:45 (18,185)	
Casey, Mark	4:00:01 (12,091)	
Casey, Michael	4:38:14 (21,636)	
Casey, Paul	4:01:20 (12,399)	
Casey, Paul	5:00:31 (26,379)	
Casey, Peter	4:20:53 (17,083)	
Casey, Peter	4:48:34 (24,141)	
Casey, Russell	3:30:25 (4,935)	
Casey, Stephen	3:55:56 (10,882)	
Casey, Stewart	4:08:36 (14,059)	
Cash, Christopher	5:06:06 (27,176)	
Cash, David	4:03:27 (12,873)	
Cash, Jonny	3:55:38 (10,792)	
Cashman, Michael	4:25:13 (18,312)	
Cashmore, Jeremy	5:19:30 (28,817)	
Cass, John	3:49:43 (9,103)	
Cass, Warren	4:47:08 (23,840)	
Cassar, Andreas	4:26:36 (18,680)	
Cassells, Michael	4:50:53 (24,590)	
Casselton, Stephen	3:55:05 (10,619)	
Casserley, Rob	3:39:43 (6,671)	
Cassidy, Andrew	3:25:45 (4,106)	
Cassidy, Bernard	3:12:18 (2,330)	
Cassidy, Bill	3:44:01 (7,661)	
Cassidy, Frank	3:58:00 (11,508)	
Cassidy, Mark	4:15:02 (15,582)	
Cassidy, Michael	4:33:06 (20,375)	
Cassidy, Paul	3:56:57 (11,192)	
Cassie, Paul	4:53:25 (25,054)	
Cassina, Matteo	3:23:51 (3,784)	
Casson, Keith	4:35:39 (21,001)	
Castagna, Giuseppe	3:42:31 (7,291)	
Castanheira, Nuno	4:32:05 (20,105)	
Castell, Clive	5:28:33 (29,660)	
Castell, Phil	3:41:52 (7,125)	
Castellano, Giovanni	3:20:36 (3,325)	
Castillo-Calcerrada, José	4:31:26 (19,940)	
Castle, Matthew	4:59:34 (26,236)	
Castle, Steve	5:07:13 (27,335)	
Castledine, Kenneth	3:07:40 (1,783)	
Catalfamo, Salvatore	5:10:00 (27,690)	
Catanach, David	4:36:18 (21,153)	
Catanzaro, Vincenzo	5:02:34 (26,681)	
Catchpole, Phil	3:37:58 (6,307)	
Catena-Asunsolo, Angel	3:11:43 (2,229)	
Cates, Michael	2:52:18 (588)	
Catling, Ian	4:43:22 (22,927)	
Catmull, Julian	2:59:28 (1,129)	
Cator, Ralph	4:09:11 (14,183)	
Cattell, Michael	6:17:37 (32,022)	
Catterall, Andrew	4:47:00 (23,811)	
Catterall, Donald	4:41:39 (22,513)	
Cattermole, Andrew	4:56:08 (25,618)	
Catto, David	2:52:28 (595)	
Catton, John	4:44:10 (23,099)	
Catton, Neill	4:35:10 (20,866)	
Caudron, Bernard	2:56:10 (841)	
Caulder, Graham	3:14:54 (2,657)	
Caulfield, David	3:46:25 (8,258)	
Caulfield, Robert	4:28:47 (19,252)	
Caulton, Tony	2:54:22 (696)	
Caulwell, Wayne	5:08:20 (27,474)	
Causley, Benjamin	4:34:58 (20,823)	
Cavagna, Antonello	4:39:29 (21,965)	
Cavagna, Gian	4:22:44 (17,618)	
Cavalla, Paul	4:28:05 (19,051)	
Cavallaro, Gianni	4:52:55 (24,963)	
Cavalli, Gaetano	4:22:30 (17,545)	
Cavanagh, Mark	4:39:49 (22,062)	
Cavanagh, Russell	3:32:05 (5,204)	
Cavanagh, Sean	4:31:18 (19,900)	
Cavanaugh, Jim	3:56:35 (11,078)	
Cavannagh, Lance	3:53:39 (10,197)	
Cavedasca, Paul	4:36:35 (21,241)	
Caveney, Terry	3:01:38 (1,266)	
Cavers, Dave	2:28:51 (54)	
Cawdron, Danny	3:42:36 (7,305)	
Cawkwell, Robert	3:49:14 (8,950)	
Cawood, Kevin	4:11:34 (14,759)	
Cawood, Simon	4:05:53 (13,407)	
Cawston, Edmund	4:41:29 (22,472)	
Cayton, Neil	2:33:54 (88)	
Ceccardi, Vanni	3:57:49 (11,455)	
Cecchini, Paolo	3:38:28 (6,416)	
Centeno, Roberto	3:50:08 (9,196)	
Cerezo, Jean-Paul	2:50:58 (532)	
César De Sa, Nuno	3:52:20 (9,790)	
Ceulemans, Koen	4:10:19 (14,464)	
Chabot, Jean	3:25:36 (4,081)	
Chacko, Jacob	4:11:30 (14,747)	
Chacksfield, Mark	4:14:14 (15,377)	

Chadha, Gad 4:08:21 (13,976)
Chadha, Sutish 5:55:16 (31,363)
Chadwick, Alexander 3:53:15 (10,061)
Chadwick, Christopher 4:41:52 (22,574)
Chadwick, Mark 3:43:21 (7,489)
Chadwick, Nicholas 4:07:21 (13,761)
Chadwick, Paul 5:11:00 (27,812)
Chadwick, Peter 4:54:50 (25,349)
Chadwick, Stephen 3:41:18 (7,030)
Chadwick, Steve 4:19:55 (16,840)
Chaffe, Gary 5:00:53 (26,441)
Chaffer, Peter 2:51:48 (571)
Chaffin, John 4:38:49 (21,796)
Chagger, Balbinder 5:54:46 (31,341)
Chahal, Tim 4:27:47 (18,978)
Chairon, Laurent 2:34:12 (92)
Chalcroft, Anthony 4:37:09 (21,348)
Chalfont, Roger 5:35:47 (30,255)
Chaline, Christian 3:57:11 (11,256)
Chalk, Ian 4:18:44 (16,530)
Chalk, Jason 3:18:01 (3,010)
Chalk, Stephen 4:44:11 (23,104)
Chalke, Daniel 4:39:33 (21,985)
Chalke, Robert 4:15:39 (15,739)
Chalke, Steve 3:44:26 (7,780)
Challis, Raymond 3:38:18 (6,370)
Challoner, Michael 4:50:38 (24,529)
Chalmers, Alexander 4:25:41 (18,436)
Chalmers, Charles 4:32:06 (20,109)
Chalmers, Ian 4:24:01 (17,985)
Chalmin, Christophe 3:48:13 (8,677)
Chalners, Matt 4:24:04 (18,001)
Chamberlain, Brian 4:23:09 (17,738)
Chamberlain, Ken 3:02:56 (1,365)
Chamberlain, Mark 2:50:32 (513)
Chamberlain, Martin 4:19:42 (16,778)
Chamberlain, Matthew 3:01:15 (1,245)
Chamberlain, Paul 4:25:02 (18,274)
Chamberlain, Paul 7:26:27 (32,773)
Chamberlain, Simon 3:51:56 (9,657)
Chamberlin, Andrew 5:19:55 (28,861)
Chambers, Andrew 4:02:35 (12,675)
Chambers, Anthony 4:21:31 (17,255)
Chambers, Brian 4:17:14 (16,179)
Chambers, Bryan 4:18:34 (16,501)
Chambers, Carl 3:48:32 (8,757)
Chambers, Carl 3:58:36 (11,678)
Chambers, James 4:52:50 (24,944)
Chambers, Joseph 4:22:40 (17,596)
Chambers, Paul 4:43:58 (23,058)
Chambers, Peter 4:31:40 (20,003)
Chambers, Simon 5:13:15 (28,108)
Chambers, Stephen 4:59:29 (26,215)
Chamley, Brian 5:35:33 (30,233)
Champagne, Jean-Louis 3:28:03 (4,523)
Chamunoita, Reuben 4:32:51 (20,320)
Chan, Aaron 4:32:11 (20,136)
Chan, Chong 3:04:34 (1,509)
Chan, Shun-On 3:30:53 (5,006)
Chana, Jaswant 3:39:10 (6,559)
Chandler, Anthony 4:34:33 (20,710)
Chandler, David 4:09:54 (14,363)
Chandler, David 4:21:39 (17,297)
Chandler, Jim 3:16:40 (2,859)
Chandler, Keith 5:53:47 (31,304)
Chandler, Michael 3:09:52 (2,023)
Chandler, Paul 3:58:34 (11,664)
Chandler, Peter 3:59:47 (12,019)
Chandler, Peter 4:01:51 (12,535)
Chandler, Ross 4:06:21 (13,529)
Chandley, Paul 3:56:24 (11,017)
Chandley, Peter 3:26:38 (4,257)
Chandor, Benjamin 3:23:53 (3,795)
Chandramdhan, Vayramuthu 6:32:39 (32,316)
Changela, Nitin 5:00:42 (26,411)
Channing, Geoffrey 5:12:15 (27,984)
Channings, George 4:17:33 (16,253)
Channon, Amos 4:43:09 (22,881)
Channon, David 4:46:02 (23,579)
Chant, Doug 3:29:14 (4,738)
Chant, Ian 3:37:00 (6,118)
Chant, Nicholas 4:04:42 (13,135)
Chantler, Danny 4:21:31 (17,255)
Chantreux, Domnique 3:03:42 (1,442)
Chant-Sempill, Ian 4:27:37 (18,941)
Chantyaz, Mimprasad 4:11:28 (14,737)
Chapel, Jerome 3:49:17 (8,965)
Chaplin, Ben 5:01:55 (26,590)
Chaplin, Graham 5:14:28 (28,242)
Chaplin, Ian 2:58:18 (1,031)
Chaplin, Neil 3:26:41 (4,269)
Chaplin, Simon 4:30:04 (19,615)
Chaplin, Stephen 3:27:21 (4,385)
Chaplin, Stephen 4:13:28 (15,181)
Chapman, Anthony 4:21:50 (17,349)
Chapman, Ashley 4:04:06 (13,008)
Chapman, Brian 4:40:59 (22,350)
Chapman, Clive 5:27:33 (29,580)
Chapman, Colin 3:32:55 (5,341)
Chapman, Colin 4:21:14 (17,174)
Chapman, Frederick 6:35:35 (32,369)
Chapman, Gary 3:56:09 (10,942)
Chapman, Graham 4:38:35 (21,730)
Chapman, Ian 3:41:57 (7,143)
Chapman, Ian 4:08:41 (14,076)
Chapman, James 5:33:56 (30,104)
Chapman, Jamie 4:38:15 (21,642)
Chapman, Jason 3:57:01 (11,214)
Chapman, Jeff 4:29:03 (19,335)
Chapman, Jonathan 4:39:40 (22,009)
Chapman, Kevin 4:28:38 (19,208)
Chapman, Leslie 2:54:42 (723)
Chapman, Leslie 5:40:34 (30,588)
Chapman, Mark 3:25:47 (4,111)
Chapman, Neil 3:09:16 (1,961)
Chapman, Neil 3:55:32 (10,758)
Chapman, Nigel 3:41:56 (7,137)
Chapman, Nigel 4:18:15 (16,427)
Chapman, Nigel 5:14:00 (28,195)
Chapman, Paul 3:57:54 (11,476)
Chapman, Peter 3:49:17 (8,965)
Chapman, Peter 4:23:14 (17,755)
Chapman, Reg 3:19:25 (3,191)
Chapman, Richard 4:17:14 (16,179)
Chapman, Robert 3:49:00 (8,896)
Chapman, Robert 4:05:29 (13,324)
Chapman, Simon 3:35:16 (5,758)
Chapman, Simon 3:58:02 (11,522)
Chapman, Steven 3:53:08 (10,025)
Chapman, Stewart 3:48:35 (8,773)
Chapman, Tim 4:47:25 (23,900)
Chapman, William 4:33:23 (20,438)
Chappell, Aaron 3:50:42 (9,347)
Chappell, Stephen 4:23:27 (17,814)
Charbonnier, Paul 3:34:27 (5,610)
Chard, Stephen 3:45:01 (7,929)
Charge, Terence 6:29:46 (32,270)
Charles, Alan 4:39:20 (21,930)
Charles, Anthony 4:16:20 (15,924)
Charles, Bryan 4:56:43 (25,718)
Charles, Chris 4:27:39 (18,951)
Charles, Edward 5:25:40 (29,418)
Charles, Martin 5:30:53 (29,857)
Charles, Michel 4:04:34 (13,104)
Charles, Paul 3:05:16 (1,563)
Charles, Paul 3:48:41 (8,807)
Charles, Paul 4:19:40 (16,765)
Charlesworth, Mike 4:59:59 (26,307)
Charlesworth, Paul 4:59:56 (26,296)
Charley, Richard 3:36:54 (6,093)
Charlton, Alan 4:14:49 (15,529)
Charlton, Alan 6:29:09 (32,259)
Charlton, David 5:12:36 (28,037)
Charlton, Martin 4:05:32 (13,335)
Charlton, Roger 5:17:31 (28,631)
Charlton, Trevor 4:46:16 (23,635)
Charluteau, Nicholas 3:34:18 (5,583)
Charman, Gary 4:22:20 (17,493)
Charman, Jon 4:36:11 (21,129)
Charman, Kevin 3:45:30 (8,044)
Charman, Philip 4:01:39 (12,482)
Charmasson, Bernard 3:37:28 (6,203)
Charpentier, Pascal 3:37:11 (6,146)
Chart, Robert 3:21:38 (3,455)
Charter, John 3:15:34 (2,731)
Charters, Paul 4:41:08 (22,382)
Chase, Anthony 3:36:08 (5,942)
Chatburn, Chris 4:27:29 (18,915)
Chatburn, Dean 3:42:19 (7,236)
Chatelain, Ronan 3:05:34 (1,600)
Chater, Andrew 4:43:59 (23,062)
Chater, Christopher 4:01:38 (12,476)
Chater, Nick 3:45:24 (8,021)
Chatfield, Gerald 4:35:33 (20,960)
Chatfield, Mark 3:37:30 (6,217)
Chattell, Steven 3:57:17 (11,288)
Chatten, Malcolm 4:06:16 (13,509)
Chauhan, Anil 4:48:40 (24,161)
Chausset, Christophe 3:22:30 (3,581)
Chauvin, Patrice 3:08:46 (1,902)
Chavasse, Steven 5:34:35 (30,156)
Chavda, Gordhan 5:27:03 (29,527)
Chedotal, David 4:47:10 (23,849)
Cheek, Nicholas 3:39:19 (6,592)
Cheesebrough, Timothy 4:18:43 (16,529)
Cheeseman, Darren 4:23:19 (17,781)
Cheeseman, Robin 2:43:19 (249)
Cheesman, Alan 4:49:00 (24,234)
Cheesman, Charles 4:54:47 (25,337)
Cheesman, Christopher 3:55:51 (10,855)
Cheesman, Tony 4:34:33 (20,710)
Cheesmur, Stephen 4:29:16 (19,405)
Cheetham, Christopher 4:33:36 (20,494)
Cheetham, David 3:55:31 (10,750)
Cheetham, Gregg 3:46:49 (8,349)
Cheetham, Robert 4:42:45 (22,782)
Chell, Brian 3:40:06 (6,762)
Chell, Philip 4:33:50 (20,541)
Chelton, Lee 5:08:20 (27,474)
Chen, Theodore 3:28:18 (4,568)
Chenery, Mark 3:52:01 (9,693)
Cheney, David 3:35:28 (5,799)
Cheney, Les 5:05:10 (27,040)
Chennell, David 4:36:27 (21,200)
Cherrett, Andy 4:22:46 (17,628)
Cherry, David Bruce 4:53:41 (25,102)
Cherry, Gareth 4:24:56 (18,234)
Cherry, Robert 3:43:00 (7,390)
Cheseaux, Gerard 3:52:23 (9,808)
Cheshire, Thomas 4:08:15 (13,961)
Chesmore, Rupert 5:48:19 (31,051)
Chessa, Antonio 5:17:02 (28,569)
Chester, Symon 3:00:57 (1,223)
Chesters, Alan 3:53:32 (10,157)
Chesters, Graham 3:19:24 (3,185)
Chetelat, Bernard 3:40:34 (6,867)
Cheung, Andrew 3:40:44 (6,900)
Cheung, Peter 4:57:52 (25,925)
Cheval, Thierry 4:17:16 (16,192)
Cheyne, Brian 5:37:24 (30,375)
Cheyne, Giles 3:54:19 (10,404)
Chiari, Pelle 3:59:36 (11,969)
Chicheportiche, Gerard 4:32:27 (20,207)
Chick, Roger 5:41:35 (30,660)
Chidgey, Christopher 4:40:37 (22,257)
Chidley, Tim 3:55:04 (10,614)
Chidwick, Ian 3:17:01 (2,906)
Chilcott, Pete 5:28:35 (29,663)
Child, John 5:24:41 (29,338)
Child, Keith 3:17:39 (2,970)
Childerhouse, Erik 4:37:37 (21,471)
Childs, Andrew 3:46:33 (8,300)
Childs, Daniel 3:52:02 (9,700)
Childs, David 4:27:38 (18,947)
Childs, Gary 3:54:44 (10,529)
Childs, Leslie 4:20:09 (16,905)
Childs, Mark 3:58:00 (11,508)
Childs, Phillip 3:10:32 (2,108)
Childs, Roger 3:58:10 (11,558)
Childs, Shaun 4:22:02 (17,405)
Chiles, Andrew 3:55:50 (10,850)
Chilton, Andy 4:17:45 (16,310)
Chilver, Chris 4:37:37 (21,471)
Chimejczuk, Michael 4:59:03 (26,142)
Chinery, Neale 4:10:48 (14,576)
Chinoda, Jenki 5:28:38 (29,668)
Chioke, Ike 4:28:57 (19,309)
Chiplin, Terry 3:44:21 (7,757)
Chippendale, Simon 5:18:53 (28,764)

Chisholm, Andrew	5:00:12	(26,337)
Chisholm, Barry	3:06:35	(1,698)
Chisholm, David	3:40:18	(6,811)
Chisholm Batten, Roderick	3:52:08	(9,736)
Chislett, David	3:24:18	(3,877)
Chissell, Kevin	4:36:44	(21,266)
Chittell, Christopher	4:05:56	(13,420)
Chittem, David	3:45:05	(7,950)
Chittenden, Tim	4:57:11	(25,809)
Chittendon, Oliver	3:55:26	(10,732)
Chitticks, Richard	6:09:01	(31,814)
Chivers, Adam	4:44:19	(23,134)
Chivers, Francis	4:50:29	(24,502)
Chivers, Hugh	4:54:33	(25,292)
Chiverton, Mark	4:32:49	(20,306)
Chmara, Edward	4:39:54	(22,080)
Chodzko Zajko, Piotr	3:53:21	(10,094)
Chohan, Gavin	3:52:55	(9,955)
Chong, Gerald	5:15:31	(28,367)
Chopra, Raj	4:27:27	(18,905)
Chou, Alfred	2:56:14	(851)
Choudhury, Sajal	5:24:47	(29,343)
Chow, Franklin	5:15:28	(28,357)
Chow, Richard	5:39:36	(30,522)
Chownes-Dove, Paul	3:54:38	(10,494)
Christensen, Per	3:53:01	(9,985)
Christensen, Peter	4:10:28	(14,505)
Christer, James	5:29:30	(29,736)
Christian, David	4:13:51	(15,272)
Christiansen, Peter	6:25:20	(32,187)
Christie, Campbell	3:35:46	(5,859)
Christie, Emlyn	3:54:20	(10,409)
Christie, Graham	3:57:06	(11,235)
Christie, Iain	3:04:21	(1,491)
Christinet, Stephan	3:57:00	(11,210)
Christison, Clive	4:02:16	(12,609)
Christison, Colin	3:02:44	(1,353)
Christopher, David	4:13:31	(15,192)
Christopher, David	4:56:03	(25,594)
Christopher, John	3:32:48	(5,316)
Christopher, Leonard	2:49:50	(480)
Chrysostomou, Vasos	4:27:23	(18,886)
Chubb, Richard	4:12:35	(14,992)
Chung, Alan	4:08:23	(13,990)
Chung, Sandy	4:02:36	(12,681)
Churaman, Roger	5:03:58	(26,884)
Church, Andrew	3:58:59	(11,796)
Church, Charles	4:03:48	(12,943)
Church, Colin	4:26:55	(18,764)
Church, David	4:39:54	(22,080)
Church, Jerome	4:47:36	(23,925)
Church, Martin	3:54:49	(10,547)
Church, Michael	4:32:39	(20,261)
Church, Richard	6:18:16	(32,044)
Churcher, Steve	2:56:46	(897)
Churchill, Nigel	3:32:03	(5,198)
Churchill, Roger	3:45:15	(7,989)
Chutter, Anthony	3:00:07	(1,178)
Chynoweth, Stephen	5:12:14	(27,979)
Ciacci, Claudio	5:12:16	(27,989)
Ciaccia, Peter	3:19:43	(3,223)
Cicutti, Ambrose	4:47:07	(23,834)
Cilliers, Stephan	4:29:42	(19,506)
Cimino, Carmelo	3:37:27	(6,195)
Cinque, Giulio	3:53:04	(10,003)
Cinque, Giuseppe	4:35:40	(21,008)
Civico, Reynaldo	3:55:31	(10,750)
Clack, James	4:42:16	(22,665)
Clack, Paul	3:55:47	(10,835)
Clack, Philip	3:56:10	(10,948)
Clamp, Paul	4:30:54	(19,808)
Clancy, Danny	5:42:52	(30,743)
Clannachan, Gordon	4:41:41	(22,526)
Clapham, Jeremy	3:16:57	(2,897)
Clapham, Peter	4:45:45	(23,503)
Clapp, Franchot	4:27:48	(18,983)
Clapp, Matthew	2:43:56	(266)
Clapp, William	3:14:24	(2,599)
Clapson, Martin	3:50:19	(9,256)
Clarabut, Raymond	3:27:15	(4,368)
Clarasso, Jean Jacques	3:50:37	(9,327)
Clare, Jonathan	2:58:11	(1,021)
Clare-Brown, Keith	4:16:44	(16,045)
Claret, Eric	4:37:39	(21,477)
Claridge, Alan	5:02:33	(26,679)
Claridge, Robert	3:22:39	(3,598)
Clark, Adrian	3:47:47	(8,584)
Clark, Allan	4:21:06	(17,140)
Clark, Allister	4:49:00	(24,234)
Clark, Andrew	2:54:15	(691)
Clark, Andrew	4:40:47	(22,304)
Clark, Benjamin	3:56:31	(11,059)
Clark, Christopher	3:51:01	(9,433)
Clark, Colin	5:40:20	(30,573)
Clark, Daniel	4:15:12	(15,621)
Clark, Daniel	4:39:07	(21,877)
Clark, Darrin	4:54:42	(25,323)
Clark, David	3:41:15	(7,025)
Clark, David	3:56:08	(10,940)
Clark, David	3:56:39	(11,097)
Clark, David	3:59:27	(11,930)
Clark, Derek	3:39:24	(6,603)
Clark, Duncan	4:53:24	(25,049)
Clark, Frank	4:33:07	(20,383)
Clark, Gary	4:09:09	(14,170)
Clark, Gary	4:55:39	(25,504)
Clark, Geoffrey	3:12:17	(2,326)
Clark, Graeme	4:24:44	(18,182)
Clark, Ian	3:16:35	(2,851)
Clark, Ian	3:52:17	(9,779)
Clark, Ian	4:35:48	(21,028)
Clark, Jeff	4:13:45	(15,251)
Clark, John	3:20:00	(3,254)
Clark, John	6:53:14	(32,572)
Clark, Jonathan	4:35:37	(20,993)
Clark, Jonathan	5:32:37	(30,001)
Clark, Joseph	3:57:45	(11,440)
Clark, Julian	3:56:53	(11,168)
Clark, Mark	3:14:46	(2,635)
Clark, Michael	3:24:50	(3,961)
Clark, Neil	3:08:29	(1,869)
Clark, Paul	3:04:06	(1,475)
Clark, Paul	4:10:35	(14,532)
Clark, Paul	5:15:05	(28,309)
Clark, Peter	4:01:24	(12,417)
Clark, Peter	4:12:17	(14,919)
Clark, Richard	4:00:09	(12,118)
Clark, Richard	4:07:53	(13,890)
Clark, Robert	3:52:32	(9,849)
Clark, Rod	5:06:30	(27,230)
Clark, Roger	4:01:45	(12,505)
Clark, Ron	4:49:59	(24,419)
Clark, Russell	4:07:38	(13,826)
Clark, Simon	4:40:39	(22,266)
Clark, Simon	5:33:36	(30,077)
Clark, Stephen	4:19:08	(16,627)
Clark, Stephen	4:28:35	(19,187)
Clark, Stephen	4:29:08	(19,361)
Clark, Steven	4:58:48	(26,096)
Clark, Toby	4:06:57	(13,662)
Clark, William	3:03:18	(1,404)
Clark III, Franklin	5:37:30	(30,385)
Clarke, Andrew	3:10:03	(2,045)
Clarke, Andrew	4:08:25	(13,997)
Clarke, Andy	3:52:12	(9,754)
Clarke, Anthony	3:46:35	(8,309)
Clarke, Anthony	5:01:20	(26,508)
Clarke, Barry	4:30:32	(19,715)
Clarke, Brian	4:13:16	(15,143)
Clarke, Bruce	3:05:33	(1,596)
Clarke, Chris	3:59:30	(11,938)
Clarke, Chris	5:31:46	(29,932)
Clarke, Christopher	4:05:31	(13,329)
Clarke, Christopher	4:51:12	(24,654)
Clarke, Christopher	5:59:52	(31,540)
Clarke, Craig	4:08:34	(14,045)
Clarke, Dan	5:11:15	(27,845)
Clarke, David	3:27:40	(4,451)
Clarke, Dominic	4:02:49	(12,733)
Clarke, Eric	3:33:05	(5,366)
Clarke, Gregory	3:09:22	(1,980)
Clarke, Ian	4:55:57	(25,576)
Clarke, John	3:53:18	(10,081)
Clarke, Kenneth	3:52:58	(9,967)
Clarke, Martin	3:00:54	(1,218)
Clarke, Martin	3:19:58	(3,252)
Clarke, Matthew	4:11:01	(14,633)
Clarke, Matthew	4:32:00	(20,085)
Clarke, Maurice	7:26:18	(32,771)
Clarke, Michael	5:12:47	(28,054)
Clarke, Nicholas	3:08:19	(1,842)
Clarke, Nicholas	4:52:56	(24,970)
Clarke, Paul	3:16:39	(2,857)
Clarke, Paul	4:39:04	(21,862)
Clarke, Paul	5:20:26	(28,933)
Clarke, Paul	5:51:21	(31,206)
Clarke, Peter	4:11:42	(14,796)
Clarke, Peter	4:55:25	(25,469)
Clarke, Peter	7:04:26	(32,666)
Clarke, Phil	4:06:47	(13,627)
Clarke, Phillip	6:07:11	(31,766)
Clarke, Robert	3:12:20	(2,337)
Clarke, Robert	3:53:02	(9,994)
Clarke, Robert	5:05:51	(27,135)
Clarke, Robert	6:36:30	(32,386)
Clarke, Robin	5:07:12	(27,328)
Clarke, Roger	3:00:50	(1,217)
Clarke, Russell	2:55:51	(816)
Clarke, Sean	3:54:42	(10,516)
Clarke, Simon	3:59:04	(11,825)
Clarke, Stephen	3:58:13	(11,571)
Clarke, Steven	4:08:41	(14,076)
Clarke, Steven	5:00:48	(26,421)
Clarke, Timothy	4:29:10	(19,373)
Clarke, Toby	3:50:22	(9,268)
Clarkson, Bob	4:10:22	(14,479)
Clarkson, David	3:13:13	(2,466)
Clarkson, Frank	4:05:25	(13,305)
Clarkson, Matthew	3:55:26	(10,732)
Clarkson, Simon	4:56:21	(25,671)
Clarkson, Stewart	3:44:16	(7,731)
Clasper, Craig	4:53:04	(24,988)
Clatot, Didier	3:36:39	(6,049)
Claxton, Coral	3:55:35	(10,778)
Claxton, Kevin	4:28:38	(19,208)
Clay, Adrian	4:22:57	(17,689)
Clay, Toby	2:58:39	(1,065)
Clayden, Matthew	3:53:31	(10,150)
Clayden, Stephen	5:23:51	(29,267)
Claydon, Paul	4:48:23	(24,097)
Clayson, Edward	4:27:17	(18,858)
Clayton, Andrew	5:03:07	(26,766)
Clayton, Ian	2:36:55	(126)
Clayton, Ian	4:42:03	(22,622)
Clayton, John	3:45:02	(7,933)
Clayton, Jonathan	3:50:22	(9,268)
Clayton, Jonathan	3:59:45	(12,007)
Clayton, Mark	4:46:43	(23,738)
Clayton, Shaun	4:28:23	(19,131)
Clazey, Graeme	3:15:43	(2,758)
Clearkin, Peter	3:29:38	(4,818)
Cleary, Andrew	2:58:49	(1,076)
Cleary, Christopher	3:21:52	(3,497)
Cleary, David	4:19:17	(16,665)
Cleary, Michael	3:49:43	(9,103)
Cleary, Paul	4:24:45	(18,185)
Cleator, Christopher	5:05:15	(27,051)
Clee, Adrian	4:35:20	(20,909)
Clegg, Gavin	3:00:05	(1,174)
Clegg, Mark	3:20:32	(3,319)
Clegg, Peter	3:27:46	(4,411)
Clegg, William	4:16:19	(15,921)
Clemence, Grant	3:29:17	(4,744)
Clemens, Claude	4:44:28	(23,162)
Clemens, John	3:13:50	(2,543)
Clemens, Nigel	3:01:43	(1,274)
Clement, Gerald	3:34:10	(5,557)
Clements, Andrew	2:39:42	(177)
Clements, Gary	4:24:16	(18,059)
Clements, Gary	4:28:51	(19,278)
Clements, John	4:36:27	(21,200)
Clements, Jonathan	3:54:07	(10,351)
Clements, Martin	3:08:35	(1,879)
Clements, Martin	3:41:21	(7,038)
Clements, Martyn	3:44:18	(7,742)
Clements, Paul	3:03:14	(1,394)
Clements, Paul	4:27:53	(19,000)
Clements, Peter	4:12:46	(15,034)
Clements, Simon	4:25:55	(18,493)

Clements, Tony 3:41:32 (7,070)
Clements, Trevor 3:13:35 (2,515)
Clemo, Bill 5:14:14 (28,216)
Clenaghan, Stuart 4:16:10 (15,881)
Clerc, Thierry 3:46:21 (8,236)
Clerc, Thierry 3:51:37 (9,576)
Clerc-Renaud, Denis 5:00:44 (26,415)
Cleves, Andrew 2:50:42 (521)
Clewley, Adam 3:43:12 (7,442)
Cliff, Lee 5:44:22 (30,846)
Cliff, Paul 4:00:18 (12,153)
Cliffe, Tom 4:50:31 (24,512)
Clifford, Daniel 3:12:25 (2,348)
Clifford, John 4:03:02 (12,782)
Clifford, Les 3:45:14 (7,983)
Clifford, Peter 3:14:49 (2,641)
Clifford, Stephen 3:41:30 (7,066)
Clifford, Stephen 5:14:06 (28,205)
Clifford, Tim 3:41:01 (6,966)
Clifford, Tom 3:51:11 (9,479)
Clifford Jones, Paul 4:00:21 (12,158)
Clift, Dominick 5:25:42 (29,420)
Clifton, Andrew 4:35:12 (20,881)
Clifton, Ivo 4:13:05 (15,100)
Clifton, Michael 3:01:49 (1,284)
Clifton, Toby 4:46:19 (23,639)
Climent, Francesc 3:55:14 (10,675)
Clinch, Peter 4:11:31 (14,751)
Clish, Simon 4:38:38 (21,749)
Cloke, Ian 4:56:54 (25,745)
Clothier, Ben 3:45:50 (8,127)
Clough, David 4:10:27 (14,497)
Cloux, Pierre 4:20:01 (16,866)
Clover, David 4:00:52 (12,273)
Clover, James 4:39:17 (21,921)
Clowes, Andrew 5:24:13 (29,298)
Clulee, John 5:35:34 (30,236)
Cluley, David 4:54:17 (25,240)
Clune, Joe 4:04:27 (13,078)
Clunie, Jason 3:05:24 (1,580)
Clutterbuck, Barnaby 5:23:33 (29,226)
Clynes, Declan 2:53:54 (675)
Coad, Gilmour 5:09:15 (27,599)
Coade, David 3:26:09 (4,174)
Coate, Clive 4:15:30 (15,697)
Coates, Alan 5:49:05 (31,105)
Coates, Brian 3:12:47 (2,396)
Coates, David 2:56:35 (880)
Coates, Glen 3:36:05 (5,924)
Coates, Jonathon 3:46:42 (8,330)
Coates, Nigel 2:57:52 (996)
Coates, Peter 5:00:46 (26,418)
Coates, Phil 5:08:31 (27,498)
Coates, Phillip 3:40:50 (6,925)
Coats, Brian 6:57:46 (32,607)
Coats, James 4:22:57 (17,689)
Coats, Jim 3:56:17 (10,983)
Coats, John 3:30:41 (4,976)
Cobain, David 4:42:25 (22,701)
Cobb, George 4:19:41 (16,775)
Cobb, Paul 6:36:56 (32,393)
Cobbe, Henry 3:47:22 (8,480)
Cobbett, Peter 4:19:34 (16,741)
Cobbold, Alex 3:56:24 (11,017)
Cobbold, Matthew 4:32:12 (20,141)
Cobbold, Richard 3:41:38 (7,087)
Cobill, Sebastian 3:26:31 (4,234)
Coburn, Daniel 3:46:01 (8,163)
Cocaud, Olivier 3:34:36 (5,636)
Cochrane, Ian 4:54:50 (25,349)
Cochrane, Jason 4:27:20 (18,873)
Cochrane, Robert 3:10:43 (2,124)
Cock, Stuart 4:34:18 (20,649)
Cockbain, Mark 3:10:51 (2,139)
Cockburn, Ben 4:07:29 (13,793)
Cockburn, Jason 3:52:06 (9,723)
Cocker, Daniel 4:11:25 (14,715)
Cockings, Alexander 4:28:24 (19,139)
Cocklin, Alan 4:55:06 (25,391)
Cockram, Nigel 3:45:12 (7,975)
Coe, Gordon 3:59:59 (12,080)
Coffey, Damian 3:10:28 (2,095)
Coffey, John 4:09:33 (14,281)
Coffey, Simon 4:40:20 (22,195)
Coggan, Benjamin 4:21:50 (17,349)
Coggan, Robert 4:17:51 (16,337)
Coggan, Thomas 4:21:51 (17,356)
Coggin, Robert 5:50:51 (31,177)
Cogman, David 3:39:13 (6,574)
Cogolludo, José 4:39:41 (22,016)
Cohen, Carl 4:55:38 (25,499)
Cohen, Howard 3:23:36 (3,743)
Cohen, Julius 4:00:02 (12,092)
Cohen, Lee 4:24:17 (18,062)
Cohen, Oliver 4:03:12 (12,813)
Coker, Kevin 4:29:49 (19,543)
Coke-Smyth, Tom 3:06:33 (1,694)
Colagiovanni, Antonio 4:37:29 (21,445)
Colbert, Alan 5:41:30 (30,655)
Colbourne, George 3:55:17 (10,687)
Colbourne, Richard 3:25:51 (4,124)
Colby, Geoffrey 4:58:14 (25,989)
Colclough, Nicholas 3:57:35 (11,389)
Colcombe, Paul 5:14:22 (28,234)
Coldicott, Allan 3:52:58 (9,967)
Coldman, Trevor 4:03:15 (12,827)
Cole, Brian 4:20:56 (17,090)
Cole, Chris 3:40:42 (6,895)
Cole, David 3:56:26 (11,025)
Cole, David 5:22:32 (29,136)
Cole, Ed 4:46:38 (23,720)
Cole, Ian 4:40:35 (22,252)
Cole, James 5:35:05 (30,190)
Cole, Jeremy 5:00:29 (26,371)
Cole, Julian 3:55:04 (10,614)
Cole, Marc 4:06:26 (13,550)
Cole, Mark 3:37:28 (6,203)
Cole, Marlon 3:26:59 (4,327)
Cole, Martin 4:18:08 (16,394)
Cole, Michael 3:18:57 (3,130)
Cole, Michael 3:47:41 (8,558)
Cole, Neil 4:49:47 (24,376)
Cole, Nick 3:46:54 (8,367)
Cole, Paul 3:34:16 (5,572)
Cole, Paul 4:29:26 (19,444)
Cole, Paul 7:20:47 (32,758)
Cole, Shaun 4:48:45 (24,178)
Cole, Stephen 3:58:24 (11,621)
Cole, Terence 3:34:20 (5,587)
Cole, Terry 6:04:33 (31,675)
Cole, Wesley 4:57:35 (25,877)
Colebrook, Julian 5:01:49 (26,571)
Colebrook, Martyn 4:44:15 (23,115)
Coleman, Adam 5:01:53 (26,585)
Coleman, Brian 4:04:42 (13,135)
Coleman, Clinton 4:09:55 (14,367)
Coleman, Glen 2:52:31 (599)
Coleman, Glenn 4:57:02 (25,774)
Coleman, Jamie 4:12:39 (15,012)
Coleman, John 4:49:47 (24,376)
Coleman, John 6:11:48 (31,876)
Coleman, Kevin 4:30:39 (19,745)
Coleman, Martin 5:36:46 (30,329)
Coleman, Paul 3:35:23 (5,778)
Coleman, Richard 4:24:33 (18,131)
Coleman, Simon 4:34:54 (20,803)
Coleman, Simon 5:10:22 (27,734)
Coleman, Stanley 2:59:56 (1,164)
Coleman, Tony 5:02:19 (26,643)
Colepio Filoteo, Giuseppe 3:51:31 (9,550)
Colerick, Arthur 6:21:33 (32,115)
Coles, Brian 4:28:01 (19,038)
Coles, Daryl 4:31:54 (20,057)
Coles, David 2:57:33 (963)
Coles, Jason 4:40:12 (22,159)
Coles, Lee 4:15:47 (15,778)
Coles, Terence 3:16:59 (2,903)
Coley, Edward 4:06:02 (13,442)
Coley, Philip 4:17:11 (16,166)
Coley-Smith, Nigel 4:05:34 (13,343)
Colfer, James 3:28:34 (4,616)
Colfor, Jim 3:27:03 (4,339)
Colgate, Cyril 4:35:33 (20,960)
Colin, Bruno 4:16:56 (16,100)
Colin, Etienne 3:18:45 (3,106)
Colin, Olivier 3:46:12 (8,201)
Collacott, Christopher 3:54:03 (10,326)
Collell-Riera, Xavier 4:14:01 (15,316)
Collenette, John 4:36:26 (21,196)
Collerton, Liam 4:03:48 (12,943)
Collett, Ray 5:46:41 (30,975)
Colley, David 3:48:34 (8,766)
Colley, John 4:00:37 (12,209)
Collie, John 3:35:00 (5,710)
Collier, David 2:44:06 (274)
Collier, John 4:18:27 (16,476)
Collier, Jonathan 4:24:37 (18,152)
Collier, Matt 6:08:19 (31,792)
Collier, Paul 3:23:13 (3,680)
Collier, Paul 4:31:52 (20,047)
Collier, Stuart 5:23:38 (29,240)
Colligan, Grant 4:19:07 (16,621)
Colliingham, John 2:43:27 (252)
Collingbine, Danny 4:14:02 (15,324)
Collingbourne, Alan 4:05:56 (13,420)
Collingbourne, Michael 3:05:09 (1,556)
Collingbourne, Robert 3:59:02 (11,819)
Collings, Charles 4:44:31 (23,181)
Collings, Philip 3:24:15 (3,869)
Collingwood, Edwin 3:50:30 (9,302)
Collini, Stefan 3:50:45 (9,363)
Collins, Alan 4:27:11 (18,839)
Collins, Andy 3:06:27 (1,678)
Collins, Anthony 5:22:00 (29,093)
Collins, Barry 2:54:17 (693)
Collins, Benjamin 3:52:21 (9,797)
Collins, Chris 4:31:06 (19,855)
Collins, Gary 3:00:23 (1,195)
Collins, Gavin 3:45:34 (8,065)
Collins, Gilbert 5:53:07 (31,282)
Collins, Graham 3:11:44 (2,234)
Collins, Graham 3:43:53 (7,630)
Collins, James 4:20:50 (17,073)
Collins, John 3:59:23 (11,914)
Collins, John 5:45:30 (30,910)
Collins, Justin 3:46:04 (8,172)
Collins, Mark 4:37:12 (21,370)
Collins, Mark 4:52:42 (24,915)
Collins, Martin 4:47:02 (23,823)
Collins, Matthew 4:27:53 (19,000)
Collins, Michael 3:45:28 (8,034)
Collins, Nicholas 4:49:36 (24,342)
Collins, Patrick 3:35:55 (5,886)
Collins, Patrick 4:05:18 (13,273)
Collins, Paul 3:24:55 (3,975)
Collins, Philip 3:44:16 (7,731)
Collins, Piers 4:34:44 (20,758)
Collins, Richard 4:07:40 (13,831)
Collins, Robert 4:45:33 (23,454)
Collins, Scott 3:53:16 (10,071)
Collins, Stephen 3:23:01 (3,660)
Collins, Terry 5:04:47 (26,997)
Collins, Tim 4:40:09 (22,145)
Collinson, Andrew 3:04:41 (1,516)
Collinson, Anthony 5:31:15 (29,891)
Collis, Brian 4:01:23 (12,415)
Collis, David 4:47:46 (23,965)
Collis, James 3:29:09 (4,720)
Collison, Nick 9:04:50 (32,893)
Collison, Nigel 3:43:41 (7,568)
Colls, David 4:52:09 (24,805)
Colls, David 6:26:10 (32,205)
Colls, Stewart 3:58:27 (11,635)
Collyer, Daniel 4:33:14 (20,412)
Collyer, Dean 4:39:31 (21,973)
Colman, Barry 4:40:46 (22,300)
Colman, Ivan 3:10:30 (2,102)
Colon, William 6:04:13 (31,666)
Coltman, Guy 5:00:18 (26,347)
Coltman, Jason 4:32:24 (20,188)
Colven, David 5:09:13 (27,597)
Colverson, Nigel 4:40:58 (22,348)
Colwell, Stephen 4:21:04 (17,131)
Colyer, Barry 4:30:04 (19,615)
Comas-Trayter, Albert 4:14:01 (15,316)
Combalbert, Maurice 3:46:02 (8,167)
Combe, Stephen 2:58:22 (1,034)
Combes, George 4:54:44 (25,334)
Combes, Neal 4:46:52 (23,777)

Combstock, Emerson	2:56:36	(882)
Comer, James	3:27:42	(4,457)
Comerford, Paul	4:17:58	(16,365)
Comette, Allan	4:47:38	(23,935)
Comfort, Alan	5:41:49	(30,678)
Comley, Robert	3:55:59	(10,892)
Commbs, Ian	4:58:50	(26,104)
Commins, Paul	4:11:25	(14,715)
Comper, Paul	3:17:15	(2,929)
Compton, David	4:31:57	(20,071)
Compton, Jeff	5:13:34	(28,152)
Compton-Cook, Adrian	4:09:20	(14,228)
Comrie, John	2:51:34	(564)
Comte, Xavier	3:38:25	(6,404)
Conaghan, James	3:44:23	(7,769)
Conaghan, Michael	4:40:18	(22,183)
Conchinha, José	4:01:07	(12,341)
Condliff, Anthony	3:49:19	(8,977)
Condliffe, Honor	4:29:45	(19,524)
Condliffe, James	5:34:39	(30,162)
Condon, David	5:07:03	(27,302)
Condon, Edward	4:52:32	(24,882)
Condren, Patrick	4:37:20	(21,408)
Coney, Charlie	3:57:22	(11,307)
Coney, Richard	3:36:24	(6,004)
Confalonieri, Elio	4:04:01	(12,993)
Conibear, Stuart	3:14:43	(2,629)
Coniglio, Tony	3:59:20	(11,896)
Coningham, Matthew	2:52:48	(619)
Conlin, Steve	3:46:25	(8,258)
Conlon, John	3:50:12	(9,215)
Conlon, Michael	3:10:10	(2,054)
Conn, David	4:34:52	(20,795)
Conn, Peter	3:16:07	(2,799)
Connaghton, Michael	4:17:40	(16,284)
Connaughton, Peter	4:39:54	(22,080)
Connell, Philip	3:31:12	(5,064)
Connell, Robin	3:33:52	(5,490)
Connelly, David	4:26:38	(18,696)
Connelly, Martin	4:41:35	(22,491)
Connelly, Simon	4:57:23	(25,839)
Conners, Kevin	3:34:39	(5,649)
Connolly, Barry	4:47:23	(23,894)
Connolly, Brendan	4:40:11	(22,154)
Connolly, David	3:24:32	(3,925)
Connolly, Dermot	3:23:13	(3,680)
Connolly, Gabriel	3:37:25	(6,192)
Connolly, James	5:31:07	(29,874)
Connolly, Kevin	4:02:34	(12,669)
Connolly, Matthew	5:24:58	(29,367)
Connolly, Shane	2:52:30	(596)
Connolly, Wayne	2:55:14	(760)
Connoly, Charles	4:19:06	(16,617)
Connor, Damian	5:13:18	(28,114)
Connor, Frank	4:42:24	(22,698)
Connor, Hadley	5:03:24	(26,811)
Connor, Ian	4:44:15	(23,115)
Connor, Lee	3:11:29	(2,202)
Connor, Norman	4:02:42	(12,704)
Connor, Paul	3:14:23	(2,597)
Connor, Paul	4:01:04	(12,330)
Connor, Roger	3:36:40	(6,051)
Connor-Stead, Philip	3:48:49	(8,845)
Conquest, Johnny	3:31:49	(5,167)
Conradie, Arno	4:12:33	(14,980)
Conroy, Kieron	3:40:51	(6,929)
Conroy, Paul	5:51:24	(31,209)
Conroy Harris, Michael	3:16:15	(2,816)
Considine, John	3:49:37	(9,074)
Constable, Darren	5:01:07	(26,467)
Constable, Piers	3:51:18	(9,502)
Constable, Tim	4:12:23	(14,937)
Contant, Ludo	4:15:31	(15,700)
Conte, Marcel	3:20:58	(3,359)
Contentin, Nicolas	3:32:49	(5,320)
Convery, Marc	4:21:57	(17,376)
Convey, Michael	4:24:37	(18,152)
Conway, Richard	3:42:58	(7,380)
Conway, Stuart	3:39:56	(6,720)
Coogan, Eamonn	3:50:25	(9,281)
Cook, Alan	2:49:12	(454)
Cook, Albert	4:31:25	(19,935)
Cook, Alistair	4:44:45	(23,236)

Cook, Andrew	3:05:00	(1,545)
Cook, Andrew	3:50:13	(9,228)
Cook, Arthur	4:33:57	(20,569)
Cook, Barry	4:22:53	(17,668)
Cook, Christopher	3:17:13	(2,922)
Cook, Christopher	4:41:53	(22,581)
Cook, Colin	3:40:24	(6,833)
Cook, David	2:56:21	(860)
Cook, David	4:25:51	(18,471)
Cook, David	5:54:14	(31,323)
Cook, Desmond	4:25:38	(18,428)
Cook, Gary	4:32:46	(20,294)
Cook, Gary	5:43:59	(30,818)
Cook, Geoff	3:39:36	(6,646)
Cook, Graham	4:35:35	(20,982)
Cook, Halsey	4:22:40	(17,596)
Cook, Hugh	3:21:25	(3,423)
Cook, Ivan	3:26:16	(4,200)
Cook, James	3:16:43	(2,866)
Cook, James	3:18:35	(3,082)
Cook, John	3:42:51	(7,349)
Cook, John	4:25:23	(18,358)
Cook, John	5:04:43	(26,981)
Cook, Jonathan	3:40:02	(6,739)
Cook, Jonathan	4:41:46	(22,549)
Cook, Keith	3:09:18	(1,967)
Cook, Len	4:47:01	(23,815)
Cook, Michael	3:41:05	(6,984)
Cook, Nicholas	4:46:41	(23,734)
Cook, Nik	3:40:16	(6,803)
Cook, Peter	4:06:58	(13,668)
Cook, Phil	3:14:38	(2,621)
Cook, Philip	4:42:54	(22,815)
Cook, Richard	3:28:03	(4,523)
Cook, Richard	4:38:18	(21,655)
Cook, Robert	6:53:42	(32,578)
Cook, Roy	4:45:53	(23,537)
Cook, Roy	5:06:24	(27,213)
Cook, Stephen	5:23:48	(29,261)
Cook, Steve	4:20:30	(16,990)
Cook, Trevor	2:45:57	(325)
Cook, William	3:12:50	(2,407)
Cooke, Alan	4:06:29	(13,562)
Cooke, Andrew	4:09:54	(14,363)
Cooke, Barry	4:06:39	(13,601)
Cooke, Chris	4:38:50	(21,804)
Cooke, Daniel	3:54:28	(10,450)
Cooke, David	5:05:51	(27,135)
Cooke, David	5:16:15	(28,475)
Cooke, Edward	4:15:13	(15,629)
Cooke, Howard	3:44:26	(7,780)
Cooke, Jason	2:42:14	(231)
Cooke, Kevin	4:00:17	(12,150)
Cooke, Mark	4:24:39	(18,159)
Cooke, Paul	3:17:52	(2,996)
Cooke, Peter	3:41:44	(7,102)
Cooke, Peter	4:00:55	(12,281)
Cooke, Roger	4:43:27	(22,948)
Cook-Radmore, Adrian	4:09:08	(14,160)
Cooksey, Andrew	3:51:03	(9,442)
Cooley, Anthony	2:57:18	(937)
Cooley, John	3:54:01	(10,314)
Coomb, Peter	5:02:49	(26,713)
Coombe, Nicholas	3:58:31	(11,654)
Coomber, Richard	3:40:11	(6,779)
Coombes, Nick	4:28:20	(19,119)
Coombes, Paul	3:49:34	(9,059)
Coombs, Philip	3:24:16	(3,870)
Coombs, Robin	4:07:28	(13,790)
Coon, Alexander	3:52:20	(9,790)
Cooney, Andrew	2:54:20	(694)
Cooper, Aaron	4:35:54	(21,049)
Cooper, Adrian	3:16:01	(2,790)
Cooper, Allan	3:10:41	(2,121)
Cooper, Andrew	2:54:34	(711)
Cooper, Andy	4:28:32	(19,178)
Cooper, Arthur	5:12:13	(27,975)
Cooper, Ashley	3:36:34	(6,034)
Cooper, Barry	5:58:24	(31,492)
Cooper, Carl	2:56:08	(837)
Cooper, Carl	4:11:25	(14,715)
Cooper, Charlie	2:56:08	(837)
Cooper, Chris	3:43:18	(7,480)

Cooper, Clive	3:40:42	(6,895)
Cooper, Daniel	5:17:00	(28,557)
Cooper, David	2:59:18	(1,116)
Cooper, David	3:11:27	(2,198)
Cooper, David	3:21:48	(3,483)
Cooper, David	3:43:17	(7,467)
Cooper, David	4:24:33	(18,131)
Cooper, David	4:35:29	(20,942)
Cooper, David	4:49:21	(24,296)
Cooper, David	5:05:19	(27,065)
Cooper, Gerwyn	4:05:39	(13,358)
Cooper, Gordon	3:36:18	(5,978)
Cooper, Huw	3:49:23	(8,998)
Cooper, Ian	3:19:24	(3,185)
Cooper, Ian	3:49:31	(9,048)
Cooper, Ian	4:00:52	(12,273)
Cooper, Jason	4:51:23	(24,680)
Cooper, John	3:23:28	(3,719)
Cooper, John	5:00:50	(26,433)
Cooper, Jon	4:42:19	(22,675)
Cooper, Malcolm	3:23:21	(3,703)
Cooper, Mark	4:57:00	(25,769)
Cooper, Martin	3:11:59	(2,273)
Cooper, Martin	4:35:48	(21,028)
Cooper, Matthew	4:03:16	(12,831)
Cooper, Michale	5:09:34	(27,642)
Cooper, Neil	3:32:41	(5,301)
Cooper, Neil	3:54:27	(10,443)
Cooper, Nicholas	3:18:27	(3,062)
Cooper, Nigel	3:56:28	(11,033)
Cooper, Oliver	4:22:25	(17,527)
Cooper, Paul	4:19:02	(16,602)
Cooper, Paul	4:29:30	(19,458)
Cooper, Peter	4:20:46	(17,061)
Cooper, Ralph	5:35:19	(30,210)
Cooper, Richard	4:01:30	(12,441)
Cooper, Richard	5:01:12	(26,481)
Cooper, Robert	3:51:50	(9,632)
Cooper, Robert	4:43:04	(22,856)
Cooper, Rodney	3:48:42	(8,812)
Cooper, Simon	3:48:25	(8,728)
Cooper, Simon	4:21:30	(17,250)
Cooper, Stanley	4:40:01	(22,109)
Cooper, Stefan	4:32:46	(20,294)
Cooper, Stephen	4:05:47	(13,390)
Cooper, Stephen	4:48:19	(24,089)
Cooper, Steven	5:04:33	(26,958)
Cooper, Timothy	4:24:08	(18,017)
Cooper, Vincent	4:58:23	(26,012)
Coopman, Christopher	5:07:00	(27,295)
Cooreman, Dirk	3:26:36	(4,247)
Coote, Shaun	3:20:18	(3,292)
Copcutt, Nicholas	3:39:42	(6,667)
Cope, Jason	5:08:54	(27,557)
Cope, Paul	5:08:54	(27,557)
Cope, Trevor	3:34:47	(5,673)
Copeland, Gary	2:54:54	(735)
Copeland, Maurice	5:24:05	(29,287)
Copeland, Stephen	5:04:50	(27,005)
Copeman, Julian	4:54:50	(25,349)
Copeman, Mark	4:20:34	(17,014)
Copeman, Stuart	4:43:14	(22,897)
Copland, Christopher	4:14:10	(15,349)
Copleston, Edward	4:41:54	(22,585)
Coplestone, Peter	3:28:38	(4,631)
Copley, Donald	5:10:37	(27,765)
Copp, Alan	5:32:35	(29,998)
Coppeard, Patrick	5:41:48	(30,677)
Coppell, Richard	3:58:51	(11,749)
Copping, Paul	4:58:31	(26,035)
Coppock, John	5:30:28	(29,819)
Coppock, Mick	4:34:44	(20,758)
Copsey, Richard	4:08:29	(14,014)
Copsey, Simon	3:47:01	(8,384)
Copus, Christopher	3:04:41	(1,516)
Coquet, Joel	4:04:04	(13,001)
Coram, Steve	5:16:59	(28,553)
Coram-Wright, Edward	4:54:54	(25,362)
Corbae, Gerald	5:11:00	(27,812)
Corbelli, Giuseppe	4:41:03	(22,362)
Corbett, Anthony	5:32:19	(29,980)
Corbett, Clive	4:45:53	(23,537)
Corbett, Iain	3:12:07	(2,296)

Corbett, Richard 4:40:18 (22,183)
Corbett, Ron....6:09:00 (31,812)
Corbett Jones, Andrew....4:12:37 (15,002)
Corbin, Andrew....4:05:51 (13,400)
Corbould, Percy....7:22:10 (32,763)
Corby, Nicholas....3:51:51 (9,638)
Corcoran, Andrew....4:05:28 (13,317)
Corcoran, Gary....4:36:28 (21,208)
Cordall, Michael....3:28:50 (4,667)
Corder, Michael....4:09:44 (14,328)
Cordery, Gary....4:30:28 (19,705)
Cordes, James....4:55:46 (25,539)
Cordiner, Mark....5:42:53 (30,748)
Cordiner, Martin....4:47:21 (23,885)
Cordiner, Nicky....4:05:15 (13,262)
Cording, Stephen....3:41:24 (7,046)
Cordingley, Jason....5:34:43 (30,168)
Cordingley, Simon....5:56:42 (31,430)
Corfield, James....3:16:30 (2,844)
Corinovis, Michele....4:07:58 (13,900)
Cork, Geoffrey....3:51:17 (9,498)
Corke, Andrew....5:05:38 (27,101)
Corke, Simon....4:23:16 (17,768)
Corker, David....4:01:06 (12,337)
Corkindale, Timothy....4:07:41 (13,836)
Corless, Stephen....3:59:47 (12,019)
Corlett, David....3:58:40 (11,695)
Corlett, Michael....4:33:30 (20,466)
Corlett, Neil....3:32:56 (5,344)
Corlett, William....3:39:58 (6,725)
Cormack, David....4:32:22 (20,181)
Cornec, Patrick....4:16:06 (15,864)
Corneille, Dean....5:16:58 (28,551)
Cornelis, Harry....4:04:18 (13,046)
Cornelis, Olivier....4:04:19 (13,049)
Cornelius, Donald....4:41:18 (22,425)
Corner, Christopher....3:29:41 (4,824)
Corner, Dale....2:54:43 (725)
Corner, John....4:29:49 (19,543)
Corner, Richard....3:42:22 (7,252)
Cornetta, Roberto....4:42:46 (22,784)
Cornewall Walker, James....3:46:16 (8,215)
Corney, Donald....4:08:47 (14,089)
Corney, Paul....3:45:17 (7,996)
Cornish, Alan....3:22:46 (3,627)
Cornish, Jeremy....5:13:06 (28,092)
Cornish, Lee....4:42:51 (22,801)
Cornish, Peter....4:22:20 (17,493)
Cornish, Steven....5:11:08 (27,829)
Cornwall, Adrian....3:20:39 (3,332)
Cornwall, Leslie....3:10:26 (2,092)
Cornwall, Michael....3:30:12 (4,894)
Corongiu, Giuseppe....3:23:20 (3,700)
Corp, Jonathan....3:15:38 (2,742)
Corpe, Robin....5:13:11 (28,099)
Corr, Michael....5:34:39 (30,162)
Correvon, Michel....2:50:19 (501)
Corriette, Michael....4:35:33 (20,960)
Corrigan, Christopher....4:12:42 (15,025)
Corrigan, John....4:53:30 (25,068)
Corrigan, Kevin....4:21:34 (17,270)
Corrigan, Patrik....3:41:19 (7,034)
Corrigan, Tony....4:53:06 (24,998)
Corten, Michael....6:10:49 (31,854)
Corti, Dominic....4:46:17 (23,636)
Cortis, Daniel....4:22:08 (17,431)
Corton, Mark....3:44:42 (7,852)
Cortvriend, Martin....3:22:40 (3,602)
Cosgrave, James....3:12:24 (2,345)
Cosh, Adrian....4:31:24 (19,929)
Cosham, Derek....4:52:10 (24,809)
Cosier, Andrew....6:00:01 (31,542)
Cossar, Anthony....3:51:12 (9,482)
Cossey, Graham....5:02:30 (26,668)
Costa, Nannel....3:23:50 (3,776)
Costas, Paraskeva....3:11:41 (2,228)
Costas, Paul....3:02:15 (1,320)
Costella, Marco....4:04:35 (13,109)
Costello, Darren....6:08:38 (31,804)
Costello, Kevin....4:54:24 (25,265)
Costello, Michael....3:41:12 (7,017)
Costello, Stephen....3:40:37 (6,877)
Costello, Warren....5:07:09 (27,321)
Coster, Malcolm....3:04:08 (1,479)
Coster, Paul....4:44:51 (23,257)
Costidell, Peter....3:46:30 (8,285)
Costley, Simon....4:09:43 (14,321)
Coston, Neil....4:29:02 (19,330)
Cosulich, Augusto....4:22:18 (17,476)
Cote, Dalton....3:18:36 (3,083)
Cottam, Anthony....3:53:12 (10,044)
Cotter, Trevor....3:53:27 (10,128)
Cotterell, Jeremy....4:34:30 (20,700)
Cotterill, Mark....3:13:26 (2,496)
Cotterill, Phillip....3:09:02 (1,936)
Cotterill, Trevor....3:29:43 (4,829)
Cotterrell, Eugene....4:00:25 (12,170)
Cottingham, David....4:56:35 (25,701)
Cottington, Ryan....5:30:19 (29,805)
Cottis, John....2:52:40 (607)
Cottis, Roy....3:40:18 (6,811)
Cottle, James....3:40:30 (6,850)
Cottle, Royston....6:08:14 (31,788)
Cotton, Andrew....4:19:45 (16,793)
Cotton, Anthony....3:17:43 (2,979)
Cotton, Paul....4:05:30 (13,327)
Cotton, Robert....3:43:42 (7,574)
Cottrell, Andrew....5:17:47 (28,649)
Cottrell, Michael....4:09:15 (14,201)
Cottrell, Peter....5:22:06 (29,100)
Cottrell, Thomas....5:35:49 (30,257)
Cottrill, Gary....4:14:06 (15,339)
Cottrill, Philip....4:14:06 (15,339)
Cotty, Hubert....4:14:40 (15,487)
Cotty, Michael....3:40:44 (6,900)
Couch, John....3:35:06 (5,732)
Couchman, Kevin....4:11:02 (14,639)
Coull, Andrew....3:58:45 (11,718)
Coull, David....5:16:09 (28,460)
Coulson, Adrian....4:45:13 (23,361)
Coulson, Benjamin....3:37:31 (6,223)
Coulson, Jeffrey....3:50:33 (9,311)
Coulson, Stephen....4:31:30 (19,968)
Coulson, Wayne....3:00:40 (1,207)
Coultart, Gary....4:14:26 (15,433)
Coulter, Gary....3:43:25 (7,502)
Coulter, John....4:07:59 (13,903)
Coultrup, Timothy....3:52:28 (9,829)
Coupe, Michael....3:26:28 (4,223)
Coupe, Paul....3:36:41 (6,055)
Couper, William....4:14:02 (15,324)
Coupland, Andrew....4:43:54 (23,044)
Coupland, Terry....4:09:24 (14,254)
Courcol, Gilles....4:45:00 (23,304)
Courivaud, Jacques....3:53:27 (10,128)
Courivaud, Jean....5:29:46 (29,759)
Court, Alan....3:30:15 (4,901)
Court, Phil....5:17:52 (28,658)
Court, Simon....6:01:06 (31,581)
Court, Stuart....5:22:27 (29,127)
Courtice, Nic....4:31:54 (20,057)
Courtier, Robert....4:30:07 (19,630)
Courtman, Simon....4:17:12 (16,171)
Courtney, Denis....3:52:10 (9,744)
Courtney, John....5:21:35 (29,053)
Courtney, Joseph....3:41:10 (7,003)
Courtney, Kevin....2:41:38 (222)
Courtney, Patrick....4:21:45 (17,324)
Courts, Andrew....4:37:52 (21,536)
Cousens, Charles....4:32:15 (20,149)
Cousineau, Paul....4:24:15 (18,054)
Cousins, Darren....4:17:05 (16,139)
Cousins, David....3:49:41 (9,094)
Cousins, David....5:04:06 (26,898)
Cousins, Gordon....4:20:41 (17,044)
Cousins, John....3:41:03 (6,977)
Cousins, Paul....2:51:36 (565)
Cousins, Stephen....3:49:04 (8,915)
Cousins, William....3:55:53 (10,869)
Coutant, Patrick....2:55:38 (792)
Coveney, Martin....4:21:11 (17,162)
Covey, Sean....3:18:27 (3,062)
Covus, Steve....5:23:25 (29,211)
Cowan, Christopher....4:46:19 (23,639)
Cowan, James....3:12:25 (2,348)
Cowan, Justin....4:29:34 (19,473)
Coward, Edgar....3:39:43 (6,671)
Coward, John....4:43:41 (22,994)
Cowderoy, Andrew....4:33:38 (20,500)
Cowdrill, Gary....4:11:28 (14,737)
Cowell, Adam....4:03:24 (12,859)
Cowell, Robert....2:39:26 (173)
Cowen, Dave....4:57:31 (25,864)
Cowie, Bevan....4:03:01 (12,778)
Cowie, Douglas....2:45:03 (301)
Cowie, Edwin....3:41:37 (7,084)
Cowie, Michael....3:32:36 (5,289)
Cowley, Keith....3:16:11 (2,806)
Cowley, Nicholas....3:30:42 (4,979)
Cowley, Peter....5:09:18 (27,605)
Cowley, Philip....5:17:52 (28,658)
Cowling, Andrew....3:49:50 (9,137)
Cowling, Jonathan....3:57:58 (11,496)
Cowling, Scott....3:47:35 (8,537)
Cowper-Smith, Adam....3:03:41 (1,439)
Cox, Alan....3:22:52 (3,644)
Cox, Alexander....3:42:27 (7,276)
Cox, Andrew....3:12:20 (2,337)
Cox, Andrew....3:22:23 (3,569)
Cox, Andrew....4:15:35 (15,718)
Cox, Brian....4:40:13 (22,162)
Cox, Christopher....4:16:03 (15,851)
Cox, Clive....3:34:14 (5,568)
Cox, Dennis....4:03:25 (12,867)
Cox, Edward....3:42:33 (7,298)
Cox, Elwyn....5:34:58 (30,183)
Cox, Guy....4:35:50 (21,036)
Cox, John....2:37:49 (141)
Cox, John....5:03:44 (26,847)
Cox, Jonathan....3:48:19 (8,700)
Cox, Jonathan....3:48:23 (8,718)
Cox, Jonathan....3:50:07 (9,192)
Cox, Jonathan....6:33:38 (32,334)
Cox, Mark....3:46:44 (8,334)
Cox, Martin....4:36:21 (21,178)
Cox, Michael....5:31:09 (29,885)
Cox, Nick....4:13:04 (15,096)
Cox, Nigel....5:13:22 (28,122)
Cox, Philip....4:38:40 (21,756)
Cox, Richard....4:28:53 (19,284)
Cox, Richard....4:36:06 (21,102)
Cox, Richard....4:38:32 (21,713)
Cox, Richard....5:27:44 (29,601)
Cox, Robert....3:40:45 (6,909)
Cox, Simon....4:35:25 (20,927)
Cox, Stephen....4:25:56 (18,498)
Cox, Stephen....4:41:42 (22,534)
Coxhead, Ian....2:49:41 (471)
Coxhead, Neil....4:59:44 (26,270)
Coy, Gerard....3:19:05 (3,148)
Coy, Julian....3:39:41 (6,661)
Coyle, Christopher....4:34:42 (20,750)
Coyle, David....4:14:40 (15,487)
Coyle, Eddie....3:13:31 (2,509)
Coyle, Jeff....3:13:47 (2,541)
Coyle, John....4:02:05 (12,573)
Coyle, William....2:32:54 (80)
Coyne, Andrew....5:31:30 (29,917)
Coyne, Colin....3:19:43 (3,223)
Coyne, Michael....4:34:58 (20,823)
Coyne, Niall....4:56:53 (25,744)
Coyne, Stephen....4:04:35 (13,109)
Cozens, Christopher....5:06:35 (27,241)
Cozens, Paul....6:32:04 (32,307)
Crabb, David....4:50:30 (24,507)
Crabb, Jonathan....3:49:25 (9,014)
Crabb, Stephen....5:05:19 (27,065)
Crabb, Wayne....3:29:04 (4,707)
Crabeil, Jean-Yves....5:58:02 (31,476)
Crabtree, Ian....3:07:51 (1,798)
Crabtree, Mark....2:54:23 (699)
Crader, Michael....4:00:00 (12,085)
Crafer, Gary....4:33:40 (20,511)
Craft, Alan....4:20:02 (16,870)
Craft, David....3:59:56 (12,066)
Cragg, Melvyn....3:12:00 (2,275)
Cragg, Stephen....3:23:38 (3,749)
Craggs, Douglas....3:55:54 (10,872)
Craggs, Jamie....4:32:26 (20,200)

Craggs, Roger	4:12:06 (14,880)	
Craib, Michael	3:17:25 (2,951)	
Craig, Gary	3:43:52 (7,625)	
Craig, Geoffrey	4:26:32 (18,664)	
Craig, Jim	3:08:21 (1,846)	
Craig, John	5:12:36 (28,037)	
Craig, Mark	3:28:00 (4,516)	
Craig, Michael	4:53:42 (25,104)	
Craig, Scott	3:46:56 (8,368)	
Craig, William	3:27:12 (4,361)	
Craik, Nick	4:01:00 (12,308)	
Crake, Matthew	6:12:08 (31,883)	
Cramer, Matthias	3:19:00 (3,132)	
Cramp, Richard	5:11:43 (27,909)	
Cramphorn, John	3:44:23 (7,769)	
Cranage, Ian	4:58:37 (26,061)	
Crandell, Stephen	3:52:18 (9,783)	
Crane, Graham	4:47:48 (23,978)	
Crane, Michael	4:59:53 (26,286)	
Crane, Patrick	4:38:20 (21,669)	
Crane, Robert	3:22:03 (3,533)	
Crane, William	3:09:10 (1,948)	
Cranfield, Nicholas	4:17:38 (16,277)	
Crang, Paul	4:21:01 (17,117)	
Cranham, Nick	3:19:54 (3,245)	
Crank, David	5:17:27 (28,621)	
Crank, Jamie	4:02:58 (12,770)	
Crank, Steven	5:04:29 (26,955)	
Crankshaw, Andrew	5:42:58 (30,756)	
Crankshaw, David	4:55:34 (25,491)	
Crann, Philip	3:36:44 (6,061)	
Cranston, Andrew	4:01:26 (12,423)	
Cranston, David	4:52:39 (24,906)	
Cranston, Jonathan	4:46:51 (23,772)	
Crass, Peter	3:30:13 (4,898)	
Craswell, Mark	4:11:32 (14,752)	
Craven, Paul	4:23:29 (17,821)	
Crawford, Adam	4:42:00 (22,607)	
Crawford, Mark	5:11:01 (27,818)	
Crawford, Paul	4:07:14 (13,728)	
Crawford, Richard	4:27:02 (18,798)	
Crawford, Victor	3:48:47 (8,839)	
Crawford, Ward	3:38:55 (6,505)	
Crawley, David	4:24:14 (18,048)	
Crawley, George	4:58:06 (25,964)	
Crawley, Ian	3:25:08 (4,006)	
Crawley, Joe	4:37:05 (21,333)	
Crawshaw, Fyfe	4:16:21 (15,930)	
Creak, Will	5:15:48 (28,412)	
Creaney-Birch, Neil	3:46:16 (8,215)	
Crease, Gregory	3:57:02 (11,220)	
Creasey, Robert	4:20:26 (16,980)	
Creasy, Justin	3:35:44 (5,853)	
Cree, Timothy	5:35:42 (30,251)	
Cree, Weir	6:06:11 (31,736)	
Creech, Stuart	3:03:59 (1,465)	
Creed, Jeremy	3:21:44 (3,469)	
Creed, Mike	5:08:13 (27,461)	
Creedon, Patrick	6:06:21 (31,741)	
Creedy, Colin	6:01:56 (31,603)	
Creese, Richard	3:43:25 (7,502)	
Creighton, Peter	4:22:20 (17,493)	
Crellin, Ken	5:59:07 (31,516)	
Cremin, James	5:15:56 (28,434)	
Crenn, Patrice	5:29:28 (29,734)	
Crenol, Kevin	2:36:47 (120)	
Crespo, José	3:59:01 (11,810)	
Cresswell, Gary	4:26:51 (18,751)	
Cresswell, Jonathan	4:46:39 (23,724)	
Cresswell, Paul	4:57:53 (25,932)	
Crewe, David	3:36:14 (5,965)	
Crewe, Maxim	3:44:01 (7,661)	
Cribbin, Peter	4:49:58 (24,417)	
Cribbis, Michael	5:09:43 (27,666)	
Crick, Jonathan	3:26:30 (4,228)	
Criddle, Richard	3:34:09 (5,554)	
Crimble, David	4:44:46 (23,240)	
Crimmen, Daniel	3:21:28 (3,430)	
Crimmen, David	4:11:05 (14,654)	
Cripps, David	5:01:58 (26,601)	
Cripps, Timothy	4:42:20 (22,683)	
Crisp, Andrew	5:41:42 (30,665)	
Crisp, John	3:43:29 (7,517)	

Crisp, John	5:15:30 (28,362)
Crisp, Robert	3:30:36 (4,963)
Crispie, Gerard	2:48:05 (405)
Crispini, Stefano	4:45:43 (23,497)
Crissall, Steven	4:58:17 (25,997)
Critchley, Chad	4:23:48 (17,919)
Critchley, Richard	3:17:20 (2,937)
Critchlow, Julian	5:41:16 (30,639)
Crittenden, Robert	3:32:22 (5,243)
Croager, Alan	4:30:46 (19,776)
Croal, Jeremy	4:32:07 (20,114)
Croasdale, Mark	2:21:09 (24)
Crock, Andy	3:05:51 (1,626)
Crocker, Darren	4:26:07 (18,556)
Crocker, Edward	3:57:11 (11,256)
Crocker, Robert	3:37:27 (6,195)
Crocker, Robin	4:36:30 (21,221)
Crockett, Jonathan	4:48:55 (24,218)
Crockett, Mark	3:55:18 (10,696)
Crockford, John	2:47:43 (390)
Crockford, Thomas	3:57:11 (11,256)
Croft, Brian	4:51:44 (24,733)
Croft, Brian	6:03:08 (31,641)
Croft, David	3:37:02 (6,126)
Croft, Dominic	3:13:38 (2,519)
Croft, Jared	3:10:58 (2,151)
Croft, Roger	3:58:22 (11,607)
Crofts, Gary	3:40:44 (6,900)
Crofts, Joe	4:21:59 (17,389)
Croise, Jean	3:51:56 (9,657)
Crompton, Neil	2:49:54 (483)
Cronen, David	4:08:51 (14,102)
Cronin, Denis	4:16:18 (15,913)
Cronin, Geoff	4:09:18 (14,218)
Cronin, Mark	4:45:26 (23,424)
Cronin, William	4:09:24 (14,254)
Cronk, Antony	3:27:36 (4,435)
Crook, Andrew	3:42:31 (7,291)
Crook, David	3:34:54 (5,695)
Crook, David	5:09:11 (27,593)
Crook, Graham	4:49:35 (24,339)
Crook, Keith	4:35:41 (21,011)
Crook, Richard	4:03:14 (12,822)
Crook, Simon	3:41:11 (7,013)
Crook, Warren	2:55:13 (759)
Crooke, Alex	4:14:13 (15,368)
Crookes, Derek	4:28:22 (19,128)
Crooks, Melvyn	5:08:57 (27,564)
Croot, Matthew	2:55:26 (775)
Cropley, Edward	3:39:58 (6,725)
Cropley, Nigel	4:28:40 (19,213)
Cropper, John	3:46:57 (8,373)
Crosbie, Donald	4:17:37 (16,273)
Crosby, Angus	3:16:58 (2,899)
Crosby, Peter	3:14:10 (2,570)
Cross, Anthony	3:14:02 (2,559)
Cross, Howard	4:24:02 (17,990)
Cross, Ian	4:20:58 (17,102)
Cross, Ivan	3:57:01 (11,214)
Cross, Jim	4:38:13 (21,631)
Cross, John	3:45:10 (7,962)
Cross, Matt	3:38:55 (6,505)
Cross, Paul	4:09:10 (14,178)
Cross, Peter	4:42:28 (22,714)
Cross, Peter	5:04:08 (26,904)
Cross, Philip	3:17:35 (2,962)
Cross, Stanley	4:21:02 (17,123)
Cross, Tim	4:37:19 (21,404)
Crosse, Matthew	3:36:26 (6,012)
Crossing, Anthony	4:36:09 (21,121)
Crossing, Leigh	4:41:39 (22,513)
Crossland, Paul	4:55:04 (25,385)
Crossley, Anthony	3:20:05 (3,263)
Crossley, Colin	4:25:52 (18,475)
Crossley, Frederick	3:54:36 (10,487)
Crossley, Hugh	3:30:36 (4,963)
Crossley, Hugh	3:44:35 (7,818)
Crossley, Joe	6:05:22 (31,710)
Crossley, Jonathan	5:23:11 (29,193)
Crossley, Patrick	4:25:29 (18,381)
Crossley Cooke, Charlie	4:01:44 (12,502)
Crothers, Alastair	4:44:16 (23,123)
Crouch, David	4:31:21 (19,918)

Crouch, Garry	3:47:23 (8,484)
Crouch, Iain	5:33:12 (30,043)
Crouch, John	5:05:46 (27,121)
Crouch, Nicholas	3:36:47 (6,074)
Crouch, Robin	6:24:26 (32,177)
Crouch, Steven	5:59:42 (31,535)
Crouch, Thomas	3:12:12 (2,312)
Crouchman, Paul	4:24:53 (18,226)
Croud, Nigel	5:30:51 (29,852)
Crout, Michael	3:54:54 (10,570)
Crow, Peter	3:15:40 (2,751)
Crowder, Michael	3:50:26 (9,284)
Crowe, David	4:07:03 (13,686)
Crowe, Nicholas	4:49:46 (24,372)
Crowell, Pete	3:55:59 (10,892)
Crowley, David	3:48:06 (8,650)
Crowley, Kieran	3:26:37 (4,252)
Crowley, Vincent	2:53:31 (655)
Crown, Simon	3:27:19 (4,379)
Crowther, Benjamin	3:47:02 (8,390)
Crowther, Gary	5:33:30 (30,074)
Crowther, Gordon	3:34:09 (5,554)
Crowther, John	4:10:02 (14,393)
Croydon, David	4:44:28 (23,162)
Crozier, Peter	3:30:15 (4,901)
Crudgington, James	4:18:49 (16,551)
Crudgington, Tommy	4:21:39 (17,297)
Cruickshank, Darren	4:55:45 (25,533)
Cruickshank, David	5:24:55 (29,359)
Cruickshank, George	4:17:57 (16,359)
Cruickshank, Sandy	3:08:39 (1,885)
Cruise, Richard	5:10:57 (27,804)
Crumley, Euan	3:50:50 (9,382)
Crummett, Stephen	3:54:57 (10,580)
Crummie, John	5:27:59 (29,616)
Cruse, Michael	4:16:01 (15,842)
Crush, Graham	4:27:29 (18,915)
Crush, Peter	4:57:17 (25,824)
Crutchley, Paul	2:55:02 (744)
Cruttenden, Duncan	4:31:31 (19,972)
Cruz, Augusto	2:46:12 (330)
Cryer, Mark	3:56:18 (10,989)
Crystal, Alan	4:07:09 (13,708)
Csillag, David	4:43:01 (22,843)
Cubillos, Manuel	3:13:08 (2,453)
Cubitt, Fred	3:49:45 (9,112)
Cuddihy, Marc	3:35:56 (5,891)
Cuddy, Richard	5:36:55 (30,344)
Cuffe, John	5:31:05 (29,870)
Cufi-Colomer, Josep	3:30:46 (4,985)
Cugliari, Guiseppe	4:27:03 (18,805)
Culkin, John	4:36:41 (21,257)
Cull, Mark	4:37:15 (21,390)
Cull, Matthew	4:05:42 (13,368)
Cull, Stephen	5:06:49 (27,272)
Cullen, Allen	5:27:17 (29,549)
Cullen, Daniel	3:36:46 (6,069)
Cullen, John	4:00:54 (12,278)
Cullen, Martin	4:07:42 (13,842)
Cullern, Doug	4:29:01 (19,325)
Cullern, Paul	3:42:19 (7,236)
Cullimore, Philip	3:51:35 (9,569)
Cullingworth, Ian	3:16:02 (2,792)
Cullis, Jonathan	3:38:31 (6,429)
Cullis, Stephen	3:11:16 (2,183)
Cullis, Timothy	4:08:31 (14,027)
Culpan, Philip	3:05:23 (1,578)
Culsham, John	4:43:24 (22,932)
Culver, Lance	4:48:24 (24,104)
Culver, Simon	4:43:49 (23,022)
Culwick, John	3:44:46 (7,878)
Culwin, Fintan	4:16:13 (15,895)
Cumber, Geoffrey	2:53:24 (651)
Cumberworth, Paul	4:21:22 (17,210)
Cumming, Kevin	4:26:11 (18,569)
Cumming, Mark	3:48:30 (8,747)
Cumming, Robert	5:08:23 (27,480)
Cummings, Alvin	5:21:09 (29,014)
Cummings, Dennis	4:54:22 (25,257)
Cummings, Frankie	3:38:23 (6,394)
Cummings, Tony	2:33:42 (86)
Cummins, Kevin	4:42:02 (22,617)
Cummins, Nicholas	4:25:55 (18,493)

Cummins, Paul 3:52:48 (9,926)
Cummins, Vern 5:07:05 (27,310)
Cumper, Stephen 3:58:47 (11,729)
Cumpsty, Brian 3:45:29 (8,039)
Cundell, Ian 4:24:51 (18,213)
Cundy, Andrew 3:56:07 (10,937)
Cundy, Robert 4:57:04 (25,782)
Cunliffe, John 6:11:32 (31,871)
Cunliffe, Luke 4:16:11 (15,889)
Cunliffe, Neil 4:27:37 (18,941)
Cunnane, John 5:34:21 (30,137)
Cunnell, Andrew 3:35:25 (5,785)
Cunniffe, Dean 3:36:19 (5,981)
Cunningham, Colin 3:47:13 (8,443)
Cunningham, Craig 3:54:31 (10,463)
Cunningham, Darren 4:55:54 (25,561)
Cunningham, David 4:23:22 (17,791)
Cunningham, Gary 5:05:45 (27,116)
Cunningham, Ian 4:22:50 (17,652)
Cunningham, James 3:21:51 (3,493)
Cunningham, John 2:50:02 (494)
Cunningham, Michael 4:42:14 (22,657)
Cunningham, Nick 4:58:34 (26,049)
Cunningham, Nigel 5:30:05 (29,783)
Cunningham, Paul 4:36:21 (21,178)
Cunningham, Peter 2:57:36 (969)
Cunningham, Roderick 5:11:15 (27,845)
Cunningham, Steve 2:46:26 (338)
Cupitt, Edward 3:48:32 (8,757)
Curd, Paul 3:53:06 (10,018)
Curd, Paul 4:05:59 (13,432)
Curle, Richard 5:21:19 (29,026)
Curless, Brent 3:50:28 (9,294)
Curley, John 3:55:32 (10,758)
Curley, Laurence 2:53:38 (660)
Curnick, Simon 4:56:28 (25,687)
Curnock, Michael 4:57:58 (25,949)
Curphey, Paul 2:46:19 (336)
Currams, Neil 3:28:03 (4,523)
Curran, Andrew 4:40:34 (22,248)
Curran, David 4:40:47 (22,304)
Curran, Dominic 4:11:36 (14,768)
Curran, Malcolm 3:45:19 (8,003)
Curran, Martin 6:45:03 (32,487)
Curran, Patrick 4:15:03 (15,585)
Curran, Quentin 3:37:36 (6,244)
Currant, Steven 3:49:51 (9,143)
Currell, Geoffrey 3:39:23 (6,601)
Currie, David 4:45:55 (23,545)
Currie, Donald 3:07:30 (1,769)
Currie, John 3:23:28 (3,719)
Currie, Mark 4:05:20 (13,283)
Currie, Patrick 3:59:46 (12,013)
Currie, Ross 7:43:05 (32,835)
Currie, Simon 3:30:59 (5,022)
Currie, Stuart 3:30:25 (4,935)
Currier, Stanely 4:53:35 (25,084)
Currington, Jonathan 3:34:07 (5,546)
Curry, Denis 5:15:19 (28,340)
Curry, Edward 3:24:31 (3,923)
Curry, Joe 3:42:13 (7,204)
Curry, John 4:00:51 (12,267)
Curry, William 4:21:35 (17,274)
Curtin, Brendan 3:58:26 (11,629)
Curtin, Jeff 2:49:58 (490)
Curtin, Thomas 3:16:53 (2,891)
Curtis, Andrew 3:47:40 (8,551)
Curtis, Anthony 4:54:13 (25,229)
Curtis, Daniel 4:32:57 (20,345)
Curtis, David 4:41:34 (22,487)
Curtis, Derrick 6:47:28 (32,511)
Curtis, Graham 5:46:12 (30,946)
Curtis, James 4:20:25 (16,974)
Curtis, Jason 3:29:57 (4,864)
Curtis, Jason 5:12:41 (28,046)
Curtis, Paul 2:55:51 (816)
Curtis, Paul 4:39:04 (21,862)
Curtis, Peadar 3:48:44 (8,822)
Curtis, Simon 4:16:31 (15,984)
Curtis, Trevor 3:25:51 (4,124)
Curtis-Raleigh, Guy 4:17:31 (16,246)
Curtis-Raleigh, Nick 4:17:31 (16,246)
Curwood, Keith 4:54:31 (25,289)

Curzon, David 4:09:06 (14,153)
Cusack, Dermot 3:25:56 (4,142)
Cusack, Jake 4:45:40 (23,484)
Cush, Harry 4:53:55 (25,160)
Cush, Terrence 4:53:55 (25,160)
Cushway, Paul 3:35:33 (5,811)
Cusimano, Rick 6:57:18 (32,604)
Custodio, Antonio 3:25:12 (4,015)
Cutbill, Richard 4:05:12 (13,254)
Cuthbert, Christopher 4:18:34 (16,501)
Cuthbert, George 5:02:30 (26,668)
Cuthbert, Jim 4:16:27 (15,969)
Cuthbert, Kevin 3:49:47 (9,125)
Cuthbert, Matthew 3:48:36 (8,782)
Cutler, David 4:25:11 (18,305)
Cutting, Graham 3:47:21 (8,472)
Cutting, Stephen 4:18:17 (16,431)
Cuviello, Stephen 5:19:42 (28,839)
Cuville, Serge 3:35:17 (5,760)
Cuypers, Philip 4:07:43 (13,845)
Czyzyk, Matthew 5:03:15 (26,792)
Dable, Thomas 3:25:49 (4,114)
Daborn, David 3:54:14 (10,379)
Dabrowski, Barry 3:39:17 (6,586)
Dade, Neil 3:35:26 (5,789)
Dadswell, Jonathan 4:42:13 (22,651)
Dady, Stephen 3:56:18 (10,989)
Daeche, Gavin 4:21:20 (17,200)
Dael, Simon 4:01:00 (12,308)
Daelemans, Ronald 4:01:34 (12,461)
Daffy, Sean 4:37:08 (21,345)
Dagon, Claude 5:25:29 (29,400)
Dagorn, Christian 4:32:55 (20,339)
Dahbi, Yacing 5:45:00 (30,883)
Dahill, Brendan 4:03:59 (12,985)
Daines, Mark 4:25:11 (18,305)
Daines, Michael 4:02:20 (12,623)
Dainton, Stephen 3:57:22 (11,307)
Dainty, Andrew 4:06:33 (13,577)
Daisley, Jamie 5:02:34 (26,681)
Dajlid, James 3:16:38 (2,856)
Dakin, Keith 3:52:55 (9,955)
Dalbret, Marc 7:01:46 (32,644)
Daldry, Simon 4:30:58 (19,823)
Dale, Adrian 2:57:00 (914)
Dale, Andrew 3:48:18 (8,693)
Dale, Jeremy 3:59:30 (11,938)
Dale, Nicolas 4:00:31 (12,190)
Dale, Richard 3:28:31 (4,606)
Dale, Rupert 4:40:11 (22,154)
Dale, Russell 4:36:27 (21,200)
Dale, Stuart 4:07:20 (13,754)
Daley, John 4:03:05 (12,795)
Daley, Kevin 3:57:53 (11,472)
Daley, Nigel 4:23:23 (17,798)
Dalgleish, Andrew 3:27:21 (4,385)
Dalkins, Jason 3:57:13 (11,269)
D'All, Gordon 4:01:07 (12,341)
Dall'Ava, Bernard 3:44:32 (7,804)
Dalley, Alexander 3:45:28 (8,034)
Dalley, David 4:27:22 (18,881)
Dalley, Robert 4:54:19 (25,246)
Dally, Paul 4:00:33 (12,196)
Dalmeijer, Philip 5:21:39 (29,063)
Daloia, Antonio 4:22:05 (17,419)
Dalton, James 5:34:11 (30,121)
Dalton, Laurie 3:55:51 (10,855)
Dalton, Mark 2:54:23 (699)
Dalton, Nick 4:31:57 (20,071)
Dalton, Robert 5:50:43 (31,169)
Dalton, Simon 4:11:32 (14,752)
Dalton, William 3:16:46 (2,873)
Daly, Anthony 4:07:18 (13,748)
Daly, Dean 3:57:24 (11,325)
Daly, John 3:40:16 (6,803)
Daly, Martin 4:38:48 (21,792)
Daly, Peter 3:25:19 (4,033)
Dalzell, John 3:09:49 (2,019)
Dalziel, Ian 4:42:11 (22,646)
D'Ambrosio, Gino 3:47:12 (8,441)
Dampney, Hugh 3:55:44 (10,823)
Dams, Richard 3:51:09 (9,472)
Danaher, Mark 4:55:21 (25,447)

Danby, James 3:44:17 (7,739)
Dance, Richard 4:20:29 (16,988)
Danciger, Simon 2:45:01 (300)
Dando, Mark 4:21:00 (17,110)
Dandridge, Neil 4:59:57 (26,300)
Daniel, Andrew 5:31:08 (29,882)
Daniel, Jeremy 4:09:44 (14,328)
Daniell, Edward 4:10:02 (14,393)
Daniels, Chris 5:24:33 (29,330)
Daniels, Clive 4:21:04 (17,131)
Daniels, Gary 4:30:20 (19,679)
Daniels, Hugh 4:37:05 (21,333)
Daniels, Jason 4:07:18 (13,748)
Daniels, Jonathan 4:57:55 (25,939)
Daniels, Michael 3:27:34 (4,428)
Daniels, Peter 4:23:43 (17,893)
Daniels, Sasha 2:44:27 (280)
Daniels, Terence 5:27:17 (29,549)
Dann, Geoff 3:47:51 (8,600)
Dann, Peter 4:43:26 (22,940)
Dannatt, Edward 3:56:04 (10,918)
Danvers, Benjamin 3:08:26 (1,857)
Dany, Poelaert 3:27:01 (4,331)
D'Apice, Crispin 3:46:05 (8,178)
Darbin, Kevin 4:13:35 (15,201)
Darby, John 4:28:56 (19,297)
Darby, Mark 4:25:01 (18,270)
Darby, Paul 3:58:55 (11,767)
Darbyshire, Malcolm 3:14:46 (2,635)
Darbyshire, Peter 4:28:35 (19,187)
Darbyshire, Simon 3:27:15 (4,368)
Darch, Frank 4:16:37 (16,016)
Darch, Richard 4:01:38 (12,476)
Darcy, John 4:07:21 (13,761)
D'Arcy, Andrew 7:21:51 (32,760)
Dare, Martin 3:31:35 (5,121)
Dare, Stuart 4:00:26 (12,175)
Dargue, Karl 5:31:40 (29,927)
Dargue, Robert 4:25:46 (18,454)
Darius, Simon 3:04:06 (1,475)
Dark, Anthony 4:28:24 (19,139)
Dark, Christopher 4:28:36 (19,197)
Dark, Michael 4:13:17 (15,145)
Darke, Antony 4:21:45 (17,324)
Darke, Neil 3:04:50 (1,527)
Darker, Barry 4:17:02 (16,129)
Darkes, Stephen 4:31:51 (20,040)
Darling, Barry 5:35:27 (30,220)
Darlington, Daniel 3:16:09 (2,803)
Darnbrook, Bob 6:00:00 (31,541)
Darnell, Jon 5:25:57 (29,442)
Darnery, Bryan 5:13:29 (28,138)
Dart, Kenneth 3:43:27 (7,513)
Darvell, Jack 4:38:49 (21,796)
Da-Silva-Mota, Manuel 3:06:07 (1,652)
Dauchy, Eric 3:35:03 (5,719)
Daugherty, Brian 3:45:32 (8,054)
Dauncey, Chris 3:15:39 (2,748)
Dauncey, Timothy 3:19:35 (3,212)
Dauvergne, Regis 3:46:27 (8,265)
Daveney, Steven 4:55:11 (25,417)
Davenport, Danny 4:09:14 (14,198)
Davenport, Hugh 4:40:05 (22,129)
Davenport, Robert 4:16:25 (15,956)
Davey, Peter 3:42:57 (7,376)
Davey, Simon 3:43:24 (7,496)
David, Edward 4:45:21 (23,393)
David, Gareth 3:41:35 (7,080)
David, Giles 4:34:24 (20,673)
David, Robert 5:15:12 (28,324)
Davids, Anthony 5:15:43 (28,397)
Davids, Peter 6:15:34 (31,969)
Davidson, Bruce 5:47:48 (31,028)
Davidson, Christopher 4:46:51 (23,772)
Davidson, Clive 4:36:00 (21,080)
Davidson, David 5:34:54 (30,175)
Davidson, Doug 4:08:20 (13,974)
Davidson, George 3:35:57 (5,893)
Davidson, Ian 6:55:09 (32,587)
Davidson, James 5:44:16 (30,837)
Davidson, John 3:56:11 (10,957)
Davidson, Ken 3:43:24 (7,496)
Davidson, Neil 4:47:11 (23,855)

Davidson, Paul 3:50:10 (9,205)
Davidson, Peter 4:46:52 (23,777)
Davidson, Robert 5:25:42 (29,420)
Davidson, Stuart 2:52:31 (599)
Davie, Allan 3:37:04 (6,133)
Davie, Benedict 5:16:36 (28,511)
Davie, Roy 4:20:25 (16,974)
Davies, Adam 4:23:21 (17,786)
Davies, Adam 5:34:10 (30,120)
Davies, Adrian 3:39:12 (6,567)
Davies, Andrew 2:54:22 (696)
Davies, Andrew 3:56:31 (11,059)
Davies, Anthony 4:54:17 (25,240)
Davies, Barry 4:40:17 (22,176)
Davies, Brian 3:24:33 (3,929)
Davies, Brian 4:19:12 (16,646)
Davies, Carl 3:22:59 (3,655)
Davies, Carwyn 3:52:21 (9,797)
Davies, Christopher 4:14:55 (15,554)
Davies, Colin 3:27:02 (4,336)
Davies, Craig 5:00:29 (26,371)
Davies, Dave 3:57:18 (11,293)
Davies, David 4:22:13 (17,449)
Davies, David 4:44:51 (23,257)
Davies, David 4:53:30 (25,068)
Davies, David 4:55:26 (25,472)
Davies, Dawn 4:06:54 (13,649)
Davies, Dennis 4:36:14 (21,136)
Davies, Derek 4:48:02 (24,041)
Davies, Dilwyn 5:13:50 (28,174)
Davies, Duncan 5:13:56 (28,180)
Davies, Euryl 3:59:51 (12,041)
Davies, Gareth 3:31:38 (5,135)
Davies, Gareth 3:36:42 (6,059)
Davies, Gareth 3:37:44 (6,271)
Davies, Gareth 3:59:48 (12,024)
Davies, Gareth 5:09:40 (27,656)
Davies, Geoffrey 4:05:44 (13,376)
Davies, Henry 4:07:59 (13,903)
Davies, Howard 5:08:29 (27,494)
Davies, Hywel 3:39:41 (6,661)
Davies, James 2:55:50 (815)
Davies, James 3:57:01 (11,214)
Davies, Jamie 4:00:55 (12,281)
Davies, Jeff 4:13:59 (15,308)
Davies, John 3:10:05 (2,047)
Davies, John 3:27:57 (4,508)
Davies, John 3:36:35 (6,039)
Davies, John 3:59:38 (11,977)
Davies, John 4:09:12 (14,189)
Davies, John 4:48:51 (24,206)
Davies, John 5:07:48 (27,406)
Davies, Jon 4:37:28 (21,439)
Davies, Jon 4:51:30 (24,700)
Davies, Jonathan 3:03:57 (1,461)
Davies, Julian 4:27:42 (18,962)
Davies, Julian 5:09:58 (27,686)
Davies, Justin 5:48:53 (31,089)
Davies, Karl 3:38:40 (6,468)
Davies, Keith 2:53:35 (658)
Davies, Kevin 3:44:17 (7,739)
Davies, Kevin 4:36:55 (21,300)
Davies, Lawrence 4:04:51 (13,172)
Davies, Lee 3:39:55 (6,714)
Davies, Leighton 3:06:22 (1,671)
Davies, Lewis 2:55:45 (805)
Davies, Marc 4:44:20 (23,138)
Davies, Mark 4:42:15 (22,659)
Davies, Mark 4:46:10 (23,613)
Davies, Martin 3:55:40 (10,798)
Davies, Martyn 4:19:16 (16,657)
Davies, Mathew 3:45:27 (8,029)
Davies, Matthew 4:16:38 (16,019)
Davies, Matthew 4:35:50 (21,036)
Davies, Michael 3:19:53 (3,242)
Davies, Michael 4:15:14 (15,631)
Davies, Michael 5:27:33 (29,580)
Davies, Mike 5:21:48 (29,078)
Davies, Nicholas 2:49:16 (455)
Davies, Nicholas 4:50:50 (24,575)
Davies, Nick 3:59:22 (11,906)
Davies, Nick 4:43:04 (22,856)
Davies, Nigel 3:32:26 (5,259)
Davies, Nigel 3:36:21 (5,992)
Davies, Paul 2:46:19 (336)
Davies, Paul 2:52:22 (593)
Davies, Paul 3:17:02 (2,907)
Davies, Paul 3:50:52 (9,396)
Davies, Paul 4:13:25 (15,170)
Davies, Paul 4:27:59 (19,029)
Davies, Peter 5:43:39 (30,793)
Davies, Philip 4:13:07 (15,106)
Davies, Philip 5:11:55 (27,940)
Davies, Ray 4:31:51 (20,040)
Davies, Richard 3:09:04 (1,939)
Davies, Richard 3:51:28 (9,535)
Davies, Richard 3:51:42 (9,593)
Davies, Richard 3:53:32 (10,157)
Davies, Richard 4:03:41 (12,914)
Davies, Richard 4:44:20 (23,138)
Davies, Richard 5:48:48 (31,081)
Davies, Rob 6:40:59 (32,444)
Davies, Robin 4:05:45 (13,380)
Davies, Roger 3:46:59 (8,378)
Davies, Roger 4:19:37 (16,754)
Davies, Roy 4:35:06 (20,855)
Davies, Shane 3:35:45 (5,855)
Davies, Simon 3:26:20 (4,208)
Davies, Simon 5:06:35 (27,241)
Davies, Stephen 2:38:51 (164)
Davies, Stephen 3:51:24 (9,521)
Davies, Stephen 4:26:21 (18,615)
Davies, Stephen 4:30:38 (19,739)
Davies, Stuart 4:37:02 (21,323)
Davies, Stuart 4:37:27 (21,438)
Davies, Stuart 4:46:55 (23,796)
Davies, Stuart 5:10:25 (27,739)
Davies, Terry 3:59:41 (11,989)
Davies, Thomas 2:46:27 (340)
Davies, Thomas 3:08:07 (1,817)
Davies, Thomas 3:19:32 (3,206)
Davies, Thomas 3:50:32 (9,306)
Davies, Thomas 4:23:38 (17,857)
Davies, Timothy 3:12:07 (2,296)
Davies, Tom 3:56:34 (11,075)
Davies, Tony 3:12:40 (2,381)
Davies, Trevor 3:10:58 (2,151)
Davies, Vincent 3:28:30 (4,604)
Davies, Wayne 3:46:17 (8,223)
Davies, Wayne 5:23:44 (29,255)
Davies, Wyn 4:44:20 (23,138)
Davis, Adrian 2:36:47 (120)
Davis, Adrian 4:21:38 (17,293)
Davis, Anthony 7:31:39 (32,795)
Davis, Brian 5:06:08 (27,179)
Davis, Frank 4:20:07 (16,891)
Davis, Hugh 3:30:47 (4,990)
Davis, James 5:35:26 (30,218)
Davis, Jevin 3:58:40 (11,695)
Davis, Joe 3:57:54 (11,476)
Davis, Jonathan 3:54:20 (10,409)
Davis, Kevin 3:53:50 (10,261)
Davis, Marcus 4:22:38 (17,583)
Davis, Mark 3:18:52 (3,119)
Davis, Mark 4:10:00 (14,385)
Davis, Martin 2:50:26 (507)
Davis, Martin 3:11:45 (2,237)
Davis, Nathaniel 4:11:40 (14,791)
Davis, Nicholas 3:47:34 (8,530)
Davis, Paul 4:05:29 (13,324)
Davis, Phillip 4:23:15 (17,760)
Davis, Richard 4:46:25 (23,667)
Davis, Robert 3:46:13 (8,206)
Davis, Robin 4:54:46 (25,336)
Davis, Simon 3:38:37 (6,453)
Davis, Stephen 4:24:24 (18,091)
Davis, Steve 2:43:43 (261)
Davis, Timothy 3:59:43 (11,998)
Davis, Tony 6:17:34 (32,021)
Davis, Wynn 3:36:19 (5,981)
Davison, Alan 3:22:33 (3,590)
Davison, Ian 4:56:02 (25,589)
Davison, John 5:23:41 (29,253)
Davison, Malcolm 5:54:16 (31,324)
Davison, Philip 4:56:54 (25,745)
Davison, Robert 3:17:22 (2,943)
Davison, Robin 4:59:28 (26,212)
Davison, Stephen 5:37:10 (30,360)
Davitt, Patrick 3:18:42 (3,098)
Davoren, Patrick 3:02:20 (1,328)
Davren, Paul 3:29:02 (4,698)
Davy, Alan 3:02:26 (1,335)
Davy, John 5:27:16 (29,547)
Daw, Alasdair 5:44:48 (30,875)
Dawber, Nigel 3:12:42 (2,387)
Dawes, Alex 4:21:46 (17,328)
Dawes, Duncan 3:00:00 (1,170)
Dawes, William 4:35:50 (21,036)
Dawkin, Stuart 4:09:15 (14,201)
Dawkins, Russell 3:14:53 (2,654)
Dawney, Kevin 5:16:49 (28,529)
Daws, Peter 2:54:32 (708)
Dawson, Alan 3:01:28 (1,257)
Dawson, Alex 3:54:18 (10,401)
Dawson, Andy 3:26:45 (4,285)
Dawson, Carl 4:38:08 (21,609)
Dawson, Christopher 4:31:32 (19,978)
Dawson, Douglas 3:57:46 (11,444)
Dawson, Fraser 2:55:48 (809)
Dawson, John 3:42:52 (7,353)
Dawson, Mark 4:23:46 (17,907)
Dawson, Mark 5:15:30 (28,362)
Dawson, Peter 4:32:50 (20,314)
Dawson, Richard 3:43:08 (7,426)
Dawson, Richard 3:43:51 (7,620)
Dawson, Simon 3:43:46 (7,591)
Dawson, William 4:00:14 (12,140)
Day, Alistair 4:02:27 (12,642)
Day, Andrew 4:24:11 (18,029)
Day, Brian 4:21:53 (17,363)
Day, Colin 2:57:45 (983)
Day, David 3:23:38 (3,749)
Day, David 3:33:40 (5,450)
Day, David 4:33:58 (20,572)
Day, Jason 4:43:16 (22,901)
Day, John 3:53:39 (10,197)
Day, Kenneth 4:36:55 (21,300)
Day, Laurence 4:23:41 (17,872)
Day, Michael 3:59:29 (11,937)
Day, Michael 4:10:16 (14,452)
Day, Nicholas 3:12:33 (2,368)
Day, Norman 3:32:54 (5,338)
Day, Paul 4:13:27 (15,177)
Day, Peter 4:29:49 (19,543)
Day, Philip 3:41:09 (7,000)
Day, Richard 4:08:05 (13,931)
Day, Richard 4:25:14 (18,317)
Day, Rob 3:44:54 (7,906)
Day, Stephen 3:54:20 (10,409)
Day, Steve 3:20:31 (3,316)
Day, Thomas 3:08:12 (1,824)
Day, Tony 4:27:18 (18,864)
Dayman, Graham 5:03:19 (26,800)
Daynes, Christopher 5:09:35 (27,644)
Days, Anthony 4:58:04 (25,959)
Dayus, Geoffrey 4:25:59 (18,513)
De Barton-Watson, James 4:15:03 (15,585)
De Beuyelaen, Gunther 4:33:26 (20,448)
De Boer, Sake 3:21:36 (3,453)
De Bondt, Jan 3:54:00 (10,309)
De Carle, Stewart 4:10:03 (14,401)
De Cherisey, Jean 3:37:40 (6,258)
De Courcy-Grylls, Christopher 3:52:45 (9,909)
De Dios-Gomez, Bernardo 3:51:30 (9,543)
De Filippo, Armand 4:02:37 (12,685)
De Frateschi, Michael 3:28:06 (4,532)
De Gois, Jean 3:48:19 (8,700)
De Groot, Coenie 5:27:36 (29,589)
De Jager, André 3:57:35 (11,389)
De Jager, Jaco 3:05:14 (1,561)
De Jong, Maarten 3:05:30 (1,591)
De Jong, Rolandus 4:23:19 (17,781)
De Kesel, Dimitri 2:58:57 (1,088)
De Klerk, Charl 4:14:09 (15,345)
De La Fuente, Enrique 4:28:29 (19,166)
De La Hoz-Parrondo, Juan 3:20:24 (3,299)
De La Kethulle, José 3:52:36 (9,870)
De Lisle, John 4:55:12 (25,423)
De Luca, Paolo 3:18:46 (3,108)

Dickinson, Tobyn 4:24:25 (18,094)
Dicklemente, Alan 3:02:45 (1,355)
Dickman, Andrew 4:22:42 (17,608)
Dicks, Jamie 3:57:23 (11,317)
Dicks, Jeff 4:29:58 (19,587)
Dickson, Alex 5:32:48 (30,011)
Dickson, Andrew 4:22:53 (17,668)
Dickson, George 3:35:37 (5,829)
Dickson, Jim 4:47:37 (23,930)
Dickson, Richard 4:38:54 (21,819)
Dickson, Robert 3:12:04 (2,284)
Dickson, Trevor 5:48:11 (31,045)
Dickson, William 4:43:00 (22,838)
Dicruz, Gerry 4:14:54 (15,553)
Didcott, Martyn 3:33:46 (5,469)
Didier, Charles 5:11:04 (27,820)
Didier, Gaetan 4:21:00 (17,110)
Diedrick, Kevin 4:24:35 (18,143)
Diem, Peter 3:53:43 (10,212)
Diesner, Stephen 3:22:05 (3,535)
Dietl, Berndt 5:06:36 (27,244)
Dietz, Antony 3:36:25 (6,008)
Diez-Gilabert, José 4:34:20 (20,654)
Differding, Christian 3:32:51 (5,330)
Digby-Baker, Hugh 4:26:15 (18,588)
Diggens, Nigel 6:14:48 (31,951)
Diggins, Jess 4:58:21 (26,005)
Diggles, Bob 3:24:41 (3,942)
Dijkhuis, Elzo 3:55:40 (10,798)
Dijkstra, S. 4:00:55 (12,281)
Dilley, Robert 3:29:33 (4,807)
Dillon, Barry 3:54:04 (10,334)
Dillon, Steven 4:54:43 (25,328)
Dilloway, Luke 3:43:58 (7,654)
Dilworth, Mark 4:36:23 (21,189)
Dimambro, Franco 6:58:39 (32,612)
Dimarco, Ben 4:22:41 (17,603)
Dimbleby, Nick 4:17:08 (16,154)
Dimelow, Geoffrey 3:38:19 (6,378)
Dimmock, Graeme 6:14:19 (31,936)
Dimmock, Matthew 3:36:27 (6,018)
Dimmock, Paul 3:08:21 (1,846)
Dimond, Steven 3:38:38 (6,459)
Dinan, Mike 4:10:12 (14,437)
D'Incalci, Attilio 3:29:58 (4,867)
Dine, Roger 3:29:23 (4,774)
Dingley, Peter 4:57:39 (25,887)
Dingwall, Basil 7:40:57 (32,826)
Dingwall, Jim 2:52:01 (579)
Dinham, Geoffrey 4:41:56 (22,593)
Dinham, Martin 3:54:21 (10,415)
Dinicola, Peter 5:08:56 (27,561)
Dinnage, Martin 3:59:26 (11,926)
Dinsdale, Elliot 4:22:02 (17,405)
Dinsmore, David 5:18:52 (28,759)
Dinwoodie, Mark 3:38:24 (6,400)
Dion, Marco 4:22:55 (17,677)
Dionisio, José 3:44:57 (7,919)
Dionisio, Tiago 3:06:40 (1,705)
Ditch, Matthew 4:27:18 (18,864)
Ditch, Neil 4:38:58 (21,834)
Dittrich, Lee 4:24:09 (18,023)
Diventura, Angelo 4:09:13 (14,193)
Dixon, Clem 8:00:51 (32,862)
Dixon, Colin 3:16:55 (2,892)
Dixon, Garry 3:15:12 (2,687)
Dixon, Gary 3:32:14 (5,220)
Dixon, Gary 3:50:38 (9,334)
Dixon, Gordon 2:36:53 (125)
Dixon, Keith 4:31:14 (19,887)
Dixon, Kevin 3:47:07 (8,409)
Dixon, Martin 4:05:10 (13,245)
Dixon, Matt 3:39:43 (6,671)
Dixon, Michael 3:54:44 (10,529)
Dixon, Reginald 6:28:38 (32,248)
Dixon, Richard 3:44:07 (7,683)
Dixon, Stephen 3:29:01 (4,696)
Dixon, Timothy 4:05:02 (13,216)
Djan, Kwabena 5:56:29 (31,422)
Djavanian, Hassan 4:19:56 (16,846)
Dobbie, David 3:47:13 (8,443)
Dobbs, Andrew 4:15:40 (15,747)
Dobbs, Gary 4:38:05 (21,596)
Dobbs, Michael 4:58:08 (25,970)
Dobbs, Patrick 2:58:08 (1,015)
Dobbs, Paul 4:05:03 (13,223)
Dobbs, Simon 2:40:54 (202)
Dobedoe, Richard 2:57:59 (1,005)
Dobie, Ronald 4:16:21 (15,930)
Doble, Simon 5:27:24 (29,568)
Dobson, Barry 4:17:55 (16,349)
Dobson, Jamie 3:57:32 (11,372)
Dobson, Jeffrey 3:45:14 (7,983)
Dobson, Malcolm 5:53:55 (31,308)
Dobson, Mark 3:49:02 (8,906)
Dobson, Noel 4:07:34 (13,811)
Dobson, Richard 4:29:58 (19,587)
Docherty, David 4:07:52 (13,884)
Docherty, Douglas 4:54:57 (25,370)
Docwra-Chapman, Paul 4:33:26 (20,448)
Dodanis, Christos 2:57:31 (959)
Dodd, Alan 4:27:25 (18,893)
Dodd, Andrew 4:46:36 (23,715)
Dodd, Bruce 5:28:28 (29,652)
Dodd, David 3:29:04 (4,707)
Dodd, Jason 4:31:31 (19,972)
Dodd, Keith 4:10:10 (14,430)
Dodd, Michael 3:43:36 (7,550)
Dodd, Michel 4:13:41 (15,229)
Dodd, Stephen 3:44:32 (7,804)
Dodd, Toby 4:34:25 (20,676)
Dodds, Andrew 3:53:02 (9,994)
Dodds, George 3:33:25 (5,419)
Dodds, Jamie 4:30:03 (19,608)
Dodds, Nigel 4:09:47 (14,336)
Dodds, Rupert 2:59:40 (1,144)
Dodge, James 3:39:41 (6,661)
Dodoo, Eddie 2:58:25 (1,041)
Dods, Michael 4:47:04 (23,828)
Dodson, Andrew 3:38:31 (6,429)
Dodson, Edward 3:40:22 (6,828)
Dodsworth, Ian 4:19:55 (16,840)
Dodwell, Alan 7:17:54 (32,751)
Dodwell, David 4:04:48 (13,160)
Dodwell, Leslie 7:30:02 (32,787)
Doe, Andrew 4:26:23 (18,620)
Doe, Digby 4:28:18 (19,109)
Doe, Don 3:03:31 (1,424)
Doe, Jesse 5:22:37 (29,142)
Doegl, Josef 3:51:44 (9,603)
Doelling, Volker 4:41:55 (22,590)
Doets, Robert 4:05:08 (13,238)
Dogglis, Colin 4:27:27 (18,905)
Dogna, Vincent 3:21:44 (3,469)
Doherty, Danny 4:31:03 (19,842)
Doherty, Hugh 5:09:09 (27,589)
Doherty, James 3:32:11 (5,216)
Doherty, Michael 3:08:36 (1,881)
Doherty, Oliver 4:35:17 (20,898)
Doherty, Paul 3:13:57 (2,553)
Doherty, Rory 3:28:46 (4,652)
Dohler, Mischa 4:00:57 (12,295)
Doidge, William 3:32:23 (5,247)
Doig, Martin 3:59:48 (12,024)
Doikajarvi, Juha 3:27:12 (4,361)
Dolan, Aidan 3:54:50 (10,551)
Dolan, John 5:49:47 (31,135)
Dolan, Robert 3:08:30 (1,873)
Dolley, Alan 3:43:14 (7,454)
Dolling, Michael 3:18:23 (3,056)
Dolman, Antony 4:12:06 (14,880)
Dolphin, Christopher 3:33:10 (5,377)
Dolphin, Huw 3:26:21 (4,210)
Dolphin, Oliver 3:59:41 (11,989)
Doman, Carl 4:15:24 (15,665)
Domenech, Francisco 4:30:43 (19,764)
Dominguez-Lopez, Jorge 3:30:52 (5,000)
Domjan, Mihaly 3:27:09 (4,352)
Dommett, Christopher 4:27:21 (18,875)
Domnick, Clive 4:27:07 (18,822)
Domokos, Michael 4:36:03 (21,092)
Donachie, David 4:00:36 (12,207)
Donaghey, Michael 5:47:22 (31,006)
Donaghy, James 5:30:09 (29,795)
Donaire Del Yerro, Manuel 2:54:23 (699)
Donald, Ian 3:56:29 (11,044)
Donaldson, Alex 4:56:22 (25,673)
Donaldson, Andrew 3:45:32 (8,054)
Donaldson, Andrew 4:12:29 (14,967)
Donaldson, Drew 2:57:37 (971)
Donaldson, Iain 4:14:18 (15,391)
Donkin, Neil 3:43:35 (7,546)
Donne, George 4:11:16 (14,685)
Donne, Tudor 4:04:38 (13,118)
Donohoe, Patrick 3:28:48 (4,662)
Donohue, Ralph 4:41:05 (22,371)
Donovan, Daniel 5:27:17 (29,549)
Donovan, Len 3:39:29 (6,625)
Donovan, Roy 4:35:33 (20,960)
Donovan, Stephen 4:29:33 (19,467)
Donovan, William 4:14:31 (15,449)
Dood, Tom 4:23:14 (17,755)
Doody, Andrew 4:55:55 (25,567)
Doolan, James 3:53:00 (9,976)
Doole, Stuart 4:19:30 (16,726)
Dooley, John 3:42:01 (7,158)
Dooley, Kieran 4:37:34 (21,461)
Dooley, Stephen 3:33:58 (5,513)
Doorbeejah, Chris 4:28:56 (19,297)
Doran, Martin 3:58:37 (11,684)
Dordoy, Laurence 4:55:17 (25,437)
Dorfman, Robert 4:23:25 (17,806)
Doring, Peter 4:06:43 (13,618)
Dorling, John 5:16:07 (28,456)
Dorrian, Brendan 4:30:43 (19,764)
Dorrian, John 4:49:27 (24,311)
Dorrill, Robert 4:32:35 (20,239)
Dorrington, John 3:53:57 (10,293)
Dorrington, Keith 5:29:35 (29,745)
Dorward, Iain 4:37:13 (21,378)
Dorward, Neil 3:39:31 (6,629)
Dosanjh, Paul 5:03:08 (26,771)
Dossett, David 4:19:11 (16,641)
Dossetter, Alan 5:21:54 (29,088)
Doubell, Wessel 4:41:05 (22,371)
Double, Michael 4:43:58 (23,058)
Douchet, Jean-Luc 3:43:47 (7,601)
Dougherty, Andrew 4:29:26 (19,444)
Dougherty, Christopher 3:41:00 (6,964)
Dougherty, Phillip 5:09:07 (27,585)
Doughty, Barry 5:01:11 (26,479)
Doughty, Garry 4:11:25 (14,715)
Doughty, Martin 3:15:38 (2,742)
Douglas, David 3:52:19 (9,785)
Douglas, Dick 6:06:56 (31,759)
Douglas, Donal 7:01:10 (32,639)
Douglas, Donald 4:50:42 (24,544)
Douglas, Ian 4:58:14 (25,989)
Douglas, John 6:17:59 (32,037)
Douglas, Neil 2:48:58 (445)
Douglas, Paul 2:53:59 (682)
Douglas, Philip 3:05:50 (1,624)
Douglas, Robert 4:24:38 (18,154)
Douglas, Robin 4:59:54 (26,290)
Douglas, Stuart 2:45:26 (308)
Douglas, Timothy 4:50:54 (24,591)
Douglas, Tony 2:50:19 (501)
Douglas Browne, Roger 3:52:16 (9,771)
Douglas-Jones, Alexander 3:28:41 (4,639)
Douglass, Chippy 4:16:36 (16,010)
Douglass, Harry 4:19:00 (16,589)
Dovedi, Stephen 3:31:54 (5,175)
Dovey, Andrew 4:25:33 (18,404)
Dow, Colin 4:14:00 (15,313)
Dowd, Charlie 4:31:36 (19,995)
Dowd, David 2:53:22 (648)
Dowdall, Jim 7:30:03 (32,788)
Dowdall, Robert 5:03:18 (26,797)
Dowdell, Steven 4:24:04 (18,001)
Dowding, Nicholas 5:22:55 (29,168)
Dowdy, John 3:15:55 (2,782)
Dowdy, Michael 4:15:32 (15,704)
Dowdy, Simon 4:20:54 (17,086)
Dowling, David 4:03:41 (12,914)
Dowling, Jason 3:59:48 (12,024)
Dowling, Jonathan 3:16:23 (2,829)
Dowling, Shaun 4:57:02 (25,774)
Down, Cameron 3:10:48 (2,135)
Down, Craig 3:46:04 (8,172)

Down, James	3:49:36 (9,069)	
Down, Nicholas	4:38:35 (21,730)	
Down, Patrick	4:05:16 (13,267)	
Downer, Matthew	4:29:56 (19,581)	
Downer, Michael	3:57:20 (11,302)	
Downes, Antony	4:11:02 (14,639)	
Downes, Henry	4:30:55 (19,813)	
Downes, Jason	4:33:11 (20,397)	
Downey, Desmond	4:41:08 (22,382)	
Downey, Eric	3:15:08 (2,681)	
Downey, Kevin	5:37:35 (30,392)	
Downham, Paul	5:01:07 (26,467)	
Downing, Oliver	3:12:07 (2,296)	
Downing, Terence	4:29:25 (19,440)	
Downs, Simon	4:18:54 (16,569)	
Dowse, Stephen	4:26:28 (18,642)	
Dowsett, Frederick	3:55:34 (10,772)	
Dowsett, Kevin	4:09:09 (14,170)	
Dowsett, Lawrie	4:37:53 (21,542)	
Dowsett, Matthew	3:26:42 (4,275)	
Dowsett, Peter	3:16:06 (2,798)	
Dowson, Simon	3:26:09 (4,174)	
Dowthwaite, Neil	3:36:02 (5,911)	
Doyen, Jacques	4:42:32 (22,733)	
Doyle, Alan	4:22:38 (17,583)	
Doyle, Alastair	2:58:55 (1,086)	
Doyle, Brendan	3:20:39 (3,332)	
Doyle, Christopher	4:22:33 (17,560)	
Doyle, Edmund	5:30:06 (29,784)	
Doyle, James	4:08:01 (13,916)	
Doyle, John	3:47:51 (8,600)	
Doyle, John	4:07:41 (13,836)	
Doyle, Julian	4:25:06 (18,286)	
Doyle, Kevin	4:14:57 (15,559)	
Doyle, Mark	3:07:41 (1,786)	
Doyle, Michael	5:48:03 (31,040)	
Doyle, Noel	5:11:19 (27,856)	
Doyle, Peter	5:48:03 (31,040)	
Doyle, Philip	3:36:08 (5,942)	
Doyle, Richard	4:11:11 (14,673)	
Doyle, Simon	2:57:18 (937)	
Doyle, Steven	4:11:10 (14,668)	
Doyle, Tommy	4:14:18 (15,391)	
Drabwell, Alan	4:29:12 (19,380)	
Drabwell, Lee	4:14:21 (15,409)	
Drage, Graham	3:27:28 (4,410)	
Dragicevich, Anthony	4:25:21 (18,348)	
Drake, Gary	4:12:34 (14,984)	
Drake, Martin	4:51:15 (24,660)	
Drake, Robin	5:40:50 (30,602)	
Drane, Paul	3:56:47 (11,138)	
Dransfield, Paul	4:26:00 (18,518)	
Draper, Daniel	4:50:21 (24,472)	
Draper, David	4:07:11 (13,718)	
Draper, Dennis	4:29:14 (19,394)	
Draper, Hedde	3:46:29 (8,272)	
Draper, Kevin	3:51:51 (9,638)	
Draper, Martin	4:13:26 (15,173)	
Draper, Nicholas	4:30:29 (19,707)	
Draper, Nick	3:33:12 (5,382)	
Draycott, Michael	4:08:28 (14,010)	
Drayson, Geoffry	4:02:36 (12,681)	
Drechsler, Thomas	3:17:55 (3,001)	
Dreelan, Ian	3:37:06 (6,134)	
Dreelan, Mark	4:12:40 (15,020)	
Dresner, Martin	3:21:29 (3,434)	
Drew, Anthony	5:53:56 (31,309)	
Drew, Christopher	5:24:52 (29,351)	
Drew, David	3:43:30 (7,525)	
Drew, David	4:16:56 (16,100)	
Drew, David	4:23:43 (17,893)	
Drew, David	4:52:45 (24,926)	
Drew, David	5:38:10 (30,422)	
Drew, Gary	5:11:38 (27,899)	
Drew, Mark	3:31:00 (5,028)	
Drew, Stephen	3:50:49 (9,379)	
Drewett, Graeme	3:56:53 (11,168)	
Drewienkiewicz, Robert	4:22:00 (17,393)	
Drewitt, Kevin	3:42:56 (7,366)	
Drews, Franz	3:56:19 (10,994)	
Dreyer, Jonathan	3:40:33 (6,863)	
Dreyer, Leonhard	4:03:21 (12,843)	
Dridge, Gareth	3:42:57 (7,376)	

Driessen, Chris	3:09:14 (1,956)
Driscoll, Douglas	5:51:00 (31,187)
Driscoll, Michael	4:06:17 (13,516)
Driver, Chris	5:04:59 (27,017)
Driver, Christopher	4:14:31 (15,449)
Driver, David	5:57:19 (31,451)
Driver, Gary	3:24:47 (3,956)
Driver, Marlon	4:13:18 (15,147)
Drobac, Gavin	5:15:49 (28,416)
Drouet, Christophe	3:44:47 (7,884)
Drummie, David	3:25:54 (4,139)
Drummond, Jamie	3:19:40 (3,218)
Drummond, Michael	3:37:34 (6,239)
Drummond, Paul	3:27:40 (4,451)
Drummond, Samuel	2:48:05 (405)
Drummond, Stephen	3:46:19 (8,229)
Drury, Darren	4:08:04 (13,929)
Drury, John	5:14:28 (28,242)
Drury, Mark	4:49:53 (24,404)
Drury, Warren	5:43:13 (30,769)
Drybala, Gary	3:36:13 (5,960)
Drysdale, Richard	3:37:19 (6,167)
Drzewiecki, Patrick	3:36:20 (5,985)
D'Souza, Derrick	4:06:14 (13,498)
D'Souza, Robin	5:28:01 (29,618)
Du Chastel, Nicolas	3:51:32 (9,555)
Du Feu, Ian	4:33:21 (20,429)
Du Toit, André	3:31:34 (5,117)
Du Toit, François	3:42:20 (7,246)
Du Toit, Gerhardus	4:28:00 (19,032)
Du Toit, Pieter	5:03:19 (26,800)
Dubec, Daniel	5:00:39 (26,401)
Dubois, James	4:18:05 (16,385)
Dubois, Tony	3:48:26 (8,732)
Duboscq, Eric	4:40:56 (22,339)
Duby, Samuel	5:15:25 (28,350)
Duca, Giovanni	3:20:54 (3,352)
Ducheny, Laurent	4:02:45 (12,713)
Duck, Christopher	4:07:06 (13,697)
Duck, Gary	4:57:55 (25,939)
Duck, Philip	3:59:00 (11,806)
Duck, Terry	5:19:04 (28,783)
Duckett, Ewan	4:11:16 (14,685)
Duckworth, Caleb	5:30:49 (29,849)
Duckworth, Kevin	3:02:41 (1,347)
Duddell, Stephen	2:53:00 (629)
Dudding, Lyndon	4:42:55 (22,818)
Duddy, Gerald	3:13:04 (2,442)
Dudfield, Philip	3:02:30 (1,338)
Dudfield, Stephen	4:55:41 (25,516)
Dudhill, John	3:00:25 (1,198)
Dudley, Dennis	3:45:45 (8,100)
Dudley, George	4:38:42 (21,761)
Dudley, Martin	4:05:24 (13,298)
Dudley, Michael	3:44:31 (7,797)
Dudman, Richard	4:24:54 (18,227)
Dudok, John	4:10:45 (14,562)
Dudzis, Drzysztof	2:56:13 (847)
Duell, Kevin	3:06:17 (1,664)
Duff, James	4:57:30 (25,856)
Duff, Kenneth	4:53:37 (25,088)
Duff, Nigel	4:01:09 (12,352)
Duff, Peter	4:05:17 (13,270)
Duffell, John	3:23:59 (3,818)
Duffield, Geoff	5:16:52 (28,537)
Duffield, Michael	7:32:06 (32,797)
Duffy, Brian	3:07:39 (1,779)
Duffy, David	4:58:04 (25,959)
Duffy, Eugene	3:35:11 (5,747)
Duffy, Lee	4:07:23 (13,771)
Duffy, Michael	3:47:13 (8,443)
Duffy, Paul	3:23:49 (3,772)
Duffy, Philip	3:49:16 (8,959)
Duffy, Thomas	5:18:37 (28,734)
Dufour, Robert	4:28:26 (19,152)
Dugdale, Ian	4:06:07 (13,465)
Dugdale, Jonathan	3:49:07 (8,928)
Dugdale, Richard	4:36:40 (21,256)
Duggan, Anthony	3:37:18 (6,163)
Duggan, Markis	3:21:03 (3,374)
Duhamel, David	5:08:19 (27,473)
Duke, Bernie	4:23:21 (17,786)
Duke, Chris	4:05:50 (13,398)

Duke, Nolan	4:57:04 (25,782)
Duke, Trevor	5:26:26 (29,485)
Dul, Slawomir	4:18:47 (16,541)
Dulai, Gurinderjit	3:54:26 (10,439)
Dulake, David	3:53:21 (10,094)
Duley, Russello	4:24:08 (18,017)
Dumbleton, Andrew	4:52:17 (24,841)
Dummer, Henry	4:03:47 (12,936)
Dumortier, Cedric	4:38:18 (21,655)
Dumper, Alan	2:52:21 (592)
Dunbabin, Richard	3:16:32 (2,849)
Duncan, Andrew	3:25:56 (4,142)
Duncan, David	4:21:02 (17,123)
Duncan, George	5:02:43 (26,700)
Duncan, Jamie	4:44:56 (23,348)
Duncan, Mark	3:16:35 (2,851)
Duncan, Paul	3:47:01 (8,384)
Duncan, Tyler	4:45:10 (23,348)
Duncton, Roger	4:00:37 (12,209)
Dunford, Christopher	4:41:59 (22,603)
Dungate, Keith	3:50:30 (9,302)
Dungate, Paul	3:07:44 (1,789)
Dungate, Paul	4:54:38 (25,307)
Dunham, Robert	4:11:16 (14,685)
Dunkel, Wolfgang	3:39:37 (6,649)
Dunkerley, Guy	4:35:52 (21,045)
Dunkley, Graeme	4:02:05 (12,573)
Dunkley, Neil	3:49:41 (9,094)
Dunkley, Simon	3:26:57 (4,321)
Dunlea, Brian	4:36:29 (21,214)
Dunleavy, James	5:12:46 (28,052)
Dunleavy, Marc	5:08:50 (27,541)
Dunleavy, Mark	4:21:33 (17,267)
Dunleavy, Michael	5:26:05 (29,453)
Dunlop, Brien	5:29:36 (29,748)
Dunlop, Paul	3:35:54 (5,884)
Dunlop, Stuart	3:44:16 (7,731)
Dunmall, Peter	4:25:17 (18,330)
Dunn, Andrew	5:41:10 (30,632)
Dunn, Barrie	3:27:28 (4,410)
Dunn, Benedict	5:37:34 (30,389)
Dunn, Carl	6:02:55 (31,636)
Dunn, Chris	4:32:23 (20,184)
Dunn, Colin	3:13:43 (2,534)
Dunn, David	4:12:24 (14,943)
Dunn, Gary	3:51:32 (9,555)
Dunn, Geoff	4:10:55 (14,612)
Dunn, James	4:10:07 (14,414)
Dunn, Kim	3:38:26 (6,410)
Dunn, Mark	3:35:36 (5,828)
Dunn, Matthew	5:41:10 (30,632)
Dunn, Peter	4:21:35 (17,274)
Dunn, Roger	3:14:25 (2,603)
Dunn, Simon	4:11:43 (14,798)
Dunn, Stephen	3:08:27 (1,860)
Dunn, Stephen	3:13:05 (2,444)
Dunn, Steve	5:05:16 (27,055)
Dunn, William	2:57:35 (968)
Dunne, Ciaran	4:21:35 (17,274)
Dunne, Gerard	3:45:15 (7,989)
Dunne, Gerard	4:17:08 (16,154)
Dunne, James	3:18:12 (3,033)
Dunne, Jeff	3:36:49 (6,079)
Dunne, Paul	4:32:58 (20,351)
Dunne, Sean	3:25:42 (4,099)
Dunne, Stephen	5:14:33 (28,253)
Dunnett, James	3:57:06 (11,235)
Dunnicliffe, James	4:44:09 (23,093)
Dunning, Guy	4:27:45 (18,972)
Dunning, Steve	4:18:42 (16,526)
Dunningham, James	5:02:00 (26,605)
Dunphy, Martin	4:56:25 (25,679)
Dunscombe, Mark	3:11:14 (2,179)
Dunsmuir, Scott	4:56:03 (25,594)
Dunstone, Philip	3:10:54 (2,142)
Dunton, Ian	4:21:36 (17,283)
Dunton, Simon	5:35:39 (30,245)
Dunwell, Philip	4:43:16 (22,901)
Dunwoody, Guy	3:27:40 (4,451)
Dunwoody, Richard	3:10:21 (2,085)
Dupain, Nigel	4:04:11 (13,022)
Dupont, Sebastien	3:47:08 (8,414)
Duportal, Franck	2:35:24 (103)

Dupoy, Gavin	3:32:23	(5,247)
Dupuis, Gerald	4:29:14	(19,394)
Durack, Conor	3:28:48	(4,662)
Durcan, Micheal	3:51:56	(9,657)
Durdy, Steven	3:00:06	(1,176)
Durkin, Adrian	4:36:37	(21,244)
Durkin, Barry	4:44:29	(23,170)
Durling, Daniel	3:44:12	(7,715)
Durnin, David	3:26:47	(4,290)
Durr, Sean	4:57:31	(25,864)
Du-Sartel, André	4:11:17	(14,690)
Dussard, Philip	4:05:24	(13,298)
Dussart, Herve	3:31:22	(5,086)
Dutch, James	4:58:53	(26,112)
Dutfield, Tim	3:48:31	(8,751)
Dutton, Bryan	4:27:08	(18,826)
Dutton, Martin	4:17:09	(16,160)
Dutton, Philip	4:17:10	(16,165)
Dutton, Terry	5:38:12	(30,425)
Duune, Sean	5:27:15	(29,546)
Duvall, Steve	3:53:36	(10,178)
Duxbury, Robert	3:08:25	(1,852)
Duyvestein, Ronny	3:10:31	(2,103)
Dwarakanath, Deepak	5:53:43	(31,303)
Dweh, Garry	4:22:40	(17,596)
Dwelly, Mark	4:12:27	(14,960)
Dwight, Simon	5:25:21	(29,392)
Dwivedi, Sanjay	4:55:29	(25,477)
Dwyer, John	5:48:28	(31,060)
Dwyer, Kevin	3:42:43	(7,319)
Dwyer, Maurice	4:58:49	(26,100)
Dwyer, Paul	4:57:17	(25,824)
Dwyer, Sean	4:43:08	(22,876)
Dyckes, John	3:10:28	(2,095)
Dyde, Martin	2:45:38	(316)
Dye, Richard	3:30:41	(4,976)
Dye, Tim	5:46:16	(30,953)
Dyer, Andrew	5:57:22	(31,454)
Dyer, Andrew	7:01:32	(32,642)
Dyer, Colin	3:55:05	(10,619)
Dyer, David	4:46:46	(23,750)
Dyer, Glen	5:33:25	(30,063)
Dyer, John	4:43:45	(23,004)
Dyer, Nicholas	3:48:52	(8,859)
Dyer, Peter	3:18:42	(3,098)
Dyer, Terry	2:40:59	(205)
Dyet, William	3:15:28	(2,720)
Dyke, Antony	4:57:45	(25,907)
Dyke, David	4:02:38	(12,688)
Dykes, Steve	4:48:37	(24,149)
Dylla, Walter	4:30:45	(19,775)
Dymond, Graeme	3:52:22	(9,805)
Dymott, Michael	3:47:29	(8,505)
Dyson, Adam	3:56:52	(11,165)
Dyson, Matt	4:42:46	(22,784)
Dyton, Richard	3:55:59	(10,892)
Dziubak, Stefan	4:16:45	(16,052)
Eachus, Peter	4:37:23	(21,418)
Eade, Gary	3:38:11	(6,340)
Eade, James	3:05:21	(1,573)
Eades, Graham	3:29:05	(4,709)
Eades, Paul	4:06:05	(13,455)
Eadie, James	3:52:21	(9,797)
Eagle, Roger	4:06:34	(13,581)
Eaglestone, William	3:28:29	(4,600)
Eagnin, Graziano	3:17:04	(2,911)
Eales, Nicholas	3:13:06	(2,449)
Eales, Paul	4:36:33	(21,236)
Ealing, Stuart	4:19:16	(16,657)
Eames, John	3:48:24	(8,721)
Eames, John	4:12:29	(14,967)
Eames, Paul	3:47:34	(8,530)
Eardley-Taylor, Paul	3:15:46	(2,765)
Earl, Derek	3:52:21	(9,797)
Earl, Dvaid	3:55:32	(10,758)
Earl, Graham	5:00:11	(26,334)
Earl, Martin	3:24:41	(3,942)
Earl, Martyn	4:08:24	(13,994)
Earl, Thomas	3:58:46	(11,722)
Earle, Ken	4:10:07	(14,414)
Earles, Paul	3:25:22	(4,039)
Earley, David	4:00:46	(12,249)
Early, Adrian	4:52:32	(24,882)

Earney, David	3:32:08	(5,211)
Earnshaw, Adam	3:39:55	(6,714)
Earnshaw, Tom	4:44:50	(23,253)
Eason, Alex	3:55:14	(10,675)
Eason, Ben	4:25:47	(18,459)
East, Daniel	4:16:06	(15,864)
East, David	3:58:41	(11,701)
East, Grant	3:15:02	(2,668)
East, Richard	5:51:34	(31,219)
Eastabrook, Paul	4:11:52	(14,828)
Easteal, Christopher	4:36:30	(21,221)
Easter, Stephen	4:34:46	(20,766)
Easterbrook, Tristan	4:31:02	(19,834)
Eastham, Fred	4:38:44	(21,774)
Eastham, Graeme	4:58:12	(25,984)
Eastham, John	4:30:11	(19,648)
Eastham, Keith	3:10:19	(2,079)
Easthope, David	3:36:10	(5,953)
Easthope, James	4:13:05	(15,100)
Eastlake, Jonathan	3:53:50	(10,261)
Eastley, Philip	3:00:40	(1,207)
Easto, Simon	3:08:45	(1,900)
Easton, Mark	5:01:16	(26,495)
Easton, Michael	5:20:19	(28,919)
Easton, Robert	3:42:31	(7,291)
Eastwood, Hywel	5:12:08	(27,967)
Easy, Jason	3:31:48	(5,165)
Eaton, Ben	3:42:30	(7,287)
Eaton, Henry	4:28:35	(19,187)
Eaton, Mark	3:20:28	(3,308)
Eaton, Richard	5:35:18	(30,208)
Eaton, Russell	5:15:23	(28,344)
Eaton, Simon	4:32:08	(20,122)
Eaton, Tony	5:34:16	(30,130)
Ebdell, Martin	4:23:39	(17,859)
Ebden, Paddy	5:47:09	(30,995)
Eberhardt, Volker	4:03:38	(12,907)
Ebrahim, Nazir	6:49:05	(32,531)
Eccles, John	3:04:05	(1,473)
Eccles, Michael	5:01:45	(26,565)
Eccleshare, William	3:39:28	(6,617)
Eccleston, Christopher	2:57:19	(939)
Eccleston, John	3:52:03	(9,709)
Eckleben, Wolfgang	3:57:48	(11,449)
Ecochard, Laurent	4:38:23	(21,681)
Ecochard, Patrick	4:53:54	(25,147)
Eddy, Martin	3:27:48	(4,480)
Ede, Anthony	3:49:43	(9,103)
Ede, David	4:53:36	(25,085)
Ede, Philip	4:22:40	(17,596)
Edelmann, Anton	4:07:26	(13,783)
Eden, Craig	4:36:10	(21,128)
Eden, Michael	4:41:50	(22,565)
Eden, Reg	3:23:56	(3,807)
Eden, Tim	4:06:24	(13,546)
Edensor, Ray	4:36:25	(21,194)
Edgar, Hamish	3:02:03	(1,305)
Edgar, James	5:06:10	(27,184)
Edgar, Jonty	3:02:04	(1,307)
Edgar, Stephen	3:09:49	(2,019)
Edge, Andrew	5:38:46	(30,462)
Edge, Eric	3:29:31	(4,800)
Edge, James	4:05:58	(13,431)
Edge, Michael	4:53:27	(25,057)
Edge, Shane	3:03:39	(1,436)
Edgell, Jonathan	3:48:01	(8,633)
Edgell, Rhys	4:51:48	(24,744)
Edgings, Steven	3:44:18	(7,742)
Edgington, Adrian	3:30:21	(4,920)
Ediker, Simon	4:55:42	(25,520)
Edington, Paul	3:52:01	(9,693)
Edmeades, Allan	3:57:57	(11,491)
Edmiston, James	4:47:40	(23,945)
Edmond, Ian	2:52:05	(584)
Edmonds, Ian	3:35:57	(5,893)
Edmonds, Neil	4:38:21	(21,672)
Edmonds, Peter	4:17:18	(16,203)
Edmonds, Richard	3:49:43	(9,103)
Edmondson, Colin	3:54:44	(10,529)
Edmondson, David	5:10:25	(27,739)
Edmondson, Ian	3:44:40	(7,839)
Edmondson, Raymond	4:41:41	(22,526)
Edmondson, Tony	4:02:37	(12,685)

Edney, David	4:20:42	(17,047)
Edney, Simon	2:37:56	(143)
Edney, Trevor	4:18:53	(16,566)
Edser, Jonathan	4:36:28	(21,208)
Edvardsen, Magne	4:49:05	(24,255)
Edvardsen, Marius	3:47:00	(8,381)
Edwards, Adam	3:57:36	(11,396)
Edwards, Allan	4:00:56	(12,289)
Edwards, Andrew	4:34:35	(20,719)
Edwards, Barry	4:51:35	(24,715)
Edwards, Ben	5:22:15	(29,114)
Edwards, Benjamin	3:41:11	(7,013)
Edwards, Brendan	4:40:49	(22,313)
Edwards, Bruce	5:33:42	(30,085)
Edwards, Chris	2:54:22	(696)
Edwards, Chris	3:53:09	(10,030)
Edwards, Christopher	5:08:11	(27,451)
Edwards, Crispin	4:49:39	(24,350)
Edwards, David	3:39:25	(6,606)
Edwards, David	3:42:19	(7,236)
Edwards, David	3:48:31	(8,751)
Edwards, David	4:07:34	(13,811)
Edwards, David	4:39:20	(21,930)
Edwards, David	5:03:29	(26,820)
Edwards, David	6:37:48	(32,409)
Edwards, Dean	4:22:25	(17,527)
Edwards, Delon	4:54:18	(25,243)
Edwards, Derek	4:22:23	(17,512)
Edwards, Duncan	5:38:15	(30,428)
Edwards, Gareth	4:04:19	(13,049)
Edwards, Gary	4:51:35	(24,715)
Edwards, George	5:16:13	(28,470)
Edwards, Giles	4:17:42	(16,294)
Edwards, Graham	3:44:15	(7,722)
Edwards, Gregory	5:03:26	(26,815)
Edwards, Hans	3:35:21	(5,769)
Edwards, Ian	2:45:12	(305)
Edwards, Jeremy	4:34:03	(20,595)
Edwards, John	4:01:15	(12,379)
Edwards, Jonathan	4:41:25	(22,451)
Edwards, Joseph	4:39:21	(21,936)
Edwards, Keith	4:08:35	(14,051)
Edwards, Laurence	4:15:21	(15,653)
Edwards, Leonard	3:37:51	(6,288)
Edwards, Lewis	3:55:11	(10,658)
Edwards, Luke	4:07:09	(13,708)
Edwards, Malcolm	3:44:55	(7,912)
Edwards, Mark	3:57:46	(11,444)
Edwards, Mark	4:00:39	(12,214)
Edwards, Mark	4:49:03	(24,245)
Edwards, Mark	4:50:39	(24,531)
Edwards, Martin	3:48:41	(8,807)
Edwards, Martin	4:47:30	(23,912)
Edwards, Matthew	4:07:49	(13,876)
Edwards, Mike	4:19:29	(16,720)
Edwards, Myles	4:24:18	(18,067)
Edwards, Neil	3:10:17	(2,073)
Edwards, Niall	4:58:24	(26,016)
Edwards, Nicholas	4:23:04	(17,723)
Edwards, Nicholas	4:32:21	(20,173)
Edwards, Nicholas	5:05:52	(27,141)
Edwards, Paul	3:20:12	(3,277)
Edwards, Paul	3:37:01	(6,125)
Edwards, Paul	5:05:38	(27,101)
Edwards, Philip	4:16:10	(15,881)
Edwards, Richard	3:56:26	(11,025)
Edwards, Rik	4:00:09	(12,118)
Edwards, Robert	3:44:49	(7,892)
Edwards, Robert	4:13:20	(15,151)
Edwards, Robert	4:51:49	(24,746)
Edwards, Russell	3:46:23	(8,246)
Edwards, Sean	4:05:59	(13,432)
Edwards, Simon	4:30:25	(19,697)
Edwards, Simon	4:55:07	(25,400)
Edwards, Stephen	4:08:30	(14,021)
Edwards, Steve	3:29:40	(4,822)
Edwards, Steven	5:49:17	(31,113)
Edwards, Stuart	4:15:59	(15,833)
Edwards, Tim	3:49:19	(8,977)
Edwards, Tony	5:41:46	(30,669)
Edwards, Trevor	4:42:16	(22,665)
Edwards, Wayne	5:15:08	(28,311)
Effer, Jonathan	4:32:39	(20,261)

Efthimiou, Panikos 3:56:10 (10,948)
Egan, Andy 4:16:00 (15,839)
Egan, Arthur 3:09:21 (1,978)
Egan, Christopher 3:19:54 (3,245)
Egan, James 4:18:18 (16,439)
Egan, Marcus 3:53:37 (10,182)
Egan, Thomas 3:54:06 (10,343)
Egerton, Simon 4:38:24 (21,685)
Egeskov, Mogens 3:40:14 (6,794)
Eggbeer, Peter 3:12:19 (2,332)
Eggett, Christopher 4:40:23 (22,209)
Eggleton, Tony 4:07:23 (13,771)
Eglinton, David 4:07:36 (13,816)
Ehenulo, Chuma 4:26:11 (18,569)
Ehrenburg, Marcus 4:08:21 (13,976)
Ehrhart, Andrew 3:49:14 (8,950)
Ehteshani, Mani 4:01:48 (12,522)
Eisenberger, Harald 3:23:25 (3,710)
Eisenhut, Konrad 4:17:01 (16,121)
Eke, Christopher 5:02:48 (26,712)
Eke, Paul 3:14:18 (2,592)
El Hattab, Mohammed 2:11:49 (10)
El Mouaziz, Abdelkader 2:06:50 (4)
Elbro, Matthew 3:01:42 (1,273)
Elby, Stepehn 4:38:42 (21,761)
Elder, Carl 4:09:01 (14,135)
Elder, Richard 5:02:36 (26,686)
Elder, Russell 6:02:02 (31,610)
Eldernbosch, Olaf 3:56:11 (10,957)
Eldred, Grant 4:19:52 (16,827)
Eldred, Mark 3:00:42 (1,210)
Eldred, Norman 3:43:15 (7,459)
Eldridge, Christopher 4:25:18 (18,333)
Eldridge, Peter 4:54:52 (25,358)
Elford, John 3:56:44 (11,117)
Elford, Peter 3:21:46 (3,476)
El-Ghazouani, Mohamed 3:58:59 (11,796)
Elgie, Neil 4:43:06 (22,865)
El-Hadouchi, Kamel 3:47:13 (8,443)
El-Haram, Mohamed 3:47:43 (8,565)
Elkan, Stephen 4:37:45 (21,503)
Elleman, Mark 3:18:22 (3,053)
Elleman, Peter 5:50:56 (31,184)
Ellerby, Roger 3:35:46 (5,859)
Ellerby, Vincent 2:59:51 (1,161)
Ellery, John 3:25:48 (4,113)
Elletson, Hope 4:01:30 (12,441)
Ellicock, Mike 4:08:28 (14,010)
Elliff, Stephen 4:25:14 (18,317)
Elling, Mark 4:46:45 (23,747)
Ellingford, Ray 3:53:44 (10,218)
Elliot, Ian 4:38:35 (21,730)
Elliott, Alexander 3:08:05 (1,813)
Elliott, Alistair 4:14:18 (15,391)
Elliott, Andrew 3:42:38 (7,310)
Elliott, Brett 4:00:57 (12,295)
Elliott, Bryan 3:29:13 (4,731)
Elliott, Christopher 5:11:07 (27,828)
Elliott, Craig 3:44:43 (7,861)
Elliott, Daniel 3:49:29 (9,036)
Elliott, Graham 4:56:26 (25,681)
Elliott, Hugh 4:22:52 (17,661)
Elliott, Hugo 3:03:36 (1,430)
Elliott, James 4:01:30 (12,441)
Elliott, John 3:42:58 (7,380)
Elliott, Jonathan 5:12:48 (28,057)
Elliott, Mark 3:23:53 (3,795)
Elliott, Mrak 3:01:46 (1,280)
Elliott, Neill 3:22:44 (3,621)
Elliott, Peter 4:40:27 (22,222)
Elliott, Richard 3:58:55 (11,767)
Elliott, Roger 3:56:00 (10,897)
Elliott, Simon 3:37:49 (6,282)
Elliott, Stephen 4:26:28 (18,642)
Elliott, Stephen 5:11:51 (27,930)
Elliott, Steven 5:26:27 (29,486)
Elliott, Wayne 3:44:53 (7,899)
Ellis, Adam 4:49:53 (24,404)
Ellis, Alan 4:12:12 (14,903)
Ellis, Anthony 4:34:17 (20,645)
Ellis, Arron 3:45:23 (8,017)
Ellis, Barnaby 5:11:16 (27,850)
Ellis, Brian 6:33:53 (32,338)
Ellis, Carl 3:40:04 (6,752)
Ellis, Daniel 4:28:26 (19,152)
Ellis, David 5:25:42 (29,420)
Ellis, Eamonn 4:27:53 (19,000)
Ellis, Garry 4:58:06 (25,964)
Ellis, Ian 4:11:26 (14,727)
Ellis, Ieuan 2:29:19 (62)
Ellis, Jeremy 4:05:20 (13,283)
Ellis, John 3:36:06 (5,932)
Ellis, John 4:11:43 (14,798)
Ellis, Joseph 5:48:54 (31,091)
Ellis, Keith 4:28:59 (19,318)
Ellis, Kenneth 4:14:21 (15,409)
Ellis, Kevin 3:52:20 (9,790)
Ellis, Mark 3:57:14 (11,274)
Ellis, Mark 4:02:27 (12,642)
Ellis, Martin 4:56:02 (25,589)
Ellis, Matthew 4:38:33 (21,720)
Ellis, Matthew 5:05:03 (27,029)
Ellis, Peter 6:19:30 (32,071)
Ellis, Richard 3:30:43 (4,982)
Ellis, Richard 4:49:03 (24,245)
Ellis, Robert 3:03:35 (1,428)
Ellis, Robert 3:52:47 (9,922)
Ellis, Shaun 6:34:26 (32,347)
Ellis, Simon 3:11:08 (2,171)
Ellis, Simon 3:53:38 (10,190)
Ellis, Simon 4:31:24 (19,929)
Ellis, Simon 5:47:00 (30,986)
Ellis, Stephen 4:29:11 (19,378)
Ellis, Steve 3:23:50 (3,776)
Ellis, Steven 4:06:07 (13,465)
Ellis, Thomas 4:52:11 (24,813)
Ellis, Tim 4:33:20 (20,426)
Ellison, Mark 3:09:51 (2,021)
Ellison, Mark 3:53:37 (10,182)
Ellison, Stuart 3:48:12 (8,675)
Ellison, Wayne 3:55:43 (10,818)
Ellithorn, Mark 2:55:40 (795)
Ellsmore, David 4:55:45 (25,533)
Ellsmore, Michael 2:44:39 (287)
Ellwood, Alexandre 3:39:19 (6,592)
Ellwood, Brian 3:27:25 (4,400)
Ellwood, Tim 3:58:08 (11,553)
Elmasry, Hassan 4:33:52 (20,551)
Elmer, Jimmy 3:51:16 (9,493)
Elmer, Philip 4:20:15 (16,926)
Elmer, Timothy 4:07:29 (13,793)
Elmhirst, Tristram 3:54:30 (10,459)
El-Moubarak, Brahim 2:49:27 (463)
Elms, Gareth 4:28:52 (19,282)
Elmy, Matthew 3:18:02 (3,013)
Eloi, Robinson 4:11:56 (14,841)
Elphick, Andrew 3:53:09 (10,030)
Elphick, Richard 4:20:02 (16,870)
Elphinstone, Angus 4:05:22 (13,290)
Elrick, Peter 4:38:57 (21,832)
Elsawy, Magdy 3:54:43 (10,519)
Elsby, Dominic 3:04:41 (1,516)
Elsdon, Phillip 4:55:07 (25,400)
Else, Bernard 4:57:29 (25,854)
Elsey, Timothy 4:07:24 (13,777)
Elsmere, Alan 3:01:36 (1,264)
Elsmere, Frank 5:34:13 (30,125)
Elson, Mark 3:05:03 (1,549)
Elson, Michael 3:21:11 (3,396)
Elston, Barry 4:11:41 (14,794)
Elves, Rupert 4:06:06 (13,460)
Elvidge, Jon 4:33:47 (20,534)
Elvin, Mark 4:22:13 (17,449)
Elvin, Steven 2:47:37 (385)
Elwell, Adam 4:05:57 (13,425)
Emblem, Edward 4:12:48 (15,039)
Emerson, Andrew 4:46:28 (23,685)
Emery, Andrew 2:57:57 (1,002)
Emery, Jonathan 3:16:58 (2,899)
Emery, Michael 4:37:51 (21,532)
Emery, Peter 3:19:04 (3,146)
Emery, Robert 4:57:32 (25,868)
Emery, Robert 5:29:16 (29,721)
Emery, Simon 5:29:16 (29,721)
Emirali, Kenan 3:49:23 (8,998)
Emly, Timothy 7:16:42 (32,741)
Emmerson, Bob 3:23:18 (3,694)
Emmerson, Brian 5:02:38 (26,693)
Emmerson, Duncan 3:27:21 (4,385)
Emmerson, Steven 3:49:02 (8,906)
Emmett, Mark 3:31:49 (5,167)
Emmines, Jim 2:56:15 (853)
Emmins, David 5:08:57 (27,564)
Empsall, David 4:10:41 (14,551)
Emsall, Nicholas 4:56:05 (25,601)
Emsley, Derek 2:55:47 (806)
Emsley, Simon 4:27:07 (18,822)
Endersby, Adrian 4:22:42 (17,608)
Enfield, David 5:34:32 (30,152)
Engel, Bob 4:16:32 (15,988)
Engel, Mark 4:37:12 (21,370)
Engel, Sebastien 3:15:28 (2,720)
Engeltjes, Roel 4:16:46 (16,056)
England, John 4:01:11 (12,361)
England, John 4:08:35 (14,051)
England, Marc 5:14:56 (28,298)
England, Paul 4:32:54 (20,335)
England, Paul 4:58:15 (25,991)
England, Phil 3:19:34 (3,209)
Englefield, Duncan 4:41:50 (22,565)
English, Andrew 5:19:47 (28,851)
English, Bryan 3:36:17 (5,975)
English, Luc 2:52:38 (604)
English, Paul 4:19:53 (16,831)
English, Robert 3:17:46 (2,985)
English, Stephen 4:22:15 (17,462)
Engmann, Robert 4:10:26 (14,494)
Ennis, Darren 4:46:01 (23,569)
Ennis, Kevin 3:45:33 (8,062)
Ennis, Patrick 3:33:03 (5,359)
Enoch, Paul 4:00:22 (12,160)
Enskat, Neil 4:52:28 (24,868)
Enston, Charles 5:17:08 (28,582)
Entwistle, David 4:01:38 (12,476)
Entwistle, Nicholas 4:55:05 (25,387)
Entwistle, Peter 2:47:24 (377)
Epifori, Luciano 3:43:55 (7,635)
Epino, Henry 3:46:36 (8,314)
Eppel, Karl 4:11:56 (14,841)
Epsom, Joseph 3:38:26 (6,410)
Eriksson, Mikael 4:47:38 (23,935)
Ermisz, Gregory 5:17:52 (28,658)
Ernst, Guenter 2:42:59 (243)
Ernstsson, Sveinn 2:37:27 (133)
Erol, Rasim 3:47:50 (8,597)
Erskine, James 4:41:44 (22,540)
Erturk, Yash 4:33:22 (20,432)
Erwart, Bodern 3:24:00 (3,820)
Esajas, Oscar 5:26:01 (29,446)
Escalera, Juan 5:29:13 (29,714)
Escobar, Carlos 3:32:31 (5,272)
Escott, Harry 3:49:28 (9,033)
Eshelby, Mark 3:11:14 (2,179)
Espey, Robert 3:35:34 (5,817)
Esposito, Ciro 3:08:52 (1,918)
Essery, John 3:52:48 (9,926)
Essex, Jonathan 3:44:02 (7,667)
Essex-Crosby, Chris 3:13:50 (2,543)
Estall, Jim 3:13:07 (2,450)
Estall, Mark 5:17:00 (28,557)
Esteban, Emilio 5:20:30 (28,940)
Etchells, Bob 4:45:23 (23,404)
Etchenou, Arnaud 3:45:16 (7,992)
Etherington, Andrew 4:04:18 (13,046)
Etherington, David 3:44:27 (7,784)
Etherington, James 4:24:15 (18,054)
Etherington, John 3:48:35 (8,773)
Etherington, Philip 3:45:03 (7,940)
Ettery, David 4:36:19 (21,164)
Ettlinger, Anthony 4:05:45 (13,380)
Eustis, Roger 4:22:55 (17,677)
Evangelista, Joe 5:07:57 (27,430)
Evans, Adrian 4:41:45 (22,543)
Evans, Alexander 5:22:52 (29,163)
Evans, Alun 3:21:53 (3,502)
Evans, Andrew 2:53:18 (642)
Evans, Andrew 4:29:23 (19,432)
Evans, Andrew 4:30:09 (19,641)
Evans, Andy 4:39:10 (21,890)

Evans, Anthony	3:41:59 (7,149)	
Evans, Anthony	4:14:14 (15,377)	
Evans, Anthony	4:41:04 (22,367)	
Evans, Ben	4:27:23 (18,886)	
Evans, Brian	4:10:49 (14,586)	
Evans, Bruce	3:29:42 (4,827)	
Evans, Chris	4:31:48 (20,031)	
Evans, Christopher	4:10:18 (14,460)	
Evans, Christopher	4:21:48 (17,335)	
Evans, Christopher	5:01:00 (26,449)	
Evans, Cliff	3:14:26 (2,606)	
Evans, Clive	3:29:47 (4,840)	
Evans, Dan	3:36:14 (5,965)	
Evans, Daniel	4:50:44 (24,546)	
Evans, David	3:32:22 (5,243)	
Evans, David	3:42:16 (7,226)	
Evans, David	3:45:11 (7,969)	
Evans, David	4:40:10 (22,150)	
Evans, David	5:09:25 (27,624)	
Evans, Des	4:19:07 (16,621)	
Evans, Edwin	3:13:11 (2,462)	
Evans, Elfyn	4:42:47 (22,789)	
Evans, Francis	3:49:20 (8,981)	
Evans, Gareth	3:45:34 (8,065)	
Evans, Gareth	4:09:06 (14,153)	
Evans, Gareth	5:22:12 (29,107)	
Evans, Gary	4:35:31 (20,951)	
Evans, Gavin	2:56:15 (853)	
Evans, Glynn	4:14:04 (15,333)	
Evans, Howard	3:15:32 (2,726)	
Evans, Hugh	3:30:26 (4,937)	
Evans, Ian	3:13:46 (2,539)	
Evans, James	4:32:31 (20,219)	
Evans, Jean-Louis	4:04:16 (13,040)	
Evans, John	4:00:51 (12,267)	
Evans, John	4:34:27 (20,682)	
Evans, John	4:46:32 (23,699)	
Evans, Jonathan	6:04:48 (31,688)	
Evans, Julian	3:52:01 (9,693)	
Evans, Julian	5:00:58 (26,447)	
Evans, Keith	5:48:51 (31,087)	
Evans, Kenneth	4:11:25 (14,715)	
Evans, Kenneth	5:01:55 (26,590)	
Evans, Kevin	4:06:40 (13,606)	
Evans, Kevin	4:39:58 (22,096)	
Evans, Leonard	5:27:53 (29,608)	
Evans, Mark	3:13:09 (2,456)	
Evans, Mark	3:28:36 (4,626)	
Evans, Mark	3:51:11 (9,479)	
Evans, Mark	4:48:47 (24,190)	
Evans, Mark	5:34:18 (30,132)	
Evans, Martyn	4:25:44 (18,448)	
Evans, Matthew	5:15:26 (28,353)	
Evans, Mervyn	2:57:59 (1,005)	
Evans, Michael	2:37:26 (132)	
Evans, Michael	3:17:37 (2,964)	
Evans, Michael	4:13:56 (15,291)	
Evans, Michael	4:44:42 (23,220)	
Evans, Michael	5:03:06 (26,762)	
Evans, Neil	4:22:13 (17,449)	
Evans, Nicholas	4:00:11 (12,127)	
Evans, Nicholas	5:17:18 (28,602)	
Evans, Nick	3:46:39 (8,321)	
Evans, Nick	4:34:55 (20,807)	
Evans, Nigel	4:00:11 (12,127)	
Evans, Paul	3:54:43 (10,519)	
Evans, Peter	4:23:58 (17,965)	
Evans, Peter	4:27:43 (18,964)	
Evans, Peter	6:27:19 (32,231)	
Evans, Ray	4:52:35 (24,899)	
Evans, Richard	5:28:08 (29,625)	
Evans, Robert	5:34:11 (30,121)	
Evans, Sankie	2:40:07 (183)	
Evans, Simon	3:34:11 (5,561)	
Evans, Simon	3:38:14 (6,351)	
Evans, Simon	6:14:55 (31,957)	
Evans, Sion	4:50:52 (24,586)	
Evans, Stefan	6:05:21 (31,709)	
Evans, Steven	3:08:25 (1,852)	
Evans, Thomas	4:30:10 (19,645)	
Evans, Tim	3:37:28 (6,203)	
Evans, Timothy	4:03:57 (12,976)	
Evans, Tomos	5:00:53 (26,441)	

Evans, Tony	4:10:32 (14,518)	
Evans, Tony	4:12:31 (14,975)	
Evans, Trent	4:23:24 (17,802)	
Evans-Pollard, Chris	4:37:56 (21,558)	
Eve, Kevin	6:04:02 (31,664)	
Eve, Stuart	3:32:08 (5,211)	
Eveleigh, Paul	4:05:45 (13,380)	
Evemy, Richard	4:31:53 (20,053)	
Everard, Alan	4:03:13 (12,819)	
Everard, James	3:52:46 (9,916)	
Everard, Roger	2:58:48 (1,075)	
Everest, Eric	5:07:26 (27,364)	
Everett, Barry	4:04:24 (13,069)	
Everett, Jerry	4:29:48 (19,534)	
Everett, Michael	4:19:50 (16,810)	
Everett, Paul	3:59:56 (12,066)	
Everett, Wayne	3:57:27 (11,347)	
Everington, Daniel	3:45:31 (8,048)	
Everitt, Geoffrey	4:10:21 (14,471)	
Everitt, Matt	3:43:31 (7,533)	
Everitt, Michael	4:12:29 (14,967)	
Everitt, Simon	5:07:12 (27,328)	
Everson, Desmond	3:47:20 (8,467)	
Everson, Matthew	4:38:24 (21,685)	
Every, Keith	4:26:02 (18,527)	
Eves, Peter	4:04:48 (13,160)	
Evison, Michael	4:29:33 (19,467)	
Evrard, Eric	3:29:35 (4,811)	
Ewart, David	3:25:41 (4,097)	
Ewen, Robert	3:47:08 (8,414)	
Ewing, Tom	5:14:32 (28,251)	
Ewins, James	3:56:50 (11,149)	
Ex, Gustav	4:47:31 (23,915)	
Exall, David	5:04:13 (26,919)	
Exall, Mark	3:50:27 (9,290)	
Excell, Paul	4:29:49 (19,543)	
Exposito, Christian	4:22:15 (17,462)	
Extence, John	4:37:48 (21,522)	
Extremera, Francisco	4:30:48 (19,785)	
Exworth, Matthew	3:16:15 (2,816)	
Eyre, David	5:38:17 (30,432)	
Eyre, Joseph	4:34:04 (20,598)	
Eyre, Martin	4:23:21 (17,786)	
Eyre, Simon	3:53:30 (10,145)	
Eyre, Timothy	5:36:17 (30,295)	
Fabregat, Marc	3:26:57 (4,321)	
Fabricius, Michael	4:08:59 (14,127)	
Fachadas, Fernando	4:02:10 (12,588)	
Facherty, Michael	5:07:24 (27,357)	
Fackrell, Steven	3:56:29 (11,044)	
Facon, Jean	4:57:22 (25,836)	
Fadiora, George	3:06:56 (1,729)	
Faes, Daniel	3:47:27 (8,497)	
Fagan, Jamie	3:30:03 (4,880)	
Fagan, Sean	3:43:50 (7,616)	
Fagernas, Kai	4:49:51 (24,395)	
Fagernes, Vebjoern	3:37:02 (6,126)	
Faherty, Paul	4:52:53 (24,958)	
Fahey, Barry	4:49:25 (24,304)	
Fahy, Brian	3:48:43 (8,816)	
Fahy, Seamus	3:38:15 (6,357)	
Faichney, Edward	4:15:36 (15,722)	
Faint, Keith	3:29:25 (4,780)	
Faint, Richard	6:30:08 (32,280)	
Fairbrace, Brian	6:37:39 (32,408)	
Fairclough, John	3:37:00 (6,118)	
Fairclough, Thomas	4:15:46 (15,774)	
Faires, Christian	4:31:37 (19,996)	
Fairfield, Andrew	4:03:05 (12,795)	
Fairfoull, Andrew	3:53:51 (10,268)	
Fairhurst, John	4:05:40 (13,362)	
Fairhurst, Wayne	3:08:30 (1,873)	
Fairlcough, Matthew	3:57:56 (11,483)	
Fairman, Ian	3:52:18 (9,783)	
Fairweather, Andrew	5:31:21 (29,897)	

Fairweather, Michael	4:38:03 (21,584)	
Fairweather, Trevor	4:18:49 (16,551)	
Fairweather, Walter	5:28:45 (29,677)	
Fakande, Olubenga	6:04:53 (31,690)	
Fakhry, Husam	5:04:37 (26,967)	
Falconer, James	4:12:52 (15,054)	
Fallacara, Gaetano	3:18:28 (3,067)	
Fallis, Jonathan	5:29:55 (29,772)	
Fallon, Tom	3:03:22 (1,409)	
Falloon, Ian	4:42:06 (22,634)	
Fane, Patrick	5:23:31 (29,223)	
Fanfoni, Andrea	4:38:56 (21,827)	
Fanning, Alastair	3:23:53 (3,795)	
Fanning, David	4:45:08 (23,343)	
Fanning, Jerome	2:59:57 (1,166)	
Fanning, Martin	4:25:47 (18,459)	
Fantis, Costas	4:50:12 (24,452)	
Farago, Robert	3:55:10 (10,653)	
Farbotko, Shay	4:49:24 (24,299)	
Farina, Franco	4:27:01 (18,792)	
Farina, Jonathan	5:43:20 (30,776)	
Farley, Anthony	5:43:20 (30,776)	
Farley, Nick	3:25:24 (4,048)	
Farmer, Adrian	4:04:13 (13,032)	
Farmer, Andrew	4:19:05 (16,614)	
Farmer, Chris	4:34:02 (20,591)	
Farmer, Conrad	4:13:01 (15,088)	
Farmer, John	3:52:16 (9,771)	
Farmer, Marc	5:18:39 (28,737)	
Farmer, Mark	4:45:07 (23,339)	
Farmer, Michael	4:23:11 (17,747)	
Farmer, Samuel	4:27:01 (18,792)	
Farmer, Stuart	4:20:02 (16,870)	
Farmilo, Reece	4:13:06 (15,104)	
Farnell, Mark	2:56:11 (843)	
Farnell, Robert	4:24:31 (18,124)	
Farnes, Jeffrey	4:35:20 (20,909)	
Faro, Geoffrey	4:28:31 (19,175)	
Farquhar, Ian	3:59:20 (11,896)	
Farquharson, Andrew	2:31:39 (72)	
Farquharson, Stuart	4:45:00 (23,304)	
Farr, Raymond	4:13:10 (15,113)	
Farrajota, Francisco	3:17:48 (2,992)	
Farrant, Giles	4:04:12 (13,027)	
Farrant, Paul	4:29:32 (19,464)	
Farrar, Alasdair	4:44:53 (23,266)	
Farrar, Andrew	3:08:56 (1,928)	
Farrar, Bill	3:48:08 (8,658)	
Farrar, Malcolm	4:28:00 (19,032)	
Farrar, Mark	3:59:06 (11,830)	
Farrel, Gary	5:02:28 (26,662)	
Farrell, Bernard	3:40:57 (6,949)	
Farrell, Brendan	4:27:12 (18,841)	
Farrell, David	3:45:35 (8,069)	
Farrell, David	4:39:52 (22,076)	
Farrell, Edward	3:59:02 (11,819)	
Farrell, John	4:00:09 (12,118)	
Farrell, Matthew	4:31:18 (19,900)	
Farrell, Robert	3:19:14 (3,165)	
Farrell, Tony	4:10:21 (14,471)	
Farrelly, Kevin	4:14:20 (15,405)	
Farrelly, Vincent	4:03:54 (12,963)	
Farren, Bobby	2:37:23 (131)	
Farren, Christopher	4:54:07 (25,202)	
Farrer, Tyrone	4:49:05 (24,255)	
Farrimond, John	5:40:29 (30,582)	
Farrin, Dennis	5:47:22 (31,006)	
Farrington, Andrew	3:52:01 (9,693)	
Farrow, Andrew	3:46:52 (8,358)	
Farrow, Jim	4:37:52 (21,536)	
Farrow, Nigel	3:43:46 (7,591)	
Farsides, Tom	3:26:16 (4,200)	
Farthing, David	3:51:25 (9,525)	
Fasse, Matthias	4:07:36 (13,816)	
Fasting, Tonny	3:52:56 (9,958)	
Fataky, Joseph	4:54:39 (25,314)	
Fatemi, Nader	3:08:33 (1,876)	
Faucon, Jean-Christophe	3:56:58 (11,200)	
Faulkner, Andrew	4:26:27 (18,637)	
Faulkner, Anthony	4:43:59 (23,062)	
Faulkner, Christian	4:39:17 (21,921)	
Faulkner, David	4:54:05 (25,198)	
Faulkner, Edward	3:48:36 (8,782)	

LONDON MARATHON

Faulkner, James	3:54:30 (10,459)
Faulkner, Joe	3:36:34 (6,034)
Faulkner, Jon	4:24:27 (18,106)
Faulkner, Matthew	5:45:03 (30,885)
Faulkner, Michael	4:08:29 (14,014)
Faulkner, Patrick	5:08:37 (27,509)
Faulkner, Robert	3:45:37 (8,074)
Faulkner, Roger	3:48:40 (8,802)
Faulkner, Russell	4:17:44 (16,304)
Faure, Wynton	3:15:24 (2,714)
Faure Walker, Teddy	4:35:04 (20,846)
Fauset, Paul	4:09:52 (14,355)
Fawbert, Jeremy	3:11:37 (2,215)
Fawcett, Andrew	4:38:16 (21,645)
Fawcett, Derrick	4:23:59 (17,976)
Fawcett, John	3:56:35 (11,078)
Fawcett, Steven	3:33:09 (5,375)
Fawkes, Richard	4:19:46 (16,797)
Fayau, Yves	4:45:03 (23,323)
Fazackerley, Leslie	4:30:34 (19,725)
Feakes, Kieren	3:39:03 (6,537)
Feakins, Richard	4:23:43 (17,893)
Fear, Richard	4:33:35 (20,486)
Fear, William	3:07:41 (1,786)
Fearn, Jon	3:38:54 (6,501)
Fearn, Mark	4:32:07 (20,114)
Fearnhead, Gary	3:24:47 (3,956)
Fearnley, Darren	3:11:44 (2,234)
Fearns, Donald	5:02:10 (26,624)
Fearns, Stuart	3:38:49 (6,486)
Fearon, Alex	4:12:26 (14,955)
Featley, Colin	5:47:32 (31,019)
Febery, Grant	3:42:11 (7,196)
Fee, Graeme	3:10:33 (2,111)
Fegan, Mark	5:55:47 (31,391)
Fegan, Timothy	4:16:22 (15,938)
Fehsenfeld, Burkhard	3:16:21 (2,825)
Feige, Dieter	4:34:55 (20,807)
Fekih, Lahcene	4:10:26 (14,494)
Feld, David	3:28:30 (4,604)
Feld, Steven	4:57:28 (25,850)
Felici, Aldo	3:44:10 (7,698)
Feliks, Michael	3:49:40 (9,086)
Fell, Adrian	3:58:49 (11,742)
Fell, Andrew	4:02:43 (12,705)
Fell, James	4:26:38 (18,696)
Fell, Samuel	3:50:57 (9,411)
Fell, Simon	3:57:45 (11,440)
Fell, Stephan	5:31:35 (29,919)
Feller, James	4:56:21 (25,671)
Fellowes-Freeman, Malcolm	4:45:36 (23,475)
Fellows, Stephen	5:13:05 (28,090)
Feltham, Barry	4:28:46 (19,248)
Feltham, Peter	4:40:35 (22,252)
Felton, Clive	3:41:52 (7,125)
Felton, Jonathan	4:14:52 (15,542)
Felxas-Portella, Miquel	4:14:00 (15,313)
Fenby, James	3:51:43 (9,599)
Fender, Thomas	4:52:48 (24,939)
Fenech, Clinton	4:46:49 (23,762)
Fenet, Daniel	4:08:27 (14,003)
Fenlon, Mark	4:32:14 (20,147)
Fenlon, Stephen	3:57:26 (11,339)
Fenn, Alec	4:49:17 (24,286)
Fenn, Ian	4:19:08 (16,627)
Fenn, Paul	4:25:21 (18,348)
Fenn, Russell	4:25:07 (18,292)
Fennell, Jonathan	4:38:59 (21,841)
Fennelly, John	5:49:38 (31,128)
Fenson, Graham	3:45:20 (8,006)
Fenton, Andrew	4:18:19 (16,444)
Fenton, Christopher	4:25:52 (18,475)
Fenton, Dave	2:56:17 (857)
Fenton, Les	3:02:52 (1,362)
Fenwick, Andrew	4:32:11 (20,136)
Fenwick, Jonathan	4:11:48 (14,817)
Fereday, David	3:46:17 (8,223)
Fereday, David	4:43:13 (22,890)
Ferel, Dieter	4:22:35 (17,568)
Fergus, Adam	4:23:48 (17,919)
Ferguson, Carl	4:08:22 (13,982)
Ferguson, David	3:49:49 (9,135)
Ferguson, Duncan	4:34:49 (20,777)
Ferguson, Iain	3:21:49 (3,487)
Ferguson, James	3:39:42 (6,667)
Ferguson, Mark	4:18:13 (16,417)
Ferguson, Mark	4:27:57 (19,022)
Ferguson, Michael	3:12:37 (2,375)
Ferguson, Neil	4:35:39 (21,001)
Ferguson, Paul	5:52:23 (31,246)
Ferguson, Rory	3:39:12 (6,567)
Ferguson, Samuel	4:11:03 (14,647)
Ferguson, William	4:05:55 (13,417)
Fergusson, Bruce	6:07:54 (31,779)
Fermi, Guissepe	4:16:02 (15,847)
Fern, Neil	4:35:54 (21,049)
Fernall, Robert	4:09:29 (14,266)
Fernandes, Alan	6:18:12 (32,040)
Fernandes, Ivan	5:11:59 (27,949)
Fernandez, José	4:40:01 (22,109)
Fernando, Michael	4:21:17 (17,186)
Fernee, Ronald	3:49:05 (8,919)
Ferner Robson, Kristian	5:02:18 (26,641)
Ferns, Alex	4:50:29 (24,502)
Ferns, Douglas	4:37:11 (21,365)
Ferns, Gerard	3:27:37 (4,440)
Ferraiolo, Raymond	4:15:10 (15,609)
Ferrar, Ian	4:48:23 (24,097)
Ferrar, Mark	4:48:23 (24,097)
Ferrar, Philip	4:02:16 (12,609)
Ferrar, Richard	4:26:07 (18,556)
Ferrari, Attilio	4:33:21 (20,429)
Ferrario, Mark	5:13:25 (28,127)
Ferrario, Paolo	3:58:59 (11,796)
Ferreira, Leopold	5:35:29 (30,226)
Ferre-Lite, Ferran	3:59:20 (11,896)
Ferreno, Diego	3:09:52 (2,023)
Ferretti, Pasqualino	4:41:43 (22,536)
Ferri, Andrea	3:50:22 (9,268)
Ferrier, Graham	3:36:05 (5,924)
Ferrington, John	4:57:44 (25,904)
Ferris, Steven	2:53:51 (670)
Ferrman, Vaughan	4:28:16 (19,102)
Ferro, Bruno	3:48:08 (8,658)
Fether, Harold	5:15:13 (28,330)
Feunteun, Tristan	5:34:56 (30,180)
Feurer, Daniel	4:00:24 (12,165)
Few, Joseph	4:39:46 (22,047)
Fewllows, Mark	4:51:25 (24,682)
Feys, Hans	4:10:39 (14,545)
Ffoulkes-Mollis, Gareth	3:45:21 (8,012)
Fichoux, Jean	4:52:02 (24,787)
Fiddis, Richard	4:24:48 (18,198)
Fidge, John	3:50:58 (9,418)
Field, Andrew	2:55:34 (786)
Field, Andrew	4:37:32 (21,454)
Field, Frank	4:07:47 (13,866)
Field, Geoffrey	3:52:01 (9,693)
Field, Ivan	3:51:45 (9,610)
Field, Mark	4:14:18 (15,391)
Field, Martyn	4:57:37 (25,881)
Field, Matthew	5:55:56 (31,395)
Field, Michael	4:21:00 (17,110)
Field, Robert	3:43:28 (7,516)
Field, Stephen	3:01:59 (1,300)
Field, Terry	5:50:15 (31,149)
Fielden, Simon	5:40:44 (30,599)
Fielder, Rick	3:24:44 (3,951)
Fielder, Simon	3:08:12 (1,824)
Fieldhouse, David	3:27:56 (4,505)
Fielding, David	4:35:17 (20,898)
Fielding, Kevin	4:06:11 (13,484)
Fielding, Paul	2:54:07 (685)
Fielding, Paul	4:39:37 (21,996)
Fields, Andrew	3:43:15 (7,459)
Fields, Leon	4:35:44 (21,015)
Fields, Steven	3:43:15 (7,459)
Fiennes, Ran	3:48:44 (8,822)
Fiesal, Emir	4:06:51 (13,638)
Fievez, Andrew	4:53:12 (25,014)
Fifield, John	3:37:44 (6,271)
Filkin, Neil	4:46:11 (23,618)
Fillenwarth, Edward Jnr	5:18:31 (28,730)
Filler, Paul	5:18:10 (28,686)
Fillette, Sylvain	4:19:26 (16,700)
Filmer, Mark	4:35:31 (20,951)

The Ever Presents

A small number of runners, known as the 'Ever Presents', have completed every London since 1981. By 2010 their number was down to 20. The oldest are 76-year-olds Kenneth Jones and Jeffrey Gordon, while the youngest is 51-year-old Chris Finill who amazingly has run every London Marathon in less than three hours. His fastest time in London was 2:28:27 in 1985. In 2010 he could still do 2:52:05. In 1981, one of them, Jeff Aston was hit by crippling cramp 40 yards from the finish. 'I couldn't quit', he said, 'so I hopped to the finish.' Aston's battle with pain was reported the following day in *The Times*. Aston is still an 'Ever Present' and at the age of 62 ran 4:18:34.

Finbow, Mark	4:25:28 (18,377)
Finch, Darren	6:03:28 (31,650)
Finch, Edward	5:35:58 (30,267)
Finch, Lewis	3:21:03 (3,374)
Finch, Simon	3:33:43 (5,462)
Fincham, Daron	4:13:22 (15,159)
Findel Hawkins, David	3:03:13 (1,393)
Finden Crofts, Christian	3:41:56 (7,137)
Finding, Antony	4:43:40 (22,990)
Findon, Gerald	4:34:05 (20,603)
Fine, Martin	3:46:39 (8,321)
Fine, Nathaniel	4:24:11 (18,029)
Finerty, Bernard	3:50:57 (9,411)
Finill, Chris	2:55:02 (744)
Fink, Chris	4:20:33 (17,006)
Finlay, David	4:19:10 (16,636)
Finlayson, Gordon	4:58:02 (25,954)
Finlayson, John	4:00:00 (12,085)
Finley, Aidan	4:45:10 (23,348)
Finn, Andy	3:07:48 (1,793)
Finn, Geoffrey	4:05:25 (13,305)
Finn, Jim	5:32:05 (29,957)
Finn, Julian	4:14:33 (15,457)
Finn, Patrick	4:37:18 (21,400)
Finn, Rupert	3:53:15 (10,061)
Finnegan, David	5:38:42 (30,460)
Finnegan, Michael	3:52:11 (9,747)
Finnegan, Stephen	3:59:55 (12,063)
Finney, Mark	3:42:22 (7,252)
Finniear, Kevin	6:03:46 (31,656)
Fiocco, Gilberto	3:53:14 (10,055)
Fiolka, Helmut	4:08:01 (13,916)
Fioriti, Luigi	3:49:42 (9,099)
Firdose, Tariq	5:08:27 (27,492)
Firkin, Richard	4:35:14 (20,893)
Firmager, Gary	4:50:45 (24,550)
Firmin, Barry	3:51:59 (9,678)
Firmin, Michael	3:31:41 (5,148)
Firmin, Paul	2:59:11 (1,109)
Firth, Andrew	4:07:13 (13,725)
Firth, Benjamin	3:35:47 (5,862)
Firth, Clive	4:53:07 (25,000)
Firth, Graham	4:05:53 (13,407)
Firth, James	4:37:25 (21,428)
Firth, Mark	4:51:04 (24,619)
Firth, Martin	2:45:41 (318)
Firth, Richard	3:23:00 (3,657)
Fischer, Alan	4:15:49 (15,783)
Fischer, Greg	3:32:49 (5,320)
Fischer, Kai	3:58:43 (11,712)
Fischer, Mark	3:40:33 (6,863)

Fischer, Michael	4:28:56 (19,297)	
Fischer, Oliver	3:49:19 (8,977)	
Fischer, Ulrich	3:30:35 (4,958)	
Fish, Andrew	3:53:14 (10,055)	
Fish, Jonathan	3:14:36 (2,619)	
Fish, Michael	3:40:30 (6,850)	
Fish, Ralph	5:31:55 (29,946)	
Fisher, Adrian	4:06:04 (13,452)	
Fisher, Andrew	4:36:03 (21,092)	
Fisher, Crispin	3:20:57 (3,356)	
Fisher, David	3:43:32 (7,537)	
Fisher, Derek	4:49:34 (24,337)	
Fisher, Edward	3:45:59 (8,157)	
Fisher, Gary	3:45:29 (8,039)	
Fisher, Ian	2:22:07 (27)	
Fisher, James	4:44:10 (23,099)	
Fisher, John	3:42:53 (7,358)	
Fisher, John	5:05:54 (27,144)	
Fisher, John	5:56:24 (31,417)	
Fisher, Jonah	5:12:20 (28,004)	
Fisher, Lee	3:44:42 (7,852)	
Fisher, Marcus	5:03:10 (26,774)	
Fisher, Mark	4:21:14 (17,174)	
Fisher, Martyn	2:44:08 (276)	
Fisher, Michael	4:00:31 (12,190)	
Fisher, Neil	4:07:44 (13,850)	
Fisher, Nicholas	3:48:36 (8,782)	
Fisher, Richard	4:54:19 (25,246)	
Fisher, Robert	3:19:20 (3,178)	
Fisher, Robin	3:39:41 (6,661)	
Fisher, Roderick	3:46:44 (8,334)	
Fisher, Simon	3:46:02 (8,167)	
Fisher, Stephen	3:40:39 (6,885)	
Fisher, Stephen	4:19:30 (16,726)	
Fisher, Stephen	4:40:44 (22,286)	
Fisher, Steven	3:44:44 (7,867)	
Fisher, Todd	3:56:14 (10,975)	
Fishpool, Sean	3:11:55 (2,259)	
Fishwick, Ian	5:11:24 (27,874)	
Fiske, Mathew	4:12:15 (14,915)	
Fitch, Davey	3:43:48 (7,606)	
Fitch, Greg	3:39:16 (6,585)	
Fitch, Will	3:54:17 (10,396)	
Fitchen, Michael	4:34:07 (20,611)	
Fitchett, Allan	3:56:54 (11,174)	
Fitt, James	3:17:56 (3,002)	
Fitt, John	5:47:58 (31,037)	
Fitter, Gary	3:21:04 (3,379)	
Fitzgerald, Ben	4:34:34 (20,714)	
Fitzgerald, Brian	5:25:24 (29,395)	
Fitzgerald, Jack	5:39:57 (30,545)	
Fitzgerald, Lawrence	4:04:04 (5,533)	
Fitzgerald, Lloyd	5:01:59 (26,603)	
Fitzgerald, Richard	3:41:07 (6,994)	
Fitzhugh, William	4:59:17 (26,172)	
Fitzjohn, Ben	3:32:24 (5,252)	
Fitzpatrick, Craig	3:52:00 (9,683)	
Fitzpatrick, David	3:46:56 (8,368)	
Fitzpatrick, David	3:55:22 (10,714)	
Fitzpatrick, John	3:55:05 (10,619)	
Fitzpatrick, Mark	5:09:17 (27,603)	
Fitzsimmons, Thomas	5:20:05 (28,890)	
Fitzsimons, Timothy	3:22:41 (3,606)	
Fitzwilliams, Piers	4:41:48 (22,556)	
Flack, Richard	3:50:56 (9,406)	
Flaherty, Mark	3:41:13 (7,019)	
Flaherty, Patrick	4:08:31 (14,027)	
Flanagan, Brian	4:05:43 (13,372)	
Flanagan, John	4:01:41 (12,489)	
Flanagan, Martin	4:14:59 (15,570)	
Flanagan, Raymond	4:04:39 (13,123)	
Flanagan, Sean	4:18:55 (16,571)	
Flanaghan, John	4:38:56 (21,827)	
Flanders, Robert	5:41:27 (30,649)	
Flannery, Kevin	5:25:18 (29,385)	
Flashman, Keith	4:57:59 (25,950)	
Flavell, Christopher	2:51:14 (547)	
Flavell, Julian	4:20:34 (17,014)	
Flaye, Stuart	3:58:21 (11,601)	
Flear, Christopher	4:48:10 (24,066)	
Fleck, Michael	3:28:22 (4,583)	
Fleckney, Paul	5:26:06 (29,456)	
Flegg, Tony	5:11:08 (27,829)	

Fleischer, Georg	4:08:05 (13,931)	
Fleischer, Herbert	3:17:41 (2,972)	
Fleming, Clin	4:00:20 (12,157)	
Fleming, Frank	4:47:29 (23,910)	
Fleming, James	3:21:25 (3,423)	
Fleming, Mark	3:09:12 (1,953)	
Fleming, Mark	4:45:49 (23,520)	
Fleming, Timothy	3:55:51 (10,855)	
Flesher, Roy	2:54:51 (732)	
Fletcher, Andrew	2:50:15 (499)	
Fletcher, Andrew	5:04:19 (26,938)	
Fletcher, Ben	4:47:01 (23,815)	
Fletcher, Cedric	2:56:34 (878)	
Fletcher, Chris	3:27:12 (4,361)	
Fletcher, Dale	5:11:38 (27,899)	
Fletcher, David	4:06:53 (13,645)	
Fletcher, Euan	4:24:33 (18,131)	
Fletcher, Gary	4:23:54 (17,948)	
Fletcher, James	3:30:29 (4,941)	
Fletcher, Kevin	4:24:58 (18,254)	
Fletcher, Martin	4:47:05 (23,830)	
Fletcher, Neil	3:43:41 (7,568)	
Fletcher, Nicholas	4:21:19 (17,197)	
Fletcher, Paul	4:30:15 (19,662)	
Fletcher, Paul	5:11:46 (27,918)	
Fletcher, Richard	3:28:31 (4,606)	
Fletcher, Stephen	3:35:57 (5,893)	
Fletcher, Stephen	4:08:53 (14,109)	
Fletcher, Stephen	5:20:49 (28,978)	
Flew, Nicholas	4:21:58 (17,382)	
Flint, Andrew	3:19:06 (3,150)	
Flint, Anthony	3:15:22 (2,711)	
Flint, Gary	4:02:37 (12,685)	
Flint, Robert	5:06:15 (27,191)	
Flint, Russell	3:55:00 (10,596)	
Flood, Christopher	3:36:07 (5,940)	
Flook, Alan	4:18:51 (16,558)	
Flook, Brett	2:43:28 (253)	
Flor, Antonio	4:09:16 (14,206)	
Florek, Joseph	4:26:03 (18,529)	
Florent, Didier	3:25:58 (4,149)	
Flotve, Ole	4:19:55 (16,840)	
Flower, John	4:57:38 (25,884)	
Flower, Mark	5:42:39 (30,733)	
Flowers, Karl	4:56:54 (25,745)	
Flowers, Mark	3:43:02 (7,396)	
Flowers, Michael	3:43:32 (7,537)	
Floyd, Geoffrey	5:26:02 (29,447)	
Floyd, Giles	3:50:51 (9,392)	
Floyd, Robert	3:32:17 (5,231)	
Flute, Edward	4:54:42 (25,323)	
Flyckt, Geir	4:29:46 (19,527)	
Flynn, Anthony	4:58:27 (26,024)	
Flynn, Brian	3:54:02 (10,320)	
Flynn, Fred	3:34:46 (5,668)	
Flynn, Gareth	4:22:36 (17,576)	
Flynn, John	3:02:20 (1,328)	
Flynn, John	3:34:24 (5,598)	
Flynn, Matthew	4:51:39 (24,725)	
Flynn, Paul	4:50:57 (24,600)	
Flynn, Peter	3:38:29 (6,418)	
Flynn, Sean	3:39:00 (6,523)	
Flynn, Tommy	2:59:29 (1,132)	
Foden, Matt	4:06:15 (13,504)	
Foerster, Horst	3:58:50 (11,745)	
Fogarty, Terry	3:29:37 (4,817)	
Fogg, William	3:46:52 (8,358)	
Foley, Jerome	3:55:07 (10,637)	
Folkard, Melvyn	3:25:41 (4,097)	
Folkerd, David	4:49:49 (24,383)	
Follows, Dominic	3:52:06 (9,723)	
Fontaine, Guillaume	4:17:41 (16,288)	
Fontana, Pietro	4:26:41 (18,714)	
Fontyn, Barry	4:20:12 (16,913)	
Foo, Kim	3:54:25 (10,435)	
Foo, Shane	3:18:41 (3,095)	
Foody, Peter	2:52:53 (624)	
Foord, Gary	3:12:08 (2,301)	
Foord, Roger	3:39:05 (6,544)	
Foot, Michael	4:13:28 (15,181)	
Forbes, Craig	2:51:09 (540)	
Forbes, Stuart	4:13:51 (15,272)	
Forbes, Will	3:55:01 (10,600)	

Ford, Andrew	3:44:37 (7,827)	
Ford, Andrew	3:48:38 (8,796)	
Ford, Brian	4:47:55 (24,010)	
Ford, Christian	4:35:08 (20,861)	
Ford, Christopher	3:56:04 (10,918)	
Ford, Christopher	4:09:11 (14,183)	
Ford, Daniel	4:48:30 (24,126)	
Ford, David	5:39:21 (30,493)	
Ford, Don	4:19:44 (16,785)	
Ford, Graham	4:28:11 (19,079)	
Ford, Jonathan	4:29:43 (19,510)	
Ford, Jonathan	4:31:13 (19,886)	
Ford, Kevin	4:07:11 (13,718)	
Ford, Martin	4:56:35 (25,701)	
Ford, Matt	4:06:31 (13,571)	
Ford, Richard	2:47:18 (372)	
Ford, Robert	3:53:10 (10,036)	
Ford, Ross	4:11:55 (14,837)	
Ford, Russell	3:32:20 (5,237)	
Ford, Thomas	4:40:18 (22,183)	
Ford, Timothy	4:08:59 (14,127)	
Forde, Rufus	4:33:47 (20,534)	
Forder, Kevin	3:41:01 (6,966)	
Forder, Nigel	7:02:43 (32,656)	
Fordham, Alan	4:05:11 (13,248)	
Fordham, Craig	3:32:20 (5,237)	
Fordham, David	3:59:52 (12,046)	
Fordham, David	4:13:53 (15,281)	
Fordham, Joseph	4:20:41 (17,044)	
Fordham, Mark	4:23:46 (17,907)	
Fordyce, Bruce	4:19:32 (16,733)	
Foreman, Colin	3:35:38 (5,833)	
Foreman, James	4:17:37 (16,273)	
Foreman, Neil	4:25:35 (18,410)	
Foreman, Robert	4:46:57 (23,803)	
Foreman, Tim	4:04:08 (13,014)	
Forfar, Rob	3:41:40 (7,094)	
Forgrave, Martyn	3:42:10 (7,193)	
Forman, Alasdair	4:17:41 (16,288)	
Forman, David	3:53:29 (10,139)	
Forman, Ian	3:42:41 (7,313)	
Fornasari, Rossano	3:40:51 (6,929)	
Forner, Helmut	3:52:41 (9,893)	
Forrest, Abie	3:36:44 (6,061)	
Forrest, Ewan	3:39:21 (6,596)	
Forrest, Gordon	4:15:33 (15,708)	
Forrest, Ian	3:49:39 (9,083)	
Forrester, David	3:49:11 (8,941)	
Forrester, Graham	3:48:37 (8,789)	
Forrester, James	5:07:25 (27,360)	
Forrester, Michael	4:33:15 (20,415)	
Forrester, Peter	3:49:34 (9,059)	
Forsdick, David	3:49:33 (9,053)	
Forsey, Keith	4:21:48 (17,335)	
Forsham, Glyn	3:38:16 (6,362)	
Forshaw, Lee	4:36:17 (21,147)	
Forshaw, Lee	4:55:45 (25,533)	
Forshaw, Robert	3:42:57 (7,376)	
Forsteinsson, Gudmundur	3:41:28 (7,059)	
Forster, Adrian	5:18:54 (28,766)	
Forster, Andrew	2:58:47 (1,073)	
Forster, David	3:40:09 (6,772)	
Forster, Nicholas	3:50:40 (9,338)	
Forster, Nicholas	3:30:07 (4,887)	
Forster, Paul	3:56:21 (11,003)	
Forster, Paul	5:18:57 (28,773)	
Forster, Peter	2:37:57 (145)	
Forster, Stephen	4:15:48 (15,780)	
Forster-Jones, Paul	3:23:56 (3,807)	
Forster-Knight, Eddie	4:52:10 (24,809)	
Forsyth, Andrew	3:49:40 (9,086)	
Forsyth, Gordon	3:51:54 (9,650)	
Forsyth, Jamie	4:01:48 (12,522)	
Forsyth, Malcolm	4:53:24 (25,049)	
Forsyth, Samuel	4:27:35 (18,933)	
Forsyth, Stewart	3:35:57 (5,893)	
Forte, Philip	2:57:45 (983)	
Fortin, Christian	3:50:24 (9,276)	
Fortino, Giovanni	3:29:10 (4,724)	
Fortune, Stephen	3:35:22 (5,772)	
Forty, Mark	4:18:21 (16,455)	
Foskett, Geoff	3:46:16 (8,215)	
Foster, Alan	4:10:35 (14,532)	

Foster, Andy	3:35:29 (5,802)
Foster, Ben	4:04:22 (13,062)
Foster, Christopher	4:28:41 (19,220)
Foster, Dave	4:01:26 (12,423)
Foster, David	3:11:51 (2,252)
Foster, David	4:36:18 (21,153)
Foster, David	4:57:29 (25,854)
Foster, David	5:02:15 (26,634)
Foster, Eric	3:51:47 (9,621)
Foster, Gary	4:36:14 (21,136)
Foster, Howard	3:50:58 (9,418)
Foster, James	4:32:58 (20,351)
Foster, John	3:59:41 (11,989)
Foster, John	4:17:26 (16,229)
Foster, John	4:28:09 (19,071)
Foster, Kevin	3:49:27 (9,027)
Foster, Lee	5:12:09 (27,968)
Foster, Mark	4:23:52 (17,937)
Foster, Martin	3:20:26 (3,304)
Foster, Michael	4:13:15 (15,134)
Foster, Neil	5:32:20 (29,982)
Foster, Paul	4:47:55 (24,010)
Foster, Paul	4:50:51 (24,580)
Foster, Paul	5:09:41 (27,659)
Foster, Peter	3:35:50 (5,871)
Foster, Peter	3:51:40 (9,587)
Foster, Peter	4:11:44 (14,801)
Foster, Richard	3:30:59 (5,022)
Foster, Richard	3:42:04 (7,170)
Foster, Richard	5:19:58 (28,872)
Foster, Stephen	3:51:09 (9,472)
Foster, Stephen	5:54:08 (31,317)
Foster, Steven	4:18:51 (16,558)
Foster, Stuart	3:26:15 (4,197)
Foster, Timothy	4:29:45 (19,524)
Fotherby, Kenneth	2:47:37 (385)
Fothergill, Simon	4:30:08 (19,635)
Fothergill, Tom	3:53:44 (10,218)
Fotheringham, William	3:45:16 (7,992)
Foulds, Daniel	3:17:25 (2,951)
Foulds, John	3:55:40 (10,798)
Foulds, John	4:30:43 (19,764)
Foulger, Richard	5:45:08 (30,888)
Foulger, Stanley	3:58:39 (11,691)
Foulkes, Andrew	4:46:01 (23,569)
Foulos, Matthew	4:23:34 (17,840)
Foulston, Robert	4:27:57 (19,022)
Fountain, Colin	3:38:50 (6,491)
Fountain, Peter	4:17:29 (16,240)
Fourcade, Edouard	4:20:21 (16,955)
Fourneaux, Stephane	4:20:47 (17,066)
Fournet, Dominique	3:42:06 (7,180)
Fournier, Marc	3:31:07 (5,054)
Fowkes, Gary	4:25:15 (18,323)
Fowkes, Roger	3:06:29 (1,682)
Fowler, Craig	3:38:16 (6,362)
Fowler, David	4:02:54 (12,755)
Fowler, David	4:40:55 (22,336)
Fowler, Kenneth	2:56:00 (829)
Fowler, Martin	3:10:45 (2,127)
Fowler, Richard	3:04:57 (1,538)
Fowler, Stephen	3:15:05 (2,675)
Fowler, Steven	3:31:36 (5,124)
Fowler, Tom	3:42:46 (7,335)
Fowles, Stephen	3:27:08 (4,349)
Fox, Andrew	4:40:41 (22,270)
Fox, David	5:24:45 (29,341)
Fox, Edward	4:10:22 (14,479)
Fox, Graham	4:58:48 (26,096)
Fox, Gregory	4:05:28 (13,317)
Fox, James	4:44:56 (23,283)
Fox, Martin	3:30:22 (4,924)
Fox, Matthew	5:01:31 (26,527)
Fox, Mervyn	5:08:56 (27,561)
Fox, Nick	4:58:48 (26,096)
Fox, Paul	4:41:14 (22,408)
Fox, Robin	4:41:27 (22,463)
Fox, Thomas	5:44:16 (30,837)
Fox, Trevor	3:57:15 (11,278)
Fox, William	3:31:17 (5,075)
Foxall, Ian	4:58:42 (26,079)
Foxall, Peter	3:03:00 (1,368)
Foxley, Eric	4:34:21 (20,658)

Foxwell, Andrew	4:44:23 (23,149)
Foxwell, Pete	3:41:56 (7,137)
Fragner, Frederic	3:02:14 (1,316)
Fragola, Anthony	4:20:57 (17,098)
Frain, Dennis	3:55:53 (10,869)
Frame, John	4:30:14 (19,658)
Frampton, Duncan	2:50:30 (509)
Frampton, Nigel	4:15:44 (15,764)
France, Peter	4:24:36 (18,149)
France, Richard	5:00:24 (26,359)
France, Steven	4:17:55 (16,349)
Francirek, Tomas	3:47:30 (8,510)
Francis, Andrew	5:11:11 (27,838)
Francis, David	3:57:57 (11,491)
Francis, David	4:58:08 (25,970)
Francis, Dominic	4:38:48 (21,792)
Francis, Emrys	2:57:33 (963)
Francis, Glyn	3:44:01 (7,661)
Francis, John	4:37:29 (21,445)
Francis, Kevin	3:32:23 (5,247)
Francis, Lee	3:57:07 (11,238)
Francis, Mark	3:36:38 (6,047)
Francis, Mark	4:20:25 (16,974)
Francis, Michael	3:56:28 (11,033)
Francis, Nick	2:22:26 (28)
Francis, Oliver	3:58:53 (11,757)
Francis, Peter	3:26:58 (4,325)
Francis, Raymond	2:52:18 (588)
Francis, Richard	3:12:55 (2,421)
Francis, Richard	3:27:09 (4,352)
Francis, Stephen	3:59:16 (11,873)
Francke, Mark	5:28:35 (29,663)
François, Eric	3:40:41 (6,892)
Frank, Jason	4:32:36 (20,243)
Frank, Joachim	4:14:34 (15,460)
Frankland, Anthony	5:44:34 (30,862)
Frankland, Paul	4:06:49 (13,632)
Franklin, Alan	4:54:40 (25,318)
Franklin, Clive	5:14:38 (28,266)
Franklin, Colin	4:17:43 (16,299)
Franklin, David	4:45:07 (23,339)
Franklin, Jeremy	4:00:04 (12,097)
Franklin, Kevin	3:45:57 (8,148)
Franklin, Simon	5:04:12 (26,917)
Franks, Glyn	5:32:43 (30,006)
Franks, Iain	3:57:19 (11,298)
Franks, Jason	4:15:07 (15,599)
Franks, Kieron	5:40:53 (30,605)
Franks, Martin	3:53:26 (10,116)
Franks, Simon	4:41:50 (22,565)
Frankum, Martin	4:26:23 (18,620)
Franz, Dean	4:31:25 (19,935)
Franzen, Christopher	4:08:12 (13,950)
Frary, Dale	5:17:32 (28,634)
Fraser, Andrew	4:15:39 (15,739)
Fraser, Derek	2:56:39 (885)
Fraser, Edward	3:45:21 (8,012)
Fraser, Ian	4:39:05 (21,869)
Fraser, James	5:08:39 (27,515)
Fraser, Kevin	3:03:30 (1,422)
Fraser, Mark	3:33:25 (5,419)
Fraser, Matthew	4:48:48 (24,197)
Fraser, Simon	3:29:58 (4,867)
Fratter, Carl	3:52:57 (9,960)
Frau, Bernardo	3:40:19 (6,817)
Frau, José	4:17:52 (16,341)
Frawley, Mike	3:39:32 (6,632)
Frazer, Michael	3:44:54 (7,906)
Freaney, Alan	4:23:28 (17,817)
Frearson, Paul	4:03:34 (12,895)
Fredericks, Schalf	4:49:31 (24,325)
Frediani, Edoardo	4:05:39 (13,358)
Fredrick Chapman, Colin	6:25:56 (32,200)
Freedman, Paul	4:53:20 (25,034)
Freeland, John	4:43:20 (22,918)
Freeland, Lee	3:21:51 (3,493)
Freeland, Lee	5:17:00 (28,557)
Freeman, Ben	4:19:10 (16,636)
Freeman, David	2:59:39 (1,142)
Freeman, Dennis	3:26:39 (4,262)
Freeman, Euan	4:23:42 (17,883)
Freeman, Gary	5:17:16 (28,596)
Freeman, Glenn	4:34:56 (20,814)

Freeman, Guy	4:15:37 (15,728)
Freeman, Julian	4:08:22 (13,982)
Freeman, Martin	3:59:39 (11,984)
Freeman, Michael	5:53:38 (31,299)
Freeman, Michael	5:58:28 (31,495)
Freeman, Paul	4:00:15 (12,143)
Freeman, Paul	4:04:18 (13,046)
Freeman, Peter	4:18:05 (16,385)
Freeman, Robert	4:58:44 (26,088)
Freeman, Robin	3:26:51 (4,301)
Freeman, Samuel	3:52:02 (9,700)
Freemantle, Mark	5:10:03 (27,694)
Freer, David	4:32:42 (20,277)
Freer, John	4:54:53 (25,360)
Freestone, Charles	6:01:08 (31,583)
Freestone, Martin	4:04:39 (13,123)
Freeth, Robin	3:45:10 (7,962)
Frei, Peter	3:26:12 (4,187)
Frei, Reto	3:08:42 (1,889)
Freir, John	3:40:10 (6,776)
Freire, Gualdino	3:58:08 (11,553)
Freman, Laurence	4:06:57 (13,662)
French, Alan	4:37:07 (21,339)
French, Chris	5:50:57 (31,185)
French, David	3:38:24 (6,400)
French, Jason	3:12:27 (2,353)
French, Jeffrey	3:52:29 (9,831)
French, Jeremy	3:38:18 (6,370)
French, Jonathan	4:47:49 (23,982)
French, Lester	4:40:50 (22,316)
French, Michael	3:17:49 (2,994)
French, Neal	3:24:18 (3,877)
French, Nicholas	5:02:03 (26,608)
French, Paul	5:51:39 (31,220)
French, Peter	3:50:01 (9,171)
French, Peter	5:16:17 (28,480)
French, Richard	2:56:25 (866)
French, Tim	3:43:11 (7,437)
French, Tim	4:12:28 (14,963)
Freshwater, Ross	4:37:07 (21,339)
Fresle, Kirk	4:03:21 (12,843)
Fresu, Giovanni	4:44:49 (23,252)
Fretigny, Patrick	5:11:08 (27,829)
Fretwell, Andrew	3:48:31 (8,751)
Fretwell, Jason	4:12:11 (14,897)
Frew, Colin	3:06:47 (1,710)
Frew, Stuart	3:46:53 (8,364)
Frewer, Jeremy	3:49:42 (9,099)
Frewer, Jeremy	4:06:01 (13,439)
Frewer, Martyn	3:58:21 (11,601)
Frey, Marcel	5:16:19 (28,488)
Frey-Davies, Christopher	4:20:38 (17,027)
Fricker, Coln	3:16:12 (2,807)
Fricker, Tom	3:21:52 (3,497)
Friday, Antony	3:23:50 (3,776)
Friday, Gary	3:37:51 (6,288)
Friedrichsen, Erk	4:17:13 (16,176)
Friel, Desmond	5:11:35 (27,892)
Friend, Bryan	3:09:37 (2,002)
Friend, Michael	4:55:37 (25,495)
Friend, Richard	5:03:24 (26,811)
Friery, Andy	4:34:32 (20,706)
Frigieri, Nicolas	4:31:45 (20,023)
Frimmel, Bernold	3:24:29 (3,915)
Frimmel, Erwin	3:34:46 (5,668)
Frimpong, Keith	4:01:30 (12,441)
Frimpong, Patrick	4:08:10 (13,943)
Frisby, David	6:05:36 (31,715)
Frisby, Stephen	6:05:36 (31,715)
Frisino, Antony	6:23:22 (32,157)
Frith, Alan	6:06:47 (31,750)
Frith, Ewan	4:00:45 (12,247)
Fritsch, Jens	4:05:04 (13,227)
Frodsham, Paul	2:58:57 (1,088)
Froggatt, Mark	4:24:51 (18,213)
Frohawk McLucas, Andy	4:14:21 (15,409)
Fromage, Stephen	4:55:54 (25,561)
Fromme, Jan	3:15:38 (2,742)
Frondella, Luigi	2:48:11 (411)
Frosch, Gerd	3:14:46 (2,635)
Frosdick, Roland	4:13:58 (15,301)
Frossard, Pierre	2:31:55 (74)
Frost, Andrew	4:17:58 (16,365)

Frost, Duncan 3:49:42 (9,099)
Frost, Gary 5:14:10 (28,210)
Frost, Graham 4:46:44 (23,742)
Frost, Kevin 6:27:13 (32,226)
Frost, Nicholas 2:47:45 (391)
Frost, Paul 4:06:07 (13,465)
Frost, Raymond 4:06:28 (13,558)
Frost, Richard 4:38:18 (21,655)
Frost, Robert 3:51:16 (9,493)
Frost, Thomas 3:30:04 (4,883)
Frost, Tony 3:30:51 (4,998)
Froud, Michael 4:09:38 (14,300)
Froude, Andrew 3:33:18 (5,401)
Froude, Philip 4:51:56 (24,772)
Frrow, Michael 3:57:43 (11,430)
Frutuoso, Jorge 4:06:03 (13,445)
Fry, Adrian 5:04:45 (26,987)
Fry, Christopher 3:39:37 (6,649)
Fry, Clifton 4:10:38 (14,541)
Fry, Malcolm 4:34:46 (20,766)
Fry, Peter 4:20:21 (16,955)
Fry, Simon 4:01:28 (12,430)
Fryer, Ivan 4:53:30 (25,068)
Fryer, Jack 3:16:00 (2,788)
Fryer, Laurence 4:05:19 (13,277)
Fryer, Michael 4:46:30 (23,692)
Fryer, Peter 5:15:30 (28,362)
Fuchs, René 4:05:53 (13,407)
Fudge, Keith 5:41:23 (30,645)
Fudge, Malcolm 4:41:44 (22,540)
Fuentes, Antonio 3:49:26 (9,021)
Fuesselberger, Johannes 2:50:30 (509)
Fugistier, Bernard 4:47:07 (23,834)
Fuhrer, Ernst 2:58:26 (1,043)
Fuhrmann, Andreas 3:44:54 (7,906)
Fujita, Toshiaki 4:31:16 (19,892)
Fukuzawa, Kiyoshi 5:35:23 (30,213)
Full, Philip 3:36:30 (6,026)
Fullbrook, Richard 3:39:11 (6,565)
Fullegar, Gary 3:39:59 (6,731)
Fuller, Adrian 3:11:27 (2,198)
Fuller, Andrew 4:59:56 (26,296)
Fuller, Chris 2:42:09 (228)
Fuller, Chris 4:00:03 (12,095)
Fuller, Gary 3:57:28 (11,350)
Fuller, John 3:12:02 (2,277)
Fuller, Jon 7:02:01 (32,647)
Fuller, Jonathon 3:48:10 (8,665)
Fuller, Keith 5:08:31 (27,498)
Fuller, Matthew 5:29:36 (29,748)
Fuller, Michael 3:58:47 (11,729)
Fuller, Robert 3:44:07 (7,683)
Fuller, Stephen 4:19:02 (16,602)
Fuller, Steve 4:00:32 (12,194)
Fullerton, Paul 4:41:19 (22,433)
Fullman, Kurt 5:40:13 (30,565)
Fulls, Neal 5:11:06 (27,824)
Fulong, Andrew 5:03:57 (26,882)
Fulton, James 4:37:14 (21,380)
Fulton, Matthew 5:02:56 (26,730)
Fulton, Michael 5:27:01 (29,523)
Fulton, Paul 4:28:08 (19,065)
Fulton, Roger 3:23:15 (3,687)
Fung, Lewis 3:56:54 (11,174)
Funk, Pascal 2:56:16 (856)
Funnell, Ian 4:31:52 (20,047)
Furber, Jeremy 4:48:27 (24,116)
Furhoff, Bjorn 3:05:52 (1,627)
Furlan, Oliviero 3:26:47 (4,290)
Furlonger, Ian 5:02:47 (26,708)
Furlonger, Kevin 3:54:00 (10,309)
Furneaux, Daniel 3:44:36 (7,820)
Furness, Brian 4:34:15 (20,641)
Furness, Tom 4:11:24 (14,710)
Furniss, Andrew 4:55:58 (25,577)
Furniss, Malcolm 3:43:51 (7,620)
Furniss, Michael 5:18:21 (28,709)
Furniss, Robert 4:29:24 (19,436)
Fursey, Karl 4:31:51 (20,040)
Fursey, Robert 3:00:02 (1,172)
Fursman, Mark 4:38:05 (21,596)
Furuichi, Sei 4:39:54 (22,080)
Fury, Mark 4:33:07 (20,383)
Furze, Jim 3:37:28 (6,203)
Fusco, Domenico 2:44:02 (273)
Futter, Nigel 3:47:19 (8,464)
Fyfe, Jonathan 4:42:01 (22,610)
Fyfe, Ralph 4:06:57 (13,662)
Fysh, Robert 4:36:14 (21,136)
Gabellone, Gaetano 5:03:49 (26,859)
Gabriel, Julian 4:10:10 (14,430)
Gabriel, Steven 3:44:19 (7,747)
Gabrielli, Silvano 4:41:39 (22,513)
Gabrielli, William 5:25:14 (29,382)
Gadal, Bruno 3:48:07 (8,656)
Gaddum, Giles 3:47:17 (8,454)
Gadgil, Devendra 5:57:31 (31,459)
Gadian, David 4:33:56 (20,564)
Gaetjens, Charles 4:23:41 (17,872)
Gaffney, James 4:15:45 (15,769)
Gage, Ricky 4:12:34 (14,984)
Gage, Trevor 3:01:07 (1,237)
Gageot, Pascal 3:10:12 (2,063)
Gahagan, Martin 4:37:32 (21,454)
Gaillard, Didier 4:09:15 (14,201)
Gaillard, Jean 3:23:43 (3,761)
Gaimster, Paul 4:10:17 (14,456)
Gaines, Mark 3:50:12 (9,215)
Gainsborough, Martin 2:37:04 (128)
Gair, Geoff 4:48:00 (24,029)
Gair, Jonathan 3:18:43 (3,101)
Gaisburgh-Watkyn, Graham 4:27:04 (18,810)
Gaiser, Kurt-Jorg 4:21:03 (17,127)
Gaitskell, Andrew 4:44:52 (23,263)
Gajbutowicz, Andrzej 4:53:54 (25,147)
Gajraj, Haroun 3:58:53 (11,757)
Galagher, Colin 3:12:05 (2,289)
Galan, Manuel 3:11:43 (2,229)
Gale, Andrew 4:39:50 (22,067)
Gale, Brian 5:21:57 (29,090)
Gale, Dean 3:39:25 (6,606)
Gale, Matthew 3:21:24 (3,420)
Gale, Philip 4:34:30 (20,700)
Galentino, Antonio 3:54:02 (10,320)
Gall, Allan 3:58:16 (11,584)
Gall, Nicholas 4:54:09 (25,215)
Gall, Robert 3:45:04 (7,946)
Gall, Stuart 4:56:55 (25,749)
Gallacher, Jim 5:01:04 (26,459)
Gallacher, Russell 3:58:15 (11,580)
Gallagher, Daniel 5:25:12 (29,378)
Gallagher, David 4:26:00 (18,518)
Gallagher, John 4:07:17 (13,743)
Gallagher, Kevin 4:48:28 (24,118)
Gallagher, Kieran 3:21:48 (3,483)
Gallagher, Mark 4:18:26 (16,473)
Gallagher, Matthew 3:32:13 (5,218)
Gallagher, Paul 4:08:00 (13,911)
Gallagher, Shaun 5:56:44 (31,433)
Gallagher, Spencer 4:58:33 (26,041)
Gallant, Peter 4:15:22 (15,657)
Gallazzi, Giulio 4:22:20 (17,493)
Galley, André 3:20:06 (3,266)
Gallimore, Dean 3:45:54 (8,134)
Gallivan, John 6:53:35 (32,577)
Gallo, Simon 4:41:22 (22,444)
Galloway, Ben 3:48:59 (8,891)
Galloway, Peter 3:21:32 (3,446)
Galloway, Richard 3:47:51 (8,600)
Galloway, Tom 4:45:19 (23,384)
Gallus, John 4:40:42 (22,277)
Galuschky, Christian 3:27:48 (4,480)
Galvany, Jef 3:16:42 (2,862)
Galvao Rogers, John 5:06:00 (27,155)
Galvez-Garcia, José 3:33:57 (5,509)
Galvin, Jeff 5:31:28 (29,913)
Galvin, Tim 4:46:26 (23,674)
Gamble, Keith 5:11:37 (27,895)
Gamble, Lee 4:17:00 (16,116)
Gamble, Paul 3:54:14 (10,379)
Gamble, Paul 4:26:37 (18,688)
Gamble, Tony 4:47:41 (23,949)
Gambrill, Michael 5:28:17 (29,635)
Game, Stephen 3:22:40 (3,602)
Game, Steven 2:39:11 (169)
Gammon, Carl 4:03:19 (12,838)
Gammon, Vincent 3:33:31 (5,429)
Gammons, Paul 5:09:49 (27,673)
Gamston, Paul 2:56:14 (851)
Gan, Andrew 3:15:20 (2,707)
Gan, Heng 4:58:12 (25,984)
Gan, Yona 4:32:43 (20,282)
Gander, Frank 3:39:49 (6,691)
Ganderton, Anthony 4:48:00 (24,029)
Ganderton, Ian 5:16:04 (28,451)
Gandon, Andrew 3:41:18 (7,030)
Gane, Jeremy 4:01:33 (12,457)
Ganguly, Stephen 3:16:10 (2,805)
Gannon, Andrew 3:35:27 (5,794)
Gannon, Daniel 4:26:07 (18,556)
Gannon, Martin 3:47:49 (8,591)
Gannon, Timothy 3:57:28 (11,350)
Gannon, Walter 3:55:07 (10,637)
Ganpatsingh, Roger 4:06:33 (13,577)
Gant, Nicholas 3:05:23 (1,578)
Garbet, Jamie 3:50:20 (9,258)
Garbett, Anthony 5:09:18 (27,605)
Garcha, Parvinder 5:37:28 (30,382)
Garcia, Dario 3:40:52 (6,933)
Garcia, Edson 5:07:19 (27,346)
Garcia De Quiros, José 2:46:26 (338)
Garcia-Atance, Salvador 5:37:16 (30,366)
Garcia-Guerrero, Mario 4:09:11 (14,183)
Garcia-Medina, Valentin 4:11:48 (14,817)
Garcia-Rubio, Gonzalo 4:08:45 (14,086)
Garcia-Woods, Julian 3:34:29 (5,616)
Garcis, David 2:38:48 (163)
Gardam, Matthew 5:34:18 (30,132)
Garderen, Jac 4:22:45 (17,621)
Gardetto, Roberto 5:04:26 (26,951)
Gardien, Peter 4:23:55 (17,953)
Gardiner, Frank 4:41:05 (22,371)
Gardiner, Gary 3:51:03 (9,442)
Gardiner, John 3:12:09 (2,303)
Gardiner, Kevin 3:57:44 (11,434)
Gardiner, Malcolm 5:39:24 (30,505)
Gardiner, Neill 4:55:27 (25,473)
Gardiner, Richard 2:23:18 (34)
Gardiner, Robert 4:32:25 (20,194)
Gardner, Andrew 3:53:10 (10,036)
Gardner, Douglas 4:17:36 (16,268)
Gardner, Leroy 4:16:12 (15,891)
Gardner, Mark 4:21:14 (17,174)
Gardner, Michael 4:36:06 (21,102)
Gardner, Nicholas 4:42:05 (22,629)
Gardner, Rupert 4:09:17 (14,209)
Gardner, Stephen 3:57:57 (11,491)
Gardner, William 2:50:34 (516)
Garessus, Gerard 3:46:34 (8,303)
Garland, Andy 5:55:57 (31,396)
Garland, Michael 3:26:35 (4,246)
Garland, Michael 4:06:18 (13,520)
Garland, Richard 4:50:06 (24,439)
Garlick, Jeff 4:32:18 (20,161)
Garlick, Nick 3:28:49 (4,665)
Garner, Andrew 3:35:28 (5,799)
Garner, Darren 4:38:35 (21,730)
Garner, Kristian 4:28:56 (19,297)
Garner, Martin 4:15:23 (15,662)
Garner, Michael 4:23:58 (17,965)
Garner, Neil 4:02:40 (12,695)
Garner, Paul 4:38:46 (21,787)
Garner, Peter 5:03:11 (26,778)
Garner, Richard 3:56:28 (11,033)
Garner, Simon 4:05:23 (13,293)
Garner, Stephen 3:00:34 (1,204)
Garner, Tony 4:00:44 (12,240)
Garner, William 2:48:54 (441)
Garnett, Andrew 4:23:49 (17,922)
Garnett, Simon 4:39:48 (22,058)
Garnish, Jeffrey 4:18:23 (16,460)
Garo, Roland 3:38:58 (6,515)
Garrard, Philip 3:52:34 (9,864)
Garratt, Christopher 3:14:54 (2,657)
Garratt, Mark 2:43:58 (269)
Garratt, Martin 5:41:13 (30,635)
Garrett, Anthony 3:13:46 (2,539)
Garrett, Anthony 3:35:14 (5,751)
Garrett, Charles 4:46:24 (23,664)

Garrett, Jeremy....4:12:28 (14,963)
Garrett, Martin....3:47:09 (8,423)
Garrett, Paul....4:41:52 (22,574)
Garrett, Phil....5:46:16 (30,953)
Garrity, Troy....2:38:02 (147)
Garro, Patrick....3:21:26 (3,425)
Garrod, Henry....5:17:00 (28,557)
Garrod, Mark....3:28:15 (4,560)
Garry, Michael....3:50:36 (9,322)
Garside, Christopher....4:57:24 (25,845)
Garside, James....3:53:46 (10,228)
Garside, Robert....3:40:45 (6,909)
Garstang, Malcolm....4:41:01 (22,358)
Garth, George....4:39:48 (22,058)
Garthwaite, Henry....4:48:31 (24,129)
Garvey, Dennis....5:46:17 (30,955)
Garvey, Robert....4:27:35 (18,933)
Garvey, Stephen....3:15:29 (2,723)
Garwood, Fergus....3:08:20 (1,843)
Gascoigne-Pees, Edward....4:14:58 (15,565)
Gashe, Erence....3:40:23 (6,831)
Gaskell, Chris....4:44:13 (23,110)
Gaskell, Giles....5:15:54 (28,430)
Gaskell, Philip....4:18:20 (16,452)
Gaskin, John....5:19:20 (28,808)
Gaskin, Teymour....4:42:23 (22,691)
Gasper, Matthew....5:15:33 (28,373)
Gass, Barry....5:39:44 (30,534)
Gassmann, Martin....4:30:38 (19,739)
Gaston, Reginald....5:25:37 (29,413)
Gatens, John....3:46:48 (8,343)
Gatepain, Ron....5:33:01 (30,023)
Gates, Andrew....4:12:51 (15,050)
Gates, Christopher....4:35:53 (21,047)
Gateshill, Daniel....5:48:38 (31,072)
Gatfield, Mark....3:54:27 (10,443)
Gatiss, Ian....5:12:15 (27,984)
Gatley, David....4:45:33 (23,454)
Gaudion, René....3:39:47 (6,682)
Gaudion, Richard....4:18:41 (16,522)
Gaudreau, Robert....3:54:22 (10,417)
Gaukroger, Stephen....5:36:46 (30,329)
Gaulder, Nicholas....3:42:15 (7,220)
Gault, Alan....4:52:11 (24,813)
Gault, Ian....4:01:00 (12,308)
Gaunt, Mike....3:51:26 (9,528)
Gaunt, Paul....5:21:39 (29,063)
Gaunt-Edwards, Stephen....4:46:35 (23,712)
Gauthier, Laurent....3:34:25 (5,602)
Gauthier, Nicolas....3:46:26 (8,263)
Gautrey, Jamie....4:34:01 (20,582)
Gautrey, Norman....3:06:25 (1,673)
Gavaghan, Kevin....4:43:58 (23,058)
Gavasso, Lucio....3:38:15 (6,357)
Gavelle, Daniel....3:02:43 (1,351)
Gavelle, Joseph....2:48:54 (441)
Gavigan, Stephen....3:55:25 (10,727)
Gavin, Matthew....4:30:38 (19,739)
Gavin, Oliver....3:27:49 (4,487)
Gavini, David....5:10:36 (27,764)
Gawley, Marc....3:04:29 (1,502)
Gay, Christopher....4:20:48 (17,069)
Gay, Gary....4:35:35 (20,982)
Gay, James....4:17:08 (16,154)
Gay, Richard....2:36:20 (112)
Gay, Richard....3:25:33 (4,072)
Gay, Richard....4:28:25 (19,142)
Gayleard, Matt....4:32:16 (20,152)
Gayner, Oliver....3:44:10 (7,698)
Gaynor, Denis....4:16:45 (16,052)
Gaze, Stevie....4:31:50 (20,037)
Gazizov, Anton....3:24:26 (3,906)
Geaney, John....4:11:58 (14,851)
Gearing, Daniel....3:47:33 (8,523)
Geary, Darin....4:59:00 (26,130)
Geary, Dave....4:51:27 (24,692)
Geary, Kevin....5:26:34 (29,499)
Gebauer, André....3:54:16 (10,392)
Gebrselassie, Haile....2:06:35 (3)
Geddes, Mike....4:20:10 (16,907)
Geden, Stephen....3:53:10 (10,036)
Gedin, Mats....2:38:21 (151)
Gee, Gary....4:14:50 (15,533)
Gee, Kevin....3:35:47 (5,862)
Gee, Raymond....3:43:41 (7,568)
Gee, Richard....5:30:33 (29,828)
Gee, Toby....3:34:40 (5,655)
Geen, Peter....4:39:01 (21,850)
Geeraert, Kris....3:48:48 (8,842)
Geeraert, Philip....3:30:57 (5,015)
Geffroy, Philippe....4:33:34 (20,477)
Geggie, Stuart....2:59:41 (1,148)
Gehrig, Michael....3:57:39 (11,411)
Gehrig, Urs....3:40:06 (6,762)
Geiger, Georg....4:23:50 (17,925)
Geikie-Cobb, Peter....4:58:36 (26,055)
Geldeart, Paul....3:38:10 (6,335)
Gellard, Barry....4:27:04 (18,810)
Geller, Laurence....4:03:07 (12,800)
Gelling, Alan....4:24:26 (18,100)
Gelson, William....3:55:52 (10,864)
Gemmill, Tristan....5:07:18 (27,345)
Genes, Christopher....3:32:24 (5,252)
Geneve, Christophe....3:11:02 (2,160)
Genge, Leigh....4:15:10 (15,609)
Gennari, Fabio....4:42:59 (22,834)
Gensane, Alain....4:51:32 (24,707)
Gent, Andrew....3:04:35 (1,510)
Gent, John....4:39:11 (21,892)
Gent, Richard....4:29:06 (19,348)
Gent, Robert....4:12:34 (14,984)
Gent, Tom....4:19:57 (16,848)
Gentilhomme, Damien....4:19:29 (16,720)
George, Ben....2:55:25 (774)
George, Bruce....4:22:08 (17,431)
George, David....3:12:15 (2,322)
George, Michael....3:53:32 (10,157)
George, Nicholas....4:52:40 (24,908)
George, Richard....3:13:12 (2,465)
George, Richard....4:12:14 (14,909)
George, Stephen....5:48:50 (31,083)
Georgeson, Paul....3:57:22 (11,307)
Georgiadis, Nicolas....3:28:04 (4,529)
Georgieff, Fabien....3:48:08 (8,658)
Georgiou, Luke....3:57:25 (11,333)
Geraghty, Robert....4:09:29 (14,266)
Geraghty, Roger....2:44:56 (296)
Gerard, Jacques....4:22:30 (17,545)
Gerber, Andrew....3:57:51 (11,464)
Gerber, Marius....4:33:13 (20,407)
Gerencser, Stephen....4:20:17 (16,937)
Gerges, Ahdy....3:57:58 (11,496)
Gerhardt, Peter....4:23:22 (17,791)
Gerkins, Dene....5:39:19 (30,489)
German, Mark....4:13:12 (15,121)
Germon, Paul....3:32:48 (5,316)
Gernert, Karl....5:54:37 (31,336)
Gerrelli, Martin....4:48:54 (24,216)
Gershon, Robert....4:49:27 (24,311)
Gershon, Steve....4:11:06 (14,659)
Gesiot, Michael....3:23:11 (3,676)
Gethin, David....5:15:15 (28,333)
Gething, Dominic....5:05:03 (27,029)
Gevaux, Martin....5:15:33 (28,373)
Gevrey, Claude....3:19:15 (3,166)
Ghani, Irfan....5:28:56 (29,689)
Ghanmouni, Rachid....2:15:27 (12)
Ghassemi, Fardjad....4:08:57 (14,121)
Ghazi-Tabatabai, Yousef....5:12:17 (27,995)
Gheuens, Eric....4:08:49 (14,094)
Ghosh, Mrinal....6:34:56 (32,351)
Ghosh, Sanjay....5:14:34 (28,255)
Giacche, Robert....4:38:08 (21,609)
Giacomazzi, Daniele....4:25:11 (18,305)
Gianesini, Luciano....6:00:15 (31,552)
Gianoli, Diego....3:39:07 (6,551)
Giarolo, Filippo....4:06:29 (13,562)
Gibb, Andrew....3:45:34 (8,065)
Gibb, William....4:33:22 (20,432)
Gibbard, Mark....4:22:37 (17,580)
Gibbon, Anthony....4:20:08 (16,896)
Gibbon, Dale....3:25:27 (4,056)
Gibbon, Ian....2:49:19 (458)
Gibbon, Mark....3:55:36 (10,783)
Gibbons, Andrew....4:20:49 (17,071)
Gibbons, Anthony....4:47:13 (23,859)
Gibbons, Carl....3:47:00 (8,381)
Gibbons, Jeremy....3:52:24 (9,812)
Gibbons, John....4:01:21 (12,407)
Gibbons, John....4:17:07 (16,148)
Gibbons, Nigel....4:09:55 (14,367)
Gibbons, Oliver....4:40:15 (22,170)
Gibbons, Philip....5:24:57 (29,365)
Gibbons, Thomas....4:25:29 (18,381)
Gibbs, Andrew....4:21:18 (17,191)
Gibbs, David....3:55:23 (10,719)
Gibbs, Glyn....3:38:25 (6,404)
Gibbs, Hugh....3:14:03 (2,561)
Gibbs, John....3:38:10 (6,335)
Gibbs, Jonathan....5:33:17 (30,052)
Gibbs, Scott....3:23:52 (3,789)
Gibbs, Sidney....5:01:22 (26,515)
Gibbs, Timothy....3:56:29 (11,044)
Gibbs-Seymour, Richard....4:55:11 (25,417)
Gibby, Robert....4:00:22 (12,160)
Giblin, Paul....3:23:28 (3,719)
Giboin, Xavier....3:22:09 (3,544)
Gibson, Andrew....4:45:04 (23,325)
Gibson, Barry....3:07:01 (1,737)
Gibson, Craig....3:52:57 (9,960)
Gibson, Craig....4:57:42 (25,898)
Gibson, David....4:42:04 (22,625)
Gibson, David....4:42:23 (22,691)
Gibson, David....6:39:41 (32,434)
Gibson, Davis....6:06:52 (31,755)
Gibson, Dean....3:41:36 (7,082)
Gibson, Eric....4:48:38 (24,152)
Gibson, John....3:51:31 (9,550)
Gibson, John....6:24:17 (32,170)
Gibson, Mark....4:22:24 (17,522)
Gibson, Martin....6:34:14 (32,342)
Gibson, Paul....4:33:29 (20,459)
Gibson, Peter....3:25:23 (4,043)
Gibson, Phililp....5:18:43 (28,746)
Gibson, Stephen....4:12:39 (15,012)
Gibson, Will....4:14:37 (15,473)
Gicquel, Pascal....3:05:33 (1,596)
Giemza-Pipe, Jonathon....5:04:35 (26,963)
Giertsen, Bjoern....4:08:34 (14,045)
Gifford, Alan....5:10:21 (27,731)
Gifford, Bryson....4:42:43 (22,773)
Gifford, Roger....3:42:48 (7,342)
Gigerl, Thomas....4:33:14 (20,412)
Gil, John....3:51:32 (9,555)
Gilabert-Monllor, Bravlio....3:15:25 (2,716)
Gilardi, Paolo....4:19:00 (16,589)
Gilbert, Aaron....4:17:01 (16,121)
Gilbert, Brian....5:27:22 (29,565)
Gilbert, Carl....4:33:03 (20,368)
Gilbert, David....4:15:46 (15,774)
Gilbert, Jonathan....3:34:17 (5,578)
Gilbert, Laurent....3:47:15 (8,449)
Gilbert, Mark....4:29:09 (19,367)
Gilbert, Nicholas....4:15:24 (15,665)
Gilbert, Pascal....4:52:55 (24,963)
Gilbert, Richard....3:11:32 (2,207)
Gilbert, Stephen....6:09:10 (31,817)
Gilbey, Kenneth....3:54:34 (10,478)
Gilbey, Pete....3:38:22 (6,389)
Gilbey, Peter....3:03:16 (1,401)
Gilby, Keith....6:21:02 (32,105)
Gilchrist, Tyrone....4:49:11 (24,273)
Gilderdale, Philip....5:48:09 (31,043)
Giles, David....3:58:37 (11,684)
Giles, Ian....3:53:01 (9,985)
Giles, Mark....4:12:38 (15,005)
Giles, Martin....2:37:55 (142)
Giles, Peter....5:19:36 (28,829)
Giles, Timothy....3:58:00 (11,508)
Gilham, Ian....4:59:02 (26,137)
Gilkes, Phil....2:56:17 (857)
Gill, Alan....3:59:11 (11,849)
Gill, Alan....4:35:26 (20,932)
Gill, Amarjit....5:12:14 (27,979)
Gill, Brendan....4:47:26 (23,904)
Gill, Colin....3:43:17 (7,467)
Gill, Colin....4:37:51 (21,532)
Gill, James....3:23:49 (3,772)
Gill, Jonathan....4:08:31 (14,027)

Gill, Keith	3:10:13 (2,066)	Gleeson, Ian	4:35:07 (20,857)	Goldstone, Barry	4:22:13 (17,449)
Gill, Ken	5:21:43 (29,070)	Gleeson, Timothy	4:04:30 (13,088)	Goldstone, Robert	4:47:10 (23,849)
Gill, Mathew	4:24:27 (18,106)	Gleiwitz, Roy	5:42:30 (30,726)	Goldwenko, Alexander	3:57:34 (11,386)
Gill, Mike	3:50:27 (9,290)	Glen, Andrew	3:22:41 (3,606)	Golesworthy, Keith	5:29:21 (29,726)
Gill, Paul	4:04:22 (13,062)	Glencross, Philip	4:25:44 (18,448)	Golfetto, Dan	4:11:14 (14,680)
Gill, Paul	5:42:55 (30,752)	Glendinning, Kevin	3:29:27 (4,784)	Golightly, Michael	3:01:17 (1,248)
Gill, Peter	3:57:21 (11,305)	Glenister, Stuart	4:30:09 (19,641)	Golla, Steve	3:32:49 (5,320)
Gill, Robert	3:06:47 (1,710)	Glenn, Clive	4:21:28 (17,238)	Golland, Clive	3:42:14 (7,214)
Gill, Robert	4:50:03 (24,435)	Glew, Mark	4:47:14 (23,862)	Gollins, Simon	4:28:35 (19,187)
Gill, Roy	4:41:07 (22,381)	Glew, Roy	4:47:15 (23,869)	Gomes, Joao	3:24:50 (3,961)
Gill, Sean	4:36:09 (21,121)	Gley, Gerrit	3:48:22 (8,714)	Gomez, Antonio	4:14:08 (15,342)
Gillam, Michael	5:11:09 (27,835)	Gliddon, Paul	4:12:18 (14,920)	Gomez, Rodolfo	3:46:32 (8,294)
Gillam, Stephen	4:06:09 (13,478)	Glockshuber, Rudolf	3:16:46 (2,873)	Gomez, Rodolfo	4:16:33 (15,991)
Gillard, Ian	4:54:23 (25,263)	Glover, Adrian	4:50:48 (24,564)	Gomoluch, Tadeusz	3:44:16 (7,731)
Gillard, Kevin	4:54:22 (25,257)	Glover, Brian	4:12:34 (14,984)	Gonde, Chris	3:39:10 (6,559)
Gillard, Nigel	5:11:41 (27,904)	Glover, Brian	4:15:25 (15,671)	Gonzalez, José	4:42:15 (22,659)
Gillard, Richard	4:04:09 (13,017)	Glover, Carl	4:44:48 (23,249)	Gonzalez Urrutia, José	2:51:37 (566)
Gillard, Terence	3:42:28 (7,282)	Glover, Michael	4:17:36 (16,268)	Gonzalez-Llanos, Carlos	3:37:16 (6,158)
Gillemon, Franz	4:43:59 (23,062)	Glover, Stuart	4:30:22 (19,687)	Gooch, Leonard	4:03:55 (12,968)
Gillen, Patrick	4:13:40 (15,222)	Glover, Toby	3:56:04 (10,918)	Good, Eric	4:14:10 (15,349)
Gillen, Timothy	3:18:19 (3,048)	Gluckman, Robert	3:37:42 (6,260)	Good, Peter	5:19:27 (28,815)
Gillespie, Alex	4:57:37 (25,881)	Gluyas, Jon	4:58:09 (25,973)	Goodacre, Darren	4:15:41 (15,750)
Gillespie, Jamie	5:49:35 (31,127)	Glyn-Owen, Julian	4:01:27 (12,425)	Goodacre, David	5:40:57 (30,611)
Gillespie, John	3:24:18 (3,877)	Goad, James	3:46:29 (8,272)	Goodair, Andrew	2:57:22 (944)
Gillespie, Michael	3:04:04 (1,471)	Goadsby, Bill	4:59:17 (26,172)	Goodall, David	4:18:09 (16,403)
Gillett, Edward	3:33:33 (5,436)	Goater, Nicholas	4:44:15 (23,115)	Goodall, Gareth	5:10:24 (27,736)
Gillett, Kevin	3:34:39 (5,649)	Gobetti, Bruno	5:14:37 (28,264)	Goodall, Graeme	3:23:49 (3,772)
Gillett, Philip	4:04:29 (13,085)	Goble, Richard	4:53:41 (25,102)	Goodall, Graham	3:54:10 (10,366)
Gillett, Simon	3:59:15 (11,868)	Godard, Jean	3:48:51 (8,853)	Goodall, John	7:12:26 (32,719)
Gillford, Paddy	5:38:51 (30,469)	Godbee, James	4:33:53 (20,555)	Goodall, Malcolm	5:29:31 (29,738)
Gillham, Greg	4:35:12 (20,881)	Godbee, Peter	3:53:09 (10,030)	Gooday, Stephen	4:12:27 (14,960)
Gillian, David	4:09:24 (14,254)	Goddard, Barry	3:55:48 (10,840)	Goodchild, Colum	3:52:12 (9,754)
Gilliard, Nicolas	3:53:38 (10,190)	Goddard, Brian	4:55:16 (25,432)	Goodchild, Edward	4:46:10 (23,613)
Gillibrand, Simon	4:37:47 (21,517)	Goddard, Christopher	3:39:31 (6,629)	Gooddie, Chris	3:43:46 (7,591)
Gillick, Matthew	3:47:41 (8,558)	Goddard, George	4:03:47 (12,936)	Gooddy, John	4:21:31 (17,255)
Gillies, Clint	6:15:51 (31,976)	Goddard, James	4:40:21 (22,199)	Goode, Barry	3:57:19 (11,298)
Gilliland, Crawford	5:58:01 (31,475)	Goddard, Peter	6:06:25 (31,742)	Goode, Jonny	4:10:02 (14,393)
Gilliland, David	4:18:11 (16,411)	Goddard, Steve	3:56:21 (11,003)	Goode, Scott	3:44:15 (7,722)
Gillings, Garry	4:18:35 (16,506)	Goddard, Trevor	3:03:37 (1,433)	Goode, Timothy	3:41:14 (7,023)
Gillings, Stephen	5:59:26 (31,529)	Godden, Oliver	4:19:40 (16,765)	Goodenough, Paul	3:56:31 (11,059)
Gillingwater, Paul	3:43:36 (7,550)	Godding, Neil	4:51:15 (24,660)	Goodfellow, Stephen	5:01:50 (26,572)
Gilliott, Adam	4:25:42 (18,439)	Godfrey, Christopher	4:12:38 (15,005)	Goodfield, Paul	4:03:44 (12,926)
Gillison, Matthew	4:57:32 (25,868)	Godfrey, Darren	4:10:32 (14,518)	Goodhart, William	3:49:30 (9,041)
Gillman, Clive	3:27:45 (4,467)	Godfrey, David	6:10:53 (31,855)	Gooding, John	4:15:51 (15,791)
Gillott, Martin	4:39:15 (21,910)	Godfrey, Keith	5:14:33 (28,253)	Goodlad, Chris	3:34:03 (5,531)
Gillson, James	5:29:31 (29,738)	Godfrey, Liam	5:18:56 (28,769)	Goodlad, Robin	4:50:57 (24,600)
Gillson, Stephen	3:09:03 (1,937)	Godfrey, Malcolm	3:12:47 (2,396)	Goodluck, Jerome	5:06:31 (27,233)
Gilmartin, Noel	4:27:38 (18,947)	Godfrey, Nicholas	5:21:29 (29,042)	Goodman, Kevin	4:40:13 (22,162)
Gilmour, James	4:45:02 (23,319)	Godfrey, Richard	3:59:02 (11,819)	Goodman, Mark	4:16:41 (16,035)
Gilmour, Rory	3:56:50 (11,149)	Godfrey, Russell	5:49:54 (31,139)	Goodman, Mark	4:29:36 (19,482)
Gilpin, James	2:48:07 (408)	Godier, Neil	4:26:37 (18,688)	Goodricke, Paul	4:54:27 (25,275)
Gilroy, Robson	5:00:05 (26,320)	Godinho, Jacinto	4:32:03 (20,101)	Goodridge, Mark	2:31:40 (73)
Gimenez, Sebastien	3:20:36 (3,325)	Godman, Michael	3:32:31 (5,272)	Goodridge, Michael	4:58:32 (26,038)
Gimson, Ashley	2:57:11 (928)	Godsmark, Philip	4:08:17 (13,969)	Goodson, Ben	5:18:32 (28,731)
Gingell, Kevin	4:34:45 (20,764)	Goff, Daniel	3:24:57 (3,982)	Goodwill, Robin	4:11:53 (14,831)
Ginns, Jonathan	3:49:06 (8,924)	Goggin, Stephen	4:20:10 (16,907)	Goodwill, Tony	4:36:08 (21,115)
Ginocchio, Paul	4:28:45 (19,244)	Gohar, Marcus	2:47:21 (374)	Goodwin, Andrew	5:55:32 (31,379)
Giorgetti, Jean	3:44:30 (7,793)	Golby, Robert	5:07:34 (27,383)	Goodwin, Colin	4:06:30 (13,568)
Giorgini, Patrizio	4:07:22 (13,767)	Gold, Adam	4:41:26 (22,455)	Goodwin, David	4:27:11 (18,839)
Giovannoni, Gavin	3:13:27 (2,498)	Gold, David	4:14:13 (15,368)	Goodwin, David	5:22:33 (29,138)
Girard, Laurent	3:51:19 (9,506)	Gold, Jonathan	5:05:02 (27,027)	Goodwin, Dominic	3:25:58 (4,149)
Giraud, Anson	3:32:37 (5,294)	Gold, Lawrence	3:42:32 (7,296)	Goodwin, Edward	4:40:50 (22,316)
Girdler, Ian	4:15:58 (15,831)	Gold, Mark	3:22:59 (3,655)	Goodwin, Kevin	4:19:37 (16,754)
Gire, Georges	4:45:17 (23,379)	Goldberg, Arthur	4:22:33 (17,560)	Goodwin, Mark	4:04:36 (13,115)
Girling, Simon	3:42:26 (7,269)	Golder, Terence	4:23:44 (17,899)	Goodwin, Michael	5:33:40 (30,083)
Gisby, Alan	4:20:24 (16,964)	Goldfarb, Simon	4:31:54 (20,057)	Goodwin, Nick	4:54:03 (25,192)
Gjini, James	3:24:27 (3,910)	Goldie, Jack	4:18:47 (16,541)	Goodwin, Peter	4:31:07 (19,860)
Gladman, Alan	3:45:43 (8,094)	Golding, Andrew	4:48:19 (24,089)	Goodwin, Philip	4:21:50 (17,349)
Gladman, Andrew	5:09:05 (27,581)	Golding, Frank	5:57:49 (31,471)	Goodwin, Robert	3:04:51 (1,528)
Gladwell, Aran	5:38:34 (30,454)	Golding, Graham	4:30:25 (19,697)	Googe, Michael	4:57:13 (25,813)
Gladwell, Chris	5:06:54 (27,281)	Golding, Nick	5:10:30 (27,750)	Goold, Andrew	4:07:18 (13,748)
Gladwin, David	4:15:47 (15,778)	Golding, Peter	2:58:37 (1,058)	Goold, John	4:22:45 (17,621)
Glaister, Thomas	4:26:57 (18,775)	Golding, Shaun	4:10:20 (14,468)	Goosen, Jacobus	4:44:11 (23,104)
Glass, Colin	4:21:29 (17,248)	Goldman, Andrew	4:45:47 (23,512)	Goossens, Johan	3:22:45 (3,625)
Glasson, Richard	3:51:44 (9,603)	Goldmsith, Jerry	3:45:18 (7,999)	Gordon, Bob	3:56:50 (11,149)
Glasspell, Michael	5:11:51 (27,930)	Golds, Andrew	5:55:40 (31,387)	Gordon, Darren	3:23:13 (3,680)
Glazebrook, Martin	6:01:34 (31,597)	Golds, Richard	4:14:26 (15,433)	Gordon, David	4:16:55 (16,095)
Glazier, David	4:01:28 (12,430)	Goldsack, Leon	4:52:43 (24,918)	Gordon, Frank	3:25:22 (4,039)
Gleadell, Roger	5:30:44 (29,843)	Goldsmith, Christopher	4:11:20 (14,699)	Gordon, Garron	3:41:04 (6,980)
Gleave, Graham	4:16:21 (15,930)	Goldsmith, Paul	3:18:39 (3,092)	Gordon, Glenn	3:57:09 (11,246)
Gledhill, Tim	4:12:55 (15,066)	Goldsmith, Paul	4:47:29 (23,910)	Gordon, Jeffrey	4:09:55 (14,367)
Gleeson, Daniel	3:59:41 (11,989)	Goldsmith, Stuart	3:42:13 (7,204)	Gordon, Marc	4:03:51 (12,954)
Gleeson, Declan	3:56:27 (11,030)	Goldspink, David	2:59:24 (1,121)	Gordon, Matthew	3:49:36 (9,069)

Gordon, Neil	4:15:38 (15,733)	
Gordon, Peter	3:15:19 (2,704)	
Gordon, Phil	5:23:55 (29,275)	
Gordon, Richard	5:20:46 (28,971)	
Gordon, Robert	4:22:58 (17,696)	
Gordon, Robert	5:04:10 (26,912)	
Gordon, Steven	3:53:00 (9,976)	
Gordon Lennox, Anthony	5:12:23 (28,010)	
Gore, Michael	3:36:02 (5,911)	
Gorman, Gregg	4:44:16 (23,123)	
Gorman, Mark	2:47:33 (381)	
Gorman, Michael	4:32:07 (20,114)	
Gorman, Thomas	4:42:23 (22,691)	
Gormley, David	3:56:02 (10,906)	
Gorostiaga-Urrutia, Asier	3:13:54 (2,550)	
Gorostiaga-Urrutia, Iker	3:01:15 (1,245)	
Gorrie, Thomas	4:41:09 (22,389)	
Gorrod, Mark	4:46:41 (23,734)	
Gorrod, Nicholas	2:46:09 (328)	
Gorton, Daniel	4:12:05 (14,878)	
Gosling, Christopher	4:42:06 (22,634)	
Gosling, Darren	4:51:10 (24,643)	
Gosling, Geoff	4:26:38 (18,696)	
Gosling, Michael	4:26:38 (18,696)	
Goslyn, David	4:39:01 (21,850)	
Goss, Jonathan	3:12:02 (2,277)	
Goss, Jonathan	4:06:59 (13,674)	
Goswell, Philip	4:00:12 (12,132)	
Gotkine, Elliott	4:25:16 (18,325)	
Gott, Clive	3:33:34 (5,440)	
Gottlieb, Craig	5:37:53 (30,406)	
Gotts, Jason	3:52:45 (9,909)	
Gotts, Nigel	2:47:33 (381)	
Goubet, Didier	3:36:08 (5,942)	
Goucher, David	5:06:16 (27,195)	
Goudenege, Didier	4:03:45 (12,928)	
Gough, Adrian	3:10:28 (2,095)	
Gough, Andrew	5:31:23 (29,904)	
Gough, Brian	5:24:34 (29,332)	
Gough, Des	3:56:36 (11,086)	
Gough, Ginge	2:36:51 (124)	
Gough, James	5:21:09 (29,014)	
Goulborn, Keith	4:26:44 (18,726)	
Goulbourn, Mark	3:49:24 (9,005)	
Gould, Andrew	4:33:51 (20,548)	
Gould, Antony	3:00:30 (1,202)	
Gould, Bruce	9:01:28 (32,891)	
Gould, Daniel	4:10:58 (14,625)	
Gould, Elliot	5:27:09 (29,535)	
Gould, Martin	3:08:25 (1,852)	
Gould, Neil	4:33:33 (20,472)	
Gould, Norman	9:01:28 (32,891)	
Gould, Paul	4:18:18 (16,439)	
Gould, Philip	4:10:09 (14,428)	
Gould, Robert	6:01:57 (31,604)	
Gould, Stephen	5:19:39 (28,831)	
Gould, Thomas	3:55:32 (10,758)	
Gould, William	4:26:15 (18,588)	
Goulder, Christopher	4:27:17 (18,858)	
Goulder, Stephen	3:11:03 (2,162)	
Gouldin, Michael	4:42:02 (22,617)	
Goulding, Andrew	5:35:29 (30,226)	
Goulding, Mark	3:26:06 (4,165)	
Goulet, Michel	3:29:19 (4,757)	
Gouret, Jean	3:45:50 (8,127)	
Gournay, Kevin	4:20:41 (17,044)	
Gouveia, Alex	3:56:37 (11,090)	
Gouveia, José	5:23:38 (29,240)	
Gouwy, Diego	4:04:14 (13,037)	
Govindan, Vikram	4:07:16 (13,737)	
Gow, Elliot	4:16:23 (15,945)	
Gowans, Peter	4:16:04 (15,855)	
Gowda, Thimme	5:38:50 (30,467)	
Gowdy, Harry	4:08:16 (13,966)	
Gower, Simon	4:03:21 (12,843)	
Gowers, Ian	3:58:31 (11,654)	
Gowing, Michael	3:42:14 (7,214)	
Goyvaerts, Erik	4:15:39 (15,739)	
Graaf, Klaus	5:20:00 (28,879)	
Grabham, Mark	4:28:09 (19,071)	
Grabowski, Simon	3:59:19 (11,887)	
Grace, David	4:40:03 (22,120)	
Grace, Kevin	5:15:26 (28,353)	
Grace, Matthew	4:15:00 (15,576)	
Gracey, John	3:44:15 (7,722)	
Grady, John	3:54:32 (10,467)	
Grady, Oswin	4:14:20 (15,405)	
Graf, Gabinus	4:36:27 (21,200)	
Grafton, Graham	4:17:36 (16,268)	
Graham, Alan	5:19:58 (28,872)	
Graham, Alistair	3:12:35 (2,371)	
Graham, Aubyn	5:45:00 (30,883)	
Graham, Brian	6:59:38 (32,624)	
Graham, Geoff	4:50:47 (24,556)	
Graham, Hugh	4:18:47 (16,541)	
Graham, Ian	3:07:57 (1,803)	
Graham, Ian	4:04:10 (13,019)	
Graham, James	4:21:34 (17,270)	
Graham, Peter	4:15:12 (15,621)	
Graham, Peter	5:23:53 (29,270)	
Graham, Raymond	2:57:10 (926)	
Graham, Scott	3:39:21 (6,596)	
Graham, Stewart	4:46:55 (23,796)	
Graham, Stuart	3:49:09 (8,934)	
Graham, Thomas	4:10:05 (14,408)	
Graham, Warren	3:58:59 (11,796)	
Grahamme, Andrew	4:44:57 (23,287)	
Grail, Chris	4:48:51 (24,206)	
Grainge, Duncan	4:45:33 (23,454)	
Grainge, Matthew	3:06:12 (1,658)	
Grainger, Jason	3:48:34 (8,766)	
Grainger, John	5:59:17 (31,525)	
Grainger, Steve	3:44:36 (7,820)	
Grammaticas, Dominic	4:10:34 (14,527)	
Granday, Nicolas	4:24:48 (18,198)	
Grandjean, Luc	4:31:29 (19,962)	
Granelli, André	3:45:33 (8,062)	
Graney, Barry	3:12:42 (2,387)	
Grange, Ian	3:58:35 (11,671)	
Grange, Stuart	5:22:35 (29,140)	
Granger, Del	4:10:38 (14,541)	
Granier, Florent	4:49:11 (24,273)	
Granier, Guillaume	3:38:12 (6,344)	
Granier, Jean	4:13:43 (15,242)	
Grant, Alexander	4:42:48 (22,791)	
Grant, Andrew	3:36:34 (6,034)	
Grant, Andrew	3:49:50 (9,137)	
Grant, Andrew	4:21:28 (17,238)	
Grant, Andrew	5:04:47 (26,997)	
Grant, David	4:29:07 (19,354)	
Grant, Keith	5:19:10 (28,790)	
Grant, Kenneth	5:13:48 (28,169)	
Grant, Matthew	3:26:05 (4,161)	
Grant, Neil	4:47:02 (23,823)	
Grant, Peter	4:45:21 (23,393)	
Grant, Richard	4:31:26 (19,940)	
Grant, Sean	4:41:45 (22,543)	
Grant, Simon	4:44:58 (23,290)	
Grant, Stuart	4:03:04 (12,793)	
Grantham, Peter	3:22:48 (3,636)	
Granzow, John	3:28:14 (4,558)	
Grassby, Dean	3:52:16 (9,771)	
Grassick, Richard	4:26:59 (18,782)	
Gratton, Jonathan	3:51:04 (9,447)	
Grauballe, Morten	3:28:45 (4,646)	
Gravatt, Christopher	4:16:29 (15,976)	
Gravel, Andrew	3:53:28 (10,135)	
Graveling, Martin	4:46:46 (23,750)	
Graven, Michael	3:37:18 (6,163)	
Graves, Dan	3:56:36 (11,086)	
Graves, Dean	3:44:44 (7,867)	
Graves, Mark	4:45:35 (23,467)	
Graves, Markus	4:18:55 (16,571)	
Graves, Paul	3:05:42 (1,607)	
Gravestock, Mic	4:01:23 (12,415)	
Gravett, Tom	4:47:17 (23,874)	
Gravis, Craig	4:24:19 (18,073)	
Gray, Adam	4:17:51 (16,337)	
Gray, Anthony	3:03:49 (1,451)	
Gray, Barnaby	3:32:49 (5,320)	
Gray, Brian	4:51:46 (24,736)	
Gray, Christopher	4:57:17 (25,824)	
Gray, Colin	3:04:04 (1,471)	
Gray, Craig	3:43:00 (7,390)	
Gray, Davd	4:15:44 (15,764)	
Gray, David	3:18:02 (3,013)	
Gray, David	3:42:41 (7,313)	
Gray, Denis	4:02:49 (12,733)	
Gray, Garry	4:16:18 (15,913)	
Gray, George	4:56:12 (25,636)	
Gray, Ian	3:27:20 (4,383)	
Gray, James	4:14:31 (15,449)	
Gray, John	3:43:17 (7,467)	
Gray, John	4:14:22 (15,417)	
Gray, John	4:24:35 (18,143)	
Gray, Kevin	5:31:43 (29,928)	
Gray, Lloyd	4:12:50 (15,045)	
Gray, Malcolm	5:52:57 (31,273)	
Gray, Michael	3:37:27 (6,195)	
Gray, Michael	6:02:12 (31,615)	
Gray, Mitchell	5:11:24 (27,874)	
Gray, Neil	4:42:06 (22,634)	
Gray, Nigel	3:21:08 (3,391)	
Gray, Nigel	4:21:22 (17,210)	
Gray, Nigel	4:52:16 (24,836)	
Gray, Paul	4:09:40 (14,309)	
Gray, Philip	4:09:36 (14,293)	
Gray, Rob	4:42:55 (22,818)	
Gray, Robert	4:25:12 (18,309)	
Gray, Robert	4:38:02 (21,578)	
Gray, Stephen	3:50:01 (9,171)	
Gray, Stephen	4:17:03 (16,133)	
Gray, Steven	4:31:24 (19,929)	
Gray, Steven	4:48:45 (24,178)	
Grayling, Kenneth	4:58:21 (26,005)	
Grayshon, Paul	4:25:46 (18,454)	
Grayson, James	4:28:38 (19,208)	
Grayson, Robert	4:56:31 (25,692)	
Grayston, Alan	4:16:46 (16,056)	
Graystone, Peter	7:15:47 (32,740)	
Greagsby, David	4:23:16 (17,768)	
Grealy, Michael	3:44:23 (7,769)	
Greasby, Peter	4:15:56 (15,824)	
Greaves, Jon	3:34:16 (5,572)	
Greaves, Jonathan	5:25:31 (29,402)	
Greaves, Martyn	3:54:21 (10,415)	
Greco, Carlo	4:28:12 (19,081)	
Grecu, Serban	4:40:08 (22,143)	
Gredler, Markus	3:50:24 (9,276)	
Greedy, Philip	3:44:42 (7,852)	
Greeff, Johan	3:39:26 (6,610)	
Green, Alan	3:18:52 (3,119)	
Green, Andrew	2:56:31 (873)	
Green, Andy	4:56:59 (25,763)	
Green, Ashley	4:40:42 (22,277)	
Green, Barry	4:54:06 (25,200)	
Green, Charles	2:59:59 (1,167)	
Green, Chris	6:06:20 (31,969)	
Green, Christopher	4:24:38 (18,154)	
Green, Damian	3:28:31 (4,606)	
Green, Daniel	3:57:38 (11,406)	
Green, Darren	3:15:36 (2,735)	
Green, David	3:09:59 (2,039)	
Green, David	3:56:30 (11,053)	
Green, David	4:11:29 (14,741)	
Green, David	5:47:33 (31,021)	
Green, David	7:15:45 (32,739)	
Green, Francis	4:32:51 (20,320)	
Green, Gary	4:27:59 (19,029)	
Green, Gary	5:40:05 (30,552)	
Green, Ivan	5:03:34 (26,831)	
Green, James	4:44:58 (23,290)	
Green, John	3:08:39 (1,885)	
Green, John	3:35:43 (5,851)	
Green, John	4:18:21 (16,455)	
Green, Jonathan	4:45:24 (23,413)	
Green, Julian	5:01:56 (26,594)	
Green, Laurence	3:15:32 (2,726)	
Green, Leo	3:44:57 (7,919)	
Green, Mark	7:31:31 (32,794)	
Green, Martyn	6:58:28 (32,611)	
Green, Matthew	4:13:07 (15,106)	
Green, Michael	3:19:17 (3,169)	
Green, Michael	3:32:37 (5,294)	
Green, Michael	3:45:31 (8,048)	
Green, Mick	3:05:43 (1,610)	
Green, Nathan	3:58:04 (11,531)	
Green, Nicholas	3:53:23 (10,103)	
Green, Nicholas	3:58:06 (11,544)	

Green, Oliver	3:30:22	(4,924)
Green, Patrick	3:23:33	(3,735)
Green, Paul	4:04:04	(13,001)
Green, Paul	4:43:53	(23,036)
Green, Paul	5:02:49	(26,713)
Green, Paul	5:58:13	(31,484)
Green, Peter	3:55:41	(10,803)
Green, Peter	4:26:59	(18,782)
Green, Peter	4:34:20	(20,654)
Green, Philip	5:11:54	(27,938)
Green, Richard	3:27:33	(4,423)
Green, Richard	4:14:08	(15,342)
Green, Richard	4:26:20	(18,606)
Green, Richard	7:30:04	(32,789)
Green, Robert	3:40:58	(6,958)
Green, Robert	4:17:19	(16,209)
Green, Robert	5:54:33	(31,333)
Green, Sam	4:28:40	(19,213)
Green, Scott	4:07:46	(13,861)
Green, Simon	3:17:48	(2,992)
Green, Stephen	4:28:50	(19,269)
Green, Stephen	4:43:01	(22,843)
Green, Steve	4:56:11	(25,628)
Green, Stuart	3:43:34	(7,543)
Green, Thomas	3:59:52	(12,046)
Green, Tony	4:19:44	(16,785)
Greenan, Alastair	4:36:49	(21,280)
Greenaway, Christopher	5:08:40	(27,517)
Greenaway, Martyn	4:52:44	(24,920)
Greenaway, Richard	4:59:04	(26,143)
Greenaway, Stephen	3:28:43	(4,641)
Greene, Brendan	2:55:43	(801)
Greene, Bruce	5:38:18	(30,433)
Greene, Graham	4:07:42	(13,842)
Greene, Harvey	5:33:53	(30,097)
Greene, Kevin	4:45:07	(23,339)
Greene, Mike	4:04:38	(13,118)
Greenhalgh, Andrew	4:53:54	(25,147)
Greenhalgh, Andy	4:41:13	(22,403)
Greenhalgh, Ian	3:08:14	(1,828)
Greenhalgh, Mark	4:41:14	(22,408)
Greenhalgh, Myles	5:03:22	(26,807)
Greenhalgh, Peter	4:15:04	(15,590)
Greenham, David	4:27:47	(18,978)
Greenham, Peter	4:47:49	(23,982)
Greenhill, Julian	4:12:24	(14,943)
Greenhough, Craig	3:23:52	(3,789)
Greenin, Daniel	5:15:53	(28,426)
Greenland, Edward	3:40:41	(6,892)
Greenleaf, Daniel	3:40:06	(6,762)
Greenlees, Scott	3:52:16	(9,771)
Greenrod, James	3:34:33	(5,626)
Greenshields, Richard	4:40:57	(22,345)
Greensitt-Black, Steven	4:10:39	(14,545)
Greenslade, Heath	4:35:10	(20,866)
Greenway, Patrick	5:40:37	(30,591)
Greenwell, Charles	4:04:59	(13,204)
Greenwood, Andrew	5:29:25	(29,731)
Greenwood, Charles	4:12:19	(14,925)
Greenwood, Charlie	4:29:31	(19,460)
Greenwood, David	3:44:11	(7,707)
Greenwood, Jason	3:18:21	(3,051)
Greenwood, Jonathan	3:58:03	(11,528)
Greenwood, Keith	5:02:27	(26,660)
Greenwood, Martin	6:42:40	(32,453)
Greenwood, Michael	5:23:08	(29,191)
Greenwood, Paul	4:24:32	(18,129)
Greenwood, Peter	5:27:56	(29,612)
Greenwood, Richard	4:14:12	(15,361)
Greenwood, Richard	4:42:15	(22,659)
Greenyer, Dominic	4:23:25	(17,806)
Greer, Ken	3:19:56	(3,248)
Greer, Richard	3:30:55	(5,013)
Greet, James	3:57:33	(11,381)
Greet, Wayne	3:16:40	(2,859)
Greeves, Jerry	2:37:57	(145)
Greevy, John	3:28:55	(4,684)
Gregg, Edward	4:03:34	(12,895)
Gregg, Wesley	4:06:46	(6,940)
Gregg, William	3:53:37	(10,182)
Gregg, William	5:29:05	(29,701)
Gregory, Adrian	4:00:28	(12,180)
Gregory, Anthony	3:33:56	(5,504)

Gregory, Chris	5:03:12	(26,781)
Gregory, Clive	3:45:18	(7,999)
Gregory, David	2:48:35	(430)
Gregory, Dean	3:19:13	(3,164)
Gregory, John	5:02:18	(26,641)
Gregory, Jonathan	4:05:09	(13,240)
Gregory, Keith	4:44:11	(23,104)
Gregory, Keith	5:04:48	(27,002)
Gregory, Mostyn	5:04:46	(26,994)
Gregory, Neil	4:10:55	(14,612)
Gregory, Peter	3:45:44	(8,096)
Gregory, Simon	4:50:51	(24,580)
Gregory, Stuart	5:31:00	(29,861)
Gregory, Tom	5:04:46	(26,994)
Gregory-Peake, Brett	4:32:37	(20,251)
Gregson, Andrew	4:04:35	(13,109)
Grehan, Mark	3:39:00	(6,523)
Greif, Thorsten	4:05:54	(13,411)
Greig, Alan	3:27:47	(4,474)
Greig, David	6:22:20	(32,131)
Greig, Steven	4:28:47	(19,252)
Gremo, Chris	4:23:45	(17,905)
Gremo, Stuart	4:52:46	(24,931)
Greves, John	5:06:46	(27,266)
Grew, Roy	3:25:52	(4,128)
Grewal, Hardeep	3:52:11	(9,747)
Grewal, Harjeet	4:59:39	(26,253)
Grewcock, Duncan	4:06:58	(13,668)
Grey, Christopher	3:52:40	(9,887)
Grey, Stephen	2:43:51	(265)
Grey, Stephen	4:26:39	(18,702)
Gribben, Lawrence	3:52:38	(9,877)
Grice, Benjamin	3:43:57	(7,643)
Grice, David	4:11:48	(14,817)
Grice, Neil	4:32:48	(20,303)
Grice, Nigel	4:13:50	(15,267)
Grice, Robert	3:25:46	(4,109)
Gridley, David	3:20:00	(3,254)
Gridley, David	4:15:52	(15,798)
Griffies, Miles	4:20:46	(17,061)
Griffin, Allen	3:52:40	(9,887)
Griffin, Andrew	3:51:34	(9,564)
Griffin, Andrew	6:02:06	(31,612)
Griffin, Bob	3:47:24	(8,488)
Griffin, Bruce	3:40:34	(6,867)
Griffin, Gareth	4:29:33	(19,467)
Griffin, Geoffrey	4:09:48	(14,344)
Griffin, James	4:26:42	(18,717)
Griffin, Jonathan	3:55:11	(10,658)
Griffin, Mark	3:03:15	(1,396)
Griffin, Nick	4:19:53	(16,831)
Griffin, Paul	4:22:47	(17,631)
Griffin, Richard	3:35:54	(5,884)
Griffin, Richard	4:05:27	(13,313)
Griffin, Roger	3:30:42	(4,979)
Griffin, Timothy	4:09:47	(14,336)
Griffin, William	3:55:06	(10,628)
Griffith, Dorian	4:09:49	(14,346)
Griffith, Jonathan	4:36:44	(21,266)
Griffith, Stephen	3:49:13	(8,946)
Griffiths, Alistair	3:33:45	(5,465)
Griffiths, Andrew	4:16:39	(16,028)
Griffiths, Brian	3:46:23	(8,246)
Griffiths, Bryn	3:40:05	(6,756)
Griffiths, Chris	3:20:47	(3,343)
Griffiths, Christopher	4:38:07	(21,605)
Griffiths, Clive	3:39:13	(6,574)
Griffiths, David	2:55:34	(786)
Griffiths, David	3:46:29	(8,272)
Griffiths, Dean	3:59:58	(12,076)
Griffiths, Graeme	3:09:16	(1,961)
Griffiths, Huw	3:58:49	(11,742)
Griffiths, Ian	4:11:12	(14,674)
Griffiths, John	4:00:12	(12,132)
Griffiths, Keith	4:37:55	(21,553)
Griffiths, Mark	3:43:02	(7,396)
Griffiths, Matthew	4:00:33	(12,196)
Griffiths, Michael	3:46:38	(8,317)
Griffiths, Mike	4:03:54	(12,928)
Griffiths, Neil	3:30:03	(4,880)
Griffiths, Neville	3:12:06	(2,293)
Griffiths, Peter	3:42:45	(7,326)
Griffiths, Peter	4:10:49	(14,586)

Griffiths, Peter	4:55:21	(25,447)
Griffiths, Phil	5:04:20	(26,940)
Griffiths, Phillip	5:03:12	(26,781)
Griffiths, Richard	3:08:17	(1,836)
Griffiths, Simon	3:57:56	(11,483)
Griffiths, Stephen	3:57:52	(11,469)
Griffiths, Stephen	4:38:18	(21,655)
Grigg, Andy	4:52:18	(24,843)
Griggs, David	5:34:34	(30,154)
Griggs, Justin	5:12:22	(28,007)
Grigoleit, Peter	3:59:07	(11,833)
Grigoletti, Enzo	4:22:14	(17,459)
Grigor, Duncan	5:18:30	(28,727)
Grillo, Rob	3:18:48	(3,112)
Grimes, Andrew	3:43:29	(7,517)
Grimes, Anthony	4:12:13	(14,905)
Grimes, Philip	2:52:04	(582)
Grimes, Robert	5:27:05	(29,531)
Grimison, Steve	4:20:31	(16,994)
Grimley, Noel	4:09:13	(14,193)
Grimmer, Harold	5:04:50	(27,005)
Grimsdale, Martin	3:24:22	(3,901)
Grimsey, James	4:26:55	(18,764)
Grimsey, William	3:27:09	(4,352)
Grimshaw, Antony	5:08:02	(27,439)
Grimsley, Paul	5:44:24	(30,849)
Grimster, William	4:58:10	(25,979)
Grimwade, Mark	4:51:43	(24,732)
Grinberg, Simon	3:53:46	(10,228)
Grindell, Dean	4:01:52	(12,541)
Grindley-Ferris, Graham	4:48:13	(24,074)
Grindu, Louis	3:55:06	(10,628)
Grinham, Rick	5:49:00	(31,098)
Grinsell, Terry	4:37:52	(21,536)
Gristwood, Andrew	3:26:36	(4,247)
Gristwood, William	2:33:18	(82)
Grivot, Pascal	2:41:09	(208)
Grocock, Neil	4:19:16	(16,657)
Grocott, Ian	4:00:46	(12,249)
Groen, John	4:41:26	(22,455)
Groenli, Sture	2:37:12	(129)
Grogan, Timothy	4:34:32	(20,706)
Groom, Eddie	4:20:51	(17,075)
Groom, Kristian	3:41:38	(7,087)
Groombridge, Jason	3:25:58	(4,149)
Groombridge, Jeremy	4:46:37	(23,718)
Groombridge, Stephen	2:42:57	(242)
Groothedde, Arco	3:42:01	(7,158)
Grose, Geoffrey	3:56:44	(11,117)
Grosse, Howard	4:03:09	(12,804)
Grosse Homann, Bernhard	6:48:13	(32,524)
Grossi, Mario	5:15:25	(28,350)
Grossiels, Dirk	4:01:14	(12,374)
Grostate, Ian	4:59:57	(26,300)
Grove, Andrew	3:11:09	(2,172)
Grove, Shaun	4:41:59	(22,603)
Groves, Anthony	4:21:11	(17,162)
Groves, Carl	3:22:05	(3,535)
Groves, David	4:26:06	(18,549)
Groves, Ivor	5:05:40	(27,109)
Groves, James	4:44:16	(23,123)
Groves, Jason	5:06:40	(27,252)
Groves, Mark	4:17:54	(16,346)
Groves, Patrick	5:04:13	(26,919)
Groves, Peter	4:35:09	(20,968)
Grubb, Andrew	3:11:10	(2,173)
Grubb, Nick	4:48:23	(24,097)
Gruendler, Matthias	4:37:02	(21,323)
Gruettner, Donald	4:24:05	(18,005)
Grugan, John	3:55:08	(10,646)
Grundy, Brian	5:41:15	(30,637)
Grundy, David	4:45:59	(23,560)
Grundy, Mark	3:34:24	(5,598)
Grundy, Norman	5:22:13	(29,108)
Grundy, Steve	4:41:00	(22,355)
Grundy, Steven	3:27:01	(4,331)
Gryson, Herve	4:03:25	(12,867)
Guard, Stephen	4:09:20	(14,228)
Guarini, Davide	4:22:42	(17,608)
Gubbins, Matthew	5:18:45	(28,750)
Gubbins, Shamus	6:07:25	(31,770)
Gudgion, David	3:21:38	(3,455)
Gudjonsson, Sigbjorn	3:53:51	(10,268)

Gudka, Piyush	4:22:20	(17,493)
Gudmundsson, Egill	4:02:52	(12,747)
Gudmundsson, Hilmar	3:41:28	(7,059)
Gueguen, Christian	3:39:24	(6,603)
Guendouz, Omar	4:44:04	(23,080)
Guerin, James	4:57:25	(25,848)
Guerinoni, Luigi	4:10:42	(14,552)
Guerreiro, Goncalo	5:11:45	(27,915)
Guerrero, Nicholas	4:28:42	(19,224)
Guerrier, Chris	2:54:38	(718)
Guest, Andrew	5:01:15	(26,492)
Guest, Graham	4:52:55	(24,963)
Guest, Ian	4:06:07	(13,465)
Guest, Michael	4:14:16	(15,382)
Guest, Paul	3:50:17	(9,248)
Guest, Richard	4:24:49	(18,205)
Guest, Robert	4:39:40	(22,009)
Guest, Steve	4:59:59	(26,307)
Guest, Stuart	2:38:22	(152)
Guest, Tim	4:33:58	(20,572)
Gugalka, Raphael	4:19:20	(16,673)
Guglielmini, Paolo	4:41:37	(22,507)
Guidez, Richard	3:44:07	(7,683)
Guidotti, Alessandro	3:36:25	(6,008)
Guillot, Bernard	4:04:43	(13,143)
Guilloux, Laurent	4:02:52	(12,747)
Guinan, Paul	2:50:47	(525)
Guinard, Denis	5:05:49	(27,126)
Guinard, Patrick	3:37:00	(6,118)
Guinness, Edward	5:36:10	(30,288)
Guire, Craig	4:42:06	(22,634)
Guite, Lee	3:44:53	(7,899)
Guittard, Didier	3:52:37	(9,873)
Guli, Pascal	2:59:49	(1,160)
Gulland, Matt	4:40:19	(22,187)
Gulliford, Mark	4:16:33	(15,991)
Gullis, Peter	3:26:53	(4,309)
Gulliver, David	4:22:51	(17,658)
Gumbley, Edward	3:39:59	(6,731)
Gummery, Keith	3:41:44	(7,102)
Gunda, Satyanarayana	5:23:40	(29,246)
Gunn, David	4:14:43	(15,500)
Gunn, Graham	4:05:04	(13,227)
Gunn, James	4:10:48	(14,576)
Gunn, Mark	4:05:03	(13,223)
Gunning, Lionel	5:19:39	(28,831)
Gunputh, Burmanun	6:28:01	(32,238)
Gunston, Ian	3:03:47	(1,448)
Gunter, Jack	8:33:29	(32,877)
Gunther, Martin	2:58:09	(1,016)
Guppy, Simon	3:51:13	(9,485)
Gupta, Sanjeev	4:17:16	(16,192)
Gurd, James	4:02:06	(12,575)
Gurd, Richard	3:26:02	(4,154)
Gurney, Giles	4:30:42	(19,755)
Gurr, David	5:23:07	(29,189)
Gurr, Simon	4:38:29	(21,697)
Gurung, Mahendra	4:02:30	(12,654)
Guruwg, Khem	4:40:37	(22,257)
Gurving, Nagendra	4:09:23	(14,245)
Gutenstein, Dennis	3:11:23	(2,191)
Guthrie, Adrian	3:26:27	(4,222)
Guthrie, Matthew	3:49:30	(9,041)
Guthrie, Thomas	3:40:01	(6,737)
Gutierrez-Bujalance, Antonio	4:39:47	(22,051)
Gutierrez-Gallemi, Albert	4:00:04	(12,097)
Guttenplan, Don	4:45:13	(23,361)
Guy, Anthony	4:17:09	(16,160)
Guy, Damian	3:58:10	(11,558)
Guy, Dominic	5:00:41	(26,407)
Guy, John	4:28:23	(19,131)
Guy, Mark	4:05:41	(13,366)
Guy, Nigel	4:13:27	(15,177)
Guy, Richard	3:51:40	(9,587)
Guyet, Emmanuel	3:24:38	(3,934)
Guyot, Daniel	2:49:07	(452)
Guzman, Fernando	3:04:17	(1,488)
Gwillam, Andy	2:46:40	(348)
Gwillim, John	3:26:03	(4,157)
Gwizdala, Peter	5:16:13	(28,470)
Gwynne, David	4:40:03	(22,120)
Gwynne, Mark	4:02:18	(12,616)
Gymer, Alexander	4:02:30	(12,654)
Gynn, Trevor	2:48:01	(402)
Gyprien, Michel	2:58:23	(1,037)
Gyte, Barry	2:57:19	(939)
Haaksma, Jacques	4:52:29	(24,870)
Haan, Herman	3:51:53	(9,646)
Haars, Jan	4:11:25	(14,715)
Haase, James	4:29:57	(19,584)
Habershon, Stephen	4:07:24	(13,777)
Hacker, Peter	4:11:16	(14,685)
Hackett, Alan	4:31:50	(20,037)
Hackett, John	3:29:36	(4,813)
Hackett, Kevin	4:35:19	(20,905)
Hackett, Martin	3:32:14	(5,220)
Hackett, Ray	4:50:46	(24,553)
Hackney, Roger	2:42:13	(230)
Hacquebord, Louwrens	3:28:22	(4,583)
Hadaway, David	3:08:43	(1,891)
Hadberg, Preben	4:37:04	(21,331)
Haddouche, Marc	3:27:51	(4,492)
Haddow, Reid	3:33:53	(5,493)
Haddrell, Rod	3:45:32	(8,054)
Haden, Tony	2:50:53	(529)
Hadfield, Charles	4:18:05	(16,385)
Hadfield, Hugh	4:04:07	(13,012)
Hadfield, John	4:35:55	(21,057)
Hadfield, Tom	2:42:02	(226)
Hadley, Anthony	5:39:30	(30,518)
Hadley, Ian	3:39:52	(6,705)
Hadley, Peter	3:20:49	(3,346)
Hadlington, Steve	3:31:14	(5,069)
Hadorn, Martin	3:57:00	(11,210)
Hadwen, Nicholas	5:35:33	(30,233)
Haertel, Rainer	5:27:28	(29,574)
Haest, Roland	3:35:05	(5,725)
Haetta, Nils	2:44:06	(274)
Haetzman, Andrew	3:46:47	(8,339)
Hagan, Robert	4:18:31	(16,489)
Hagar, Richard	3:26:10	(4,181)
Hageman, Mark	4:35:48	(21,028)
Haggas, Neil	2:47:23	(376)
Hagger, Graham	5:32:08	(29,963)
Hagger, Nicholas	4:31:58	(20,075)
Haggerty, Steven	3:10:34	(2,112)
Haggett, Christopher	4:21:18	(17,191)
Haggett, Jonathan	4:35:22	(20,914)
Hagman, Christer	4:04:06	(13,008)
Hagon, Timothy	3:24:07	(3,840)
Hagon-Powley, Clive	5:10:17	(27,723)
Hague, Kevin	3:09:40	(2,006)
Hague, Martin	4:35:55	(21,057)
Hague-Holmes, Gerard	3:43:38	(7,559)
Hahn, Jens	2:56:10	(841)
Haig, Peter	3:54:42	(10,516)
Haigh, Adrian	4:11:02	(14,639)
Haigh, Ashley	4:03:25	(12,867)
Haigh, James	4:00:42	(12,227)
Haigh, Michael	4:09:12	(14,189)
Haigh, Michael	4:39:16	(21,916)
Haigh, Peter	4:03:28	(12,877)
Haigh, Simon	3:29:17	(4,744)
Hailes, Roger	3:30:59	(5,022)
Hails, Philip	2:55:06	(751)
Hain, John	4:02:22	(12,628)
Haines, Simon	3:45:19	(8,003)
Haines, Stephen	3:24:17	(3,873)
Haining, William	3:15:08	(2,681)
Hains, Kevin	3:50:33	(9,311)
Hainsworth, Jon	4:02:59	(12,771)
Hainsworth, Paul	3:02:07	(1,310)
Hairon, Keith	4:43:01	(22,843)
Haisaid, Francis	4:35:11	(20,875)
Haisley, Matthew	3:53:26	(10,116)
Haissat, Gilles	4:14:23	(15,421)
Haith, Kenneth	3:33:42	(5,457)
Haitzmann, Martin	3:57:22	(11,307)
Hajjaj, Mustapha	3:43:57	(7,643)
Hakkola, Terrence	3:14:52	(2,651)
Halcomb, Anthony	5:06:10	(27,184)
Haldane, Richard	5:10:38	(27,766)
Hale, Garry	3:53:29	(10,139)
Hale, Joe	5:35:40	(30,246)
Hale, John	4:18:14	(16,422)
Hale, Kenneth	3:50:26	(9,284)
Hale, Mike	3:50:05	(9,186)
Hale, Richard	4:27:08	(18,826)
Hale, Richard	5:28:48	(29,683)
Hale, Robert	4:46:36	(23,715)
Hale, Tony	3:40:10	(6,776)
Hales, Roger	3:29:29	(4,793)
Halewyck, Bart	3:29:17	(4,744)
Halfpenny, Brett	4:29:09	(19,367)
Hall, Alan	5:12:17	(27,995)
Hall, Alex	3:22:41	(3,606)
Hall, Alun	3:42:06	(7,180)
Hall, Andrew	3:44:59	(7,923)
Hall, Anthony	3:36:26	(6,012)
Hall, Arnold	6:01:30	(31,589)
Hall, Brian	2:34:02	(90)
Hall, Bruce	2:50:47	(525)
Hall, Chris	2:49:18	(457)
Hall, Chris	3:27:34	(4,428)
Hall, Christopher	3:47:01	(8,384)
Hall, Christopher	4:35:21	(20,912)
Hall, David	2:59:40	(1,144)
Hall, David	4:01:49	(12,526)
Hall, David	4:09:30	(14,270)
Hall, Edward	4:14:40	(15,487)
Hall, Frederick	4:14:59	(15,570)
Hall, Gareth	3:13:28	(2,501)
Hall, Geoffrey	4:42:18	(22,671)
Hall, Ian	3:29:22	(4,773)
Hall, Ian	4:53:49	(25,124)
Hall, James	3:06:59	(1,732)
Hall, James	4:58:29	(26,030)
Hall, Jamie	4:37:33	(21,456)
Hall, Jamie	5:55:35	(31,384)
Hall, Jason	3:12:30	(2,360)
Hall, John	3:35:12	(5,748)
Hall, John	3:55:11	(10,658)
Hall, John	3:59:23	(11,914)
Hall, John	6:30:45	(32,291)
Hall, Jonathan	5:46:29	(30,962)
Hall, Joseph	4:14:43	(15,500)
Hall, Kieran	4:47:48	(23,978)
Hall, Malcolm	4:16:25	(15,956)
Hall, Mark	5:02:24	(26,654)
Hall, Martin	3:38:54	(6,501)
Hall, Martin	4:13:42	(15,232)
Hall, Matthew	3:08:14	(1,828)
Hall, Matthew	3:33:39	(5,447)
Hall, Michael	4:29:01	(19,325)
Hall, Michael	5:36:22	(30,301)
Hall, Neil	3:06:04	(1,647)
Hall, Nicky	2:56:33	(875)
Hall, Patrick	2:51:15	(548)
Hall, Paul	4:37:05	(21,333)
Hall, Peter	4:00:57	(12,295)
Hall, Peter	4:10:47	(14,571)
Hall, Raymond	2:58:11	(1,021)
Hall, Rob	2:46:42	(349)
Hall, Robert	3:15:04	(2,670)
Hall, Robert	3:22:25	(3,573)
Hall, Robert	3:24:28	(3,913)
Hall, Roger	4:10:27	(14,497)
Hall, Stephen	4:07:44	(13,850)
Hall, Stephen	4:52:58	(24,975)
Hall, Stephen	5:03:42	(26,841)
Hall, Steven	5:40:17	(30,571)
Hall, Steven	6:00:58	(31,577)
Hall, Stuart	3:51:43	(9,599)
Hall, Thomas	3:51:02	(9,438)
Hall, Timothy	6:03:32	(31,651)
Hall, Tom	3:23:40	(3,755)
Hall, William	4:12:38	(15,005)
Hall Taylor, Michael	5:13:33	(28,148)
Halladay, Andy	3:44:16	(7,731)
Hallam, Matthew	3:41:54	(7,132)
Hallam, Simon	4:23:34	(17,840)
Hallas, Adrian	3:35:42	(5,846)
Hallauer, Marc	3:27:23	(4,396)
Hallcrow, Alastair	4:26:05	(18,544)
Haller, Josef	3:49:17	(8,965)
Hallett, Mark	3:27:51	(4,492)
Hallett, Martin	5:02:41	(26,698)
Halliday, James	3:16:23	(2,829)
Halliday, John	3:57:31	(11,368)

Halliday, Neil 4:14:55 (15,554)
Halliday, Roy 5:28:26 (29,647)
Halliday, Scott 4:08:02 (13,923)
Halliwell, Jonathan 3:44:27 (7,784)
Halliwell, Tom 4:29:54 (19,575)
Hall-McNair, Robert 3:16:51 (2,887)
Hallows, Richard 3:50:56 (9,406)
Halpin, Francis 4:36:54 (21,297)
Halpin, Stuart 3:37:09 (6,140)
Halsall, Dean 5:55:23 (31,370)
Halse, Tristan 3:50:15 (9,235)
Halsey, Andrew 4:52:40 (24,908)
Halther, Eberhard 4:47:30 (23,912)
Haltmeier, Thomas 4:20:40 (17,038)
Halton, Andrew 4:31:10 (19,874)
Halton, Clifford 4:14:01 (15,316)
Halton, Mark 5:04:43 (26,981)
Halvatzis, Nicos 3:21:05 (3,384)
Halvey, Martin 2:47:13 (368)
Hamblen, Richard 5:15:32 (28,370)
Hambleton, Stephen 4:08:22 (13,982)
Hamblin, Alan 4:00:16 (12,149)
Hamblin, Steven 3:59:10 (11,845)
Hambly, Darren 5:38:50 (30,467)
Hamby, Glynn 3:51:35 (9,569)
Hamer, Garry 6:34:16 (32,344)
Hamer, Graham 4:45:57 (23,552)
Hamer, Jon 5:12:23 (28,010)
Hamer, Philip 3:49:02 (8,906)
Hamer, Steve 3:21:56 (3,511)
Hames, Richard 4:24:26 (18,100)
Hamill, Geoffrey 3:30:31 (4,949)
Hamill, Lee 4:22:13 (17,449)
Hamill, Stefan 4:23:38 (17,857)
Hamilton, Alex 5:22:03 (29,096)
Hamilton, Alexander 4:19:21 (16,677)
Hamilton, Allan 4:01:47 (12,514)
Hamilton, Brian 3:48:44 (8,822)
Hamilton, Edward 3:08:10 (1,820)
Hamilton, James 4:34:53 (20,798)
Hamilton, Jeremy 4:12:26 (14,955)
Hamilton, Lee 5:48:53 (31,089)
Hamilton, Mark 3:37:26 (6,194)
Hamilton, Martin 4:15:55 (15,816)
Hamilton, Nicholas 4:01:42 (12,493)
Hamilton, Robert 4:03:13 (12,819)
Hamilton, Stephen 4:51:47 (24,741)
Hamilton, Steve 3:15:33 (2,729)
Hamilton-Brown, Robert 5:53:11 (31,285)
Hamilton-Smith, Kevin 4:37:41 (21,488)
Hamlet, Colin 3:22:00 (3,526)
Hamlin, Phillip 4:19:43 (16,781)
Hamlin, Tony 4:56:45 (25,725)
Hammer, Matthias 4:45:35 (23,467)
Hammerton, Robbie 5:25:46 (29,426)
Hammet, Paul 3:28:11 (4,548)
Hammond, Ben 4:16:06 (15,864)
Hammond, Christopher 4:58:28 (26,027)
Hammond, Edward 4:13:57 (15,297)
Hammond, John 3:42:14 (7,214)
Hammond, John 4:27:17 (18,858)
Hammond, Mark 2:58:00 (1,008)
Hammond, Matthew 4:36:31 (21,226)
Hammond, Michael 4:31:00 (19,828)
Hammond, Nicholas 4:51:05 (24,625)
Hammond, Paul 3:38:55 (6,505)
Hammond, Paul 4:06:46 (13,624)
Hammond, Robert 4:08:05 (13,931)
Hammond, Scott 4:00:09 (12,118)
Hammond, Simon 4:39:51 (22,070)
Hammond, Stephen 4:59:27 (26,207)
Hammond, Tim 4:03:56 (12,971)
Hammond, Warren 4:35:05 (20,851)
Hammonds, Nigel 4:38:01 (21,575)
Hamon, Maxime 2:34:45 (95)
Hampi, Ronald 2:40:49 (200)
Hampson, Michael 4:06:53 (13,645)
Hampton, Brian 3:10:07 (2,051)
Hampton, Chris 3:56:02 (10,906)
Hampton, James 5:58:18 (31,487)
Hampton, Ray 3:39:03 (6,537)
Hamsher, Mark 4:11:56 (14,841)
Hancock, Alan 4:51:49 (24,746)
Hancock, Alistair 5:59:13 (31,521)
Hancock, Anthony 3:23:43 (3,761)
Hancock, Brian 3:27:45 (4,467)
Hancock, Cliff 4:13:00 (15,082)
Hancock, Hartley 3:52:11 (9,747)
Hancock, Keith 4:50:59 (24,606)
Hancox, Grenville 3:59:58 (12,076)
Hancox, Michael 4:29:33 (19,467)
Hand, Michael 3:15:15 (2,694)
Hand, Richard 4:49:56 (24,412)
Hand, Rob 2:31:25 (70)
Handford, John 3:51:33 (9,563)
Handley, Brian 4:07:30 (13,799)
Handley, Derek 5:16:39 (28,518)
Handley, Gary 4:09:08 (14,160)
Handley, Nick 3:49:46 (9,121)
Handley, Phillip 3:55:34 (10,772)
Handley, Ray 3:16:32 (2,849)
Hands, Raymond 5:06:15 (27,191)
Handslip, Nicholas 3:10:23 (2,089)
Handy, Lionel 3:05:53 (1,631)
Hanison, Darren 5:06:24 (27,213)
Hankey, Paul 4:31:48 (20,031)
Hanley, Dean 4:16:04 (15,855)
Hanley, Liam 2:56:28 (869)
Hanley, Paul 4:10:43 (14,556)
Hanlon, David 5:13:16 (28,110)
Hann, Charles 3:51:21 (9,511)
Hann, Jeremy 3:49:12 (8,944)
Hann, Ottmar 4:10:07 (14,414)
Hannah, David 3:48:29 (8,744)
Hannah, Kevin 3:38:44 (6,477)
Hannah, Samuel 4:00:51 (12,267)
Hannah, Tom 3:26:41 (4,269)
Hannam, Laurence 3:29:53 (4,856)
Hannequin, Patrick 3:50:25 (9,281)
Hanney, Andrew 4:04:23 (13,067)
Hanney, David 3:03:28 (1,417)
Hanscomb, John 3:59:35 (11,962)
Hansen, Adam 3:13:29 (2,507)
Hansen, David 4:56:07 (25,614)
Hansen, Knud 2:57:39 (975)
Hansen, Paul 3:12:23 (2,344)
Hansen, Paul 4:59:04 (26,143)
Hansen, Piers 4:46:54 (23,786)
Hansen, Poul 3:51:34 (9,564)
Hansen, Richard 5:09:59 (27,688)
Hansen, Scott 5:17:28 (28,625)
Hansford, Jerry 4:38:12 (21,626)
Hanson, Carl 4:19:26 (16,700)
Hanson, David 3:10:09 (2,052)
Hanson, David 4:10:06 (14,410)
Hanson, David 4:22:38 (17,583)
Hanson, Gareth 3:25:12 (4,015)
Hanson, Mark 3:36:19 (5,981)
Hanson, Paul 3:11:15 (2,182)
Hantzsch, Helmut 2:53:33 (657)
Hanz, Detlef 3:23:25 (3,710)
Happel, Erich 3:55:13 (10,668)
Haragan, Scott 4:52:37 (24,901)
Haran, Michael 3:54:50 (10,551)
Harasse, Daniel 5:23:38 (29,240)
Harbon, Richard 3:01:08 (1,238)
Harbour, Joseph 4:11:05 (14,654)
Harbour, Peter 3:53:57 (10,293)
Harby, Alan 4:01:34 (12,461)
Harcombe, Ian 3:53:53 (10,274)
Harcourt, David 4:37:24 (21,422)
Hard, Newman 5:14:48 (28,282)
Hardcastle, David 5:15:42 (28,394)
Hardcastle, Ian 2:51:33 (563)
Hardcastle, Kenneth 3:31:29 (5,105)
Hardcastle, Richard 4:27:28 (18,911)
Harden-Sweetnam, Andrew 4:06:23 (13,540)
Harder, Michael 4:35:58 (21,071)
Hardicre, Steven 4:48:20 (24,093)
Hardie, Duncan 5:54:10 (31,318)
Hardie, Michel 3:25:26 (4,051)
Hardiman, Michael 4:27:43 (18,964)
Harding, Alan 4:14:37 (15,473)
Harding, Anthony 5:14:14 (28,216)
Harding, Brian 3:56:57 (11,192)
Harding, Craig 3:45:46 (8,104)
Harding, Derek 5:12:17 (27,995)
Harding, Ian 2:53:46 (666)
Harding, James 3:14:18 (2,592)
Harding, Jeffrey 3:33:16 (5,392)
Harding, John 4:49:12 (24,276)
Harding, John 5:26:41 (29,502)
Harding, Jonathan 5:10:05 (27,698)
Harding, Keith 4:26:59 (18,782)
Harding, Mark 3:54:32 (10,467)
Harding, Norman 5:41:29 (30,653)
Harding, Peter 4:24:51 (18,213)
Harding, Peter 4:53:44 (25,110)
Harding, Robert 4:11:55 (14,837)
Hardman, Bob 3:31:19 (5,080)
Hardman, James 4:09:16 (14,206)
Hardman, Paul 5:30:36 (29,832)
Hardman, Roger 4:23:56 (17,958)
Hardman, Timothy 5:56:22 (31,414)
Hards, Neil 4:50:48 (24,564)
Hardwell, Keith 3:54:04 (10,334)
Hardwick, Andrew 4:34:09 (20,618)
Hardwick, Kevin 3:57:06 (11,235)
Hardwick, Matthe 2:56:38 (884)
Hardwidge, Stephen 4:07:16 (13,737)
Hardy, Andrew 3:31:23 (5,091)
Hardy, Anthony 5:06:57 (27,288)
Hardy, Damian 6:25:34 (32,194)
Hardy, Gary 4:49:30 (24,323)
Hardy, Lance 4:26:24 (18,623)
Hardy, Luc 3:46:40 (8,327)
Hardy, Martin 3:56:56 (11,187)
Hardy, Ruari 3:33:46 (5,469)
Hare, David 4:29:21 (19,422)
Harel, Zvi 4:20:58 (17,102)
Harfield, Patrick 5:59:14 (31,522)
Harfield, Stephen 5:59:12 (31,520)
Harford, Mark 3:14:51 (2,648)
Hargate, Paul 4:28:25 (19,142)
Hargis, Brian 6:24:14 (32,168)
Hargraves, Ben 4:13:53 (15,281)
Hargreaves, David 4:35:46 (21,021)
Hargreaves, Mark 5:58:54 (31,509)
Harison, Marc 4:16:35 (16,002)
Harker, Joseph 3:52:22 (9,805)
Harkin, Kevin 4:26:39 (18,702)
Harkness, Jack 3:43:10 (7,434)
Harkus, Gavin 2:46:09 (328)
Harland, Cameron 3:43:57 (7,643)
Harland, Colin 3:55:35 (10,778)
Harland, Jonathon 4:34:43 (20,754)
Harland, Philip 4:26:24 (18,623)
Harle, Colin 3:35:00 (5,710)
Harlick, Julian 4:57:42 (25,898)
Harling, Joseph 4:30:34 (19,725)
Harlock, Peter 5:14:36 (28,262)
Harlow, Derek 4:42:32 (22,733)
Harlow, Steven 3:48:22 (8,714)
Harlow, Thomas 6:49:13 (32,533)
Harman, Gary 3:20:26 (3,304)
Harman, Matthew 3:52:09 (9,741)
Harman, Paul 5:26:50 (29,511)
Harman, Steven 4:42:52 (22,807)
Harmening, Manfred 3:30:59 (5,022)
Harms, Timothy 3:54:24 (10,427)
Harmundal, Thomas 3:05:54 (1,634)
Harnden, Jon 4:24:01 (17,985)
Harness, Nicholas 4:48:04 (24,053)
Harnett, Ricci 4:32:37 (20,251)
Harney, Brian 3:02:35 (1,342)
Harney, Mark 3:26:49 (4,296)
Harney, Mark 4:32:39 (20,261)
Harper, Benjamin 4:30:53 (19,801)
Harper, Charles 3:08:45 (1,900)
Harper, Chris 4:02:07 (12,583)
Harper, Clive 3:53:48 (10,249)
Harper, Dai 4:16:48 (16,064)
Harper, Dale 3:55:19 (10,701)
Harper, Iain 4:28:08 (19,065)
Harper, Ian 3:41:47 (7,112)
Harper, Ian 4:27:01 (18,792)
Harper, Kerry 4:20:15 (16,926)
Harper, Martin 4:02:48 (12,729)
Harper, Michael 4:15:26 (15,676)

Harper, Michael	4:30:28 (19,705)	
Harper, Neil	4:45:37 (23,478)	
Harper, Nigel	3:53:48 (10,249)	
Harper, Paul	5:46:00 (30,934)	
Harper, Steven	3:39:12 (6,567)	
Harpin, Michael	4:45:20 (23,389)	
Harragan, Stuart	4:31:57 (20,071)	
Harrap, John	3:17:20 (2,937)	
Harrasser, Reinhard	2:38:03 (148)	
Harrigan, Joseph	5:14:16 (28,226)	
Harriman, David	5:58:54 (31,509)	
Harrington, Alexander	4:08:44 (14,085)	
Harrington, Ciaran	4:56:19 (25,658)	
Harrington, David	3:39:55 (6,714)	
Harrington, George	5:19:02 (28,781)	
Harrington, Neil	3:43:54 (7,633)	
Harrington, Neil	3:55:49 (10,844)	
Harrington, Patrick	5:08:45 (27,530)	
Harrington, Peter	5:00:38 (26,393)	
Harrington, Roy	5:06:06 (27,176)	
Harrington, Sarah	6:04:04 (31,665)	
Harris, Adrian	3:54:59 (10,592)	
Harris, Alasdair	3:47:21 (8,472)	
Harris, Alex	3:29:21 (4,766)	
Harris, Andrew	3:44:28 (7,790)	
Harris, Andrew	4:09:08 (14,160)	
Harris, Andrew	4:28:23 (19,131)	
Harris, Andrew	4:55:55 (25,567)	
Harris, Chris	3:56:03 (10,913)	
Harris, Chris	4:54:56 (25,364)	
Harris, Clifford	4:39:20 (21,930)	
Harris, Colin	5:57:40 (31,465)	
Harris, Damian	4:49:58 (24,417)	
Harris, Damian	4:54:50 (25,349)	
Harris, Damon	2:20:42 (20)	
Harris, Damon	2:58:33 (1,055)	
Harris, Daniel	4:11:25 (14,715)	
Harris, David	3:40:11 (6,779)	
Harris, David	3:54:44 (10,529)	
Harris, David	4:26:36 (18,680)	
Harris, David	4:29:32 (19,464)	
Harris, Donald	6:36:21 (32,378)	
Harris, Garry	3:55:36 (10,783)	
Harris, Graham	4:18:25 (16,469)	
Harris, Howard	5:39:26 (30,508)	
Harris, Jason	3:15:23 (2,713)	
Harris, Jason	5:58:16 (31,485)	
Harris, Jeremy	4:25:25 (18,364)	
Harris, John	4:52:55 (24,963)	
Harris, Jon	4:30:41 (19,752)	
Harris, Jonathan	3:55:34 (10,772)	
Harris, Justin	4:47:52 (23,996)	
Harris, Keith	5:03:37 (26,837)	
Harris, Keith	5:34:55 (30,177)	
Harris, Leon	3:54:48 (10,541)	
Harris, Leon	6:19:46 (32,075)	
Harris, Mark	3:07:59 (1,806)	
Harris, Mark	3:25:51 (4,124)	
Harris, Mark	5:49:23 (31,117)	
Harris, Martin	2:57:17 (934)	
Harris, Martin	4:34:29 (20,688)	
Harris, Michael	4:41:24 (22,447)	
Harris, Michael	6:35:19 (32,361)	
Harris, Neil	4:00:15 (12,143)	
Harris, Neil	5:34:52 (30,172)	
Harris, Nigel	3:58:01 (11,517)	
Harris, Paul	3:55:02 (10,603)	
Harris, Paul	4:29:23 (19,432)	
Harris, Paul	5:34:52 (30,172)	
Harris, Peter	3:12:54 (2,417)	
Harris, Peter	5:34:49 (30,170)	
Harris, Phil	5:46:10 (30,942)	
Harris, Richard	3:24:01 (3,824)	
Harris, Richard	4:18:25 (16,469)	
Harris, Richard	4:44:10 (23,099)	
Harris, Richard	6:24:27 (32,178)	
Harris, Robin	3:23:57 (3,814)	
Harris, Ross	3:36:05 (5,924)	
Harris, Ryan	4:22:30 (17,545)	
Harris, Sean	4:16:52 (16,082)	
Harris, Simon	3:23:34 (3,736)	
Harris, Simon	3:34:04 (5,533)	
Harris, Simon	5:34:55 (30,177)	
Harris, Stanley	4:40:37 (22,257)	
Harris, Steven	4:21:37 (17,287)	
Harris, Tim	4:45:25 (23,419)	
Harris, Timothy	4:13:26 (15,173)	
Harrison, Andrew	3:22:47 (3,632)	
Harrison, Andy	3:59:12 (11,859)	
Harrison, Charles	3:41:02 (6,973)	
Harrison, Darren	4:09:09 (14,170)	
Harrison, David	4:33:44 (20,523)	
Harrison, Derek	3:36:49 (6,079)	
Harrison, Derek	3:46:39 (8,321)	
Harrison, Doug	5:06:49 (27,272)	
Harrison, Graeme	4:52:46 (24,931)	
Harrison, Ian	4:48:19 (24,089)	
Harrison, John	3:19:03 (3,144)	
Harrison, John	3:54:06 (10,343)	
Harrison, Jonathan	3:51:20 (9,507)	
Harrison, Julian	4:36:00 (21,080)	
Harrison, Mark	3:43:26 (7,508)	
Harrison, Mark	4:31:55 (20,061)	
Harrison, Martin	4:15:46 (15,774)	
Harrison, Matthew	2:47:00 (360)	
Harrison, Michael	4:04:08 (13,014)	
Harrison, Neil	4:14:03 (15,332)	
Harrison, Richard	4:06:27 (13,556)	
Harrison, Robert	3:45:26 (8,027)	
Harrison, Robert	5:08:44 (27,526)	
Harrison, Simon	4:23:34 (17,840)	
Harrison, Simon	4:55:15 (25,430)	
Harrison, Timothy	3:42:53 (7,358)	
Harrison, Trevor	3:56:35 (11,078)	
Harrison, William	3:59:19 (11,887)	
Harrison-Church, John	3:46:23 (8,246)	
Harrod, Craig	4:01:41 (12,489)	
Harrold, Martin	3:19:02 (3,140)	
Harron, Christopher	3:07:24 (1,762)	
Harrop, Andrew	3:31:02 (5,036)	
Harrop, Samuel	4:02:50 (12,741)	
Harrop, Simon	4:12:37 (15,002)	
Harrow, Lee	3:29:50 (4,845)	
Harrow, Martin	3:09:17 (1,965)	
Harrowell, Jonathan	5:56:03 (31,403)	
Harrower, Andy	3:09:18 (1,967)	
Harrowen, Craig	4:53:54 (25,147)	
Harry, Dave	4:11:49 (14,822)	
Hart, Alexander	4:20:10 (16,907)	
Hart, Christopher	3:13:38 (2,519)	
Hart, Christopher	4:28:12 (19,081)	
Hart, David	3:16:21 (2,825)	
Hart, David	3:42:02 (7,164)	
Hart, Gary	4:46:34 (23,706)	
Hart, George	2:49:58 (490)	
Hart, Jon	3:14:39 (2,625)	
Hart, Kevin	4:22:50 (17,652)	
Hart, Matthew	4:06:19 (13,522)	
Hart, Matthew	4:27:13 (18,847)	
Hart, Patrick	4:33:50 (20,541)	
Hart, Paul	3:49:35 (9,066)	
Hart, Paul	4:25:21 (18,348)	
Hart, Peter	2:58:01 (1,009)	
Hart, Simon	4:22:47 (17,631)	
Hart, Terence	4:21:22 (17,210)	
Harte, Declan	3:49:11 (8,941)	
Harte, John	3:38:20 (6,381)	
Harte, Tony	3:59:15 (11,868)	
Hartham, Peter	4:10:19 (14,464)	
Hartigan, Paul	3:54:51 (10,557)	
Hartland, Paul	3:03:52 (1,455)	
Hartle, Peter	5:16:54 (28,543)	
Hartley, Alexander	4:34:14 (20,636)	
Hartley, Jalaal	3:38:25 (6,404)	
Hartley, John	4:50:13 (24,454)	
Hartley, Jonathan	3:46:22 (8,244)	
Hartley, Paul	4:34:48 (20,773)	
Hartley, Richard	3:26:16 (4,200)	
Hartley, Simon	4:20:40 (17,038)	
Hartley, Stuart	3:41:45 (7,109)	
Hartley Bowker, Richard	2:54:33 (709)	
Hartmann, Henrik	4:10:11 (14,435)	
Hartmann, Thierry	3:11:11 (2,174)	
Hartmans, Ceed	3:32:27 (5,262)	
Hartmut, Vogt	3:52:07 (9,726)	
Hartnell, Stephen	3:17:23 (2,947)	
Hartwright, Stephen	5:58:33 (31,500)	
Harty, Andrew	3:39:00 (6,523)	
Harvatt, Neil	4:07:48 (13,872)	
Harvey, Andrew	5:15:37 (28,385)	
Harvey, Christopher	3:10:46 (2,131)	
Harvey, David	5:00:17 (26,344)	
Harvey, Douglas	3:32:16 (5,229)	
Harvey, Edward	4:54:39 (25,314)	
Harvey, Gareth	3:20:24 (3,299)	
Harvey, Glen	3:25:53 (4,133)	
Harvey, Ian	3:06:20 (1,669)	
Harvey, James	2:48:20 (420)	
Harvey, Kenneth	4:52:10 (24,809)	
Harvey, Luke	4:04:47 (13,155)	
Harvey, Ory	3:33:02 (5,357)	
Harvey, Paul	3:41:34 (7,076)	
Harvey, Paul	4:02:11 (12,595)	
Harvey, Paul	4:41:18 (22,425)	
Harvey, Peter	3:13:20 (2,480)	
Harvey, Peter	3:25:01 (3,987)	
Harvey, Philip	4:14:00 (15,313)	
Harvey, Richard	4:54:20 (25,254)	
Harvey, Robert	3:14:56 (2,664)	
Harvey, Robert	4:16:59 (16,112)	
Harwood, Chris	3:12:21 (2,341)	
Harwood, Clive	3:06:26 (1,676)	
Harwood, Jeff	3:41:31 (7,067)	
Harwood, Jeff	3:56:39 (11,097)	
Harwood, Lee	3:26:28 (4,223)	
Harwood, Mark	4:22:39 (17,588)	
Harwood, Neil	3:58:18 (11,590)	
Harwood, Paul	2:35:57 (105)	
Haseley, Harry	5:30:33 (29,828)	
Haslam, Andrew	4:12:53 (15,058)	
Haslett, Francis	5:07:14 (27,340)	
Hassan, William	3:39:44 (6,676)	
Hassan Hicks, Turgay	3:40:13 (6,792)	
Hassell, Desmond	3:50:40 (9,338)	
Hasslacher, Mark	4:48:42 (24,168)	
Hastie, David	4:32:36 (20,243)	
Hastie, James	3:44:27 (7,784)	
Hastings, Andrew	4:02:54 (12,755)	
Hastings, Gavin	3:54:26 (10,439)	
Hastings, Robert	4:57:35 (25,877)	
Hastings, Steven	3:28:15 (4,560)	
Haston, Charles	3:56:05 (10,923)	
Hatch, David	4:44:03 (23,074)	
Hatch, James	4:09:58 (14,377)	
Hatfield, Edward	4:03:22 (12,849)	
Hatfield, Paul	4:01:44 (12,502)	
Hathway, Christopher	4:31:14 (19,887)	
Hatje, Dominic	4:27:51 (18,996)	
Hatter, Anthony	3:40:52 (6,933)	
Hattersley, Andrew	5:20:42 (28,961)	
Hattersley, David	3:29:25 (4,780)	
Hatton, David	3:48:28 (8,739)	
Hatton, Philip	3:38:53 (6,499)	
Hattrill, Wayne	4:03:54 (12,963)	
Haughey, John	4:10:10 (14,430)	
Haughton, Jack	3:23:58 (3,817)	
Haus, Jens	3:45:03 (7,940)	
Hausch, Eberhard	4:15:53 (15,804)	
Hausmann, Andreas	3:14:15 (2,587)	
Hautebas, Jerome	3:21:49 (3,487)	
Havelin, Fintan	3:41:16 (7,027)	
Hawcroft, Gareth	3:32:19 (5,236)	
Hawdon, Darren	4:31:26 (19,940)	
Hawe, Terry	5:22:27 (29,127)	
Hawes, Dougie	4:56:38 (25,708)	
Hawes, Steven	4:13:35 (15,201)	
Hawes, William	2:59:05 (1,101)	
Hawken, Archie	3:38:16 (6,362)	
Hawken, Gareth	3:30:39 (4,972)	
Hawker, Jeff	3:48:37 (8,789)	
Hawker, Simon	2:56:01 (833)	
Hawkes, Alec	3:54:14 (10,379)	
Hawkes, Andy	3:28:55 (4,684)	
Hawkes, David	3:35:13 (5,749)	
Hawkes, Jeff	5:09:19 (27,608)	
Hawkins, Ben	4:41:27 (22,463)	
Hawkins, Christopher	3:56:19 (10,994)	
Hawkins, Jeff	4:03:24 (12,859)	
Hawkins, Jim	5:35:08 (30,193)	

Hawkins, John	3:54:20 (10,409)	
Hawkins, John	5:31:03 (29,868)	
Hawkins, Michael	3:56:09 (10,942)	
Hawkins, Norman	5:23:23 (29,208)	
Hawkins, Paul	3:07:35 (1,774)	
Hawkins, Peter	3:12:04 (2,284)	
Hawkins, Peter	3:13:44 (2,536)	
Hawkins, Peter	5:09:30 (27,632)	
Hawkins, Richard	3:46:15 (8,211)	
Hawkins, Robert	3:00:12 (1,182)	
Hawkins, Ross	3:52:45 (9,909)	
Hawkins, Simon	4:55:58 (25,577)	
Hawkins, Stephen	4:02:16 (12,609)	
Hawkins, Stephen	4:03:21 (12,843)	
Hawkshaw, Paul	3:59:07 (11,833)	
Hawkshaw-Burn, Charles	3:28:35 (4,622)	
Hawksworth, Nicholas	4:41:16 (22,418)	
Hawley, Graham	4:33:38 (20,500)	
Hawliczek, Eddie	3:16:56 (2,895)	
Hawman, George	4:22:40 (17,596)	
Haworth, John	3:22:52 (3,644)	
Haworth, Nick	4:33:55 (20,560)	
Haworth, Simon	4:32:26 (20,200)	
Haworth-Booth, Luke	4:16:04 (15,855)	
Hawthorn, Jamie	4:20:08 (16,896)	
Hawthorne, Jerry	4:17:23 (16,220)	
Hay, Alastair	4:00:42 (12,227)	
Hay, Alexander	4:53:37 (25,088)	
Hay, Andrew	4:23:06 (17,728)	
Hay, Andy	3:33:32 (5,430)	
Hay, David	3:52:25 (9,815)	
Hay, David	4:04:11 (13,022)	
Hay, David	4:10:01 (14,389)	
Hay, Dominic	3:27:09 (4,352)	
Hay, John	4:21:03 (17,127)	
Hay, Mark	5:23:22 (29,206)	
Hay, Paul	3:24:40 (3,938)	
Hay, Richard	3:42:50 (7,347)	
Hay, Stephen	3:25:47 (4,111)	
Haycock, David	3:39:12 (6,567)	
Haycock, Gavin	3:58:08 (11,553)	
Haycock, Richard	4:46:40 (23,731)	
Haycock, Stewart	5:29:10 (29,707)	
Hayday, Marcus	4:11:36 (14,768)	
Hayden, Mark	4:41:50 (22,565)	
Haydon, Andrew	3:02:07 (1,310)	
Haydon, David	3:01:28 (1,257)	
Hayes, Andrew	3:16:55 (2,892)	
Hayes, Andrew	4:21:57 (17,376)	
Hayes, Brian	4:39:49 (22,062)	
Hayes, Brendon	4:27:00 (18,790)	
Hayes, Charles	3:53:30 (10,145)	
Hayes, Christopher	4:27:45 (18,972)	
Hayes, Curt-Lee	3:51:48 (9,624)	
Hayes, Dennis	4:50:40 (24,537)	
Hayes, Gavin	4:59:37 (26,247)	
Hayes, Paul	3:26:47 (4,290)	
Hayes, Philip	6:18:19 (32,045)	
Hayes, Richard	5:11:51 (27,930)	
Hayes, Robert	4:06:40 (13,606)	
Hayes, Robert	4:53:09 (25,002)	
Hayes, Roger	3:02:42 (1,349)	
Hayes, Russ	4:25:26 (18,370)	
Hayes, Shaun	4:32:16 (20,152)	
Hayes, Stephen	3:39:58 (6,725)	
Hayes, Stephen	4:34:06 (20,608)	
Hayes, Steven	3:46:04 (8,172)	
Hayes, Tony	3:37:18 (6,163)	
Hayhurst, John	3:54:25 (10,435)	
Hayhurst, Stephen	4:59:52 (26,284)	
Hayler, Colin	3:34:52 (5,688)	
Hayler, Ian	4:35:10 (20,866)	
Haylett, Philip	3:46:34 (8,303)	
Hayllar, Crispin	3:49:01 (8,902)	
Haylock, Keith	5:02:25 (26,655)	
Haylock, Nick	3:33:40 (5,450)	
Haylor, David	4:14:02 (15,324)	
Hayman, Mark	2:44:20 (279)	
Haymes, Anthony	4:13:08 (15,109)	
Haymes, Chris	3:32:01 (5,193)	
Hayne, Guy	3:48:14 (8,681)	
Haynes, Anthony	4:43:47 (23,011)	
Haynes, Lee	4:10:04 (14,403)	

Haynes, Matthew	3:26:42 (4,275)	
Haynes, Neil	4:16:27 (15,969)	
Haynes-Oliver, Simon	5:02:23 (26,652)	
Hayter, Edward	4:23:59 (17,976)	
Hayter, Quinton	3:47:30 (8,510)	
Hayter, Sam	3:52:00 (9,683)	
Haythornthwaite, James	4:20:02 (16,870)	
Hayton, Joseph	4:34:46 (20,766)	
Hayward, Adrian	3:41:00 (6,964)	
Hayward, Alastair	4:02:25 (12,633)	
Hayward, Alexander	4:56:31 (25,692)	
Hayward, Andrew	4:19:58 (16,852)	
Hayward, Anthony	6:34:08 (32,340)	
Hayward, Daniel	4:27:07 (18,822)	
Hayward, Kevin	4:18:36 (16,513)	
Hayward, Mike	4:55:20 (25,443)	
Hayward, Pau	4:43:08 (22,876)	
Hayward, Paul	3:33:52 (5,490)	
Hayward, Paul	5:52:00 (31,234)	
Hayward, Peter	3:21:53 (3,502)	
Hayward, Philip	4:12:21 (14,931)	
Hayward, Rhys	5:20:46 (28,971)	
Hayward, Robert	3:47:04 (8,399)	
Hayward, Trevor	4:20:38 (17,027)	
Haywood, Andrew	3:42:50 (7,347)	
Haywood, Arthur	5:20:17 (28,914)	
Haywood, Glenn	3:59:05 (11,827)	
Haywood, Marcus	3:30:00 (4,874)	
Haywood, Russell	3:46:38 (8,317)	
Hayworth, Scott	3:48:32 (8,757)	
Hazan, Jonathan	4:05:37 (13,352)	
Hazard, John	3:31:36 (5,124)	
Hazeldine, Bryan	5:16:47 (28,526)	
Hazeldine, Rex	4:55:22 (25,453)	
Hazelgrove, Roy	4:13:04 (15,096)	
Hazell, Graham	3:55:26 (10,732)	
Hazell, Martin	5:15:46 (28,406)	
Hazell, Stephen	4:36:48 (21,276)	
Hazell, Tony	2:44:10 (278)	
Hazelwood, Justin	3:52:58 (9,967)	
Hazlewood, Paul	3:43:43 (7,580)	
Head, David	3:55:32 (10,758)	
Head, Edward	3:53:02 (9,994)	
Head, Stephen	3:53:50 (10,261)	
Head, William	4:32:39 (20,261)	
Heade, Stuart	4:46:54 (23,786)	
Headland, Darren	3:42:07 (7,184)	
Headley, Finbar	5:44:31 (30,856)	
Headon, Andrew	3:46:07 (8,186)	
Headon, David	2:52:48 (619)	
Headridge, Keith	4:44:25 (23,154)	
Heal, Chris	3:26:37 (4,252)	
Heal, David	4:17:14 (16,179)	
Heal, David	4:23:19 (17,781)	
Heal, Richard	4:25:45 (18,453)	
Heald, Nigel	4:03:02 (12,782)	
Heald, Richard	4:03:02 (12,782)	
Heale, Nicholas	3:27:00 (4,330)	
Heale, Simon	3:28:34 (4,616)	
Heales, Richard	4:11:56 (14,841)	
Healey, Andrew	4:09:19 (14,224)	
Healey, David	6:09:54 (31,835)	
Healey, Martin	4:48:48 (24,197)	
Healey, Nick	5:19:06 (28,786)	
Healey, Pat	4:41:41 (22,526)	
Healy, Danny	4:51:12 (24,654)	
Healy, Dominic	3:51:29 (9,539)	
Healy, Ken	5:14:48 (28,282)	
Healy, Lee	4:16:50 (16,075)	
Healy, Paul	3:46:24 (8,254)	
Healy, Philip	4:50:45 (24,550)	
Healy, Sean	4:21:32 (17,264)	
Heap, Carl	3:12:47 (2,396)	
Heap, Michael	3:32:14 (5,220)	
Heard, David	3:36:15 (5,968)	
Heard, Neil	3:49:02 (8,906)	
Hearn, Austen	4:30:05 (19,620)	
Hearn, Colin	6:05:06 (31,696)	
Hearn, David	4:29:09 (19,367)	
Hearn, Derek	4:35:09 (20,862)	
Hearn, Graham	5:09:28 (27,629)	
Hearn, John	4:28:52 (19,282)	
Hearne, Matthew	3:53:10 (10,036)	

Hearst, Aidan	3:12:38 (2,377)	
Heasman, Jonathon	3:31:57 (5,178)	
Heath, Bary	4:01:20 (12,399)	
Heath, Charles	4:57:53 (25,932)	
Heath, Damon	4:18:17 (16,431)	
Heath, David	3:56:44 (11,117)	
Heath, Frederick	3:41:15 (7,025)	
Heath, Gary	5:15:04 (28,307)	
Heath, Les	2:56:21 (860)	
Heath, Oliver	3:46:12 (8,201)	
Heath, Peter	4:44:56 (23,283)	
Heath, Richard	4:46:40 (23,731)	
Heath, Terence	5:13:13 (28,105)	
Heathcoat-Amory, David	3:58:18 (11,590)	
Heathcock, Robert	4:22:25 (17,527)	
Heathcote, Aidan	4:16:38 (16,019)	
Heather, Craig	4:00:31 (12,190)	
Heathfield, Adrian	3:53:23 (10,103)	
Heatley, Gareth	5:03:07 (26,766)	
Heaton, David	3:54:48 (10,541)	
Heaton, David	3:57:38 (11,406)	
Heaton, Martin	3:58:00 (11,508)	
Heaton Armstrong, Alistair	3:55:00 (10,596)	
Heaton-Ellis, David	4:48:51 (24,206)	
Heaven, Chris	4:30:24 (19,693)	
Heaver, Donald	3:36:28 (6,020)	
Heaver, Matthew	6:04:38 (31,681)	
Hebbes, David	4:05:56 (13,420)	
Hebborn, Ian	3:06:45 (1,707)	
Hebden, John	4:38:12 (21,626)	
Hebels, Niels	5:05:24 (27,077)	
Heber, Andrew	3:52:45 (9,909)	
Hebert, Thierry	4:42:16 (22,665)	
Hechinger, Robert	3:26:49 (4,296)	
Heckmann, Pierre	3:23:17 (3,693)	
Hedderman, Jamie	4:44:11 (23,104)	
Hedgecox, Richard	4:42:31 (22,730)	
Hedger, Graham	2:59:04 (1,100)	
Hedgley, Adrian	4:41:35 (22,491)	
Hedley, David	4:42:24 (22,698)	
Hedley, Don	4:45:49 (23,520)	
Hedmann, Lindsay	4:00:15 (12,143)	
Heel, Robin	5:01:07 (26,467)	
Heeley, David	4:16:47 (16,060)	
Heeley, Peter	5:04:45 (26,987)	
Heeney, Roy	3:47:42 (8,562)	
Heer, Balbir	5:15:10 (28,317)	
Heer, Hermaish	4:45:33 (23,454)	
Heeren, John	4:11:34 (14,759)	
Heeringa, Ronald	3:24:21 (3,893)	
Heffernan, Terry	3:56:01 (10,902)	
Hegarty, Damian	4:52:44 (24,920)	
Hegarty, George	3:54:52 (10,562)	
Hegarty, Martin	3:59:35 (11,962)	
Hegarty, Paul	4:28:13 (19,088)	
Hegarty, Shawn	5:16:58 (28,551)	
Hehir, Gerard	3:28:38 (4,631)	
Heidler, Gerd-Michael	3:58:34 (11,664)	
Heimolainen, Patrik	4:06:22 (13,536)	
Heine, Carl	3:26:47 (4,290)	
Heinen, Dale	3:13:01 (2,434)	
Heinrich, Andreas	3:31:57 (5,178)	
Heissig, Andrew	4:18:29 (16,482)	
Hellen, Richard	4:58:21 (26,005)	
Heller, Douglas	3:46:08 (8,189)	
Helleux, André	3:06:26 (1,676)	
Hellin, Jonathan	3:56:50 (11,149)	
Hellin, Stany	4:03:12 (12,813)	
Hellings, Christopher	4:01:04 (12,330)	
Helliwell, Simon	3:36:39 (6,049)	
Helm, David	4:32:17 (20,157)	
Helmbold, Laurent	3:30:46 (4,985)	
Helmer, Jamie	3:24:09 (3,848)	
Helmer, Joerg	5:19:55 (28,861)	
Helyar, Robert	5:31:55 (29,946)	
Hemingway, Wayne	3:22:47 (3,632)	
Hemley, Dale	2:59:25 (1,126)	
Hemming, Graham	3:43:25 (7,502)	
Hemming, Martin	3:48:29 (8,744)	
Hemming, Norman	3:48:44 (8,822)	
Hemmings, Adam	4:24:49 (18,205)	
Hemmings, Andrew	2:56:46 (897)	
Hemmings, Lance	2:43:34 (256)	

Hemmings, Neil	3:58:00 (11,508)	Hermann, Udo	5:10:35 (27,761)	Hickmott, Patrick	4:29:14 (19,394)
Hemmings, Stephen	4:39:47 (22,051)	Hermsen, Mark	3:55:14 (10,675)	Hicks, Alan	3:38:40 (6,468)
Hemmings, Stuart	3:57:55 (11,480)	Hern, John	4:47:37 (23,930)	Hicks, Andy	4:41:05 (22,371)
Hemmington, James	4:44:48 (23,249)	Hernandez, Ruben	4:49:02 (24,242)	Hicks, David	3:49:24 (9,005)
Hemmington, Richard	4:27:49 (18,987)	Herne, David	3:07:01 (1,737)	Hicks, Jamie	4:43:37 (22,980)
Hempstead, Charles	4:24:25 (18,094)	Heron, Alex	3:04:58 (1,540)	Hicks, Kevin	4:02:31 (12,659)
Hemsley, Colin	3:38:32 (6,436)	Herren, Nicholas	2:45:26 (308)	Hicks, Lee	4:26:27 (18,637)
Hemson, Robert	5:45:37 (30,916)	Herring, David	4:44:33 (23,190)	Hicks, Stephen	3:03:16 (1,401)
Hemsworth, Kieran	4:59:33 (26,234)	Herring, James	4:33:19 (20,423)	Hicks, Thomas	4:22:05 (17,419)
Hemus, Clive	3:26:09 (4,174)	Herring, Ray	3:27:47 (4,474)	Hidalgo, Patrick	3:57:12 (11,263)
Hemy, Vaughan	2:57:41 (979)	Herring, Simon	4:07:29 (13,793)	Hiddleston, Mark	3:05:16 (1,563)
Henchie, Richard	4:19:08 (16,627)	Herrington, Kevin	5:59:20 (31,526)	Hide, Philip	3:07:36 (1,778)
Hender, Justin	3:42:56 (7,366)	Herriot, Nicholas	4:43:26 (22,940)	Hiest, Daniel	4:52:02 (24,787)
Hender, Nicholas	3:28:25 (4,591)	Hertenstein, Bernd	4:09:26 (14,261)	Higdon, Simon	3:51:38 (9,580)
Henderson, Angus	3:02:44 (1,353)	Hertz, David	4:19:55 (16,840)	Higgins, Alastair	3:44:20 (7,753)
Henderson, Angus	3:23:55 (3,803)	Herzmark, Adrian	3:59:30 (11,938)	Higgins, Andrew	3:31:21 (5,085)
Henderson, Billy	3:44:39 (7,837)	Hesketh, Benjamin	4:47:47 (23,971)	Higgins, Ben	4:14:13 (15,368)
Henderson, Colin	4:11:53 (14,831)	Hesketh, Tony	3:08:34 (1,877)	Higgins, Bernard	3:25:38 (4,090)
Henderson, David	4:21:27 (17,232)	Hesler, Ian	3:53:55 (10,283)	Higgins, David	3:36:05 (5,924)
Henderson, Gordon	4:07:11 (13,718)	Hesling, Peter	5:13:27 (28,133)	Higgins, Eamonn	5:18:24 (28,716)
Henderson, Ian	4:35:54 (21,049)	Heslop, Alan	3:44:38 (7,831)	Higgins, Gareth	4:01:02 (12,319)
Henderson, James	3:58:46 (11,722)	Heslop, John	7:32:13 (32,798)	Higgins, John	3:46:06 (8,182)
Henderson, James	4:30:54 (19,808)	Heslop, Ronald	3:34:25 (5,602)	Higgins, John	3:46:08 (8,189)
Henderson, Jim	4:00:35 (12,203)	Hesp, Robert	2:56:56 (908)	Higgins, John	4:18:18 (16,439)
Henderson, Mark	4:08:21 (13,976)	Hess, Claus	3:52:14 (9,762)	Higgins, Mark	4:39:07 (21,877)
Henderson, Martin	4:57:42 (25,898)	Hession, Darren	4:11:19 (14,696)	Higgins, Matthew	5:11:26 (27,877)
Henderson, Nicholas	3:24:06 (3,837)	Hester, André	4:21:39 (17,297)	Higgins, Michael	3:13:38 (2,519)
Henderson, Steven	5:05:14 (27,048)	Hester, David	3:55:21 (10,713)	Higgins, Ryan	4:10:13 (14,440)
Henderson, Stuart	3:47:20 (8,467)	Hester, Liam	3:19:22 (3,181)	Higgins, Shaun	4:28:35 (19,187)
Hendicott, John	3:51:56 (9,657)	Hester, Mark	3:57:36 (11,396)	Higgins, Stuart	5:11:23 (27,866)
Hendon, Bruce	3:32:57 (5,346)	Heuchert, Dirk	3:48:02 (8,634)	Higgins, Thomas	4:50:09 (24,448)
Hendrick, Paul	3:29:55 (4,860)	Hewes, Colin	3:56:21 (11,003)	Higgins, Vincent	3:47:05 (8,405)
Hendrikx, Antoine	4:30:48 (19,785)	Hewetson, Edward	4:19:28 (16,713)	Higginson, Martin	3:58:27 (11,635)
Hendry, Andrew	5:13:56 (28,180)	Hewett, Alan	4:05:31 (13,329)	Higglesden, Matthew	3:44:47 (7,884)
Hendry, Neil	3:50:34 (9,314)	Hewett, Tim	3:53:06 (10,018)	Higgs, Martin	3:48:56 (8,875)
Hendry, Philip	4:06:03 (13,445)	Hewison, Matt	4:26:57 (18,775)	High, Charles	4:33:04 (20,370)
Hendy, Mike	4:49:00 (24,234)	Hewison, Philip	4:08:14 (13,957)	Highfield, Colin	3:56:46 (11,131)
Hendy, Paul	4:01:01 (12,314)	Hewitson, Robert	3:49:30 (9,041)	Higho, Allen	4:02:03 (12,568)
Hendy, Peter	3:53:50 (10,261)	Hewitt, Antony	5:42:34 (30,730)	Higson, Gary	4:07:42 (13,842)
Henfrey, Philip	4:27:18 (18,864)	Hewitt, Clive	3:40:35 (6,872)	Higson, Rennie	3:35:04 (5,722)
Henkel, André	3:09:25 (1,983)	Hewitt, David	4:42:35 (22,744)	Higton, Mark	3:56:45 (11,128)
Henley, Wayne	3:10:01 (2,044)	Hewitt, Dennis	6:15:38 (31,970)	Hilal, Tariq	5:09:06 (27,583)
Henn, Heinz	3:21:31 (3,438)	Hewitt, Graham	3:40:24 (6,833)	Hilberdinu, Willem	5:03:07 (26,766)
Hennah, Richard	5:10:47 (27,782)	Hewitt, Ian	3:57:20 (11,302)	Hilborne, Steve	3:09:20 (1,973)
Hennell, Martin	5:04:10 (26,912)	Hewitt, John	3:13:28 (2,501)	Hildage, Justin	4:47:42 (23,955)
Henness, Mark	4:43:17 (22,905)	Hewitt, Michael	4:20:33 (17,006)	Hilderbrand, Bruce	4:06:20 (13,524)
Hennessey, David	3:43:31 (7,533)	Hewitt, Phil	3:56:24 (11,017)	Hilditch, Steven	2:53:42 (665)
Hennessy, James	4:03:20 (12,841)	Hewitt, Simon	3:11:05 (2,166)	Hildreth, Jan	4:41:16 (22,418)
Hennessy, Nick	4:24:41 (18,167)	Hewlett, Mark	3:31:38 (5,135)	Hildyard, Michael	3:25:04 (3,999)
Hennessy, Tony	3:51:15 (9,487)	Hewlitt, Rob	3:09:19 (1,970)	Hiles, Stephen	6:11:21 (31,866)
Henry, Martin	3:58:13 (11,571)	Hewson, Alistair	3:43:38 (7,559)	Hiley, Keith	3:53:11 (10,040)
Henry, Michael	5:53:01 (31,277)	Hewson, Tony	4:10:55 (14,612)	Hill, Adrian	3:39:26 (6,610)
Henry, Simon	3:23:40 (3,755)	Hexley, Gary	4:53:04 (24,988)	Hill, Alistair	3:54:22 (10,417)
Henry, Stephen	4:28:16 (19,102)	Hey, James	3:25:10 (4,009)	Hill, Anthony	3:03:10 (1,385)
Henshall, David	5:33:04 (30,030)	Heyden, Andrew	3:01:05 (1,232)	Hill, Barrie	4:09:08 (14,160)
Henshall, Richard	4:51:47 (24,741)	Heyes, Colin	4:09:41 (14,313)	Hill, Brian	5:43:55 (30,812)
Henshall, Tim	4:15:28 (15,684)	Heyes, Peter	3:29:09 (4,720)	Hill, Christopher	4:20:46 (17,061)
Henshaw, Gary	3:54:58 (10,586)	Heyward, Daniel	3:22:37 (3,596)	Hill, Christopher	5:27:56 (29,612)
Henson, Russell	5:05:21 (27,071)	Heywood, Kevin	2:58:35 (1,056)	Hill, Daniel	3:34:37 (5,641)
Henson, Stuart	4:31:16 (19,892)	Heywood, Mark	3:47:26 (8,494)	Hill, Dave	3:16:14 (2,812)
Henwood, Simon	4:24:12 (18,037)	Heywood, Paul	4:23:43 (17,893)	Hill, Fraser	3:09:30 (1,989)
Heppell, Duncan	5:17:47 (28,649)	Hibberd, Richard	3:26:37 (4,252)	Hill, Graham	4:09:33 (14,281)
Heppenstall, Robert	3:27:41 (4,455)	Hibberd, Roy	3:53:48 (10,249)	Hill, Ian	4:12:54 (15,062)
Hepples, Norman	4:18:36 (16,513)	Hibbert, Andrew	4:00:34 (12,200)	Hill, Ian	4:42:58 (22,894)
Hepworth, Ian	3:29:36 (4,813)	Hibbert, Christopher	4:55:29 (25,477)	Hill, Ivan	4:21:53 (17,363)
Hepworth, Jeremy	3:37:44 (6,271)	Hibbert, Grant	3:48:43 (8,816)	Hill, Jason	3:54:24 (10,427)
Hepworth, Kevin	5:12:27 (28,020)	Hibbert, Paul	5:35:34 (30,236)	Hill, Jeremy	5:24:27 (29,320)
Hepworth, Richard	4:06:53 (13,645)	Hick, Martin	5:01:47 (26,568)	Hill, John	5:39:04 (30,475)
Herbert, Adam	3:33:45 (5,465)	Hickey, Barry	3:35:23 (5,778)	Hill, Justin	3:11:33 (2,211)
Herbert, Alex	4:01:42 (12,493)	Hickey, Colm	4:01:12 (12,365)	Hill, Keith	2:56:48 (902)
Herbert, Brendan	4:49:42 (24,361)	Hickey, Graham	5:45:29 (30,909)	Hill, Kenneth	3:07:35 (1,774)
Herbert, Chris	3:13:03 (2,441)	Hickey, Patrick	5:17:26 (28,620)	Hill, Leslie	3:26:05 (4,161)
Herbert, Neil	3:10:09 (2,052)	Hickie, Stephen	3:32:20 (5,237)	Hill, Malcolm	4:52:30 (24,877)
Herbert, Paul	4:40:35 (22,252)	Hickish, Angus	3:37:29 (6,211)	Hill, Mark	2:46:37 (344)
Herbert, Raymond	4:40:06 (22,137)	Hickish, Tamas	2:56:00 (829)	Hill, Mark	3:16:35 (2,851)
Herbert, Stephen	3:18:08 (3,028)	Hickling, Gary	4:03:57 (12,976)	Hill, Mark	4:38:56 (21,827)
Herchet, Robert	3:57:57 (11,491)	Hickling, Graham	3:58:45 (11,718)	Hill, Matthew	4:16:58 (16,108)
Herdman, Dominic	5:35:17 (30,207)	Hickman, James	4:14:34 (15,460)	Hill, Michael	3:39:44 (6,676)
Herledant, Jean	3:58:53 (11,757)	Hickman, Matthew	5:41:45 (30,668)	Hill, Miguel	4:14:19 (15,398)
Herman, Keith	4:02:11 (12,595)	Hickman, Mitchell	5:01:31 (26,527)	Hill, Peter	3:26:32 (4,238)
Herman, Mark	4:47:26 (23,904)	Hickman, Reginald	6:13:06 (31,910)	Hill, Peter	4:46:27 (23,680)
Hermann, Josef	4:25:35 (18,410)	Hickman, Stephen	4:06:42 (13,614)	Hill, Raymond	3:12:04 (2,284)
Hermann, Raiver	3:34:36 (5,636)	Hickman, Stephen	5:18:24 (28,716)	Hill, Richard	4:09:08 (14,160)

Hill, Richard	4:19:51 (16,821)	
Hill, Richard	4:41:34 (22,487)	
Hill, Robert	4:52:25 (24,861)	
Hill, Roger	3:10:32 (2,108)	
Hill, Simon	4:40:44 (22,286)	
Hill, Stephen	4:08:02 (13,923)	
Hill, Steve	3:21:35 (3,452)	
Hill, Steve	3:56:47 (11,138)	
Hill, Stewart	5:26:39 (29,501)	
Hill, Stuart	3:30:21 (4,920)	
Hill, Stuart	4:19:34 (16,741)	
Hill, Thomas	7:04:10 (32,664)	
Hill, Tim	3:19:56 (3,248)	
Hill, Tim	4:09:02 (14,140)	
Hill, Tim	4:38:13 (21,631)	
Hill, Tom	3:16:21 (2,825)	
Hill, Tom	4:28:25 (19,142)	
Hill, Walter	2:53:40 (663)	
Hill, William	4:56:19 (25,658)	
Hillan, Alex	3:56:47 (11,138)	
Hillary, Ian	5:56:53 (31,442)	
Hillary, Thomas	5:18:25 (28,720)	
Hilliard, James	3:46:05 (8,178)	
Hillier, Jeffrey	5:49:11 (31,108)	
Hillier, Neil	3:57:51 (11,464)	
Hillier, Noel	3:46:23 (8,246)	
Hillier, Stephen	4:07:17 (13,743)	
Hillman, Christopher	4:00:13 (12,137)	
Hillman, David	4:45:32 (23,449)	
Hills, Christopher	8:48:55 (32,885)	
Hills, Peter	4:50:47 (24,556)	
Hills, Steven	4:28:25 (19,142)	
Hillson, Martin	4:00:41 (12,220)	
Hilsow, Alan	5:42:33 (30,729)	
Hilton, James	3:23:26 (3,713)	
Hilton, Leonard	3:39:09 (6,557)	
Hilton, Martin	2:20:53 (22)	
Hilton, Peter	5:23:38 (29,240)	
Hilton, Steve	2:54:12 (690)	
Hinchcliffe, Alan	6:06:52 (31,755)	
Hinchcliffe, Glynn	4:30:21 (19,681)	
Hinchcliffe, Simon	4:30:21 (19,681)	
Hincks, Alexander	4:51:06 (24,629)	
Hind, Nick	5:10:11 (27,715)	
Hinde, Martin	4:37:07 (21,339)	
Hindell, James	3:47:11 (8,433)	
Hindle, Barry	2:52:39 (605)	
Hindle, Richard	4:01:42 (12,493)	
Hindle, Robert	4:17:35 (16,265)	
Hindley, Jon	5:19:01 (28,779)	
Hindmarch, Andrew	4:45:05 (23,328)	
Hindmarch, Nick	4:37:35 (21,466)	
Hinds, Carlos	5:25:33 (29,406)	
Hinds, John	4:31:20 (19,912)	
Hindson, Paul	5:18:11 (28,689)	
Hine, Frank	5:15:31 (28,367)	
Hines, David	4:30:42 (19,755)	
Hing, Dennis	4:57:05 (25,790)	
Hing, Robert	4:23:39 (17,859)	
Hingston, Martin	4:31:46 (20,026)	
Hinks, Stuart	6:08:30 (31,801)	
Hinojosa-Bareas, Gregorio	3:20:31 (3,316)	
Hinshelwood, James	4:51:54 (24,766)	
Hinsley, David	3:21:46 (3,476)	
Hinson, Robert	4:28:58 (19,313)	
Hinterhoelzl, Robert	3:54:04 (10,334)	
Hinton, Geoff	3:19:23 (3,184)	
Hinton, Jeremy	4:53:05 (24,994)	
Hintze, Martin	3:31:42 (5,151)	
Hinves, Jules	3:41:50 (7,120)	
Hinze, Joern	3:34:26 (5,607)	
Hiom, Robert	4:25:43 (18,446)	
Hipkin, John	4:10:23 (14,487)	
Hipkin, Laurence	4:35:41 (21,011)	
Hircock, Geoffrey	3:35:51 (5,872)	
Hird, Frank	3:08:36 (1,881)	
Hirons, Steve	3:28:40 (4,636)	
Hirota, Naoto	4:07:01 (13,683)	
Hirschfield, Robert	5:37:14 (30,364)	
Hirshler, Gilon	3:57:32 (11,372)	
Hirshler, Jonathan	4:33:02 (20,360)	
Hirst, David	4:11:24 (14,710)	
Hirst, David	4:50:15 (24,458)	

Hirst, John	5:02:47 (26,708)	
Hirst, Karl	3:14:49 (2,641)	
Hirst, Robert	3:39:15 (6,583)	
Hirt, Stephan	3:53:22 (10,100)	
Hirtz, Bernard	3:27:17 (4,374)	
Hiscock, Graham	5:00:38 (26,393)	
Hiscox, John	3:18:12 (3,033)	
Hiscox, Trevor	3:16:47 (2,878)	
Hislop, Tim	4:27:26 (18,896)	
Hissett, Graham	4:26:16 (18,594)	
Histead, Donald	3:59:01 (11,810)	
Hita-Hita, Luis	3:12:07 (2,296)	
Hitch, Alan	4:37:23 (21,418)	
Hitch, Michael	4:54:49 (25,345)	
Hitch, Richard	4:31:31 (19,972)	
Hitch, Robin	3:37:39 (6,253)	
Hitchcock, Aaron	5:41:21 (30,643)	
Hitchcock, Ben	3:31:00 (5,028)	
Hitchcock, Ben	3:44:25 (7,778)	
Hitchcock, Jamie	4:21:21 (17,203)	
Hitchcock, Mark	4:26:03 (18,529)	
Hitchcock, William	4:37:00 (21,315)	
Hitchinson, Mark	4:01:45 (12,505)	
Hitman, Oliver	4:59:58 (26,305)	
Hivart, Pascal	4:48:22 (24,096)	
Hives, Rob	4:11:30 (14,747)	
Hizette, Laurent	2:56:15 (853)	
Hnson, Miles	4:54:17 (25,240)	
Hoad, Martin	3:56:15 (10,978)	
Hoad, Michael	3:59:20 (11,896)	
Hoadley, Nicholas	4:43:06 (22,865)	
Hoar, Andrew	4:28:17 (19,105)	
Hoare, Jeff	4:13:42 (15,232)	
Hoare, Michael	4:52:29 (24,870)	
Hoare, Nicholas	4:45:03 (23,323)	
Hoare, Paul	5:09:22 (27,620)	
Hoare, Timothy	4:45:00 (23,304)	
Hobbes, Graham	5:25:06 (29,373)	
Hobbs, Anthony	4:15:59 (15,833)	
Hobbs, Bernard	3:52:23 (9,808)	
Hobbs, Darren	4:27:31 (18,922)	
Hobbs, Derek	3:47:02 (8,390)	
Hobbs, Desmond	4:08:33 (14,041)	
Hobbs, Duncan	5:30:39 (29,838)	
Hobbs, John	4:28:50 (19,269)	
Hobbs, Mark	4:28:44 (19,236)	
Hobbs, Mark	4:37:21 (21,412)	
Hobbs, Stephen	3:26:59 (4,327)	
Hobbs, Stephen	3:51:03 (9,442)	
Hobby, Philip	4:51:06 (24,629)	
Hobson, Malcolm	3:49:59 (9,168)	
Hobson, Steve	4:38:25 (21,689)	
Hochgerner, Markus	4:16:24 (15,952)	
Hochreiter, Werner	2:43:42 (259)	
Hockenhull, Robert	3:54:10 (10,366)	
Hockey, Jason	3:59:45 (12,007)	
Hockey, Paul	4:17:35 (16,265)	
Hockin, Peter	2:29:14 (60)	
Hocking, Christopher	3:31:05 (5,043)	
Hockings Thompson, Steve	2:53:28 (654)	
Hockley, Barry	3:39:32 (6,632)	
Hockley, Stephen	3:21:47 (3,481)	
Hockmayr, Klaus	3:53:16 (10,071)	
Hoddell, David	2:56:26 (867)	
Hodenberg, Justin	4:26:02 (18,527)	
Hodey, Russell	3:12:24 (2,345)	
Hodge, Bobby	5:47:32 (31,019)	
Hodge, Carl	3:22:30 (3,581)	
Hodge, Ian	4:29:23 (19,432)	
Hodge, Nigel	2:58:09 (1,016)	
Hodge, Steve	4:47:38 (23,935)	
Hodge, Tony	2:57:31 (959)	
Hodges, Anthony	3:58:58 (11,787)	
Hodges, Christopher	5:07:13 (27,335)	
Hodges, Darren	4:15:11 (15,614)	
Hodges, Gary	4:15:11 (15,614)	
Hodges, John	3:58:44 (11,716)	
Hodges, Jonathan	4:33:29 (20,459)	
Hodges, Michael	4:28:05 (19,051)	
Hodges, Nicholas	2:57:48 (987)	
Hodges, Paul	3:40:03 (6,744)	
Hodges, Peter	3:42:04 (7,170)	
Hodges, Richard	3:50:21 (9,263)	

Hodges, Robert	3:57:26 (11,339)	
Hodges, Stephen	4:49:54 (24,407)	
Hodgins, David	3:41:49 (7,117)	
Hodgins, Joseph	4:53:43 (25,107)	
Hodgkins, Martin	3:29:28 (4,790)	
Hodgkins, Paul	4:21:25 (17,224)	
Hodgkinson, James	3:45:42 (8,090)	
Hodgkinson, Mark	3:50:07 (9,192)	
Hodgkinson, Thomas	3:51:01 (9,433)	
Hodgkiss, Brian	5:34:50 (30,171)	
Hodgson, Adrian	4:43:56 (23,051)	
Hodgson, Christopher	3:19:11 (3,158)	
Hodgson, Jeff	3:39:39 (6,657)	
Hodgson, Jonathan	4:31:06 (19,855)	
Hodgson, Julian	3:50:16 (9,242)	
Hodgson, Keith	5:34:59 (30,186)	
Hodgson, Michael	4:01:13 (12,370)	
Hodgson, Michael	4:43:44 (23,001)	
Hodgson, Paul	3:40:41 (6,892)	
Hodgson, Peter	4:07:43 (13,845)	
Hodgson, Philip	3:49:05 (8,919)	
Hodgson, Tim	5:12:40 (28,043)	
Hodgson, Timothy	3:44:46 (7,878)	
Hodgson, Tony	3:12:53 (2,415)	
Hodkinson, Adam	5:23:07 (29,189)	
Hodkinson, Matt	4:06:16 (13,509)	
Hodson, David	3:46:23 (8,246)	
Hodson, Richard	4:53:39 (25,095)	
Hoelig, Gerd	3:30:16 (4,909)	
Hoerte, Ronny	5:25:05 (29,370)	
Hoeschler, Helmut	5:24:16 (29,302)	
Hoexter, Sam	3:57:31 (11,368)	
Hoey, Anthony	4:15:29 (15,689)	
Hoey, Joe	3:44:53 (7,899)	
Hoez, Jean Luc	4:16:22 (15,938)	
Hoff, Martin	2:58:53 (1,084)	
Hoff, Svein	4:45:32 (23,449)	
Hoffman, Jonathan	5:27:31 (29,578)	
Hoffman, Stephen	3:42:46 (7,335)	
Hoffmann, Jocrq	3:48:33 (8,762)	
Hofmeister, Rainer	3:58:06 (11,544)	
Hofwolt, Daryl	4:03:22 (12,849)	
Hogan, Charles	4:23:14 (17,755)	
Hogan, James	4:26:21 (18,615)	
Hogan, James	4:40:52 (22,329)	
Hogan, John	4:27:12 (18,841)	
Hogan, Tom	3:52:52 (9,942)	
Hogarth, Stephen	2:58:45 (1,070)	
Hogben, Marcus	4:08:59 (14,127)	
Hogben, Neil	4:49:02 (24,242)	
Hogben, Peter	4:10:51 (14,592)	
Hogg, Allen	4:36:50 (21,286)	
Hogg, Richard	3:35:33 (5,811)	
Hogg, Simon	3:16:08 (2,802)	
Hoggan, Brent	3:00:22 (1,192)	
Hoggard, John	3:38:37 (6,453)	
Hogger, Chris	3:44:04 (7,669)	
Hoimeyer, Guido	4:31:08 (19,867)	
Hoiom, Runar	2:20:34 (19)	
Holberry, Miles	3:35:25 (5,785)	
Holbrook, Andy	3:32:23 (5,247)	
Holburn, James	5:00:20 (26,349)	
Holcomb, Scott	4:11:45 (14,806)	
Holcombe, John	5:09:08 (27,588)	
Holden, Ben	3:59:54 (12,057)	
Holden, Clive	4:02:00 (12,560)	
Holden, Darren	3:44:24 (7,773)	
Holden, David	3:58:47 (11,729)	
Holden, Frank	5:51:18 (31,203)	
Holden, Granville	5:47:44 (31,025)	
Holden, Mark	4:54:25 (25,267)	
Holden, Stephen	3:10:17 (2,073)	
Holden, Wayne	4:50:58 (24,604)	
Holden-Brown, Nicholas	4:05:25 (13,305)	
Holder, John	4:56:48 (25,732)	
Holder, Matthew	3:57:41 (11,419)	
Holder, Tim	4:24:47 (18,193)	
Holder, Timothy	3:44:37 (7,827)	
Holderness, Barry	3:49:34 (9,059)	
Holding, Neil	2:54:25 (703)	
Holdstock, Paul	3:09:57 (2,036)	
Holdsworth, Greg	3:52:08 (9,736)	
Holdsworth, John	3:42:00 (7,155)	

Holdsworth, Neil	2:57:58 (1,003)
Holdway, John	3:35:24 (5,781)
Hole, Chris	4:20:31 (16,994)
Hole, Mark	4:36:56 (21,305)
Holford, Timothy	4:58:01 (25,951)
Holgate, Christopher	3:48:46 (8,835)
Holgate, Paul	3:55:50 (10,850)
Holicky, Bernard	5:19:56 (28,867)
Holiday, David	4:23:02 (17,713)
Holladay, Norman	4:55:40 (25,511)
Holland, Alex	3:55:45 (10,827)
Holland, David	3:24:40 (3,938)
Holland, Graham	4:24:48 (18,198)
Holland, James	4:43:03 (22,849)
Holland, John	3:47:44 (8,569)
Holland, Kevin	3:08:55 (1,924)
Holland, Kevin	3:43:24 (7,496)
Holland, Kevin	5:00:51 (26,437)
Holland, Martin	4:35:33 (20,960)
Holland, Neil	3:54:34 (10,478)
Holland, Richard	3:31:29 (5,105)
Holland, Robert	4:11:29 (14,741)
Holland, Robert	4:20:14 (16,922)
Holland, Scot	4:46:29 (23,688)
Holland, Shane	5:20:38 (28,953)
Holland, Simon	4:46:29 (23,688)
Holland, Terence	4:02:06 (12,575)
Holland, Vincent	4:31:11 (19,877)
Hollands, Kenneth	5:28:08 (29,625)
Hollands, Neil	4:02:47 (12,725)
Hollenstein, Roger	3:50:44 (9,356)
Holleron, Les	4:24:41 (18,167)
Holley, David	4:48:12 (24,072)
Holley, Greg	5:19:54 (28,858)
Holliday, Ian	4:21:58 (17,382)
Hollier, Jeremy	4:04:53 (13,179)
Hollier, Stephen	2:54:29 (704)
Holliman, Richard	4:54:04 (25,197)
Hollingdale, Matthew	5:24:29 (29,322)
Hollingsworth, Alan	4:41:40 (22,519)
Hollingsworth, Andrew	4:23:29 (17,821)
Hollingsworth, John	2:58:19 (1,032)
Hollins, Dan	3:58:25 (11,625)
Hollinshead, Andrew	5:58:36 (31,501)
Hollis, Christopher	3:55:19 (10,701)
Hollis, Graham	4:38:08 (21,609)
Hollis, Iain	3:48:37 (8,789)
Hollis, Nigel	5:04:00 (26,889)
Hollis, Simon	4:02:50 (12,741)
Hollister, Michael	4:49:04 (24,250)
Holloran, Darren	4:38:04 (21,589)
Holloway, Adrian	4:07:54 (13,894)
Holloway, Alan	4:23:31 (17,830)
Holloway, Andrew	3:36:16 (5,969)
Holloway, Daniel	4:15:31 (15,700)
Holloway, Darren	4:53:06 (24,998)
Holloway, Jason	4:19:29 (16,720)
Holloway, John	5:37:28 (30,382)
Holloway, Mark	5:16:33 (28,507)
Holloway, Melvyn	3:10:05 (2,047)
Holloway, Patrick	5:16:57 (28,550)
Holloway, Peter	4:49:41 (24,357)
Holloway, William	6:02:47 (31,632)
Hollywood, David	3:56:58 (11,200)
Holm, Carsten	3:50:03 (9,178)
Holman, James	4:18:44 (16,530)
Holmans, Michael	4:50:40 (24,537)
Holmes, Adam	4:15:28 (15,684)
Holmes, Alexander	4:27:55 (19,011)
Holmes, Andrew	4:00:12 (12,132)
Holmes, Darren	4:37:21 (21,412)
Holmes, David	4:55:20 (25,443)
Holmes, Francis	3:01:09 (1,241)
Holmes, Gary	3:38:32 (6,436)
Holmes, Graham	3:29:12 (4,727)
Holmes, Ian	3:32:02 (5,196)
Holmes, Jamie	4:10:46 (14,566)
Holmes, Lawrie	4:29:10 (19,373)
Holmes, Malcolm	5:02:26 (26,658)
Holmes, Mark	4:55:19 (25,442)
Holmes, Mike	2:49:02 (447)
Holmes, Paul	4:08:30 (14,021)
Holmes, Peter	3:58:58 (11,787)

Holmes, Richard	3:12:41 (2,385)
Holmes, Robert	3:26:05 (4,161)
Holmes, Stanley	5:23:34 (29,229)
Holmes, Stephen	4:22:00 (17,393)
Holmes, Steven	3:34:46 (5,668)
Holmes, Terry	4:38:34 (21,727)
Holmes, Warren	3:51:57 (9,671)
Holmquist, Edwin	3:19:19 (3,173)
Holness, Stuart	4:59:36 (26,243)
Holopainen, Pekka	4:25:55 (18,493)
Holpin, Stuart	5:46:08 (30,941)
Holroyd, John	4:19:37 (16,754)
Holst, Martin	3:51:48 (9,624)
Holt, Alan	3:29:46 (4,838)
Holt, Jared	5:08:45 (27,530)
Holt, John	4:28:39 (19,212)
Holt, Keith	2:58:45 (1,070)
Holt, Richard	3:50:42 (9,347)
Holt, Robin	4:15:39 (15,739)
Holt, Simon	4:28:18 (19,109)
Holt, Spencer	4:09:30 (14,270)
Holt, Tim	4:37:12 (21,370)
Holt, Tony	3:18:15 (3,039)
Holton, John	3:57:02 (11,220)
Holtzer, Anthony	4:32:24 (20,188)
Holwill, Derek	3:40:44 (6,900)
Holyday, Mark	3:28:26 (4,594)
Holz, Bernaard	4:21:40 (17,305)
Home, Steven	3:10:12 (2,063)
Homer, Scott	5:35:30 (30,230)
Homma, Hisashi	4:09:24 (14,254)
Hone, Andrew	4:22:02 (17,405)
Honey, Richard	5:07:00 (27,295)
Honeychurch, Jamie	5:00:36 (26,388)
Hood, Christopher	3:30:17 (4,912)
Hood, Mike	3:02:14 (1,316)
Hood, Ray	3:19:44 (3,227)
Hoodless, Robert	3:32:42 (5,306)
Hoogelander, Nico	4:15:04 (15,590)
Hook, Alan	4:19:25 (16,697)
Hook, David	3:29:58 (4,867)
Hook, Trevor	2:57:14 (932)
Hooker, Andrew	3:56:14 (10,975)
Hooker, Jonathan	4:53:52 (25,136)
Hookins, Julian	3:48:39 (8,799)
Hoole, Philip	3:13:05 (2,444)
Hooley, Paul	3:52:50 (9,933)
Hooper, Ashley	4:30:23 (19,690)
Hooper, Barnaby	3:41:02 (6,973)
Hooper, Gareth	4:09:59 (14,380)
Hooper, John	5:00:52 (26,438)
Hooper, Martin	3:47:21 (8,472)
Hooper, Michael	4:28:15 (19,099)
Hooper, Michael	4:42:28 (22,714)
Hooper, Paul	3:47:45 (8,577)
Hooper, Paul	3:51:15 (9,487)
Hooper, Philip	3:11:46 (2,240)
Hooper, Steven	2:53:21 (647)
Hooper, Tony	3:32:43 (5,307)
Hooton, David	3:27:12 (4,361)
Hooton, James	4:19:10 (16,636)
Hooton, Michael	5:43:18 (30,775)
Hooton, Nigel	4:00:23 (12,163)
Hoover, Roderick	3:47:47 (8,584)
Hopcraft, Andrew	4:41:32 (22,481)
Hope, Christopher	3:26:26 (4,217)
Hope, Jonathan	3:13:25 (2,494)
Hope, Lee	6:19:54 (32,080)
Hope, Richard	4:17:13 (16,176)
Hopes, Timothy	4:29:36 (19,482)
Hopgood, Martin	4:30:06 (19,627)
Hopkins, Graham	5:08:03 (27,440)
Hopkins, Graham	5:43:03 (30,758)
Hopkins, Greg	3:52:30 (9,838)
Hopkins, James	3:27:29 (4,415)
Hopkins, Kevin	4:20:47 (17,066)
Hopkins, Kevin	7:41:51 (32,827)
Hopkins, Lee	3:51:30 (9,543)
Hopkins, Martin	4:15:55 (15,816)
Hopkins, Michael	3:44:34 (7,813)
Hopkins, Peter	5:04:01 (26,890)
Hopkins, Simon	3:56:52 (11,165)
Hopkins, Stuart	5:22:44 (29,155)

Hopley, Peter	3:11:45 (2,237)
Hopper, Andrew	4:13:08 (15,109)
Hopperton, Edward	3:27:05 (4,344)
Hopperton, James	3:42:08 (7,186)
Hopps, Peter	3:15:17 (2,699)
Hopwood, Simon	3:51:59 (9,678)
Horan, John	3:55:47 (10,835)
Horan, Philip	4:12:38 (15,005)
Hordell, Peter	5:58:32 (31,499)
Horder, Kevin	3:59:36 (11,969)
Horetti, Filippo	5:04:13 (26,919)
Horler, David	4:07:23 (13,771)
Horn, Derek	3:06:04 (1,647)
Horn, Peter	4:52:44 (24,920)
Horn, Steven	4:37:10 (21,355)
Hornall, Alex	6:28:54 (32,256)
Hornby, Keith	4:46:12 (23,623)
Hornby, Philip	4:16:12 (15,891)
Horne, Bernard	4:17:14 (16,179)
Horne, Jason	3:40:11 (6,779)
Hornegold, John	4:53:22 (25,044)
Horner, Justin	3:55:51 (10,855)
Horner, Liam	3:34:26 (5,607)
Horner, Michael	3:09:03 (1,937)
Horner, Robin	3:52:10 (9,744)
Hornsby, Danny	4:26:26 (18,631)
Hornsby, Richard	4:43:13 (22,890)
Hornsey, Paul	4:35:45 (21,020)
Horrell, Peter	4:01:01 (12,314)
Horrex, Stuart	4:46:29 (23,688)
Horridge, Dean	4:42:05 (22,629)
Horridge, Mark	4:32:18 (20,161)
Horrox, Mark	5:17:06 (28,577)
Horsefield, Robin	4:38:36 (21,742)
Horsell, Edwin	3:35:42 (5,846)
Horsfall, Christopher	3:09:31 (1,992)
Horsfall, Mark	4:37:38 (21,474)
Horsfall-Turner, Ivan	2:55:01 (743)
Horsley, Andrew	4:37:26 (21,434)
Horsley, Graham	3:15:14 (2,692)
Horsley, Paul	3:44:11 (7,707)
Horsman, Gary	4:13:44 (15,248)
Horsman, Joseph	3:26:10 (4,181)
Horsthuis, John	3:40:55 (6,944)
Horstschaefer, Michael	3:08:26 (1,857)
Horton, Andrew	3:50:12 (9,215)
Horton, Christopher	3:38:20 (6,381)
Horton, John	3:17:44 (2,982)
Horton, John	4:58:36 (26,055)
Horton, Martyn	5:24:55 (29,359)
Horton, Peter	3:03:10 (1,385)
Horton, Peter	4:40:40 (22,268)
Horton, Richard	4:17:34 (16,259)
Horton, Richard	5:37:54 (30,407)
Horton, Tod	3:37:56 (6,300)
Horvath, Paul	2:55:09 (754)
Horwood, Mike	3:17:05 (2,912)
Hosey, Richard	3:31:46 (5,162)
Hoshino, Takateru	5:27:08 (29,534)
Hoskin, David	2:49:36 (467)
Hoskings, Paul	4:01:02 (12,319)
Hossain, Syed	5:31:08 (29,882)
Hotchkiss, David	4:20:19 (16,948)
Hotchkiss, Paul	3:24:55 (3,975)
Houchell, David	5:59:45 (31,536)
Houden, Jon	3:29:17 (4,744)
Hough, Andrew	2:49:06 (451)
Hough, Barry	4:09:30 (14,270)
Hough, David	5:50:25 (31,157)
Hough, Martin	3:36:22 (5,996)
Hough, Stephen	4:19:01 (16,597)
Houghton, Anthony	4:42:39 (22,758)
Houghton, Benjamin	4:03:45 (12,928)
Houghton, David	4:27:01 (18,792)
Houghton, Mark	6:17:12 (32,010)
Houghton, Peter	5:47:05 (30,992)
Houghton, Philip	4:18:27 (16,476)
Houghton, Rick	3:04:48 (1,524)
Houghton, Toby	3:16:22 (2,828)
Houghton, Tony	3:52:46 (9,916)
Houing, Peter	4:23:58 (17,965)
Hoult, Colin	4:11:59 (14,859)
Hoult, Michael	3:49:02 (8,906)

Houlton, Nicholas 3:18:25 (3,059)
Hounsell, David 4:13:21 (15,155)
Houquet, Patrick 4:15:34 (15,712)
House, Andrew 3:11:55 (2,259)
House, David 5:06:36 (27,244)
House, Kenneth 6:33:19 (32,326)
House, Richard 3:51:26 (9,528)
Housego, Stephen 5:26:30 (29,491)
Houseman, Paul 5:01:36 (26,544)
Housley, Alex 3:50:49 (9,379)
Housley, David 4:21:17 (17,186)
Houson, Neil 4:17:16 (16,192)
Houston, Charles 3:58:37 (11,684)
Houston, James 5:13:30 (28,140)
Houston, John 4:51:10 (24,643)
Houtby, John 4:05:32 (13,335)
How, Christopher 4:37:16 (21,394)
How, David 4:17:44 (16,304)
How, Michael 5:20:28 (28,934)
Howard, Andrew 3:40:49 (6,923)
Howard, Charles 4:49:04 (24,250)
Howard, Christopher 3:30:24 (4,933)
Howard, Colin 4:08:42 (14,079)
Howard, David 3:21:48 (3,483)
Howard, David 3:55:15 (10,679)
Howard, David 4:42:38 (22,755)
Howard, George 7:13:04 (32,724)
Howard, Ian 3:34:02 (5,524)
Howard, Ivor 3:09:47 (2,015)
Howard, John 4:40:24 (22,216)
Howard, Mark 4:34:34 (20,714)
Howard, Martin 5:39:42 (30,530)
Howard, Michael 2:59:06 (1,103)
Howard, Michael 4:25:19 (18,341)
Howard, Paul 3:20:49 (3,346)
Howard, Peter 3:21:16 (3,402)
Howard, Peter 3:26:30 (4,228)
Howard, Philip 3:21:30 (3,436)
Howard, Richard 3:57:55 (11,480)
Howard, Roger 3:58:46 (11,722)
Howard, Stephen 3:12:47 (2,396)
Howard, Stephen 3:37:12 (6,150)
Howard, Steven 4:00:56 (12,289)
Howard, Stuart 4:10:04 (14,403)
Howarth, Peter 4:32:57 (20,345)
Howarth, Philip 3:52:27 (9,823)
Howarth, Philip 4:14:52 (15,542)
Howarth, Raymond 2:55:38 (792)
Howat, Peter 3:55:49 (10,844)
Howcroft, Tom 4:02:19 (12,619)
Howden, David 5:15:44 (28,399)
Howe, Adrian 4:08:29 (14,014)
Howe, Gary 2:59:18 (1,116)
Howe, Jacob 3:17:08 (2,916)
Howe, John 4:39:59 (22,099)
Howe, John 5:07:52 (27,419)
Howe, Mark 3:53:42 (10,208)
Howe, Martin 4:29:08 (19,361)
Howe, Michael 3:46:19 (8,229)
Howe, Peter 3:26:14 (4,193)
Howe, Robert 3:25:26 (4,051)
Howe, Scott 4:25:52 (18,475)
Howe, Stephen 3:49:43 (9,103)
Howell, Christopher 6:50:07 (32,542)
Howell, Craig 4:09:13 (14,193)
Howell, David 5:35:27 (30,220)
Howell, Gareth 4:50:51 (24,580)
Howell, Huw 3:17:54 (3,000)
Howell, James 3:41:20 (7,036)
Howell, Peter 5:18:22 (28,712)
Howell, Richard 5:27:24 (29,568)
Howell, Rob 2:38:54 (165)
Howell, Robin 3:20:46 (3,341)
Howell, Scott 2:59:38 (1,141)
Howell, Stephen 3:39:50 (6,693)
Howell, Tony 5:24:06 (29,288)
Howell-Jones, Julian 5:04:08 (26,904)
Howells, Andy 3:26:36 (4,247)
Howells, David 3:28:56 (4,690)
Howells, David 3:31:57 (5,178)
Howells, David 6:33:20 (32,327)
Howells, Malcolm 3:07:45 (1,790)
Howells, Phllip 5:20:07 (28,892)
Howells, Tony 5:17:05 (28,575)
Howes, John 3:46:45 (8,336)
Howes, Malcolm 5:09:25 (27,624)
Howes, Scott 3:50:48 (9,377)
Howes, Simon 5:27:17 (29,549)
Howes, Toby 3:55:11 (10,658)
Howes, William 3:30:30 (4,945)
Howie, Neil 4:15:35 (15,718)
Howland, Doug 3:48:00 (8,630)
Howle, Clifford 4:52:01 (24,785)
Howlett, Kevin 3:12:50 (2,407)
Howlett, Steven 4:23:15 (17,760)
Howlett, Timothy 3:51:51 (9,638)
Howorth, Craig 4:10:22 (14,479)
Howorth, Keith 3:44:44 (7,867)
Howse, Martin 4:40:44 (22,286)
Howson, Edward 5:32:22 (29,985)
Howson, Philip 4:55:15 (25,430)
Hoy, John 2:52:03 (581)
Hoy, Lane 3:49:24 (9,005)
Hoy, Stephen 4:23:59 (17,976)
Hoyle, Jonathan 3:53:59 (10,305)
Hoyle, Michael 4:26:19 (18,601)
Hoyle, Raymond 6:15:11 (31,963)
Huard, Patrick 4:29:46 (19,527)
Hubbard, David 4:04:54 (13,183)
Hubbard, Jason 4:13:24 (15,167)
Hubbard, John 3:21:28 (3,430)
Hubbard, Robert 5:02:59 (26,736)
Hubbard, Robert 6:06:05 (31,735)
Hubbard, Ross 4:09:40 (14,309)
Hubbard, Tony 3:51:07 (9,463)
Huber, Patrick 4:05:06 (13,231)
Hubner, Nick 4:54:28 (25,279)
Hubschmid, Roger 3:43:17 (7,467)
Huc, Ewan 4:35:33 (20,960)
Huchinson, Peter 3:38:14 (6,351)
Huck, Dave 2:51:02 (533)
Huck, Ernest 3:18:43 (3,101)
Huckenpahler, Robert 5:45:49 (30,925)
Huckett, Simon 3:11:11 (2,174)
Hucknall, Jon 4:38:33 (21,720)
Huckstepp, Mark 6:28:49 (32,253)
Huddart, Andrew 3:50:23 (9,274)
Hudson, Alan 3:03:33 (1,425)
Hudson, Ben 3:19:28 (3,199)
Hudson, Damian 4:25:20 (18,346)
Hudson, Darren 4:26:28 (18,642)
Hudson, Gary 3:29:44 (4,835)
Hudson, Guy 3:56:44 (11,117)
Hudson, Ian 5:03:18 (26,797)
Hudson, James 6:59:03 (32,617)
Hudson, Jeremy 4:48:11 (24,070)
Hudson, Kenneth 3:56:40 (11,101)
Hudson, Kevin 3:42:46 (7,335)
Hudson, Kevin 5:25:46 (29,426)
Hudson, Kieron 5:50:53 (31,179)
Hudson, Mark 3:10:32 (2,108)
Hudson, Michael 4:40:05 (22,129)
Hudson, Raymond 7:42:05 (32,828)
Hudson, Ronald 5:22:17 (29,115)
Hudson, Sean 3:29:52 (4,852)
Hudspith, John 3:03:02 (1,374)
Huesken, Joerg 5:02:45 (26,702)
Huey, Bryan 3:38:42 (6,475)
Huffadine, Derek 5:30:06 (29,784)
Huggins, James 3:34:50 (5,681)
Huggins, Mervyn 3:40:04 (6,752)
Hughes, Barry 4:29:52 (19,560)
Hughes, Bernard 3:35:58 (5,899)
Hughes, Billy 4:52:05 (24,796)
Hughes, Brian 5:51:18 (31,203)
Hughes, Bruce 4:43:03 (22,849)
Hughes, Carl 4:29:05 (19,344)
Hughes, Chris 3:39:12 (6,567)
Hughes, Clifford 3:27:25 (4,400)
Hughes, David 4:12:56 (15,073)
Hughes, David 4:38:32 (21,713)
Hughes, David 4:57:30 (25,856)
Hughes, David 5:28:25 (29,646)
Hughes, Gareth 4:32:31 (20,219)
Hughes, Gareth 4:49:57 (24,414)
Hughes, Glyn 3:57:59 (11,506)
Hughes, Harri 7:30:38 (32,791)
Hughes, Ian 3:25:18 (4,032)
Hughes, Ian 3:41:03 (6,977)
Hughes, James 3:54:06 (10,343)
Hughes, James 3:56:59 (11,203)
Hughes, James 5:21:35 (29,053)
Hughes, Jason 4:21:38 (17,293)
Hughes, John 4:46:07 (23,594)
Hughes, Ken 3:59:50 (12,036)
Hughes, Kenneth 4:50:34 (24,517)
Hughes, Kevin 5:30:27 (29,816)
Hughes, Kevin 5:36:25 (30,306)
Hughes, Leslie 4:23:30 (17,825)
Hughes, Malcom 3:32:33 (5,278)
Hughes, Mark 3:32:41 (5,301)
Hughes, Mark 4:57:39 (25,887)
Hughes, Martin 3:47:58 (8,620)
Hughes, Neil 4:28:51 (19,278)
Hughes, Nigel 3:56:10 (10,948)
Hughes, Patrick 3:54:43 (10,519)
Hughes, Paul 5:05:51 (27,135)
Hughes, Peter 2:48:00 (401)
Hughes, Peter 5:12:12 (27,972)
Hughes, Philip 4:06:04 (13,452)
Hughes, Richard 3:52:53 (9,945)
Hughes, Robert 4:19:24 (16,688)
Hughes, Sean 5:23:44 (29,255)
Hughes, Sion 3:53:54 (10,278)
Hughes, Stephen 3:42:53 (7,358)

Hughes, Steven 3:32:49 (5,320)

Every year my Mum used to love to watch the London Marathon. Sadly, in 1990, she died of cancer. At that time I was quite a heavy smoker and her last words to me were 'be happy and try to give up smoking, and then one day you might be able to run the London Marathon!' This I decided to do for her to raise money for the Christie Hospital in Manchester.

I have now completed 5 London Marathons, all in under 4 hours, and have loved every minute. The crowds certainly keep you going.

Hughes, Tim 4:10:56 (14,621)
Hughes, Tony 4:59:02 (26,137)
Hughes, Trevor 4:24:28 (18,110)
Hughes, Warren 3:50:37 (9,327)
Hughes, Wayne 4:34:01 (20,582)
Hughes Daeth, Paul 3:47:32 (8,519)
Hughson, Steve 4:22:24 (17,522)
Hugill, Gary 3:24:52 (3,966)
Hugill, Martyn 5:14:38 (28,266)
Huguet, Dominique 3:55:40 (10,798)
Huish, Nigel 3:52:13 (9,758)
Huizengh, Henk 4:49:20 (24,293)
Hulburd, Jack 4:39:38 (21,999)
Hulcoop, Simon 4:12:22 (14,932)
Hulcoop, Stephen 4:30:00 (19,592)
Hulett, Bruce 3:56:00 (10,897)

Hulin, Barry	5:56:34 (31,425)	Hunter, Stephen	3:30:58 (5,019)	Hyland, Anthony	3:05:03 (1,549)
Hull, Greg	2:31:55 (74)	Hunter, Stephen	3:31:02 (5,036)	Hyland, Daniel	3:21:53 (3,502)
Hull, Keith	3:10:39 (2,117)	Huntingdon, Peter	5:01:21 (26,514)	Hyland, Terence	3:06:53 (1,722)
Hull, Peter	6:01:32 (31,591)	Huntley, Ian	3:40:31 (6,856)	Hylton, Kenneth	4:43:24 (22,932)
Hull, Steven	4:40:33 (22,244)	Huntsman, Mark	5:37:26 (30,379)	Hymans, Michael	3:43:30 (7,525)
Hull, Steven	4:51:26 (24,686)	Hurchalla, Gregory	4:12:29 (14,967)	Hymers, John	3:48:43 (8,816)
Hulley, Mike	5:33:16 (30,050)	Hurcom, Melvin	4:11:12 (14,674)	Hynard, Mark	3:42:18 (7,232)
Hulme, Anthony	3:50:29 (9,297)	Hurdle, Paul	6:00:33 (31,561)	Hynes, Andrew	3:44:46 (7,878)
Hulme, Anthony	4:51:39 (24,725)	Hurley, Kevin	5:01:37 (26,548)	Hynes, John	3:24:46 (3,954)
Hulme, Michael	4:21:03 (17,127)	Hurley, Paul	5:00:27 (26,367)	Hynes, Marcellus	3:07:40 (1,783)
Hulme, Stephen	5:14:51 (28,289)	Hurley, Rupert	4:54:02 (25,188)	Hynes, Peter	3:34:39 (5,649)
Hulse, Mark	4:53:38 (25,092)	Hurley, Steve	4:03:42 (12,918)	Hynes, Simon	3:22:09 (3,544)
Human, Roy	4:55:13 (25,425)	Hurrell, Geoff	3:40:12 (6,786)	Hyoms, Mark	3:55:24 (10,721)
Humber, Matthew	4:52:51 (24,948)	Hurrell, Martin	4:24:57 (18,242)	Iball, John	4:14:27 (15,441)
Humble, Brian	4:43:02 (22,847)	Hurrell, Richard	4:56:41 (25,715)	Iball, Steve	4:27:42 (18,962)
Humby, Kevin	4:52:04 (24,791)	Hurren, John	5:33:03 (30,028)	Ibanez, Yvan	3:12:48 (2,404)
Humm, Joby	4:31:14 (19,887)	Hurren, Matthew	4:28:55 (19,294)	Ibberson, Alan	3:27:22 (4,391)
Humm, Mike	4:49:49 (24,383)	Hurst, Howard	4:59:13 (26,165)	Ibbotson, David	3:40:00 (6,733)
Hummel, Martin	3:35:53 (5,880)	Hurst, Jon	3:36:21 (5,992)	Ibrahim, Huseyin	2:34:31 (94)
Hummerson, James Edward	4:59:02 (26,137)	Hurst, Robert	4:25:18 (18,333)	Ibrahim, Sam	5:15:45 (28,402)
Hummerson, Jonathan	4:59:02 (26,137)	Hurt, Tim	4:21:39 (17,297)	Ide, Philip	3:09:13 (1,954)
Humpherston, Tor	4:48:09 (24,062)	Hurtado-Bernabe, Antonio	4:34:21 (20,658)	Idowy, Fidelis	4:35:09 (20,862)
Humphrey, Jeremy	4:11:42 (14,796)	Husain, Sadruddin	4:01:54 (12,545)	Iffland, Colin	6:05:12 (31,702)
Humphrey, Simon	4:16:38 (16,019)	Husband, Noel	3:17:58 (3,005)	Iffland, Steven	4:44:04 (23,080)
Humphrey, Stuart	4:45:24 (23,413)	Husbands, Mark	4:39:38 (21,999)	Iijima, Shigeru	4:16:04 (15,855)
Humphrey, Tom	3:38:30 (6,423)	Hussain, Azhar	6:36:46 (32,390)	Ikeda, Yoji	5:01:20 (26,508)
Humphreys, Mark	3:20:15 (3,283)	Hussain, Khasraw	5:44:54 (30,878)	Ikoli, Tandy	4:30:55 (19,813)
Humphreys, Nicholas	5:02:23 (26,652)	Hussain, Sajid	4:40:49 (22,313)	Iland, Mike	3:55:17 (10,687)
Humphreys, Steve	3:28:55 (4,684)	Hussey, Bill	3:53:04 (10,003)	Ilchshyn, Andrew	4:16:55 (16,095)
Humphries, Andrew	3:14:08 (2,568)	Hussey, Matthew	5:06:08 (27,179)	Iles, Rupert	4:04:22 (13,062)
Humphries, David	5:03:39 (26,838)	Hussey, Sean	3:53:44 (10,218)	Iles, Stephen	3:47:17 (8,454)
Humphries, John	3:44:54 (7,906)	Husseyin, Fadil	4:19:01 (16,597)	Iles, Toby	3:39:21 (6,596)
Humphries, Kevin	4:15:41 (15,750)	Husson, Philippe	4:01:46 (12,511)	Ilett, Doug	4:25:15 (18,323)
Humphries, Mervyn	4:24:47 (18,193)	Huston, Mike	5:36:23 (30,304)	Illidge, Clive	3:19:27 (3,196)
Humphries, Nicholas	4:48:09 (24,062)	Hutcheon, Keith	3:43:46 (7,591)	Illing, Paul	2:51:31 (562)
Humphries, Peter	3:35:18 (5,764)	Hutcheson, Adam	3:56:27 (11,030)	Illingworth, Colin	5:01:36 (26,544)
Humphries, Robert	4:38:55 (21,824)	Hutcheson, Christopher	4:05:10 (13,245)	Illingworth, John	4:08:19 (13,973)
Humphries, Stephen	3:52:33 (9,858)	Hutchin, Anthony	3:30:50 (4,994)	Illsley, John	5:42:19 (30,714)
Humphryes, Edmund	3:11:39 (2,222)	Hutchings, Andrew	3:26:09 (4,174)	Ilott, Martin	2:55:30 (782)
Hunger, Siegfried	2:59:05 (1,101)	Hutchings, Bryan	3:54:31 (10,463)	Ilott, Paul	4:07:48 (13,872)
Hunns, Andrew	4:59:17 (26,172)	Hutchings, Gerard	3:58:41 (11,701)	Imeri, Fadil	3:37:07 (6,137)
Hunt, Alex	5:04:17 (26,933)	Hutchins, Charles	3:47:10 (8,426)	Inaba, Akimichi	3:56:00 (10,897)
Hunt, Andrew	3:34:04 (5,533)	Hutchins, Wayne	4:15:34 (15,712)	Ince, David	3:57:09 (11,246)
Hunt, Andrew	4:56:38 (25,708)	Hutchinson, Adrian	4:50:54 (24,591)	Ince, Ian	3:24:20 (3,891)
Hunt, Anthony	4:17:31 (16,246)	Hutchinson, Brett	2:40:37 (195)	Inchley, Andrew	3:01:10 (1,242)
Hunt, Carl	4:00:44 (12,240)	Hutchinson, Chris	4:13:11 (15,118)	Inchley, Richard	3:52:30 (9,838)
Hunt, Christopher	3:04:35 (1,510)	Hutchinson, David	4:17:21 (16,215)	Inchley, Thomas	3:03:36 (1,430)
Hunt, David	3:12:13 (2,316)	Hutchinson, Deryck	4:12:15 (14,915)	Inchley, Timothy	3:02:20 (1,328)
Hunt, David	4:07:48 (13,872)	Hutchinson, Douglas	3:05:59 (1,639)	Ind, Andy	3:35:26 (5,789)
Hunt, David	4:25:09 (18,299)	Hutchinson, Mark	3:21:59 (3,520)	Inett, David	4:43:53 (23,036)
Hunt, Denzil	3:06:31 (1,688)	Hutchinson, Micheal	3:39:40 (6,659)	Ing, John	3:18:03 (3,017)
Hunt, Ian	3:17:21 (2,941)	Hutchinson, Tim	3:32:47 (5,315)	Ing, Will	4:23:49 (17,922)
Hunt, James	7:03:21 (32,663)	Hutchison, Bill	3:20:52 (3,350)	Inggall, James	4:52:47 (24,937)
Hunt, Julian	3:46:20 (8,233)	Hutchison, Mark	3:43:42 (7,574)	Ingham, Mark	3:14:51 (2,648)
Hunt, Lee	5:42:46 (30,736)	Hutchison, Robert	3:53:32 (10,157)	Ingham, Richard	4:15:55 (15,816)
Hunt, Lester	3:54:37 (10,491)	Hutchison, Ross	3:35:10 (5,744)	Ingle, Simon	4:12:25 (14,950)
Hunt, Mark	3:22:37 (3,596)	Hutchison, Tom	3:21:33 (3,448)	Ingleby, David	4:02:31 (12,659)
Hunt, Nathan	3:50:16 (9,242)	Huteson, Alwyn	4:51:05 (24,625)	Ingleby, Geoffrey	3:25:36 (4,081)
Hunt, Neil	4:11:38 (14,777)	Hutson, Alan	4:17:15 (16,187)	Inglesfield, Jonathan	3:53:18 (10,081)
Hunt, Oliver	4:15:27 (15,679)	Hutson, John	4:05:32 (13,335)	Inglis, Gary	4:31:28 (19,953)
Hunt, Phil	4:44:59 (23,297)	Hutt, Clive	3:51:14 (9,486)	Inglis, Jack	3:46:14 (8,209)
Hunt, Reuben	3:56:12 (10,964)	Hutt, Raymond	4:51:33 (24,711)	Inglis, Jon	4:31:09 (19,870)
Hunt, Richard	3:43:43 (7,580)	Hutt, Simon	4:25:27 (18,371)	Inglis, Warren	3:48:51 (8,853)
Hunt, Richard	4:26:40 (18,711)	Hutton, George	4:21:28 (17,238)	Ingoe, Phil	2:58:14 (1,027)
Hunt, Robert	4:19:18 (16,667)	Hutton, Gordon	5:57:35 (31,461)	Ingold, Alex	6:15:54 (31,979)
Hunt, Ross	4:31:32 (19,978)	Hutton, Kenneth	3:28:52 (4,673)	Ingold, Richard	6:15:54 (31,979)
Hunt, Simon	2:43:42 (259)	Hutton, Robert	4:33:55 (20,560)	Ingram, Chris	3:47:17 (8,454)
Hunt, Simon	3:07:58 (1,805)	Huws, Llion	3:21:18 (3,408)	Ingram, David	4:39:40 (22,009)
Hunt, Steve	3:05:42 (1,607)	Huwyler, Walter	4:52:57 (24,972)	Ingram, Kevin	5:04:13 (26,919)
Hunt, Stewart	4:36:28 (21,208)	Huxham, Hamilton	4:18:51 (16,558)	Ingram, Lawrence	4:35:37 (20,993)
Hunt, Terry	5:07:24 (27,357)	Huxley, Andrew	5:08:53 (27,551)	Ingram, Michael	3:46:32 (8,294)
Hunt, Tom	3:44:46 (7,878)	Huzinel, Michael	4:28:15 (19,099)	Ingram, Richard	4:33:34 (20,477)
Hunt, William	3:26:38 (4,257)	Hyams, David	4:24:10 (18,027)	Ingram, Stewart	3:58:27 (11,635)
Hunt, William	3:52:13 (9,758)	Hyams, Maurice	5:56:46 (31,435)	Ings, Ross	3:51:11 (9,479)
Hunter, Alistair	3:42:19 (7,236)	Hyatt, Gary	3:14:12 (2,577)	Inker, Gareth	4:08:51 (14,102)
Hunter, Andrew	3:50:30 (9,302)	Hyatt, Paul	5:15:33 (28,373)	Inman, Simon	4:52:24 (24,860)
Hunter, Dick	5:02:39 (26,694)	Hyde, Christopher	3:51:04 (9,447)	Innes, Duncan	4:01:17 (12,384)
Hunter, Donald	5:07:57 (27,430)	Hyde, Danny	4:50:37 (24,527)	Innes, Nyn	4:05:13 (13,258)
Hunter, Gareth	3:59:02 (11,819)	Hyde, Gordon	6:39:30 (32,431)	Innes, Richard	3:55:25 (10,727)
Hunter, James	5:29:13 (29,714)	Hyde, Nick	4:13:15 (15,134)	Innocent, Ben	5:26:00 (29,445)
Hunter, Justin	4:42:13 (22,651)	Hyde, Philip	4:19:43 (16,781)	Inns, Neil	3:26:39 (4,262)
Hunter, Martin	5:51:16 (31,202)	Hyett, Steven	5:20:22 (28,923)	Inskip, Michael	4:13:43 (15,242)
Hunter, Richard	3:10:35 (2,114)	Hylaire, Michel	3:50:56 (9,406)	Inskip, William	3:54:15 (10,386)

Instance, Kevin	3:29:28 (4,790)	
Instone, Jonathan	4:38:02 (21,578)	
Ioannou, Anthony	5:36:00 (30,271)	
Ion, Peter	3:15:22 (2,711)	
Ioni, Giampaolo	2:56:49 (903)	
Irchad, Abdelmounaim	3:31:39 (5,139)	
Ireland, Christopher	5:23:03 (29,180)	
Ireland, Gordon	5:48:30 (31,062)	
Ireland, Graham	4:02:53 (12,751)	
Ireland, Kevin	3:30:12 (4,894)	
Ireland, Peter	3:39:10 (6,559)	
Ironside, Alexander	3:06:32 (1,691)	
Irvine, Andy	4:43:07 (22,871)	
Irvine, Bill	5:02:56 (26,730)	
Irvine, Dale	4:50:01 (24,428)	
Irvine, Ian	3:38:45 (6,478)	
Irvine, James	3:53:30 (10,145)	
Irvine, Stewart	4:48:44 (24,175)	
Irvine, Stuart	3:18:42 (3,098)	
Irving, Daniel	5:01:45 (26,565)	
Irving, Geoffrey	3:29:23 (4,774)	
Irving, Gordon	4:34:35 (20,719)	
Irving, Greg	4:32:08 (20,122)	
Irving, Paul	4:25:06 (18,286)	
Irving, Roger	3:03:58 (1,462)	
Irwin, Allan	4:02:01 (12,563)	
Isaac, Bruce	4:26:34 (18,670)	
Isaac, Meirion	5:01:20 (26,508)	
Isaac, Nicholas	3:09:32 (1,993)	
Isaacs, David	3:59:24 (11,919)	
Isaacs, Graham	4:46:39 (23,724)	
Isaacs, Scott	4:52:32 (24,882)	
Iseke, Hans	3:34:22 (5,597)	
Isherwood, Christopher	4:15:07 (15,599)	
Isomora, Kabuo	4:06:56 (13,657)	
Ison, Peter	4:06:40 (13,606)	
Israel, John	6:22:30 (32,133)	
Issitt, David	3:42:05 (7,174)	
Isted, Darren	4:15:31 (15,700)	
Iszatt, Adrian	2:35:07 (99)	
Ito, Mitsugi	4:02:10 (12,588)	
Ito, Toshiyuki	4:16:48 (16,064)	
Ive, Martin	3:21:28 (3,430)	
Ivens, Gareth	4:19:28 (16,713)	
Ives, Spencer	5:34:40 (30,165)	
Ivison, Tim	5:49:27 (31,118)	
Iwanow, Jean	3:58:01 (11,517)	
Iwasawa, Toshiaki	5:09:30 (27,632)	
Izon, Neil	3:54:26 (10,439)	
Jack, Michael	3:35:42 (5,846)	
Jack, Rodney	7:39:06 (32,821)	
Jackett, Mark	2:53:11 (637)	
Jacklin, Dave	4:48:52 (24,212)	
Jackman, Dominic	4:43:53 (23,036)	
Jackman, Gavin	4:20:16 (16,932)	
Jackson, Adam	4:34:05 (20,603)	
Jackson, Alan	4:15:53 (15,804)	
Jackson, Angus	3:45:10 (7,962)	
Jackson, Aubrey	5:53:05 (31,280)	
Jackson, Carl	3:51:21 (9,511)	
Jackson, Chris	3:57:31 (11,368)	
Jackson, Chris	4:36:05 (21,098)	
Jackson, Christopher	3:11:19 (2,186)	
Jackson, Christopher	3:44:55 (7,912)	
Jackson, Cliff	4:02:25 (12,633)	
Jackson, Colin	3:13:41 (2,529)	
Jackson, David	4:07:10 (13,711)	
Jackson, David	5:17:30 (28,628)	
Jackson, Dean	3:10:18 (2,077)	
Jackson, Duncan	3:36:59 (6,114)	
Jackson, Earl	4:29:26 (19,444)	
Jackson, Garry	4:03:42 (12,918)	
Jackson, George	3:10:28 (2,095)	
Jackson, Ian	4:43:32 (22,968)	
Jackson, John	4:32:07 (20,114)	
Jackson, John	4:47:20 (23,883)	
Jackson, Leslie	3:40:20 (6,819)	
Jackson, Leslie	4:35:12 (20,881)	
Jackson, Mark	4:35:31 (20,951)	
Jackson, Martin	3:08:47 (1,906)	
Jackson, Martin	4:11:25 (14,715)	
Jackson, Martyn	3:29:21 (4,766)	
Jackson, Martyn	4:52:51 (24,948)	

Jackson, Melvyn	4:40:24 (22,216)	
Jackson, Michael	3:42:51 (7,349)	
Jackson, Mike	3:36:59 (6,114)	
Jackson, Neil	2:59:59 (1,167)	
Jackson, Neil	4:47:20 (23,883)	
Jackson, Nick	3:27:39 (4,447)	
Jackson, Nigel	3:17:14 (2,926)	
Jackson, Nigel	4:17:49 (16,329)	
Jackson, Nigel	4:44:16 (23,123)	
Jackson, Paul	3:16:09 (2,803)	
Jackson, Paul	3:49:36 (9,069)	
Jackson, Peter	3:34:59 (5,709)	
Jackson, Peter	3:54:41 (10,511)	
Jackson, Philip	3:30:45 (4,983)	
Jackson, Philip	3:33:32 (5,430)	
Jackson, Richard	4:19:50 (16,810)	
Jackson, Richard	4:24:14 (18,048)	
Jackson, Roger	3:39:25 (6,606)	
Jackson, Stephen	2:58:19 (1,032)	
Jackson, Steven	3:54:50 (10,551)	
Jackson, Terence	5:12:06 (27,965)	
Jackson, Trevor	4:14:23 (15,421)	
Jackson, Vincent	3:56:19 (10,994)	
Jackson, William	5:36:35 (30,319)	
Jacob, Andrew	3:53:59 (10,305)	
Jacob, Kevin	3:24:12 (3,861)	
Jacobs, Alan	4:52:50 (24,944)	
Jacobs, Andrew	3:14:44 (2,632)	
Jacobs, Barry	4:57:21 (25,883)	
Jacobs, Callum	4:14:59 (15,570)	
Jacobs, Julian	3:04:26 (1,499)	
Jacobs, Marcus	4:47:53 (24,002)	
Jacobs, Martin	4:08:13 (13,954)	
Jacobs, Philip	3:28:19 (4,571)	
Jacobs, Robert	2:37:38 (136)	
Jacobs, Terry	3:55:22 (10,714)	
Jacomb, Thomas	4:25:08 (18,295)	
Jacombs, James	5:08:12 (27,454)	
Jacomet, Martin	4:45:50 (23,523)	
Jacques, Richard	5:18:52 (28,759)	
Jacquin, Kenneth	3:59:23 (11,914)	
Jaeger, Falk	3:57:11 (11,256)	
Jaffe, Peter	3:19:01 (3,135)	
Jaffer, Arif	6:08:28 (31,797)	
Jaffre, Pierrick	2:42:35 (239)	
Jagger, Cristopher	4:19:06 (16,617)	
Jagger, Mark	4:50:08 (24,443)	
Jahans, Stephen	4:30:30 (19,712)	
Jahn, Matthias	3:15:19 (2,704)	
Jaines, John	4:00:59 (12,304)	
Jallal, Craig	5:03:13 (26,785)	
Jalloh, Amadu	2:51:13 (545)	
Jalloh, Ibrahim	3:12:12 (2,312)	
James, Adrian	4:33:57 (20,569)	
James, Alan	4:14:26 (15,433)	
James, Alexander	4:15:55 (15,816)	
James, Andrew	2:40:07 (183)	
James, Andrew	3:23:55 (3,803)	
James, Brian	4:38:18 (21,655)	
James, Chris	5:27:19 (29,561)	
James, Christopher	4:41:15 (22,413)	
James, Christopher	4:46:00 (23,566)	
James, Daniel	5:01:37 (26,548)	
James, David	3:31:18 (5,077)	
James, David	3:39:21 (6,596)	
James, David	3:48:05 (8,646)	
James, Gilbert	5:47:14 (30,998)	
James, Hywel	3:26:13 (4,190)	
James, Iain	4:10:30 (14,510)	
James, Ian	3:57:14 (11,274)	
James, Julian	2:55:48 (809)	
James, Keith	4:59:22 (26,190)	
James, Kevin	3:24:03 (3,831)	
James, Kevin	3:36:07 (5,940)	
James, Laurence	3:49:21 (8,985)	
James, Lee	4:50:50 (24,575)	
James, Martyn	3:51:37 (9,576)	
James, Melvyn	4:40:03 (22,120)	
James, Michael	4:30:01 (19,597)	
James, Paul	4:05:01 (13,212)	
James, Pete	3:53:48 (10,249)	
James, Philip	3:56:11 (10,957)	
James, Philippe	3:29:19 (4,757)	

James, Robert	5:41:02 (30,621)	
James, Simon	6:04:42 (31,685)	
James, Timothy	4:04:46 (13,152)	
James, Wendell	3:46:51 (8,355)	
James, William	4:22:48 (17,639)	
James, William	5:18:28 (28,723)	
James, Wyn	3:49:24 (9,005)	
James-Crook, Neal	3:31:37 (5,132)	
Jameson, Andrew	4:02:22 (12,628)	
Jameson, David	2:59:24 (1,121)	
Jameson, John	4:30:42 (19,755)	
Jameson, Paul	3:57:22 (11,307)	
Jameson, William	5:58:09 (31,478)	
Jamieson, Derek	4:34:52 (20,795)	
Jamieson, Fraser	3:00:05 (1,174)	
Jamieson, George	3:05:47 (1,614)	
Jamieson, Gordon	3:48:57 (8,881)	
Jamieson, Ian	4:33:25 (20,445)	
Jamieson, Robin	4:38:44 (21,774)	
Jamssen, Jan	3:04:23 (1,494)	
Janaway, Andrew	5:50:28 (31,159)	
Janaway, Richard	5:15:34 (28,377)	
Janaway, Stuart	5:15:34 (28,377)	
Janes, Jeremy	3:01:53 (1,292)	
Janes, Murray	3:56:28 (11,033)	
Jani, Harsh	5:15:59 (28,441)	
Janikiewicz, Stefan	3:44:40 (7,839)	
Janowski, Georges	4:11:27 (14,733)	
Jans, Ruud	4:21:22 (17,210)	
Jansen, Christian	5:17:22 (28,613)	
Jansen, first name unknown	4:16:20 (15,924)	
Jansma, Albert	3:58:38 (11,688)	
Janvier, Nicolas	2:27:00 (47)	
Jardaneh, Kamal	3:57:22 (11,307)	
Jardine, Charles	6:09:25 (31,821)	
Jardine, Howard	3:15:06 (2,676)	
Jardine, Ian	4:36:38 (21,249)	
Jarmain, Dominic	4:44:45 (23,236)	
Jarman, Brian	4:03:27 (12,873)	
Jarman, Charles	4:13:20 (15,151)	
Jarman, Ian	4:19:28 (16,713)	
Jarman, Jim	3:27:54 (4,501)	
Jarman, Jonathan	3:46:32 (8,294)	
Jarrett, David	5:17:28 (28,625)	
Jarrett, Neale	3:26:45 (4,285)	
Jarrold, Darren	3:07:39 (1,779)	
Jarvis, Andrew	3:50:15 (9,235)	
Jarvis, Bill	6:17:08 (32,008)	
Jarvis, Christopher	3:55:54 (10,872)	
Jarvis, Christopher	4:32:09 (20,129)	
Jarvis, John	3:24:43 (3,950)	
Jarvis, Jonathan	4:16:49 (16,071)	
Jarvis, Luke	3:48:43 (8,816)	
Jarvis, Mark	3:21:02 (3,371)	
Jarvis, Michael	3:28:43 (4,641)	
Jarvis, Neil	3:56:22 (11,009)	
Jarvis, Neil	4:47:48 (23,978)	
Jarvis, Nic	5:27:09 (29,535)	
Jarvis, Nigel	4:06:13 (13,496)	
Jarvis, Peter	3:33:18 (5,401)	
Jarvis, Robert	4:41:55 (22,590)	
Jary, Jonathan	4:21:54 (17,368)	
Jasnoch, Paul	3:08:02 (1,807)	
Jason, Trevor	2:56:34 (878)	
Jasper, Andrew	4:21:03 (17,127)	
Jaspers, Edward	3:42:06 (7,180)	
Jaswal, Kulbir	3:37:37 (6,246)	
Jaubert, François	4:55:23 (25,461)	
Jauncey, Lee	4:04:39 (13,123)	
Javens, Barrie	5:21:23 (29,034)	
Jeacock, Paul	4:04:44 (13,145)	
Jeal, Christopher	3:06:46 (1,709)	
Jeal, Nick	5:04:40 (26,973)	
Jeal, Stephen	4:01:46 (12,511)	
Jeeves, Brian	4:51:53 (24,760)	
Jefcoate, Simon	3:47:22 (8,480)	
Jeff, Steven	3:41:09 (7,000)	
Jefferies, Graham	5:15:03 (28,304)	
Jefferies, Michael	4:32:30 (20,215)	
Jefferies, Paul	4:15:07 (15,599)	
Jefferis, Christopher	6:05:09 (31,699)	
Jefferson, Nick	4:39:09 (21,886)	
Jeffery, Andrew	3:38:30 (6,423)	

Jeffery, Ben	4:31:56 (20,066)	
Jeffery, Colin	4:29:31 (19,460)	
Jeffery, Graham	5:04:08 (26,904)	
Jeffery, James	4:01:29 (12,437)	
Jeffery, Peter	4:48:07 (24,058)	
Jeffery, Sheridan	5:19:43 (28,841)	
Jefford, Andrew	4:00:23 (12,163)	
Jefford, Mark	3:09:15 (1,960)	
Jeffrey, Ian	4:01:39 (12,482)	
Jeffrey, James	3:57:30 (11,365)	
Jeffrey, John	3:53:43 (10,212)	
Jeffrey, Keith	4:01:02 (12,319)	
Jeffrey, Kevin	5:05:54 (27,144)	
Jeffrey, Malcolm	5:04:01 (26,890)	
Jeffrey, Michael	3:42:27 (7,276)	
Jeffrey, Noel	4:42:44 (22,775)	
Jeffrey, Peter	3:47:07 (8,409)	
Jeffries, Stacey	2:58:29 (1,046)	
Jeffries, Stuart	4:10:00 (14,385)	
Jeffs, Peter	4:06:30 (13,568)	
Jeffs, Richard	4:12:59 (15,076)	
Jeffs, Richard	4:57:55 (25,939)	
Jeffs, Stephen	3:56:10 (10,948)	
Jekyll, Paul	4:24:02 (17,990)	
Jelkeby, Peter	3:57:51 (11,464)	
Jelley, David	3:00:00 (1,170)	
Jelley, Hugh	4:25:22 (18,355)	
Jellicoe, David	3:15:16 (2,696)	
Jellis, David	4:58:57 (26,121)	
Jellows, Lawrie	4:59:41 (26,263)	
Jenei, Tamas	6:32:43 (32,317)	
Jenkin, Daniel	4:30:23 (19,690)	
Jenkin, Neil	4:15:57 (15,828)	
Jenkings, Kenneth	3:59:52 (12,046)	
Jenkins, Alun	3:48:18 (8,693)	
Jenkins, Andrew	3:11:31 (2,205)	
Jenkins, Chris	3:41:50 (7,120)	
Jenkins, Chris	3:54:38 (10,494)	
Jenkins, Christopher	3:57:03 (11,224)	
Jenkins, Clifford	4:01:17 (12,384)	
Jenkins, Colin	4:50:05 (24,437)	
Jenkins, David	5:09:20 (27,612)	
Jenkins, Dominic	3:36:06 (5,932)	
Jenkins, Harvey	4:03:58 (12,983)	
Jenkins, Ian	6:08:45 (31,806)	
Jenkins, John	4:15:12 (15,621)	
Jenkins, John	4:48:21 (24,094)	
Jenkins, John	7:32:55 (32,800)	
Jenkins, Jonathan	4:47:50 (23,986)	
Jenkins, Mark	4:09:50 (14,348)	
Jenkins, Neil	3:30:04 (4,883)	
Jenkins, Paul	3:23:30 (3,727)	
Jenkins, Paul	3:23:49 (3,772)	
Jenkins, Paul	4:13:49 (15,264)	
Jenkins, Paul	4:37:25 (21,428)	
Jenkins, Philip	4:42:21 (22,687)	
Jenkins, Richard	3:48:52 (8,859)	
Jenkins, Robert	4:22:54 (17,671)	
Jenkins, Robert	4:27:53 (19,000)	
Jenkins, Robert	4:37:48 (21,522)	
Jenkinson, Kate	4:00:52 (12,273)	
Jenkinson, Lee	3:56:37 (11,090)	
Jenkinson, Neil	4:32:24 (20,188)	
Jenkinson, Richard	3:43:17 (7,467)	
Jenkinson, Shaun	3:36:23 (6,002)	
Jenkinson, Tony	3:47:03 (8,394)	
Jenks, John	4:07:05 (13,692)	
Jenn, Dieter	5:11:43 (27,909)	
Jenner, Chris	4:10:18 (14,460)	
Jenner, Jason	3:59:32 (11,947)	
Jenner, Marc	4:56:14 (25,643)	
Jenner, Peter	7:15:05 (32,737)	
Jenner, Roger	5:11:27 (27,880)	
Jennings, Colin	5:40:04 (30,550)	
Jennings, David	4:11:00 (14,631)	
Jennings, Duncan	4:20:08 (16,896)	
Jennings, Keith	5:08:01 (27,438)	
Jennings, Mark	3:35:22 (5,772)	
Jennings, Nik	7:00:25 (32,630)	
Jennings, Paul	4:30:06 (19,627)	
Jennings, Perry	4:22:10 (17,445)	
Jennings, Ross	4:45:21 (23,393)	
Jennings, Roy	5:16:11 (28,466)	
Jennings, Steven	4:48:46 (24,182)	
Jennings, Terence	4:12:18 (14,920)	
Jennions, Chris	3:30:33 (4,952)	
Jenny, François	3:20:48 (3,345)	
Jensen, Christian	4:22:37 (17,580)	
Jensen, Jesper Hahn	3:03:23 (1,412)	
Jensen, Kurt	4:22:56 (17,682)	
Jerome, Anthony	4:08:09 (13,941)	
Jerrard, Peter	5:23:14 (29,197)	
Jerrit, Giles	6:00:25 (31,558)	
Jervis, John	4:29:39 (19,495)	
Jervis, John	5:30:22 (29,809)	
Jespersen, Benedikte	5:12:33 (28,032)	
Jess, Trevor	3:20:08 (3,270)	
Jessop, Simon	4:13:56 (15,291)	
Jessop, Tony	6:03:59 (31,662)	
Jest, Andrew	3:36:26 (6,012)	
Jetley, Luke	4:46:10 (23,613)	
Jetmani, Yogesh	5:28:58 (29,690)	
Jewell, Guy	4:24:23 (18,087)	
Jewell, Paul	2:56:01 (833)	
Jewell, Ray	5:44:08 (30,829)	
Jeynes, James	5:18:52 (28,759)	
Jeynes, Richard	4:15:36 (15,722)	
Jifar, Tesfaye	2:09:49 (9)	
Jimenez, Miguel	4:31:09 (19,870)	
Jimenez-Blanco, David	4:04:50 (13,167)	
Jinks, Steven	4:17:01 (16,121)	
Jobanputra, Sanjay	5:15:27 (28,355)	
Jobling, Jeremy	3:54:23 (10,422)	
Jobson, Pau	4:40:51 (22,322)	
Jochem, Michael	3:56:59 (11,203)	
Joejima, Kazuya	5:19:55 (28,861)	
Joel, Gareth	4:02:50 (12,741)	
Joel, Rupert	4:26:16 (18,594)	
Jogia, Sanjay	5:16:00 (28,446)	
Johansen, Paul	3:52:43 (9,897)	
Johansen-Allison, Nathanael	4:04:57 (13,197)	
Johansson, Daniel	3:02:57 (1,367)	
Johansson, Goran	3:57:16 (11,280)	
Johansson, Stig	4:20:56 (17,090)	
John, Antony	4:17:43 (16,299)	
John, Chris	7:21:52 (32,761)	
John, Christopher	4:25:42 (18,439)	
John, Daryl	4:02:17 (12,613)	
John, David	5:26:20 (29,468)	
John, Gilbert	3:35:27 (5,794)	
John, Nigel	3:17:22 (2,943)	
John, Paul	3:09:38 (2,004)	
John, Paul	4:47:33 (23,919)	
John, Peter	3:41:38 (7,087)	
Johnbeck, Djarne	3:09:33 (1,995)	
Johnes, John	5:16:18 (28,482)	
John-Lewis, Johnson	4:05:28 (13,317)	
Johns, Arthur	2:53:55 (678)	
Johns, Cedric	5:44:48 (30,875)	
Johns, Michael	4:14:47 (15,520)	
Johns, Paul	4:01:28 (12,430)	
Johns, Paul	4:52:00 (24,783)	
Johns, Peter	4:53:53 (25,141)	
Johns, Robin	4:24:02 (17,990)	
Johns, Stephen	3:19:36 (3,216)	
Johns, Tim	3:24:16 (3,870)	
Johnson, Aiden	4:22:31 (17,550)	
Johnson, Allan	4:22:06 (17,424)	
Johnson, Andrew	3:04:19 (1,489)	
Johnson, Andrew	3:40:20 (6,819)	
Johnson, Andrew	3:42:03 (7,167)	
Johnson, Andrew	4:37:20 (21,408)	
Johnson, Ben	4:11:38 (14,777)	
Johnson, Bob	3:04:12 (1,483)	
Johnson, Carl	5:32:55 (30,017)	
Johnson, Christopher	3:54:37 (10,491)	
Johnson, Christopher	4:48:18 (24,084)	
Johnson, Christopher	5:23:37 (29,236)	
Johnson, Damian	3:32:24 (5,252)	
Johnson, David	3:56:22 (11,009)	
Johnson, David	6:23:33 (32,159)	
Johnson, Dean	4:25:17 (18,330)	
Johnson, Fraser	4:28:07 (19,058)	
Johnson, Geoff	4:48:44 (24,175)	
Johnson, Glen	2:58:24 (1,038)	
Johnson, Graham	4:50:09 (24,448)	
Johnson, Graham	5:12:39 (28,041)	
Johnson, Guy	3:37:33 (6,232)	
Johnson, Guy	4:35:15 (20,895)	
Johnson, Harvey	4:37:55 (21,553)	
Johnson, Howard	3:50:13 (9,228)	
Johnson, Howard	4:07:03 (13,686)	
Johnson, Ian	2:36:05 (107)	
Johnson, Ian	4:08:16 (13,966)	
Johnson, James	4:24:11 (18,029)	
Johnson, James	5:10:07 (27,703)	
Johnson, John	3:15:42 (2,754)	
Johnson, Jonathan	4:51:11 (24,652)	
Johnson, Josph	4:50:23 (24,478)	
Johnson, Kevin	3:48:30 (8,747)	
Johnson, Kevin	5:02:03 (26,608)	
Johnson, Kevin	6:08:54 (31,810)	
Johnson, Lee	2:54:55 (736)	
Johnson, Mark	3:36:13 (5,960)	
Johnson, Mark	4:04:22 (13,062)	
Johnson, Mark	4:16:16 (15,904)	
Johnson, Nicholas	4:24:59 (18,258)	
Johnson, Nicholas	4:29:53 (19,569)	
Johnson, Paul	3:48:35 (8,773)	
Johnson, Paul	3:49:42 (9,099)	
Johnson, Paul	4:40:50 (22,316)	
Johnson, Paul	4:50:59 (24,606)	
Johnson, Pete	2:39:47 (180)	
Johnson, Peter	4:44:20 (23,138)	
Johnson, Philip	4:44:19 (23,134)	
Johnson, Ray	3:24:03 (3,831)	
Johnson, Raymond	4:26:55 (18,764)	
Johnson, Richard	2:58:50 (1,078)	
Johnson, Richard	3:45:14 (7,983)	
Johnson, Robert	4:28:30 (19,172)	
Johnson, Robert	5:07:46 (27,403)	
Johnson, Roger	4:09:46 (14,334)	
Johnson, Scott	4:09:57 (14,373)	
Johnson, Stephen	4:41:10 (22,394)	
Johnson, Walter	5:34:36 (30,158)	
Johnston, Adam	5:11:44 (27,913)	
Johnston, David	5:01:48 (26,570)	
Johnston, Gordon	4:46:25 (23,667)	
Johnston, Graham	4:09:47 (14,336)	
Johnston, Ian	4:46:05 (23,589)	
Johnston, John	4:34:01 (20,582)	
Johnston, Neil	4:41:36 (22,498)	
Johnston, Sim	3:44:53 (7,899)	
Johnston, Stephen	3:38:09 (6,332)	
Johnstone, Andrew	4:00:08 (12,115)	
Johnstone, Iain	4:03:17 (12,835)	
Johnstone, James	3:43:06 (7,410)	
Johnstone, Peter	4:02:20 (12,623)	
Jokidii, Kim	4:38:24 (21,685)	
Jokstad, Asbjoern	2:55:17 (764)	
Jolain, Bruno	4:34:02 (20,591)	
Jolley, Alastair	3:50:12 (9,215)	
Jolliff, Philip	4:47:10 (23,849)	
Jolliffe, David	4:42:55 (22,818)	
Jolly, Max	3:17:46 (2,985)	
Jolly, Nathan	3:28:55 (4,684)	
Jolly, Richard	3:45:51 (8,131)	
Joly, Rob	4:04:53 (13,179)	
Jonas, Leland	3:22:39 (3,598)	
Jones, Adrian	5:36:10 (30,288)	
Jones, Alan	3:43:39 (7,564)	
Jones, Alex	3:49:45 (9,112)	
Jones, Allen	2:46:14 (333)	
Jones, Alun	4:24:54 (18,227)	
Jones, Andrew	3:02:26 (1,335)	
Jones, Andrew	3:37:31 (6,223)	
Jones, Andrew	3:40:12 (6,786)	
Jones, Andrew	3:43:09 (7,431)	
Jones, Andrew	4:51:37 (24,721)	
Jones, Arwel	3:16:46 (2,873)	
Jones, Barry	3:26:11 (4,185)	
Jones, Barry	4:03:02 (12,782)	
Jones, Ben	3:57:49 (11,455)	
Jones, Bernard	3:36:05 (5,924)	
Jones, Bob	4:46:34 (23,706)	
Jones, Bradley	3:38:05 (6,327)	
Jones, Brian	3:47:24 (8,488)	
Jones, Brian	4:13:47 (15,258)	
Jones, Brian	4:59:01 (26,134)	

Jones, Brian	5:19:52	(28,856)
Jones, Charles	4:02:14	(12,604)
Jones, Chris	4:23:41	(17,872)
Jones, Chris	5:33:08	(30,039)
Jones, Christopher	3:40:40	(6,889)
Jones, Christopher	3:56:07	(10,937)
Jones, Christopher	4:43:37	(22,980)
Jones, Christopher	4:45:01	(23,312)
Jones, Christopher	4:58:31	(26,035)
Jones, Clive	3:36:56	(6,104)
Jones, Colin	3:25:29	(4,062)
Jones, Colin	3:30:57	(5,015)
Jones, Colin	4:06:59	(13,674)
Jones, Colin	4:33:31	(20,468)
Jones, Colwyn	4:05:27	(13,313)
Jones, Conrad	3:27:40	(4,451)
Jones, Craig	5:19:26	(28,814)
Jones, Dan	4:58:39	(26,067)
Jones, Daniel	4:03:09	(12,804)
Jones, Daniel	4:03:55	(12,968)
Jones, Darren	2:48:50	(440)
Jones, Darren	5:29:16	(29,721)
Jones, Daryl	4:28:19	(19,114)
Jones, Dave	3:47:14	(8,448)
Jones, David	3:02:30	(1,338)
Jones, David	3:03:10	(1,385)
Jones, David	3:15:45	(2,761)
Jones, David	3:48:30	(8,747)
Jones, David	4:12:15	(14,915)
Jones, David	4:23:59	(17,976)
Jones, David	4:24:52	(18,222)
Jones, David	4:47:39	(23,943)
Jones, David	5:00:38	(26,393)
Jones, Derek	3:20:35	(3,323)
Jones, Derek	3:29:13	(4,731)
Jones, Derek	3:54:06	(10,343)
Jones, Dewi	3:10:50	(2,138)
Jones, Donald	4:10:02	(14,393)
Jones, Dylan	5:47:26	(31,015)
Jones, Edwin	3:47:44	(8,569)
Jones, Eurwyn	3:39:18	(6,589)
Jones, Frank	4:25:57	(18,502)
Jones, Frank	4:33:02	(20,360)
Jones, Gareth	3:07:39	(1,779)
Jones, Gareth	3:43:14	(7,454)
Jones, Gareth	4:09:03	(14,146)
Jones, Gareth	4:18:08	(16,394)
Jones, Gareth	4:21:13	(17,168)
Jones, Gareth	4:22:41	(17,603)
Jones, Gareth	4:52:22	(24,856)
Jones, Gary	3:54:07	(10,351)
Jones, Gary	4:19:07	(16,621)
Jones, Gary	4:54:26	(25,272)
Jones, Geoffrey	3:18:11	(3,029)
Jones, George	4:35:55	(21,057)
Jones, Geraint	4:16:35	(16,002)
Jones, Glyn	3:51:29	(9,539)
Jones, Glyn	4:54:38	(25,307)
Jones, Graham	5:50:17	(31,151)
Jones, Hadyn	2:57:51	(994)
Jones, Haydn	3:04:25	(1,498)
Jones, Henry	3:49:29	(9,036)
Jones, Herbert	5:00:58	(26,447)
Jones, Horace	4:09:48	(14,344)
Jones, Howard	3:53:15	(10,061)
Jones, Ian	3:40:46	(6,913)
Jones, Ian	4:47:28	(23,907)
Jones, Ieuan	2:55:24	(773)
Jones, Irfon	3:31:01	(5,031)
Jones, James	5:20:11	(28,903)
Jones, Jeffrey	5:11:11	(27,838)
Jones, John	3:58:32	(11,657)
Jones, John	4:16:29	(15,976)
Jones, John	4:21:08	(17,151)
Jones, John	4:21:20	(17,200)
Jones, John	4:43:18	(22,909)
Jones, John	4:46:30	(23,692)
Jones, John	4:52:29	(24,870)
Jones, Jonathan	4:39:43	(22,030)
Jones, Keith	3:03:12	(1,390)
Jones, Keith	4:06:40	(13,606)
Jones, Keith	4:41:19	(22,433)
Jones, Kenneth	4:15:27	(15,679)
Jones, Kenneth	4:17:02	(16,129)
Jones, Kevin	3:09:16	(1,961)
Jones, Lee	4:28:22	(19,128)
Jones, Lee	4:50:07	(24,442)
Jones, Lloyd	3:49:29	(9,036)
Jones, Malcolm	4:09:45	(14,332)
Jones, Mark	3:36:08	(5,942)
Jones, Mark	3:40:59	(6,961)
Jones, Mark	3:43:09	(7,431)
Jones, Mark	3:58:56	(11,772)
Jones, Mark	4:16:06	(15,864)
Jones, Mark	4:25:30	(18,390)
Jones, Mark	4:43:00	(22,838)
Jones, Mark	4:56:10	(25,623)
Jones, Mark	5:13:58	(28,185)
Jones, Mark	5:28:31	(29,656)
Jones, Mark	5:40:31	(30,586)
Jones, Martin	4:02:41	(12,701)
Jones, Matthew	3:29:43	(4,829)
Jones, Matthew	4:07:14	(13,728)
Jones, Matthew	4:20:48	(17,069)
Jones, Matthew	4:58:34	(26,049)
Jones, Max	6:09:38	(31,826)
Jones, Michael	2:59:53	(1,162)
Jones, Michael	3:18:34	(3,080)
Jones, Michael	3:41:07	(6,994)
Jones, Michael	4:25:09	(18,299)
Jones, Michael	4:55:05	(25,387)
Jones, Neil	3:54:00	(10,309)
Jones, Neil	3:56:44	(11,117)
Jones, Niall	4:24:03	(17,996)
Jones, Nicholas	4:19:18	(16,667)
Jones, Nicholas	4:48:48	(24,197)
Jones, Nicholas	4:50:27	(24,496)
Jones, Nick	3:30:24	(4,933)
Jones, Nigel	3:26:28	(4,223)
Jones, Nigel	4:16:39	(16,028)
Jones, Paul	4:00:42	(12,227)
Jones, Paul	4:13:30	(15,189)
Jones, Peter	3:12:55	(2,421)
Jones, Peter	3:23:15	(3,687)
Jones, Peter	3:31:36	(5,124)
Jones, Peter	4:19:50	(16,810)
Jones, Peter	5:06:19	(27,198)
Jones, Peter	5:17:46	(28,647)
Jones, Philip	3:49:21	(8,985)
Jones, Philip	3:58:40	(11,695)
Jones, Philip	4:07:28	(13,790)
Jones, Ralph	3:50:24	(9,276)
Jones, Raymond	3:27:43	(4,459)
Jones, Rex	4:03:50	(12,952)
Jones, Rhodri	4:28:54	(19,289)
Jones, Richard	2:53:16	(640)
Jones, Richard	3:40:54	(6,940)
Jones, Richard	4:31:32	(19,978)
Jones, Richard	5:06:42	(27,259)
Jones, Richard	5:49:04	(31,103)
Jones, Robert	3:43:22	(7,491)
Jones, Robert	4:27:37	(18,941)
Jones, Robert	4:48:56	(24,225)
Jones, Robert	5:01:31	(26,527)
Jones, Robert	7:38:41	(32,820)
Jones, Robin	3:56:44	(11,117)
Jones, Rodri	2:22:54	(32)
Jones, Russell	3:10:55	(2,144)
Jones, Simon	3:16:30	(2,844)
Jones, Simon	3:50:36	(9,322)
Jones, Simon	3:53:00	(9,976)
Jones, Simon	4:15:24	(15,665)
Jones, Simon	4:41:51	(22,570)
Jones, Simon	4:52:11	(24,813)
Jones, Spencer	4:54:31	(25,289)
Jones, Stephen	3:18:00	(3,009)
Jones, Stephen	3:31:12	(5,064)
Jones, Stephen	3:36:29	(6,023)
Jones, Stephen	3:38:58	(6,515)
Jones, Stephen	3:49:25	(9,014)
Jones, Stephen	3:59:36	(11,969)
Jones, Stephen	4:22:16	(17,470)
Jones, Stephen	5:32:17	(29,977)
Jones, Stephen	6:21:54	(32,118)
Jones, Steve	4:11:57	(14,848)
Jones, Steven	3:46:32	(8,294)
Jones, Steven	5:22:09	(29,103)
Jones, Stuart	3:32:48	(5,316)
Jones, Stuart	3:59:43	(11,998)
Jones, Stuart	4:29:50	(19,551)
Jones, Stuart	6:26:26	(32,207)
Jones, Terry	4:08:17	(13,969)
Jones, Thomas	3:58:04	(11,531)
Jones, Thomas	5:34:29	(30,147)
Jones, Tim	2:54:55	(736)
Jones, Tim	3:31:45	(5,160)
Jones, Tim	4:31:44	(20,018)
Jones, Timothy	4:41:36	(22,498)
Jones, Toby	4:10:39	(14,545)
Jones, Tudur	3:56:42	(11,109)
Jones, Vince	4:29:16	(19,405)
Jones, Wyn	4:30:17	(19,669)
Jonsson, Magnus	3:15:12	(2,687)
Jooste, Pierre	4:26:36	(18,680)
Jordaan, Danie	4:14:25	(15,429)
Jordaan, Theodorus	2:50:10	(496)
Jordan, Andrew	4:16:18	(15,913)
Jordan, Andy	3:59:10	(11,845)
Jordan, Anthony	4:33:50	(20,541)
Jordan, Dean	3:34:42	(5,660)
Jordan, Gary	4:22:43	(17,614)
Jordan, Ian	3:57:31	(11,368)
Jordan, Jamie	4:09:37	(14,295)
Jordan, Matthew	4:14:17	(15,385)
Jordan, Matthew	4:35:11	(20,875)
Jordan, Michael	3:04:27	(1,501)
Jordan, Noel	4:51:32	(24,707)
Jordan, Peter	4:19:31	(16,730)
Jordan, Peter	4:41:05	(22,371)
Jordan, Philip	3:56:35	(11,078)
Jordan, Regis	3:21:36	(3,453)
Jordan, Robert	4:44:26	(23,157)
Jordan, Stephen	3:35:26	(5,789)
Jordan, Tony	4:53:27	(25,057)
Jordan, William	3:08:34	(1,877)
Jorgensen, Bo	3:33:47	(5,474)
Jory, Richard	3:23:28	(3,719)
Jose, Jemy	4:50:39	(24,531)
Josefsson, Roland	4:17:12	(16,171)
Joseph, Carl	3:44:40	(7,839)
Joseph, Ian	5:37:41	(30,399)
Joseph, Patrick	3:23:50	(3,776)
Joseph, Revanie	4:01:10	(12,356)
Joseph, Simeon	5:55:23	(31,370)
Joseph, Stephen	4:33:02	(20,360)
Josephs, Merrick	3:57:23	(11,317)
Josephs, Robin	4:44:30	(23,172)
Joshi, Kamaleshkumar	5:58:28	(31,495)
Joshi, Raj	6:27:07	(32,219)
Joslin, Alan	4:52:55	(24,963)
Joslin, Shaun	3:43:11	(7,437)
Josso, Michel	4:06:39	(13,601)
Jost, Robert	3:09:04	(1,939)
Jouan, Patrice	3:10:46	(2,131)
Joubert, André	4:40:01	(22,109)
Joubert, Daniel	4:10:09	(14,428)
Jouin, Hoann	5:47:20	(31,005)
Jowett, Jeremy	5:21:49	(29,079)
Jowett, Stephen	4:33:34	(20,477)
Joy, Chris	3:26:07	(4,169)
Joy, Peter	5:01:50	(26,572)
Joyce, Andrew	4:35:34	(20,978)
Joyce, Christopher	3:33:20	(5,406)
Joyce, Ciaran	3:43:31	(7,533)
Joyce, Dean	3:15:07	(2,677)
Joyce, John	5:55:13	(31,360)
Joyce, Michael	4:41:36	(22,498)
Joyce, Paul	3:16:26	(2,835)
Joyce, Philip	3:05:01	(1,546)
Joyce, Richad	4:55:02	(25,381)
Joyles, Philip	4:43:08	(22,876)
Joynson, Gerard	4:23:17	(17,772)
Juan, Lopez	3:14:29	(2,611)
Jubb, Chris	3:42:12	(7,201)
Jubb, Mike	2:28:08	(50)
Judd, Benjamin	4:38:01	(21,575)
Judd, Chris	5:26:09	(29,460)
Judd, John	4:30:53	(19,801)
Judge, Bruce	2:40:57	(204)

Judge, Clifford	4:57:23 (25,839)	
Judge, Gergory	3:50:10 (9,205)	
Judson, Robert	7:08:58 (32,692)	
Juergens, Rainer	3:33:47 (5,474)	
Jugadoe, Roshan	5:45:58 (30,932)	
Juignet, François	3:30:41 (4,976)	
Jukes, David	4:27:13 (18,847)	
Jukes, Frank	3:32:36 (5,289)	
Jukes, Jonathan	5:13:03 (28,086)	
Jukes, Paul	5:39:57 (30,545)	
Jukes, Paul	5:53:47 (31,304)	
Jukes, Richard	5:00:13 (26,338)	
Julien, James	5:54:56 (31,348)	
Julier, Derek	4:09:27 (14,263)	
Jummon, Arnold	3:50:22 (9,268)	
Juniper, Graham	4:57:16 (25,822)	
Jupp, Anthony	3:52:33 (9,858)	
Jupp, David	5:22:13 (29,108)	
Jupp, Keith	4:58:06 (25,964)	
Jupp MBE, Paul	4:50:43 (24,545)	
Jurgens, Werner	5:19:35 (28,827)	
Juster, Geoffrey	5:41:02 (30,621)	
Juster, Peter	4:34:28 (20,687)	
Justice, Timothy	5:09:24 (27,623)	
Kaczmarek, Zbigniew	3:19:03 (3,144)	
Kadish, Mark	4:19:55 (16,840)	
Kagdadia, Ashwin	6:51:33 (32,555)	
Kahlow, Edward	3:28:46 (4,652)	
Kaiser, Ken	3:12:11 (2,309)	
Kaiser, Kristian	3:58:02 (11,522)	
Kakoullis, Panos	3:46:07 (8,186)	
Kalar, Mark	3:12:17 (2,326)	
Kalema, Stephen	5:04:10 (26,912)	
Kalinsky, Sydney	6:48:16 (32,525)	
Kalma, Jacob	5:51:25 (31,210)	
Kalss, Reinhard	3:40:30 (6,850)	
Kaluba, Mbachi	4:53:44 (25,110)	
Kalyan, Gurcharan	7:04:46 (32,668)	
Kalynij, Raymond	3:58:24 (11,621)	
Kamil, Eren	4:38:10 (21,616)	
Kamminga, Jacob	4:20:31 (16,994)	
Kamp, Raimund	4:42:45 (22,782)	
Kan, Tokio	4:32:41 (20,272)	
Kandola, Amrik	5:38:22 (30,435)	
Kandunias, Jim	4:51:30 (24,700)	
Kane, Alastair	4:58:21 (26,005)	
Kane, Andrew	4:08:27 (14,003)	
Kane, John	3:11:25 (2,193)	
Kane, Jonathan	3:48:28 (8,739)	
Kane, Nicholas	3:23:02 (3,662)	
Kane, Peter	4:37:07 (21,339)	
Kang, Kamaljit	5:44:56 (30,880)	
Kanji, Aneez	3:59:49 (12,028)	
Kanning, Klaas	3:57:32 (11,372)	
Kantorowicz, Donald	5:41:49 (30,678)	
Kanumilli, Naresh	4:28:08 (19,065)	
Kanzler, Thorsten	3:46:29 (8,272)	
Kapadia, Cyrus	6:00:46 (31,571)	
Kapadia, Hatim	4:25:37 (18,424)	
Kapoor, Neil	3:07:05 (1,742)	
Kapoor, Palwinder	4:43:21 (22,919)	
Kapur, Krishan	3:06:10 (1,654)	
Kara, Recep	3:29:12 (4,727)	
Karagiannidis, Emanouil	4:24:29 (18,117)	
Karavis, Graeme	3:24:08 (3,844)	
Karjalainen, Niko	4:31:00 (19,828)	
Karlas, Richard	4:04:31 (13,090)	
Karle, Werner	4:56:15 (25,648)	
Karlsons, Paul	4:03:36 (12,903)	
Karlsson, Henrik	3:13:41 (2,529)	
Karmali, Ramzan	3:55:17 (10,687)	
Karnfalt, Anders	2:48:39 (433)	
Karp, Julian	3:37:19 (6,167)	
Karrasch, Stephen	3:32:35 (5,285)	
Karrenbeld, Arend	3:15:53 (2,777)	
Karsson, Ingemar	3:13:05 (2,444)	
Kasket, Alan	3:59:16 (11,873)	
Kasolter, Benoit	3:54:00 (10,309)	
Kass, Mark	3:20:58 (3,359)	
Kat, Gregory	3:11:25 (2,193)	
Katavic, Dejan	5:01:51 (26,577)	
Katchour, Vladimir	3:55:36 (10,783)	
Katechia, Bhagesh	3:08:21 (1,846)	
Katkhuoa, Sebastian	3:33:11 (5,380)	
Katkov, Gennady	3:52:33 (9,858)	
Katri, Edmond	3:45:16 (7,992)	
Katz, Jonathan	3:47:23 (8,484)	
Kavanagh, John	4:54:41 (25,320)	
Kavanagh, Kevin	4:20:43 (17,049)	
Kavanagh, Larry	4:14:45 (15,515)	
Kavanagh, Paul	6:20:58 (32,103)	
Kavanagh, Terence	4:30:42 (19,755)	
Kawakani, Morie	4:03:59 (12,985)	
Kay, Alasdair	3:38:49 (6,486)	
Kay, Danny	3:28:25 (4,591)	
Kay, George	3:15:20 (2,707)	
Kay, Matthew	3:05:16 (1,563)	
Kay, Michael	4:16:47 (16,060)	
Kay, Samuel	3:12:14 (2,318)	
Kay, Tom	2:52:42 (611)	
Kaye, Adam	4:27:39 (18,951)	
Kaye, David	3:38:03 (6,322)	
Kaye, Martin	4:34:49 (20,777)	
Kaye, Michael	4:07:40 (13,831)	
Kaye Krzeczkowsks, Henry	6:05:51 (31,727)	
Kayes, Daniel	4:47:36 (23,925)	
Kayley, Mark	4:44:09 (23,093)	
Kayley, Mick	4:11:39 (14,782)	
Kazalbash, Imran	4:12:23 (14,937)	
Kazan, Elie	4:46:09 (23,607)	
Kazemi, Tawab	4:27:36 (18,939)	
Kazimierski, Michael	2:40:35 (193)	
Keal, Ian	3:25:57 (4,148)	
Keane, Glenn	4:38:06 (21,599)	
Keane, Glenn	6:39:41 (32,434)	
Keane, Peter	4:11:10 (14,668)	
Keane, Simon	4:05:40 (13,362)	
Keaney, Dominic	3:48:36 (8,782)	
Kear, Neil	3:34:36 (5,636)	
Kearn, Richard	3:03:33 (1,425)	
Kearney, Chris	4:00:08 (12,115)	
Kearney, Michael	4:07:02 (13,684)	
Kearney, Patrick	4:57:10 (25,805)	
Kearns, Adrian	3:27:55 (4,504)	
Kearns, Bryan	4:06:13 (13,496)	
Kearns, Sean	4:15:22 (15,657)	
Keast, Mark	4:12:51 (15,050)	
Keast, Robert	4:01:54 (12,545)	
Keat, Rodney	4:33:11 (20,397)	
Keating, Kenneth	5:11:00 (27,812)	
Keating, Niall	3:46:48 (8,343)	
Keating, Patrick	4:20:33 (17,006)	
Keating, Rory	4:05:01 (13,212)	
Keay, Frank	4:30:56 (19,819)	
Keay, Kevin	4:23:29 (17,821)	
Kececioglu, Deniz	3:25:42 (4,099)	
Kedward, Neil	4:02:40 (12,695)	
Kee, Howard	3:30:35 (4,958)	
Keeble, Tony	3:40:35 (6,872)	
Keech, Steven	5:00:05 (26,320)	
Keech, Tony	3:28:10 (4,544)	
Keefe, David	4:16:26 (15,963)	
Keeffe, Andrew	4:51:31 (24,703)	
Keegan, Christian	4:22:42 (17,608)	
Keeling, David	4:15:57 (15,828)	
Keely, Patrick	4:55:27 (25,473)	
Keem, Nicholas	4:31:28 (19,953)	
Keen, Andrew	4:46:49 (23,762)	
Keen, Buster	4:45:47 (23,512)	
Keen, Howard	4:09:25 (14,258)	
Keen, Peter	4:52:13 (24,830)	
Keen, Robert	3:24:29 (3,915)	
Keen, Tim	5:13:12 (28,103)	
Keenaghan, Shaun	4:01:02 (12,319)	
Keenan, John	4:53:48 (25,121)	
Keenan, Paul	4:24:08 (18,017)	
Keenan, Steven	5:50:16 (31,150)	
Keene, Huw	3:53:40 (10,201)	
Keenes, Colin	4:15:11 (15,614)	
Keep, Trevor	3:12:17 (2,326)	
Keeson, Rick	4:03:56 (12,971)	
Keet, Wayne	3:08:47 (1,906)	
Kefford, Andrew	4:44:03 (23,074)	
Keightley, Tim	4:08:06 (13,935)	
Keilloh, Richard	5:23:28 (29,217)	
Keily, Lee	2:38:54 (165)	
Keino, Kip	4:59:20 (26,185)	
Keith, Philip	5:02:50 (26,719)	
Kelf, David	3:38:31 (6,429)	
Kelf, Jon	3:45:48 (8,120)	
Kelland, Peter	3:19:06 (3,150)	
Kellaway, Andrew	2:46:13 (332)	
Kellaway, Roy	3:07:06 (1,744)	
Kellaway, Thomas	3:25:21 (4,038)	
Kelleher, Cornelius	2:58:13 (1,024)	
Kelleher, Joe	3:34:12 (5,564)	
Kelleher, Neale	4:35:33 (20,960)	
Kelleher, Sean	6:36:58 (32,396)	
Kelleher, Stephen	3:02:48 (1,357)	
Keller, Clayton	5:04:12 (26,917)	
Keller, Max	3:53:33 (10,165)	
Kellett, Michael	5:03:23 (26,809)	
Kelley, Philip	3:10:49 (2,136)	
Kelly, Adrian	4:13:40 (15,222)	
Kelly, Andrew	7:37:14 (32,813)	
Kelly, Anthony	3:57:40 (11,416)	
Kelly, Chris	4:22:09 (17,439)	
Kelly, Christopher	4:15:43 (15,758)	
Kelly, Christopher	5:15:16 (28,335)	
Kelly, Conleth	4:37:16 (21,394)	
Kelly, David	3:53:33 (10,165)	
Kelly, David	5:11:17 (27,853)	
Kelly, Geoffrey	4:51:07 (24,631)	
Kelly, Gerard	3:38:56 (6,510)	
Kelly, Gerrard	4:59:22 (26,190)	
Kelly, Graham	6:30:09 (32,283)	
Kelly, Hugh	3:08:17 (1,836)	
Kelly, Ian	3:30:40 (4,975)	
Kelly, James	4:31:39 (20,000)	
Kelly, John	4:08:39 (14,066)	
Kelly, John	4:42:22 (22,689)	
Kelly, Joseph	4:17:07 (16,148)	
Kelly, Keith	3:26:40 (4,268)	
Kelly, Kevin	3:19:08 (3,154)	
Kelly, Laim	6:02:12 (31,615)	
Kelly, Liam	4:40:06 (22,137)	
Kelly, Martin	4:18:48 (16,548)	
Kelly, Neil	4:13:11 (15,118)	
Kelly, Paul	3:58:01 (11,517)	
Kelly, Paul	5:26:48 (29,510)	
Kelly, Peter	3:40:00 (6,733)	
Kelly, Peter	4:41:34 (22,487)	
Kelly, Philip	5:02:13 (26,630)	
Kelly, Raymond	4:00:59 (12,304)	
Kelly, Russell	4:39:46 (22,047)	
Kelly, Sean	4:05:24 (13,298)	
Kelly, Simon	4:41:11 (22,398)	
Kelly, Stefan	4:28:31 (19,175)	
Kelly, Stephen	3:15:58 (2,783)	
Kelly, Stephen	4:14:23 (15,421)	
Kelly, Stephen	5:06:31 (27,233)	
Kelly, Steve	2:53:38 (660)	
Kelly, Steven	5:10:38 (27,766)	
Kelly, Terence	3:47:01 (8,384)	
Kelly, Thomas	5:07:55 (27,425)	
Kelly, Tim	2:59:45 (1,154)	
Kelly, Tom	4:28:06 (19,054)	
Kelly, William	4:08:47 (14,089)	
Kelly-Noakes, Stuart	5:17:21 (28,612)	
Kelsall, Mike	5:19:46 (28,847)	
Kelsey, Tim	4:27:37 (18,941)	
Kelting, John	3:51:59 (9,678)	
Kemble, Peter	3:47:43 (8,565)	
Kemboly, M.	4:42:55 (22,818)	
Kemmett, Gavin	3:50:44 (9,356)	
Kemmis, Luke	3:59:32 (11,947)	
Kemp, Adrian	3:24:19 (3,887)	
Kemp, Andrew	3:25:01 (3,987)	
Kemp, Christopher	3:24:01 (3,824)	
Kemp, David	4:31:52 (20,047)	
Kemp, Jon	2:55:36 (790)	
Kemp, Kabir	3:17:26 (2,954)	
Kemp, Marcus	4:45:27 (23,430)	
Kemp, Mark	4:55:47 (25,540)	
Kemp, Martin	4:22:16 (17,470)	
Kemp, Martin	4:34:49 (20,777)	
Kemp, Martyn	3:51:22 (9,514)	
Kemp, Michael	5:54:24 (31,328)	
Kemp, Nick	4:22:19 (17,486)	

Kemp, Philip 4:16:53 (16,086)
Kemp, Richard 4:39:47 (22,051)
Kempen, Andrew 3:33:10 (5,377)
Kempgens, Arndt 4:03:53 (12,961)
Kemple, Terence 4:12:22 (14,932)
Kempster, Anthony 5:31:01 (29,864)
Kempton, Stephen 4:42:52 (22,807)
Kempton, Stuart 4:47:40 (23,945)
Kenchington, Christopher 3:00:37 (1,206)
Kenchington, Nicholas 2:41:15 (211)
Kendal, Mark 4:22:35 (17,568)
Kendall, Benjamin 3:46:57 (8,373)
Kendall, Ian 4:48:49 (24,202)
Kendall, Jason 4:05:54 (13,411)
Kendall, Kevin 3:56:38 (11,094)
Kendall, Lee 3:36:24 (6,004)
Kendall, Matthew 5:07:05 (27,310)
Kendrick, Brian 3:30:51 (4,998)
Kennard, Christopher 3:01:25 (1,254)
Kennard, Stephen 5:00:29 (26,371)
Kennedy, Andrew 3:23:12 (3,677)
Kennedy, Andrew 4:05:15 (13,262)
Kennedy, Angus 4:54:09 (25,215)
Kennedy, Anthony 4:00:06 (12,107)
Kennedy, George 3:55:50 (10,850)
Kennedy, Ian 3:14:13 (2,581)
Kennedy, Ian 3:34:35 (5,633)
Kennedy, John 4:45:08 (23,343)
Kennedy, John 4:50:24 (24,479)
Kennedy, Leslie 3:43:03 (7,400)
Kennedy, Mark 3:46:48 (8,343)
Kennedy, Nicholas 4:19:51 (16,821)
Kennedy, Paul 4:31:19 (19,906)
Kennedy, Richard 3:12:26 (2,351)
Kennedy, Richard 3:27:03 (4,339)
Kennedy, Richard 4:47:25 (23,900)
Kennedy, Ryan 4:12:34 (14,984)
Kennedy, Tim 4:15:19 (15,644)
Kenneth, Barry 3:45:47 (8,110)
Kenneth, Robert 4:18:59 (16,584)
Kennett, Adrian 4:28:28 (19,159)
Kennett, Craig 4:25:13 (18,312)
Kenny, Chris 5:15:33 (28,373)
Kenny, Jack 3:48:31 (8,751)
Kenny, John 4:32:08 (20,122)
Kenny, Luke 3:20:45 (3,339)
Kenny, Michael 3:52:16 (9,771)
Kenny, Neil 3:05:58 (1,638)
Kenny, Triss 3:19:08 (3,154)
Kensett, Martin 3:37:42 (6,260)
Kensington, Nick 3:18:11 (3,029)
Kent, Andrew 4:33:00 (20,356)
Kent, Lee 4:23:25 (17,806)
Kent, Paul 3:15:07 (2,677)
Kenward, Ian 4:46:50 (23,769)
Kenyon, Craig 3:58:42 (11,707)
Kenyon, Michael 3:10:34 (2,112)
Kenyon, Stephen 3:14:11 (2,572)
Kenyon-Muir, Nick 3:32:27 (5,262)
Keogh, David 4:48:55 (24,218)
Keogh, Donovan 4:05:02 (13,216)
Keogh, Eamonn 4:55:33 (25,490)
Keppie, Adam 4:13:32 (15,195)
Ker, Neil 3:33:39 (5,447)
Ker, Robert 4:23:40 (17,864)
Kerbey, Philip 3:48:35 (8,773)
Kerins, Garvin 5:16:18 (28,482)
Kermode, Brad 4:32:11 (20,136)
Kermode, Nigel 6:14:08 (31,933)
Kern, Thierry 4:20:32 (17,000)
Kernan, Charles 4:49:49 (24,383)
Kernn, Uwe 3:08:41 (1,888)
Kerr, Alan 5:58:22 (31,491)
Kerr, Alistair 5:02:15 (26,634)
Kerr, Desmond 4:26:58 (18,779)
Kerr, Haydn 4:18:47 (16,541)
Kerr, John 3:57:09 (11,246)
Kerr, Jules 6:12:24 (31,892)
Kerr, Malcolm 4:00:04 (12,097)
Kerr, Matthew 5:19:55 (28,861)
Kerr, Stewart 3:22:14 (3,557)
Kerr, William 3:48:28 (8,739)
Kerrigan, John 4:28:44 (19,236)

Kerry, Patrick 4:28:42 (19,224)
Kerry, Simon 4:10:08 (14,424)
Kershaw, Craig 3:27:38 (4,444)
Kershaw, Daniel 5:06:38 (27,250)
Kershaw, John 3:46:52 (8,358)
Kershaw, Keith 4:46:00 (23,566)
Kershaw, Robin 3:56:42 (11,109)
Kershaw, Steven 5:23:37 (29,236)
Kerslake, Justin 4:24:13 (18,041)
Kerslake, Robert 4:05:53 (13,407)
Kerslake, William 4:33:24 (20,443)
Kersley, William 4:38:02 (21,578)
Kesby, Robert 5:20:49 (28,978)
Kesterton, Rob 3:55:33 (10,767)
Kestle, Michael 3:19:31 (3,205)
Kestle, Ryan 3:09:42 (2,007)
Ketchell, Robert 3:47:22 (8,480)
Ketchin, Ian 3:16:19 (2,821)
Kettle, Aidan 4:30:05 (19,620)
Kettle, Simon 3:54:03 (10,326)
Kettlewell, William 4:26:15 (18,588)
Kettridge, Robert 4:07:26 (13,783)
Keun, Andries 4:46:27 (23,680)
Kew, Wayne 3:09:26 (1,985)
Key, Colin 4:37:48 (21,522)
Key, Timothy 4:55:12 (25,423)
Keyes, Jason 5:11:08 (27,829)
Keylock, Robert 3:49:45 (9,112)
Keymer, Simon 4:53:19 (25,031)
Keymer, Stefan 4:51:08 (24,635)
Keys, Jason 3:26:56 (4,317)
Keys, John 3:56:05 (10,923)
Keys, Leon 5:44:10 (30,832)
Keys, Stephen 3:32:41 (5,301)
Khagram, Ilesh 4:47:14 (23,862)
Khan, Naveed 5:40:57 (30,611)
Khan, Shakeel 5:01:28 (26,523)
Khan, Syed 4:35:48 (21,028)
Khan, Tariq 3:48:20 (8,705)
Khan, Zahair 6:20:29 (32,095)
Khan-Lodhi, Jamal 6:39:37 (32,433)
Khanna, Paul 6:21:58 (32,122)

Khannouchi, Khalid...................2:05:38 (1)

Khalid Khannouchi is a Moroccan-born American marathon runner. He is the former world record holder for the marathon and held the former road world best for 20km. His marathon best is 2:05:38. His marathon wins include Chicago and London 2002. He finished fourth at the Olympic Marathon Trials in 2007. Khannouchi was born in Meknes, Morocco on 22 December 1971. After the Moroccan track federation turned down his request for financial assistance for training expenses he immigrated to Brooklyn, New York City, and found work washing dishes. In September 1996, he married Sandra Inoa, an American distance runner who became his coach and agent. Khannouchi ran well in minor road races in the US before running the fastest debut marathon in history to win the 1997 Chicago Marathon. In 1999 he ran the fastest time to date in the marathon at Chicago (2:05:42). He became a US citizen on May 2, 2000. Khannouchi returned to marathon competition in 2006 with a fourth-place finish in the London Marathon. His 2006 London time of 2:07:04 marked the fourth time as an American that he has bettered the 2:08.00 barrier.

Khomsi, Aymen 4:27:49 (18,987)
Khoory, Mithal 4:46:07 (23,594)
Kidd, Jonathan 4:36:16 (21,142)
Kidd, Malcolm 3:33:51 (5,486)
Kidd, Peter 4:37:28 (21,439)
Kidger, Sam 3:40:14 (6,794)
Kidner, Simon 3:52:38 (9,877)
Kidwell, Peter 3:06:31 (1,688)
Kielmann, Oliver 3:25:36 (4,081)
Kielty, Cahal 4:24:56 (18,234)
Kielty, John 4:24:57 (18,242)
Kielty, Patrick 4:24:57 (18,242)
Kiely, Dennis 4:11:04 (14,651)
Kiely, Philip 4:01:06 (12,337)
Kiennast, Michael 4:44:30 (23,172)
Kiennast, Raimund 4:44:30 (23,172)
Kiernan, Jason 3:36:12 (5,957)
Kiesling, Andreas 3:57:14 (11,274)
Kiff, Alan 4:59:19 (26,181)
Kilbane, Dominic 4:00:04 (12,097)
Kilcullen, Seamus 5:11:22 (27,864)
Kilkenny, Kevin 3:26:12 (4,187)
Killbe, Robert 5:18:56 (28,769)
Kille, Anthony 6:13:35 (31,920)
Killeen, Oliver 4:43:34 (22,972)
Kilminster, Gary 4:02:29 (12,651)
Kilpin, Jim 4:24:45 (18,185)
Kilsby, Gary 3:53:12 (10,044)
Kiltie, David 3:32:53 (5,335)
Kim, Christopher 3:49:15 (8,953)
Kimber, Andrew 4:30:39 (19,745)
Kimber, Nick 3:47:52 (8,604)
Kimber, Philip 4:32:35 (20,239)
Kimber, Robert 4:34:55 (20,807)
Kimman, Peter 4:51:09 (24,638)
Kimtai, Julius 2:18:13 (16)
Kinchin-Smith, Alex 4:37:07 (21,339)
Kincla, George 6:00:42 (31,570)
Kindell, Matthew 3:56:33 (11,070)
Kinder, Julian 4:03:17 (12,835)
Kindler, Thomas 3:47:03 (8,394)
Kindred, Robert 4:17:26 (16,229)
Kinenrsley, Matthew 5:42:54 (30,750)
Kinet, Lawrence 5:29:33 (29,742)
King, Alan 4:22:17 (17,472)
King, Anthony 4:40:04 (22,127)
King, Bradley 4:52:31 (24,879)
King, Brian 5:14:34 (28,255)
King, Bryan 3:27:44 (4,465)
King, Chris 5:16:03 (28,449)
King, Christopher 5:52:26 (31,248)
King, Daniel 5:17:39 (28,640)
King, Daniel 5:26:27 (29,486)
King, David 3:09:47 (2,015)
King, David 3:26:32 (4,238)
King, Edgar 3:23:50 (3,776)
King, Gerard 4:17:01 (16,121)
King, Graham 3:21:08 (3,391)
King, Ian 2:52:37 (603)
King, James 3:06:19 (1,665)
King, Jeremy 4:40:21 (22,199)
King, John 5:53:56 (31,309)

King, Justin 3:44:53 (7,899)
King, Kevin 5:17:57 (28,665)
King, Leslie 4:57:18 (25,829)
King, Malcolm 4:36:07 (21,106)
King, Martin 4:26:45 (18,731)
King, Matthew 3:06:12 (1,658)
King, Matthew 3:48:34 (8,766)
King, Matthew 5:36:05 (30,282)
King, Nicholas 4:17:55 (16,349)
King, Philip 3:47:30 (8,510)
King, Philip 4:31:40 (20,003)
King, Phillip 3:44:27 (7,784)
King, Richard 3:31:43 (5,154)
King, Richard 4:01:15 (12,379)
King, Richard 4:22:40 (17,596)
King, Robert 3:40:05 (6,756)
King, Roy 4:48:33 (24,133)
King, Simon 3:49:40 (9,086)
King, Stephen 3:32:22 (5,243)
King, Stephen 4:14:36 (15,471)
King, Thomas 5:39:28 (30,511)
King, Tony 4:39:05 (21,869)
King, Trevor 6:11:39 (31,874)
Kingdon, Adam 3:49:48 (9,133)
Kinghorn, Graeme 4:13:42 (15,232)
Kingscott, Paul 3:34:41 (5,659)
Kingsford, Jonathan 3:43:25 (7,502)
Kingsley, John 5:03:01 (26,746)
Kingstad, Richard 2:48:11 (411)
Kingston, Andrew 4:30:03 (19,608)
Kingston, Gerald 3:09:24 (1,982)
Kingston, Richard 4:12:05 (14,878)
Kingston, Simon 4:16:34 (15,996)
King-Underwood, Gregory 4:20:46 (17,061)
Kinoshita, Hiromitsu 4:19:00 (16,589)
Kinsell, Paul 5:14:11 (28,212)
Kinsey, Nicholas 2:37:29 (135)
Kinsey, William 5:05:27 (27,078)
Kintoff, Clive 3:43:44 (7,585)
Kinzel, Ernst 4:21:47 (17,332)
Kiplagat, William 2:15:58 (13)
Kipling, Gerry 5:03:14 (26,788)
Kipping, Bernie 4:03:49 (12,947)
Kipps, Courtney 3:59:59 (12,080)
Kirby, Alex 5:00:38 (26,393)
Kirby, Andrew 3:46:30 (8,285)
Kirby, Andrew 4:16:44 (16,045)
Kirby, Christopher 4:16:49 (16,071)
Kirby, Graham 3:14:11 (2,572)
Kirby, Ian 5:05:48 (27,125)
Kirby, James 4:52:41 (24,911)
Kirby, John 5:44:31 (30,856)
Kirby, Martin 3:04:59 (1,542)
Kirby, Michael 3:42:59 (7,385)
Kirby, Nicholas 5:24:01 (29,281)
Kirby, Oliver 5:53:03 (31,278)
Kirby, Paul 4:22:01 (17,401)
Kirby, Raymond 5:44:24 (30,849)
Kirby, Robert 4:24:55 (18,230)
Kirby, Roger 4:21:21 (17,203)
Kirby, Steven 3:20:21 (3,295)
Kirchhoff, Martin 3:35:51 (5,872)
Kirk, Alan 4:02:43 (12,705)
Kirk, Angus 4:23:42 (17,883)
Kirk, David 3:40:59 (6,961)
Kirk, Leslie 3:29:42 (4,827)
Kirk, Michael 4:44:56 (23,283)
Kirk, Paul 3:38:40 (6,468)
Kirk, Richard 3:47:43 (8,565)
Kirkby, Gary 4:20:11 (16,911)
Kirkby, Lee 4:35:59 (21,077)
Kirkby, Leonard 3:53:03 (10,000)
Kirkdale, Brian 3:19:56 (3,248)
Kirkham, Colin 4:23:53 (17,946)
Kirkham, David 3:46:50 (8,351)
Kirkham, Jonathan 4:15:53 (15,804)
Kirkham, Stan 4:21:22 (17,210)
Kirkland, Alastair 4:31:45 (20,023)
Kirkpatrick, Matthew 4:14:10 (15,349)
Kirkpatrick, Neven 5:42:30 (30,726)
Kirkum, Michael 5:57:07 (31,446)
Kirlew, Lance 2:53:31 (655)
Kirrage, Nicholas 4:56:04 (25,599)
Kirrage, Philip 6:16:09 (31,990)
Kirsten, Keith 3:57:42 (11,422)
Kirtland, Edward 4:04:47 (13,155)
Kirtley, Paul 4:57:18 (25,829)
Kirton, Ian 3:42:59 (7,385)
Kirton, Steven 4:48:40 (24,161)
Kirwan, Stephen 5:12:32 (28,027)
Kiss, Szilard 5:15:48 (28,412)
Kissell, Bruce 3:44:58 (7,922)
Kistner, Martin 3:33:15 (5,388)
Kitchen, Neil 3:31:59 (5,186)
Kitchen, Richard 6:01:25 (31,588)
Kitchener, Steven 3:26:56 (4,317)
Kitchener, Tristan 3:49:18 (8,972)
Kitcher, Stephen 4:43:18 (22,909)
Kitching, Ian 2:43:35 (258)
Kitching, Leslie 4:39:43 (22,030)
Kite, Benedict 4:24:08 (18,017)
Kite, Simon 5:48:23 (31,056)
Kiteley, Mark 5:05:49 (27,126)
Kitley, Richard 3:56:31 (11,059)
Kittle, Ian 4:00:49 (12,258)
Kivikoski, Jouni 4:07:44 (13,850)
Kjaernsno, Reidar 6:23:33 (32,159)
Klabe, Neil 4:14:35 (15,467)
Klatt, Dirk 4:30:27 (19,701)
Klausler, Peter 4:38:18 (21,655)
Kleemann, Marcio 3:11:47 (2,242)
Klein, Adam 4:59:17 (26,172)
Klein, Juergen 3:58:29 (11,648)
Klein, Peter 3:36:34 (6,034)
Kleinecke-Pohl, Uwe 4:44:47 (23,248)
Kleinschnitker, Ludger 3:33:07 (5,368)
Kleister, Roy 4:17:26 (16,229)
Klement, Valery 3:01:32 (1,262)
Klenerman, Paul 4:21:52 (17,359)
Klompmaker, Ruben 3:46:04 (8,172)
Kloot, Colin 4:46:06 (23,592)
Kluck, Jan 4:45:46 (23,508)
Klunder, Hans 4:14:12 (15,361)
Knaggs, Christopher 3:49:55 (9,155)
Knapman, Barrie 3:53:54 (10,278)
Knapp, Allan 4:34:00 (20,579)
Knapp, Edward 3:16:44 (2,868)
Knapp, Neil 3:29:02 (4,698)
Knauder, Gerhard 4:29:07 (19,354)
Kneissl, Ruediger 4:08:02 (13,923)
Knibb, John 2:53:38 (660)
Knibbs, Alec 5:43:45 (30,799)
Knight, Alan 3:43:41 (7,568)
Knight, Alan 4:56:32 (25,696)
Knight, Andrew 3:38:49 (6,486)
Knight, Andrew 4:14:50 (15,533)
Knight, Andrew 4:45:23 (23,404)
Knight, Barry 4:04:31 (13,090)
Knight, Barry 6:00:22 (31,555)
Knight, Brian 6:34:53 (32,350)
Knight, Bruce 4:00:35 (12,203)
Knight, Chris 2:51:04 (535)
Knight, Dave 3:48:09 (8,663)
Knight, David 3:38:49 (6,486)
Knight, Derek 3:50:45 (9,363)
Knight, Gary 5:10:33 (27,756)
Knight, James 3:20:52 (3,350)
Knight, John 4:23:45 (17,905)
Knight, John 4:55:29 (25,477)
Knight, Kevin 3:48:13 (8,677)
Knight, Kevin 4:24:46 (18,192)
Knight, Malcolm 3:27:36 (4,435)
Knight, Mark 3:23:48 (3,769)
Knight, Mark 3:42:03 (7,167)
Knight, Mark 3:58:41 (11,701)
Knight, Michael 4:13:32 (15,195)
Knight, Peter 4:18:41 (16,522)
Knight, Philip 4:12:53 (15,058)
Knight, Richard 6:38:42 (32,417)
Knight, Rob 5:48:23 (31,056)
Knight, Ronald 4:13:40 (15,222)
Knight, Sebastian 4:12:24 (14,943)
Knight, Steve 4:20:15 (16,926)
Knight, Steven 3:27:35 (4,433)
Knight, Steven 4:38:21 (21,672)
Knighton, Barry 2:58:49 (1,076)
Knights, Christopher 5:11:23 (27,866)
Knights, Jim 5:01:37 (26,548)
Knill, Richard 4:24:45 (18,185)
Knipprath, Johannes 3:46:13 (8,206)
Knoll, Jerome 3:17:37 (2,964)
Knopp, Simon 4:22:27 (17,535)
Knott, Andrew 3:48:39 (8,799)
Knott, Charles 4:23:49 (17,922)
Knott, John 4:41:26 (22,455)
Knott, Kevin 4:41:27 (22,463)
Knott, Mike 4:22:45 (17,621)
Knowles, Gareth 5:42:03 (30,699)
Knowles, Roy 4:06:16 (13,509)
Knox, Graeme 3:53:43 (10,212)
Knox, Simon 4:17:17 (16,197)
Knox-Macaulay, Ian 5:08:26 (27,491)
Koch, James 5:06:36 (27,244)
Koe, Richard 3:18:29 (3,072)
Koe, Simon 4:19:50 (16,810)
Koehler, Jens 4:02:10 (12,588)
Koehler, Martin 2:39:44 (178)
Kohama, Hiroshige 4:21:58 (17,382)
Kohl, Russell 3:57:23 (11,317)
Kohlmannhuber, Dietmar 4:09:35 (14,287)
Kok, Arnout 4:43:29 (22,958)
Kok, Ed 4:21:55 (17,371)
Kokoruwe, Benjamin 6:11:01 (31,859)
Kokri, Manmohan 5:34:31 (30,150)
Koliopulos, Thanos 6:23:19 (32,154)
Koller, Philip 4:09:42 (14,318)
Kollnberger, Adrian 3:53:52 (10,272)
Konderla, Christopher 4:07:58 (13,900)
Kondo, Takayoshi 5:00:26 (26,364)
Kondragunta, Satya 4:41:20 (22,438)
Kong, Matthew 4:57:10 (25,805)
Koninx, Jack 3:45:02 (7,933)
Konopelski, Andrew 3:11:05 (2,166)
Koolen, Adrianus 3:58:19 (11,593)
Kopec, Chris 6:39:19 (32,425)
Kopp, Christoph 3:18:13 (3,037)
Korndoerfer, Frank 4:20:26 (16,980)
Korro, Barry 3:45:49 (8,124)
Kors, Frank 4:37:28 (21,439)
Kosak, Miha 5:42:16 (30,709)
Koscielny, Joerg 3:28:13 (4,554)
Kose, Mufit 5:13:49 (28,172)
Koshy, Ommen 4:47:22 (23,891)
Kotb, Arlan 4:33:43 (20,519)
Koukos, Spyros 3:19:26 (3,193)
Kovacs, Andrea 2:35:18 (100)
Kovats, Steven 2:46:48 (352)
Kowal, David 4:19:59 (16,858)
Kowalczyk, Andy 4:57:30 (25,856)
Kowollik, Niels 3:48:06 (8,650)
Kraemer, Herbert 4:58:28 (26,027)
Kramer, Graham 3:32:57 (5,346)
Krause, John 3:49:02 (8,906)
Krause, Ludwig 3:15:29 (2,723)
Krause, Victor 4:25:14 (18,317)
Krauss, Joachin 4:55:31 (25,483)
Kreckeler, Kevin 4:20:37 (17,024)
Kresse, Kai 4:39:35 (21,993)
Kretzschmar, Shane 4:35:22 (20,914)
Kreusler, Hans 4:27:58 (19,027)
Kreutner, Walter 3:49:32 (9,051)
Krishnamurthy, Arun 3:49:41 (9,094)
Kristensen, Kaj 3:08:56 (1,928)
Kristiansen, Torstein 2:55:22 (768)
Kristjansson, Johann 3:07:31 (1,770)
Kronberger, Benedikt 2:58:10 (1,018)
Kronberger, Daniel 3:18:02 (3,013)
Kruk, Marcus 4:02:06 (12,575)
Kruppa, Robert 4:53:15 (25,020)
Kualsvik, Ole 4:35:55 (21,057)
Kuberuwa, Gray 2:56:53 (906)
Kubota, Tetsuya 2:28:56 (55)
Kuczynski, Stuart 4:17:55 (16,349)
Kuebler, Florian 3:27:30 (4,418)
Kuellmer, Herrmann 4:56:14 (25,643)
Kugel, Gunter 3:38:30 (6,423)
Kuijken, Stefan 3:35:59 (5,901)
Kuklinski, Conrad 3:34:54 (5,695)
Kulot, Holger 3:44:16 (7,731)

Kumar, Sanjeen 4:19:46 (16,797)
Kumar Patel, Vijay 5:16:00 (28,446)
Kunert, Egbert 3:18:57 (3,130)
Kunin, Seth 4:02:11 (12,595)
Kunz, Gregor 4:27:56 (19,018)
Kunz, Reinhard 3:47:41 (8,558)
Kunze, Erwin 4:26:15 (18,588)
Kuoppamaki, Mikko 3:36:27 (6,018)
Kuosmanen, Pasi 4:00:04 (12,097)
Kuronen, Mikko 2:57:21 (942)
Kurse, Alfred 4:00:39 (12,214)
Kusche, Rainer 3:54:52 (10,562)
Kusel, John 5:52:45 (31,266)
Kushner, Jason 4:49:55 (24,409)
Kwarteng, Eric 4:21:06 (17,140)
Kyd, Laurence 3:57:02 (11,220)
Kyle, Richard 3:45:14 (7,983)
Kyritsis, Nick 4:41:49 (22,561)
Kysela, Boris 3:54:48 (10,541)
La Ballois, Frederic 3:50:50 (9,382)
Labanowski, Stanley 4:39:46 (22,047)
Labarr, Winston 4:31:33 (19,988)
Labram, Henry 4:19:12 (16,646)
Labuschagne, Timothy 3:09:48 (2,018)
Lacaze, Daniel 3:43:57 (7,643)
Lacey, Mark 2:47:26 (379)
Lacey, Sean 4:50:02 (24,429)
Lacey, Simon 3:16:46 (2,873)
Lacey, Stephen 4:27:24 (18,890)
Lach, Roman 3:56:39 (11,097)
Lackey, Thomas 4:48:47 (24,190)
Lacoursiere, Jeffrey 4:39:29 (21,965)
Lad, Jeetan 3:30:57 (5,015)
Lad, Mahesh 6:48:57 (32,530)
Ladd, Julian 3:30:02 (4,878)
Ladner, Kevin 3:52:24 (9,812)
Ladrange, Nicolas 3:33:08 (5,371)
Lafferty, Brooke 3:14:39 (2,625)
Lafferty, Clive 4:15:33 (15,708)
Lafferty, Stephen 3:58:42 (11,707)
Laffineur, Olivier 3:52:07 (9,726)
Lafforgue, Guy 3:22:58 (3,653)
Lagacherie, Frederic 3:45:00 (7,926)
Lagan, Paul 6:47:40 (32,515)
Lagoute, Alain 3:26:52 (4,303)
Lahmar, Stephane 4:26:56 (18,771)
Laing, Stewart 3:51:32 (9,555)
Lainsbury, Raymond 3:23:43 (3,761)
Lake, Carl 3:22:42 (3,610)
Lake, David 7:18:49 (32,752)
Lake, Mark 4:21:41 (17,309)
Lake, Reginald 4:11:28 (14,737)
Lake, Richard 3:52:50 (9,933)
Lakey, Daniel 3:43:57 (7,643)
Lakey, Stuart 4:54:36 (25,303)
Lakin, David 3:57:49 (11,455)
Laking, George 3:54:24 (10,427)
Lam, Alex 5:11:18 (27,855)
Lam, David 4:27:08 (18,826)
Lam, Man Biu 3:39:44 (6,676)
Lam, Wayne 4:46:21 (23,652)
Lamb, Andy 2:43:57 (267)
Lamb, Brian 4:29:19 (19,416)
Lamb, Ian 3:05:01 (1,546)
Lamb, James 4:04:21 (13,057)
Lamb, Jamie 5:05:11 (27,042)
Lamb, Jeremy 3:23:51 (3,784)
Lamb, John 4:11:54 (14,833)
Lamb, Michael 3:36:35 (6,039)
Lamb, Philip 4:11:36 (14,768)
Lamb, Rod 4:29:00 (19,322)
Lamb, Steven 4:32:24 (20,188)
Lamb, Terry 3:45:54 (8,134)
Lambden, Murray 2:59:32 (1,138)
Lambert, Andrew 5:26:20 (29,468)
Lambert, Brian 3:56:10 (10,948)
Lambert, Christophe 3:26:04 (4,159)
Lambert, David 3:58:15 (11,580)
Lambert, John 4:24:13 (18,041)
Lambert, Jonathan 4:32:54 (20,335)
Lambert, Kevin 3:21:31 (3,438)
Lambert, Kim 4:04:44 (13,145)
Lambert, Paul 5:23:36 (29,235)
Lambert, Sebastian 3:24:35 (3,931)
Lambert, Simon 5:28:32 (29,657)
Lambert, Stuart 5:41:52 (30,687)
Lambert, Toby 2:34:02 (90)
Lamberti, Sergio 3:29:11 (4,726)
Lamble, Robert 5:01:34 (26,537)
Lambournme, Martin 4:24:28 (18,110)
Lambrigts, Wim 4:33:30 (20,466)
Lamford, Russell 5:23:18 (29,202)
Laming, Ian 3:55:23 (10,719)
Lamley, Jonathan 4:39:39 (22,003)
Lammali, Aziouz 2:44:37 (286)
Lammiman, Chris 3:53:58 (10,299)
Lamont, Christopher 4:38:48 (21,792)
Lamont, Paul 3:42:55 (7,365)
Lamothe, Michel 3:32:48 (5,316)
Lamplough, George 3:50:37 (9,327)
Lamplough, Ian 3:35:56 (5,891)
Lamy, Lionel 4:28:48 (19,257)
Lanahan, Paul 4:58:21 (26,005)
Lanaway, Stephen 5:11:52 (27,935)
Lancashire, Paul 7:05:42 (32,677)
Lancaster, Dave 3:55:38 (10,792)
Lancaster, Gregory 4:21:46 (17,328)
Lancaster, Kenneth 4:55:44 (25,527)
Lancaster, Matthew 4:15:41 (15,750)
Lance, Ian 4:09:43 (14,321)
Lanckham, Kevin 2:58:57 (1,088)
Land, Jonathon 3:28:48 (4,662)
Landale, Jamie 4:41:56 (22,593)
Landau, David 5:24:06 (29,288)
Landells, Stephen 3:58:25 (11,625)
Lander, Christopher 4:07:12 (13,723)
Lander, Peter 3:16:13 (2,811)
Landgraf, Werner 2:59:15 (1,112)
Landman, Olivier 3:47:33 (8,523)
Landon, Guy 3:17:11 (2,917)
Landowski, Paul 3:43:39 (7,564)
Landowski, Richard 4:08:34 (14,045)
Landsberger, Richard 4:13:59 (15,308)
Landy, Adam 4:17:16 (16,192)
Lane, Alasdair 3:33:58 (5,513)
Lane, Andrew 3:03:56 (1,460)
Lane, Barnard 4:51:42 (24,730)
Lane, Ben 3:50:04 (9,184)
Lane, Brian 3:19:43 (3,223)
Lane, Christopher 3:42:13 (7,204)
Lane, David 4:25:33 (18,404)
Lane, Jason 4:08:28 (14,010)
Lane, John 4:42:57 (22,827)
Lane, Kevin 4:35:22 (20,914)
Lane, Michael 3:49:35 (9,066)
Lane, Michael 4:12:36 (15,000)
Lane, Michael 4:42:55 (22,818)
Lane, Peter 4:23:05 (17,726)
Lane, Richard 3:46:06 (8,182)
Lane, Ronald 3:06:30 (1,685)
Lane, Stephen 3:59:51 (12,041)
Lang, Brian 4:07:02 (13,684)
Lang, Karl 4:35:10 (20,866)
Langdell, David 3:23:34 (3,736)
Langdon, Ben 4:14:12 (15,361)
Langdon, Dean 5:15:15 (28,333)
Langdon, Jack 4:20:04 (16,882)
Langella, André 4:10:22 (14,479)
Langer, Roger 4:02:14 (12,604)
Langford, Andy 5:54:12 (31,320)
Langford, Brian 5:23:01 (29,177)
Langford, Simon 4:47:59 (24,024)
Langham, Brian 3:21:11 (3,396)
Langham, George 7:23:05 (32,764)
Langhorn, Michael 3:20:29 (3,311)
Langler, Ian 3:06:11 (1,655)
Langley, Kevin 4:55:21 (25,447)
Langley, Mark 4:19:58 (16,852)
Langley, Robert 2:57:22 (944)
Langley, Toby 3:28:24 (4,588)
Langlois, Jean 2:44:08 (276)
Langman, Chris 3:59:24 (11,919)
Langman, Michael 3:47:58 (8,620)
Langrish, David 5:42:59 (30,757)
Langrish, Ray 4:57:45 (25,907)
Langton, Alan 4:47:31 (23,915)
Langton, Barry 6:11:24 (31,868)
Langton, William 3:45:22 (8,015)
Lanham, James 4:15:05 (15,592)
Lanigan, Graham 4:58:39 (26,067)
Lanigan, Rodney 5:06:58 (27,290)
Lankester, Peter 4:46:42 (23,736)
Lankshear, Richard 3:44:08 (7,691)
Lannigan, Michael 4:09:56 (14,372)
Lannoye, Richard 3:58:07 (11,550)
Lansaque-Sautaux, Jean 4:20:08 (16,896)
Lansdown, Nick 4:27:19 (18,869)
Lansell, Mark 3:31:31 (5,113)
Lant, Steven 4:25:44 (18,448)
Laplain, Trevor 5:29:59 (29,780)
Lapping, Grant 3:21:16 (3,402)
Lapworth, David 3:54:51 (10,557)
Large, Simon 4:20:56 (17,090)
Large, Steven 2:56:41 (888)
Larham, Kevin 3:21:50 (3,491)
Larkham, Richard 4:04:27 (13,078)
Larkin, Hadyn 5:26:29 (29,488)
Larkin, Jamie 2:54:50 (731)
Larkin, Kevin 4:59:06 (26,153)
Larkin, Lee 4:29:14 (19,394)
Larkins, James 5:51:13 (31,196)
Larkins, Simon 3:11:11 (2,174)
Larner, Daniel 5:13:23 (28,124)
Larner, Simon 4:14:29 (15,446)
Larsen, Philip 4:02:18 (12,616)
Larter, Philip 4:13:48 (15,262)
Lashayas Madariaga, Aitor 2:41:23 (214)
Laskow-Pooley, Kurt 3:59:38 (11,977)
Lasky, Paul 4:42:37 (22,750)
Lassen, Michael 4:16:08 (15,873)
Lasseter, David 4:21:49 (17,342)
Lasseur, Claude 4:06:51 (13,638)
Lassise, Mark 5:00:09 (26,328)
Lassus, Neil 4:32:49 (20,306)
Last, Daniel 3:49:51 (9,143)
Last, David 4:40:36 (22,256)
Last, Howard 4:34:36 (20,726)
Latcham, Dean 3:49:26 (9,021)
Latham, Andrew 4:56:07 (25,614)
Latham, Frederick 4:43:17 (22,905)
Latham, Kevin 5:07:31 (27,379)
Latham, Philip 5:49:33 (31,123)
Latter, Andy 4:01:06 (12,337)
Latter, John 3:14:38 (2,621)
Lattimore, Alan 4:24:17 (18,062)
Latto, Brian 3:38:51 (6,495)
Latton, Greg 3:44:05 (7,675)
Latty, Shane 4:12:59 (15,076)
Lau, Cheung 5:13:57 (28,183)
Lau, Keith 4:27:31 (18,922)
Lau, Yuk Lun 4:49:37 (24,345)
Lauber, Hans 4:11:19 (14,696)
Lauder, Simon 4:56:01 (25,587)
Lauffer, Jonathan 5:45:42 (30,922)
Lauren, Markku 2:55:42 (798)
Laurence, Garry 4:13:51 (15,272)
Laurence, Peter 4:01:17 (12,384)
Laurence, William 3:02:51 (1,361)
Laurent, Frederic 3:24:56 (3,980)
Laurent, Jean 3:58:19 (11,593)
Laurent, Michel 5:52:40 (31,261)
Laurie, Graham 3:17:13 (2,922)
Laurie, John 4:45:10 (23,348)
Laurieux, Patrick 2:54:30 (705)
Lauwen, Joost 5:11:27 (27,880)
Lavender, Frederick 5:38:02 (30,416)
Lavender, Richard 3:01:49 (1,284)
Laver, Toby 2:45:42 (319)
Laverick, Peter 5:24:54 (29,354)
Laverty, John 6:06:26 (31,743)
Laverty, Martin 4:47:42 (23,955)
Lavery, Joe 5:54:59 (31,349)
Laviers, Paul 3:55:05 (10,619)
Laville, René 3:33:23 (5,415)
Lavin, Andy 4:40:37 (22,257)
Lavin, Stephen 5:12:52 (28,063)
Lavy, Nicholas 4:28:28 (19,159)
Lavy, Timothy 3:57:50 (11,461)
Law, Eric 5:59:26 (31,529)

Law, Gary	5:17:12 (28,589)	Lazos, Antonios	4:32:14 (20,147)	Lee, Keith	7:13:24 (32,728)
Law, Graham	4:00:34 (12,200)	Le Beuvant, Sean	3:22:39 (3,598)	Lee, Kevin	4:06:17 (13,516)
Law, Matthew	3:56:46 (11,131)	Le Brun, Ian	3:49:39 (9,083)	Lee, Koon Leung	6:59:18 (32,619)
Law, Peter	4:49:24 (24,299)	Le Cocq, Nick	3:45:46 (8,104)	Lee, Martin	2:34:49 (96)
Law, Simon	3:09:18 (1,967)	Le Floch, Herve	2:48:39 (433)	Lee, Melvyn	4:31:47 (20,028)
Lawes, Leslie	4:54:38 (25,307)	Le Gendre, Philippe	3:26:05 (4,161)	Lee, Michael	4:08:15 (13,961)
Lawler, Nicholas	3:58:58 (11,787)	Le Grice, Marcus	3:38:54 (6,501)	Lee, Nicholas	3:47:27 (8,497)
Lawless, Peter	7:16:59 (32,743)	Le Huray, Mathew	3:54:33 (10,472)	Lee, Nigel	3:13:15 (2,467)
Lawless, Philip	4:44:06 (23,086)	Le Jeune, Martin	4:22:04 (17,415)	Lee, Richard	3:18:17 (3,042)
Lawley, Rob	3:56:12 (10,964)	Le Maire, Andrew	3:51:49 (9,628)	Lee, Richard	3:26:07 (4,169)
Lawlor, Kevin	4:28:19 (19,114)	Le Mette, Didier	3:55:31 (10,750)	Lee, Robert	4:30:19 (19,676)
Lawlor, Paul	3:10:46 (2,131)	Le Moing, Lucien	2:41:32 (220)	Lee, Roger	4:49:43 (24,364)
Lawlor, Sean	3:36:32 (6,030)	Le Pelley, Philip	3:57:29 (11,359)	Lee, Stephen	3:23:10 (3,674)
Lawn, Christopher	4:37:58 (21,568)	Le Quesne, John	4:27:19 (18,869)	Lee, Stephen	3:27:14 (4,367)
Lawn, Robert	4:57:43 (25,902)	Le Sueur, Oliver	4:18:06 (16,391)	Lee, Steven	3:44:31 (7,797)
Lawne, James	3:17:22 (2,943)	Le Sueur, Vernon	3:48:35 (8,773)	Lee, Stuart	4:42:44 (22,775)
Lawrence, Adrian	3:54:59 (10,592)	Lea, Jeffrey	3:46:36 (8,314)	Lee, Trevor	3:53:05 (10,013)
Lawrence, Alan	4:55:31 (25,483)	Lea, Peter	5:02:57 (26,734)	Lee-Browne, Patrick	3:49:00 (8,896)
Lawrence, Andrew	3:43:01 (7,392)	Lea Gerrard, Andrew	4:00:12 (12,132)	Leech, Terry	3:10:17 (2,073)
Lawrence, Andrew	4:22:08 (17,431)	Leach, Alan	3:49:46 (9,121)	Leedham, David	4:33:02 (20,360)
Lawrence, Clifford	4:21:18 (17,191)	Leach, David	3:19:32 (3,206)	Lee-Jones, Peter	4:44:43 (23,226)
Lawrence, David	5:16:52 (28,537)	Leach, Eric	5:19:50 (28,855)	Leek, Jonathan	2:53:47 (668)
Lawrence, Francis	5:15:09 (28,315)	Leach, Jonathan	4:34:32 (20,706)	Leek, Steve	3:35:01 (5,714)
Lawrence, Frank	5:11:42 (27,906)	Leach, Mark	4:25:10 (18,302)	Leeks, Clinton	3:42:51 (7,349)
Lawrence, Gary	4:49:41 (24,357)	Leach, Robert	4:01:49 (12,526)	Leeming, Michael	5:27:54 (29,610)
Lawrence, Ian	3:27:26 (4,404)	Leacock, Herman	4:39:54 (22,080)	Leeper, Patrick	5:28:10 (29,629)
Lawrence, Keith	3:27:21 (4,385)	Leadbetter, Ian	4:02:44 (12,709)	Leerink, Hans	3:55:17 (10,687)
Lawrence, Mark	4:49:39 (24,350)	Leader, David	3:23:01 (3,660)	Lees, Bruce	3:35:30 (5,804)
Lawrence, Michael	3:08:51 (1,915)	Leafe, Richard	3:37:13 (6,151)	Lees, Christopher	3:45:31 (8,048)
Lawrence, Michael	4:09:10 (14,178)	Leahy, Ian	3:15:37 (2,738)	Lees, Fraser	3:37:34 (6,239)
Lawrence, Michael	5:11:14 (27,842)	Leahy, Justin	3:47:56 (8,614)	Lees, Robin	4:23:37 (17,851)
Lawrence, Neil	4:48:55 (24,218)	Leahy, Richard	3:27:11 (4,359)	Lees, Wayne	3:58:52 (11,754)
Lawrence, Peter	4:32:43 (20,282)	Leak, Christopher	4:16:38 (16,019)	Leesing, Paul	3:22:32 (3,587)
Lawrence, Robert	3:14:40 (2,627)	Leak, Peter	3:41:23 (7,043)	Lee-Smith, Richard	4:30:16 (19,664)
Lawrence, Robin	5:12:22 (28,007)	Leake, David	3:28:45 (4,646)	Leeves, Paul	3:50:02 (9,175)
Lawrence, Ronnie	3:56:36 (11,086)	Leake, Martin	3:04:59 (1,542)	Lefevre, Jean	5:16:59 (28,553)
Lawrence, Scott	5:21:37 (29,058)	Leakey, Kegan	4:13:36 (15,207)	Legard, Ian	3:58:10 (11,558)
Lawrence, Simon	4:46:46 (23,750)	Leal, Raj	4:08:31 (14,027)	Legg, John	4:48:18 (24,084)
Lawrence, Stephen	4:58:59 (26,128)	Leaning, Sean	4:31:06 (19,855)	Legg, Timothy	3:09:26 (1,985)
Lawrence, Tonh	5:20:25 (28,931)	Lear, Daniel	4:22:30 (17,545)	Leggate, Rees	3:46:21 (8,236)
Lawrence, Tony	4:44:59 (23,297)	Lear, David	2:47:40 (389)	Legge, Jon	3:21:20 (3,411)
Lawrenson, Matthew	4:12:46 (15,034)	Learmont, James	4:37:47 (21,517)	Legge, Timothy	2:55:09 (754)
Lawrie, Denis	4:29:33 (19,467)	Learmonth, David	3:45:58 (8,153)	Leggett, Dominic	3:01:44 (1,275)
Lawrie, Mark	3:42:58 (7,380)	Leary, Colin	5:03:00 (26,738)	Leggett, Simon	3:59:15 (11,868)
Lawry, Alistair	3:39:00 (6,523)	Leather, Giles	4:46:04 (23,587)	Leggett, Theo	4:27:09 (18,832)
Laws, Allan	3:03:51 (1,454)	Leather, Stephen	4:33:38 (20,500)	Legrand, Philippe	3:20:30 (3,312)
Laws, Andrew	4:27:39 (18,951)	Leatherbarrow, Derek	3:42:35 (7,304)	Le-Guen, Jacques	3:45:07 (7,956)
Laws, John	3:25:11 (4,012)	Leatherbarrow, Peter	5:09:31 (27,634)	Lehane, William	4:22:54 (17,671)
Laws, Keith	4:59:08 (26,158)	Leathers, Raymond	4:22:08 (17,431)	Lehmann, Michael	3:48:29 (8,744)
Laws, Richard	5:23:06 (29,185)	Leathley, Nicholas	3:35:37 (5,829)	Lehner, Christoph	3:39:58 (6,725)
Lawson, Adam	3:32:59 (5,351)	Leavesley, James	4:31:02 (19,834)	Lehner, Markos	3:28:40 (4,636)
Lawson, Craig	6:08:52 (31,809)	Leavy, Drew	5:13:51 (28,176)	Lehner, Stefan	3:43:33 (7,540)
Lawson, Ian	3:32:39 (5,297)	Lebidineuse, Jason	5:12:24 (28,014)	Lehner, Ulrich	4:39:43 (22,030)
Lawson, Ian	4:41:04 (22,367)	Le-Bihan, Patrick	4:09:21 (14,232)	Lehoter, Guenter	4:55:40 (25,511)
Lawson, Jonathan	3:57:12 (11,263)	Le-Blanc, Jean	4:22:09 (17,439)	Leib, Robert	5:12:33 (28,032)
Lawson, Jonathan	4:13:12 (15,121)	Leclerc, Lionel	3:30:46 (4,985)	Leifsson, Thorberguv	3:41:24 (7,046)
Lawson, Mark	2:59:41 (1,148)	Lecolle, Christophe	3:37:16 (6,158)	Leigh, Edward	4:16:08 (15,873)
Lawson, Mark	5:28:33 (29,660)	Lederer, Joachim	3:01:50 (1,288)	Leigh, John	4:49:32 (24,327)
Lawson, Matthew	3:27:07 (4,348)	Ledson, Andrew	3:35:42 (5,846)	Leigh, Jon	3:32:26 (5,259)
Lawson, Matthew	4:04:55 (13,189)	Ledwidge, Alan	3:41:26 (7,051)	Leigh, Keith	4:47:46 (23,965)
Lawson, Shaun	3:43:27 (7,513)	Lee, Adrian	3:17:51 (2,995)	Leigh, Nigel	5:18:10 (28,686)
Lawson, Simon	3:27:17 (4,374)	Lee, Alex	4:49:29 (24,318)	Leigh, Robert	3:29:41 (4,824)
Lawther, Dennis	4:06:01 (13,439)	Lee, Allan	2:39:15 (171)	Leinster, Robert	3:47:51 (8,600)
Lawton, Alasdair	3:33:02 (5,357)	Lee, Brian	3:06:59 (1,732)	Leinvuo, Joni	4:24:09 (18,023)
Lawton, Bryan	3:19:20 (3,178)	Lee, Bryan	4:50:39 (24,531)	Leitch, David	3:57:01 (11,214)
Lawton, Oliver	4:24:56 (18,234)	Lee, Christopher	3:57:20 (11,302)	Leitch, Kenny	2:43:24 (251)
Lawton, Peter	3:35:09 (5,742)	Lee, Christopher	5:36:07 (30,285)	Leith, Robin	3:57:11 (11,256)
Lawton, Robert	4:21:07 (17,148)	Lee, Darren	3:28:07 (4,535)	Leitl, Claus	3:18:55 (3,127)
Lawton, William	3:53:19 (10,086)	Lee, David	3:48:27 (8,735)	Lejeune, Erich	4:57:21 (25,833)
Lay, David	4:59:38 (26,250)	Lee, David	4:07:43 (13,845)	Lekanet, Nguliya	3:09:42 (2,007)
Lay, Duncan	4:36:29 (21,214)	Lee, Edward	3:01:05 (1,232)	Leleu, Serge	3:52:07 (9,726)
Laycock, Andrew	2:52:30 (596)	Lee, Eric	4:36:24 (21,190)	Leliard, Troy	3:47:34 (8,530)
Laycock, Grant	4:17:08 (16,154)	Lee, Francis	4:49:04 (24,250)	Lemanski, Philip	3:58:13 (11,571)
Layland, Andrew	3:46:12 (8,201)	Lee, Geoffrey	2:59:03 (1,097)	Lemmermann, Kurt	4:22:21 (17,506)
Layley, Christopher	5:16:59 (28,553)	Lee, Ian	4:07:10 (13,711)	Lemmon, Paul	3:56:35 (11,078)
Layne, William	4:36:19 (21,164)	Lee, James	3:46:06 (8,182)	Lemon, Ben	5:24:28 (29,321)
Lazarus, Joel	4:32:01 (20,088)	Lee, James	4:13:02 (15,092)	Lemon, Darren	4:40:59 (22,350)
Lazell, Luke	3:15:04 (2,670)	Lee, Jayson	2:57:56 (1,001)	Lemon, Mark	3:55:35 (10,778)
Lazell, Richard	3:14:49 (2,641)	Lee, Jeremy	4:32:21 (20,173)	Lemon, Mark	4:07:08 (13,707)
Lazenbury, Neil	4:36:07 (21,106)	Lee, Jeremy	4:51:50 (24,750)	Lemon, Mark	4:47:38 (23,935)
Lazenby, Peter	5:26:25 (29,483)	Lee, John	3:52:29 (9,831)	Lemon, Richard	4:32:41 (20,272)
Lazetera, Giuseppe	4:29:03 (19,335)	Lee, Johnson	3:47:04 (8,399)	Lenaghan, John	3:16:57 (2,897)
Lazo, Pablo	2:56:45 (892)	Lee, Kai	4:35:28 (20,936)	Lennock, Ian	4:12:35 (14,992)

Lennon, Christopher 3:56:51 (11,159)
Lennon, Christopher 4:32:47 (20,298)
Lennox, Gordon 3:03:45 (1,446)
Lenz, Christian 5:17:08 (28,582)
Lenz, Nicholas 3:54:01 (10,314)
Leon, Clement 4:06:26 (13,550)
Leon, Peter 3:54:05 (10,341)
Leonard, Andrew 3:57:53 (11,472)
Leonard, Christopher 3:41:01 (6,966)
Leonard, Eamonn 4:19:07 (16,621)
Leonard, Frank 3:53:03 (10,000)
Leonard, Gary 6:30:08 (32,280)
Leonard, Guy 3:27:54 (4,501)
Leonard, Paul 3:41:36 (7,082)
Leonard, Raymond 4:58:55 (26,115)
Leonard, Stephen 4:30:53 (19,801)
Leonard, Steven 4:56:10 (25,623)
Leonard, Stuart 2:47:35 (384)
Le-Pape, Guenole 4:19:16 (16,657)
Lepere, Patrick 3:54:35 (10,484)
Leppard, Mark 4:28:49 (19,261)
Lescornez, Gerald 3:58:02 (11,522)
Lescott, Charles 3:29:23 (4,774)
Leslie, Glen 3:52:16 (9,771)
Leslie, Julian 3:36:13 (5,960)
Leslie, Karl 4:06:37 (13,592)
Leslie, Luke 4:47:13 (23,859)
Leslie, Tony 5:17:31 (28,631)
Lesoif, Joel 5:47:12 (30,997)
Lespeare, Trevor 3:43:22 (7,491)
Lester, Andrew 3:46:16 (8,215)
Leszek, Mark 4:29:31 (19,460)
Letchford, Darren 3:58:20 (11,600)
Letchworth, Nicholas 3:07:29 (1,767)
Lethaby, Raymond 3:52:45 (9,909)
Lethenet, Didier 3:48:03 (8,639)
Letheren, Michael 3:26:43 (4,281)
Letourneur, Joel 5:47:07 (30,994)
Letsome, Mark 3:52:46 (9,916)
Letwenjuk, Michael 3:30:28 (4,938)
Leuzinger, Walter 3:11:57 (2,267)
Leveau, Lars 3:09:14 (1,956)
Lever, Ian 4:14:47 (15,520)
Leverton, Jack 3:12:19 (2,332)
Levey, Mark 4:49:12 (24,276)
Levick, Paul 2:44:58 (298)
Levin, Lance 3:58:42 (11,707)
Levin, Michael 4:13:15 (15,134)
Levinson, Jeffrey 4:46:56 (23,798)
Levison, John 2:53:15 (639)
Leviten, David 6:05:24 (31,712)
Levitt, Julian 3:53:53 (10,274)
Levitt, Justin 3:52:52 (9,942)
Levoir, Andrew 4:11:39 (14,782)
Levy, Alon 4:16:57 (16,103)
Levy, David 4:26:35 (18,675)
Levy, Jason 4:54:34 (25,301)
Lewin, Bernard 4:53:21 (25,037)
Lewin, Michael 4:17:50 (16,333)
Lewin, Robert 5:03:21 (26,805)
Lewin, Rodolfo 4:43:21 (22,919)
Lewis, Adrian 3:53:06 (10,018)
Lewis, Adrian 4:04:50 (13,167)
Lewis, Alan 3:01:05 (1,232)
Lewis, Alan 4:09:22 (14,242)
Lewis, Alan 4:22:27 (17,535)
Lewis, Allan 5:42:09 (30,702)
Lewis, Andrew 4:24:16 (18,059)
Lewis, Andrew 4:34:16 (20,643)
Lewis, Avid 4:21:20 (17,200)
Lewis, Benjamin 5:07:27 (27,367)
Lewis, Brian 4:06:18 (13,520)
Lewis, Brian 5:20:03 (28,886)
Lewis, Christopher 3:43:11 (7,437)
Lewis, Clive 3:38:12 (6,344)
Lewis, Clive 3:57:04 (11,227)
Lewis, Colin 4:33:11 (20,397)
Lewis, David 3:37:56 (6,300)
Lewis, David 3:58:46 (11,722)
Lewis, David 4:25:00 (18,266)
Lewis, David 4:36:33 (21,236)
Lewis, David 4:39:22 (21,939)
Lewis, David 5:39:29 (30,514)
Lewis, Gary 3:28:19 (4,571)
Lewis, Geoffrey 4:20:12 (16,913)
Lewis, Graham 5:06:31 (27,233)
Lewis, Grahame 5:15:52 (28,423)
Lewis, Gwynfor 4:50:22 (24,473)
Lewis, Ian 4:24:13 (18,041)
Lewis, Ivan 3:54:07 (10,351)
Lewis, James 4:30:59 (19,826)
Lewis, Mark 2:44:36 (285)
Lewis, Martin 3:47:39 (8,546)
Lewis, Matthew 3:50:56 (9,406)
Lewis, Matthew 4:04:00 (12,989)
Lewis, Matthew 5:39:30 (30,518)
Lewis, Michael 3:55:38 (10,792)
Lewis, Neil 4:04:06 (13,008)
Lewis, Neil 4:37:46 (21,509)
Lewis, Patrick 5:03:42 (26,841)
Lewis, Paul 3:11:14 (2,179)
Lewis, Paul 3:33:58 (5,513)
Lewis, Paul 4:21:04 (17,131)
Lewis, Paul 4:46:43 (23,738)
Lewis, Paul 4:51:56 (24,772)
Lewis, Peter 5:01:44 (26,563)
Lewis, Philip 3:43:32 (7,537)
Lewis, Piers 3:09:19 (1,970)
Lewis, Raymond 5:24:56 (29,362)
Lewis, Richard 4:06:20 (13,524)
Lewis, Richard 6:08:15 (31,789)
Lewis, Robert 4:49:19 (24,290)
Lewis, Simon 4:06:14 (13,498)
Lewis, Simon 4:57:55 (25,939)
Lewis, Stephen 4:24:57 (18,242)
Lewis, Steven 4:29:33 (19,467)
Lewis, Steven 5:51:40 (31,222)
Lewis, Timothy 5:19:14 (28,801)
Lewis, Tracy 3:34:32 (5,624)
Lewis, Trevor 4:37:35 (21,466)
Lewis-Azayear, Gerald 7:02:46 (32,658)
Lewis-Manning, Robert 4:23:59 (17,976)
Lewton, Sean 4:38:19 (21,663)
Leyden, Tristan 4:47:13 (23,859)
Leyenda, Manuel 3:33:21 (5,409)
Leyland, Alex 4:26:42 (18,717)
Leyland, Edward 5:10:43 (27,777)
Leyland, Ralph 5:18:40 (28,740)
Leymonie, Philippe 3:54:59 (10,592)
Lherm, Thierry 3:22:51 (3,643)
Lhote, Arnaud 4:14:13 (15,368)
Li, Sammy 3:53:16 (10,071)
Libeau, Hagen 5:13:32 (28,144)
Licata, Antony 3:26:55 (4,315)
Liddiard, Peter 4:47:37 (23,930)
Liddle, Alexander 3:04:26 (1,499)
Liddle, George 3:34:43 (5,662)
Liddle, Ian 4:01:14 (12,374)
Liddle, Robert 2:56:03 (835)
Liddle, Stephen 4:20:00 (16,860)
Liebeskind, Kenneth 3:38:13 (6,348)
Liedags, Ingars 5:02:42 (26,699)
Liedke, Klaus 4:36:39 (21,254)
Life, Alan 3:20:15 (3,283)
Liggett, Daniel 4:36:53 (21,296)
Light, Ian 4:56:28 (25,687)
Light, Stephen 4:38:42 (21,761)
Light, Tim 3:32:44 (5,308)
Lightfoot, Alan 3:18:07 (3,025)
Lightfoot, Jonathan 3:50:18 (9,253)
Lightfoot, Philip 3:37:11 (6,146)
Lightfoot, Thomas 4:27:59 (19,029)
Lightman, Shaun 4:55:56 (25,572)
Lighton, John 6:11:02 (31,860)
Lightwood, Barry 5:16:29 (28,499)
Ligios, Vincenzo 4:21:15 (17,180)
Liljegren, Mats 2:57:44 (982)
Lilley, Chris 5:04:36 (26,965)
Lilley, David 4:15:25 (15,671)
Lilley, Jon 3:38:14 (6,351)
Lilley, Michael 4:51:25 (24,682)
Lilley, Nick 5:16:49 (28,529)
Lilley, Tim 4:33:53 (20,555)
Lilleystone, Roger 6:00:48 (31,573)
Lillico, Ronald 4:18:10 (16,404)
Lilly, John 4:47:07 (23,834)
Lilly, Martin 3:45:36 (8,071)
Lim, Eng 4:11:12 (14,674)
Lim, Guan 4:27:04 (18,810)
Lim, Mark 4:58:12 (25,984)
Limb, Alan 5:31:21 (29,897)
Limb, David 3:09:30 (1,989)
Linares Saiz, José 4:05:52 (13,403)
Lincoln, Brian 3:52:26 (9,820)
Lincoln, Timothy 3:41:11 (7,013)
Lindell, Robert 3:50:35 (9,317)
Linden, Juergen 3:34:51 (5,682)
Lindford, Maurice 3:25:35 (4,075)
Lindgken, Tommy 4:19:52 (16,827)
Lindgren, Ake 3:33:04 (5,362)
Lindholm, Erik 4:41:24 (22,447)
Lindley, Brian 4:22:12 (17,447)
Lindley, Colin 4:06:58 (13,668)
Lindley, Gray 4:01:08 (12,345)
Lindley, Paul 3:16:41 (2,861)
Lindley, Tim 3:27:23 (4,396)
Lindsay, David 4:40:32 (22,239)
Lindsay, Donald 3:11:16 (2,183)
Lindsay, James 3:54:27 (10,443)
Lindsay, John 7:10:03 (32,702)
Lindsay, Patrick 4:28:44 (19,236)
Lindsay, Paul 5:10:33 (27,756)
Lindsay, William 5:10:29 (27,747)
Line, Ian 4:04:44 (13,145)
Line, Matthew 3:44:51 (7,897)
Lineham, Jeremy 4:45:06 (23,333)
Linehan, Kevin 3:25:28 (4,058)
Lines, Chris 4:01:51 (12,535)
Lines, Derek 2:49:20 (459)
Lines, Jason 4:13:41 (15,229)
Liney, Ian 5:31:18 (29,894)
Linforth, Adrian 4:53:04 (24,988)
Ling, Martin 4:21:06 (17,140)
Ling, Robin 4:05:51 (13,400)
Ling, Terry 6:12:11 (31,885)
Ling, Trevor 5:05:59 (27,153)
Lingard, Alex 3:54:09 (10,361)
Lingard, Andrew 4:28:06 (19,054)
Lingard, John 3:06:49 (1,715)
Link, Paul 4:49:50 (24,393)
Linnane, Mark 5:08:51 (27,543)
Linnane, Neil 4:49:37 (24,345)
Linsell, Robin 5:42:31 (30,728)
Linstead, Andrew 4:43:53 (23,036)
Linstead, Michael 5:11:39 (27,901)
Linstow, Jonathan 3:31:41 (5,148)
Lintern, Marc 3:35:14 (5,751)
Linton, Perry 4:41:13 (22,403)
Lintschnig, Peter 4:29:22 (19,424)
Lion, Daniel 4:47:32 (23,917)
Lipczynski, Nicholas 3:55:12 (10,663)
Lipman, Gideon 4:50:17 (24,463)
Lippiett, Adam 3:06:47 (1,710)
Lips, Heinz 5:01:57 (26,598)
Lipsky, Andrew 4:46:56 (23,798)
Li-Rocchi, Rosario 3:16:14 (2,812)
Lisi, Daniel 3:48:04 (8,643)
List, Peter 3:12:59 (2,429)
Lister, Charles 4:15:52 (15,798)
Lister, Ewart 3:34:17 (5,578)
Lister, John 4:55:20 (25,443)
Lister, Nicholas 4:12:18 (14,920)
Liston, Ian 3:40:56 (6,948)
Litchfield, Andrew 4:19:13 (16,649)
Litchfield, David 3:44:34 (7,813)
Litherland, Colin 2:53:50 (669)
Little, Andrew 5:52:55 (31,271)
Little, Dave 4:01:33 (12,457)
Little, Ian 3:11:50 (2,248)
Little, James 5:49:30 (31,120)
Little, Kelvin 4:28:20 (19,119)
Little, Mark 3:53:46 (10,228)
Little, Stewart 2:58:25 (1,041)
Littlechild, Justin 3:04:33 (1,506)
Littlechild, Raymond 4:25:50 (18,468)
Littlecott, Gary 4:05:54 (13,411)
Littlecott, Stephen 3:41:28 (7,059)
Littlefair, John 3:24:16 (3,870)
Littlefield, Daniel 4:19:46 (16,797)

Littlefield, Des 4:37:29 (21,445)
Littler, Frank 3:50:38 (9,334)
Littler, Jules 4:07:25 (13,781)
Littler, Steve 2:39:33 (175)
Littlewood, Graham 4:23:30 (17,825)
Littlewood, Mike 4:06:49 (13,632)
Littlewood, Stephen 3:11:00 (2,154)
Littlewood, Tom 4:19:56 (16,846)
Litton, Thomas 5:18:00 (28,668)
Liu, David 4:26:24 (18,623)
Liu, Yip Kein 5:35:57 (30,264)
Liusso, Piergiorgio 3:48:17 (8,690)
Livermore, Ernest 5:53:03 (31,278)
Livesey, Paul 4:53:28 (25,065)
Livesey, Richard 3:36:00 (5,905)
Livet, Dominique 3:28:05 (4,531)
Livett, Peter 4:41:32 (22,481)
Livingstone, Stuart 5:41:52 (30,687)
Livingstone-Learmont, Max 3:40:02 (6,739)
Lize, François 4:15:00 (15,576)
Llanos-Madrigal, José 3:33:12 (5,382)
Llewellyn, Mark 4:00:24 (12,165)
Llewellyn-Jones, Ivor 3:48:24 (8,721)
Llibre-Pous, Jaume 5:13:58 (28,185)
Llorente, José 3:06:11 (1,655)
Lloyd, Andrew 4:23:52 (17,937)
Lloyd, Andrew 5:03:57 (26,882)
Lloyd, Benjamin 3:14:42 (2,628)
Lloyd, Chris 5:02:00 (26,605)
Lloyd, David 4:37:11 (21,365)
Lloyd, Edward 4:45:50 (23,523)
Lloyd, Gareth 3:20:57 (3,356)
Lloyd, Gareth 4:11:13 (14,678)
Lloyd, Gary 4:16:35 (16,002)
Lloyd, Glyndwr 4:40:54 (22,332)
Lloyd, Gwyn 3:40:21 (6,824)
Lloyd, Ian 3:13:07 (2,450)
Lloyd, Ian 4:01:32 (12,452)
Lloyd, Jonathan 4:04:42 (13,135)
Lloyd, Michael 3:56:13 (10,972)
Lloyd, Nigel 4:44:01 (23,068)
Lloyd, Paul 3:43:01 (7,392)
Lloyd, Peter 4:30:49 (19,792)
Lloyd, Ralph 3:46:15 (8,211)
Lloyd, Rhodri 4:25:53 (18,482)
Lloyd, Rhys 4:25:53 (18,482)
Lloyd, Robin 3:29:50 (4,845)
Lloyd, Roger 6:05:46 (31,724)
Lloyd, Simon 3:22:02 (3,531)
Lloyd, Steve 5:05:45 (27,116)
Lloyd-Brennan, Andrew 4:34:21 (20,658)
Lloyd-Edwards, Thomas 4:45:09 (23,345)
Lluch, Josep 3:32:41 (5,301)
Loach, Simon 3:16:55 (2,892)
Loader, Joe 2:25:20 (42)
Loaiza, Alejandro 2:54:05 (684)
Lobb, Bill 4:03:22 (12,849)
Lobb, Huw 2:21:15 (25)
Lobb, William 3:32:22 (5,243)
Lobley, David 3:56:53 (11,168)
Lobo, Darryl 4:57:36 (25,879)
Lochray, Ian 3:22:07 (3,538)
Lock, Alan 4:11:23 (14,704)
Lock, Anthony 3:32:15 (5,226)
Lock, David 4:18:10 (16,404)
Lock, David 6:09:21 (31,820)
Lock, Gary 4:33:25 (20,445)
Lock, Gary 5:19:23 (28,809)
Lock, Ricky 4:06:11 (13,484)
Locke, Gary 4:22:03 (17,412)
Locker, Robert 4:39:33 (21,985)
Lockey, Paul 4:46:43 (23,738)
Lockie, Derek 4:14:50 (15,533)
Lockie, Gordon 3:24:32 (3,925)
Lockley, Nigel 5:02:35 (26,684)
Lockley, Robin 5:23:12 (29,194)
Lockwood, Andrew 4:52:03 (24,790)
Lockwood, Michael 3:01:57 (1,296)
Lockwood, Paul 4:26:56 (18,771)
Lockwood, Robert 3:46:29 (8,272)
Lockwood, Robert 4:32:49 (20,306)
Lockwood, Robert 5:12:42 (28,047)
Lockwood, Stephen 3:28:43 (4,641)
Lockwood, Steven 5:07:25 (27,360)
Lockyer, Andrew 4:36:00 (21,080)
Lockyer, Charlie 3:53:46 (10,228)
Lockyer, Derek 2:49:51 (482)
Lockyer, Jeremy 3:18:27 (3,062)
Loder, Adam 3:54:52 (10,562)
Loder, Robert 3:53:13 (10,048)
Lodge, Alain 3:40:21 (6,824)
Lodge, Jonathan 4:38:58 (21,834)
Lodge, Stephen 4:59:39 (26,253)
Lofthouse, Gary 5:37:27 (30,381)
Loftus, Carl 3:31:27 (5,100)
Loftus, Kevin 3:02:43 (1,351)
Logan, Michael 4:06:47 (13,627)
Logan, Stuart 2:48:07 (408)
Lohner, Andreas 4:30:17 (19,669)
Loiffait, Louis 4:11:22 (14,701)
Loizou, Christopher 2:55:43 (801)
Loizou, Stavros 4:16:00 (15,839)
Loker, Vernon 4:46:42 (23,736)
Lomas, Gary 3:50:07 (9,192)
Lomas, Gary 4:13:50 (15,267)
Lomas, Gregory 3:25:08 (4,006)
Lomas, Kenneth 5:19:54 (28,858)
Lommaert, Cyril 4:19:50 (16,810)
Loncke, Mark 6:14:04 (31,930)
Londra, Thomas 4:15:06 (15,597)
Lonergan, Ian 3:43:39 (7,564)
Lonergan, John 2:55:44 (803)
Long, Christopher 3:40:28 (6,846)
Long, Darrel 3:50:30 (9,302)
Long, Darrell 3:59:00 (11,806)
Long, David 3:10:20 (2,084)
Long, David 4:19:34 (16,741)
Long, David 4:48:55 (24,218)
Long, Ian 4:28:50 (19,269)
Long, Jean 3:46:21 (8,236)
Long, John 4:45:46 (23,508)
Long, Joseph 4:58:09 (25,973)
Long, Martin 4:58:24 (26,016)
Long, Rupert 3:59:01 (11,810)
Long, Stephen 3:47:01 (8,384)
Long, Stephen 4:40:19 (22,187)
Long, William 4:41:35 (22,491)
Long, Robert Jnr 4:05:42 (13,368)
Longbone, Garry 4:19:27 (16,708)
Longbottom, James 4:37:05 (21,333)
Longbottom, Matthew 3:33:57 (5,509)
Longhurst, Martin 3:20:04 (3,261)
Longhurst, Paul 3:53:23 (10,103)
Longhurst, Raymond 5:01:16 (26,495)
Longman, Dominic 3:47:21 (8,472)
Longstaff, Martyn 3:50:16 (9,242)
Longstaff, Tony 3:55:57 (10,884)
Longsworth, Frank 4:42:56 (22,825)
Longthorp, Andrew 4:16:50 (16,075)
Longworth, Ben 3:44:21 (7,757)
Lonsdale, Ian 4:19:17 (16,665)
Lonsdale, William 3:36:59 (6,114)
Loock, Xavier 4:02:10 (12,588)
Looker, Philip 3:43:30 (7,525)
Loom, Jason 6:03:45 (31,655)
Looney, Richard 3:43:01 (7,392)
Loong, Hing Tong 5:31:52 (29,942)
Loosley, David 4:45:59 (23,560)
Lopeman, Kevan 3:03:21 (1,408)
Lopez, Gerard 5:53:13 (31,289)
Lopez, Sergio 4:39:37 (21,996)
Lopez Cascante, Juan 2:56:45 (892)
Lopez-Gomez, Nicolas 3:01:45 (1,277)
Lord, Christopher 3:01:49 (1,284)
Lord, John 4:06:07 (13,465)
Lord, Shaun 4:41:22 (22,444)
Lorenc, Ronald 4:28:00 (19,032)
Lorenz, Michael 3:44:56 (7,915)
Lorimer, Ray 4:10:35 (14,532)
Lorking, Trevor 4:23:10 (17,742)
Los, Peter 3:40:00 (6,733)
Loscul, Frederic 3:31:14 (5,069)
Loskant, Klaus 3:27:56 (4,505)
Loubon, Micheal 5:19:55 (28,861)
Louca, Cos 3:25:31 (4,067)
Louesdon, Alain 4:38:31 (21,707)
Lougborough, Geoff 3:54:17 (10,396)
Loughlan, D 4:31:22 (19,921)
Loughman, David 4:23:54 (17,948)
Loughnane, Martin 3:05:26 (1,583)
Loughney, Vincent 5:14:52 (28,292)
Loughran, Raymond 3:45:03 (7,940)
Loughrey, Matthew 3:40:47 (6,917)
Louis, Freddy 3:04:45 (1,522)
Lourdel, Florent 3:33:46 (5,469)
Lourie, David 4:09:52 (14,355)
Louw, Mark 4:07:45 (13,858)
Louw, Wynand 4:46:28 (23,685)
Love, Andrew 4:21:13 (17,168)
Love, Andrew 4:35:22 (20,914)
Love, Martin 3:25:35 (4,075)
Love, Nicholas 4:58:02 (25,954)
Love, Stuart 3:42:25 (7,265)
Love, Wesley 5:12:32 (28,027)
Loveday, Christopher 3:33:16 (5,392)
Loveday, Mark 5:26:32 (29,495)
Loveday, Trevor 5:18:20 (28,707)
Lovegrove, James 3:43:36 (7,550)
Lovejoy, Gary 4:18:14 (16,422)
Lovelace, Philip 3:42:56 (7,366)
Loveless, Martin 3:15:42 (2,754)
Lovell, Alistair 3:09:55 (2,029)
Lovell, Ashley 4:07:40 (13,831)
Lovell, Christopher 5:02:08 (26,619)
Lovell, David 3:57:56 (11,483)
Lovell, David 4:54:29 (25,282)
Lovell, Jonathan 4:59:51 (26,282)
Lovell, Peter 3:45:10 (7,962)
Lovell, Simon 4:26:40 (18,711)
Lovell, Stuart 3:36:18 (5,978)
Lovely, Colin 4:26:43 (18,721)
Lovesey, Williams 3:09:19 (1,970)
Lovett, Alan 3:53:46 (10,228)
Lovewell, Peter 4:59:53 (26,286)
Lovewell, Roger 3:33:17 (5,398)
Lovick, John 3:46:04 (8,172)
Low, Brendan 4:00:54 (12,278)
Low, Daniel 4:03:16 (12,831)
Low, Nick 4:03:15 (12,827)
Low, Roger 3:28:09 (4,541)
Lowe, Andrew 4:12:34 (14,984)
Lowe, Craig 5:03:49 (26,859)
Lowe, David 5:30:07 (29,789)
Lowe, Ian 3:48:35 (8,773)
Lowe, Karl 3:36:46 (6,069)
Lowe, Matthew 3:03:49 (1,451)
Lowe, Nicholas 4:27:21 (18,875)
Lowe, Paul 3:40:01 (6,737)
Lowe, Peter 4:10:00 (14,385)
Lowe, Robert 3:58:21 (11,601)
Lower, Dorian 4:11:55 (14,837)
Lower, Rob 3:08:09 (1,819)
Lowis, Stephen 4:45:54 (23,541)
Lowitt, Saul 6:11:22 (31,867)
Lown, Brian 5:31:52 (29,942)
Lowndes, Nigel 4:44:46 (23,240)
Lowndes, Paul 3:56:23 (11,015)
Lowndes, Simon 4:16:46 (16,056)
Lowrie, Martyn 4:10:42 (14,552)
Lowry, Kevin 4:42:29 (22,719)
Lowry, Robert 4:27:51 (18,996)
Lowson, Richard 3:33:32 (5,430)
Loxton, Paul 3:21:02 (3,371)
Loxton-Edwards, Piers 4:36:12 (21,130)
Loydall, Mark 5:29:11 (29,710)
Luby, Michael 5:41:52 (30,687)
Lucas, Adrian 5:32:54 (30,014)
Lucas, Alan 3:29:21 (4,766)
Lucas, Bernard 3:20:12 (3,277)
Lucas, Daniel 4:43:25 (22,938)
Lucas, David 3:41:49 (7,117)
Lucas, John 3:25:22 (4,039)
Lucas, Martin 2:56:53 (906)
Lucas, Mike 4:38:29 (21,697)
Lucas, Richard 5:59:39 (31,534)
Lucas, Victor 4:40:42 (22,277)
Lucbereilh, Regis 3:49:10 (8,939)
Luce, John 5:15:50 (28,418)
Luchinger, Peter 3:59:52 (12,046)

Maddocks, Jason 3:52:07 (9,726)
Maddocks, Joseph 5:58:18 (31,487)
Maddox, Colin 3:51:42 (9,593)
Madeira, Pedro 3:52:53 (9,945)
Maderecker, Michael 3:05:33 (1,596)
Madgett, Oliver 4:19:20 (16,673)
Madura, Percy 5:18:42 (28,745)
Maes, Bart 4:30:13 (19,655)
Magalhaes, Paulo 2:43:22 (250)
Magan, Bryan 5:16:26 (28,495)
Magee, Ken 3:41:37 (7,084)
Magellan, Jon 4:54:52 (25,358)
Maggs, Adrian 2:58:50 (1,078)
Maggs, Keith 4:12:08 (14,887)
Maggs, Simon 3:11:54 (2,258)
Magill, Colin 4:46:02 (23,579)
Magnall, Philip 4:00:32 (12,194)
Magner, Christopher 4:51:04 (24,619)
Magnus, Daniel 3:39:54 (6,710)
Magnus, Serge 3:11:07 (2,170)
Magnusson, Voggur 3:31:30 (5,109)
Magona, Steven 4:05:03 (13,223)
Magor, Ian 3:35:40 (5,837)
Magro Servet, Vicente 3:28:38 (4,631)
Maguire, Aidan 4:11:33 (14,756)
Maguire, Chris 4:53:27 (25,057)
Maguire, Corrigan 5:20:28 (28,934)
Maguire, Gerry 3:42:45 (7,326)
Maguire, Graham 3:32:38 (5,296)
Maguire, Kevin 5:23:14 (29,197)
Maguire, Paul 3:15:15 (2,694)
Maguire, Terence 6:03:08 (31,641)
Mahadevan, Louis 4:39:51 (22,070)
Mahaffey, Simon 4:50:22 (24,473)
Maher, Derek 4:21:10 (17,161)
Maher, Patrick 3:33:28 (5,425)
Maher, Peter 3:20:18 (3,292)
Maheswaran, Shanmaga 5:33:49 (30,094)
Mahmood, Mazhar 4:02:19 (12,619)
Mahmood, Tariq 6:27:38 (32,235)
Mahon, Michael 3:46:11 (8,196)
Mahoney, Andrew 2:55:29 (779)
Mahoney, Gerard 5:01:50 (26,572)
Mahoney, James 3:56:28 (11,033)
Mahoney, Mark 4:48:24 (24,104)
Mahoney, Shaun 5:25:52 (29,434)
Mahoney, Simon 4:29:22 (19,424)
Mahoney, Terry 4:12:46 (15,034)
Mahony, Michael 5:21:02 (28,994)
Mahta, Paresh 3:54:39 (10,501)
Maidman, Terry 3:55:12 (10,663)
Maillard, Edmund 4:51:46 (24,736)
Mailley Smith, Wesley 3:33:47 (5,474)
Mainguet, Jacques 2:55:53 (818)
Mainini, Max 5:28:05 (29,623)
Mainix, Christian 3:09:26 (1,985)
Mainix, Christian 3:52:29 (9,831)
Maiquez, Marc 4:36:52 (21,292)
Maisey, Colin 4:39:39 (22,003)
Maisey, Peter 2:50:25 (505)
Maitland-Titterton, Rupert 4:31:20 (19,912)
Majer, Raymond 4:36:22 (21,182)
Major, Alan 3:30:29 (4,941)
Major, David 3:52:08 (9,736)
Major, Paul 2:45:27 (311)
Makanjvola, Taiwo 4:43:55 (23,048)
Makemson, Nick 5:12:22 (28,007)
Makepeace, Jeremy 4:23:40 (17,864)
Makin, Dick 4:01:50 (12,531)
Makin, Frank 3:42:42 (7,316)
Makin, Mark 4:22:59 (17,702)
Makinson, Barrie 3:30:23 (4,931)
Makonnen, John 3:27:18 (4,378)
Mal, Firouz 3:12:54 (2,417)
Malaterre, Gilles 4:44:10 (23,099)
Malcolm, David 3:47:48 (8,589)
Malcolm, Graeme 3:57:22 (11,307)
Malcolm, Thomas 3:17:29 (2,956)
Malcolm-Smith, Michael 3:28:53 (4,676)
Malcolmson, Angus 4:14:18 (15,391)
Male, Tony 4:45:01 (23,312)
Males, Anthony 3:25:35 (4,075)
Males, Stuart 3:04:38 (1,513)
Malherbe, Jacky 4:39:38 (21,999)
Malherbe, Martin 3:26:19 (4,207)
Malik, Adam 3:28:51 (4,671)
Malik, Adnan 4:08:27 (14,003)
Malik, Karam 3:56:18 (10,989)
Malinowski, Thomas 4:33:01 (20,357)
Mall, Mark 5:05:34 (27,093)
Mall, Patrick 4:09:10 (14,178)
Mallalieu, David 4:44:14 (23,112)
Mallandaine, Michael 4:25:04 (18,277)
Mallard, Andy 4:45:01 (23,312)
Mallen, Garry 4:28:55 (19,294)
Mallender, Mark 4:30:04 (19,615)
Mallery, Phillip 3:18:21 (3,051)
Mallett, Matthew 6:30:04 (32,278)
Mallett, Michael 4:42:26 (22,706)
Mallett, Paul 6:21:00 (32,104)
Mallett, Ross 3:38:55 (6,505)
Mallon, Andrew 4:28:28 (19,159)
Maloingne, Sebastien 3:25:01 (3,987)
Malone, Ian 2:25:09 (40)
Malone, Sean 5:12:01 (27,955)
Maloney, Derek 3:46:16 (8,215)
Maloney, John 3:47:08 (8,414)
Malpass, Ian 4:46:19 (23,639)
Malyan, Paul 4:54:42 (25,323)
Malyon, Ashley 5:20:22 (28,923)
Man, Tony 3:41:42 (7,099)
Manda, Michel 2:59:25 (1,126)
Mandel, Neil 4:53:01 (24,978)
Manders, Tom 3:20:19 (3,294)
Mandi, Rupert 3:58:57 (11,779)
Mandron, Pierre 4:16:19 (15,921)
Manfrini, Pierluigi 4:42:59 (22,834)
Mangeot, Andrew 3:12:37 (2,375)
Manger, Garth 3:27:01 (4,331)
Mangon, Ted 4:12:33 (14,980)
Manicom, Grant 4:22:35 (17,568)
Manion, Martin 3:40:20 (6,819)
Manir, Mohammed 2:36:23 (114)
Maniscalco, Jean 3:20:33 (3,321)
Mankee, Grant 3:14:18 (2,592)
Manley, David 3:57:38 (11,406)
Manley, Neale 5:02:05 (26,614)
Manly, Ronan 3:20:31 (3,316)
Mann, Adrian 4:09:32 (14,275)
Mann, Andrew 4:43:10 (22,885)
Mann, Brian 5:20:36 (28,949)
Mann, Christopher 4:57:13 (25,813)
Mann, Darren 3:48:20 (8,705)
Mann, Dave 3:20:15 (3,283)
Mann, David 3:26:56 (4,317)
Mann, David 4:03:49 (12,947)
Mann, David 4:54:18 (25,243)
Mann, Dennis 4:21:01 (17,117)
Mann, Gian 3:47:10 (8,426)
Mann, James 4:18:48 (16,548)
Mann, James 5:20:42 (28,961)
Mann, Lionel 6:07:32 (31,774)
Mann, Mark 2:49:07 (452)
Mann, Paul 3:03:15 (1,396)
Mann, Paul 3:07:14 (1,753)
Mann, Pete 3:02:14 (1,316)
Mann, Peter 3:41:24 (7,046)
Mann, Phil 3:56:54 (11,174)
Mann, Simon 4:33:04 (20,370)
Mann, Stephen 4:48:36 (24,147)
Mann, Steve 4:25:05 (18,281)
Mann, Stuart 3:07:56 (1,802)
Mann, Stuart 4:50:58 (24,604)
Mann, Tom 4:27:31 (18,922)
Mannering, Stuart 3:31:34 (5,117)
Manners, Richard 3:36:57 (6,107)
Manners, Rick 3:36:21 (5,992)
Manning, Bruce 3:30:15 (4,901)
Manning, Dennis 4:19:24 (16,688)
Manning, Gary 3:31:38 (5,135)
Manning, Jason 3:04:48 (1,524)
Manning, Julian 2:57:51 (994)
Manning, Lee 4:21:58 (17,382)
Manning, Mark 4:44:26 (23,157)
Manning, Rodger 2:57:33 (963)
Mannion, Christopher 4:10:53 (14,601)
Mannion, Daniel 3:21:22 (3,414)
Mannion, Robert 4:51:38 (24,723)
Mansergh, Andrew 3:10:19 (2,079)
Mansfield, Angus 4:21:52 (17,359)
Mansfield, Brian 7:28:47 (32,781)
Mansfield, David 3:30:22 (4,924)
Mansfield, John 4:51:33 (24,711)
Mansfield, John 4:59:34 (26,236)
Mansfield, Matthew 4:44:17 (23,128)
Mansfield, Philip 5:05:12 (27,044)
Mansfield, Stephen 3:40:38 (6,878)
Mansfield, William 3:43:08 (7,426)
Mansfield, William 4:31:40 (20,003)
Manship, David 3:39:28 (6,617)
Mansi, Andrew 2:57:34 (966)
Manson, Alex 5:19:34 (28,826)
Manson, Hamish 4:43:42 (22,997)
Manson, Nicholas 3:55:41 (10,803)
Mansworth, Russell 4:26:13 (18,578)
Mantel, David 4:32:21 (20,173)
Mantel, Rob 3:41:22 (7,041)
Mantell, Darren 4:46:40 (23,731)
Mantell, Jonathan 3:44:22 (7,765)
Mantell, Stephen 3:41:01 (6,966)
Mantle, David 3:52:07 (9,726)
Mantovani, Giorgio 4:04:26 (13,076)
Manuel, David 4:43:55 (23,048)
Manuel, Harry 4:47:14 (23,862)
Manwaring, Mark 4:45:14 (23,366)
Manzoor, Asif 4:46:22 (23,660)
Maout, Yann 2:59:24 (1,121)
Mape, Jonathan 4:55:56 (25,572)
Mapp, George 4:59:32 (26,227)
Mappin, James 4:28:49 (19,261)
Maquillen, Gordon 3:34:54 (5,695)
Maran, Matthew 3:42:47 (7,339)
Marcelle, Nicholas 3:58:47 (11,729)
March, Steve 3:28:55 (4,684)
Marchak, Chris 3:30:17 (4,912)
Marchant, Barry 6:36:57 (32,395)
Marchant, James 3:44:45 (7,874)
Marchmont, Richard 5:08:16 (27,467)
Marchon, Gerard 3:16:27 (2,837)
Marci, Valerio 2:45:42 (319)
Marcinkiewicz, Henry 6:53:13 (32,571)
Marcolini, Fracnesco 4:04:15 (13,039)
Marcolongo, Claudid 6:23:22 (32,157)
Marculewicz, Michel 4:08:22 (13,982)
Marcus, Ian 4:33:39 (20,506)
Marcus, Neil 4:10:21 (14,471)
Margelisch, David 5:27:14 (29,543)
Margereson, Matt 4:08:00 (13,911)
Margo, Gideon 4:34:37 (20,731)
Maric, Peter 4:26:30 (18,653)
Marie, Antonio 5:12:24 (28,014)
Marie, Cyprien 4:56:55 (25,749)
Mariette, Serge 3:10:26 (2,092)
Marigold, Robert 4:32:59 (20,355)
Maris, Graham 4:11:01 (14,633)
Mariutto, Phil 4:58:45 (26,091)
Marjoram, Edward 4:03:42 (12,918)
Marke, Neil 3:03:17 (1,403)
Markham, David 4:28:07 (19,058)
Markham, Derek 5:21:42 (29,068)
Markham, Michael 3:29:50 (4,845)
Markham, Steve 4:07:30 (13,799)
Marklew, Steve 2:48:20 (420)
Marks, Anthony 4:56:44 (25,723)
Marks, Hugh 4:31:02 (19,834)
Marks, Philip 2:55:42 (798)
Marks, Stuart 3:20:35 (3,323)
Markusson, Markus 3:27:30 (4,418)
Markwell, Kevin 4:39:34 (21,989)
Markwell, Nick 4:34:31 (20,704)
Marland, Richard 3:26:31 (4,234)
Marler, Stephen 5:30:47 (29,848)
Marles, Ben 4:36:02 (21,088)
Marles, Paul 4:31:05 (19,852)
Marlow, Gary 4:12:35 (14,992)
Marmarchi, Laith 4:30:16 (19,664)
Marmifero, Dario 3:28:49 (4,665)
Marniquet, Cyril 4:16:35 (16,002)
Marpole, Andrew 4:17:57 (16,359)

Marques, Arsenio	3:25:05 (4,000)
Marques, Joao	3:53:01 (9,985)
Marquet, André	4:36:45 (21,268)
Marquis-Jones, Peter	4:14:27 (15,441)
Marr, James	4:19:01 (16,597)
Marrall, Grant	3:40:03 (6,744)
Marriage, Benjamin	4:22:17 (17,472)
Marriott, Alan	5:16:38 (28,516)
Marriott, Craig	3:25:37 (4,085)
Marriott, David	4:15:23 (15,662)
Marriott, Neil	3:10:54 (2,142)
Marriott, Richard	3:53:23 (10,103)
Marriott Reynolds, Anthony	5:03:29 (26,820)
Marris, Roger	4:05:16 (13,267)
Marrison, Andrew	3:03:41 (1,439)
Marron, Stephen	3:55:18 (10,696)
Marrs, Thomas	3:55:57 (10,884)
Marsden, Brian	4:34:42 (20,750)
Marsden, Christian	4:22:20 (17,493)
Marsden, George	4:05:57 (13,425)
Marsden, John	4:41:24 (22,447)
Marsden, Joseph	4:40:28 (22,225)
Marsden, Keith	4:49:55 (24,409)
Marsden, Paul	3:26:34 (4,243)
Marsden-Huggins, Tudor	4:30:35 (19,729)
Marseille, Eric	4:56:10 (25,623)
Marsh, Alan	5:01:51 (26,577)
Marsh, Brett	3:56:50 (11,149)
Marsh, Daniel	3:35:27 (5,794)
Marsh, David	5:01:54 (26,588)
Marsh, Gary	4:30:55 (19,813)
Marsh, Gavin	3:52:12 (9,754)
Marsh, Guy	5:13:59 (28,188)
Marsh, James	4:25:23 (18,358)
Marsh, Jonathan	3:29:44 (4,835)
Marsh, Nicholas	3:22:16 (3,561)
Marsh, Nigel	3:39:28 (6,617)
Marsh, Oliver	3:59:06 (11,830)
Marsh, Richard	3:47:39 (8,546)
Marsh, Sam	3:33:51 (5,486)
Marsh, Stephen	4:03:24 (12,859)
Marsh, Stephen	5:34:40 (30,165)
Marshall, Alasdair	3:37:28 (6,203)
Marshall, Alexander	4:25:31 (18,393)
Marshall, Andrew	3:11:46 (2,240)
Marshall, Andrew	3:53:03 (10,000)
Marshall, Andrew	4:07:04 (13,691)
Marshall, Andrew	4:51:18 (24,669)
Marshall, Brian	3:58:57 (11,779)
Marshall, Christian	3:33:22 (5,412)
Marshall, Christopher	3:35:07 (5,736)
Marshall, Colin	4:30:17 (19,669)
Marshall, Craig	3:38:32 (6,436)
Marshall, Daniel	3:53:17 (10,075)
Marshall, David	3:45:54 (8,134)
Marshall, David	5:21:05 (29,008)
Marshall, Dean	5:12:19 (28,003)
Marshall, Gary	4:41:36 (22,498)
Marshall, Graeme	3:51:00 (9,425)
Marshall, Ian	3:16:50 (2,885)
Marshall, Jason	4:10:30 (14,510)
Marshall, Jason	5:12:14 (27,979)
Marshall, John	3:31:16 (5,072)
Marshall, John	5:06:24 (27,213)
Marshall, Kevin	3:57:34 (11,386)
Marshall, Kevin	4:08:53 (14,109)
Marshall, Lee	3:56:54 (11,174)
Marshall, Les	4:41:46 (22,549)
Marshall, Matthew	3:46:30 (8,285)
Marshall, Nicholas	3:39:06 (6,548)
Marshall, Nigel	4:16:43 (16,041)
Marshall, Paul	4:10:13 (14,440)
Marshall, Paul	4:46:09 (23,607)
Marshall, Peter	5:08:23 (27,480)
Marshall, Shaun	3:48:40 (8,802)
Marshall, Simon	4:16:06 (15,864)
Marshall-Andrew, Angus	4:08:51 (14,102)
Marsham, Jeffrey	3:55:54 (10,872)
Marshlain, Guy	4:15:18 (15,638)
Marston, Glyn	3:45:40 (8,086)
Marston, Paul	3:55:22 (10,714)
Martel, Alain	4:50:55 (24,594)
Martell, Paul	3:47:11 (8,433)

Martelli, Simon	3:22:11 (3,548)
Marti, Markus	3:30:54 (5,011)
Martin, Alan	5:16:55 (28,545)
Martin, Alistair	3:48:16 (8,688)
Martin, Andrew	4:16:29 (15,976)
Martin, Andrew	5:03:59 (26,887)
Martin, Barry	4:42:14 (22,657)
Martin, Barry	4:56:47 (25,729)
Martin, Ben	4:47:56 (24,018)
Martin, Bob	3:02:39 (1,344)
Martin, Bob	3:20:04 (3,261)
Martin, Bruce	4:03:42 (12,918)
Martin, Clive	4:25:19 (18,341)
Martin, Daniel	3:48:20 (8,705)
Martin, Danny	3:33:10 (5,377)
Martin, David	3:56:55 (11,181)
Martin, David	4:15:50 (15,786)
Martin, David	5:23:58 (29,278)
Martin, Dean	4:52:43 (24,918)
Martin, Don	6:05:22 (31,710)
Martin, Edward	3:43:57 (7,643)
Martin, Ernie	4:20:32 (17,000)
Martin, Francis	2:55:22 (768)
Martin, Gary	3:20:13 (3,281)
Martin, Gary	4:02:24 (12,632)
Martin, Gary	4:55:23 (25,461)
Martin, Graeme	5:14:54 (28,295)
Martin, Ian	5:16:49 (28,529)
Martin, Jean	3:45:58 (8,153)
Martin, Jeff	3:42:41 (7,313)
Martin, Jim	4:25:19 (18,341)
Martin, Joe	4:47:08 (23,840)
Martin, John	4:26:13 (18,578)
Martin, Kenneth	3:33:37 (5,445)
Martin, Kevin	3:32:01 (5,193)
Martin, Kevin	3:44:25 (7,778)
Martin, Kevin	4:53:13 (25,017)
Martin, Lee	3:31:33 (5,116)
Martin, Mark	3:59:01 (11,810)
Martin, Michael	3:55:11 (10,658)
Martin, Michael	5:05:45 (27,116)
Martin, Nick	3:14:02 (2,559)
Martin, Nick	4:50:08 (24,443)
Martin, Paul	4:10:55 (14,612)
Martin, Paul	4:46:21 (23,652)
Martin, Paul	5:22:47 (29,158)
Martin, Philip	3:53:00 (9,976)
Martin, Philip	10:39:28 (32,899)
Martin, Richard	4:14:10 (15,349)
Martin, Richard	5:04:17 (26,933)
Martin, Ricki	4:35:40 (21,008)
Martin, Robin	4:23:21 (17,786)
Martin, Ron	4:15:05 (15,592)
Martin, Simon	3:36:55 (6,099)
Martin, Simon	4:12:57 (15,074)
Martin, Stephen	3:34:17 (5,578)
Martin, Strutz	4:04:03 (12,998)
Martindale, Roger	3:39:48 (6,686)
Martin-Dye, Benjamin	3:16:36 (2,854)
Martinez, Octavio	4:42:20 (22,683)
Martinez Gomez, Diego	4:16:34 (15,996)
Martinez-Perez, Vicente	3:30:33 (4,952)
Martino, Antonio	4:21:13 (17,168)
Martins, Antonio	4:20:38 (17,027)
Martorell-Aymerich, Joaquim	4:09:23 (14,245)
Martyn, Nick	2:30:17 (66)
Maru, Tony	2:58:38 (1,063)
Maruzzi, Lino	5:07:12 (27,328)
Marven, Roger	4:04:57 (13,197)
Marx, Wolfram	3:25:19 (4,033)
Maryan, David	4:26:59 (18,782)
Marzian, Wolfgang	5:22:04 (29,097)
Marzolini, Dan	4:18:31 (16,489)
Masango, Michael	6:07:58 (31,781)
Masefield, Ian	4:50:51 (24,580)
Masignan, Bertillo	5:01:31 (26,527)
Maskell, Paul	5:21:22 (29,032)
Maslanka, Laurence	4:05:11 (13,248)
Maslen, Robert	4:11:23 (14,704)
Masley, Christopher	3:48:23 (8,718)
Masley, Joseph	3:59:33 (11,951)
Mason, Anthony	4:52:21 (24,851)
Mason, Christian	3:19:24 (3,185)

Mason, Christopher	4:39:13 (21,905)
Mason, Christopher	5:45:05 (30,886)
Mason, David	4:47:55 (24,010)
Mason, Jack	3:31:05 (5,043)
Mason, Jake	4:09:37 (14,295)
Mason, James	4:11:36 (14,768)
Mason, Jim	4:01:10 (12,356)
Mason, John	3:28:26 (4,594)
Mason, Keith	3:05:25 (1,582)
Mason, Leslie	3:33:17 (5,398)
Mason, Marc	3:03:09 (1,384)
Mason, Mark	3:58:57 (11,779)
Mason, Martin	4:10:13 (14,440)
Mason, Simon	4:10:37 (14,539)
Mason, Paul	3:37:18 (6,163)
Mason, Paul	4:09:40 (14,309)
Mason, Peter	4:07:08 (13,701)
Mason, Richard	2:48:57 (444)
Mason, Simon	3:49:09 (8,934)
Mason, Stanley	5:07:28 (27,370)
Mason, Stephen	3:44:08 (7,691)
Mason, Terry	3:44:24 (7,773)
Mass, James	4:39:07 (21,877)
Massarella, Mark	5:17:50 (28,654)
Masse, Pierre	3:34:30 (5,618)
Massey, Adrian	2:58:10 (1,018)
Massey, Brynnen	3:37:17 (6,160)
Massey, Darren	4:01:08 (12,345)
Massey, Kevin	5:02:46 (26,704)
Massimi, Amedeo	3:40:11 (6,779)
Massini, Fulvio	4:58:32 (26,038)
Massjuk, Malcolm	5:24:49 (29,345)
Masson, Dave	4:30:08 (19,635)
Masson, François	3:28:15 (4,560)
Masson, James	4:16:33 (15,991)
Masson, William	4:26:19 (18,601)
Massoulie, Fabrice	3:12:20 (2,337)
Mast, Johannes	3:54:56 (10,574)
Masters, Andrew	3:44:10 (7,698)
Masters, Gary	3:50:28 (9,294)
Masters, Harry	3:58:22 (11,607)
Masters, Michael	4:53:56 (25,168)
Masterson, Michael	4:01:38 (12,476)
Mastin, Jonathan	3:59:57 (12,073)
Mathe, Jean	3:17:13 (2,922)
Mather, Colin	5:29:11 (29,710)
Mather, David	2:59:28 (1,129)
Mather, Frank	3:47:04 (8,399)
Mather, Godfrey	4:19:38 (16,759)
Mather, Nick	5:08:57 (27,564)
Mather, Paul	5:29:11 (29,710)
Mather, Peter	4:20:22 (16,959)
Mathers, Frank	4:36:56 (21,305)
Mathers, Ian	6:04:51 (31,689)
Mathers, Simon	3:34:44 (5,666)
Matheson, Andrew	4:39:45 (22,044)
Matheson, Iain	4:21:02 (17,123)
Mathew, Malcolm	3:24:18 (3,877)
Mathews, Ian	4:08:51 (14,102)
Mathews, Rupert	3:52:54 (9,952)
Mathias, Thomas	4:04:05 (13,005)
Mathieson, Grant	3:56:59 (11,203)
Mathieson, Muir	3:40:26 (6,841)
Mathieson, Paul	4:16:20 (15,924)
Mathieson, Peter	2:58:47 (1,073)
Mathieson, Simon	3:55:12 (10,663)
Mathieu, Frederic	3:41:46 (7,111)
Mathurin, Mark	4:02:00 (12,560)
Matijuk, Stephen	4:52:56 (24,970)
Matkin, Neil	4:07:40 (13,831)
Maton, Nicholas	3:55:16 (10,684)
Matsak, Vladimir	4:29:12 (19,380)
Matson, Alistair	3:13:40 (2,526)
Matson, Andrew	5:44:32 (30,859)
Matson De Laurier, Peter	5:41:51 (30,685)
Matsuda, Tetsuaki	2:43:31 (255)
Matt, Bernhard	4:02:06 (12,575)
Matthews, Paul	4:13:12 (15,121)
Matthews, Sean	3:26:39 (4,262)
Mattens, Gunther	3:14:06 (2,563)
Mattern, Georg	3:45:04 (7,946)
Matthams, David	4:13:50 (15,267)
Matthew, Lindsay	4:46:44 (23,742)

Matthews, Allen 4:42:40 (22,760)
Matthews, Andrew 3:43:12 (7,442)
Matthews, Carl 4:38:05 (21,596)
Matthews, Darren 3:48:18 (8,693)
Matthews, David 3:24:09 (3,848)
Matthews, Edward 4:17:52 (16,341)
Matthews, Graham 3:57:18 (11,293)
Matthews, Hamilton 3:22:47 (3,632)
Matthews, Karl 4:56:30 (25,691)
Matthews, Kenneth 4:37:14 (21,380)
Matthews, Kev 4:55:51 (25,550)
Matthews, Mark 5:35:55 (30,262)
Matthews, Martin 4:21:22 (17,210)
Matthews, Michael 3:29:43 (4,829)
Matthews, Montague 3:48:36 (8,782)
Matthews, Paul 3:39:50 (6,693)
Matthews, Phil 4:06:32 (13,576)
Matthews, Ricky 5:22:54 (29,167)
Matthews, Robert 3:40:50 (6,925)
Matthews, Robert 4:39:31 (21,973)
Matthews, Ryan 3:21:49 (3,487)
Matthews, Stephen 4:23:21 (17,786)
Matthews, Stephen 4:42:29 (22,719)
Matthews, Steve 4:22:51 (17,658)
Matthews, Stuart 4:13:59 (15,308)
Mattick, Johnathan 4:45:48 (23,518)
Mattinson, John 4:47:33 (23,919)
Mattison, Michael 2:59:30 (1,135)
Mattock, Robert 4:10:27 (14,497)
Mattocks, Darryl 4:56:36 (25,704)
Matueson, Donald 3:14:43 (2,629)
Matuku, Rohan 4:27:35 (18,933)
Maud, Greg 3:43:03 (7,400)
Maude, Jason 5:08:35 (27,506)
Maude, Stephen 3:34:20 (5,587)
Maude-Roxby, William 4:40:48 (22,310)
Maugham, Barry 3:16:07 (2,799)
Maughan, Christopher 4:25:28 (18,377)
Maughan, David 4:22:31 (17,550)
Mauldon, Kenneth 3:43:35 (7,546)
Maunder, John 4:35:36 (20,987)
Maunder, Neil 5:01:34 (26,537)
Mavani, Aakash 5:28:01 (29,618)
Mavromihales, Michael 2:38:39 (159)
Maw, Patrick 4:18:49 (16,551)
Mawer, Roger 4:08:15 (13,961)
Mawgan, Stephen 6:59:01 (32,615)
Maxl, Martin 3:26:48 (4,294)
Maxted, Malcolm 4:22:13 (17,449)
Maxwell, Nigel 5:10:39 (27,768)
Maxwell, Paul 4:36:16 (21,142)
Maxwell, Peter 3:42:27 (7,276)
Maxwell, Ross 3:42:10 (7,193)
Maxwell, Stephen 3:38:23 (6,394)
May, Darran 4:29:53 (19,569)
May, Douglas 5:22:14 (29,110)
May, Gavin 2:48:29 (426)
May, Gavin 4:12:14 (14,909)
May, Graham 4:01:33 (12,457)
May, Howard 3:48:17 (8,690)
May, John 4:33:37 (20,498)
May, Jonathan 4:39:09 (21,886)
May, Kieron 4:10:01 (14,389)
May, Martin 4:40:11 (22,154)
May, Michael 4:23:58 (17,965)
May, Pau 5:32:56 (30,019)
May, Philip 4:22:51 (17,658)
May, Philip 4:27:43 (18,964)
May, Richard 4:27:41 (18,959)
May, Simon 4:24:27 (18,106)
May, Tom 2:51:04 (535)
Mayall, Robert 6:18:40 (32,053)
Maybin, Christopher 4:22:55 (17,677)
Maydew, Jonathan 4:50:48 (24,564)
Mayer, Christopher 3:24:54 (3,972)
Mayer, Olivier 2:43:17 (247)
Mayer, Raymond 5:31:00 (29,861)
Mayers, Toby 3:59:55 (12,063)
Mayes, Emerson 4:17:25 (16,227)
Mayes, Paul 4:39:16 (21,916)
Mayfield, Oliver 6:06:39 (31,744)
Mayhead, John 3:59:07 (11,833)
Mayhook, Mark 3:47:15 (8,449)
Maylor, Richard 4:16:11 (15,889)
Maynard, Alan 5:20:49 (28,978)
Maynard, Graham 3:05:22 (1,576)
Maynard, Philip 5:21:19 (29,026)
Mayne, Christopher 5:25:53 (29,437)
Mayne, Jonathan 3:59:50 (12,036)
Mayne, Richard 4:20:20 (16,951)
Mayo, Alan 4:28:56 (19,297)
Mayo, Duncan 4:38:36 (21,742)
Mayo, Simon 3:22:47 (3,632)
Mayr, Josef 3:30:36 (4,963)
Maystone, Martin 4:07:23 (13,771)
Maytham, Gary 3:51:56 (9,657)
Mayward, Mark 4:41:21 (22,439)
Maza, Rico 4:40:19 (22,187)
Mazouni, Ali 4:16:08 (15,873)
Mazurkiewicz, Colin 4:15:27 (15,679)
Mazzera, Davide 3:26:09 (4,174)
Mazzone, Pierino 4:53:05 (24,994)
McAinsh, Andy 4:14:57 (15,559)
McAliece, Craig 4:37:24 (21,422)
McAlister, Kieron 3:48:51 (8,853)
McAllister, Christopher 3:05:48 (1,618)
McAllister, Martin 4:14:46 (15,517)
McAllister, Stuart 3:42:19 (7,236)
McAllister, William 3:54:50 (10,551)
McAlpin, Dave 2:57:01 (918)
McAlpine, Colin 3:34:27 (5,610)
McAndrew, Tom 5:17:16 (28,596)
McArdle, Patrick 6:08:02 (31,785)
McAteer, Michael 3:28:56 (4,690)
McAulay, Tom 5:06:24 (27,213)
McAuley, John 4:47:55 (24,010)
McAuley, Kevin 4:33:38 (20,500)
McAuley, Marc 5:51:12 (31,195)
McAuley, Marcus 3:15:46 (2,765)
McBain, Peter 3:10:11 (2,057)
McBride, Bernard 4:24:28 (18,110)
McBride, Hugh 6:44:29 (32,481)
McBride, Stephen 4:01:16 (12,381)
McBride, Thomas 3:06:29 (1,682)
McCabe, Andy 4:22:20 (17,493)
McCabe, Christopher 4:37:14 (21,380)
McCabe, Martin 4:20:43 (17,049)
McCabe, Terence 4:01:41 (12,489)
McCafferty, Samuel 5:57:17 (31,450)
McCaffrey, Patrick 5:20:24 (28,929)
McCall, Jeffrey 4:10:53 (14,601)
McCall, Neil 3:58:37 (11,684)
McCall, Steven 3:53:00 (9,976)
McCallen, Brian 3:34:02 (5,524)
McCallion, Seamus 3:19:17 (3,169)
McCallum, Hamish 4:58:10 (25,979)
McCallum, Sean 4:48:29 (24,123)
McCammon, David 4:18:10 (16,404)
McCann, Alastair 3:48:18 (8,693)
McCann, Dermot 4:35:11 (20,875)
McCann, Gerard 2:57:34 (966)
McCann, John 3:34:16 (5,572)
McCarney, Martin 4:28:12 (19,081)
McCarrick, Cian 5:35:31 (30,232)
McCarrick, John 4:05:23 (13,293)
McCarroll, Rodger 3:52:51 (9,939)
McCarron, Andrew 5:30:31 (29,822)
McCart, Kevin 4:54:57 (25,370)
McCarter, Dominic 2:52:02 (580)
McCarthy, Bernard 5:48:50 (31,083)
McCarthy, Brian 3:43:06 (7,410)
McCarthy, Colin 4:57:55 (25,939)
McCarthy, Craig 4:22:02 (17,405)
McCarthy, David 3:44:22 (7,765)
McCarthy, David 3:54:29 (10,453)
McCarthy, Gareth 4:37:22 (21,414)
McCarthy, John 3:32:55 (5,341)
McCarthy, John 4:04:37 (13,117)
McCarthy, John 4:19:53 (16,831)
McCarthy, Keith 4:54:47 (25,337)
McCarthy, Martin 4:26:07 (18,556)
McCarthy, Michael 5:53:10 (31,284)
McCarthy, Michael 5:55:23 (31,370)
McCarthy, Robert 4:04:38 (13,118)
McCarthy, Stephen 4:16:53 (16,086)
McCarthy, Trevor 3:38:35 (6,446)
McCartney, Peter 3:30:35 (4,958)
McCashey, Ian 4:11:47 (14,814)
McCauley, Paul 4:01:32 (12,452)
McCaw, William 4:32:33 (20,228)
McCawghey, Thomas 4:38:50 (21,804)
McCay, Patrick 4:50:26 (24,491)
McChesney, Alyn 5:47:48 (31,028)
McChesney, Angus 3:56:29 (11,044)
McCheyne, Ian 5:35:45 (30,253)
McClellan, Alan 3:27:28 (4,410)
McClelland, Ross 2:53:20 (645)
McClintock, Neil 4:38:12 (21,626)
McCluskey, Neil 4:02:17 (12,613)
McCluskey, Peter 4:25:18 (18,333)
McCole, Feilim 4:31:24 (19,929)
McColgan, Ashley 2:52:43 (615)
McColl, Ewen 2:59:17 (1,115)
McColl, Gavin 3:50:20 (9,258)
McColl, Malachy 5:45:11 (30,894)
McConachie, James 4:28:18 (19,109)
McConalogue, Ian 5:56:00 (31,398)
McConalogue, James 5:02:37 (26,692)
McCondichie, Mark 5:39:28 (30,511)
McConnel, David 3:31:42 (5,151)
McConnell, Joseph 3:24:49 (3,959)
McConnell, Kym 3:34:39 (5,649)
McConville, Cathal 3:38:01 (6,316)
McConville, John 2:59:16 (1,113)
McConville, Kevin 3:44:30 (7,793)
McCorkell, Michael 3:54:24 (10,427)
McCormack, Ben 3:19:45 (3,228)
McCormack, Richard 4:11:40 (14,791)
McCormack, Sean 3:15:07 (2,677)
McCormack, William 5:05:20 (27,070)
McCormick, Andrew 3:19:43 (3,223)
McCormick, Andrew 4:02:39 (12,691)
McCormick, David 4:16:07 (15,870)
McCormick, Peter 4:40:20 (22,195)
McCosker-Smith, James 4:26:32 (18,664)
McCourt, Adrian 4:46:54 (23,786)
McCourt, William 4:39:12 (21,900)
McCowen, Paul 5:07:07 (27,317)
McCoy, Andrew 2:44:53 (295)
McCoy, Colm 2:57:04 (920)
McCoy, Edward 4:24:57 (18,242)
McCoy, Philip 2:46:56 (356)
McCoy, Robin 3:03:20 (1,407)
McCracken, Andrew 4:01:39 (12,482)
McCracken, Joseph 3:56:04 (10,918)
McCreadie, Brian 4:29:53 (19,569)
McCreadie, Ian 3:58:45 (11,718)
McCreanor, Phillip 4:38:43 (21,768)
McCreath, Mark 5:27:00 (29,522)
McCrindle, Ewen 4:26:07 (18,556)
McCrohon, Daniel 4:40:44 (22,286)
McCrone, Derek 3:53:33 (10,165)
McCrory, Michael 4:53:21 (25,037)
McCuaig, Ian 3:04:08 (1,479)
McCubbins, Phillip 3:12:05 (2,289)
McCullich, Nick 5:26:23 (29,480)
McCullie, John 4:18:29 (16,482)
McCulloch, Richard 5:06:54 (27,281)
McCurdy, Ray 5:17:06 (28,577)
McCurley, Tony 3:50:53 (9,398)
McCusker, Eamonn 3:26:16 (4,200)
McCutcheon, Murray 3:00:02 (1,172)
McCutcheon, William 4:03:33 (12,890)
McDaid, Anthony 3:48:24 (8,721)
McDaid, Stephen 2:55:54 (819)
McDermot, Dominic 3:40:48 (6,920)
McDermott, Brian 3:56:44 (11,117)
McDermott, Brian 4:03:26 (12,870)
McDermott, Damian 3:53:56 (10,287)
McDermott, Gary 3:47:42 (8,562)
McDermott, Gavin 3:44:42 (7,852)
McDermott, Nigel 3:32:03 (5,198)
McDonald, Alan 3:07:24 (1,762)
McDonald, Christopher 2:51:29 (561)
McDonald, Daniel 4:11:27 (14,733)
McDonald, David 4:53:11 (25,010)
McDonald, Iain 4:30:42 (19,755)
McDonald, John 4:04:57 (13,197)
McDonald, Keith 3:46:34 (8,303)

McDonald, Lawrence 3:18:28 (3,067)
McDonald, Malcolm 4:06:55 (13,651)
McDonald, Mark 2:52:20 (591)
McDonald, Mark 4:22:34 (17,564)
McDonald, Neil 3:22:30 (3,581)
McDonald, Peter 3:09:44 (2,010)
McDonald, Robert 3:14:27 (2,609)
McDonald Liggins, Anthony 3:35:35 (5,822)
McDonnell, James 2:54:53 (733)
McDonnell, Matthew 4:37:00 (21,315)
McDonnell, Ryan 4:25:18 (18,333)
McDonnell, William 4:02:46 (12,719)
McDonough, Alister 4:47:47 (23,971)
McDonough, Martin 3:36:31 (6,028)
McDougal, George 3:12:22 (2,342)
McDougal, Richard 3:52:05 (9,715)
McDougall, Campbell 5:26:07 (29,458)
McDougall, Julian 4:48:00 (24,029)
McDowall, Alan 3:55:44 (10,823)
McDowall, Jamie 4:10:53 (14,601)
McDowell, Alan 5:07:48 (27,406)
McDowell, Brian 3:37:00 (6,118)
McDowell, Gregory 3:04:51 (1,528)
McDowell, Paul 4:36:24 (21,190)
McDowell, Robert 3:50:29 (9,297)
McDowell, Simon 4:53:40 (25,097)
McElhinney, David 2:43:57 (267)
McElhinney, Frank 4:45:45 (23,503)
McElwee, Michael 4:24:17 (18,062)
McEniry, Andrew 5:10:49 (27,789)
McEntagart, Gerry 3:45:24 (8,021)
McEntee, Colin 3:21:10 (3,395)
McErlain, Phil 4:54:33 (25,292)
McEvitt, Mark 3:55:17 (10,687)
McEvoy, Richard 5:32:10 (29,967)
McEvoy, Sean 5:08:32 (27,502)
McEwan, Alastair 4:04:19 (13,049)
McEwan, Bryon 4:45:31 (23,446)
McEwan, Robert 3:21:46 (3,476)
McEwen, Malcolm 3:56:46 (11,131)
McEwen, Terence 3:40:03 (6,744)
McFadden, Cornelius 2:56:47 (900)
McFarlane, Bruce 4:39:54 (22,080)
McFarlane, David 3:52:51 (9,939)
McFarlane, Gregg 4:52:34 (24,895)
McFarlane, Winston 5:15:59 (28,441)
McFaulds, Gideon 5:13:45 (28,162)
McFaull, Mark 5:32:39 (30,004)
McFerran, Jack 3:34:00 (5,519)
McGahey, Andrew 4:26:20 (18,606)
McGahey, Timothy 3:17:58 (3,005)
McGale, John 5:43:06 (30,762)
McGarr, Gerard 3:46:40 (8,327)
McGarr, Tim 5:07:43 (27,401)
McGarrity, Charles 5:06:20 (27,201)
McGarry, Kevin 3:21:17 (3,405)
McGarry, Michael 4:34:07 (20,611)
McGarva, Greig 4:29:42 (19,506)
McGaughey, James 2:29:40 (65)
McGaughey, Robert 3:02:54 (1,364)
McGeary, Paul 3:59:14 (11,866)
McGee, Craig 4:31:54 (20,057)
McGee, David 5:59:16 (31,523)
McGee, Gareth 4:41:39 (22,513)
McGee, Patrick 3:59:12 (11,859)
McGeoch, Mick 2:36:20 (112)
McGhee, Carl 3:47:08 (8,414)
McGhie, Keith 3:00:22 (1,192)
McGibbon, Alastair 4:02:48 (12,729)
McGibbon, Thomas 4:37:06 (21,337)
McGillan, David 4:28:35 (19,187)
McGillicuddy, Chris 4:07:20 (13,754)
McGilloway, Frederick 6:01:07 (31,582)
McGinn, Nicholas 3:56:41 (11,104)
McGirr, Conor 4:26:28 (18,642)
McGivern, Damian 3:47:08 (8,414)
McGivern, James 3:06:09 (1,653)
McGivern, James 4:38:32 (21,713)
McGivney, James 4:41:09 (22,389)
McGlade, David 3:59:49 (12,028)
McGlennon, David 2:50:20 (503)
McGloin, Barry 4:41:53 (22,581)
McGlynn, Joe 3:44:04 (7,669)
McGlynn, Peter 4:39:56 (22,088)
McGougan, Angus 3:57:19 (11,298)
McGovern, David 4:21:35 (17,274)
McGovern, Hugh 4:00:46 (12,249)
McGovern, Paul 4:23:43 (17,893)
McGovern, Peter 5:02:31 (26,672)
McGow, William 5:00:05 (26,320)
McGowan, Daniel 5:04:15 (26,929)
McGowan, Mervyn 3:47:11 (8,433)
McGowan, Stuart 3:47:49 (8,591)
McGowan, Thomas 4:56:48 (25,732)
McGrath, Chris 5:14:17 (28,228)
McGrath, Daniel 3:28:52 (4,673)
McGrath, David 3:15:45 (2,761)
McGrath, Kevin 5:09:16 (27,601)
McGrath, Michael 3:03:15 (1,396)
McGrath, Stephen 4:12:23 (14,937)
McGregor, Andrew 4:30:33 (19,721)
McGregor, Campbell 3:39:23 (6,601)
McGregor, David 2:30:28 (67)
McGregor, Ian 5:59:34 (31,533)
McGregor, Philip 4:29:15 (19,398)
McGroarty, Alan 3:42:22 (7,252)
McGroarty, Michael 5:06:11 (27,187)
McGroarty, Patrick 3:05:18 (1,568)
McGrory, Andrew 7:29:54 (32,785)
McGuigan, Philip 3:31:53 (5,173)
McGuiness, Stephen 2:44:39 (287)
McGuinness, Harold 3:56:22 (11,009)
McGuinness, Michael 4:14:40 (15,487)
McGuinness, Tony 4:01:08 (12,345)
McGuire, Colum 4:31:19 (19,906)
McGuire, Danny 4:56:09 (25,622)
McGuire, Robert 4:48:00 (24,029)
McGuire White, Richard 2:40:11 (186)
McGurk, Joe 2:51:25 (556)
McHale, Francis 3:23:31 (3,729)
McHarrie, Allister 4:06:48 (13,631)
McHaughton, Brian 5:26:22 (29,476)
McHugh, Noel 4:17:20 (16,213)
McIlhagger, Peter 3:56:30 (11,053)
McIllmurray, Raymond 2:49:43 (472)
McIlroy, John 5:30:12 (29,799)
McIlvride, John 4:53:21 (25,037)
McIlwaine, Adam 5:02:46 (26,704)
McInally, Ian 4:25:06 (18,286)
McInerney, Michael 3:29:52 (4,852)
McInnes, Brett 4:45:38 (23,481)
McInnes, Duncan 3:57:00 (11,210)
McInnes, Matthew 4:19:11 (16,641)
McInnes, Tom 4:14:22 (15,417)
McIntosh, Andrew 4:07:10 (13,711)
McIntosh, Christopher 3:20:15 (3,283)
McIntosh, David 7:08:46 (32,691)
McIntosh, Don 3:49:54 (9,151)
McIntosh, Doug 4:20:12 (16,913)
McIntosh, Graeme 4:10:13 (14,440)
McIntosh, Mark 3:26:08 (4,171)
McIntosh, Robbie 3:58:38 (11,688)
McIntyre, Brendan 4:47:50 (23,986)
McIntyre, Connor 2:49:16 (455)
McIntyre, Daryl 4:52:44 (24,920)
McIntyre, Edward 4:29:48 (19,534)
McIntyre, Graham 2:53:55 (678)
McIntyre, Graham 3:28:00 (4,516)
McIntyre, Robert 3:36:58 (6,113)
McKane, Christopher 4:44:32 (23,184)
McKay, Graig 3:11:56 (2,262)
McKay, Kevin 4:43:18 (22,909)
McKay, Peter 4:42:59 (22,834)
McKay, Robert 3:08:46 (1,902)
McKay, Sandy 4:35:07 (20,857)
McKay, Stuart 3:45:38 (8,077)
McKean, Ian 4:44:39 (23,206)
McKeating, Neil 3:55:54 (10,872)
McKechnie, Andrew 3:41:04 (6,980)
McKechnie, James 4:29:43 (19,510)
McKee, Dennis 7:09:59 (32,701)
McKee, Gavin 4:36:54 (21,297)
McKee, Robert 4:52:57 (24,972)
McKeever, Justin 3:54:55 (10,573)
McKeever, Stephen 3:56:45 (11,128)
McKell, Tim 4:03:40 (12,911)
McKellar, James 4:09:15 (14,201)
McKelvey, David 5:13:59 (28,188)
McKendrick, Craig 4:21:49 (17,342)
McKenna, Christopher 4:26:29 (18,649)
McKenna, Graham 3:37:27 (6,195)
McKenna, John 3:52:20 (9,790)
McKenna, Keith 5:41:03 (30,624)
McKenna, Paul 3:19:52 (3,238)
McKenna, Paul 5:51:14 (31,197)
McKenna, Seamus 4:20:50 (17,073)
McKenna, Sean 4:28:56 (19,297)
McKenna, Shaymus 4:19:14 (16,650)
McKenny, Chad 3:15:31 (2,725)
McKenzie, Callum 4:43:46 (23,008)
McKenzie, Eric 5:54:49 (31,344)
McKenzie, Gavin 4:39:20 (21,930)
McKenzie, Grahame 3:27:19 (4,379)
McKenzie, Jeremy 5:35:08 (30,193)
McKenzie, John 4:49:38 (24,347)
McKenzie, Lee 4:25:52 (18,475)
McKeon, David 4:23:58 (17,965)
McKeown, Kieran 3:53:59 (10,305)
McKeown, Peter 3:12:29 (2,357)
McKerr, Liam 3:33:03 (5,359)
McKidd, Lawrence 3:29:15 (4,740)
McKie, Alexander 4:26:34 (18,670)
McKinley, Andrew 4:21:56 (17,374)
McKinley, John 3:27:08 (4,349)
McKinney, James 3:11:37 (2,215)
McKinnon, Lachlan 4:31:02 (19,834)
McLachlan, Robert 4:39:20 (21,930)
McLaren, Bruce 3:54:12 (10,374)
McLaren, Christopher 5:57:36 (31,462)
McLaren, David 4:20:02 (16,870)
McLaren, Duncan 3:31:06 (5,049)
McLaren, Lawrence 5:14:06 (28,205)
McLaughlen, Peter 4:06:15 (13,504)
McLaughlin, Colin 4:52:50 (24,944)
McLaughlin, Daniel 4:20:24 (16,964)
McLaughlin, James 4:31:59 (20,081)
McLaughlin, Michael 3:24:57 (3,982)
McLaughlin, Paul 3:43:26 (7,508)
McLaughlin, Philip 5:25:52 (29,434)
McLean, Angus 3:35:13 (5,749)
McLean, Charles 4:28:18 (19,109)
McLean, Ian 3:29:27 (4,784)
McLean, Julian 3:53:37 (10,182)
McLean, Kevin 5:16:52 (28,537)
McLean, Stephen 4:04:28 (13,081)
McLean, Will 4:05:57 (13,425)
McLellan, Michael 4:20:00 (16,860)
McLelland, David 3:19:49 (3,233)
McLelland, James 4:29:43 (19,510)
McLelland, Steve 3:41:39 (7,091)
McLeod, Allen 4:14:59 (15,570)
McLeod, Christopher 3:47:26 (8,494)
McLeod, John 4:03:26 (12,870)
McLeod, Justin 4:46:07 (23,594)
McLeod, Roderick 3:39:31 (6,629)
McLintic, Morgan 3:53:26 (10,116)
McLoughlin, Brian 4:48:58 (24,228)
McLoughlin, James 4:53:01 (24,978)
McLoughlin, Liam 5:29:55 (29,772)
McLoughlin, Peter 4:41:05 (22,371)
McLoughlin, Roy 3:59:42 (11,996)
McLoughlin, Simon 4:42:06 (22,634)
McLoughlin, Steven 4:32:53 (20,329)
McLuckie, Kenneth 5:23:54 (29,273)
McMahon, Bernard 3:55:55 (10,877)
McMahon, Neil 3:56:57 (11,192)
McMahon, Paul 4:08:01 (13,916)
McManus, Kevin 2:56:57 (910)
McMaster, Philip 3:28:34 (4,616)
McMeekin, Lee 2:50:04 (495)
McMillan, Ashley 4:10:21 (14,471)
McMillan, Fraser 3:54:11 (10,371)
McMillan, Russell 5:17:19 (28,606)
McMonagle, Derek 5:03:17 (26,795)
McMorrow, Dermot 4:36:03 (21,092)
McMullen, Philip 4:38:35 (21,730)
McMurdo, Alan 3:50:19 (9,256)
McMyler, Sean 2:50:56 (531)
McNab, Gary 4:08:40 (14,074)

McNally, Brian	6:16:26 (31,997)	
McNally, John	3:01:54 (1,295)	
McNally, Rory	3:00:26 (1,200)	
McNamara, Martin	5:17:28 (28,625)	
McNamara, Peter	4:35:39 (21,001)	
McNamee, Gerry	4:52:18 (24,843)	
McNamee, Ryan	4:28:19 (19,114)	
McNamee, Stephen	5:33:50 (30,095)	
McNaugher, Ivor	4:16:30 (15,980)	
McNaughton, David	4:19:44 (16,785)	
McNaughton, Gavin	4:36:45 (21,268)	
McNaughton, Peter	3:34:34 (5,630)	
McNealy, Steve	3:11:04 (2,164)	
McNee, Bradley	5:02:36 (26,686)	
McNee, David	5:53:29 (31,297)	
McNeice, Stephen	4:12:35 (14,992)	
McNeil, Alan	5:57:10 (31,448)	
McNeil, Ian	3:23:05 (3,666)	
McNeil, Michael	4:45:02 (23,319)	
McNeill, Alan	3:48:06 (8,650)	
McNeill, Andrew	2:36:14 (109)	
McNeill, Simon	3:35:21 (5,769)	
McNelis, Robin	3:12:06 (2,293)	
McNelliey, John	3:59:22 (11,906)	
McNicoll, Craig	4:23:40 (17,864)	
McNulty, David	4:17:45 (16,310)	
McNulty, Michael	3:46:19 (8,229)	
McNulty, Michael	4:55:23 (25,461)	
McNulty, Trevor	4:25:51 (18,471)	
McParland, Gerard	3:03:03 (1,377)	
McParland, John	3:21:16 (3,402)	
McPaul, Robert	4:14:34 (15,460)	
McPetrie, Rupert	4:07:50 (13,879)	
McPhee, Michael	3:26:28 (4,223)	
McPherson, Judah	5:16:31 (28,501)	
McPherson, Richard	3:18:06 (3,020)	
McQuade, Graham	5:19:10 (28,790)	
McQuade, Joseph	3:46:29 (8,272)	
McQueen, Simon	4:06:58 (13,668)	
McQuillan, Peter	4:25:58 (18,510)	
McRobb, Douglas	3:42:23 (7,259)	
McRobb, Neil	4:09:21 (14,232)	
McRoberts, Dermot	4:07:59 (13,903)	
McRoberts, Neil	4:21:22 (17,210)	
McShane, Desmond	3:16:25 (2,833)	
McShane, James	5:13:57 (28,183)	
McShane, Michael	3:42:00 (7,155)	
McSharry, Philip	4:12:42 (15,025)	
McSkimming, John	3:04:36 (1,512)	
McSweeney, Charles	5:23:40 (29,246)	
McSweeney, Rodney	6:13:25 (31,915)	
McTaggart, John	4:03:07 (12,800)	
McVeigh, Robert	3:22:16 (3,561)	
McVey, Anthony	3:38:03 (6,322)	
McVey, Geoffrey	4:04:38 (13,118)	
McVitie, Russell	3:40:33 (6,863)	
McWhir, Andrew	4:40:58 (22,348)	
McWilliam, Gary	4:37:14 (21,380)	
McWilliam, Richard	4:47:41 (23,949)	
McWilliams, Alan	3:41:10 (7,003)	
Mea, Christian	4:15:01 (15,580)	
Meaby, Andrew	4:57:05 (25,790)	
Meacher, Barrington	4:28:06 (19,054)	
Mead, Adrian	2:58:57 (1,088)	
Mead, Alexander	3:43:07 (7,418)	
Mead, Andrew	3:11:52 (2,257)	
Mead, Colin	4:41:29 (22,472)	
Mead, David	4:07:52 (13,884)	
Mead, Gary	3:47:18 (8,461)	
Mead, Glenn	4:22:40 (17,596)	
Mead, Lee	4:05:14 (13,260)	
Mead, Marc	4:35:44 (21,015)	
Mead, Steve	2:47:00 (360)	
Meade, Ian	3:53:26 (10,116)	
Meadows, Chris	4:50:35 (24,520)	
Meadows, David	4:23:09 (17,738)	
Meadows, Jonathan	3:53:48 (10,249)	
Meadows, Thomas	3:47:59 (8,625)	
Meads, Geoffrey	3:55:42 (10,812)	
Meads, John	3:23:57 (3,814)	
Meagher, Ben	5:49:17 (31,113)	
Meagor, David	3:36:55 (6,099)	
Meagor, Lucas	4:11:19 (14,696)	

Meakin, Billy	3:24:12 (3,861)	
Meakin, Paul	4:09:21 (14,232)	
Meakins, Christopher	5:11:06 (27,824)	
Mealey, John	3:45:02 (7,933)	
Mean, Scott	3:43:57 (7,643)	
Meaney, David	3:52:07 (9,726)	
Meaning, David	4:53:00 (24,977)	
Meanwell, John	5:06:04 (27,168)	
Mear, Paul	3:56:41 (11,104)	
Mearns, Graeme	3:52:27 (9,823)	
Mearns, Trevor	4:52:44 (24,920)	
Mears, David	4:37:16 (21,394)	
Mears, Phillip	4:23:43 (17,893)	
Measures, Keith	3:58:23 (11,614)	
Mecklenburg, Frank	4:10:59 (14,627)	
Medcraft, Peter	4:05:31 (13,329)	
Medhurst, David	6:14:15 (31,934)	
Medley, Ray	3:47:17 (8,454)	
Medlycott, Jonathan	4:19:10 (16,636)	
Mee, Christopher	3:47:49 (8,591)	
Mee, Colin	2:58:28 (1,045)	
Meegan, Kevin	4:05:09 (13,240)	
Meehan, Brian	4:26:27 (18,637)	
Meehan, John	4:20:17 (16,937)	
Meehan, Mark	4:19:32 (16,733)	
Meehan, Neil	4:25:32 (18,396)	
Meek, Andrew	4:19:51 (16,821)	
Meek, Clive	3:35:40 (5,837)	
Meek, Richard	5:06:22 (27,207)	
Meeke, James	4:12:08 (14,887)	
Meerloo, Ricki	3:25:01 (3,987)	
Meert, Walter	3:13:49 (2,542)	
Meese, Martin	5:55:03 (31,353)	
Meeson, David	3:24:01 (3,824)	
Meg, Terry	3:47:57 (8,617)	
Megali, Aldo	4:24:36 (18,149)	
Megilley, Grahame	4:29:17 (19,405)	
Mehta, Mukesh	5:05:51 (27,135)	
Mehta, Nicholas	3:48:39 (8,799)	
Mehta, Saahil	4:41:27 (22,463)	
Meisland, Oddvar	3:35:15 (5,756)	
Mei-Tal, Eldad	3:24:00 (3,820)	
Mekonen, Desta	3:16:04 (2,795)	
Melander, Per-Erik	3:58:51 (11,749)	
Melander, Todd	4:50:48 (24,564)	
Meldrum, Duncan	5:05:27 (27,078)	
Melik, Richard	2:59:03 (1,097)	
Melis, Paul	4:12:44 (15,029)	
Meller, David	2:51:25 (556)	
Meller, Nicholas	4:41:01 (22,358)	
Mellett, Peter	4:29:48 (19,534)	
Melling, Anthony	4:31:43 (20,015)	
Melling, Paul	4:17:17 (16,197)	
Mellon, Alastair	4:32:43 (20,282)	
Mellon, James	4:52:45 (24,926)	
Mellon, Paul	4:22:09 (17,439)	
Mellor, Charles	3:14:25 (2,603)	
Mellor, Clive	3:31:50 (5,170)	
Mellor, Edward	4:17:38 (16,277)	
Mellor, Ian	3:48:40 (8,802)	
Mellor, Rex	3:52:13 (9,758)	
Mellor, Stuart	4:33:07 (20,383)	
Mellor, Wayne	3:50:15 (9,235)	
Mellors, Benjamin	3:53:07 (10,024)	
Mellows, Steven	4:34:07 (20,611)	
Melly, Serge	3:29:36 (4,813)	
Melman, Joseph	3:34:02 (5,524)	
Melms, Ulrich	3:37:39 (6,253)	
Melrose, Graham	2:58:46 (1,072)	
Melunsky, Jonathan	4:27:52 (18,998)	
Melven, Derek	3:43:23 (7,495)	
Melville, Alvin	4:24:55 (18,230)	
Melville, Colin	4:11:13 (14,678)	
Melville, Stuart	4:16:49 (16,071)	
Melville, Tomas	4:12:38 (15,005)	
Melvin, David	4:52:19 (24,846)	
Melvin, Lindsay	4:20:54 (17,086)	
Melvin, Scott	5:06:32 (27,237)	
Menard, Vincent	3:22:26 (3,574)	
Menday, Graeme	4:07:36 (13,816)	
Mendelssohn, Christopher	5:30:07 (29,789)	
Mendez, Alvaro	4:09:00 (14,133)	
Mendham, Gavin	3:03:01 (1,370)	

Mendham, Robin	4:25:57 (18,502)	
Mendoza Pacheco, Juan	3:40:39 (6,885)	
Menin, Andrew	3:39:39 (6,657)	
Mennell, Simon	3:40:34 (6,867)	
Mennen, Joachim	4:00:43 (12,233)	
Menozzi, Guido	2:55:14 (760)	
Mensley, Peter	3:04:53 (1,533)	
Menzies, Alan	3:24:10 (3,855)	
Menzies, Ian	5:25:19 (29,388)	
Mepani, Vasant	4:26:20 (18,606)	
Mepham, Derek	3:54:38 (10,494)	
Meraviglia, Giorgio	3:52:40 (9,887)	
Mercadal, Christian	3:35:38 (5,833)	
Mercanzin, Giampaolo	4:48:46 (24,182)	
Mercer, Andrew	4:19:35 (16,753)	
Mercer, Anthony	5:36:53 (30,342)	
Mercer, Ian	3:38:35 (6,446)	
Mercer, Philip	4:23:35 (17,845)	
Merchant, Warren	4:03:51 (12,954)	
Merckel, Daniel	3:42:26 (7,269)	
Meredew, Paul	4:45:23 (23,404)	
Meredith, Julian	4:09:18 (14,218)	
Meredith, Michael	3:35:23 (5,778)	
Meredith, Sean	4:12:28 (14,963)	
Meredith, Simon	2:36:43 (119)	
Meredith, Tim	4:44:06 (23,086)	
Mereweather, Ian	3:54:09 (10,361)	
Merfield, Gordon	3:39:13 (6,574)	
Merino, Victor	3:29:13 (4,731)	
Merkli, Peter	3:27:36 (4,435)	
Merle, Francis	4:03:57 (12,976)	
Merlini, Juan	4:43:06 (22,865)	
Mermagen, Patrick	2:58:32 (1,053)	
Merrett, Anthony	3:27:42 (4,457)	
Merrick, Clive	3:31:39 (5,139)	
Merridan, David	5:50:01 (31,143)	
Merrifield, Jeffrey	4:18:59 (16,584)	
Merrifield, Patrick	3:47:25 (8,492)	
Merriman, Andrew	3:48:44 (8,822)	
Merrington, Ian	4:40:09 (22,145)	
Merritt, Anthony	3:53:57 (10,293)	
Merritt, David	3:44:57 (7,919)	
Merry, Edward	3:51:05 (9,453)	
Meryon, Angus	4:00:56 (12,289)	
Messer, Christopher	5:27:37 (29,591)	
Messer, Dario	3:42:30 (7,287)	
Messer, Laurence	3:50:32 (9,306)	
Metcalf, Adrian	4:52:32 (24,882)	
Metcalf, Alan	2:55:22 (768)	
Metcalf, Len	4:33:12 (20,403)	
Metcalf, Lester	4:06:51 (13,638)	
Metcalf, Michael	5:55:15 (31,362)	
Metcalf, Richard	4:27:32 (18,928)	
Metcalfe, Anthony	3:02:16 (1,322)	
Metcalfe, Christopher	5:25:03 (29,369)	
Metcalfe, John	3:45:25 (8,025)	
Metcalfe, Stuart	5:08:18 (27,470)	
Metcalfe, Thomas	3:40:55 (6,944)	
Metheringham, Daniel	4:38:26 (21,692)	
Metraux, Claude	4:43:09 (22,881)	
Meurice, Nicholas	4:20:30 (16,990)	
Mewis, Marc	4:02:12 (12,599)	
Mewyer, Alex	4:01:12 (12,365)	
Mexted, Gordon	3:26:52 (4,303)	
Meyer, Pierre	2:55:56 (822)	
Meyer, Rudiger	3:01:40 (1,270)	
Meyer, Tobie	2:42:59 (243)	
Meyer, Tom	4:20:44 (17,053)	
Meykens, Mark	4:35:50 (21,036)	
Miah, Ahad	4:42:53 (22,811)	
Miaoulis, Nikolas	3:47:44 (8,569)	
Micallef, Andrew	4:55:55 (25,567)	
Micallef, James	3:52:35 (9,865)	
Micallef, Rocco	3:31:46 (5,162)	
Michael, Dennis	2:59:25 (1,126)	
Michael, Magdi	6:10:14 (31,844)	
Michael, Nick	5:11:51 (27,930)	
Michalak, Richard	3:48:20 (8,705)	
Michalitsianos, Jeremy	4:12:38 (15,005)	
Michalski, Antony	4:47:41 (23,949)	
Michel, Pierre	3:14:34 (2,615)	
Michell, Nick	4:06:02 (13,442)	
Michell, Oliver	4:07:26 (13,783)	

LONDON MARATHON

Michell, Piers	4:45:24 (23,413)
Michie, James	2:57:50 (991)
Mickleborough, Timothy	2:50:36 (517)
Micklethwait, James	3:02:18 (1,327)
Middle, Christopher	4:41:15 (22,413)
Middlebrook, Richard	5:23:22 (29,206)
Middleditch, Andrew	4:05:44 (13,376)
Middleman, Keith	3:34:10 (5,557)
Middlemiss, George	3:44:55 (7,912)
Middleton, Adam	5:03:08 (26,771)
Middleton, Anthony	2:53:16 (640)
Middleton, Barry	3:22:07 (3,538)
Middleton, Bill	4:12:26 (14,955)
Middleton, Brian	3:13:11 (2,462)
Middleton, Colin	3:31:24 (5,092)
Middleton, Graham	3:55:07 (10,637)
Middleton, Howard	5:08:45 (27,530)
Middleton, Ian	3:10:46 (2,131)
Middleton, Ian	3:12:53 (2,415)
Middleton, James	5:07:28 (27,370)
Middleton, John	4:29:36 (19,482)
Middleton, Laurie	4:30:58 (19,823)
Middleton, Michael	3:51:31 (9,550)
Middleton, Roger	3:36:44 (6,061)
Midgley, Martin	2:58:41 (1,068)
Midgley, Richard	3:39:38 (6,654)
Midmer, Michael	2:57:23 (946)
Midwinter, Mark	4:22:35 (17,568)
Mifsud, Selwyn	3:35:58 (5,899)
Migeot, Philippe	3:20:02 (3,257)
Mihara, Taiji	4:06:39 (13,601)
Mikelsons, Kristians	3:11:16 (2,183)
Mikustiak, Martin	2:54:42 (723)
Milazzo, Joe	5:11:28 (27,883)
Milbride, Michael	3:49:00 (8,896)
Milburn, Alastair	4:17:01 (16,121)
Milburn, Ian	3:28:23 (4,586)
Milburn, Ian	6:26:27 (32,209)
Milburn, Paul	4:44:28 (23,162)
Miles, Adam	3:47:40 (8,551)
Miles, Alastair	4:20:06 (16,888)
Miles, Albert	4:30:00 (19,592)
Miles, Christopher	3:23:27 (3,714)
Miles, Christopher	4:18:59 (16,584)
Miles, Christopher	4:36:20 (21,174)
Miles, David	3:57:42 (11,422)
Miles, Dyfed	4:08:25 (13,997)
Miles, Graham	5:55:46 (31,390)
Miles, Kevin	4:22:09 (17,439)
Miles, Larry	5:33:46 (30,088)
Miles, Neil	4:48:51 (24,206)
Miles, Paul	4:43:27 (22,948)
Miles, Robert	3:40:39 (6,885)
Miles, Robert	4:26:00 (18,518)
Miles, Stan	6:44:54 (32,486)
Miles, Steven	4:30:23 (19,690)
Miles, Stuart	4:56:11 (25,628)
Miles, Tony	5:43:28 (30,787)
Milington, Robert	3:57:28 (11,350)
Millar, Andrew	4:00:26 (12,175)
Millar, Barry	5:10:40 (27,771)
Millar, Campbell	3:54:31 (10,463)
Millar, Clive	3:19:25 (3,191)
Millar, Gordon	4:19:30 (16,726)
Millar, Graham	5:00:16 (26,343)
Millar, James	3:46:56 (8,368)
Millar, James	5:15:17 (28,337)
Millar, Steve	4:15:43 (15,758)
Millard, Duncan	3:35:30 (5,804)
Millard, Iain	5:09:04 (27,577)
Millard, Paul	4:56:05 (25,601)
Miller, Adrian	5:08:52 (27,546)
Miller, Allan	4:30:00 (19,592)
Miller, Anthony	4:07:13 (13,725)
Miller, Carl	6:58:20 (32,610)
Miller, Craig	4:42:38 (22,755)
Miller, Daniel	4:11:35 (14,763)
Miller, David	2:35:21 (102)
Miller, David	4:40:46 (22,300)
Miller, David	5:06:03 (27,165)
Miller, Edward	4:53:02 (24,983)
Miller, Gary	4:53:19 (25,031)
Miller, Glenn	3:31:29 (5,105)

Miller, Graeme	3:12:47 (2,396)
Miller, Grant	3:52:06 (9,723)
Miller, James	3:49:04 (8,915)
Miller, John	3:37:02 (6,126)
Miller, John	4:23:44 (17,899)
Miller, Justin	4:24:42 (18,173)
Miller, Kenneth	4:23:47 (17,913)
Miller, Lee	5:45:11 (30,894)
Miller, Leon	5:31:04 (29,869)
Miller, Les	5:01:10 (26,478)
Miller, Leslie	4:28:20 (19,119)
Miller, Matthew	4:03:45 (12,928)
Miller, Nigel	3:31:46 (5,162)
Miller, Patrick	4:24:34 (18,138)
Miller, Paul	3:19:42 (3,221)
Miller, Paul	5:09:21 (27,617)
Miller, Philip	5:39:21 (30,493)
Miller, Richard	4:00:09 (12,118)
Miller, Ricky	3:43:49 (7,612)
Miller, Robert	3:05:47 (1,614)
Miller, Robert	4:45:22 (23,398)
Miller, Stephen	3:29:13 (4,731)
Millership, Anthony	3:28:53 (4,676)
Millett, Christopher	4:27:34 (18,931)
Millican, Keith	3:36:03 (5,915)
Millichamp, Alan	3:58:58 (11,787)
Milligan, Ian	6:57:25 (32,605)
Milligan, Jonathan	4:49:25 (24,304)
Milligan, Mark	3:50:16 (9,242)
Milliken Smith, Mark	5:47:24 (31,010)
Millings, Terence	3:43:16 (7,465)
Millington, John	4:07:08 (13,701)
Millington, Mark	5:16:38 (28,516)
Millington, Paul	3:29:33 (4,807)
Millington, Simon	3:55:41 (10,803)
Millman-Outten, Kyle	6:02:08 (31,613)
Milloch, William	3:27:37 (4,440)
Millot, Christophe	3:47:11 (8,433)
Mills, Adrian	4:13:56 (15,291)
Mills, Alan	5:03:15 (26,792)
Mills, Andrew	3:55:50 (10,850)
Mills, Andrew	3:56:17 (10,983)
Mills, Andrew	4:24:31 (18,124)
Mills, Andrew	4:56:57 (25,756)
Mills, Brian	4:11:05 (14,654)
Mills, Brian	4:14:37 (15,473)
Mills, Brian	5:14:29 (28,247)
Mills, Clive	5:39:21 (30,493)
Mills, Daniel	3:30:58 (5,019)
Mills, David	4:39:03 (21,860)
Mills, David	4:45:05 (23,328)
Mills, Duncan	5:24:42 (29,339)
Mills, Fred	4:30:05 (19,620)
Mills, Graham	3:29:02 (4,698)
Mills, Ian	4:39:48 (22,058)
Mills, Jon	3:31:19 (5,080)
Mills, Joseph	4:08:26 (14,001)
Mills, Nathan	4:08:24 (13,994)
Mills, Nicholas	4:21:50 (17,349)
Mills, Peter	3:47:19 (8,464)
Mills, Richard	4:20:40 (17,038)
Mills, Simon	3:22:48 (3,636)
Mills, Simon	3:39:13 (6,574)
Mills, Stephen	4:22:58 (17,696)
Mills, Stuart	3:27:31 (4,421)
Mills, Trevor	3:59:58 (12,076)
Millward, Piers	3:11:49 (2,247)
Milne, Bruce	4:42:47 (22,789)
Milne, Colin	4:32:12 (20,141)
Milne, David	5:01:03 (26,456)
Milne, Garry	4:13:00 (15,082)
Milne, Gordon	5:03:58 (26,884)
Milne, Kenneth	4:31:41 (20,008)
Milne, Michael	4:25:19 (18,341)
Milne, Peter	5:45:09 (30,889)

Milne, Stephen	3:04:12 (1,483)
Milner, Adrian	5:24:51 (29,349)
Milner, David	3:33:57 (5,509)
Milner, James	3:55:29 (10,741)
Milner, Simon	3:57:22 (11,307)
Milner, Stephen	4:49:55 (24,409)
Milns, Leon	3:47:39 (8,546)
Milton, Daren	5:33:41 (30,084)
Milton, David	3:02:17 (1,324)
Milton, Nigel	4:51:58 (24,778)
Milton, Richard	4:25:31 (18,393)
Milton, Trevor	3:57:52 (11,469)
Minagana, Tatsuya	2:50:47 (525)
Mines, Ben	3:37:27 (6,195)
Minett, Terrence	3:41:34 (7,076)
Minkus, Guenter	3:43:51 (7,620)
Minshull, Darren	4:23:41 (17,872)
Minshull, Neil	3:49:04 (8,915)
Minter, Michael	4:46:01 (23,569)
Minton, Kevin	4:35:00 (20,833)
Mires, Robert	4:01:12 (12,365)
Miron, Paul	3:20:21 (3,295)
Misselbrook, Michael	5:10:29 (27,747)
Misselbrook, Nigel	3:04:24 (1,495)
Missin, Jon	4:06:08 (13,473)
Misson, Michael	5:09:06 (27,583)
Mistry, Ajay	4:09:06 (14,153)
Mistry, Hitesh	3:12:45 (2,393)
Mistry, Jayanti	4:15:10 (15,609)
Mitates, Julio	5:00:09 (26,328)
Mitchell, Alasdair	3:46:10 (8,193)
Mitchell, Andrew	3:44:11 (7,707)
Mitchell, Andrew	4:11:47 (14,814)
Mitchell, Andrew	4:46:01 (23,569)
Mitchell, Anthony	4:48:10 (24,066)
Mitchell, Brian	4:27:09 (18,832)
Mitchell, Darren	4:10:33 (14,523)
Mitchell, David	3:45:54 (8,134)
Mitchell, David	4:32:05 (20,105)
Mitchell, Derek	5:07:10 (27,324)
Mitchell, Gareth	4:52:57 (24,972)
Mitchell, George	2:52:39 (605)
Mitchell, Gordon	4:46:48 (23,757)
Mitchell, Graham	3:25:44 (4,103)
Mitchell, Gregor	3:43:06 (7,410)
Mitchell, Ian	3:49:10 (8,939)
Mitchell, James	3:37:24 (6,189)
Mitchell, James	4:41:35 (22,491)
Mitchell, Jason	5:32:59 (30,021)
Mitchell, John	3:55:58 (10,889)
Mitchell, Jonathan	6:30:00 (32,276)
Mitchell, Karl	4:24:57 (18,242)
Mitchell, Keith	4:40:41 (22,270)
Mitchell, Keith	4:47:54 (24,005)
Mitchell, Mark	5:08:44 (27,526)
Mitchell, Michael	3:06:32 (1,691)
Mitchell, Nicholas	3:48:52 (8,859)
Mitchell, Paul	3:16:49 (2,883)
Mitchell, Paul	4:25:42 (18,439)
Mitchell, Peter	3:32:36 (5,289)
Mitchell, Peter	4:43:21 (22,919)
Mitchell, Robert	3:07:34 (1,772)
Mitchell, Robert	3:59:00 (11,806)
Mitchell, Robert	3:59:16 (11,873)
Mitchell, Stephen	4:39:22 (21,939)
Mitchell, Stuart	3:23:22 (3,706)
Mitchell, Stuart	5:28:39 (29,670)
Mitchell, Teddy	2:41:31 (219)
Mitchell, Tim	3:02:24 (1,334)
Mitchell, Tim	4:19:24 (16,688)
Mitchell, Tim	4:45:36 (23,475)
Mitchell, Tony	4:26:35 (18,675)
Mitchell, William	3:37:39 (6,253)
Mitchell Smith, Timothy	3:55:10 (10,653)
Mitchener, Paul	3:58:34 (11,664)
Mitchinson, David	4:22:50 (17,652)
Mithcell, Carl	3:54:16 (10,392)
Mithen, Anthony	4:05:06 (13,231)
Mitterer, Michael	4:21:23 (17,218)
Mitterhuber, Paul	4:32:29 (20,214)
Mlambo, Donald	3:39:40 (6,659)
Moat, Darren	3:18:52 (3,119)
Mobbs, Timothy	3:33:30 (5,427)

Moberly, Thomas	3:58:11 (11,564)	
Mocaer, Alain	3:20:03 (3,260)	
Mocevic, Blazenko	4:35:38 (20,998)	
Mochan, Mike	5:08:07 (27,444)	
Mochrlein, Johannes	5:20:16 (28,911)	
Mockel, Guido	4:32:30 (20,215)	
Modaher, Jasvir	5:17:18 (28,602)	
Model, Bjorn	4:13:10 (15,113)	
Modley, Paul	3:35:26 (5,789)	
Moffat, Jonathan	3:56:01 (10,902)	
Moffatt, John	4:25:25 (18,364)	
Moffett, David	3:04:14 (1,486)	
Moffett, James	4:29:13 (19,384)	
Mogan, John	4:24:33 (18,131)	
Mogg, David	4:15:41 (15,750)	
Mohamed, André	5:16:32 (28,503)	
Mohamed, Tarek	5:04:25 (26,950)	
Mohammad, Naeem	4:14:10 (15,349)	
Mohan, Robert	4:22:34 (17,564)	
Mohiuddine, Lawrence	5:07:29 (27,372)	
Mohun, Timothy	3:27:23 (4,396)	
Moir, Alexander	3:25:28 (4,058)	
Moir, David	5:51:15 (31,201)	
Moir, Robbie	4:29:43 (19,510)	
Moisley, Dave	3:47:49 (8,591)	
Mojsa, Peter	4:33:22 (20,432)	
Mold, Graham	5:35:36 (30,239)	
Mole, David	4:09:01 (14,135)	
Molenkamp, Aad	4:27:17 (18,858)	
Molesworth, Tony	3:53:44 (10,218)	
Molgora, Alessandro	3:35:51 (5,872)	
Molin, Patrick	4:28:35 (19,187)	
Molinier, Fabien	4:17:34 (16,259)	
Molitor, Lutz	4:09:41 (14,313)	
Moll, Simon	4:15:20 (15,651)	
Molloy, Adrian	3:26:36 (4,247)	
Molloy, Carrissa	5:15:57 (28,436)	
Molloy, Peter	3:37:19 (6,167)	
Molloy, Sean	3:00:23 (1,195)	
Molloy, Tony	4:37:52 (21,536)	
Moloney, Jeremiah	3:32:32 (5,276)	
Moloney, William	4:38:52 (21,812)	
Mols, Alain	3:45:06 (7,953)	
Molyneux, Sidney	4:25:21 (18,348)	
Molyneux, Simon	4:32:40 (20,269)	
Momcilovic, George	4:18:34 (16,501)	
Monaghan, Francis	4:58:38 (26,065)	
Monaghan, Phil	3:36:17 (5,975)	
Moncad, Richard	4:49:41 (24,357)	
Moncaster, Christopher	3:14:12 (2,577)	
Mondello, Mario	3:17:47 (2,988)	
Mondrup, Jens	3:45:59 (8,157)	
Mones, Giancarlo	4:46:04 (23,587)	
Monington, Paul	4:17:05 (16,139)	
Monk, Arthur	3:20:10 (3,274)	
Monk, Barry	4:41:23 (22,446)	
Monk, Colin	3:53:32 (10,157)	
Monk, John	4:42:19 (22,675)	
Monk, Jonathan	4:22:59 (17,702)	
Monk, Rowland	3:58:29 (11,648)	
Monk, William	4:43:58 (23,058)	
Monnery, Anthony	3:12:19 (2,332)	
Monniot, Edward	4:11:56 (14,841)	
Monod, Yann	3:17:23 (2,947)	
Mons-Ribas, Carles	4:38:30 (21,703)	
Montagnon, Giles	4:24:59 (18,258)	
Montague, Gary	4:59:27 (26,207)	
Montague, Ian	3:31:37 (5,132)	
Montague, Peter	5:56:01 (31,400)	
Montanri, Olivero	4:10:35 (14,532)	
Montaque, Peter	4:04:57 (13,197)	
Monteiro, Joaquim	3:29:25 (4,780)	
Monteith, Craig	3:20:38 (3,329)	
Monteith, Maurice	4:38:58 (21,834)	
Montgomery, David	5:10:11 (27,715)	
Montgomery, Neil	4:44:28 (23,162)	
Montgomery, Sean	4:19:22 (16,684)	
Montgomery, Simon	3:34:21 (5,594)	
Monti, John	3:57:42 (11,422)	
Montlaur, Pierrre	4:18:05 (16,385)	
Moody, Adrian	3:31:34 (5,117)	
Moody, Colin	3:03:47 (1,448)	
Moody, David	4:38:25 (21,689)	
Moody, Douglas	3:55:05 (10,619)	
Moody, Jerome	3:39:18 (6,589)	
Moody, Paul	4:47:10 (23,849)	
Moojen, Karel	4:20:18 (16,940)	
Moon, Chris	4:52:11 (24,813)	
Moon, John	3:38:16 (6,362)	
Moon, Michael	4:38:23 (21,681)	
Moon, Richard	3:28:07 (4,535)	
Mooney, Allan	3:33:40 (5,450)	
Mooney, Noel	5:13:16 (28,110)	
Mooney, Patrick	4:10:48 (14,576)	
Mooney, Sean	4:48:06 (24,056)	
Mooney, Stephen	5:15:57 (28,436)	
Moorby, Vinny	3:32:30 (5,269)	
Moorcroft, Johnny	4:46:54 (23,786)	
Moore, Alex	4:15:34 (15,712)	
Moore, Andrew	3:26:26 (4,217)	
Moore, Anthony	3:56:56 (11,187)	
Moore, Brendan	4:00:55 (12,281)	
Moore, Brendan	4:33:53 (20,555)	
Moore, Colin	4:23:48 (17,919)	
Moore, Craig	3:48:37 (8,789)	
Moore, David	3:52:20 (9,790)	
Moore, David	4:10:13 (14,440)	
Moore, David	4:28:25 (19,142)	
Moore, David	4:29:13 (19,384)	
Moore, Edwin	4:12:38 (15,005)	
Moore, Gerry	3:18:47 (3,111)	
Moore, Graeme	3:27:05 (4,344)	
Moore, Graham	3:13:28 (2,501)	
Moore, Greane	3:34:52 (5,688)	
Moore, Ian	4:26:44 (18,726)	
Moore, Ian	5:34:58 (30,183)	
Moore, Ivan	5:10:06 (27,702)	
Moore, James	4:32:11 (20,136)	
Moore, Jimmy	4:13:02 (15,092)	
Moore, John	5:12:12 (27,972)	
Moore, Karl	4:32:27 (20,207)	
Moore, Lee	4:24:59 (18,258)	
Moore, Martin	4:01:14 (12,374)	
Moore, Melwyn	3:41:29 (7,064)	
Moore, Michael	3:59:52 (12,046)	
Moore, Michael	4:45:23 (23,404)	
Moore, Nicholas	5:50:39 (31,167)	
Moore, Nick	4:46:26 (23,674)	
Moore, Nigel	5:24:09 (29,291)	
Moore, Patrick	4:12:37 (15,002)	
Moore, Paul	5:33:25 (30,063)	
Moore, Peter	4:28:27 (19,157)	
Moore, Philip	4:13:45 (15,251)	
Moore, Ray	4:56:57 (25,756)	
Moore, Richard	3:35:06 (5,732)	
Moore, Robert	3:51:58 (9,674)	
Moore, Robert	3:52:53 (9,945)	
Moore, Robert	3:56:59 (11,203)	
Moore, Stephen	4:11:32 (14,752)	
Moore, Steven	3:16:27 (2,837)	
Moore, Steven	4:30:48 (19,785)	
Moore, Timothy	3:47:44 (8,569)	
Moore, Trevor	3:18:22 (3,053)	
Moore, William	5:01:09 (26,475)	
Moore Doherty, Paddy	2:41:21 (213)	
Moore-Gillon, John	3:57:08 (11,243)	
Moores, Jame	4:40:02 (22,117)	
Moores, Nigel	5:13:07 (28,095)	
Moorhouse, Graham	2:55:59 (827)	
Moorhouse, Stephen	4:35:54 (21,049)	
Moorthy, Siva	6:02:14 (31,622)	
Moosbrugger, Stephen	3:16:02 (2,792)	
Moraghan, John	4:50:11 (24,450)	
Morales, Alexander	3:52:21 (9,797)	
Moran, Christopher	3:30:08 (4,889)	
Moran, David	2:54:36 (714)	
Moran, James	3:11:50 (2,248)	
Moran, Paschal	3:25:06 (4,002)	
Moran, Stuart	4:07:59 (13,903)	
Morant, William	4:45:37 (23,478)	
Morciano, Simon	4:38:02 (21,578)	
Morck, Per-Erik	3:45:28 (8,034)	
Mordue, Stefan	4:23:08 (17,734)	
More, Gerry	4:15:25 (15,671)	
Moreau, Tony	4:45:05 (23,328)	
Moreira, Carlos	3:40:05 (6,756)	
Moreira, Gary	4:39:05 (21,869)	
More-King, William	5:25:05 (29,370)	
Morel, Philip	4:01:16 (12,381)	
Moreland, Alan	4:39:50 (22,067)	
Moreland, Paul	2:52:44 (616)	
Moreman, Keith	3:45:46 (8,104)	
More-Molyneux, Michael	5:27:06 (29,533)	
Morenas, Ransley	3:53:15 (10,061)	
Moreno, Manuel	4:27:43 (18,964)	
Moreno-Galvez, Angel	4:25:40 (18,434)	
Moreton, Adrian	2:54:34 (711)	
Moreton, Adrian	3:43:20 (7,483)	
Moreton, Andrew	4:37:07 (21,339)	
Moreton, Gary	3:49:34 (9,059)	
Moreton, Lloyd	4:56:19 (25,658)	
Moreton, Neil	3:53:26 (10,116)	
Moreton, Patrick	4:45:22 (23,398)	
Moretti, Massimo	4:24:43 (18,178)	
Moretto, Gerardo	4:43:57 (23,055)	
Morgan, Ben	4:11:54 (14,833)	
Morgan, Brenan	2:57:24 (947)	
Morgan, Bryan	3:34:33 (5,626)	
Morgan, Christopher	4:17:34 (16,259)	
Morgan, Colin	4:42:24 (22,698)	
Morgan, David	4:00:13 (12,137)	
Morgan, David	4:17:46 (16,320)	
Morgan, David	4:41:25 (22,451)	
Morgan, Derrick	2:54:34 (711)	
Morgan, Gareth	3:49:21 (8,985)	
Morgan, Gareth	4:40:27 (22,222)	
Morgan, Graham	3:45:11 (7,969)	
Morgan, Howard	3:51:27 (9,532)	
Morgan, Huw	4:07:55 (13,895)	
Morgan, Jacob	4:01:31 (12,451)	
Morgan, James	3:47:17 (8,454)	
Morgan, John	4:27:32 (18,928)	
Morgan, John	4:31:53 (20,053)	
Morgan, Jonathan	3:25:28 (4,058)	
Morgan, Kenneth	3:06:12 (1,658)	
Morgan, Matthew	4:24:33 (18,131)	
Morgan, Michael	4:38:39 (21,753)	
Morgan, Nigel	4:17:37 (16,273)	
Morgan, Oliver	3:34:46 (5,668)	
Morgan, Paul	3:37:29 (6,211)	
Morgan, Peter	3:03:25 (1,413)	
Morgan, Rhys	3:51:37 (9,576)	
Morgan, Robert	3:22:54 (3,406)	
Morgan, Robert	4:54:37 (25,305)	
Morgan, Russell	4:01:53 (12,543)	
Morgan, Stephen	4:30:39 (19,745)	
Morgan, Steve	4:01:34 (12,461)	
Morgan, Steven	3:54:13 (10,376)	
Morgan, Thomas	5:30:32 (29,824)	
Morgan, Tim	3:29:18 (4,752)	
Morgan, Wesley	3:40:24 (6,833)	
Morgan, William	4:42:26 (22,706)	
Morgans, David	5:38:51 (30,469)	
Morgans, John	4:00:50 (12,262)	
Morgan-Smith, Graham	4:51:02 (24,613)	
Morganti, Adam	3:48:34 (8,766)	
Moriand, Gerry	4:08:28 (14,010)	
Moriarty, Alexander	2:55:26 (775)	
Morio, Gilbert	3:32:36 (5,289)	
Moris, Joel	2:55:48 (809)	
Morley, David	4:04:13 (13,032)	
Morley, David	4:28:59 (19,318)	
Morley, David	5:48:22 (31,055)	
Morley, Derek	4:15:50 (15,786)	
Morley, Eric	3:58:19 (11,593)	
Morley, Gary	3:16:05 (2,796)	
Morley, Julian	4:43:41 (22,994)	
Morley, Paul	3:57:33 (11,381)	
Morley, Philip	2:56:59 (913)	
Morley, Richard	4:18:59 (16,584)	
Morley, Simon	5:46:22 (30,958)	
Morley, Stephen	4:27:03 (18,805)	
Morley, Steven	4:06:56 (13,657)	
Morley-Fletcher, Peter	3:47:08 (8,414)	
Moroney, Simon	3:55:48 (10,840)	
Moroz, David	4:59:51 (26,282)	
Morpuss, Guy	3:38:18 (6,370)	
Morreale, Calogero	3:19:46 (3,230)	
Morreale, Joe	4:18:01 (16,375)	

Morrell, David 4:00:44 (12,240)
Morrell, Nicholas 4:14:08 (15,342)
Morrell, Stephen 3:57:01 (11,214)
Morrin, Joe 5:18:27 (28,722)
Morris, Aaron 4:02:35 (12,675)
Morris, Alan 3:33:16 (5,392)
Morris, Alun 3:51:20 (9,507)
Morris, Andrew 4:26:20 (18,606)
Morris, Andy 3:45:30 (8,044)
Morris, Barry 4:12:14 (14,909)
Morris, Barry 4:13:35 (15,201)
Morris, Ben 3:41:10 (7,003)
Morris, Bob 5:36:47 (30,334)
Morris, Chris 3:06:51 (1,719)
Morris, Chris 4:21:59 (17,389)
Morris, Christopher 3:45:50 (8,127)
Morris, David 4:44:25 (23,154)
Morris, Garth 2:49:03 (448)
Morris, Garwyn 3:58:15 (11,580)
Morris, Gary 3:44:16 (7,731)
Morris, Gary 5:16:16 (28,478)
Morris, James 6:24:42 (32,180)
Morris, Jean 3:14:07 (2,566)
Morris, John 5:05:41 (27,112)
Morris, Jonathan 3:36:50 (6,081)
Morris, Kevin 3:26:38 (4,257)
Morris, Kevin 3:45:50 (8,127)
Morris, Leighton 4:16:41 (16,035)
Morris, Leighton 4:39:10 (21,890)
Morris, Leonard 5:04:50 (27,005)
Morris, Mark 3:59:07 (11,833)
Morris, Michael 5:02:36 (26,686)
Morris, Peter 4:45:16 (23,374)
Morris, Philip 3:13:42 (2,532)
Morris, Richard 3:27:16 (4,372)
Morris, Richard 3:50:11 (9,210)
Morris, Robert 3:55:06 (10,628)
Morris, Ron 5:43:37 (30,791)
Morris, Shaun 6:01:05 (31,580)
Morris, Simon 5:39:07 (30,478)
Morris, Stephen 3:38:45 (6,478)
Morris, Stephen 3:49:05 (8,919)
Morris, Stephen 3:56:55 (11,181)
Morris, Stephen 4:55:53 (25,554)
Morris, Terence 4:17:47 (16,325)
Morris, Timothy 3:36:54 (6,093)
Morrison, Alastair 4:10:16 (14,452)
Morrison, Christopher 2:48:14 (417)
Morrison, Clark 4:02:34 (12,669)
Morrison, Darren 8:45:50 (32,884)
Morrison, David 3:10:14 (2,068)
Morrison, Digby 4:55:49 (25,542)
Morrison, George 3:27:08 (4,349)
Morrison, James 3:47:46 (8,580)
Morrison, James 4:34:57 (20,818)
Morrison, Joe 3:26:39 (4,262)
Morrison, Jon 3:28:46 (4,652)
Morrison, Nick 3:58:59 (11,796)
Morrison, Paul 3:38:11 (6,340)
Morrison, Robert 4:32:48 (20,303)
Morriss, James 6:14:45 (31,950)
Morrissey, Richard 4:33:47 (20,534)
Mors, Barnhard 4:37:41 (21,488)
Morse, David 3:11:29 (2,202)
Morse, David 3:52:41 (9,893)
Morson, Roger 3:51:07 (9,463)
Mort, Allan 4:25:35 (18,410)
Mort, Nick 3:29:57 (4,864)
Mort, Nick 3:57:47 (11,448)
Mortazavi, Mahmood 3:38:48 (6,484)
Mortensen, Svend 3:32:35 (5,285)
Mortimer, Ian 4:31:30 (19,968)
Mortimer, Richard 5:01:40 (26,557)
Mortimer, Rob 4:37:28 (21,439)
Mortimer, Roger 5:33:26 (30,067)
Mortin, John 3:57:25 (11,333)
Morton, Alan 5:42:29 (30,724)
Morton, Andrew 3:49:53 (9,148)
Morton, Brian 4:38:11 (21,621)
Morton, Christopher 3:28:02 (4,521)
Morton, Clive 3:41:41 (7,097)
Morton, Colin 4:41:46 (22,549)
Morton, Derek 4:54:07 (25,202)
Morton, Geraint 4:27:56 (19,018)
Morton, Jamie 3:51:25 (9,525)
Morton, Jonathan 4:17:24 (16,224)
Morton, Nick 4:04:49 (13,166)
Morton, Robin 4:41:40 (22,519)
Morton, Steve 3:21:00 (3,364)
Morton, Steven 3:12:40 (2,381)
Morton, Tim 4:17:55 (16,349)
Moruzzi, Carlos 3:22:57 (3,651)
Mosby, Derek 4:19:50 (16,810)
Moseley, Andrew 3:51:41 (9,591)
Moseley, Daniel 3:31:42 (5,151)
Moseley, Michael 3:52:00 (9,683)
Moseley, Oliver 3:39:06 (6,548)
Moseley, Paul 4:36:54 (21,297)
Moseley, Roger 4:26:37 (18,688)
Moseley, Silvanus 5:01:11 (26,479)
Moseling, Chris 3:44:18 (7,742)
Moses, Ephraim 6:07:13 (31,767)
Moses, Moddy 3:36:50 (6,081)
Mosley, Ian 3:38:13 (6,348)
Mosley, Paul 5:09:51 (27,677)
Mosobbir, Misbah 3:46:10 (8,193)
Moss, Carl 4:20:57 (17,098)
Moss, Charles 4:52:09 (24,805)
Moss, Colin 4:51:56 (24,772)
Moss, Edward 4:34:21 (20,658)
Moss, Jonathan 4:10:48 (14,576)
Moss, Keith 3:44:48 (7,889)
Moss, Kevin 4:04:24 (13,069)
Moss, Neale 3:56:03 (10,913)
Moss, Peter 3:13:53 (2,548)
Moss, Philip 4:42:37 (22,750)
Moss, Raymond 5:15:43 (28,397)
Moss, Rob 3:56:50 (11,149)
Moss, Roger 3:21:31 (3,438)
Moss, Steven 3:29:06 (4,711)
Mossman, Charles 3:05:31 (1,592)
Moston, Andrew 4:49:33 (24,332)
Motley, Michael 4:42:19 (22,675)
Mottershead, Dean 4:58:23 (26,012)
Mottram Jones, Robert 3:39:37 (6,649)
Mouat, Paul 4:27:08 (18,826)
Moufarrige, Philip 4:56:07 (25,614)
Moul, Stuart 3:59:54 (12,057)
Mouland, James 4:25:30 (18,390)
Mould, Alan 2:57:29 (955)
Mould, Andrew 3:34:38 (5,645)
Mould, John 2:58:13 (1,024)
Mould, John 4:19:55 (16,840)
Moulding, Craig 3:40:57 (6,949)
Moult, James 6:39:28 (32,430)
Moulton, Benjamin 4:53:56 (25,168)
Moulton, Clifford 5:26:21 (29,472)
Moulton, Paul 4:28:20 (19,119)
Mouncey, David 3:59:43 (11,998)
Mounde, David 3:51:15 (9,487)
Mounichetty, Max 2:59:56 (1,164)
Mounsey, Ben 3:52:58 (9,967)
Mountain, David 4:30:21 (19,681)
Mourant, Anthony 4:10:06 (14,410)
Mourey, Thierry 4:02:19 (12,619)
Mousdale, Anthony 3:44:41 (7,848)
Mousnier, Geraud 3:50:33 (9,311)
Mowbray, Roger 5:42:16 (30,709)
Mowle, Lee 2:57:21 (942)
Moxon, David 3:39:03 (6,537)
Moxon, Dean 5:36:33 (30,313)
Moye, Andrew 3:50:08 (9,196)
Moyes, Martin 4:53:34 (25,081)
Moyes, Peter 4:23:08 (17,734)
Moylan, William 4:12:50 (15,045)
Moyo, Shep 5:27:26 (29,573)
Mozesh, David 3:37:50 (6,285)
Mozzer, Todd 4:21:50 (17,349)
Mrkaic, Savo 4:13:32 (15,195)
Muckersie, Steven 5:19:13 (28,796)
Muckett, Jeff 4:14:13 (15,368)
Muddimer, Dave 4:05:57 (13,425)
Mudge, Jason 4:55:09 (25,411)
Mudie, Robert 4:32:40 (20,269)
Mueksch, Herbert 5:12:17 (27,995)
Mueller, Dirk 4:28:02 (19,043)
Mueller, Jurrgen 4:48:49 (24,202)
Mueller, Peter 3:59:27 (11,930)
Mueller, Theo 4:14:42 (15,495)
Muenster, Karl 4:53:45 (25,114)
Mugford, Clifford 4:19:34 (16,741)
Muggleton, Keith 3:52:19 (9,785)
Mughal, Mohammed 4:34:48 (20,773)
Mugridge, Wayne 5:11:58 (27,948)
Muhr, Christian 5:46:10 (30,942)
Muino, Steve 3:45:47 (8,110)
Muir, Graham 3:48:18 (8,693)
Muir, Malcolm 3:44:00 (7,658)
Muir, Matthew 4:20:47 (17,066)
Muir, Roger 5:17:27 (28,621)
Muir, Tim 4:17:44 (16,304)
Muirhead, John 4:59:58 (26,305)
Mukhtar, Christopher 4:01:42 (12,493)
Mulcahy, John 4:50:00 (24,423)
Mulcahy, Paul 4:33:12 (20,403)
Mulcahy, Vincent 2:50:46 (524)
Mulder, Pieter 5:03:07 (26,766)
Mulgrew, Gerry 4:14:21 (15,409)
Mulgrew, Paul 3:53:04 (10,003)
Mulholland, Patrick 4:34:29 (20,688)
Mulholland, Peter 4:56:16 (25,650)
Mullally, Paul 4:20:17 (16,937)
Mullan, Liam 5:36:42 (30,327)
Mullan, Rowan 3:40:16 (6,803)
Mullane, Danny 4:07:36 (13,816)
Mullard, Gavin 3:19:12 (3,162)
Mullen, Brian 3:55:57 (10,884)
Mullen, James 4:12:00 (14,862)
Mullen, Patrick 3:21:04 (3,379)
Mullender, Timothy 4:25:38 (18,428)
Muller, Daniel 4:51:25 (24,682)
Mullery, Peter 3:08:16 (1,833)
Mullett, Lee 4:28:09 (19,071)
Mulley, James 3:47:54 (8,606)
Mullin, Brian 4:25:32 (18,396)
Mullin, Frank 3:52:43 (9,897)
Mullin, Fursey 4:56:11 (25,628)
Mullin, Peter 5:13:01 (28,083)
Mullin, Tim 4:34:48 (20,773)
Mullings, Delroy Junior 4:42:00 (22,607)
Mullings, Jason 4:06:33 (13,577)
Mulock Houwer, Jan 3:45:47 (8,110)
Multon, Richard 3:53:26 (10,116)
Mulvaney, Paul 4:24:59 (18,258)
Mulvaney, Trevor 5:04:45 (26,987)
Mulvey, Graeme 4:18:41 (16,522)
Mumberson, Robert 5:07:13 (27,335)
Mumby, Matthew 5:11:16 (27,850)
Mumford, Justin 3:27:17 (4,374)
Mumford, Richard 5:49:16 (31,111)
Mummery, Robert 3:45:17 (7,996)
Munafo, Paolo 3:03:07 (1,382)
Muncila, Paul 4:24:25 (18,094)
Munday, Bob 3:37:33 (6,232)
Munday, Warren 5:13:25 (28,127)
Mundel, Toby 3:58:56 (11,772)
Munden, Grant 4:14:13 (15,368)
Mundy, David 4:21:25 (17,224)
Mundy, Denis 5:23:32 (29,225)
Mundzar, Ivan 3:40:03 (6,744)
Munelly, Dominic 2:41:24 (216)
Munford, John 5:00:10 (26,331)
Mungavin, Richard 4:01:09 (12,352)
Munn, James 11:31:03 (32,903)
Munn, John 4:45:43 (23,497)
Munnery, David 3:19:00 (3,132)
Munns, Robert 4:03:14 (12,822)
Munro, Colin 3:22:09 (3,544)
Munro, David 3:04:02 (1,469)
Munro, Iain 3:47:45 (8,577)
Munro, Neil 5:41:44 (30,667)
Munro, William 3:17:41 (2,972)
Munson, William 4:45:41 (23,488)
Munster, Paul 4:43:14 (22,897)
Munt, Jonathan 4:22:17 (17,472)
Muorah, Mordi 4:16:22 (15,938)
Muraro, Anthony 3:54:09 (10,361)
Murat, John 3:49:00 (8,896)
Murat, Joseph 3:48:59 (8,891)

Newcombe, Frank........................3:57:59 (11,506)
Newcombe, Ian............................3:32:35 (5,285)
Newell, Christopher....................4:48:19 (24,089)
Newell, Jeremy............................4:24:47 (18,193)
Newell, John................................5:28:26 (29,647)
Newell, Julian...............................3:19:48 (3,231)
Newell, Mark...............................3:47:55 (8,608)
Newell, Mark...............................6:36:25 (32,383)
Newell, Paul.................................5:44:04 (30,824)
Newell, Terry...............................5:24:48 (29,344)
Newing, Andrew...........................3:48:28 (8,739)
Newing, Rodney...........................4:24:16 (18,059)
Newitt, Joe...................................3:44:27 (7,784)
Newland, Simon............................4:02:40 (12,695)
Newlands, Alistair........................3:26:42 (4,275)
Newlands, Roy..............................3:39:19 (6,592)
Newlin, Anthony...........................3:56:25 (11,024)
Newman, Alan...............................4:54:22 (25,257)
Newman, Chris..............................4:44:58 (23,290)
Newman, Craig..............................3:24:22 (3,901)
Newman, Daniel............................3:11:56 (2,262)
Newman, Darren...........................5:06:40 (27,252)
Newman, David.............................3:58:58 (11,787)
Newman, David.............................4:03:23 (12,855)
Newman, Dominic.........................3:59:22 (11,906)
Newman, Guy................................4:46:21 (23,652)
Newman, Patrick...........................3:49:37 (9,074)
Newman, Paul...............................4:54:56 (25,364)
Newman, Ralph.............................3:24:19 (3,887)
Newman, Raymond........................6:23:43 (32,162)
Newman, Richard..........................3:09:44 (2,010)
Newman, Robert...........................4:48:50 (24,205)
Newman, Ron................................3:40:34 (6,867)
Newman, Trevor............................4:07:53 (13,890)
Newmarch, Mark...........................4:59:32 (26,227)
Newport, John...............................3:42:56 (7,366)
Newsham, Lee...............................4:26:00 (18,518)
Newsome, Christopher..................4:40:13 (22,162)
Newsome, Paul..............................3:49:34 (9,059)
Newson, David..............................4:09:21 (14,232)
Newstone, David...........................3:40:32 (6,859)
Newsum, Jeremy............................4:18:50 (16,556)
Newton, Alastair............................4:55:41 (25,516)
Newton, Alex.................................3:24:20 (3,891)
Newton, Brian................................3:24:27 (3,910)
Newton, Edward............................5:27:42 (29,596)
Newton, Joseph.............................5:15:41 (28,393)
Newton, Michael............................4:13:50 (15,267)
Newton, Nick.................................3:05:19 (1,569)
Newton, Phillip..............................5:25:58 (29,443)
Newton, Ronald.............................4:46:38 (23,720)
Newton, Simon..............................2:58:52 (1,082)
Newton, Tony.................................5:19:24 (28,810)
Newton, Vicky................................4:50:47 (24,556)
Nezosi, Giocondo..........................2:55:31 (783)
Ng, Ronald.....................................4:20:00 (16,860)
Nganga, Henry...............................4:39:44 (22,037)
Niblett, Trebor...............................4:52:41 (24,911)
Niblock, Ian...................................6:10:46 (31,851)
Nice, Richard.................................5:02:33 (26,679)
Nichol, Donald...............................4:00:57 (12,295)
Nichol, Philip.................................2:42:27 (236)
Nichol, Robert...............................3:42:58 (7,380)
Nicholaou, Nicholas......................5:00:48 (26,421)
Nicholas, Adrian............................5:30:07 (29,789)
Nicholas, David.............................6:07:30 (31,773)
Nicholas, Kevin.............................3:48:05 (8,646)
Nicholas, Martin............................5:08:36 (27,508)
Nicholl, Gary.................................4:34:35 (20,719)
Nicholl, Matthew............................4:20:16 (16,932)
Nicholls, Alan................................4:08:32 (14,036)
Nicholls, Alistair...........................4:14:20 (15,405)
Nicholls, Andrew...........................3:12:45 (2,393)
Nicholls, Ashley.............................4:43:00 (22,838)
Nicholls, Dan.................................5:04:31 (26,956)
Nicholls, David..............................3:53:32 (10,157)
Nicholls, David..............................4:04:21 (13,057)
Nicholls, David..............................4:22:29 (17,541)
Nicholls, Garry..............................5:23:24 (29,209)
Nicholls, Gavin..............................5:16:07 (28,456)
Nicholls, Michael...........................4:31:32 (19,978)
Nicholls, Raymond.........................5:21:29 (29,042)
Nicholls, Ron.................................3:18:39 (3,092)
Nicholls, Sebastian........................4:04:59 (13,204)
Nichols, Carl..................................4:29:28 (19,452)
Nichols, David...............................4:01:24 (12,417)
Nichols, David...............................4:39:42 (22,026)
Nichols, Derek...............................4:55:39 (25,504)
Nichols, Jack.................................4:23:36 (17,847)
Nichols, John.................................4:16:59 (16,112)
Nichols, John.................................4:21:33 (17,267)
Nichols, John.................................5:28:45 (29,677)
Nichols, Martin..............................4:18:31 (16,489)
Nichols, Oliver...............................4:45:22 (23,398)
Nichols, Stephen............................3:37:38 (6,251)
Nichols, Stephen............................4:34:26 (20,678)
Nichols, Trevor..............................4:05:54 (13,411)
Nicholson, Angus...........................4:08:42 (14,079)
Nicholson, Barry............................4:31:31 (19,972)
Nicholson, Daniel..........................3:45:54 (8,134)
Nicholson, James...........................5:06:29 (27,229)
Nicholson, Mark.............................5:33:46 (30,088)
Nicholson, Mark.............................5:46:05 (30,938)
Nicholson, Michael........................3:56:12 (10,964)
Nicholson, Murray.........................4:38:11 (21,621)
Nicholson, Oliver...........................4:32:50 (20,314)
Nicholson, Rupert..........................3:40:52 (6,933)
Nicholson, Steve............................4:19:32 (16,733)
Nicholson, Steven..........................4:40:20 (22,195)
Nicholson, Steven..........................6:08:04 (31,786)
Nickau, Hanno...............................2:55:40 (795)
Nickells, Paul.................................2:55:04 (749)
Nicklin, Brian................................3:44:56 (7,915)
Nicklin, Garry................................3:50:11 (9,210)
Nicklin, Nicholas............................5:10:00 (27,690)
Nickson, Peter...............................2:59:23 (1,120)
Nicol, Brian...................................4:51:26 (24,686)
Nicol, Bruce..................................3:32:50 (5,327)
Nicol, David..................................4:05:37 (13,352)
Nicol, Jerry....................................3:54:17 (10,396)
Nicol, Simon..................................3:27:43 (4,459)
Nicolet, Fabien..............................6:22:41 (32,142)
Nicoll, David..................................4:46:10 (23,613)
Nicoll, Kenneth..............................3:36:53 (6,090)
Nie, Douglas..................................4:50:56 (24,596)
Niedojadlo, Mietek.........................3:49:21 (8,985)
Niedojadlo, Stephen.......................4:53:54 (25,147)
Nielsen, Alex.................................5:04:06 (26,898)
Nielsen, Ole...................................3:13:15 (2,467)
Nielsen, Per...................................3:36:54 (6,093)
Nielsen, Rolf..................................4:15:10 (15,609)
Nielson, Paul..................................4:14:10 (15,349)
Niemarkt, Bert...............................4:02:26 (12,638)
Nightingale, Jason.........................3:48:18 (8,693)
Nightingale, Mark..........................5:28:20 (29,642)
Nijjar, Nairinderpall.......................6:57:50 (32,608)
Nijland, Jeroen..............................4:24:26 (18,100)
Nikiforov, Peter.............................3:21:46 (3,476)
Nilsand, Bo....................................4:13:54 (15,286)
Nilsson, Karl..................................2:43:58 (269)
Nimmegeers, Johan........................3:18:07 (3,025)
Ninch, Dolan..................................3:20:21 (3,295)
Ninet, Jacques...............................4:01:47 (12,514)
Ninham, Richard.............................4:14:29 (15,446)
Nisbet, Angus................................6:19:23 (32,067)
Nisbet, Richmond...........................3:33:20 (5,406)
Nissen, Tom...................................4:08:32 (14,036)
Nitescu, Tiberiu.............................3:54:56 (10,574)
Nitsch, Roger.................................3:54:38 (10,494)
Niven, Mark...................................4:23:37 (17,851)
Nix, William....................................4:20:05 (16,886)
Nixon, Arum...................................4:00:44 (12,240)
Nixon, David..................................3:52:49 (9,929)
Nixon, George................................3:25:53 (4,133)
Nixon, John....................................4:19:21 (16,677)
Nixon, Joseph................................3:07:49 (1,796)
Noad, Peter....................................3:20:45 (3,339)
Nobbs, Dean...................................3:17:00 (2,905)
Nobbs, Martin.................................3:10:22 (2,087)
Noble, Angus..................................4:05:33 (13,341)
Noble, Darren.................................5:00:09 (26,328)
Noble, Paul.....................................3:36:11 (5,955)
Noble, Tim......................................4:50:27 (24,496)
Noblett, Damian..............................4:27:57 (19,022)
Nock, Graham.................................3:35:53 (5,880)
Nock, Michael.................................3:16:14 (2,812)
Noel, Casey.....................................4:45:02 (23,319)
Noel, Ralph.....................................6:06:45 (31,746)
Noel, Selwyn...................................4:53:47 (25,118)
Noering, Jared.................................3:57:41 (11,419)
Nohira, Soichiro..............................3:38:18 (6,370)
Noirjean, Roger...............................4:07:44 (13,850)
Nokes, Ernest..................................6:13:59 (31,928)
Nolan, Christopher...........................5:05:17 (27,058)
Nolan, Colin.....................................4:23:46 (17,907)
Nolan, James...................................4:05:18 (13,273)
Nolan, Karl.......................................5:19:09 (28,789)
Nolan, Nev..5:18:21 (28,709)
Nolan, Paul.......................................3:44:19 (7,747)
Nolan, Richard..................................2:48:36 (432)
Nolan, Robert...................................4:06:55 (13,651)
Nolan, Sean......................................3:43:40 (7,567)
Nolan, Shane.....................................5:19:10 (28,790)
Noonan, Eamonn...............................5:05:49 (27,126)
Noonan, John....................................3:38:09 (6,332)
Noone, Jim..3:50:37 (9,327)
Noor, Saqib.......................................4:38:07 (21,605)
Norbury, Antony................................3:50:32 (9,306)
Norbury, Gary...................................3:52:45 (9,909)
Norcott, James..................................4:19:27 (16,708)
Nordang, Kjell...................................5:53:27 (31,295)
Nordlund, Lars...................................4:57:13 (25,813)
Norgett, Graham................................4:10:01 (14,389)
Norkett, Geoffrey...............................4:59:49 (26,277)
Norman, David...................................2:21:00 (23)
Norman, Dene....................................4:34:02 (20,591)
Norman, Keith....................................5:31:44 (29,929)
Norman, Mark.....................................3:47:48 (8,589)
Norman, Tim.......................................3:53:20 (10,090)
Norman, Trevor...................................3:56:21 (11,003)
Normington, Luke...............................4:08:50 (14,100)
Norrey, Sheridan................................4:04:20 (13,053)
Norridge, Christopher.........................4:21:00 (17,110)
Norris, Andrew...................................2:43:30 (254)
Norris, Andrew...................................3:30:30 (4,945)
Norris, Antony....................................4:44:48 (23,249)
Norris, Benedict.................................3:55:30 (10,745)
Norris, Colin.......................................4:29:34 (19,473)
Norris, Duncan...................................3:09:59 (2,039)
Norris, Gary..5:03:00 (26,738)
Norris, Geoff.......................................3:32:52 (5,333)
Norris, Ian..3:37:28 (6,203)
Norris, Ian..3:54:15 (10,386)
Norris, James.....................................3:10:11 (2,057)
Norris, John.......................................3:42:56 (7,366)
Norris, John.......................................3:55:13 (10,668)
Norris, Keith......................................4:32:34 (20,234)
Norris, Leigh......................................4:03:09 (12,804)
Norris, Louis.......................................3:57:46 (11,444)
Norris, Peter.......................................3:24:07 (3,840)
Norster, David.....................................4:54:56 (25,364)
Norsworthy, Gary................................4:28:10 (19,078)
North, Adam.......................................4:49:57 (24,414)
North, Andrew....................................4:05:10 (13,245)
North, Jonathan..................................4:03:47 (12,936)
North, Martin......................................3:27:52 (4,498)
North, Matthew...................................2:56:19 (859)
North, Michael....................................4:33:04 (20,370)
North, Neil..4:54:48 (25,342)
North, Shaun.......................................2:38:04 (149)
Northcott, Adrian.................................3:28:14 (4,558)
Northcott, Alexander...........................3:45:49 (8,124)
Northern, Paul.....................................4:06:05 (13,455)
Northey, Michael.................................2:40:25 (192)
North-Lewis, David.............................3:26:49 (4,296)
Northmore, Alan..................................4:38:16 (21,645)
Northover, William...............................4:33:37 (20,498)
Northwood, David................................3:25:11 (4,012)
Northwood, Robert..............................4:58:42 (26,079)
Norton, Christopher.............................4:54:39 (25,314)
Norton, Michael...................................5:35:14 (30,203)
Norton, Nick..4:09:17 (14,209)
Norton, Paul..4:23:40 (17,864)
Norton, Phillip.....................................4:49:17 (24,286)
Norton, Roger......................................5:01:55 (26,590)
Noschese, Guiseppe............................5:07:51 (27,414)
Nosworthy, Tim...................................3:48:04 (8,643)
Nothard, John......................................4:32:25 (20,194)
Notridge, Malcolm...............................4:16:16 (15,904)

Nott, David 3:23:46 (3,767)
Nott, James 4:04:31 (13,090)
Nottage, Jason 4:29:37 (19,490)
Notz, Markus 4:14:44 (15,508)
Novacek, Gerhard 3:31:50 (5,170)
Novik, Guy 5:25:13 (29,380)
Novis, Rupert 3:27:49 (4,487)
Nowacki, Wies 2:56:09 (839)
Noya-Noya, José 4:34:43 (20,754)
Noyce, Avid 4:14:44 (15,508)
Nuckcheddy, Iqbal 3:57:39 (11,411)
Nudd, Peter 3:40:38 (6,878)
Nuechtern, Martin 4:47:16 (23,871)
Nugent, Brendan 4:27:58 (19,027)
Nugent, Graham 3:51:55 (9,655)
Nugent, John 4:09:10 (14,178)
Nugent, Ross 3:12:07 (2,296)
Nunn, Bob 3:34:10 (5,557)
Nunn, Christopher 4:52:55 (24,963)
Nunn, David 3:57:28 (11,350)
Nunn, Gregory 3:47:08 (8,414)
Nunn, Robert 3:55:03 (10,611)
Nunn, Simon 3:53:52 (10,272)
Nunn, Steve 3:28:35 (4,622)
Nunns, Roger 4:55:51 (25,550)
Nunny, Mark 4:18:51 (16,558)
Nurse, Matthew 4:41:41 (22,526)
Nuss, Charles 3:38:35 (6,446)
Nutley, Gary 5:00:20 (26,349)
Nutley, Julian 5:00:20 (26,349)
Nuttall, Mark 6:11:33 (31,872)
Nuttall, Paul 4:16:15 (15,899)
Nuttall, Sean 5:04:51 (27,008)
Nuttall, Warrick 5:04:59 (27,017)
Nutter, George 4:11:38 (14,777)
Nutter, Paul 4:33:13 (20,407)
Nuzzaco, Joseph 4:05:59 (13,432)
Nye, André 4:35:58 (21,071)
Nye, Howard 3:14:53 (2,654)
Nye, John 4:37:08 (21,345)
Nye, Philip 3:58:13 (11,571)
Nykolyszyr, Roman 3:36:19 (5,981)
Nyland, Paul 3:01:05 (1,232)
Oak, Simon 3:56:30 (11,053)
Oakes, Mark 2:41:26 (217)
Oakes, Peter 5:06:57 (27,288)
Oakes, Wally 5:01:52 (26,580)
Oakes, Wayne 3:35:04 (5,722)
Oakham, Stephen 5:50:06 (31,145)
Oakley, Alan 4:19:40 (16,765)
Oakley, Andrew 3:47:11 (8,433)
Oakley, Richard 4:28:33 (19,181)
Oakley, Stuart 4:09:02 (14,140)
Oates, David 4:18:25 (16,469)
Oates, Michael 5:01:50 (26,572)
Oatts, Andrew 3:06:31 (1,688)
O'Beirne, Edward 5:42:01 (30,696)
Oberst, Robin 3:52:04 (9,714)
Oborski, Andrzej 4:34:07 (20,611)
Obre, Emmanuel 3:43:49 (7,612)
O'Brien, Bern Ie 5:02:22 (26,649)
O'Brien, Denis 3:49:23 (8,998)
O'Brien, John 3:10:56 (2,147)
O'Brien, John 3:40:45 (6,909)
O'Brien, John 4:59:48 (26,275)
O'Brien, Michael 3:21:59 (3,520)
O'Brien, Richard 5:37:49 (30,402)
O'Brien, Robert 4:34:54 (20,803)
O'Brien, Shannon 3:59:56 (12,066)
O'Brien, Simon 6:23:03 (32,149)
O'Brien, Thomas 3:29:16 (4,742)
O'Brien, Tim 4:08:23 (13,990)
O'Brien, Wesley 4:53:49 (25,124)
O'Brien Brackenburey, Brendan 4:46:09 (23,607)
O'Byrne, Edward 4:03:49 (12,947)
O'Callaghan, Paul 3:54:23 (10,422)
O'Carroll, Christopher 3:46:19 (8,229)
O'Carroll, Michael 4:14:49 (15,529)
O'Carroll, Tim 4:30:44 (19,770)
Occleshaw, Simon 5:20:48 (28,976)
Ochsner, Walter 4:08:37 (14,062)
Ockenden, Richard 4:11:06 (14,659)
Ockwell, Christopher 4:42:28 (22,714)
O'Connell, John 4:47:34 (23,923)
O'Connell, Maurice 3:54:02 (10,320)
O'Connell, Michael 4:22:01 (17,401)
O'Connor, Charles 3:54:15 (10,386)
O'Connor, David 3:55:43 (10,818)
O'Connor, Edward 3:10:12 (2,063)
O'Connor, Edward 4:52:16 (24,836)
O'Connor, Fintan 4:56:39 (25,712)
O'Connor, John 3:41:01 (6,966)
O'Connor, Judd 5:53:58 (31,311)
O'Connor, Liam 3:50:20 (9,258)
O'Connor, Maurice 3:44:19 (7,747)
O'Connor, Martin 3:54:15 (10,386)
O'Connor, Martin 3:54:45 (10,537)
O'Connor, Michael 4:01:30 (12,441)
O'Connor, Philip 3:09:56 (2,032)
O'Connor, Raymond 4:41:13 (22,403)
O'Connor, Rory 3:45:25 (8,025)
O'Connor, Ross 3:15:18 (2,701)
O'Connor, Steven 4:25:44 (18,448)
O'Connor, William 3:44:21 (7,757)
Oddy, Huw 4:36:30 (21,221)
Oddy, Jonathan 3:39:07 (6,551)
Oddy, Philip 4:52:19 (24,846)
O'Dell, Benoit 3:21:06 (3,387)
O'Donnell, Ben 3:44:44 (7,867)
O'Donnell, Eamon 3:53:08 (10,025)
O'Donnell, John 3:21:17 (3,405)
O'Donnell, John 3:51:28 (9,535)
O'Donnell, John 4:05:28 (13,317)
O'Donnell, Kevin 3:48:53 (8,869)
O'Donnell, Kevin 4:06:08 (13,473)
O'Donnell, Kieron 3:31:12 (5,064)
O'Donoghue, Daniel 2:45:13 (306)
O'Donoghue, James 4:04:50 (13,167)
O'Donoghue, Philip 4:46:17 (23,636)
O'Donoghue, Thomas 2:59:12 (1,111)
O'Donovan, Timothy 3:07:53 (1,799)
O'Driscoll, Andrew 4:38:00 (21,573)
O'Driscoll, Patrick 5:39:29 (30,514)
O'Driscoll, Robert 4:38:17 (21,651)
Odum, Marvin 4:23:50 (17,925)
Oduneye, Adeyemi 4:58:29 (26,030)
O'Dwyer, David 4:48:57 (24,226)
Oeglaend, Jan 3:40:51 (6,929)
O'Farrell, Daniel 5:03:06 (26,762)
Office, Michael 3:41:10 (7,003)
Offord, Christopher 3:28:45 (4,646)
Offord, David 4:42:51 (22,801)
Offord, Matthew 3:56:28 (11,033)
Offord, Paul 4:44:13 (23,110)
O'Gara, Kevin 4:50:35 (24,520)
Ogata, Tsuyoshi 2:25:02 (39)
Ogden, Andrew 6:17:37 (32,022)
Ogden, Neil 3:32:11 (5,216)
Ogden, Peter 4:17:47 (16,325)
Ogden, Rick 4:54:56 (25,364)
Ogg, Billy 4:54:07 (25,202)
Ogg, Steven 2:38:56 (167)
Oggiano, Andrea 3:43:13 (7,450)
Ogier, Geoff 4:15:07 (15,599)
Oglesby, Mark 2:49:54 (483)
Oglesby, Steven 5:26:41 (29,502)
Ogley, Andrew 3:24:39 (3,936)
Ogoe, Bernard 4:39:40 (22,009)
O'Gorman, Tom 4:34:02 (20,591)
O'Grady, David 3:54:18 (10,401)
O'Grady, Paul 4:09:06 (14,153)
O'Grady, Vincent 3:59:24 (11,919)
Oh, Marcus 5:07:30 (27,377)
O'Hagan, John 3:39:27 (6,612)
O'Hanlon, Eddie 4:00:25 (12,170)
O'Hara, Christopher 5:07:50 (27,411)
O'Hara, Michael 4:03:45 (12,928)
O'Hara, Noel 4:45:51 (23,530)
Ohare, Brian 4:22:13 (17,449)
O'Hare, Michael 3:44:24 (7,773)
O'Hare, Sam 3:54:33 (10,472)
Ohl, Eugene 3:55:34 (10,772)
Ohnstad, Ian 4:14:44 (15,508)
Okane, Joe 4:51:21 (24,672)
O'Keefe, Dennis 4:50:51 (24,580)
O'Keefe, Kevin 4:02:09 (12,586)
O'Keeffe, Derek 4:38:32 (21,713)
O'Keeffe, Jimmy 5:03:17 (26,795)
O'Keeffe, Paul 6:19:28 (32,070)
O'Keeffe, Terence 3:58:00 (11,508)
Okell, Tim 4:49:59 (24,419)
O'Kelly, Steven 3:30:17 (4,912)
Okely, Peter 3:33:57 (5,509)
Okoh, Tony 4:30:05 (19,620)
Oku, Katsuhiko 4:52:02 (24,787)
Olafsson, Dall 4:04:17 (13,042)
Olaisen, Oeivind 3:22:29 (3,579)
Olaleye, Bode 5:25:54 (29,439)
Olaribigbe, Robert 4:04:59 (13,204)
Olchawa, Piotr 3:04:24 (1,495)
Old, David 3:31:28 (5,102)
Oldaker, David 4:41:55 (22,590)
Olden, Christian 2:44:50 (293)
Oldenburger, Rutgert 4:17:06 (16,145)
Older, Paul 4:33:29 (20,459)
Olderhsaw, Glen 5:32:39 (30,004)
Oldfield, Mark 3:53:40 (10,201)
Oldfield, Richard 4:17:12 (16,171)
Oldfield, Richard 4:26:33 (18,668)
Oldfield, Russell 3:30:22 (4,924)
Olding, Keith 3:47:36 (8,538)
Oldland, Christopher 5:16:32 (28,503)
Oldman, Daniel 3:47:09 (8,423)
Oldman, Matthew 3:36:03 (5,915)
O'Leary, Brian 4:10:31 (14,517)
O'Leary, James 4:19:46 (16,797)
O'Leary, Jerome 4:17:43 (16,299)
O'Leary, John 5:05:08 (27,038)
O'Leary, Mark 4:16:58 (16,108)
O'Leary, Paul 3:51:02 (9,438)
O'Leary, Sean 4:23:16 (17,768)
Olejak, Jens 3:53:43 (10,212)
Oley, John 3:50:56 (9,406)
Oliphant, David 3:48:02 (8,634)
Olivant, Vernon 3:55:41 (10,803)
Olive, Gary 3:55:35 (10,778)
Oliveira, Silvi 3:52:25 (9,815)
Oliver, Alan 4:28:43 (19,231)
Oliver, Alan 4:35:40 (21,008)
Oliver, David 4:42:15 (22,659)
Oliver, Geoffrey 3:21:58 (3,516)
Oliver, John 4:41:40 (22,519)
Oliver, Michael 3:15:37 (2,738)
Oliver, Michael 4:25:33 (18,404)
Oliver, Michael 4:42:13 (22,651)
Oliver, Neil 6:26:27 (32,209)
Oliver, Paul 4:41:09 (22,389)
Oliver, Roland 4:16:52 (16,082)
Oliver, Steven 4:02:57 (12,766)
Olivier, Cedric 3:53:35 (10,175)
Olivieri, Valter 3:13:55 (2,552)
Ollerhead, Colin 6:13:34 (31,919)
Ollier, Marc 4:28:58 (19,313)
Ollis, Stephen 3:56:51 (11,159)
Olloman, Paul 5:25:36 (29,412)
Olney, Alan 6:14:31 (31,943)
O'Lone, Marcus 5:34:13 (30,125)
O'Loughlin, Ben 4:52:51 (24,948)
Olsen, Mark 5:03:56 (26,876)
Olson, Richard 5:24:34 (29,332)
Olson, Victor 4:26:36 (18,680)
Olszewski, Krzysztof 3:07:06 (1,744)
O'Mahony, Mark 4:19:00 (16,589)
O'Malley, Mark 3:46:18 (8,225)
Omana, Chester 3:49:27 (9,027)
O'Mara, Robert 3:35:33 (5,811)
O'Mathena, Fiachra 4:02:07 (12,583)
O'Meara, Pat 4:05:05 (13,229)
Omland, Morten 3:14:54 (2,657)
Omtzigt, Dirk-Jan 3:46:21 (8,236)
O'Neill, Aidan 3:46:11 (8,196)
O'Neill, James 3:39:54 (6,710)
O'Neill, James 4:53:51 (25,134)
O'Neill, Patrick 4:38:16 (21,645)
O'Neill, Stephen 4:44:03 (23,074)
O'Neill, Stuart 5:08:05 (27,443)
O'Neill, Tony 4:16:36 (16,010)
O'Neill-Egan, John 3:05:47 (1,614)
Onions, Terence 3:42:31 (7,291)

Onions, Tom 3:21:18 (3,408)
Onita, Tommy 4:07:09 (13,708)
Ono, Kazuo 4:01:18 (12,391)
Oohollo, Laurent 4:00:28 (12,180)
Opperman, Manie 5:03:12 (26,781)
Oppliger, Etienne 4:19:41 (16,775)
Or Kam Fat, Patrick 4:19:14 (16,650)
Oragano, Anthony 4:09:34 (14,284)
Oram, Derek 4:56:42 (25,717)
O'Rawe, Alan 4:32:55 (20,339)
Orchard, Mark 5:16:56 (28,547)
Orde, Hugh 3:56:26 (11,025)
O'Reilly, Barry 4:50:24 (24,479)
O'Reilly, Edward 3:25:12 (4,015)
O'Reilly, James 4:49:48 (24,380)
O'Reilly, John 4:10:20 (14,468)
O'Reilly, John 4:35:06 (20,855)
O'Reilly, Kevin 4:26:48 (18,744)
O'Reilly, Peter 5:11:48 (27,921)
O'Reilly, Richard 3:52:17 (9,779)
Orfanos, Michael 5:20:41 (28,960)
Organ, Rodney 4:40:03 (22,120)
Orgill, Andrew 5:02:20 (26,646)
O'Riordan, David 4:45:41 (23,488)
O'Riordan, James 4:01:49 (12,526)
Orloff, Simon 4:52:38 (24,904)
Orlowski, Andrew 3:53:44 (10,218)
Orme, John 6:31:31 (32,298)
Orme, Jonathan 3:44:00 (7,658)
Orme, Peter 3:02:56 (1,365)
Orme, Peter 3:15:51 (2,773)
Ormerod, Stephen 5:21:38 (29,061)
Ormesher, Kevan 4:14:57 (15,559)
Orme-Smith, James 3:12:04 (2,284)
Ormiston, Ian 3:40:15 (6,799)
Ormond, Paul 4:17:28 (16,237)
O'Rourke, Leo 6:20:27 (32,094)
O'Rourke, Michael 4:36:42 (21,261)
Orpwood, Peter 5:36:33 (30,313)
Orr, Alan 5:05:16 (27,055)
Orr, Billy 2:44:41 (289)
Orr, David 3:45:13 (7,981)
Orr, James 3:12:50 (2,407)
Orr, Lewis 3:13:02 (2,437)
Orr, Mark 3:45:47 (8,110)
Orridge, Christian 3:26:30 (4,228)
Orrock, Andrew 3:58:23 (11,614)
Ortega Erazo, Ivan 4:24:31 (18,124)
Orthmann, Thorsten 4:33:23 (20,438)
Orthouse, Stephen 4:43:16 (22,901)
Ortiz, Jorge 3:34:07 (5,546)
Ortner, Peter 4:58:20 (26,002)
Orton, Stewart 3:28:12 (4,551)
Orton, Trevor 4:29:31 (19,460)
Oruc, Ibrahim 4:26:56 (18,771)
Osabe, Shizuo 3:44:38 (7,831)
Osborn, Andrew 4:20:39 (17,032)
Osborn, Barry 5:04:14 (26,926)
Osborn, Duncan 5:19:41 (28,837)
Osborn, Mark 3:26:13 (4,190)
Osborne, Bruce 3:28:59 (4,694)
Osborne, Dale 3:29:34 (4,809)
Osborne, David 5:10:42 (27,774)
Osborne, Duncan 5:04:33 (26,958)
Osborne, Matthew 4:25:52 (18,475)
Osborne, Neil 4:08:49 (14,094)
Osborne, Nicholas 3:59:12 (11,859)
Osborne, Nick 3:50:45 (9,363)
Osborne, Patrick 3:49:45 (9,112)
Osborne, Paul 5:33:26 (30,067)
Osborne, Peter 2:55:18 (765)
Osborne, Russell 4:07:32 (13,806)
Osborne, Stephen 5:48:23 (31,056)
Osborne, Stuart 6:02:33 (31,627)
Osbourne, Matthew 3:30:52 (5,000)
Oscroft, Martin 4:19:39 (16,763)
O'Shaughnessy, Damian 4:01:04 (12,330)
O'Shea, Jamie 3:54:00 (10,309)
O'Shea, Keld 4:46:33 (23,702)
O'Shea, Matthew 6:20:40 (32,098)
O'Shea, Nigel 5:13:38 (28,155)
O'Shea, Paul 3:50:34 (9,314)
O'Shea, Timothy 3:49:12 (8,944)
Osinowo, Remi 3:25:44 (4,103)
Osman, Rick 4:17:50 (16,333)
Ossege, Ferdinand 4:05:56 (13,420)
Ostermeyer, Daniel 4:27:03 (18,805)
Ostermeyer, Marcel 3:03:30 (1,422)
Osterwalder, Martin 2:56:52 (905)
Ostle, Steve 4:01:08 (12,345)
Ostrowski, Stephen 5:44:35 (30,864)
O'Sullivan, Christopher 5:16:37 (28,514)
O'Sullivan, Daniel 4:37:33 (21,456)
O'Sullivan, Donal 3:04:21 (1,491)
O'Sullivan, John 4:47:02 (23,823)
O'Sullivan, Kevin 3:43:56 (7,638)
O'Sullivan, Michael 3:25:49 (4,114)
O'Sullivan, Michael 3:32:25 (5,258)
O'Sullivan, Michael 4:34:26 (20,678)
O'Sullivan, Patrick 4:56:01 (25,587)
O'Sullivan, Paul 7:08:38 (32,690)
O'Sullivan, Sean 3:47:07 (8,409)
O'Sullivan, Steven 3:45:44 (8,096)
Oswald, David 6:16:43 (31,998)
Oswald, Richard 3:49:23 (8,998)
Oswick, Darren 5:41:09 (30,630)
Oswin, Michael 3:55:03 (10,611)
Oswin, Raymond 3:58:13 (11,571)
Otim, Richard 4:24:40 (18,164)
Otmane, Farid 3:04:38 (1,513)
O'Toole, Martin 4:58:07 (25,968)
Ottavi, Jacques 4:32:41 (20,272)
Ottaway, Bob 5:16:37 (28,514)
Ottesen, Lars 4:02:10 (12,588)
Ottey, Lee 4:29:24 (19,436)
Ottey, Martin 4:08:35 (14,051)
Ottley, Simon 4:04:24 (13,069)
Otto, Kevin 4:09:21 (14,232)
Otto, Pieter 4:28:40 (19,213)
Otto, Rolf 4:04:11 (13,022)
Ottoy, Marcel 3:27:06 (4,346)
Ouastani, Said 3:53:14 (10,055)
Oudijk, Redeeris 5:40:55 (30,608)
Oui, Seng 4:07:36 (13,816)
Oulton, Simon 4:33:06 (20,375)
Ousey, Richard 3:49:21 (8,985)
Outhwaite, Jeffrey 3:26:14 (4,193)
Outhwaite, John 3:05:53 (1,631)
Outten, Simon 3:53:53 (10,274)
Ovenden, Timothy 4:56:38 (25,708)
Overbeek, Sjaak 3:09:51 (2,021)
Overend, Charlie 6:00:40 (31,567)
Overgaard, Jan 4:15:33 (15,708)
Overvoorde, Peter 3:41:07 (6,994)
Owen, Aled 3:59:40 (11,986)
Owen, Chris 5:17:02 (28,569)
Owen, Craig 5:03:11 (26,778)
Owen, Daniel 4:18:22 (16,458)
Owen, David 4:21:21 (17,203)
Owen, Derek 4:07:05 (13,692)
Owen, Dylan 3:04:07 (1,478)
Owen, Eugene 3:47:50 (8,597)
Owen, Gareth 3:57:28 (11,350)
Owen, Gareth 4:37:57 (21,564)
Owen, Graham 4:35:36 (20,987)
Owen, Harry 3:42:16 (7,226)
Owen, Ian 3:27:51 (4,492)
Owen, Ian 3:53:48 (10,249)
Owen, John 3:31:27 (5,100)
Owen, Jonathan 4:39:15 (21,910)
Owen, Julian 2:50:25 (505)
Owen, Keith 4:09:52 (14,355)
Owen, Kevin 2:51:07 (539)
Owen, Lee 4:12:33 (14,980)
Owen, Liam 3:58:14 (11,577)
Owen, Matthew 3:02:08 (1,313)
Owen, Nick 3:47:11 (8,433)
Owen, Nigel 4:54:26 (25,272)
Owen, Paul 4:26:47 (18,739)
Owen, Paul 4:37:57 (21,564)
Owen, Paul 4:58:57 (26,121)
Owen, Richard 2:51:25 (556)
Owen, Richard 4:27:18 (18,864)
Owen, Simon 3:59:54 (12,057)
Owen, Stanley 4:01:35 (12,466)
Owen, Steven 3:43:20 (7,483)
Owen, Terence 3:43:56 (7,638)
Owen, William 3:30:55 (5,013)
Owens, Bob 4:20:04 (16,882)
Owens, David 3:27:43 (4,459)
Owens, David 3:32:05 (5,204)
Owens, Gareth 3:27:45 (4,467)
Owens, Ivor 7:39:07 (32,822)
Owens, Phillip 3:42:32 (7,296)
Owens, Simon 4:20:39 (17,032)
Owers, Ian 4:59:12 (26,163)
Oxberry, Kevin 4:45:21 (23,393)
Oxberry, Paul 4:44:15 (23,115)
Oxenham, Phillip 3:06:57 (1,731)
Oxley, David 3:28:44 (4,645)
Oxley, Neil 4:11:35 (14,763)
Oxley, William 4:21:41 (17,309)
Paccapelo, Enrico 5:08:10 (27,448)
Pace, Kevin 3:18:30 (3,074)
Pache, Bernard 2:58:56 (1,087)
Pachod, Patrick 3:43:02 (7,396)
Pachoud, André 3:42:56 (7,366)
Pack, Andrew 3:08:44 (1,896)
Packer, Dean 3:43:12 (7,442)
Packer, Malcolm 2:43:44 (262)
Packer, Stephen 5:00:45 (26,417)
Packer, Stephen 5:55:26 (31,375)
Packford, Ian 7:02:34 (32,655)
Packham, Christopher 4:14:42 (15,495)
Packham, Daren 4:10:16 (14,452)
Paddeo, Giovanni 3:54:57 (10,580)
Padwick, Nick 4:19:37 (16,754)
Paetzold, Falko 3:09:47 (2,015)
Page, Aaron 3:37:42 (6,260)
Page, Andrew 3:05:09 (1,556)
Page, Anthony 5:35:08 (30,193)
Page, Bob 5:43:57 (30,815)
Page, Carl 3:04:45 (1,522)
Page, Daniel 4:29:17 (19,410)
Page, Gary 4:59:25 (26,202)
Page, James 4:53:34 (25,081)
Page, Jeremy 3:33:48 (5,479)
Page, John 4:27:53 (19,000)
Page, Nicholas 2:46:53 (353)
Page, Nicholas 4:36:29 (21,214)
Page, Richard 4:50:41 (24,540)
Page, Simon 4:07:00 (13,678)
Page, Steven 4:24:45 (18,185)
Pageot, Vincent 5:07:47 (27,404)
Paget, Martin 4:14:39 (15,485)
Paget, Michael 3:19:19 (3,173)
Paice, David 4:44:12 (23,108)
Pain, Robert 5:04:09 (26,908)
Paine, Clive 4:01:13 (12,370)
Paine, Nigel 4:40:17 (22,176)
Paine, Richard 4:11:12 (14,674)
Paine, Richard 4:56:48 (25,732)
Paine, Ron 3:52:02 (9,700)
Painter, Andrew 4:26:15 (18,588)
Painter, Danny 3:55:45 (10,827)
Painter, Ian 3:21:54 (3,507)
Paintin, Edward 4:24:39 (18,159)
Paintin, Ian 4:58:40 (26,070)
Paiva, Carlos 4:13:27 (15,177)
Paiva De Brito, Edvaldo 4:32:23 (20,184)
Pakenham, Dermot 5:14:15 (28,222)
Palee, René 5:11:36 (27,894)
Paley, James 3:59:01 (11,810)
Palfi, Xavier 2:44:52 (294)
Palfrey, Daryl 3:03:22 (1,409)
Palfreyman, Dean 4:40:12 (22,159)
Pallant, Robert 3:43:13 (7,450)
Pallister, Gerald 5:18:00 (28,668)
Pallister, Stephen 3:56:49 (11,148)
Pallone, Francesco 3:39:34 (6,638)
Palmer, Alex 3:58:09 (11,556)
Palmer, Andrew 3:53:49 (10,258)
Palmer, Andrew 4:23:37 (17,851)
Palmer, Christopher 4:24:12 (18,037)
Palmer, Daniel 3:28:37 (4,628)
Palmer, David 3:11:32 (2,207)
Palmer, David 3:39:50 (6,693)
Palmer, Eric 3:18:19 (3,048)
Palmer, Joseph 4:43:50 (23,027)

Palmer, Julie 5:35:33 (30,233)
Palmer, Kenneth 3:08:06 (1,814)
Palmer, Liam 3:47:37 (8,541)
Palmer, Lloyd 2:42:02 (226)
Palmer, Mark 3:08:15 (1,831)
Palmer, Mark 4:03:40 (12,911)
Palmer, Mark 4:16:21 (15,930)
Palmer, Martin 4:19:34 (16,741)
Palmer, Nigel 5:17:14 (28,592)
Palmer, Paul 3:29:20 (4,761)
Palmer, Paul 4:31:41 (20,008)
Palmer, Peter 6:02:35 (31,630)
Palmer, Roy 2:36:49 (123)
Palmer, Stephen 4:08:11 (13,947)
Palmer, Steven 4:51:13 (24,658)
Palmer, Stuart 3:02:23 (1,333)
Palmer, Stuart 4:36:29 (21,214)
Palmer, Tim 4:02:50 (12,741)
Palmer, Timothy 3:29:53 (4,856)
Palmieri, Sauro 3:06:02 (1,644)
Palser, Tristan 3:34:42 (5,660)
Pampanini, Sebastian 4:23:13 (17,754)
Pamplin, John 4:01:19 (12,396)
Panayiotou, Yiannis 4:11:39 (14,782)
Pancrazi, Robert 3:58:47 (11,729)
Panesar, Harpal 4:01:02 (12,319)
Paniagua, Fernando 4:26:37 (18,688)
Paniagua, Rafael 4:26:43 (18,721)
Panien, Marc 5:03:00 (26,738)
Panis, Walter 5:24:02 (29,283)
Pankhania, Mahendra 5:53:24 (31,294)
Pannell, Alexander 4:21:08 (17,151)
Pannett, Peter 4:46:54 (23,786)
Panter, David 4:17:14 (16,179)
Pantlin, Tim 3:41:05 (6,984)
Papa, Gerald 5:35:21 (30,212)
Papillon, Franck 3:26:34 (4,243)
Papst, Sepp 4:05:18 (13,273)
Papworth, Mark 3:56:38 (11,094)
Paramor, Jon 3:31:10 (5,061)
Paramore, Ian 2:51:24 (554)
Parczuk, Mike 5:08:03 (27,440)
Pardey, James 3:34:39 (5,649)
Pardon, Justin 3:12:31 (2,364)
Parekh, Bhupesh 7:17:16 (32,747)
Parekh, Sandip 7:17:16 (32,747)
Parello, Salvatore 3:08:49 (1,910)
Parfitt, David 4:55:22 (25,453)
Parfitt, Kevin 3:31:30 (5,109)
Parham, Christopher 4:24:10 (18,027)
Parham, Martin 4:18:08 (16,394)
Parise, Stefano 4:53:14 (25,018)
Park, Andrew 4:08:55 (14,116)
Park, Derek 4:33:58 (20,572)
Park, Gary 5:02:05 (26,614)
Park, John 3:22:44 (3,621)
Park, Mungo 3:59:56 (12,066)
Park, Thomas 4:06:28 (13,558)
Parker, Aaron 4:35:26 (20,932)
Parker, Allan 3:55:31 (10,750)
Parker, Alun 4:28:36 (19,197)
Parker, Andrew 3:32:05 (5,204)
Parker, Benjamin 4:25:10 (18,302)
Parker, Brian 3:37:46 (6,275)
Parker, Charles 4:08:12 (13,950)
Parker, Chris 4:43:03 (22,849)
Parker, Christopher 5:06:46 (27,266)
Parker, Colin 3:34:51 (5,682)
Parker, Duncan 3:44:00 (7,658)
Parker, Garrie 3:22:02 (3,531)
Parker, George 3:59:03 (11,823)
Parker, George 5:03:00 (26,738)
Parker, Jon 4:55:43 (25,526)
Parker, Jonathan 4:41:42 (22,534)
Parker, Mark 4:04:34 (13,104)
Parker, Mike 3:43:41 (7,568)
Parker, Paul 3:30:47 (4,990)
Parker, Richard 3:23:34 (3,736)
Parker, Robert 5:02:26 (26,658)
Parker, Simon 4:18:18 (16,439)
Parker, Stephen 3:03:55 (1,458)
Parker, Stephen 3:24:04 (3,833)
Parker, Terence 5:14:21 (28,233)
Parker-Mead, Gary 4:43:00 (22,838)
Parkes, Adrian 4:59:47 (26,272)
Parkes, Benjamin 4:03:21 (12,843)
Parkes, Keith 3:43:17 (7,467)
Parkes, Roy 3:56:19 (10,994)
Parkin, Daniel 4:42:10 (22,642)
Parkin, David 3:01:52 (1,290)
Parkington, David 3:49:44 (9,111)
Parkins, David 2:56:09 (839)
Parkins, Derek 3:31:24 (5,092)
Parkinson, Brendan 3:37:17 (6,160)
Parkinson, Colin 4:55:07 (25,400)
Parkinson, Edward 4:14:22 (15,417)
Parkinson, James 3:28:40 (4,636)
Parkinson, Kevin 4:12:25 (14,950)
Parkinson, Paul 3:12:12 (2,312)
Parkinson, Peter 3:51:59 (9,678)
Parkinson, Roy 3:16:28 (2,842)
Parkinson, Stuart 4:25:32 (18,396)
Parkinson, Timothy 5:08:23 (27,480)
Parkyn, Giles 3:45:12 (7,975)
Parlato, Shane 4:29:45 (19,524)
Parmar, Arvind 4:45:14 (23,366)
Parmar, Rupesh 5:27:43 (29,599)
Parmenter, Dale 5:27:13 (29,541)
Parnell, Chris 4:54:48 (25,342)
Parnell, Derek 3:58:23 (11,614)
Parnell, Lee 4:18:02 (16,377)
Parnell, Leonard 4:46:56 (23,798)
Parnell, Robert 3:31:04 (5,041)
Parnell, Rupert 3:59:09 (11,841)
Parr, Richard 4:25:49 (18,465)
Parrish, James 5:43:37 (30,791)
Parrish, Robert 4:22:19 (17,486)
Parrock, Neil 4:06:34 (13,581)
Parrott, Brian 4:39:49 (22,062)
Parry, Alister 3:54:23 (10,422)
Parry, Andrew 5:08:47 (27,537)
Parry, Colin 3:49:45 (9,112)
Parry, Haydn 4:45:49 (23,520)
Parry, John 3:26:34 (4,243)
Parry, John 4:08:42 (14,079)
Parry, Martyn 3:44:17 (7,739)
Parry, Matthew 5:28:27 (29,651)
Parry, Paul 5:44:22 (30,846)
Parry, Richard 3:27:38 (4,444)
Parry, Stephen 3:56:57 (11,192)
Parry, Stephen 4:03:44 (12,926)
Parry, Vaughan 4:05:11 (13,248)
Parry Jones, Ashley 4:31:18 (19,900)
Parry-Jones, Michael 5:05:03 (27,029)
Parsley, Derek 5:41:25 (30,647)
Parsley, Elvis 2:39:30 (174)
Parsley, Stephen 4:50:28 (24,500)
Parslow, Stephen 3:54:04 (10,334)
Parson, George 4:44:09 (23,093)
Parsons, Andy 3:50:17 (9,248)
Parsons, Chris 4:50:28 (24,500)
Parsons, Ian 3:21:08 (3,391)
Parsons, Ian 3:52:35 (9,865)
Parsons, James 4:48:38 (24,152)
Parsons, Jason 3:29:21 (4,766)
Parsons, Michael 3:40:48 (6,920)
Parsons, Neil 4:34:03 (20,595)
Parsons, Robert 5:32:04 (29,956)
Parsons, Ronald 5:33:53 (30,097)
Parsons, Stephen 4:33:43 (20,519)
Parsons, Stephen 4:44:50 (23,253)
Partington, Jonathan 4:13:00 (15,082)
Partington, Shaun 3:45:01 (7,929)
Partner, Nick 4:14:17 (15,385)
Parton, Adam 3:57:30 (11,365)
Parton, Terence 3:05:14 (1,561)
Partridge, Edward 4:30:03 (19,608)
Partridge, Graham 3:59:19 (11,887)
Partridge, Greg 4:11:58 (14,851)
Partridge, James 3:44:31 (7,797)
Partridge, Kenneth 7:22:00 (32,762)
Partridge, Mark 3:07:40 (1,783)
Partridge, Nicholas 4:03:01 (12,778)
Partridge, Simon 3:00:19 (1,186)
Pascoe, Barry 3:35:38 (5,833)
Pascoe, Robert 4:14:11 (15,357)
Pascoe, Simon 5:04:11 (26,915)
Pashley, Scott 5:28:30 (29,654)
Pask, Michael 3:07:11 (1,749)
Paskins, Paul 3:15:24 (2,714)
Pasquale, Paul 5:04:28 (26,953)
Pass, Ian 3:59:12 (11,859)
Passant, Colin 4:45:52 (23,533)
Passey, Duncan 3:00:31 (1,203)
Passfield, David 3:57:29 (11,359)
Passinger, Michael 4:23:14 (17,755)
Passingham, Leonard 3:05:29 (1,589)
Passot, André 4:45:53 (23,537)
Passway, Norry 2:57:50 (991)
Pastor, David 2:48:28 (425)
Pastore, Francesco 3:39:17 (6,586)
Pastori, Alessandro 4:42:05 (22,629)
Pastori, Antonio 4:05:37 (13,352)
Patania, Giuseppe 3:13:43 (2,534)
Patch, Martin 5:03:00 (26,738)
Patch, Michael 3:54:40 (10,506)
Patching, Graham 4:02:15 (12,607)
Patel, Amish 4:31:26 (19,940)
Patel, Anant 5:34:59 (30,186)
Patel, Anver 3:54:57 (10,580)
Patel, Ashok 3:18:38 (3,089)
Patel, Balwant 5:46:34 (30,968)
Patel, Bhupendra 4:41:01 (22,358)
Patel, Dee 3:00:42 (1,210)
Patel, Hitesh 6:19:55 (32,082)
Patel, Jaykumar 3:45:06 (7,953)
Patel, Minesh 4:34:50 (20,788)
Patel, Praful 5:11:27 (27,880)
Patel, Ramesh 5:58:17 (31,486)
Patel, Sanjay 5:11:15 (27,845)
Patel, Shilew 6:24:12 (32,167)
Patel, Siraj 4:17:41 (16,288)
Patel, Sumantlal 2:53:55 (678)
Patel, Sunil 5:36:44 (30,328)
Patel, Vijay 4:46:20 (23,649)
Paterson, Anthony 3:40:46 (6,913)
Paterson, Cameron 4:42:49 (22,796)
Paterson, James 4:31:48 (20,031)
Paterson, Marshall 3:55:19 (10,701)
Paterson, Simon 4:13:56 (15,291)
Paterson, Stephen 6:36:19 (32,376)
Paterson, Tom 5:12:04 (27,961)
Patey, Danny 5:55:59 (31,397)
Patey, Steven 3:56:48 (11,144)
Patey, Toby 5:25:26 (29,399)
Pathmanathan, Gajan 4:39:52 (22,076)
Pathmanathan, Kangesh 6:29:17 (32,260)
Pathmanathan, Pratheepan 4:02:32 (12,663)
Patience, Kevin 3:57:16 (11,280)
Patient, David 4:22:18 (17,476)
Patient, Peter 3:09:17 (1,965)
Patjens, Benedikt 3:40:05 (6,756)
Patmore, Hector 3:51:02 (9,438)
Paton, Colin 2:38:31 (157)
Paton, Dean 4:45:59 (23,560)
Paton, Malcolm 3:33:42 (5,457)
Paton, Philip 3:51:54 (9,650)
Paton, Tim 5:04:18 (26,937)
Patrick, Maurice 4:46:48 (23,757)
Patrick, Oliver 4:27:02 (18,798)
Patrick, Paul 3:56:09 (10,942)
Patrick, Stanley 4:40:51 (22,322)
Patrick, Thomas 4:00:08 (12,115)
Patten, Russell 4:55:07 (25,400)
Patten, Stefan 2:44:56 (296)
Patten, William 4:48:59 (24,232)
Patterson, David 3:19:53 (3,242)
Patterson, Iain 3:29:06 (4,711)
Patterson, John 5:16:39 (28,518)
Patterson, Paul 3:57:53 (11,472)
Patterson, Paul 6:09:54 (31,835)
Pattimore, Nathan 5:29:08 (29,705)
Pattinson, Carl 3:30:03 (4,880)
Pattison, Andrew 4:18:49 (16,551)
Pattison, Jonathan 4:38:56 (21,827)
Pattison, Lloyd 5:18:52 (28,759)
Pattison, Tristan 4:40:14 (22,168)
Pauk, Thomas 4:10:34 (14,527)
Paul, Darren 5:28:26 (29,647)

Paul, Douglas....4:00:28 (12,180)
Paul, Jonathan....4:40:03 (22,120)
Paul, Jonny....3:58:44 (11,716)
Paul, Josef....2:55:29 (779)
Paul, Ken....3:56:23 (11,015)
Paul, Matthew....4:37:45 (21,503)
Paul, Patrick....4:06:53 (13,645)
Paul, Philippe....3:31:16 (5,072)
Paul, Ric....4:20:04 (16,882)
Paul, Rupert....3:29:21 (4,766)
Paul, Stephen....3:34:55 (5,700)
Paul, Stephen....4:34:59 (20,828)
Paul, Stuart....4:38:51 (21,808)
Paulett, Gregory....4:34:44 (20,758)
Paull, Stephen....3:35:34 (5,817)
Paull, Stephen....5:08:38 (27,512)
Paulsen, Jeff....4:28:36 (19,197)
Paumier, Jean....3:28:13 (4,554)
Pavey, Giles....3:56:55 (11,181)
Pavlis, Terry....3:43:15 (7,459)
Pawlak, Andrew....3:51:45 (9,610)
Pawlowski, Francis....4:25:12 (18,309)
Pawluk, Ivan....4:53:27 (25,057)
Pawsey, Edward....4:26:00 (18,518)
Pawson, Mark....6:39:01 (32,422)
Paxman, Anthony....5:50:40 (31,168)
Paxman, Keith....5:22:28 (29,129)
Paxman, Oliver....4:45:11 (23,353)
Pay, Darren....5:30:51 (29,852)
Pay, Iain....3:13:38 (2,519)
Pay, Nick....4:14:44 (15,508)
Pay, Richard....4:02:50 (12,741)
Payan, Yves....3:45:21 (8,012)
Payne, Anthony....3:00:21 (1,189)
Payne, Chris....3:05:19 (1,569)
Payne, Colin....3:38:59 (6,520)
Payne, Darren....4:23:33 (17,838)
Payne, Darren....5:01:20 (26,508)
Payne, David....3:10:53 (2,141)
Payne, David....5:11:56 (27,943)
Payne, Garry....2:33:02 (81)
Payne, Gary....3:28:03 (4,523)
Payne, Gary....4:56:06 (25,611)
Payne, Gary....5:05:33 (27,091)
Payne, Gerald....4:10:45 (14,562)
Payne, Ian....4:01:01 (12,314)
Payne, Kenneth....3:56:06 (10,929)
Payne, Kevin....4:16:57 (16,103)
Payne, Kevin....4:17:15 (16,187)
Payne, Matthew....4:33:34 (20,477)
Payne, Michael....4:13:29 (15,183)
Payne, Nigel....2:36:03 (106)
Payne, Paul....4:22:02 (17,405)
Payne, Richard....3:35:22 (5,772)
Payne, Robert....4:21:32 (17,264)
Payne, Robin....3:40:44 (6,900)
Payne, Ronald....3:48:58 (8,886)
Payne, Simon....3:57:33 (11,381)
Payne, Simon....4:26:31 (18,662)
Payne, Stephen....4:38:14 (21,636)
Payne, Steve....2:30:28 (67)
Payne, Steven....4:10:14 (14,446)
Payne, Timothy....5:36:39 (30,323)
Payne, William....4:54:10 (25,220)
Paynter, Richard....5:06:23 (27,211)
Peabody, Ian....3:56:18 (10,989)
Peace, Michael....2:52:41 (609)
Peace, Simon....5:32:38 (30,002)
Peach, David....5:07:39 (27,392)
Peach, Robert....5:21:03 (28,999)
Peachey, Michael....3:10:56 (2,147)
Peachey, Richard....3:45:59 (8,157)
Peacock, Carl....4:20:58 (17,102)
Peacock, Chris....6:37:01 (32,397)
Peacock, David....4:44:40 (23,209)
Peacock, Gary....4:16:08 (15,873)
Peacock, Graeme....4:20:33 (17,006)
Peacock, John....4:01:57 (12,554)
Peacock, Kieron....4:01:56 (12,549)
Peacock, Kim....5:21:01 (28,991)
Peacock, Richard....4:39:30 (21,968)
Peacock, Ryan....4:49:49 (24,383)
Peacock, Stephen....2:38:27 (156)
Pead, Andrew....2:34:15 (93)
Pead, Mark....3:15:42 (2,754)
Peak, James....4:39:13 (21,905)
Peake, John....5:31:57 (29,950)
Peake, Jonathan....2:53:20 (645)
Peakman, Matthew....3:55:13 (10,668)
Peaks, Stephen....3:11:40 (2,224)
Peaple, Derek....3:03:59 (1,465)
Pearce, Andrew....4:33:07 (20,383)
Pearce, Ben....4:42:46 (22,784)
Pearce, Christian....3:50:36 (9,322)
Pearce, Christopher....4:09:34 (14,284)
Pearce, Daniel....4:57:23 (25,839)
Pearce, David....2:37:02 (127)
Pearce, David....4:02:45 (12,713)
Pearce, David....4:15:15 (15,633)
Pearce, David....5:08:31 (27,498)
Pearce, Dean....3:06:53 (1,722)
Pearce, Gareth....3:48:26 (8,732)
Pearce, Gary....4:01:36 (12,469)
Pearce, Ian....5:16:14 (28,472)
Pearce, James....4:21:43 (17,315)
Pearce, Justin....4:32:39 (20,261)
Pearce, Matthew....4:55:13 (25,425)
Pearce, Michael....4:22:15 (17,462)
Pearce, Neil....4:51:21 (24,672)
Pearce, Nicholas....4:16:03 (15,851)
Pearce, Paul....5:08:53 (27,551)
Pearce, Peter....4:00:50 (12,262)
Pearce, Peter....4:17:06 (16,145)
Pearce, Raymond....2:42:37 (240)
Pearce, Robert....3:22:44 (3,621)
Pearce, Robert....3:29:34 (4,809)
Pearce, Stephen....3:49:34 (9,059)
Pearce, Stephen....4:41:47 (22,553)
Pearce, Steve....4:13:02 (15,092)
Pearce, Stewart....4:08:54 (14,112)
Pearce, Toby....4:00:13 (12,137)
Pearce, Warren....4:28:50 (19,269)
Pearcey, David....3:55:22 (10,714)
Pearcey, Joshua....3:56:26 (11,025)
Pearch, Sam....3:06:33 (1,694)
Pearsall, Quenten....4:22:02 (17,405)
Pearse, Simon....4:58:02 (25,954)
Pearson, Alex....3:52:30 (9,838)
Pearson, Alexander....4:58:44 (26,088)
Pearson, Andrew....4:19:20 (16,673)
Pearson, Andrew....5:07:06 (27,314)
Pearson, Anthony....3:43:50 (7,616)
Pearson, Charles....4:36:38 (21,249)
Pearson, Christopher....3:20:54 (3,352)
Pearson, Christopher....3:23:51 (3,784)
Pearson, David....5:03:14 (26,788)
Pearson, Gary....4:51:19 (24,670)
Pearson, Kevin....3:10:39 (2,117)
Pearson, Mark....3:13:00 (2,431)
Pearson, Mark....4:09:38 (14,300)
Pearson, Michael....4:14:23 (15,421)
Pearson, Neil....3:57:58 (11,496)
Pearson, Robert....3:59:14 (11,866)
Pearson, Simon....5:01:32 (26,534)
Pearson, Tobias....5:08:24 (27,487)
Peat, Dan....4:36:09 (21,121)
Peatfield, Toby....3:56:09 (10,942)
Peck, Cris....3:29:59 (4,870)
Peck, David....3:56:10 (10,948)
Peck, Gordon....4:09:22 (14,242)
Peck, Ian....4:46:49 (23,762)
Peck, Ian....4:48:58 (24,228)
Peck, Lee....5:01:44 (26,563)
Peck, Mark....4:22:35 (17,568)
Peckham, David....7:16:57 (32,742)
Pecoraro, Antonio....2:42:19 (234)
Pedder, Alan....4:05:36 (13,348)
Pedder, David....3:41:07 (6,994)
Pedder-Smith, Stephen....3:21:01 (3,368)
Pedersen, Susan....4:19:57 (16,848)
Pedersen, Verner....5:30:17 (29,802)
Pederzolli, Mario....4:40:29 (22,230)
Pedlar, Charlie....3:03:42 (1,442)
Pedlow, Martin....3:08:23 (1,850)
Peebles, Murray....3:36:40 (6,051)
Peed, Mike....3:55:51 (10,855)
Peel, Edward....4:28:06 (19,054)
Peel, John....4:26:11 (18,569)
Peel, Mike....3:42:44 (7,323)
Peel, Stephen....3:22:23 (3,569)
Peel, Stephen....5:09:21 (27,617)
Peene, Franky....3:41:23 (7,043)
Peers, Alan....4:22:20 (17,493)
Peers, Kenneth....3:45:54 (8,134)
Peeters, Dirk....4:59:32 (26,227)
Pegg, David....4:47:24 (23,898)
Pegg, Roland....4:29:02 (19,330)
Pegoraro, Federico....5:26:30 (29,491)
Pegram, Ian....4:30:17 (19,669)
Peiris, Anthony....5:32:54 (30,014)
Pekar, Zsolt....3:35:29 (5,802)
Pekkas, Jean-François....3:43:42 (7,574)
Pelizza, Stefano....3:56:54 (11,174)
Pelizzari, Maurizio....3:36:54 (6,093)
Pell, David....4:11:16 (14,685)
Pell, Gary....4:35:00 (20,833)
Pell, Max....3:41:58 (7,144)
Pellecchia, Pasquale....3:01:19 (1,249)
Pelley, Mark....3:42:48 (7,342)
Pelzer, Horst....3:24:34 (3,930)
Pemberton, Alan....2:56:21 (860)
Pemberton, Anthony....4:54:50 (25,349)
Pemberton, Gareth....3:02:14 (1,316)
Pemberton, Michael....3:40:29 (6,847)
Pemberton, Robert....4:05:43 (13,372)
Pemble, Doug....3:38:13 (6,348)
Pendleton, Alan....4:40:30 (22,232)
Pendleton, Nick....3:54:51 (10,557)
Pendleton, Peter....5:07:37 (27,388)
Pendrill, Jim....3:06:47 (1,710)
Penfold, David....3:57:44 (11,434)
Penfold, Keith....4:24:03 (17,996)
Penfold, Richard....3:44:04 (7,669)
Penfold, Stephen....5:21:02 (28,994)
Pengelley, Ian....4:32:49 (20,306)
Pengelly, Gary....4:29:17 (19,410)
Pengelly, Laurence....3:16:50 (2,885)
Pengelly, Peter....4:52:31 (24,879)
Pengelly, Steve....4:52:31 (24,879)
Penhale, Bruce....2:57:52 (996)
Penhallow, Russell....2:52:40 (607)
Penman, Jeffrey....5:10:50 (27,794)
Penn, John....4:29:17 (19,410)
Penn, Richard....5:13:24 (28,126)
Penneck, Graham....3:50:24 (9,276)
Pennell, Ian....3:44:43 (7,861)
Penney, Simon....2:55:34 (786)
Pennicott, Derek....3:44:42 (7,852)
Pennington, Ian....4:25:54 (18,488)
Pennington, Martyn....3:42:13 (7,204)
Pennington, Michael....3:55:33 (10,767)
Penniston, Chris....4:44:01 (23,068)
Penny, Andrew....3:56:33 (11,070)
Penny, Bryan....3:50:55 (9,402)
Penny, Kenton....4:48:00 (24,029)
Penny, Nigel....5:36:06 (30,284)
Penny, Stephen....3:02:15 (1,320)
Pennycook, David....4:36:05 (21,098)
Penrose, John....4:26:23 (18,620)
Penrose, Noel....3:26:21 (4,210)
Penson, James....3:27:57 (4,508)
Pentecost, Matthew....5:08:14 (27,465)
Pentin, Richard....3:17:41 (2,972)
Pentland, Bob....3:09:14 (1,956)
Penwell, Scott....3:27:12 (4,361)
Peppe, Alasdair....5:03:42 (26,841)
Pepper, Jon....4:24:42 (18,173)
Pepper, Keith....5:11:14 (27,842)
Peppiatt, Tim....3:51:17 (9,498)
Perales-Candela, Manuel....4:07:59 (13,903)
Perarnau, Joan....3:10:16 (2,069)
Peray, Michel....4:01:14 (12,374)
Percy, Donald....3:12:11 (2,309)
Percy, Robin....4:55:02 (25,381)
Perdesi, Sohan....3:09:38 (2,004)
Pere, Stephane....3:47:33 (8,523)
Pereira, Norman....4:45:45 (23,503)
Perel, Moshe....5:03:56 (26,876)
Perez Avellaneda, Marino....4:32:45 (20,289)

Pinto, Antonio.................2:09:09 (7)
Pinto, Tomas.................4:13:24 (15,167)
Pipe, Alan.................5:25:15 (29,384)
Pipe, John.................3:33:19 (5,403)
Pipe, Jonathan.................3:39:28 (6,617)
Piper, David.................5:28:14 (29,632)
Piper, Robin.................4:00:33 (12,196)
Piper, Tim.................5:04:28 (26,953)
Piper Hunter, Allistair.................4:13:27 (15,177)
Pires, Artur.................2:50:15 (499)
Piret, Ronald.................4:24:41 (18,167)
Piron, Gregory.................3:47:44 (8,569)
Pirotto, Pierpaolo.................4:39:46 (22,047)
Pitcaithly, Mark.................3:06:19 (1,665)
Pitcher, Guy.................3:55:19 (10,701)
Pitcher, Jason.................3:40:25 (6,839)
Pitchley, Danny.................4:40:18 (22,183)
Pitman, Paul.................4:00:41 (12,220)
Pitman, Simon.................3:21:00 (3,364)
Pitman, Timothy.................4:55:06 (25,391)
Pitt, Bernard.................5:52:49 (31,269)
Pitt, Chris.................4:10:15 (14,449)
Pitt, Mark.................4:32:06 (20,109)
Pitt, Simon.................5:12:50 (28,059)
Pitt, Will.................3:40:18 (6,811)
Pittman, Anthony.................4:11:26 (14,727)
Pitts, Crombie.................4:53:55 (25,160)
Pitts, Michael.................3:37:59 (6,310)
Piwonski, Marcin.................3:29:29 (4,793)
Place, Jeff.................3:30:18 (4,915)
Place, Michael.................4:31:52 (20,047)
Plaistowe, Richard.................4:06:00 (13,437)
Plank, Anthony.................3:27:13 (4,366)
Planner, Donald.................5:26:20 (29,468)
Plant, Michael.................5:36:18 (30,296)
Plant, Ray.................2:23:14 (33)
Plant, Stephen.................4:37:53 (21,542)
Planzer, Martin.................3:11:05 (2,166)
Plaskett, Gary.................4:57:28 (25,850)
Plater, Darren.................4:54:20 (25,254)
Platt, Austin.................4:00:11 (12,127)
Platt, David.................4:31:07 (19,860)
Platt, Robert.................5:09:27 (27,628)
Platts, Michael.................4:46:24 (23,664)
Platts, Rob.................2:40:13 (188)
Player, Howard.................3:58:28 (11,643)
Playfair, Ben.................4:22:32 (17,557)
Plaza, Luis.................6:03:40 (31,653)
Pleasance, Neal.................4:04:31 (13,090)
Plenderleith, Scott.................3:34:30 (5,618)
Plesner, Marcel.................4:54:43 (25,328)
Plesner, Mark.................4:54:42 (25,323)
Plested, Neil.................3:48:56 (8,875)
Plimsall, Ray.................3:51:48 (9,624)
Plowman, Peter.................3:12:39 (2,379)
Plowright, Tony.................3:33:09 (5,375)
Plumb, Keith.................3:30:30 (4,945)
Plumb, Roland.................4:07:17 (13,743)
Plumbly, Gregory.................4:21:18 (17,191)
Plummer, Bradley.................3:25:37 (4,085)
Plummer, Martin.................5:00:57 (26,445)
Plummer, Matthew.................3:51:45 (9,610)
Plummer, Simon.................4:45:21 (23,393)
Plumstead, Mark.................3:01:57 (1,296)
Plumstead, Pat.................3:00:13 (1,183)
Plunkett, Mark.................3:44:44 (7,867)
Plush, Christopher.................5:06:36 (27,244)
Pluves, Steven.................5:16:51 (28,535)
Pluvinage, Jean.................3:06:54 (1,725)
Pochin, Michael.................5:55:27 (31,377)
Pockler, Uwe.................4:19:03 (16,607)
Pocock, Frank.................4:45:13 (23,361)
Pocock, John.................3:44:11 (7,707)
Pocock, Victor.................4:03:48 (12,943)
Podbery, Adrian.................3:12:41 (2,385)
Podbury, John.................4:30:24 (19,693)
Podeur, Marcel.................3:57:13 (11,269)
Podmilsak, Joseph.................2:47:05 (364)
Poell, Thomas.................3:54:06 (10,343)
Poeschel, Ralf.................4:17:45 (16,310)
Poirier, Jean.................3:26:52 (4,303)
Poisson, Stephane.................5:52:59 (31,274)
Polglase, Mark.................4:09:11 (14,183)

Polglase, Patrick.................3:44:22 (7,765)
Polhill, Dean.................3:59:04 (11,825)
Poli, Graziano.................2:26:07 (43)
Pollard, Gary.................4:24:15 (18,054)
Pollard, Ian.................3:11:48 (2,244)
Pollard, Kenton.................3:58:30 (11,651)
Pollard, Lionel.................4:47:25 (23,900)
Pollard, Peter.................4:58:09 (25,973)
Pollard, Simon.................4:26:09 (18,566)
Pollard, Simon.................4:35:11 (20,875)
Pollard, Simon.................5:07:49 (27,409)
Pollard, William.................5:37:38 (30,395)
Polleichtner, Josef.................3:55:06 (10,628)
Pollen, Richard.................3:20:58 (3,359)
Pollen, Richard.................4:04:47 (13,155)
Pollet, Stephane.................3:21:57 (3,515)
Pollett, Derek.................3:57:00 (11,210)
Polley, Keith.................4:25:01 (18,270)
Pollitt, John.................5:03:51 (26,865)
Pollock, Glen.................4:20:19 (16,948)
Pollock, Robert.................3:07:27 (1,764)
Polonini, Pietrantonio.................3:40:57 (6,949)
Pomario, Sean.................4:24:47 (18,193)
Pond, Alex.................4:11:24 (14,710)
Pond, Chris.................3:57:42 (11,422)
Ponsonby, Clive.................3:11:55 (2,259)
Ponsonby, Fred.................4:03:35 (12,900)
Pontefract, Lee.................3:49:15 (8,953)
Pontifex, Nick.................3:26:09 (4,174)
Ponting, David.................3:41:26 (7,051)
Ponting, Geoff.................4:50:27 (24,496)
Poole, Alistair.................4:08:43 (14,083)
Poole, Andrew.................4:54:16 (25,236)
Poole, Antony.................3:52:46 (9,916)
Poole, Damian.................3:31:30 (5,109)
Poole, David.................4:40:52 (22,329)
Poole, Iain.................3:39:10 (6,559)
Poole, John.................3:21:38 (3,455)
Poole, Jonathan.................5:32:06 (29,960)
Poole, Kenneth.................5:58:27 (31,494)
Poole, Simon.................3:53:28 (10,135)
Poole, Timothy.................4:51:29 (24,697)
Pooley, Jim.................3:21:46 (3,476)
Popat, Sachin.................5:01:16 (26,495)
Pope, Chris.................4:47:24 (23,898)
Pope, Christopher.................3:46:34 (8,303)
Pope, David.................4:09:01 (14,135)
Pope, Ian.................4:47:54 (24,005)
Pope, Richard.................4:00:55 (12,281)
Pope, Robert.................2:59:03 (1,097)
Pope, Sean.................3:28:26 (4,594)
Pophan, Craig.................5:16:12 (28,468)
Popman, Keith.................5:19:58 (28,872)
Popp, Bernd.................3:31:36 (5,124)
Popplestone, Alan.................3:27:26 (4,404)
Poppleton, Ben.................4:35:38 (20,998)
Popplestone, Benjamin.................4:28:44 (19,236)
Popplewell, Andrew.................5:04:54 (27,010)
Porchet, Manuel.................3:36:01 (5,907)
Porge, William.................4:32:57 (20,345)
Porier, Christopher.................3:57:29 (11,359)
Portat, Pierre.................4:14:31 (15,449)
Porte, Samuel.................3:44:06 (7,681)
Porteous, Henry.................3:14:52 (2,651)
Porter, Andy.................6:21:16 (32,114)
Porter, Arthur.................4:01:30 (12,441)
Porter, Brian.................4:11:45 (14,806)
Porter, James.................3:48:41 (8,807)
Porter, John.................3:05:43 (1,610)
Porter, John.................3:49:23 (8,998)
Porter, John.................7:13:59 (32,730)
Porter, Keith.................4:03:40 (12,911)
Porter, Kerry.................6:18:40 (32,053)
Porter, Pete.................5:04:41 (26,978)
Porter, Richard.................3:37:51 (6,288)
Porter, Robert.................3:25:50 (4,121)
Porter, Robert.................5:39:26 (30,508)
Porter, Rod.................4:27:28 (18,911)
Porter, Roger.................3:13:26 (2,496)
Porter, Roger.................3:32:07 (5,210)
Porter, Stephen.................4:49:53 (24,404)
Porter, Sturt.................3:55:19 (10,701)
Porter-Hough, Darren.................3:56:35 (11,078)

Porteus, Thomas.................3:34:49 (5,679)
Porthault, Jean Bernard.................3:47:02 (8,390)
Posgate, Robert.................4:20:52 (17,080)
Posner, Keith.................4:56:23 (25,675)
Postill, Adam.................5:03:52 (26,868)
Potgieter, David.................4:19:48 (16,804)
Potter, Alan.................4:16:44 (16,045)
Potter, Andrew.................3:29:18 (4,752)
Potter, Andrew.................5:08:23 (27,480)
Potter, Andrew.................5:23:39 (29,245)
Potter, Christopher.................4:29:12 (19,380)
Potter, Christopher.................4:58:30 (26,033)
Potter, David.................3:20:51 (3,348)
Potter, Howard.................4:03:24 (12,859)
Potter, Ian.................4:02:25 (12,633)
Potter, Ian.................4:28:34 (19,184)
Potter, James.................3:48:00 (8,630)
Potter, James.................4:02:09 (12,586)
Potter, Karl.................3:49:43 (9,103)
Potter, Keith.................3:49:40 (9,086)
Potter, Marc.................4:58:57 (26,121)
Potter, Mark.................5:54:38 (31,337)
Potter, Oliver.................4:16:51 (16,079)
Potter, Stephen.................5:29:10 (29,707)
Pottinger, Gavin.................5:15:59 (28,441)
Potts, David.................4:02:56 (12,763)
Potts, Ian.................4:17:15 (16,187)
Potts, Paul.................4:36:39 (21,254)
Potts, Richard.................3:57:42 (11,422)
Potze, Freerk.................3:58:53 (11,757)
Poulter, Stuart.................4:31:56 (20,066)
Poulton, Andrew.................4:44:41 (23,214)
Poulton, Gavin.................2:45:24 (307)
Poulton, John.................4:44:41 (23,214)
Poulton, Lee.................5:07:42 (27,399)
Poulton, Timothy.................3:52:50 (9,933)
Pouly, Gilbert.................4:12:06 (14,880)
Pounder, Nicholas.................4:23:03 (17,717)
Pounsberry, Christopher.................4:30:38 (19,739)
Povey, John.................7:42:53 (32,833)
Povey, Kenneth.................4:40:05 (22,129)
Povinelli, Ray.................4:02:11 (12,595)
Pow, Jim.................3:35:59 (5,901)
Powditch, Vincent.................5:58:40 (31,503)
Powell, Alun.................4:12:55 (15,066)
Powell, Andrew.................3:16:27 (2,837)
Powell, Ben.................3:54:02 (10,320)
Powell, Christopher.................5:42:51 (30,741)
Powell, Dean.................5:47:22 (31,006)
Powell, Glyn.................3:36:35 (6,039)
Powell, Gregg.................3:40:50 (6,925)
Powell, James.................4:20:44 (17,053)
Powell, Jason.................3:35:20 (5,767)
Powell, John.................3:50:39 (9,337)
Powell, John.................4:24:22 (18,086)
Powell, John.................4:32:06 (20,109)
Powell, Jon.................3:33:16 (5,392)
Powell, Martin.................2:54:37 (717)
Powell, Michael.................3:12:54 (2,417)
Powell, Nathan.................3:42:15 (7,220)
Powell, Ray.................3:37:02 (6,126)
Powell, Richard.................3:14:36 (2,619)
Powell, Robert.................4:57:56 (25,946)
Powell, Ron.................4:04:01 (12,993)
Powell, Sion.................4:21:37 (17,287)
Powell, Stephen.................4:42:33 (22,737)
Powell, Steven.................3:07:13 (1,750)
Powell, Thomas.................3:55:53 (10,869)
Powell, Thomas.................4:11:39 (14,782)
Powell, Vince.................7:15:23 (32,738)
Power, Brian.................3:55:29 (10,741)
Power, John.................4:25:49 (18,465)
Power, Michael.................4:00:15 (12,143)
Power, Niall.................5:25:25 (29,397)
Power, Tyrone.................5:01:26 (26,521)
Powers, Scott.................4:35:35 (20,982)
Powers, Howard Jnr.................3:26:54 (4,313)
Powis, Ian.................4:43:56 (23,051)
Powles, James.................4:43:18 (22,909)
Powlesland, Paul.................4:36:49 (21,280)
Powleson, Sean.................4:38:53 (21,815)
Powne, Simon.................3:59:40 (11,986)
Powrie, Duncan.................4:24:08 (18,017)

Poynton, Ian	4:35:32 (20,957)
Poyntz, Glenn	4:46:23 (23,662)
Poyser, Michael	4:18:05 (16,385)
Prabakaran, Perampalam	4:31:17 (19,897)
Prasad, Vikash	5:01:20 (26,508)
Pratheepan, Thavarajah	5:12:33 (28,032)
Prati, Carlo	4:27:28 (18,911)
Prato, Eduardo	3:37:57 (6,303)
Prato, Luis	3:37:59 (6,310)
Pratt, Alan	3:13:24 (2,491)
Pratt, Christopher	3:06:51 (1,719)
Pratt, Dean	3:53:46 (10,228)
Pratt, Ian	3:06:38 (1,703)
Pratt, Kenneth	3:10:19 (2,079)
Pratt, Nick	3:44:07 (7,683)
Pratt, Paul	4:15:24 (15,665)
Pratt, Robert	3:39:27 (6,612)
Pratt, Simon	5:32:08 (29,963)
Pratt, Stephen	3:36:06 (5,932)
Prebble, John	3:50:00 (9,169)
Precelton, Jeremy	3:25:26 (4,051)
Preece, Andrew	4:02:39 (12,691)
Preece, Barry	4:43:17 (22,905)
Preece, Brian	5:19:44 (28,844)
Preece, David	3:09:05 (1,941)
Preece, David	3:17:03 (2,910)
Preece, David	3:28:45 (4,646)
Preece, Jim	3:29:27 (4,784)
Preece, Roland	3:54:34 (10,478)
Preece, Stephen	4:54:19 (25,246)
Prendergast, Ian	4:36:03 (21,092)
Prendergast, Matthew	3:49:05 (8,919)
Prentice, Stuart	4:07:51 (13,881)
Prescott, Alan	4:32:50 (20,314)
Prescott, Christian	5:26:09 (29,460)
Prescott, David	3:50:49 (9,379)
Prescott-Frost, Matthew	4:38:59 (21,841)
Presland, Philip	3:08:46 (1,902)
Press, Michael	4:22:36 (17,576)
Pressman, Bernard	5:07:17 (27,343)
Preston, Craig	3:30:07 (4,887)
Preston, David	4:25:56 (18,498)
Preston, Gary	2:36:30 (116)
Preston, Gavin	4:59:59 (26,307)
Preston, Graham	5:07:04 (27,306)
Preston, John	4:15:14 (15,631)
Preston, Matthew	3:51:10 (9,476)
Preston, Robert	3:59:37 (11,973)
Preston, Tim	7:04:10 (32,664)
Preston, Uel	4:10:54 (14,605)
Preston-Jones, Jeremy	3:58:57 (11,779)
Prestridge, Jeffrey	3:48:59 (8,891)
Pretorius, Rion	4:52:47 (24,937)
Prevost, Ivan	4:31:58 (20,075)
Prewer, Rodney	4:28:13 (19,088)
Price, Allan	3:46:11 (8,196)
Price, Andrew	3:20:16 (3,288)
Price, Andrew	5:46:13 (30,948)
Price, Bryn	5:15:08 (28,311)
Price, Carl	2:51:39 (568)
Price, Ceris	4:45:29 (23,433)
Price, Chris	4:17:09 (16,160)
Price, Colin	4:03:47 (12,936)
Price, Darren	4:11:30 (14,747)
Price, Darrin	4:57:33 (25,872)
Price, David	3:07:28 (1,766)
Price, David	3:28:12 (4,551)
Price, David	4:24:30 (18,121)
Price, David	4:33:41 (20,513)
Price, Derek	3:07:07 (1,747)
Price, Derek	5:28:43 (29,676)
Price, Greg	4:39:15 (21,910)
Price, Howard	3:06:54 (1,725)
Price, Howard	3:25:29 (4,062)
Price, Ian	3:22:45 (3,625)
Price, Ian	3:54:27 (10,443)
Price, Jeremy	4:25:00 (18,266)
Price, Jim	4:46:54 (23,786)
Price, Jonathan	4:01:03 (12,328)
Price, Jonathan	4:08:39 (14,066)
Price, Jonathan	4:20:06 (16,888)
Price, Lawrence	4:04:24 (13,069)
Price, Martin	2:44:35 (284)
Price, Michael	3:29:25 (4,780)
Price, Michael	4:18:15 (16,427)
Price, Michael	4:37:18 (21,400)
Price, Richard	3:48:53 (8,869)
Price, Rupert	3:41:04 (6,980)
Price, Sean	3:43:43 (7,580)
Price, Sean	3:54:25 (10,435)
Price, Simon	5:29:55 (29,772)
Price, Simon	5:38:40 (30,458)
Price, Stephen	3:10:58 (2,151)
Price, Stephen	4:53:18 (25,024)
Price, Stewart	3:55:39 (10,795)
Price, Stuart	3:54:06 (10,343)
Price, Tim	4:36:22 (21,182)
Price, Vincent	4:32:08 (20,122)
Price, Wayne	3:59:57 (12,073)
Priday, Bruce	6:53:12 (32,570)
Priday, Joseph	4:51:08 (24,635)
Priddle, Matt	3:49:34 (9,059)
Pridmore, John	4:21:54 (17,368)
Priesner, Rico	3:22:50 (3,640)
Priest, Darren	2:45:35 (315)
Priest, Donald	3:41:55 (7,134)
Priestley, Donald	3:37:09 (6,140)
Priestley, Mark	3:13:24 (2,491)
Priestly, Scott	4:50:56 (24,596)
Prieto, José	3:14:49 (2,641)
Prikkel, Ate	4:28:32 (19,178)
Prime, David	4:22:41 (17,603)
Primrose, Noel	3:48:06 (8,650)
Prince, Adam	3:04:11 (1,482)
Prince, Andrew	4:35:34 (20,978)
Prince, David	3:40:52 (6,933)
Prince, Joseph	4:22:45 (17,621)
Prince, Kelvin	4:25:13 (18,312)
Pringle, Ian	4:56:50 (25,739)
Pringle, Lee	4:00:56 (12,289)
Pringle, Scott	4:03:08 (12,802)
Pringle, Simon	5:44:20 (30,843)
Pringle, Stuart	5:00:20 (26,349)
Prior, Andrew	3:57:16 (11,280)
Prior, Danny	3:36:09 (5,950)
Prior, David	3:43:42 (7,574)
Prior, Stephen	4:23:44 (17,899)
Prior, Tony	4:35:46 (21,021)
Pritchard, Andrew	5:27:33 (29,580)
Pritchard, Ashley	3:23:29 (3,724)
Pritchard, Christopher	4:59:16 (26,170)
Pritchard, Hugh	6:06:53 (31,758)
Pritchard, Iain	4:32:45 (20,289)
Pritchard, James	3:12:10 (2,305)
Pritchard, James	4:57:46 (25,911)
Pritchard, John	3:43:30 (7,525)
Pritchard, John	4:36:26 (21,196)
Pritchard, Jonathan	4:49:51 (24,395)
Pritchard, Keith	3:43:48 (7,606)
Pritchard, Mike	5:19:39 (28,831)
Pritchard, Nigel	4:38:41 (21,758)
Pritchard, Owen	4:10:22 (14,479)
Pritchard, Paul	5:19:39 (28,831)
Pritchard, Peter	4:21:40 (17,305)
Pritchard, Robert	3:38:29 (6,418)
Pritchard, Simon	2:39:14 (170)
Pritchard Jones, Dilwyn	5:36:39 (30,323)
Probets, Robert	4:28:35 (19,187)
Procope, Robert	3:57:23 (11,317)
Procter, Dave	3:23:15 (3,687)
Procter, Kent	3:12:29 (2,357)
Procter, Scott	3:16:39 (2,857)
Proctor, Gregory	4:44:31 (23,181)
Proctor, Peter	4:35:05 (20,851)
Proctor, Tony	3:58:23 (11,614)
Proffitt, Stephen	4:46:09 (23,607)
Proffitt-White, John	3:37:30 (6,217)
Proietti, Roberto	4:14:20 (15,405)
Prokopiuk, Aleksander	3:48:58 (8,886)
Prosperino, Michael	4:22:24 (17,522)
Prosser, Paul	2:36:23 (114)
Prothero, Jonathan	4:44:17 (23,128)
Prothero, Robert	2:47:13 (368)
Proud, Matthew	4:15:50 (15,786)
Proudfoot, Trevor	4:54:10 (25,220)
Proudley, Gavin	3:12:50 (2,407)
Prowse, Simeon	4:13:38 (15,213)
Pruden, John	5:23:44 (29,255)
Prudham, Joseph	3:27:47 (4,474)
Pruschwitz, Suergen	4:26:30 (18,653)
Pryce, Thomas	4:35:39 (21,001)
Pryer, Anthony	5:15:23 (28,344)
Pryer, William	4:34:36 (20,726)
Pryke, Robert	4:51:36 (24,719)
Pryor, John	4:26:21 (18,615)
Puccio, Bruno	4:13:32 (15,195)
Puckey, Steve	3:53:38 (10,190)
Puddicombe, Vince	4:46:25 (23,667)
Puevi, Margus	3:11:38 (2,220)
Pugh, Adrian	4:01:34 (12,461)
Pugh, Eddie	4:29:15 (19,398)
Pugh, Graham	3:51:01 (9,433)
Pugh, Harvey	4:11:17 (14,690)
Pugh, John	3:38:30 (6,423)
Pugh, Martin	5:30:18 (29,803)
Pugh, Martyn	4:08:07 (13,936)
Pugh, Pattrick	3:24:14 (3,867)
Pugh, Richard	4:36:46 (21,271)
Pugh, Roderick	3:10:13 (2,066)
Pugh, Wayne	3:26:18 (4,204)
Pulham, Tim	5:03:02 (26,749)
Puliatti, Carmelo	3:23:07 (3,669)
Pullen, Andrew	4:30:02 (19,603)
Pullen, Dan	3:49:40 (9,086)
Pullen, Geoffrey	3:33:04 (5,362)
Pullen, Graham	3:30:52 (5,000)
Pullen, Leslie	4:26:26 (18,631)
Pullen, Matthew	4:39:11 (21,892)
Pullen, Terry	4:00:09 (12,118)
Pullinger, Stephen	3:44:40 (7,839)
Punkka, Veikko	4:45:41 (23,488)
Punt, David	4:37:26 (21,434)
Punton, Stephen	4:48:45 (24,178)
Pupo, Carlos	3:23:38 (3,749)
Purcell, Edward	5:14:10 (28,210)
Purcell, Jim	8:38:27 (32,882)
Purcell, Sean	4:00:02 (12,092)
Purchase, Nick	3:55:46 (10,832)
Purchese, Adrian	4:28:36 (19,197)
Purdon, Christopher	3:07:18 (1,754)
Purdue, Paul	4:34:49 (20,777)
Purdy, Richard	4:32:09 (20,129)
Purdy, Vincent	4:32:07 (20,114)
Purewal, Pars	3:56:57 (11,192)
Puri, Aman	6:47:31 (32,512)
Puri, Lee	3:44:59 (7,923)
Purkiss, Simon	4:15:49 (15,783)
Purser, David	4:49:36 (24,342)
Purser, Marcus	3:47:45 (8,577)
Purslow, Philip	3:48:11 (8,670)
Purvis, Darren	2:59:55 (1,163)
Purvis, Ian	3:53:58 (10,299)
Purvis, Keith	2:41:29 (218)
Pussard, Gerry	5:01:28 (26,523)
Pussard, Marc	5:01:25 (26,517)
Putman, Ian	4:30:47 (19,780)
Putman, Stephen	5:34:28 (30,144)
Puttick, Andrew	3:44:20 (7,753)
Puttock, Simon	3:19:50 (3,235)
Puyenchet, Cedric	3:30:08 (4,889)
Pyatt, Francis	4:32:48 (20,303)
Pycock, Graham	3:52:56 (9,958)
Pye, Alan	2:59:36 (1,139)
Pye, Alexander	4:07:11 (13,718)
Pye, Andy	6:09:55 (31,839)
Pye, David	4:52:32 (24,882)
Pye, Derek	4:03:31 (12,885)
Pye, Peter	5:14:43 (28,275)
Pyle, Michael	3:40:21 (6,824)
Pyne, Michael	4:13:12 (15,121)
Pyniger, Ian	3:56:02 (10,906)
Pynn, Harvey	3:34:05 (5,537)
Pyper, Darryl	4:48:46 (24,182)
Pyper, George	3:57:03 (11,224)
Pza, Pranav	4:32:02 (20,096)
Qizilbash, Trevor	4:48:01 (24,037)
Quantrill, Clive	4:21:30 (17,250)
Quartermaine, Mark	4:32:22 (20,181)
Quartermaine, Richard	4:04:05 (13,005)

Quarterman, Bruce......4:05:13 (13,258)
Quee, Michael......4:11:03 (14,647)
Quelch, Christopher......4:03:05 (12,795)
Quelch, Paul......4:40:31 (22,234)
Quemard, Peter......3:44:45 (7,874)
Quentel, Olivier......4:04:52 (13,175)
Quevillon, Jean-Claude......5:47:15 (31,001)
Quezada, Luis......3:17:15 (2,929)
Quick, Andrew......3:35:07 (5,736)
Quick, James......2:51:22 (552)
Quick, Michael......4:23:46 (17,907)
Quigg, Robin......4:43:28 (22,956)
Quigley, John......3:47:49 (8,591)
Quiles, Patrick......3:59:30 (11,938)
Quilley, Anthony......4:13:33 (15,200)
Quimby, Craig......4:22:28 (17,538)
Quin, Thomas......4:59:09 (26,160)
Quince, Jason......3:52:48 (9,926)
Quinlan, Liam......4:14:14 (15,377)
Quinlan, Mark......4:04:59 (13,204)
Quinlivan, David......3:31:34 (5,117)
Quinn, Anthony......3:39:14 (6,579)
Quinn, Barry......3:29:14 (4,738)
Quinn, Bob......4:22:35 (17,568)
Quinn, Daniel......5:24:11 (29,295)
Quinn, David......3:04:24 (1,495)
Quinn, Jack......4:38:49 (21,796)
Quinn, Malcolm......4:14:32 (15,455)
Quinn, Neil......4:57:02 (25,774)
Quinn, Patrick......4:45:09 (23,345)
Quinn, Raymond......3:48:46 (8,835)
Quinton, David......4:22:54 (17,671)
Quinton, Terry......5:12:01 (27,955)
Quiroga, Rafael......3:37:31 (6,223)
Quoirin, Sebastien......2:57:55 (999)
Raasch, Karsten......3:13:09 (2,456)
Rabino, Giuseppe......4:00:59 (12,304)
Rabinowitz, Gideon......4:45:35 (23,467)
Rabjohns, Peter......2:59:47 (1,156)
Raby, Alan......5:03:13 (26,785)
Raby Smith, Phil......4:11:48 (14,817)
Racke, Trevor......4:12:59 (15,076)
Rackind, Kevin......3:42:11 (7,196)
Racklyeft, Nick......5:00:48 (26,421)
Racz, Sandor......3:45:36 (8,071)
Radauer, Hermann......3:43:17 (7,467)
Radbourne, Mathew......3:21:33 (3,448)
Radcliffe, Nigel......4:26:37 (18,688)
Radcliffe, Rodney......2:52:04 (582)
Radcliffe, Stewart......4:19:24 (16,688)
Raddenbury, Adrian......4:39:59 (22,099)
Radebe, Lucky......4:06:42 (13,614)
Radford, Neil......4:27:55 (19,011)
Radford, Tim......4:14:24 (15,427)
Radley, Alan......5:51:08 (31,191)
Radley, Dean......3:45:47 (8,110)
Radley, Rob......3:54:29 (10,453)
Radosevic, Slavo......3:25:40 (4,096)
Raducanu, Bernard......3:47:30 (8,510)
Rae, Angus......3:52:07 (9,726)
Rae, Ian......6:39:20 (32,427)
Rae, Neil......3:08:24 (1,851)
Rae, Richard......4:06:50 (13,636)
Raeburn, Oliver......4:37:12 (21,370)
Rafferty, David......4:41:21 (22,439)
Rafferty, James......3:34:43 (5,662)
Raffington, John......3:10:37 (2,116)
Rafter, Josh......5:43:17 (30,774)
Raftery, Edward......3:15:37 (2,738)
Ragg, Peter......4:35:48 (21,028)
Rahilly, Curtis......4:04:52 (13,175)
Rahim, Paul......4:05:19 (13,277)
Rahman, Anthony......5:17:24 (28,617)
Rahman, Maabubur......4:57:08 (25,798)
Raichle, Joerg......3:37:08 (6,138)
Railton, Duncan......3:59:28 (11,935)
Raine, Kevin......3:43:46 (7,591)
Raines, Stephen......5:17:49 (28,652)
Rains, John......3:48:14 (8,681)
Rains, Kevin......3:49:54 (9,151)
Rainsby, Alec......2:49:20 (459)
Raithatha, Nickyl......3:58:56 (11,772)
Raithby, Christopher......3:32:18 (5,232)

Rajski, Richard......5:23:48 (29,261)
Rakusen, Lloyd......4:13:53 (15,281)
Ralph, Ian......3:21:01 (3,368)
Ralph, John......3:44:30 (7,793)
Ralph, Omar......4:44:46 (23,240)
Ramalhal, Rus......3:50:58 (9,418)
Ramil, Ahmed......6:19:46 (32,075)
Ramirez, René......3:10:31 (2,103)
Ramirez-Espané, Maximiliano......3:56:51 (11,159)
Ramm, Duncan......6:11:33 (31,872)
Rammell, David......4:03:51 (12,954)
Ramon, Ray......3:34:31 (5,622)
Ramos, Abel......4:08:29 (14,014)
Rampley, Philip......3:14:24 (2,599)
Rampling, Laurence......4:38:01 (21,575)
Ramsay, Gordon......4:27:06 (18,818)
Ramsay, Grant......2:49:54 (483)
Ramsay, Norrie......4:14:11 (15,357)
Ramsay, Patrick......3:35:52 (5,878)
Ramsay, Peter......3:21:56 (3,511)
Ramsay, Robert......4:40:34 (22,248)
Ramsbottom, Paul......3:51:18 (9,502)
Ramsden, Dominic......4:02:04 (12,571)
Ramsden, Stephen......4:28:42 (19,224)
Ramsell, Chris......2:53:03 (630)
Ramsey, Charles......6:43:47 (32,472)
Ramsey, Desmond......3:57:43 (11,430)
Ramsey, John......3:14:53 (2,654)
Ramsey, Mark......3:52:29 (9,831)
Ramsey, Michael......4:04:56 (13,194)
Ramsey, Nathan......4:21:18 (17,191)
Ramsler, Andreas......4:10:54 (14,605)
Ramzan, Nadim......5:14:36 (28,262)
Rance, Jon......4:48:26 (24,115)
Rance, Keith......3:31:07 (5,054)
Randall, André......3:37:20 (6,173)
Randall, Andrew......3:56:41 (11,104)
Randall, David......4:26:49 (18,746)
Randall, John......3:49:09 (8,934)
Randall, Jonathan......5:06:08 (27,179)
Randall, Kevin......5:09:15 (27,599)
Randall, Michael......4:20:22 (16,959)
Randall, Michael......5:29:39 (29,755)
Randall, Rhys......4:47:01 (23,815)
Randall, Sean......3:58:10 (11,558)
Randall, Timothy......4:47:50 (23,986)
Randell, Chris......4:14:26 (15,433)
Randell, Craig......4:37:09 (21,348)
Randerson, Irvin......3:55:19 (10,701)
Randhawa, Kuldip......4:31:07 (19,860)
Randle, Richard......2:56:40 (887)
Randlers, Stephen......3:48:35 (8,773)
Randles, Michael......4:04:12 (13,027)
Randles, Steven......4:43:40 (22,990)
Rands, Mark......4:00:05 (12,104)
Rands, Martin......3:32:27 (5,262)
Rang, Simon......3:40:42 (6,895)
Rankin, Geoffrey......3:30:52 (5,000)
Rankin, James......3:56:32 (11,067)
Rankin, Tom......4:40:44 (22,286)
Rankin, Vinton......6:47:59 (32,519)
Ransome, Daniel......5:43:27 (30,786)
Ranson, Ashleigh......3:48:00 (8,630)
Ranson, Lee......3:46:21 (8,236)
Ranson, Scott......3:46:20 (8,233)
Ranyard, Robert......6:56:03 (32,592)
Rao, Krishna......7:56:01 (32,856)
Raphael, Andrew......3:53:42 (10,208)
Raphael, Derek......5:32:09 (29,965)
Raphael, Lee......3:21:15 (3,399)
Raphaely, Adam......4:15:51 (15,791)
Rapley, Colin......4:16:48 (16,064)
Rapley, David......3:59:35 (11,962)
Rapley, James......3:53:54 (10,278)
Rapley, Nick......3:53:57 (10,293)
Rapson, Ian......5:30:26 (29,814)
Rash, Edward......3:24:27 (3,910)
Rashdi, Martin......5:27:11 (29,538)
Rashid, Maqsood......3:52:32 (9,849)
Rasmussen, Jorgen......4:58:19 (26,000)
Ratcliff, Chris......4:01:36 (12,469)
Ratcliff, Ian......4:54:01 (25,186)
Ratcliff, Martin......4:35:17 (20,898)

Ratcliffe, David......3:47:08 (8,414)
Ratcliffe, Terry......5:00:49 (26,430)
Rathbone, Garry......3:46:27 (8,265)
Rathbone, Mark......3:25:25 (4,050)
Ratliffe, Robert......3:45:55 (8,144)
Ratnasuriya, Vishanka......4:03:10 (12,808)
Ratnayake, Madduma......3:50:12 (9,215)
Rattigan, Dean......4:30:22 (19,687)
Ratwage, Alan......5:31:38 (29,924)
Rau, Jonathan......4:31:40 (20,003)
Rauch, Rudi......3:31:09 (5,059)
Ravai, Henry......4:56:03 (25,594)
Ravarani, Mirko......3:27:36 (4,435)
Rave, Bert......3:40:38 (6,878)
Raven, Andrew......5:23:34 (29,229)
Raven, Malcolm......4:43:01 (22,843)
Rawbone, Colin......3:43:29 (7,517)
Rawbone, Raymond......3:28:51 (4,671)
Rawles, Jason......3:54:24 (10,427)
Rawlings, Keith......3:43:08 (7,426)
Rawlings, Kenny......5:39:15 (30,485)
Rawlings, Leonard......5:40:07 (30,556)
Rawlings, Stephen......3:56:57 (11,192)
Rawlins, Craig......5:10:07 (27,703)
Rawlinson-Plant, Matt......3:31:20 (5,083)
Rawson, David......3:31:36 (5,124)
Rawson, Trevor......4:49:24 (24,299)
Ray, Bill......4:47:34 (23,923)
Ray, Duncan......4:04:13 (13,032)
Ray, Paul......3:36:06 (5,932)
Ray, Paul......4:26:37 (18,688)
Ray, Sanjit......4:17:46 (16,320)
Ray, Simon......3:21:15 (3,399)
Raybould, Mark......5:30:29 (29,821)
Rayfield, David......2:57:37 (971)
Rayment, Steven......5:30:28 (29,819)
Raymond, Benn......5:12:15 (27,984)
Raymond, Byron......3:08:53 (1,919)
Raymond, Jon......3:46:02 (8,167)
Rayner, Paul......4:20:22 (16,959)
Rayner, Simon......3:12:17 (2,326)
Rayner, Simon......4:26:39 (18,702)
Rayner, Steven......4:45:02 (23,319)
Rayner, Trevor......2:52:58 (628)
Raynes, Andrew......3:47:34 (8,530)
Raynor, Leonard......3:14:46 (2,635)
Raynor, Maurice......4:55:09 (25,411)
Raynor, Paul......3:56:34 (11,075)
Raynor, Tony......4:01:54 (12,545)
Rayson, William......5:02:36 (26,686)
Rea, Anthony......3:34:54 (5,695)
Rea, Paul......3:23:51 (3,784)
Rea, Robert......3:25:52 (4,128)
Read, Alfred......4:23:56 (17,958)
Read, Anthony......3:53:01 (9,985)
Read, Anthony......4:55:48 (25,541)
Read, Brian......3:33:54 (5,496)
Read, Eric......4:39:59 (22,099)
Read, Graham......5:06:09 (27,183)
Read, Graham......5:20:22 (28,923)
Read, John......4:25:00 (18,266)
Read, Jonathan......3:54:26 (10,439)
Read, Julian......3:03:48 (1,450)
Read, Julian......3:04:42 (1,520)
Read, Malcolm......3:19:53 (3,242)
Read, Matt......4:39:39 (22,003)
Read, Matthew......3:47:18 (8,461)
Read, Paul......5:08:29 (27,494)
Read, Ronald......3:33:32 (5,430)
Read, Simon......3:50:08 (9,194)
Read, Steven......3:23:37 (3,745)
Reade, Steve......4:26:29 (18,649)
Reader, Frank......5:46:54 (30,981)
Reader, Richard......4:10:50 (14,590)
Reader, Robert......4:58:24 (26,016)
Reading, David......3:41:26 (7,051)
Reading, Graham......4:43:11 (22,888)
Reading, Steven......4:02:17 (12,613)
Readings, Gavin......6:05:42 (31,720)
Readman, Benjamin......3:42:28 (7,282)
Readman, Leo......4:36:49 (21,280)
Reakes, John......3:30:18 (4,915)
Realff, Justin......3:03:26 (1,415)

Reardon, Michael 5:13:27 (28,133)
Reay, Gordon 3:50:51 (9,392)
Reay, Jonathan 3:59:51 (12,041)
Reay, Phil 3:48:25 (8,728)
Rebbeck, Hugh 3:56:40 (11,101)
Rebbeck, James 3:50:21 (9,263)
Rebello, Wayne 3:31:13 (5,068)
Reck, André 3:42:08 (7,186)
Redaelli, Maurizio 3:34:20 (5,587)
Redden, Phil 2:57:52 (996)
Reddin, David 3:38:11 (6,340)
Redding, Jonathan 3:34:00 (5,519)
Reddy, André 4:29:49 (19,543)
Redfearn, David 5:13:32 (28,144)
Redfern, Graham 5:26:25 (29,483)
Redford, Roy 6:55:52 (32,590)
Redhead, Darryl 3:48:32 (8,757)
Redhead, James 5:22:57 (29,172)
Redhouse, Mark 4:41:26 (22,455)
Redmond, Alasdair 3:31:12 (5,064)
Redmond, John 2:35:06 (98)
Redmond, Laurence 4:14:52 (15,542)
Redmond, Robert 4:22:43 (17,614)
Redmond, Ronan 4:28:07 (19,058)
Redo, Franck 3:03:01 (1,370)
Redpath, Alan 4:56:19 (25,658)
Redpath, David 3:44:36 (7,820)
Redpath, Giles 3:27:03 (4,339)
Redpath, John 3:53:54 (10,278)
Redwood, Leslie 3:35:43 (5,851)
Reed, Alan 3:04:51 (1,528)
Reed, Andrew 4:31:57 (20,071)
Reed, Chris 3:45:45 (8,100)
Reed, Christopher 3:25:09 (4,008)
Reed, Colin 6:47:40 (32,515)
Reed, David 2:42:14 (231)
Reed, David 4:02:55 (12,758)
Reed, David 4:09:50 (14,348)
Reed, David 6:17:53 (32,030)
Reed, James 4:24:56 (18,234)
Reed, Jeremy 3:47:59 (8,625)
Reed, John 3:53:44 (10,218)
Reed, Peter 4:47:21 (23,885)
Reed, Philip 5:31:18 (29,894)
Reed, Stephen 5:21:35 (29,053)
Reed, Stuart 4:18:23 (16,460)
Reeder, Roy 2:42:55 (241)
Reeh, Christopher 3:51:39 (9,583)
Reek, Philipp 3:36:28 (6,020)
Reekie, Grant 4:03:14 (12,822)
Reeks, Mark 3:41:10 (7,003)
Rees, Alun 4:45:45 (23,503)
Rees, Andrew 3:08:02 (1,807)
Rees, Chris 5:14:46 (28,281)
Rees, Christopher 4:21:14 (17,174)
Rees, Colin 3:01:14 (1,244)
Rees, Daryl 3:49:35 (9,066)
Rees, Gareth 4:07:18 (13,748)
Rees, Howard 4:03:35 (12,900)
Rees, Huw 3:52:46 (9,916)
Rees, James 4:52:29 (24,870)
Rees, Jeff 2:55:47 (806)
Rees, John 3:27:58 (4,512)
Rees, Joseph 4:55:41 (25,516)
Rees, Martyn 3:45:38 (8,077)
Rees, Matthew 5:06:25 (27,219)
Rees, Michael 3:52:39 (9,881)
Rees, Nigel 3:58:27 (11,635)
Rees, Paul 5:21:19 (29,026)
Rees, Raymond 6:21:10 (32,110)
Rees, Stephen 4:26:54 (18,760)
Reeve, Bill 4:18:20 (16,452)
Reeve, David 4:49:39 (24,350)
Reeve, Nathan 4:06:11 (13,484)
Reeve, Peter 4:30:18 (19,675)
Reeves, Colin 3:39:53 (6,707)
Reeves, Daragh 4:48:24 (24,104)
Reeves, Gavin 4:52:29 (24,870)
Reeves, Gerald 4:08:27 (14,003)
Reeves, Ian 3:50:47 (9,373)
Regan, Daniel 3:36:56 (6,104)
Regan, Ronald 5:49:54 (31,139)
Regelouse, Paul 3:29:06 (4,711)
Regereau, Pascal 4:17:44 (16,304)
Reho, Petteri 3:26:25 (4,216)
Reichel, Bernd 3:14:12 (2,577)
Reichel, Hannes 3:16:02 (2,792)
Reid, Chris 3:56:50 (11,149)
Reid, Clive 2:57:49 (988)
Reid, Dave 4:38:06 (21,599)
Reid, Dean 4:08:00 (13,911)
Reid, George 4:23:47 (17,913)
Reid, Ian 4:57:10 (25,805)
Reid, James 3:14:29 (2,611)
Reid, James 4:28:58 (19,313)
Reid, James 4:31:51 (20,040)
Reid, John 4:10:54 (14,605)
Reid, Karl 3:59:46 (12,013)
Reid, Mark 3:15:38 (2,742)
Reid, Mark 3:46:01 (8,163)
Reid, Neil 3:08:25 (1,852)
Reid, Peter 3:08:55 (1,924)
Reid, Peter 3:52:27 (9,823)
Reid, Peter 3:52:45 (9,909)
Reid, William 4:15:50 (15,786)
Reide, Peter 3:50:42 (9,347)
Reidy, Kevin 4:54:02 (25,188)
Reilly, Gerard 3:28:07 (4,535)
Reilly, Jason 3:50:35 (9,317)
Reilly, Michael 3:33:35 (5,441)
Reilly, Stephen 3:08:46 (1,902)
Rein, Jonathan 4:04:28 (13,081)
Reinert, Richard 3:44:08 (7,691)
Reiss, Joshua 5:01:02 (26,453)
Reiten, Jan 3:12:30 (2,360)
Rej, Edek 4:23:15 (17,760)
Relph, James 3:50:35 (9,317)
Remaud, Alain 5:19:56 (28,867)
Remichi, David 3:28:46 (4,652)
Renak, Leigh 4:56:16 (25,650)
Rendell, John 3:56:48 (11,144)
Rendell, Malcolm 4:31:51 (20,040)
Renna, Onofrio 5:02:01 (26,607)
Rennicks, James 3:39:29 (6,625)
Rennie, David 3:49:11 (8,941)
Rennie, Gavin 3:50:47 (9,373)
Rennie, Jamie 3:34:02 (5,524)
Rennie, Stephen 2:37:47 (140)
Rennison, Steve 4:01:59 (12,557)
Rennolds, Steven 5:07:55 (27,425)
Renny, Steven 3:03:46 (1,447)
Renshaw, Patrick 4:00:06 (12,107)
Renton, Alan 4:55:22 (25,453)
Renton, Neil 2:51:59 (576)
Renwick, Rory 3:27:33 (4,423)
Repellini, Carmelo 4:07:52 (13,884)
Reskelly, Dave 3:47:27 (8,497)
Resta, Carlo 3:17:46 (2,985)
Reuben, Nigel 3:28:07 (4,535)
Reusch, Matthias 3:51:39 (9,583)
Revill, John 4:48:43 (24,173)
Reynard, Christopher 3:53:00 (9,976)
Reynolds, Andrew 4:34:44 (20,758)
Reynolds, Anthony 4:35:32 (20,957)
Reynolds, Ben 4:29:40 (19,499)
Reynolds, Christopher 3:43:30 (7,525)
Reynolds, Christopher 5:03:14 (26,788)
Reynolds, David 3:21:23 (3,418)
Reynolds, David 4:15:48 (15,780)
Reynolds, Giles 3:29:00 (4,695)
Reynolds, Huw 4:17:32 (16,250)
Reynolds, James 3:03:34 (1,427)
Reynolds, Joe 3:53:29 (10,139)
Reynolds, Jon 3:25:16 (4,026)
Reynolds, Karl 3:34:12 (5,564)
Reynolds, Luke 5:03:14 (26,788)
Reynolds, Matthew 4:16:21 (15,930)
Reynolds, Peter 3:39:00 (6,523)

LONDON MARATHON

Reynolds, Rhon 4:11:27 (14,733)
Reynolds, Robert 4:09:39 (14,307)
Rhimes, Godfrey 2:39:35 (176)
Rhodes, Andrew 4:10:02 (14,393)
Rhodes, David 3:20:02 (3,257)
Rhodes, David 4:00:41 (12,220)
Rhodes, Jonathan 3:42:36 (7,305)
Rhodes, Jonathan 4:17:51 (16,337)
Rhodes, Lee 4:13:31 (15,192)
Rhodes, Malcolm 3:49:22 (8,993)
Rhodes, Michael 3:38:33 (6,440)
Rhodes, Nigel 4:53:33 (25,079)
Rhodes, Philip 4:01:47 (12,514)
Rhodes, Stephen 3:08:20 (1,843)
Rhodes, Stuart 3:49:06 (8,924)
Rhodes-Edwards, Paul 7:37:23 (32,817)
Rhys, Andrew 5:21:43 (29,070)
Ribbeck, Nick 3:55:02 (10,603)
Ribeiro, Abilio 3:13:34 (2,513)
Ricardson, Paul 5:41:33 (30,659)
Riccardi, Roberto 4:10:44 (14,560)
Ricci, Antonio 3:26:48 (4,294)
Ricciardi, Ferdinando 3:47:29 (8,505)
Rice, Alex 3:52:32 (9,849)
Rice, Charles 4:07:14 (13,728)
Rice, Darren 3:54:23 (10,422)
Rice, John 4:14:11 (15,357)
Rice, Michael 3:45:09 (7,959)
Rice, Patrick 4:06:36 (13,586)
Rice, Peter 4:40:03 (22,120)
Rice, Philip 5:32:57 (30,020)
Rice, Stephen 3:42:01 (7,158)
Rice, Stephen 3:55:15 (10,679)
Rice, Tim 5:09:20 (27,612)
Rich, Andrew 3:56:46 (11,131)
Rich, Michael 5:06:15 (27,191)
Rich, Nick 4:57:30 (25,856)
Rich, Stephen 3:46:11 (8,196)
Richard, Frederic 4:21:15 (17,180)
Richards, Adam 4:39:55 (22,087)
Richards, Andrew 3:36:55 (6,099)
Richards, Angus 4:43:21 (22,919)
Richards, Anthony 5:18:30 (28,727)
Richards, Clive 4:12:55 (15,066)
Richards, David 4:59:17 (26,172)
Richards, Gary 3:32:58 (5,348)
Richards, Glyn 3:49:33 (9,053)
Richards, Gordon 3:01:08 (1,238)
Richards, Jeremy 4:18:23 (16,460)
Richards, Ken 3:56:31 (11,059)
Richards, Kenneth 6:26:39 (32,213)
Richards, Kevin 4:20:24 (16,964)
Richards, Leonard 3:53:26 (10,116)
Richards, Mark 4:20:21 (16,955)
Richards, Matthew 5:21:34 (29,048)
Richards, Matthew 6:40:15 (32,438)
Richards, Neil 3:56:06 (10,929)
Richards, Paul 2:40:47 (199)
Richards, Paul 3:29:28 (4,790)
Richards, Philip 5:08:12 (27,454)
Richards, Rhodri 4:23:55 (17,953)
Richards, Stephen 4:50:02 (24,429)
Richards, Timothy 3:50:46 (9,371)
Richards, Toby 4:07:51 (13,881)
Richardson, Alan 3:46:31 (8,290)
Richardson, Andrew 4:25:25 (18,364)
Richardson, Bryn 5:47:00 (30,986)
Richardson, Clive 3:28:18 (4,568)
Richardson, Colin 2:55:02 (744)
Richardson, David 4:17:18 (16,203)
Richardson, David 4:31:44 (20,018)
Richardson, Dean 3:38:39 (6,465)
Richardson, Gary 5:09:05 (27,581)
Richardson, Graham 3:44:48 (7,889)
Richardson, Graham 4:16:48 (16,064)
Richardson, Ian 3:51:53 (9,646)
Richardson, James 3:13:31 (2,509)
Richardson, John 6:35:00 (32,353)
Richardson, Kenneth 4:58:02 (25,954)
Richardson, Lance 3:24:41 (3,942)
Richardson, Mark 4:54:33 (25,292)
Richardson, Mark 4:56:37 (25,705)
Richardson, Martin 4:50:20 (24,470)

Richardson, Michael	3:59:24 (11,919)	
Richardson, Miles	3:05:38 (1,604)	
Richardson, Raymond	5:18:25 (28,720)	
Richardson, Robert	3:12:52 (2,414)	
Richardson, Roger	3:38:05 (6,327)	
Richardson, Scott	3:57:24 (11,325)	
Richardson, Simon	2:51:02 (533)	
Richardson, Simon	3:58:30 (11,651)	
Richardson, Steve	8:02:31 (32,863)	
Richardson, Tim	4:53:28 (25,065)	
Richardson, Timothy	3:53:45 (10,225)	
Richardson, Timothy	4:24:43 (18,178)	
Richardson Perks, Tim	3:37:25 (6,192)	
Riches, Christopher	3:54:58 (10,586)	
Riches, Christopher	3:58:35 (11,671)	
Richmond, Adrian	4:53:49 (25,124)	
Richmond, Andrew	4:37:36 (21,468)	
Richmond, David	3:45:23 (8,017)	
Richmond, James	4:50:34 (24,517)	
Richmond, Nicholas	4:11:10 (14,668)	
Richter, Bernard	3:54:24 (10,427)	
Richter, Lutz	3:26:11 (4,185)	
Rickard, John	4:07:31 (13,802)	
Rickards, James	3:29:08 (4,716)	
Ricketts, Dean	3:21:42 (3,463)	
Ricketts, Graham	3:59:43 (11,998)	
Ricklow, Dean	3:41:40 (7,094)	
Riddaway, Robert	3:12:03 (2,282)	
Riddell, Don	4:07:43 (13,845)	
Riddoch, Neil	3:49:03 (8,912)	
Ride, Michael	4:46:59 (23,806)	
Rideout, James	3:27:43 (4,459)	
Rider, Jerry	5:16:59 (28,553)	
Rider, Nicholas	4:32:24 (20,188)	
Rider, Tim	3:40:24 (6,833)	
Ridge, Bill	4:27:14 (18,851)	
Ridgeon, Jon	3:26:38 (4,257)	
Ridgeway, Paul	3:12:29 (2,357)	
Ridgwell, Matthew	6:04:40 (31,684)	
Ridler, Adam	4:02:34 (12,669)	
Ridler, Christopher	4:16:41 (16,035)	
Ridler, Mark	4:52:09 (24,805)	
Ridley, Matthew	3:32:54 (5,338)	
Ridley, Michael	4:47:05 (23,830)	
Ridley, Paul	3:29:51 (4,849)	
Ridout, Andrew	3:26:21 (4,210)	
Ridout, Glen	3:10:31 (2,103)	
Ridout, John	3:13:54 (2,550)	
Ridout, Marc	4:36:25 (21,194)	
Riedel, David	3:58:47 (11,729)	
Riedl, Johann	4:06:20 (13,524)	
Rief, Michael	3:25:10 (4,009)	
Riefer, Markus	2:53:07 (634)	
Rifat, Jeffrey	3:51:45 (9,610)	
Rigby, Billy	5:41:57 (30,693)	
Rigby, Carl	3:49:56 (9,158)	
Rigby, Christopher	5:05:06 (27,034)	
Rigby, Colin	2:40:39 (196)	
Rigby, David	3:24:01 (3,824)	
Rigby, Michael	4:56:56 (25,753)	
Rigby, Paul	5:11:16 (27,850)	
Rigby, Robert	3:22:42 (3,610)	
Rigg, Grahame	4:24:23 (18,087)	
Rigg, Nigel	3:02:03 (1,305)	
Righton, Edward	4:28:54 (19,289)	
Rigney, Noel	5:45:18 (30,901)	
Riley, Brian	3:23:48 (3,769)	
Riley, Carl	3:05:50 (1,624)	
Riley, James	4:37:33 (21,456)	
Riley, Jim	4:19:54 (16,836)	
Riley, Mark	4:05:02 (13,216)	
Riley, Martyn	4:29:32 (19,464)	
Riley, Martyn	4:43:43 (23,000)	
Riley, Paul	5:08:37 (27,509)	
Riley, Peter	5:12:29 (28,022)	
Riley, Simon	2:59:39 (1,142)	
Riley, Warren	3:54:18 (10,401)	
Rimmer, John	5:19:40 (28,835)	
Rimmer, Mark	4:13:57 (15,297)	
Rimmer, Mike	3:12:15 (2,322)	
Rimmer, Peter	4:23:23 (17,798)	
Rimmington, Andrew	4:27:04 (18,810)	
Rinchey, Alan	5:00:38 (26,393)	

Rinder, Christopher	4:24:57 (18,242)
Rindlisbacher, Daniel	3:08:32 (1,875)
Riobueno, Luis	3:18:56 (3,128)
Riordan, Tony	4:10:27 (14,497)
Rios, Moncho	4:46:19 (23,639)
Ripley, Chris	3:56:21 (11,003)
Risby, Floyd	3:28:25 (4,591)
Risdale, Neil	2:54:21 (695)
Rissi, Serge	4:32:01 (20,088)
Rissom, Kay	4:11:45 (14,806)
Ritchie, Alan	5:11:25 (27,876)
Ritchie, Craig	4:22:32 (17,557)
Ritchie, John	4:43:19 (22,913)
Ritchie, Keith	4:26:59 (18,782)
Ritchie, Stephen	5:17:14 (28,592)
Ritchie, William	4:21:35 (17,274)
Ritson, Martin	4:16:37 (16,016)
Rittiger, Klaus	4:42:19 (22,675)
Rivero, Jean	3:36:45 (6,068)
Rivers, Brian	3:12:26 (2,351)
Rivers, Jeremy	3:19:40 (3,218)
Rivers, Roderick	4:19:43 (16,781)
Rivers, Sydney	4:12:39 (15,012)
Rivers, Tony	3:57:38 (11,406)
Rivett, Graeme	4:55:07 (25,400)
Rixon, David	3:35:27 (5,794)
Rixon, Paul	4:00:56 (12,289)
Rizzitelli, Michele	4:36:18 (21,153)
Rizzo, Franco	3:32:18 (5,232)
Roach, John	4:16:40 (16,032)
Roach, Justin	4:33:36 (20,494)
Roach, Michael	3:52:05 (9,715)
Roach, Stephen	4:56:58 (25,759)
Roach, Stuart	4:39:00 (21,846)
Roach, Timothy	4:35:30 (20,946)
Road, Tom	4:26:03 (18,529)
Robb, Andrew	3:35:48 (5,866)
Robb, Chris	3:47:21 (8,472)
Robben, Jef	3:26:06 (4,165)
Robbens, Wayne	6:14:24 (31,938)
Robberts, Geoffrey	2:57:49 (988)
Robbesom, Henny	4:26:06 (18,549)
Robbie, Hamish	4:16:23 (15,945)
Robbins, Fred	3:49:52 (9,145)
Robbins, Jason	2:58:50 (1,078)
Robbins, Jonathan	3:36:09 (5,950)
Robbins, Keith	4:17:17 (16,197)
Robbins, Mark	3:01:21 (1,251)
Robbins, Michael	5:50:53 (31,179)
Robe, Alec	4:56:11 (25,628)
Robein, Etienne	3:52:23 (9,808)
Roberson, Clive	3:53:17 (10,075)
Roberts, Alan	3:33:23 (5,415)
Roberts, Alan	5:13:21 (28,121)
Roberts, Aled	3:54:01 (10,314)
Roberts, Alf	4:28:20 (19,119)
Roberts, Alun	4:22:36 (17,576)
Roberts, Andrew	3:41:24 (7,046)
Roberts, Andrew	3:42:28 (7,282)
Roberts, Austin	4:13:01 (15,088)
Roberts, Bernard	4:14:01 (15,316)
Roberts, Blane	5:00:36 (26,388)
Roberts, Craig	5:20:24 (28,929)
Roberts, David	3:25:38 (4,090)
Roberts, David	3:44:43 (7,861)
Roberts, David	3:56:59 (11,203)
Roberts, David	4:41:18 (22,425)
Roberts, David	5:01:58 (26,601)
Roberts, Derek	4:09:59 (14,380)
Roberts, Derlwyn	4:21:30 (17,250)
Roberts, Emyr	3:20:07 (3,268)
Roberts, Graham	3:55:36 (10,783)
Roberts, Howard	2:54:38 (718)
Roberts, Hugh	4:55:45 (25,533)
Roberts, Ian	4:03:55 (12,968)
Roberts, Ifor	3:47:05 (8,405)
Roberts, Ifor	4:56:26 (25,681)
Roberts, James	3:45:41 (8,088)
Roberts, James	4:36:41 (21,257)
Roberts, John	3:58:48 (11,737)
Roberts, John	9:24:51 (32,896)
Roberts, Johnny	3:42:52 (7,353)
Roberts, Jonathan	3:15:17 (2,699)

Roberts, Jonathan	4:41:39 (22,513)
Roberts, Lawrence	4:03:06 (12,799)
Roberts, Lee	4:38:32 (21,713)
Roberts, Mark	3:26:26 (4,217)
Roberts, Mark	3:39:50 (6,693)
Roberts, Mark	4:08:30 (14,021)
Roberts, Mark	4:51:54 (24,766)
Roberts, Mark	5:11:52 (27,935)
Roberts, Matt	5:09:55 (27,683)
Roberts, Matthew	5:08:18 (27,470)
Roberts, Nicholas	3:09:16 (1,961)
Roberts, Nick	4:31:26 (19,940)
Roberts, Oliver	3:37:47 (6,277)
Roberts, Pat	3:43:14 (7,454)
Roberts, Peter	4:25:01 (18,270)
Roberts, Peter	5:27:10 (29,537)
Roberts, Philip	2:59:02 (1,096)
Roberts, Raymond	3:37:42 (6,260)
Roberts, Richard	3:18:17 (3,042)
Roberts, Richard	4:43:38 (22,983)
Roberts, Rodney	3:44:46 (7,878)
Roberts, Scott	4:02:48 (12,729)
Roberts, Shane	4:18:37 (16,517)
Roberts, Simon	3:52:53 (9,945)
Roberts, Stephen	3:18:18 (3,047)
Roberts, Stephen	3:35:31 (5,807)
Roberts, Stephen	4:09:57 (14,373)
Roberts, Steve	4:07:21 (13,761)
Roberts, Thomas	4:15:44 (15,764)
Roberts, Tim	3:52:01 (9,693)
Roberts, William	4:13:11 (15,118)
Robertshaw, Andrew	2:36:35 (117)
Robertshaw, Philip	4:16:26 (15,963)
Robertshaw, Tom	3:01:53 (1,292)
Robertson, Adrian	3:15:40 (2,751)
Robertson, Allan	4:46:23 (23,662)
Robertson, Andrew	4:34:10 (20,621)
Robertson, Andrew	4:47:21 (23,885)
Robertson, Colin	4:22:52 (17,661)
Robertson, David	2:27:10 (48)
Robertson, David	3:58:22 (11,607)
Robertson, David	4:48:59 (24,232)
Robertson, David	5:05:31 (27,086)
Robertson, Derek	4:16:01 (15,842)
Robertson, Duncan	4:23:23 (17,798)
Robertson, Gordon	5:24:29 (29,322)
Robertson, Iain	3:46:32 (8,294)
Robertson, Iain	4:48:07 (24,058)
Robertson, Mark	5:53:06 (31,281)
Robertson, Paul	4:28:47 (19,252)
Robertson, Sami	4:05:23 (13,293)
Robertson, Stewart	4:13:01 (15,088)
Robertson, Stewart	4:22:49 (17,648)
Robertson, Stuart	3:24:21 (3,893)
Robertson, William	4:32:31 (20,219)
Robins, Shaun	5:01:02 (26,453)
Robins, Stephen	5:14:15 (28,222)
Robinson, Andrew	3:34:40 (5,655)
Robinson, Andy	3:48:45 (8,829)
Robinson, Antony	4:01:09 (12,352)
Robinson, Brent	4:48:33 (24,133)
Robinson, Dan	2:17:50 (15)
Robinson, David	3:45:14 (7,983)
Robinson, David	4:31:51 (20,040)
Robinson, David	4:39:52 (22,076)
Robinson, David	4:41:41 (22,526)
Robinson, David	4:53:04 (24,988)
Robinson, Dean	4:06:31 (13,571)
Robinson, Dean	4:18:55 (16,571)
Robinson, Derek	4:03:02 (12,782)
Robinson, Desmond	5:30:36 (29,832)
Robinson, Gareth	3:59:35 (11,962)
Robinson, Glenn	3:12:32 (2,366)
Robinson, Gordon	4:06:22 (13,536)
Robinson, Graham	4:11:28 (14,737)
Robinson, Henry	4:22:22 (17,507)
Robinson, James	4:06:23 (13,540)
Robinson, James	4:16:59 (16,112)
Robinson, Jonathan	3:46:58 (8,377)
Robinson, Julian	4:35:11 (20,875)
Robinson, Justin	3:47:55 (8,608)
Robinson, Kevin	5:00:08 (26,326)
Robinson, Malcolm	5:05:12 (27,044)

Rossi, Giuseppe	7:27:13 (32,779)	
Rossiter, Graham	7:26:23 (32,772)	
Ross-Jones, John	5:57:48 (31,469)	
Ross-Jones, William	5:57:48 (31,469)	
Ross-Jordan, Gary	4:04:32 (13,099)	
Rostad, Hans	3:25:02 (3,991)	
Rostron, Hanno	4:59:30 (26,216)	
Rota, Giuseppe	4:34:35 (20,719)	
Rothe, Dieter	4:21:27 (17,232)	
Rothin, Keith	5:16:29 (28,499)	
Rothwell, Alan	3:48:33 (8,762)	
Rothwell, Colin	3:55:30 (10,745)	
Rothwell, Lee	3:11:26 (2,196)	
Rothwell, Paul	3:35:07 (5,736)	
Roud, Pete	4:10:47 (14,571)	
Round, Simon	3:47:24 (8,488)	
Rountree, Frederick	2:32:41 (79)	
Rourke, Simon	4:02:55 (12,758)	
Rous, James	3:35:26 (5,789)	
Rouse, Anthony	4:03:24 (12,859)	
Rouse, David	3:32:36 (5,289)	
Rouse, Stephen	3:19:11 (3,158)	
Rousseau, Guy	5:30:06 (29,784)	
Rout, Russell	3:15:13 (2,691)	
Routh, Alan	4:30:27 (19,701)	
Routier, Paul	5:20:30 (28,940)	
Routledge, Jonathan	4:41:18 (22,425)	
Routledge, Richard	3:15:12 (2,687)	
Routledge, William	3:34:11 (5,561)	
Rowan, Matthew	3:35:55 (5,886)	
Rowbotham, Ian	2:51:23 (553)	
Rowcroft, Stephen	4:43:52 (23,034)	
Rowe, Antony	3:48:21 (8,710)	
Rowe, Brandon	3:59:59 (12,080)	
Rowe, Christopher	5:03:33 (26,827)	
Rowe, Colin	6:09:54 (31,835)	
Rowe, David	3:50:37 (9,327)	
Rowe, Kevin	5:17:00 (28,557)	
Rowe, Martin	3:33:56 (5,504)	
Rowe, Oliver	3:55:45 (10,827)	
Rowe, Peter	4:13:47 (15,258)	
Rowe, Philip	5:14:23 (28,235)	
Rowe, Phillip	3:10:10 (2,054)	
Rowe, Simon	3:35:32 (5,809)	
Rowe, Timothy	3:18:37 (3,088)	
Rowell, Barry	4:25:38 (18,428)	
Rowell, Jonathan	3:59:51 (12,041)	
Rowell, Stephen	4:54:08 (25,208)	
Rowland, Alan	3:56:46 (11,131)	
Rowland, Darren	7:12:37 (32,721)	
Rowland, Gareth	5:27:14 (29,543)	
Rowland, Martyn	5:29:07 (29,704)	
Rowland, Michael	5:27:45 (29,602)	
Rowland, Stewart	4:41:45 (22,543)	
Rowlands, Anthony	3:53:33 (10,165)	
Rowlands, Ben	3:36:38 (6,047)	
Rowlands, David	5:48:21 (31,054)	
Rowlands, Peter	4:11:57 (14,848)	
Rowlatt, Gary	4:26:11 (18,569)	
Rowley, Alistair	3:49:56 (9,158)	
Rowley, Andrew	4:40:28 (22,225)	
Rowley, Jody	4:29:34 (19,473)	
Rowley, Ray	5:11:08 (27,829)	
Rowlinson, Jonathan	5:13:11 (28,099)	
Rowlson, Mark	3:11:34 (2,212)	
Rowsell, David	4:17:57 (16,359)	
Rowson, David	4:13:16 (15,143)	
Roy, Bratin	4:33:50 (20,541)	
Roy, David	5:41:30 (30,655)	
Roy, Malcolm	4:32:37 (20,251)	
Roy, Prasanta	5:46:13 (30,948)	
Roy, Ramses	4:15:56 (15,824)	
Roy, Steve	4:44:40 (23,209)	
Royal, Paul	3:24:52 (3,966)	
Royce, William	4:29:50 (19,551)	
Royle, John	4:46:03 (23,584)	
Royle, Neil	4:32:15 (20,149)	
Rozes, Jean	3:38:49 (6,486)	
Ruane, Anthony	4:28:49 (19,261)	
Rubery, Jonathan	4:03:38 (12,907)	
Rudd, Andrew	3:27:52 (4,498)	
Rudd, Graham	6:34:24 (32,345)	
Rudd, Matthew	3:06:47 (1,710)	
Rudd, Phil	2:52:42 (611)	
Rudder, Jim	4:08:23 (13,990)	
Rudder, Simon	4:46:59 (23,806)	
Ruddock, David	5:14:52 (28,292)	
Rudge, David	4:08:39 (14,066)	
Rudkin, Jason	4:45:30 (23,436)	
Rudolf, James	4:41:53 (22,581)	
Rudrum, Martyn	5:26:58 (29,520)	
Ruff, Keith	3:33:07 (5,368)	
Ruffle, Richard	4:13:13 (15,126)	
Ruffle, Steve	4:01:25 (12,421)	
Ruffles, John	5:03:02 (26,749)	
Rugg, Paul	4:08:35 (14,051)	
Ruggles, Paul	5:15:17 (28,337)	
Rugman, Stanley	4:51:53 (24,760)	
Ruia, Alok	3:50:45 (9,363)	
Ruia, Sunil	4:11:52 (14,828)	
Rulten, Brian	5:00:48 (26,421)	
Rumary, Brian	3:24:04 (3,833)	
Rumary, David	5:14:44 (28,276)	
Rumbelow, Nicholas	3:10:16 (2,069)	
Rumbles, Christopher	4:22:23 (17,512)	
Rummery, Ian	5:36:52 (30,340)	
Rumney, Kevin	3:35:17 (5,760)	
Rumpf, Markus	3:38:23 (6,394)	
Rumsey, Paul	3:01:49 (1,284)	
Runacres, Mark	3:38:11 (6,340)	
Rundle, Daniel	4:50:59 (24,606)	
Rundle, David	6:30:19 (32,287)	
Rundle, Kevin	4:07:21 (13,761)	
Rundle, Mike	3:36:35 (6,039)	
Rundle, Paul	4:09:09 (14,170)	
Ruparelia, Milan	4:58:05 (25,962)	
Rupp, Daniel	4:11:30 (14,747)	
Rupp, Peter	4:05:00 (13,210)	
Rusga, Daniel	3:34:34 (5,630)	
Rush, Timothy	4:28:50 (19,269)	
Rushby, John	4:34:27 (20,682)	
Rushby, Phillip	3:51:00 (9,425)	
Rushmer, Martin	4:13:13 (15,126)	
Rushton, Mark	4:12:55 (15,066)	
Rushton, Paul	3:43:43 (7,580)	
Rushworth, Paul	3:03:25 (1,413)	
Russ, David	5:07:48 (27,406)	
Russ, Mark	4:37:49 (21,525)	
Russell, Darren	3:54:34 (10,478)	
Russell, David	3:42:09 (7,191)	
Russell, Duncan	3:34:44 (5,666)	
Russell, Ian	4:17:29 (16,240)	
Russell, Jim	3:12:16 (2,324)	
Russell, Jimmy	4:40:44 (22,286)	
Russell, John	3:18:50 (3,116)	
Russell, John	3:23:52 (3,789)	
Russell, John	3:29:01 (4,696)	
Russell, John	4:19:03 (16,607)	
Russell, John	4:33:22 (20,432)	
Russell, Jonathan	5:27:32 (29,579)	
Russell, Joseph	4:36:18 (21,153)	
Russell, Keith	5:03:45 (26,850)	
Russell, Kelvin	2:55:29 (779)	
Russell, Kevin	4:15:29 (15,689)	
Russell, Malcolm	4:36:19 (21,164)	
Russell, Mark	3:23:40 (3,755)	
Russell, Mark	4:51:37 (24,721)	
Russell, Mike	2:57:50 (991)	
Russell, Mike	3:22:11 (3,548)	
Russell, Neil	4:37:04 (21,331)	
Russell, Niall	4:38:44 (21,774)	
Russell, Nigel	2:55:11 (758)	
Russell, Norman	4:40:25 (22,218)	
Russell, Paul	4:26:04 (18,539)	
Russell, Paul	7:59:41 (32,860)	
Russell, Peter	2:42:32 (238)	
Russell, Phillip	3:30:15 (4,901)	
Russell, Shane	5:09:39 (27,655)	
Russell, Shaune	3:00:08 (1,180)	
Russell, Simon	2:55:49 (813)	
Russell, Stephen	3:19:00 (3,132)	
Rust, James	3:04:12 (1,483)	
Ruston, Philip	4:45:04 (23,325)	
Ruston, Robin	2:58:40 (1,066)	
Ruston, Ron	4:53:50 (25,131)	
Ruth, Sean	3:47:37 (8,541)	
Rutherford, Neil	3:58:10 (11,558)	
Rutherford, Simon	3:49:52 (9,145)	
Rutherford, Stephen	3:49:47 (9,125)	
Ruthven, Christopher	3:49:30 (9,041)	
Rutland, Ian	3:25:52 (4,128)	
Rutnam, John	4:14:37 (15,473)	
Rutter, David	5:04:57 (27,013)	
Rutter, Julian	4:45:30 (23,436)	
Rutter, Kenneth	4:30:03 (19,608)	
Rutter, Mark	4:40:22 (22,207)	
Rutter, Neil	4:08:17 (13,969)	
Rutter, Paul	3:48:42 (8,812)	
Rutter, Tom	4:22:23 (17,512)	
Ruxton, David	3:57:42 (11,422)	
Ryalls, Terry	3:42:28 (7,282)	
Ryan, Anthony	4:45:19 (23,384)	
Ryan, Charles	3:58:39 (11,691)	
Ryan, David	4:26:13 (18,578)	
Ryan, Denny	3:10:31 (2,103)	
Ryan, James	4:40:42 (22,277)	
Ryan, Jeremy	5:00:23 (26,356)	
Ryan, Joseph	3:39:56 (6,720)	
Ryan, Mark	5:37:55 (30,411)	
Ryan, Paul	4:02:49 (12,733)	
Ryan, Sean	4:45:26 (23,424)	
Ryan, Steve	4:11:39 (14,782)	
Ryan, Terence	4:30:21 (19,681)	
Ryce, Mark	4:22:47 (17,631)	
Ryde, Edward	6:01:50 (31,602)	
Rydell, Jamie	6:22:38 (32,139)	
Ryder, David	3:31:38 (5,135)	
Ryder, Kevin	3:43:20 (7,483)	
Rye, Joseph	2:44:01 (272)	
Ryeland, John	5:21:52 (29,084)	
Ryffel, Markus	2:55:23 (771)	
Ryssel, Christian	3:54:58 (10,586)	
Sacco, Renato	3:56:15 (10,978)	
Saccoh, Teddy	3:22:18 (3,563)	
Sackett, Martin	5:12:40 (28,043)	
Sacks, Brian	3:58:56 (11,772)	
Sacks, Daniel	3:46:16 (8,215)	
Sadler, Adrian	3:49:22 (8,993)	
Sadler, Benjamin	3:43:36 (7,550)	
Sadler, David	4:17:34 (16,259)	
Sadler, Dexter	4:43:39 (22,986)	
Sadler, James	5:37:26 (30,379)	
Sadler, Kevin	2:53:07 (634)	
Sadler, Phillip	4:44:24 (23,151)	
Sadler, Richard	3:49:03 (8,912)	
Sadrian, Luke	3:28:10 (4,544)	
Saether, Hans-Joergen	3:38:26 (6,410)	
Saffman, Andrew	4:01:45 (12,505)	
Safford, Robert	4:13:58 (15,301)	
Sagar, Nicholas	3:41:53 (7,129)	
Sage, Graham	5:24:03 (29,284)	
Sage, Peter	5:49:27 (31,118)	
Saha, Sanjoy	5:14:45 (28,280)	
Sainsbury, Clive	4:41:24 (22,447)	
Saint, Tom	3:55:02 (10,603)	
Saiz Nistal, José	3:29:15 (4,740)	
Sakai, Katsuhiko	5:34:39 (30,162)	
Saker, Andrew	3:53:50 (10,261)	
Saker, Graeme	3:23:34 (3,736)	
Sakol, Gordon	4:43:27 (22,948)	
Saladin, Patrick	3:16:58 (2,899)	
Sale, Alan	3:40:53 (6,937)	
Sale, Antonio	4:05:28 (13,317)	
Sale, Graham	4:30:53 (19,801)	
Sale, Tony	3:52:26 (9,820)	
Salem, Jonathan	4:41:28 (22,470)	
Sales, Roger	3:58:01 (11,517)	
Salinger, Joseph	4:41:21 (22,439)	
Salisbury, Alan	5:00:39 (26,401)	
Salisbury, Graham	5:03:27 (26,817)	
Salisbury, Martin	3:42:05 (7,174)	
Salisbury, Philip	4:06:43 (13,618)	
Salkeld, Edwin	3:36:05 (5,924)	
Salkeld, Michael	3:24:22 (3,901)	
Sallis, Stephen	4:24:14 (18,048)	
Sallnow, Gavin	5:25:34 (29,407)	
Salman, Paul	4:42:23 (22,691)	
Salmon, Geoffrey	4:47:07 (23,834)	
Salmon, Keith	5:02:14 (26,632)	

Salmon, Matthew	4:47:07 (23,834)	
Salmon, Michael	3:37:06 (6,134)	
Salmond, George	3:26:06 (4,165)	
Salmons, Nigel	4:58:51 (26,107)	
Salsbury, Grendan	4:00:24 (12,165)	
Salt, Anthony	3:55:18 (10,696)	
Salt, Jonathan	4:49:11 (24,273)	
Salt, Philip	3:55:03 (10,611)	
Salter, Daniel	5:04:45 (26,987)	
Salter, Dennis	3:48:11 (8,670)	
Salter, Jules	3:42:03 (7,167)	
Salter, Neil	3:20:37 (3,328)	
Salter, Richard	4:01:35 (12,466)	
Salter, Tim	4:45:29 (23,433)	
Salts, Philip	3:58:14 (11,577)	
Salueddin, Rasheed	3:34:58 (5,707)	
Salway, Eric	4:43:44 (23,001)	
Samat, Daren	4:32:28 (20,213)	
Sambhi, Davinder	4:29:13 (19,384)	
Sambridge, Ron	4:55:32 (25,487)	
Sambrook, Stuart	3:09:29 (1,988)	
Sami, Talat	3:59:53 (12,053)	
Samler, Charles	3:39:37 (6,649)	
Sammons, Robert	4:46:10 (23,613)	
Sammut, Anthony	5:39:55 (30,543)	
Samothrakis, Paulo	3:36:44 (6,061)	
Sampas, George	4:17:14 (16,179)	
Sampson, Nigel	5:26:05 (29,453)	
Sampson, Richard	4:28:28 (19,159)	
Sams, Chris	5:23:59 (29,279)	
Samson, Edward	3:57:58 (11,496)	
Samuel, Derek	6:46:47 (32,502)	
Samuel, Japhet	3:38:34 (6,443)	
Samuel, Jon	3:57:04 (11,227)	
Samuel, Mark	4:05:57 (13,425)	
Samuel, Michael	4:16:08 (15,873)	
Samuel, Sammy	4:34:36 (20,726)	
Samways, Shane	4:05:42 (13,368)	
Sanano, José	3:06:00 (1,642)	
Sanchez, Vincent	5:10:26 (27,745)	
Sanchez, Xavier	4:46:27 (23,680)	
Sanchez Irizo, José	2:44:46 (291)	
Sanchez-Vidal, Roberto	3:39:03 (6,537)	
Sanctuary, Colin	3:46:51 (8,355)	
Sand, Augus	3:04:33 (1,506)	
Sanday, John	4:30:10 (19,645)	
Sandells, Charles	4:26:21 (18,615)	
Sandeman, Donald	3:20:17 (3,290)	
Sandercombe, Robert	3:31:08 (5,057)	
Sanders, David	4:12:28 (14,963)	
Sanders, Eddie	3:12:35 (2,371)	
Sanders, Kevin	3:43:17 (7,467)	
Sanders, Leigh	4:52:32 (24,882)	
Sanders, Richard	4:10:30 (14,510)	
Sanders, Steve	3:27:48 (4,480)	
Sanders, Steve	4:28:01 (19,038)	
Sanders, William	4:39:00 (21,846)	
Sanderson, Brian	4:24:51 (18,213)	
Sanderson, Gareth	4:36:31 (21,226)	
Sanderson, Mark	3:55:47 (10,835)	
Sanderson, Mark	5:22:18 (29,117)	
Sanderson, Neil	4:05:40 (13,362)	
Sanderson, Paul	3:44:15 (7,722)	
Sanderson, Terence	3:57:33 (11,381)	
Sandford, Mark	3:55:59 (5,901)	
Sandham, David	4:34:30 (20,700)	
Sandham, Francis	4:14:57 (15,559)	
Sandhu, David	4:44:30 (23,172)	
Sandhu, John	4:30:05 (19,620)	
Sandmann, Johannes	4:31:20 (19,912)	
Sandoe, Anthony	4:32:42 (20,277)	
Sandon, Adrian	3:53:47 (10,237)	
Sandre, Samuel	3:29:59 (4,870)	
Sands, Matthew	3:24:30 (3,918)	
Sands, Richard	3:59:38 (11,977)	
Sandy, Tom	2:58:22 (1,034)	
Sanger, Mark	4:34:18 (20,649)	
Sanghera, Kirn	4:13:29 (15,183)	
Sanham, Robert	4:03:45 (12,928)	
Sankey, Mark	3:16:56 (2,895)	
Sankey, Richard	4:54:59 (25,374)	
Sano, Hiroaki	4:34:14 (20,636)	
Sansom, Matthew	3:53:37 (10,182)	

Sansome, Gary	4:04:42 (13,135)	
Sansum, Mark	5:26:21 (29,472)	
Santamaria, Carlos	3:52:29 (9,831)	
Santini, Nazzareno	3:49:05 (8,919)	
Santos, Martin	4:46:52 (23,777)	
Sanz, Jorge	3:44:29 (7,791)	
Saouli, Mohammed	4:23:10 (17,742)	
Sapey, Tony	4:13:40 (15,222)	
Sapienza, Dominique	3:43:57 (7,643)	
Sarakinsky, Atholl	5:18:23 (28,713)	
Sardone, Francesco	3:45:12 (7,975)	
Sargant, Harry	3:27:02 (4,336)	
Sargeant, Kevin	4:24:28 (18,110)	
Sargeant, Malcolm	4:29:28 (19,452)	
Sargeant, Philip	3:49:40 (9,086)	
Sargeant, Scott	4:22:43 (17,614)	
Sargeant, Steve	3:25:15 (4,024)	
Sargeant, Trevor	4:15:25 (15,671)	
Sargeant, William	3:41:10 (7,003)	
Sargent, Dale	3:53:28 (10,135)	
Sargent, David	3:26:14 (4,193)	
Sargent, Matthew	4:32:49 (20,306)	
Sargent, Peter	2:59:21 (1,119)	
Sarra, Gino	4:02:30 (12,654)	
Sarson, Peter	2:50:31 (511)	
Sartain, John	3:51:44 (9,603)	
Sartin, Rob	3:00:58 (1,225)	
Sartorelli, Raffaele	4:52:51 (24,948)	
Saru, Rewat	3:49:15 (8,953)	
Sasaki, Daizo	3:50:29 (9,297)	
Sasaki, Jiro	6:21:59 (32,124)	
Sasaki, Kazvati	6:21:57 (32,121)	
Sasson, Nathaniel	4:18:23 (16,460)	
Sassone, Joseph	3:45:27 (8,029)	
Sathasivam, Sivakumar	5:56:14 (31,409)	
Sattentau, Quentin	3:53:42 (10,208)	
Satterly, James	4:37:24 (21,422)	
Sattler, Christopher	3:48:47 (8,839)	
Sauer, Ulrich	3:29:27 (4,784)	
Saunders, Alan	5:18:23 (28,713)	
Saunders, Andrew	3:28:10 (4,544)	
Saunders, Andrew	4:38:35 (21,730)	
Saunders, Barry	4:32:16 (20,152)	
Saunders, David	3:36:16 (5,969)	
Saunders, David	5:26:18 (29,466)	
Saunders, John	3:24:11 (3,857)	
Saunders, John	3:47:10 (8,426)	
Saunders, John	3:59:06 (11,830)	
Saunders, Julian	4:31:04 (19,844)	
Saunders, Keith	4:51:11 (24,652)	
Saunders, Kenneth	3:03:12 (1,390)	
Saunders, Lee	3:33:15 (5,388)	
Saunders, Mark	4:09:23 (14,245)	
Saunders, Mark	5:05:00 (27,021)	
Saunders, Martin	4:18:44 (16,530)	
Saunders, Nigel	3:49:20 (8,981)	
Saunders, Richard	3:19:35 (3,212)	
Saunders, Stephen	4:23:00 (17,708)	
Saunders, Steve	3:37:33 (6,232)	
Saunders, Steven	3:46:13 (8,206)	
Savage, Ian	4:33:13 (20,407)	
Savage, James	3:01:46 (1,280)	
Savage, Philip	4:13:51 (15,272)	
Savage, Sean	4:09:23 (14,245)	
Savage, Terry	4:14:52 (15,542)	
Savary, Michel	4:28:23 (19,131)	
Savas, Andreas	4:22:00 (17,393)	
Saverwald, Johannes	3:56:06 (10,929)	
Savides, Sean	4:00:41 (12,220)	
Savill, David	3:47:04 (8,399)	
Savill, Philip	4:12:00 (14,862)	
Savill, Tim	3:59:49 (12,028)	
Saville, Mike	5:56:31 (31,424)	
Saville, Philip	4:08:48 (14,092)	
Saville, Steve	4:40:50 (22,316)	
Savory, Charlie	4:24:51 (18,213)	
Savvides, Andrew	4:01:17 (12,384)	
Sawamura, Keiji	4:09:11 (14,183)	
Sawer, Martin	3:14:47 (2,640)	
Sawford, Glyn	3:04:29 (1,502)	
Sawtell, John	4:11:41 (14,794)	
Sawyer, Adam	4:15:59 (15,833)	
Sawyer, Edward	3:19:22 (3,181)	

Sawyer, John	3:40:13 (6,792)	
Sawyer, Keith	3:35:17 (5,760)	
Sawyer, Matthew	4:16:01 (15,842)	
Sawyer, Neil	3:48:06 (8,650)	
Sawyer, Steven	3:53:15 (10,061)	
Saxby, Adrian	5:11:22 (27,864)	
Saxelby, Jai	3:12:01 (2,276)	
Saxton, Jonathan	3:34:43 (5,662)	
Saxton, Michael	5:24:09 (29,291)	
Saya, Jacques	4:02:56 (12,763)	
Sayer, John	3:54:19 (10,404)	
Sayer, Philip	4:22:06 (17,424)	
Sayer, Timothy	4:32:33 (20,228)	
Sayers, Brian	4:33:35 (20,486)	
Sayers, John	4:32:53 (20,329)	
Sayers, Robert	3:41:07 (6,994)	
Sayers, Simon	4:49:39 (24,350)	
Sayers, Steve	3:59:47 (12,019)	
Sayers, Victor	3:06:20 (1,669)	
Sayle, Mark	4:23:18 (17,776)	
Saywell, Michael	3:35:52 (5,878)	
Scadden, Mark	4:22:00 (17,393)	
Scaglioni, Francesco	4:29:07 (19,354)	
Scaife, Michael	3:48:37 (8,789)	
Scaife, Raymond	4:01:47 (12,514)	
Scales, Dean	6:43:10 (32,461)	
Scales, Peter	4:08:54 (14,112)	
Scales, Robin	3:47:36 (8,538)	
Scalzo, Enzo	4:06:03 (13,445)	
Scambler, Neal	4:32:23 (20,184)	
Scamman, Jon	4:30:32 (19,715)	
Scampton, Gary	3:36:06 (5,932)	
Scandrett-Smith, Graeme	3:34:38 (5,645)	
Scane, Gary	4:35:13 (20,891)	
Scanlan, Christopher	4:04:09 (13,017)	
Scarles, Philip	2:47:51 (395)	
Scarrott, Pete	4:59:01 (26,134)	
Scarzello, Giancarlo	3:58:56 (11,772)	
Scase, Douglas	4:34:55 (20,807)	
Scatola, Nino	4:23:00 (17,708)	
Schaaf, William	3:25:50 (4,121)	
Schab, Karl	4:54:25 (25,267)	
Schaefer, Wolfgang	3:33:17 (5,398)	
Schaerer, Juerg	3:48:49 (8,845)	
Schaffer, Thomas	3:47:36 (8,538)	
Schall, Markus	3:58:19 (11,593)	
Scharfe, Dieter	5:31:06 (29,872)	
Schartner, David	3:46:48 (8,343)	
Schartner, Manfred	3:49:16 (8,959)	
Schatt, Hans-Jorg	4:25:48 (18,462)	
Schawinski, Roger	3:45:10 (7,962)	
Scheers, Kurt	3:06:50 (1,717)	
Schenk, Bernhard	3:24:40 (3,938)	
Schenk, Kurt	4:30:02 (19,603)	
Schepp, Manfred	4:15:03 (15,585)	
Schepp, Markus	4:03:02 (12,782)	
Scheunemann, Dirk	3:57:43 (11,430)	
Schiattarella, Biagio	5:22:44 (29,155)	
Schiavottiello, Vincenzo	2:54:33 (709)	
Schick, Harald	3:26:55 (4,315)	
Schidlowski, Volker	3:09:36 (2,000)	
Schiller, Burkhard	4:29:41 (19,502)	
Schisano, Francesco	3:23:18 (3,694)	
Schlamm, John	4:00:10 (12,125)	
Schlender, Marek	3:49:47 (9,125)	
Schlesser, Cyril	4:26:36 (18,680)	
Schleuchter, Marcus	4:07:15 (13,734)	
Schleuder, Wolfram	4:01:21 (12,407)	
Schlosser, Darren	4:43:04 (22,856)	
Schmeitzky, Mathieu	3:55:51 (10,855)	
Schmetzer, Paulo	4:43:31 (22,964)	
Schmidt, Lutz	4:24:25 (18,094)	
Schmidt, Matthias	3:55:33 (10,767)	
Schmidt, Paul	4:45:01 (23,312)	
Schmidt-Mende, Lukas	4:19:32 (16,733)	
Schmitt, Marc Timo	4:25:27 (18,371)	
Schmitz, Klaus	3:29:40 (4,822)	
Schneck, Dietmar	4:21:48 (17,335)	
Schneider, Daniel	4:28:57 (19,309)	
Schneider, Jwerg	4:01:21 (12,407)	
Schneider, Mark-Dominik	2:52:53 (624)	
Schneider, Matthew	4:28:58 (19,313)	
Schneider, Peter	4:23:26 (17,811)	

Schneider, Robert 3:13:50 (2,543)
Schneider, Walter 2:57:26 (953)
Schnetzer, Markus 3:37:10 (6,144)
Schnizer, Friedrich 4:34:54 (20,803)
Schoenherr, Allan 4:18:57 (16,580)
Schofield, Darren 4:35:39 (21,001)
Schofield, Graham 3:18:44 (3,103)
Schofield, John 5:25:49 (29,431)
Schofield, Mark 3:15:04 (2,670)
Schofield, Nigel 3:43:20 (7,483)
Schofield, Peter 3:49:09 (8,934)
Schofield, Peter 4:17:45 (16,310)
Schofield, Peter 6:50:45 (32,550)
Schokman, Tony 4:43:30 (22,961)
Scholey, James 4:50:33 (24,515)
Scholey, Mark 5:10:48 (27,784)
Scholte, Ben 4:08:49 (14,094)
Scholtes, Mark 5:14:31 (28,250)
Schooling, Steven 2:50:31 (511)
Schoonderwoerd, Thom 3:39:00 (6,523)
Schoy, Rolf 3:02:01 (1,301)
Schrade, Gernot 4:39:18 (21,924)
Schray, Joseph 3:21:00 (3,364)
Schroder-Nielsen, Soren 3:33:39 (5,447)
Schroeder, Wolfram 3:34:52 (5,688)
Schroedes-Davis, Steve 4:29:07 (19,354)
Schuett, Andreas 4:23:16 (17,768)
Schuiling, Koen 4:09:37 (14,295)
Schuler, Benedict 3:16:19 (2,821)
Schuller Tot Peursum, Vincent 3:39:02 (6,535)
Schulot, Michael 4:26:35 (18,675)
Schulte-Eversum, Dirk 3:08:26 (1,857)
Schultz, Larry 4:47:54 (24,005)
Schultz, Torben 4:13:19 (15,149)
Schulz, Klaus 4:39:34 (21,989)
Schumann, Joerg 3:00:54 (1,218)
Schumann, Paul 2:56:27 (868)
Schumann, Steven 3:53:36 (10,178)
Schuppan, Knut 3:55:41 (10,803)
Schurmann, Jason 5:19:06 (28,786)
Schuster, Eugene 4:38:43 (21,768)
Schutte, Andrew 4:20:38 (17,027)
Schuurmans, Rini 3:12:56 (2,425)
Schvartz, Clement 4:19:31 (16,730)
Schwald, André 2:59:47 (1,156)
Schwartz, Serge 4:15:43 (15,758)
Schwarz, Erwin 3:55:10 (10,653)
Schwarz, Karl 3:38:06 (6,330)
Schweighofer, Helmut 2:56:45 (892)
Schweinzer, Paul 4:21:15 (17,180)
Schwerch, Stefan 3:29:57 (4,864)
Schweter, Andreas 4:01:57 (12,554)
Scoffham, Alastair 4:02:36 (12,681)
Scoins, Daniel 3:39:28 (6,617)
Scorer, Gregory 4:28:45 (19,244)
Scoresby, Neil 4:48:28 (24,118)
Scotchford, Colin 3:09:00 (1,933)
Scotney, Lee 4:45:09 (23,345)
Scotney, Paul 4:42:25 (22,701)
Scott, Andrew 3:34:06 (5,543)
Scott, Anthony 3:47:32 (8,519)
Scott, Anthony 4:10:54 (14,605)
Scott, Barry 5:04:11 (26,915)
Scott, Bruce 4:27:05 (18,816)
Scott, Cameron 3:31:40 (5,145)
Scott, Charles 5:17:25 (28,619)
Scott, Christopher 4:08:33 (14,041)
Scott, Christopher 4:47:38 (23,935)
Scott, Damian 3:18:38 (3,089)
Scott, Danny 2:52:09 (586)
Scott, Douglas 3:14:14 (2,585)
Scott, Gary 3:41:22 (7,041)
Scott, Gavin 5:15:55 (28,431)
Scott, George 3:36:11 (5,955)
Scott, Graeme 3:48:59 (8,891)
Scott, Graham 5:22:39 (29,148)
Scott, Ian 4:02:01 (12,563)
Scott, Ian 4:08:01 (13,916)
Scott, Jim 3:43:04 (7,406)
Scott, Jonathan 5:26:18 (29,466)
Scott, Justin 3:41:58 (7,144)
Scott, Lloyd 128:29:46 (32,897)
Scott, Matthew 4:19:25 (16,697)
Scott, Peter 3:52:44 (9,905)
Scott, Peter 4:15:35 (15,718)
Scott, Philip 3:30:12 (4,894)
Scott, Richard 5:05:50 (27,131)
Scott, Robert 3:51:00 (9,425)
Scott, Robin 3:00:22 (1,192)
Scott, Rupert 4:28:44 (19,236)
Scott, Steven 4:25:35 (18,410)
Scott, Stuart 4:39:44 (22,037)
Scott, Ty 4:34:46 (20,766)
Scott, William 4:13:13 (15,126)
Scott Ralphs, David 3:53:04 (10,003)
Scotting, Andrew 3:48:38 (8,796)
Scrase, Thomas 3:16:24 (2,832)
Scriber, Keith 4:14:38 (15,481)
Scrini, Alex 3:31:45 (5,160)
Scripps, Elliot 4:20:03 (16,880)
Scriven, Lloyd 3:57:40 (11,416)
Scriven, Marcos 3:19:19 (3,173)
Scriven, Tom 4:36:38 (21,249)
Scrivener, Chris 3:24:07 (3,840)
Scrivener, Richard 4:30:39 (19,745)
Scrivens, Alexander 4:42:26 (22,706)
Scullard, Jonathan 3:24:55 (3,975)
Scullion, David 4:27:00 (18,790)
Scurlock, Jamie 3:58:50 (11,745)
Scuto, Franco 3:48:08 (8,658)
Scutt, Graham 5:09:29 (27,630)
Scutt, Michael 3:51:00 (9,425)
Scyner, Mark 4:31:24 (19,929)
Seaborn, George 4:59:43 (26,268)
Seabrook, Joe 3:50:45 (9,363)
Seager, Jerry 4:13:39 (15,216)
Seager, Neil 4:54:19 (25,246)
Seager, Nick 4:55:01 (25,378)
Seal, Jonathan 4:26:46 (18,736)
Seal, Julian 4:58:56 (26,119)
Sealey, Robert 6:05:57 (31,730)
Seaman, David 3:59:53 (12,053)
Seaman, Kelvin 4:52:26 (24,864)
Seamark, Jamie 3:11:02 (2,160)
Sear, John 2:47:22 (375)
Searl, John 4:37:53 (21,542)
Searle, Adrian 4:29:53 (19,569)
Searle, Andrew 4:34:57 (20,818)
Searle, Greg 3:29:07 (4,714)
Searle, Ian 4:53:26 (25,055)
Searle, Jonny 3:08:43 (1,891)
Sears, John 3:50:26 (9,284)
Seaton, Graham 3:39:55 (6,714)
Seaton, Mark 4:17:36 (16,268)
Seaton, Mike 3:15:48 (2,769)
Seaton, Steven 4:15:51 (15,791)
Sebban, Samuel 3:32:28 (5,266)
Sebbar, Abdelhalim 4:28:20 (19,119)
Secrett, Jonathan 3:51:04 (9,447)
Seddon, Andrew 5:17:08 (28,582)
Seddon, Daniel 4:36:37 (21,244)
Seddon, Stephen 4:14:51 (15,540)
Sedge, Martyn 2:54:53 (733)
Sedgley, David 3:36:25 (6,008)
Sedgwick, Alan 3:46:05 (8,178)
Sedgwick, Stephen 3:57:17 (11,288)
Sedgwick, Stephen 4:25:53 (18,482)
Seear, John 4:19:26 (16,700)
Seebauer, Manfred 2:51:59 (576)
Seebauer, Mark 3:03:41 (1,439)
Seed, David 3:34:29 (5,616)
Seelandt, Frank 3:29:24 (4,777)
Seels, Douglas 4:37:10 (21,355)
Segust, Richard 3:43:06 (7,410)
Sehon, Scot 2:37:42 (138)
Seidel, Mirko 3:48:16 (8,688)
Seifert, Hubert 4:59:23 (26,197)
Seifried, Kai 3:25:31 (4,067)
Seifried, Wolfgang 4:28:16 (19,102)
Seiller, Didier 3:26:31 (4,234)
Seini, Ian 3:35:51 (5,872)
Sekhon, Parwinder 4:36:34 (21,238)
Selby, Darren 4:02:34 (12,669)
Selby, Greg 3:16:15 (2,816)
Selby, Joseph 3:23:48 (3,769)
Selby, Marc 3:31:19 (5,080)
Selby, Martin 5:06:53 (27,279)
Selby, Nick 3:11:34 (2,212)
Selcuk, Miko 4:33:11 (20,397)
Seldon, Keith 3:49:50 (9,137)
Self, Richard 3:55:16 (10,684)
Seller, Paul 3:44:40 (7,839)
Sellers, David 3:47:23 (8,484)
Sellers, James 4:24:49 (18,205)
Sellick, Brian 4:47:44 (23,959)
Sellick, Ken 4:24:20 (18,077)
Sellwood, Guy 3:05:49 (1,620)
Selmes, Colin 5:13:55 (28,179)
Selway, Philip 4:35:33 (20,960)
Selwyn, Raymond 3:09:00 (1,933)
Semeraro, John 5:04:59 (27,017)
Semple, Aidan 3:45:30 (8,044)
Semple, John 3:59:01 (11,810)
Senda, Keizo 5:28:37 (29,666)
Senior, Ian 4:35:12 (20,881)
Senior, Michael 3:06:04 (1,647)
Sentner, Robert 4:57:48 (25,915)
Sercombe, Stephen 3:47:50 (8,597)
Serenelli, Stephen 3:49:01 (8,902)
Seretis, Spiro 6:37:35 (32,407)
Serey, Guillaume 3:53:31 (10,150)
Sergeant, Graeme 3:12:25 (2,348)
Sergeant, Kevin 3:35:08 (5,740)
Serjeant, James 4:32:21 (20,173)
Serneels, Lucien 3:19:26 (3,193)
Serra, Gerolamo 4:44:51 (23,257)
Serrano, Alexandre 3:40:04 (6,752)
Servaes, Michael 4:37:38 (21,474)
Severs, James 4:39:57 (22,090)
Severs, Jonathan 4:49:39 (24,350)
Seward, Ed 3:38:36 (6,450)
Sewell, Andrew 3:08:02 (1,807)
Sewell, Ian 4:10:54 (14,605)
Sewell, Jonathan 5:11:21 (27,860)
Sewell, Kevin 4:22:05 (17,419)
Sewell, Liam 4:58:41 (26,074)
Sewell, Peter 4:54:50 (25,349)
Sewell, Richard 3:24:11 (3,857)
Sewell, Robert 3:25:53 (4,133)
Sexton, John 4:39:02 (21,854)
Sexton, Paul 4:24:44 (18,182)
Seymoor, Mark 5:18:13 (28,693)
Seymour, Andrew 3:22:39 (3,598)
Seymour, Mark 5:27:33 (29,580)
Seymour, Peter 3:49:57 (9,163)
Sgariglia, Marino 4:00:14 (12,140)
Shaarup, Nils 4:22:00 (17,393)
Shachar, Tal 3:05:52 (1,627)
Shackleton, John 4:10:26 (14,494)
Shackleton, Peter 4:28:13 (19,088)
Shackleton, Stephen 7:00:43 (32,634)
Shadbolt, Oliver 3:11:56 (2,262)
Shadie, Damian 6:36:08 (32,374)
Shaffer, Robert 5:33:05 (30,034)
Shaffner, Philip 3:59:22 (11,906)
Shah, Amit 4:31:12 (19,883)
Shah, Andrew 4:02:45 (12,713)
Shah, Harshad 5:58:24 (31,492)
Shah, Jitu 5:30:56 (29,860)
Shah, Sanjay 4:17:41 (16,288)
Shah, Sanjay 5:39:10 (30,481)
Shah, Shamin 4:20:34 (17,014)
Shah, Vijay 4:34:49 (20,777)
Shah, Vishal 5:32:13 (29,971)
Shah, Yashovardhan 4:27:39 (18,951)
Shaikh, Nadeem 3:14:13 (2,581)
Shailes, Joseph 3:23:44 (3,764)
Shakeshaft, Andrew 2:57:47 (986)
Shakesheaf, Michael 4:37:39 (21,477)
Shan, Barry 3:26:12 (4,187)
Shankar, Oma 5:41:46 (30,669)
Shanley, Paul 4:44:52 (23,263)
Shanley, William 2:45:43 (322)
Shannon, Anthony 4:17:30 (16,245)
Shannon, David 3:43:49 (7,612)
Shannon, Philip 4:42:05 (22,629)
Shannon, Robert 2:51:09 (540)
Shapira, Haggai 4:26:52 (18,753)
Shapland, John 3:09:36 (2,000)

Shapley, Roger.................4:47:53 (24,002)
Shard, Norman.................3:15:37 (2,738)
Sharkey, Jonathan 3:10:39 (2,117)
Sharkey, Seamus...............4:22:29 (17,541)
Sharkey, Thomas...............3:35:41 (5,842)
Sharland, Mick.................3:03:15 (1,396)
Sharland, Roger...............3:39:42 (6,667)
Sharma, Sanjai.................3:15:32 (2,726)
Sharma, Sushil.................4:55:36 (25,493)
Sharman, Charlie..............4:06:21 (13,529)
Sharman, Michael..............5:07:47 (27,404)
Sharman, Nicholas.............3:53:17 (10,075)
Sharman, Paul.................3:23:34 (3,736)
Sharp, Aaron 4:10:57 (14,623)
Sharp, Anthony................5:39:17 (30,488)
Sharp, Ben....................3:39:12 (6,567)
Sharp, David..................5:03:09 (26,773)
Sharp, Duncan.................4:58:28 (26,027)
Sharp, Edward.................4:29:56 (19,581)
Sharp, Geoff..................3:50:11 (9,210)
Sharp, Ian....................3:51:07 (9,463)
Sharp, Jason..................3:51:53 (9,646)
Sharp, Jeremy.................3:12:46 (2,395)
Sharp, John...................4:21:37 (17,287)
Sharp, Kenneth................4:03:59 (12,985)
Sharp, Malcolm................4:18:31 (16,489)
Sharp, Mick...................4:37:43 (21,493)
Sharp, Richard................3:00:56 (1,222)
Sharp, Robin..................4:31:42 (20,013)
Sharp, Steven.................3:25:12 (4,015)
Sharp, Tim....................5:13:18 (28,114)
Sharp, William................4:22:45 (17,621)
Sharpe, Anthony...............4:22:57 (17,689)
Sharpe, Gary..................5:02:53 (26,725)
Sharpe, Richard 4:14:21 (15,409)
Sharpe, Richard...............4:42:34 (22,742)
Sharpe, Tony..................3:57:58 (11,496)
Sharples, Nick................5:21:23 (29,034)
Sharples, Stephen 4:23:53 (17,946)
Sharples, Stephen 4:36:18 (21,153)
Sharratt, Martin..............4:25:36 (18,418)
Sharrock, Robert..............3:57:12 (11,263)
Shatford, Jeremy..............4:19:40 (16,765)
Shattock, Gerry 4:18:13 (16,417)
Shattock, Simon...............6:17:13 (32,011)
Shatz, Anthony................4:21:38 (17,293)
Shaul, Chris 3:25:17 (4,031)
Shaw, Adam....................6:06:46 (31,747)
Shaw, Alan 4:50:49 (24,572)
Shaw, Alex....................3:38:37 (6,453)
Shaw, Andrew..................3:57:56 (11,483)
Shaw, Ben.....................4:13:14 (15,132)
Shaw, Darren..................4:16:55 (16,095)
Shaw, David...................3:26:33 (4,241)
Shaw, David...................4:03:41 (12,914)
Shaw, David...................4:22:33 (17,560)
Shaw, Donald..................4:36:59 (21,309)
Shaw, Gary....................2:51:54 (573)
Shaw, Gerry...................3:07:05 (1,742)
Shaw, Greg....................4:40:02 (22,117)
Shaw, Jonathan................3:45:10 (7,962)
Shaw, Mark....................4:40:47 (22,304)
Shaw, Matt....................4:14:23 (15,421)
Shaw, Mike....................3:09:57 (2,036)
Shaw, Mike....................3:54:20 (10,409)
Shaw, Neil....................3:19:30 (3,203)
Shaw, Nicholas................4:22:18 (17,476)
Shaw, Nigel...................4:06:16 (13,509)
Shaw, Patrick.................3:55:30 (10,745)
Shaw, Paul....................3:37:19 (6,167)
Shaw, Paul....................3:41:18 (7,030)
Shaw, Peter...................3:04:56 (1,537)
Shaw, Phillip.................4:18:46 (16,538)
Shaw, Phillip.................5:21:50 (29,081)
Shaw, Richard.................4:46:37 (23,718)
Shaw, Richard.................5:35:36 (30,239)
Shaw, Simon...................4:22:48 (17,639)
Shaw, Stuart..................2:40:40 (197)
Shaw, Stuart..................3:30:50 (4,994)
Shaw, Timothy.................5:03:06 (26,762)
Shea, Nicholas................3:57:16 (11,280)
Shea Simonds, Duncan..........3:20:24 (3,299)
Shead, Michael................4:34:44 (20,758)

Sheaf, John 6:13:33 (31,916)
Sheahan, John.................3:51:46 (9,616)
Sheal, Stephen 4:23:37 (17,851)
Shealy, Tommy.................4:49:51 (24,395)
Sheard, Jeremy................4:22:30 (17,545)
Sheard, Nicholas..............3:19:02 (3,140)
Shearman, Anthony.............5:29:50 (29,766)
Shearn, Nick..................3:53:05 (10,013)
Shears, Joe...................4:18:04 (16,383)
Shears, Keith.................5:28:45 (29,677)
Shears, Roderick 4:48:07 (24,058)
Sheath, Kevin.................4:40:01 (22,109)
Shed, Nigel...................4:42:57 (22,827)
Sheehan, David................4:05:25 (13,305)
Sheehan, David................4:19:07 (16,621)
Sheehan, Eamon................4:15:56 (15,824)
Sheehan, Jonathan.............3:35:45 (5,855)
Sheehan, Martin...............3:44:41 (7,848)
Sheehan, Matthew..............3:23:37 (3,745)
Sheehan, Nicholas.............4:39:47 (22,051)
Sheehan, Richard..............5:11:39 (27,901)
Sheehy, Leigh 4:18:10 (16,404)
Sheehy, Michael...............3:36:26 (6,012)
Sheen, Graham 4:41:58 (22,601)
Sheern, Martin................3:58:07 (11,550)
Sheffield, Andrew.............5:24:56 (29,362)
Sheibani, Sahand 4:35:33 (20,960)
Sheikh, Nabil.................4:48:21 (24,094)
Sheker, Jim 3:20:32 (3,319)
Shekle, Raymond 6:23:05 (32,151)
Shelbourne, Stephen 3:57:24 (11,325)
Sheldon, Anthony..............2:57:06 (923)
Sheldon, Ian..................5:23:37 (29,236)
Shellard, Michael 3:51:56 (9,657)
Shelley, Alexander............6:38:48 (32,419)
Shelley, Arnot................4:46:52 (23,777)
Shellito, David 5:15:45 (28,402)
Shelly, Simon 4:42:51 (22,801)
Shelswell, Richard............4:07:27 (13,788)
Shelton, Andrew...............2:55:57 (825)
Shelton, David................3:16:37 (2,855)
Shenstone, Ian 3:34:54 (5,695)
Shephard, David...............3:08:06 (1,814)
Shepheard, Peter 5:15:58 (28,440)
Shepherd, Adam 4:05:46 (13,386)
Shepherd, Ben 3:35:53 (5,880)
Shepherd, Ben 4:16:17 (15,909)
Shepherd, David 5:07:09 (27,321)
Shepherd, Paul................4:30:47 (19,780)
Shepherd, Ralph...............5:55:23 (31,370)
Shepherd, Terence.............3:21:00 (3,364)
Shepherd, Warren..............4:37:45 (21,503)
Shepley, Sebastian 2:28:30 (51)
Sheppard, David...............4:10:18 (14,460)
Sheppard, Denis 4:43:04 (22,856)
Sheppard, Michael.............5:11:23 (27,866)
Sheppard, Stephen 5:00:25 (26,360)
Sheppard, Steve...............5:14:08 (28,208)
Sher, Cecil...................5:04:05 (26,895)
Sher, David...................4:26:07 (18,556)
Sheridan, Chris 3:59:55 (12,063)
Sheridan, David...............3:49:30 (9,041)
Sheridan, Jonathan 3:36:41 (6,055)
Sheridan, Thomas..............3:07:23 (1,761)
Sheridan, Tony................3:45:08 (7,957)
Sherlock, Keith...............3:23:56 (3,807)
Sherman, Danny................4:22:55 (17,677)
Sherman, Elliot...............3:04:48 (1,524)
Sherman, Wiliam...............3:26:41 (4,269)
Sherratt, Craig...............4:10:22 (14,479)
Sherriff, John................4:21:37 (17,287)
Sherriff, Mark................2:54:46 (726)
Sherrington, Paul.............3:58:46 (11,722)
Shervington, Michael..........3:27:11 (4,359)
Sherwin, Gregory 4:01:05 (12,336)
Sherwood, Colin 4:43:53 (23,036)
Sherwood, Roland..............4:01:28 (12,430)
Shewan, Garry.................5:36:00 (30,271)
Shield, Jerry.................3:13:18 (2,473)
Shields, Christopher 4:25:06 (18,286)
Shields, Dennis...............4:12:35 (14,992)
Shields, Gordon...............3:33:01 (5,354)
Shields, John 3:17:38 (2,967)

Shields, John 4:15:12 (15,621)
Shier, Carl...................4:35:37 (20,993)
Shilland, David...............4:07:21 (13,761)
Shillcutt, Samuel.............3:50:26 (9,284)
Shilling, Michael.............3:04:06 (1,475)
Shilton, Colin 3:03:04 (1,378)
Shilvock, Matthew.............4:13:56 (15,291)
Shimmin, Greg.................3:50:50 (9,382)
Shimura, Kira.................4:15:40 (15,747)
Shinnick, Mathis..............4:04:30 (13,088)
Shipley, David................4:55:11 (25,417)
Shipley, Malcolm..............3:53:26 (10,116)
Shipman, John.................5:16:56 (28,547)
Shipton, Brian................5:01:01 (26,450)
Shipton, Mark.................3:32:08 (5,211)
Shirkie, Alan.................4:56:03 (25,594)
Shirley, Peter................3:27:03 (4,339)
Shoare, David.................4:44:54 (23,271)
Shoebridge, Tony..............3:59:17 (11,878)
Shoesmith, Edward 3:09:20 (1,973)
Shone, Grahame 2:59:18 (1,116)
Shooter, Robert...............4:47:36 (23,925)
Shore, Andrew.................4:34:48 (20,773)
Shore, Harry..................4:55:21 (25,447)
Shore, Richard 3:56:43 (11,113)
Shore, Roger..................5:17:45 (28,646)
Shorrock, Lee.................6:11:03 (31,861)
Shorrocks, David 3:49:37 (9,074)
Short, Arthur.................3:05:31 (1,592)
Short, Dominik................5:11:21 (27,860)
Short, Edward.................2:59:29 (1,132)
Short, Garry..................3:03:05 (1,379)
Shortt, Martin................4:29:52 (19,560)
Shosarski, Christopher........6:26:00 (32,203)
Shotton, Neil.................4:42:30 (22,725)
Shotton, Richard..............3:39:36 (6,646)
Shoults, Will.................3:17:22 (2,943)
Shout, Anoy...................4:08:02 (13,923)
Shreeve, Simon 4:06:36 (13,586)
Shrubsall, James 3:40:53 (6,937)
Shuck, Stephen................3:27:51 (4,492)
Shuckard, Ronald 3:52:05 (9,715)
Shucksmith, David 4:05:32 (13,335)
Shucksmith, James 4:14:42 (15,495)
Shugar, Nicolas...............4:19:47 (16,803)
Shujja-Ud-Din, Omar 3:59:09 (11,841)
Shuker, John..................4:38:00 (21,573)
Shuker, Richard...............3:34:55 (5,700)
Shukla, Nitin.................4:06:14 (13,498)
Shuter, Peter.................5:20:45 (28,968)
Shutte, Sandro................4:32:33 (20,228)
Shuttle, David................5:29:35 (29,745)
Siapatis, John................6:05:04 (31,694)
Sibbering, Ken................4:31:53 (20,053)
Siboulotte, Christophe........3:55:30 (10,745)
Sibun, Andrew.................4:01:25 (12,421)
Sidarow, Yvan.................4:01:04 (12,330)
Siddall, Chris................5:50:18 (31,152)
Siddall, Stuart...............4:06:46 (13,624)
Sidders, Stuart...............5:47:28 (31,016)
Siddle, Garry.................4:40:28 (22,225)
Siddle, Paul..................4:15:44 (15,764)
Siddon, Tony..................3:35:05 (5,725)
Siddon, Tony..................4:25:24 (18,362)
Siddons, Barrie...............3:55:33 (10,767)
Sidebotham, John 3:02:04 (1,307)
Siderfin, Robert..............4:44:55 (23,274)
Sidgwick, David...............3:31:24 (5,092)
Sidi-Moussa, Abdelkader 3:13:58 (2,554)
Sidwick, Bob 3:19:01 (3,135)
Siegel, Norbert...............2:56:28 (869)
Sieger, Franz.................4:15:42 (15,755)
Sierra, Penafiel..............5:31:05 (29,870)
Sierra-Lopez, José............4:07:26 (13,783)
Sievewright, Alan.............3:15:42 (2,754)
Siewertsen, George 4:42:27 (22,711)
Signerin, François............3:52:38 (9,877)
Silk, Alan....................4:57:44 (25,904)
Silk, Jonathan................4:32:31 (20,219)
Sillers, Jonny................4:19:12 (16,646)
Sillett, Ian..................4:13:43 (15,242)
Sillitoe, Michael.............3:27:47 (4,474)
Sills, Robin..................4:30:29 (19,707)

Silmon, Mark	4:12:49 (15,041)
Silver, Anthony	4:36:07 (21,106)
Silver, Matthew	3:48:44 (8,822)
Silver, Michael	3:53:13 (10,048)
Silver, Sean	5:33:54 (30,101)
Silverthorn, Kevin	3:52:05 (9,715)
Silverthorn, Lee	5:03:28 (26,819)
Silvester, Robin	3:35:41 (5,842)
Silvestro, Enzo	3:34:12 (5,564)
Sim, Derek	3:59:25 (11,924)
Simcott, Andrew	3:07:35 (1,774)
Simcox, Ean	4:42:50 (22,799)
Simcox, Mark	3:04:15 (1,487)
Simkins, Edward	4:19:06 (16,617)
Simm, Terry	3:23:13 (3,680)
Simmonds, Alan	4:27:25 (18,893)
Simmonds, Christopher	4:04:36 (13,115)
Simmonds, Guy	5:07:56 (27,428)
Simmonds, Richard	3:51:58 (9,674)
Simmonds, Richard	4:33:46 (20,528)
Simmons, Andrew	5:24:09 (29,291)
Simmons, David	3:06:37 (1,701)
Simmons, Keith	4:30:40 (19,750)
Simmons, Keith	5:05:31 (27,086)
Simmons, Mark	4:45:35 (23,467)
Simmons, Nolan	5:04:45 (26,987)
Simmons, Steven	3:37:21 (6,176)
Simmons, Tom	4:30:33 (19,721)
Simms, Andrew	3:55:02 (10,603)
Simms, Michael	4:41:39 (22,513)
Simms, Peter	6:11:24 (31,868)
Simms, William	5:36:55 (30,344)
Simnett, John	3:30:47 (4,990)
Simon, Alberto	3:29:54 (4,858)
Simon, Jonathan	4:13:29 (15,183)
Simonet, Paul	4:09:35 (14,287)
Simonet, Philippe	3:21:29 (3,434)
Simons, John	4:01:24 (12,417)
Simpkin, David	5:25:18 (29,385)
Simpkins, Lee	4:00:27 (12,179)
Simpkins, Rick	4:28:43 (19,231)
Simpkins, Vaughan	4:44:53 (23,266)
Simpson, Andrew	4:57:45 (25,907)
Simpson, Brian	4:48:38 (24,152)
Simpson, Colin	2:57:41 (979)
Simpson, David	3:16:07 (2,799)
Simpson, David	3:53:56 (10,287)
Simpson, David	3:58:33 (11,660)
Simpson, David	4:13:23 (15,162)
Simpson, David	4:26:25 (18,629)
Simpson, David	6:43:03 (32,458)
Simpson, Dennis	4:39:36 (21,994)
Simpson, Donald	5:08:52 (27,546)
Simpson, Gareth	3:12:19 (2,332)
Simpson, Gary	3:22:01 (3,528)
Simpson, George	3:10:57 (2,150)
Simpson, Gordon	4:51:08 (24,635)
Simpson, Hugh	3:58:57 (11,779)
Simpson, Iain	3:53:25 (10,113)
Simpson, Jeremy	3:29:30 (4,795)
Simpson, John	4:39:56 (22,088)
Simpson, John	6:20:49 (32,099)
Simpson, Kim	4:04:01 (12,993)
Simpson, Martin	4:44:04 (23,080)
Simpson, Matthew	4:08:25 (13,997)
Simpson, Michael	3:45:29 (8,039)
Simpson, Michael	4:35:04 (20,846)
Simpson, Richard	3:53:17 (10,075)
Simpson, Robert	3:13:40 (2,526)
Simpson, Robert	3:29:02 (4,698)
Simpson, Russell	5:09:13 (27,597)
Simpson, Scott	4:48:47 (24,190)
Simpson, Stewart	5:38:08 (30,421)
Simpson, Timothy	4:30:42 (19,755)
Simpson, Tom	4:19:16 (16,657)
Simpson, Wayne	4:31:16 (19,892)
Sims, Daniel	4:14:23 (15,421)
Sims, Daniel	5:27:52 (29,606)
Sims, Paul	7:13:05 (32,725)
Sims, Ray	4:27:41 (18,959)
Sims, Stuart	4:03:15 (12,827)
Sims, Terence	4:29:50 (19,551)
Simson, Matthew	4:34:30 (20,700)
Sinadino, Alex	5:57:34 (31,460)
Sincalir, Steven	4:24:09 (18,023)
Sinclair, Alastair	3:17:24 (2,949)
Sinclair, Charles	4:42:44 (22,775)
Sinclair, Daniel	4:56:20 (25,667)
Sinclair, Donald	3:37:37 (6,246)
Sinclair, Graeme	5:33:55 (30,103)
Sinclair, James	4:45:41 (23,488)
Sinclair, Kevin	4:28:04 (19,048)
Sinclair, Malcolm	2:59:29 (1,132)
Sinclair, Michael	4:01:06 (12,337)
Sinclair, Nigel	3:12:09 (2,303)
Sinclair, Robert	3:58:24 (11,621)
Sinclair, Simon	3:43:46 (7,591)
Sinclair, Terence	3:23:21 (3,703)
Sinclair, Thomas	4:03:30 (12,881)
Sinclair, Thomas	4:50:00 (24,423)
Sinden, Matthew	4:43:07 (22,871)
Sinfield, Robert	5:22:41 (29,151)
Singer, Gareth	4:28:32 (19,178)
Singer, Stuart	3:50:21 (9,263)
Singh, Amrik	5:21:26 (29,039)
Singh, Amritpal	4:42:18 (22,671)
Singh, Bill	5:11:21 (27,860)
Singh, Fauja	6:45:31 (32,492)
Singh, George	4:24:44 (18,182)
Singh, Harbagh	3:53:17 (10,075)
Singh, Harmander	5:52:59 (31,274)
Singh, Ranjit	5:34:58 (30,183)
Singh, Ravindra	4:30:11 (19,648)
Singh, Resham	3:39:14 (6,579)
Singh, Steven	3:46:11 (8,196)
Singh, Surinder	4:54:47 (25,337)
Singleton, Andrew	5:35:34 (30,236)
Singleton, David	3:25:37 (4,085)
Singleton, Jonathan	4:55:16 (25,432)
Singleton, Joseph	4:25:36 (18,418)
Singleton, Mark	5:07:19 (27,346)
Sinik, John	3:13:45 (2,538)
Sinnott, David	3:35:05 (5,725)
Sinnott, Stephen	2:48:13 (416)
Sirett, John	4:01:46 (12,511)
Sirett, Michael	3:18:05 (3,018)
Sirett, Paul	4:22:59 (17,702)
Sironik, Ndorriany	4:14:40 (15,487)
Sirrell, Brett	3:25:58 (4,149)
Sirs, Nicholas	2:37:21 (130)
Sissens, David	5:34:59 (30,186)
Sisson, Gary	4:03:00 (12,775)
Siu, Jason	5:46:48 (30,979)
Sivewright, David	3:13:09 (2,456)
Siviter, Mike	4:45:34 (23,461)
Sivry, Eric	4:29:25 (19,440)
Sivyer, Stephen	4:53:58 (25,179)
Sjoen, Jan	3:22:44 (3,621)
Skailes, Andrew	2:45:48 (323)
Skattkjaer, Fredrik	2:59:08 (1,107)
Skeet, John	3:11:13 (2,177)
Skegg, Stephen	3:33:56 (5,504)
Skelly, Daniel	3:25:32 (4,070)
Skelton, Andy	4:31:28 (19,953)
Skelton, Colin	4:00:05 (12,104)
Skelton, Nick	4:57:52 (25,925)
Skelton, Raymond	2:57:40 (977)
Skelton, Wayne	4:34:13 (20,631)
Skene, Richard	4:59:52 (26,284)
Skett, Mark	4:33:59 (20,576)
Skevington, John	3:29:18 (4,752)
Skidmore, Guy	4:35:09 (20,862)
Skidmore, Jonathan	3:48:55 (8,873)
Skidmore, Paul	4:13:58 (15,301)
Skillborg, Hans	4:30:58 (19,823)
Skimming, James	6:33:26 (32,331)
Skingley, Daniel	5:10:02 (27,693)
Skingley, Ian	3:13:19 (2,476)
Skinner, Antony	3:50:44 (9,356)
Skinner, David	3:57:44 (11,434)
Skinner, James	3:38:40 (6,468)
Skinner, John	4:33:39 (20,506)
Skinner, John	6:18:15 (32,041)
Skinner, Martyn	4:27:19 (18,869)
Skinner, Matthew	3:23:13 (3,680)
Skinner, Matthew	4:51:34 (24,714)
Skinner, Neil	4:20:54 (17,086)
Skinner, Steve	5:15:40 (28,390)
Skinner, Timothy	4:37:09 (21,348)
Skipper, Michael	4:19:52 (16,827)
Skipworth, Gary	4:06:11 (13,484)
Skitt, Richard	6:22:43 (32,143)
Skivington, Bernard	4:53:05 (24,994)
Skjelbred, Harald	4:49:07 (24,263)
Skjelbred, Karl	4:43:49 (23,022)
Skov, Henrik	2:45:58 (326)
Skrzypecki, Anthony	3:24:19 (3,887)
Skuse, Geraint	3:30:21 (4,920)
Skwara, Stefan	3:30:59 (5,022)
Slabber, Adriaan	4:37:44 (21,499)
Slack, Gordon	3:39:51 (6,701)
Slack, Jonathan	3:49:15 (8,953)
Slack, Martin	3:45:01 (7,929)
Sladdin, James	5:25:52 (29,434)
Slade, Michael	4:20:10 (16,907)
Slade, Paul	3:40:02 (6,739)
Slade, Peter	3:53:58 (10,299)
Slade, Richard	4:03:37 (12,904)
Slade, Russell	4:21:01 (17,117)
Slade, Stephen	4:15:09 (15,604)
Slade, Stephen	4:34:20 (20,654)
Slagel, Craig	3:49:13 (8,946)
Slaney, Mark	3:22:08 (3,542)
Slate, Darren	4:49:46 (24,372)
Slater, Andrew	3:48:10 (8,665)
Slater, Ben	5:59:08 (31,518)
Slater, David	3:25:03 (3,993)
Slater, Deryck	4:37:41 (21,488)
Slater, Graham	4:40:23 (22,209)
Slater, John	3:53:33 (10,165)
Slater, John	4:31:07 (19,860)
Slater, John	5:35:57 (30,264)
Slater, John	5:57:28 (31,455)
Slater, Justin	4:23:32 (17,834)
Slater, Karl	3:59:27 (11,930)
Slater, Keith	3:55:49 (10,844)
Slater, Mark	4:28:12 (19,081)
Slater, Peter	3:52:02 (9,700)
Slater, Peter	6:01:02 (31,578)
Slater, Philip	3:32:50 (5,327)
Slater, William	5:15:25 (28,350)
Slatford, Paul	4:41:40 (22,519)
Slator, Tim	3:52:33 (9,858)
Slatter, Tim	5:21:02 (28,994)
Slattery, Stephen	3:51:27 (9,532)
Slaven, Richard	4:22:59 (17,702)
Slaymaker, Rob	4:57:48 (25,915)
Slayne, Andrew	4:27:03 (18,805)
Sleap, Jason	4:35:10 (20,866)
Sleath, Tim	4:13:51 (15,272)
Slee, Barrie	3:25:55 (4,140)
Sleep, Christopher	4:08:27 (14,003)
Slegg, Christopher	4:07:47 (13,866)
Sleightholme, Jon	5:12:11 (27,970)
Slemko, Terry	4:30:19 (19,676)
Sletten, Roald	4:31:51 (20,040)
Slevin, Martin	2:43:49 (263)
Slimani, Abdelah	2:47:20 (373)
Slinger, Andrew	3:59:07 (11,833)
Sloan, Brian	4:31:43 (20,015)
Sloan, Christopher	4:42:30 (22,725)
Sloan, Ian	4:12:55 (15,066)
Sloan, Ian	5:22:58 (29,174)
Sloan, Jonathan	4:08:01 (13,916)
Sloan, Mathew	4:06:11 (13,484)
Sloan, Ron	3:31:28 (5,102)
Sloane, Jeffrey	4:20:14 (16,922)
Sloane, Scott	4:12:52 (15,054)
Sloman, Alan	3:49:27 (9,027)
Sloper, Chris	4:41:31 (22,479)
Slow, Gareth	3:51:45 (9,610)
Slowly, Daniel	4:25:18 (18,333)
Sluman, Jon	4:11:47 (14,814)
Slyfield, Edward	3:15:04 (2,670)
Smailes, Michael	3:42:22 (7,252)
Smaje, Benjamin	4:51:20 (24,671)
Smales, Keith	3:52:17 (9,779)
Small, Anthony	4:28:47 (19,252)
Small, Iain	4:03:37 (12,904)

Small, James	4:57:39	(25,887)
Small, Jamieson	3:45:47	(8,110)
Smalley, Alan	4:19:02	(16,602)
Smallman, Christopher	3:22:58	(3,653)
Smart, Anthony	3:55:51	(10,855)
Smart, Chris	3:55:51	(10,855)
Smart, Darren	4:33:52	(20,551)
Smart, David	4:17:08	(16,154)
Smart, David	4:32:39	(20,261)
Smart, Grant	5:08:12	(27,454)
Smart, Ian	4:12:02	(14,871)
Smart, Jonathan	4:25:22	(18,355)
Smart, Kevin	3:08:28	(1,866)
Smart, Neil	6:36:20	(32,377)
Smart, Robert	3:46:28	(8,269)
Smart, Simon	4:19:18	(16,667)
Smeaton, Barry	5:33:23	(30,061)
Smeddle, Jeremy	4:11:04	(14,651)
Smedley, Andrew	5:02:03	(26,608)
Smee, Tim	3:32:24	(5,252)
Smeeth, Stephen	3:57:28	(11,350)
Smelt, David	4:44:55	(23,274)
Smethurst, Andrew	4:44:44	(23,230)
Smiddy, Andrew	4:00:44	(12,240)
Smillie, Darren	4:23:51	(17,928)
Smit, Stephan	4:23:32	(17,834)
Smith, Adrain	5:45:37	(30,916)
Smith, Adrian	4:00:29	(12,184)
Smith, Alan	3:39:28	(6,617)
Smith, Alan	4:36:17	(21,147)
Smith, Alexander	5:17:46	(28,647)
Smith, Alexander	5:24:23	(29,313)
Smith, Alun	3:57:49	(11,455)
Smith, André	4:07:20	(13,754)
Smith, Andrew	3:08:15	(1,831)
Smith, Andrew	3:26:52	(4,303)
Smith, Andrew	3:35:45	(5,855)
Smith, Andrew	3:43:30	(7,525)
Smith, Andrew	3:50:21	(9,263)
Smith, Andrew	3:54:06	(10,343)
Smith, Andrew	4:10:17	(14,456)
Smith, Andrew	4:12:14	(14,909)
Smith, Andrew	4:15:11	(15,614)
Smith, Andrew	4:15:54	(15,810)
Smith, Andrew	4:23:28	(17,817)
Smith, Andrew	4:26:17	(18,597)
Smith, Andrew	4:29:10	(19,373)
Smith, Andrew	4:35:41	(21,011)
Smith, Andrew	4:40:19	(22,187)
Smith, Andrew	4:44:41	(23,214)
Smith, Andrew	5:37:19	(30,372)
Smith, Anthony	3:36:24	(6,004)
Smith, Anthony	4:02:35	(12,675)
Smith, Anthony	4:19:04	(16,610)
Smith, Anthony	4:51:58	(24,778)
Smith, Ashley	4:26:47	(18,739)
Smith, Barry	4:00:35	(12,203)
Smith, Barry	4:11:49	(14,822)
Smith, Barry	5:23:26	(29,213)
Smith, Barry	5:33:27	(30,069)
Smith, Ben	3:46:25	(8,258)
Smith, Brian	3:19:19	(3,173)
Smith, Chris	3:34:20	(5,587)
Smith, Christian	4:10:27	(14,497)
Smith, Christopher	3:47:43	(8,565)
Smith, Christopher	3:55:22	(10,714)
Smith, Christopher	7:02:58	(32,660)
Smith, Cliff	3:15:46	(2,765)
Smith, Clifford	4:13:42	(15,232)
Smith, Clive	5:18:45	(28,750)
Smith, Colin	3:58:04	(11,531)
Smith, Colin	4:00:56	(12,289)
Smith, Colin	4:17:00	(16,116)
Smith, Colin	4:28:57	(19,309)
Smith, Colin	4:34:54	(20,803)
Smith, Dale	4:32:53	(20,329)
Smith, Dan	4:05:02	(13,216)
Smith, Daniel	3:40:06	(6,762)
Smith, Darios	4:14:01	(15,316)
Smith, Darren	4:55:08	(25,408)
Smith, David	3:25:14	(4,021)
Smith, David	3:37:31	(6,223)
Smith, David	3:41:44	(7,102)
Smith, David	3:43:38	(7,559)
Smith, David	3:43:52	(7,625)
Smith, David	4:03:32	(12,888)
Smith, David	4:54:08	(25,208)
Smith, David	5:37:05	(30,354)
Smith, David	5:40:31	(30,586)
Smith, Dean	4:06:56	(13,657)
Smith, Derek	3:49:50	(9,137)
Smith, Derek	5:11:19	(27,856)
Smith, Douglas	4:14:35	(15,467)
Smith, Duncan	4:49:17	(24,286)
Smith, Duncan	4:50:52	(24,586)
Smith, Edwin	3:39:10	(6,559)
Smith, Erik	3:29:09	(4,720)
Smith, Francis	4:35:54	(21,049)
Smith, Gareth	4:10:00	(14,385)
Smith, Gary	3:57:55	(11,480)
Smith, Gary	4:10:33	(14,523)
Smith, Gary	5:55:14	(31,361)
Smith, Geoff	4:56:19	(25,658)
Smith, Gerald	3:07:35	(1,774)
Smith, Gerry	2:46:37	(344)
Smith, Glen	4:46:01	(23,569)
Smith, Glynn	3:30:15	(4,901)
Smith, Gordon	4:27:48	(18,983)
Smith, Graham	4:00:43	(12,233)
Smith, Graham	4:06:16	(13,509)
Smith, Graham	4:11:45	(14,806)
Smith, Graham	4:41:15	(22,413)
Smith, Graham	4:48:42	(24,168)
Smith, Iain	3:58:21	(11,601)
Smith, Ian	2:47:45	(391)
Smith, Ian	3:09:14	(1,956)
Smith, Ian	4:00:42	(12,227)
Smith, Ian	4:02:32	(12,663)
Smith, Ian	4:37:37	(21,471)
Smith, Jake	3:56:55	(11,181)
Smith, James	3:09:10	(1,948)
Smith, James	3:35:05	(5,725)
Smith, James	3:36:54	(6,093)
Smith, James	3:49:18	(8,972)
Smith, James	4:25:35	(18,410)
Smith, James	5:20:31	(28,945)
Smith, Jamie	3:22:23	(3,569)
Smith, Jason	3:30:46	(4,985)
Smith, Jason	4:10:58	(14,625)
Smith, Jason	4:18:51	(16,558)
Smith, Jeffrey	5:13:47	(28,168)
Smith, Jeremy	3:40:08	(6,771)
Smith, Jeremy	5:41:08	(30,629)
Smith, Jim	4:36:09	(21,121)
Smith, John	3:46:04	(8,172)
Smith, John	3:52:44	(9,905)
Smith, John	4:08:39	(14,066)
Smith, John	4:13:42	(15,232)
Smith, John	4:30:43	(19,764)
Smith, John	5:09:04	(27,577)
Smith, Jonathan	3:21:26	(3,425)
Smith, Jonathan	3:43:03	(7,400)
Smith, Jonathan	3:56:12	(10,964)
Smith, Jonathan	3:59:18	(11,885)
Smith, Jonathan	4:14:51	(15,540)
Smith, Joseph	3:31:10	(5,061)
Smith, Josh	4:40:22	(22,207)
Smith, Julisn	3:30:59	(5,022)
Smith, Kenny	6:11:49	(31,878)
Smith, Kevin	3:52:43	(9,897)
Smith, Kevin	3:54:48	(10,541)
Smith, Lee	4:00:40	(12,216)
Smith, Liam	3:57:32	(11,372)
Smith, Malcolm	3:45:58	(8,153)
Smith, Mark	3:12:36	(2,373)
Smith, Mark	3:42:27	(7,276)
Smith, Mark	3:47:28	(8,503)
Smith, Mark	3:54:01	(10,314)
Smith, Mark	3:56:01	(10,902)
Smith, Mark	4:22:00	(17,393)
Smith, Mark	4:35:19	(20,905)
Smith, Mark	5:05:35	(27,095)
Smith, Marshall	5:45:38	(30,918)
Smith, Martin	4:16:34	(15,996)
Smith, Martin	4:34:56	(20,814)
Smith, Martin	5:06:04	(27,168)
Smith, Matthew	2:48:25	(424)
Smith, Matthew	2:51:42	(569)
Smith, Michael	2:29:02	(58)
Smith, Michael	3:15:35	(2,733)
Smith, Michael	3:39:00	(6,523)
Smith, Michael	3:46:57	(8,373)
Smith, Michael	4:05:07	(13,235)
Smith, Michael	4:06:39	(13,601)
Smith, Michael	4:28:01	(19,038)
Smith, Neil	3:59:46	(12,013)
Smith, Neil	4:03:27	(12,873)
Smith, Neil	4:22:25	(17,527)
Smith, Neil	4:49:01	(24,237)
Smith, Nicholas	3:30:01	(4,876)
Smith, Nicholas	3:42:13	(7,204)
Smith, Nicholas	4:33:27	(20,452)
Smith, Nicholas	4:46:44	(23,742)
Smith, Nicholas	4:58:20	(26,002)
Smith, Nicholas	5:56:14	(31,409)
Smith, Nigel	4:16:23	(15,945)
Smith, Nigel	4:30:22	(19,687)
Smith, Norman	3:44:42	(7,852)
Smith, Norman	3:57:45	(11,440)
Smith, Owen	4:21:57	(17,376)
Smith, Patrick	5:19:13	(28,796)
Smith, Patrick	6:22:18	(32,130)
Smith, Paul	3:11:28	(2,201)
Smith, Paul	3:21:59	(3,520)
Smith, Paul	3:28:19	(4,571)
Smith, Paul	3:54:54	(10,570)
Smith, Paul	4:20:03	(16,880)
Smith, Paul	4:54:58	(25,373)
Smith, Paul	5:15:00	(28,303)
Smith, Paul	5:28:30	(29,654)
Smith, Peter	3:35:01	(5,714)
Smith, Peter	3:37:49	(6,282)
Smith, Peter	4:08:13	(13,954)
Smith, Peter	5:08:27	(27,492)
Smith, Peter	5:19:18	(28,806)
Smith, Peter	5:31:01	(29,864)
Smith, Peter	5:55:19	(31,366)
Smith, Philip	3:22:50	(3,640)
Smith, Philip	3:42:39	(7,311)
Smith, Philip	3:58:27	(11,635)
Smith, Ray	3:13:28	(2,501)
Smith, Richard	3:51:04	(9,447)
Smith, Richard	4:01:18	(12,391)
Smith, Richard	4:01:56	(12,549)
Smith, Richard	4:08:14	(13,957)
Smith, Richard	4:19:48	(16,804)
Smith, Richard	4:38:13	(21,631)
Smith, Robert	2:48:40	(436)
Smith, Robert	3:01:21	(1,251)
Smith, Robert	3:41:52	(7,125)
Smith, Robert	3:56:06	(10,929)
Smith, Robert	4:14:34	(15,460)
Smith, Robert	4:37:43	(21,493)
Smith, Robert	4:39:15	(21,910)
Smith, Robert	5:03:51	(26,865)
Smith, Robin	4:20:20	(16,951)
Smith, Roderick	4:26:19	(18,601)
Smith, Ronald	5:20:23	(28,926)
Smith, Ross	4:32:08	(20,122)
Smith, Roy	4:23:58	(17,965)
Smith, Royston	3:12:16	(2,324)
Smith, Royston	4:36:21	(21,178)
Smith, Ryan	3:52:15	(9,769)
Smith, Sean	4:24:03	(17,996)
Smith, Shaun	4:08:07	(13,936)
Smith, Sidney	3:45:23	(8,017)
Smith, Simon	3:05:28	(1,586)
Smith, Simon	3:28:36	(4,667)
Smith, Simon	3:44:23	(7,769)
Smith, Simon	4:00:46	(12,249)
Smith, Simon	4:16:17	(15,909)
Smith, Simon	5:51:32	(31,217)
Smith, Stephen	2:38:43	(160)
Smith, Stephen	3:36:21	(5,992)
Smith, Stephen	3:45:13	(7,981)
Smith, Stephen	3:53:01	(9,985)
Smith, Stephen	4:16:14	(15,897)
Smith, Stephen	4:25:46	(18,454)
Smith, Stephen	4:40:41	(22,270)

Smith, Stephen	4:46:54 (23,786)	
Smith, Stephen	6:25:20 (32,187)	
Smith, Steve	3:19:52 (3,238)	
Smith, Steven	3:38:47 (6,482)	
Smith, Steven	3:45:36 (8,071)	
Smith, Stuart	4:10:17 (14,456)	
Smith, Stuart	4:30:54 (19,808)	
Smith, Terrance	3:45:39 (8,082)	
Smith, Thomas	3:12:50 (2,407)	
Smith, Thomas	3:41:29 (7,064)	
Smith, Thomas	4:06:55 (13,651)	
Smith, Timothy	5:06:41 (27,257)	
Smith, Toby	4:47:00 (23,811)	
Smith, Tom	2:59:40 (1,144)	
Smith, Tony	4:04:31 (13,090)	
Smith, Trevor	3:35:10 (5,744)	
Smith, Trevor	3:48:24 (8,721)	
Smith, Trevor	5:03:49 (26,859)	
Smith, Uriah	3:30:33 (4,952)	
Smith, Wayne	3:36:54 (6,093)	
Smith, Wayne	4:42:02 (22,617)	
Smith, William	3:23:27 (3,714)	
Smith, William	3:23:50 (3,776)	
Smith, William	4:00:43 (12,233)	
Smith, William	4:19:29 (16,720)	
Smitham, Kelvin	3:38:15 (6,357)	
Smithson, Ian	3:53:38 (10,190)	
Smithson, James	6:09:31 (31,822)	
Smithson, Martin	4:19:27 (16,708)	
Smithson, Russell	2:46:12 (330)	
Smoughton, David	6:21:05 (32,107)	
Smout, Craig	4:34:31 (20,704)	
Smth, Russell	4:39:57 (22,090)	
Smyth, Gavin	4:51:50 (24,750)	
Smyth, James	5:36:16 (30,293)	
Smyth, Kevin	3:32:27 (5,262)	
Smyth, Michael	3:44:42 (7,852)	
Smythe, Jonathan	3:21:50 (3,491)	
Smythe, Stephen	2:57:49 (988)	
Snailum, Gary	3:50:08 (9,196)	
Snaith, David	3:18:29 (3,072)	
Snape, Carl	3:44:49 (7,892)	
Snary, Martin	4:17:49 (16,329)	
Sneddon, John	3:40:22 (6,828)	
Snelgrove, William	2:49:33 (465)	
Snell, George	3:43:07 (7,418)	
Snell, John	4:58:05 (25,962)	
Snelling, Steve	4:34:34 (20,714)	
Snodgrass, James	2:36:15 (110)	
Snook, Christopher	5:44:00 (30,819)	
Snook, John	4:04:03 (12,998)	
Snook, Peter	4:44:23 (23,149)	
Snook, Steven	3:27:19 (4,379)	
Snooks, Mark	5:19:03 (28,782)	
Snow, Kieron	3:36:04 (5,919)	
Snowball, Derek	4:57:39 (25,887)	
Snowden, Ben	5:06:40 (27,252)	
Snowden, Craig	5:43:09 (30,765)	
Snowden, Phillip	3:56:37 (11,090)	
Snowdon, Brian	4:48:35 (24,146)	
Snowdon, Les	4:16:36 (16,010)	
Snowdon, Rouven	4:29:08 (19,361)	
Snowdon, Tim	4:48:37 (24,149)	
Soane, Anthony	5:23:01 (29,177)	
Sobowale, Junior	6:20:02 (32,086)	
Soenens, Joris	3:41:56 (7,137)	
Soerensen, Stig	3:59:37 (11,973)	
Solan, Kevin	4:15:09 (15,604)	
Solberg, John	3:29:30 (4,795)	
Solenni, Davide	4:15:38 (15,733)	
Soley, David	4:01:35 (12,466)	
Soley, Paul	5:37:12 (30,363)	
Solomons, Alan	3:44:33 (7,811)	
Solomons, Gary	3:55:29 (10,741)	
Solomou, Anthony	5:57:05 (31,444)	
Somers, Alan	3:57:26 (11,339)	
Somerville, Joe	6:26:13 (32,206)	
Somerville, Peter	4:15:19 (15,644)	
Somerville, Simon	3:56:15 (10,978)	
Somes-Charlton, Christopher	4:20:15 (16,926)	
Sommerlad, Michael	6:36:51 (32,392)	
Sommers, Paul	4:40:28 (22,225)	
Sommers, Rupert	3:35:35 (5,822)	

Sommerville, Roger	4:55:49 (25,542)	
Sonander, Johan	4:21:52 (17,359)	
Sonnenstein, Keith	4:34:49 (20,777)	
Soole, Brian	3:06:34 (1,696)	
Soole, Ivor	4:26:12 (18,575)	
Soper, John	6:29:50 (32,272)	
Sore, Mervyn	5:48:45 (31,075)	
Sortino, Mike	4:18:30 (16,486)	
Sossick, Alex	4:37:19 (21,404)	
Soulsby, Martin	4:18:53 (16,566)	
Sousa, Luis	2:59:07 (1,106)	
Soustrade, Jacques	4:12:07 (14,885)	
South, Stewart	4:18:46 (16,538)	
Southcott, Mark	5:35:19 (30,210)	
Southern, Anthony	4:22:27 (17,535)	
Southern, Neil	3:54:09 (10,361)	
Southerton, Clive	4:00:24 (12,165)	
Southgate, Edward	4:18:33 (16,497)	
Southwell, David	3:58:23 (11,614)	
Southwell, Geoffrey	4:54:43 (25,328)	
Southwell, Niall	4:05:32 (13,335)	
Southwick, Andrew	4:21:48 (17,335)	
Southworth, Anthony	4:33:41 (20,513)	
Sovegjarto, Peter	3:33:53 (5,493)	
Sovelet, Frederic	4:02:31 (12,659)	
Soverini, Stefano	3:33:21 (5,409)	
Sovocool, John	3:01:02 (1,227)	
Sowden, Richard	3:27:47 (4,474)	
Sowery, Andrew	2:40:18 (190)	
Spackman, Ian	5:20:47 (28,974)	
Spaety, Eric	3:30:53 (5,006)	
Spagnol, Jean	4:48:41 (24,165)	
Spagnol, Serge	4:09:23 (14,245)	
Spalding, Ben	3:50:48 (9,377)	
Spalding, David	4:01:48 (12,522)	
Spanke, Karl	4:53:53 (25,141)	
Sparey, Kevin	2:56:49 (903)	
Spark, Ronald	3:23:37 (3,745)	
Sparke, Kevin	4:14:19 (15,398)	
Sparke, Paul	5:39:50 (30,537)	
Sparkes, Malcolm	5:43:21 (30,779)	
Sparks, Chris	4:28:59 (19,318)	
Sparks, David	3:36:22 (5,996)	
Sparks, Ian	4:52:29 (24,870)	
Sparks, Steve	3:56:21 (11,003)	
Sparrow, Nigel	4:23:40 (17,864)	
Sparrow, Roger	3:59:59 (12,080)	
Sparsis, Andrew	7:00:14 (32,629)	
Spaul, Graham	5:30:55 (29,859)	
Speadborough, David	5:28:39 (29,670)	
Speake, Doug	2:54:57 (738)	
Speake, Malcolm	4:07:55 (13,895)	
Speake, Peter	2:47:34 (383)	
Speake, Williams	2:26:47 (44)	
Spear, David	3:48:05 (8,646)	
Spear, Derk	4:17:24 (16,224)	
Spearing, Matthew	4:32:31 (20,219)	
Spearpoint, Paul	3:46:41 (8,329)	
Spears, James	3:51:35 (9,569)	
Spears, Robert	3:12:04 (2,284)	
Specht, Andrew	5:05:41 (27,112)	
Speechley, Tom	4:37:28 (21,439)	
Speed, David	3:38:20 (6,381)	
Speed, Fergus	4:10:25 (14,490)	
Speed, Russell	5:14:32 (28,251)	
Speedy, David	4:27:29 (18,915)	
Speer, Gavin	3:50:47 (9,373)	
Spegele, John	4:31:38 (19,999)	
Speight, Anthony	3:38:24 (6,400)	
Speight, Ralph	4:15:32 (15,704)	
Speirs, Rodney	4:39:30 (21,968)	
Speller, Stephen	4:29:25 (19,440)	
Spelman, Peter	4:01:52 (12,541)	
Spence, David	3:09:45 (2,012)	
Spence, Graham	3:52:25 (9,815)	
Spence, Joseph	6:07:23 (31,769)	
Spence, Marcus	5:17:00 (28,557)	
Spence, Matthew	3:44:40 (7,839)	
Spence, Max	5:17:00 (28,557)	
Spence, Michael	6:55:43 (32,589)	
Spence, Peter	3:52:43 (9,897)	
Spence, Simon	4:18:23 (16,460)	
Spence, Simon	5:20:04 (28,888)	

Spence, Stephen	2:48:49 (439)	
Spence, Trevor	4:47:36 (23,925)	
Spence, Will	3:49:45 (9,112)	
Spencer, Adrian	3:18:32 (3,077)	
Spencer, Adrian	5:15:32 (28,370)	
Spencer, Andrew	3:02:41 (1,347)	
Spencer, Brian	3:51:58 (9,674)	
Spencer, Chris	4:22:47 (17,631)	
Spencer, Christian	6:05:27 (31,713)	
Spencer, Colin	3:36:01 (5,907)	
Spencer, Danny	4:50:31 (24,512)	
Spencer, David	3:43:10 (7,434)	
Spencer, Gavin	4:28:42 (19,224)	
Spencer, Ian	3:01:06 (1,236)	
Spencer, Jeremy	2:51:20 (551)	
Spencer, Jeremy	5:23:00 (29,176)	
Spencer, John	4:20:43 (17,049)	
Spencer, Keith	3:13:39 (2,524)	
Spencer, Kevin	2:56:46 (897)	
Spencer, Kevin	5:05:27 (27,078)	
Spencer, Matthew	3:26:59 (4,327)	
Spencer, Melvyn	3:37:21 (6,176)	
Spencer, Paul	4:32:52 (20,327)	
Spencer, Raymond	3:59:54 (12,057)	
Spencer, Robert	4:26:29 (18,649)	
Spencer, Roger	4:38:16 (21,645)	
Spencer, Simon	4:27:12 (18,841)	
Spencer, Steven	4:14:12 (15,361)	
Spencer, Timothy	4:09:39 (14,307)	
Spender, Barney	4:28:31 (19,175)	
Spensley, Mark	4:03:28 (12,877)	
Spensley, Robert	5:44:25 (30,851)	
Spicer, Garry	4:59:32 (26,227)	
Spicer, Mark	3:55:26 (10,732)	
Spiess, Sven	3:02:32 (1,340)	
Spillane, Micky	3:39:54 (6,710)	
Spilsbury, Ian	2:48:48 (437)	
Spindler, Andrew	4:37:25 (21,428)	
Spink, Bob	4:31:37 (19,996)	
Spink, Chris	3:51:00 (9,425)	
Spink, George	4:34:40 (20,742)	
Spink, Patrick	4:12:39 (15,012)	
Spinke, Oliver	5:34:29 (30,147)	
Spinks, Chrales	4:15:19 (15,644)	
Spinks, Roger	3:55:06 (10,628)	
Spiro, Gary	4:32:21 (20,173)	
Spissu, Tony	4:46:07 (23,594)	
Spitzer, Edward	4:39:52 (22,076)	
Spofforth, Kevin	4:37:34 (21,461)	
Spooner, Paul	4:21:43 (17,315)	
Sportillo, Roberto	3:09:33 (1,995)	
Spouse, Iain	3:01:34 (1,263)	
Spranklen, Brendan	5:30:27 (29,816)	
Sprason, David	4:36:04 (21,096)	
Spratt, Norman	3:37:35 (6,243)	
Spray, Michael	4:16:02 (15,847)	
Spray, Richard	5:09:52 (27,680)	
Sprich, Adrian	3:19:11 (3,158)	
Spriggs, Andrew	4:00:22 (12,160)	
Spriggs, Chris	5:29:15 (29,718)	
Spring, Andrew	6:38:46 (32,418)	
Springall, Gary	5:15:34 (28,377)	
Springall, Kevin	6:07:20 (31,768)	
Springate, Glenn	3:42:18 (7,232)	
Springer, Gideon	3:37:42 (6,260)	
Springer, Marcellus	2:58:07 (1,014)	
Springett, Adrian	4:18:50 (16,556)	
Springett, David	3:43:51 (7,620)	
Springford, Patrick	5:00:11 (26,334)	
Sprules, Christopher	3:05:33 (1,596)	
Spurr, Graeme	4:41:09 (22,389)	
Squibb, Rick	4:35:23 (20,921)	
Squibb, Robert	3:16:12 (2,807)	
Squire, Anthony	3:19:04 (3,146)	
Squires, Rupert	4:13:39 (15,216)	
Squires, Thomas	6:28:35 (32,247)	
Squires, Warren	3:32:34 (5,282)	
Srikandakumar, Anton	5:16:43 (28,521)	
St Croix, Dennis	3:36:06 (5,932)	
St George, Peter	3:46:29 (8,272)	
St John, James	3:05:55 (1,635)	
St John, Wayne	4:13:35 (15,201)	
St Martin, Daniel	6:23:54 (32,165)	

St Quinton, Nicholas 4:41:26 (22,455)
Stabb, Matthew 4:06:47 (13,627)
Stabbins, Richard 4:38:47 (21,790)
Stabler, David 4:24:14 (18,048)
Stables, David 3:42:25 (7,265)
Stables, Kenneth 3:15:18 (2,701)
Stables, Thomas 3:53:05 (10,013)
Stace, Nick 4:46:01 (23,569)
Stacey, David 5:31:22 (29,903)
Stacey, Ed 4:32:51 (20,320)
Stacey, Geoffrey 3:22:28 (3,578)
Stacey, John 5:29:43 (29,757)
Stacey, Jonathan 3:45:23 (8,017)
Stacey, Jonathan 3:48:18 (8,693)
Stacey, Mark 3:09:08 (1,945)
Stacey, Michael 4:36:09 (21,121)
Stacey, Philip 4:05:47 (13,390)
Stacey, Robert 4:37:11 (21,365)
Stachel, Siegfried 3:08:27 (1,860)
Stack, David 4:50:47 (24,556)
Stack, Greg 4:49:29 (24,318)
Stack, Mark 5:05:12 (27,044)
Stack, Richard 4:09:02 (14,140)
Staddon, Ian 4:19:54 (16,836)
Staddon, Nicholas 4:20:39 (17,032)
Stadler, Nicolas 2:41:14 (210)
Staff, Gary 4:33:06 (20,375)
Staff, Granville 5:07:15 (27,342)
Staff, Neil 5:23:06 (29,185)
Stafford, Christopher 3:53:23 (10,103)
Stafford, Darren 4:50:14 (24,456)
Stafford, Thomas 4:07:46 (13,861)
Stagg, Michael 2:47:02 (362)
Stagg, Michael 4:12:23 (14,937)
Stagg, Patrick 4:58:03 (25,958)
Staggs, Jason 5:15:57 (28,436)
Stainer, David 4:16:26 (15,963)
Stainer, Gordon 4:28:48 (19,257)
Stainer, Peter 2:47:14 (370)
Staines, Michael 3:48:11 (8,670)
Stainton, Roger 4:51:35 (24,715)
Staley, Graham 4:46:12 (23,623)
Stallard, Brian 3:32:32 (5,276)
Stallard, Jaron 3:08:28 (1,866)
Stallard, Philip 3:54:04 (10,334)
Stamper, Iain 3:57:26 (11,339)
Stamper, Michael 4:30:46 (19,776)
Stanbridge, Michael 3:15:34 (2,731)
Stanbridge, Philip 3:38:50 (6,491)
Stanbury, Darren 3:24:09 (3,848)
Stander, Rudolf 4:13:05 (15,100)
Standing, Deano 5:00:10 (26,331)
Standing, Peter 3:19:49 (3,233)
Standley, Robert 2:50:41 (520)
Standring, Graham 3:34:57 (5,706)
Stanex, Robert 5:36:01 (30,275)
Stanfield, Charlie 4:43:47 (23,011)
Stanford, Patrick 3:21:53 (3,502)
Stanford, Paul 3:39:25 (6,606)
Stanhope, Ian 3:57:32 (11,372)
Stanhope, Raymond 4:40:42 (22,277)
Stanier, Bev 4:43:51 (23,029)
Staniforth, Adam 4:25:05 (18,281)
Staniland, Anthony 3:34:14 (5,568)
Stanley, Frank 5:44:16 (30,837)
Stanley, Gordon 4:49:21 (24,296)
Stanley, Kenneth 3:22:52 (3,644)
Stanley, Neil 3:09:08 (1,945)
Stanley, Paul 4:16:18 (15,913)
Stanley, Roger 4:12:20 (14,927)
Stanley, Roger 4:15:20 (15,651)
Stanmore, Carl 3:35:49 (5,868)
Stanmore, Nigel 3:41:45 (7,109)
Stannard, Richard 5:29:47 (29,761)
Stannek, Peter 3:49:00 (8,896)
Stanner, Philip 5:36:01 (30,275)
Stannett, Charlie 6:17:26 (32,018)
Stanton, David 3:43:26 (7,508)
Stanton, Michael 4:56:20 (25,667)
Stanton, Mitchell 4:03:33 (12,890)
Stanworth, James 3:45:32 (8,054)
Stanyer, Stephen 4:23:28 (17,817)
Staple, Oliver 3:33:08 (5,371)
Staples, Francis 6:01:32 (31,591)
Staples, James 4:08:57 (14,121)
Stapleton, John 3:29:05 (4,709)
Starbrook, Samuel 4:43:48 (23,021)
Stark, Adrian 3:45:06 (7,953)
Stark, David 3:18:26 (3,060)
Stark, Donald 4:59:22 (26,190)
Stark, Greig 4:04:40 (13,127)
Stark, Stephen 3:05:46 (1,612)
Starkie, Timothy 3:59:15 (11,868)
Starling, Shane 3:13:17 (2,472)
Starmer-Smith, Charles 4:45:23 (23,404)
Starr, Archie 6:27:04 (32,217)
Starr, Michael 3:16:59 (2,903)
Starr, Michael 3:48:46 (8,835)
Starr, Thomas 3:25:53 (4,133)
Starrett, Joseph 4:41:31 (22,479)
Start, David 4:12:06 (14,880)
Stasinski, Paul 4:16:34 (15,996)
Statham, Christopher 4:29:39 (19,495)
Statham, Malcolm 3:18:34 (3,080)
Staton, Mark 3:20:30 (3,312)
Staton, Oliver 4:03:34 (12,895)
Statter, Ian 4:49:33 (24,332)
Stavri, Anthony 4:08:58 (14,125)
Stead, Guy 3:39:06 (6,548)
Stead, Jonathan 3:51:05 (9,453)
Stead, Martin 4:02:23 (12,631)
Stead, Matthew 5:53:41 (31,301)
Stead, Robert 6:16:03 (31,984)
Steadman, Karl 3:41:42 (7,099)
Steadman, Mark 4:11:03 (14,647)
Steadman, Martin 5:30:43 (29,842)
Steadman, Terry 3:20:55 (3,354)
Stearn, Martyn 4:31:18 (19,900)
Stearn, Nicholas 3:36:18 (5,978)
Steatham, James 4:00:58 (12,301)
Steatham, Royston 4:16:47 (16,060)
Stebbing, Nick 4:04:17 (13,042)
Steeansson, Siguraur 5:48:54 (31,091)
Steel, Alexander 3:51:00 (9,425)
Steel, Barry 4:23:18 (17,776)
Steel, David 3:18:06 (3,020)
Steel, David 4:05:52 (13,403)
Steele, David 2:57:43 (981)
Steele, Kevin 7:59:59 (32,861)
Steele, Morgan 3:15:54 (2,781)
Steele, Nigel 5:04:36 (26,965)
Steele, Robert 4:57:42 (25,898)
Steele, Roy 2:59:30 (1,135)
Steeman, Michiel 4:08:40 (14,074)
Steenhuisen, Frederik 3:09:23 (1,981)
Steenson, Andrew 5:02:20 (26,646)
Steeples, Trevor 3:33:54 (5,496)
Steer, Mark 3:49:29 (9,036)
Steere, Peter 4:13:40 (15,222)
Stefani, Jean 4:38:38 (21,749)
Stefansson, Stefan 3:18:51 (3,118)
Steffen, Clive 3:43:34 (7,543)
Steffensen, Morten 4:26:28 (18,642)
Steib, Michael 3:58:03 (11,528)
Steibelt, Chris 4:18:34 (16,501)
Steiger, André 2:53:23 (650)
Steiger, Malcolm 3:52:41 (9,893)
Stein, Karsten 3:34:58 (5,707)
Stein, Neil 4:18:33 (16,497)
Stein, Philip 6:49:55 (32,540)
Steinberg, Jeffrey 4:05:48 (13,393)
Steiner, Helmut 3:56:28 (11,033)
Steiner, Uno 4:46:35 (23,712)
Steinle, Mark 2:09:16 (8)
Stelfox, Andrew 3:28:13 (4,554)
Stell, Alan 3:55:19 (10,701)
Stendall, Chris 5:27:48 (29,603)
Stenner, Roger 3:24:41 (3,942)
Stennett, James 4:10:43 (14,556)
Stepanek, Frantisek 3:05:48 (1,618)
Stephane, Didier 3:39:49 (6,691)
Stephen, Ian 3:47:03 (8,394)
Stephen, Keith 3:33:19 (5,403)
Stephens, Alan 4:21:28 (17,238)
Stephens, Christopher 3:55:51 (10,855)
Stephens, Christopher 5:05:54 (27,144)
Stephens, Cliff 3:53:48 (10,249)
Stephens, Colin 4:17:02 (16,129)
Stephens, Dean 4:27:56 (19,018)
Stephens, Desmond 4:59:30 (26,216)
Stephens, Ed 4:19:45 (16,793)
Stephens, Gwyn 5:00:00 (26,310)
Stephens, Neale 3:08:29 (1,869)
Stephens, Neil 4:00:42 (12,227)
Stephens, Nicholas 2:51:26 (559)
Stephens, Richard 4:24:01 (17,985)
Stephens, Timothy 5:16:31 (28,501)
Stephens, Toby 4:03:22 (12,849)
Stephens, Tony 3:57:26 (11,339)
Stephenson, Charlie 4:14:11 (15,357)
Stephenson, David 4:44:37 (23,199)
Stephenson, Gary 4:25:54 (18,488)
Stephenson, Keith 4:42:12 (22,649)
Stephenson, Mark 3:58:19 (11,593)
Stephenson, Mark 4:42:44 (22,775)
Stephenson, Matthew 5:04:39 (26,971)
Stephenson, Oliver 2:53:51 (670)
Stephenson, Philip 4:24:24 (18,091)
Steptoe, Colin 2:40:36 (194)
Sterkenburg, Ben 3:24:47 (3,956)
Sternfeld, Thomas 3:49:04 (8,915)
Sterry, Andrew 3:46:24 (8,254)
Steven, Dave 6:50:28 (32,547)
Stevenage, Hugh 3:58:49 (11,742)
Stevenette, Simon 4:38:02 (21,578)
Stevens, Andrew 3:23:45 (3,765)
Stevens, Anthony 3:27:51 (4,492)
Stevens, Anthony 3:45:54 (8,134)
Stevens, Anthony 4:49:27 (24,311)
Stevens, Brian 3:12:33 (2,368)
Stevens, Brian 4:12:58 (15,075)
Stevens, Conrad 4:07:46 (13,861)
Stevens, Daniel 5:18:39 (28,737)
Stevens, Darren 3:28:31 (4,606)
Stevens, David 3:07:32 (1,771)
Stevens, David 4:36:50 (21,286)
Stevens, Glenn 5:37:16 (30,366)
Stevens, Graham 2:48:12 (415)
Stevens, Graham 3:43:17 (7,467)
Stevens, Greg 2:38:44 (161)
Stevens, Jamie 4:26:05 (18,544)
Stevens, Mark 3:50:16 (9,242)
Stevens, Mark 4:28:30 (19,172)
Stevens, Neil 4:39:16 (21,916)
Stevens, Paul 3:40:57 (6,949)
Stevens, Peter 5:10:32 (27,754)
Stevens, Philip 3:57:25 (11,333)
Stevens, Philip 4:11:36 (14,768)
Stevens, Ross 4:45:24 (23,413)
Stevens, Roy 3:29:43 (4,829)
Stevens, Scott 4:34:06 (20,608)
Stevens, Simon 2:39:46 (179)
Stevens, Thomas 4:04:54 (13,183)
Stevens, Tim 3:58:04 (11,531)
Stevenson, Andrew 3:12:42 (2,387)
Stevenson, Chris 5:43:51 (30,808)
Stevenson, Craig 4:45:47 (23,512)
Stevenson, Gordon 2:58:10 (1,018)
Stevenson, Gordon 3:24:08 (3,844)
Stevenson, John 4:46:25 (23,667)
Stevenson, Mark 3:40:05 (6,756)
Stevenson, Mark 3:58:34 (11,664)
Stevenson, Michael 4:23:30 (17,825)
Stevenson, Paul 2:57:00 (914)
Stevenson, Robert 4:41:51 (22,570)
Stevenson, Ross 4:37:56 (21,558)
Stevenson, Timothy 5:07:29 (27,372)
Stevenson, Trevor 5:46:30 (30,963)
Stevinson, David 5:06:02 (27,162)
Steward, Mark 3:37:29 (6,211)
Steward, Robin 3:45:46 (8,104)
Stewart, Alan 3:33:32 (5,430)
Stewart, Andrew 3:16:45 (2,870)
Stewart, Andrew 4:06:11 (13,484)
Stewart, Colin 4:37:34 (21,461)
Stewart, David 3:12:10 (2,305)
Stewart, David 3:45:56 (8,145)
Stewart, Douglas 4:52:58 (24,975)
Stewart, Gary 3:23:51 (3,784)

Stewart, Graham	3:08:10 (1,820)	
Stewart, Iain	3:30:57 (5,015)	
Stewart, Ian	3:00:58 (1,225)	
Stewart, Ian	3:55:32 (10,758)	
Stewart, Innes	4:55:16 (25,432)	
Stewart, James	3:38:05 (6,327)	
Stewart, James	4:38:14 (21,636)	
Stewart, James	5:07:50 (27,411)	
Stewart, Michael	3:06:14 (1,662)	
Stewart, Michael	6:28:02 (32,239)	
Stewart, Peter	4:56:05 (25,601)	
Stewart, Philip	4:51:10 (24,643)	
Stewart, Richard	3:54:43 (10,519)	
Stewart, William	3:25:05 (4,000)	
Stewart-Mole, Edmunds	5:26:31 (29,494)	
Stick, Anthony	5:39:41 (30,529)	
Stickings, Paul	3:19:42 (3,221)	
Stickland, David	4:14:12 (15,361)	
Stickley, Duncan	5:53:11 (31,285)	
Stidder, Gary	5:35:15 (30,204)	
Stiefel, Juerg	3:23:54 (3,799)	
Stiefvater, Hansjoerg	3:01:52 (1,290)	
Stiff, Kevin	4:15:54 (15,810)	
Stiff, Michael	2:46:15 (334)	
Stileman, Mark	2:54:16 (692)	
Stiles, Andrew	2:57:17 (934)	
Stiles, Andrew	3:01:26 (1,255)	
Stiles, Lee	4:32:49 (20,306)	
Still, Stuart	4:06:12 (13,494)	
Stillman, Richard	5:17:36 (28,639)	
Stillwell, Robert	3:17:36 (2,963)	
Stimpson, Dean	5:08:38 (27,512)	
Stimpson, George	3:53:29 (10,139)	
Stimpson, Paul	3:40:14 (6,794)	
Stinchcombe, Nigel	3:26:50 (4,300)	
Stirling, Alexander	4:02:34 (12,669)	
Stirling, Chris	4:22:45 (17,621)	
Stirling, William	4:41:43 (22,536)	
Stittle, Neil	4:04:20 (13,053)	
Stkinson, Christopher	4:34:17 (20,645)	
Stoat, Antony	3:30:52 (5,000)	
Stoate, Howard	3:57:32 (11,372)	
Stobie, William	4:36:18 (21,153)	
Stock, Andrew	3:37:28 (6,203)	
Stock, Paul	5:40:20 (30,573)	
Stock, Russell	4:46:05 (23,589)	
Stocking, Peter	3:59:01 (11,810)	
Stockman, Barton	2:57:04 (920)	
Stockman, David	4:52:42 (24,915)	
Stocks, Andrew	5:56:48 (31,440)	
Stocks, Martin	2:58:40 (1,066)	
Stocks, Martin	5:25:12 (29,378)	
Stocks, Terence	4:22:53 (17,668)	
Stockwell, Michael	5:07:22 (27,350)	
Stoddard, Mark	3:11:22 (2,190)	
Stoddart, Mark	6:38:07 (32,412)	
Stoddart, Richard	4:03:37 (12,904)	
Stoffer, Dietrich	3:35:15 (5,756)	
Stojanovic, Marco	3:52:11 (9,747)	
Stoker, Michael	3:00:45 (1,215)	
Stoker, Stephen	4:20:12 (16,913)	
Stokes, Antony	4:06:38 (13,596)	
Stokes, Christopher	4:00:48 (12,256)	
Stokes, Craig	5:00:03 (26,315)	
Stokes, Ian	4:27:12 (18,841)	
Stokes, John	4:23:03 (17,717)	
Stokes, John	5:56:02 (31,401)	
Stokes, Neil	3:58:58 (11,787)	
Stokes, Patrick	5:19:54 (28,858)	
Stokes, Peter	4:30:25 (19,697)	
Stokes, Tim	3:54:19 (10,404)	
Stokes, Wayne	3:24:57 (3,982)	
Stokoe, David	3:56:29 (11,044)	
Stokoe, Matthew	4:22:42 (17,608)	
Stolk, Piet	4:30:35 (19,729)	
Stolk, Rien	4:03:00 (12,775)	
Stollery, Michael	4:16:41 (16,035)	
Stone, Andrew	3:52:25 (9,815)	
Stone, Andrew	4:09:36 (14,293)	
Stone, Barry	3:50:43 (9,352)	
Stone, Chris	4:35:10 (20,866)	
Stone, David	2:34:51 (97)	
Stone, Derek	3:12:20 (2,337)	
Stone, Desmond	5:10:53 (27,799)	
Stone, Gavin	5:15:08 (28,311)	
Stone, Geoffrey	4:15:26 (15,676)	
Stone, Ian	4:30:50 (19,793)	
Stone, John	3:09:33 (1,995)	
Stone, Jonathan	4:10:52 (14,597)	
Stone, Kevin	5:33:47 (30,090)	
Stone, Martin	7:01:46 (32,644)	
Stone, Matt	3:59:17 (11,878)	
Stone, Matthew	3:57:09 (11,246)	
Stone, Michael	6:33:11 (32,324)	
Stone, Patrick	4:30:57 (19,821)	
Stone, Paul	5:16:09 (28,460)	
Stone, Richard	4:59:37 (26,247)	
Stone, Roger	3:08:10 (1,820)	
Stone, Timothy	3:48:58 (8,886)	
Stone, William	4:18:10 (16,404)	
Stoneham, Christian	4:35:31 (20,951)	
Stonehouse, Andrew	4:29:51 (19,557)	
Stoneley, Jonathan	3:05:03 (1,549)	
Stoneley, Norman	4:13:15 (15,134)	
Stoneman, James	3:16:45 (2,870)	
Stoneman-Merret, Jonathan	3:59:25 (11,924)	
Stonham, Colin	5:00:56 (26,444)	
Stonham, Mark	6:17:55 (32,034)	
Stonier, Christopher	3:05:46 (1,612)	
Stopher, Louis	3:22:32 (3,587)	
Storer, Christopher	4:06:29 (13,562)	
Storer, Mick	3:51:15 (9,487)	
Storer, Terry	4:28:00 (19,032)	
Storey, Jim	5:06:00 (27,155)	
Storey, John	5:20:30 (28,940)	
Storey, Kenneth	3:26:23 (4,215)	
Storey, Les	4:21:21 (17,203)	
Storey, Matthew	3:32:21 (5,242)	
Storey, Michael	4:10:51 (14,592)	
Storey, Phlip	3:48:12 (8,675)	
Storey, Simon	3:45:56 (8,145)	
Storey, Stuart	3:28:35 (4,622)	
Storey, Walter	6:09:14 (31,818)	
Storf, Christopher	5:53:13 (31,289)	
Stork, Robert	3:57:24 (11,325)	
Storrie, John	3:42:02 (7,164)	
Storrie, Martin	3:48:21 (8,710)	
Storrs, Michael	5:02:12 (26,628)	
Storry, Terence	3:39:12 (6,567)	
Stossberger, Udo	3:17:31 (2,959)	
Stoten, Terry	4:29:13 (19,384)	
Stott, Douglas	3:47:44 (8,569)	
Stott, Lee	5:12:05 (27,963)	
Stout, Richard	4:18:26 (16,473)	
Stow, Mark	4:35:28 (20,936)	
Straccamore, Amedeo	4:20:08 (16,896)	
Strachan, Graham	5:12:00 (27,950)	
Strain, Ian	4:53:09 (25,002)	
Stranaghan, Simon	4:18:29 (16,482)	
Strandberg, Roland	4:58:53 (26,112)	
Strange, Adam	4:23:42 (17,883)	
Strange, Gareth	3:48:36 (8,782)	
Strange, Peter	4:04:48 (13,160)	
Strange, Peter	4:23:42 (17,883)	
Strangeway, David	4:59:27 (26,207)	
Stratford, John	3:38:02 (6,320)	
Stratford, John	4:01:24 (12,417)	
Stratford, Lawrie	4:31:32 (19,978)	
Strathearn, Daniel	4:09:18 (14,218)	
Strathie, Gavin	4:47:46 (23,965)	
Stratton, Edward	3:59:44 (12,003)	
Stratton, Lester	4:17:50 (16,333)	
Straw, Kevin	2:53:18 (642)	
Straw, Michael	4:16:01 (15,842)	
Straw, Neil	4:15:56 (15,824)	
Street, Christopher	3:52:03 (9,709)	
Street, Daniel	5:18:48 (28,756)	
Street, Darren	3:33:14 (5,386)	
Street, Paul	2:42:26 (235)	
Street, Steve	4:32:03 (20,101)	
Street, William	3:48:30 (8,747)	
Strelt, Ulrich	4:36:16 (21,142)	
Streng, Chris	4:07:57 (13,898)	
Stretch, Keith	3:54:08 (10,358)	
Stretton, Matt	4:34:10 (20,621)	
Stribling, David	4:22:35 (17,568)	
Strick, Nigel	5:34:09 (30,118)	
Stricker, Ronald	5:30:46 (29,847)	
Stringer, Gary	4:20:11 (16,911)	
Stringer, Mark	4:13:13 (15,126)	
Stringer, Richard	4:01:50 (12,531)	
Stringer, Sean	4:43:53 (23,036)	
Stringer, Thomas	3:43:05 (7,408)	
Stringer, Will	4:10:43 (14,556)	
Strivens, Martin	4:28:41 (19,220)	
Strode, Richard	2:55:59 (827)	
Strohmaier, Charles	3:40:40 (6,889)	
Stromsoe, Michael	3:44:43 (7,861)	
Stronach, James	3:13:33 (2,512)	
Strong, Christian	3:56:31 (11,059)	
Strong, Darryl	4:54:28 (25,279)	
Strong, Gary	5:29:36 (29,748)	
Strong, Gary	5:45:31 (30,912)	
Strong, Jim	3:17:40 (2,971)	
Stroud, Richard	3:54:42 (10,516)	
Stroud, Robert	3:57:15 (11,278)	
Strowbridge, Andy	3:40:34 (6,867)	
Struck, Gustav	3:35:09 (5,742)	
Strudwick, Andrew	4:25:05 (18,281)	
Strugnell, Anthony	4:41:34 (22,487)	
Struthers, Kevin	4:15:39 (15,739)	
Struthers, Michael	4:46:57 (23,803)	
Strutt, Barry	4:34:19 (20,652)	
Strutt, Jeremy	4:50:25 (24,487)	
Stuart, Brenner	4:46:43 (23,738)	
Stuart, Brian	4:31:29 (19,962)	
Stuart, Bruce	3:57:16 (11,280)	
Stuart, James	4:48:06 (24,056)	
Stuart, James	5:21:34 (29,048)	
Stuart, Matthew	5:39:14 (30,484)	
Stuart, Michael	4:24:40 (18,164)	
Stuart, Paul	5:05:19 (27,065)	
Stuart-Smith, Innes	4:14:52 (15,542)	
Stubbs, Bernard	3:50:55 (9,402)	
Stubbs, David	3:04:19 (1,489)	
Stubbs, Denis	6:14:17 (31,935)	
Stubbs, Edward	4:01:07 (12,341)	
Stubbs, Edward	5:17:36 (28,628)	
Stubley, Andy	4:25:37 (18,424)	
Studd, Darren	3:01:39 (1,268)	
Studd, Paul	3:29:17 (4,744)	
Studds, Philip	3:15:20 (2,707)	
Studer, Ueli	2:53:08 (636)	
Stump, David	6:13:18 (31,912)	
Stupple, Gerry	4:30:38 (19,739)	
Sturdgess, Ian	4:55:06 (25,391)	
Sturdy, Paul	3:30:22 (4,924)	
Sturgeon, Ian	5:18:41 (28,742)	
Sturgess, Simon	4:13:31 (15,192)	
Sturla, Timothy	4:09:35 (14,287)	
Sturley, Hugh	3:28:01 (4,519)	
Sturrock, Stewart	4:54:15 (25,233)	
Sturton, Peter	3:47:10 (8,426)	
Stutchbury, James	5:01:17 (26,500)	
Styler, Paul	5:05:00 (27,021)	
Suarez, Fernando	4:57:03 (25,779)	
Suc, Thierry	4:18:41 (16,522)	
Suda, Hiroyuki	4:23:15 (17,760)	
Suddards, David	4:22:56 (17,682)	
Suffield, Tim	4:36:08 (21,115)	
Suffling, Norford	4:44:39 (23,206)	
Sugarman, Alan	4:37:15 (21,390)	
Sugden, Gavin	3:26:52 (4,303)	
Sugden, John	4:24:11 (18,029)	
Suleman, Aarif	4:48:02 (24,041)	
Suleyman, Erol	4:54:50 (25,349)	
Sullens, John	4:01:51 (12,535)	
Sullivan, Daniel	3:27:30 (4,418)	
Sullivan, David	4:10:33 (14,523)	
Sullivan, Diter	5:28:10 (29,629)	
Sullivan, Gordon	3:58:00 (11,508)	
Sullivan, John	4:16:18 (15,913)	
Sullivan, John	4:43:26 (22,940)	
Sullivan, Mike	4:51:53 (24,760)	
Sullivan, Neil	4:51:31 (24,703)	
Sullivan, Peter	4:10:22 (14,479)	
Sullivan, Raymond	3:25:55 (4,140)	
Sullivan, Richard	4:39:24 (21,953)	
Sullivan, Sam	3:23:16 (3,691)	

Sullivan, Stephen	4:16:21 (15,930)
Sullivan, Stuart	5:19:44 (28,844)
Summerfield, Richard	3:17:30 (2,958)
Summers, Anthony	3:11:50 (2,248)
Summers, Christopher	5:02:45 (26,702)
Summers, Clark	4:06:47 (13,627)
Summers, David	3:25:00 (3,986)
Summers, David	5:23:50 (29,265)
Summers, David	5:47:10 (30,996)
Summers, Derek	3:32:15 (5,226)
Summers, Jeremy	5:44:14 (30,835)
Summers, Mark	4:31:04 (19,844)
Summers, Martin	3:11:43 (2,229)
Summers, Norman	4:54:00 (25,184)
Summers, Peter	3:17:31 (2,959)
Summers, Scott	6:22:51 (32,147)
Summers, Stephen	3:52:00 (9,683)
Summers, Wayne	4:41:32 (22,481)
Summerscales, Simon	3:45:00 (7,926)
Summerson, Mark	4:22:52 (17,661)
Summerton, John	5:27:43 (29,599)
Sumner, Gary	5:20:54 (28,984)
Sumner, John	5:55:22 (31,369)
Sumner, Mark	3:57:48 (11,449)
Sumners, Simon	3:24:06 (3,837)
Sumpter, James	2:48:55 (443)
Sumpter, Michael	4:30:17 (19,669)
Sunderland, Oliver	3:08:43 (1,891)
Sunderland, Phil	3:34:31 (5,622)
Sundovist, Anders	3:42:30 (7,287)
Sundvik, Harri	3:38:59 (6,520)
Supri, Nalinder	4:58:29 (26,030)
Surace, Vincenzo	4:28:44 (19,236)
Suriano, Vito	5:25:21 (29,392)
Surman, David	4:34:33 (20,710)
Surman, William	3:39:32 (6,632)
Surrey, Samuel	3:35:35 (5,822)
Surridge, Lewis	5:40:57 (30,611)
Sushams, Anthony	5:37:42 (30,400)
Sussman, David	4:21:09 (17,156)
Sustins, Gordon	4:20:56 (17,090)
Sutcliffe, Alistair	4:24:56 (18,234)
Sutcliffe, Dale	4:44:54 (23,271)
Sutcliffe, David	3:17:52 (2,996)
Sutcliffe, David	3:52:23 (9,808)
Sutcliffe, David	4:27:47 (18,978)
Sutcliffe, Martin	3:55:37 (10,789)
Sutcliffe, Richard	3:12:18 (2,330)
Suter, Anthony	3:29:31 (4,800)
Suter, Yvan	3:05:52 (1,627)
Sutherland, Alex	4:07:30 (13,799)
Sutherland, Alistair	3:43:08 (7,426)
Sutherland, David	4:44:14 (23,112)
Sutherland, Graeme	4:17:14 (16,179)
Sutherland, Graham	3:43:35 (7,546)
Sutherland, Graham	3:55:55 (10,877)
Sutherland, James	3:43:37 (7,555)
Sutherland, Leslie	4:39:25 (21,956)
Sutherland, Michael	3:34:05 (5,537)
Sutherland, Scott	5:50:36 (31,165)
Sutterby, Philip	4:39:26 (21,961)
Suttle, David	4:09:38 (14,300)
Sutton, Anthony	6:03:12 (31,646)
Sutton, Darren	3:28:34 (4,616)
Sutton, Dominic	4:25:17 (18,330)
Sutton, Errol	5:38:15 (30,428)
Sutton, Jeremy	4:06:45 (13,621)
Sutton, John	5:06:42 (27,259)
Sutton, Malcolm	3:54:41 (10,511)
Sutton, Mark	3:28:54 (4,679)
Sutton, Mark	3:50:23 (9,274)
Sutton, Mark	4:04:35 (13,109)
Sutton, Paul	4:17:00 (16,116)
Sutton, Philip	4:18:45 (16,536)
Sutton, Richard	3:51:21 (9,511)
Sutton, Tim	5:50:57 (31,185)
Svoboda, Jared	3:28:20 (4,579)
Swaby, GJ	4:35:33 (20,960)
Swaffield, James	4:39:32 (21,978)
Swain, Alan	5:04:56 (27,011)
Swain, Anthony	4:23:54 (17,948)
Swain, David	4:33:27 (20,452)
Swain, Luke	4:26:33 (18,668)

Swain, Matthew	4:44:46 (23,240)
Swaine, Alan	4:24:58 (18,254)
Swaine, Kevin	5:16:09 (28,460)
Swainson, Christopher	3:55:04 (10,614)
Swallow, Peter	4:09:52 (14,355)
Swan, Charles	3:47:22 (8,480)
Swan, David	3:52:00 (9,683)
Swan, Kim	3:58:53 (11,757)
Swan, Stephen	4:23:41 (17,872)
Swann, Graham	4:17:39 (16,280)
Swann, Jonathan	3:52:05 (9,715)
Swann, Philip	3:46:12 (8,201)
Swannell, Matthew	4:26:21 (18,615)
Swanson, Adam	5:09:00 (27,572)
Swarbrick, Michael	4:22:34 (17,564)
Swarts, David	4:16:28 (15,973)
Swateridge, Andrew	3:43:44 (7,585)
Swatton, Iain	4:57:27 (25,849)
Swatton, Neville	3:22:05 (3,535)
Sweeney, Iain	4:30:35 (19,729)
Sweeney, Robert	4:34:09 (20,618)
Sweet, Christopher	5:00:28 (26,370)
Sweet, David	3:41:47 (7,112)
Sweet, Michael	3:52:57 (9,960)
Sweet, Timothy	4:29:03 (19,335)
Sweeting, Ian	6:03:57 (31,661)
Sweeting, Paul	4:39:11 (21,892)
Sweetlove, Malcolm	3:38:57 (6,512)
Sweny, Dominic	3:23:50 (3,776)
Sweny, Paul	3:33:53 (5,493)
Swerling, Robert	3:58:24 (11,621)
Swift, Brian	3:34:12 (5,564)
Swift, Edward	3:57:12 (11,263)
Swift, Marcus	4:56:27 (25,684)
Swift, Tom	4:46:56 (23,798)
Swindells, Paul	4:03:42 (12,918)
Swindlehurst, Mark	4:01:04 (12,330)
Swingler, David	3:26:39 (4,262)
Swinhoe, Alan	3:49:56 (9,158)
Swordy, Peter	3:46:35 (8,309)
Syang-Thomsen, Helge	4:44:06 (23,086)
Sycamore, Paul	5:45:28 (30,908)
Sydenham, Gareth	3:29:12 (4,727)
Sydenham, Jonathan	3:59:57 (12,073)
Sykes, Andrew	3:35:40 (5,837)
Sykes, Charlie	5:02:52 (26,723)
Sykes, Christopher	4:11:25 (14,715)
Sykes, David	4:00:55 (12,281)
Sykes, John	4:40:43 (22,284)
Sykes, Wayne	3:41:11 (7,013)
Sylvester, Martin	4:38:41 (21,758)
Sylvester, Matthew	3:29:52 (4,852)
Symington, Ian	3:13:24 (2,491)
Symington, Neil	4:32:01 (20,088)
Symonds, Andrew	2:38:11 (150)
Symonds, Barrie	3:22:50 (3,640)
Symonds, Colin	3:52:21 (9,797)
Symonds, David	4:19:11 (16,641)
Symonds, Neil	4:12:13 (14,905)
Symons, David	2:33:27 (83)
Syms, David	4:42:13 (22,651)
Synan, John	4:27:01 (18,792)
Syster, Ian	2:07:04 (5)
Sysum, Mark	3:17:41 (2,972)
Szczepanek, Antonio	3:46:21 (8,236)
Szechenyi, Robert	3:30:37 (4,966)
Szkoda, Les	5:03:53 (26,870)
Szostak, Jerzy	2:46:28 (341)
Szpak, Mike	4:47:51 (23,990)
Tabb, Chris	4:27:05 (18,816)
Tabenor, Peter	3:00:13 (1,183)
Tabet, Jean	3:48:09 (8,663)
Tabiner, Ben	4:18:44 (16,530)
Tabor, Frank	4:38:43 (21,768)
Tabor, Paul	3:08:39 (1,885)
Tabor, Raymond	4:22:31 (17,550)
Tabraham, Adam	3:41:38 (7,087)
Tabrett, Daniel	4:54:12 (25,225)
Tack, Joe	5:18:11 (28,689)
Taft, Kevin	4:00:19 (12,156)
Tagand, Patrick	3:24:51 (3,964)
Tagg, Gavin	4:06:36 (13,586)
Taggart, James	4:20:56 (17,090)

Tagney, Gregory	3:22:26 (3,574)
Tagt, Anders	4:43:57 (23,055)
Tague, Stephen	3:14:07 (2,566)
Taheri, Peyman	3:30:58 (5,019)
Tahmassebi, Arman	3:57:36 (11,396)
Tailor, Dennis	3:55:17 (10,687)
Tailor, Navin	3:22:15 (3,560)
Tailor, Navnit	4:55:07 (25,400)
Tait, Graham	5:15:39 (28,388)
Tait, Paul	3:04:42 (1,520)
Takacs, Mark	5:49:43 (31,131)
Takahashi, Kenki	4:28:37 (19,205)
Takahashi, Sadao	4:38:04 (21,589)
Takahashi, Yukio	4:47:18 (23,877)
Takamura, Kenji	4:16:42 (16,040)
Takano, Satoshi	3:31:59 (5,186)
Takeda, Akihiko	5:28:38 (29,668)
Taki, Mohamed	3:18:01 (3,010)
Talamonti, Sergio	4:25:33 (18,404)
Talbot, Simon	3:09:08 (1,945)
Talbott, Mark	4:54:54 (25,362)
Tallan, William	3:50:51 (9,392)
Tallio, Jean	3:16:51 (2,887)
Talloh, Mohammed	4:29:16 (19,405)
Tam, Patrick	3:47:20 (8,467)
Tamagni, David	4:12:41 (15,022)
Tamang, Saran	3:32:40 (5,299)
Tamas, Walter	3:12:47 (2,396)
Tamura, Kazayoshi	4:14:47 (15,520)
Tamura, Morio	4:12:10 (14,894)
Tanaka, Koji	4:57:14 (25,818)
Tancock, Stephen	2:52:00 (578)
Tancos, Timothy	3:21:58 (3,516)
Tande, Jean-Yves	5:47:15 (31,001)
Taniguchi, Koji	2:23:44 (37)
Tanini, Andrea	4:03:47 (12,936)
Tannahill, William	5:00:49 (26,430)
Tanner, Adrian	2:41:33 (221)
Tanner, Colin	4:09:23 (14,245)
Tanner, Martin	3:49:50 (9,137)
Tanner, Neil	4:46:30 (23,692)
Tanqueray, John	3:37:13 (6,151)
Tansey, Michael	3:45:47 (8,110)
Tanzey, Sean	4:09:17 (14,209)
Taplin, David	3:17:12 (2,920)
Taplin, Derek	4:21:48 (17,335)
Taplin, Steve	4:13:29 (15,183)
Tapper, Tyrone	6:08:48 (31,807)
Tapster, Alan	5:07:04 (27,306)
Tarbares, John	4:41:54 (22,585)
Tarbyat, Mahmoud	5:35:40 (30,246)
Tardy, Michel	3:13:18 (2,473)
Tari-Alonso, José	3:29:41 (4,824)
Tarling, Stephen	3:31:37 (5,132)
Tarpey, Christopher	3:15:58 (2,783)
Tarpey, Michael	4:04:00 (12,989)
Tarragano, Joe	4:34:04 (20,598)
Tarrant, Matthew	4:09:58 (14,377)
Tarrant, Steve	3:32:34 (5,282)
Tarrantino, Giovanni	4:28:48 (19,257)
Tarratt, Christopher	3:42:05 (7,174)
Tarren, David	4:33:45 (20,526)
Tarver, Andrew	3:40:15 (6,799)
Tarver, Jason	3:58:12 (11,570)
Tasker, David	4:26:52 (18,753)
Tasker, John	3:15:04 (2,670)
Tasker, John	4:02:41 (12,701)
Tasker, Kevin	4:35:57 (21,067)
Tasker, Lewis	4:12:24 (14,943)
Tasker, Simon	4:47:21 (23,885)
Tassell, Nicholas	3:46:25 (8,258)
Tassell, Steven	3:58:21 (11,607)
Tate, Andrew	3:17:07 (2,914)
Tate, Douglas	4:30:29 (19,707)
Tate, Mark	3:31:24 (5,092)
Tate, Simon	4:28:44 (19,236)
Tate, Simon	5:37:03 (30,352)
Tatham, Alasdair	2:36:05 (107)
Tatham, David	4:30:46 (19,776)
Tatham, Joe	4:28:13 (19,088)
Tatham, John	5:30:06 (29,784)
Tatibouet, Erwan	4:04:35 (13,109)
Tattersall, Alan	3:59:33 (11,951)

Tattersall, Toby 3:42:53 (7,358)
Tattershall, Darren 3:44:14 (7,720)
Tattum, David 3:34:17 (5,578)
Tattum, Paul 3:51:45 (9,610)
Taun, Alastair 5:17:49 (28,652)
Tavender, Graham 2:59:16 (1,113)
Taverner, Mark 4:47:37 (23,930)
Tavner, David 4:12:35 (14,992)
Tayler, Daniel 3:54:51 (10,557)
Taylor, Adam 4:45:44 (23,502)
Taylor, Alan 3:13:23 (2,490)
Taylor, Alan 3:18:11 (3,029)
Taylor, Alan 3:53:18 (10,081)
Taylor, Alan 5:00:54 (26,443)
Taylor, Alan 5:28:18 (29,638)
Taylor, Andrew 3:38:38 (6,459)
Taylor, Arron 4:06:55 (13,651)
Taylor, Ben 3:51:08 (9,466)
Taylor, Ben 4:31:08 (19,867)
Taylor, Ben 5:00:08 (26,326)
Taylor, Brant 3:06:36 (1,699)
Taylor, Brian 3:45:46 (8,104)
Taylor, Bruce 3:24:41 (3,942)
Taylor, Bruce 4:07:57 (13,898)
Taylor, Bryon 4:58:27 (26,024)
Taylor, Christopher 4:10:12 (14,437)
Taylor, Christopher 4:23:52 (17,937)
Taylor, Colin 3:58:55 (11,767)
Taylor, Darren 3:27:21 (4,385)
Taylor, David 3:06:29 (1,682)
Taylor, David 3:54:11 (10,371)
Taylor, David 4:05:01 (13,212)
Taylor, David 4:17:21 (16,215)
Taylor, David 4:23:40 (17,864)
Taylor, David 4:30:00 (19,592)
Taylor, David 4:38:06 (21,599)
Taylor, David 5:25:46 (29,426)
Taylor, David 6:06:14 (31,738)
Taylor, Derek 4:08:22 (13,982)
Taylor, Duncan 4:02:36 (12,681)
Taylor, Frank 5:30:22 (29,809)
Taylor, Gareth 4:53:43 (25,107)
Taylor, Glenn 4:29:06 (19,348)
Taylor, Graham 3:00:45 (1,215)
Taylor, Graham 5:24:12 (29,297)
Taylor, Greig 4:42:46 (22,784)
Taylor, Howard 4:54:57 (25,370)
Taylor, Iain 6:05:11 (31,700)
Taylor, Ian 4:02:59 (12,771)
Taylor, Ian 4:09:47 (14,336)
Taylor, James 3:43:35 (7,546)
Taylor, James 5:55:39 (31,386)
Taylor, John 3:39:51 (6,701)
Taylor, John 3:49:06 (8,924)
Taylor, John 3:59:11 (11,849)
Taylor, John 4:00:40 (12,216)
Taylor, John 4:32:34 (20,234)
Taylor, John 4:40:54 (22,332)
Taylor, John 5:36:02 (30,279)
Taylor, Jonathan 4:25:27 (18,371)
Taylor, Keith 3:49:57 (9,163)
Taylor, Keith 4:07:24 (13,777)
Taylor, Kevin 3:53:33 (10,165)
Taylor, Kevin 4:19:58 (16,852)
Taylor, Lee 4:45:25 (23,419)
Taylor, Malcolm 3:41:39 (7,091)
Taylor, Mark 3:06:25 (1,673)
Taylor, Mark 4:59:22 (26,190)
Taylor, Mark 6:36:21 (32,378)
Taylor, Martin 3:50:10 (9,205)
Taylor, Martin 4:52:39 (24,906)
Taylor, Martyn 7:50:55 (32,848)
Taylor, Matthew 3:19:45 (3,228)
Taylor, Matthew 3:42:58 (7,380)
Taylor, Matthew 4:10:45 (14,562)
Taylor, Matthew 4:39:22 (21,939)
Taylor, Matthew 5:02:30 (26,668)
Taylor, Matthew 5:16:01 (28,448)
Taylor, Melvyn 3:24:07 (3,840)
Taylor, Michael 3:08:27 (1,860)
Taylor, Michael 3:44:11 (7,707)
Taylor, Michael 3:47:15 (8,449)
Taylor, Michael 4:28:14 (19,095)

Taylor, Neale 4:21:34 (17,270)
Taylor, Neil 3:32:14 (5,220)
Taylor, Nicholas 3:41:28 (7,059)
Taylor, Nick 3:46:51 (8,355)
Taylor, Nick 4:29:49 (19,543)
Taylor, Orlando 4:05:24 (13,298)
Taylor, Patrick 4:11:01 (14,633)
Taylor, Paul 3:50:07 (9,192)
Taylor, Paul 3:53:18 (10,081)
Taylor, Paul 4:16:51 (16,079)
Taylor, Paul 4:25:24 (18,362)
Taylor, Paul 4:41:26 (22,455)
Taylor, Paul 4:55:09 (25,411)
Taylor, Paul 5:17:32 (28,634)
Taylor, Peter 3:05:53 (1,631)
Taylor, Philip 2:43:50 (264)
Taylor, Philip 3:14:46 (2,635)
Taylor, Philip 3:49:40 (9,086)
Taylor, Phillip 2:57:25 (950)
Taylor, Phillip 4:27:55 (19,011)
Taylor, Phillip 4:41:30 (22,476)
Taylor, Richard 3:05:27 (1,584)
Taylor, Richard 3:56:24 (11,017)
Taylor, Richard 4:44:54 (23,271)
Taylor, Robert 4:29:52 (19,560)
Taylor, Robin 3:48:34 (8,766)
Taylor, Rupert 4:58:43 (26,082)
Taylor, Saul 3:34:01 (5,522)
Taylor, Scott 4:25:42 (18,439)
Taylor, Scott 4:58:52 (26,110)
Taylor, Simon 4:15:43 (15,758)
Taylor, Simon 4:20:45 (17,059)
Taylor, Stephen 3:56:30 (11,053)
Taylor, Stephen 4:10:42 (14,552)
Taylor, Steve 3:32:52 (5,333)
Taylor, Steven 3:18:27 (3,062)
Taylor, Steven 4:44:42 (23,220)
Taylor, Steven 4:47:55 (24,010)
Taylor, Stuart 4:35:55 (21,057)
Taylor, Stuart 5:18:05 (28,680)
Taylor, Stuart 5:24:54 (29,354)
Taylor, Warrick 4:05:15 (13,262)
Taylor-Schofield, Nigel 4:44:31 (23,181)
Taylorson, Simon 4:16:02 (15,847)
Tcholakian, David 4:31:59 (20,081)
Te Velthuis, Gerben 3:46:29 (8,272)
Teague, Dominic 4:47:01 (23,815)
Teal, Lee 4:19:03 (16,607)
Teare, Ivan 3:28:23 (4,586)
Teasdale, David 5:11:23 (27,866)
Teasel, Sheridan 4:53:32 (25,078)
Tebb, Rupert 5:07:19 (27,346)
Tebbutt, David 3:47:15 (8,449)
Tecchi, Marcello 3:18:44 (3,103)
Tee, George 3:56:11 (10,957)
Tee, Julian 3:38:31 (6,429)
Tee, Paul 2:57:39 (975)
Teideman, Ian 4:19:53 (16,831)
Teles, Francisco 4:54:30 (25,286)
Telfer, Charlie 4:38:29 (21,697)
Telfer, Robert 3:29:54 (4,858)
Telford, Brian 4:10:43 (14,556)
Telford, David 5:24:35 (29,334)
Telling, Barry 4:19:24 (16,688)
Temple, Geoffrey 3:39:08 (6,554)
Temple, Neil 4:06:23 (13,540)
Templeman, Paul 5:18:11 (28,689)
Templer, Mark 4:08:08 (13,939)
Templer, Tristan 4:14:34 (15,460)
Ten Berge, Job 4:07:44 (13,850)
Ten Doornkaat, Fritz 4:45:43 (23,497)
Tengattini, Ezio 3:28:47 (4,658)
Tennant, Brian 3:44:15 (7,722)
Tennant, John 3:08:55 (1,924)
Tennant, Jonathan 4:52:11 (24,813)
Tennant, Mark 3:32:49 (5,320)
Tennant, Paul 4:07:38 (13,826)
Tephaine, Sean 3:50:20 (9,258)
Tergat, Paul 2:05:48 (2)
Terrell, Kevin 5:21:19 (29,026)
Terrell, Stuart 3:40:11 (6,779)
Terriill, Chris 3:42:56 (7,366)
Terrill, Paul 4:59:33 (26,234)

Terrington, Simon 4:52:21 (24,851)
Terry, Andrew 3:58:21 (11,601)
Terry, Christopher 5:10:07 (27,703)
Terry, Colin 5:11:37 (27,895)
Terry, Craig 5:09:41 (27,659)
Terry, Kenneth 4:10:10 (14,430)
Terry, Warren 3:53:47 (10,237)
Tester, Philip 5:41:50 (30,680)
Tester, Victor 4:07:11 (13,718)
Tetley, Christopher 5:15:12 (28,324)
Tetlow, Paul 2:58:50 (1,078)
Tetsill, Ian 4:34:29 (20,688)
Tetstall, Peter 3:58:19 (11,593)
Teubes, Bruce 3:52:20 (9,790)
Thackeray, Brian 4:54:56 (25,364)
Thackeray, Stephen 3:38:51 (6,495)
Thackray, Richard 3:36:08 (5,942)
Thake, Andrew 2:35:48 (104)
Tharme, Gary 3:36:40 (6,051)
Thatcher, Gary 3:45:35 (8,069)
Thatcher, Gary 5:14:51 (28,289)
Thatcher, Mark 5:09:25 (27,624)
Thaw, George 5:40:46 (30,600)
Thawani, Arjun 5:07:38 (27,390)
Theakston, Simon 5:16:51 (28,535)
Theakstone, Ian 3:19:38 (3,217)
Theivendram, Anuraj 4:53:18 (25,024)
Thelen, Karl Heinz 3:35:07 (5,736)
Theobald, Keith 3:57:49 (11,455)
Theobald, Kevin 3:55:59 (10,892)
Theodoulides, Andy 3:29:03 (4,703)
Thers, Soren 3:15:39 (2,748)
Thethi, Paul 4:46:52 (23,777)
Thiebault, Alain 4:09:11 (14,183)
Thiel, Martin 4:36:28 (21,208)
Thiele, Holger 2:45:08 (304)
Thimbleby, Richard 5:06:02 (27,162)
Thing, James 3:59:39 (11,984)
Thirlwell, Paul 5:38:11 (30,423)
Thistlethwaite, Trevor 3:21:59 (3,520)
Thistleton, Terry 5:04:14 (26,926)
Thobhani, Rakesh 4:49:27 (24,311)
Thom, Graham 3:37:29 (6,211)
Thomas, Adrian 4:28:15 (19,099)
Thomas, Alan 2:58:15 (1,028)
Thomas, Alan 4:34:22 (20,664)
Thomas, Alan 5:03:56 (26,876)
Thomas, Alex 4:29:07 (19,354)
Thomas, Andrew 2:59:24 (1,121)
Thomas, Andrew 4:20:01 (16,866)
Thomas, Andrew 4:42:36 (22,748)
Thomas, Andrew 4:48:46 (24,182)
Thomas, Andy 3:53:51 (10,268)
Thomas, Aubrey 3:31:32 (5,114)
Thomas, Barry 4:14:52 (15,542)
Thomas, Bob 3:55:20 (10,710)
Thomas, Bobby 4:11:35 (14,763)
Thomas, Carl 4:24:34 (18,138)
Thomas, Clive 3:12:22 (2,342)
Thomas, Colin 5:13:54 (28,178)
Thomas, Craig 4:52:25 (24,861)
Thomas, Dale 4:40:39 (22,266)
Thomas, Darren 3:05:35 (1,602)
Thomas, David 2:57:16 (933)
Thomas, David 3:11:03 (2,162)
Thomas, David 3:43:47 (7,601)
Thomas, David 3:54:11 (10,371)
Thomas, David 4:10:34 (14,527)
Thomas, David 4:18:48 (16,548)
Thomas, David 4:39:39 (22,003)
Thomas, David 4:45:45 (23,503)
Thomas, David 5:57:59 (31,474)
Thomas, David 6:40:46 (32,442)
Thomas, Eddie 5:10:48 (27,784)
Thomas, Francis 3:49:48 (9,133)
Thomas, Frank 3:18:54 (3,125)
Thomas, Gareth 2:55:34 (786)
Thomas, Gary 3:58:05 (11,536)
Thomas, Gary 5:10:25 (27,739)
Thomas, George 4:18:03 (16,380)
Thomas, Glyn 4:24:33 (18,131)
Thomas, Glyn 5:30:50 (29,851)
Thomas, Graham 4:08:49 (14,094)

Thomas, Graham	4:10:47 (14,571)	
Thomas, Graham	4:43:54 (23,044)	
Thomas, Howard	4:17:35 (16,265)	
Thomas, Huw	3:44:36 (7,820)	
Thomas, Huw	4:37:36 (21,468)	
Thomas, Huw	5:18:53 (28,764)	
Thomas, Iain	3:43:24 (7,496)	
Thomas, Iain	3:49:21 (8,985)	
Thomas, Ian	3:23:38 (3,749)	
Thomas, Ian	3:53:41 (10,205)	
Thomas, Ian	3:58:38 (11,688)	
Thomas, Ian	4:16:10 (15,881)	
Thomas, Ian	4:21:28 (17,238)	
Thomas, Jeff	3:38:47 (6,482)	
Thomas, Jeremy	3:51:09 (9,472)	
Thomas, John	3:45:57 (8,148)	
Thomas, John	4:57:10 (25,805)	
Thomas, Julian	5:41:47 (30,673)	
Thomas, Justin	3:05:16 (1,563)	
Thomas, L	3:10:45 (2,127)	
Thomas, Lea	4:49:54 (24,407)	
Thomas, Leighton	3:16:31 (2,846)	
Thomas, Leighton	3:27:43 (4,459)	
Thomas, Leon	4:24:29 (18,117)	
Thomas, Malcolm	4:17:40 (16,284)	
Thomas, Mark	5:55:08 (31,359)	
Thomas, Matthew	3:54:44 (10,529)	
Thomas, Matthew	4:38:42 (21,761)	
Thomas, Michael	3:27:51 (4,492)	
Thomas, Michael	3:45:40 (8,086)	
Thomas, Neil	4:37:10 (21,355)	
Thomas, Nicholas	4:02:49 (12,733)	
Thomas, Nick	4:20:07 (16,891)	
Thomas, Nigel	3:55:06 (10,628)	
Thomas, Pau	3:24:45 (3,952)	
Thomas, Paul	4:37:10 (21,355)	
Thomas, Paul	4:38:04 (21,589)	
Thomas, Paul	4:55:32 (25,487)	
Thomas, Paul	5:58:43 (31,505)	
Thomas, Peter	3:17:17 (2,931)	
Thomas, Peter	3:44:24 (7,773)	
Thomas, Peter	4:21:12 (17,165)	
Thomas, Peter	5:20:58 (28,988)	
Thomas, Richard	2:56:28 (869)	
Thomas, Richard	4:02:10 (12,588)	
Thomas, Richard	4:10:12 (14,437)	
Thomas, Richard	4:36:59 (21,309)	
Thomas, Robert	4:05:26 (13,311)	
Thomas, Robert	4:49:49 (24,383)	
Thomas, Ron	5:22:50 (29,160)	
Thomas, Ronald	4:15:54 (15,810)	
Thomas, Roy	3:05:35 (1,602)	
Thomas, Russell	2:55:21 (767)	
Thomas, Simon	3:49:45 (9,112)	
Thomas, Simon	4:23:03 (17,717)	
Thomas, Steve	4:39:06 (21,875)	
Thomas, Steven	5:03:56 (26,876)	
Thomas, Trevor	4:13:44 (15,248)	
Thomas, Wayne	3:22:43 (3,615)	
Thomas-Bourgneur, Jacques	3:42:26 (7,269)	
Thomason, Alan	5:03:33 (26,827)	
Thomason, Francis	3:14:33 (2,614)	
Thompson, Alan	4:01:38 (12,476)	
Thompson, Anders	4:39:19 (21,925)	
Thompson, Andrew	3:23:45 (3,765)	
Thompson, Andrew	3:46:15 (8,211)	
Thompson, Andrew	4:18:34 (16,501)	
Thompson, Andrew	4:51:31 (24,703)	
Thompson, Andy	3:24:37 (3,932)	
Thompson, Andy	5:03:18 (26,797)	
Thompson, Barry	3:02:16 (1,322)	
Thompson, Charlie	6:04:37 (31,679)	
Thompson, Chris	3:56:28 (11,033)	
Thompson, Chris	5:11:48 (27,921)	
Thompson, Chris	5:26:51 (29,512)	
Thompson, Christopher	3:38:36 (6,450)	
Thompson, Colin	3:29:13 (4,731)	
Thompson, Darren	3:54:36 (10,487)	
Thompson, Dave	4:16:31 (15,984)	
Thompson, David	2:57:32 (962)	
Thompson, David	4:29:22 (19,424)	
Thompson, David	4:58:34 (26,049)	
Thompson, David	5:54:25 (31,330)	

Thompson, Garth	3:29:07 (4,714)	
Thompson, Gary	3:39:55 (6,714)	
Thompson, Howard	4:33:02 (20,360)	
Thompson, Iain	3:14:15 (2,587)	
Thompson, Iain	3:43:45 (7,589)	
Thompson, Ian	3:35:45 (5,855)	
Thompson, Ian	4:06:20 (13,524)	
Thompson, Ian	4:39:19 (21,925)	
Thompson, James	2:49:46 (475)	
Thompson, James	3:50:22 (9,268)	
Thompson, James	4:01:30 (12,441)	
Thompson, Jamie	3:54:12 (10,374)	
Thompson, John	4:01:44 (12,502)	
Thompson, John	4:26:53 (18,757)	
Thompson, Jon	3:55:05 (10,619)	
Thompson, Jonathan	4:43:30 (22,961)	
Thompson, Keith	4:20:33 (17,006)	
Thompson, Kenneth	5:00:39 (26,401)	
Thompson, Kenneth	5:02:27 (26,660)	
Thompson, Kevin	4:15:28 (15,684)	
Thompson, Laurence	3:44:45 (7,874)	
Thompson, Mark	2:46:57 (358)	
Thompson, Mark	3:03:02 (1,374)	
Thompson, Mark	3:59:23 (11,914)	
Thompson, Mark	4:04:48 (13,160)	
Thompson, Martin	3:18:50 (3,116)	
Thompson, Matt	4:37:24 (21,422)	
Thompson, Mel	4:22:44 (17,618)	
Thompson, Neil	5:18:55 (28,768)	
Thompson, Nick	3:57:03 (11,224)	
Thompson, Nigel	3:07:48 (1,793)	
Thompson, Nigel	4:20:32 (17,000)	
Thompson, Patrick	4:38:35 (21,730)	
Thompson, Paul	3:11:51 (2,252)	
Thompson, Paul	3:25:56 (4,142)	
Thompson, Paul	4:17:52 (16,341)	
Thompson, Peter	3:26:10 (4,181)	
Thompson, Phillip	4:22:03 (17,412)	
Thompson, Richard	4:24:34 (18,138)	
Thompson, Richard	4:24:38 (18,154)	
Thompson, Robert	3:37:19 (6,167)	
Thompson, Robert	3:53:11 (10,040)	
Thompson, Robert	4:21:41 (17,309)	
Thompson, Ron	4:28:40 (19,213)	
Thompson, Roy	4:49:14 (24,281)	
Thompson, Scott	3:56:28 (11,033)	
Thompson, Simon	5:04:38 (26,970)	
Thompson, Stephen	2:48:06 (407)	
Thompson, Stephen	4:39:32 (21,978)	
Thompson, Stuart	3:44:32 (7,804)	
Thompson, Stuart	4:10:27 (14,497)	
Thompson, Tom	4:25:27 (18,371)	
Thompson, Tony	3:08:35 (1,879)	
Thompson, Victor	3:35:37 (5,829)	
Thompstone, George	3:46:10 (8,193)	
Thompstone, Rodger	3:14:11 (2,572)	
Thoms, Kenneth	3:51:35 (9,569)	
Thomsett, Martin	5:34:32 (30,152)	
Thomson, Adam	2:47:48 (394)	
Thomson, Bob	3:58:00 (11,508)	
Thomson, Colin	4:36:18 (21,153)	
Thomson, David	3:52:02 (9,700)	
Thomson, Denis	3:26:38 (4,257)	
Thomson, Gary	4:44:51 (23,257)	
Thomson, George	3:37:00 (6,118)	
Thomson, Iain	5:08:13 (27,461)	
Thomson, Ian	4:20:35 (17,019)	
Thomson, James	4:32:25 (20,194)	
Thomson, Michael	2:57:36 (969)	
Thomson, Michael	3:57:29 (11,359)	
Thomson, Paul	3:12:02 (2,277)	
Thomson, Paul	3:22:14 (3,557)	
Thomson, Paul	4:33:56 (20,564)	
Thomson, Peter	3:58:09 (11,556)	
Thomson, Peter	3:59:49 (12,028)	
Thomson, Richard	4:06:51 (13,638)	
Thomson, Robert	3:41:26 (7,051)	
Thomson, Robert	3:53:58 (10,299)	
Thomson, Robert	4:54:40 (25,318)	
Thomson, Robin	4:20:16 (16,932)	
Thomson, Roger	4:43:26 (22,940)	
Thomson, Simon	3:32:29 (5,267)	
Thomson, Stewart	4:54:29 (25,282)	

Thomson, Stuart	5:23:56 (29,277)	
Thomson, Wayne	3:52:02 (9,700)	
Thong, James	5:00:26 (26,364)	
Thorburn, Peter	3:49:32 (9,051)	
Thoren, Bjorn	4:32:22 (20,181)	
Thorn, David	3:52:14 (9,762)	
Thorn, Michael	3:30:11 (4,893)	
Thorn, Sidney	6:22:02 (32,125)	
Thornby, David	3:21:02 (3,371)	
Thorne, Colin	4:44:03 (23,074)	
Thorne, David	3:43:31 (7,533)	
Thorne, Ian	5:12:15 (27,984)	
Thorne, Nigel	5:57:39 (31,464)	
Thorne, Simon	4:33:33 (20,472)	
Thorne-Jones, Stuart	5:08:31 (27,498)	
Thornhill, Andy	3:56:50 (11,149)	
Thornhill, Ernest	3:31:44 (5,158)	
Thornley, Andrew	4:20:36 (17,022)	
Thorns, David	3:24:05 (3,836)	
Thornton, Andrew	4:39:31 (21,973)	
Thornton, Dean	3:07:04 (1,741)	
Thornton, James	4:27:27 (18,905)	
Thornton, Jason	4:43:06 (22,865)	
Thornton, Myles	5:54:16 (31,324)	
Thornton, Stanley	4:25:32 (18,396)	
Thorogood, Andrew	5:06:21 (27,204)	
Thorp, Philip	3:34:07 (5,546)	
Thorpe, Andrew	3:58:26 (11,629)	
Thorpe, Barry	3:18:36 (3,083)	
Thorpe, Barry	3:46:23 (8,246)	
Thorpe, Benjamin	5:21:03 (28,999)	
Thorpe, David	4:18:55 (16,571)	
Thorpe, Glenn	4:10:15 (14,449)	
Thorpe, Graham	4:15:15 (15,633)	
Thorpe, Ian	3:39:11 (6,565)	
Thorpe, James	4:56:58 (25,759)	
Thorpe, Nigel	5:18:14 (28,695)	
Thorpe, Roger	4:01:36 (12,469)	
Thorpe, Stuart	3:50:12 (9,215)	
Thorsteinsson, Gautur	3:03:58 (1,164)	
Thorsteinsson, Orn	3:50:55 (9,402)	
Thouless, Gavin	4:07:03 (13,686)	
Thraves, Jonathan	3:38:58 (6,515)	
Thraves, Peter	4:06:31 (13,571)	
Threadgold, Colin	4:45:12 (23,356)	
Threlfall, Kevin	4:47:01 (23,815)	
Thrower, Edward	5:15:04 (28,307)	
Thrower, Steve	2:56:35 (880)	
Thurgar-Dawson, Chris	4:48:00 (24,029)	
Thurgood, Geoffrey	5:17:50 (28,654)	
Thurgood, Hugh	4:14:44 (15,508)	
Thurgood, Lyndon	4:23:15 (17,760)	
Thurlow, Ivan	5:20:18 (28,915)	
Thurlow, Robert	4:58:36 (26,055)	
Thurston, Colin	2:50:44 (522)	
Thurston, Ian	3:44:09 (7,695)	
Thurston, Philip	4:29:40 (19,499)	
Thury, Werner	4:28:50 (19,269)	
Thusan, Viv	4:27:06 (18,818)	
Thust, Wolfgang	4:32:42 (20,277)	
Thwaite, Paul	3:44:39 (7,837)	
Thwaites, Jeremy	4:04:42 (13,135)	
Tibbs, Gary	4:39:51 (22,070)	
Tibbs, Stephen	2:47:54 (400)	
Tichbon, Peter	5:29:58 (29,778)	
Tickle, Andrew	5:49:09 (31,106)	
Tidder, Anthony	4:22:34 (17,564)	
Tideswell, Simon	3:52:47 (9,922)	
Tidiman, Steve	3:29:03 (4,703)	
Tie, Daniell	3:25:23 (4,043)	
Tiernan, Patrick	3:12:13 (2,316)	
Tierney, Roy	3:44:15 (7,722)	
Tietz, Karl	3:17:14 (2,926)	
Tieulie, Alain	4:21:08 (17,151)	
Tighe, Mark	3:14:38 (2,621)	
Tighe, Michael	4:05:25 (13,305)	
Tighe, Patrick	5:51:58 (31,230)	
Tiley, David	4:06:14 (13,498)	
Tilke, Warren	4:23:03 (17,717)	
Till, David	5:13:00 (28,081)	
Till, Stephen	3:15:25 (2,716)	
Tillbrooke, Tony	4:09:38 (14,300)	
Tiller, Brian	4:51:33 (24,711)	

Tiller, David	4:35:36 (20,987)	
Tiller, Mark	3:18:07 (3,025)	
Tillery, Andrew	2:58:31 (1,052)	
Tilley, Ian	3:51:15 (9,487)	
Tilley, Jonathan	3:54:40 (10,506)	
Tilley, Kevin	2:45:39 (317)	
Tilley, Richard	3:48:31 (8,751)	
Tilling, Martin	3:27:02 (4,336)	
Tillotson, Marcus	3:14:38 (2,621)	
Tilly, Alan	4:11:29 (14,741)	
Tilsley, Andrew	2:55:41 (797)	
Tilton, Mike	4:36:14 (21,136)	
Timanti, Claudio	5:10:05 (27,698)	
Timmis, Brian	4:32:15 (20,149)	
Timms, Adrian	4:46:20 (23,649)	
Timms, Geoffrey	4:09:00 (14,133)	
Timms, Mitchell	4:14:26 (15,433)	
Tindal, Peter	4:38:11 (21,621)	
Tindale, Ian	2:39:18 (172)	
Tindall, David	4:32:45 (20,289)	
Tindall, Steven	4:09:02 (14,140)	
Tindell, Benjamin	5:23:55 (29,275)	
Tindill, Michael	4:10:08 (14,424)	
Tindle, Vincent	2:59:28 (1,129)	
Tingle, Christopher	3:59:03 (11,823)	
Tinham, Andrew	4:11:25 (14,715)	
Tinker, Andrew	3:53:44 (10,218)	
Tinker, Brian	4:59:22 (26,190)	
Tinker, Kenneth	4:13:58 (15,301)	
Tinkler, Alan	5:03:04 (26,755)	
Tinkler, Sean	4:22:18 (17,476)	
Tinnyunt, Robert	4:09:42 (14,318)	
Tinsley, Andrew	4:51:17 (24,665)	
Tinsley, Anthony	5:00:32 (26,382)	
Tinsley, David	3:02:45 (1,355)	
Tinsley, Ian	6:12:11 (31,885)	
Tinsley, Maurice	3:58:41 (11,701)	
Tinsley, Paul	3:25:03 (3,993)	
Tinson, Adam	4:41:05 (22,371)	
Tipler, Philip	3:17:41 (2,972)	
Tipp, Daniel	4:30:01 (19,597)	
Tippen, Ian	4:26:26 (18,631)	
Tipper, Andrew	4:34:23 (20,668)	
Tipple, Richard	4:25:42 (18,439)	
Tipson, Russell	3:36:42 (6,059)	
Titchener, Frank	4:46:39 (23,724)	
Titcomb, Mark	3:57:12 (11,263)	
Titcomb, Paul	3:50:57 (9,411)	
Titcombe, Graham	3:58:00 (11,508)	
Titley, John	5:07:27 (27,367)	
Titmaa, Alan-John	4:37:52 (21,536)	
Titmarsh, Jeffrey	4:42:50 (22,799)	
Tjakkes, Geerten-Has	3:53:13 (10,048)	
Tjakkes, Tjakko	3:53:13 (10,048)	
Tng, Chin Tzong	5:42:19 (30,714)	
Toach, Terence	4:11:38 (14,777)	
Tobin, Daniel	4:17:37 (16,273)	
Tobin, David	6:05:19 (31,708)	
Tobin, Ray	5:31:07 (29,874)	
Tobin, Thomas	6:37:54 (32,410)	
Toby, Jackson	3:40:12 (6,786)	
Todd, David	3:37:43 (6,269)	
Todd, Edward	3:18:12 (3,033)	
Todd, Michael	5:25:43 (29,423)	
Todd, Paul	2:55:03 (747)	
Todd, Perry	3:22:01 (3,528)	
Todman, William	4:27:17 (18,858)	
Toffolo, Stefano	4:16:56 (16,100)	
Toft, Adam	4:56:28 (25,687)	
Tola, Tesfaye	2:29:21 (63)	
Tolan, Brendon	3:24:18 (3,877)	
Tole, Christopher	4:00:45 (12,247)	
Tolentino, Sandro	2:59:11 (1,109)	
Tolfree, Andrew	4:21:39 (17,297)	
Tolfrey, Neil	3:12:12 (2,312)	
Toller, Simon	3:49:38 (9,078)	
Tolley, David	3:52:32 (9,849)	
Tolley, Vivian	2:48:02 (403)	
Tollfree, John	4:21:26 (17,228)	
Tollit, Ryan	4:08:04 (13,929)	
Tomas, Albino	3:10:10 (2,054)	
Tomassini, Michele	4:46:56 (23,798)	
Tomblin, David	3:53:13 (10,048)	

Tombs, Jonathan	3:47:31 (8,515)	
Tomin, Valentine	3:52:22 (9,805)	
Tomkins, Kevin	3:57:19 (11,298)	
Tomkinson, Aaron	4:10:03 (14,401)	
Tomkinson-Hill, Nicholas	4:02:46 (12,719)	
Tomley, James	3:43:34 (7,543)	
Tomlin, Peter	3:56:37 (11,090)	
Tomlin, Peter	4:58:13 (25,987)	
Tomlins, Andrew	4:27:14 (18,851)	
Tomlinson, Alan	5:35:16 (30,206)	
Tomlinson, Dennis	3:03:52 (1,455)	
Tomlinson, Frederick	6:51:02 (32,552)	
Tomlinson, Geoffrey	2:51:13 (545)	
Tomlinson, Howard	4:36:50 (21,286)	
Tomlinson, Ian	4:31:02 (19,834)	
Tomlinson, James	2:48:35 (430)	
Tomlinson, James	4:33:47 (20,534)	
Tomlinson, John	4:19:37 (16,754)	
Tomlinson, Mark	3:14:13 (2,581)	
Tomlinson, Sam	4:08:16 (13,966)	
Tomlinson, Warren	3:31:05 (5,043)	
Tompkins, Bill	5:04:34 (26,960)	
Toms, David	3:57:42 (11,422)	
Toms, David	4:26:13 (18,578)	
Toms, Roy	6:00:12 (31,550)	
Toner, Hugo	5:18:17 (28,700)	
Tones, Darran	4:24:50 (18,210)	
Tong, Michael	4:54:08 (25,208)	
Tonge, David	3:28:54 (4,679)	
Tonks, Henry	5:00:11 (26,334)	
Tonna, David	4:31:16 (19,892)	
Tooke, Stephen	3:37:21 (6,176)	
Toolan, John	3:43:05 (7,408)	
Toolan, Nicholas	3:42:11 (7,196)	
Tooley, Mark	4:18:02 (16,377)	
Toone, Simon	4:44:51 (23,257)	
Tooth, Paul	4:59:38 (26,250)	
Tooze, Paul	3:56:03 (10,913)	
Toplis, Paul	4:37:59 (21,571)	
Topol, Adam	4:07:47 (13,866)	
Topolewski, Jan	4:17:04 (16,135)	
Topper, Simon	3:08:58 (1,932)	
Topps, Jonathan	4:13:21 (15,155)	
Topps, Jonathan	4:13:21 (15,155)	
Tordoff, Mark	3:51:34 (9,564)	
Torelli, Giovanni	2:51:12 (543)	
Torgersen, Tommy	2:47:03 (363)	
Torre, Peter	4:39:42 (22,026)	
Torres, Hector	3:35:46 (5,859)	
Torresi, Massimo	3:06:03 (1,645)	
Torseillo, Antonino	3:39:05 (6,544)	
Torz, Edmunds	3:48:42 (8,812)	
Toseland, Gary	6:12:44 (31,902)	
Toseland, Peter	4:12:59 (15,076)	
Toson, Dino	4:00:59 (12,304)	
Totterdell, Graham	5:01:15 (26,492)	
Tottman, Philip	6:23:42 (32,161)	
Toudic, Gerald	2:58:11 (1,021)	
Tourle, Kevin	3:24:58 (3,985)	
Touse, Kevin	4:41:59 (22,603)	
Tovey, Christopher	3:49:27 (9,027)	
Tovey, Gerald	5:18:01 (28,674)	
Tovey, Jacob	3:44:31 (7,797)	
Tow, Kelvyn	4:51:26 (24,686)	
Toward, Evan	5:27:25 (29,571)	
Towell, Derrick	4:25:36 (18,418)	
Towers, Geoffrey	3:29:27 (4,784)	
Towler, Colin	5:11:30 (27,886)	
Town, Jamie	3:49:26 (9,021)	
Townend, Richard	3:36:57 (6,107)	
Townley, Matt	4:04:17 (13,042)	
Townrow, Michael	5:28:32 (29,657)	
Townsend, David	4:21:00 (17,110)	
Townsend, Gary	4:25:40 (18,434)	
Townsend, Martin	3:24:04 (3,833)	
Townsend, Nicolas	6:29:23 (32,262)	
Townsend, Robin	3:40:29 (6,847)	
Townsend, Steven	4:14:19 (15,398)	
Townsend, Ted	3:21:19 (3,410)	
Townsend, Victor	5:38:40 (30,458)	
Townsley, Christopher	4:43:19 (22,913)	
Townson, Matthew	4:16:53 (16,086)	
Tozer, Don	4:50:55 (24,594)	

Tozer, Ross	2:55:00 (741)	
Tracey, Thomas	3:21:21 (3,413)	
Tracy, Simon	4:07:22 (13,767)	
Trafford, Brian	5:40:35 (30,590)	
Trafford, Peter	3:53:01 (9,985)	
Trafford, Stephen	4:47:12 (23,856)	
Train, Paul	4:43:56 (23,051)	
Traini, Giancarlo	4:25:08 (18,295)	
Trainor, Chris	4:21:13 (17,168)	
Tran, Tho	5:57:54 (31,472)	
Tranter, Carl	4:39:41 (22,016)	
Tranter, Chris	4:39:41 (22,016)	
Tranter, Paul	3:48:27 (8,735)	
Travers, Duncan	3:58:23 (11,614)	
Travers, Glen	4:14:53 (15,550)	
Travers, Rob	4:29:44 (19,520)	
Trawinski, Dieter	3:45:19 (8,003)	
Treacher, Christopher	3:21:22 (3,414)	
Treacy, Glenn	2:56:45 (892)	
Treadwell, Andrew	4:16:48 (16,064)	
Treadwell, Robert	3:24:52 (3,966)	
Trebilcock, Mark	3:22:35 (3,592)	
Trebilcock, Norman	4:52:30 (24,877)	
Tredgett, John	3:07:29 (1,767)	
Tregoning, John	4:01:45 (12,505)	
Trehearne, Edward	4:20:32 (17,000)	
Treherne, Jonathan	4:29:48 (19,534)	
Treleaven, David	3:44:36 (7,820)	
Trelfa-McHardy, Keith	5:10:42 (27,774)	
Trelogan, Michael	4:45:20 (23,389)	
Tremain, Andrew	4:03:22 (12,849)	
Tremble, Philip	3:50:34 (9,314)	
Trennery, David	4:38:19 (21,663)	
Trent, Timothy	3:36:56 (6,104)	
Trenter, Russell	5:12:57 (28,075)	
Tresias, Andrew	3:55:30 (10,745)	
Tresidder, Charles	3:51:59 (9,678)	
Trevett, Gordon	4:47:51 (23,990)	
Trevett, Terry	4:40:11 (22,154)	
Trevillion, Phil	4:11:58 (14,851)	
Trevis, Charles	4:33:39 (20,506)	
Trevithick, Nigel	4:39:44 (22,037)	
Trew, Paul	5:07:14 (27,340)	
Tribe, Barrie	3:44:04 (7,669)	
Tricker, Colin	3:49:39 (9,083)	
Trigg-Graynoth, Gary	5:02:40 (26,695)	
Triggs, Jeff	3:56:58 (11,200)	
Triggs, Simon	4:13:51 (15,272)	
Trigiani, Giuseppe	6:04:18 (31,668)	
Trilk, Nigel	3:53:15 (10,061)	
Trill, Gerard	4:12:49 (15,041)	
Trill, Robert	3:10:24 (2,090)	
Trim, Benjamin	5:13:27 (28,133)	
Trim, Mark	5:14:48 (28,282)	
Trim, Nick	5:13:27 (28,133)	
Trimarco, Costantino	3:22:46 (3,627)	
Trimming, James	3:41:08 (6,999)	
Trindell, Daniel	4:24:52 (18,222)	
Trinham, Francis	6:36:44 (32,388)	
Trinks, Immo	4:40:27 (22,222)	
Tristram, Andrew	4:05:25 (13,305)	
Trivett, Jeremy	4:33:59 (20,576)	
Trodd, Ron	4:16:15 (15,899)	
Trollope, Neil	3:27:59 (4,515)	
Tromans, Benjamin	3:06:28 (1,680)	
Tromans, Stuart	3:27:46 (4,471)	
Tromboni, Alessio	3:50:24 (9,276)	
Troni, Alberto	3:31:59 (5,186)	
Troop, Nicholas	4:36:22 (21,182)	
Trory, John	3:43:17 (7,467)	
Trotman, Michael	4:11:09 (14,666)	
Trott, Mark	3:52:24 (9,812)	
Trott, Michael	5:39:21 (30,493)	
Trott, Stuart	5:49:21 (31,116)	
Trotter, Douglas	4:42:59 (22,834)	
Trotter, Ian	4:14:31 (15,449)	
Troup, Mike	3:10:11 (2,057)	
Trowsdale, John	4:50:24 (24,479)	
Troy, Malcolm	4:21:47 (17,332)	
Truby, Karl	4:01:02 (12,319)	
Trucco, Lorenzo	3:59:56 (12,066)	
Trudgeon, Kevin	5:49:02 (31,102)	
Truelove, Michael	3:51:52 (9,644)	

Trueman, Neil	6:03:00 (31,639)	
Truman, Daniel	3:30:10 (4,892)	
Truman, Matthew	3:48:24 (8,721)	
Trumble, Christopher	4:53:11 (25,010)	
Trumper, Paul	5:20:29 (28,937)	
Truscott, James	4:07:53 (13,890)	
Trusler, Neil	4:56:47 (25,729)	
Trustram, Paul	3:43:06 (7,410)	
Truswell, Nigel	3:18:49 (3,114)	
Try, Chris	2:43:08 (246)	
Tsanga, Tendai	3:14:08 (2,568)	
Tsavliris, George	5:11:54 (27,938)	
Tse, Kenny	4:37:16 (21,394)	
Tse, Ricky	3:13:02 (2,437)	
Tse, Yincent	4:39:23 (21,946)	
Tsouvallaris, Peter	5:09:33 (27,638)	
Tsunomiya, Kazumitsu	3:45:47 (8,110)	
Tubb, James	4:49:43 (24,364)	
Tubb, Robert	5:12:36 (28,037)	
Tubby, James	3:53:55 (10,283)	
Tuck, Stephen	4:06:15 (13,504)	
Tuck, Steven	2:56:00 (829)	
Tucker, Andrew	6:14:36 (31,946)	
Tucker, Christopher	4:02:02 (12,566)	
Tucker, Clifford	4:56:07 (25,614)	
Tucker, Colin	4:56:41 (25,715)	
Tucker, Darren	4:47:51 (23,990)	
Tucker, David	3:09:54 (2,027)	
Tucker, Edward	4:21:40 (17,305)	
Tucker, Graham	4:21:49 (17,342)	
Tucker, Jeremy	3:26:56 (4,317)	
Tucker, Peter	5:01:12 (26,481)	
Tucker, Stephen	3:53:51 (10,268)	
Tucker, Steve	4:16:27 (15,969)	
Tueter, Trygue	3:39:50 (6,693)	
Tuffnell, Shaun	4:03:30 (12,881)	
Tuffs, Simon	5:33:13 (30,045)	
Tufnell, Raoul	3:17:17 (2,931)	
Tufton, Grant	5:10:58 (27,811)	
Tugwell, Peter	4:25:05 (18,281)	
Tulip, Alan	2:59:40 (1,144)	
Tull, Andrew	3:27:44 (4,465)	
Tull, Danny	3:52:49 (9,929)	
Tull, David	3:18:01 (3,010)	
Tulloch, Gordon	4:33:19 (20,423)	
Tully, Christopher	5:08:20 (27,474)	
Tully, Glyn	3:45:27 (8,029)	
Tunana, Luke	4:35:01 (20,839)	
Tunley, Roger	3:43:55 (7,635)	
Tunstall, Paul	3:44:26 (7,780)	
Tunstall-Pedoe, Hugh	4:40:05 (22,129)	
Tunvor, Pradip	3:58:39 (11,691)	
Tuohy, Marcus	3:52:12 (9,754)	
Tupling, Steve	4:44:20 (23,138)	
Turfus, Colin	3:36:36 (6,043)	
Turk, David	4:03:02 (12,782)	
Turk, Stephen	3:28:46 (4,652)	
Turley, Richard	4:42:01 (22,610)	
Turnbull, Christopher	4:17:02 (16,129)	
Turnbull, John	4:17:01 (16,121)	
Turnbull, Matthew	4:22:47 (17,631)	
Turnbull, Rory	4:15:52 (15,798)	
Turnbull, Stuart	5:08:00 (27,435)	
Turner, Adrian	3:55:31 (10,750)	
Turner, Alan	4:53:57 (25,176)	
Turner, Alistair	3:48:24 (8,721)	
Turner, Andrew	3:05:28 (1,586)	
Turner, Andrew	3:21:31 (3,438)	
Turner, Andrew	3:42:22 (7,252)	
Turner, Andrew	4:11:32 (14,752)	
Turner, Ben	6:34:49 (32,349)	
Turner, Benjamin	4:28:23 (19,131)	
Turner, Benjamin	4:52:52 (24,954)	
Turner, Brian	3:01:02 (1,227)	
Turner, Charles	5:33:15 (30,049)	
Turner, Christopher	4:55:44 (25,527)	
Turner, Dale	4:47:59 (24,024)	
Turner, Dean	4:53:24 (25,049)	
Turner, Derek	4:24:34 (18,138)	
Turner, Edward	4:46:07 (23,594)	
Turner, Geoff	3:13:10 (2,460)	
Turner, Geoff	3:39:38 (6,654)	
Turner, Glen	4:27:18 (18,864)	
Turner, Graham	4:35:46 (21,021)	
Turner, Grahame	4:19:24 (16,688)	
Turner, Guy	4:48:42 (24,168)	
Turner, Hugh	5:10:05 (27,698)	
Turner, Ian	3:48:42 (8,812)	
Turner, James	4:30:48 (19,785)	
Turner, James	4:44:35 (23,195)	
Turner, John	3:19:52 (3,238)	
Turner, John	4:14:48 (15,526)	
Turner, John	4:20:30 (16,990)	
Turner, Julian	3:13:27 (2,498)	
Turner, Keith	2:40:10 (185)	
Turner, Kevin	4:09:19 (14,224)	
Turner, Lee	3:50:50 (9,382)	
Turner, Mark	3:21:03 (3,374)	
Turner, Matthew	3:42:27 (7,276)	
Turner, Matthew	5:42:18 (30,712)	
Turner, Matthew	6:08:16 (31,790)	
Turner, Michael	3:57:51 (11,464)	
Turner, Michael	4:28:58 (19,313)	
Turner, Neil	6:16:05 (31,986)	
Turner, Norman	4:37:58 (21,568)	
Turner, Peter	2:49:05 (449)	
Turner, Philip	5:27:01 (29,523)	
Turner, Richard	4:33:41 (20,513)	
Turner, Richard	4:50:08 (24,443)	
Turner, Richard	5:55:44 (31,389)	
Turner, Robert	4:05:52 (13,403)	
Turner, Roger	3:41:02 (6,973)	
Turner, Samuel	5:44:43 (30,871)	
Turner, Simon	4:43:28 (22,956)	
Turner, Stephen	3:43:07 (7,418)	
Turner, Stephen	5:09:20 (27,612)	
Turner, Stephen	6:16:08 (31,988)	
Turner, Steve	5:04:52 (27,009)	
Turner, Steven	3:57:16 (11,280)	
Turner, Terry	3:34:52 (5,688)	
Turner, Thomas	4:43:24 (22,932)	
Turpin, Geoff	4:11:37 (14,774)	
Turpin, John	3:56:59 (11,203)	
Turton, Brian	3:08:56 (1,908)	
Turton, Les	3:05:52 (1,627)	
Turvey, Brian	4:50:02 (24,429)	
Turvey, Matthew	3:20:07 (3,268)	
Turvey, Peter	4:00:25 (12,170)	
Tuson, Neil	4:58:33 (26,041)	
Tuson, William	4:08:34 (14,045)	
Tutt, Graham	3:18:06 (3,020)	
Tutt, Kevin	4:01:32 (12,452)	
Tutt, Michael	5:56:00 (31,398)	
Tvohy, Stephen	4:35:04 (20,846)	
Twaite, Peter	5:02:32 (26,674)	
Tweed, Andrew	3:45:15 (7,989)	
Tweed, Kevin	4:25:35 (18,410)	
Tweeddale, Eoin	4:56:13 (25,639)	
Tweedie, Alex	3:29:31 (4,800)	
Tweedie, Daniel	4:04:29 (13,085)	
Twigger-Ross, Malcolm	4:02:39 (12,691)	
Twilley, John	4:36:20 (21,174)	
Twilton, David	3:52:39 (9,881)	
Twiner, Richard	4:34:23 (20,668)	
Twite, Paul	4:31:17 (19,897)	
Twomey, Eamonn	3:22:43 (3,615)	
Twomey, Ray	3:10:45 (2,127)	
Twort, Christopher	3:51:51 (9,638)	
Tyabji, Adil	4:17:07 (16,148)	
Tyalor, Euan	3:59:52 (12,046)	
Tyalor, Laurence	4:42:49 (22,796)	
Tyas, Adrian	3:38:21 (6,386)	
Tyas, Christopher	5:30:18 (29,803)	
Tyas, Stephen	4:27:20 (18,873)	
Tychowski, Georges	5:03:05 (26,759)	
Tye, Colin	3:54:58 (10,586)	
Tyler, John	3:08:50 (1,913)	
Tyler, Keith	5:56:03 (31,403)	
Tyler, Robert	4:52:18 (24,843)	
Tyler, Simon	4:45:57 (23,552)	
Tyler, Stephen	4:29:27 (19,449)	
Tyler, Steven	4:26:10 (18,568)	
Tym, Colin	3:58:11 (11,564)	
Tyrer, Nick	4:54:19 (25,246)	
Tyrer, Paddy	4:54:19 (25,246)	
Tyrer, Richard	3:28:19 (4,571)	
Tyrrell, Alex	3:20:24 (3,299)	
Tyrrell, Bryan	4:39:17 (21,921)	
Tyrrell, Christopher	3:30:22 (4,924)	
Tyrrell, Christopher	4:52:11 (24,813)	
Tyrrell, Colin	6:43:57 (32,476)	
Tyrrell, Michael	5:06:25 (27,219)	
Tyson, Evan	4:06:06 (13,460)	
Tyson, Michael	3:53:35 (10,175)	
Tyson, Neil	4:59:23 (26,197)	
Tyson, Peter Jnr	4:31:39 (20,000)	
Tyszkiewicz, John	3:51:50 (9,632)	
Tytherleigh, Martin	3:47:33 (8,523)	
Tyzack, David	4:19:41 (16,775)	
Ubaldino, Pascal	2:58:27 (1,044)	
Ubsdell, Simon	2:55:38 (792)	
Ucko, Manfred	3:30:16 (4,909)	
Ufert, Stefan	4:06:38 (13,596)	
Uff, Frederick	3:58:55 (11,767)	
Uff, Stephen	4:57:37 (25,881)	
Ufken, Tobias	3:53:26 (10,116)	
Ugelstad, Ole-Jonny	4:23:25 (17,806)	
Ukiah, Bob	4:22:22 (17,507)	
Ulislam, Noor	5:45:30 (30,910)	
Ullman, James	4:36:31 (21,226)	
Ullmann, Tibor	3:15:53 (2,777)	
Ulrich, Kai-Uwe	3:34:48 (5,676)	
Umbers, Douglas	4:15:31 (15,700)	
Underdown, Marc	4:19:24 (16,688)	
Underhill, Christian	5:20:21 (28,922)	
Underhill, Roger	4:32:34 (20,234)	
Underhill, William	3:28:31 (4,606)	
Underwood, Dennis	4:05:19 (13,277)	
Underwood, Peter	3:16:01 (2,790)	
Underwood, Victor	4:34:14 (20,636)	
Unerman, Martin	4:06:57 (13,662)	
Ungi, Thomas	4:21:35 (17,274)	
Unnerstall, Ronald	4:11:22 (14,701)	
Unsted, Paul	3:58:15 (11,580)	
Unsworth, Andrew	3:51:20 (9,507)	
Unsworth, David	7:02:31 (32,653)	
Unsworth, Mark	4:20:08 (16,896)	
Unvois, Arnaud	4:34:22 (20,664)	
Unwin, Andrew	4:51:29 (24,697)	
Unwin, David	3:44:01 (7,661)	
Unwin, James	3:22:18 (3,563)	
Unwin, Mark	4:17:18 (16,203)	
Unwin, Nigel	3:34:05 (5,537)	
Upple, Janinder	4:37:53 (21,542)	
Upston-Hooper, Karl	3:23:02 (3,662)	
Upton, Brian	3:13:21 (2,485)	
Upton, Chris	3:22:49 (3,638)	
Upton, Chris	3:48:43 (8,816)	
Upton, Darren	3:37:34 (6,239)	
Upton, James	4:46:48 (23,757)	
Upton, Kevin	3:59:19 (11,887)	
Upton, Paul	4:03:48 (12,943)	
Upton, Simon	4:32:18 (20,161)	
Upton, Stephen	4:53:18 (25,024)	
Urand, Kevin	5:00:18 (26,347)	
Urbanowski, Frank	3:57:56 (11,483)	
Urch, Tyrone	3:44:11 (7,707)	
Ureeswgk, Paul	3:58:28 (11,643)	
Urigoitia-Amorrortu, Pedro	3:44:18 (7,714)	
Urschel, Harold	5:48:33 (31,065)	
Urwin, Gail	6:50:45 (32,550)	
Urwin, Kenneth	4:18:32 (16,496)	
Urwin, Robert	3:44:10 (7,698)	
Urwin, Roger	4:56:11 (25,628)	
Usher, Geraint	4:13:00 (15,082)	
Usher, Richard	3:54:03 (10,326)	
Usher, Tim	4:46:36 (23,715)	
Uter, John	3:47:20 (8,467)	
Utterson, Colin	3:33:48 (5,479)	
Uttin, Robin	4:29:42 (19,506)	
Uttley, Paul	4:49:51 (24,395)	
Uttley, Simon	5:10:41 (27,773)	
Utton, Damian	2:56:31 (873)	
Uzzell, Kevin	3:06:03 (1,645)	
Vaaben, Peter	3:12:38 (2,377)	
Vaananen, Jukka	3:27:58 (4,512)	
Vaananen, Pentti	4:28:56 (19,297)	
Vackenburg, Martin	4:44:40 (23,209)	

Vadapolas, Einius 2:47:25 (378)
Vadgama, Nilesh 4:46:11 (23,618)
Vaidyanathan, Raju 6:05:13 (31,704)
Vaillant, Benoit 3:46:45 (8,336)
Vala, Ramesh 4:37:36 (21,468)
Vale, Peter 2:55:07 (752)
Vale, Richard 5:08:00 (27,435)
Valek, Paul 2:48:31 (427)
Valentine, David 4:37:20 (21,408)
Valentini, Michael 2:57:05 (922)
Valeri, Valerio 4:38:53 (21,815)
Vallance, Andrew 3:10:04 (2,046)
Vallario, Antony 5:08:57 (27,564)
Valley, Kenneth 3:28:20 (4,579)
Vallis, Keith 2:45:48 (323)
Van Aardenne, Cas 3:27:48 (4,480)
Van Bommel, Victor 3:57:26 (11,339)
Van Caster, Eric 3:13:08 (2,453)
Van De Watering, Frans 5:34:57 (30,181)
Van Den Berg, Brian 3:05:47 (1,614)
Van Den Berg, Len 5:34:05 (30,115)
Van Den Bergh, David 4:12:59 (15,076)
Van Den Heuvel, Roger 3:55:49 (10,844)
Van Der Ande, Rudolk 4:05:20 (13,283)
Van Der Heij, Bernard 4:40:46 (22,300)
Van Der Horst, Richard 3:02:50 (1,358)
Van Der Kwast, Johny 3:41:27 (7,058)
Van Der Meer, Hendrik 4:23:51 (17,928)
Van Der Meer, Peter 5:04:47 (26,997)
Van Der Merwe, George 5:01:12 (26,481)
Van Der Ploeg, Klaas 4:42:42 (22,768)
Van Der Steeg, René 5:03:35 (26,833)
Van Der Tol, Martijn 4:26:40 (18,711)
Van Der Velpen, Patrick 4:16:10 (15,881)
Van Driel, Philip 3:51:56 (9,657)
Van Ek, Edwin 6:04:28 (31,673)
Van Espen, Erik 4:14:09 (15,345)
Van Eyk, Craig 3:24:46 (3,954)
Van Groenestijn, Wouter 4:04:47 (13,155)
Van Haght, Vincent 3:47:12 (8,441)
Van Hal, Erik 3:22:33 (3,590)
Van Hal, Job 4:05:43 (13,372)
Van Heerden, Anton 3:25:37 (4,085)
Van Heerden, Deon 4:59:17 (26,172)
Van Hogezand, Menno 4:58:43 (26,082)
Van Holland, Richard 5:23:05 (29,182)
Van Hussen, Marc 4:04:24 (13,069)
Van Impe, Joseph 5:03:33 (26,827)
Van Klooster, Richard 4:07:39 (13,829)
Van Leeuwen, Sander 3:48:40 (8,802)
Van Lyl, Yves 3:59:01 (11,810)
Van Mechelen, Johan 4:07:06 (13,697)
Van Merrienboer, Ron 4:41:57 (22,598)
Van Nispen, Emile 3:52:59 (9,972)
Van Noort, Benjamin 4:19:18 (16,667)
Van Olmen, Erik 4:28:12 (19,081)
Van Oppen, Guy 3:02:17 (1,324)
Van Overeem, Frank 5:32:48 (30,011)
Van Rooyen, Innis 4:37:26 (21,434)
Van Straalen, Adriaan 5:23:50 (29,265)
Van Straubenzee, Thomas 3:34:18 (5,583)
Van Winckel, Koen 3:41:33 (7,074)
Van Wyck, Paul 4:55:05 (25,387)
Van Wyk, Riaan 4:36:07 (21,106)
Van Wyk, Stephan 4:21:26 (17,228)
Van Zyl, Adrian 4:26:45 (18,731)
Vandemlindemloof, Erwin 3:50:05 (9,186)
Vanden Heuvel, John 4:18:02 (16,377)
Vandendriessche, Kris 3:06:34 (1,696)
Vandeperre, Danny 3:42:05 (7,174)
Vandyk, Johannes 5:21:44 (29,074)
Vanhoucke, Freddy 4:06:03 (13,445)
Vanmeensel, François 3:53:53 (10,274)
Van-Moerkercke, Bruno 3:36:46 (6,069)
Vannozzi, Christopher 5:19:59 (28,877)
Vanstone, Neil 5:46:59 (30,985)
Varah, Andrew 5:01:52 (26,580)
Varden, Mark 3:20:11 (3,276)
Varin, Gerard 3:29:32 (4,805)
Varley, Philip 4:20:56 (17,090)
Varney, David 4:08:05 (13,931)
Varney, Steven 2:54:30 (705)
Varsani, Harshad 6:10:06 (31,842)
Varsani, Ramesh 4:42:37 (22,750)
Vassiliades, Steven 2:50:55 (530)
Vat, Ruud 4:10:07 (14,414)
Vaughan, Adam 3:35:02 (5,717)
Vaughan, Andrew 4:59:47 (26,272)
Vaughan, Anthony 6:41:39 (32,445)
Vaughan, Bryan 2:39:07 (168)
Vaughan, Bryan 3:31:02 (5,036)
Vaughan, Daniel 2:39:57 (182)
Vaughan, Daniel 3:38:22 (6,389)
Vaughan, David 3:21:07 (3,389)
Vaughan, Philip 5:26:30 (29,491)
Vaughan, Simon 4:41:58 (22,601)
Vaughan, Tim 4:09:18 (14,218)
Vdberg, Jack 5:44:32 (30,859)
Veal, Gareth 3:54:40 (10,506)
Veale, Lee 3:53:31 (10,150)
Vecchi, Claudio 5:44:07 (30,826)
Veillard, Antony 4:19:42 (16,778)
Vekaria, Mitesh 4:52:14 (24,831)
Vekic, John 4:14:26 (15,433)
Velazquez Aguilar, Ernesto 4:43:03 (22,849)
Velazquez Aguilar, Jorge 4:06:23 (13,540)
Velazquez Aguilar, Mauricio 3:52:00 (9,683)
Veldt, Johannes 3:11:19 (2,186)
Vellupillaz, Anandasothy 5:29:45 (29,758)
Velthuis, Peter 4:58:27 (26,024)
Venables, Edward 3:55:08 (10,646)
Venables, Neil 3:58:10 (11,558)
Veneman, Freddy 3:55:01 (10,600)
Venoey, Jan 4:18:07 (16,392)
Venters, John 4:13:06 (15,104)
Ventress, Paul 4:19:54 (16,836)
Venus, Michael 4:15:46 (15,774)
Vera Bacallado, Juan 4:40:49 (22,313)
Vercaemst, Joost 3:32:26 (5,259)
Verdier, Pascal 5:08:59 (27,570)
Verdon, Jonathan 4:28:59 (19,318)
Verdoodt, Ignace 3:39:50 (6,693)
Verdult, Peter 3:32:18 (5,232)
Vere, Derek 4:43:44 (23,001)
Vere-Nicholl, Alastair 3:56:38 (11,094)
Verhees, Caspar 5:11:00 (27,812)
Verheij, Louis 4:52:48 (24,939)
Verheij, Steef 4:41:48 (22,556)
Verhulst, Georges 3:39:56 (6,720)
Verhulst, Maxime 4:43:46 (23,008)
Verity, Stephen 5:22:29 (29,132)
Verleyen, Norbert 4:03:24 (12,859)
Vermeere, Daniel 3:24:18 (3,877)
Vernon, Darren 3:01:53 (1,292)
Vernon, David 3:27:48 (4,480)
Vernon, Mike 4:10:39 (14,545)
Vernon, Peter 3:35:42 (5,846)
Vero, Alexander 4:21:27 (17,232)
Verrill, Ian 4:19:31 (16,730)
Verry, Jonathon 4:45:01 (23,312)
Vesentini, Damiano 4:20:00 (16,860)
Vessey, Duncan 3:23:15 (3,687)
Vettorazzo, Maurizio 3:48:50 (8,849)
Veyes, Andrew 3:06:59 (1,732)
Veys, Alexander 3:52:35 (9,865)
Vezzu, Loris 2:56:57 (910)
Vial, Tony 3:55:02 (10,603)
Vicker, Thomas 4:19:34 (16,741)
Vickers, Luke 3:28:03 (4,523)
Vickers, Neil 4:14:37 (15,473)
Vickers, Robert 3:04:00 (1,467)
Vickers, Ryan 3:09:53 (2,025)
Vickers, Tony 3:49:45 (9,112)
Vickery, Adrian 4:08:31 (14,027)
Vickery, James 4:09:08 (14,160)
Vickery, James 4:34:11 (20,625)
Victoros, John 5:14:07 (28,207)
Vidler, James 5:00:48 (26,421)
Vieille, Claude 3:41:05 (6,984)
Vierling, Stefan 4:17:55 (16,349)
Vierschilling, Leander 3:15:07 (2,677)
Vieuille, Marc 3:50:50 (9,382)
Vige, François 4:55:23 (25,461)
Vigier, Jean-François 4:43:47 (23,011)
Vigne, Gerard 3:28:47 (4,658)
Vilanova, Jordi 3:11:59 (2,273)
Vildary, Patrick 3:09:59 (2,039)
ViliIer, Robert 4:46:54 (23,786)
Villa-Clarke, David 4:37:45 (21,503)
Villari, Antonio 4:39:39 (22,003)
Ville, Harold 4:28:50 (19,269)
Villeneuve, Michel 3:26:51 (4,301)
Vinall, Chris 4:00:07 (12,113)
Vincent, Charles 5:30:14 (29,801)
Vincent, Dean 3:43:37 (7,555)
Vincent, Edward 3:33:40 (5,450)
Vincent, Gregory 4:48:37 (24,149)
Vincent, Ian 3:26:54 (4,313)
Vincent, Joseph 5:00:46 (26,418)
Vincent, Kevin 4:23:51 (17,928)
Vincent, Mark 3:46:31 (8,290)
Vincent, Martin 5:29:24 (29,728)
Vincent, Peter 4:28:12 (19,081)
Vincent, Ronald 4:41:21 (22,439)
Vincent, Stephen 4:33:12 (20,403)
Vine, Andrew 3:36:47 (6,074)
Vine, Desmond 3:25:23 (4,043)
Vine, Terry 3:57:48 (11,449)
Vines, Mark 4:04:04 (13,001)
Vines, Timothy 4:40:37 (22,257)
Viney, Nicholas 4:49:52 (24,401)
Vinnicombe, Thomas 3:19:29 (3,201)
Vinter, Philip 3:48:08 (8,658)
Viola, Luigi 3:29:17 (4,744)
Vipulanandarajah, Shankar 4:06:57 (13,662)
Virama, Jean 3:39:28 (6,617)
Virdee, Manmohan 4:55:09 (25,411)
Virgo, Ryan 4:47:19 (23,881)
Virk, Jaswant 4:01:41 (12,489)
Viveash, Joe 5:28:46 (29,680)
Vivian, Charles 4:03:33 (12,890)
Vivian, Lee 4:17:07 (16,148)
Viviani, Luigi 4:45:35 (23,467)
Vizard, William 4:33:31 (20,468)
Vizern, Daniel 3:11:56 (2,262)
Vlaming, Paul 3:16:18 (2,820)
Vlok, David 4:19:32 (16,733)
Vlok, Deon 3:12:10 (2,305)
Vock, Walter 3:30:35 (4,958)
Vogel, John 3:49:36 (9,069)
Vogel, Richard 4:57:23 (25,839)
Vogel, William 3:14:55 (2,662)
Vogler, Volker 4:01:36 (12,469)
Vogt, Jim 4:02:29 (12,651)
Voice, Dan 3:53:27 (10,128)
Voisey, Ian 4:37:59 (21,571)
Voitin, John 4:30:39 (19,745)
Volk, Ulrich 4:12:24 (14,943)
Vollentine, Brian 3:11:26 (2,196)
Voller, Paul 4:20:23 (16,962)
Vollgraf, Guenter 4:11:23 (14,704)
Von Buchwaldt, Chrstian 4:31:08 (19,867)
Von Daehne, Niklas 3:35:01 (5,714)
Von Falkenhayn, York 4:56:33 (25,700)
Von Felten, Stephan 4:34:24 (20,673)
Von Hirschberg, Murray 3:45:49 (8,124)
Von Thadden, Goetz 3:53:27 (10,128)
Vondra, Philip 3:06:11 (1,655)
Vonlanthen, Marc 5:11:05 (27,822)
Vooght, Stephen 4:02:55 (12,758)
Voos, John 3:37:57 (6,303)
Vosper, Peter 5:53:54 (31,307)
Voss, Stacey 3:27:33 (4,423)
Vout, Tony 3:19:19 (3,173)
Vowles, Jayson 4:04:46 (13,152)
Voyantzis, Hari 5:08:34 (27,505)
Voyce, Ian 5:48:17 (31,048)
Voysey, Joel 4:24:34 (18,138)
Vyas, Anant 6:42:33 (32,451)
Waddams, Alan 3:52:21 (9,797)
Waddell, Arthur 6:32:27 (32,312)
Waddell, Bruce 3:54:59 (10,592)
Waddell, David 4:59:18 (26,179)
Waddingham, Elton 3:36:36 (6,043)
Waddingham, Keith 3:18:53 (3,123)
Waddington, David 3:21:56 (3,511)
Waddington, Nigel 4:14:59 (15,570)
Waddington, Philip 4:06:40 (13,606)
Waddington, Richard 4:13:23 (15,162)

Wade, Alexander	5:08:50 (27,541)	
Wade, Alvin	5:36:32 (30,312)	
Wade, Antony	5:20:07 (28,892)	
Wade, Daniel	3:38:57 (6,512)	
Wade, Darrell	3:54:32 (10,467)	
Wade, David	6:25:49 (32,196)	
Wade, Graeme	6:00:02 (31,543)	
Wade, James	3:42:12 (7,201)	
Wade, Julian	4:21:07 (17,148)	
Wade, Mark	4:21:07 (17,148)	
Wade, Matthew	5:02:47 (26,708)	
Wade, Nicholas	4:22:19 (17,486)	
Wade, Nick	3:27:34 (4,428)	
Wade, Rex	3:40:55 (6,944)	
Wade, Spencer	5:08:52 (27,546)	
Wade, Steven	4:19:30 (16,726)	
Wade, William	3:28:18 (4,568)	
Wadeley, Kevin	3:05:59 (1,639)	
Wadey, Ian	3:12:03 (2,282)	
Wadley, Mark	3:52:32 (9,849)	
Wadman, Richard	4:29:27 (19,449)	
Wadrup, Richard	5:11:50 (27,927)	
Wadsworth, Adrian	3:43:44 (7,585)	
Wadsworth, Paul	4:16:20 (15,924)	
Wadsworth, Tony	5:33:56 (30,104)	
Waelkens, Jean	4:51:26 (24,686)	
Waggett, Colin	3:51:43 (9,599)	
Waggott, George	4:26:55 (18,764)	
Waghorn, Arthur	3:49:25 (9,014)	
Wagner, Conre	4:28:23 (19,131)	
Wagner, Magnus	3:39:48 (6,686)	
Wagstaff, John	3:04:30 (1,504)	
Wagstaff, Michael	4:54:28 (25,279)	
Waide, Ivan	3:44:20 (7,753)	
Wain, Chris	3:18:30 (3,074)	
Wain, Jim	5:19:05 (28,785)	
Wain, John	4:00:40 (12,216)	
Waine, Kerry	3:40:07 (6,768)	
Waine, Michael	2:48:16 (419)	
Wainewright, David	4:50:48 (24,564)	
Wainman, Paul	5:31:15 (29,891)	
Wainwright, Philip	3:51:39 (9,583)	
Wainwright, David	5:46:40 (30,973)	
Wainwright, Liam	4:04:33 (13,101)	
Wairimu, Andrew	4:47:08 (23,840)	
Waistell, David	4:27:35 (18,933)	
Waite, David	4:29:09 (19,367)	
Waite, Kenneth	6:17:11 (32,009)	
Waite, Mark	3:42:49 (7,346)	
Waite, Paul	5:26:22 (29,476)	
Waite, Richard	3:14:52 (2,651)	
Waites, Matthew	3:37:50 (6,285)	
Waites, Stephen	4:59:25 (26,202)	
Wake, Adam	3:57:28 (11,350)	
Wakefield, Andy	5:16:18 (28,482)	
Wakefield, Paul	3:19:15 (3,166)	
Wakefield, Paul	4:13:36 (15,207)	
Wakefield, Robert	3:46:47 (8,339)	
Wakeford, Thomas	4:06:08 (13,473)	
Wakeham, Simon	4:56:46 (25,726)	
Wakem, Terence	3:40:57 (6,949)	
Wakenshaw, Trevor	3:41:25 (7,050)	
Walbank, Andrew	5:09:07 (27,585)	
Walbank, Benjamin	4:47:45 (23,961)	
Walburn, Matthew	4:33:33 (20,472)	
Walcroft, Graham	6:47:16 (32,510)	
Walden, Mark	3:51:49 (9,628)	
Waldram, Stephen	3:11:27 (2,198)	
Waldron, Christopher	4:20:25 (16,974)	
Wales, Ben	4:25:04 (18,277)	
Walford, David	4:23:39 (17,859)	
Waligorski, Hermann	5:21:01 (28,991)	
Walkden, Hugh	4:10:08 (14,424)	
Walker, Andrew	3:12:32 (2,366)	
Walker, Andrew	3:50:05 (9,186)	
Walker, Andrew	4:51:54 (24,766)	
Walker, Andy	5:17:08 (28,582)	
Walker, Charles	4:44:42 (23,220)	
Walker, Christopher	3:36:06 (5,932)	
Walker, Christopher	4:01:56 (12,549)	
Walker, Christopher	4:18:12 (16,414)	
Walker, Christopher	7:45:00 (32,841)	
Walker, Colin	3:35:41 (5,842)	
Walker, Daniel	4:45:30 (23,436)	
Walker, Darren	2:42:11 (229)	
Walker, Darren	4:30:13 (19,655)	
Walker, Dave	3:51:50 (9,632)	
Walker, David	3:08:14 (1,828)	
Walker, David	3:41:58 (7,144)	
Walker, David	4:08:54 (14,112)	
Walker, Donald	5:13:33 (28,148)	
Walker, Doug	3:52:27 (9,823)	
Walker, Duncan	3:01:58 (1,299)	
Walker, Eddie	4:19:44 (16,785)	
Walker, Gary	4:11:00 (14,631)	
Walker, Gary	4:17:41 (16,288)	
Walker, Geoffrey	4:18:12 (16,414)	
Walker, George	3:04:58 (1,540)	
Walker, Gerald	3:36:50 (6,081)	
Walker, Giles	4:34:05 (20,603)	
Walker, Greig	4:44:38 (23,202)	
Walker, Ian	3:33:47 (5,474)	
Walker, Ian	5:16:24 (28,492)	
Walker, Jack	3:25:39 (4,095)	
Walker, James	4:07:29 (13,793)	
Walker, James	4:08:55 (14,116)	
Walker, John	4:08:56 (14,119)	
Walker, Julian	5:42:01 (30,696)	
Walker, Jurjuan	2:40:12 (187)	
Walker, Justin	5:18:06 (28,682)	
Walker, Marc	3:26:18 (4,204)	
Walker, Mark	3:38:33 (6,440)	
Walker, Mark	5:43:29 (30,788)	
Walker, Martin	3:11:35 (2,214)	
Walker, Martyn	4:47:16 (23,871)	
Walker, Max	3:31:39 (5,139)	
Walker, Michael	3:26:22 (4,214)	
Walker, Michael	4:21:17 (17,186)	
Walker, Michael	5:13:23 (28,124)	
Walker, Mike	2:57:00 (914)	
Walker, Nick	4:41:03 (22,362)	
Walker, Oliver	4:34:39 (20,739)	
Walker, Peter	3:03:22 (1,409)	
Walker, Richard	3:37:37 (6,246)	
Walker, Richard	4:55:44 (25,527)	
Walker, Robert	4:25:38 (18,428)	
Walker, Robert	5:32:00 (29,953)	
Walker, Roger	3:42:19 (7,236)	
Walker, Russell	5:13:50 (28,174)	
Walker, Simon	3:29:12 (4,727)	
Walker, Stephen	4:00:46 (12,249)	
Walker, Steven	2:59:00 (1,093)	
Walker, Steven	4:19:40 (16,765)	
Walker, Stewart	4:44:55 (23,274)	
Walker, Stuart	2:59:09 (1,108)	
Walker, William	4:52:11 (24,813)	
Walker-Buckton, Tristan	3:37:47 (6,277)	
Walkey, Matthew	4:30:13 (19,655)	
Walkley, Anthony	4:41:53 (22,581)	
Wall, Colin	4:46:26 (23,674)	
Wall, David	4:34:05 (20,603)	
Wall, Michael	3:46:12 (8,201)	
Wall, Stephen	3:25:23 (4,043)	
Wall, Tony	4:55:30 (25,481)	
Wallace, Andrew	4:04:57 (13,197)	
Wallace, Andrew	4:15:09 (15,604)	
Wallace, Iain	3:03:44 (1,445)	
Wallace, Jason	3:51:30 (9,543)	
Wallace, Jerry	3:20:51 (3,348)	
Wallace, Joe	3:35:24 (5,781)	
Wallace, Michael	4:50:56 (24,596)	
Wallace, Richard	4:46:35 (23,712)	
Wallace, Robert	3:13:20 (2,480)	
Wallace, Spencer	3:33:54 (5,496)	
Wallace, Steve	3:47:44 (8,569)	
Wallace, Steven	3:29:21 (4,766)	
Wallace, Victor	3:50:36 (9,322)	
Wallach, Dennis	6:05:52 (31,728)	
Walland, John	5:39:36 (30,522)	
Wallbank, Robert	3:53:56 (10,287)	
Wallenberg, Bo	5:04:09 (26,908)	
Waller, Anthony	4:21:44 (17,321)	
Waller, Douglas	3:37:23 (6,185)	
Waller, Gary	4:26:05 (18,544)	
Waller, Justin	4:19:08 (16,627)	
Waller, Nicholas	5:38:46 (30,462)	
Waller, Patrick	4:01:56 (12,549)	
Waller, Richard	4:25:35 (18,410)	
Walley, Nigel	4:55:38 (25,499)	
Wallington, James	3:36:57 (6,107)	
Wallington, Martin	4:04:52 (13,175)	
Wallington, Richard	4:06:03 (13,445)	
Wallis, Colin	3:54:56 (10,574)	
Wallis, Dean	4:35:30 (20,946)	
Wallis, Gordon	4:40:35 (22,252)	
Wallis, Graham	3:47:55 (8,608)	
Wallis, James	3:23:18 (3,694)	
Wallis, John	2:47:29 (380)	
Wallis, Mike	4:25:43 (18,446)	
Wallis, Simon	5:56:10 (31,408)	
Wallis, Steve	5:30:37 (29,837)	
Walmsley, David	5:04:58 (27,015)	
Walpole, Christopher	4:53:40 (25,097)	
Walpole, Scott	5:06:07 (27,178)	
Walser, Andrew	4:05:09 (13,240)	
Walsgrove, Ben	4:38:03 (21,584)	
Walsgrove, John	3:34:47 (5,673)	
Walsh, Antony	3:10:28 (2,095)	
Walsh, Chris	5:06:00 (27,155)	
Walsh, Colman	4:45:32 (23,449)	
Walsh, David	3:04:52 (1,532)	
Walsh, Duncan	4:00:41 (12,220)	
Walsh, Gary	3:59:34 (11,958)	
Walsh, Graeme	2:50:27 (508)	
Walsh, Ian	4:16:04 (15,855)	
Walsh, James	3:58:40 (11,695)	
Walsh, John	6:56:52 (32,602)	
Walsh, Matthew	3:45:53 (8,133)	
Walsh, Michael	3:21:49 (3,487)	
Walsh, Michael	4:46:49 (23,762)	
Walsh, Peter	3:50:32 (9,306)	
Walsh, Peter	4:15:34 (15,712)	
Walsh, Peter	4:43:35 (22,975)	
Walsh, Peter	5:10:19 (27,729)	
Walsh, Sean	3:34:06 (5,543)	
Walsh, Steve	3:07:19 (1,755)	
Walsh, Timothy	4:55:22 (25,453)	
Walsham, James	3:11:48 (2,244)	
Walshaw, John	3:56:03 (10,913)	
Walshe, Sean	4:12:35 (14,992)	
Walter, Alex	4:56:43 (25,718)	
Walters, Alan	4:55:42 (25,520)	
Walters, Alan	5:15:09 (28,315)	
Walters, David	5:06:41 (27,257)	
Walters, Gary	4:56:11 (25,628)	
Walters, Humphrey	4:39:00 (21,846)	
Walters, James	4:52:32 (24,882)	
Walters, Martin	4:02:39 (12,691)	
Walters, Matthew	5:29:56 (29,776)	
Walters, Matthew	5:50:54 (31,182)	
Walters, Meirion	4:07:41 (13,836)	
Walters, Michael	4:25:06 (18,286)	
Walters, Morgan	3:01:39 (1,268)	
Walters, Paul	7:02:19 (32,650)	
Walters, Peter	4:41:13 (22,403)	
Walters, Spencer	3:52:00 (9,683)	
Walton, Andrew	5:54:12 (31,320)	
Walton, Bradley	3:36:13 (5,960)	
Walton, Darren	3:21:31 (3,438)	
Walton, David	3:15:48 (2,769)	
Walton, David	4:43:21 (22,919)	
Walton, David	4:51:22 (24,676)	
Walton, James	5:04:08 (26,904)	
Walton, Jim	4:12:39 (15,012)	
Walton, John	4:19:38 (16,759)	
Walton, Mark	4:06:24 (13,546)	
Walton, Michael	3:15:51 (2,773)	
Walton, Philip	4:33:39 (20,506)	
Walton, Simon	3:46:01 (8,163)	
Walton, Stephen	5:20:00 (28,879)	
Walton, Stuart	7:00:33 (32,632)	
Walton, Tim	3:39:13 (6,574)	
Walvius, Joop	3:22:29 (3,579)	
Wan, Jung	4:26:01 (18,525)	
Wang, Roal	5:29:35 (29,745)	
Want, Paul	4:49:49 (24,383)	
Waples, Justin	5:04:17 (26,933)	
Warburton, Nigel	3:40:27 (6,843)	
Ward, Adam	4:22:39 (17,588)	

Ward, Alan 3:36:44 (6,061)
Ward, Alan 3:38:23 (6,394)
Ward, Alan 3:51:50 (9,632)
Ward, Allan 5:16:43 (28,521)
Ward, Andrew 3:10:19 (2,079)
Ward, Andrew 3:40:30 (6,850)
Ward, Andrew 4:30:21 (19,681)
Ward, Anthony 3:53:34 (10,171)
Ward, Barry 4:32:01 (20,088)
Ward, Charlie 4:16:20 (15,924)
Ward, Christopher 4:46:01 (23,569)
Ward, Christopher 5:15:27 (28,355)
Ward, David 3:05:40 (1,606)
Ward, David 4:07:36 (13,816)
Ward, David 4:40:21 (22,199)
Ward, David 5:47:01 (30,988)
Ward, Gavin 4:12:45 (15,033)
Ward, Ian 3:12:05 (2,289)
Ward, John 4:23:32 (17,834)
Ward, John 5:20:02 (28,883)
Ward, John 5:55:04 (31,354)
Ward, Mark 3:22:21 (3,568)
Ward, Martin 3:27:36 (4,435)
Ward, Matthew 3:29:08 (4,716)
Ward, Michael 3:36:41 (6,055)
Ward, Michael 3:39:48 (6,686)
Ward, Neil 3:24:18 (3,877)
Ward, Paul 4:18:27 (16,476)
Ward, Paul 4:59:19 (26,181)
Ward, Peter 3:13:00 (2,431)
Ward, Peter 3:48:33 (8,762)
Ward, Richard 4:42:03 (22,622)
Ward, Richard 5:14:28 (28,242)
Ward, Robert 3:59:49 (12,028)
Ward, Robin 4:18:19 (16,444)
Ward, Ross 4:08:03 (13,928)
Ward, Roy 3:21:27 (3,427)
Ward, Sean 3:19:51 (3,236)
Ward, Simon 3:30:29 (4,941)
Ward, Simon 4:01:39 (12,482)
Ward, Simon 4:44:44 (23,230)
Ward, Steven 6:12:23 (31,891)
Ward, Timothy 5:33:33 (30,076)
Wardell, Chris 3:34:19 (5,586)
Wardell, Stephen 3:42:39 (7,311)
Warden, Alan 3:27:15 (4,368)
Warden, Brian 4:07:00 (13,678)
Warden, Martin 5:44:22 (30,846)
Warden, Paul 4:34:19 (20,652)
Wardill, Devin 3:53:49 (10,258)
Wardlaw, Robert 3:09:05 (1,941)
Wardlaw, Steve 3:48:54 (8,871)
Wardle, Charlie 4:46:52 (23,777)
Wardle, Daniel 4:33:44 (20,523)
Wardle, Kim 3:48:27 (8,735)
Wardle, Nicholas 5:44:39 (30,868)
Wardle, Steve 3:40:17 (6,809)
Ward-Lilley, James 4:06:51 (13,638)
Ward-Lowery, Nicholas 4:05:43 (13,372)
Wardrope, David 3:42:54 (7,363)
Wardy, David 4:11:08 (14,664)
Ware, Anthony 3:16:29 (2,843)
Ware, Michael 6:21:43 (32,116)
Ware, Robert 4:03:54 (12,963)
Ware, Thomas 3:44:15 (7,722)
Wareham, Michael 2:52:05 (584)
Wareham, Sean 4:06:23 (13,540)
Wareing, Brian 3:10:21 (2,085)
Wareing, David 4:38:59 (21,841)
Wareing, Nathan 4:37:09 (21,348)
Warfield, Anthony 4:35:33 (20,960)
Waring, Keith 3:27:49 (4,487)
Warland, Gary 4:05:15 (13,262)
Warland, Graham 4:16:14 (15,897)
Warn, Derek 3:14:26 (2,606)
Warn, Timothy 3:19:01 (3,135)
Warne, Philip 4:38:58 (21,834)
Warne, Richard 5:15:47 (28,409)
Warne, Stephen 7:00:45 (32,635)
Warner, Anthony 3:13:41 (2,529)
Warner, Anthony 4:38:51 (21,808)
Warner, David 4:01:17 (12,384)
Warner, Edmond 3:26:31 (4,234)
Warner, James 4:21:18 (17,191)
Warner, John 4:31:31 (19,972)
Warner, Kevon 4:38:49 (21,796)
Warner, Kim 3:34:36 (5,636)
Warner, Martin 3:38:20 (6,381)
Warner, Michael 3:15:53 (2,777)
Warner, Michael 3:21:01 (3,368)
Warner, Michael 3:54:50 (10,551)
Warner, Nigel 3:37:53 (6,295)
Warner, Phillip 4:44:55 (23,274)
Warner, Stephen 3:26:30 (4,228)
Warnes, Richard 5:15:10 (28,317)
Warnock, Dennis 5:21:41 (29,067)
Warnock, Jim 3:38:30 (6,423)
Warnock, John 4:02:03 (12,568)
Warnock, Michael 4:26:44 (18,726)
Warren, Andrew 4:09:18 (14,218)
Warren, Andrew 4:43:50 (23,027)
Warren, Huw 3:26:15 (4,197)
Warren, Michael 3:37:11 (6,146)
Warren, Michael 5:10:13 (27,721)
Warren, Peter 3:58:05 (11,536)
Warren, Peter 4:06:37 (13,592)
Warren, Phil 3:57:26 (11,339)
Warren, Philip 3:49:00 (8,896)
Warren, Robert 4:27:45 (18,972)
Warren, Terence 3:56:17 (10,983)
Warren-Tape, Jonathan 4:02:41 (12,701)
Warrick, Nicholas 4:49:06 (24,261)
Warriner, Alan 3:45:34 (8,065)
Warriner, David 4:44:07 (23,090)
Warrington, Anthony 3:57:35 (11,389)
Warsaw, Harris 4:43:37 (22,980)
Warton, Paul 3:03:02 (1,374)
Warwick, Barry 3:27:37 (4,440)
Warwick, Kennedy 3:58:56 (11,772)
Warwick, Lee 5:13:19 (28,118)
Washer, Regan 3:55:48 (10,840)
Washington, Darren 3:03:00 (1,368)
Wasilewski, Charles 3:50:40 (9,338)
Wasley, David 4:19:16 (16,657)
Wasmer, Kilian 3:05:13 (1,560)
Wason, Ian 4:24:21 (18,080)
Wass, David 3:47:32 (8,519)
Wass, Martin 5:02:51 (26,721)
Wassall, Stephen 5:37:24 (30,375)
Wassell, Brian 5:10:50 (27,794)
Wasserman, Ian 5:13:48 (28,169)
Watari, Tadayoshi 4:35:12 (20,881)
Waterfield, Dickon 3:27:01 (4,331)
Waterfield, John 5:07:04 (27,306)
Waterfield, Richard 5:00:31 (26,379)
Waterhouse, Daniel 4:03:08 (12,802)
Waterhouse, John 4:23:24 (17,802)
Waterhouse, Nathan 3:33:50 (5,484)
Waterman, David 3:29:27 (4,784)
Waterman, David 3:36:29 (6,023)
Waterman, Ian 3:46:16 (8,215)
Waters, Cedric 5:08:46 (27,535)
Waters, Daniel 4:57:06 (25,793)
Waters, David 5:28:11 (29,631)
Waters, James 5:29:04 (29,699)
Waters, Jeremy 4:13:49 (15,264)
Waters, Matthew 4:19:40 (16,765)
Waters, Philip 5:40:04 (30,550)
Waters, Richard 3:52:14 (9,762)
Waters, Rodney 4:52:21 (24,851)
Waters, William 4:04:56 (13,194)
Waterson, David 5:44:43 (30,871)
Waterston, Kevin 3:54:07 (10,351)
Waterston, Laughlan 4:00:52 (12,273)
Waterton, Joe 4:33:18 (20,420)
Waterworth, James 3:40:12 (6,786)
Wates, Phillip 5:31:54 (29,945)
Watkin, Nigel 3:13:39 (2,524)
Watkins, Christopher 4:32:03 (20,101)
Watkins, Daniel 3:28:52 (4,673)
Watkins, David 3:54:35 (10,484)
Watkins, Gene 5:03:56 (26,876)
Watkins, Geoffrey 4:14:48 (15,526)
Watkins, James 3:21:30 (3,436)
Watkins, James 4:16:55 (16,095)
Watkins, John 4:44:30 (23,172)
Watkins, Jonathan 5:59:09 (31,519)
Watkins, Matthew 3:56:02 (10,906)
Watkins, Stephen 3:08:48 (1,909)
Watkins, Stephen 4:48:01 (24,037)
Watkinson, Peter 3:11:31 (2,205)
Watling, Shuan 4:08:39 (14,066)
Watmough, Craig 4:03:23 (12,855)
Watmough, Micah 4:16:22 (15,938)
Watson, Adrian 4:54:38 (25,307)
Watson, Alan 6:19:01 (32,061)
Watson, Alex 4:15:54 (15,810)
Watson, Andrew 2:55:49 (813)
Watson, Andrew 4:32:50 (20,314)
Watson, Aubrey 3:53:27 (10,128)
Watson, Bob 3:42:23 (7,259)
Watson, Bruce 4:12:08 (14,887)
Watson, Colin 3:41:35 (7,080)
Watson, Craig 4:25:41 (18,436)
Watson, David 3:03:42 (1,442)
Watson, David 5:27:05 (29,531)
Watson, Dudley 5:07:54 (27,423)
Watson, Ian 4:32:13 (20,145)
Watson, Keith 4:07:28 (13,790)
Watson, Kevin 3:23:21 (3,703)
Watson, Kevin 4:46:39 (23,724)
Watson, Lewis 4:52:50 (24,944)
Watson, Martin 5:04:45 (26,987)
Watson, Neil 3:50:35 (9,317)
Watson, Neil 4:33:22 (20,432)
Watson, Nicholas 3:49:18 (8,972)
Watson, Paul 4:17:04 (16,135)
Watson, Paul 4:48:46 (24,182)
Watson, Peter 3:17:47 (2,988)
Watson, Philip 3:32:41 (5,301)
Watson, Philip 3:38:37 (6,453)
Watson, Rory 4:39:32 (21,978)
Watson, Roy 4:01:02 (12,319)
Watson, Shaun 3:34:56 (5,703)
Watson, Simon 3:39:51 (6,701)
Watson, Simon 4:35:33 (20,960)
Watson, Simon 4:53:28 (25,065)
Watson, Stephen 3:56:41 (11,104)
Watson, Stephen 4:46:51 (23,772)
Watson, Stephen 4:55:05 (25,387)
Watson, Thomas 3:39:27 (6,612)
Watson, Thomas 3:45:41 (8,088)
Watson, William 3:51:08 (9,466)
Watson-Thorp, Patrick 3:59:34 (11,958)
Watt, Alexander 3:50:21 (9,263)
Watt, Brian 3:32:51 (5,330)
Watt, Cameron 4:28:03 (19,047)
Watt, David 4:26:20 (18,606)
Watt, Glen 3:56:11 (10,957)
Watt, Guy 4:19:59 (16,858)
Watt, Peter 4:57:31 (25,864)
Watteevn, Carl 3:23:27 (3,714)
Watters, Dominic 4:17:33 (16,253)
Watterson, Robert 3:59:44 (12,003)
Wattley, Travis 3:55:27 (10,737)
Watton, Matthew 4:38:42 (21,761)
Watts, Allen 5:40:23 (30,577)
Watts, Andrew 2:59:01 (1,094)
Watts, Andrew 3:33:15 (5,388)
Watts, Andrew 4:36:19 (21,164)
Watts, Andy 3:37:22 (6,181)
Watts, Barry 3:40:44 (6,900)
Watts, Darren 4:14:06 (15,339)
Watts, Gavin 4:42:15 (22,659)
Watts, Graham 3:50:46 (9,371)
Watts, Graham 4:12:03 (14,874)
Watts, Graham 5:10:39 (27,768)
Watts, Harris 4:27:10 (18,837)
Watts, Lee 4:38:21 (21,672)
Watts, Lee 4:51:02 (24,613)
Watts, Lewis 5:04:40 (26,973)
Watts, Nigel 3:57:04 (11,227)
Watts, Paul 3:32:06 (5,209)
Watts, Paul 4:25:30 (18,390)
Watts, Paul 4:40:05 (22,129)
Watts, Robert 3:12:24 (2,345)
Watts, Robert 4:11:58 (14,851)
Watts, Robert 4:23:56 (17,958)
Watts, Stephen 3:25:35 (4,075)

Watts, Stephen 3:50:12 (9,215)
Watts, Stephen 4:29:34 (19,473)
Waudby, Forrest 4:02:27 (12,642)
Waudby, Joseph 3:43:29 (7,517)
Waudby, Trevor 4:56:19 (25,658)
Waugh, Daniel 3:43:36 (7,550)
Waugh, Steven 4:21:42 (17,313)
Waumsley, Peter 3:09:13 (1,954)
Waving, Steven 4:57:17 (25,824)
Waxman, Jonathan 4:14:47 (15,520)
Way, Charles 3:21:55 (3,508)
Way, Gregory 3:38:28 (6,416)
Way, Martin 3:43:08 (7,426)
Way, Pete 4:22:56 (17,682)
Way, Steven 5:55:19 (31,366)
Waye, Oswald 6:49:20 (32,535)
Wayland, John 3:51:42 (9,593)
Wayland, William 4:34:29 (20,688)
Wayne, Carl 3:37:17 (6,160)
Wayne, Simon 5:29:20 (29,725)
Weale, Charles 3:59:50 (12,036)
Weatherall, Mark 4:42:35 (22,744)
Weatherhead, Craig 5:12:14 (27,979)
Weaver, Andrew 3:29:32 (4,805)
Weaver, Anthony 3:11:51 (2,252)
Weaver, Ian 3:47:56 (8,614)
Weavers, Keith 5:13:29 (28,138)
Weaving, Peter 2:56:28 (869)
Webb, Alex 3:08:12 (1,824)
Webb, Christopher 3:12:14 (2,318)
Webb, Christopher 3:44:05 (7,675)
Webb, Clinton 4:21:52 (17,359)
Webb, Daniel 4:17:51 (16,337)
Webb, David 4:14:53 (15,550)
Webb, David 4:25:14 (18,317)
Webb, David 6:06:46 (31,747)
Webb, Gary 3:45:31 (8,048)
Webb, Graham 4:50:33 (24,515)
Webb, Jason 3:40:42 (6,895)
Webb, Justin 3:58:26 (11,629)
Webb, Mark 4:47:14 (23,862)
Webb, Matthew 4:15:55 (15,816)
Webb, Maurice 4:43:30 (22,961)
Webb, Nick 3:55:17 (10,687)
Webb, Nigel 3:47:31 (8,515)
Webb, Peter 4:41:51 (22,570)
Webb, Peter 4:47:51 (23,990)
Webb, Robert 3:43:55 (7,635)
Webb, Robert 4:47:14 (23,862)
Webb, Stephen 4:26:46 (18,736)
Webb, Steve 4:58:33 (26,041)
Webb, Stuart 3:12:11 (2,309)
Webb, Timothy 2:58:13 (1,024)
Webber, Bryn 4:01:59 (12,557)
Webber, Ian 4:40:45 (22,295)
Webber, John 4:20:02 (16,870)
Webber, Philip 4:19:45 (16,793)
Webber, Roger 3:26:06 (4,165)
Webber, Simon 4:23:51 (17,928)
Webborn, Martin 3:07:22 (1,758)
Webdale, Paul 5:34:09 (30,118)
Webelguenne, Ruediger 3:43:06 (7,410)
Weber, Daniel 4:58:18 (25,999)
Weber, Vincent 3:39:05 (6,544)
Websdale, Philip 4:42:52 (22,807)
Webster, Andrew 3:37:39 (6,253)
Webster, Andrew 3:44:30 (7,793)
Webster, Cedric 5:30:22 (29,809)
Webster, Christopher 7:09:01 (32,695)
Webster, Gary 6:27:20 (32,232)
Webster, Gavin 4:16:52 (16,082)
Webster, Ian 3:27:28 (4,410)
Webster, James 3:01:30 (1,260)
Webster, James 4:29:06 (19,348)
Webster, John 5:09:01 (27,574)
Webster, John 5:34:26 (30,142)
Webster, Jon 3:23:22 (3,706)
Webster, Keith 4:35:46 (21,021)
Webster, Matthew 3:50:12 (9,215)
Webster, Neil 3:21:45 (3,474)
Webster, Nigel 4:43:27 (22,948)
Webster, Paul 5:18:18 (28,701)
Webster, Peter 4:08:26 (14,001)
Webster, Peter 4:41:18 (22,425)
Webster, Richard 3:07:54 (1,801)
Webster, Simon 3:24:11 (3,857)
Webster, Stephen 3:27:33 (4,423)
Webster, Stuart 4:44:04 (23,080)
Webster, Stuart 5:18:18 (28,701)
Webster, Terry 4:14:19 (15,398)
Webster, William 4:04:23 (13,067)
Wedderburn, Peter 3:56:59 (11,203)
Wedge, Marcus 4:06:11 (13,484)
Wedrychowski, Kazek 3:49:55 (9,155)
Weed, Gareth 4:09:44 (14,328)
Weedon, Paul 4:49:25 (24,304)
Weedon, Warren 4:57:55 (25,939)
Weekes, Robin 3:46:23 (8,246)
Weekly, Christopher 4:11:48 (14,817)
Weeks, David 3:54:58 (10,586)
Weeks, David 4:27:38 (18,947)
Weeks, Stuart 4:36:48 (21,276)
Weeks, Thomas 4:00:26 (12,175)
Weet, John 4:36:19 (21,164)
Weetman, Martin 3:49:41 (9,094)
Wegg, Terry 3:31:02 (5,036)
Wegmueller, Bernhard 4:29:22 (19,424)
Weh, Ludwig 4:56:05 (25,601)
Wehrle, Jean-Claude 3:23:08 (3,670)
Wehrle, Stephen 4:12:26 (14,955)
Weide Van Der, Bert 3:55:39 (10,795)
Weighell, Ian 3:38:23 (6,394)
Weighill, Mark 5:45:09 (30,889)
Weighill, Robert 3:31:01 (5,031)
Weight, Andrew 3:12:55 (2,421)
Weight, Christopher 5:20:47 (28,974)
Weiner, Alex 5:20:01 (28,882)
Weinstein, Jeffrey 5:55:34 (31,383)
Weir, Barry 3:12:02 (2,277)
Weir, George 4:33:34 (20,477)
Weir, Paul 4:25:56 (18,498)
Weir, Peter 4:30:52 (19,798)
Welburn, Martyn 4:20:00 (16,860)
Welburn, Robert 4:08:32 (14,036)
Welch, Alan 2:43:17 (247)
Welch, Alastair 5:47:02 (30,991)
Welch, Dick 4:27:40 (18,958)
Welch, Neil 3:34:16 (5,572)
Welch, Paul 4:23:54 (17,948)
Welch, Stephen 3:28:29 (4,600)
Welch, Tom 3:45:09 (7,959)
Weldin, Jonathan 3:24:18 (3,877)
Weldon, David 3:53:31 (10,150)
Welham, Grant 3:36:02 (5,911)
Welham, Lee 3:07:53 (1,799)
Weller, David 5:33:13 (30,045)
Weller, David 5:39:20 (30,490)
Weller, Geoffrey 5:11:42 (27,906)
Weller, Martin 3:49:15 (8,953)
Weller, Ulrich 3:16:20 (2,824)
Wellings, Ian 4:22:18 (17,476)
Wellings, Keith 5:03:30 (26,824)
Wellington, Christopher 4:04:45 (13,148)
Wellman, Steven 3:09:05 (1,941)
Wells, Angus 3:25:56 (4,142)
Wells, Ben 3:19:24 (3,185)
Wells, Benjamin 3:01:13 (1,243)
Wells, Charles 3:41:47 (7,112)
Wells, Colin 4:50:47 (24,556)
Wells, Craig 4:15:27 (15,679)
Wells, Darren 5:18:11 (28,689)
Wells, Gary 5:39:26 (30,508)
Wells, Graham 3:12:19 (2,332)
Wells, James 3:43:13 (7,450)
Wells, Jeffrey 4:36:01 (21,084)
Wells, John 4:59:47 (26,272)
Wells, Kevin 4:38:26 (21,692)
Wells, Kevin 5:09:45 (27,668)
Wells, Lawrence 4:32:36 (20,243)
Wells, Michael 6:28:29 (32,246)
Wells, Neil 4:18:42 (16,526)
Wells, Peter 4:30:38 (19,739)
Wells, Richard 4:21:14 (17,174)
Wells, Richard 4:38:42 (21,761)
Wells, Steven 6:17:50 (32,028)
Wellstead, Charles 4:13:30 (15,189)
Welsh, Charlie 3:33:43 (5,462)
Welsh, Hadaian 6:56:14 (32,594)
Welsh, Irvine 5:19:16 (28,803)
Welsh, Neil 4:24:48 (18,198)
Welsh, Neil 4:37:52 (21,536)
Welsh, Robert 5:11:34 (27,891)
Welsh, Stephen 4:26:58 (18,779)
Welshman, Andrew 2:45:04 (303)
Welton, Duncan 4:17:44 (16,304)
Wendleken, Dylan 3:51:08 (9,466)
Wendleken, Edward 5:18:41 (28,742)
Wendt-Larsen, Henrik 3:00:16 (1,185)
Wenger, Urs 3:57:17 (11,288)
Wengraf-Townsend, James 4:53:12 (25,014)
Wenlock, Tony 4:11:17 (14,690)
Wensley, Ben 5:03:50 (26,862)
Wentland, Gregory 4:21:12 (17,165)
Wentworth, Daniel 3:36:57 (6,107)
Wentworth, Douglas 4:10:18 (14,460)
Wernli, Beat 4:16:26 (15,963)
Wescomb, Christopher 3:08:16 (1,833)
Weske, Helmut 3:49:06 (8,924)
Wesley, Nicholas 3:52:28 (9,829)
Wessinghage, Thomas 2:55:23 (771)
Wesson, Simon 4:46:50 (23,769)
West, Andrew 3:42:15 (7,220)
West, Carl 4:44:57 (23,287)
West, Christopher 3:05:16 (1,563)
West, Christopher 3:51:57 (9,671)
West, Clint 4:05:30 (13,327)
West, Colin 2:59:01 (1,094)
West, Darin 3:40:30 (6,850)
West, David 3:03:05 (1,379)
West, David 4:20:24 (16,964)
West, Kenneth 4:50:08 (24,443)
West, Kevin 3:13:20 (2,480)
West, Lee 4:16:37 (16,016)
West, Martyn 4:31:42 (20,013)
West, Matthew 3:14:43 (2,629)
West, Michael 4:05:46 (13,386)
West, Michael 5:02:36 (26,686)
West, Nicholas 3:49:40 (9,086)
West, Niel 4:38:06 (21,599)
West, Paul 4:55:16 (25,432)
West, Richard 2:50:14 (498)
West, Richard 4:31:00 (19,828)
West, Robert 3:59:07 (11,833)
West, Robert 5:23:41 (29,253)
West, Stephen 3:59:21 (11,903)
West, Stephen 4:48:05 (24,054)
West, Thomas 5:04:37 (26,967)
Westbrook, Ernest 4:27:48 (18,983)
Westcott, Christopher 4:20:19 (16,948)
Westcough, Steven 4:02:22 (12,628)
Wester, Robert 4:44:50 (23,253)
Westerhout, Kees 3:41:50 (7,120)
Westerman, Trevor 4:19:34 (16,741)
Western, Andrew 4:31:21 (19,918)
Westgate, Mark 5:05:58 (27,150)
Westgate, Stuart 3:26:43 (4,281)
Westhead, Robert 3:57:07 (11,238)
Westhead, Roger 3:48:11 (8,670)
Westhead, Terence 3:27:22 (4,391)
Westlake, Graham 3:56:08 (10,940)
Westlake, Nick 4:14:50 (15,533)
Westman, Jason 3:57:42 (11,422)
Westoby, Guy 5:52:05 (31,238)
Westoby-Brooks, Ben 4:57:56 (25,946)
Weston, Andrew 4:26:37 (18,688)
Weston, David 4:38:18 (21,655)
Weston, James 4:54:03 (25,192)
Weston, Jeff 4:54:09 (25,215)
Weston, Keith 4:20:05 (16,886)
Weston, Mark 4:57:04 (25,782)
Weston, Nick 4:46:25 (23,667)
Weston, Stephen 3:01:45 (1,277)
Westwell, Michael 4:06:24 (13,546)
Westwood, Maurice 5:25:35 (29,410)
Westwood, Roger 5:18:48 (28,756)
Wetheridge, Nicholas 2:19:40 (18)
Wetherilt, Timothy 4:14:46 (15,517)
Wethers, Nigel 3:45:57 (8,148)
Wetmore, Tim 2:50:32 (513)

LONDON MARATHON

Weyell, Peter	4:48:38	(24,152)
Weyers, Peter	3:13:34	(2,513)
Whale, Chris	5:34:21	(30,137)
Whale, Colin	4:18:17	(16,431)
Whalley, Adrian	3:02:36	(1,343)
Whannel, George	3:28:19	(4,571)
Whannel, James	3:58:42	(11,707)
Wharmby, Nicholas	4:40:03	(22,120)
Wharton, Roy	5:48:47	(31,078)
Whatford, Howard	4:34:40	(20,742)
Whatley, David	4:47:08	(23,840)
Whawell, Michael	5:16:16	(28,478)
Wheatley, David	5:40:39	(30,593)
Wheatley, Dennis	3:27:34	(4,428)
Wheatley, Graham	5:40:38	(30,592)
Wheatley, Iain	4:08:20	(13,974)
Wheaton, Antony	4:09:44	(14,328)
Wheddon, Charles	3:27:57	(4,508)
Wheeldon, Brian	4:17:27	(16,233)
Wheeldon, Matthew	4:27:31	(18,922)
Wheeldon, Scott	4:22:39	(17,588)
Wheele, James	4:36:16	(21,142)
Wheeler, Alan	3:29:24	(4,777)
Wheeler, Ben	4:58:33	(26,041)
Wheeler, Benjamin	6:31:56	(32,305)
Wheeler, Bradley	4:21:05	(17,136)
Wheeler, David	4:53:56	(25,168)
Wheeler, John	3:34:10	(5,557)
Wheeler, Michael	3:53:35	(10,175)
Wheeler, Michael	4:32:27	(20,207)
Wheeler, Paul	4:14:27	(15,441)
Wheeler, Robert	3:33:54	(5,496)
Wheeler, Simon	4:39:06	(21,875)
Wheeler, Sydney	3:29:24	(4,777)
Wheeler, Tim	4:29:29	(19,456)
Whelan, Andrew	5:27:29	(29,575)
Whelan, Dominic	4:06:46	(13,624)
Whelan, Joseph	3:59:33	(11,951)
Whelan, Kevin	4:51:17	(24,665)
Whelan, Michael	4:01:17	(12,384)
Whelan, Paul	3:51:37	(9,556)
Whelehan, Oliver	3:47:04	(8,399)
Wheller, Stephen	5:41:54	(30,691)
Whetman, James	2:54:36	(714)
Whetter, Richard	4:19:28	(16,713)
Whiles, Mick	4:57:45	(25,907)
Whiley, Neil	4:41:21	(22,439)
Whillier, Roy	4:39:25	(21,956)
Whilock, Stacey	3:42:14	(7,214)
Whisnant, Stephen	3:55:52	(10,864)
Whitaker, John	6:12:11	(31,885)
Whitaker, Keith	3:44:21	(7,757)
Whitaker, Martin	4:25:04	(18,277)
Whitcher, Jeremy	5:05:15	(27,051)
Whitchurch, Chris	5:15:21	(28,341)
White, Adam	4:24:13	(18,041)
White, Alec	3:34:25	(5,602)
White, Andrew	3:41:31	(7,067)
White, Anthony	3:05:07	(1,555)
White, Anthony	4:02:49	(12,733)
White, Anthony	4:11:34	(14,759)
White, Barry	3:06:38	(1,703)
White, Bijan	3:49:21	(8,985)
White, Brian	2:46:28	(341)
White, Charles	4:54:30	(25,286)
White, Chris	3:50:20	(9,258)
White, Christopher	5:56:41	(31,428)
White, Colin	5:37:51	(30,404)
White, Daniel	3:58:59	(11,796)
White, Darren	3:51:30	(9,543)
White, Darren	4:52:46	(24,931)
White, David	3:36:46	(6,069)
White, David	4:19:01	(16,597)
White, David	4:25:32	(18,396)
White, David	4:25:51	(18,471)
White, David	6:06:44	(31,745)
White, Dean	4:11:24	(14,710)
White, Derek	3:08:27	(1,860)
White, Douglas	5:13:45	(28,162)
White, George	4:19:10	(16,636)
White, Graham	3:42:52	(7,353)
White, Graham	5:18:04	(28,678)
White, Ian	4:24:05	(18,005)

White, James	3:12:47	(2,396)
White, John	3:05:32	(1,594)
White, John	3:54:48	(10,541)
White, John	5:19:32	(28,823)
White, Jonathan	3:24:32	(3,925)
White, Jos	3:43:26	(7,508)
White, Kenneth	4:37:30	(21,449)
White, Kevin	4:44:02	(23,071)
White, Malcolm	3:58:18	(11,590)
White, Mark	3:33:42	(5,457)
White, Mark	3:38:31	(6,429)
White, Mark	4:07:53	(13,890)
White, Martin	3:54:56	(10,574)
White, Martin	4:55:02	(25,381)
White, Martin	5:25:45	(29,424)
White, Martin	5:32:46	(30,010)
White, Nick	4:27:47	(18,978)
White, Nigel	3:00:21	(1,189)
White, Peter	2:54:58	(739)
White, Peter	3:15:47	(2,768)
White, Philip	3:31:56	(5,177)
White, Robert	3:35:05	(5,725)
White, Robert	3:48:45	(8,829)
White, Robert	3:53:18	(10,081)
White, Robert	3:59:44	(12,003)
White, Robert	5:44:45	(30,873)
White, Stan	4:40:56	(22,339)
White, Stanley	4:59:31	(26,221)
White, Stephen	3:05:42	(1,607)
White, Stephen	3:43:56	(7,638)
White, Stephen	3:56:43	(11,113)
White, Stephen	4:06:29	(13,562)
White, Stephen	4:43:47	(23,011)
White, Steve	3:09:37	(2,002)
White, Steven	3:50:29	(9,297)
White, Stewart	3:49:22	(8,993)
White, Stuart	4:46:38	(23,720)
White, Thomas	3:17:18	(2,933)
White, Thomas	4:39:51	(22,070)
White, Tony	3:03:18	(1,404)
White, Victor	5:32:17	(29,977)
White, William	4:39:36	(21,994)
White, Willy	3:44:43	(7,861)
Whitefield, Chris	4:21:27	(17,232)
Whitefield, Peter	3:28:19	(4,571)
Whiteford, James	5:12:30	(28,026)
Whitehand, Mark	3:27:49	(4,487)
Whitehead, Alistair	3:33:25	(5,419)
Whitehead, Christopher	3:51:12	(9,482)
Whitehead, David	3:48:04	(8,643)
Whitehead, David	5:51:25	(31,210)
Whitehead, Malcolm	3:35:40	(5,837)
Whitehead, Mark	4:39:23	(21,946)
Whitehead, Martyn	5:02:11	(26,627)
Whitehead, Nigel	4:15:36	(15,722)
Whitehead, Richard	4:45:14	(23,366)
Whitehead, Richard	4:45:23	(23,404)
Whitehead, Sean	4:12:50	(15,045)
Whitehead, Simon	3:49:08	(8,931)
Whitehead, Simon	3:52:50	(9,933)
Whitehouse, Alan	4:40:48	(22,310)
Whitehouse, Andy	5:05:36	(27,099)
Whitehouse, James	4:22:48	(17,639)
Whitehouse, Joseph	4:07:52	(13,884)
Whitelan, Mark	3:33:54	(5,496)
Whitelegg, Richard	2:38:34	(158)
Whiteley, Alan	4:54:07	(25,202)
Whiteley, James	3:34:07	(5,546)
Whiteley, Stephen	3:17:02	(2,907)
Whitelock, Neil	3:37:00	(6,118)
Whiten, Mark	5:04:43	(26,981)
Whiteoak, Brett	2:54:36	(714)
Whiter, George	4:19:20	(16,673)
Whiteside, Christopher	4:18:19	(16,444)
Whiteside, David	3:49:52	(9,145)

Whiteway, Martin	4:03:57	(12,976)
Whiteway, Philip	3:45:38	(8,077)
Whitfield, Dean	3:35:34	(5,817)
Whitfield, Hugh	3:54:04	(10,334)
Whitfield, Matthew	3:17:45	(2,983)
Whitford, Frank	3:08:25	(1,852)
Whitford, Richard	4:10:27	(14,497)
Whitham, Stephen	4:31:02	(19,834)
Whiting, John	7:44:43	(32,840)
Whiting, Richard	3:26:46	(4,288)
Whiting, Richard	4:40:02	(22,117)
Whitley, David	4:07:05	(13,692)
Whitley, John	3:27:26	(4,404)
Whitlock, Marc	4:07:18	(13,748)
Whitlock, Russell	3:22:24	(3,572)
Whitlock, Tony	3:27:34	(4,428)
Whitmarsh, Jim	3:43:52	(7,625)
Whitmarsh, Richard	5:09:36	(27,649)
Whitmarsh-Knight, Simon	4:32:32	(20,225)
Whitmee, Timothy	3:43:50	(7,616)
Whitmer, Stephen	4:30:16	(19,664)
Whitmill, Martin	5:23:18	(29,202)
Whitmore, Ceri	3:33:49	(5,482)
Whitmore, Ivon	2:56:13	(847)
Whitmore, Kris	4:17:09	(16,160)
Whitmore, Simon	4:21:06	(17,140)
Whitmore, Simon	5:10:52	(27,798)
Whitney, Peter	3:03:27	(1,416)
Whitrow, Andrew	3:35:03	(5,719)
Whittaker, David	3:20:30	(3,312)
Whittaker, John	4:30:16	(19,664)
Whittaker, Michael	4:16:57	(16,103)
Whittaker, Michael	4:38:24	(21,685)
Whittaker, Phil	3:54:14	(10,379)
Whittaker, Samuel	3:08:44	(1,896)
Whittam, Michael	4:57:14	(25,818)
Whittell, Stuart	3:38:03	(6,322)
Whittemore, Michael	5:27:42	(29,596)
Whitten, Robert	4:33:07	(20,383)
Whitten, Stephen	5:02:25	(26,655)
Whittingham, Dylan	3:43:27	(7,513)
Whittingham, Matthew	4:43:45	(23,004)
Whittington, Bruce	4:36:18	(21,153)
Whittle, Ben	3:25:31	(4,067)
Whittle, David	4:48:40	(24,161)
Whittle, Gareth	6:47:01	(32,507)
Whittle, John	3:40:43	(6,899)
Whittle, John	4:08:08	(13,939)
Whittle, Stephen	3:27:58	(4,512)
Whittle, Stuart	4:35:12	(20,881)
Whittle, Stuart	4:46:46	(23,750)
Whittley, Shane	3:37:42	(6,260)
Whitton, Mark	4:54:03	(25,192)
Whitty, Iain	3:41:41	(7,097)
Whitworth, Bill	3:51:22	(9,514)
Whitworth, Peter	3:39:01	(6,532)
Wholey, Paul	5:18:24	(28,716)
Whoriskey, William	7:47:53	(32,845)
Whyatt, Christopher	4:17:29	(16,240)
Whybourn, Jean	4:22:22	(17,507)
Whyndham, Matthew	3:44:10	(7,698)
Whysall, Michael	3:43:43	(7,580)
Whyte, Alistair	3:55:07	(10,637)
Whyte, Lloyd	3:53:55	(10,283)
Whyte, Mark	7:06:46	(32,681)
Wickenden, Richard	4:51:03	(24,616)
Wickenden, Stephen	3:54:01	(10,314)
Wickens, Paul	3:28:39	(4,635)
Wickens, Robert	5:25:09	(29,376)
Wickham, Henry	4:06:05	(13,455)
Wickham, Stephen	3:33:06	(5,367)
Wicks, Douglas	4:46:26	(23,674)
Wicks, Edward	4:31:59	(20,081)
Wicks, Pete	3:21:43	(3,466)
Wicks, Philip	3:24:32	(3,925)
Wicks, Stephen	4:42:40	(22,760)
Wictome, Matthew	4:27:22	(18,881)
Widdop, John	3:27:45	(4,467)
Widdows, Terence	4:02:40	(12,695)
Widdowson, James	4:14:02	(15,324)
Widdowson, Philip	3:51:54	(9,650)
Widmann, Armand	3:57:56	(11,483)
Wiecano, Werver	3:47:55	(8,608)

Williams, Red....4:47:33 (23,919)
Williams, Rhodri....3:42:15 (7,220)
Williams, Richard....3:48:52 (8,859)
Williams, Richard....4:36:59 (21,309)
Williams, Richard....4:49:14 (24,281)
Williams, Robert....4:15:12 (15,621)
Williams, Robert....4:17:59 (16,368)
Williams, Rodney....3:40:48 (6,920)
Williams, Ronald....3:10:11 (2,057)
Williams, Rowland....3:18:06 (3,020)
Williams, Royston....3:09:55 (2,029)
Williams, Simon....3:40:16 (6,803)
Williams, Simon....3:47:16 (8,453)
Williams, Simon....4:43:34 (22,972)
Williams, Sion....5:10:00 (27,690)
Williams, Stephen....2:49:57 (489)
Williams, Stephen....3:25:45 (4,106)
Williams, Stephen....7:05:08 (32,671)
Williams, Steven....3:28:45 (4,646)
Williams, Steven....5:01:51 (26,577)
Williams, Thomas....4:10:55 (14,612)
Williams, Thomas....4:34:05 (20,603)
Williams, Tim....3:36:29 (6,023)
Williams, Tim....3:36:33 (6,031)
Williams, Timothy....5:07:51 (27,414)
Williams, Trevor....4:34:13 (20,631)
Williams, Trevor....4:35:23 (20,921)
Williams, Vernon....5:22:32 (29,136)
Williams, Vincent....2:59:47 (1,156)
Williams, William....4:32:27 (20,207)
Williams, Wyn....5:20:19 (28,919)
Williamson, Alex....4:33:06 (20,375)
Williamson, Anthony....4:25:21 (18,348)
Williamson, Blair....4:06:40 (13,606)
Williamson, Brian....5:39:10 (30,481)
Williamson, Colin....3:44:47 (7,884)
Williamson, Craig....4:00:51 (12,267)
Williamson, Darren....3:32:49 (5,320)
Williamson, David....4:17:57 (16,359)
Williamson, Dennis....5:19:46 (28,847)
Williamson, Derek....5:01:59 (26,603)
Williamson, Keith....4:19:11 (16,641)
Williamson, Mark....3:25:03 (3,993)
Williamson, Neil....4:08:30 (14,021)
Williamson, Neil....5:59:25 (31,528)
Williamson, Paul....3:59:17 (11,878)
Williamson, Peter....3:53:09 (10,030)
Williamson, Rupert....4:27:26 (18,896)
Williamson, Steven....3:46:42 (8,330)
Willie, Trevor....4:19:58 (16,852)
Willink, Patrick....4:04:40 (13,127)
Willis, Adrian....4:37:39 (21,477)
Willis, Alan....4:21:35 (17,274)
Willis, Andrew....4:16:47 (16,060)
Willis, Andrew....5:12:14 (27,979)
Willis, Bob....4:13:50 (15,267)
Willis, Darren....4:44:28 (23,162)
Willis, David....4:31:05 (19,852)
Willis, David....4:34:29 (20,688)
Willis, David....4:36:58 (21,307)
Willis, Edward....3:31:11 (5,063)
Willis, Gordon....3:57:17 (11,288)
Willis, James....5:51:27 (31,213)
Willis, Jason....4:02:26 (12,638)
Willis, John....3:08:53 (1,919)
Willis, John....4:07:59 (13,903)
Willis, Mark....5:06:30 (27,230)
Willis, Paul....7:01:43 (32,643)
Willis, Richard....3:49:24 (9,005)
Willis, Russell....4:08:02 (13,923)
Willmitt, William....3:07:57 (1,803)
Willmott, Dan....5:56:47 (31,437)
Willmott, Ian....4:53:01 (24,978)
Willmott, Roy....5:36:02 (30,279)
Willoughby, Gary....3:25:19 (4,033)
Willoughby, Rae....4:52:04 (24,791)
Willoughby, Stefan....6:05:58 (31,732)
Willoughby, Terence....4:52:04 (24,791)
Willows, Peter....4:47:52 (23,996)
Wills, Andrew....3:00:25 (1,198)
Wills, Andrew....3:33:15 (5,388)
Wills, Garry....4:27:35 (18,933)
Wills, Paul....4:09:06 (14,153)
Wills, Ron....2:41:06 (207)
Wills, Sidney....4:14:58 (15,565)
Wills, Thomas....6:02:09 (31,614)
Willsher, Brian....3:53:20 (10,090)
Willsher, Neil....3:19:12 (3,162)
Willson, Jonathan....3:38:00 (6,313)
Willson, Timothy....3:29:31 (4,800)
Wills-Wilson, Graham....5:19:52 (28,856)
Wilmer, Duncan....4:10:07 (14,414)
Wilmeringer, Stefan....5:46:43 (30,976)
Wilmot, Andrew....3:17:07 (2,914)
Wilmot, Andrew....3:31:16 (5,072)
Wilmot, Timothy....3:38:35 (6,446)
Wilmshurst, Andrew....2:53:13 (638)
Wilsmore, Paul....3:12:40 (2,381)
Wilson, Alan....3:34:16 (5,572)
Wilson, Allan....3:42:56 (7,366)
Wilson, Andrew....3:03:10 (1,385)
Wilson, Andrew....3:38:16 (6,362)
Wilson, Andrew....4:02:25 (12,633)
Wilson, Andrew....5:05:52 (27,141)
Wilson, Andrew....5:10:21 (27,731)
Wilson, Andy....4:33:58 (20,572)
Wilson, Andy....4:56:39 (25,712)
Wilson, Anthony....4:40:01 (22,109)
Wilson, Anthony....4:42:38 (22,755)
Wilson, Barry....2:47:52 (398)
Wilson, Brian....3:27:15 (4,368)
Wilson, Brian....3:59:09 (11,841)
Wilson, Craig....4:44:16 (23,123)
Wilson, Craig....5:43:56 (30,813)
Wilson, David....3:02:34 (1,341)
Wilson, David....3:25:53 (4,133)
Wilson, David....3:34:03 (5,531)
Wilson, David....4:05:22 (13,290)
Wilson, David....4:28:34 (19,184)
Wilson, David....4:29:48 (19,534)
Wilson, Donough....6:39:25 (32,429)
Wilson, Duncan....3:45:52 (8,132)
Wilson, Duncan....5:30:20 (29,807)
Wilson, Dylan....3:36:12 (5,957)
Wilson, Geoff....3:22:13 (3,556)
Wilson, Glisson....3:37:37 (6,246)
Wilson, Graham....4:23:03 (17,717)
Wilson, Graham....4:36:19 (21,164)
Wilson, Ian....4:15:50 (15,786)
Wilson, Ian....4:43:19 (22,913)
Wilson, Joe....4:07:36 (13,816)
Wilson, Jonathan....4:46:31 (23,698)
Wilson, Jonathan....6:14:33 (31,945)
Wilson, Kenneth....3:23:00 (3,657)
Wilson, Leigh....3:47:47 (8,584)
Wilson, Malcolm....4:28:08 (19,065)
Wilson, Mark....3:55:05 (10,619)
Wilson, Mark....5:03:55 (26,873)
Wilson, Martin....3:32:05 (5,204)
Wilson, Martin....5:06:40 (27,252)
Wilson, Matthew....4:05:59 (13,432)
Wilson, Michael....3:15:36 (2,735)
Wilson, Michael....3:42:29 (7,286)
Wilson, Neil....3:45:45 (8,100)
Wilson, Neil....4:06:14 (13,498)
Wilson, Nicholas....2:58:29 (1,046)
Wilson, Nicholas....4:16:49 (16,071)
Wilson, Paul....3:40:32 (6,859)
Wilson, Paul....3:43:14 (7,454)
Wilson, Paul....3:48:44 (8,822)
Wilson, Paul....4:05:54 (13,411)
Wilson, Paul....4:15:34 (15,712)
Wilson, Paul....5:32:30 (29,994)
Wilson, Peter....3:30:46 (4,985)
Wilson, Philip....5:28:22 (29,645)
Wilson, Ramon....4:10:21 (14,471)
Wilson, Richard....3:55:19 (10,701)
Wilson, Robert....2:45:33 (313)
Wilson, Robert....3:02:10 (1,314)
Wilson, Robert....3:28:34 (4,616)
Wilson, Robert....4:01:37 (12,475)
Wilson, Robert....4:10:22 (14,479)
Wilson, Robin....3:40:09 (6,772)
Wilson, Robin....4:16:44 (16,045)
Wilson, Sean....3:31:05 (5,043)
Wilson, Stephen....4:17:42 (16,294)
Wilson, Stephen....4:44:26 (23,157)
Wilson, Stephen....5:03:07 (26,766)
Wilson, Stuart....3:43:17 (7,467)
Wilson, Stuart....3:55:28 (10,739)
Wilson, T....4:21:28 (17,238)
Wilson, Tim....4:20:32 (17,000)
Wilson, Timothy....3:48:56 (8,875)
Wilson, Toby....4:10:04 (14,403)
Wilson, Victor....3:27:17 (4,374)
Wilson, Wayne....5:48:57 (31,097)
Wilton, Matthew....3:47:27 (8,497)
Wiltshire, Tim....4:15:21 (15,653)
Winchester, Kenneth....4:06:29 (13,562)
Winchester, Rob....3:40:05 (6,756)
Winchester, Terry....3:52:47 (9,922)
Winclawski, Wlodzimierz....4:13:56 (15,291)
Wind, Kevan....3:25:45 (4,106)
Winder, Bill....6:27:13 (32,226)
Winder, Mark....4:48:16 (24,081)
Winder, Richard....3:28:57 (4,692)
Windibank, Paul....3:45:42 (8,090)
Windisch, Viktor....3:44:01 (7,661)
Windle, John....4:42:27 (22,711)
Windley, Joseph....3:34:04 (5,533)
Windmill, Stephen....3:34:28 (5,613)
Windsor, Mike....4:26:07 (18,556)
Winfield, Brian....4:43:59 (23,062)
Winfield, David....3:51:16 (9,493)
Winfield, David....5:30:06 (29,784)
Winfield, Matthew....3:57:23 (11,317)
Winfield, Nicholas....3:23:04 (3,665)
Winfield, Peter....3:13:38 (2,519)
Winfield, Russell....3:52:07 (9,726)
Winfield, Stephen....3:58:52 (11,754)
Wing, John....3:57:26 (11,339)
Wingfield, Mike....3:42:18 (7,232)
Wingfield, Tom....4:26:55 (18,764)
Wingrave, Kenny....5:03:03 (26,752)
Wingrove, Nicholas....4:56:39 (25,712)
Wingrove, Oliver....6:26:07 (32,204)
Wingrove, Simon....4:59:23 (26,197)
Winkelmann, Jorg....4:06:19 (13,522)
Winkenbach, Frank....3:42:45 (7,326)
Winkfield, Dave....6:47:05 (32,508)
Winkle, Dewi....3:45:29 (8,039)
Winnister, Les....5:03:29 (26,820)
Winslow, Michael....3:49:33 (9,053)
Winstanley, Andrew....4:53:44 (25,110)
Winstanley, Gareth....4:24:09 (18,023)
Winstanley, Ian....3:18:54 (3,125)
Winstanley, Ian....4:33:28 (20,455)
Winston, Roger....3:43:47 (7,601)
Wint, Owen....5:20:13 (28,906)
Winter, Guy....4:20:31 (16,994)
Winter, James....4:22:26 (17,531)
Winter, Martin....3:54:43 (10,519)
Winter, Peter....4:44:17 (23,128)
Winter, Stephen....2:59:06 (1,103)
Winter, Tim....3:36:52 (6,088)
Winterflood, Ian....2:37:39 (137)
Winterflood, Ross....4:29:18 (19,415)
Wintermantel, Oliver....5:30:34 (29,830)
Winters, John....3:50:11 (9,210)
Winters, Oliver....4:06:10 (13,480)
Winters, Stephen....4:24:28 (18,110)
Winther, Max....4:12:01 (14,867)
Wintle, George....4:06:55 (13,651)
Wintrip, Clive....2:51:49 (572)
Winward, John....3:54:24 (10,427)
Wisbey, Andrew....4:44:15 (23,115)
Wisbey, Andrew....6:15:09 (31,961)
Wisdom, John....5:48:10 (31,044)
Wisdom, Martin....3:30:28 (4,938)
Wise, Alan....3:36:14 (5,965)
Wise, James....4:17:59 (16,368)
Wise, Paul....5:37:34 (30,389)
Wise, Robert....4:22:13 (17,449)
Wisely, Jonathan....4:51:10 (24,643)
Wiseman, Guy....3:44:14 (7,720)
Wiseman, John....4:14:24 (15,427)
Wiseman, William....6:47:13 (32,509)
Wishart, James....3:48:50 (8,849)
Wisken, Mark....4:42:39 (22,758)

Wright, Darren 3:47:53 (8,605)
Wright, David 2:55:28 (778)
Wright, David 4:14:25 (15,429)
Wright, Dennis 5:14:14 (28,216)
Wright, Derek 3:17:31 (2,959)
Wright, Derek 3:32:00 (5,191)
Wright, Gary 3:00:19 (1,186)
Wright, Gary 3:54:28 (10,450)
Wright, Gary 4:17:01 (16,121)
Wright, Geoffrey 4:21:44 (17,321)
Wright, Geoffrey 5:14:38 (28,266)
Wright, Gordon 3:43:44 (7,585)
Wright, James 3:46:29 (8,272)
Wright, John 4:38:19 (21,663)
Wright, Ken 4:58:43 (26,082)
Wright, Lee 6:22:22 (32,132)
Wright, Marcus 3:44:07 (7,683)
Wright, Michael 3:42:37 (7,307)
Wright, Michael 5:30:25 (29,813)
Wright, Mitchell 4:17:25 (16,227)
Wright, Nathon 2:49:49 (477)
Wright, Nicholas 4:50:44 (24,546)
Wright, Nick 4:57:43 (25,902)
Wright, Nick 5:19:10 (28,790)
Wright, Oliver 3:23:55 (3,803)
Wright, Paul 3:35:37 (5,829)
Wright, Paul 4:05:38 (13,357)
Wright, Paul 4:10:25 (14,490)
Wright, Paul 4:32:36 (20,243)
Wright, Peter 2:53:59 (682)
Wright, Peter 3:19:34 (3,209)
Wright, Peter 3:54:36 (10,487)
Wright, Phillip 4:56:32 (25,696)
Wright, Ralph 3:59:49 (12,028)
Wright, Robert 4:30:07 (19,630)
Wright, Robert 4:34:13 (20,631)
Wright, Ronald 4:53:23 (25,046)
Wright, Ross 3:58:06 (11,544)
Wright, Selwyn 4:14:02 (15,324)
Wright, Simon 3:26:18 (4,204)
Wright, Simon 4:49:29 (24,318)
Wright, Stephen 3:08:43 (1,891)
Wright, Stephen 4:15:39 (15,739)
Wright, Stephen 4:26:54 (18,760)
Wright, Stephen 4:33:08 (20,391)
Wright, Steve 4:28:50 (19,269)
Wright, Steven 4:07:19 (13,753)
Wright, Steven 4:59:00 (26,130)
Wright, Steven 5:10:40 (27,771)
Wright, Stuart 4:27:53 (19,000)
Wright, Stuart 4:29:04 (19,341)
Wright, Tim 6:02:56 (31,638)
Wright, Timothy 3:59:11 (11,849)
Wright, Tony 4:54:14 (25,231)
Wright, William 3:49:43 (9,103)
Wright, William 5:37:09 (30,357)
Wrighton, Christopher 2:49:20 (459)
Wrighton, James 4:18:23 (16,460)
Wrigley, Colin 4:31:44 (20,018)
Wuensch, Ulrich 3:49:38 (9,078)
Wyatt, Andrew 4:31:04 (19,844)
Wyatt, Dean 4:44:36 (23,196)
Wyatt, Keith 3:53:34 (10,171)
Wyatt, Philip 3:41:10 (7,003)
Wyatt, Stephen 4:11:02 (14,639)
Wyatt, Steve 5:33:06 (30,035)
Wye, Mark 5:13:12 (28,103)
Wyer, Martin 3:57:35 (11,389)
Wyeth, Andrew 4:30:37 (19,737)
Wyhler, Marco 3:18:26 (3,060)
Wyldes, Mark 4:03:24 (12,859)
Wyles, William 4:27:24 (18,890)
Wylie, Patrick 5:00:23 (26,356)
Wyllie, Andrew 4:40:13 (22,162)
Wyllie, Darren 3:55:13 (10,668)
Wyllie, Peter 4:11:54 (14,833)
Wyman, Glyn 4:44:01 (23,068)
Wyncoll, James 4:47:43 (23,958)
Wynne, Gareth 3:40:57 (6,949)
Wynne, Mike 4:34:00 (20,579)
Wynne, Peter 3:42:07 (7,184)
Wynne, Rob 2:44:29 (281)
Wynne-Jones, Gareth 4:24:11 (18,029)
Wyre, David 3:50:25 (9,281)
Yadave, Rush 4:09:57 (14,373)
Yagishita, Go 2:36:48 (122)
Yallop, Tony 4:25:29 (18,381)
Yamada, Kensuke 4:25:10 (18,302)
Yamazaki, Toshio 3:58:51 (11,749)
Yan, Andrew 3:54:31 (10,463)
Yandell, John 3:47:24 (8,488)
Yang, Xiao 4:30:01 (19,597)
Yard, Maurice 5:34:14 (30,127)
Yarde, Eddie 4:24:59 (18,258)
Yardley, Walter 3:53:58 (10,299)
Yarrow, Christopher 5:26:04 (29,450)
Yarrow, Nigel 3:47:41 (8,558)
Yasuhara, Kazunari 4:50:22 (24,473)
Yasumatsu, Kazuhiko 4:31:14 (19,887)
Yates, Anthony 3:27:27 (4,408)
Yates, Chris 3:27:16 (4,372)
Yates, Damian 5:42:52 (30,743)
Yates, Eric 4:22:49 (17,648)
Yates, Gary 3:06:19 (1,665)
Yates, John 3:00:57 (1,223)
Yates, Jonathan 4:28:22 (19,128)
Yates, Neville 3:38:48 (6,484)
Yates, Nicholas 3:59:15 (11,868)
Yates, Nicholas 4:27:28 (18,911)
Yates, Paul 4:23:34 (17,840)
Yates, Roger 3:48:51 (8,853)
Yeadon, Simon 5:13:04 (28,088)
Yearwood, Nicholas 4:07:15 (13,734)
Yeatman, Richard 3:43:49 (7,612)
Yeats, Andy 3:36:55 (6,099)
Yeats, Gavin 3:41:44 (7,102)
Yellop, David 4:35:47 (21,025)
Yellop, Tim 4:36:08 (21,115)
Yeo, John 3:21:27 (3,427)
Yeo, Keith 4:20:26 (16,980)
Yeo, Nigel 4:45:00 (23,304)
Yeoman, Mark 3:24:08 (3,844)
Yeomans, Martin 2:57:30 (956)
Yeomans, Stephen 3:44:33 (7,811)
Yeomans, Stephen 3:47:56 (8,614)
Yeung, Simon 3:25:38 (4,090)
Yianni, George 3:58:54 (11,764)
Yianni, Nicolas 6:13:33 (31,916)
Yiannouzis, Andrew 4:02:54 (12,755)
Yin, Peter 5:07:03 (27,302)
Yokota, Taneatsu 4:24:56 (18,234)
Yonge, Toby 3:38:38 (6,459)
York, David 3:55:24 (10,721)
York, Michael 4:49:46 (24,372)
York, Scott 4:10:57 (14,623)
Yorke, Keith 4:31:20 (19,912)
Yoshida, Akihiro 4:10:55 (14,612)
Yoshida, Tamotsu 3:59:17 (11,878)
Yost, Shaun 4:51:27 (24,692)
Youds, Martin 4:09:43 (14,321)
Youens, Robert 3:42:13 (7,204)
Youlden, James 3:37:23 (6,185)
Young, Alan 4:15:39 (15,739)
Young, Andy 5:51:07 (31,190)
Young, Angus 3:41:21 (7,038)
Young, Clinton 3:30:15 (4,901)
Young, David 3:43:16 (7,465)
Young, David 4:25:23 (18,358)
Young, Dean 4:14:53 (15,550)
Young, Findlay 3:54:56 (10,574)
Young, Gavin 3:51:42 (9,593)
Young, Ian 4:17:33 (16,253)
Young, James 3:23:32 (3,733)
Young, Jeremy 3:53:47 (10,237)
Young, John 3:41:16 (7,027)
Young, John 4:35:57 (21,067)
Young, Jonathan 3:23:56 (3,807)
Young, Leon 4:02:02 (12,566)
Young, Lester 3:06:14 (1,662)
Young, Michael 4:43:40 (22,990)
Young, Mickey 5:12:23 (28,010)
Young, Nigel 3:36:22 (5,996)
Young, Paul 4:19:29 (16,720)
Young, Peter 3:47:29 (8,505)
Young, Richard 3:18:17 (3,042)
Young, Robert 4:26:46 (18,736)
Young, Roy 3:54:43 (10,519)
Young, Simon 3:25:24 (4,048)
Young, Simon 4:15:51 (15,791)
Young, Stephen 4:29:36 (19,482)
Young, Steven 4:37:45 (21,503)
Young, Timothy 3:22:20 (3,566)
Yousuf, Zahed 4:00:21 (12,158)
Yuill, Charles 4:44:39 (23,206)
Yule, Brian 3:26:57 (4,321)
Yusuf, Yusuf 5:27:35 (29,587)
Zabari, Yehuda 3:37:45 (6,274)
Zabeli, Brahim 4:33:59 (20,576)
Zaczek, Karl 5:49:40 (31,130)
Zalesskiy, Vladimir 3:02:52 (1,362)
Zambrano, Marco 3:08:51 (1,915)
Zammit, Arthur 3:45:03 (7,940)
Zamova, Daniel 4:09:09 (14,170)
Zampieri, Maurizio 3:50:16 (9,242)
Zang, James 4:57:46 (25,911)
Zanini, Luigi 3:23:29 (3,724)
Zanon, Luigi 4:23:36 (17,847)
Zanoni, Aldo 4:50:35 (24,520)
Zante, André 4:10:33 (14,523)
Zazulak, Stefan 6:28:49 (32,253)
Zech, Christian 4:22:52 (17,661)
Zeederberg, Butch 4:09:20 (14,228)
Zegers Reyes, Rodrigo 2:49:55 (486)
Zeh, Glenn 5:03:16 (26,794)
Zehmke, Volker 3:53:22 (10,100)
Zehnder, Peter 4:00:24 (12,165)
Zerbib, Yves 4:15:09 (15,604)
Zhang, Skee 4:00:57 (12,295)
Zielinski, Jeremy 3:10:18 (2,077)
Zielinski, Steven 6:04:27 (31,671)
Zikusoka, Moses 3:43:53 (7,630)
Zilka, Jeffrey 4:18:23 (16,460)
Zimmermann, Herbert 3:56:31 (11,059)
Zimmern, Nicholas 5:29:31 (29,738)
Zipperlen, Peder 4:09:43 (14,321)
Zirngast, Philip 3:57:10 (11,252)
Zuccherato, Piero 4:29:06 (19,348)
Zugic, Richard 4:27:26 (18,896)
Zulliger, Ricardo 3:57:24 (11,325)

FEMALE RUNNERS

Abbas, Angeli 5:23:30 (29,221)
Abbey, Gail 4:04:28 (13,081)
Abbott, Kim 5:21:02 (28,994)
Abbott, Lisa 3:59:16 (11,873)
Abraham, Beverley 4:13:42 (15,232)
Abraham, Eileen 4:15:36 (15,722)
Abrahams, Corinne 4:28:45 (19,244)
Abrahams, Maggie 5:02:08 (26,619)
Abram, Clare 4:05:16 (13,267)
Abran, Louise 4:01:29 (12,437)
Abson, Jean 5:07:03 (27,302)
Abson, Jean 6:02:55 (31,636)
Acher, Louise 4:38:30 (21,703)
Achieng Ogot, Annex 5:12:00 (27,950)
Ackerman, Claire 5:15:50 (28,418)
Ackermann, Mia 4:14:10 (15,349)
Acklam, Anna-Liese 4:29:13 (19,384)
Ackland, Sacha 4:12:50 (15,045)
Acloque, Laura 5:00:14 (26,340)
Acton, Jane 3:22:43 (3,615)
Acton, Samantha 4:09:50 (14,348)
Adam, Catherine 4:45:59 (23,560)
Adam-Rapin, Martine 4:41:03 (22,362)
Adams, Anne 6:36:26 (32,384)
Adams, Claire 5:35:12 (30,200)
Adams, Elaine 5:42:25 (30,719)
Adams, Jacqui 4:04:17 (13,042)
Adams, Jane 6:13:05 (31,909)
Adams, Jeanette 6:46:34 (32,499)
Adams, Karen 4:52:41 (24,911)
Adams, Kim 4:40:01 (22,109)
Adams, Melanie 4:31:11 (19,877)
Adams, Paula 3:25:23 (4,043)
Adams, Rebecca 4:17:39 (16,280)
Adams, Ros 4:52:16 (24,836)
Adams, Susan 4:45:25 (23,419)
Adams, Tracey 4:16:31 (15,984)
Adams, Victoria 4:11:37 (14,774)

Adams, Victoria	5:36:00 (30,271)	
Adamson, Caron	4:56:55 (25,749)	
Adamson, Louise	3:57:08 (11,243)	
Adaramola, Ayodele	5:03:53 (26,870)	
Adedeji, Lola	4:20:44 (17,053)	
Adlard, Sarah	3:19:20 (3,178)	
Affleck, Patricia	2:58:38 (1,063)	
Agnew, Sarah	4:23:02 (17,713)	
Ahearn, Clem	5:17:44 (28,644)	
Ahearn, Rob	4:21:43 (17,315)	
Ahearne, Linda	5:36:49 (30,336)	
Aherne, Aisling	6:59:04 (32,618)	
Aherne, Christine	4:00:30 (12,188)	
Ainsworth, Pat	4:42:23 (22,691)	
Ainsworth, Susan	5:54:17 (31,327)	
Airey, Karen	4:15:54 (15,810)	
Airey, Virginia	4:35:58 (21,071)	
Aitken, Claire	4:21:09 (17,156)	
Aitken, Elizabeth	5:15:36 (28,383)	
Aitken, Janet	3:57:29 (11,359)	
Aitken, Susan	4:13:37 (15,209)	
Akehurst, Christine	6:32:03 (32,306)	
Akeroyd, Suzanne	3:14:10 (2,570)	
Akintoye, Toyin	5:22:31 (29,134)	
Albert, Linda	5:10:11 (27,715)	
Albrow, Shirley	4:54:08 (25,208)	
Albury, Michelle	4:12:44 (15,029)	
Alder, Claire	4:51:07 (24,631)	
Alder, Louise	5:14:58 (28,301)	
Aldous, Caroline	5:32:49 (30,013)	
Aldred, Caroline	5:01:43 (26,562)	
Aldridge, Gemma	5:36:10 (30,288)	
Aldridge, Jayne	5:43:16 (30,772)	
Alexander, Caroline	4:32:19 (20,165)	
Alexander, Michala	4:34:10 (20,621)	
Alexander, Rosalyn	2:56:56 (908)	
Alexandrou, Tracey	3:27:29 (4,415)	
Ali, Beverley	4:57:07 (25,797)	
Ali, Christine	5:27:37 (29,591)	
Ali, Ruksana	4:05:02 (13,216)	
Ali Khan, Shirley	5:18:20 (28,707)	
Alker, Kathryn	3:29:50 (4,845)	
Allali, Nora	5:18:02 (28,676)	
Allan, Deborah	5:52:50 (31,270)	
Allan, Elaine	3:49:26 (9,021)	
Allan, Juliet	4:36:28 (21,208)	
Allan, Tania	6:01:13 (31,584)	
Allaway, Ellen	5:41:40 (30,662)	
Allcock, Alison	4:26:14 (18,586)	
Allcock, Sophie	4:15:59 (15,833)	
Allday, Gill	6:08:21 (31,794)	
Allen, Amanda	4:44:43 (23,226)	
Allen, Angela	2:55:36 (790)	
Allen, Barbara	4:54:41 (25,320)	
Allen, Catherine	3:52:00 (9,683)	
Allen, Charlotte	3:44:26 (7,780)	
Allen, Donna	4:20:39 (17,032)	
Allen, Heather	3:40:02 (6,739)	
Allen, Jenny	11:34:00 (32,904)	
Allen, Joan	4:34:13 (20,631)	
Allen, Linda	3:50:10 (9,205)	
Allen, Rachel	4:03:23 (12,855)	
Allen, Susan	3:47:54 (8,606)	
Allen, Vanessa	4:34:04 (20,598)	
Allen, Wendy	4:24:36 (18,149)	
Allinson, Elizabeth	5:04:13 (26,919)	
Allison, Fiona	5:11:23 (27,866)	
Allison, Melanie	4:39:41 (22,016)	
Allison, Rebecca	5:07:27 (27,367)	
Allitt, Beverley	4:36:13 (21,134)	
Allsopp, Beverley	4:43:29 (22,958)	
Allsopp, Samantha	4:35:32 (20,957)	
Allum, Laura	5:27:37 (29,591)	
Allworthy, Karen	4:17:42 (16,294)	
Almosawi, Thikriat	6:42:14 (32,447)	
Alston, Margi	6:00:50 (31,574)	
Altoft, Maria	6:09:53 (31,833)	
Alton, Susan	7:43:19 (32,836)	
Altran, Francesca	4:31:11 (19,877)	
Alves, Virginia	4:57:31 (25,864)	
Alves De Sousa, Sarah	4:16:36 (16,010)	
Amara, Fabiola	5:17:27 (28,621)	
Ambrose, Jane	4:38:13 (21,631)	
Amey, Brenda	5:35:28 (30,224)	
Amos, Clare	4:24:21 (18,080)	
Amos, Louise	4:53:58 (25,179)	
Amos, Sally	4:24:21 (18,080)	
Amrani, Aicha	3:55:29 (10,741)	
Amy, Chris	4:42:32 (22,733)	
Anders, Rachael	4:37:43 (21,493)	
Anders, Sandra	7:14:56 (32,736)	
Andersen, Anne-Marie	5:15:17 (28,337)	
Anderson, Alyson	4:45:51 (23,530)	
Anderson, Amanda	6:09:46 (31,831)	
Anderson, Angela	4:29:26 (19,444)	
Anderson, Anna-Marie	4:21:26 (17,228)	
Anderson, Carolyn	4:38:55 (21,824)	
Anderson, Hilary	5:52:35 (31,259)	
Anderson, Irene	3:48:35 (8,773)	
Anderson, Jackie	3:57:07 (11,238)	
Anderson, Jane	5:08:44 (27,526)	
Anderson, Lisa	4:28:09 (19,071)	
Anderson, Margot	6:28:16 (32,244)	
Anderson, Melanie	4:14:38 (15,481)	
Anderson, Rachel	5:14:01 (28,199)	
Anderson, Sue-Ann	5:01:04 (26,459)	
Anderson, Susan	3:57:35 (11,389)	
Anderson, Tracey	5:05:38 (27,101)	
Anderson-Marsh, Lorraine	6:44:23 (32,478)	
Andrew, Jane	4:04:12 (13,027)	
Andrews, Annalisa	5:48:34 (31,066)	
Andrews, Denise	4:29:44 (19,520)	
Andrews, Jane	3:53:19 (10,086)	
Andrews, Joanne	4:43:40 (22,990)	
Andrews, Lynne	4:59:40 (26,259)	
Andrews, Sue	4:37:58 (21,568)	
Angel, Melanie	4:24:32 (18,129)	
Angell-Williams, Clare	4:17:33 (16,253)	
Anjo, Benilde	6:54:26 (32,585)	
Ankers, Elaine	4:24:45 (18,185)	
Anne, Kerie	5:54:54 (31,347)	
Annis, Victoria	5:09:49 (27,673)	
Ansell, Lizbeth	3:35:30 (5,804)	
Ansell, Maddalaine	3:48:14 (8,681)	
Anson, Frances	3:55:57 (10,884)	
Anstey, Judith	5:08:37 (27,509)	
Antell, Helen	4:40:56 (22,339)	
Anthonisz, Francine	5:17:11 (28,587)	
Anthony, Christine	4:35:44 (21,015)	
Antolik, Olivia	3:48:56 (8,875)	
Antoniou, Angela	5:15:35 (28,380)	
Antoniou, Marina	4:21:31 (17,255)	
Appavoo, Olive	4:31:24 (19,929)	
Appleby, Bonny	3:41:56 (7,137)	
Appleton, Angie	4:58:09 (25,973)	
Appleton, Janice	4:42:35 (22,744)	
Appleton, Rachel	3:44:11 (7,707)	
Applin, Helen	6:32:44 (32,320)	
Apps, Tracey	3:26:43 (4,281)	
Arbon, Fay	4:44:58 (23,290)	
Archbold, Karen	4:55:07 (25,400)	
Archer, Caroline	4:53:54 (25,147)	
Archer, Juliet	5:49:49 (31,137)	
Ardron, Susie	4:00:03 (12,095)	
Arena, Maud	4:00:00 (12,085)	
Arend, Leann	3:53:27 (10,128)	
Arey, Molly	4:09:10 (14,178)	
Argue, Paulette	6:03:14 (31,647)	
Argyle, Katherine	4:22:50 (17,652)	
Arimont Lincoln, Carla	6:23:04 (32,150)	
Arkinstall, Melissa	3:05:55 (1,635)	
Armand Smith, Penelope	4:43:17 (22,905)	
Armfield, Abigail	5:26:22 (29,476)	
Armiger, Sally	4:32:43 (20,282)	
Armour, Elizabeth	5:33:08 (30,039)	
Armstrong, Clare	5:07:22 (27,350)	
Armstrong, Debbie	5:09:04 (27,577)	
Armstrong, Janet	4:06:27 (13,556)	
Armstrong, Pamela	4:48:31 (24,129)	
Armstrong-Smith, Samantha	4:46:49 (23,762)	
Armytage, Gee	3:21:51 (3,493)	
Arnold, Gina	3:27:26 (4,404)	
Arnold, Janice	6:16:12 (31,993)	
Arnold, Katerina	4:06:11 (13,484)	
Arnold-MacCuish, Helen	3:55:07 (10,637)	
Arthur, Catherine	4:58:49 (26,100)	
Arundale-Burns, Lisa	3:01:40 (1,270)	
Ashcroft, Cynthia	4:09:08 (14,160)	
Asher, Carolyn	5:56:03 (31,403)	
Ashley, Susan	3:13:52 (2,547)	
Ashmall, Linda	6:16:09 (31,990)	
Ashman, Linda	4:42:43 (22,773)	
Ashton, Nicola	5:04:20 (26,940)	
Ashworth, Sarah	3:53:36 (10,178)	
Askew, Gerida	4:56:49 (25,737)	
Askwith, Celia	5:22:56 (29,170)	
Aspinall, Suzanne	4:17:11 (16,166)	
Asquith, Marlene	5:32:06 (29,960)	
Astley, Jenny	4:11:36 (14,768)	
Astley, Laura	4:29:52 (19,560)	
Aston, Karen	4:40:15 (22,170)	
Atac, Berna	4:51:03 (24,616)	
Atherton, Helen	5:37:37 (30,393)	
Atherton, Jane	4:27:52 (18,998)	
Athow, Sandie	3:23:56 (3,807)	
Atkin, Amelia	5:43:12 (30,768)	
Atkins, Christine	7:10:27 (32,708)	
Atkins, Emma	5:35:09 (30,197)	
Atkins, Joanne	6:12:08 (31,883)	
Atkins, Julie	4:10:06 (14,410)	
Atkins, Michelle	5:26:02 (29,447)	
Atkins, Tracey	4:49:36 (24,342)	
Atkinson, Andrea	6:33:32 (32,332)	
Atkinson, Cathy	4:08:31 (14,027)	
Atkinson, Ellen	5:35:49 (30,257)	
Atkinson, Jan	5:33:04 (30,030)	
Attwood, Helen	3:48:55 (8,873)	
Attwood, Karen	5:35:46 (30,254)	
Attwood, Katie	4:39:24 (21,953)	
Aubry, Christelle	3:59:37 (11,973)	
Auckland, Diane	4:18:26 (16,473)	
Audenshaw, Anthony	3:14:11 (2,572)	
Audis, Patricia	5:29:34 (29,743)	
Aughton, Hazel	5:30:11 (29,798)	
Augustus, Diane	4:23:36 (17,847)	
Aussenberg, Glenda	7:52:35 (32,849)	
Austen, Alison	6:11:09 (31,864)	
Austin, Angela	4:12:41 (15,022)	
Austin, Kelly	4:14:59 (15,570)	
Austin, Kelly	4:50:59 (24,606)	
Austin, Linda	3:50:58 (9,418)	
Austin, Naomi	4:00:44 (12,240)	
Austin, Sandra	5:13:09 (28,098)	
Aves, Susan	3:41:37 (7,084)	
Avon, Katie	3:52:37 (9,873)	
Awty, Elizabeth	4:16:03 (15,851)	
Axelrod, Nell	4:51:26 (24,686)	
Axton, Louise	5:40:14 (30,568)	
Aycinena, Karen	5:01:57 (26,598)	
Aylward, Colleen	3:56:22 (11,009)	
Aylward, Heather	5:43:36 (30,789)	
Aynge, Katie	4:18:17 (16,431)	
Ayres, Janet	4:36:26 (21,196)	
Ayres, Joanne	6:21:08 (32,109)	
Azenma, Celia	4:39:04 (21,862)	
Azim, Nadine	3:58:42 (11,707)	
Azlan, Sofia	5:04:22 (26,946)	
Azzuri, Pia	4:32:06 (20,109)	
Babb, Kim	5:23:40 (29,246)	
Backlin, Karin	4:02:56 (12,763)	
Bacon, Anny	4:58:08 (25,970)	
Bacon, Fiona	3:54:49 (10,547)	
Bacon, Pauline	4:59:49 (26,277)	
Bacon, Teresa	4:10:50 (14,590)	
Badin, Claudine	5:50:25 (31,157)	
Baekers-Dirven, Miranda	4:28:02 (19,043)	
Bagenal, Jessamy	3:29:10 (4,724)	
Baggio, Beverley	4:04:21 (13,057)	
Baggott, Kerry	3:45:30 (8,044)	
Bagwell, Sarah	5:08:40 (27,517)	
Baikovitch, Gilda	3:58:02 (11,522)	
Bailey, Claire	4:39:41 (22,016)	
Bailey, Clare	4:43:47 (23,011)	
Bailey, Estima	4:15:24 (15,665)	
Bailey, Fiona	5:52:10 (31,243)	
Bailey, Helen	5:10:48 (27,784)	
Bailey, Jayne	5:15:57 (28,436)	
Bailey, Marion	4:17:44 (16,304)	
Bailey, Sheila	3:26:58 (4,325)	

Bailey, Victoria 4:10:08 (14,424)
Bailey, Wanda 5:16:05 (28,452)
Baillie, Kathy 6:05:46 (31,724)
Baillie-Gage, Ailsa 4:09:55 (14,367)
Bain, Carol 5:10:57 (27,804)
Bain, Natasha 4:44:59 (23,297)
Bainbridge, Wendy 5:11:55 (27,940)
Bains, Ranju 5:15:40 (28,390)
Baird, Janet 10:48:09 (32,901)
Baird, Linda 4:08:21 (13,976)
Baird, Margaret 10:48:08 (32,900)
Baker, Amanda 4:19:29 (16,720)
Baker, Ann 6:03:50 (31,658)
Baker, Anna-Louise 5:23:05 (29,182)
Baker, Bonnie 5:05:28 (27,082)
Baker, Caroline 5:40:46 (30,600)
Baker, Charlotte 4:50:29 (24,502)
Baker, Deana 3:44:09 (7,695)
Baker, Jennifer 3:51:02 (9,438)
Baker, Laura 5:38:31 (30,451)
Baker, Lucy 5:06:19 (27,198)
Baker, Michelle 5:21:07 (29,010)
Baker, Ngaire 3:23:29 (3,724)
Baker, Nicola 5:33:53 (30,097)
Baker, Rachel 4:33:23 (20,438)
Baker, Sally 3:11:38 (2,220)
Baker, Sarah 5:17:18 (28,602)
Baker, Sharon 4:28:07 (19,058)
Baker, Stella 6:05:13 (31,704)
Bakmit, Helen 5:30:22 (29,809)
Baldassand, Roberta 6:44:23 (32,478)
Baldino, Maria 5:36:31 (30,309)
Baldrey, Charlotte 3:18:28 (3,067)
Baldwin, Ase 4:13:13 (15,126)
Baldwin, Carol 4:38:17 (21,651)
Baldwin, Emma 4:44:36 (23,196)
Bale, Christine 4:17:27 (16,233)
Bales, Rowena 3:26:32 (4,238)
Balfour, Jacky 3:53:21 (10,094)
Ball, Becky 4:37:49 (21,525)
Ball, Charlotte 4:29:43 (19,510)
Ball, Debbie 7:44:26 (32,839)
Ball, Joanna 3:35:17 (5,760)
Ball, Marni 4:08:21 (13,976)
Ball, Valarie 4:21:23 (17,218)
Ballard, Eleanor 4:16:33 (15,991)
Ballinger, Anne 4:08:01 (13,916)
Balossi, Ermelinda 4:35:48 (21,028)
Bambridge, Jackie 5:07:26 (27,364)
Banaghan, Maria 5:22:05 (29,098)
Banasco, Gloria 4:34:01 (20,582)
Banbury, Elizabeth 5:37:54 (30,407)
Bandeen, Bonnie 5:02:03 (26,608)
Bandey, Terrie 6:27:06 (32,218)
Bangham, Kirsty 4:45:32 (23,449)
Banks, Elizabeth 4:32:03 (20,101)
Banks, Wendy 5:01:07 (26,467)
Bannat, Heather 4:24:13 (18,041)
Banner, Andrea 3:08:53 (1,919)
Banner, Heather 3:53:55 (10,283)
Banneville, Angela 7:17:00 (32,744)
Bannister, Julie 4:50:44 (24,546)
Banwister, Roselyn 3:39:00 (6,523)
Baptist, Victoria 4:30:57 (19,821)
Barba-Soler, Lourdes 4:14:42 (15,495)
Barber, Cathryn 4:27:55 (19,011)
Barber, Julia 5:59:16 (31,523)
Barber, Kenwynne 5:22:38 (29,146)
Barber, Mary 5:06:59 (27,292)
Barber, Sue 3:57:32 (11,372)
Barber, Suzanne 3:24:51 (3,964)
Barclay, Janice 3:42:05 (7,174)
Barclay, Joanna 4:50:50 (24,575)
Bardon, Angela 4:40:23 (22,209)
Bareille, Marie 4:35:59 (21,077)
Barfield, Abigail 5:13:26 (28,131)
Barker, Angela 5:32:12 (29,968)
Barker, Ann 3:11:56 (2,262)
Barker, Debbie 6:27:10 (32,222)
Barker, Della 4:22:47 (17,631)
Barker, Emma 4:27:26 (18,896)
Barker, Helen 5:42:18 (30,712)
Barker, Jackie 3:26:10 (4,181)
Barker, Kate 5:32:12 (29,968)
Barker, Margaret 5:10:07 (27,703)
Barker, Tracey 5:11:26 (27,877)
Barkman, Sally 5:04:21 (26,944)
Barley, Julie 3:16:31 (2,846)
Barlow, Rachel 3:48:03 (8,639)
Barnaby, Sophie 4:37:38 (21,474)
Barnard, Janice 4:53:16 (25,022)
Barnard, Laura 5:24:19 (29,309)
Barnes, Ann 5:35:27 (30,220)
Barnes, Emma 4:07:59 (13,903)
Barnes, Emma 6:26:38 (32,212)
Barnes, Heidi 5:19:24 (28,810)
Barnes, Helen 4:29:01 (19,325)
Barnes, Helen 4:58:24 (26,016)
Barnes, Jenny 5:27:17 (29,549)
Barnes, Joanne 4:25:07 (18,292)
Barnes, Nicola 4:12:54 (15,062)
Barnes, Sue 3:38:14 (6,351)
Barnes, Wendy 3:27:33 (4,423)
Barnett, Alison 4:01:59 (12,557)
Barnett, Alison 5:15:50 (28,418)
Barnett, Christina 5:21:01 (28,991)
Barnett, Gillian 5:42:07 (30,701)
Barnett, Lyndsay 4:55:53 (25,554)
Barnett, Marion 7:08:31 (32,689)
Barnett, Susan 3:51:05 (9,453)
Barnett, Trudi 6:49:40 (32,538)
Barnsley, Susan 5:07:39 (27,392)
Baron-Hall, Amy 5:38:27 (30,443)
Barratt, Joanne 4:48:46 (24,182)
Barrett, Anita 4:08:37 (14,062)
Barrett, Caroline 4:21:50 (17,349)
Barrett, Esther 4:11:29 (14,741)
Barrett, Fiona 4:14:21 (15,409)
Barrett, Katie 5:44:11 (30,833)
Barrett, Teresa 4:20:24 (16,964)
Barrett, Victoria 3:14:13 (2,581)
Barrinton, Belinda 5:16:06 (28,454)
Barritt, Pamela 6:08:24 (31,795)
Barrosa, Celia 3:49:24 (9,005)
Barrow, Georgina 4:41:10 (22,394)
Barrow, Lauren 5:10:57 (27,804)
Barrow Green, June 3:34:00 (5,519)
Barrowclough, Catherine 4:59:39 (26,253)
Barry, Carole 5:12:52 (28,063)
Barry, Jane 3:31:57 (5,178)
Barss, Julia 3:24:21 (3,893)
Barstow, Bel 3:25:22 (4,039)
Bartels, Maureen 3:19:41 (3,220)
Barter, Pat 4:18:20 (16,452)
Bartlett, Anna 3:50:03 (9,178)
Bartlett, Jocelyn 4:41:38 (22,510)
Bartley, Ann 5:51:46 (31,227)
Bartoli, Josee 4:49:51 (24,395)
Barton, Gail 5:37:25 (30,378)
Barton, Joan 5:32:15 (29,974)
Barton-Smith, John 5:46:35 (30,970)
Bartrum, Jenny 4:16:35 (16,002)
Bartrum, Sue 5:00:33 (26,385)
Barwood, Marilyn 3:51:23 (9,517)
Basford, Sarah 4:58:31 (26,035)
Baskerville, Erica 4:16:54 (16,093)
Bass, Irenie 3:34:37 (5,641)
Bassett, Gillian 4:29:16 (19,405)
Batchelor, Jackie 5:40:21 (30,575)
Bateman, Claire 6:56:22 (32,596)
Bateman, Judith 3:23:59 (3,818)
Bates, Angela 3:37:52 (6,292)
Bates, Brenda 4:23:32 (17,834)
Bates, Helen 4:18:07 (16,392)
Bates, Jane 4:37:23 (21,418)
Bath, Doreen 4:07:44 (13,850)
Batty, Jane 4:04:10 (13,019)
Batty, Laura 4:32:58 (20,351)
Battye, Susan 4:52:41 (24,911)
Baudains, Sue 4:38:17 (21,651)
Bauer, Martha 4:45:06 (23,333)
Baumgaertner, Gabriela 5:04:17 (26,933)
Bawden, Julia 6:02:13 (31,619)
Baxter, Clare 3:18:32 (3,077)
Baxter, Jacqueline 4:09:09 (14,170)
Baxter, Kay 4:33:52 (20,551)
Baylay, Sharon 4:09:32 (14,275)
Bayliss, Hannah 3:54:40 (10,506)
Bayliss, Tina 6:07:57 (31,780)
Bayly, Sara 4:23:50 (17,925)
Baynard, Sarah 6:16:12 (31,993)
Bays, Lorna 4:30:52 (19,798)
Beadle, Deborah 4:53:03 (24,986)
Beagley, Tania 5:02:35 (26,684)
Beal, Samantha 4:57:51 (25,922)
Bear, Angie 3:36:25 (6,008)
Beard, Lucy 4:26:09 (18,566)
Beart, Laura 5:17:13 (28,590)
Beasant, Julie 4:26:20 (18,606)
Beasley, Beverley 5:17:43 (28,641)
Beasley, Kathryn 4:35:18 (20,904)
Beattie, Julie 4:59:36 (26,243)
Beaumont, Amanda 3:23:31 (3,729)
Beaumont, Geraldine 6:48:06 (32,520)
Beaumont, Joanna 6:03:35 (31,652)
Beaumont, Victoria 4:52:11 (24,813)
Beawlieu, Madeleine 5:01:13 (26,487)
Bebbington, Jan 3:56:17 (10,983)
Becconsall, Sue 3:33:24 (5,417)
Becherucci, Barbara 4:21:31 (17,255)
Beck, Rachel 4:57:40 (25,893)
Beckett, Patricia 4:40:41 (22,270)
Beckwith, Claire 5:17:34 (28,637)
Beckwith, Clare 5:23:53 (29,270)
Beckwith, Julie Linda 4:03:26 (12,870)
Beckwith, Laura 5:17:34 (28,637)
Bedd, Kate 4:56:43 (25,718)
Beddows, Amanda 5:02:09 (26,623)
Bedford, Rosalind 4:33:55 (20,560)
Bedford, Suzanne 3:41:18 (7,030)
Bedingfield, Alexandra 4:24:05 (18,005)
Bedingham, Emma 4:33:17 (20,419)
Beeching, Valerie 7:19:32 (32,754)
Beeke, Vikki 4:31:19 (19,906)
Beer, Kim 4:39:05 (21,869)
Beese, Fay 4:22:44 (17,618)
Beesley, Katherine 4:58:43 (26,082)
Begg, Pauline 6:17:21 (32,013)
Begum, Rusna 7:29:46 (32,784)
Belcham, Kay 5:01:06 (26,464)
Bell, Brona 4:48:14 (24,076)
Bell, Carla 3:57:44 (11,434)
Bell, Carolyn 4:24:51 (18,213)
Bell, Charlotte 4:34:57 (20,818)
Bell, Fiona 4:53:54 (25,147)
Bell, Fiona 5:30:44 (29,843)
Bell, Hazel 4:16:16 (15,904)
Bell, Karen 4:32:41 (20,272)
Bell, Kimberley 6:00:37 (31,563)
Bell, Louise 4:47:19 (23,881)
Bell, Maura 5:30:36 (29,832)
Bell, Susan 3:58:45 (11,718)
Bellamy, Vanessa 5:11:48 (27,921)
Bellaris, Wendy 5:46:45 (30,978)
Benbow, Claire 4:50:46 (24,553)
Bench, Allison 5:07:29 (27,372)
Bending, Karen 4:38:04 (21,589)
Bendix, Candida 4:11:56 (14,841)
Benjamin, Angela 5:00:27 (26,367)
Benjamin, Floella 5:13:41 (28,158)
Benjaminsson, Camilla 2:50:37 (519)
Bennett, Elettra 5:09:04 (27,577)
Bennett, Jane 5:15:28 (28,357)
Bennett, Kelly 5:35:53 (30,260)
Bennett, Patricia 4:06:10 (13,480)
Bennett, Patricia 4:07:13 (13,725)
Bennett, Paul 4:25:36 (18,418)
Bennett, Sara 4:40:57 (22,345)
Bennett, Stephen 4:03:43 (12,925)
Bennett, Susan 3:26:15 (4,197)
Bennett, Susan 5:14:44 (28,276)
Bennett, Vanessa 6:19:21 (32,065)
Bennett-Hornsey, Lindsay 3:42:56 (7,366)
Bensusan, Iona 6:16:03 (31,984)
Bent, Clare 4:18:57 (16,580)
Bentham, Caroline 5:41:07 (30,627)
Bentham, Karen 4:16:50 (16,075)
Bentley, Gina 4:45:01 (23,312)
Bentley, Helen 4:35:53 (21,047)

Benton, Jane	5:33:17	(30,052)
Benton, Tara	4:15:22	(15,657)
Benz, Petra	5:40:58	(30,614)
Berdusco, Kimberley	5:31:36	(29,921)
Berisford, Lucy	3:55:32	(10,758)
Bernard, Jennifer	4:56:43	(25,718)
Bernstein, Lucy	5:23:13	(29,196)
Berridge, Marilyn	4:32:01	(20,088)
Berriman, Lindsey	3:40:27	(6,843)
Berriman, Pamela	4:03:14	(12,822)
Berry, Catherine	4:17:12	(16,171)
Berry, Cheryle	6:44:33	(32,482)
Berry, Elizabeth	5:53:20	(31,292)
Berry, Jakki	3:57:37	(11,400)
Berry, Lesley	4:55:08	(25,408)
Berry, Rachel	6:29:29	(32,264)
Berry, Sheila	5:13:32	(28,144)
Berry, Vicky	5:56:34	(31,425)
Besley, Sally	3:54:19	(10,404)
Best, Alison	4:22:31	(17,550)
Best, Zdena	4:48:31	(24,129)
Bethune, Deirdre	3:49:23	(8,998)
Bett, Marinella	4:09:13	(14,193)
Betts, Carol	3:37:32	(6,229)
Betts, Fiona	3:48:28	(8,739)
Betts, Jackie	3:43:12	(7,442)
Betts, Katie	5:08:25	(27,489)
Bevan, Julie	3:53:50	(10,261)
Bevier, Gail	3:54:23	(10,422)
Bhahra, Billy	4:58:41	(26,074)
Bi, Sania	6:36:21	(32,378)
Bianchini, Sandra	5:11:44	(27,913)
Bibby, Dinah	5:17:43	(28,641)
Bickell, Susan	5:56:38	(31,427)
Bickers, Tara	4:51:07	(24,631)
Bidd, Heena	4:30:25	(19,697)
Biderre, Martine	3:41:39	(7,091)
Bidgood, Karen	4:36:22	(21,182)
Bidnell, Alison	5:36:31	(30,309)
Bidston, Joanna	3:41:59	(7,149)
Bielby, Patricia	4:04:51	(13,172)
Bienek, Jadwiga	3:42:48	(7,342)
Bienenstock, Robin	4:39:03	(21,860)
Bieri, Yvonne	4:24:15	(18,054)
Biglioli, Monioa	3:59:09	(11,841)
Bilbrough, Rachael	4:35:30	(20,946)
Bilcock, Heather	5:09:23	(27,621)
Biles, Sylvia	5:46:06	(30,940)
Bilham, Deborah	4:33:35	(20,486)
Billett, Lynda	5:44:20	(30,843)
Billington, Jody	4:02:49	(12,733)
Bimson, Karen	5:24:25	(29,317)
Bingham, Stephanie	4:09:43	(14,321)
Binns, Clare	4:31:43	(20,015)
Binns, Karen	4:53:50	(25,131)
Binns, Samantha	3:45:10	(7,962)
Binsted, Nicola	4:29:03	(19,335)
Binstock, Abbe	4:16:39	(16,028)
Birakos, Jane	6:05:04	(31,694)
Birch, Francesca	5:09:51	(27,677)
Birch, Jan	5:07:12	(27,328)
Birch, Katherine	6:14:52	(31,956)
Birch, Maria	4:45:43	(23,497)
Birch, Tracie	4:30:02	(19,603)
Birch, Zoe	4:53:54	(25,147)
Bircher, Carolyn	5:09:31	(27,634)
Bird, Hayley	3:46:33	(8,300)
Bird, Heather	5:35:23	(30,213)
Bird, Justine	5:31:55	(29,946)
Bird, Norma	3:23:35	(3,742)
Birkenhead, Kate	3:20:01	(3,256)
Birkett, Ailsa	4:36:43	(21,264)
Birkett, Christine	5:03:46	(26,852)
Birkett, Louise	5:17:07	(28,580)
Birkhead, Lucy	4:06:51	(13,638)
Birkhead, Sue	3:50:09	(9,202)
Birkinshaw, Hilary	4:15:19	(15,644)
Birtwell, Susan	4:36:22	(21,182)
Birtwistle, Esther	3:44:22	(7,765)
Bisgaard-Frantzen, Anita	4:15:41	(15,750)
Bishop, Deborah	5:48:29	(31,061)
Bishop, Elizabeth	5:10:11	(27,715)
Bishop, Kirsty	4:14:29	(15,446)
Bishop, Lucy	3:59:22	(11,906)
Bishop, Pauline	4:00:41	(12,220)
Bishop, Robyn	6:50:12	(32,543)
Bishop, Sarah	3:37:29	(6,211)
Bishopp, Sara	3:38:31	(6,429)
Bisset-Smith, Anne	5:14:41	(28,272)
Bjorneke, Britt	5:09:11	(27,593)
Black, Amanda	5:11:10	(27,837)
Black, Angus	4:12:35	(14,992)
Black, Giselle	4:06:44	(13,620)
Black, Kathryn	3:27:06	(4,346)
Black, Lisette	3:48:40	(8,802)
Black, Maggie	4:56:46	(25,726)
Black, Mairead	4:10:48	(14,576)
Blackbourn, Shirley	6:07:35	(31,775)
Blackburn, Linda	4:34:29	(20,688)
Blackburn, Marie	3:53:45	(10,225)
Blackburne, Helen	4:58:30	(26,033)
Blacker, Jane	5:42:25	(30,719)
Blackford, Robyne	4:36:09	(21,121)
Blackham, Catherine	4:21:24	(17,222)
Blackiston, Jo	4:43:47	(23,011)
Blackmore, Ruth	4:41:32	(22,481)
Blackshaw, Victoria	3:54:32	(10,467)
Blackwell, Pauline	4:09:32	(14,275)
Blackwell, Victoria	6:09:00	(31,812)
Blagbrough, Donna	4:22:54	(17,671)
Blair, Sophie	4:21:35	(17,274)
Blake, Ann Maree	4:16:43	(16,041)
Blake, Caroline	4:29:00	(19,322)
Blake, Elizabeth	4:35:56	(21,063)
Blake, Maureen	7:10:26	(32,706)
Blakemore, Jayne	4:17:23	(16,220)
Blanc-Surel, Mireille	3:48:10	(8,665)
Bland, Madeleine	4:48:43	(24,173)
Blandford, Sarah	6:13:02	(31,907)
Blaney, Pamela	3:56:09	(10,942)
Blanford, Fleur	4:26:47	(18,739)
Blann, Janet	4:48:13	(24,074)
Blasby, Anne	4:16:55	(16,095)
Blaydes, Sarah	4:30:31	(19,713)
Blaylock, Sue	5:23:15	(29,200)
Blazey, Lindsey	6:15:45	(31,974)
Bleaken, Marianne	3:13:09	(2,456)
Bleasdale, Gillian	5:33:18	(30,056)
Blenkin, Harriet	3:54:13	(10,376)
Blethyn, Brenda	6:43:33	(32,470)
Blewett, Jenni	5:03:20	(26,804)
Blinko, Lyn	3:23:39	(3,753)
Bliss, Elizabeth	4:40:21	(22,199)
Blocksidge, Jane	5:14:15	(28,222)
Blofield, Janice	5:59:07	(31,516)
Blondel, Anne	4:21:16	(17,183)
Bloomfield, Anna	5:22:06	(29,100)
Blore Mitchell, Carolyn	4:07:10	(13,711)
Blumenthal, Laura-Ann	5:20:38	(28,953)
Blundn, Sophie	5:07:22	(27,350)
Blunt, Emma	3:27:35	(4,433)
Blyth, Christine	4:07:14	(13,728)
Blyth, Sarah	5:09:33	(27,638)
Boardman, Elizabeth	5:23:24	(29,209)
Boardman, Marie	4:47:01	(23,815)
Boase, Alison	5:00:30	(26,377)
Boast, Nicola	5:13:52	(28,177)
Boast, Rebecca	4:26:17	(18,597)
Boby, Fay	5:31:28	(29,913)
Boddington, Julie	4:55:27	(25,473)
Bodemeaid, Amanda	6:12:19	(31,890)
Boeckl-Kudrna, Edith	4:04:54	(13,183)
Boelee, Scotia	4:32:05	(20,105)
Bogdanovic, Ana	6:29:57	(32,274)
Boggid, Julia	5:05:39	(27,105)
Boggis, Michele	4:51:46	(24,736)
Bolam, Anita	5:06:00	(27,155)
Bolton, Carrie	4:10:34	(14,527)
Bolton, Danille	3:55:43	(10,818)
Bolton, Jill	4:28:18	(19,109)
Bolton, Mary	5:48:50	(31,083)
Bond, Donna	3:36:20	(5,985)
Bond, Sarah	4:05:55	(13,417)
Bond, Sharon	6:46:57	(32,505)
Bond, Susan	4:14:38	(15,481)
Bonfield, Wendy	6:13:01	(31,906)
Bongers, Paula	3:29:59	(4,870)
Bonner, Joanna	8:19:56	(32,871)
Bonney, Joanne	4:27:17	(18,858)
Bonninga, Shelagh	5:11:57	(27,945)
Boorman, Josephine	4:56:06	(25,611)
Booth, Geraldine	3:40:57	(6,949)
Booth, Jamie	5:25:24	(29,395)
Booth, Lesley	5:20:53	(28,982)
Booth, Mariola	4:41:54	(22,585)
Booth, Sarah	4:26:31	(18,662)
Bore, Caroline	4:20:26	(16,980)
Borg, Colette	4:40:54	(22,332)
Borja, José	4:41:41	(22,526)
Borridge, Frances	4:55:04	(25,385)
Borrs, Edda	3:24:00	(3,820)
Bosley, Helen	4:35:17	(20,898)
Bosque-Oliva, Elisa	4:08:23	(13,990)
Bostock, Christine	5:00:27	(26,367)
Boston, Sue	7:07:02	(32,682)
Bottoms, Dawn	4:04:22	(13,062)
Bouck-Standen, Victoria	3:56:02	(10,906)
Boughton, Sarah	3:39:08	(6,554)
Boult, Deborah	3:30:33	(4,952)
Bourgalay, Brigitte	4:52:37	(24,901)
Bourne, Joanna	3:40:24	(6,833)
Bourne-Lange, Lesley	5:53:27	(31,295)
Bourne-Lange, Mandy	4:28:49	(19,261)
Bowater, Marina	4:37:03	(21,330)
Bowden, Hannah	4:19:24	(16,688)
Bowden, Suzanne	4:35:39	(21,001)
Bowdler, Sarah	4:19:05	(16,614)
Bowen, Caroline	4:31:55	(20,061)
Bowen, Claire	4:24:20	(18,077)
Bowen, Samantha	5:15:36	(28,383)
Bowen, Sandra	4:37:45	(21,503)
Bowers, Emma	4:52:46	(24,931)
Bowker, Margot	3:55:56	(10,783)
Bowles, Ann	3:38:20	(6,381)
Bowles, Victoria	3:34:46	(5,668)
Bowlt-Rasor, Joanne	4:10:47	(14,571)
Bowman, Louisa	4:41:57	(22,598)
Bowsnead, Joanne	3:59:38	(11,977)
Bowyer, Janet	4:40:55	(22,336)
Boxx, Jacqueline	6:32:57	(32,322)
Boyd, Fiona	5:04:06	(26,898)
Boyer, Julia	5:12:17	(27,995)
Boyes, Heather	6:37:05	(32,398)
Boylan, Shirley	5:16:44	(28,524)
Boyle, Deborah	5:36:53	(30,342)
Boyle, Susan	5:18:16	(28,699)
Boynton, Gillian	3:36:40	(6,051)
Boynton, Patricia	7:33:22	(32,802)
Brackley, Janet	5:06:51	(27,275)
Brackley, Sharon	4:01:36	(12,469)
Bradburn, Margaret	3:56:13	(10,972)
Bradford, Lynda	4:25:32	(18,396)
Bradford, Victoria	4:25:29	(18,381)
Bradley, Alexa	4:23:56	(17,958)
Bradley, Amanda	4:37:31	(21,451)
Bradley, Catherine	4:03:01	(12,778)
Bradley, Jayne	5:12:53	(28,065)
Bradley, Karen	3:21:27	(3,427)
Bradley, Lynn	4:15:38	(15,733)
Bradley, Sally	4:11:25	(14,715)
Bradley-Smith, Jane	5:12:50	(28,059)
Bradwell, Helen	4:19:00	(16,589)
Brady, Denise	4:50:06	(24,439)
Brady, Theresa	3:12:55	(2,421)
Bragg, Chloe	4:46:13	(23,628)
Bragg, Emma-Jane	4:48:28	(24,118)
Bragg, Hannah	5:09:41	(27,659)
Braham, Julie	4:25:01	(18,270)
Brailsford, Julie	4:37:22	(21,414)
Braker, Julie	4:31:18	(19,900)
Bramble, Jane	5:46:40	(30,973)
Bramhall, Sally	5:56:43	(31,432)
Bramley, Joanne	3:41:40	(7,094)
Brandon, Elizabeth	3:38:25	(6,404)
Brandt, Stacy	5:35:47	(30,255)
Branford, Jennifer	4:30:24	(19,693)
Brangan, Mary	5:00:29	(26,371)
Brannan, Susan	6:16:51	(32,002)
Brant, Claire	3:55:41	(10,803)

Brass, Zoe	4:56:20 (25,667)	
Brassfield, Emily	4:01:30 (12,441)	
Braund, Diana	5:47:45 (31,026)	
Bray, Brydie	4:01:01 (12,314)	
Bray, Dria	5:44:26 (30,852)	
Bray, Lorraine	4:25:51 (18,471)	
Bray, Sarah	4:37:14 (21,380)	
Braybrook, Alison	5:21:56 (29,089)	
Breeze, Hilary	4:55:50 (25,544)	
Bremner, Jane	3:21:41 (3,460)	
Brenchley, Nicola	3:09:43 (2,009)	
Breniere, Claudine	5:25:54 (29,439)	
Brennan, Rebecca	3:59:19 (11,887)	
Brennan, Susan	4:03:12 (12,813)	
Brennan, Theresa	4:05:02 (13,216)	
Brent, Katherine	4:41:57 (22,598)	
Brentall, Claire	3:40:40 (6,889)	
Bretherick, Samantha	2:50:33 (515)	
Bretherton, Serena	3:48:46 (8,835)	
Brewitt, Debbie	3:52:02 (9,700)	
Brewster, Claire	3:52:57 (9,960)	
Brewster, Vanessa	4:12:39 (15,012)	
Brickell, Lucy	3:56:53 (11,168)	
Brickwood, Elli	3:29:30 (4,795)	
Bridge, Teresa	6:39:19 (32,425)	
Bridot-Stoessel, Laurence	4:33:05 (20,373)	
Briefel, Terri	4:32:07 (20,114)	
Briers, Helen	4:23:28 (17,817)	
Briffett, Jane	5:30:52 (29,855)	
Briggs, Gial	4:42:58 (22,830)	
Brigham, Barbara	5:37:02 (30,351)	
Bright, Daniela	4:59:56 (26,296)	
Bright, Hetty	4:26:04 (18,539)	
Bright, Jenny Louise	5:21:05 (29,008)	
Bright, Meg	5:05:58 (27,150)	
Brightman, Pat	5:25:58 (29,443)	
Brighton, Susan	3:51:56 (9,657)	
Brightwell, Louise	4:43:51 (23,029)	
Brightwell, Wendy	4:43:51 (23,029)	
Brinck, Gaby	5:37:57 (30,412)	
Brindal, Anna	4:19:53 (16,831)	
Brindley, Elizabeth	4:30:56 (19,819)	
Bringlow, Véronique	2:59:37 (1,140)	
Brinicombe, Lucy	4:34:35 (20,719)	
Brinklow, Patricia	5:33:12 (30,043)	
Brinkmann, Stephanie	4:35:33 (20,960)	
Brinksma, Margaretha	4:38:04 (21,589)	
Britnell, Karen	5:20:43 (28,963)	
Britten, Caroline	4:21:09 (17,156)	
Britten, Victoria	4:59:35 (26,240)	
Broad, Joanna	4:35:58 (21,071)	
Broadbent, Anne	6:14:25 (31,939)	
Broadbent, Helen	4:40:31 (22,234)	
Broadhurst, Tracy	4:06:05 (13,455)	
Broatch, Cherry	5:27:58 (29,615)	
Brock, Stephanie	4:09:21 (14,232)	
Brockett, Clare	3:38:50 (6,491)	
Brocklesby, Edwina	3:48:52 (8,859)	
Broderick, Shelley	5:18:39 (28,737)	
Brodie, Jaime	4:46:29 (23,688)	
Brodie, Jennifer	3:44:10 (7,698)	
Brodie, Natalie	4:39:27 (21,962)	
Brokenshire, Ethel	3:41:05 (6,984)	
Bromfield, Sharon	4:30:51 (19,797)	
Brook, Catherine	5:10:24 (27,736)	
Brook, Tracy	4:39:49 (22,062)	
Brooke, Sophie	5:16:32 (28,503)	
Brooker, Mandy	5:05:59 (27,153)	
Brooker, Virginia	4:02:32 (12,663)	
Brookhouse, Jane	4:24:42 (18,173)	
Brooks, Fiona	6:43:12 (32,464)	
Brooks, Gillian	4:40:47 (22,304)	
Brooks, Lucy	4:40:38 (22,263)	
Brooks, Sarah	5:05:19 (27,065)	
Brooksbank, Nicola	4:57:20 (25,831)	
Brookshaw, Lucy	3:36:00 (5,905)	
Broome, Anita	6:10:35 (31,847)	
Brophy, Emma	5:16:43 (28,521)	
Brosnan, Jacqueline	5:46:01 (30,936)	
Brosnan, Julie	4:01:02 (12,319)	
Brosnan, Leila	3:18:31 (3,076)	
Brough, Elaine	6:36:49 (32,391)	
Brough, Lesley	3:31:01 (5,031)	
Broughton, Andrea	4:18:47 (16,541)	
Broughton, Susan	6:38:23 (32,414)	
Broughton, Susannah	4:57:28 (25,850)	
Broughton, Wendy	4:29:48 (19,534)	
Brown, Amanda	4:31:44 (20,018)	
Brown, Ana	4:21:46 (17,328)	
Brown, Angie	4:20:21 (16,955)	
Brown, Ann	4:35:10 (20,866)	
Brown, Caroline	4:13:55 (15,289)	
Brown, Cathy	5:23:28 (29,217)	
Brown, Danielle	6:46:30 (32,498)	
Brown, Deborah	4:22:04 (17,415)	
Brown, Elizabeth	5:18:10 (28,686)	
Brown, Emma	4:40:50 (22,316)	
Brown, Emma	4:55:24 (25,466)	
Brown, Estelle	3:38:04 (6,326)	
Brown, Glen	5:23:40 (29,246)	
Brown, Jacky	5:44:27 (30,853)	
Brown, Jacqueline	5:10:25 (27,739)	
Brown, Janet	5:01:56 (26,594)	
Brown, Johanna	4:20:24 (16,964)	
Brown, Joy	5:23:40 (29,246)	
Brown, Judy	2:56:06 (836)	
Brown, Kate	4:51:22 (24,676)	
Brown, Lisa	4:25:54 (18,488)	
Brown, Lorna	5:05:01 (27,025)	
Brown, Lynne	5:06:33 (27,238)	
Brown, Michelle	5:14:14 (28,216)	
Brown, Rebecca	4:34:01 (20,582)	
Brown, Rebecca	5:19:44 (28,844)	
Brown, Sandra	5:17:48 (28,651)	
Brown, Susan	3:41:58 (7,144)	
Brown, Susan	4:15:11 (15,614)	
Brown, Valerie	4:13:53 (15,281)	
Brown, Wendy	3:55:06 (10,628)	
Browne, Heather	4:13:10 (15,113)	
Browne, Helena	5:31:24 (29,905)	
Browne, Henrietta	4:51:56 (24,772)	
Brown-Shaw, Elizabeth	4:31:25 (19,935)	
Bruce, Madaleine	4:14:36 (15,471)	
Bruce, Susan	3:11:43 (2,229)	
Bruce, Zoe	4:23:44 (17,899)	
Bruno, Ellen	5:40:30 (30,584)	
Brussels, Linzi	4:29:15 (19,398)	
Bruton, Carey	5:19:25 (28,813)	
Bruun, Natasha	5:37:57 (30,412)	
Bryan, Delyth	3:31:57 (5,178)	
Bryan, Lorraine	5:27:37 (29,591)	
Bryan, Terri	4:21:24 (17,222)	
Bryan, Theresa	4:42:05 (22,629)	
Bryant, Andrea	5:36:46 (30,329)	
Bryant, Carol	5:32:45 (30,007)	
Bryant, Jane	4:17:15 (16,187)	
Bryant, Nicola	4:20:43 (17,049)	
Brydson, Kara	5:01:33 (26,536)	
Bryer, Kathryn	3:57:13 (11,269)	
Bubloz, Hazel	6:10:57 (31,857)	
Buck, Gloria	4:26:39 (18,702)	
Buck, Grete	4:11:02 (14,639)	
Buck, Kate	4:46:09 (23,607)	
Buck, Susan	6:32:31 (32,313)	
Buckenham, Sarah	4:56:26 (25,681)	
Buckingham, Clare	4:36:05 (21,098)	
Buckland, Alexandra	4:08:43 (14,083)	
Buckley, Diane	4:23:30 (17,825)	
Buckley, Joan	5:01:12 (26,481)	
Buckley, Kathy	5:22:18 (29,117)	
Buckley, Lucy	4:29:08 (19,361)	
Buckley, Nikola	3:36:37 (6,046)	
Buckley, Susan	4:00:25 (12,170)	
Buckley-Jones, Clare	3:47:06 (8,408)	
Budd, Luisa	4:40:53 (22,331)	
Budd, Vivien	5:24:30 (29,325)	
Bukojets, Liese	4:18:52 (16,563)	
Bulcock, Ann-Marie	3:46:39 (8,321)	
Bulgin, Amanda	4:32:51 (20,320)	
Bull, Alexis	4:33:06 (20,375)	
Bull, Alison	4:05:42 (13,368)	
Bull, Calire	4:24:12 (18,037)	
Bull, Helen	4:34:59 (20,828)	
Bull, Joan	4:41:05 (22,371)	
Bull, Maqry	4:02:46 (12,719)	
Bulliar, Sharon	4:07:39 (13,829)	
Bullingham, Maria	5:43:42 (30,796)	
Bullivant, Jayne	5:06:26 (27,224)	
Bullock, Caroline	4:34:41 (20,747)	
Bullock, Joanne	5:45:41 (30,921)	
Bullock, Sarah	4:21:31 (17,255)	
Bulow, Kathryn	3:38:29 (6,418)	
Bunch, Diane	4:19:21 (16,677)	
Bundock, Amanda	4:51:05 (24,625)	
Bunten, Susan	3:39:15 (6,583)	
Buquet, Esther	5:12:13 (27,975)	
Burchfield, Jo-Anne	4:16:32 (15,988)	
Burd, Amanda	4:45:35 (23,467)	
Burden, Diane	5:01:17 (26,500)	
Burford, Louisa	5:38:46 (30,462)	
Burgess, Juliette	5:07:25 (27,360)	
Burgess, Lucinda	5:07:25 (27,360)	
Burgess, Paula	4:13:09 (15,112)	
Burgess, Suzanna	5:07:22 (27,350)	
Burgoyne, Dionne	5:16:23 (28,490)	
Burke, Angela	4:53:18 (25,024)	
Burke, Deborah	4:34:01 (20,582)	
Burke, Eileen	4:45:50 (23,523)	
Burke, Helen	3:45:02 (7,933)	
Burke, Lisa	4:02:38 (12,688)	
Burke, Lorette	6:02:50 (31,635)	
Burke, Rachel	6:14:56 (31,958)	
Burles, Gail	3:06:13 (1,661)	
Burling, Alison	5:31:49 (29,936)	
Burmeister, Beverley	3:59:53 (12,053)	
Burnett, Barbara	4:06:55 (13,651)	
Burnett, Joanne	5:05:01 (27,025)	
Burnett-Armstrong, Olivia	4:41:36 (22,498)	
Burnham, Emma	4:07:16 (13,737)	
Burnill, Claire	3:53:48 (10,249)	
Burns, Jacqueline	4:46:12 (23,623)	
Burns, Sarah	4:45:30 (23,436)	
Burr, Alison	5:24:07 (29,290)	
Burrell, Noeleen	4:21:43 (17,315)	
Burrells, Jillian	4:32:20 (20,171)	
Burroughs, Kate	6:55:09 (32,587)	
Burroughs, Rebecca	5:36:34 (30,317)	
Burrow, Emma	4:38:23 (21,681)	
Burrows, Barbara	4:36:47 (21,273)	
Burton, Cathy	3:38:43 (6,476)	
Burton, Christine	4:47:14 (23,862)	
Burton, Karen	4:29:13 (19,384)	
Burton, Karen	5:47:54 (31,034)	
Burton, Sandra	5:24:30 (29,325)	
Burton, Teresa	3:50:45 (9,363)	
Bushell, Claire	4:16:52 (16,082)	
Bushell, Nicky	3:22:57 (3,651)	
Bussey, Amanda	3:41:59 (7,149)	
Bussey, Christine	6:14:25 (31,939)	
Butland, Olly	4:15:51 (15,791)	
Butland, Orlanda	5:21:00 (28,989)	
Butler, Angela	6:25:08 (32,183)	
Butler, Audrey	5:44:14 (30,835)	
Butler, Barbara	4:45:30 (23,436)	
Butler, Bridget	3:40:30 (6,850)	
Butler, Kate	3:57:39 (11,411)	
Butler, Lynnette	4:05:06 (13,231)	
Butler, Margaret	4:10:07 (14,414)	
Butler, Patricia	5:57:46 (31,467)	
Butler, Sandra	4:39:22 (21,939)	
Butler, Sarah	6:08:16 (31,790)	
Butler, Stephen	4:42:30 (22,725)	
Butler, Vanessa	4:09:18 (14,218)	
Butt, Laura	4:03:45 (12,928)	
Butter, Jenny	3:22:43 (3,615)	
Butterfield, Caroline	6:30:10 (32,284)	
Butterfield, Kate	4:25:25 (18,364)	
Butterill, Carol	4:20:25 (16,974)	
Butterworth, Alison	3:47:27 (8,497)	
Buttfield, Kirsten	5:07:31 (27,379)	
Buttle, Ann	4:57:52 (25,925)	
Button, Linda	5:14:56 (28,298)	
Buzzeo, Kathie	3:51:46 (9,616)	
Byrne, Diane	3:30:37 (4,966)	
Byrne, Niamh	5:24:17 (29,303)	
Byrne, Sharon	4:30:33 (19,721)	
Byrne, Sheila	4:55:40 (25,511)	
Byrne, Sue	5:06:48 (27,270)	
Byrom, Diane	5:14:16 (28,226)	

Byron, Hannah 5:36:00 (30,271)
Bytheway, Helen 3:55:39 (10,795)
Byzia, Julie 5:42:10 (30,703)
Cadman, Samantha 4:16:12 (15,891)
Cadwgan, Rachel 4:41:38 (22,510)
Cahn, Julie 4:31:01 (19,831)
Caig, Joanne 4:44:14 (23,112)
Caile, Sharon 3:28:29 (4,600)
Caine, Christine 4:39:14 (21,908)
Calcott, Sarah 4:45:25 (23,419)
Calcutta, Jacqueline 6:49:11 (32,532)
Caldeira, Allison 4:58:50 (26,104)
Calder, Helen 3:26:42 (4,275)
Calder, Selena 3:41:55 (7,134)
Caldicott, Lesley 6:22:44 (32,145)
Caldwell, Gillian 5:15:55 (28,431)
Callaghan, Amanda 4:07:33 (13,808)
Callan, Anne-Marie 5:14:15 (28,222)
Callan, Doreen 4:19:57 (16,848)
Calliste, Gillian 4:23:18 (17,776)
Calnan, Ann 4:54:22 (25,257)
Calnan, Stephanie 3:50:43 (9,352)
Calton, Patsy 6:05:49 (31,726)
Calvert, Carrie 4:16:04 (15,855)
Calvert, Jane 3:52:46 (9,916)
Calvert, Sue 3:41:13 (7,019)
Calvet, Caroline 4:52:32 (24,882)
Calvo-Boveda, Consuelo 4:31:26 (19,940)
Camecho, Charlotte 5:23:19 (29,205)
Cameron, Eleanor 4:56:13 (25,639)
Cameron, Joan 6:24:30 (32,179)
Cameron, Lindsey 4:44:41 (23,214)
Cameron, Shirley 4:41:17 (22,423)
Cameron, Susan 4:12:03 (14,874)
Camp, Deborah 5:19:35 (28,827)
Campbell, Celia 5:07:12 (27,328)
Campbell, Claire 5:27:34 (29,585)
Campbell, Ilidia 4:05:31 (13,329)
Campbell, Irene 4:49:04 (24,250)
Campbell, Karen 4:50:41 (24,540)
Campbell, Kirsty 4:44:55 (23,274)
Campbell, Lisa 3:26:53 (4,309)
Campbell, Lorraine 5:44:07 (30,826)
Campbell, Marian 4:46:32 (23,699)
Campbell, Morag 3:14:23 (2,597)
Campbell, Rachel 4:37:50 (21,528)
Campbell, Sarah 2:51:24 (554)
Campbell, Sylvia 6:16:54 (32,003)
Campbell, Victoria 4:51:46 (24,736)
Campbell-Scott, Renée 3:58:16 (11,584)
Campbell-Stanway, Camilla 4:34:10 (20,621)
Campitelli, Anna 4:25:50 (18,468)
Canavan, Lisa 4:41:56 (22,593)
Candy, Susan 3:10:49 (2,136)
Cank, Diane 5:25:48 (29,429)
Cannell, Linda 5:42:12 (30,704)
Canning, Judith 5:33:07 (30,036)
Cannings, Sharron 4:52:23 (24,858)
Cannon, Sarah 6:05:36 (31,715)
Canter, Harriet 3:39:53 (6,707)
Cantley, Louise 4:47:59 (24,024)
Cantwell, Berna 4:48:08 (24,061)
Capel, Sarah 4:32:31 (20,219)
Cappart, Sue 4:20:53 (17,083)
Cappelman, Georgina 8:38:16 (32,881)
Capperauld, Anneline 5:13:59 (28,188)
Carden, Kitty 4:32:44 (20,286)
Cardwell, Elaine 5:21:18 (29,023)
Carfineto, Julie 4:46:00 (23,566)
Cargill, Caroline 4:06:08 (13,473)
Cariss, Sue 3:03:06 (1,381)
Carlisle, Janet 4:37:25 (21,428)
Carlson, Bethany 5:35:38 (30,244)
Carlson, Sheila 6:12:40 (31,898)
Carlton, Ellen 5:39:08 (30,480)
Carmichael, Barbara 5:40:16 (30,569)
Carn, Felicity 5:48:31 (31,063)
Carney, Treena 3:01:19 (1,249)
Carolan, Cristie 4:06:26 (13,550)
Carpenter, Chrstine 4:20:52 (17,080)
Carpenter, Lisa 4:59:13 (26,165)
Carpenter, Vivien 4:17:09 (16,160)
Carpineto, Amy 4:46:03 (23,584)
Carpinteiro, Anne 5:14:39 (28,269)
Carr, Caroline 4:53:36 (25,085)
Carrington, Catherine 4:27:15 (18,855)
Carrington, Jackie 3:57:04 (11,227)
Carroll, Christina 3:48:45 (8,829)
Carroll, Gail 5:20:08 (28,897)
Carruthers, Dawn 5:55:04 (31,354)
Carson, Eileen 5:38:06 (30,418)
Carson, Suzanne 3:01:16 (1,247)
Carter, Charlotte 4:29:52 (19,560)
Carter, Christine 4:15:27 (15,679)
Carter, Diane 5:05:40 (27,109)
Carter, Gemma 4:22:48 (17,639)
Carter, Janet 3:42:33 (7,298)
Carter, Janet 4:01:51 (12,535)
Carter, Johanne 6:48:56 (32,527)
Carter, Karen 3:56:05 (10,923)
Cartledge, Margaret 4:51:53 (24,760)
Cartwright, Helen 3:53:30 (10,145)
Cartwright, Izzie 5:43:47 (30,801)
Cartwright, Linda 4:16:38 (16,019)
Carvalho, Regina 3:34:53 (5,693)
Carvello, Claire 3:16:00 (2,788)
Carver, Alison 4:35:35 (20,982)
Casbon, Marie 5:33:57 (30,107)
Casco, Samantha 4:40:28 (22,225)
Casey, Elizabeth 4:18:21 (16,455)
Cash, Caroline 5:00:35 (26,387)
Cash, Rebecca 4:03:57 (12,976)
Cashell, Nuala 5:03:34 (26,831)
Casile, Anne 4:17:29 (16,240)
Cassar, Ilona 3:55:04 (10,614)
Cassidy, Viv 6:09:19 (31,819)
Casson, Jennifer 5:03:55 (26,873)
Castera, Marie 5:18:38 (28,735)
Castle, Emma 3:22:42 (3,610)
Castle, Virginia 5:02:49 (26,713)
Castledine, Eileen 4:01:22 (12,413)
Castles, Dawn 4:03:39 (12,909)
Castree, Fiona 4:27:09 (18,832)
Caswell, Katherine 4:06:23 (13,540)
Catchpole, Christine 4:03:02 (12,782)
Catchpole, Victoria 3:57:41 (11,419)
Cater, Fiona 4:31:58 (20,075)
Cathalin, Evelyn 7:55:35 (32,855)
Catlin, Guillian 5:09:21 (27,617)
Catling, Melanie 4:33:12 (20,403)
Catling, Sarah 4:28:01 (19,038)
Catlow, Gillian 5:35:29 (30,226)
Catmur, Caroline 7:38:39 (32,819)
Catt, Vicky 5:12:53 (28,065)
Cauchy, Guylaine 4:15:57 (15,828)
Caunter, Janice 4:31:15 (19,891)
Cavanagh, Helen 5:18:15 (28,697)
Cavill, Clare-Ann 5:06:40 (27,252)
Cawdery, Deborah 3:30:38 (4,969)
Cawte, Jill 10:03:52 (32,898)
Cawthorne, Helen 2:49:36 (467)
Cendrowioz, Natasha 3:19:02 (3,140)
Chadburn, Katharine 4:46:34 (23,706)
Chadney, Clare 4:46:38 (23,720)
Chadwick, Jackie 4:27:12 (18,841)
Chadwick, Joanne 4:30:36 (19,734)
Chadwick, Michaela 5:38:45 (30,461)
Chalkley, Sharon 3:38:23 (6,394)
Challens, Caroline 4:41:33 (22,486)
Chalton, Joyce 6:03:46 (31,656)
Chamberlain, Carol 3:57:52 (11,469)
Chamberlain, Christine 5:45:20 (30,903)
Chamberlain, Diane 5:06:58 (27,290)
Chamberlain, Jane 4:45:30 (23,436)
Chamberlain, Rebecca 6:48:49 (32,526)
Chambers, Kirsten 4:32:05 (20,105)
Chambers, Miranda 4:39:43 (22,030)
Chambers, Rosie-Jo 6:09:58 (31,840)
Chambers, Sally 5:12:29 (28,022)
Chambers, Samanatha 4:59:54 (26,290)
Chan, Ling 4:11:37 (14,774)
Chandler, Julia 5:05:54 (27,144)
Chaney, Sarah 5:18:30 (28,727)
Chantler, Claire 4:38:49 (21,796)
Chantler, Mary 4:02:12 (12,599)
Chaplin, Ann 5:14:28 (28,242)
Chapman, Ann-Maria 5:08:10 (27,448)
Chapman, Deirdre 5:30:52 (29,855)
Chapman, Jacqueline 4:56:17 (25,652)
Chapman, Jemma 4:51:10 (24,643)
Chapman, Linda 5:20:54 (28,984)
Chapman, Mary 3:33:54 (5,496)
Chapman, Pauline 4:20:13 (16,918)
Chapman, Sally 3:34:32 (5,624)
Chapman, Sharon 4:34:23 (20,668)
Chapman, Victoria 3:49:08 (8,931)
Chapman Jones, Catherine 5:22:40 (29,149)
Chapple, Alice 3:53:41 (10,205)
Chapple, Emily 4:36:00 (21,080)
Chapple, Jemma 4:08:41 (14,076)
Chapple, Kate 3:57:14 (11,274)
Chard, Lucy 4:14:49 (15,529)
Chare, Elizabeth 5:25:31 (29,402)
Charkiewicz, Angela 5:56:02 (31,401)
Charles, Maureen 5:25:41 (29,419)
Charles, Odile 7:02:32 (32,654)
Charles, Sandra 4:20:18 (16,940)
Charlesworth, Marian 5:51:30 (31,216)
Charlton, Deborah 5:03:10 (26,774)
Charlwood, Carol 5:40:53 (30,605)
Charnock, Kirstie 4:56:31 (25,692)
Charrington, Holly 6:34:30 (32,348)
Charter, Helen 4:19:16 (16,657)
Chase, Hilary 4:10:39 (14,545)
Chasokela, Zodwa 6:42:16 (32,448)
Chastell, Joyce 5:13:59 (28,188)
Chatfield, Joanne 5:27:36 (29,589)
Chatoo, Ayn 5:31:07 (29,874)
Chavasse, Diane 5:34:35 (30,156)
Chen, Wendy 4:38:20 (21,669)
Chepchumba, Joyce 2:26:52 (45)
Chepkemei, Susan 2:23:18 (34)
Cherney, Carrie 4:48:09 (24,062)
Cherry, Elizabeth 4:58:37 (26,061)
Cherry, Ruth 4:22:02 (17,405)
Chetwode, Alexandra 4:26:39 (18,702)
Cheshire, Lorna 5:04:23 (26,947)
Chesser, Paula 4:06:58 (13,668)
Chester, Lorna 4:27:49 (18,987)
Cheung, Lynn 5:08:41 (27,520)
Chevallier, Chrystelle 5:26:24 (29,481)
Chiappinelli, Susan 4:24:29 (18,117)
Chick, Joanna 3:55:25 (10,727)
Chick, Louise 5:37:29 (30,384)
Child, Elisabeth 3:51:52 (9,644)
Childerstone, Amanda 4:32:56 (20,344)
Childs, Hannah 4:40:37 (22,257)
Childs, Joanna 3:31:59 (5,186)
Chilvers, Kerry 5:44:29 (30,854)
Ching, Tessa 3:37:15 (6,155)
Chipperfield, Christine 5:00:32 (26,382)
Chipperfield, Lisa 4:11:51 (14,825)
Chisholm, Helen 3:53:25 (10,113)
Chittock, Susan 4:50:05 (24,437)
Chivers, Sharyn 4:29:48 (19,534)
Choi, Cecile 5:15:30 (28,362)
Choi, Lisa 5:51:29 (31,215)
Chrascina, Nicola 4:38:28 (21,696)
Chrispin, Pamela 4:49:28 (24,316)
Christian, Nicola 4:51:55 (24,770)
Christiansen, Doreen 6:25:20 (32,187)
Christianson, Teresa 4:37:57 (21,564)
Christie, Erica 3:06:30 (1,685)
Christie, Nathalie 3:19:16 (3,168)
Christie, Susanne 4:48:25 (24,108)
Christina, Judith 4:35:02 (20,842)
Christmas, Helen 4:22:01 (17,401)
Christophers, Irene 4:43:53 (23,036)
Chuah, Ju Mai 5:10:04 (27,696)
Church, Jo 3:51:46 (9,616)
Church, Polly 5:25:54 (29,439)
Churchill, Clare 4:57:01 (25,773)
Churchill, Helen 4:37:56 (21,558)
Churm, Marina 4:36:45 (21,268)
Cicone, Lou 6:18:48 (32,059)
Cilia, Anne 3:55:13 (10,668)
Cimaschi, Antonella 3:40:58 (6,958)
Clack, Jacqueline 4:47:05 (23,830)
Clancy, Juliette 5:02:50 (26,719)

Clapham, Jennifer	5:36:51 (30,338)	
Clapham, Penelope	4:43:00 (22,838)	
Clare, Halina	4:21:59 (17,389)	
Clare, Sylvia	4:44:59 (23,297)	
Clare, Valerie	3:58:43 (11,712)	
Clark, Abbie	4:11:38 (14,777)	
Clark, Angela	4:39:30 (21,968)	
Clark, Denise	5:06:02 (27,162)	
Clark, Diana	6:56:59 (32,603)	
Clark, Elinor	4:49:52 (24,401)	
Clark, Elspeth	4:49:51 (24,395)	
Clark, Emma	5:05:55 (27,148)	
Clark, Georgina	5:01:16 (26,495)	
Clark, Hannah	5:28:07 (29,624)	
Clark, Helen	4:45:32 (23,449)	
Clark, Helen	5:07:10 (27,324)	
Clark, Janet	4:17:19 (16,209)	
Clark, Jenny	5:11:50 (27,927)	
Clark, Juliette	2:52:11 (587)	
Clark, Lucy	6:01:16 (31,585)	
Clark, Melissa	5:34:11 (30,121)	
Clark, Pauline	4:41:05 (22,371)	
Clark, Penelope	4:17:18 (16,203)	
Clark, Sharon	4:42:55 (22,818)	
Clark, Victoria	4:41:02 (22,361)	
Clark, Wendy	4:02:35 (12,675)	
Clarke, Amanda	3:12:02 (2,277)	
Clarke, Amanda	3:20:58 (3,359)	
Clarke, Amanda	5:24:23 (29,313)	
Clarke, Amanda	7:21:20 (32,759)	
Clarke, Anna	5:41:50 (30,680)	
Clarke, Carole	4:23:56 (17,958)	
Clarke, Georgina	5:33:36 (30,077)	
Clarke, Irene	6:13:04 (31,908)	
Clarke, Joan	3:29:08 (4,716)	
Clarke, Joan	5:52:56 (31,272)	
Clarke, Joanna	3:59:11 (11,849)	
Clarke, Kathy	5:40:24 (30,578)	
Clarke, Katie	4:47:52 (23,996)	
Clarke, Lucy	4:44:44 (23,230)	
Clarke, Michelle	5:23:33 (29,226)	
Clarke, Naomi	5:31:36 (29,921)	
Clarke, Sonia	4:09:16 (14,206)	
Clarke, Susan	4:57:51 (25,922)	
Clarke, Tina	4:12:12 (14,903)	
Clarkson, Caroline	4:28:57 (19,309)	
Clarry, Cynthia	4:22:19 (17,486)	
Clayden, Olwyn	4:00:55 (12,281)	
Claymore, Fiona	4:56:43 (25,718)	
Clayton, Cherilyn	3:25:43 (4,101)	
Clayton, Joanna	4:37:43 (21,493)	
Cleary, Paula	5:14:48 (28,282)	
Cleary, Stephanie	4:13:07 (15,106)	
Cleaver, Lisa	4:13:22 (15,159)	
Cleaver, Margaret	5:04:40 (26,973)	
Clement, Rebecca	4:31:18 (19,900)	
Clements, Denise	4:54:38 (25,307)	
Clements, Michelle	7:11:05 (32,712)	
Clendinnen, Natasha	5:21:23 (29,034)	
Cleverly, Elizabeth	5:11:20 (27,859)	
Clews, Nickola	4:14:04 (15,333)	
Clifford, Jennifer	3:22:35 (3,592)	
Clifford, Tracey	4:35:56 (21,063)	
Clifton, Cathy	5:32:12 (29,968)	
Clifton, Julie	4:47:38 (23,935)	
Clifton-Smith, Ellen	4:32:34 (20,234)	
Clinch, Emma	4:39:08 (21,883)	
Clinton, Jane	3:44:40 (7,839)	
Clinton, Vera	4:38:13 (21,631)	
Close, Julia	3:36:33 (6,031)	
Clough, Fiona	4:48:29 (24,123)	
Clough, Hazel	4:50:29 (24,502)	
Clout, Charlotte	4:13:59 (15,308)	
Clowes, Sophie	3:48:02 (8,634)	
Clubley, Victoria	4:10:10 (14,430)	
Cluley, Susan	3:48:19 (8,700)	
Clutton, Diana	4:11:23 (14,704)	
Coates, Caroline	4:24:39 (18,159)	
Coats, Caroline	4:13:42 (15,232)	
Cobain, Katherine	4:23:51 (17,928)	
Cobby, Janet	3:16:42 (2,862)	
Cobby, Jennifer	5:03:47 (26,855)	
Coburn, Helen	3:26:42 (4,275)	
Cochrane, Lynette	5:33:07 (30,036)	
Cockayne, Alison	3:52:43 (9,897)	
Cockman, Nia	5:19:01 (28,779)	
Cockroft, Judith	6:30:07 (32,279)	
Codd, Tabitha	4:59:04 (26,143)	
Codling, Rachel	3:59:17 (11,878)	
Cody, Rachel	5:27:17 (29,549)	
Coe, Alexandra	3:42:24 (7,262)	
Coen, Fionnuala	4:08:53 (14,109)	
Coffey, Rachel	5:48:34 (31,066)	
Coggan, Delia	4:56:50 (25,739)	
Coggins, Claire	5:09:09 (27,589)	
Cognet, Mylene	4:43:38 (22,983)	
Cohen, Carol	4:12:02 (14,871)	
Cohen, Karen	6:56:45 (32,601)	
Coker, Eleanor	3:50:59 (9,423)	
Colasanti, Meghan	4:46:14 (23,630)	
Cole, Hayley	5:25:34 (29,407)	
Cole, Julie	4:34:53 (20,798)	
Cole, Phillipa	4:50:18 (24,466)	
Cole, Sally	4:55:59 (25,583)	
Cole, Trudi	4:28:49 (19,261)	
Colee, Julie	4:46:26 (23,674)	
Coleman, Melanie	4:38:58 (21,834)	
Colenutt, Margaret	5:32:32 (29,995)	
Colguhoun, Christine	4:24:04 (18,001)	
Collen, Agnes	4:47:36 (23,925)	
Collet, Sarah	4:05:37 (13,352)	
Colling, Frances	4:38:27 (21,694)	
Collinge, Maddy	3:31:20 (5,083)	
Collins, Cherry	7:09:52 (32,700)	
Collins, Dee	4:19:50 (16,810)	
Collins, Emma	5:19:06 (28,786)	
Collins, Gwen	3:40:14 (6,794)	
Collins, Hilary	4:02:13 (12,601)	
Collins, Jacky	4:18:38 (16,518)	
Collins, Julia	5:07:50 (27,411)	
Collins, Katherine	4:38:12 (21,626)	
Collins, Louise	5:01:03 (26,456)	
Collins, Penny	5:20:40 (28,957)	
Collins, Sarah	4:52:52 (24,954)	
Collins, Suzanne	5:43:16 (30,772)	
Collinson, Audrey	5:18:35 (28,732)	
Collison, Sue	4:57:54 (25,935)	
Colston, Julia	5:36:01 (30,275)	
Colville, Joanne	5:08:23 (27,480)	
Colyer, Sophie	4:29:57 (19,584)	
Combes, Georgina	4:11:01 (14,633)	
Comerford, Anna	4:37:22 (21,414)	
Comeskey, Jane	4:45:40 (23,484)	
Compton, Joanna	5:27:22 (29,565)	
Conaghan, Isabel	4:32:33 (20,228)	
Conan, Joelle	3:22:30 (3,581)	
Conceicao, Maria	5:43:49 (30,807)	
Conen, Helena	4:17:59 (16,368)	
Coney, Diane	3:53:48 (10,249)	
Confrey, Tara	4:39:11 (21,892)	
Conley, Julie	4:28:25 (19,142)	
Conn, Karin	5:09:40 (27,656)	
Conneally, Florence	5:24:30 (29,325)	
Connelly, Jaqueline	5:50:38 (31,166)	
Connolly, Angela	5:52:40 (31,261)	
Connolly, Michelle	4:56:11 (25,628)	
Connolly, Rachel	3:49:28 (9,033)	
Connor, Kerry	4:21:05 (17,136)	
Conroy, Mairon	4:12:09 (14,891)	
Constable, Sarah	3:38:45 (6,478)	
Constant, Kelly	4:14:01 (15,316)	
Contreas, Julie	4:14:02 (15,324)	
Conway, Claire	3:40:27 (6,843)	
Cooil, Janice	4:23:14 (17,755)	
Cook, Ann	4:05:34 (13,343)	
Cook, Elaine	3:44:50 (7,896)	
Cook, Esther	5:23:06 (29,185)	
Cook, Helen	5:00:42 (26,411)	
Cook, Jennifer	5:26:16 (29,464)	
Cook, Loretta	4:12:18 (14,920)	
Cook, Paula	4:57:52 (25,925)	
Cook, Rosemary	5:05:49 (27,126)	
Cook, Shirley	5:22:52 (29,163)	
Cook, Susan	4:56:49 (25,737)	
Cook, Tonia	4:23:52 (17,937)	
Cook, Tracey	5:07:10 (27,324)	
Cooke, Elizabeth	5:18:44 (28,748)	
Cooke, Frances	3:52:08 (9,736)	
Cooke, Sarah	4:31:03 (19,842)	
Cooke, Sharon	4:06:07 (13,465)	
Cooke-Simmons, Julia	3:47:39 (8,546)	
Cookson, Lisa	4:46:34 (23,706)	
Cooling, Susanna	4:44:05 (23,085)	
Coomber, Diana	5:05:30 (27,084)	
Coomber, Manuela	4:56:02 (25,589)	
Coombs, Joan	4:18:19 (16,444)	
Coomes, Sarah	5:50:31 (31,161)	
Cooney, Emma-Jane	8:36:41 (32,879)	
Cooper, Andrea	5:42:02 (30,698)	
Cooper, Angela	5:33:25 (30,063)	
Cooper, Carol	5:35:18 (30,208)	
Cooper, Heidi	4:27:35 (18,933)	
Cooper, Jackie	3:21:44 (3,469)	
Cooper, Jacqui	4:40:17 (22,176)	
Cooper, Janelle	3:43:57 (7,643)	
Cooper, Janet	5:38:29 (30,448)	
Cooper, Joanna	4:41:47 (22,553)	
Cooper, Justine	4:40:17 (22,176)	
Cooper, Katherine	4:34:15 (20,641)	
Cooper, Kerri	5:18:45 (28,750)	
Cooper, Lindsay	4:45:56 (23,547)	
Cooper, Louise	3:06:23 (1,672)	
Cooper, Ruth	4:08:30 (14,021)	
Cooper, Sandra	3:49:31 (9,048)	
Cooper, Sue	7:47:57 (32,847)	
Cooper, Valerie	4:50:37 (24,527)	
Cooper, Wendy	4:53:10 (25,005)	
Cope, Anna	5:09:38 (27,654)	
Cope, Linda	6:07:25 (31,770)	
Cope, Stacey	5:23:52 (29,268)	
Copeland, Caroline	5:12:28 (28,021)	
Copland, Maxine	5:12:58 (28,077)	
Copp, Rhona	4:08:39 (14,066)	
Copsey, Julie	4:08:33 (14,041)	
Copsey, Kate	4:57:40 (25,893)	
Copsey-Blake, Debbie	5:20:38 (28,953)	
Cora, Elizabetta	3:57:23 (11,317)	
Corben, Angela	4:04:11 (13,022)	
Corbet, Carmel	4:56:27 (25,684)	
Corbett, Michelle	4:09:23 (14,245)	
Corbett, Sallyanne	4:24:14 (18,048)	
Corbett, Sarah	4:57:38 (25,884)	
Corbin, Francine	4:32:30 (20,215)	
Corbin, Julie	4:05:51 (13,400)	
Corble, Gillian	5:07:03 (27,302)	
Corby, Catherine	4:45:05 (23,328)	
Corby, Joan	5:35:57 (30,264)	
Corcoran, Beverley	4:39:30 (21,968)	
Corcoran, Bridie	4:06:00 (13,437)	
Cordery, Karen	4:57:06 (25,793)	
Cordy, Lynne	4:55:58 (25,577)	
Corfield, Jane	4:50:30 (24,507)	
Cornforth, Carolyn	4:10:47 (14,571)	
Cornwell, Helen	3:47:58 (8,620)	
Corp, Jan	5:01:07 (26,467)	
Corrie, Jeannette	3:33:55 (5,502)	
Corriette, Jane	5:29:37 (29,752)	
Corrigan, Jennifer	3:51:54 (9,650)	
Corsini, Francesca	5:34:12 (30,124)	
Cortvrvriend, Victoria	5:44:05 (30,825)	
Cosman, Sue	5:21:22 (29,032)	
Costa, Fiona	4:54:50 (25,349)	
Costello, Elizabeth	4:26:43 (18,721)	
Costello, Janice	5:33:13 (30,045)	
Coster, Lorraine	4:37:24 (21,422)	
Coster, Pat	4:14:09 (15,345)	
Costiff, Christine	3:26:30 (4,228)	
Coston, Teresa	3:41:53 (7,129)	
Cotes, Viviane	4:32:17 (20,157)	
Cotterall, Katrina	5:11:41 (27,904)	
Cotterell, Christina	4:50:30 (24,507)	
Cotterill, Brenda	5:28:55 (29,688)	
Cotterill, Caroline	4:03:22 (12,849)	
Cotterill, Jane	5:58:48 (31,507)	
Cotterill, Sandra	4:25:05 (18,281)	
Cottrell, Maureen	5:41:50 (30,680)	
Cotty, Martine	4:39:04 (21,862)	
Coty, Alexia	5:10:45 (27,780)	
Coubrough, Virginia	4:20:37 (17,024)	

Coulson, Vicki	5:42:13 (30,706)	
Coulter, Jessica	4:38:50 (21,804)	
Coulthard, Amanda	4:38:45 (21,782)	
Courrier, Marie-Odile	6:13:09 (31,911)	
Court, Amanda	7:26:30 (32,776)	
Courtauld, Sarah	4:42:20 (22,683)	
Cousen, Sharon	3:46:02 (8,167)	
Cousin, Kate	4:27:46 (18,976)	
Cousins, Elizabeth	5:04:06 (26,898)	
Cousins, Karen	5:25:19 (29,388)	
Cousins, Lucy	4:38:19 (21,663)	
Coutts, Lydia	4:34:58 (20,823)	
Coutts, Philippa	3:54:49 (10,547)	
Coutts-Wood, Emma	4:44:07 (23,090)	
Couturier, Lucille	5:42:48 (30,737)	
Cove, Jenny	4:19:08 (16,627)	
Coventry, Sheila	4:37:18 (21,400)	
Cowan, Jacqueline	4:38:54 (21,819)	
Cowan, Kari	3:52:51 (9,939)	
Cowdy, Mary-Lou	4:59:53 (26,286)	
Cowell, Jane	5:13:13 (28,105)	
Cowell, Sasha	4:55:11 (25,417)	
Cowen, Samantha	3:49:33 (9,053)	
Cowey, Jill	4:20:18 (16,940)	
Cowlard, Caroline	6:19:44 (32,074)	
Cowlard, Nicky	4:30:29 (19,707)	
Cowley, Annie	3:56:30 (11,053)	
Cowling, Gert	4:40:13 (22,162)	
Cowup, Phyllis	3:53:40 (10,201)	
Cox, Anne	5:06:15 (27,191)	
Cox, Ann-Gaelle	4:12:00 (14,862)	
Cox, Catherine	6:10:34 (31,846)	
Cox, Christine	6:02:12 (31,615)	
Cox, June	7:04:55 (32,669)	
Cox, Kathryn	4:27:27 (18,905)	
Cox, Lorraine	4:32:13 (20,145)	
Cox, Lynda	5:17:44 (28,644)	
Cox, Maureen	5:06:59 (27,292)	
Cox, Michelle	4:39:23 (21,946)	
Cox, Sarah	4:32:39 (20,261)	
Cox, Sarah	5:05:34 (27,093)	
Cox, Stephanie	4:11:22 (14,701)	
Cox, Wendy	5:22:09 (29,103)	
Cozens, Philippa	4:31:01 (19,831)	
Crabb, Hayley	7:43:20 (32,837)	
Crabb, Mary	5:02:40 (26,695)	
Cracknell, Joanna	4:54:30 (25,286)	
Craft, Sheila	4:54:08 (25,208)	
Craig, Jenny	3:33:22 (5,412)	
Craig, Sarah	5:28:26 (29,647)	
Craig, Theresa	5:22:28 (29,129)	
Craigie, Dominique	4:45:34 (23,461)	
Cramp, Helen	3:26:30 (4,228)	
Crane, Denise	5:07:34 (27,383)	
Crane, Jacqueline	3:42:22 (7,252)	
Crane, Victoria	4:14:18 (15,391)	
Cranmer, Angela	4:06:10 (13,480)	
Cranwell, Vic	4:23:41 (17,872)	
Crawford, Fabiola	3:57:56 (11,483)	
Crawford, Janet	3:34:09 (5,554)	
Crawford, Mary	3:37:33 (6,232)	
Crawford, Rebecca	5:21:07 (29,010)	
Crawley, Anita	4:02:03 (12,568)	
Crawley, Catherine	4:40:01 (22,109)	
Crawley, Vanessa	6:04:36 (31,676)	
Crawshaw, Jennie	4:23:09 (17,738)	
Creegan, Lindsey	4:57:23 (25,839)	
Crepin, Virginie	6:52:19 (32,562)	
Cresswell, Fiona	4:15:12 (15,621)	
Crick, Judy	4:19:15 (16,653)	
Crideford, Freda	4:29:37 (19,490)	
Crilley, Kathy	5:19:30 (28,817)	
Criso, Rachael	4:46:09 (23,607)	
Crisp, Jodie	4:13:39 (15,216)	
Critchell, Dawn	3:39:54 (6,710)	
Critchley, Marlene	4:32:20 (20,171)	
Crocker, Jacqueline	4:43:31 (22,964)	
Crockford, Janet	4:25:42 (18,439)	
Croft, Shirley	6:15:01 (31,959)	
Crofton, Sue	6:19:24 (32,068)	
Crook, Hazel	6:41:56 (32,446)	
Crook, Sarah-Louise	4:32:26 (20,200)	
Cropper, Louise	5:31:39 (29,925)	

Cross, Anne	4:15:34 (15,712)	
Cross, Caroline	4:22:54 (17,671)	
Cross, Catherine	4:01:29 (12,437)	
Cross, Felicity	4:28:45 (19,244)	
Cross, Heidi	5:33:29 (30,073)	
Cross, Katrina	4:24:59 (18,258)	
Cross, Michelle	3:40:47 (6,917)	
Cross, Philippa	4:02:29 (12,651)	
Cross, Sarah	3:52:57 (9,960)	
Cross, Sheila	6:24:14 (32,168)	
Crossley, Anna	4:55:50 (25,544)	
Crossley, Jane	3:55:12 (10,663)	
Crossman, Denise	5:09:48 (27,671)	
Crouch, Andrea	4:57:08 (25,798)	
Crouchman, Susan	4:13:29 (15,183)	
Crowe, Chantal	4:30:44 (19,770)	
Crowe, Margaret	3:53:26 (10,116)	
Crowe, Suzy	3:48:21 (8,710)	
Crowle, Revis	3:06:32 (1,691)	
Crowley, Sharon	4:39:07 (21,877)	
Crowley, Sue	4:55:00 (25,376)	
Crowther, Helen	4:34:12 (20,628)	
Croxford, Tracie	3:32:35 (5,285)	
Croxon, Paula	3:41:52 (7,125)	
Crozier, Lisa	5:12:33 (28,032)	
Crudgington, Hannah	3:58:05 (11,536)	
Cruickshank, Irene	4:53:56 (25,168)	
Crump, Alexandra	4:38:42 (21,761)	
Cryer, Jackie	4:20:20 (16,951)	
Cuddy, Karen	4:56:13 (25,639)	
Cudmore, Lauren	4:26:34 (18,670)	
Cudworth, Jennifer	5:39:21 (30,493)	
Cullen, Alison	4:16:29 (15,976)	
Cullen, Jennie	4:21:30 (17,250)	
Cullen, Wendy	5:50:31 (31,161)	
Cullip, Sheila	4:24:48 (18,198)	
Cullum, Gail	4:22:19 (17,486)	
Culshaw, Sian	4:24:58 (18,254)	
Cumberbatch, Ersin	6:23:19 (32,154)	
Cuming, Lyndsay	4:28:20 (19,119)	
Cummings, Susan	4:42:34 (22,742)	
Cummins, Fiona	3:42:05 (7,174)	
Cummins, Jacqueline	3:38:38 (6,459)	
Cummins, Kelly	3:21:42 (3,463)	
Cunningham, Pauline	4:01:21 (12,407)	
Cunnington, Lisa	7:01:46 (32,644)	
Cunti, Loredana	4:38:54 (21,819)	
Cuoghi, Rachel	4:11:58 (14,851)	
Curl, Tracey	3:02:42 (1,349)	
Curran, Tracey	4:12:54 (15,062)	
Curry, Lena	4:45:52 (23,533)	
Curtis, Eleanor	4:45:12 (23,356)	
Curtis, Helen	4:42:25 (22,701)	
Curtis, Jason	4:43:27 (22,948)	
Curtis, Sarah	4:12:49 (15,041)	
Curtis, Sarah	4:26:43 (18,721)	
Curtis, Shelley	4:24:48 (18,198)	
Curtis, Trudy	4:47:46 (23,965)	
Cushen, Alison	4:01:22 (12,413)	
Cussens, Hazel	5:02:03 (26,608)	
Cust, Jodie	4:02:25 (12,633)	
Cutmore, Michaela	4:13:00 (15,082)	
Cutmore, Nicola	4:57:06 (25,793)	
Cutter, Jacqueline	5:15:31 (28,367)	
Cutting, Emily	4:49:38 (24,347)	
Cyprien, Monique	4:23:40 (17,864)	
Da Silva, Kate	4:37:00 (21,315)	
D'Agosto, Tiziana	3:46:31 (8,290)	
Dahl, Fiona	3:35:33 (5,811)	
Dainty, Julia	4:08:10 (13,943)	
Dainty, Margery	3:57:23 (11,317)	
Dalby, Maj	4:49:02 (24,242)	
Dale, Jean	6:11:07 (31,862)	
Dale, Sue	3:36:20 (5,985)	
Daley, Susan	6:31:54 (32,304)	
Dalley, Kathy	4:22:20 (17,493)	
Dallimore, Kate	5:42:55 (30,752)	
Dalton, Elizabeth	5:13:28 (28,137)	
Dalton, Laura	4:31:56 (20,066)	
Dalton, Marjory	7:00:46 (32,637)	
Daly, Janet	4:22:23 (17,512)	
Daly, Marie-Louise	4:50:15 (24,458)	
Daly, Sandra	5:32:45 (30,007)	

Damiral, Katrina	5:00:43 (26,414)	
Daniel, Elizabeth	4:22:23 (17,512)	
Daniel, Jackie	5:12:00 (27,950)	
Daniel, Julia	4:33:08 (20,391)	
Daniel, June	6:29:48 (32,271)	
Daniel, Linda	4:23:07 (17,729)	
Daniel, Teresa	3:12:14 (2,318)	
Daniels, Amanda	3:53:06 (10,018)	
Darsey, Katrina	4:23:51 (17,928)	
Dart, Susan	4:13:45 (15,251)	
Dartnell, Mary	6:17:55 (32,034)	
Darwin, Elizabeth	4:54:12 (25,225)	
Darwin, Ruth	4:47:52 (23,996)	
Dashper, Susan	5:08:11 (27,451)	
Davenport, Claire	4:52:15 (24,833)	
Davenport, Judy	5:07:39 (27,392)	
Davenport, Nicola	4:39:51 (22,070)	
Davenport, Sara	3:21:34 (3,450)	
Davey, Fran	5:43:22 (30,781)	
Davey, Juliet	3:47:02 (8,390)	
Davey, Louise	4:50:47 (24,556)	
Davey, Nicola	4:37:02 (21,323)	
Davey, Nicola	6:43:12 (32,464)	
Davey, Rebecca	4:23:54 (17,948)	
Davey Thomas, Nicola	4:51:28 (24,696)	
David, Ghazala	5:30:41 (29,840)	
David, Karen	5:15:12 (28,324)	
David, Maria	4:07:35 (13,813)	
David, Soran	4:17:45 (16,310)	
Davie, Julia	4:33:11 (20,397)	
Davie, Mary	4:02:59 (12,771)	
Davies, Caroline	3:53:08 (10,025)	
Davies, Charlotte	5:05:06 (27,034)	
Davies, Claire	4:26:34 (18,670)	
Davies, Dianne	3:59:11 (11,849)	
Davies, Elizabeth	3:49:22 (8,993)	
Davies, Elizabeth	5:19:47 (28,851)	
Davies, Emma	5:01:38 (26,555)	
Davies, Eryllois	4:29:11 (19,378)	
Davies, Gina	3:52:03 (9,709)	
Davies, Hannah	5:40:07 (30,556)	
Davies, Hilary	4:01:39 (12,482)	
Davies, Hilary	4:38:23 (21,681)	
Davies, Jane	4:39:15 (21,910)	
Davies, Jo	4:43:49 (23,022)	
Davies, Joanna	5:14:39 (28,269)	
Davies, Karen	3:59:56 (12,066)	
Davies, Laura	5:17:50 (28,654)	
Davies, Maria	3:52:44 (9,905)	
Davies, Natalie	4:12:13 (14,905)	
Davies, Nia Ann	4:38:29 (21,697)	
Davies, Pam	3:39:51 (6,701)	
Davies, Patricia	5:09:41 (27,659)	
Davies, Rhiannon	4:52:51 (24,948)	
Davies, Sarah-Jane	5:35:26 (30,218)	
Davies, Sian	4:26:30 (18,653)	
Davies, Susan	4:53:10 (25,005)	
Davies, Tryphena	4:18:19 (16,444)	
Davies, Wendy	3:09:59 (2,039)	
Davis, Carol	5:37:10 (30,360)	
Davis, Christina	4:41:41 (22,526)	
Davis, Hazel	3:43:46 (7,591)	
Davis, Julia	4:41:35 (22,491)	
Davis, Lee	5:04:16 (26,930)	
Davis, Margaret	5:32:45 (30,007)	
Davis, Mary	5:15:30 (28,362)	
Davis, Sandy	4:41:13 (22,403)	
Davis, Sarah	4:46:49 (23,762)	
Davis, Susan	4:13:37 (15,209)	
Davis, Zoe	4:42:01 (22,610)	
Daw, Sharon	3:21:22 (3,414)	
Dawes, Helen	4:01:39 (12,482)	
Dawkins, Margaret	4:53:54 (25,147)	
Dawrant, Kate	4:29:58 (19,587)	
Dawson, Jayne	4:48:02 (24,041)	
Dawson, Mia	5:09:55 (27,683)	
Dawson, Rebecca	3:56:05 (10,923)	
Dawson, Sally	3:21:56 (3,511)	
Dawson, Sarah	4:27:10 (18,837)	
Dawson, Sharon	5:11:31 (27,888)	
Day, Alison	5:16:26 (28,495)	
Day, Anne	4:31:29 (19,962)	
Day, April	4:23:41 (17,872)	

Day, Julia	3:25:34 (4,073)	
Day, Karen	4:13:39 (15,216)	
Day, Kevan	3:39:00 (6,523)	
Day, Marilyn	4:27:39 (18,951)	
Day, Penny	4:35:38 (20,998)	
Day-Lewis, Tamasin	4:45:35 (23,467)	
D'Cruze, Suzanne	5:41:46 (30,669)	
De Beer, Debbie	4:21:45 (17,324)	
De Boick, Wendy	4:58:07 (25,968)	
De Fusco, Louise	6:14:04 (31,930)	
De Gois, Chantal	4:11:15 (14,682)	
De Groote, Francine	4:14:43 (15,500)	
De La Haye, Samantha	4:14:15 (15,380)	
De La Rue, Nicola	4:22:20 (17,493)	
De Lumley-Santrot, Marie	5:24:57 (29,365)	
De Maria, Sophia	3:37:24 (6,189)	
De Silva, Priyanthi	4:27:30 (18,919)	
De Souza, Christina	6:06:11 (31,736)	
De Vantier, Angela	4:48:10 (24,066)	
De Verdiere, Morgane	4:23:47 (17,913)	
De Vries-Veenbaas, Thekla	5:34:17 (30,131)	
De Winton, Elizabeth	4:48:30 (24,126)	
De Wit-Ybema, Luc	3:50:43 (9,352)	
Deacy, Lorraine	4:31:32 (19,978)	
Deakin, Lindsay	4:29:51 (19,557)	
Deal, Jayne	4:39:33 (21,985)	
Dean, Catherine	6:59:30 (32,620)	
Dean, Elizabeth	5:11:32 (27,890)	
Dean, Freda	4:46:59 (23,806)	
Dean, Helen	4:18:33 (16,497)	
Dean, Helen	5:19:13 (28,796)	
Dean Hart, Sarah	4:13:32 (15,195)	
Deans, Sandra	4:57:11 (25,809)	
Dear, Karen	5:21:03 (28,999)	
Dearing, Anna	3:56:10 (10,948)	
Dearman, Zoe	4:25:54 (18,488)	
Dearness, Susan	4:23:44 (17,899)	
Deas, Margaret	4:28:40 (19,213)	
Debnam, Madelaine	4:03:30 (12,881)	
Debney, Christine	5:34:42 (30,167)	
Debs, Laila	4:45:56 (23,547)	
Decovemacker, Christine	3:56:35 (11,078)	
Deeks, Katrine	4:40:19 (22,187)	
Defis, Cartin	4:33:01 (20,357)	
Defoe, Doris	3:40:03 (6,744)	
Degoumois, Andrée	5:03:31 (26,825)	
Dejaeghere, Valerie	3:51:09 (9,472)	
De-La-Hunty, Noreen	8:13:09 (32,869)	
Delaney, Dympna	5:54:28 (31,332)	
Delaney, Emma	4:18:14 (16,422)	
Delaney, Heather	4:26:42 (18,717)	
D'Elisa, Vera	4:10:24 (14,489)	
Dell, Michelle	5:46:34 (30,968)	
Dellacherie, Sylvette	3:23:02 (3,662)	
Dellaway, Lucy	5:48:56 (31,095)	
Delmar, Clare	4:23:52 (17,937)	
Delmar-Morgan, Alice	4:29:39 (19,495)	
Delport, Leonie	4:22:39 (17,588)	
Deluca, Antonella	3:38:22 (6,389)	
Dematteo, Julie	4:22:58 (17,696)	
Dempsey, Emma	5:00:31 (26,379)	
Dempster, Jill	3:48:14 (8,681)	
Dendurent, Catherine	4:10:59 (14,627)	
Denley, Katrine	4:35:59 (21,077)	
Denley, Sarah	4:24:03 (17,996)	
Dennis, Christine	6:14:50 (31,952)	
Dennis, Helen	4:48:25 (24,108)	
Dennis, Julie	9:06:00 (32,894)	
Dennis, Mandy	4:39:12 (21,900)	
Dennison, Andrea	3:01:46 (1,280)	
Dennison, Julie	5:45:25 (30,906)	
Dennison, Tania	4:56:56 (25,753)	
Denny, Dionne	4:59:39 (26,253)	
Depagne, Monique	3:49:25 (9,014)	
Derbyshire, Lesley	4:29:13 (19,384)	
Derbyshire, Susan	4:46:19 (23,639)	
Dering, Jo	2:55:33 (784)	
Dernis, Sarah	4:26:53 (18,757)	
Derrick, Sarah	3:26:21 (4,210)	
Desbaux, Carole	5:31:46 (29,932)	
Dethick, Lisa	3:51:27 (9,532)	
Deutscher, Waltraud	3:21:31 (3,438)	
Devine, Andrea	3:02:02 (1,304)	
Devine, Mary	4:41:26 (22,455)	
Devoys, Shannon	5:27:25 (29,571)	
Dewar, Hazel	5:18:01 (28,674)	
Dewarrat, Anilda	3:56:56 (11,187)	
Dewberry, Julie	4:00:43 (12,233)	
Dewinter, Margaret	4:22:56 (17,682)	
Dewynter, Alison	3:47:28 (8,503)	
Dhanani, Anne	5:01:23 (26,516)	
Dhell, Marinder Pal	5:19:41 (28,837)	
Dhillon, Manjit	4:07:37 (13,824)	
Di Benedetto, Angela	4:04:01 (12,993)	
Di Gaetano, Giovanna	4:08:27 (14,003)	
Diamanti, Gabriella	4:44:46 (23,240)	
Dibble, Liza	4:24:43 (18,178)	
Dick, Eleanor	4:22:48 (17,639)	
Dick, Lesley	4:30:14 (19,658)	
Dick, Patricia	3:29:20 (4,761)	
Dicker, Faye	4:42:28 (22,714)	
Dickerson, Maureen	5:10:18 (27,726)	
Dickinson, Becky	3:57:46 (11,444)	
Dickinson, Bernadette	3:29:20 (4,761)	
Dickinson, Jean	6:16:01 (31,983)	
Dicks, Alison	4:03:49 (12,947)	
Dickson, Sonia	5:39:25 (30,507)	
Digby, Helen	3:37:13 (6,151)	
Digney, Lindsay	6:37:17 (32,404)	
Dillon, Ursula	5:15:38 (28,387)	
Diment, Gemma	6:42:48 (32,456)	
Dimmock, Charlie	4:18:45 (16,536)	
Dimond, Gillian	7:31:47 (32,796)	
Dingley, Anna	4:57:38 (25,884)	
Dingwall, Susie	5:37:33 (30,388)	
Dinnage, Tracy	5:06:03 (27,165)	
Disney, Glennys	3:08:55 (1,924)	
Ditchfield, Angela	5:00:30 (26,377)	
Ditheridge, Elizabeth	5:01:25 (26,517)	
Dittadi, Iolanda	4:49:08 (24,266)	
Dives, Helen	5:34:34 (30,154)	
Dixon, Andrea	5:15:59 (28,441)	
Dixon, Debra	3:35:22 (5,772)	
Dixon, Dorothy	3:46:00 (8,161)	
Dixon, Elaine	5:00:03 (26,315)	
Dixon, Karen	3:26:41 (4,269)	
Dixon, Karen	4:55:42 (25,520)	
Dixon, Kirsten	5:44:55 (30,879)	
Dixon, Marion	3:49:01 (8,902)	
Dixon, Pearl	4:15:58 (15,831)	
Dixon, Sally	7:14:20 (32,732)	
Dixon, Sharon	2:45:03 (301)	
Dixon, Zoe	5:03:44 (26,847)	
Djemil-Ysif, Denise	6:17:28 (32,020)	
Dobbie, Shona	3:50:08 (9,196)	
Dobie, Amelia	4:35:19 (20,905)	
Dobinson, Nichola	4:59:32 (26,227)	
Dobson, Emma	5:34:28 (30,144)	
Dobson, Judith	3:33:47 (5,474)	
Dobson, Katie	4:37:01 (21,319)	
Dobson, Mary	3:58:57 (11,779)	
Docherty, Caroline	4:53:45 (25,114)	
Dockling, Margaret	3:36:36 (6,043)	
Dodd, Adele	5:08:51 (27,543)	
Dodd, Catherine	4:07:47 (13,866)	
Dodd, Joanne	4:50:22 (24,473)	
Dodd, Katherine	3:50:54 (9,399)	
Dodds, Aileen	4:31:21 (19,918)	
Dodds, Beatrice	5:33:01 (30,023)	
Dodds, Zoe	5:42:13 (30,706)	
Doel, Juliette	5:44:07 (30,826)	
Doerffer, Tina	4:10:04 (14,403)	
Doga, Elaine	4:05:59 (13,432)	
Doherty, Brenda	4:59:14 (26,169)	
Doherty, Colette	4:52:09 (24,805)	
Doherty, Keri	4:24:41 (18,167)	
Dolan, Susan	2:56:33 (875)	
Dollery, Alison	6:29:25 (32,263)	
Dolphin, Ella	4:52:19 (24,846)	
Donald, Rachel	5:40:34 (30,588)	
Donaldson, Emma	3:38:37 (6,453)	
Donaldson, Hazel	3:39:27 (6,612)	
Donaldson, Meghan	4:20:20 (16,951)	
Donkin, Ann	4:32:12 (20,141)	
Donkin, Sally	5:57:20 (31,452)	
Donnelly, Ann Maria	4:47:28 (23,907)	
Donnelly, Eve	5:48:37 (31,071)	
Donnelly, Sham	5:30:45 (29,845)	
Donnelly, Sharon	3:12:47 (2,396)	
Donnelly, Susan	4:29:20 (19,418)	
Donoghue, Paula	3:37:43 (6,269)	
Donohoe, Diane	4:38:39 (21,753)	
Donohoe, Elizabeth	4:35:51 (21,042)	
Donohoe, Tara	5:19:48 (28,853)	
Donora, Jayne	4:15:43 (15,758)	
Donovan, Ceri	3:51:31 (9,550)	
Donovan, Emily	5:13:42 (28,159)	
Donovan, Kimberley	3:51:43 (9,599)	
Donovan, Shannon	4:36:22 (21,182)	
Doran, Martina	6:14:30 (31,942)	
Dorarinsdottir, Sigrum	4:53:54 (25,147)	
Dore, Pauline	3:46:21 (8,236)	
Dormer, Sally	4:05:21 (13,287)	
Dorrell, Patricia	4:37:01 (21,319)	
Dorrity, Miriam	5:08:33 (27,504)	
Dorsett, Po	4:40:01 (22,109)	
Dorward, Lesley	4:39:08 (21,883)	
Dosanjh, Rajinder	5:03:50 (26,862)	
Dossa, Cressida	4:39:44 (22,037)	
Double, Alison	5:41:53 (30,690)	
Dougan, Sheila	3:14:54 (2,657)	
Doughty, Georgina	4:25:14 (18,317)	
Doughty, Karla	5:31:44 (29,929)	
Doughty, Sara	4:02:43 (12,705)	
Doughty, Susan	5:21:20 (29,031)	
Douglas, Alice	5:05:33 (27,091)	
Douglas, Maureen	3:40:44 (6,900)	
Douglas, Sasha	5:40:51 (30,603)	
Douglas, Teresa	3:26:39 (4,262)	
Douglass, Carolyn	4:16:35 (16,002)	
Dowds, Esther	4:36:30 (21,221)	
Dowell, Melissa	3:25:03 (3,993)	
Dowle, Julie	5:05:28 (27,082)	
Dowler, Edwina	5:09:37 (27,651)	
Downes, Anna	4:37:49 (21,525)	
Downie, Marie	4:00:11 (12,127)	
Downie, Sally	4:15:55 (15,816)	
Downs, Mel	4:21:33 (17,267)	
Downton, Pamela	5:55:51 (31,392)	
Dowton, Patricia	6:35:11 (32,356)	
Doyle, Emma	4:31:33 (19,988)	
Doyle, Fiona	5:38:25 (30,439)	
Doyle, Judith	4:17:45 (16,310)	
Doyle, Mary	3:15:38 (2,742)	
Doyle, Sylvia	3:48:45 (8,829)	
Drake, Amanda	4:15:54 (15,810)	
Drake, Julie	3:29:43 (4,829)	
Drake, Susan	5:09:36 (27,649)	
Draper, Eleanor	4:24:13 (18,041)	
Draycott, Carol	4:30:32 (19,715)	
Draycott, Lindsay	4:57:39 (25,887)	
Drayton, Linda	4:11:39 (14,782)	
Dreier, Melanie	4:55:31 (25,483)	
Drew, Courtney	4:55:37 (25,495)	
Drew, Penny	4:21:36 (17,283)	
Drewett, Cereta	4:34:33 (20,710)	
Drinkwater, Ann	3:49:56 (9,158)	
Drinkwater, Julia	4:44:06 (23,086)	
Driscoll, Jean	5:17:18 (28,602)	
Driscoll, Sara	4:24:13 (18,041)	
Driver, Carol	5:34:04 (30,113)	
Driver, Debbie	5:34:04 (30,113)	
Driver, Sabrina	4:19:28 (16,713)	
Driver, Tracy	3:44:05 (7,675)	
Drost, Kristina	4:47:47 (23,971)	
Drovandi, Simona	4:46:22 (23,660)	
Drummond, Henrietta	3:14:54 (2,657)	
Druon, Manuelle	4:04:42 (13,135)	
Druvaskalns, Lina	5:21:43 (29,070)	
Du Plessis, Adeline	4:52:46 (24,931)	
Du Plessis, Carien	4:12:11 (14,897)	
Du Toit, Susanne	5:03:19 (26,800)	
Dubois, Ann	4:06:26 (13,510)	
Duce, Lisa	4:21:32 (17,264)	
Duchesne, Carole	4:34:04 (20,598)	
Duckett, Kate	4:53:04 (24,988)	
Duckworth, Clare	4:04:45 (13,148)	
Duckworth, Nicole	4:24:17 (18,062)	
Dudgeon, Sarah	3:41:06 (6,988)	

Dudziak, Malgorzata 5:29:05 (29,701)
Duff, Jenny 4:24:45 (18,185)
Duffy, Fiona 3:35:27 (5,794)
Duffy, Marie 7:33:53 (32,803)
Duffy, Therezia 3:37:27 (6,195)
Duggan, Andrea 5:24:03 (29,284)
Duggan, Sara 4:12:07 (14,885)
Dummer, Sophie 5:29:02 (29,697)
Duncan, June 4:37:30 (21,449)
Duncan, Yvonne 6:09:04 (31,815)
Dunford, Lindsey 5:38:26 (30,441)
Dungey, Claire 5:02:30 (26,668)
Dunham, Emma 3:45:42 (8,090)
Dunkley, Kerry 4:23:52 (17,937)
Dunleaven, Elizabeth 4:16:07 (15,870)
Dunmall, Julietta 4:25:16 (18,325)
Dunn, Angela 4:19:51 (16,821)
Dunn, Carol 4:05:12 (13,254)
Dunn, Pandie 4:21:21 (17,203)
Dunne, Victoria 3:55:57 (10,884)
Dunster, Carol 5:22:23 (29,123)
Dupland, Celia 3:49:41 (9,094)
Durcan, Siobhan 4:55:54 (25,561)
Durdy, Helen 4:46:30 (23,692)
Durnford, Sally 4:20:30 (16,990)
Duroe, Fiona 3:40:29 (6,847)
Durrant, Nicola 4:59:22 (26,190)
Duxbury, Amanda 4:23:19 (17,781)
Dwarakanatu, Asha 4:48:58 (24,228)
Dwyer, Brenda 4:51:12 (24,654)
Dyde, Lorraine 4:48:46 (24,182)
Dyer, Danielle 4:28:36 (19,197)
Dyer, Judith 4:28:11 (19,079)
Dyer, Lucy 5:33:48 (30,092)
Dyett, Audrey 3:44:36 (7,820)
Dyke, Carole 3:48:23 (8,718)
Dykes, Madeline 3:25:15 (4,024)
Dymond, Penni 4:00:06 (12,107)
Dymore-Brown, Linda 4:00:04 (12,097)
Dzialdow, Resi 4:07:46 (13,861)
Eades, Joanna 3:46:07 (8,186)
Eagle, Kelly 4:38:49 (21,796)
Eagleson, Holly 4:40:38 (22,263)
Eagleton, Karen 4:15:26 (15,676)
Eakins, Colette 4:28:17 (19,105)
Eales, Louise 4:06:31 (13,571)
Earl, Rowan 5:23:05 (29,182)
Eason, Sharon 6:17:18 (32,012)
East, Sheila 5:36:36 (30,320)
Easter, Gemma 4:32:19 (20,165)
Easton, Anna 4:54:16 (25,236)
Eastwood, Kathryn 3:21:05 (3,384)
Eaton, Helen 5:39:58 (30,548)
Eaton, Sally 6:07:05 (31,764)
Ebert, Jane 3:56:53 (11,168)
Ebreuil, Rachel 5:18:19 (28,704)
Eckford, Sophie 3:58:36 (11,678)
Eckland, Joanna 4:56:38 (25,708)
Eclery, Nicole 4:45:33 (23,454)
Ecoffey, Laurence 5:06:30 (27,230)
Edbrooke, Rowan 4:47:15 (23,869)
Ede, Natasha 4:36:22 (21,182)
Edelsten, Marika 4:33:34 (20,477)
Eden, Emily 4:02:00 (12,560)
Eden, Pamela 4:39:09 (21,886)
Edge, Dawn 5:37:39 (30,397)
Edge, Sarah 4:16:06 (15,864)
Edgings, Ruth 3:36:16 (5,969)
Edney, Edith 5:23:27 (29,216)
Edrich, Janet 5:57:43 (31,466)
Edwards, Alice 3:53:15 (10,061)
Edwards, Aveline 4:40:50 (22,316)
Edwards, Beverley 2:59:46 (1,155)
Edwards, Caroline 3:55:49 (10,844)
Edwards, Christine 7:32:47 (32,799)
Edwards, Felicity 5:39:04 (30,475)
Edwards, Joanne 5:32:59 (30,021)
Edwards, Jude 5:14:25 (28,237)
Edwards, Julia 7:37:19 (32,814)
Edwards, Kath 5:12:10 (27,969)
Edwards, Kathryn 4:31:52 (20,047)
Edwards, Kathryn 5:05:39 (27,105)
Edwards, Kelly 6:26:48 (32,214)
Edwards, Lisa 5:02:32 (26,674)
Edwards, Mair 4:23:11 (17,747)
Edwards, Natalie 4:17:42 (16,294)
Edwards, Penelope 7:02:01 (32,647)
Edwards, Sara 5:15:44 (28,399)
Edwards, Sian 5:18:46 (28,754)
Edwards, Susan 3:57:37 (11,400)
Edwards, Traci 4:10:07 (14,414)
Edwards, Val 5:52:27 (31,251)
Edwards, Wendy 3:19:24 (3,185)
Edwardson, Jane 3:52:49 (9,929)
Effhert, Felizitas 4:29:35 (19,478)
Efford, Jane 5:26:07 (29,458)
Eggleston, Diana 4:51:02 (24,613)
Eggleston, Elizabeth 5:37:32 (30,386)
Ehteshani, Kay 4:34:57 (20,818)
Eilbeck, Sandra 4:51:07 (24,631)
Einarsdottir, Gunnur 3:53:11 (10,040)
Ekman, Katrina 4:22:19 (17,486)
Elackman, Anita 5:06:26 (27,224)
Elcome, Lorraine 5:33:21 (30,058)
Elder, Glenda 3:42:21 (7,248)
Elder, Rachel 5:02:36 (26,686)
Eldred, Lynn 4:49:01 (24,237)
Eldridge, Joy 4:49:01 (24,237)
Eldridge, Marian 3:51:16 (9,493)
Eldridge, Sharon 3:36:04 (5,919)
Eley, Maria 6:00:02 (31,543)
Elford, Madeline 6:18:29 (32,049)
Elger, Victoria 5:21:52 (29,084)
Elias, Amanda 3:59:11 (11,849)
Elkington, Susan 4:55:22 (25,453)
Ellins, Samantha 4:32:36 (20,243)
Elliot, Marie 3:23:19 (3,698)
Elliot-Pyle, Emma 5:28:59 (29,691)
Elliott, Charlotte 5:54:36 (31,335)
Elliott, Clare 3:48:57 (8,881)
Elliott, Clare 4:46:53 (23,784)
Elliott, Helena 6:05:57 (31,730)
Elliott, Jenny 3:45:17 (7,996)
Elliott, Linda 5:01:31 (26,527)
Elliott, Louise 4:59:53 (26,286)
Ellis, Denise 3:59:37 (11,973)
Ellis, Francis 6:27:43 (32,236)
Ellis, Jacqueline 5:43:52 (30,809)
Ellis, Mandy 3:54:22 (10,417)
Ellis, Sundy 4:49:08 (24,266)
Ellis, Tracey 4:27:44 (18,969)
Ellsmore, Kate 4:55:45 (25,533)
Elsensohn, Laura 3:37:42 (6,260)
Elsmore, Catherine 4:01:50 (12,531)
Elsworth, Diane 7:06:28 (32,679)
Elton, Jane 4:39:02 (21,854)
Elton-Farr, Jane 4:05:03 (13,223)
Elvidge, Elaine 5:09:33 (27,638)
Elwell, Samantha 5:03:05 (26,759)
Elwig, Catherine 4:05:36 (13,348)
Elworthy, Natasha 4:25:08 (18,295)
Embleton, Fiona 5:52:14 (31,242)
Emblin, Sarah 4:47:55 (24,010)
Emery, Carol 3:34:25 (5,602)
Emery, Shirley 5:52:32 (31,256)
Emmerson, Frances 4:52:04 (24,791)
Emmett, Maureen 3:23:42 (3,760)
Emms, Sarah 4:42:01 (22,610)
Enbom, Benedicte 3:32:45 (5,311)
Endres, Christine 5:17:19 (28,606)
Enger, Susan 5:51:22 (31,208)
England, Maureen 5:01:16 (26,495)
English, Amanda 4:30:08 (19,635)
English, Louise 4:19:34 (16,741)
Ennis, Christina 4:13:13 (15,126)
Enright, Penny 4:44:44 (23,230)
Ensor, Diana 3:42:45 (7,326)
Eperon, Carrie 5:01:09 (26,475)

LONDON MARATHON

Epstein, Michelle 4:16:28 (15,973)
Erhardt, Louise 5:06:39 (27,251)
Erskine, Joanne 4:18:57 (16,580)
Escolme, Mary 4:45:05 (23,328)
Eskdale, Jacki 4:21:57 (17,376)
Essex, Julia 6:00:23 (31,556)
Etheridge, Kate 4:37:42 (21,491)
Etter, Ann 6:05:18 (31,707)
Euridge, Alyson 5:52:34 (31,258)
Evans, Amanda 4:29:24 (19,436)
Evans, Angela 3:40:18 (6,811)
Evans, April 6:04:46 (31,686)
Evans, Debbie 4:14:43 (15,500)
Evans, Deborah 3:20:34 (3,322)
Evans, Diane 4:54:25 (25,267)
Evans, Eurgain 5:08:45 (27,530)
Evans, Geraldine 3:55:42 (10,812)
Evans, Gillian 4:01:08 (12,345)
Evans, Jacqueline 7:36:21 (32,811)
Evans, Jane 4:49:33 (24,332)
Evans, Jane 5:20:10 (28,898)
Evans, Jayne 4:38:22 (21,679)
Evans, Karen 5:27:52 (29,606)
Evans, Kate 4:16:43 (16,041)
Evans, Laura 5:44:38 (30,866)
Evans, Lisa 4:16:30 (15,980)
Evans, Lisa 4:46:48 (23,757)
Evans, Lorraine 4:19:34 (16,741)
Evans, Lynne 4:35:19 (20,905)
Evans, Mary 5:01:54 (26,588)
Evans, Maureen 5:26:04 (29,450)
Evans, Meinir 5:01:12 (26,481)
Evans, Mikala 3:59:45 (12,007)
Evans, Polly 3:39:29 (6,625)
Evans, Rebecca 4:53:49 (25,124)
Evans, Sally 3:46:18 (8,225)
Evans, Sharon 4:59:04 (26,143)
Evans, Sheila 5:11:49 (27,924)
Evans, Shirley 4:54:21 (25,256)
Evans, Siobhan 3:13:19 (2,476)
Evans, Susan 4:28:42 (19,224)
Evans, Valerie 4:08:35 (14,051)
Evans, Victoria 6:28:52 (32,255)
Evans, Wendy 5:32:18 (29,979)
Evans, Wendy 6:30:47 (32,292)
Evason, Cheryl 4:27:44 (18,969)
Eve, Susan 5:19:58 (28,872)
Evensen, Susanne 4:24:31 (18,124)
Everatt, Joann 3:24:52 (3,966)
Everden, Shona 4:26:39 (18,702)
Everest, Barbara 4:11:05 (14,654)
Everett, Christina 6:10:36 (31,848)
Everett, Katherine 6:03:00 (31,639)
Everke-Mecheln, Magdalene 4:37:15 (21,390)
Every, Caroline 3:46:47 (8,339)
Eves, Celina 4:25:54 (18,488)
Ewens, Karen 5:16:54 (28,543)
Ewer, Jodi 5:35:40 (30,246)
Ewin, Rachel 6:29:22 (32,261)
Ewing, Alison 4:53:11 (25,010)
Ewins, Tiffany Alice 4:43:07 (22,871)
Facer, Lucy 3:44:46 (7,878)
Fahy, Sally 5:38:19 (30,434)
Fair, Sue 4:39:59 (22,099)
Fairclough, Allison 4:37:40 (21,484)
Fairhead, Jane 6:00:39 (31,565)
Fairhurst, Dorothy 4:33:54 (20,558)
Fairtlough, Amapola 4:20:40 (17,038)
Falconer, Ailsa 4:16:34 (15,996)
Falconer, Fay 3:55:02 (10,603)
Fall, Sara 5:07:35 (27,386)
Fallon, Bethan 3:39:34 (6,638)
Fallon, Lynne 3:50:14 (9,232)
Fane, Suzanne 3:43:51 (7,620)
Farcey, Alison 4:07:00 (13,678)
Farey, Joan 5:01:05 (26,462)
Farley, Angela 3:56:35 (11,078)
Farley, Susan 5:41:09 (30,630)
Farman, Michelle 3:35:38 (5,833)
Farmer, Adele 4:24:42 (18,173)
Farmer, Diane 4:34:55 (20,807)
Farmer, Gayle 5:54:40 (31,338)
Farmer, Maureen 4:26:26 (18,631)

Farmiloe, Clare	4:16:25 (15,956)	
Farnan, Jane	4:58:53 (26,112)	
Farnsworth, Christine	4:10:32 (14,518)	
Farquhar, Helen	4:20:01 (16,866)	
Farr, Kristina	3:15:51 (2,773)	
Farr, Natasha	4:23:55 (17,953)	
Farrall, Ali	4:33:50 (20,541)	
Farrant, Catriona	5:49:48 (31,136)	
Farr-Davies, Esme	4:44:44 (23,230)	
Farrell, Aileen	6:09:43 (31,828)	
Farrell, Fiona	4:06:45 (13,621)	
Farrell, Frances	4:52:11 (24,813)	
Farrell, Jacqueline	4:19:33 (16,739)	
Farrelly, Elizabeth	5:48:17 (31,048)	
Farrington, Debby	3:34:07 (5,546)	
Farris, Jane	4:57:28 (25,850)	
Fasolino, Jennie	4:16:32 (15,988)	
Fasquelle, Delphine	4:06:41 (13,613)	
Faulkner, Angela	3:46:52 (8,358)	
Faulkner, Dawn	4:21:04 (17,131)	
Faulkner, Elizabeth	5:40:13 (30,565)	
Faulkner, Janet	6:50:15 (32,545)	
Faulkner, Samantha	4:35:16 (20,896)	
Fawcett, Kirsty	5:16:49 (28,529)	
Fawcett, Linda	3:51:25 (9,525)	
Faye, Maria	4:50:38 (24,529)	
Fearis, Teresa	4:35:01 (20,839)	
Fearn, Liane	5:16:07 (28,456)	
Feasey, Nikki	4:59:48 (26,275)	
Feather, Sarah	4:27:53 (19,000)	
Feek, Olivia	4:05:27 (13,313)	
Feldman, Sue	3:35:22 (5,772)	
Felix, Jamie	3:14:24 (2,599)	
Fell, Carol	6:19:39 (32,073)	
Fellows, Julie	4:25:44 (18,448)	
Feltwell, Anne	4:36:19 (21,164)	
Feneley, Jane	4:24:06 (18,011)	
Fenn, Aimée	4:50:40 (24,537)	
Fenn, Susan	5:02:14 (26,632)	
Fennell, Clare	3:15:25 (2,716)	
Fenton, Ann	3:45:46 (8,104)	
Fenttiman, Rosemarie	4:45:36 (23,475)	
Fenwick, Alison	4:46:02 (23,579)	
Fenwick, Rachel	6:28:15 (32,242)	
Fergus, Doris	4:45:52 (23,533)	
Ferguson, Amanda	4:23:44 (17,899)	
Ferguson, Tamara	4:27:46 (18,976)	
Fernandez, Dolores	4:19:42 (16,778)	
Ferreira, Elizka	3:22:36 (3,594)	
Ferreira, Rita	4:53:11 (25,010)	
Ferrelly, Katherine	3:56:06 (10,929)	
Feys, Monique	4:16:22 (15,938)	
Ffoulkes, Julia	6:25:56 (32,200)	
Ficenec, Lucy	4:43:54 (23,044)	
Fiddes, Elizabeth	5:14:01 (28,199)	
Fiddes, Gemma	3:02:39 (1,344)	
Fidler, Vicky	4:00:02 (12,092)	
Field, Anna	4:14:12 (15,361)	
Field, Debbie	4:30:53 (19,801)	
Field, Deborah	6:28:17 (32,245)	
Field, Heidi	3:50:45 (9,363)	
Field, Ruth	4:48:40 (24,161)	
Field, Vanessa	4:13:42 (15,232)	
Fielder, Jodie	3:24:55 (3,975)	
Fielder, Tanya	5:15:24 (28,347)	
Figard, Angelique	5:00:17 (26,344)	
File, Hayley	5:12:03 (27,960)	
Filkins, Terri	4:24:50 (18,210)	
Fillus, Dawn	4:36:29 (21,214)	
Finch, Corrinne	4:11:09 (14,666)	
Finch, Janet	4:30:08 (19,635)	
Finch, Vicky	4:39:59 (22,099)	
Finlay, Grainne	4:47:39 (23,943)	
Finnegan, Vicki	4:15:45 (15,769)	
Finnerty, Nicola	4:50:48 (24,564)	
Finnigan, Sarah	4:02:52 (12,747)	
Firth, Mellissa	4:32:50 (20,314)	
Fish, Allison	5:31:56 (29,949)	
Fisher, Claire	3:52:27 (9,823)	
Fisher, Jane	4:27:44 (18,969)	
Fisher, Jane	4:51:47 (24,741)	
Fisher, Kay	4:28:49 (19,261)	
Fisher, Lyn-Si	4:05:28 (13,317)	
Fisher, Nicola	5:40:39 (30,593)	
Fisher, Rachel	4:34:52 (20,795)	
Fisher, Sarah	3:35:49 (5,868)	
Fishpool, Susan	5:30:10 (29,796)	
Fisk, Marie	4:33:18 (20,420)	
Fitzgerald, Maureen	4:56:58 (25,759)	
Fitzgerald, Sarah	4:56:59 (25,763)	
Fitzmaurice-Cotton, Heather	3:24:18 (3,877)	
Fitzpatrick, Anne	5:27:35 (29,587)	
Fitzpatrick, Jayne	5:29:01 (29,695)	
Fitzsimmons, Susan	4:34:44 (20,758)	
Flaherty, Angela	4:28:35 (19,187)	
Flaherty, Sian	4:38:16 (21,645)	
Flannery, Anne	5:55:06 (31,356)	
Fleming, Clara	5:14:00 (28,195)	
Fleming, Shona	6:11:14 (31,865)	
Fletcher, Alison	2:44:41 (289)	
Fletcher, Amanda	5:41:00 (30,617)	
Fletcher, Emily	4:53:18 (25,024)	
Fletcher, Helen	4:48:16 (24,081)	
Fletcher, Sandra	4:37:08 (21,345)	
Fletcher, Susan	4:21:58 (17,382)	
Fletcher, Tracy	6:49:32 (32,537)	
Fletcher, Vivienne	6:11:48 (31,876)	
Fleville, Sinead	7:42:18 (32,829)	
Flint, Amanda	5:37:22 (30,374)	
Flockhart, Lindsay	7:03:01 (32,661)	
Flood, Jane	5:46:58 (30,984)	
Flook, Jackie	5:46:31 (30,965)	
Florent, Valerie	4:39:02 (21,854)	
Flores-Laird, Dorina	5:34:03 (30,111)	
Flynn, Eunice	5:27:54 (29,610)	
Flynn, Judith	5:37:37 (30,393)	
Flynn, Kathleen	5:44:20 (30,843)	
Flynn, Zoe	5:57:29 (31,457)	
Folcan (Williams), Anne	3:35:19 (5,766)	
Foley, Niamh	4:12:00 (14,862)	
Foley, Nicola	4:12:01 (14,867)	
Folland, Sally-Anne	4:07:41 (13,836)	
Fontaine, Aline	4:56:10 (25,623)	
Fontaine, Marie	5:02:22 (26,649)	
Fontana, Catherine	4:29:29 (19,456)	
Foot, Lisa	4:35:55 (21,057)	
Foot, Susan	3:55:34 (10,772)	
Forbank, Anne	3:37:34 (6,239)	
Forbes, Valery	3:34:35 (5,633)	
Ford, Deborah	4:52:17 (24,841)	
Ford, Diane	5:20:45 (28,968)	
Ford, Fiona	3:20:09 (3,273)	
Ford, Josephine	3:57:21 (11,305)	
Ford, Julia	4:16:44 (16,045)	
Ford, Keri	4:33:56 (20,564)	
Ford, Liz	5:13:17 (28,112)	
Ford, Nicola	5:25:51 (29,432)	
Ford, Sarah	4:14:19 (15,398)	
Ford, Susan	4:30:41 (19,752)	
Forde, Anne	4:56:18 (25,656)	
Forder, Jeanette	4:37:14 (21,380)	
Foreman, Mary	4:18:19 (16,444)	
Foreman, Samantha	4:51:53 (24,760)	
Forman, Christine	4:35:54 (21,049)	
Forrest, Allison	4:21:21 (17,203)	
Forrest, Claire	4:20:18 (16,940)	
Forrester, Emma	4:33:46 (20,528)	
Forrester, Jan	3:50:01 (9,171)	
Forrester, Trudy	5:48:15 (31,047)	
Forss, Sarah	4:49:19 (24,290)	
Forster, Nicol	4:53:23 (25,046)	
Forsyth, Rosalind	4:59:07 (26,156)	
Forte, Wendy	5:50:12 (31,148)	
Fortes Mayer, Gail	3:14:34 (2,615)	
Forth, Elaine	5:42:52 (30,743)	
Forth, Judi	4:25:25 (18,364)	
Forth, Tamara	4:39:42 (22,026)	
Fosker, Denise	4:48:03 (24,047)	
Fossey, Janine	6:11:50 (31,879)	
Foster, Ann	6:21:12 (32,112)	
Foster, Jackie	5:06:16 (27,195)	
Foster, Lyn	5:09:41 (27,659)	
Foster, Nicola	4:58:23 (26,012)	
Foster, Rachel	4:30:07 (19,630)	
Foster, Sharon	3:35:00 (5,710)	
Foster-Devine, Carmel	5:31:11 (29,887)	
Foswhene, Amelia	6:12:45 (31,903)	
Foubert, Anne-Marie	3:46:50 (8,351)	
Foulger, Lindsay	6:03:40 (31,653)	
Fountain, Hannah	5:00:14 (26,340)	
Fountain, Leslie	3:43:04 (7,406)	
Fountain, Sandra	4:03:52 (12,959)	
Fountan, Emily	4:40:56 (22,339)	
Foux, Melissa	4:59:10 (26,161)	
Fovargue, Kathryn	3:57:54 (11,476)	
Fowler, Claire	3:38:12 (6,344)	
Fowler, Louise	4:42:49 (22,796)	
Fowler, Michelle	4:18:30 (16,486)	
Fox, Joanne	6:01:42 (31,599)	
Fox, Lisa	4:50:44 (24,546)	
Fox, Simone	4:07:20 (13,754)	
Fox-Pitt, Alicia	4:09:53 (14,360)	
Frake, Anne-Marie	4:15:18 (15,638)	
Frake, Karen	4:34:59 (20,828)	
Frampton, Ann	6:04:58 (31,692)	
France, Cinead	5:26:21 (29,472)	
France, Jacqueline	3:11:37 (2,215)	
Francis, Fiona	4:34:55 (20,807)	
Francis, Janine	3:21:04 (3,379)	
Francis, Molly	4:40:00 (22,106)	
Francis, Nikki	4:56:06 (25,611)	
Frangs, Shirley	3:52:44 (9,905)	
Frank, Flora	6:00:19 (31,553)	
Frank, Rebecca	4:32:38 (20,258)	
Frankcom, Pamela	4:06:49 (13,632)	
Franklin, Jo	4:29:22 (19,424)	
Franklin, Paula	4:15:11 (15,614)	
Franklin, Roberta	3:40:32 (6,859)	
Franks, Helen	4:25:59 (18,513)	
Franks, Hilary	4:28:54 (19,289)	
Franks, Imogen	4:42:31 (22,730)	
Franks, Mavis	5:55:02 (31,352)	
Franses, Tania	5:15:10 (28,317)	
Franz, Julia	4:49:47 (24,376)	
Franzel, Cindy	4:36:01 (21,084)	
Fraser, Claire	5:59:48 (31,538)	
Fraser, Dorothy	5:06:20 (27,201)	
Fraser, Eileen	4:18:11 (16,411)	
Fraser, Fiona	4:52:14 (24,831)	
Fraser, Katherine	4:39:05 (21,869)	
Fraser, Lorna	4:56:32 (25,696)	
Fraser, Zoe	4:30:01 (19,597)	
Frater, Alison	4:52:45 (24,926)	
Freathy, Morag	4:41:49 (22,561)	
Freelove, Lynn	5:56:42 (31,430)	
Freeman, Nicola	4:55:41 (25,516)	
Freeman, Susan	4:42:16 (22,665)	
Freeman, Wendy	3:39:46 (6,680)	
Frei Fellmann, Marianne	5:13:25 (28,127)	
French, Dawn	3:50:02 (9,175)	
French, Natalie	3:58:28 (11,643)	
French, Stephanie	3:30:39 (4,972)	
French, Valerie	4:37:02 (21,323)	
French, Yvonne	4:17:59 (16,368)	
Freshwatr, Dawn	4:58:44 (26,088)	
Fretwell, Tiffany	3:56:41 (11,104)	
Frewin, Bentyn	4:12:25 (14,950)	
Friar, Maureen	5:31:37 (29,923)	
Fridlington, Elizabeth	5:09:01 (27,574)	
Fridriksdottir, Rosa	3:55:31 (10,750)	
Frisby, Rebecca	4:40:38 (22,263)	
Frith, Susan	4:46:50 (23,769)	
Frith, Victoria	4:40:07 (22,140)	
Frommer, Beth	4:06:56 (13,657)	
Frost, Anne	4:06:07 (13,465)	
Frost, Janet	3:55:06 (10,628)	
Frost, Katharine	5:01:36 (26,544)	
Fry, Emma	5:04:48 (27,002)	
Fry, Lisa	6:25:57 (32,202)	
Fryer, Rebecca	4:04:47 (13,155)	
Fuentes, Teresa	4:14:47 (15,520)	
Fuggle, Caroline	4:15:36 (15,722)	
Fugler, Dannie	4:27:22 (18,881)	
Fukuzawa, Yuriko	5:35:24 (30,215)	
Fulbrook, Mary	4:59:35 (26,240)	
Fuller, Michelle	3:49:18 (8,972)	
Fuller, Sarah	5:05:15 (27,051)	
Fuller, Sue	4:19:58 (16,852)	
Fulton, Melanie	5:29:48 (29,764)	

Funnell, Ellen	4:28:41 (19,220)	
Furbank, Valerie	4:59:55 (26,294)	
Furlong, Jayne	5:10:03 (27,694)	
Furlong, Lindsey	6:35:23 (32,365)	
Furlong, Suzanne	5:33:02 (30,026)	
Furnage, Alaine	4:34:12 (20,628)	
Furniss, Helena	5:25:32 (29,404)	
Furzer, Penny	4:16:10 (15,881)	
Fyfe, Helen	4:07:00 (13,678)	
Fyffe-Roberts, Maxine	4:51:54 (24,766)	
Fynn, Michelle	5:10:13 (27,721)	
Gable, Candy	4:39:12 (21,900)	
Gadd, Patricia	4:44:28 (23,162)	
Gaffney, Monica	3:58:53 (11,757)	
Gage, Karen	5:30:40 (29,839)	
Gale, Jennifer	6:33:25 (32,330)	
Gallagher, Susan	4:55:58 (25,577)	
Gallazzi, Giulia	4:54:07 (25,202)	
Galley, Nicola	3:58:36 (11,678)	
Galpin, Anna	5:41:39 (30,661)	
Galpin, Vivienne	5:41:40 (30,662)	
Gamble, Claire	6:19:14 (32,064)	
Gamble, Hawa	5:42:52 (30,743)	
Gamblen, Susan	4:31:11 (19,877)	
Gambles, Janine	4:10:20 (14,468)	
Gander, Mary	5:44:03 (30,823)	
Gannon, Isobel	4:32:35 (20,239)	
Gannon, Sharon	3:05:03 (1,549)	
Gapp, Joanna	4:13:01 (15,088)	
Garatin, Véronique	6:22:43 (32,143)	
Garcia, Glenn	5:17:31 (28,631)	
Gard, Caroline	4:55:18 (25,441)	
Gardiner, Amy	4:00:17 (12,150)	
Gardiner, Anna	5:31:21 (29,897)	
Gardiner, Georgina	4:59:05 (26,149)	
Gardiner, Jennifer	3:52:43 (9,897)	
Gardiner, Julie	6:04:26 (31,670)	
Gardiner, Kate	4:35:34 (20,978)	
Gardiner, Sally	5:24:19 (29,309)	
Garfoot, Jean	4:46:27 (23,680)	
Gargano, Angela	4:36:17 (21,147)	
Gargaro, Caroline	6:26:48 (32,214)	
Gargrave, Alexandra	5:10:57 (27,804)	
Garner, Alison	5:01:19 (26,504)	
Garner, Claire	4:07:14 (13,728)	
Garner, Patricia	5:03:29 (26,820)	
Garnett, Kathleen	4:20:33 (17,006)	
Garonzi, Isabelle	4:09:23 (14,245)	
Garratt, Anna	4:27:43 (18,964)	
Garrett, Laura	6:02:46 (31,631)	
Garrod, Lorna	3:42:11 (7,196)	
Garrod, Nicola	6:13:58 (31,927)	
Garry, Jane	4:23:31 (17,830)	
Garside, Cathryn	5:04:13 (26,919)	
Garside, Lisa	3:48:37 (8,789)	
Gartland, Dorothea	4:08:35 (14,051)	
Garton, Elaine	4:48:52 (24,212)	
Garvey, Jill	4:48:55 (24,218)	
Garvey, Joanne	6:00:38 (31,564)	
Garvie, Bridget	4:08:00 (13,911)	
Gaskell, Kate	3:41:56 (7,137)	
Gasper, Teresa	4:14:39 (15,485)	
Gass, Josephine	5:39:43 (30,532)	
Gassor, Erica	5:14:14 (28,216)	
Gates, Catherine	5:30:45 (29,845)	
Gates, Dominique	5:58:09 (31,478)	
Gates, Nicol	5:58:10 (31,480)	
Gates, Serena	3:44:12 (7,715)	
Gatrell, Hazel	5:10:49 (27,789)	
Gauden-Ing, Lisa	7:05:40 (32,676)	
Gaulter, Julie	5:14:53 (28,294)	
Gaulton, Amy	4:36:05 (21,098)	
Gautier, Sue	4:20:36 (17,022)	
Gawor, Edyta	4:35:26 (20,932)	
Gay, Alexandra	4:06:20 (13,524)	
Gayle, Joanna	5:14:09 (28,209)	
Gaylor, Elizabeth	5:15:48 (28,412)	
Gaynor, Claire	4:41:43 (22,536)	
Gaytten, Lorraine	5:07:09 (27,321)	
Gedge, Sarah	5:12:57 (28,075)	
Gedney, Polly	4:31:33 (19,988)	
Gee, Belinda	4:11:54 (14,833)	
Gee, Emily	5:33:25 (30,063)	
Geear, Lorraine	4:53:45 (25,114)	
Gemechu, Shitaye	2:28:56 (55)	
Gemmill, Pippa	3:40:23 (6,831)	
Genisans-Seveto, Margarita	4:38:31 (21,707)	
Gennard, Joanne	6:56:17 (32,595)	
Gent, Christine	3:39:46 (6,680)	
Gent, Karen	3:36:47 (6,074)	
Gent, Sarah	3:41:26 (7,051)	
George, Ann	5:51:59 (31,231)	
George, Jane	3:47:13 (8,443)	
George, Susan	3:43:12 (7,442)	
Georghiou, Dorothy	3:22:01 (3,528)	
Georgiou, Georgina	5:31:27 (29,908)	
Gerard, Denise	4:45:26 (23,424)	
Gerard-Pearse, Jane	6:13:40 (31,921)	
German, Lisa	5:18:35 (28,732)	
Gerrard, Mandy	5:51:21 (31,206)	
Gerstrom, Donna	5:48:19 (31,051)	
Gestetner, Sarah	3:31:05 (5,043)	
Geyle, Zosia	5:06:25 (27,219)	
Giann, Susan	5:24:53 (29,352)	
Giannotto, Pina	5:29:54 (29,769)	
Gibbeson, Sally	5:54:25 (31,330)	
Gibbins, Deborah	5:38:26 (30,441)	
Gibbon, Sahra	4:31:19 (19,906)	
Gibbons, Kate	5:04:43 (26,981)	
Gibbs, Dawn	3:10:11 (2,057)	
Giblett, Jane	4:24:19 (18,073)	
Gibson, Beverley	3:29:03 (4,703)	
Gibson, Caley	4:52:05 (24,796)	
Gibson, Dawn	4:10:55 (14,612)	
Gibson, Diana	3:39:41 (6,661)	
Gibson, Helena	5:23:33 (29,226)	
Gibson, Joanne	4:22:38 (17,583)	
Gibson, Julie-Anne	4:52:07 (24,804)	
Gibson, Louise	4:31:52 (20,047)	
Gibson, Lucy	4:20:58 (17,102)	
Gibson, Shirley	4:16:51 (16,079)	
Gicquel, Claire	3:22:43 (3,615)	
Giddings, Emma	4:32:02 (20,096)	
Giddings, Michelle	5:11:47 (27,919)	
Giddings, Naomi	4:50:13 (24,454)	
Gierhart, Christine	5:29:15 (29,718)	
Giffin, Corrine	6:12:26 (31,893)	
Gilbert, Dolly	5:49:39 (31,129)	
Gilbert, Faith	4:59:05 (26,149)	
Gilbert, Gerty	7:05:21 (32,675)	
Gilbert, Kevin	7:35:06 (32,806)	
Gilbride, Bridget	6:35:03 (32,354)	
Gilby, Sue	3:41:32 (7,070)	
Gild, Nady	4:21:08 (17,151)	
Giles, Abigail	4:10:32 (14,518)	
Giles, Jeannette	4:40:42 (22,277)	
Giles, Kelley	5:09:35 (27,644)	
Gilfillan, Laura	5:51:40 (31,222)	
Gilham, Wendy	5:16:18 (28,482)	
Gilkes, Lisa	3:56:19 (10,994)	
Gill, Gillian	4:37:46 (21,509)	
Gill, Tessa	4:44:30 (23,172)	
Gillam, Leanne	5:39:37 (30,524)	
Gillemon, Marie-Pascale	3:37:46 (6,275)	
Gillen, Jacqueline	5:28:04 (29,621)	
Gillespie, Martine	5:15:03 (28,304)	
Gillford, Cara	4:22:10 (17,445)	
Gilliard, Patricia	3:43:20 (7,483)	
Gillibrand, Helen	4:37:50 (21,528)	
Gillies, Sarah	4:03:46 (12,935)	
Gillies, Wendy	4:39:41 (22,016)	
Gilliland, Annette	4:07:26 (13,783)	
Gillingwater, Barbara	4:11:23 (14,704)	
Gilpin, Jasmine	6:08:33 (31,803)	
Gimber, Sophie	4:16:19 (15,921)	
Ginbey, Sarah-Jane	5:29:53 (29,767)	
Gisborne, Sally	3:44:27 (7,784)	
Gist, Niki	4:53:42 (25,104)	
Gitting, Sylvia	4:59:01 (26,134)	
Gittins, Shereen	6:34:24 (32,345)	
Giudici, Cinzia	4:58:32 (26,038)	
Gladwin, Sarah Jane	4:27:37 (18,941)	
Glairon, Susan	5:49:16 (31,111)	
Glazebrook, Jacqueline	6:01:31 (31,590)	
Glazier, Hayley	5:02:29 (26,663)	
Gleeson, Julia	3:51:36 (9,573)	
Glen, Kate	5:26:46 (29,506)	
Glover, Linda	4:52:37 (24,901)	
Glynn, Arlene	4:47:10 (23,849)	
Glynn, Diane	3:44:59 (7,913)	
Glynn, Sarah	3:57:58 (11,496)	
Godber, Helen	7:27:40 (32,780)	
Goddard, Janet	5:06:22 (27,207)	
Goddard, Joanne	6:14:50 (31,952)	
Goddard, Maria	4:46:11 (23,618)	
Godding-Feltham, Lisa	3:00:21 (1,189)	
Godfrey, Audrey	7:12:36 (32,720)	
Godfrey, Charlotte	4:17:57 (16,359)	
Godfrey, Dawn	4:48:34 (24,141)	
Godfrey, Joanne	4:45:34 (23,461)	
Godfrey, Susan	5:14:05 (28,203)	
Godwin, Lisa	4:39:12 (21,900)	
Goedhart, Annelies	3:57:18 (11,293)	
Goess-Saurau, Susie	4:23:07 (17,729)	
Goff, Anne	3:57:30 (11,365)	
Gohani, Bindi	7:36:14 (32,810)	
Gold, Lorna	5:56:47 (31,437)	
Gold, Stephanie	5:58:11 (31,482)	
Goldsmith, Gail	3:51:50 (9,632)	
Goldstein, Nathalie	4:11:01 (14,633)	
Gollnau, Sigune	4:33:07 (20,383)	
Goman, Nicola	5:29:56 (29,776)	
Gomer, Anne	4:05:26 (13,311)	
Gomez, Maria	4:06:04 (13,452)	
Gonzalez, Amy	3:50:54 (9,399)	
Gonzalez, Isabel	3:40:49 (6,923)	
Good, Sarah	5:19:14 (28,801)	
Goodall, Greta	4:44:42 (23,220)	
Goodall, Sharon	4:51:52 (24,756)	
Goodchild, Alice	4:30:10 (19,645)	
Gooding, Melanie	4:16:01 (15,842)	
Goodman, Christina	4:15:37 (15,728)	
Goodman, Sophie	6:19:24 (32,068)	
Goodridge, Catherine	6:18:15 (32,041)	
Goodship, Susan	4:09:28 (14,264)	
Goodwin, Helen	4:43:31 (22,964)	
Goodwin, Julie	4:34:38 (20,736)	
Goodwin, Justin	4:15:35 (15,718)	
Goodwin, Sarah	4:45:22 (23,398)	
Goodwin, Sarah	5:31:24 (29,905)	
Goodwin, Vivien	3:52:31 (9,842)	
Goossens, Martine	4:21:28 (17,238)	
Gordon, Diane	4:46:39 (23,724)	
Gordon, Janet	4:43:04 (22,856)	
Gordon, Jo	4:39:28 (21,963)	
Gordon, Laura	5:20:10 (28,898)	
Gordon, Louisa	5:15:40 (28,390)	
Gordon, Megan	4:46:02 (23,579)	
Goren, Silvia	4:41:25 (22,451)	
Gorga, Cheryl	6:22:37 (32,138)	
Goring, Ruth	4:00:15 (12,143)	
Gorman, Barbara	5:01:19 (26,504)	
Gormley, Julie	6:51:45 (32,556)	
Gormley, Teresa	4:38:04 (21,589)	
Gornall, Diana	4:50:26 (24,491)	
Gorse, Louise	5:27:41 (29,595)	
Gosling, Louise	4:34:40 (20,742)	
Goss, Elizabeth	5:44:41 (30,869)	
Gotrel, Rosy	4:08:52 (14,036)	
Gott, Sara	4:43:03 (22,849)	
Gottwald, Mary	4:23:39 (17,859)	
Gough, Bridget	5:11:50 (27,927)	
Gough, Jean	4:38:43 (21,768)	
Gough, Terri	4:57:48 (25,915)	
Gould, Caroline	5:17:20 (28,608)	
Gould, Jane	3:37:33 (6,232)	
Gould, Joanna	5:50:32 (31,163)	
Gould, Louise	5:33:16 (30,050)	
Goulding, Mary	4:12:40 (15,020)	
Gouldstone, Emma	4:49:03 (24,245)	
Goulston, Lyndsey	4:46:25 (23,667)	
Gourlay, Susan	4:52:48 (24,939)	
Gowans, Jenny	3:43:14 (7,454)	
Gowens, Denise	4:09:40 (14,309)	
Gower, Kerrie	4:44:55 (23,274)	
Gowland, Kate	4:27:36 (18,939)	
Goya-Perez, Louise	4:50:50 (24,575)	
Grabham, Verity	4:47:01 (23,815)	
Graham, Adeline	3:39:35 (6,643)	

Graham, Debbie 4:00:17 (12,150)
Graham, Eleanor 4:11:29 (14,741)
Graham, Janice 3:51:44 (9,603)
Graham, Janine 5:00:48 (26,421)
Graham, Joanna 5:00:41 (26,407)
Graham, Julia 4:05:19 (13,277)
Graham, Karen 4:17:46 (16,320)
Graham, Susan 4:14:43 (15,500)
Grahamslaw, Margaret 4:40:51 (22,322)
Grahn, Kath 3:28:11 (4,548)
Grail, Julie 4:48:49 (24,202)
Grainger, Jennifer 4:22:42 (17,608)
Graley, Joanne 4:58:41 (26,074)
Grandjean, Elizabeth 4:31:26 (19,940)
Grandy, Sarah 3:21:07 (3,389)
Grant, Christine 4:17:53 (16,345)
Grant, Jean 5:20:15 (28,909)
Grant, Julie 4:18:57 (16,580)
Grant, Julie 5:10:57 (27,804)
Grant, Karen 3:47:46 (8,580)
Grant, Naomi 4:12:24 (14,943)
Grant, Pamela 3:51:15 (9,487)
Grant, Pamela 6:46:52 (32,503)
Grantham, Lizzy 3:47:21 (8,472)
Grant-Ives, Anna 5:40:10 (30,560)
Grant-Ives, Bonnie 5:40:10 (30,560)
Graves, Katharine 6:10:10 (31,843)
Gray, Belinda 5:42:50 (30,738)
Gray, Elizabeth 5:22:31 (29,134)
Gray, Isobel 3:32:01 (5,193)
Gray, Janet 6:02:13 (31,619)
Gray, Jenny 3:07:20 (1,757)
Gray, Juanita 4:45:57 (23,552)
Gray, Laura 4:07:29 (13,793)
Gray, Lesley 4:47:12 (23,856)
Gray, Marian 4:24:15 (18,054)
Gray, Melanie 4:25:02 (18,274)
Gray, Rosaire 4:04:48 (13,160)
Gray, Samantha 6:45:18 (32,488)
Gray, Steff 5:12:26 (28,017)
Gready, Julia 4:57:53 (25,932)
Greatorex, Emma 4:34:12 (20,628)
Greaves, Hilary 3:25:49 (4,114)
Green, Anne 5:31:48 (29,935)
Green, Carol 4:44:15 (23,115)
Green, Cathy 5:22:55 (29,168)
Green, Christine 4:38:36 (21,742)
Green, Denise 3:30:52 (5,000)
Green, Emma 4:58:38 (26,065)
Green, Heather 4:16:02 (15,847)
Green, Helen 4:26:30 (18,653)
Green, Jacqueline 4:26:39 (18,702)
Green, Julie 5:00:02 (26,314)
Green, Kathryn 6:17:40 (32,025)
Green, Laura 5:28:09 (29,628)
Green, Patricia 5:00:23 (26,356)
Green, Pauline 4:26:03 (18,529)
Green, Rachel 5:33:54 (30,101)
Green, Stacey 4:40:23 (22,209)
Green, Sylvia 7:07:28 (32,683)
Green, Tara 3:51:49 (9,628)
Green, Tracey 4:29:09 (19,367)
Green, Tracey 5:08:39 (27,515)
Greenbank, Emma 4:17:39 (16,280)
Greene, Bernadette 4:32:26 (20,200)
Greenfield, Rachel 5:41:28 (30,651)
Greenhall, Clair 5:26:17 (29,465)
Greenhill, Melanie 4:35:16 (20,896)
Greenland, Samantha 5:17:53 (28,661)
Greenough, Glynis 3:40:07 (6,768)
Greenway, Carol 5:40:25 (30,579)
Greenway, Gillian 5:12:18 (28,001)
Greenway, Rachel 6:05:36 (31,715)
Greenwell, Monica 4:04:58 (13,202)
Greenwood, Carol 4:21:30 (17,250)
Greenwood, Celia 3:49:57 (9,163)
Greenwood, Laura 4:33:34 (20,477)
Greenwood, Valerie 4:28:38 (19,208)
Gregory, Fiona 5:51:42 (31,225)
Gregory, Joanna 4:07:45 (13,858)
Gregory, Sarah 4:40:09 (22,145)
Gregurec, Julia 4:44:02 (23,071)
Greneski, Angela 4:34:51 (20,791)
Grenfell, Nicola 6:39:01 (32,422)
Gribble, Emmie 3:27:28 (4,410)
Grice, Nicole 5:25:07 (29,374)
Grierson, Debra 5:47:14 (30,998)
Griffin, Anna 5:12:32 (28,027)
Griffin, Betty 5:36:46 (30,329)
Griffin, Jennie 4:31:07 (19,860)
Griffin, Kathryn 4:54:18 (25,243)
Griffin, Leah 4:29:02 (19,330)
Griffin, Yvonne 4:45:54 (23,541)
Griffith, Emma 5:34:05 (30,115)
Griffiths, Bernadette 4:33:10 (20,394)
Griffiths, Carole 6:19:59 (32,085)
Griffiths, Eirlys 5:34:53 (30,174)
Griffiths, Evelyn 4:33:48 (20,539)
Griffiths, Geraldine 3:46:29 (8,272)
Griffiths, Jane 3:32:31 (5,272)
Griffiths, Jennifer 4:15:37 (15,728)
Griffiths, Joy 3:39:58 (6,725)
Griffiths, Judith 4:38:11 (21,621)
Griffiths, Katie 4:30:03 (19,608)
Griffiths, Kerry 4:57:04 (25,782)
Griffiths, Lisa 4:13:42 (15,232)
Griffiths, Madeline 3:54:53 (10,568)
Griffiths, Rebekah 3:47:17 (8,454)
Griffiths, Rosalie 5:43:42 (30,796)
Griffiths, Sally 4:22:48 (17,639)
Griffiths, Sharon 4:58:37 (26,061)
Griffiths, Vanessa 3:48:17 (8,690)
Grigsby, Tracey 4:35:07 (20,857)
Grimes, Julie 4:34:37 (20,731)
Grimshaw, Sarah 4:59:42 (26,265)
Grindrod, Clare 4:04:00 (12,989)
Grindu, Christiane 4:10:48 (14,576)
Grinhaff, Rachel 5:28:54 (29,686)
Gristwood, Julia 3:39:33 (6,636)
Gristwood, Shelley 4:38:14 (21,636)
Groom, Michelle 4:45:29 (23,433)
Groothedde, Kitty 3:42:01 (7,158)
Grose, Katherine 3:35:47 (5,862)
Grosle, Michelle 6:23:19 (32,154)
Grossman, Ruth 5:43:10 (30,766)
Groucott, Lindsey 4:27:34 (18,931)
Grover, Claire 4:22:24 (17,522)
Grover, Clare 6:14:02 (31,929)
Grover, Sonia 5:05:58 (27,150)
Groves, Brooke 5:01:15 (26,492)
Groves, Joanne 4:11:03 (14,647)
Grozier, Sue 4:36:49 (21,280)
Grylls, Elaine 4:51:53 (24,760)
Guard, Maureen 4:22:18 (17,476)
Guck, Kathryn 5:47:24 (31,010)
Guegan, Denise 4:24:02 (17,990)
Guelpa, Nathalie 4:47:08 (23,840)
Guest, Janet 6:02:00 (31,608)
Guilding, Anne 3:41:51 (7,124)
Guillot, Isabelle 4:45:27 (23,430)
Guiney, Barbara 5:43:44 (30,798)
Guinness, Sally 4:16:57 (16,103)
Gulliver, Zoe 3:34:20 (5,587)
Gunawardhana, Ishanka 4:41:10 (22,394)
Gunn, Felicidade 4:56:59 (25,763)
Gunn, Sarah 4:24:06 (18,011)
Gunn, Tracy 4:42:48 (22,791)
Gunnardsdottir, Erla 3:29:18 (4,752)
Gunther, Tanya 4:16:08 (15,873)
Gunton, Georgine 5:46:31 (30,965)
Gurnell, Julie 3:59:17 (11,878)
Gurr, Karen 4:32:47 (20,298)
Gurrin, Claire 5:09:07 (27,585)
Gutch, Clare 3:44:21 (7,757)
Guthrie, Sylvia 4:09:25 (14,258)
Guy, Kerry 7:35:30 (32,807)
Guyot, Anne-Marie 3:53:17 (10,075)
Gwaderi, Razia 6:16:46 (31,999)
Gwerder, Cornelia 4:07:05 (13,692)
Gylfadottir, Thorey 3:53:02 (9,994)
Hackett, Shirley 4:17:17 (16,197)
Haden, Kay 5:45:54 (30,930)
Haeger, Astrid 5:01:40 (26,557)
Hagan, Davida 4:17:42 (16,294)
Haggarty, Elaine 5:32:26 (29,991)
Hagger, Cherie 5:32:05 (29,957)
Hague, Deborah 5:43:22 (30,781)
Hahnemann, Amanda 4:49:35 (24,339)
Hahury, Norma 5:09:57 (27,685)
Haigh, Amanda 3:48:38 (8,796)
Haigh, Dawn 4:54:53 (25,360)
Haigh, Jane 4:58:33 (26,041)
Haigh, Nova 4:11:02 (14,639)
Hailey, Dee 3:41:59 (7,149)
Haillay, Emma 3:44:01 (7,661)
Haines, Lesley 3:19:27 (3,196)
Haines, Natalie 4:41:49 (22,561)
Haines, Sarah 4:02:43 (12,705)
Haining, Rachel 3:15:36 (2,735)
Hairsine, Janet 3:27:31 (4,421)
Hake, Louise 3:44:13 (7,719)
Hale, Mary 5:56:22 (31,414)
Hale, Sarah 4:56:32 (25,696)
Hales, Martine 5:09:54 (27,681)
Halford, Charlotte 4:28:48 (19,257)
Hall, Beverley 4:33:06 (20,375)
Hall, Elizabeth 4:11:44 (14,801)
Hall, Emily 5:55:51 (31,392)
Hall, Gayle 5:12:55 (28,071)
Hall, Gillian 3:59:45 (12,007)
Hall, Joanne 3:43:26 (7,508)
Hall, Kate 5:12:18 (28,001)
Hall, Linda 3:57:22 (11,307)
Hall, Mary 6:33:14 (32,325)
Hall, Michelle 4:06:37 (13,592)
Hall, Pauline 3:52:59 (9,972)
Hall, Rebecca 3:36:06 (5,932)
Hall, Rebecca 5:38:22 (30,435)
Hall, Sarah 3:41:32 (7,070)
Hall, Suzanne 3:43:59 (7,655)
Hallam, Denise 4:21:04 (17,131)
Hallam, Kathryn 3:40:59 (6,961)
Hallecker, Andrea 3:39:33 (6,636)
Haller, Maureen 4:29:58 (19,587)
Hallett, Lorraine 4:10:46 (14,566)
Halliday, Freja 3:37:15 (6,155)
Halligan, Ruth 4:38:14 (21,636)
Halloran, Louise 4:38:03 (21,584)
Hall-Taylor, Clare 5:13:30 (28,140)
Halstead, Tracey 3:55:02 (10,603)
Ham, Paula 4:50:56 (24,596)
Hamer, Beverley 5:12:24 (28,014)
Hamer, Sara 5:28:59 (29,691)
Hamilton, Jenny 3:43:11 (7,437)
Hamilton, Marie 4:21:40 (17,305)
Hamilton-Smith, Joanna 5:41:07 (30,627)
Hamlett, Sue 5:37:54 (30,407)
Hammersley, Emma 3:42:57 (7,376)
Hammerton, Delia 4:35:37 (20,993)
Hammerton, Louise 3:48:19 (8,700)
Hammerton, Wendy 4:34:41 (20,747)
Hammett, Suzie 3:57:05 (11,232)
Hammond, Chloe 3:57:35 (11,389)
Hammond, Lesley 4:14:13 (15,368)
Hammond, Susan 4:45:04 (23,325)
Hammond-Chambers, Claire 4:28:13 (19,088)
Hampshire, Vanessa 5:22:56 (29,170)
Hampson, Karen 7:09:08 (32,697)
Hampson, Samantha 4:56:58 (25,759)
Hampton, Jacqueline 5:15:45 (28,402)
Hamson, Alison 4:22:29 (17,541)
Hamson, Clare 4:21:51 (17,356)
Hanbury, Susanna 3:58:51 (11,749)
Hanby, Tracey 4:45:59 (23,560)
Hancock, Helen 3:54:14 (10,379)
Hancock, Nicola 5:25:14 (29,382)
Hancox, Emma 5:46:18 (30,956)
Hand, Julie 7:26:29 (32,774)
Handford, Kathryn 4:29:20 (19,418)
Handley, Carol 3:38:21 (6,386)
Hankins, Marie 4:44:53 (23,266)
Hanley, Lynn 3:50:38 (9,334)
Hanlon, Meryl 5:03:46 (26,852)
Hanna, Lynn 6:13:33 (31,916)
Hannam, Denise 5:38:07 (30,419)
Hanning, Nadia 4:01:20 (12,399)
Hansell, Clare 5:47:25 (31,013)
Hanshaw, Geraldine 4:43:08 (22,876)
Hanson, Emma 4:50:24 (24,479)

Hanson, Janet	6:53:15 (32,573)	
Hanson, Shona	4:35:33 (20,960)	
Hanson, Zoe	5:22:45 (29,157)	
Hanway, Kate	3:30:20 (4,919)	
Happs, Gillian	4:38:35 (21,730)	
Harbron, Christina	4:06:11 (13,484)	
Harding, Alison	3:55:00 (10,596)	
Harding, Belinda	5:01:04 (26,459)	
Harding, Catriona	4:39:59 (22,099)	
Harding, Lucinda	4:14:50 (15,533)	
Harding, Paula	5:54:11 (31,319)	
Harding, Sheena	4:55:58 (25,577)	
Harding, Tracy	5:47:18 (31,004)	
Hardman, Christine	4:53:52 (25,136)	
Hardy, Alison	3:45:00 (7,926)	
Hardy, Joanne	5:29:47 (29,761)	
Hardy, Karen	4:15:32 (15,704)	
Hardy, Lorraine	3:15:49 (2,771)	
Hardy, Louise	4:42:55 (22,818)	
Harford, Julie	6:56:38 (32,599)	
Hargadon, Susan	4:42:42 (22,768)	
Hargie, Patricia	4:56:48 (25,732)	
Hargreaves, Lucy	4:28:36 (19,197)	
Haris, Dianne	4:07:03 (13,686)	
Harker, Julie	4:17:00 (16,116)	
Harkness, Ann	6:18:25 (32,047)	
Harkness, Mary	4:44:42 (23,220)	
Harlow, Beverley	4:36:52 (21,292)	
Harnett, Sarah	4:19:02 (16,602)	
Harnwell, Sally	4:23:03 (17,717)	
Harold, Ruth	4:11:44 (14,801)	
Harper, Ann	4:26:08 (18,563)	
Harper, Kay	6:35:20 (32,363)	
Harratt, Nicola	4:02:21 (12,626)	
Harries, Barbara	3:24:56 (3,980)	
Harries, Heather	3:58:34 (11,664)	
Harrigan, Kathleen	5:24:50 (29,346)	
Harrigan, Sarah	5:37:11 (30,362)	
Harrington, Olivia	4:53:55 (25,160)	
Harris, Abi	4:46:19 (23,639)	
Harris, Ali	4:05:19 (13,277)	
Harris, Andrea	4:29:35 (19,478)	
Harris, Beverley	4:26:28 (18,642)	
Harris, Cheryl	4:51:09 (24,638)	
Harris, Claire	6:09:43 (31,828)	
Harris, Deborah	5:28:29 (29,653)	
Harris, Dill	6:42:22 (32,449)	
Harris, Gillian	4:33:32 (20,471)	
Harris, Hilary	5:55:06 (31,356)	
Harris, Jacqueline	5:26:36 (29,500)	
Harris, Jane	4:22:09 (17,439)	
Harris, Jennifer	4:11:58 (14,851)	
Harris, Jody	3:32:54 (5,338)	
Harris, Lena	5:21:44 (29,074)	
Harris, Lucy	4:15:37 (15,728)	
Harris, Lynne	4:12:49 (15,041)	
Harris, Mandy	4:13:08 (15,109)	
Harris, Mary	4:27:33 (18,930)	
Harris, Nicola	5:30:32 (29,824)	
Harris, Sandra	5:31:35 (29,919)	
Harris, Stephanie	6:36:23 (32,381)	
Harris, Vanessa	4:54:43 (25,328)	
Harrison, Claire	4:41:08 (22,382)	
Harrison, Elaine	5:15:11 (28,322)	
Harrison, Gill	3:58:52 (11,754)	
Harrison, Jane	5:11:19 (27,856)	
Harrison, Joy	4:01:45 (12,505)	
Harrison, Julie	4:08:59 (14,127)	
Harrison, Margaret	5:04:37 (26,967)	
Harrison, Michelle	5:34:03 (30,111)	
Harrison, Phillippa	4:38:36 (21,742)	
Harrison, Samantha	4:42:04 (22,625)	
Harrison, Shirley	5:24:13 (29,298)	
Harrison, Susanna	3:02:22 (1,331)	
Harrow, Alison	3:44:21 (7,757)	
Harshman, Catherine	4:53:52 (25,136)	
Hart, Denece	6:12:43 (31,900)	
Hart, Gail	4:35:28 (20,936)	
Hart, Heledd	3:55:07 (10,637)	
Hart, Melanie	4:04:40 (13,127)	
Hart, Susie	5:52:10 (31,239)	
Harte, Karen	3:57:56 (11,483)	
Hartfield, Julie	4:36:32 (21,231)	
Hartley, Julia	3:42:42 (7,316)	
Hartley, Lisa	4:39:59 (22,099)	
Hartley, Maureen	3:53:49 (10,258)	
Hartley, Pollie	3:49:46 (9,121)	
Hartwright, Jayne	4:20:28 (16,987)	
Harvey, Diana	3:24:21 (3,893)	
Harvey, Gwen	3:44:31 (7,797)	
Harvey, Loretto	5:00:15 (26,342)	
Harvey, Naomi	4:19:44 (16,785)	
Harvey, Paula	4:54:19 (25,246)	
Harvey, Zoe	5:00:32 (26,382)	
Harvey-Jones, Martha	4:23:27 (17,814)	
Harwood, Jane	4:23:11 (17,747)	
Harwood, Lesley	5:25:22 (29,394)	
Harwood, Pauline	6:00:41 (31,569)	
Harwood, Sue	5:42:21 (30,718)	
Haselhurst, Sally	3:52:09 (9,741)	
Hasler, Victoria	4:25:29 (18,381)	
Hassan, Selin	5:30:36 (29,832)	
Hastings, Jayne	7:20:13 (32,755)	
Hastings, Karie	3:50:55 (9,402)	
Hatch, Ann-Marie	5:31:27 (29,908)	
Hatfield, Lizzie	3:56:45 (11,128)	
Hatfull, Janice	5:16:09 (28,460)	
Hatherley, Marilyn	4:02:33 (12,667)	
Hattam, Victoria	5:29:46 (29,759)	
Hautmann, Andrea	4:35:00 (20,833)	
Hawes, Diane	5:27:53 (29,608)	
Hawes, Yvette	5:03:04 (26,755)	
Hawken, Valerie	5:14:30 (28,248)	
Hawker, Lyn	5:54:41 (31,339)	
Hawkes, Jane	6:56:23 (32,598)	
Hawkes, Paulien	3:47:05 (8,405)	
Hawkins, Helen	7:11:06 (32,713)	
Hawkins, Margaret	5:22:18 (29,117)	
Hawkins, Patricia	3:52:03 (9,709)	
Hawkins, Sharon	3:11:01 (2,156)	
Hawkins, Victoria	4:02:28 (12,648)	
Hawkridge, Nikki	6:02:12 (31,615)	
Hawthorn, Claire	5:26:33 (29,497)	
Hawthorne, Olivia	5:37:54 (30,407)	
Hawton, Maria	4:36:32 (21,231)	
Hay, Debz	4:23:58 (17,965)	
Hay, Melanie	3:39:04 (6,542)	
Hayburn, Gaynor	5:43:04 (30,759)	
Hayes, Annabel	4:26:19 (18,601)	
Hayes, Carol	4:26:03 (18,529)	
Hayes, Elizabeth	6:22:10 (32,127)	
Hayes, Gillian	4:40:17 (22,176)	
Hayes, Liz	5:34:19 (30,135)	
Hayes, Philippa	4:59:05 (26,149)	
Hayhow, Prunella	3:24:11 (3,857)	
Haynes, Elizabeth	4:17:36 (16,268)	
Haynes, Jane	4:13:14 (15,132)	
Haynes, Susan	5:45:27 (30,907)	
Haynes, Vivien	4:12:11 (14,897)	
Haystead, Jennifer	4:38:15 (21,642)	
Hayter, Annie	4:10:30 (14,510)	
Hayward, Jan	5:21:42 (29,068)	
Hayward, Nikki	3:27:25 (4,400)	
Hayward, Sarah	3:36:05 (5,924)	
Hayward, Sarah	5:25:19 (29,388)	
Hayward, Susan	6:51:53 (32,557)	
Hayward, Victoria	4:48:58 (24,228)	
Hazell, Johanna	4:06:35 (13,583)	
Hazenfratz, Susanne	4:32:51 (20,320)	
Hazle, Kate	4:31:26 (19,940)	
Head, Joanna	4:27:50 (18,992)	
Heal, Tanya	4:58:40 (26,070)	
Healey, Janice	6:09:54 (31,835)	
Heap, Philippa	5:29:25 (29,731)	
Heard, Sandra	6:23:13 (32,152)	
Heard, Sharon	3:54:52 (10,562)	
Hearfield, Tessa	4:14:35 (15,467)	
Hearn, Angela	5:36:36 (30,320)	
Hearn, Suzanne	4:52:12 (24,824)	
Heasman, Lindsay	3:37:32 (6,229)	
Heath, Caroline	4:15:19 (15,644)	
Heath, Natalie	4:28:51 (19,278)	
Heath, Nicola	5:22:47 (29,158)	
Heath, Rachel	4:11:39 (14,782)	
Heath, Sarah	4:06:07 (13,465)	
Heath-Downey, Susan	5:10:07 (27,703)	
Heathfield-Eliott, Lynette	3:35:48 (5,866)	
Heaton, Mathilde	3:05:24 (1,580)	
Heaton, Sandra	3:54:17 (10,396)	
Heaven, Sharon	4:40:51 (22,322)	
Heavey, Judith	4:53:48 (25,121)	
Heckel, Sally	4:18:56 (16,578)	
Hedberg, Maj	4:04:40 (13,127)	
Hedgecock, Michelle	7:26:29 (32,774)	
Hedges, Hannah	4:39:40 (22,009)	
Hedley, Lesley	6:22:07 (32,126)	
Hegenbarth, Sally	4:30:48 (19,785)	
Hegetschweiler, Christa	3:56:29 (11,044)	
Heinrich, Dorothea	5:21:43 (29,070)	
Helker, Elke	3:28:16 (4,564)	
Hellen, Jennifer	6:03:09 (31,643)	
Hellevang, Wanda	5:08:22 (27,478)	
Hellicar, Edna	4:24:08 (18,017)	
Hellier, Lindsay	3:41:06 (6,988)	
Helliwell, Brenda	4:44:30 (23,172)	
Helm, Laura	5:59:03 (31,513)	
Helsing, Anna	4:21:50 (17,349)	
Helyer, Nicola	3:51:40 (9,587)	
Hemmings, Susan	4:39:48 (22,058)	
Henderson, Amanda	4:05:28 (13,317)	
Henderson, Carla	5:21:18 (29,023)	
Henderson, Demelza	4:01:28 (12,430)	
Henderson, Emma	4:00:34 (12,200)	
Henderson, Jenny	4:10:29 (14,507)	
Henderson, Joanne	4:10:51 (14,592)	
Henderson, Josephine	5:06:49 (27,272)	
Henderson, Laura	4:10:28 (14,505)	
Henderson, Lisa	3:45:18 (7,999)	
Henderson, Sheena	3:50:10 (9,205)	
Henderson, Susan	5:01:42 (26,560)	
Hendrie, Jacqueline	4:28:29 (19,166)	
Hendrie, Linda	4:31:22 (19,921)	
Hendry, Allison	5:08:09 (27,446)	
Henley, Denise	4:56:05 (25,601)	
Hennessy, Annabel	6:44:02 (32,477)	
Hennicke, Bettina	3:30:15 (4,901)	
Henry, Majorie	5:50:21 (31,156)	
Henry, Sue	4:09:42 (14,318)	
Hensby, Denise	4:21:25 (17,224)	
Hensen, Caroline	3:42:13 (7,204)	
Henshilwood, Elizabeth	3:51:29 (9,539)	
Hepburn, Angela	3:42:12 (7,201)	
Heppner, Jane	4:09:17 (14,209)	
Heppner, Louise	3:49:08 (8,931)	
Heppner, Louise	4:09:17 (14,209)	
Hepworth, Claire	5:05:10 (27,040)	
Hepworth, Karen	4:23:56 (17,958)	
Herbert, Jayne	3:49:17 (8,965)	
Herbert, Penelope	4:30:16 (19,664)	
Herbert, Sarah	5:19:30 (28,817)	
Herbert, Yvonne	5:47:31 (31,018)	
Hercock, Lisa	5:06:24 (27,213)	
Heritage, Julie Ann	4:36:31 (21,226)	
Hermannsdottir, Matthilour	4:24:55 (18,230)	
Herring, Louise	4:29:46 (19,527)	
Herring, Patricia	4:54:25 (25,267)	
Hershey, Julie	4:53:56 (25,168)	
Hester, Angela	3:55:20 (10,710)	
Hett, Tanja	4:09:35 (14,287)	
Hewett, Karen	3:48:35 (8,773)	
Hewis, Sharon	3:34:25 (5,602)	
Hewison, Caroline	4:40:30 (22,232)	
Hewitson, Denise	7:43:35 (32,838)	
Hewitson-Bevis, Bridgette	5:43:21 (30,779)	
Hewitt, Angela	4:25:16 (18,325)	
Hewitt, Catherine	3:38:26 (6,410)	
Hewitt, Emma	5:29:54 (29,769)	
Hewitt, Kirsty	4:38:40 (21,756)	
Hewitt, Mary	4:31:55 (20,061)	
Hewitt, Sally	4:35:39 (21,001)	
Hewlett, Henrietta	4:02:57 (12,766)	
Hewlett, Ingrid	4:09:08 (14,160)	
Hext, Jane	4:26:43 (18,721)	
Hibberd, Pam	5:14:11 (28,212)	
Hibbert, Jennifer	5:54:54 (31,334)	
Hibbitt, Cathy	5:54:12 (31,320)	
Hibble, Patricia	4:25:34 (18,409)	
Hickey, Maria	4:45:24 (23,413)	
Hickling, Marianne	4:24:02 (17,990)	

Hickman, Carol	4:56:19 (25,658)	
Hicks, Carolyn	5:31:21 (29,897)	
Hicks, Jo	3:53:42 (10,208)	
Hicks, Monique	5:01:50 (26,572)	
Hicks, Wendy	4:53:37 (25,088)	
Hickson, Barbara	3:40:54 (6,940)	
Hier, Diane	3:34:51 (5,682)	
Higgins, Elizabeth	5:39:07 (30,478)	
Higgins, Nicky	4:18:19 (16,444)	
Higgins, Susan	3:59:56 (12,066)	
Higgins, Vanessa	6:43:55 (32,475)	
Higgs, Lynsey	4:53:42 (25,104)	
Higgs, Miranda	5:26:24 (29,481)	
Higson, Carolyn	5:54:49 (31,344)	
Higson, Rob	5:54:49 (31,344)	
Hildebrand, Christina	3:23:50 (3,776)	
Hill, Alicia	3:34:07 (5,546)	
Hill, Andrea	3:16:47 (2,878)	
Hill, Catherine	4:22:31 (17,550)	
Hill, Catherine	4:31:55 (20,061)	
Hill, Claire	4:47:23 (23,894)	
Hill, Debra	4:21:31 (17,255)	
Hill, Frances	6:11:00 (31,858)	
Hill, Janet	4:09:59 (14,380)	
Hill, Joanne	5:09:58 (27,686)	
Hill, Judy	5:01:19 (26,504)	
Hill, Julie	3:28:54 (4,679)	
Hill, Karen	4:18:15 (16,427)	
Hill, Laura	4:28:56 (19,297)	
Hill, Lesley	4:49:52 (24,401)	
Hill, Louise	5:05:16 (27,055)	
Hill, Lucy	3:51:40 (9,587)	
Hill, Paula	3:19:11 (3,158)	
Hill, Rebecca	3:45:11 (7,969)	
Hill, Tracey	4:35:28 (20,936)	
Hill, Victoria	3:35:55 (5,886)	
Hill, Zoe	6:03:22 (31,649)	
Hillary, Judith	5:56:53 (31,442)	
Hillcox-Smith, Alexandra	6:36:27 (32,385)	
Hillier, Sonia	4:53:43 (25,107)	
Hillman, Maria	4:35:10 (20,866)	
Hillman, Sallie	5:12:29 (28,022)	
Hills, Amelia	3:48:19 (8,700)	
Hills, Delwyn	4:35:20 (20,909)	
Hillyer, Margaret	4:59:13 (26,165)	
Hilton, Lindsay	5:12:17 (27,995)	
Hinchliffe, Sara	4:25:28 (18,377)	
Hinchliffe, Sarah	4:13:00 (15,082)	
Hind, Julie	5:10:11 (27,715)	
Hindle, Carol	4:38:10 (21,616)	
Hindle, Emma	6:13:41 (31,923)	
Hinds, Rebecca	4:42:51 (22,801)	
Hinksman, Sarah	4:13:57 (15,297)	
Hinsehelwood, Linda	4:44:00 (23,066)	
Hipkin, Sharon	4:45:30 (23,436)	
Hirons, Sarah	4:25:27 (18,371)	
Hirotsuna, Shoko	5:55:33 (31,382)	
Hirst, Katherine	3:58:29 (11,648)	
Hiscock, Kerryn	4:43:14 (22,897)	
Hitch, Helen	3:38:39 (6,465)	
Hitchcock, Nicola	4:29:25 (19,440)	
Ho, Francesca	7:17:09 (32,746)	
Hoad-Reddick, Sarah	4:45:51 (23,530)	
Hoare, Nicki	3:52:55 (9,955)	
Hochfeld, Kim	4:16:31 (15,984)	
Hock, Antze	3:51:28 (9,535)	
Hocking, Michelle	5:13:15 (28,108)	
Hodge, Emma	4:35:52 (21,045)	
Hodge, Lynne	3:45:31 (8,048)	
Hodges, Claire	3:49:17 (8,965)	
Hodgkins, Amanda	5:37:32 (30,386)	
Hodgkiss, Michelle	5:28:15 (29,633)	
Hodgson, Catherine	4:17:17 (16,197)	
Hodgson, Julia	4:11:07 (14,661)	
Hodgson, Lucy	5:21:28 (29,041)	
Hodjatoleslami, Jean	5:06:25 (27,219)	
Hodkinson, Gemma	6:28:47 (32,251)	
Hodman, Flo	4:55:34 (25,491)	
Hodnett, Nicola	5:29:54 (29,769)	
Hodson, Nichola	5:37:00 (30,346)	
Hoffmann, Leane	4:56:50 (25,739)	
Hofstee, Brigitte	4:52:42 (24,915)	
Hoga, Michelle	3:28:34 (4,616)	
Hogan, Emma	5:49:34 (31,125)	
Hogan, Susan	3:32:44 (5,308)	
Hogben, Christine	5:39:45 (30,535)	
Hoker, Lynda	5:59:49 (31,539)	
Holburn, Anna	5:20:05 (28,890)	
Holden, Dorothy	4:45:25 (23,419)	
Holden, Emma	5:22:25 (29,125)	
Holden, Tracey	4:32:38 (20,258)	
Holder, Jeanette	6:32:59 (32,323)	
Holland, Katrina	5:15:23 (28,344)	
Holland, Laura	5:39:24 (30,505)	
Holland, Sally	5:08:13 (27,461)	
Hollingsworth, Kelly	4:03:54 (12,963)	
Hollinshead, Monique	3:01:57 (1,296)	
Hollis, Claire	4:47:17 (23,874)	
Hollmann, Victoria	3:38:07 (6,331)	
Holloway, Catherine	3:09:20 (1,973)	
Holloway, Esther	4:47:49 (23,982)	
Holloway, Naomi	4:45:00 (23,304)	
Holloway, Rosie	5:22:06 (29,100)	
Holloway, Sally	4:28:56 (19,297)	
Holman, Catherine	4:30:42 (19,755)	
Holman, Ronata	5:07:26 (27,364)	
Holmes, Catherine	4:55:17 (25,437)	
Holmes, Deborah	4:21:48 (17,335)	
Holmes, Lesley	3:54:33 (10,472)	
Holmstrup, Thérèse	4:12:50 (15,045)	
Holst, Sabine	4:15:01 (15,580)	
Holt, Angela	4:27:56 (19,018)	
Holt, Jennifer	5:11:00 (27,812)	
Holt, Julia	3:33:26 (5,422)	
Holt, Linda	5:06:25 (27,219)	
Holter, Kristin	4:08:00 (13,911)	
Holthaus, Joan	5:33:59 (30,108)	
Holton, Kate	4:39:37 (21,996)	
Homer, Britta	3:24:26 (3,906)	
Homer, Jae	4:41:15 (22,413)	
Homes, Gill	5:41:30 (30,655)	
Hone, Michael	4:05:35 (13,345)	
Hones, Michaela	5:42:50 (30,738)	
Hood, Janet	6:13:45 (31,924)	
Hood, Joanna	5:38:05 (30,417)	
Hood, Marion	6:22:34 (32,135)	
Hooper-Smith, Rachel	6:08:28 (31,797)	
Hooton, Mary	5:28:53 (29,685)	
Hope, Alison	4:43:19 (22,913)	
Hope-Smith, Victoria	4:20:27 (16,984)	
Hopkins, Diane	4:33:11 (20,397)	
Hopkins, Jaimie	6:05:00 (31,693)	
Hopkins, Jennifer	3:38:22 (6,389)	
Hopkins, Lisa	5:12:26 (28,017)	
Hopkins, Lucy	5:36:01 (30,275)	
Hopkins, Sarah	5:33:18 (30,056)	
Hopkinson, Nicola	3:40:46 (6,913)	
Hopkinson, Susan	5:34:37 (30,161)	
Hopper, Lucy	5:03:48 (26,858)	
Horne, Margo	3:45:38 (8,077)	
Horne-Hilgers, Barbara	6:05:42 (31,720)	
Horner, Nicola	5:05:52 (27,141)	
Hornsby, Mya	4:08:07 (13,936)	
Hornshaw, Claire	5:21:03 (28,999)	
Horris, Michelle	6:02:04 (31,611)	
Horsfall, Vanessa	5:08:44 (27,526)	
Horsley, Karen	5:40:41 (30,595)	
Horsman, Kathleen	3:21:04 (3,379)	
Horsman-Gray, Kerry	5:09:20 (27,612)	
Horton, Lesley	4:39:30 (21,968)	
Horton, Lindsay	4:03:34 (12,895)	
Horton, Sue	5:25:18 (29,385)	
Horton, Tania	5:21:11 (29,017)	
Horwitz, Shelley	3:47:07 (8,409)	
Hosken, Taryn Ann	3:45:45 (8,100)	
Hosking, Mary	5:13:33 (28,148)	
Hoskins, Caroline	4:07:08 (13,701)	
Hotta, Makiko	2:49:56 (487)	
Houden, Aase	3:29:17 (4,744)	
Hough, Grace	3:47:33 (8,523)	
Hough, Lindsay	5:13:00 (28,081)	
Hough, Pamela	4:44:55 (23,274)	
Hough, Taflyn	5:00:13 (26,338)	
Houghton, Angela	5:24:40 (29,337)	
Houghton, Elizabeth	3:51:51 (9,638)	
Houghton, Jane	4:52:38 (24,904)	
Houldey, Julie	4:46:15 (23,633)	
Houlihan, Geraldine	4:50:12 (24,452)	
Houliston, Laura	4:04:39 (13,123)	
Hounsell, Anne	4:48:39 (24,156)	
House, Wendy	4:58:34 (26,049)	
Househam, Elizabeth	4:46:54 (23,786)	
Houtman, Gonny	3:55:43 (10,818)	
Houvenaghel, Wendy	3:44:15 (7,722)	
Howard, Belinda	5:08:12 (27,454)	
Howard, Carole	4:19:22 (16,684)	
Howard, Caroline	3:23:54 (3,799)	
Howard, Deborah	4:59:42 (26,265)	
Howard, Hazel	4:18:01 (16,375)	
Howard, Jacqueline	4:58:33 (26,041)	
Howard, Joyce	6:22:45 (32,146)	
Howard, Orla	4:28:07 (19,058)	
Howard, Susan	5:18:28 (28,723)	
Howard, Suzette	3:45:37 (8,074)	
Howe, Anne	3:53:40 (10,201)	
Howe, Fiona	4:50:17 (24,463)	
Howell, Anushka	4:30:03 (19,608)	
Howell, Deborah	4:47:41 (23,949)	
Howell, Debra	4:02:10 (12,588)	
Howell, Katrina	5:37:07 (30,355)	
Howells, Margaret	5:38:34 (30,454)	
Howie, Laura	3:34:33 (5,626)	
Howland, Clare	5:39:20 (30,490)	
Howson, Paula	3:51:53 (9,646)	
Howson, Susan	4:18:35 (16,506)	
Hoy, Kate	4:55:50 (25,544)	
Hoye, Jacqueline	4:58:36 (26,055)	
Hoyland, Joanne	4:48:53 (24,215)	
Hrstich, Natasha	3:37:30 (6,217)	
Hubbard, Penelope	3:52:39 (9,881)	
Hubbard, Sandra	6:35:17 (32,357)	
Huber, Kelly	4:15:18 (15,638)	
Huck, Susan	4:26:54 (18,760)	
Hucker, Catherine	5:57:05 (31,444)	
Hudson, Allison	6:15:06 (31,960)	
Hudson, Andrea	6:35:58 (32,373)	
Hudson, Jill	4:27:13 (18,847)	
Hudson, Nicola	3:42:30 (7,287)	
Hudson, Nina	5:37:18 (30,371)	
Hudson, Sheena	4:26:44 (18,726)	
Huffen, Sandra	4:24:35 (18,143)	
Huffman, Binney	3:39:47 (6,682)	
Hufton, Elizabeth	3:52:03 (9,709)	
Huggett, Bridget	5:31:46 (29,932)	
Huggett, Nicola	4:37:51 (21,532)	
Huggett, Sylvia	3:43:07 (7,418)	
Huggins, Melanie	5:50:54 (31,182)	
Huggins, Samantha	4:20:18 (16,940)	
Hugh, Deborah	4:59:56 (26,296)	
Hughes, Ann	4:02:50 (12,741)	
Hughes, Anna	4:11:39 (14,782)	
Hughes, Anna	4:31:12 (19,883)	
Hughes, Anne	6:00:11 (31,548)	
Hughes, Chloe	4:51:23 (24,680)	
Hughes, Clare	4:28:56 (19,297)	
Hughes, Jane	3:59:36 (11,969)	
Hughes, Janice	4:42:58 (22,830)	
Hughes, Jean	4:37:12 (21,370)	
Hughes, Jean	4:50:14 (24,456)	
Hughes, Jeanette	5:24:17 (29,303)	
Hughes, Keturah	3:57:58 (11,496)	
Hughes, Lorraine	5:41:00 (30,617)	
Hughes, Maria	3:59:20 (11,896)	
Hughes, Rebekah	5:00:50 (26,433)	
Hughes, Sarah	4:32:19 (20,165)	
Hughes, Sarah	5:43:13 (30,769)	
Hughes, Sarah	6:52:52 (32,566)	
Hughes, Shirley	4:35:36 (20,987)	
Hughes, Suzanne	4:23:01 (17,711)	
Hughes, Tara	6:00:51 (31,575)	
Hughes, Vicki	4:55:17 (25,437)	
Hugh-Jones, Pia	4:25:57 (18,502)	
Hukins, Caroline	4:11:26 (14,727)	
Hulett, Angela	3:50:13 (9,228)	
Hull, Sarah	4:20:13 (16,918)	
Hulland, Gaynor	4:20:38 (17,027)	
Hulse, Denise	5:20:38 (28,953)	
Humber, Caroline	5:00:52 (26,438)	
Humbert, Alison	4:48:03 (24,047)	

Jones, Azure	5:38:33	(30,452)
Jones, Belinda	4:39:11	(21,892)
Jones, Carol	5:02:43	(26,700)
Jones, Charlotte	4:25:52	(18,475)
Jones, Christine	3:42:19	(7,236)
Jones, Claire	5:31:21	(29,897)
Jones, Dianne	3:59:05	(11,827)
Jones, Elizabeth	4:48:11	(24,070)
Jones, Hazel	3:33:11	(5,380)
Jones, Helen	3:45:47	(8,110)
Jones, Jackie	5:18:08	(28,684)
Jones, Jacqueline	5:01:34	(26,537)
Jones, Janice	5:55:07	(31,358)
Jones, Jennifer	5:28:00	(29,617)
Jones, Jenny	6:38:48	(32,419)
Jones, Jessica	3:37:22	(6,181)
Jones, Johanna	5:07:08	(27,320)
Jones, Judith	3:44:10	(7,698)
Jones, Judith	3:52:47	(9,922)
Jones, Justine	5:09:54	(27,681)
Jones, Karen	3:34:56	(5,703)
Jones, Karen	5:31:27	(29,908)
Jones, Kim	5:48:54	(31,091)
Jones, Laurel	4:27:53	(19,000)
Jones, Lesley	3:45:09	(7,959)
Jones, Lesley	5:32:34	(29,996)
Jones, Linda	4:17:11	(16,166)
Jones, Lowri	4:09:17	(14,209)
Jones, Lynda	4:26:47	(18,739)
Jones, Lyndsey	4:07:20	(13,754)
Jones, Marie	5:24:01	(29,281)
Jones, Mary	6:26:26	(32,207)
Jones, Melanie	5:49:04	(31,103)
Jones, Melinda	3:59:26	(11,926)
Jones, Mererid	4:44:09	(23,093)
Jones, Natalie	5:16:25	(28,493)
Jones, Paddy	4:50:30	(24,507)
Jones, Rachel	5:07:30	(27,377)
Jones, Rachel	5:20:18	(28,915)
Jones, Rebecca	4:39:20	(21,930)
Jones, Rosanna	7:40:42	(32,825)
Jones, Sally	5:16:52	(28,537)
Jones, Sandra	5:10:27	(27,746)
Jones, Sarah	3:35:47	(5,862)
Jones, Sarah	4:08:22	(13,982)
Jones, Sarah	4:37:02	(21,323)
Jones, Shan	3:39:43	(6,671)
Jones, Sharon	3:49:25	(9,014)
Jones, Sian	4:43:41	(22,994)
Jones, Susan	3:54:03	(10,326)
Jones, Tamsyn	3:52:32	(9,849)
Jones, Tessa	3:51:08	(9,466)
Jones, Tina	5:28:21	(29,643)
Jones, Yvonne	5:06:47	(27,269)
Jones, Zandra	5:17:03	(28,573)
Jones, Zoe	3:56:43	(11,113)
Jordaan, Noreen	4:51:41	(24,729)
Jordan, Aishling	4:58:40	(26,070)
Jordan, Deborah	4:39:23	(21,946)
Jordan, Dineen-Mari	5:40:30	(30,584)
Jordan, Louise	4:17:57	(16,359)
Jordan, Moyra	3:12:10	(2,305)
Jordan, Vicki	3:45:11	(7,969)
Jordanova, Alix	5:09:40	(27,656)
Joseph-Hazell, Jacqui	5:40:16	(30,569)
Josselyn, Eileen	4:29:01	(19,325)
Jourdier, Jessica	3:34:16	(5,572)
Joy, Sheila	7:06:28	(32,679)
Joyce, Deirdre	4:29:13	(19,384)
Joyce, Jacqueline	4:27:30	(18,919)
Joyce, Kerry	4:22:08	(17,431)
Joyce, Susan	4:23:00	(17,708)
Joynson, Seonaid	5:14:42	(28,273)
Judd, Clare	4:53:10	(25,005)
Judd, Laura	4:27:49	(18,987)
Judson, Amy	7:08:58	(32,692)
Judson, Jill	4:23:09	(17,738)
Judson, Maureen	7:08:58	(32,692)
Julian, Jenny	5:42:53	(30,748)
Jupp, Lucy	4:44:29	(23,170)
Kaddu, Celine	5:26:29	(29,488)
Kail, Dorian	3:56:47	(11,138)
Kail, Nancy	4:53:53	(25,141)

Kaiser, Kathy	3:08:20	(1,843)
Kaiser, Muriel	4:30:55	(19,813)
Kalashnikoff, Maria	5:14:26	(28,238)
Kaldor, Ellen	4:13:39	(15,216)
Kalisz, Helen	4:01:49	(12,526)
Kalkanzi, Nisha	5:38:07	(30,419)
Kaming, Christine	5:10:49	(27,789)
Kandler, Petra	4:18:10	(16,404)
Kane, Emma	5:42:16	(30,709)
Kane, Justine	6:17:07	(32,007)
Kane, Louise	4:02:48	(12,729)
Kane, Rachel	5:58:49	(31,508)
Kantorowicz, Melanie	4:37:34	(21,461)
Kapadia, Shiraz	3:58:27	(11,635)
Kapila, Rajini	4:56:03	(25,594)
Karabiyik, Ozee	5:12:56	(28,073)
Karsten, Beatrice	3:52:54	(9,952)
Kashey, Lois	6:48:11	(32,521)
Katrusiak, Ewa	3:46:39	(8,321)
Kavanagh, Donna	7:37:20	(32,815)
Kay, Angela	4:53:27	(25,057)
Kay, Heather	4:34:49	(20,777)
Kay, Michelle	3:58:48	(11,737)
Keaney, Jennifer	5:36:46	(30,329)
Kear, Barbara	4:01:20	(12,399)
Kearney, Nuala	5:24:26	(29,319)
Keasley, Jacqueline	3:31:40	(5,145)
Keaton, Helen	4:05:31	(13,329)
Keegan, Patricia	4:24:05	(18,005)
Keegan, Sam	6:47:31	(32,512)
Keeling, Emma	4:52:26	(24,864)
Keen, Emma	4:29:43	(19,510)
Keen, Joanna	5:37:38	(30,395)
Keenan, Nicola	4:50:20	(24,470)
Keenan, Sarah	5:57:09	(31,447)
Keeping, Christel	5:52:41	(31,263)
Keet-Marsh, Lorayne	3:43:59	(7,655)
Keevill, Heather	4:37:46	(21,509)
Keighley, Lesley	4:11:59	(14,859)
Keith, Anya	3:59:11	(11,849)
Keith, Gillean	4:13:48	(15,262)
Keith, Irene	4:23:41	(17,872)
Keith, Louise	3:44:42	(7,852)
Kelleher, Grace	5:14:28	(28,242)
Kellett, Sally	4:29:20	(19,418)
Kelly, Anne-Louise	3:30:32	(4,951)
Kelly, Diana	4:38:57	(21,832)
Kelly, Diana	4:40:07	(22,140)
Kelly, Diane	3:29:51	(4,849)
Kelly, Holly	4:34:57	(20,818)
Kelly, Jacqueline	4:36:04	(21,096)
Kelly, Lorna	4:30:21	(19,681)
Kelsall, Emma	5:59:47	(31,537)
Kemble, Sheila	4:36:14	(21,136)
Kemp, Linda	4:25:57	(18,502)
Kemp, Michelle	4:34:49	(20,777)
Kemp, Rebecca	4:09:17	(14,209)
Kemp, Thomasin	4:44:32	(23,184)
Kendall, Rebecca	3:36:23	(6,002)
Kenden, Fran	3:42:01	(7,158)
Kendrick, Charlotte	4:47:38	(23,935)
Kenee, Paula	7:14:20	(32,732)
Kenna, Diane	3:10:16	(2,069)
Kennealy, Trisha	5:24:24	(29,315)
Kennedy, Hilary	4:07:17	(13,743)
Kennedy, Maria	5:12:23	(28,010)
Kennedy, Susan	5:35:29	(30,226)
Kennedy, Vida	5:00:52	(26,438)
Kennelly, Catherine	5:20:25	(28,931)
Kennerdale, Victoria	5:58:07	(31,477)
Kenniford, Audrey	6:35:19	(32,361)
Kennington-Arnold, Jayne	4:37:00	(21,315)
Kenny, Gail	4:25:57	(18,502)
Kenny, Gillian	5:15:32	(28,370)
Kenny, Helen	3:44:12	(7,715)
Kenny, Tara	4:42:33	(22,737)
Kent, Alma	7:58:01	(32,858)
Kent, Carina	4:41:25	(22,451)
Kent, Claire	4:53:15	(25,020)
Kent, Katrina	6:25:12	(32,184)
Kent, Nicola	4:56:05	(25,601)
Kent, Philippa	4:59:19	(26,181)
Kenworthy, Ruth	4:24:51	(18,213)

Kenwright, Dawn	3:06:00	(1,642)
Kenyon, Katy	4:28:53	(19,284)
Keogh, Pettrina	6:08:42	(31,805)
Kerley, Ruth	5:59:00	(31,511)
Kern, Tracey	5:52:59	(31,274)
Kerr, Elaine	5:07:37	(27,388)
Kerr, Elizabeth	5:09:50	(27,676)
Kerr, Fiona	4:43:08	(22,876)
Kerr, Linda	4:14:50	(15,533)
Kerr, Lyndsay	5:11:26	(27,877)
Kerr, Val	3:33:28	(5,425)
Kers, Margo	5:24:11	(29,295)
Kershaw, Lynne	4:31:58	(20,075)
Kershaw, Michelle	4:18:17	(16,431)
Kershaw, Rachel	3:23:05	(3,666)
Kessel, Anne	3:51:38	(9,580)
Kessell, Nicola	4:43:47	(23,011)
Kesteven, Joanna	5:33:56	(30,104)
Ketilsdottir, Bara	3:30:30	(4,945)
Ketley, Fern	3:50:13	(9,228)
Kettle, Sally	5:15:16	(28,335)
Kettleborough, Christine	4:35:25	(20,927)
Keys, Christine	5:39:00	(30,472)
Khalwa, Rahila	6:59:57	(32,626)
Khan, Eleanor	4:46:49	(23,762)
Khan, Patricia	4:44:36	(23,196)
Kidd, Chico	5:26:46	(29,506)
Kidd, Sue	5:44:30	(30,855)
Kift, Penny	5:07:34	(27,383)
Kight, Kim	4:08:49	(14,094)
Kilby, Helen	4:08:29	(14,014)
Kilby, Sharon	5:27:14	(29,543)
Kilgour, Kirsteen	4:46:21	(23,652)
Killick, Elizabeth	3:50:41	(9,343)
Killner, Louise	5:08:48	(27,539)
Kilmartin, Jane	4:29:08	(19,361)
Kim, Young-Hee	4:47:59	(24,024)
Kimman-Van Wyk, Mieke	5:06:27	(27,227)
Kimpton, Patricia	5:08:47	(27,537)
King, Clair-Annette	4:31:07	(19,860)
King, Deborah	6:54:10	(32,583)
King, Elisabeth	4:26:35	(18,675)
King, Ellen	5:52:27	(31,251)
King, Jane	3:45:59	(8,157)
King, Kerry	4:20:02	(16,870)
King, Lucy	4:29:03	(19,335)
King, Nadine	3:38:57	(6,512)
King, Sally	3:46:38	(8,317)
King, Sally	5:17:55	(28,663)
King, Sarah	4:33:25	(20,445)
King, Shirley	5:51:14	(31,197)
King, Stephanie	5:38:14	(30,427)
King, Susan	5:31:09	(29,885)
King, Tracey	5:15:29	(28,360)
Kingdon, Jennie	3:33:20	(5,406)
Kingdon, Paula	4:06:15	(13,504)
Kinghorn, Barbara	4:30:09	(19,641)
Kingston, Nicola	5:19:00	(28,778)
Kinnear, Holly	4:22:15	(17,462)
Kinney, Gillian	4:50:25	(24,487)
Kipps, Megan	4:22:08	(17,431)
Kirby, Amanda	6:18:36	(32,052)
Kirby, Julie	4:45:41	(23,488)
Kirby, Maureen	4:16:10	(15,881)
Kirby, Ruth	5:06:53	(27,279)
Kirby, Sue	4:21:39	(17,297)
Kirk, Elizabeth	4:35:03	(20,844)
Kirk, Lesley	3:23:22	(3,706)
Kirk, Richard	4:57:30	(25,856)
Kirkby, Kathleen	4:21:43	(17,315)
Kirton, Jean	5:25:39	(29,416)
Kirton, Lena	3:50:09	(9,202)
Kirwan, Carmel	5:15:48	(28,412)
Kirwan, Elaine	5:12:32	(28,027)
Kitching, Margaret	4:21:37	(17,287)
Kitching D'Lima, Anna	3:45:22	(8,015)
Kite, Barbara	5:08:59	(27,570)
Kitto, Angie	4:13:18	(15,147)
Klabe, Nicola	3:10:27	(2,094)
Klammer, Janessa	4:31:10	(19,874)
Klatt, Mechthild	4:30:27	(19,701)
Klausen, Karin	4:24:29	(18,117)
Kleinknecht, Lisa	4:30:05	(19,620)

Klisz, Maria	4:37:33 (21,456)	
Klumpers-Jongenotter, Cornelia	3:33:48 (5,479)	
Knapper, Sarah	4:57:22 (25,836)	
Knee, Wendy	4:14:42 (15,495)	
Knight, Carol	3:58:58 (11,787)	
Knight, Carol	5:25:19 (29,388)	
Knight, Deborah	5:00:05 (26,320)	
Knight, Diana	3:38:37 (6,453)	
Knight, Joanna	4:50:48 (24,564)	
Knight, Julie	5:58:10 (31,480)	
Knight, Lynda	5:39:01 (30,473)	
Knight, Sophie	5:01:01 (26,450)	
Knighton, Joanne	4:33:20 (20,426)	
Knights, Caroline	5:37:17 (30,368)	
Knopp, Rosalind	3:55:10 (10,653)	
Knott, Charlotte	6:04:36 (31,676)	
Knott, Sarah	3:52:32 (9,849)	
Knowles, Julie	4:55:38 (25,499)	
Knowlson, Suzanne	3:40:26 (6,841)	
Knuth, Helen	4:24:25 (18,094)	
Koch, Marion	3:51:04 (9,447)	
Koehler, Brigitte	3:58:33 (11,660)	
Koehn, Jenifer	4:19:15 (16,653)	
Koeth, Melanie	4:04:31 (13,090)	
Kohli, Pia	4:07:44 (13,850)	
Koneaasdottir, Sigrun	4:53:54 (25,147)	
Konieczna, Yvonne	5:28:42 (29,674)	
Korenjak, Ulla	3:50:09 (9,202)	
Korpanec, Jaroslava	3:26:20 (4,208)	
Koumendourou, Maria	5:46:12 (30,946)	
Koutson, Sacha	4:07:49 (13,876)	
Koutsoudis, Marina	4:27:41 (18,959)	
Kowi, Beth	6:14:50 (31,952)	
Kraemer, Ingrid	4:19:00 (16,589)	
Krajewski, Rebecca	4:32:25 (20,194)	
Kribben, Kathrin	4:09:01 (14,135)	
Krieger, Heide	4:47:23 (23,894)	
Kristensen, Kitty	3:21:31 (3,438)	
Kronenburg, Renate	5:56:26 (31,420)	
Kruklinski, Jadzia	4:28:33 (19,181)	
Krupowicz, Laura	4:51:09 (24,638)	
Kugel, Erika	3:57:27 (11,347)	
Kuhm, Daniela	3:36:17 (5,975)	
Kuhn, Trudy	3:50:12 (9,215)	
Kumar, Harjit	3:51:18 (9,502)	
Kumar, Nandana	5:59:28 (31,531)	
Kusche, Gabriele	4:35:49 (21,034)	
Kynaston, Diane	4:14:17 (15,385)	
Kysela, Maria	4:51:22 (24,676)	
Laban, Chrissie	4:33:19 (20,423)	
Laband, Caroline	3:52:02 (9,700)	
Labes, Lucinda	5:43:06 (30,762)	
Lacey, Rachael	5:16:47 (28,526)	
Lacey, Rebecca	4:17:17 (16,197)	
Lacey, Sandra	4:27:48 (18,983)	
Lachs, Lynn	4:39:01 (21,850)	
Laddiman, Hazel	4:18:24 (16,467)	
Ladlow, Diana	5:29:31 (29,738)	
Lafforgue-Puyot, Jacqueline	5:20:45 (28,968)	
Laidlaw, Hazel	4:13:10 (15,113)	
Laidlaw, Linda	4:09:47 (14,336)	
Lake, Jaime	6:05:58 (31,732)	
Laking, Anne	3:54:25 (10,435)	
Lam, Fong	4:54:10 (25,220)	
Lam, Stephanie	4:32:07 (20,114)	
Lamb, Jacqueline	3:34:47 (5,673)	
Lamb, Robyn	5:02:06 (26,617)	
Lambert, Sue	3:32:46 (5,313)	
Lambert, Wendy	4:40:45 (22,295)	
Lambert-Julmy, Marie	4:30:47 (19,780)	
Lamont, Janet	4:57:24 (25,845)	
Lan, Tracy	4:51:16 (24,662)	
Lancashire, Gaye	7:05:42 (32,677)	
Lancaster, Andrea	4:10:48 (14,576)	
Lancaster, Kristin	4:56:12 (25,636)	
Lancaster, Wendy	5:16:44 (28,524)	
Land, Denise	4:34:49 (20,777)	
Land, Elaine	6:22:51 (32,147)	
Landale, Miranda	5:42:28 (30,723)	
Landers, Gayle	4:37:39 (21,477)	
Lane, Emma	4:35:25 (20,927)	
Lane, Jessica	3:59:43 (11,998)	
Lane, Kellie	5:59:03 (31,513)	

Lane, Sam	4:45:17 (23,379)	
Lang, Beate	4:33:07 (20,383)	
Lang, Caroline	5:43:04 (30,759)	
Langdon, Rachel	5:00:25 (26,360)	
Langebrink, Katherine	4:56:00 (25,585)	
Langham, Chris	7:23:05 (32,764)	
Langley, Carole	4:31:47 (20,028)	
Langley, Irene	5:31:52 (29,942)	
Langley, Julie	4:31:30 (19,968)	
Langridge, Claire	8:04:59 (32,865)	
Langridge, Heather	8:04:59 (32,865)	
Langston, Belinda	7:05:08 (32,671)	
Langston, Caroline	5:27:16 (29,547)	
Langston, Denise	3:31:01 (5,031)	
Langston, Kate	5:27:18 (29,558)	
Langston, Tamsin	7:11:00 (32,711)	
Langton, Carole	6:18:57 (32,060)	
Langton, Clementine	5:28:47 (29,682)	
Laraman, Catherine	5:01:34 (26,537)	
Largan, Sandra	5:12:53 (28,065)	
Larkins, Rachel	6:15:53 (31,978)	
Larmour, Veryan	4:54:59 (25,374)	
Latham, Libby	4:42:04 (22,625)	
Latham, Lisa	5:49:33 (31,123)	
Latham, Sarah	5:00:22 (26,355)	
Lathwell, Christine	3:39:34 (6,638)	
Latter, Karen	5:40:22 (30,576)	
Lattey, Alison	3:58:36 (11,678)	
Latto, Elizabeth	6:00:39 (31,565)	
Latto, Emma	3:03:53 (1,457)	
Latto, Sheila	4:45:42 (23,494)	
Laud, Carolyn	4:06:06 (13,460)	
Laughlin, Deirdre	3:44:53 (7,899)	
Laurance, Wynne	5:15:53 (28,426)	
Laurence, Janet	4:29:43 (19,510)	
Lavelle, Helen	6:06:47 (31,750)	
Laver, Beverley	5:00:50 (26,433)	
Law, Barbara	3:37:51 (6,288)	
Law, Katherine	5:07:36 (27,387)	
Law, Larin	7:01:23 (32,640)	
Law, Nicola	5:36:20 (30,298)	
Law, Penny	7:07:38 (32,684)	
Lawrence, Helen	5:24:50 (29,346)	
Lawrence, Jane	5:32:03 (29,955)	
Lawrence, Joanna	3:56:29 (11,044)	
Lawrence, Melissa	5:51:28 (31,214)	
Lawrence, Nicola	4:23:46 (17,907)	
Lawrence, Susan	4:37:54 (21,547)	
Lawrence, Suzanne	4:26:25 (18,629)	
Lawrence, Wendy	4:03:50 (12,952)	
Lawrenson, Joy	5:31:28 (29,913)	
Lawson, Paula	4:30:12 (19,652)	
Lawson, Vanessa	4:04:51 (13,172)	
Lawton, Janice	5:11:37 (27,895)	
Lawton, Linda	5:39:37 (30,524)	
Lawton, Susan	4:53:10 (25,005)	
Laxton, Katie	4:49:50 (24,393)	
Lay, Felicity	5:24:18 (29,307)	
Lay, Natalie	5:33:03 (30,028)	
Layne, Helen	4:21:37 (17,287)	
Layne, Susan	4:01:20 (12,399)	
Lazarowitz, Michele	6:49:46 (32,539)	
Le Baigue, Angela	4:14:16 (15,382)	
Le Cocq, Heather	5:51:59 (31,231)	
Le Cocq, Jenny	5:13:11 (28,099)	
Le Good, Vivien	4:14:26 (15,433)	
Le Masurier, Claire	5:11:55 (27,940)	
Le Roux, Monique	3:53:59 (10,305)	
Leach, Edith	4:42:51 (22,801)	
Leach, Nicola	5:33:17 (30,052)	
Leach, Susan	4:31:32 (19,978)	
Leadbetter, Katherine	5:34:02 (30,110)	
Leader, Elizabeth	3:31:48 (5,165)	
Leadley, Karen	5:16:17 (28,480)	
Leadley, Lenka	3:53:24 (10,112)	
Leafe, Kathryn	4:54:38 (25,307)	
Leahy, Jacqueline	6:02:34 (31,629)	
Lear, Jenit	4:57:15 (25,820)	
Learoyd, Alison	4:55:44 (25,527)	
Leavy, Paula	3:48:03 (8,659)	
Lederer, Regina	3:59:26 (11,926)	
Ledwidge, Angela	5:51:44 (31,226)	
Lee, Anne	5:06:44 (27,264)	

Lee, Frances	4:33:06 (20,375)	
Lee, Katie	4:21:19 (17,197)	
Lee, Michelle	2:53:03 (630)	
Lee, Sally	4:20:07 (16,891)	
Lee, Young	4:54:25 (25,267)	
Leegood, Emma	5:34:22 (30,139)	
Lee-Potter, Charlie	5:20:14 (28,907)	
Lees, Susan	4:02:47 (12,725)	
Leete, Jenny	4:09:35 (14,287)	
Legg, Helen	4:45:27 (23,430)	
Legrand, Nathalie	4:01:07 (12,341)	
Lehmann, Hayley	7:24:41 (32,768)	
Leibbrant, Dedj	4:53:37 (25,088)	
Leigh, Anne	6:21:02 (32,105)	
Leigh, Karen	4:46:15 (23,633)	
Leigh, Kerin	4:25:18 (18,333)	
Leigh, Lucy	4:22:52 (17,661)	
Leigh, Samantha	5:33:28 (30,072)	
Leitch, Jessica	3:13:25 (2,494)	
Leleu, Roselyne	3:37:33 (6,232)	
Lendon, Karen	5:37:07 (30,355)	
Lendon, Sarah	5:00:39 (26,401)	
Lennon, Caroline	4:03:42 (12,918)	
Lennon, Susan	4:05:06 (13,231)	
Lenoel, Valerie	4:54:10 (25,220)	
Lenz, Anja	3:47:58 (8,620)	
Leoffeler, Julia	4:19:34 (16,741)	
Leonard, Angela	5:28:34 (29,662)	
Leonard, Catherine	3:24:09 (3,848)	
Leonard, Vanessa	4:04:31 (13,090)	
Leslie, Alison	5:05:40 (27,109)	
Leslie, Caroline	3:42:25 (7,265)	
Letch, Wendy	5:03:00 (26,738)	
Letsinger, Katherine	4:23:22 (17,791)	
Letts, Rachel	4:42:04 (22,625)	
Lever, Susan	4:09:05 (14,151)	
Levinson, Nancy	6:48:12 (32,522)	
Levy, Elizabeth	4:30:50 (19,793)	
Levy, Margaret	3:38:40 (6,468)	
Lewin, Joy	4:41:00 (22,355)	
Lewis, Ebi	5:14:50 (28,288)	
Lewis, Fiona	4:31:33 (19,988)	
Lewis, Georgia	4:23:18 (17,776)	
Lewis, Georgia	5:41:40 (30,662)	
Lewis, Kate	5:45:24 (30,905)	
Lewis, Melanie	4:54:26 (25,272)	
Lewis, Nicky	4:33:40 (20,511)	
Lewis, Pamela	6:46:42 (32,501)	
Lewis, Sally-Anne	4:32:53 (20,329)	
Lewis, Samantha	4:40:44 (22,286)	
Lewis, Sarah	4:21:55 (17,371)	
Lewis, Sue	5:47:46 (31,027)	
Lewis, Susanne	5:02:29 (26,663)	
Lewis, Trudi	4:30:36 (19,734)	
Lewis, Valerie	6:35:18 (32,358)	
Lewis-Meredith, Michelle	4:25:33 (18,404)	
Lewittes, Adina	4:28:00 (19,032)	
Leyton, Kellie Anne	4:46:54 (23,786)	
Li, May Fay	3:21:44 (3,469)	
Li, Rita	4:16:23 (15,945)	
Li, Sylvia	5:33:39 (30,082)	
Lichty-Engmann, Laurel	4:39:21 (21,936)	
Liddell, Kirsten	4:06:01 (13,439)	
Liebman, Joanna	5:00:40 (26,406)	
Life, Carol	3:51:56 (9,657)	
Liggett, Sarah	5:00:50 (26,438)	
Light, Esther	4:13:41 (15,229)	
Lighton, Sarah	5:33:24 (30,062)	
Li-Kwai-Cheung, Anne-Marie	4:33:44 (20,523)	
Limmer, Hollie	5:20:10 (28,898)	
Limond, Stephanie	4:11:45 (14,806)	
Limouzin, Sandra	3:50:37 (9,327)	
Lind, Mette	4:20:40 (17,038)	
Lindley, Nicola	4:22:12 (17,447)	
Lindner, Dianne	5:13:36 (28,153)	
Lindop, Trina	3:23:56 (3,807)	
Lindow, Ginny	5:21:19 (29,026)	
Lindsay, Kate	3:52:36 (9,870)	
Lindsay, Olga	7:10:03 (32,702)	
Lindsay, Sally	4:38:33 (21,720)	
Lines, Anne	5:16:56 (28,547)	
Lingley, Elizabeth	4:00:38 (12,212)	
Link, Abigail	4:28:20 (19,119)	

Linley, Elizabeth	4:12:31 (14,975)	
Lipede, Kehinde	3:48:52 (8,859)	
Lippett, Karen	4:07:36 (13,816)	
Lipscombe, Emma	6:01:33 (31,595)	
Liptrott, Katrina	6:18:27 (32,048)	
Litchfield, Kellie	4:43:51 (23,029)	
Litchfield, Nikki	4:43:51 (23,029)	
Litman, Lucy	3:59:46 (12,013)	
Litterick, Emma	3:33:21 (5,409)	
Little, Cheryl	6:08:32 (31,802)	
Little, Clemency	4:47:54 (24,005)	
Little, Deborah	4:17:26 (16,229)	
Little, Emma	5:43:20 (30,776)	
Little, Hayley	6:30:40 (32,289)	
Little, Maureen	3:44:21 (7,757)	
Little, Sue	4:58:56 (26,119)	
Little, Zoe	4:57:00 (25,769)	
Littler, Victoria	4:23:58 (17,965)	
Liukkonen, Anna	3:43:38 (7,559)	
Liversidge, Yvonne	5:32:02 (29,954)	
Livesey, Belinda	3:19:02 (3,140)	
Livesley, Rebecca	3:42:19 (7,236)	
Livingston, Gwen	5:20:23 (28,926)	
Livingstone, Catherine	4:48:25 (24,108)	
Livingstone, Lisa	4:17:34 (16,259)	
Llewellyn, Helen	4:24:40 (18,164)	
Llewellyn, Judith	3:23:40 (3,755)	
Llewellyn, Rhian	4:20:57 (17,098)	
Lloyd, Alison	4:22:48 (17,639)	
Lloyd, Catherine	4:25:36 (18,418)	
Lloyd, Emma	6:09:41 (31,827)	
Lloyd, Gillian	4:39:57 (22,090)	
Lloyd, Helen	4:03:10 (12,808)	
Lloyd, Philippa	5:22:42 (29,153)	
Lloyd, Sharon	4:25:18 (18,333)	
Lloyd, Sheilah	4:03:16 (12,831)	
Lloyd, Susan	5:05:45 (27,116)	
Lloyd Jones, Sarah	5:35:08 (30,193)	
Lloyd-Jones, Jenny	3:29:31 (4,800)	
Loader, Carole	4:23:07 (17,729)	
Loades, Carol	4:35:00 (20,833)	
Lobban, Fiona	4:02:44 (12,709)	
Locher, Emily	3:51:46 (9,616)	
Lock, Lynne	4:32:06 (20,109)	
Lock, Maria	3:57:29 (11,359)	
Lockhart, Ruth	5:30:19 (29,805)	
Locklin, Janet	4:54:07 (25,202)	
Lockton, Lara	5:40:43 (30,598)	
Lockwood, Linda	4:26:57 (18,775)	
Lockyer, Janice	4:37:10 (21,355)	
Lodge, Aileen	4:46:24 (23,664)	
Lodge, Jo	2:38:24 (154)	
Loftus, Eileen	6:17:58 (32,036)	
Loftus, Sandra	4:35:02 (20,842)	
Loftus, Sarah	4:26:03 (18,529)	
Logan, Caroline	4:49:40 (24,355)	
Logan, Patricia	5:43:41 (30,795)	
Logan, Samantha	5:21:33 (29,045)	
Lohman, Lyndall	4:46:21 (23,652)	
Lomax, Estelle	4:29:13 (19,384)	
Lomax, Rachel	5:40:07 (30,556)	
Long, Caroline	7:02:24 (32,651)	
Long, Christine	5:15:42 (28,394)	
Long, Donna	6:17:23 (32,016)	
Long, Emma	5:11:31 (27,888)	
Long, Erin	6:24:25 (32,175)	
Long, Helen	4:32:21 (20,173)	
Long, Janet	4:24:35 (18,143)	
Long, Jennifer	4:38:03 (21,584)	
Long, Kirstie	5:49:31 (31,122)	
Long, Lisa	4:36:46 (21,271)	
Long, Sally	4:43:36 (22,976)	
Long, Sheila	5:08:52 (27,546)	
Long, Susan	4:35:57 (21,067)	
Long, Susan	4:41:36 (22,498)	
Long, Susan	6:29:41 (32,268)	
Longhurst, Deanne	5:44:37 (30,865)	
Lonsdale, Rachel	4:30:34 (19,725)	
Lonsdale-Hands, Tiffany	5:32:35 (29,998)	
Loomes, Lynda	6:11:47 (31,875)	
Loose, Phillippa	5:18:28 (28,723)	
Loosemore, Rachel	3:53:46 (10,228)	
Lopes, Teresa	3:39:01 (6,532)	
Lorant, Hedy	5:03:12 (26,781)	
Lorch, Heidi	4:34:53 (20,798)	
Lord, Carol	4:55:17 (25,437)	
Lord, Evelyn	7:42:40 (32,831)	
Lord, Jo	4:31:29 (19,962)	
Lord, Mary	5:08:55 (27,559)	
Louesdon, Maryvonne	4:38:31 (21,707)	
Loughlin, Gillian	3:54:27 (10,443)	
Loughran, Jill	4:55:02 (25,381)	
Louis, Guylyne	3:13:28 (2,501)	
Louis-Hodebar, Yannick	4:16:48 (16,064)	
Love, Chris	4:22:14 (17,459)	
Love, Nicola	4:59:38 (26,250)	
Lovell, Emily	4:50:57 (24,600)	
Lovell, Sally	3:51:05 (9,453)	
Loveridge, Trudie	4:32:00 (20,085)	
Lovesey, Jennifer	3:18:36 (3,083)	
Lovett, Saskia	4:56:19 (25,658)	
Low, Cheng Ee	5:34:28 (30,144)	
Lowe, Breesha	5:56:30 (31,423)	
Lowe, Helen	4:28:37 (19,205)	
Lowe, Rochelle	4:45:33 (23,454)	
Lowe, Sarah	4:28:37 (19,205)	
Lower, Mandy	5:29:34 (29,743)	
Lowes, Kim	4:44:59 (23,297)	
Lowndes, Sally	5:13:02 (28,085)	
Lowson, Maureen	4:12:23 (14,937)	
Lowthorpe, Michal	4:04:48 (13,160)	
Loynd, Natalie	5:33:36 (30,077)	
Lubbock, Lucy	4:52:12 (24,824)	
Lubbock, Tracey	5:11:06 (27,824)	
Lucas, Alison	5:01:03 (26,456)	
Lucas, Pauline	3:55:17 (10,687)	
Lucas, Sue	4:58:36 (26,055)	
Lucas, Suzanne	6:27:15 (32,228)	
Lueck-Wheeler, Jennifer	3:24:55 (3,975)	
Lueginger, Julia	5:10:09 (27,713)	
Luffman, Carolyn	4:53:55 (25,160)	
Lugton, Helen	3:51:32 (9,555)	
Luji Ross, Latifah	3:48:52 (8,859)	
Luke, Anne	3:09:59 (2,039)	
Luker, Katrina	5:25:13 (29,380)	
Lumb, Valerie	4:45:33 (23,454)	
Lumsden, Gro	4:31:28 (19,953)	
Lunnon, Jayne	4:26:03 (18,529)	
Lusignani, Nicola	5:16:41 (28,520)	
Luternauer-Harnett, Tanya	4:32:37 (20,251)	
Luton, Sophie	4:29:22 (19,424)	
Luxford, Katherine	3:58:50 (11,745)	
Luxton, Anne	5:42:50 (30,738)	
Lyden, Lorraine	5:07:12 (27,328)	
Lyle, Lucy	4:08:17 (13,969)	
Lynch, Kara	4:43:21 (22,919)	
Lynch, Katherine	4:53:03 (24,986)	
Lynch, Nichola	4:33:50 (20,541)	
Lynch, Sinead	3:49:16 (8,959)	
Lynch-Aird, Jeanne	4:57:54 (25,935)	
Lynton, Patricia	6:24:17 (32,170)	
Lyon, Anita	4:13:24 (15,167)	
Ma, Justina	3:51:41 (9,591)	
Maag, Barbara	4:41:35 (22,491)	
Maby, Julie	7:10:23 (32,704)	
Macaro, Paola	3:46:15 (8,211)	
MacAskill, Bronwyn	4:00:07 (12,113)	
MacCabe, Gillian	4:54:16 (25,236)	
Mac Cana, Liadan	4:31:02 (19,834)	
Maccariello, Bettina	3:43:48 (7,606)	
Macdonald, Davina	4:06:12 (13,494)	
Macdonald, Hazel	5:40:09 (30,559)	
Macdonald, Maria	4:26:50 (18,748)	
Macdonald, Patricia	4:52:32 (24,882)	
MacEchern, Tatianna	4:13:15 (15,134)	
MacGregor, Sylvia	6:20:04 (32,087)	
MacHale, Tania	3:41:34 (7,076)	
Machell, Ingrid	3:48:05 (8,646)	
MacInnes, Joy	3:46:30 (8,285)	
MacInnes, Louise	4:28:13 (19,088)	
MacInnes, Maureen	3:43:47 (7,601)	
MacIver Clark, Mairi	4:03:39 (12,909)	
Mack, Elizabeth	4:24:28 (18,110)	
Mack, Kathryn	4:21:49 (17,342)	
Mack, Lynda	3:56:19 (10,994)	
Mackay, Helen	5:10:25 (27,739)	
Mackay, Sharon	4:43:53 (23,036)	
MacKellow, Karen	5:32:27 (29,992)	
Mackenzie, Catherine	5:03:23 (26,809)	
Mackenzie, Delia	3:51:44 (9,603)	
Mackenzie, Henrietta	3:49:38 (9,078)	
Mackenzie, Jacqueline	4:14:10 (15,349)	
Mackenzie, Sylvia	4:47:46 (23,965)	
MacKeown, Stephanie	3:51:56 (9,657)	
Mackie, Anne	6:00:33 (31,561)	
Mackie, Jennifer	4:17:05 (16,139)	
Mackinney, Beccy	4:58:55 (26,115)	
Mackley, Veronica	3:35:34 (5,817)	
MacLachlan, Karina	4:20:18 (16,940)	
MacLannan, Ruth	4:22:52 (17,661)	
Maclean, Lorna	3:59:35 (11,962)	
Macleod, Rebecca	4:01:32 (12,452)	
Macleod-Smith, Anna	3:53:15 (10,061)	
MacLynn, Catherine	4:49:42 (24,361)	
MacLynn, Louise	4:49:44 (24,368)	
MacOvaghie, Diane	4:44:32 (23,184)	
Macpherson, Alyson	3:53:09 (10,030)	
Macpherson, Anna	4:26:20 (18,606)	
Madden, Carol	5:02:12 (26,628)	
Madden, Catherine	4:13:58 (15,301)	
Madden, Oonagh	4:48:42 (24,168)	
Madden, Sarah	6:01:47 (31,601)	
Maddock, Jayne	4:48:57 (24,226)	
Maddocks, Jan	5:14:24 (28,236)	
Madel, Lynne	4:59:57 (26,300)	
Madsen, Mia	4:09:08 (14,160)	
Maeda, Taeko	4:44:17 (23,128)	
Maggs, Julie	5:39:16 (30,486)	
Magnier, Katherine	4:50:11 (24,450)	
Maguire, Fiona	3:58:01 (11,517)	
Maguire, Frederica	6:35:18 (32,358)	
Maguire, Marie	5:30:41 (29,840)	
Maguire, Paula	4:54:03 (25,192)	
Mahal, Anita	5:27:12 (29,540)	
Mahobah, Lydia	3:55:42 (10,812)	
Maillard, Joan	5:23:28 (29,217)	
Maino, Pamela	4:55:53 (25,554)	
Maitland, Emma	5:48:34 (31,066)	
Maizey, Laren	3:56:02 (10,906)	
Major, Caroline	5:03:59 (26,887)	
Major, Pippa	3:06:30 (1,685)	
Makin, Laura	3:59:31 (11,942)	
Malard, Nadine	3:51:16 (9,493)	
Malcolm, Ann	4:22:49 (17,648)	
Malcolm, Judith	4:34:20 (20,654)	
Maleney, Catherine	4:28:53 (19,284)	
Malherbe, Christiane	4:39:11 (21,892)	
Malhotra, Surbhi	4:25:48 (18,462)	
Malik, Jasmin	6:05:12 (31,702)	
Malik, Yasmin	4:51:59 (24,782)	
Malkin, Jessica	4:40:51 (22,322)	
Mallery, Lynne	4:59:21 (26,186)	
Mallett, Zoe	6:30:03 (32,277)	
Mallin, Katharine	5:22:19 (29,121)	
Malone, Emily	3:39:24 (6,603)	
Malone, Julie	4:18:08 (16,394)	
Maltby, Diana	4:08:13 (13,954)	
Maltin, Lydie	3:32:00 (5,191)	
Mandausch, Luce	5:56:06 (31,407)	
Mander, Amy	4:19:52 (16,827)	
Manfield, Mary	5:47:53 (31,032)	
Manfield, Nicci	4:55:56 (25,572)	
Manly, Georgie	5:20:23 (28,926)	
Manly, Rita	3:23:27 (3,714)	
Mann, Catherine	5:38:39 (30,457)	
Mann, Elies	4:11:27 (14,733)	
Mann, Louisa	5:12:45 (28,051)	
Mann, Sally	4:38:45 (21,782)	
Mann-Heer, Pritpal	5:15:55 (28,431)	
Manning, Sharon	4:44:25 (23,154)	
Manning Benson, Samantha	3:51:18 (9,502)	
Manole, Monica	3:50:06 (9,190)	
Mansbridge, Christine	5:50:19 (31,154)	
Mansbridge, Rebecca	5:01:35 (26,542)	
Mansbridge, Sue	4:30:50 (19,793)	
Manser, Sonya	4:35:12 (20,881)	
Mansergh, Jane	5:02:20 (26,646)	
Mansfield, Lynn	3:44:54 (7,906)	
Mansie, Roseline	4:13:26 (15,173)	

McLaughlan, Louise 5:29:10 (29,707)
McLaughlin, Alison 5:03:11 (26,778)
McLaughlin, Anna 4:07:44 (13,850)
McLaughlin, Frances 3:23:32 (3,733)
McLaughlin, Sharon 4:12:01 (14,867)
McLay, Natalie 4:32:09 (20,129)
McLean, Jennifer 4:03:00 (12,775)
McLeod, Joanne 4:46:05 (23,589)
McLindon, Laura 3:24:45 (3,952)
McLoughlin, Sarah 3:12:57 (2,426)
McMahon, Patricia 5:20:03 (28,886)
McMahon Turner, Abigail 5:39:22 (30,500)
McMann, Jennifer 5:03:26 (26,815)
McManus, Claire 3:15:43 (2,758)
McManus, Leigh 4:51:40 (24,727)
McMaster, Katharine 5:37:17 (30,368)
McMenamin, Myra 4:11:55 (14,837)
McMillan, Carys 3:58:23 (11,614)
McMillan, Isobel 4:47:57 (24,022)
McMonagle, Jacqueline 4:17:54 (16,346)
McMorran, Cynthia 3:55:12 (10,663)
McMurtrie, Sarah 4:59:21 (26,186)
McNaney, Sarah 4:03:47 (12,936)
McNeillie, Janice 4:57:21 (25,833)
McNeilly, Angela 4:39:02 (21,854)
McNiece, Heidi 5:53:49 (31,306)
McPaul, Carol 3:48:22 (8,714)
McPherson, Beth 4:49:40 (24,355)
McPherson, Trish 4:39:25 (21,956)
McQuaid, Jennifer 6:05:59 (31,734)
McQueston, Eileen 5:26:47 (29,508)
McQuitty, Fiona 4:00:29 (12,184)
McRae, Isla 4:32:21 (20,173)
McRoberts, Morag 5:14:00 (28,195)
McSharry, Peta 4:19:11 (16,641)
McSporran, Mandy 8:49:24 (32,886)
McSweeney, Donna 5:00:10 (26,331)
McVeigh, Sheila 3:23:31 (3,729)
McVicker, Clare 4:39:38 (21,999)
McWhir, Celia 5:57:28 (31,455)
Meachem, Lisa 5:26:43 (29,504)
Mead, Ann 5:08:22 (27,478)
Mead, Helen 4:57:54 (25,935)
Mead, Sherrie 5:02:08 (26,619)
Meade, Natasha 4:26:00 (18,518)
Mears, Sarah 4:14:41 (15,493)
Meechan, Annie 4:28:34 (19,184)
Meek, Helen 5:06:22 (27,207)
Meheran, Lynda 3:50:26 (9,284)
Mehta, Susan 4:45:15 (23,371)
Meikle, Sally 4:41:56 (22,593)
Meldrum, Judy 4:49:03 (24,245)
Mellis, Susan 5:02:32 (26,674)
Mellodew, Anita 2:56:43 (889)
Mellotte, Louise 4:48:36 (24,147)
Melrose, Janis 5:56:28 (31,421)
Melrose, Maria 4:01:28 (12,430)
Melvin, Deirdre 4:59:06 (26,153)
Melvin, Helen 4:25:41 (18,436)
Menchenton, Erika 4:46:02 (23,579)
Mendelssohn, Jane 4:24:57 (18,242)
Mendham, Lorrain 4:15:05 (15,592)
Mendlow, Frances 5:21:07 (29,010)
Mendoza, Ruth 5:07:51 (27,414)
Mennen, Petronell 5:01:41 (26,559)
Menzies-Gow, Sarah 3:42:34 (7,302)
Menzies-Sacher, Rosemary 5:09:19 (27,608)
Merali, Lina 4:42:51 (22,801)
Mercer, Margaret 4:45:43 (23,497)
Mercer-Rees, Alixandra 4:19:19 (16,671)
Meredith, Catherine 4:45:26 (23,424)
Meredith, Jean 4:27:12 (18,841)
Merley, Jean 4:14:18 (15,391)
Merrill, Carol 3:52:15 (9,769)
Messenger, Amanda 4:33:06 (20,375)
Messerli-Gerhards, Daniela 2:55:20 (766)
Messinger, Kim 5:07:01 (27,300)
Meston, Niki 3:29:21 (4,766)
Metcalfe, Danae 4:40:31 (22,234)
Metcalfe, Margaret 3:44:34 (7,813)
Metcalfe, Rachel 4:22:15 (17,462)
Metherell, Claire 5:16:55 (28,545)
Metherll, Phillipa 4:23:42 (17,883)
Meyer, Hannelore 4:06:28 (13,558)
Meyer, Jennfer 4:00:33 (12,196)
Micco, Nicole 4:37:29 (21,445)
Michael, Thoraval 5:15:35 (28,380)
Michel, Louise 3:51:32 (9,555)
Michell, Rebecca 4:40:41 (22,270)
Michie, Rosemary 4:50:15 (24,458)
Mickley, Nita 3:37:20 (6,173)
Middlehurst, Susan 4:37:54 (21,547)
Middleman, Sharon 4:04:29 (13,085)
Middleton, Lisa 4:19:34 (16,741)
Middleton, Liz 5:08:41 (27,520)
Middleton, Sarah 5:19:16 (28,803)
Middlewick, Gillian 4:33:38 (20,500)
Midwood, Rachel 4:23:27 (17,814)
Migliorini, Gabriella 4:47:53 (24,002)
Mihara, Keiko 4:27:16 (18,856)
Milan, Lisa 3:47:23 (8,484)
Miles, Nicola 4:52:06 (24,800)
Miles, Rebecca 4:41:37 (22,507)
Miles, Ruth 3:23:27 (3,714)
Miles, Wendy 5:33:09 (30,041)
Millac, Sarah 3:24:01 (3,824)
Millar, Patricia 4:31:58 (20,075)
Millar, Philippa 6:13:40 (31,921)
Millar, Rowena 4:55:06 (25,391)
Millard, Lynette 4:48:15 (24,080)
Millen, Emma 4:32:26 (20,200)
Miller, Angie 5:05:49 (27,126)
Miller, Anne 4:23:42 (17,883)
Miller, Annette 5:17:03 (28,573)
Miller, Carol 3:26:49 (4,296)
Miller, Gabrielle 3:39:35 (6,643)
Miller, Heather 4:50:26 (24,491)
Miller, Janet 4:58:33 (26,041)
Miller, Joanna 4:42:41 (22,763)
Miller, Karen 4:58:19 (26,000)
Miller, Lisa 5:09:20 (27,612)
Miller, Melanie 4:23:07 (17,729)
Miller, Naomi 4:29:10 (19,373)
Miller, Rachel 4:55:37 (25,495)
Miller, Sharon 8:14:53 (32,870)
Miller, Shawna 4:22:15 (17,462)
Miller, Sheryn 3:51:55 (9,655)
Miller, Stephanie 3:45:43 (8,094)
Miller-Wright, Deborah 4:21:39 (17,297)
Millet, Evelyne 4:17:39 (16,280)
Milligan, Elaine 4:53:58 (25,179)
Millin, Amanda 6:40:31 (32,439)
Millin, Rosemary 6:40:31 (32,439)
Millington, Hazel 4:59:17 (26,172)
Mills, Alexandra 3:36:10 (5,953)
Mills, Annette 4:13:57 (15,297)
Mills, Carol 4:23:22 (17,791)
Mills, Cynthia 5:43:36 (30,789)
Mills, Deirdre 6:05:06 (31,696)
Mills, Eleanor 5:22:50 (29,160)
Mills, Helen 5:29:36 (29,748)
Mills, Jacqueline 4:05:36 (13,348)
Mills, Jane 3:58:54 (11,764)
Mills, Marie 5:13:32 (28,144)
Milne, Anne 4:58:52 (26,110)
Milne, Claire 4:41:16 (22,418)
Milne, Linda 5:45:09 (30,889)
Milner, Charlotte 4:09:38 (14,300)
Milner, Janine 5:18:54 (28,766)
Milton, Alison 3:45:57 (8,148)
Mincher, Lynsey 5:17:43 (28,641)
Mindelsohn, Katie 5:21:33 (29,045)
Mindenhall, Lucinda 4:23:11 (17,747)
Minford, Louise 4:05:11 (13,248)
Minty, Joan 4:12:53 (15,058)
Miramontes, Sara 3:48:10 (8,665)
Mirams, M. 4:43:06 (22,865)
Mistry, Manisha 4:53:18 (25,024)
Mitchard, Sheila 5:17:22 (28,613)
Mitchell, Adele 4:33:23 (20,438)
Mitchell, Annie 5:45:07 (30,887)
Mitchell, Avril 4:30:37 (19,737)
Mitchell, Catherine 5:07:13 (27,335)
Mitchell, Clare 3:52:39 (9,881)
Mitchell, Donna 5:05:19 (27,065)
Mitchell, Elaine 4:01:19 (12,396)
Mitchell, Heather 3:50:40 (9,338)
Mitchell, Joanne 3:56:48 (11,144)
Mitchell, Judith 5:46:26 (30,959)
Mitchell, Kate 5:28:21 (29,643)
Mitchell, Kay 3:27:24 (4,399)
Mitchell, Libby 3:52:05 (9,715)
Mitchell, Marian 6:16:14 (31,995)
Mitchell, Marion 6:43:11 (32,463)
Mitchell, Natalie 3:55:24 (10,721)
Mitchell, Natasha 6:27:07 (32,219)
Mitchell, Pamela 5:48:47 (31,078)
Mitchell, Rebecca 4:16:07 (15,870)
Mitchell, Tracey 4:04:05 (13,005)
Mitchell, Tricia 5:05:30 (27,084)
Mitten, Denise 4:44:30 (23,172)
Mizen, Angela 4:17:14 (16,179)
Moeljadi, Christine 4:36:37 (21,244)
Moffett, Jennifer 4:27:09 (18,832)
Moisson, Sabine 4:05:33 (13,341)
Mokra, Joanna 5:29:05 (29,701)
Mollin, Stefanie 4:04:40 (13,127)
Molloy, Sarah 4:46:21 (23,652)
Moloney, Claire 4:30:46 (19,776)
Molyneux, Anne 3:31:50 (5,170)
Monahan, Irene 6:08:29 (31,800)
Monk, Emma 4:22:58 (17,696)
Monk, Margarett 4:04:13 (13,032)
Monks, Amanda 4:43:49 (23,022)
Montague, Ruth 4:34:51 (20,791)
Montalto, Annabel 3:58:31 (11,654)
Montgomery, Alison 5:00:48 (26,421)
Montgomery, Joanne 4:44:28 (23,162)
Montgomery Miller, Juliana 4:37:09 (21,348)
Montwill, Jacqueline 7:20:13 (32,755)
Monza, Carol 4:01:28 (12,430)
Moody, Alison 5:26:58 (29,520)
Moolman, Sandi 3:36:26 (6,012)
Moon, Clare 4:32:55 (20,339)
Moon, Gillian 5:40:52 (30,604)
Mooney, Carole 3:28:32 (4,613)
Mooney, Mary 4:38:56 (21,827)
Mooney, Nicola 3:55:33 (10,767)
Moorcroft, Fiona 4:16:00 (15,839)
Moore, Debbie 4:29:52 (19,560)
Moore, Debbie 5:01:31 (26,527)
Moore, Elaine 5:30:36 (29,832)
Moore, Helen 5:28:32 (29,657)
Moore, Jessica 3:47:49 (8,591)
Moore, Kate 4:05:40 (13,362)
Moore, Louise 5:22:40 (29,149)
Moore, Maria 3:30:38 (4,969)
Moore, Nancy 5:37:17 (30,368)
Moore, Natasha 5:30:12 (29,799)
Moore, Sacha 5:19:58 (28,872)
Moore, Suki 5:13:25 (28,127)
Moores-Coram, Glynis 5:17:00 (28,557)
Moorhouse, Karen 4:27:19 (18,869)
Morales, Rebecca 4:34:55 (20,807)
Moran, Abigail 5:09:25 (27,624)
Moran, first name unknown 4:13:38 (15,213)
Moran, Sharon 6:17:03 (32,004)
Morck, Lotta 4:13:46 (15,256)
Moreau, Linda 3:16:47 (2,878)
Morecroft, Debbie 4:10:01 (14,389)
More-Molyneux, Katrina 5:09:03 (27,576)
Moreton, Amanda 3:31:39 (5,139)
Moreton, Esther 5:18:14 (28,695)
Moreton, Penny 4:48:14 (24,076)
Moretta, Nicola 4:51:10 (24,643)
Morgan, Alison 4:30:15 (19,662)
Morgan, Becky 5:21:25 (29,037)
Morgan, Carys 4:27:02 (18,798)
Morgan, Clare 4:08:31 (14,027)
Morgan, Cressida 4:15:45 (15,769)
Morgan, Edwina 6:01:32 (31,591)
Morgan, Gail 4:34:39 (20,739)
Morgan, Helen 4:23:37 (17,851)
Morgan, Helen 4:51:40 (24,727)
Morgan, Hilary 5:00:25 (26,360)
Morgan, Karen 4:31:28 (19,953)
Morgan, Kathyrn 5:43:11 (30,767)
Morgan, Mary 5:43:04 (30,759)
Morgan, Melanie 4:57:33 (25,872)

Morgan, Michelle....4:09:52 (14,355)
Morgan, Nicola....5:07:12 (27,328)
Morgan, Philippa....5:00:39 (26,401)
Morgan, Rachel....4:40:07 (22,140)
Morgan, Tamsyn....4:23:37 (17,851)
Morgan, Tracey....3:14:49 (2,641)
Moriarty, Louise....3:56:44 (11,117)
Morley, Jo....4:13:03 (15,095)
Morrell, Elizabeth....3:26:26 (4,217)
Morrell-Glenister, Diana....6:31:42 (32,301)
Morrewski, Karen....5:24:25 (29,317)
Morrin, Gillian....5:06:28 (27,228)
Morris, Alison....5:32:36 (30,000)
Morris, Anne....5:21:37 (29,058)
Morris, Cheryl....4:21:49 (17,342)
Morris, Deborah....4:38:51 (21,808)
Morris, Emma....4:50:52 (24,586)
Morris, Esther....4:08:49 (14,094)
Morris, Helen....3:42:52 (7,353)
Morris, Jennifer....4:06:59 (13,674)
Morris, Jennifer....4:55:55 (25,567)
Morris, Kelly....4:06:38 (13,596)
Morris, Linda....3:55:47 (10,835)
Morris, Maggie....4:24:31 (18,124)
Morris, Patricia....6:06:58 (31,761)
Morris, Tessa....4:51:32 (24,707)
Morrison, Angela....3:17:43 (2,979)
Morrison, Carol....4:24:41 (18,167)
Morrison, Jane....3:30:33 (4,952)
Morrissey, Clare....5:20:43 (28,963)
Morse, Marie....4:38:15 (21,642)
Mortimer, Sandra....4:49:13 (24,278)
Mortimer, Susan....5:08:45 (27,530)
Mortimer-Ford, Zoe....4:26:41 (18,714)
Morton, Susanne....3:24:08 (3,844)
Mosley, Helen....5:09:51 (27,677)
Moss, Alicia....5:23:12 (29,194)
Moss, Amanda....4:33:42 (20,517)
Moss, Caroline....3:21:41 (3,460)
Moss, Dena....5:02:22 (26,649)
Moss, Kim....4:22:06 (17,424)
Moss, Nicky....4:31:04 (19,844)
Mossberg, Helene....3:45:03 (7,940)
Mostyn, Alison....5:35:25 (30,216)
Mothersille, Sheryl....6:53:26 (32,576)
Motley, Hilary....4:42:19 (22,675)
Motley, Margaret....4:26:20 (18,606)
Motley, Michaleen....4:14:46 (15,517)

Mott, Paula....4:58:16 (25,992)

I ran the London Marathon in 2002 in memory of my brother, Ben Thorn. He had died suddenly in his sleep only 7 months before. He was 24 years old. I chose to support the charity Cardiac Risk in the Young and ran in a giant foam heart. It was a warm, spring day, made warmer by my cumbersome costume. The crowd support was incredible and it was great to see my family supporting me around the course. I found the run very difficult, emotionally and physically but I was determined to finish. The elation of crossing the finishing line was tarnished with the injustice I felt from losing my brother. I managed to raise about £5,000 in total for CRY, and I feel proud of my achievement.

Mottram, Joanne....4:36:34 (21,238)
Mottram, Rachel....4:46:44 (23,742)
Mottram, Virgina....4:18:59 (16,584)
Moullin, Alison....7:17:00 (32,744)
Moulton, Elaine....5:24:35 (29,334)
Mountford, Angela....4:59:36 (26,243)
Mounty, Maureen....4:34:35 (20,719)
Mouradian, Jackie....3:44:07 (7,683)
Mourisse, Silvie....4:51:27 (24,692)
Mowbray, Donna....7:01:23 (32,640)
Mowle, Linda....4:46:45 (23,747)
Moxham, Justine....4:31:48 (20,031)
Moxon, Elizabeth....3:49:58 (9,167)
Moyle, Camilla....3:43:18 (7,480)
Mozley, Hannah....5:06:10 (27,184)
Muckenfuss, Hedwig....4:11:44 (14,801)
Muenster, Julia....4:53:46 (25,117)
Muggleton, Dawn....3:52:19 (9,785)
Muirhead, Sarah....4:27:54 (19,009)
Muldoon, Sterrin....4:13:25 (15,170)
Mulholland, Louise....4:28:07 (19,058)
Muller, Zoe....3:59:41 (11,989)
Mulqueen, Katharine....4:54:08 (25,208)
Mulryne, Ruth....5:13:59 (28,188)
Mulvenna, Claire....5:55:40 (31,387)
Mumby, Benita....6:52:36 (32,563)
Munday, Cheryl....4:24:01 (17,985)
Munday, Sarah....4:58:16 (25,992)
Munnelly, Tora....3:31:18 (5,077)
Munnings, Sarah....5:07:24 (27,357)
Munoz, Gabriela....4:05:46 (13,386)
Murch, Jennifer....4:47:42 (23,955)
Murdoch, Helen....4:47:45 (23,961)
Murdoch, Jane....3:25:50 (4,121)
Murland, Alexandra....3:38:38 (6,459)
Murphy, Angela....5:02:40 (26,695)
Murphy, Bernadette....4:23:07 (17,729)
Murphy, Beth....3:46:47 (8,339)
Murphy, Bridget....5:01:07 (26,467)
Murphy, Chris....5:05:23 (27,075)
Murphy, Diane....7:12:47 (32,722)
Murphy, Edel....4:34:27 (20,682)
Murphy, Helen....4:07:33 (13,808)
Murphy, Marisa....4:48:54 (24,216)
Murphy, Michelle....4:10:46 (14,566)
Murphy, Michelle....4:58:57 (26,121)
Murphy, Patricia....4:54:02 (25,188)
Murphy, Penny....4:58:01 (25,951)
Murphy, Samantha....3:42:52 (7,353)
Murray, Alison....6:28:05 (32,241)
Murray, Angela....3:29:55 (4,860)
Murray, Anne....4:42:31 (22,730)
Murray, Louise....6:27:28 (32,234)
Murray, Sandra....4:38:33 (21,720)
Murray, Valerie....5:33:27 (30,069)
Murrell, Sue....5:05:18 (27,062)
Musgrave, Gill....4:33:47 (20,534)
Musgrave, Kathryn....4:36:02 (21,088)
Mussell, Christine....5:18:18 (28,701)
Musson, Sally....3:13:42 (2,532)
Myatt, Julia....3:07:02 (1,739)
Mycroft, Elizabeth....2:49:36 (467)
Mycroft, Nicola....4:31:37 (19,996)
Myers, Brenda....4:20:44 (17,053)
Myers, Jenny....4:20:33 (17,006)
Myerscough, Lindsey....5:02:56 (26,730)
Naden, Isobel....6:22:14 (32,129)
Nadin, Louise....4:39:05 (21,869)
Nairn, Janet....4:15:42 (15,755)
Nance, Sharron....6:21:13 (32,113)
Nankivell, Cathryn....3:42:53 (7,358)
Napier, Susan....6:21:06 (32,108)
Naquin, Christine....4:47:07 (23,834)
Nasehi, Kereshmeh....5:52:47 (31,267)
Nash, Joanna....3:59:22 (11,906)
Nathan, Linda....6:11:53 (31,880)
Nau, Susanne....3:53:19 (10,086)
Naude, Debbie....4:28:05 (19,051)
Naude, Susan....5:02:19 (26,643)
Naylor, Catherine....4:57:33 (25,872)
Neal, Belinda....4:25:29 (18,381)
Neal, Jennifer....6:17:38 (32,024)
Neal, Sharon....6:20:51 (32,100)

Neal, Susan....4:03:17 (12,835)
Neale, Caroline....4:36:32 (21,231)
Neale, Rebecca....4:46:59 (23,806)
Nedza, Alyson....4:21:31 (17,255)
Needley, Dorothy....4:53:38 (25,092)
Neenan, Jacqueline....4:42:01 (22,610)
Negre-Wolneringer, Muriel....4:34:34 (20,714)
Neill, Judy....3:44:47 (7,884)
Neilson, Carolyn....4:54:42 (25,323)
Nell, Madre....4:25:46 (18,454)
Nelson, Mary....4:00:43 (12,233)
Nelson, Paula....4:24:23 (18,087)
Nerinckx, Christel....3:39:03 (6,537)
Nerurkar, Gail....3:15:08 (2,681)
Neubauer, Britta....4:30:44 (19,770)
Neve, Caroline....5:37:03 (30,352)
Neville, Dominique....5:17:54 (28,662)
Nevin, Catherine....3:22:26 (3,574)
Nevin, Joan....5:23:06 (29,185)
Newark, Kim....3:49:56 (9,158)
Newborough, Kathryn....4:41:15 (22,413)
Newbould, Nicola....5:33:02 (30,026)
Newbury, Christine....5:29:49 (29,765)
Newbury, Joanne....4:04:41 (13,132)
Newby, Deborah....3:52:36 (9,870)
Newcomb, Helen....3:42:47 (7,339)
Newell, Claire....4:29:52 (19,560)
Newill, Karen....5:56:44 (31,433)
Newlands, Ellie....5:14:34 (28,255)
Newman, Angela....6:28:54 (32,256)
Newman, Annette....4:56:28 (25,687)
Newman, Clare....3:32:08 (5,211)
Newman, Gill....3:53:58 (10,299)
Newman, Rebecca....3:49:07 (8,928)
Newman, Tracey....5:18:02 (28,676)
Newman, Victoria....4:23:33 (17,838)
Newstead, Johanne....4:49:48 (24,380)
Newton, Andrea....4:02:07 (12,583)
Newton, Jenni....3:21:20 (3,411)
Newton, Julie....6:25:21 (32,190)
Newton, Rebecca....4:56:55 (25,749)
Newton, Sarah....3:17:13 (2,922)
Nias, Helen....8:08:22 (32,867)
Nice, Lorraine....5:22:28 (29,129)
Nichol, Dianne....3:49:24 (9,005)
Nichol, Melanie....3:49:07 (8,928)
Nicholls, Karen....4:29:28 (19,452)
Nicholls, Sally....5:21:49 (29,079)
Nicholls, Sarah....3:15:59 (2,785)
Nichols, Florence....6:00:23 (31,556)
Nichols, Maggie....4:15:22 (15,657)
Nicholson, Tracey....5:46:05 (30,938)
Nickson, Nathalie....4:04:55 (13,189)
Nicol, Eileen....3:38:31 (6,429)
Nicoll, Carole....3:55:09 (10,650)
Nicoll, Catherine....5:35:54 (30,261)
Nicoll, Katherine....6:54:18 (32,584)
Nielsen, Annelise....4:28:26 (19,152)
Nielsen, Lindsay....4:50:26 (24,491)
Nilola, Georgina....5:19:59 (28,877)
Nippard, Janet....4:08:09 (13,941)
Nitsch, Janina....3:58:34 (11,664)
Noble, Claire....4:36:14 (21,136)
Noble, Eileen....4:59:18 (26,179)
Noble, Lucy....4:42:41 (22,763)
Noble, Sally....4:35:35 (20,982)
Nobles, Margaret....4:32:49 (20,306)
Noblet, Fiona....4:16:18 (15,913)
Nock, Tracey....4:18:08 (16,394)
Noden, Cindy....5:21:58 (29,091)
Noghani, Angela....4:38:58 (21,834)
Noher, Angelique....4:25:59 (18,513)
Nokes, Stephanie....4:43:26 (22,940)
Nolan, Kathleen....3:52:05 (9,715)
Nolan, Sheila....3:52:05 (9,715)
Norbury, Clare....4:59:50 (26,279)
Nordin, Breege....3:28:17 (4,565)
Nordlun, Birgitta....4:57:13 (25,813)
Nordqvist, Cecilia....4:17:47 (16,325)
Norgett, Elizabeth....4:47:50 (23,986)
Norlyk-Goulding, Bente....4:47:18 (23,877)
Norman, Julie....4:01:21 (12,407)
Norman, Katie....5:35:37 (30,243)

Norris, Allison	3:44:44 (7,867)	
Norris, Angela	3:38:40 (6,468)	
Norris, Christine	4:40:10 (22,150)	
Norris, Helen	4:36:07 (21,106)	
Norris, Kim	4:01:11 (12,361)	
Norris, Patricia	4:48:28 (24,118)	
Norris, Tracy	4:24:57 (18,242)	
North, Alison	4:37:33 (21,456)	
North, Carol	3:52:49 (9,929)	
North, Lisa	3:37:11 (6,146)	
North, Margaret	5:36:40 (30,326)	
North, Sheila	7:19:25 (32,753)	
Northcott, Jennifer	4:22:06 (17,424)	
Norton, Deborah	4:40:23 (22,209)	
Norton, Vivienne	5:32:15 (29,974)	
Notley, Joanna	5:09:35 (27,644)	
Noury, Ana	3:15:10 (2,684)	
Novacek, Sabine	4:47:01 (23,815)	
Novak, Pamela	4:39:13 (21,905)	
Novle, Kate	5:17:59 (28,666)	
Nowacki, Lee	4:23:25 (17,806)	
Nowell, Lucille	5:32:14 (29,972)	
Nowell, Stella	4:31:04 (19,844)	
Nuernberg, Maria	3:30:53 (5,006)	
Nunn, Gill	3:58:06 (11,544)	
Nunn, Leigh-Ann	4:39:42 (22,026)	
Nutt, Joanna	4:51:17 (24,665)	
Nutting, Judy	3:22:14 (3,557)	
Nyman, Britt	4:38:43 (21,768)	
Oakes, Kathleen	5:24:30 (29,325)	
Oakley, Carolyn	4:22:48 (17,639)	
Oakley, Katrina	4:58:39 (26,067)	
Oatts, Elizabeth	3:46:01 (8,163)	
Oberkofler, Monica	4:53:27 (25,057)	
Oborn, Rachael	5:56:41 (31,428)	
O'Brien, Della	5:54:45 (31,340)	
O'Brien, Jane	5:12:42 (28,047)	
O'Brien, Jo	3:22:40 (3,602)	
O'Brien, Julia	5:03:04 (26,755)	
O'Brien, Kathleen	6:53:08 (32,569)	
O'Bryan, Louisa	4:16:25 (15,956)	
O'Callaghan, Christine	5:13:22 (28,122)	
Ochiltree, Elaine	5:25:38 (29,415)	
Ochiltree, Lorna	4:31:47 (20,028)	
O'Connell, Joanne	4:44:53 (23,266)	
O'Connor, Aine	5:51:09 (31,192)	
O'Connor, Gill	3:00:24 (1,197)	
O'Connor, Helen	4:15:24 (15,665)	
O'Connor, Jacinta	5:19:56 (28,867)	
O'Connor, Melanie	5:20:07 (28,892)	
O'Connor, Sue	3:55:24 (10,721)	
O'Connor, Susie	4:33:41 (20,513)	
O'Connor, Theresa	6:24:25 (32,175)	
O'Daly, Imogen	5:27:01 (29,523)	
Odams, Suzanne	5:21:51 (29,083)	
Odbratt, Annette	4:39:25 (21,956)	
O'Donnell, Christine	3:57:24 (11,325)	
O'Donnell, Renata	4:55:21 (25,447)	
O'Donovan, Fiona	4:17:16 (16,192)	
O'Dowd, Joanne	3:24:00 (3,820)	
O'Dwyer, Maureen	6:09:59 (31,841)	
O'Farrell, Elizabeth	4:57:44 (25,904)	
Offer, Caroline	4:57:47 (25,914)	
Offredi, Doreen	5:43:07 (30,764)	
Ogden, Corinne	6:25:13 (32,185)	
Ogden, Diane	4:29:19 (19,416)	
Ogden, Karen	4:49:06 (24,261)	
Ogden, Louise	5:58:21 (31,490)	
Ogilvie, Catherine	7:24:16 (32,766)	
O'Gorman, Sinead	4:31:49 (20,035)	
O'Hagan, Collette	5:12:58 (28,077)	
O'Hara, Pauline	5:14:14 (28,216)	
O'Hare, Emily	4:19:27 (16,708)	
Ojugo, Sarah Jane	9:10:01 (32,895)	
O'Kane, Anne	5:42:43 (30,734)	
O'Kane, Karen	4:01:10 (12,356)	
O'Keefe, Patricia	3:38:01 (6,316)	
O'Keeffe, Natalie	5:19:46 (28,847)	
Okine, Priscilla	4:22:47 (17,631)	
Olafsdottir, Lilja	4:08:57 (14,121)	
Olcer, Sibel	6:22:11 (32,128)	
Oldfield, Julie	4:55:39 (25,504)	
Oldham, Nicola	3:55:56 (10,882)	

O'Leary, Cornelia	6:01:32 (31,591)	
O'Leary, Louise	6:29:58 (32,275)	
O'Leary, Tracy	4:10:30 (14,510)	
Olhfsoottir, Helga	3:57:49 (11,455)	
Oliver, Catherine	4:27:50 (18,992)	
Ollerenshaw, Cherry	5:27:13 (29,541)	
Olley, Katherine	5:23:35 (29,233)	
Ollivier, Louise	3:43:07 (7,418)	
Olney, Dita	4:09:47 (14,336)	
Ologunro, Charlotte	3:47:42 (8,562)	
Olsen, Gitte	6:00:13 (31,551)	
Olsen, Pia	6:24:23 (32,174)	
O'Mahony, Jane	4:14:28 (15,445)	
O'Mahony, Teresa	4:38:21 (21,672)	
Ombler, Sharon	4:28:02 (19,043)	
Omerod, Jean	6:15:22 (31,965)	
O'Neill, Grainne	4:19:58 (16,852)	
O'Neill, Helen	4:42:10 (22,642)	
O'Neill, Janet	6:51:58 (32,559)	
O'Neill, Jenny	5:16:36 (28,511)	
O'Neill, Natalie	4:24:38 (18,154)	
Opara, Semirah	3:18:44 (3,103)	
Orban, Mary	3:49:03 (8,912)	
Ord, Louise	6:15:26 (31,967)	
O'Regan, Catherine	3:53:05 (10,013)	
O'Regan, Davina	3:48:56 (8,875)	
O'Regan-Reidy, Susan	7:07:56 (32,685)	
O'Reilly, Debra	4:57:04 (25,782)	
O'Reilly, Jane	4:34:06 (20,608)	
O'Reilly, Pauline	4:26:30 (18,653)	
Orford, Jennifer	4:58:06 (25,964)	
O'Rourke, Janet	5:51:14 (31,197)	
O'Rourke, Sandra	5:52:26 (31,248)	
Orpin, Janet	5:20:15 (28,909)	
Orr, Jenny	4:03:33 (12,890)	
Orr, Pearl	4:01:42 (12,493)	
Orth, Barbara	3:39:48 (6,686)	
Ortstad, Jenny	4:46:46 (23,750)	
Osborn, Jodie	7:09:10 (32,698)	
Osborn, Stephanie	5:00:00 (26,310)	
Osborn, Teresa	5:00:47 (26,420)	
Osborne, Janette	4:08:10 (13,943)	
O'Shea, Hilary	4:40:12 (22,159)	
O'Shea, Bettina	5:24:19 (29,309)	
Oshisanya, Dola	6:03:10 (31,644)	
Osmond, Kerry	4:35:56 (21,063)	
Osowska, Francesca	3:29:47 (4,840)	
Osterjerhuus, Anette	4:25:58 (18,510)	
O'Sullivan, Katy	4:21:53 (17,363)	
O'Sullivan, Kira	4:02:44 (12,709)	
O'Sullivan, Monica	4:59:22 (26,190)	
O'Sullivan, Rhonda	6:42:45 (32,454)	
O'Sullivan, Susan	5:39:48 (30,536)	
Oswald, Claire	5:22:37 (29,142)	
Oswald, Julie	4:36:27 (21,200)	
Oswin, Linda	4:14:44 (15,508)	
Ottaway, Julia	6:43:23 (32,469)	
Oudendijk, Mari	3:52:53 (9,945)	
Outram, Kathryn	5:03:52 (26,868)	
Ovens, Janet	3:41:23 (7,043)	
Overson, Victoria	5:39:54 (30,541)	
Overy, Nicolette	3:52:33 (9,858)	
Owen, Dianne	5:15:12 (28,324)	
Owen, Emma	3:59:41 (11,989)	
Owen, Fleur	5:39:50 (30,537)	
Owen, Helen	5:30:08 (29,794)	
Owen, Joanne	6:19:54 (32,080)	
Owen, Rachel	3:59:58 (12,076)	
Owen, Rhian	4:50:36 (24,524)	
Owen, Sue	6:33:41 (32,335)	
Owen, Susan	4:37:14 (21,380)	
Owens, Christine	5:12:55 (28,071)	
Owers, Gillian	4:10:30 (14,510)	
Oxley, Victoria	4:45:31 (23,446)	
Oxton, Margaret	4:32:17 (20,157)	
Oyemade, Kemi	4:46:19 (23,639)	
Oyre, Tamara	3:52:27 (9,823)	
Ozanne, Rachel	4:21:31 (17,255)	
Ozanne, Sally-Ann	4:50:57 (24,600)	
Pacheco, Beth	4:42:35 (22,744)	
Paczer, Rebekah	4:17:59 (16,368)	
Padmore, Jacqueline	4:45:26 (23,424)	
Pagan, Carol	3:11:20 (2,188)	

Page, Andrea	4:48:03 (24,047)	
Page, Anna	4:49:46 (24,372)	
Page, Anna	5:21:10 (29,016)	
Page, Joy	7:13:05 (32,725)	
Page, Julie	4:58:51 (26,107)	
Page, Louise	4:29:27 (19,449)	
Page, Susan	4:30:41 (19,752)	
Paget, Janice	4:44:15 (23,115)	
Pahlsson, Anna	6:19:21 (32,065)	
Pain, Ruth	4:32:17 (20,157)	
Paine, Doreen	4:33:52 (20,551)	
Painter, Penelope	4:38:10 (21,616)	
Paisley-Chisholm, Carol	6:17:54 (32,033)	
Pakenham, Johanna	5:38:22 (30,435)	
Pakenham-Walsh, Tara	3:56:18 (10,989)	
Pakes, Kirsten	4:53:30 (25,068)	
Paley, Pauline	5:56:17 (31,411)	
Pallister, Deborah	5:18:00 (28,668)	
Palm, Carolyn	5:04:02 (26,893)	
Palmer, Alexandra	6:17:53 (32,030)	
Palmer, Ann	5:55:00 (31,350)	
Palmer, Anna	4:19:34 (16,741)	
Palmer, Carol	5:12:53 (28,065)	
Palmer, Fiona	5:10:25 (27,739)	
Palmer, Janice	3:33:55 (5,502)	
Palmer, Jean	4:40:05 (22,129)	
Palmer, Judith	4:56:05 (25,601)	
Palmer, Julia	3:27:48 (4,480)	
Palmer, Marion	5:25:25 (29,397)	
Palmer, Mary	4:44:53 (23,266)	
Palmer, Olivia	5:32:23 (29,987)	
Palmer, Sarah	5:39:37 (30,524)	
Palmer, Susan	5:03:45 (26,850)	
Palmer, Vicky	6:25:55 (32,199)	
Pamplin, Diane	3:44:29 (7,791)	
Panayiotou, Athena	5:46:14 (30,950)	
Pannell, Sarah	4:31:20 (19,912)	
Papougnot, Sophie	5:47:24 (31,010)	
Papworth, Annette	4:47:09 (23,847)	
Papworth, Lisa	5:31:45 (29,931)	
Pare, Mona	3:53:04 (10,003)	
Parfitt, Dena	3:48:51 (8,853)	
Park, Jacqueline	6:03:21 (31,648)	
Parke, Kay	4:58:17 (25,997)	
Parker, Beverley	4:47:08 (23,840)	
Parker, Carmel	3:52:14 (9,762)	
Parker, Daz	3:45:28 (8,034)	
Parker, Eleanor	4:55:14 (25,427)	
Parker, Jill	3:27:19 (4,379)	
Parker, Kim	4:28:29 (19,166)	
Parker, Kristina	5:44:01 (30,821)	
Parker, Lucy	4:40:16 (22,174)	
Parker, Patricia	3:34:51 (5,682)	
Parker, Sally	4:38:25 (21,689)	
Parker, Tessa	4:08:32 (14,036)	
Parkes, Karen	5:47:54 (31,034)	
Parkes, Penelope	5:11:57 (27,945)	
Parkin, Juliette	3:52:57 (9,960)	
Parkin, Samantha	4:04:27 (13,078)	
Parkinson, Joanne	3:58:34 (11,664)	
Parkinson, Michelle	5:20:29 (28,937)	
Parkinson, Nicola	4:24:06 (18,011)	
Parlett, Alyson	3:08:36 (1,881)	
Parmee, Jacqueline	4:18:35 (16,506)	
Parnell, Marilyn	5:52:00 (31,234)	
Parnham, Gayle	4:12:36 (15,000)	
Parr, Laura	4:28:49 (19,261)	
Parratt, Lesley	6:59:37 (32,623)	
Parris, Eva	3:14:45 (2,634)	
Parrott, Moira	5:20:53 (28,982)	
Parry, Clare	4:48:34 (24,141)	
Parry, Helen	4:35:03 (20,844)	
Parry, Rachel	3:50:37 (9,327)	
Parry-Jones MBE, Jemima	5:50:33 (31,164)	
Parsons, Alison	4:22:03 (17,412)	
Parsons, Connie	5:34:15 (30,129)	
Parsons, Joanne	5:55:32 (31,379)	
Parsons, Julie	3:58:11 (11,564)	
Parsons, Lucy	4:01:33 (12,457)	
Parsons, Naomi	3:30:02 (4,878)	
Parsons, Norah	5:22:14 (29,110)	
Parsons, Victoria	5:25:37 (29,413)	
Partington, Nicole	4:41:09 (22,389)	

Parton, Lynne 4:29:57 (19,584)
Partridge, Isobel 3:18:17 (3,042)
Partridge, Jenny 3:57:58 (11,496)
Parveen, Roseena 6:14:20 (31,937)
Pascall-Toppin, Julietta 4:59:00 (26,130)
Pascoe, Angela 5:06:16 (27,195)
Pasian, Alessandra 3:58:56 (11,772)
Pasquale, Alison 8:09:02 (32,868)
Pasquini, Annamaria 4:34:56 (20,814)
Passingham, Charlotte 4:52:33 (24,893)
Passot, Murielle 4:51:16 (24,662)
Passway, Tracey 3:31:26 (5,098)
Pastorino, Jodi 5:45:18 (30,901)
Pate, Karen 3:49:25 (9,014)
Patel, Dimple 4:32:44 (20,286)
Patel, Heena 5:16:35 (28,509)
Patel, Ninan 5:51:14 (31,197)
Patel, Parul 4:59:19 (26,181)
Patel, Priya 7:24:58 (32,769)
Patel, Roshni 4:35:47 (21,025)
Patel, Swati 6:59:55 (32,625)
Paterson, Elaine 4:22:00 (17,393)
Paterson, Gail 4:27:02 (18,798)
Paterson, Hazel 3:53:39 (10,197)
Paterson, Samantha 5:10:11 (27,715)
Paterson, Sarah 7:55:00 (32,854)
Paterson, Shona 3:54:38 (10,494)
Patmore, Caroline 5:19:43 (28,841)
Paton, Gloria 5:31:14 (29,890)
Paton, Linda 4:43:29 (22,958)
Paton, Naomi 3:52:14 (9,762)
Patrick, Julie 4:15:09 (15,604)
Patrick, Linda 7:14:18 (32,731)
Patterson, Rachel 4:44:32 (23,184)
Pattison, Janine 3:49:09 (8,934)
Patton, Teresa 4:53:40 (25,097)
Paul, Carol 4:31:28 (19,953)
Paul, Georgina 6:43:15 (32,467)
Paul, Sally 4:48:02 (24,041)
Paul, Sally 4:57:34 (25,875)
Paull, Charlotte 4:39:11 (21,892)
Pauzers, Clare 2:49:24 (462)
Pawley, Claire 6:31:43 (32,302)
Pawley, Kate 5:12:13 (27,975)
Pay, Claire 5:42:54 (30,750)
Payne, Claire 3:31:06 (5,049)
Payne, Daphne 5:05:03 (27,029)
Payne, Gisela 3:16:48 (2,881)
Payne, Julie 3:45:02 (7,933)
Payne, Karen 3:54:10 (10,366)
Payne, Kathleen 4:30:44 (19,770)
Payne, Stephanie 7:10:24 (32,705)
Payton, Susan 3:58:59 (11,796)
Peace, Heather 4:26:38 (18,696)
Peace, Sevita 5:01:05 (26,462)
Peacock, Claire 3:16:49 (2,883)
Peacock, Jenny 6:20:06 (32,090)
Peacock, Michelle 5:25:39 (29,416)
Peacock, Philippa 5:31:08 (29,882)
Pead, Vikki 5:08:08 (27,445)
Peagram, Rebecca 4:35:33 (20,960)
Peapell, Elizabeth 4:10:52 (14,597)
Pearce, Ann 4:46:01 (23,569)
Pearce, Beverley 5:14:27 (28,239)
Pearce, Deborah 4:29:07 (19,354)
Pearce, Ellen 5:05:21 (27,071)
Pearce, Janie 3:35:31 (5,807)
Pearce, Joanna 5:05:17 (27,058)
Pearce, Katherine 5:08:42 (27,523)
Pearce, Kathleen 5:44:41 (30,869)
Pearce, Katie 4:09:03 (14,146)
Pearce, Nicola 5:36:09 (30,287)
Pearce, Samantha 3:45:32 (8,054)
Pearce, Susan 4:41:45 (22,543)
Pearle, Deborah 4:07:21 (13,761)
Pearson, Alexandra 4:38:58 (21,834)
Pearson, Allison 4:55:28 (25,476)
Pearson, Dawn 3:40:24 (6,833)
Pearson, Emma 5:11:08 (27,829)
Pearson, Jill 4:22:26 (17,531)
Pearson, Katie 6:33:22 (32,329)
Pearson, Mary 4:49:34 (24,337)
Pearson, Sarah 3:53:31 (10,150)
Pearson, Sylvia 4:36:47 (21,273)
Peatfield, Lisa 4:04:55 (13,189)
Pecchia, Nicole 4:56:17 (25,652)
Peck, Charlie 5:02:32 (26,674)
Peck, Jane 4:03:21 (12,843)
Peck, Jaqueline 6:43:54 (32,474)
Peck, Rita 4:09:23 (14,245)
Pecriaux, Delphine 3:51:17 (9,498)
Peddle, Samantha 5:31:20 (29,896)
Pedersen, Birthe 5:30:20 (29,807)
Pedersen, Shirley 5:07:55 (27,425)
Pederzolli, Amanda 3:49:24 (9,005)
Peek, Lynn 6:47:50 (32,517)
Pegg, Julia 5:10:30 (27,750)
Pegram, Tracey 7:10:59 (32,710)
Pel, Gysbertha 4:20:34 (17,014)
Pellard, Sarah 5:46:01 (30,936)
Pelling, Mandy 5:14:34 (28,255)
Pendleton, Elaine 6:54:05 (32,582)
Penfold, Emma 4:06:15 (13,504)
Penfound, Natasha 4:44:58 (23,290)
Penn, Emma 4:07:25 (13,781)
Pennanen, Mia 3:31:03 (5,040)
Pennell, Brenda 3:35:04 (5,722)
Pennell, Christine 4:13:29 (15,183)
Pennock, Sarah 3:31:57 (5,178)
Pentland, Debbie 5:13:19 (28,118)
Penwington, Anastasia 6:00:11 (31,548)
Pepe, Laurie 5:01:53 (26,585)
Perazza, Sabrina 3:47:03 (8,394)
Percival, Mo 4:13:42 (15,232)
Peretti, Donatella 3:37:30 (6,217)
Perez, Sonia 3:49:18 (8,972)
Perez, Sylvia 3:56:50 (11,149)
Perinparajah, Prashantha 6:17:59 (32,037)
Perkins, Christine 6:06:52 (31,755)
Perkins, Jemma 3:54:19 (10,404)
Perlhagen, Jenny 5:11:45 (27,915)
Perowne, Clemmie 7:00:38 (32,633)
Perrin, Tash 6:32:37 (32,315)
Perrott, Valerie 4:54:02 (25,188)
Perry, Caroline 4:37:56 (21,558)
Perry, Christine 3:58:11 (11,564)
Perry, Donna 5:44:38 (30,866)
Perry, Margaret 5:10:47 (27,782)
Perry, Patricia 6:38:40 (32,416)
Perry, Victoria 3:00:20 (1,188)
Persaud, Marcia 5:02:51 (26,721)
Pestka, Debbie 4:24:12 (18,037)
Peters, Christina 3:43:12 (7,442)
Peters, Emma 4:16:53 (16,086)
Peters, Harriet 6:17:22 (32,015)
Peters, Jane 4:02:13 (12,601)
Peters, Louise 4:13:40 (15,222)
Peters, Nicky 3:17:58 (3,005)
Peters, Rachel 4:54:33 (25,292)
Peeters, Rita 4:35:58 (21,071)
Peters, Valerie 5:55:52 (31,394)
Petersen, Laila 4:41:06 (22,380)
Peterson, Sara 5:15:21 (28,341)
Petitt, Claire 5:24:24 (29,315)
Petrova, Lyudmila 2:22:32 (30)
Pett, Mariette 4:54:29 (25,282)
Pett, Rebecca 6:00:06 (31,546)
Pettett, Jane 6:32:19 (32,311)
Pettifer, Jean 4:18:35 (16,506)
Pettinger, Arlene 5:14:58 (28,301)
Pettinger, Colleen 5:31:07 (29,874)
Pettipher, Georgia 3:59:35 (11,962)
Pettit, Michelle 6:25:50 (32,197)
Pettit, Natascha 4:42:56 (22,825)
Pettitt, Bridget 4:29:36 (19,482)
Petty, Wendy 5:29:17 (29,724)
Pfannebecker, Mareile 4:13:43 (15,242)
Phelan, Georgia 5:03:41 (26,840)
Philips, Linda 4:43:04 (22,856)
Phillips, Anna Teresa 4:06:54 (13,649)
Phillips, Clare 3:31:22 (5,086)
Phillips, Cynthia 4:57:40 (25,893)
Phillips, Dina 3:53:12 (10,044)
Phillips, Jean 6:19:55 (32,082)
Phillips, Katherine 4:25:20 (18,346)
Phillips, Lesley 5:39:29 (30,514)
Phillips, Liane 5:05:35 (27,095)
Phillips, Lindsey 5:46:14 (30,950)
Phillips, Lorraine 5:11:04 (27,820)
Phillips, Lorraine 5:52:15 (31,243)
Phillips, Rachel 5:14:54 (28,295)
Phillips, Renée 3:57:54 (11,476)
Phillips, Sandra 5:15:12 (28,324)
Phillips, Sonia 3:15:39 (2,748)
Phillips, Tanya 5:47:25 (31,013)
Phillips, Wendy 4:32:01 (20,088)
Philp, Katherine 5:08:51 (27,543)
Philpott, Linda 4:45:50 (23,523)
Phipps, Deborah 4:49:08 (24,266)
Pickard, Emma 4:34:29 (20,688)
Pickering, Denise 4:03:27 (12,873)
Pickering, Lorraine 4:24:48 (18,198)
Pickett, Helen 3:42:45 (7,326)
Pickett, Jill 4:46:19 (23,639)
Pickett, Sheila 4:29:10 (19,373)
Pickford, Marilyn 4:38:04 (21,589)
Pickford, Nicola 7:14:21 (32,734)
Pickvance, Ruth 2:45:33 (313)
Pidcock, Carmen 3:46:31 (8,290)
Pidgeley, Michelle 4:46:32 (23,699)
Piekos, Laura 7:29:34 (32,783)
Pienaar, Nerine 4:34:13 (20,631)
Pierce, Bridget 6:19:49 (32,077)
Pierce, Sandra 4:37:14 (21,380)
Pierce, Stacy 3:26:46 (4,288)
Piggot, Katie 3:47:31 (8,515)
Pigott, Kathryn 4:45:34 (23,461)
Pike, Judith 5:49:45 (31,133)
Pike, Linda 5:29:03 (29,698)
Pike, Lucy 4:34:26 (20,678)
Pike, Trudi 3:34:05 (5,537)
Pike, Zoe 3:07:10 (1,748)
Pilkington, Sheena 6:44:47 (32,484)
Pilling, Victoria 4:49:08 (24,266)
Pim, Deborah 4:37:14 (21,380)
Pinder, Susan 3:30:31 (4,949)
Pini, Daniela 4:58:41 (26,074)
Pinney, Gina 5:43:54 (30,811)
Pinnock, Nicola 5:21:37 (29,058)
Pio-Serrano, Rosa 4:38:29 (21,697)
Piper, Valerie 7:03:13 (32,662)
Pipes, Jo 5:36:33 (30,313)
Pirro, Alexandra 4:38:08 (21,609)
Pitcairn, Alison Anne 4:46:46 (23,750)
Pitcher, Katie 4:34:43 (20,754)
Pitt, Nicola 5:09:19 (27,608)
Pittman, Rebecca 3:38:51 (6,495)
Pittman, Sarah 4:11:26 (14,727)
Pitzpatrick, Jennifer 5:08:58 (27,568)
Plant, Marilyn 5:14:42 (28,273)
Platt, Jayne 3:31:41 (5,148)
Playford, Marie 3:47:46 (8,580)
Plent, Christine 6:28:55 (32,258)
Plested, Barbara 4:28:08 (19,065)
Pluckrose, Claire 4:31:41 (20,008)
Plumpton, Lyn 7:09:44 (32,699)
Plumtree, Adele 5:18:00 (28,668)
Plush, Lynn 5:06:35 (27,241)
Pocker, Lara 4:54:43 (25,328)
Pocock, Rosie 3:54:43 (10,519)
Pocock, Valerie 4:45:14 (23,366)
Pogson, Linda 4:29:36 (19,482)
Poke, Celia 4:55:39 (25,504)
Pole, Judith 6:43:51 (32,473)
Poling, Samantha 5:40:58 (30,614)
Poll, Sarah 3:27:22 (4,391)
Pollack, Grace 4:03:52 (12,959)
Pollard, Deborah 5:23:53 (29,270)
Pollex, Katharina 4:59:39 (26,253)
Pollock, Susan 4:26:06 (18,549)
Pomeroy, Jane 5:59:33 (31,532)

Pontin, Karen 5:01:06 (26,464)
Pook, Susannah 4:31:19 (19,906)
Pooke, Nicola 3:41:13 (7,019)
Poole, Alice 5:22:01 (29,094)
Poole, Anne 4:15:29 (15,689)
Poole, Emma 5:41:24 (30,646)
Poole, Helen 4:50:18 (24,466)
Poole, Jackie 4:32:32 (20,225)
Poole, Janet 4:40:44 (22,286)
Poole, Pauline 6:52:40 (32,564)
Pope, Judith 4:56:25 (25,679)
Pope, Rebecca 5:49:13 (31,109)
Pope, Suzanne 6:12:42 (31,899)
Pople, Larissa 3:45:01 (7,929)
Pople, Melanie 4:09:46 (14,334)
Popp, Catherine 5:20:48 (28,976)
Port, Louise 4:36:06 (21,102)
Porter, Claire 3:32:02 (5,196)
Porter, Honor 4:53:27 (25,057)
Porter, Karen 3:16:42 (2,862)
Porter, Karen 5:15:52 (28,423)
Porter, Lynn 4:46:14 (23,630)
Porter, Sarah 4:53:38 (25,092)
Porter, Sara-Louise 5:04:42 (26,979)
Potgieter, Lori 4:11:51 (14,825)
Potier, Beatrice 3:57:11 (11,256)
Potter, Janet 3:22:55 (3,650)
Potter, Kate 3:21:04 (3,379)
Potts, Genevieve 4:57:16 (25,822)
Poulter, Donna Renea 4:02:27 (12,642)
Pounds, Carolyn 4:13:21 (15,155)
Powditch, Nicola 5:58:40 (31,503)
Powdrill, Julia 4:30:43 (19,764)
Powell, Alison 4:55:20 (25,443)
Powell, Carol 5:50:47 (31,173)
Powell, Clare 4:38:09 (21,615)
Powell, Debra 4:39:25 (21,956)
Powell, Emma 4:57:22 (25,836)
Powell, Helen 4:42:37 (22,750)
Powell, Jennifer 5:43:48 (30,806)
Powell, Karen 4:55:25 (25,469)
Powell, Rosemary 4:53:53 (25,141)
Powell, Rosie 3:49:21 (8,985)
Powell, Sarah 6:32:43 (32,317)
Powell, Su 6:05:15 (31,706)
Powell, Zoe 4:58:09 (25,973)
Power, Anne 2:58:54 (1,085)
Power, Anne 5:12:54 (28,069)
Power, Jan 4:26:32 (18,664)
Power, Sarah 5:14:02 (28,201)
Pownall, Gill 4:18:13 (16,417)
Pownall, Jo-Anne 4:27:21 (18,875)
Pownall, Karen 4:32:45 (20,289)
Powney, Frances 4:42:26 (22,706)
Poynter Smith, Sylvia 7:53:34 (32,850)
Praekelt, Uta 4:42:29 (22,719)
Prance, Carole 3:23:00 (3,657)
Pratt, Jennie 4:36:32 (21,231)
Pratt, Kerri 4:37:22 (21,414)
Pratt, Mary 5:38:24 (30,438)
Pratt, Sarah 4:20:14 (16,922)
Pratten, Kate 4:04:41 (13,132)
Precious, Kim 5:23:10 (29,192)
Preece, Samantha 4:38:10 (21,616)
Preedy, Clare 3:57:04 (11,227)
Preiner, Heidi 5:02:15 (26,634)
Prescott, Caroline 3:55:18 (10,696)
Prested, Christine 4:47:56 (24,018)
Prestoe, Andrea 5:10:05 (27,698)
Preston, Christine 3:23:16 (3,691)
Preston-Low, Deborah 5:16:05 (28,452)
Pretious, Alison 3:48:26 (8,732)
Pretorius, Karen 4:19:44 (16,785)
Pretorius, Susan 4:28:23 (19,131)
Pretty, Charlotte 4:46:11 (23,618)
Pretty, Helen 4:40:21 (22,199)
Prevett, Fiona 7:08:00 (32,686)
Pribil, Natalie 4:27:21 (18,875)
Price, Abigail 4:19:00 (16,589)
Price, Annabel 4:32:55 (20,339)
Price, Ashley 5:28:17 (29,635)
Price, Cathy 4:06:58 (13,668)
Price, Gail 4:32:44 (20,286)
Price, Jayne 4:36:55 (21,300)
Price, Judith 5:50:43 (31,169)
Price, Karen 3:56:51 (11,159)
Price, Lara 4:37:54 (21,547)
Price, Madeleine 4:08:11 (13,947)
Price, Nicola 5:20:33 (28,946)
Price, Paula 5:23:17 (29,201)
Price, Simone 5:34:06 (30,117)
Price, Suzanne 4:42:02 (22,617)
Price, Venetia 4:39:32 (21,978)
Price, Verena 6:07:04 (31,762)
Prichard, Hannah 5:21:13 (29,021)
Prichard, Julienne 5:02:13 (26,630)
Priday, Gillian 3:48:25 (8,728)
Prideaux, Louise 4:41:04 (22,367)
Prien, Kirsten 4:01:45 (12,505)
Priestley, Carole 4:26:13 (18,578)
Priestley, Leanne 5:21:39 (29,063)
Prifti, Helen 4:23:42 (17,883)
Pringle, Dawn 4:21:14 (17,174)
Pringle, Linda 5:03:56 (26,876)
Prior, Liz 4:24:52 (18,222)
Pritchard, Diana 5:18:13 (28,693)
Pritchard, Helen 5:16:25 (28,493)
Pritchard, Louisa 3:25:51 (4,124)
Pritchard, Victoria 4:32:49 (20,306)
Pritchett, Bernadine 5:41:47 (30,673)
Probert, Natasha 3:22:54 (3,648)
Procter, Sarah 3:43:57 (7,643)
Proctor, Amanda 3:06:37 (1,701)
Proctor, Michele 6:14:37 (31,948)
Proctor, Michelle 6:14:37 (31,948)
Proffitt, Diana 4:36:42 (21,261)
Prosser, Alicia 4:49:14 (24,281)
Prosser, Gwyneth 6:27:45 (32,237)
Pruden, Ann 4:49:07 (24,263)
Pryce, Joanna 3:46:26 (8,263)
Pryce, Karen 5:15:13 (28,330)
Pryke, Gail 3:21:06 (3,387)
Pryke, Sara 5:45:43 (30,923)
Pryne, Sandra 4:45:16 (23,374)
Psatha, Maria 3:37:27 (6,195)
Puckeridge, Jayne 4:05:44 (13,376)
Pude, Michelle 4:02:06 (12,575)
Pugh, Caroline 4:54:37 (25,305)
Pugh, Gillian 3:21:03 (3,374)
Pugh, Janice 4:51:49 (24,746)
Pullen, Gillian 4:55:11 (25,417)
Punshon, Donna 5:16:18 (28,482)
Puolo, Emily 5:39:34 (30,521)
Purcell, Laura 3:35:25 (5,785)
Purkiss, Lisa 3:42:08 (7,186)
Purnell, Jacqueline 4:40:32 (22,239)
Purshouse, Sharon 4:31:04 (19,844)
Purslow, Sara 5:13:33 (28,148)
Purssord, Charlotte 5:10:19 (27,729)
Pusterla, Anna 4:30:43 (19,764)
Puttock, Sarah 5:28:01 (29,618)
Pye, Catherine 4:18:35 (16,506)
Pye, Hazel 4:40:40 (22,268)
Pye, Lisa 4:18:30 (16,486)
Pyett, Judith 4:41:40 (22,519)
Pyke, Yvonne 6:22:40 (32,140)
Pykett, Clare 7:30:40 (32,792)
Pyle, May 5:17:07 (28,580)
Pyne, Janet 4:36:32 (21,231)
Pyper, Jennifer 3:51:23 (9,517)
Quann, Susan 4:13:35 (15,201)
Quarry, Janet 4:53:10 (25,005)
Quayle, Anna 4:43:46 (23,008)
Quayle, Ruth 4:43:47 (23,011)
Quek, Ai Ling 4:30:55 (19,813)
Quick, Miriam 4:13:58 (15,301)
Quigley, Marian 4:36:59 (21,309)
Quinlan, Toni 5:12:29 (28,022)
Quinn, Aisling 3:57:08 (11,243)
Quinn, Brigid 4:02:04 (12,571)
Quinn, Emma-Jane 4:33:28 (20,455)
Quinn, Kerry 4:04:33 (13,101)
Quinn, Laura 4:58:24 (26,016)
Quinton, Caty 3:28:29 (4,600)
Quirk, Lisa 6:01:58 (31,605)
Quirke, Deborah 4:16:26 (15,963)
Quismorio, Anne 4:54:33 (25,292)
Quoirin, Meabh 5:06:00 (27,155)
Raanan-Brown, Sally 4:20:44 (17,053)
Rackstraw, Lisa 4:36:37 (21,244)

Radcliffe, Paula 2:18:56 (17)

Paula Radcliffe MBE (born 17 December 1973) has been hailed as arguably the greatest female distance runner of all time. Her amazing run of record-breaking victories in 2002 and 2003, including smashing the women's world record in Chicago and London showed an athlete at the peak of her power and her popularity. Her dominance was such that winning gold at the 2004 Athens Olympics seemed to many of her fans a formality. But that race ended in tears and despair on a kerbside. She had long been an underdog, and her lack of a sprint finish had long hampered her. He fans longed for her to win, but since her breakthrough year of 2002, she has made it to the start line of only three leading championships. And after her collapse in Athens she could finish only 23rd at the 2008 Beijing Olympic marathon (her training had been ruined by a stress fracture). Her failure never to have won an Olympic medal is a situation she is determined to rectify in 2012. Despite this, Paula has run the three fastest times by a woman over 26.2 miles, climaxed by her world record of 2:15:25 in 2003.

Radcliffe was born in Northwich, Cheshire, but she grew up in Bedfordshire and is a member of Bedford Athletic Club. She studied French, German and economics at Loughborough University. Her early running success was in cross-country events, including the 1992 World Junior title, beating Wang Junxia. Radcliffe also has three European titles to her name, winning at the European Cross Country Championships in 1999 and 2003 and also over 10,000m on the track at the 2002 European Athletics Championships. Paula and her husband and manager, Gary Lough, gave birth to their first child, a daughter, Isla, on 17 January 2007. She hopes to increase her family before the 2012 Olympics. Paula says she is excited at the prospect of winning gold in the country of her birth. 'I have a massive desire to win gold in 2012,' she said. 'The fact that it is in London on home soil makes you want to go out and perform well.'

Radema, Jet 4:40:47 (22,304)
Raeburn, Gail 4:37:12 (21,370)
Raffetto, Deborah 5:04:05 (26,895)
Raglione-Hall, Jean 4:30:53 (19,801)
Rahman, Huma 3:37:20 (6,173)
Raiker, Andrea 5:23:30 (29,221)

On course for a record

Paula Radcliffe made the fastest debut by a woman in London in 2002 and set a world record of 2:15:25 a year later. The world record for the marathon distance is held by Haile Gebrselassie, who ran 2:03:59 in Berlin. The course record for the London Marathon is 2:05:10, set by Sammy Wanjiru, the Bejing Olympic champion, in the 2009 race.

Rainbird, Katy 4:49:24 (24,299)
Rainbow, Sarah 4:22:22 (17,507)
Raine, Jane 5:49:14 (31,110)
Rajani, Shital 4:57:08 (25,798)
Rajarathna, Kanchana 3:36:28 (6,020)
Ralph, Barbara 3:16:45 (2,870)
Ralph, Karen 4:44:26 (23,157)
Raman, Tanja 4:37:11 (21,365)
Ramos-Vasconcelos, Noelle 6:25:47 (32,195)
Ramsden, Anne 4:25:37 (18,424)
Ramshaw, Sara 3:53:47 (10,237)
Rana, Naheed 4:20:00 (16,860)
Rance, Bunty 4:30:36 (19,734)
Rand, Emma 4:57:08 (25,798)
Randall, Helen 6:09:07 (31,816)
Randall, Louisa 5:18:19 (28,704)
Randall, Louise 5:51:59 (31,231)
Randell, Jessica 4:36:19 (21,164)
Randle, Heidi 4:33:24 (20,443)
Randle, Sally 5:05:14 (27,048)
Raney, Elisa 5:51:09 (31,192)
Rankin, Aileen 5:38:27 (30,443)
Rannard, Gillian 4:54:03 (25,192)
Ranyard, Lynda 6:56:02 (32,591)
Rasmussen, Davina 3:54:53 (10,568)
Rasmussen, Louise 5:42:51 (30,741)
Ratcliffe, Allison 4:07:16 (13,737)
Ratcliffe, Helen 4:09:03 (14,146)
Ratcliffe, Victoria 5:48:31 (31,063)
Ratnarajah, Anne 4:08:22 (13,982)
Ratner, Katie 6:34:14 (32,342)
Rattigan, Carol 4:35:28 (20,936)
Raub-Segal, Elke 4:55:22 (25,453)
Rawdon Smith, Kate 4:35:12 (20,881)
Rawlings, Sarah 5:19:55 (28,861)
Rawlinson, Fay 4:43:42 (22,997)
Rawson, Amanda 3:24:19 (3,887)
Raybone, Sophie 4:47:52 (23,996)
Raye, Katherine 4:16:53 (16,086)
Rayner, Elizabeth 4:31:28 (19,953)
Rayner, Marion 3:10:39 (2,117)
Raynes, Deborah 3:47:34 (8,530)
Read, Avril 3:54:10 (10,366)
Read, Melanie 5:20:00 (28,879)
Read, Nicola 5:04:20 (26,940)
Reader, Jacqueline 5:46:54 (30,981)
Reading, Avril 6:02:26 (31,623)
Reading, Jill 4:20:56 (17,090)
Readman, Tamzin 5:03:47 (26,855)
Realmuto, Sarah 4:08:58 (14,125)
Rebollo Meira, Laura 4:52:00 (24,783)
Recaldin, Paola 4:59:25 (26,202)
Reddig, Alexandra 5:21:12 (29,018)
Reddy, Aushandrie 4:29:49 (19,543)
Redfern, Judith 4:03:16 (12,831)
Redfern, Sally 3:40:44 (6,900)
Redhead, Abigail 5:03:04 (26,755)
Redman, Janet 5:46:10 (30,942)
Redmond, Christine 6:24:55 (32,181)
Redmond, Rosemary 6:00:26 (31,559)
Redpath, Janet 3:45:12 (7,975)
Reed, Christine 4:43:31 (22,964)
Reed, Gaynor 4:37:57 (21,564)
Rees, Angela 5:54:02 (31,313)
Rees, Caron 4:16:25 (15,956)
Rees, Elen 4:40:16 (22,174)
Rees, Hannah 4:19:50 (16,810)
Rees, Joanne 4:45:47 (23,512)
Rees, Lisa 3:47:40 (8,551)
Rees, Samantha 3:55:52 (10,864)
Rees, Sandra 4:37:44 (21,499)
Rees, Yvonne 3:33:33 (5,436)
Reeve, Sheena 5:46:43 (30,976)
Reeves, Claire 3:43:56 (7,638)
Reeves, Emma 4:00:49 (12,258)
Regan, Katy 4:17:46 (16,320)
Regan, Maura 4:57:55 (25,939)
Regan, Paulette 5:30:02 (29,782)
Regel, Linda 4:51:29 (24,697)
Reggiani, Lucia 5:31:50 (29,937)
Register, Dawn 4:05:21 (13,287)
Rehn, Anne 4:24:39 (18,159)
Reid, Carol 3:28:12 (4,551)
Reid, Jacqueline 4:17:07 (16,148)
Reid, Jan 4:14:50 (15,533)
Reid, Janet 5:04:20 (26,940)
Reid, Kirsten 4:24:49 (18,205)
Reid, Stephanie 4:30:09 (19,641)
Reilly, Catherine 5:40:25 (30,579)
Reilly, Cynthia 5:55:20 (31,368)
Reilly, Valery 3:54:03 (10,326)
Reinertsen, Sarah 5:27:04 (29,529)
Relle, Angela 5:51:05 (31,188)
Renmant, Beverley 4:26:36 (18,680)
Renner, Caroline 4:39:04 (21,862)
Rennie, Anita 3:38:14 (6,351)
Rennison, Charlotte 5:10:53 (27,799)
Renson, Jill 3:48:27 (8,735)
Restall, Julie 4:13:10 (15,113)
Reudy, Kirsty 4:13:37 (15,209)
Reutersward, Anna 3:38:32 (6,436)
Revell, Bethany 6:20:39 (32,097)
Revell, Clare 4:56:56 (25,753)
Revell, Josephine 5:01:57 (26,598)
Revill, Julia 4:43:06 (22,865)
Revill, Kate 4:49:33 (24,332)
Rew, Susan 4:02:26 (12,638)
Rexin, Julia 4:45:58 (23,555)
Reyes, Monica 4:09:14 (14,198)
Reynolds, Alison 4:23:55 (17,953)
Reynolds, Ann 4:47:57 (24,022)
Reynolds, Elizabeth 6:25:03 (32,182)
Reynolds, Frances 4:45:18 (23,382)
Reynolds, Jacqueline 4:38:06 (21,599)
Reynolds, Julie 4:05:52 (13,403)
Reynolds, Julie 5:40:41 (30,595)
Reynolds, Maria 5:01:09 (26,475)
Reynolds, Suzanne 3:47:58 (8,620)
Rhodes, Eileen 3:58:36 (11,678)
Rhodes, Karen 5:49:00 (31,098)
Rhodes, Maxine 6:53:51 (32,580)
Rhodes, Victoria 5:01:32 (26,534)
Rhone-Adrien, Paula 4:40:45 (22,295)
Rhymes, Natasha 3:42:16 (7,226)
Rice, Amanda 3:45:54 (8,134)
Rice, Sheila 5:31:16 (29,893)
Rich, Jo 4:25:18 (18,333)
Richards, Abigail 4:39:23 (21,946)
Richards, Claire 5:00:42 (26,411)
Richards, Emma 3:37:30 (6,217)
Richards, Jackie 3:25:10 (4,009)
Richards, Joanna 5:32:34 (29,996)
Richards, Joanna 5:45:10 (30,892)
Richards, Linda 5:49:00 (31,098)
Richards, Tammy 4:50:15 (24,458)
Richardson, Jane 4:33:29 (20,459)
Richardson, Lesley 6:32:16 (32,310)
Richardson, Lucinda 5:40:19 (30,572)
Richardson, Sarah 6:05:52 (31,728)
Richardson, Susan 5:02:17 (26,640)
Riches, Clare 4:45:18 (23,382)
Richmond, Alexandra 3:22:42 (3,610)
Richmond, Denise 4:35:51 (21,042)
Richmond, Jennifer 4:07:59 (13,903)
Richmond, Nicola 4:59:06 (26,153)
Richmond, Wendy 4:34:23 (20,668)
Richoz, Teresa 3:43:37 (7,555)
Richter, Letizia 4:18:17 (16,431)
Rickett, Lucy 3:46:38 (8,317)
Ridge, Sheila 4:57:49 (25,921)
Ridgway, Hayley 4:22:56 (17,682)
Riding, Samantha 4:54:23 (25,263)
Ridley, Christine 6:06:57 (31,760)
Ridley, Diane 4:22:41 (17,603)
Ridout, Anne 4:35:22 (20,914)
Rigby, Jane 5:39:28 (30,511)
Rigby, Louise 4:48:25 (24,108)
Rigg, Janine 4:20:07 (16,891)
Riggott, Emma 4:01:38 (12,476)
Rikardsdottir, Hildur 3:44:54 (7,906)
Riley, Andrea 4:06:28 (13,558)
Riley, Claire 4:03:30 (12,881)
Riley, Jacqueline 5:11:43 (27,909)
Riley, Sian 4:53:55 (25,160)
Rimington, Dawn 4:33:33 (20,472)
Rimmer, Dawn 4:49:13 (24,278)
Rimmer, Patsy 5:19:40 (28,835)
Rimmington, Carole 4:29:06 (19,348)
Rinchey, Gail 5:00:38 (26,393)
Riner, Janine 7:02:27 (32,652)
Ringer, Samantha 6:39:21 (32,428)
Ringham, Gay 6:31:43 (32,302)
Riordan-Askin, Lisa 6:28:46 (32,249)
Ripley, Helen 4:38:35 (21,730)
Riseley, Katie 5:22:42 (29,153)
Ritchie, Amanda 3:53:29 (10,139)
Ritchie, Miriam 4:24:57 (18,242)
Ritchie, Sally 5:32:28 (29,993)
Rivett, Pamela 5:27:11 (29,538)
Robb, Veronica 4:40:45 (22,295)
Robbins, Anita 4:54:35 (25,302)
Robbins, Jane 6:47:51 (32,518)
Roberts, Angela 4:25:56 (18,498)
Roberts, Annabel 5:03:44 (26,847)
Roberts, Anne 4:50:34 (24,517)
Roberts, Brenda 4:27:26 (18,896)
Roberts, Christine 4:04:33 (13,101)
Roberts, Elaine 5:51:49 (31,228)
Roberts, Emma 3:47:21 (8,472)
Roberts, Emma 4:24:18 (18,067)
Roberts, Emma 4:40:32 (22,239)
Roberts, Helen 4:20:40 (17,038)
Roberts, Helen 4:57:04 (25,782)
Roberts, Jane 4:17:50 (16,333)
Roberts, Jill 4:37:16 (21,394)
Roberts, Karen 4:56:17 (25,652)
Roberts, Karen 5:45:58 (30,932)
Roberts, Kathryn 4:43:36 (22,976)
Roberts, Katie 4:27:53 (19,000)
Roberts, Kelly 7:05:15 (32,673)
Roberts, Paula 4:48:34 (24,141)
Roberts, Penelope 4:40:09 (22,145)
Roberts, Rhoslyn 4:53:36 (25,085)
Roberts, Rosemary 4:52:28 (24,868)
Roberts, Sandy 3:59:48 (12,024)
Roberts, Sarah 3:47:59 (8,625)
Roberts, Sheenagh 4:40:59 (22,350)
Roberts, Sian 5:45:51 (30,926)
Roberts, Sylvia 3:34:33 (5,626)
Roberts, Vikki 4:44:34 (23,193)
Robertshaw, Kathleen 3:50:44 (9,356)
Roberts-Jones, Bethan 4:42:29 (22,719)
Robertson, Bridget 3:59:31 (11,942)
Robertson, Esther 5:32:06 (29,960)
Robertson, Helen 4:37:46 (21,509)
Robertson, Sarah 4:14:57 (15,559)
Robins, Andrea 3:34:14 (5,568)
Robins, Jenny 4:54:27 (25,275)
Robinson, Annette 4:54:51 (25,357)
Robinson, Christine 4:55:50 (25,544)
Robinson, Dawn 4:53:31 (25,075)
Robinson, Denise 5:33:04 (30,030)
Robinson, Elizabeth 4:42:54 (22,815)
Robinson, Karen 4:04:55 (13,189)
Robinson, Kate 4:01:30 (12,441)
Robinson, Laura 6:18:32 (32,050)
Robinson, Liz 3:42:47 (7,339)
Robinson, Louise 4:46:30 (23,692)
Robinson, Lynda 7:11:27 (32,716)

Robinson, Lynn 3:59:20 (11,896)
Robinson, Margaret 4:58:11 (25,982)
Robinson, Patricia 4:33:08 (20,391)
Robinson, Paula 4:19:44 (16,785)
Robinson, Rosemary 4:40:10 (22,150)
Robjohns, Karen 4:43:13 (22,890)
Robson, Amanda 7:30:33 (32,790)
Robson, Barbara 6:07:04 (31,762)
Robson, Dany 3:36:01 (5,907)
Robson, Heather 4:05:47 (13,390)
Robson, Jacqueline 3:20:05 (3,263)
Robson, Kate 4:14:33 (15,457)
Robson, Liz 4:38:35 (21,730)
Rock, Nichola 5:21:26 (29,039)
Rodda, Lisa 3:24:14 (3,867)
Roddy, Donna 5:29:38 (29,754)
Rodgers, Carolann 4:03:05 (12,795)
Rodgers, Fiona 4:45:39 (23,483)
Rodgers, Gillian 4:55:06 (25,391)
Rodgers, Linda 4:21:09 (17,156)
Rodgers, Nicole 5:39:22 (30,500)
Rodgerson, Elinor 4:54:39 (25,314)
Rodriguez, Joanna 4:50:02 (24,429)
Rodriguez, Silvia 4:05:35 (13,345)
Roebuck, Wendy 4:03:57 (12,976)
Rogan, Emma 4:06:39 (13,601)
Rogan, Marion 4:26:06 (18,549)
Rogers, Alexandra 3:44:19 (7,747)
Rogers, Audrey 5:12:50 (28,059)
Rogers, Danielle 4:33:42 (20,517)
Rogers, Emma 5:52:00 (31,234)
Rogers, Helen 5:31:11 (29,887)
Rogers, Jakki 6:33:53 (32,338)
Rogers, Jamie 3:27:47 (4,474)
Rogers, Joanne 5:56:19 (31,413)
Rogers, Zoe 4:30:31 (19,713)
Rogerson, Donna 3:37:28 (6,203)
Rogger, Sara 5:13:49 (28,172)
Rohner, Dinah 4:32:57 (20,345)
Rolfe, Melanie 5:17:16 (28,596)
Rollings, Ann 3:28:15 (4,560)
Rolliston, Joanne 5:20:16 (28,911)
Rolt, Georgina 3:53:14 (10,055)
Romagnoli, Caroline 5:07:17 (27,343)
Romain, Sarah 4:43:36 (22,976)
Roman, Marit 4:18:08 (16,394)
Ronayne-Dubock, Natasha 4:30:55 (19,813)
Ronco, Vivien 4:34:21 (20,658)
Roodt, Joan 4:58:01 (25,951)
Rooke, Ruth 7:13:14 (32,727)
Rookes, Julie 4:52:52 (24,954)
Rooney, Sharon 6:52:49 (32,565)
Roper, Alison 4:36:20 (21,174)
Rose, Cathy 5:04:26 (26,951)
Rose, Charlotte 5:10:32 (27,754)
Rose, Elizabeth 5:43:57 (30,815)
Rose, Emma 4:33:13 (20,407)
Rose, Julie 4:52:34 (24,895)
Rose, Kelly 5:24:33 (29,330)
Rose, Sally 4:57:46 (25,911)
Rosenberg, Holly 4:04:42 (13,135)
Rosen-Nash, Ilkay 4:25:59 (18,513)
Rosenthal, Gaby 3:26:42 (4,275)
Rosmer, Sandra 4:50:54 (24,591)
Ross, Jenny 4:48:25 (24,108)
Ross, Jessica 3:28:02 (4,521)
Ross, Lara 6:22:32 (32,134)
Ross, Namuni 4:20:12 (16,913)
Ross, Paulette 6:45:42 (32,496)
Ross, Wendy 3:50:41 (9,343)
Rosser, Heidi 5:37:49 (30,402)
Rosser, Leanne Jayne 5:46:54 (30,981)
Rossi, Benedetta 3:58:02 (11,522)
Rossiter, Carolyn 4:52:52 (24,954)
Rossouw, Pamela 4:26:24 (18,623)
Rossouw, Yolande 5:01:12 (26,481)
Rostant, Deborah 5:44:31 (30,856)
Rothwell, Linda 4:17:11 (16,166)
Rothwell, Lindzi 5:17:16 (28,596)
Roue, Katy 4:46:28 (23,685)
Roug, Tanja 4:46:01 (23,569)
Rourke, Anne 5:08:43 (27,525)
Rousseau, Marie-Helene 4:28:17 (19,105)
Roussel, Kay 7:11:10 (32,714)
Roussy, Daniele 4:01:47 (12,514)
Routledge, Alison 3:41:26 (7,051)
Routledge, Deborah 4:32:47 (20,298)
Routley-Driver, Elizabeth 3:35:16 (5,758)
Rowbotham, Johanne 4:53:24 (25,049)
Rowbottom, Claire 4:31:12 (19,883)
Rowe, Amanda 7:47:36 (32,843)
Rowe, Jill 4:07:52 (13,884)
Rowe, Laura 4:17:32 (16,250)
Rowe, Peggy 7:02:05 (32,649)
Rowe-Wakeling, Pippa 4:25:42 (18,439)
Rowlands, Rachel 3:54:52 (10,562)
Rowlands, Sue 4:15:16 (15,636)
Rowley, Alison 4:36:08 (21,115)
Rowlinson, Marie-Claire 5:09:59 (27,688)
Rowntree, Karen 4:32:51 (20,320)
Roworth, Wendy 4:44:38 (23,202)
Rowswell, Kathryn 4:19:46 (16,797)
Rowswell, Trudie 5:29:24 (29,728)
Royall, Lorraine 5:44:50 (30,877)
Royce, Brigget 6:42:52 (32,457)
Royles, Deborah 5:24:13 (29,298)
Royston, Claire 5:57:21 (31,453)
Rubidge, Tina 4:35:23 (20,921)
Rudd, Nadine 5:11:29 (27,885)
Rudin, Kaye 5:31:02 (29,866)
Rudrum, Stefanie 5:26:57 (29,518)
Ruffle, Catherine 4:22:58 (17,696)
Ruffle, Dinae 4:45:06 (23,333)
Rufus, Zoe 4:43:27 (22,948)
Rule, Lorraine 4:21:01 (17,117)
Runeckles, Nicky 5:31:27 (29,908)
Runnalls, Lucie 3:50:15 (9,235)
Rusby, Louise 3:47:40 (8,551)
Ruscio, Mirella 5:06:24 (27,213)
Rushby, Maia 3:38:24 (6,400)
Rushton, Kirsty 4:16:35 (16,002)
Rushworth, Catherine 5:36:48 (30,335)
Rusling, Barbara 3:58:40 (11,695)
Russell, Christine 4:09:25 (14,258)
Russell, Elizabeth 4:26:24 (18,623)
Russell, Jenny 4:38:29 (21,697)
Russell, Judith 4:10:15 (14,449)
Russell, Lenore 4:47:56 (24,018)
Russell, Teresa 3:58:58 (11,787)
Russo, Deborah 4:21:55 (17,371)
Russouw, Tonia 5:26:53 (29,513)
Ruston, Rachelle 4:53:51 (25,134)
Ruthven, Stephanie 3:49:31 (9,048)
Rutland, Fiona 4:09:41 (14,313)
Rutter, Helen 4:01:48 (12,522)
Rutter, Jackie 4:49:57 (24,414)
Rutter, Joanna 5:04:58 (27,015)
Ruzewicz, Patsie 4:57:09 (25,802)
Ryan, Julie 5:29:13 (29,714)
Ryan, Lea 5:15:44 (28,399)
Ryan, Lisa 6:46:56 (32,504)
Ryan, Lynda 4:07:52 (13,884)
Ryan, Mary 3:18:14 (3,038)
Ryan, Phyllis 3:51:22 (9,514)
Ryan, Sheena 5:02:57 (26,734)
Ryan, Sian 5:08:40 (27,517)
Ryssel, Maria 4:07:41 (13,836)
Sabharmal, Laura 3:27:01 (4,331)
Sabin, Anna 5:08:10 (27,448)
Sacher, Chloe 5:15:35 (28,380)
Saddler, Janet 6:37:05 (32,398)
Sadler, Angela 3:08:44 (1,896)
Sadler, Ruth 6:16:09 (31,990)
Safarova, Irina 2:29:18 (61)
Safran Sentner, Vicki 4:57:48 (25,915)
Sail, Annette 5:41:50 (30,680)
Saiman, Nathalie 4:51:10 (24,643)
Saint, Debbie 4:28:28 (19,159)
Saise, Shannon 5:32:21 (29,984)
Sakamoto, Sawako 5:22:37 (29,142)
Sakol, Marissa 4:43:27 (22,948)
Salam, Bilquis 6:50:34 (32,548)
Sale, Fiona 5:28:46 (29,680)
Sales, Charlene 5:09:42 (27,665)
Salkeld, Lynda 4:34:46 (20,766)
Salkeld, Nadine 3:48:32 (8,757)
Sallis, Caroline 4:54:47 (25,337)
Salmon, Agnes 3:30:53 (5,006)
Salmon, Elaine 4:04:45 (13,148)
Salway, Sarah 4:40:54 (22,332)
Sambell, Suzanne 4:22:32 (17,557)
Sammons, Rita 4:34:59 (20,828)
Samuel, Gloria 4:57:40 (25,893)
Samuels, Dawn 3:50:03 (9,178)
Samworth, Victoria 4:59:16 (26,170)
Sandberg, Rhona 3:33:32 (5,430)
Sandberg, Ruth 4:18:35 (16,506)
Sanders, Gillian 4:55:54 (25,561)
Sanders, Helena 4:42:37 (22,750)
Sanders, Sarah 7:54:49 (32,853)
Sanderson, Diane 4:53:22 (25,044)
Sandford, Cathie 5:04:45 (26,987)
Sandilands, Julie 3:43:30 (7,525)
Sandle, Sarah 5:00:01 (26,313)
Sandmann, Barbara 4:31:32 (19,978)
Sando, Anneke 3:52:26 (9,820)
Sands, Bronagh 5:02:29 (26,663)
Sands, Laura 5:02:29 (26,663)
Sands, Martina 6:07:59 (31,783)
Sands, Rebecca 5:08:13 (27,461)
Sanghera, Amy 4:48:44 (24,175)
Sansom-Smith, Jayne 4:08:36 (14,059)
Santos, Cristina 4:41:35 (22,491)
Sare, Kirsten 5:10:33 (27,756)
Sargeant, Bina 4:09:54 (14,363)
Sargent, Joanna 4:18:22 (16,458)
Sarsfield, Jennifer 5:09:34 (27,642)
Sasaki, Yukiko 6:50:40 (32,549)
Sato, Norko 4:10:51 (14,592)
Sauchenko, Nadya 4:22:05 (17,419)
Saunders, Angie 4:54:29 (25,282)
Saunders, Caryn 4:57:54 (25,935)
Saunders, Clare 5:27:51 (29,604)
Saunders, Deborah 4:26:47 (18,739)
Saunders, Donna 4:12:29 (14,967)
Saunders, Ellen 3:57:50 (11,461)
Saunders, Judy 3:50:29 (9,297)
Saunders, Lynne 3:51:50 (9,632)
Saunders, Rachel 5:00:00 (26,310)
Saunders, Sharon 4:36:02 (21,088)
Savill, Anna 3:23:52 (3,789)
Sawdon, Margaret 4:53:21 (25,037)
Sawyer, Catriona 5:27:17 (29,549)
Sawyer, Emma 4:28:27 (19,157)
Sawyer, Suzanne 4:50:24 (24,479)
Saxon, Joan 4:02:55 (12,758)
Sayer, Nicholette 4:18:03 (16,380)
Sayers, Innys 4:09:21 (14,232)
Sayle, Nicola 4:48:17 (24,083)
Sayles, Louisa 4:54:56 (25,364)
Scadden, Emma 4:37:46 (21,509)
Scaife, Ann 5:45:10 (30,892)
Scaife, Clair 4:46:25 (23,667)
Scamman, Helen 4:30:32 (19,715)
Scampion, Patricia 6:32:06 (32,308)
Scarf, Jackie 4:34:40 (20,742)
Scarr, Antonia 4:03:58 (12,983)
Scarr, Michelle 4:27:30 (18,919)
Scarr, Nikki 4:42:13 (22,651)
Schaerer, Patricia 3:45:11 (7,969)
Schaffner, Daniela 4:20:16 (16,932)
Schelbert, Heidy 4:53:56 (25,168)
Schleuder, Nicole 4:17:11 (16,166)
Schneider, Angelika 4:59:28 (26,212)
Schneider, Fiona 4:43:27 (22,948)
Schneider, Gerlinde 4:00:00 (12,085)
Schnitger, Miranda 4:42:25 (22,701)
Schoch, Alex 4:43:21 (22,919)
Schofield, Jennifer 4:40:48 (22,310)
Schollaert, Arlene 4:04:20 (13,053)
Schooling, Tessa 3:46:28 (8,269)
Schultz, Fern 4:02:44 (12,709)
Schwarzkopp, Annette 4:37:13 (21,378)
Schwederle, Juliane 3:45:11 (7,969)
Scoffham, Sarah 4:32:38 (20,258)
Scoles, Susan 6:18:33 (32,051)
Scoot, Ninette 4:45:59 (23,560)
Scorer, Ann 6:00:07 (31,547)
Scorer, Maggie 5:29:53 (29,767)

Scotland, Brenda	4:43:32 (22,968)	
Scott, Amanda	4:16:22 (15,938)	
Scott, Angela	5:34:19 (30,135)	
Scott, Anne	5:48:50 (31,083)	
Scott, Carol	4:23:41 (17,872)	
Scott, Charlotte	4:59:40 (26,259)	
Scott, Clare	3:42:14 (7,214)	
Scott, Clarissa	4:46:08 (23,602)	
Scott, Eleanor	4:18:52 (16,563)	
Scott, Helen	5:42:00 (30,695)	
Scott, Katherine	4:03:31 (12,885)	
Scott, Kirstie	4:46:08 (23,602)	
Scott, Nichola	4:53:40 (25,097)	
Scott, Sarah	4:13:04 (15,096)	
Scott, Vanessa	6:35:23 (32,365)	
Scott, Zoe	4:22:45 (17,621)	
Scougall, Kyla	4:22:33 (17,560)	
Scowcroft, Cora	4:44:45 (23,236)	
Scrivener, Sarah	4:23:52 (17,937)	
Scrivens, Natasha	3:42:54 (7,363)	
Scroggins, Janella	3:47:10 (8,426)	
Scully, Pat	4:37:39 (21,477)	
Scutt, Sophie	4:37:10 (21,355)	
Seabright, Vivienne	6:45:40 (32,495)	
Seabrook, Patricia	4:27:06 (18,818)	
Seal, Annabel	6:04:37 (31,679)	
Seale, Debbie	4:44:59 (23,297)	
Seaman, Cheryl	6:38:31 (32,415)	
Seamark, Sarah	6:53:18 (32,574)	
Searl, Chloe	4:45:34 (23,461)	
Searle, Caroline	4:41:52 (22,574)	
Searle, Lisa	4:01:10 (12,356)	
Sebastiani, Milena	3:51:30 (9,543)	
Sebastiani, Simona	4:28:14 (19,095)	
Secker, Caroline	4:46:51 (23,772)	
Seddon, Amanda	5:20:19 (28,919)	
Sedgwick, Thérèse	3:57:11 (11,256)	
Seguro, Caroline	4:47:14 (23,862)	
Seidler, Petra	4:13:51 (15,272)	
Seims, Amanda	3:55:20 (10,710)	
Seldon, Kim	4:47:47 (23,971)	
Sellek, Yoko	4:24:26 (18,100)	
Selman, Natasha	5:32:22 (29,985)	
Selous-Hodges, Rosslynne	5:22:35 (29,140)	
Selsby, Tracy	4:21:36 (17,283)	
Selway, Linda	6:16:46 (31,999)	
Semenova, Zinaida	2:27:43 (49)	
Semple, Lorna	5:56:24 (31,417)	
Sen Gupta, Piya	5:29:30 (29,736)	
Sendlhofer, Britta	4:44:32 (23,184)	
Senior, Jane	4:06:05 (13,455)	
Senogles, Leigh	3:25:52 (4,128)	
Sergeant, Ann	4:20:02 (16,870)	
Sethi, Karen	5:24:20 (29,312)	
Setter, Kathy	3:24:30 (3,918)	
Setterfield, Emma	5:22:37 (29,142)	
Settle, Jan	3:41:02 (6,973)	
Setty, Mani	5:35:10 (30,198)	
Sewell, Maria	5:38:16 (30,430)	
Seydell, Nina	4:59:37 (26,247)	
Seymour, Carol	5:37:15 (30,365)	
Seymour, Rachael	4:55:37 (25,495)	
Seymour, Rebecca	4:20:57 (17,098)	
Shackel, Clare	5:40:56 (30,609)	
Shahzad, Abida	5:43:47 (30,801)	
Shand, Claudia	5:55:24 (31,374)	
Shand, Sally	4:35:56 (21,063)	
Shannon, Audrey	5:12:40 (28,043)	
Shannon, Carole	4:02:28 (12,648)	
Shapter, Philippa	5:22:59 (29,175)	
Sharkey, Shauna	4:39:47 (22,051)	
Sharland, Joanne	4:21:46 (17,328)	
Sharma, Rajni	4:41:28 (22,470)	
Sharman, Suzanne	5:52:26 (31,248)	
Sharp, Anne	5:01:02 (26,453)	
Sharp, Gemma	3:40:47 (6,917)	
Sharp, Jacqueline	3:47:11 (8,433)	
Sharp, Kirsty	4:26:13 (18,578)	
Sharp, Renata	4:31:41 (20,008)	
Sharp, Sally Anne	4:46:08 (23,602)	
Sharp, Susan	3:38:29 (6,418)	
Sharpe, Jill	4:13:25 (15,170)	
Sharrap, Eva	6:15:31 (31,968)	
Sharrock, Gaynor	3:24:40 (3,938)	
Shaw, Beverley	8:28:47 (32,875)	
Shaw, Caroline	5:16:53 (28,541)	
Shaw, Chriselda	4:04:20 (13,053)	
Shaw, Helen	5:43:13 (30,769)	
Shaw, Jacqueline	4:51:44 (24,733)	
Shaw, Joanne	4:40:59 (22,350)	
Shaw, Karen	4:58:37 (26,061)	
Shaw, Margaret	4:36:48 (21,276)	
Shawcroft, Kathleen	5:36:24 (30,305)	
Shawyer, Helen	4:11:02 (14,639)	
Shayne, Kim	3:55:44 (10,823)	
Shea, Teresa	6:15:21 (31,964)	
Shean, Zena	3:59:20 (11,896)	
Sheardown, Phillipa	5:09:12 (27,595)	
Shedden, Felicity	5:27:03 (29,527)	
Shelbourne, Helen	5:24:17 (29,303)	
Shelbourne, Lori	5:45:33 (30,913)	
Sheldon, Marion	4:44:08 (23,092)	
Sheldon, Valentine	4:55:59 (25,583)	
Shelton, Friday	4:36:09 (21,121)	
Shemetras, Naso	5:25:30 (29,401)	
Shenton, Emily	4:28:26 (19,152)	
Shepherd, Catherine	4:47:28 (23,907)	
Shepherd, Jet Jon	4:02:35 (12,675)	
Shepherd, Rachel	4:23:41 (17,872)	
Sheppard, Jennifer	4:19:05 (16,610)	
Sheridan, Margaret	3:47:55 (8,608)	
Sheriston, Kay	4:46:14 (23,630)	
Sherlock, Pamela	5:20:56 (28,987)	
Sherriff, Imogen	5:28:42 (29,674)	
Sherrington, Sue	4:49:03 (24,245)	
Sherwin, Sharon	6:18:45 (32,058)	
Sherwood, Katie	3:40:07 (6,768)	
Sherwood, Patricia	5:14:49 (28,287)	
Shields, Diane	4:15:25 (15,671)	
Shields, Hannah	3:19:28 (3,199)	
Shier, Gillian	3:34:39 (5,649)	
Shim, Christine	4:39:02 (21,854)	
Shingles, Frances	4:39:07 (21,877)	
Shipley, Chris	5:33:21 (30,058)	
Shirtcliff, Martine	4:28:04 (19,048)	
Shivaji, Tara	5:22:19 (29,121)	
Shivarattan, Tara	4:39:39 (22,003)	
Shoebridge, Polly	3:55:34 (10,772)	
Short, Andrea	6:25:27 (32,191)	
Short, Elizabeth	4:38:34 (21,727)	
Short, Natalie	4:59:08 (26,158)	
Short, Susan	4:52:12 (24,824)	
Shread, Jaqueline	4:40:00 (22,106)	
Shrimpton, Deborah	4:02:15 (12,607)	
Shrimpton, Karen	3:58:51 (11,749)	
Shrine, Katharine	4:39:40 (22,009)	
Shute, Madia	6:04:23 (31,669)	
Siao, Diane	3:37:30 (6,217)	
Sibbald, Deborah	4:57:11 (25,809)	
Sibley, Carol	5:03:36 (26,835)	
Sickling, Sarah-Jayne	5:13:38 (28,155)	
Siderfin, Catherine	5:36:02 (30,279)	
Sieloff, Cheryl	5:04:34 (26,960)	
Sier, Jacqueline	3:57:27 (11,347)	
Signy, Helen	5:03:27 (26,817)	
Sigurdson, Leslie	4:25:23 (18,358)	
Sillito, Christine	5:18:58 (28,775)	
Sills, Ruth	3:41:16 (7,027)	
Silva, Ximena	4:28:25 (19,142)	
Silva-Fletcher, Ayona	4:44:32 (23,184)	
Silverthorne, Jillian	4:01:27 (12,425)	
Silvester, Naomi	3:40:46 (6,913)	
Silvester, Wendy	5:29:08 (29,705)	
Silvey, Carolyn	3:07:13 (1,750)	
Silvey, Jane	5:01:56 (26,594)	
Simber, Jane	4:21:00 (17,110)	
Simmie, Linda	4:10:52 (14,597)	
Simmons, Helen	4:56:04 (25,599)	
Simmons, Katie	4:40:05 (22,129)	
Simms, Jenny	5:21:34 (29,048)	
Simms, June	6:11:24 (31,868)	
Simms, Kathryn	4:24:52 (18,222)	
Simons, Susan	4:11:33 (14,756)	
Simpson, Angie	5:31:32 (29,918)	
Simpson, Fiona	8:51:40 (32,887)	
Simpson, Joanna	3:55:31 (10,750)	
Simpson, Julie	3:55:26 (10,732)	
Simpson, Kate	4:56:37 (25,705)	
Simpson, Liz	4:12:10 (14,894)	
Simpson, Lucy	4:44:19 (23,134)	
Simpson, Simone	3:56:06 (10,929)	
Simpson, Victoria	4:09:12 (14,189)	
Sims, Pearl	4:45:50 (23,523)	
Sinclair, Alison	3:37:22 (6,181)	
Sinclair, Judith	4:22:29 (17,541)	
Sinclair, Nina	3:54:24 (10,427)	
Sinfield, Sharon	4:32:55 (20,339)	
Sinturel, Michelle	3:50:43 (9,352)	
Sipos, Sue	4:20:13 (16,918)	
Skelton, Joy	4:36:07 (21,106)	
Skelton, Susan	4:50:50 (24,575)	
Skelton, Vicky	3:08:51 (1,915)	
Sketchley, Karen	5:02:10 (26,624)	
Skidmore, Flora	3:35:10 (5,744)	
Skinner, Claire	3:46:27 (8,265)	
Skinner, Claire	5:23:31 (29,223)	
Skinner, Corrina	4:24:03 (17,996)	
Skinner, Hayley	5:01:55 (26,590)	
Skinsley, Helen	4:32:07 (20,114)	
Skvortsova, Silvia	2:27:06 (46)	
Slade, Debbie	5:15:22 (28,343)	
Slamon, Lynne	4:18:53 (16,566)	
Slater, Deborah	4:26:54 (18,760)	
Slater, Tracy	4:54:36 (25,303)	
Slater, Victoria	4:00:49 (12,258)	
Slator, Ann	4:49:49 (24,383)	
Slaughter, Helen	4:08:11 (13,947)	
Sleath, Sue	3:15:35 (2,733)	
Slevin, Sally	4:28:19 (19,114)	
Slivington, Sharon	3:31:22 (5,086)	
Slocombe, Lindsey	6:07:43 (31,777)	
Smale, Dee	3:03:29 (1,419)	
Small, Emma	6:42:46 (32,455)	
Smallbone, Lucy	4:45:15 (23,371)	
Smallman, Joanna	4:59:23 (26,197)	
Smallwood, James	4:52:44 (24,920)	
Smallwood, Karen	4:40:34 (22,248)	
Smart, Jennifer	4:02:21 (12,626)	
Smart, Michelle	5:05:31 (27,086)	
Smart, Natalie-Marie	5:43:45 (30,799)	
Smart, Stephanie	3:59:47 (12,019)	
Smeed, Alex	4:32:54 (20,335)	
Smelt-Webb, Caroline	4:23:58 (17,965)	
Smethurst, Helen	3:07:00 (1,735)	
Smith, Alexandra	5:09:37 (27,651)	
Smith, Ali	5:31:39 (29,925)	
Smith, Alison	4:11:45 (14,806)	
Smith, Alison	4:38:07 (21,605)	
Smith, Alison	4:38:44 (21,774)	
Smith, Alison	5:39:31 (30,520)	
Smith, Amanda	4:23:58 (17,965)	
Smith, Amanda	5:28:41 (29,672)	
Smith, Angela	5:30:32 (29,824)	
Smith, Anne	4:28:49 (19,261)	
Smith, Armorel	6:01:45 (31,600)	
Smith, Barbara	4:50:41 (24,540)	
Smith, Brenda	4:33:55 (20,560)	
Smith, Charlotte	4:45:23 (23,404)	
Smith, Charlotte	5:00:37 (26,390)	
Smith, Chris	4:31:55 (20,061)	
Smith, Claire	5:12:43 (28,049)	
Smith, Eleanor	6:04:38 (31,681)	
Smith, Elizabeth	6:14:32 (31,944)	
Smith, first name unknown	4:38:11 (21,621)	
Smith, Frances	4:49:49 (24,383)	
Smith, Gillian	4:26:45 (18,731)	
Smith, Gillian	5:40:58 (30,614)	
Smith, Glenys	4:39:33 (21,985)	
Smith, Hannah	4:20:15 (16,926)	
Smith, Hayley	4:16:25 (15,956)	
Smith, Hazel	4:08:30 (14,021)	
Smith, Heather	6:15:56 (31,981)	
Smith, Helen	4:15:10 (15,609)	
Smith, Helen	4:18:03 (16,380)	
Smith, Helen	5:35:11 (30,199)	
Smith, Helen	5:48:19 (31,051)	
Smith, Helen	5:51:06 (31,189)	
Smith, Jackie	3:53:01 (9,985)	
Smith, Jackie	5:07:23 (27,354)	

Smith, Jackie....5:11:49 (27,924)
Smith, Jane....4:30:14 (19,658)
Smith, Janet....5:00:04 (26,318)
Smith, Janet....5:51:39 (31,220)
Smith, Jennifer....4:21:51 (17,356)
Smith, Joan....5:11:13 (27,841)
Smith, Jodie....6:42:39 (32,452)
Smith, Josephine....6:01:19 (31,587)
Smith, Joy....4:24:30 (18,121)
Smith, June....5:05:04 (27,033)
Smith, Karen....3:44:51 (7,897)
Smith, Karen....4:17:29 (16,240)
Smith, Karen....4:20:46 (17,061)
Smith, Kathryn....5:05:27 (27,078)
Smith, Keely....5:14:48 (28,282)
Smith, Leisa....3:09:35 (1,998)
Smith, Linda....6:25:32 (32,193)
Smith, Linda....6:43:20 (32,468)
Smith, Lorraine....4:59:32 (26,227)
Smith, Lucy....4:29:43 (19,510)
Smith, Maggie....4:55:06 (25,391)
Smith, Mandy....4:59:35 (26,240)
Smith, Mark....3:34:56 (5,703)
Smith, Maureen....4:44:57 (23,287)
Smith, Melanie....4:44:18 (23,133)
Smith, Michelle....5:17:13 (28,590)
Smith, Nina....4:56:47 (25,729)
Smith, Norma....4:01:53 (12,543)
Smith, Rachel....3:35:57 (5,893)
Smith, Rachel....4:58:21 (26,005)
Smith, Rachel....5:05:46 (27,121)
Smith, Sally....6:12:49 (31,905)
Smith, Samantha....5:49:10 (31,107)
Smith, Sandra....5:41:06 (30,626)
Smith, Sara....4:14:58 (15,565)
Smith, Sara....5:34:31 (30,150)
Smith, Sheila....4:03:56 (12,971)
Smith, Sian....6:48:56 (32,527)
Smith, Susan....4:41:16 (22,418)
Smith, Susan....4:47:21 (23,885)
Smith, Suzanne....6:30:42 (32,290)
Smith, Valerie....5:18:45 (28,750)
Smith, Vicky....4:30:44 (19,770)
Smith, Wendy....4:08:15 (13,961)
Smith, Wendy....4:39:15 (21,910)
Smith, Zoe....4:52:04 (24,791)
Smith, Zoe....7:11:31 (32,717)
Smithers, Min....4:54:49 (25,345)
Smithson, Sonia....6:09:31 (31,822)
Smits, Ann....7:33:59 (32,804)
Smolyansky, Julie....5:10:57 (27,804)
Smyth, Annette....5:39:37 (30,524)
Smyth, Cara....5:27:34 (29,585)
Smyth, Loretta....5:43:25 (30,783)
Smyth, Vyvyenne....7:13:56 (32,729)
Smythe, Elizabeth....6:36:12 (32,375)
Snaith, Susan....3:44:34 (7,813)
Snape, Sandra....3:28:08 (4,540)
Sneddon, Fiona....5:48:49 (31,082)
Snee, Sarah....3:59:00 (11,806)
Snell, Gail....4:59:28 (26,212)
Snell, Rebecca....5:07:58 (27,433)
Snellgrove, Kirstie....5:17:01 (28,565)
Snelling, Emma....4:08:27 (14,003)
Snelling, Jean....4:35:50 (21,036)
Snook, Philomena....5:08:52 (27,546)
Snook, Susan....5:44:00 (30,819)
Snow, Jenny....4:34:29 (20,688)
Soar, Susan....4:06:21 (13,529)
Sobolewska, Magdalema....4:47:51 (23,990)
Soldevila, Belen....4:58:47 (26,094)
Solomon, Penny....5:54:24 (31,328)
Sone, Tracey....4:33:38 (20,500)
Sonebridge-Foster, Vicki....6:15:47 (31,975)
Soper, Kerry....5:38:29 (30,448)
Sophoclides, Sarah....4:32:10 (20,133)
Sore, Kerry....5:48:47 (31,078)
Sorenson, Kory....4:23:36 (17,847)
Sott, Andrea....3:55:24 (10,721)
Soul, Frances....4:42:16 (22,665)
Soulsby, Clare....4:22:39 (17,588)
Soulsby, Linda....5:47:41 (31,023)
Sousa, Rute....3:36:08 (5,942)

Southen, Julie-Maree....4:33:48 (20,539)
Southern, Tanya....4:07:20 (13,754)
Sowerby, Jeanie....7:30:57 (32,793)
Spacey, Joanna....4:39:12 (21,900)
Spackman, Lynne....4:07:16 (13,737)
Spada, Isabella....3:50:44 (9,356)
Spagnol, Françoise....4:48:39 (24,156)
Spagnol, Viviane....4:20:27 (16,984)
Spalla, Karen....4:01:18 (12,391)
Spanswick, Catherine....4:57:57 (25,948)
Spark, Julia....3:08:29 (1,869)
Sparkes, Kay....5:47:55 (31,036)
Sparks, Katharine....4:10:35 (14,532)
Sparks, Yvonne....5:41:51 (30,685)
Sparrow, Eileen....4:36:12 (21,130)
Sparrow, Monica....4:49:21 (24,296)
Speake, Janet....4:09:09 (14,170)
Speake, Rachel....4:09:09 (14,170)
Spear, Jo....5:14:00 (28,195)
Spedding, Helen....4:54:47 (25,337)
Speers, Rebecca....4:22:04 (17,415)
Spence, Ruth....5:14:44 (28,276)
Spencer, Joaanne....4:59:30 (26,216)
Spencer, Joanne....3:24:01 (3,824)
Spencer, Maxine....4:34:11 (20,625)
Spencer, Nicola....5:26:02 (29,447)
Spencer, Vicki....5:23:01 (29,177)
Spencer, Victoria....4:06:06 (13,460)
Spencer-Cusick, Susan....2:58:32 (1,053)
Sperry, Beverly....5:45:23 (30,904)
Sperry, Nicholas....4:24:17 (18,062)
Spiller, Amy....4:45:00 (23,304)
Spink, Jane....4:56:17 (25,652)
Spink, Miranda....7:33:06 (32,801)
Spires, Hattie....5:20:16 (28,911)
Spong, Sue....3:10:22 (2,087)
Spooner, Jeannie....4:00:09 (12,118)
Spooner, Karen....5:16:09 (28,460)
Spratt-Dawson, Josephine....6:57:40 (32,606)
Spray, Michelle....4:29:02 (19,330)
Spriggs, Lisa....4:48:33 (24,133)
Springell, Clare....6:37:06 (32,400)
Springfield, Sharon....4:03:11 (12,811)
St Ledger, Jeannette....4:57:09 (25,802)
Stables, Julie....4:50:29 (24,502)
Stacey, Julie....4:46:26 (23,674)
Stach Kevitz, Adele....3:36:52 (6,088)
Staerck, Moira....6:26:58 (32,216)
Stafford, Lisa....4:53:57 (25,176)
Stafford, Roberta....4:54:19 (25,246)
Staley, Phillipa....6:34:56 (32,351)
Stalker, Sherry....4:10:29 (14,507)
Stallard, Joy....4:47:04 (23,828)
Stamat, Jocelyn....5:12:49 (28,058)
Stamp, Margaret....4:33:36 (20,494)
Standing, Angie....5:00:41 (26,407)
Standring, Jacquetta....4:00:46 (12,249)
Standring, Lucy....3:49:57 (9,163)
Staniforth, Kerry....5:15:06 (28,310)
Stanley, Carol....4:45:50 (23,523)
Stanley, Marie....4:39:16 (21,916)
Stannett, Jennifer....4:27:22 (18,881)
Stannett, Kate....4:15:02 (15,582)
Stanton, Josephine....5:23:26 (29,213)
Stapleton, Julie....4:27:26 (18,896)
Stapleton, Laura....4:26:08 (18,563)
Starbuck, Helen....4:23:15 (17,760)
Stasic, Ria....5:11:11 (27,838)
State, Marie....5:37:48 (30,401)
Staveley-Dick, Joanna....5:12:11 (27,970)
Stead, Deborah....5:46:37 (30,972)
Stead, Deborah....5:53:41 (31,301)
Stead, Helen....3:51:56 (9,657)
Stead, Sarah....5:06:13 (27,188)

LONDON MARATHON

Steadman, Elanor....4:39:31 (21,973)
Steadman, Susan....4:12:27 (14,960)
Stearns, Annabelle....5:10:04 (27,696)
Steed, Amy....4:25:11 (18,305)
Steel, Gillian....5:09:41 (27,659)
Steel, Philippa....4:39:40 (22,009)
Steele, Julia....3:44:35 (7,818)
Steele, Julie....6:05:42 (31,720)
Steele, Kathelen....4:09:41 (14,313)
Steenkamp, Bronwyn....3:35:22 (5,772)
Steer, Deborah....3:19:34 (3,209)
Steer, Rebecca....4:30:47 (19,780)
Stein, Julia....4:39:01 (21,850)
Steinberg, Mara....4:37:10 (21,355)
Steinbrecher, Irene....5:12:04 (27,961)
Steinfeld, Jutta....4:37:01 (21,319)
Stendall, Helen....5:10:50 (27,794)
Stengel, Kim....4:32:27 (20,207)
Stepan, Polly....3:54:14 (10,379)
Stephen, Lynne....3:39:41 (6,661)
Stephenson, Jaine....3:46:35 (8,309)
Stephenson, Kim....4:32:16 (20,152)
Stevens, Alison....5:27:20 (29,562)
Stevens, Amanda....5:35:05 (30,190)
Stevens, Caroline....5:19:43 (28,841)
Stevens, Caron....4:14:41 (15,493)
Stevens, Cheryl....8:25:47 (32,873)
Stevens, Christine....4:51:04 (24,619)
Stevens, Donna....6:01:58 (31,605)
Stevens, Ericka....6:46:34 (32,499)
Stevens, Kay....5:06:05 (27,171)
Stevens, Mary....3:53:08 (10,025)
Stevens, Ondine....5:15:53 (28,426)
Stevens, Sarah....4:13:43 (15,242)
Stevens, Tina....4:55:16 (25,432)
Steward, Ruth....3:59:19 (11,887)
Stewart, Ada....3:41:54 (7,132)
Stewart, Alexandra....3:14:24 (2,599)
Stewart, Jane....4:37:19 (21,404)
Stewart, Jennifer....5:14:35 (28,261)
Stewart, Kirsty....6:16:49 (32,001)
Stewart, Laura....5:22:10 (29,105)
Stewart, Liesel....4:28:43 (19,231)
Stewart, Lindsey....5:25:11 (29,377)
Stewart, Lisa....4:19:32 (16,733)
Stewart, Rozelle....4:26:27 (18,637)
Stewart, Sue....3:43:48 (7,606)
Stewart, Victoria....6:16:08 (31,988)
Stiles, Carol....5:19:49 (28,854)
Stilting, Jolande....4:30:24 (19,693)
Stimpson, Christine....4:14:57 (15,559)
Stimpson, Lucy....6:06:48 (31,752)
Stirling, Alison....4:52:06 (24,800)
Stirton, Janis....4:45:56 (23,547)
Stirton, Zoe....4:13:55 (15,289)
Stnley, Maria....4:40:11 (22,154)
Stobart, Sara....3:54:39 (10,501)
Stobbart, Gloria....5:08:35 (27,506)
Stobie, Carla....3:54:46 (10,539)
Stock, Julie....3:52:29 (9,831)
Stocker, Lisa....5:52:35 (31,259)
Stockham, Elizabeth....4:47:27 (23,906)
Stockham, Jacqui....3:46:24 (8,254)
Stoddard, Amy....5:07:33 (27,382)
Stoddart, Joanna....4:27:47 (18,978)
Stokes, Liz....6:31:04 (32,296)
Stokes, Rachel....6:33:45 (32,337)
Stokes, Reana....4:43:03 (22,849)
Stoll, Barbara....3:59:46 (12,013)
Stone, Gina....3:57:18 (11,293)
Stone, Katherine....5:07:42 (27,399)
Stone, Maria....4:41:38 (22,510)
Stone, Veronica....4:19:49 (16,809)
Stoneham, Elizabeth....5:15:03 (28,304)
Stonehill, Claire....6:27:10 (32,222)
Stoneman, Samantha....4:53:24 (25,049)
Stoner, Ceri....4:19:15 (16,653)
Stones, Sharon....4:42:25 (22,701)
Stoppard, Tracey....4:45:52 (23,533)
Storey, Andrea....6:05:45 (31,723)
Stothard, Helen....3:42:45 (7,326)
Stowell, Camilla....5:22:14 (29,110)
Stowell, Kathryn....4:42:28 (22,714)

Strachan, Caroline 4:37:40 (21,484)
Strachan, Claire 5:12:00 (27,950)
Strachan, Jackie 4:53:05 (24,994)
Strafford, Lesley 4:52:12 (24,824)
Strain, Catriona 5:02:53 (26,725)
Strang, Louise 4:44:26 (23,157)
Strange, Nicolas 5:08:30 (27,496)
Stranks, Elizabeth 4:48:05 (24,054)
Strassle, Claudia 4:17:34 (16,259)
Stratford, Angela 3:54:44 (10,529)
Strauss, Sophie 4:46:27 (23,680)
Stravato, Susan 4:11:45 (14,806)
Strayer, Patty 5:32:25 (29,990)
Stroem, Vibeke 4:57:52 (25,925)
Strohl, Karen 5:19:30 (28,817)
Stronach, Marie 3:44:38 (7,831)
Strong, Hilary 4:55:58 (25,577)
Stropnik, Sigrid 4:33:51 (20,548)
Stroud, Sian 4:40:04 (22,127)
Strover, Hannah 5:12:20 (28,004)
Stuart, Barbara 5:47:52 (31,031)
Stuart, Joanne 4:50:59 (24,606)
Stuart, Pamela 3:53:27 (10,128)
Sturdy, Julia 4:45:22 (23,398)
Sturgeon, Marguerite 4:04:52 (13,175)
Sturgeon, Tina 5:18:43 (28,746)
Sturt, Ruth 4:18:36 (16,513)
Stuttard, Rosalind 4:49:43 (24,364)
Styles, Amber 5:10:45 (27,780)
Styles, Giorgina 4:41:19 (22,433)
Suckling, Alison 5:06:03 (27,165)
Suda, Kimiko 4:23:18 (17,776)
Suldo, Tara 3:52:11 (9,747)
Sullivan, Charlotte 4:53:21 (25,037)
Sullivan, Elizabeth 6:49:28 (32,536)
Sullivan, Jo 4:39:09 (21,886)
Sullivan, Kathryn 4:56:54 (25,745)
Sullivan, Kim 6:52:01 (32,560)
Sullivan, Laura 4:44:28 (23,162)
Summers, Caroline 6:02:33 (31,627)
Sunderland, Wendy 4:25:57 (18,502)
Sundovist, Magdalena 4:45:35 (23,467)
Sunstrum, Deirdre 5:48:40 (31,074)
Suquet, Nathalie 3:14:35 (2,618)
Surrell, Lisa 6:18:23 (32,046)
Surry, Sarah 4:17:13 (16,176)
Sutcliff, Emma 3:50:40 (9,338)
Sutcliffe, Denise 4:41:56 (22,593)
Suter, Christa 4:49:05 (24,255)
Suter, Mirjam 4:22:06 (17,424)
Sutherland, Fiona 3:23:23 (3,709)
Sutton, Catherine 4:15:45 (15,769)
Sutton, Heidi 4:42:07 (22,639)
Sutton, Jane 5:08:53 (27,551)
Sutton, Jasmine 5:02:46 (26,704)
Sutton, Tiffany 4:29:05 (19,344)
Swain, Jane 4:48:47 (24,190)
Swain, Nancy 4:28:23 (19,131)
Swaine, June 5:16:09 (28,460)
Swaine, Tessa 4:32:10 (20,133)
Swan, Eileen 5:01:53 (26,585)
Swan, Victoria 7:56:30 (32,857)
Swanson, Katherine 3:48:57 (8,881)
Swanson, Sandy 3:38:59 (6,520)
Sweatman, Elizabeth 4:21:13 (17,168)
Sweeney, Anne 3:19:07 (3,152)
Sweeney, Elizabeth 5:12:58 (28,077)
Sweetenham, Caroline 4:59:31 (26,221)
Sweetham, Pamela 4:22:39 (17,588)
Sweeting, Joanne 5:15:52 (28,423)
Swinhoe, Yvonne 3:20:56 (3,355)
Switala, Ewa 4:21:53 (17,363)
Swithenby, Margaret 3:24:09 (3,848)
Sykes, Christine 4:36:34 (21,238)
Sykes, Lucy 4:09:41 (14,313)
Sylvester, Ruth 4:49:15 (24,285)
Symes, Eleanor 6:38:00 (32,411)
Symonds, Karen 4:07:10 (13,711)
Symonds, Lynn 5:09:00 (27,572)
Syrett, Joan 3:53:09 (10,030)
Szostak, Teresa 5:00:57 (26,445)
Tabaksert, Leyla 6:56:43 (32,600)
Tabenor, Patricia 5:15:46 (28,406)
Taber, Heather 5:34:22 (30,139)
Taddonio, Karin 6:52:56 (32,568)
Tadecicco, Louise 4:55:39 (25,504)
Tafoya, Nancy 5:50:46 (31,172)
Tait, Gillian 3:08:44 (1,896)
Takac, Angelina 4:31:06 (19,855)
Takahashi, Tomoe 4:39:32 (21,978)
Takenami, Yoko 4:29:20 (19,418)
Talleux, Françoise 4:36:17 (21,147)
Tam, Judy 4:52:49 (24,943)
Tamas, Gabriele 4:14:13 (15,368)
Tamblyn, Debra 7:10:35 (32,709)
Tamplin, Fiona 5:52:31 (31,255)
Tande, Sylvie 5:47:14 (30,998)
Tang, Alice 6:37:11 (32,402)
Tanner, Anita 6:38:14 (32,413)
Tapper, Rosie 4:08:01 (13,916)
Tappin, Anna Maria 4:31:05 (19,852)
Tarling, Serena 4:38:03 (21,584)
Tarpey, Mary 6:21:54 (32,118)
Tarr, Samantha 3:50:51 (9,392)
Tarrant, Hazel 6:47:35 (32,514)
Tarry, Beverley 4:42:27 (22,711)
Tasker, Lisa 4:55:45 (25,533)
Tatam, Margaret 6:12:11 (31,885)
Tate, Emily 4:05:36 (13,348)
Tatum, Dawn 4:23:59 (17,976)
Taun, Margaret 5:58:11 (31,482)
Tavener, Diane 4:28:54 (19,289)
Tawney, Susie 3:35:51 (5,872)
Tay, Regina 5:18:04 (28,678)
Tayler, Caroline 4:00:50 (12,262)
Taylor, Alison 4:35:13 (20,891)
Taylor, Angie 6:43:08 (32,460)
Taylor, Ann 5:28:19 (29,640)
Taylor, Ann 5:33:48 (30,092)
Taylor, Annette 4:15:18 (15,638)
Taylor, Bridgeen 4:54:15 (25,233)
Taylor, Clare 3:46:39 (8,321)
Taylor, Deborah 4:15:55 (15,816)
Taylor, Emma 5:44:47 (30,874)
Taylor, Gill 4:37:31 (21,451)
Taylor, Imogen 4:50:30 (24,507)
Taylor, Jacqueline 5:36:21 (30,299)
Taylor, Jane 4:55:52 (25,553)
Taylor, Janet 5:29:01 (29,695)
Taylor, Jenni 3:47:37 (8,541)
Taylor, Judith 5:16:12 (28,468)
Taylor, Juleen 4:07:35 (13,813)
Taylor, Karen 3:27:48 (4,480)
Taylor, Karen 5:18:50 (28,758)
Taylor, Kate 4:35:12 (20,881)
Taylor, Kim 4:08:15 (13,961)
Taylor, Laura 5:36:31 (30,309)
Taylor, Linda 5:23:04 (29,181)
Taylor, Linda 5:57:30 (31,458)
Taylor, Margaret 5:25:32 (29,404)
Taylor, Michele 5:02:32 (26,674)
Taylor, Nicola 5:13:45 (28,162)
Taylor, Patricia 3:35:14 (5,751)
Taylor, Patricia 5:49:43 (31,131)
Taylor, Penny 5:05:11 (27,042)
Taylor, Ruth 6:48:12 (32,522)
Taylor, Samantha 6:08:25 (31,796)
Taylor, Sandra 7:42:51 (32,832)
Taylor, Sarah 4:34:01 (20,582)
Taylor, Sarah 5:17:59 (28,666)
Taylor, Sarah 6:00:54 (31,576)
Taylor, Siana 10:01:28 (32,897)
Taylor, Sophie 4:52:45 (24,926)
Taylor, Stella 6:20:05 (32,089)
Taylor, Sue 4:17:33 (16,253)
Taylor, Susan 4:46:08 (23,602)
Taylor, Tara 3:31:30 (5,109)
Taylor, Vicky 6:45:25 (32,490)
Taylor-Dowding, Stella 6:20:04 (32,087)
Taylor-Smith, Joanna 4:54:12 (25,225)
Teague, Celina 4:58:49 (26,100)
Teal, Julie 4:51:56 (24,772)
Teale, Carol 5:14:11 (28,212)
Tearis, Beverley 4:29:43 (19,510)
Teasel, Michelle 3:46:22 (8,244)
Teebay, Maxine 5:05:56 (27,149)
Tegner, Ginny 3:25:56 (4,142)
Telfer, Irene 7:59:01 (32,859)
Telford, Christine 4:08:39 (14,066)
Telling, Catharine 6:35:55 (32,372)
Temowo, Bimpe 4:48:30 (24,126)
Temperton, Carol 4:26:24 (18,623)
Temple, Andrea 5:11:23 (27,866)
Templeman, Clare 4:45:48 (23,518)
Templeman, Sharie 5:05:51 (27,135)
Templeman, Sue 5:15:47 (28,409)
Tennant, Andrea 5:06:48 (27,270)
Tennant, Ann 4:41:36 (22,498)
Terjesen, Siri 3:05:32 (1,594)
Terris, Jane 4:34:42 (20,750)
Terry, Rebecca 4:55:07 (25,400)
Tetley, Fiona 5:15:12 (28,324)
Tetley, Julia 5:05:39 (27,105)
Thackray, Jane 3:39:28 (6,617)
Tham, Alice 4:09:50 (14,348)
Thatcher, Joanne 5:52:13 (31,241)
Thatcher, Sarah 4:43:47 (23,011)
Thelen, Jennifer 4:27:02 (18,798)
Thelwell, Belinda 4:52:15 (24,833)
Thevenet-Smith, Ramona 3:23:18 (3,694)
Thirlwell, Christina 4:56:02 (25,589)
Thistleton, Heather 4:18:27 (16,476)
Thom, Julia 5:47:29 (31,017)
Thomas, Alison 5:53:58 (31,311)
Thomas, Antoinette 3:53:23 (10,103)
Thomas, Bernadette 5:20:07 (28,892)
Thomas, Beverley 4:27:55 (19,011)
Thomas, Caroline 5:17:32 (28,634)
Thomas, Cheryl 3:54:09 (10,361)
Thomas, Claire 4:34:17 (20,645)
Thomas, Debbie 3:32:31 (5,272)
Thomas, Denise 4:59:31 (26,221)
Thomas, Edwina 4:08:21 (13,976)
Thomas, Eleanor 4:41:51 (22,570)
Thomas, Elizabeth 5:05:39 (27,105)
Thomas, Emma 5:06:31 (27,233)
Thomas, Faye 4:44:59 (23,297)
Thomas, Frances 4:49:32 (24,327)
Thomas, Georgina 4:45:46 (23,508)
Thomas, Jeanette 3:18:23 (3,056)
Thomas, Joanna 4:53:20 (25,034)
Thomas, Judith 4:00:26 (12,175)
Thomas, Lindsey 4:40:56 (22,339)
Thomas, Lisa 4:38:53 (21,815)
Thomas, Lynn 5:40:10 (30,560)
Thomas, Mary 5:22:17 (29,115)
Thomas, Nicola 4:04:13 (13,032)
Thomas, Patricia 4:02:14 (12,604)
Thomas, Rose 4:13:17 (15,145)
Thomas, Sara 7:30:01 (32,786)
Thomas, Sarah 3:27:37 (4,440)
Thomas, Sarah 4:58:25 (26,021)
Thomas, Sue 4:07:10 (13,711)
Thomi, Muriel 3:30:06 (4,886)
Thompson, Allison 5:00:03 (26,315)
Thompson, Angela 4:16:10 (15,881)
Thompson, Anna 5:39:22 (30,500)
Thompson, Annabel 4:14:47 (15,520)
Thompson, Clare 4:58:34 (26,049)
Thompson, Donna 4:38:33 (21,720)
Thompson, Dorothy 4:37:12 (21,370)
Thompson, Geraldine 5:03:06 (26,762)
Thompson, Gillian 3:52:43 (9,897)
Thompson, Jane 3:32:44 (5,308)
Thompson, Jane 4:15:43 (15,758)
Thompson, Judith 4:58:34 (26,049)
Thompson, Karen 4:11:44 (14,801)
Thompson, Kirsty 4:22:57 (17,689)
Thompson, Lucy 3:16:17 (2,819)
Thompson, Nicola 3:06:55 (1,727)
Thompson, Rachel 4:18:08 (16,394)
Thompson, Ruth 5:08:18 (27,470)
Thompson, Sarah 4:53:12 (25,014)
Thompson, Sharon 4:42:41 (22,763)
Thompson, Tessa 5:00:26 (26,364)
Thompson, Vivienne 3:09:56 (2,032)
Thomson, Beverley 4:49:18 (24,289)
Thomson, Ellen 4:10:42 (14,552)
Thomson, Hazel 4:59:57 (26,300)

Thomson, Margaret	3:56:00 (10,897)
Thomson, Margaret	5:33:53 (30,097)
Thomson, Nicola	4:26:28 (18,642)
Thomson, Nicola	5:39:22 (30,500)
Thomson, Nicola	6:56:22 (32,596)
Thomson, Sarah	5:22:38 (29,146)
Thorley, Bernice	4:54:06 (25,200)
Thorn, Jacqueline	3:11:00 (2,154)
Thorn, Lisa	4:35:10 (20,866)
Thorn, Pauline	5:04:32 (26,957)
Thorn, Sarah	5:43:26 (30,785)
Thornby, Jo-Ann	5:27:29 (29,575)
Thorne, Christine	3:54:41 (10,511)
Thorne, Margaret	6:14:36 (31,946)
Thorne, Sarah	4:10:06 (14,410)
Thornhill, Anna	3:42:26 (7,269)
Thornton, Dawn	4:53:19 (25,031)
Thornton, Jana	5:34:29 (30,147)
Thornton, Juliet	5:54:16 (31,324)
Thornton, Lesley	5:15:14 (28,332)
Thorogood, Wendy	4:55:36 (25,493)
Thorpe, Gaye	5:21:04 (29,006)
Thorvaldsdottir, Marta	4:53:53 (25,141)
Tibbott, Catherine	5:16:53 (28,541)
Tidswell, Beth	5:24:55 (29,359)
Tidy, Julianne	4:04:03 (12,998)
Tiekstka, Wilma	5:48:04 (31,042)
Tier, Grace	4:10:21 (14,471)
Till, Eileen	4:37:50 (21,528)
Tilley, Karen	4:29:48 (19,534)
Tillman, Ulrika	4:55:01 (25,378)
Tilly, Liz	4:52:48 (24,939)
Tilney, Kirsten	3:45:20 (8,006)
Timms, Mandy	5:42:26 (30,721)
Tingle, Alison	3:54:36 (10,487)
Tingle, Gladys	5:55:31 (31,378)
Tingy, Sarah	3:41:48 (7,115)
Tinn, Charlotte	4:44:43 (23,226)
Tinnirello, Guiseppina	4:43:34 (22,972)
Tinsley, Judith	3:28:20 (4,579)
Tinsley, Victoria	6:02:00 (31,608)
Tipping, Julie	4:41:10 (22,394)
Tiptaft, Emma	3:38:15 (6,357)
Tipton, Jacqueline	6:46:57 (32,505)
Titley, Jane	5:03:10 (26,774)
Tock, Sarah	5:09:12 (27,595)
Tocknell, Susan	7:12:47 (32,722)
Todd, Amanda	4:05:45 (13,380)
Todd, Angela	5:25:34 (29,407)
Todd, Carolin	3:54:20 (10,409)
Todd, Nicola	4:46:52 (23,777)
Tokota, Taeko	5:50:04 (31,144)
Toland, Susan	7:14:22 (32,735)
Tolbart, Ruth	4:38:36 (21,742)
Toman, Jan	4:33:23 (20,438)
Tomaszczyk, Barbara	3:33:08 (5,371)
Tombs, Amanda	4:10:05 (14,408)
Tomkins, Jeanette	5:27:17 (29,549)
Tomkins, Mandy	4:04:53 (13,179)
Tomkinson-Hill, Louise	4:38:32 (21,713)
Tomlin, Helen	3:57:58 (11,496)
Tomlinson, Diane	3:31:35 (5,121)
Tomlinson, Jane	4:53:09 (25,002)
Tomlinson, Lee	3:42:31 (7,291)
Tompkin, Diana	3:53:56 (10,287)
Toms, Vivien	4:00:48 (12,256)
Tondolo, Isabella	4:45:12 (23,356)
Tonelli, Susan	4:34:29 (20,688)
Tonge, Jerusha	4:46:34 (23,706)
Tongs, Amanda	4:46:06 (23,592)
Tonking, Lesley	4:53:21 (25,037)
Tonnetot, Lise	3:56:53 (11,168)
Toof, Louise	4:12:09 (14,891)
Toogood, Clare	4:34:45 (20,764)
Toombs, Lesley	5:18:57 (28,773)
Toomey, Emma	6:27:11 (32,225)
Toop, Claire	4:57:00 (25,769)
Toozs-Hobson, Gillian	3:35:33 (5,811)
Topham, Anna	5:00:06 (26,324)
Topham, Kathryn	4:34:18 (20,649)
Tordoff, Abigail	4:46:33 (23,702)
Torn, Helen	5:10:42 (27,774)
Tornare, Edith	4:39:08 (21,883)

Torrent-Marre, Maria	4:39:45 (22,044)
Tosa, Reiko	2:22:46 (31)
Tourniaire, Regine	4:15:05 (15,592)
Towle, Katherine	5:06:44 (27,264)
Towner, Hannah	4:09:29 (14,266)
Townsend, Diane	5:31:07 (29,874)
Townsend, Karen	4:04:26 (13,076)
Townsend, Lucy	3:07:22 (1,758)
Towse, Hilary	4:54:08 (25,208)
Tozer, Sarah	3:45:56 (8,145)
Trabia, Stephanie	4:54:22 (25,257)
Tracey, Lynda	4:06:26 (13,550)
Tracy, Barbara	6:20:11 (32,091)
Travaglino, Marilena	4:46:03 (23,584)
Travis, Jane	4:19:50 (16,810)
Treadwell, Gill	3:46:21 (8,236)
Tregaskes, Sarah	4:43:49 (23,022)
Tresler, Gabrielle	4:33:29 (20,459)
Trevena, Niki Marie	4:24:58 (18,254)
Trewin, Elaine	4:45:56 (23,547)
Tribe, Julie	4:21:27 (17,232)
Tricker, Mary	4:56:27 (25,684)
Trigger, Adrienne	6:52:55 (32,567)
Trikic, Jessica	6:20:11 (32,091)
Trocherie, Ginette	3:54:30 (10,459)
Trodd-Pomeroy, Jane	5:03:10 (26,774)
Trollen, Carole	3:57:37 (11,400)
Trollope, Kellie	3:08:54 (1,922)
Tropeano, Mandy	4:27:21 (18,875)
Troughton, Marina	3:39:29 (6,625)
Trow, Lisa	5:41:20 (30,641)
Trowbridge, Caroline	4:24:30 (18,121)
Trowbridge, Tracy	5:14:40 (28,271)
Trucy, Laura	5:10:34 (27,760)
Truesdale, Jan	4:51:49 (24,746)
Trump, Amanda	4:20:53 (17,083)
Truscott, Helen	7:00:01 (32,628)
Truscott, Jane	7:37:20 (32,815)
Truswell, Sandra	4:15:53 (15,804)
Tse, Tania	3:49:47 (9,125)
Tucker, Susan	5:06:43 (27,261)
Tucker, Terry	4:57:52 (25,925)
Tuckett, Kate	5:00:41 (26,407)
Tuellmann, Jutta	5:18:00 (28,668)
Tuffen, Lynn	4:40:09 (22,145)
Tuffin, Tracie	3:35:35 (5,822)
Tuite, Helen	4:18:42 (16,526)
Tull, Jane	5:04:40 (26,973)
Tullett, Anne	5:41:47 (30,673)
Tully, Anne	4:13:59 (15,308)
Tulu, Derartu	2:28:35 (52)
Tunstall, Rebecca	3:50:57 (9,411)
Turley, Elizabeth	4:32:21 (20,173)
Turley, Susan	4:33:35 (20,486)
Turnbull, Bridgit	5:39:22 (30,500)
Turnbull, Charlotte	4:44:46 (23,240)
Turnbull, Lone	4:44:41 (23,214)
Turnbull, Tina	4:48:27 (24,116)
Turner, Alison	3:17:02 (2,907)
Turner, Christina	6:29:29 (32,264)
Turner, Helen	4:31:19 (19,906)
Turner, Helen	4:33:35 (20,486)
Turner, Jenny	5:36:08 (30,286)
Turner, Katherine	6:10:47 (31,853)
Turner, Nicola	4:21:16 (17,183)
Turner, Rosslyn	6:05:38 (31,719)
Turner, Sarah	4:18:12 (16,414)
Turner, Sarah	4:28:17 (19,105)
Turner, Sharron	6:02:28 (31,624)
Turner, Teena	4:43:24 (22,932)
Turner, Wendy	4:27:02 (18,798)
Turnill, Lucy	6:44:51 (32,485)
Turpin, Anna	4:35:25 (20,927)
Turpin, Claire	5:08:03 (27,440)
Turrell, Tracy	4:53:50 (25,131)
Turton, Elizabeth	3:59:44 (12,003)
Turton, Helen	3:31:43 (5,154)
Tweed, Daveena	3:56:50 (11,149)
Tweed, Katharine	4:15:59 (15,833)
Twelvetree, Yvonne	3:58:40 (11,695)
Twomey, Catherine	3:23:56 (3,807)
Twyman, Lucy	5:04:47 (26,997)
Tyas, Diane	6:31:41 (32,299)

Tye, Victoria	4:58:59 (26,128)
Tyler, Deborah	5:13:56 (28,180)
Tyler, Laura	4:51:46 (24,736)
Tyler, Pat	5:20:46 (28,971)
Tyler, Victoria	4:22:38 (17,583)
Tyrrell, Rebecca	4:52:11 (24,813)
Tysoe, Julia	3:54:15 (10,386)
Ullrich, Viola	4:43:24 (22,932)
Underwood, Jane	7:05:01 (32,670)
Underwood, Karen	4:10:07 (14,414)
Underwood, Rachel	3:32:04 (5,202)
Upton, Jane	5:06:05 (27,171)
Urban, Sonja	3:58:46 (11,722)
Urquhart, Flora	8:41:10 (32,883)
Urrutia, Vanessa	4:46:45 (23,747)
Urschel, Christina	5:46:52 (30,980)
Urwin, Jackie	4:52:06 (24,800)
Usher, Donna	4:53:27 (25,057)
Usher, Elizabeth	3:39:14 (6,579)
Usher, Judith	5:04:56 (27,011)
Usher, Lindsey	5:06:55 (27,283)
Utting, Jane	4:04:10 (13,019)
Vaccari, Luisa	4:22:18 (17,476)
Vagniez, Fleur	3:59:33 (11,951)
Vaillant, Claire	4:31:49 (20,035)
Vaillant, Sandrine	5:35:41 (30,250)
Vakil, Zarina	5:31:57 (29,950)
Vakildour, Janet	4:02:45 (12,713)
Valentine, Charley	4:32:19 (20,165)
Vallance, Justine	4:32:02 (20,096)
Vam Lamoen, Ellen	4:09:43 (14,321)
Van De Zande, Janice	4:18:00 (16,374)
Van Den Bergh, Sophie	4:56:24 (25,678)
Van Der Merwe, Mauneen	4:54:05 (25,198)
Van Der Welle, Sian	5:06:55 (27,283)
Van Dijk, Simone	5:50:29 (31,160)
Van Eck, Sylvia	6:12:30 (31,895)
Van Gough, Ruth	4:57:00 (25,769)
Van Hove, Thesesa	4:44:19 (23,134)
Van Ouwerkerk, Monique	4:41:49 (22,561)
Van Ryssen, Frances	5:40:56 (30,609)
Van Wyk, Bernette	4:26:36 (18,680)
Van Zyl, Anna	3:52:19 (9,785)
Vandamme, Helene	4:52:22 (24,856)
Vandepeear, Linda	3:56:57 (11,192)
Vanes, Rita	4:20:18 (16,940)
Vanhatalo, Emmi	3:59:34 (11,958)
Varah, Lesley	5:01:52 (26,580)
Varley, Charlotte	3:55:48 (10,840)
Vartan, Jennie	3:24:25 (3,904)
Vasey, Joanne	5:17:20 (28,608)
Vassall, Jacqui	5:12:54 (28,069)
Vaughan, Diane	4:38:54 (21,819)
Vaughan, Pauline	5:08:46 (27,535)
Vaughan, Susan	3:49:29 (9,036)
Vaughan, Susan	4:01:00 (12,308)
Veneer, Georgia	7:43:02 (32,834)
Venn, Kerry	3:44:40 (7,839)
Venn, Wendy	4:30:32 (19,715)
Verdini, Serena	3:51:32 (9,555)
Vere Hodge, Stephanie	4:55:39 (25,504)
Verjee, Sabrina	4:23:15 (17,760)
Verlander, Lucy	6:20:53 (32,102)
Verma, Misty	4:36:29 (21,214)
Vernon, Emma	4:37:01 (21,319)
Vernon, Natalie	4:45:20 (23,389)
Versteynen, Jeanne	4:10:48 (14,576)
Vezzu, Joanna	5:11:35 (27,892)
Viatge, Jo	4:46:48 (23,757)
Vick, Sarah	4:46:11 (23,618)
Vicker, Paula	3:11:37 (2,215)
Vickers, Lynn	4:21:35 (17,274)
Vickers, Mary	4:20:56 (17,090)
Victor, Christina	4:24:38 (18,154)
Vidler, Nikki	4:09:19 (14,224)
Vietz, Heidi	5:32:23 (29,987)
Vigfusdottir, Kristin	4:07:03 (13,686)
Vila-Mercader, Elena	3:51:30 (9,543)
Vildosola, Paula	3:26:02 (4,154)
Vincent, Laura	4:23:52 (17,937)
Vincent, Pam	6:05:32 (31,714)
Vincent Smith, Pamela	6:48:56 (32,527)
Vine, Debbie	4:49:25 (24,304)

Vines, Lisa 3:55:52 (10,864)
Virgo, Avril 4:45:30 (23,436)
Visser, Marina 4:32:52 (20,327)
Vitale Cumper, Giulietta 3:34:20 (5,587)
Vocanson, Valerie 5:37:52 (30,405)
Voitin, Clare 3:27:22 (4,391)
Voller, Karin 3:25:02 (3,991)
Von Dem Hagen, Beatrix 4:10:04 (14,403)
Vosloo, Lee-Anne 5:54:46 (31,341)
Vosper-Brown, Rachael 3:58:03 (11,528)
Vranic, Dragica 4:21:42 (17,313)
Vuagniaux, Alison 2:58:24 (1,038)
Vynnycky, Emilia 3:44:38 (7,831)
Vyse, Denise 5:52:20 (31,245)
Waddell, Sarah 6:43:12 (32,464)
Wade, Maxine 3:52:11 (9,747)
Wade, Melanie 4:04:42 (13,135)
Wadey, Elizabeth 4:22:20 (17,493)
Wadforth, Catherine 3:27:22 (4,391)
Waeber, Chantal 4:25:09 (18,299)
Wagman, Debra 4:36:20 (21,174)
Wagner, Helga 4:39:34 (21,989)
Wagstaff, Dorothy 4:21:45 (17,324)
Wain, Michelle 5:24:32 (29,329)
Wainwright, Jean 4:32:57 (20,345)
Waite, Diane 4:29:09 (19,367)
Waite, Elizabeth 4:36:07 (21,106)
Waite, Pauline 5:20:07 (28,892)
Wakabayashi, Naoko 4:35:21 (20,912)
Wake, Nina 4:29:38 (19,494)
Walcroft, Freda 6:59:00 (32,614)
Walder, Antonia 3:52:31 (9,842)
Walder, Julia 3:52:31 (9,842)
Waldmeyer, Irene 6:15:41 (31,971)
Walker, Alexandra 5:03:03 (26,752)
Walker, Alison 4:41:40 (22,519)
Walker, Amanda 3:49:13 (8,946)
Walker, Angela 3:10:24 (2,090)
Walker, Charlotte 4:01:01 (12,314)
Walker, Claire 4:10:46 (14,566)
Walker, Emma 4:46:58 (23,805)
Walker, Georgie 7:17:34 (32,749)
Walker, Hilary 3:29:20 (4,761)
Walker, Lucy 4:41:30 (22,476)
Walker, Lynsey 4:40:21 (22,199)
Walker, Merryl 3:57:43 (11,430)
Walker, Rachel 4:44:45 (23,236)
Walker, Sharon 4:23:58 (17,965)
Walker, Susan 3:40:00 (6,733)
Walker, Susan 4:58:42 (26,079)
Walker, Sylvia 5:22:18 (29,117)
Walker, Yvonne 4:56:37 (25,705)
Wallace, Alana 4:32:36 (20,243)
Wallace, Anna 3:50:18 (9,253)
Wallace, Dawn 4:13:23 (15,162)
Wallace, Hannah 6:59:30 (32,620)
Wallace, Shirley 4:51:09 (24,638)
Wallace, Susan 5:12:56 (28,073)
Wallen, Brigid 3:22:20 (3,566)
Waller, Annie 4:58:50 (26,104)
Waller, Jane 5:34:57 (30,181)
Wallis, Elizabeth 4:26:57 (18,775)
Wallis, Victoria 4:08:46 (14,087)
Walmsley, Elsie 5:00:29 (26,371)
Walpole, Tina 4:53:40 (25,097)
Walsh, Catherine 5:45:39 (30,920)
Walsh, Christine 4:51:00 (24,611)
Walsh, Clara 4:53:52 (25,136)
Walsh, Joanne 5:01:52 (26,580)
Walsh, Joyce 4:45:56 (23,547)
Walsh, Monica 4:48:14 (24,076)
Walsh, Victoria 4:41:46 (22,549)
Walter, Lise 4:38:20 (21,669)
Walters, Karen 4:40:33 (22,244)
Walton, Beverley 4:25:16 (18,325)
Walton, Valerie 3:29:39 (4,820)
Walton, Valerie 4:36:35 (21,241)
Walton, Wendy Jane 3:39:43 (6,671)
Wanniaratchy, Linda 3:56:54 (11,174)
Wapper, Patricia 5:16:11 (28,466)
Warburton, Pauline 4:07:08 (13,701)
Ward, Annette 3:33:33 (5,436)
Ward, Caroline 3:36:47 (6,074)
Ward, Davina 4:26:12 (18,575)
Ward, Elan 4:51:55 (24,770)
Ward, Elizabeth 3:53:23 (10,103)
Ward, Jane 3:36:51 (6,086)
Ward, Joanne 4:16:38 (16,019)
Ward, Joanne 5:10:35 (27,761)
Ward, Mina 6:02:47 (31,632)
Ward, Rebecca 5:05:15 (27,051)
Ward, Sarah 5:14:27 (28,239)
Ward, Susan 5:47:01 (30,988)
Ward, Tracy 4:07:48 (13,872)
Ward, Zietta 5:38:27 (30,443)
Wardlaw, Susan 6:36:56 (32,393)
Wardle, Sarah 6:12:43 (31,900)
Ware, Ann 5:04:43 (26,981)
Wareing, Hazel 4:15:32 (15,704)
Warenius, Eleanor 6:01:17 (31,586)
Waring, Gabrielle 3:21:59 (3,520)
Waring, June 5:16:06 (28,454)
Warne, Julie 4:12:42 (15,025)
Warner, Anne 4:46:12 (23,623)
Warner, Denise 4:12:13 (14,905)
Warner, Gail 3:43:33 (7,540)
Warner, Julie 4:12:14 (14,909)
Warner, Kathryn 4:32:47 (20,298)
Warnke, Emily 4:48:02 (24,041)
Warrell, Althea 5:58:37 (31,502)
Warren, Alexandra 4:38:19 (21,663)
Warren, Karen 3:56:17 (10,983)
Warren, Karen 6:31:41 (32,299)
Warren, Sara 4:04:41 (13,132)
Warren, Sarah 4:34:29 (20,688)
Warren, Suzanne 5:58:20 (31,489)
Warren, Zoe 6:16:05 (31,986)
Warrington, Sarah 4:55:53 (25,554)
Warville, Colleen 6:36:43 (32,387)
Warwick, Cindy 4:13:12 (15,121)
Warwick, Lin 4:22:26 (17,531)
Washington, Michelle 4:23:15 (17,760)
Wastnage, Rachel 3:42:08 (7,186)
Waterhouse, Jane 5:00:20 (26,349)
Waterhouse, Larraine 5:12:58 (28,077)
Waterman, Patricia 4:31:11 (19,877)
Waterman, Sarah 4:37:55 (21,553)
Waters, Beatriz 5:23:34 (29,229)
Waters, Emma 5:21:34 (29,048)
Waters, Joan 7:20:31 (32,757)
Wates, Melanie 4:00:11 (12,127)
Watkins, Adele 4:32:30 (20,215)
Watkins, Beth 5:46:36 (30,971)
Watkins, Marina 6:10:24 (31,845)
Watkinson, Lynne 3:16:27 (2,837)
Watkinson, Rebecca 5:40:13 (30,565)
Watson, Alicia 3:41:03 (6,977)
Watson, Andrea 3:20:15 (3,283)
Watson, Christina 4:18:46 (16,538)
Watson, Claire 4:24:04 (18,001)
Watson, Denise 5:02:10 (26,624)
Watson, Diane 4:44:34 (23,193)
Watson, Emma 4:16:12 (15,891)
Watson, Janet 3:39:52 (6,705)
Watson, Jason 5:01:37 (26,548)
Watson, Joanne 4:48:46 (24,182)
Watson, Laura 3:52:39 (9,881)
Watson, Nicola 6:49:14 (32,534)
Watson, Pamela 4:19:05 (16,614)
Watson, Pippa 4:37:54 (21,547)
Watson, Valerie 3:53:26 (10,116)
Watt, Caroline 4:01:16 (12,381)
Watt, Glenys 5:27:29 (29,575)
Watts, Amelia 3:54:39 (10,501)
Watts, Carolyn 4:25:21 (18,348)
Watts, Heather 5:04:24 (26,948)
Watts, Heidi 5:23:54 (29,273)
Watts, Laura 5:00:48 (26,421)
Watts, Nicky 4:42:16 (22,665)
Watts, Paula 4:31:06 (19,855)
Waugh, Carol 5:23:44 (29,255)
Wawn, Sarah 4:25:57 (18,502)
Way, Fiona 5:30:51 (29,852)
Waylen, Kate 4:52:36 (24,900)
Wear, Rachel 4:07:45 (13,858)
Wearmouth, Kaye 4:45:14 (23,366)
Weaver, Clair 4:17:48 (16,328)
Weaver, Pauline 4:42:13 (22,651)
Webb, Anne 3:12:39 (2,379)
Webb, Dawn 6:24:20 (32,172)
Webber, Kate 3:47:40 (8,551)
Webbon, Victoria 5:48:51 (31,087)
Weber, Monique 5:21:50 (29,081)
Webster, Camilla 5:56:47 (31,437)
Webster, Catherine 4:22:28 (17,538)
Webster, Catherine 4:41:36 (22,498)
Webster, Deborah 5:15:53 (28,426)
Webster, Emma 5:01:34 (26,537)
Webster, Evelyn 3:25:20 (4,037)
Weekes, Lisa 4:39:44 (22,037)
Wehrli, Barbara 5:09:09 (27,589)
Weil, Corinne 3:22:53 (3,647)
Weipers, Estelle 4:24:14 (18,048)
Weir, Veta 3:42:37 (7,307)
Welch, Rebecca 4:43:13 (22,890)
Weldon, Sarah 6:33:20 (32,327)
Weller, Cheryl 5:03:31 (26,825)
Weller, Susan 4:55:24 (25,466)
Wellington, Christine 3:08:17 (1,836)
Wells, Diane 4:53:18 (25,024)
Wells, Heather 4:16:34 (15,996)
Wells, Jenny 5:19:11 (28,795)
Wells, Jill 4:43:38 (22,983)
Wells, Philippa 5:23:14 (29,197)
Wells, Sita 4:53:23 (25,046)
Welman, Karen 6:39:15 (32,424)
Welsh, Stephanie 3:27:56 (4,505)
Welstead, Samantha 4:35:24 (20,926)
Wemyss, Sarah 4:25:16 (18,325)
Wenck, Mary 4:04:54 (13,183)
Wensley, Suzanne 4:54:41 (25,320)
Went, Angela 3:55:14 (10,675)
Werro, Carmen 4:26:59 (18,782)
Wescott, Sandra 4:22:48 (17,639)
West, Amanda 4:30:02 (19,603)
West, Dawn 6:28:15 (32,242)
West, Joan 5:33:17 (30,052)
West, Julie 4:31:11 (19,877)
West, Julie 4:42:10 (22,642)
West, Leander 4:19:28 (16,713)
West, Lilly 4:51:14 (24,659)
West, Nicola 4:44:12 (23,108)
West, Tracey 3:09:01 (1,935)
West, Zoe 3:53:16 (10,071)
Westerlund, Tina 4:51:52 (24,756)
Weston, Denise 3:53:04 (10,003)
Weston, Joanne 5:42:36 (30,732)
Weston, Judith 4:02:13 (12,601)
Weston, Pauline 4:37:47 (21,517)
Weston, Tracy 5:24:43 (29,340)
Westrop, Clare 6:08:12 (31,787)
Westrop, Lindsey 6:07:58 (31,781)
Westwood, Sally 4:31:44 (20,018)
Whalley, Sarah 5:22:25 (29,125)
Whalley, Susie 3:54:30 (10,459)
Wharam, Hilary 4:17:03 (16,133)
Wharton, Celia 5:06:05 (27,171)
Wharton, Emma 3:31:58 (5,184)
Wharton, Teresa 4:33:57 (20,569)
Wheatley, Andrée 4:09:37 (14,295)
Wheatley, Samantha 4:14:09 (15,345)
Wheatley, Sarah 4:09:02 (14,140)
Wheeler, Emma 5:12:16 (27,989)
Wheeler, Jennifer 5:41:31 (30,658)
Wheeler, Lorraine 3:58:07 (11,550)
Wheeler, Mary 4:43:42 (22,997)
Wheeler, Sarah 4:58:57 (26,121)
Wherry, Becky 5:41:46 (30,669)
Whiley, Lesley 2:55:58 (826)
Whisenhunt, Elizabeth 4:09:58 (14,377)
Whitbourn-Hughes, Rachel 3:59:17 (11,878)
White, Angela 4:15:38 (15,733)
White, Anna 4:31:50 (20,037)
White, Berry 5:22:14 (29,110)
White, Caroline 3:30:16 (4,909)
White, Catherine 4:32:36 (20,243)
White, Dawn 4:26:17 (18,597)
White, Elaine 5:48:35 (31,069)
White, Gillian 4:17:41 (16,288)

White, Ian....4:15:49 (15,783)
White, Jane....5:19:31 (28,821)
White, Janine....4:35:44 (21,015)
White, Jenny....4:05:05 (13,229)
White, Jessica....4:41:47 (22,553)
White, Katherine....4:49:32 (24,327)
White, Kay....5:31:57 (29,950)
White, Laura....4:49:32 (24,327)
White, Louise....4:19:21 (16,677)
White, Madeline....5:32:20 (29,982)
White, Melanie....4:36:50 (21,286)
White, Nicola....4:25:36 (18,418)
White, Odette....4:07:43 (13,845)
White, Sarah....4:43:39 (22,986)
White, Sharon....4:03:41 (12,914)
White, Sheila....3:45:37 (8,074)
White, Sonia....4:59:13 (26,165)
White, Stephanie....5:39:06 (30,477)
Whitefield, Lynda....5:17:11 (28,587)
Whitehead, Sarah....3:27:09 (4,352)
Whitehouse, Angela....3:17:20 (2,937)
Whitehouse, Gillian....4:24:43 (18,178)
Whitehouse, Zoe....5:42:26 (30,721)
Whiteley, Emma....4:37:40 (21,484)
Whiteman, Rosemary....6:30:28 (32,288)
Whitemore, Helen....4:06:40 (13,606)
Whiteside, Helen....4:36:49 (21,280)
Whitfield, Diane....4:34:14 (20,636)
Whitfield, Georgina....4:36:48 (21,276)
Whitfield, Lesley....4:52:16 (24,836)
Whitman, Elizabeth....4:49:35 (24,339)
Whitmore, Naomi....4:51:26 (24,686)
Whitmore, Samantha....4:37:14 (21,380)
Whitney, Kate....3:48:31 (8,751)
Whittaker, Alexandra....5:30:26 (29,814)
Whittaker, Alexandra....6:37:17 (32,404)
Whittaker, Beth....3:52:53 (9,945)
Whittaker, Diana....7:11:55 (32,718)
Whittaker, Geraldine....4:43:57 (23,055)
Whittaker, Nadezhda....4:13:15 (15,134)
Whittaker, Samantha....4:57:48 (25,915)
Whittall, Liz....5:42:19 (30,714)
Whittenbury, Alison....4:28:47 (19,252)
Whittet, Sally....5:08:25 (27,489)
Whittington, Jelica....4:31:59 (20,081)
Whittle, Carrie....4:53:49 (25,124)
Whittle, Gillian....5:13:43 (28,160)
Whittle, Tracy....5:19:04 (28,783)
Whittome, Sarah....7:26:33 (32,777)
Whitty, Catherine....3:49:53 (9,148)
Why, Christina....4:34:22 (20,664)
Whysall, Hannah....4:08:35 (14,051)
Whysall, Polly....4:37:39 (21,477)
Whyte, Margaret....3:35:57 (5,893)
Whyte, Rebecca....3:55:25 (10,727)
Wickbold, Kirsten....4:32:25 (20,194)
Wickens, Janet....5:10:29 (27,747)
Wicks, Kay....3:16:42 (2,862)
Widdop, Anne....5:07:52 (27,419)
Widdowson, Karen....3:48:50 (8,849)
Widdowson, Sue....5:46:21 (30,957)
Wiegank, Susanne....4:07:23 (13,771)
Wieringa-Nienhuis, Fenny....4:48:33 (24,133)
Wigan, Louise....6:59:32 (32,622)
Wigger, Barbara....4:56:10 (25,623)
Wiggill, Lee-Anne....4:15:21 (15,653)
Wiggins, Ruth....4:18:05 (16,385)
Wightwick, Juliet....5:00:06 (26,324)
Wijsman, Katharine....4:05:48 (13,393)
Wilcocks, Patricia....5:49:34 (31,125)
Wild, Clare....4:48:01 (24,037)
Wild, Margaret....3:34:11 (5,561)
Wiles, Julia....3:52:57 (9,960)
Wilkerson, Leonie....5:41:01 (30,619)
Wilkes, Cindy....3:35:44 (5,853)
Wilkes, Denese....6:45:26 (32,491)
Wilkie, Caroline....5:07:00 (27,295)
Wilkie, Gillian....4:15:08 (15,603)
Wilkie, Rose....3:59:13 (11,865)
Wilkin, Susan....4:11:17 (14,690)
Wilkins, Christine....4:33:34 (20,477)
Wilkinson, Anne....4:14:17 (15,385)
Wilkinson, Carolyn....4:17:04 (16,135)
Wilkinson, Dorothy....3:32:53 (5,335)
Wilkinson, Francine....4:32:53 (20,329)
Wilkinson, Joy....3:39:50 (6,693)
Wilkinson, Karen....4:57:41 (25,897)
Wilkinson, Melanie....4:48:34 (24,141)
Wilkinson, Sarah....4:32:47 (20,298)
Wilkinson, Sharon....4:38:54 (21,819)
Willer, Lucy....4:37:46 (21,509)
Willett, Christina....4:33:29 (20,459)
Williams, Affa....3:16:52 (2,890)
Williams, Amber....3:54:22 (10,417)
Williams, Anita....5:37:00 (30,346)
Williams, Ann....3:59:10 (11,845)
Williams, Anna....4:15:29 (15,689)
Williams, Dawn....4:09:17 (14,209)
Williams, Donna....4:34:49 (20,777)
Williams, Eileen....4:52:54 (24,960)
Williams, Emma....4:37:10 (21,355)
Williams, Esta....4:10:32 (14,518)
Williams, Frances....3:34:02 (5,524)
Williams, Frances....3:37:10 (6,144)
Williams, Frances....6:15:41 (31,971)
Williams, Helen....4:43:02 (22,847)
Williams, Helen....4:46:07 (23,594)
Williams, Jacqueline....4:20:25 (16,974)
Williams, Jenny....6:30:48 (32,294)
Williams, Jessica....5:07:23 (27,354)
Williams, Justine....4:55:53 (25,554)
Williams, Kate....4:17:04 (16,135)
Williams, Katherine....5:03:25 (26,813)
Williams, Madeleine....4:39:23 (21,946)
Williams, Margaret....5:41:22 (30,644)
Williams, Marian....6:39:31 (32,432)
Williams, Mary....3:55:32 (10,758)
Williams, Melanie....5:04:34 (26,960)
Williams, Nina....4:53:33 (25,079)
Williams, Pamla....4:56:59 (25,763)
Williams, Rebecca....5:23:25 (29,211)
Williams, Regina....4:12:52 (15,054)
Williams, Rochelle....4:33:46 (20,528)
Williams, Rosalind....5:59:01 (31,512)
Williams, Ruth....4:38:45 (21,782)
Williams, Safina....4:42:23 (22,691)
Williams, Sally....5:21:02 (28,994)
Williams, Sarah....3:11:05 (2,166)
Williams, Sarah....4:20:01 (16,866)
Williams, Sharon....5:26:56 (29,516)
Williams, Sian....4:50:35 (24,520)
Williams, Silifa....4:56:59 (25,763)
Williams, Susan....3:53:41 (10,205)
Williams, Susan....3:53:47 (10,237)
Williams, Teresa....3:51:00 (9,425)
Williams, Vanessa....4:39:11 (21,892)
Williamson, Chris....4:42:42 (22,768)
Williamson, Deborah....4:45:19 (23,384)
Williamson, Doreen....6:45:35 (32,493)
Williamson, Julia....5:59:23 (31,527)
Williamson, Rae....4:42:29 (22,719)
Williamson, Sue....3:25:46 (4,109)
Willis, Christine....5:12:16 (27,989)
Willis, Claire....3:41:01 (6,966)
Willis, Debbie....5:16:36 (28,511)
Willis, Gemma....3:55:43 (10,818)
Willis, Judith....5:18:00 (28,668)
Willis, Katrina....3:54:43 (10,519)
Willis, Nicola....4:59:00 (26,130)
Willis, Sharon....6:23:45 (32,163)
Willix, Helene....2:40:23 (191)
Willmott, Nikki....4:53:01 (24,978)
Wills, Ruth....5:44:02 (30,822)
Wills, Sabrina....6:37:20 (32,406)
Wills, Sarah....5:18:06 (28,682)
Willson, Lea....6:18:00 (32,039)
Wilsmore, Karen....5:18:59 (28,776)
Wilson, Anita....3:53:00 (9,976)
Wilson, Anne....3:38:18 (6,370)
Wilson, Anne....4:11:57 (14,848)
Wilson, Beverley....2:59:42 (1,151)
Wilson, Caroline....3:54:07 (10,351)
Wilson, Dawn....4:35:12 (20,881)
Wilson, Denise....6:35:18 (32,358)
Wilson, Diana....4:49:26 (24,309)
Wilson, Dinah....4:48:51 (24,206)
Wilson, Elizabeth....4:50:06 (24,439)
Wilson, Freda....4:53:52 (25,136)
Wilson, Georgina....4:44:55 (23,274)
Wilson, Heidi....3:22:46 (3,627)
Wilson, Helen....3:58:28 (11,643)
Wilson, Irene....5:16:34 (28,508)
Wilson, Janet....3:34:37 (5,641)
Wilson, Janis....3:38:10 (6,335)
Wilson, Jean....4:55:31 (25,483)
Wilson, Joy....5:11:06 (27,824)
Wilson, Louise....5:13:13 (28,105)
Wilson, Louise....5:45:36 (30,915)
Wilson, Mandy....4:26:42 (18,717)
Wilson, Nicole....5:33:32 (30,075)
Wilson, Petra....4:01:18 (12,391)
Wilson, Phyl....4:43:39 (22,986)
Wilson, Rosemary....3:40:57 (6,949)
Wilson, Sally....4:28:28 (19,159)
Wilson, Sally....5:11:37 (27,895)
Wilson, Sara....7:34:33 (32,805)
Wilson, Sarah....4:15:22 (15,657)
Wilson, Simone....3:50:15 (9,235)
Wilson, Tracey....4:04:11 (13,022)
Wiltshire, Brenda....4:26:12 (18,575)
Wiltshire, Rachel....6:17:26 (32,018)
Windeers, Catherine....4:38:49 (21,796)
Winder, Mel....5:18:24 (28,716)
Windus, Barbara....6:00:46 (31,571)
Winearls, Lyn....5:09:43 (27,666)
Wing, Julia....4:49:14 (24,281)
Wing, Rebecca....4:44:24 (23,151)
Wingrove, Esme....5:58:30 (31,497)
Winkelmann, Simone....4:35:49 (21,034)
Winkfield, Hazel....6:40:31 (32,439)
Winner, Angelika....3:50:35 (9,317)
Winter, Anne-Marie....4:24:02 (17,990)
Winter, Carol....4:46:19 (23,639)
Winter, Wendy....7:47:45 (32,844)
Winterburn, Jayne....5:15:08 (28,311)
Winterburn, Sandra....3:35:28 (5,799)
Wisbey, Michelle....6:15:10 (31,962)
Wise, Julie....4:16:44 (16,045)
Wise, Kirsty....4:10:19 (14,464)
Wiser, Joanna....5:01:37 (26,548)
Wishart, Caroline....3:46:50 (8,351)
Witham, Helen....3:40:12 (6,786)
Withers, Hilary....3:54:39 (10,501)
Withers, Karen....6:08:51 (31,808)
Withey, Jill....7:53:53 (32,851)
Witte, Stefanie....4:07:49 (13,876)
Wixley, Judith....4:13:44 (15,248)
Wogan, Christine....4:23:22 (17,791)
Wojta, Andrea....4:02:53 (12,751)
Wolfe, Paula....7:08:15 (32,687)
Wolfendale, Vivienne....3:42:51 (7,349)
Wolfrom, Annette....2:46:56 (356)
Wolfson, Jacqueline....4:41:16 (22,418)
Wolkowski, Sally....5:22:23 (29,123)
Wong, Jean....6:10:46 (31,851)
Wong, Melinda....3:54:38 (10,494)
Wong, Suzie....3:34:38 (5,645)
Wood, Charlotte....4:05:45 (13,380)
Wood, Emma....5:17:16 (28,596)
Wood, Gaynor....4:24:35 (18,143)
Wood, Geraldine....5:10:31 (27,752)
Wood, Jo....4:56:14 (25,643)
Wood, Juliette....5:05:23 (27,075)
Wood, Kate....4:32:46 (20,294)
Wood, Michelle....5:19:33 (28,825)
Wood, Michelle....5:49:52 (31,138)
Wood, Nicola....4:17:18 (16,203)
Wood, Pauline....4:58:04 (25,959)
Wood, Rachel....4:22:23 (17,512)
Wood, Rebecca....4:27:02 (18,798)
Wood, Rebecca....4:38:35 (21,730)
Wood, Sara....5:16:14 (28,472)
Wood, Zoe....4:51:21 (24,672)
Woodard, Fran....4:14:37 (15,473)
Woodburn, Jane....4:16:35 (16,002)
Woodcock, Mary....6:12:39 (31,896)
Woodford, Gloria....5:13:17 (28,112)
Woodham, Heather....6:30:08 (32,280)
Woodhams, Emma....4:10:23 (14,487)

Wooding, Teresa.....................5:02:49 (26,713)
Woodroffe, Nikki.....................5:11:03 (27,819)
Woods, Alison.....................5:08:21 (27,477)
Woods, Anna.....................4:56:08 (25,618)
Woods, Helen.....................4:10:02 (14,393)
Woods, Joanna.....................5:20:40 (28,957)
Woods, Lynn.....................3:34:30 (5,618)
Woodward, Eliza.....................4:12:59 (15,076)
Woodward, Julie.....................3:19:26 (3,193)
Woolcott, Sarah.....................5:20:02 (28,883)
Woolf, Mary.....................8:35:07 (32,878)
Woolford, Elizabeth.....................4:42:54 (22,815)
Woollatt, Caroline.....................4:18:47 (16,541)
Wooller, Diane.....................3:57:45 (11,440)
Woolley, Catherine.....................6:19:58 (32,084)
Woolley, Sue.....................4:02:40 (12,695)
Woolliscroft, Rachel.....................4:43:14 (22,897)
Woolner, Karen.....................4:51:04 (24,619)
Woolner, Suzanna.....................3:58:39 (11,691)
Wootton, Jacqueline.....................4:34:08 (20,616)
Wootton, Ruth.....................6:15:41 (31,971)
Workman, Hayley.....................4:51:22 (24,676)
Worland, Suzanne.....................6:32:36 (32,314)
World, Susan.....................4:09:12 (14,189)
Worledge, Claire.....................5:21:47 (29,077)
Worley, Joanne.....................4:43:52 (23,034)
Worman, Justine.....................3:51:51 (9,638)
Worrell, Claire.....................5:44:17 (30,841)
Worsfold, Clare.....................5:39:43 (30,532)
Worthy, Diana.....................3:54:03 (10,326)
Wotton, Dawn.....................5:16:14 (28,472)
Wotton, Irene.....................4:34:23 (20,668)
Wozniak, Julie.....................4:59:54 (26,290)
Wren, Jackie.....................4:28:29 (19,166)
Wren, Laura.....................4:17:12 (16,171)
Wrenn, Fiona.....................4:55:53 (25,554)
Wright, Alice.....................4:09:53 (14,360)
Wright, Alison.....................5:24:17 (29,303)
Wright, Annette.....................5:26:11 (29,462)
Wright, Gael.....................5:01:25 (26,517)
Wright, Linda.....................4:58:40 (26,070)
Wright, Lisa.....................4:24:07 (18,015)
Wright, Louise.....................4:46:46 (23,750)
Wright, Lucy.....................5:11:00 (27,812)
Wright, Marie.....................4:30:48 (19,785)
Wright, Michelle.....................5:13:06 (28,092)
Wright, Nichole.....................4:53:49 (25,124)
Wright, Nicola.....................5:44:08 (30,829)
Wright, Nicole.....................5:10:18 (27,726)
Wright, Rachel.....................4:19:38 (16,759)
Wright, Samantha.....................3:15:59 (2,785)
Wright, Sara.....................4:49:49 (24,383)
Wright, Sharon.....................6:24:22 (32,173)
Wright, Stephanie.....................5:06:05 (27,171)
Wright, Suzy.....................4:18:55 (16,571)
Wright, Tracey.....................4:43:16 (22,901)
Wyatt, Jill.....................6:35:33 (32,368)
Wyatt-Davies, Patricia.....................5:37:59 (30,414)
Wynn, Annalise.....................4:57:02 (25,774)
Yanagisawa, Kumi.....................5:20:49 (28,978)
Yardley, Catherine.....................5:12:46 (28,052)
Yates, Joanne.....................4:26:30 (18,653)
Yates, Sylvia.....................5:33:07 (30,036)
Yearley, Lesley.....................4:21:38 (17,293)
Yeates, Julie.....................3:22:12 (3,553)
Yeldon, Judith.....................5:14:17 (28,228)
Yendley, Susan.....................3:37:15 (6,155)
Yeo, Sandra.....................5:10:07 (27,703)
Yeoman, Deborah.....................5:03:33 (26,827)
Yeomans, Maggie.....................6:33:41 (32,335)
Yesson, Caroline.....................5:06:37 (27,249)
Yevko, Nicola.....................3:20:13 (3,281)
Yirrell, Sara.....................8:31:12 (32,876)
York, Marie.....................3:42:44 (7,323)
Young, Amanda.....................4:22:13 (17,449)
Young, Andie.....................6:36:44 (32,388)
Young, Anna.....................4:06:36 (13,586)
Young, Elaine.....................5:43:47 (30,801)
Young, Fiona.....................5:01:01 (26,450)
Young, Helen.....................5:28:41 (29,672)
Young, Jemma.....................5:40:06 (30,554)
Young, Julie.....................3:46:29 (8,272)
Young, Julie.....................5:17:08 (28,582)

Young, Lesley.....................5:41:25 (30,647)
Young, Nicola.....................4:21:21 (17,203)
Young, Rachael.....................5:37:34 (30,389)
Young, Vivien.....................6:03:53 (31,660)
Youngman, Sarah.....................4:26:03 (18,529)
Young-Norris, Karen.....................4:19:33 (16,739)
Yuill, Margaret.....................5:27:17 (29,549)
Yule, Helen.....................3:06:25 (1,673)
Zagni, Gina.....................4:11:40 (14,791)
Zakharova, Svetlana.....................2:22:31 (29)
Zaman, Hasina.....................4:19:46 (16,797)
Zamperini, Sylvia.....................4:13:40 (15,222)
Zanoline, Barbara.....................5:07:49 (27,409)
Zarat, Elena.....................5:06:08 (27,179)
Zasikowska, Susan.....................4:32:35 (20,239)
Zegewitz, Rosemarie.....................4:47:33 (23,919)
Zeytin, Simone.....................3:42:18 (7,232)
Zhuge Wilson, Julie.....................7:39:48 (32,823)
Zielina, Katarzyna.....................5:44:57 (30,882)
Zimmerman, Debbie.....................5:01:06 (26,464)
Zissimatou, Anna.....................5:19:31 (28,821)
Zoellner, Sheila.....................4:14:17 (15,385)
Zolikoff, Mary.....................6:04:13 (31,666)
Zorzi, Raffaella.....................3:49:15 (8,953)
Zuber, Julita.....................5:02:08 (26,619)
Zuckerman, Rachel.....................4:20:27 (16,984)
Zulver, Allyn.....................4:06:06 (13,460)
Zwart, Jannie.....................4:40:43 (22,284)
Zylstra, Susan.....................4:20:34 (17,014)

WHEELCHAIR ENTRANTS

Abrutat, David.....................2:22:54 (24)
Allen, Geoff.....................2:24:00 (25)
Carruthers, Peter.....................2:53:11 (33)
Cassell, Ric.....................3:06:28 (36)
Cheek, Andrew.....................2:11:27 (17)
Craig, Paula.....................2:48:53 (31)
De Neve, Jurgen.....................2:14:59 (19)
Derwin, Steve.....................3:07:54 (37)
Downing, Peter.....................3:00:44 (35)
Echevarria, Angel.....................3:20:50 (39)
Fairbank, Pierre.....................1:57:48 (7)
Forde, Jerry.....................3:24:59 (40)
Gilbert, Joseph.....................2:55:29 (34)
Gill, Jason.....................1:56:49 (6)

Grey-Thompson, Tanni.....................2:22:51 (23)

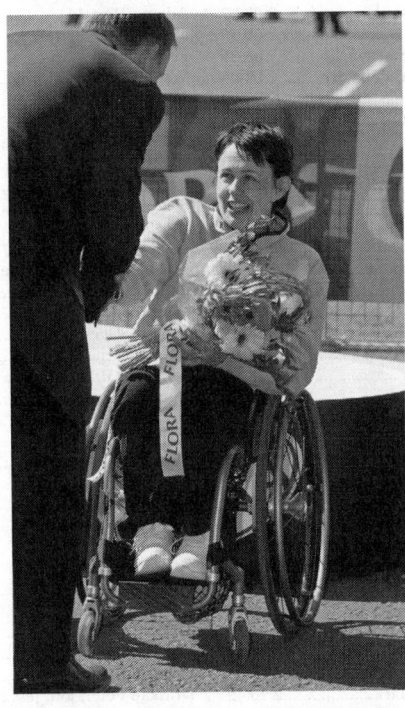

Hallam, James.....................2:40:18 (30)

Hanks, John.....................2:01:39 (8)
Herriot, Kenny.....................2:02:01 (12)
Hickey, Andrew.....................2:37:06 (28)
Hunt, Paul.....................2:03:27 (13)
Issorat, Claude.....................2:25:13 (26)
Lemeunier, Denis.....................1:41:17 (3)
Leray, Gregory.....................2:01:41 (9)
Lewis, Michelle.....................2:37:07 (29)
Londono, Oscar.....................3:30:36 (41)
Madden, Chris.....................1:55:57 (5)
Nevitt, Michael.....................2:21:32 (20)
Norrman, Carl.....................3:50:30 (43)
Nunnari, Paul.....................1:41:17 (4)
O'Connor, Gerald.....................2:22:46 (22)
Patel, Tushar.....................1:41:17 (2)
Pierre, François.....................2:13:09 (18)
Powell, Richie.....................2:01:45 (10)
Ramirez, Freddy.....................3:16:40 (38)
Rappe, Guy.....................2:03:44 (14)
Raulea, David.....................2:22:26 (21)
Richards, Jason.....................2:01:50 (11)
Riggs, Stuart.....................2:36:42 (27)
Telford, Mark.....................2:04:31 (15)
Wainwright, Brett.....................2:52:42 (32)
Watson, Wally.....................3:44:42 (42)

Weir, David.....................1:39:44 (1)

David Weir MBE (born 5 June 1979) is a British athlete with amazing versatility. He has won four London Marathon titles (2002, 2006, 2007, 2008). He came third in the 2010 London Marathon after being four minutes ahead of the field, a victim of flat tyres on his new chair. Weir currently holds the British records at all track distances up to 5,000m, as well as on the road at 10km, half marathon, and marathon. Weir won four medals (two gold, one silver and one bronze) at the 2008 Summer Paralympics Games, which were his third Games. He also won a silver medal and a bronze at the 2004 Summer Paralympics in Athens. He races for Kingston AC & Polytechnic Harriers and is coached by Christine Parsloe and Jenny Archer of the Velocity Wheelchair Racing Club. He started racing when he was 8, and at age 17 he was placed seventh in the 100m at the 1996 Paralympics in Atlanta.

Worrell, Wesley.....................2:05:20 (16)

The 2003 London Marathon

This was the year of Paula Radcliffe – and probably the greatest marathon race anyone had witnessed. The men's race was won in a fierce five-man sprint finish by the world and Olympic champion, Gezahegne Abera. But it was overshadowed by Paula, who ran faster than all the British men.

No woman could keep up with her, and Paula tackled the race with the aid of two male Kenyan pacemakers and set a sensational world record of 2:15:25. She tore an astonishing 1 minute 53 seconds from the time she set in Chicago in October 2002. Catherine Ndereba finished second, more than 4 minutes adrift, with America's Deena Drossin third.

There had been fears that Radcliffe wouldn't even make the starting line after she had dislocated her jaw and suffered severe cuts to her knees, hands and shoulders when colliding with a cyclist during training at Albuquerque, New Mexico. Her rapid recovery, according to her physical therapist Gerard Hartman, was hastened by emu oil, supposed to have powers to heal wounds, reduce swelling, soften skin and banish wrinkles. Hartman set Paula on an intensive regimen, which included applying emu oil on the wounds four to five times a day. In three weeks the wounds had healed. The three-toed emu is also a remarkable runner and can reach speeds of up to 31mph.

Marathon day dawned with almost perfect conditions. The temperature was a cool 10°C at the start, and rose just six degrees during the race. Radcliffe clearly wanted a fast time, latching onto the two pacemakers who had been asked to run a 2:16:00 pace. In fact they started at a much faster tempo – the third mile was covered in an amazing 4 minutes 57 seconds.

One of the pacemakers, Christopher Kandie called it a day at 19 miles, leaving only Samson Loywapet, whose personal best stood at just 2:12:00, to chaperone Radcliffe home. She passed 20 miles in 1:43:34 and only then took off the gloves she had been wearing from the start. With the crowd roaring her on, the 29-year-old Radcliffe sprinted across the line in 2:15:25, almost a mile ahead of Ndereba.

Both races were a great testimony to Chris Brasher, as is the event itself. This was the first London Marathon staged after he had died in February that year. Thousands remained silent in tribute before the start to remember him. Brasher's widow Shirley was the official starter for the race.

The women's and men's marathons were two very different races; Paula against the clock and the men's race that was in the balance until the final few yards. Radcliffe won by four and a half minutes in her race, but the 24-year-old Ethiopian Gezahegne Abera had not a moment to spare in his victory.

For much of the race Abera formed part of the crocodile of athletes who followed a Kenyan pacemaker. Eventually, five runners closed in on the finish line together. When Stefano Baldini made a dash for the line, Abera, who had looked comfortable throughout the race, shortened his stride to sprint past him. They were both given the same time, 2:07:56, while Ngolepus was just a second back in third. The first eight finished in under 2:09:00.

Frenchman Joel Jeannot won the wheelchair marathon, beating the course record by more than three minutes in 1:32:02. The 2002 winner David Weir beat Denis Lemeunier (France) for second in a sprint, clocking 1:34:48 and 1:34:50 respectively.

Italian Francesca Porcellato won the women's race in 2:04:21. Porcellato and Tanni Grey-Thompson were together until the cobbles at the Tower of London when the Italian opened a gap that she increased to more than 30 seconds by the finish.

Former boxer Michael Watson walked just over four miles a day to raise funds for the Brain and Spine Foundation. Watson was accompanied on the final leg by Chris Eubank – the fighter who left him with the injuries that almost cost his life. Before setting out with 33,000 other competitors, Watson received messages of support from Muhammad Ali and Lennox Lewis.

Watson finally lurched across the line into the arms of his mother Joan, who hung the finisher's medal around his neck. The clock showed 6 days, 2 hours, 27 minutes and 6 seconds. Dave Bedford rates this as one of the Marathon's great achievements: 'I've never seen anyone so challenged by so much. He showed everyone what the Marathon is all about.'

Explanation of placing system

Each London Marathon year in this register is divided up into four categories: first, a summary of the **Elite Athletes**, containing names (last, first) and times (hours : minutes : seconds) of the top 50 male runners, top 50 female runners, top 3 male and top 2 female wheelchair entrants; then **Male Runners, Female Runners** and **Wheelchair Entrants**. These last three sections display the individual names and times of *every* entrant, including elite athletes, alphabetically and with their overall finishing position in that year's Marathon displayed in brackets alongside.

Some entrants have chosen to enhance past London Marathon entries with photos and recollections online at www.aubreybooks.com. Please visit the website to find out more about appearing in future editions.

ELITE ATHLETES

Top 50 male runners

Abera, Gezahegne	2:07:56
Baldini, Stefano	2:07:56
Ngolepus, Joseph	2:07:57
Tergat, Paul	2:07:59
Ramadhani, Samson	2:08:01
El Mouaziz, Abdelkadre	2:08:03
Bong-Ju, Lee	2:08:10
Ramaala, Hendrick	2:08:58
Syster, Ian	2:09:18
Corters, Javier	2:10:39
Kehugu, Joseph	2:13:17
Makori, David	2:13:24
Tolossa, Ambesse	2:13:33
Kilonzo, Onesmus	2:13:56
Loywapet, Samson	2:15:24
Bezabeh, Sisay	2:16:09
Cariss, Chris	2:17:57
Letherby, Andrew	2:18:25
Lobb, Huw	2:18:30
Guery, Olivier	2:18:56
Yatich, Mark	2:19:52
Mitej, Ibrahim	2:19:53
Bilton, Darran	2:20:50
Norman, David	2:21:00
Kiprono, John	2:21:14
Proudlove, Michael	2:23:11
Kanda, Paul	2:23:13
McGaughey, James	2:23:49
Chelule, Wesley	2:24:00
Fattore, Mario	2:24:09
Altmann, Nicholas	2:24:11
Janvier, Nick	2:24:59
Weir, Andrew	2:25:00
Plant, Ray	2:26:02
Hargreaves, Mark	2:26:42
Reynolds, Ben	2:26:47
Prokopcuks, Alexander	2:26:52
Galpin, Peter	2:26:56
Martyn, Nicholas	2:27:11
Adams, Ronald	2:27:21
Macdonald, Stewart	2:28:00
Fisher, Ian	2:28:10
Van Zyl, Anton	2:28:12
Lincoln, Wayne	2:28:29
Williams, Gareth	2:28:35
Cockerell, William	2:28:43
Payne, Garry	2:29:08
Wetherill, Andrew	2:29:18
Littler, Stephen	2:29:19
Eckstein, Klaus	2:29:32

Top 50 female runners

Radcliffe, Paula	2:15:25
Ndereba, Catherine	2:19:55
Drossin, Deena	2:21:16
Chepkemei, Susan	2:23:12
Petrova, Ludmila	2:23:14
Dita, Constantina	2:23:43
Prokocuka, Jelena	2:24:01
Alemu, Elfenesh	2:24:56
Botezan, Michaela	2:25:32
Tulu, Derartu	2:26:33
Zousko, Larissa	2:28:05
Fernandez, Adriana	2:29:54
Semenova, Zinaid	2:32:37
Genovese, Bruna	2:32:58
Pouchkina, Rimma	2:38:00
McCallum, Michaela	2:41:57
Towler, Karen	2:43:00
Lee, Michelle	2:43:41
Fletcher, Alison	2:45:10
Draskau-Petersson, Jess	2:46:10
Angell, Margaret	2:46:20

Watson, Louise	2:48:11
Burrell, Helen	2:52:14
Redfern, Vicki	2:53:28
Mellodew, Anita	2:53:54
Deasy, Margaret	2:53:57
Aitken, Nicola	2:54:01
Marot, Véronique	2:55:01
Cawthorne, Helen	2:56:35
Alexander, Rosalyn	2:56:46
Knights, Lisa	2:56:57
Letherby, Margaret	2:58:09
Dennison, Andrea	2:58:14
Shenton, Fiona	2:58:34
Perry, Victoria	2:58:40
Richardson, Dawn	2:58:45
Bruce, Susan	2:59:12
Gerrard, Adrienne	2:59:23
Engdahl, Elin	2:59:25
Cheverton, Dinah	2:59:26
Yule, Helen	2:59:37
Christie, Nathalie	2:59:51
Hills, Nicola	3:00:25
Fines, Helen	3:00:35
Pike, Zoe	3:00:54
Dering, Jo	3:00:58
Wilyman, Lisa	3:01:34
Harrison, Susanna	3:01:57
Macmaster, Jennifer	3:02:09
Carson, Suzanne	3:02:25

Top 3 male and top 2 female wheelchair entrants

Jeannot, Joel	1:32:02
Weir, David	1:34:48
Lemeunier, Denis	1:34:50
Porcellato, Francesca	2:04:21
Grey-Thompson, Tanni	2:04:54

MALE RUNNERS

Aaronson, Joel...........................6:36:03 (31,476)
Abauna, Harold........................3:32:42 (4,560)
Abbey, Nick.............................4:16:42 (13,905)
Abbott, Benton........................3:28:42 (3,943)
Abbott, Chris...........................5:43:42 (29,283)
Abbott, Colin...........................6:17:50 (30,922)
Abbott, Frankie........................4:00:32 (10,336)
Abbott, Gordon........................5:57:47 (30,154)
Abbott, Jon..............................4:37:27 (18,972)
Abbott, Matthew.......................3:34:56 (4,896)
Abbott, Peter............................4:29:31 (17,123)
Abbott, Trevor..........................4:55:39 (23,065)
Abdulraheem, Adeyemi.............5:01:29 (24,229)
Abdy Collins, Henry..................3:29:30 (4,092)
Abel, Jeremy............................4:12:12 (12,819)
Abel, Lawrence.........................2:55:54 (642)
Abels, Michael..........................5:07:25 (25,166)
Ab-Elwyn, Rhys.......................2:51:02 (419)

Abera, Gezahegne....................2:07:56 (1)

Gezahegne Abera, from Ethiopia, (born 23 April 1978) was winner of the marathon at the 2000 Olympics in Sydney. At 22 years old, he was the youngest marathon champion in Olympic history. Born in Etya, Arsi Province (home to almost 90 percent of Ethiopia's runners), Abera's first international competition was the 1999 Los Angeles Marathon, where he finished fourth, behind three Kenyans. That earned him a place in the Ethiopian 1999 World Championships team, where he finished eleventh. Later in the 1999 season, Abera won his first international marathon by finishing first at Fukuoka. He won this marathon again in 2001 and 2002. In 2000, Abera finished second in the Boston Marathon.

In 2001, Abera won the World Championships to become the first person to achieve an Olympics-World Championships marathon double. Running has made him a millionaire in a land where annual incomes average $150, and Geza – his nickname – has given more in donations to famine relief than most of his compatriots will live long enough to earn. He has an American agent, Japanese sponsors, and a splendid bungalow in Ethiopia's capital city, Addis Ababa. Abera is a simple country boy. He worked in the fields on his father's subsistence-farm and was brought up on tales of Abebe Bikila – the winner of two Olympic marathons, 1960 and 1964, and the father of Ethiopian running.

Abernethy, Peter 4:47:53 (21,394)
Abeyta, Paul............................5:54:41 (29,977)
Ablett, Justin...........................3:50:40 (7,879)
Abraham, Paul..........................2:43:31 (208)
Abraham, William.....................4:17:15 (14,045)
Abrahams, Michael...................3:43:48 (6,506)
Abram, Andy............................3:12:47 (1,964)
Abram, Barry............................3:00:58 (999)
Abram, Ricky............................5:18:56 (26,748)
Abramowitz, David....................5:07:17 (25,140)
Absalom, Michael......................3:30:32 (4,249)
Abson, Michael.........................5:18:05 (26,624)
Absolon, Christopher.................3:39:35 (5,713)
Accleton, Robert 3:25:20 (3,447)
Ackerman, Richard....................4:55:20 (22,985)
Ackers, Matthew.......................5:18:08 (26,640)
Acreman, Alex..........................5:55:19 (30,016)
Acton, Robert...........................3:17:22 (2,472)
Acton, Timothy.........................4:25:39 (16,168)
Adair, Carl...............................4:24:20 (15,829)
Adam, Bob...............................4:22:00 (15,241)
Adam, David.............................3:25:51 (3,519)
Adam, Doug..............................5:02:16 (24,357)
Adams, Adrian..........................4:03:54 (11,036)
Adams, Brian............................6:22:32 (31,087)
Adams, Christian.......................4:26:06 (16,278)
Adams, David............................3:59:17 (10,034)
Adams, David............................4:17:11 (14,030)
Adams, Douglas........................4:10:13 (12,401)
Adams, Gary.............................4:41:46 (19,935)
Adams, Graham.........................4:27:35 (16,621)
Adams, Guy..............................4:31:36 (17,639)
Adams, James 3:49:07 (7,537)
Adams, James 3:55:42 (9,107)
Adams, James 4:17:22 (14,074)
Adams, Jeffrey..........................5:25:10 (27,566)
Adams, John.............................4:13:25 (13,100)
Adams, John.............................4:43:52 (20,475)
Adams, Keatley.........................4:23:15 (15,560)
Adams, Keith............................4:55:07 (22,944)
Adams, Kevin............................4:24:29 (15,864)
Adams, Leslie 3:42:24 (6,219)
Adams, Michael........................4:31:44 (17,676)
Adams, Mike.............................3:54:49 (8,870)
Adams, Paul.............................5:33:00 (28,374)
Adams, Peter 4:52:56 (22,491)
Adams, Phil..............................3:04:33 (1,216)
Adams, Philip...........................3:33:30 (4,678)
Adams, Philip...........................4:24:20 (15,829)
Adams, Richard.........................3:51:29 (8,068)
Adams, Richard.........................5:22:41 (27,231)
Adams, Robert..........................4:04:15 (11,120)
Adams, Robert..........................4:05:02 (11,299)
Adams, Ronald..........................2:27:21 (50)
Adams, Russell..........................4:32:28 (17,826)
Adams, Steve............................6:45:39 (31,636)
Adams, Steven..........................3:57:06 (9,478)
Adams, Terry.............................4:21:11 (15,030)
Adams, Thomas.........................2:54:34 (565)
Adams, Tony.............................4:30:29 (17,364)
Adams, William.........................4:06:43 (11,630)
Adamson, David........................3:27:13 (3,704)
Adamson, Harry........................4:05:46 (11,447)
Adby, Terry 5:33:32 (28,426)
Adcock, Matthew......................2:30:54 (67)
Adcock, Norman.......................4:55:15 (22,965)
Adderley, Philip........................3:53:43 (8,593)
Addis, Peter..............................5:13:31 (26,047)
Addison, Guy............................4:29:47 (17,190)
Addison, Mark...........................4:52:56 (22,491)
Addison, Paul............................3:50:52 (7,919)
Addoh, Seb...............................5:29:39 (28,057)
Addy, David...............................5:47:31 (29,537)
Addy, John................................3:12:33 (1,938)
Addy, Paul................................3:51:51 (8,165)
Addy, Timothy...........................5:09:31 (25,476)
Adediran, Stephen.....................5:19:51 (26,865)
Adelizzi, Stephano.....................4:30:20 (17,319)
Adey, Michael...........................4:47:09 (21,218)
Adeyemi, Latif...........................5:01:49 (24,284)
Adiouban, Othman.....................4:33:16 (17,998)
Adkin, Andy..............................3:51:55 (8,178)
Adkins, Davids..........................3:07:07 (1,421)

Adkins, Peter 3:16:34 (2,382)
Adkinson, Des...........................3:21:47 (2,962)
Adlard, Simon...........................3:14:07 (2,145)
Adler, Thomas...........................4:24:42 (15,915)
Adley, James............................3:54:09 (8,691)
Adnitt, Robert...........................4:17:35 (14,132)
Adradi, Dris..............................5:46:36 (29,470)
Adshead, Simon 4:18:53 (14,473)
Adu, Stephen............................4:58:10 (23,621)
Affleck, Michael........................3:36:40 (5,175)
Afonso, Joao............................3:38:20 (5,462)
Afshar, Dan..............................3:38:51 (5,569)
Agar, Alexander........................3:58:19 (9,788)
Agarwal, Ravi...........................3:55:57 (9,165)
Agasse, Remi............................3:26:00 (3,543)
Agate, Paul...............................3:55:20 (9,003)
Agbo, Celestine........................3:17:25 (2,478)
Ager, Mark...............................4:46:24 (21,070)
Agnarson, Dan..........................2:42:09 (183)
Agostini, Marco.........................3:26:57 (3,669)
Aguirre, David...........................5:27:42 (27,857)
Aguirre, John............................6:12:54 (30,763)
Ahearne, Robert........................3:29:36 (4,111)
Ahearne, Scott..........................3:34:49 (4,882)
Aherne, Brian............................4:24:34 (15,879)
Ahmed, Ismael..........................4:20:34 (14,883)
Ahmed, Jahangir.......................4:26:35 (16,375)
Ahmed, Rashed.........................5:00:34 (24,081)
Ahmed, Shabbir........................4:54:18 (22,770)
Ahmed, Tahir............................4:12:32 (12,894)
Ahnien, Mario...........................3:49:15 (7,576)
Ahsunollah, Paul.......................3:54:25 (8,759)
Aimable, Michael......................6:06:27 (30,513)
Ainge, Damian..........................4:30:43 (17,422)
Ainger, Shaun...........................4:35:45 (18,580)
Ainscough, William....................4:55:40 (23,072)
Ainslie, Ian...............................5:11:14 (25,727)
Ainslie, Paul.............................3:16:12 (2,348)
Ainsworth, Andrew....................5:18:28 (26,695)
Ainsworth, James......................3:59:34 (10,112)
Ainsworth, James......................4:05:11 (11,327)
Ainsworth, Mark........................4:10:05 (12,369)
Aird, Robert..............................3:13:52 (2,109)
Airey, Michael...........................4:31:21 (17,582)
Airlie, Brian..............................4:08:40 (12,055)
Airs, Paul.................................4:35:09 (18,431)
Ait-Braham, Aziz.......................3:09:32 (1,634)
Aitken, Jamie............................4:43:16 (20,309)
Aitken, Matthew........................3:48:20 (7,381)
Aitken, Michael.........................3:38:08 (5,432)
Aitken, Robert...........................4:36:16 (18,702)
Aitken, William.........................3:26:06 (3,551)
Aitkenhead, Euan......................3:20:11 (2,783)
Aizawa, Hiroshi 4:47:59 (21,424)
Aizlewood, Stephen 6:07:58 (30,565)
Aked, Peter...............................2:42:53 (193)
Akenhead, David.......................5:56:59 (30,106)
Akhurst, Graeme.......................4:00:12 (10,271)
Akiens, Mark.............................5:13:10 (25,995)
Akinfe, Francis..........................6:28:25 (31,283)
Akpufure, Oni............................6:41:47 (31,563)
Alamazani, Jeremie....................4:11:08 (12,560)
Alaoui Soulailani, Mohamed........4:18:35 (14,387)
Alb, Johannes...........................3:59:41 (10,146)
Albert, Dominique......................3:54:05 (8,680)
Albert, Harold...........................4:59:08 (23,834)
Alberti, Terry............................4:51:51 (22,278)
Albon, John..............................4:51:22 (22,173)
Al-Dahhan, Omar.......................3:38:54 (5,581)
Alday, Dion...............................4:24:57 (15,981)
Alder, John...............................5:22:12 (27,166)
Aldersley, Mark.........................3:35:47 (5,037)
Alderson, David.........................5:38:07 (28,820)
Aldouri, Amer 4:54:06 (22,730)
Aldred, Geoffrey........................4:32:04 (17,746)
Aldred, Simon...........................4:40:53 (19,723)
Aldreidge, Adrian 5:39:42 (28,963)
Aldridge, Nigel..........................3:46:10 (6,966)
Alessi, Christiano.......................4:51:01 (22,075)
Alexander, Andrew 3:53:23 (8,510)
Alexander, David.......................5:12:37 (25,923)
Alexander, Eddie.......................5:43:49 (29,293)
Alexander, James......................4:08:25 (11,984)

Alexander, Mark	3:11:29 (1,802)	
Alexander, Robert	3:38:09 (5,434)	
Alexander, Roger	5:23:01 (27,288)	
Alexander, Rohan	3:52:06 (8,223)	
Alexander, Scott	3:48:59 (7,511)	
Alford, Andrew	4:43:40 (20,423)	
Alford, Bryce	3:00:39 (985)	
Alford, Robert	4:53:43 (22,652)	
Alford, Stephen	4:33:55 (18,147)	
Algacs, Dezso	7:13:30 (32,026)	
Algeo, Nicholas	3:35:49 (5,044)	
Algie, Robert	3:26:57 (3,669)	
Ali, Imran	4:02:02 (10,642)	
Alibert, Marc	3:08:34 (1,554)	
Alibocus, Del	5:49:27 (29,672)	
Allam, Keith	3:37:41 (5,362)	
Allan, Derek	3:50:31 (7,844)	
Allan, John	3:51:06 (7,976)	
Allan, Peter	3:43:06 (6,387)	
Allan, Ross	5:18:33 (26,707)	
Allan, Simon	4:08:56 (12,117)	
Allan, Stephen	3:53:28 (8,531)	
Allancy, Paul	3:52:40 (8,347)	
Allard, Charles Jnr	3:04:31 (1,212)	
Allared, Mats	4:03:33 (10,957)	
Allaway, Jason	6:12:54 (30,763)	
Allday, James	4:24:46 (15,941)	
Allder, Colin	4:27:55 (16,693)	
Allen, Barrie	4:06:06 (11,515)	
Allen, Bernard	6:41:43 (31,562)	
Allen, Bradley	3:54:22 (8,743)	
Allen, Brian	3:35:36 (5,011)	
Allen, Brian	5:20:00 (26,888)	
Allen, Chris	3:57:00 (9,458)	
Allen, Christopher	3:53:32 (8,555)	
Allen, Christopher	5:56:40 (30,087)	
Allen, Daren	5:36:37 (28,701)	
Allen, David	3:43:58 (6,539)	
Allen, David	4:34:23 (18,259)	
Allen, Dean	4:43:18 (20,322)	
Allen, Derek	5:44:19 (29,324)	
Allen, Gareth	4:30:41 (17,414)	
Allen, Gary	4:30:19 (17,312)	
Allen, Gavin	3:43:08 (6,393)	
Allen, Graham	2:56:03 (652)	
Allen, Greg	3:40:16 (5,838)	
Allen, Greg	5:55:58 (30,039)	
Allen, Hugh	3:48:08 (7,345)	
Allen, Ivan	7:12:14 (32,015)	
Allen, Jack	4:35:46 (18,588)	
Allen, James	3:08:14 (1,516)	
Allen, James	4:13:47 (13,195)	
Allen, James	4:29:12 (17,039)	
Allen, James	4:32:00 (17,730)	
Allen, Jamie	4:38:00 (19,088)	
Allen, Jeff	3:47:40 (7,251)	
Allen, John	4:05:51 (11,467)	
Allen, Karl	3:59:49 (10,180)	
Allen, Kevin	3:09:09 (1,598)	
Allen, Kevin	4:13:22 (13,086)	
Allen, Malcolm	4:42:29 (20,104)	
Allen, Mark	3:22:39 (3,063)	
Allen, Mark	3:49:55 (7,719)	
Allen, Mark	4:57:12 (23,430)	
Allen, Martin	4:35:10 (18,436)	
Allen, Matthew	4:33:03 (17,963)	
Allen, Michael	5:08:59 (25,401)	
Allen, Michael	5:55:24 (30,019)	
Allen, Michael	5:59:05 (30,212)	
Allen, Neil	5:31:30 (28,245)	
Allen, Paul	3:27:57 (3,810)	
Allen, Paul	3:58:38 (9,867)	
Allen, Peter	4:47:47 (21,368)	
Allen, Richard	4:52:51 (22,470)	
Allen, Robert	3:52:22 (8,281)	
Allen, Rodney	3:52:05 (8,219)	
Allen, Sean	3:47:33 (7,223)	
Allen, Simon	4:09:46 (12,291)	
Allen, Simon	5:27:26 (27,824)	
Allen, Stephen	4:07:19 (11,763)	
Allen, Steve	3:31:33 (4,421)	
Allen, Terry	5:33:40 (28,433)	
Allen, Tim	3:42:16 (6,199)	
Allen, Tom	4:35:23 (18,492)	
Allen, Tony	3:52:21 (8,276)	
Allen, Trace	3:58:12 (9,755)	
Allen, Tristan	5:12:30 (25,897)	
Alley, Stuart	5:47:32 (29,542)	
Allford, Simon	3:44:38 (6,655)	
Alli, Graeme	5:49:28 (29,674)	
Allibone, Mark	4:56:38 (23,294)	
Allin, Howard	3:30:34 (4,255)	
Allingham, Richard	5:12:47 (25,942)	
Allisat, Wolf	4:18:25 (14,334)	
Allison, Arthur	6:28:49 (31,298)	
Allison, David	6:03:30 (30,394)	
Allison, Derek	5:13:57 (26,094)	
Allison, George	6:31:27 (31,360)	
Allitt, Matthew	4:46:15 (21,032)	
Allonby, Ross	4:26:50 (16,436)	
Allott, Timothy	4:07:14 (11,745)	
Allport, Trevor	3:40:07 (5,816)	
Allsop, Giles	5:27:44 (27,864)	
Allsop, Paul	4:30:58 (17,485)	
Allsopp, Jonathan	4:17:06 (14,010)	
Almond, Colin	4:39:26 (19,427)	
Almond, Martin	4:32:41 (17,875)	
Almond, Michael	5:42:47 (29,228)	
Almond, Stephen	2:56:33 (678)	
Almond, Steve	3:31:00 (4,327)	
Al-Ohahir, Haitham	4:26:22 (16,330)	
Alpert, John	3:11:29 (1,802)	
Alptekin, Seref	4:18:30 (14,359)	
Alqueres, Pedro	4:00:48 (10,386)	
Alsop, Roger	2:34:10 (93)	
Alsworth, Michael	4:09:55 (12,329)	
Altmann, Nicholas	2:24:11 (38)	
Altoft, Colin	6:52:42 (31,776)	
Alty, Steven	4:16:03 (13,750)	
Aluko, Olalekan	5:37:36 (28,782)	
Alvaree Meijide, José Luis	3:20:26 (2,821)	
Alvarez, Floreal	3:58:53 (9,939)	
Alvarez, Miguel	4:34:12 (18,213)	
Alvarez-Marcos, Pedro	3:25:28 (3,461)	
Alvarez-Padilla, Alejandro	3:29:44 (4,132)	
Alveranga, Raymond	3:55:49 (9,132)	
Alves Da Costa, Pedro José	5:22:46 (27,250)	
Amato, Manlio	4:31:19 (17,570)	
Ambler, Richard	4:54:42 (22,866)	
Ambrose, Carl	4:22:07 (15,267)	
Ambrose, Ian	4:51:18 (22,152)	
Ambrose, Robert	4:09:42 (12,274)	
Ambrose, Robert	5:01:50 (24,288)	
Ambrosini, Orlando	5:11:46 (25,798)	
Ameel, Johan	4:26:08 (16,282)	
Ameer, Sam	5:25:13 (27,578)	
Amer, Paul	5:56:16 (30,068)	
Amer, Stephen	5:56:15 (30,066)	
Amero, Carlos	4:36:59 (18,872)	
Amery, Nathan	3:57:50 (9,658)	
Ames, Tim	4:17:11 (14,030)	
Ames, Tony	5:33:07 (28,379)	
Amin, Kanubhai	6:34:46 (31,442)	
Amirahmadi, Afshin	4:44:37 (20,637)	
Amiri, Manoochehr	4:31:38 (17,652)	
Amiss, Peter	5:30:50 (28,178)	
Amlot, Richard	4:31:53 (17,705)	
Amoils, Matthew	2:58:01 (768)	
Amos, John	4:18:04 (14,266)	
Amos, Nigel	4:33:29 (18,055)	
Amos, Peter	3:39:57 (5,773)	
Anastasakis, Yannis	6:23:58 (31,133)	
Andell, Nick	3:58:11 (9,748)	
Anders, Julian	5:58:50 (30,193)	
Andersen, Franck	3:38:55 (5,584)	
Andersen, Karsten	3:47:47 (7,276)	
Andersen, Knut	3:52:07 (8,229)	
Andersen, Per	3:48:08 (7,345)	
Andersen, Stig	4:22:28 (15,355)	
Anderson, Alan	4:26:24 (16,334)	
Anderson, Brian	4:03:03 (10,855)	
Anderson, Charles	5:18:32 (26,701)	
Anderson, Christopher	3:45:50 (6,895)	
Anderson, David	4:13:10 (13,041)	
Anderson, David	5:42:40 (29,223)	
Anderson, Graham	4:04:05 (11,084)	
Anderson, Ian	2:36:01 (107)	
Anderson, Ian	4:56:47 (23,334)	
Anderson, John	5:22:16 (27,181)	
Anderson, John	5:25:11 (27,568)	
Anderson, Lindsay	3:34:26 (4,824)	
Anderson, Mark	4:30:47 (17,442)	
Anderson, Mark	6:34:13 (31,428)	
Anderson, Michael	4:06:33 (11,601)	
Anderson, Neil	3:54:57 (8,906)	
Anderson, Neil	4:18:47 (14,442)	
Anderson, Paul	3:19:22 (2,686)	
Anderson, Paul	5:35:47 (28,619)	
Anderson, Peter	4:03:43 (10,987)	
Anderson, Ray	3:28:34 (3,913)	
Anderson, Richard	3:01:47 (1,041)	
Anderson, Richard	3:23:14 (3,144)	
Anderson, Robert	3:56:23 (9,288)	
Anderson, Rupert	3:37:07 (5,257)	
Anderson, Thomas	4:26:02 (16,254)	
Anderson, William	4:12:25 (12,864)	
Andersson, Conny	3:57:08 (9,488)	
Andersson, Eddy	4:25:23 (16,113)	
Andersson, Morgan	4:50:11 (21,900)	
Anderton-Tyers, Roy	5:36:05 (28,645)	
Andesilic, Luka	3:56:43 (9,381)	
Andrade, Luis	5:44:19 (29,324)	
Andreis, Alex	4:40:16 (19,594)	
Andretto, Flemming	3:07:44 (1,477)	
Andrew, Kevin	3:52:50 (8,377)	
Andrew, Mark	6:00:11 (30,261)	
Andrew, Paul	4:31:18 (17,566)	
Andrews, Adam	6:03:27 (30,391)	
Andrews, Alan	3:40:24 (5,857)	
Andrews, Bekir	4:02:35 (10,754)	
Andrews, Chris	4:43:12 (20,286)	
Andrews, David	4:51:05 (22,099)	
Andrews, Douglas	3:44:12 (6,584)	
Andrews, Ian	4:55:37 (23,058)	
Andrews, Jason	4:23:26 (15,595)	
Andrews, John	3:58:47 (9,914)	
Andrews, Jonathan	3:44:52 (6,698)	
Andrews, Mark	3:18:05 (2,561)	
Andrews, Mark	4:57:57 (23,571)	
Andrews, Mark	5:22:08 (27,157)	
Andrews, Martin	5:42:17 (29,190)	
Andrews, Neil	5:18:06 (26,630)	
Andrews, Paul	3:29:00 (4,001)	
Andrews, Philip	3:56:56 (9,439)	
Andrews, Roger	5:24:22 (27,457)	
Andrews, Ross	4:51:38 (22,231)	
Andrzejewski, Stanley	5:30:50 (28,178)	
Anemene, Leonard	6:49:23 (31,699)	
Angel, Alan	4:38:31 (19,200)	
Angelaki-King, Darren	4:40:30 (19,653)	
Angell, Kevin	4:42:20 (20,062)	
Angold, Ben	5:42:31 (29,210)	
Angus, Martin	4:58:49 (23,768)	
Angus, Terry	6:14:02 (30,799)	
Anholm, Kevin	4:01:41 (10,576)	
Anibaba, Deji	5:11:21 (25,743)	
Anichkin, Alexander	3:36:28 (5,137)	
Ankers, James	4:35:25 (18,501)	
Annals, Marc	3:44:41 (6,664)	
Annandale, Jerry	4:45:49 (20,919)	
Annema, Jouke	3:32:14 (4,501)	
Anning, Stephen	3:49:07 (7,537)	
Anorve, Jesus	3:28:10 (3,841)	
Anscombe, Matthew	4:17:23 (14,082)	
Ansell, Antony	4:28:40 (16,902)	
Ansell, David	4:40:26 (19,640)	
Ansell, Martin	4:14:45 (13,434)	
Ansell, Richard	2:46:13 (266)	
Ansell, Stephen	5:10:57 (25,686)	
Anson, Dave	3:58:57 (9,955)	
Anstead, Matthew	3:48:31 (7,405)	
Anstee, Nick	4:05:12 (11,330)	
Anstes, Julian	4:17:04 (14,004)	
Anstey, Adam	4:44:00 (20,497)	
Antcliffe, Mark	3:20:20 (2,807)	
Anteyi, Alex	6:44:49 (31,617)	
Anthony, Lawrence	4:30:09 (17,269)	
Anthony, Roger	4:57:02 (23,389)	
Antill, Paul	6:48:20 (31,682)	

Antonini, André	4:04:34 (11,191)	
Antoniou, Anthony	4:33:30 (18,060)	
Antrobus, Mark	4:15:33 (13,652)	
Anwyl, Martyn	5:28:07 (27,902)	
Ap Garth, Garmon	3:18:34 (2,615)	
Apaya-Gadabya, Yves	4:51:51 (22,278)	
Apple, Paul	4:32:28 (17,826)	
Appleboam, Andrew	3:15:07 (2,252)	
Appleby, Alan	3:00:20 (957)	
Appleby, Glenn	4:02:39 (10,769)	
Appleby, Matthew	5:00:35 (24,083)	
Appleby, Paul	4:40:15 (19,591)	
Appleford, Robert	5:16:40 (26,447)	
Applegate, Christopher	2:56:06 (654)	
Applegate, Jeffrey	4:35:24 (18,495)	
Appleton, Robert	3:53:39 (8,579)	
Appleton, Steven	5:10:12 (25,582)	
Applewhaite, Paul	5:30:36 (28,153)	
Appleyard, Andrew	5:09:32 (25,481)	
Apps, Dan	4:24:55 (15,975)	
Aquilina, Jonathan	5:38:31 (28,858)	
Arakliti, Zak	3:30:12 (4,199)	
Aram, Paul	5:27:46 (27,867)	
Aran Iglesia, Alfredo	3:26:14 (3,572)	
Arbenz, Andreas	4:19:19 (14,576)	
Arbery, Giles	5:00:55 (24,141)	
Arbouine, Mark	4:37:54 (19,065)	
Archbold, Martin	3:42:48 (6,315)	
Archer, Michael	4:47:13 (21,230)	
Archer, Nicholas	4:49:08 (21,655)	
Archer, Richard	5:17:30 (26,544)	
Archer, Robert	3:20:26 (2,821)	
Archer, Steven	4:17:14 (14,041)	
Archer-Perkins, James	4:58:43 (23,737)	
Archer-Perkins, Simon	4:58:43 (23,737)	
Ard, Jonathan	3:15:10 (2,257)	
Arden, Bazil	3:50:52 (7,919)	
Ardura, Alberto	3:37:40 (5,358)	
Arena, Giuseppe	3:28:24 (3,884)	
Arendse, Roger	5:22:19 (27,190)	
Arens, Kerrin	3:36:39 (5,170)	
Argent, Alan	4:28:34 (16,878)	
Argent, Dean	3:47:59 (7,316)	
Argent, Simon	4:26:41 (16,398)	
Arghandawi, Shah	4:31:03 (17,513)	
Arghebant, Edward	4:58:14 (23,633)	
Ariatti, Paolo	4:05:35 (11,415)	
Ariss, Stephen	4:49:33 (21,761)	
Ark, Bahadar	3:54:23 (8,748)	
Arkell, Ben	4:21:09 (15,020)	
Arkinstall, Ivan	3:48:45 (7,453)	
Arlington, Michael	4:43:43 (20,435)	
Armellini, Armando	5:21:04 (27,030)	
Armenti, Gianluca	5:54:27 (29,968)	
Armist, Ronnie	3:52:04 (8,213)	
Armitage, Christopher	4:28:07 (16,740)	
Armitage, Michael	4:49:13 (21,679)	
Armitage, Neil	3:40:29 (5,866)	
Armitage, Nick	2:57:56 (761)	
Armitage, Richard	5:04:50 (24,767)	
Armitage, Robert	4:04:32 (11,185)	
Armstead, Christopher	4:26:39 (16,391)	
Armstrong, Neil	3:51:09 (7,995)	
Armstrong, James	5:22:57 (27,278)	
Armstrong, John	4:32:06 (17,752)	
Armstrong, John	4:52:04 (22,323)	
Armstrong, Mark	7:01:45 (31,903)	
Armstrong, Neil	3:46:03 (6,943)	
Armstrong, Peter	3:15:37 (2,303)	
Armstrong, Quinton	4:46:50 (21,154)	
Armstrong, Richard	6:00:01 (30,267)	
Armstrong, Stuart	3:41:03 (5,968)	
Armstrong, Stuart	5:24:10 (27,431)	
Armstrong, Thomas	6:05:16 (30,467)	
Arnell, Ben	4:44:49 (20,682)	
Arnell, Geoff	3:14:02 (2,133)	
Arnell, Kevin	4:58:45 (23,745)	
Arnell, Robert	4:53:17 (22,569)	
Arnold, Andrew	4:18:20 (14,309)	
Arnold, Antony	3:56:40 (9,365)	
Arnold, Dave	3:15:41 (2,307)	
Arnold, David	4:32:39 (17,868)	
Arnold, Geoffrey	5:22:30 (27,212)	
Arnold, Jim	5:02:45 (24,426)	
Arnold, Martin	2:47:09 (304)	
Arnold, Matthew	3:24:06 (3,267)	
Arnold, Peter	5:22:29 (27,210)	
Arnold, Ralph	3:55:20 (9,003)	
Arnold, Tim	3:37:41 (5,362)	
Arnold, Wayne	3:39:14 (5,642)	
Arnott, Alan	3:59:41 (10,146)	
Arnott, Francis	4:36:49 (18,841)	
Arnott, Stuart	5:11:54 (25,812)	
Arntzen, Carl	3:18:16 (2,584)	
Aronsson, Henrik	3:15:18 (2,271)	
Arrgon, Michael	4:56:05 (23,166)	
Arrol, Alec	4:51:13 (22,137)	
Arrowsmith, Shaun	4:52:01 (22,312)	
Arsenyev, Sergei	4:02:24 (10,718)	
Arthofer, Klaus	3:56:59 (9,451)	
Arthur, Nicholas	4:46:07 (20,999)	
Arthur, Robert	3:54:38 (8,827)	
Arthurton, Tony	4:35:13 (18,449)	
Artus, Tim	2:35:39 (105)	
Arundel, Stuart	5:11:32 (25,763)	
Ash, Chris	4:15:22 (13,607)	
Ash, David	5:05:47 (24,933)	
Ash, Graeme	5:29:44 (28,064)	
Ash, James	4:31:01 (17,502)	
Ash, Jason	5:34:47 (28,536)	
Ashburner, Alan	3:20:31 (2,828)	
Ashby, Charles	3:35:04 (4,921)	
Ashby, Edward	4:24:12 (15,797)	
Ashby, Gerald	4:16:31 (13,860)	
Ashby, John	5:32:08 (28,300)	
Ashby, Jonathan	4:36:01 (18,654)	
Ashby, Mark	2:56:46 (688)	
Ashby, Michael	3:50:33 (7,854)	
Ashby, Nick	3:31:55 (4,460)	
Ashby, Paul	3:47:58 (7,311)	
Ashby, Steve	4:38:04 (19,108)	
Ashcroft, Anthony	4:38:02 (19,099)	
Ashcroft, Geoffrey	4:55:52 (23,122)	
Ashcroft, Martin	4:01:28 (10,533)	
Ashdown, Gordon	5:07:57 (25,262)	
Ashfield, Robert	4:46:21 (21,061)	
Ashford, Justyn	3:45:42 (6,868)	
Ashford, Mark	4:48:47 (21,588)	
Ashford, Richard	4:09:33 (12,241)	
Ashford-Smith, Darryl	4:22:02 (15,247)	
Ashforth, Alan	3:03:21 (1,139)	
Ashley, James	3:44:30 (6,635)	
Ashley, James	4:18:29 (14,351)	
Ashman, Christopher	4:54:27 (22,803)	
Ashman, Michael	4:59:06 (23,824)	
Ashman, Richard	4:15:11 (13,563)	
Ashman, Rod	4:40:01 (19,539)	
Ashman-Lee, Tom	4:26:45 (16,417)	
Ashmore, Simon	4:05:43 (11,435)	
Ashton, Craig	4:01:20 (10,505)	
Ashton, David	4:43:43 (20,435)	
Ashton, Dudley	4:45:38 (20,876)	
Ashton, Jeffrey	3:37:40 (5,358)	
Ashton, John	4:38:43 (19,257)	
Ashton, Peter	6:17:14 (30,898)	
Ashton, Richard	3:44:52 (6,698)	
Ashton, Timothy	3:17:50 (2,532)	
Ashwood, John	4:37:15 (18,937)	
Ashwood, Keith	3:48:56 (7,499)	
Ashwood, Roger	3:50:29 (7,838)	
Ashworth, Howard	4:42:00 (19,993)	
Ashworth, Nathan	3:51:26 (8,057)	
Asiedu, Eric	3:56:09 (9,225)	
Askew, Duncan	4:50:30 (21,968)	
Askew, Michael	4:10:05 (12,369)	
Askew, Philip	4:13:25 (13,100)	
Askew, Robert	3:10:50 (1,742)	
Askwith, Andrew	5:02:09 (24,335)	
Aspey, Neil	4:09:01 (12,134)	
Aspinall, David	5:13:11 (25,997)	
Aspinall, Emmanuel	4:44:43 (20,663)	
Aspinall, Michael	3:17:22 (2,472)	
Aspinall, Steven	5:35:10 (28,568)	
Aspinall-O'Dea, Mark	5:12:27 (25,888)	
Asplund, Torvald	4:01:26 (10,525)	
Asquith, Antony	3:20:25 (2,819)	
Asquith, Gary	3:57:02 (9,464)	
Asser, Gregory	3:33:58 (4,742)	
Asser, Jeffrey	3:00:31 (976)	
Astell, Trevor	4:08:31 (12,014)	
Astill, Jonathan	4:04:04 (11,079)	
Astle, Thomas	3:22:51 (3,092)	
Astles, Peter	4:01:45 (10,589)	
Aston, Alan	5:10:36 (25,635)	
Aston, Andrew	3:01:23 (1,017)	
Aston, Christopher	4:21:51 (15,194)	
Aston, Darran	3:32:04 (4,478)	
Aston, David	3:51:46 (8,138)	
Aston, Jeffrey	3:28:21 (3,874)	
Aston, John	4:53:43 (22,652)	
Aston, Stephen	6:18:09 (30,940)	
Athawes, Jon	3:52:58 (8,412)	
Atherton, Alex	5:13:37 (26,059)	
Atherton, Joseph	3:33:25 (4,669)	
Atherton, Paul	4:41:49 (19,949)	
Atienza-Rodriguez, Ricardo	4:06:11 (11,533)	
Atkin, James	4:30:04 (17,257)	
Atkins, Gary	4:16:25 (13,838)	
Atkins, Graham	3:51:00 (7,953)	
Atkins, Jeremy	4:00:55 (10,411)	
Atkins, Kevin	4:07:51 (11,884)	
Atkins, Nicky	4:37:45 (19,036)	
Atkins, Paul	3:53:17 (8,491)	
Atkins, Peter	4:09:09 (12,163)	
Atkins, Richard	3:25:31 (3,463)	
Atkins, Richard	5:01:50 (24,288)	
Atkins, Robert	4:49:24 (21,724)	
Atkins, Simon	4:06:00 (11,502)	
Atkinson, Alexis	3:17:55 (2,538)	
Atkinson, Andrew	3:59:21 (10,053)	
Atkinson, Carl	3:40:40 (5,897)	
Atkinson, Chris	5:12:35 (25,917)	
Atkinson, Christopher	4:33:25 (18,036)	
Atkinson, David	2:46:32 (278)	
Atkinson, Dean	3:41:27 (6,055)	
Atkinson, James	5:16:42 (26,451)	
Atkinson, Kevin	4:17:47 (14,206)	
Atkinson, Mark	5:23:18 (27,331)	
Atkinson, Michael	4:47:53 (21,394)	
Atkinson, Peter	3:40:18 (5,843)	
Atkinson, Tony	4:04:43 (11,230)	
Atraghji, David	5:05:41 (24,917)	
Attala, Claude	5:33:15 (28,397)	
Attanasio, Fabio	4:01:07 (10,451)	
Attard, Kevin	4:19:59 (14,737)	
Attenborough, Charlie	4:29:34 (17,127)	
Atter, Adrian	4:58:34 (23,711)	
Attewell, Gary	3:15:09 (2,255)	
Attfield, Brian	4:47:47 (21,368)	
Attreed, Kristian	3:12:10 (1,878)	
Attridge, Joseph	3:25:09 (3,417)	
Attrill, Raymond	3:29:10 (4,021)	
Attrill, Rick	3:37:32 (5,330)	
Attwell, Clinton	5:49:00 (29,639)	
Attwell, Steve	3:55:16 (8,983)	
Attwood, Tom	4:09:39 (12,264)	
Attwood-Smith, Nicholas	3:53:10 (8,464)	
Atwal, Jodh	5:50:07 (29,724)	
Atwal, Kulwant	4:45:48 (20,913)	
Atya, Khalil	3:11:36 (1,811)	
Aubree, Yvon	4:13:22 (13,086)	
Aubry, Hubert	3:59:02 (9,971)	
Auckland, John	3:49:38 (7,665)	
Aucott, Michael	3:26:57 (3,669)	
Audas, Allen	3:22:21 (3,029)	
Audenshaw, Tony	3:08:20 (1,527)	
Audrain, Timothy	5:17:18 (26,512)	
Audsley, Marc	5:03:34 (24,543)	
Auer, Dietrich	3:56:50 (9,407)	
Augo, Ochieng	3:09:09 (1,598)	
Auguet, Jacques	4:07:44 (11,859)	
Augustin, Franz	2:55:33 (622)	
Augustine, Anto	4:54:42 (22,866)	
Aujla, Jagdeep	6:03:23 (30,388)	
Aukett, John	5:05:24 (24,857)	
Ault, John	4:22:44 (15,425)	
Auskern, Barry	3:06:00 (1,322)	
Austen, Graham	4:00:56 (10,417)	
Auster, Paul	5:10:50 (25,666)	

Austin, Alan 4:47:28 (21,293)
Austin, Alex 5:17:22 (26,522)
Austin, Christopher 3:23:49 (3,214)
Austin, Douglas 6:32:17 (31,387)
Austin, Edward 3:18:41 (2,625)
Austin, Huw 3:56:13 (9,249)
Austin, Jon 4:32:57 (17,935)
Austin, Leslie 4:05:49 (11,461)
Austin, Michael 5:24:48 (27,508)
Austin, Richard 3:07:47 (1,486)
Austin, Steve 3:58:18 (9,782)
Avander, Kent 3:38:29 (5,492)
Avanzato, Roberto 2:59:21 (885)
Aver, Karl 3:05:21 (1,275)
Averell, James 5:02:59 (24,454)
Averill, Tim 3:31:16 (4,373)
Avery, Joe 5:55:01 (29,999)
Avery, Paul 4:23:17 (15,571)
Aves, Clayton 3:19:05 (2,661)
Avey, Terry 4:04:39 (11,210)
Aveyard, Darren 4:13:47 (13,195)
Avigad, Daniel 3:28:35 (3,919)
Avis, Charles 4:54:39 (22,849)
Avrahampour, Eli 5:54:13 (29,944)
Avrili, Walter 4:24:44 (15,928)
Axsel, Fred 4:04:07 (11,096)
Axtell, Adrian 4:28:40 (16,902)
Axton, Matthew 2:41:59 (180)
Ayers, Robert 4:10:33 (12,476)
Aylett, Paul 3:31:57 (4,465)
Ayliffe, Dave 5:41:26 (29,109)
Ayling, Giles 4:48:19 (21,499)
Ayling, Paul 4:02:57 (10,835)
Aylmore, James 3:13:37 (2,073)
Aylott, Wayne 3:57:35 (9,591)
Aylward, Robin 4:13:21 (13,083)
Aymes, Philip 5:45:12 (29,384)
Ayres, Arthur 3:52:53 (8,393)
Ayres, Douglas 4:31:27 (17,602)
Ayres, Duncan 4:31:01 (17,502)
Ayres, Laurie 5:15:36 (26,333)
Ayres, Lee 4:52:19 (22,362)
Ayres, Mark 5:03:30 (24,530)
Baalham, Simon 5:14:50 (26,224)
Babb, Steven 3:04:08 (1,191)
Babbs, Antony 3:28:03 (3,827)
Babecki, Julio 2:55:48 (636)
Baber, Guy 3:53:30 (8,541)
Babicz, Nicholas 3:54:19 (8,732)
Babington, Nick 3:55:59 (9,173)
Bacallado, Juan Manuel 4:28:53 (16,961)
Bacchus, Feizal 4:38:50 (19,285)
Bach, Oliver 3:53:58 (8,664)
Bache, Robert 4:32:32 (17,840)
Bachelet, Guillaume 3:59:39 (10,136)
Baci, Arber 2:54:56 (586)
Back, David 4:43:28 (20,367)
Back, Terry 3:20:08 (2,775)
Backer, Daniel 7:02:57 (31,911)
Backhouse, Paul 4:20:26 (14,854)
Backhouse, Timothy 5:36:56 (28,730)
Backstrand, Tommy 6:12:29 (30,749)
Bacon, Alan 4:33:16 (17,998)
Bacon, Alan 6:26:34 (31,219)
Bacon, Clive 4:11:50 (12,727)
Bacon, Colin 6:35:47 (31,469)
Bacon, Craig 3:55:15 (8,978)
Bacon, Gary 4:19:04 (14,521)
Bacon, John 4:38:00 (19,088)
Bacon, Peter 6:34:48 (31,444)
Bacon, Steven 4:31:12 (17,549)
Bader, Christian 3:35:39 (5,021)
Badger, Glenn 5:35:37 (28,607)
Badillo, José 3:40:49 (5,930)
Badinka, Paul 4:33:39 (18,089)
Badstuber, Paul 3:38:37 (5,521)
Baga, Barry 6:15:41 (30,846)
Baga, Steve 5:41:35 (29,128)
Bagnall, Stuart 4:52:02 (22,316)
Bahier, Lauren 3:10:41 (1,727)
Bai, Jerome 3:24:53 (3,383)
Bai, Laurent 3:03:02 (1,117)
Baigent, Derek 2:58:41 (819)
Baiguera, Marco 2:57:16 (721)
Bailey, Adrian 3:46:56 (7,112)
Bailey, Alan 4:50:51 (22,043)
Bailey, Alastair 3:10:34 (1,720)
Bailey, Andrew 4:22:09 (15,276)
Bailey, Andrew 4:30:57 (17,481)
Bailey, Bart 3:56:11 (9,234)
Bailey, Chris 2:52:22 (463)
Bailey, Chris 3:52:20 (8,273)
Bailey, Colin 4:39:45 (19,488)
Bailey, David 3:18:16 (2,584)
Bailey, David 5:35:07 (28,564)
Bailey, David 5:45:55 (29,435)
Bailey, Derek 4:19:31 (14,619)
Bailey, Edward 4:12:18 (12,832)
Bailey, Frank 3:45:46 (6,883)
Bailey, Gareth 4:48:15 (21,482)
Bailey, Gary 4:42:15 (20,039)
Bailey, Guy 4:03:13 (10,884)
Bailey, John 5:18:00 (26,611)
Bailey, Mark 4:50:50 (22,038)
Bailey, Nick 4:09:06 (12,153)
Bailey, Peter 3:30:00 (4,167)
Bailey, Peter 4:19:39 (14,652)
Bailey, Robert 5:00:15 (24,027)
Bailey, Robert 5:09:41 (25,504)
Bailey, Robin 3:49:17 (7,587)
Bailey, Robin 4:52:13 (22,344)
Bailey, Roger 4:50:13 (21,905)
Bailey, Stuart 3:19:52 (2,739)
Bailey, Thomas 3:23:16 (3,147)
Baillie, Edward 3:44:36 (6,649)
Baillie, Michael 2:46:53 (292)
Baily, Stephen 4:49:17 (21,698)
Bain, Alan 5:31:58 (28,289)
Bain, Daibhidh 5:02:44 (24,425)
Bain, David 4:45:41 (20,884)
Bain, David 5:26:19 (27,715)
Bain, Derek 4:12:00 (12,762)
Bains, Diljit 4:49:15 (21,689)
Bains, Gurdeep 4:44:13 (20,548)
Bains, Narinder 4:32:01 (17,736)
Baird, Andrew 4:42:25 (20,088)
Baird, James 3:00:26 (968)
Baird, Paul 3:13:18 (2,034)
Baird, Timothy 2:54:32 (562)
Baisden, Kevin 5:00:24 (24,050)
Baker, Alexander 4:19:08 (14,538)
Baker, Andrew 4:16:24 (13,833)
Baker, Andrew 4:33:18 (18,007)
Baker, Andrian 4:14:51 (13,466)
Baker, Brendan 4:39:46 (19,490)
Baker, Carl 2:56:25 (672)
Baker, Christopher 4:10:25 (12,449)
Baker, Cliff 5:15:25 (26,306)
Baker, Clive 3:05:10 (1,264)
Baker, Colin 6:04:34 (30,432)
Baker, Damian 4:39:06 (19,343)
Baker, Ed 6:09:38 (30,624)
Baker, Eric 3:52:28 (8,300)
Baker, Euan 4:34:58 (18,388)
Baker, Gerald 6:14:37 (30,815)
Baker, Graham 2:59:08 (866)
Baker, Henry 6:09:38 (30,624)
Baker, John 4:49:35 (21,776)
Baker, Kevin 5:58:00 (30,163)
Baker, Kim 3:11:41 (1,819)
Baker, Mark 3:53:09 (8,460)
Baker, Mark 4:11:44 (12,702)
Baker, Mark 4:48:33 (21,542)
Baker, Mark 4:58:02 (23,591)
Baker, Mat 4:24:25 (15,844)
Baker, Michael 4:34:05 (18,192)
Baker, Michael 5:19:47 (26,860)
Baker, Mickey 5:31:37 (28,250)
Baker, Nathan 4:31:50 (17,697)
Baker, Nicholas 4:15:49 (13,707)
Baker, Nicholas 4:45:07 (20,748)
Baker, Nicola 5:31:37 (28,250)
Baker, Nigel 3:38:52 (5,573)
Baker, Paul 5:24:34 (27,485)
Baker, Peter 5:57:49 (30,156)
Baker, Philip 4:27:06 (16,497)
Baker, Russell 3:49:58 (7,729)
Baker, Stephen 4:02:51 (10,817)
Baker, Stephen 4:56:01 (23,150)
Baker, Steven 3:58:18 (9,782)
Baker, Stuart 5:29:36 (28,054)
Baker, Wayne 4:18:23 (14,325)
Bakker, Carlos 3:37:13 (5,277)
Bakrania, Rajesh 7:11:09 (32,000)
Balchin, Ivan 3:02:15 (1,076)
Balcon, Simon 5:11:53 (25,811)
Balczar, Guillermo 4:04:17 (11,134)
Baldaro, John 4:01:10 (10,465)
Balden, David 5:33:01 (28,375)
Baldini, Stefano 2:07:56 (1)
Baldock, Nick 4:35:49 (18,603)
Baldry, Jon 4:21:40 (15,149)
Baldwin, David 2:58:11 (783)
Baldwin, Kevin 4:35:44 (18,570)
Baldwin, Mark 4:19:33 (14,626)
Baldwin, Paul 5:28:33 (27,946)
Baldwin, Richard 4:51:55 (22,296)
Baldwin, Robert 4:54:20 (22,776)
Bale, Mons 2:57:36 (744)
Balfour, Ian 3:32:26 (4,520)
Balfour, Scott 2:53:35 (511)
Balfourth, Winston 3:07:05 (1,410)
Ball, Adrian 3:19:23 (2,689)
Ball, Andrew 3:06:18 (1,338)
Ball, Andrew 3:50:42 (7,886)
Ball, Andrew 4:13:12 (13,049)
Ball, Christopher 5:42:25 (29,200)
Ball, David 4:45:11 (20,767)
Ball, Graham 2:54:56 (586)
Ball, Ian 4:01:05 (10,448)
Ball, James 4:48:05 (21,448)
Ball, Martin 4:19:43 (14,673)
Ball, Martin 4:52:44 (22,449)
Ball, Michael 5:21:49 (27,126)
Ball, Nigel 6:05:18 (30,469)
Ball, Paul 3:57:05 (9,472)
Ball, Peter 3:57:27 (9,569)
Ball, Philip 3:21:53 (2,971)
Ball, Stephen 3:53:20 (8,504)
Ball, Stephen 4:08:50 (12,093)
Ball, Steve 4:43:28 (20,367)
Ball, Welsey 4:17:08 (14,018)
Balladon, Paul 5:21:00 (27,021)
Ballagher, Bruce 5:14:29 (26,172)
Ballam, Paul 4:08:25 (11,984)
Ballantine, Ewan 3:14:46 (2,215)
Ballantyne, Andrew 4:47:23 (21,269)
Ballard, David 4:49:39 (21,793)
Ballard, Neil 3:13:38 (2,077)
Ballett, Leighton 3:09:18 (1,615)
Ballinger, Christopher 4:09:01 (12,134)
Balmer, David 3:26:08 (3,558)
Balmer, Malcolm 3:29:18 (4,044)
Baltierrez-Saus, Jordi 4:44:05 (20,517)
Bamber, Stephen 5:19:12 (26,782)
Bamberough, Roger 4:21:30 (15,113)
Bamford, David 3:09:55 (1,668)
Bamford, David 4:20:40 (14,899)
Bamford, Karl 4:21:33 (15,119)
Bamford, Nicholas 3:52:10 (8,237)
Bamford, Steven 4:36:15 (18,698)
Bamforth, Richard 4:23:06 (15,512)
Bampton, Paul 3:27:51 (3,798)
Bampton, Richard 3:58:54 (9,942)
Bamsey, Jonathan 3:26:47 (3,641)
Bamsey, Simon 4:45:51 (20,926)
Bance, Elliott 4:08:28 (12,002)
Bancewicz, Tony 4:45:23 (20,817)
Bancroft, David 4:26:21 (16,326)
Bancroft, Tony 3:59:26 (10,073)
Banfi, Michael 3:10:56 (1,751)
Banfield, Mark 4:36:31 (18,775)
Banfield, Philip 4:01:03 (10,439)
Banfield, Simon 3:57:35 (9,591)
Bangert, Alexander 3:16:46 (2,402)
Banham, Richard 4:48:59 (21,627)
Banister, Michael 3:29:18 (4,044)
Banks, John 4:28:51 (16,951)
Banks, Julian 5:07:27 (25,172)

Banks, Mark 3:49:19 (7,593)
Banks, Paul 4:19:59 (14,737)
Banks, Peter 5:10:42 (25,648)
Banks, Phil 3:08:21 (1,530)
Banks, Philip 6:10:03 (30,645)
Banks, Simon 5:59:08 (30,216)
Banks, Steve 4:00:02 (10,229)
Banks, Timothy 4:35:49 (18,603)
Banner, Charles 4:05:31 (11,403)
Bannerman, Keith 3:28:18 (3,866)
Banning, Fred 4:32:57 (17,935)
Bannister, John 4:30:05 (17,259)
Bannister, Mark 4:44:28 (20,608)
Bannister, Michael 3:28:44 (3,952)
Bannister, Nick 3:54:45 (8,850)
Bannister, Peter 3:57:21 (9,542)
Bannister, Stuart 3:03:26 (1,146)
Banwell, Kevin 4:11:45 (12,707)
Baple, Jonathan 6:15:24 (30,841)
Barback, David 4:09:27 (12,215)
Barback, Neil 4:16:50 (13,941)
Barber, Andrew 4:28:30 (16,858)
Barber, Anthony 4:42:59 (20,229)
Barber, Charles 4:41:10 (19,790)
Barber, Clive 4:59:16 (23,852)
Barber, Ian 4:15:01 (13,512)
Barber, Jon 4:30:06 (17,263)
Barber, Nick 3:53:56 (8,653)
Barber, Oliver 4:23:49 (15,700)
Barber, Steven 5:04:47 (24,757)
Barber, Timothy 4:14:50 (13,461)
Barberio, Daniel 4:07:54 (11,888)
Barbour, Laurence 4:54:14 (22,753)
Barcham, Daniel 4:17:01 (13,989)
Barclay, Andy 4:48:11 (21,465)
Barclay, Bob 5:02:41 (24,415)
Barclay, Ibrahim 4:26:59 (16,465)
Barclay, Luke 4:17:02 (13,993)
Barclay, Raymond 3:25:59 (3,540)
Barclay, Richard 3:55:05 (8,933)
Barclay, Simon 3:43:10 (6,399)
Barclay, Simon 4:08:16 (11,953)
Bardell, Graham 3:52:00 (8,197)
Barden, David 3:58:29 (9,830)
Barden, Stuart 5:52:53 (29,874)
Barder, Owen 3:12:20 (1,908)
Bargues, Dominique 5:32:48 (28,356)
Barham, Jeff 5:05:59 (24,955)
Barham, Malcolm 3:50:26 (7,829)
Barke, Christopher 4:41:47 (19,938)
Barke, Norman 5:37:55 (28,804)
Barker, Andrew 5:09:51 (25,521)
Barker, Charles 4:05:28 (11,395)
Barker, Christopher 4:59:03 (23,812)
Barker, Christopher 5:29:22 (28,025)
Barker, David 3:55:37 (9,081)
Barker, David 4:47:57 (21,412)
Barker, James 3:49:24 (7,610)
Barker, James 3:53:38 (8,574)
Barker, John 3:54:52 (8,885)
Barker, Jonathan 3:55:51 (9,144)
Barker, Jonathan 4:39:31 (19,444)
Barker, Matthew 5:55:06 (30,006)
Barker, Michael 3:37:09 (5,264)
Barker, Michael 3:52:30 (8,310)
Barker, Michael 4:19:25 (14,599)
Barker, Michael 4:48:06 (21,451)
Barker, Philip 5:12:21 (25,872)
Barker, Rob 5:22:09 (27,160)
Barker, Steven 5:01:45 (24,269)
Barker, Timothy 4:31:39 (17,658)
Barker, Victor 4:08:54 (12,108)
Barker, William 3:40:42 (5,903)
Barklam, Anthony 3:53:31 (8,548)
Barkley, Andrew 5:07:48 (25,238)
Barkley, Ian 4:53:19 (22,574)
Barley, Allan 5:50:57 (29,784)
Barley, Laurence 4:23:23 (15,588)
Barley, Victor 5:29:33 (28,045)
Barlow, Alex 3:26:25 (3,593)
Barlow, Andrew 4:08:09 (11,928)
Barlow, David 5:26:42 (27,753)
Barlow, Geoff 5:53:33 (29,909)
Barlow, Howard 3:49:15 (7,576)
Barlow, Jeremy 4:04:28 (11,171)
Barlow, Lawrence 6:29:34 (31,315)
Barlow, Lee 3:25:39 (3,481)
Barlow, Nicholas 4:18:02 (14,257)
Barlow, Paul 3:48:40 (7,434)
Barlow, Richard 4:35:52 (18,613)
Barlow, Robin 4:16:25 (13,838)
Barlow, Roger 3:48:20 (7,381)
Barlow, Thomas 4:34:16 (18,230)
Barltrop, Verne 3:49:04 (7,529)
Barnaby, Simon 6:49:50 (31,714)
Barnard, Carl 4:28:18 (16,789)
Barnard, Edward 4:02:55 (10,828)
Barnardiston, Nathaniel 5:11:03 (25,700)
Barne, Alasdair 5:24:01 (27,410)
Barnert, Paul 3:23:52 (3,226)
Barnes, Andrew 3:48:28 (7,395)
Barnes, Andy 3:19:18 (2,678)
Barnes, Arthur 3:07:29 (1,451)
Barnes, Colin 5:49:57 (29,710)
Barnes, David 3:14:34 (2,193)
Barnes, Frederick 6:25:31 (31,179)
Barnes, Gary 3:16:22 (2,363)
Barnes, Gary 4:20:42 (14,903)
Barnes, Gary 4:33:47 (18,112)
Barnes, James 6:04:04 (30,412)
Barnes, Kerry 4:04:54 (11,270)
Barnes, Michael 3:02:22 (1,081)
Barnes, Michael 4:08:39 (12,052)
Barnes, Nigel 4:25:18 (16,086)
Barnes, Peter 3:23:55 (3,235)
Barnes, Peter 5:31:07 (28,208)
Barnes, Phil 5:14:09 (26,114)
Barnes, Robert 5:48:28 (29,603)
Barnes, Roy 3:34:57 (4,901)
Barnes, Steven 4:26:29 (16,351)
Barnes, Trevor 3:42:56 (6,349)
Barnes, William 4:40:50 (19,712)
Barnett, Charles 5:23:07 (27,303)
Barnett, David 5:21:30 (27,081)
Barnett, Gary 3:57:07 (9,481)
Barnett, Graham 4:05:35 (11,415)
Barnett, Hugh 4:03:16 (10,906)
Barnett, Jonathan 4:44:23 (20,591)
Barnett, Mark 3:23:30 (3,178)
Barnett, Michael 4:56:46 (23,329)
Barnett, Paul 4:03:22 (10,925)
Barnett, Robert 4:01:24 (10,519)
Barnett, Simon 3:27:40 (3,762)
Barnett, Stewart 3:54:12 (8,705)
Barney, Steve 4:42:58 (20,222)
Barnham, Darren 4:49:02 (21,640)
Barningham, Richard 4:57:43 (23,524)
Barnish, Stephen 7:21:48 (32,086)
Barns, John 3:35:50 (5,048)
Barnwell, Tim 3:43:13 (6,410)
Baron, Stuart 3:37:57 (5,405)
Baroncini, Nello 4:38:44 (19,263)
Barot, Krishna 6:05:42 (30,491)
Barot, Sanjay 4:59:01 (23,804)
Barr, David 3:32:07 (4,486)
Barr, Jacob 6:01:00 (30,295)
Barr, James 3:39:38 (5,717)
Barr, Jonathan 3:55:31 (9,052)
Barr, Richard 3:54:29 (8,776)
Barr, Robert 4:48:01 (21,433)
Barr, Roger 2:47:16 (307)
Barraclough, Roger 5:10:34 (25,630)
Barrance, Steven 4:46:48 (21,146)
Barrance, Tony 4:23:44 (15,680)
Barrance, Tony 5:01:42 (24,257)
Barrand, Peter 4:13:58 (13,251)
Barrass, Barnaby 3:13:37 (2,073)
Barrass, Malcolm 5:18:40 (26,723)
Barratt, Clinton 4:05:03 (11,303)
Barratt, Martin 7:07:09 (31,960)
Barrell, David 4:28:51 (16,951)
Barrell, James 7:35:32 (32,187)
Barrell, Stuart 5:01:45 (24,269)
Barrett, Andrew 4:27:47 (16,671)
Barrett, Anthony 6:00:08 (30,260)
Barrett, Bill 3:02:11 (1,073)
Barrett, Craig 3:46:38 (7,058)
Barrett, Daniel 4:36:57 (18,866)
Barrett, Gerard 4:07:04 (11,703)
Barrett, Gordon 3:04:45 (1,228)
Barrett, James 4:37:42 (19,020)
Barrett, John 4:01:44 (10,586)
Barrett, Lloyd 4:52:20 (22,365)
Barrett, Mark 5:55:00 (29,998)
Barrett, Mark 6:56:04 (31,844)
Barrett, Neil 4:55:15 (22,965)
Barrett, Nicholas 4:14:46 (13,437)
Barrett, Paul 4:04:50 (11,252)
Barrett, Simon 4:38:45 (19,268)
Barrett, Stuart 4:33:27 (18,047)
Barretto, Dominic 4:25:47 (16,198)
Barrie, Tim 3:29:28 (4,083)
Barringer, Scott 5:01:17 (24,202)
Barron, Edward 4:16:19 (13,809)
Barron, Robert 3:46:57 (7,115)
Barron, Robert 4:43:10 (20,277)
Barrow, Christopher 4:57:48 (23,542)
Barrow, David 4:48:20 (21,501)
Barrow, Martin 4:56:18 (23,221)
Barrow, Michael 6:42:11 (31,569)
Barrow, Paul 5:54:25 (29,966)
Barrow, Richard 5:18:52 (26,740)
Barrowclough, Nicholas 4:56:28 (23,251)
Barrs, Gary 4:37:06 (18,902)
Barry, Alexander 4:40:27 (19,643)
Barry, Andrew 3:39:34 (5,706)
Barry, David 5:46:35 (29,467)
Barry, Jason 3:34:30 (4,839)
Barry, Julian 2:56:23 (669)
Barry, Keith 3:36:39 (5,170)
Barry, Michael 3:54:02 (8,673)
Barry, Neal 4:01:59 (10,630)
Barry, Stephen 3:46:30 (7,028)
Barry, Tony 3:57:46 (9,638)
Barsley, Jason 4:45:09 (20,757)
Barstow, Michael 5:41:59 (29,161)
Bartell, Matthew 4:02:55 (10,828)
Barter, Alex 4:15:56 (13,728)
Bartl, Guenther-Hans 3:52:15 (8,255)
Bartle, Darryl 5:49:54 (29,708)
Bartlett, Anthony 4:20:31 (14,873)
Bartlett, Ben 3:35:53 (5,053)
Bartlett, Brian 5:05:24 (24,857)
Bartlett, Charles 4:31:30 (17,616)
Bartlett, David 4:23:40 (15,662)
Bartlett, Edwin 5:18:12 (26,653)
Bartlett, Gareth 5:45:18 (29,389)
Bartlett, Greg 3:55:18 (8,996)
Bartlett, Ian 3:47:06 (7,141)
Bartlett, Ian 4:45:38 (20,876)
Bartlett, James 3:35:19 (4,960)
Bartlett, John 4:41:35 (19,889)
Bartlett, Nicholas 3:26:55 (3,664)
Bartlett, Peter 4:47:26 (21,283)
Bartlett, Richard 4:31:00 (17,498)
Bartlett, Simon 5:21:43 (27,112)
Bartlett, Steve 6:01:01 (30,299)
Barton, Christopher 4:04:49 (11,250)
Barton, David 4:48:03 (21,441)
Barton, Dick 5:42:26 (29,202)
Barton, Gary 4:47:39 (21,333)
Barton, James 4:52:51 (22,470)
Barton, Ken 3:41:30 (6,067)
Barton, Michael 3:57:28 (9,574)
Barton, Michael 4:58:45 (23,745)
Barton, Nigel 4:31:39 (17,658)
Barton, Patrick 4:14:01 (13,264)
Barton, Paul 4:22:57 (15,482)
Barton, Stuart 4:44:13 (20,548)
Bartram, Andrew 4:54:21 (22,779)
Bartram, Bruce 5:48:52 (29,625)
Bartram, Douglas 4:48:37 (21,554)
Barwell, Michael 3:13:55 (2,118)
Barzee, Darren 3:54:43 (8,840)
Baseggio, Paolo 3:33:43 (4,707)
Basetti, Marco 3:06:32 (1,364)
Basham, Leslie 4:34:02 (18,172)
Bashford, Kevin 4:14:06 (13,282)
Bashford, Richard 3:38:46 (5,555)

Belcher, Simon	3:39:43	(5,731)
Belderbos, Edward	4:08:43	(12,068)
Belding, Hamish	5:26:03	(27,680)
Belgaumkar, Ajay	4:41:52	(19,966)
Belkin, Paul	4:03:25	(10,933)
Bell, Alan	5:55:11	(30,010)
Bell, André	4:04:12	(11,112)
Bell, Anthony	4:03:00	(10,839)
Bell, Ashley	4:51:53	(22,287)
Bell, Colin	4:23:24	(15,590)
Bell, Damian	4:43:06	(20,263)
Bell, David	3:25:02	(3,399)
Bell, David	3:33:17	(4,643)
Bell, David	4:11:54	(12,741)
Bell, David	5:21:10	(27,043)
Bell, Douglas	4:22:36	(15,394)
Bell, Duncan	3:50:09	(7,765)
Bell, Gary	4:59:54	(23,967)
Bell, Gavin	3:54:26	(8,763)
Bell, Geoffrey	3:21:41	(2,951)
Bell, Graham	3:03:22	(1,142)
Bell, Ian	4:21:04	(14,997)
Bell, James	3:43:41	(6,486)
Bell, John	2:57:07	(712)
Bell, John	5:47:22	(29,522)
Bell, Kevin	4:37:48	(19,045)
Bell, Mark	5:02:26	(24,379)
Bell, Martin	3:19:33	(2,705)
Bell, Martin	3:42:34	(6,272)
Bell, Martyn	4:53:12	(22,545)
Bell, Matthew	5:07:29	(25,179)
Bell, Michael	3:40:47	(5,922)
Bell, Michael	6:08:31	(30,591)
Bell, Mike	3:28:01	(3,818)
Bell, Nick	4:41:03	(19,767)
Bell, Pete	4:05:30	(11,401)
Bell, Philip	3:40:55	(5,946)
Bell, Russell	3:27:23	(3,718)
Bell, Sean	4:53:11	(22,541)
Bell, Simon	2:36:45	(117)
Bell, Stephen	4:25:36	(16,158)
Bell, Steven	5:04:33	(24,714)
Bell, Wayne	2:57:00	(703)
Bell, William	4:52:26	(22,384)
Bell, Williams	3:47:36	(7,237)
Bellacosa, Maurizio	3:47:50	(7,289)
Bellal, Sedki	5:40:01	(28,995)
Bellamy, Darren	5:32:16	(28,312)
Bellars, Tim	3:45:31	(6,836)
Bellen, Marcel	4:09:36	(12,249)
Bellis, Stephen	3:02:16	(1,077)
Bello, Sylvain	3:46:41	(7,063)
Belsom, Robin	3:15:48	(2,314)
Belt, Keith	3:36:40	(5,175)
Belton, Chris	3:05:15	(1,272)
Ben Mlih, Nourredine	3:34:34	(4,847)
Benabdellah, Mehdi	3:28:42	(3,943)
Benbow, Martin	4:03:56	(11,044)
Bence, Matthew	4:09:45	(12,285)
Bendall, Jeffrey	4:46:51	(21,161)
Bendall, Michael	5:35:05	(28,561)
Bendelow, Keith	4:22:38	(15,406)
Bendle, Simon	4:21:57	(15,224)
Bendle, Stephen	4:05:15	(11,342)
Benedict, Daniel	3:31:23	(4,390)
Benetti, Fulvio	3:42:59	(6,364)
Beneventi, Mario	5:23:56	(27,401)
Benfredj, Sacha	4:09:32	(12,237)
Benger, Alexander	3:39:28	(5,686)
Benger, Nicholas	3:27:52	(3,799)
Benghalem, Abdelhamid	4:19:39	(14,652)
Bengtsson, Jan	5:15:59	(26,377)
Bengtsson, Joakim	5:00:11	(24,009)
Bengtsson, Jonas	5:07:33	(25,195)
Benham, David	4:46:47	(21,143)
Benham, Kevin	4:19:08	(14,538)
Benjamin, Adam	4:47:49	(21,380)
Benjamin, Eric	5:58:51	(30,194)
Benjamin, Peter	3:17:21	(2,469)
Benjamin, Trevor	3:39:26	(5,683)
Benn, Andrew	3:08:57	(1,582)
Bennani, Amal	3:20:54	(2,875)
Bennanni, Rachid	3:44:23	(6,618)
Ben-Nathan, Marc	3:52:46	(8,367)
Bennell, Kevin	4:27:05	(16,494)
Bennet, David	3:13:32	(2,065)
Bennett, Ben	2:56:57	(697)
Bennett, Brian	4:26:02	(16,254)
Bennett, Brian	5:11:45	(25,792)
Bennett, Colin	4:01:50	(10,607)
Bennett, David	4:57:54	(23,561)
Bennett, Digby	4:16:09	(13,773)
Bennett, Gary	7:30:58	(32,160)
Bennett, Harold	4:44:09	(20,527)
Bennett, Harvey	4:18:00	(14,251)
Bennett, Jeremy	4:06:37	(11,611)
Bennett, Kevin	2:49:24	(376)
Bennett, Kevin	5:18:17	(26,670)
Bennett, Mark	4:53:44	(22,663)
Bennett, Martin	5:09:36	(25,491)
Bennett, Michael	5:02:57	(24,449)
Bennett, Mike	3:44:51	(6,696)
Bennett, Nic	5:06:33	(25,025)
Bennett, Nigel	5:24:12	(27,437)
Bennett, Peter	4:00:34	(10,340)
Bennett, Peter	4:13:47	(13,195)
Bennett, Raymond	4:02:56	(10,832)
Bennett, Richard	2:56:45	(686)
Bennett, Richard	3:48:53	(7,486)
Bennett, Richard	4:57:46	(23,537)
Bennett, Roger	2:58:04	(770)
Bennett, Spencer	5:05:03	(24,801)
Bennett, Stephen	3:57:01	(9,461)
Bennett, Stephen	4:23:40	(15,662)
Bennett, Stephen	5:27:38	(27,853)
Bennett, Steven	3:07:11	(1,426)
Bennett, Tony	3:43:47	(6,504)
Bennett, Tony	5:15:15	(26,286)
Bennett-Smith, Lloyd	4:15:34	(13,656)
Benning, Christopher	3:56:06	(9,206)
Benning, Joseph	3:56:05	(9,203)
Bennion, Chris	3:28:41	(3,940)
Bennis, Rachid	3:52:21	(8,276)
Benns, Will	3:58:06	(9,730)
Benott, Metais	3:50:24	(7,825)
Benskin, Ian	2:59:00	(851)
Benson, Ian	3:10:10	(1,692)
Benson, James	3:23:25	(3,164)
Benson, Mark	3:59:19	(10,040)
Benson, Richard	3:49:04	(7,529)
Benson, Richard	4:16:32	(13,864)
Benson, Stephen	3:32:06	(4,483)
Benson, Timothy	4:20:49	(14,931)
Benson, Tom	4:45:48	(20,913)
Bent, Alan	3:53:35	(8,564)
Bent, Christopher	4:37:16	(18,942)
Bent, Daniel	3:36:22	(5,125)
Bentahila, Saad	3:31:40	(4,429)
Bentham, Stephen	4:09:28	(12,219)
Bentley, Alex	4:27:10	(16,516)
Bentley, Christopher	4:17:27	(14,102)
Bentley, Christopher	4:25:41	(16,177)
Bentley, James	6:27:33	(31,249)
Bentley, Lee	4:01:46	(10,593)
Bentley, Mark	3:05:28	(1,285)
Bentley, Steve	3:55:41	(9,103)
Bentley, Stuart	3:13:34	(2,069)
Benton, Andy	4:39:08	(19,353)
Benton, Brian	4:28:31	(16,861)
Benton, Brian	4:42:52	(20,199)
Benton, Carl	4:06:39	(11,614)
Benton, David	4:04:15	(11,120)
Benton, Steven	4:20:14	(14,802)
Benvenuti, Andrea	4:32:51	(17,913)
Benzakour, Amal	2:58:33	(804)
Benzakour, Khalid	2:58:33	(804)
Beqqali, Nourredine	3:36:46	(5,191)
Berengue, Roland	5:13:52	(26,087)
Beresford, Jeff	4:11:20	(12,606)
Beresford, Jonathan	4:11:42	(12,696)
Beresford-Green, Paul	4:34:55	(18,376)
Berg, Harald	3:08:45	(1,567)
Berg, Niels	3:48:58	(7,507)
Berg, Ty	3:08:41	(1,561)
Bergamaschi, Gianpiero	4:31:20	(17,579)
Bergaust, Ole Peter	2:58:14	(785)
Bergdahl, Mark	4:32:47	(17,894)
Bergen, Marcus	3:16:59	(2,428)
Berger, Joerg	3:47:41	(7,254)
Bergin, Ian	3:55:46	(9,120)
Bergin, Mark	4:23:35	(15,635)
Bergin, Matt	3:31:35	(4,423)
Bergius, Max	3:45:04	(6,746)
Bergly, Haakon	3:54:56	(8,902)
Bergman, Jan	4:29:28	(17,107)
Bergmann, Henning	3:45:23	(6,806)
Bergot, Remy	4:04:19	(11,137)
Bergvall, Karl-Gustav	6:23:06	(31,107)
Berisford, Andrew	3:37:19	(5,293)
Berkely, Aidan	4:20:04	(14,761)
Berkhold, Patrick	3:24:13	(3,287)
Berks, Graham	4:06:54	(11,672)
Berland, Dominique	3:21:00	(2,886)
Berleen, Abdi-Karim	3:42:50	(6,324)
Bernabei, Bruno	4:44:51	(20,686)
Bernard, Ralph	4:38:17	(19,156)
Bernaudeau, Eric	4:35:47	(18,594)
Bernhardt, Mark	3:23:49	(3,214)
Bernigaud, Gerard	3:29:15	(4,034)
Berrada, Tahar	4:28:39	(16,897)
Berry, Anthony	4:19:49	(14,695)
Berry, Christopher	3:34:40	(4,863)
Berry, Dale	3:26:29	(3,607)
Berry, David	3:59:35	(10,115)
Berry, David	4:10:47	(12,508)
Berry, David	4:56:13	(23,200)
Berry, David	5:11:35	(25,777)
Berry, Gavin	3:30:45	(4,290)
Berry, George	4:43:31	(20,382)
Berry, Glynn	6:05:58	(30,501)
Berry, Jolyon	3:58:57	(9,955)
Berry, Malcolm	4:15:41	(13,671)
Berry, Mark	4:13:36	(13,153)
Berry, Martin	5:25:29	(27,605)
Berry, Matthew	4:22:19	(15,321)
Berry, Michael	3:45:55	(6,917)
Berry, Mike	3:06:22	(1,346)
Berry, Paul	3:32:27	(4,524)
Berry, Paul	4:10:02	(12,356)
Berry, Peter	4:26:13	(16,300)
Berry, Rob	2:33:38	(88)
Berry, Robert	3:50:56	(7,928)
Bertagnolio, Huges	4:09:31	(12,230)
Bertenthal, Samuel	4:06:37	(11,611)
Berthelemy, Raymond	4:40:38	(19,672)
Bertho, Daniel	3:08:01	(1,500)
Bertram, Neil	4:41:11	(19,797)
Berwald, Anthony	4:41:49	(19,949)
Berwick, Christopher	4:04:32	(11,185)
Berwick, Paul	4:20:57	(14,965)
Berwick, Peter	5:11:02	(25,699)
Besa'a, Daniel	3:52:28	(8,300)
Besley, Mark	3:26:26	(3,595)
Best, Andrew	7:24:08	(32,101)
Best, Nigel	4:53:58	(22,708)
Best, Richard	3:28:25	(3,888)
Bestley, Russell	3:37:02	(5,239)
Best-Shaw, Hugh	5:45:09	(29,380)
Beteridge, Darren	4:53:13	(22,550)
Bethell, Cyril	5:12:31	(25,899)
Bethell, Mark	3:42:51	(6,330)
Bethell, Peter	5:27:24	(27,822)
Bethell, Trevor	4:14:59	(13,505)
Betsworth, Glyn	4:16:43	(13,911)
Bett, Tim	4:04:36	(11,198)
Bettag, Urban	3:08:34	(1,554)
Betti, Marco	4:25:56	(16,238)
Bettinelli, Bruno	3:14:06	(2,140)
Bettington, Gordon	5:01:11	(24,181)
Bettini, Enrico	4:14:19	(13,333)
Bettis, Lee	4:57:20	(23,449)
Betts, Delmont	3:31:52	(4,454)
Betts, Gary	3:44:58	(6,727)
Betts, Les	3:46:46	(7,077)
Betts, Mark	3:17:38	(2,507)
Betts, Philip	4:31:37	(17,646)
Betts, Timothy	4:17:20	(14,064)
Bettsworth, Richard	4:40:43	(19,687)
Bevan, Albert	4:26:02	(16,254)

Bevan, Dave	4:43:58 (20,489)	
Bevan, Graham	4:21:49 (15,188)	
Bevan, John	3:54:23 (8,748)	
Bevan, Joseph	4:28:53 (16,961)	
Bevan, Martyn	5:16:20 (26,407)	
Bevan, Neil	3:25:42 (3,496)	
Bevan, Paul	3:55:12 (8,966)	
Bevan, Robin	3:49:05 (7,532)	
Bevan, Steve	3:34:44 (4,872)	
Beveridge, David	4:39:06 (19,343)	
Beverley, Andrew	4:01:57 (10,624)	
Bevil, Robert	5:04:03 (24,642)	
Bevington, Victor	3:46:21 (7,005)	
Bexon, Brian	4:01:14 (10,478)	
Beynon, Robert	4:55:39 (23,065)	
Bezabeh, Sisay	2:16:09 (17)	
Bezodis, Mark	5:14:23 (26,156)	
Bhachu, Jas	5:06:45 (25,066)	
Bhagalia, Yogesh	4:40:36 (19,668)	
Bhakar, Surinder	4:31:58 (17,721)	
Bhalla, Ajay	4:31:18 (17,566)	
Bhamber, Satbinder	6:19:32 (30,993)	
Bhamra, Harmesh	3:50:24 (7,825)	
Bhogal, Amreek	4:13:52 (13,220)	
Bhoja, Narshi	5:12:00 (25,826)	
Bhukhureea, Virsingh	5:04:25 (24,695)	
Biagini, Fabio	3:43:16 (6,418)	
Biagiotti, Stefano	4:12:57 (12,994)	
Bianchi, Massimiliano	3:47:23 (7,192)	
Bianco, Roberto	3:27:48 (3,780)	
Bianda, North-Pole	4:37:04 (18,892)	
Bibby, Peter	5:59:09 (30,217)	
Bibby, Trevor	4:18:13 (14,288)	
Biche, Sean	3:52:59 (8,422)	
Bickerdike, Leigh	3:28:22 (3,878)	
Bickers, Andrew	4:19:21 (14,580)	
Bickerstaffe, Simon	4:24:50 (15,959)	
Bickerton, David	3:48:23 (7,389)	
Bickmore, Angus	6:45:16 (31,625)	
Bicknell, Andrew	4:58:36 (23,718)	
Bicknell, Colin	4:41:00 (19,752)	
Bicknell, Richard	4:04:08 (11,098)	
Bidaux, Pascal	2:38:45 (141)	
Bidder, Paul	4:41:01 (19,754)	
Biddick, Dominic	2:45:04 (236)	
Biddiscombe, Martyn	4:29:47 (17,190)	
Biddiscombe, Peter	4:03:03 (10,855)	
Biddle, Edward	3:30:16 (4,216)	
Bidmead, Howard	3:49:28 (7,624)	
Bidmead, Richard	5:11:26 (25,757)	
Bidston, Mark	3:36:43 (5,184)	
Bieber, Tom	4:04:50 (11,252)	
Biebinger, Andreas	4:09:41 (12,272)	
Bier, Nicholas	5:05:14 (24,832)	
Bieris, Stan	3:48:35 (7,420)	
Bigg, Christopher	5:27:23 (27,820)	
Biggs, Gerard	4:44:24 (20,596)	
Biggs, Roger	4:20:31 (14,873)	
Biggs-Hayes, Thomas	5:26:18 (27,710)	
Bigland, Phil	4:49:22 (21,719)	
Bigley, Andrew	5:41:56 (29,155)	
Bignell, Alister	3:07:11 (1,426)	
Bignold, Jonathan	5:12:32 (25,901)	
Bigwood, John	4:02:14 (10,682)	
Bigwood, Robert	4:40:01 (19,539)	
Bilby, Nick	5:53:18 (29,893)	
Bilclough, David	4:40:10 (19,575)	
Bilcock, Graham	4:55:20 (22,985)	
Biles, Gavin	2:45:19 (242)	
Biles, Kevin	4:16:26 (13,843)	
Bilinske, Walter	3:20:11 (2,783)	
Bill, Lam	4:10:32 (12,473)	
Billiar, John	4:56:14 (23,205)	
Billing, Nigel	3:28:38 (3,933)	
Billing, Shaun	3:18:05 (2,561)	
Billingham, Ian	4:28:49 (16,939)	
Billingham, Paul	4:05:18 (11,351)	
Billinghurst, Keith	4:12:03 (12,772)	
Billman, Mark	5:58:49 (30,192)	
Billson, Simon	3:28:09 (3,838)	
Billy, Andrew	5:02:57 (24,449)	
Bilton, Darran	2:20:50 (25)	
Bimson, Kevin	4:02:57 (10,835)	

Binder, Horst	3:36:18 (5,115)	
Binder, James	4:50:45 (22,023)	
Binder, Richard	4:36:02 (18,659)	
Bing, Derek	4:31:04 (17,517)	
Bing, Steven	3:55:36 (9,076)	
Bingham, Hugh	2:58:59 (849)	
Bingham, John	5:54:13 (29,944)	
Bingham, Miles	3:44:52 (6,698)	
Bingham, Stuart	3:28:48 (3,970)	
Bingley, Kenneth	3:57:22 (9,548)	
Binks, Graham	4:21:04 (14,997)	
Binks, Richard	3:59:12 (10,004)	
Binney, Adam	4:54:42 (22,866)	
Binni, Paolo	3:45:50 (6,895)	
Binnington, Tim	4:07:06 (11,708)	
Binns, Charles	5:24:47 (27,506)	
Binns, Dave	4:52:18 (22,357)	
Binns, Stewart	5:20:04 (26,896)	
Binysh, Howard	4:21:22 (15,075)	
Birch, Alexander	4:38:59 (19,322)	
Birch, Allan	4:28:07 (16,740)	
Birch, Frank	6:06:14 (30,510)	
Birch, Graeme	5:19:06 (26,770)	
Birch, John	3:18:42 (2,626)	
Birch, Kevin	4:35:58 (18,642)	
Birch, Nathan	4:56:21 (23,230)	
Birch, Tom	3:10:58 (1,753)	
Birck, Rainer	3:55:46 (9,120)	
Bird, Adrian	4:17:39 (14,158)	
Bird, Alan	3:45:10 (6,769)	
Bird, Bryn	5:16:42 (26,451)	
Bird, Chris	4:06:40 (11,620)	
Bird, Colin	5:26:35 (27,742)	
Bird, Danny	2:55:17 (607)	
Bird, David	3:29:47 (4,138)	
Bird, Geoff	3:38:58 (5,595)	
Bird, James	5:56:44 (30,088)	
Bird, Jamie	3:27:48 (3,780)	
Bird, Jamie	3:28:35 (3,919)	
Bird, Jason	3:14:02 (2,133)	
Bird, Kevin	4:25:14 (16,067)	
Bird, Mark	3:10:23 (1,710)	
Bird, Matt	4:13:36 (13,153)	
Bird, Philip	3:49:44 (7,684)	
Bird, Samuel	5:22:43 (27,239)	
Bird, Thomas	3:37:41 (5,362)	
Bire, Jan	4:35:46 (18,588)	
Birkel, Jeffrey	3:12:31 (1,933)	
Birkens, John	4:12:33 (12,902)	
Birkenshaw, Mark	4:53:41 (22,649)	
Birkett, Fred	4:59:22 (23,868)	
Birkett, Harry	5:47:31 (29,537)	
Birks, Ben	3:52:29 (8,306)	
Birmingham, Andrew	6:47:59 (31,675)	
Birnbaum, Oliver	4:30:36 (17,391)	
Birrane, Michael	4:08:32 (12,019)	
Birss, Anthony	5:46:43 (29,477)	
Birt, Andrew	3:55:22 (9,014)	
Birt, Neil	4:53:02 (22,509)	
Biscomb, Geoffrey	3:11:22 (1,786)	
Bisconti, Natale	3:59:57 (10,211)	
Bish-Jones, Trevor	4:54:38 (22,846)	
Bishop, Andrew	5:48:57 (29,634)	
Bishop, Andy	5:19:32 (26,832)	
Bishop, Daniel	2:51:59 (442)	
Bishop, Darren	3:02:51 (1,104)	
Bishop, Jeremy	5:43:18 (29,261)	
Bishop, John	2:53:29 (507)	
Bishop, Paul	4:11:24 (12,621)	
Bishop, Paul	4:25:05 (16,021)	
Bishop, Paul	4:43:03 (20,246)	
Bishop, Peter	6:36:03 (31,476)	
Bishop, Simon	4:37:34 (19,000)	
Bishop, Steve	3:24:04 (3,261)	
Bishop, Tim	3:59:59 (10,220)	
Bishop, Tristram	3:35:12 (4,942)	
Bisoni, David	4:36:23 (18,740)	
Bissenden, Thomas	3:51:37 (8,110)	
Bisset, Paul	5:02:27 (24,382)	
Bissett, Mark	3:52:15 (8,255)	
Bissett, Timothy	4:06:47 (11,650)	
Bittner, Maximilian	4:11:50 (12,727)	
Bizby, David	4:28:05 (16,731)	

Bizley, David	4:23:37 (15,643)	
Bizzini, Angelo	3:24:27 (3,325)	
Bjarnoe, Ole	5:30:25 (28,133)	
Bjerrum, Michael	3:56:08 (9,219)	
Bjoerkhaug, Hans Mikal	4:28:19 (16,794)	
Bjornerud, Kai	4:05:56 (11,494)	
Blaboll, Gerhard	4:29:50 (17,203)	
Black, Alistair	3:57:31 (9,582)	
Black, Brian	4:55:54 (23,132)	
Black, David	4:28:53 (16,961)	
Black, David	4:56:25 (23,242)	
Black, Ewan	5:56:01 (30,044)	
Black, Ian	5:25:59 (27,669)	
Black, Kliffton	4:44:15 (20,557)	
Black, Kyle	3:48:50 (7,475)	
Black, Martin	4:02:06 (10,656)	
Black, Stephen	3:53:19 (8,501)	
Blackall, Graham	6:15:24 (30,841)	
Blackbourn, Simon	4:52:11 (22,335)	
Blackburn, Alan	5:44:56 (29,359)	
Blackburn, Duncan	4:28:32 (16,868)	
Blackburn, Gary	4:43:46 (20,444)	
Blackburn, Graham	3:14:40 (2,205)	
Blackburn, Graham	4:57:57 (23,571)	
Blackburn, Ian	3:03:16 (1,133)	
Blackburn, Paul	4:10:38 (12,491)	
Blacker, Mark	5:05:41 (24,917)	
Blackford, Robert	5:26:01 (27,677)	
Blackham, Paul	4:22:09 (15,276)	
Blackie, Brian	3:24:28 (3,328)	
Blacklaw, William	4:15:17 (13,585)	
Blackman, Clive	3:26:54 (3,658)	
Blackman, Robert	4:06:52 (11,662)	
Blackmore, Michael	4:13:56 (13,242)	
Blackmore, Peter	3:54:49 (8,870)	
Blackmore, Stuart	3:58:11 (9,748)	
Blackshaw, Kevin	4:00:43 (10,373)	
Blackshaw, Phillip	4:07:47 (11,867)	
Blackshaw, Trevor	4:04:04 (11,079)	
Blackstock, Alanzo	5:23:34 (27,351)	
Blackstock, Larry	5:23:34 (27,351)	
Blackwell, Graham	4:42:17 (20,050)	
Blackwell, Kevin	3:37:43 (5,369)	
Blackwell, Luke	4:56:59 (23,378)	
Blackwell, Martin	4:14:24 (13,361)	
Blackwell, Niall	4:53:02 (22,509)	
Blackwell, Nicholas	3:00:04 (941)	
Blackwell, Timothy	5:06:22 (25,004)	
Blackwood, Gilbert	3:22:50 (3,089)	
Blackwood, Neal	4:45:33 (20,858)	
Blacoe, Andrew	4:30:01 (17,243)	
Bladen, Alan	4:35:34 (18,533)	
Blades, Kenneth	4:28:53 (16,961)	
Blaine, John	3:05:24 (1,282)	
Blair, Iain	4:08:23 (11,977)	
Blair, John	3:50:06 (7,752)	
Blair, Magnus	4:05:56 (11,494)	
Blair, Murray	4:22:14 (15,304)	
Blair, Steven	4:21:14 (15,040)	
Blake, Adrian	3:44:19 (6,600)	
Blake, Alistair	3:44:20 (6,605)	
Blake, Anthony	4:44:28 (20,608)	
Blake, Christopher	3:22:19 (3,023)	
Blake, Dominic	3:11:14 (1,777)	
Blake, Geoffrey	3:34:29 (4,835)	
Blake, Jonathan	3:59:25 (10,068)	
Blake, Stephen	3:14:45 (2,212)	
Blake, Steve	4:04:00 (11,062)	
Blakeman, Neil	4:23:59 (15,746)	
Blakemore, Richard	3:54:18 (8,730)	
Blakey, Brian	4:30:11 (17,282)	
Blamphin, Mark	3:12:16 (1,893)	
Blanc, Gilles	3:58:32 (9,844)	
Blanc, Pierre	3:39:09 (5,621)	
Blanchard, Alex	4:28:30 (16,858)	
Blanchard, Tristan	4:29:01 (16,994)	
Blanchfield, Phillip	2:47:11 (306)	
Bland, David	4:25:04 (16,019)	
Bland, Philip	4:40:22 (19,623)	
Blandford, Andrew	4:22:13 (15,299)	
Blandford, Rowan	3:52:38 (8,338)	
Blankley, Simon	4:33:24 (18,032)	
Blantz, Andrew	4:36:03 (18,662)	

Blatcher, James	4:45:32 (20,855)	
Blatchford, Ian	4:15:38 (13,665)	
Blattmann, Thomas	4:10:08 (12,382)	
Blaymires, Dave	4:33:00 (17,952)	
Blaze, Adam	5:29:40 (28,058)	
Blazier, Darren	3:03:28 (1,148)	
Blazier, Edgar	5:33:52 (28,463)	
Bleaken, Daniel	5:14:32 (26,183)	
Bleby, Richard	4:33:11 (17,983)	
Bleckwehl, Joachim	3:30:24 (4,231)	
Blee, Simon	5:38:09 (28,824)	
Blehaut, Thierry	3:54:59 (8,917)	
Blew, Adam	6:45:29 (31,630)	
Blight, Andrew	3:58:55 (9,946)	
Blin, Emmanuel	3:08:26 (1,538)	
Blincow, Andrew	4:30:56 (17,476)	
Bliszko, Ferenc	5:29:31 (28,039)	
Blitz, Leon	5:14:03 (26,103)	
Block, Robert	3:23:03 (3,116)	
Bloemendaal, Gerrit	5:45:43 (29,421)	
Blofeld, Roger	4:19:30 (14,616)	
Blois, Richard	5:47:37 (29,547)	
Blokker, Piet	3:45:25 (6,811)	
Blom, Johannes	4:25:24 (16,117)	
Blomley, Nick	4:59:31 (23,891)	
Blood, John	2:50:53 (416)	
Bloom, Curt	6:11:03 (30,695)	
Bloomfield, Barry	3:51:27 (8,062)	
Bloomfield, Colin	4:24:36 (15,888)	
Bloomfield, Daniel	4:18:29 (14,351)	
Bloor, Kenneth	3:46:04 (6,946)	
Bloor, Mark	6:16:26 (30,874)	
Blowey, Malcolm	4:19:52 (14,708)	
Blowing, Michael	4:40:16 (19,594)	
Blows, Anthony	4:08:10 (11,932)	
Bloxham, Clifford	4:19:34 (14,631)	
Bloxham, Clive	5:30:34 (28,147)	
Bloy, Stephen	4:38:39 (19,238)	
Bloye, Graham	5:34:59 (28,551)	
Blue, Neil	4:41:10 (19,790)	
Bluer, David	4:29:29 (17,112)	
Blum, Stephan	4:19:14 (14,559)	
Blundell, Ian	4:53:33 (22,627)	
Blundell, Mark	4:15:01 (13,512)	
Blundell, Paul	4:33:35 (18,075)	
Blundell, Rodger	3:42:10 (6,182)	
Blunden, Jason	6:00:50 (30,288)	
Blunden, Mark	7:58:21 (32,253)	
Blunden, Martin	3:31:06 (4,342)	
Blunden, Philip	3:54:33 (8,803)	
Blunt, Francis	3:33:48 (4,718)	
Blyth, Charles	5:49:07 (29,645)	
Blyth, Richard	4:02:30 (10,742)	
Blythe, Terence	3:17:53 (2,534)	
Blythen, Toby	5:16:49 (26,462)	
Board, Andrew	5:00:01 (23,983)	
Board, Philip	5:02:35 (24,404)	
Boardley, Ian	3:06:44 (1,379)	
Boardman, Allan	4:32:38 (17,859)	
Boast, Peter	3:50:33 (7,854)	
Boast, Simon	3:38:36 (5,517)	
Bober, Richard	3:11:25 (1,796)	
Bockenheim, Zygmunt	3:31:14 (4,365)	
Boczek, Axel	3:08:14 (1,516)	
Boddy, James	5:22:18 (27,189)	
Boddy, John	5:51:42 (29,818)	
Boddy, Michael	3:24:32 (3,339)	
Boden, James	6:27:29 (31,247)	
Boden, Mark	4:39:27 (19,430)	
Bodin, Dominique	3:56:30 (9,318)	
Bodkin, Simon	5:20:38 (26,976)	
Bodman, Ian	5:17:21 (26,520)	
Body, Paul	3:09:52 (1,663)	
Bodycomb, Russell	5:32:26 (28,329)	
Boehm, Christian	3:39:35 (5,713)	
Boehm, Gerhard	3:19:36 (2,710)	
Boen, Ges	4:34:57 (18,383)	
Boennec, Guillaume	2:54:59 (591)	
Boers, Rudi	3:58:52 (9,934)	
Boettcher, René	4:18:55 (14,489)	
Boettcher, Ulrich	4:40:23 (19,626)	
Bofill, Cristian	4:09:01 (12,134)	
Boga, Robert	5:01:37 (24,248)	
Bogg, Keith	5:19:15 (26,795)	
Bogue, Adam	4:48:20 (21,501)	
Bohling, Adam	4:07:38 (11,841)	
Boifava, Armando	2:55:46 (632)	
Boissonnet, Herve	4:47:06 (21,203)	
Boiston, Justin	3:41:44 (6,097)	
Bol, Michael	5:21:31 (27,085)	
Bola, Raj	4:45:52 (20,931)	
Bolam, Kevin	4:46:26 (21,078)	
Bold, Christopher	3:35:47 (5,037)	
Boldero, Richard	3:45:54 (6,912)	
Boley, Stephen	4:15:47 (13,697)	
Bolling, Scott	6:00:02 (30,258)	
Bolster, Ian	4:11:11 (12,572)	
Bolt, Nigel	3:05:51 (1,309)	
Bolton, Andrew	5:21:42 (27,108)	
Bolton, Andrew	5:39:24 (28,936)	
Bolton, Christopher	4:45:28 (20,837)	
Bolton, Christopher	4:53:39 (22,643)	
Bolton, David	4:14:07 (13,290)	
Bolton, David	5:13:34 (26,052)	
Bolton, Ian	4:36:17 (18,707)	
Bolton, Philip	4:53:07 (22,525)	
Bolton, Richard	3:17:33 (2,496)	
Bolton, Ross	4:17:26 (14,097)	
Bolton, Wayne	4:00:55 (10,411)	
Bonaventura, Jordi	3:46:30 (7,028)	
Bond, Alex	5:25:02 (27,543)	
Bond, David	4:20:32 (14,881)	
Bond, Graham	2:58:40 (817)	
Bond, Gregory	4:25:07 (16,031)	
Bond, Julian	3:56:23 (9,288)	
Bond, Michael	2:46:20 (269)	
Bond, Michael	4:44:23 (20,591)	
Bond, Neale	3:22:16 (3,020)	
Bond, Phil	5:10:06 (25,567)	
Bond, Simon	3:45:59 (6,926)	
Bond, Stephen	4:14:37 (13,405)	
Bond, Terence	4:22:27 (15,351)	
Bondy, Michael	5:10:18 (25,593)	
Bone, Brooke	3:30:52 (4,307)	
Bone, Garry	4:04:21 (11,146)	
Bone, John	6:03:17 (30,386)	
Bone, Jonathan	4:46:04 (20,982)	
Bonet-Bibiloni, Juan	3:52:43 (8,357)	
Bonfield, Nick	3:22:49 (3,087)	
Bongiorno, Carlo	4:55:52 (23,122)	
Bong-Ju, Lee	2:08:10 (7)	
Bongwalt, Udo	4:14:08 (13,293)	
Boniface, Michael	6:26:48 (31,224)	
Bonner, Guy	3:37:24 (5,311)	
Bonner, Nick	3:50:59 (7,946)	
Bonnet, Alain	3:50:31 (7,844)	
Bonnet, Joseph	3:20:24 (2,816)	
Bonnet, Olivier	4:07:02 (11,691)	
Bonsall, Damian	4:04:11 (11,108)	
Bonser, Derek	5:07:15 (25,134)	
Bonser, Guy	4:34:38 (18,316)	
Bonthron, Marc	4:19:30 (14,616)	
Bontoft, Alan	2:56:08 (655)	
Bontoux, Jerome	3:10:16 (1,700)	
Boogert, D Van Den	3:02:41 (1,094)	
Booker, Alex	4:30:09 (17,269)	
Booker, Lee	5:00:53 (24,135)	
Booker, Simon	5:34:59 (28,551)	
Boole, Barry	3:39:52 (5,764)	
Boon, John	5:18:01 (26,612)	
Boon, Richard	4:12:11 (12,813)	
Boon, Robert	2:58:33 (804)	
Boorer, Bryan	4:23:06 (15,512)	
Boorer, David	3:04:10 (1,194)	
Boorman, Bill	6:22:17 (31,082)	
Booter, Joel	5:48:27 (29,601)	
Booth, Adrian	4:00:15 (10,278)	
Booth, Brian	4:14:57 (13,492)	
Booth, Clive	3:25:25 (3,455)	
Booth, Gordon	5:11:30 (25,760)	
Booth, Richard	3:35:43 (5,027)	
Booth, Roger	3:31:42 (4,435)	
Booth, Shane	3:38:49 (5,561)	
Booth, Simon	3:39:47 (5,747)	
Boothby, Giles	4:10:24 (12,444)	
Boothroyd, Alan	4:16:44 (13,914)	
Bootland, Duncan	4:38:29 (19,194)	
Bootland, Harvey	6:53:19 (31,797)	
Borck, Chris	6:24:42 (31,151)	
Bord, Alain	4:22:13 (15,299)	
Bordas, Vincent	4:31:56 (17,716)	
Bordon, Paolo	4:13:57 (13,244)	
Bore, Georges	4:28:56 (16,976)	
Boreham, Samuel	4:13:24 (13,093)	
Borghi, Emilio	4:31:41 (17,670)	
Borgund, Ole Jan	4:23:59 (15,746)	
Borkett, Nigel	4:54:13 (22,752)	
Borland, John	4:41:43 (19,925)	
Borley, Peter	4:26:06 (16,278)	
Borns, Dieter	4:48:37 (21,554)	
Borondy, Steve	5:01:06 (24,168)	
Borrego, Christobal	4:52:01 (22,312)	
Borrill, Andrew	4:27:28 (16,593)	
Borthwick, Robert	3:52:23 (8,284)	
Borusiak, Peter	4:13:55 (13,239)	
Bosch, Ulf	3:13:59 (2,125)	
Bose, Anil	4:34:34 (18,298)	
Bosley, Stuart	3:57:06 (9,478)	
Boss, Matthew	3:55:17 (8,988)	
Bosson, Paul	3:51:16 (8,024)	
Boster, Carl	4:04:26 (11,161)	
Bostock, Fergus	5:16:00 (26,379)	
Bostock, Malcolm	2:59:40 (916)	
Boston, David	4:23:31 (15,619)	
Bosustow, Steven	4:00:53 (10,403)	
Boswell, Guy	3:35:08 (4,931)	
Boswell, Stuart	3:03:17 (1,135)	
Bosworth, Jim	4:12:38 (12,925)	
Botello, Carlos	4:49:44 (21,809)	
Botfield, Glyn	4:18:12 (14,286)	
Botifoll-Castejon, Antoni	4:39:36 (19,459)	
Botros, Andrew	5:17:10 (26,500)	
Bott, Matthew	4:45:02 (20,725)	
Bottaro, Mauro	3:52:03 (8,206)	
Botteley, Mark	3:18:57 (2,650)	
Botting, Brian	4:23:58 (15,741)	
Bottomley, Jamie	4:22:12 (15,295)	
Bottoms, Edward	5:08:25 (25,328)	
Bouaird, Chris	5:09:58 (25,536)	
Bouchier, Richard	3:50:34 (7,861)	
Boudet, Henri	3:45:54 (6,912)	
Bougaud, Thierry	3:59:45 (10,165)	
Boughton, Brian	5:47:31 (29,537)	
Bouhaddioui, Abderahmane	2:57:03 (706)	
Bouldin, Christopher	5:13:00 (25,973)	
Boult, David	6:37:37 (31,501)	
Boult, John	4:58:10 (23,621)	
Boulter, Adam	4:18:50 (14,457)	
Boulton, Jude	4:12:55 (12,987)	
Boulton, Kevin	3:08:28 (1,541)	
Boulton, Leigh	5:05:01 (24,794)	
Bouman, Koen	3:48:40 (7,454)	
Bourdrel, Jean-Marc	3:55:10 (8,958)	
Bourgeois, Jean-Marie	4:19:50 (14,701)	
Bourgeois, Mark	3:58:37 (9,862)	
Bourke, Colin	4:32:30 (17,835)	
Bourkia, Lahcen	5:26:54 (27,769)	
Bourne, David	3:35:05 (4,924)	
Bourne, Marcus	4:46:35 (21,104)	
Bourne, Richard	5:52:33 (29,858)	
Bourne, Robert	6:14:47 (30,821)	
Bourne, Simon	3:31:20 (4,386)	
Bourne, William	3:11:24 (1,791)	
Bourner, Graham	5:39:04 (28,908)	
Bourquin, Marc	3:07:18 (1,437)	
Bourrouillou, Georges	4:32:50 (17,909)	
Bouston, Paul	3:41:08 (5,983)	
Boutcher, Jonathan	4:01:20 (10,505)	
Bouteille, Christian	3:47:53 (7,299)	
Bouttell, Christopher	3:27:27 (3,731)	
Bouveng, Stuart	2:49:23 (375)	
Bouwmeester, Fred	4:18:49 (14,452)	
Bovey, Frederic	3:35:10 (4,937)	
Boville, Matt	3:36:19 (5,118)	
Bowal, Paul	4:24:33 (15,875)	
Bowden, Alexander	4:06:52 (11,662)	
Bowden, Christopher	6:38:30 (31,512)	
Bowden, John	4:31:36 (17,639)	
Bowden, Jon	3:57:47 (9,642)	

Bowden, Keir.................5:05:31 (24,885)
Bowden, Nigel................5:06:51 (25,088)
Bowden, Paul.................3:12:29 (1,927)
Bowden, Paul.................4:20:50 (14,938)
Bowden, Rodney..............3:56:55 (9,428)
Bowden, Simon...............3:52:30 (8,310)
Bowden, Trevor..............3:14:36 (2,198)
Bowdery, Roy................3:53:15 (8,487)
Bowdler, Richard............3:06:22 (1,346)
Bowe, Matthew...............4:29:48 (17,195)
Bowen, Alan.................3:46:20 (7,000)
Bowen, Anthony..............4:22:55 (15,475)
Bowen, David................3:16:05 (2,335)
Bowen, John.................4:37:45 (19,036)
Bowen, Matthew..............5:30:46 (28,173)
Bowen, Paul.................4:13:03 (13,016)
Bowen, Sam..................6:18:21 (30,954)
Bowen, Sean.................2:57:53 (759)
Bowen, Spencer..............4:09:01 (12,134)
Bowen, William..............4:32:00 (17,730)
Bower, Allan................6:17:50 (30,922)
Bower, John.................3:15:35 (2,298)
Bower, Lachlan..............3:38:53 (5,577)
Bower, Peter................3:16:13 (2,352)
Bower, Robert...............3:56:09 (9,225)
Bowers, Nicholas............4:56:52 (23,355)
Bowes, Jamie................7:07:09 (31,960)
Bowes-Cavanagh, Mark........4:00:16 (10,283)
Bowie, Ian..................4:46:48 (21,146)
Bowie, Robert...............4:20:13 (14,798)
Bowker, David...............4:18:05 (14,269)
Bowker, Stuart..............4:40:02 (19,546)
Bowker, Tim.................4:41:51 (19,960)
Bowkett, Andrew.............4:58:18 (23,653)
Bowler, Dean................4:49:34 (21,766)
Bowler, Tim.................4:58:33 (23,709)
Bowler, William.............4:32:44 (17,888)
Bowles, Alan................4:58:04 (23,599)
Bowles, John................5:34:01 (28,479)
Bowles, Karl................4:39:38 (19,465)
Bowles, Pauline.............5:07:36 (25,201)
Bowles, Steve...............4:00:01 (10,226)
Bowman, Andrew..............4:07:37 (11,838)
Bowman, Gary................5:04:49 (24,765)
Bowman, Geoff...............3:44:30 (6,635)
Bowman, Graham..............3:28:24 (3,884)
Bowman, Mark................5:03:10 (24,485)
Bowmer, Martin..............4:28:05 (16,731)
Bown, Nicholas..............4:40:53 (19,723)
Bowring, James..............4:23:51 (15,708)
Bowser, Phillip.............4:32:13 (17,779)
Bowyer, Keith...............5:35:10 (28,568)
Bowyer, Malcolm.............2:59:18 (881)
Bowyer, Richard.............4:12:00 (12,762)
Box, Mark...................3:58:52 (9,934)
Boxall, Gordon..............4:17:25 (14,094)
Boxall, John................4:37:33 (18,995)
Boxer, Brian................5:50:18 (29,739)
Boxer, Richard..............4:18:37 (14,399)
Boxhall, Richard............6:10:58 (30,688)
Boy, Graeme.................5:03:53 (24,612)
Boyask, Richard.............5:25:09 (27,561)
Boyce, Edward...............3:40:04 (5,803)
Boyce, Gavin................6:50:03 (31,719)
Boyce, Wayne................4:22:13 (15,299)
Boyd, Adrian................5:13:44 (26,072)
Boyd, Christopher...........5:05:59 (24,955)
Boyd, Craig.................4:11:19 (12,601)
Boyden, Scott...............4:39:06 (19,343)
Boyer, James................3:56:01 (9,184)
Boyes, David................4:11:22 (12,616)
Boylan, Patrick.............3:47:39 (7,247)
Boyle, Ciaran...............5:49:08 (29,647)
Boyle, Gerard...............3:33:03 (4,606)
Boyle, Glen.................4:33:01 (17,956)
Boyle, John.................4:36:30 (18,769)
Boyle, John.................4:52:43 (22,441)
Boyle, Liam.................4:52:43 (22,441)
Boyle, Mark.................4:29:49 (17,199)
Boyle, Michael..............5:00:44 (24,113)
Boyle, Peter................5:17:17 (26,511)
Boyle, Stephen..............4:37:42 (19,020)
Boynes, Chris...............4:36:07 (18,674)

Boyson, James...............5:25:42 (27,630)
Boyson, Rickie..............5:25:43 (27,633)
Bozza, John.................4:23:10 (15,537)
Braadalen, Arild............3:37:40 (5,358)
Brace, Gavin................4:58:15 (23,638)
Bracey, Nick................4:12:21 (12,847)
Brachaniec, Peter...........5:44:30 (29,334)
Bracher, Charles............4:06:15 (11,545)
Brackstone, Richard.........4:40:21 (19,620)
Bradbourne, Jonathan........6:17:16 (30,900)
Bradburn, Albert............4:42:53 (20,203)
Bradburn, Tim...............5:02:34 (24,400)
Bradbury, Alan..............3:18:15 (2,583)
Bradbury, Gareth............3:55:16 (8,983)
Bradbury, Geoff.............6:35:45 (31,468)
Bradbury, Lloyd.............5:08:45 (25,363)
Bradbury, Nick..............4:07:36 (11,832)
Bradbury, Shawn.............3:36:09 (5,085)
Bradbury, Stan..............3:44:11 (6,577)
Bradfield, Stephen..........3:41:00 (5,957)
Bradford, Charles...........4:27:59 (16,703)
Bradford, Paul..............3:40:06 (5,809)
Bradford, William...........3:49:31 (7,637)
Bradley, Anthony............4:26:13 (16,300)
Bradley, Barrington.........4:35:22 (18,486)
Bradley, Dave...............5:07:43 (25,226)
Bradley, Gerard.............4:22:24 (15,342)
Bradley, Harvey.............3:52:22 (8,281)
Bradley, John...............4:40:01 (19,539)
Bradley, Kyran..............3:51:59 (8,191)
Bradley, Malcolm............4:16:51 (13,947)
Bradley, Matthew............4:33:20 (18,013)
Bradley, Michael............4:04:25 (11,157)
Bradley, Michael............4:25:34 (16,150)
Bradley, Mike...............4:47:17 (21,243)
Bradley, Mikk...............2:49:09 (367)
Bradley, Patrick............3:50:22 (7,817)
Bradley, Peter..............3:43:56 (6,533)
Bradley, Sam................3:29:31 (4,098)
Bradley, Stephen............3:11:45 (1,828)
Bradley, Terence............6:23:23 (31,114)
Bradman, Anthony............5:01:41 (24,255)
Bradnam, Stephen............3:28:53 (3,984)
Bradney, Stuart.............4:43:11 (20,281)
Bradshaw, Andrew............4:07:18 (11,756)
Bradshaw, David.............5:25:24 (27,597)
Bradshaw, Jonathan..........3:18:32 (2,611)
Bradshaw, Mark..............4:09:56 (12,336)
Bradshaw, Miles.............3:46:54 (7,103)
Bradshaw, Neil..............3:56:26 (9,300)
Bradshaw, Paul..............3:24:25 (3,320)
Bradshaw, Shaun.............4:00:22 (10,307)
Bradshaw, Stephen...........5:09:58 (25,536)
Bradwell, Andrew............5:03:36 (24,550)
Brady, Anthony..............4:17:36 (14,139)
Brady, Bryan................4:10:25 (12,449)
Brady, Daniel...............5:16:51 (26,464)
Brady, David................2:40:29 (158)
Brady, David................4:01:53 (10,618)
Brady, Edward...............3:56:42 (9,375)
Brady, George...............3:41:44 (6,097)
Brady, Harold...............6:07:10 (30,536)
Brady, John.................4:04:59 (11,284)
Brady, Joseph...............3:35:14 (4,947)
Brady, Nigel................4:30:59 (17,491)
Brady, Peter................4:30:52 (17,459)
Brady, Peter................4:58:27 (23,687)
Brady, Shaun................4:17:02 (13,993)
Bragantini, Paolo...........4:28:16 (16,783)
Bragg, Stephen..............3:39:45 (5,738)
Braham, Rollo...............3:27:32 (3,745)
Braham-Everett, Daniel......4:44:34 (20,626)
Braidwood, Billy............3:42:09 (6,178)
Brailsford, David...........3:03:32 (1,154)
Brain, Alun.................4:28:29 (16,850)
Brain, John.................5:11:14 (25,727)
Brain, Robert...............3:50:29 (7,838)
Braithwaite, Dean...........3:35:16 (4,952)
Braithwaite, Mark...........4:31:25 (17,595)
Braithwaite, Michael........4:33:59 (18,162)
Brakenhoff, Jean............4:00:22 (10,307)
Braker, Robert..............3:59:00 (9,966)
Brakes, William.............5:12:33 (25,909)

Bral, Eddy..................4:10:22 (12,431)
Brambley, Steven............4:02:48 (10,807)
Bramham, Richard............4:14:37 (13,405)
Bramwell, Nicholas..........3:49:20 (7,596)
Branagh, Noel...............4:40:54 (19,727)
Branch, Paul................3:03:21 (1,139)
Brand, Douglas..............4:08:50 (12,093)
Brand, Ian..................5:00:47 (24,123)
Brand, Julian...............3:12:50 (1,972)
Brand, Paul.................5:47:27 (29,526)
Brand, Peter................8:02:02 (32,258)
Brand, Philip...............4:29:05 (17,010)
Brand, Roger................3:53:07 (8,453)
Brandon, Mark...............4:03:02 (10,850)
Brandon, Simon..............4:28:43 (16,915)
Brandt, David...............3:45:33 (6,842)
Brandwood, Tim..............4:17:38 (14,152)
Branigan, Heath.............4:08:07 (11,924)
Brankling, Alan.............5:17:32 (26,549)
Brannelly, John.............3:33:42 (4,701)
Brannon, Tim................4:34:41 (18,325)
Branson, Jonathan...........5:05:30 (24,883)
Branson, Michael............3:43:33 (6,455)
Brash, Christian............5:24:45 (27,501)
Brasher, Hugh...............3:38:22 (5,472)
Bratt, Steve................4:19:33 (14,626)
Braud, Francis..............3:52:36 (8,332)
Braude, Jonathan............4:48:54 (21,614)
Braun, Markus...............3:35:30 (4,999)
Braunton, David.............4:54:55 (22,906)
Bray, Andrew................5:02:49 (24,434)
Bray, Chris.................3:41:31 (6,072)
Bray, David.................4:45:25 (20,824)
Bray, Gareth................3:57:38 (9,603)
Bray, Michael...............4:18:03 (14,260)
Bray, Paul..................4:34:09 (18,204)
Bray, Vivian................4:46:11 (21,012)
Braybrook, Gerard...........5:30:28 (28,138)
Brayne, Adam................3:30:41 (4,273)
Brayshaw, James.............3:12:04 (1,869)
Brayshaw, Jeremy............3:56:13 (9,249)
Brazewell, Peter............4:46:40 (21,119)
Brazier, Alan...............5:16:07 (26,388)
Brazier, Anthony............3:29:24 (4,069)
Brazil, Simon...............3:07:25 (1,445)
Breakspear, Andrew..........3:49:00 (7,518)
Brealey, Bruce..............4:20:57 (14,965)
Brealey, Ian................4:24:19 (15,822)
Bream, Nicholas.............5:15:53 (26,360)
Brearley, Matthew...........3:42:31 (6,255)
Brearley, Michael...........3:03:56 (1,179)
Brearley, Tony..............4:03:13 (10,884)
Brechner, Miguel............4:24:49 (15,954)
Breckner, Johann............3:46:55 (7,108)
Bredhurst, Christopher......5:53:36 (29,913)
Bredow, David...............5:10:22 (25,602)
Breen, Christopher..........4:13:29 (13,122)
Breen, David................4:07:38 (11,841)
Breen, Graham...............2:57:08 (714)
Breger, David...............4:42:33 (20,123)
Breivik, Simon..............3:07:46 (1,482)
Brekelmans, Rob.............3:05:56 (1,316)
Bremner, Stuart.............5:18:04 (26,620)
Brench, Andrew..............4:17:46 (14,200)
Brench, Darren..............3:38:51 (5,569)
Brench, Michael.............5:07:30 (25,181)
Brenchley, John.............5:06:04 (24,965)
Brencio, Roberto............3:19:35 (2,708)
Brennan, Christopher........6:27:25 (31,238)
Brennan, Ian................4:00:31 (10,333)
Brennan, Joseph.............3:56:35 (9,341)
Brennan, Kevin..............3:14:15 (2,158)
Brennan, Michael............4:19:26 (14,603)
Brennan, Pete...............4:12:19 (12,838)
Brent, Peter................4:53:21 (22,586)
Bresland, Noel..............4:13:18 (13,075)
Bressolles, Christian.......3:53:28 (8,531)
Brett, Derek................5:38:24 (28,851)
Brett, Eric.................4:40:35 (19,664)
Brett, Gavin................4:42:58 (20,222)
Brett, Jon..................6:04:42 (30,442)
Brett, Reginald.............3:04:59 (1,245)
Brett, Stephen..............3:43:05 (6,383)

Brew, Sean ...5:23:16 (27,320)
Brewer, John ...3:57:09 (9,494)
Brewer, Jonathan ...3:33:53 (4,730)
Brewer, Paul ...5:50:52 (29,774)
Brewer, Phillip ...7:14:48 (32,035)
Brewis, Laurie ...5:10:38 (25,640)
Brewster, Matt ...4:55:23 (22,999)
Brian, Mark ...5:10:53 (25,670)
Brian, Paul ...4:13:42 (13,176)
Briathwaite, Paul ...4:51:12 (22,132)
Brice, Chris ...4:33:20 (18,013)
Brick, Chris ...3:58:44 (9,892)
Brick, Shaun ...3:12:41 (1,955)
Brickland, Garry ...8:10:38 (32,267)
Brickman, Andrew ...3:49:28 (7,624)
Bridge, Adrian ...4:05:18 (11,351)
Bridge, Adrian ...4:42:55 (20,210)
Bridge, Kevin ...4:59:59 (23,979)
Bridge, Robert ...5:01:05 (24,163)
Bridger, Andrew ...4:22:05 (15,261)
Bridges, Anthony ...3:13:42 (2,087)
Bridges, Christopher ...5:19:35 (26,837)
Bridges, George ...5:41:31 (29,117)
Bridges, Russell ...4:09:57 (12,340)
Bridgewater, Mark ...3:56:55 (9,428)
Bridgman, William ...4:19:49 (14,695)
Bridgwater, Chris ...6:12:11 (30,737)
Bridgwater, Christopher ...6:12:11 (30,737)
Briegel, Bruno ...3:43:05 (6,383)
Brien, Gareth ...3:27:39 (3,760)
Brier, Tony ...4:57:27 (23,468)
Brierley, Andrew ...3:32:26 (4,520)
Brierley, Danny ...4:20:49 (14,931)
Brierley, Graham ...3:55:29 (9,044)
Brierley, Peter ...4:41:22 (19,839)
Brierly, William ...5:49:39 (29,693)
Briffett, Philip ...4:13:04 (13,019)
Briffett, Stephen ...4:34:16 (18,230)
Briggs, Charles ...3:56:41 (9,372)
Briggs, Charles ...5:29:11 (28,003)
Briggs, Edd ...4:23:16 (15,565)
Briggs, Michael ...3:54:51 (8,879)
Briggs, Peter ...3:50:16 (7,792)
Briggs, Simon ...4:55:06 (22,939)
Briggs, Simon ...5:47:35 (29,546)
Briggs, Steven ...2:54:59 (591)
Brighouse, John ...3:55:20 (9,003)
Bright, Barry ...3:36:04 (5,075)
Bright, Ian ...4:03:20 (10,919)
Bright, Jeremy ...3:50:20 (7,813)
Bright, Stephen ...4:46:03 (20,977)
Brightley, Leo ...3:49:37 (7,661)
Brighton, Sam ...3:55:06 (8,941)
Brightwell, Terence ...3:12:49 (1,968)
Briley, Gary ...4:59:54 (23,967)
Brill, Luke ...5:27:57 (27,888)
Brimble, Peter ...4:32:58 (17,944)
Brimble, Stuart ...3:57:49 (9,650)
Brims, Craig ...5:14:49 (26,220)
Brims, Keith ...5:14:48 (26,217)
Brimson, Mark ...4:39:15 (19,386)
Brindley, Paul ...3:42:57 (6,354)
Brine, Martin ...3:18:04 (2,559)
Brink, Chris ...3:50:07 (7,757)
Brinklow, David ...5:25:03 (27,546)
Brinn, Chris ...4:31:23 (17,589)
Briody, Donal ...3:31:13 (4,362)
Brisco, Douglas ...3:05:29 (1,286)
Briscoe, Stuart ...4:19:40 (14,658)
Briscombe, Stephen ...4:33:09 (17,979)
Brisland, Mark ...3:49:08 (7,543)
Briston, Jim ...4:32:06 (17,752)
Bristow, Jamie ...4:51:29 (22,206)
Bristow, John ...2:56:48 (692)
Bristow, Mark ...4:10:22 (12,431)
Britcliffe, Mark ...4:02:55 (10,828)
Brito, Matt ...3:50:20 (7,813)
Britt, Andi ...3:38:57 (5,591)
Britt, Paul ...4:18:27 (14,344)
Brittain, Mathew ...4:14:51 (13,466)
Brittain, Stephen ...5:45:32 (29,409)
Britten, Tony ...3:17:19 (2,463)
Brittleton, Paul ...6:54:40 (31,823)

Britton, Alan ...4:02:44 (10,789)
Britton, Cai ...3:13:22 (2,046)
Britton, Christopher ...4:37:25 (18,967)
Britton, Lee ...3:14:52 (2,223)
Britton, Matthew ...4:26:12 (16,296)
Britton, Toby ...3:59:40 (10,141)
Broadbent, Clive ...3:47:38 (7,245)

Broadbent, Steve ...3:04:36 (1,222)

2010 saw the completion of my 21st consecutive London Marathon. Each one has been a memorable experience. Probably one of the most notable was 2003 when I ran from Paris to London. I completed the Paris Marathon in 2 hours 55 minutes then ran four marathons through France, crossed the channel and ran two more marathons through southern England before arriving at Blackheath. After 200 miles of running I completed the London Marathon in 3 hours 04 minutes, only nine minutes slower than in Paris one week earlier. I also raised over £500 for the 'PDSA' charity! The London Marathon must be the best marathon in the world and I hope my 30th in 2020 will be my 100th Marathon in my 60th year!

Broadfoot, Keith ...3:41:29 (6,060)
Broadhurst, Carl ...3:41:17 (6,010)
Broadway, Andrew ...4:23:34 (15,633)
Brock, Graham ...5:17:36 (26,560)
Brockbank, Richard ...4:58:11 (23,625)
Brockhurst, Daniel ...4:45:58 (20,952)
Brocklebank, Jason ...3:55:05 (8,933)
Brocklehurst, Aaron ...4:06:22 (11,566)
Brocklehurst, Richard ...4:49:23 (21,722)
Brockway, Albert ...5:27:04 (27,784)
Brockway, Darren ...4:47:17 (21,243)
Brockwell, Darren ...4:39:50 (19,508)
Brodie, Andrew ...3:07:01 (1,405)
Brodrick-Ward, Oliver ...3:31:29 (4,407)
Broell, Wolfgang ...5:11:22 (25,747)
Brogan, Christopher ...2:57:10 (715)
Bromage, Gary ...4:28:01 (16,708)
Bromley, Alec ...4:40:42 (19,684)
Bromley, Nigel ...3:57:11 (9,502)
Bromley, Stephen ...5:32:29 (28,334)
Brompton, Michael ...3:15:39 (2,305)
Bromuro, Fabrizio ...3:11:28 (1,801)
Brook, Jim ...4:20:35 (14,887)
Brook, John ...5:48:53 (29,628)
Brook, Nigel ...5:04:15 (24,672)
Brooke, Craig ...3:14:50 (2,220)
Brooke, David ...3:38:33 (5,504)
Brooke, David ...6:28:18 (31,282)
Brooke, Ian ...4:44:26 (20,602)
Brooker, Curt ...4:31:46 (17,682)
Brooker, John ...3:43:10 (6,399)
Brooker, Martin ...5:15:27 (26,309)
Brooker, Philip ...3:39:19 (5,658)
Brooker, Simon ...3:34:04 (4,756)
Brooker, Simon ...4:10:22 (12,431)
Brooker, Thomas ...3:59:58 (10,217)
Brookes, Anthony ...4:03:27 (10,934)

Brookes, Anthony ...4:53:15 (22,556)
Brookes, Chris ...3:13:59 (2,125)
Brookes, David ...5:46:05 (29,444)
Brookes, Nigel ...3:16:59 (2,428)
Brookes, Steven ...2:58:15 (788)
Brooking, Ian ...6:08:58 (30,604)
Brookling, Ryan ...3:30:18 (4,219)
Brookman, Mike ...5:12:10 (25,844)
Brooks, Antony ...3:22:30 (3,048)
Brooks, Arthur ...3:37:36 (5,346)
Brooks, David ...4:22:56 (15,478)
Brooks, David ...4:42:01 (19,995)
Brooks, David ...6:11:53 (30,722)
Brooks, Duncan ...5:11:19 (25,737)
Brooks, Edward ...3:22:50 (3,089)
Brooks, Gary ...3:11:36 (1,811)
Brooks, John ...4:18:26 (14,341)
Brooks, Jon ...5:56:36 (30,086)
Brooks, Lyndon ...4:45:29 (20,847)
Brooks, Melvyn ...4:13:37 (13,156)
Brooks, Michael ...3:22:11 (3,007)
Brooks, Paul ...4:15:04 (13,529)
Brooks, Paul ...4:21:02 (14,988)
Brooks, Richard ...3:31:07 (4,345)
Brooks, Roger ...3:28:28 (3,897)
Brooks, Roger ...4:18:40 (14,412)
Brooksbank, Nicholas ...4:21:04 (14,997)
Brooksby, Dorian ...4:44:38 (20,644)
Broom, John ...2:49:38 (382)
Broom, Richard ...4:39:31 (19,444)
Broome, George ...4:56:14 (23,205)
Broome, Marcus ...3:41:27 (6,055)
Broomhead, Rob ...3:04:34 (1,219)
Brophy, Laurence ...5:54:40 (29,976)
Brosnan, Martin ...5:55:15 (30,012)
Brost, Henry ...3:54:29 (8,776)
Broster, Chris ...5:27:35 (27,845)
Broster, Gary ...4:04:37 (11,201)
Brotawek, Timur ...4:28:13 (16,773)
Brothwell, Ben ...4:06:21 (11,562)
Brough, Christopher ...4:00:38 (10,355)
Brough, Oliver ...4:06:50 (11,656)
Brough, Paul ...3:21:13 (2,900)
Broughton, Alan ...2:45:12 (240)
Broughton, James ...3:51:47 (8,144)
Broughton, Richard ...5:40:13 (29,011)
Broughton, Stephen ...3:42:50 (6,324)
Brouillet, Mickael ...3:56:47 (9,393)
Brown, Adrian ...5:47:17 (29,513)
Brown, Alan ...3:36:13 (5,098)
Brown, Alan ...3:57:21 (9,542)
Brown, Alexander ...4:11:40 (12,683)
Brown, Allan ...5:41:33 (29,122)
Brown, Andrew ...4:06:27 (11,583)
Brown, Andrew ...4:43:14 (20,296)
Brown, Andrew ...5:16:55 (26,472)
Brown, Anthony ...5:35:17 (28,579)
Brown, Chris ...3:45:35 (6,846)
Brown, Christian ...3:30:13 (4,203)
Brown, Christopher ...3:24:26 (3,323)
Brown, Christopher ...3:37:11 (5,274)
Brown, Christopher ...3:55:00 (8,921)
Brown, Clive ...4:42:40 (20,150)
Brown, Colin ...4:22:57 (15,482)
Brown, Craig ...4:39:07 (19,348)
Brown, Daniel ...4:56:10 (23,189)
Brown, Daniel ...7:23:44 (32,097)
Brown, David ...3:23:37 (3,194)
Brown, David ...4:09:44 (12,280)
Brown, David ...4:17:17 (14,053)
Brown, David ...4:30:55 (17,473)
Brown, David ...4:42:18 (20,053)
Brown, David ...4:56:13 (23,200)
Brown, David ...4:58:40 (23,727)
Brown, David ...5:27:52 (27,875)
Brown, Derek ...2:54:11 (547)
Brown, Derek ...4:40:28 (19,648)
Brown, Derek ...4:42:14 (20,035)
Brown, Derek ...5:15:14 (26,282)
Brown, Derek ...5:50:07 (29,942)
Brown, Dominic ...4:38:47 (19,278)
Brown, Drew ...6:08:24 (30,583)
Brown, Edward ...5:03:00 (24,457)

Brown, Francis	5:12:40 (25,929)	
Brown, Gareth	4:03:20 (10,919)	
Brown, Gary	3:46:46 (7,077)	
Brown, Gary	5:57:21 (30,128)	
Brown, Graeme	3:57:45 (9,632)	
Brown, Graham	5:42:16 (29,188)	
Brown, Gregor	4:21:17 (15,054)	
Brown, Gregory	3:14:21 (2,172)	
Brown, Henry	2:40:10 (154)	
Brown, Iain	5:39:23 (28,935)	
Brown, Ian	2:58:08 (776)	
Brown, Ian	4:33:43 (18,100)	
Brown, James	3:13:26 (2,052)	
Brown, James	3:56:08 (9,219)	
Brown, James	4:17:20 (14,064)	
Brown, James	4:53:56 (22,702)	
Brown, Jamie	4:27:20 (16,555)	
Brown, Jamie	5:43:02 (29,238)	
Brown, John	3:57:16 (9,522)	
Brown, John	5:17:20 (26,518)	
Brown, Justin	4:10:11 (12,389)	
Brown, Kenneth	4:07:38 (11,841)	
Brown, Lawrence	4:28:01 (16,708)	
Brown, Malcolm	5:09:45 (25,514)	
Brown, Mark	3:34:11 (4,774)	
Brown, Mark	4:40:45 (19,694)	
Brown, Martin	3:45:09 (6,767)	
Brown, Martin	4:12:50 (12,966)	
Brown, Martin	4:36:45 (18,823)	
Brown, Matthew	3:23:26 (3,169)	
Brown, Matthew	4:28:58 (16,984)	
Brown, Matthew	4:42:30 (20,109)	
Brown, Michael	4:42:30 (20,109)	
Brown, Michael	5:07:39 (25,212)	
Brown, Mike	3:13:47 (2,094)	
Brown, Mike	3:48:51 (7,477)	
Brown, Neil	4:49:50 (21,832)	
Brown, Nicholas	3:21:42 (2,954)	
Brown, Nick	4:47:28 (21,293)	
Brown, Nigel	4:14:31 (13,384)	
Brown, Oliver	5:53:56 (29,927)	
Brown, Paul	4:03:49 (11,017)	
Brown, Paul	4:18:58 (14,498)	
Brown, Paul	4:36:30 (18,769)	
Brown, Paul	5:04:27 (24,699)	
Brown, Paul	5:05:20 (24,847)	
Brown, Paul	5:06:39 (25,044)	
Brown, Paul	5:29:48 (28,070)	
Brown, Per-Elvind	4:37:52 (19,060)	
Brown, Peter	4:55:43 (23,083)	
Brown, Peter	5:50:36 (29,760)	
Brown, Phil	4:11:24 (12,621)	
Brown, Philip	4:13:42 (13,176)	
Brown, Richard	3:06:42 (1,377)	
Brown, Richard	3:14:30 (2,184)	
Brown, Richard	4:11:28 (12,636)	
Brown, Robert	4:35:41 (18,558)	
Brown, Robert	5:18:09 (26,642)	
Brown, Roger	2:57:05 (708)	
Brown, Roger	4:30:45 (17,431)	
Brown, Roger	5:20:17 (26,926)	
Brown, Rory	3:27:02 (3,686)	
Brown, Simon	4:17:08 (14,018)	
Brown, Stephen	3:43:12 (6,409)	
Brown, Stephen	7:06:20 (31,946)	
Brown, Steve	4:43:59 (20,494)	
Brown, Steven	3:06:17 (1,336)	
Brown, Steven	3:39:10 (5,623)	
Brown, Stuart	3:37:35 (5,342)	
Brown, Stuart	3:57:38 (9,603)	
Brown, Terry	4:08:26 (11,989)	
Brown, Tim	4:15:29 (13,635)	
Brown, Timothy	2:59:45 (923)	
Brown, Timothy	4:04:55 (11,274)	
Brown, Timothy	4:12:55 (12,987)	
Brown, Timothy	4:14:20 (13,341)	
Brown, Trevor	3:15:06 (2,248)	
Brown, Vincent	4:32:37 (17,856)	
Brown, Warren	7:23:45 (32,098)	
Brownbill, Roger	4:53:45 (22,672)	
Browne, Christopher	4:06:31 (11,593)	
Browne, Danny	5:32:22 (28,324)	
Browne, Edward	3:52:57 (8,409)	

Browne, Erik	4:19:22 (14,584)	
Browne, Michael	4:43:29 (20,371)	
Browne, Mike	4:18:34 (14,380)	
Browne, Patrick	4:38:54 (19,305)	
Browne, Paul	4:18:34 (14,380)	
Browne, Peter	3:47:04 (7,135)	
Browne, Peter	4:33:53 (18,138)	
Browne, Richard	2:34:08 (92)	
Browne, Sean	4:24:10 (15,789)	
Browne, Winston	4:56:33 (23,275)	
Browner, Simon	5:20:55 (27,014)	
Brownhill, George	3:55:49 (9,132)	
Browning, Andrew	4:45:00 (20,717)	
Browning, David	3:29:27 (4,079)	
Browning, Goeff	4:15:45 (13,685)	
Browning, John	4:36:50 (18,842)	
Browning, Michael	4:12:47 (12,956)	
Browning, Neil	3:19:54 (2,743)	
Browning, Nick	3:05:17 (1,273)	
Browning, Paul	3:26:15 (3,573)	
Browning, Paul	4:11:04 (12,551)	
Browning, Simon	4:19:51 (14,704)	
Browning, Steven	3:57:55 (9,685)	
Brownlie, Allan	3:55:58 (9,168)	
Brownlie, Colin	5:14:51 (26,227)	
Brownlie, John	4:21:39 (15,143)	
Broxton, Keith	3:20:15 (2,798)	
Bruce, Alexander	4:20:20 (14,824)	
Bruce, Andrew	3:40:45 (5,914)	
Bruce, Andrew	3:43:14 (6,413)	
Bruce, Anthony	5:32:05 (28,296)	
Bruce, Malcolm	6:08:06 (30,569)	
Bruce, Nigel	4:15:48 (13,702)	
Bruce, Richard	4:03:38 (10,970)	
Bruford, Edward	4:34:03 (18,176)	
Bruggeman, Stephen	3:51:59 (8,191)	
Brulin, Didier	3:46:41 (7,063)	
Brun, Christian	3:28:47 (3,966)	
Brun, Theodore	3:15:50 (2,316)	
Brunaux, Patrice	4:19:02 (14,513)	
Brundle, Michael	4:36:40 (18,800)	
Bruneau, Dominic	4:11:20 (12,606)	
Bruneaux, Michel	3:52:15 (8,255)	
Brunell, Paul	3:29:42 (4,125)	
Brunke, Klaus-Dieter	3:48:20 (7,381)	
Brunner, John	3:39:45 (5,738)	
Brunskill, Iain	4:34:56 (18,380)	
Brunskill, Melvyn	3:56:03 (9,194)	
Brunskill, Michael	3:10:30 (1,718)	
Brunt, Martyn	5:19:45 (26,855)	
Brunton, Jerym	3:53:49 (8,623)	
Bruree, Kevin	3:37:06 (5,253)	
Bruton, Paul	4:48:12 (21,471)	
Brutsch, Benny	5:00:01 (23,983)	
Bruwer, Gideon	4:31:35 (17,636)	
Bruyninckx, Rudy	2:56:57 (697)	
Bruyns, François	3:22:25 (3,039)	
Bryan, Jerry	3:40:56 (5,949)	
Bryan, John	6:30:52 (31,346)	
Bryan, Michael	5:07:59 (25,267)	
Bryan, Peter	3:59:16 (10,027)	
Bryan, Peter	5:07:30 (25,181)	
Bryan, Roger	2:59:59 (939)	
Bryan, Rory	3:43:00 (6,369)	
Bryant, Alexander	5:22:24 (27,202)	
Bryant, Gary	4:35:48 (18,598)	
Bryant, James	3:27:16 (3,709)	
Bryant, John	4:51:00 (22,070)	
Bryant, John	4:51:03 (22,083)	
Bryant, Kevin	4:01:11 (10,470)	
Bryant, Mark	3:20:06 (2,770)	
Bryant, Nicholas	4:59:14 (23,848)	
Bryant, Nick	4:34:54 (18,372)	
Bryant, Richard	3:30:43 (4,282)	
Bryant, Rory	3:54:35 (8,813)	
Bryant, Tony	4:02:19 (10,698)	
Bryant, Wayne	4:17:44 (14,189)	
Brynie, Jens Graham	4:30:38 (17,399)	
Bryson, Patrick	4:11:26 (12,627)	
Brzeskwinski, Simon	3:47:37 (7,241)	
Bubb, Nick	4:11:15 (12,589)	
Bubloz, Nigel	5:14:45 (26,207)	
Buchan, Ian	3:38:11 (5,440)	

Buchan, Kevin	4:03:37 (10,969)	
Buchan, Paul	5:04:12 (24,661)	
Buchan, Stuart	2:41:50 (176)	
Buchanan, Ben	5:01:12 (24,183)	
Buchanan, Ian	4:28:07 (16,740)	
Buchanan, John	4:47:20 (21,254)	
Buchanan, Stanley	3:37:03 (5,241)	
Buck, David	4:12:10 (12,805)	
Buck, Karl	4:25:55 (16,234)	
Buck, Paul	4:25:39 (16,168)	
Buckenham, Clive	4:31:15 (17,558)	
Buckerfield, David	4:03:14 (10,891)	
Buckingham, Ian	3:12:27 (1,921)	
Buckingham, Jonathan	3:57:03 (9,469)	
Buckingham, Phil	4:26:41 (16,398)	
Buckingham, Richard	5:14:30 (26,177)	
Buckingham, Warren	4:59:36 (23,903)	
Buckland, Charles	4:21:28 (15,104)	
Buckland, Michael	6:18:20 (30,950)	
Buckley, Allan	4:01:51 (10,612)	
Buckley, Anthony	4:59:46 (23,935)	
Buckley, Daniel	4:27:10 (16,516)	
Buckley, George	4:33:17 (18,001)	
Buckley, Ian	4:39:39 (19,467)	
Buckley, Jason	4:09:40 (12,268)	
Buckley, Jonathan	3:35:13 (4,944)	
Buckley, Oliver	4:23:59 (15,746)	
Buckley, Paul	4:20:05 (14,765)	
Buckley, Steven	3:38:41 (5,538)	
Buckman, Shaun	5:49:23 (29,668)	
Budd, Edward	4:44:11 (20,538)	
Budd, Ian	4:46:58 (21,177)	
Budd, John	4:01:18 (10,495)	
Budd, Martin	3:55:17 (8,988)	
Budd, Stephen	5:18:05 (26,624)	
Budden, Martin	4:40:39 (19,674)	
Budden, Neil	8:22:38 (32,277)	
Budge, Nicholas	4:11:39 (12,677)	
Budworth, Martin	3:40:33 (5,873)	
Buerger, Rainer	4:37:40 (19,012)	
Buetler, Marcel	3:40:05 (5,807)	
Buffery, Brynley	5:03:39 (24,557)	
Buffham, Peter	5:18:18 (26,673)	
Bufton, Richard	3:55:24 (9,022)	
Bugby, Anthony	5:34:00 (28,478)	
Bugg, John	3:29:07 (4,017)	
Bugh, Kevin	5:00:09 (24,001)	
Bugler, Paul	3:20:13 (2,789)	
Buick, James	3:12:16 (1,893)	
Buis, Nick	3:22:56 (3,101)	
Buitendijk, Piet	3:39:19 (5,658)	
Bulaitis, Peter	4:02:42 (10,781)	
Bull, Anthony	4:58:04 (23,599)	
Bull, Ian	4:56:15 (23,212)	
Bull, Ian	6:04:39 (30,439)	
Bull, James	4:17:36 (14,139)	
Bull, Martyn	7:26:49 (32,126)	
Bull, Michael	3:45:13 (6,777)	
Bull, Michael	5:43:56 (29,303)	
Bull, Nicholas	3:32:08 (4,489)	
Bull, Nicholas	4:45:44 (20,893)	
Bull, Peter	3:41:02 (5,967)	
Bull, Peter	4:23:21 (15,581)	
Bull, Roland	4:28:30 (16,858)	
Bull, Steve	4:38:50 (19,285)	
Bull, Steve	4:47:39 (21,333)	
Bullen, Nigel	4:05:39 (11,427)	
Bullivant, Peter	4:35:42 (18,562)	
Bull-Larsen, Thomas	3:47:58 (7,311)	
Bullock, Alastair	3:17:26 (2,482)	
Bullock, Bernard	4:10:47 (12,508)	
Bullock, Paul	3:05:36 (1,293)	
Bullock, Peter	4:28:19 (16,794)	
Bullock, Phillip	4:25:04 (16,019)	
Bullock, Stephen	4:16:50 (13,941)	
Bulmer, Hugo	4:44:04 (20,513)	
Bumstead, Robert	4:45:08 (20,755)	
Bunbury, Anthony	4:18:34 (14,380)	
Bunce, Anthony	5:51:23 (29,802)	
Bunce, James	4:35:49 (18,603)	
Bunce, Malcolm	4:26:05 (16,272)	
Bunce, Stephen	4:27:07 (16,502)	
Bunclark, Nick	3:35:52 (5,052)	

Byrne, Mark	4:21:16	(15,049)
Byrne, Matthew	4:20:19	(14,820)
Byrne, Matthew	4:29:08	(17,022)
Byrne, Paul	3:27:23	(3,718)
Byrne, Philip	3:54:03	(8,674)
Byrne, Robert	4:40:18	(19,608)
Byrne, Sean	4:11:14	(12,584)
Byrnes, Damian	3:41:27	(6,055)
Byrom, Christopher	4:32:58	(17,944)
Byworth, Bryan	3:51:30	(8,074)
Byworth, Matthew	3:02:19	(1,078)
Cabiddu, Demetrio	4:02:45	(10,793)
Cable, Geoffrey	5:21:17	(27,061)
Cable, Stephen	3:07:02	(1,406)
Cable, Stephen	4:36:26	(18,753)
Cabras, Piergianni	3:50:16	(7,792)
Cabrita, Mark	3:08:41	(1,561)
Caceffo, Renzo	4:30:45	(17,431)
Cacioli, Riccardo	4:19:55	(14,717)
Caddy, James	4:50:23	(21,939)
Cadman, John	3:55:26	(9,032)
Cadman, Karl	3:44:10	(6,575)
Cadman, Matthew	4:16:48	(13,936)
Cado, Antoine	4:50:40	(22,005)
Cadogan, Martin	4:25:39	(16,168)
Cadogan, Patrick	5:31:05	(28,202)
Cadogan, Sean	5:31:05	(28,202)
Cadu, Christian	3:50:14	(7,785)
Caffrey, Stephen	4:42:41	(20,154)
Cahill, Barry	3:38:40	(5,535)
Caie, Matthew	3:33:54	(4,734)
Cain, Douglas	4:34:53	(18,369)
Cain, Scott	3:49:22	(7,601)
Cain, Simon	3:44:58	(6,727)
Caira, David	4:25:12	(16,056)
Caird, Gordon	3:36:58	(5,227)
Cairns, Alan	3:26:54	(3,658)
Cairns, William	3:27:14	(3,706)
Caisley, Alastair	4:10:34	(12,478)
Cakebread, John	3:20:15	(2,798)
Calabro, Anthony	4:30:36	(17,391)
Caldecott, Peter	5:16:14	(26,396)
Caldecott, Timothy	5:16:14	(26,396)
Calder, Gavin	4:18:56	(14,492)
Calder, Ian	4:07:30	(11,811)
Calder, Steve	3:49:23	(7,608)
Calderwood, Lee	5:44:08	(29,312)
Calderwood, William	4:48:39	(21,561)
Caldicott, Steven	4:07:48	(11,871)
Caldon, Dean	4:57:41	(23,519)
Caldwell, Alan	3:52:48	(8,374)
Caldwell, George	4:42:14	(20,035)
Caldwell, Philip	4:32:40	(17,871)
Caldwell, Ronald	4:57:11	(23,426)
Caleno, Mark	4:18:00	(14,251)
Cali, Maurizio	4:17:15	(14,045)
Calicibete, Ricardo	5:12:56	(25,967)
Calkins, Samuel	3:34:36	(4,852)
Calladine-Smith, Gregory	3:44:30	(6,635)
Callaghan, Andrew	3:50:06	(7,752)
Callaghan, Andrew	6:25:12	(31,169)
Callaghan, David	4:28:24	(16,828)
Callaghan, James	6:26:57	(31,229)
Callaghan, Robert	4:43:48	(20,453)
Callaghan, Thomas	4:51:02	(22,079)
Callaghan, Toby	4:33:04	(17,968)
Callanan, Gerry	3:58:09	(9,743)
Calleja-Martin, Miguel	4:06:34	(11,605)
Callen, David	5:03:41	(24,567)
Caller, Mark	4:48:25	(21,520)
Callis, Sam	5:26:07	(27,689)
Callow, Geoffrey	5:19:23	(26,812)
Callow, Leo	4:08:05	(11,921)
Calnon, Robert	4:13:35	(13,146)
Calvert, Gerald	3:28:07	(3,834)
Calvert, Mark	4:10:50	(12,516)
Calvert, Michael	4:02:06	(10,656)
Calvert, Neil	3:14:19	(2,165)
Calvey, John	4:29:29	(17,112)
Camara, Paulo	4:42:08	(20,018)
Cambiano, Dario	3:33:01	(4,602)
Cambridge, Gary	4:58:56	(23,789)
Cameron, Alastair	5:06:50	(25,084)

Cameron, Andrew	3:35:37	(5,015)
Cameron, Anthony	5:02:45	(24,426)
Cameron, David	2:51:23	(428)
Cameron, Ian	5:36:25	(28,675)
Cameron, Jamie	4:05:37	(11,419)
Cameron, Paul	3:25:21	(3,448)
Cameron, Paul	4:09:50	(12,310)
Cameron, Pyers	4:07:13	(11,743)
Cameron, Stuart	4:12:06	(12,786)
Camfield, Bryan	3:28:46	(3,962)
Camp, Brian	6:38:23	(31,510)
Camp, Vernon	6:00:51	(30,289)
Campbell, Adrian	5:04:29	(24,705)
Campbell, Alastair	3:53:06	(8,451)
Campbell, Brian	3:52:06	(8,223)
Campbell, Charles	3:44:59	(6,733)
Campbell, Chris	2:55:17	(607)
Campbell, Christopher	3:53:56	(8,653)
Campbell, Colin	6:19:33	(30,994)
Campbell, David	4:12:52	(12,973)
Campbell, Duncan	4:12:32	(12,894)
Campbell, Gary	3:17:47	(2,526)
Campbell, Gavin	4:15:45	(13,685)
Campbell, Graeme	5:00:26	(24,057)
Campbell, Iain	3:31:42	(4,435)
Campbell, Iain	4:30:51	(17,454)
Campbell, Lee	4:28:20	(16,801)
Campbell, Leroy	3:38:16	(5,456)
Campbell, Michael	4:20:49	(14,931)
Campbell, Paul	4:39:51	(19,512)
Campbell, Richard	3:19:56	(2,748)
Campbell, Richard	4:57:55	(23,564)
Campbell, Robert	4:26:13	(16,300)
Campbell, Russell	4:21:33	(15,119)
Campbell, Simon	4:20:51	(14,944)
Campbell, Steven	3:47:48	(7,277)
Campbell, Stuart	4:01:42	(10,580)
Campbell-Reid, Ludo	4:48:13	(21,475)
Campen, James	4:36:28	(18,762)
Campion, Robert	5:19:16	(26,797)
Campion, Stephen	3:28:48	(3,970)
Campo, Aldo	3:06:58	(1,400)
Campolungo, Giovanni	4:25:11	(16,051)
Camsell, Brian	4:16:06	(13,763)
Canavan, Clifford	3:09:24	(1,622)
Canavan, Kevin	4:19:15	(14,568)
Cando, Luis	3:26:22	(3,587)
Candy, Owen	4:50:46	(22,025)
Candy, Robin	3:12:35	(1,943)
Caneva, Richard	6:54:28	(31,817)
Canham, Paul	3:44:12	(6,584)
Cann, Nicholas	6:50:04	(31,720)
Cann, S	3:25:49	(3,514)
Cannell, Mark	4:04:12	(11,112)
Canning, Cerne	4:24:25	(15,844)
Canning, Charles	4:12:42	(12,937)
Canning, Mark	4:09:41	(12,272)
Canning, Nigel	4:04:01	(11,070)
Canning, Oliver	4:50:03	(21,871)
Cannon, Andrew	3:25:40	(3,486)
Cannon, Antony	4:48:11	(21,465)
Cannon, Ben	4:25:28	(16,135)
Cannon, Charles	4:29:42	(17,162)
Cannon, David	4:03:57	(11,048)
Cannon, David	5:22:45	(27,248)
Cannon, Gary	4:08:00	(11,905)
Cannon, John	3:47:04	(7,135)
Cannon, Martin	3:54:21	(8,738)
Cannon, Russell	4:17:23	(14,082)
Cannon, Sean	3:40:32	(5,871)
Canovas-Sanchez, José	4:01:57	(10,624)
Cant, Christopher	5:50:23	(29,743)
Cant, Cliff	3:57:54	(9,677)
Canterbury, Daniel	3:15:34	(2,295)
Cantero Paredes, Francisco	3:37:05	(5,249)
Cantu, Jesus	4:39:13	(19,377)
Cantwell, Gerard	2:59:05	(864)
Capdeville, Robert	3:48:24	(7,391)
Capes, Ian	4:20:25	(14,864)
Capewell, Graham	4:13:51	(13,216)
Capitan-Silva, Francisco	4:00:54	(10,407)
Caplin, Heath	4:55:01	(22,925)
Capper, Matthew	4:48:33	(21,542)

Be prepared

Hugh Jones, first British winner of the London in 1982 in 2:09:24, is living proof that preparing for this race starts long before the day. As a boy he ran to and from primary school, often four times a day. He popped up again in 2003 as coach to Alastair Campbell, Tony Blair's spin-doctor. Campbell ran to his work at No 10 Downing Street as part of his training. 'You've got to get the miles in somehow,' says Jones. 'That's the secret.'

Cappetta, Diego	3:08:39	(1,558)
Capps, Christopher	4:00:45	(10,378)
Capretti, Gino	3:09:03	(1,592)
Capriotti, Nino	4:09:18	(12,197)
Capuano, Anthony	4:14:48	(13,453)
Carbury, Giles	5:07:39	(25,212)
Carbury, Timothy	5:07:39	(25,212)
Carder, Adrian	4:25:05	(16,021)
Carder, Richard	5:20:44	(26,990)
Cardon, Clive	3:44:37	(6,653)
Cardoza, Pio	4:26:44	(16,413)
Cardwell, Mark	4:36:46	(18,826)
Cardy, David	4:35:36	(18,541)
Cardy, Ian	4:07:30	(11,811)
Cardy, Mark	4:06:22	(11,566)
Carey, Christopher	3:19:56	(2,748)
Carey, John	5:04:01	(24,633)
Carey, Moray	4:08:43	(12,068)
Carey, Stephen	5:24:30	(27,475)
Cargill, Jamie	4:58:56	(23,789)
Cargill, Robbie	4:58:55	(23,784)
Carim, Enver	4:58:23	(23,667)
Cariss, Chris	2:17:57	(18)
Carlen, Rolf	5:09:19	(25,452)
Carlin, Brian	2:42:52	(192)
Carlin, Hugo	4:27:17	(16,546)
Carlin, Ian	4:02:54	(10,827)
Carling, Lee	6:39:47	(31,536)
Carlino, Jacques	5:02:59	(24,454)
Carlisle, Richard	3:55:53	(9,150)
Carlson, Burton	5:40:05	(29,004)
Carlsson, Toby	4:29:36	(17,139)
Carlucci, Donato	4:28:37	(16,890)
Carlucci, Francesco	3:06:25	(1,350)
Carmagnani, Filippo	4:29:21	(17,071)
Carmel, Edmund	4:42:56	(20,213)
Carmichael, Stuart	4:05:55	(11,487)
Carmody, James	4:07:13	(11,743)
Carmody, John	4:29:39	(17,150)
Carne, Andrew	4:24:38	(15,897)
Carnegie, Malcolm	4:05:17	(11,349)
Carnegie, William	6:53:07	(31,789)
Carnell, Miles	6:09:21	(30,614)
Carnell, Robert	5:27:59	(27,891)
Carnell, Thomas	4:17:07	(14,015)
Carnevale, Luigi	4:42:14	(20,035)
Carney, Michael	4:42:15	(20,039)
Carney, Michael	4:53:19	(22,574)
Carney, Robert	4:11:39	(12,677)
Caroe, Chris	3:59:07	(9,986)
Carol, Riel	4:17:19	(14,060)
Carolan, Peter	5:11:55	(25,816)
Carpenter, Colin	5:41:52	(29,148)
Carpenter, Graham	4:30:24	(17,344)
Carpenter, Howard	3:08:26	(1,538)
Carpenter, Jason	5:07:27	(25,172)
Carpenter, John	4:20:14	(14,802)
Carpenter, John	4:30:27	(17,357)
Carpenter, Neil	4:27:34	(16,617)
Carpenter, Richard	3:59:42	(10,154)
Carpenter, Trevor	4:48:34	(21,545)
Carr, Andy	4:55:36	(23,053)

Carr, David 4:15:18 (13,592)
Carr, Geoffrey 4:51:37 (22,228)
Carr, Gordon 5:36:52 (28,724)
Carr, Jason 4:34:45 (18,338)
Carr, Joe 4:09:38 (12,256)
Carr, John 6:33:59 (31,423)
Carr, Kenneth 5:17:33 (26,553)
Carr, Mike 4:09:09 (12,163)
Carr, Paul 4:44:20 (20,577)
Carr, Robert 4:35:17 (18,468)
Carr, Scott 4:03:39 (10,973)
Carr, Sean 4:28:34 (16,878)
Carr, Stephen 4:34:23 (18,259)
Carr, Stephen 4:49:31 (21,754)
Carrad, Stephen 3:58:36 (9,857)
Carraro, Andrea 2:57:31 (736)
Carrasco, Jean-Pierre 3:50:22 (7,817)
Carrera, Fernando 4:15:46 (13,690)
Carrick, Paul 5:03:44 (24,582)
Carrington, Alex 3:39:19 (5,658)
Carrington, Michael 5:21:52 (27,132)
Carrington, Simon 4:03:44 (10,992)
Carrivick, Daniel 2:59:16 (877)
Carroll, Antony 3:55:09 (8,951)
Carroll, Bradley 3:29:17 (4,040)
Carroll, Craig 4:33:41 (18,094)
Carroll, Gerry 3:43:38 (6,473)
Carroll, John 4:22:03 (15,252)
Carroll, Lee 3:49:32 (7,639)
Carroll, Mark 4:16:43 (13,911)
Carroll, Michael 4:17:22 (14,074)
Carroll, Mike 5:01:38 (24,251)
Carroll, Paul 3:52:52 (8,386)
Carroll, Paul 4:26:59 (16,465)
Carroll, Paul 4:36:53 (18,849)
Carroll, Raymond 4:35:53 (18,617)
Carroll, Rob 3:09:50 (1,658)
Carroll, Sean 3:49:08 (7,543)
Carroll, Vincent 2:51:03 (421)
Carrotte, Greg 3:49:04 (7,529)
Carrouee, Pierre-Alexis 3:46:04 (6,946)
Carslaw, Neil 5:17:34 (26,556)
Carson, James 4:03:30 (10,942)
Carson, Jon 4:33:02 (17,960)
Carson, Roger 4:21:47 (15,180)
Carson, Rory 4:21:47 (15,180)
Carson, Scott 4:34:47 (18,348)
Carson, Thomas 4:07:12 (11,737)
Carstairs, Timothy 4:34:03 (18,176)
Cartailler, Mathias 2:46:54 (295)
Carter, Adam 4:47:47 (21,368)
Carter, Alastair 4:09:11 (12,171)
Carter, Andrew 3:29:30 (4,092)
Carter, Andrew 4:48:52 (21,602)
Carter, Andrew 4:50:07 (21,884)
Carter, Andrew 6:23:00 (31,104)
Carter, Avid 3:28:32 (3,909)
Carter, Daniel 4:45:48 (20,913)
Carter, Darryl 3:22:15 (3,019)
Carter, David 2:54:45 (579)
Carter, David 5:44:51 (29,349)
Carter, Eric 3:56:31 (9,327)
Carter, Harden 4:36:01 (18,654)
Carter, James 3:59:46 (10,167)
Carter, James 5:29:50 (28,072)
Carter, Jason 4:30:54 (17,468)
Carter, Jonathan 4:25:20 (16,096)
Carter, Kevin 3:02:46 (1,100)
Carter, Lee 3:41:50 (6,120)
Carter, Les 3:28:02 (3,820)
Carter, Mark 3:34:48 (4,879)
Carter, Martin 4:08:09 (11,928)
Carter, Michael 3:17:46 (2,525)
Carter, Michael 5:11:08 (25,713)
Carter, Paul 3:04:47 (1,233)
Carter, Paul 4:41:17 (19,819)
Carter, Paul 5:10:44 (25,652)
Carter, Richard 3:44:42 (6,672)
Carter, Rob 5:04:45 (24,747)
Carter, Robert 4:18:32 (14,368)
Carter, Sean 4:58:48 (23,766)
Carter, Stephen 4:27:00 (16,470)
Carter, Steven 5:31:11 (28,216)
Carter, Stuart 3:39:22 (5,671)
Carter-Hume, David 7:35:31 (32,185)
Carter-White, Richard 4:27:31 (16,605)
Cartin, Michael 3:23:58 (3,244)
Cartledge, Ian 4:36:10 (18,682)
Cartlidge, Barry 3:15:27 (2,282)
Cartlidge, Bernard 4:44:20 (20,577)
Cartmale, Thomas 4:10:09 (12,384)
Cartner, James 4:26:19 (16,317)
Cartwright, Adrian 3:38:53 (5,577)
Cartwright, Darren 4:23:29 (15,611)
Cartwright, David 2:44:15 (224)
Cartwright, Gordon 4:36:47 (18,833)
Cartwright, James 4:21:23 (15,080)
Cartwright, Malcolm 5:35:04 (28,559)
Carty, Nick 4:02:25 (10,723)
Caruana, John 4:48:11 (21,465)
Caruana, Paul 5:19:13 (26,783)
Caruso, Pier Paolo 4:26:38 (16,389)
Carver, James 3:45:32 (6,837)
Casara, Giuseppe Maria 3:51:14 (8,016)
Cascarina, Michael 6:25:57 (31,201)
Case, Anthony 5:29:13 (28,009)
Casement, William 3:59:48 (10,176)
Case-Upton, Stephen 4:36:21 (18,733)
Casey, Anthony 2:57:01 (705)
Casey, Ashley 6:01:32 (30,325)
Cash, Jamie 4:26:34 (16,370)
Cashmore, Paul 5:07:26 (25,168)
Casini, Vincenzo 4:15:36 (13,660)
Casley, Dan 3:42:41 (6,295)
Cass, Warren 5:26:03 (27,680)
Casselton, Stephen 3:44:11 (6,577)
Cassidy, Bernard 3:10:57 (1,752)
Cassidy, Steven 4:08:58 (12,124)
Cassidy, William 3:38:00 (5,413)
Cassie, Paul 4:19:06 (14,530)
Casson, Peter 5:56:51 (30,095)
Castagnola, Barry 4:25:11 (16,051)
Castaldo, Paul 3:28:14 (3,854)
Castana, Salvatore 3:26:13 (3,570)
Castell, Andrew 4:08:03 (11,913)
Castell, Martin 3:37:35 (5,342)
Castiglioni, Jorge 4:22:50 (15,449)
Castillo, Carlos 3:01:30 (1,024)
Castle, Christopher 3:13:19 (2,037)
Castle, David 4:55:20 (22,985)
Castle, John 2:40:48 (163)
Castle, Nick 4:33:23 (18,028)
Castle, Toby 3:33:10 (4,623)
Castrey, Gary 3:07:26 (1,448)
Castro, José 5:06:27 (25,012)
Caswell, Edward 5:47:09 (29,501)
Caswell, Steve 3:07:43 (1,475)
Catanach, David 4:41:55 (19,977)
Catanzaro, Vincenzo 5:25:55 (27,655)
Catchlove, Neil 4:14:11 (13,302)
Catchpole, Andrew 4:43:12 (20,286)
Catchpole, Charles 3:51:28 (8,066)
Catchpole, Phil 3:57:54 (9,677)
Catchpole, Robin 4:30:39 (17,402)
Cates, Michael 3:06:18 (1,338)
Cates, Patrick 3:24:16 (3,299)
Cathcart, Nigel 6:05:09 (30,458)
Cathcart, Paul 4:09:35 (12,246)
Catherall, Michael 5:15:41 (26,339)
Cathro, David 3:17:47 (2,526)
Catling, Howard 5:14:00 (26,099)
Catling, Michael 4:36:38 (18,793)
Catlow, Ian 4:14:01 (13,264)
Catmull, Jeremy 3:22:28 (3,046)
Catmull, Julian 3:01:44 (1,034)
Catsaras, Zamir 3:50:24 (7,825)
Cattell, Michael 8:11:13 (32,269)
Cattell, Richard 5:00:01 (23,983)
Cattermole, David 4:27:02 (16,480)
Catton, Christopher 3:12:42 (1,958)
Catton, Rodney 4:55:44 (23,091)
Caudrelier, Jean-Pierre 4:21:53 (15,203)
Caulder, Graham 3:24:07 (3,270)
Caulfield, Daniel 4:30:45 (17,431)
Caulfield, Matt 4:15:01 (13,512)
Caulley, Allan 5:12:49 (25,945)
Caunce, Peter 4:28:39 (16,897)
Caunter, Ben 3:22:33 (3,053)
Causer, Fred 5:39:38 (28,959)
Causon, Roger 4:53:47 (22,675)
Caussinus, Nicolas 4:57:35 (23,499)
Cavanagh, David 4:33:37 (18,079)
Cavanagh, Kenneth 5:02:22 (24,371)
Cavanagh, Mark 5:05:31 (24,885)
Cavanagh, Sean 4:19:55 (14,717)
Cavanagh, Shaun 4:36:02 (18,659)
Cavara, Massimiliano 3:17:05 (2,437)
Cavazza, Marcello 3:27:46 (3,777)
Cave, Brett 6:42:40 (31,584)
Cavill, Anthony 4:11:41 (12,687)
Cawdron, Danny 4:26:13 (16,300)
Cawdron, Dave 5:22:54 (27,267)
Cawley, Robert 5:51:24 (29,806)
Cawood, Kevin 4:24:58 (15,990)
Cayley, Christopher 4:01:03 (10,439)
Cayton, Neil 2:38:34 (139)
Cazenove, George 3:57:44 (9,628)
Cazes, Jean-Marie 4:47:03 (21,190)
Cazzato, Danny 4:52:49 (22,466)
Celal, Devrim 3:21:45 (2,959)
Cerely, Peter 4:09:02 (12,142)
Ceresa, Pascal 3:42:35 (6,273)
César de Sa, Nuno 4:15:27 (13,627)
Cesari, Frederic 3:41:29 (6,060)
Cespedes, Marcelo 4:23:54 (15,720)
Cespedes, Steven 4:46:39 (21,116)
Chacksfield, Mark 3:50:57 (7,933)
Chadderton, Derek 4:32:30 (17,835)
Chadwick, Dan 3:32:12 (4,497)
Chadwick, David 4:31:52 (17,701)
Chadwick, Nick 3:38:20 (5,462)
Chadwick, Simon 5:40:43 (29,057)
Chadwick, Steven 4:25:53 (16,224)
Chadwick, Steven 6:02:00 (30,341)
Chaffe, Richard 3:20:55 (2,877)
Chaffey, John 3:59:13 (10,007)
Chaffin, John 5:21:29 (27,079)
Chairon, Laurent 3:20:49 (2,862)
Chait, Bradley 3:42:31 (6,255)
Chakrabarti, Debasish 4:23:05 (15,508)
Chalfen, David 2:59:14 (875)
Chalk, Duncan 4:33:15 (17,993)
Chalk, Trevor 3:12:10 (1,878)
Chalke, Steve 3:55:46 (9,120)
Chalker, Stanley 5:36:14 (28,657)
Chalklen, Steven 3:11:45 (1,828)
Challen, John 4:36:48 (18,835)
Challinor, Craig 5:27:03 (27,783)
Challis, Ross 6:13:10 (30,772)
Chalmers, Alan 4:59:50 (23,955)
Chalmers, Alexander 4:40:28 (19,648)
Chalmers, Ian 5:16:24 (26,414)
Chalmers, James 4:07:27 (11,796)
Chalmers, Stephen 5:08:29 (25,333)
Chalmers, Thomas 3:51:00 (7,953)
Chalmers, Vince 4:01:31 (10,543)
Chalmers, William 3:56:32 (9,330)
Chaloner, Paul 5:06:58 (25,100)
Chamberlain, Brian 4:39:34 (19,453)
Chamberlain, Graham 5:28:42 (27,960)
Chamberlain, Martin 3:53:52 (8,637)
Chamberlain, Matthew 5:05:43 (24,925)
Chamberlain, Michael 3:31:32 (4,417)
Chamberlain, Peter 6:31:08 (31,352)
Chamberlin, Simon 4:21:56 (15,217)
Chambers, Alistair 2:58:45 (828)
Chambers, Ben 4:05:47 (11,454)
Chambers, Darren 5:56:04 (30,054)
Chambers, Dean 4:26:04 (16,269)
Chambers, John 3:45:58 (6,925)
Chambers, Joseph 4:15:30 (13,640)
Chambers, Keith 3:12:25 (1,918)
Chambers, Lindley 4:35:41 (18,558)
Chambers, Michael 5:32:10 (28,306)
Chambers, Paul 6:36:36 (31,486)
Chambers, Robert 4:28:21 (16,807)
Chambers, Troy 6:12:14 (30,740)
Champion, Charles 4:52:39 (22,431)
Champion, Stephen 5:20:24 (26,941)

Chamulewicz, Paul 4:31:21 (17,582)
Chan, Chi Pan 4:16:25 (13,838)
Chan, Chong 2:59:32 (905)
Chan, David 4:19:14 (14,559)
Chan, Johnathan 5:05:50 (24,938)
Chan, Siu 3:34:36 (4,852)
Chan, Wing 3:57:58 (9,698)
Chana, Jaswant 4:13:13 (13,055)
Chana, Ravinder 5:30:51 (28,181)
Chandler, Christian 4:42:39 (20,142)
Chandler, Gary 3:17:25 (2,478)
Chandler, Jim 3:11:41 (1,819)
Chandler, Keith 6:04:13 (30,417)
Chandler, Lee 4:02:15 (10,686)
Chandler, Mark 4:52:37 (22,417)
Chandler, Michael 3:06:51 (1,390)
Chandler, Paul 4:36:21 (18,733)
Chandler, Peter 4:03:31 (10,945)
Chandler, Stephen 3:27:17 (3,711)
Chandler, Steven 4:49:43 (21,806)
Chandley, Paul 4:44:46 (20,673)
Chandra-Mohan, Alagar 6:29:28 (31,314)
Changer, Daniel 5:05:29 (24,880)
Channing, Kevin 5:13:01 (25,976)
Chant, Daniel 5:50:33 (29,756)
Chant, Doug 3:16:12 (2,348)
Chantrey, David 6:09:59 (30,640)
Chant-Sempill, Ian 4:41:08 (19,783)
Chapel, Jerome 3:27:42 (3,769)
Chaplin, Ian 2:54:30 (559)
Chaplin, Michael 4:13:01 (13,008)
Chaplin, Neil 3:28:20 (3,872)
Chaplin, Robert 3:39:59 (5,782)
Chapman, Christopher 4:12:40 (12,933)
Chapman, Christopher 4:27:45 (16,666)
Chapman, David 4:00:20 (10,301)
Chapman, David 7:52:44 (32,239)
Chapman, George 5:11:49 (25,805)
Chapman, Ian 4:05:09 (11,321)
Chapman, Jamie 4:27:44 (16,660)
Chapman, Jason 3:51:01 (7,957)
Chapman, Jason 4:19:33 (14,626)
Chapman, Keith 4:53:27 (22,609)
Chapman, Kevin 3:57:02 (9,464)
Chapman, Leslie 6:20:11 (31,022)
Chapman, Mark 4:51:42 (22,246)
Chapman, Neil 3:07:36 (1,460)
Chapman, Neil 3:39:45 (5,738)
Chapman, Neil 5:34:23 (28,516)
Chapman, Neville 3:31:42 (4,435)
Chapman, Peter 3:49:35 (7,652)
Chapman, Richard 3:35:44 (5,031)
Chapman, Robert 4:12:45 (12,949)
Chapman, Robert 4:18:35 (14,387)
Chapman, Simon 3:55:39 (9,091)
Chapman-Sheath, Philip 5:17:46 (26,574)
Chappell, Michael 3:19:12 (2,671)
Chappell, Stephen 3:54:56 (8,902)
Chapple, Stephen 3:05:20 (1,274)
Chapple, Stephen 4:06:29 (11,587)
Charbonnier, Gilbert 4:07:14 (11,745)
Charles, Danny 4:18:38 (14,403)
Charles, Lee 4:28:06 (16,735)
Charles, Paul 3:04:57 (1,243)
Charles, Paul 4:22:54 (15,471)
Charles, Paul 5:04:18 (24,677)
Charles, Peter 5:43:03 (29,243)
Charlett, Gwyn 4:32:18 (17,792)
Charlton, Adam 3:57:57 (9,694)
Charlton, Christopher 5:19:38 (26,841)
Charlton, David 5:38:02 (28,813)
Charlton, Raymond 3:39:59 (5,782)
Charluteau, Nicolas 3:57:31 (9,582)
Charlwood, Martyn 4:30:53 (17,464)
Charnock, Graham 4:47:57 (21,412)
Charp, Erik 3:55:33 (9,062)
Charters, Matthew 4:18:53 (14,473)
Charters, Paul 4:35:44 (18,570)
Chase, David 5:27:29 (27,828)
Chase, Jeremy 3:50:31 (7,844)
Chase, Mark 4:18:06 (14,272)
Chaseling, Jeff 2:54:38 (570)
Chatburn, Dean 3:51:05 (7,974)
Chater, Paul 4:43:11 (20,281)
Chatfield, Daniel 3:31:59 (4,470)
Chatfield, Darren 5:23:35 (27,354)
Chatfield, Gary 4:49:51 (21,838)
Chatfield, Guy 4:53:43 (22,652)
Chatfield, Mark 3:38:54 (5,581)
Chatte, Yannick 3:55:37 (9,081)
Chattenton, Michael 3:41:33 (6,079)
Chatterton, Mark 5:22:17 (27,184)
Chatwin, Edward 3:57:55 (9,685)
Chauhan, Abhishek 5:22:48 (27,255)
Chauhan, Arun 3:58:02 (9,717)
Chaundy, Neil 4:53:47 (22,675)
Chaundy, Robert 4:09:48 (12,301)
Chauveau, Patrice 3:08:39 (1,558)
Chauviere, Arnaud 3:51:44 (8,132)
Chavasse, Steven 4:00:59 (10,426)
Cheal, John 3:32:41 (4,556)
Cheal, Paul 5:51:18 (29,799)
Cheatham, Mark 4:22:37 (15,401)
Cheema, Irfan Ul Haq 4:56:29 (23,255)
Cheesman, Charles 4:46:27 (21,081)
Cheetham, John 5:04:01 (24,633)
Cheevers, Colm 4:06:58 (11,679)
Chell, Philip 4:49:38 (21,786)
Chelton, Neil 5:17:26 (26,531)
Chelule, Wesley 2:24:00 (35)
Chen, Theodore 3:34:38 (4,860)
Chenery, Cliff 4:05:47 (11,454)
Cheney, Les 4:22:17 (15,313)
Chernack, Leon 5:52:28 (29,851)
Cherrett, Andrew 5:09:33 (25,488)
Cherriman, David 4:36:20 (18,722)
Cherry, Jason 4:40:59 (19,748)
Cherry, Robert 3:47:25 (7,196)
Chersich, Matthew 5:49:28 (29,674)
Cheseldine, Noel 4:38:52 (19,295)
Cheshire, David 4:28:27 (16,839)
Cheshire, Nick 4:09:44 (12,280)
Chester, John 4:00:42 (10,367)
Chester, Martin 3:11:53 (1,847)
Chester Master, Richard 5:13:47 (26,081)
Chesterton, Lee 3:55:42 (9,107)
Chesterton, Peter 4:38:08 (19,114)
Cheuens, Eric 4:34:44 (18,335)
Cheung, Anthony 5:11:32 (25,763)
Cheung, Delon 4:43:12 (20,286)
Cheung, Desmond 5:35:54 (28,628)
Cheung, Vincent 4:47:34 (21,310)
Cheval, Thierry 3:41:00 (5,957)
Chevassut, Timothy 4:21:54 (15,207)
Cheyne, Brian 5:19:28 (26,827)
Chhabra, Ajay 5:44:41 (29,341)
Chhetri, Gautam 4:56:58 (23,371)
Chick, David 4:58:19 (23,655)
Chick, Jonathan 4:43:23 (20,347)
Chico, Ben 4:39:11 (19,370)
Chilcott, Peter 5:49:09 (29,648)
Child, Keith 3:40:06 (5,809)
Child, Robert 3:21:29 (2,929)
Childerhouse, Erik 6:57:58 (31,873)
Children, Simon 4:00:43 (10,373)
Childs, David 4:52:58 (22,499)
Childs, Gary 3:49:41 (7,679)
Childs, Gordon 4:18:52 (14,468)
Childs, Mark 4:24:40 (15,906)
Childs, Nicholas 4:50:34 (21,979)
Childs, Peter 3:51:06 (7,976)
Childs, Shaun 4:10:19 (12,419)
Childs, Steven 6:17:55 (30,928)
Chillery, Richard 3:33:17 (4,643)
Chilton, John 5:37:03 (28,743)
Chilton, Jonathan 4:12:10 (12,805)
Chilton, Mark 5:34:53 (28,545)
Chilvers, Andrew 3:33:12 (4,629)
Chilvers, Ben 4:00:08 (10,257)
Chin, Ambrose 4:41:52 (19,966)
Chinn, Rod 3:54:23 (8,748)
Chippendale, Mark 3:22:24 (3,035)
Chippendale, Neil 3:12:39 (1,953)
Chipperfield, Marcus 4:07:28 (11,799)
Chirume, Charles 4:31:48 (17,687)
Chisholm, Barry 3:06:28 (1,356)
Chisholm, David 4:44:30 (20,615)
Chisholm, Paul 4:50:35 (21,987)
Chislett, Bradley 3:19:19 (2,681)
Chisnall, Nigel 4:47:24 (21,274)
Chittell, Christopher 4:16:04 (13,759)
Chivers, Matthew 4:58:47 (23,762)
Chivers, Michael 5:49:47 (29,699)
Choat, Matthew 4:23:56 (15,734)
Chochoy, Alain 3:21:55 (2,974)
Chodzko-Zajko, Piotr 3:41:09 (5,985)
Choi, Shing 3:46:51 (7,093)
Chong, Heong 3:21:22 (2,919)
Choppen, Greg 3:47:20 (7,179)
Chopra, Narinder 4:27:24 (16,572)
Chorlton, Gordon 4:02:26 (10,727)
Chorn, Justin 3:44:26 (6,625)
Chouaib, Mohamed 3:45:04 (6,746)
Choules, David 3:36:33 (5,152)
Chow, Gary 4:18:09 (14,279)
Chowings, Kevin 4:48:28 (21,529)
Chraibi, Fouad 4:29:57 (17,229)
Chraibi, Salah-Eddine 3:51:44 (8,132)
Christensen, Jon 4:52:19 (22,362)
Christensen, Martin 3:41:32 (6,075)
Christensen, Morten 3:36:51 (5,204)
Christensen, Per 4:34:50 (18,355)
Christensen, Thomas 3:49:15 (7,576)
Christian, David 4:54:52 (22,898)
Christian, Marc 3:07:41 (1,473)
Christiansen, Mikkel 3:50:52 (7,919)
Christie, David 4:28:23 (16,817)
Christie, Ian 4:50:13 (21,905)
Christie, Neil 3:40:34 (5,878)
Christie, Rupert 3:56:24 (9,294)
Christie, Sandy 3:28:02 (3,820)
Christmas, Paul 3:59:21 (10,053)
Christophe, Laurent 3:50:11 (7,773)
Christophers, Philip 5:28:44 (27,962)
Christopherson, Kevin 4:16:04 (13,759)
Christov, Mick 5:01:17 (24,202)
Chu, Chi 4:01:25 (10,523)
Chubb, Geoffrey 4:36:34 (18,781)
Chubb, Karl 3:59:36 (10,119)
Chui, Wai 4:02:55 (10,828)
Chukwuemeka, Victor 4:52:54 (22,484)
Chung, Kam 3:17:16 (2,457)
Chung, Sandy 3:47:28 (7,207)
Church, Anthony 4:01:42 (10,580)
Church, Graham 4:54:16 (22,761)
Church, Jerome 4:25:22 (16,107)
Church, Martin 4:08:33 (12,024)
Churchill, Carl 5:20:23 (26,937)
Churchill, Nigel 3:38:22 (5,472)
Churchill, Stephen 5:35:28 (28,591)
Churchward, David 3:52:58 (8,412)
Churn, Peter 3:09:23 (1,620)
Chusseau, Christophe 3:31:55 (4,460)
Cicalese, Luca 5:27:55 (27,886)
Cicognini, Mariangelo 4:23:17 (15,571)
Cicutti, Ambrose 3:59:45 (10,165)
Cicutti, Nic 5:41:28 (29,114)
Ciereszko, Richard 4:50:59 (22,065)
Cierocki, David 4:02:20 (10,703)
Cifuentes, José 4:58:20 (23,656)
Cinque, Giulio 3:34:26 (4,824)
Cinque, Giuseppe 4:36:44 (18,814)
Cinturel, Bruno 3:04:16 (1,199)
Ciotti, Dino 4:41:18 (19,825)
Ciriaco, Carlos 3:27:46 (3,777)
Citron, Marc 3:18:14 (2,580)
Clack, Tony 5:14:33 (26,185)
Clague, James 4:05:34 (11,414)
Clapham, Jeremy 3:13:50 (2,100)
Clapp, Matthew 2:56:16 (658)
Clapp, Michael 4:48:57 (21,621)
Clapshaw, James 7:25:26 (32,111)
Clapson, Barrie 3:46:08 (6,959)
Clapton, Roland 5:34:55 (28,547)
Clar, Robert 4:58:23 (23,667)
Clarasso, Jean 5:09:00 (25,407)
Clare, Anthony 4:55:11 (22,959)
Clare, Daniel 5:25:11 (27,568)
Clare, Jonathan 3:04:27 (1,208)

Cobourne, Stuart	4:51:20 (22,165)	
Coburn, Anthony	3:28:44 (3,952)	
Cockayne, Andrew	3:35:25 (4,977)	
Cockbain, Mark	3:18:27 (2,607)	
Cockburn, Ben	3:40:30 (5,867)	
Cockburn, Mike	4:23:52 (15,712)	
Cocker, Andrew	4:15:20 (13,602)	
Cockerell, Barnaby	3:46:53 (7,100)	
Cockerell, William	2:28:43 (57)	
Cockerton, Paul	5:36:47 (28,715)	
Cockle, Ray	3:37:37 (5,349)	
Cockroft, Martin	4:16:18 (13,808)	
Coddington, Russell	4:21:33 (15,119)	
Code, Peter	3:36:02 (5,069)	
Codling, Stuart	4:50:58 (22,063)	
Codrington, Barry	6:17:27 (30,905)	
Codrington, Charles	3:29:48 (4,144)	
Coe, Kevin	3:25:39 (3,481)	
Coe, Rob	4:22:29 (15,359)	
Coe, Robert	4:43:54 (20,481)	
Coey, Stephen	3:52:34 (8,322)	
Coffey, Damian	3:04:05 (1,188)	
Coffey, Ivor	3:49:32 (7,639)	
Coffey, Kieran	4:31:19 (17,570)	
Coggan, Robert	4:28:10 (16,756)	
Cognolato, Alessandro	3:32:59 (4,596)	
Cohen, Adam	4:23:35 (15,635)	
Cohen, Howard	3:17:22 (2,472)	
Cohen, Oliver	4:16:54 (13,964)	
Cohen, Simon	4:55:18 (22,977)	
Cohen, Stuart	5:37:31 (28,777)	
Cohring, John	6:27:23 (31,236)	
Coic, Pascal	4:00:07 (10,253)	
Cointreau, François	4:39:56 (19,524)	
Coker, Andrew	3:52:02 (8,203)	
Coke-Smyth, Thomas	3:16:11 (2,346)	
Colaianni, Scipione	2:59:10 (868)	
Colas, Michel	3:09:15 (1,605)	
Colbourne, Steve	2:59:21 (885)	
Colbridge, Ian	5:55:51 (30,034)	
Coldicott, Allan	4:32:21 (17,801)	
Coldman, Brian	4:52:46 (22,452)	
Coldron, Andrew	3:59:52 (10,193)	
Cole, Alan	3:37:00 (5,229)	
Cole, Clive	4:55:33 (23,037)	
Cole, David	4:43:35 (20,396)	
Cole, David	4:51:27 (22,195)	
Cole, David	4:59:01 (23,804)	
Cole, Ernie	3:55:05 (8,933)	
Cole, Jeremy	3:56:38 (9,358)	
Cole, Matthew	3:43:54 (6,527)	
Cole, Richard	4:09:53 (12,318)	
Cole, Richard	4:24:39 (15,904)	
Cole, Rob	3:20:01 (2,763)	
Cole, Shaun	6:22:48 (31,097)	
Cole, Simon	5:39:50 (28,974)	
Cole, Stephen	4:29:40 (17,153)	
Cole-Bludau, Daniel	6:02:43 (30,364)	
Colebrook, Martyn	4:41:06 (19,777)	
Coleby, William	3:54:46 (8,859)	
Colegate-Stone, Toby	4:44:17 (20,569)	
Coleman, Christopher	5:10:09 (25,575)	
Coleman, Glen	3:32:26 (4,520)	
Coleman, Glenn	4:53:50 (22,686)	
Coleman, Jason	4:29:21 (17,071)	
Coleman, John	6:30:13 (31,334)	
Coleman, Leighton	5:04:28 (24,703)	
Coleman, Richard	3:41:58 (6,142)	
Coleman, Rory	4:21:30 (15,113)	
Coleman, Shaun	5:50:31 (29,754)	
Coleman, Stanley	3:19:17 (2,677)	
Coleman, Stephen	5:14:20 (26,143)	
Coles, Alan	3:51:50 (8,159)	
Coles, Daryl	4:10:29 (12,460)	
Coles, David	2:57:34 (743)	
Coles, Ian	4:59:48 (23,951)	
Coles, James	6:15:50 (30,854)	
Coles, Philip	4:35:56 (18,633)	
Coles, Scott	4:02:27 (10,732)	
Coles, Terence	3:17:31 (2,491)	
Coles, Vernon	6:03:35 (30,399)	
Coleshill, Stephen	4:04:30 (11,180)	
Coley, David	4:26:46 (16,421)	

Coley, James	3:26:31 (3,610)	
Coley, Philip	4:18:42 (14,423)	
Colfer, James	4:04:16 (11,127)	
Colgin, Everard	3:47:14 (7,161)	
Colin, Etienne	3:04:32 (1,213)	
Colings, Stuart	5:54:18 (29,957)	
Collard, Mark	5:54:37 (29,973)	
Collenette, John	4:40:51 (19,716)	
Collett, Andrew	5:20:23 (26,937)	
Collett, Les	4:16:20 (13,815)	
Colley, Ian	4:56:04 (23,161)	
Colley, James	4:17:14 (14,041)	
Colley, John	4:00:49 (10,390)	
Colley, Mark	7:34:09 (32,180)	
Colley, Russell	6:12:09 (30,734)	
Collie, Neil	4:55:49 (23,114)	
Collie, Philip	5:02:14 (24,352)	
Collier, Andrew	4:33:58 (18,158)	
Collier, Andrew	5:54:43 (29,981)	
Collier, David	2:46:24 (273)	
Collier, Douglas	4:30:17 (17,305)	
Collier, Jeffrey	3:53:12 (8,474)	
Collier, John	4:02:26 (10,727)	
Collier, Jonathan	4:38:08 (19,114)	
Collier, Lloyd	3:22:52 (3,096)	
Collier, Michael	3:35:24 (4,972)	
Collier, Paul	3:42:24 (6,219)	
Collier, Peter	5:01:41 (24,255)	
Collier, Scott	4:49:08 (21,655)	
Colligan, Martin	4:39:20 (19,409)	
Collinge, Andrew	3:00:30 (974)	
Collingham, Steven	6:15:55 (30,856)	
Collings, Andrew	3:20:03 (2,766)	
Collings, Robert	4:37:57 (19,075)	
Collingwood, John	4:49:49 (21,827)	
Collingwood, Paul	3:16:53 (2,416)	
Collins, Adam	4:11:54 (12,741)	
Collins, Andy	2:55:33 (622)	
Collins, Barrie	4:38:50 (19,285)	
Collins, Chris	4:43:44 (20,440)	
Collins, David	3:47:19 (7,177)	
Collins, David	4:30:01 (17,243)	
Collins, Dennis	3:23:42 (3,204)	
Collins, Gary	2:57:43 (750)	
Collins, Gerard	3:24:38 (3,347)	
Collins, Gilbert	4:41:03 (19,767)	
Collins, Graham	3:13:30 (2,061)	
Collins, James	4:17:46 (14,200)	
Collins, James	4:42:57 (20,217)	
Collins, John	4:23:50 (15,703)	
Collins, John	5:02:33 (24,397)	
Collins, Jonathan	5:18:50 (26,738)	
Collins, Malcolm	3:35:36 (5,011)	
Collins, Mark	3:36:09 (5,085)	
Collins, Martin	5:17:32 (26,549)	
Collins, Martyn	6:11:26 (30,709)	
Collins, Matthew	3:59:34 (10,112)	
Collins, Matthew	4:59:06 (23,824)	
Collins, Maurice	2:46:38 (283)	
Collins, Michael	3:00:31 (976)	
Collins, Michael	3:34:11 (4,774)	
Collins, Michael	5:30:13 (28,099)	
Collins, Nathaniel	3:12:37 (1,950)	
Collins, Paul	5:14:30 (26,177)	
Collins, Peter	3:23:55 (3,235)	
Collins, Phil	3:19:09 (2,665)	
Collins, Robert	4:34:58 (18,388)	
Collins, Sean	3:45:29 (6,828)	
Collins, Shaun	3:42:48 (6,315)	
Collins, Stephen	5:34:06 (28,488)	
Collins, Steve	4:51:13 (22,137)	
Collins, Steven	5:11:40 (25,784)	
Collinson, Daniel	4:15:12 (13,567)	
Collinson, Julian	4:56:05 (23,166)	
Collinson, Malcolm	4:31:14 (17,553)	
Collis, Adrian	6:19:03 (30,975)	
Collis, Andrew	4:44:23 (20,591)	
Collis, Benjamin	4:33:11 (17,983)	
Collis, Brian	3:34:20 (4,800)	
Collis, James	3:21:58 (2,980)	
Collis, James	3:29:30 (4,092)	
Collodel, Adrien	3:12:41 (1,955)	
Collyer, Daniel	3:51:08 (7,989)	

Collyer, Richard	3:58:28 (9,826)
Colman, Edward	3:57:27 (9,569)
Colman, Ivan	3:15:35 (2,298)
Colman, Mark	3:45:25 (6,811)
Colombage, Don Marcel	4:28:51 (16,951)
Colombo, Matteo	4:27:37 (16,628)
Colquhoun, Adrian	5:13:15 (26,005)
Colquhoun, Ian	3:54:32 (8,793)
Coltman, Geoff	4:47:03 (21,190)
Coltman, Jason	4:31:09 (17,541)
Colton, Eric	5:02:36 (24,409)
Colton, Ivan	3:38:34 (5,507)
Colton, John	3:55:37 (9,081)
Colton, Kevin	5:02:35 (24,404)
Colverson, Nigel	6:53:07 (31,789)
Colville, Edward	6:57:02 (31,859)
Colville, Johnny	4:10:20 (12,425)
Colville, Robert	4:26:36 (16,383)
Colvin, Graham	3:20:17 (2,802)
Colvin, Paul	4:29:53 (17,215)
Colwell, Alistair	4:39:19 (19,403)
Colwell, Nick	4:37:52 (19,060)
Colwell, Stephen	4:00:35 (10,342)
Colyer, Barry	4:54:21 (22,779)
Colyer, Richard	5:30:19 (28,120)
Comb, John	4:39:32 (19,448)
Combe, Ross	4:02:22 (10,711)
Combes, Christian	4:02:10 (10,671)
Combes, Neal	4:37:05 (18,899)
Comer, Royston	5:30:35 (28,150)
Comette, Allan	4:37:09 (18,909)
Commons, Sean	4:22:13 (15,299)
Comninos, Michael	3:07:38 (1,466)
Compean, Aurelio	3:23:50 (3,219)
Compton, Patrick	5:20:30 (26,957)
Comyn, Paul	3:48:56 (7,499)
Concannon, Graham	4:07:09 (11,725)
Concannon, Peter	3:44:00 (6,544)
Concroft, Peter	5:09:03 (25,416)
Condell, John	3:39:32 (5,698)
Condie, Williams	5:24:09 (27,427)
Condon, Edward	5:10:41 (25,645)
Condon, Kieran	4:09:02 (12,142)
Condon, Richard	4:01:43 (10,583)
Condra, Terrence	7:02:53 (31,910)
Coney, Howard	3:46:43 (7,069)
Coney, Richard	3:50:10 (7,767)
Coney, William	4:52:47 (22,457)
Congdon, Andrew	4:42:58 (20,222)
Congram, Derek	3:03:19 (1,136)
Conibear, Stuart	3:09:53 (1,666)
Conisbee, Peter	4:30:15 (17,299)
Conlin, Geoffrey	3:22:21 (3,029)
Conlin, Stephen	3:42:14 (6,193)
Conlon, Michael	3:22:33 (3,053)
Conn, Matthew	6:03:27 (30,391)
Conn, Peter	3:12:08 (1,875)
Conn, Russell	4:58:39 (23,726)
Connaughton, Peter	4:51:03 (22,083)
Connell, Anthony	3:55:48 (9,129)
Connell, Anthony	5:49:58 (29,711)
Connell, Edward	4:18:44 (14,432)
Connell, Martin	4:52:35 (22,411)
Connell, Simon	3:31:35 (4,423)
Connelley, James	4:30:39 (17,402)
Connelly, James	6:16:45 (30,887)
Connett, David	4:28:42 (16,910)
Connick, Brian	4:36:10 (18,682)
Connolly, Brendan	5:18:27 (26,692)
Connolly, Craig	4:07:14 (11,745)
Connolly, Dermot	3:00:33 (978)
Connolly, Gary	3:49:29 (7,629)
Connolly, James	4:39:23 (19,418)
Connolly, John	4:08:13 (11,942)
Connolly, Kevin	3:28:28 (3,897)
Connolly, Kevin	3:31:00 (4,327)
Connolly, Mark	4:41:35 (19,889)
Connolly, Phil	2:59:58 (935)
Connolly, Shane	2:48:41 (353)
Connolly, Stephen	4:16:45 (13,922)
Connolly, Wayne	4:51:32 (22,214)
Connoly, Charles	3:54:11 (8,699)
Connop, David	4:22:12 (15,295)

Connor, Colin....3:23:33 (3,185)
Connor, Dennis....3:30:29 (4,245)
Connor, Hadley....4:47:32 (21,304)
Connor, James....4:52:08 (22,330)
Connor, John....4:16:40 (13,897)
Connor, Matthew....4:11:54 (12,741)
Connor, Paul....3:15:54 (2,328)
Connor, Paul....3:51:11 (8,008)
Connor, Roger....3:23:34 (3,189)
Connor-Stead, Philip....4:09:31 (12,230)
Conquest, Johnny....3:56:10 (9,228)
Conres, Stuart....5:57:01 (30,108)
Consamaro, Michele....3:41:17 (6,010)
Constable, Tim....3:56:15 (9,259)
Constance, Neil....4:21:03 (14,995)
Constantinou, Andreas....5:43:49 (29,293)
Constantinou, Antonios....5:41:21 (29,102)
Conte, Orlando....5:04:01 (24,633)
Conti, Francesco....3:37:18 (5,289)
Contreras, Gabriel....4:51:27 (22,195)
Convers, Jean-Luc....3:29:32 (4,101)
Convery, Paul....5:56:27 (30,077)
Convey, Christopher....4:14:02 (13,270)
Convey, Michael....4:01:39 (10,570)
Conway, John....3:26:36 (3,619)
Conway, Malcolm....4:33:19 (18,008)
Conway, Paul....4:04:27 (11,163)
Conway, Stephen....4:17:36 (14,139)
Conway, Stephen....5:21:37 (27,100)
Conway, Stewart....3:38:55 (5,584)
Conway, Stuart....3:39:16 (5,647)
Conway-Hughes, Ben....4:00:33 (10,339)
Cook, Adrian....4:28:35 (16,883)
Cook, Andrew....4:24:14 (15,805)
Cook, Barry....3:13:11 (2,016)
Cook, Ben....4:10:19 (12,419)
Cook, Cardell....5:10:09 (25,575)
Cook, Christian....4:12:51 (12,971)
Cook, Christopher....3:47:42 (7,255)
Cook, Colin....4:12:59 (13,000)
Cook, Darren....4:12:48 (12,959)
Cook, David....3:21:42 (2,954)
Cook, David....4:14:28 (13,371)
Cook, David....4:23:25 (15,591)
Cook, David....5:23:41 (27,367)
Cook, Dominic....4:56:38 (23,294)
Cook, Douglas....5:07:17 (25,140)
Cook, Gary....3:17:40 (2,512)
Cook, Gary....3:46:12 (6,973)
Cook, Ian....3:35:51 (5,049)
Cook, James....3:53:21 (8,507)
Cook, Jonathan....3:57:50 (9,658)
Cook, Jonathan....4:37:12 (18,923)
Cook, Kenneth....4:09:30 (12,228)
Cook, Lee....6:22:01 (31,075)
Cook, Mark....3:58:38 (9,867)
Cook, Nigel....2:53:57 (530)
Cook, Nigel....3:38:34 (5,507)
Cook, Nikalas....3:48:31 (7,405)
Cook, Paul....3:51:14 (8,016)
Cook, Peter....3:59:25 (10,068)
Cook, Phil....2:40:01 (152)
Cook, Rob....3:16:19 (2,359)
Cook, Robert....4:24:57 (15,981)
Cook, Robert....5:11:49 (25,805)
Cook, Robin....3:52:59 (8,422)
Cook, Roy....5:29:19 (28,020)
Cook, Simon....3:55:13 (8,969)
Cook, Terry....5:38:56 (28,892)
Cook, Tony....5:00:06 (23,994)
Cook, William....5:23:16 (27,320)
Cooke, Alex....3:56:15 (9,259)
Cooke, David....4:39:07 (19,348)
Cooke, David....5:50:32 (29,755)
Cooke, Howard....4:40:48 (19,703)
Cooke, Jason....2:47:48 (324)
Cooke, Jonathan....4:29:24 (17,089)
Cooke, Kevin....3:35:26 (4,984)
Cooke, Michael....6:04:34 (30,432)
Cooke, Peter....5:12:09 (25,842)
Cooke, Richard....3:46:30 (7,028)
Cooksey, Andrew....3:56:45 (9,387)
Cookson, William....4:15:30 (13,640)
Cooley, Anthony....3:00:56 (997)
Cooley, Brian....4:28:43 (16,915)
Coombe, Nick....4:03:53 (11,033)
Coombes, Mike....6:10:35 (30,665)
Coombes, Paul....4:20:12 (14,794)
Coombs, David....5:13:02 (25,980)
Coombs, Michael....4:29:58 (17,234)
Coombs, Philip....3:30:24 (4,231)
Coombs, Richard....3:30:24 (4,231)
Coombs, Robin....3:54:13 (8,712)
Coombs, Stephen....5:20:18 (26,927)
Coop, Harvey....4:17:40 (14,165)
Coope, Adam....3:47:37 (7,241)
Cooper, Alan....3:15:44 (2,310)
Cooper, Allan....3:28:36 (3,925)
Cooper, Andrew....2:44:52 (233)
Cooper, Barry....4:28:56 (16,976)
Cooper, Brian....4:33:38 (18,080)
Cooper, Christopher....4:27:02 (16,480)
Cooper, Colin....4:58:38 (23,725)
Cooper, Craig....3:45:40 (6,863)
Cooper, Daniel....4:43:39 (20,417)
Cooper, David....3:27:54 (3,801)
Cooper, David....5:32:14 (28,310)
Cooper, Douglas....3:00:43 (989)
Cooper, Douglas....5:13:36 (26,057)
Cooper, Gary....5:08:41 (25,356)
Cooper, Gary....5:33:07 (28,379)
Cooper, Glenn....5:05:24 (24,857)
Cooper, Graeme....4:12:20 (12,845)
Cooper, Huw....4:15:52 (13,720)
Cooper, Ian....3:17:24 (2,477)
Cooper, Jason....4:11:49 (12,723)
Cooper, Jay....4:24:47 (15,948)
Cooper, Jeff....5:03:55 (24,622)
Cooper, John....3:52:04 (8,213)
Cooper, Lee....4:16:07 (13,766)
Cooper, Mark....2:34:50 (97)
Cooper, Matthew....4:52:36 (22,415)
Cooper, Michael....3:31:56 (4,463)
Cooper, Mike....4:44:02 (20,504)
Cooper, Neil....3:21:35 (2,939)
Cooper, Neil....3:44:11 (6,577)
Cooper, Neil....3:59:21 (10,053)
Cooper, Neil....4:57:20 (23,449)
Cooper, Nicholas....3:25:48 (3,513)
Cooper, Nigel....4:40:27 (19,643)
Cooper, Paul....4:23:40 (15,662)
Cooper, Paul....4:53:39 (22,643)
Cooper, Philip....3:10:43 (1,730)
Cooper, Robert....3:51:51 (8,165)
Cooper, Robert....4:16:36 (13,876)
Cooper, Robert....4:34:03 (18,176)
Cooper, Roger....4:26:55 (16,453)
Cooper, Stephen....4:15:30 (13,640)
Cooper, Stephen....4:16:35 (13,872)
Cooper, Stephen....5:29:58 (28,083)
Cooper, Vincent....5:50:56 (29,782)
Coopey, Simon....4:17:39 (14,158)
Copas, Robert....3:57:51 (9,663)
Cope, Paul....4:42:52 (20,199)
Cope, Robin....5:34:21 (28,511)
Cope, Trevor....3:46:30 (7,028)
Copeland, Maurice....5:28:46 (27,964)
Copeland, Peter....4:16:57 (13,981)
Copeland, Peter....5:29:57 (28,081)
Copeman, Julian....4:25:52 (16,219)
Copestake, Chris....3:52:11 (8,241)
Copestick, Robin....2:52:42 (481)
Copland, Christopher....4:26:28 (16,347)
Copland, James....3:23:20 (3,153)
Copland, Malcolm....4:56:11 (23,195)
Copleston, Edward....3:38:13 (5,445)
Copley, Ben....3:12:26 (1,919)
Coppack, Ian....4:23:28 (15,607)
Coppelov, Wally....3:20:40 (2,842)
Coppen, Dean....4:42:48 (20,180)
Copping, Paul....5:08:11 (25,295)
Copsey, Simon....4:00:30 (10,327)
Copus, Chris....3:10:45 (1,737)
Coquelin, Philippe....3:28:46 (3,962)
Coram, Tony....5:28:16 (27,921)
Corbett, Brian....4:16:32 (13,864)
Corbett, Oliver....3:47:15 (7,171)
Corbett, Paul....4:51:13 (22,137)
Corbett, Richard....4:49:21 (21,716)
Corbett, Ron....4:20:23 (14,842)
Corbin, Daniel....4:48:07 (21,456)
Corbin, Stuart....4:07:27 (11,796)
Corbould, Stephen....4:06:21 (11,562)
Corby, Nick....4:21:51 (15,194)
Corcoran, James....5:06:41 (25,049)
Corcut, Thomas....3:53:23 (8,510)
Cordall, Michael....3:14:06 (2,140)
Corder, Michael....3:29:25 (4,072)
Cordery, Gary....3:59:33 (10,105)
Cordes, James....4:25:24 (16,117)
Cordiner, Nicky....3:58:33 (9,849)
Cordle, Calvin....3:27:10 (3,700)
Cordwell, James....2:43:00 (199)
Cordwell, Jeff....3:51:50 (8,159)
Corena, Mario....5:57:04 (30,111)
Corfe, Andrew....3:40:34 (5,878)
Coringley, Simon....4:42:52 (20,199)
Cork, David....4:11:22 (12,616)
Cork, Geoffrey....4:25:12 (16,056)
Cork, John....4:40:17 (19,599)
Corke, Adrian....5:09:18 (25,446)
Corlett, Michael....4:43:48 (20,453)
Cormack, David....4:05:49 (11,461)
Cormell, Richard....5:55:43 (30,027)
Cormier, Vincent....4:30:49 (17,449)
Cornelius, Gary....3:57:52 (9,669)
Cornell, Mark....3:48:46 (7,457)
Corner, Dale....3:12:28 (1,923)
Corner, Duncan....5:49:36 (29,689)
Corney, Glenn....3:41:30 (6,067)
Corney, John....4:35:06 (18,414)
Cornish, Alan....3:24:05 (3,263)
Cornish, David....5:25:42 (27,630)
Cornish, Mark....3:25:41 (3,491)
Cornish, Simon....4:15:46 (13,690)
Cornwall, Michael....3:38:30 (5,494)
Cornwall, Paul....5:03:42 (24,574)
Cornwell, Peter....3:39:33 (5,704)
Coronel, Jacques....3:55:55 (9,158)
Corp, Jonathan....3:37:23 (5,305)
Corpe, Jonathan....3:28:33 (3,910)
Correal, Marc....5:25:48 (27,641)
Corrigan, Christopher....4:26:54 (16,448)
Corrigan, John....4:47:08 (21,212)
Corringham, Barry....3:54:16 (8,723)
Corrington, Kevin....5:10:39 (25,643)
Corry, Edward....3:12:26 (1,919)
Corry, James....5:08:50 (25,381)
Corscaden, Antony....5:38:27 (28,853)
Cortat, Bernard....3:29:18 (4,044)
Corters, Javier....2:10:39 (10)
Cortese, Michael....4:14:32 (13,389)
Cortizo, José....4:30:02 (17,248)
Corton, Mark....4:08:40 (12,055)
Cosby, Scott....4:35:45 (18,580)
Cosgrave, James....3:30:50 (4,300)
Cosher, Jamie....4:41:47 (19,938)
Costa, Daniel....4:39:36 (19,459)
Costain, Michael....3:38:56 (5,588)
Costain, Nigel....3:26:43 (3,637)
Costas, Paraskeva....3:08:03 (1,506)
Costas, Paul....3:05:22 (1,278)
Costello, John....5:08:37 (25,350)
Costello, Neil....3:26:41 (3,630)
Costello, Simon....4:50:04 (21,876)
Costellow, Robert....3:39:23 (5,675)
Coster, Malcolm....3:12:06 (1,872)
Costes, Etienne....3:57:39 (9,607)
Costin, Haydn....3:55:45 (9,119)
Cosway, David....4:35:16 (18,465)
Cosway, Mark....5:07:31 (25,186)
Cotin, Arnaud....3:26:30 (3,608)
Cottam, John....4:13:31 (13,130)
Cottam, Mark....3:27:42 (3,769)
Cotterell, Alan....3:47:57 (7,307)
Cotterell, Neil....3:52:01 (8,200)
Cotterill, Mark....3:08:30 (1,547)
Cottis, John....2:58:47 (833)
Cottis, Luke....4:20:31 (14,873)

Cottis, Roy 3:58:05 (9,726)
Cottle, Terry 5:17:55 (26,600)
Cotton, Anthony 3:24:38 (3,347)
Cotton, Chris 4:56:00 (23,148)
Cotton, Ian 4:21:15 (15,044)
Cotton, Simon 3:51:24 (8,051)
Cottrell, David 5:22:20 (27,193)
Cottrell, Michael 4:01:43 (10,583)
Cottrell, Michael 4:05:25 (11,379)
Cottrill, Mark 3:25:17 (3,443)
Couch, Simon 3:45:25 (6,811)
Coudron, Vincent 5:33:28 (28,419)
Coughlan, Matthew 4:11:38 (12,671)
Coull, Graham 4:05:10 (11,325)
Coull, John 3:58:00 (9,706)
Coulson, Andrew 3:04:47 (1,233)
Coulson, Andrew 4:03:43 (10,987)
Coulson, Daniel 3:55:08 (8,947)
Coulson, Jeffrey 3:40:02 (5,793)
Coulson, Joe 5:18:22 (26,680)
Coulson, Paul 5:25:40 (27,627)
Coulson, Stephen 5:18:12 (26,653)
Coulson, Steve 4:52:18 (22,357)
Coulson, Wayne 3:03:13 (1,131)
Coultas, Andrew 7:13:41 (32,027)
Coulthard, William 4:38:50 (19,285)
Counsell, John 5:20:05 (26,899)
Coupe, Michael 3:27:30 (3,738)
Coupe, Paul 3:28:27 (3,893)
Coupe, Richard 6:20:16 (31,024)
Coupland, James 4:28:04 (16,725)
Court, Alistair 4:44:59 (20,711)
Court, Andrew 4:28:43 (16,915)
Court, Ben 4:33:57 (18,153)
Court, Jamie 5:47:04 (29,496)
Court, Kenneth 3:38:44 (5,549)
Court, Michael 3:17:03 (2,433)
Court, Robert 5:31:06 (28,205)
Court, Stephen 5:04:08 (24,654)
Court, Steve 3:24:23 (3,314)
Courtman-Stock, Paul 4:16:12 (13,785)
Courtney, John 5:42:12 (29,185)
Courtney, Kevin 2:57:36 (744)
Courtney, Patrick 4:47:09 (21,218)
Courtney, Sean 3:47:25 (7,196)
Cousens, Charles 4:40:46 (19,696)
Cousens, Matthew 3:52:35 (8,328)
Cousin, Tony 5:10:22 (25,602)
Cousins, Anthony 4:40:55 (19,732)
Cousins, Jason 3:44:43 (6,674)
Cousins, Jeremy 3:48:21 (7,386)
Cousins, Paul 2:56:43 (683)
Cousins-Jenvey, Bengt 4:07:26 (11,788)
Coutts, David 4:32:10 (17,767)
Coutts-Wood, Charles 3:02:32 (1,089)
Cova Caiazzo, Silverio 2:57:43 (750)
Covell, David 4:16:54 (13,964)
Coventry, Andrew 4:03:03 (10,855)
Coventry, James 4:13:35 (13,146)
Coventry, Neil 6:33:42 (31,417)
Coventry, Paul 6:34:16 (31,431)
Covey, Sean 3:28:02 (3,820)
Covey, Wayne 5:04:42 (24,733)
Covi Stolfa, Franco 3:12:02 (1,865)
Covington, Neil 3:17:07 (2,441)
Cowan, Andrew 4:31:29 (17,612)
Cowan, Christopher 4:58:37 (23,722)
Cowan, Elliot 3:49:56 (7,723)
Cowan, Kevin 5:10:09 (25,575)
Cowan, Nicholas 4:23:37 (15,643)
Cowan, Paul 3:53:43 (8,593)
Coward, Andrew 3:53:07 (8,453)
Cowburn, Chris 4:43:48 (20,453)
Cowdrey, Paul 4:39:19 (19,403)
Cowdrill, Gary 4:20:02 (14,757)
Cowell, Clayden 4:48:24 (21,517)
Cowell, Courtney 4:29:05 (17,010)
Cowell, Peter 4:38:27 (19,190)
Cowell, Philip 3:47:59 (7,316)
Cowen, Stephen 4:53:21 (22,586)
Cowland, Dan 4:35:05 (18,411)
Cowley, Ian 3:23:10 (3,132)
Cowley, James 6:17:20 (30,901)
Cowley, John 4:26:47 (16,427)
Cowley, John 5:42:48 (29,229)
Cowley, Julian 4:52:49 (22,466)
Cowley, Shane 5:25:19 (27,590)
Cowling, Jeff 3:57:07 (9,481)
Cowls, Stephen 4:19:54 (14,716)
Cox, Andrew 3:16:11 (2,346)
Cox, Andrew 4:09:07 (12,156)
Cox, Andrew 4:49:03 (21,644)
Cox, Bob 5:33:19 (28,403)
Cox, Chris 4:50:22 (21,935)
Cox, Darren 4:31:07 (17,533)
Cox, Darryl 4:51:39 (22,235)
Cox, David 3:26:26 (3,595)
Cox, David 3:49:53 (7,706)
Cox, David 4:40:12 (19,584)
Cox, Garry 5:20:36 (26,973)
Cox, George 4:54:04 (22,723)
Cox, Glen 2:47:10 (305)
Cox, Ian 4:05:13 (11,333)
Cox, James 3:34:27 (4,830)
Cox, John 2:43:19 (204)
Cox, John 4:28:48 (16,935)
Cox, John 5:22:24 (27,202)
Cox, Jon 3:18:17 (2,589)
Cox, Jonathan 5:38:28 (28,854)
Cox, Marcus 5:56:01 (30,044)
Cox, Mark 4:21:07 (15,011)
Cox, Mark 4:48:53 (21,609)
Cox, Nicholas 6:53:07 (31,789)
Cox, Oliver 3:45:22 (6,799)
Cox, Peter 5:53:43 (29,917)
Cox, Peter 5:58:56 (30,205)
Cox, Raymond 3:51:17 (8,025)
Cox, Raymond 4:34:58 (18,388)
Cox, Richard 4:51:21 (22,167)
Cox, Richard 5:25:07 (27,557)
Cox, Robert 3:50:00 (7,734)
Cox, Simon 3:54:29 (8,776)
Cox, Stephen 3:41:12 (5,988)
Cox, Stephen 4:14:19 (13,333)
Cox, Stewart 3:03:57 (1,181)
Cox, Timothy 4:05:26 (11,390)
Cox, Troy 5:18:10 (26,647)
Cox, Vivion 3:58:59 (9,962)
Coxhead, Ian 3:01:49 (1,042)
Coxon, Christopher 5:49:03 (29,643)
Coyle, Bernard 4:01:11 (10,470)
Coyle, Brendan 4:24:10 (15,789)
Coyle, Eddie 3:17:48 (2,530)
Coyle, Graham 5:19:38 (26,841)
Coyle, John 4:02:49 (10,811)
Coyle, Stephen 4:59:51 (23,959)
Coyle, Terence 2:55:27 (615)
Coyne, Andrew 4:45:37 (20,874)
Coyne, Dominic 4:38:21 (19,175)
Coyne, Michael 4:14:14 (13,312)
Coyne, Timothy 5:13:19 (26,014)
Cozens, Christopher 5:30:43 (28,168)
Cozens, Colin 4:17:14 (14,041)
Crabb, Jonathan 6:25:06 (31,163)
Crabbe, Martin 4:51:21 (22,167)
Crabtree, Ian 3:12:50 (1,972)
Crabtree, Ian 4:59:46 (23,935)
Crabtree, Mark 2:55:58 (648)
Crabtree, Michael 3:10:13 (1,696)
Crabtree, Nicholas 3:51:23 (8,045)
Crabtree, Peter 3:50:11 (7,773)
Cradden, Brendan 3:30:09 (4,193)
Craddock, Peter 3:49:38 (7,665)
Crader, Michael 3:49:47 (7,696)
Cradock, Jonas 4:56:11 (23,195)
Crafer, Gary 4:07:34 (11,824)
Craft, David 4:07:32 (11,819)
Cragg, Melvyn 3:14:13 (2,155)
Cragg, Stephen 4:17:36 (14,139)
Cragg, Stephen 4:37:58 (19,080)
Craggs, Douglas 4:15:49 (13,707)
Craig, Andrew 3:44:54 (6,707)
Craig, Jim 3:11:41 (1,819)
Craig, John 4:32:47 (17,894)
Craig, Michael 5:50:05 (29,722)
Craig, Robert 3:12:00 (1,861)
Craig, Scott 4:50:04 (21,876)
Craig, Wayne 4:59:03 (23,812)
Cramer, Wil 4:21:36 (15,132)
Cramery, Anthony 3:40:51 (5,932)
Cramp, Howard 4:54:54 (22,903)
Crampton, Ian 2:31:48 (73)
Crampton, Paul 4:19:53 (14,714)
Crandon, Stephen 4:18:45 (14,438)
Crane, Dean 6:22:14 (31,081)
Crane, Robert 4:52:19 (22,362)
Crane, Terence 4:22:39 (15,409)
Crane, Timothy 4:15:28 (13,631)
Crane, William 3:31:41 (4,432)
Cranfield, Nicholas 5:00:26 (24,057)
Cranford, Wayne 4:58:14 (23,633)
Crank, David 5:12:33 (25,909)
Cranmer, Jason 4:55:49 (23,114)
Cranston, Mark 5:12:32 (25,901)
Craplet, Xavier 4:34:53 (18,369)
Cratchley, Neil 4:13:42 (13,176)
Craven, Paul 4:40:04 (19,552)
Craven, Philip 4:09:25 (12,211)
Craven, Richard 4:22:46 (15,434)
Cravo E Silva, Rui 4:51:56 (22,297)
Crawford, Bruce 4:09:38 (12,256)
Crawford, Daniel 4:44:29 (20,612)
Crawford, David 4:25:18 (16,086)
Crawford, Desmond 4:36:57 (18,866)
Crawford, Graham 3:44:48 (6,690)
Crawford, James 4:17:27 (14,102)
Crawford, Peter 4:27:16 (16,539)
Crawford, Robert 3:55:29 (9,044)
Crawley, Ian 3:12:15 (1,891)
Crawley, Mark 3:56:10 (9,228)
Crawley, Matthew 4:51:24 (22,178)
Crawley, Michael 4:12:42 (12,937)
Crawley, Stephen 3:25:50 (3,516)
Crawley, Steven 3:34:45 (4,873)
Crawley, Steven 4:55:45 (23,097)
Crawley, William 3:47:34 (7,228)
Crawshaw, Andrew 4:13:25 (13,100)
Crawshaw, John 4:24:47 (15,948)
Cray, Matthew 3:57:07 (9,481)
Crease, Gregory 3:46:41 (7,063)
Creasey, Daniel 3:59:14 (10,014)
Creech, Stuart 3:04:00 (1,184)
Creedon, Patrick 3:41:12 (5,988)
Creer, Dean 3:36:00 (5,064)
Creer, Matthew 6:48:43 (31,688)
Creese, John 4:05:01 (11,294)
Creese, Lee 4:25:02 (16,010)
Creighton, David 5:28:07 (27,902)
Creighton, Stephen 4:50:15 (21,909)
Cremonini, William 3:50:57 (7,933)
Crenol, Kevin 2:43:44 (214)
Creric, Vincent 5:23:08 (27,305)
Cressman, David 4:18:24 (14,330)
Cressot, Dominique 4:22:59 (15,489)
Creus, Paul 5:38:37 (28,869)
Crew, Danny 3:30:50 (4,300)
Crew, Kevin 3:05:02 (1,255)
Crewe, Ian 5:14:49 (26,220)
Cribbis, Michael 4:59:17 (23,855)
Crichton, Daniel 3:32:01 (4,475)
Cripps, Graham 5:06:54 (25,094)
Cripps, Kevin 4:33:08 (17,976)
Cripps, Paul 3:52:06 (8,223)
Cripps, Stephen 3:52:05 (8,219)
Criscuolo, Ciro 5:40:02 (28,998)
Crisp, Jim 2:55:10 (603)
Crisp, John 3:14:42 (2,206)
Crisp, Matthew 4:21:50 (15,190)
Crispie, Gerard 2:51:59 (442)
Critchell, Norman 3:48:31 (7,405)
Critchfield, John 3:49:19 (7,593)
Critchley, David 4:18:34 (14,380)
Critchley, Lee 5:15:23 (26,302)
Critchley, Mark 5:10:24 (25,608)
Critchley, Matthew 5:07:55 (25,254)
Croal, Jeremy 4:02:38 (10,766)
Crocker, Jeremy 4:28:10 (16,756)
Crockett, Geoffrey 5:06:26 (25,011)
Crockford, John 2:52:40 (479)

Croft, Anthony 3:23:51 (3,221)
Croft, Colin 3:42:23 (6,216)
Croft, Stuart 5:09:31 (25,476)
Croft, Tim 4:55:33 (23,037)
Crofts, Alexander 4:53:07 (22,525)
Crofts, Joe 4:42:17 (20,050)
Crole-Rees, Matt 4:44:01 (20,500)
Cromby, Michael 3:54:07 (8,684)
Crompton, Matthew 5:14:12 (26,120)
Crompton, Neil 2:42:43 (189)
Cromwell, Darren 6:25:41 (31,190)
Crone, Colin 4:03:51 (11,025)
Cronin, Brian 4:22:15 (15,306)
Cronin, Damien 3:48:35 (7,420)
Cronin, David 4:59:35 (23,900)
Cronin, John 4:31:05 (17,520)
Cronk, David 3:23:53 (3,230)
Cronshaw, John 3:59:57 (10,211)
Crook, David 3:33:36 (4,692)
Crook, Mark 5:45:26 (29,401)
Crook, Warren 3:18:51 (2,641)
Crookes, Philip 3:59:22 (10,060)
Crooks, Alistair 3:25:37 (3,478)
Crooks, Melvyn 3:57:26 (9,564)
Crooks, Neil 3:21:15 (2,905)
Crooks, Robert 6:17:54 (30,927)
Croom, Robert 6:18:22 (30,955)
Croome, Jonathan 3:07:30 (1,452)
Cropper, Neil 4:00:47 (10,381)
Crosby, Kenneth 3:39:43 (5,731)
Crosby, Peter 3:44:00 (6,544)
Crosby, Trevor 3:57:29 (9,576)
Cross, Anthony 3:11:57 (1,857)
Cross, Daniel 4:08:32 (12,019)
Cross, David 4:26:35 (16,375)
Cross, Gary 5:05:57 (24,947)
Cross, Jonathan 4:27:16 (16,539)
Cross, Julian 3:30:06 (4,186)
Cross, Mark 3:38:37 (5,521)
Cross, Michael 3:27:08 (3,697)
Cross, Michael 4:57:16 (23,439)
Cross, Peter 3:30:31 (4,247)
Cross, Peter 5:21:33 (27,089)
Cross, Richard 4:51:48 (22,267)
Cross, Stephen 5:03:19 (24,507)
Cross, Stewart 5:24:45 (27,501)
Cross, William 3:58:09 (9,743)
Crosse, Matthew 3:29:10 (4,021)
Crosse, Roger 3:55:16 (8,983)
Crossing, Leigh 3:27:48 (3,780)
Crossley, Anthony 3:24:09 (3,273)
Crossley, Mark 4:32:26 (17,820)
Crossman, David 3:51:06 (7,976)
Crosswell, Julian 6:16:25 (30,873)
Crotaz, Gary 4:33:44 (18,104)
Crothers, Alastair 4:35:25 (18,501)
Crouch, Alan 4:18:42 (14,423)
Crouch, Blake 4:17:22 (14,074)
Crouch, Nicholas 4:45:38 (20,876)
Crouch, Nicholas 5:27:35 (27,845)
Crouch, Steven 4:35:13 (18,449)
Crouch, Thomas 3:23:23 (3,160)
Croucher, Alan 5:32:49 (28,359)
Crough, Andrew 3:42:50 (6,324)
Crow, Christopher 5:33:30 (28,421)
Crow, George 4:25:53 (16,224)
Crow, Graham 4:35:33 (18,527)
Crow, Gregory 5:49:06 (29,644)
Crow, Ian 4:44:09 (20,527)
Crow, Mike 6:50:37 (31,735)
Crow, Paul 4:20:38 (14,895)
Crow, Peter 3:25:42 (3,496)
Crowder, David 4:37:15 (18,937)
Crowder, John 4:46:50 (21,154)
Crowe, David 3:44:40 (6,661)
Crowe, Leslie 5:40:57 (29,073)
Crowe, Quentin 4:28:06 (16,735)
Crowfoot, Geoff 5:00:33 (24,078)
Crowhurst, Colin 5:22:07 (27,155)
Crowley, David 4:10:22 (12,431)
Crowley, Gregory 3:17:55 (2,538)
Crowley, James 6:07:27 (30,553)
Crowley, John 3:32:50 (4,572)
Crowley, Peter 4:59:43 (23,927)
Crowley, Vincent 2:54:03 (539)
Crowther, Bill 2:32:29 (76)
Crowther, George 6:01:31 (30,323)
Crowther, Mark 5:26:44 (27,756)
Crozier, John 3:46:09 (6,962)
Crozier, Peter 3:13:03 (1,998)
Crudgington, Neil 4:58:17 (23,645)
Cruickshank, Andrew 2:55:46 (632)
Cruickshank, Darren 5:14:23 (26,156)
Cruickshank, George 4:47:37 (21,322)
Cruickshank, Kevin 3:41:09 (5,985)
Cruickshank, Mike 3:12:30 (1,929)
Cruickshank, Sandy 3:26:41 (3,630)
Crump, Jason 4:56:42 (23,316)
Crumpler, Russell 3:48:59 (7,511)
Crumpton, Anthony 4:08:45 (12,078)
Crunp, Graham 3:53:48 (8,618)
Cruse, Peter 3:01:55 (1,048)
Crush, Graham 4:36:40 (18,800)
Crush, Peter 5:18:43 (26,730)
Crutch, Nicholas 3:37:46 (5,381)
Cruz, Carlos 3:37:32 (5,330)
Cryer, Simon 5:05:37 (24,905)
Crystal, Roger 4:39:35 (19,454)
Cubbon, Andrew 5:18:09 (26,642)
Cubley, Simon 4:05:36 (11,418)
Cudahy, Mark 3:23:12 (3,136)
Cuddihy, Marc 3:32:07 (4,486)
Cuerden, John 5:22:30 (27,212)
Cuff, Paul 3:22:06 (2,995)
Cuffe, James 3:29:23 (4,062)
Cuffe, John 5:30:15 (28,106)
Cugliari, Giuseppe 5:02:56 (24,448)
Cull, Alan 5:16:21 (26,410)
Cull, Matt 3:27:48 (3,780)
Cullen, Martin 4:13:13 (13,055)
Cullen, Tom 4:18:30 (14,359)
Cullern, Doug 4:51:18 (22,152)
Culling, Adam 3:59:36 (10,119)
Cullis, Stephen 3:07:36 (1,460)
Culmer, Glen 5:11:34 (25,770)
Culwin, Fintan 4:42:12 (20,029)
Cumber, Geoffrey 2:57:30 (733)
Cumbers, Leonard 5:06:29 (25,014)
Cumberworth, Paul 4:21:49 (15,188)
Cumming, Colin 5:56:12 (30,061)
Cumming, Richard 5:14:51 (26,227)
Cummings, Dennis 4:43:22 (20,342)
Cummings, Graham 4:38:07 (19,113)
Cummings, Grant 2:50:54 (417)
Cummings, Stuart 4:03:13 (10,884)
Cummins, Barry 5:22:27 (27,205)
Cummins, Brian 4:54:24 (22,795)
Cummins, Jaime 4:14:08 (13,293)
Cummins, Kevin 4:48:00 (21,427)
Cummins, Nicholas 4:49:50 (21,832)
Cummins, Paul 4:20:51 (14,944)
Cummins, Tim 4:48:06 (21,451)
Cumpsty, Samuel 4:23:57 (15,737)
Cunliffe, Graham 2:48:53 (362)
Cunliffe, Thomas 5:13:30 (26,042)
Cunningham, Colin 3:46:38 (7,058)
Cunningham, Darren 4:34:18 (18,241)
Cunningham, Graham 5:51:08 (29,792)
Cunningham, John 2:50:41 (406)
Cunningham, John 4:06:33 (11,601)
Cunningham, Justin 3:21:22 (2,919)
Cunningham, Lindsay 3:01:07 (1,010)
Cunningham, Michael 3:20:50 (2,864)
Cunningham, Michael 4:40:55 (19,732)
Cunningham, Nigel 4:49:55 (21,849)
Cunningham, Patrick 4:43:05 (20,256)
Cunningham, Paul 3:26:36 (3,619)
Cunningham, Paul 4:08:06 (11,923)
Cunningham, Philip 3:03:01 (1,116)
Cunningham, Richard 5:10:21 (25,601)
Cunningham, Simon 5:14:22 (26,153)
Cunningham, Steve 3:02:45 (1,099)
Curial, Christian 4:26:55 (16,453)
Curless, Brent 4:17:38 (14,152)
Curley, Paul 4:42:25 (20,088)
Curling, Nick 4:39:17 (19,391)
Curnow, Anthony 4:59:03 (23,812)
Curphey, Paul 2:48:34 (350)
Curran, Mike 5:01:39 (24,252)
Curran, Patrick 2:32:23 (75)
Curran, Philip 3:24:05 (3,263)
Curran, Ray 3:02:41 (1,094)
Curran, Stephen 4:41:24 (19,848)
Curran, Thomas 4:30:37 (17,396)
Curran, Tony 3:47:39 (7,247)
Currell, Andrew 4:19:44 (14,679)
Currell, Geoffrey 3:53:56 (8,653)
Curren, Gerard 4:21:17 (15,054)
Currie, Andy 6:23:06 (31,107)
Currie, John 3:25:47 (3,509)
Currie, Lyndon 3:30:23 (4,230)
Curry, John 4:00:55 (10,411)
Curson, Robin 4:16:20 (13,815)
Curtin, Jeff 2:55:57 (647)
Curtin, Thomas 3:14:00 (2,129)
Curtis, Adrian 4:58:29 (23,696)
Curtis, Dan 6:00:46 (30,286)
Curtis, Derrick 6:59:43 (31,883)
Curtis, John 4:05:42 (11,433)
Curtis, Martyn 4:42:20 (20,062)
Curtis, Michael 5:03:46 (24,587)
Curtis, Peter 4:39:28 (19,434)
Curtis, Raymond 4:23:16 (15,565)
Curtis, Richard 4:38:15 (19,143)
Curtis, Robert 3:31:56 (4,463)
Curtis, Sean 4:15:08 (13,550)
Curtis, Steven 2:55:08 (601)
Curtis, Stuart 4:51:58 (22,303)
Curtis, Tony 3:57:45 (9,632)
Curzon, Frank 4:36:57 (18,866)
Curzon-Hope, Steven 4:22:40 (15,412)
Cusack, Martin 5:16:30 (26,427)
Cushing, Andrew 3:47:24 (7,195)
Cushing, George 4:30:45 (17,431)
Cushion, Robert 3:02:57 (1,111)
Cuthbert, Kevin 3:59:05 (9,977)
Cuthbert, Matthew 3:34:24 (4,819)
Cuthbert, Philip 3:03:05 (1,123)
Cutin, Noel 2:58:49 (835)
Cutler, Darren 4:47:27 (21,287)
Cutler, John 4:25:54 (16,231)
Czaja, Alan 4:05:53 (11,478)
Czarnocki, Chris 3:53:47 (8,613)
Czerwinski, David 4:38:14 (19,142)
Dabbs, Jonathan 3:29:13 (4,030)
Dable, Thomas 4:53:16 (22,564)
Daborn, David 4:04:47 (11,245)
Dabrowski, Barry 3:40:42 (5,903)
Dack, Paul 4:34:34 (18,298)
Dacre, James 4:08:07 (11,924)
Dadge, Lucia 6:25:28 (31,177)
Dadge, Michael 6:51:35 (31,752)
Dadge, Nigel 4:30:09 (17,269)
Dadge, Steven 6:25:29 (31,178)
Dadomo, Robert 3:46:15 (6,983)
Dady, Stephen 3:41:48 (6,113)
Daelemans, Ronald 3:47:45 (7,267)
Daelemans, Vincent 3:55:04 (8,929)
Daffarn, Oliver 3:41:21 (6,025)
Dagnan, Emmanuel 5:10:22 (25,602)
Dagnell, Adam 5:05:27 (24,867)
Dagnin, Sean 5:05:24 (24,857)
Dagonnot, Peter 4:51:03 (22,083)
Dagwell, Andrew 6:37:46 (31,503)
Dahabiyeh, Hassan 4:18:48 (14,446)
Dahl, Jan Inge 2:46:01 (256)
Dahlborg, Gunnar 3:02:19 (1,078)
Dahlen, Arne 5:05:41 (24,917)
Dahlgaard, Karsten 3:26:28 (3,602)
Daines, Colin 4:57:27 (23,468)
Dakin, Andrew 4:58:07 (23,611)
Dakin, Philip 4:24:42 (15,915)
Dal Cero, Michele 3:11:01 (1,758)
Dal Pra, Luca 5:00:35 (24,083)
D'Albertanson, Stephen 5:12:50 (25,949)
Dalby, Peter 4:27:18 (16,550)
Dalby, Robin 4:55:59 (23,144)
Dale, Adrian 3:07:06 (1,416)
Dale, David 4:17:23 (14,082)

Dale, Jonathan	4:18:54	(14,479)
Dale, Peter	7:08:39	(31,979)
Dale, Richard	3:29:00	(4,001)
Daley, John	5:21:28	(27,076)
Daley, Kevin	4:24:35	(15,883)
Daley, Nigel	5:26:52	(27,764)
Daley, Nik	5:25:26	(27,601)
Daley, Tony	4:34:32	(18,295)
Daley, Trev	6:17:45	(30,915)
Dalgleish, Duncan	5:34:32	(28,525)
Dalglish, Kenneth	3:58:27	(9,823)
Dallal, Yasser	5:39:20	(28,926)
Dalling, Kevin	4:23:48	(15,695)
Dallman, Neil	3:47:48	(7,277)
Dally, James	4:27:50	(16,677)
Dally, Paul	4:21:06	(15,004)
Dalton, Andrew	4:25:26	(16,126)
Dalton, Anthony	4:29:17	(17,057)
Dalton, Mark	4:37:57	(19,075)
Dalton, Nicholas	4:12:44	(12,946)
Daly, Fergus	4:43:48	(20,453)
Daly, Ian	6:18:42	(30,961)
Daly, James	4:21:19	(15,066)
Daly, Jon	4:31:29	(17,612)
Daly, Mark	3:24:12	(3,285)
Daly, Neil	4:28:51	(16,951)
Daly, Stephen	2:43:50	(215)
Dalziel, Andrew	7:22:27	(32,088)
D'Ambrosio, Gino	4:17:54	(14,230)
Damianopoulos, Andrew	4:47:48	(21,375)
Damon, Peter	2:33:12	(84)
Dampier, James	4:22:49	(15,447)
Dance, David	4:41:52	(19,966)
Dance, John	5:09:31	(25,476)
Dance, Nigel	4:59:17	(23,855)
Dance, Richard	3:13:51	(2,107)
Danciger, Simon	2:45:04	(236)
Dand, James	5:37:01	(28,739)
Dangauthier, Jean-Philippe	5:14:46	(26,212)
Dangerfield, Andrew	4:05:06	(11,309)
Daniel, David	4:01:48	(10,598)
Daniel, George	4:24:22	(15,835)
Daniel, Gil	3:38:35	(5,511)
Daniel, Jeremy	4:55:00	(22,921)
Daniel, Richard	3:56:29	(9,313)
Daniel, Roger	7:11:24	(32,006)
Daniel, Yves	3:30:25	(4,237)
Daniell, Alexander	4:32:24	(17,816)
Daniels, Andrew	4:18:28	(14,347)
Daniels, Clive	4:03:19	(10,916)
Daniels, Duncan	3:58:41	(9,882)
Daniels, Gary	4:53:16	(22,564)
Daniels, Hugh	4:27:02	(16,480)
Daniels, Kevin	4:07:28	(11,799)
Daniels, Michael	4:08:55	(12,112)
Daniels, Phelim	4:00:30	(10,327)
Daniels, Steven	4:15:07	(13,544)
Danielsen, Claus	4:50:00	(21,856)
Danks, Peter	5:42:28	(29,207)
Danks, Simon	3:31:09	(4,351)
Dann, Peter	4:10:01	(12,353)
Dannatt, Oliver	5:23:09	(27,310)
Danquah, Ben	3:47:11	(7,155)
Dansey, Martin	5:21:29	(27,079)
Danskin, Ian	3:17:09	(2,444)
D'Antona, Giovanni	4:00:15	(10,278)
Danvers, Benjamin	2:51:44	(438)
Darbon, Clive	5:55:01	(29,999)
Darby, Gareth	5:57:07	(30,115)
Darby, Paul	4:36:17	(18,707)
Darby, Paul	4:46:12	(21,018)
Darbyshire, Malcolm	3:14:15	(2,158)
D'Arcy, Lee	4:13:51	(13,216)
Dargaville, Sheldon	4:21:17	(15,054)
Darius, Simon	2:58:57	(846)
Darke, Tony	4:16:29	(13,854)
Darker, Laurence	4:47:12	(21,226)
Dart, James	5:29:45	(28,065)
Darvill, Matthew	5:12:13	(25,859)
Das, Bidan	4:00:46	(10,379)
D'Asero, Carmelo	4:00:15	(10,278)
Dash, Elliot	5:01:44	(24,266)
Dashper, Wayne	2:31:13	(69)

Dattani, Dilip	3:52:03	(8,206)
Dattani, Kunal	6:05:21	(30,471)
Dauchez, Julien	3:43:55	(6,530)
Daugherty, Brian	3:40:57	(5,950)
Daugherty, Duane	3:48:16	(7,371)
Daultrey, Paul	3:56:58	(9,444)
Daum, Peter	5:08:24	(25,327)
Daunay, Jean-Jacques	3:36:50	(5,199)
Dauncey, Stephen	4:55:52	(23,122)
Daurat, Alain	3:46:30	(7,028)
Davaney, Martin	4:04:12	(11,112)
Davenhill, Jason	3:10:50	(1,742)
Davenny, William	5:38:54	(28,889)
Davenport, Dan	3:52:58	(8,412)
Davenport, Richard	5:07:34	(25,197)
Davenport, Robert	4:30:46	(17,438)
Davenport, Will	5:39:53	(28,979)
Daversa, Tomano	3:03:02	(1,117)
Davey, Andrew	4:58:17	(23,645)
Davey, Christopher	4:34:03	(18,176)
Davey, Clement	4:03:08	(10,871)
Davey, Clive	4:58:48	(23,766)
Davey, Howard	3:11:04	(1,763)
Davey, Ian	5:24:51	(27,513)
Davey, John	4:14:51	(13,466)
Davey, Keiron	3:44:49	(6,691)
Davey, Kevin	2:58:09	(780)
Davey, Mark	3:56:29	(9,313)
Davey, Matthew	3:06:56	(1,396)
Davey, Michael	5:39:38	(28,959)
Davey, Patrick	4:58:18	(23,653)
Davey, Richard	5:54:13	(29,944)
Davey-Sinclair, John	6:30:24	(31,338)
Davey-Sinclair, Matthew	5:19:50	(26,863)
David, George	4:40:56	(19,736)
David, Paul	4:20:44	(14,914)
Davidge, James	4:40:17	(19,599)
Davidson, Adrian	4:34:08	(18,198)
Davidson, Alistair	5:13:33	(26,050)
Davidson, Chris	4:17:41	(14,172)
Davidson, Crawford	4:08:28	(12,002)
Davidson, David	4:03:32	(10,953)
Davidson, David	5:16:17	(26,400)
Davidson, George	3:43:37	(6,469)
Davidson, George	4:20:30	(14,868)
Davidson, James	5:35:58	(28,637)
Davidson, John	3:59:13	(10,007)
Davidson, Kenneth	3:20:00	(2,760)
Davidson, Kent	3:49:32	(7,639)
Davidson, Leonard	5:36:15	(28,659)
Davidson, Michael	4:44:20	(20,577)
Davidson, Paul	5:54:03	(29,934)
Davidson, Peter	4:03:31	(10,945)
Davidson, Sean	5:00:42	(24,106)
Davie, Barry	4:01:03	(10,439)
Davies, Adam	4:54:40	(22,857)
Davies, Adrian	4:24:19	(15,822)
Davies, Adrian	4:31:38	(17,652)
Davies, Alan	4:15:07	(13,544)
Davies, Alan	5:36:19	(28,665)
Davies, Alan	6:22:59	(31,103)
Davies, Andrew	3:56:05	(9,203)
Davies, Andrew	4:20:23	(14,842)
Davies, Andrew	4:59:19	(23,859)
Davies, Ben	4:49:08	(21,655)
Davies, Brian	3:55:50	(9,139)
Davies, Carl	4:13:47	(13,195)
Davies, Charles	4:32:09	(17,764)
Davies, Chris	5:11:14	(25,727)
Davies, Christopher	3:51:34	(8,097)
Davies, Clive	2:50:07	(391)
Davies, Conrad	4:05:00	(11,289)
Davies, Daniel	4:59:43	(23,927)
Davies, Daniel	5:02:36	(24,409)
Davies, David	4:25:41	(16,177)
Davies, Desmond	3:49:33	(7,642)
Davies, Dilwyn	4:47:16	(21,237)
Davies, Gareth	3:37:14	(5,278)
Davies, Gareth	3:38:37	(5,521)
Davies, Gareth	4:15:05	(13,536)
Davies, Gareth	4:39:26	(19,427)
Davies, Gareth	4:42:28	(20,101)
Davies, Gary	7:06:35	(31,951)

Davies, Gavin	4:53:40	(22,647)
Davies, Gawain	3:35:14	(4,947)
Davies, Geraint	4:00:54	(10,407)
Davies, Glynn	5:35:03	(28,556)
Davies, Gregory	4:32:51	(17,913)
Davies, Haydn	5:40:24	(29,029)
Davies, Huw	3:59:14	(10,014)
Davies, Ian	4:12:34	(12,907)
Davies, James	5:34:04	(28,484)
Davies, John	3:11:37	(1,815)
Davies, John	4:03:33	(10,957)
Davies, John	4:06:45	(11,643)
Davies, John	4:49:34	(21,766)
Davies, Jonathan	3:17:33	(2,496)
Davies, Keith	2:53:42	(514)
Davies, Kevin	4:07:35	(11,830)
Davies, Lee	4:34:14	(18,220)
Davies, Leighton	3:29:55	(4,155)
Davies, Leslie	4:31:25	(17,595)
Davies, Lewis	2:54:19	(554)
Davies, Malcolm	4:34:35	(18,301)
Davies, Mark	3:39:50	(5,754)
Davies, Mark	3:41:20	(6,023)
Davies, Martin	5:13:16	(26,009)
Davies, Matt	5:46:43	(29,477)
Davies, Matthew	4:07:29	(11,808)
Davies, Michael	3:13:21	(2,041)
Davies, Michael	3:25:15	(3,440)
Davies, Michael	4:57:01	(23,384)
Davies, Neal	4:19:12	(14,551)
Davies, Neil	5:37:00	(28,737)
Davies, Neville	5:01:47	(24,279)
Davies, Nicholas	3:02:10	(1,071)
Davies, Nicholas	4:39:41	(19,471)
Davies, Nicholas	4:54:41	(22,861)
Davies, Nigel	3:34:23	(4,814)
Davies, Nigel	3:40:44	(5,909)
Davies, Paul	3:54:12	(8,705)
Davies, Paul	4:02:03	(10,647)
Davies, Paul	4:42:06	(20,009)
Davies, Paul	4:48:01	(21,433)
Davies, Peter	4:14:14	(13,312)
Davies, Rhys	4:43:01	(20,241)
Davies, Richard	3:54:38	(8,827)
Davies, Richard	3:57:46	(9,638)
Davies, Richard	4:41:14	(19,810)
Davies, Richard	4:46:42	(21,124)
Davies, Robert	4:19:39	(14,652)
Davies, Robert	4:31:45	(17,680)
Davies, Robert	4:56:42	(23,316)
Davies, Roger	3:53:34	(8,561)
Davies, Roger	4:20:06	(14,770)
Davies, Samuel	4:35:11	(18,438)
Davies, Sean	4:02:47	(10,803)
Davies, Shaun	3:59:12	(10,004)
Davies, Shaun	5:39:57	(28,989)
Davies, Simon	3:13:15	(2,028)
Davies, Stuart	4:37:04	(18,892)
Davies, Thomas	3:26:11	(3,564)
Davies, Thomas	3:41:43	(6,094)
Davies, Tom	4:22:01	(15,244)
Davies, Trevor	3:19:36	(2,710)
Davies, Vivian	6:04:47	(30,446)
Davies, Wil	3:46:15	(6,983)
Davies, William	3:30:27	(4,243)
Davies, Wyn	5:10:56	(25,685)
Davis, Adrian	4:19:18	(14,572)
Davis, Andrew	3:11:57	(1,857)
Davis, Andrew	4:13:24	(13,093)
Davis, Anthony	3:24:24	(3,319)
Davis, Chris	5:25:24	(27,597)
Davis, Faye	6:03:06	(30,379)
Davis, Ivan	4:01:35	(10,558)
Davis, James	3:26:15	(3,573)
Davis, James	3:41:12	(5,988)
Davis, James	4:52:52	(22,477)
Davis, Joe	3:50:29	(7,838)
Davis, John	4:35:13	(18,449)
Davis, Kenneth	5:24:01	(27,410)
Davis, Kevin	3:56:54	(9,422)
Davis, Lee	5:34:08	(28,490)
Davis, Mark	2:57:46	(755)
Davis, Mark	4:18:24	(14,330)

Davis, Mark 4:18:46 (14,440)
Davis, Mark 4:53:49 (22,684)
Davis, Mark 5:11:07 (25,709)
Davis, Mark 5:13:27 (26,034)
Davis, Martin 2:53:13 (499)
Davis, Martin 3:40:39 (5,891)
Davis, Matthew 3:58:30 (9,837)
Davis, Michael 5:15:43 (26,346)
Davis, Oliver 5:30:21 (28,125)
Davis, Paul 4:12:35 (12,909)
Davis, Richard 3:27:54 (3,801)
Davis, Richard 3:59:07 (9,986)
Davis, Robert 3:38:20 (5,462)
Davis, Robert 5:18:11 (26,651)
Davis, Scott 3:23:50 (3,219)
Davis, Simon 3:44:58 (6,727)
Davis, Simon 4:34:24 (18,266)
Davis, Stephen 4:44:44 (20,668)
Davison, Alan 3:33:03 (4,606)
Davison, John 6:16:24 (30,871)
Davison, Mark 3:21:17 (2,909)
Davison, Robert 4:32:55 (17,928)
Davison, Robin 5:26:12 (27,700)
Davison, Stephen 4:41:28 (19,866)
Davitt, Patrick 3:47:19 (7,177)
Davy, Jason 6:17:44 (30,914)
Davy, John 4:50:30 (21,968)
Davy, Paul 3:30:24 (4,231)
Dawber, Nigel 3:21:40 (2,949)
Dawe, James 6:30:53 (31,347)
Dawe, Nicholas 4:24:44 (15,928)
Dawes, Paul 3:42:38 (6,280)
Dawes, Paul 5:12:50 (25,949)
Dawes, Peter 3:42:53 (6,337)
Dawes, Timothy 5:18:04 (26,620)
Dawkins, Jonathan 5:00:56 (24,144)
Dawkins, Neil 3:51:35 (8,100)
Dawney, Kevin 5:07:43 (25,226)
Dawson, Alan 3:03:08 (1,127)
Dawson, Anthony 4:56:05 (23,166)
Dawson, Christophe 4:22:09 (15,276)
Dawson, Daniel 4:19:09 (14,541)
Dawson, David 4:05:52 (11,473)
Dawson, Garth 3:33:15 (4,639)
Dawson, Glen 4:18:47 (14,442)
Dawson, Gordon 5:39:33 (28,953)
Dawson, Ian 4:30:54 (17,468)
Dawson, Jamie 4:53:35 (22,635)
Dawson, Jeremy 3:53:40 (8,585)
Dawson, Mark 3:51:18 (8,032)
Dawson, Max 5:22:50 (27,258)
Dawson, Neil 4:43:53 (20,478)
Dawson, Patrick 3:57:41 (9,613)
Dawson, Paul 4:11:20 (12,606)
Dawson, Paul 4:18:22 (14,322)
Dawson, Paul 4:24:57 (15,981)
Dawson, Peter 4:44:09 (20,527)
Dawson, Philip 3:51:30 (8,074)
Dawson, Robert 4:42:29 (20,104)
Dawson, Roger 4:47:07 (21,208)
Dawson, Stephen 3:37:00 (5,229)
Dawson, Steve 3:05:01 (1,250)
Dawson, Steven 4:55:43 (23,083)
Dawson, Stuart 5:10:06 (25,567)
Day, Barry 3:41:16 (6,000)
Day, Barry 4:56:04 (23,161)
Day, Brian 5:33:48 (28,452)
Day, Christopher 5:11:46 (25,798)
Day, Colin 3:33:42 (4,701)
Day, David 3:19:30 (2,701)
Day, David 4:29:26 (17,098)
Day, Grant 3:45:42 (6,868)
Day, Harry 3:43:59 (6,541)
Day, Jim 6:18:53 (30,969)
Day, John 3:52:52 (8,386)
Day, Kevin 4:04:50 (11,252)
Day, Nicholas 5:04:47 (24,757)
Day, Norman 3:44:22 (6,615)
Day, Russell 5:05:58 (24,948)
Day, Steve 3:32:33 (4,534)
Day, Tom 3:28:28 (3,897)
Day, Warren 3:54:40 (8,831)
Day, William 4:33:11 (17,983)
Daykin, Eric 5:41:40 (29,133)
Dayman, Graham 5:28:21 (27,925)
D'Conceicao, Glenn 5:40:31 (29,035)
De Baene, Edwin 3:28:29 (3,900)
De Bruyn, Marino 5:03:15 (24,500)
De Charentenay, Ghislain 3:51:27 (8,062)
De Clerk, Jason 5:03:04 (24,467)
De Courcy-Grylls, Christopher 3:39:03 (5,607)
De Coverly, Marcus 5:12:04 (25,836)
De Ferry Forster, Harry 4:52:58 (22,499)
De Frateschi, Michael 3:33:23 (4,663)
De Guelle, Basil 4:27:36 (16,624)
De Jong, Theo 4:02:02 (10,642)
De Jonge, Michiel 3:48:53 (7,486)
De Klerk, Stijn 4:04:30 (11,180)
De Kock, Johannes 5:23:27 (27,344)
De La Hoz-Vega, Fernando 4:11:26 (12,627)
De La Torre-Arce, Rodrigo 4:00:50 (10,396)
De Lange, Leyton 3:50:59 (7,946)
De Las Morenas, Enrique 5:32:42 (28,350)
De Luca, Paolo 3:08:58 (1,583)
De Luca, Patrick 3:19:41 (2,723)
De Montfort, John 3:23:55 (3,235)
De Nul, Dirk 4:50:11 (21,900)
De Oliveira, José 2:54:02 (537)
De Pao, Andrew 3:45:22 (6,799)
De Rienzo, Roberto 4:56:29 (23,255)
De Roeper, Simon 4:54:42 (22,866)
De Silva, Lester 4:46:58 (21,177)
De Swardt, Arnold 4:33:42 (18,098)
De Swardt, Frans 4:22:28 (15,355)
De Turckheim, Eric 4:36:18 (18,713)
De Wan, Peregrine 5:13:47 (26,081)
De Willbois, Ian W Van Der Does 4:18:02 (14,257)
Deacon, James 4:05:24 (11,373)
Deacon, Richard 6:45:31 (31,631)
Deacon, Scott 4:26:20 (16,323)
Deakin, Andrew 5:06:59 (25,103)
Deakin, Nicholas 3:44:18 (6,598)
Dean, Gary 2:58:31 (800)
Dean, Jonathan 3:48:59 (7,511)
Dean, Joseph 3:39:57 (5,773)
Dean, Ken 4:21:59 (15,236)
Dean, Kevin 4:34:48 (18,351)
Dean, Mark 3:22:12 (3,011)
Dean, Mark 3:39:18 (5,655)
Dean, Martin 4:09:47 (12,295)
Dean, Michael 3:25:58 (3,537)
Dean, Paul 4:07:03 (11,698)
Dean, Philip 3:51:42 (8,128)
Dean, Philip 4:18:36 (14,392)
Dean, Rupert 4:05:06 (11,309)
Dean, Russell 4:56:21 (23,230)
Dean, Sean 6:01:20 (30,317)
Dean, Shaun 5:49:51 (29,704)
Dean, Stephen 6:10:24 (30,654)
Dean, Stuart 4:23:16 (15,565)
Dean, Trevor 3:18:20 (2,595)
Deane, Alan 4:54:49 (22,885)
Deane, James 3:25:27 (3,458)
Deans, Jamie 3:57:13 (9,509)
Deans, Martin 4:00:17 (10,291)
Dear, Graham 7:05:58 (31,941)
Dear, Jay 5:08:41 (25,356)
Dear, Richard 4:48:15 (21,482)
Dear, Richard 5:09:51 (25,521)
Dear, Simon 4:55:45 (23,097)
Deardon, Raymond 7:16:21 (32,047)
Deards, Sam 4:54:04 (22,723)
Dearsley, Tony 3:10:37 (1,724)
Debekker, Alain 5:09:40 (25,499)
Debney, Graham 4:53:23 (22,591)
Debney, Richard 4:26:40 (16,395)
Debney, Richard 4:56:38 (23,294)
Debricon, Jean-Marc 4:59:42 (23,925)
Debruyne, Lieven 3:51:04 (7,971)
Debruyne, Patrick 3:30:05 (4,180)
Decent, Michael 5:12:35 (25,917)
Declerck, Guido 3:19:41 (2,723)
Decourcy, Graham 3:17:55 (2,538)
Dector-Vega, German 4:22:36 (15,394)
De-Dieuleveult, Emmanuel 3:09:15 (1,605)
Deding, Jan 3:21:19 (2,915)
Dee, Jonathon 4:58:40 (23,727)
Dee, William 2:50:22 (397)
Deegan, John 3:33:21 (4,652)
Deegan, Richard 3:24:45 (3,364)
Deehan, Packy 3:10:36 (1,723)
Deely, James 4:28:45 (16,922)
Deeprose, William 3:30:15 (4,210)
Deery, Mark 3:32:29 (4,528)
Deetlefs, Eduan 3:59:43 (10,160)
Degnarain, Ashvin 4:17:57 (14,241)
Dehayen, Alexander 4:43:47 (20,449)
Deighton, Matthew 3:27:56 (3,807)
Deken, Simon 3:23:47 (3,211)
Delafollie, Gerard 4:11:18 (12,598)
De-La-Garde, Eric 3:39:44 (5,734)
Delahay, Mark 5:32:19 (28,321)
Delahyes, Michel 4:29:03 (17,004)
Delamare, Paul 5:14:27 (26,167)
Delaney, John 5:03:49 (24,597)
Delaney, Mark 5:20:35 (26,971)
Delaney, Patrick 5:18:05 (26,624)
Delano, Julian 2:58:45 (828)
Delany, John 3:11:22 (1,786)
Delaross, Paul 4:41:38 (19,896)
Delauney, Michael 4:46:34 (21,100)
Delbue, Guido 4:56:25 (23,242)
Delcroix, Jean-Guy 5:37:36 (28,782)
Delderfield, Martin 4:14:19 (13,333)
Delessio, Michael 4:07:32 (11,819)
Delgado-Peralta, Eugenio 3:33:11 (4,627)
Delgardo-Criado, Manuel 2:48:19 (346)
Delhoy, Mark 4:49:44 (21,809)
Dell, Andrew 3:23:37 (3,194)
Dell, Graeme 5:23:08 (27,305)
Dell, Gregory 2:37:41 (128)
Della Mea, Ennio 3:36:27 (5,135)
Dellar, Peter 3:09:07 (1,595)
Dellen, David 2:59:21 (885)
Deller, John 4:43:25 (20,354)
Dell'Oro, Dean 3:11:27 (1,800)
Delmaine, John 5:00:10 (24,004)
Delmas, Nicolas 3:50:19 (7,805)
Delpierre, Yann 3:36:13 (5,098)
Delsol, Thierry 4:41:59 (19,987)
Deluca, Jean-François 4:11:33 (12,656)
Delves-Broughton, Alex 4:38:18 (19,161)
Demaine, Michael 4:31:16 (17,561)
Demarest, Philippe 6:05:14 (30,466)
Denbow, Nicholas 5:24:09 (27,427)
Denby, Nigel 4:19:37 (14,647)
Dench, Gary 2:52:02 (444)
Dench, John 5:09:15 (25,439)
Denelly, Jon 4:10:35 (12,480)
Denham, Paul 3:48:13 (7,362)
Denham, Simon 3:38:56 (5,588)
Denis, Daniel 4:20:43 (14,907)
Denison, Paul 5:44:15 (29,322)
Denman, Stephen 6:16:00 (30,859)
Dennett, Peter 3:44:01 (6,553)
Denning, Jason 5:39:51 (28,976)
Dennington, Paul 3:39:42 (5,727)
Dennis, Paul 3:28:34 (3,913)
Dennis, Paul 5:30:14 (28,102)
Dennis, Paul 6:02:59 (30,372)
Dennison, Carl 4:57:42 (23,522)
Dennison, Mark 4:05:29 (11,399)
Denny, Mark 3:59:09 (9,991)
Denny, Mark 4:11:30 (12,649)
Denny, Paul 4:18:07 (14,274)
Denny, Paul 4:55:10 (22,956)
Denny, Reg 4:39:08 (19,353)
Densham, Stephen 4:35:50 (18,608)
Dent, Adrian 5:21:42 (27,108)
Dent, Andrew 3:33:21 (4,652)
Dent, Andrew 4:25:18 (16,086)
Dent, David 3:37:07 (5,257)
Denton, Chris 3:13:54 (2,115)
Denton, Keith 4:04:20 (11,142)
Denton, Paul 4:22:20 (15,324)
Denwood, Tom 3:17:57 (2,543)
Denyer, Billy 3:11:04 (1,763)
Depaoli, Andrea 3:44:09 (6,571)
Derbyshire, Stephen 5:14:42 (26,203)

Derda, Patrick 4:46:21 (21,061)
Derksen, Adrianus 4:34:02 (18,172)
Derrett, Don 4:40:08 (19,565)
Derrett, Joseph 4:40:52 (19,721)
Derrick, Ian 3:52:10 (8,237)
Derube, Alain 4:43:21 (20,336)
De-Rugy, Laurent 3:46:52 (7,097)
De-Ryck, Xavier 4:55:28 (23,021)
Des Forges, Rupert 4:29:17 (17,057)
Descamps, Daniel 3:41:16 (6,000)
Descamps, Fabrice 3:29:10 (4,021)
Desforges, Malcolm 5:11:45 (25,792)
Dessoy, Craig 3:46:26 (7,017)
D'Esteve-De-Pradel, Luc 3:23:05 (3,125)
Detante, Gilles 3:50:33 (7,854)
Deutschmann, Werner 5:35:49 (28,620)
Devane, Timothy 3:48:58 (7,507)
Devaney, Michael 3:33:24 (4,666)
Deverell, Mark 5:02:17 (24,359)
Deverill, Kevin 5:28:04 (27,897)
Devine, Brian 3:49:31 (7,637)
Devine, Joseph 4:23:48 (15,695)
Devine, Michael 3:42:21 (6,209)
Devine, Robert 4:23:26 (15,595)
Devine, Stephen 4:23:19 (15,578)
Devine, William 5:01:07 (24,171)
Devitt, Russell 3:18:45 (2,629)
Devlin, Brian 3:19:50 (2,737)
Devlin, Giles 4:18:33 (14,372)
Dewar, David 3:41:06 (5,979)
Dewar, Paul 3:17:09 (2,444)
Dewhurst, Brian 2:44:16 (225)
Dewhurst, John 4:38:01 (19,093)
Dewick, Bill 4:54:24 (22,795)
Dewsbury, Glyn 4:01:48 (10,598)
Dewsbury, Stephen 4:27:03 (16,488)
Dexter, Colin 5:28:03 (27,895)
Dhar, Zeeshan 4:41:30 (19,870)
Dhellin, Alain 3:46:10 (6,966)
Dherbecourt, Gerard 3:23:24 (3,162)
Dhondt, Peter 4:44:44 (20,668)
Di Fabio, Sergio 3:55:21 (9,008)
Di Turi, Leonardo 3:20:08 (2,775)
Diab, Amr 4:55:42 (23,079)
Diallo, Zakaria 4:13:41 (13,170)
Diamond, Mark 7:09:15 (31,983)
Diamond, Peter 3:28:15 (3,857)
Diaper, Thomas 3:42:41 (6,295)
Diaz, Fernand 4:23:12 (15,547)
Diaz Barriga Herrero, David 3:26:02 (3,544)
Diaz Barriga Quiroz, David 3:35:20 (4,963)
Diaz Orbegoso, Nelson 3:38:33 (5,504)
Dibble, Harley 3:28:34 (3,913)
Dibble, Kevin 4:59:34 (23,897)
Dick, Andrew 3:30:35 (4,258)
Dick, Michael 3:10:43 (1,730)
Dickens, Stephen 2:59:40 (916)
Dickens, Theo 4:43:49 (20,464)
Dickenson, Andrew 2:45:43 (249)
Dickenson, David 3:55:14 (8,974)
Dickenson, Robert 3:05:02 (1,255)
Dicker, Clive 4:17:18 (14,057)
Dickerson, Joseph 3:47:53 (7,299)
Dickinson, Christopher 4:03:10 (10,875)
Dickinson, David 5:13:13 (26,002)
Dickinson, David 6:49:51 (31,715)
Dickinson, John 3:46:55 (7,108)
Dickinson, Jonathan 3:48:49 (7,469)
Dickinson, Justin 4:03:12 (10,881)
Dickinson, Mary 3:38:17 (5,458)
Dickinson, Paul 3:25:19 (3,445)
Dickinson, Robert 2:57:38 (747)
Dickinson, Stephen 4:31:20 (17,579)
Dickinson, Stephen 4:49:05 (21,648)
Dickson, Alan 4:22:42 (15,420)
Dickson, Colin 3:19:45 (2,728)
Dickson, Graham 3:57:51 (9,663)
Dickson, Hugh 5:26:44 (27,756)
Dickson, Kevin 3:43:04 (6,380)
Dickson, Robert 3:13:34 (2,069)
Diddams, Greg 3:02:54 (1,106)
Diegnan, Lee 4:12:09 (12,799)
Diego, Clifford 4:01:18 (10,495)
Dielen, Thom 4:19:24 (14,594)
Diemer, Christopher 4:05:46 (11,447)
Dietsch, Sebastien 3:40:54 (5,943)
Dietsch, Serge 4:13:59 (13,258)
Diffey, Peter 5:18:24 (26,683)
Diffley, James 5:24:25 (27,461)
Digby-Baker, Hugh 3:35:48 (5,040)
Diggins, Jess 5:15:18 (26,290)
Diggle, Tim 4:46:41 (21,122)
Dill, John 4:13:24 (13,093)
Dillane, Stephen 3:58:46 (9,909)
Dilley, Stephen 4:55:36 (23,053)
Dillin, Jason 3:37:51 (5,392)
Dillon, Donal 3:37:58 (5,409)
Dillon, Geoff 4:43:48 (20,453)
Dillon, James 4:52:49 (22,466)
Dillon, Kevin 5:25:20 (27,592)
Dillon, Max 3:19:58 (2,757)
Dillon, Nick 4:48:55 (21,618)
Dillon, Oliver 4:34:28 (18,281)
Dills, Robert 4:02:46 (10,798)
Dimbleby, Peter 3:07:33 (1,458)
Dimelow, Geoffrey 3:39:28 (5,686)
Dimmock, Howard 4:37:51 (19,058)
Dimmock, Paul 3:20:49 (2,862)
Dinan, Dominic 3:52:29 (8,306)
Dine, Roger 3:38:29 (5,492)
Dines, Mick 4:15:06 (13,539)
Dines, Ross 4:02:40 (10,774)
Dingwall, James 2:47:30 (316)
Dinsdale, Paul 4:28:17 (16,785)
Dinsey, Eric 4:42:42 (20,159)
Dinsmore, David 4:01:23 (10,516)
Dinsmore, Edward 4:25:46 (16,190)
Dinter, Martin 4:30:53 (17,464)
Dintner, Norbert 4:15:44 (13,679)
Dionisio, Tiago 4:51:34 (22,217)
Dipede, Ryan 4:15:02 (13,520)
Dipple, Robert 4:08:25 (11,984)
Dipple, Stephen 4:54:23 (22,790)
Dipre, Stephen 3:12:45 (1,962)
Diprose, Jan 3:57:30 (9,580)
Dirubba, Domenico 4:02:12 (10,678)
Dischinger, Karl-Heinz 3:54:35 (8,813)
Diston, David 7:18:14 (32,058)
Dite, Chris 5:48:38 (29,613)
Dittrich, Lee 4:07:58 (11,899)
Divialle, David 3:27:29 (3,736)
Dix, Peter 4:23:02 (15,500)
Dixon, Alistair 4:38:34 (19,213)
Dixon, Andrew 3:46:31 (7,035)
Dixon, Charles 3:37:28 (5,321)
Dixon, Christopher 4:45:57 (20,948)
Dixon, Clem 3:02:06 (1,061)
Dixon, Davey 5:13:52 (26,087)
Dixon, David 4:21:19 (15,066)
Dixon, Declan 4:50:23 (21,939)
Dixon, Garry 3:33:05 (4,611)
Dixon, Geoff 5:27:07 (27,792)
Dixon, Graeme 3:51:32 (8,086)
Dixon, Huw 3:40:49 (5,930)
Dixon, Marcel 6:57:03 (31,860)
Dixon, Mark 4:31:24 (17,592)
Dixon, Michael 5:28:22 (27,928)
Dixon, Paul 4:17:30 (14,112)
Dixon, Peter 3:41:55 (6,135)
Dixon, Stuart 3:56:30 (9,318)
Dixon, Thomas 3:50:38 (7,871)
Dixon-Gough, Richard 3:55:41 (9,103)
Djelil, Dino 5:14:50 (26,224)
Djemal, Jay 4:56:05 (23,166)
Doak, Ian 4:31:06 (17,525)
Dobbie, David 4:23:40 (15,662)
Dobbie, James 3:48:30 (7,400)
Dobbs, Andrew 3:55:15 (8,978)
Dobbs, Gary 5:08:06 (25,280)
Dobbs, Patrick 2:57:36 (744)
Dobbs, Simon 2:40:34 (160)
Dobby, Brett 4:32:48 (17,898)
Dobie, Ronald 4:16:01 (13,746)
Doble, Malcolm 4:27:22 (16,563)
Doble, Paul 3:34:32 (4,843)
Dobson, Alan 4:16:35 (13,872)
Dobson, Andrew 4:38:35 (19,221)
Dobson, Andrew 5:01:09 (24,176)
Dobson, Glen 4:03:31 (10,945)
Dobson, John 4:43:40 (20,423)
Dobson, Jonathan 4:48:17 (21,491)
Dobson, Spencer 3:31:03 (4,337)
Docherty, Brian 3:49:55 (7,719)
Docherty, Hugh 4:14:46 (13,437)
Docherty, Stephen 4:33:08 (17,976)
Dodanis, Christos 3:03:58 (1,183)
Dodaro, Gianfranco 6:53:45 (31,802)
Dodd, Andrew 3:07:12 (1,430)
Dodd, David 3:41:39 (6,087)
Dodd, Jason 5:09:45 (25,514)
Dodd, John 5:33:43 (28,438)
Dodd, Richard 5:52:47 (29,871)
Dodd, Simon 5:05:32 (24,890)
Dodd, Toby 4:43:57 (20,487)
Doddington, Steve 4:48:21 (21,509)
Dodgson, Arthur 5:17:47 (26,577)
Dodsley, Stuart 4:04:08 (11,098)
Dodson, Edward 3:48:54 (7,489)
Dodson, Martin 3:06:18 (1,338)
Dodson, Richard 5:41:34 (29,125)
Dodwell, Edward 3:01:21 (1,015)
Dodwell, Stephen 4:12:35 (12,909)
Doggett, Christopher 4:35:19 (18,476)
Doherty, Andrew 5:20:58 (27,019)
Doherty, Barney 5:55:52 (30,037)
Doherty, Danny 4:17:53 (14,225)
Doherty, Frank 4:51:10 (22,125)
Doherty, Ian 3:00:20 (957)
Doherty, Jackie 3:26:31 (3,610)
Doherty, James 4:40:22 (19,623)
Doherty, Johnny 5:55:51 (30,034)
Doherty, Martin 5:46:58 (29,487)
Doherty, Neil 3:29:34 (4,105)
Doherty, Patrick 4:11:26 (12,627)
Doherty, Paul 5:05:49 (24,935)
Doherty, Peter 5:33:51 (28,459)
Doherty, Stephen 4:59:19 (23,859)
Dohollo, Laurent 4:12:46 (12,953)
Doig, Gavin 4:13:31 (13,130)
Doig, Ross 4:22:00 (15,241)
Doktor, Bernd 4:35:11 (18,438)
Dolan, James 7:35:31 (32,185)
Dolan, Patrick 4:10:42 (12,500)
Dolan, Robert 3:16:04 (2,334)
Dolan, Robert 3:50:19 (7,805)
Dolan, Timothy 5:01:01 (24,159)
Dolan, Vincent 4:33:38 (18,080)
Dolby, Richard 3:57:27 (9,569)
Dolby, Stuart 5:23:49 (27,384)
Dolman, Antony 4:49:17 (21,698)
Dolphin, Christopher 3:47:49 (7,285)
Domenget, Jean Pierre 5:21:30 (27,081)
Dominikowski, Jerzy 3:05:23 (1,280)
Dommett, Robert 6:29:44 (31,321)
Don, Ian 5:40:25 (29,031)
Donaghey, Douglas 7:03:31 (31,918)
Donaghey, Michael 6:20:43 (31,037)
Donaghy, Colin 4:28:04 (16,725)
Donaghy, James 5:03:31 (24,532)
Donaghy, James 5:13:39 (26,062)
Donaghy, Simon 4:46:05 (20,990)
Donaire, Manuel 3:19:19 (2,681)
Donald, Chris 3:43:17 (6,422)
Donald, Ian 3:45:43 (6,876)
Donald, John 4:17:31 (14,115)
Donald, Stephen 4:51:34 (22,217)
Donaldson, Drew 2:56:21 (663)
Donaldson, James 4:05:44 (11,440)
Donaldson, Neil 4:38:09 (19,124)
Donaldson, Ray 3:16:36 (2,385)
Donaldson, Robert 4:10:26 (12,454)
Donaldson, Sam 5:52:35 (29,859)
Donegan, Jeremy 5:54:23 (29,963)
Donegan, Paul 3:53:44 (8,598)
Donegan, Stephen 4:19:29 (14,611)
Donkin, Arthur 4:45:14 (20,776)
Donkin, David 3:58:28 (9,826)
Donkin, Robert 3:35:15 (4,951)
Donnachie, Jim 4:41:42 (19,919)

Donnan, Graeme	3:24:27 (3,325)	
Donnan, James	6:29:21 (31,309)	
Donne, Tudor	4:27:07 (16,502)	
Donnell-Jones, David	5:09:32 (25,481)	
Donnelly, Andrew	3:18:09 (2,574)	
Donnelly, Fintan	3:31:22 (4,388)	
Donoghue, Christopher	3:10:05 (1,683)	
Donoghue, Fergal	4:05:01 (11,294)	
Donoghue, Gary	4:26:24 (16,334)	
Donoghue, John	3:47:49 (7,285)	
Donoghue, John	5:19:53 (26,869)	
Donoghue, Kevin	4:31:13 (17,550)	
Donohoe, James	4:47:50 (21,385)	
Donohoe, Matthew	4:39:21 (19,414)	
Donohue, Brendan	5:21:44 (27,117)	
Donohue, Richard	5:39:14 (28,923)	
Donougher, Ian	3:45:42 (6,868)	
Donovan, Alan	4:14:47 (13,445)	
Donovan, James	5:19:13 (26,783)	
Donovan, Peter	3:30:31 (4,247)	
Donovan, Ray	3:25:11 (3,425)	
Donovan, Richard	4:07:24 (11,784)	
Donovan, Roy	4:37:40 (19,012)	
Donovan, Sean	4:30:11 (17,282)	
Dooey, John	5:01:19 (24,209)	
Doolan, James	4:01:40 (10,572)	
Doolan, Philip	3:38:40 (5,535)	
Dooley, Andrew	4:25:07 (16,031)	
Dooley, Brian	4:24:46 (15,941)	
Dooley, John	3:54:04 (8,678)	
Doran, Colin	5:31:54 (28,279)	
Doran, Peter	4:33:46 (18,108)	
Dordoy, Laurence	4:51:02 (22,079)	
Doris, William	4:10:38 (12,491)	
Dorman, Edgar	4:29:06 (17,014)	
Dornan, Mark	3:27:00 (3,681)	
Dornbusch, Vincent	4:10:57 (12,532)	
Dorr, Martyn	4:52:21 (22,369)	
Dorrill, Martin	3:00:45 (991)	
Dorrity, Barry	5:28:32 (27,943)	
Dorsett, Mark	4:56:54 (23,361)	
Dorsey, William	3:55:04 (8,929)	
Dorward, Neil	3:38:32 (5,502)	
Dos Ramos, Roy	5:26:06 (27,686)	
Doshi, Anish	5:56:50 (30,091)	
Doshi, Rajen	4:24:03 (15,766)	
Dossett, Steve	4:34:33 (18,296)	
Dotterweich, Werner	2:54:35 (566)	
Doubie, Steve	3:23:38 (3,197)	
Double, Michael	4:43:22 (20,342)	
Double, Neil	4:20:07 (14,774)	
Doucelin, Daniel	4:47:00 (21,184)	
Dougherty, Simon	5:18:07 (26,639)	
Douglas, Keith	4:16:44 (13,914)	
Douglas, Neil	2:46:44 (287)	
Douglas, Patrick	4:00:44 (10,376)	
Douglas, Paul	2:54:21 (555)	
Douglas, Paul	5:40:33 (29,038)	
Douglas, Philip	3:09:52 (1,663)	
Douglas, Richard	3:54:42 (8,837)	
Douglas, Robert	4:21:56 (15,217)	
Douglas, Roger	6:20:43 (31,037)	
Douglas, Stephen	6:34:13 (31,428)	
Douglas, Stuart	4:39:25 (19,423)	
Douglas, William	3:40:35 (5,883)	
Douglas-Browne, Roger	3:52:05 (8,219)	
Douglass, Paul	4:53:11 (22,541)	
Douglass, Simon	3:15:30 (2,289)	
Douguet, Eric	3:09:15 (1,605)	
Dourlen, Jean-Marie	3:01:35 (1,029)	
Douse, Chris	4:49:10 (21,667)	
Doust, Tom	4:40:19 (19,614)	
Dove, Chris	4:51:54 (22,291)	
Dove, Christopher	4:19:41 (14,665)	
Dovedi, Stephen	3:36:26 (5,133)	
Dover, Terry	3:14:44 (2,209)	
Dow, Colin	4:04:27 (11,163)	
Dow, Iain	4:46:45 (21,136)	
Dow, James	4:29:34 (17,127)	
Dowall, Matthew	4:46:20 (21,054)	
Dowd, Christopher	4:14:47 (13,445)	
Dowd, David	3:00:09 (949)	
Dowdall, William	7:11:22 (32,005)	
Dowden, Anthony	3:28:29 (3,900)	
Dowdeswell, Phillip	5:16:20 (26,407)	
Dowell, Perry	6:13:45 (30,790)	
Dowley, Nicholas	3:49:54 (7,712)	
Dowling, Andrew	4:47:59 (21,424)	
Dowling, Eurene	4:06:51 (11,659)	
Dowling, Michael	3:36:31 (5,146)	
Dowling, Paul	3:50:15 (7,788)	
Down, Craig	3:43:36 (6,465)	
Downer, Dave	4:45:25 (20,824)	
Downer, Michael	3:44:54 (6,707)	
Downes, Chris	4:47:50 (21,385)	
Downes, Henry	4:30:12 (17,287)	
Downes, Ryk	5:18:02 (26,614)	
Downey, Colin	4:43:36 (20,404)	
Downey, James	5:30:41 (28,162)	
Downey, Kevin	5:22:08 (27,157)	
Downham, Ian	3:44:45 (6,684)	
Downie, David	4:30:59 (17,491)	
Downie, Peter	3:47:07 (7,145)	
Downing, David	5:23:55 (27,397)	
Downing, Michael	6:37:35 (31,499)	
Downing, Nick	4:40:45 (19,694)	
Downing, Simon	4:42:46 (20,172)	
Downing, Terence	3:48:38 (7,430)	
Downs, David	4:30:39 (17,402)	
Downs, Simon	5:32:36 (28,339)	
Downton, Brendan	4:08:55 (12,112)	
Dowse, Ian	3:51:44 (8,132)	
Dowsett, Darren	5:51:21 (29,801)	
Dowsett, Frederick	3:30:47 (4,294)	
Dowsett, Matthew	3:27:32 (3,745)	
Dowson, Jason	2:58:14 (785)	
Doyle, Alan	3:56:41 (9,372)	
Doyle, Alastair	2:58:31 (800)	
Doyle, Andrew	4:19:23 (14,589)	
Doyle, Dennis	4:00:53 (10,403)	
Doyle, Gavin	5:00:57 (24,145)	
Doyle, James	3:46:32 (7,041)	
Doyle, James	4:17:11 (14,030)	
Doyle, Michael	4:08:46 (12,084)	
Doyle, Noel	5:04:37 (24,718)	
Doyle, Patrick	4:08:46 (12,084)	
Doyle, Simon	4:02:56 (10,832)	
Doyle, Tim	4:34:50 (18,355)	
Doyle, Timothy	5:07:44 (25,230)	
Doyle, Tony	3:55:40 (9,098)	
Dragazis, Dimitri	6:16:13 (30,863)	
Drain, Paul	3:58:16 (9,775)	
Drake, Gavin	5:47:18 (29,515)	
Drake, Justin	4:37:02 (18,887)	
Drake, Sean	4:46:14 (21,026)	
Drakesmith, Timon	3:42:01 (6,153)	
Dransfield, Lee	4:09:47 (12,295)	
Dransfield, Paul	4:15:41 (13,671)	
Draper, Kevin	4:10:21 (12,428)	
Draper, Martin	4:06:21 (11,562)	
Draper, Nicholas	4:04:25 (11,157)	
Draper, Robert	5:17:26 (26,531)	
Draper, Tim	3:51:34 (8,097)	
Dray, Alan	5:16:18 (26,404)	
Dray, Philip	5:09:07 (25,424)	
Dray, Philip	5:31:46 (28,260)	
Draycott, Gerald	4:24:19 (15,822)	
Drebold, Jors	4:29:58 (17,234)	
Dreher, Garry	4:24:00 (15,751)	
Drennan, Wesley	3:33:12 (4,629)	
Drever, Jason	6:23:24 (31,117)	
Drew, Barrington	5:12:35 (25,917)	
Drew, Chris	5:17:11 (26,502)	
Drew, Christopher	4:34:37 (18,311)	
Drew, David	4:27:46 (16,669)	
Drew, James	4:30:23 (17,336)	
Drew, Nathan	4:29:28 (17,107)	
Drew, Peter	4:28:08 (16,748)	
Drew, Philip	4:56:58 (23,371)	
Drew, Philip	5:09:54 (25,527)	
Drewell, Daniel	5:31:04 (28,198)	
Drewery, Ian	4:37:42 (19,020)	
Drewett, James	4:20:10 (14,788)	
Drewett, Nicholas	3:53:18 (8,496)	
Drexler, Hans	5:00:35 (24,083)	
Driehuijs, Sander	4:56:44 (23,324)	
Drigani, Flavio	3:19:01 (2,656)	
Drinkell, Andrew	4:14:55 (13,482)	
Drinkwater, Anthony	3:23:52 (3,226)	
Driscoll, Craig	4:31:40 (17,663)	
Driver, Andrew	3:58:19 (9,788)	
Driver, Gary	3:44:52 (6,698)	
Driver, Marlon	4:18:20 (14,309)	
Driver, Ronnie	4:31:05 (17,520)	
Driza, Wolfgang	3:14:33 (2,190)	
Drouillard, John	4:04:03 (11,075)	
Drozario, Paul-John	3:50:44 (7,894)	
Druce, Edward	4:10:06 (12,373)	
Druet Ampuero, José Maria	3:40:10 (5,826)	
Drumm, Brian	3:46:27 (7,020)	
Drumm, Paul	4:09:58 (12,345)	
Drummond, James	4:23:11 (15,541)	
Drummond, Matthew	4:38:58 (19,318)	
Drummond, Michael	3:59:14 (10,014)	
Drummond, Samuel	2:54:08 (544)	
Drury, Chris	6:03:02 (30,377)	
Drury, Richard	4:22:44 (15,425)	
Dry, Peter	3:52:56 (8,402)	
Dryden, Marc	4:07:18 (11,756)	
Dsouza, Derrick	4:16:21 (13,820)	
Du Plessis, Jaco	3:39:41 (5,724)	
Du Plessis, Michael	3:37:52 (5,394)	
Du Plessis, Nico	5:58:51 (30,194)	
Du Toit, Hendrik	3:11:00 (1,756)	
Dubbey, Martin	4:25:58 (16,242)	
Dubey, Elliot	5:08:33 (25,342)	
Dubos, Gilbert	4:01:48 (10,598)	
Dubrevil, Pascal	3:16:49 (2,405)	
Duck, Alex	3:39:50 (5,754)	
Duck, Christopher	4:11:39 (12,677)	
Duckworth, Kevin	2:52:44 (482)	
Duckworth, Myles	5:01:12 (24,183)	
Duckworth, Philip	4:16:46 (13,927)	
Duckworth-Chad, James	3:39:59 (5,782)	
Dudack, Lee	5:15:35 (26,329)	
Duddell, Michael	5:26:15 (27,706)	
Duddell, Stephen	2:49:46 (386)	
Duddridge, Mark	5:14:45 (26,207)	
Duddy, Brendan	3:54:42 (8,837)	
Dudek, Bree	4:01:34 (10,555)	
Dudfield, John	4:18:08 (14,278)	
Dudfield, Philip	3:33:01 (4,602)	
Dudley, Dennis	4:22:13 (15,299)	
Dudney, Alan	5:09:41 (25,504)	
Dudok, John	4:02:08 (10,664)	
Duell, Kevin	3:32:27 (4,524)	
Duff, Christopher	5:48:45 (29,617)	
Duff, Peter	4:13:27 (13,111)	
Duff, Tom	5:03:54 (24,615)	
Duffelen, Ian	3:46:00 (6,928)	
Duffelen, Mark	4:29:18 (17,061)	
Duffin, Vincent	6:28:34 (31,287)	
Duffy, Anthony	4:08:43 (12,068)	
Duffy, Brian	3:05:01 (1,250)	
Duffy, David	3:41:28 (6,059)	
Duffy, David	6:17:49 (30,920)	
Duffy, Eugene	5:46:21 (29,458)	
Duffy, John	4:54:00 (22,714)	
Duffy, Paul	3:21:58 (2,980)	
Duffy, Philip	3:57:16 (9,522)	
Duffy, Shaun	3:37:20 (5,296)	
Dufty, Philip	4:32:12 (17,775)	
Dugan, Jeffrey	3:48:59 (7,511)	
Duggan, Cyril	4:39:10 (19,368)	
Duggan, James	7:16:20 (32,046)	
Duggan, Martin	4:21:43 (15,163)	
Duggan, Neil	4:41:31 (19,871)	
Dugos, Vincent	3:25:30 (3,462)	
Duivenvoorden, Hans	5:07:09 (25,125)	
Duivenvoorden, Hen	4:36:19 (18,717)	
Duke, Trevor	6:54:10 (31,810)	
Dulai, Gurinderjit	4:30:57 (17,481)	
Dullage, Richard	4:31:29 (17,612)	
Duly, Patrick	3:28:39 (3,936)	
Dumalle, Florian	3:01:52 (1,045)	
Dumartin, Jerome	4:35:38 (18,545)	
Dumbleton, Andrew	4:32:22 (17,807)	
Dumper, Alan	3:12:22 (1,911)	
Dun, Craig	3:39:03 (5,607)	

Dunbabin, Richard	3:15:11	(2,261)
Dunbar, Graeme	3:15:52	(2,322)
Duncan, Adrian	4:38:19	(19,167)
Duncan, Anthony	3:59:20	(10,047)
Duncan, Colin	4:43:48	(20,453)
Duncan, Ian	4:04:51	(11,257)
Duncan, James	4:12:50	(12,966)
Duncan, James	5:16:36	(26,438)
Duncan, Mark	3:37:34	(5,338)
Duncan, Paul	3:49:45	(7,686)
Dunford, John	4:53:15	(22,556)
Dungate, Keith	3:32:12	(4,497)
Dungate, Paul	2:54:31	(560)
Dunglas, Stephane	5:23:08	(27,305)
Dungley, Kevin	5:01:08	(24,173)
Dunham, Glen	2:48:18	(344)
Dunham, Paul	4:26:09	(16,288)
Dunham, Robert	4:36:05	(18,666)
Dunkerley, John	3:59:15	(10,021)
Dunkin, Stephen	4:48:36	(21,552)
Dunkley, Timothy	4:42:48	(20,180)
Dunlea, Brian	4:40:14	(19,586)
Dunlea, Gerard	3:21:25	(2,926)
Dunleavy, David	4:17:32	(14,125)
Dunleavy, James	4:33:01	(17,956)
Dunleavy, Mark	4:27:51	(16,680)
Dunleavy, Martin	5:26:21	(27,717)
Dunleavy, Michael	4:58:36	(23,718)
Dunleavy, Rory	4:46:02	(20,971)
Dunlop, Andrew	4:44:30	(20,615)
Dunlop, Craig	4:31:54	(17,707)
Dunlop, Peter	3:48:25	(7,392)
Dunn, Andrew	4:12:04	(12,777)
Dunn, Andrew	5:11:51	(25,808)
Dunn, David	3:21:37	(2,943)
Dunn, Derek	3:26:37	(3,626)
Dunn, Greg	4:39:56	(19,524)
Dunn, Ian	5:15:32	(26,316)
Dunn, John	6:12:03	(30,730)
Dunn, Kim	3:00:51	(994)
Dunn, Matthew	3:39:13	(5,633)
Dunn, Matthew	3:56:01	(9,184)
Dunn, Peter	4:38:55	(19,308)
Dunn, Robert	4:00:41	(10,361)
Dunn, Roger	3:55:59	(9,173)
Dunn, Scott	4:53:38	(22,641)
Dunn, Simon	4:42:51	(20,194)
Dunn, Stephen	3:49:22	(7,601)
Dunn, Stuart	4:01:18	(10,495)
Dunn, Thomas	4:29:29	(17,112)
Dunn, Tom	4:48:38	(21,558)
Dunne, Gerard	3:42:58	(6,358)
Dunne, Jeff	3:18:16	(2,584)
Dunne, Mark	5:06:38	(25,039)
Dunne, Mark	5:07:47	(25,237)
Dunnet, James	4:36:29	(18,768)
Dunnett, Keith	4:56:16	(23,214)
Dunnett, Robert	4:41:32	(19,874)
Dunnicliffe, James	4:22:45	(15,429)
Dunning, Guy	4:19:52	(14,708)
Dunning, Thomas	3:54:55	(8,899)
Dunnington, Gary	4:26:08	(16,282)
Dunphy, Brian	5:45:37	(29,412)
Dunscombe, Mark	3:23:13	(3,139)
Dunstan, Bruce	4:01:30	(10,539)
Dunstan, Richard	4:46:51	(21,161)
Dunstone, Philip	3:17:21	(2,469)
Dupont, Nigel	4:42:25	(20,088)
Dupre, Nicolas	4:19:36	(14,639)
Durairaj, Pattu	5:59:21	(30,231)
Durance, Richard	3:47:22	(7,183)
Durand, Patrick	4:23:27	(15,603)
Durant, Brett	4:34:35	(18,301)
Durante, Carlo	3:20:08	(2,775)
Duray, Claude	3:33:19	(4,648)
Durbin, James	4:28:44	(16,919)
Durcan, Michael	3:39:28	(5,686)
Durdy, Steven	3:17:32	(2,493)
Durell, David	6:39:19	(31,529)
Durham, Andrew	5:02:03	(24,320)
Durham, Peter	4:48:34	(21,545)
Durham, William	5:19:09	(26,778)
Durie, Douglas	5:28:07	(27,902)
Durkin, Brendan	4:42:19	(20,059)
Durnin, David	3:15:30	(2,289)
Durrani, Amer	5:21:47	(27,124)
Dursley, Paul	3:38:13	(5,445)
Durston, Alan	3:36:41	(5,179)
Dury, Michael	3:46:31	(7,035)
Duscha, Arnulf	4:36:52	(18,846)
Dusnter, Stuart	3:24:38	(3,347)
Dutch, Steffan	5:13:18	(26,012)
Duthie, Ian	5:00:59	(24,150)
Dutoit, René	3:29:16	(4,036)
Dutta, Jamie	4:08:10	(11,932)
Dutton, Bryan	4:11:14	(12,584)
Dutton, Robin	3:48:11	(7,354)
Dutton, Timothy	6:57:19	(31,863)
Duvall, Steve	3:48:17	(7,376)
Dux, John	6:10:46	(30,676)
Dux, Timothy	3:56:10	(9,228)
Duzbeyaz, Goksel	5:02:52	(24,440)
Dwaah, Derek	4:56:52	(23,355)
Dwan, Ricky	7:10:50	(31,996)
Dwyer, Brennan	3:44:17	(6,595)
Dwyer, Daniel	5:43:29	(29,269)
Dwyer, Nick	3:30:41	(4,273)
Dyble, Glen	4:37:44	(19,029)
Dyckes, John	3:09:27	(1,629)
Dyde, Jon	4:36:26	(18,753)
Dyde, Mark	4:44:11	(20,538)
Dyde, Martin	2:59:46	(924)
Dyde, Robert	3:41:45	(6,101)
Dyer, Arthur	3:42:03	(6,160)
Dyer, David	5:20:49	(27,002)
Dyer, Graham	7:18:33	(32,061)
Dyer, John	5:08:49	(25,377)
Dyer, Nicholas	3:29:46	(4,137)
Dyer, Paul	4:42:10	(20,022)
Dyer, Roderick	4:00:05	(10,240)
Dyer, Terry	4:09:01	(12,134)
Dyke, Rupert	4:55:08	(22,949)
Dykes, Nigel	4:14:47	(13,445)
Dyment, Anthony	4:50:24	(21,943)
Dyrmose, Morten	4:14:29	(13,377)
Dyson, Greg	4:52:48	(22,460)
Dyson, Ian	4:40:08	(19,565)
Dyson, John	4:52:03	(22,320)
Dziemianko, Andrzej	4:05:53	(11,478)
Dzikowski, Raymond	3:06:25	(1,350)
Dzivbak, Stefan	4:35:39	(18,551)
Dzurinda, Mikulas	3:36:24	(5,130)
Eade, Benjamin	4:57:35	(23,499)
Eade, David	4:47:28	(21,293)
Eades, Andrew	4:31:10	(17,543)
Eadie, Nigel	4:46:15	(21,032)
Eagle, Paul	4:35:47	(18,594)
Eaglesham, Robert	4:32:07	(17,755)
Ealand, Nigel	4:09:11	(12,171)
Eames, Joseph	6:18:01	(30,934)
Eames, Michael	3:59:41	(10,146)
Eames, Norman	3:21:13	(2,900)
Eames, Peter	4:57:49	(23,546)
Eardley, Donald	5:26:11	(27,698)
Eardley-Taylor, Paul	3:27:25	(3,724)
Earl, Adrian	4:45:47	(20,908)
Earl, David	4:57:23	(23,456)
Earl, Derek	4:02:33	(10,749)
Earl, Jared	4:06:10	(11,532)
Earl, Martin	3:49:37	(7,661)
Earl, Simon	4:25:11	(16,051)
Earl, Thomas	4:11:45	(12,707)
Earland, Paul	3:58:39	(9,875)
Earley, Gordon	3:35:37	(5,015)
Early, Richard	4:53:19	(22,574)
Earney, Mark	4:00:00	(10,224)
Earp, Blieu	6:13:41	(30,789)
Earp, Craig	6:33:39	(31,415)
Earp, Daniel	4:45:49	(20,919)
Eason, Paul	4:38:56	(19,311)
Easson, David	3:51:52	(8,169)
Easson, James	3:16:17	(2,358)
East, Gary	4:21:42	(15,158)
East, Jonathan	3:15:06	(2,248)
East, Michael	4:59:31	(23,891)
East, Stephen	4:41:04	(19,770)
Eastaugh, Chris	3:48:49	(7,469)
Eastgate, Michael	4:09:17	(12,190)
Eastham, Fred	4:25:03	(16,015)
Eastham, John	4:15:51	(13,719)
Eastlake, Simon	2:59:01	(855)
Easton, Mark	5:25:02	(27,543)
Easton, Murray	4:59:25	(23,873)
Easton, Terry	4:24:25	(15,844)
Eastwood, Clive	3:16:21	(2,361)
Eastwood, Ian	3:34:53	(4,889)
Eastwood, Kevin	4:08:57	(12,122)
Eastwood, Mark	4:56:44	(23,324)
Eastwood, Mark	5:24:04	(27,419)
Easy, Jason	3:56:21	(9,284)
Eaton, Alan	4:27:55	(16,693)
Eaton, Colin	3:35:55	(5,059)
Eaton, Dom	3:11:29	(1,802)
Eaton, James	4:22:44	(15,425)
Eaton, John	4:43:50	(20,466)
Eaton, Kevin	4:14:37	(13,405)
Eaton, Paul	3:45:56	(6,919)
Eaton, Paul	3:55:57	(9,165)
Eaton, Philip	3:47:14	(7,161)
Eaton, Richard	6:32:49	(31,396)
Eaton, Robert	3:48:45	(7,453)
Eaton, Simon	5:31:03	(28,196)
Eaton, Steve	5:49:19	(29,664)
Eaton, Tony	5:47:47	(29,558)
Eaves, Richard	4:25:02	(16,010)
Eavis, Jeremy	4:23:22	(15,583)
Ebanks, Mark	3:24:25	(3,320)
Ebbs, Charles	4:37:14	(18,934)
Ebden, Albert	6:09:08	(30,608)
Ebdon, Ben	3:57:28	(9,574)
Ebdon, Nicholas	4:38:02	(19,099)
Eberlein, Robert	4:48:02	(21,437)
Ebert, Erhard	5:12:28	(25,891)
Eccles, David	3:42:27	(6,231)
Eccles, John	4:09:04	(12,148)
Eccles, John-Paul	3:47:27	(7,204)
Eccles, Phil	3:57:46	(9,638)
Eccleston, John	3:32:41	(4,556)
Eckersley, Andrew	5:02:18	(24,361)
Eckersley, Roger	4:06:43	(11,630)
Eckstein, Klaus	2:29:32	(61)
Eddie, Gordon	4:49:28	(21,743)
Eddy, Peter	4:29:00	(16,991)
Ede, David	4:27:09	(16,511)
Ede, David	5:09:16	(25,441)
Edelmann, Anton	3:52:57	(8,409)
Edelsten, Simon	4:23:02	(15,500)
Edelston, Philip	4:02:12	(10,678)
Eden, David	5:11:40	(25,784)
Eden, Paul	4:02:56	(10,832)
Eden, Scott	5:20:48	(26,999)
Edensor, Ray	4:49:27	(21,737)
Edgar, James	3:38:00	(5,413)
Edgar, Jonathon	2:46:56	(296)
Edgar, Stephen	3:12:20	(1,908)
Edge, Michael	4:43:24	(20,351)
Edge, Shane	3:33:31	(4,681)
Edgecliffe-Johnson, Robin	4:49:11	(21,673)
Edgington, Adrian	3:38:15	(5,452)
Edginton, Mark	4:22:38	(15,406)
Edington, Paul	5:33:17	(28,401)
Edington, Peter	3:30:03	(4,172)
Edis, Anthony	5:05:52	(24,941)
Edis, Jamyn	4:09:58	(12,345)
Edlund, Roger	3:24:10	(3,277)
Edmands, Simon	4:21:56	(15,217)
Edmans, Alex	3:56:43	(9,381)
Edmond, Chris	3:29:57	(4,158)
Edmond, Kenneth	4:21:13	(15,037)
Edmond, Ross	5:22:19	(27,190)
Edmonds, Matthew	4:27:00	(16,470)
Edmonds, Neil	5:22:56	(27,274)
Edmonds, Yogi	3:52:58	(8,412)
Edmondson, Bryan	4:51:12	(22,132)
Edmondson, Frederick	4:00:02	(10,229)
Edmondson, Ian	3:43:56	(6,533)
Edmunds, Peter	4:44:22	(20,587)
Edney, Colin	4:34:54	(18,372)
Edonds, Steven	4:20:30	(14,868)

Edridge, Norman	3:42:16 (6,199)	
Edwards, Alex	4:27:20 (16,555)	
Edwards, Andrew	3:50:44 (7,894)	
Edwards, Andrew	4:26:35 (16,375)	
Edwards, Andrew	7:26:18 (32,117)	
Edwards, Anthony	3:51:58 (8,186)	
Edwards, Antony	3:56:34 (9,338)	
Edwards, Ben	6:00:31 (30,274)	
Edwards, Chris	4:51:08 (22,115)	
Edwards, Chris	5:19:07 (26,773)	
Edwards, Christopher	7:26:20 (32,122)	
Edwards, Daniel	4:24:57 (15,981)	
Edwards, Darren	5:15:26 (26,308)	
Edwards, David	3:05:58 (1,318)	
Edwards, David	3:06:18 (1,338)	
Edwards, David	4:16:50 (13,941)	
Edwards, Gavin	4:34:41 (18,325)	
Edwards, George	5:36:50 (28,718)	
Edwards, Graham	3:54:40 (8,831)	
Edwards, Graham	4:22:04 (15,256)	
Edwards, Huw	5:15:32 (26,316)	
Edwards, Jason	4:04:00 (11,062)	
Edwards, Jim	3:15:41 (2,307)	
Edwards, Keith	4:34:19 (18,246)	
Edwards, Ken	3:47:36 (7,237)	
Edwards, Kenneth	6:05:10 (30,461)	
Edwards, Lewis	3:58:28 (9,826)	
Edwards, Luke	4:26:46 (16,421)	
Edwards, Lyndon	5:00:41 (24,105)	
Edwards, Mark	4:34:55 (18,376)	
Edwards, Mark	4:38:44 (19,263)	
Edwards, Martin	4:44:33 (20,622)	
Edwards, Matthew	4:36:20 (18,722)	
Edwards, Matthew	4:38:11 (19,127)	
Edwards, Michael	3:31:41 (4,432)	
Edwards, Michael	4:07:59 (11,902)	
Edwards, Mike	4:22:52 (15,458)	
Edwards, Neil	3:02:09 (1,066)	
Edwards, Neil	7:26:18 (32,117)	
Edwards, Paul	5:16:37 (26,439)	
Edwards, Peter	7:26:18 (32,117)	
Edwards, Richard	4:31:05 (17,520)	
Edwards, Rik	3:43:18 (6,424)	
Edwards, Robert	4:18:06 (14,272)	
Edwards, Rupert	7:26:18 (32,117)	
Edwards, Scott	4:17:18 (14,057)	
Edwards, Stephen	3:41:46 (6,107)	
Edwards, Stephen	6:15:20 (30,838)	
Edwards, Steve	5:03:12 (24,492)	
Edwards, Steven	6:03:08 (30,380)	
Edwards, Wayne	5:25:57 (27,659)	
Edwards, William	7:26:18 (32,117)	
Edwards-Geary, Tony	4:30:11 (17,282)	
Edwardson, Patrick	3:50:10 (7,767)	
Edye, Simon	3:17:20 (2,464)	
Efthimiou, Panikos	4:23:29 (15,611)	
Egan, Anthony	5:11:34 (25,770)	
Egan, Arthur	3:04:47 (1,233)	
Egan, Christopher	3:20:20 (2,807)	
Egan, Daniel	4:38:20 (19,172)	
Egan, David	5:18:05 (26,624)	
Egan, John	4:34:17 (18,234)	
Egan, Paul	5:25:48 (27,641)	
Egan, Shaun	4:34:59 (18,393)	
Egan, Stuart	4:47:16 (21,237)	
Egan, Thomas	3:55:31 (9,052)	
Egan, William	3:49:35 (7,652)	
Egdell, Roger	2:48:59 (365)	
Egelie, Eduard	3:04:35 (1,220)	
Egerton, Henry	4:38:34 (19,213)	
Eggenberger, Herbert	3:40:45 (5,914)	
Eggesvik, Svein Magnar	3:13:30 (2,061)	
Eggett, Christopher	4:06:06 (11,515)	
Eggleston, Andy	4:29:45 (17,178)	
Eggleston, Peter	4:26:13 (16,300)	
Eggleston, Stuart	4:07:21 (11,766)	
Egglestone, Timothy	5:21:38 (27,104)	
Eggleton, Bernard	3:47:48 (7,277)	
Eggleton, Tony	3:53:14 (8,485)	
Egstrand, Claus	3:46:08 (6,959)	
Ehm, Christian	3:44:28 (6,632)	
Ehm, Friedhelm	3:39:12 (5,631)	
Ehren, Gary	4:29:43 (17,166)	

Ehrhart, Andrew	4:10:05 (12,369)	
Eichert, Bryan	5:53:47 (29,920)	
Eikill, Gunnar	4:20:39 (14,897)	
Eilers, Wolfgang	3:47:35 (7,232)	
Eilles, Paul	3:21:12 (2,898)	
Eitner, Michael	3:17:06 (2,438)	
Eki, Hiroaki	4:37:43 (19,025)	
El Marwani, Mohammed	3:31:21 (4,387)	
El Mouaziz, Abdelkadre	2:08:03 (6)	
El Mrah, Said	4:07:41 (11,852)	
El Ouazzani, Driss	4:18:16 (14,294)	
Eland, Marc	3:51:53 (8,173)	
Elbro, Matthew	2:56:56 (696)	
Elder, Brian	4:29:31 (17,123)	
Elder, Mark	4:03:15 (10,899)	
Elderfield, Colin	4:40:21 (19,620)	
Elderkin, William	3:39:20 (5,664)	
Eldon, Peter	5:34:42 (28,530)	
Eldred, Nigel	4:46:45 (21,136)	
El-Gadi, Saleh	4:39:01 (19,327)	
Elgar, Jamie	4:38:54 (19,305)	
Elgie, Darren	4:47:44 (21,353)	
Elgie, Neil	5:02:26 (24,379)	
El-Hajji, Yasser	4:43:01 (20,241)	
Elikwu, Charles	3:36:10 (5,091)	
Elkington, Jason	3:01:23 (1,017)	
Elkington, Timothy	3:14:00 (2,129)	
Elkins, John	4:36:05 (18,666)	
Elkins, Peter	5:21:53 (27,136)	
Elleman, Peter	6:08:27 (30,589)	
Ellen, John	5:16:12 (26,394)	
Ellenberger, Chris	4:21:09 (15,020)	
Ellenrieder, Tom	4:33:53 (18,138)	
Ellens, David	5:05:11 (24,826)	
Ellerby, John	3:31:00 (4,327)	
Ellerby, Julian	4:40:49 (19,706)	
Ellerby, Roger	3:50:10 (7,767)	
Ellerby, Vincent	3:03:52 (1,172)	
Elliman, Peter	4:26:37 (16,386)	
Elliot, Christopher	3:34:53 (4,889)	
Elliot, Reginald	3:50:45 (7,899)	
Elliott, Adrian	4:14:26 (13,365)	
Elliott, Adrian	4:38:34 (19,213)	
Elliott, Alexander	3:29:07 (4,017)	
Elliott, Andrew	3:09:28 (1,631)	
Elliott, Andrew	3:42:52 (6,333)	
Elliott, David	4:14:23 (13,353)	
Elliott, Giles	4:27:11 (16,521)	
Elliott, Graham	5:41:50 (29,145)	
Elliott, James	4:09:17 (12,190)	
Elliott, Keith	3:27:58 (3,812)	
Elliott, Malcolm	3:38:28 (5,489)	
Elliott, Mathew	4:45:06 (20,743)	
Elliott, Matt	3:09:23 (1,620)	
Elliott, Miles	4:35:23 (18,492)	
Elliott, Neill	3:51:12 (8,011)	
Elliott, Peter	3:40:58 (5,952)	
Elliott, Peter	6:37:14 (31,492)	
Elliott, Richard	5:04:14 (24,668)	
Elliott, Ross	3:34:56 (4,896)	
Elliott, Ruan	4:41:05 (19,775)	
Elliott, Simon	3:11:24 (1,791)	
Elliott, Simon	5:10:03 (25,558)	
Elliott, Stuart	3:32:22 (4,516)	
Elliott, Stuart	4:22:11 (15,291)	
Elliott, Tom	6:54:23 (31,815)	
Ellis, Ben	4:16:45 (13,922)	
Ellis, Carl	3:24:48 (3,372)	
Ellis, Chris	3:50:01 (7,740)	
Ellis, Christopher	4:33:34 (18,071)	
Ellis, Daniel	3:48:55 (7,494)	
Ellis, David	3:29:34 (4,105)	
Ellis, David	3:37:59 (5,410)	
Ellis, David	6:05:59 (30,503)	
Ellis, Duncan	4:08:40 (12,055)	
Ellis, Garry	4:32:52 (17,918)	
Ellis, Gethin	3:44:57 (6,724)	
Ellis, Harry	5:30:01 (28,088)	
Ellis, Ian	4:22:26 (15,348)	
Ellis, James	4:08:32 (12,019)	
Ellis, Jeremy	3:55:46 (9,120)	
Ellis, John	3:21:51 (2,967)	
Ellis, John	4:23:10 (15,537)	

Ellis, Keith	4:24:38 (15,897)	
Ellis, Kevan	3:29:01 (4,005)	
Ellis, Martin	4:49:14 (21,685)	
Ellis, Matthew	4:27:28 (16,593)	
Ellis, Michael	4:23:41 (15,670)	
Ellis, Morne	4:50:01 (21,862)	
Ellis, Paul	4:14:01 (13,264)	
Ellis, Robert	3:13:47 (2,094)	
Ellis, Roger	4:15:43 (13,676)	
Ellis, Shaun	4:08:31 (12,014)	
Ellis, Simon	3:06:30 (1,359)	
Ellis, Steve	3:17:42 (2,517)	
Ellis, Stuart	3:25:37 (3,478)	
Ellis, Tim	2:56:17 (659)	
Ellis, William	3:55:35 (9,070)	
Ellison, Mark	3:03:53 (1,174)	
Ellison, Stuart	3:59:36 (10,119)	
Elliston, Robert	4:37:02 (18,887)	
Ellithorn, Mark	2:53:49 (520)	
Ellner, Andrew	3:46:20 (7,000)	
Ellsmore, Michael	2:46:34 (281)	
Ellson, Nicholas	4:59:29 (23,883)	
Ellwood, Scott	4:13:35 (13,146)	
Ellwood, Timothy	3:38:22 (5,472)	
Elmes, Alan	4:42:19 (20,059)	
Elmes, Gregory	4:31:30 (17,616)	
Elmes, Jeffrey	4:49:08 (21,655)	
Elmes, Michael	4:31:14 (17,553)	
Eloi, Robinson	4:30:11 (17,282)	
Elrick, James	3:56:30 (9,318)	
Elrick, Peter	5:32:31 (28,335)	
Elsby, Dominic	2:53:53 (526)	
Else, Bernard	4:56:22 (23,236)	
Eslander, Arnaud	4:17:08 (14,018)	
Elsmere, Alan	2:56:51 (694)	
Elsom, David	4:08:35 (12,035)	
Elson, Stephen	4:14:06 (13,282)	
Elson, William	3:42:36 (6,276)	
Elston, Barry	4:01:26 (10,525)	
Elston, Paul	3:24:58 (3,390)	
Elsworth, Lester	4:40:17 (19,599)	
Elton, Colin	5:03:19 (24,507)	
Elvidge, Rusty	4:09:48 (12,301)	
Elvin, Andrew	4:36:13 (18,692)	
Elvin, Craig	3:51:19 (8,037)	
Elvin, Kenneth	3:53:09 (8,460)	
Elwell, Nicholas	5:06:30 (25,016)	
Elwin, Don	4:30:32 (17,318)	
Elwood, John	3:42:28 (6,240)	
Emberson, Iain	3:39:21 (5,666)	
Emerson, Paul	6:16:11 (30,862)	
Emery, David	3:57:50 (9,658)	
Emery, Neil	5:00:35 (24,083)	
Emery, Peter	3:11:53 (1,847)	
Emirali, Bulent	4:31:07 (17,533)	
Emirali, Kenan	3:50:37 (7,870)	
Emm, Martin	3:34:48 (4,879)	
Emmerson, Andrew	6:05:22 (30,472)	
Emmerson, Bob	4:40:34 (19,661)	
Emmet, Anthony	3:48:00 (7,319)	
Emmett, Mark	3:27:35 (3,755)	
Emorfopoulos, George	4:12:50 (12,966)	
Empson, Gary	3:57:32 (9,585)	
Emsden, John	3:52:08 (8,230)	
Emsley, Andrew	4:20:49 (14,931)	
Emsley, Derek	3:28:42 (3,943)	
Emson, James	4:45:35 (20,863)	
Emus, Jonathan	4:04:15 (11,120)	
Emus, William	4:10:02 (12,356)	
Encke, Jochen	5:54:29 (29,966)	
Enderby, Geoff	4:31:27 (17,602)	
England, Anthony	3:55:22 (9,014)	
England, Graham	3:59:29 (10,090)	
England, Paul	5:38:21 (28,846)	
England, Phil	3:51:39 (8,120)	
Englerth, Juergen	4:32:18 (17,792)	
English, Bobby	5:43:27 (29,266)	
English, Jolyon	4:03:28 (10,936)	
English, Philip	5:06:40 (25,044)	
English, Richard	4:21:23 (15,080)	
Enoch, Paul	4:20:21 (14,829)	
Enright, Daniel	5:05:52 (24,941)	

Ensart, Peter	3:39:17 (5,651)	
Enskat, Richard	4:29:26 (17,098)	
Enthoven, Richard	4:01:37 (10,563)	
Epifori, Luciano	3:56:55 (9,428)	
Epin, Yannick	3:50:31 (7,844)	
Eplett, Liam	4:35:19 (18,476)	
Epsom, Joseph	4:01:07 (10,451)	
Erb, Jean	3:57:26 (9,564)	
Erdal, Helge Magnus	4:41:52 (19,966)	
Erdhuetter, Alfons	4:32:41 (17,875)	
Erdweg, Walter	4:32:04 (17,746)	
Eriksson, Henrig	4:37:34 (19,000)	
Eriksson, Roger	3:07:39 (1,468)	
Erith, Mike	3:34:05 (4,758)	
Errey, John	5:12:49 (25,945)	
Erridge, Ian	5:47:59 (29,575)	
Erritt, Andrew	3:51:32 (8,086)	
Erskine, Stuart	6:32:21 (31,390)	
Esam, John	4:14:14 (13,312)	
Eschholz, Helmut	3:14:30 (2,184)	
Escobar, Carlos	3:27:27 (3,731)	
Escott, Gavin	3:56:11 (9,234)	
Escott-Watson, Andrew	4:55:49 (23,114)	
Eskandari, Roobik	5:26:15 (27,706)	
Eskinazi, Robert	4:15:18 (13,592)	
Espedal, Gunnar	4:46:52 (21,165)	
Espey, Lin	4:27:25 (16,575)	
Espinosa, Manuel	5:05:22 (24,852)	
Essery, John	4:10:53 (12,524)	
Essilfie, Henry	5:42:00 (29,165)	
Esslemont, Paul	4:35:30 (18,517)	
Estanislao, José	4:11:14 (12,584)	
Estaugh, Mark	7:44:01 (32,220)	
Esteban-Lasa, Peter	4:13:40 (13,167)	
Estrada, Agustin	4:03:50 (11,021)	
Esward, Sam	5:21:11 (27,047)	
Etheridge, Dan	5:01:34 (24,240)	
Etheridge, Ian	5:27:53 (27,881)	
Etheridge, Paul	3:12:32 (1,937)	
Etherington, David	4:48:17 (21,491)	
Etherington, Michael	4:32:12 (17,775)	
Etherton, Steve	4:14:15 (13,319)	
Etienne, Jean-Marie	5:06:38 (25,039)	
Ettlinger, Anthony	4:37:28 (18,975)	
Etty, Steven	4:31:11 (17,546)	
Eva, David	4:21:09 (15,020)	
Evamy, Philip	3:46:00 (6,928)	
Evangelou, Costakis	5:13:18 (26,012)	
Evans, Adam	5:10:53 (25,670)	
Evans, Adrian	6:01:22 (30,318)	
Evans, Aled	3:43:09 (6,396)	
Evans, Alex	6:59:51 (31,887)	
Evans, Andrew	2:44:10 (220)	
Evans, Andrew	3:56:17 (9,268)	
Evans, Anthony	3:48:47 (7,462)	
Evans, Anthony	5:07:27 (25,172)	
Evans, Barrie	4:24:07 (15,781)	
Evans, Barry	3:52:42 (8,354)	
Evans, Barry	4:41:19 (19,830)	
Evans, Benjamin	3:47:26 (7,199)	
Evans, Bill	3:46:00 (6,928)	
Evans, Bryan	5:12:36 (25,921)	
Evans, Bryn	4:29:01 (16,994)	
Evans, Christopher	4:17:39 (14,158)	
Evans, Christopher	4:53:34 (22,632)	
Evans, Christopher	5:12:14 (25,862)	
Evans, Christopher	5:13:26 (26,029)	
Evans, Clifford	5:34:08 (28,490)	
Evans, Clive	3:26:52 (3,651)	
Evans, Colin	3:34:33 (4,845)	
Evans, Colin	4:24:13 (15,800)	
Evans, Colin	4:30:09 (17,269)	
Evans, Daren	4:13:38 (13,160)	
Evans, Dave	5:43:02 (29,238)	
Evans, David	3:39:31 (5,697)	
Evans, David	5:03:22 (24,515)	
Evans, David	5:42:45 (29,227)	
Evans, David	5:58:07 (30,166)	
Evans, Emyr	5:14:27 (26,167)	
Evans, Gareth	3:52:50 (8,377)	
Evans, Gareth	5:08:09 (25,291)	
Evans, Gary	4:44:12 (20,545)	
Evans, Gavin	3:09:04 (1,593)	
Evans, Geraint	3:56:56 (9,439)	
Evans, Graham	3:06:10 (1,332)	
Evans, Graham	3:46:57 (7,115)	
Evans, Ian	3:12:05 (1,871)	
Evans, Ian	3:47:57 (7,307)	
Evans, Liam	4:05:51 (11,467)	
Evans, James	4:01:15 (10,483)	
Evans, James	4:04:54 (11,270)	
Evans, James	4:59:06 (23,824)	
Evans, Jamie	3:57:16 (9,522)	
Evans, John	4:10:54 (12,528)	
Evans, Jonathan	3:34:09 (4,768)	
Evans, Keith	2:57:12 (719)	
Evans, Lee	6:22:57 (31,102)	
Evans, Lee-Stuart	5:48:00 (29,578)	
Evans, Marc	2:46:53 (292)	
Evans, Marcus	3:35:21 (4,966)	
Evans, Mark	3:57:20 (9,536)	
Evans, Martin	5:16:35 (26,434)	
Evans, Matthew	5:20:11 (26,912)	
Evans, Michael	2:39:12 (147)	
Evans, Michael	3:01:59 (1,052)	
Evans, Michael	4:12:57 (12,994)	
Evans, Mike	4:14:04 (13,278)	
Evans, Mike	4:34:52 (18,367)	
Evans, Nick	5:10:53 (25,670)	
Evans, Nigel	4:49:13 (21,679)	
Evans, Paul	3:47:37 (7,241)	
Evans, Paul	4:26:03 (16,264)	
Evans, Paul	4:36:19 (18,717)	
Evans, Paul	5:23:24 (27,340)	
Evans, Peter	4:20:42 (14,903)	
Evans, Rhodri	4:45:56 (20,942)	
Evans, Richard	3:49:36 (7,656)	
Evans, Richard	4:54:24 (22,795)	
Evans, Richard	4:59:19 (23,859)	
Evans, Richard	6:14:26 (30,807)	
Evans, Richard	7:25:04 (32,109)	
Evans, Ricky	4:32:32 (17,840)	
Evans, Royston	4:55:58 (23,143)	
Evans, Ryan	4:27:37 (16,628)	
Evans, Simon	3:46:20 (7,000)	
Evans, Simon	4:23:34 (15,633)	
Evans, Sion	5:28:55 (27,979)	
Evans, Stephen	4:35:05 (18,411)	
Evans, Tim	4:25:20 (16,096)	
Evans, Vaughan	3:52:03 (8,206)	
Evanson, Leslie	5:24:34 (27,485)	
Eve, Kevin	6:35:24 (31,458)	
Evenett, Glyn	3:42:58 (6,358)	
Evenson, Simon	4:17:40 (14,165)	
Everard, Roger	2:57:05 (708)	
Everdell, Warren	4:59:04 (23,820)	
Everett, Barry	3:57:45 (9,632)	
Everett, Jerry	4:29:58 (17,234)	
Everett, Thomas	3:17:45 (2,524)	
Everett-Pride, Christian	5:04:13 (24,665)	
Everitt, Matthew	6:19:31 (30,991)	
Everson, Colin	3:17:33 (2,496)	
Everson, Desmond	3:41:27 (6,055)	
Everson, Eugene	4:30:25 (17,350)	
Eves, Peter	3:38:10 (5,437)	
Eveson, Norman	4:09:10 (12,167)	
Evett, Christopher	3:42:30 (6,248)	
Ewan, James	5:31:50 (28,267)	
Ewart, Harry	3:46:20 (7,000)	
Ewen, George	4:21:07 (15,011)	
Ewen, Richard	5:47:10 (29,503)	
Ewing, Mark	3:52:24 (8,288)	
Exall, Philip	6:10:51 (30,684)	
Exarchos, Nicholas	4:23:04 (15,506)	
Exarheas, Nick	5:47:44 (29,554)	
Excell, Paul	4:28:08 (16,748)	
Exley, David	5:29:08 (27,999)	
Exley, Jonathan	3:08:54 (1,578)	
Extence, John	5:04:45 (24,747)	
Exton, Graham	5:40:48 (29,062)	
Eynon, Mark	4:03:14 (10,891)	
Eynon, Nicholas	3:44:13 (6,587)	
Eyole-Monono, Lloney	4:46:36 (21,109)	
Eyre, Douglas	4:23:31 (15,619)	
Eyre, Richard	6:18:30 (30,957)	
Eyre, Torbjorn	4:18:21 (14,316)	
Eyres, Anthony	3:48:58 (7,507)	
Eyres, Iain	3:50:56 (7,928)	
Ezure, Seiyo	5:16:34 (26,432)	
Fabbri, Gary	5:08:12 (25,300)	
Fabel, Martin	4:20:55 (14,957)	
Fabry, Hein	3:36:26 (5,133)	
Facchin, Mario	5:29:31 (28,039)	
Faccini, Vic	3:37:23 (5,305)	
Facey, Mark	4:11:29 (12,643)	
Facon, Jean	5:16:35 (26,434)	
Fadden, Alastair	3:14:58 (2,234)	
Fadiora, George	3:16:10 (2,342)	
Faerber, Steffen	3:18:18 (2,591)	
Faherty, Aidan	4:05:51 (11,467)	
Fahy, Dominic	6:22:05 (31,077)	
Faiers, Gray	4:27:22 (16,563)	
Fainchney, Edward	4:12:04 (12,777)	
Fairbairn, Warren	4:57:33 (23,490)	
Fairbrass, Andrew	4:13:03 (13,016)	
Fairbrass, Keith	4:43:37 (20,407)	
Fairbrass, Niegel	4:48:52 (21,602)	
Fairbrother, Paul	4:34:46 (18,341)	
Fairchild, Jonathan	4:45:54 (20,936)	
Fairclough, John	5:38:18 (28,837)	
Fairclough, Paul	3:49:24 (7,610)	
Fairclough, Thomas	4:03:28 (10,936)	
Fairey, Anthony	5:26:25 (27,728)	
Fairhead, John	5:01:17 (24,202)	
Fairhurst, Robin	4:44:13 (20,548)	
Fairlcough, Mark	4:46:06 (20,992)	
Fairley, Jon	3:33:11 (4,627)	
Fajimolu, Tony	3:55:19 (8,999)	
Fakhry, Husan	4:53:42 (22,651)	
Falasca, Marco	4:14:28 (13,371)	
Falch, Franz	3:39:21 (5,666)	
Falk, Christopher	2:42:55 (195)	
Falk, Richard	4:14:05 (13,280)	
Fallon, Niall	6:07:19 (30,546)	
Fallon, Thomas	4:36:05 (18,666)	
Fallon, Tom	3:29:13 (4,030)	
Falvin, Laurence	4:46:59 (21,182)	
Falzone, Martino	5:58:36 (30,185)	
Fane, Peter	3:32:03 (4,477)	
Fanouillere, Mickael	4:33:43 (18,100)	
Fanstone, Spencer	5:52:18 (29,846)	
Farabolini, Marco	4:30:19 (17,312)	
Farag, Ben	3:11:38 (1,817)	
Farago, Peter	4:49:46 (21,818)	
Farazi, Dilawer	5:04:09 (24,656)	
Fardell, Michael	4:14:32 (13,389)	
Farmer, Owen	4:09:38 (12,256)	
Farmer, Roger	4:03:01 (10,846)	
Farmer, Stephen	4:42:15 (20,039)	
Farmery, Ian	3:31:43 (4,440)	
Farndale, Martin	4:25:42 (16,183)	
Farnell, Mark	2:51:56 (440)	
Farneti, Stefano	3:31:57 (4,465)	
Farnham, Malcolm	4:47:25 (21,279)	
Farnham, Robert	4:01:30 (10,539)	
Farnie, Stephen	5:01:54 (24,294)	
Farnsworth, Graham	3:15:50 (2,316)	
Farnworth, Eric	3:30:04 (4,178)	
Farnworth, Kevin	5:17:47 (26,577)	
Farquhar, Barry	3:39:57 (5,773)	
Farquhar, Charles	4:18:56 (14,492)	
Farquhar, Graham	5:55:58 (30,039)	
Farquharson, Andrew	3:24:58 (3,390)	
Farquharson, David	3:52:46 (8,367)	
Farr, Anthony	4:13:49 (13,205)	
Farr, Jason	3:46:43 (7,069)	
Farr, Paul	4:48:12 (21,471)	
Farr, Raymond	4:10:51 (12,519)	
Farrall, Andrew	4:33:14 (17,990)	
Farrar, Alasdair	4:45:04 (20,737)	
Farrar, David	4:44:55 (20,700)	
Farrar, John	4:03:39 (10,973)	
Farrar, Mark	3:56:10 (9,228)	
Farre, Jean-Michel	4:34:57 (18,383)	
Farrell, Andrew	3:58:49 (9,921)	
Farrell, Douglas	4:56:12 (23,199)	
Farrell, John	5:42:27 (29,205)	
Farrell, Michael	4:45:59 (20,956)	
Farrell, Michael	5:22:17 (27,184)	

Farrelly, Simon	4:57:08 (23,411)	
Farrimond, Nicholas	5:22:28 (27,207)	
Farrin, Dennis	6:20:45 (31,040)	
Farrington, Derek	3:30:03 (4,172)	
Farrow, David	4:25:35 (16,153)	
Farrow, John	3:39:06 (5,618)	
Farrow, Nigel	3:30:15 (4,210)	
Fasse, Steffan	4:21:57 (15,224)	
Fassett, Andy	5:24:01 (27,410)	
Fattore, Luciano	2:46:42 (286)	
Fattore, Mario	2:24:09 (37)	
Fauchart, Michel	4:33:56 (18,149)	
Faucheur, Jean	5:12:53 (25,956)	
Faughy, David	5:35:54 (28,628)	
Faulkner, David	4:13:26 (13,107)	
Faulkner, John	4:17:38 (14,152)	
Faulkner, Jon	4:55:52 (23,122)	
Faulkner, Kevin	3:35:44 (5,031)	
Faulkner, Kevin	4:46:03 (20,977)	
Faulkner, Paul	5:57:35 (30,142)	
Faulkner, Richard	4:40:44 (19,690)	
Faunce, John	5:17:02 (26,483)	
Faust, Stuart	4:25:07 (16,031)	
Faux, Darryl	5:42:03 (29,168)	
Favereau, Xavier	4:35:13 (18,449)	
Fawcett, Colin	4:05:08 (11,319)	
Fawcett, Michael	3:37:53 (5,397)	
Fawcett, Richard	4:01:26 (10,525)	
Fawkner, Alan	3:27:03 (3,688)	
Fayle, Matt	3:52:08 (8,230)	
Fayle, Tom	3:28:22 (3,878)	
Feakes, Duncan	4:53:53 (22,694)	
Fear, Jamie	5:20:38 (26,976)	
Fear, Richard	4:11:59 (12,756)	
Fearfield, Terry	4:35:48 (18,598)	
Fearn, Kevin	5:05:27 (24,867)	
Fearn, Mark	3:58:37 (9,862)	
Fearn, Neil	4:22:31 (15,369)	
Fearns, Donald	5:19:43 (26,851)	
Fearns, Stuart	3:29:02 (4,007)	
Fearon, Alex	4:17:50 (14,215)	
Featherstone, Lee	3:44:19 (6,600)	
Febvin, Mickael	3:41:00 (5,957)	
Feddeck, Volker	4:06:34 (11,605)	
Fedi, Daniele	3:53:01 (8,429)	
Fee, Graeme	3:36:49 (5,195)	
Feeney, Patrick	4:08:28 (12,002)	
Feeney, Paul	3:49:53 (7,706)	
Feeney, Scott	3:49:54 (7,712)	
Feher, Richard	4:30:18 (17,311)	
Feibelman, Robert	3:13:07 (2,008)	
Feingold, Limor	5:36:11 (28,653)	
Fell, Russell	3:49:53 (7,706)	
Fell, Samuel	3:43:16 (6,418)	
Fell, Stephan	5:29:33 (28,045)	
Feller, Robert	4:45:59 (20,956)	
Fellingham, Richard	3:51:36 (8,105)	
Fellows, Mark	3:45:50 (6,895)	
Fellows, Mark	5:20:53 (27,006)	
Fellows, Stephen	5:14:06 (26,107)	
Feltham, Andrew	4:41:48 (19,943)	
Feltham, Barry	5:10:25 (25,611)	
Feltham, Peter	5:02:20 (24,366)	
Felton, David	5:34:19 (28,509)	
Fender, Thomas	4:49:31 (21,754)	
Fendick, Gareth	4:53:07 (22,525)	
Fenech, Michael	5:32:40 (28,344)	
Fenech Pisani, Clinton	5:23:22 (27,335)	
Fenn, Nick	5:13:28 (26,037)	
Fenn, Patrick	4:56:14 (23,205)	
Fenn, Richard	3:29:44 (4,132)	
Fennell, Donald	6:45:35 (31,634)	
Fennell, Jim	4:53:31 (22,621)	
Fenner, Ceri	5:05:41 (24,917)	
Fenner, Simon	4:41:48 (19,943)	
Fenney, Eric	3:15:10 (2,257)	
Fent, Martin	3:48:14 (7,364)	
Fenton, Dave	3:09:56 (1,670)	
Fenton, David	4:40:25 (19,635)	
Fenton, John	3:42:05 (6,165)	
Fenton, John	4:54:38 (22,846)	
Fenton, Les	3:06:37 (1,370)	
Fenton, Simon	4:19:30 (14,616)	
Fenton, William	5:21:14 (27,056)	
Fenwick, Paul	4:35:04 (18,410)	
Ferebee, David	4:14:11 (13,302)	
Fereday, David	3:37:53 (5,397)	
Ferguson, Andrew	4:33:24 (18,032)	
Ferguson, Cameron	3:07:14 (1,432)	
Ferguson, Carl	3:31:27 (4,399)	
Ferguson, Euan	3:14:26 (2,178)	
Ferguson, Frank	3:24:11 (3,280)	
Ferguson, Gary	3:23:11 (3,133)	
Ferguson, Gordon	4:37:46 (19,039)	
Ferguson, John	3:55:47 (9,127)	
Ferguson, Larry	4:42:27 (20,098)	
Ferguson, Paul	3:51:27 (8,062)	
Ferguson, Paul	6:53:47 (31,805)	
Ferguson, Robert	3:49:09 (7,548)	
Ferguson, Stephen	4:46:10 (21,009)	
Fermi, Giuseppe	3:55:17 (8,988)	
Fern, Neil	4:58:52 (23,773)	
Fernandes, Blaise	4:35:07 (18,417)	
Fernandez, Alberto	3:50:39 (7,873)	
Fernandez, Alesandro	4:23:35 (15,635)	
Fernandez, John	4:34:21 (18,252)	
Fernandez, Lee	5:30:46 (28,173)	
Fernandez–Gil, Juan	3:33:16 (4,640)	
Fernandez-Gonzalez, German	4:35:16 (18,465)	
Fernee, Ron	4:08:38 (12,047)	
Ferrar, Ian	5:09:05 (25,419)	
Ferrar, Mark	5:09:05 (25,419)	
Ferrar, Philip	3:56:07 (9,214)	
Ferrario, Mark	4:00:13 (10,274)	
Ferreira E Sousa, Armenio	4:15:48 (13,702)	
Ferrelly, Neil	4:03:15 (10,899)	
Ferres, Peter	3:12:18 (1,904)	
Ferriday, Ernest	4:53:01 (22,505)	
Ferrie, John	5:40:59 (29,075)	
Ferrier, Andrew	4:14:20 (13,341)	
Ferris, Ian	3:49:45 (7,686)	
Ferris MBE, Peter	5:53:35 (29,912)	
Ferry, Paul	4:32:52 (17,918)	
Ferson, Gregory	4:46:16 (21,035)	
Festini, Marco	4:03:04 (10,862)	
Fettah, Allan	3:49:40 (7,672)	
Fewings, Ian	4:59:27 (23,878)	
Fewster, David	6:29:17 (31,306)	
Fewtrell, Malcolm	5:39:25 (28,938)	
Fiander, Jamie	4:36:20 (18,722)	
Fiander, Mark	3:37:54 (5,400)	
Fiandri, Giorgio	3:51:07 (7,981)	
Ficchi, Thomas	4:04:16 (11,127)	
Ficek, George	6:22:53 (31,099)	
Fichardt, Gustav	4:42:30 (20,109)	
Fiddes, Gary	3:56:42 (9,375)	
Fidge, John	3:57:29 (9,576)	
Field, Adam	4:10:30 (12,462)	
Field, Alan	3:33:21 (4,652)	
Field, Andrew	2:58:30 (798)	
Field, Anthony	4:18:15 (14,291)	
Field, Christopher	3:46:48 (7,083)	
Field, Daniel	5:04:00 (24,628)	
Field, David	4:22:18 (15,315)	
Field, Donald	3:14:39 (2,203)	
Field, Geoffrey	4:07:21 (11,766)	
Field, John	5:45:42 (29,419)	
Field, Kevin	4:14:59 (13,505)	
Field, Paul	6:26:02 (31,206)	
Field, Richard	4:27:26 (16,578)	
Field, Stephen	3:46:35 (7,051)	
Field, Steven	3:44:04 (6,560)	
Field, Stuart	5:00:25 (24,053)	
Fielder, Simon	3:34:22 (4,811)	
Fieldhouse, Philip	5:29:22 (28,025)	
Fielding, Alan	5:07:17 (25,140)	
Fifield, Alan	5:53:26 (29,903)	
Fifield, John	3:48:55 (7,494)	
Figg, Dale	5:51:16 (29,797)	
Figuero Fernandez, Joaquin	4:00:06 (10,244)	
Filali, Saad	4:07:43 (11,854)	
Filby, Justin	4:03:14 (10,891)	
Filby, Richard	5:00:23 (24,048)	
Filby, Richard	5:52:13 (29,843)	
Fildes, Colin	4:19:23 (14,589)	
Filer, Mark	4:24:00 (15,751)	
Filkins, Paul	4:30:13 (17,291)	
Filmer, Greg	4:16:37 (13,884)	
Finch, Jonathan	4:25:36 (16,158)	
Finch, Simon	4:06:57 (11,677)	
Fincham, Chris	4:41:39 (19,906)	
Fincham, Daron	3:44:44 (6,679)	
Findlater, Andrew	4:56:51 (23,352)	
Findlay, Alistair	5:10:10 (25,579)	
Findlay, Gordon	3:38:09 (5,434)	
Findlay, Leigh	4:17:22 (14,074)	
Findley, Michael	5:14:16 (26,136)	
Fine, Martin	5:17:22 (26,522)	
Fine, Stephen	4:57:08 (23,411)	
Finegan, Ross	3:36:16 (5,108)	
Finer, Roland	4:02:47 (10,803)	
Finill, Chris	2:42:00 (181)	
Finlay, Jack	4:01:48 (10,598)	
Finlayson, Andrew	4:41:32 (19,874)	
Finn, Andrew	2:56:49 (693)	
Finn, Conor	4:53:44 (22,663)	
Finn, Jonathan	3:48:42 (7,440)	
Finn, Julian	4:25:25 (16,123)	
Finn, Matthew	4:50:03 (21,871)	
Finnegan, Denis	5:32:51 (28,365)	
Finnemore, Alan	6:02:53 (30,369)	
Finnemore, Chris	4:29:08 (17,022)	
Finney, Colin	3:41:29 (6,060)	
Finney, John	4:01:00 (10,429)	
Finney, Kevin	3:24:31 (3,333)	
Finney, Mark	4:10:04 (12,366)	
Finney, Simon	4:58:51 (23,772)	
Finnie, Lorin	4:12:01 (12,769)	
Finnie, Wayne	4:36:04 (18,665)	
Finnigan, Alun	4:42:54 (20,206)	
Finnigan, Justin	5:13:33 (26,050)	
Finnigan, Rupert	5:11:33 (25,767)	
Fioravanti, Andreas	3:58:45 (9,901)	
Fiore, Gary	3:39:08 (5,620)	
Firaw, Dagmani	3:12:17 (1,901)	
Firebrace, Patrick	4:21:24 (15,088)	
Firman, Ian	4:52:00 (22,308)	
Firman, Marco	4:18:58 (14,498)	
Firmin, Patrick	4:07:21 (11,766)	
Firth, Andrew	4:35:46 (18,588)	
Firth, Colin	3:59:51 (10,187)	
Firth, Richard	4:28:45 (16,922)	
Firth, Simon	5:02:42 (24,419)	
Fischer, Dan	3:46:43 (7,069)	
Fischer, Johannes	3:54:49 (8,870)	
Fish, Adam	5:26:01 (27,677)	
Fish, Andrew	4:05:05 (11,487)	
Fish, Jonathan	3:23:03 (3,116)	
Fish, Michael	3:37:29 (5,323)	
Fish, Tom	3:45:07 (6,759)	
Fish, Tony	4:51:13 (22,137)	
Fishburn, Andrew	3:34:26 (4,824)	
Fishenden, Paul	4:32:11 (17,770)	
Fisher, Charles	4:12:30 (12,887)	
Fisher, Christopher	3:28:58 (3,998)	
Fisher, Dave	4:45:17 (20,792)	
Fisher, David	3:36:13 (5,098)	
Fisher, David	4:57:24 (23,460)	
Fisher, Derek	5:08:51 (25,385)	
Fisher, Drew	2:31:34 (71)	
Fisher, Grant	4:55:41 (23,074)	
Fisher, Ian	2:28:10 (53)	
Fisher, Ian	3:15:13 (2,264)	
Fisher, John	2:50:01 (389)	
Fisher, John	5:36:52 (28,724)	
Fisher, Mark	4:21:27 (15,100)	
Fisher, Martin	3:53:02 (8,433)	
Fisher, Mattehw	5:56:54 (30,101)	
Fisher, Nicholas	3:28:36 (3,925)	
Fisher, Nigel	3:08:01 (1,500)	
Fisher, Paul	4:53:39 (22,643)	
Fisher, Philip	3:59:51 (10,187)	
Fisher, Roderick	3:50:52 (7,919)	
Fisher, Simon	3:18:05 (2,561)	
Fishleigh, Andrew	4:21:57 (15,224)	
Fishlock, Chris	4:14:01 (13,264)	
Fishpoool, Sean	3:51:51 (8,165)	
Fisk, Kristofor	4:39:19 (19,403)	
Fisse, Gregory	2:54:45 (579)	

Fitch, Chris 4:56:58 (23,371)
Fitchett, Andrew 4:05:12 (11,330)
Fitchew, Michael 4:57:36 (23,503)
Fitt, Richard 6:42:57 (31,590)
Fitter, Carl 3:12:13 (1,887)
Fitter, Gary 3:41:21 (6,025)
Fitzgerald, Charles 4:53:25 (22,599)
Fitzgerald, Jack 6:54:41 (31,824)
Fitzgerald, Mark 3:49:07 (7,537)
Fitzgerald, Michael 3:32:39 (4,550)
Fitzgerald, Michael 4:54:44 (22,872)
Fitzgerald, Michael 5:00:49 (24,125)
Fitzgerald, Paul 4:41:48 (19,943)
Fitzgerald, Warren 5:51:34 (29,810)
Fitzhugh, Martin 3:43:06 (6,387)
Fitzjohn, Graeme 3:24:03 (3,254)
Fitzmaurice, James 4:13:20 (13,080)
Fitzmaurice, Wessan 3:52:56 (8,402)
Fitzpatrick, Craig 3:37:10 (5,269)
Fitzpatrick, John 3:56:14 (9,255)
Fitzpatrick, Paul 3:43:57 (6,537)
Fitzpatrick, Paul 4:44:29 (20,612)
Fitzpatrick, Peter 5:04:21 (24,684)
Fitzpatrick, Sam 4:54:36 (22,837)
Fitzpatrick, Tom 4:17:54 (14,230)
Fitzsimmonds, Andrew 5:15:56 (26,366)
Fitzsimmons, Keith 5:00:11 (24,009)
Fitzsimmons, Thomas 5:16:37 (26,439)
Fitzsimons, Andrew 4:10:12 (12,399)
Fitzsimons, Timothy 3:26:59 (3,678)
Fixter, Stephen 4:17:28 (14,108)
Flack, Colin 5:17:53 (26,592)
Flanagan, Brian 3:46:13 (6,978)
Flanagan, Matthew 3:25:02 (3,399)
Flanagan, Tadhg 3:15:07 (2,252)
Flanaghan, David 4:19:14 (14,559)
Flannery, Hugh 3:16:51 (2,410)
Flannery, Kevin 5:01:12 (24,183)
Flannery, William 3:26:21 (3,586)
Flashman, Mark 5:56:04 (30,054)
Flavell, Christopher 2:46:21 (271)
Flavell, Julian 3:54:34 (8,809)
Flaxton, Stuart 3:52:50 (8,377)
Flello, Robert 5:26:03 (27,680)
Fleming, Albert 4:27:27 (16,581)
Fleming, John 4:06:09 (11,526)
Fleming, Mark 3:11:15 (1,779)
Fleming, Peter 3:58:48 (9,918)
Fleming, Rupert 4:35:31 (18,521)
Fleming, Tony 4:19:18 (14,572)
Flemyng, Jason 3:47:39 (7,247)
Flesher, Roy 3:06:35 (1,367)
Fletcher, Alan 4:24:42 (15,915)
Fletcher, Andrew 3:22:05 (2,993)
Fletcher, Andrew 3:43:49 (6,511)
Fletcher, Cedric 2:53:15 (500)
Fletcher, Chris 3:13:58 (2,123)
Fletcher, David 4:01:37 (10,563)
Fletcher, Gary 5:26:25 (27,728)
Fletcher, George 4:39:35 (19,454)
Fletcher, Kevin 3:19:46 (2,730)
Fletcher, Marc 4:00:06 (10,244)
Fletcher, Mark 3:01:30 (1,024)
Fletcher, Matthew 5:09:26 (25,465)
Fletcher, Robert 5:34:35 (28,527)
Fletcher, Robin 3:29:47 (4,138)
Fletcher, Robin 4:47:39 (21,333)
Fletcher, Simon 4:03:31 (10,945)
Fletcher, Stephen 4:43:10 (20,277)
Fletcher, Steve 4:19:04 (14,521)
Fleuchaus, Uwe 3:16:32 (2,378)
Fleurisson, Didier 3:57:07 (9,481)
Flint, Duncan 4:01:16 (10,486)
Flint, John 3:43:48 (6,506)
Flint, Michael 4:18:49 (14,452)
Flint, Russell 3:45:36 (6,849)
Flitney, Paul 4:22:42 (15,420)
Flood, Douglas 6:39:44 (31,534)
Flood, William 5:34:15 (28,500)
Flores, Raul 5:14:24 (26,159)
Florey, Richard 4:17:02 (13,993)
Florida-James, Peter 3:13:33 (2,067)
Florio, John 6:17:49 (30,920)
Flotman, Jacobus 3:04:39 (1,225)
Flouris, Floros 5:49:31 (29,680)
Flower, Mark 6:29:40 (31,319)
Flowerday, Matthew 4:08:35 (12,035)
Floyd, David 5:23:17 (27,322)
Floyd, Dominic 5:20:29 (26,954)
Floyd, Geoffrey 4:18:21 (14,316)
Floyd, Robert 3:34:12 (4,781)
Floyd, Warren 4:50:08 (21,887)
Fluck, Steven 4:58:58 (23,792)
Flynn, Christopher 4:17:47 (14,206)
Flynn, John 4:15:13 (13,571)
Flynn, Paul 4:23:44 (15,680)
Foad, Martin 4:54:10 (22,738)
Foard, Martyn 3:46:13 (6,978)
Foden, John 5:53:23 (29,899)
Fogden, Terry 4:17:19 (14,060)
Fogg, Brian 4:08:01 (11,908)
Fogg, Steven 3:59:05 (9,977)
Fokinther, Roger 3:18:33 (2,613)
Folbigg, Jack 3:39:24 (5,678)
Foley, Anthony 4:59:30 (23,886)
Foley, Benjamin 3:54:51 (8,879)
Foley, Conor 3:42:41 (6,295)
Foley, James 5:21:33 (27,089)
Foley, John 4:35:28 (18,510)
Folkman, David 3:39:46 (5,744)
Follan, Michael 3:43:22 (6,432)
Folland, Mike 4:54:23 (22,790)
Folland, Nicholas 3:56:08 (9,219)
Follett, Barry 5:16:54 (26,469)
Fong, Tak 3:27:49 (3,787)
Fonseca Seco, Pedro 6:33:01 (31,400)
Fontaine, Francis 3:23:11 (3,133)
Fontana, Giovanni 5:29:30 (28,038)
Fontana, Peter 4:06:01 (11,503)
Fontimpe, Marc 3:20:20 (2,807)
Fontyn, Barry 4:36:09 (18,679)
Foody, Peter 2:50:26 (400)
Foord, Richard 4:00:09 (10,260)
Foord, Roger 4:14:52 (13,471)
Foord, Timothy 4:51:53 (22,287)
Foot, Gary 4:59:16 (23,852)
Foot, Paul 4:59:16 (23,852)
Foot, Peter 5:52:41 (29,868)
Foran, Ian 5:22:55 (27,271)
Forber, Timothy 6:09:38 (30,624)
Forbes, Angus 3:56:20 (9,280)
Forbes, Craig 3:34:20 (4,800)
Forbes, Mark 4:51:19 (22,159)
Forbes, Thomas 3:38:36 (5,517)
Forbes, Wayne 5:28:54 (27,976)
Force, Steven 3:40:23 (5,855)
Ford, Christopher 4:27:43 (16,657)
Ford, David 5:23:10 (27,312)
Ford, Graham 3:11:02 (1,761)
Ford, Graham 4:22:41 (15,417)
Ford, Jonathan 5:15:43 (26,346)
Ford, Mark 3:58:34 (9,853)
Ford, Martin 2:59:55 (933)
Ford, Michael 3:53:45 (8,603)
Ford, Nicholas 4:32:27 (17,821)
Ford, Peter 4:06:59 (11,684)
Ford, Robert 3:52:37 (8,335)
Ford, Russell 3:29:57 (4,158)
Ford, Simon 3:33:47 (4,717)
Ford, Stephen 3:34:11 (4,774)
Ford, Timothy 4:28:17 (16,785)
Forde, Gerry 4:14:22 (13,349)
Forde, Kevin 3:30:11 (4,197)
Fordham, Benjamin 4:07:55 (11,890)
Fordham, Colin 3:40:52 (5,937)
Fordham, David 4:17:10 (14,027)
Fordham, Stuart 3:43:34 (6,457)
Fordyce, Bruce 3:52:04 (8,213)
Foreman, Timothy 3:50:23 (7,822)
Foreman, Tony 4:10:29 (12,460)
Forey, Simon 4:05:26 (11,390)
Forgan, Jamie 5:21:27 (27,073)
Form, Aubrey 4:49:13 (21,679)
Forman, Ian 4:05:40 (11,429)
Forni, Jacques 3:18:20 (2,595)
Forrest, Aaron 4:46:09 (21,006)
Forrest, Abraham 4:29:34 (17,127)
Forrest, Christopher 3:29:11 (4,025)
Forrest, Ian 4:24:58 (15,990)
Forrest, Les 5:00:28 (24,063)
Forrest, Roy 5:46:06 (29,445)
Forrest, Siomn 4:58:14 (23,633)
Forrest, Stephen 5:11:03 (25,700)
Forrester, Bob 4:21:06 (15,004)
Forrester, Craig 4:11:10 (12,567)
Forrestill, Rod 6:51:32 (31,751)
Forrest-Jones, Ian 4:39:19 (19,403)
Forrow, Alastair 3:33:59 (4,747)
Forsberg, Lars 5:55:32 (30,023)
Forsberg, Morgan 4:37:34 (19,000)
Forsdyke, David 5:20:16 (26,923)
Forshaw, Glyn 3:45:38 (6,856)
Forshaw, James 4:01:26 (10,525)
Forster, Adrian 3:56:16 (9,263)
Forster, David 4:01:07 (10,451)
Forster, Michael 4:23:48 (15,695)
Forster, Peter 2:46:11 (265)
Forster, Stephen 4:25:29 (16,139)
Forster, Tim 3:53:37 (8,570)
Forsyth, Andrew 3:53:49 (8,623)
Forsyth, Ewan 3:51:47 (8,144)
Forsyth, Stephen 4:51:26 (22,188)
Forsyth, Stewart 3:46:27 (7,020)
Fortescue, Jeff 6:00:56 (30,292)
Forth, Michael 3:58:13 (9,760)
Fortin, Julien 4:33:26 (18,043)
Fortune, David 4:38:12 (19,133)
Fortune, William 4:25:41 (16,177)
Fortuny-Clotet, Jordi 3:46:46 (7,077)
Forward, Richard 4:19:52 (14,708)
Fosse, Gaute 3:59:40 (10,141)
Fossett, James 3:30:43 (4,282)
Fossi, Paolo 4:38:51 (19,292)
Foster, Alan 3:51:26 (8,057)
Foster, Alexander 4:17:48 (14,210)
Foster, Andrew 3:09:00 (1,586)
Foster, Andrew 4:37:35 (19,005)
Foster, Andy 3:34:35 (4,851)
Foster, Anthony 3:42:12 (6,191)
Foster, Christopher 4:25:16 (16,074)
Foster, Christopher 4:45:05 (20,739)
Foster, Colin 5:12:13 (25,859)
Foster, Dave 4:10:15 (12,408)
Foster, David 3:13:11 (2,016)
Foster, David 3:39:44 (5,734)
Foster, David 4:22:50 (15,449)
Foster, David 4:53:30 (22,617)
Foster, David 5:33:53 (28,465)
Foster, Eric 4:03:03 (10,855)
Foster, Gary 4:48:32 (21,537)
Foster, Gregory 5:31:42 (28,257)
Foster, Jamie 3:26:33 (3,616)
Foster, John 4:16:36 (13,876)
Foster, Jonathan 4:29:54 (17,220)
Foster, Mark 4:01:40 (10,572)
Foster, Mark 5:03:06 (24,475)
Foster, Mark 5:54:13 (29,944)
Foster, Michael 4:28:12 (16,766)
Foster, Paul 2:46:04 (262)
Foster, Paul 4:13:18 (13,075)
Foster, Peter 5:15:33 (26,324)
Foster, Richard 3:57:49 (9,650)
Foster, Robert 3:06:52 (1,391)
Foster, Robert 3:36:37 (5,167)
Foster, Robert 4:08:16 (11,953)
Foster, Simon 4:05:01 (11,294)
Foster, Stephen 3:48:59 (7,511)
Foster, Terence 3:46:50 (7,090)
Foster, Tim 4:18:37 (14,399)
Fotherby, Kenneth 2:44:52 (233)
Fotheringham, Bill 3:58:50 (9,927)
Fouilett, Christian 3:44:54 (6,707)
Foulds, Daniel 2:52:16 (456)
Foulds, John 3:32:55 (4,584)
Foulkes, Carl 3:06:58 (1,400)
Foulkes, James 4:24:41 (15,911)
Foulkes, Jonathan 4:28:04 (16,725)
Foulkes, Simon 4:39:03 (19,331)
Foulkes-Arnold, Malcolm 4:25:28 (16,135)

Foulston, Robert 4:13:59 (13,258)
Fountain, Colin 3:34:41 (4,867)
Fourie, Paul 3:47:18 (7,175)
Fourier, Laurent 3:20:14 (2,795)
Fowden, Sean 5:31:41 (28,255)
Fowell, Mark 4:39:29 (19,437)
Fower, Malcolm 3:53:53 (8,642)
Fowkes, Julian 5:03:03 (24,464)
Fowle, David 4:36:45 (18,823)
Fowle, Lee 6:20:23 (31,029)
Fowler, Charles 4:09:02 (12,142)
Fowler, Christopher 4:05:00 (11,289)
Fowler, George 4:09:47 (12,295)
Fowler, Graham 6:32:43 (31,394)
Fowler, Mark 3:45:42 (6,868)
Fowler, Mark 4:10:41 (12,497)
Fowler, Stephen 3:51:40 (8,124)
Fowler, William 4:17:20 (14,064)
Fox, Albie 5:40:37 (29,045)
Fox, Brian 3:59:59 (10,220)
Fox, David 3:58:08 (9,739)
Fox, Fred 3:34:12 (4,781)
Fox, Gary 4:27:41 (16,643)
Fox, John 4:47:46 (21,364)
Fox, Jonathan 4:44:01 (20,500)
Fox, Kieran 4:18:04 (14,266)
Fox, Martin 3:10:39 (1,725)
Fox, Martin 3:10:43 (1,730)
Fox, Michael 3:49:33 (7,642)
Fox, Neil 5:08:38 (25,352)
Fox, Robert 3:26:41 (3,630)
Fox, Thomas 5:17:02 (26,483)
Fox, Tim 3:08:02 (1,504)
Fox, Tim 4:43:59 (20,494)
Fox, Trevor 4:54:16 (22,761)
Fox, William 3:39:19 (5,658)
Foxall, Peter 3:09:55 (1,668)
Foy, John 5:04:26 (24,698)
Foyster, Richard 3:42:53 (6,337)
Fozard, Dean 3:55:28 (9,039)
Fradin, Louis 2:55:29 (618)
Fragniere, Roger 5:11:21 (25,743)
Frain, John 4:55:34 (23,042)
Fraine, Kevin 4:57:12 (23,430)
Frame, Paul 4:05:43 (11,435)
Frampton, Brian 3:34:17 (4,791)
Frampton, Jeremy 4:55:50 (23,118)
Frampton, Robert 3:41:54 (6,130)
France, Colin 4:52:47 (22,457)
France, Kelvin 5:42:03 (29,168)
France, Mark 4:22:55 (15,475)
France, Patrice 2:58:25 (795)
France, Paul 5:47:47 (29,558)
France, Peter 3:58:03 (9,722)
France, Shaun 6:12:54 (30,763)
France, Victor 4:15:11 (13,563)
Francelle, Hubert 3:53:14 (8,485)
Franceschini, Fabrizio 3:09:20 (1,618)
Franceschini, Franco 5:18:15 (26,664)
Franchi, Mark 7:09:26 (31,986)
Francis, Emrys 2:59:10 (868)
Francis, Glyn 3:37:55 (5,403)
Francis, John 8:01:19 (32,257)
Francis, Jon 5:01:36 (24,242)
Francis, Kevin 3:12:51 (1,975)
Francis, Lee 3:46:56 (7,112)
Francis, Leslie 4:46:20 (21,054)
Francis, Richard 2:55:56 (645)
Francis, Richard 3:06:44 (1,379)
Francis, Richard 3:23:24 (3,162)
Francis, Robert 5:07:31 (25,186)
Francis, Roger 4:40:01 (19,539)
Francis, Stephen 4:12:45 (12,949)
Francis, Thomas 2:53:08 (498)
Franco, Luca 4:09:38 (12,256)
Franco, Marco 3:04:52 (1,240)
Franco, Rocco 4:02:44 (10,789)
Franey, James 4:41:04 (19,770)
Frank, Steven 3:42:15 (6,194)
Frankel, Christopher 3:48:02 (7,326)
Frankland, Anthony 5:40:21 (29,022)
Franklin, David 5:24:10 (27,431)
Franklin, Kevin 3:35:07 (4,927)
Franklin, Mark 3:48:56 (7,499)
Franklin, Mark 4:38:12 (19,133)
Franklin, Simon 5:38:33 (28,860)
Franks, Keith 3:50:51 (7,916)
Franks, Paul 3:26:53 (3,656)
Fransson, Claes 3:56:40 (9,365)
Fraquelli, Andrea 4:09:38 (12,256)
Fraser, Alec 5:06:36 (25,033)
Fraser, Anthony 3:57:20 (9,536)
Fraser, Derek 3:05:55 (1,315)
Fraser, Douglas 5:14:13 (26,129)
Fraser, Gavin 3:44:41 (6,664)
Fraval, Bruno 3:39:42 (5,727)
Frearson, Paul 3:46:22 (7,009)
Fredrick Chapman, Colin 5:31:51 (28,270)
Freedman, Clive 4:43:20 (20,328)
Freedman, Paul 5:20:09 (26,910)
Freeland, Hugh 4:03:56 (11,044)
Freeman, Adrian 4:26:32 (16,362)
Freeman, Colin 4:32:33 (17,846)
Freeman, David 3:25:57 (3,535)
Freeman, David 5:17:54 (26,596)
Freeman, Dick 4:48:54 (21,614)
Freeman, Jason 4:21:02 (14,988)
Freeman, Mark 4:27:28 (16,593)
Freeman, Mark 5:12:21 (25,872)
Freeman, Mark 5:31:08 (28,211)
Freeman, Martin 4:27:41 (16,643)
Freeman, Patrick 4:54:52 (22,898)
Freeman, Paul 3:53:57 (8,661)
Freeman, Peter 3:43:10 (6,399)
Freeman, Peter 4:12:09 (12,799)
Freeman, Peter 4:37:48 (19,045)
Freeman, Robin 3:20:12 (2,786)
Freeman, Scott 5:03:42 (24,574)
Freeman, William 4:24:42 (15,915)
Freemantle, Andrew 4:56:50 (23,347)
Freemantle, Paul 3:52:10 (8,237)
Freer, Art 3:06:18 (1,338)
French, Andrew 4:39:48 (19,501)
French, Brian 5:16:42 (26,451)
French, Clive 5:12:50 (25,949)
French, David 3:46:15 (6,983)
French, Guy 4:29:29 (17,112)
French, Jason 3:24:41 (3,356)
French, Kevin 3:44:17 (6,595)
French, Kevin 4:21:56 (15,217)
French, Lester 4:32:10 (17,767)
French, Michael 3:43:38 (6,473)
French, Peter 3:50:15 (7,788)
French, Peter 4:13:20 (13,080)
French, Peter 4:54:51 (22,891)
French, Richard 4:43:34 (20,393)
French, Rob 5:02:34 (24,400)
French, Steven 5:45:05 (29,376)
French, William 4:05:07 (11,315)
Frenzel, Christian 3:43:50 (6,514)
Frett, Kevin 3:52:13 (8,247)
Fretwell, Andrew 3:35:58 (5,061)
Frew, Marcus 4:52:53 (22,481)
Frew, Ryan 4:11:35 (12,663)
Friar, Darren 3:25:46 (3,504)
Fribbins, Michael 5:00:29 (24,065)
Fricker, Colin 3:22:43 (3,071)
Fricker, Thomas 3:20:06 (2,770)
Fridd, Derek 3:41:04 (5,971)
Friedman, Gary 6:53:05 (31,784)
Friedrich, James 3:53:33 (8,558)
Friend, Glyn 4:38:21 (19,175)
Friend, Simon 3:47:50 (7,289)
Frigerio, Andrea 2:48:01 (335)
Frigoli, Luca Gregorio 6:23:12 (31,109)
Frisby, Andrew 4:12:43 (12,941)
Frisby, Charles 3:13:17 (2,033)
Frisby, David 7:06:21 (31,947)
Frisby, Stephen 7:06:24 (31,948)
Frischholz, Juergen 3:16:33 (2,381)
Frith, Robert 5:38:31 (28,858)
Frith, Stuart 5:02:20 (24,366)
Fritz, Jurgen 4:23:15 (15,560)
Fritzer, Friedrich 5:10:30 (25,624)
Frizzel, Peter 3:42:26 (6,228)
Froeschle, Guenter 4:03:34 (10,962)
Froggatt, Stephen 4:47:12 (21,226)
Frogley, George 6:06:34 (30,515)
Frohlick, Friedrick 2:48:03 (337)
Fromage, Stephen 5:00:58 (24,148)
Fromme, Paul 2:58:41 (819)
Frondella, Luigi 2:52:53 (491)
Frost, Allan 3:31:57 (4,465)
Frost, Charles 3:56:30 (9,318)
Frost, Colin 4:47:57 (21,412)
Frost, David 4:42:57 (20,217)
Frost, Gary 5:56:18 (30,071)
Frost, John 3:53:44 (8,598)
Frost, Jonathan 4:19:43 (14,673)
Frost, Les 4:36:30 (18,769)
Frost, Robert 5:13:34 (26,052)
Frost, Stephens 5:14:38 (26,193)
Fry, Andrew 4:57:08 (23,411)
Fry, Anthony 4:25:27 (16,130)
Fry, Christopher 3:35:36 (5,011)
Fry, Edward 4:35:55 (18,625)
Fry, Malcolm 4:35:08 (18,427)
Fry, Martin 4:49:00 (21,633)
Fry, Sheldon 4:20:58 (14,968)
Fry, Simon 5:40:26 (29,033)
Fry, Tim 4:27:54 (16,689)
Fry, William 4:27:09 (16,511)
Fryer, Andrew 3:24:01 (3,249)
Fryer, Conan 3:13:12 (2,022)
Fryer, Matthew 4:27:49 (16,675)
Fryer, Richard 4:43:31 (20,382)
Fryer, Richard 5:02:30 (24,386)
Fryman, Neil 5:32:48 (28,356)
Fudge, Paul 4:21:06 (15,004)
Fuentes, Antonio 3:50:50 (7,915)
Fugistier, Bernard 4:28:12 (16,766)
Fulbrook, Julian 4:30:45 (17,431)
Fulford, David 4:38:49 (19,282)
Fullard, Ashley 4:30:32 (17,375)
Fullbrook, Richard 3:48:54 (7,489)
Fuller, Adrian 3:13:33 (2,067)
Fuller, Andrew 4:40:58 (19,746)
Fuller, Chris 2:38:12 (134)
Fuller, Edd 6:43:34 (31,604)
Fuller, John 3:37:08 (5,261)
Fuller, Mark 4:30:59 (17,491)
Fuller, Matthew 4:04:13 (11,117)
Fuller, Neil 5:50:43 (29,766)
Fuller, Peter 4:45:03 (20,728)
Fuller, Richard 2:59:19 (884)
Fuller, Stephen 4:28:40 (16,902)
Fuller, Stephen 4:31:36 (17,639)
Fullerton, Angus 4:53:33 (22,627)
Fulton, Mark 4:02:28 (10,736)
Fulton, Matthew 4:59:12 (23,843)
Fulton, Rick 3:00:43 (989)
Fulton, Rorie 6:09:35 (30,619)
Fumoso, Gerard 3:33:54 (4,734)
Funcks, Derek 4:08:26 (11,989)
Fung, Luen 3:21:49 (2,965)
Funk, Christian 4:16:43 (13,911)
Funnell, Mark 4:31:04 (17,517)
Funnell, Simon 3:44:27 (6,628)
Furber, Garry 4:48:34 (21,545)
Furey, Damian 4:47:04 (21,194)
Furhoff, Bjorn 3:08:47 (1,571)
Furhuraire, Ranjeet 6:27:42 (31,255)
Furness, Paul 3:12:39 (1,953)
Furness, Peter 3:24:10 (3,277)
Furniss, Henry 3:32:34 (4,535)
Furnival, Michael 5:41:53 (29,151)
Furno, Jonathan 4:45:32 (20,855)
Fursey, Karl 3:55:50 (9,139)
Fursey, Robert 3:09:50 (1,658)
Furzeman, Matthew 4:33:44 (18,104)
Fussell, Barry 6:53:50 (31,807)
Futcher, Ian 4:48:53 (21,609)
Futrell, Rodney 3:25:14 (3,432)
Futter, Nigel 3:53:26 (8,524)
Futter, Toby 2:59:27 (896)
Gabrael, Admon 4:55:25 (23,008)
Gabriel, Simon 4:14:34 (13,397)
Gabriel, Steven 3:38:51 (5,569)
Gabrielli, Giovanni 4:40:28 (19,648)

Gad, Neil....3:57:55 (9,685)
Gadd, Christopher....5:15:24 (26,304)
Gadd, Ron....4:40:13 (19,585)
Gaddes, Jimmy....4:11:31 (12,650)
Gaddie, Andrew....4:25:06 (16,026)
Gaddu, Amrit....7:18:43 (32,062)
Gadestedt, Kenneth....3:37:00 (5,229)
Gadgil, Devendra....6:00:42 (30,284)
Gage, Trevor....3:07:43 (1,475)
Gahagan, James....5:23:17 (27,322)
Gahunia, Jiwan....4:18:36 (14,392)
Gailer, Giles....3:31:43 (4,440)
Gain, Alastair....3:41:54 (6,130)
Gaines, Michael....6:06:06 (30,508)
Gainsborough, Martin....2:37:56 (131)
Gaitely, Christopher....5:54:05 (29,936)
Gaitley, Mark....5:06:22 (25,004)
Gajbutowicz, Andrzej....4:57:17 (23,443)
Galbraith, Roddy....3:29:57 (4,158)
Gale, Anthony....4:52:59 (22,502)
Gale, Clifford....3:11:21 (1,785)
Gale, John....4:04:28 (11,171)
Gale, Robin....3:36:00 (5,064)
Gall, Robert....3:56:37 (9,352)
Gallacher, Jim....4:49:10 (21,667)
Gallagher, Colin....3:26:11 (3,564)
Gallagher, Daniel....4:16:03 (13,750)
Gallagher, David....4:01:29 (10,536)
Gallagher, David....4:10:06 (12,373)
Gallagher, Francis....5:04:39 (24,723)
Gallagher, James....3:50:02 (7,741)
Gallagher, Kevin....4:14:37 (13,405)
Gallagher, Leslie....5:20:59 (27,020)
Gallagher, Matthew....4:01:03 (10,439)
Gallagher, Michael....4:16:33 (13,867)
Gallagher, Michael....4:51:51 (22,278)
Gallagher, Paul....3:45:47 (6,889)
Gallagher, Paul....4:26:45 (16,417)
Gallagher, Shaun....6:11:50 (30,719)
Gallard, Richard....3:32:29 (4,528)
Gallarotti, Giuseppe....4:46:14 (21,026)
Gallenschutz, Thomas....3:46:19 (6,997)
Gallichan, Richard....4:19:42 (14,667)
Gallie, Alexander....5:11:13 (25,725)
Galliford, Neil....4:04:44 (11,238)
Gallimore, Clive....4:58:21 (23,662)
Gallimore, Steven....5:48:11 (29,591)
Gallivan, John....7:11:52 (32,010)
Gallo, Nardino....2:56:25 (672)
Gallo, Simon....6:48:20 (31,682)
Gallop, Matthew....4:12:43 (12,941)
Galpin, Peter....2:26:56 (48)
Galvin, Mark....4:13:28 (13,116)
Galvin, Tim....4:56:50 (23,347)
Galway, Craig....3:25:08 (3,413)
Galway, Keith....4:28:36 (16,886)
Gambier, Jean Claude....3:46:01 (6,935)
Gambier, Nicolas....4:20:25 (14,851)
Gamble, David....4:56:51 (23,352)
Gamble, Ian....5:40:35 (29,041)
Gamble, John....4:36:54 (18,854)
Gamble, Paul....3:36:36 (5,160)
Gambles, Tracey....5:45:39 (29,416)
Gamble-Thompson, Mark....2:51:04 (422)
Game, Robert....4:12:14 (12,823)
Game, Steven....2:39:11 (146)
Gameson, Philip....3:59:37 (10,125)
Gammie, Neil....4:21:51 (15,194)
Gammon, Carl....4:00:48 (10,386)
Gammon, Malcolm....3:37:03 (5,241)
Gammon, Vincent....3:52:06 (8,223)
Gamston, Paul....3:04:17 (1,200)
Gan, Yona....5:09:15 (25,439)
Gander, Frank....3:43:36 (6,465)
Ganderton, Anthony....4:51:36 (22,225)
Gandolfo, Ronald....4:38:27 (19,190)
Gandon, Andrew....3:32:55 (4,584)
Gane, William....4:49:38 (21,786)
Ganguly, Stephen....3:16:56 (2,424)
Ganier, Vincent....4:20:37 (14,892)
Gannicliffe, Christopher....4:12:09 (12,799)
Gannon, Brian....5:08:15 (25,306)
Gannon, David....4:14:43 (13,429)
Gannon, Peter....3:56:16 (9,263)
Gannon, Sean....7:27:43 (32,137)
Gara, Fergal....3:23:52 (3,226)
Garbarino, Renato....4:36:55 (18,858)
Garbett, Lloyd....5:46:37 (29,472)
Garbett, Simon....3:55:29 (9,044)
Garbutt, Frank....4:06:42 (11,625)
Garbutt, Will....3:54:54 (8,893)
Garcha, Kultar....6:28:07 (31,274)
Garcha, Parvinder....6:28:07 (31,274)
Garcia, Francisco....4:29:21 (17,071)
Garcia, Kester....4:57:03 (23,392)
Garcia, Raphael....2:57:40 (748)
Garcia-Salcedo, Isais....3:33:54 (4,734)
Gard, Matthew....4:28:05 (16,731)
Gard, Peter....3:47:07 (7,145)
Gardam, Matthew....5:22:14 (27,171)
Garden, Andrew....5:31:18 (28,226)
Gardener, Alex....3:33:56 (4,740)
Gardener, John....3:35:07 (4,927)
Gardiner, Frank....4:19:00 (14,509)
Gardiner, Glenn....3:30:50 (4,300)
Gardiner, John....3:12:49 (1,968)
Gardiner, John....4:15:23 (13,615)
Gardiner, Matthew....4:17:02 (13,993)
Gardiner, Roy....3:37:46 (5,381)
Gardiner, Shaun....3:37:46 (5,381)
Gardiner, Stephen....4:44:35 (20,629)
Gardiner, Will....5:26:27 (27,732)
Gardner, Andrew....4:45:19 (20,798)
Gardner, Andrew....5:03:33 (24,539)
Gardner, Anthony....4:07:43 (11,854)
Gardner, Bruce....6:32:25 (31,391)
Gardner, Dave....3:43:36 (6,465)
Gardner, David....3:03:56 (1,179)
Gardner, David....3:53:30 (8,541)
Gardner, David....4:06:17 (11,553)
Gardner, Graham....5:07:35 (25,199)
Gardner, Keith....4:51:01 (22,075)
Gardner, Mark....4:55:07 (22,944)
Gardner, Martin....4:51:07 (22,108)
Gardner, Paul....4:59:15 (23,850)
Gardner, Peter....4:36:08 (18,676)
Gardner, Peter....4:49:09 (21,662)
Gardner, Stuart....3:37:33 (5,334)
Garfroth, Anthony....3:43:40 (6,480)
Gargard, Vincent....4:22:21 (15,327)
Gargin, Philip....3:29:37 (4,114)
Garland, Christopher....3:48:01 (7,323)
Garner, Alan....4:08:30 (12,011)
Garner, Andrew....5:03:19 (24,507)
Garner, David....5:24:15 (27,445)
Garner, Jeremy....3:32:41 (4,556)
Garner, Martin....5:05:45 (24,928)
Garner, Michael....4:35:09 (18,431)
Garner, Paul....4:14:13 (13,311)
Garner, Richard....4:42:29 (20,104)
Garner, Robert....4:03:14 (10,891)
Garner, Tony....4:08:13 (11,942)
Garner, William....3:10:11 (1,693)
Garnett, Bob....4:24:41 (15,911)
Garnett, Dennis....4:47:15 (21,235)
Garnett, James....4:04:21 (11,146)
Garnett, Lee....5:41:14 (29,095)
Garney, James....5:15:44 (26,349)
Garnier, Pierre-Philippe....4:11:38 (12,671)
Garratt, Christopher....3:10:11 (1,693)
Garratt, David....4:32:27 (17,821)
Garratt, John....4:46:47 (21,143)
Garrett, Mark....3:05:48 (1,307)
Garrett, Paul....6:01:56 (30,339)
Garrett, Philip....5:26:28 (27,733)
Garrett, Richard....5:41:01 (29,078)
Garrido, Joseph....3:29:17 (4,040)
Garrity, Adrian....4:22:51 (15,455)
Garrity, Roger....3:46:45 (7,075)
Garrod, Adrian....4:11:25 (12,625)
Garrood, Steve....4:28:02 (16,715)
Garside, Duncan....5:29:12 (28,005)
Garside, Simon....3:23:32 (3,184)
Garth, Crispian....3:59:15 (10,021)
Garth, Robert....6:16:41 (30,884)
Gartland, David....5:09:31 (25,476)
Gartside, Jamie....2:54:31 (560)
Gartside, Simon....4:28:14 (16,776)
Garvey, Clem....3:54:12 (8,705)
Garvey, Stephen....3:28:48 (3,970)
Garza, Gerardo....6:00:37 (30,279)
Garza, Gerardo Jnr....4:58:37 (23,722)
Gascoigne, Martin....5:38:09 (28,824)
Gascoigne, Timothy....4:24:28 (15,860)
Gascoigne-Pees, Edward....4:34:19 (18,246)
Gashe, Terry....3:48:30 (7,400)
Gaskarth, Andrew....3:12:28 (1,923)
Gaskell, Alex....2:51:23 (428)
Gaskell, Ben....4:28:11 (16,761)
Gaskell, Robert....4:50:57 (22,059)
Gaskell, Tony....3:57:22 (9,548)
Gaskin, Damian....4:12:12 (12,819)
Gaskin, Edward....3:45:25 (6,811)
Gasparini, Tiziano....2:44:48 (232)
Gasty, Urs....4:28:36 (16,886)
Gates, Anthony....4:08:38 (12,047)
Gateson, Gary....4:46:51 (21,161)
Gatfield, Christopher....3:54:54 (8,893)
Gatherer, William....4:07:18 (11,756)
Gatiss, Ian....5:25:20 (27,592)
Gatley, David....4:55:54 (23,132)
Gatward, David....3:25:33 (3,468)
Gaucher, George....6:15:48 (30,851)
Gaughan, John....6:17:43 (30,911)
Gaukroger, Antony....5:02:20 (24,366)
Gaul, Stephen....5:04:41 (24,730)
Gauld, Sid....3:35:00 (4,912)
Gault, Ian....3:59:02 (9,971)
Gault, Robert....3:03:37 (1,162)
Gaunt, Alex....3:56:18 (9,271)
Gaunt, David....5:16:39 (26,445)
Gaunt, John....4:11:40 (12,683)
Gaunt, Martin....2:57:59 (765)
Gaunt, Mike....4:50:20 (21,930)
Gaunt, Nicholas....3:59:33 (10,105)
Gaunt, Oliver....5:02:04 (24,323)
Gaunt-Edwards, Stephen....3:53:53 (8,642)
Gautrey-Pijpker, David....5:07:50 (25,243)
Gavaghan, James....5:21:08 (27,041)
Gavelle, Daniel....3:12:59 (1,987)
Gavigan, Martin....5:39:26 (28,942)
Gavilli, Alain....5:33:54 (28,470)
Gavin, Ciaran....4:45:16 (20,788)
Gavin, Dominic....5:03:11 (24,488)
Gavin, John....3:54:54 (8,893)
Gavin, John....4:25:48 (16,201)
Gavin, Lee....4:13:01 (13,008)
Gavins, Neil....3:30:37 (4,260)
Gawley, James....5:30:20 (28,121)
Gawn, Richard....5:15:32 (26,316)
Gay, Andrew....4:27:41 (16,643)
Gay, Andrew....4:58:15 (23,638)
Gay, Christopher....4:19:51 (14,704)
Gay, Christopher....4:26:57 (16,458)
Gay, David....4:07:00 (11,687)
Gaylard, Jonathan....4:36:12 (18,691)
Gaylor, Ryan....3:42:53 (6,337)
Gaynor, Colin....5:05:35 (24,898)
Gaynor, James....3:31:14 (4,365)
Gaze, Stevie....4:50:28 (21,956)
Gazeley, Andrew....4:51:21 (22,167)
Gazzard, Nathan....5:13:23 (26,024)
Geake, William....3:31:47 (4,450)
Geal, Tim....4:35:07 (18,417)
Gear, Alistair....4:02:20 (10,703)
Gear, Allan....5:35:45 (28,617)
Gearing, Alan....4:05:51 (11,467)
Geary, Richard....4:57:15 (23,437)
Geary, Vivian....5:27:57 (27,888)
Gebbie, Martyn....3:59:35 (10,115)
Geddes, Alan....4:17:43 (14,183)
Geddes, Gordon....3:40:08 (5,820)
Geddes, Tom....4:44:30 (20,615)
Geddes, Will....5:14:36 (26,189)
Gedge, Tony....3:47:57 (7,307)
Gee, David....3:48:30 (7,400)
Gee, Geoffrey....3:05:39 (1,296)
Gee, Raymond....4:13:16 (13,068)
Geen, Peter....4:31:00 (17,498)

Geers, Tom	4:05:24 (11,373)	
Geggie, Stuart	4:41:15 (19,814)	
Gehrke, Ingo	3:45:52 (6,906)	
Geisler, Lars	3:30:06 (4,186)	
Geitner, Joseph	3:12:16 (1,893)	
Gellard, Barry	5:57:28 (30,135)	
Gellatly, Stephen	4:14:32 (13,389)	
Geller, James	4:51:21 (22,167)	
Gelson, Stephen	4:04:42 (11,225)	
Generalczyk, Wiestaw	4:48:07 (21,456)	
Genever, Mark	5:30:52 (28,182)	
Genower, Peter	4:31:56 (17,716)	
Gent, Christopher	5:05:58 (24,948)	
Gentle, Kevin	5:01:25 (24,224)	
Gentot, Rodolphe	3:14:22 (2,174)	
Geoghegan, Peter	3:10:43 (1,730)	
George, Clive	5:29:28 (28,033)	
George, David	3:12:17 (1,901)	
George, Jon	4:49:39 (21,793)	
George, Michael	4:20:00 (14,743)	
George, Neil	4:11:44 (12,702)	
George, Nicholas	3:51:32 (8,086)	
George, Richard	3:05:37 (1,295)	
George, Richard	4:20:47 (14,923)	
George, Robin	5:36:02 (28,641)	
George, Russell	5:22:41 (27,231)	
George, Zane	4:42:49 (20,188)	
Georgiadis, Vassos	3:43:35 (6,460)	
Georgiou, George	6:27:33 (31,249)	
Geraghty, Roger	2:47:42 (320)	
Gerakaris, Yiannis	3:16:47 (2,404)	
Gerhardt, Manfred	3:07:05 (1,410)	
German, Robin	6:48:04 (31,676)	
Germanis, Nikolaos	3:48:36 (7,425)	
Germann, Alfres	3:16:10 (2,342)	
Gerrard, Scott	4:16:52 (13,954)	
Gerrard, Stuart	5:59:59 (30,256)	
Gerrity, Tony	3:17:39 (2,509)	
Gershlick, Anthony	4:52:39 (22,431)	
Gerundini, Anthony	3:16:06 (2,336)	
Gervaise-Jones, Henry	5:20:28 (26,951)	
Gerweck, James	4:41:51 (19,960)	
Gething, Dominic	4:27:28 (16,593)	
Gething, Fraser	3:39:46 (5,744)	
Gething, Mark	5:53:28 (29,904)	
Geyton, Barry	5:14:29 (26,172)	
Gfiffiths, Mike	3:50:54 (7,926)	
Gharoomi, Mohamad	4:56:41 (23,313)	
Ghazvinian, John	6:05:30 (30,478)	
Ghermezian, Romano Ramin	2:43:59 (216)	
Gholkar, Santosh	5:36:13 (28,655)	
Ghosh, Robin	3:44:11 (6,577)	
Giangiacomi, Luigino	4:01:06 (10,449)	
Giangrossi, Bruno	5:09:40 (25,499)	
Gianquitto, John	5:09:00 (25,407)	
Giansiracusa, Salvatore	3:38:41 (5,538)	
Gibb, Andy	3:34:39 (4,862)	
Gibb, Simon	3:42:57 (6,354)	
Gibb, Tom	4:52:11 (22,335)	
Gibbard, Mark	4:17:48 (14,210)	
Gibbens, Philip	5:02:06 (24,327)	
Gibbins, David	4:16:17 (13,804)	
Gibbins, Nick	3:59:26 (10,073)	
Gibbins, Richard	3:58:57 (9,955)	
Gibbon, Adrian	4:01:44 (10,586)	
Gibbons, Alan	5:52:35 (29,859)	
Gibbons, Alastair	3:43:44 (6,497)	
Gibbons, Andrew	3:59:48 (10,176)	
Gibbons, Andrew	5:14:50 (26,224)	
Gibbons, Chris	4:10:30 (12,462)	
Gibbons, Clyde	4:25:48 (16,201)	
Gibbons, Gary	4:37:31 (18,987)	
Gibbons, Ian	4:03:47 (11,007)	
Gibbons, John	4:22:36 (15,394)	
Gibbons, Peter	3:23:25 (3,164)	
Gibbons, Philip	6:18:15 (30,946)	
Gibbons, Robert	4:42:09 (20,019)	
Gibbons, Robert	4:44:15 (20,557)	
Gibbons, Stuart	3:46:19 (6,997)	
Gibbs, Alexander	4:55:08 (22,949)	
Gibbs, Andrew	3:14:23 (2,175)	
Gibbs, Anthony	3:31:18 (4,381)	
Gibbs, Edward	3:39:59 (5,782)	
Gibbs, Glyn	3:31:32 (4,417)	
Gibbs, Graham	3:41:31 (6,072)	
Gibbs, James	4:50:00 (21,856)	
Gibbs, James	4:56:31 (23,266)	
Gibbs, John	3:30:25 (4,237)	
Gibbs, Jonathan	5:39:58 (28,990)	
Gibbs, Keith	4:49:48 (21,823)	
Gibbs, Stephen	4:31:59 (17,724)	
Gibbs, Timothy	3:27:09 (3,699)	
Gibby, Rob	4:09:48 (12,301)	
Giblin, John	6:44:52 (31,620)	
Giboin, Xavier	3:42:33 (6,265)	
Gibson, Alan	4:06:11 (11,533)	
Gibson, David	3:22:20 (3,028)	
Gibson, David	4:24:04 (15,771)	
Gibson, Dean	3:15:48 (2,314)	
Gibson, Glyn	5:05:39 (24,909)	
Gibson, John	3:47:14 (7,161)	
Gibson, John	5:12:00 (25,826)	
Gibson, John	6:46:36 (31,650)	
Gibson, Mark	4:45:18 (20,796)	
Gibson, Mark	4:47:14 (21,232)	
Gibson, Matthew	3:55:38 (9,088)	
Gibson, Nicholas	4:12:28 (12,876)	
Gibson, Paul	4:54:07 (22,732)	
Gibson, Paul	5:05:39 (24,909)	
Gibson, Peter	4:32:42 (17,879)	
Gibson, Tony	4:59:32 (23,893)	
Gibson, William	5:41:12 (29,091)	
Gidalla, Lee	4:06:45 (11,643)	
Giertsen, Bjorn	4:29:22 (17,081)	
Gifford, Christopher	5:01:22 (24,216)	
Gijs, Bruno	3:29:12 (4,026)	
Gilares, Jean-Pierre	3:32:20 (4,514)	
Gilbank, Neale	5:35:11 (28,571)	
Gilbert, Andrew	3:10:03 (1,681)	
Gilbert, Andrew	4:25:16 (16,074)	
Gilbert, Barry	4:30:23 (17,336)	
Gilbert, Brendon	3:43:35 (6,460)	
Gilbert, David	3:29:21 (4,055)	
Gilbert, James	4:18:52 (14,468)	
Gilbert, Jonathan	3:44:30 (6,635)	
Gilbert, Mark	3:55:11 (8,962)	
Gilbert, Paul	3:48:32 (7,409)	
Gilbert, Paul	4:15:04 (13,529)	
Gilbert, Reginald	4:02:53 (10,824)	
Gilbert, Richard	3:23:29 (3,176)	
Gilbert, Richard	5:01:47 (24,279)	
Gilbert, Robert	3:14:05 (2,139)	
Gilbert, Robert	4:29:17 (17,057)	
Gilbert, Roger	5:17:52 (26,590)	
Gilbert, Steve	6:28:25 (31,283)	
Gilbertson, John	3:45:43 (6,876)	
Gilbey, Ken	4:14:12 (13,308)	
Gilbody, Keith	4:59:58 (23,977)	
Gilby, Pete	3:47:12 (7,157)	
Gilchrist, Tyrone	4:43:11 (20,281)	
Gildea, Richard	5:18:28 (26,695)	
Giles, Adrian	3:42:15 (6,194)	
Giles, Christopher	4:04:07 (11,096)	
Giles, Kevin	3:28:44 (3,952)	
Giles, Martin	2:49:18 (372)	
Giles, Matthew	2:54:56 (586)	
Giles, Matthew	5:06:47 (25,073)	
Giles, Simon	3:56:30 (9,318)	
Gilg, Jerome	3:36:07 (5,081)	
Gilks, Robert	3:36:53 (5,209)	
Gill, Amarjit	5:41:23 (29,106)	
Gill, Colin	3:55:32 (9,058)	
Gill, Dave	3:54:32 (8,793)	
Gill, Gavin	4:04:43 (11,230)	
Gill, James	3:47:28 (7,207)	
Gill, Keith	3:04:45 (1,228)	
Gill, Mark	5:03:31 (24,532)	
Gill, Merrick	4:49:25 (21,726)	
Gill, Mike	4:14:38 (13,409)	
Gill, Nicholas	3:58:41 (9,882)	
Gill, Paul	3:51:47 (8,144)	
Gill, Ray	4:48:22 (21,512)	
Gill, Robert	3:56:35 (9,341)	
Gill, Robert	4:45:55 (20,939)	
Gill, Roy	5:07:18 (25,147)	
Gill, Timothy	3:59:42 (10,154)	
Gill, Trevor	5:48:22 (29,596)	
Gillard, Vernon	4:16:09 (13,773)	
Gillbanks, Matthew	3:18:11 (2,576)	
Gillen, Timothy	3:15:41 (2,307)	
Gillespie, Angus	3:20:07 (2,773)	
Gillespie, John	3:40:34 (5,878)	
Gillespie, Neil	3:19:32 (2,703)	
Gillespie, Norman	4:17:41 (14,172)	
Gillett, Lee	5:21:14 (27,056)	
Gillham, Tom	4:51:38 (22,231)	
Gillian, David	4:09:30 (12,228)	
Gillies, Crawford	4:13:22 (13,086)	
Gillies, Michael	5:43:34 (29,276)	
Gillies, Richard	4:19:23 (14,589)	
Gilligan, Eddie	3:00:23 (964)	
Gilling, Jonathan	2:54:23 (556)	
Gillings, Garry	4:13:30 (13,125)	
Gillingwater, Paul	3:54:58 (8,911)	
Gillman, Clive	3:19:37 (2,714)	
Gillon, Thomas	3:23:00 (3,110)	
Gillott, Paul	4:40:56 (19,736)	
Gillson, Stephen	3:10:44 (1,735)	
Gilmartin, Chris	4:56:58 (23,371)	
Gilmartin, James	3:57:43 (9,622)	
Gilmartin, Noel	4:11:17 (12,594)	
Gilmour, Charles	4:44:20 (20,577)	
Gilmour, James	3:55:05 (8,933)	
Gilmour, Jamie	5:58:22 (30,177)	
Gilmour, Rory	3:50:40 (7,877)	
Gilson, Kenneth	3:31:04 (4,339)	
Gilson, Richard	5:41:27 (29,111)	
Gilson, Thomas	4:07:50 (11,879)	
Ginesy, Albert	4:12:11 (12,813)	
Giovannini, Fabio	4:30:21 (17,322)	
Girlanda, Raffaele	3:46:09 (6,962)	
Girling, David	4:37:59 (19,084)	
Girling, Stephen	4:18:29 (14,351)	
Girling, Stuart	4:43:06 (20,263)	
Giro-Cata, Jordi	3:01:49 (1,042)	
Gisby, Alan	3:48:11 (7,354)	
Gittos, Kenneth	4:54:43 (22,870)	
Giudici, Kevin	3:44:22 (6,615)	
Giuli, Claudio	3:58:17 (9,776)	
Glackin, Brian	3:23:51 (3,221)	
Gladikowski, Jens	3:50:13 (7,783)	
Gladwell, Nathan	4:29:36 (17,139)	
Gladwin, John	5:52:56 (29,877)	
Glaister, Joseph	3:59:56 (10,210)	
Glaister, Warren	5:21:13 (27,052)	
Glanville, Richard	4:24:45 (15,937)	
Glardon, Daniel	2:59:04 (863)	
Glass, Andy	3:35:59 (5,063)	
Glass, Garry	3:29:58 (4,162)	
Glass, Martyn	4:19:42 (14,667)	
Glasspool, Justin	3:31:11 (4,357)	
Glatman, Mark	7:07:14 (31,964)	
Glaysher, Nicholas	5:08:23 (25,322)	
Glazebrook, Jamie	4:20:47 (14,923)	
Glazebrook, Joe	5:33:53 (28,465)	
Glazebrook, Martin	5:07:14 (25,132)	
Glazin, Jeffrey	4:50:08 (21,887)	
Gleave, Oliver	3:58:55 (9,946)	
Gleaves, Alexander	4:50:25 (21,944)	
Gleaves, Peter	4:03:48 (11,014)	
Gleeson, Darren	4:30:22 (17,328)	
Gleeson, Declan	5:49:39 (29,693)	
Gleeson, Gerard	5:04:02 (24,640)	
Gleeson, James	3:59:47 (10,173)	
Gleeson, Luke	3:26:48 (3,644)	
Glen, Andrew	3:23:01 (3,112)	
Glen, Graham	3:56:18 (9,701)	
Glen, Jonathan	5:33:18 (28,402)	
Glendenning, David	3:52:31 (8,314)	
Glendinning, Kevin	3:30:42 (4,277)	
Glendinning, Paul	3:06:36 (1,368)	
Glendinning, Ross	3:10:39 (1,725)	
Glenn, Alistair	4:08:12 (11,938)	
Glenn, Barry	4:58:13 (23,629)	
Glennie, Christian	4:23:32 (15,625)	
Glenville, David	4:43:51 (20,470)	
Glew, Paul	4:38:16 (19,150)	
Glew, Peter	5:27:02 (27,778)	
Glew, Steve	3:55:44 (9,116)	

Glibbery, Robert	5:19:59 (26,884)
Glick, Peter-Anthony	4:30:12 (17,287)
Glide, Michael	4:41:38 (19,896)
Glinn, Paul	4:54:30 (22,814)
Glossop, Nigel	3:45:50 (6,895)
Gloster, James	4:13:19 (13,078)
Glover, Adrian	4:31:00 (17,498)
Glover, Christopher	5:59:20 (30,228)
Glover, Davey	6:40:38 (31,551)
Glover, James	4:19:40 (14,658)
Glover, John	4:58:54 (23,781)
Glover, Jonathan	4:15:47 (13,697)
Glover, Lee	3:37:25 (5,318)
Glover, Mark	4:53:45 (22,672)
Glover, Peter	4:48:24 (21,517)
Glynne-Jones, Jeremy	4:52:55 (22,487)
Gnatiuk, Stefan	5:28:25 (27,933)
Goarnisson, Luc	3:24:09 (3,273)
Godbee, Peter	3:44:35 (6,647)
Godber, James	5:09:26 (25,465)
Goddard, Barry	3:55:14 (8,974)
Goddard, Ian	4:58:04 (23,599)
Goddard, Matthew	4:37:11 (18,919)
Goddard, Michael	3:24:03 (3,254)
Goddard, Pete	4:45:09 (20,757)
Goddard, Steve	4:36:20 (18,722)
Goddard, Trevor	3:08:20 (1,527)
Godden, Iain	4:15:57 (13,733)
Godden, Ian	3:04:59 (1,245)
Godden, Oliver	4:02:19 (10,698)
Godfray, Tim	4:43:42 (20,431)
Godfrey, Andrew	3:56:28 (9,310)
Godfrey, Christopher	4:57:01 (23,384)
Godfrey, David	4:35:07 (18,417)
Godfrey, David	6:09:37 (30,622)
Godfrey, Ronald	4:49:26 (21,733)
Godfrey, Ryan	5:25:12 (27,574)
Godfrey, William	3:57:35 (9,591)
Godier, Neil	4:45:14 (20,776)
Godrich, Shane	3:04:33 (1,216)
Godwin, David	3:47:44 (7,263)
Godwin, Graham	5:03:48 (24,592)
Godwin, Mark	4:39:47 (19,497)
Godwin, Steven	3:40:03 (5,799)
Godwin, William	3:58:36 (9,857)
Goebbels, Sean	4:21:29 (15,107)
Goebel, Matthias	2:56:34 (679)
Goessweiner, Herwig	4:54:12 (22,747)
Goetschi, Rolf	4:06:42 (11,625)
Goff, Matthew	3:49:46 (7,691)
Goffin, Philippe	4:45:04 (20,737)
Goggin, Brad	2:44:23 (227)
Goh, Eng	6:02:53 (30,369)
Gold, Adam	4:10:30 (12,462)
Gold, David	3:55:35 (9,070)
Gold, Joel	4:13:03 (13,016)
Gold, Jon	4:59:01 (23,804)
Gold, Lindsay	3:59:52 (10,193)
Gold, Mark	5:42:26 (29,202)
Gold, Nick	5:40:37 (29,045)
Gold, Paul	3:58:27 (9,823)
Golder, Andrew	5:21:34 (27,093)
Goldie, Christopher	5:46:34 (29,466)
Golding, Graham	4:46:28 (21,085)
Golding, John	4:35:33 (18,527)
Golding, Nick	4:15:00 (13,507)
Golding, Stephen	5:10:54 (25,678)
Goldingham, Alexander	3:26:54 (3,658)
Goldman, Paul	4:16:51 (13,947)
Golds, Nigel	6:53:44 (31,801)
Goldsmid, Graham	3:29:23 (4,062)
Goldsmith, James	3:54:19 (8,732)
Goldsmith, Paul	3:31:16 (4,373)
Goldsmith, Peter	7:36:56 (32,191)
Goldsmith, Stuart	3:30:52 (4,307)
Goldsworthy, Gary	4:34:00 (18,168)
Goldup, Reginald	6:40:19 (31,544)
Golla, Steve	3:34:45 (4,873)
Golliker, Stephen	5:27:06 (27,789)
Gomer, Lindsay	3:34:08 (4,766)
Gomez, Luis	3:19:21 (2,684)
Gomez, Matthew	3:54:46 (8,859)
Gomeze, Jason	3:58:40 (9,877)

Gomm, Philip	3:37:00 (5,229)
Gommers, Kees	5:22:20 (27,193)
Gomperts, Larry	4:31:49 (17,692)
Gompertz, Gary	5:32:09 (28,303)
Gonbar, Gabor	3:55:31 (9,052)
Goncalves, José	5:23:31 (27,350)
Gonde, Chris	3:56:12 (9,242)
Gonsalves, Victor	4:18:02 (14,257)
Gonzalez, Edilberto	4:01:52 (10,613)
Gonzalez, Espiridion	3:54:32 (8,793)
Gonzalez, Joaquin	3:11:19 (1,782)
Gonzalez, Pablo	3:29:43 (4,129)
Gonzalez-Alvarex, Antonio	4:04:06 (11,090)
Gonzalez-Gallardo, José	4:57:47 (23,540)
Good, Christopher	4:45:19 (20,798)
Good, Michael	4:27:00 (16,470)
Goodair, Andrew	2:56:03 (652)
Goodall, Graham	4:09:48 (12,301)
Goodall, Malcolm	3:46:21 (7,005)
Goodall, Martin	4:29:05 (17,010)
Goodchild, Mark	3:46:23 (7,012)
Goode, Alan	4:12:50 (12,966)
Goode, Darren	4:56:48 (23,337)
Goode, Tom	6:02:09 (30,346)
Gooden, Steven	5:50:08 (29,728)
Goodenough, Gary	5:22:27 (27,205)
Goodenough, Robert	5:17:52 (26,590)
Gooderham, Howard	5:25:14 (27,582)
Goodey, David	5:05:04 (24,806)
Goodfellow, Andrew	5:30:40 (28,160)
Goodfellow, Christopher	5:18:17 (26,670)
Goodfellow, Richard	4:30:35 (17,386)
Goodger, Gary	3:36:40 (5,175)
Goodhand, Martyn	4:01:34 (10,555)
Gooding, Simon	4:31:59 (17,724)
Goodison, Joel	4:13:50 (13,210)
Goodlad, Robin	3:55:18 (8,996)
Goodman, Alan	4:32:08 (17,759)
Goodman, Andrew	5:12:33 (25,909)
Goodman, Kevin	6:06:57 (30,528)
Goodman, Paul	5:01:10 (24,179)
Goodman, Peter	3:21:31 (2,936)
Goodman, Tim	3:49:16 (7,582)
Goodrich, Luke	3:51:31 (8,080)
Goodsall, James	3:55:49 (9,132)
Goodship, Antony	4:19:18 (14,572)
Goodson, Andrew	3:50:00 (7,734)
Goodspeed, Ray	3:55:39 (9,091)
Goodwill, James	4:23:51 (15,708)
Goodwin, Barry	3:14:08 (2,146)
Goodwin, Brian	4:55:41 (23,074)
Goodwin, Colin	4:18:25 (14,334)
Goodwin, David	3:40:35 (5,883)
Goodwin, David	4:07:50 (11,879)
Goodwin, Edward	5:09:51 (25,521)
Goodwin, Graham	4:49:20 (21,711)
Goodwin, Ian	3:41:58 (6,142)
Goodwin, Lee	4:27:59 (16,703)
Goodwin, Leon	3:08:28 (1,541)
Goodwin, Michael	5:20:22 (26,933)
Goodwin, Ron	4:54:51 (22,891)
Goodwin, Simon	4:33:21 (18,019)
Goodwin, Stephen	3:29:09 (4,020)
Goodwin, Terry	4:21:18 (15,060)
Goodworth, David	3:35:26 (4,984)
Goody, Christopher	5:12:43 (25,934)
Goodyear, Clive	3:52:42 (8,354)
Goodyer, Stephen	4:30:16 (17,302)
Googe, Michael	5:04:00 (24,628)
Goole, Brian	3:31:42 (4,435)
Goossens, John	3:40:05 (5,807)
Gordine, Alan	5:19:24 (26,818)
Gordon, Alex	4:38:32 (19,206)
Gordon, Andrew	5:29:35 (28,049)
Gordon, Anthony	4:24:02 (15,761)
Gordon, Bradley	5:08:36 (25,346)
Gordon, Chris	4:21:01 (14,983)
Gordon, Christopher	5:53:32 (29,906)
Gordon, Eric	3:04:56 (1,242)
Gordon, Glenn	3:50:39 (7,873)
Gordon, Ian	4:22:57 (15,482)
Gordon, James	4:07:18 (11,756)
Gordon, Jeffrey	4:22:54 (15,471)

Gordon, Jonathan	4:23:30 (15,616)
Gordon, Richard	5:07:44 (25,230)
Gordon-Brown, Paul	4:05:46 (11,447)
Gordon-Smith, Giles	3:56:13 (9,249)
Gordon-Wilkin, Gareth	4:23:19 (15,578)
Gore, Amos	2:55:34 (624)
Gore, Andy	2:30:51 (66)
Gore, Jason	4:20:18 (14,819)
Gore, Jeremy	5:58:46 (30,189)
Gorie, Georges	3:19:46 (2,730)
Gorman, Garrett	4:06:45 (11,643)
Gorman, Kieran	4:44:41 (20,655)
Gorman, Mark	3:44:03 (6,555)
Gorman, Michael	4:12:10 (12,805)
Gormley, Gerard	3:23:12 (3,136)
Gorrie, Tomas	4:46:54 (21,169)
Gorrod, Nicholas	3:08:45 (1,567)
Gorry, Paul	4:41:52 (19,966)
Gorton, Carl	4:28:49 (16,939)
Gosbee, Norman	4:14:09 (13,298)
Gosling, Christopher	4:46:24 (21,070)
Gosling, Peter	3:48:12 (7,359)
Goss, Ernest	3:29:29 (4,090)
Gossage, Michael	5:33:45 (28,445)
Goss-Custard, John	4:22:50 (15,449)
Gothard, Alan	5:23:07 (27,303)
Gothard, Jeremy	4:08:59 (12,127)
Gotobed, Benjamin	5:06:44 (25,061)
Gott, Adrian	5:05:20 (24,847)
Gottfredsson, Magnus	3:07:31 (1,454)
Gotts, Nigel	3:13:02 (1,996)
Gotts, Terry	3:47:35 (7,232)
Goubert, Carey	4:08:45 (12,078)
Goucher, Dave	4:48:02 (21,437)
Gough, Christopher	5:00:36 (24,090)
Gough, Dan	4:36:37 (18,792)
Gough, James	5:17:08 (26,497)
Gough, John	3:33:50 (4,723)
Goulbourne, Hugh	4:19:17 (14,570)
Goulbourne, Patrick	4:26:15 (16,308)
Gould, Andrew	4:32:54 (17,924)
Gould, Christopher	4:41:43 (19,925)
Gould, Daniel	3:48:46 (7,457)
Gould, Jason	3:56:30 (9,318)
Gould, Martin	3:13:21 (2,041)
Gould, Simon	3:49:54 (7,712)
Gould, Stuart	5:06:42 (25,056)
Goulding, Jon	5:15:42 (26,344)
Goulding, Mark	3:13:37 (2,073)
Goundry, William	3:35:21 (4,966)
Gourdon, Patrick	4:39:02 (19,328)
Gouriff, Yann	3:53:05 (8,447)
Gournay, Kevin	4:20:01 (14,748)
Gousse-Brickman, Eric	3:35:24 (4,972)
Govi, Gabriele	5:40:01 (28,995)
Govier, Adrian	5:18:06 (26,630)
Govier, Gordon	4:32:43 (17,885)
Govier, Neil	3:36:48 (5,193)
Govier, Steven	4:58:01 (23,583)
Gow, Bryn	4:49:50 (21,832)
Gow, Chris	4:13:58 (13,251)
Gow, James	4:17:44 (14,189)
Goward, Luke	5:07:49 (25,241)
Gowda, Nanda	4:08:58 (12,124)
Gowdy, Michael	4:25:07 (16,031)
Gower, Matthew	3:28:47 (3,966)
Gower, Simon	4:00:47 (10,381)
Gowers, Ian	3:07:30 (1,452)
Goyvaerts, Eric	4:08:36 (12,042)
Grabham, Mark	4:20:33 (14,882)
Grace, Ian	3:44:03 (6,555)
Grace, Kevin	5:09:19 (25,452)
Grace, Ray	4:40:03 (19,549)
Grace, Samuel	4:03:16 (10,906)
Gradshaw, John	6:26:53 (31,226)
Grady, John	3:40:25 (5,863)
Grady, Matthew	4:01:29 (10,536)
Grafton, Graham	5:30:06 (28,094)
Grafton, Jonathan	4:59:22 (23,868)
Graham, Colin	5:17:26 (26,531)
Graham, David	3:30:46 (4,292)
Graham, Dominic	4:50:00 (21,856)
Graham, Hugh	4:12:06 (12,786)

Graham, Ian 4:25:35 (16,153)
Graham, John 4:25:53 (16,224)
Graham, John 5:17:29 (26,541)
Graham, Joseph 5:11:40 (25,784)
Graham, Leigh 4:45:48 (20,913)
Graham, Mark 3:14:35 (2,195)
Graham, Michael 3:54:29 (8,776)
Graham, Michael 4:34:23 (18,259)
Graham, Paul 4:22:23 (15,336)
Graham, Ray 4:20:29 (14,864)
Graham, Raymond 2:39:43 (151)
Graham, Richard 4:19:13 (14,555)
Graham, Richard 4:45:00 (20,717)
Graham, Robbie 4:19:33 (14,626)
Graham, Robert 4:54:34 (22,831)
Graham, Stuart 4:11:34 (12,660)
Graham, Tom 4:29:42 (17,162)
Grailard, Joel 4:36:26 (18,753)
Grain, Alastair 4:40:08 (19,565)
Grainge, Nigel 3:55:08 (8,947)
Grainger, Alan 4:56:38 (23,294)
Grainger, Andrew 3:36:02 (5,069)
Grainger, Matt 4:28:20 (16,801)
Grainger, Nick 4:47:22 (21,261)
Grainger, Rod 3:49:36 (7,656)
Grainger, Steve 3:39:21 (5,666)
Grajetzki, Dieter 4:11:50 (12,727)
Graney, Barry 3:05:25 (1,283)
Granger, Derek 4:30:05 (17,259)
Granger, Steve 5:15:27 (26,309)
Granieri, Richard 5:46:57 (29,486)
Grann, Joergen 3:17:09 (2,444)
Grant, Andrew 5:41:57 (29,156)
Grant, Andrew 5:50:14 (29,736)
Grant, Gareth 5:02:46 (24,430)
Grant, Iain 4:30:25 (17,350)
Grant, Ian 4:17:09 (14,024)
Grant, Karl 5:04:45 (24,747)
Grant, Kenneth 4:58:04 (23,599)
Grant, Lewis 4:17:15 (14,045)
Grant, Michael 3:44:10 (6,575)
Grant, Neil 5:00:14 (24,022)
Grant, Patrick 3:35:53 (5,053)
Grant, Peter 3:58:55 (9,946)
Grant, Shaun 4:20:25 (14,851)
Grant, William 2:37:04 (123)
Gras, Harry 3:52:44 (8,361)
Grasso, Angelo 3:37:43 (5,369)
Grater, Adrian 4:19:14 (14,559)
Grattan, John 4:16:09 (13,773)
Gratton, Kenneth 4:16:52 (13,954)
Gravatt, Christopher 4:36:42 (18,809)
Graves, Dean 3:34:20 (4,800)
Graves, Malcolm 4:40:07 (19,561)
Graves, Matthew 3:35:56 (5,060)
Graves, Sam 5:44:24 (29,328)
Graves, William 6:26:50 (31,225)
Gravis, Craig 4:51:00 (22,070)
Gray, Adam 3:11:55 (1,853)
Gray, Adam 5:17:53 (26,592)
Gray, Alastair 3:14:12 (2,152)
Gray, Anthony 3:08:10 (1,514)
Gray, Brett 3:19:03 (2,659)
Gray, Brian 4:26:24 (16,334)
Gray, Cliff 4:14:12 (13,308)
Gray, Colin 3:08:22 (1,533)
Gray, Colin 5:27:20 (27,813)
Gray, Conor 4:52:42 (22,439)
Gray, David 3:28:34 (3,913)
Gray, Dean 4:35:41 (18,558)
Gray, Dennis 4:29:45 (17,178)
Gray, Douglas 5:33:48 (28,452)
Gray, Hamish 3:50:17 (7,796)
Gray, Ian 3:29:02 (4,007)
Gray, James 5:19:36 (26,839)
Gray, John 3:51:31 (8,080)
Gray, John 4:54:17 (22,767)
Gray, Jonathan 3:59:37 (10,125)
Gray, Keith 5:25:00 (27,536)
Gray, Kelvin 3:47:31 (7,216)
Gray, Malcolm 5:53:56 (29,927)
Gray, Matthew 3:42:21 (6,209)
Gray, Matthew 4:07:43 (11,854)
Gray, Myles 4:50:40 (22,005)
Gray, Nick 3:35:53 (5,053)
Gray, Nigel 4:55:45 (23,097)
Gray, Paul 3:39:34 (5,706)
Gray, Paul 4:15:08 (13,550)
Gray, Paul 5:27:02 (27,778)
Gray, Peter 3:54:22 (8,743)
Gray, Peter 4:26:56 (16,456)
Gray, Philip 5:06:11 (24,981)
Gray, Richard 4:41:01 (19,754)
Gray, Robin 4:28:45 (16,922)
Gray, Samuel 3:24:52 (3,380)
Gray, Simon 4:29:41 (17,159)
Gray, Stephen 4:41:01 (19,754)
Gray, Steve 4:53:15 (22,556)
Gray, Stuart 3:19:19 (2,681)
Gray, Stuart 4:58:02 (23,591)
Gray, Tony 4:13:07 (13,026)
Gray, Tony 5:17:58 (26,604)
Gray, Vincent 3:54:10 (8,696)
Graydon, Simon 3:29:26 (4,075)
Graysmark, Richard 3:53:38 (8,574)
Graysmark, Robin 4:19:32 (14,624)
Grayson, Robert 4:58:05 (23,606)
Graziano, Giovanni 4:22:52 (15,458)
Grealis, Kevin 3:17:47 (2,526)
Grealy, Vince 3:47:26 (7,199)
Greasby, Olliver 4:32:57 (17,935)
Greatorex, Ben 3:56:11 (9,234)
Greaves, Barry 3:12:18 (1,904)
Greaves, Colin 4:15:24 (13,620)
Greaves, Ian 5:00:09 (24,001)
Greaves, Marcus 3:55:04 (8,929)
Greaves, Mark 3:07:27 (1,450)
Greaves, Michael 4:31:03 (17,513)
Grecian, Peter 3:56:12 (9,242)
Greco, Marco 3:14:55 (2,230)
Gredka, Jacek 4:17:43 (14,183)
Greedy, Philip 4:01:58 (10,629)
Green, Andrew 2:44:36 (229)
Green, Andrew 4:56:23 (23,238)
Green, Andrew 5:47:41 (29,550)
Green, Andy 4:04:08 (11,098)
Green, Aron 4:07:51 (11,884)
Green, Ashley 4:13:53 (13,226)
Green, Ben 4:04:27 (11,163)
Green, Brett 4:51:21 (22,167)
Green, Charles 3:00:40 (986)
Green, Chris 4:48:02 (21,437)
Green, Colin 3:51:04 (7,971)
Green, Colin 3:57:14 (9,513)
Green, Daniel 4:12:59 (13,000)
Green, David 3:13:09 (2,012)
Green, David 3:14:10 (2,149)
Green, David 3:24:23 (3,314)
Green, David 3:28:17 (3,861)
Green, David 4:14:03 (13,275)
Green, David 4:58:36 (23,718)
Green, David 5:18:24 (26,683)
Green, Dominic 5:16:35 (26,434)
Green, Donald 3:42:46 (6,312)
Green, Gary 4:53:40 (22,647)
Green, Gavin 4:33:14 (17,990)
Green, James 4:15:03 (13,525)
Green, James 4:43:56 (20,483)
Green, James 5:09:10 (25,432)
Green, John 3:11:00 (1,756)
Green, John 3:34:52 (4,886)
Green, John 3:51:20 (8,039)
Green, Jonathan 5:15:54 (26,361)
Green, Jonathan 5:24:30 (27,475)
Green, Karl 3:54:40 (8,831)
Green, Laurence 2:54:51 (583)
Green, Mark 4:13:17 (13,072)
Green, Michael 3:25:59 (3,540)
Green, Michael 4:19:40 (14,658)
Green, Michael 4:34:25 (18,271)
Green, Michael 4:35:55 (18,625)
Green, Mick 3:03:33 (1,155)
Green, Neil 3:21:07 (2,893)
Green, Nicholas 4:18:54 (14,479)
Green, Norman 4:01:12 (10,472)
Green, Paul 5:04:07 (24,652)
Green, Phil 6:51:20 (31,748)
Green, Philip 3:43:17 (6,422)
Green, Robert 3:26:45 (3,639)
Green, Robert 4:23:12 (15,547)
Green, Robert 6:16:34 (30,880)
Green, Roger 6:37:50 (31,505)
Green, Simon 3:29:28 (4,083)
Green, Stephen 4:48:54 (21,614)
Green, Steven 3:14:37 (2,200)
Green, Stuart 4:55:39 (23,065)
Green, Timothy 3:54:28 (8,771)
Green, Trevor 4:42:10 (20,022)
Green, Vincent 4:00:42 (10,367)
Greenaway, Andy 4:04:11 (11,108)
Greenbank, Martin 4:06:34 (11,605)
Greenbaum, Marc 4:45:28 (20,837)
Greene, Brendan 3:17:10 (2,449)
Greene, David 4:18:20 (14,309)
Greene, Harvey 5:48:18 (29,595)
Greene, John 3:04:39 (1,225)
Greene, Michael 4:56:52 (23,355)
Greene, Mike 4:22:21 (15,327)
Greenhalgh, David 4:10:03 (12,362)
Greenhalgh, Ian 3:32:26 (4,520)
Greenhalgh, John 4:25:09 (16,043)
Greenhalgh, Mike 4:07:36 (11,832)
Greenhalgh, Paul 4:37:10 (18,912)
Greenhalgh, Steven 4:08:04 (11,917)
Greenham, David 4:09:09 (12,163)
Greenhill, Simon 4:06:07 (11,519)
Greenleaf, Andrew 2:45:08 (238)
Greensill, Mark 3:45:03 (6,741)
Greenslade, David 3:58:17 (9,776)
Greenway, Andrew 2:39:32 (149)
Greenwell, Charles 4:29:37 (17,144)
Greenwell, Robert 5:45:10 (29,382)
Greenwood, Adam 6:03:55 (30,409)
Greenwood, Adrian 5:49:27 (29,672)
Greenwood, Howard 4:46:48 (21,146)
Greenwood, John 3:18:57 (2,650)
Greenwood, Paul 3:32:27 (4,524)
Greenwood, Richard 4:52:46 (22,452)
Greer, Jeremy 3:51:17 (8,025)
Greer, Joseph 3:41:22 (6,034)
Greer, Mark 3:02:00 (1,053)
Greet, Mark 3:15:04 (2,244)
Greeves, Jerry 2:37:43 (129)
Greevy, John 3:40:02 (5,793)
Gregg, John 6:28:53 (31,300)
Gregg, William 3:45:23 (6,806)
Greggio, Davide 4:47:05 (21,198)
Gregoire, Peter 3:21:59 (2,983)
Gregor, John 3:48:48 (7,466)
Gregory, Anthony 4:13:53 (13,226)
Gregory, Brian 5:18:39 (26,718)
Gregory, Bruce 4:56:33 (23,275)
Gregory, Christopher 4:50:45 (22,023)
Gregory, Fraser 4:09:44 (12,280)
Gregory, Geoffrey 3:40:33 (5,873)
Gregory, Kevin 4:22:45 (15,429)
Gregory, Mark 3:11:32 (1,806)
Gregory, Michael 4:16:38 (13,885)
Gregory, Nicholas 3:12:58 (1,986)
Gregory, Paul 4:17:42 (14,176)
Gregory, Ronan 5:00:04 (23,991)
Gregory, Russell 5:24:19 (27,453)
Gregory, Stephen 4:30:42 (17,420)
Gregory, Trevor 3:29:48 (4,144)
Gregson, Jonathan 5:22:06 (27,154)
Grehan, Michael 3:34:11 (4,774)
Greif, Daniel 4:13:26 (13,107)
Greig, Barry 4:27:27 (16,581)
Greiner, Reinhard 3:42:56 (6,349)
Gremo, Adam 4:16:22 (13,823)
Gremo, Christopher 4:16:22 (13,823)
Gremo, Stuart 5:02:08 (24,332)
Grendon, Jaymes 6:16:03 (30,860)
Grenfell, Nigel 3:28:25 (3,888)
Grenson, Freddy 4:45:19 (20,798)
Grenwood, Michael 3:25:40 (3,486)
Gretton, Victor 5:01:59 (24,311)
Greve, Carsten 4:54:05 (22,728)
Grew, Fergus 4:57:52 (23,554)

Grew, Roy 3:53:36 (8,567)
Grewal, Varinder 5:35:56 (28,633)
Grewar, Donald 4:06:13 (11,539)
Grewar, Guy 3:56:55 (9,428)
Grey, Garry 3:35:49 (5,044)
Grey, Jack 4:29:23 (17,084)
Grey, Paul 5:46:33 (29,465)
Grey, Robert 4:57:37 (23,505)
Gribben, Michael 3:53:36 (8,567)
Grice, Benjamin 3:29:34 (4,105)
Grice, David 4:12:43 (12,941)
Gridley, David 4:22:07 (15,267)
Griethe, Wolfgang 4:14:22 (13,349)
Grieve, Graham 3:56:03 (9,194)
Griffen, Richard 4:37:20 (18,954)
Griffin, Anthony 5:57:55 (30,160)
Griffin, Evan 4:17:06 (14,010)
Griffin, Gareth 4:02:17 (10,694)
Griffin, John 5:27:30 (27,832)
Griffin, Kieran 4:59:50 (23,955)
Griffin, Liam 4:27:28 (16,593)
Griffin, Mark 3:49:13 (7,568)
Griffin, Martin 6:33:55 (31,422)
Griffin, Richard 5:52:11 (29,839)
Griffin, Rob 5:06:42 (25,056)
Griffin, Roger 3:36:04 (5,075)
Griffin, Thomas 3:31:29 (4,407)
Griffin, Thomas 4:00:47 (10,381)
Griffith, Barry 3:39:52 (5,764)
Griffith, Chris 3:19:22 (2,686)
Griffith, Jackson 4:21:08 (15,014)
Griffith, John 4:02:16 (10,692)
Griffith, Owen 4:30:46 (17,438)
Griffith, Stephen 3:30:16 (4,216)
Griffith, Timothy 4:08:15 (11,947)
Griffiths, Alan 4:55:13 (22,962)
Griffiths, Alistair 3:20:33 (2,832)
Griffiths, Andrew 4:22:34 (15,379)
Griffiths, Andrew 4:26:05 (16,272)
Griffiths, Andrew 5:10:54 (25,678)
Griffiths, Anthony 3:17:57 (2,543)
Griffiths, Brian 3:47:26 (7,199)
Griffiths, Bryn 3:45:04 (6,746)
Griffiths, Clem 4:58:32 (23,704)
Griffiths, Colin 4:20:01 (14,748)
Griffiths, David 4:16:39 (13,892)
Griffiths, David 4:19:36 (14,639)
Griffiths, Graham 3:19:21 (2,684)
Griffiths, Huw 4:56:35 (23,283)
Griffiths, John 4:29:45 (17,178)
Griffiths, John 6:03:25 (30,389)
Griffiths, Jonathan 5:42:51 (29,231)
Griffiths, Keith 3:31:23 (4,390)
Griffiths, Mark 3:08:33 (1,552)
Griffiths, Mark 5:24:30 (27,475)
Griffiths, Martin 4:14:36 (13,403)
Griffiths, Michael 3:18:04 (2,559)
Griffiths, Neville 3:07:56 (1,495)
Griffiths, Nicholas 4:42:25 (20,088)
Griffiths, Paul 4:30:03 (17,252)
Griffiths, Paul 4:58:26 (23,683)
Griffiths, Peter 3:52:59 (8,422)
Griffiths, Peter 4:17:25 (14,094)
Griffiths, Peter 5:31:55 (28,281)
Grigg, Iain 4:38:46 (19,274)
Griggs, Jeremy 3:58:20 (9,793)
Griggs, Martyn 4:29:46 (17,188)
Grigor, Thomas 5:27:57 (27,888)
Grigsby, Jeffrey 4:28:25 (16,832)
Grigson, Edward 4:17:08 (14,018)
Grimaux, Thierry 4:45:09 (20,757)
Grimes, Matthew 4:07:45 (11,862)
Grimes, Philip 2:48:10 (339)
Grimes, Richard 4:28:37 (16,890)
Grimley, Martyn 4:43:52 (20,475)
Grimmer, Harold 5:25:09 (27,561)
Grimmer, Lothar 5:01:33 (24,239)
Grimsey, William 3:45:08 (6,762)
Grimshaw, Kevin 4:33:27 (18,047)
Grimwood, Paul 4:32:51 (17,913)
Grindrod, Martin 4:21:50 (15,190)
Grindu, Louis 4:11:27 (12,632)
Grist, Rogert 3:45:23 (6,806)
Gristock, David 3:47:42 (7,255)
Gristwood, Andrew 3:11:46 (1,832)
Groenewald, Andrew 3:30:49 (4,298)
Groet, Jurgen 3:36:47 (5,192)
Grondona, Pietro 3:21:56 (2,976)
Gronow, Richard 3:38:47 (5,558)
Groocock, Ian 4:15:48 (13,702)
Groom, Michael 4:21:54 (15,207)
Groom, Nigel 5:24:01 (27,410)
Groom, Simon 4:25:10 (16,047)
Groombridge, Nick 3:54:06 (8,681)
Groombridge, Stephen 2:51:38 (436)
Groombridge, Thomas 4:58:22 (23,664)
Grose, Crispin 3:34:52 (4,886)
Grose, Glen 4:39:48 (19,501)
Gross, Geoffrey 4:25:03 (16,015)
Gross, Iain 4:12:03 (12,772)
Gross, Michel 3:52:15 (8,255)
Gross, Ray 4:29:44 (17,171)
Grosse, Howard 4:08:45 (12,078)
Grosse, Pagrick 3:49:12 (7,562)
Grosse-Lembeck, Josef 3:33:29 (4,675)
Grossman, Doron 3:46:26 (7,017)
Grossman, Kevin 4:42:50 (20,192)
Grossman, Marc 7:02:42 (31,909)
Grosvenor, Iain 4:53:50 (22,686)
Groth, Stefan 4:04:51 (11,257)
Grothusen, Peter 3:08:01 (1,500)
Grout, Paul 4:49:35 (21,776)
Grove, Andrew 3:20:40 (2,842)
Grove, Carl 2:58:51 (836)
Grove, Darren 4:14:01 (13,264)
Grove, Jason 4:47:55 (21,403)
Grove, Nigel 2:57:00 (703)
Grover, Colin 4:17:41 (14,172)
Grover, David 3:06:05 (1,327)
Grover, Simon 5:07:44 (25,230)
Groves, Nick 3:03:36 (1,161)
Groves, Richard 3:10:06 (1,686)
Groves, Rik 3:39:44 (5,734)
Grubb, Matthew 4:10:31 (12,468)
Gruenes, Walter 4:08:18 (11,961)
Gruffydd, Alun 4:58:26 (23,683)
Grumet, Bernhard 3:39:00 (5,598)
Grummitt, Richard 4:23:14 (15,554)
Grundy, Adrian 4:59:46 (23,935)
Grundy, Trevor 3:42:06 (6,168)
Grundy-Wheeler, Henry 5:25:47 (27,638)
Gruner, David 3:49:59 (7,732)
Gruson, Didier 4:56:44 (23,324)
Grutsch, Peter 3:34:24 (4,819)
Guarducci, Luigi 4:32:22 (17,807)
Gubler, Peter 4:16:09 (13,773)
Gudka, Diptan 5:43:45 (29,286)
Gueguen, Jean-Pierre 4:09:02 (12,142)
Guendouz, Omar 4:57:09 (23,424)
Guenebaut, Jean-Michel 3:19:06 (2,662)
Guerra, Patrick 3:24:38 (3,347)
Guerraoui, Salim 3:36:21 (5,124)
Guerra-Zubiaga, David 3:53:41 (8,586)
Guerrerio, Gwaldino 6:29:39 (31,318)
Guerrier, Chris 2:54:06 (542)
Guerrieri, Vincent 5:37:57 (28,807)
Guerrieria, Martin 4:22:09 (15,276)
Guery, Olivier 2:18:56 (21)
Guesnet, Thierry 2:55:00 (593)
Guest, Christopher 5:57:27 (30,134)
Guest, Glyn 3:25:08 (3,413)
Guest, Graham 4:26:49 (16,433)
Guest, Martin 4:32:07 (17,755)
Guest, Paul 3:53:12 (8,474)
Guest, Richard 3:45:18 (6,788)
Guest, Stephen 4:57:45 (23,529)
Guffie, Kenneth 4:57:47 (23,540)
Guffroy, Thomas 4:09:42 (12,274)
Gugger, Christophe 3:09:15 (1,605)
Guichard, Mark 2:46:14 (268)
Guiden, Noel 3:32:10 (4,491)
Guignard, Philippe 3:58:26 (9,818)
Guild, Barry 4:27:23 (16,567)
Guillemot, Herve 3:27:49 (3,787)
Guiney, Aaron 5:45:28 (29,402)
Guisset, Georges 3:57:33 (9,587)
Guivarch, Stephane 4:24:55 (15,975)
Gullefer, Paul 5:02:10 (24,341)
Gullick, Peter 4:23:38 (15,654)
Gulliver, Keith 6:05:13 (30,463)
Gumbleton, David 6:26:15 (31,211)
Gunawardena, Harsha 3:49:21 (7,599)
Gunn, Anthony 4:12:06 (12,786)
Gunn, David 4:35:44 (18,570)
Gunn, Mark 3:55:52 (9,148)
Gunn, Richard 5:00:35 (24,083)
Gunn, Simon 4:28:25 (16,832)
Gunnell, Julian 4:21:26 (15,098)
Gunning, David 4:20:21 (14,829)
Gunning, Simon 4:22:10 (15,288)
Gunning, Tony 4:22:29 (15,359)
Gunston, Ian 3:27:40 (3,762)
Gunther, Lee 4:35:35 (18,536)
Gunther, Mattens 3:03:22 (1,142)
Gunther, Werner 4:53:19 (22,574)
Guppy, Neil 4:14:06 (13,282)
Gupta, Anil 6:16:56 (30,891)
Gupta, Sunil 5:19:23 (26,812)
Gupwell, Alan 5:40:33 (29,038)
Guram, Charanjit 5:26:30 (27,737)
Gurd, Richard 3:23:41 (3,203)
Gurr, Simon 4:56:24 (23,240)
Guschke, Dietger 3:56:08 (9,219)
Gustafsson, Lars 4:53:12 (22,545)
Guthrie, Adrian 3:55:32 (9,058)
Guthrie, Duncan 3:31:42 (4,435)
Gutierrez, Carlos 4:33:53 (18,138)
Guttenplan, Don 4:39:44 (19,484)
Guy, Darren 6:31:54 (31,377)
Guy, Despeghel 4:27:15 (16,534)
Guy, Graham 4:39:11 (19,370)
Gwillam, Andy 2:58:05 (773)
Gwillam, Martin 4:31:40 (17,663)
Gwillam, Peter 4:30:46 (17,438)
Gwilliams, David 6:04:32 (30,430)
Gwizdala, Peter 5:08:07 (25,282)
Gwozdcki, Pawel 4:08:16 (11,953)
Gwynne, David 4:50:36 (21,993)
Gwynne, Mark 4:03:51 (11,025)
Gyles, Peter 4:19:42 (14,667)
Gymer, Alexander 4:01:47 (10,594)
Gynn, Trevor 2:54:09 (545)
Gyte, Barry 3:06:49 (1,387)
Haak, Wim 3:39:34 (5,706)
Haapala, Juha 3:49:24 (7,610)
Haarer, Peter 2:42:15 (184)
Haas, Otto 3:02:04 (1,058)
Habgood, John 4:06:58 (11,679)
Hacker, Peter 3:56:12 (9,242)
Hackett, Alan 4:44:22 (20,587)
Hackett, Kevin 4:49:33 (21,761)
Hackl, Bruno 5:15:58 (26,374)
Hackl, Fritz 3:31:45 (4,446)
Hackl, Manfred 3:48:34 (7,415)
Hackland, Mark 4:31:03 (17,513)
Hackleton, John 3:49:38 (7,665)
Hackman, Graeme 4:33:15 (17,993)
Hadavi, Hamid 6:02:17 (30,352)
Hadaway, Dave 3:02:55 (1,108)
Hadaway, Mark 4:04:37 (11,201)
Haddon, John 5:58:56 (30,205)
Haddow, Ross 5:42:17 (29,190)
Haden, Paul 5:50:23 (29,743)
Hadfield, Frank 3:50:06 (7,752)
Hadfield, Hugh 4:15:08 (13,550)
Hadfield, Jenny 5:54:13 (29,944)
Hadfield, Stefan 4:48:46 (21,580)
Hadler, Darryl 4:00:07 (10,253)
Hadley, James 3:48:14 (7,364)
Hadley, Peter 3:16:52 (2,412)
Hadley, Richard 4:00:03 (10,233)
Hadley, Ricky 4:21:46 (15,176)
Hadlington, Nigel 5:19:33 (26,835)
Hadlow, Edward 3:25:35 (3,473)
Haefliger, Bernhard 4:14:58 (13,500)
Haefliger, Eugen 4:25:22 (16,107)
Haesaert, Ronny 4:58:46 (23,755)
Hafeez, Yousaf 5:12:43 (25,934)
Hafkemeyer, Christof 3:36:53 (5,209)

Hagan, Robert	4:05:54 (11,483)	
Hagar, Richard	3:24:22 (3,311)	
Hagerman, Thomas	6:00:40 (30,280)	
Haggart, Robin	3:51:29 (8,068)	
Hagger, Simon	4:16:06 (13,763)	
Haggett, Stephen	4:56:26 (23,245)	
Hagon-Powley, Clive	5:47:18 (29,515)	
Hague, Joseph	5:24:36 (27,489)	
Hague, Nicholas	3:50:18 (7,801)	
Hague, Peter	3:43:08 (6,393)	
Hague-Holmes, Gerard	3:48:11 (7,354)	
Hague-Moss, Nicholas	3:29:25 (4,072)	
Haigh, Edwin	5:49:44 (29,698)	
Haigh, Gary	5:10:53 (25,670)	
Haigh, James	3:37:31 (5,326)	
Haigh, Jason	3:22:18 (3,022)	
Haigh, Philip	3:32:36 (4,540)	
Haigh, Robert	4:16:02 (13,748)	
Haigh, Steven	3:44:52 (6,698)	
Haigh, Stewart	4:22:45 (15,429)	
Haigh-Brown, Nigel	3:53:46 (8,608)	
Haigney, Nicholas	4:47:36 (21,319)	
Hailes, Roger	3:25:46 (3,504)	
Hails, Stephen	3:41:12 (5,988)	
Hain, John	3:51:49 (8,153)	
Haines, Kenneth	6:02:21 (30,354)	
Haines, Mark	4:09:24 (12,208)	
Haines, Martin	3:42:30 (6,248)	
Haines, Stephen	3:36:51 (5,204)	
Hains, Kevin	3:37:24 (5,311)	
Hainsworth, David	3:33:43 (4,707)	
Hainsworth, Paul	3:10:48 (1,741)	
Hainsworth, Paul	3:54:57 (8,906)	
Hairon, Keith	4:50:23 (21,939)	
Haisaid, Francis	4:33:43 (18,100)	
Hakki, Hassan	3:52:35 (8,328)	
Hakvoort, Jos	3:02:22 (1,081)	
Hal, Wilco	4:05:46 (11,447)	
Halbert, Jay	4:47:14 (21,232)	
Haldin, Benjamin	4:44:03 (20,508)	
Hale, Anthony	4:01:14 (10,478)	
Hale, Christopher	4:40:14 (19,586)	
Hale, Gareth	5:12:28 (25,891)	
Hale, John	4:37:32 (18,993)	
Hale, Michael	3:20:00 (2,760)	
Hale, Robert	5:04:25 (24,695)	
Hales, Alexander	6:34:07 (31,425)	
Hales, Colin	4:59:35 (23,900)	
Hales, Pete	5:37:56 (28,806)	
Halestrap, Peter	5:09:36 (25,491)	
Haley, Lee	5:46:59 (29,488)	
Haley, Peter	4:46:03 (20,977)	
Haley, Tim	5:46:11 (29,450)	
Haliday, Philip	3:58:25 (9,813)	
Halkett, Angus	3:45:03 (6,741)	
Halkyard, David	3:56:55 (9,428)	
Hall, Alexander	3:18:03 (2,556)	
Hall, Andrew	3:26:57 (3,669)	
Hall, Andrew	4:30:43 (17,422)	
Hall, Andrew	4:45:02 (20,725)	
Hall, Andrew	4:45:57 (20,948)	
Hall, Anthony	3:20:27 (2,824)	
Hall, Arnold	6:36:12 (31,480)	
Hall, Benjamin	5:00:50 (24,128)	
Hall, Brian	2:37:07 (124)	
Hall, Bruce	3:00:05 (942)	
Hall, Christian	3:38:41 (5,538)	
Hall, Christopher	3:30:02 (4,170)	
Hall, Colin	4:54:39 (22,849)	
Hall, Darren	4:47:11 (21,223)	
Hall, David	3:20:24 (2,816)	
Hall, David	3:49:10 (7,555)	
Hall, David	4:41:06 (19,777)	
Hall, David	5:34:46 (28,534)	
Hall, Douglas	4:21:42 (15,158)	
Hall, Frederick	4:41:31 (19,871)	
Hall, Gareth	4:17:17 (14,053)	
Hall, Gary	4:07:18 (11,756)	
Hall, Gavin	3:27:19 (3,715)	
Hall, Gerard	4:31:11 (17,546)	
Hall, Graeme	3:18:00 (2,551)	
Hall, Ian	3:15:14 (2,265)	
Hall, Ian	4:56:37 (23,291)	
Hall, James	4:10:36 (12,482)	
Hall, James	4:15:07 (13,544)	
Hall, John	3:29:23 (4,062)	
Hall, John	3:43:19 (6,429)	
Hall, John	3:52:38 (8,338)	
Hall, John	4:34:14 (18,220)	
Hall, Julian	4:50:43 (22,018)	
Hall, Lee	4:29:45 (17,178)	
Hall, Leigh	3:43:28 (6,448)	
Hall, Leslie	5:05:40 (24,912)	
Hall, Mark	4:25:49 (16,205)	
Hall, Mark	6:12:20 (30,745)	
Hall, Martin	3:20:04 (2,768)	
Hall, Martin	3:33:22 (4,657)	
Hall, Matt	3:42:30 (6,248)	
Hall, Matthew	2:53:50 (523)	
Hall, Michael	4:05:43 (11,435)	
Hall, Michael	4:23:03 (15,504)	
Hall, Neil	3:13:50 (2,100)	
Hall, Neil	4:23:54 (15,720)	
Hall, Nicky	2:53:58 (532)	
Hall, Nigel	3:35:10 (4,937)	
Hall, Nigel	4:16:20 (13,815)	
Hall, Patrick	2:59:15 (876)	
Hall, Peter	3:26:02 (3,544)	
Hall, Peter	5:00:50 (24,128)	
Hall, Richard	3:35:46 (5,033)	
Hall, Richard	4:07:10 (11,731)	
Hall, Richard	4:08:35 (12,035)	
Hall, Robert	3:14:12 (2,152)	
Hall, Robert	4:51:59 (22,305)	
Hall, Russell	4:55:35 (23,048)	
Hall, Sam	4:34:27 (18,280)	
Hall, Scott	6:01:47 (30,332)	
Hall, Steve	3:39:22 (5,671)	
Hall, Stuart	3:54:45 (8,850)	
Hall, Tim	3:46:46 (7,077)	
Hall, William	3:34:14 (4,787)	
Hallam, Neil	5:07:48 (25,238)	
Hallam, Paul	3:06:52 (1,391)	
Hallard, Richard	5:03:04 (24,467)	
Hallauer, Mark	3:35:00 (4,912)	
Hallett, Ian	3:49:13 (7,568)	
Hallett, James	4:02:02 (10,642)	
Hallett, Martin	4:56:10 (23,189)	
Hallett, Roy	5:35:29 (28,593)	
Halliday, John	3:58:05 (9,726)	
Halliday, Paul	3:59:55 (10,206)	
Halliday, Stuart	5:00:59 (24,150)	
Hallinan, Neil	3:39:49 (5,751)	
Hallissey, Daniel	4:44:32 (20,620)	
Hallitt, Andrew	4:33:15 (17,993)	
Halls, Mark	3:13:21 (2,041)	
Halls, Nicholas	5:03:29 (24,526)	
Hallson, David	3:28:05 (3,830)	
Hallward, Charles	4:40:14 (19,586)	
Halpenny, Kieran	4:43:16 (20,309)	
Halpenny, Richard	3:36:37 (5,167)	
Halpin, Shawn	4:53:02 (22,509)	
Halsey, Michael	5:13:46 (26,080)	
Halsey, Stephen	3:35:29 (4,996)	
Halson, Adrian	4:25:23 (16,113)	
Halvatzis, Nicos	3:18:46 (2,632)	
Halvey, Martin	2:47:42 (320)	
Hamard, André	4:59:46 (23,935)	
Hamard, Cedric	4:59:46 (23,935)	
Hamblen, Colin	5:24:13 (27,440)	
Hamblett, Stuart	5:13:29 (26,039)	
Hambley, Michael	4:22:52 (15,458)	
Hambling, David	3:57:21 (9,542)	
Hambling, Stuart	4:07:05 (11,705)	
Hambly, James	4:24:06 (15,779)	
Hambly, Rupert	4:52:21 (22,369)	
Hambrey, Oliver	3:49:33 (7,642)	
Hamer, Andrew	4:14:32 (13,389)	
Hamer, Graham	4:14:31 (13,384)	
Hamer, Hans	6:05:58 (30,501)	
Hamer, Michael	3:10:02 (1,677)	
Hamer, Sean	4:40:17 (19,599)	
Hamer, Steve	3:31:28 (4,403)	
Hamer, Warren	5:09:11 (25,433)	
Hamill, Eric	4:26:54 (16,448)	
Hamill, Richard	3:14:45 (2,212)	
Hamilton, Alex	5:03:36 (24,550)	
Hamilton, Alistair	3:23:37 (3,194)	
Hamilton, Brian	3:31:26 (4,395)	
Hamilton, Craig	3:47:11 (7,155)	
Hamilton, David	4:56:09 (23,182)	
Hamilton, Derren	4:29:47 (17,190)	
Hamilton, Edward	3:11:54 (1,851)	
Hamilton, Elliot	4:45:58 (20,952)	
Hamilton, Graham	3:12:49 (1,968)	
Hamilton, Ian	3:58:06 (9,730)	
Hamilton, James	4:14:00 (13,263)	
Hamilton, Jim	6:05:06 (30,455)	
Hamilton, Keith	4:10:45 (12,503)	
Hamilton, Richard	4:08:10 (11,932)	
Hamilton, Robert	3:30:52 (4,307)	
Hamilton, Robert	4:24:59 (15,999)	
Hamilton, Robert	5:22:31 (27,217)	
Hamilton, Robert	5:36:59 (28,734)	
Hamilton, Roderick	4:09:28 (12,219)	
Hamilton, Stephen	3:10:54 (1,747)	
Hamilton, Stephen	5:32:49 (28,359)	
Hamilton-Brown, Robert	5:49:43 (29,697)	
Hamilton-Jones, Cecil	4:31:59 (17,724)	
Hamlin, Tony	4:28:40 (16,902)	
Hammell, William	5:36:51 (28,719)	
Hammick, Paul	6:18:59 (30,973)	
Hammond, Andrew	4:44:11 (20,538)	
Hammond, Brendan	5:12:39 (25,927)	
Hammond, Brian	4:42:58 (20,222)	
Hammond, Chris	3:46:35 (7,051)	
Hammond, Darren	3:39:02 (5,604)	
Hammond, David	4:09:57 (12,340)	
Hammond, Dominic	4:16:33 (13,867)	
Hammond, James	3:48:07 (7,342)	
Hammond, James	4:34:13 (18,216)	
Hammond, Jason	4:17:03 (14,001)	
Hammond, John	3:39:59 (5,782)	
Hammond, John	4:30:32 (17,375)	
Hammond, Mark	2:54:03 (539)	
Hammond, Michael	6:45:11 (31,623)	
Hammond, Nicky	3:30:00 (4,167)	
Hammond, Paul	3:56:58 (9,444)	
Hammond, Robert	3:48:39 (7,432)	
Hammond, Robert	4:14:30 (13,382)	
Hammond, Stephen	3:28:49 (3,974)	
Hammond, Steve	3:35:27 (4,990)	
Hamoen, Niels	5:08:49 (25,377)	
Hamon, Patrick	3:16:07 (2,337)	
Hampson, Brian	5:07:38 (25,210)	
Hampson, Christopher	4:01:56 (10,623)	
Hampson, Michael	3:36:06 (5,078)	
Hampton, Chris	4:27:46 (16,669)	
Hampton, Simon	4:56:02 (23,152)	
Hamsher, Mark	4:17:59 (14,249)	
Hamshere, Stephen	6:20:26 (31,032)	
Hanburger, Jade	4:04:57 (11,280)	
Hance, Fred	7:28:03 (32,143)	
Hancock, Glen	4:03:29 (10,941)	
Hancock, Graham	3:50:21 (7,816)	
Hancock, Graham	4:30:13 (17,291)	
Hancock, Hamish	5:14:18 (26,141)	
Hancock, Roland	3:12:22 (1,911)	
Hancock, Tim	4:11:16 (12,591)	
Hancorn, Christopher	3:59:28 (10,086)	
Hancox, Robert	3:27:29 (3,736)	
Hand, Geoffrey	3:32:29 (4,528)	
Hand, Michael	3:05:56 (1,316)	
Hand, Terence	3:51:17 (8,025)	
Handel, Paul	5:10:05 (25,565)	
Handley, Mark	4:49:17 (21,698)	
Handley, Nicholas	3:52:56 (8,445)	
Handley, Philip	4:43:52 (20,475)	
Handley, Simon	4:31:13 (17,550)	
Handley, Stuart	5:31:56 (28,285)	
Handley, Tristan	3:33:31 (4,681)	
Handley-Greaves, Chris	3:42:38 (6,280)	
Hands, Richard	4:23:31 (15,619)	
Handscombe, Clive	3:53:04 (8,442)	
Handscombe, Paul	3:57:10 (9,498)	
Handslip, Rhodri	3:26:12 (3,567)	
Hankinson, Karl	3:29:28 (4,083)	
Hanks, Michael	4:22:24 (15,342)	

Hanlan, Hugo 4:06:03 (11,510)
Hanley, Alan 3:33:20 (4,650)
Hanley, Frank 4:58:46 (23,755)
Hanlon, John 4:59:58 (23,977)
Hanlon, Stephen 4:37:24 (18,963)
Hanna, Martin 3:42:56 (6,349)
Hanna, Paul 4:18:09 (14,279)
Hannaford, Alex 3:52:40 (8,347)
Hannah, Errick 4:09:06 (12,153)
Hannah, Kenneth 4:41:42 (19,919)
Hannah, Malcolm 4:13:08 (13,030)
Hannam, Nicholas 5:27:54 (27,883)
Hanney, Mark 5:17:54 (26,596)
Hannon, Jason 4:10:21 (12,428)
Hannon, Patrick 4:19:01 (14,511)
Hannum, John 3:36:30 (5,142)
Hanraham, Colin 3:30:58 (4,323)
Hanrahan, Mark 4:00:49 (10,390)
Hanratty, James 3:52:51 (8,384)
Hanreck, Michael 3:44:52 (6,698)
Hans, Carol 3:41:16 (6,000)
Hanscomb, John 4:07:07 (11,713)
Hansegger, Wolfgang 3:57:43 (9,622)
Hansen, Adam 3:07:44 (1,477)
Hansen, Daniel 5:14:12 (26,120)
Hansen, David 4:38:18 (19,161)
Hansen, Mads 4:13:54 (13,233)
Hansen, Paul 3:23:04 (3,122)
Hansen, Paul 3:44:40 (6,661)
Hansen, Torben 3:13:26 (2,052)
Hansford, John 5:06:44 (25,061)
Hanson, Anton 3:57:31 (9,582)
Hanson, David 3:13:39 (2,080)
Hanson, Eric 4:59:06 (23,824)
Hanson, Mark 4:41:21 (19,837)
Hanson, Neil 6:35:32 (31,463)
Hanson, Paul 3:36:13 (5,098)
Hanson, Richard 5:22:04 (27,149)
Hanson, Stephen 3:44:21 (6,611)
Hanson, Trevor 6:03:51 (30,407)
Hansson, Leif 2:57:16 (721)
Happel, Erich 3:33:13 (4,635)
Happersberger, Reinhold 2:50:01 (389)
Harault, Sylvain 3:36:27 (5,135)
Harbage, Noel 4:05:50 (11,465)
Harber, Mark 3:53:48 (8,618)
Harbert, Barrie 3:52:37 (8,335)
Harbon, Richard 3:03:34 (1,160)
Harbour, Jason 2:42:45 (191)
Harbour, Joseph 4:07:09 (11,725)
Harbron, Christopher 3:28:02 (3,820)
Harcombe, Ian 4:24:49 (15,954)
Harcourt, David 4:03:47 (11,007)
Hard, Newman 5:01:18 (24,205)
Hardaker, Christopher 4:17:36 (14,139)
Hardcastle, Kenneth 3:37:05 (5,249)
Hardcastle, Matthew 3:55:55 (9,158)
Hardie, Carl 4:16:52 (13,954)
Hardie, Mark 3:48:22 (7,387)
Hardie, Robert 5:03:40 (24,560)
Hardiman, Paul 5:45:48 (29,429)
Harding, Anthony 5:11:01 (25,694)
Harding, Brian 3:52:15 (8,255)
Harding, David 4:09:38 (12,256)
Harding, Fred 3:11:24 (1,791)
Harding, James 3:13:57 (2,122)
Harding, James 5:25:26 (27,601)
Harding, Jeffrey 2:58:43 (823)
Harding, Lee 2:53:48 (517)
Harding, Louis 5:04:00 (24,628)
Harding, Nigel 4:49:32 (21,758)
Harding, Peter 4:17:32 (14,125)
Harding, Peter 5:12:53 (25,956)
Harding, Stephen 5:12:28 (25,891)
Harding, Victor 7:34:45 (32,183)
Hardman, Andrew 4:53:19 (22,574)
Hardman, Bob 3:46:03 (6,943)
Hardman, Darren 4:41:42 (19,919)
Hards, Ashley 4:38:51 (19,292)
Hards, Neil 5:14:30 (26,177)
Hards, Peter 3:32:34 (4,535)
Hardstaff, Ian 3:00:42 (987)
Hardwell, Keith 3:43:03 (6,377)
Hardwick, Charles 4:37:47 (19,041)
Hardwick, Matthew 3:10:44 (1,735)
Hardwidge, Stephen 5:06:51 (25,088)
Hardy, Colin 5:49:28 (29,674)
Hardy, Holt 2:41:04 (167)
Hardy, Jim 4:30:34 (17,384)
Hardy, John 3:14:48 (2,216)
Hardy, Martin 4:11:31 (12,650)
Hardy, Nicholas 4:11:20 (12,606)
Hardy, Paul 5:55:07 (30,007)
Hardy, Philip 5:10:22 (25,602)
Hardy, Thomas 3:59:40 (10,141)
Hare, Keith 4:20:59 (14,974)
Hare, Sohan 4:49:21 (21,716)
Hares, James 4:16:13 (13,787)
Harfield, Patrick 6:27:25 (31,238)
Harfield, Robert 4:11:50 (12,727)
Harford, Mark 3:11:13 (1,776)
Hargreaves, Craig 4:02:05 (10,654)
Hargreaves, Cristopher 4:21:24 (15,088)
Hargreaves, Jason 4:50:46 (22,025)
Hargreaves, John 3:07:23 (1,443)
Hargreaves, Mark 2:26:42 (45)
Hargreaves, Michael 4:51:05 (22,099)
Hargreaves, Nigel 4:36:05 (18,666)
Hargreaves, Paul 4:11:16 (12,591)
Hargreaves, Stuart 5:09:01 (25,411)
Haring, Stuart 4:02:46 (10,798)
Harker, Andrew 3:06:07 (1,330)
Harker, James 4:34:23 (18,259)
Harker, Joseph 4:19:32 (14,624)
Harker, Robert 3:27:49 (3,787)
Harkus, Gavin 2:50:51 (415)
Harland, Alan 3:02:50 (1,102)
Harland, Joseph 5:24:10 (27,431)
Harley, Colin 3:32:35 (4,539)
Harley, James 4:04:06 (11,090)
Harling, Graham 3:59:33 (10,105)
Harling, Joseph 5:00:38 (24,100)
Harlow, John 5:18:32 (26,701)
Harlow, Steven 4:07:45 (11,862)
Harman, Alan 3:33:42 (4,701)
Harman, Gary 3:27:43 (3,772)
Harmer, Chris 5:05:13 (24,829)
Harmer, Timothy 3:25:07 (3,411)
Harne, Jason 3:00:24 (965)
Harnett, Howard 3:44:19 (6,600)
Harney, Mark 4:45:55 (20,939)
Harney, Steve 4:28:04 (16,725)
Harold, Alexander 3:55:09 (8,951)
Harold, Christopher 3:47:18 (7,175)
Harper, Andrew 5:16:48 (26,459)
Harper, Andy 3:01:04 (1,008)
Harper, Charles 3:01:26 (1,021)
Harper, Clive 4:35:38 (18,545)
Harper, Craig 5:26:04 (27,683)
Harper, John 4:13:59 (13,258)
Harper, Kenneth 4:25:18 (16,086)
Harper, Kevin 3:12:22 (1,911)
Harper, Martin 4:02:15 (10,686)
Harper, Martin 4:15:04 (13,529)
Harper, Michael 4:25:54 (16,231)
Harper, Nicholas 4:14:41 (13,420)
Harper, Stuart 4:47:40 (21,339)
Harrap, John 3:26:43 (3,637)
Harrap, Paul 3:38:39 (5,531)
Harrhy, Alan 4:57:57 (23,571)
Harries, Geraint 4:45:01 (20,721)
Harrild, Mark 5:25:00 (27,536)
Harrington, Michael 5:18:34 (26,710)
Harrington, Paul 4:20:58 (14,968)
Harrington, Stephen 4:23:51 (15,708)
Harriott, Gilmore 6:10:00 (30,642)
Harris, Adam 4:30:23 (17,336)
Harris, Alastair 4:55:06 (22,939)
Harris, Andrew 3:52:36 (8,332)
Harris, Andrew 3:58:17 (9,776)
Harris, Andrew 4:28:21 (16,807)
Harris, Chris 4:00:30 (10,327)
Harris, David 3:24:15 (3,296)
Harris, David 3:53:26 (8,524)
Harris, David 3:57:30 (9,580)
Harris, David 5:56:35 (30,085)
Harris, Derrick 4:43:31 (20,382)
Harris, Dominic 3:31:23 (4,390)
Harris, Garry 2:55:07 (600)
Harris, Graham 5:41:20 (29,101)
Harris, Howard 4:51:44 (22,250)
Harris, Ian 5:05:31 (24,885)
Harris, Ian 6:14:47 (30,821)
Harris, Jill 5:31:04 (28,198)
Harris, John 3:09:51 (1,661)
Harris, Mark 3:12:13 (1,887)
Harris, Mark 5:39:46 (28,967)
Harris, Mark 5:47:38 (29,548)
Harris, Martin 3:43:18 (6,424)
Harris, Martin 4:54:45 (22,877)
Harris, Michael 3:40:48 (5,925)
Harris, Michael 5:41:46 (29,142)
Harris, Mike 4:15:24 (13,620)
Harris, Mike 4:35:12 (18,442)
Harris, Paul 3:56:48 (9,398)
Harris, Paul 4:00:20 (10,301)
Harris, Paul 5:21:44 (27,117)
Harris, Paul 5:48:22 (29,596)
Harris, Paul 6:08:52 (30,601)
Harris, Paul 6:28:06 (31,271)
Harris, Peter 3:54:32 (8,793)
Harris, Peter 4:17:13 (14,036)
Harris, Peter 4:56:02 (23,152)
Harris, Peter 6:16:31 (30,876)
Harris, Philip 3:21:51 (2,967)
Harris, Philip 3:43:23 (6,434)
Harris, Philip 4:06:22 (11,566)
Harris, Phill 4:36:46 (18,826)
Harris, Richard 4:15:59 (13,738)
Harris, Richard 4:21:46 (15,176)
Harris, Richard 4:49:17 (21,698)
Harris, Ronald 5:31:55 (28,281)
Harris, Ross 3:29:47 (4,138)
Harris, Ryan 3:42:33 (6,265)
Harris, Simon 3:02:10 (1,071)
Harris, Simon 3:23:33 (3,185)
Harris, Simon 4:55:15 (22,965)
Harris, Stephen 5:20:11 (26,912)
Harris, Steven 4:22:59 (15,489)
Harris, Timothy 3:11:43 (1,825)
Harris, Timothy 4:11:24 (12,621)
Harris, William 3:41:49 (6,118)
Harrison, Andrew 4:52:27 (22,388)
Harrison, Barry 3:24:54 (3,384)
Harrison, Christopher 5:22:41 (27,231)
Harrison, David 3:56:29 (9,313)
Harrison, Derek 3:27:47 (3,779)
Harrison, Gary 4:27:28 (16,593)
Harrison, Graeme 4:08:48 (12,089)
Harrison, James 5:19:32 (26,832)
Harrison, James 6:56:28 (31,850)
Harrison, John 5:47:27 (29,526)
Harrison, Jonathan 3:58:34 (9,853)
Harrison, Julian 4:24:26 (15,850)
Harrison, Martyn 5:00:06 (23,994)
Harrison, Matthew 2:38:53 (143)
Harrison, Michael 4:16:07 (13,766)
Harrison, Michael 5:03:05 (24,472)
Harrison, Neil 5:11:23 (25,751)
Harrison, Paul 3:56:46 (9,388)
Harrison, Paul 4:54:29 (22,810)
Harrison, Richard 3:18:36 (2,617)
Harrison, Robert 3:14:21 (2,172)
Harrison, Scott 3:34:45 (4,873)
Harrison, Simon 3:22:27 (3,044)
Harrison, Tim 4:28:44 (16,919)
Harrison, William 3:27:04 (3,691)
Harrison, William 4:16:15 (13,797)
Harrod, Douglas 5:52:02 (29,832)
Harrold, Geoffrey 3:19:18 (2,678)
Harron, Gareth 4:31:54 (17,707)
Harrop, Mark 5:33:44 (28,440)
Harrowven, Craig 4:31:51 (17,699)
Harry, Mark 5:13:03 (25,981)
Harryman, Michael 4:44:02 (20,504)
Hart, Andy 2:52:37 (476)
Hart, Andy 4:39:18 (19,398)
Hart, Barry 4:18:18 (14,303)
Hart, Christopher 4:20:22 (14,838)

Hickman, Gavin	5:01:20	(24,213)
Hickman, John	5:29:43	(28,062)
Hickman, Karl	3:03:30	(1,150)
Hickman, Michael	4:02:24	(10,718)
Hickman, Paul	3:43:36	(6,465)
Hickman, Stephen	3:49:09	(7,548)
Hickmott, Patrick	4:34:20	(18,251)
Hicks, Brian	3:37:42	(5,365)
Hicks, Chris	5:15:47	(26,357)
Hicks, Jamie	4:36:28	(18,762)
Hicks, Lloyd	6:27:50	(31,260)
Hicks, Paul	4:12:52	(12,973)
Hicks, Paul	5:54:09	(29,940)
Hicks, Robert	4:23:16	(15,565)
Hicks, Russell	5:04:43	(24,738)
Hicks, Stephen	3:10:42	(1,728)
Hicks, Stephen	3:36:13	(5,098)
Hicks, Timothy	3:36:22	(5,125)
Hide, George	2:45:53	(253)
Hider, Justin	5:08:47	(25,373)
Hides, Nick	2:55:47	(634)
Higginbotham, John	4:31:39	(17,658)
Higginbottom, Robert	3:22:25	(3,039)
Higgins, Andrew	4:14:18	(13,327)
Higgins, Bernard	3:27:16	(3,709)
Higgins, Daniel	3:02:30	(1,088)
Higgins, George	3:35:32	(5,002)
Higgins, Robert	2:58:27	(797)
Higgins, William	5:20:26	(26,945)
Higginson, Martin	3:49:55	(7,719)
Higginson, Phillip	5:07:24	(25,161)
Higgs, David	3:17:39	(2,509)
Higgs, John	3:50:45	(7,899)
Higgs, Simon	4:27:31	(16,605)
Higgs-Howson, Andrew	5:02:17	(24,359)
High, Charles	4:23:59	(15,746)
Higham, Ian	4:25:17	(16,081)
Higham, Matthew	4:01:13	(10,474)
Highfield, Mark	3:33:10	(4,623)
Highfield, Paul	4:47:40	(21,339)
Hignell, Stephen	4:25:34	(16,150)
Higson, Andrerw	3:17:29	(2,488)
Hilaire, John	3:54:35	(8,813)
Hilary, David	3:34:57	(4,901)
Hildebrand, Jeffery	4:22:23	(15,336)
Hildesley, Simon	4:11:06	(12,553)
Hildreth, Jan	5:23:51	(27,390)
Hildreth, Richard	4:27:45	(16,666)
Hiley, Keith	3:44:55	(6,713)
Hiley, Paul	3:01:44	(1,034)
Hiley, Philip	5:56:19	(30,073)
Hill, Adrian	3:20:19	(2,805)
Hill, Adrian	3:54:33	(8,803)
Hill, Adrian	5:22:45	(27,248)
Hill, Alan	5:32:57	(28,371)
Hill, Antony	3:04:45	(1,228)
Hill, Calvin	3:36:44	(5,187)
Hill, Christopher	4:28:59	(16,986)
Hill, Clive	3:52:55	(8,399)
Hill, Clive	4:01:03	(10,439)
Hill, Daniel	4:07:08	(11,721)
Hill, Dave	2:54:37	(568)
Hill, David	4:14:19	(13,333)
Hill, David	4:29:26	(17,098)
Hill, David	4:31:54	(17,707)
Hill, Fraser	3:06:44	(1,379)
Hill, Gavin	4:47:20	(21,254)
Hill, Geoffrey	4:31:40	(17,663)
Hill, Gregory	3:34:17	(4,791)
Hill, Iain	4:01:01	(10,435)
Hill, Ian	3:40:13	(5,835)
Hill, Ian	4:08:25	(11,984)
Hill, John	4:12:07	(12,791)
Hill, John	5:03:54	(24,615)
Hill, Joseph	4:51:17	(22,150)
Hill, Justin	6:07:07	(30,534)
Hill, Kenneth	3:30:39	(4,265)
Hill, Len	4:25:10	(16,047)
Hill, Leslie	2:52:57	(494)
Hill, Malcolm	4:42:39	(20,142)
Hill, Mark	3:35:33	(5,005)
Hill, Mark	4:12:21	(12,847)
Hill, Martin	3:40:34	(5,878)
Hill, Martin	3:43:27	(6,443)
Hill, Martin	3:53:31	(8,548)
Hill, Michael	5:06:11	(24,981)
Hill, Nathaniel	4:24:44	(15,928)
Hill, Patrick	3:52:02	(8,203)
Hill, Patrick	4:19:19	(14,576)
Hill, Paul	4:50:59	(22,065)
Hill, Peter	3:03:06	(1,126)
Hill, Peter	3:05:35	(1,290)
Hill, Peter	3:22:24	(3,035)
Hill, Peter	3:50:58	(7,941)
Hill, Raymond	3:04:09	(1,192)
Hill, Raymond	3:53:26	(8,524)
Hill, Raymond	4:37:42	(19,020)
Hill, Richard	3:46:34	(7,049)
Hill, Richard	4:20:02	(14,757)
Hill, Robert	4:10:02	(12,356)
Hill, Robert	5:37:44	(28,792)
Hill, Robin	3:52:59	(8,422)
Hill, Roger	3:22:11	(3,007)
Hill, Roger	3:25:49	(3,514)
Hill, Shaun	4:34:37	(18,311)
Hill, Simon	3:50:23	(7,822)
Hill, Stephen	4:20:00	(14,743)
Hill, Stephen	5:21:19	(27,063)
Hill, Stephen	6:12:58	(30,768)
Hill, Steven	4:47:50	(21,385)
Hill, Stewart	5:39:24	(28,936)
Hill, Stuart	4:46:42	(21,124)
Hill, Thomas	3:27:44	(3,773)
Hill, Tony	4:57:17	(23,443)
Hillary, Ian	5:25:36	(27,621)
Hillary, Phil	3:50:32	(7,852)
Hillary, Thomas	5:19:22	(26,809)
Hille, Christian	3:54:06	(8,681)
Hillgaertner, Kurt	4:57:37	(23,505)
Hillier, Noel	3:53:20	(8,504)
Hilliker, Grant	5:05:22	(24,852)
Hillman, Andrew	4:46:28	(21,085)
Hillman, Stuart	5:28:45	(27,963)
Hills, Neil	5:57:25	(30,130)
Hills, Richard	5:17:25	(26,530)
Hills, Steven	4:14:48	(13,453)
Hills, Trevor	5:25:31	(27,612)
Hillson, Martin	4:02:07	(10,658)
Hilmi, Mahmut	4:31:44	(17,676)
Hilson, Richard	3:45:12	(6,773)
Hilson, Steven	3:24:13	(3,287)
Hilton, David	3:57:49	(9,650)
Hilton, John	4:50:54	(22,054)
Hilton, Peter	5:08:45	(25,363)
Hime, David	4:52:28	(22,390)
Hinchcliffe, Anthony	4:55:41	(23,074)
Hinchelwood, Richard	5:24:13	(27,440)
Hinchliffe, Robert	3:54:34	(8,809)
Hind, James	4:15:16	(13,583)
Hindell, James	4:50:09	(21,894)
Hinderling, Hans	3:45:28	(6,825)
Hindes, Sean	4:53:24	(22,596)
Hindle, Adrian	5:48:47	(29,620)
Hindley, Mark	3:44:09	(6,571)
Hindmarch, David	4:18:23	(14,325)
Hindmarsh, Paul	5:18:39	(26,718)
Hinds, Andrew	3:56:12	(9,242)
Hinds, Carlos	5:14:32	(26,183)
Hinds, James	5:07:45	(25,235)
Hinds, John	4:37:00	(18,878)
Hine, Toby	5:18:06	(26,630)
Hing, Robert	4:52:27	(22,388)
Hingston, Martin	5:14:42	(26,203)
Hinningan, Guy	3:55:39	(9,091)
Hinns, Kevin	3:19:54	(2,743)
Hinshaw, Ron	4:36:44	(18,814)
Hinton, Gary	4:54:51	(22,891)
Hiorns, Andrew	4:41:16	(19,816)
Hipf, Gerhard	3:46:34	(7,049)
Hipsley, Stephen	4:29:10	(17,031)
Hirani, Surendra	5:44:54	(29,355)
Hirji, Aly	6:34:13	(31,428)
Hirons, Philip	4:58:44	(23,742)
Hirons, Steven	3:46:29	(7,026)
Hirst, Alastair	3:07:06	(1,416)
Hirst, John	5:14:07	(26,109)
Hirst, John	5:23:56	(27,401)
Hirst, Martin	5:40:23	(29,025)
Hirst, Matthew	5:23:56	(27,401)
Hirst, Michael	3:11:45	(1,828)
Hirst, Philip	4:37:31	(18,987)
Hirst, Richard	3:46:10	(6,966)
Hirst, Simon	5:38:04	(28,817)
Hirst, Stephen	3:10:15	(1,699)
Hirst, Wally	6:27:37	(31,251)
Hirt, Shlomo	4:58:59	(23,795)
Hiscock, Jonathan	3:07:52	(1,491)
Hiscox, John	3:15:35	(2,298)
Hiscox, Trevor	4:28:50	(16,945)
Hislop, John	4:42:23	(20,078)
Hitchcock, Ben	3:51:00	(7,953)
Hitchcock, John	5:26:06	(27,686)
Hitchcock, Martin	5:07:38	(25,210)
Hitchens, John	3:59:49	(10,180)
Hitchings, Stephen	4:17:18	(14,057)
Hitchman, Grant	4:56:31	(23,266)
Hitman, Graham	5:10:55	(25,684)
Hitt, Neil	5:25:01	(27,540)
Hitz, René	4:21:28	(15,104)
Hixon, John	5:20:11	(26,912)
Hixson, Richard	4:47:16	(21,237)
Ho, Kui	3:23:57	(3,240)
Hoad, Mark	3:29:38	(4,117)
Hoadley, James	6:32:02	(31,380)
Hoare, Andrew	4:00:07	(10,253)
Hoare, Ian	3:25:26	(3,456)
Hoare, Mark	5:04:01	(24,633)
Hoare, Oliver	5:50:06	(29,723)
Hoban, Andrew	3:56:48	(9,398)
Hobbs, Barrie	3:56:16	(9,263)
Hobbs, Blake	6:01:34	(30,326)
Hobbs, Christopher	3:24:13	(3,287)
Hobbs, John	3:39:28	(5,686)
Hobbs, Martin	5:19:54	(26,870)
Hobbs, Stephen	3:11:24	(1,791)
Hobby, Philip	4:34:19	(18,246)
Hobday, Michael	3:33:42	(4,701)
Hobden, Greg	3:28:52	(3,982)
Hobin, Mark	3:36:01	(5,068)
Hobson, Leslie	4:09:01	(12,134)
Hobson, Martyn	5:56:52	(30,104)
Hobson, Matt	3:24:17	(3,300)
Hobson, Simon	4:20:19	(14,820)
Hock, Michael	2:58:32	(802)
Hockedy, Mark	3:29:18	(4,044)
Hockenhull, Neil	5:48:00	(29,578)
Hockenhull, Robert	3:45:39	(6,861)
Hockett, Michael	3:56:22	(9,287)
Hockett, Stephen	3:11:42	(1,824)
Hockey, Paul	3:36:33	(5,152)
Hockey, Paul	4:12:22	(12,850)
Hockin, Peter	2:38:13	(135)
Hockings-Thompson, Steve	2:56:26	(674)
Hockley, Ryan	4:30:45	(17,431)
Hockley, Stephen	3:32:04	(4,478)
Hoda, Feroz	4:26:16	(16,311)
Hoddell, David	2:57:44	(754)
Hodder, Bryan	4:14:50	(13,461)
Hodder, Gareth	3:44:47	(6,685)
Hodder, Mark	3:42:39	(6,285)
Hodey, Russell	3:58:45	(9,901)
Hodge, Paul	5:16:00	(26,379)
Hodge, Tim	4:36:59	(18,872)
Hodges, Colin	5:34:56	(28,548)
Hodges, David	4:00:46	(10,379)
Hodges, Gary	5:44:13	(29,318)
Hodges, Kevan	4:30:22	(17,328)
Hodges, Michael	4:39:24	(19,421)
Hodges, Nicholas	3:17:53	(2,534)
Hodges, Paul	3:29:36	(4,111)
Hodges, Robert	3:18:46	(2,632)
Hodges, Robert	4:57:41	(23,519)
Hodges, Rufus	3:35:32	(5,002)
Hodges, Stephen	3:55:25	(9,027)
Hodgetts, Peter	3:48:55	(7,494)
Hodgkins, Martin	3:23:05	(3,125)
Hodgkins, Norman	5:41:07	(29,086)
Hodgkins, Paul	4:28:55	(16,973)
Hodgkins, Thomas	4:46:21	(21,061)

Hodgkinson, John	4:31:20 (17,579)
Hodgkiss, Brian	5:57:43 (30,151)
Hodgkiss, Richard	3:18:11 (2,576)
Hodgman, Paul	5:21:04 (27,030)
Hodgskiss, Brin	3:11:33 (1,807)
Hodgson, Ben	3:30:13 (4,203)
Hodgson, Kieran	2:58:56 (844)
Hodgson, Mark	4:48:42 (21,570)
Hodgson, Ross	5:03:23 (24,516)
Hodgson, Tim	5:33:44 (28,440)
Hodgson, Tony	3:14:53 (2,224)
Hodkin, Jack	4:09:20 (12,204)
Hodkinson, Matt	4:03:01 (10,846)
Hodson, Alan	6:13:55 (30,794)
Hodson, Rupert	4:30:27 (17,357)
Hoedemaker, Paul-Gerard	5:44:41 (29,341)
Hoeks, Frans	3:35:29 (4,996)
Hoekstra, Jan	4:35:34 (18,533)
Hoey, Kenneth	2:58:36 (812)
Hofer, Bruno	2:55:23 (613)
Hoff, Alan	3:47:41 (7,263)
Hoff, Karsten	6:14:46 (30,820)
Hoffmann, Didier	4:17:38 (14,152)
Hofmann, Gert	4:31:01 (17,502)
Hofmann, Patrick	5:31:06 (28,205)
Hogan, Charles	3:36:48 (5,193)
Hogan, Grant	4:02:44 (10,789)
Hogan, James	4:19:37 (14,647)
Hogan, James	5:11:01 (25,694)
Hogan, Mike	3:35:39 (5,021)
Hogan, Patrick	4:14:18 (13,327)
Hogan, Peter	6:29:50 (31,326)
Hogan, Tom	3:47:29 (7,211)
Hogarth, Martin	4:02:40 (10,774)
Hogervorst, Cok	3:35:34 (5,007)
Hogg, David	5:12:33 (25,909)
Hogg, Rodney	3:49:37 (7,661)
Hoggan, Brent	3:07:40 (1,472)
Hohmann, Stefan	3:18:29 (2,608)
Hohol, Michael	4:25:55 (16,234)
Holbrook, Andrew	3:46:01 (6,935)
Holbrook, Philip	3:20:53 (2,871)
Holcroft, Glyn	3:35:29 (4,996)
Hold, Daniel	4:21:08 (15,014)
Holdaway, Les	4:10:35 (12,480)
Holdcroft, Dean	2:50:37 (405)
Holden, Alan	5:07:26 (25,168)
Holden, Christopher	4:39:21 (19,414)
Holden, Clive	4:22:27 (15,351)
Holden, David	4:09:19 (12,202)
Holden, David	4:35:35 (18,536)
Holden, Frank	4:47:04 (21,194)
Holden, Ian	4:27:41 (16,643)
Holden, James	4:28:11 (16,761)
Holden, John	4:21:57 (15,224)
Holden, Peter	4:14:07 (13,290)
Holden, Ryan	5:41:33 (29,122)
Holden, Stephen	3:13:23 (2,048)
Holder, Andrew	2:59:48 (926)
Holder, Christopher	4:24:08 (15,785)
Holder, Paul	5:02:32 (24,394)
Holder, Peter	6:38:18 (31,508)
Holding, Niel	3:14:29 (2,182)
Holding, Rudy	5:41:32 (29,120)
Holditch, Karl	4:16:13 (13,787)
Holdrick, Paul	5:43:19 (29,262)
Holdrick, Wayne	5:47:31 (29,537)
Holdsworth, Andrew	4:24:06 (15,779)
Holdsworth, Daniel	3:35:07 (4,927)
Holdsworth, David	4:44:37 (20,637)
Holdsworth, Greg	3:43:16 (6,418)
Holdsworth, John	4:26:28 (16,347)
Holdsworth, Neil	2:52:26 (466)
Holdway, John	4:31:45 (17,680)
Hole, Andrew	4:18:18 (14,303)
Hole, Gordon	4:40:24 (19,633)
Hole, James	4:42:21 (20,067)
Hole, Paul	4:45:53 (20,934)
Holifield, Nigel	5:06:09 (24,976)
Holladay, Rob	2:33:34 (87)
Holland, Kevin	3:04:32 (1,213)
Holland, Kevin	5:26:07 (27,689)
Holland, Mark	4:19:07 (14,534)

Holland, Martin	5:03:38 (24,555)
Holland, Oliver	3:41:15 (5,998)
Holland, Paul	4:00:28 (10,324)
Holland, Robert	4:48:32 (21,537)
Holland, Shane	5:35:31 (28,594)
Holland, Stephen	5:15:42 (26,344)
Holland, Tony	5:22:05 (27,150)
Holland, Vincent	4:13:57 (13,244)
Holland, William	3:55:36 (9,076)
Hollands, Mark	4:39:09 (19,360)
Hollands, Richard	4:08:24 (11,980)
Hollands, Richard	6:34:07 (31,425)
Holliday, Simon	4:14:53 (13,475)
Hollidge, Thomas	5:27:52 (27,875)
Hollier, Steve	2:47:53 (331)
Hollingdale, Ross	5:08:13 (25,302)
Hollings, Kevin	3:53:46 (8,608)
Hollingsworth, Andrew	4:38:01 (19,093)
Hollingsworth, David	6:06:41 (30,517)
Hollingsworth, Martin	3:39:17 (5,651)
Hollingsworth, Noel	3:39:51 (5,761)
Hollington, Allan	5:05:11 (24,826)
Hollington, Dean	3:47:34 (7,228)
Hollington, Peter	5:13:05 (25,984)
Hollinshead, Christopher	3:10:24 (1,713)
Hollinworth, Lee	3:54:58 (8,911)
Hollis, Dafydd	3:37:51 (5,392)
Hollis, Gideon	4:34:12 (18,213)
Hollis, Ian	4:44:49 (20,682)
Hollis, Tim	4:33:36 (18,077)
Holloway, Arthur	4:16:59 (13,985)
Holloway, Jason	4:00:17 (10,291)
Holloway, Paul	4:35:44 (18,570)
Holloway, Peter	5:26:40 (27,749)
Holloway, Stephen	4:23:14 (15,554)
Hollywood, Adam	4:43:48 (20,453)
Hollywood, Bernard	4:18:28 (14,347)
Holman, Clive	4:35:15 (18,459)
Holman, Mark	3:53:30 (8,541)
Holmes, Adam	3:46:25 (7,015)
Holmes, Albert	4:49:52 (21,840)
Holmes, Andrew	5:37:35 (28,781)
Holmes, Arthur	4:41:25 (19,853)
Holmes, Charles	4:18:00 (14,251)
Holmes, Craig	3:42:07 (6,171)
Holmes, Darren	4:54:33 (22,823)
Holmes, Darren	5:18:10 (26,647)
Holmes, David	4:22:07 (15,267)
Holmes, David	4:45:07 (20,748)
Holmes, Graham	4:24:02 (15,761)
Holmes, Karl	5:01:47 (24,279)
Holmes, Leigh	4:33:54 (18,144)
Holmes, Mark	4:44:13 (20,548)
Holmes, Nicholas	3:08:18 (1,524)
Holmes, Nicholas	3:54:43 (8,840)
Holmes, Patrick	4:20:26 (14,854)
Holmes, Peter	5:36:21 (28,668)
Holmes, Richard	3:07:05 (1,410)
Holmes, Steven	3:36:10 (5,091)
Holmes, Steven	3:51:45 (8,136)
Holmes, Tam	3:43:31 (6,451)
Holmes, Trevor	4:38:22 (19,180)
Holness, Andrew	4:57:49 (23,546)
Holness, Tim	5:49:51 (29,704)
Holohan, James	4:09:21 (12,205)
Holroyd, Thomas	5:04:55 (24,782)
Holt, Adrian	4:37:54 (19,065)
Holt, Alan	3:30:42 (4,277)
Holt, Andrew	2:48:16 (343)
Holt, John	5:17:07 (26,493)
Holt, Jon	5:18:19 (26,674)
Holt, Keith	2:54:57 (589)
Holt, Michael	4:29:12 (17,039)
Holt, Richard	3:38:10 (5,437)
Holter, Anthony	4:27:09 (16,511)
Holtorp, Gavin	5:42:27 (29,205)
Holzinger, Erik	3:22:35 (3,059)
Homan, Andrew	4:20:07 (14,774)
Homan, Guy	3:30:11 (4,197)
Home, Steven	2:58:46 (831)
Homeier, Lars	4:25:33 (16,147)
Homer, Daniel	4:18:33 (14,372)
Homer, Mark	3:09:33 (1,637)

Homer, Paul	5:43:17 (29,260)
Homer, Stephen	4:34:09 (18,204)
Homewood, Gordon	4:20:21 (14,829)
Homewood, Stephen	3:45:56 (6,919)
Hone, Michael	4:03:57 (11,048)
Hone, Spencer	5:14:53 (26,231)
Hones, Stephen	3:26:12 (3,567)
Honess, Nathan	4:14:02 (13,230)
Honess, Richard	5:11:04 (25,703)
Honey, Michael	5:18:31 (26,700)
Honeyball, Stephen	5:28:31 (27,942)
Honour, Andrew	3:38:00 (5,413)
Honour, Mark	4:23:46 (15,688)
Hoo, Jonathan	4:13:58 (13,251)
Hood, Andrew	5:39:31 (28,948)
Hood, Andy	3:48:46 (7,457)
Hood, Mike	3:09:49 (1,656)
Hoods, Karl	5:26:20 (27,716)
Hook, Alastair	4:57:15 (23,437)
Hook, Christopher	3:44:41 (6,664)
Hook, David	3:19:02 (2,658)
Hook, Matthew	3:20:09 (2,779)
Hook, Philip	3:49:33 (7,642)
Hook, Scott	5:02:41 (24,415)
Hook, Trevor	2:56:58 (700)
Hooker, Bob	3:47:45 (7,267)
Hooker, Malcolm	4:53:48 (22,682)
Hooker, Michael	3:37:33 (5,334)
Hooks, Gary	5:00:10 (24,004)
Hooper, Dave	4:59:11 (23,841)
Hooper, Philip	3:16:35 (2,383)
Hooper, Ronald	4:10:15 (12,408)
Hooper, Tom	4:10:13 (12,401)
Hooton, Glenn	4:32:40 (17,871)
Hooton, Michael	4:54:51 (22,891)
Hope, David	3:13:06 (2,005)
Hope, Jonathan	2:59:35 (909)
Hope, Lee	4:00:21 (10,306)
Hope, Lee	6:03:00 (30,374)
Hope, Richard	4:15:55 (13,725)
Hopegood, James	5:02:58 (24,453)
Hopes, Ben	4:25:57 (16,240)
Hopgood, Martin	4:13:42 (13,176)
Hopkin, David	5:27:21 (27,814)
Hopkin, Kyle	5:57:19 (30,121)
Hopkins, Darren	4:55:55 (23,135)
Hopkins, Gareth	3:48:05 (7,336)
Hopkins, Gareth	4:55:28 (23,021)
Hopkins, Greg	4:09:45 (12,285)
Hopkins, Jame	4:52:12 (22,340)
Hopkins, Jason	4:30:33 (17,382)
Hopkins, Lee	6:12:14 (30,740)
Hopkins, Martin	4:14:20 (13,341)
Hopkins, Martin	4:54:32 (22,881)
Hopkins, Philip	5:37:12 (28,753)
Hopkins, Stephen	3:42:04 (6,162)
Hopkins, Tristan	4:19:59 (14,737)
Hopkinson, James	3:36:19 (5,118)
Hopkinson, Neil	3:55:40 (9,098)
Hopla, Simon	4:33:24 (18,032)
Hopley, Nicholas	4:30:49 (17,449)
Hopley, Peter	3:27:37 (3,756)
Hopper, Graham	4:28:46 (16,928)
Hopperton, Edward	3:19:34 (2,706)
Hopperton, James	4:04:42 (11,225)
Hoppitt, Graeme	3:55:40 (9,098)
Hopwood, Anthony	4:53:38 (22,641)
Hopwood, Duncan	3:53:25 (8,521)
Hopwood, George	5:20:36 (26,973)
Hopwood, Martyn	3:25:50 (3,516)
Hopwood, Simon	4:20:47 (14,923)
Horan, David	3:17:56 (2,541)
Horan, Iwan	3:58:25 (9,813)
Horgan, Paul	3:54:48 (8,868)
Horgan, Paul	4:42:39 (20,142)
Horgan, Shane	3:37:45 (5,376)
Horgan, Tim	5:30:18 (28,117)
Horn, Christopher	4:11:38 (12,671)
Horn, Darryl	4:35:09 (18,431)
Horn, Ian	3:38:39 (5,531)
Horn, Jason	4:42:15 (20,039)
Horn, Steven	4:44:35 (20,629)
Hornby, Keith	4:58:10 (23,621)

Hornby, Mark	7:24:18 (32,104)	
Horne, Andrew	5:17:51 (26,588)	
Horne, Chad	3:47:14 (7,161)	
Horne, Doug	5:15:20 (26,295)	
Horne, Liam	5:03:19 (24,507)	
Horne, Matthew	5:15:35 (26,329)	
Horne, Neil	4:40:58 (19,746)	
Horne, Robert	3:45:23 (6,806)	
Horner, Michael	3:17:20 (2,464)	
Hornung, Klaus	5:14:54 (26,232)	
Horsburgh, Barrie	3:32:52 (4,579)	
Horsewood, Stuart	4:26:25 (16,339)	
Horsfall, Chris	3:14:58 (2,234)	
Horsfield, Craig	4:09:13 (12,175)	
Horsley, Alex	3:52:20 (8,273)	
Horsley, Graham	3:16:39 (2,390)	
Horsley, Paul	3:33:58 (4,742)	
Horsley, Philip	7:45:34 (32,224)	
Horsman, Joseph	3:27:50 (3,792)	
Horspool, John	5:26:07 (27,689)	
Horton, Andrew	4:14:02 (13,270)	
Horton, David	4:24:35 (15,883)	
Horton, Jamie	4:42:53 (20,203)	
Horton, Lee	6:18:11 (30,942)	
Horton, Peter	3:09:57 (1,671)	
Horton, Stephen	6:16:37 (30,882)	
Horwood, Mike	3:29:12 (4,026)	
Hosack, Samuel	4:10:40 (12,493)	
Hosemann, Paul	4:12:56 (12,992)	
Hosie, John	4:03:46 (11,002)	
Hosier, Joshua	4:36:16 (18,702)	
Hosker, Michael	4:42:21 (20,067)	
Hoskin, Dave	2:50:15 (394)	
Hoskyn, John	4:56:50 (23,347)	
Hosmer, Richard	3:26:37 (3,626)	
Hossack, Stuart	6:18:53 (30,969)	
Hostetler, Thomas	3:16:29 (2,374)	
Hotelin, Gilles	3:34:28 (4,833)	
Hotz, Roland	4:38:18 (19,161)	
Houdart, Didier	2:45:24 (244)	
Houdin, Pascal	3:28:58 (3,998)	
Hough, Martin	4:53:56 (22,702)	
Houghton, David	4:20:56 (14,963)	
Houghton, Guy	3:42:33 (6,265)	
Houghton, Ian	4:40:51 (19,716)	
Houghton, James	6:05:47 (30,493)	
Houghton, Jonathan	3:56:48 (9,398)	
Houghton, Philip	4:07:21 (11,766)	
Houghton, Ricky	4:44:48 (20,679)	
Houghton, Robert	4:02:36 (10,756)	
Houghton, Robin	2:39:37 (150)	
Houghton, Thomas	3:56:35 (9,341)	
Houlahan, Oliver	4:29:02 (17,003)	
Hould, Christopher	5:27:46 (27,867)	
Houlgrave, Paul	4:38:09 (19,124)	
Houlihane, Thomas	5:10:02 (25,555)	
Houlton, Matthew	4:07:22 (11,772)	
Houlton, Nicholas	2:51:36 (435)	
Hounsell, Bryan	4:39:32 (19,448)	
Hounsell, Kevin	5:37:06 (28,746)	
Hounsfield, Nicholas	4:03:47 (11,007)	
Hourigan, James	4:36:08 (18,676)	
Hourston, Neil	3:38:35 (5,511)	
House, David	4:39:50 (19,508)	
House, Julian	4:19:04 (14,521)	
House, Kevin	4:07:23 (11,778)	
House, Tim	4:47:58 (21,419)	
Housego, Stephen	5:24:37 (27,495)	
Houston, Angus	3:42:22 (6,214)	
Houtepen, Ton	4:36:53 (18,849)	
Hovden, Jon	3:25:40 (3,486)	
Hoverd, Bruce	5:41:29 (29,115)	
Hovey, Ian	5:25:45 (27,635)	
How, Nicholas	4:04:39 (11,210)	
Howaniets, Helmuth	3:26:28 (3,602)	
Howard, Alistair	4:23:58 (15,741)	
Howard, Allan	4:29:44 (17,171)	
Howard, Chris	2:52:19 (460)	
Howard, Clive	4:25:35 (16,153)	
Howard, David	3:38:24 (5,479)	
Howard, David	5:37:14 (28,758)	
Howard, David	5:44:36 (29,338)	
Howard, Kenneth	3:01:24 (1,020)	
Howard, Mark	4:00:16 (10,283)	
Howard, Mark	4:46:12 (21,018)	
Howard, Martin	4:50:34 (21,979)	
Howard, Martin	5:37:24 (28,768)	
Howard, Michael	3:17:23 (2,475)	
Howard, Michael	3:58:23 (9,804)	
Howard, Michael	4:43:44 (20,440)	
Howard, Nigel	4:58:23 (23,667)	
Howard, Philip	3:29:28 (4,083)	
Howard, Ray	3:59:27 (10,083)	
Howard, Robin	3:41:33 (6,079)	
Howard, Roger	4:21:14 (15,040)	
Howard, Stephen	3:18:08 (2,568)	
Howard, Stephen	3:28:11 (3,845)	
Howard, Steven	3:54:23 (8,748)	
Howard, Timothy	3:40:06 (5,809)	
Howard-Kishi, Michael	5:46:22 (29,459)	
Howarth, Philip	4:42:23 (20,078)	
Howarth, Raymond	3:18:51 (2,641)	
Howarth, Roger	5:11:44 (25,790)	
Howarth, Steve	4:46:17 (21,040)	
Howchin, Neil	4:09:26 (12,212)	
Howden, Peter	4:15:22 (13,607)	
Howe, Andrew	4:15:25 (13,622)	
Howe, David	4:32:08 (17,759)	
Howe, Gary	3:00:56 (997)	
Howe, Jacob	3:32:39 (4,550)	
Howe, Jonathan	6:28:39 (31,294)	
Howe, Robert	3:25:58 (3,537)	
Howe, Stewart	4:51:52 (22,283)	
Howe, Trevor	3:50:22 (7,817)	
Howell, Chris	3:15:29 (2,287)	
Howell, Christopher	6:33:37 (31,413)	
Howell, Jonathan	3:09:37 (1,647)	
Howell, Michael	6:23:41 (31,127)	
Howell, Nicholas	7:28:56 (32,145)	
Howell, Peter	5:37:59 (28,808)	
Howell, Scott	3:08:17 (1,522)	
Howell-Jones, Julian	4:57:52 (23,554)	
Howells, David	3:20:32 (2,829)	
Howells, Don	5:27:19 (27,811)	
Howells, Gareth	4:00:01 (10,226)	
Howells, Gareth	4:36:09 (18,679)	
Howells, Malcolm	3:08:22 (1,533)	
Howells, Nigel	4:08:34 (12,029)	
Howells, Robert	3:23:42 (3,204)	
Howells, Trevor	3:33:41 (4,699)	
Howes, Alan	5:22:05 (27,150)	
Howes, Alexander	5:21:51 (27,131)	
Howes, Andrew	4:14:18 (13,327)	
Howes, Greg	2:48:59 (365)	
Howes, Simon	3:53:59 (8,666)	
Howes, Stuart	5:31:56 (28,285)	
Howes, Toby	4:34:35 (18,301)	
Howes, William	3:10:01 (1,675)	
Howett, Ian	3:24:14 (3,293)	
Howie, Douglas	3:57:11 (9,502)	
Howie, John	4:34:51 (18,359)	
Howie, Kevin	5:37:38 (28,786)	
Howieson, Robert	3:35:16 (4,952)	
Howitt, Stuart	4:43:05 (20,256)	
Howkins, Alex	5:36:43 (28,708)	
Howle, Clifford	5:07:58 (25,265)	
Howlett, Alan	3:24:03 (3,254)	
Howlett, Kevin	3:22:58 (3,108)	
Howlett, Neil	4:17:50 (14,215)	
Howley, Paul	4:27:48 (16,672)	
Howling, Darren	3:56:43 (9,381)	
Howsam, Nicolas	5:23:45 (27,378)	
Howson, Andrew	3:17:57 (2,543)	
Howson, Eugene	3:39:02 (5,604)	
Hoy, David	3:33:04 (4,609)	
Hoy, Kristian	4:58:34 (23,711)	
Hoya Martinez, Victor	4:41:38 (19,896)	
Hoyle, Michael	3:49:01 (7,523)	
Hoyle, Nick	3:46:09 (6,962)	
Hoyle, Raymond	6:48:15 (31,681)	
Hrastic, Martin	5:23:05 (27,298)	
Hrstic, Andrew	4:51:15 (22,144)	
Hrynczak, Stephen	4:44:56 (20,704)	
Huband, Geoff	4:21:01 (14,983)	
Hubbard, Craig	6:54:29 (31,818)	
Hubbard, John	3:22:24 (3,035)	
Hubbard, John	4:03:04 (10,862)	
Hubbard, Robert	3:51:35 (8,100)	
Hubbard, Ross	4:06:52 (11,662)	
Huberich, Markus	4:14:55 (13,482)	
Hubert, Eric	4:07:26 (11,788)	
Huck, Dave	2:54:37 (568)	
Huck, Ernest	3:17:38 (2,507)	
Huck, Philippe	4:48:49 (21,595)	
Huckett, James	4:45:17 (20,792)	
Huckett, Simon	3:12:12 (1,885)	
Huckle, Alan	3:30:49 (4,298)	
Huddart, Andrew	3:48:49 (7,469)	
Hudgell, David	5:51:41 (29,816)	
Hudson, Alan	2:54:38 (570)	
Hudson, Andrew	5:57:16 (30,118)	
Hudson, Barry	5:41:34 (29,125)	
Hudson, Damian	4:52:37 (22,417)	
Hudson, Daniel	4:56:49 (23,342)	
Hudson, Danny	6:12:39 (30,757)	
Hudson, David	3:26:28 (3,602)	
Hudson, David	3:47:30 (7,213)	
Hudson, Graham	4:08:03 (11,913)	
Hudson, Hugh	4:32:29 (17,830)	
Hudson, Ian	5:01:54 (24,294)	
Hudson, Jeff	3:55:34 (9,065)	
Hudson, John	4:48:52 (21,602)	
Hudson, Leslie	3:08:45 (1,567)	
Hudson, Mark	3:19:39 (2,719)	
Hudson, Matt	4:18:48 (14,446)	
Hudson, Paul	3:30:50 (4,300)	
Hudson, Paul	3:54:43 (8,840)	
Hudson, Paul	4:46:28 (21,085)	
Hudson, Paul	4:53:44 (22,663)	
Hudson, Paul	5:59:29 (30,239)	
Hudson, Peter	3:43:27 (6,443)	
Hudson, Ronald	5:45:09 (29,380)	
Hudson, Shaun	3:37:30 (5,325)	
Hudson, Simon	3:41:48 (6,113)	
Hudson, Stephen	4:41:13 (19,804)	
Hudson, Tony	3:04:00 (1,184)	
Hudson-Sieg, Jonathan	6:27:54 (31,262)	
Hudspeth, William	4:33:45 (18,106)	
Hudspith, John	2:57:56 (761)	
Huebler, Thomas	4:49:16 (21,694)	
Hueger, Bernhard	3:51:07 (7,981)	
Hufton, Tim	4:35:46 (18,588)	
Huggett, Ronald	5:12:12 (25,856)	
Huggins, James	3:24:40 (3,354)	
Huggins, Mervyn	3:46:20 (7,000)	
Huggins, Richard	5:15:18 (26,290)	
Hughes, Adam	5:18:37 (26,716)	
Hughes, Adrian	5:47:55 (29,567)	
Hughes, Chris	4:33:34 (18,071)	
Hughes, Christopher	4:18:39 (14,407)	
Hughes, Dafydd	4:13:27 (13,111)	
Hughes, Daniel	3:55:03 (8,927)	
Hughes, David	3:42:49 (6,318)	
Hughes, David	4:20:10 (14,788)	
Hughes, David	4:46:42 (21,124)	
Hughes, David	5:47:18 (29,515)	
Hughes, David	6:00:41 (30,883)	
Hughes, Frank	3:09:58 (1,672)	
Hughes, Gareth	4:30:38 (17,399)	
Hughes, Gareth	5:11:03 (25,700)	
Hughes, Gareth	5:53:14 (29,889)	
Hughes, Gerad	4:30:10 (17,277)	
Hughes, Geraint	2:57:48 (756)	
Hughes, Geraint	5:17:07 (26,493)	
Hughes, Geraint	5:29:40 (28,058)	
Hughes, Gqvin	3:25:51 (3,519)	
Hughes, Graeme	4:51:27 (22,195)	
Hughes, Graham	3:40:51 (5,932)	
Hughes, Gwyn	4:13:24 (13,093)	
Hughes, James	4:39:17 (19,391)	
Hughes, James	4:57:45 (23,259)	
Hughes, Jason	6:42:01 (31,565)	
Hughes, Jeremy	4:53:16 (22,564)	
Hughes, John	3:26:48 (3,644)	
Hughes, Jonathan	4:31:48 (17,687)	
Hughes, Kelli	4:57:01 (23,384)	
Hughes, Kevin	4:17:39 (14,158)	
Hughes, Kevin	4:43:19 (20,325)	
Hughes, Les	3:54:44 (8,847)	

Hughes, Malcolm	3:47:55 (7,304)	
Hughes, Marc	4:20:55 (14,957)	
Hughes, Mark	3:12:50 (1,972)	
Hughes, Mark	3:27:38 (3,759)	
Hughes, Mark	3:59:34 (10,112)	
Hughes, Mark	4:40:33 (19,659)	
Hughes, Mark	5:38:19 (28,841)	
Hughes, Michael	3:15:52 (2,322)	
Hughes, Mitchell	4:14:06 (13,282)	
Hughes, Neil	4:07:23 (11,778)	
Hughes, Nicholas	5:21:06 (27,034)	
Hughes, Paul	4:00:15 (10,278)	
Hughes, Paul	4:06:26 (11,578)	
Hughes, Paul	4:10:20 (12,425)	
Hughes, Peter	2:57:49 (757)	
Hughes, Peter	3:34:56 (4,896)	
Hughes, Peter	5:15:05 (26,259)	
Hughes, Philip	4:32:14 (17,782)	
Hughes, Robert	3:43:43 (6,494)	
Hughes, Robert	4:54:20 (22,776)	
Hughes, Robert	5:42:25 (29,200)	
Hughes, Rodger	2:48:44 (356)	
Hughes, Sean	5:05:28 (24,874)	
Hughes, Simon	3:57:15 (9,517)	
Hughes, Simon	4:38:45 (19,268)	
Hughes, Stephen	3:36:06 (5,078)	
Hughes, Stephen	4:49:30 (21,750)	
Hughes, Steven	3:30:17 (4,218)	
Hughes, Steven	4:13:24 (13,093)	
Hughes, Stuart	3:05:23 (1,280)	
Hughes, Tony	6:15:52 (30,855)	
Hughes MBE, Evan	3:42:52 (6,333)	
Hughes-Jones, Geoffrey	5:30:42 (28,166)	
Hugo, Jeremy	5:55:17 (30,015)	
Huiberts, Chris	4:41:32 (19,874)	
Huille, Alexandre	3:44:19 (6,600)	
Huille, Matthew	3:58:14 (9,764)	
Hukin, Danny	3:19:57 (2,754)	
Hulbert, George	4:38:22 (19,180)	
Hulbert, Martin	3:50:12 (7,777)	
Hulcoop, Stephen	4:34:19 (18,246)	
Hull, Darren	7:21:02 (32,077)	
Hull, Jamie	4:41:45 (19,931)	
Hull, John	3:46:40 (7,061)	
Hull, Peter	4:29:29 (17,112)	
Hull, Richard	5:40:08 (29,006)	
Hulme, Anthony	3:41:58 (6,142)	
Hulme, Ged	5:26:55 (27,771)	
Hulme, Stephen	5:17:29 (26,541)	
Hulme, Tom	5:16:29 (26,424)	
Hulse, Christopher	4:09:55 (12,329)	
Hulse, Michael	3:17:36 (2,503)	
Humber, Steven	3:58:14 (9,764)	
Humberstone, David	3:22:08 (3,000)	
Humbert, James	3:55:53 (9,150)	
Humbert, Michael	4:52:46 (22,452)	
Humbert-Droz, Laurent	3:17:43 (2,520)	
Humble, Brian	3:33:06 (4,614)	
Hume, Adam	3:36:25 (5,131)	
Hume, Nicol	3:58:44 (9,892)	
Hume, Richard	4:11:59 (12,756)	
Hume, Robin	4:47:18 (21,247)	
Humfrey, Tim	3:53:33 (8,558)	
Hummel, Martin	3:38:17 (5,458)	
Humphrey, Adam	3:24:57 (3,389)	
Humphrey, Alun	3:58:31 (9,839)	
Humphrey, Andrew	4:52:37 (22,417)	
Humphrey, Mike	5:16:17 (26,400)	
Humphrey, Richard	4:28:58 (16,984)	
Humphrey, Stuart	3:58:12 (9,755)	
Humphrey, Tim	4:23:05 (15,508)	
Humphreys, Allan	3:58:00 (9,706)	
Humphreys, David	4:07:06 (11,708)	
Humphreys, Duncan	4:28:45 (16,922)	
Humphreys, Mark	3:19:38 (2,715)	
Humphreys, Martin	4:43:04 (20,250)	
Humphreys, Martin	5:16:02 (26,383)	
Humphreys, Matt	5:56:51 (30,095)	
Humphreys, Paul	4:43:14 (20,296)	
Humphreys, Steve	3:21:37 (2,943)	
Humphries, Benjamin	4:50:43 (22,018)	
Humphries, John	3:55:41 (9,103)	
Humphries, Paul	3:33:40 (4,697)	

Humphries, Paul	4:59:57 (23,975)	
Humphries, Robert	5:17:06 (26,492)	
Hunt, Alex	5:01:56 (24,302)	
Hunt, Andrew	5:03:54 (24,615)	
Hunt, Anthony	3:50:07 (7,757)	
Hunt, Chris	5:07:53 (25,249)	
Hunt, Christopher	2:58:01 (768)	
Hunt, Clinton	4:04:52 (11,264)	
Hunt, David	3:20:02 (2,765)	
Hunt, David	3:36:32 (5,150)	
Hunt, David	3:57:05 (9,472)	
Hunt, Edward	5:55:01 (29,999)	
Hunt, Gary	4:14:46 (13,437)	
Hunt, George	4:21:48 (15,185)	
Hunt, Graham	3:55:06 (8,941)	
Hunt, Mark	3:53:39 (8,579)	
Hunt, Martin	4:03:32 (10,953)	
Hunt, Michael	3:08:16 (1,521)	
Hunt, Michael	5:12:40 (25,929)	
Hunt, Micky	3:17:57 (2,543)	
Hunt, Nathan	3:24:34 (3,344)	
Hunt, Neil	5:41:15 (29,097)	
Hunt, Peter	4:43:00 (20,236)	
Hunt, Robert	3:36:32 (5,150)	
Hunt, Russell	5:06:13 (24,988)	
Hunt, Steven	3:18:26 (2,605)	
Hunt, Timothy	4:37:04 (18,892)	
Hunt, Timothy	4:37:40 (19,012)	
Hunt, Toby	3:44:47 (6,685)	
Hunt, Tom	3:42:36 (6,276)	
Hunter, Andrew	3:14:44 (2,209)	
Hunter, Andrew	3:30:43 (4,282)	
Hunter, Ben	3:11:59 (1,859)	
Hunter, David	3:36:43 (5,184)	
Hunter, David	6:03:48 (30,405)	
Hunter, Dick	4:04:35 (11,196)	
Hunter, Edward	6:23:36 (31,125)	
Hunter, Graham	5:06:40 (25,046)	
Hunter, Ian	3:40:39 (5,891)	
Hunter, Jonathan	4:08:11 (11,936)	
Hunter, Matthew	3:52:39 (8,344)	
Hunter, Nicholas	4:26:18 (16,316)	
Hunter, Paul	5:11:09 (25,715)	
Hunter, Richard	4:00:03 (10,233)	
Hunter, Robert	3:41:17 (6,010)	
Hunter, Robert	4:22:46 (15,434)	
Hunter, Simon	4:04:31 (11,183)	
Huntington, Tim	4:22:03 (15,252)	
Huntley, David	4:30:30 (17,366)	
Huntley, George	5:24:54 (27,520)	
Hunton, Chris	3:30:05 (4,180)	
Hunton, Geoff	3:32:40 (4,553)	
Hurd, Andrew	4:20:42 (14,903)	
Hurley, Arthur	3:51:43 (8,130)	
Hurley, James	5:31:14 (28,218)	
Hurley, Joe	3:09:31 (1,632)	
Hurley, Mark	3:53:56 (8,653)	
Hurley, Michael	3:30:58 (4,323)	
Hurn, Mike	5:50:10 (29,731)	
Hurry, Andy	4:21:04 (14,997)	
Hurse, John	4:26:39 (16,391)	
Hurst, Alan	4:37:11 (18,919)	
Hurst, Andrew	3:50:59 (7,946)	
Hurst, Anthony	4:35:36 (18,541)	
Hurst, David	4:36:41 (18,806)	
Hurst, Graham	4:15:14 (13,576)	
Hurst, Nigel	3:51:01 (7,957)	
Hurst, Philip	4:56:28 (23,251)	
Hurt, Garry	4:19:44 (14,679)	
Hurtig, Michael	4:47:38 (21,328)	
Hurtley, Charles	4:38:17 (19,156)	
Husband, Eryl	2:48:58 (363)	
Huser, Thomas	4:03:28 (10,936)	
Huseyin, Turan	5:10:26 (25,617)	
Huss, Hans-Hoachim	4:41:02 (19,763)	
Hussain, Pervez	7:30:12 (32,153)	
Hussain, Soleman	4:45:23 (20,817)	
Hussein, Rafiq	5:23:04 (27,295)	
Hussey, Alex	3:10:02 (1,677)	
Hussey, Andrew	2:32:50 (80)	
Hussey, Scott	4:01:18 (10,495)	
Huston, James	4:53:04 (22,514)	
Hutcheson, Adam	3:57:21 (9,542)	

Hutcheson, Christopher	4:27:51 (16,680)	
Hutchin, Anthony	3:20:30 (2,826)	
Hutchings, Clive	4:15:30 (13,640)	
Hutchings, Raymond	5:15:07 (26,266)	
Hutchings, Terence	7:58:03 (32,250)	
Hutchings, Terence	8:33:53 (32,279)	
Hutchins, Philip	4:30:10 (17,277)	
Hutchins, Steven	3:50:39 (7,873)	
Hutchinson, Alan	2:55:12 (604)	
Hutchinson, Douglas	3:18:56 (2,649)	
Hutchinson, Garry	4:08:39 (12,052)	
Hutchinson, Gordon	5:23:05 (27,298)	
Hutchinson, Philip	3:59:15 (10,021)	
Hutchinson, Stephen	3:17:13 (2,453)	
Hutchinson, Steve	6:14:43 (30,818)	
Hutchinson, Tony	4:40:24 (19,633)	
Hutchinson, Tony	5:13:25 (26,026)	
Hutchison, Mark	3:28:37 (3,929)	
Hutchison, Robert	3:53:18 (8,496)	
Hutison, David	5:48:09 (29,588)	
Hutsby, Ian	5:40:37 (29,045)	
Hutson, Giles	4:03:02 (10,850)	
Hutt, Alasdair	4:17:32 (14,125)	
Hutt, Graham	4:51:03 (22,083)	
Hutter, Jonathan	4:45:46 (20,905)	
Hutton, Alexander	3:40:53 (5,941)	
Hutton, Craig	4:06:26 (11,578)	
Hutton, David	4:11:56 (12,749)	
Hutton, Guy	3:10:42 (1,728)	
Hutton, Mark	5:15:13 (26,279)	
Hutton, Peter	3:27:32 (3,745)	
Hutton, Peter	3:30:18 (4,219)	
Hutton, Toby	4:36:53 (18,849)	
Huws, Llion	3:09:26 (1,627)	
Huxley, Mark	6:33:53 (31,421)	
Huxtable, Richard	4:46:50 (21,154)	
Hyam, Richard	3:50:32 (7,852)	
Hyatt, Gary	3:25:14 (3,432)	
Hybertsen, Tage	4:27:40 (16,641)	
Hyde, Brian	4:50:02 (21,868)	
Hyde, Daniel	4:52:15 (22,350)	
Hyde, Gordon	4:53:47 (22,675)	
Hyde, Gordon	6:29:05 (31,304)	
Hyde, Richard	4:57:00 (23,382)	
Hyer, Jonathan	4:57:23 (23,456)	
Hyer, Stephen	5:04:45 (24,747)	
Hyland, Anthony	3:10:16 (1,700)	
Hyland, Edward	4:01:41 (10,576)	
Hyland, Martin	3:51:50 (8,159)	
Hyland, Terence	3:00:28 (971)	
Hynard, Mark	4:00:16 (10,283)	
Hynds, Andy	3:37:16 (5,286)	
Hynes, Andrew	3:25:52 (3,523)	
Hynes, John	4:27:19 (16,553)	
Hynes, Peter	3:52:57 (8,409)	
Hyson, Terry	6:08:05 (30,568)	
Iacono, Gaspare	4:05:39 (11,427)	
Iacuzzi, Nico	4:07:52 (11,886)	
Iannilli, Carlo	2:45:47 (251)	
Ibberson, Mark	4:13:27 (13,111)	
Ibbitson, Martin	4:34:02 (18,172)	
Ibbitson, Michael	4:34:02 (18,172)	
Ibbotson, Alan	3:54:38 (8,827)	
Ibnabdeljalil, Nacer	3:49:57 (7,726)	
Ibn-Ibrahim, Mustapha	5:51:04 (29,789)	
Iceton, Ben	3:37:50 (5,390)	
Iddles, Chris	3:54:26 (8,763)	
Idelenburg, Frank	4:32:27 (17,821)	
Idle, Jonathan	3:16:49 (2,405)	
Idriss, Mohammed	4:34:26 (18,275)	
Idsoe, Asbjoern	3:30:33 (4,253)	
Igo, Gareth	4:27:43 (16,657)	
Ii, Yasushi	4:52:24 (22,376)	
Ilabaca, Prudencio	4:52:51 (22,470)	
Ilchyshyn, Andrew	5:09:38 (25,494)	
Iley, Paul	5:15:04 (26,256)	
Iliff, Christopher	3:53:43 (8,593)	
Iliffe, Edward	5:18:42 (26,729)	
Illing, Paul	2:55:51 (639)	
Illingworth, Andrew	4:45:19 (20,798)	
Illingworth, Colin	5:17:42 (26,568)	
Illingworth, Kenneth	3:54:33 (8,803)	
Ilsley, Mark	4:47:50 (21,385)	

Janjuha, Sohail	4:38:30 (19,198)	
Jannaty, Yunus	4:22:53 (15,466)	
Janoff, Daniel	5:21:22 (27,068)	
Jantzen, Gerd	5:05:15 (24,835)	
Janvier, Nick	2:24:59 (40)	
Jaques, Mark	4:24:44 (15,928)	
Jaramillo, Juan	4:11:41 (12,687)	
Jardine, Gary	4:01:09 (10,461)	
Jardine, Howard	3:39:19 (5,658)	
Jarman, Guy	4:31:25 (17,595)	
Jarman, Mark	4:54:19 (22,772)	
Jarman, Matthew	5:03:38 (24,555)	
Jarmin, Ricky	3:59:51 (10,187)	
Jarmyn, Ray	4:54:34 (22,831)	
Jarratt, Jeremy	4:24:58 (15,990)	
Jarrett, Andrew	4:26:03 (16,264)	
Jarrey, Michael	4:49:13 (21,679)	
Jarrold, Darren	3:15:53 (2,326)	
Jarrold, Paul	4:57:08 (23,411)	
Jarrot, Olivier	3:23:55 (3,235)	
Jarry, John	3:57:29 (9,576)	
Jarvie, James	3:56:39 (9,364)	
Jarvie, Stephen	5:08:49 (25,377)	
Jarvis, Duncan	5:01:42 (24,257)	
Jarvis, Luke	4:00:06 (10,244)	
Jarvis, Nicholas	4:52:42 (22,439)	
Jarvis, Robert	3:39:50 (5,754)	
Jarvis, Robin	5:36:43 (28,708)	
Jarvis, Stephen	3:47:14 (7,161)	
Jarvis, Stephen	3:51:31 (8,080)	
Jarvis, Timothy	3:43:40 (6,480)	
Jarvis, Tony	6:15:27 (30,843)	
Jasnoch, Paul	3:31:08 (4,347)	
Jasper, Richard	3:56:31 (9,327)	
Jaspers, Geert	4:09:45 (12,285)	
Javaudin, Regis	4:05:15 (11,342)	
Jay, Gary	4:42:02 (19,998)	
Jay, Paul	4:47:20 (21,254)	
Jay, Stephen	3:58:29 (9,830)	
Jay, Stephen	5:04:11 (24,659)	
Jay, Tim	4:44:03 (20,508)	
Jeal, Nicholas	4:36:17 (18,707)	
Jeanes, Ben	3:36:13 (5,098)	
Jean-Paul, Desmond	3:51:41 (8,127)	
Jeans, Nicholas	4:00:20 (10,301)	
Jeeves, Brian	4:58:34 (23,711)	
Jeeves, Jamie	3:12:11 (1,882)	
Jefcoate, Simon	3:43:35 (6,460)	
Jefferies, Jonathan	4:30:37 (17,396)	
Jefferies, Roger	4:32:32 (17,840)	
Jefferson, Neil	3:58:38 (9,867)	
Jeffery, Christopher	3:58:00 (9,706)	
Jeffery, James	3:56:00 (9,178)	
Jeffery, John	4:06:16 (11,549)	
Jeffery, Michael	5:42:21 (29,196)	
Jeffery, Stephen	2:52:45 (485)	
Jefford, Mark	2:58:43 (823)	
Jeffreson, Nigel	7:40:46 (32,209)	
Jeffrey, Adam	3:49:38 (7,665)	
Jeffrey, Gordon	4:27:14 (16,529)	
Jeffrey, Neill	3:55:02 (8,926)	
Jeffrey, Thomas	4:00:00 (10,224)	
Jeffreys, Jeff	4:57:29 (23,479)	
Jeffries, Alan	4:47:40 (21,339)	
Jeffries, Brian	5:21:33 (27,089)	
Jeffries, Derrek	6:10:25 (30,657)	
Jeffries, Lee	3:27:07 (3,695)	
Jeffries, Stacey	3:07:50 (1,490)	
Jeffs, Leslie	5:02:51 (24,438)	
Jeffs, Mark	3:44:21 (6,611)	
Jeffs, Richard	4:14:14 (13,312)	
Jegu, Frederic	2:54:12 (550)	
Jelley, David	2:59:37 (911)	
Jemmett, Thomas	4:10:23 (12,438)	
Jenden, Richard	4:33:46 (18,108)	
Jenkin, Huw	3:10:08 (1,688)	
Jenkins, Andy	3:17:26 (2,482)	
Jenkins, Andy	3:48:11 (7,354)	
Jenkins, Benjamin	4:29:50 (17,203)	
Jenkins, Christopher	3:57:09 (9,494)	
Jenkins, Clive	4:42:07 (20,014)	
Jenkins, Colin	4:27:37 (16,628)	
Jenkins, David	3:22:43 (3,071)	

Jenkins, David	5:09:31 (25,476)	
Jenkins, Huw	3:26:20 (3,581)	
Jenkins, Ian	6:28:14 (31,279)	
Jenkins, Jonathan	4:11:28 (12,636)	
Jenkins, Nicholas	4:54:10 (22,738)	
Jenkins, Nicholas	4:59:55 (23,972)	
Jenkins, Paul	3:20:13 (2,789)	
Jenkins, Paul	5:08:08 (25,288)	
Jenkins, Paul	5:15:57 (26,369)	
Jenkins, Peter	3:29:26 (4,075)	
Jenkins, Philip	3:56:54 (9,422)	
Jenkins, Robert	4:41:34 (19,885)	
Jenkins, Stephen	4:32:00 (17,730)	
Jenkins, Timothy	4:59:49 (23,952)	
Jenkins, Trevor	4:28:25 (16,832)	
Jenkinson, Gary	4:21:23 (15,080)	
Jenkinson, Robert	4:39:04 (19,335)	
Jenks, John	4:27:30 (16,603)	
Jenks, Philip	5:07:24 (25,161)	
Jenner, Blaise	5:25:33 (27,618)	
Jenner, Chris	4:17:31 (14,115)	
Jenner, David	5:10:04 (25,561)	
Jenner, Jason	3:27:54 (3,801)	
Jenner, Marc	4:49:10 (21,667)	
Jenner, Oliver	5:15:43 (26,346)	
Jenner, Peter	6:20:58 (31,050)	
Jennings, Barrie	4:27:23 (16,567)	
Jennings, Barry	4:38:56 (19,311)	
Jennings, Derek	4:58:27 (23,687)	
Jennings, Frank	6:02:51 (30,368)	
Jennings, Ken	4:31:27 (17,602)	
Jennings, Mark	4:10:24 (12,444)	
Jennings, Mark	4:19:18 (14,572)	
Jennings, Nik	6:18:49 (30,967)	
Jennings, Odran	3:56:36 (9,346)	
Jennings, Paul	4:58:45 (23,745)	
Jennings, Peter	3:06:47 (1,385)	
Jennings, Robert	3:23:42 (3,204)	
Jennings, Stephen	3:46:25 (7,015)	
Jennings, Stephen	4:07:12 (11,737)	
Jennings, Terry	4:58:54 (23,781)	
Jennings, Timothy	4:16:03 (13,750)	
Jennison, Phillip	5:20:20 (26,929)	
Jennison, Toby	3:54:49 (8,870)	
Jenny, Seth	2:58:36 (812)	
Jensen, Bjarne	3:13:29 (2,060)	
Jensen, Kristian	4:34:36 (18,307)	
Jensen, Martin	3:23:04 (3,122)	
Jensen, Martin	4:50:52 (22,050)	
Jensen, Nicki	3:53:47 (8,613)	
Jensen, William	3:53:00 (8,426)	
Jeoffroy, Matthew	3:12:57 (1,981)	
Jeremy, Mike	4:39:42 (19,476)	
Jerome, Richard	6:12:21 (30,746)	
Jervis, Graeme	2:52:33 (471)	
Jervis, Graham	6:00:04 (30,259)	
Jespersen, Ulrik	2:59:17 (878)	
Jessop, Benjamin	4:31:42 (17,672)	
Jessop, Julian	4:24:18 (15,820)	
Jette, Michael	3:58:50 (9,927)	
Jevons, Steve	4:00:31 (10,333)	
Jewell, Andrew	3:15:11 (2,261)	
Jewell, Mark	3:45:03 (6,741)	
Jewell, Neville	3:18:18 (2,591)	
Jewson, Anthony	3:51:39 (8,120)	
Jeyes, Oliver	4:08:12 (11,938)	
Jim, Jackie	4:55:46 (23,103)	
Jinks, Alan	7:00:17 (31,891)	
Jno-Lewis, Spencer	3:56:00 (9,178)	
Joachin, Steffan	2:58:04 (770)	
Joad, David	4:00:41 (10,361)	
Job, Barry	4:50:29 (21,963)	
Jobes, Heath	5:12:30 (25,897)	
Jobling, David	3:56:01 (9,184)	
Jobling, John	4:42:49 (20,188)	
Jobling, Paul	4:47:22 (21,261)	
Jochym, Bogdan	4:48:20 (21,501)	
Joehring, Jochen	3:55:53 (9,150)	
Johannesen, Stein	3:34:53 (4,889)	
Johannknecht, Raphael	3:25:10 (3,420)	
Johansson, Anders	4:30:20 (17,319)	
Johansson, Christer	3:07:16 (1,436)	
Johansson, Kent	4:00:43 (10,373)	

Johansson, Lennart	5:08:31 (25,340)	
Johansson, Mikael	4:11:11 (12,572)	
John, Andrew	5:02:04 (24,323)	
John, Antony	4:13:12 (13,049)	
John, Dean	2:58:07 (775)	
John, Dewi	4:07:48 (11,871)	
John, Gilbert	3:41:21 (6,025)	
John, Marcus	3:50:57 (7,933)	
John, Nigel	3:12:51 (1,975)	
John, Paul	3:43:50 (6,514)	
John, Spencer	5:24:07 (27,424)	
Johnes, Michael	5:55:16 (30,013)	
John-Lewis, Allan	5:12:09 (25,842)	
Johns, Alun	3:16:16 (2,356)	
Johns, Barnaby	5:28:40 (27,957)	
Johns, Lance	3:28:43 (3,949)	
Johns, Marcus	3:58:41 (9,882)	
Johns, Nigel	3:24:23 (3,314)	
Johns, Paul	3:54:14 (8,714)	
Johns, Paul	4:07:08 (11,721)	
Johns, Robert	5:37:04 (28,745)	
Johnsen, Trond-Rolf	4:52:38 (22,428)	
Johnsey, Paul	3:53:45 (8,603)	
Johnson, Adam	3:55:55 (9,158)	
Johnson, Adrian	5:49:20 (29,667)	
Johnson, Alex	5:44:07 (29,310)	
Johnson, Allan	4:31:52 (17,701)	
Johnson, Andrew	3:16:16 (2,356)	
Johnson, Andrew	3:45:06 (6,755)	
Johnson, Andrew	4:31:32 (17,626)	
Johnson, Andrew	5:15:14 (26,282)	
Johnson, Andy	4:26:05 (16,272)	
Johnson, Andy	4:57:50 (23,550)	
Johnson, Anthony	4:54:53 (22,901)	
Johnson, Ben	3:38:35 (5,511)	
Johnson, Christopher	3:41:59 (6,147)	
Johnson, Christopher	3:56:44 (9,385)	
Johnson, Christopher	4:41:29 (19,869)	
Johnson, Christopher	5:31:40 (28,254)	
Johnson, Craig	5:19:49 (26,861)	
Johnson, David	3:55:01 (8,923)	
Johnson, David	4:16:54 (13,964)	
Johnson, David	5:39:39 (28,961)	
Johnson, Declan	4:36:24 (18,744)	
Johnson, Dominic	4:23:06 (15,512)	
Johnson, Gary	4:28:56 (16,976)	
Johnson, Gavin	4:27:58 (16,701)	
Johnson, Geoff	5:38:36 (28,867)	
Johnson, Geoffrey	3:06:40 (1,375)	
Johnson, Geoffrey	4:02:09 (10,666)	
Johnson, Graham	5:12:40 (25,929)	
Johnson, Greg	5:34:02 (28,481)	
Johnson, Harry	6:29:44 (31,321)	
Johnson, Harvey	4:19:11 (14,548)	
Johnson, Ian	4:18:39 (14,407)	
Johnson, James	4:52:38 (22,428)	
Johnson, James	5:00:14 (24,022)	
Johnson, John	4:09:13 (12,175)	
Johnson, Kevin	3:29:19 (4,048)	
Johnson, Kevin	4:04:16 (11,127)	
Johnson, Kevin	5:16:40 (26,447)	
Johnson, Lee	3:12:11 (1,882)	
Johnson, Mark	4:23:12 (15,547)	
Johnson, Mark	4:50:52 (22,050)	
Johnson, Michael	3:42:05 (6,165)	
Johnson, Michael	4:57:03 (23,392)	
Johnson, Neil	4:55:47 (23,107)	
Johnson, Nigel	4:21:33 (15,119)	
Johnson, Paul	3:24:17 (3,300)	
Johnson, Paul	3:49:46 (7,691)	
Johnson, Paul	4:52:48 (22,460)	
Johnson, Paul	5:29:56 (28,077)	
Johnson, Paul	7:06:12 (31,943)	
Johnson, Peter	3:32:10 (4,491)	
Johnson, Ray	3:33:28 (4,674)	
Johnson, Raymond	4:37:15 (18,937)	
Johnson, Richard	2:58:25 (795)	
Johnson, Richard	3:11:22 (1,786)	
Johnson, Richard	5:18:54 (26,742)	
Johnson, Robert	2:55:16 (610)	
Johnson, Robert	3:41:59 (6,147)	
Johnson, Robert	5:47:55 (29,567)	
Johnson, Ross	3:53:34 (8,561)	

Johnson, Scott	3:54:33 (8,803)	
Johnson, Simon	3:55:01 (8,923)	
Johnson, Simon	4:11:46 (12,713)	
Johnson, Stuart	5:44:27 (29,333)	
Johnson, Tim	5:31:07 (28,208)	
Johnston, Andy	4:12:45 (12,949)	
Johnston, Andy	4:54:39 (22,849)	
Johnston, Barry	2:55:22 (612)	
Johnston, Ben	4:27:08 (16,506)	
Johnston, Chris	4:24:58 (15,990)	
Johnston, Forbes	3:50:03 (7,743)	
Johnston, Jason	3:55:15 (8,978)	
Johnston, Jeremy	4:04:28 (11,171)	
Johnston, Nicholas	4:32:42 (17,879)	
Johnston, Paul	5:37:45 (28,795)	
Johnston, Robert	4:09:52 (12,315)	
Johnston, Stephen	3:42:40 (6,288)	
Johnston, Timothy	4:17:42 (14,176)	
Johnston, William	4:25:00 (16,003)	
Johnstone, Douglas	3:27:32 (3,745)	
Johnstone, James	3:45:11 (6,771)	
Johnstone, Oliver	4:14:38 (13,409)	
Johnstone, Rodney	4:29:31 (17,123)	
Johnstone, Sean	3:43:10 (6,399)	
Johnstone, Victor	4:00:31 (10,333)	
Jokat, Brian	4:31:40 (17,663)	
Jolley, David	5:07:28 (25,177)	
Jolly, Richard	4:18:26 (14,341)	
Jolly, Stephen	4:24:41 (15,911)	
Joly, Robin	4:23:55 (15,724)	
Jonasar, Sigurgeir	4:58:26 (23,683)	
Joncoux, Benoit	4:00:23 (10,310)	
Jones, Adrian	4:29:55 (17,225)	
Jones, Alan	2:50:48 (411)	
Jones, Alan	3:53:49 (8,623)	
Jones, Alan	5:46:26 (29,463)	
Jones, Aled	3:18:21 (2,598)	
Jones, Aled	3:33:30 (4,678)	
Jones, Allen	2:42:05 (182)	
Jones, Alun	6:09:35 (30,619)	
Jones, Andrew	3:28:53 (3,984)	
Jones, Andrew	3:58:29 (9,830)	
Jones, Andrew	4:02:30 (10,742)	
Jones, Andrew	4:16:45 (13,922)	
Jones, Andrew	4:50:47 (22,031)	
Jones, Andrew	4:51:28 (22,204)	
Jones, Andrew	5:14:38 (26,193)	
Jones, Andrew	6:53:17 (31,795)	
Jones, Anthony	4:19:43 (14,673)	
Jones, Anthony	4:52:40 (22,436)	
Jones, Anthony	4:58:40 (23,727)	
Jones, Anthony	5:09:51 (25,521)	
Jones, Arwel	3:07:41 (1,473)	
Jones, Arwel	3:24:59 (3,393)	
Jones, Austin	5:49:16 (29,660)	
Jones, Barrie	3:46:11 (6,969)	
Jones, Barry	6:50:45 (31,739)	
Jones, Ben	3:45:38 (6,856)	
Jones, Ben	4:37:04 (18,892)	
Jones, Benjamin	4:07:22 (11,772)	
Jones, Benjamin	4:17:36 (14,139)	
Jones, Bernard	3:36:10 (5,091)	
Jones, Brian	4:18:59 (14,504)	
Jones, Brian	4:39:51 (19,512)	
Jones, Brian	5:03:07 (24,477)	
Jones, Brian	5:25:48 (27,641)	
Jones, Bruce	3:53:17 (8,491)	
Jones, Bryn	5:15:54 (26,361)	
Jones, Carlos	4:04:52 (11,264)	
Jones, Chris	4:46:21 (21,061)	
Jones, Christopher	4:52:30 (22,396)	
Jones, Christopher	4:58:46 (23,755)	
Jones, Christopher	5:07:41 (25,221)	
Jones, Clifford	4:56:19 (23,224)	
Jones, Clive	4:38:34 (19,213)	
Jones, Colin	3:16:53 (2,416)	
Jones, Colin	4:33:51 (18,126)	
Jones, Dan	4:02:11 (10,675)	
Jones, Danial	5:19:57 (26,879)	
Jones, Daniel	3:40:23 (5,855)	
Jones, Daniel	4:54:04 (22,723)	
Jones, Darren	4:13:59 (13,258)	
Jones, Daryl	4:48:12 (21,471)	
Jones, David	2:48:15 (342)	
Jones, David	3:13:41 (2,086)	
Jones, David	3:21:39 (2,946)	
Jones, David	3:23:26 (3,169)	
Jones, David	4:00:26 (10,319)	
Jones, David	4:04:03 (11,075)	
Jones, David	4:19:06 (14,530)	
Jones, David	4:41:42 (19,919)	
Jones, David	5:20:41 (26,984)	
Jones, David	5:28:26 (27,935)	
Jones, Dennis	5:02:18 (24,361)	
Jones, Derek	4:52:22 (22,373)	
Jones, Dewi	3:03:46 (1,168)	
Jones, Donald	4:07:32 (11,819)	
Jones, Douglas	4:33:38 (18,080)	
Jones, Duncan	3:10:01 (1,675)	
Jones, Emyr	4:53:05 (22,517)	
Jones, Eurwyn	4:30:03 (17,252)	
Jones, Gareth	3:25:52 (3,523)	
Jones, Gareth	4:09:17 (12,190)	
Jones, Gareth	4:15:09 (13,554)	
Jones, Gareth	4:18:25 (14,334)	
Jones, Gareth	4:28:17 (16,785)	
Jones, Gareth	4:52:48 (22,460)	
Jones, Gareth	5:59:16 (30,224)	
Jones, Gary	4:11:12 (12,578)	
Jones, George	4:49:53 (21,842)	
Jones, George	6:09:58 (30,639)	
Jones, Geraint	5:49:47 (29,699)	
Jones, Graham	3:15:45 (2,312)	
Jones, Graham	4:05:37 (11,419)	
Jones, Graham	4:40:37 (19,670)	
Jones, Graham	5:34:01 (28,479)	
Jones, Graham	5:42:19 (29,194)	
Jones, Gwyn	4:04:43 (11,230)	
Jones, Hadyn	2:53:48 (517)	
Jones, Hume	3:52:24 (8,288)	
Jones, Huw	3:56:33 (9,335)	
Jones, Ian	3:07:14 (1,432)	
Jones, Ian	3:59:57 (10,211)	
Jones, Ian	4:16:28 (13,850)	
Jones, James	4:46:45 (21,136)	
Jones, Jeffrey	4:55:08 (22,949)	
Jones, John	3:08:58 (1,583)	
Jones, John	4:09:31 (12,230)	
Jones, Keith	3:30:01 (4,169)	
Jones, Keith	4:42:05 (20,004)	
Jones, Kenneth	4:42:30 (20,109)	
Jones, Kenton	3:59:26 (10,073)	
Jones, Kevin	3:58:52 (9,934)	
Jones, Kevin	4:37:08 (18,906)	
Jones, Kevin	4:41:13 (19,804)	
Jones, Kevin	5:09:59 (25,546)	
Jones, Lawrence	3:01:53 (1,046)	
Jones, Lee	5:21:16 (27,060)	
Jones, Malcolm	4:32:47 (17,894)	
Jones, Mark	3:31:07 (4,345)	
Jones, Mark	3:51:08 (7,989)	
Jones, Mark	4:04:27 (11,163)	
Jones, Mark	4:11:41 (12,687)	
Jones, Mark	4:15:12 (13,567)	
Jones, Mark	5:14:14 (26,132)	
Jones, Mark	5:22:49 (27,256)	
Jones, Martin	4:13:32 (13,134)	
Jones, Martin	4:30:12 (17,287)	
Jones, Martin	4:35:45 (18,580)	
Jones, Martin	4:44:46 (20,673)	
Jones, Martin	5:30:20 (28,121)	
Jones, Matthew	4:14:22 (13,349)	
Jones, Matthew	5:01:14 (24,191)	
Jones, Matthew	5:36:41 (28,706)	
Jones, Michael	3:50:40 (7,879)	
Jones, Michael	4:17:19 (14,060)	
Jones, Michael	4:20:47 (14,923)	
Jones, Michael	4:23:26 (15,595)	
Jones, Murray	4:08:30 (12,011)	
Jones, Neil	3:48:50 (7,475)	
Jones, Nicholas	5:37:24 (28,768)	
Jones, Nigel	2:54:43 (575)	
Jones, Nigel	3:27:50 (3,792)	
Jones, Paul	4:12:00 (12,762)	
Jones, Paul	4:27:32 (16,610)	
Jones, Paul	4:38:52 (19,295)	
Jones, Peter	5:07:33 (25,195)	
Jones, Philip	3:37:18 (5,289)	
Jones, Philip	5:15:29 (26,312)	
Jones, Quentin	3:38:15 (5,452)	
Jones, Raymond	3:37:10 (5,269)	
Jones, Richard	2:48:00 (334)	
Jones, Richard	2:50:18 (395)	
Jones, Richard	3:37:43 (5,369)	
Jones, Richard	4:36:52 (18,846)	
Jones, Richard	4:41:26 (19,858)	
Jones, Richard	4:41:51 (19,960)	
Jones, Richard	5:21:31 (27,085)	
Jones, Rob	4:04:16 (11,127)	
Jones, Robert	4:16:44 (13,914)	
Jones, Robert	4:38:22 (19,180)	
Jones, Robert	4:49:21 (21,716)	
Jones, Robert	6:38:22 (31,509)	
Jones, Robin	4:06:08 (11,522)	
Jones, Roger	5:21:06 (27,034)	
Jones, Russell	3:39:48 (5,748)	
Jones, Sean	4:49:47 (21,820)	
Jones, Shane	5:43:53 (29,296)	
Jones, Simon	3:13:12 (2,022)	
Jones, Simon	3:46:18 (6,994)	
Jones, Simon	4:59:56 (23,974)	
Jones, Simon	5:01:13 (24,189)	
Jones, Stephen	3:30:42 (4,277)	
Jones, Stephen	3:42:16 (6,199)	
Jones, Stephen	4:02:02 (10,642)	
Jones, Stephen	4:05:28 (11,395)	
Jones, Stephen	4:32:57 (17,935)	
Jones, Stephen	4:33:05 (17,971)	
Jones, Stephen	4:48:33 (21,542)	
Jones, Stephen	4:52:30 (22,396)	
Jones, Stephen	5:07:43 (25,226)	
Jones, Steve	4:57:26 (23,463)	
Jones, Steve	5:07:56 (25,255)	
Jones, Steve	5:35:09 (28,567)	
Jones, Steven	3:10:09 (1,690)	
Jones, Steven	4:11:25 (12,625)	
Jones, Steven	4:28:37 (16,890)	
Jones, Steven	4:49:53 (21,842)	
Jones, Steven	5:01:22 (24,216)	
Jones, Stuart	3:42:44 (6,306)	
Jones, Terry	3:28:02 (3,820)	
Jones, Thomas	3:41:32 (6,075)	
Jones, Thomas	4:21:06 (15,004)	
Jones, Tim	3:35:11 (4,939)	
Jones, Timothy	3:17:10 (2,449)	
Jones, Timothy	3:56:48 (9,398)	
Jones, Timothy	4:35:22 (18,486)	
Jones, Timothy	4:50:08 (21,887)	
Jones, Tod	5:44:24 (29,328)	
Jones, Tom	3:34:21 (4,805)	
Jones, Trevor	4:01:41 (10,576)	
Jones, Tudor	3:39:34 (5,706)	
Jones, Vernon	4:06:08 (11,522)	
Jones, William	4:13:44 (13,184)	
Jones, William	4:23:38 (15,654)	
Jones, Zachary	4:54:02 (22,716)	
Jones Parry, Paul	5:24:06 (27,423)	
Jonsson, Stefan	5:10:34 (25,630)	
Jooste, Charles	4:21:54 (15,207)	
Jooste, Conrad	3:43:45 (6,499)	
Jopling, Alan	4:28:49 (16,939)	
Jordaan, Bernard	3:55:48 (9,129)	
Jordan, Anthony	5:21:27 (27,073)	
Jordan, Colin	4:19:42 (14,667)	
Jordan, Frenny	5:05:10 (24,822)	
Jordan, Graham	4:47:55 (21,403)	
Jordan, Ian	3:51:08 (7,989)	
Jordan, John	4:16:21 (13,820)	
Jordan, Lee	4:05:23 (11,368)	
Jordan, Mark	3:29:55 (4,155)	
Jordan, Mark	4:28:01 (16,708)	
Jordan, Mike	4:16:55 (13,975)	
Jordan, Nicholas	3:49:06 (7,536)	
Jordan, Percy	4:37:42 (19,020)	
Jordan, Philip	5:06:42 (25,056)	
Jordan, Richard	3:49:48 (7,700)	
Jordan, Stephen	4:18:49 (14,452)	
Jordan, William	4:35:08 (18,427)	
Jose, Jemy	3:49:09 (7,548)	

Joseph, David 3:39:12 (5,631)
Josephs, David 4:05:49 (11,461)
Josephs, Merrick 4:09:32 (12,237)
Josey, Gary 3:42:15 (6,194)
Joshi, Deepak 4:34:18 (18,241)
Joshi, Kamaleshkumar 5:57:28 (30,135)
Jost, Robert 3:07:46 (1,482)
Joundy, Hassan 3:26:37 (3,626)
Jowett, David 6:21:46 (31,069)
Jowett, Guy 3:50:28 (7,832)
Jowett, Mark 4:19:23 (14,589)
Joy, David 3:46:01 (6,935)
Joy, Geoffrey 5:49:55 (29,709)
Joyce, Andrew 4:01:16 (10,486)
Joyce, Andrew 4:55:23 (22,999)
Joyce, Ciaran 3:26:53 (3,656)
Joyce, Dean 3:10:07 (1,687)
Joyce, Paul 3:29:10 (4,021)
Joyce, Philip 3:22:57 (3,105)
Joyce, Philip 4:43:03 (20,246)
Joynson, Mark 3:37:38 (5,351)
Joynson, Richard 6:08:22 (30,580)
Juan, Bernard 4:19:49 (14,695)
Juarez, Christopher 2:40:18 (155)
Juarez, Victor 4:04:51 (11,257)
Juchems, Alex 3:31:59 (4,470)
Judd, Garry 2:34:18 (94)
Judd, Nicholas 4:34:22 (18,256)
Judd, Ricky 4:25:17 (16,081)
Judd, Simon 3:44:11 (6,577)
Judge, Alastair 4:04:28 (11,171)
Judge, David James 4:01:47 (10,594)
Judge, James 4:55:48 (23,112)
Judge, Rupert 3:22:35 (3,059)
Judkins, Steven 4:29:19 (17,065)
Juett, Michael 5:56:03 (30,051)
Jukes, Tim 3:45:37 (6,853)
Julian, Ben 3:34:24 (4,819)
Julian, John 4:36:54 (18,854)
Julian, Paul 3:45:44 (6,880)
Juliano, Angelo 4:13:32 (13,134)
Julien, James 5:09:23 (25,461)
Julier, Derek 4:03:55 (11,039)
July, Colin 4:07:02 (11,691)
Julyan, Michael 4:04:02 (11,073)
Jumpertz, Peter 4:34:17 (18,234)
Jupp, Ian 4:37:50 (19,050)
Jurasinski, Marek 3:30:25 (4,237)
Jurek, Barteomiej 3:40:41 (5,901)
Jurgens, Mark 3:25:47 (3,509)
Jury, Tim 5:16:00 (26,379)
Justeau, Christophe 4:14:48 (13,453)
Justice, William 5:58:12 (30,169)
Juveli, Ole-Arthur 3:02:57 (1,111)
Juwara, Ebou 5:29:35 (28,049)
Kabbaj, Amine 3:29:22 (4,060)
Kabbaj, Mohamed 3:12:36 (1,945)
Kadir, Muhammed 4:21:25 (15,095)
Kagezi, Thomas 3:52:37 (8,335)
Kaikini, Robert 4:18:23 (14,325)
Kainth, Ranjiet 3:07:54 (1,494)
Kaiser, Neil 3:48:19 (7,378)
Kakoullis, Panos 3:52:40 (8,347)
Kalema, Stephen 5:00:31 (24,073)
Kalinauckas, Mark 4:56:53 (23,360)
Kalinski, Pawel 5:24:36 (27,489)
Kalka, John 5:04:44 (24,742)
Kamil, Ahmed 5:44:51 (29,349)
Kaminski-Morrow, David 5:24:44 (27,499)
Kamis, Adrian 4:08:12 (11,938)
Kana, Ketan 4:10:24 (12,444)
Kanda, Paul 2:23:13 (31)
Kane, Andrew 4:33:30 (18,060)
Kane, John 3:18:55 (2,646)
Kane, John 4:51:11 (22,128)
Kane, Jonathan 3:24:03 (3,254)
Kanouni, Karim 4:22:28 (15,355)
Kantarjian, Berj 3:55:20 (9,003)
Kantor, Leszek 3:54:24 (8,756)
Kanumilli, Naresh 4:10:45 (12,503)
Kaplankiran, Ihsan 5:51:17 (29,798)
Kapoor, Neil 3:06:55 (1,395)
Kapoor, Vivak 3:46:57 (7,115)
Kappel, Mathias 2:47:41 (319)
Kappenstein, Bernd 5:19:25 (26,820)
Kapur, Krishan 3:03:45 (1,166)
Kara, Altaf 5:21:52 (27,132)
Karagic, Alek 3:24:31 (3,333)
Karim, Mustapha 4:08:29 (12,008)
Karlsson, Krister 3:49:03 (7,527)
Karlsson, Nicklas 3:42:05 (6,165)
Karn, James 4:28:51 (16,951)
Karni Cohen, Adam 4:57:37 (23,505)
Karstens, Thorsten 3:28:43 (3,949)
Karthaus, Roland 4:08:27 (11,995)
Karunarajah, Rohan 5:54:45 (29,984)
Kashmiri, Musadiq 5:14:09 (26,114)
Kast, Martin 4:23:11 (15,541)
Kat, Gregory 3:33:51 (4,724)
Katechia, Bhagesh 3:38:00 (5,413)
Katkov, Gennady 4:05:26 (11,390)
Kato, Isunehiro 4:34:34 (18,298)
Kattenhorn, Stuart 4:20:03 (14,759)
Katz, Jonathan 3:25:11 (3,425)
Kaufmann, Volker 3:31:30 (4,412)
Kauntze, Anthony 3:40:33 (5,873)
Kavanagh, Richard 4:16:54 (13,964)
Kavanagh, Stephen 4:44:51 (20,686)
Kavanagh, Steve 4:47:45 (21,361)
Kavanagh, Terence 4:45:49 (20,919)
Kawamura, Takafumi 3:05:31 (1,288)
Kay, Andy 4:35:25 (18,501)
Kay, Danny 3:30:03 (4,172)
Kay, David 4:27:36 (16,624)
Kay, Gavin 4:24:49 (15,954)
Kay, Martin 4:35:24 (18,495)
Kay, Matthew 2:57:32 (737)
Kay, Peter 4:25:08 (16,037)
Kay, Peter 4:41:20 (19,833)
Kayakan, Ayhan 5:12:21 (25,872)
Kaye, Adam 3:51:03 (7,967)
Kaye, Martin 4:20:11 (14,792)
Kaye, Ryan 4:01:28 (10,533)
Kayonga, Tom 5:19:26 (26,825)
Kazalbash, Imran 4:12:14 (12,823)
Kazalbash, Kamran 4:55:20 (22,985)
Kazimierski, Michael 2:50:48 (411)
Keable, Richard 4:49:14 (21,685)
Keal, Ian 3:26:34 (3,617)
Kean, Alasdair 2:36:18 (111)
Keane, Damien 4:11:07 (12,556)
Keane, Glenn 6:33:23 (31,411)
Keane, Michael 4:17:40 (14,165)
Keane, Paul 3:39:28 (5,686)
Keane, Paul 6:21:22 (31,059)
Kear, Neil 4:37:04 (18,892)
Kearn, Richard 3:05:53 (1,312)
Kearney, Peter 3:47:55 (7,304)
Kearns, Andrew 3:49:38 (7,665)
Kearns, Kevin 3:46:30 (7,028)
Kearns, Kevin 4:18:16 (14,294)
Kearsley, Mark 5:53:56 (29,927)
Kearsley, Stewart 4:38:40 (19,245)
Keast, John 2:51:14 (426)
Keating, Paul 4:24:15 (15,810)
Keats, Peter 4:50:07 (21,884)
Keaveney, Alison 4:26:54 (16,448)
Keay, Richard 4:38:12 (19,133)
Keayes, Spencer 4:57:32 (23,487)
Keddie, Andrew 4:20:29 (14,864)
Keddie, Anthony 5:19:13 (26,783)
Keeble, Christopher 4:25:39 (16,168)
Keeble, Ford 4:57:51 (23,551)
Keefe, Joshua 3:21:30 (2,933)
Keegan, Paul 4:21:44 (15,166)
Keeler, Andy 3:23:49 (3,214)
Keeley, Andrew 2:54:54 (585)
Keeley, Simon 5:31:52 (28,271)
Keeling, Colin 3:52:23 (8,284)
Keeling, David 4:20:42 (14,903)
Keen, Blair 3:48:47 (7,462)
Keenaghan, Shaun 2:52:39 (477)
Keenan, Alexander 4:25:16 (16,074)
Keenan, Iain 4:59:05 (23,823)
Keenan, Noel 3:49:39 (7,671)
Keenan, Wayne 3:21:29 (2,929)
Keepence, Stephen 5:14:39 (26,196)
Keers, Alexander 5:47:29 (29,532)
Keet, Wayne 2:59:33 (907)
Keeves, Colin 3:38:20 (5,462)
Kefford, Matthew 4:16:52 (13,954)
Kehugu, Joseph 2:13:17 (11)
Keighley, Michael 4:13:10 (13,041)
Keilloh, Richard 5:15:35 (26,329)
Keilty, Sean 4:51:26 (22,188)
Keirs, James 3:33:10 (4,623)
Kekus, Nick 4:23:39 (15,658)
Kelchtermans, Peter 2:30:18 (65)
Kelf, David 3:52:43 (8,357)
Kelf, Jason 3:45:48 (6,893)
Kelf, Jon 3:34:29 (4,835)
Kelham, Christopher 3:20:42 (2,848)
Kell, James 4:11:47 (12,720)
Kellas, Gary 4:51:11 (22,128)
Kellaway, Andrew 2:48:42 (354)
Kellaway, David 3:24:44 (3,363)
Kellaway, Roy 2:59:24 (891)
Kelleher, Cornelious 2:58:34 (807)
Kelleher, Stephen 3:02:42 (1,098)
Keller, Gale 6:02:42 (30,362)
Keller, Holger 2:58:24 (793)
Keller, Philip 3:38:06 (5,427)
Kellett, David 4:24:59 (15,999)
Kellett, Gary 3:03:02 (1,117)
Kellett, Neil 3:47:14 (7,161)
Kelley, John 3:33:48 (4,718)
Kelley, Kevin 7:22:29 (32,089)
Kellow, Robert 4:48:19 (21,499)
Kellow, Robert 5:03:36 (24,550)
Kelly, Anthony 3:22:33 (3,053)
Kelly, Christopher 3:25:39 (3,481)
Kelly, Christopher 3:40:52 (5,937)
Kelly, Colin 4:42:20 (20,062)
Kelly, Conleth 4:35:52 (18,613)
Kelly, Daniel 6:09:49 (30,633)
Kelly, David 3:55:27 (9,035)
Kelly, David 3:55:58 (9,168)
Kelly, David 4:12:21 (12,847)
Kelly, Dean 4:06:40 (11,620)
Kelly, Edward 3:31:57 (4,465)
Kelly, Francis 4:24:56 (15,979)
Kelly, Ian 3:20:35 (2,835)
Kelly, John 3:54:27 (8,768)
Kelly, Joseph 4:03:13 (10,884)
Kelly, Julian 3:30:59 (4,325)
Kelly, Kevin 3:17:31 (2,491)
Kelly, Lee 4:02:22 (10,711)
Kelly, Lee 4:13:08 (13,030)
Kelly, Mark 3:48:03 (7,328)
Kelly, Mark 4:00:17 (10,291)
Kelly, Mark 4:11:57 (12,751)
Kelly, Oliver 5:08:25 (25,328)
Kelly, Peter 3:34:21 (4,805)
Kelly, Peter 4:37:16 (18,942)
Kelly, Richard 3:37:09 (5,264)
Kelly, Shaun 3:51:30 (8,074)
Kelly, Simon 3:43:56 (6,533)
Kelly, Stephen 3:22:04 (2,992)
Kelly, Stephen 4:01:02 (10,438)
Kelly, Stephen 4:12:37 (12,920)
Kelly, Stephen 5:18:21 (26,679)
Kelly, Steve 3:15:50 (2,316)
Kelly, Steven 3:06:29 (1,358)
Kelly, Stuart 5:35:07 (28,564)
Kelly, Terence 4:03:48 (11,014)
Kelly, Tim 3:07:32 (1,457)
Kelm, Wolfgang 3:46:04 (6,946)
Kelsall, Mike 5:31:14 (28,218)
Kelsall, Thomas 4:20:23 (14,842)
Kelsey, Johnny 5:03:11 (24,488)
Kelsey, Russell 3:52:54 (8,397)
Kember, Julian 4:36:48 (18,835)
Kemboly, Mpay 4:25:18 (16,086)
Kemmett, Gavin 3:50:18 (7,801)
Kemp, Adrian 3:30:13 (4,203)
Kemp, Alex 4:26:37 (16,386)
Kemp, Attie 4:34:51 (18,359)
Kemp, Christopher 4:01:09 (10,461)
Kemp, David 4:18:37 (14,399)

Kemp, David 4:36:44 (18,814)
Kemp, Graham 3:28:45 (3,959)
Kemp, Jon 3:00:30 (974)
Kemp, Jonathan 5:27:42 (27,857)
Kemp, Martyn 4:11:45 (12,707)
Kemp, Nicholas 3:53:45 (8,603)
Kemp, Nicholas 5:36:07 (28,648)
Kemp, Nick 4:31:19 (17,570)
Kemp, Peter 5:01:12 (24,183)
Kempf, Walter 4:30:35 (17,386)
Kempgens, Arnot 4:02:01 (10,639)
Kemsley, Benjamin 6:05:09 (30,458)
Kemsley, Neil 6:05:09 (30,458)
Kenchington, Andrew 2:51:02 (419)
Kenchington, Chris 3:06:27 (1,355)
Kenchington, Nicholas 2:46:44 (287)
Kendall, David 4:06:44 (11,637)
Kendall, John 3:00:25 (966)
Kendall, Paul 3:09:35 (1,642)
Kendall, Richard 3:23:30 (3,178)
Kenderdine, Robert 3:36:30 (5,142)
Kendrick, Anthony 4:12:06 (12,786)
Kendrick, Philip 2:52:45 (485)
Kendrick, Stephen 4:13:04 (13,019)
Kenn, Christopher 4:21:08 (15,014)
Kennair, Jonathan 4:27:56 (16,698)
Kennard, Graham 5:06:58 (25,100)
Kennard, Martin 4:22:21 (15,327)
Kennard, Stephen 5:14:46 (26,212)
Kennaugh, Simon 3:00:18 (956)
Kennaway, Hugh 4:17:30 (14,112)
Kennedy, Andrew 4:11:20 (12,606)
Kennedy, Andrew 4:49:25 (21,726)
Kennedy, Andrew 5:42:26 (29,202)
Kennedy, Anthony 3:57:15 (9,517)
Kennedy, Benedict 4:50:34 (21,979)
Kennedy, Colin 4:00:06 (10,244)
Kennedy, Daniel 5:13:45 (26,079)
Kennedy, David 3:54:01 (8,670)
Kennedy, Donald 3:10:26 (1,715)
Kennedy, Duncan 5:01:29 (24,229)
Kennedy, George 3:15:22 (2,276)
Kennedy, George 4:02:48 (10,807)
Kennedy, Ian 4:14:55 (13,482)
Kennedy, Ian 4:15:46 (13,690)
Kennedy, Ian 5:56:02 (30,047)
Kennedy, John 3:48:44 (7,448)
Kennedy, John 4:27:44 (16,660)
Kennedy, John 5:12:46 (25,941)
Kennedy, Les 3:47:17 (7,174)
Kennedy, Marcus 4:29:45 (17,178)
Kennedy, Nicholas 4:46:46 (21,141)
Kennedy, Peter 3:32:14 (4,501)
Kennedy, Richard 3:02:08 (1,065)
Kennedy, Richard 3:35:22 (4,970)
Kennedy, Roy 4:09:40 (12,268)
Kennedy, Russell 4:40:01 (19,539)
Kennedy, Terry 5:36:33 (28,694)
Kennedy, Tim 4:45:24 (20,821)
Kenneth, Paul 3:44:03 (6,555)
Kenneth, Robert 3:39:32 (5,698)
Kennett, Ainsley 4:12:23 (12,852)
Kennett, Roland 4:55:02 (22,928)
Kenning, George 4:24:14 (15,805)
Kenny, Alex 4:01:30 (10,539)
Kenny, Cormac 3:51:05 (7,974)
Kenny, David 7:27:33 (32,136)
Kenny, Jack 3:56:26 (9,300)
Kenny, Jimmy 3:54:14 (8,714)
Kenny, Liam 4:19:03 (14,517)
Kenny, Michael 3:42:40 (6,288)
Kenny, Neil 3:12:59 (1,987)
Kenny, Triss 3:27:41 (3,767)
Kent, Alex 5:34:06 (28,488)
Kent, Daniel 3:53:13 (8,479)
Kent, Donald 4:27:18 (16,550)
Kent, John 6:15:16 (30,833)
Kent, Kev 3:55:09 (8,951)
Kent, Paul 3:08:51 (1,575)
Kent, Stephen 5:01:29 (24,229)
Kent, Steve 5:27:32 (27,834)
Kenton, Benjamin 3:24:10 (3,277)
Kenton, Peter 3:39:34 (5,706)

Kenworthy, David 4:15:00 (13,507)
Kenwright, Mike 3:53:23 (8,510)
Kenyon, Stephen 3:14:42 (2,206)
Keogh, Craig 3:41:24 (6,041)
Keogh, David 4:55:18 (22,977)
Keogh, Michael 5:25:57 (27,659)
Keogh, Nigel 4:50:16 (21,915)
Keogh, Sean 3:15:38 (2,304)
Keough, Colin 3:23:25 (3,164)
Keown, Michael 4:15:31 (13,645)
Kerhornou, Thierry 4:27:23 (16,567)
Kermally, Sultan 6:21:33 (31,064)
Kermisch, Charles 3:16:30 (2,376)
Kermode, Nigel 6:20:34 (31,034)
Kernick, Vincent 4:36:31 (18,775)
Kerns, Grant 4:56:04 (23,161)
Kerr, Andrew 3:41:52 (6,126)
Kerr, Duncan 4:38:52 (19,295)
Kerr, Paul 4:20:19 (14,820)
Kerr, Richard 3:56:58 (9,444)
Kerr, Scott 4:32:38 (17,859)
Kerr, Will 2:49:19 (373)
Kerridge, Alan 4:16:58 (13,982)
Kerrigan, John 4:10:16 (12,413)
Kerrison, Martin 5:29:36 (28,054)
Kerry, Simon 4:14:08 (13,293)
Kershaw, Christopher 3:35:27 (4,990)
Kershaw, Craig 3:23:47 (3,211)
Kershaw, Graham 4:30:01 (17,243)
Kershaw, Sally 4:33:45 (18,106)
Kershaw, Steven 5:16:54 (26,469)
Kershaw, Thomas 4:54:10 (22,738)
Kerslake, Geoffrey 5:09:43 (25,510)
Kerslake, Jonathan 5:07:54 (25,250)
Kerwin, John 4:23:12 (15,547)
Kerwood, Richard 5:00:29 (24,065)
Kestle, Michael 3:13:50 (2,100)
Kestle, Ryan 3:14:02 (2,133)
Ketchell, Robert 3:51:06 (7,976)
Ketchin, Ian 3:15:08 (2,254)
Ketley, John 3:07:06 (1,416)
Kett, Brian 4:46:40 (21,119)
Kettani, Ali 5:18:03 (26,617)
Ketteringham, Darren 6:16:33 (30,878)
Kettlewell, Jonathan 4:18:59 (14,504)
Keukelaar, Jos 3:45:53 (6,909)
Kevill, Russell 3:57:05 (9,472)
Key, Tim 4:00:47 (10,381)
Keyes, Gary 6:37:32 (31,496)
Keyes, Jason 6:07:52 (30,562)
Khachikian, André 7:54:37 (32,245)
Khaihra, Harvey 3:21:11 (2,897)
Khairul, Abid 5:23:19 (27,334)
Khakha, Raghbir 4:22:50 (15,449)
Khan, Ahmed 4:48:46 (21,580)
Khan, Amjid 4:52:32 (22,405)
Khan, Derrick 4:48:46 (21,580)
Khan, Nabiel 5:05:36 (24,900)
Khan, Rahman 6:12:13 (30,739)
Khan, Raz 5:16:29 (26,424)
Khan, Saqib 4:44:24 (20,596)
Khan, Shakeel 5:19:31 (26,831)
Khasidy, Garry 4:12:00 (12,762)
Khatri, Dinesh 5:49:17 (29,661)
Khella, Kalvinder 6:50:07 (31,724)
Kho, Stephen 4:20:51 (14,944)
Khonsaraki, Behrodz 4:48:00 (21,427)
Kibble, James 4:02:22 (10,711)
Kibblewhite, Michael 4:38:13 (19,138)
Kidd, Alex 3:57:05 (9,472)
Kidd, David 5:24:33 (27,482)
Kidd, James 4:26:42 (16,403)
Kidd, Pete 2:58:41 (819)
Kidd, Tarquin 3:40:11 (5,829)
Kidd, Thomas 3:50:17 (7,796)
Kidner, Quentin 4:04:15 (11,120)
Kiehlmann, Mark 4:40:38 (19,672)
Kielty, Michael 5:14:49 (26,220)
Kieniewicz, Tim 4:33:28 (18,051)
Kiernan, Patrick 3:11:52 (1,844)
Kiersey, Neil 4:42:07 (20,014)
Kihara, Stanley 6:00:45 (30,285)
Kijima, Nagayoshi 3:29:55 (4,155)

Kilbey, Alexander 5:20:03 (26,895)
Kilbride, Colin 3:55:05 (8,933)
Kilday, John 6:14:07 (30,802)
Kilgour, Kenneth 4:29:53 (17,215)
Kilgour, Stephen 5:57:44 (30,153)
Kilkenny, Gavin 3:56:46 (9,388)
Kilkenny, Kevin 3:36:11 (5,095)
Killeen, Martin 4:02:22 (10,711)
Killelea, David 4:37:09 (18,909)
Killen, David 4:47:34 (21,310)
Killian, Mark 5:10:01 (25,552)
Killigrew, Steve 5:33:12 (28,391)
Killington, Lee 4:29:28 (17,107)
Kilner, Chris 3:59:43 (10,160)
Kilner, John 3:44:59 (6,733)
Kilner, Mark 3:48:18 (7,377)
Kilonzo, Onesmus 2:13:56 (14)
Kilsby, Gary 4:07:46 (11,865)
Kilshaw, Ian 3:20:24 (2,816)
Kiltie, David 3:42:19 (6,205)
Kilzer, Josef 4:03:55 (11,039)
Kim, Joung Ho 3:41:26 (6,052)
Kimber, Geoff 4:06:05 (11,512)
Kimber, John 5:40:26 (29,033)
Kimber, Nick 3:35:02 (4,918)
Kimpton, Nigel 2:46:01 (256)
Kincaid, Sam 2:50:48 (411)
Kind, Scott 5:10:59 (25,690)
King, Alan 5:14:51 (26,227)
King, Andy 4:13:15 (13,063)
King, Barry 5:38:47 (28,881)
King, Brian 5:52:09 (29,836)
King, Chris 4:24:44 (15,928)
King, Daniel 4:29:13 (17,044)
King, Danny 5:46:25 (29,461)
King, David 3:15:10 (2,257)
King, David 3:29:23 (4,062)
King, David 5:34:47 (28,536)
King, Donald 4:30:39 (17,402)
King, Douglas 5:37:15 (28,760)
King, Edgar 3:20:48 (2,859)
King, Ellis 4:54:58 (22,913)
King, Gerry 3:17:51 (2,533)
King, Ian 3:29:04 (4,013)
King, Malcolm 4:52:51 (22,470)
King, Michael 4:13:32 (13,134)
King, Nicholas 4:22:52 (15,458)
King, Nigel 3:42:59 (6,364)
King, Paul 3:30:41 (4,273)
King, Paul 3:34:36 (4,852)
King, Paul 4:43:12 (20,286)
King, Paul 5:28:09 (27,908)
King, Peter 4:22:49 (15,447)
King, Philip 6:53:27 (31,799)
King, Richard 5:04:29 (24,705)
King, Seamus 4:17:44 (14,189)
King, Simon 3:54:31 (8,788)
King, Stephen 5:22:01 (27,144)
King, Steve 4:27:03 (16,488)
King, Steven 6:10:47 (30,678)
King, Stuart 4:51:11 (22,128)
King, Toby 4:53:43 (22,652)
King, Tony 5:19:11 (26,781)
Kingdon, Adam 4:01:38 (10,566)
Kingon, Ian 4:13:00 (13,005)
Kingsley, Anthony 4:57:14 (23,435)
Kingsley, Nicolas 5:24:03 (27,415)
Kingston, Adrian 4:18:20 (14,309)
Kingston, Anthony 3:57:40 (9,611)
Kingston, Gerry 3:12:36 (1,945)
Kingston, Matthew 4:18:44 (14,432)
Kingston, Robin 3:41:36 (6,085)
Kingston, Simon 3:40:04 (5,803)
Kingston-Lee, Toby 3:06:03 (1,325)
Kinka, Geoffrey 4:54:40 (22,857)
Kinnane, Brian 5:30:00 (28,085)
Kinnear, Daniel 4:27:50 (16,677)
Kinsella, Gary 4:31:27 (17,602)
Kinsey, Nicholas 2:36:54 (119)
Kinsman, Alexander 4:48:07 (21,456)
Kioufi, Niazy 6:25:10 (31,164)
Kipling, Richard 4:58:02 (23,591)
Kiprono, John 2:21:14 (27)

Kirby, Angus 3:48:47 (7,462)
Kirby, Christopher 3:59:31 (10,098)
Kirby, David 4:46:36 (21,109)
Kirby, Graham 3:22:22 (3,031)
Kirby, Jason 4:45:15 (20,785)
Kirby, Michael 3:50:28 (7,832)
Kirby, Oliver 6:30:07 (31,331)
Kirby, Richard 3:56:34 (9,338)
Kirby, Steven 3:13:45 (2,092)
Kiritharanathan, Kailayanathan 5:52:52 (29,873)
Kirk, David 5:23:04 (27,295)
Kirk, Elliott 3:54:22 (8,743)
Kirk, Jason 3:44:15 (6,593)
Kirk, Mark 3:11:26 (1,798)
Kirk, Michael 5:24:49 (27,510)
Kirk, Neil 2:53:42 (514)
Kirk, Richard 4:27:48 (16,672)
Kirkbride, David 4:53:24 (22,596)
Kirkconel, Andrew 4:53:43 (22,652)
Kirkdale, Brian 3:28:40 (3,939)
Kirkham, Colin 3:28:18 (3,866)
Kirkwood, Trevor 3:19:54 (2,743)
Kirland, James 4:15:03 (13,525)
Kirlew, Lance 2:55:54 (642)
Kirsopp, Grahame 5:05:12 (24,828)
Kirton, Akira 4:13:14 (13,058)
Kirwan, Eric 4:55:16 (22,973)
Kirwan, Robert 3:50:59 (7,946)
Kirwan, Stephen 5:24:13 (27,440)
Kirwin, Peter 3:14:35 (2,195)
Kisbee, Murray 3:16:32 (2,378)
Kiser, Uwe 3:59:26 (10,073)
Kitchen, Christopher 4:23:44 (15,680)
Kitchen, Gavin 3:31:14 (4,365)
Kitchen, Jim 4:47:12 (21,226)
Kitchen, Jonathan 3:55:49 (9,132)
Kitchener, Simon 5:05:14 (24,832)
Kitchener, Tristan 5:11:43 (25,788)
Kitchin, Graham 4:41:41 (19,915)
Kitching, Andrew 3:56:51 (9,413)
Kitching, Ian 2:52:17 (457)
Kitromilides, Alex 3:10:04 (1,682)
Kitt, Jeremy 4:26:57 (16,458)
Kitteridge, Shayne 4:39:18 (19,398)
Kittle, Ian 3:47:43 (7,259)
Kitton, Daniel 5:20:57 (27,018)
Kivijervi, Trond 4:29:01 (16,994)
Kivlehan, David 4:20:05 (14,765)
Kiy, Timothy 4:35:50 (18,608)
Kjell, Johan 4:29:27 (17,105)
Klaber, Robert 4:50:42 (22,011)
Klaproth, Renke 3:45:18 (6,788)
Klein, Adam 4:45:05 (20,739)
Klein, Anthony 4:19:05 (14,525)
Klein, Duncan 4:13:09 (13,037)
Klein, Hans 3:30:38 (4,263)
Klein, Manfred 3:58:29 (9,830)
Klein, Mark 5:10:08 (25,571)
Klein, Stuart 3:42:47 (6,314)
Kleinau, Bernd 3:28:07 (3,834)
Kleinman, Dan 4:27:33 (16,614)
Kleipool, Arthur 3:42:25 (6,227)
Kloepfer, Michael 3:29:39 (4,118)
Kloosterman, Jan 4:16:22 (13,823)
Klos, Karl 3:45:47 (6,889)
Kluge, Harald 3:23:39 (3,198)
Kluth, Richard 3:38:54 (5,581)
Kmetyko, Peter 3:48:00 (7,319)
Knapman, John 5:16:42 (26,451)
Knapp, Colin 4:25:21 (16,104)
Knapp, Neil 3:31:28 (4,403)
Knattress, Stephen 4:41:46 (19,935)
Knell, Robert 3:24:52 (3,380)
Knellwolf, Walter 3:57:37 (9,599)
Knibb, John 2:42:56 (196)
Knibbs, Alec 5:29:58 (28,083)
Knight, Andrew 3:57:10 (9,498)
Knight, Anthony 4:21:22 (15,075)
Knight, Charles 3:52:52 (8,386)
Knight, David 3:55:27 (9,035)
Knight, David 4:32:59 (17,949)
Knight, Derek 4:03:55 (11,039)
Knight, Gary 4:28:56 (16,976)
Knight, Howard 4:54:37 (22,841)
Knight, Ian 5:31:21 (28,235)
Knight, Jim 4:24:03 (15,766)
Knight, John 4:09:45 (12,285)
Knight, John 5:24:29 (27,473)
Knight, Kevin 3:47:01 (7,128)
Knight, Kevin 5:02:06 (24,327)
Knight, Lee 4:17:45 (14,193)
Knight, Mark 3:37:02 (5,239)
Knight, Mark 6:00:24 (30,270)
Knight, Matthew 3:17:32 (2,493)
Knight, Paul 5:00:27 (24,060)
Knight, Peter 3:30:12 (4,199)
Knight, Raymond 5:40:50 (29,066)
Knight, Richard 8:18:21 (32,274)
Knight, Robert 3:54:45 (8,850)
Knight, Stephen 4:02:17 (10,694)
Knight, Steve 4:16:47 (13,933)
Knight, Stuart 4:38:45 (19,268)
Knight, Timothy 3:48:49 (7,469)
Knight-Baker, Martin 4:23:37 (15,643)
Knighton, Barry 4:21:42 (15,158)
Knighton, Simon 4:22:08 (15,274)
Knights, Bruce 4:49:56 (21,850)
Knights, Jim 5:52:20 (29,848)
Knights, Lewis 5:33:24 (28,411)
Knights, Neville 3:06:36 (1,368)
Knoll, Thomas 4:00:37 (10,348)
Knott, Andrew 4:07:19 (11,763)
Knott, Patrick 3:38:38 (5,529)
Knott, Peter 4:20:11 (14,792)
Knott, Raymond 4:54:39 (22,849)
Knowles, John 3:53:03 (8,437)
Knowles, Matthew 4:13:58 (13,251)
Knowles, Peter 3:55:14 (8,974)
Knox, David 4:09:01 (12,134)
Knox, Douglas 4:11:23 (12,618)
Knox, Ian 4:45:56 (20,942)
Knox, Roger 2:47:50 (327)
Knox, Tom 4:22:34 (15,379)
Knudsen, Sebastian 4:00:18 (10,297)
Knupfer, Anton 3:35:43 (5,027)
Kobayashi, Akira 4:40:23 (19,626)
Kobayshi-Hillary, Mark 4:56:48 (23,337)
Kobrak, Paul 4:13:20 (13,080)
Koch, Emno 3:59:29 (10,090)
Koch De Gooreynd, Alexander 5:35:36 (28,602)
Koczkar, Robert 3:44:58 (6,727)
Koe, Digby 4:15:04 (13,529)
Koeth, Klaus 5:09:14 (25,438)
Kohler, André 3:48:34 (7,415)
Kok, Arnout 5:13:05 (25,984)
Kolic, Davorin 4:31:21 (17,582)
Koller, Harold 4:04:56 (11,278)
Koloi, Paul 4:55:50 (23,118)
Kolvin, Philip 5:57:19 (30,121)
Konan, Ismail 4:10:06 (12,373)
Kondic, Chris 5:37:48 (28,798)
Konopelski, Andrew 3:36:36 (5,160)
Koolen, Theo 4:29:26 (17,098)
Koot, Richard 3:20:13 (2,789)
Koozehkanani, Alaeddin 5:53:22 (29,898)
Kopas, Ronald 3:24:35 (3,345)
Kopp, Jean-Claude 4:45:52 (20,931)
Kor, Michael 4:50:17 (21,919)
Korff, Schaun 5:04:03 (24,642)
Korro, Barry 3:22:51 (3,092)
Kos, Marc 4:17:38 (14,152)
Koster, David 4:54:52 (22,898)
Kostka, Helge 5:19:43 (26,851)
Koszegi, Istvan 4:08:31 (12,014)
Kot, Antoni 2:49:09 (367)
Kotecha, Pratish 4:42:16 (20,046)
Kouwenhoven, Adrianus 3:42:43 (6,301)
Kovats, Steven 2:47:03 (301)
Kowolik, David 5:10:12 (25,582)
Kracht, Olaf 3:27:40 (3,762)
Kraft, Jonas 3:58:55 (9,946)
Kraft, Thomas 4:41:32 (19,874)
Kramer, Achim 3:38:48 (5,559)
Kramer, Bradley 6:01:50 (30,333)
Kramer, Graham 3:30:22 (4,226)
Kramer, James 6:01:53 (30,337)
Kraus, Elmar 4:11:37 (12,668)
Krause, John 3:56:26 (9,300)
Krelle, Jonathan 5:57:26 (30,133)
Krelle, Matthew 2:49:25 (377)
Kretschmer, Wolfgang 3:07:11 (1,426)
Kreusler, Hans-Ernst 4:43:19 (20,325)
Kreutziger, Bernd 3:12:57 (1,981)
Krischka, Peter 4:35:27 (18,507)
Krishnan, Venkataraman 5:02:20 (24,366)
Kristan, Pavel 4:15:50 (13,713)
Kristensen, Mark 3:21:41 (2,951)
Kristensen, Soren 3:07:31 (1,454)
Kristiansen, Verner 4:05:05 (11,307)
Kristoffersen, Ola 3:58:18 (9,782)
Kroeller, Gerhard 4:34:10 (18,208)
Krollig, Sharon 5:07:00 (25,107)
Kruk, Marcus 3:31:06 (4,342)
Kruk, Nigel 4:00:05 (10,240)
Kruppa, Robert 4:21:44 (15,166)
Kruspel, Walter 4:43:21 (20,336)
Krzossok, Stefan 3:19:08 (2,664)
Kualvaag, Robert 4:05:43 (11,435)
Kubica, Krzysztof 3:13:25 (2,051)
Kueberuwa, Gray 3:00:16 (953)
Kugener, Henri 3:53:10 (8,464)
Kuhn, Lawrence 4:11:19 (12,601)
Kuhn, Max 3:12:02 (1,865)
Kuhnle, Hans-Juergen 4:03:17 (10,911)
Kuijper, Willem 5:00:59 (24,150)
Kulik, Waldemar 3:45:43 (6,876)
Kumar, Sam 5:31:54 (28,279)
Kumararajan, Annalingam 5:24:18 (27,451)
Kunin, Seth 3:49:15 (7,576)
Kunst, Heiko 3:24:09 (3,273)
Kuosmanen, Pasi 4:50:30 (21,968)
Kupse, John 5:56:09 (30,059)
Kurihara, Shigeru 6:44:22 (31,612)
Kuronen, Mikko 2:46:47 (291)
Kustow, Jonathan 4:40:41 (19,680)
Kutmar, Dusan 5:22:54 (27,267)
Kvisgaard, Jon Anders 4:41:59 (19,987)
Kwarteng, Eric 3:34:55 (4,894)
Kwaterski, Joe 5:09:18 (25,446)
Kybert, Mark 5:25:07 (27,557)
Kydd, Gerald 4:15:15 (13,581)
Kyebler, Florian 3:35:01 (4,916)
Kyle, Andrew 5:48:01 (29,581)
Kyle, Greg 4:49:12 (21,677)
Kyle, Martyn 3:43:02 (6,375)
Kyle, Peter 4:10:50 (12,516)
Kyle, Richard 5:29:09 (28,001)
Kyriacou, Andros 5:48:54 (29,631)
Kyriakides, Costas 4:43:42 (20,431)
Kyriakides, Lakis 5:32:13 (28,309)
Labarr, Winston 4:56:27 (23,248)
Labaschagne, Timothy 3:42:29 (6,243)
Labbe, Francis 5:19:02 (26,759)
Labrom, Brad 6:03:44 (30,402)
Lacaze, Bernard 3:21:37 (2,943)
Lacey, Alan 4:17:04 (14,004)
Lacey, Drewe 4:06:29 (11,587)
Lacey, Kevin 6:24:19 (31,141)
Lacey, Mark 3:21:40 (2,949)
Lacey, Simon 3:55:17 (8,988)
Lacey, Stephen 4:22:05 (15,261)
Lach, Roman 4:54:22 (22,786)
Lack, Andy 3:12:18 (1,904)
Lackey, Peter 3:47:33 (7,223)
Lacome-Shaw, Ashley 5:12:50 (25,949)
Lacoste, Michel 3:45:07 (6,759)
Lacoste, Xavier 3:08:30 (1,547)
Lacy, Christopher 4:35:54 (18,620)
Lacy, David 3:36:41 (5,179)
Lacy, David 4:54:58 (22,913)
Lad, Mahesh 5:34:40 (28,529)
Ladanowski, John 3:32:17 (4,504)
Ladd, Julian 3:27:11 (3,703)
Lado-Devesa, Alan 6:10:30 (30,660)
Laeuffer, Denis 4:35:13 (18,449)
Lafferty, Brooke 3:23:05 (3,125)
Lafferty, Stephen 4:01:09 (10,461)
Lafuente Leston, Fernando 3:42:08 (6,174)
Lagan, Mark 3:26:36 (3,619)

Lagan, Paul.................7:15:54 (32,041)
Lagarde, Denis.................4:20:34 (14,883)
Lagger, Philipp.................3:52:31 (8,314)
Lahbabi, Abdelouahhab.................3:12:36 (1,945)
Lahbabi, Najib.................3:34:36 (4,852)
Lai, Simon.................4:56:52 (23,355)
Laidlaw, James.................4:26:43 (16,405)
Laidler, Kenneth.................5:13:53 (26,089)
Lain, Frank.................4:12:04 (12,777)
Laine, Courtney.................5:03:39 (24,557)
Laing, George.................3:43:02 (6,375)
Laing, Stewart.................4:46:18 (21,045)
Lainsbury, Raymond.................4:49:05 (21,648)
Laird, Alexander.................4:11:14 (12,584)
Laird, Ian.................4:49:34 (21,766)
Laisby, Gavin.................3:39:24 (5,678)
Laishley, Matthew.................3:31:24 (4,393)
Lake, David.................4:15:47 (13,697)
Lake, Neil.................4:06:44 (11,637)
Lake, Philip.................4:25:15 (16,070)
Lake, Reginald.................4:42:52 (20,199)
Lake, Steve.................4:28:14 (16,776)
Lakeman, Raymond.................4:54:19 (22,772)
Laker, Andrew.................3:22:41 (3,068)
Lakey, Daniel.................3:51:10 (8,002)
Lakha, Gulamabbas.................4:21:32 (15,117)
Lakhloufi, Ali.................3:21:16 (2,907)
Lakhmiri, Salam.................3:15:06 (2,248)
Lakin, Paul.................5:26:15 (27,706)
Lam, Bart.................4:30:58 (17,485)
Lam, Edward.................4:33:49 (18,121)
Lamarche, Didier.................3:14:09 (2,147)
Lamb, Adrian.................4:15:01 (13,512)
Lamb, Andy.................2:54:47 (581)
Lamb, George.................3:49:34 (7,646)
Lamb, Jamie.................4:28:51 (16,951)
Lamb, Ken.................4:12:19 (12,838)
Lamb, Nicholas.................4:50:26 (21,947)
Lamb, Nicholas.................5:00:14 (24,022)
Lamb, Peter.................4:52:51 (22,470)
Lamb, Philip.................3:59:31 (10,098)
Lamb, Richard.................3:15:52 (2,322)
Lamb, Terry.................3:29:13 (4,030)
Lamb, William.................5:04:43 (24,738)
Lambden, Keith.................3:49:30 (7,634)
Lambe, Jason.................5:21:32 (27,087)
Lambe, Mark.................5:43:19 (29,262)
Lambert, Andrew.................3:54:25 (8,759)
Lambert, Clive.................4:13:51 (13,216)
Lambert, David.................4:05:52 (11,473)
Lambert, Jon.................4:23:08 (15,526)
Lambert, Nigel.................4:18:07 (14,274)
Lambert, Toby.................3:02:55 (1,108)
Lambillion-Jameson, Peter.................3:32:06 (4,483)
Lambourne, Martin.................4:42:29 (20,104)
Lamburn, David.................3:36:30 (5,142)
Lamerton, Carl.................4:27:12 (16,526)
Laming, Paul.................3:57:59 (9,703)
Lammali, Aziouz.................2:52:53 (491)
Lammens, Dominique.................3:46:01 (6,935)
Lammer, Bernd.................4:21:42 (15,158)
Lamont, Clinton.................4:12:16 (12,831)
Lamont, Neil.................3:26:18 (3,578)
Lampard, Ben.................3:43:52 (6,522)
Lamper, James.................4:44:58 (20,706)
Lamplough, Ian.................4:30:59 (17,491)
Lamprell, James.................4:12:29 (12,880)
Lamprey, Philip.................4:59:59 (23,979)
Lamptey, Jonathan.................6:24:48 (31,156)
Lancashire, Steve.................3:56:27 (9,305)
Lancaster, David.................6:21:17 (31,056)
Lancaster, Kenneth.................5:52:03 (29,833)
Lance, Andy.................5:03:16 (24,503)
Lance, Timothy.................4:44:13 (20,548)
Lanchas-Gomez, Luis.................3:53:10 (8,464)
Lanchbury, Richard.................4:12:19 (12,838)
Lancon, Phillippe.................3:08:19 (1,526)
Land, John.................3:49:25 (7,613)
Landells, Martin.................3:51:46 (8,138)
Lander, Graham.................5:37:22 (28,765)
Lander, Paul.................5:07:30 (25,181)
Lander, Stuart.................3:28:46 (3,962)
Landsman, Paul.................4:40:40 (19,676)

Lane, Andrew.................3:00:20 (957)
Lane, Anthony.................4:54:16 (22,761)
Lane, Barnard.................5:12:29 (25,895)
Lane, Brian.................4:06:02 (11,506)
Lane, Christopher.................5:54:45 (29,984)
Lane, Cliff.................3:55:37 (9,081)
Lane, David.................2:46:26 (275)
Lane, Derrick.................4:04:42 (11,225)
Lane, Gareth.................4:59:08 (23,834)
Lane, James.................4:47:22 (21,261)
Lane, Jason.................4:25:48 (16,201)
Lane, Matthew.................4:33:01 (17,956)
Lane, Michael.................5:35:50 (28,624)
Lane, Peter.................4:28:42 (16,910)
Lane, Philip.................6:21:10 (31,055)
Lane, Richard.................6:18:45 (30,963)
Lane, Ronald.................3:11:56 (1,854)
Lane, Stuart.................5:47:03 (29,494)
Lang, Angus.................4:57:48 (23,542)
Lang, Benjamin.................2:59:50 (929)
Lang, John.................4:20:26 (14,854)
Langdell, David.................3:27:01 (3,684)
Langdon, Ben.................4:09:40 (12,268)
Langdon, Benjamin.................4:03:10 (10,875)
Lange, Fritz.................2:34:26 (95)
Langeweg, Segert.................4:15:09 (13,554)
Langford, Mark.................5:40:33 (29,038)
Langford, Michael.................4:26:31 (16,358)
Langford, Nicholas.................3:53:48 (8,618)
Langham, Garry.................4:42:05 (20,004)
Langham, Neil.................3:09:24 (1,622)
Langlands, Jeff.................4:08:22 (11,973)
Langler, Ian.................2:59:00 (851)
Langley, Clive.................3:51:02 (7,963)
Langley, Kelly.................4:59:09 (23,838)
Langley, Manfred.................4:50:26 (21,947)
Langley, Paul.................4:16:35 (13,872)
Langley, Philip.................4:39:08 (19,353)
Langley, Robert.................2:59:58 (935)
Langley, Trevor.................5:39:32 (28,951)
Langman, Rodney.................5:44:06 (29,308)
Langmyren, Ole Kjell.................2:47:16 (307)
Langner, Andrew.................4:23:26 (15,595)
Langridge, John.................4:28:22 (16,814)
Langridge, Simon.................4:10:25 (12,449)
Langroo, Raj.................5:47:20 (29,521)
Langsford, Arthur.................4:37:50 (19,050)
Langston, Brian.................3:52:29 (8,306)
Langton, Alan.................5:02:09 (24,335)
Lanham, James.................3:58:43 (9,889)
Lanham, Tim.................4:35:12 (18,442)
Lannagan, Patrick.................5:41:37 (29,130)
Lansdell, Denham.................4:29:29 (17,112)
Lansley, Mark.................5:07:57 (25,262)
Lantinga, Herman.................3:29:00 (4,001)
Lantos, David.................3:27:26 (3,728)
Laperna, Paul.................5:35:56 (28,633)
Lapinskis, Jeffrey.................5:49:32 (29,684)
Laplain, Trevor.................6:42:35 (31,583)
Laplante, George.................3:58:44 (9,892)
Lapping, Grant.................3:08:20 (1,527)
Laraki, Ghali.................4:35:24 (18,495)
Larby, Kenneth.................6:05:57 (30,499)
Larcombe, Peter.................4:21:18 (15,060)
Larcombe, William.................4:28:12 (16,766)
Large, Phillip.................3:23:45 (3,208)
Large, Simon.................4:29:44 (17,171)
Large, Steven.................3:10:17 (1,702)
Largemain, Pascal.................2:59:23 (889)
Largou, Mohamed.................3:46:42 (7,068)
Larkin, Brian.................4:28:25 (16,832)
Larkin, Kevin.................4:39:04 (19,335)
Larkins, Stuart.................4:51:32 (22,214)
Larminier, Claude.................4:03:09 (10,873)
Larnach, Alastair.................5:56:52 (30,098)
Larner, Daniel.................5:22:13 (27,168)
Larner, Ian.................5:22:14 (27,171)
Larotonda, Francesco.................4:09:53 (12,318)
Larrieu, Bernard.................3:29:30 (4,092)
Larsen, Jonhard.................2:58:15 (788)
Larsen, Nils Ivar.................3:45:46 (6,883)
Larter, Andrew.................4:45:54 (20,936)
Larter, Simon.................5:32:43 (28,352)

Larter, William.................4:41:05 (19,775)
Lartigue, Michel.................3:24:01 (3,249)
Lartigue, Philippe.................4:52:37 (22,417)
Larvin, Philip.................4:45:07 (20,748)
Lashbrook, Alan.................4:57:01 (23,384)
Lashmar, Anthony Paul.................2:47:20 (311)
Lashmar, Ben.................4:00:27 (10,321)
Laskow-Pooley, Kurt.................4:24:38 (15,897)
Lasne, Dominique.................3:20:07 (2,773)
Lasserre, Jean-André.................3:59:23 (10,063)
Last, David.................4:57:04 (23,394)
Last, Rob.................4:56:19 (23,224)
Latchford, Ian.................5:04:42 (24,733)
Latham, Andrew.................4:36:23 (18,740)
Latham, Benn.................4:23:25 (15,591)
Latham, Christopher.................3:00:08 (947)
Latham, Ronald.................4:36:55 (18,858)
Latham, Stan.................4:36:53 (18,849)
Lathbury, David.................3:31:16 (4,373)
Lathwell, Simon.................3:28:34 (3,913)
Latorre, Antonio.................3:56:23 (9,288)
Latourte, Ludovic.................3:58:02 (9,717)
Lattimore, Alan.................3:57:49 (9,650)
Lau, Chris.................5:01:27 (24,228)
Laubis, Hans.................4:27:41 (16,643)
Laubscher, Xavier.................3:44:00 (6,544)
Lauffs, Teja.................5:32:41 (28,345)
Laurence, Garry.................4:25:39 (16,168)
Laurent, Stephane.................3:42:56 (6,349)
Laurie, Graham.................3:28:21 (3,874)
Laursen, Anders.................2:57:25 (729)
Lavelle, Edward.................3:49:16 (7,582)
Lavelle, Gareth.................3:53:47 (8,613)
Lavelle, Jon.................3:54:20 (8,735)
Lavender, Tony.................5:01:36 (24,242)
Laver, Timothy.................4:27:08 (16,506)
Lavery, Adrian.................3:27:55 (3,805)
Lavigne, James.................3:18:24 (2,602)
Lavrit, Yvan.................3:40:31 (5,868)
Lavy, Jeremy.................4:14:42 (13,423)
Law, Alastair.................6:47:34 (31,664)
Law, Albert.................3:59:19 (10,040)
Law, Alexander.................3:34:31 (4,841)
Law, Andrew.................3:25:39 (3,481)
Law, Andrew.................4:45:31 (20,851)
Law, Angus.................4:28:27 (16,839)
Law, David.................4:49:19 (21,707)
Law, Edward.................4:10:22 (12,431)
Law, Graham.................3:46:13 (6,978)
Law, Kwong-Wing.................6:04:49 (30,448)
Law, Nigel.................4:44:04 (20,513)
Law, Simon.................3:01:37 (1,031)
Lawer, Paul.................4:38:33 (19,210)
Lawes, Cameron.................4:41:17 (19,819)
Lawes, Richard.................2:56:31 (675)
Lawes, Timothy.................2:55:06 (599)
Lawfull, Mark.................4:11:21 (12,612)
Lawler, Christopher.................3:51:58 (8,186)
Lawler, Tony.................4:40:21 (19,620)
Lawless, Patrick.................4:49:30 (21,750)
Lawless, Richard.................5:40:23 (29,025)
Lawley, Rob.................4:06:45 (11,643)
Lawlor, John.................4:56:36 (23,287)
Lawlor, Kevin.................4:34:50 (18,355)
Lawlor, Paul.................3:09:10 (1,600)
Lawlor, Shaun.................3:16:53 (2,416)
Lawlor, Warren.................4:24:57 (15,981)
Lawrance, Richard.................4:47:27 (21,287)
Lawrence, Alan.................4:44:00 (20,497)
Lawrence, Anton.................3:49:25 (7,613)
Lawrence, Colin.................4:25:13 (16,063)
Lawrence, Creswell.................5:28:05 (27,901)
Lawrence, David.................3:38:25 (5,480)
Lawrence, Francis.................4:18:53 (14,473)
Lawrence, Ivor.................3:38:14 (5,449)
Lawrence, John.................5:08:50 (25,381)
Lawrence, Lee.................4:36:20 (18,722)
Lawrence, Mark.................4:12:36 (12,914)
Lawrence, Mark.................4:17:06 (14,010)
Lawrence, Michael.................4:10:08 (12,382)
Lawrence, Nigel.................3:53:53 (8,642)
Lawrence, Peter.................4:57:07 (23,404)
Lawrence, Raymond.................4:18:56 (14,492)

Lawrence, Sam 4:57:18 (23,446)
Lawrence, Scott 4:56:48 (23,337)
Lawrence, Simon 4:23:37 (15,643)
Lawrence, Thomas 3:44:03 (6,555)
Lawrence, Tim 3:41:25 (6,047)
Lawry, Mathew 5:25:00 (27,536)
Lawry, Steve 5:25:03 (27,546)
Lawson, James 4:16:55 (13,975)
Lawson, Mark 2:53:24 (503)
Lawson, Matthew 3:44:23 (6,618)
Lawson, Matthew 4:40:40 (19,676)
Lawson, Nic 3:47:10 (7,154)
Lawson, Nick 4:32:38 (17,859)
Lawson, Richard 4:42:43 (20,163)
Lawton, Bryan 3:41:45 (6,101)
Lawton, David 3:42:20 (6,207)
Lawton, Nicholas 4:17:52 (14,224)
Lawton, Peter 3:43:15 (6,414)
Lax, James 4:51:00 (22,070)
Lay, David 6:04:44 (30,444)
Lay, John 4:39:04 (19,335)
Laycock, Andrew 4:07:37 (11,838)
Laycock, Jon 5:01:18 (24,205)
Laycock, Marcus 3:51:23 (8,045)
Laycock, Peter 4:46:19 (21,050)
Layfield, Kieran 4:18:53 (14,473)
Layton, David 4:53:01 (22,505)
Layzell, Simeon 4:58:20 (23,656)
Lazarus, Alan 5:08:46 (25,367)
Lazarus, Robert 5:12:52 (25,954)
Lazarz, Zbigniew 3:18:59 (2,652)
Lazell, Sebastian 4:44:13 (20,548)
Lazou, Peter 3:45:50 (6,895)
Lazrak, Abdelfatah 3:24:11 (3,280)
Le Bihan, Jacques 3:01:04 (1,008)
Le Bihan, Neil 4:45:57 (20,948)
Le Breton, Timothy 4:06:32 (11,596)
Le Cocq, Nick 3:50:47 (7,905)
Le Fevre, Chris 4:44:37 (20,637)
Le Grange, Eugene 4:37:44 (19,029)
Le Grelle, Matthieu 5:02:16 (24,357)
Le Jeune, Martin 4:21:12 (15,034)
Le Maire, Andrew 3:59:46 (10,167)
Le Marrec, Patrick 3:59:54 (10,200)
Le May, Chris 4:02:11 (10,675)
Le Merdy, François 5:38:03 (28,816)
Le Quesne, John 4:43:37 (20,407)
Le Roy, Robert 6:52:10 (31,764)
Le Tacon, Philippe 3:48:48 (7,466)
Le Vagueres, Didier 4:14:44 (13,432)
Lea, Andrew 5:23:59 (27,406)
Lea, Timothy 5:04:20 (24,682)
Leach, Anthony 5:10:13 (25,586)
Leach, David 3:55:17 (8,988)
Leach, Gregory 4:32:52 (17,918)
Leach, Mark 3:55:13 (8,969)
Leach, Mark 4:27:16 (16,539)
Leach, Robert 4:45:43 (20,889)
Leach, Ronald 3:13:21 (2,041)
Leach, Simon 4:35:39 (18,551)
Leach, Timothy 5:19:08 (26,776)
Leach, Tony 4:42:17 (20,050)
Leacy, James 4:47:19 (21,251)
Leadbetter, Ian 3:50:18 (7,801)
Leadbetter, Martin 3:51:02 (7,963)
Leader, Gary 3:22:08 (3,000)
Leafe, Jonathan 5:12:03 (25,833)
Leak, Andrew 5:21:06 (27,034)
Leake, David 3:40:13 (5,835)
Leal, Raj 4:14:05 (13,280)
Leale, Nicholas 4:52:29 (22,393)
Leane, Andrew 4:28:02 (16,715)
Leard, Dennis 3:40:12 (5,832)
Learmonth, Ian 4:37:11 (18,919)
Leather, Giles 4:41:38 (19,896)
Leatherdale, Malcolm 3:29:32 (4,101)
Leathes, Simon 4:06:32 (11,596)
Leaver, Andy 4:42:41 (20,154)
Leaver, Marcus 4:47:46 (21,364)
Lebair, Benoit 2:52:48 (488)
Lebeau, Yann 4:58:23 (23,667)
Leck, Andrew 2:47:48 (324)
Leckenby, David 3:32:34 (4,535)
Leckie, Roy 4:18:11 (14,285)
Leclerc, Emmanuel 3:48:00 (7,319)
Lecoanet, Philippe 5:30:16 (28,110)
Lecolle, Thierry 4:31:39 (17,658)
Ledger, Clare 5:43:22 (29,264)
Ledwidge, Alan 3:50:52 (7,919)
Lee, Allan 2:32:36 (77)
Lee, Charles 3:49:46 (7,691)
Lee, Christopher 4:14:43 (13,429)
Lee, Christopher 5:28:32 (27,943)
Lee, Daniel 4:08:42 (12,066)
Lee, Daniel 4:14:42 (13,423)
Lee, Daniel 4:38:38 (19,234)
Lee, Dave 5:01:15 (24,194)
Lee, David 3:24:31 (3,333)
Lee, David 3:59:00 (9,966)
Lee, David 4:39:58 (19,533)
Lee, David 4:50:21 (21,933)
Lee, David 5:05:46 (24,930)
Lee, Ewe 4:58:01 (23,583)
Lee, Francis 4:58:53 (23,777)
Lee, Freddie 4:16:58 (13,982)
Lee, Gary 4:09:28 (12,219)
Lee, James 4:03:39 (10,973)
Lee, James 4:09:09 (12,163)
Lee, Jason 4:09:17 (12,190)
Lee, John 4:03:44 (10,992)
Lee, Johnson 4:09:50 (12,310)
Lee, Jonathan 4:04:17 (11,134)
Lee, Jonathan 6:28:16 (31,281)
Lee, Keith 7:31:59 (32,167)
Lee, Malcolm 3:34:21 (4,805)
Lee, Martyn 5:26:12 (27,700)
Lee, Nicholas 3:35:05 (4,924)
Lee, Nigel 3:13:46 (2,093)
Lee, Philip 3:35:04 (4,921)
Lee, Phong Thuan 3:57:45 (9,632)
Lee, Richard 3:57:56 (9,690)
Lee, Richard 4:32:36 (17,855)
Lee, Richard 5:11:57 (25,823)
Lee, Robert 4:58:28 (23,692)
Lee, Robert 5:23:42 (27,369)
Lee, Royston 2:55:34 (624)
Lee, Stephen 3:31:18 (4,381)
Lee, Trevor 4:28:19 (16,794)
Lee, Wei Lam 4:31:24 (17,592)
Leech, Terry 3:06:49 (1,387)
Leeder, Daniel 4:01:08 (10,457)
Leedham, Ian 4:26:14 (16,306)
Lee-Edghill, John 4:03:21 (10,923)
Leefe, Simon 3:54:08 (8,687)
Leek, Jonathan 2:46:39 (284)
Leek, Steven 3:39:26 (5,683)
Leeming, John 4:37:28 (18,975)
Leeming, Malcolm 4:12:10 (12,805)
Leemker, Robert 4:39:25 (19,423)
Leeper, Patrick 5:56:53 (30,100)
Lees, Allan 3:44:24 (6,622)
Lees, Chris 3:38:35 (5,511)
Lees, George 3:52:45 (8,363)
Lees, Jim 6:47:36 (31,668)
Lees, Martin 4:38:11 (19,127)
Lees, Matthew 4:57:35 (23,499)
Lees, Nick 4:22:33 (15,375)
Lees, Simon 4:12:08 (12,795)
Leese, Gareth 3:47:22 (7,183)
Leeson, John 3:33:08 (4,618)
Leeson, John 4:40:48 (19,703)
Leeuwangh, Jonathan 5:26:41 (27,750)
Le-Faye, Nicholas 4:04:52 (11,264)
Lefer, Hughes 3:14:45 (2,212)
Lefeure, Olivier 5:20:46 (26,993)
Legassick, David 4:53:23 (22,591)
Leggate, Thomas 3:59:33 (10,105)
Legge, John 4:05:52 (11,473)
Legge, Rex 3:41:44 (6,097)
Legge, Timothy 2:53:05 (496)
Lehmann, Michael 3:36:18 (5,115)
Leidel, Charlie 2:38:06 (133)
Leigh, John 4:44:01 (20,500)
Leigh, Peter 4:31:33 (17,630)
Leigh, Robert 4:53:14 (22,552)
Leigh, Vincent 3:38:06 (5,427)
Leighton, Guy 5:18:17 (26,670)
Leinster, Robert 4:49:53 (21,842)
Leinvuo, Joni 4:18:38 (14,403)
Leitch, Graham 4:45:55 (20,939)
Leitch, Jonathan 4:21:44 (15,166)
Leitch, Malcolm 3:30:55 (4,317)
Leknes, Tim 3:26:57 (3,669)
Leland, Howard 4:04:58 (11,282)
Lelean, Ross 5:16:52 (26,466)
Lelliott, Stephen 2:55:42 (630)
Lemar, Andrew 4:43:06 (20,263)
Lemke, Grant 3:15:16 (2,269)
Lemon, James 5:14:28 (26,170)
Lemon, Paul 4:34:49 (18,354)
Le-Mons, Michel 3:29:19 (4,048)
Lemoulec, Roger 4:26:08 (16,282)
Lendon, Jason 3:02:22 (1,081)
Lenegan, Neville 5:38:21 (28,846)
Leniconi, Paolo 3:34:11 (4,774)
Lennon, Brad 4:34:57 (18,383)
Lennon, Clifford 4:52:35 (22,411)
Lennox, Gordon 3:11:49 (1,838)
Lennox, Graeme 5:07:24 (25,161)
Lenti, Marcelo 3:37:24 (5,311)
Lenton, Wayne 4:27:35 (16,621)
Leon, Clement 4:21:16 (15,049)
Leon, Mauricio 5:10:54 (25,678)
Leonard, Andrew 4:18:43 (14,429)
Leonard, Christopher 4:19:03 (14,517)
Leonard, Jaimie 4:51:52 (22,283)
Leonard, Michael 4:39:06 (19,343)
Leonard, Paul 4:13:58 (13,251)
Leonard, Simon 5:48:52 (29,625)
Leonard, Stephen 4:34:55 (18,376)
Leonhardmair, Josef 3:17:15 (2,456)
Le-Pape, Regis 3:29:25 (4,072)
Le-Quere, Jean-Pierre 3:23:22 (3,159)
Leray, Thierry 3:19:23 (2,689)
Lerche, Eric 3:28:11 (3,845)
Lerkegaard, Niels 4:50:16 (21,915)
Lerman, Antony 3:48:43 (7,443)
Leroux, Bruno 3:54:16 (8,723)
Leroux, Edouard 4:20:31 (14,873)
Lery, Laurent 4:31:49 (17,692)
Leskinen, Seppo Tapio 4:13:55 (13,239)
Lesley, Michael 4:41:10 (19,790)
Leslie, Barry 4:50:57 (22,059)
Leslie, Mike 5:23:43 (27,371)
Leslie Melville, Jake 4:37:56 (19,071)
Lesser, Scott 5:36:37 (28,701)
Lessey, Kevin 5:23:18 (27,331)
Lessware, Christopher 4:13:50 (13,210)
Lester, David 5:54:20 (29,959)
Lester, Jonathon 3:31:27 (4,399)
Lester, Mel 4:51:41 (22,243)
Lester, Shaun 4:13:00 (13,005)
Letang, Joseph 4:59:59 (23,979)
Lethaby, Raymond 3:57:19 (9,533)
Letherby, Andrew 2:18:25 (19)
Letourneau, Luc 3:59:54 (10,200)
Letschert, Peter 3:58:08 (9,739)
Leuther, Johann 4:44:58 (20,706)
Leuw, Peter 3:56:58 (9,444)
Levan, David 3:41:07 (5,982)
Lever, Nicholas 4:57:04 (23,394)
Leverett, Iain 4:48:00 (21,427)
Levermore, Paul 4:15:09 (13,554)
Levett, Peter 4:23:46 (15,688)
Levick, John 3:42:31 (6,255)
Levin, Maurice 5:22:51 (27,261)
Levine, Mark 4:55:05 (22,938)
Levison, John 3:12:27 (1,921)
Levy, Jason 4:36:25 (18,750)
Levy, Ori 3:55:10 (8,958)
Levy, Stuart 5:49:32 (29,684)
Lewendon, John 5:19:20 (26,806)
Lewes, James 3:51:01 (7,957)
Lewin, Michael 4:11:02 (12,546)
Lewin, Richard 4:58:17 (23,645)
Lewin, Robert 3:49:18 (7,590)
Lewington, Colin 4:53:34 (22,632)
Lewis, Adrian 3:27:33 (3,751)
Lewis, Alan 3:02:29 (1,086)

MacAskill, Andy 2:48:18 (344)
Macauglan, Ian 3:42:55 (6,347)
Macaulay, John 5:08:58 (25,395)
Macbean, Andrew 5:13:34 (26,052)
Macbeath, Niall 3:44:36 (6,649)
MacCallum, Alistair 3:55:32 (9,058)
Mac Coille, Conall 5:02:00 (24,316)
Macdonald, Alexander 3:37:46 (5,381)
Macdonald, Alistair 4:25:37 (16,162)
Macdonald, Andrew 4:20:53 (14,950)
Macdonald, Colin 5:14:38 (26,193)
Macdonald, David 3:34:22 (4,811)
Macdonald, Gavin 5:08:48 (25,374)
Macdonald, Gordon 4:49:49 (21,827)
Macdonald, Graeme 3:48:07 (7,342)
Macdonald, James 4:00:48 (10,386)
Macdonald, John 4:06:25 (11,575)
Macdonald, John 5:04:03 (24,642)
Macdonald, Julian 3:08:31 (1,550)
Macdonald, Kevin 4:17:58 (14,244)
Macdonald, Malcolm 4:54:03 (22,720)
Macdonald, Robert 4:59:38 (23,910)
Macdonald, Rory 4:54:03 (22,720)
Macdonald, Scott 5:05:32 (24,890)
Macdonald, Stewart 2:28:00 (51)
Macdonald, Stuart 4:32:37 (17,856)
Mace, Andrew 5:13:20 (26,018)
Macefield, Anthony 6:00:35 (30,276)
Macenhill, Justin 2:55:04 (598)
Macer, Dugald 4:05:24 (11,373)
Mac Ewan, Colin 4:51:06 (22,107)
Macey, Andrew 5:18:26 (26,687)
Macey, Christian 5:00:25 (24,053)
Macey, Mark 4:35:07 (18,417)
Macey, Terence 4:15:19 (13,599)
Macfadyen, Brian 3:25:14 (3,432)
Macfarlane, Fraser 4:55:12 (22,961)
Macfarlane, John 3:41:43 (6,094)
Macfarlane, Paul 4:26:26 (16,342)
MacGregor, Martin 3:34:11 (4,774)
MacGregor, Niall 3:46:48 (7,083)
MacGregor, Simon 4:16:52 (13,954)
Macheret, Dominique 3:49:37 (7,661)
Machin, Tony 5:27:08 (27,793)
Machray, Simon 3:56:25 (9,297)
Maciariello, Patrick 3:25:47 (3,509)
MacIldowie, Paul 4:33:28 (18,051)
MacInnes, Chris 5:00:21 (24,044)
MacInnes, John 3:59:19 (10,040)
MacInnes, Roddy 3:47:48 (7,277)
Macintosh, John 3:50:02 (7,741)
Macintyre, Donal 4:34:14 (18,220)
Macintyre, Donal 4:34:15 (18,226)
Macintyre, John 4:26:03 (16,264)
MacIver, Ray 5:14:17 (26,138)
MacIver, Robert 3:43:32 (6,453)
Mack, Adam 3:34:57 (4,901)
Mack, Darren 2:54:39 (573)
Mack, Jeffrey 3:39:53 (5,768)
Mack, Julian 4:32:15 (17,784)
Mack, Steven 4:20:43 (14,907)
Mackaness, Sam 6:43:36 (31,605)
Mackay, Bain 4:29:13 (17,044)
Mackay, Colin 3:30:56 (4,318)
Mackay, David 5:12:23 (25,879)
Mackay, Garry 4:42:46 (20,172)
Mackay, Mike 6:49:45 (31,712)
Mackay, Steve 3:49:53 (7,706)
Macken, Shaun 3:54:11 (8,699)
Mackender, James 5:36:22 (28,669)
Mackenzie, Barry 6:16:33 (30,878)
Mackenzie, John 5:09:47 (25,519)
Mackenzie, Norman 5:47:24 (29,524)
Mackenzie, Robert 4:46:54 (21,169)
Mackenzie, Vincent 3:22:29 (3,047)
Mackenzie Smith, Hugo 4:32:49 (17,905)
Mackervoy, Stephen 4:57:45 (23,529)
Mackey, Jim 6:32:41 (31,393)
Mackie, Alan 4:08:42 (12,066)
Mackie, Baird 5:01:45 (24,269)
Mackie, Ian 4:49:14 (21,685)
Mackie, Peter 4:01:22 (10,509)
Mackinnon, Angus 3:43:22 (6,432)
Mackintosh, Jamie 5:29:32 (28,043)
Mackintosh, Julian 3:48:03 (7,328)
Mackintosh, Nicholas 4:05:58 (11,498)
Mackley, Dan 5:36:25 (28,675)
Mackness, Anthony 3:37:34 (5,338)
MacLachlan, Alastair 2:50:30 (402)
MacLachlan, James 4:10:37 (12,486)
Maclean, Colin 4:33:03 (17,963)
Maclean, Duncan 5:09:32 (25,481)
Maclean, Edward 4:26:02 (16,254)
MacLellan, Sean 3:32:38 (4,547)
Maclennan, Colin 3:44:37 (6,653)
Macleod, Andrew 3:46:45 (7,075)
Macleod, Douglas 4:37:17 (18,946)
Macleod, Duncan 3:55:39 (9,091)
Macleod, Jamie 4:43:13 (20,292)
Macleod, Mark 4:45:32 (20,855)
Macmahon, Tim 4:23:22 (15,583)
Macmillan, Euan 3:45:51 (6,901)
Macmillan, Jim 3:59:37 (10,125)
Macmillan, Mark 4:57:32 (23,487)
Macmillan, Richard 4:28:27 (16,839)
Macmillan, Robert 5:25:11 (27,568)
MacNamara, Paul 4:34:59 (18,393)
MacNaughton, Iain 3:54:28 (8,771)
MacNaughton, Robert 3:58:54 (9,942)
Macpherson, Andrew 4:44:10 (20,533)
Macpherson, Anthony 3:53:50 (8,628)
Macpherson, Daniel 3:28:46 (3,962)
Macpherson, David 3:55:14 (8,974)
Macpherson, William 4:21:56 (15,217)
MacQueen, Ian 3:48:20 (7,381)
Macrae, Donald 3:37:15 (5,282)
Macrae, Duncan 3:41:32 (6,075)
Macrae, Gordon 5:54:42 (29,979)
MacShane, Denis 4:51:46 (22,258)
MacTavish, Ian 4:11:18 (12,598)
MacVicar, Alexander 4:17:23 (14,082)
MacVicar, Richard 5:00:10 (24,004)
Maddams, Michael 5:42:34 (29,213)
Maddams, Russell 2:34:52 (98)
Madden, Adrian 3:51:46 (8,138)
Madden, Dean 4:46:59 (21,182)
Madden, Gary 5:39:22 (28,929)
Madden, Jerry 3:27:55 (3,805)
Maddern, Peter 5:03:07 (24,477)
Maddick, Simon 4:14:47 (13,445)
Maddison, Ian 3:50:35 (7,864)
Maddock, Alistair 4:46:58 (21,177)
Maddocks, Jason 3:17:34 (2,500)
Maddocks, Jon 4:38:01 (19,093)
Maddocks, Terry 4:19:09 (14,541)
Maddox, Colin 4:13:41 (13,170)
Madeley, Sean 4:40:09 (19,571)
Maderecker, Michael 3:29:45 (4,134)
Madgett, Oliver 6:27:39 (31,252)
Madiba, James 3:04:05 (1,188)
Madsen, Anders 3:59:58 (10,217)
Madsen, Harald 4:52:37 (22,417)
Madsen, Vagn 4:17:20 (14,064)
Maestri, Stefano 3:50:34 (7,861)
Mafham, Paul 4:01:17 (10,491)
Mafico, Christopher 4:30:21 (17,322)
Magee, Ken 3:52:14 (8,254)
Mager, Robin 4:13:12 (13,049)
Maggini, Vasco 5:38:14 (28,832)
Maggs, Adrian 3:04:09 (1,192)
Magnier, Stephan 3:41:24 (6,041)
Magot, Stephane 4:39:06 (19,343)
Magoulianiti, Arthur 4:10:40 (12,493)
Magson, Paul 4:43:34 (20,393)
Maguire, Alex 5:15:35 (26,329)
Maguire, Anthony 4:53:58 (22,708)
Maguire, David 4:15:19 (13,599)
Maguire, Graham 3:36:34 (5,156)
Maguire, Liam 4:47:03 (21,190)
Maguire, Michael 4:33:38 (18,080)
Maguire, Paul 3:17:53 (2,534)
Mahadevaiah, Kailas 4:22:05 (15,261)
Mahajan, Vinay 4:34:28 (18,281)
Maher, Derek 5:03:32 (24,536)
Maher, Martin 3:56:52 (9,417)
Maher, Terry 5:28:40 (27,957)
Maheswaran, Akeeban 5:22:14 (27,171)
Mahil, Manminder 5:52:39 (29,867)
Mahon, Dominic 2:52:34 (472)
Mahon, John 4:42:11 (20,027)
Mahoney, Ayodeji 3:47:13 (7,160)
Mahoney, Mark 3:47:35 (7,232)
Mahoney, Mark 4:47:22 (21,261)
Mahoney, Paul 3:56:55 (9,428)
Mahoney, Paul 5:00:36 (24,090)
Maide, José 5:57:04 (30,111)
Maier, Andreas 3:05:11 (1,267)
Maier, Dieter 5:22:00 (27,143)
Mailer, Greg 3:31:14 (4,365)
Mailey, Craig 4:24:13 (15,800)
Maillard, Edmund 5:18:41 (26,725)
Maillard, Joel 3:40:38 (5,888)
Maille, Philippe 3:43:07 (6,390)
Mailloux, William 3:41:19 (6,017)
Mainelli, Michael 5:29:53 (28,074)
Maini, Raj 3:31:18 (4,381)
Mainwaring, Stuart 3:43:32 (6,453)
Mainwaring, Wyn 6:55:07 (31,833)
Mainwood, Christopher 4:43:16 (20,309)
Mair, David 3:55:37 (9,081)
Mair, Grant 3:56:27 (9,305)
Mair, Richard 5:22:49 (27,256)
Maironis, Darren 3:00:20 (957)
Maisani, Andrea 3:32:55 (4,584)
Maisey, Colin 4:46:01 (20,964)
Maitland, Graham 3:27:44 (3,773)
Maitland-M-Crichton, William 3:59:17 (10,034)
Maitre, Michel 3:57:38 (9,603)
Majer, Raymond 4:38:40 (19,245)
Major, John 5:14:07 (26,109)
Major, Paul 2:46:59 (299)
Major, Scott 4:18:32 (14,368)
Makin, Paul 4:37:17 (18,946)
Makin, Stuart 5:16:17 (26,400)
Makins, Ronald 5:34:19 (28,509)
Makonnen, John 3:33:40 (4,697)
Makori, David 2:13:24 (12)
Mal, Firouz 3:22:57 (3,105)
Malachard, Victor 4:48:52 (21,602)
Malanga, Riccardo 4:54:29 (22,810)
Malcolm, Richard 3:36:16 (5,108)
Malcolm, Solomon 4:38:28 (19,193)
Malcolm, Thomas 3:27:59 (3,813)
Maldar, Alec 4:01:36 (10,560)
Maldonado, Gregorio 3:33:52 (4,726)
Male, Chris 5:03:28 (24,524)
Male, David 4:20:16 (14,813)
Male, Nathony 4:40:32 (19,657)
Malet, Jean-Michel 4:50:46 (22,025)
Malherbe, Johann 4:37:18 (18,948)
Malhomme, Nicholas 4:27:31 (16,605)
Malik, Waqas 4:57:22 (23,453)
Malin, Robert 3:42:28 (6,240)
Malin, William 3:54:29 (8,776)
Maliney, Keith 3:34:16 (4,790)
Malins, Gary 3:33:49 (4,720)
Malkin, Anthony 3:56:42 (9,375)
Mallet, Mickael 3:55:31 (9,052)
Mallett, Sean 4:37:10 (18,912)
Mallison, Peter 2:47:16 (307)
Mallon, John 3:19:34 (2,706)
Malon, Jean-Luc 3:02:09 (1,066)
Malone, Ken 5:35:11 (28,571)
Malone, Lawrence 3:15:12 (2,263)
Malone, Sean 5:29:12 (28,005)
Maloney, Liam 3:25:14 (3,432)
Malpass, Arran 5:41:41 (29,136)
Maltby, Christopher 4:21:26 (15,098)
Malthouse, Iain 4:49:37 (21,784)
Maltman, James 5:06:37 (25,036)
Malyan, Paul 4:36:43 (18,812)
Man, Kwok 4:34:13 (18,216)
Man, Tony 4:06:42 (11,625)
Mancer, Jez 2:44:55 (235)
Mander, Gary 4:11:43 (12,699)
Mander, Peter 4:27:06 (16,497)
Mander, Richard 6:57:19 (31,863)
Manfrini, Leonardo 3:11:01 (1,758)
Mangeot, Andrew 3:14:18 (2,164)

Manger, Garth....3:55:42 (9,107)
Mangion, Stuart....4:17:05 (14,007)
Manister, Paul....3:58:17 (9,776)
Manjlai, Abdul....4:52:37 (22,417)
Manjlai, Mansoor....4:52:34 (22,407)
Mankee, Grant....3:13:30 (2,061)
Manktelon, Alexander....4:46:43 (21,129)
Manktelow, Anthony....4:54:30 (22,814)
Manley, Paul....5:21:28 (27,076)
Mann, Andrew....4:31:19 (17,570)
Mann, Barry....4:46:29 (21,091)
Mann, Bradley....5:40:37 (29,045)
Mann, Christopher....4:30:44 (17,429)
Mann, Dave....3:56:36 (9,346)
Mann, David....4:20:13 (14,798)
Mann, James....3:23:05 (3,125)
Mann, Jason....4:23:45 (15,686)
Mann, John....4:23:50 (15,703)
Mann, Malvin....4:29:09 (17,026)
Mann, Martin....4:10:23 (12,438)
Mann, Nicholas....4:10:07 (12,378)
Mann, Paul....3:20:13 (2,789)
Mann, Pete....2:58:06 (774)
Mann, Raj....4:22:22 (15,331)
Mann, Shane....6:28:07 (31,274)
Mann, Steven....3:38:02 (5,421)
Mannan, Nazrul....4:10:37 (12,486)
Mannering, Ryan....4:40:02 (19,546)
Manners, Paul....3:05:59 (1,320)
Mannier, Didier....3:51:23 (8,045)
Manning, Dennis....4:50:22 (21,935)
Manning, Douglas....3:58:56 (9,951)
Manning, Greg....4:18:53 (14,473)
Manning, Jason....3:03:21 (1,139)
Manning, John....4:01:00 (10,429)
Manning, Julian....3:06:50 (1,389)
Manning, Paul....3:31:39 (4,427)
Manning, Peter....5:18:46 (26,735)
Manning, Roger....2:55:47 (634)
Mannion, Chris....3:47:45 (7,267)
Mannion, Daniel....4:53:49 (22,684)
Mannion, Liam....6:25:40 (31,188)
Manns, Shaun....4:58:28 (23,692)
Mansell, Thomas....4:48:44 (21,575)
Manser, Reg....3:54:59 (8,917)
Mansfield, Andrew....3:59:51 (10,187)
Mansfield, Angus....4:24:51 (15,962)
Mansfield, David....3:36:55 (5,215)
Mansfield, David....3:46:33 (7,045)
Mansfield, Derek....3:42:36 (6,276)
Mansfield, John....5:07:41 (25,221)
Mansfield, Paul....5:25:01 (27,540)
Mansfield, Peter....4:08:15 (11,947)
Mansfield, Philip....5:11:00 (25,692)
Mansfield, Stephen....3:23:13 (3,139)
Mansi, Andrew....3:11:07 (1,768)
Mansi, Savino....2:52:52 (490)
Mansley, Joseph....5:56:21 (30,074)
Mansley, Paul....6:14:24 (30,805)
Manson, Alex....4:48:06 (21,451)
Manson, Andrew....3:49:13 (7,568)
Manson, Christopher....3:12:34 (1,942)
Manson, Ian....3:59:20 (10,047)
Manson, Justin....4:37:52 (19,060)
Mansoori, Sasson....5:00:20 (24,041)
Mansour, Dominic....4:25:17 (16,081)
Mansukhani, Raoul....4:41:31 (19,871)
Mansworth, Russell....4:34:26 (18,275)
Mantell, Stephen....3:48:08 (7,345)
Mantle, Derek....4:56:10 (23,189)
Mapes, Robert....7:19:10 (32,064)
Mapleston, John....5:06:37 (25,036)
Mapstone, Colin....5:21:20 (27,064)
Marabelli, Enzo....4:06:12 (11,537)
Marais, Ernest....3:34:18 (4,795)
Marais, Marnus....3:35:25 (4,977)
Marand, Johan....4:38:38 (19,234)
Marat, Ludwig....3:20:43 (2,849)
Marcelle, Nicholas....3:44:44 (6,679)
March, David....4:00:52 (10,398)
March, Michael....6:13:18 (30,776)
Marchand, Trevor....3:11:50 (1,841)
Marchant, Andrew....5:14:04 (26,104)
Marchant, Greville....6:50:05 (31,722)
Marchant, Kevin....4:44:41 (20,655)
Marchant, Nicholas....3:53:08 (8,457)
Marchant, Richard....4:16:54 (13,964)
Marchant, Warwick....5:28:58 (27,983)
Marchl, Ernmst....5:28:11 (27,916)
Marchmont, Richard....6:42:26 (31,580)
Marciniak, Szymon....4:04:12 (11,112)
Marcinowicz, Adam....3:34:37 (4,857)
Marechaud, Richard....4:43:02 (20,243)
Marescia, Brandon....4:27:55 (16,693)
Marfell, Ian....3:47:09 (7,152)
Margo, Gideon....3:41:15 (5,998)
Margolis, Geoffrey....4:04:22 (11,150)
Margolis, Stephen....5:33:54 (28,470)
Margulies, Daniel....3:23:51 (3,221)
Maric, Peter....4:56:07 (23,175)
Mariner, Tim....4:00:13 (10,274)
Marini, Marino....4:06:46 (11,648)
Maris, Graham....3:52:13 (8,247)
Marjoram, Brian....3:36:13 (5,098)
Marklew, Stephen....2:56:22 (667)
Markley, Simon....3:21:58 (2,980)
Markowicz, Stephen....3:37:49 (5,388)
Markowski, Kevin....3:30:21 (4,225)
Marks, Alex....4:08:17 (11,959)
Marks, Bill....4:26:02 (16,254)
Marks, David....4:21:58 (15,234)
Marks, Paul....4:29:25 (17,094)
Marks, Richard....3:45:10 (6,769)
Marks, Richard....4:06:02 (11,506)
Marks, Stuart....3:12:35 (1,943)
Markwell, Kevin....4:33:58 (18,158)
Markwell, Nicholas....4:52:24 (22,376)
Marley, Bob....4:52:24 (22,376)
Marley, Graham....4:54:23 (22,790)
Marlow, Stephen....5:18:09 (26,642)
Marnell, Stephen....3:49:40 (7,672)
Marner, Matthew....4:09:29 (12,225)
Marns, Jason....3:58:18 (9,782)
Marotta, Charlie....4:16:33 (13,867)
Marotti, Germano....4:26:15 (16,308)
Marques, Albertino....3:19:13 (2,673)
Marques, Rafael....4:07:59 (11,902)
Marques da Silva, Eloi....4:02:34 (10,751)
Marquis, Alex....5:12:10 (25,844)
Marr, Graham....4:02:44 (10,789)
Marr, Peter....3:04:23 (1,205)
Marr, Richard....3:13:05 (2,004)
Marr, Thomas....3:49:00 (7,518)
Marriage, David....3:59:24 (10,064)
Marriott, Alan....5:21:44 (27,117)
Marriott, Kevin....4:30:40 (17,411)
Marriott, Neil....3:03:03 (1,120)
Marritt, Chris....3:53:20 (8,504)
Marron, Stephen....5:20:53 (27,006)
Marrow, Phil....5:12:33 (25,909)
Marrs, Stuart....4:23:43 (15,676)
Marrs, Tony....4:25:55 (16,234)
Marsden, Duncan....2:50:46 (410)
Marsden, John....4:47:05 (21,198)
Marsden, Nicholas....3:38:46 (5,555)
Marsden, Paul....3:24:00 (3,247)
Marsden, Peter....4:43:39 (20,417)
Marsden, Roger....4:43:53 (20,478)
Marseglia, Pasquale....2:49:31 (379)
Marsh, Alan....4:08:13 (11,942)
Marsh, Alan....4:12:41 (12,935)
Marsh, Alan....4:16:44 (13,914)
Marsh, Colin....4:33:21 (18,019)
Marsh, Daniel....3:57:12 (9,506)
Marsh, David....4:01:45 (10,589)
Marsh, Ian....4:18:58 (14,498)
Marsh, Justin....4:16:41 (13,900)
Marsh, Paul....2:58:58 (848)
Marsh, Paul....3:45:47 (6,889)
Marsh, Paul....5:20:07 (26,907)
Marsh, Pete....3:13:26 (2,052)
Marsh, Roland....4:10:03 (12,362)
Marsh, Roy....5:31:10 (28,214)
Marsh, Stephen....4:44:55 (20,700)
Marsh, Stuart....4:39:12 (19,374)
Marsh, Toby....4:14:24 (13,361)
Marsh, William....5:04:01 (24,633)
Marshall, Alex....3:43:48 (6,506)
Marshall, Andrew....4:24:15 (15,810)
Marshall, Gary....4:26:10 (16,289)
Marshall, Ian....3:17:17 (2,459)
Marshall, Jack....4:28:04 (16,725)
Marshall, James....4:14:54 (13,479)
Marshall, Jason....4:52:29 (22,393)
Marshall, John....3:56:37 (9,352)
Marshall, John....3:57:11 (9,502)
Marshall, Justin....4:56:45 (23,328)
Marshall, Kris....4:36:40 (18,800)
Marshall, Lloyd....2:40:24 (156)
Marshall, Matthew....5:11:45 (25,792)
Marshall, Phil....5:36:47 (28,715)
Marshall, Robert....5:03:32 (24,536)
Marshall, Roy....5:10:57 (25,686)
Marshall, Stephen....4:56:46 (23,329)
Marshall, Stuart....3:50:08 (7,761)
Marshall, Stuart....4:23:26 (15,595)
Marshall, Tim....3:51:53 (8,173)
Marson, John....4:28:49 (16,939)
Marston, Clive....3:39:15 (5,645)
Marston, Glyn....3:52:13 (8,247)
Martell, Paul....3:53:54 (8,646)
Martello, Sabio....5:17:50 (26,583)
Martens, Eric....3:57:16 (9,522)
Martensson, Goran....3:20:48 (2,859)
Martensson, Hakan....2:46:40 (285)
Martensson, Lars....3:20:48 (2,859)
Martin, Alan....5:03:42 (24,574)
Martin, Alan....5:24:04 (27,419)
Martin, Andrew....4:45:43 (20,889)
Martin, Andy....3:24:47 (3,371)
Martin, Andy....4:48:45 (21,577)
Martin, Barry....5:12:49 (25,945)
Martin, Ben....4:16:09 (13,773)
Martin, Bob....3:20:57 (2,878)
Martin, Christian....4:56:37 (23,291)
Martin, Colin....3:36:22 (5,125)
Martin, Daniel....3:24:17 (3,300)
Martin, Daniel....3:40:17 (5,839)
Martin, David....3:37:43 (5,369)
Martin, David....3:58:52 (9,934)

Martin, David....4:23:41 (15,670)

It's hard to imagine why running 26 miles should make you feel so exhilarated, and indeed after 17 miles that initial exhilaration gives way to an overwhelming feeling of tiredness as I hit the wall going around Docklands. Seeing a fellow runner carrying a house on his shoulders (running for Shelter) makes you realise that perhaps you needed a few more longer training runs. But with the help of the great London support, and a handful of jelly beans, those final few miles along the Embankment still live clear in the memory. A finish time of 4hrs 23mins could have been better, but I am so proud of the money I managed to raise for Cancer Research. My knees, however, have never been the same since.

Martin, David....5:40:55 (29,070)
Martin, Dean....4:41:19 (19,830)
Martin, Dennis....4:14:23 (13,353)
Martin, Denzil....4:37:30 (18,984)
Martin, Don....6:35:50 (31,470)
Martin, Edward....3:30:43 (4,282)
Martin, Eric....3:52:33 (8,320)
Martin, Erich....5:09:13 (25,437)
Martin, Gary....3:38:26 (5,483)
Martin, Gary....5:09:27 (25,468)
Martin, Hugh....3:50:17 (7,796)
Martin, Ian....4:24:48 (15,951)
Martin, James....4:16:15 (13,797)
Martin, James....5:52:55 (29,876)
Martin, Jeffrey....4:14:11 (13,302)
Martin, Jeffrey....4:55:37 (23,058)
Martin, Jim....4:57:25 (23,461)
Martin, John....5:43:30 (29,270)

Martin, John 6:03:54 (30,408)
Martin, Kenneth..............5:20:12 (26,915)
Martin, Kevin..............4:59:08 (23,834)
Martin, Lee..............4:58:54 (23,781)
Martin, Michael..............3:45:29 (6,828)
Martin, Michael..............4:22:47 (15,440)
Martin, Morgan..............4:48:45 (21,577)
Martin, Nicholas..............3:38:44 (5,549)
Martin, Nick..............4:55:56 (23,138)
Martin, Olivier..............2:58:57 (846)
Martin, Paul..............3:27:24 (3,722)
Martin, Paul..............3:32:34 (4,535)
Martin, Paul..............4:12:00 (12,762)
Martin, Peter..............4:13:42 (13,176)
Martin, Peter..............4:57:35 (23,499)
Martin, Philip..............3:45:14 (6,780)
Martin, Richard..............3:27:34 (3,753)
Martin, Ricky..............3:45:54 (6,912)
Martin, Russell..............4:31:59 (17,724)
Martin, Samuel..............3:41:06 (5,979)
Martin, Seon..............4:10:03 (12,362)
Martin, Sergio..............4:42:10 (20,022)
Martin, Simon..............4:00:24 (10,312)
Martin, Tony..............4:52:12 (22,340)
Martin Hobson, Garry..............3:47:08 (7,148)
Martindale, Roger..............3:20:03 (2,766)
Martindale, Will..............4:08:24 (11,980)
Martin-Dye, Ben..............3:20:53 (2,871)
Martineau, Mike..............5:09:58 (25,536)
Martinelli, Alessio..............3:55:28 (9,039)
Martinez, José..............3:20:32 (2,829)
Martinez Gomez, Diego..............4:01:14 (10,478)
Martinez-Garcia, Pedro..............3:16:43 (2,399)
Martins, José..............3:14:57 (2,232)
Marti-Reverte, Eloi..............3:21:29 (2,929)
Martyn, Nicholas..............2:27:11 (49)
Maruzzi, Lino..............5:30:22 (28,128)
Marven, Roger..............4:08:44 (12,076)
Marx, Peter..............4:31:49 (17,692)
Maryan, David..............4:39:49 (19,504)
Mascarenhas, Nigel..............4:16:36 (13,876)
Maselli, Mauro..............3:42:24 (6,219)
Maselli, Raffaele..............3:42:27 (6,231)
Mash, Raymond..............6:28:34 (31,287)
Maskell, Christopher..............4:01:34 (10,555)
Maskell, Robert..............4:22:01 (15,244)
Maskell, Roger..............4:35:59 (18,646)
Maskell, Simon..............4:13:39 (13,165)
Maskens, David..............4:04:38 (11,207)
Maslen, Andy..............3:58:38 (9,867)
Mason, Adam..............5:13:00 (25,973)
Mason, Christopher..............2:53:17 (502)
Mason, Christopher..............3:48:35 (7,420)
Mason, Daniel..............5:33:10 (28,389)
Mason, David..............5:14:58 (26,242)
Mason, Glenn..............6:01:18 (30,314)
Mason, Gregory..............4:21:27 (15,100)
Mason, Harry..............4:46:16 (21,035)
Mason, Jack..............3:24:12 (3,285)
Mason, James..............4:15:43 (13,676)
Mason, James..............4:20:50 (14,938)
Mason, John..............3:18:08 (2,568)
Mason, John..............3:41:55 (6,135)
Mason, Mark..............3:20:51 (2,865)
Mason, Mark..............4:20:08 (14,779)
Mason, Martin..............4:31:23 (17,589)
Mason, Mike..............3:37:09 (5,264)
Mason, Neil..............4:45:51 (20,926)
Mason, Pete..............3:59:13 (10,007)
Mason, Peter..............3:56:20 (9,280)
Mason, Peter..............4:03:43 (10,987)
Mason, Philip..............4:36:21 (18,733)
Mason, Richard..............2:58:30 (798)
Mason, Richard..............4:35:49 (18,603)
Mason, Russell..............4:13:08 (13,030)
Mason, Russell..............4:27:44 (16,660)
Mason, Simon..............3:51:38 (8,116)
Mason, Simon..............5:17:53 (26,592)
Mason, Stephen..............5:02:54 (24,444)
Mason, Steve..............3:55:13 (8,969)
Mason, Tom..............3:57:16 (9,522)
Mason, Trevor..............6:46:59 (31,654)
Massaloux, Christopher..............3:23:21 (3,156)

Massei, Ennio..............4:48:05 (21,448)
Massey, Adrian..............3:15:00 (2,238)
Massey, Daniel..............3:22:12 (3,011)
Massey, Graeme..............3:54:31 (8,788)
Massey, Ian..............4:01:47 (10,594)
Massey, Ian..............5:35:25 (28,589)
Massey, Jim..............4:37:13 (18,925)
Massey, Julian..............5:01:32 (24,236)
Massey, Raymond..............4:16:54 (13,964)
Massey, Stephen..............4:11:28 (12,636)
Massie, Keith..............4:55:34 (23,042)
Massier, Stephane..............3:07:38 (1,466)
Massingham, George..............4:01:21 (10,508)
Massingham, Paul..............2:59:58 (935)
Masterman, Darren..............5:06:30 (25,016)
Masterman, Kerrin..............4:21:53 (15,203)
Masters, Dominic..............3:27:40 (3,762)
Masters, Julian..............3:54:27 (8,768)
Masters, Neil..............4:21:52 (15,199)
Masterson, Antony..............3:41:13 (5,995)
Masterson, David..............4:28:31 (16,861)
Masterson, John..............3:55:44 (9,116)
Mastrini, Gianni..............4:44:43 (20,663)
Mastrodicasa, Andrea..............2:44:03 (219)
Masuto, Hiroshi..............3:10:00 (1,673)
Matcham, Chris..............4:56:30 (23,263)
Mather, Christopher..............5:54:14 (29,950)
Mather, Miles..............5:53:01 (29,880)
Mathers, Ian..............5:27:02 (27,778)
Mathias, Michael..............4:41:23 (19,844)
Mathieson, Charles..............5:06:05 (24,966)
Mathieson, Colin..............3:02:20 (1,080)
Mathieson, Grant..............3:54:15 (8,716)
Mathieson, Neil..............4:06:13 (11,539)
Mathieson, Steven..............3:31:54 (4,458)
Mathieu, Mark..............4:27:01 (16,478)
Mathurin, Mark..............4:10:11 (12,389)
Maton, David..............4:26:53 (16,444)
Matson, Alistair..............3:13:37 (2,073)
Matsunaga, Shiro..............3:39:14 (5,642)
Mattera Junior, Mimmo..............4:42:07 (20,014)
Matthams, David..............4:35:15 (18,459)
Matthews, Alan..............3:27:54 (3,801)
Matthews, Alan..............3:54:48 (8,868)
Matthews, Andrew..............3:42:27 (6,231)
Matthews, Barry..............3:25:50 (3,516)
Matthews, Christopher..............4:12:53 (12,978)
Matthews, Christopher..............4:13:58 (13,251)
Matthews, David..............3:29:59 (4,163)
Matthews, David..............5:06:35 (25,031)
Matthews, Dene..............5:40:32 (29,036)
Matthews, Dominic..............5:25:57 (27,659)
Matthews, Dylan..............4:23:27 (15,603)
Matthews, Gerry..............5:34:15 (28,500)
Matthews, James..............4:22:12 (15,295)
Matthews, Julian..............4:27:29 (16,600)
Matthews, Kevin..............4:32:49 (17,905)
Matthews, Mark..............3:35:19 (4,960)
Matthews, Raymond..............5:07:39 (25,212)
Matthews, Richard..............4:21:47 (15,180)
Matthews, Robin..............4:05:13 (11,333)
Matthews, Ryan..............3:37:01 (5,235)
Matthews, Sean..............4:40:08 (19,565)
Mattingley, Chris..............4:09:05 (12,150)
Mattison, Michael..............2:50:26 (400)
Mattocks, Craig..............3:00:58 (999)
Matus, Phil..............4:49:04 (21,646)
Matyska, Tomas..............3:29:45 (4,134)
Maude, Christian..............4:14:31 (13,384)
Mauduit, G..............4:39:40 (19,469)
Mauer, Florian..............4:19:35 (14,636)
Mauger, St John..............4:44:44 (20,668)
Maughan, Gary..............4:19:25 (14,599)
Maughan-Brown, Anthony..............4:04:41 (11,222)
Mauldon, Kenneth..............4:08:34 (12,029)
Maund, Bill..............3:47:51 (7,293)
Maurer, Daniel..............5:04:13 (24,665)
Maurer, Walter..............3:16:52 (2,412)
Mauret, Louis..............3:28:47 (3,966)
Maury, Neil..............3:45:04 (6,746)
Mautschke, Brendon..............4:03:39 (10,973)
Maw, Tim..............4:52:25 (22,381)
Mawby, Edward..............3:11:45 (1,828)

Mawby, Stephen..............4:27:39 (16,638)
Mawer, Richard..............4:10:23 (12,438)
Mawer, Roger..............4:15:59 (13,738)
Mawhinney, Patrick..............5:27:15 (27,807)
Mawle, Edward..............4:13:49 (13,205)
Mawle, Roger..............4:21:10 (15,027)
Mawson, Julian..............2:41:12 (169)
Maxwell, Gregor..............4:50:01 (21,862)
Maxwell, Marcus..............2:57:11 (716)
May, Andrew..............3:42:30 (6,248)
May, Bryan..............3:42:09 (6,178)
May, Christopher..............4:44:35 (20,629)
May, David..............3:29:41 (4,124)
May, David..............5:21:48 (27,125)
May, Dean..............5:03:57 (24,624)
May, Douglas..............4:16:24 (13,833)
May, Gavin..............2:56:59 (702)
May, Geoff..............5:25:12 (27,574)
May, Giles..............3:12:16 (1,893)
May, Graham..............3:00:38 (984)
May, Graham..............5:19:14 (26,789)
May, Ian..............4:03:05 (10,865)
May, Kevin..............3:03:51 (1,171)
May, Kieron..............4:23:47 (15,692)
May, Philip..............4:34:36 (18,307)
May, Stephen..............4:05:17 (11,349)
May, William..............3:57:50 (9,658)
Mayard, Didier..............3:41:35 (6,084)
Maybury, Paul..............4:30:19 (17,312)
Maydew, James..............4:44:52 (20,689)
Maye, Alan..............3:11:14 (1,777)
Mayer, Johann..............4:11:29 (12,643)
Mayer, Raoul..............3:39:51 (5,761)
Mayer, Wolfgang..............3:41:50 (6,120)
Mayers, Douglas..............5:29:45 (28,065)
Mayers, Nick..............4:20:04 (14,761)
Mayers, Richard..............3:41:41 (6,090)
Mayes, Colin..............7:00:43 (31,897)
Mayes, Stephen..............5:44:55 (29,357)
Mayfield, Oliver..............5:59:47 (30,248)
Mayhew, Adam..............4:26:35 (16,375)
Mayhew, Joseph..............4:16:38 (13,885)
Mayhook, Mark..............3:41:25 (6,047)
Maynard, Graham..............3:19:40 (2,721)
Mayne, James..............3:37:22 (5,300)
Mayo, Simon..............6:32:07 (31,383)
Mays, Bob..............4:17:05 (14,007)
Maywood, Bryan..............5:00:50 (24,128)
Mazzarini, Pascal..............3:38:46 (5,555)
Mbuyi, Joseph..............4:06:56 (11,675)
McAdam, William..............4:38:52 (19,295)
McAleer, Richard..............5:26:00 (27,672)
McAllister, Mark..............4:13:26 (13,107)
McAllister, Richard..............5:07:43 (25,226)
McAllister, William..............3:51:29 (8,068)
McAlpine, Daniel..............5:32:16 (28,312)
McAlpine, Stephen..............4:39:12 (19,374)
McAra, Adrian..............3:51:50 (8,159)
McArthur, Antony..............4:24:04 (15,771)
McAteer, Michael..............3:32:28 (4,527)
McAuley, Jason..............6:54:36 (31,820)
McAuley, Michael..............4:29:57 (17,229)
McAvoy, John..............4:52:52 (22,477)
McAvoy, Stephen..............4:31:52 (17,701)
McBoyle, Andrew..............5:29:02 (27,994)
McBride, David..............4:38:43 (19,257)
McBride, Gavin..............5:21:02 (27,027)
McBride, Hugh..............6:53:23 (31,798)
McBride, Thomas..............3:12:00 (1,861)
McBrien, James..............4:06:08 (11,522)
McCabe, Alan..............4:38:16 (19,150)
McCabe, Edward..............3:32:37 (4,544)
McCabe, Harry..............4:56:49 (23,344)
McCaffery, Paul..............5:12:22 (25,876)
McCaffery, Stephen..............3:13:04 (2,001)
McCaffrey, Robert..............3:50:33 (7,854)
McCaig, Colan..............3:15:01 (2,241)
McCall, Stephen..............4:17:35 (14,132)
McCallion, Seamus..............3:18:36 (2,617)
McCallum, Iain..............4:30:56 (17,476)
McCallum, John..............3:49:28 (7,624)
McCann, Alastair..............4:32:01 (17,736)
McCann, Alec..............3:37:09 (5,264)

McCann, Joe 2:55:49 (638)
McCann, John 3:48:03 (7,328)
McCann, John 3:55:33 (9,062)
McCann, John 5:13:34 (26,052)
McCann, Joseph 4:53:27 (22,609)
McCann, Neil 4:15:33 (13,652)
McCann, Patrick 5:13:22 (26,019)
McCann, Sean 4:52:43 (22,441)
McCann, Stephen 5:51:53 (29,824)
McCann, Thomas 5:22:34 (27,222)
McCarrick, Cian 3:44:47 (6,685)
McCarrick, Derek 6:07:47 (30,560)
McCarter, Dominic 2:43:03 (201)
McCarthy, Bernard 6:37:32 (31,496)
McCarthy, Brian 4:45:47 (20,908)
McCarthy, Colin 6:32:52 (31,398)
McCarthy, Gregory 6:57:53 (31,872)
McCarthy, Hugh 4:34:29 (18,286)
McCarthy, Martin 3:57:47 (9,642)
McCarthy, Michael 3:24:59 (3,393)
McCarthy, Michael 4:22:11 (15,291)
McCarthy, Michael 5:12:03 (25,833)
McCarthy, Neil 5:13:04 (25,982)
McCarthy, Paul 4:06:43 (11,630)
McCarthy, Peter 5:46:20 (29,456)
McCarthy, Robert 4:08:04 (11,917)
McCarthy, Stephen 4:46:56 (21,172)
McCarthy, Trevor 3:59:47 (10,173)
McCartney, David 3:33:22 (4,657)
McCartney, Peter 3:28:29 (3,900)
McCartney, Samuel 4:32:58 (17,944)
McCauley, Jason 4:14:15 (13,319)
McCavera, Kevin 4:12:28 (12,876)
McCaw, Andrew 3:54:15 (8,716)
McCay, Patrick 5:18:56 (26,748)
McClelland, John 3:39:13 (5,633)
McClelland, Paul 2:52:21 (462)
McClintock, Neil 4:33:59 (18,162)
McCloskey, Emyr 4:46:35 (21,104)
McCloskey, Michael 3:54:21 (8,738)
McClure, Charlie 3:46:05 (6,950)
McCluskey, Brian 4:36:34 (18,781)
McCluskey, Mark 4:26:51 (16,439)
McCole, Andrew 5:09:22 (25,459)
McColl, Christopher 5:52:03 (29,833)
McColl, Ewen 3:01:58 (1,051)
McCombie, Derek 3:43:41 (6,486)
McConalogue, Ian 6:08:19 (30,577)
McConville, John 3:11:51 (1,842)
McCoo, Alastair 4:31:25 (17,595)
McCorkell, Michael 3:40:40 (5,897)
McCormack, Alan 4:49:33 (21,761)
McCormack, Ben 4:12:48 (12,959)
McCormack, David 5:48:39 (29,614)
McCormack, James 3:54:52 (8,885)
McCormack, Sean 3:15:56 (2,329)
McCormack, Steven 3:32:30 (4,532)
McCormick, Andrew 3:17:58 (2,550)
McCormick, Andrew 4:31:14 (17,553)
McCormick, Bernard 4:30:02 (17,248)
McCormick, Brian 4:49:32 (21,758)
McCormick, Duncan 4:16:50 (13,941)
McCormick, Graham 3:07:25 (1,445)
McCosh, Gavin 4:43:42 (20,431)
McCosker, Albert 4:15:29 (13,635)
McCoy, Andrew 2:42:53 (193)
McCoy, David 3:18:37 (2,620)
McCoy, Robin 3:09:45 (1,652)
McCoy, Trevor 5:20:27 (26,947)
McCreadie, Duane 4:11:34 (12,660)
McCreanor, Andrew 5:35:13 (28,574)
McCrorie, Thomas 6:52:36 (31,772)
McCrossin, Paul 3:22:56 (3,101)
McCubbing, Mark 4:48:25 (21,520)
McCullagh, Nicholas 4:19:19 (14,576)
McCullagh, Peter 7:03:49 (31,920)
McCullagh, Rolf 3:43:01 (6,372)
McCulley, Donald 7:04:49 (31,930)
McCulloch, David 3:55:05 (8,933)
McCulloch, Howard 3:37:53 (5,397)
McCullough, Alexander 5:42:35 (29,215)
McCusker, Charles 4:07:12 (11,737)
McDade, Gary 4:47:46 (21,364)
McDade, Malcolm 4:53:52 (22,691)
McDade, Norman 4:50:42 (22,011)
McDaid, Gerard 3:25:08 (3,413)
McDermott, Damian 4:00:15 (10,278)
McDermott, David 5:16:37 (26,439)
McDermott, Dominic 3:09:46 (1,653)
McDermott, Ian 4:33:32 (18,066)
McDermott, Ian 4:35:45 (18,580)
McDermott, John 3:08:52 (1,576)
McDermott, Michael 5:38:23 (28,849)
McDermott, Paul 3:00:48 (992)
McDermott, Stephen 6:24:47 (31,155)
McDonagh, Barry 3:45:22 (6,799)
McDonagh, John 4:55:26 (23,013)
McDonagh, Nicholas 3:23:17 (3,148)
McDonald, Andrew 4:04:34 (11,191)
McDonald, Andy 4:44:33 (20,622)
McDonald, Christopher 5:39:36 (28,958)
McDonald, Damien 4:54:48 (22,882)
McDonald, Glynn 3:36:34 (5,156)
McDonald, Lee 4:01:06 (10,449)
McDonald, Mark 4:45:48 (20,913)
McDonald, Neil 3:13:39 (2,080)
McDonald, Steven 6:04:32 (30,430)
McDonald, Thomas 4:28:33 (16,874)
McDonald, Tony 4:05:32 (11,406)
McDonald, Liam 4:13:31 (13,130)
McDonald-Liggins, Anthony 3:53:11 (8,470)
McDonnell, Bill 3:52:53 (8,393)
McDonnell, Christopher 3:03:05 (1,123)
McDonnell, Fergal 3:52:55 (8,399)
McDonnell, James 2:50:54 (417)
McDonnell, Matthew 4:24:32 (15,871)
McDonnell, Padraig 3:05:13 (1,270)
McDonnell, Terence 5:08:05 (25,276)
McDougal, George 3:10:24 (1,713)
McDougal, Richard 3:43:09 (6,396)
McDowall, Alastair 3:20:19 (2,805)
McDowall, Ewan 4:51:34 (22,217)
McDowell, Andrew 4:32:48 (17,898)
McDuff, Michael 4:26:58 (16,462)
McElheron, Michael 4:31:28 (17,607)
McElhill, Jonathan 4:09:51 (12,313)
McElhinney, Dermot 4:53:23 (22,591)
McElhinney, Martin 4:55:16 (22,973)
McElhinney, Philip 3:57:44 (9,628)
McElroy, Thomas 3:45:19 (6,794)
McEntee, Colin 4:14:09 (13,298)
McEntee, Scott 4:14:11 (13,302)
McEntegart, Damian 4:54:28 (22,808)
McEvoy, Anthony 5:00:26 (24,057)
McEvoy, Ciaran 5:05:02 (24,796)
McEvoy, Peter 4:47:51 (21,391)
McEvoy, Sean 4:48:51 (21,600)
McEwan, Jock 4:36:40 (18,800)
McEwan, Joe 4:16:28 (13,850)
McEwen, Daniel 4:17:24 (14,090)
McEwen, Thomas 3:58:14 (9,764)
McFadden, Stephen 4:29:12 (17,039)
McFadyen, Iain 4:50:43 (22,018)
McFadyen, James 4:42:58 (20,222)
McFall, Scott 5:41:46 (29,142)
McFarland, Eric 4:48:32 (21,537)
McFarlane, Callum 4:35:29 (18,515)
McFarlane, Frank 4:51:04 (22,091)
McFarlane, Jamie 4:12:26 (12,867)
McFarlane, John 3:35:58 (5,061)
McFarlane, Lindsay 4:12:26 (12,867)
McFarnon, Gregory 4:38:39 (19,238)
McFeat, Ian 4:49:44 (21,809)
McGaffin, Philip 4:02:00 (10,634)
McGannan, Joseph 5:55:59 (30,041)
McGarr, Gerry 3:34:32 (4,843)
McGarry, Christopher 3:38:52 (5,573)
McGarry, Frank 3:38:37 (5,521)
McGarry, Kevin 3:39:05 (5,613)
McGarty, William 4:55:49 (23,114)
McGaughey, James 2:23:49 (34)
McGavigan, Peter 4:28:54 (16,968)
McGee, David 4:08:26 (11,989)
McGee, Gareth 2:57:58 (764)
McGee, Kevin 4:14:03 (13,275)
McGee, Philip 4:45:02 (20,725)
McGee, Christopher 3:47:06 (7,141)
McGeever, Keith 5:58:15 (30,171)
McGeoch, William 5:39:06 (28,910)
McGeorge, Alistair 4:41:01 (19,754)
McGeough, Peter 3:19:06 (2,662)
McGhee, Gary 3:15:32 (2,294)
McGibbon, Thomas 4:12:29 (12,880)
McGill, Clive 4:55:07 (22,944)
McGill, Gordon 4:29:24 (17,089)
McGill, Hugh 3:41:00 (5,957)
McGill, James 3:55:46 (9,120)
McGillan, David 4:10:24 (12,444)
McGillivray, Gordon 3:56:50 (9,407)
McGinley, Mark 4:26:48 (16,430)
McGinley, Stephen 5:47:30 (29,534)
McGinn, Eoin 3:22:54 (3,098)
McGinn, Nicholas 4:11:55 (12,747)
McGinn, Patrick 4:01:16 (10,486)
McGinnigle, John 5:14:26 (26,164)
McGinnity, Nigel 5:32:58 (28,372)
McGirr, Conor 3:55:51 (9,144)
McGivern, Jeremy 3:28:34 (3,913)
McGivern, Mark 3:20:59 (2,882)
McGlachie, Steven 4:17:10 (14,027)
McGlade, David 3:57:39 (9,607)
McGlennon, David 2:59:48 (926)
McGlone, Adam 4:16:19 (13,809)
McGlynn, James 3:29:22 (4,060)
McGlynn, Peter 4:53:05 (22,517)
McGlynn, Robert 3:28:49 (3,974)
McGlynn, Stephen 3:15:27 (2,282)
McGovern, Andrew 3:52:04 (8,213)
McGovern, John 5:30:41 (28,162)
McGovern, Stephen 4:37:10 (18,912)
McGovern, Tony 3:45:03 (6,741)
McGowan, John 6:06:48 (30,523)
McGowan, Michael 3:18:43 (2,627)
McGowan, Paul 6:58:04 (31,874)
McGowan, Peter 5:34:50 (28,543)
McGowan, Robert 7:34:39 (32,181)
McGowan, Roy 5:25:48 (27,641)
McGowan, Stuart 3:28:52 (3,982)
McGowan, Glen 3:36:02 (5,069)
McGranaghan, Sean 4:32:21 (17,801)
McGrath, Chris 5:16:31 (26,428)
McGrath, Martin 4:47:17 (21,243)
McGrath, Michael 3:02:09 (1,066)
McGrath, Richard 3:27:03 (3,688)
McGrath, Stephen 4:45:29 (20,847)
McGraw, Paul 4:56:47 (23,334)
McGregor, Campbell 3:13:28 (2,059)
McGregor, David 2:31:30 (70)
McGregor, Ian 3:52:12 (8,243)
McGregor, John 5:27:13 (27,804)
McGregor, Stuart 4:21:38 (15,139)
McGroarty, Andrew 3:56:17 (9,268)
McGuckin, Ultan 4:19:04 (14,521)
McGuigan, Malachy 3:58:21 (9,796)
McGuigan, Paul 3:19:10 (2,667)
McGuiness, Stephen 2:47:04 (302)
McGuinness, Michael 5:30:45 (28,172)
McGuinness, Pat 4:35:55 (18,625)
McGuire, Danny 4:59:46 (23,935)
McGuire, Raymond 6:37:17 (31,494)
McGuire, Robert 4:24:28 (15,860)
McGuone, Paul 4:36:19 (18,717)
McGurk, Joe 2:53:15 (500)
McHale, Barry 6:02:36 (30,360)
McHale, Philip 5:11:45 (25,792)
McHollan, Nigel 5:19:32 (26,832)
McHugh, Bernard 3:42:17 (6,202)
McHugh, Cian 3:39:00 (5,598)
McHugh, Duncan 5:47:18 (29,515)
McHugh, Michael 4:07:44 (11,859)
McHugh, Noel 4:37:28 (18,975)
McHugh, Peter 3:31:30 (4,412)
McHugh, Ray 7:26:52 (32,127)
McHugh, Stephen 3:29:50 (4,149)
McHugh, Timothy 4:30:31 (17,370)
McIlveen-Wright, David 4:59:30 (23,886)
McInerney, John 4:06:09 (11,526)
McInerney, Michael 4:03:19 (10,916)
McInnes, Andrew 3:28:21 (3,874)

McInnes, Duncan 4:30:48 (17,447)
McInteer, Warren 5:08:05 (25,276)
McIntosh, Doug 4:22:56 (15,478)
McIntosh, Graeme 4:04:39 (11,210)
McIntosh, Mark 3:20:08 (2,775)
McIntyre, Andrew 4:01:49 (10,605)
McIntyre, Angus 3:39:58 (5,777)
McIntyre, Eddie 4:03:39 (10,973)
McIntyre, James 4:58:14 (23,633)
McIntyre, Russell 3:36:56 (5,218)
McIntyre, Stewart 3:37:46 (5,381)
McIntyre, Toby 5:09:58 (25,536)
McIntyre, William 5:14:41 (26,200)
McInulty, David 4:53:26 (22,602)
McIver, Duncan 3:31:13 (4,362)
McIver, Neil 4:58:09 (23,617)
McIvor, Stephen 4:26:46 (16,421)
McKane, Christopher 4:59:36 (23,903)
McKanna, Donald 4:32:49 (17,905)
McKay, Chris 4:39:54 (19,518)
McKay, Robert 3:18:10 (2,575)
McKay, Sinclair 3:56:21 (9,284)
McKay, Steven 4:18:29 (14,351)
McKechnie, James 4:32:52 (17,918)
McKee, Robert 5:17:03 (26,486)
McKell, Tim 4:17:42 (14,176)
McKellar, James 4:04:25 (11,157)
McKenna, Gerard 4:11:21 (12,612)
McKenna, Martin 4:50:51 (22,043)
McKenna, Michael 5:57:29 (30,138)
McKenning, Matthew 4:56:16 (23,214)
McKenzie, Duncan 4:05:50 (11,465)
McKenzie, Gerard 5:26:57 (27,774)
McKenzie, Grahame 3:15:51 (2,320)
McKenzie, Ian 3:57:36 (9,597)
McKenzie, Matthew 4:00:57 (10,419)
McKenzie, Rob 4:56:11 (23,195)
McKenzie, Robert 4:19:27 (14,605)
McKenzie-Cook, Terrence 6:01:04 (30,301)
McKeon, David 4:06:55 (11,674)
McKeown, Brendan 3:39:19 (5,658)
McKeown, Jeremy 3:58:32 (9,844)
McKeown, Michael 4:11:31 (12,650)
McKeown, Peter 3:37:28 (5,321)
McKerr, Gary 3:56:56 (9,439)
McKerracher, John 4:16:17 (13,804)
McKevith, James 4:50:42 (22,011)
McKidd, Laurence 3:40:19 (5,847)
McKie, Richard 4:49:38 (21,786)
McKinlay, Mark 5:24:36 (27,489)
McKinlay, Michael 4:17:59 (14,249)
McKinley, John 3:21:46 (2,961)
McKinney, Charles 5:33:20 (28,405)
McKinney, Robert 5:01:06 (24,168)
McKnight, Simon 4:51:12 (22,132)
McLachlan, Hamish 5:01:49 (24,284)
McLachlan, Robert 4:53:27 (22,609)
McLaren, Bruce 3:32:17 (4,504)
McLaren, Duncan 3:57:02 (9,464)
McLaren, Iain 3:49:35 (7,652)
McLaren, John 4:46:33 (21,098)
McLaren, Larry 4:54:55 (22,906)
McLaughlin, Andrew 3:59:09 (9,991)
McLaughlin, Ciaran 4:49:23 (21,722)
McLaughlin, Clifton 5:12:47 (25,942)
McLaughlin, David 4:19:58 (14,731)
McLaughlin, David 5:30:18 (28,117)
McLaughlin, Gary 3:54:37 (8,824)
McLaughlin, Liam 5:33:42 (28,436)
McLaughlin, Paul 3:54:08 (8,687)
McLaughlin, Simon 3:41:30 (6,067)
McLean, Craig 4:09:10 (12,167)
McLean, David 3:46:11 (6,969)
McLean, Warren 6:32:03 (31,381)
McLeese, Leslie 6:46:43 (31,651)
McLennan, Norman 2:51:35 (434)
McLennan, Ross 4:04:59 (11,284)
McLennon, David 4:25:53 (16,224)
McLeod, Alastair 4:03:35 (10,964)
McLeod, Benjamin 4:34:18 (18,241)
McLeod, Chad 3:24:48 (3,372)
McLeod, Gary 5:12:34 (25,916)
McLeod, Roderick 3:39:04 (5,611)
McLeod, John 4:15:02 (13,520)
McLoughlin, Liam 5:32:50 (28,363)
McLoughlin, Rob 4:17:37 (14,147)
McLoughlin, Stephen 3:55:28 (9,039)
McLoughlin, Steven 4:11:02 (12,546)
McLullick, Richard 4:30:27 (17,357)
McMahon, Bernard 4:21:57 (15,224)
McMahon, Damon 4:31:02 (17,510)
McManus, Brendan 3:40:40 (5,897)
McManus, Gary 5:15:46 (26,352)
McManus, Graham 3:59:49 (10,180)
McManus, Kevin 3:57:57 (9,694)
McMenanin, William 4:10:47 (12,508)
McMillan, Charlie 6:04:55 (30,452)
McMillan, David 4:41:34 (19,885)
McMillan, David 4:55:21 (22,991)
McMillan, Duncan 3:28:20 (3,872)
McMillan, Michael 4:35:27 (18,507)
McMillan, Stephen 5:10:42 (25,648)
McMillan, David 3:15:30 (2,289)
McMinn, Andrew 3:54:49 (8,870)
McMonagle, Jamie 2:59:00 (851)
McMonagle, Noel 3:28:41 (3,940)
McMullan, Edward 4:27:37 (16,628)
McMullan, John 3:38:33 (5,504)
McMullan, Tristan 6:13:15 (30,774)
McMullen, Thomas 4:21:06 (15,004)
McMyler, Sean 2:54:33 (563)
McNally, John 3:57:03 (9,469)
McNally, John 4:07:26 (11,788)
McNally, Joseph 4:37:14 (18,934)
McNally, Simon 5:12:25 (25,883)
McNamara, Paul 3:22:40 (3,067)
McNamara, Peter 4:30:40 (17,411)
McNaught, Keith 4:39:30 (19,439)
McNaull, Allisdhair 3:55:12 (8,966)
McNealy, Steve 3:30:03 (4,172)
McNeil, James 3:44:11 (6,577)
McNeill, Andrew 4:24:41 (15,911)
McNeill, Edward 5:27:34 (27,842)
McNeill, Mark 4:31:54 (17,707)
McNelis, Robin 3:04:33 (1,216)
McNicholas, Vincent 4:55:34 (23,042)
McNicoll, Keith 3:50:59 (7,946)
McNish, Michael 5:00:47 (24,123)
McNulty, Micheal 4:27:29 (16,600)
McNutt, James 4:35:07 (18,417)
McParland, Gerard 3:05:04 (1,259)
McParland, John 3:27:10 (3,700)
McPetrie, Rupert 4:20:49 (14,931)
McPhail, Stuart 3:57:42 (9,617)
McPherson, Dick 5:50:11 (29,732)
McQueen, Gregor 4:17:46 (14,200)
McQuillan, Ross 4:21:52 (15,199)
McRobb, Douglas 3:43:51 (6,521)
McShane, Desmond 3:07:47 (1,486)
McSherry, John 4:34:37 (18,311)
McSorley, Eugene 4:44:52 (20,689)
McSparron, Paul 4:37:44 (19,029)
McSweeney, Brian 4:43:25 (20,354)
McSweeney, Christopher 4:15:07 (13,544)
McSweeney, Rodney 6:11:43 (30,716)
McSwiggan, Christopher 3:55:40 (9,098)
McTeare, Andrew 4:27:02 (16,480)
McVea, Darrell 5:05:54 (24,944)
McVey, Geoffrey 4:11:53 (12,735)
McWilliam, Craig 3:09:46 (1,653)
McWilliams, David 4:38:52 (19,295)
Meacher, Barrington 4:45:20 (20,807)
Mead, Adrian 2:56:58 (700)
Mead, Michael 6:06:01 (30,504)
Mead, Paul 4:18:56 (14,492)
Mead, Richard 4:06:38 (11,613)
Mead, Stephen 4:47:18 (21,247)
Meade, Mike 3:51:19 (8,037)
Meadow, Alan 4:33:50 (18,123)
Meadowcroft, Jonathan 4:19:38 (14,650)
Meadows, Chris 4:50:22 (21,935)
Meadows, David 4:27:07 (16,502)
Meadows, Geoffrey 4:13:07 (13,026)
Meadows, Lee 4:14:45 (13,434)
Meads, Jason 4:52:21 (22,369)
Meadwell, Andrew 5:40:00 (28,992)
Meagor, David 3:28:00 (3,814)
Meakin, Anthony 4:36:31 (18,775)
Meakin, Paul 4:13:42 (13,176)
Meaking, Billy 3:24:20 (3,307)
Mealing, Barry 3:50:15 (7,788)
Meaney, Damon 6:19:45 (31,007)
Mears, David 4:05:54 (11,483)
Mears, Matthew 4:55:08 (22,949)
Measham, Hayden 4:55:45 (23,097)
Measures, Christopher 4:18:39 (14,407)
Measures, Keith 4:24:43 (15,924)
Medcraft, Peter 4:33:48 (18,115)
Meddeman, Kevin 4:03:14 (10,891)
Medici, Giuliano 3:31:10 (4,355)
Medley, Malcolm 3:49:47 (7,696)
Medlock, Richard 4:42:56 (20,213)
Medway, Jim 3:51:10 (8,002)
Mee, Colin 3:01:30 (1,024)
Mee, John 4:43:11 (20,281)
Mee, Paul 3:14:36 (2,198)
Mee, Terry 3:54:03 (8,674)
Meehan, Leonard 3:23:33 (3,185)
Meehl, Greg 3:26:20 (3,581)
Meek, Andrew 4:39:40 (19,469)
Meek, David 4:53:26 (22,602)
Meek, Graham 5:14:25 (26,161)
Meek, Jonathan 3:15:39 (2,305)
Meeks, Vincent 5:38:37 (28,869)
Meek-Welsh, Andrew 4:09:14 (12,181)
Meenan, Niall 4:56:58 (23,371)
Meering, Richard 5:28:39 (27,954)
Meeser, Michael 4:21:18 (15,060)
Meier, Robert 3:39:11 (5,626)
Meiklejohn, Steven 3:49:22 (7,601)
Mein, Trevor 3:52:41 (8,353)
Mein, William 5:14:25 (26,161)
Meisterjahn, Thomas 5:42:04 (29,171)
Mekouar, Faycal 4:49:19 (21,707)
Melbourne, John 5:07:52 (25,244)
Melbourne, Steven 4:36:36 (18,789)
Melby, Brage 3:19:25 (2,693)
Meldrum, Julian 3:08:18 (1,524)
Meldrum, Samuel 4:18:48 (14,446)
Melhuish, David 6:56:19 (31,846)
Melia, Simon 6:38:39 (31,513)
Melik, Richard 3:06:16 (1,335)
Melindo, Giuseppe 5:05:01 (24,794)
Meller, David 2:49:42 (383)
Mello, Roberto 4:46:38 (21,112)
Mellon, James 3:51:03 (7,967)
Mellon, James 6:17:46 (30,916)
Mellon, Mark 3:07:26 (1,448)
Mellor, Aaron 4:31:01 (17,502)
Mellor, Charles 3:30:52 (4,307)
Mellor, Ian 4:06:23 (11,570)
Mellows, Steve 5:05:22 (24,852)
Melville, Derek 5:50:37 (29,761)
Mende, Thomas 3:45:44 (6,880)
Mendel, Rikard 3:22:42 (3,069)
Mendes, Aldo 3:14:02 (2,133)
Mendez, Pierre 3:21:44 (2,958)
Mendham, Gavin 3:07:58 (1,496)
Mends, Daniel 3:48:16 (7,371)
Menendez-Ros, Javier 3:49:59 (7,732)
Menken, Lars 4:21:56 (15,217)
Menon, David 4:11:46 (12,713)
Mensley, Peter 3:05:58 (1,318)
Mentis, Louis 4:47:38 (21,328)
Menzies, Paul 4:30:36 (17,391)
Mepham, Derek 4:13:47 (13,195)
Meppenstall, David 5:02:54 (24,444)
Mepstead, Sid 5:12:26 (25,885)
Mepsted, James 3:16:19 (2,359)
Mercer, Darren 4:03:31 (10,945)
Mercer, David 3:36:19 (5,118)
Mercer, David 4:36:22 (18,739)
Merckel, Daniel 3:08:47 (1,571)
Meredew, Paul 4:19:37 (14,647)
Meredith, Adrian 3:35:11 (4,939)
Meredith, Duncan 5:43:38 (29,280)
Meredith, Roy 3:44:28 (6,632)
Meredith, Sean 4:05:29 (11,399)
Meredith, Simon 2:49:52 (388)

Meredith, Tim 4:26:19 (16,317)
Meredith Jones, Daniel 4:25:01 (16,007)
Meregalli, Giuseppe 4:35:12 (18,442)
Mereweather, Ian 3:59:05 (9,977)
Merigeau, Eric 3:57:49 (9,650)
Merino, Victor 4:05:52 (11,473)
Merison, Paul 6:27:56 (31,263)
Merlin, Sam 3:28:25 (3,888)
Merrall, Grant 3:11:41 (1,819)
Merrath, Juergen 3:18:16 (2,584)
Merrell, Stephen 3:58:56 (9,951)
Merrels, Jason 4:52:29 (22,393)
Merrett, Edward 4:23:06 (15,512)
Merrick, Andrew 4:39:24 (19,421)
Merrick, Dean 3:57:08 (9,488)
Merricks, Joe 5:43:15 (29,258)
Merrics, Brian 5:18:27 (26,692)
Merrifield, Jeffrey 4:12:06 (12,786)
Merriman, Huw 4:54:30 (22,814)
Merrington, Michael 5:43:57 (29,304)
Merriott, Colin 3:07:46 (1,482)
Merritt, Anthony 4:46:50 (21,154)
Merritt, Keith 3:51:48 (8,149)
Merry, Nicholas 4:34:08 (18,198)
Merry, Thomas 4:34:08 (18,198)
Mersie, Wim 4:03:17 (10,911)
Mertens, Daniel 3:31:30 (4,412)
Mesney, Peter 4:04:02 (11,073)
Messa, José 5:07:23 (25,156)
Messinger, William 4:14:39 (13,413)
Meston, James 4:51:49 (22,270)
Meston, Thomas 3:12:24 (1,916)
Metanomski, Erik 4:41:26 (19,858)
Metcalf, Adrian 4:39:45 (19,488)
Metcalf, Alan 2:45:48 (252)
Metcalf, David 5:21:44 (27,117)
Metcalf, Lester 4:03:39 (10,973)
Metcalf, Richard 5:08:44 (25,360)
Metcalf, Robert 4:17:51 (14,218)
Metcalfe, Barry 3:47:08 (7,148)
Metcalfe, Chris 5:11:34 (25,770)
Metcalfe, John 3:50:28 (7,832)
Metcalfe, Len 3:57:58 (9,698)
Metcalfe, Robert 5:38:11 (28,828)
Metcalfe, Sam 4:52:13 (22,344)
Metherell, Timothy 4:35:08 (18,427)
Methley, David 4:20:05 (14,765)
Metraux, Claude 4:51:00 (22,070)
Mets, Martin 5:38:17 (28,835)
Mettler, René 3:58:47 (9,914)
Mewes, Lother 4:46:09 (21,006)
Meyer, Jacky 3:24:48 (3,372)
Meyer, Martin 5:41:04 (29,081)
Meyer, Rudiger 3:01:13 (1,012)
Meyer, Tobie 4:35:24 (18,495)
Meyer, Vaugan 4:13:24 (13,093)
Meyer Higgins, Matthew 5:54:46 (29,986)
Meziani, Fabrice 4:24:29 (15,864)
Mialhes, Olivier 4:10:59 (12,539)
Miao, Philip 4:43:26 (20,361)
Micallef, David 4:44:39 (20,649)
Micallef, Jean-Louis 4:28:54 (16,968)
Michael, Douglas 4:24:28 (15,860)
Michael, Simon 4:39:41 (19,471)
Michalitsianos, Jeremy 4:20:09 (14,783)
Michell, Ian 4:29:14 (17,049)
Michels, Stefaan 3:35:49 (5,044)
Michhiana, Ravinder 3:54:01 (8,670)
Mickleburgh, Trevor 3:48:54 (7,489)
Middendorp, Herman 4:21:19 (15,066)
Middleman, Steve 5:19:21 (26,807)
Middlemiss, Colin 4:34:56 (18,380)
Middleton, Andrew 3:56:00 (9,178)
Middleton, Clifford 3:37:11 (5,274)
Middleton, Clive 2:59:44 (921)
Middleton, Craig 4:01:38 (10,566)
Middleton, David 4:01:33 (10,549)
Middleton, Graham 4:12:38 (12,925)
Middleton, Ian 3:06:06 (1,329)
Middleton, James 5:03:42 (24,574)
Middleton, Kevan 3:53:26 (8,524)
Middleton, Mark 4:28:31 (16,861)
Middleton, Michael 3:54:54 (8,893)
Middleton, Neil 3:33:53 (4,730)
Middleton, Nicholas 4:28:21 (16,807)
Middleton, Paul 4:08:02 (11,911)
Middleton, Phil 4:24:23 (15,839)
Middleton, Simon 3:58:48 (9,918)
Middleton, Steven 4:07:57 (11,895)
Middleton, Stuart 4:07:34 (11,824)
Middleton, Thomas 3:13:23 (2,048)
Middleton, Timothy 5:03:00 (24,457)
Middlewick, Andrew 4:48:48 (21,590)
Midgley, David 4:14:26 (13,365)
Midgley, Martin 3:04:14 (1,198)
Midgley, Matthew 6:12:37 (30,754)
Midgley, Paul 4:23:05 (15,508)
Midgley, Richard 3:44:07 (6,567)
Miefret, Alain 3:55:21 (9,008)
Milburn, Alistair 4:19:53 (14,714)
Milburn, David 4:10:47 (12,508)
Milburn, Martin 6:29:35 (31,316)
Mildenhall, Mat 4:43:02 (20,243)
Mildon, Paul 4:15:58 (13,734)
Miles, Brian 3:57:17 (9,528)
Miles, Christopher 4:38:57 (19,315)
Miles, David 3:10:17 (1,702)
Miles, David 4:13:08 (13,030)
Miles, Jason 5:39:48 (28,970)
Miles, Mark 4:31:19 (17,570)
Miles, Neil 4:19:51 (14,704)
Miles, Nicholas 3:15:56 (2,329)
Miles, Paul 3:01:20 (1,014)
Miles, Paul 4:25:26 (16,126)
Miles, Robert 3:40:17 (5,839)
Miles, Robin 4:11:44 (12,702)
Miles, Stan 5:56:55 (30,102)
Miles, Stephen 4:24:00 (15,751)
Miles, Tim 4:09:32 (12,237)
Miles, Tom 4:29:44 (17,171)
Mileusnic, Christopher 3:38:42 (5,544)
Milford, Bruce 5:22:50 (27,258)
Milford, Simon 4:44:19 (20,576)
Milgate, Darren 4:38:31 (19,200)
Milici, Giuseppe 5:35:20 (28,583)
Milikowsky, Matthew 3:09:13 (1,601)
Milke, Ralf 2:56:23 (669)
Mill, Paul 4:38:06 (19,112)
Milla-Canals, Marti 3:49:34 (7,646)
Milla-Canals, Pau 3:49:35 (7,652)
Milla-Iglesis, Pere 3:49:34 (7,646)
Millan Formica, Matias 6:17:24 (30,904)
Millar, Colin 5:10:41 (25,645)
Millar, David 4:16:41 (13,900)
Millar, Gordon 4:13:47 (13,195)
Millar, James 4:13:54 (13,233)
Millar, James 5:03:47 (24,589)
Millar, Nicholas 3:03:53 (1,174)
Millar, Philip 5:02:50 (24,436)
Millard, Christopher 5:20:32 (26,960)
Millard, David 5:15:10 (26,274)
Millard, Iain 4:56:59 (23,378)
Millard, Jonathan 3:51:03 (7,967)
Millard, Ross 3:27:30 (3,738)
Millen, Reginald 4:43:25 (20,354)
Miller, Alan 3:33:42 (4,701)
Miller, Alan 5:30:14 (28,102)
Miller, Brian 5:45:46 (29,425)
Miller, Christopher 3:47:05 (7,140)
Miller, David 2:32:39 (79)
Miller, David 3:30:42 (4,277)
Miller, Frank 3:53:28 (8,531)
Miller, Graeme 3:08:07 (1,511)
Miller, Graham 4:12:37 (12,920)
Miller, Grant 4:26:29 (16,351)
Miller, Howard 3:50:57 (7,933)
Miller, Ian 3:15:21 (2,275)
Miller, James 3:46:13 (6,978)
Miller, James 4:03:53 (11,033)
Miller, Jim 4:01:57 (10,624)
Miller, Keith 4:24:05 (15,775)
Miller, Kenneth 4:22:07 (15,267)
Miller, Les 5:19:14 (26,789)
Miller, Michael 4:02:41 (10,779)
Miller, Michael 4:54:04 (22,723)
Miller, Paul 3:43:24 (6,437)
Miller, Paul 4:07:48 (11,871)
Miller, Paul 5:56:14 (30,063)
Miller, Philip 3:29:31 (4,098)
Miller, Philip 3:43:47 (6,504)
Miller, Richard 4:35:45 (18,580)
Miller, Roy 5:51:25 (29,807)
Miller, Stephen 3:43:48 (6,506)
Miller, Stephen 5:16:12 (26,394)
Miller, Steve 3:53:02 (8,433)
Miller, Toby 4:21:16 (15,049)
Millership, Stephen 5:10:47 (25,658)
Millican, Graham 3:45:21 (6,797)
Millican, Keith 3:45:22 (6,799)
Millichamp, Edward 5:11:38 (25,781)
Milligan, Ben 4:03:46 (11,002)
Milligan, Robert 3:28:15 (3,857)
Milligan, Steve 4:37:13 (18,925)
Millingen, Magnus 4:59:57 (23,975)
Millington, Mike 4:13:57 (13,244)
Millman, Geoffrey 5:14:55 (26,236)
Millross, Nigel 4:42:48 (20,180)
Mills, Alan 5:20:34 (26,965)
Mills, Andrew 3:58:33 (9,849)
Mills, Andrew 4:15:05 (13,536)
Mills, Christopher 3:49:30 (7,634)
Mills, Christopher 4:13:08 (13,030)
Mills, Christopher 6:01:07 (30,305)
Mills, Dane 4:56:13 (23,200)
Mills, Darren 4:29:51 (17,207)
Mills, David 4:12:27 (12,873)
Mills, David 4:29:34 (17,127)
Mills, Edward 3:36:53 (5,209)
Mills, Gerald 5:16:46 (26,458)
Mills, Glyn 5:29:52 (28,073)
Mills, Graham 4:49:17 (21,698)
Mills, Jeremy 3:56:28 (9,310)
Mills, Jon 3:47:14 (7,161)
Mills, Jonathan 3:44:06 (6,564)
Mills, Jonathan 4:50:43 (22,018)
Mills, Keith 4:35:07 (18,417)
Mills, Michael 4:13:37 (13,156)
Mills, Mike 4:24:09 (15,786)
Mills, Nathan 3:59:41 (10,146)
Mills, Nigel 4:08:48 (12,089)
Mills, Paul 3:58:54 (9,942)
Mills, Peter 5:23:00 (27,287)
Mills, Peter 5:39:40 (28,962)
Mills, Philip 5:20:21 (26,930)
Mills, Robert 4:36:00 (18,650)
Mills, Stuart 2:39:13 (148)
Mills, Stuart 3:14:11 (2,151)
Mills, Stuart 4:58:33 (23,709)
Mills, Terry 4:39:25 (19,423)
Mills, Tim 4:22:24 (15,342)
Mills, Victor 4:50:49 (22,034)
Millsip, David 5:21:43 (27,112)
Millward, Guy 4:58:22 (23,664)
Millward, Ian 4:40:00 (19,537)
Millward, Richard 5:03:41 (24,567)
Milne, Alex 4:48:32 (21,537)
Milne, Christopher 3:27:00 (3,681)
Milne, Colin 5:06:54 (25,094)
Milne, John 2:53:53 (526)
Milne, Simon 4:53:06 (22,521)
Milne, Stephen 3:29:06 (4,015)
Milner, David 3:31:09 (4,351)
Milner, Hartley 4:36:20 (18,722)
Milner, James 3:58:25 (9,813)
Milner, Rob 4:15:33 (13,652)
Milner, William 4:11:00 (12,543)
Milnes, Christopher 3:39:39 (5,720)
Milnes, Richard 4:06:15 (11,545)
Milone, Vito 4:19:13 (14,555)
Milsom, Peter 7:26:24 (32,124)
Milsom, Richard 4:33:17 (18,001)
Milton, Ben 3:38:59 (5,596)
Milton, Richard 3:38:42 (5,544)
Mine, Teiji 6:10:50 (30,682)
Mines, Ben 3:38:59 (5,596)
Minford, Mark 4:48:56 (21,620)
Minhall, Martin 4:25:13 (16,063)
Minihane, Jerry 5:03:21 (24,513)
Minihane, Ross 5:03:21 (24,513)

Minion, Chris	4:22:23 (15,336)	
Minkus, Christian	3:21:48 (2,964)	
Minnis, Jonathan	5:52:47 (29,871)	
Minnis, Mark	5:35:18 (28,581)	
Minnis, Michael	5:33:03 (28,377)	
Minogue, Ben	4:16:52 (13,954)	
Minor, James	5:03:49 (24,597)	
Minshull, Ian	4:05:04 (11,306)	
Minter, David	3:23:20 (3,153)	
Minton, Kevin	4:56:09 (23,182)	
Minty, Kevin	2:45:12 (240)	
Mioulane, Bernard	4:56:22 (23,236)	
Miramont, Frederick	3:33:26 (4,672)	
Miron, Paul	3:29:20 (4,050)	
Mirza, Rozib	4:11:47 (12,720)	
Miskell, Peter	3:06:39 (1,373)	
Miskin, Clive	3:31:53 (4,455)	
Misselbrook, Nigel	2:59:31 (904)	
Missirian, Carlo	4:28:39 (16,897)	
Mistry, Bharat	4:27:33 (16,614)	
Mistry, Bipinchandra	4:13:21 (13,083)	
Mistry, Janak	4:13:56 (13,242)	
Mistry, Jayanti	4:23:54 (15,720)	
Mitchell, Andy	2:59:01 (855)	
Mitchell, Anthony	4:54:48 (22,882)	
Mitchell, Bernard	4:36:14 (18,696)	
Mitchell, Bernie	3:55:53 (9,150)	
Mitchell, Cameron	4:19:31 (14,619)	
Mitchell, Carl	4:54:38 (22,846)	
Mitchell, Christopher	4:28:07 (16,740)	
Mitchell, Damian	3:55:41 (9,103)	
Mitchell, Ewan	3:03:26 (1,146)	
Mitchell, Gary	2:54:15 (552)	
Mitchell, Glen	3:58:31 (9,839)	
Mitchell, Ian	3:35:33 (5,005)	
Mitchell, Ian	5:16:53 (26,467)	
Mitchell, James	3:58:42 (9,886)	
Mitchell, James	4:45:14 (20,776)	
Mitchell, Jeremy	5:05:27 (24,867)	
Mitchell, Jonathan	4:09:29 (12,225)	
Mitchell, Jonathan	4:50:00 (21,856)	
Mitchell, Karl	4:22:28 (15,355)	
Mitchell, Mark	6:42:44 (31,586)	
Mitchell, Neil	3:30:32 (4,249)	
Mitchell, Neil	5:00:30 (24,069)	
Mitchell, Nick	4:41:35 (19,889)	
Mitchell, Paul	4:11:46 (12,713)	
Mitchell, Paul	5:36:59 (28,734)	
Mitchell, Robert	4:13:26 (13,107)	
Mitchell, Scott	2:41:05 (168)	
Mitchell, Simon	4:21:00 (14,979)	
Mitchell, Stephen	4:47:37 (21,322)	
Mitchell, Stephen	5:14:08 (26,112)	
Mitchell, Steve	3:38:07 (5,430)	
Mitchell, Vince	4:41:45 (19,931)	
Mitchell, Wayne	3:43:50 (6,514)	
Mitchelmore, David	4:18:54 (14,479)	
Mitchener, Paul	3:51:59 (8,191)	
Mitchinson, Jim	5:15:38 (26,335)	
Mitchinson, Russell	4:35:05 (18,411)	
Mitej, Ibrahim	2:19:53 (23)	
Mitford, Timothy	4:18:09 (14,279)	
Mitton, Alan	6:17:46 (30,916)	
Mlambo, Donald	4:06:25 (11,575)	
Mnomiya, Steven	4:48:58 (21,624)	
Moakes, David	4:26:19 (16,317)	
Moakes, Graham	4:55:17 (22,976)	
Moat, Andrew	3:55:49 (9,132)	
Moat, Chris	5:30:16 (28,110)	
Moaven, Amir	5:01:05 (24,163)	
Mobbs, Timothy	4:28:17 (16,785)	
Mocevic, Micha	4:29:47 (17,190)	
Modaher, Jasvir	5:26:37 (27,744)	
Moden, Ian	4:28:39 (16,897)	
Modi, Chetan	4:16:03 (13,750)	
Modley, Paul	3:43:52 (6,522)	
Moeller, Thor	4:06:50 (11,656)	
Moennig, Bernhard	3:46:50 (7,090)	
Moerk, Jacob	4:29:42 (17,162)	
Moffat, Stephen	2:47:59 (332)	
Moffatt, Alistair	3:37:15 (5,282)	
Moffatty, James	4:46:39 (21,116)	
Moffett, David	3:14:17 (2,161)	

Mogridge, Simon	5:07:41 (25,221)	
Mohamed, Omar	5:39:58 (28,990)	
Mohamed, Simon	5:13:27 (26,034)	
Mohammed, Adel	4:43:28 (20,367)	
Mohan, Bernard	4:22:23 (15,336)	
Mohan Raj, Prem	4:10:34 (12,478)	
Mohr, Dierk	4:35:52 (18,613)	
Moiba, Nathaniel	4:20:24 (14,848)	
Moir, Cameron	5:09:58 (25,536)	
Moisan, David	4:35:37 (18,544)	
Mokete, Moeketsi	5:39:22 (28,929)	
Mole, Denis	4:55:34 (23,042)	
Moles, David	4:55:33 (23,037)	
Mollart, Nicholas	4:00:09 (10,260)	
Moller-Butcher, Kristian	3:36:16 (5,108)	
Molloy, Anthony	4:13:10 (13,041)	
Molloy, Benjamin	3:32:18 (4,507)	
Molloy, Bernard	5:07:58 (25,265)	
Molloy, Lee	4:32:47 (17,894)	
Molloy, Michael	4:37:00 (18,878)	
Molloy, Peter	3:09:33 (1,637)	
Moloney, Der	3:31:27 (4,399)	
Molyneaux, Paul	3:58:10 (9,745)	
Molyneux, Alastair	5:08:23 (25,322)	
Molyneux, Damian	4:21:53 (15,203)	
Molyneux, Graham	3:14:44 (2,209)	
Molyneux, Paul	3:00:08 (947)	
Molyneux, Sidney	4:34:17 (18,234)	
Mommersteeg, Sjaak	3:48:58 (7,507)	
Monab, Kevin	4:16:51 (13,947)	
Monachon, Jean-Claude	3:54:32 (8,793)	
Monaghan, Andrew	5:30:32 (28,143)	
Monaghan, John	4:56:30 (23,263)	
Monahan, Daniel	4:04:51 (11,257)	
Monander, Sven	5:17:35 (26,558)	
Monasteri, Santi	3:46:07 (6,955)	
Moncrief, Edward	4:23:00 (15,494)	
Mondy, Didier	2:56:52 (695)	
Mone, Olaf	4:02:51 (10,817)	
Money, David	3:00:07 (946)	
Monger, Desmond	4:01:10 (10,465)	
Monin, Bernard	3:21:57 (2,978)	
Monk, Daniel	6:11:49 (30,718)	
Monk, Harold	4:56:55 (23,363)	
Monk, Paul	4:22:52 (15,458)	
Monk, Scott	4:07:43 (11,854)	
Monkhouse, Andrew	4:19:06 (14,530)	
Monks, Douglas	4:28:52 (16,958)	
Monks, Lewis	3:42:27 (6,231)	
Monks, Simon	5:42:03 (29,168)	
Monksq, Joseph	2:57:24 (728)	
Mons, Dieter	4:07:18 (11,756)	
Montague, John	3:02:12 (1,074)	
Montague, Peter	6:08:22 (30,580)	
Montague, Robin	6:55:20 (31,837)	
Montague, Tyree	3:22:01 (2,988)	
Montaner Gimenez, Juan A.	5:06:45 (25,066)	
Montet, Jean-Pierre	4:03:02 (10,850)	
Montgomerie, Raymond	4:54:27 (22,803)	
Montgomery, Edward	4:31:40 (17,663)	
Montgomery, Hugh	4:30:52 (17,459)	
Montgomery, James	6:22:20 (31,084)	
Montgomery, Kevin	4:15:09 (13,554)	
Montgomery, Malcolm	3:33:34 (4,690)	
Montgomery, Paul	4:13:08 (13,030)	
Montgomery, Simon	3:43:07 (6,390)	
Monticelli, Massimo	4:25:57 (16,240)	
Montorsi, Giuliano	4:17:46 (14,200)	
Monvoisin, François	4:09:50 (12,310)	
Moodie, Roland	4:39:43 (19,481)	
Moody, Colin	3:00:22 (963)	
Moody, David	4:16:38 (13,885)	
Moody, Douglas	3:18:30 (2,609)	
Moody, Ian	5:44:58 (29,364)	
Moody, John	6:37:38 (31,502)	
Moody, Paul	4:49:43 (21,806)	
Moody, Steve	3:53:35 (8,564)	
Moon, Chris	5:12:11 (25,851)	
Moonen, Tim	3:19:29 (2,699)	
Mooney, Christopher	4:16:51 (13,947)	
Mooney, Richard	5:56:44 (30,088)	
Moorby, Vinny	3:46:55 (7,108)	
Moorcraft, Robert	4:59:21 (23,866)	

Moore, Alex	5:13:16 (26,009)	
Moore, Allan	4:28:23 (16,817)	
Moore, Andrew	3:25:35 (3,473)	
Moore, Andrew	3:45:18 (6,788)	
Moore, Andrew	3:47:40 (7,251)	
Moore, Andrew	4:00:30 (10,327)	
Moore, Andrew	6:07:39 (30,556)	
Moore, Anthony	3:37:23 (5,305)	
Moore, Brett	3:32:57 (4,589)	
Moore, Brian	5:38:54 (28,889)	
Moore, Daniel	4:30:36 (17,391)	
Moore, David	3:35:13 (4,944)	
Moore, Donald	4:27:24 (16,572)	
Moore, Douglas	4:23:03 (15,504)	
Moore, Gary	3:10:02 (1,677)	
Moore, Gerry	3:24:03 (3,254)	
Moore, Graham	3:17:13 (2,453)	
Moore, Ian	4:07:03 (11,698)	
Moore, Ivan	4:28:53 (16,961)	
Moore, John	5:02:50 (24,436)	
Moore, Julian	3:39:13 (5,633)	
Moore, Kevin	2:55:39 (628)	
Moore, Kevin	3:05:54 (1,313)	
Moore, Leroy	4:24:11 (15,794)	
Moore, Mark	3:17:40 (2,512)	
Moore, Matthew	3:59:51 (10,187)	
Moore, Melwyn	3:55:23 (9,018)	
Moore, Michael	2:45:43 (249)	
Moore, Mick	3:11:46 (1,832)	
Moore, Neil	4:33:56 (18,149)	
Moore, Nicholas	4:26:52 (16,441)	
Moore, Nigel	5:47:27 (29,526)	
Moore, Nigel	6:35:40 (31,465)	
Moore, Paul	3:39:29 (5,693)	
Moore, Paul	3:59:15 (10,021)	
Moore, Paul	4:07:41 (11,852)	
Moore, Paul	4:58:35 (23,716)	
Moore, Peter	3:56:36 (9,346)	
Moore, Ralph	3:25:53 (3,529)	
Moore, Richard	3:14:06 (2,140)	
Moore, Richard	3:42:27 (6,231)	
Moore, Richard	3:48:06 (7,339)	
Moore, Richard	4:40:18 (19,608)	
Moore, Richard	5:58:07 (30,166)	
Moore, Robert	4:09:45 (12,285)	
Moore, Robert	5:04:47 (24,757)	
Moore, Scott	4:47:32 (21,304)	
Moore, Simon	3:50:19 (7,805)	
Moore, Stephen	3:53:54 (8,646)	
Moore, Stephen	4:31:35 (17,636)	
Moore, Stephen	5:17:27 (26,536)	
Moore, Tony	4:19:34 (14,631)	
Moore, Trevor	3:19:42 (2,726)	
Moore, Tristram	3:57:51 (9,663)	
Moore, Wayne	4:32:23 (17,813)	
Moorhead, Michael	4:41:28 (19,866)	
Moorhouse, Graham	3:04:13 (1,197)	
Moorhouse, Nicholas	5:19:55 (26,874)	
Moorley, Rupert	3:55:23 (9,018)	
Moosantl, Heinz	3:33:33 (4,687)	
Mora, Ricardo	3:54:11 (8,699)	
Morabito, Alfredo	3:49:54 (7,712)	
Moralee, Simon	3:44:50 (6,694)	
Morales, Alexandre	3:51:23 (8,045)	
Moran, Christopher	3:12:48 (1,967)	
Moran, David	3:03:57 (1,181)	
Moran, David	5:07:52 (25,244)	
Moran, John	4:58:53 (23,777)	
Moran, John	5:18:11 (26,651)	
Moran, John-Paul	3:47:26 (7,199)	
Moran, Mark	3:47:45 (7,267)	
Moran, Michael	3:31:00 (4,327)	
Moran, Michael	3:48:56 (7,499)	
Moran, Patrick	3:39:42 (5,727)	
Moran, Stephen	3:24:35 (3,345)	
Moran, Stephen	3:59:06 (9,984)	
Morano-Abril, Victor	4:45:10 (20,764)	
Morcombe, Andy	3:37:59 (5,410)	
Mordaunt, Jonathan	5:26:28 (27,733)	
Moreau, Camille	3:47:45 (7,267)	
Moreau, Xavier	4:34:42 (18,330)	
Moreaux, René	3:28:45 (3,959)	
Morel, Rick	5:42:58 (29,235)	

Moreland, David 3:56:15 (9,259)
More-Molyneux, Alexander 5:07:11 (25,129)
More-Molyneux, Mike 5:34:08 (28,490)
Morenas, Ransley 3:44:54 (6,707)
Moreno Olmedo, Fernando 3:33:42 (4,701)
Moreton, Andrew 5:28:33 (27,946)
Moreton, Lloyd 5:09:40 (25,499)
Morey, Keith 3:40:17 (5,839)
Morfey, Michael 5:03:01 (24,460)
Morgan, Ben 4:35:56 (18,633)
Morgan, Bernard 4:19:57 (14,729)
Morgan, Byron 4:33:32 (18,066)
Morgan, Chris 4:14:44 (13,432)
Morgan, Christopher 3:59:07 (9,986)
Morgan, Christopher 4:53:34 (22,632)
Morgan, Colin 4:42:35 (20,131)
Morgan, Darren 5:33:40 (28,433)
Morgan, Dave 3:18:08 (2,568)
Morgan, David 4:00:18 (10,297)
Morgan, David 4:17:43 (14,183)
Morgan, David 4:44:16 (20,565)
Morgan, David 4:48:46 (21,580)
Morgan, Derrick 3:15:27 (2,282)
Morgan, Dewi 4:14:09 (13,298)
Morgan, Gareth 3:56:27 (9,305)
Morgan, Gareth 4:10:58 (12,535)
Morgan, Gareth 5:37:38 (28,786)
Morgan, Iain 4:14:57 (13,492)
Morgan, Jason 5:15:10 (26,274)
Morgan, Keith 5:08:10 (25,293)
Morgan, Kenneth 4:08:40 (12,055)
Morgan, Mark 3:55:21 (9,008)
Morgan, Mark 5:51:57 (29,830)
Morgan, Martin 3:43:18 (6,424)
Morgan, Mike 5:36:22 (28,669)
Morgan, Neill 3:54:04 (8,678)
Morgan, Nigel 3:53:24 (8,517)
Morgan, Patrick 3:42:53 (6,337)
Morgan, Paul 7:27:56 (32,142)
Morgan, Richard 3:43:03 (6,377)
Morgan, Robert 3:50:51 (7,916)
Morgan, Robert 4:18:55 (14,489)
Morgan, Ross 5:00:43 (24,108)
Morgan, Simon 5:11:01 (25,694)
Morgan, Stephen 4:01:33 (10,549)
Morgan, Stuart 4:23:49 (15,700)
Morgan, Timothy 5:50:51 (29,773)
Morgan-Warren, Peter 4:31:56 (17,716)
Moriarty, Steve 5:33:13 (28,394)
Morillon, Samuel 3:38:27 (5,485)
Morland, Charles 4:21:01 (14,983)
Morley, Alex 3:49:00 (7,518)
Morley, David 4:12:10 (12,805)
Morley, David 4:48:21 (21,509)
Morley, Don 5:16:38 (26,443)
Morley, Kevin 4:37:24 (18,963)
Morley, Paul 3:42:32 (6,260)
Morley, Phil 2:54:02 (537)
Morley, Philip 4:17:51 (14,218)
Morley, Simon 3:14:50 (2,220)
Morley, Stephen 3:49:16 (7,582)
Morley, Stephen 3:57:35 (9,591)
Morley, Steven 3:42:32 (6,260)
Morlin, Gino 3:22:30 (3,048)
Moroney, Gerard 4:22:10 (15,288)
Moroney, Phil 4:58:46 (23,755)
Moroni, Giuseppe 3:07:46 (1,482)
Morosits, Michael 3:05:11 (1,267)
Morpuss, Guy 4:30:32 (17,375)
Morrell, Alexander 3:22:56 (3,101)
Morrell, Stephen 3:53:16 (8,490)
Morrell, Stephen 3:57:08 (9,488)
Morrey, St John 4:27:24 (16,572)
Morrin, Damian 5:19:19 (26,803)
Morrin, Kieran 5:19:19 (26,803)
Morris, Aaron 4:34:51 (18,359)
Morris, Andrew 4:01:03 (10,439)
Morris, Bennet 3:33:29 (4,675)
Morris, Christopher 4:07:26 (11,788)
Morris, Christopher 5:49:02 (29,642)
Morris, Clive 4:46:25 (21,077)
Morris, Colin 4:18:33 (14,372)
Morris, David 4:58:20 (23,656)
Morris, Dean 4:01:52 (10,613)
Morris, Garwyn 3:45:08 (6,762)
Morris, Gary 6:04:49 (30,448)
Morris, Gregory 4:49:46 (21,818)
Morris, Ian 4:23:50 (15,703)
Morris, Ian 4:24:39 (15,904)
Morris, James 4:30:22 (17,328)
Morris, John 4:13:30 (13,125)
Morris, John 4:29:57 (17,229)
Morris, Jonathan 4:37:16 (18,942)
Morris, Keith 4:10:57 (12,532)
Morris, Kevin 3:27:50 (3,792)
Morris, Mark 2:48:47 (358)
Morris, Mark 4:34:23 (18,259)
Morris, Martyn 3:37:18 (5,289)
Morris, Neil 4:37:45 (19,036)
Morris, Paul 4:28:50 (16,945)
Morris, Paul 5:12:01 (25,830)
Morris, Peter 3:36:17 (5,113)
Morris, Philip 3:05:51 (1,309)
Morris, Philip 3:14:26 (2,178)
Morris, Phill 4:30:54 (17,468)
Morris, Richard 3:29:05 (4,014)
Morris, Richard 5:14:29 (26,172)
Morris, Robert 3:58:46 (9,909)
Morris, Robert 4:51:12 (22,132)
Morris, Robin 3:20:45 (2,851)
Morris, Shaun 3:54:45 (8,850)
Morris, Spero 5:30:21 (28,125)
Morris, Stephen 3:37:54 (5,400)
Morris, Stephen 4:01:32 (10,545)
Morris, Timothy 4:44:03 (20,508)
Morris, Wayne 6:32:43 (31,394)
Morris-Adams, Damian 4:08:47 (12,088)
Morrish, James 4:57:08 (23,411)
Morrison, Alan 3:44:41 (6,664)
Morrison, Barry 3:13:16 (2,032)
Morrison, Christopher 2:51:26 (430)
Morrison, Darren 5:21:35 (27,097)
Morrison, David 5:30:53 (28,183)
Morrison, Derek 3:41:12 (5,988)
Morrison, Ian 3:50:30 (7,842)
Morrison, Ian 8:21:39 (32,275)
Morrison, James 4:02:46 (10,798)
Morrison, James 4:34:59 (18,393)
Morrison, Joseph 3:33:58 (4,742)
Morrison, Mark 5:19:23 (26,812)
Morrison, Sid 3:50:14 (7,785)
Morrison, Simon 3:38:55 (5,584)
Morrissey, Jason 5:04:22 (24,688)
Morrod, Andrew 4:15:46 (13,690)
Morse, David 3:05:48 (1,307)
Morsley, John 3:28:22 (3,878)
Morsund, Geir 4:07:39 (11,848)
Mort, Allan 5:26:31 (27,740)
Mortazavi, Mahmood 3:46:54 (7,103)
Mortensen, Michael 3:49:29 (7,629)
Mortimer, Alistair 4:01:57 (10,624)
Mortimer, Ian 4:29:45 (17,178)
Mortimer, John 4:52:04 (22,323)
Mortimer, Matthew 4:45:10 (20,764)
Mortimer, Roger 5:36:34 (28,697)
Mortimore, Andrew 3:47:06 (7,141)
Mortimore, David 5:38:10 (28,827)
Mortin, John 4:10:14 (12,406)
Morton, Alan 5:44:47 (29,345)
Morton, Andrew 4:58:31 (23,702)
Morton, Bernard 5:26:58 (27,775)
Morton, Brian 4:51:53 (22,287)
Morton, Christopher 5:05:34 (24,894)
Morton, Colin 4:41:15 (19,814)
Morton, David 4:58:27 (23,687)
Morton, Iain 4:01:33 (10,549)
Morton, James 7:26:23 (32,123)
Morton, Steven 3:15:26 (2,281)
Moscrop, David 4:07:27 (11,796)
Moscrop, Mark 5:17:19 (26,516)
Mosedale, Wayne 3:29:28 (4,083)
Moseley, James 4:28:46 (16,928)
Moseley, Oliver 3:50:07 (7,757)
Moseley, Peter 4:23:44 (15,680)
Moseley, Simon 3:06:39 (1,373)
Moseley, Simon 4:13:05 (13,022)
Moseley-Williams, Mark 5:06:47 (25,073)
Moser, Richard 4:24:20 (15,829)
Moses, Ephraim 7:21:16 (32,079)
Moses, Moddy 4:04:44 (11,238)
Mosley, Ian 3:43:54 (6,527)
Mosley, Paul 4:14:42 (13,423)
Mosobbir, Misbah 3:59:05 (9,977)
Moss, Andrew 3:45:42 (6,868)
Moss, Anthony 3:57:13 (9,509)
Moss, Graham 5:28:21 (27,925)
Moss, Jason 3:53:23 (8,510)
Moss, Jeremy 5:04:39 (24,723)
Moss, Neil 4:33:51 (18,126)
Moss, Spencer 3:51:45 (8,136)
Moss, Trevor 4:02:26 (10,727)
Mossakowski, Marek 4:37:38 (19,008)
Motha, Marlon 5:02:32 (24,394)
Motson, Christopher 3:39:16 (5,647)
Mott, Michael 4:42:40 (20,150)
Mottershead, Nick 5:28:30 (27,941)
Mould, Alan 2:59:03 (862)
Mould, Andrew 3:23:27 (3,172)
Mould, Nathan 3:50:10 (7,767)
Moulder, Kevin 5:26:06 (27,686)
Moulding, Jon 3:58:42 (9,886)
Moule, Daniel 4:47:49 (21,380)
Moule, John 5:18:41 (26,725)
Moule, Steve 4:07:16 (11,751)
Moulton, Robert 3:12:23 (1,914)
Mouncey, David 3:41:48 (6,113)
Mound, David 5:02:07 (24,331)
Mounde, David 4:19:58 (14,731)
Mounsey, Ben 3:40:24 (5,857)
Mountain, Joe 3:52:25 (8,292)
Mountain, Matthew 4:05:19 (11,358)
Mountford, Edward 6:37:17 (31,494)
Moura, Victor 4:58:28 (23,692)
Mournian, David 4:22:31 (15,369)
Moussi, Mo 5:47:28 (29,529)
Mouzard, Laurent 3:18:47 (2,635)
Mowle, Lee 3:00:06 (944)
Moxon, Andrew 5:23:23 (27,339)
Moya, Carlos 4:07:59 (11,902)
Moyes, Peter 4:09:59 (12,349)
Moynihan, Kevin 5:08:08 (25,288)
Moyse, Gary 4:40:53 (19,723)
Moyse, Graham 2:57:30 (733)
Mozeson, Mark 4:47:00 (21,184)
Msith, David 5:58:52 (30,196)
Muci, Maurizio 4:05:15 (11,342)
Muddiman, Dean 4:37:58 (19,080)
Muddimer, Andrew 3:45:46 (6,883)
Mudge, Ian 3:36:56 (5,218)
Muehling, Veit 4:11:29 (12,643)
Mueller, Armin 4:03:31 (10,945)
Mueller, Peter 4:19:09 (14,541)
Mueller, Theo 4:18:03 (14,260)
Muff, Hugo 4:34:36 (18,307)
Muga, Ramon 5:31:08 (28,211)
Mugford, Ryan 4:06:28 (11,586)
Muhammad, Darren 5:18:23 (26,681)
Muhammad, Lloyd 4:21:19 (15,066)
Muhammad, Michael 5:05:42 (24,921)
Muir, Alistair 4:29:52 (17,213)
Muir, Colin 4:40:25 (19,635)
Muir, Craig 3:29:28 (4,083)
Muir, Graham 3:55:30 (9,049)
Muir, Gregor 3:44:56 (6,718)
Muir, Ian 3:54:17 (8,728)
Muir, Ian 3:58:13 (9,760)
Muir, James 4:04:40 (11,216)
Muir, Jonathan 3:08:30 (1,547)
Muirhead, Graeme 3:32:05 (4,480)
Mujinga, John 4:17:53 (14,225)
Mulcahy, John 5:11:09 (25,715)
Mulcahy, Kenneth 2:54:29 (557)
Mulchinock, Paul 4:33:00 (17,952)
Mulhern, Mark 3:37:03 (5,241)
Mulholland, John 3:46:15 (6,983)
Mullan, Rowan 4:03:45 (10,997)
Mullane, Paul 4:30:52 (17,459)
Mullaney, Christopher 4:11:38 (12,671)
Mullaruey, Peter 4:16:14 (13,792)

Mullee, James	4:49:27 (21,737)	
Mullen, James	4:53:33 (22,627)	
Mullen, Michael	4:41:04 (19,770)	
Mullen, Patrick	3:28:35 (3,919)	
Mullen, Philip	3:58:51 (9,930)	
Mullens, Brian	4:53:20 (22,581)	
Muller, Jason	5:29:45 (28,065)	
Muller, Zsolt	5:19:05 (26,768)	
Mullery, Peter	3:13:04 (2,001)	
Mullett, Rob	5:57:43 (30,151)	
Mulley, Jim	3:57:12 (9,506)	
Mulligan, Michael	4:42:42 (20,159)	
Mulliner, Stephen	4:29:26 (17,098)	
Mullings, Delroy	4:32:07 (17,755)	
Mullins, Andrew	3:56:29 (9,313)	
Mullins, Michael	3:40:43 (5,905)	
Mullins, Patrick	4:24:14 (15,805)	
Mullins, Roger	2:47:49 (326)	
Mulqueen, John	4:19:24 (14,594)	
Mulrooney, Chris	4:13:38 (13,160)	
Multon, Richard	3:49:51 (7,704)	
Mulvihill, Peter	4:29:11 (17,036)	
Mumberson, Bob	5:18:53 (26,741)	
Mumford, Alex	5:02:30 (24,386)	
Mumford, Kenneth	3:50:56 (7,928)	
Mummery, Neil	5:54:46 (29,986)	
Munday, Paul	3:58:49 (9,921)	
Munday, Paul	6:01:00 (30,295)	
Munday, Richard	3:53:46 (8,608)	
Munday, Simon	4:24:26 (15,850)	
Munden, Barry	4:33:29 (18,055)	
Munden, Tony	5:10:57 (25,686)	
Mundy, Bob	4:25:24 (16,117)	
Mundy, Gordon	4:36:18 (18,713)	
Mundy, Scott	3:57:17 (9,528)	
Mundzar, Ivan	4:07:54 (11,888)	
Mungai, Maurizio	3:57:13 (9,509)	
Mun-Gavin, Anthony	4:11:17 (12,594)	
Mungin-Jenkins II, Escye	4:55:25 (23,008)	
Munim, Abdul	6:34:40 (31,439)	
Munn, Christopher	3:50:46 (7,902)	
Munn, Jame	3:07:18 (1,437)	
Munn, James	5:20:27 (26,947)	
Munnery, David	3:30:41 (4,273)	
Munns, Brian	3:21:15 (2,905)	
Munro, Bruce	3:47:38 (7,245)	
Munro, Bruce	4:41:08 (19,783)	
Munro, Darren	5:01:54 (24,294)	
Munro, David	3:13:09 (2,012)	
Munro, Neil	4:01:52 (10,613)	
Munro, Phillip	3:26:59 (3,678)	
Munro, William	3:58:49 (9,921)	
Munroe, Andrew	3:38:45 (5,552)	
Munsey, Dean	5:23:27 (27,344)	
Munslow, Gary	2:55:00 (593)	
Munslow, Haydon	5:32:08 (28,300)	
Munson, William	5:18:54 (26,742)	
Muoio, Thomas	4:16:56 (13,979)	
Muorah, Mordi	3:58:22 (9,801)	
Murat, Joseph	4:08:21 (11,969)	
Muray, John	3:53:59 (8,666)	
Murch, Gordon	6:53:03 (31,782)	
Murch, Jonny	3:25:52 (3,523)	
Murchison, Andrew	4:55:04 (22,936)	
Murdey, Ian	2:46:03 (259)	
Murdoch, Gerry	6:18:33 (30,959)	
Murdoch, Graeme	3:03:22 (1,142)	
Murdock, Richard	3:37:47 (5,386)	
Murenu, Peter	4:40:42 (19,684)	
Murfin, Andrew	3:13:22 (2,046)	
Murfitt, Darren	3:08:42 (1,563)	
Murison, Kevin	2:58:10 (782)	
Murkin, Robert	6:10:32 (30,663)	
Murphy, Alan	4:59:36 (23,903)	
Murphy, Darren	5:09:32 (25,481)	
Murphy, David	4:41:01 (19,754)	
Murphy, Eddie	6:07:28 (30,554)	
Murphy, Eddy	5:59:13 (30,222)	
Murphy, Jeff	4:14:06 (13,282)	
Murphy, John	3:19:14 (2,675)	
Murphy, John	4:06:58 (11,679)	
Murphy, John	4:08:03 (11,913)	
Murphy, John	4:18:29 (14,351)	
Murphy, Karl	5:58:01 (30,164)	
Murphy, Kevin	3:54:40 (8,831)	
Murphy, Kevin	4:22:27 (15,351)	
Murphy, Lorcan	4:18:50 (14,457)	
Murphy, Mark	4:38:31 (19,200)	
Murphy, Martin	2:53:44 (516)	
Murphy, Martin	4:11:28 (12,636)	
Murphy, Michael	3:38:15 (5,452)	
Murphy, Michael	4:39:09 (19,360)	
Murphy, Patrick	2:53:49 (520)	
Murphy, Paul	3:19:10 (2,667)	
Murphy, Peter	3:17:08 (2,442)	
Murphy, Phillip	4:26:20 (16,323)	
Murphy, Ryan	4:08:41 (12,063)	
Murphy, Shaun	6:24:26 (31,145)	
Murphy, Stephen	3:35:25 (4,977)	
Murphy, Steve	4:20:21 (14,829)	
Murphy, Terrence	4:08:25 (11,984)	
Murphy, Terry	4:02:48 (10,807)	
Murphy, Thomas	4:10:24 (12,444)	
Murphy, Thomas	5:31:50 (28,267)	
Murray, Adrian	4:48:39 (21,561)	
Murray, Alan	4:24:59 (15,999)	
Murray, Alastair	3:40:03 (5,799)	
Murray, Alex	3:41:34 (6,082)	
Murray, Alistair	4:59:40 (23,917)	
Murray, Andrew	4:57:08 (23,411)	
Murray, Duncan	4:22:50 (15,449)	
Murray, Frank	3:54:32 (8,793)	
Murray, Gary	3:33:12 (4,629)	
Murray, Graeme	4:54:56 (22,908)	
Murray, Harry	5:00:46 (24,121)	
Murray, Hugh	3:42:32 (6,260)	
Murray, Iain	2:57:53 (759)	
Murray, James	3:04:37 (1,223)	
Murray, James	4:36:09 (18,679)	
Murray, Joe	5:05:18 (24,840)	
Murray, John	3:43:45 (6,499)	
Murray, Ken	5:12:32 (25,901)	
Murray, Kevan	5:29:48 (28,070)	
Murray, Neil	4:52:02 (22,316)	
Murray, Robert	3:58:39 (9,875)	
Murray, Robert	4:24:46 (15,941)	
Murray, Scott	6:17:38 (30,909)	
Murray, Stephen	3:58:29 (9,830)	
Murray, Stephen	4:07:31 (11,813)	
Murray, Stephen	3:16:51 (2,410)	
Murray, Steven	4:03:23 (10,928)	
Murray, Vincent	3:51:02 (7,963)	
Murray, William	4:40:49 (19,706)	
Murray, William	5:12:00 (25,826)	
Mursell, Ian	4:37:21 (18,956)	
Mursell, Steven	5:28:11 (27,916)	
Murta, Jack	5:46:39 (29,476)	
Murtagh, Dominic	4:40:17 (19,599)	
Murtagh, Simon	5:49:17 (29,661)	
Murton, Alexander	3:51:36 (8,105)	
Muscolo, Gerardo	3:12:59 (1,987)	
Musgrove, Eric	3:26:38 (3,629)	
Muskett, Alan	4:14:11 (13,302)	
Muskett, Charles	4:12:58 (12,997)	
Muspratt-Williams, Alexander	4:43:25 (20,354)	
Mussi, Paul	2:54:52 (584)	
Mutch, Graeme	3:57:09 (9,494)	
Mutter, Dave	6:26:15 (31,211)	
Mutton, Karl	3:33:52 (4,726)	
Muzikants, Peter	5:44:26 (29,331)	
Muzio, Steven	2:54:35 (566)	
Muzzetto, Giuseppe	4:29:43 (17,166)	
Mwaniki, Antony	4:10:28 (12,456)	
Mwanje, Barnabas	3:56:01 (9,184)	
Myatt, James	4:25:12 (16,056)	
Mycock, Simon	4:01:22 (10,509)	
Myers, Christopher	4:00:22 (10,307)	
Myers, Clive	4:16:12 (13,785)	
Myers, John	3:28:51 (3,977)	
Myers, Jonathan	4:12:18 (12,832)	
Myers, Terry	3:26:08 (3,558)	
Myhill, Andrew	3:42:59 (6,364)	
Myhill, Douglas	5:14:42 (26,203)	
Myint, Ye Kyaw	4:38:29 (19,194)	
Mylchreest, Peter	4:32:38 (17,859)	
Myler, Alan	3:08:49 (1,574)	
Mynard, Andrew	3:58:26 (9,818)	
Mynett, Michael	4:00:03 (10,233)	
Mytton, Graham	2:36:17 (110)	
Mytton, Neil	3:44:23 (6,618)	
Nabarro, Mike	5:03:40 (24,560)	
Nagel, David	3:11:24 (1,791)	
Nagel, Stefan	3:29:40 (4,123)	
Nagle, Joseph	8:07:16 (32,264)	
Nah, Kay	5:16:04 (26,385)	
Naicker, Rajandren	4:52:52 (22,477)	
Nairn, Andrew	4:33:07 (17,973)	
Nairn, Craig	3:44:06 (6,564)	
Naish, Keith	4:44:42 (20,658)	
Naldrett, Andrew	3:08:53 (1,577)	
Nally, Martin	5:25:04 (27,549)	
Nanayakkara, Edgar	4:06:01 (11,503)	
Nanfra, David	3:21:59 (2,983)	
Nannetti, Mauro	5:15:15 (26,286)	
Nannini, Giancarlo	3:39:24 (5,678)	
Nanton, Carl	5:06:32 (25,022)	
Napp, Jerome	5:33:09 (28,385)	
Naqui, Samar	5:03:40 (24,560)	
Nar, Satbinder	3:34:03 (4,755)	
Narcisi, Joe	5:54:42 (29,979)	
Nash, Darren	3:20:36 (2,837)	
Nash, David	4:02:32 (10,747)	
Nash, Ian	5:00:52 (24,132)	
Nash, Paul	5:36:23 (28,671)	
Nash, Paul	4:27:43 (16,657)	
Nash, Peter	3:22:11 (3,007)	
Nash, Philip	3:51:29 (8,068)	
Nash, Richard	4:17:40 (14,165)	
Nash, Stephen	3:19:23 (2,689)	
Nash, Trevor	4:21:53 (15,203)	
Nash, William	5:17:32 (26,549)	
Nasir, Abizer	4:38:34 (19,213)	
Nasman, Emil	6:30:29 (31,341)	
Nason, Christopher	6:05:55 (30,497)	
Nastri, Philip	3:35:20 (4,963)	
Natale, Tony	4:50:01 (21,862)	
Nathan, Elliott	7:29:15 (32,147)	
Nathan, Michael	3:39:05 (5,613)	
Nathwani, Hitesh	4:30:42 (17,420)	
Naughton, Brendan	3:42:41 (6,295)	
Naughton, Joe	4:00:59 (10,426)	
Naughton, Sebastian	6:04:28 (30,429)	
Nauta, Maurice	3:35:16 (4,952)	
Navarro-Magan, Manuel	4:01:17 (10,491)	
Navesey, Ged	3:43:28 (6,448)	
Navrady, Jeremy	5:46:49 (29,484)	
Nawaz, Ack	4:30:54 (17,468)	
Nawaz, Qasim	3:43:01 (6,372)	
Naya-Diez, Oscar	3:47:00 (7,124)	
Nayler, Mark	3:55:35 (9,070)	
Naylor, Barney	4:05:23 (11,368)	
Naylor, Chris	6:23:00 (31,104)	
Naylor, Christopher	3:46:50 (7,090)	
Naylor, Dave	5:05:21 (24,849)	
Naylor, Paul	3:54:23 (8,748)	
Ndlovu, Mandla	4:04:47 (11,245)	
Neads, Kevin	4:45:07 (20,748)	
Neal, David	3:34:46 (4,877)	
Neal, Garry	4:22:41 (15,417)	
Neal, Kevin	3:19:42 (2,726)	
Neal, Simon	4:19:42 (14,667)	
Neale, Colin	3:28:49 (3,974)	
Neale, Darren	3:09:36 (1,645)	
Neale, David	3:52:26 (8,296)	
Neale, Mark	5:48:41 (29,615)	
Neale, Mark	5:03:15 (24,500)	
Neale, Paul	3:33:35 (4,691)	
Neale, Robert	3:07:18 (1,437)	
Neale, Simon	4:34:39 (18,321)	
Neale, Tony	3:48:54 (7,489)	
Neal-Hopes, Timothy	4:41:11 (19,797)	
Nealon, Duncan	3:34:09 (4,768)	
Nealon, Nick	4:26:43 (16,405)	
Nealon, Paul	4:45:52 (20,931)	
Neary, Aiden	4:48:52 (21,602)	
Neate, Philip	4:36:50 (18,842)	
Neate-Stidson, Simon	5:16:25 (26,418)	
Neave, Robert	5:10:36 (25,635)	
Neaves, Roger	4:58:32 (23,704)	
Nebioglu, Erdal		

Needham, David	3:46:14	(6,982)
Needham, David	4:51:37	(22,228)
Needham, John	5:05:28	(24,874)
Needham, Kevin	4:24:51	(15,962)
Neenan, Peter	4:12:44	(12,946)
Neergaard, Jens	4:11:09	(12,561)
Neighbour, Paul	5:04:48	(24,762)
Neill, Brian	3:53:19	(8,501)
Neill, Lawrence	3:14:06	(2,140)
Neill, Thomas	3:47:52	(7,296)
Neill, Timothy	4:26:40	(16,395)
Neilly, Gordon	4:28:31	(16,861)
Neilson, Christopher	4:18:31	(14,365)
Nel, Daniel	5:09:46	(25,516)
Nel, Dirk	4:48:53	(21,609)
Nel, Douglas	5:29:15	(28,012)
Nelhams, Michael	2:48:25	(348)
Nelis, Jan	3:40:38	(5,888)
Nell, André	4:18:22	(14,322)
Nell, Michael	4:42:34	(20,127)
Nelligan, Bernard	4:15:37	(13,663)
Nellins, Christopher	3:05:47	(1,304)
Nellis, Joseph	4:43:00	(20,236)
Nelson, Adam	3:01:13	(1,012)
Nelson, Asa	3:29:21	(4,055)
Nelson, Barry	5:11:34	(25,770)
Nelson, Christopher	4:05:02	(11,299)
Nelson, Dennis	4:36:59	(18,872)
Nelson, Gerald	4:06:08	(11,522)
Nelson, Gregory	3:32:17	(4,504)
Nelson, James	4:01:15	(10,483)
Nelson, Kevin	4:34:23	(18,259)
Nelson, Mark	5:27:21	(27,814)
Nelson, Paul	3:18:45	(2,629)
Nelson, Paul	4:30:01	(17,243)
Nelson, Roy	3:58:07	(9,733)
Nelson, Sean	5:13:26	(26,029)
Nelson, Shaun	6:16:59	(30,893)
Nelson, Stephen	4:15:37	(13,663)
Nelson, Stuart	3:27:23	(3,718)
Nelson, Tim	4:19:05	(14,525)
Nelson-Judd, Michael	6:50:37	(31,735)
Nepean, Nigel	3:39:13	(5,633)
Nesbit, Simon	5:30:17	(28,113)
Nesbitt, Guy	4:23:44	(15,680)
Nesbitt, Keith	5:33:53	(28,465)
Nesbitt, Russ	7:03:06	(31,916)
Nesbitt, Tristan	4:48:59	(21,627)
Ness, Andrew	4:15:20	(13,602)
Nester, Michael	2:46:13	(266)
Nettelfield, David	4:58:25	(23,679)
Nettleton, Mike	5:15:44	(26,349)
Netuschill, Karl	4:15:39	(13,666)
Neufville, Gillian	4:53:14	(22,552)
Nevill, Gary	4:45:54	(20,936)
Neville, Michael	3:43:59	(6,541)
Nevin, Michael	4:24:26	(15,850)
Nevin, Paul	3:44:18	(6,598)
New, Edward	4:50:32	(21,974)
New, Stephen	4:09:07	(12,156)
Newall, Justin	5:04:58	(24,787)
Newall, Oliver	4:51:59	(22,305)
Newbery, William	3:22:22	(3,031)
Newbould, Harry	5:01:21	(24,215)
Newbury, Adam	5:20:05	(26,899)
Newbury, Duncan	3:46:01	(6,935)
Newbury, Sean	3:28:03	(3,827)
Newby, Alan	3:54:23	(8,748)
Newby, Christopher	2:42:34	(187)
Newby, Jonathan	3:50:49	(7,912)
Newcombe, Colin	4:04:33	(11,188)
Newell, Frank	5:21:35	(27,097)
Newell, Ian	3:34:02	(4,753)
Newell, John	5:44:09	(29,314)
Newell, Mark	3:54:09	(8,691)
Newell, Mark	6:09:57	(30,637)
Newell, Matthew	4:54:04	(22,723)
Newell, Michael	5:26:07	(27,689)
Newell, Quinton	4:17:19	(14,060)
Newell, Stephen	4:43:46	(20,444)
Newell, Terry	5:56:46	(30,090)
Newing, Andy	3:40:02	(5,793)
Newing, John	4:23:00	(15,494)

Newlands, Alistair	3:21:47	(2,962)
Newland-Smith, Richard	4:10:28	(12,456)
Newling, Dan	4:32:04	(17,746)
Newman, Adam	2:51:10	(424)
Newman, Anthony	5:18:59	(26,754)
Newman, Craig	5:00:30	(24,069)
Newman, David	3:12:30	(1,929)
Newman, David	4:31:30	(17,616)
Newman, Denis	2:36:20	(113)
Newman, James	5:05:25	(24,863)
Newman, John	4:12:36	(12,914)
Newman, Jonathan	3:43:49	(6,511)
Newman, Matthew	3:54:32	(8,793)
Newman, Matthew	4:47:44	(21,353)
Newman, Maurice	3:36:39	(5,170)
Newman, Michael	4:12:15	(12,828)
Newman, Neville	4:53:15	(22,556)
Newman, Peter	6:01:53	(30,337)
Newman, Philip	3:47:54	(7,301)
Newman, Philip	4:22:22	(15,331)
Newman, Richard	3:12:21	(1,910)
Newman, Richard	3:50:03	(7,743)
Newman, Richard	4:05:25	(11,379)
Newman, Robin	4:07:26	(11,788)
Newman, Terry	4:03:15	(10,899)
Newport, Alan	5:05:19	(24,845)
Newport, Gary	4:28:20	(16,801)
Newport, Lee	5:02:09	(24,335)
Newsham, John	4:48:53	(21,609)
Newson, Stephen	5:12:08	(25,841)
Newstead, Peter	4:53:47	(22,675)
Newsway, Jason	5:26:24	(27,727)
Newth, Tom	4:39:44	(19,484)
Newton, Adrian	3:57:08	(9,488)
Newton, Ben	3:58:58	(9,960)
Newton, Brian	3:34:42	(4,868)
Newton, Christopher	4:13:47	(13,195)
Newton, Darren	3:38:42	(5,544)
Newton, David	5:15:09	(26,271)
Newton, Gavin	3:40:46	(5,918)
Newton, Harry	4:05:15	(11,342)
Newton, Matthew	4:28:09	(16,752)
Newton, Peter	3:44:30	(6,635)
Newton, Robert	3:50:54	(7,926)
Newton, Simon	2:58:46	(831)
Newton, Stephen	5:18:44	(26,732)
Newton-Brown, James	5:30:39	(28,159)
Neylan, Michael	3:56:30	(9,318)
Neyra, Michel	4:22:18	(15,315)
Ng, Chun	4:01:04	(10,446)
Ng, Hok	3:35:40	(5,024)
Ng, Wing	3:11:44	(1,827)
Ngan, Siong-Kin	4:53:06	(22,521)
Ngethi, James	5:33:03	(28,377)
Ngilo, Seiso	3:26:20	(3,581)
Ngo, Chan	4:26:43	(16,405)
Ngolepus, Joseph	2:07:57	(3)
Nguyen, Giac	3:06:40	(1,375)
Niazi, Tabrez	3:52:09	(8,234)
Niblock, Brian	3:06:23	(1,348)
Niblock, David	4:29:44	(17,171)
Nicel, John	4:06:02	(11,506)
Nichol, Christopher	5:25:35	(27,620)
Nicholaou, Nicholas	4:52:55	(22,487)
Nicholas, Adam	4:05:15	(11,342)
Nicholas, David	6:28:47	(31,297)
Nicholas, William	3:13:09	(2,012)
Nicholl, James	5:50:22	(29,741)
Nicholls, Andrew	3:53:05	(8,447)
Nicholls, Andrew	3:17:48	(2,530)
Nicholls, Clive	3:59:24	(10,064)
Nicholls, David	3:47:27	(7,204)
Nicholls, Edward	4:25:50	(16,211)
Nicholls, Enda	4:37:21	(18,956)
Nicholls, Eric	4:16:26	(13,843)
Nicholls, Gary	4:16:58	(13,982)
Nicholls, Ian	4:09:02	(12,142)
Nicholls, Jason	4:15:11	(13,563)
Nicholls, Jonathan	4:15:30	(13,640)
Nicholls, Nicholas	4:55:06	(22,939)
Nicholls, Paul	4:58:31	(23,702)
Nicholls, Phil	4:16:36	(13,876)
Nicholls, Spencer	4:32:41	(17,875)

Nichols, Carl	4:31:59	(17,724)
Nichols, Dave	4:20:57	(14,965)
Nichols, Paul	4:06:58	(11,679)
Nichols, Stephen	3:59:09	(9,991)
Nicholson, Andrew	3:48:52	(7,482)
Nicholson, Angus	4:24:24	(15,841)
Nicholson, Anthony	6:17:13	(30,897)
Nicholson, Charlie	4:31:06	(17,525)
Nicholson, Chris	3:49:46	(7,691)
Nicholson, David	3:38:51	(5,569)
Nicholson, Ian	3:49:44	(7,684)
Nicholson, James	5:06:38	(25,039)
Nicholson, John	4:29:23	(17,084)
Nicholson, Magnus	5:08:50	(25,381)
Nicholson, Murray	4:43:50	(20,466)
Nicholson, Rob	3:50:57	(7,933)
Nicholson, Roy	3:36:50	(5,199)
Nickerson, Jere	4:39:52	(19,514)
Nickerson, Stuart	3:54:55	(8,899)
Nicklas, David	4:02:48	(10,807)
Nicklin, Simon	4:13:58	(13,251)
Nickson, Peter	3:21:51	(2,967)
Nicolas, Darren	5:18:45	(26,733)
Nicoll, David	5:33:27	(28,417)
Nicoll, Robert	3:23:19	(3,150)
Niederhauser, Rolf	4:06:16	(11,549)
Niedermaier-Reed, Robert	4:59:07	(23,830)
Niedrist, Markus	2:44:02	(218)
Nielsen, Henrik	4:48:39	(21,561)
Nielsen, John	5:21:28	(27,076)
Nielsen, Jorgen	4:26:54	(16,448)
Niemeier, Joachim	3:43:34	(6,457)
Nieuwenhuizen, Marcus	3:31:12	(4,358)
Nightingale, Adrian	3:50:30	(7,842)
Nightingale, Colin	4:06:21	(11,562)
Nightingale, David	3:56:23	(9,288)
Nightingale, Jonathan	3:39:45	(5,738)
Nikiforov, Peter	3:24:55	(3,386)
Nilsson, Martin	4:10:33	(12,476)
Nimbley, Graham	5:05:24	(24,857)
Nimmey, David	4:46:16	(21,035)
Nimmo, David	4:38:31	(19,200)
Ninham, Andy	4:45:46	(20,905)
Ninpenny, Andrew	3:56:02	(9,189)
Nisbet, Jack	3:20:41	(2,845)
Nisbett, Michael	4:03:39	(10,973)
Niven, Christopher	5:12:10	(25,844)
Niwa, Hironobu	4:43:04	(20,250)
Nixon, Craig	3:57:24	(9,560)
Nixon, Craig	5:13:19	(26,014)
Nixon, David	4:33:51	(18,126)
Nixon, Roy	3:38:02	(5,421)
Noad, Ian	3:01:00	(1,003)
Nobbs, Martin	3:18:02	(2,554)
Noble, Alexander	4:35:34	(18,533)
Noble, Bob	5:05:34	(24,894)
Noble, Derrick	3:26:48	(3,644)
Noble, Elliott	4:22:53	(15,466)
Noble, Iain	3:35:02	(4,918)
Noble, Ian	3:34:45	(4,873)
Noble, Mike	4:03:12	(10,881)
Noble, Pete	3:06:28	(1,356)
Noble, Raymond	3:07:08	(1,423)
Noble, William	4:29:07	(17,017)
Nock, Graham	3:19:53	(2,742)
Nock, Michael	3:08:54	(1,578)
Noda, Michael	4:23:26	(15,595)
Noel, Thomas	5:20:06	(26,904)
Noffki, Gavin	4:42:44	(20,165)
Nogues, Jerome	3:45:51	(6,901)
Nolan, Brian	3:12:36	(1,945)
Nolan, Chris	5:10:33	(25,628)
Nolan, Fergal	3:43:34	(6,457)
Nolan, Lewis	4:34:29	(18,286)
Nolan, Mike	3:06:25	(1,350)
Nolan, Shane	3:34:33	(4,845)
Noll, Peter	4:42:29	(20,104)
Noonan, Patrick	3:09:25	(1,625)
Noortman, William	4:09:36	(12,249)
Norburn, Jonathan	4:47:55	(21,443)
Norbury, Anthony	4:08:37	(12,044)
Norbury, Stephen	4:34:48	(18,351)
Norcup, Derek	5:39:00	(28,903)

Nordam, Odd	4:30:22 (17,328)	
Nordin, Andrew	4:13:49 (13,205)	
Nordstrand, Malvin	4:24:22 (15,835)	
Norfolk, Guy	4:33:29 (18,055)	
Norgate, Andrew	5:20:42 (26,988)	
Norgrove, John	4:18:54 (14,479)	
Norman, Adam	4:47:08 (21,212)	
Norman, Andrew	4:01:43 (10,583)	
Norman, Andrew	4:08:51 (12,098)	
Norman, Billy	4:17:23 (14,082)	
Norman, David	2:21:00 (26)	
Norman, Keith	6:04:35 (30,435)	
Norman, Nigel	4:03:10 (10,875)	
Norman, Richard	4:15:06 (13,539)	
Norris, Andrew	2:39:06 (145)	
Norris, Andrew	3:30:53 (4,312)	
Norris, Christopher	4:56:59 (23,378)	
Norris, Craig	4:22:56 (15,478)	
Norris, David	4:24:20 (15,829)	
Norris, Gary	5:08:07 (25,282)	
Norris, James	3:27:56 (3,807)	
Norris, Jason	3:56:35 (9,341)	
Norris, Jason	4:31:17 (17,563)	
Norris, Kerry	4:36:14 (18,696)	
Norris, Matt	3:29:21 (4,055)	
Norris, Paul	5:52:07 (29,835)	
Norris, Richard	2:56:44 (685)	
Norris, Simon	5:47:34 (29,545)	
Norris-Grey, Robert	4:04:37 (11,201)	
North, Colin	4:01:45 (10,589)	
North, Ernest	4:35:12 (18,442)	
North, Shaun	2:35:02 (101)	
North, Thomas	6:34:32 (31,436)	
Northam, Roger	4:03:03 (10,855)	
Northcroft, Jonathan	5:22:52 (27,264)	
Northey, Edgar	4:02:11 (10,675)	
Northrop, Kevin	4:33:48 (18,115)	
Northwood, John	4:57:28 (23,474)	
Norton, Andrew	4:32:21 (17,801)	
Norton, Bernard	6:03:01 (30,375)	
Norton, Dru	5:53:09 (29,885)	
Norton, Eric	5:18:19 (26,674)	
Norton, Francis	3:59:14 (10,014)	
Norton, Paul	5:50:47 (29,771)	
Norton, Roger	4:51:18 (22,152)	
Norwood, Daniel	4:06:53 (11,667)	
Norwood, Simon	3:02:28 (1,085)	
Nott, Gregory	4:34:43 (18,332)	
Nottidge, Richard	4:05:41 (11,430)	
Notton, Christopher	4:07:21 (11,766)	
Nougaoui, Abdelwahab	3:26:22 (3,587)	
Nouillan, Bill	4:37:19 (18,952)	
Nowacki, Wies	2:58:24 (793)	
Nowak, Herbert	3:22:34 (3,058)	
Nowosielski, Andrzej	3:43:07 (6,390)	
Nufer, Martin	3:31:03 (4,337)	
Nugent, Brian	4:57:51 (23,551)	
Nugent, John	4:19:21 (14,580)	
Nunn, Gregory	5:53:32 (29,906)	
Nunn, Paul	5:47:06 (29,497)	
Nunn, Terry	4:29:40 (17,153)	
Nurcombe, Tim	3:49:54 (7,712)	
Nurse, Robert	4:04:16 (11,127)	
Nurtman, Michael	4:49:05 (21,648)	
Nutt, Matthew	3:12:09 (1,876)	
Nuttall, Alan	4:08:46 (12,084)	
Nuttall, Chris	5:44:30 (29,334)	
Nuttall, Paul	4:51:27 (22,195)	
Nutter, George	4:17:22 (14,074)	
Nutton, David	3:40:46 (5,918)	
Nuttycombe, Bill	5:23:35 (27,354)	
Nyarko, Michael	4:42:22 (20,074)	
Nyarko, Stephen	4:16:40 (13,897)	
Nye, Alan	4:09:53 (12,318)	
Nye, Howard	3:37:06 (5,253)	
Nye, John	5:04:42 (24,733)	
Nye, Keith	3:34:14 (4,787)	
Nygren, Tuomas	4:23:08 (15,526)	
Nyindo, Patrick	3:41:21 (6,025)	
Nyland, Paul	3:00:35 (981)	
Nys, Vincent	3:34:47 (4,878)	
Nystroem, Patrik	2:47:43 (322)	
Oak, Makarand	5:45:49 (29,430)	
Oakes, Anthony	5:32:24 (28,326)	
Oakes, Harold	4:57:37 (23,505)	
Oakes, Mark	2:50:36 (404)	
Oakes, Mike	3:26:56 (3,665)	
Oakes, Philip	4:40:51 (19,716)	
Oakes, Terry	4:47:33 (21,308)	
Oakley, Alan	4:19:29 (14,611)	
Oakley, Andrew	3:51:37 (8,110)	
Oakley, David	4:31:51 (17,699)	
Oakley, James	4:12:43 (12,941)	
Oakley, John	4:41:35 (19,889)	
Oakley, Robert	4:22:07 (15,267)	
Oakshott, Angus	4:21:57 (15,224)	
Oates, David	4:29:45 (17,178)	
Oatham, Philip	3:21:06 (2,892)	
Oatts, Andrew	3:05:01 (1,250)	
Obagi, Nadeem	4:06:09 (11,526)	
Obaidi, David	6:42:53 (31,588)	
O'Beirne, Andy	3:09:17 (1,611)	
Oborne, Jordan	4:45:03 (20,728)	
Obrador-Medina, Antonio	5:38:52 (28,886)	
O'Bree, Michael	5:16:54 (26,469)	
O'Brien, Adrian	4:53:13 (22,550)	
O'Brien, Anthony	5:33:13 (28,394)	
O'Brien, Bernard	5:13:22 (26,019)	
O'Brien, Brian	5:02:24 (24,373)	
O'Brien, Chris	4:36:16 (18,702)	
O'Brien, Dave	3:41:16 (6,000)	
O'Brien, David	6:03:33 (30,398)	
O'Brien, Fergal	5:02:24 (24,373)	
O'Brien, Frank	5:27:42 (27,857)	
O'Brien, Jack	4:59:30 (23,886)	
O'Brien, Jason	5:50:07 (29,724)	
O'Brien, John	4:07:26 (11,788)	
O'Brien, Justin	3:58:17 (9,776)	
O'Brien, Kelvin	3:25:09 (3,417)	
O'Brien, Kevin	4:21:06 (15,004)	
O'Brien, Michael	3:42:53 (6,337)	
O'Brien, Michael	4:10:02 (12,356)	
O'Brien, Neil	4:52:38 (22,428)	
O'Brien, Paul	3:00:55 (996)	
O'Brien, Peter	3:58:25 (9,813)	
O'Brien, Peter	5:36:34 (28,697)	
O'Brien, Robert	4:03:57 (11,048)	
O'Brien, Simon	4:46:20 (21,054)	
O'Brien, Stephen	4:08:18 (11,961)	
O'Brien-Brackenburey, Brendan	4:44:23 (20,591)	
O'Bryan, Lee	4:10:53 (12,524)	
Ocakli, Hasan	4:22:47 (15,440)	
O'Callaghan, Mark	4:48:46 (21,580)	
O'Callaghan, Sean	5:33:16 (28,398)	
Occhilupo, Sandro	3:03:33 (1,155)	
Ockenden, James	4:59:39 (23,914)	
Ockwell, Christopher	4:59:52 (23,965)	
Ockwell, Edward	7:41:28 (32,213)	
O'Connell, Eoin	2:33:44 (89)	
O'Connell, John	6:12:36 (30,753)	
O'Connell, Liam	4:24:22 (15,883)	
O'Connell, Michael	3:53:03 (8,437)	
O'Connell, Stephen	4:35:25 (18,501)	
O'Connell, Tony	3:58:37 (9,862)	
O'Connor, Breffni	3:53:31 (8,548)	
O'Connor, Brendan	4:19:46 (14,687)	
O'Connor, Denis	3:20:59 (2,882)	
O'Connor, Denis	4:59:46 (23,935)	
O'Connor, Drew	4:11:21 (12,612)	
O'Connor, Edward	3:07:31 (1,454)	
O'Connor, Geoff	4:19:28 (14,609)	
O'Connor, Hubert	4:43:02 (20,243)	
O'Connor, John	4:05:25 (11,379)	
O'Connor, John	5:22:36 (27,225)	
O'Connor, John	5:27:37 (27,850)	
O'Connor, Michael	4:22:32 (15,373)	
O'Connor, Milo	4:47:47 (21,368)	
O'Connor, Ray	4:30:25 (17,350)	
O'Connor, Rory	3:58:47 (9,914)	
O'Connor, Ross	3:16:39 (2,390)	
O'Connor, Sean	3:33:55 (4,739)	
O'Connor, Terence	4:39:31 (19,444)	
O'Connor, William	3:32:50 (4,572)	
Oddy, Huw	5:03:24 (24,518)	
Oddy, Simon	3:22:07 (2,999)	
Odell, Michael	3:14:27 (2,180)	
Odell, Neil	3:53:51 (8,633)	
Odey, Loyd	4:27:51 (16,680)	
Odihiri, Rusty	6:55:45 (31,843)	
Odling, William	4:33:35 (18,075)	
O'Doherty, Kieran	4:24:09 (15,786)	
O'Doherty, Michael	3:02:14 (1,075)	
O'Doherty, Paul	2:57:05 (708)	
O'Donnell, Benjamin	3:54:03 (8,674)	
O'Donnell, Debbie	5:24:03 (27,415)	
O'Donnell, Eamon	4:24:35 (15,883)	
O'Donnell, Kevin	4:12:25 (12,864)	
O'Donnell, Kieron	3:20:26 (2,821)	
O'Donnell, Mark	4:02:15 (10,686)	
O'Donoghue, Daniel	2:48:47 (358)	
O'Donoghue, David	3:21:36 (2,942)	
O'Donoghue, David	4:17:29 (14,110)	
O'Donoghue, James	4:55:48 (23,112)	
O'Donoghue, Thomas	3:25:10 (3,420)	
O'Donoghue, Thomas	5:27:06 (27,789)	
O'Donovan, Darragh	4:44:38 (20,644)	
O'Donovan, Ian	3:48:51 (7,477)	
O'Donovan, Paul	5:32:41 (28,345)	
O'Donovan, Timothy	3:24:03 (3,254)	
O'Driscoll, Martin	3:52:21 (8,276)	
O'Driscoll, Pat	4:22:37 (15,401)	
O'Driscoll, Patrick	3:52:35 (8,328)	
Odurny, Allan	3:40:15 (5,837)	
O'Dwyer, David	5:03:45 (24,584)	
Oertig, Pius	3:44:52 (6,698)	
Oestberg, Bjarki	3:36:41 (5,179)	
Oestberg, Eirik	4:49:25 (21,726)	
O'Farrell, Paul	4:20:14 (14,802)	
O'Farrell, Sean	4:37:15 (18,937)	
Ofee, Gary	4:18:52 (14,468)	
Offer, Justin	4:05:53 (11,478)	
Offermann, Eric	4:43:31 (20,382)	
Offiah, Christian	7:10:13 (31,991)	
Offler, Gordon	3:48:28 (7,395)	
Offord, Malcolm	5:39:48 (28,905)	
Oficialdegui, Javier	3:49:47 (7,696)	
O'Flaherty, Lee	4:33:30 (18,060)	
O'Flanagan, Sean	4:45:56 (20,942)	
O'Flynn, Nicholas	3:53:24 (8,517)	
Ogata, Joe	3:38:14 (5,449)	
Ogborn, Steve	2:59:13 (873)	
Ogden, David	2:45:25 (246)	
Ogden, Paul	5:31:24 (28,239)	
Ogg, David	2:59:02 (859)	
Ogilvie, Daniel	3:43:03 (6,377)	
Ogilvie, Stuart	4:54:39 (22,849)	
Ogle, Nigel	4:06:30 (11,590)	
Oglesby, Mark	2:52:39 (477)	
O'Gorman, Barry	3:32:06 (4,483)	
O'Gorman, Will	4:04:51 (11,257)	
O'Grady, Daniel	3:57:32 (9,585)	
O'Grady, John	3:48:32 (7,409)	
O'Grady, Geoff	3:20:12 (2,786)	
O'Grady, Paul	4:24:57 (15,981)	
O'Grady, Sean	4:24:44 (15,928)	
O'Gunyemi, Jackson	4:45:39 (20,881)	
O'Hanlon, John	6:29:50 (31,326)	
O'Hara, Andy	4:43:56 (20,483)	
O'Hara, Brendan	3:59:39 (10,136)	
O'Hara, Ian	4:17:51 (14,218)	
O'Hare, Christian	5:47:08 (29,498)	
O'Hare, Sam	4:38:35 (19,221)	
Ojagh, Parvis	3:10:28 (1,716)	
O'Kane, James	4:53:20 (22,581)	
O'Kane, Steven	5:08:05 (25,276)	
Okantey, Edward	5:08:35 (25,343)	
O'Kearney, Geoff	4:41:01 (19,754)	
O'Keefe, Christopher	4:07:35 (11,830)	
O'Keefe, Daniel	4:49:17 (21,698)	
O'Keefe, Steven	6:58:16 (31,875)	
O'Keefe, Wilf	4:48:18 (21,496)	
O'Keeffe, Jeremiah	3:39:05 (5,614)	
O'Keeffe, Patrick	3:35:34 (5,007)	
O'Keeffe, Terence	3:57:06 (9,478)	
Okin, Andrew	6:00:52 (30,290)	
Olcese, Franco	3:56:38 (9,358)	
Olden, Christian	2:42:28 (186)	
Older, Paul	5:10:46 (25,657)	
Older, Tim	3:12:01 (1,863)	

Oldfield, Christopher 3:40:28 (5,865)
Oldfield, David 3:39:38 (5,717)
Oldfield, Gerry 2:33:13 (85)
Oldfield, Richard 4:40:46 (19,696)
Oldroyd, Paul 4:56:05 (23,166)
O'Leary, Benedict 3:06:31 (1,361)
O'Leary, Brad 3:33:00 (4,601)
O'Leary, Dermot 4:08:34 (12,029)
O'Leary, James 4:08:00 (11,905)
O'Leary, Paul 3:36:54 (5,213)
O'Leary, Thomas 5:46:00 (29,441)
Olejak, Jens 4:03:51 (11,025)
Oleofse, Marthinus 4:56:57 (23,368)
Oletzky, Torsten 4:02:07 (10,658)
Oliveira, Carlos 4:53:01 (22,505)
Oliveira, Silvi 3:56:44 (9,385)
Oliver, James 5:57:40 (30,148)
Oliver, Laurence 3:28:36 (3,925)
Oliver, Michael 4:05:12 (11,330)
Oliver, Victor 4:28:49 (16,939)
Olivier, Guinard 4:57:42 (23,522)
Olivier, Philippe 3:24:46 (3,367)
Olivier, Richard 3:51:20 (8,039)
Ollington, Michael 4:45:51 (20,926)
Ollis, Graham 4:20:58 (14,968)
Ollive, Ian 4:28:09 (16,752)
Olliver, Andrew 4:27:16 (16,539)
Olney, Sam 4:30:59 (17,491)
Olorunshola, Bandele 3:51:25 (8,055)
O'Loughlin, Andrew 5:04:46 (24,752)
O'Loughlin, Michael 3:06:17 (1,336)
O'Loughlin Irwin, Naoise 3:34:00 (4,749)
Olower, Crispin 2:52:08 (447)
Olsen, Erik 4:38:15 (19,143)
Olsen, Henning 3:01:31 (1,027)
Olsson, John 5:33:20 (28,405)
Olsson, Lars 4:06:39 (11,614)
Oluborode, Anthony 4:07:01 (11,690)
Olusanya, Tunde 4:41:13 (19,804)
Olver, George 3:37:33 (5,334)
O'Mahoney, Dan 4:31:37 (17,646)
O'Mahoney, Kevin 3:50:12 (7,777)
O'Mahony, Brendan 4:33:48 (18,115)
O'Malley, Christopher 5:03:42 (24,574)
O'Malley, John 4:16:07 (13,766)
O'Maonaigh-Lennon, Neil 3:50:43 (7,890)
Ommerborn, Stephen 4:36:46 (18,826)
Omotayo, Sammy 6:02:05 (30,343)
O'Neal, Patrick 4:50:10 (21,897)
O'Neill, Adam 4:22:22 (15,331)
O'Neill, Charles 5:04:12 (24,661)
O'Neill, Douglas 3:57:59 (9,703)
O'Neill, Gary 5:25:11 (27,568)
O'Neill, Ian 3:07:21 (1,441)
O'Neill, Kevin 4:21:42 (15,158)
O'Neill, Michael 3:49:13 (7,568)
O'Neill, Michael 5:33:56 (28,474)
O'Neill, Patrick 4:20:40 (14,899)
O'Neill, Paul 3:28:30 (3,903)
O'Neill, Paul 5:13:05 (25,984)
O'Neill, Richard 4:16:41 (13,900)
O'Neill, Robert 3:08:17 (1,522)
O'Neill, Robin 3:56:19 (9,276)
O'Neill, Stephen 4:02:15 (10,686)
O'Neill, Stephen 5:00:53 (24,135)
Onions, Terence 3:46:52 (7,097)
Onita, Tommy 4:06:17 (11,553)
Onodera, Akio 5:57:00 (30,107)
Onslow, Richard 4:40:35 (19,664)
Opbroek, Jean-Claude 4:42:46 (20,172)
Openshaw, Steven 4:41:51 (19,960)
Opfer, Lothar 3:41:26 (6,052)
Oppenheim, Max 3:17:27 (2,486)
Or Kam Fat, Patrick 5:09:21 (25,456)
Oram, William 3:47:51 (7,293)
Orange, Jon 2:29:51 (63)
Orchard, Gerald 4:36:17 (18,707)
Orchard, Lawrence 5:43:13 (29,256)
Orchard, Mark 4:04:40 (11,216)
Orde, Hugh 4:08:14 (11,946)
Ordish, Ian 4:21:20 (15,072)
Oregan, David 4:38:43 (19,257)
O'Reilly, Bob 4:38:34 (19,213)
O'Reilly, Eamonn 4:49:22 (21,719)
O'Reilly, Edward 3:24:22 (3,311)
O'Reilly, Michael 4:38:08 (19,114)
O'Reilly, Michael 4:45:06 (20,743)
O'Reilly, Simon 4:33:52 (18,135)
Orenes-Bo, Francisco 3:24:31 (3,333)
Orfano, Giulio 2:56:22 (667)
Organ, Philip 3:18:38 (2,622)
Organ, Rodney 4:09:01 (12,134)
Organ, Roy 3:29:20 (4,050)
Orme, Richard 3:14:57 (2,232)
Ormerod, Timothy 4:58:02 (23,591)
Ormisher, Richard 4:59:41 (23,922)
Ormiston, Paul 4:33:57 (18,153)
Ormond, Paul 3:45:38 (6,856)
Ornstein, Kenneth 4:13:57 (13,244)
O'Rourke, Phil 4:25:05 (16,021)
Orpin, Mark 4:46:27 (21,081)
Orr, Adam 4:48:15 (21,482)
Orr, Billy 2:58:59 (849)
Orr, David 3:53:02 (8,433)
Orr, Douglas 4:47:07 (21,208)
Orr, James 3:22:46 (3,081)
Orrell, Andrew 4:22:51 (15,455)
Orrock, Duncan 4:37:34 (19,000)
Ort, Peter 4:51:19 (22,159)
Ortega, Ivan 5:17:50 (26,583)
Ortega, Pierre 3:53:27 (8,530)
Orth, Dieter 4:46:20 (21,054)
Orth, Lars 3:38:39 (5,531)
Orton, Ian 6:31:29 (31,361)
Orton, Sebastian 4:16:55 (13,975)
Osborn, David 4:24:40 (15,906)
Osborn, Giaran 2:47:05 (303)
Osborn, Peter 5:12:36 (25,921)
Osborn, Roger 3:50:03 (7,743)
Osborne, Andrew 4:29:24 (17,089)
Osborne, Bruce 3:38:43 (5,548)
Osborne, Chris 4:00:53 (10,403)
Osborne, David 4:31:38 (17,652)
Osborne, Dennis 4:37:24 (18,963)
Osborne, Derek 3:13:11 (2,016)
Osborne, Jamie 4:24:35 (15,883)
Osborne, Jarrod 3:34:59 (4,908)
Osborne, Mark 5:18:32 (26,701)
Osborne, Matthew 3:50:19 (7,805)
Osborne, Michael 4:49:17 (21,698)
Osborne, Nicholas 4:58:30 (23,699)
Osborne, Nicolas 3:49:55 (7,719)
Osborne, Peter 3:51:33 (8,092)
Osborne, Stephen 5:11:15 (25,731)
Osgood, Paul 4:58:21 (23,662)
O'Shaughnessy, Damian 3:59:20 (10,047)
O'Shea, Andrew 4:52:20 (22,365)
O'Shea, James 4:42:03 (20,001)
O'Shea, Paul 4:03:59 (11,059)
Osinowo, Remi 3:58:52 (9,934)
Osman, Adib 4:55:23 (22,999)
Osmond, Paul 6:25:52 (31,198)
Ost, Andrew 4:42:39 (20,142)
Osterdahl, Anthony 4:12:32 (12,894)
Ostermeyer, Marcel 3:04:30 (1,210)
O'Sullivan, Andrew 3:47:00 (7,124)
O'Sullivan, Donal 4:19:55 (14,717)
O'Sullivan, Gareth 5:02:08 (24,332)
O'Sullivan, Hugh 3:53:50 (8,628)
O'Sullivan, Martin 3:49:56 (7,723)
O'Sullivan, Michael 3:23:28 (3,174)
O'Sullivan, Paul 3:56:27 (9,305)
O'Sullivan, Paul 4:21:29 (15,107)
O'Sullivan, Steven 4:14:18 (13,327)
O'Sullivan, Tim 3:36:06 (5,078)
O'Sullivan, Tim 4:12:18 (12,832)
O'Sullivan, Wayne 5:04:46 (24,752)
Oswald, David 6:11:54 (30,723)
Oswald, James 3:35:24 (4,972)
Oswald, Richard 3:53:45 (8,603)
Oswin, Raymond 4:07:10 (11,731)
O'Toole, Michael 5:05:04 (24,806)
Ott, Dan 4:16:09 (13,773)
Ott, Keith 5:39:10 (28,917)
Ottemoller, Lars 2:48:38 (352)
Otterburn, Frederick 3:59:19 (10,040)
Ottley, Ken 4:54:40 (22,857)
Otto, Heiko 3:23:51 (3,221)
Ottosson, Anders 4:49:48 (21,823)
Otwal, Mukhtiar 5:08:45 (25,363)
Oubib, Mohamed 3:31:26 (4,395)
Oudghiri, Moulay Idriss 3:16:49 (2,405)
Oudshoorn, Ben 4:26:53 (16,444)
Outhwaite, Jeff 3:20:16 (2,800)
Outhwaite, John 3:08:28 (1,541)
Ovenstone, Keith 4:19:36 (14,639)
Over, Robert 4:53:33 (22,627)
Overall, Geoffrey 3:29:20 (4,050)
Overney, Thierry 3:07:04 (1,409)
Overstall, Oliver 5:06:42 (25,056)
Overy, Terence 3:38:22 (5,472)
Owen, Andrew 3:08:03 (1,506)
Owen, Andrew 4:26:46 (16,421)
Owen, Chris 4:23:58 (15,741)
Owen, Colin 6:18:01 (30,934)
Owen, David 4:31:48 (17,687)
Owen, Doug 4:04:05 (11,084)
Owen, Dylan 3:06:26 (1,353)
Owen, Eugene 3:44:09 (6,571)
Owen, Gareth 4:36:11 (18,689)
Owen, Gary 5:01:59 (24,311)
Owen, Glyn 6:47:50 (31,671)
Owen, Ian 5:26:39 (27,747)
Owen, James 5:11:44 (25,790)
Owen, Jon 6:53:46 (31,804)
Owen, Kevin 3:37:22 (5,300)
Owen, Matthew 3:13:43 (2,089)
Owen, Matthew 5:01:30 (24,233)
Owen, Paul 3:51:21 (8,043)
Owen, Paul 4:24:36 (15,888)
Owen, Richard 2:54:06 (542)
Owen, Richard 5:03:49 (24,597)
Owen, Robert 4:13:33 (13,141)
Owen, Robert 4:26:33 (16,366)
Owen, Stanley Ewart 4:06:47 (11,650)
Owen, Stephen 4:20:29 (14,864)
Owen, Steven 3:46:28 (7,024)
Owen, Stuart 4:53:59 (22,711)
Owens, Christopher 4:10:45 (12,503)
Owens, Ivor 8:06:54 (32,263)
Owens, Martin 5:18:05 (26,624)
Owens, Phillip 4:06:43 (11,630)
Owens, Stuart 4:53:10 (22,537)
Owens, Terry 5:22:30 (27,212)
Owens, Thomas 2:58:08 (776)
Owers, Andrew 4:12:19 (12,838)
Oxberry, Paul 5:15:52 (26,359)
Oxborough, Craig 5:26:59 (27,776)
Oxbrow, Darren 4:28:57 (16,982)
Oxenham, Lawrence 4:07:21 (11,766)
Oxer, Matthew 5:50:27 (29,745)
Oxford, Stewart 5:38:57 (28,894)
Oxley, Alan 4:50:04 (21,876)
Oxley, Christopher 3:43:50 (6,514)
Oxley, James 5:25:26 (27,601)
Oxley, Neil 4:20:34 (14,883)
Oza, Pranav 4:15:00 (13,507)
Pabila, Lalit 4:19:58 (14,731)
Pace, Andrew 3:10:50 (1,742)
Pace, Kevin 3:39:48 (5,748)
Pachatz, Markus 4:16:49 (13,939)
Pachmann, Matthias 4:15:23 (13,615)
Pacillo, Francesco 4:03:20 (10,919)
Packer, Leigh 3:27:10 (3,700)
Packer, Malcolm 2:42:44 (190)
Packer, Scott 4:37:13 (18,925)
Packman, Kieran 4:46:30 (21,094)
Packwood, Samuel 4:11:57 (12,751)
Paco, Joao 5:22:46 (27,250)
Padden, Eamonn 6:40:17 (31,543)
Paddock, Lloyd 4:53:09 (22,530)
Paden, Edward 4:16:22 (13,823)
Padhiar, Nat 6:16:17 (30,865)
Padley, Paul 5:50:35 (29,759)
Padou, Mickael 3:42:35 (6,273)
Padwick, Steuart 4:51:54 (22,291)
Paffendorf, Gilbert 4:10:11 (12,389)
Paganini, Giorgio 4:58:56 (23,789)
Page, Andrew 3:54:29 (8,776)

Page, Ashley 3:37:45 (5,376)
Page, David 5:13:26 (26,029)
Page, Geoffrey 6:57:52 (31,871)
Page, Gordon 4:53:09 (22,530)
Page, Ian 5:36:04 (28,644)
Page, Jeremy 3:49:16 (7,582)
Page, Mark 4:57:27 (23,468)
Page, Martin 3:55:21 (9,008)
Page, Mick 2:46:46 (290)
Page, Neal 3:14:32 (2,188)
Page, Nicholas 4:55:54 (23,132)
Page, Nick 2:47:52 (330)
Page, Richard 3:55:34 (9,065)
Page, Serge 3:24:13 (3,287)
Page, Stephen 4:52:48 (22,460)
Page, William 5:58:35 (30,183)
Page-Brown, Christian 4:39:46 (19,490)
Paget, David 4:16:02 (13,748)
Pagett, James 6:37:47 (31,504)
Pagnamenta, Robert 3:31:12 (4,358)
Pagnotta, Michael 3:44:56 (6,718)
Pagotto, Jean-Michel 3:42:10 (6,182)
Pagura, Marcel 3:06:31 (1,361)
Pailor, Stuart 4:26:24 (16,334)
Pailthorpe, Stewart 3:30:40 (4,268)
Pain, John 6:50:36 (31,734)
Paina, Claude 4:29:59 (17,239)
Paine, Ron 3:59:00 (9,966)
Paine, Thomas 4:51:34 (22,217)
Painet, Patrick 4:09:07 (12,156)
Painter, Andrew 4:35:36 (18,541)
Painter, Daniel 4:40:34 (19,661)
Painter, Paul 4:18:53 (14,473)
Paintin, Edward 4:20:46 (14,918)
Pairman, John 3:58:49 (9,921)
Paisley, David 4:25:00 (16,003)
Pajak, Lee 3:45:06 (6,755)
Paletta, Fabrizio 3:28:01 (3,818)
Paley, Sean 4:43:20 (20,328)
Palfrey, Daryl 2:59:37 (911)
Palladini, Massimo 3:22:11 (3,007)
Pallant, Robert 3:52:58 (8,412)
Pallas Font, Joan 4:27:02 (16,480)
Pallister, Andrew 4:27:17 (16,546)
Pallister, David 4:15:40 (13,668)
Palm, Jonas 3:48:34 (7,415)
Palmer, Andrew 4:26:30 (16,355)
Palmer, Craig 5:31:02 (28,194)
Palmer, David 3:47:15 (7,171)
Palmer, David 3:47:32 (7,220)
Palmer, Ian 5:17:59 (26,607)
Palmer, Jeremy 3:31:00 (4,327)
Palmer, John 3:48:03 (7,328)
Palmer, Jonny 4:50:03 (21,871)
Palmer, Karl 3:34:11 (4,774)
Palmer, Kenneth 3:01:23 (1,017)
Palmer, Kevin 4:24:04 (15,771)
Palmer, Lee 4:58:53 (23,777)
Palmer, Lloyd 2:46:00 (255)
Palmer, Mark 4:25:17 (16,081)
Palmer, Mark 5:13:01 (25,976)
Palmer, Michael 4:24:28 (15,860)
Palmer, Michael 4:56:49 (23,342)
Palmer, Neil 4:33:19 (18,008)
Palmer, Paul 3:42:06 (6,168)
Palmer, Richard 4:49:20 (21,711)
Palmer, Robert 4:35:55 (18,625)
Palmer, Roy 2:35:34 (104)
Palmer, Russell 4:39:30 (19,439)
Palmer, Stuart 3:02:36 (1,091)
Palmer, Stuart 4:43:22 (20,342)
Palmer, Stuart 5:32:54 (28,367)
Palmer, Tim 3:52:51 (8,384)
Palmer, Wayne 4:22:09 (15,276)
Palomo, Francisco 3:39:46 (5,744)
Palpacuer, Claude 3:37:42 (5,365)
Palser, Tristan 3:08:43 (1,565)
Pan, Ramon 4:49:59 (21,854)
Pancaldi, Matthew 4:48:26 (21,524)
Pandit, Stephane 4:16:27 (13,846)
Panesar, Harpal 4:08:11 (11,936)
Pang, Anthony 4:47:05 (21,198)
Pang, Richard 4:41:22 (19,839)
Pankhania, Mahendra 6:52:28 (31,768)
Pannell, James 4:33:19 (18,008)
Pannell, Mark 4:38:08 (19,114)
Panni, Franco 3:44:47 (6,685)
Panter, Anthony 5:11:41 (25,787)
Pantlin, Andrew 5:00:19 (24,038)
Pantlin, Tim 4:16:23 (13,829)
Paosila-Jones, Martin 4:12:14 (12,823)
Papa, Francesco 6:10:24 (30,654)
Papadimitriou, Alex 4:05:44 (11,440)
Papaloizou, Christopher 4:56:03 (23,158)
Papani, Darren 5:05:13 (24,829)
Papay, Barnaby 4:48:51 (21,600)
Pape, Christopher 6:33:47 (31,419)
Pape, Michael 5:46:49 (29,484)
Pappernigg, Hermann 2:57:11 (716)
Pappini, James 4:20:15 (14,809)
Papst, Bernd 4:55:31 (23,031)
Paramor, Graham 3:35:28 (4,993)
Paramor, Jon 3:38:49 (5,561)
Paramore, Ian 2:47:22 (313)
Parasram, Anthony 4:23:33 (15,630)
Parcell, Bob 4:08:33 (12,024)
Pardey, James 3:32:51 (4,577)
Parekh, Bhupesh 6:22:03 (31,076)
Parello, Salvatore 3:12:52 (1,977)
Pares, John 3:05:59 (1,320)
Parfitt, James 4:23:11 (15,541)
Parigi, Fabio 3:41:30 (6,067)
Parish, Andrew 4:11:52 (12,733)
Parish, Brian 4:50:42 (22,011)
Parish, Daniel 4:15:26 (13,624)
Parish, Ian 3:56:28 (9,310)
Parish, Stuart 4:54:54 (22,903)
Park, David 5:50:21 (29,740)
Park, Graham 3:27:32 (3,745)
Park, Grahame 4:34:46 (18,341)
Park, Gregor 3:32:08 (4,489)
Park, Iain 4:33:25 (18,036)
Park, Kenny 4:24:03 (15,766)
Park, Mungo 3:54:30 (8,784)
Parke, Aaron 3:59:27 (10,083)
Parke, Kevin 3:53:22 (8,509)
Parker, Adam 3:52:42 (8,354)
Parker, Anthony 3:55:58 (9,168)
Parker, Anthony 4:34:04 (18,186)
Parker, Charles 4:12:49 (12,963)
Parker, David 5:36:52 (28,724)
Parker, Geoffrey 3:37:14 (5,278)
Parker, Graham 4:17:55 (14,235)
Parker, Matthew 3:23:18 (3,149)
Parker, Richard 3:11:22 (1,786)
Parker, Robert 4:04:55 (11,274)
Parker, Robert 4:59:17 (23,855)
Parker, Robert 5:35:02 (28,554)
Parker, Roger 4:49:41 (21,799)
Parker, Shaun 3:48:14 (7,364)
Parker, Stephen 4:25:08 (16,037)
Parker, Stephen 4:33:20 (18,013)
Parker, Terence 4:58:15 (23,638)
Parker-Mead, Gary 4:44:26 (20,602)
Parkes, Bradley 7:15:54 (32,041)
Parkes, John 4:00:36 (10,345)
Parkes, Keith 4:13:44 (13,184)
Parkes, Mike 4:33:16 (17,998)
Parkes, Roy 3:50:41 (7,884)
Parkhouse, Andy 5:23:03 (27,292)
Parkin, Barry 5:14:29 (26,172)
Parkin, David 5:17:15 (26,509)
Parkin, Dean 4:08:22 (11,973)
Parkin, George 4:37:33 (18,995)
Parkin, Gregory 4:27:11 (16,521)
Parkin, Ian 4:21:03 (14,995)
Parkin, Keith 2:57:32 (737)
Parkington, David 3:13:52 (2,109)
Parkins, David 3:27:26 (3,728)
Parkins, Ian 3:26:41 (3,630)
Parkinson, Alastair 5:25:59 (27,669)
Parkinson, Brendan 3:48:25 (7,392)
Parkinson, Edward 4:09:27 (12,215)
Parkinson, James 4:56:35 (23,283)
Parkinson, Paul 2:59:27 (896)
Parkinson, Peter 3:49:05 (7,532)
Parkinson, Roy 3:12:44 (1,961)
Parkinson, Simon 4:27:13 (16,527)
Parks, Floyd 4:23:30 (15,616)
Parks, Peter 5:23:06 (27,300)
Parks, Sydney 4:49:54 (21,847)
Parmley, Andrew 5:21:49 (27,126)
Parnell, Leonard 4:54:11 (22,744)
Parnell, Lloyd 3:57:26 (9,564)
Parnell, Philip 5:03:14 (24,498)
Parnell, Richard 4:50:56 (22,058)
Parnell, Rupert 4:34:35 (18,301)
Parnum, Alan 3:42:18 (6,204)
Parr, Guy 4:13:15 (13,063)
Parr, James 6:19:50 (31,010)
Parr, John 3:35:14 (4,947)
Parr, Richard 4:29:18 (17,061)
Parr, Richard 5:53:33 (29,909)
Parrenin, Patrick 3:25:46 (3,504)
Parrett, Leslie 5:22:17 (27,184)
Parrin, Robert 3:52:58 (8,412)
Parris, Noel 4:54:10 (22,738)
Parrish, Keith 3:38:00 (5,413)
Parrish, Paul 5:08:01 (25,268)
Parrott, Jeremy 5:16:06 (26,387)
Parrott, Nick 4:21:29 (15,107)
Parry, Andrew 4:35:59 (18,646)
Parry, Anthony 4:50:35 (21,987)
Parry, Antony 3:15:51 (2,320)
Parry, David 3:48:15 (7,368)
Parry, Graham 4:47:23 (21,269)
Parry, Keith 3:15:15 (2,267)
Parry, Mark 3:53:01 (8,429)
Parry, Martin 4:29:51 (17,207)
Parry, Owain 4:29:08 (17,022)
Parry, Steve 4:00:16 (10,283)
Parry, Tony 3:17:03 (2,433)
Parry, Walter 5:04:38 (24,721)
Parsell, Daniel 4:19:11 (14,548)
Parsison, Keith 4:30:33 (17,382)
Parsley, Elvis 2:59:40 (916)
Parslow, Stephen 3:52:49 (8,375)
Parson, Mark 5:39:48 (28,970)
Parsonage, Andrew 4:43:03 (20,246)
Parsonaut, Garry 4:13:28 (13,116)
Parsons, Andrew 3:19:56 (2,748)
Parsons, Carl 5:52:20 (29,848)
Parsons, Clive 4:14:50 (13,461)
Parsons, Howard 6:04:58 (30,453)
Parsons, Jonathan 4:27:15 (16,534)
Parsons, Neil 5:30:17 (28,113)
Parsons, Stephen 3:41:01 (5,962)
Parsons, Steve 4:14:09 (13,298)
Parsons, Steven 5:22:26 (27,204)
Parsons, Thomas 2:57:18 (725)
Partington, Christopher 4:55:22 (22,994)
Parton, Christopher 4:40:46 (19,696)
Parton, David 4:19:02 (14,513)
Partridge, Duncan 4:51:50 (22,275)
Partridge, Edward 2:45:34 (248)
Partridge, Graham 3:50:11 (7,773)
Partridge, Keith 3:12:15 (1,891)
Partridge, Nicholas 4:08:05 (11,921)
Partridge, Simon 3:14:58 (2,234)
Partridge, Stephen 4:52:47 (22,457)
Partridge, Stewart 4:01:57 (10,624)
Partridge, Toby 4:55:01 (22,925)
Parvin, Philip 4:07:00 (11,687)
Pasandin, Francisco 2:37:27 (126)
Pascal, Monin 3:40:51 (5,932)
Pascazio, Alessandro 3:25:52 (3,523)
Pascoe, Barry 3:19:56 (2,748)
Pascoe, Kevin 4:26:01 (16,251)
Pascucci, Alessandro 3:02:03 (1,055)
Pashley, Howard 4:51:47 (22,264)
Pask, Andrew 3:51:09 (7,995)
Pask, Michael 3:13:38 (2,077)
Pasola, Richard 4:47:54 (21,399)
Pasquinelli, Claudio 4:19:27 (14,605)
Pass, Colin 4:27:05 (16,494)
Passacantilli, Francesco 3:58:54 (9,942)
Passer, Andrew 4:04:14 (11,118)
Passingham, Leonard 2:49:42 (383)
Pastorini, Giancarlo 3:33:08 (4,618)

Pilarski, Richard	4:33:59 (18,162)	
Pilcher, Martin	3:37:17 (5,288)	
Pile, Gareth	4:10:11 (12,389)	
Pile, Robert	5:07:36 (25,201)	
Pilfold, Mike	5:26:08 (27,693)	
Pilkington, Adrian	2:58:08 (776)	
Pill, Stephen	3:38:49 (5,561)	
Pilley, Richard	5:24:47 (27,506)	
Pilling, Kristian	3:53:08 (8,457)	
Pilling, Michael	4:14:27 (13,369)	
Pillinger, Chris	4:53:09 (22,530)	
Pilnik, Graham	4:11:31 (12,650)	
Pim, Brian	3:23:31 (3,181)	
Pim, Jonathan	3:53:29 (8,536)	
Pincepoche, David	3:49:11 (7,561)	
Pinchbeck, Christopher	3:42:39 (6,285)	
Pinckney, Charles	4:21:10 (15,027)	
Pinder, George	3:25:35 (3,473)	
Pinder, Richard	4:56:52 (23,355)	
Pineda Gil, Juan Pedro	5:33:37 (28,431)	
Pinhorne, Jan	3:57:18 (9,531)	
Pink, Anthony	3:43:50 (6,514)	
Pink, Robert	3:09:02 (1,590)	
Pink, Stuart	3:56:59 (9,451)	
Pinkerton, Charles	3:06:38 (1,371)	
Pinnell, Andrew	5:10:01 (25,552)	
Pinner, Barnaby	5:19:25 (26,820)	
Pinner, John	5:05:06 (24,814)	
Pinney, Mark	6:17:43 (30,911)	
Pinnick, David	4:14:29 (13,377)	
Pinnion, Clive	3:14:01 (2,131)	
Pinnock, James	3:58:50 (9,927)	
Pinnock, Mark	4:22:16 (15,309)	
Pinto de Abreu, Carlos	4:00:55 (10,411)	
Piotrowski, Marek	3:59:57 (10,211)	
Piovan, Renzo	5:42:08 (29,180)	
Piovesana, Martin	3:58:53 (9,939)	
Pipe, John	4:16:44 (13,914)	
Pipe, Steven	4:20:49 (14,931)	
Pipe, Timothy	4:01:19 (10,503)	
Piper, Chris	3:01:12 (1,011)	
Piper, Christopher	4:29:15 (17,053)	
Piper, Colin	4:53:48 (22,682)	
Piper, Patrick	4:07:49 (11,875)	
Pippard, Mark	5:25:29 (27,605)	
Pires, Artur	2:52:22 (463)	
Pironet, Ewald	5:06:05 (24,966)	
Pirozzolo, Mario	4:29:07 (17,017)	
Pirt, Nathan	4:27:54 (16,689)	
Pirttikangas, Kari	5:24:52 (27,514)	
Pisaneschi, Adriano	4:15:13 (13,571)	
Pita Andreu, José	3:25:09 (3,417)	
Pitcaithly, Mark	2:57:11 (716)	
Pitcher, Mike	4:45:23 (20,817)	
Pitcock, Richard	4:54:12 (22,747)	
Pitman, Donald	3:10:46 (1,738)	
Pitman, James	3:59:26 (10,073)	
Pitman, Steve	4:05:41 (11,430)	
Pitron, David	4:58:29 (23,696)	
Pitt, Alan	3:13:56 (2,121)	
Pitt, Frank	4:56:25 (23,242)	
Pitt, Graeme	3:44:21 (6,611)	
Pitt, Stephen	4:36:30 (18,769)	
Pittaccio, Michael	4:17:58 (14,244)	
Pittock, Mark	4:29:26 (17,098)	
Pitts, David	3:47:45 (7,267)	
Piunti, Pietro	3:26:17 (3,576)	
Place, Kevin	4:48:59 (21,627)	
Plaice, Christopher	5:25:53 (27,651)	
Plaistowe, Andrew	4:02:29 (10,738)	
Plane, Terrance	4:37:39 (19,009)	
Plank, Anthony	3:29:00 (4,001)	
Plank, Michael	4:08:52 (12,102)	
Plant, David	4:17:21 (14,072)	
Plant, Douglas	4:40:51 (19,716)	
Plant, Gareth	3:31:59 (4,470)	
Plant, James	5:27:08 (27,793)	
Plant, Ray	2:26:02 (43)	
Plaskett, Gary	4:59:13 (23,846)	
Plaskowski, Bron	4:57:27 (23,468)	
Plastow, Robert	4:44:15 (20,557)	
Platt, Austin	3:51:13 (8,014)	
Platt, Gregory	4:10:53 (12,524)	

Platt, Mark	5:04:42 (24,733)	
Platt, Robert	5:54:15 (29,951)	
Platts, Glen	3:58:00 (9,706)	
Platts, Rob	2:48:07 (338)	
Playdon, Andrew	4:26:50 (16,436)	
Player, Geoff	4:36:39 (18,797)	
Player, Howard	3:53:00 (8,426)	
Playford-Smith, Terry	4:18:23 (14,325)	
Pleasance, Neal	4:18:27 (14,344)	
Pledger, Stephen	3:41:29 (6,060)	
Pleming, Aled	4:07:08 (11,721)	
Plenderleith, Scott	3:33:26 (4,672)	
Plessl, Karl	2:55:03 (597)	
Plews, Kevin	4:27:40 (16,641)	
Pleydell-Bouverie, Nicholas	3:48:38 (7,430)	
Plind, Joanthan	3:44:02 (6,554)	
Plitt, Timm	3:56:00 (9,178)	
Plowman, Barry	3:36:08 (5,084)	
Plowman, Peter	3:28:00 (3,814)	
Plowright, Tony	3:35:48 (5,040)	
Pluck, Mark	3:39:30 (5,696)	
Plum, Hans-Joachim	3:26:25 (3,593)	
Plumb, Alan	4:29:30 (17,120)	
Plumb, David	6:06:07 (30,509)	
Plumb, Giles	3:27:04 (3,691)	
Plummer, Barry	5:25:09 (27,561)	
Plummer, Matthew	4:11:33 (12,656)	
Plumpton, Andrew	4:37:41 (19,016)	
Plumpton, Graham	3:24:54 (3,384)	
Plumstead, Mark	3:24:13 (3,287)	
Plumstead, Pat	3:13:43 (2,089)	
Plumtree, Matthew	4:14:47 (13,445)	
Plunkett, Mark	4:04:01 (11,070)	
Plunkett, Stuart	4:29:01 (16,994)	
Pocklington, Andy	3:54:22 (8,743)	
Pocock, Frank	4:00:28 (10,324)	
Pocock, Jeremy	4:53:14 (22,552)	
Pocock, John	3:36:33 (5,152)	
Pocock, John	4:36:56 (18,863)	
Pocock, Michael	4:07:49 (11,875)	
Podowski, Jan	3:09:32 (1,634)	
Poesio, Massimo	4:18:16 (14,294)	
Poffley, Vincent	7:12:22 (32,017)	
Pogson, Andrew	4:56:32 (23,270)	
Pogson, Charles	5:30:27 (28,137)	
Pointon, Darol	5:17:33 (26,553)	
Pointon, Philip	3:39:38 (5,717)	
Poirier, Didier	3:56:52 (9,417)	
Pol, Chrisjan	4:52:53 (22,481)	
Poland, Patrick	4:29:01 (16,994)	
Polden, Robert	4:10:56 (12,531)	
Poli, Marzio	4:08:19 (11,963)	
Politi, Domenico	3:41:21 (6,025)	
Poll, Stuart	4:27:11 (16,521)	
Pollard, Christopher	3:58:24 (9,810)	
Pollard, Christopher	4:19:10 (14,546)	
Pollard, Gary	4:20:26 (14,854)	
Pollard, Lionel	4:41:12 (19,800)	
Pollard, Michael	4:17:05 (14,007)	
Pollard, Michael	4:47:44 (21,353)	
Pollard, Nicholas	3:38:10 (5,437)	
Pollard, Philip	4:00:06 (10,244)	
Pollard, Simon	4:04:37 (11,201)	
Pollett, Derek	4:19:58 (14,731)	
Polley, Ian	5:08:22 (25,320)	
Polley, Keith	4:46:26 (21,078)	
Pollock, Andrew	4:55:07 (22,944)	
Pollock, Jeremy	3:18:07 (2,566)	
Pollock, Robert	3:16:24 (2,367)	
Pomario, Sean	4:01:08 (10,457)	
Pomeroy, Richard	4:28:56 (16,976)	
Pomfret, Robert	4:21:25 (15,095)	
Pommeret, Laurent	3:56:47 (9,393)	
Pomo, Giuseppe	3:07:00 (1,402)	
Pomposo-Galbarriartu, Pedro	3:13:47 (2,094)	
Pomroy, Jonathan	4:29:49 (17,199)	
Ponchelle, Jerome	4:26:43 (16,405)	
Pond, Chris	4:01:41 (10,576)	
Pond, Graham	4:44:18 (20,571)	
Ponder, Carl	5:17:32 (26,549)	
Ponder, Nigel	5:35:55 (28,630)	
Poneskis, John	6:00:13 (30,264)	
Ponet, Alain	4:17:38 (14,152)	

Ponsonby, Clive	3:45:29 (6,828)	
Pont, David	5:40:10 (29,009)	
Pontefract, Lee	4:41:09 (19,788)	
Pontt, Nicholas	3:47:20 (7,179)	
Poole, Daniel	4:40:06 (19,556)	
Poole, Edward	5:12:37 (25,923)	
Poole, Graham	5:14:45 (26,207)	
Poole, John	3:28:00 (3,814)	
Poole, Julie	5:08:20 (25,316)	
Poole, Lee	4:47:44 (21,353)	
Poole, Matthew	4:25:10 (16,047)	
Poole, Robert	4:20:48 (14,929)	
Poole, Stephen	3:47:21 (7,182)	
Poole, Terry	4:56:19 (23,224)	
Poole, Thomas	4:20:59 (14,974)	
Pooley, Roger	4:54:25 (22,801)	
Poolman, Ian	3:46:43 (7,069)	
Poolman, Robert	4:21:15 (15,044)	
Poon, Andrew	4:38:34 (19,213)	
Poon, Simon	4:52:50 (22,469)	
Poonian, Satnam	6:15:41 (30,846)	
Poot, Dirk	4:34:28 (18,281)	
Poot, Hans	4:29:56 (17,227)	
Pope, Christopher	4:13:37 (13,156)	
Pope, Dennis	3:32:18 (4,507)	
Pope, Eric	4:12:07 (12,791)	
Pope, Matthew	3:38:41 (5,538)	
Pope, Michael	4:11:51 (12,732)	
Pope, Robert	3:52:03 (8,206)	
Pope, Roger	6:35:36 (31,464)	
Pope, Timothy	5:19:03 (26,763)	
Popham, Andrew	4:05:07 (11,315)	
Popham, Brett	3:22:44 (3,075)	
Pople, Clive	4:18:07 (14,274)	
Popov, Mikhail	3:21:03 (2,890)	
Poppleton, Ben	4:44:35 (20,629)	
Popplewell, Alex	4:27:55 (16,693)	
Porrini, Luigi	3:54:58 (8,911)	
Porritt, André	3:27:52 (3,799)	
Port, Leslie	4:03:51 (11,025)	
Portall, Bertie	3:57:45 (9,632)	
Portanier, Daniel	3:42:21 (6,209)	
Porteous, Andrew	2:57:21 (727)	
Porteous, Andy	4:12:40 (12,933)	
Porteous, Harry	3:14:35 (2,195)	
Porteous, Robert	5:05:54 (24,944)	
Porter, Andrew	3:24:33 (3,341)	
Porter, Brian	3:53:42 (8,591)	
Porter, Garry	4:09:17 (12,190)	
Porter, Garry	4:25:52 (16,219)	
Porter, Ian	3:46:28 (7,024)	
Porter, John	3:09:25 (1,625)	
Porter, Jonathan	4:58:55 (23,784)	
Porter, Keith	4:37:50 (19,050)	
Porter, Mark	4:41:41 (19,915)	
Porter, Matthew	5:00:25 (24,053)	
Porter, Patrick	4:26:35 (16,375)	
Porter, Ray	3:51:43 (8,130)	
Porter, Richard	4:04:55 (11,274)	
Porter, Roger	3:11:34 (1,809)	
Porter, Roger	3:37:34 (5,338)	
Porter, Russell	4:11:13 (12,581)	
Porter, Stephen	4:22:20 (15,324)	
Portnoi, Gershon	4:57:58 (23,576)	
Porto, Santiago	3:35:35 (5,010)	
Portsmouth, Barry	4:58:24 (23,676)	
Possegger, Franz	3:39:17 (5,651)	
Postans, Dean	5:20:10 (26,911)	
Postans, Neil	4:06:11 (11,533)	
Postlethwaite, David	4:40:41 (19,680)	
Postmus, John	5:27:52 (27,875)	
Potter, Adam	5:21:02 (27,027)	
Potter, Alan	4:17:55 (14,235)	
Potter, Cliff	4:56:43 (23,320)	
Potter, Craig	5:15:00 (26,248)	
Potter, Darren	4:05:06 (11,308)	
Potter, David	5:14:05 (26,106)	
Potter, Edward	3:52:45 (8,363)	
Potter, John	5:36:30 (28,683)	
Potter, John	5:39:56 (28,987)	
Potter, Jolyon	5:07:48 (25,238)	
Potter, Jonothan	4:01:10 (10,465)	
Potter, Karl	3:25:27 (3,458)	

Potter, Matthew	4:28:54 (16,968)	
Potter, Simon	4:52:31 (22,399)	
Potter, Stephen	4:57:30 (23,482)	
Potter, Stuart	5:30:22 (28,128)	
Potter, William	4:38:46 (19,274)	
Pottinger, Gavin	5:26:25 (27,728)	
Pottle, Tim	4:32:35 (17,852)	
Potts, Andrew	4:49:34 (21,766)	
Potts, John	4:32:34 (17,848)	
Potts, Martin	4:55:11 (22,959)	
Potts, Richard	3:13:15 (2,028)	
Poulain, Alastair	4:23:55 (15,724)	
Poulton, Simon	3:35:25 (4,977)	
Pouncey, David	3:23:36 (3,191)	
Pounder, Nicholas	3:50:05 (7,751)	
Pouplin, Benoit	3:16:31 (2,377)	
Pouplin, Jean-Pierre	3:45:51 (6,901)	
Powell, Adam	5:16:25 (26,418)	
Powell, Adrian	3:14:54 (2,228)	
Powell, Adrian	4:17:15 (14,045)	
Powell, Alan	4:21:46 (15,176)	
Powell, Alan	6:51:04 (31,744)	
Powell, Alun	4:09:27 (12,215)	
Powell, Chris	4:31:13 (17,550)	
Powell, David	3:37:49 (5,388)	
Powell, David	6:48:49 (31,690)	
Powell, Eliot	3:42:01 (6,153)	
Powell, Greg	3:42:11 (6,187)	
Powell, Ian	3:55:50 (9,139)	
Powell, James	4:21:17 (15,054)	
Powell, Jason	5:19:38 (26,841)	
Powell, John	4:41:54 (19,974)	
Powell, John	4:55:37 (23,058)	
Powell, Martin	3:37:40 (5,358)	
Powell, Michael	2:57:03 (706)	
Powell, Michael	5:02:24 (24,373)	
Powell, Nathan	3:30:48 (4,297)	
Powell, Nigel	3:39:59 (5,782)	
Powell, Raymond	3:34:59 (4,908)	
Powell, Robert	5:42:22 (29,197)	
Powell, Russell	4:59:01 (23,804)	
Powell, Stephen	4:47:04 (21,194)	
Powell, Stephen	5:36:43 (28,708)	
Powell, Steven	4:11:31 (12,650)	
Powell, Tarquin	4:08:10 (11,932)	
Powell, Thomas	3:51:01 (7,957)	
Powell, Timothy	3:24:58 (3,390)	
Powell, Toby	4:26:44 (16,413)	
Powell, Wayne	3:47:23 (7,192)	
Power, Andrew	5:10:53 (25,670)	
Power, Andy	2:52:45 (485)	
Power, Brian	3:51:38 (8,116)	
Power, David	5:40:20 (29,020)	
Power, Matthew	5:25:53 (27,651)	
Power, Michael	3:58:44 (9,892)	
Power, Nick	6:54:22 (31,813)	
Power, Richard	3:40:57 (5,950)	
Power, Robert	4:06:58 (11,679)	
Power, Sean	5:38:22 (28,848)	
Power, Stuart	2:59:59 (939)	
Powers, Sean	4:06:05 (11,512)	
Powles, Grant	3:24:59 (3,393)	
Powles, Sean	4:35:18 (18,471)	
Powling, Mark	5:09:57 (25,532)	
Pownall, Richard	3:27:50 (3,792)	
Powner, Geoffrey	3:12:02 (1,865)	
Powolny, Roderick	4:30:27 (17,357)	
Powter, David	4:43:51 (20,470)	
Powter, Seth	4:17:12 (14,034)	
Poynter, Jonathan	4:12:52 (12,973)	
Prabhakar, Sajiv	4:59:54 (23,967)	
Prady, Clive	3:49:45 (7,686)	
Prankerd, Henry	4:46:19 (21,050)	
Pranner, Christian	5:08:23 (25,322)	
Pratt, Dean	3:37:07 (5,257)	
Pratt, Derek	3:45:04 (6,746)	
Pratt, Gary	4:53:21 (22,586)	
Pratt, Ian	3:09:51 (1,661)	
Pratten, Kenneth	4:03:55 (11,039)	
Pready, Nicholas	4:51:01 (22,075)	
Prebble, John	3:57:59 (9,703)	
Prechtl, Wolfgang	3:26:51 (3,649)	
Precious, John	3:57:37 (9,599)	
Preddy, Robert	3:33:44 (4,710)	
Preece, Brian	5:25:29 (27,605)	
Preece, David	3:08:08 (1,513)	
Preedy, Mark	4:37:56 (19,071)	
Preitschopf, Michael	4:17:13 (14,036)	
Prendegast, Matt	3:28:18 (3,866)	
Prendergast, Craig	6:05:42 (30,491)	
Prendergast, Martin	4:03:40 (10,981)	
Prendergast, Paul	4:54:35 (22,833)	
Prendergast, Thomas	3:43:13 (6,410)	
Prentice, Iain	3:57:00 (9,458)	
Prescott, Alan	4:34:05 (18,192)	
Prescott, Richard	4:47:57 (21,412)	
Prescott, Richard	5:23:29 (27,347)	
Presland, Geoff	5:06:00 (24,960)	
Pressey, Martin	4:39:14 (19,380)	
Pressley, David	5:26:36 (27,743)	
Pressling, Jon	4:37:10 (18,912)	
Prest, Michael	4:43:47 (20,449)	
Preston, Bamber	3:41:01 (5,962)	
Preston, Ben	5:58:35 (30,183)	
Preston, Chris	4:11:07 (12,556)	
Preston, David	4:57:08 (23,411)	
Preston, Edward	4:10:48 (12,513)	
Preston, Gareth	3:12:54 (1,979)	
Preston, Gary	5:56:06 (30,057)	
Preston, Kevin	3:51:26 (8,057)	
Preston, Marc	5:18:04 (26,620)	
Preston, Mark	4:20:00 (14,743)	
Preston, Neil	4:06:39 (11,614)	
Preston, Stephen	3:15:18 (2,271)	
Preston, Stuart	3:24:52 (3,380)	
Preston, Timothy	4:19:38 (14,650)	
Prestridge, Jeff	4:18:25 (14,334)	
Prestwich, David	5:10:34 (25,630)	
Pretty, Simon	5:10:08 (25,571)	
Preuvot, Didier	3:36:43 (5,184)	
Prevost, Ivan	5:05:02 (24,796)	
Prevost, Jean	3:30:53 (4,312)	
Prew, Maurice	4:30:32 (17,375)	
Price, Alexander	3:42:11 (6,187)	
Price, Andrew	4:43:44 (20,440)	
Price, Ashley	4:24:29 (15,864)	
Price, Barrie	4:59:53 (23,966)	
Price, Carl	2:46:25 (274)	
Price, Colin	4:00:49 (10,390)	
Price, David	4:56:42 (23,316)	
Price, Frederick	5:31:30 (28,245)	
Price, Howard	3:22:54 (3,098)	
Price, Iain	5:08:11 (25,295)	
Price, Ian	3:04:04 (1,187)	
Price, James	5:08:05 (25,276)	
Price, John	4:55:07 (22,944)	
Price, Jonathan	4:52:12 (22,340)	
Price, Joseph	4:48:39 (21,561)	
Price, Luke	4:34:13 (18,216)	
Price, Neil	3:31:15 (4,372)	
Price, Paul	3:37:15 (5,282)	
Price, Paul	4:17:25 (14,094)	
Price, Paul	5:12:16 (25,867)	
Price, Rod	4:31:23 (17,589)	
Price, Simon	3:28:33 (3,910)	
Price, Simon	5:22:51 (27,261)	
Price, Stan	3:16:46 (2,402)	
Price, Stephen	3:13:48 (2,098)	
Price, Stewart	3:52:53 (8,393)	
Price-Wallace, Edward	5:58:53 (30,199)	
Prichard, Euan	5:26:42 (27,753)	
Pridding, Simon	3:44:23 (6,618)	
Prideaux, Paul	4:00:16 (10,283)	
Prieels, Frank	4:45:19 (20,798)	
Priekulis, Bernie	3:10:20 (1,708)	
Priem, Arno	3:22:31 (3,050)	
Priest, Andrew	4:00:53 (10,403)	
Priest, Darren	2:54:43 (575)	
Priest, Jonathan	3:22:48 (3,086)	
Priest, Mark	4:13:50 (13,210)	
Priest, Samuel	5:15:31 (26,315)	
Priest, Steve	5:38:23 (28,849)	
Priestley, Donald	3:36:15 (5,106)	
Priestley, Spencer	4:22:59 (15,489)	
Priestly, Scott	4:50:51 (22,043)	
Priestman, Paul	5:04:49 (24,765)	
Prieur-Garroust, Yves	4:25:07 (16,031)	
Primas, Christian	2:57:07 (712)	
Primetzhofer, Helmut	2:40:30 (159)	
Primo, Giorgio	3:44:00 (6,544)	
Primrose, Noel	3:46:16 (6,988)	
Prince, Alexander	3:25:05 (3,407)	
Prince, Keith	4:35:07 (18,417)	
Prince, Nicholas	3:57:10 (9,498)	
Pringle, John	6:31:42 (31,370)	
Pringle, Simon	5:05:58 (24,948)	
Prior, Ben	5:20:39 (26,979)	
Prior, Leslie	4:49:50 (21,832)	
Prior, Stephen	4:28:22 (16,814)	
Pritchard, Andrew	2:38:55 (144)	
Pritchard, Andrew	4:20:00 (14,743)	
Pritchard, Brian	3:27:32 (3,745)	
Pritchard, Colin	4:46:08 (21,003)	
Pritchard, Daniel	3:28:30 (3,903)	
Pritchard, Keith	3:28:23 (3,882)	
Pritchard, Martin	5:24:26 (27,465)	
Pritchard, Nigel	3:21:18 (2,914)	
Pritchard, Nigel	3:58:36 (9,857)	
Pritchard, Philip	5:45:16 (29,388)	
Pritchard, Robert	3:25:33 (3,468)	
Pritchard, Roger	3:54:47 (8,863)	
Pritchett, Nigel	3:55:21 (9,008)	
Probert, Peter	5:53:20 (29,895)	
Probst, Stefan	3:59:35 (10,115)	
Probyn, Simon	5:22:44 (27,244)	
Procter, Andrew	5:07:42 (25,225)	
Procter, Michael	5:46:18 (29,454)	
Proctor, Lawrance	4:47:54 (21,399)	
Proctor, Peter	5:16:04 (26,385)	
Proctor, Richard	4:55:28 (23,021)	
Proger, William	3:55:35 (9,070)	
Proietti, Massimo	2:50:12 (392)	
Prokopcuks, Alexander	2:26:52 (47)	
Pronk, Martin	3:21:17 (2,909)	
Prosperino, Michael	3:36:34 (5,156)	
Prosser, Kevin	4:56:08 (23,177)	
Prosser, Paul	3:02:37 (1,092)	
Prothero, Robert	2:52:10 (449)	
Protheroe, David	5:18:03 (26,617)	
Protheroe, Mark	3:44:33 (6,644)	
Protheroe, Richard	4:08:24 (11,980)	
Proud, David	3:57:27 (9,569)	
Proudfoot, Duncan	4:00:20 (10,301)	
Proudfoot, Trevor	4:46:07 (20,999)	
Proudlove, Michael	2:23:11 (29)	
Proudlove, Richard	3:45:57 (6,924)	
Provan, Robert	4:41:25 (19,853)	
Provot, Pascal	3:56:36 (9,346)	
Pruckner, Alexander	5:40:56 (29,072)	
Prudham, Joseph	3:44:53 (6,706)	
Prunty, John	6:21:25 (31,063)	
Prutton, Geoffrey	6:13:56 (30,795)	
Pryce, Charles	4:45:36 (20,867)	
Pryde, Mark	5:09:20 (25,455)	
Pryke, Matthew	4:30:56 (17,476)	
Pryor, Benjamin	4:18:25 (14,334)	
Prytherch, David	4:25:02 (16,010)	
Puchala, Lee	4:50:11 (21,900)	
Puech-Samson, Pierre	4:01:00 (10,429)	
Puffette, Kevin	4:31:26 (17,601)	
Pugh, Andrew	4:29:21 (17,071)	
Pugh, Eddie	4:23:09 (15,532)	
Pugh, John	3:44:58 (6,727)	
Pugh, Mike	5:02:35 (24,404)	
Pugh, Nick	5:03:47 (24,589)	
Pugh, Richard	4:24:12 (15,797)	
Pugh, Roderick	3:37:23 (5,305)	
Pugh, Stuart	3:37:23 (5,305)	
Pugh, Tom	3:48:34 (7,415)	
Pugsley, Simon	4:37:46 (19,039)	
Pullan, Rupert	4:58:25 (23,679)	
Pullen, Geoffrey	3:33:31 (4,681)	
Pullen, Graham	3:50:17 (7,796)	
Pullen, Lee	4:18:26 (14,341)	
Pullen, Leslie	4:49:35 (21,776)	
Pullen, Timothy	3:38:12 (5,442)	
Pullinger, Stephen	3:46:00 (6,928)	
Pullman, David	4:13:35 (13,146)	
Pulman, Darren	4:26:05 (16,272)	

Pund, Nathan	3:46:36 (7,055)	
Punyer, Clive	5:43:45 (29,286)	
Purcell, Gregor	4:29:11 (17,036)	
Purcell, Jason	5:23:17 (27,322)	
Purcell, Peter	4:52:31 (22,399)	
Purcell, Stuart	5:44:17 (29,323)	
Purcell, Tom	4:21:37 (15,136)	
Purdy, Alan	4:00:49 (10,390)	
Purdy, John	4:30:27 (17,357)	
Purdy, Nick	4:52:13 (22,344)	
Puri, Aman	5:23:30 (27,349)	
Purkiss, Mark	3:44:39 (6,658)	
Purnell, Garry	4:31:43 (17,674)	
Purnell, Jeremy	4:11:21 (12,612)	
Purnell, Richard	6:04:43 (30,443)	
Purser, Richard	4:45:44 (20,893)	
Pursey, Jonathan	3:19:31 (2,702)	
Purslow, Matthew	7:37:31 (32,193)	
Purton, Kevin	6:11:37 (30,713)	
Purves-Hume, Ian	4:57:39 (23,514)	
Purvis, Darren	2:59:27 (896)	
Purvis, David	4:53:43 (22,652)	
Purvis, Derek	3:49:13 (7,568)	
Purvis, Keith	2:41:26 (170)	
Purvis, Stanley	4:14:21 (13,345)	
Pusch, Andreas	3:07:06 (1,416)	
Putley, Colin	3:28:10 (3,841)	
Putman, Ashley	4:14:42 (13,423)	
Putman, Stephen	5:08:38 (25,352)	
Putt, Ashley	4:24:46 (15,941)	
Puttick, Michael	4:50:53 (22,052)	
Puttick, Neil	5:29:33 (28,045)	
Puzio, Jan	3:59:59 (10,220)	
Pycock, Graham	4:25:34 (16,150)	
Pye, Alan	2:57:32 (737)	
Pye, Christopher	3:17:57 (2,543)	
Pye, Derek	3:54:07 (8,684)	
Pye, Roy	3:49:12 (7,562)	
Pykett, Daniel	4:23:01 (15,498)	
Pykett, Geoffrey	5:27:22 (27,819)	
Pyle, Christopher	3:23:11 (3,133)	
Pynacker, Maarten	4:19:02 (14,513)	
Pyne, Daniel	4:51:07 (22,108)	
Pyne-O'Donnell, Sean	4:05:22 (11,366)	
Pyrah, James	4:58:52 (23,773)	
Qadri, Emile	4:20:22 (14,838)	
Quaedvlieg, Maurice	3:12:10 (1,878)	
Quaife, Nicholas	3:38:08 (5,432)	
Quaintance, Paul	4:32:45 (17,891)	
Quali, Larry	3:44:35 (6,647)	
Quantrill, Philip	3:02:03 (1,055)	
Quarmby, Richard	4:58:47 (23,762)	
Quarry, Jamie	3:37:43 (5,369)	
Quartermain, Glen	4:59:01 (23,804)	
Quartermaine, Alan	4:03:24 (10,929)	
Quarterman, Bruce	4:36:24 (18,744)	
Quartly, Leonard	4:03:45 (10,997)	
Quayle, Peter	4:36:44 (18,814)	
Quayle, Stephen	5:05:10 (24,822)	
Queenan, John	3:43:27 (6,443)	
Quelch, Steven	4:13:14 (13,058)	
Quessada, Nicolas	3:33:53 (4,730)	
Quick, James	3:03:30 (1,150)	
Quick, Michael	6:45:27 (31,629)	
Quicke, Andrew	4:00:24 (10,312)	
Quigley, Graham	4:00:57 (10,419)	
Quigley, James	4:47:36 (21,319)	
Quigley, Justin	4:46:06 (20,992)	
Quigley, Kevin	4:10:54 (12,528)	
Quigley, Robert	5:28:53 (27,974)	
Quin, David	3:47:22 (7,183)	
Quin, Paul	5:20:25 (26,943)	
Quin, Thomas	4:39:03 (19,331)	
Quiney, Nial	4:25:46 (16,190)	
Quinlan, Raymond	3:36:51 (5,204)	
Quinlivan, David	4:08:32 (12,019)	
Quinlivan, Michael	4:46:24 (21,070)	
Quinn, Andrew	5:38:58 (28,896)	
Quinn, Bob	4:42:21 (20,067)	
Quinn, Darren	3:28:00 (3,814)	
Quinn, David	3:21:54 (2,973)	
Quinn, Eamonn	5:54:09 (29,940)	
Quinn, Greg	3:13:36 (2,072)	

Quinn, Malcolm	4:20:44 (14,914)	
Quinn, Mike	3:15:09 (2,255)	
Quinn, Sean	4:07:23 (11,778)	
Quinn, Simon	7:12:22 (32,017)	
Quinn, Thomas	3:21:41 (2,951)	
Quintanal, Victor	3:43:40 (6,480)	
Quintelier, Tom	4:08:21 (11,969)	
Quinton, Stuart	3:59:30 (10,097)	
Quirke, Andrew	4:37:29 (18,981)	
Qushair, Hani	4:11:38 (12,671)	
Rabbah, Abdelatif	4:19:46 (14,687)	
Rabbetts, Alex	5:00:07 (23,997)	
Rabbetts, Mark	3:30:26 (4,242)	
Rabin, David	3:44:26 (6,625)	
Rabin, Matthew	4:05:47 (11,454)	
Rabjohns, Peter	3:09:13 (1,601)	
Rabut, Patrice	2:44:01 (217)	
Raby, John	3:28:45 (3,959)	
Rackham, Nigel	3:12:01 (1,863)	
Rackley, Benjamin	3:35:32 (5,002)	
Radama, Jean-Marc	4:28:06 (16,735)	
Radbone, Shane	4:28:28 (16,847)	
Radbourne, Mathew	3:19:38 (2,715)	
Radburn, Ian	4:14:40 (13,416)	
Radcliffe, Neil	5:35:49 (28,620)	
Radcliffe, Richard	3:22:14 (3,015)	
Radcliffe, Stephen	3:50:19 (7,805)	
Radford, Andrew	3:48:01 (7,323)	
Radford, Max	3:51:27 (8,062)	
Radford, Philip	6:10:43 (30,673)	
Radford, Tom	4:42:18 (20,053)	
Radosevic, Slavo	3:44:43 (6,674)	
Rae, Alexander	4:27:49 (16,675)	
Raeburn, Oliver	4:38:34 (19,213)	
Rafferty, Adrian	4:32:25 (17,818)	
Rafi, Driss	4:08:56 (12,117)	
Rafter, Stewart	4:04:19 (11,137)	
Ragget, Ian	4:31:18 (17,566)	
Raggett, Jeremy	5:02:49 (24,434)	
Rahman, Luthfur	4:48:04 (21,444)	
Raimondo, Marco	5:03:54 (24,615)	
Rainbow, Richard	4:17:36 (14,139)	
Rainey, Ralph	5:02:52 (24,440)	
Rains, Simon	4:02:35 (10,754)	
Rainsden, Jeff	4:07:02 (11,691)	
Raiser, Sylvain	5:03:54 (24,615)	
Raith, Peter	3:05:46 (1,302)	
Raja, Maqsood	4:54:53 (22,901)	
Rakshit, Kinshuk	3:54:09 (8,691)	
Rakusen, David	4:15:01 (13,512)	
Rakusen, Lloyd	4:15:01 (13,512)	
Ralfs, Andrew	3:12:45 (1,962)	
Ralph, Andrew	3:50:46 (7,902)	
Ralph, Chris	3:29:43 (4,129)	
Ralph, David	4:45:28 (20,837)	
Ralston, James	4:49:45 (21,815)	
Ralton, Paul	3:29:03 (4,009)	
Ramaala, Hendrick	2:08:58 (8)	
Ramadhani, Samson	2:08:01 (5)	
Ramage, Alan	3:11:01 (1,758)	
Ramage, Stephen	5:31:50 (28,267)	
Ramakrishna, Suresha	5:53:11 (29,888)	
Ramanathan, Uthaya	5:35:42 (28,612)	
Ramanauskas, Stephen	4:39:36 (19,459)	
Ramon, Ray	3:58:22 (9,801)	
Ramos, Abel	4:04:43 (11,230)	
Rampling, Laurence	4:30:36 (17,391)	
Ramsay, Grant	2:49:20 (374)	
Ramsay, Hamish	4:32:57 (17,935)	
Ramsden, John	3:46:06 (6,952)	
Ramsden, John	3:47:30 (7,213)	
Ramsden, Kevin	3:57:53 (9,673)	
Ramsden, Paul	5:09:41 (25,504)	
Ramsden, Stephen	4:20:36 (14,888)	
Ramsell, Chris	3:12:16 (1,893)	
Ramsey, Gordon	3:51:26 (8,057)	
Ramsey, Mark	3:47:45 (7,267)	
Ramsey, Nathan	4:44:55 (20,700)	
Ramsey, Timothy	3:55:30 (9,049)	
Ramzan, Nadim	3:40:19 (5,847)	
Rance, Anthony	5:57:02 (30,110)	
Rance, Daniel	5:57:01 (30,108)	
Rance, Keith	4:35:32 (18,524)	

Rance, Mark	3:53:03 (8,437)	
Rand, Chris	5:17:51 (26,588)	
Randall, Carl	3:10:35 (1,721)	
Randall, Gary	4:36:16 (18,702)	
Randall, Ian	4:48:03 (21,441)	
Randall, James	5:24:27 (27,468)	
Randall, Michael	4:43:50 (20,466)	
Randall, Peter	5:24:28 (27,471)	
Randall, Simon	3:49:53 (7,706)	
Randall, Stephen	4:53:12 (22,545)	
Randall, Timothy	4:40:19 (19,614)	
Randall, Trevor	4:32:09 (17,764)	
Randle, Colin	5:01:06 (24,168)	
Randles, Stephen	3:47:22 (7,183)	
Rang, David	4:08:09 (11,928)	
Rang, Simon	3:27:20 (3,716)	
Rankin, James	4:40:36 (19,668)	
Ranking, Stuart	3:45:16 (6,784)	
Rann, Philip	5:54:31 (29,970)	
Ranpura, Kirit	4:57:27 (23,468)	
Ransley-Warnes, Chris	5:27:33 (27,840)	
Ransom, Matthew	3:50:22 (7,817)	
Ransome, Jeremy	3:29:33 (4,103)	
Ranson, Stuart	4:38:45 (19,268)	
Rantell, David	3:26:58 (3,677)	
Raper, John	3:24:18 (3,305)	
Raphael, Derek	4:50:28 (21,956)	
Rapley, Nicholas	3:33:02 (4,605)	
Rapson, Ian	5:12:45 (25,939)	
Rasmussen, Finn	3:22:57 (3,105)	
Rasmussen, Frank	4:09:44 (12,280)	
Rasmussen, Henrik	4:33:57 (18,153)	
Ratcliff, Ian	5:16:35 (26,434)	
Ratcliffe, Bruce	3:52:09 (8,234)	
Ratcliffe, David	3:42:24 (6,219)	
Ratcliffe, John	3:28:33 (3,910)	
Ratcliffe, John	4:15:50 (13,713)	
Ratcliffe, Nigel	5:09:58 (25,536)	
Ratcliffe, Robert	3:25:45 (3,503)	
Ratcliffe, Sam	3:56:13 (9,249)	
Rathbone, Colin	3:11:53 (1,847)	
Rathbone, Mark	3:28:42 (3,943)	
Ratnage, Alan	5:18:19 (26,674)	
Ratti, Tommy	5:23:15 (27,318)	
Rattray, Rab	6:24:31 (31,146)	
Rauber, Dietmar	3:29:03 (4,009)	
Rauscher, Thomas	4:33:00 (17,952)	
Rauschnabel, Markus	3:55:54 (9,154)	
Ravagnani, Paolo	4:10:51 (12,519)	
Raven, James	3:51:18 (8,032)	
Raven, James	3:54:03 (8,674)	
Raven, Malcolm	4:49:07 (21,652)	
Raveney, Samuel	4:05:46 (11,447)	
Rawat, Feroz	4:56:33 (23,275)	
Rawat, Ravinder	4:16:24 (13,833)	
Rawcliffe, Ian	4:27:41 (16,643)	
Rawling, William	4:17:22 (14,074)	
Rawlings, Gary	5:24:50 (27,511)	
Rawlings, Ian	3:47:08 (7,148)	
Rawlings, Len	4:28:27 (16,839)	
Rawlings, Matthew	4:39:54 (19,518)	
Rawlins, Colin	5:19:34 (26,836)	
Rawlins, Richard	5:12:15 (25,863)	
Rawlinson, Anthony	4:24:16 (15,816)	
Rawlinson, David	4:09:16 (12,187)	
Rawlinson, Nigel	5:32:38 (28,342)	
Rawlinson, Paul	3:54:34 (8,809)	
Rawson, David	4:10:09 (12,384)	
Rawson, Steven	4:01:24 (10,519)	
Ray, Alistair	5:33:23 (28,410)	
Ray, Geoffrey	4:01:03 (10,439)	
Ray, Philip	4:39:44 (19,484)	
Ray, Simon	3:04:20 (1,203)	
Raybould, Frank	4:26:19 (16,317)	
Rayfield, David	2:58:34 (807)	
Rayment, Paul	5:51:14 (29,795)	
Raymer, Trevor	4:56:00 (23,148)	
Raymond, Benn	4:36:06 (18,671)	
Raymond, Byron	2:59:35 (909)	
Raymond, Michel	3:32:36 (4,540)	
Rayner, Martin	3:56:32 (9,330)	
Rayner, Mike	3:51:33 (8,092)	
Rayner-Cook, Chris	4:28:14 (16,776)	

Raynes, Andrew	4:06:30 (11,590)	
Raynes, David	4:04:39 (11,210)	
Raynor, Leonard	3:27:39 (3,760)	
Raynor, Maurice	4:55:04 (22,936)	
Raynor, Paul	4:12:33 (12,902)	
Rayson, Chris	4:32:15 (17,784)	
Re, Adamo	4:15:44 (13,679)	
Rea, Andrew	5:05:40 (24,912)	
Rea, Martin	2:44:42 (231)	
Rea, Paul	3:39:40 (5,722)	
Read, Antony	4:38:53 (19,301)	
Read, Brian	3:47:42 (7,255)	
Read, Chris	4:25:28 (16,135)	
Read, Chris	4:43:00 (20,236)	
Read, David	5:16:14 (26,396)	
Read, Jeremy	5:15:10 (26,274)	
Read, John	3:37:19 (5,293)	
Read, John	6:53:06 (31,786)	
Read, Keith	3:48:55 (7,494)	
Read, Malcolm	3:25:59 (3,540)	
Read, Nick	4:05:25 (11,379)	
Read, Nick	4:37:04 (18,892)	
Read, Nick	4:39:14 (19,380)	
Read, Ronald	3:27:14 (3,706)	
Read, Thomas	3:48:19 (7,378)	
Reade, Steve	4:13:52 (13,220)	
Reader, Frank	5:36:41 (28,706)	
Reading, Gary	5:32:56 (28,369)	
Reading, Paul	4:46:18 (21,045)	
Readings, Glynn	5:23:22 (27,335)	
Readman, Andrew	4:58:27 (23,687)	
Readman, Benjamin	3:56:15 (9,259)	
Readman, Christopher	3:40:43 (5,905)	
Rean, Peter	3:51:24 (8,051)	
Reaney, Patrick	3:59:09 (9,991)	
Reardon, James	6:09:39 (30,627)	
Reavey, Matthew	3:48:06 (7,339)	
Reay, Ken	5:00:13 (24,020)	
Rebert, Alain	3:38:19 (5,461)	
Rebora, Paolo	3:48:10 (7,353)	
Reburn, William	3:21:13 (2,900)	
Recko, Rudy	4:23:43 (15,676)	
Record, Matthew	3:53:10 (8,464)	
Redden, Philip	3:16:44 (2,400)	
Reddicliffe, Alexander	4:08:50 (12,093)	
Redding, Derek	5:20:47 (26,996)	
Reddrop, Richard	6:27:39 (31,252)	
Reddy, André	4:24:58 (15,990)	
Reddy, Jim	3:56:55 (9,428)	
Reddyhoff, Richard	3:50:53 (7,925)	
Redfearn, Darren	4:00:19 (10,300)	
Redfern, John	4:24:48 (15,951)	
Redford, Roy	6:42:16 (31,571)	
Redgrave, Gerald	4:51:26 (22,188)	
Redhead, Darryl	3:38:41 (5,538)	
Redhead, John	6:10:50 (30,682)	
Redick, Bryan	4:49:15 (21,689)	
Redman, Christopher	4:19:49 (14,695)	
Redman, Tim	4:21:00 (14,979)	
Redmayne, William	4:37:21 (18,956)	
Redmile, Andrew	4:41:47 (19,938)	
Redmond, Alasdair	3:35:04 (4,921)	
Redmond, John	5:22:30 (27,212)	
Redmond, Martin	4:01:13 (10,474)	
Redmond, Michael	4:17:45 (14,193)	
Redmond, Michael	4:46:04 (20,982)	
Redmond, Robert	4:08:56 (12,117)	
Redon, Laurent	2:48:02 (336)	
Redpath, David	3:53:28 (8,531)	
Redwood, Paul	4:20:07 (14,774)	
Reed, Alan	3:01:42 (1,033)	
Reed, Andrew	6:05:29 (30,476)	
Reed, Charly	3:50:48 (7,908)	
Reed, Christopher	4:34:57 (18,383)	
Reed, David	2:41:58 (179)	
Reed, Edward	3:18:45 (2,629)	
Reed, Fraser	4:59:29 (23,883)	
Reed, George	4:59:49 (23,952)	
Reed, Howard	5:39:54 (28,981)	
Reed, James	4:10:49 (12,514)	
Reed, Jeremy	4:41:55 (19,977)	
Reed, John	3:43:42 (6,489)	
Reed, Jonathan	4:01:20 (10,505)	
Reed, Paul	3:22:46 (3,081)	
Reed, Peter	4:04:03 (11,075)	
Reed, Rory	3:29:34 (4,105)	
Reed, Simon	3:30:08 (4,190)	
Reed, Simon	4:59:43 (23,927)	
Reed, William	3:16:10 (2,342)	
Reekie, Grant	3:59:55 (10,206)	
Reeks, Mark	3:47:55 (7,304)	
Reel, Sean	4:33:23 (18,028)	
Rees, Alan	4:55:19 (22,982)	
Rees, Andrew	3:24:21 (3,308)	
Rees, Anthony	4:47:59 (21,424)	
Rees, Ben	5:30:00 (28,085)	
Rees, Christopher	3:47:01 (7,128)	
Rees, Christopher	3:57:19 (9,533)	
Rees, Edward	4:24:42 (15,915)	
Rees, Gerith	4:06:04 (11,511)	
Rees, Gwynn	5:35:10 (28,568)	
Rees, James	5:24:56 (27,528)	
Rees, Jeffrey	2:47:50 (327)	
Rees, John	4:41:22 (19,839)	
Rees, Larry	3:54:41 (8,836)	
Rees, Nick	3:54:43 (8,840)	
Rees, Nigel	4:38:25 (19,186)	
Reeve, Chris	4:48:15 (21,482)	
Reeve, Damon	3:37:22 (5,300)	
Reeve, Neil	4:53:44 (22,663)	
Reeve, Stuart	4:30:25 (17,350)	
Reeve, Tim	5:09:25 (25,463)	
Reeves, Alan	3:58:37 (9,862)	
Reeves, John	3:54:12 (8,705)	
Reeves, Martin	3:48:40 (7,434)	
Reeves, Matthew	5:01:54 (24,294)	
Reeves, Richard	4:39:08 (19,353)	
Reeves, Robb	3:54:43 (8,840)	
Reeves, Stuart	3:33:16 (4,640)	
Regan, Maurice	3:36:45 (5,189)	
Regnaud, Didier	3:24:08 (3,271)	
Rehu, Martti	4:36:20 (18,722)	
Rehu, Petteri	3:20:22 (2,813)	
Reid, Ben	4:47:19 (21,251)	
Reid, Clive	3:14:20 (2,169)	
Reid, David	4:35:07 (18,417)	
Reid, Fraser	3:31:29 (4,407)	
Reid, Gordon	4:49:38 (21,786)	
Reid, Graeme	2:45:22 (243)	
Reid, Guy	3:33:16 (4,640)	
Reid, Iain	4:21:41 (15,152)	
Reid, James	3:33:25 (4,669)	
Reid, John	5:33:14 (28,396)	
Reid, Malcolm	4:06:20 (11,561)	
Reid, Neil	3:34:00 (4,749)	
Reid, Paul	4:33:19 (18,008)	
Reid, Peter	3:50:00 (7,734)	
Reid, Stephen	3:39:15 (5,645)	
Reidy, Kevin	5:02:57 (24,449)	
Reilly, Damian	5:00:19 (24,038)	
Reilly, Daniel	3:58:38 (9,867)	
Reilly, Jonathan	5:02:43 (24,422)	
Reilly, Leonard	2:34:03 (91)	
Reilly, Michael	3:47:33 (7,223)	
Reilly, Patrick	6:27:28 (31,244)	
Reilly, Stephen	3:28:37 (3,929)	
Reina, James	5:13:22 (26,019)	
Reinecke, John	4:21:14 (15,040)	
Reis, Francis	3:10:09 (1,690)	
Reiter, Robert	2:34:01 (90)	
Reith, Douglas	5:40:48 (29,062)	
Rej, Edward	3:54:15 (8,716)	
Remy, Didier	3:51:34 (8,097)	
Renault, Christian	4:31:07 (17,533)	
Rendall, Jason	5:06:12 (24,984)	
Render, Simon	3:58:10 (9,745)	
Rennick, Shane	4:36:40 (18,800)	
Rennicks, James	3:20:12 (2,786)	
Rennie, Gavin	3:34:20 (4,800)	
Rennie, James	4:59:08 (23,834)	
Rennie, Robert	6:49:18 (31,698)	
Rennie, Stephen	2:41:01 (166)	
Renny, Stephen	5:41:31 (29,117)	
Renny, Steven	2:54:40 (574)	
Rensham, Ian	5:12:02 (25,832)	
Renshaw, Andrew	4:48:52 (21,602)	
Renshaw, Arthur	3:49:53 (7,706)	
Renshaw, Benedict	4:48:59 (21,627)	
Renshaw, Steven	4:28:23 (16,817)	
Renton, David	4:24:54 (15,972)	
Renyard, Malcolm	5:40:00 (28,992)	
Repper, James	3:26:24 (3,591)	
Rescorla, Philip	4:25:17 (16,081)	
Reseigh, Peter	4:18:45 (14,438)	
Retalic, Ronald	4:14:25 (13,364)	
Reuben, Nigel	3:56:47 (9,393)	
Revell, Andrew	3:51:30 (8,074)	
Revemont, Cedric	4:08:17 (11,959)	
Revilla-Saavedra, Francisco	3:38:20 (5,462)	
Rew, Nicholas	3:51:08 (7,989)	
Rew, Simon	3:49:10 (7,555)	
Rewcastle, Michael	4:07:44 (11,859)	
Reynolds, Andrew	5:50:37 (29,761)	
Reynolds, Anthony	4:08:38 (12,047)	
Reynolds, Anthony	4:52:11 (22,335)	
Reynolds, Ben	2:26:47 (46)	
Reynolds, Benjamin	4:11:11 (12,572)	
Reynolds, Bryan	4:24:27 (15,857)	
Reynolds, Chris	3:42:50 (6,324)	
Reynolds, Christopher	3:53:00 (8,426)	
Reynolds, Daniel	4:10:50 (12,516)	
Reynolds, David	4:20:04 (14,761)	
Reynolds, David	4:32:03 (17,743)	
Reynolds, David	4:32:56 (17,932)	
Reynolds, Geoff	3:12:28 (1,923)	
Reynolds, Glen	4:06:18 (11,555)	
Reynolds, Jeremy	5:14:58 (26,242)	
Reynolds, Jon	3:32:45 (4,567)	
Reynolds, Jonathan	4:15:26 (13,624)	
Reynolds, Kevin	4:21:29 (15,107)	
Reynolds, Mark	3:42:56 (6,349)	
Reynolds, Matthew	4:05:14 (11,339)	
Reynolds, Neil	4:24:27 (15,857)	
Reynolds, Nicholas	4:25:20 (16,096)	
Reynolds, Paul	3:10:12 (1,695)	
Reynolds, Shaun	3:41:46 (6,107)	
Reynolds, Stephen	3:39:05 (5,613)	
Reynolds, Steve	5:12:26 (25,885)	
Reynolds, Thomas	3:30:03 (4,172)	
Reynolds, Thomas	4:31:21 (17,582)	
Rheims, Didier	4:25:20 (16,096)	
Rheinberger, Stephen	3:44:33 (6,644)	
Rhoades, Andrew	4:12:58 (12,997)	
Rhoden, Cyril	5:11:39 (25,782)	
Rhodes, Andrew	5:50:53 (29,777)	
Rhodes, Arthur	6:47:53 (31,672)	
Rhodes, Barton	3:58:07 (9,733)	
Rhodes, David	3:56:08 (9,219)	
Rhodes, Steven	5:09:40 (25,499)	
Riad, Mohamed	3:55:39 (9,091)	
Riba-Satorra, Jordi	3:56:48 (9,398)	
Ribeiro, Luiz Mazagao	4:06:23 (11,570)	
Ricaud, Alain	4:22:24 (15,342)	
Riccardi, Roberto	3:28:43 (3,949)	
Rice, Brian	4:24:17 (15,818)	
Rice, Christopher	3:51:06 (7,976)	
Rice, Jim	4:33:47 (18,112)	
Rice, John	4:19:39 (14,652)	
Rice, Joseph	4:12:32 (12,894)	
Rice, Mark	4:57:08 (23,411)	
Rice, Michael	3:06:24 (1,349)	
Rice, Regan	4:02:45 (10,793)	
Rice, Xan	4:19:31 (14,619)	
Rich, Andrew	4:42:31 (20,116)	
Rich, Andrew	5:14:48 (26,217)	
Rich, Geoff	3:36:16 (5,108)	
Rich, Stephen	4:05:28 (11,395)	
Rich, William	4:44:59 (20,711)	
Richaards, Leonard	3:45:40 (6,863)	
Richard, Eric	3:26:07 (3,554)	
Richards, Anthony	5:31:46 (28,260)	
Richards, Barry	3:09:32 (1,634)	
Richards, Christopher	4:59:44 (23,931)	
Richards, Clive	5:17:00 (26,480)	
Richards, Clive	6:39:09 (31,525)	
Richards, Darren	5:10:31 (25,625)	
Richards, David	4:39:47 (19,497)	
Richards, David	5:12:13 (25,859)	
Richards, David	7:30:12 (32,153)	

Richards, Gareth	3:55:59 (9,173)	
Richards, Geoff	3:18:07 (2,566)	
Richards, Gordon	3:06:53 (1,393)	
Richards, Gwilym	4:50:03 (21,871)	
Richards, James	4:46:17 (21,040)	
Richards, Jonathan	4:47:42 (21,346)	
Richards, Jonathon	4:50:34 (21,979)	
Richards, Julius	4:56:21 (23,230)	
Richards, Karl	3:59:44 (10,162)	
Richards, Keith	3:52:00 (8,197)	
Richards, Kelvin	5:57:58 (30,162)	
Richards, Ken	4:28:09 (16,752)	
Richards, Kevin	3:57:54 (9,677)	
Richards, Mark	4:19:22 (14,584)	
Richards, Martin	4:07:56 (11,892)	
Richards, Nigel	5:33:52 (28,463)	
Richards, Paul	3:30:15 (4,210)	
Richards, Sean	5:05:04 (24,806)	
Richards, Simon	3:48:59 (7,511)	
Richards, Tom	4:00:48 (10,386)	
Richardson, Alan	4:14:16 (13,323)	
Richardson, Andrew	3:51:37 (8,110)	
Richardson, Colin	3:05:21 (1,275)	
Richardson, David	3:42:06 (6,168)	
Richardson, Francis	5:00:17 (24,033)	
Richardson, Glen	3:43:53 (6,525)	
Richardson, Graham	3:35:17 (4,955)	
Richardson, Hilary	4:30:45 (17,431)	
Richardson, Ian	3:13:55 (2,118)	
Richardson, Ian	4:52:18 (22,357)	
Richardson, John	3:38:37 (5,521)	
Richardson, John	5:05:38 (24,907)	
Richardson, Kevin	3:50:42 (7,886)	
Richardson, Kevin	5:14:34 (26,187)	
Richardson, Mark	3:16:38 (2,388)	
Richardson, Mark	4:38:40 (19,245)	
Richardson, Michael	4:15:00 (13,507)	
Richardson, Murray	4:03:50 (11,021)	
Richardson, Nigel	4:07:02 (11,691)	
Richardson, Paul	3:58:45 (9,901)	
Richardson, Paul	5:38:17 (28,835)	
Richardson, Roger	3:56:04 (9,198)	
Richardson, Simon	2:53:32 (510)	
Richardson, Stephen	3:40:06 (5,809)	
Richardson, Stephen	4:43:30 (20,375)	
Richardson, Stephen	4:49:25 (21,726)	
Richardson, Steve	6:21:55 (31,071)	
Richer, Paul	4:39:57 (19,528)	
Riches, Tim	3:25:22 (3,449)	
Richings, Matthew	4:32:51 (17,913)	
Richmond, Andy	4:55:43 (23,083)	
Richmond, Nigel	4:05:18 (11,351)	
Richmond, William	4:18:51 (14,463)	
Richter, Frank	3:49:26 (7,616)	
Richter, Ralf	4:13:49 (13,205)	
Rickard, John	4:55:53 (23,129)	
Rickelton, Paul	4:14:27 (13,369)	
Rickers, Stuart	4:41:46 (19,935)	
Rickett, Peter	4:56:48 (23,337)	
Ricketts, Andrew	3:59:53 (10,197)	
Ricketts, Derek	3:56:55 (9,428)	
Rickis, Victor	5:44:04 (29,307)	
Ricks, Matthew	4:58:47 (23,762)	
Rickwood, Simon	5:32:24 (28,326)	
Ridd, Sebastian	3:36:09 (5,085)	
Riddell, Brian	3:31:53 (4,455)	
Riddell, David	4:41:48 (19,943)	
Riddell, Lachlan	3:43:49 (6,511)	
Riddell, Robert	4:28:50 (16,945)	
Riddick, Danny	3:47:14 (7,161)	
Riddiford, Andrew	3:54:30 (8,784)	
Ridding, John	3:50:04 (7,749)	
Riddle, Benjamin	3:20:14 (2,795)	
Riddoch, Neil	3:14:48 (2,216)	
Rider, Alex	4:14:21 (13,345)	
Rider, Paul	3:58:01 (9,712)	
Ridge, Brendan	3:58:38 (9,867)	
Ridgeway, Paul	3:00:27 (970)	
Ridgewell, Stanley	3:13:50 (2,100)	
Ridgway, Mark	3:46:31 (7,035)	
Ridgway, Mark	4:36:26 (18,753)	
Ridgwell, Alan	4:45:24 (20,821)	
Riding, George	3:52:13 (8,247)	

Ridler, Adam	4:52:43 (22,441)	
Ridley, Andrew	5:09:35 (25,490)	
Ridley, Andrew	6:03:17 (30,386)	
Ridout, Glen	3:25:15 (3,440)	
Ridout, John	3:14:19 (2,165)	
Ridout, Nick	4:00:37 (10,348)	
Rielander, Ian	4:17:30 (14,112)	
Ries, Egbert	4:45:15 (20,785)	
Rigby, Billy	5:02:31 (24,391)	
Rigby, Christopher	7:27:49 (32,140)	
Rigby, Colin	2:36:02 (108)	
Rigby, David	3:24:45 (3,364)	
Rigby, Michael	4:57:28 (23,474)	
Rigby, Stefan	3:38:31 (5,501)	
Rigg, Nigel	3:11:12 (1,773)	
Rigg, Peter	4:56:28 (23,251)	
Rigg, Warren	4:25:22 (16,107)	
Riggs, Adrian	4:31:14 (17,553)	
Riggs, Barnaby	5:37:06 (28,746)	
Rigney, Noel	5:33:55 (28,473)	
Rigoin, Serge	3:23:04 (3,122)	
Rijn, Laurens	4:41:20 (19,833)	
Rijs, Christian	5:50:41 (29,763)	
Riley, Alex	4:59:04 (23,820)	
Riley, Carl	3:31:17 (4,378)	
Riley, Christopher	5:21:50 (27,129)	
Riley, Colin	3:41:03 (5,968)	
Riley, Daniel	3:16:41 (2,395)	
Riley, Gerard	4:52:04 (22,323)	
Riley, Jim	4:30:22 (17,328)	
Riley, John	3:43:10 (6,399)	
Riley, John	5:25:41 (27,629)	
Riley, Richard	5:09:06 (25,423)	
Riley, Simon	3:01:00 (1,003)	
Riley, Simon	5:45:30 (29,404)	
Riley, Thomas	4:23:05 (15,508)	
Rimford, Ben	3:19:47 (2,733)	
Rimmer, John	4:48:35 (21,550)	
Rimmer, Paul	4:39:58 (19,533)	
Rimmer, Simon	4:34:17 (18,234)	
Rindlisbacher, Daniel	3:25:00 (3,397)	
Ring, Hans	4:09:54 (12,328)	
Ringsing, Martin	3:48:09 (7,351)	
Riordan, Clement	4:59:14 (23,848)	
Riordan, Patrick	4:09:56 (12,336)	
Ripley, William	3:57:55 (9,685)	
Rissel, Mathias	3:42:32 (6,260)	
Risslegger, Gregor	4:56:21 (23,230)	
Ritchie, Duncan	3:36:42 (5,182)	
Ritchie, Keith	4:45:06 (20,743)	
Ritchie, William	4:43:21 (20,336)	
Ritson, Martin	4:52:18 (22,357)	
Rivers, Brian	3:21:22 (2,919)	
Rivers, Christopher	4:31:37 (17,646)	
Rivers, Jack	4:16:51 (13,947)	
Rivers, Roderick	4:51:09 (22,119)	
Rivet, Pascal	3:16:58 (2,427)	
Rivett, Kelvin	5:15:41 (26,339)	
Rix, Jonathan	3:14:23 (2,175)	
Rixon, David	3:58:45 (9,901)	
Rizvi, Ashraf	4:53:20 (22,581)	
Roach, Mark	4:28:20 (16,801)	
Roach, William	4:07:20 (11,765)	
Roast, Barrie	4:57:37 (23,505)	
Robathan, Kevin	4:40:23 (19,626)	
Robb, Adam	4:11:07 (12,556)	
Robb, Andrew	3:39:58 (5,777)	
Robb, Paul	5:13:42 (26,067)	
Robb, Stephen	3:53:39 (8,579)	
Robb, Stuart	5:41:37 (29,130)	
Robbins, Fred	3:57:49 (9,650)	
Robbins, George	5:07:37 (25,208)	
Robbins, Glyn	4:07:28 (11,799)	
Robbins, Jason	3:04:28 (1,209)	
Robbins, Jonathan	3:07:39 (1,468)	
Robbins, Kevin	4:04:57 (11,280)	
Robbins, Michael	4:25:09 (16,043)	
Robe, Alec	5:05:49 (24,935)	
Roberts, Adrian	3:52:13 (8,247)	
Roberts, Alan	3:33:18 (4,645)	
Roberts, Alan	5:06:20 (24,998)	
Roberts, Aled	3:49:22 (7,601)	
Roberts, Alex	4:45:51 (20,926)	

Roberts, Andrew	3:46:47 (7,081)	
Roberts, Andrew	4:21:52 (15,199)	
Roberts, Andrew	5:22:02 (27,145)	
Roberts, Anthony	4:18:16 (14,294)	
Roberts, Arthur	3:07:14 (1,432)	
Roberts, Bamikole	6:09:10 (30,610)	
Roberts, Barry	4:04:39 (11,210)	
Roberts, Barry	4:25:33 (16,147)	
Roberts, Brian	5:23:03 (27,292)	
Roberts, Colin	2:35:26 (103)	
Roberts, Colin	5:23:43 (27,371)	
Roberts, Coyle	3:28:21 (3,874)	
Roberts, Daniel	6:31:46 (31,374)	
Roberts, Darren	6:02:15 (30,349)	
Roberts, David	3:02:46 (1,100)	
Roberts, David	3:42:54 (6,345)	
Roberts, David	4:40:31 (19,654)	
Roberts, David	4:42:23 (20,078)	
Roberts, Duncan	5:30:17 (28,113)	
Roberts, Emyr	2:59:01 (855)	
Roberts, Gareth	5:15:55 (26,365)	
Roberts, Greg	4:40:57 (19,741)	
Roberts, Hugh	4:02:36 (10,756)	
Roberts, Ian	5:24:03 (27,415)	
Roberts, Ifor	4:53:44 (22,663)	
Roberts, Jason	4:52:57 (22,494)	
Roberts, John	4:35:18 (18,471)	
Roberts, Jonathan	3:39:23 (5,675)	
Roberts, Justin	4:53:09 (22,530)	
Roberts, Justin	4:59:27 (23,878)	
Roberts, Kenneth	3:26:02 (3,544)	
Roberts, Lawrence	4:08:50 (12,093)	
Roberts, Lee	4:13:46 (13,191)	
Roberts, Lee	4:40:48 (19,703)	
Roberts, Liam	4:18:15 (14,291)	
Roberts, Malcolm	2:56:37 (681)	
Roberts, Mark	3:23:21 (3,156)	
Roberts, Mark	3:48:03 (7,328)	
Roberts, Mark	4:00:09 (10,260)	
Roberts, Mark	4:49:58 (21,852)	
Roberts, Martin	3:31:45 (4,446)	
Roberts, Mathew	4:09:33 (12,241)	
Roberts, Michael	3:45:20 (6,795)	
Roberts, Michael	3:54:46 (8,859)	
Roberts, Neirin	5:16:28 (26,422)	
Roberts, Oliver	3:39:50 (5,754)	
Roberts, Paul	6:53:06 (31,786)	
Roberts, Raymond	3:51:31 (8,080)	
Roberts, Raymond	4:53:44 (22,663)	
Roberts, Richard	3:34:23 (4,814)	
Roberts, Richard	4:38:39 (19,238)	
Roberts, Richard	5:57:36 (30,144)	
Roberts, Robert	4:22:25 (15,346)	
Roberts, Roger	5:25:32 (27,614)	
Roberts, Russell	4:08:50 (12,093)	
Roberts, Sean	5:56:55 (30,102)	
Roberts, Simon	3:01:29 (1,023)	
Roberts, Steiner	4:16:38 (13,885)	
Roberts, Stephen	4:53:24 (22,596)	
Roberts, Steve	3:01:01 (1,005)	
Roberts, Tim	4:22:43 (15,422)	
Roberts, Tony	3:30:52 (4,307)	
Roberts, Vaughan	3:13:15 (2,028)	
Roberts, William	3:51:08 (7,989)	
Robertshaw, Philip	4:15:20 (13,602)	
Robertson, Andrew	3:31:14 (4,365)	
Robertson, Andrew	4:58:43 (23,737)	
Robertson, Angus	3:58:14 (9,764)	
Robertson, Anthony	3:36:10 (5,091)	
Robertson, Callum	4:21:37 (15,136)	
Robertson, David	2:29:45 (62)	
Robertson, Frazer	4:26:29 (16,351)	
Robertson, Graeme	5:32:01 (28,291)	
Robertson, Iain	3:27:57 (3,810)	
Robertson, Ian	5:23:43 (27,371)	
Robertson, Lex	3:45:02 (6,738)	
Robertson, Paul	3:04:53 (1,241)	
Robertson, Peter	4:14:46 (13,437)	
Robertson, Stewart	3:36:09 (5,085)	
Robertson, Struan	4:35:47 (18,594)	
Robertson, Trevor	4:22:52 (15,458)	
Robertson, Wally	4:46:13 (21,022)	
Robin, Loic	3:52:56 (8,402)	

Ross, Alastair	4:44:08 (20,525)
Ross, Andrew	5:03:13 (24,495)
Ross, Brian	3:42:17 (6,202)
Ross, Charles	4:12:18 (12,832)
Ross, Christopher	3:56:12 (9,242)
Ross, Christopher	5:00:21 (24,044)
Ross, David	3:28:17 (3,861)
Ross, David	3:51:07 (7,981)
Ross, Donald	4:07:07 (11,713)
Ross, Dougal	3:46:54 (7,103)
Ross, Douglas	3:58:44 (9,892)
Ross, Duncan	4:59:07 (23,830)
Ross, Ian	5:18:39 (26,718)
Ross, James	3:53:01 (8,429)
Ross, James	5:23:26 (27,343)
Ross, Jeremy	4:27:59 (16,703)
Ross, Joseph	5:54:54 (29,991)
Ross, Mark	5:08:32 (25,341)
Ross, Michael	3:54:53 (8,889)
Ross, Niall	5:06:09 (24,976)
Ross, Nick	5:11:48 (25,801)
Ross, Paul	2:58:00 (767)
Ross, Rick	3:12:07 (1,874)
Ross, Stephen	3:34:06 (4,762)
Ross, Stephen	5:06:10 (24,980)
Ross, Steven	4:24:44 (15,928)
Rossel, André	4:11:00 (12,543)
Rossi, Alessandro	4:33:27 (18,047)
Rossi, Giuseppe	7:17:49 (32,056)
Rossiter, Robert	5:07:03 (25,113)
Rossor, Alexander	3:26:20 (3,581)
Rossouw, François	4:33:58 (18,158)
Rostad, Hans	3:38:20 (5,462)
Rostern, Paul	3:05:03 (1,257)
Rostron, Robert	4:18:18 (14,303)
Rota, Maurizio	4:27:38 (16,633)
Roth, Alexander	3:17:57 (2,543)
Roth, David	4:47:45 (21,361)
Rothbart, Jonathan	6:13:50 (30,791)
Rothe, Carsten	4:13:50 (13,210)
Rothwell, Alan	4:23:57 (15,737)
Rothwell, William	4:29:05 (17,010)
Rottenburg, Alexander	5:38:50 (28,884)
Rouasnel, Franck	3:51:35 (8,100)
Rouault, Gillies	3:59:46 (10,167)
Roukin, Danny	5:39:51 (28,976)
Round, John	5:55:07 (30,007)
Round, Matt	3:40:10 (5,826)
Round, Neil	4:12:14 (12,823)
Rous, John	3:34:29 (4,835)
Rouse, Adam	2:53:31 (509)
Rouse, Anthony	4:09:43 (12,277)
Rousell, Lee	4:53:44 (22,663)
Rousseau, André	4:15:02 (13,520)
Rout, Adam	4:03:15 (10,899)
Rout, David	4:43:24 (20,351)
Routledge, Allen	4:10:23 (12,438)
Routledge, George	5:22:23 (27,198)
Routledge, John	3:05:43 (1,298)
Routledge, Jonathan	4:52:01 (22,312)
Routledge, Nigel	5:07:57 (25,262)
Routley, Miles	2:58:38 (814)
Roux, Michel	3:20:54 (2,875)
Rouyer, Thierry	4:44:36 (20,633)
Row, Paul	3:53:23 (8,510)
Rowan, Philip	4:57:59 (23,580)
Rowbotham, Andrew	3:25:26 (3,456)
Rowbotham, Malcolm	3:38:41 (5,538)
Rowbottom, Steven	4:27:21 (16,561)
Rowden, Jay	3:25:08 (3,413)
Rowe, Adam	4:23:29 (15,611)
Rowe, Alex	2:37:13 (125)
Rowe, Clifford	5:41:58 (29,158)
Rowe, Clive	6:46:02 (31,645)
Rowe, Ian	5:07:03 (25,113)
Rowe, John	3:44:40 (6,661)
Rowe, Jonathan	4:55:44 (23,091)
Rowe, Mark	4:14:16 (13,323)
Rowe, Mark	4:48:22 (21,512)
Rowe, Mark	5:19:45 (26,855)
Rowe, Michael	4:03:06 (10,869)
Rowe, Philip	5:34:24 (28,518)
Rowe, Roger	2:52:30 (470)

Rowe, Thomas	4:19:07 (14,534)
Rowe-Ham, Gerry	4:26:59 (16,465)
Rowell, Alan	3:24:31 (3,333)
Rowell, Barry	4:35:51 (18,611)
Rowell, Ben	3:54:21 (8,738)
Rowell, James	4:16:11 (13,782)
Rowett, Malcolm	6:27:25 (31,238)
Rowland, Adam	5:38:12 (28,829)
Rowland, Colin	3:51:01 (7,957)
Rowland, Ian	4:03:47 (11,007)
Rowland, Matthew	5:55:03 (30,004)
Rowland, Michael	5:30:34 (28,147)
Rowland, Paul	5:13:26 (26,029)
Rowland, Robert	3:24:11 (3,280)
Rowland, Shaun	6:17:50 (30,922)
Rowland, Stephen	4:46:11 (21,012)
Rowland, Stewart	4:55:15 (22,965)
Rowland-Bowen, Dafydd	4:22:02 (15,247)
Rowland-Jones, Nicholas	3:44:56 (6,718)
Rowlands, Dan	3:24:17 (3,300)
Rowlands, Gary	4:30:59 (17,491)
Rowlands, Graham	4:17:16 (14,052)
Rowlands, Peter	4:14:38 (13,409)
Rowlandson, Daniel	4:24:58 (15,990)
Rowley, Adrian	6:49:47 (31,713)
Rowley, David	4:25:05 (16,021)
Rowley, Dean	3:05:06 (1,261)
Rowley, Gavin	4:48:34 (21,545)
Rowley, Mark	5:20:40 (26,983)
Rowley, Neil	4:36:35 (18,785)
Rowley, Neil	5:10:47 (25,658)
Rowley, Peter	3:56:53 (9,420)
Rowlinson, Leslie	4:23:09 (15,532)
Rowntree, Timothy	4:16:00 (13,743)
Roxburgh, Bruce	4:05:55 (11,487)
Roy, Shaun	5:00:49 (24,125)
Royden, Mark	4:19:00 (14,509)
Royle, Mark	3:45:37 (6,853)
Royle, Simon	5:53:47 (29,920)
Rozes, Sebastien	4:20:08 (14,779)
Rozewicz, Leon	4:42:23 (20,078)
Rozier, Edward	4:44:20 (20,577)
Ruane, Anthony	4:20:58 (14,968)
Rubenstein, Brian	5:07:17 (25,140)
Rubery, Jonathan	4:20:55 (14,957)
Rucinski, Jacek	4:30:31 (17,370)
Ruck Keene, Alexander	4:56:40 (23,306)
Ruda, Robert	4:38:05 (19,110)
Rudd, Andrew	3:29:47 (4,138)
Rudd, Keith	2:58:53 (839)
Rudd, Lee	4:41:56 (19,979)
Rudd, Michael	4:42:58 (20,222)
Rudd, Phil	2:52:28 (469)
Rudder, Simon	4:11:34 (12,660)
Rudderow, Preston	3:37:29 (5,323)
Ruddle, Jason	4:48:20 (21,501)
Ruddle, Paul	3:00:59 (1,002)
Ruddock, Ian	4:17:07 (14,015)
Ruddy, Lee	3:54:11 (8,699)
Rudemalm, Bo	4:28:23 (16,817)
Rudge, Anthony	5:19:02 (26,759)
Rudge, David	4:35:24 (18,495)
Rudland, Oliver	4:12:00 (12,762)
Rudrof, Thomas	3:25:51 (3,519)
Ruedisueli, Henny	3:58:10 (9,745)
Ruehl, Hans	5:00:49 (24,125)
Rueppel, Henner	3:16:22 (2,363)
Ruetten, Hartmut	3:41:23 (6,037)
Ruff, Elliot	4:12:36 (12,914)
Ruff, Keith	4:12:36 (12,914)
Ruffell, Richard	3:07:11 (1,426)
Ruffles, John	4:50:27 (21,952)
Ruffley, Stephen	3:58:00 (9,706)
Rufus, Josh	4:11:53 (12,735)
Ruia, Alok	3:53:04 (8,442)
Ruia, Sunil	5:11:15 (25,731)
Ruivaj May, Marco	4:22:59 (15,489)
Ruiz, Miguel	4:13:41 (13,170)
Ruiz-Jimenez, José	3:27:02 (3,686)
Rule, Brian	4:09:56 (12,336)
Rumary, David	3:41:19 (6,017)
Rumbelow, Nicholas	3:29:26 (4,075)
Rumble, John	4:19:29 (14,611)

Rumbles, Christopher	4:56:36 (23,287)
Rumsey, Paul	2:57:32 (737)
Runacres, Mark	3:46:49 (7,089)
Ruparelia, Kalpesh	6:17:33 (30,907)
Rushby, Philip	4:31:15 (17,558)
Rushby, Sonia	3:51:12 (8,011)
Rushmer, Gary	4:35:32 (18,524)
Rushmer, Martin	4:27:10 (16,516)
Rushton, Christopher	3:47:48 (7,277)
Rushton, David	5:18:26 (26,687)
Russ, Mark	4:25:08 (16,037)
Russell, Al	5:12:31 (25,899)
Russell, Brian	3:46:31 (7,035)
Russell, Charles	4:12:05 (12,780)
Russell, David	3:52:58 (8,412)
Russell, Duncan	5:02:18 (24,361)
Russell, Edward	3:50:40 (7,879)
Russell, Gareth	3:57:47 (9,642)
Russell, Ian	2:59:58 (935)
Russell, Ian	3:42:40 (6,288)
Russell, Jimmy	4:59:03 (23,812)
Russell, John	3:16:52 (2,412)
Russell, John	3:30:56 (4,318)
Russell, John	3:32:21 (4,515)
Russell, John	4:24:10 (15,789)
Russell, Jonathan	4:11:07 (12,556)
Russell, Jonathan	5:33:30 (28,421)
Russell, Mark	3:55:24 (9,022)
Russell, Mark	4:27:14 (16,529)
Russell, Michael	3:49:26 (7,616)
Russell, Nic	3:53:12 (8,474)
Russell, Paul	4:27:20 (16,555)
Russell, Peter	2:37:01 (120)
Russell, Philip	4:14:52 (13,471)
Russell, Phillip	3:35:53 (5,053)
Russell, Richard	5:02:06 (24,327)
Russell, Robert	4:28:23 (16,817)
Russell, Ronald	4:17:37 (14,147)
Russell, Shane	5:41:58 (29,158)
Russell, Simon	2:58:44 (825)
Russell, Stephen	4:43:47 (20,449)
Russell, Steven	4:29:19 (17,065)
Russell, Terence	3:41:06 (5,979)
Russell-Smith, Charles	5:07:06 (25,118)
Russo, Antonio	3:34:51 (4,885)
Russo, Jean-Marc	3:52:45 (8,363)
Russsell, Bob	6:20:22 (31,027)
Rust, Adam	4:50:28 (21,956)
Rustem, Robert	5:55:48 (30,030)
Rutherford, Craig	5:13:44 (26,072)
Rutherford, Scott	3:57:47 (9,642)
Rutland, Andrew	5:12:04 (25,836)
Rutledge, Richard	4:49:00 (21,633)
Rutt, Carl	4:23:40 (15,662)
Rutter, John	3:19:45 (2,728)
Rutter, Mark	4:52:31 (22,399)
Rutter, Simon	3:49:27 (7,621)
Rutter, Simon	4:10:58 (12,535)
Rutter, Tod	2:54:49 (582)
Ruvalcaba, Santiago	4:43:06 (20,263)
Ruxton, David	3:57:23 (9,552)
Ryall, Frank	5:11:22 (25,747)
Ryan, Andrew	4:20:21 (14,829)
Ryan, Graham	4:18:42 (14,423)
Ryan, James	5:24:19 (27,453)
Ryan, James	5:36:02 (28,641)
Ryan, John	2:46:04 (262)
Ryan, Kevin	3:08:40 (1,560)
Ryan, Kyril	5:41:05 (29,082)
Ryan, Lewis	4:00:55 (10,411)
Ryan, Michael	3:24:14 (3,293)
Ryan, Paul	4:06:02 (11,506)
Ryan, Paul	5:01:43 (24,262)
Ryan, Richard	5:37:26 (28,714)
Ryan, Sean	5:07:23 (25,156)
Ryan, Thomas	5:50:00 (29,713)
Ryan, Tim	3:50:47 (7,905)
Ryder, Kevin	3:46:26 (7,017)
Ryder, Mark	3:53:26 (8,524)
Rye, Joseph	2:46:58 (297)
Ryffel, Markus	3:13:07 (2,008)
Rykens, Alasdair	3:43:25 (6,441)
Rylance, Tom	4:15:13 (13,571)

Ryland, John 6:23:30 (31,121)
Rymer, Christoher 5:13:57 (26,094)
Rymer, Timothy 3:35:17 (4,955)
Rytter, Jens 4:33:25 (18,036)
Sabanathan, Rajan 3:57:51 (9,663)
Sabatino, Anthony 5:12:52 (25,954)
Sabbatini, Gianluca 3:25:52 (3,523)
Sabharwal, Ravi 5:16:03 (26,384)
Sachau, Thomas 2:43:36 (211)
Sackett, Derek 5:16:44 (26,457)
Sacks, Daniel 3:03:43 (1,165)
Sacre, Denis 4:26:30 (16,355)
Sadiq, Michael 4:52:34 (22,407)
Sadler, Chris 6:08:39 (30,594)
Sadler, Christopher 5:05:58 (24,948)
Sadler, James 3:15:17 (2,270)
Sadler, Kevin 2:52:44 (482)
Sadler, Kevin 3:52:22 (8,281)
Sadley, Stephen 6:17:42 (30,910)
Saeed, Nadeem 4:26:08 (16,282)
Saes, Karl-Heinz 4:35:17 (18,468)
Saether, Bjoern 4:39:11 (19,370)
Safranek, Jan 4:22:18 (15,315)
Sagar, Neal 4:49:25 (21,726)
Sagar, Nicholas 3:49:12 (7,562)
Sagaran, Stephen 4:28:39 (16,897)
Sage, David 5:03:49 (24,597)
Sage, Gary 3:36:12 (5,097)
Saggers, Martin 3:38:11 (5,440)
Sagone, Alessandro 2:56:21 (663)
Sagot, Philippe 3:38:13 (5,445)
Said, Yahia 4:45:07 (20,748)
Saint, Alastair 5:00:54 (24,139)
Saint, Nick 4:44:49 (20,682)
Saker, Andrew 3:57:52 (9,669)
Salam, Kwame 4:02:22 (10,711)
Salas, Vicente 6:48:38 (31,685)
Salgues, Serve 3:11:33 (1,807)
Salih, Mustafa 2:55:34 (624)
Salina, Ludovico 5:06:08 (24,974)
Salisbury, Alan 4:10:22 (12,431)
Salisbury, Mark 5:52:37 (29,863)
Salisbury, Paul 4:42:14 (20,035)
Salkeld, Michael 3:12:52 (1,977)
Salmon, Carl 4:38:58 (19,318)
Salmon, Geoffrey 4:56:08 (23,177)
Salmon, Nick 4:39:27 (19,430)
Salsbury, Phillip 6:08:52 (30,601)
Salt, Nicholas 4:20:59 (14,974)
Salter, Andrew 3:40:51 (5,932)
Salter, Dennis 4:04:06 (11,090)
Saltmarsh, Robin 5:37:11 (28,751)
Salton, Christopher 3:48:16 (7,371)
Saltrick, Christopher 4:17:35 (14,132)
Sambhi, Sarwjit 4:49:43 (21,806)
Sami, Nour-Eddine 3:03:00 (1,114)
Sammes, Mark 5:38:05 (28,818)
Sampas, George 3:58:15 (9,773)
Sampson, Paul 6:47:34 (31,664)
Sampson, Stuart 5:06:50 (25,084)
Samra, Parminderjit 5:05:18 (24,840)
Samro, Oli 4:00:52 (10,398)
Sams, Ronald 5:10:51 (25,669)
Samson, Antony 5:13:44 (26,072)
Samuel, Jody 3:35:39 (5,021)
Samuel, Nicolas 3:41:24 (6,041)
Samuels, Blake 4:18:52 (14,468)
Samways, Robin 3:37:05 (5,249)
Samworth, James 3:28:56 (3,994)
Sanchez, Joe 3:29:53 (4,152)
Sanchez, Vincent 5:07:36 (25,201)
Sanchez Bermejo, Pedro Juan 4:02:50 (10,815)
Sancto, Steve 3:23:31 (3,181)
Sandall, David 4:09:46 (12,291)
Sandall, Mick 5:03:36 (24,550)
Sanders, Christopher 4:43:38 (20,413)
Sanders, Dave 4:45:07 (20,748)
Sanders, Gerald 4:17:20 (14,064)
Sanders, Ian 6:03:25 (30,389)
Sanders, Mark 4:14:57 (13,492)
Sanders, Richard 4:55:27 (23,015)
Sanders, Richard 5:36:28 (28,681)
Sanders, Simon 4:08:40 (12,055)

Sanders, Stephen 5:32:01 (28,291)
Sanders, Steve 3:47:04 (7,135)
Sanderson, Gavin 4:13:16 (13,068)
Sanderson, Mark 5:24:46 (27,505)
Sanderson, Michael 3:16:40 (2,394)
Sanderson, Paul 5:24:18 (27,451)
Sanderson, Terence 3:46:02 (6,940)
Sandford, Adam 3:44:55 (6,713)
Sandford-Hart, John 7:40:48 (32,210)
Sandhu, John 4:21:12 (15,034)
Sandilands, Paul 4:26:07 (16,280)
Sandison, Ron 4:18:40 (14,412)
Sandrin, Andrea 5:06:46 (25,069)
Sands, Mark 5:01:37 (24,248)
Sandstrom, Ulrik 3:45:28 (6,825)
Sanger, Neil 5:19:08 (26,776)
Sanghera, Jas 4:16:33 (13,867)
Sanghera, Kirn 4:18:44 (14,432)
Sanghera, Lember 6:11:27 (30,711)
Sankey, Stuart 5:49:32 (29,684)
Sano, Hiroaki 4:43:10 (20,277)
Sansom, Ahmos 5:18:55 (26,746)
Sansom, Derek 3:03:45 (1,166)
Sansome, Andrew 3:55:31 (9,052)
Sansoni, Edoardo 4:02:15 (10,686)
Santolin, Demetrio 4:39:10 (19,368)
Santos, Fernando 3:03:54 (1,176)
Santos, Ramiro 4:25:42 (16,183)
Santos-Martin, Martin 4:38:44 (19,263)
Sanz, Antonio 3:22:06 (2,995)
Sanz-Garcia, Carlos 4:04:04 (11,079)
Saouli, Mohammed 5:02:12 (24,349)
Sappor, Henry 4:00:04 (10,237)
Sapsford, Kevin 4:31:48 (17,687)
Sapsworth, Derek 4:22:29 (15,359)
Sapte, Matthew 3:26:54 (3,658)
Saraiva, Carlos 3:20:45 (2,851)
Sarakinsky, Atholl 5:05:43 (24,925)
Sarbah, Mensah 4:14:35 (13,399)
Sarbutts, John 6:08:24 (30,583)
Sardina-Costa, Luis 4:26:34 (16,370)
Sardis, Fragkiskos 5:47:51 (29,565)
Sargeant, Robert 3:23:13 (3,139)
Sargeant, Steven 3:42:44 (6,306)
Sargeant, Steven 3:48:57 (7,503)
Sargent, Darren 5:58:44 (30,187)
Sargent, Nicholas 5:42:08 (29,180)
Sargent, Nigel 3:52:52 (8,386)
Sargent, Robert 3:45:18 (6,788)
Sarmini, Sehdi 3:39:29 (5,693)
Sarson, Peter 2:51:07 (423)
Sartain, William 3:38:52 (5,573)
Sartin, Rob 2:58:11 (783)
Sassone, Matthew 4:11:12 (12,578)
Sastry, Sanjay 4:49:49 (21,827)
Satchell, Orlando 4:45:07 (20,748)
Satchwill, David 3:56:40 (9,365)
Sattler, Christoph 4:05:25 (11,379)
Sauer, Reiner 4:52:45 (22,450)
Saunders, Andy 5:08:46 (25,367)
Saunders, Angus 3:25:27 (3,458)
Saunders, Arran 4:02:09 (10,666)
Saunders, Barry 4:52:57 (22,494)
Saunders, Bernard 5:46:46 (29,483)
Saunders, Carl 3:57:15 (9,517)
Saunders, Charles 3:45:15 (6,783)
Saunders, David 4:23:06 (15,512)
Saunders, David 4:35:21 (18,483)
Saunders, Gavin 3:33:33 (4,687)
Saunders, Ivan 5:07:52 (25,244)
Saunders, Jason 4:38:47 (19,278)
Saunders, Mark 4:18:41 (14,419)
Saunders, Michael 5:18:32 (26,701)
Saunders, Neil 3:49:28 (7,624)
Saunders, Peter 4:28:22 (16,814)
Saunders, Richard 3:50:58 (7,941)
Saunders, Robert 3:56:20 (9,280)
Saunders, Simon 4:33:22 (18,024)
Saunders, Steve 6:28:36 (31,292)
Saunders, Tony 4:02:50 (10,815)
Saunderson, Robert 4:22:18 (15,315)
Sauvary, Kelvyn 5:05:31 (24,885)
Savage, Brian 3:48:52 (7,482)

Savage, Christopher 4:21:27 (15,100)
Savage, Damien 4:54:30 (22,814)
Savage, David 3:07:02 (1,406)
Savage, Kevin 4:55:50 (23,118)
Savage, Malcolm 5:15:22 (26,300)
Savage, Paul 4:41:54 (19,974)
Savage, Sean 4:19:17 (14,570)
Savery, Justin 5:04:03 (24,642)
Savill, John 3:57:48 (9,648)
Savill, Mathew 4:17:42 (14,176)
Saville, Kevin 3:50:31 (7,844)
Saville, Niall 4:04:29 (11,177)
Saville, Philip 4:48:45 (21,577)
Saville, Stephen 4:22:04 (15,256)
Savimaki, Ilkka 4:53:47 (22,675)
Savin, Guy 6:53:05 (31,784)
Savio, Gastone 5:32:23 (28,325)
Savry, Philippe 3:03:33 (1,155)
Saw, Bjorn 4:29:48 (17,195)
Sawday, David 4:24:57 (15,981)
Sawer, Martin 3:28:36 (3,925)
Sawford, Paul 3:28:54 (3,987)
Sawyer, Adam 4:39:27 (19,430)
Sawyer, Clive 5:19:19 (26,803)
Sawyer, Gary 3:36:25 (5,131)
Sawyer, Jason 3:29:17 (4,040)
Saxelby, Jai 3:06:47 (1,385)
Saxton, Jon 3:37:25 (5,318)
Sayburn, Ronan 4:04:33 (11,188)
Sayce, Alastair 3:32:58 (4,591)
Sayer, Ian 3:51:59 (8,191)
Sayer, James 4:46:57 (21,174)
Sayer, Philip 4:58:22 (23,664)
Sayer, Trevor 3:50:16 (7,792)
Sayers, Brian 5:13:00 (25,973)
Sayle, Mark 4:35:28 (18,510)
Sayles, Terence 4:51:36 (22,225)
Saywell, Mark 5:39:03 (28,906)
Saywell, Stephen 5:03:41 (24,567)
Scadden, Mark 3:58:17 (9,776)
Scaife, Michael 3:55:36 (9,076)
Scaife, Paul 4:43:06 (20,263)
Scally, Brian 4:01:48 (10,598)
Scalza, Louis 5:04:12 (24,661)
Scammell, Steve 4:58:15 (23,638)
Scamp, George 4:52:55 (22,487)
Scanlan, Thomas 4:18:38 (14,403)
Scanlon, Alex 4:09:18 (12,197)
Scanlon, Bernard 5:07:17 (25,140)
Scanlon, Mike 5:44:26 (29,331)
Scanlon, Peter 4:32:11 (17,770)
Scarborough, Derek 2:46:33 (280)
Scarborough, John 4:22:14 (15,304)
Scarborough, Neil 5:23:41 (27,367)
Scarfe, Geoff 3:59:05 (9,977)
Scarisbrick, Alan 4:46:49 (21,150)
Scarisbrick, Paul 4:23:26 (15,595)
Scarr-Hall, Ian 5:47:03 (29,494)
Scawthorn, Jason 4:11:26 (12,627)
Schachter, Norbert 4:29:25 (17,094)
Schaeferbarthold, Martin 4:52:25 (22,381)
Schaerer, Juerg 3:59:57 (10,211)
Schaerer, Peter 4:42:02 (19,998)
Schafer, Christian 3:59:38 (10,130)
Schafer, Danny 4:01:35 (10,558)
Schaffhauser, Daniel 3:30:50 (4,300)
Schapira, Paul 4:24:25 (15,844)
Schat-Holm, Rolf 3:53:17 (8,491)
Schaufler, Siegfried 4:51:20 (22,165)
Scheepbouwer, Aat 5:01:05 (24,163)
Scheepers, Dawie 4:04:43 (11,230)
Scheffold, Thomas 4:02:36 (10,756)
Scheib, Robert 4:53:43 (22,652)
Schenk, Kurt 5:13:43 (26,069)
Scheubert, Johannes 3:09:33 (1,637)
Scheuring, Joachim 3:27:31 (3,740)
Scheuring, Steffen 3:45:17 (6,787)
Schiel, Chris 3:43:27 (6,443)
Schildermans, Johan 2:37:33 (127)
Schillinger, Michael 4:55:28 (23,021)
Schimmel, Nicholas 5:33:57 (28,476)
Schippel, John 6:27:26 (31,243)
Schipper, Jan 4:24:01 (15,756)

Schlosser, Jens	3:55:07 (8,944)	
Schmidders, Ralph	3:51:32 (8,086)	
Schmidt, Andreas	4:16:42 (13,905)	
Schmidt, Christian	4:32:03 (17,743)	
Schmidt, Hans	5:25:19 (27,590)	
Schmidt, Jacob	3:42:40 (6,288)	
Schmidt, Jens	3:58:03 (9,722)	
Schmidt, Karlheinz	4:16:44 (13,914)	
Schmunz, Ralf	3:30:40 (4,268)	
Schneider, Matthew	5:09:30 (25,474)	
Schoeb, Chris	4:34:57 (18,383)	
Schofield, Darren	4:36:48 (18,835)	
Schofield, David	3:07:44 (1,477)	
Schofield, Graham	3:18:48 (2,638)	
Schofield, James	5:03:14 (24,498)	
Schofield, Jason	4:40:11 (19,581)	
Schofield, Malcolm	3:03:38 (1,163)	
Schofield, Mark	3:41:59 (6,147)	
Schofield, Philip	4:25:18 (16,086)	
Schokman, Tony	4:57:57 (23,571)	
Scholes, David	4:58:40 (23,727)	
Scholes, Glenn	3:49:17 (7,587)	
Scholey, Alan	3:56:18 (9,271)	
Scholl, Reinhard	5:06:43 (25,060)	
Schollum, Stephan	3:55:09 (8,951)	
Scholtalbers, Johan	4:17:14 (14,041)	
Scholz, Thomas	3:42:38 (6,280)	
Schonfeld, Romvald	3:04:32 (1,213)	
Schorah, Noel	3:25:03 (3,401)	
Schrauwen, Dominiek	3:03:29 (1,149)	
Schreiber-Michael, Reiner	5:03:33 (24,539)	
Schroeder, Gunnar	4:15:09 (13,554)	
Schroeder-Davis, Stephen	4:03:00 (10,839)	
Schtonbrunn, Helmut	3:16:55 (2,422)	
Schuetz, Hans	4:06:22 (11,566)	
Schultz, John	3:19:56 (2,748)	
Schumann, Paul	3:01:01 (1,005)	
Schumm, Volker	3:58:08 (9,739)	
Schuster, Arne	4:53:46 (22,674)	
Schuster, Roland	3:32:19 (4,510)	
Schwaberl, Lukas	3:36:29 (5,139)	
Schwaiger, Georg	3:34:26 (4,824)	
Schwank, Samuel	4:42:23 (20,078)	
Schwarte, Rainer	3:55:36 (9,076)	
Schwartz, Steven	4:04:09 (11,105)	
Schwarz, Rob	3:54:29 (8,776)	
Schwarz, Stefan	3:21:56 (2,976)	
Schweer, Marco	3:24:38 (3,347)	
Schweicke, Georg	4:08:51 (12,098)	
Schweitzer, Heindieter	4:15:55 (13,725)	
Sciberras, Alan	5:15:27 (26,309)	
Scicluna, Christopher	5:33:11 (28,390)	
Scileppi, Greg	3:59:50 (10,184)	
Sciorilli Borrelli, Filippo	4:23:07 (15,521)	
Scoarnec, Franck	4:15:10 (13,561)	
Scoble, Mark	4:33:07 (17,973)	
Scoble, Wayne	5:37:29 (28,775)	
Scogings, Andrew	3:37:16 (5,286)	
Scothern, Mark	5:01:56 (24,302)	
Scothern, Martin	6:07:17 (30,540)	
Scotney, Lee	4:56:19 (23,224)	
Scotney, Paul	4:58:05 (23,606)	
Scotson, Paul	4:04:53 (11,268)	
Scott, Adam	3:28:35 (3,919)	
Scott, Alan	4:56:02 (23,152)	
Scott, Alexander	4:56:02 (23,152)	
Scott, André	4:58:05 (23,606)	
Scott, Andrew	4:51:05 (22,099)	
Scott, Anthony	3:49:00 (7,518)	
Scott, Asa	4:40:26 (19,640)	
Scott, Brough	4:05:58 (11,498)	
Scott, Charles	5:49:09 (29,648)	
Scott, Chris	3:58:45 (9,901)	
Scott, Cyril	5:06:30 (25,016)	
Scott, David	3:27:28 (3,735)	
Scott, David	4:55:02 (22,928)	
Scott, Douglas	3:34:58 (4,905)	
Scott, Gary	5:12:48 (25,944)	
Scott, Geoffrey	6:23:01 (31,106)	
Scott, George	3:13:26 (2,052)	
Scott, Grae	3:10:52 (1,745)	
Scott, Guy	4:10:00 (12,352)	
Scott, Haydn	4:43:46 (20,444)	

Scott, Hugo	3:23:45 (3,208)	
Scott, Ian	2:57:57 (763)	
Scott, Ian	3:52:01 (8,200)	
Scott, Ian	4:02:43 (10,786)	
Scott, James	4:03:49 (11,017)	
Scott, John	4:33:09 (17,979)	
Scott, Kenneth	3:25:14 (3,432)	
Scott, Lloyd	5:27:10 (27,801)	
Scott, Martin	4:42:32 (20,121)	
Scott, Murray	3:42:54 (6,345)	
Scott, Paul	4:13:49 (13,205)	
Scott, Philip	3:41:59 (6,147)	
Scott, Philip	4:19:43 (14,673)	
Scott, Richard	3:54:47 (8,863)	
Scott, Richard	4:05:24 (11,373)	
Scott, Robin	3:10:18 (1,706)	
Scott, Ronald	4:46:28 (21,085)	
Scott, Russell	4:08:21 (11,969)	
Scott, Simon	4:24:37 (15,892)	
Scott, Stephen	5:03:26 (24,522)	
Scott, Steve	4:45:05 (20,739)	
Scott, Stuart	4:41:14 (19,810)	
Scott, Terry	5:31:18 (28,226)	
Scott, William	4:28:59 (16,986)	
Scott-Tomlin, Oliver	5:23:24 (27,340)	
Scovil, Richard	3:54:58 (8,911)	
Scowcroft, Michael	3:37:31 (5,326)	
Scrini, Alex	4:03:42 (10,986)	
Scripps, Elliot	4:27:10 (16,516)	
Scriven, Harvey	4:14:32 (13,389)	
Scrivener, Aaron	4:47:44 (21,353)	
Scrivener, Christopher	3:16:25 (2,368)	
Scrivener, Michael	4:40:43 (19,687)	
Scrivener, Paul	4:02:07 (10,658)	
Scroggins, Jay	4:40:57 (19,741)	
Scroop, Marcus	4:49:34 (21,766)	
Scrope, Harry	3:23:09 (3,130)	
Scruton, Neil	2:53:49 (520)	
Scudamore, Keith	3:30:40 (4,268)	
Scudds, Paul	4:21:10 (15,027)	
Scurlock, Andrew	4:17:42 (14,176)	
Scurr, Andrew	4:16:44 (13,914)	
Scutt, Martin	3:32:14 (4,501)	
Scutt, Oliver	3:37:06 (5,253)	
Scutt, Sean	4:34:04 (18,186)	
Seaborn, Geroge	4:59:26 (23,877)	
Seabrook, Joe	4:04:40 (11,216)	
Seabrook, Mark	4:15:36 (13,660)	
Seaden-Jones, Peter	4:51:30 (22,211)	
Seager, Barry	7:39:15 (32,199)	
Seagrave, James	4:07:09 (11,725)	
Seal, David	3:33:22 (4,657)	
Seal, Julian	4:48:13 (21,475)	
Sealey, Michael	5:24:27 (27,468)	
Seals, Douglas	4:38:59 (19,322)	
Seaman, David	3:59:08 (9,990)	
Seaman, Kelly	4:34:31 (18,290)	
Seaman, Paul	5:39:26 (28,942)	
Seamark, Jamie	2:59:28 (899)	
Sear, Barry	5:06:13 (24,988)	
Sear, James	4:18:59 (14,504)	
Sear, Lawrence	4:41:16 (19,816)	
Sear, Paul	4:20:51 (14,944)	
Searil, David	3:40:04 (5,803)	
Searle, Adrian	4:15:50 (13,713)	
Searle, Alastair	3:28:54 (3,987)	
Searle, Kevin	5:28:17 (27,922)	
Searle, Paul	3:54:31 (8,788)	
Sear-Mayes, David	5:06:13 (24,988)	
Seaton, Steven	4:20:01 (14,748)	
Sebborn, Peter	5:19:01 (26,758)	
Sebley, Nick	3:21:24 (2,924)	
Secker, Ian	3:49:14 (7,574)	
Secrett, Jonathan	3:36:49 (5,195)	
Sector, Gary	4:39:35 (19,454)	
Seddon, Adrian	4:19:40 (14,658)	
Seddon, Gary	7:30:16 (32,155)	
Seddon, Gerald	4:51:39 (22,235)	
Seddon, Mike	4:34:53 (18,369)	
Sedge, Martin	3:20:47 (2,855)	
Sedgemore, Edward	3:57:23 (9,552)	
Sedgewick, Benjamin	4:40:52 (19,721)	
Sedgley, David	4:21:35 (15,126)	

Sedgmond, Andrew	4:04:21 (11,146)	
Sedgwick, Alan	3:52:17 (8,263)	
Sedgwick, Keith	6:05:35 (30,483)	
Sedgwick, Stephen	4:23:40 (15,662)	
Sedman, Nigel	3:09:02 (1,590)	
Seelandt, Frank	3:28:26 (3,891)	
Sees, Robert	4:12:03 (12,772)	
Sefton, Paul	3:26:59 (3,678)	
Segal, Steven	4:32:28 (17,826)	
Segall, Alan	4:07:00 (11,687)	
Seglow, Jonathan	4:59:01 (23,804)	
Segrera, Rafael	5:25:32 (27,614)	
Sehn, Marc	3:55:51 (9,144)	
Seifert, Andreas	4:46:05 (20,990)	
Seifert, Christian	3:34:53 (4,889)	
Seigal-James, Ian	6:23:28 (31,120)	
Seini, Ian	3:46:48 (7,083)	
Sekeram, Ranjan	5:45:59 (29,439)	
Sekkat, Said	3:32:07 (4,486)	
Sekula, Mark	4:43:27 (20,363)	
Selby, Gregory	3:11:43 (1,825)	
Selby, Paul	3:43:59 (6,541)	
Self, Graeme	4:57:05 (23,398)	
Sell, Alexander	3:38:04 (5,425)	
Sell, James	3:45:36 (6,849)	
Sellar, Benjamin	3:26:36 (3,619)	
Sellars, Neil	4:51:49 (22,270)	
Sellathurai, Jeganivasan	7:41:59 (32,216)	
Sellen, Steve	4:57:38 (23,511)	
Sellers, Ian	5:17:09 (26,498)	
Sellers, Michael	4:34:03 (18,176)	
Sellick, James	4:07:11 (11,735)	
Selow, Paul	4:30:53 (17,464)	
Selves, Stephen	5:07:56 (25,255)	
Selway, Richard	4:51:07 (22,108)	
Selwyn, Raymond	3:16:57 (2,425)	
Semmens, Brian	6:36:21 (31,481)	
Sen, Paul	4:45:24 (20,821)	
Senac-Sansano, Antonio	3:47:22 (7,183)	
Sendall, Nicholas	3:44:24 (6,622)	
Sengl, Otto	3:45:40 (6,863)	
Senior, Christopher	5:49:26 (29,670)	
Senner, Freddie	6:07:03 (30,532)	
Sephton, Michael	4:13:48 (13,203)	
Seret, Jean	4:18:29 (14,351)	
Seretis, Spiro	6:14:42 (30,817)	
Serge, Choquet	4:53:43 (22,652)	
Sergeant, Stephen	4:03:00 (10,839)	
Serres, Jean-Marie	2:48:12 (341)	
Sessions, Jason	4:53:18 (22,573)	
Setford, John	4:26:13 (16,300)	
Seth, Jai	4:39:46 (19,490)	
Seth-Smith, Edward	4:26:31 (16,358)	
Severini, Giovanni	3:08:14 (1,516)	
Sevink, Eddie	3:38:30 (5,494)	
Sevink, Marco	3:38:30 (5,494)	
Sevitt, Timothy	4:13:31 (13,130)	
Seward, Colin	3:49:49 (7,702)	
Seward, Leonard	4:45:00 (20,717)	
Sewell, Andrew	3:06:57 (1,398)	
Sewell, Andrew	5:18:34 (26,710)	
Sewell, Anthony	3:46:31 (7,035)	
Sewell, Colin	3:22:37 (3,062)	
Sewell, Mark	5:17:23 (26,525)	
Sewell, Nigel	3:14:51 (2,222)	
Sewell, Paul	4:25:55 (16,234)	
Sexton, John	5:45:18 (29,389)	
Sexton, Mark	4:37:48 (19,045)	
Sexton, Mark	5:00:18 (24,045)	
Sexton, Noel	5:59:54 (30,254)	
Sexty, Roger	3:04:48 (1,237)	
Seyfried, Max	3:53:56 (8,653)	
Seymour, Mark	3:49:42 (7,680)	
Seymour, Michael	5:17:00 (26,480)	
Seymour, Tony	4:03:49 (11,017)	
Shackleton, Peter	4:06:39 (11,614)	
Shackleton, Philip	4:37:55 (19,069)	
Shackleton, Raymond	5:27:21 (27,814)	
Shadbolt, Chris	4:29:53 (17,215)	
Shaddock, John	3:13:44 (2,091)	
Shaffrey, Len	3:33:54 (4,734)	
Shafier, Lawrence	3:03:19 (1,136)	
Shah, Amit	5:22:44 (27,244)	

Shah, Jatin 4:30:02 (17,248)
Shah, Kaushik 4:28:50 (16,945)
Shah, Kavit....................4:42:28 (20,101)
Shah, Neel 4:53:06 (22,521)
Shah, Paresh 5:24:55 (27,524)
Shah, Rumit...................7:00:23 (31,893)
Shah, Sailesh 6:18:32 (30,958)
Shah, Sunil 4:17:01 (13,989)
Shakeshaft, Andrew 2:59:01 (855)
Shakespeare, Stephen.......3:59:54 (10,200)
Shallcross, Rowland 5:14:31 (26,182)
Shalon, Dan 4:01:28 (10,533)
Shan, Nazam..................5:17:09 (26,498)
Shand, Ian 4:20:07 (14,774)
Shand, Wayne.................5:46:43 (29,477)
Shankland, Tony 5:42:35 (29,215)
Shanks, Alexander 4:50:48 (22,032)
Shanks, Jonathan 3:26:13 (3,570)
Shanks, Stephen 3:00:34 (980)
Shanley, Joseph 5:54:33 (29,971)
Shannon, Mark................3:45:29 (6,828)
Shannon, Simon 3:46:07 (6,955)
Shanyer, Richard 6:02:07 (30,344)
Shapland, Martin 3:11:56 (1,854)
Share, Richard.................3:23:57 (3,240)
Sharif, Basharat 5:49:52 (29,707)
Sharkey, Jonathan 3:20:04 (2,768)
Sharland, David 4:38:17 (19,156)
Sharland, Mick 3:12:59 (1,987)
Sharland, Paul 4:27:55 (16,693)
Sharland, Roger 3:42:58 (6,358)
Sharma, Kishore..............3:51:17 (8,025)
Sharma, Rajnesh 6:21:55 (31,071)
Sharma, Sanjai 3:18:46 (2,632)
Sharma, Vikesh 4:39:46 (19,490)
Sharman, Ben 4:25:00 (16,003)
Sharman, Neil 4:14:56 (13,488)
Sharp, Aaron 4:28:33 (16,874)
Sharp, Charles 3:36:36 (5,160)
Sharp, David 3:32:45 (4,567)
Sharp, David 4:51:46 (22,258)
Sharp, Jeremy 3:26:32 (3,613)
Sharp, Ken 3:58:12 (9,755)
Sharp, Michael................6:19:01 (30,974)
Sharp, Neil 3:52:40 (8,347)
Sharp, Paul 4:48:32 (21,537)
Sharp, Richard 3:03:20 (1,138)
Sharp, Robert.................3:23:57 (3,240)
Sharp, Stephen 6:34:38 (31,438)
Sharpe, David 7:11:12 (32,003)
Sharpe, George 6:11:57 (30,725)
Sharpe, Jonathan 3:15:52 (2,322)
Sharpe, Martyn 4:00:56 (10,417)
Sharpe, Richard 3:57:23 (9,552)
Sharpe, Richard 4:21:46 (15,176)
Sharples, Ian 2:57:26 (730)
Sharples, Jon 3:48:42 (7,440)
Sharrock, James..............5:08:22 (25,320)
Shatford, Jeremy 4:20:14 (14,802)
Shaughnessy, Alan 4:12:53 (12,978)
Shaughnessy, John 3:55:09 (8,951)
Shaw, Adam 5:48:33 (29,609)
Shaw, Alan 4:49:54 (21,847)
Shaw, Andrew 3:59:13 (10,007)
Shaw, Andrew 4:33:25 (18,036)
Shaw, Anthony................3:30:59 (4,325)
Shaw, Carl 4:36:05 (18,666)
Shaw, Christopher 4:44:43 (20,663)
Shaw, Darren 4:24:11 (15,794)
Shaw, David 3:02:41 (1,094)
Shaw, David 3:35:46 (5,033)
Shaw, David 4:07:08 (11,721)
Shaw, Edward 6:27:58 (31,264)
Shaw, Gary 4:51:56 (22,297)
Shaw, Geoffrey...............4:32:21 (17,801)
Shaw, Gerry 3:03:12 (1,130)
Shaw, Ian 4:10:06 (12,373)
Shaw, James 3:53:55 (8,652)
Shaw, John 5:25:29 (27,605)
Shaw, Jonathan 4:22:16 (15,309)
Shaw, Michael.................3:32:51 (4,577)
Shaw, Michael.................4:40:16 (19,594)
Shaw, Neil 3:13:03 (1,998)

Shaw, Peter 3:12:24 (1,916)
Shaw, Peter 4:29:51 (17,207)
Shaw, Steven 3:54:26 (8,763)
Shaw, Steven 4:20:19 (14,820)
Shaw, Tom....................3:58:11 (9,748)
Shaw, Tom....................5:08:39 (25,354)
Shaw, Tony 3:54:11 (8,699)
Shaw, Will 5:05:02 (24,796)
Shaw, William 3:36:33 (5,152)
Shawcroft, Graham 3:50:08 (7,761)
Shaya, Darrin 4:06:24 (11,573)
Shaya, Paul 3:47:46 (7,274)
Shayler, Mark 5:20:46 (26,993)
Shead, Mark 4:17:03 (14,001)
Sheard, Colin 4:02:08 (10,664)
Shearman, Cliff 4:04:19 (11,137)
Shearman, Peter 4:17:45 (14,193)
Shearn, Mark 3:50:43 (7,890)
Shears, Russell 4:50:15 (21,909)
Sheckleford, Ashley..........3:24:11 (3,280)
Sheehan, Andrew 4:15:42 (13,675)
Sheehan, Barry 3:40:59 (5,953)
Sheehan, Dermot 4:49:31 (21,754)
Sheehan, Eamon 4:31:21 (17,582)
Sheehan, James 2:55:30 (620)
Sheehan, Jeremiah 5:01:50 (24,288)
Sheehan, Jonathan 5:30:00 (28,085)
Sheehan, Martin...............3:45:42 (6,868)
Sheehan, Nicholas 4:53:28 (22,616)
Sheen, Austen 3:56:02 (9,189)
Sheen, Geoffrey...............5:30:14 (28,102)
Shegog, Andrew 3:34:13 (4,783)
Sheibani, Askar................3:48:14 (7,364)
Sheibani, Mohammad 5:00:19 (24,038)
Sheikh, Nabil 4:17:17 (14,053)
Sheil, Peter 6:36:21 (31,481)
Sheild, Jerry...................3:22:13 (3,013)
Shek, Duncan 5:22:42 (27,235)
Sheldon, Geoffrey............3:39:40 (5,722)
Sheldon, Leonard 3:55:47 (9,127)
Sheldon, Marcus 4:27:00 (16,470)
Sheldon, Michael..............4:06:44 (11,637)
Shellard, Neil..................4:49:47 (21,820)
Shelley, Kevin 5:50:09 (29,730)
Shelton, Michael 3:12:18 (1,904)
Shenton, Peter 4:52:21 (22,369)
Shephard, Hamish 4:13:44 (13,184)
Shephard, Richard 3:25:22 (3,449)
Shepheard, Peter 5:25:12 (27,574)
Shephedrd, Scott 4:01:32 (10,545)
Shepherd, Adam 4:03:16 (10,906)
Shepherd, Alec 3:47:04 (7,135)
Shepherd, Alister 4:57:05 (23,398)
Shepherd, André..............3:17:44 (2,522)
Shepherd, Ben 3:45:34 (6,843)
Shepherd, David 3:48:43 (7,443)
Shepherd, David 5:00:15 (24,027)
Shepherd, Guy 3:40:33 (5,873)
Shepherd, James 7:21:38 (32,083)
Shepherd, John 5:41:52 (29,148)
Shepherd, Michael............5:08:30 (25,338)
Shepherd, Michael............7:41:48 (32,215)
Shepherd, Peter 4:36:21 (18,733)
Shepherd, Ralph 6:11:18 (30,701)
Shepherd, Roger 3:41:16 (6,000)
Sheppard, Adrian 5:03:45 (24,584)
Sheppard, Andrew 3:50:12 (7,777)
Sheppard, Daniel 5:23:50 (27,388)
Sheppard, David 5:26:18 (27,710)
Sheppard, Stephen 4:51:27 (22,195)
Shepperson, Mark 4:45:28 (20,837)
Sherbrooke, Tom 3:49:21 (7,599)
Shercliff, Hugh 4:36:26 (18,753)
Shergill, Iqbal.................6:00:36 (30,278)
Shergill, Sukhpal 6:00:35 (30,276)
Sheridan, Christopher 5:41:40 (29,133)
Sheridan, Pat 6:10:38 (30,669)
Sheridan, Paul 4:09:38 (12,256)
Sheridan, Thomas.............3:04:06 (1,190)
Sheriff, Antony 6:30:29 (31,341)
Sherlock, Mark 4:11:10 (12,567)
Sherlock, Steven 3:49:09 (7,548)
Sherriff, Stuart................4:23:13 (15,551)

Sherwen, Peter 4:55:08 (22,949)
Sherwin, Graham 5:54:07 (29,939)
Sherwin, Nick 4:22:52 (15,458)
Sherwin, Terence 5:14:13 (26,129)
Sherwood, Mark 4:18:35 (14,387)
Shew, Peter 5:02:15 (24,353)
Shewbridge, Paul.............4:38:08 (19,114)
Shiel, Stephen 4:01:36 (10,560)
Shiel, Terence.................4:24:02 (15,761)
Shields, Brian 6:01:08 (30,308)
Shields, Hugh 3:46:53 (7,100)
Shields, Jim 4:28:02 (16,715)
Shields, Martin 5:11:11 (25,719)
Shields, Nicholas 4:09:14 (12,181)
Shields, Steven 5:20:12 (26,915)
Shields, Timothy 3:41:24 (6,041)
Shiels, Michael 6:05:41 (30,489)
Shillabeer, Edmund 5:02:15 (24,353)
Shillitto, Martin 4:36:01 (18,654)
Shilston, Stuart 3:17:47 (2,526)
Shimakage, Sam 3:45:54 (6,912)
Shimizu, Yoji 4:38:55 (19,308)
Shimmin, Andrew 7:27:48 (32,139)
Shimmin, Greg 3:56:59 (9,451)
Shimmin, Robert..............3:43:06 (6,387)
Shimwell, Robert..............3:29:30 (4,092)
Shingler, Jason 4:34:28 (18,281)
Shinmar, Rajinder 6:57:22 (31,866)
Shipley, Craig.................4:14:29 (13,377)
Shipman, Alan 3:42:39 (6,285)
Shipp, Kevin 3:44:08 (6,569)
Shipton, Mark 3:28:22 (3,878)
Shipway, Mike 3:18:22 (2,600)
Shipway, Rich.................3:08:13 (1,515)
Shires, Neil 3:09:13 (1,601)
Shires, Stuart 4:05:53 (11,478)
Shirley, David 6:04:17 (30,422)
Shirley, Peter 4:01:10 (10,465)
Shivji, Sharif 3:39:02 (5,604)
Shockley, Bernard 4:31:40 (17,663)
Shomer, Gabi 4:25:35 (16,153)
Shore, Andrew................4:31:46 (17,682)
Shore, Justin 4:15:08 (13,550)
Shore, Keith 5:06:41 (25,049)
Shorey, Andrew 3:39:24 (5,678)
Shorney, Stephen 4:51:29 (22,206)
Shorrock, Lee 5:25:42 (27,630)
Short, Arthur 3:39:09 (5,621)
Short, Garry 3:21:29 (2,929)
Short, Murray 5:19:23 (26,812)
Short, Paul 3:51:32 (8,086)
Short, Richard 4:23:29 (15,611)
Short, Tony 4:52:20 (22,365)
Shotton, William 5:22:28 (27,207)
Shotwell, Jay..................5:22:23 (27,198)
Shout, Andy 4:20:30 (14,868)
Showell, John 4:11:15 (12,589)
Shread, Darren 4:36:46 (18,826)
Shreeve, Phil..................3:39:04 (5,611)
Shrestha, Subir 5:04:24 (24,692)
Shropshire, Mark 3:38:32 (5,502)
Shrourou, Tareq 4:35:54 (18,620)
Shute, Jeremy 4:38:57 (19,315)
Shutler, Mark 4:29:52 (17,213)
Shutler, Matthew 3:01:44 (1,034)
Shuttlewood, Simon 4:15:18 (13,592)
Shuttleworth, Christopher....4:30:35 (17,386)
Shuttleworth, Matthew 3:49:01 (7,523)
Siapatis, John 5:49:26 (29,670)
Sibbett, Peter 2:54:44 (578)
Sibley, Graham 4:29:55 (17,225)
Sidaway, Paul 2:50:22 (397)
Siddall, Stuart 4:16:07 (13,766)
Siddans, Richard 4:46:14 (21,026)
Siddons, Barrie 4:13:01 (13,008)
Sidebotham, John 3:05:03 (1,257)
Sides, Wayne 5:38:07 (28,820)
Sidher, Sunil 3:50:42 (7,886)
Sidhu, Amandeep 4:50:04 (21,876)
Sidhu, Sanjeev 4:52:37 (22,417)
Sidwick, Bob 3:20:00 (2,760)
Siegert, Bernd 4:20:58 (14,968)
Sievewright, Kevin 3:18:21 (2,598)

Siewertsen, George	5:42:06 (29,174)	
Sigley, Philip	3:56:32 (9,330)	
Sikandar, Zulqarnan	5:13:26 (26,029)	
Silasi, Octavian	5:34:09 (28,493)	
Silcock, Jonathan	3:36:57 (5,223)	
Silcock, Peter	3:35:00 (4,912)	
Silcock, Richard	3:58:02 (9,717)	
Silk, Tim	5:23:17 (27,322)	
Sills, Matthew	3:47:44 (7,263)	
Sills, Russell	4:31:36 (17,639)	
Silvani, Christian	4:22:03 (15,252)	
Silver, Gavin	4:59:19 (23,859)	
Silverton, Ross	3:44:59 (6,733)	
Silverwood, Karl	4:30:21 (17,322)	
Silvester, Matthew	4:38:02 (19,099)	
Silvester, Paul	4:21:36 (15,132)	
Silvester, Paul	5:26:15 (27,706)	
Silvester, Richard	3:59:16 (10,027)	
Silvester, Robin	3:54:40 (8,831)	
Silvestrini, Giovanni	6:28:13 (31,278)	
Silvey, Adrian	4:38:36 (19,228)	
Sim, Craig	4:17:45 (14,193)	
Sim, Toby	4:18:42 (14,423)	
Simister, Gareth	4:39:54 (19,518)	
Simkins, Paul	3:52:18 (8,267)	
Simkins, Paul	4:19:39 (14,652)	
Simlinger, Michael	3:28:27 (3,893)	
Simm, Michael	4:14:19 (13,333)	
Simmonds, Ian	3:28:51 (3,977)	
Simmonds, Martin	3:44:43 (6,674)	
Simmonds, Richard	4:26:23 (16,332)	
Simmonds, Richard	4:50:50 (22,038)	
Simmonds, Robert	4:51:05 (22,099)	
Simmonds, Ron	5:22:11 (27,164)	
Simmons, David	3:01:22 (1,016)	
Simmons, Grant	4:46:44 (21,134)	
Simmons, John	5:45:04 (29,373)	
Simmons, Kevin	3:53:44 (8,598)	
Simmons, Scott	3:46:07 (6,955)	
Simmons, Steven	3:27:40 (3,762)	
Simmons, Trevor	3:22:33 (3,053)	
Simms, Andrew	4:14:36 (13,403)	
Simms, Henry	4:34:59 (18,393)	
Simms, Stephen	4:18:30 (14,359)	
Simner, Wayne	5:15:04 (26,256)	
Simon, Clement	2:46:29 (277)	
Simon, Lloyd	4:46:04 (20,982)	
Simon, Rodney	5:17:37 (26,565)	
Simonet, Paul	4:08:35 (12,035)	
Simons, Andrew	4:42:36 (20,134)	
Simons, David	3:53:44 (8,598)	
Simons, Giles	5:18:06 (26,630)	
Simons, Martin	4:44:39 (20,649)	
Simons, Richard	4:36:35 (18,785)	
Simons, Stephen	4:13:52 (13,220)	
Simonsen, Henrik	5:18:28 (26,695)	
Simpkins, Vaughan	4:31:32 (17,626)	
Simpson, Adrian	4:26:52 (16,441)	
Simpson, Andrew	3:44:30 (6,635)	
Simpson, Andy	4:19:25 (14,599)	
Simpson, Benjamin	4:16:31 (13,860)	
Simpson, Brian	4:16:28 (13,850)	
Simpson, Clark	5:32:17 (28,317)	
Simpson, Colin	3:25:55 (3,532)	
Simpson, Daron	4:30:23 (17,336)	
Simpson, Dave	3:53:52 (8,637)	
Simpson, David	3:26:36 (3,619)	
Simpson, David	4:26:21 (16,326)	
Simpson, Donald	6:32:54 (31,399)	
Simpson, Fraser	5:01:43 (24,262)	
Simpson, Gareth	3:12:13 (1,887)	
Simpson, Gary	3:22:56 (3,101)	
Simpson, George	5:49:09 (29,648)	
Simpson, Graham	4:00:11 (10,268)	
Simpson, John	3:38:45 (5,552)	
Simpson, John	4:29:20 (17,068)	
Simpson, John	5:11:01 (25,694)	
Simpson, Mark	3:24:49 (3,375)	
Simpson, Mark	3:40:48 (5,925)	
Simpson, Mark	3:53:17 (8,491)	
Simpson, Peter	4:20:50 (14,938)	
Simpson, Peter	4:23:57 (15,737)	
Simpson, Raymond	3:59:16 (10,027)	
Simpson, Richard	4:04:52 (11,264)	
Simpson, Richard	4:10:41 (12,497)	
Simpson, Robert	3:25:42 (3,496)	
Simpson, Robert	3:39:11 (5,626)	
Simpson, Stuart	4:04:29 (11,177)	
Simpson, Timothy	4:30:47 (17,442)	
Sims, Daniel	4:11:49 (12,723)	
Sims, Darren	5:35:16 (28,577)	
Sims, David	5:30:32 (28,143)	
Sims, Paul	4:33:26 (18,043)	
Sims, Steven	5:39:08 (28,914)	
Sincere, Michel	4:46:01 (20,964)	
Sinclair, John	4:31:36 (17,639)	
Sinclair, Malcolm	2:59:29 (900)	
Sinclair, Mark	5:29:19 (28,020)	
Sinclair, Nicholas	4:23:14 (15,554)	
Sinclair, Paul	4:03:51 (11,025)	
Sinclair, Phillip	3:32:58 (4,591)	
Sinclair, Richard	4:55:38 (23,062)	
Sinclair, Russell	4:43:30 (20,375)	
Sinclair, Terence	3:11:48 (1,836)	
Singer, Mark	4:58:55 (23,784)	
Singh, Ahrik	5:41:12 (29,091)	
Singh, Ajit	5:45:32 (29,409)	
Singh, Fauja	6:02:43 (30,364)	
Singh, George	4:21:41 (15,152)	
Singh, Gurdev	5:18:06 (26,630)	
Singh, Harbhag	3:55:51 (9,144)	
Singh, Harmander	6:02:43 (30,364)	
Singh, Makhan	4:59:03 (23,812)	
Singh, Resham	3:20:23 (2,814)	
Singh, Surinder	4:50:26 (21,947)	
Singleton, James	4:50:55 (22,055)	
Singleton, Michael	3:53:30 (8,541)	
Sinton, James	3:50:19 (7,805)	
Sirett, Nicholas	7:06:46 (31,953)	
Sirimalwatta, Uplai	4:41:39 (19,906)	
Sirs, Nicholas	2:38:42 (140)	
Sisto, Egidio	6:01:19 (30,315)	
Sitch, John	5:05:38 (24,907)	
Sitch, Mark	3:19:13 (2,673)	
Sithole, Patrick	3:54:24 (8,756)	
Siu, Chung	3:03:54 (1,176)	
Sivakumar, Branavan	5:57:35 (30,142)	
Sivry, Eric	4:36:40 (18,800)	
Skaarup, Steen	3:59:36 (10,119)	
Skagerlind, Lars	4:21:11 (15,030)	
Skalli Houssaini, Mohamed	4:12:49 (12,963)	
Skaper, George	4:00:47 (10,381)	
Skeates, Edward	3:44:32 (6,642)	
Skedsmo, Stein	3:56:00 (9,178)	
Skeet, John	3:23:40 (3,200)	
Skeet, Martin	3:06:19 (1,344)	
Skeffington, John	3:59:25 (10,068)	
Skehan, Gerard	5:37:39 (28,788)	
Skellern, Christopher	4:47:08 (21,212)	
Skelton, Andrew	4:59:01 (23,804)	
Skelton, David	4:10:11 (12,389)	
Skelton, George	4:01:47 (10,594)	
Skelton, John	4:40:47 (19,700)	
Skelton, Ray	3:11:09 (1,771)	
Skeoch, Aidan	4:28:03 (16,721)	
Skerry, Peter	4:31:59 (17,724)	
Skewes, John	6:20:25 (31,031)	
Skidmore, Jonathan	3:02:03 (1,055)	
Skidmore, Paul	4:14:38 (13,409)	
Skillborg, Hans	4:26:43 (16,405)	
Skingley, Ian	3:19:46 (2,730)	
Skinner, Antony	3:57:47 (9,642)	
Skinner, Mark	4:17:39 (14,158)	
Skinner, Matthew	3:50:31 (7,844)	
Skinner, Nigel	4:03:38 (10,970)	
Skinner, Robert	3:47:48 (7,277)	
Skipidarov, Oleg	5:03:23 (24,516)	
Skipp, Paul	3:07:09 (1,424)	
Skipper, Michael	4:23:48 (15,695)	
Skipper, Nicholas	3:05:45 (1,300)	
Skrabal, Philipp	4:03:21 (10,923)	
Skrimshire, Chris	3:53:04 (8,442)	
Slack, Martin	3:32:44 (4,564)	
Sladden, Charles	4:51:12 (22,132)	
Sladden, James	3:59:31 (10,098)	
Slade, Francis	5:51:00 (29,785)	
Slade, Nick	3:56:50 (9,407)	
Slade, Stuart	4:48:24 (21,517)	
Slama, Serge	3:26:52 (3,651)	
Slaney, Andrew	3:43:41 (6,486)	
Slaoui, Abdallah	5:39:07 (28,912)	
Slaoui, Nabil	3:34:21 (4,805)	
Slaoui, Omar	3:16:32 (2,378)	
Slate, Richard	5:23:44 (27,375)	
Slate, Terry	6:34:40 (31,439)	
Slater, Alfred	4:11:36 (12,667)	
Slater, Iain	4:19:21 (14,580)	
Slater, Richard	3:42:48 (6,315)	
Slater, Stephen	4:54:41 (22,861)	
Slater, Terence	4:30:21 (17,322)	
Slatford, Richard	4:24:44 (15,928)	
Slatter, Keith	5:44:12 (29,315)	
Slaughter, Courtenay	5:41:34 (29,125)	
Slayford, Leslie	4:58:13 (23,629)	
Sledon, Keith	5:16:25 (26,418)	
Slee, Alan	5:35:17 (28,579)	
Sleep, Martin	3:53:32 (8,555)	
Slegg, Christopher	4:28:34 (16,878)	
Sleight, James	4:58:01 (23,583)	
Slingsby, Jason	3:42:52 (6,333)	
Sloan, Jonathan	4:06:29 (11,587)	
Sloane, Sidney	5:09:39 (25,496)	
Slocock, Julian	4:01:42 (10,580)	
Slocombe, Colin	4:06:23 (11,570)	
Slomke, Roger	2:52:44 (482)	
Slootweg, Kees	5:12:26 (25,885)	
Sloper, Nicholas	4:32:29 (17,830)	
Slowik, Michael	4:24:53 (15,970)	
Slowikowski, Mark	5:22:15 (27,178)	
Sluman, John	3:34:19 (4,797)	
Slutter, Benjamin	4:32:06 (17,752)	
Sly, Andy	3:21:13 (2,900)	
Sly, Christopher	5:10:25 (25,611)	
Slysz, Martin	2:38:48 (142)	
Smales, Jonathan	4:55:15 (22,965)	
Small, Edward	4:59:38 (23,910)	
Small, Kevin	4:27:08 (16,506)	
Smalley, Alan	4:17:39 (14,158)	
Smalley, Michael	4:57:53 (23,557)	
Smallridge, James	3:27:45 (3,776)	
Smalls, Allen	2:43:40 (212)	
Smallwood, Ian	3:02:06 (1,061)	
Smallwood, Timothy	4:16:53 (13,963)	
Smart, Andy	4:13:06 (13,023)	
Smart, Christopher	3:20:51 (2,865)	
Smart, Christopher	4:56:54 (23,361)	
Smart, Darren	3:59:26 (10,073)	
Smart, David	4:05:15 (11,342)	
Smart, David	4:06:35 (11,608)	
Smart, George	4:56:31 (23,266)	
Smart, Ian	3:27:17 (3,711)	
Smart, Ian	3:56:20 (9,280)	
Smart, Rhoderick	4:33:09 (17,979)	
Smart, Roy	4:04:00 (11,062)	
Smart, Simon	6:04:10 (30,415)	
Smart, Trevor	3:45:26 (6,818)	
Smeath, David	3:34:27 (4,830)	
Smeddle, Jeremy	3:57:08 (9,488)	
Smekens, Olivier	5:03:31 (24,532)	
Smethurst, James	3:22:43 (3,071)	
Smid, Ilya	3:59:48 (10,176)	
Smikle, Hugh	4:28:20 (16,801)	
Smiles, Karl	3:52:58 (8,412)	
Smiley, Jamie	3:48:33 (7,412)	
Smith, Adam	4:09:49 (12,309)	
Smith, Adrian	4:30:11 (17,282)	
Smith, Adrian	7:40:44 (32,208)	
Smith, Alan	3:14:31 (2,186)	
Smith, Alan	3:24:21 (3,308)	
Smith, Alan	3:41:19 (6,017)	
Smith, Alan	3:47:12 (7,157)	
Smith, Alan	3:58:07 (9,733)	
Smith, Alastair	5:23:08 (27,305)	
Smith, Alex	3:46:17 (6,991)	
Smith, Andrew	3:36:57 (5,223)	
Smith, Andrew	3:47:40 (7,251)	
Smith, Andrew	3:52:21 (8,276)	
Smith, Andrew	3:55:43 (9,113)	
Smith, Andrew	3:59:31 (10,098)	

Smith, Andrew	4:19:34	(14,631)
Smith, Andrew	4:33:39	(18,089)
Smith, Andrew	5:07:54	(25,250)
Smith, Andrew	5:47:28	(29,529)
Smith, Andrew	5:49:33	(29,688)
Smith, Andy	3:30:20	(4,223)
Smith, Anthony	4:24:31	(15,868)
Smith, Anthony	4:25:06	(16,026)
Smith, Anthony	5:01:36	(24,242)
Smith, Anthony	5:45:04	(29,373)
Smith, Antony	3:52:30	(8,310)
Smith, Barry	3:22:51	(3,092)
Smith, Barry	4:22:12	(15,295)
Smith, Barry	4:40:34	(19,661)
Smith, Barry	5:27:35	(27,845)
Smith, Brett	3:55:46	(9,120)
Smith, Brian	4:09:39	(12,264)
Smith, Carl	3:56:55	(9,428)
Smith, Carl	4:26:49	(16,433)
Smith, Carl	4:38:29	(19,194)
Smith, Charles	3:40:12	(5,832)
Smith, Chris	4:11:54	(12,741)
Smith, Christopher	3:07:49	(1,488)
Smith, Christopher	3:19:25	(2,693)
Smith, Christopher	3:30:09	(4,193)
Smith, Christopher	3:41:22	(6,034)
Smith, Christopher	4:30:10	(17,277)
Smith, Cliff	3:26:20	(3,581)
Smith, Colin	3:14:17	(2,161)
Smith, Colin	4:48:20	(21,501)
Smith, Colin	6:53:35	(31,800)
Smith, Craig	4:50:34	(21,979)
Smith, Daniel	4:11:10	(12,567)
Smith, Daniel	4:33:34	(18,071)
Smith, Darren	4:40:03	(19,549)
Smith, Darren	6:11:38	(30,714)
Smith, Darren	6:11:54	(30,723)
Smith, Darren	6:23:23	(31,114)
Smith, Dave	3:45:16	(6,784)
Smith, David	3:26:07	(3,554)
Smith, David	3:43:23	(6,434)
Smith, David	3:46:04	(6,946)
Smith, David	3:56:21	(9,284)
Smith, David	3:59:14	(10,014)
Smith, David	5:30:26	(28,134)
Smith, David	5:42:07	(29,179)
Smith, Derek	5:31:38	(28,252)
Smith, Derek	5:58:57	(30,207)
Smith, Dominic	4:02:47	(10,803)
Smith, Douglas	4:04:34	(11,191)
Smith, Dyfed	6:10:21	(30,653)
Smith, Earl	6:56:52	(31,858)
Smith, Eddie	3:25:43	(3,500)
Smith, Garry	4:43:39	(20,417)
Smith, Gary	5:05:40	(24,912)
Smith, Geoff	5:09:16	(25,441)
Smith, Geoffrey	2:55:44	(631)
Smith, Giles	3:51:46	(8,138)
Smith, Glyn	4:40:09	(19,571)
Smith, Graham	4:54:27	(22,803)
Smith, Grant	3:40:52	(5,937)
Smith, Grant	5:05:13	(24,829)
Smith, Harry	4:52:45	(22,450)
Smith, Hayden	6:04:27	(30,427)
Smith, Huw	4:38:51	(19,292)
Smith, Ian	2:54:11	(547)
Smith, Ian	3:26:31	(3,610)
Smith, Ian	3:48:08	(7,345)
Smith, Ian	3:50:46	(7,902)
Smith, Ian	4:17:35	(14,132)
Smith, Ian	4:25:59	(16,248)
Smith, Ian	4:38:42	(19,252)
Smith, Ian	4:51:46	(22,258)
Smith, Ian	5:03:54	(24,615)
Smith, Jack	5:16:24	(26,414)
Smith, James	3:12:28	(1,923)
Smith, James	3:38:49	(5,561)
Smith, James	3:50:28	(7,832)
Smith, James	4:53:44	(22,663)
Smith, Jamie	3:14:20	(2,169)
Smith, Jason	3:42:19	(6,205)
Smith, Jason	3:49:20	(7,596)
Smith, Jeff	5:22:19	(27,190)
Smith, Jeffrey	4:50:41	(22,010)
Smith, Jeremy	4:29:35	(17,134)
Smith, Jim	5:55:39	(30,025)
Smith, John	3:21:07	(2,893)
Smith, John	3:52:54	(8,397)
Smith, John	4:07:38	(11,841)
Smith, John	5:39:42	(28,963)
Smith, Jonathan	3:56:59	(9,451)
Smith, Jonathan	4:22:04	(15,256)
Smith, Keith	3:02:58	(1,113)
Smith, Keith	4:08:53	(12,105)
Smith, Keith	4:41:47	(19,938)
Smith, Kevin	2:53:58	(532)
Smith, Kevin	3:48:44	(7,448)
Smith, Kevin	3:51:11	(8,008)
Smith, Kim	4:29:21	(17,071)
Smith, Lee	3:49:03	(7,527)
Smith, Lester	4:12:29	(12,880)
Smith, Lyndon	3:57:11	(9,502)
Smith, Mal	3:42:30	(6,248)
Smith, Marius	5:08:53	(25,387)
Smith, Mark	3:10:43	(1,730)
Smith, Mark	3:23:46	(3,210)
Smith, Mark	4:10:28	(12,456)
Smith, Mark	4:34:43	(18,332)
Smith, Mark	4:38:19	(19,167)
Smith, Mark	5:25:58	(27,667)
Smith, Martin	3:40:45	(5,914)
Smith, Martin	3:55:48	(9,129)
Smith, Martin	5:48:29	(29,605)
Smith, Martyn	5:51:03	(29,788)
Smith, Matt	3:25:31	(3,463)
Smith, Matthew	4:19:58	(14,731)
Smith, Matthew	4:59:50	(23,955)
Smith, Matthew	5:45:58	(29,438)
Smith, Michael	3:30:38	(4,263)
Smith, Michael	3:47:58	(7,311)
Smith, Michael	3:57:57	(9,694)
Smith, Michael	3:58:03	(9,722)
Smith, Michael	4:05:25	(11,379)
Smith, Michael	4:07:49	(11,875)
Smith, Michael	4:35:57	(18,637)
Smith, Michael	4:37:56	(19,071)
Smith, Michael	4:53:17	(22,569)
Smith, Michael	5:31:57	(28,288)
Smith, Mike	3:12:23	(1,914)
Smith, Nathan	3:48:33	(7,412)
Smith, Neil	4:01:23	(10,516)
Smith, Neil	4:21:35	(15,126)
Smith, Nicholas	2:55:24	(614)
Smith, Nicholas	5:38:59	(28,900)
Smith, Patrick	3:53:11	(8,470)
Smith, Paul	3:13:52	(2,109)
Smith, Paul	4:07:31	(11,813)
Smith, Paul	4:34:59	(18,393)
Smith, Paul	4:49:16	(21,694)
Smith, Paul	6:33:15	(31,405)
Smith, Peter	2:47:31	(317)
Smith, Peter	3:12:49	(1,968)
Smith, Peter	3:18:39	(2,624)
Smith, Peter	3:50:28	(7,832)
Smith, Peter	3:58:02	(9,717)
Smith, Peter	4:06:15	(11,545)
Smith, Peter	4:29:44	(17,171)
Smith, Peter	5:05:07	(24,818)
Smith, Phil	5:33:57	(28,476)
Smith, Philip	4:28:49	(16,939)
Smith, Ray	4:39:30	(19,439)
Smith, Raymond	4:13:15	(13,063)
Smith, Raymond	4:32:17	(17,791)
Smith, Raymond	5:28:36	(27,949)
Smith, Regan	3:53:18	(8,496)
Smith, Richard	3:08:25	(1,536)
Smith, Richard	4:37:57	(19,075)
Smith, Richard	5:54:16	(29,952)
Smith, Robert	3:22:03	(2,991)
Smith, Robert	3:56:38	(9,358)
Smith, Robert	4:29:10	(17,031)
Smith, Robert	4:45:44	(20,893)
Smith, Robert	4:58:17	(23,645)
Smith, Robert	5:14:29	(26,172)
Smith, Robert	5:29:43	(28,062)
Smith, Robin	3:57:44	(9,628)
Smith, Robin	4:49:40	(21,796)
Smith, Roger	5:18:14	(26,661)
Smith, Ronald	3:31:54	(4,458)
Smith, Rowan	4:38:00	(19,088)
Smith, Roy	3:06:13	(1,333)
Smith, Roy	3:29:39	(4,118)
Smith, Sam	5:22:13	(27,168)
Smith, Sean	3:24:11	(3,280)
Smith, Simon	3:28:56	(3,994)
Smith, Simon	3:56:04	(9,198)
Smith, Simon	4:04:50	(11,252)
Smith, Simon	4:16:19	(13,809)
Smith, Simon	4:29:53	(17,215)
Smith, Simon	6:12:09	(30,734)
Smith, Stan	4:07:57	(11,895)
Smith, Stephen	2:52:23	(465)
Smith, Stephen	3:20:38	(2,839)
Smith, Stephen	4:25:01	(16,007)
Smith, Stephen	4:45:45	(20,899)
Smith, Stephen	5:17:47	(26,577)
Smith, Stephen	5:41:33	(29,122)
Smith, Steve	6:18:46	(30,964)
Smith, Steven	3:07:23	(1,443)
Smith, Steven	3:43:18	(6,424)
Smith, Steven	5:19:25	(26,820)
Smith, Stuart	4:25:36	(16,158)
Smith, Sullivan	2:31:42	(72)
Smith, Terence	5:08:59	(25,401)
Smith, Terrence	3:19:41	(2,723)
Smith, Terry	3:42:41	(6,295)
Smith, Thomas	3:11:46	(1,832)
Smith, Thomas	3:52:15	(8,255)
Smith, Timothy	4:24:46	(15,941)
Smith, Timothy	4:57:37	(23,505)
Smith, Tom	4:24:02	(15,761)
Smith, Tony	4:11:45	(12,707)
Smith, Tony	4:31:16	(17,561)
Smith, Tony	4:37:48	(19,045)
Smith, Trevor	4:08:01	(11,908)
Smith, Trevor	6:10:07	(30,648)
Smith, Warren	4:22:18	(15,315)
Smith, Wayne	3:26:11	(3,564)
Smith, Wayne	5:02:05	(24,326)
Smith, William	3:39:53	(5,768)
Smitham, David	4:42:31	(20,116)
Smith-Bosanquet, Samuel	4:46:58	(21,177)
Smither, Richard	4:29:21	(17,071)
Smithers, Keith	5:20:48	(26,999)
Smithson, David	4:46:02	(20,971)
Smithson, James	3:42:02	(6,158)
Smithyes, Richard	4:41:01	(19,754)
Smy, Jamie	3:59:49	(10,180)
Smyth, Cecil	3:20:59	(2,882)
Smyth, Damian	5:04:21	(24,684)
Smyth, James	5:45:20	(29,393)
Smyth, Kevin	3:26:08	(3,558)
Smyth, Russell	4:00:57	(10,419)
Smyth, Stephen	5:25:13	(27,578)
Smyth, Thomas	3:22:51	(3,092)
Smythe, Jonathan	3:36:19	(5,118)
Smythe, Stephen	3:22:26	(3,042)
Snaith, Darren	4:16:39	(13,892)
Snaith, David	3:22:31	(3,050)
Snaith, Derek	3:38:45	(5,552)
Snaith, William	5:27:09	(27,797)
Snalune, Philip	5:11:00	(25,692)
Snashfold, Paul	4:25:19	(16,094)
Snelgrove, William	2:50:20	(396)
Snell, Daniel	3:59:06	(9,984)
Snell, David	3:14:12	(2,152)
Snell, John	5:37:59	(28,808)
Snellgrove, Adrian	3:54:56	(8,902)
Snellgrove, Thomas	5:10:47	(25,658)
Snelson, Marc	3:58:32	(9,844)
Snoddy, Paul	4:33:15	(17,993)
Snodgrass, James	2:35:57	(106)
Snook, Peter	4:45:22	(20,813)
Snook, Philip	6:18:12	(30,943)
Snooks, Mark	5:46:43	(29,477)
Snoussi, Khalid	3:11:25	(1,796)
Snow, Ian	5:45:25	(29,398)
Snowden, Craig	6:00:25	(30,271)
Snowden, Martin	5:11:32	(25,763)

Snowdon, Les	3:51:15 (8,019)	
Snowdon, Peter	3:13:42 (2,087)	
Snutch, Mark	5:41:21 (29,102)	
Soanes, John	5:14:23 (26,156)	
Soares, Dominic	4:41:50 (19,957)	
Soden, Christopher	4:00:37 (10,348)	
Soekeland, Georg	4:23:53 (15,716)	
Soerensen, Karsten	4:16:54 (13,964)	
Soffritti, Corrado	3:53:54 (8,646)	
Softleigh, Stanislaus	3:28:14 (3,854)	
Softley, Peter	4:45:56 (20,942)	
Solanki, Vinay	4:59:20 (23,865)	
Solbu, Anders	3:30:08 (4,190)	
Sole, Ben	5:38:35 (28,864)	
Sole, Joe	4:45:11 (20,767)	
Solender, Neil	4:18:33 (14,372)	
Solly, John	3:07:36 (1,460)	
Soloman, Nick	5:22:14 (27,171)	
Solomon, David	6:20:23 (31,029)	
Solomons, Daniel	3:06:54 (1,394)	
Somers, Tim	5:45:38 (29,414)	
Somers, Vincent	4:44:15 (20,557)	
Somerville, Peter	3:37:39 (5,354)	
Somes-Charlton, Christopher	4:19:29 (14,611)	
Sommer, Benjamin	4:36:27 (18,760)	
Sommerlad, Michael	5:55:48 (30,030)	
Sommers, Peter	3:35:09 (4,934)	
Sommerville, Ian	5:39:54 (28,981)	
Sonara, Chandrakant	5:23:52 (27,394)	
Sonara, Deepak	6:25:17 (31,170)	
Sonnenfeld, Joseph	4:51:41 (22,243)	
Sonnenstein, Keith	5:15:33 (26,324)	
Soole, Ivor	5:22:57 (27,278)	
Soon, Derek	4:16:15 (13,797)	
Soper, David	3:32:22 (4,516)	
Soper, John	5:01:34 (24,240)	
Sorensen, Torben	4:53:11 (22,541)	
Soresi, Domenico	4:24:31 (15,868)	
Sorrell, Paul	5:23:36 (27,358)	
Sossick, Matthew	3:58:56 (9,951)	
Sothisrihari, Saranga	4:28:44 (16,919)	
Soulabaail, Christian	3:48:31 (7,405)	
Soulier, Louis	4:24:10 (15,789)	
South, Les	4:58:59 (23,795)	
South, Stewart	4:34:16 (18,230)	
Southall, Roger	4:13:17 (13,072)	
Southam, Christopher	2:56:21 (663)	
Southard, Andy	5:33:51 (28,459)	
Southcombe, Jonathan	4:31:07 (17,533)	
Southern, John	5:22:42 (27,235)	
Southerton, Clive	4:04:35 (11,196)	
Southey, Alastair	4:26:50 (16,436)	
Southey, Nicolas	3:55:52 (9,148)	
Southwell, Alastair	3:40:11 (5,829)	
Southwell, Christopher	3:38:57 (5,591)	
Southwell, Nathan	4:26:02 (16,254)	
Southwell, Philip	3:48:53 (7,486)	
Southwell-Sander, Tim	4:01:30 (10,539)	
Southwood, Stephen	4:03:13 (10,884)	
Soutif, Arnaud	4:15:49 (13,707)	
Soutif, Eric	3:59:01 (9,970)	
Sowerby, James	5:45:46 (29,379)	
Sowerby, Kay	5:18:04 (26,620)	
Spacie, Daniel	3:43:27 (6,443)	
Spain, Victor	3:35:26 (4,984)	
Spangenberg, Jonas	4:47:07 (21,208)	
Sparber, Jan	4:56:39 (23,303)	
Sparey, Simon	4:58:03 (23,596)	
Sparkes, Stephen	5:09:27 (25,468)	
Sparkes, Steve	4:50:59 (22,065)	
Sparks, David	3:48:42 (7,440)	
Sparks, David	4:32:57 (17,935)	
Sparks, Ian	4:50:50 (22,038)	
Sparks, Karl	5:22:15 (27,178)	
Sparks, Steve	3:54:43 (8,840)	
Sparling, Gari	4:30:06 (17,263)	
Sparrey, Graham	3:16:38 (2,388)	
Sparrow, Matthew	3:21:24 (2,924)	
Sparrow, Roger	4:08:04 (11,917)	
Sparsis, Andrew	7:49:18 (32,228)	
Spaul, Graham	4:49:22 (21,719)	
Spayne, Nicholas	4:44:48 (20,679)	
Speake, Malcolm	4:33:03 (17,963)	
Speake, Peter	2:40:02 (153)	
Speakman, Ian	4:49:26 (21,733)	
Speakman, James	3:38:55 (5,584)	
Spear, Michael	3:36:58 (5,227)	
Spears, Robert	2:59:18 (881)	
Spector, Michael	4:50:40 (22,005)	
Spedding, Simon	2:59:37 (911)	
Speed, Christopher	3:35:08 (4,931)	
Speed, David	3:38:06 (5,427)	
Speed, David	4:26:10 (16,289)	
Speed, Marcus	5:12:54 (25,962)	
Speed, Michael	5:37:14 (28,758)	
Speed, Morley	3:27:13 (3,704)	
Speed, Russell	4:43:15 (20,303)	
Speed, Simon	3:40:06 (5,809)	
Speers, Gary	4:38:35 (19,221)	
Speirs, Rodney	4:45:34 (20,862)	
Speller, Mathew	5:28:38 (27,951)	
Speller, Michael	4:40:25 (19,635)	
Spelman, Peter	3:44:49 (6,691)	
Spence, Darren	3:53:13 (8,479)	
Spence, Lincoln	6:49:30 (31,709)	
Spencer, Andrew	3:05:22 (1,278)	
Spencer, Bert	5:20:34 (26,965)	
Spencer, Colin	3:50:33 (7,854)	
Spencer, Edward	3:54:16 (8,723)	
Spencer, Gary	4:57:29 (23,479)	
Spencer, Gavin	4:20:37 (14,892)	
Spencer, Geoffrey	3:56:07 (9,214)	
Spencer, Graham	4:15:59 (13,738)	
Spencer, Ian	3:06:42 (1,377)	
Spencer, Ian	3:17:11 (2,451)	
Spencer, James	5:08:02 (25,271)	
Spencer, John	4:08:45 (12,078)	
Spencer, John	6:34:07 (31,425)	
Spencer, Keith	3:18:33 (2,613)	
Spencer, Kevin	3:12:29 (1,927)	
Spencer, Lee	4:26:49 (16,433)	
Spencer, Martin	4:38:49 (19,282)	
Spencer, Paul	3:58:23 (9,804)	
Spencer, Philip	3:23:03 (3,116)	
Spencer, Robert	4:41:44 (19,928)	
Spencer, Stuart	3:39:17 (5,651)	
Spender, Barney	4:55:41 (23,074)	
Spendlove, Mark	3:52:03 (8,206)	
Spensley, Martin	4:08:55 (12,112)	
Spensley, Robert	5:25:04 (27,549)	
Sperinde, Massimo	3:12:31 (1,933)	
Sperrfechter, Dirk	3:57:58 (9,698)	
Spicer, Brian	5:42:42 (29,224)	
Spicer, Graham	4:25:00 (16,003)	
Spicer, Lloyd	4:24:37 (15,892)	
Spicer, Thomas	4:23:35 (15,635)	
Spiegel, Hugo	4:29:06 (17,014)	
Spiers, Adam	5:03:15 (24,500)	
Spiertz, Herbert	4:03:09 (10,873)	
Spiess, Sven	2:57:59 (765)	
Spillane, Darrell	3:48:55 (7,494)	
Spillane, John	3:18:00 (2,551)	
Spiller, Mark	5:07:16 (25,138)	
Spindler, Andrew	4:52:37 (22,417)	
Spindler, Matthias	3:46:18 (6,994)	
Spink, Andrew	5:27:45 (27,866)	
Spink, Darren	5:06:32 (25,022)	
Spink, Jonathan	3:56:38 (9,358)	
Spink, Roger	3:41:01 (5,962)	
Spinks, Marc	4:03:27 (10,934)	
Spinks, Roger	4:16:39 (13,892)	
Spiteri, John	3:44:27 (6,628)	
Spiteri, Robert	6:20:35 (31,035)	
Spitz, Graham	4:02:14 (10,682)	
Spitzhorn, Heiko	3:52:46 (8,367)	
Spivey, Garry	3:56:59 (9,451)	
Splain, Mark	4:22:46 (15,434)	
Spoerer, Peter	5:20:54 (27,013)	
Spokes, Graham	4:09:38 (12,256)	
Spooner, Cliff	5:19:42 (26,848)	
Spooner, Martin	5:17:07 (26,493)	
Sporri, Georg	2:54:33 (563)	
Spotswood, Robert	3:36:19 (5,118)	
Spottiswoode, Mark	4:36:16 (18,702)	
Spragg-Thomas, Carl	4:50:59 (22,065)	
Spratley, Andrew	4:14:39 (13,413)	
Spratt, Graham	5:33:33 (28,428)	
Spratt, Norman	3:18:55 (2,646)	
Spreadbury, Kevin	3:44:55 (6,713)	
Sprekeler, Une	4:36:48 (18,835)	
Spriggs, Andrew	4:06:09 (11,526)	
Spriggs, Gary	4:47:57 (21,412)	
Spring, Jeffrey	3:27:31 (3,740)	
Springall, Colin	7:05:42 (31,935)	
Springer, Marcellus	3:13:49 (2,099)	
Springett, Adrian	3:55:56 (9,162)	
Sprules, Christopher	3:01:49 (1,042)	
Spruyt, Stephen	4:21:16 (15,049)	
Spurgeon, Joe	4:24:35 (15,883)	
Spurgeon, Simon	4:13:12 (13,049)	
Spurlin, William	4:07:31 (11,813)	
Spurling, Gavin	4:23:07 (15,521)	
Sque, Craig	4:52:26 (22,384)	
Squibb, Robert	3:46:19 (6,997)	
Squibb, Roderick	4:54:16 (22,761)	
Squire, Anthony	3:20:09 (2,779)	
Squire, Danny	4:56:31 (23,266)	
Squire, Henry	4:07:07 (11,713)	
Squires, Andy	3:40:09 (5,824)	
Squires, Graham	4:57:09 (23,424)	
Squires, Stuart	5:34:44 (28,533)	
Ssajjabbi, Mark	5:23:01 (27,288)	
Ssali, Gerald	4:07:38 (11,841)	
St Croix, Dennis	3:35:19 (4,960)	
St George, Julian	4:09:47 (12,295)	
St John, Anthony	4:00:51 (10,397)	
St Pier, Edward	3:29:45 (4,134)	
Stables, Craig	5:26:53 (27,765)	
Stacey, Graham	4:15:25 (13,622)	
Stack, Christopher	4:23:07 (15,521)	
Stack, David	4:59:07 (23,830)	
Stack, John	6:51:50 (31,761)	
Staddon, Luke	4:50:51 (22,043)	
Stafford, Andrew	3:37:20 (5,296)	
Stafford, Christopher	4:18:43 (14,429)	
Stafford, John	3:37:44 (5,375)	
Stafford, Jonathan	4:01:18 (10,495)	
Stafford, Leon	4:29:17 (17,057)	
Stafford, Thomas	4:30:14 (17,295)	
Stafford, Timothy	3:40:38 (5,888)	
Staggs, Robert	3:55:28 (9,039)	
Stainer, David	4:12:53 (12,978)	
Stainer, Peter	2:44:27 (228)	
Stainforth, John	3:45:27 (6,820)	
Stalker, Ian	6:48:08 (31,679)	
Stallard, Paul	4:58:52 (23,773)	
Stallard, Tim	4:07:49 (11,875)	
Stalley, Andrew	3:20:32 (2,829)	
Stals, Peter	5:00:32 (24,076)	
Stamford, Gerard	4:04:47 (11,245)	
Stamp, Gordon	4:57:08 (23,411)	
Stamp, James	3:36:56 (5,218)	
Stamp, Richard	3:38:28 (5,489)	
Stamper, Iain	4:06:51 (11,659)	
Stanbridge, John	4:27:05 (16,494)	
Stanbridge, Phillip	4:37:16 (18,942)	
Stanbridge, Simon	3:56:11 (9,234)	
Stancliffe, Ian	3:33:09 (4,622)	
Stancombe, Dominic	5:45:29 (29,403)	
Standen, Melvin	3:37:39 (5,354)	
Standing, Chris	4:28:28 (16,847)	
Standing, Deano	4:35:01 (18,402)	
Standing, Peter	3:17:39 (2,509)	
Standish, Mark	4:38:36 (19,228)	
Standley, Mark	4:34:24 (18,266)	
Standring, Anthony	3:49:01 (7,523)	
Standring, Graham	3:54:56 (8,902)	
Standvoss, Heinrich	4:00:11 (10,268)	
Stanfield, Eugene	3:38:53 (5,577)	
Stanfield, Paul	4:34:03 (18,176)	
Staniard, Bill	4:25:15 (16,070)	
Stanier, Bev	5:32:32 (28,336)	
Stanley, Andrew	5:15:32 (26,316)	
Stanley, David	4:39:05 (19,341)	
Stanley, Mark	4:47:24 (21,274)	
Stanley, Michael	6:45:56 (31,644)	
Stanley, Peter	4:22:33 (15,375)	
Stanley, Roger	4:42:24 (20,085)	
Stannard, Matthew	4:02:29 (10,738)	

Stannard, Michael	5:02:09 (24,335)	
Stannett, Charlie	5:08:08 (25,288)	
Stanton, Nigel	4:12:57 (12,994)	
Stanton, Richard	4:39:20 (19,409)	
Stanway, Robert	4:02:09 (10,666)	
Stapleton, Giles	4:15:17 (13,585)	
Stapleton, Richard	3:44:05 (6,562)	
Starbrook, Samuel	6:02:32 (30,359)	
Starcevic, Andrey	3:51:37 (8,110)	
Stares, David	4:39:14 (19,380)	
Stark, Chris	5:00:46 (24,121)	
Stark, Christopher	4:45:44 (20,893)	
Stark, Fraser	4:05:41 (11,430)	
Stark, Peter	3:45:28 (6,825)	
Stark, Stephen	3:15:46 (2,313)	
Stark, Warren	4:55:18 (22,977)	
Starkey, Dominic	3:56:04 (9,198)	
Starkey, Simon	5:05:07 (24,818)	
Starkie, Timothy	4:33:54 (18,144)	
Starks, Gordon	3:47:28 (7,207)	
Starling, Robert	3:59:32 (10,104)	
Starr, Michael	3:08:06 (1,509)	
Statham, Malcolm	4:33:04 (17,968)	
Stather, Michael	3:53:49 (8,623)	
Statton, Peter	3:56:58 (9,444)	
Staub, Simon	3:57:05 (9,472)	
Staubli, Oliver	3:42:40 (6,288)	
Staunton, Charles	5:03:35 (24,545)	
Staveley, Andrew	3:21:19 (2,915)	
Stead, Andrew	4:11:10 (12,567)	
Stead, John	3:32:05 (4,480)	
Steadman, Mark	3:56:05 (9,203)	
Steadman, Terry	3:27:25 (3,724)	
Steane, Richard	5:07:31 (25,186)	
Steans, Nicholas	4:59:12 (23,843)	
Stearn, Derek	5:47:16 (29,510)	
Stearn, Martyn	4:11:46 (12,713)	
Stearn, Nicholas	3:30:24 (4,231)	
Stearn, Tom	3:45:47 (6,889)	
Stearne, Neil	5:29:26 (28,031)	
Steatham, James	4:22:39 (15,409)	
Stedeford, John	6:32:49 (31,396)	
Steed, Jason	4:07:25 (11,786)	
Steed, Jeff	5:34:22 (28,513)	
Steedman, Chris	3:48:03 (7,328)	
Steel, Andrew	4:29:48 (17,195)	
Steel, David	3:20:13 (2,789)	
Steel, Glenn	3:42:30 (6,248)	
Steel, Harry	5:00:15 (24,027)	
Steel, Robert	4:02:09 (10,666)	
Steel, Robert	4:44:05 (20,517)	
Steel, Wade	3:53:03 (8,437)	
Steele, Alfie	5:09:09 (25,429)	
Steele, Cameron	3:43:13 (6,410)	
Steele, Duncan	4:31:31 (17,621)	
Steele, Fraser	4:47:49 (21,380)	
Steele, Kenneth	3:23:54 (3,234)	
Steele, Morgan	3:12:36 (1,945)	
Steele, Nigel	5:23:45 (27,378)	
Steele, Paul	6:26:13 (31,210)	
Steele, Ray	5:06:27 (25,012)	
Steele, Roger	4:01:14 (10,478)	
Steele, Roy	3:09:24 (1,622)	
Steen, Paul	4:57:49 (23,546)	
Steene, Marc	3:36:09 (5,085)	
Steenson, Colin	5:35:36 (28,602)	
Steeples, Trevor	3:44:41 (6,664)	
Steer, Andrew	4:19:44 (14,679)	
Steer, Michael	4:20:21 (14,829)	
Steer, Richard	3:18:00 (2,551)	
Stefaniak, Edmond	5:16:21 (26,410)	
Steffen, Clive	3:57:42 (9,617)	
Steffens, Hans-Hermann	5:26:18 (27,710)	
Steffny, Nik	3:23:15 (3,146)	
Steggles, Roger	4:37:20 (18,954)	
Steiger, David	4:41:58 (19,986)	
Steiger, Juergen	3:25:11 (3,425)	
Steiger, Malcolm	3:30:14 (4,208)	
Stein, Peter	2:59:49 (928)	
Steiner, Andy	3:42:53 (6,337)	
Steinpress, Laurence	4:43:36 (20,404)	
Stell, Patrick	4:55:45 (23,097)	
Stender, Emil	5:07:39 (25,212)	

Stenhouse, Jamieson	4:33:54 (18,144)	
Stennett, Stewart	5:42:16 (29,188)	
Stenning, James	4:55:46 (23,103)	
Stensland-Bugge, Erlend	3:47:00 (7,124)	
Stenson, Michael	5:39:33 (28,953)	
Stenzel, Jurgen	3:59:57 (10,211)	
Step, Randal	6:10:59 (30,690)	
Stepanek, Frantisek	3:45:14 (6,780)	
Steph, James	4:44:11 (20,538)	
Stephan, Helal	5:21:10 (27,043)	
Stephane, Miquel	3:57:13 (9,509)	
Stephens, Adam	2:59:37 (911)	
Stephens, Alan	4:55:53 (23,129)	
Stephens, Andrew	3:12:57 (1,981)	
Stephens, Andrew	4:56:16 (23,214)	
Stephens, Andrew	5:14:12 (26,120)	
Stephens, Chris	5:13:09 (25,994)	
Stephens, Christopher	4:00:52 (10,398)	
Stephens, Daniel	4:28:59 (16,986)	
Stephens, David	3:02:05 (1,059)	
Stephens, Garry	4:28:48 (16,935)	
Stephens, George	2:53:01 (495)	
Stephens, Graham	2:46:53 (292)	
Stephens, James	5:23:56 (27,401)	
Stephens, Malcolm	5:20:21 (26,930)	
Stephens, Mark	3:28:51 (3,977)	
Stephens, Nicholas	2:53:40 (512)	
Stephens, Rhidian	4:10:09 (12,384)	
Stephenson, Andrew	3:03:08 (1,127)	
Stephenson, Brian	6:19:31 (30,991)	
Stephenson, Jeremy	3:17:20 (2,464)	
Stephenson, Lawrence	3:53:32 (8,555)	
Stephenson, Simon	3:58:18 (9,782)	
Steptoe, Colin	2:43:35 (210)	
Sterland, Paul	3:44:38 (6,655)	
Sterling, Darren	4:43:30 (20,375)	
Sterling, Robert	3:56:24 (9,294)	
Sterling, Simon	4:08:26 (11,989)	
Stern, Philip	5:13:30 (26,042)	
Sternkopf, Stefan	2:59:17 (878)	
Sterz, Klaus	3:04:25 (1,206)	
Steurbaut, Adi	4:41:49 (19,949)	
Steveney, Rupert	4:48:53 (21,609)	
Stevens, Andrew	4:24:19 (15,822)	
Stevens, Anthony	5:19:18 (26,799)	
Stevens, Christopher	4:20:15 (14,809)	
Stevens, Dave	3:18:03 (2,556)	
Stevens, David	3:57:02 (9,464)	
Stevens, Graham	3:13:39 (2,080)	
Stevens, Graham	5:47:25 (29,525)	
Stevens, Greg	2:37:03 (122)	
Stevens, James	4:45:45 (20,899)	
Stevens, John-Paul	4:43:35 (20,396)	
Stevens, Leslie	5:03:40 (24,560)	
Stevens, Malcolm	4:22:48 (15,442)	
Stevens, Matthew	7:10:15 (31,992)	
Stevens, Peter	4:15:49 (13,707)	
Stevens, Philip	4:06:51 (11,659)	
Stevens, Philip	4:30:09 (17,269)	
Stevens, Richard	4:48:25 (21,520)	
Stevens, Richard	5:26:56 (27,773)	
Stevens, Robert	5:23:17 (27,322)	
Stevens, Roy	3:32:42 (4,560)	
Stevens, Rupert	4:35:38 (18,545)	
Stevens, Tom	5:01:44 (24,266)	
Stevenson, Andrew	2:58:52 (837)	
Stevenson, Clive	3:29:47 (4,138)	
Stevenson, Colin	4:22:35 (15,387)	
Stevenson, Darryl	3:50:26 (7,829)	
Stevenson, Gareth	6:09:34 (30,618)	
Stevenson, Gary	3:48:43 (7,443)	
Stevenson, Graeme	3:26:04 (3,547)	
Stevenson, Graham	5:47:29 (29,532)	
Stevenson, John	4:16:27 (13,846)	
Stevenson, Nathan	5:30:37 (28,155)	
Stevenson, Robert	4:47:46 (21,364)	
Stevenson, Robert	4:53:15 (22,556)	
Stevenson, Ross	3:33:19 (4,648)	
Stevenson, Trevor	6:12:41 (30,759)	
Steward, Clive	3:24:50 (3,376)	
Steward, Mark	3:37:27 (5,320)	
Steward, Robin	3:58:44 (9,892)	
Stewart, Alan	3:24:31 (3,333)	

Stewart, Alan	4:30:19 (17,312)	
Stewart, Alan	5:29:05 (27,996)	
Stewart, Alexander	4:34:38 (18,316)	
Stewart, Alistair	3:30:44 (4,287)	
Stewart, Alistair	3:56:10 (9,228)	
Stewart, Ashley	3:56:42 (9,375)	
Stewart, Christopher	3:16:12 (2,348)	
Stewart, Colin	4:53:55 (22,699)	
Stewart, Derek	3:53:10 (8,464)	
Stewart, Douglas	5:23:35 (27,354)	
Stewart, Duncan	3:54:43 (8,840)	
Stewart, Dwayne	3:13:06 (2,005)	
Stewart, Iain	4:55:56 (23,138)	
Stewart, Jackie	3:16:09 (2,341)	
Stewart, James	3:59:24 (10,064)	
Stewart, James	4:18:16 (14,294)	
Stewart, James	5:03:05 (24,472)	
Stewart, Kenneth	3:46:09 (6,962)	
Stewart, Marcus	4:18:40 (14,412)	
Stewart, Murray	3:41:29 (6,060)	
Stewart, Peter	4:21:44 (15,166)	
Stewart, Richard	4:25:24 (16,117)	
Steweart, Richard	4:02:52 (10,819)	
Stichler, Alexander	3:09:38 (1,648)	
Stickings, Kevin	4:09:00 (12,129)	
Stickland, Charlie	3:31:28 (4,403)	
Stickley, Lyndon	5:16:53 (26,467)	
Stidwell, Ray	4:54:07 (22,732)	
Stieber, Reinhard	4:27:35 (16,621)	
Stiff, Dudley	4:24:02 (15,761)	
Stiff, Michael	2:56:18 (660)	
Stigner, Simon	4:21:55 (15,214)	
Stiles, Andrew	2:57:06 (711)	
Stiles, Andrew	3:28:02 (3,820)	
Still, Len	5:38:35 (28,864)	
Stimpson, Dean	4:51:10 (22,125)	
Stimson, Timothy	5:31:15 (28,221)	
Stinchcombe, Nigel	3:20:10 (2,782)	
Stirling, Peter	4:39:09 (19,360)	
Stobbs, Timothy	2:59:44 (921)	
Stock, Jonathan	3:29:21 (4,055)	
Stock, Leonard	4:19:29 (14,611)	
Stock, Mark	5:12:53 (25,956)	
Stockenius, Silvio	4:44:17 (20,569)	
Stocker, Julian	5:23:49 (27,384)	
Stockert, Nicholas	3:56:04 (9,198)	
Stockley, Antony	4:19:50 (14,701)	
Stocks, Adrian	4:16:22 (13,823)	
Stocks, Paul	4:48:57 (21,621)	
Stoddard, Jason	3:03:23 (1,145)	
Stoddard, Mark	3:31:37 (4,426)	
Stoddard, Michael	3:56:42 (9,375)	
Stoddart, Andrew	3:40:07 (5,816)	
Stokc, Stephen	4:15:43 (13,676)	
Stokell, Robert	4:26:01 (16,251)	
Stoker, Geoffrey	4:20:01 (14,748)	
Stoker, Michael	3:24:55 (3,386)	
Stokes, Christopher	2:59:56 (934)	
Stokes, Christopher	3:52:55 (8,399)	
Stokes, Clifford	4:33:05 (17,971)	
Stokes, Gavin	3:56:53 (9,420)	
Stokes, George	3:59:25 (10,068)	
Stokes, Michael	5:09:32 (25,481)	
Stokes, Nik	4:29:12 (17,039)	
Stokes, Robert	4:18:54 (14,479)	
Stokes, Steve	5:33:41 (28,435)	
Stokes, Trevor	4:35:42 (18,562)	
Stokes, William	5:37:34 (28,780)	
Stokoe, David	5:21:56 (27,142)	
Stollery, Michael	4:43:20 (20,328)	
Stone, Alex	3:34:54 (4,893)	
Stone, Barry	3:48:52 (7,482)	
Stone, Barry	3:49:23 (7,608)	
Stone, Bernard	5:01:44 (24,266)	
Stone, Chris	2:55:48 (636)	
Stone, Christopher	4:47:47 (21,368)	
Stone, Christopher	5:13:36 (26,057)	
Stone, Conor	4:50:08 (21,887)	
Stone, David	2:36:25 (114)	
Stone, Ethan	3:31:59 (4,470)	
Stone, Gaby	5:18:20 (26,677)	
Stone, John	3:19:55 (2,746)	
Stone, Jonathan	4:28:52 (16,958)	

Stone, Mark	3:58:44	(9,892)
Stone, Matthew	6:22:35	(31,089)
Stone, Michael	4:02:20	(10,703)
Stone, Paul	4:35:48	(18,598)
Stone, Roger	3:02:09	(1,066)
Stone, Timothy	4:24:57	(15,981)
Stoneham, Alan	5:17:28	(26,538)
Stoneham, Paul	4:47:09	(21,218)
Stoneman, Christopher	5:00:24	(24,050)
Stoneman, Matthew	4:38:36	(19,228)
Stoneman-Merret, Jonathan	3:52:35	(8,328)
Stones, Jonathan	5:18:06	(26,630)
Stonier, Christopher	3:13:59	(2,125)
Storck, Christian	2:59:17	(878)
Storer, David	4:00:11	(10,268)
Storer, Joseph	3:52:33	(8,320)
Storer, Mark	5:16:48	(26,459)
Storey, John	5:31:55	(28,281)
Storey, Michael	4:21:36	(15,132)
Storey, Miles	4:31:02	(17,510)
Storey, Stephen	5:14:41	(26,200)
Storie, Chris	4:51:39	(22,235)
Storr, Martin	4:57:21	(23,451)
Storrie, Martin	4:03:35	(10,964)
Storry, Terry	3:53:56	(8,653)
Story, Thomas	4:35:45	(18,580)
Stothard, Damian	4:26:08	(16,282)
Stothard, Peter	4:42:33	(20,123)
Stothard, Simon	3:54:32	(8,793)
Stott, Charles	4:18:21	(14,316)
Stott, Joshua	3:23:26	(3,169)
Stott, Julian	4:44:52	(20,689)
Stott, Peter	4:37:50	(19,050)
Stotter-Brooks, Andrew	4:30:58	(17,485)
Stout, Richard	3:59:50	(10,184)
Stoute, Colin	5:22:02	(27,145)
Stow, Philip	5:04:10	(24,657)
Strachan, Gordon	3:15:15	(2,267)
Strain, David	4:43:43	(20,435)
Strain, John	4:29:20	(17,068)
Straker, Simon	4:14:23	(13,353)
Strange, John	3:53:18	(8,496)
Strange, Kit	5:30:56	(28,187)
Stranger-Jones, Anthony	3:05:01	(1,250)
Stranks, Robert	3:56:54	(9,422)
Strasser, Michael	4:02:46	(10,798)
Stratford, John	5:16:24	(26,414)
Stratful, Ian	4:28:55	(16,973)
Strathdee, Andrew	3:17:11	(2,451)
Strathearn, Daniel	3:51:30	(8,074)
Stratten, Lester	4:41:37	(19,894)
Stratton, Iain	4:43:55	(20,482)
Straughan, Ross	4:20:21	(14,829)
Straw, Kevin	2:53:51	(524)
Streek, Simon	4:17:51	(14,218)
Street, Christopher	4:01:12	(10,472)
Street, Gavin	4:24:07	(15,781)
Street, Jon	3:59:59	(10,220)
Street, Jonathan	3:26:57	(3,669)
Street, Neil	5:30:17	(28,113)
Street, René	4:12:23	(12,852)
Street, Wiliam	3:59:42	(10,154)
Street, William	3:57:23	(9,552)
Streets, Colin	4:25:59	(16,248)
Strelitz, Jason	4:02:49	(10,811)
Stretch, Keith	3:53:01	(8,429)
Strevens, Nigel	3:25:16	(3,442)
Strickland, John	5:46:08	(29,446)
Strickland, Mark	5:52:42	(29,869)
Strickland, Steven	4:27:51	(16,680)
Stringer, Carl	4:48:03	(21,441)
Stringer, Heath	4:27:44	(16,660)
Stringer, Roy	5:57:37	(30,146)
Stringer, Thomas	3:25:57	(3,535)
Stritter, Josef	4:24:55	(15,975)
Stromback, Per	4:13:21	(13,083)
Strong, Freddie	4:39:04	(19,335)
Stross, Robert	6:22:28	(31,086)
Stroud, Andrew	4:15:17	(13,585)
Stroud, Mark	6:05:57	(30,499)
Stroud, Michael	4:16:54	(13,964)
Stroud, Robert	4:15:15	(13,581)
Stroud, Steve	5:01:59	(24,311)

Strover, Richard	3:40:21	(5,852)
Strowbridge, Andy	3:57:49	(9,650)
Stroyberg, Karsten	3:49:49	(7,702)
Strozzo, Philip	6:16:17	(30,865)
Strunc, Pierre	3:45:09	(6,767)
Strutt, Barry	4:45:03	(20,728)
Strutt, Benjamin	3:52:17	(8,263)
Strutt, Nigel	5:28:35	(27,948)
Struyve, Lambertus	3:59:19	(10,040)
Strzoda, Paul	4:01:18	(10,495)
Stuart, James	3:15:20	(2,274)
Stuart, Stephen	3:42:21	(6,209)
Stuart, Steven	4:16:24	(13,833)
Stuart, Tony	4:02:18	(10,697)
Stuart-William, Mark	4:05:21	(11,363)
Stubberfield, Jonathan	5:33:49	(28,455)
Stubbs, Andrew	2:49:49	(387)
Stubbs, Bernard	6:21:24	(31,060)
Stubbs, Christopher	3:53:30	(8,541)
Stubbs, David	2:58:44	(825)
Stubbs, Gareth	3:13:50	(2,100)
Stubbs, Nigel	4:24:59	(15,999)
Stubbs, Peter	5:04:47	(24,757)
Studd, Darren	3:29:49	(4,146)
Studer, Ueli	3:05:05	(1,260)
Stuemer, Uwe	3:57:42	(9,617)
Sturdy, Greg	3:47:09	(7,152)
Sturdy, Phil	4:01:27	(10,529)
Sturgeon, Michael	6:54:12	(31,811)
Sturges, Robert	4:27:38	(16,633)
Sturla, Timothy	3:39:35	(5,713)
Sturley, John	4:48:37	(21,554)
Sturm, Niels	4:17:00	(13,987)
Sturman, Darren	4:35:32	(18,524)
Sturrock, Lindsay	4:24:42	(15,915)
Sturrock, Stewart	4:54:37	(22,841)
Stybbs, Edward	3:39:32	(5,698)
Styles, Simon	4:53:23	(22,591)
Stylianou, Andrew	3:20:40	(2,842)
Stylianou, Mark	4:41:04	(19,770)
Stylo, Adam	5:06:48	(25,082)
Styring, Nicholas	3:22:55	(3,100)
Subbiani, Gary	3:58:46	(9,909)
Suckling, Adam	4:19:07	(14,534)
Suddens, Robin	3:51:29	(8,068)
Sudwell, Philip	3:41:16	(6,000)
Suett, Andrew	3:53:05	(8,447)
Sugars, Clive	4:53:10	(22,537)
Sugden, Andrew	4:22:34	(15,379)
Sugden, Ben	3:12:31	(1,933)
Sugden, David	3:36:31	(5,146)
Sugden, George	4:43:13	(20,292)
Sugden, Jason	4:35:57	(18,637)
Suggitt, Neil	4:13:43	(13,182)
Suggitt, Paul	4:41:12	(19,800)
Sugrue, Toby	4:30:31	(17,370)
Sullivan, Dieter	4:02:09	(10,666)
Sullivan, Gary	4:16:09	(13,773)
Sullivan, Gary	4:17:07	(14,015)
Sullivan, James	3:22:39	(3,063)
Sullivan, Joseph	4:19:21	(14,580)
Sullivan, Kevin	5:14:27	(26,167)
Sullivan, Matthew	5:00:59	(24,150)
Sullivan, Michael	4:48:48	(21,590)
Sullivan, Neil	4:36:50	(18,842)
Sullivan, Patrick	4:25:18	(16,086)
Sullivan, Richard	5:06:41	(25,049)
Sullivan, Sam	3:09:16	(1,610)
Sullivan, Stuart	5:14:49	(26,220)
Sully, Andrew	4:24:32	(15,871)
Sully, Steven	4:45:58	(20,952)
Summerfield, Richard	3:21:23	(2,922)
Summers, Andrew	4:57:44	(23,527)
Summers, Darrell	4:43:38	(20,413)
Summers, David	5:07:06	(25,118)
Summers, Derek	3:52:34	(8,322)
Summers, Mark	3:33:39	(4,696)
Summers, Martin	3:22:00	(2,987)
Summers, Paul	3:55:43	(9,113)
Summers, Paul	6:25:33	(31,182)
Summers, Peter	3:13:01	(1,992)
Summers, Russell	4:31:55	(17,712)
Summerton, Phillip	5:04:18	(24,677)

Sumner, Matthew	4:37:00	(18,878)
Sumner, Peter	3:12:30	(1,929)
Sundberg, Fredrik	2:49:34	(380)
Sundermann, Uwe	5:54:41	(29,977)
Sundstrom, Henrik	4:27:27	(16,581)
Sundvik, Harri	3:42:03	(6,160)
Sunley, Richard	4:17:17	(14,053)
Sunner, Jasbir	3:41:21	(6,025)
Sunner, Joe	5:06:21	(25,002)
Sunshine, Daniel	4:17:43	(14,183)
Supple, Martin	4:38:12	(19,133)
Suriano, Francesco	4:41:56	(19,979)
Surmacz, Karl	3:44:20	(6,605)
Surman, David	4:16:32	(13,864)
Surplice, Andy	3:23:25	(3,164)
Surrey, Mike	4:47:09	(21,218)
Surrey, Samuel	3:11:19	(1,782)
Surridge, Mark	3:35:46	(5,033)
Surridge, Stephen	5:12:10	(25,844)
Surtees, Roger	6:15:17	(30,837)
Sussman, Paul	4:53:26	(22,602)
Suster, Mark	3:57:07	(9,481)
Sutcliffe, Alistair	4:22:34	(15,379)
Sutcliffe, Dale	4:57:30	(23,482)
Sutcliffe, Nathan	4:15:52	(13,720)
Sutherland, Alistair	3:54:57	(8,906)
Sutherland, David	4:25:36	(16,158)
Sutherland, Graham	4:51:16	(22,148)
Sutherland, Grant	3:21:01	(2,887)
Sutherland, Leslie	4:53:27	(22,609)
Sutherland, Liam	4:05:09	(11,321)
Sutherland, Mark	5:07:56	(25,255)
Sutherland, Vaughan	3:39:28	(5,686)
Sutherland, William	2:48:47	(358)
Sutherns, Robin	4:43:40	(20,423)
Sutter, Mike	3:40:44	(5,909)
Suttle, Stephen	3:13:18	(2,034)
Sutton, Andrew	5:34:28	(28,521)
Sutton, Daniel	4:54:35	(22,833)
Sutton, Errol	5:51:54	(29,827)
Sutton, Graham	5:06:50	(25,084)
Sutton, Jonathan	3:33:12	(4,629)
Sutton, Peter	5:01:19	(24,209)
Sutton, Roger	5:46:36	(29,470)
Sutton, Ryan	4:43:23	(20,347)
Suzuki, Takao	4:00:25	(10,317)
Suzuki, Yorio	3:52:56	(8,402)
Svensson, Bjorn	3:40:18	(5,843)
Svensson, Karl	5:26:38	(27,746)
Swagemakers, Marcel	3:50:57	(7,933)
Swain, Chris	3:18:16	(2,584)
Swain, John	3:53:43	(8,593)
Swain, Keith	3:40:19	(5,847)
Swain, Peter	6:05:13	(30,463)
Swaine, Alan	4:39:35	(19,454)
Swaine, Kevin	4:08:39	(12,052)
Swainson, Michael	4:46:26	(21,078)
Swaley, Harminder	5:33:45	(28,445)
Swallow, Ian	4:22:35	(15,387)
Swallow, Neil	5:39:42	(28,963)
Swallow, Robert	3:48:44	(7,448)
Swallow, Shaun	3:10:08	(1,688)
Swan, Alasdair	5:24:39	(27,496)
Swan, Graeme	5:10:28	(25,619)
Swan, Jason	2:51:13	(425)
Swan, Jonathan	4:06:49	(11,652)
Swan, Kim	3:51:39	(8,120)
Swan, Stephen	5:02:10	(24,341)
Swanevelder, Justus	3:52:29	(8,306)
Swann, John	5:17:18	(26,512)
Swann, Jonathan	3:51:55	(8,178)
Swann, Roger	4:22:37	(15,401)
Swansborough, Dan	3:38:20	(5,462)
Swarbrick, Terry	4:16:17	(13,804)
Swarbrick, Terry	5:42:54	(29,233)
Swart, André	3:35:37	(5,015)
Swart, Jaco	5:07:56	(25,255)
Swateridge, Andrew	3:40:44	(5,909)
Swatman, Jason	4:26:12	(16,296)
Swatton, Duncan	5:44:07	(29,310)
Swatton, Neville	3:06:18	(1,338)
Swaysland, Ian	3:49:57	(7,726)
Sweeney, Anthony	5:02:29	(24,384)

Sweeney, Christian	4:13:38	(13,160)
Sweeney, Raymond	4:17:35	(14,132)
Sweet, David	3:28:24	(3,884)
Sweetlove, Malcolm	4:06:07	(11,519)
Sweetlove, Malcolm	4:38:53	(19,301)
Sweetman, Tim	4:12:07	(12,791)
Sweny, Paul	4:18:40	(14,412)
Swerling, Robert	4:11:33	(12,656)
Swift, Brian	4:02:29	(10,738)
Swift, Daniel	3:53:29	(8,536)
Swift, Derrick	3:09:52	(1,663)
Swift, Marcus	5:05:49	(24,935)
Swift, Simon	3:31:08	(4,347)
Swindells, Paul	4:16:54	(13,964)
Swindley, Ian	3:29:24	(4,069)
Swindon, Jason	3:54:20	(8,735)
Swingler, David	3:34:52	(4,886)
Swinhoe, Yvonne	3:22:06	(2,995)
Swinnerton, John	4:15:48	(13,702)
Swinney, Anthony	4:20:55	(14,957)
Swinney, Jonathan	4:14:52	(13,471)
Sydenham, Christopher	3:59:36	(10,119)
Sydenham, Christopher	4:56:56	(23,364)
Sydenham, Gareth	4:37:43	(19,025)
Sykes, Adam	3:08:14	(1,516)
Sykes, Andrew	4:07:36	(11,832)
Sykes, Christopher	3:44:17	(6,595)
Sykes, Christopher	4:41:33	(19,882)
Sykes, David	3:54:00	(8,669)
Sykes, David	4:00:41	(10,361)
Sykes, John	5:43:36	(29,277)
Sykes, Justin	4:17:58	(14,244)
Sykes, Peter	5:17:03	(26,486)
Sykes, Peter-John	3:57:43	(9,622)
Sylvester, Peter	4:49:58	(21,852)
Symes, John	5:37:26	(28,771)
Symes, Jonathan	4:44:53	(20,695)
Symington, Mark	4:21:08	(15,014)
Symmonds, Mark	3:17:40	(2,512)
Symns, Paul	3:25:41	(3,491)
Symonds, Lee	4:30:51	(17,454)
Symonds, Matthew	4:44:11	(20,538)
Symonds, Neil	3:38:25	(5,480)
Symonds, Stephen	3:44:36	(6,649)
Symons, Andrew	6:03:02	(30,377)
Symons, Christopher	3:58:47	(9,914)
Symons, David	4:14:28	(13,371)
Symons, Marcus	3:34:40	(4,863)
Symons, Matt	4:08:52	(12,102)
Syre, Guido	3:55:44	(9,116)
Syrett, Jason	3:56:27	(9,305)
Syson, Albert	6:12:37	(30,754)
Syster, Ian	2:09:18	(9)
Szadorkski, David	5:33:46	(28,447)
Szczerbicki, Stephen	3:26:30	(3,608)
Sztendur, Jarek	4:06:18	(11,555)
Szymczak, Tomasz	4:29:54	(17,220)
Tabatabaian, Seyed	6:05:06	(30,455)
Tabenor, Peter	3:15:35	(2,298)
Tabiner, Ben	4:36:42	(18,809)
Tabor, Kevin	3:43:04	(6,380)
Tabor, Paul	3:12:16	(1,893)
Tack, Ian	3:09:19	(1,617)
Tadd, Philip	3:51:08	(7,989)
Tadeo Folch, Alberto	4:23:47	(15,692)
Tadgell, Hamish	4:27:36	(16,624)
Taft, Kevin	4:28:23	(16,817)
Tagand, Patrick	3:40:44	(5,909)
Tagney, Gregory	3:28:26	(3,891)
Taheri, Peyman	3:28:11	(3,845)
Tahir, Abdeslam	3:10:17	(1,702)
Tai, Wai-Land	3:53:37	(8,570)
Tait, James	4:47:10	(21,222)
Takano, Satoshi	4:12:22	(12,850)
Takenaka, Satoshi	5:38:02	(28,813)
Takhar, Jatinder	5:42:36	(29,219)
Talbot, Andrew	4:56:39	(23,303)
Talbot, Andrew	5:19:18	(26,799)
Talbot, Andrew	5:40:16	(29,014)
Talbot, Colin	3:10:55	(1,750)
Talbot, Dean	5:22:30	(27,212)
Talbot, Marc	5:41:41	(29,136)
Talbot, Peter	3:57:36	(9,597)
Talbot, Simon	3:25:41	(3,491)
Talbot, Stephen	5:37:13	(28,755)
Tallick, Simon	4:38:15	(19,143)
Tallon, Paul	4:48:42	(21,570)
Tam, Kelvin	4:19:03	(14,517)
Tamagni, David	4:19:51	(14,704)
Tambling, Mark	5:53:50	(29,923)
Tamblyn, Ben	4:42:21	(20,067)
Tammaro, Adrian	4:05:45	(11,445)
Tan, Christopher	3:44:55	(6,713)
Tan, Yee-Seng	4:39:04	(19,335)
Tanae, Fumiuaki	3:52:13	(8,247)
Tancock, Stephen	2:51:29	(433)
Tancos, Timothy	2:55:21	(611)
Tandon, Rakesh	4:26:25	(16,339)
Tanguy, Michel	3:51:59	(8,191)
Tanini, Andrea	4:33:11	(17,983)
Tank, Gavin	4:08:35	(12,035)
Tann, Garry	3:58:36	(9,857)
Tann, Nicholas	3:49:22	(7,601)
Tanner, Adrian	2:43:27	(206)
Tanner, Anthony	5:08:54	(25,388)
Tanner, Gregory	5:14:12	(26,120)
Tanner, John	4:11:42	(12,696)
Tanner, Nigel	4:57:41	(23,519)
Tansey, Eugene	5:19:18	(26,799)
Tansey, James	5:20:08	(26,909)
Tapie, Jaques	4:09:29	(12,225)
Tapley, Peter	4:18:44	(14,432)
Taplin, Alan	3:51:57	(8,182)
Taplin, Derek	3:58:43	(9,889)
Taplin, Richard	4:41:27	(19,861)
Taplin, Steve	4:11:41	(12,687)
Tapnack, Jonathan	6:56:20	(31,848)
Tapp, Ed	4:11:41	(12,687)
Tapp, Nigel	3:58:02	(9,717)
Tapper, Humphrey	4:00:49	(10,390)
Taptiklis, Benjamin	5:14:56	(26,239)
Taranik, Dan	6:26:16	(31,213)
Tarantino, Giovanni	4:35:57	(18,637)
Tardieu, Frederic	3:42:10	(6,182)
Tarkanyi, John	2:59:30	(902)
Tarkow, David	4:32:55	(17,928)
Tarpey, Chris	3:24:05	(3,263)
Tarrant, Nick	3:52:23	(8,284)
Tarrier, Peter	3:03:52	(1,172)
Tarring, Keith	4:01:14	(10,478)
Tarver, Andrew	3:31:04	(4,339)
Tarver, Jason	3:54:37	(8,824)
Tasker, Adrian	4:57:30	(23,482)
Tasker, Grahame	3:57:45	(9,632)
Tasker, Julian	3:23:49	(3,214)
Tasker, Mark	4:51:58	(22,303)
Tasker, Simon	4:51:57	(22,301)
Tasquier, Nick	3:59:29	(10,090)
Tatam, Peter	5:49:28	(29,674)
Tate, Andrew	4:27:15	(16,534)
Tate, Chris	3:28:06	(3,833)
Tate, Ian	5:00:36	(24,090)
Tate, Ian	5:03:05	(24,472)
Tate, Jeffrey	5:34:22	(28,513)
Tate, Stephen	3:37:24	(5,311)
Tatham, Joe	4:30:52	(17,459)
Tatia, Joel	4:37:21	(18,956)
Tattersall, Alan	3:59:15	(10,021)
Tattersall, Andrew	4:17:26	(14,097)
Tattershall, Darren	3:41:52	(6,126)
Tatum, David	4:15:45	(13,685)
Taub, Robert	6:12:21	(30,746)
Tavelli, Alberto	5:40:01	(28,995)
Tavender, Graham	3:18:24	(2,602)
Tavernor, Jack	4:40:40	(19,676)
Tayabali, Imran	4:37:44	(19,029)
Tayler, Martin	3:46:32	(7,041)
Taylor, Alan	3:25:37	(3,478)
Taylor, Alan	3:29:47	(4,138)
Taylor, Alan	4:16:52	(13,954)
Taylor, Alan	5:20:32	(26,960)
Taylor, Alasdair	3:45:22	(6,799)
Taylor, Alwyn	4:17:53	(14,225)
Taylor, Andrew	5:14:12	(26,120)
Taylor, Andrew	5:44:19	(29,324)
Taylor, Barry	4:50:42	(22,011)
Taylor, Ben	3:58:23	(9,804)
Taylor, Benjamin	4:34:45	(18,338)
Taylor, Bridgeen	5:51:23	(29,802)
Taylor, Bryan	5:04:12	(24,661)
Taylor, Byron	6:07:01	(30,531)
Taylor, Cameron	4:43:05	(20,256)
Taylor, Charles	3:33:44	(4,710)
Taylor, Charles	3:53:37	(8,570)
Taylor, Chris	3:37:39	(5,354)
Taylor, Chris	4:55:36	(23,053)
Taylor, Christopher	3:54:16	(8,723)
Taylor, Colin	3:59:17	(10,034)
Taylor, Colin	4:03:18	(10,913)
Taylor, Colin	5:03:35	(24,545)
Taylor, Darren	4:18:50	(14,457)
Taylor, David	2:58:54	(841)
Taylor, David	3:31:16	(4,373)
Taylor, David	3:42:20	(6,207)
Taylor, David	4:00:16	(10,283)
Taylor, David	4:01:27	(10,529)
Taylor, David	7:07:15	(31,965)
Taylor, Dean	4:57:07	(23,404)
Taylor, Derek	5:29:15	(28,012)
Taylor, Derek	6:52:38	(31,775)
Taylor, Desmond	3:44:39	(6,658)
Taylor, Duncan	4:10:17	(12,414)
Taylor, Eric	3:13:47	(2,094)
Taylor, Frank	5:50:27	(29,745)
Taylor, Gary	3:59:14	(10,014)
Taylor, Geoff	5:19:14	(26,789)
Taylor, George	2:45:24	(244)
Taylor, Glenn	4:49:30	(21,750)
Taylor, Gordon	3:52:18	(8,267)
Taylor, Graeme	5:37:26	(28,771)
Taylor, Graham	2:56:01	(650)
Taylor, Graham	5:08:36	(25,346)
Taylor, Grant	4:42:30	(20,109)
Taylor, Grant	6:00:53	(30,291)
Taylor, Iain	4:13:39	(13,165)
Taylor, Ian	4:47:51	(21,391)
Taylor, Ian	4:48:59	(21,627)
Taylor, Ian	5:03:26	(24,522)
Taylor, James	4:32:59	(17,949)
Taylor, James	4:44:14	(20,554)
Taylor, James	4:49:12	(21,677)
Taylor, James	4:53:05	(22,517)
Taylor, James	5:13:30	(26,042)
Taylor, James	6:31:10	(31,354)
Taylor, Jeffrey	4:20:43	(14,907)
Taylor, Jeremy	4:06:26	(11,578)
Taylor, Jim	5:12:45	(25,939)
Taylor, John	3:11:36	(1,811)
Taylor, John	3:34:22	(4,811)
Taylor, John	4:08:27	(11,995)
Taylor, John	5:01:03	(24,161)
Taylor, John	5:30:16	(28,110)
Taylor, Jonathan	3:30:36	(4,259)
Taylor, Keith	3:40:39	(5,891)
Taylor, Keith	4:29:08	(17,022)
Taylor, Kevin	3:30:37	(4,260)
Taylor, Kevin	3:56:06	(9,206)
Taylor, Kevin	4:24:49	(15,954)
Taylor, Kevin	5:01:03	(24,161)
Taylor, Laurence	5:41:16	(29,099)
Taylor, Lee	4:00:35	(10,342)
Taylor, Lee	4:38:11	(19,127)
Taylor, Lee	4:41:06	(19,777)
Taylor, Lindsay	4:44:15	(20,557)
Taylor, Luke	4:21:15	(15,044)
Taylor, Mark	3:07:58	(1,496)
Taylor, Mark	3:13:00	(1,991)
Taylor, Mark	3:14:48	(2,216)
Taylor, Mark	3:16:42	(2,396)
Taylor, Mark	4:18:33	(14,372)
Taylor, Mark	5:23:51	(27,390)
Taylor, Mark	5:25:00	(27,536)
Taylor, Mark	5:38:28	(28,854)
Taylor, Martin	4:15:23	(13,615)
Taylor, Martin	4:28:47	(16,932)
Taylor, Martin	5:30:15	(28,106)
Taylor, Matthew	3:34:48	(4,879)
Taylor, Matthew	4:34:24	(18,266)
Taylor, Mel	2:58:32	(802)

Taylor, Michael 3:39:49 (5,751)
Taylor, Michael 3:41:34 (6,082)
Taylor, Michael 4:35:14 (18,457)
Taylor, Neil 3:59:16 (10,027)
Taylor, Neil 4:36:20 (18,722)
Taylor, Neil 4:47:58 (21,419)
Taylor, Neil 5:53:59 (29,931)
Taylor, Nicholas 4:13:41 (13,170)
Taylor, Nick 4:46:06 (20,992)
Taylor, Nigel 3:39:58 (5,777)
Taylor, Norman 4:50:37 (21,995)
Taylor, Patrick 4:02:49 (10,811)
Taylor, Paul 4:04:20 (11,142)
Taylor, Paul 4:07:04 (11,703)
Taylor, Paul 4:14:23 (13,353)
Taylor, Paul 4:34:03 (18,176)
Taylor, Paul 4:45:49 (20,919)
Taylor, Paul 5:20:50 (27,003)
Taylor, Paul 5:21:45 (27,122)
Taylor, Peter 4:31:33 (17,630)
Taylor, Peter 5:24:53 (27,517)
Taylor, Peter 5:36:45 (28,712)
Taylor, Philip 2:55:29 (618)
Taylor, Phillip 3:05:41 (1,297)
Taylor, Raymond 5:25:01 (27,540)
Taylor, Richard 3:54:36 (8,817)
Taylor, Richard 3:55:31 (9,052)
Taylor, Richard 4:11:45 (12,707)
Taylor, Richard 5:03:52 (24,608)
Taylor, Robert 3:44:22 (6,615)
Taylor, Robert 4:43:14 (20,296)
Taylor, Robert 5:28:08 (27,906)
Taylor, Robert 5:33:25 (28,414)
Taylor, Rory 4:11:03 (12,550)
Taylor, Scott 4:56:33 (23,275)
Taylor, Simon 4:02:07 (10,658)
Taylor, Stephen 3:57:07 (9,481)
Taylor, Stephen 4:42:39 (20,142)
Taylor, Steve 3:41:56 (6,139)
Taylor, Steve 3:45:36 (6,849)
Taylor, Steven 4:46:27 (21,081)
Taylor, Stuart 4:45:27 (20,834)
Taylor, Stuart 5:55:16 (30,013)
Taylor, Tim 3:40:25 (5,863)
Taylor, Tink 5:06:02 (24,963)
Taylor, Warrick 4:43:21 (20,336)
Taylor, Wayne 3:36:04 (5,075)
Taylor-Schofield, Nigel 5:25:36 (27,621)
Taylorson, Simon 4:08:40 (12,055)
Teague, Stephen 3:40:46 (5,918)
Teal, Alexander 4:50:31 (21,972)
Tear, Alfred 4:05:18 (11,351)
Teare, Eddie 4:27:44 (16,660)
Teare, Ivan 3:30:37 (4,260)
Teasdale, David 4:46:11 (21,012)
Teasdale, Graham 3:39:00 (5,598)
Teather, Keith 4:45:03 (20,728)
Tebbitt, Steve 5:25:49 (27,646)
Tebbs, Alexander 3:49:20 (7,596)
Tebbutt, David 3:52:52 (8,386)
Tebbutt, Michael 4:28:45 (16,922)
Tedcastle, Robert 5:19:10 (26,779)
Tedder, Constant 3:50:28 (7,832)
Tedham, James 4:24:23 (15,839)
Tee, Kenneth 5:25:55 (27,655)
Tee, Paul 3:04:35 (1,220)
Tee, Wayne 5:24:12 (27,437)
Teixeira, Pedro 5:03:43 (24,580)
Telfer, Phil 3:17:18 (2,460)
Telfer, Robert 3:25:00 (3,397)
Telford, Andrew 3:59:26 (10,073)
Telford, James 4:01:59 (10,630)
Tellem, Geraint 3:27:08 (3,697)
Telling, Barry 4:23:43 (15,676)
Tempest, Mark 3:17:26 (2,482)
Templar, Martin 4:13:14 (13,058)
Temple, Neil 3:52:47 (8,371)
Temple, Paul 6:52:37 (31,773)
Ten Klooster, Roel 3:52:40 (8,347)
Tene, Claude 5:03:13 (24,495)
Tennant, Mark 3:35:54 (5,057)
Tennant, Richard 3:36:53 (5,209)
Tergat, Paul 2:07:59 (4)

Terhorst, Michael 3:25:44 (3,502)
Termaat, Adri 2:47:39 (318)
Terrell, Scott 4:26:26 (16,342)
Terrett, Seamus 8:03:35 (32,260)
Terrill, Chris 3:56:12 (9,242)
Terrington, Andrew 5:39:08 (28,914)
Terrone, Paolo 3:37:38 (5,351)
Terry, Nicholas 3:39:43 (5,731)
Terry, Nick 4:51:19 (22,159)
Tertrin, Jean Paul 4:52:09 (22,331)
Teryl, James 3:19:00 (2,654)
Terzic, Mario 3:11:22 (1,786)
Teschl, Franz 4:11:33 (12,656)
Tester, Michel 4:05:01 (11,294)
Teunissen, Lyn 3:42:58 (6,358)
Tevebring, Mads 3:28:27 (3,893)
Tevenan, John 4:16:14 (13,792)
Tew, Shaun 3:07:05 (1,410)
Thacker, Brian 5:24:30 (27,475)
Thacker, Simon 3:12:31 (1,933)
Thackeray, Charles 4:07:28 (11,799)
Thackeray, Richard 3:16:21 (2,361)
Thackray, Charles 4:20:20 (14,824)
Thain, Rob 4:43:38 (20,413)
Tham, An Liang 3:51:48 (8,149)
Tharby, Kevin 4:49:59 (21,854)
Thatcher, Bob 4:55:18 (22,977)
Thatcher, Gary 4:34:48 (18,351)
Thatcher, Gary 5:11:51 (25,808)
Thatcher, Steve 3:57:40 (9,611)
Thavenot, Alexander 3:29:39 (4,118)
Thavenot, William 4:39:41 (19,471)
Thay, Michael 4:08:44 (12,076)
Thear, Adrian 4:03:28 (10,936)
Theobald, Lionel 3:03:31 (1,152)
Theodoulou, Orthodoxos 5:46:10 (29,447)
Thewlis, Andrew 3:53:19 (8,501)
Thibeault, Colin 4:41:44 (19,928)
Thickett, Keith 3:26:52 (3,651)
Thing, James 3:42:35 (6,273)
Thirsk, Michael 4:51:19 (22,159)
Thiruvengadam, Thiagaraja 4:39:53 (19,516)
Thistlethwaite, Anthony 3:25:10 (3,420)
Thistlewood, David 4:42:45 (20,169)
Tholen, Peter 4:15:47 (13,697)
Tholome, Luc 4:04:43 (11,230)
Thoma, Nigel 5:27:19 (27,811)
Thomas, Adrian 3:15:01 (2,241)
Thomas, Alan 2:59:21 (885)
Thomas, Alan 3:44:54 (6,707)
Thomas, Alan 4:16:46 (13,927)
Thomas, Alan 4:33:20 (18,013)
Thomas, Alan 6:33:16 (31,406)
Thomas, Alan 6:33:17 (31,407)
Thomas, Alasdair 3:29:51 (4,150)
Thomas, Alex 4:38:54 (19,305)
Thomas, Andrew 3:07:15 (1,435)
Thomas, Andrew 3:57:42 (9,617)
Thomas, Andrew 4:13:23 (13,091)
Thomas, Andrew 4:15:23 (13,615)
Thomas, Andrew 4:26:22 (16,330)
Thomas, Andy 5:34:47 (28,536)
Thomas, Bobby 4:56:13 (23,200)
Thomas, Brian 3:25:23 (3,452)
Thomas, Calvin 2:59:10 (868)
Thomas, Clive 3:24:06 (3,267)
Thomas, Colin 4:35:41 (18,558)
Thomas, Craig 4:05:06 (11,309)
Thomas, Craig 4:46:00 (20,959)
Thomas, Craig 5:24:55 (27,524)
Thomas, Damon 4:58:24 (23,676)
Thomas, Daniel 5:35:49 (28,620)
Thomas, David 3:32:11 (4,495)
Thomas, David 3:35:28 (4,993)
Thomas, David 3:52:56 (8,402)
Thomas, David 3:56:51 (9,413)
Thomas, David 5:01:26 (24,226)
Thomas, Dean 4:12:13 (12,822)
Thomas, Deri 3:07:05 (1,410)
Thomas, Eddie 3:39:16 (5,647)
Thomas, Emrys 3:30:12 (4,199)
Thomas, Eric 3:03:46 (1,168)
Thomas, Frank 3:33:22 (4,657)

Thomas, Gareth 2:49:36 (381)
Thomas, Gavin 4:25:14 (16,067)
Thomas, George 3:53:58 (8,664)
Thomas, Graham 2:57:26 (730)
Thomas, Henry 3:12:38 (1,951)
Thomas, Huw 4:12:10 (12,805)
Thomas, Huw 5:22:44 (27,244)
Thomas, Ian 3:53:46 (8,608)
Thomas, Ian 4:30:46 (17,438)
Thomas, Iwan 6:03:01 (30,375)
Thomas, James 3:29:34 (4,105)
Thomas, Jamie 4:35:44 (18,570)
Thomas, Jeff 3:54:10 (8,696)
Thomas, Jeff 4:59:41 (23,922)
Thomas, John 6:42:54 (31,589)
Thomas, Justin 2:57:29 (732)
Thomas, Kevin 3:44:26 (6,625)
Thomas, Kevin 5:29:35 (28,049)
Thomas, Kevin 6:05:48 (30,495)
Thomas, Kevin 6:58:33 (31,877)
Thomas, Leigh 4:31:38 (17,652)
Thomas, Leighton 3:50:48 (7,908)
Thomas, Lenny 3:12:16 (1,893)
Thomas, Leon 4:10:32 (12,473)
Thomas, Marcus 3:42:27 (6,231)
Thomas, Mark 4:46:56 (21,172)
Thomas, Martin 6:33:17 (31,407)
Thomas, Martyn 4:03:33 (10,957)
Thomas, Neal 4:15:32 (13,646)
Thomas, Neil 4:13:00 (13,005)
Thomas, Neville 4:21:35 (15,126)
Thomas, Nicholas 4:21:57 (15,224)
Thomas, Nick 3:53:51 (8,633)
Thomas, Nigel 5:29:17 (28,016)
Thomas, Paul 4:18:55 (14,489)
Thomas, Paul 4:21:34 (15,123)
Thomas, Paul 6:42:22 (31,579)
Thomas, Peter 3:07:00 (1,402)
Thomas, Richard 3:39:58 (5,777)
Thomas, Richard 4:04:06 (11,090)
Thomas, Richard 5:04:41 (24,730)
Thomas, Richard 5:06:44 (25,061)
Thomas, Robert 3:33:04 (4,609)
Thomas, Robert 4:44:36 (20,633)
Thomas, Roger 4:49:07 (21,652)
Thomas, Roy 3:17:09 (2,444)
Thomas, Russell 3:06:15 (1,334)
Thomas, Sam 4:02:05 (10,654)
Thomas, Simon 3:08:22 (1,533)
Thomas, Simon 5:18:36 (26,714)
Thomas, Stephen 5:04:44 (24,742)
Thomas, Stuart 4:25:45 (16,189)
Thomas-Haynes, Martin 4:51:05 (22,099)
Thomason, Francis 3:13:13 (2,026)
Thompkins, Richard 4:06:56 (11,675)
Thompson, Adam 4:08:56 (12,117)
Thompson, Aidan 5:56:16 (30,068)
Thompson, Alan 5:42:01 (29,166)
Thompson, Alistair 5:37:28 (28,774)
Thompson, Andrew 2:47:26 (314)
Thompson, Andrew 3:58:25 (9,813)
Thompson, Andrew 4:16:09 (13,773)
Thompson, Andy 4:10:52 (12,521)
Thompson, Andy 5:01:57 (24,306)
Thompson, Barry 3:13:18 (2,034)
Thompson, Brian 4:51:04 (22,091)
Thompson, Chris 3:53:24 (8,517)
Thompson, Colin 3:18:08 (2,568)
Thompson, Craig 4:26:27 (16,345)
Thompson, David 2:52:03 (445)
Thompson, David 3:05:36 (1,293)
Thompson, David 5:04:19 (24,680)
Thompson, Derek 4:25:47 (16,198)
Thompson, Donald 5:13:15 (26,005)
Thompson, Gary 3:57:41 (9,613)
Thompson, Gary 4:58:25 (23,679)
Thompson, Geoff 3:36:49 (5,195)
Thompson, Graham 3:18:05 (2,561)
Thompson, Grant 3:26:12 (3,567)
Thompson, Ian 4:45:56 (20,942)
Thompson, Johnnie 4:18:48 (14,446)
Thompson, Jonathan 4:32:55 (17,928)
Thompson, Keith 4:01:40 (10,572)

Thompson, Laurence	3:46:24 (7,013)	
Thompson, Marjorie	5:27:29 (27,828)	
Thompson, Martin	4:31:19 (17,570)	
Thompson, Michael	3:56:03 (9,194)	
Thompson, Michael	4:31:48 (17,687)	
Thompson, Michael	4:56:18 (23,221)	
Thompson, Nigel	2:52:14 (452)	
Thompson, Nigel	4:42:24 (20,085)	
Thompson, Paul	3:42:46 (6,312)	
Thompson, Paul	5:41:45 (29,139)	
Thompson, Peter	4:15:04 (13,529)	
Thompson, Philip	4:14:43 (13,429)	
Thompson, Philip	4:34:51 (18,359)	
Thompson, Richard	4:03:31 (10,945)	
Thompson, Robert	5:03:59 (24,626)	
Thompson, Shaun	5:53:16 (29,892)	
Thompson, Stewart	3:52:50 (8,377)	
Thompson, Stewart	4:55:00 (22,921)	
Thompson, Trevor	4:36:57 (18,866)	
Thompson, Victor	5:19:43 (26,851)	
Thomsett, Martin	5:20:43 (26,989)	
Thomsett, Roger	4:46:01 (20,964)	
Thomson, Adam	2:50:22 (397)	
Thomson, Adrian	5:30:26 (28,134)	
Thomson, Alistair	5:09:38 (25,494)	
Thomson, Gary	5:21:14 (27,056)	
Thomson, John	3:25:56 (3,533)	
Thomson, Mark	3:10:23 (1,710)	
Thomson, Mark	5:56:02 (30,047)	
Thomson, Martin	3:58:57 (9,955)	
Thomson, Melville	5:58:33 (30,180)	
Thomson, Michael	3:56:32 (9,330)	
Thomson, Paul	3:11:40 (1,818)	
Thomson, Paul	4:48:15 (21,482)	
Thomson, Peter	3:29:07 (4,017)	
Thomson, Peter	4:14:02 (13,270)	
Thomson, Richard	3:51:18 (8,032)	
Thomson, Robert	4:13:50 (13,210)	
Thomson, Robert	5:00:17 (24,033)	
Thomson, Rod	3:39:20 (5,664)	
Thomson, Stephen	3:20:30 (2,826)	
Thoresen, Yngue	4:05:14 (11,339)	
Thorley, David	5:54:17 (29,955)	
Thorn, Keith	4:40:54 (19,727)	
Thorn, Michael	3:48:27 (7,394)	
Thorn, Richard	3:12:12 (1,885)	
Thornby, David	3:50:24 (7,825)	
Thorndyke, Steven	5:08:56 (25,392)	
Thorne, Colin	5:22:34 (27,222)	
Thorne, Reuben	7:30:16 (32,155)	
Thornett, Lee	7:11:10 (32,001)	
Thornewell, Ian	5:36:32 (28,689)	
Thornhill, Justin	5:11:59 (25,825)	
Thornton, Clifford	3:12:55 (1,980)	
Thornton, Daniel	4:04:45 (11,242)	
Thornton, David	5:25:30 (27,611)	
Thornton, Dean	3:04:19 (1,202)	
Thornton, Jason	4:38:13 (19,138)	
Thornton, Peter	4:43:16 (20,309)	
Thornton, Philip	4:16:47 (13,933)	
Thornton, Sean	5:34:53 (28,545)	
Thornton, Stanley	4:32:58 (17,944)	
Thorogood, Mitzi	6:07:20 (30,547)	
Thorold, Marcus	4:14:33 (13,394)	
Thorp, Andrew	5:22:43 (27,239)	
Thorp, Anthony	4:53:25 (22,599)	
Thorp, Richard	3:47:32 (7,220)	
Thorpe, Andrew	4:58:17 (23,645)	
Thorpe, Benjamin	5:10:59 (25,690)	
Thorpe, Colin	3:28:11 (3,845)	
Thorpe, James	5:31:52 (28,271)	
Thorpe, Philip	4:03:58 (11,056)	
Thorpe, Simon	4:29:09 (17,026)	
Thorpe, Walter	4:43:32 (20,388)	
Threadgold, Robin	3:09:31 (1,632)	
Thresher, Timothy	4:02:36 (10,756)	
Thrisk, David	4:54:14 (22,753)	
Throp, Jonathan	4:45:12 (20,772)	
Throssell, Stephen	3:04:44 (1,227)	
Thrupp, William	3:51:03 (7,967)	
Thubron, Neil	3:12:43 (1,960)	
Thuiller, Serve	3:21:30 (2,933)	
Thurgood, Geoffrey	5:37:16 (28,761)	

Thurgood, Hugh	4:10:20 (12,425)	
Thurgood, Mark	3:42:43 (6,301)	
Thurlow, James	4:19:05 (14,525)	
Thurtle, Gary	4:07:10 (11,731)	
Thwaites, David	3:44:12 (6,584)	
Thwaites, George	4:21:36 (15,132)	
Thwaites, Laurie	3:37:42 (5,365)	
Thyfa, Hassan	4:31:28 (17,607)	
Tibble, Anthony	5:06:55 (25,096)	
Tibbles, Clive	4:32:15 (17,784)	
Tibbles, David	5:03:44 (24,582)	
Tibbs, Christopher	3:49:12 (7,562)	
Tidd, Graham	3:52:21 (8,276)	
Tidd, Patrick	4:59:40 (23,917)	
Tidder, Anthony	4:17:49 (14,214)	
Tidiman, Steve	3:06:38 (1,371)	
Tiernan, Patrick	3:11:12 (1,773)	
Tiernan, Paul	5:10:15 (25,590)	
Tierney, John	5:09:02 (25,415)	
Tierney, Patrick	6:29:14 (31,305)	
Tietz, Joachim	3:54:23 (8,748)	
Tiffin, Ian	4:20:31 (14,873)	
Tiffney, Christopher	3:43:35 (6,460)	
Tighe, William	6:35:16 (31,453)	
Tilbrook, John	4:50:21 (21,933)	
Tiley, Daniel	3:31:25 (4,394)	
Till, Richard	3:39:05 (5,613)	
Till, Simon	4:10:09 (12,384)	
Till, Stephen	3:27:31 (3,740)	
Till, Steven	5:08:30 (25,338)	
Tillbrooke, Tony	4:32:48 (17,898)	
Tiller, Brian	4:54:14 (22,753)	
Tiller, David	4:05:56 (11,494)	
Tillery, Andrew	2:59:30 (902)	
Tillett, Charles	4:47:24 (21,274)	
Tillett, Ian	3:13:31 (2,064)	
Tilley, Ian	4:54:17 (22,767)	
Tilley, Kevin	2:49:16 (371)	
Tilley, Nicholas	4:55:21 (22,991)	
Tilley, Stuart	4:47:22 (21,261)	
Tilling, Martin	3:25:53 (3,529)	
Tillyer, Andrew	4:10:30 (12,462)	
Tilney, Hugo	4:22:59 (15,489)	
Tilsley, Andrew	3:05:21 (1,275)	
Timanti, Claudio	4:23:55 (15,724)	
Timewell, Andy	3:37:10 (5,269)	
Timmermann, Till	5:00:59 (24,150)	
Timmins, Gary	3:53:05 (8,447)	
Timonen Alsing, Pauli	4:02:52 (10,819)	
Timossi, Luca	4:18:28 (14,347)	
Tims, Edward	3:46:33 (7,045)	
Timson, Andrew	4:19:46 (14,687)	
Tinat, Eric	3:05:29 (1,286)	
Tindall, David	5:05:29 (24,880)	
Tindell, Henry	4:42:30 (20,109)	
Tindell, Richard	4:27:08 (16,506)	
Tiner, Peter	3:46:21 (7,005)	
Tinham, Andrew	4:29:50 (17,203)	
Tink, Andy	4:13:41 (13,170)	
Tinnyunt, Robert	4:26:40 (16,395)	
Tinsley, Paul	4:05:07 (11,315)	
Tinsley, Peter	3:34:23 (4,814)	
Tinson, Adam	4:48:42 (21,570)	
Tinston, Gary	3:25:47 (3,509)	
Tiplady, David	4:07:36 (11,832)	
Tipper, Tom	3:48:51 (7,477)	
Tipping, John	4:15:22 (13,607)	
Titchener, Frank	5:03:53 (24,612)	
Titley, Andy	3:17:29 (2,488)	
Titterton, Lawrence	3:52:08 (8,230)	
Titus, Martin	5:33:51 (28,459)	
To, Chun Kwong	6:12:34 (30,751)	
To, Kam	4:29:33 (3,341)	
Tobin, Andrew	3:48:02 (7,326)	
Tod, Jonathan	3:42:49 (6,318)	
Todd, Adrian	4:21:24 (15,088)	
Todd, Andrew	3:42:26 (6,228)	
Todd, David	2:58:04 (770)	
Todd, Jason	5:39:22 (28,929)	
Todd, Joseph	7:07:45 (31,972)	
Todd, Michael	5:37:39 (28,788)	
Todd, Paul	2:44:13 (222)	
Todd, Rory	4:42:44 (20,165)	

Todi, Mauro	3:23:30 (3,178)	
Tofts, John	5:42:29 (29,208)	
Tojeiro, Robert	3:05:10 (1,264)	
Tolan, Brendon	3:29:27 (4,079)	
Tolan, Daniel	4:51:53 (22,287)	
Tolboom, Leo	3:21:14 (2,904)	
Tolchard, Edward	3:17:37 (2,505)	
Tole, Reginald	5:22:08 (27,157)	
Tolfrey, Neil	3:16:23 (2,366)	
Toller, Christopher	6:43:36 (31,605)	
Tolley, John	3:48:32 (7,409)	
Tolley, Paul	5:27:23 (27,820)	
Tollhurst, Paul	4:53:14 (22,552)	
Tolman, Barry	4:01:44 (10,586)	
Tolossa, Ambesse	2:13:33 (13)	
Tolotta, Giovanni	2:59:12 (871)	
Toman, Sean	4:42:06 (20,009)	
Tomaschko, Daniel	3:58:56 (9,951)	
Tombling, Anthony	4:59:33 (23,895)	
Tombs, Jonathan	3:35:48 (5,040)	
Tomiak, Richard	4:41:19 (19,830)	
Tominey, Joel	4:16:11 (13,782)	
Tomkins, Kevin	3:47:43 (7,259)	
Tomkinson, Aaron	4:36:44 (18,814)	
Tomkinson, Michael	4:40:10 (19,575)	
Tomkinson-Hill, Nicholas	3:37:08 (5,261)	
Tomlin, James	3:36:36 (5,160)	
Tomlin, James	5:13:29 (26,039)	
Tomlin, Mark	3:31:02 (4,335)	
Tomlin, Stephen	5:07:09 (25,125)	
Tomlin, Stuart	5:46:20 (29,456)	
Tomlinson, Dennis	3:02:55 (1,108)	
Tomlinson, Frederick	7:26:47 (32,125)	
Tomlinson, Howard	4:41:38 (19,896)	
Tomlinson, Mark	2:56:47 (690)	
Tomlinson, Michael	5:45:31 (29,408)	
Tomlinson, Stephen	3:49:40 (7,672)	
Tomlinson, Stephen	5:10:00 (25,547)	
Tompkins, Matthew	4:36:30 (18,769)	
Toms, David	4:02:24 (10,718)	
Tomsett, Peter	4:59:35 (23,900)	
Toney, Glenn	4:25:24 (16,117)	
Tong, Andrew	3:50:39 (7,873)	
Tong, Yau	3:22:10 (3,004)	
Tonge, Peter	3:03:50 (1,170)	
Tonkin, Andrew	4:43:08 (20,270)	
Tonkin, Kenneth	4:02:34 (10,751)	
Tonkin, Richard	4:49:34 (21,766)	
Tonni, Davide	3:28:08 (3,836)	
Tooke, Daniel	3:49:09 (7,548)	
Tooke, Stephen	3:46:48 (7,083)	
Toomer, John	4:29:43 (17,166)	
Toomey, Ricky	4:17:35 (14,132)	
Toone, Richard	3:26:26 (3,595)	
Tootal, Thomas	4:38:41 (19,250)	
Tooth, Barrie	6:59:48 (31,886)	
Tooze, Paul	3:50:16 (7,792)	
Topliffe, David	4:18:44 (14,432)	
Topolewski, Jan	4:05:03 (11,303)	
Topper, Stephen	3:54:44 (8,847)	
Topper, Timothy	3:44:00 (6,544)	
Topping, Nigel	3:42:57 (6,354)	
Topping, Paul	3:56:35 (9,341)	
Topps, Jonathan	4:14:28 (13,371)	
Torre, Marcos	4:37:59 (19,084)	
Torres, Hector-David	3:31:14 (4,365)	
Torsiello, Antonino	4:06:32 (11,596)	
Tortiger, Eric	4:10:46 (12,506)	
Tortiger, Guy	4:00:14 (10,277)	
Toseland, Keith	5:53:57 (29,930)	
Toss, Robert	2:48:24 (347)	
Tott, Greg	4:18:50 (14,457)	
Totten, Gerard	5:10:25 (25,611)	
Totterdell, Graham	5:08:18 (25,311)	
Tougher, Phil	7:26:17 (32,116)	
Touhami, Mohamed	3:42:15 (6,194)	
Touhey, Brendan	4:38:43 (19,257)	
Toulme, Christian	5:46:01 (29,443)	
Touw, Simon	5:59:01 (30,210)	
Tovey, Benjamin	4:40:59 (19,748)	
Tovey, Jacob	3:38:22 (5,472)	
Towe, James	3:46:30 (7,028)	
Towell, Mark	4:16:04 (13,759)	

Towers, Geoffrey	3:41:42 (6,093)	
Towers, Paul	4:59:19 (23,859)	
Towlson, Carl	4:29:16 (17,056)	
Town, Trevor	7:45:05 (32,222)	
Townley, Stephen	4:16:36 (13,876)	
Townsend, Andrew	3:59:28 (10,086)	
Townsend, David	6:09:16 (30,612)	
Townsend, Martin	3:40:18 (5,843)	
Townsend, Peter	3:57:04 (9,471)	
Townsend, Peter	4:44:37 (20,637)	
Townsend, Peter	5:17:26 (26,531)	
Towse, Kevin	4:55:35 (23,048)	
Toye, Matthew	4:20:01 (14,748)	
Toyn, Greg	6:08:07 (30,572)	
Trace, Jonathan	3:54:27 (8,768)	
Tracey, Francis	3:40:37 (5,887)	
Traenk, Jonas	4:04:16 (11,127)	
Traeris, Andreas	3:50:19 (7,805)	
Train, Terence	5:05:34 (24,894)	
Trainor, Christopher	4:30:49 (17,449)	
Tran, Henry	5:06:44 (25,061)	
Tran, Phong	4:37:13 (18,925)	
Tran, Van	3:55:22 (9,014)	
Tranelsi, Sascha	4:33:59 (18,162)	
Tranter, Ian	5:00:05 (23,993)	
Tranter, John	4:35:29 (18,515)	
Tranter, Paul	3:26:50 (3,648)	
Trapp, Neil	4:16:24 (13,833)	
Trasler, Kieran	4:47:42 (21,346)	
Traynor, Mark	2:52:17 (457)	
Treadgold, Simon	4:03:38 (10,970)	
Treadwell, Brian	5:28:22 (27,928)	
Treadwell, Gregory	4:06:45 (11,643)	
Treadwell, Paul	3:55:38 (9,088)	
Treanor, Francis	4:31:58 (17,721)	
Treanor, Matt	3:51:59 (8,191)	
Trebern, René	4:13:33 (13,141)	
Trebilcock, Norman	4:37:28 (18,975)	
Tredget, Gary	5:04:53 (24,775)	
Tredget, Richard	5:04:53 (24,775)	
Tredget, Ross	5:04:53 (24,775)	
Tree, Daniel	4:50:14 (21,907)	
Tree, Stuart	3:50:11 (7,773)	
Tregaskes, Andrew	3:45:49 (6,894)	
Tregubov, Victor	3:17:41 (2,515)	
Trehearne, Edward	4:15:48 (13,702)	
Treiber, Andreas	5:03:25 (24,519)	
Trembirth, Anthony	4:09:47 (12,295)	
Tremblais, Peter	3:24:08 (3,271)	
Trenary, Albert	5:32:50 (28,363)	
Trenga, Laurent	6:10:24 (30,654)	
Trenkel, Christian	3:26:32 (3,613)	
Trennery, David	4:38:33 (19,210)	
Trent, Alan	3:26:15 (3,573)	
Tresca, Arnaud	3:22:45 (3,077)	
Treves, Michael	4:49:27 (21,737)	
Trevithick, David	3:58:14 (9,764)	
Treweek, William	5:11:36 (25,779)	
Trexler, Adam	4:45:03 (20,728)	
Tribe, Mark	4:17:31 (14,115)	
Trice, Ian	3:23:58 (3,244)	
Trice, Robert	4:18:50 (14,457)	
Trichot, Alex	4:29:07 (17,017)	
Trick, Robert	4:41:20 (19,833)	
Tride, Barrie	4:28:04 (16,725)	
Trigg, Nick	4:44:27 (20,606)	
Triggs, Alan	3:59:10 (9,997)	
Triggs, Chris	4:35:55 (18,625)	
Trigle, Alan	4:32:49 (17,905)	
Trim, Benjamin	5:27:21 (27,814)	
Trim, Chris	4:09:58 (12,345)	
Trimble, Gareth	4:06:59 (11,684)	
Trinder, Patrick	4:33:53 (18,138)	
Triner, Steve	3:15:05 (2,247)	
Trinham, Francis	6:51:59 (31,762)	
Tripp, Nick	3:53:50 (8,628)	
Trippanera, Mario	4:55:02 (22,928)	
Trodd, Ron	4:25:02 (16,010)	
Trofimczuk, Darren	6:22:35 (31,089)	
Trofimczuk, Jason	6:22:36 (31,092)	
Trombert, Christian	3:34:37 (4,857)	
Troop, Nicholas	5:16:49 (26,462)	
Trory, John	3:35:21 (4,966)	

Trotman, Michael	4:23:11 (15,541)	
Trott, Dennis	4:49:36 (21,783)	
Trott, Michael	4:56:29 (23,255)	
Troup, Mike	3:20:41 (2,845)	
Trowbridge, Christopher	4:21:40 (15,149)	
Trowell, Ian	3:46:41 (7,063)	
Trowsdale, John	4:47:27 (21,287)	
Troy, Christopher	4:51:45 (22,252)	
Troy, Malcolm	4:24:54 (15,972)	
Truby, David	4:55:42 (23,079)	
Trudgill, Alan	5:27:55 (27,886)	
Truelove, Michael	4:13:09 (13,037)	
Trueman, Kevin	3:53:39 (8,579)	
Trueman, Neil	5:56:05 (30,056)	
Truepenny, David	2:56:32 (677)	
Trujillo, Manuel	3:46:08 (6,959)	
Trules, Max	3:14:10 (2,149)	
Truman, Ian	4:26:32 (16,362)	
Truman, Mike	4:23:55 (15,724)	
Truman, Robert	3:39:00 (5,598)	
Trundle, Gary	3:55:42 (9,107)	
Trup, Danny	5:00:59 (24,150)	
Trupiano, Franck	3:32:44 (4,564)	
Truran, Martin	3:16:22 (2,363)	
Trusler, Neil	4:46:49 (21,150)	
Trustram, Paul	4:04:11 (11,108)	
Try, Christopher	3:55:55 (9,158)	
Tsang, Gein	4:01:38 (10,566)	
Tsavalos, John	4:16:31 (13,860)	
Tschapeller, Werner	3:15:00 (2,238)	
Tschirk, Wolfgang	3:19:40 (2,721)	
Tuach, James	4:57:34 (23,497)	
Tubb, Robert	4:47:37 (21,322)	
Tubbs, Trevor	3:56:50 (9,407)	
Tuck, Matthew	6:11:42 (30,715)	
Tuck, Steven	3:06:20 (1,345)	
Tucker, Allan	4:07:15 (11,749)	
Tucker, Andy	2:58:42 (822)	
Tucker, Christopher	4:03:05 (10,865)	
Tucker, David	3:22:08 (3,000)	
Tucker, David	3:59:31 (10,098)	
Tucker, Graham	3:16:10 (2,342)	
Tucker, Martin	6:22:32 (31,087)	
Tucker, Paul	3:44:20 (6,605)	
Tucker, Stephen	3:14:54 (2,228)	
Tucker, William	4:34:04 (18,186)	
Tuckey, Andrew	3:30:04 (4,178)	
Tuff, Andrew	4:54:23 (22,790)	
Tuffnell, Shaun	3:55:10 (8,958)	
Tufton, Grant	5:06:41 (25,049)	
Tuhill, Paul	3:55:50 (9,139)	
Tuitama, Godfrey	6:00:40 (30,280)	
Tuite, Patrick	2:55:12 (604)	
Tuller, Yvan	4:18:12 (14,286)	
Tullett, Peter	3:13:38 (2,077)	
Tullo, Peter	4:02:49 (10,811)	
Tulloch, James	5:14:20 (26,143)	
Tulloch, Kevin	2:53:30 (508)	
Tully, John	6:16:43 (30,886)	
Tunga, Kutetana	3:28:15 (3,857)	
Tunnicliffe, Gary	5:27:30 (27,832)	
Tunnicliffe, John	4:39:11 (19,370)	
Tunstall, Stephen	4:43:29 (20,371)	
Turk, David	4:45:41 (20,884)	
Turkington, Richard	2:33:03 (83)	
Turley, Carl	3:31:04 (4,339)	
Turley, James	3:28:18 (3,866)	
Turley, William	5:15:06 (26,261)	
Turnbull, Alexander	3:12:33 (1,938)	
Turnbull, David	3:46:35 (7,051)	
Turnbull, Kenneth	3:30:22 (4,226)	
Turnbull, Matthew	3:44:16 (6,594)	
Turnbull, Matthew	4:09:28 (12,219)	
Turnbull, Ray	5:15:32 (26,316)	
Turner, Alan	3:04:45 (1,228)	
Turner, Alex	3:36:49 (5,195)	
Turner, Andrew	3:17:20 (2,464)	
Turner, Andrew	3:47:02 (7,132)	
Turner, Barry	6:57:25 (31,867)	
Turner, Carl	3:28:41 (3,940)	
Turner, Christian	4:36:54 (18,854)	
Turner, Colin	4:18:24 (14,330)	
Turner, Craig	4:03:52 (11,031)	

Turner, Daniel	3:43:19 (6,429)	
Turner, David	3:56:02 (9,189)	
Turner, David	4:37:33 (18,995)	
Turner, David	4:37:50 (19,050)	
Turner, David	4:55:44 (23,091)	
Turner, Dean	4:23:11 (15,541)	
Turner, Edward	5:06:09 (24,976)	
Turner, Geoff	3:29:14 (4,033)	
Turner, Glyn	4:24:07 (15,781)	
Turner, Graham	5:08:18 (25,311)	
Turner, Hugh	4:43:25 (20,354)	
Turner, Ian	3:33:56 (4,740)	
Turner, Ian	4:02:14 (10,682)	
Turner, James	3:29:21 (4,055)	
Turner, Jeff	3:18:55 (2,646)	
Turner, John	3:21:16 (2,907)	
Turner, John	4:38:32 (19,206)	
Turner, Keith	3:49:09 (7,548)	
Turner, Keith	4:28:32 (16,868)	
Turner, Kenneth	4:35:43 (18,565)	
Turner, Lee	5:13:11 (25,997)	
Turner, Mark	4:10:37 (12,486)	
Turner, Mark	4:40:08 (19,565)	
Turner, Mark	6:12:07 (30,733)	
Turner, Matthew	4:10:28 (12,456)	
Turner, Matthew	4:52:57 (22,494)	
Turner, Mickey	4:37:43 (19,025)	
Turner, Nigel	3:47:34 (7,228)	
Turner, Nigel	4:17:23 (14,082)	
Turner, Paul	4:36:39 (18,797)	
Turner, Peter	2:46:03 (259)	
Turner, Raymond	6:25:45 (31,193)	
Turner, Richard	4:33:17 (18,001)	
Turner, Roger	5:39:55 (28,983)	
Turner, Simon	3:58:51 (9,930)	
Turner, Simon	4:10:19 (12,419)	
Turner, Spencer	3:50:59 (7,946)	
Turner, Stewart	4:32:01 (17,736)	
Turner, Thomas	4:02:42 (10,781)	
Turner, Warren	3:29:49 (4,146)	
Turney, Lee	4:28:53 (16,961)	
Turnpenny, Peter	3:13:34 (2,069)	
Turp, Paul	3:53:09 (8,460)	
Turpton, Dave	3:34:37 (4,857)	
Turquer, Romuald	4:50:36 (21,993)	
Turrell, James	3:46:00 (6,928)	
Turrell, Paul	4:44:07 (20,522)	
Turrell, Peter	2:54:29 (557)	
Turton, Brian	2:52:50 (489)	
Turton, Les	3:13:11 (2,016)	
Turvey, Andrew	4:15:12 (13,567)	
Turvey, George	4:06:35 (11,608)	
Turvey, Matthew	3:16:39 (2,390)	
Tuson, David	6:44:22 (31,612)	
Tuson, Neil	4:18:50 (14,457)	
Tutt, Kevin	3:56:52 (9,417)	
Tuttle, Peter	3:00:16 (953)	
Tveter, Trygue	3:26:26 (3,595)	
Twamley, Richard	5:55:42 (30,026)	
Tweed, Kevin	4:32:23 (17,813)	
Tweed, Mark	3:36:00 (5,064)	
Tweedie, Mark	4:04:47 (11,245)	
Twigger, Andrew	4:50:16 (21,915)	
Twilley, John	4:25:52 (16,219)	
Twiner, Richard	4:58:53 (23,777)	
Twinn, Jason	4:33:20 (18,013)	
Twist, John	4:58:59 (23,795)	
Twittey, Kevin	5:05:04 (24,806)	
Twomey, Eamon	3:14:27 (2,180)	
Twomey, Patrick	3:28:18 (3,866)	
Twyford, Harry	5:31:43 (28,258)	
Twyford, Ross	3:41:32 (6,075)	
Tyas, Adrian	3:49:40 (7,672)	
Tychowski, Georges	5:24:45 (27,501)	
Tye, Geoffrey	5:04:44 (24,742)	
Tye, Philip	3:33:22 (4,657)	
Tye, Ronald	4:32:30 (17,853)	
Tyler, Anthony	4:48:29 (21,532)	
Tyler, Benjamin	4:00:44 (10,376)	
Tyler, David	4:44:00 (20,497)	
Tyler, David	4:57:53 (23,557)	
Tyler, Kevin	3:57:23 (9,552)	
Tyler, Richard	3:25:31 (3,463)	

Tyler, Robert	4:53:36 (22,639)	
Tyler, Roger	4:32:54 (17,924)	
Tyler, Simon	4:48:15 (21,482)	
Tyler, Simon	5:12:50 (25,949)	
Tyler, Stephen	4:55:47 (23,107)	
Tyler, Terry	4:05:48 (11,458)	
Tymms, Andrew	3:31:00 (4,327)	
Tymms, Leigh	4:37:10 (18,912)	
Tyre, Mark	6:45:51 (31,642)	
Tyrer, Paddy	4:31:08 (17,538)	
Tyrrell, Bryan	4:05:47 (11,454)	
Tyrrell, Michael	5:02:25 (24,376)	
Tyrrell-Evans, Ben	4:28:40 (16,902)	
Tyson, Graham	4:13:25 (13,100)	
Tyszkiewicz, John	4:21:09 (15,020)	
Ubaldi, Giovanni	3:45:43 (6,876)	
Ubsdell, Simon	2:59:25 (893)	
Uden, Barry	4:48:18 (21,496)	
Uden, Lois	4:29:51 (17,207)	
Uerschels, Guido	4:03:46 (11,002)	
Uglow, John	3:53:23 (8,510)	
Ugoala, Nwabu	4:01:18 (10,495)	
Ulbricht, Armin	2:53:26 (505)	
Ulfik, Victor	3:40:40 (5,897)	
Ulivieri, Roberto	3:54:13 (8,712)	
Ullah, Anis	4:24:05 (15,775)	
Ullman, James	4:28:03 (16,721)	
Ulrich, Herbert	3:28:53 (3,984)	
Ulrich, Kai-Uwe	3:23:53 (3,230)	
Umpleby, Mark	4:30:35 (17,386)	
Umpleby, Philip	6:47:23 (31,659)	
Underdown, Kevin	3:33:20 (4,650)	
Underhill, Tim	3:20:52 (2,869)	
Underwood, Robin	4:06:31 (11,593)	
Underwood, Simon	5:04:59 (24,791)	
Underwood, Stuart	2:55:34 (624)	
Underwood, Tom	3:44:21 (6,611)	
Unerman, David	5:39:25 (28,938)	
Unerman, Martin	3:56:25 (9,297)	
Ung, Hy	3:38:21 (5,469)	
Ungi, Tom	4:51:48 (22,267)	
Ungi, Tom	4:51:49 (22,270)	
Unterhalter, David	5:04:31 (24,708)	
Unvin, David	3:37:33 (5,334)	
Unwin, Andy	5:06:44 (25,061)	
Unwin, Ashley	3:35:51 (5,049)	
Unwin, James	7:00:18 (31,892)	
Upson, Christopher	3:13:12 (2,022)	
Upton, Chris	3:29:43 (4,129)	
Upton, Ed	4:25:12 (16,056)	
Upton, James	5:08:23 (25,322)	
Upton, Michael	4:53:27 (22,609)	
Upton, Simon	4:34:31 (18,290)	
Urbanowski, Frank	4:07:24 (11,784)	
Urron, Geoffrey	4:12:05 (12,780)	
Urwin, Jeremy	4:28:08 (16,748)	
Urwin, Robert	3:32:53 (4,580)	
Urwin, Roger	4:50:38 (21,997)	
Urwin, Stephen	5:18:28 (26,695)	
Urwin, Steven	5:12:32 (25,901)	
Usher, Ian	5:15:00 (26,248)	
Usher, John	6:29:01 (31,302)	
Usher, Kevin	2:49:30 (378)	
Usher, Mark	4:09:13 (12,175)	
Usmar, Shaun	4:40:10 (19,575)	
Uter, John	3:31:26 (4,395)	
Utterson, Colin	3:27:50 (3,792)	
Utting, James	6:43:26 (31,599)	
Uzzell, Philip	4:26:28 (16,347)	
Vacalopoulos, Robert	3:18:08 (2,568)	
Vachon, Paul	5:33:07 (28,379)	
Valbonesi, Michael	2:56:18 (660)	
Valdinger, Stefan	4:57:34 (23,497)	
Vale, Paul	4:49:26 (21,733)	
Vale, Richard	5:37:16 (28,761)	
Valentin, Patrick	4:06:16 (11,549)	
Valentine, Malcolm	4:59:15 (23,850)	
Valkenburg, Martin	3:50:45 (7,899)	
Vallance, Andrew	3:10:02 (1,677)	
Vallentin, Uwe	4:32:50 (17,909)	
Vallis, John	3:30:34 (4,255)	
Valvona, Ian	4:19:24 (14,594)	
Vamben, Eric	2:36:12 (109)	
Van Alebeek, Hans	3:24:26 (3,323)	
Van Alphen, Wil	3:48:00 (7,319)	
Van Asperen, Rob	2:56:43 (683)	
Van Beek, Hans	4:41:38 (19,896)	
Van Blommestein, Andrew	4:07:12 (11,737)	
Van Campenhout, Jos	3:59:53 (10,197)	
Van Caster, Eric	3:17:29 (2,488)	
Van De Griendt, Rob	4:43:45 (20,443)	
Van De Kuil, Marinus	4:16:14 (13,792)	
Van De Velde, Charles	3:54:58 (8,911)	
Van De Vyver, Herman	4:09:11 (12,171)	
Van Den Abbeele, Hans	4:05:19 (11,358)	
Van Den Bergh, David	4:27:18 (16,550)	
Van Den Berghen, Jan	4:44:59 (20,711)	
Van Den Bosch, Alex	3:54:33 (8,803)	
Van Den Bosch, Paul	4:04:00 (11,062)	
Van Den Engel, Etienne	4:22:54 (15,471)	
Van Den Heever, Peter	4:50:01 (21,862)	
Van Den Oever, Harco	4:36:59 (18,872)	
Van Der Horst, Rupert	3:57:37 (9,599)	
Van Der Lee, Paul	4:11:44 (12,702)	
Van Der Linden, Eric	4:04:08 (11,098)	
Van Der Linden, Rob	5:08:55 (25,390)	
Van Der Linden, Sjaak	3:37:32 (5,330)	
Van Der Merwe, George	4:51:10 (22,125)	
Van Der Merwe, Robert	4:43:29 (20,371)	
Van Der Vliet, Bart	4:10:59 (12,539)	
Van Der Wal, Johannes	4:22:35 (15,387)	
Van Der Zee, Pieter	3:37:36 (5,346)	
Van Dijk, Nico	3:31:14 (4,365)	
Van Dorth, Wim	4:09:44 (12,280)	
Van Dyk, Eugene	3:42:51 (6,330)	
Van Elkan, Dean	4:13:01 (13,008)	
Van Eyk, Craig	3:22:39 (3,063)	
Van Eyssen, Wade	5:18:06 (26,630)	
Van Hal, Erik	3:29:33 (4,103)	
Van Katwijk, Jan	3:28:02 (3,820)	
Van Kessel, Hans	3:57:20 (9,536)	
Van Kets, Werner	3:56:40 (9,365)	
Van Leuck, Thomas	3:44:20 (6,605)	
Van Lint, Koen	3:42:42 (6,300)	
Van Nieuwpoort, Albert	3:58:23 (9,804)	
Van Oosten, Aad	4:27:27 (16,581)	
Van Os, Eddie	4:02:19 (10,698)	
Van Rensburg, Jacques	3:59:13 (10,007)	
Van Riet, Stefan	3:16:08 (2,339)	
Van Rinjn, Jasper	5:07:18 (25,147)	
Van Rossum, Leonard	3:27:50 (3,792)	
Van Schoor, Bob	3:45:38 (6,856)	
Van Straalen, Adriaan	3:20:25 (2,839)	
Van Twest, Rohan	4:47:14 (21,232)	
Van Ulzen, Vincent	4:42:48 (20,180)	
Van Velzen, Cees	4:31:18 (17,566)	
Van Waard, Hans	4:39:57 (19,528)	
Van Werkum, Frank	3:59:40 (10,141)	
Van Wijk, Gert-Jan	4:50:04 (21,876)	
Van Woerkom, Alfons	4:21:13 (15,037)	
Van Zuylen, Stephen	4:16:51 (13,947)	
Van Zyl, Anton	2:28:12 (54)	
Van Zyl, Charl	3:25:13 (3,431)	
Vanda, Vincenzo	4:47:05 (21,198)	
Vandaele, Michel	3:18:34 (2,615)	
Vandelli, Emilio	4:03:28 (10,936)	
Vandenbert, Jacob	6:18:14 (30,945)	
Vandenplas, Marc	3:39:58 (5,777)	
Vandepeear, Magnus	4:07:38 (11,841)	
Vanderbiest, Paul	4:20:23 (14,842)	
Vandoros, Mark	3:42:11 (6,187)	
Vanhinsbergh, Mark	4:37:31 (18,987)	
Vankuyk, Daniel	5:03:07 (24,477)	
Vanlangenhoven, Robert	3:05:46 (1,302)	
Van-Loveren, Michel	3:45:50 (6,895)	
Vanner, Terry	3:05:35 (1,290)	
Vanneste, Pol	3:45:27 (6,820)	
Vanstone, Martin	5:21:20 (27,064)	
Vanweesep, Jeroen	3:27:48 (3,780)	
Varachaud, Christian	4:29:14 (17,049)	
Varah, Paul	3:40:39 (5,891)	
Varden, Mark	2:59:47 (925)	
Varndell, Andrew	5:09:00 (25,407)	
Varney, Adrian	3:34:09 (4,768)	
Varney, Kenneth	6:30:25 (31,339)	
Varney, Richard	4:15:04 (13,529)	
Varney, Steven	3:10:00 (1,673)	
Varnham, Thomas	4:41:17 (19,819)	
Varsani, Surya	4:45:44 (20,893)	
Varzi, Raniero	4:43:04 (20,250)	
Vasey, Peter	4:15:49 (13,707)	
Vasili, Alexi	6:15:16 (30,833)	
Vassallo, James	3:19:22 (2,686)	
Vassiliades, Steven	2:52:26 (466)	
Vastenhout, Ferguson	4:25:41 (16,177)	
Vaughan, Andrew	3:40:08 (5,820)	
Vaughan, Bryan	3:49:08 (7,543)	
Vaughan, David	4:22:23 (15,336)	
Vaughan, Ian	3:26:54 (3,658)	
Vaughan, John	7:35:52 (32,189)	
Vaughan, Michael	4:10:17 (12,414)	
Vaughton, David	4:39:57 (19,528)	
Vautier, Lionel	3:27:27 (3,731)	
Veal, Peter	4:37:10 (18,912)	
Vebezgunne, Detlef-Rudiger	4:05:48 (11,458)	
Vecchie, Giuliano	5:25:11 (27,568)	
Veevers, Charles	5:17:48 (26,581)	
Veiga, Jaime	3:45:27 (6,820)	
Veit, Martin	4:44:12 (20,545)	
Veitch, Paul	3:20:18 (2,803)	
Vekaria, Pritam	5:21:11 (27,047)	
Vela, José	3:51:11 (8,008)	
Velasco, David	3:14:09 (2,147)	
Veldkamp, Lex	4:42:16 (20,046)	
Velho, Helder	5:03:41 (24,567)	
Vella, Felix	3:32:54 (4,582)	
Vella, Mark	5:30:11 (28,098)	
Vella, Simon	4:20:58 (14,968)	
Venables, Edward	5:18:32 (26,701)	
Venderpump, William	4:36:10 (18,682)	
Veness, Ian	3:58:07 (9,733)	
Veness, Martyn	4:30:22 (17,328)	
Vengadasalam, Ganesh	4:36:26 (18,753)	
Venkataraman, Ramamurthy	5:16:08 (26,391)	
Venturi, Stefano	4:33:25 (18,036)	
Verburgh, André	3:36:02 (5,069)	
Vercauteren, Marc	3:49:29 (7,629)	
Verdu-Berenguer, Ismael	6:07:46 (30,559)	
Vere, Derek	5:35:31 (28,594)	
Vergalito, Aurelio	4:04:23 (11,153)	
Verheijen, Guy	3:13:14 (2,027)	
Verhoef, Emil	3:45:53 (6,909)	
Verhulst, Georges	3:49:54 (7,712)	
Vermigle, Terence	5:04:01 (24,633)	
Vermot, Arnaud	2:56:31 (675)	
Vernon, Darren	2:51:47 (439)	
Vernon, Mark	4:09:15 (12,184)	
Vernon, Nigel	4:10:53 (12,524)	
Vernon, Peter	4:55:27 (23,015)	
Vero, Alexander	3:53:41 (8,586)	
Véronique, Maurice	5:09:01 (25,411)	
Verougstraete, Mathieu	4:28:11 (16,761)	
Verri, William	3:59:03 (9,975)	
Vester, Tommy	3:36:54 (5,213)	
Vestli, Espen	5:32:32 (28,336)	
Vezzu, Loris	2:57:17 (724)	
Viard, Phil	3:53:41 (8,586)	
Vice, Jeremy	3:26:35 (3,618)	
Vicente Do Souto, Carlos	3:43:35 (6,460)	
Vickers, Bernard	2:54:11 (547)	
Vickers, David	5:25:55 (27,655)	
Vickers, Donald	4:04:38 (11,207)	
Vickers, Mark	4:07:23 (11,778)	
Vickers, Peter	3:58:23 (9,804)	
Vickery, Anthony	4:34:59 (4,747)	
Vickeus, Marcuz	4:32:57 (17,935)	
Victory, Patrick	4:49:28 (21,743)	
Vidal, Clidd	4:33:17 (18,001)	
Vidler, James	5:05:37 (24,905)	
Vigano, Federico	4:54:51 (22,891)	
Vigne, James	3:22:59 (3,109)	
Vigrass, Brian	4:45:29 (20,847)	
Vigurs, Robert	3:39:52 (5,764)	
Vilajeti, Paulin	5:24:54 (27,520)	
Vile, Martin	3:31:16 (4,373)	
Vilhelhsen, Robert	3:34:58 (4,905)	
Villa, Piergiorgio	4:47:06 (21,203)	
Villain, Norbert	3:51:49 (8,153)	
Villalpando, Andrés	3:28:58 (3,998)	

Villaume, Daniel	4:05:33 (11,410)	
Villet, John	4:13:11 (13,044)	
Vinall, Thomas	4:57:51 (23,551)	
Vinay, Michel	4:49:19 (21,707)	
Vince, Phil	4:43:04 (20,250)	
Vincent, Alain	3:53:25 (8,521)	
Vincent, Andrew	5:18:54 (26,742)	
Vincent, Edward	3:28:30 (3,903)	
Vincent, George	4:11:11 (12,572)	
Vincent, Heliard	3:51:57 (8,182)	
Vincent, Ian	3:29:26 (4,075)	
Vincent, Ian	4:12:35 (12,909)	
Vincent, Martyn	4:49:49 (21,827)	
Vincent, Paul	5:46:24 (29,460)	
Vincent, Wayne	3:02:29 (1,086)	
Vine, Desmond	3:54:30 (8,784)	
Vine, Laurence	4:54:03 (22,720)	
Vine, Phillip	5:15:05 (26,259)	
Vine, Raymond	4:51:30 (22,211)	
Viner, John	4:52:23 (22,375)	
Vines, Jason	4:28:38 (16,894)	
Viney, Craig	4:41:14 (19,810)	
Vinken, Adrian	3:42:50 (6,324)	
Violanti, Adriano	4:48:05 (21,448)	
Virk, Jaswant	4:49:32 (21,758)	
Vita, Aldo	4:54:41 (22,861)	
Vitellozzi, Dean	4:42:43 (20,163)	
Vivent, Eric	3:54:51 (8,879)	
Vivian, Richard	3:53:54 (8,646)	
Vivier, Jean-Luc	4:12:53 (12,978)	
Vlaanderen, Romke	4:00:09 (10,260)	
Vlasblom, Xander	3:23:23 (3,160)	
Vlierboom, Dirk	3:47:43 (7,259)	
Vlk, Werner	3:26:36 (3,619)	
Vlok, Deon	3:39:22 (5,671)	
Vogan, Ian	4:29:03 (17,004)	
Vogel, William	3:25:31 (3,463)	
Vogt, Jim	4:14:35 (13,399)	
Vohra, Rajiv	5:41:11 (29,089)	
Voight, Michael	4:43:53 (20,478)	
Voirin, Francis	3:31:27 (4,399)	
Volkov, Shane	4:42:31 (20,116)	
Vollands, Arthur	4:49:08 (21,655)	
Vollentine, Brian	3:15:22 (2,276)	
Voller, Paul	3:56:08 (9,219)	
Vollmer, Justin	3:42:01 (6,153)	
Voltolini, Rino	4:04:43 (11,230)	
Von Dahl, Philipp	3:48:41 (7,437)	
Von Hoesslin, Denis	4:37:44 (19,029)	
Von Kalckreuth, Goetz	4:38:18 (19,161)	
Von Westenholz, Nicholas	4:46:57 (21,174)	
Vondra, Philip	3:09:08 (1,596)	
Vonk, Ronald	3:42:26 (6,228)	
Vonwiller, Hans-Martin	3:52:50 (8,377)	
Vooght, Haydn	3:56:36 (9,346)	
Vooght, Stephen	3:57:54 (9,677)	
Vorley, Brett	4:45:22 (20,813)	
Vorres, Dimitri	2:44:17 (226)	
Vose, Colin	4:22:22 (15,331)	
Voskoboinikoff, Stephan	4:22:37 (15,401)	
Vosper, Andy	4:40:54 (19,727)	
Voss, Axel	4:33:43 (18,100)	
Voss, Peter	6:18:46 (30,964)	
Vote, William	3:42:33 (6,265)	
Vout, Tony	3:14:04 (2,138)	
Vowell, Darrin	4:32:04 (17,746)	
Vowles, Jayson	4:03:24 (10,929)	
Vrijenhoek, Jan	4:30:09 (17,269)	
Vye, Alan	5:09:16 (25,441)	
Waddell, Ian	5:51:34 (29,810)	
Waddingham, Michael	4:30:17 (17,305)	
Waddington, Ashley	3:41:48 (6,113)	
Waddington, Simon	3:42:50 (6,324)	
Wade, Calvin	5:12:27 (25,888)	
Wade, David	6:56:20 (31,848)	
Wade, Gary	4:16:00 (13,743)	
Wade, Ian	4:19:56 (14,723)	
Wade, James	3:34:05 (4,758)	
Wade, Michael	5:09:57 (25,532)	
Wade, Neil	4:09:55 (12,329)	
Wade, Richard	4:58:17 (23,645)	
Wade, Stuart	5:20:46 (26,993)	
Wade, Tim	3:59:28 (10,086)	

Wade-Thomas, Martin	3:13:06 (2,005)	
Wadey, Graham	5:26:01 (27,677)	
Wadey, Ian	3:24:51 (3,378)	
Wadey, Jeff	5:15:46 (26,352)	
Wadey, Robert	4:46:49 (21,150)	
Wadley, Mark	3:31:41 (4,432)	
Wadsley, Nick	3:57:20 (9,536)	
Wadsworth, Adrian	3:15:25 (2,280)	
Wagemann, Eberhard	3:41:47 (6,109)	
Wagenknecht, Robert	3:35:25 (4,977)	
Wager, Ashley	3:58:46 (9,909)	
Waghorn, Hayden	3:40:12 (5,832)	
Waghorn, Nick	3:39:48 (5,748)	
Wagland, Gareth	3:16:49 (2,405)	
Wagner, Andrew	4:36:11 (18,689)	
Wagner, Gunter	4:43:07 (20,268)	
Wagner, Helmut	3:05:10 (1,264)	
Wagner, Martin	5:24:59 (27,533)	
Wagner, Stuart	5:24:59 (27,533)	
Wagstaff, Peter	3:59:13 (10,007)	
Wagstaff, Steve	5:10:02 (25,555)	
Wah, Li	3:29:12 (4,026)	
Wahl, Jochen	3:18:14 (2,580)	
Wahlberg, Anders	4:27:51 (16,680)	
Wain, Francis	4:28:54 (16,968)	
Wain, Gary	3:53:38 (8,574)	
Wain, Robert	4:04:03 (11,075)	
Wain, Timothy	3:59:54 (10,200)	
Waine, Michael	2:41:28 (171)	
Wainer, Alan	4:12:24 (12,858)	
Wainewright, David	5:35:42 (28,612)	
Wainwright, Benjamin	6:17:22 (30,903)	
Wainwright, Bruce	3:27:17 (3,711)	
Wainwright, David	5:17:30 (26,544)	
Wainwright, Jake	4:13:32 (13,134)	
Wainwright, Jason	3:58:38 (9,867)	
Waistell, Lee	4:20:41 (14,902)	
Waite, Alfred	3:44:05 (6,562)	
Waite, Christopher	4:21:24 (15,088)	
Waite, James	4:18:30 (14,359)	
Waite, Jeffrey	4:37:06 (18,902)	
Waite, Mark	3:28:54 (3,987)	
Waite, Mark	3:41:25 (6,047)	
Waite, Mark	4:43:47 (20,449)	
Waite, Richard	3:51:17 (8,025)	
Waite, Stephen	4:18:29 (14,351)	
Waites, Andrew	3:00:29 (972)	
Waites, David	4:28:02 (16,715)	
Waites, Stephen	3:45:25 (6,811)	
Wake, Alan	4:35:44 (18,570)	
Wake, Martyn	5:38:14 (28,832)	
Wake, Paul	4:04:46 (11,243)	
Wake, Steven	4:12:15 (12,828)	
Wakefield, Andy	5:38:50 (28,884)	
Wakefield, Charles	5:35:03 (28,556)	
Wakefield, Nigel	3:50:26 (7,829)	
Wakefield, Ollie	4:20:09 (14,783)	
Wakefield, Robin	5:01:19 (24,209)	
Wakefield, Simon	3:37:01 (5,235)	
Wakefield, William	4:04:36 (11,198)	
Wakeford, Martin	3:24:22 (3,311)	
Wakeford, Stephen	3:25:04 (3,404)	
Wakeford, Thomas	4:31:31 (17,621)	
Wakeham, Stephen	3:39:07 (5,619)	
Wakely, David	4:46:29 (21,091)	
Wakem, Jamie	4:05:15 (11,342)	
Wakem, Terry	4:14:47 (13,445)	
Wakeman, Mark	4:40:27 (19,643)	
Walbert, Bernd	3:44:14 (6,589)	
Walbridge, John	6:01:08 (30,308)	
Walburn, Kenneth	5:51:54 (29,827)	
Walden, James	4:25:49 (16,205)	
Walder, David	4:25:16 (16,074)	
Waldie, Brian	3:13:20 (2,039)	
Walding, James	5:19:18 (26,799)	
Waldram, Simon	4:52:56 (22,491)	
Waldram, Stephen	3:15:30 (2,289)	
Waldren, Daniel	4:59:25 (23,873)	
Waldron, David	3:11:49 (1,838)	
Waldron, Julian	4:22:06 (15,265)	
Waldrop, William	2:41:53 (177)	
Wale, Charles	3:39:42 (5,727)	
Waler, David	4:22:02 (15,247)	

Wales, Brian	5:56:30 (30,081)	
Wales, David	4:48:02 (21,437)	
Walker, Alex	4:26:10 (16,289)	
Walker, Andrew	3:43:26 (6,442)	
Walker, Andrew	4:21:51 (15,194)	
Walker, Angus	3:41:12 (5,988)	
Walker, Anthony	3:55:42 (9,107)	
Walker, Anthony	4:03:05 (10,865)	
Walker, Brendan	4:42:15 (20,039)	
Walker, Bruce	3:48:15 (7,368)	
Walker, Christopher	4:07:39 (11,848)	
Walker, Christopher	6:00:56 (30,292)	
Walker, David	3:30:33 (4,253)	
Walker, David	4:08:56 (12,117)	
Walker, David	4:38:19 (19,167)	
Walker, Derek	2:59:18 (881)	
Walker, Eddie	4:22:09 (15,276)	
Walker, Gary	5:18:16 (26,669)	
Walker, Geof	4:28:06 (16,735)	
Walker, George	3:09:01 (1,587)	
Walker, Giles	3:31:09 (4,351)	
Walker, Graham	4:48:25 (21,520)	
Walker, Howard	4:42:41 (20,154)	
Walker, Ian	3:41:19 (6,017)	
Walker, Ian	5:19:42 (26,848)	
Walker, Ian	6:07:17 (30,540)	
Walker, John	3:57:53 (9,673)	
Walker, John	4:55:28 (23,021)	
Walker, John	7:10:12 (31,990)	
Walker, Keith	4:52:57 (22,494)	
Walker, Kevin	3:12:42 (1,958)	
Walker, Lee	3:26:10 (3,516)	
Walker, Lee	4:42:21 (20,067)	
Walker, Marc	3:33:06 (4,614)	
Walker, Mark	5:09:43 (25,510)	
Walker, Mark	5:36:23 (28,671)	
Walker, Martin	3:13:50 (2,100)	
Walker, Martin	5:13:11 (25,997)	
Walker, Martin	5:28:01 (27,894)	
Walker, Mike	2:59:52 (932)	
Walker, Oliver	4:16:16 (13,802)	
Walker, Paul	4:08:38 (12,047)	
Walker, Paul	5:14:39 (26,196)	
Walker, Peter	4:15:53 (13,722)	
Walker, Philip	5:40:04 (29,002)	
Walker, Ray	3:17:41 (2,515)	
Walker, Richard	3:55:13 (8,969)	
Walker, Richard	4:41:49 (19,949)	
Walker, Richard	5:09:08 (25,427)	
Walker, Robert	3:23:28 (3,174)	
Walker, Robert	3:47:36 (7,237)	
Walker, Robert	5:00:54 (24,139)	
Walker, Scott	3:42:49 (6,318)	
Walker, Scott	5:06:38 (25,039)	
Walker, Scott	6:27:00 (31,230)	
Walker, Shaun	4:45:16 (20,788)	
Walker, Steven	3:05:01 (1,250)	
Walker, Steven	3:39:00 (5,598)	
Walker, Stuart	3:00:29 (972)	
Walker, Stuart	3:52:38 (8,338)	
Walker, Thomas	5:59:09 (30,217)	
Walker, William	3:35:42 (5,026)	
Walker, William	4:05:27 (11,394)	
Walker, William	4:29:18 (17,061)	
Walker-Buckton, Tristan	3:31:30 (4,412)	
Walkerdine, Martin	3:44:56 (6,718)	
Walkey, Nathan	4:23:54 (15,720)	
Walkingshaw, Grahame	5:06:51 (25,088)	
Walkley, Darrell	4:29:54 (17,220)	
Wall, Colin	4:21:58 (15,234)	
Wall, David	4:17:51 (14,218)	
Wall, David	5:41:59 (29,161)	
Wall, Ivan	3:22:14 (3,015)	
Wall, Jonathan	4:44:16 (20,565)	
Wall, Matthew	4:41:27 (19,861)	
Wall, Michael	5:28:22 (27,928)	
Wall, Nick	3:43:23 (6,434)	
Wall, Tony	4:36:44 (18,814)	
Wallace, Andrew	2:53:41 (513)	
Wallace, Clark	4:13:51 (13,216)	
Wallace, Colin	3:24:39 (3,353)	
Wallace, David	3:29:17 (4,040)	
Wallace, David	4:08:38 (12,047)	

Wallace, Dean 2:58:56 (844)
Wallace, Jim 2:58:35 (811)
Wallace, John 6:26:18 (31,215)
Wallace, Malcolm 4:34:21 (18,252)
Wallace, Mark 3:59:44 (10,162)
Wallace, Michael 4:39:14 (19,380)
Wallace, Paul 4:57:27 (23,468)
Wallace, Philip 3:59:41 (10,146)
Wallace, Richard 4:54:31 (22,820)
Wallace, Steve 3:58:41 (9,882)
Wallace, Stewart 5:57:06 (30,114)
Walland, John 4:40:47 (19,700)
Wallbank, Peter 4:31:19 (17,570)
Wallbank, Robert 3:37:23 (5,305)
Waller, Andrew 4:16:38 (13,885)
Waller, Ian 3:11:35 (1,810)
Waller, Lee 5:07:32 (25,192)
Wallhead, Ian 3:42:24 (6,219)
Walliker, Alexander 3:42:43 (6,301)
Wallington, Paul 4:52:46 (22,452)
Wallis, Angus 3:53:52 (8,637)
Wallis, Gordon 4:28:50 (16,945)
Wallis, John 3:59:15 (10,021)
Wallis, Nigel 4:26:24 (16,334)
Wallis, Philip 3:42:08 (6,174)
Wallis, Shaun 4:54:51 (22,891)
Wallis, Simon 4:46:02 (20,971)
Wallis, Simon 4:59:25 (23,873)
Wallman, Scott 3:53:06 (8,451)
Walmsley, Dennis 2:31:59 (74)
Walmsley, Mark 3:33:25 (4,669)
Walmsley, Paul 3:51:36 (8,105)
Walmsley, Paul 4:16:16 (13,802)
Walmsley, William 4:10:52 (12,521)
Walpole, David 3:20:47 (2,855)
Walsgrove, John 3:17:06 (2,438)
Walsh, A 6:11:52 (30,721)
Walsh, Chris 4:57:08 (23,411)
Walsh, Colman 4:30:07 (17,266)
Walsh, David 2:52:14 (452)
Walsh, Gary 4:09:08 (12,162)
Walsh, George 4:54:36 (22,837)
Walsh, James 3:32:39 (4,550)
Walsh, John 6:45:36 (31,635)
Walsh, Kevin 4:09:39 (12,264)
Walsh, Kieran 4:49:08 (21,655)
Walsh, Martin 4:10:07 (12,378)
Walsh, Matthew 3:56:48 (9,398)
Walsh, Matthew 4:00:04 (10,237)
Walsh, Neil 4:52:03 (22,320)
Walsh, Nicel 3:47:49 (7,285)
Walsh, Paul 4:03:43 (10,987)
Walsh, Paul 4:49:40 (21,796)
Walsh, Raymond 3:42:28 (6,240)
Walsh, Timothy 4:21:19 (15,066)
Walsh, Wayne 4:40:10 (19,575)
Walshaw, John 4:16:42 (13,905)
Walsh-de-Serrant, Henry 3:39:45 (5,738)
Walshe, Anthony 3:41:59 (6,147)
Walter, Richard 3:34:55 (4,894)
Walters, David 5:01:43 (24,262)
Walters, Eric 5:14:45 (26,207)
Walters, Humphrey 4:36:41 (18,806)
Walters, Kennth 4:24:45 (15,937)
Walters, Matthew 3:41:23 (6,037)
Walters, Meirion 4:18:40 (14,412)
Walters, Michael 3:56:23 (9,288)
Walters, Mitchell 6:42:50 (31,587)
Walters, Paul 4:15:41 (13,671)
Walters, Paul 4:18:03 (14,260)
Walters, Peter 4:14:21 (13,345)
Walters, Philip 3:08:26 (1,538)
Walters, Spencer 4:19:56 (14,723)
Walters, Stuart 3:41:47 (6,109)
Walton, Chris 4:19:22 (14,584)
Walton, David 3:30:05 (4,180)
Walton, Dennis 4:42:01 (19,995)
Walton, Grahame 5:00:36 (24,090)
Walton, James 4:33:36 (18,077)
Walton, Jim 4:13:11 (13,044)
Walton, Kevin 4:14:57 (13,492)
Walton, Mark 5:20:06 (26,904)
Walton, Michael 3:12:10 (1,878)
Walton, Michael 4:47:31 (21,302)
Walton, Michael 4:50:38 (21,997)
Walton, Nigel 3:56:58 (9,444)
Walton, Peter 4:35:22 (18,486)
Walton, Phillip 5:19:59 (26,884)
Walton, Simon 4:16:21 (13,820)
Wan, Rob 4:16:54 (13,964)
Wan, Yum 4:07:03 (11,698)
Wane, Adam 4:27:10 (16,516)
Warburton, Lance 4:51:04 (22,091)
Warburton, Robert 4:08:35 (12,035)
Warburton, Thomas 5:00:21 (24,044)
Warburton-Smith, Brett 5:01:16 (24,201)
Ward, Alan 3:51:12 (8,011)
Ward, Andrew 3:43:15 (6,414)
Ward, Anthony 3:42:49 (6,318)
Ward, Anthony 4:35:53 (18,617)
Ward, Charles 4:11:50 (12,727)
Ward, Charles 5:25:48 (27,641)
Ward, Colin 3:18:36 (2,617)
Ward, Colin 4:02:04 (10,651)
Ward, Damien 3:41:43 (6,094)
Ward, Daniel 4:06:49 (11,652)
Ward, David 2:59:08 (866)
Ward, David 4:27:29 (16,600)
Ward, Des 5:47:22 (29,522)
Ward, Graham 4:50:20 (21,930)
Ward, Ian 3:10:47 (1,739)
Ward, Ian 4:24:46 (15,941)
Ward, James 4:11:18 (12,598)
Ward, John 3:06:30 (1,359)
Ward, John 3:34:19 (4,797)
Ward, John 3:41:45 (6,101)
Ward, John 3:51:37 (8,110)
Ward, John 4:41:56 (19,979)
Ward, John 5:14:45 (26,207)
Ward, John 5:41:45 (29,139)
Ward, Jonathan 5:43:39 (29,281)
Ward, Kevin 4:54:19 (22,772)
Ward, Kim 4:32:43 (17,885)
Ward, Mark 3:19:29 (2,699)
Ward, Martin 4:32:22 (17,807)
Ward, Martin 4:44:39 (20,649)
Ward, Martin 5:07:15 (25,134)
Ward, Matthew 3:40:03 (5,799)
Ward, Matthew 4:20:13 (14,798)
Ward, Melvin 3:44:49 (6,691)
Ward, Neil 4:29:06 (17,014)
Ward, Neil 4:48:41 (21,569)
Ward, Nigel 5:40:14 (29,013)
Ward, Peter 4:26:27 (16,345)
Ward, Philip 4:25:53 (16,224)
Ward, Ralph 3:27:15 (3,708)
Ward, Richard 4:38:33 (19,210)
Ward, Roy 3:47:59 (7,316)
Ward, Simon 4:22:33 (15,375)
Ward, Stephen 4:48:54 (21,614)
Ward, Steven 4:22:04 (15,256)
Ward, Timothy 5:31:19 (28,231)
Ward, William 5:34:09 (28,493)
Wardale, Terry 3:17:37 (2,505)
Ward-Booth, Alex 4:12:59 (13,000)
Wardell, Robert 4:16:03 (13,750)
Warden, Martin 6:30:03 (31,329)
Wardlaw, Robert 3:28:30 (3,903)
Wardle, Kim 4:02:45 (10,793)
Wardle, Steve 3:50:08 (7,761)
Ward-Thomas, Ewan 5:49:28 (29,674)
Ware, James 3:42:07 (6,171)
Ware, John 4:25:08 (16,037)
Ware, Martin 5:20:44 (26,990)
Ware, Nicholas 4:05:46 (11,447)
Ware, Robert 5:39:21 (28,927)
Ware, Thomas 4:18:54 (14,479)
Wareham, Bruce 3:55:17 (8,988)
Wareham, Sean 3:53:15 (8,487)
Wareing, Brian 2:56:21 (663)
Wareing, Peter 3:58:07 (9,733)
Warham, Roger 3:58:40 (9,877)
Waring, Carl 3:35:37 (5,015)
Warman, Cliff 4:32:45 (17,891)
Warman, Johnny 5:44:03 (29,306)
Warn, David 4:09:15 (12,184)
Warn, Timothy 3:24:32 (3,339)
Warne, Mark 4:41:49 (19,949)
Warne, Pete 3:37:10 (5,269)
Warne, Robert 3:33:52 (4,726)
Warne, Stephen 6:18:50 (30,968)
Warner, Aidan 4:44:46 (20,673)
Warner, Andrew 4:06:33 (11,601)
Warner, Anthony 3:14:06 (2,140)
Warner, Anthony 4:55:03 (22,934)
Warner, Charles 5:47:00 (29,490)
Warner, Daniel 5:11:20 (25,739)
Warner, David 2:32:57 (81)
Warner, David 4:03:24 (10,929)
Warner, Geoffrey 5:18:40 (26,723)
Warner, Kevin 4:39:07 (19,348)
Warner, Kim 3:22:49 (3,087)
Warner, Mark 4:04:49 (11,250)
Warner, Mark 6:10:05 (30,647)
Warner, Michael 3:25:46 (3,504)
Warnes, Peter 5:30:43 (28,168)
Warne-Thomas, Stephen 4:07:03 (11,698)
Warnock, Jim 3:20:51 (2,865)
Warnock, John 4:10:07 (12,378)
Warnock, Martin 4:25:11 (16,051)
Warnock, Michael 4:45:26 (20,829)
Warnock, Peter 3:54:25 (8,759)
Warre, Caspar 4:04:34 (11,191)
Warren, Andrew 3:33:10 (4,623)
Warren, Andrew 4:10:18 (12,417)
Warren, Carl 2:31:10 (68)
Warren, David 6:14:05 (30,800)
Warren, Edward 6:21:02 (31,052)
Warren, Mark 3:37:20 (5,296)
Warren, Mark 5:19:03 (26,763)
Warren, Peter 3:38:15 (5,452)
Warren, Peter 4:23:55 (15,724)
Warren, Richard 6:21:03 (31,053)
Warren, Stephen 4:07:17 (11,754)
Warrender, Benjamin 4:06:07 (11,519)
Warrick, Michael 3:05:35 (1,290)
Warriner, Keith 4:17:40 (14,165)
Warrington, Anthony 5:24:53 (27,517)
Warrington, Ian 4:49:28 (21,743)
Warrington, James 5:03:18 (24,505)
Warwick, Douglas 6:29:43 (31,320)
Warwick, Gary 5:04:27 (24,699)
Washbrook, Ian 4:40:41 (19,680)
Washington, Darren 3:09:08 (1,596)
Wasley, David 4:02:31 (10,746)
Wasley, Matt 4:02:30 (10,742)
Wasp, Gareth 4:10:05 (12,369)
Wass, Chris 5:02:21 (24,370)
Wassall, Peter 4:59:47 (23,947)
Watanabe, Toshinori 5:04:39 (24,723)
Watari, Makio 5:06:13 (24,988)
Watcham, Kevin 5:29:55 (28,076)
Waterfield, Alan 4:07:28 (11,799)
Waterfield, Hubert 5:14:58 (26,242)
Waterfield, Keith 5:05:03 (24,801)
Waterhouse, Andrew 3:40:46 (5,918)
Waterhouse, David 3:41:41 (6,090)
Waterman, David 3:35:49 (5,044)
Waterman, Lawrence 4:02:41 (10,779)
Waterman, Richard 4:38:02 (19,099)
Waterman, Ryan 3:09:18 (1,615)
Waterman, Stuart 3:52:12 (8,243)
Waters, Darren 4:21:44 (15,166)
Waters, Graham 4:33:51 (18,126)
Waterworth, Stephen 4:31:49 (17,692)
Wathan, Navin 4:54:57 (22,910)
Watkins, Benjamin 4:55:31 (23,031)
Watkins, Gavin 3:06:45 (1,382)
Watkins, Jonathan 6:22:49 (31,098)
Watkins, Mark 5:23:36 (27,358)
Watkins, Michael 4:47:16 (21,237)
Watkins, Simon 4:23:52 (15,712)
Watkinson, Brian 6:04:19 (30,424)
Watkinson, Peter 3:15:44 (2,310)
Watkinson, Robert 3:41:26 (6,052)
Watling, Christopher 3:30:53 (4,312)
Watling, Kenneth 5:52:10 (29,837)
Watmore, William 5:23:06 (27,300)
Watmough, Craig 3:49:57 (7,726)

Watsn, Hugh..............................4:53:52 (22,691)
Watson, Andrew 5:32:46 (28,353)
Watson, Andrew 6:03:45 (30,403)
Watson, Bill...............................4:15:41 (13,671)
Watson, Brian............................6:17:57 (30,932)
Watson, Caleb............................4:49:26 (21,733)
Watson, Clive.............................4:27:02 (16,480)
Watson, Daniel 4:24:52 (15,968)
Watson, Darren 3:58:21 (9,796)
Watson, Dave.............................5:08:04 (25,274)
Watson, Euan.............................6:43:15 (31,597)
Watson, Gary.............................4:51:16 (22,148)
Watson, Ian................................3:28:09 (3,838)
Watson, Ian................................4:34:23 (18,259)
Watson, James............................4:30:31 (17,370)
Watson, James............................5:13:07 (25,988)
Watson, Jerry.............................2:43:30 (207)
Watson, Keith............................4:07:31 (11,813)
Watson, Keith............................4:40:56 (19,736)
Watson, Kent..............................3:28:04 (3,829)
Watson, Kevin............................5:48:33 (29,609)
Watson, Mark.............................3:35:12 (4,942)
Watson, Mark.............................5:14:10 (26,117)
Watson, Matt..............................4:01:59 (10,630)
Watson, Michael....................146:27:06 (32,280)
Watson, Neil...............................4:10:15 (12,408)
Watson, Nicholas........................4:07:18 (11,756)
Watson, Paul..............................3:08:46 (1,570)
Watson, Paul..............................3:38:44 (5,549)
Watson, Paul..............................4:00:59 (10,426)
Watson, Paul..............................4:57:56 (23,568)
Watson, Peter 3:19:59 (2,758)
Watson, Peter 7:54:45 (32,246)
Watson, Phil...............................3:25:11 (3,425)
Watson, Robert...........................3:24:05 (3,263)
Watson, Robert...........................4:47:44 (21,353)
Watson, Simon 3:22:01 (2,988)
Watson, Simon 5:05:36 (24,900)
Watson, Stephen 5:13:07 (25,988)
Watson, Stephen 5:23:59 (27,406)
Watson, Steve.............................4:56:11 (23,195)
Watson, Steven 3:51:56 (8,180)
Watson, Stuart 3:39:13 (5,633)
Watt, Alan 4:16:19 (13,809)
Watt, Brian 3:32:44 (4,564)
Watt, David 4:15:33 (13,652)
Watt, Peter 4:07:06 (11,708)
Watt, Ritchie 5:43:01 (29,237)
Watters, Bryan 4:50:11 (21,900)
Watters, Michael........................3:55:07 (8,944)
Watterson, Mathew 4:38:46 (19,274)
Watterson, Tim...........................5:09:58 (25,536)
Wattley, Travis 4:34:06 (18,196)
Watts, Allen...............................5:43:46 (29,288)
Watts, Anthony 4:21:47 (15,180)
Watts, Christopher 5:30:13 (28,099)
Watts, David 3:54:09 (8,691)
Watts, Graham 5:47:43 (29,552)
Watts, Karl.................................3:39:41 (5,724)
Watts, Kevin 4:37:13 (18,925)
Watts, Lee 4:05:38 (11,423)
Watts, Michael 3:53:31 (8,548)
Watts, Nigel...............................4:17:53 (14,225)
Watts, Paul 4:29:10 (17,031)
Watts, Paul 4:55:32 (23,035)
Watts, Paul 5:06:33 (25,025)
Watts, Peter 3:50:58 (7,941)
Watts, Robert.............................3:03:03 (1,120)
Watts, Robert.............................4:44:09 (20,527)
Watts, Ronald 4:59:00 (23,802)
Watts, Roy.................................5:01:30 (24,233)
Watts, Stephen 5:58:58 (30,208)
Watts, Vincent 4:01:22 (10,509)
Waudby, Adrian 6:31:00 (31,350)
Waudby, Peter............................4:12:05 (12,780)
Waudby, Trevor 4:51:39 (22,235)
Waugh, Daniel 3:40:31 (5,868)
Waugh, Paul 4:48:58 (21,624)
Waumsley, Peter.........................3:42:00 (6,152)
Way, Benjamin 4:44:37 (20,637)
Way, Charles 3:16:08 (2,339)
Way, Tim 4:26:44 (16,413)
Wayland, John 6:08:25 (30,586)

Wayman, Christopher 3:40:06 (5,809)
Wayman, Tim 4:44:07 (20,522)
Wayne, Robert............................5:23:42 (27,369)
Weale, Tom................................3:51:49 (8,153)
Weatherall, Marc 3:08:35 (1,556)
Weatherall, Peter........................4:44:10 (20,533)
Weatherly, Robert.......................3:12:33 (1,938)
Weatherstone, Barry 4:55:43 (23,083)
Weaver, Derek............................3:01:57 (1,049)
Weaver, John 5:43:02 (29,238)
Weaver, Kevin 4:44:15 (20,557)
Weavers, Keith 4:50:40 (22,005)
Webb, Alan 4:09:57 (12,340)
Webb, Alan 4:24:36 (15,888)
Webb, Alex 3:00:42 (987)
Webb, Andrew 4:26:05 (16,272)
Webb, Andrew 4:53:54 (22,697)
Webb, Andy 6:19:50 (31,010)
Webb, Brian 3:46:38 (7,058)
Webb, Christopher 4:51:52 (22,283)
Webb, Colin 4:32:15 (17,784)
Webb, Darren 7:14:33 (32,034)
Webb, David 3:06:45 (1,382)
Webb, David 4:27:14 (16,529)
Webb, Derek 4:24:11 (15,794)
Webb, Gary 4:48:52 (21,602)
Webb, Joe 3:47:22 (7,183)
Webb, Martin 4:39:08 (19,353)
Webb, Matthew 5:03:54 (24,615)
Webb, Nicholas...........................4:39:30 (19,439)
Webb, Nick 4:39:16 (19,390)
Webb, Nigel 3:54:26 (8,763)
Webb, Paul 4:44:42 (20,658)
Webb, Peter 5:10:45 (25,654)
Webb, Richard 4:44:23 (20,591)
Webb, Simon 3:54:16 (8,723)
Webb, Steve 5:13:28 (26,037)
Webb, Terry 3:47:20 (7,179)
Webb, Timothy 2:59:43 (920)
Webb, Trevor 4:49:11 (21,673)
Webber, Brian 3:44:00 (6,544)
Webber, Graham 4:04:54 (11,270)
Webber, Ian 4:17:10 (14,027)
Webber, Paul 3:40:48 (5,925)
Webber, Steven 4:48:13 (21,475)
Weber-Hall, Stephen 4:14:31 (13,384)
Webster, Christopher 6:29:45 (31,324)
Webster, David 4:18:18 (14,303)
Webster, James 4:18:48 (14,446)
Webster, Jeremy 5:44:58 (29,364)
Webster, Jim 3:36:17 (5,113)
Webster, John 5:56:57 (30,104)
Webster, Jon 3:33:24 (4,666)
Webster, Lee 3:53:29 (8,536)
Webster, Mark 6:03:29 (30,393)
Webster, Peter............................4:01:27 (10,529)
Webster, Richard 4:43:08 (20,270)
Webster, Terry 3:46:43 (7,069)
Webster, Vincent 4:33:22 (18,024)
Wedderburn, Peter 4:00:39 (10,359)
Wedel, Anders 4:39:36 (19,459)
Wedge, Iain 2:58:52 (837)
Wedge, Marcus 4:12:38 (12,925)
Weedon, Paul 5:41:06 (29,084)
Weeedon, Derek..........................4:47:33 (21,308)
Weehuizen, Jan Willem................5:34:49 (28,542)
Weekes, Andrew 4:47:18 (21,247)
Weeks, Chris 3:24:45 (3,364)
Weemaes, Ronny 3:27:31 (3,740)
Weemaes, Rudy 3:50:52 (7,919)
Wegener, Karl 4:07:02 (11,691)
Wehner, Oliver 4:25:41 (16,177)
Wehrle, Stephen..........................6:39:04 (31,523)
Weidl, Norbert............................3:26:24 (3,591)
Weighill, Matthew 6:05:51 (30,496)
Weightman, Andrew 4:37:00 (18,878)
Weinel, Alastair 3:45:12 (6,773)
Weiner, Alan 5:11:10 (25,718)
Weiner, Mark 4:45:09 (20,757)
Weir, Andrew 2:25:00 (41)
Weir, Andrew 5:06:20 (24,998)
Weir, Antony 4:42:22 (20,074)
Weir, Paul..................................5:08:18 (25,311)

Weir, Peter 4:56:40 (23,306)
Weisker, Michael 3:55:54 (9,154)
Weiss, Milah 4:41:33 (19,882)
Welbourn, Brian..........................4:02:33 (10,749)
Welbourn, Matthew.....................5:40:41 (29,055)
Welbourn, Richard.......................3:22:16 (3,020)
Welby, Mark 4:26:34 (16,370)
Welch, Alan 2:41:35 (174)
Welch, Gary 4:39:48 (19,501)
Welch, Graham 5:10:20 (25,597)
Welch, Ian 4:10:14 (12,406)
Welch, James 3:58:01 (9,712)
Welch, Joseph 3:39:13 (5,633)
Welch, Stephen 4:28:55 (16,973)
Weldon, Anthony 5:47:58 (29,572)
Weldon, Brent 3:45:23 (6,806)
Welford, Justin 5:57:18 (30,120)
Welham, Lee 3:08:36 (1,557)
Welham, Robert 4:35:06 (18,414)
Welland, Mike 6:47:36 (31,668)
Weller, Allan 4:28:26 (16,837)
Weller, Bryan 6:32:33 (31,392)
Weller, Colin 3:52:19 (8,271)
Weller, Keith 4:47:58 (21,419)
Weller, Martin 3:42:13 (6,192)
Wellington, Stephen 5:41:01 (29,078)
Wellman, Edward 5:06:14 (24,993)
Wellman, Steven 3:11:51 (1,842)
Wellman, Timothy 3:30:25 (4,237)
Wells, Anthony 5:19:05 (26,768)
Wells, Daniel 3:02:05 (1,059)
Wells, Daniel 4:20:17 (14,817)
Wells, David 3:23:52 (3,226)
Wells, David 4:10:49 (12,514)
Wells, David 4:35:12 (18,442)
Wells, Donald 3:42:27 (6,231)
Wells, John 5:22:31 (27,217)
Wells, Keith 5:26:28 (27,733)
Wells, Kevin 4:47:22 (21,261)
Wells, Mark 5:15:14 (26,282)
Wells, Neil 4:22:51 (15,455)
Wells, Paul 4:35:33 (18,527)
Wells, Paul 5:17:04 (26,490)
Wells, Scott 5:22:38 (27,229)
Wells, Sean 5:05:36 (24,900)
Wells, Simon 4:16:42 (13,905)
Wells, Steven 5:02:35 (24,404)
Welsby, Christopher 7:20:41 (32,072)
Welsh, Andrew...........................3:47:44 (7,263)
Welsh, Charlie 3:26:27 (3,599)
Welsh, Christopher 3:37:24 (5,311)
Welsh, Darren.............................3:55:03 (8,927)
Welsh, Hadrian...........................7:17:35 (32,055)
Welz, Harold 3:52:52 (8,386)
Wendover, Ross 3:38:38 (5,529)
Wenlock, Tony............................3:50:44 (7,894)
Wentland, Gregory......................4:18:13 (14,288)
Wentworth, Alfred 4:38:13 (19,138)
Wentworth, Michael....................4:47:41 (21,344)
Wentworth-Stanley, Nicholas.......4:49:35 (21,776)
Wermter, Peter 4:43:26 (20,361)
Werner, Juergen 2:55:28 (617)
Werner, Schmid..........................3:26:41 (3,630)
Wersant, Joseph..........................4:44:33 (20,622)
Wescomb, Christopher 3:10:54 (1,747)
Wesel, Peter 3:12:04 (1,869)
Wesley, Stephen 4:02:47 (10,803)
Wessinghage, Thomas..................3:01:02 (1,007)
Wesson, Will 3:09:38 (1,648)
West, Andrew 3:43:04 (6,380)
West, Andrew 3:56:19 (9,276)
West, Andrew 4:08:45 (12,078)
West, Andy 5:47:19 (29,519)
West, Arnold 5:07:22 (25,155)
West, Colin 3:00:12 (951)
West, Colin 4:38:08 (19,114)
West, Daniel 5:12:27 (25,888)
West, James 4:19:41 (14,665)
West, James 4:51:46 (22,258)
West, Jason 4:09:18 (12,197)
West, Kenneth 4:42:24 (20,085)
West, Kevin 2:52:18 (459)
West, Mark 4:44:52 (20,689)

West, Michael 4:11:05 (12,552)
West, Michael 4:51:47 (22,264)
West, Morley 4:48:04 (21,444)
West, Richard 3:02:01 (1,054)
West, Rory 4:48:06 (21,451)
West, Shaun 4:25:53 (16,224)
West, Steve 5:01:09 (24,176)
West, Tim 5:07:56 (25,255)
Westcott, Christopher 4:22:50 (15,449)
Westcott, Mark 4:01:22 (10,509)
Westcough, Steven 3:45:06 (6,755)
Wester, Samuel 3:39:50 (5,754)
Westerman, Jerry 3:49:05 (7,532)
Westerman, Mick 3:36:57 (5,223)
Western, Ashley 4:04:00 (11,062)
Western, Ivan 4:56:50 (23,347)
Westgate, Nicholas 3:42:32 (6,260)
Westheimer, Danny 3:15:22 (2,276)
Westlake, Nick 4:29:01 (16,994)
Westlake, Philip 5:55:01 (29,999)
Westmancoat, Keith 6:10:37 (30,667)
Westmoreland, Jason 3:18:20 (2,595)
Weston, Barry 5:04:59 (24,791)
Weston, Greg 4:17:13 (14,036)
Weston, Mark 3:31:36 (4,425)
Weston, Stephen 3:10:23 (1,710)
Westpfel, Ashley 4:42:26 (20,093)
Westwell, Steven 5:10:01 (25,552)
Westwood, David 3:42:29 (6,243)
Westwood, Jamie 3:28:12 (3,851)
Westwood, Nigel 4:50:50 (22,038)
Westwood, Robert 4:51:23 (22,177)
Wetherill, Andrew 2:29:18 (59)
Wetmore, Tim 2:53:52 (525)
Wetton, Nicholas 4:51:40 (22,241)
Whadlock, David 5:07:00 (25,107)
Whale, Christopher 4:51:09 (22,119)
Whale, Matthew 3:11:07 (1,768)
Whale, Matthew 4:13:52 (13,220)
Whale, Richard 5:02:51 (24,438)
Whaley, Michael 6:15:42 (30,848)
Whalley, Adrian 3:27:04 (3,691)
Whalley, Peter 4:34:26 (18,275)
Whalley, Simon 3:17:23 (2,475)
Whateley-Harris, Ben 4:39:17 (19,391)
Whatford, Howard 5:01:59 (24,311)
Whatley, Andrew 4:15:09 (13,554)
Whawell, Michael 5:44:39 (29,339)
Wheable, Paul 3:40:21 (5,852)
Wheat, Alan 3:42:04 (6,162)
Wheatley, David 4:12:29 (12,880)
Wheatley, Iain 4:08:43 (12,068)
Wheatley, Ian 3:12:16 (1,893)
Wheatley, Matthew 4:30:00 (17,241)
Wheatley, Stephen 4:29:22 (17,081)
Wheeldon, Brian 3:38:21 (5,469)
Wheeldon, Dean 3:31:39 (4,427)
Wheeldon, Scott 5:19:03 (26,763)
Wheeler, Alan 3:31:51 (4,453)
Wheeler, Andrew 3:14:53 (2,224)
Wheeler, Christopher 3:27:23 (3,718)
Wheeler, Jeremy 4:52:30 (22,396)
Wheeler, Jonathan 4:20:14 (14,802)
Wheeler, Ralph 4:31:19 (17,570)
Wheeler, Simon 5:04:44 (24,742)
Wheeler, Sydney 3:36:31 (5,146)
Wheeler, Timothy 4:22:40 (15,412)
Whelan, John 5:38:39 (28,872)
Whelan, Martin 4:41:53 (19,971)
Whelan, Matthew 3:51:48 (8,149)
Whelan, Michael 4:07:05 (11,705)
Whelan, Thomas 4:32:20 (17,798)
Whelan, Timothy 5:12:53 (25,956)
Whelband, Gary 5:43:31 (29,274)
Whelehan, Oliver 3:56:47 (9,393)
Wheller, Stephen 6:22:43 (31,094)
Whiffin, Eric 5:00:12 (24,016)
Whiffin, James 3:28:37 (3,929)
Whiles, Stephen 4:43:49 (20,464)
Whillis, Simon 4:07:57 (11,895)
Whilock, Stacey 3:56:10 (9,228)
Whippy, John 4:21:08 (15,014)
Whitaker, Andrew 4:08:15 (11,947)
Whitaker, Andrew 5:41:13 (29,094)
Whitaker, Christopher 3:41:20 (6,023)
Whitaker, Keith 3:51:00 (7,953)
Whitaker, Steven 4:47:25 (21,279)
Whitaker, Timothy 4:15:58 (13,734)
Whitbread, Scott 5:02:27 (24,382)
Whitby, Adrian 4:36:28 (18,762)
Whitcombe, Paul 3:03:08 (1,127)
White, Adrian 4:41:51 (19,960)
White, Andrew 3:41:05 (5,974)
White, Andrew 4:39:13 (19,377)
White, Anthony 3:08:29 (1,545)
White, Barry 4:25:22 (16,107)
White, Bijan 3:40:41 (5,901)
White, Christopher 4:11:43 (12,699)
White, Christopher 4:23:19 (15,578)
White, Dan 4:15:07 (13,544)
White, Daniel 4:13:18 (13,075)
White, David 3:28:19 (3,871)
White, David 5:03:39 (24,557)
White, Derek 3:23:43 (3,207)
White, Derek 5:15:58 (26,374)
White, Douglas 5:36:31 (28,685)
White, Duncan 4:50:34 (21,979)
White, Frank 3:09:54 (1,667)
White, Gary 4:36:57 (18,866)
White, Geroge 4:21:30 (15,113)
White, Graham 5:20:30 (26,957)
White, Ian 2:52:40 (479)
White, Ian 3:19:39 (2,719)
White, James 3:44:14 (6,589)
White, Jamie 2:59:33 (907)
White, Jason 4:46:47 (21,143)
White, Jeremy 5:52:56 (29,877)
White, John 4:07:09 (11,725)
White, John 4:13:22 (13,086)
White, John 4:22:09 (15,276)
White, John 4:32:22 (17,807)
White, John 5:45:41 (29,418)
White, Jonathan 5:56:28 (30,078)
White, Karl 4:23:50 (15,703)
White, Mark 4:22:48 (15,442)
White, Mark 4:25:21 (16,104)
White, Martin 4:32:58 (17,944)
White, Martin 4:49:13 (21,679)
White, Nicholas 3:09:17 (1,611)
White, Paul 3:17:25 (2,478)
White, Paul 4:41:39 (19,906)
White, Peter 3:59:10 (9,997)
White, Philip 4:58:01 (23,583)
White, Richard 4:13:11 (13,044)
White, Richard 4:53:22 (22,589)
White, Robert 3:23:39 (3,198)
White, Robert 4:31:17 (17,563)
White, Robert 5:01:08 (24,173)
White, Ronald 4:01:40 (10,572)
White, Simon 4:09:53 (12,318)
White, Simon 5:02:31 (24,391)
White, Stephen 4:46:35 (21,104)
White, Steve 3:12:30 (1,929)
White, Steve 3:50:10 (7,767)
White, Steve 3:51:37 (8,110)
White, Stuart 5:41:59 (29,161)
White, Timothy 3:50:00 (7,734)
White, Tony 5:50:29 (29,752)
Whiteaker, James 5:07:31 (25,186)
Whitefield, Alan 4:31:25 (17,595)
Whiteford, Derek 3:23:53 (3,230)
Whiteford, James 5:16:39 (26,445)
Whitehall, Robert 2:48:36 (351)
Whitehead, Alan 4:55:09 (22,955)
Whitehead, Carl 4:51:08 (22,115)
Whitehead, David 4:02:01 (10,639)
Whitehead, Graham 3:25:14 (3,432)
Whitehead, Malcolm 3:51:42 (8,128)
Whitehead, Richard 5:19:58 (26,883)
Whitehorne, Hilton 3:50:58 (7,941)
Whitehouse, Andrew 4:24:13 (15,800)
Whitehouse, Joseph 4:02:28 (10,736)
Whitehouse, Lee 6:18:12 (30,943)
Whitehouse, Mark 4:23:02 (15,500)
Whitehurst, David 4:00:12 (10,271)
Whitehurst, Richard 4:33:28 (18,051)
Whiteland, Geoff 4:47:48 (21,375)
Whitelaw, Davie 3:57:56 (9,690)
Whitelaw, Mark 2:44:11 (221)
Whitelegg, Richard 2:40:35 (161)
Whiteley, Mike 3:49:08 (7,543)
Whitelock, Mark 3:16:25 (2,368)
Whitelock, Neil 3:54:52 (8,885)
Whiteman, Richard 4:20:12 (14,794)
Whiteman, Simon 4:27:26 (16,578)
Whitemore, Tom 5:26:13 (27,704)
Whiter, George 4:18:19 (14,307)
Whiter, Roger 4:28:24 (16,828)
Whiteside, Andrew 4:25:58 (16,242)
Whitesmith, Michael 4:11:23 (12,618)
Whitfield, Adam 4:33:48 (18,115)
Whitford, Frank 3:21:08 (2,895)
Whiting, Gregg 3:52:25 (8,292)
Whiting, John 6:54:47 (31,828)
Whiting, Richard 3:36:50 (5,199)
Whiting, Simeon 4:58:49 (23,768)
Whiting, Simon 3:41:52 (6,126)
Whiting, Tim 5:30:35 (28,150)
Whitley, David 4:34:31 (18,290)
Whitley, Michael 4:15:45 (13,685)
Whitley, Nat 3:29:37 (4,114)
Whitley, Richard 4:32:48 (17,898)
Whitlock, Paul 3:14:24 (2,177)
Whitlock, Russell 3:59:38 (10,130)
Whitmill, Martin 4:46:43 (21,129)
Whitmore, Ivon 2:59:02 (859)
Whitmore, John 4:06:16 (11,549)
Whitney, Lee 3:50:35 (7,864)
Whittaker, David 3:44:20 (6,605)
Whittaker, Dennis 4:09:00 (12,129)
Whittaker, Peter 5:42:44 (29,226)
Whittaker, Simon 6:23:32 (31,123)
Whittell, Stuart 4:03:24 (10,929)
Whittemore, Bill 5:01:58 (24,308)
Whittenbury, Robert 5:06:24 (25,008)
Whittingham, Conrad 5:30:32 (28,143)
Whittingham, Iain 3:37:04 (5,247)
Whittingham, Philip 4:46:10 (21,009)
Whittington, Russell 3:58:22 (9,801)
Whittle, Alan 5:38:56 (28,892)
Whittle, David 3:46:41 (7,063)
Whittle, Nigel 3:30:13 (4,203)
Whitton, Mark 4:51:54 (22,291)
Whitton, Simon 3:54:36 (8,817)
Whitworth, Bill 3:58:14 (9,764)
Whitworth, David 3:41:30 (6,067)
Whorlow, Derek 4:33:38 (18,080)
Whtington, Stephen 3:20:44 (2,850)
Whybourn, Jean 4:55:44 (23,091)
Whyman, Mark 4:42:30 (20,109)
Whyndham, Matthew 3:55:38 (9,088)
Whyte, Alistair 4:02:16 (10,692)
Whyte, Bruce 4:59:44 (23,931)
Whyte, Gregory 3:22:19 (3,023)
Whyte, Ian 3:17:25 (2,478)
Whyte, Peter 3:39:18 (5,655)
Wiazowski, Peter 3:34:13 (4,783)
Wick, Heiko 4:55:35 (23,048)
Wick, Wolfgang 3:33:05 (4,611)
Wickenden, Anthony 5:11:22 (25,747)
Wickens, James 5:27:29 (27,828)
Wickham, Graham 4:04:05 (11,084)
Wickham, Henry 4:24:01 (15,756)
Wickham, Ian 4:47:01 (21,187)
Wickham, Peter 3:52:39 (8,344)
Wickham, Stefan 5:06:31 (25,021)
Wickham, Stephen 3:13:54 (2,115)
Wicking, Andrew 6:43:49 (31,609)
Wickins, Michael 4:36:28 (18,762)
Wickramasinghe, Eranda 3:33:53 (4,730)
Wicks, Matt 4:23:02 (15,500)
Wicks, Pete 3:23:14 (3,144)
Wicks, Philip 3:03:33 (1,155)
Widmer, Bernard 3:21:35 (2,939)
Wieckowski, Paul 3:19:12 (2,671)
Wieder, Matthias 3:44:13 (6,587)
Wiegand, Klaus 3:20:23 (2,814)
Wieland, Andrew 5:05:46 (24,930)
Wigens, John 3:52:44 (8,361)

Wigg, Michael	4:45:11 (20,767)	
Wiggans, Andrew	3:58:59 (9,962)	
Wiggett, Paul	4:29:37 (17,144)	
Wiggin, Joseph	4:08:00 (11,905)	
Wiggins, Michael	3:18:49 (2,639)	
Wiggins, Norman	3:08:01 (1,500)	
Wigginton, Richard	4:07:58 (11,899)	
Wigham, David	4:14:53 (13,475)	
Wigmore, James	3:13:52 (2,109)	
Wigmore, Nick	2:36:48 (118)	
Wignall, Derek	3:55:17 (8,988)	
Wigzell, Edward	4:24:14 (15,805)	
Wilbraham, Stephen	3:34:25 (4,823)	
Wilby, Leonard	5:16:22 (26,412)	
Wilcock, Martin	2:53:58 (532)	
Wilcock, Neil	4:45:06 (20,743)	
Wilcock, Paul	3:22:45 (3,077)	
Wilcock, Philip	5:06:24 (25,008)	
Wilcock, Roger	4:30:12 (17,287)	
Wilcox, Mark	2:45:31 (247)	
Wilcox, Sean	3:56:25 (9,297)	
Wild, Andrew	4:11:35 (12,663)	
Wild, Mark	4:11:06 (12,553)	
Wild, Oscar	3:59:10 (9,997)	
Wild, Roger	4:15:27 (13,627)	
Wild, Stuart	4:32:10 (17,767)	
Wilde, Anthony	4:54:14 (22,753)	
Wilde, Ben	3:49:07 (7,537)	
Wilde, Benjamin	4:27:23 (16,567)	
Wilde, James	4:40:18 (19,608)	
Wilder, Christopher	3:45:16 (6,784)	
Wilder, Paul	4:58:32 (23,704)	
Wildgoose, Ian	5:21:42 (27,108)	
Wilding, Simon	5:06:47 (25,073)	
Wilds, Tony	4:34:01 (18,170)	
Wiles, Robert	3:44:43 (6,674)	
Wiles, Simon	3:14:53 (2,224)	
Wiles, Stephen	4:15:18 (13,592)	
Wilhelmsson, Mikael	3:21:51 (2,967)	
Wiliams, Colin	3:40:20 (5,851)	
Wiliams, Frank	3:15:04 (2,244)	
Wiliams, Ian	5:10:53 (25,670)	
Wiliams, Noel	5:01:08 (24,173)	
Wiliams, Philip	4:59:18 (23,858)	
Wiliams, Simon	4:13:35 (13,146)	
Wiliams, William	6:07:23 (30,549)	
Wiliamson, Paul	3:28:51 (3,977)	
Wilkes, Antony	4:07:50 (11,879)	
Wilkes, Bernard	3:47:22 (7,183)	
Wilkes, Jim	4:16:52 (13,954)	
Wilkes, Michael	5:07:03 (25,113)	
Wilkes, Peter	4:12:30 (12,887)	
Wilkie, Alexander	4:17:28 (14,108)	
Wilkie, David	4:14:58 (13,500)	
Wilkie, Thomas	5:11:01 (25,694)	
Wilkin, Andrew	3:52:39 (8,344)	
Wilkins, Graham	5:02:57 (24,449)	
Wilkins, Ian	4:46:19 (21,050)	
Wilkins, Nigel	5:28:23 (27,931)	
Wilkins, Paul	4:16:26 (13,843)	
Wilkins, Robert	4:47:04 (21,194)	
Wilkins, Ted	5:15:11 (26,277)	
Wilkinson, Andrew	3:43:46 (6,503)	
Wilkinson, Anrew	4:06:43 (11,630)	
Wilkinson, Anthony	3:59:52 (10,193)	
Wilkinson, Ben	5:27:46 (27,867)	
Wilkinson, Benjamin	3:30:53 (4,312)	
Wilkinson, Clifford	5:03:40 (24,560)	
Wilkinson, David	3:58:01 (9,712)	
Wilkinson, Duncan	4:16:55 (13,975)	
Wilkinson, Geoffrey	4:26:20 (16,323)	
Wilkinson, Graham	2:47:28 (315)	
Wilkinson, Graham	3:52:26 (8,296)	
Wilkinson, Henry	4:02:22 (10,711)	
Wilkinson, Ian	3:52:28 (8,300)	
Wilkinson, Ian	4:51:49 (22,270)	
Wilkinson, James	3:51:10 (8,002)	
Wilkinson, Jamie	3:47:58 (7,311)	
Wilkinson, Jerome	3:51:20 (8,039)	
Wilkinson, Jonathan	6:24:57 (31,160)	
Wilkinson, Kevin	5:13:10 (25,995)	
Wilkinson, Leslie	5:59:24 (30,233)	
Wilkinson, Martin	3:18:47 (2,635)	

Wilkinson, Michael	5:22:29 (27,210)	
Wilkinson, Neil	3:50:15 (7,788)	
Wilkinson, Nicholas	5:04:52 (24,772)	
Wilkinson, Nigel	3:31:57 (4,465)	
Wilkinson, Paul	3:53:07 (8,453)	
Wilkinson, Peter	5:20:32 (26,960)	
Wilkinson, Richard	4:25:50 (16,211)	
Wilkinson, Richard	5:27:43 (27,861)	
Wilkinson, Robert	4:00:35 (10,342)	
Wilkinson, Stephen	4:47:27 (21,287)	
Wilkinson, Steven	3:24:18 (3,305)	
Wilkinson, Trevor	4:30:55 (17,473)	
Wilklinson, Gerry	4:27:36 (16,624)	
Wilks, Derek	4:04:06 (11,090)	
Wilks, Steve	4:32:32 (17,840)	
Willard, Adrian	4:38:00 (19,088)	
Willcox, David	4:35:19 (18,476)	
Willcox, Michael	3:01:37 (1,031)	
Willett, Kevin	2:54:43 (575)	
Willett, Lee	4:31:01 (17,502)	
Willett, Raymond	3:42:33 (6,265)	
Willett, Richard	5:53:05 (29,884)	
Willett, Timothy	4:44:54 (20,697)	
Willetts, Guy	4:25:02 (16,010)	
Willetts, William	4:13:06 (13,023)	
Willey, Paul	5:47:16 (29,510)	
Willey, Timothy	4:28:15 (16,780)	
Willfratt, Kevin	4:41:39 (19,906)	
Williams, Aled	5:01:50 (24,288)	
Williams, Aled	5:09:01 (25,411)	
Williams, Alexander	4:50:32 (21,974)	
Williams, Alexander	5:20:01 (26,890)	
Williams, Alun	3:05:07 (1,263)	
Williams, Alun	4:40:14 (19,586)	
Williams, Andrew	4:27:41 (16,643)	
Williams, Andy	3:27:49 (3,787)	
Williams, Andy	4:27:20 (16,555)	
Williams, Andy	4:53:37 (22,640)	
Williams, Anthony	4:20:25 (14,851)	
Williams, Anthony	5:27:09 (27,797)	
Williams, Antony	3:50:09 (7,765)	
Williams, Ashley	3:41:04 (5,971)	
Williams, Ayo	4:47:30 (21,298)	
Williams, Barry	5:26:55 (27,771)	
Williams, Ben	3:45:14 (6,780)	
Williams, Benjamin	3:30:05 (4,180)	
Williams, Brian	5:00:36 (24,090)	
Williams, Carl	3:50:17 (7,796)	
Williams, Charles	4:00:29 (10,326)	
Williams, Chris	3:42:23 (6,216)	
Williams, Chris	3:54:36 (8,817)	
Williams, Chris	4:21:57 (15,224)	
Williams, Chris	4:29:23 (17,084)	
Williams, Chris	4:58:46 (23,755)	
Williams, Christopher	4:28:23 (16,817)	
Williams, Christopher	5:04:45 (24,747)	
Williams, Colin	3:34:26 (4,824)	
Williams, Cyril	4:50:55 (22,055)	
Williams, Dale	3:50:13 (7,783)	
Williams, Darren	2:53:05 (496)	
Williams, Darren	3:47:33 (7,223)	
Williams, David	2:33:13 (85)	
Williams, David	3:54:34 (8,809)	
Williams, David	3:58:33 (9,849)	
Williams, David	4:12:12 (12,819)	
Williams, David	4:25:07 (16,031)	
Williams, David	4:39:28 (19,434)	
Williams, David	4:45:01 (20,721)	
Williams, David	5:21:43 (27,112)	
Williams, David	5:47:14 (29,508)	
Williams, Dennis	3:25:56 (3,533)	
Williams, Dennis	5:13:40 (26,065)	
Williams, Derek	3:45:29 (6,828)	
Williams, Edward	5:00:45 (24,119)	
Williams, Frank	4:47:38 (21,328)	
Williams, Gareth	2:28:35 (56)	
Williams, Gareth	3:03:33 (1,155)	
Williams, Gareth	4:46:12 (21,018)	
Williams, Gareth	5:14:35 (26,188)	
Williams, Gareth	5:18:37 (26,716)	
Williams, Gareth	5:20:47 (26,996)	
Williams, Gary	4:01:24 (10,519)	
Williams, Gary	4:58:46 (23,755)	

Williams, Geoff	3:39:49 (5,751)	
Williams, Glyn	4:03:20 (10,919)	
Williams, Huw	3:14:19 (2,165)	
Williams, Huw	4:06:26 (11,578)	
Williams, Ian	4:40:09 (19,571)	
Williams, Iolo	4:12:41 (12,935)	
Williams, James	4:01:27 (10,529)	
Williams, James	4:34:03 (18,176)	
Williams, James	4:37:13 (18,925)	
Williams, Jason	3:23:49 (3,214)	
Williams, John	3:35:47 (5,037)	
Williams, John	4:17:37 (14,147)	
Williams, John	4:18:41 (14,419)	
Williams, John	5:21:52 (27,132)	
Williams, John	5:41:40 (29,133)	
Williams, John	5:59:20 (30,228)	
Williams, John	6:25:42 (31,191)	
Williams, Joseph	5:10:45 (25,654)	
Williams, Keith	4:47:24 (21,274)	
Williams, Ken	5:23:48 (27,383)	
Williams, Kevin	3:34:05 (4,758)	
Williams, Kevin	4:45:03 (20,728)	
Williams, Kevin	6:08:51 (30,600)	
Williams, Les	3:42:49 (6,318)	
Williams, Leslie	4:02:42 (10,781)	
Williams, Luke	3:19:18 (2,678)	
Williams, Marc	4:27:30 (16,603)	
Williams, Mark	3:20:09 (2,779)	
Williams, Mark	3:22:32 (3,052)	
Williams, Mark	3:29:23 (4,062)	
Williams, Mark	4:08:07 (11,924)	
Williams, Mark	4:12:54 (12,984)	
Williams, Mark	4:40:59 (19,748)	
Williams, Mark	4:50:15 (21,909)	
Williams, Mark	4:52:03 (22,320)	
Williams, Mark	4:59:13 (23,846)	
Williams, Mark	5:16:41 (26,449)	
Williams, Mark	5:39:10 (28,917)	
Williams, Martin	3:16:07 (2,337)	
Williams, Martin	4:46:52 (21,165)	
Williams, Martin	4:54:10 (22,738)	
Williams, Martin	8:04:34 (32,262)	
Williams, Martyn	4:45:08 (20,755)	
Williams, Matthew	5:53:32 (29,906)	
Williams, Michael	3:02:41 (1,094)	
Williams, Michael	3:49:36 (7,656)	
Williams, Michael	4:18:03 (14,260)	
Williams, Mike	4:57:08 (23,411)	
Williams, Nathan	4:21:59 (15,236)	
Williams, Neil	3:31:09 (4,351)	
Williams, Neil	3:32:45 (4,567)	
Williams, Neil	4:30:57 (17,481)	
Williams, Neville	4:13:32 (13,134)	
Williams, Nicholas	3:38:21 (5,469)	
Williams, Osian	4:25:32 (16,145)	
Williams, Paul	3:41:16 (6,000)	
Williams, Paul	3:49:34 (7,646)	
Williams, Paul	4:07:26 (11,788)	
Williams, Paul	4:29:44 (17,171)	
Williams, Paul	4:46:34 (21,100)	
Williams, Paul	4:53:10 (22,537)	
Williams, Paul	5:09:33 (25,488)	
Williams, Paul	5:14:46 (26,212)	
Williams, Paul	5:24:00 (27,409)	
Williams, Paul	6:48:06 (31,677)	
Williams, Peter	3:30:05 (4,180)	
Williams, Peter	3:52:12 (8,243)	
Williams, Peter	5:49:17 (29,661)	
Williams, Peter	7:20:44 (32,073)	
Williams, Phillip	3:46:27 (7,020)	
Williams, Ray	3:20:57 (2,878)	
Williams, Reginald	3:53:46 (8,608)	
Williams, Rhodri	3:59:16 (10,027)	
Williams, Richard	4:15:12 (13,567)	
Williams, Richard	4:20:06 (14,770)	
Williams, Robert	5:05:42 (24,921)	
Williams, Robert	5:28:54 (27,976)	
Williams, Russell	4:22:23 (15,336)	
Williams, Scott	3:49:54 (7,712)	
Williams, Sebastian	4:03:16 (10,906)	
Williams, Simon	4:00:18 (10,297)	
Williams, Simon	4:04:27 (11,163)	
Williams, Simon	4:21:02 (14,988)	

Williams, Simon 4:57:46 (23,537)	Wilson, Andy 3:23:27 (3,172)	Winfield, Stephen 3:43:40 (6,480)
Williams, Stephen 2:56:08 (655)	Wilson, Anthony 5:08:36 (25,346)	Winfield, Steven 3:25:43 (3,500)
Williams, Stephen 4:18:38 (14,403)	Wilson, Barry 2:46:23 (272)	Wing, John 3:51:07 (7,981)
Williams, Stewart 5:01:49 (24,284)	Wilson, Benjamin 7:25:26 (32,111)	Wing, Stephen 6:22:08 (31,080)
Williams, Stuart 3:18:12 (2,578)	Wilson, Charlie 4:09:37 (12,253)	Wingate, Carl 4:33:55 (18,147)
Williams, Stuart 4:59:36 (23,903)	Wilson, Chris 4:39:17 (19,391)	Wingate, Matthew 3:34:58 (4,905)
Williams, Thomas 3:31:02 (4,335)	Wilson, Christopher 2:43:25 (205)	Wingate, Thomas 5:31:26 (28,241)
Williams, Tim 3:46:17 (6,991)	Wilson, Christopher 3:42:29 (6,243)	Wingfield, Geoff 5:19:22 (26,809)
Williams, Tom 4:21:24 (15,088)	Wilson, Christopher 4:34:47 (18,348)	Wingrove, Andrew 4:42:48 (20,180)
Williams, Tom 5:15:59 (26,377)	Wilson, Christopher 5:12:53 (25,956)	Wingrove, Philip 4:20:43 (14,907)
Williams, Trevor 4:54:11 (22,744)	Wilson, Damian 3:48:36 (7,425)	Winkler, Andreas 4:35:18 (18,471)
Williams, Vincent 3:06:00 (1,322)	Wilson, Daniel 3:41:47 (6,109)	Winks, Gary 4:37:55 (19,069)
Williamson, Adrian 3:36:36 (5,160)	Wilson, David 4:43:11 (20,281)	Winn, Michael 2:54:09 (545)
Williamson, Anthony 4:50:57 (22,059)	Wilson, David 4:47:27 (21,287)	Winnery, Keith 4:28:15 (16,780)
Williamson, Bruce 3:13:27 (2,058)	Wilson, David 5:11:34 (25,770)	Winsbury, Mark 4:05:02 (11,299)
Williamson, Chris 4:12:09 (12,799)	Wilson, Derek 4:57:54 (23,561)	Winship, Stewart 5:15:57 (26,369)
Williamson, Craig 3:22:19 (3,023)	Wilson, Desmond 5:24:26 (27,465)	Winslow, Michael 3:46:21 (7,005)
Williamson, David 5:24:27 (27,468)	Wilson, Dominick 6:17:35 (30,908)	Winstanley, Andrew 4:32:57 (17,935)
Williamson, Dennis 6:08:25 (30,586)	Wilson, Donough 5:52:31 (29,853)	Winstanley, Graham 5:47:01 (29,492)
Williamson, Glen 4:03:52 (11,031)	Wilson, Duncan 3:49:40 (7,672)	Winstanley, Granville 5:03:28 (24,524)
Williamson, Malcolm 5:05:59 (24,955)	Wilson, Dylan 3:23:36 (3,191)	Winstanley, James 5:23:53 (27,396)
Williamson, Mark 3:13:20 (2,039)	Wilson, Gary 5:11:15 (25,731)	Winstanley, Peter 4:52:51 (22,470)
Williamson, Mark 5:04:01 (24,633)	Wilson, George 3:31:18 (4,381)	Winstanley, Simon 4:06:44 (11,637)
Williamson, Mark 6:21:45 (31,068)	Wilson, Graham 5:02:48 (24,432)	Winstone, Eric 3:41:48 (6,113)
Williamson, Matthew 4:54:21 (22,779)	Wilson, Hugh 3:23:20 (3,153)	Winter, Alan 4:26:02 (16,254)
Williamson, Matthew 5:48:17 (29,594)	Wilson, Ian 2:55:27 (615)	Winter, Ashley 4:27:34 (16,617)
Williamson, Neil 5:27:54 (27,883)	Wilson, Ian 4:55:31 (23,031)	Winter, Dean 3:49:25 (7,613)
Williamson, Peter 4:23:06 (15,512)	Wilson, Ian 5:20:34 (26,965)	Winter, Martin 3:42:59 (6,364)
Williamson, Rupert 3:57:14 (9,513)	Wilson, Jason 3:44:58 (6,727)	Winter, Matthew 4:46:58 (21,177)
Williamson, Wesley 4:24:00 (15,751)	Wilson, Jason 4:12:25 (12,864)	Winter, Warwick 5:55:21 (30,018)
Willis, Andrew 4:29:38 (17,146)	Wilson, Jeff 5:00:08 (23,998)	Winters, John 3:55:27 (9,035)
Willis, Darrn 5:34:47 (28,536)	Wilson, John 3:42:43 (6,301)	Winters, Michael 3:39:54 (5,770)
Willis, David 5:27:02 (27,778)	Wilson, John 3:57:58 (9,698)	Winters, Stephen 3:57:01 (9,481)
Willis, Howard 4:29:35 (17,134)	Wilson, Keith 4:18:37 (14,399)	Wintersgill, Graham 3:48:16 (7,371)
Willis, James 5:24:30 (27,475)	Wilson, Kenneth 3:43:24 (6,437)	Wintersgill, Neil 5:00:11 (24,009)
Willis, John 4:05:38 (11,423)	Wilson, Laurence 5:00:55 (24,141)	Wintle, David 3:02:54 (1,106)
Willis, Jonathan 4:32:22 (17,807)	Wilson, Lee 3:34:06 (4,762)	Wintle, George 4:21:39 (15,143)
Willis, Kevin 3:51:33 (8,092)	Wilson, Marc 3:51:26 (8,057)	Winton, Edward 4:28:06 (16,735)
Willis, Michael 3:25:40 (3,486)	Wilson, Mark 3:26:47 (3,641)	Wintour, Matthew 5:05:28 (24,874)
Willis, Nathan 4:35:15 (18,459)	Wilson, Mark 4:05:28 (11,395)	Winzer, Mirko 4:10:02 (12,356)
Willis, Paul 5:22:56 (27,274)	Wilson, Mark 4:27:45 (16,666)	Wipf, Fernand 3:59:38 (10,130)
Willis, Peter 3:19:11 (2,670)	Wilson, Mark 5:00:44 (24,113)	Wirrer, Walter 3:54:01 (8,670)
Willis, Stephen 3:17:04 (2,435)	Wilson, Martin 3:26:45 (3,639)	Wirz, Thierry 3:11:06 (1,765)
Willis, Stephen 3:46:40 (7,061)	Wilson, Matthew 4:20:34 (14,883)	Wisdish, Robert 5:58:54 (30,200)
Willis, Stuart 4:41:47 (19,938)	Wilson, Michael 3:25:54 (3,531)	Wisdom, Gareth 5:06:53 (25,093)
Willis, Tim 3:59:09 (9,991)	Wilson, Neale 5:30:29 (28,139)	Wisdom, Julian 4:37:30 (18,984)
Willmitt, William 2:58:44 (825)	Wilson, Paul 3:00:10 (950)	Wise, Alan 3:48:45 (7,453)
Willmore, Adam 5:33:08 (28,383)	Wilson, Peter 4:49:41 (21,799)	Wise, Ben 4:09:22 (12,207)
Willott, Guy 5:36:31 (28,685)	Wilson, Peter 5:01:46 (24,274)	Wise, Chris 3:31:06 (4,342)
Willoughby, Gary 3:27:24 (3,722)	Wilson, Richard 3:45:00 (6,737)	Wise, Daniel 5:06:09 (24,976)
Willoughby, Keith 6:15:16 (30,833)	Wilson, Richard 6:26:02 (31,206)	Wise, George 4:08:30 (12,011)
Willoughby, Mark 5:35:54 (28,615)	Wilson, Rob 4:07:14 (11,745)	Wise, Stephen 4:46:43 (21,129)
Willoughby, Rex 5:28:18 (27,923)	Wilson, Robert 2:43:31 (208)	Wiseman, Christian 5:43:48 (29,292)
Willows, Peter 4:53:05 (22,517)	Wilson, Robert 3:10:18 (1,706)	Wiseman, Dallas 4:10:07 (12,378)
Wills, Andrew 3:58:05 (9,726)	Wilson, Robert 4:06:36 (11,610)	Wiseman, Garry 5:29:29 (28,036)
Wills, Bernard 4:08:46 (12,084)	Wilson, Robin 4:40:42 (19,684)	Wiseman, Timothy 4:41:18 (19,825)
Wills, Craig 4:06:13 (11,539)	Wilson, Robin 4:52:14 (22,348)	Wishart, Neil 4:42:06 (20,009)
Wills, Darren 5:09:11 (25,433)	Wilson, Robin 5:19:35 (26,837)	Wishart, Robbie 4:20:31 (14,873)
Wills, David 4:15:07 (13,544)	Wilson, Scott 3:37:47 (5,386)	Wishlade, Chris 4:20:37 (14,892)
Wills, Edward 4:49:33 (21,761)	Wilson, Simon 4:53:27 (22,609)	Witham, Gary 3:58:19 (9,788)
Wills, Gordon 4:14:14 (13,312)	Wilson, Stephen 4:07:28 (11,799)	Witherick, Roger 3:03:16 (1,133)
Wills, Robin 4:58:44 (23,742)	Wilson, Stephen 5:21:53 (27,136)	Withers, David 4:40:47 (19,700)
Willsmer, Nicholas 3:48:39 (7,432)	Wilson, Taylor 4:32:21 (17,801)	Withers, Gareth 4:37:05 (18,899)
Willsmer, Phil 6:05:13 (30,463)	Wilson, Trevor 3:28:55 (3,991)	Withers, Paul 3:59:24 (10,064)
Willsmore, Andrew 4:16:30 (13,858)	Wilson, Victor 3:25:34 (3,471)	Withers, Philip 3:17:33 (2,496)
Willson, Jonathon 4:48:34 (21,545)	Wilson-Storey, Simon 4:12:39 (12,929)	Withers, Scott 3:47:42 (7,255)
Willson, William 3:58:51 (9,930)	Wilton, Daniel 4:08:16 (11,953)	Withers, Simon 5:32:03 (28,295)
Wilman, Lewis 3:29:59 (4,163)	Wilton, David 4:52:17 (22,354)	Withers, Thomas 3:54:51 (8,879)
Wilmot, Andrew 3:18:37 (2,620)	Wilton, Graham 3:05:43 (1,298)	Witherstone, Matthew 4:26:15 (16,308)
Wilmot, Terence 4:25:09 (16,043)	Wiltshire, Charles 5:15:06 (26,261)	Withey, Jonathan 3:10:47 (1,739)
Wilmot, Tom 4:24:21 (15,834)	Wiltshire, Christopher 5:33:09 (28,385)	Withnell, Toby 4:42:35 (20,131)
Wilmshurst, Andrew 2:51:26 (430)	Wiltshire, Dale 3:40:47 (5,922)	Witte, Marchel 3:05:26 (1,284)
Wilmshurst, Glyn 2:54:57 (589)	Wiltsshire, Kevin 6:06:43 (30,518)	Wittek, Ruediger 4:46:04 (20,982)
Wilmshurst, Mark 4:42:13 (20,034)	Wimble, Christopher 3:24:51 (3,378)	Witteman, Tom 4:45:14 (20,776)
Wiloman, Fraser 2:54:38 (570)	Wimborne, Paul 4:32:52 (17,918)	Wittering, Mark 2:52:08 (447)
Wilsmore, Paul 3:06:46 (1,384)	Winch, Martin 3:57:35 (9,591)	Witts, Michael 3:06:34 (1,366)
Wilson, Alan 5:03:11 (24,488)	Windebank, Mark 3:25:11 (3,425)	Wittstock, Dirk 4:09:48 (12,301)
Wilson, Alex 4:32:19 (17,795)	Winder, Garry 3:54:53 (8,889)	Wixon, Ian 4:54:28 (22,808)
Wilson, Andrew 3:38:27 (5,485)	Winder, Robert 6:27:19 (31,233)	Wodehouse, Dominic 3:40:44 (5,909)
Wilson, Andrew 4:33:39 (18,089)	Windler, Felix 2:51:21 (427)	Woelke, Joachim 3:45:39 (6,861)
Wilson, Andrew 5:00:03 (23,988)	Windoffer, Andreas 4:24:46 (15,941)	Woels, Claus 3:33:58 (4,742)
Wilson, Andrew 5:38:09 (28,824)	Window, Cameron 3:34:42 (4,868)	Wold, Richard 2:56:18 (660)
Wilson, Andrw 4:08:28 (12,002)	Winfield, Peter 3:19:47 (2,733)	Woledge, William 4:44:06 (20,520)

Wolf, Roland 4:18:05 (14,269)
Wolfe, Christopher 4:32:20 (17,798)
Wolfenden, Andrew 4:13:28 (13,116)
Wolfenden, Nick 5:47:30 (29,534)
Wolff, Ulrich 4:13:14 (13,058)
Wolfrat, Jan 3:42:10 (6,182)
Wolk, Dieter 4:55:19 (22,982)
Wolovitz, Lionel 3:18:02 (2,554)
Wolstenholme, Andrew 5:22:36 (27,225)
Wolton, Sam 3:35:48 (5,040)
Wombwell, Michael 4:05:10 (11,325)
Wong, Chi 4:46:42 (21,124)
Wong, Peter 4:43:20 (20,328)
Wong, Raymond 3:45:53 (6,909)
Wonko, Adam 3:46:36 (7,055)
Wonko, Witold 4:20:22 (14,838)
Wonnacott, Mark 4:48:28 (21,529)
Wood, Adam 4:50:15 (21,909)
Wood, Alistair 3:30:45 (4,290)
Wood, Andrew 4:23:00 (15,494)
Wood, Andrew 4:24:51 (15,962)
Wood, Andrew 4:37:04 (18,892)
Wood, Ben 4:30:23 (17,336)
Wood, Brian 4:15:56 (13,728)
Wood, Charlie 4:01:39 (10,570)
Wood, Chris 3:39:23 (5,675)
Wood, Christopher 3:57:58 (9,698)
Wood, Christopher 5:11:18 (25,736)
Wood, David 4:25:50 (16,211)
Wood, David 4:28:07 (16,740)
Wood, Dominic 3:49:34 (7,646)
Wood, Fraser 4:03:01 (10,846)
Wood, Gary 6:39:06 (31,524)
Wood, Graham 4:25:13 (16,063)
Wood, Hugo 3:21:43 (2,957)
Wood, Ian 5:26:53 (27,765)
Wood, James 3:18:59 (2,652)
Wood, John 4:17:47 (14,206)
Wood, John 4:35:44 (18,570)
Wood, Kevin 4:30:47 (17,442)
Wood, Kevin 4:50:06 (21,883)
Wood, Kevin 4:52:20 (22,365)
Wood, Mark 3:58:57 (9,955)
Wood, Mark 4:14:52 (13,471)
Wood, Matthew 5:35:03 (28,556)
Wood, Michael 3:41:51 (6,123)
Wood, Michael 4:28:35 (16,883)
Wood, Phil 4:46:09 (21,006)
Wood, Robert 3:30:02 (4,170)
Wood, Robert 4:05:26 (11,390)
Wood, Ron 4:55:14 (22,963)
Wood, Stephen 4:45:13 (20,774)
Wood, Stephen 4:53:20 (22,581)
Wood, Steve 3:46:47 (7,081)
Wood, Steven 5:03:29 (24,526)
Wood, Terence 4:08:51 (12,098)
Wood, Terry 2:42:56 (196)
Wood, Tim 4:31:32 (17,626)
Wood, Tom 4:32:31 (17,838)
Woodage, Phil 3:56:01 (9,184)
Woodall, David 4:45:19 (20,798)
Woodall, Eric 3:36:11 (5,095)
Woodall, Nicholas 4:22:11 (15,291)
Woodall, Tom 5:09:53 (25,526)
Woodcock, Andrew 5:17:58 (26,604)
Woodcock, Clive 3:54:10 (8,696)
Woodcock, Marc 3:03:00 (1,114)
Woodcock, Mark 4:21:59 (15,236)
Woodcock, Martin 4:04:56 (11,278)
Woodcock, Nicholas 4:36:38 (18,793)
Woodcroft, Mark 4:12:30 (12,887)
Woodeson, Matthew 4:14:40 (13,416)
Woodfine, Idris 5:20:21 (26,930)
Woodfine, William 4:20:16 (14,813)
Woodford, Michael 4:46:04 (20,982)
Woodham, Paul 4:45:18 (20,796)
Woodhouse, Brian 4:34:22 (18,256)
Woodhouse, James 5:12:24 (25,881)
Woodhouse, Martin 4:03:13 (10,884)
Woodhouse, Matt 4:28:03 (16,721)
Woodhouse, Paul 4:26:57 (16,458)
Woodhouse, Paul 4:43:32 (20,388)
Woodhouse, Paul 4:59:46 (23,935)
Woodhouse, Philip 3:38:52 (5,573)
Woodhouse, Simon 3:42:45 (6,310)
Woodley, Dave 3:17:53 (2,534)
Woodley, David 4:25:06 (16,026)
Woodley, Greg 5:25:36 (27,621)
Woodley, Peter 4:50:46 (22,025)
Woodley, Roger 4:44:58 (20,706)
Woodley, Thomas 5:30:57 (28,188)
Woodlock, Michael 4:34:51 (18,359)
Woodman, Grant 3:22:24 (3,035)
Woodman, Mark 2:41:32 (173)
Woodman, Nigel 5:18:06 (26,630)
Woodroof, Alan 4:23:06 (15,512)
Woodrow, Austin 4:38:40 (19,245)
Woodrow, John 3:36:56 (5,218)
Woodruff, Keith 4:17:45 (14,193)
Woodruff, Michael 3:31:46 (4,449)
Woodruff, Raymond 3:19:57 (2,754)
Woods, Alan 5:29:35 (28,049)
Woods, Alec 2:40:43 (162)
Woods, Andrew 5:08:48 (25,374)
Woods, Brian 3:38:39 (5,531)
Woods, Colin 3:56:26 (9,300)
Woods, Dennis 4:25:37 (16,162)
Woods, George 5:00:10 (24,004)
Woods, Jason 4:45:36 (20,867)
Woods, Jonathan 4:25:46 (16,190)
Woods, Keith 4:58:35 (23,716)
Woods, Kevin 4:43:39 (20,417)
Woods, Mark 4:45:36 (20,867)
Woods, Michael 4:59:46 (23,935)
Woods, Mike 3:17:36 (2,503)
Woods, Neville 5:37:24 (28,768)
Woods, Roger 4:38:35 (19,221)
Woods, Terry 5:43:04 (29,245)
Woodward, Adrian 4:29:01 (16,994)
Woodward, Andrew 4:03:59 (11,059)
Woodward, Brian 3:56:59 (9,451)
Woodward, Christopher 4:26:30 (16,355)
Woodward, David 5:39:12 (28,921)
Woodward, Harry 4:09:53 (12,318)
Woodward, Jamie 4:08:27 (11,995)
Woodward, Jason 4:53:50 (22,686)
Woodward, Peter 4:08:54 (12,108)
Woodward, Philip 4:21:35 (15,126)
Woodward, Simon 4:27:00 (16,470)
Woodward, Timothy 3:18:25 (2,604)
Woodworth, James 4:48:21 (21,509)
Wookey, David 5:05:17 (24,836)
Wookey, Nigel 4:50:01 (21,862)
Woolcock, Martin 3:59:26 (10,073)
Woolcock, Steve 4:52:36 (22,415)
Wooldridge, Iain 5:54:51 (29,989)
Wooldridge, Mark 5:03:32 (24,536)
Wooley, Alan 3:34:13 (4,783)
Woolf, Jonathan 3:55:05 (8,933)
Woolf, Matthew 5:28:58 (27,983)
Woolf, Simon 4:33:47 (18,112)
Woolford, Nathan 5:59:10 (30,219)
Woolgar, Gary 2:46:44 (287)
Woolhouse, David 4:42:12 (20,029)
Woolhouse, John 5:24:19 (27,453)
Woolhouse, Michael 4:34:11 (18,209)
Woolhouse, Neal 4:48:36 (21,552)
Woollard, Paul 4:45:43 (20,889)
Wooller, John 5:55:04 (30,005)
Woollett, Guy 3:09:42 (1,651)
Woolley, Alan 4:04:34 (11,191)
Woolley, David 5:38:52 (28,886)
Woolley, Glyn 3:55:22 (9,014)
Woolley, Ricky 3:31:08 (4,347)
Woolley, Simon 3:41:14 (5,996)
Woolley, Stephen 4:15:36 (13,660)
Woolliscroft, Philip 4:32:43 (17,885)
Woollon, Andy 4:00:20 (10,301)
Woolner, Tom 4:08:02 (11,911)
Woolston, Thomas 5:01:36 (24,242)
Woolven, David 5:49:58 (29,711)
Woolven, Tony 4:41:02 (19,763)
Woon, Jayson 3:56:02 (9,189)
Wootten, Richard 6:45:32 (31,632)
Wootton, Gary 4:02:20 (10,703)
Wootton, Neil 4:35:43 (18,565)
Wootton, Terence 3:50:10 (7,767)
Worboys, Robin 4:10:30 (12,462)
Worden, Neil 3:37:07 (5,257)
Workman, Ian 5:17:46 (26,574)
Wormald, Alex 4:00:57 (10,419)
Wormald, Mark 4:22:16 (15,309)
Worn, Tony 5:40:39 (29,050)
Worrall, Anthony 4:32:39 (17,868)
Worrall, Chris 4:29:45 (17,178)
Worrall, Paul 5:03:29 (24,526)
Worrell, Peter 5:46:14 (29,451)
Worrell, Richard 4:00:42 (10,367)
Worrow, Jeff 4:21:54 (15,207)
Worsfold, Glen 5:30:01 (28,088)
Worsfold, Lee 5:41:58 (29,158)
Worship, George 3:21:39 (2,946)
Worsley, Martin 3:38:35 (5,511)
Worsley, Peter 3:35:43 (5,027)
Worth, Austen 3:14:14 (2,156)
Worth, Daniel 4:07:16 (11,751)
Worth, Paul 3:29:03 (4,009)
Worth, William 5:20:05 (26,899)
Worthington, Andrew 4:47:25 (21,279)
Worthington, John 5:14:59 (26,245)
Worthington, Paul 5:05:27 (24,867)
Worthington, Samuel 3:15:30 (2,289)
Worthy, David 4:01:22 (10,509)
Wortley, Andrew 4:35:33 (18,527)
Wortley, Matthew 3:23:03 (3,116)
Wotherspoon, Alex 4:07:39 (11,848)
Would, Andrew 3:35:25 (4,977)
Wragg, Anthony 4:44:51 (20,686)
Wragg, Peter 5:46:45 (29,482)
Wragg, Philip 5:09:26 (25,465)
Wragg, Richard 5:23:02 (27,290)
Wraight, Anthony 5:09:09 (25,429)
Wraight, Simon 4:16:40 (13,897)
Wrangles, Paul 4:26:03 (16,264)
Wrapson, Nigel 4:00:27 (10,321)
Wrather, Jonathan 4:42:33 (20,123)
Wray, Daniel 4:59:32 (23,893)
Wray, Paul 4:32:16 (17,789)
Wray, Peter 4:23:18 (15,576)
Wren, Andrew 5:22:36 (27,225)
Wren, Stephen 5:19:54 (26,870)
Wrenn, Nicholas 3:35:08 (4,931)
Wresniwiro, Raden 5:22:41 (27,231)
Wride, Chris 4:15:27 (13,627)
Wright, Andrew 3:26:07 (3,554)
Wright, Andrew 4:40:20 (19,618)
Wright, Andrew 4:49:30 (21,750)
Wright, Andrew 4:55:43 (23,083)
Wright, Anthony 4:47:08 (21,212)
Wright, Antony 4:25:22 (16,107)
Wright, Barry 3:46:17 (6,991)
Wright, Benjamin 4:06:40 (11,620)
Wright, Brian 3:35:18 (4,958)
Wright, Christopher 3:29:20 (4,050)
Wright, Colin 4:57:28 (23,474)
Wright, Daniel 2:59:13 (873)
Wright, David 2:56:23 (669)
Wright, David 3:53:56 (8,653)
Wright, David 4:09:40 (12,268)
Wright, David 5:30:05 (28,093)
Wright, David 6:15:55 (30,856)
Wright, Dylan 3:58:49 (9,921)
Wright, Edwin 3:55:11 (8,962)
Wright, Eric 4:14:33 (13,394)
Wright, Gavin 6:21:54 (31,070)
Wright, Geoffrey 5:29:27 (28,032)
Wright, Graeme 5:23:06 (27,300)
Wright, Graham 4:13:41 (13,170)
Wright, Ian 4:36:33 (18,780)
Wright, Ian 4:47:22 (21,261)
Wright, James 3:19:52 (2,739)
Wright, Jamie 5:16:22 (26,412)
Wright, Jeffrey 6:34:55 (31,447)
Wright, John 3:57:14 (9,513)
Wright, John 4:26:31 (16,358)
Wright, John 4:41:10 (19,790)
Wright, Jonathan 2:52:15 (455)
Wright, Keith 3:51:20 (8,039)
Wright, Kenneth 4:07:23 (11,778)

Wright, Larry 3:37:35 (5,342)
Wright, Lee 5:04:57 (24,786)
Wright, Malcolm 3:55:26 (9,032)
Wright, Mark 4:04:47 (11,245)
Wright, Michael 3:46:58 (7,120)
Wright, Michael 4:38:21 (19,175)
Wright, Neal 4:07:07 (11,713)
Wright, Neil 4:03:46 (11,002)
Wright, Neil 5:30:38 (28,157)
Wright, Nicholas 4:11:27 (12,632)
Wright, Nick 4:07:47 (11,867)
Wright, Nigel 4:56:09 (23,182)
Wright, Oliver 3:21:25 (2,926)
Wright, Oliver 3:57:54 (9,677)
Wright, Owen 3:51:07 (7,981)
Wright, Patrick 3:56:57 (9,442)
Wright, Paul 4:03:57 (11,048)
Wright, Paul 4:32:34 (17,848)
Wright, Paul 5:12:49 (25,945)
Wright, Peter 2:34:45 (96)
Wright, Rob 4:53:57 (22,705)
Wright, Robert 5:47:46 (29,555)
Wright, Simon 5:26:04 (27,683)
Wright, Stephen 3:24:01 (3,249)
Wright, Stephen 4:07:34 (11,824)
Wright, Stephen 4:56:29 (23,255)
Wright, Steve 5:34:52 (28,544)
Wright, Terence 4:36:28 (18,762)
Wright, Timothy 5:09:58 (25,536)
Wright, Tony 2:47:47 (323)
Wright, William 4:48:15 (21,482)
Wrighton, Christopher 3:13:59 (2,125)
Wrigley, Mark 5:57:38 (30,147)
Wroblewski, Marek 4:27:34 (16,617)
Wroblewski, Steve 3:26:27 (3,599)
Wroe, Stephen 3:53:13 (8,479)
Wu, Shad 3:51:32 (8,086)
Wulf, Michael 3:00:33 (978)
Wulf, Thomas 2:42:20 (185)
Wurfbain, Michiel 4:40:55 (19,732)
Wyard, Eric 4:50:18 (21,925)
Wyatt, Esmond 4:28:24 (16,828)
Wyatt, Keith 3:39:33 (5,704)
Wyatt, Michael 5:04:39 (24,723)
Wyatt, Richard 5:40:18 (29,018)
Wyatt, Richard 7:05:12 (31,934)
Wyatt-Budd, Simon 5:12:15 (25,863)
Wybrant, John 4:50:39 (22,001)
Wykes, Leigh 3:30:57 (4,320)
Wykes, Richard 4:30:53 (17,464)
Wylie, Fraser 4:34:59 (18,393)
Wylie, Samuel 3:56:54 (9,422)
Wyllie, John 6:26:19 (31,216)
Wynn, Lucien 4:13:55 (13,239)
Wynne, Colin 4:26:01 (16,251)
Wynne, Murray 4:35:02 (18,406)
Wynne, Rob 2:54:13 (551)
Wysocki-Jones, Simon 4:27:09 (16,511)
Yadave, Rush 4:26:58 (16,462)
Yallop, David 3:40:08 (5,820)
Yallup, Lister 3:38:37 (5,521)
Yam, Perry 4:52:25 (22,381)
Yamamoto, Gary 4:56:17 (23,219)
Yang, Yipeng 3:39:27 (5,685)
Yannic, Arnaud 5:28:21 (27,925)
Yardley, Chris 4:23:17 (15,571)
Yardley, Graham 3:55:00 (8,921)
Yardley, Walter 3:51:31 (8,080)
Yarnold, Roger 4:54:07 (22,732)
Yarnold, Stuart 4:24:51 (15,962)
Yarranton, Nigel 4:47:06 (21,203)
Yarrow, Nigel 4:18:20 (14,309)
Yarwood, Nigel 4:50:17 (21,919)
Yateman, Robert 5:20:01 (26,890)
Yates, Alexander 4:51:18 (22,152)
Yates, Anthony 3:53:45 (8,603)
Yates, Eric 4:31:06 (17,525)
Yates, Steven 5:19:28 (26,827)
Yatich, Mark 2:19:52 (22)
Yawitch, Darrel 4:17:48 (14,210)
Yazaki, Etsuro 3:59:31 (10,098)
Ybert, Laurent 3:58:58 (9,960)
Yeaman, Robin 3:30:22 (4,226)
Yearwood, Brian 6:11:24 (30,707)
Yeates, Nigel 4:05:13 (11,333)
Yeats, Stephen 4:15:40 (13,668)
Yelding, Steven 4:34:59 (18,393)
Yelland, Stephen 3:48:36 (7,425)
Yendall, Keith 3:23:29 (3,176)
Yendole, Andrew 3:42:40 (6,288)
Yenter, Hugo 4:17:08 (14,018)
Yeo, Matthew 3:53:50 (8,628)
Yeoman, Mark 3:19:55 (2,746)
Yeomans, Arnold 3:39:29 (5,693)
Yeomans, Martin 3:28:09 (3,838)
Yeomans, Stephen 4:18:17 (14,301)
Yetts, Alan 4:16:15 (13,797)
Yetts, Trevor 6:55:42 (31,842)
Yeung, Lawrence 3:42:02 (6,158)
Yeung, Sydney 6:19:15 (30,981)
Yildiz, Nevil 4:42:12 (20,029)
Yip, Terry 4:04:44 (11,238)
Yiu, Joseph 4:03:53 (11,033)
Yolles, Bryan 4:37:53 (19,063)
Yoofoo, John 5:30:49 (28,177)
York, David 4:49:20 (21,711)
Yorke, Richard 3:56:11 (9,234)
Yorke, Simon 4:07:48 (11,871)
Yorwerth, Michael 3:40:18 (5,843)
Yoshida, Tamotsu 4:18:59 (14,504)
Youlden, James 4:56:27 (23,248)
Young, Alastair 3:21:59 (2,983)
Young, Andrew 3:28:11 (3,845)
Young, Barnaby 3:54:58 (8,911)
Young, Chris 3:34:01 (4,752)
Young, David 3:42:44 (6,306)
Young, David 4:17:27 (14,102)
Young, Graham 6:09:54 (30,636)
Young, Ian 3:55:32 (9,058)
Young, Ian 4:35:14 (18,457)
Young, James 5:15:03 (26,254)
Young, John 4:44:25 (20,599)
Young, Jonathan 4:59:40 (23,917)
Young, Keith 4:31:52 (17,701)
Young, Kevin 4:28:08 (16,748)
Young, Lester 5:54:49 (29,988)
Young, Mark 3:59:36 (10,119)
Young, Mark 5:27:40 (27,856)
Young, Michael 4:21:18 (15,060)
Young, Murray 6:37:36 (31,500)
Young, Nigel 3:42:57 (6,354)
Young, Nigel 4:50:33 (21,977)
Young, Patrick 3:41:54 (6,130)
Young, Paul 4:02:10 (10,671)
Young, Paul 5:10:37 (25,638)
Young, Peter 4:04:27 (11,163)
Young, Richard 6:13:57 (30,796)
Young, Rob 4:55:27 (23,015)
Young, Robert 5:01:12 (24,183)
Young, Roderick 6:14:32 (30,811)
Young, Roger 4:43:14 (20,296)
Young, Shaun 5:59:47 (30,248)
Young, Simon 4:28:32 (16,868)
Young, Stephen 4:14:53 (13,475)
Young, Steven 6:19:19 (30,985)
Young, Stewart 5:37:47 (28,797)
Young, William 6:51:41 (31,755)
Ysern, Ricardo 4:03:44 (10,992)
Ytreland, Kristian 5:04:16 (24,675)
Yue, Chor 3:19:25 (2,693)
Yuen, Hok 3:58:31 (9,839)
Yuill, Chick 5:17:02 (26,483)
Yuill, Paul 4:39:09 (19,360)
Yule, Michael 4:18:16 (14,294)
Yves, Rannou 2:37:02 (121)
Zaagman, Jan 3:59:19 (10,040)
Zabari, Yehuda 3:36:50 (5,199)
Zabell, Howard 5:03:02 (24,463)
Zach, Wolfgang 5:03:25 (24,519)
Zachariassen, Svein 4:12:26 (12,867)
Zahir, Rachid 4:19:42 (14,667)
Zaman, Nadim 3:59:05 (9,977)
Zaman, Nuruz 4:24:38 (15,897)
Zanardini, Vincenzo 3:07:44 (1,477)
Zander, Uwe 4:40:28 (19,648)
Zannou, Regis 4:34:38 (18,316)
Zanola, Alfredo 4:08:22 (11,973)
Zappia, Domenico 5:19:50 (26,863)
Zappulo, Giovanni 4:02:39 (10,769)
Zardet, Fausto 4:10:23 (12,438)
Zarraonandia-Ayo, Ibon 3:35:11 (4,939)
Zarza, Nik 4:39:00 (19,325)
Zavahir, Mohammed 3:28:39 (3,936)
Zaveri, Rishi 5:11:39 (25,782)
Zazzi, Michael 4:28:02 (16,715)
Zdeba, John 3:54:32 (8,793)
Zealey, David 3:43:05 (6,383)
Zeh, Jean-Noel 4:27:22 (16,563)
Zehmke, Volker 4:09:13 (12,175)
Zehnich, Didier 3:07:49 (1,488)
Zeidler, Hans 4:53:09 (22,530)
Zemlich, Michael 4:13:54 (13,233)
Zender, Willibrord 3:54:31 (8,788)
Zentner, Marcus 4:35:57 (18,637)
Zeuthen, Thomas 3:32:59 (4,596)
Zibarras, Jason 4:18:10 (14,283)
Ziegler, François 4:49:44 (21,809)
Zikmann, Robert 4:09:46 (12,291)
Zikusoka, Moses 3:44:51 (6,696)
Zimmer, Jason 4:11:44 (12,702)
Zimmerer, Eugen 3:18:14 (2,580)
Zinopoulos, André 4:32:02 (17,740)
Zomer, Konrad 3:35:24 (4,972)
Zoro, Barnaby 3:49:42 (7,680)
Zuccotto, Giancarlo 4:17:02 (13,993)
Zucker, Andrew 6:26:08 (31,209)
Zulli, Dario 3:05:00 (1,249)
Zwingel, Albert 4:55:22 (22,994)

FEMALE RUNNERS

Aaronson, Barbara 6:36:03 (31,476)
Abadzis, Natalie 5:25:31 (27,612)
Abbey, Gail 4:45:28 (20,837)
Abbiss, Donna 7:29:39 (32,150)
Abbott, Caroline 5:18:01 (26,612)
Abbott, Jacqueline 3:45:32 (6,837)
Abbott, Sally 4:57:16 (23,439)
Abell, Kathryn 4:44:01 (20,500)
Abendroth, Maria 4:52:48 (22,460)
Abington, Jane 4:18:33 (14,372)
Ablett, Davinia 4:30:41 (17,414)
Aboona, Sana 6:10:58 (30,688)
Abrahams, Nicola 3:36:40 (5,175)
Abrahamsen, Rita 3:29:36 (4,111)
Acher, Louise 4:58:45 (23,745)
Ackers, Margaret 5:06:24 (25,008)
Acton, Jane 3:28:13 (3,852)
Adam, Paula 6:56:33 (31,852)
Adams, Claire 5:24:54 (27,520)
Adams, Eve 5:15:07 (26,266)
Adams, Jacqueline 4:23:22 (15,583)
Adams, Laura 5:25:40 (27,627)
Adams, Linda 4:37:31 (18,987)
Adams, Paula 3:13:04 (2,001)
Adams, Susan 4:59:47 (23,947)
Adams, Susan 5:04:21 (24,684)
Adams, Tracey 3:54:45 (8,850)
Adams, Vicky 4:53:26 (22,602)
Adams, Victoria 4:15:17 (13,585)
Adams, Victoria 4:30:30 (17,366)
Adamson, Brenda 4:43:58 (20,489)
Adamson, Caron 4:56:21 (23,230)
Adamson, Rachel 4:10:19 (12,419)
Addison, Susan 4:03:33 (10,957)
Ademoye, Fola 5:10:11 (25,580)
Adkins, Melanie 4:42:27 (20,098)
Advani, Melissa 5:22:09 (27,160)
Aeynard, Melissa 4:57:04 (23,394)
Agasse, Yveline 4:43:23 (20,347)
Agosti, Emanuela 4:46:14 (21,026)
Aguirre, Kimberly 6:12:54 (30,763)
Aguis, Stacy 5:23:46 (27,382)
Ahearn, Ginette 5:29:25 (28,029)
Aherne, Christine 3:56:37 (9,352)
Ahmad, Sarah 4:03:08 (10,871)
Ahmed, Kirstin 4:05:03 (11,303)
Ahmed, Sameena 6:31:29 (31,361)
Ainge, Elizabeth 7:15:53 (32,040)
Ainslie, Jane 3:48:35 (7,420)

Ainsworth, Kathryn 4:27:15 (16,534)
Ainsworth, Pat 4:47:30 (21,298)
Airey, Elizabeth 4:41:13 (19,804)
Aitchison, Pauline 3:43:52 (6,522)
Aitken, Nicola 2:54:01 (535)
Aizawa, Kimiko 5:43:05 (29,246)
Aizawa, Yoshie 5:15:04 (26,256)
Akram, Amina 4:37:00 (18,878)
Albert, Justine 4:02:17 (10,694)
Alberts, Ida 4:45:14 (20,776)
Albon, Wendy 4:14:26 (13,365)
Alcock, Emma 4:01:00 (10,429)
Aldersley, Helen 4:20:50 (14,938)
Alderson, Doreen 5:08:15 (25,306)
Alderton, Jacqueline 4:22:53 (15,466)
Aldreidge, Claire 6:21:34 (31,065)
Aldridge, Lorraine 5:04:15 (24,672)
Aldridge, Sara 4:44:54 (20,697)
Alemu, Elfenesh 2:24:56 (39)
Alexander, Audri 4:59:09 (23,838)
Alexander, Caroline 4:24:55 (15,975)
Alexander, Katie 3:24:21 (3,308)
Alexander, Kristen 3:34:23 (4,814)
Alexander, Rosalyn 2:56:46 (688)
Alford, Rebecca 4:26:38 (16,389)
Allan, Dawn 4:21:41 (15,152)
Allan, Julie 5:43:03 (29,243)
Allared, Britt 4:30:35 (17,386)
Allaway, Caroline 5:12:10 (25,844)
Allen, Antonia 5:17:24 (26,527)
Allen, Barbara 5:25:50 (27,648)
Allen, Catherine 4:26:59 (16,465)
Allen, Deborah 3:52:30 (8,310)
Allen, Deborah 6:31:57 (31,379)
Allen, Heather 3:55:29 (9,044)
Allen, Indira 4:39:25 (19,423)
Allen, Julie 4:17:43 (14,183)
Allen, Kathie 4:07:45 (11,862)
Allen, Kelly 4:01:22 (10,509)
Allen, Lesley 4:23:01 (15,498)
Allen, Linda 4:57:49 (23,546)
Allen, Lynn 5:26:12 (27,700)
Allen, Rachael 5:23:11 (27,313)
Allen, Sue 5:15:57 (26,369)
Allen, Vanessa 4:22:29 (15,359)
Allerton, Caroline 5:46:00 (29,441)
Allison, Judith 5:14:22 (26,153)
Allison, Lynn 6:31:26 (31,359)
Allison, Lynne 5:05:59 (24,955)
Allison, Melanie 4:55:19 (22,982)
Allison, Vivien 4:44:59 (20,711)
Allsop, Diana 4:33:13 (17,987)
Allwood, Cressida 7:07:08 (31,959)
Almond, Janette 6:12:02 (30,727)
Alteneder, Elisabeth 4:17:35 (14,132)
Alton, Nina 4:30:24 (17,344)
Alty, Lorraine 6:41:18 (31,556)
Alty, Lynsey 6:41:17 (31,555)
Alwen, Heather 4:52:22 (22,373)
Amas, Helen 4:01:29 (10,536)
Ambler, Helen 5:25:54 (27,654)
Ambler, Sarah 5:26:46 (27,759)
Ambrose, Charlotte 5:22:11 (27,164)
Ambrose, Natalie 5:32:16 (28,312)
Ambrosio, Lara 4:04:17 (11,134)
Amer, Claire 4:28:05 (16,731)
Amicizia, Orietta 4:52:00 (22,308)
Amps, Joanne 4:08:15 (11,947)
Ancona, Ronni 4:31:11 (17,546)
Anderegg, Lise 4:40:16 (19,594)
Anderson, Aileen 4:21:40 (15,149)
Anderson, Alice 5:25:49 (27,646)
Anderson, Christine 3:48:05 (7,336)
Anderson, Irene 3:50:56 (7,928)
Anderson, Jill 4:07:34 (11,824)
Anderson, Joanne 3:32:50 (4,572)
Anderson, June 4:56:48 (23,337)
Anderson, Katie 6:04:51 (30,450)
Anderson, Kay 4:57:38 (23,511)
Anderson, Paula 6:16:20 (30,868)
Anderson, Sally 3:45:56 (6,919)
Anderton, Lesley 5:34:47 (28,536)
Andrew, Lisa 3:20:35 (2,835)
Andrews, Andrea 6:25:48 (31,195)
Andrews, Anna-Lisa 5:20:29 (26,954)
Andrews, Charlotte 4:12:50 (12,966)
Andrews, Katie 4:30:51 (17,454)
Andrews, Kirstie 4:05:11 (11,327)
Andrews, Lisa 6:14:41 (30,816)
Andrews, Sandra 5:03:33 (24,539)
Anello, Denise 4:09:36 (12,249)
Angel, Melanie 4:25:39 (16,168)
Angell, Margaret 2:46:20 (269)
Angulatta, Susan 4:07:07 (11,713)
Angus, Linda 4:56:28 (23,251)
Anigacz, Geraldine 5:28:09 (27,908)
Anken, Paula 3:49:15 (7,576)
Annals, Jacqueline 4:16:27 (13,846)
Annear, Kathryn 6:44:42 (31,615)
Ansell, Lizbeth 3:36:52 (5,208)
Anstee, Jessica 5:55:59 (30,041)
Antoine, Jacqueline 4:54:39 (22,849)
Anwyll, Catarina 4:39:32 (19,448)
Appelboam, Helen 4:00:58 (10,424)
Appleton, Andrea 5:06:12 (24,984)
Appleton, Claire 6:31:08 (31,352)
Appleton, Karen 4:42:41 (20,154)
Aquilina, Helen 5:48:22 (29,596)
Aral, Zeynep 5:01:23 (24,220)
Arapoglou, Kanella 4:45:38 (20,876)
Aravena-Imlah, Laura 3:46:57 (7,115)
Arayo, Mary 5:24:33 (27,482)
Arbon, Fay 5:40:23 (29,025)
Arch, Sarah 4:55:01 (22,925)
Archer, Barbara 6:21:07 (31,054)
Archer, Karen 4:02:40 (10,774)
Archer, Lynn 4:32:08 (17,759)
Archibald, Nicola 7:01:45 (31,903)
Arendse, Rinalda 5:19:23 (26,812)
Argent, Patricia 4:51:03 (22,083)
Argent, Sherralyn 6:45:43 (31,638)
Arkell, Katherine 5:08:58 (25,395)
Arkell, Yvonne 6:25:19 (31,173)
Armand-Smith, Penny 3:59:04 (9,976)
Armitage, Claire 4:55:00 (22,921)
Armitage, Lucy 4:05:54 (11,483)
Armstrong, Claire 4:03:04 (10,862)
Armstrong, Clare 5:09:18 (25,446)
Armstrong, Helen 4:50:02 (21,868)
Armstrong, Jane 4:14:26 (13,365)
Armstrong, Julia 3:08:29 (1,545)
Armstrong, Julie 4:29:33 (17,126)
Armstrong, Rosemary 4:09:33 (12,241)
Arnaud, Marie-Helene 3:30:46 (4,292)
Arnfield, Alison 4:08:59 (12,127)
Arnold, Charlotte 3:49:47 (7,696)
Arnold, Helen 5:58:34 (30,181)
Arora, Jessica 5:39:47 (28,968)
Arragon, Sarah 4:38:20 (19,172)
Arthofer, Michaela 3:44:44 (6,679)
Arthur, Carol 4:37:29 (18,981)
Arwell, Beverley 4:09:24 (12,208)
Asghar, Anita 5:35:49 (28,620)
Ashby, Jane 5:15:01 (26,251)
Ashby, Valerie 4:37:09 (18,909)
Ashcroft, Cynthia 4:19:24 (14,594)
Ashcroft, Joanne 3:22:39 (3,063)
Ashcroft, Julie 4:19:01 (14,511)
Ashdown, Sophie 5:04:41 (24,730)
Ashenden, Jacqueline 4:51:56 (22,297)
Asher, Carolyn 5:19:03 (26,763)
Asher, Jennifer 6:50:17 (31,728)
Asher, Joanne 6:50:17 (31,728)
Asher, Vivienne 5:19:57 (26,879)
Ashfield, Lesina 7:03:52 (31,921)
Ashfield, Pippa 4:42:44 (20,165)
Ashford-Smith, Paulette 4:22:02 (15,247)
Ashley, Sarah 6:40:21 (31,545)
Ashley, Susan 3:21:17 (2,909)
Ashmore, Joanna 3:44:54 (6,707)
Ashraf, Yasmin 4:36:23 (18,740)
Ashton, Clare 5:45:14 (29,385)
Ashton, Hannah 6:09:28 (30,616)
Ashton, Jane 6:12:56 (30,767)
Ashton, Jeanette 3:41:54 (6,130)
Ashton, Nicola 4:47:17 (21,243)
Ashton, Susan 3:40:54 (5,943)
Ashton, Tracey 4:21:21 (15,073)
Ashworth, Karike 4:27:00 (16,470)
Askwith, Celia 5:19:42 (26,848)
Astaire, Anne 5:33:54 (28,470)
Aston, Heather 4:05:35 (11,415)
Aston, Jennifer 4:29:49 (17,199)
Atherton, Amy 3:41:17 (6,010)
Atherton, Sarah 4:31:10 (17,543)
Atherton, Sereca 3:20:57 (2,878)
Atherton-Tomlin, Hilary 5:40:59 (29,075)
Atkins, Clare 6:04:40 (30,441)
Atkins, Michelle 5:43:43 (29,284)
Atkins, Nichola 3:56:26 (9,300)
Atkins, Tracey 4:38:36 (19,228)
Atkinson, Catherine 6:17:15 (30,899)
Atkinson, Ellen 5:35:31 (28,594)
Atkinson, Jan 5:04:10 (24,657)
Atkinson, Jane 4:17:33 (14,129)
Attenburrow, Ralda 5:31:01 (28,193)
Atterwill, Beth 4:40:53 (19,723)
Atton, Geraldine 4:35:38 (18,545)
Attwood, Jayne 4:28:47 (16,932)
Au, Fiona 6:00:31 (30,274)
Augur, Ann 5:24:50 (27,511)
August, Dianne 3:59:48 (10,176)
Aulsford, Elizabeth 4:12:32 (12,894)
Auroux, Annie 4:38:01 (19,093)
Ausden, Nuala 5:17:28 (26,538)
Aussenberg, Glenda 7:22:58 (32,094)
Austin, Dudleen 4:58:46 (23,755)
Austin, Joyce 5:06:38 (25,039)
Austin, Kelly 4:00:54 (10,407)
Austin, Louise 6:24:25 (31,143)
Austin, Sian 5:05:04 (24,806)
Aver, Doris 4:55:24 (23,003)
Avery, Amanda 4:26:53 (16,444)
Avery, Brenda 4:05:13 (11,333)
Axe, Rebecca 3:49:12 (7,562)
Ayers, Samantha 3:15:04 (2,244)
Ayley, Deborah 5:37:40 (28,790)
Ayres, Cheryl 4:14:54 (13,479)
Ayres, Natalie 7:26:55 (32,128)
Babajide, Addy 4:37:06 (18,902)
Babb, Kim 4:56:14 (23,205)
Back, Gabriele 3:47:49 (7,285)
Back, Karen 4:54:29 (22,810)
Backstrand, Lena 5:19:02 (26,759)
Baerselman, Tessa 4:16:38 (13,885)
Bagg, Sarah 5:41:09 (29,088)
Bagnall, Alison 4:02:22 (10,711)
Bagnall, Victoria 5:11:24 (25,753)
Bailey, Clair 5:18:36 (26,714)
Bailey, Estina 4:56:34 (23,280)
Bailey, Helen 4:23:25 (15,591)
Bailey, Lesley 4:19:22 (14,584)
Bailey, Louise 4:39:38 (19,465)
Bailey, Madeline 4:50:14 (21,907)
Bailey, Sarah 4:22:29 (15,359)
Bailey, Sharon 5:09:39 (25,496)
Bailey, Sheila 5:22:44 (27,244)
Baillie, Lucy 4:34:41 (18,325)
Bainbridge, Shelley 5:46:10 (29,447)
Bainbridge, Wendy 5:12:33 (25,909)
Bains, Randip 5:01:43 (24,262)
Baker, Bernice 6:08:19 (30,577)
Baker, Catherine 7:14:54 (32,036)
Baker, Deana 3:33:01 (4,602)
Baker, Gemma 4:37:13 (18,925)
Baker, Georgina 3:55:08 (8,947)
Baker, Georgina 5:35:13 (28,574)
Baker, Ioana 5:44:24 (29,328)
Baker, Juliette 4:44:22 (20,587)
Baker, Kirstin 4:08:16 (11,953)
Baker, Lauren 6:56:48 (31,857)
Baker, Linsy 5:02:09 (24,335)
Baker, Marnie 7:02:24 (31,907)
Baker, Meg 4:23:35 (15,635)
Baker, Odette 5:04:28 (24,703)
Baker, Sallie 6:36:24 (31,483)
Baker, Sally 3:05:34 (1,289)
Baker, Véronique 5:11:19 (25,737)
Bakkerud, Benedicte 5:20:05 (26,899)

Berry-Poole, Wendy	5:31:18 (28,226)	
Bertulis, Debra	5:38:08 (28,823)	
Berwick, Anita	4:45:56 (20,942)	
Berwick, Pauline	5:05:47 (24,933)	
Besley, Siobhan	5:18:35 (26,713)	
Bessant, Christine	5:10:54 (25,678)	
Best, Carolyn	5:33:49 (28,455)	
Best, Claire	4:27:04 (16,491)	
Best, Gael	4:13:07 (13,026)	
Best, Lisa	5:15:24 (26,304)	
Beswick, Emma	5:03:41 (24,567)	
Beswick, Joanne	4:23:37 (15,643)	
Beswick, Lauren	4:12:00 (12,762)	
Bethune, Deirdre	4:10:52 (12,521)	
Betley, Melika	3:44:09 (6,571)	
Bett, Marinella	3:59:33 (10,105)	
Betti, Eva	4:57:19 (23,448)	
Bettison, Emma	4:28:29 (16,850)	
Betts, Carol	3:35:00 (4,912)	
Betts, Fiona	3:40:24 (5,857)	
Betts, Jacqueline	3:45:46 (6,883)	
Betts, Rona	4:04:27 (11,163)	
Betts, Sally-Ann	4:48:50 (21,598)	
Beukes, Elizabeth	3:50:33 (7,854)	
Bevins, Nandini	5:12:22 (25,876)	
Bhatti, Smeera	5:33:16 (28,398)	
Bhogal, Harjit	4:21:07 (15,011)	
Bhudia, Rama	7:07:16 (31,966)	
Bibby, Rachel	4:40:26 (19,640)	
Biddel, Hannah	4:18:01 (14,255)	
Biden, Pauline	6:55:20 (31,837)	
Bidnell, Alison	5:14:15 (26,135)	
Bidston, Joanna	3:32:48 (4,570)	
Bielby, Jayne	4:21:50 (15,190)	
Biggs, Elizabeth	6:24:46 (31,152)	
Biggs, Louise	7:33:51 (32,177)	
Biggs, Melanie	5:34:30 (28,523)	
Bigham, Sarah	5:40:40 (29,052)	
Bigland, Lucy	4:26:47 (16,427)	
Bigus, Jessica	7:29:39 (32,150)	
Bilcock, Heather	4:55:20 (22,985)	
Bilham, Deborah	4:47:20 (21,254)	
Billiar, Sharon	4:56:14 (23,205)	
Billings, Joanne	3:43:53 (6,525)	
Bilsby, Wendy	5:21:24 (27,071)	
Bingham, Rachel	6:30:00 (31,328)	
Binks-Swain, Jillian	5:28:51 (27,971)	
Binstead, Julia	3:51:10 (8,002)	
Birbeck, Karen	4:35:15 (18,459)	
Birch, Chris	4:05:21 (11,363)	
Birch, Francesca	5:25:57 (27,659)	
Birch, Jan	5:25:56 (27,658)	
Birch, Julie	7:05:55 (31,939)	
Birch, Samantha	4:03:18 (10,913)	
Bircher, Katy	5:06:00 (24,960)	
Birchill, Becky	6:24:07 (31,136)	
Bird, Bridget	6:14:14 (30,803)	
Bird, Dorothy	4:10:44 (12,501)	
Bird, Maggi	6:20:57 (31,048)	
Bird, Monica	5:04:14 (24,668)	
Bird, Sara	5:40:59 (29,075)	
Bird, Sarah	4:19:56 (14,723)	
Bird, Zoe	6:20:59 (31,051)	
Birkett, Ailsa	4:25:10 (16,047)	
Birks, Katherine	4:13:30 (13,125)	
Birss, Sandra	6:38:41 (31,516)	
Bishop, Amber	5:37:31 (28,777)	
Bishop, Fiona	4:09:14 (12,181)	
Bishop, Kim	4:56:09 (23,182)	
Bishop, Rachel	5:23:38 (27,362)	
Bishop, Sara	3:32:59 (4,596)	
Bishopp, Helen	5:30:38 (28,157)	
Bissey, Sueann	4:35:35 (18,536)	
Bjorklund, Margareta	6:54:26 (31,816)	
Black, Beverley	4:08:09 (11,928)	
Black, Josephine	4:25:29 (16,139)	
Black, Julia	4:24:26 (15,850)	
Black, Linda	4:37:59 (19,084)	
Black, Louise	6:06:51 (30,525)	
Black, Rebecca	5:27:37 (27,850)	
Black, Sue	3:26:32 (3,613)	
Black, Sue	4:44:10 (20,533)	
Blackborrow, Karen	5:13:12 (26,000)	

Blackburn, Amanda	6:27:43 (31,256)	
Blackburn, Joanna	3:17:35 (2,502)	
Blackburn, Laura	6:04:39 (30,439)	
Blackler, Eileen	4:15:56 (13,728)	
Blackler, Laura	6:59:44 (31,884)	
Blackman, Melanie	3:31:13 (4,362)	
Blagg, Deborah	4:30:02 (17,248)	
Blagrove, Margaret	5:40:02 (28,998)	
Blake, Joanne	5:26:26 (27,731)	
Blake, Maureen	7:23:46 (32,099)	
Blakey, Katherine	4:11:19 (12,601)	
Blakiston, Vikki	5:26:30 (27,737)	
Blanc, Brigitte	4:26:43 (16,405)	
Bland, Debbie	4:10:15 (12,408)	
Bland, Gilly	5:33:32 (28,426)	
Blanford, Fleur	4:28:32 (16,868)	
Blayber, Nicola	4:47:28 (21,293)	
Blaydes, Sarah	3:42:31 (6,255)	
Blazey, Elizabeth	4:18:32 (14,368)	
Bleach, Daphne	4:54:19 (22,772)	
Bleaken, Marianne	3:11:52 (1,844)	
Blensted, Belinda	3:31:34 (4,422)	
Blethyn, Brenda	6:33:17 (31,407)	
Blewett, Elizabeth	4:48:49 (21,595)	
Blick, Philippa	7:49:16 (32,227)	
Bliss, Olivia	3:57:54 (9,677)	
Bliss, Wendy	7:07:17 (31,967)	
Blofield, Janice	5:16:29 (26,424)	
Blomefield, Georgina	5:15:03 (26,254)	
Bloodworth, Karen	3:37:03 (5,241)	
Bloom, Deb	4:43:58 (20,489)	
Bloom, Julie	4:45:20 (20,807)	
Bloomfield, Emma	3:25:39 (3,481)	
Bloomfield, Joanna	5:24:55 (27,524)	
Bloomfield, Tina	8:11:53 (32,271)	
Bloore, Jane	4:35:15 (18,459)	
Blount, Emma	5:24:52 (27,514)	
Blume, Alison	4:31:17 (17,563)	
Blumenthal, Elizabeth	4:57:46 (23,537)	
Blunden, Rita	7:58:15 (32,252)	
Blunt, Susan	4:49:16 (21,694)	
Blyde, Natalie	4:00:36 (10,345)	
Blyth, Christine	4:35:25 (18,501)	
Blyth, Sara	4:17:47 (14,206)	
Blyth, Sarah	5:30:36 (28,153)	
Blythe, Jaime	5:49:39 (29,693)	
Boal, Wendy	3:56:02 (9,189)	
Board, Frances	4:13:33 (13,141)	
Board, Helen	4:13:33 (13,141)	
Boardman, Kelly	4:58:32 (23,704)	
Boardman, Susan	5:49:12 (29,653)	
Boarnoe, Charlotte	4:45:05 (20,739)	
Boast, Nicola	5:12:41 (25,932)	
Boast, Rebecca	5:02:45 (24,426)	
Boatfield, Jessica	5:06:07 (24,971)	
Boden, Patricia	3:51:40 (8,124)	
Bogdanowicz, Marzena	3:32:50 (4,572)	
Bogie, Alison	4:08:27 (11,995)	
Bohmer-Laubis, Jacqueline	4:27:41 (16,643)	
Boissonnet, Marie-Laure	4:26:58 (16,462)	
Bol, Frances	5:21:32 (27,087)	
Bolam, Caroline	3:38:53 (5,577)	
Bollom, Jean	4:29:36 (17,139)	
Bolton, Caroline	4:07:46 (11,865)	
Bolton, Carolyn	4:28:28 (16,847)	
Bolwell, Vicky	4:21:35 (15,126)	
Bond, Donna	3:52:01 (8,200)	
Bond, Robyn	4:53:11 (22,541)	
Bond, Sally	5:40:35 (29,041)	
Bone, Philippa	4:13:57 (13,244)	
Bonham, Dorothy	4:34:40 (18,324)	
Bonner-Murphy, Dawn	3:53:13 (8,479)	
Bonninga, Shelagh	5:02:03 (24,320)	
Bonzon, Patricia	4:17:02 (13,993)	
Boocock, Catherine	5:52:32 (29,854)	
Boote, Philippa	3:55:16 (8,983)	
Booth, Danielle	4:44:02 (20,504)	
Booth, Helen	5:47:00 (29,490)	
Booth, Jamie	5:45:25 (29,398)	
Booth, Joanne	5:26:22 (27,719)	
Booth, Kathryn	5:34:13 (28,497)	
Booth-Fernandes, Rachel	5:14:39 (26,196)	
Bootman, Emma	6:18:04 (30,936)	

Booty, Tabitha	4:38:36 (19,228)	
Boreham, Katherine	4:06:06 (11,515)	
Born, Gabriela	3:07:07 (1,421)	
Bortoli Gnych, Rosanna	5:36:36 (28,700)	
Bosac, Creana	4:41:03 (19,767)	
Bose, Shirley	5:51:48 (29,821)	
Boston, Angela	4:43:27 (20,363)	
Boswell, Deborah	5:01:24 (24,223)	
Botezan, Michaela	2:25:32 (42)	
Bottomer, Claire	6:54:57 (31,832)	
Bottomley, Jane	4:25:16 (16,074)	
Boucher, Fiona	4:23:27 (15,603)	
Boucher, Gail	4:24:16 (15,816)	
Boughey, Louisa	5:59:33 (30,242)	
Boughtwood, Lisa	6:27:40 (31,254)	
Boulton, Jane	3:09:35 (1,642)	
Bounaud, Marie Paule	4:59:30 (23,886)	
Boune, Kate	5:18:09 (26,642)	
Bouquet, Jenny	5:56:34 (30,083)	
Bourke, Marie	5:13:12 (26,000)	
Bourke, Tracey	6:32:09 (31,384)	
Bourne, Ruth	4:26:11 (16,293)	
Bousbah-Tanner, Heidi	4:23:26 (15,595)	
Bovin, Simone	4:09:39 (12,264)	
Bowater, Helene	5:28:59 (27,988)	
Bowater, Mary	4:53:02 (22,509)	
Bowden, Nikki	3:26:56 (3,665)	
Bowen, Joanna	4:12:11 (12,813)	
Bowen, Julia	3:49:00 (7,518)	
Bowen, Samantha	5:36:59 (28,734)	
Bowers, Sarah	6:01:07 (30,305)	
Bowes, Sally	4:27:27 (16,581)	
Bowes, Shamane	3:57:37 (9,599)	
Bowie, Emily	4:33:51 (18,126)	
Bowles, Judy	4:45:40 (20,882)	
Bowles, Libby	4:36:38 (18,793)	
Bowles, Liza	4:08:29 (12,008)	
Bowman, Jean	4:39:04 (19,335)	
Bowman, Kelly	7:50:07 (32,233)	
Bowman, Melanie	4:50:42 (22,011)	
Bown, Rachel	3:34:14 (4,787)	
Bownes, Anna	5:00:31 (24,073)	
Bownes, Diane	3:51:25 (8,055)	
Bowsher, Ann-Marie	5:18:34 (26,710)	
Boxall, Fiona	4:29:38 (17,146)	
Boxall, Sarah	4:33:03 (17,963)	
Boyd, Johanna	4:42:18 (20,053)	
Boyer, Andrée	4:01:00 (10,429)	
Boyington, Claire	4:21:22 (15,075)	
Boyle, Brenda	6:04:13 (30,417)	
Boyle, Carole	5:20:53 (27,006)	
Boyle, Ellen	4:58:37 (23,722)	
Boyle, Kerry	4:52:43 (22,441)	
Boyle, Laura	4:53:58 (22,708)	
Boyle, Michelle	4:29:51 (17,207)	
Boyle, Nicola	3:37:05 (5,249)	
Boyle, Paula	4:18:35 (14,387)	
Boyles, Katy	4:45:15 (20,785)	
Boynton, Patricia	7:14:57 (32,037)	
Boys, Katie	4:46:20 (21,054)	
Bracher, Camilla	5:44:14 (29,320)	
Bradbrook, Emma	6:39:15 (31,528)	
Bradburn, Charlotte	4:12:03 (12,772)	
Bradburne, Lorna	4:39:46 (19,490)	
Bradbury, Carol	6:25:22 (31,174)	
Bradbury, Kathleen	3:49:56 (7,723)	
Bradfley, Clare	4:54:36 (22,837)	
Bradford, Elizabeth	4:33:09 (17,979)	
Bradley, Catherine	4:01:37 (10,563)	
Bradley, Judy	4:39:02 (19,328)	
Bradley, Karen	4:20:47 (14,923)	
Bradley, Tamsin	4:46:01 (20,964)	
Bradley-Watson, Amy	4:43:16 (20,309)	
Bradshaw, Ann	5:23:58 (27,405)	
Bradshaw, Margaret	6:33:46 (31,418)	
Bradwell, Helen	4:00:58 (10,424)	
Brady, Maria	3:55:04 (8,929)	
Brady, Sandra	5:06:30 (25,016)	
Brady, Theresa	3:26:05 (3,550)	
Brady, Tina	5:22:09 (27,160)	
Bragg, Amanda	4:32:19 (17,795)	
Braidwood, Rachael	5:21:25 (27,072)	
Braker, Julie	5:03:08 (24,482)	

Bran, Laurel 4:10:04 (12,366)
Branch, Ann 3:14:03 (2,137)
Branchett, Emma 5:09:16 (25,441)
Brandhorst, Fiona 5:04:37 (24,718)
Brandon, Jessica 5:06:30 (25,016)
Brandrick, Gillian 3:53:12 (8,474)
Brandt, Claudia 4:17:48 (14,210)
Brandwood, Sarah 3:56:32 (9,330)
Braun, Ines 3:58:40 (9,877)
Brause, Kerstin 3:51:40 (8,124)
Bravery, Debbie 6:59:34 (31,880)
Bray, Dominique 5:26:18 (27,710)
Bray, Elaine 5:01:07 (24,171)
Bray, Helen 5:17:50 (26,583)
Bray, Lorraine 3:47:31 (7,216)
Bray, Sarah 4:45:13 (20,774)
Bray, Stephanie 6:47:29 (31,663)
Brayford, Lucy 3:28:35 (3,919)
Brayshay, Margaret 5:41:30 (29,116)
Breadner, Jennifer 4:47:27 (21,287)
Breagan, Heidi 4:30:41 (17,414)
Brecknock, Mary 4:15:14 (13,576)
Bredin, Jane 6:34:47 (31,443)
Breen, Sara 5:39:42 (28,963)
Breeze, Elizabeth 4:16:36 (13,876)
Bremner, Aileen 3:51:30 (8,074)
Bremner, Jane 3:18:54 (2,644)
Brengdahl, Eva 3:43:55 (6,530)
Brennan, Karen 5:02:15 (24,353)
Brennan, Rebecca 3:55:58 (9,168)
Brennan, Theresa 4:24:52 (15,968)
Brenner, Sachiko 5:50:53 (29,777)
Brent, Lesley 4:53:19 (22,574)
Brentnall, Claire 3:31:17 (4,378)
Bresnahan, Cassie 4:23:27 (15,603)
Brett, Sandra 5:08:46 (25,367)
Brewer, Becky 4:51:37 (22,228)
Brewer, Caroline 4:35:54 (18,620)
Brewer, Linda 4:39:20 (19,409)
Brewer, Nicola 6:45:45 (31,639)
Brewer, Sally 4:54:47 (22,881)
Brewerton, Kerry 5:38:28 (28,854)
Brewis, Linda 3:35:43 (5,027)
Brewitt, Debbie 4:10:21 (12,428)
Brewster, Fiona 4:26:02 (16,254)
Brewster, Geraldine 4:07:03 (11,698)
Brewster, Louise 4:38:31 (19,200)
Brewster, Vanessa 4:14:20 (13,341)
Brian, Jill 5:39:21 (28,927)
Brice, Fiona 5:11:06 (25,707)
Bridge, Natasha 4:42:57 (20,217)
Bridge, Susan 3:55:24 (9,022)
Bridge, Teresa 5:57:42 (30,149)
Bridge, Tracey 4:04:41 (11,222)
Briffett, Jane 5:40:40 (29,052)
Brigger, Anna-Louise 4:54:59 (22,917)
Briggs, Camilla 3:13:01 (1,992)
Briggs, Kathryn 4:56:38 (23,294)
Briggs, Nicola 4:39:20 (19,409)
Briggs, Susan 5:23:55 (27,397)
Bright, Hetty 4:53:32 (22,625)
Bright, Meg 5:33:47 (28,450)
Brightman, Pat 5:44:45 (29,344)
Brighton, Catherine 3:23:01 (3,112)
Brighton, Susan 4:08:23 (11,977)
Brikci, Paula 4:51:45 (22,252)
Brimelow, Daniela 4:26:25 (16,339)
Brinckley, Jane 4:48:26 (21,524)
Brindley, Anne 3:33:23 (4,663)
Brindley, Jacqueline 4:58:59 (23,795)
Bringlow, Véronique 3:11:02 (1,761)
Brink, Elbie 5:53:25 (29,901)
Brink, Mary 3:57:33 (9,587)
Brink, Sandra 4:36:15 (18,698)
Brinklow, Patricia 5:25:03 (27,546)
Brinkmann, Gesa 5:28:03 (27,895)
Bristow, Celia 5:28:52 (27,972)
Bristow, Linda 5:18:41 (26,725)
Bristow, Mary 5:09:05 (25,419)
Britchford, Claire 6:37:34 (31,498)
Brittain, Susan 5:17:33 (26,553)
Brittleton, Hilda 6:54:39 (31,822)
Britton, Barbara 4:52:10 (22,333)
Britton, Toni 3:38:30 (5,494)
Britton, Trudy 5:13:49 (26,083)
Brkan, Rachelle 5:35:57 (28,635)
Broad, Joanne 4:41:27 (19,861)
Broadbent, Karen 4:44:21 (20,584)
Broadhurst, Alison 5:06:18 (24,997)
Broadwell, Nicky 4:01:00 (10,429)
Brocklehurst, Catherine 4:03:00 (10,839)
Brocklesby, Edwina 3:59:29 (10,090)
Brodie, Jennifer 4:01:52 (10,613)
Brodrick, Tessa 5:11:45 (25,792)
Broekhof, Mary 4:16:03 (13,750)
Brogan, Caroline 5:45:30 (29,404)
Brogden, Isobel 4:00:17 (10,291)
Brokenshire, Ethel 3:27:42 (3,769)
Bromham, Isabelle 6:03:32 (30,397)
Bromley, Michaela 3:42:09 (6,178)
Bromley, Patricia 4:36:17 (18,707)
Bronw, Karen 3:52:46 (8,367)
Brook, Catherine 4:50:05 (21,882)
Brooker, Joanne 4:37:18 (18,948)
Brooker, Lisa 5:25:22 (27,595)
Brooker, Teresa 3:38:50 (5,567)
Brookes, Emily 4:33:31 (18,064)
Brookes, Nicla 6:52:58 (31,781)
Brookes, Sophie 5:19:51 (26,865)
Brookhouse, Jane 4:20:23 (14,842)
Brookman, Monica 5:11:33 (25,767)
Brooks, Charlotte 6:06:29 (30,514)
Brooks, Lindsey 4:42:04 (20,002)
Brooks, Theresa 4:30:03 (17,252)
Broom, Linda 4:14:33 (13,394)
Broome, Jackie 4:41:34 (19,885)
Broome, Jayne 4:19:10 (14,546)
Broome, Sara 4:30:19 (17,312)
Brosnan, Jacqueline 4:47:11 (21,223)
Broughall, Allison 5:01:10 (24,179)
Brousse, Isabelle 5:11:48 (25,801)
Browell, Alison 4:52:40 (22,436)
Brown, Amanda 4:25:23 (16,113)
Brown, Amanda 4:33:26 (18,043)
Brown, Amanda 5:56:02 (30,047)
Brown, Ana 4:11:56 (12,749)
Brown, Angela 4:13:32 (13,134)
Brown, Angela 4:48:29 (21,532)
Brown, Anne 4:56:40 (23,306)
Brown, Barbara 4:31:42 (17,672)
Brown, Carol 3:36:30 (5,142)
Brown, Chloe 4:10:31 (12,468)
Brown, Claire 5:25:06 (27,553)
Brown, Constance 6:25:11 (31,165)
Brown, Elizabeth 4:16:56 (13,979)
Brown, Elizabeth 4:59:55 (23,972)
Brown, Emma 4:16:30 (13,858)
Brown, Georgina 4:59:45 (23,933)
Brown, Grace 5:14:25 (26,161)
Brown, Helen 4:02:07 (10,658)
Brown, Helen 4:18:09 (14,279)
Brown, Helen 7:24:31 (32,106)
Brown, Holly 5:14:30 (26,177)
Brown, Jacqueline 5:10:48 (25,663)
Brown, Jacqueline 6:21:24 (31,060)
Brown, Janet 5:17:20 (26,518)
Brown, Jennifer 4:17:01 (13,989)
Brown, Jennifer 4:47:23 (21,269)
Brown, Joanne 4:34:30 (18,289)
Brown, Joanne 4:55:46 (23,103)
Brown, Judy 3:23:40 (3,200)
Brown, Julia 4:15:02 (13,520)
Brown, Kathryn 4:28:32 (16,868)
Brown, Kerry 4:28:42 (16,910)
Brown, Lesley 4:42:25 (20,088)
Brown, Lorna 4:42:31 (20,116)
Brown, Madalaine 3:52:34 (8,322)
Brown, Marian 4:49:09 (21,662)
Brown, Melissa 5:11:54 (25,812)
Brown, Pauline 3:59:18 (10,038)
Brown, Rhona 4:21:17 (15,054)
Brown, Sally 4:15:18 (13,592)
Brown, Sally 5:11:35 (25,777)
Brown, Sandra 5:38:00 (28,812)
Brown, Sue 3:55:11 (8,962)
Brown, Sue 6:29:21 (31,309)
Brown, Susan 3:36:00 (5,064)
Brown, Susan 4:25:30 (16,142)
Brown, Susan 5:02:54 (24,444)
Brown, Trudi 5:22:59 (27,284)
Brown, Valerie 5:13:58 (26,096)
Brown, Wendy 3:52:02 (8,203)
Brown, Wendy 3:53:54 (8,646)
Brown, Wendy 4:04:32 (11,185)
Brown, Zoe 5:12:17 (25,868)
Browne, Gabrielle 3:37:36 (5,346)
Brownhill, Anne 4:05:44 (11,440)
Browning, Natalie 4:29:57 (17,229)
Brownlee, Victoria 4:49:14 (21,685)
Brownlow, Laura 4:50:53 (22,052)
Bruce, Louise 4:37:12 (18,923)
Bruce, Susan 2:59:12 (871)
Bruchez, Estelle 5:18:08 (26,640)
Bruehne, Ulrike 5:00:00 (23,982)
Brunjes, Emma 4:58:23 (23,667)
Bruno, Ludovica 3:54:22 (8,743)
Bruno, Veronica 4:56:46 (23,329)
Brunskill, Emma 4:08:40 (12,055)
Brunton, Suzanna 3:25:03 (3,401)
Brussels, Linzi 4:23:08 (15,526)
Bruton, Nicola 3:58:21 (9,796)
Bruyns, Sandra 4:45:58 (20,952)
Bryan, Delyth 3:37:14 (5,278)
Bryan, Leigh 4:30:10 (17,277)
Bryan, Louise 5:54:05 (29,936)
Bryan, Rebecca 5:47:38 (29,548)
Bryan, Sarah 6:56:31 (31,851)
Bryan, Sheila 7:05:05 (31,933)
Bryans, Fiona 4:12:24 (12,858)
Bryant, Lynn 5:57:21 (30,128)
Bryant, Margaret 4:57:39 (23,514)
Bryant-Jefferies, Lauren 4:51:27 (22,195)
Bryce, Joanna 3:28:57 (3,997)
Bryce, Rosalind 5:11:08 (25,713)
Bryce, Sarah 5:27:14 (27,805)
Bryson, Angela 4:18:30 (14,359)
Bubloz, Hazel 6:38:39 (31,513)
Buchan, Rachel 4:46:46 (21,141)
Buck, Lindsay 4:27:31 (16,605)
Buckenham, Emma 5:07:39 (25,212)
Buckingham, Louise 7:06:16 (31,944)
Buckingham, Philippa 4:42:59 (20,229)
Buckland, Suzanne 3:59:42 (10,154)
Buckle, Karen 5:10:00 (25,547)
Buckle, Sarah 4:59:30 (23,886)
Buckle, Sharon 3:34:00 (4,749)
Buckley, Andrea 5:21:39 (27,106)
Buckley, Diane 4:08:03 (11,913)
Buckley, Victoria 4:31:02 (17,510)
Bucknell, Julie 5:09:07 (25,424)
Buckton, Sandra 4:40:20 (19,618)
Budd, Judy 5:25:07 (27,557)
Budd, Vivien 6:02:23 (30,355)
Budden, Sally 5:38:42 (28,877)
Buechner, Conny 4:31:49 (17,692)
Buhlmayer, Elisabeth 3:24:00 (3,247)
Bukin, Toni 5:40:09 (29,008)
Bulcock, Ann-Marie 3:28:30 (3,903)
Bulgin, Amanda 4:08:12 (11,938)
Bull, Debra 4:53:07 (22,525)
Bull, Donna 4:50:34 (21,979)
Bull, Helen 4:33:20 (18,013)
Bull, Jill 4:45:36 (20,867)
Bull, Joanne 4:27:56 (16,698)
Bullen, Janine 6:19:52 (31,013)
Bullingham, Angela 4:20:08 (14,779)
Bullingham, Maria 5:37:36 (28,782)
Bullingham, Natalie 5:20:29 (26,954)
Bullivant, Jayne 4:34:04 (18,186)
Bullock, Carolyn 5:15:06 (26,261)
Bullock, Dawn 3:31:43 (4,440)
Bullock, Kimberley 5:53:51 (29,926)
Bullock, Sarah 4:53:26 (22,602)
Bungay, Eydna 5:48:29 (29,605)
Bunn, Lorraine 4:52:55 (22,487)
Bunning, Karen 4:47:54 (21,399)
Bunt, Deb 5:07:52 (25,244)
Bunten, Susan 3:41:57 (6,140)
Bunting, Maggie 3:46:32 (7,041)

Bunting, Tina	6:21:58 (31,074)
Bunyan, Kay	4:15:22 (13,607)
Buono, Stefania	4:31:53 (17,705)
Burbridge, Joanna	4:25:28 (16,135)
Burch, Heather	4:06:40 (11,620)
Burchmore, Carole	6:49:26 (31,700)
Burdett, Melanie	3:57:00 (9,458)
Burge, Jenny	5:08:56 (25,392)
Burgess, Harriet	4:30:14 (17,295)
Burgess, Jane	5:22:16 (27,181)
Burgess, Maxine	3:47:04 (7,135)
Burgess, Tracy	4:44:18 (20,571)
Burgin, Maria	4:50:39 (22,001)
Burke, Janet	5:26:37 (27,744)
Burke, Sinead	5:24:59 (27,533)
Burling, Laura	5:14:20 (26,143)
Burnand, Lesley	5:14:06 (26,107)
Burnett, Anita	4:43:33 (20,391)
Burnett, Jess	4:38:18 (19,161)
Burnett, Julett	5:52:13 (29,843)
Burns, Andrea	5:05:29 (24,880)
Burns, Jane	5:03:42 (24,574)
Burns, Katie	4:42:51 (20,194)
Burr, Marion	5:47:32 (29,542)
Burrage, Kellee	4:20:48 (14,929)
Burrell, Helen	2:52:14 (452)
Burrell, Jennifer	5:10:03 (25,558)
Burridge, Deborah	3:07:36 (1,460)
Burridge, Elizabeth	6:17:51 (30,925)
Burrows, Catherine	5:09:18 (25,446)
Burrows, Emma	5:23:55 (27,397)
Burrows, Katy	5:40:25 (29,031)
Burrows, Linda	5:29:20 (28,022)
Burrows, Rachel	4:04:51 (11,257)
Burrows, Wendy	4:30:21 (17,322)
Bursill, Christina	3:45:51 (6,901)
Burston, Nicola	4:56:32 (23,270)
Burton, Alexandra	4:53:43 (22,652)
Burton, Catherine	5:57:29 (30,138)
Burton, Christine	4:42:49 (20,188)
Burton, Helen	5:20:56 (27,015)
Burton, Joanne	3:49:14 (7,574)
Burton, Lesley	4:56:20 (23,228)
Burton, Linda	4:16:59 (13,985)
Burton, Ruth	5:25:46 (27,636)
Burton, Sharon	3:29:54 (4,153)
Busby, Julie	5:21:06 (27,034)
Bush, Judith	6:05:18 (30,469)
Bush, Michelle	7:21:43 (32,085)
Bushell, Julie	4:04:05 (11,084)
Bussey, Amanda	3:45:56 (6,919)
Busst, Clare	4:25:22 (16,107)
Butland, Orlanda	3:57:16 (9,522)
Butler, Ann	5:20:34 (26,965)
Butler, Bridget	4:46:34 (21,100)
Butler, Deborah	4:35:00 (18,401)
Butler, Jean	5:18:43 (26,730)
Butler, Karen	3:34:26 (4,824)
Butler, Michele	3:29:59 (4,163)
Butler, Sandra	4:54:33 (22,823)
Butter, Ruth	3:41:57 (6,140)
Butler-Stoney, Elizabeth	3:52:20 (8,273)
Butterfield, Caroline	6:48:54 (31,693)
Butterfield, Katherine	3:41:52 (6,126)
Butterworth, Janet	5:43:46 (29,288)
Butterworth, Suzanne	4:36:39 (18,797)
Byer, Elizabeth	4:10:02 (12,356)
Byers, Rachel	3:25:04 (3,404)
Bygrave, Christina	4:41:57 (19,985)
Bylsma-Hanning, Frietje	4:19:57 (14,729)
Byrd, Louise	5:55:12 (30,011)
Byre, Camilla	4:50:23 (21,939)
Byrne, Anne-Marie	5:51:42 (29,818)
Byrne, Caroline	4:24:53 (15,970)
Byrne, Catharine	4:57:59 (23,580)
Byrne, Diane	3:30:15 (4,210)
Byrne, Georgina	5:13:29 (26,039)
Byrne, Jackie	5:50:29 (29,752)
Byrne, Miranda	4:48:01 (21,433)
Byrne, Roisin	4:04:29 (11,177)
Byrom, Jenny	4:37:44 (19,029)
Cadden, Paul	4:30:26 (17,354)
Caharel, Lydie	3:21:01 (2,887)

Cahill, Lisa	4:48:20 (21,501)
Caig, Joanne	4:53:26 (22,602)
Cains, Hannah	5:37:59 (28,808)
Caira-Neeson, Susanna	5:26:50 (27,763)
Cairns, Imogen	5:22:14 (27,171)
Cajado-Ogland, Graziela	4:19:02 (14,513)
Calamari, Kimberley	6:20:49 (31,042)
Calcutt, Lisa	3:56:30 (9,318)
Calder, Mandy	4:17:12 (14,034)
Caldwell, Claire	4:51:27 (22,195)
Caldwell, Gillian	4:57:11 (23,426)
Calemard, Valerie	4:01:22 (10,509)
Caley, Paula	5:58:55 (30,204)
Callingham, Kathy	4:39:44 (19,484)
Calnan, Stephanie	4:04:58 (11,282)
Calsamiglia, Susana	4:40:27 (19,643)
Calton, Patsy	6:13:34 (30,784)
Calvert, Amanda	3:30:30 (4,246)
Calvert, Jane	4:00:26 (10,319)
Calvert, Sue	3:38:12 (5,442)
Calvin, Zita	4:23:56 (15,734)
Cameron, Joan	6:27:22 (31,235)
Cameron, Karen	4:11:19 (12,601)
Cameron, Libby	3:43:39 (6,478)
Cameron, Sarah	4:43:16 (20,309)
Camm, Joanne	4:38:58 (19,318)
Campanella, Mary	4:24:15 (15,810)
Campbell, Brenda	4:52:04 (22,323)
Campbell, Gail	4:02:45 (10,793)
Campbell, Ilidia	3:49:08 (7,543)
Campbell, Joanne	4:47:53 (21,394)
Campbell, Kate	4:55:14 (22,963)
Campbell, Kris	4:54:17 (22,767)
Campbell, Laura	4:27:32 (16,610)
Campbell, Maureen	4:22:37 (15,401)
Campbell, Nina	5:37:51 (28,800)
Campbell, Sophie	3:51:10 (8,002)
Campbell, Sylvia	3:47:50 (7,289)
Campbell-Stanway, Camilla	4:11:49 (12,723)
Campion, Stephanie	4:14:57 (13,492)
Canaday, Johanna	5:26:09 (27,696)
Candy, Susan	3:27:18 (3,714)
Cane, Claire	4:54:24 (22,795)
Canham, Jennifer	6:25:46 (31,194)
Cannell, Linda	6:28:14 (31,279)
Cannings, Pippa	4:18:34 (14,380)
Cantle, Betty	4:40:54 (19,727)
Cantos Juan, Rosario	3:54:15 (8,716)
Cantrell, Susannah	4:50:40 (22,005)
Caplan, Lucinda	6:10:25 (30,657)
Cappaert, Susan	4:12:18 (12,832)
Capps, Joanna	5:44:54 (29,355)
Carcianiga, Chiara	4:28:46 (16,928)
Cardell, Margaret	3:58:11 (9,748)
Carey, Fiona	4:53:09 (22,530)
Carey, Patricia	4:58:17 (23,645)
Cargill, Rebecca	6:34:05 (31,424)
Carleton, Meghan	3:30:12 (4,199)
Carlin, Annette	3:24:43 (3,360)
Carmichael, Linda	5:01:46 (24,274)
Carmody, Catherine	4:42:38 (20,139)
Carmody, Fiona	4:29:39 (17,150)
Carnell, Susan	3:21:23 (2,922)
Carney, Lisa	4:22:34 (15,379)
Carolan, Anne	5:00:15 (24,027)
Carpenter, Eileen	5:27:05 (27,785)
Carpenter, Maureen	4:46:36 (21,109)
Carpenter, Viki	4:50:46 (22,025)
Carr, Emma	5:17:55 (26,600)
Carr, Lesley	4:33:41 (18,094)
Carr, May	6:54:36 (31,820)
Carr, Paula	5:50:02 (29,716)
Carr, Wendy	4:38:13 (19,138)
Carr, Zoe	4:50:08 (21,887)
Carragher, Lindsey	4:56:24 (23,240)
Carrera, Elaine	4:32:29 (17,830)
Carrick, Tamara	4:40:14 (19,586)
Carrighan, Elizabeth	4:58:45 (23,745)
Carrington, Alison	5:25:38 (27,625)
Carrington, Caroline	5:01:15 (24,194)
Carrington, Shirley	4:10:10 (12,388)
Carrod, Clare	4:30:41 (17,414)
Carroll, Catherine	5:28:49 (27,969)

Carroll, Christina	3:57:52 (9,669)
Carroll, Kate	4:02:07 (10,658)
Carroll, Lucy	4:18:41 (14,419)
Carroll, Rebecca	5:59:25 (30,234)
Carroll, Sarah	4:43:31 (20,382)
Carron, Hilda	4:50:28 (21,956)
Carson, Jenny	4:30:43 (17,422)
Carson, Suzanne	3:02:25 (1,084)
Carter, Alex	4:10:06 (12,373)
Carter, Alex	4:46:29 (21,091)
Carter, Claire	5:43:25 (29,265)
Carter, Francesca	4:36:06 (18,671)
Carter, Gillian	4:28:36 (16,886)
Carter, Holly	4:15:26 (13,624)
Carter, Janet	4:04:50 (11,252)
Carter, Janice	6:25:36 (31,183)
Carter, Johanne	5:54:25 (29,966)
Carter, Lois	5:38:40 (28,873)
Carter, Ruth	5:39:27 (28,945)
Carter, Sabrina	3:56:13 (9,249)
Cartledge, Margaret	4:56:05 (23,166)
Cartmell, Sarah	4:59:03 (23,812)
Cartwright, Beth	4:38:50 (19,285)
Cartwright, Lindsey	4:31:21 (17,582)
Cartwright, Sue	3:59:38 (10,130)
Caruso, Judith	4:41:41 (19,915)
Carver, Dawn	4:00:37 (10,348)
Carver, Karen	5:30:02 (28,090)
Carver, Katie	4:35:20 (18,479)
Cary, Catherine	4:51:22 (22,173)
Casamayou, Maureen	5:40:20 (29,020)
Case, Pamela	6:05:55 (30,497)
Caseley, Ann-Marie	4:00:09 (10,260)
Caseley, Kathryn	4:09:10 (12,167)
Casely, Shona	4:17:41 (14,172)
Case-Toussaint, Margareth	4:40:49 (19,706)
Casey, Barbara	3:30:51 (4,306)
Casey, Bernadette	5:27:17 (27,808)
Cash, Nicola	4:18:51 (14,463)
Cashman, Carolyn	5:10:48 (25,663)
Cason, Julie	4:33:39 (18,089)
Cassar, Ilona	5:47:12 (29,506)
Cassidy, Mary	7:31:37 (32,164)
Cassidy, Samantha	4:55:42 (23,079)
Casson, Hilary	5:49:09 (29,648)
Castelen, Shirley	4:51:15 (22,144)
Casterton, Wendy	3:33:38 (4,695)
Castillo, Maria	4:31:58 (17,721)
Castleden, Kate	5:13:25 (26,026)
Castrogiovanni, Linda	6:24:10 (31,139)
Caterino, Anna-Maria	3:50:08 (7,761)
Catlett, Jacky	5:21:55 (27,140)
Cato, Shelley	4:27:16 (16,539)
Caton, Sophie	5:06:35 (25,031)
Caton-Hewings, Karen	7:06:17 (31,945)
Cattermole, Karen	5:35:22 (28,586)
Caudle, Claire	5:23:03 (27,292)
Caulfield, Grainne	3:43:38 (6,473)
Caunce, Melanie	5:43:52 (29,295)
Cavaliero, Nicky	5:49:14 (29,655)
Cavanagh, Meghan	4:23:44 (15,680)
Caven, Alexandra	3:48:12 (7,359)
Caven, Hannah	4:50:49 (22,034)
Caven, Sophie	4:48:17 (21,491)
Cawte, Pamela	6:39:57 (31,539)
Cawthorne, Helen	2:56:35 (680)
Cawthorne, Sarah	6:13:52 (30,792)
Ceder, Sunilla	4:11:11 (12,572)
Celenza, Elaine	6:07:26 (30,552)
Celerier, Elizabeth	4:02:46 (10,798)
César de Sa, Rebecca	3:51:24 (8,051)
Chacksfield, Felicity	5:15:40 (26,336)
Chadwick, Joanne	4:24:25 (15,844)
Chadwick, Rebecca	4:44:16 (20,565)
Chaffe, Ann	6:48:41 (31,686)
Chalkley, Sharon	3:59:54 (10,200)
Challinor-Keane, Rachel	5:41:27 (29,111)
Challis, Jan	4:23:50 (15,703)
Challis, Julie	3:55:54 (9,154)
Chamard, Sylvie	3:58:27 (9,823)
Chamberlain, Raina	4:50:29 (21,963)
Chambers, Julie	5:46:38 (29,475)
Chambers, Morgan	5:36:56 (28,730)

Chambers, Natasha 6:50:40 (31,738)
Chambers, Norah 4:59:51 (23,959)
Champion, Joy 4:27:11 (16,521)
Champion, Susan 5:15:15 (26,286)
Chan, Betty 4:04:20 (11,142)
Chandler, Julie 4:42:27 (20,098)
Chaplin, Emma 4:49:34 (21,766)
Chaplin, Nicky 5:58:03 (30,165)
Chaplin, Tina 5:45:36 (29,411)
Chapman, Ann 4:44:42 (20,658)
Chapman, Catherine 4:34:19 (18,246)
Chapman, Jayne 4:12:43 (12,941)
Chapman, Kathryn 5:49:19 (29,664)
Chapman, Lesley 3:40:31 (5,868)
Chapman, Lynne 4:28:23 (16,817)
Chapman, Philippa 3:57:02 (9,464)
Chapman, Sarah 4:25:27 (16,130)
Chapman-Sheath, Stephanie 5:17:45 (26,571)
Chapple, Janet 4:21:02 (14,988)
Charge, Kellie 6:43:42 (31,608)
Charker, Yvonne 5:59:07 (30,214)
Charkin, Natasha 4:17:09 (14,024)
Charlery, Paulette 3:39:03 (5,607)
Charles, Marvelyn 4:36:55 (18,858)
Charlesworth, Marian 5:50:43 (29,766)
Charlesworth, Susan 5:04:36 (24,717)
Charlton, Emma 4:49:01 (21,635)
Charlton, Jane 3:56:51 (9,413)
Charman, Karen 4:19:56 (14,723)
Charnock, Sarah 3:35:06 (4,926)
Chater, Ann-Marie 4:50:51 (22,043)
Chauhan, Jyoti 5:43:31 (29,274)
Chauveau, Jeanne-Marie 5:10:40 (25,644)
Chee-A-Kwai, Trina 6:01:04 (30,301)
Cheema, Mandip 5:01:42 (24,257)
Cheeseman, Kimberly 5:04:46 (24,752)
Cheeseman, Lara 4:19:43 (14,673)
Cheeseman, Rosemary 5:17:22 (26,522)
Cheifetz, Anna 3:37:59 (5,410)
Chennells, Fiona 4:38:08 (19,114)
Chepkemei, Susan 2:23:12 (30)
Chesley, Anne-Marie 4:55:56 (23,138)
Chessum, Deborah 5:01:46 (24,274)
Chettle, Dawn 6:55:20 (31,837)
Cheverton, Dinah 2:59:26 (895)
Chevis, Rebecca 7:21:00 (32,075)
Chew, Shelby 3:58:14 (9,764)
Chiaramello, Yolanda 5:12:12 (25,856)
Chib, Bindu 5:36:09 (28,651)
Chick, Stephanie 4:58:16 (23,643)
Childs, Joanna 3:27:48 (3,780)
Childs, Laura 5:06:47 (25,073)
Childs, Sarah 6:05:32 (30,480)
Chilton, Katie 5:25:16 (27,587)
Chilvers, Kerry 5:37:21 (28,763)
Chilvers, Ruth 5:18:49 (26,737)
Chittenden, Sarah 5:09:07 (25,424)
Chopping, Olivia 5:19:41 (26,846)
Choudry, Naylea 6:44:08 (31,611)
Choyce, Katy 4:07:50 (11,879)
Chrascina, Nicola 4:41:25 (19,853)
Chrismas, Nicola 5:01:54 (24,294)
Christian, Deborah 5:15:32 (26,316)
Christiansen, Susan 4:17:31 (14,115)
Christie, Erica 3:06:26 (1,353)
Christie, Nathalie 2:59:51 (931)
Christie, Ruth 7:14:03 (32,032)
Christie, Stephanie 4:20:59 (14,974)
Christie, Susanne 4:53:55 (22,699)
Christmas, Wendy 4:59:40 (23,917)
Chu, Kathryn 3:54:25 (8,759)
Chun, Julia 5:40:37 (29,045)
Chundur, Anu 7:25:04 (32,109)
Church, Jane 4:28:19 (16,794)
Church, Kathryn 4:47:30 (21,298)
Churchill, Deborah 5:00:11 (24,009)
Churchill, Jane 4:54:41 (22,861)
Churchill, Lesley 4:47:25 (21,279)
Churchill, Michelle 5:02:10 (24,341)
Chuter, Tracey 4:44:02 (20,504)
Cinturel, Jocelyne 3:17:42 (2,517)
Clack, Michaela 4:26:14 (16,306)
Claisse, Christiane 4:14:02 (13,270)
Clapham, Penelope 5:10:38 (25,640)
Clark, Anna 5:29:20 (28,022)
Clark, Candy 6:13:54 (30,793)
Clark, Caroline 5:10:20 (25,597)
Clark, Fay 5:48:02 (29,582)
Clark, Hannah 5:09:39 (25,496)
Clark, Jean 5:01:32 (24,236)
Clark, Jeanette 4:11:58 (12,754)
Clark, Jennifer 7:02:59 (31,914)
Clark, Katharine 5:31:18 (28,226)
Clark, Kerry 4:51:24 (22,178)
Clark, Linda 5:11:33 (25,767)
Clark, Lisa 6:27:51 (31,261)
Clark, Melissa 5:08:09 (25,291)
Clark, Paula 6:51:21 (31,749)
Clark, Penny 4:06:26 (11,578)
Clark, Samantha 5:08:03 (25,273)
Clark, Sandy 4:33:14 (17,990)
Clark, Sasha 4:51:15 (22,144)
Clark, Teresa 3:51:49 (8,153)
Clarke, Alison 4:37:14 (18,934)
Clarke, Amanda 3:19:28 (2,697)
Clarke, Annette 3:43:24 (6,437)
Clarke, Caroline 4:40:40 (19,676)
Clarke, Carolyn 5:15:30 (26,314)
Clarke, Debbie 4:33:48 (18,115)
Clarke, Gail 5:16:56 (26,473)
Clarke, Irene 8:15:12 (32,273)
Clarke, Joanne 4:50:19 (21,926)
Clarke, Linsey 4:03:32 (10,953)
Clarke, Pauline 4:34:46 (18,341)
Clarke, Sally 4:00:13 (10,274)
Clarke, Sally 4:17:45 (14,193)
Clarke, Sophie 4:54:16 (22,761)
Clarke, Terri 5:02:34 (24,400)
Clarke, Una 7:19:10 (32,064)
Clarke-Wareham, Sarah 4:23:48 (15,695)
Clarkson, Caroline 4:21:48 (15,185)
Clarkson, Heather 5:18:39 (26,718)
Clarkson, Julia 4:57:22 (23,453)
Clarkson, Linda 3:11:20 (1,784)
Clarkson, Penelope 5:00:03 (23,988)
Classey, Philippa 6:11:43 (30,716)
Clauson, Connie 4:00:17 (10,291)
Clawson, Julie 4:50:08 (21,887)
Claxton, Coral 4:08:16 (11,953)
Clay, Meeghan 4:24:15 (15,810)
Clay, Suzanne 5:47:16 (29,510)
Clay, Tiffany 4:20:46 (14,918)
Clayton, Bernadette 4:02:27 (10,732)
Clayton, Brenda 5:51:37 (29,812)
Clayton-Drabble, Susan 4:55:10 (22,956)
Cleary, Vivien 5:52:35 (29,859)
Cleave, Nicola 4:58:55 (23,784)
Cleaver, Lisa 5:09:12 (25,435)
Cleaver, Margaret 4:51:25 (22,182)
Cleaver, Moya 4:24:32 (15,871)
Clegg, Karly 5:20:05 (26,899)
Clemens, Linda 3:38:57 (5,591)
Clements, Angela 6:19:43 (31,005)
Clements, Joanna 5:01:47 (24,279)
Clements, Pru 3:15:50 (2,316)
Clench, Nicola 4:19:44 (14,679)
Clevely, Joanna 4:44:58 (20,706)
Clews, Nickola 4:25:15 (16,070)
Clifford, Mary 5:35:04 (28,559)
Clifton, June 5:01:45 (24,269)
Clinton, Jane 3:59:02 (9,971)
Clinton, Vera 5:04:04 (24,647)
Cloke, Yvonne 4:12:38 (12,925)
Close, Julia 3:20:59 (2,882)
Clough, Sarah 4:35:59 (18,646)
Clout, Charlotte 4:12:23 (12,852)
Cluley, Susan 3:51:28 (8,066)
Clutton, Diana 4:34:21 (18,252)
Clyde, Patricia 4:40:17 (19,599)
Coady, Emma 5:04:58 (24,787)
Cobby, Janet 4:47:55 (21,403)
Cobby, Jennifer 5:32:05 (28,296)
Cocchi, Patrizia 5:18:13 (26,657)
Cochrane, Jill 5:04:05 (24,649)
Cockroft, Karen 4:23:37 (15,643)
Codelia, Adriene 6:08:58 (30,604)
Codling, Marian 5:39:08 (28,914)
Codyre, Una 4:05:37 (11,419)
Coe, Fiona 4:26:43 (16,405)
Coen, Joanne 5:18:13 (26,657)
Coggan, Delia 5:33:22 (28,408)
Cohen, Anne 5:17:50 (26,583)
Cohen, Danielle 4:57:08 (23,411)
Coker, Wendy 5:57:20 (30,126)
Colby, Lisa 6:22:24 (31,085)
Colclough, Helen 4:46:51 (21,161)
Colcutt, Helen 4:17:36 (14,139)
Cole, Aisling 5:15:18 (26,290)
Cole, Alicia 4:22:25 (15,346)
Cole, Ann 4:53:57 (22,705)
Cole, Caroline 5:31:04 (28,198)
Cole, Dawn 6:08:47 (30,597)
Cole, Julie 4:27:57 (16,700)
Cole, Lindsey 4:58:23 (23,667)
Cole, Nicola 5:59:32 (30,240)
Cole, Susan 4:55:33 (23,037)
Cole, Theresa 5:27:39 (27,855)
Cole, Trudi 4:19:33 (14,626)
Colebourne, Ellen 5:31:39 (28,253)
Coleman, Annie 6:01:42 (30,331)
Coleman, Carolyn 4:05:30 (11,401)
Coleman, Kate 4:42:23 (20,078)
Coleman, Melanie 4:07:15 (11,749)
Coles, Snejana 6:24:51 (31,157)
Cole-Smalley, Lorna 5:16:57 (26,474)
Colgan, Anne 4:28:13 (16,773)
Colhoun, Graenia 5:45:39 (29,416)
Collen, Gillian 4:23:53 (15,716)
Collett, Teri 6:14:35 (30,812)
Colley, Sandra 6:19:54 (31,015)
Collier, Angela 5:04:53 (24,775)
Collin, Sue 3:56:19 (9,276)
Collins, Anne 4:20:56 (14,963)
Collins, Clare 5:49:36 (29,689)
Collins, Esther 4:09:58 (12,345)
Collins, Gwen 3:45:32 (6,837)
Collins, Helen 4:17:40 (14,165)
Collins, Jacky 4:57:40 (23,517)
Collins, Jane 5:59:07 (30,214)
Collins, Louise 4:29:20 (17,068)
Collins, Rita 6:01:19 (30,315)
Collins, Sandra 4:41:25 (19,853)
Collins, Tina 6:49:28 (31,705)
Collins, Virginia 4:21:50 (15,190)
Collins, Vivienne 4:38:08 (19,114)
Collinson, Audrey 5:17:18 (26,512)
Collinson, Carolyn 4:37:25 (18,967)
Collis, Victoria 5:14:14 (26,132)
Collison, Sarah 5:24:26 (27,465)
Collisson, Fiona 3:24:46 (3,367)
Colloby, Philippa 5:03:03 (24,464)
Colquhoun, Catherine 5:10:16 (25,592)
Colquhoun, Shirley 3:32:19 (4,510)
Colvill, Dawn 6:23:23 (31,114)
Colwell, Sally 4:48:04 (21,444)
Combe, Elisabeth 5:03:52 (24,608)
Combe, Marianne 5:29:53 (28,074)
Comber, Miriam 4:46:38 (21,112)
Combine, Jacqueline 4:51:18 (22,152)
Commeinhes, Marie-Helene 3:51:50 (8,159)
Compton, Linda 4:11:23 (12,618)
Conceicao, Maria 5:36:18 (28,663)
Coney, Diane 3:51:15 (8,019)
Cong, Kathy 5:21:15 (27,059)
Conklin, Tara 4:32:13 (17,779)
Conlan, Tara 6:33:33 (31,412)
Connelly, Helen 3:41:29 (6,060)
Connolly, Sheila 5:20:06 (26,904)
Connor, Anne 4:42:35 (20,131)
Connor, Emily 5:36:32 (28,689)
Connor, Sheelagh 5:17:36 (26,560)
Conquest, Lucy 3:50:12 (7,777)
Conroy, Maud 3:43:38 (6,473)
Constable, Tamsin 4:32:50 (17,909)
Conway, Darcie 4:04:30 (11,180)
Cooil, Jan 4:13:44 (13,184)
Cook, Allison 4:46:34 (21,100)
Cook, Debbie 5:35:16 (28,577)
Cook, Eliane 4:36:34 (18,781)

Cook, Fiona 4:49:11 (21,673)
Cook, Helen 3:58:26 (9,818)
Cook, Lissa 4:23:15 (15,560)
Cook, Louise 4:19:59 (14,737)
Cook, Pamela 6:11:11 (30,699)
Cook, Paula 4:59:38 (23,910)
Cook, Rachel 4:43:50 (20,466)
Cook, Sarah 6:39:51 (31,537)
Cook, Sharlene 4:14:28 (13,371)
Cook, Shirley 5:32:27 (28,331)
Cook, Stephanie 3:18:50 (2,640)
Cook, Tonia 4:12:19 (12,838)
Cooke, Camille 4:25:40 (16,174)
Cooke, Felicity 5:14:20 (26,143)
Cooke, Frances 4:20:53 (14,950)
Cooke, Helen 4:42:15 (20,039)
Cooke, Kate 3:48:51 (7,477)
Cooke, Tanya 5:00:40 (24,101)
Cooke-Simmons, Julia 3:50:42 (7,886)
Cookson, Lisa 4:36:20 (18,722)
Cooling, Susanna 4:42:05 (20,004)
Coomber, Karen 6:51:41 (31,755)
Coombs, Michell 5:38:18 (28,837)
Coope, Margaret 5:08:58 (25,395)
Cooper, Andrea 3:40:33 (5,873)
Cooper, Annick 6:31:45 (31,372)
Cooper, Claire 5:30:43 (28,168)
Cooper, Denise 4:24:27 (15,857)
Cooper, Elizabeth 4:27:09 (16,511)
Cooper, J 6:59:11 (31,878)
Cooper, Jackie 3:23:01 (3,112)
Cooper, Jane 4:19:25 (14,599)
Cooper, Karol 4:45:41 (20,884)
Cooper, Katherine 5:35:32 (28,598)
Cooper, Kathryn 5:39:52 (28,978)
Cooper, Lindsey 4:26:02 (16,254)
Cooper, Lisanne 4:09:53 (12,318)
Cooper, Louise 3:07:58 (1,496)
Cooper, Sue 5:02:37 (24,412)
Cooper, Susan 7:06:46 (31,953)
Cooper, Tina 6:39:00 (31,521)
Cooper, Toni 4:22:39 (15,409)
Coote, Annabel 3:52:53 (8,393)
Cope, Anna 5:34:23 (28,516)
Cope, Linda 6:14:35 (30,812)
Copley, Ann-Marie 7:19:04 (32,063)
Copley, Diane 4:56:49 (23,342)
Copley, Rachel 5:06:07 (24,971)
Copp, Sharon 4:15:46 (13,690)
Coray, Tania 3:59:46 (10,167)
Corbett, Tara 4:10:11 (12,389)
Corbishley, Helen 4:58:01 (23,583)
Corby, Clare 5:25:22 (27,595)
Cordal Pernas, Carmen 5:00:43 (24,108)
Corder, Maria 4:41:48 (19,943)
Cordery, Susan 6:01:34 (30,326)
Corke, Anita 7:33:09 (32,171)
Corke, Joanne 4:34:11 (18,209)
Corkill, Tracy 6:37:11 (31,490)
Cormack, Susi 4:56:04 (23,161)
Cornwell, Alix 6:02:18 (30,353)
Cornwell, Helen 3:40:52 (5,937)
Corran, Sarah 4:34:55 (18,376)
Corver, Michelle 4:56:02 (23,152)
Costello, Rebecca 5:14:37 (26,191)
Costelloe, Jenny 4:31:01 (17,502)
Costelloe, Louise 4:58:23 (23,667)
Coster, Debbie 3:56:30 (9,318)
Costiff, Christine 3:12:17 (1,901)
Costin, Sarah 3:33:37 (4,694)
Cosway, Allison 5:07:31 (25,186)
Cottaris, Tracy 4:26:35 (16,375)
Cottwald, Mary 4:33:57 (18,153)
Couchman, Hannah 5:02:48 (24,432)
Coughlan, Claire 4:29:15 (17,053)
Coull, Gemma 4:05:00 (11,289)
Coulson, Tracey 5:24:24 (27,459)
Coulter, Jenny 5:12:58 (25,971)
Coulter, Jessica 4:41:16 (19,816)
Coulthard, Sally 4:34:54 (18,372)
Coultrup, Kathleen 4:14:50 (13,461)
Couper, Suzanne 4:56:56 (23,364)
Courage, Faye 6:15:23 (30,840)
Court, Kass 4:44:59 (20,711)
Courtier, Jane 5:00:27 (24,060)
Cousen, Sharon 3:44:07 (6,567)
Cousins, Katie 6:17:55 (30,928)
Cowan, Sharon 4:46:07 (20,999)
Cowell, Angela 5:05:10 (24,822)
Cowell, Victoria 4:38:26 (19,189)
Cowen, Mary 5:47:14 (29,508)
Cowie, Tara 5:10:37 (25,638)
Cowing, Carolyn 4:51:30 (22,211)
Cowley, Laura 3:34:56 (4,896)
Cowley, Maeve 4:37:18 (18,948)
Cowling, Mary 4:36:13 (18,692)
Cox, Anita 4:50:09 (21,894)
Cox, Dorothy 5:33:19 (28,403)
Cox, Elizabeth 4:33:46 (18,108)
Cox, Emma 3:18:18 (2,591)
Cox, Emma 5:43:58 (29,305)
Cox, Evie 7:06:33 (31,950)
Cox, Janine 4:21:38 (15,139)
Cox, Jean 5:19:14 (26,789)
Cox, Karen 4:46:20 (21,054)
Cox, Kathryn 4:45:37 (20,874)
Cox, Lauren 5:03:49 (24,597)
Cox, Linda 6:33:12 (31,403)
Cox, Louise 5:23:29 (27,347)
Cox, Samantha 7:44:24 (32,221)
Cox, Simonne 4:51:39 (22,235)
Cox, Wendy 5:42:01 (29,166)
Coxall, Nicola 5:52:37 (29,863)
Coxhead, Sheena 5:08:58 (25,395)
Coxon, Alexandra 5:43:53 (29,296)
Coyne, Marilyn 5:38:49 (28,883)
Coysten Smith, Clare 4:03:57 (11,048)
Cozens, Paula Jane 5:30:43 (28,168)
Crabb, Mary 4:49:09 (21,662)
Crabtree, Sue 3:36:07 (5,081)
Cracknell, Kerensa 4:47:49 (21,380)
Crafford, Elizabeth 4:35:44 (18,570)
Craggs, Anne 5:11:20 (25,739)
Craig, Charlotte 4:12:53 (12,978)
Craig, Jennifer 4:42:33 (20,123)
Craig, Lorraine 6:33:09 (31,402)
Craig, Ruth 4:34:45 (18,338)
Craig, Sally 5:04:29 (24,705)
Craig, Sarah 5:10:45 (25,654)
Cramp, Christine 5:44:12 (29,315)
Cranbury, Nancy 5:45:56 (29,436)
Crandon, Barbara 4:56:38 (23,294)
Crane, Alison 3:44:55 (6,713)
Crane, Denise 5:04:44 (24,742)
Crane, Gemma 5:45:00 (29,369)
Crane, Wanda 7:03:23 (31,917)
Crawford, Fabiola 4:07:31 (11,813)
Crawford, Ruth 5:10:03 (25,558)
Creasey, Tanya 6:51:14 (31,746)
Creer, Claire 6:48:43 (31,688)
Cremen, Sandra 5:02:32 (24,394)
Crewe, Charity 5:23:49 (27,384)
Crideford, Freda 5:28:04 (27,897)
Crilly, Nichola 4:55:56 (23,138)
Cripps, Ruth 4:59:24 (23,871)
Crisp, Jodie 4:25:11 (16,051)
Critchell, Dawn 3:26:28 (3,602)
Critchley, Nicola 5:04:40 (24,727)
Critchley, Rebecca 4:29:51 (17,207)
Crocker, Deborah 5:48:02 (29,582)
Crocker, Pennie 5:19:25 (26,820)
Crombie, Suzanne 6:23:41 (31,127)
Crombie, Tara 6:23:42 (31,130)
Crombie Hicks, Shona 3:08:42 (1,563)
Crome, Debra 4:50:51 (22,043)
Cronin, Emma 5:59:50 (30,252)
Cronin, Kim 4:42:48 (20,180)
Cronk, Nicola 4:23:39 (15,658)
Crookes, Rachel 5:59:37 (30,246)
Crooks, Clare 4:36:00 (18,650)
Crooks, Erin 4:45:28 (20,837)
Croot, Sarah 5:09:28 (25,471)
Cross, Anne 4:07:09 (11,725)
Cross, Catherine 4:55:31 (23,031)
Cross, Diane 6:59:12 (31,879)
Cross, Felicity 4:28:47 (16,932)
Cross, Non 5:11:05 (25,705)
Cross, Philippa 5:07:27 (25,172)
Crossland, Ann 4:59:01 (23,804)
Crossman, Julie 5:14:16 (26,136)
Crossman, Sarah Jane 4:56:32 (23,270)
Crosswell, Fiona 5:06:57 (25,099)
Crouch, Andrea 4:35:13 (18,449)
Croucher, Emma 5:22:33 (27,220)
Crow, Zayne 4:05:32 (11,406)
Crowe, Katherine 4:26:12 (16,296)
Crowhurst, Maureen 6:51:36 (31,754)
Crowle, Revis 3:03:04 (1,122)
Crowson, Louisa 4:39:41 (19,471)
Crowther, Emma 6:21:36 (31,066)
Crowther, Margaret 4:15:50 (13,713)
Crowther, Nicola 4:20:27 (14,860)
Cruickshank, Fiona 4:32:40 (17,871)
Cruse, Julie 3:51:36 (8,105)
Cubberley, Rachael 3:40:55 (5,946)
Cuerden, Stephanie 6:15:05 (30,829)
Cuffie, Shirley 5:01:36 (24,242)
Cuffley, Lynn 5:25:59 (27,669)
Cull, Pamela 7:21:38 (32,083)
Cullen, Moira 4:18:17 (14,301)
Cumming, Lisa 4:20:10 (14,788)
Cummings, Joanna 4:37:25 (18,967)
Cummins, Fiona 3:37:31 (5,326)
Cunha, Andrea 7:10:52 (31,997)
Cunliffe, Judith 4:54:49 (22,885)
Cunnignham, Sarah 4:08:28 (12,002)
Cunningham, Pauline 3:59:47 (10,173)
Cunningham, Rachael 5:22:12 (27,166)
Curbishley, Lisa 4:27:04 (16,491)
Curl, Tracey 3:13:19 (2,037)
Curley, Debra 3:04:30 (1,210)
Curley, Rachel 4:20:30 (14,868)
Curry, Florence 4:08:29 (12,008)
Curtin, Sarah 5:24:10 (27,431)
Curtis, Annette 5:53:14 (29,889)
Curtis, Claire 4:01:25 (10,523)
Curtis, Eve 5:21:13 (27,052)
Curtis, Fiona 5:16:33 (26,431)
Curtis, Louise 3:33:43 (4,707)
Cusack, Niamh 4:12:30 (12,887)
Cushing, Sui 3:42:01 (6,153)
Cuthbert, Shan 3:38:42 (5,544)
Cutmore, Michaela 4:11:39 (12,677)
Cutmore, Sarah 5:15:36 (26,333)
Cutner, Christine 4:02:24 (10,718)
Dabbs, Margaret 4:06:39 (11,614)
Dable, Kristy 4:53:15 (22,556)
Daddy, Sue 4:49:28 (21,743)
Dadge, Jacky 6:51:35 (31,752)
Dahabiyeh, Nadia 4:18:49 (14,452)
Dahinten, Claire 4:43:35 (20,396)
Dahl, Halldis 3:59:27 (10,083)
Dainty, Julia 4:06:40 (11,620)
Dalbret, Pauline 7:37:56 (32,194)
Dale, Carolyn 6:35:30 (31,462)
Dale, Elisabeth 3:55:09 (8,951)
Dale, Nicola 4:05:20 (11,361)
Dale, Sarah 4:19:49 (14,695)
Dale, Sue 3:41:16 (6,000)
Daley, Susan 4:44:20 (20,577)
Daley, Susan 6:52:47 (31,779)
Dalis-Davies, Mari 5:14:21 (26,150)
Dall'Aglio, Chiara 5:55:29 (30,022)
Dallas, Nicola 5:50:11 (29,732)
Dallas, Samantha 5:18:33 (26,707)
Dalton, Laura 4:12:44 (12,946)
Dalton, Lucy 4:52:18 (22,357)
Dalton, Rebecca 5:03:41 (24,567)
Dalton, Sheryl 4:20:46 (14,918)
Dalton, Tanya 4:37:57 (19,075)
Daly, Andrea 4:51:54 (22,291)
Daly, Nancy 4:51:24 (22,178)
Damore, Maureen 4:40:39 (19,674)
Dandeker, Elyse 4:44:21 (20,584)
Dando, Isobel 5:56:28 (30,078)
Daniel, Elizabeth 4:35:20 (18,479)
Daniel, Teresa 3:07:59 (1,499)
Daniells, Christine 4:18:04 (14,266)
Daniels, Angela 3:49:15 (7,576)

Danks, Fiona 4:36:36 (18,789)
Dann, Natalie 4:45:14 (20,776)
Dannell, Sarah 4:25:29 (16,139)
Danns, Joanne 5:16:01 (26,382)
Darby, Helen 6:25:17 (31,170)
Darby, Marilyn 5:52:32 (29,854)
Darbyshire, Alex 4:33:52 (18,135)
Dargie, Lucy 4:24:45 (15,937)
Dargie, Mary 4:48:30 (21,534)
Darlow, Tara 4:25:50 (16,211)
Darrant, Leesa 4:55:53 (23,129)
Darroux, Brenda 5:42:30 (29,209)
Dart, Penny 4:42:18 (20,053)
Dartinet, Stephanie 4:10:32 (12,473)
Darwen, Carole 7:23:36 (32,096)
Dasantos-Roach, Gail 5:58:48 (30,191)
Dasey, Elizabeth 4:02:13 (10,681)
Dathan, Philippa 6:03:38 (30,401)
Daurat, Simone 4:04:37 (11,201)
Davey, Bridget 3:41:21 (6,025)
Davey, Jacqueline 5:06:21 (25,002)
Davey, Jean 3:53:47 (8,613)
Davey, Julie 4:14:23 (13,353)
Davey, Juliet 3:37:52 (5,394)
Davidoff, Vanessa 4:14:40 (13,416)
Davidson, Anne 3:59:19 (10,040)
Davidson, Pam 4:34:51 (18,359)
Davidson, Sonia 4:46:17 (21,040)
Davidson, Violet 5:19:54 (26,870)
Davies, A 3:58:13 (9,760)
Davies, Anna 5:47:47 (29,558)
Davies, Anne-Louise 4:03:50 (11,021)
Davies, Annie 5:13:30 (26,042)
Davies, Babs 5:31:48 (28,262)
Davies, Belinda 3:22:01 (2,988)
Davies, Brenda 5:03:00 (24,457)
Davies, Carys 3:47:35 (7,232)
Davies, Elizabeth 4:32:42 (17,879)
Davies, Emily 4:39:15 (19,386)
Davies, Gemma 5:03:18 (24,505)
Davies, Geraldine 4:38:20 (19,172)
Davies, Gillian 4:14:49 (13,458)
Davies, Hannah 4:51:39 (22,235)
Davies, Hazel 4:22:46 (15,434)
Davies, Jackie 6:13:16 (30,775)
Davies, Jan 4:51:25 (22,182)
Davies, Jane 4:46:39 (21,116)
Davies, Jane 5:04:52 (24,772)
Davies, Joanne 5:34:21 (28,511)
Davies, Karen 4:53:20 (22,581)
Davies, Karina 4:28:29 (16,850)
Davies, Katie 5:13:43 (26,069)
Davies, Liesl 6:05:17 (30,468)
Davies, Lorna 5:26:12 (27,700)
Davies, Lyn 4:52:26 (22,384)
Davies, Megan 4:22:04 (15,256)
Davies, Michele 3:42:23 (6,216)
Davies, Naomi 4:30:03 (17,252)
Davies, Nia 4:58:40 (23,727)
Davies, Pam 3:35:46 (5,033)
Davies, Priscilla 5:06:12 (24,984)
Davies, Sara 4:28:34 (16,878)
Davies, Sara 4:43:30 (20,375)
Davies, Sarah 4:17:42 (14,176)
Davies, Sarah-Jane 7:07:03 (31,957)
Davies, Sharon 5:45:45 (29,423)
Davies, Sian 4:30:24 (17,344)
Davies, Susan 4:48:20 (21,501)
Davies, Susan 5:31:49 (28,266)
Davies, Thelma 5:49:15 (29,658)
Davies, Tina 4:44:42 (20,658)
Davies, Tryphena 4:35:45 (18,580)
Davies, Wendy 3:08:48 (1,573)
Davies-Webster, Tracy 5:44:59 (29,367)
Davis, Gail 4:36:59 (18,872)
Davis, Gill 5:10:14 (25,588)
Davis, Hannah 5:25:25 (27,599)
Davis, Hannah 7:20:06 (32,069)
Davis, Hazel 3:51:07 (7,981)
Davis, Hazel 7:20:03 (32,068)
Davis, Helen 5:05:44 (24,927)
Davis, Janet 3:52:56 (8,402)
Davis, Katrina 4:38:16 (19,150)
Davis, Nancy 3:45:42 (6,868)
Davis, Nicola 5:01:22 (24,216)
Davis, Pamela 3:11:36 (1,811)
Davison, Patsy 5:26:41 (27,750)
Davitt, Anne 3:45:03 (6,741)
Dawes, Felicity 5:29:56 (28,077)
Dawkins, Pauline 5:29:00 (27,990)
Dawson, Caroline 5:44:44 (29,343)
Dawson, Catherine 5:50:41 (29,763)
Dawson, Donna 3:58:07 (9,733)
Dawson, Metta 4:22:36 (15,394)
Day, Anne 4:27:41 (16,643)
Day, Jane 4:13:46 (13,191)
Day, Sheila 4:31:05 (17,520)
Day, Susan 3:51:52 (8,169)
Day-Lewis, Tamasin 4:56:49 (23,342)
De Andrade, Maria 5:18:12 (26,653)
De Beer, Debbie 3:54:35 (8,813)
De Boo, Ceri 6:10:04 (30,646)
De Boo, Victoria 6:19:29 (30,989)
De Groot, Gieny Dini 3:44:57 (6,724)
De Hollander, Helma 4:33:38 (18,080)
De Jongh, Amanda 5:54:59 (29,997)
De Kock, Karen 5:23:27 (27,344)
De Luca-O'Neil, Antonella 4:36:21 (18,733)
De Max, Caroline 4:17:56 (14,238)
De Montfort, Caroline 4:03:41 (10,982)
De Reggi, Alessandra 5:53:25 (29,901)
De Sousa, Lisa 3:52:43 (8,357)
De Vos, Georgette 6:41:12 (31,554)
De Vos, Isabelle 4:25:15 (16,070)
De Wesselow, Katharine 4:42:20 (20,062)
Deacon, Angie 7:07:34 (31,969)
Deacon, Cherry 4:53:59 (22,711)
Deacon, Sharon 5:42:15 (29,187)
Deal, Pamela 5:07:08 (25,124)
Dean, Elizabeth 6:06:43 (30,518)
Dean, Emma 3:56:57 (9,442)
Dean, Juliette 4:14:58 (13,500)
Dean, Natalie 4:45:27 (20,834)
Dean, Zoe 4:18:27 (14,344)
Deane, Rebecca 4:44:04 (20,513)
Deans, Lindsay 3:49:18 (7,590)
Deans, Sarah 5:34:13 (28,497)
Dear, Sue 4:48:14 (21,478)
Dearman, Kelly 3:51:10 (8,002)
Deasy, Catherine 4:14:23 (13,353)
Deasy, Margaret 2:53:57 (530)
De'ath, Emma 5:34:47 (28,536)
Deb, Samantha 5:27:08 (27,793)
Debs, Laila 4:59:25 (23,873)
Decaillet, Ursula 4:43:36 (20,404)
Deeble, Yvonne 4:59:33 (23,895)
Deegan, Shelagh 4:50:49 (22,034)
Deeks, Katrine 3:55:34 (9,065)
Defis, Catrin 5:10:08 (25,571)
Defix, Valerie 6:55:26 (31,840)
Defoe, Doris 3:45:34 (6,843)
Defraia, Elisa 5:25:09 (27,561)
Delaney, Jacqueline 4:01:07 (10,451)
Delaney, Jessica 4:35:03 (18,407)
Delaney, Margaret 4:51:09 (22,119)
Delassus, Marie-Claude 4:52:09 (22,331)
De-Ligny, Anne 3:39:32 (5,698)
Delisser-Nuttall, Fulvia 4:51:27 (22,195)
Dell, Sally 4:00:42 (10,367)
Dell'Oro, Nadia 4:37:31 (18,987)
Delong, Carol 3:52:36 (8,332)
Demmon, Janette 6:12:03 (30,730)
Demmon, Pamela 6:12:03 (30,730)
Den Beste, Kimberly 5:26:49 (27,761)
Denby, Jayne 5:00:34 (24,081)
Dench, Jenny 7:49:51 (32,231)
Denmark, Cheryl 5:00:28 (24,063)
Denning, Jacqui 3:50:58 (7,941)
Dennis, Beth 5:00:51 (24,131)
Dennis, Christine 5:41:06 (29,084)
Dennis, Sarah 5:39:50 (28,974)
Dennis-Jones, Charlotte 4:59:46 (23,935)
Dennison, Andrea 2:58:14 (785)
Dennison, Deborah 3:40:07 (5,816)
Dennison, Maureen 5:59:14 (30,223)
Denny, Michelle 4:59:21 (23,866)
Denton, Mary 4:58:20 (23,656)
Denvir, Lucy 4:15:13 (13,571)
Dering, Jo 3:00:58 (999)
Derrick, Sara 3:55:20 (9,003)
Dervish, Sheree 6:32:14 (31,386)
Desborough, Valerie 4:15:32 (13,646)
Desilva, Gwendolyn 5:26:53 (27,765)
Despres, Emma 4:11:46 (12,713)
Devine, Lynne 4:20:44 (14,914)
Dewitt, Dorothy 3:42:51 (6,330)
Dews, Emma 3:41:19 (6,017)
Dey, Paula 5:08:35 (25,343)
Dhanani, Anne 5:11:12 (25,722)
Dhillon, Manjit 4:03:54 (11,036)
Dhupelia, Suniti 3:53:30 (8,541)
Di Luigi, Elena 4:42:39 (20,142)
Di Mambro, Hannah 4:52:53 (22,481)
Di Vita, Luisa 3:19:09 (2,665)
Diamandis, Lafina 5:25:06 (27,553)
Diani, Teresa 5:00:37 (24,097)
Dias, Hope 5:22:40 (27,230)
Dibb-Fuller, Verity 4:00:39 (10,359)
Dibley, Louise 5:08:28 (25,332)
Dick, Eleanor 6:31:44 (31,371)
Dick, Patricia 3:32:41 (4,556)
Dickenson, Patricia 4:29:45 (17,178)
Dicki, June 3:45:06 (6,755)
Dickinson, Julia 7:06:46 (31,953)
Dickinson, Lucy 4:54:06 (22,730)
Dickinson, Maxine 4:23:17 (15,571)
Dickson, Georgina 4:34:37 (18,311)
Dickson, Phyllis 4:15:56 (13,728)
Diebel, Janet 4:47:12 (21,226)
Dieckmaennken, Maria 4:12:48 (12,959)
Dietter, Kristin 3:49:58 (7,729)
Diffey, Joanna 3:54:47 (8,863)
Dillon, Elizabeth 5:58:34 (30,181)
Dillon, Jayne 4:29:39 (17,150)
Dillon, Sarah 3:56:00 (9,178)
Dinan, Gillian 5:34:16 (28,503)
D'Ingeo, Magda 5:40:39 (29,050)
Dinnage, Tracy 4:33:38 (18,080)
Dinneen, Sarah 4:04:36 (11,198)
Diprose, Valerie 4:49:04 (21,646)
Disbury, Rebecca 4:18:19 (14,307)
Dita, Constantina 2:23:43 (33)
Ditchfield, Angela 5:03:09 (24,483)
Ditmer, Lone 4:03:58 (11,056)
Dixon, Dorothy 3:28:23 (3,882)
Dixon, Jenni 5:28:56 (27,980)
Dixon, Lyn 4:49:20 (21,711)
Dixon, Maria 6:19:34 (30,996)
Dixon, Michelle 4:43:28 (20,367)
Dixon, Paula 5:10:02 (25,555)
Dixon, Pearl 4:11:27 (12,632)
Dixon, Sharon 4:10:22 (12,431)
Djsney, Glennys 3:06:05 (1,327)
Dobby, Samantha 7:16:09 (32,043)
Dobbyn, Helen 4:52:33 (22,406)
Dobinson, Lorena 4:00:24 (10,312)
Dobinson, Nichola 4:23:13 (15,551)
Dobson, Anita 4:52:31 (22,399)
Dobson, Jackie 4:51:14 (22,142)
Dobson, Katie 3:41:18 (6,014)
Dobson, Lesley 3:35:27 (4,990)
Dobson, Rachel 4:28:01 (16,708)
Docherty, Caroline 4:48:08 (21,462)
Docherty, Cheryl 3:41:01 (5,962)
Docker, Shirley 6:15:57 (30,858)
Doctor, Gillian 4:29:57 (17,229)
Dodd, Dee 7:52:32 (32,237)
Dodgson, Sarah 5:04:51 (24,769)
Doel, Sheila 4:55:47 (23,107)
Doerr, Edeltraud 3:54:57 (8,906)
Doggert, Melissa 4:14:50 (13,461)
Doherty, Bianca 6:07:09 (30,535)
Doherty, Hayley 4:18:29 (14,351)
Doherty, Katherine 4:11:09 (12,561)
Doidge, Philippa 5:19:38 (26,841)
Dolan, Annie 4:59:11 (23,841)
Dolan, Cathy 3:32:10 (4,491)
Dolman, Alison 5:11:36 (25,779)
Dolphin, Jill 5:24:14 (27,443)

Dolphin, Kirstie......6:43:28 (31,601)
Doman, Tracey......3:48:06 (7,339)
Donagh, Helen......4:52:16 (22,352)
Donald, Louise......5:25:39 (27,626)
Donaldson, Colleen......3:20:27 (2,824)
Donaldson, Gillian......7:00:34 (31,895)
Donegan, Joanna......5:54:23 (29,963)
Donkin, Charlotte......3:40:48 (5,925)
Donkin, Sasha......5:29:40 (28,058)
Donnan, Alison......5:53:24 (29,900)
Donnelly, Ann......4:43:37 (20,407)
Donnelly, Orla......5:07:06 (25,118)
Donnini, Linda......4:57:43 (23,524)
Donohoe, Mary......5:27:24 (27,822)
Donohoe, Suzanne......5:16:18 (26,404)
Donovan, Lisa......4:23:52 (15,712)
Donovan, Mary-Ellen......3:30:06 (4,186)
Donovan, Sara......5:17:28 (26,538)
Donoyou, Heather......4:19:14 (14,559)
Dooley, Alexandra......5:19:21 (26,807)
Dooley, Sarah......4:50:26 (21,947)
Doorson, Johanna......3:38:27 (5,485)
Doran, Deirdre......5:37:46 (28,796)
Doran, Martina......5:45:46 (29,425)
Dorfman, Kristina......3:13:15 (2,028)
Dorling, Josephine......4:56:01 (23,150)
Dormer, Julie......3:32:43 (4,562)
Dornan, Hayley......3:59:20 (10,047)
Dorrell, Patricia......4:20:24 (14,848)
Dorrity, Miriam......4:43:33 (20,391)
Dossa, Cressida......5:08:06 (25,280)
Dostalova, Karina......4:53:35 (22,635)
Double, Angela......5:24:58 (27,530)
Doucelin, Marie Paule......5:21:30 (27,081)
Douglas, Alice......6:38:39 (31,513)
Douglas, Charlotte......4:07:17 (11,754)
Douglas, Claire......4:46:42 (21,124)
Douglas, Jo......4:40:23 (19,626)
Douglas, Maureen......3:54:08 (8,687)
Douglas, Rebecca......5:35:11 (28,571)
Douglas, Teresa......3:33:32 (4,686)
Dove, Susan......7:25:32 (32,114)
Dow, Kirsteen......5:13:31 (26,047)
Dow, Pamela......4:53:56 (22,702)
Down, Bernadette......5:02:18 (24,361)
Downes, Beverley......4:48:11 (21,465)
Downes, Katherine......4:39:59 (19,536)
Downham, Sally......6:20:52 (31,044)
Downing, Amanda......6:20:44 (31,039)
Downs, Jessica......4:53:01 (22,505)
Downs, Mel......4:16:46 (13,927)
Doyen, Edith......3:35:13 (4,944)
Doyle, Christina......4:07:28 (11,799)
Doyle, Fiona......4:43:48 (20,453)
Doyle, Fiona......5:05:21 (24,849)
Doyle, Mary......3:23:53 (3,230)
Doyle, Pauline......5:24:08 (27,426)
Doyle, Sara......5:35:40 (28,609)
Doyle, Sylvia......3:57:52 (9,669)
Drage, Debbie......5:47:31 (29,537)
Drake, Amanda......4:17:26 (14,097)
Drake, Julie......3:20:21 (2,812)
Drake, Wendy......5:15:44 (26,349)
Draper, Alison......4:23:52 (15,712)
Draper, Eleanor......4:33:21 (18,019)
Draskau-Petersson, Jess......2:46:10 (264)
Drawbridge, Heidi......4:41:32 (19,874)
Dray, Carol......4:19:40 (14,658)
Drever, Barry......6:15:47 (30,850)
Drewe, Isabel......4:31:50 (17,697)
Drewett, Cereta......4:34:21 (18,252)
Drossin, Deena......2:21:16 (28)
Drummond, Pat......5:36:18 (28,663)
Drury, Louise......4:12:42 (12,937)
D'Souza, Lynn......5:05:17 (24,836)
Du Plooy, Sue......6:47:00 (31,655)
Duburquois, Charlotte......5:42:31 (29,210)
Ducker, Emily......3:46:12 (6,973)
Duckett, Catherine......5:17:14 (26,507)
Duckitt, Kirsten......5:27:37 (27,850)
Duckling, Louise......5:26:53 (27,765)
Dudley, Emer......3:36:23 (5,128)
Duff, Jenny......4:13:27 (13,111)

Duffield, Emma......4:29:30 (17,120)
Duffiled, Wendy......7:30:53 (32,159)
Duffner, Mary......7:00:35 (31,896)
Duffty, Lynn......4:06:39 (11,614)
Duffy, Therezia......3:37:03 (5,241)
Dufton, Patricia......3:54:54 (8,893)
Dugdale, Beatrice......5:01:49 (24,284)
Dugdale, Hannah......4:22:20 (15,324)
Dugdale, Polly......4:03:22 (10,925)
Duggan, Andrea......5:12:01 (25,830)
Duggan, Martine......5:08:54 (25,388)
Dugrenier, Marielle......3:55:42 (9,107)
Duivenvoorden, Monique......5:07:09 (25,125)
Dulout, Pascale......4:23:11 (15,541)
Duncan, Cara-Maree......5:03:51 (24,604)
Duncan, Debra......4:37:28 (18,975)
Duncan, Elaine......4:24:34 (15,879)
Duncan, June......4:15:44 (13,679)
Duncan, Natasha......4:40:16 (19,594)
Duncan, Sheila......5:48:08 (29,586)
Duncan, Tara......5:21:07 (27,039)
Duncombe, Rebecca......4:38:35 (19,221)
Dunkerley, Deborah......4:12:36 (12,914)
Dunkley, Kerry......4:09:17 (12,190)
Dunmall, Patricia......5:45:15 (29,387)
Dunn, Anita......5:58:52 (30,196)
Dunn, Dawn......4:36:07 (18,674)
Dunn, Helen......5:03:51 (24,604)
Dunn, Joanna......4:51:14 (22,142)
Dunne, Eleanor......5:10:29 (25,622)
Dunne, Lyn......4:34:09 (18,204)
Dunnett, Jane......5:37:12 (28,753)
Dunphy, Sinead......4:44:25 (20,599)
Dunstan, Julia......5:12:06 (25,840)
Dunster, Carol......5:25:20 (27,592)
Durance, Penny......3:47:22 (7,183)
Durbin, Julia......5:27:33 (27,840)
Durkin, Marina......5:27:09 (27,797)
Duroe, Fiona......3:39:24 (5,678)
Durrant, Helen......4:39:49 (19,504)
Durston, Tamsin......5:22:16 (27,181)
Dutch, Charlotte......3:52:09 (8,234)
Duthie, Claire......4:12:52 (12,973)
Dutton, Ann......4:52:02 (22,316)
Dux, Chloe......6:10:46 (30,676)
Dverio, Ann......4:25:03 (16,015)
Dyde, Lorraine......4:43:35 (20,396)
Dyer, Susan......4:02:37 (10,763)
Dyer, Zoe......4:57:55 (23,564)
Dyett, Audrey......4:08:33 (12,024)
Dykers, Joy......4:18:46 (14,440)
Dykes, Madeline......3:37:42 (5,365)
Dykes, Rita......4:31:32 (17,626)
Dymore-Brown, Lindas......3:57:10 (9,498)
Dyson, Tamsin......5:03:46 (24,587)
Dysvik, Maren......4:33:21 (18,019)
Dzialdow, Resi......4:27:48 (16,672)
Ealand, Kirsty......4:17:37 (14,147)
Ealand, Penelope......4:21:38 (15,139)
Eames, Claire......5:28:29 (27,940)
Earl, Nicole......4:42:38 (20,139)
Earle, Cherry......6:19:46 (31,008)
Eason, Susan......5:22:57 (27,278)
Easterbrook, Philippa......4:52:48 (22,460)
Eastham, Ruth......5:14:46 (26,212)
Easto, Susan......5:36:43 (28,708)
Easton, Kim......3:35:21 (4,966)
Eastwood, Kathryn......3:34:09 (4,768)
Eatenton, Joanne......6:34:49 (31,445)
Eaton, Carolyn......4:57:12 (23,430)
Eaton, Jane......3:36:35 (5,159)
Eaton, Rachel......5:32:48 (28,356)
Ebbs, Leslie......4:37:15 (18,937)
Ebert, Heike......5:12:28 (25,891)
Eburne, Vanessa......4:45:19 (20,798)
Eccles, Karen......3:59:42 (10,154)
Eckersley, Lisa......5:03:53 (24,612)
Eckersley, Louise......7:45:06 (32,223)
Eckford, Sophie......4:32:38 (17,859)
Eckles, Brenda......4:52:54 (22,484)
Eddy, Paula......6:49:27 (31,703)
Ede, Christine......4:04:19 (11,137)
Edelsten, Rosalind......4:18:52 (14,468)

Edgar, Polly......5:00:11 (24,009)
Edmans, Gail......5:07:21 (25,153)
Edmond, Jane......4:42:38 (20,139)
Edmonds, Sally......5:07:15 (25,134)
Edmondson, Deborah......3:25:58 (3,537)
Edmondson, Gail......5:13:04 (25,982)
Edmondson, Olivia......5:25:11 (27,568)
Edmondson, Tanya......5:23:34 (27,351)
Edmonson, Rebecca......4:23:22 (15,583)
Edmunds, Hannah......6:27:43 (31,256)
Edmunds, Patricia......4:49:38 (21,786)
Edwards, Adele......4:32:48 (17,898)
Edwards, Christine......7:30:31 (32,157)
Edwards, Clare......5:10:42 (25,648)
Edwards, Clare......6:31:31 (31,364)
Edwards, Emma......5:19:07 (26,773)
Edwards, Fizzy......5:20:00 (26,888)
Edwards, Helen......5:21:37 (27,100)
Edwards, Helen......5:46:35 (29,467)
Edwards, Janet......3:26:04 (3,547)
Edwards, Joanna......4:38:43 (19,257)
Edwards, Karen......3:58:42 (9,886)
Edwards, Kelly......6:03:08 (30,380)
Edwards, Kyra......6:11:50 (30,719)
Edwards, Penny......3:31:08 (4,347)
Edwards, Samantha......7:00:01 (31,889)
Edwards, Sian......7:22:52 (32,092)
Edwards, Traci......4:17:54 (14,230)
Edwards, Vicky......6:10:20 (30,652)
Edwards, Victoria......3:14:43 (2,208)
Edwards, Wendy......3:19:56 (2,748)
Efford, Jane......6:30:16 (31,335)
Eglinton, Louise......6:24:52 (31,159)
Ehrenberg, Margaret......3:32:40 (4,553)
Eilerts ce Haan, Carin......4:20:16 (14,813)
Eilledge, Amanda......4:42:12 (20,029)
Eisele, Michelle......4:22:56 (15,478)
Elderfield, Helen......3:48:57 (7,503)
Elderfield, Helen......4:37:21 (18,956)
Eldridge, Elizabeth......6:41:03 (31,553)
Elford, Nicola......5:04:51 (24,769)
Eliseou, Cassandra......3:44:00 (6,544)
Ellender, Michelle......5:50:12 (29,734)
Ellershaw, Gail......3:47:00 (7,124)
Ellins, Samantha......3:58:14 (9,764)
Elliot, Marie......3:13:26 (2,052)
Elliott, Dawn......5:01:55 (24,300)
Elliott, Elizabeth......3:30:05 (4,180)
Elliott, Jenny......3:37:31 (5,326)
Elliott, Stella......4:14:56 (13,488)
Ellis, Charlotte......5:03:48 (24,592)
Ellis, Claire......3:34:59 (4,908)
Ellis, Francis......6:50:59 (31,743)
Ellis, Jean......5:02:29 (24,384)
Ellis, Joyce......4:53:06 (22,521)
Ellis, Pauline......4:27:25 (16,575)
Ellis, Sarah......5:32:11 (28,307)
Ellison, Delia......4:25:50 (16,211)
Else, Jane......5:18:57 (26,751)
Else, Kate......3:33:31 (4,681)
Elsmore, Di......3:59:20 (10,047)
Elston, Christine......3:54:46 (8,859)
Elstone, Emma......3:53:51 (8,633)
Eltham, Patricia......4:00:38 (10,355)
Elton, Jane......4:28:42 (16,910)
Elueze, Rosaline......6:42:17 (31,572)
Elvin, Sarah......6:25:36 (31,183)
Ely, Elizabeth......6:39:01 (31,522)
Emeny, Caroline......4:35:35 (18,536)
Emmerson, Wendy......4:50:39 (22,001)
Emmett, Maureen......3:41:55 (6,135)
Emmett, Melissa......5:05:08 (24,821)
Emmett, Samantha......4:02:40 (10,774)
Emsley, Alison......4:10:40 (12,493)
Emson, Lorna......4:02:36 (10,756)
Emyr, Lindsay......3:18:08 (2,568)
Engdahl, Elin......2:59:25 (893)
Enger, Katrine......4:43:30 (20,375)
Enger, Tone......4:43:30 (20,375)
England, Debra......5:47:55 (29,567)
England, Susan......5:07:40 (25,218)
Engle, Kris......5:21:44 (27,117)
English, Anna......6:36:00 (31,473)

Ennis, Maura 5:33:53 (28,465)
Entwistle, Nicola 5:02:45 (24,426)
Erasmus, Christie 3:45:54 (6,912)
Eriksen, Fiona 4:26:04 (16,269)
Ernoult, Irene 6:06:51 (30,525)
Erskine, Linda 6:46:47 (31,652)
Escrig, Kimberley 4:17:31 (14,115)
Esler, Denise 4:07:31 (11,813)
Espedal, Louisa 4:46:52 (21,165)
Esteem, Samantha 5:19:54 (26,870)
Etan, Anne-Marie 4:39:56 (19,524)
Etches, Lisa 4:42:16 (20,046)
Etheridge, Jennifer 5:27:53 (27,881)
Etheridge, Louise 5:14:11 (26,119)
Evangelista, Elizabeth 5:20:25 (26,943)
Evans, Adelaide 4:17:57 (14,241)
Evans, Alice 5:43:10 (29,254)
Evans, Amanda 4:43:21 (20,336)
Evans, Andrea 4:38:03 (19,105)
Evans, Bernadette 4:37:03 (18,889)
Evans, Betty 7:13:41 (32,027)
Evans, Charlotte 5:11:45 (25,792)
Evans, Christine 5:45:04 (29,373)
Evans, Clair 5:55:49 (30,033)
Evans, Debbie 4:11:29 (12,643)
Evans, Esther 3:17:04 (2,435)
Evans, Gale 3:23:57 (3,240)
Evans, Gill 3:23:13 (3,139)
Evans, Gill 3:27:00 (3,681)
Evans, Gill 5:00:20 (24,041)
Evans, Isabel 4:03:00 (10,839)
Evans, Jane 4:45:45 (20,899)
Evans, Janet 7:03:52 (31,921)
Evans, Jennie 4:23:07 (15,521)
Evans, Joan 3:41:36 (6,085)
Evans, June 6:11:22 (30,705)
Evans, Kim 5:33:27 (28,417)
Evans, Kirsty 6:27:09 (31,231)
Evans, Klaire 4:25:06 (16,026)
Evans, Lorraine 4:22:03 (15,252)
Evans, Lynn 4:23:40 (15,662)
Evans, Natalie 5:04:58 (24,787)
Evans, Nicola 4:41:56 (19,979)
Evans, Patricia 4:36:18 (18,713)
Evans, Rhian 5:01:11 (24,181)
Evans, Sophie 4:32:31 (17,838)
Evans, Sue 4:11:40 (12,683)
Evans, Treena 4:40:54 (19,727)
Evans, Wendy 6:12:52 (30,761)
Evanson, Jill 5:24:33 (27,482)
Evennett, Helen 5:29:08 (27,999)
Evered, Joanna 8:02:36 (32,259)
Everett, Claire 3:58:44 (9,892)
Everett, Joanne 5:17:13 (26,505)
Everill, Elaine 4:56:26 (23,245)
Every, Sian 5:15:41 (26,339)
Eves, Katie 4:23:55 (15,724)
Evitt, Sophie 6:35:28 (31,459)
Ewins, Sharon 5:39:02 (28,905)
Exall, Annina 5:25:46 (27,636)
Eydes, Claire 5:06:47 (25,073)
Eyre, Rosalind 5:32:01 (28,291)
Fabbri, Malin 5:08:11 (25,295)
Fagan, Ciara 4:46:23 (21,067)
Fagan, Ruth 4:39:18 (19,398)
Fahy, Anne-Marie 5:57:49 (30,156)
Fairclough, Allison 5:43:28 (29,267)
Fairhead, Alison 3:47:57 (7,307)
Fairley, Nicola 4:44:46 (20,673)
Falconer, Fay 3:50:03 (7,743)
Fallon, Patricia 6:41:38 (31,559)
Fallon, Rosalind 6:41:38 (31,559)
Famiglietti, Wendy 5:22:02 (27,145)
Fantham, Lynne 5:53:02 (29,881)
Farebrother, Alice 6:25:57 (31,201)
Farebrother, Helen 6:25:57 (31,201)
Farey, Joan 5:27:29 (27,828)
Farina Lotti, Francesca 4:07:40 (11,851)
Farley, Angela 4:31:41 (17,670)
Farley, Deborah 5:08:35 (25,343)
Farley, Karen 4:19:35 (14,636)
Farley, Nichola 5:07:44 (25,230)
Farman, Michellle 3:30:57 (4,320)
Farmer, Alice 5:51:38 (29,814)
Farmer, Gayle 4:52:02 (22,316)
Farmer, Tracy 5:43:54 (29,299)
Farr, Clare 5:03:43 (24,580)
Farrall, Ali 5:21:27 (27,073)
Farrant, Catriona 4:59:46 (23,935)
Farre, Isabelle 4:37:54 (19,065)
Farrell, Ellen 4:56:08 (23,177)
Farrell, Louise 4:55:03 (22,934)
Farrelly, Taryn 5:05:58 (24,948)
Farren, Esther 7:31:57 (32,166)
Farrington, Tracy 5:24:25 (27,461)
Farrow, Pam 5:10:25 (25,611)
Faulkner, Angela 3:38:26 (5,483)
Faulkner, Jane 4:08:43 (12,068)
Faulkner, Phillippa 5:11:34 (25,770)
Faulkner, Tracey 4:02:40 (10,774)
Faunch, Ann 6:00:16 (30,265)
Faure Walker, Joanna 5:07:49 (25,241)
Fawcett, Linda 4:42:40 (20,150)
Fawcett, Tanya 6:45:41 (31,637)
Fawcett, Trudy 3:57:48 (9,648)
Fear, Belinda 4:27:02 (16,480)
Fearnley, Tracy 4:33:50 (18,123)
Fears, Melody 5:00:03 (23,988)
Featherstone, Kate 5:40:54 (29,069)
Feaver, Ayshea 5:19:38 (26,841)
Feeney, Mary 5:07:13 (25,131)
Feiven, Claire 6:10:57 (30,687)
Felix, Jamie 3:03:14 (1,132)
Fell, Carol 5:30:50 (28,178)
Feller, Emily 5:57:09 (30,116)
Fellowes, Tina 4:25:20 (16,096)
Fellows, Joanne 4:20:27 (14,860)
Feltner, Holly 4:49:41 (21,799)
Felton, Ruth 5:13:51 (26,086)
Fenelon, Patsy 3:41:18 (6,014)
Fenn, Catherine 4:34:17 (18,234)
Fenn, Maggie 4:12:55 (12,987)
Fennelly, Elizabeth 4:53:04 (22,514)
Fenton, Ann 3:54:31 (8,788)
Fenton, Lisa 6:10:10 (30,649)
Fenwick, Claire 6:21:39 (31,067)
Fenwick, Jane 4:47:43 (21,351)
Ferguson, Bridget 5:09:55 (25,531)
Ferguson, Christine 3:51:09 (7,995)
Ferguson, Claire 3:51:23 (8,045)
Ferguson, Elizabeth 3:43:45 (6,499)
Ferguson, Heather 4:18:03 (14,260)
Ferguson, Helen 3:46:02 (6,940)
Ferguson, Helen 4:52:37 (22,417)
Fernandez, Adriana 2:29:54 (64)
Ferraro, Anna 3:32:36 (4,540)
Ferreira, Elizka 3:16:52 (2,412)
Ferreira, Silvia 5:17:45 (26,571)
Ferris, Matrina 4:28:10 (16,756)
Ferriter, Josephine 4:09:00 (12,129)
Ffoulkes, Claire 6:53:47 (31,805)
Ficken, Pamela 5:49:49 (29,701)
Fiddament-Harris, Heather 3:27:33 (3,751)
Fidler, Sophie 5:12:20 (25,869)
Field, Carole 5:35:00 (28,553)
Field, Samantha 4:18:33 (14,372)
Field, Sarah 4:34:51 (18,359)
Fielden, Margaret 5:17:36 (26,560)
Fielder, Jodie 3:31:45 (4,446)
Fielding, Emma 5:42:56 (29,234)
Filby, Paula 5:52:13 (29,843)
File, Hayley 4:56:16 (23,214)
Filippetto, Luigina 4:41:26 (19,858)
Filmer, Lucy 5:00:12 (24,016)
Findlater, Jean 4:40:33 (19,659)
Findlay, Celia 3:35:26 (4,984)
Findley, Helen 5:14:17 (26,138)
Fine, Dulci 4:52:11 (22,335)
Fines, Helen 3:00:35 (981)
Finlay, Annegret 5:04:11 (24,659)
Finn, Deirdre 3:44:06 (6,564)
Finn, Gerri 3:55:28 (9,039)
Finn, Juliette 4:24:05 (15,775)
Finney, Kerri 4:52:28 (22,390)
Fippard, Katherine 4:39:18 (19,398)
Firth, Emma 5:05:18 (24,840)
Firth, Melissa 4:15:45 (13,685)
Fischer, Pauline 4:48:12 (21,471)
Fish, Sarah 5:50:33 (29,756)
Fisher, Anika 4:50:51 (22,043)
Fisher, Clare 5:38:59 (28,900)
Fisher, Janice 5:36:53 (28,728)
Fisher, Jessica 5:56:02 (30,047)
Fisher-Moody, Jan 3:24:27 (3,325)
Fishwick, Jennifer 7:13:59 (32,031)
Fitch, Sophie 4:43:58 (20,489)
Fitches, Nicola 3:41:50 (6,120)
Fitter, Diane 5:59:20 (30,228)
Fitzgerald, Julia 4:58:34 (23,711)
Fitzgerald, Julia 5:38:34 (28,863)
Fitzgerald, Sharon 3:35:02 (4,918)
Fitzgerald, Shelley 5:33:50 (28,458)
Fitzgerald, Sybi 4:35:38 (18,545)
Fitzgibbons, Teresa 4:47:39 (21,333)
Fitzmaurice, Irene 7:40:53 (32,211)
Fitzmaurice-Cotton, Heather 3:19:38 (2,715)
Fitzpatrick, Noeleen 5:02:25 (24,376)
Fitzpatrick, Rebecca 4:14:06 (13,282)
Flanagan, Terri 4:54:30 (22,814)
Flatman, Katie 5:46:59 (29,488)
Flawn, Kate 4:58:06 (23,609)
Fleet, Lorraine 6:13:19 (30,777)
Fleet, Melanie 4:53:07 (22,525)
Flegg, Joanna 4:37:43 (19,025)
Fleming, Nicola 4:16:23 (13,829)
Fletcher, Alison 2:45:10 (239)
Fletcher, Dawn 3:55:26 (9,032)
Fletcher, Emma 4:24:43 (15,924)
Fletcher, Jenny 4:34:42 (18,330)
Fletcher, Jo 4:57:55 (23,564)
Fletcher, Julie 7:21:00 (32,075)
Fletcher, Lucy 5:04:31 (24,708)
Fletcher, Susan 7:11:39 (32,008)
Fletcher, Valerie 4:54:58 (22,913)
Fletcher-Smith, Gemma 5:24:58 (27,530)
Fleton, Sarah 4:37:36 (19,007)
Flewitt, Jane 5:14:02 (26,101)
Florentine, Joanne 4:54:45 (22,877)
Flores-Laird, Dorina 7:04:51 (31,931)
Florio, Viviana 4:41:23 (19,844)
Flynn, Alison 4:44:10 (20,533)
Flynn, Hayley 6:50:08 (31,725)
Flynn, Sarah 5:22:36 (27,225)
Fogg, Gail 5:06:34 (25,028)
Foley, Niamh 4:35:10 (18,436)
Folkes, Liz 4:31:05 (17,520)
Follan, Anne 3:30:34 (4,255)
Folmert, Carola 4:50:49 (22,034)
Fontaine, Nancy 4:21:29 (15,107)
Fontaine, Reine 4:30:31 (17,370)
Fontana, Nathalie 4:32:14 (17,782)
Forbes, Jo 6:07:18 (30,544)
Forbes, Sheridan 4:08:43 (12,068)
Ford, Alison 3:42:55 (6,347)
Ford, Diane 5:35:36 (28,602)
Ford, Fiona 3:15:28 (2,285)
Ford, Helen 4:30:17 (17,305)
Ford, Janet 5:49:31 (29,680)
Ford, Nicole 4:21:23 (15,080)
Ford, Sarah 3:43:50 (6,514)
Ford, Sarah 4:21:55 (15,214)
Ford, Sharon 3:18:12 (2,578)
Ford-Dunn, Helen 5:11:52 (25,810)
Forde, Henrietta 5:15:09 (26,271)
Forder, Debora 5:37:02 (28,741)
Fordham, Jacqueline 4:39:07 (19,348)
Forrest, Dinah 5:31:20 (28,233)
Forrest, Kay 5:00:29 (24,065)
Forslund, Sofia 4:49:18 (21,706)
Forster, Micky 7:08:07 (31,974)
Forsyth, Christine 5:12:54 (25,962)
Forsyth, Wendy 6:35:28 (31,459)
Forte, Elizabeth 5:30:22 (28,128)
Fortunato, Fiorina 5:15:06 (26,261)
Fortune, Carole 3:43:01 (6,372)
Forward, Claire 4:54:57 (22,910)
Fosker, Denise 4:02:52 (10,819)
Foss, Angela 4:00:10 (10,266)
Fossey, Janine 5:57:50 (30,158)

Foster, Beverley	5:34:10 (28,495)	
Foster, Dilys	7:21:24 (32,080)	
Foster, Helen	6:24:33 (31,148)	
Foster, Joanne	4:32:12 (17,775)	
Foster, Laura	5:00:43 (24,108)	
Foster, Linda	3:59:28 (10,086)	
Foster, Lyn	4:21:04 (14,997)	
Foster, Sharon	4:52:15 (22,350)	
Fouchard, Gabriele	4:52:00 (22,308)	
Fouillet, Michelle	5:04:46 (24,752)	
Foulds, Sally	4:17:46 (14,200)	
Foulkes, Fiona	5:05:45 (24,928)	
Foundling-Hawker, Heather	3:09:17 (1,611)	
Fountain, Janine	4:55:16 (22,973)	
Fowden, Judith	4:47:11 (21,223)	
Fowle, Emma	4:36:46 (18,826)	
Fowle, Zoe	5:32:24 (28,326)	
Fowler, Caroline	5:39:04 (28,908)	
Fowler, Claire	3:20:41 (2,845)	
Fowler, Elizabeth	4:53:52 (22,691)	
Fowler, Kay	3:41:05 (5,974)	
Fowler, Mouveta	3:53:09 (8,460)	
Fowles, Nicola	4:12:39 (12,929)	
Fox, Joan	4:46:48 (21,146)	
Fox, Linda	5:10:36 (25,635)	
Fox, Margaret	4:31:35 (17,636)	
Fox, Sara-Jane	4:07:02 (11,691)	
Fox, Sue	4:02:04 (10,651)	
Fox, Susan	5:10:23 (25,606)	
Fox, Suzi	4:36:55 (18,858)	
Foyle, Una	5:44:57 (29,363)	
Foyster, Mandy	3:40:55 (5,946)	
Frame, Debra	5:50:03 (29,719)	
France, Jacqueline	3:13:39 (2,080)	
France, Rosie	4:40:17 (19,599)	
Francis, Janine	3:14:34 (2,193)	
Francis, Linda	4:50:19 (21,926)	
Frangs, Jan	4:04:40 (11,216)	
Frank, Flora	5:54:16 (29,952)	
Franklin, Elaina	4:32:00 (17,730)	
Franklin, Emma	4:43:15 (20,303)	
Franklin, Jenny	4:23:33 (15,630)	
Franklin, Kay	5:02:43 (24,422)	
Franklin, Lucy	5:35:02 (28,554)	
Franklin, Roberta	3:57:22 (9,548)	
Franklin, Sharla	5:04:47 (24,757)	
Franklin, Sylvia	4:31:09 (17,541)	
Franklyn, Sarah	4:51:29 (22,206)	
Franks, June	3:48:49 (7,469)	
Franzel, Cindy	4:39:42 (19,476)	
Frawley, Lisa	3:46:12 (6,973)	
Frecken, Kunigunde	4:04:00 (11,062)	
Frederique, Dhalluin	4:25:52 (16,219)	
Fredman, Elizabeth	4:30:55 (17,473)	
Freed, Linda	4:36:15 (18,698)	
Freeman, Caroline	5:21:20 (27,064)	
Freeman, Claire	3:29:27 (4,079)	
Freeman, Debra	5:34:57 (28,549)	
Freeman, Linda	6:03:15 (30,385)	
Freeman, Louise	7:15:23 (32,039)	
Freeman, Sally	4:29:13 (17,044)	
Freeman, Sandra	4:45:35 (20,863)	
Freeman, Sarah	5:53:18 (29,893)	
Freeman, Wendy	4:57:28 (23,474)	
Freemantle, Karen	6:06:57 (30,528)	
Freeney, Victoria	7:10:22 (31,993)	
Freer, Barbara	5:55:01 (29,999)	
French, Andrea	3:28:38 (3,933)	
French, Elspeth	4:54:16 (22,761)	
French, Ersilia	5:49:29 (29,679)	
French, Kathy	5:24:21 (27,456)	
French, Margaret	4:29:29 (17,112)	
French, Maria	5:16:34 (26,432)	
French, Natalie	4:24:15 (15,810)	
French, Stephanie	3:51:09 (7,995)	
Frenkel, Lila	3:42:59 (6,364)	
Fricker, Elizabeth	7:10:55 (31,998)	
Fridriciene, Jovita	4:57:32 (23,487)	
Friend, Sarah	6:04:35 (30,435)	
Friend, Tiffany	4:12:09 (12,799)	
Frigot, Sarah	6:39:44 (31,534)	
Frisby, Amanda	4:53:47 (22,675)	
Frisby, Rebecca	4:40:07 (19,561)	
Frith, Anne	5:51:53 (29,824)	
Fritsch, Uta	4:09:35 (12,246)	
Fritz, Karin	4:27:27 (16,581)	
Froggatt, Julie	4:39:27 (19,430)	
Froggatt, Tracy	3:20:53 (2,871)	
Frogley, Helen	4:29:21 (17,071)	
Fromings, Lara	5:09:25 (25,463)	
Frost, Roswitha	5:15:20 (26,295)	
Frost, Sarah	3:31:44 (4,444)	
Frost, Sharon	5:30:06 (28,094)	
Frost, Tina	5:56:18 (30,071)	
Froud, Helen	4:50:07 (21,884)	
Frowen, Nicola	5:10:20 (25,597)	
Fry, Melanie	7:54:31 (32,244)	
Fry, Ruth	4:49:10 (21,667)	
Fryer, Anna	3:59:58 (10,217)	
Fuggle, Caroline	4:33:23 (18,028)	
Fujii, Miho	4:49:31 (21,754)	
Fulford, Jackie	4:44:40 (20,653)	
Fulker, Yvette	3:54:15 (8,716)	
Fuller, Michelle	5:12:05 (25,839)	
Fulton, Barbara	5:07:27 (25,172)	
Fulton, Maureen	4:20:59 (14,974)	
Furbank, Valerie	5:00:20 (24,041)	
Furey, Natasha	4:44:56 (20,704)	
Furmage, Alaine	4:40:57 (19,741)	
Furner, Sue	4:07:09 (11,725)	
Furze, Helen	3:17:01 (2,431)	
Fussell, Nerida	4:21:32 (15,117)	
Fussell, Val	3:52:58 (8,412)	
Gabbott, Kim	6:39:43 (31,533)	
Gabbott, Wendy	5:10:50 (25,666)	
Gaberino, Fran	5:06:32 (25,022)	
Gaddie, Sarah	5:27:59 (27,891)	
Gadgil, Anjana	4:27:16 (16,539)	
Gaines, Maria	5:39:06 (28,910)	
Gaisford, Sophie	4:18:25 (14,334)	
Gajadhar, Howard	5:11:12 (25,722)	
Galbraith, Catherine	4:03:44 (10,992)	
Galbraith, Sarah	4:11:09 (12,561)	
Gale, Victoria	5:24:15 (27,445)	
Galeozzie, Emma	5:12:54 (25,962)	
Gallagher, Caroline	5:35:45 (28,617)	
Gallagher, Jane	5:11:27 (25,758)	
Gallagher, Tess	4:26:31 (16,358)	
Galloway, Alison	5:18:14 (26,661)	
Galloway, Julie	5:01:15 (24,194)	
Gamberoni, Martina	4:16:46 (13,927)	
Gambier, Maud	4:25:25 (16,123)	
Gamblin, Judith	3:41:58 (6,142)	
Gannon, Debbie	4:56:06 (23,172)	
Gannon, Sharon	3:14:56 (2,231)	
Gannon, Siobhan	7:27:43 (32,137)	
Gappy, Tina	3:43:54 (6,527)	
Gappy, Tracy	3:43:56 (6,533)	
Garavan, Mary	3:55:56 (9,162)	
Garavan, Rita	4:08:49 (12,091)	
Garcia, Anna	3:47:06 (7,141)	
Garcia Bouzas, Eva	4:20:26 (14,854)	
Gard, Lydia	4:46:15 (21,032)	
Gardener, Sue	4:34:05 (18,192)	
Gardiner, Christina	5:55:59 (30,041)	
Gardiner, Clare	4:29:58 (17,234)	
Gardner-Hall, Sarah	3:46:16 (6,988)	
Garman-Windsor, Wendy	5:16:59 (26,478)	
Garner, Claire	4:56:40 (23,306)	
Garner, Dalma	4:08:41 (12,063)	
Garner, Johanna	3:56:54 (9,422)	
Garner, Rachel	4:43:41 (20,429)	
Garner, Sharon	4:49:01 (21,635)	
Garner, Susan	3:54:49 (8,870)	
Garnett, Emma	4:04:21 (11,146)	
Garnett, Kathleen	4:29:03 (17,004)	
Garnham, Sandy	5:26:18 (27,710)	
Garnier, Anna	3:51:29 (8,068)	
Garnier, Sylvie	5:14:44 (26,206)	
Garratt, Amy	5:50:02 (29,716)	
Garrett, Jo-Anne	4:25:47 (16,198)	
Garrido, Kathleen	3:59:20 (10,047)	
Garrod, Lorna	3:44:57 (6,724)	
Garside, Debra	5:02:02 (24,319)	
Garside, Theresa	3:29:06 (4,015)	
Garton, Elaine	4:43:57 (20,487)	
Garvey, Colette	4:00:32 (10,336)	
Garvey, Marianne	4:49:50 (21,832)	
Garvey-Jones, Lindsay	6:31:54 (31,377)	
Garwood, Felicity	6:03:46 (30,404)	
Garwood, Lorraine	5:47:08 (29,498)	
Gaskill, Claire	4:48:17 (21,491)	
Gaskin, Bridget	4:44:03 (20,508)	
Gaskin, Leila	3:46:07 (6,955)	
Gates, Serena	3:43:55 (6,530)	
Gaunt, Kate	4:21:00 (14,979)	
Gauvin, Sarah	3:54:15 (8,716)	
Gawne-Cain, Mary	4:55:38 (23,062)	
Gaylor, Deborah	4:31:37 (17,646)	
Gaylor, Vivienne	4:46:23 (21,067)	
Gaynor, Sarah	5:05:35 (24,898)	
Gayter, Sharon	3:34:23 (4,814)	
Gaywood, Nancy	4:51:09 (22,119)	
Gazzari, Sabrina	3:43:15 (6,414)	
Gearey, Nicola	4:52:24 (22,376)	
Gearing, Lesley	4:41:38 (19,896)	
Geary, Elizabeth	4:44:16 (20,565)	
Gecaga, Soiya	4:58:59 (23,795)	
Geddes, Sarah	3:57:12 (9,506)	
Gedney, Amanda	5:07:19 (25,151)	
Gee, Elaine	4:55:33 (23,037)	
Gee, Samantha	4:24:37 (15,892)	
Geen, Jennifer	4:38:25 (19,186)	
Geiger, Brigitte	3:41:23 (6,037)	
Gelernter, Linda	5:33:37 (28,431)	
Gellard, Vanessa	5:57:25 (30,130)	
Gelling, Heather	4:41:27 (19,861)	
Gelson, Emily	4:11:52 (12,733)	
Genovese, Bruna	2:32:58 (82)	
Gent, Karen	3:37:14 (5,278)	
Gent, Manda	5:23:44 (27,375)	
Gent, Sarah	3:48:34 (7,415)	
Geoghegan, Meloney	7:29:31 (32,149)	
George, Carey	4:19:44 (14,679)	
George, Melanie	5:21:22 (27,068)	
George, Michelle	5:05:27 (24,867)	
George, Susan	4:00:52 (10,398)	
George, Susanna	4:58:08 (23,612)	
Georghiou, Dorothy	3:22:45 (3,077)	
Geraghty, Mary	5:15:15 (26,286)	
Gerard, Michele	4:50:15 (21,909)	
Gerrand, Lindsay	5:08:12 (25,300)	
Gerrard, Adrienne	2:59:23 (889)	
Gerweck, Karen	4:41:50 (19,957)	
Ghanen, Rita	4:27:25 (16,575)	
Ghazali, Dalila	3:58:29 (9,830)	
Giamarelos, Fredericka	5:04:16 (24,675)	
Gibb, Alison	4:29:22 (17,081)	
Gibbins, Deborah	4:24:58 (15,990)	
Gibbins, Sally	4:23:15 (15,560)	
Gibbon, Lisa	4:22:57 (15,482)	
Gibbons, Gemma	5:01:58 (24,308)	
Gibbons, Johanna	4:29:36 (17,139)	
Gibbs, Caroline	6:59:56 (31,888)	
Gibbs, Dawn	3:12:38 (1,951)	
Gibbs, Rebecca	5:21:01 (27,024)	
Giblin, Nichola	6:44:52 (31,620)	
Gibson, Amy	4:31:34 (17,633)	
Gibson, Caroline	6:10:56 (30,685)	
Gibson, Claire	4:30:24 (17,344)	
Gibson, Hazel	3:24:23 (3,314)	
Gibson, Joanna	4:15:58 (13,734)	
Gibson, Julie	6:22:44 (31,095)	
Gibson, Marishelle	5:36:57 (28,732)	
Gibson, Sara	4:20:15 (14,809)	
Gibson, Sarah	4:51:07 (22,108)	
Gibson, Trishy	6:34:50 (31,446)	
Gibson, Vanessa	3:33:24 (4,666)	
Giddings, Lorna	4:36:31 (18,775)	
Giehl, Andrea	4:02:19 (10,698)	
Gilbert-Denham, Georgie	4:12:36 (12,914)	
Gilbert, Anne	5:15:25 (26,306)	
Gilbert, Helen	5:57:48 (30,155)	
Gilbert, Lisha	6:33:50 (31,420)	
Gilby, Sue	3:44:59 (6,733)	
Giles, Jeanette	5:05:05 (24,812)	
Giles, Susan	4:25:48 (16,201)	
Gilham, Wendy	5:12:15 (25,863)	
Gill, Amanda	4:32:40 (17,871)	

Gill, Ann 4:35:47 (18,594)
Gill, Brenda 4:45:09 (20,757)
Gill, Gillian 4:47:18 (21,247)
Gill, Jennifer 5:36:39 (28,703)
Gill, Laura 4:17:15 (14,045)
Gillam, Leanne 4:46:17 (21,040)
Gillam, Sally....................4:05:19 (11,358)
Gilley, Wendy 4:30:43 (17,422)
Gillie, Sheila....................5:07:44 (25,230)
Gillies, Cora 4:37:31 (18,987)
Gillies, Rachel..................4:02:38 (10,766)
Gillings, Mary 4:29:43 (17,166)
Gillington, Belinda 4:48:35 (21,550)
Gillingwater, Barbara 4:21:38 (15,139)
Gillmon, Victoria.............5:04:40 (24,727)
Gillson, Sarah 5:09:19 (25,452)
Gilrowan, Clare 4:12:08 (12,795)
Gimber, Sophie................6:10:49 (30,681)
Gimeno De Estaban, Sonia.......5:10:19 (25,595)
Gingell, Deborah 5:12:37 (25,923)
Gingell, Lynne 4:43:05 (20,256)
Ginnever, Nicola 3:50:38 (7,871)
Girard, Samantha.............4:22:09 (15,276)
Girling, Jill 5:57:33 (30,140)
Girvan, Catherine 5:21:54 (27,139)
Gisborne, Sally.................3:43:10 (6,399)
Gisby, Sharon 5:36:23 (28,671)
Gitsham, Hazel.................4:38:16 (19,150)
Gladman, Kirsty................4:56:23 (23,238)
Gladwell, Katharyn 4:27:20 (16,555)
Glanville, Danielle............3:45:08 (6,762)
Glass, Caroline 5:13:22 (26,019)
Glazebrook, Clare 3:14:37 (2,200)
Glazebrook, Jacqueline......6:09:42 (30,629)
Gleave, Judith 4:43:37 (20,407)
Gleave, Maddie 4:50:01 (21,862)
Gledhill, Rachael.............4:54:59 (22,917)
Gleeson, Julia 4:09:07 (12,156)
Glen, Jennifer..................5:26:05 (27,685)
Glennie, Elizabeth 4:39:43 (19,481)
Glennie, Louise 4:37:40 (19,012)
Glennon, Gillian 4:15:28 (13,631)
Glibbery, Angela..............5:56:34 (30,083)
Gliddon, Christine 6:11:24 (30,707)
Glossop, Andrea 4:38:46 (19,274)
Glove, Sue 4:44:28 (20,608)
Glover, Catherine 4:57:05 (23,398)
Glover, Linda...................4:46:18 (21,045)
Godber, Kathleen 4:07:56 (11,892)
Goddard, Carol 4:34:24 (18,266)
Goddard, Donna 4:34:16 (18,230)
Goddard, Lizzie 4:11:27 (12,632)
Goddard, Sarah 5:42:06 (29,174)
Godfrey, Amanda 4:26:23 (16,332)
Godfrey, Joanne 4:34:37 (18,311)
Godfrey, Lesley 4:16:23 (13,829)
Godfrey, Natalie 4:24:38 (15,897)
Godfrey, Sandra 6:04:07 (30,413)
Godfrey, Susanne 3:50:43 (7,890)
Godfrey, Tracy 4:37:53 (19,063)
Godfrey, Zoe 3:50:48 (7,908)
Godwin, Dawn 3:47:54 (7,301)
Godwin, Sarah 4:22:41 (15,417)
Goeldner, Petra 4:22:58 (15,488)
Goffe, Nicky 5:01:46 (24,274)
Gold, Lorna 4:41:21 (19,837)
Gold, Stephanie 5:25:25 (27,599)
Goldblatt, Catherine 3:45:52 (6,906)
Goldie, Martha 4:23:42 (15,672)
Goldin, Nicole 4:55:40 (23,072)
Golding, Jenny 5:54:12 (29,943)
Golding, Sonja.................5:28:08 (27,906)
Goldsmith, Christy 4:46:44 (21,134)
Goldsmith, Gail 4:03:12 (10,881)
Gomer, Anne 4:27:06 (16,497)
Gomme, Frances 4:14:15 (13,319)
Good, Amanda 4:19:26 (14,603)
Goodall, Barbara 7:27:22 (32,135)
Goodall, Greta 4:50:25 (21,944)
Goodall, Patricia..............3:56:14 (9,255)
Goodchild, Heidi 4:29:09 (17,026)
Goodey, Charlotte 5:30:13 (28,099)
Goodger, Kate 4:21:14 (15,040)

Goodhind, Emma 5:18:58 (26,752)
Gooding, Carole...............6:25:31 (31,179)
Gooding, Catharina 5:29:28 (28,033)
Gooding, Melanie 5:07:54 (25,250)
Goodman, Madeline 4:28:24 (16,828)
Goodman, Rachel 4:13:15 (13,063)
Goodridge, Catherine 5:18:26 (26,687)
Goodsell, Jacqueline..........5:15:29 (26,312)
Goodwin, Beverley 6:09:44 (30,630)
Goodwin, Brenda 4:30:40 (17,411)
Goodwin, Fiona................4:23:23 (15,588)
Goodwin, Karen 4:58:44 (23,742)
Gopoulos, Claire 4:41:49 (19,949)
Gordge, Claire 4:35:48 (18,598)
Gordon, Audrey 4:19:46 (14,687)
Gordon, Eleanor 4:23:45 (15,686)
Gordon, Jo......................5:11:24 (25,753)
Gordon, Karen 4:17:20 (14,064)
Gordon, Laura 5:11:32 (25,763)
Gordon, Linda 4:38:15 (19,143)
Gordon, Shannon 5:51:52 (29,823)
Gore, Joanna...................5:02:39 (24,414)
Gorge, Angela 5:50:22 (29,741)
Gorman, Barbara 5:06:47 (25,073)
Gorman, Claire 4:26:05 (16,272)
Gorman, Gemma 6:44:51 (31,618)
Gormley, Lorraine 4:45:31 (20,851)
Gormley, Teresa 4:58:30 (23,699)
Gorski, Julia 6:05:30 (30,478)
Goscomb, Glenda..............3:57:24 (9,560)
Gosling, Cyndi 4:16:25 (13,838)
Goudge, Nicola 4:24:47 (15,948)
Goudie, Nagela 7:43:45 (32,218)
Gough, Bridget.................4:59:09 (23,838)
Gough, Nia 5:31:05 (28,202)
Gough, Suzanne 5:08:07 (25,282)
Gough, Teresa 5:05:23 (24,855)
Goulbourne, Anne.............5:02:31 (24,391)
Gould, Alice 5:02:13 (24,351)
Gould, Josephine 4:45:48 (20,913)
Goulding, Claire 4:12:15 (12,828)
Goulding, Susan 4:51:04 (22,091)
Goulston, Lyndsey.............4:30:09 (17,269)
Gourley, Catherine 4:22:34 (15,379)
Gowan, Nikki 3:43:37 (6,469)
Gowans, Eileen 3:56:40 (9,365)
Gowans, Jenny 4:42:49 (20,188)
Gowans, Samantha............5:11:46 (25,798)
Goward, Rachel 4:27:42 (16,653)
Gower, Belinda 4:00:10 (10,266)
Gower, Tanja 6:09:29 (30,617)
Gow-Smith, Julia.............3:41:23 (6,037)
Grace, Amie 6:39:11 (31,526)
Grady, Carol 3:45:02 (6,738)
Grafton, Maria.................4:57:21 (23,451)
Graham, Adele 5:28:38 (27,951)
Graham, Angela 6:05:11 (30,462)
Graham, Beth 4:51:43 (22,247)
Graham, Catherine 5:35:21 (28,584)
Graham, Danielle 5:07:36 (25,201)
Graham, Jo-Ann 3:40:19 (5,847)
Graham, Michelle 4:22:26 (15,348)
Graham, Olivia 5:02:42 (24,419)
Graham, Shivonne 5:06:55 (25,096)
Grahmslaw, Margaret 4:35:12 (18,442)
Grajetzki, Ina 4:24:48 (15,951)
Gramins, Margaret 5:15:56 (26,366)
Grandy, Sarah 3:35:17 (4,955)
Graney, Susan 7:38:34 (32,195)
Grange, Emma 5:30:57 (28,188)
Grange, Larrisa 4:59:47 (23,947)
Granger, Rachel 3:42:45 (6,310)
Gransby, Clare 4:10:55 (12,530)
Grant, Ann 5:33:53 (28,465)
Grant, Clair 5:50:04 (29,721)
Grant, Clare 4:46:43 (21,129)
Grant, Colleen 5:42:08 (29,180)
Grant, Elizabeth 3:52:23 (8,284)
Grant, Jocelyn 5:40:35 (29,041)
Grant, Josephine 6:31:00 (31,350)
Grant, Julie 5:09:09 (25,429)
Grant, Pamela..................3:46:03 (6,943)
Grant, Samantha 5:17:54 (26,596)

Gratton, Debbie 5:52:32 (29,854)
Graty, Rorie 4:42:01 (19,995)
Graves, Lynn 5:12:21 (25,872)
Gray, Cheryl 5:01:58 (24,308)
Gray, Christine.................4:06:43 (11,630)
Gray, Dawn.....................3:16:12 (2,348)
Gray, Elizabeth 6:51:06 (31,745)
Gray, Helen.....................4:22:35 (15,387)
Gray, Jacqueline 4:05:08 (11,319)
Gray, Joanne 4:30:00 (17,241)
Gray, Kaye......................5:27:02 (27,778)
Gray, Lynsey 4:41:59 (19,987)
Gray, Margaret.................4:10:13 (12,401)
Gray, Marianne 4:42:28 (20,101)
Gray, Pauline 5:04:52 (24,772)
Gray, Samantha 5:09:04 (25,417)
Graysmark, Sue 3:38:30 (5,494)
Grayson, Yvonne 4:34:07 (18,197)
Grazebrook, Clare.............5:01:40 (24,254)
Greaney, Brigid 3:56:37 (9,352)
Greatrex, Angela 5:41:50 (29,145)
Greatrex, Michelle 3:52:00 (8,197)
Greaves, Isabelle 5:03:12 (24,492)
Gredka, Tina 4:17:43 (14,183)
Green, Ana-Maria..............4:09:31 (12,230)
Green, Angela 4:27:20 (16,555)
Green, Anne 6:27:21 (31,234)
Green, Dawn....................3:57:15 (9,517)

Green, Diana 6:29:27 (31,313)

We all have 'bad news' days – mine was 18 April 2002. The bad news – breast cancer. By the next day I'd decided to run the London Marathon the following year – if I could get a place. Well I did, with the charity 'Breast Cancer Campaign' and in October after surgery and the completion of my treatment I began my training which consisted of riding my 1920s 'sit up and beg' bicycle round country lanes and by the New Year adding fast walking and jogging to my 'repertoire'. All too quickly 13 April arrived and I found myself on the start line of the 2003 LM, just ten days before my 69th birthday, and 6-and-a-half hours later crossed the finish line in The Mall. I was elated, exhausted; and never again! But aged 76 and just months after 2 total hip replacements I've completed my 8th London Marathon. I'm now training for 2011.

Green, Jacqueline 3:55:15 (8,978)
Green, Jacqueline 4:36:08 (18,676)
Green, Jan.......................5:06:58 (25,100)
Green, Jenny 4:23:53 (15,716)
Green, Joanne 4:55:39 (23,065)
Green, Karen 3:33:18 (4,645)
Green, Katherine 4:22:31 (15,369)
Green, Lucie 5:52:01 (29,831)
Green, Lynne 4:21:29 (15,107)
Green, Michelle 6:37:50 (31,505)
Green, Nichola 4:12:59 (13,000)
Green, Shelley 3:48:19 (7,378)
Green, Suzannne 5:39:56 (28,987)
Green, Tracey 4:17:13 (14,036)

Hart, Gill....4:17:58 (14,244)
Hart, Margaret....4:25:09 (16,043)
Hart, Rachel....4:12:37 (12,920)
Hartigan, Alison....5:00:17 (24,033)
Hartle, Gaynor....6:11:00 (30,693)
Hartley, Dawn....3:36:55 (5,215)
Hartley, Fiona....5:04:18 (24,677)
Hartley, Jeanette....5:13:15 (26,005)
Hartley, Jennifer....5:18:59 (26,754)
Hartley, Julia....3:31:28 (4,403)
Hartley, Julia....5:50:56 (29,782)
Hartley, Nicola....4:57:17 (23,443)
Hartley, Susan....4:21:48 (15,185)
Hartney, Rosalind....4:43:22 (20,342)
Hartridge, Ami....5:16:07 (26,388)
Hartshorn, Debbie....5:05:59 (24,955)
Hartwell, Paula....4:33:13 (17,987)
Hartz, Libby....4:22:08 (15,274)
Harvey, Angela....5:57:25 (30,130)
Harvey, Carol....4:25:51 (16,217)
Harvey, Catriona....5:12:53 (25,956)
Harvey, Sue....3:47:02 (7,132)
Harvie, Lee....4:47:34 (21,310)
Harwood, Jane....4:24:19 (15,822)
Harwood, Julia....4:38:45 (19,268)
Hasler, Emma....3:53:24 (8,517)
Hasler, Victoria....4:23:51 (15,708)
Haslip, Nicole....3:40:22 (5,854)
Hassall, Claire....4:52:43 (22,441)
Hassall, Maryvonne....3:42:33 (6,265)
Hassam, Munira....5:31:10 (28,214)
Hassan, Selin....4:44:30 (20,615)
Hassen, Diane....5:19:56 (26,877)
Hastings, Linda....4:30:52 (17,459)
Hatch, Alison....5:13:19 (26,014)
Hatcher, Ollie....4:29:53 (17,215)
Hatherley, Claire....5:02:35 (24,404)
Hathway, Denise....4:29:07 (17,017)
Hatt-Cook, Catherine....4:22:57 (15,482)
Hatton, Kay....3:46:51 (7,093)
Hau, Wendy....4:37:08 (18,906)
Hauck, Roberta....3:59:55 (10,206)
Haughton, Breda....4:51:38 (22,231)
Havers, Michelle....4:11:16 (12,591)
Hawes, Rebecca....6:19:16 (30,982)
Hawken, Valerie....5:01:32 (24,236)
Hawker, Sue....5:07:21 (25,153)
Hawkins, Antoinette....6:54:46 (31,827)
Hawkins, Emer....6:42:03 (31,567)
Hawkins, Emma....5:02:00 (24,316)
Hawkins, Emma....5:43:30 (29,270)
Hawkins, Hannah....5:16:58 (26,477)
Hawkins, Joanne....4:50:35 (21,987)
Hawkins, Kate....5:11:55 (25,816)
Hawkins, Patricia....4:15:01 (13,512)
Hawkins, Rebecca....4:01:48 (10,598)
Hawley, Sasha....4:58:16 (23,643)
Haworth, Marta....5:14:10 (26,117)
Haworth, Rachel....4:28:51 (16,951)
Haxby, Joanna....5:11:07 (25,709)
Hay, Debz....4:06:09 (11,526)
Hay, Emma....6:07:16 (30,538)
Hayashi, Mieko....4:15:35 (13,658)
Haycock, Anna....4:13:14 (13,058)
Haycock, Claire....5:12:22 (25,876)
Haycock, Jill....4:35:45 (18,580)
Hayden, Haylee....7:03:56 (31,924)
Hayden, Sally....4:08:53 (12,105)
Hayden, Valerie....7:07:11 (31,963)
Hayes, Carol....4:22:09 (15,276)
Hayes, Sue....5:53:03 (29,883)
Haylock, Kim....4:14:16 (13,323)
Haylock, Susan....7:58:14 (32,251)
Hayman, Dawn....4:33:21 (18,019)
Haynes, Jane....4:12:26 (12,867)
Haynes, Janine....4:54:33 (22,823)
Hays, Angelina....4:27:51 (16,680)
Hayward, Adel....4:24:17 (15,818)
Hayward, Amanda....7:49:54 (32,232)
Hayward, Anita....4:55:43 (23,083)
Hayward, Katharine....4:21:59 (15,236)
Hayward, Sarah....4:28:56 (16,976)
Hayward, Tamsin....3:49:22 (7,601)
Haywood, Anna....5:59:26 (30,235)
Haywood, Hettie....3:51:48 (8,149)
Hazel, Gill....3:58:13 (9,760)
Hazell, Deborah....5:37:13 (28,755)
Hazleton, Lyn....3:26:04 (3,547)
Hazlitt, Karen....3:58:11 (9,748)
Head, Elizabeth....6:18:04 (30,936)
Head, Jean....6:35:18 (31,454)
Heady, Kathy....6:11:19 (30,702)
Healey, Melanie....4:17:54 (14,230)
Healey, Wendy....5:39:31 (28,948)
Heals, Susan....4:58:45 (23,745)
Heard, Sandra....6:18:41 (30,960)
Heasman, Lindsay....3:49:19 (7,593)
Heath, Karen....5:24:16 (27,448)
Heath, Lindsay....4:21:54 (15,207)
Heath, Renée....3:35:09 (4,934)
Heath-Downey, Susan....5:12:39 (25,927)
Heavens, Lucy....7:11:24 (32,006)
Heaviside, Karen....3:48:29 (7,397)
Hebdon, Jane....5:07:56 (25,255)
Hebdon, Janet....4:40:03 (19,549)
Heck, Miranda....3:55:08 (8,947)
Hedberg, Maj....4:18:39 (14,407)
Heddon, Patricia....4:47:15 (21,235)
Hedges, Rebecca....5:04:32 (24,712)
Hedley, Lesley....6:40:28 (31,548)
Heeley, Madeleine....3:56:11 (9,234)
Heenan, Karen....7:07:09 (31,960)
Hegan, Sonia....4:13:30 (13,125)
Hegarty, Josephine....4:28:00 (16,706)
Hegenbarth, Sally....4:38:23 (19,183)
Heidkamp, Rosemarie....5:45:44 (29,422)
Heinze, Irmlind....4:07:12 (11,737)
Helbling, Anna....4:34:14 (18,220)
Helfenstein, Ruth....6:06:04 (30,506)
Hellenbrand, Julie....6:11:22 (30,705)
Hellenburgh, Susan....5:58:45 (30,188)
Hellier, Lindsay....3:30:32 (4,249)
Hellsmark, Merit....4:41:54 (19,974)
Helm, Laura....4:46:02 (20,971)
Helmsley, Julia....5:02:08 (24,332)
Hemmings, Carol....6:52:44 (31,778)
Hemsworth, Caroline....3:16:25 (2,368)
Henderson, Laura....3:59:22 (10,060)
Henderson, Lesley....5:05:03 (24,801)
Henderson-Thynne, Kate....6:05:27 (30,474)
Hendry, Allison....5:30:47 (28,176)
Hendry, Julie....5:37:13 (28,755)
Henkel, Annemarie....4:34:44 (18,335)
Henman, Amanda....6:29:44 (31,321)
Hennessy, Annabel....5:33:51 (28,459)
Hennigan, Diane....4:05:43 (11,435)
Henry, Anne....3:57:43 (9,622)
Henry, Dolores....5:16:11 (26,393)
Henry, Jean....3:24:01 (3,249)
Henry, Jo....5:07:05 (25,117)
Henry, Karen....7:12:38 (32,019)
Henry, Rita....6:54:09 (31,808)
Hensen, Frances....4:23:39 (15,658)
Hensman, Ann....4:27:54 (16,689)
Henson, Erika....4:28:12 (16,766)
Hentz, Joanne....4:40:57 (19,741)
Henwood, Sarah....4:39:37 (19,464)
Heppner, Jane....4:23:29 (15,611)
Heppner, Victoria....4:23:32 (15,625)
Herbert, Asha....4:45:30 (20,850)
Herbert, Jane....5:35:36 (28,602)
Herbert, Joanna....4:46:16 (21,035)
Herbert, Penelope....4:32:12 (17,775)
Herbert, Susie....5:08:42 (25,359)
Herbert, Victoria....4:50:10 (21,897)
Heritage, Jane....4:51:29 (22,206)
Heron, Joan....4:20:38 (14,895)
Heron, Rachel....4:30:06 (17,263)
Herring, Nicola....5:04:40 (24,727)
Herriott, Lisa....5:05:27 (24,867)
Hesketh, Brenda....4:12:30 (12,887)
Heslop, Clare....4:40:49 (19,706)
Heslop, Patricia....5:44:34 (29,336)
Heslop, Sally....4:17:27 (14,102)
Hessmer, Jennifer....4:20:09 (14,783)
Hester, Angela....6:45:45 (31,639)
Hetherington, Tracey....4:05:11 (11,327)
Heugh, Isabel....4:51:48 (22,267)
Heuze, Joanne....4:01:23 (10,516)
Heward, Sarah....4:15:21 (13,605)
Hewett, Lydia....4:23:42 (15,672)
Hewings, Suzanne....3:56:14 (9,255)
Hewis, Sharon....3:33:12 (4,629)
Hewitt, Alison....4:11:53 (12,735)
Hewitt, Catherine....3:30:03 (4,172)
Hewitt, Conagh....6:15:09 (30,831)
Hewitt, Helen....5:56:51 (30,095)
Hewitt, Paula....4:48:48 (21,590)
Hewitt, Sally....4:50:33 (21,977)
Hewson, Annabel....5:19:51 (26,865)
Hext, Jane....4:15:03 (13,525)
Heywood, Jane....5:41:32 (29,120)
Heywood, Jenny....5:06:12 (24,984)
Hick, Fiona....5:56:07 (30,058)
Hickey, Maria....3:58:19 (9,788)
Hickinson, Françoise....5:04:27 (24,699)
Hickling, Francesca....4:45:28 (20,837)
Hickling, Tania....4:28:19 (16,794)
Hickman, Charlotte....4:16:48 (13,936)
Hickmott, Janet....5:24:30 (27,475)
Hickox, Elizabeth....6:29:23 (31,311)
Hicks, Amelia....6:10:48 (30,679)
Hicks, Cheryl....5:18:33 (26,707)
Hicks, Hazel....7:53:46 (32,243)
Hicks, Toni....7:31:16 (32,162)
Hickson-Curran, Sheila....4:49:38 (21,786)
Hier, Diana....3:37:55 (5,403)
Higgins, Catherine....6:05:47 (30,493)
Higgins, Elizabeth....4:09:00 (12,129)
Higgins, Elizabeth....5:23:24 (27,340)
Higgins, Victoria....6:43:28 (31,601)
Highgate, Cath....4:30:19 (17,312)
Higson, Deborah....3:52:34 (8,322)
Hildebrand, Melinda....4:17:31 (14,115)
Hill, Amanda....5:32:56 (28,369)
Hill, Amie....5:17:31 (26,547)
Hill, Andrea....3:08:25 (1,536)
Hill, Anna....5:06:59 (25,103)
Hill, Carole....4:27:00 (16,470)
Hill, Charlotte....6:01:06 (30,304)
Hill, Claire....4:23:00 (15,494)
Hill, Cornelia....4:22:35 (15,387)
Hill, Elizabeth....5:10:25 (25,611)
Hill, Fiona....5:00:55 (24,141)
Hill, Harriet....3:42:30 (6,248)
Hill, Heather....4:55:24 (23,003)
Hill, Hjordis....4:07:36 (11,832)
Hill, Irene....6:16:41 (30,884)
Hill, Jacqueline....5:15:57 (26,369)
Hill, Janet....4:08:23 (11,977)
Hill, Julie....3:31:29 (4,407)
Hill, Kate....4:12:08 (12,795)
Hill, Lissa....4:38:38 (19,234)
Hill, Melissa....5:01:45 (24,269)
Hill, Michelle....3:50:34 (7,861)
Hill, Nicola....6:07:04 (30,533)
Hill, Olivia....6:02:58 (30,371)
Hill, Sarah....5:06:00 (24,960)
Hill, Tracey....4:30:17 (17,305)
Hill, Tracy....6:28:06 (31,271)
Hill, Tricia....5:37:44 (28,792)
Hill, Victoria....3:55:58 (9,168)
Hillenbrand, Baerbel....5:02:30 (24,386)
Hiller, Sandra....5:50:41 (29,763)
Hillman, Jill....4:55:34 (23,042)
Hillman, Maria....4:44:11 (20,538)
Hills, Jennie....3:55:19 (8,999)
Hills, Jenny....5:12:33 (25,909)
Hills, Jill....3:21:32 (2,937)
Hills, Linda....4:29:07 (17,017)
Hills, Nicola....3:00:25 (966)
Hilton, Beverley....4:57:48 (23,542)
Hilton, Caroline....3:45:04 (6,746)
Hilton, Clare....4:54:15 (22,758)
Hilton, Rosemary....5:01:22 (24,216)
Hilton, Suzanne....4:05:52 (11,473)
Hiluta, Bridget....4:55:24 (23,003)
Hinchcliffe, Emma....4:56:14 (23,205)
Hinchelwood, Carol....7:39:25 (32,200)

Hind, Tia	4:03:36 (10,967)	
Hinde, Laura	5:40:18 (29,018)	
Hindle, Caroline	3:32:56 (4,587)	
Hindlet, Lesley	5:07:17 (25,140)	
Hindley, Clare	4:56:33 (23,275)	
Hindmarch, Deborah	4:16:29 (13,854)	
Hinds, Jane	5:53:02 (29,881)	
Hindson, Joy	3:51:58 (8,186)	
Hine, Coretta	6:42:17 (31,572)	
Hinett, Zoe	5:26:08 (27,693)	
Hinshelwood, Linda	4:29:12 (17,039)	
Hinton, Jacqueline	6:28:07 (31,274)	
Hinves, Natasha	4:46:01 (20,964)	
Hipwell, Kate	6:00:22 (30,268)	
Hird, Elizabeth	4:10:37 (12,486)	
Hirons, Alison	4:58:45 (23,745)	
Hirons, Maria	5:44:47 (29,345)	
Hirotsuna, Shoko	5:56:50 (30,091)	
Hirst, Lindsey	4:19:40 (14,658)	
Hiscox, Sarah	4:12:27 (12,873)	
Hislop, Charmian	5:35:53 (28,627)	
Hitchings, Helen	5:28:38 (27,951)	
Hjort, Maren	4:43:29 (20,371)	
Hlliard, Isobel	5:39:01 (28,904)	
Hoadley, Jackie	5:03:41 (24,567)	
Hoare, Emma	4:27:15 (16,534)	
Hobbins, Catherine	4:26:32 (16,362)	
Hobbs, Lesley	4:37:59 (19,084)	
Hobbs, Margaret	5:00:43 (24,108)	
Hobbs, Rachel	5:40:53 (29,067)	
Hobday, Jacqueline	4:00:08 (10,257)	
Hochfeld, Kim	3:38:13 (5,445)	
Hocken, Anna	6:25:17 (31,170)	
Hockin, Lorayne	4:01:10 (10,465)	
Hockley, Marie	4:02:39 (10,769)	
Hoda, Fizah	4:26:16 (16,311)	
Hoddy, Leigh	4:41:06 (19,777)	
Hodges, Jo	5:38:20 (28,843)	
Hodges, Julie	4:23:39 (15,658)	
Hodgkins, Amanda	4:54:33 (22,823)	
Hodgson, Anita	4:32:28 (17,826)	
Hodgson, Lucy	5:29:01 (27,992)	
Hodson, Caroline	4:57:12 (23,430)	
Hodson, Nicola	4:44:40 (20,653)	
Hofer, Laura	4:56:09 (23,182)	
Hoffen, Kate	5:06:51 (25,088)	
Hogg, Rosie	4:12:32 (12,894)	
Hogg, Tanya	4:58:59 (23,795)	
Holberg, Eve	5:35:44 (28,615)	
Holbrook, Julia	3:54:18 (8,730)	
Holburn, Anna	5:14:20 (26,143)	
Holden, Amy	5:45:30 (29,404)	
Holden, Denise	4:25:41 (16,177)	
Holden, Louise	4:08:35 (12,035)	
Holden, Marie	4:47:54 (21,399)	
Holder, Jean	5:12:11 (25,851)	
Holdham, Caroline	6:12:51 (30,760)	
Holdsworth, Gillian	4:14:08 (13,293)	
Holes, Tracy	4:17:22 (14,074)	
Holhweller, Kristin	4:13:43 (13,182)	
Holifield, Wendy	5:06:06 (24,968)	
Holland, Andy	4:41:18 (19,825)	
Holland, Angela	5:35:39 (28,608)	
Holland, Claire	5:04:00 (24,628)	
Holland, Jennifer	4:00:06 (10,244)	
Holland, Kirsty	5:59:26 (30,235)	
Holland, Rachel	5:31:43 (28,258)	
Holland, Valerie	4:19:47 (14,692)	
Holliday, Susan	3:40:35 (5,883)	
Hollinger, Ruth	3:58:00 (9,706)	
Hollingworth, Dawn	5:22:09 (27,160)	
Hollins, Annick	5:26:39 (27,747)	
Hollinshead, Monique	3:05:14 (1,271)	
Hollis, Bridget	4:47:13 (21,230)	
Hollister, Wafaa	4:49:41 (21,799)	
Holloway, Beverley	4:44:06 (20,520)	
Holloway, Catherine	3:19:23 (2,689)	
Holloway, Lana	4:57:12 (23,430)	
Holloway, Zoe	4:50:55 (22,055)	
Hollywell, Kerri	5:04:03 (24,642)	
Holm, Elisabeth	3:42:38 (6,280)	
Holman, Katie	4:14:34 (13,397)	
Holman, Ronata	4:44:33 (20,622)	

Holmes, Beverly	4:07:56 (11,892)	
Holmes, Carol	4:30:47 (17,442)	
Holmes, Claire	4:02:14 (10,682)	
Holmes, Julie	5:42:36 (29,219)	
Holmes, Laura	3:44:38 (6,655)	
Holmes, Lorna	7:16:18 (32,045)	
Holmes, Marie	5:36:00 (28,639)	
Holmes, Patricia	6:41:24 (31,558)	
Holmes, Sandra	3:25:22 (3,449)	
Holmes, Tracey	4:20:43 (14,907)	
Holmes, Valerie	5:53:20 (29,895)	
Holt, Jacqueline	6:14:54 (30,827)	
Holt, Tina	5:17:35 (26,558)	
Holte-Smith, Sharon	6:26:35 (31,221)	
Homer, Britta	3:28:11 (3,845)	
Honeybourne, Julie	4:48:07 (21,456)	
Honeysett, Rebecca	3:47:07 (7,145)	
Hood, Alison	3:58:59 (9,962)	
Hook, Elizabeth	5:58:08 (30,168)	
Hook, Patricia	4:58:23 (23,667)	
Hooke, Amanda	3:27:21 (3,717)	
Hooker, Kelly	6:35:20 (31,455)	
Hook-Zurlino, Mariannina	4:57:16 (23,439)	
Hooley, Samantha	6:20:10 (31,021)	
Hooper, Amy	5:44:51 (29,349)	
Hooper, Clare	4:45:35 (20,863)	
Hooper, Wendy	4:05:46 (11,447)	
Hooton, Mary	5:19:07 (26,773)	
Hope, Alison	4:23:47 (15,692)	
Hope, Nicola	4:03:47 (11,007)	
Hopkins, Jennifer	3:39:03 (5,607)	
Hopkinson, Glynis	7:17:19 (32,053)	
Hopkinson, Nicola	3:31:44 (4,444)	
Hopley, Maxine	4:54:59 (22,917)	
Hopper, Fiona	4:22:44 (15,425)	
Hopper, Paula	4:51:08 (22,115)	
Horan, Jennifer	3:51:38 (8,116)	
Hornby, Carol	6:09:53 (30,635)	
Horner, Lucy	3:54:33 (8,803)	
Horsfall, Françoise	4:05:53 (11,478)	
Horsley, Helen	5:11:05 (25,705)	
Horsman, Kathleen	3:31:10 (4,355)	
Horton, Janet	5:16:51 (26,464)	
Horton, Lindsey	4:04:42 (11,225)	
Horton, Maddie	3:05:52 (1,311)	
Horton, Pauline	4:38:27 (19,190)	
Horton, Rebecca	5:10:43 (25,651)	
Horton, Vanessa	5:01:56 (24,302)	
Hoskin, Samantha	3:40:06 (5,809)	
Hosking, Amanda	3:37:23 (5,305)	
Hoskins, Caroline	4:03:45 (10,997)	
Hostombe, Clare	4:42:46 (20,172)	
Houden, Aase	3:25:40 (3,486)	
Hough, Inez	5:36:57 (28,732)	
Hough, Pamela	5:21:13 (27,052)	
Houghton, Jane	5:09:40 (25,499)	
Hourcau, Marie-Laure	4:36:24 (18,744)	
Hourigan, Rendell	4:36:10 (18,682)	
Houseman, Jacqueline	6:03:37 (30,400)	
Houston, Elizabeth	6:34:33 (31,437)	
Houston, Lorraine	4:08:24 (11,980)	
Hove, Emily	6:31:34 (31,365)	
Howard, Carol	6:56:47 (31,855)	
Howard, Charlotte	4:09:07 (12,156)	
Howard, Geraldine	4:36:19 (18,717)	
Howard, Hazel	4:10:03 (12,362)	
Howard, Joanne	5:18:15 (26,664)	
Howard, Joanne	5:50:28 (29,750)	
Howard, Joyce	6:24:14 (31,140)	
Howard, Karen	5:51:23 (29,802)	
Howard, Katie	5:39:47 (28,968)	
Howard, Lisa	3:56:06 (9,206)	
Howard, Nicolette	4:56:43 (23,320)	
Howard, Rita	6:19:50 (31,010)	
Howarth, Mary	3:47:27 (7,204)	
Howarth, Rachel	4:31:34 (17,633)	
Howarth, Sarah	4:47:34 (21,310)	
Howe, Angela	3:12:47 (1,964)	
Howe, Francesca	5:55:57 (30,038)	
Howell, Barbara	6:26:17 (31,214)	
Howell, Hazel	4:28:27 (16,839)	
Howell, Katrina	5:29:20 (28,022)	
Howell, Rachel	4:31:31 (17,621)	

Howells, Catrtiona	5:15:19 (26,293)	
Howes, Lucy	4:34:35 (18,301)	
Howieson, Jane	4:20:15 (14,809)	
Howitt, Helen	4:07:34 (11,824)	
Howland, Jacqueline	5:00:13 (24,020)	
Howles, Stephanie	4:38:56 (19,311)	
Howlett, Deborah	5:40:40 (29,052)	
Howlett, Margaret	3:54:28 (8,771)	
Howse, June	5:48:35 (29,611)	
Howton, Janice	5:03:52 (24,608)	
Hoyle, Fiona	4:52:05 (22,327)	
Hoyle, Helen	3:35:28 (4,993)	
Hoyle, Janet	4:25:52 (16,219)	
Hoyle, Stephanie	5:27:27 (27,825)	
Hppner, Louise	4:23:32 (15,625)	
Hubbard, Michelle	4:44:39 (20,649)	
Hubbard, Penelope	4:09:47 (12,295)	
Hubbard, Sandra	6:49:29 (31,706)	
Huber, Marie	5:47:11 (29,505)	
Hubert, Ciaragh	3:55:25 (9,027)	
Hubert, Victoria	4:04:28 (11,171)	
Hubery, Annette	6:00:27 (30,272)	
Huckle, Lita	5:22:47 (27,254)	
Hudgell, Cheryl	4:28:37 (16,890)	
Hudson, Claire	5:47:46 (29,555)	
Hudson, Debbie	4:41:32 (19,874)	
Hudson, Gillian	4:52:17 (22,354)	
Hudson, Heidi	6:38:56 (31,520)	
Hudson, Jane	4:36:15 (18,698)	
Hudson, Jane	4:51:28 (22,204)	
Hudson, Janice	4:20:04 (14,761)	
Hudson, Jean	4:19:14 (14,559)	
Hudson, Kirsty	4:14:51 (13,466)	
Hudson, Nicky	3:25:05 (3,407)	
Hudson, Sarah	5:25:29 (27,605)	
Hudson, Tracey	5:36:32 (28,689)	
Huebler, Hedwig	4:49:17 (21,698)	
Huesch, Kirsten	4:13:29 (13,122)	
Hufford, Sarah	4:01:49 (10,605)	
Hufnagel, Melanie	4:31:47 (17,686)	
Hugenroth, Dagmar	4:12:03 (12,772)	
Huggett, Bridget	5:51:31 (29,808)	
Hughes, Alison	4:18:39 (14,407)	
Hughes, Alison	4:56:36 (23,287)	
Hughes, Anne	4:50:20 (21,930)	
Hughes, Becky	4:57:45 (23,529)	
Hughes, Dorothy	3:57:05 (9,472)	
Hughes, Irene	4:33:27 (18,047)	
Hughes, Kendra	4:30:08 (17,267)	
Hughes, Lydia	4:58:59 (23,795)	
Hughes, Meg	4:12:11 (12,813)	
Hughes, Nicola	4:58:12 (23,626)	
Hughes, Rachel	5:54:56 (29,993)	
Hughes, Shirley	4:45:57 (20,948)	
Hughes, Suzanne	4:39:42 (19,476)	
Hughes-Jones, Gilly	5:30:42 (28,166)	
Hugh-Jones, Pia	4:38:42 (19,252)	
Huizinga, Hilde	4:35:22 (18,486)	
Hulbert, Laura	4:04:11 (11,108)	
Hulgaard, Karin	4:12:29 (12,880)	
Hulland, Gaynor	3:46:29 (7,026)	
Hulme, Lindsay	4:29:09 (17,026)	
Hulme, Susanne	6:57:13 (31,861)	
Humbert, Alison	5:13:27 (26,034)	
Hume, Elizxabeth	4:04:19 (11,137)	
Hume, Shirley	3:37:00 (5,229)	
Humpherson, Joanne	3:48:01 (7,323)	
Humphrey, Sonia	3:34:29 (4,835)	
Humphreys, Julie	7:24:17 (32,103)	
Humphreys, Lorraine	6:08:06 (30,569)	
Humphreys Elvis, Becky	5:08:21 (25,318)	
Humphries, Frances	4:37:33 (18,995)	
Humphries, Heidrun	4:58:04 (23,599)	
Hunsdon, Jo	5:46:15 (29,452)	
Hunston, Marie	4:32:37 (17,856)	
Hunt, Amanda	7:24:23 (32,105)	
Hunt, Bev	5:51:10 (29,793)	
Hunt, Caoimhe	3:56:11 (9,234)	
Hunt, Christine	4:51:24 (22,178)	
Hunt, Debbie	5:25:52 (27,650)	
Hunt, Elizabeth	4:13:08 (13,030)	
Hunt, Joanne	4:39:32 (19,448)	
Hunt, Rachel	5:41:15 (29,097)	

Hunt, Shirley...3:54:30 (8,784)
Hunter, Alyson...4:23:18 (15,576)
Hunter, Beverly...4:37:47 (19,041)
Hunter, Dawn...4:52:37 (22,417)
Hunter, Sue...6:38:05 (31,507)
Huntington, Christine...4:34:25 (18,271)
Hunwicks, Sarah...5:07:26 (25,168)
Hunziker-Muehlebach, Agnes...5:21:01 (27,024)
Hurdle, Deborah...6:11:04 (30,696)
Hurley, Karin...6:02:24 (30,356)
Hurley, Tara...5:58:17 (30,172)
Hurndall, Vanessa...7:03:41 (31,919)
Hurnell, Gillian...5:10:24 (25,608)
Hurran, Rebecca...5:27:01 (27,777)
Hurrell, Kirsten...6:35:44 (31,467)
Hurst, Alison...6:50:09 (31,726)
Hurst, Joanne...5:29:13 (28,009)
Hussein, Suzanne...6:23:13 (31,110)
Hussey, Elaine...4:12:27 (12,873)
Hutchings, Lucy...4:23:25 (15,591)
Hutchins, Catherine...5:02:10 (24,341)
Hutchinson, Susan...4:35:55 (18,625)
Hutton, Abigail...5:33:08 (28,383)
Hutton, Ceri...4:48:42 (21,570)
Hutton, Ruth...3:07:36 (1,460)
Huxley, Linda...3:44:03 (6,555)
Hyde, Lindsay...4:23:32 (15,625)
Hymas, Jane...3:45:12 (6,773)
Hynes, Caroline...3:55:23 (9,018)
Hynes, Julia...5:28:54 (27,976)
Iannelli, Sarah...3:52:45 (8,363)
Iball, Chris...4:43:22 (20,342)
Ibberson, Victoria...6:08:06 (30,569)
Illing, Anne...4:45:36 (20,867)
Ilott, Karen...5:05:05 (24,812)
Imbert, Clair...4:41:32 (19,874)
Imeson, Hazel...3:53:41 (8,586)
Immelman, Dedre...4:32:38 (17,859)
Imong, Stella...4:16:34 (13,871)
Impey, Frances...4:58:03 (23,596)
Imray, Wendy...6:10:43 (30,673)
Ind, Catherine...5:04:08 (24,654)
Ind, Katherine...4:07:26 (11,788)
Ing, Amanda...4:30:23 (17,336)
Ingham, Yvonne...4:56:10 (23,189)
Ingram, Barbara...3:57:23 (9,552)
Ingram, Claire...4:59:50 (23,955)
Ingstad, Cheryl...5:24:24 (27,459)
Inkley, Rebecca...4:12:49 (12,963)
Inman, Angela...4:52:05 (22,327)
Innes, Janice...5:30:41 (28,162)
Innes, Shauna...5:54:23 (29,963)
Inns, Natasha...6:06:02 (30,505)
Iorio, Lisa...3:36:23 (5,128)
Iredale, Lynne...5:03:48 (24,592)
Ireson, Rosa...4:51:26 (22,188)
Irlam, Lisa...5:10:54 (25,678)
Iruretagoyena, Theresa...4:12:01 (12,769)
Irvine, Kate...4:53:17 (22,569)
Irving, Abigail...8:04:30 (32,261)
Irving, Joanne...4:46:07 (20,999)
Isaacs, Susan...7:33:21 (32,172)
Isabelle, Hermes...5:47:41 (29,550)
Isham, Louise...4:50:42 (22,011)
Isherwood, Pamela...5:04:24 (24,692)
Isom-Leonard, Alison...5:59:10 (30,219)
Issatt, Belinda...3:52:58 (8,412)
Issott, Tracey...4:49:01 (21,635)
Itagaki, Sugiko...4:39:31 (19,444)
Ivory, Sharon...4:47:26 (21,283)
Iwamura, Akiko...4:29:14 (17,049)
Jack, Annette...4:12:18 (12,832)
Jack, Tanya...3:28:44 (3,952)
Jackson, Alison...5:15:20 (26,295)
Jackson, Anne...5:29:31 (28,039)
Jackson, Becky...5:29:32 (28,043)
Jackson, Catherine...4:38:59 (19,322)
Jackson, Catherine...5:20:26 (26,945)
Jackson, Cathie...4:03:01 (10,846)
Jackson, Diane...4:52:39 (22,431)
Jackson, Elizabeth...4:08:55 (12,112)
Jackson, Elizabeth...4:10:58 (12,535)
Jackson, Glen...3:41:58 (6,142)
Jackson, Hannah...4:23:15 (15,560)
Jackson, Jacqueline...4:39:46 (19,490)
Jackson, Kathy...4:52:43 (22,441)
Jackson, Marilyn...6:24:46 (31,152)
Jackson, Nikki...3:52:04 (8,213)
Jackson, Shayne...4:05:33 (11,410)
Jackson, Sonia...4:09:42 (12,274)
Jackson, Sonia...4:41:48 (19,943)
Jacobs, Margot...4:04:08 (11,098)
Jacobson, Beverley...4:09:55 (12,329)
Jafari, Shima...4:17:56 (14,238)
Jaggar, Kelly...4:32:50 (17,909)
Jagger, Betsan...3:38:49 (5,561)
Jagger, Joanne...4:11:39 (12,677)
Jakeman, Marion...4:12:10 (12,805)
James, Alison...5:11:56 (25,822)
James, Anita...4:48:04 (21,444)
James, Clair...6:13:37 (30,785)
James, Deborah...6:08:24 (30,583)
James, Donna...6:54:45 (31,826)
James, Emma...5:41:52 (29,148)
James, Hannah...6:01:57 (30,340)
James, Heulwen...4:14:03 (13,275)
James, Jane...5:17:50 (26,583)
James, Jennifer...3:56:33 (9,335)
James, Julia...4:30:56 (17,476)
James, Kathleen...5:11:07 (25,709)
James, Lysbeth...4:55:55 (23,135)
James, Melanie...5:33:30 (28,421)
James, Wendy...6:47:57 (31,674)
James-Gaut, Lisa...6:10:31 (30,661)
Jameson, Helen...6:47:26 (31,662)
James-Welsh, April...4:03:51 (11,025)
Jamieson, Susie...6:35:09 (31,452)
Jamsheer Matthews, Sophia...5:25:12 (27,574)
Jans, Chris...4:52:39 (22,431)
Jarrard, Kelli...5:15:00 (26,248)
Jarrett, Louise...4:25:16 (16,074)
Jarrett, Tessa...5:37:51 (28,800)
Jarvis, Jennie...4:57:11 (23,426)
Jaugey, Annick...4:22:21 (15,327)
Jayanetti, Naomi...6:10:00 (30,642)
Jeannette, Christine...3:24:15 (3,296)
Jefferies, Helen...5:20:16 (26,923)
Jefferies, Helen...5:49:14 (29,655)
Jeffers, Emma...5:27:34 (27,842)
Jeffery, Della...6:06:18 (30,511)
Jeffery, Tracy...4:16:54 (13,964)
Jefford, Evonne...5:19:46 (26,859)
Jeffreis, Debra...5:21:33 (27,089)
Jeffrey, Amanda...5:03:35 (24,545)
Jeffreys, Anne...4:12:19 (12,838)
Jeffs, Chris...3:46:55 (7,108)
Jeffs, Clare...3:32:48 (4,570)
Jelaca, Nada...6:12:33 (30,750)
Jelly, Alison...4:45:28 (20,837)
Jenkin, Sally...4:26:16 (16,311)
Jenking, Indra...6:19:36 (30,999)
Jenkins, Ally...6:18:20 (30,950)
Jenkins, Angela...5:30:14 (28,102)
Jenkins, Carolyn...3:36:16 (5,108)
Jenkins, Deborah...3:27:31 (3,740)
Jenkins, Elise...4:38:02 (19,099)
Jenkins, Greta...3:33:08 (4,618)
Jenkins, Helen...4:13:11 (13,044)
Jenkins, Helen...5:45:53 (29,433)
Jenkins, Janet...5:16:20 (26,407)
Jenkins, Jeanette...4:55:25 (23,008)
Jenkins, Sarah...4:25:21 (16,104)
Jenkins, Sarah...4:53:59 (22,711)
Jenkins, Sarah...5:48:53 (29,628)
Jenkins, Shelley...6:25:48 (31,195)
Jenkinson, Annie...4:07:33 (11,822)
Jenkis, Kimberly...6:13:39 (30,786)
Jennings, Clare...6:04:27 (30,427)
Jennings, Julie...5:30:33 (28,146)
Jennings, Kim...5:14:20 (26,143)
Jensen, Kirsten...4:28:16 (16,783)
Jensen, Suzanne...4:23:16 (15,565)
Jerman, Jill...4:16:25 (13,838)
Jerrett, Suzanna...4:35:44 (18,570)
Jerrom, Janice...4:18:58 (14,498)
Jervis, Sylvia...6:34:17 (31,433)
Jeschke, Stefanie...4:22:07 (15,267)
Jessah, Christina...7:05:56 (31,940)
Jewell, Rebecca...4:09:57 (12,340)
Jewett, Melanie...4:42:59 (20,229)
Jewitt, Anna...6:19:16 (30,982)
Jinivizian, Victoria...4:03:56 (11,044)
Jobey, Julie...4:07:07 (11,713)
Jobling, Julie...5:23:15 (27,318)
Jobling, Margaret...4:37:51 (19,058)
Joehr, Martina...4:15:29 (13,635)
Johannesen, Kari...3:23:33 (3,185)
John, Megan...3:19:00 (2,654)
John, Vivienne...7:55:33 (32,247)
Johnson, Christine...4:42:51 (20,194)
Johnson, Christine...4:56:46 (23,329)
Johnson, Christine...6:08:15 (30,575)
Johnson, Claudia...4:06:25 (11,575)
Johnson, Danielle...3:27:03 (3,688)
Johnson, Denise...6:08:15 (30,575)
Johnson, Diane...4:43:15 (20,303)
Johnson, Emily...4:19:31 (14,619)
Johnson, Emma...5:52:11 (29,839)
Johnson, Faye...6:13:05 (30,770)
Johnson, Hazel...4:02:34 (10,751)
Johnson, Joanne...4:42:34 (20,127)
Johnson, Joanne...6:11:04 (30,696)
Johnson, Lesley...6:24:07 (31,136)
Johnson, Linda...5:37:54 (28,803)
Johnson, Lindsay...4:11:43 (12,699)
Johnson, Marie...4:43:48 (20,453)
Johnson, Nanette...5:52:11 (29,839)
Johnson, Philippa...4:37:08 (18,906)
Johnson, Sheona...5:42:05 (29,173)
Johnson, Sue...3:32:43 (4,562)
Johnson, Yvonne...4:57:26 (23,463)
Johnston, Alison...4:24:15 (15,810)
Johnston, Alison...4:56:57 (23,368)
Johnston, Catherine...5:23:09 (27,310)
Johnston, Tracey...5:36:51 (28,719)
Johnston, Yvette...4:41:09 (19,788)
Johnstone, Dorothy...4:52:26 (22,384)
Johnstone, Janet...5:41:22 (29,104)
Johnstone, Janice...4:16:51 (13,947)
Johnstone, Mandy...4:53:31 (22,621)
Johnstone, Tracey...4:37:30 (18,984)
Jolley, Lynn...3:46:22 (7,009)
Jolly, Margaret...4:06:52 (11,662)
Joly, Ellen...4:23:55 (15,724)
Jonas, Nicola...5:45:53 (29,433)
Jones, Alison...6:12:52 (30,761)
Jones, Amanda...4:33:59 (18,162)
Jones, Angela...5:22:51 (27,261)
Jones, Barbara...4:35:49 (18,603)
Jones, Belinda...4:30:03 (17,252)
Jones, Bethan...4:29:28 (17,107)
Jones, Carol...5:29:12 (28,005)
Jones, Catherine...4:34:15 (18,226)
Jones, Charlotte...4:25:16 (16,074)
Jones, Christine...3:55:06 (8,941)
Jones, Clare...5:12:20 (25,869)
Jones, Debbie...4:29:11 (17,036)
Jones, Deirdre...3:53:57 (8,661)
Jones, Eirian...6:47:25 (31,661)
Jones, Elizabeth...4:15:23 (13,615)
Jones, Emily...5:23:59 (27,406)
Jones, Emily...6:36:26 (31,484)
Jones, Emma...4:48:00 (21,427)
Jones, Emma...5:34:36 (28,528)
Jones, Emma...6:02:42 (30,362)
Jones, Eti...7:59:10 (32,255)
Jones, Fiona...5:14:02 (26,101)
Jones, Gareth...4:23:42 (15,672)
Jones, Gwyneth...5:41:35 (29,128)
Jones, Helen...4:45:45 (20,899)
Jones, Hilary...4:44:46 (20,673)
Jones, Jennifer...4:12:10 (12,805)
Jones, Jennifer...4:58:45 (23,745)
Jones, Jenny...4:47:21 (21,259)
Jones, Jo...4:08:36 (12,042)
Jones, Judith...3:40:17 (5,839)
Jones, Judith...3:48:44 (7,448)
Jones, Judith...4:13:09 (13,037)
Jones, Justine...4:59:40 (23,917)

Jones, Kacey 5:39:53 (28,979)
Jones, Keston 4:09:59 (12,349)
Jones, Leontine 4:25:26 (16,126)
Jones, Linda 5:01:15 (24,194)
Jones, Lisa 6:22:07 (31,079)
Jones, Loraine 6:17:03 (30,895)
Jones, Lucy 4:46:17 (21,040)
Jones, Lynda 3:57:23 (9,552)
Jones, Nia 4:18:43 (14,429)
Jones, Patricia 4:56:29 (23,255)
Jones, Paula 6:05:41 (30,489)
Jones, Rachael 3:44:41 (6,664)
Jones, Rachelle 6:08:40 (30,595)
Jones, Rebecca 3:35:31 (5,000)
Jones, Rebecca 5:23:49 (27,384)
Jones, Rebecca 6:25:40 (31,188)
Jones, Rhian 4:25:23 (16,113)
Jones, Sally 4:58:28 (23,692)
Jones, Sandra 4:39:29 (19,437)
Jones, Sandra 6:07:20 (30,547)
Jones, Sarah 5:31:17 (28,224)
Jones, Sarah 5:32:42 (28,350)
Jones, Sarah 5:44:56 (29,359)
Jones, Sarah 6:42:19 (31,575)
Jones, Shannon 4:43:38 (20,413)
Jones, Sharon 4:29:19 (17,065)
Jones, Tessa 4:16:39 (13,892)
Jones, Tracy 7:16:37 (32,050)
Jones, Victoria 4:01:32 (10,545)
Jones, Yvonne 4:41:24 (19,848)
Jones, Zandra 4:50:10 (21,897)
Jonsson, Agneta 3:28:37 (3,929)
Jordan, Aileen 4:58:47 (23,762)
Jordan, Bethany 4:59:28 (23,880)
Jordan, Christine 7:08:55 (31,981)
Jordanova, Alix 4:20:01 (14,748)
José, Michelle 4:28:34 (16,878)
Jost-Carraro, Ursula 4:28:23 (16,817)
Jowett, Cristina 6:18:18 (30,947)
Joy, Johanna 4:32:52 (17,918)
Joyce, Ceara 3:43:42 (6,489)
Joyce, Kerry 4:36:45 (18,823)
Joyce, Marion 4:21:57 (15,224)
Joyce, Rebecca 4:15:56 (13,728)
Joyce, Susan 4:33:22 (18,024)
Joyner, Lesley 4:56:03 (23,158)
Jraunsoe, Ann 5:08:07 (25,282)
Judd, Lindy 6:01:00 (30,295)
Jude, Lucy 5:05:36 (24,900)
Judson, Jill 4:29:00 (16,991)
Juggins, Sandra 6:10:44 (30,675)
Julian, Rosie 4:36:54 (18,854)
Julius, Karen 5:13:59 (26,098)
Jungk, Heather 6:13:26 (30,781)
Jupp, Helen 4:37:50 (19,050)
Just, Kaye 4:08:53 (12,105)
Kabbaj, Ouadia 5:40:02 (28,998)
Kaczmarczyk, Catherine 4:10:31 (12,468)
Kaczmarek, Adela 5:30:21 (28,125)
Kadu-Baluchi, Maria 7:19:11 (32,067)
Kail, Dorian 3:44:44 (6,679)
Kail, Nancy 4:56:29 (23,255)
Kain, Joanne 6:44:04 (31,610)
Kainz, Birgit 4:32:01 (17,736)
Kairies, Kornelia 4:15:06 (13,539)
Kaiser, Kathy 3:11:59 (1,859)
Kalashnikoff, Maria 5:15:32 (26,316)
Kalawsky, Anna 7:04:00 (31,925)
Kamming, Jodi 4:43:40 (20,423)
Kane-Fane, Sandrine 4:53:27 (22,609)
Kanouni, Yasmina 3:24:41 (3,356)
Kany, Olivia 4:18:49 (14,452)
Karam, Sarah 5:29:31 (28,039)
Karlic, Heidrun 3:46:59 (7,121)
Karsten, Beatrice 4:01:33 (10,549)
Katsanis, Penny 3:57:33 (9,587)
Kavanagh, Carmel 5:10:04 (25,561)
Kavanagh, Maria 5:02:47 (24,431)
Kawahara, Rieko 5:01:09 (24,176)
Kay, Aimée 6:42:03 (31,567)
Kaye, Jennifer 5:31:53 (28,276)
Kaye, Judith 4:37:34 (19,000)
Kaye, Patricia 4:47:53 (21,394)
Kaye, Stephanie 4:51:46 (22,258)
Keane, Gill 4:17:31 (14,115)
Kearns, Angela 4:14:35 (13,399)
Kearns, Joan 4:21:00 (14,979)
Kearns, Ursula 6:31:19 (31,356)
Keasley, Jacqueline 3:31:59 (4,470)
Keates, Deanie 6:17:46 (30,916)
Keaton, Helen 3:51:39 (8,120)
Keech, Jennie 4:43:27 (20,363)
Keeling, Julie 5:00:57 (24,145)
Keen, Emma 4:20:46 (14,918)
Keen, June 4:57:33 (23,490)
Keene, Sophie 3:38:57 (5,591)
Keenleyside, Kathryn 4:36:44 (18,814)
Keeping, Jennifer 5:04:13 (24,665)
Keeping, Klara 6:43:28 (31,601)
Keer, Elizabeth 4:38:39 (19,238)
Keet Marsh, Lorayne 3:58:06 (9,730)
Kefford-Watson, Angela 3:30:07 (4,189)
Kehoe, Donna 5:24:12 (27,437)
Kehoe, Sarah 4:37:44 (19,029)
Keith, Louise 4:30:43 (17,422)
Kellar, Jennifer 5:53:50 (29,923)
Keller, Rachel 3:50:00 (7,734)
Kelley, Gill 7:22:29 (32,089)
Kellow, Emma 4:42:20 (20,062)
Kelly, Bridget 4:47:42 (21,346)
Kelly, Diane 3:28:17 (3,861)
Kelly, Elaine 5:17:15 (26,509)
Kelly, Faye 5:27:14 (27,805)
Kelly, Fiona 3:58:11 (9,748)
Kelly, Jane 4:48:48 (21,590)
Kelly, Janet 6:28:35 (31,290)
Kelly, June 4:44:18 (20,571)
Kelly, Kathryn 4:23:13 (15,551)
Kelly, Linda 6:05:34 (30,482)
Kelly, Micah 4:25:38 (16,165)
Kelly, Vicky 3:30:14 (4,208)
Kemp, Alison 6:38:41 (31,516)
Kemp, Ann 6:16:51 (30,890)
Kemp, Elaine 4:51:26 (22,188)
Kemp, Linda 4:41:43 (19,925)
Kenden, Fran 3:34:34 (4,847)
Kennah, Gwen 4:48:00 (21,427)
Kennard, Lisa 4:01:32 (10,545)
Kennedy, Carine 4:15:17 (13,585)
Kennedy, Deborah 4:48:16 (21,489)
Kennedy, Elaine 5:27:11 (27,802)
Kennedy, Evelyn 4:30:14 (17,295)
Kennedy, Ginette 4:21:09 (15,020)
Kennedy, Jenny 4:54:37 (22,841)
Kennedy, Julie 5:36:33 (28,694)
Kennedy, Linda 3:59:33 (10,105)
Kennedy, Lisa 6:09:17 (30,613)
Kennedy, Louisa 5:35:55 (28,630)
Kennedy, Trudi 3:16:28 (2,372)
Kennedy, Vida 4:02:12 (10,678)
Kennerson, Shirley 4:38:00 (19,088)
Kennet, Jane 4:17:33 (14,129)
Kennett, Mia 4:31:37 (17,646)
Kenney, Megan 4:08:27 (11,995)
Kenniford, Audrey 6:49:29 (31,706)
Kenning, Julia 4:24:50 (15,959)
Kenny, Aida 4:23:38 (15,654)
Kenny, Gillian 3:48:35 (7,420)
Kenny, Mandy 6:19:52 (31,013)
Kent, Nicola 3:48:30 (7,400)
Kent, Veronica 5:52:21 (29,850)
Kenwright, Dawn 3:15:23 (2,279)
Kenyon, Sarah 5:31:16 (28,222)
Keough, Lisa 6:01:52 (30,335)
Keppler, Anne 4:22:35 (15,387)
Kermorgant, Julie 5:18:29 (26,699)
Kerr, Felicity 4:47:58 (21,419)
Kettle, Helen 4:47:39 (21,333)
Kettler, Sheila 6:54:09 (31,808)
Kew, Beverly 7:19:10 (32,064)
Kewley, Michelle 4:30:26 (17,354)
Key, Alison 5:03:01 (24,460)
Khaihra, Mary 6:31:48 (31,375)
Khan-Orakzai, Zareena 5:00:52 (24,132)
Kibble, Carol 6:41:49 (31,564)
Kibble, Jacqueline 4:54:30 (22,814)
Kilgallon, Rachel 4:38:50 (19,285)
Kilgour, Kirsteen 4:29:35 (17,134)
Kilgour, Vivien 4:07:22 (11,772)
Killip, Amanda 3:33:22 (4,657)
Kim, Sonmi 5:31:04 (28,198)
Kimbell, Julia 7:07:34 (31,969)
Kinder, Mary 4:10:37 (12,486)
Kinder, Melanie 3:46:33 (7,045)
King, Amy 6:54:48 (31,830)
King, Andrea 5:20:01 (26,890)
King, Annette 5:14:26 (26,164)
King, April 5:08:18 (25,311)
King, Beverley 5:43:54 (29,299)
King, Caroline 3:59:42 (10,154)
King, Ele 4:53:43 (22,652)
King, Elisabeth 4:34:26 (18,275)
King, Evelyn 4:24:33 (15,875)
King, Helen 5:20:53 (27,006)
King, Jane 4:53:53 (22,694)
King, Lesley 3:51:50 (8,159)
King, Lucy 4:35:30 (18,517)
King, Nadine 3:28:48 (3,970)
King, Philippa 4:43:15 (20,303)
King, Sadie 4:26:52 (16,441)
King, Stephanie 4:06:32 (11,596)
King, Tracey 5:15:07 (26,266)
Kingdon, Jennie 3:54:59 (8,917)
Kingsley, Isabel 6:49:01 (31,695)
Kingston, Alison 3:54:08 (8,687)
Kinnard, Denise 4:38:12 (19,133)
Kinney, Gillian 4:32:08 (17,759)
Kinsella, Shannon 5:53:33 (29,909)
Kinsella-Hobbs, Anne-Marie 4:53:33 (22,627)
Kirby, Lyn 6:33:39 (31,415)
Kirby, Maureen 4:28:41 (16,907)
Kirby, Trudy 5:00:12 (24,016)
Kirby-Ashford, Claire 4:38:42 (19,252)
Kirk, Lesley 3:22:33 (3,053)
Kirk, Sally 4:21:15 (15,044)
Kirk, Sara 4:20:55 (14,957)
Kirk, Yvette 4:14:19 (13,333)
Kirkby, Tracey 4:56:14 (23,205)
Kirkley, Diane 4:12:39 (12,929)
Kirner, Karen 3:47:54 (7,301)
Kirrane, Maria 4:46:13 (21,022)
Kirrby, Lorraine 5:47:13 (29,507)
Kirton, Geraldine 5:39:07 (28,912)
Kirton, Rowena 5:33:12 (28,391)
Kirwan, Cliona 4:49:50 (21,832)
Kirwan, Elaine 4:39:26 (19,427)
Kirwan, Elizabeth 4:55:15 (22,965)
Kirwan, Emma 6:54:21 (31,812)
Kirwan, Nerys 4:02:43 (10,786)
Kitching, Lyn 4:00:16 (10,283)
Klasen, Hildegard 4:34:51 (18,359)
Kleine, Gabriele 4:54:44 (22,872)
Klerings, Daniela 3:16:13 (2,352)
Klotschkow, Sue 3:55:24 (9,022)
Kmetyko-Huber, Marianne 3:56:33 (9,335)
Kneale, Val 5:28:49 (27,969)
Knellwolf, Bettina 3:53:31 (8,548)
Knibbs, Karen 6:17:02 (30,894)
Knight, Andi 5:00:44 (24,113)
Knight, Bryn 5:02:06 (24,327)
Knight, Carol 3:44:47 (6,685)
Knight, Dawn 5:32:18 (28,319)
Knight, Donna 5:07:37 (25,208)
Knight, Ellen 4:05:45 (11,445)
Knight, Greta 3:56:37 (9,352)
Knight, Katherine 4:21:22 (15,075)
Knights, Lisa 2:56:57 (697)
Knock, Wendy 4:10:13 (12,401)
Knopp, Rosalind 3:47:35 (7,232)
Knott, Elspeth 4:20:24 (14,848)
Knouwds, Hendriette 3:31:29 (4,407)
Knowles, Diane 4:32:38 (17,859)
Knowles, Jayne 4:26:34 (16,370)
Knowles, Jennifer 5:32:08 (28,300)
Knox, Casey 4:51:50 (22,275)
Knudsen, Gry 4:47:34 (21,310)
Koch, Lisa 3:21:28 (2,928)
Koch, Rosalind 4:46:40 (21,119)
Kodish, Michala 4:48:23 (21,515)

Koen, Marilize	5:41:22 (29,104)	
Koeth, Melanie	4:18:51 (14,463)	
Korn, Nicola	3:55:10 (8,958)	
Korolova, Zarina	5:05:52 (24,941)	
Korpanec, Jaroslava	3:52:38 (8,338)	
Koster Den Hoedt, Mieke	4:49:35 (21,776)	
Kotarba, Anna	5:57:28 (30,135)	
Kramer, Kerstin	3:42:21 (6,209)	
Kramer, Michelle	4:46:45 (21,136)	
Kreitman, Petrushka	5:36:23 (28,671)	
Kristiansen, Anne Brit	4:36:03 (18,662)	
Kruk, Renata	6:15:49 (30,853)	
Kuhn, Trudy	3:45:29 (6,828)	
Kulas, Stephanie	6:08:26 (30,588)	
Kunde, Kalpita	6:04:18 (30,423)	
Kuritko, Christina	4:54:12 (22,747)	
Kwai, Jacqueline	6:54:29 (31,818)	
Kwan, Wing	4:30:34 (17,384)	
Kydd, Gillian	4:57:33 (23,490)	
Kyle, Margaret	5:47:59 (29,575)	
Kynaston, Diane	4:45:11 (20,767)	
Kyte, Lisa	4:57:40 (23,517)	
Laarmann, Martha	4:54:33 (22,823)	
Laban, Chrissie	4:06:46 (11,648)	
Ladd, Helen	4:05:31 (11,403)	
Ladlow, Diana	5:59:01 (30,210)	
Lagden, Lesley	6:09:39 (30,627)	
Lagger, Regula	5:13:01 (25,976)	
Lahbabi, Amal	5:35:55 (28,630)	
Lai, Alicia	4:37:32 (18,993)	
Lai, Martine	4:28:21 (16,807)	
Laing, Elisabeth	4:46:54 (21,169)	
Laing, Kerry	5:05:17 (24,836)	
Lainsbury, Kelly-Anne	4:49:03 (21,644)	
Laird, Lynn	4:09:28 (12,219)	
Laird, Nuala	4:35:31 (18,521)	
Lake, Emma	3:46:35 (7,051)	
Lake, Geraldine	5:10:14 (25,588)	
Lakeland, Janine	4:50:08 (21,887)	
Lakhloufi, Tam	4:09:13 (12,175)	
Lalani, Zahra	5:38:55 (28,891)	
Lalek, Angela	5:34:05 (28,485)	
Laley, Sarah	6:05:40 (30,487)	
Lam, Judy	5:42:42 (29,224)	
Lamb, Clare	5:08:26 (25,330)	
Lamb, Julie	3:14:15 (2,158)	
Lamb, Katherine	5:37:01 (28,739)	
Lamb, Rozanne	6:20:36 (31,036)	
Lambersy, Leveke	4:59:04 (23,820)	
Lambert, Clare	4:27:38 (16,633)	
Lambert, Daphne	6:01:50 (30,333)	
Lambert, Sue	3:39:21 (5,666)	
Lambert, Vicky	4:14:08 (13,293)	
Lambeth, Anneliese	3:26:18 (3,578)	
Lamerton, Elinor	4:20:52 (14,949)	
Lammens, Sonia	3:40:02 (5,793)	
Lammond, Maria	4:40:10 (19,575)	
Lampam, Julia	7:06:08 (31,942)	
Lander, Anne	5:43:06 (29,248)	
Lander, Tracey	4:17:51 (14,218)	
Landy, Anne	5:01:15 (24,194)	
Lane, Annah	5:15:02 (26,252)	
Lane, Christine	4:13:57 (13,244)	
Lane, Diane	7:00:43 (31,897)	
Lane, Elizabeth	4:12:34 (12,907)	
Lane, Emma	4:03:10 (10,875)	
Lane, Kellie	4:25:26 (16,126)	
Lane, Sandra	5:14:09 (26,114)	
Lang, Caroline	4:56:34 (23,280)	
Langan, Jane	3:58:21 (9,796)	
Langdell, Kim	3:27:01 (3,684)	
Langdon, Jean	4:47:23 (21,269)	
Lange, Emma	3:50:14 (7,785)	
Langford, Louise	4:47:40 (21,339)	
Langley, Joyce	5:57:19 (30,121)	
Langslow, Rachel	5:06:34 (25,028)	
Langston, Caroline	4:56:56 (23,364)	
Langston, Joanna	4:12:26 (12,867)	
Langton, Paula	5:48:10 (29,589)	
Lannen, Maud	5:15:20 (26,295)	
Lansdown, Wendy	4:55:06 (22,939)	
L'Anson, Penny	4:20:36 (14,888)	
Lant, Bethan	5:30:57 (28,188)	
Laperna, Rose Marie	5:35:57 (28,635)	
Lapworth, Dianne	3:57:14 (9,513)	
Larach, Alena	4:11:59 (12,756)	
Larsen, Rikke	3:40:03 (5,799)	
Larvin, Marie	4:42:51 (20,194)	
Larvin, Marie	4:50:35 (21,987)	
Lasry, Cathy	4:28:35 (16,883)	
Last, Joanna	5:29:22 (28,025)	
Latham, Gillian	5:02:22 (24,371)	
Latter, Jennifer	5:13:40 (26,065)	
Latter, Liz	4:53:39 (22,643)	
Lattey, Alison	4:11:20 (12,606)	
Lau, Kimmberly	4:56:04 (23,161)	
Laud, Carolyn	3:51:18 (8,032)	
Laurie, Emma	6:23:17 (31,111)	
Laury, Patricia	6:10:01 (30,644)	
Laver, Jan	4:18:31 (14,365)	
Law, Catherine	4:31:46 (17,682)	
Law, June	4:36:56 (18,863)	
Lawrence, Deborah	4:30:27 (17,357)	
Lawrence, Emma	4:42:45 (20,169)	
Lawrence, Janice	5:40:13 (29,011)	
Lawrence, Julie	5:10:47 (25,658)	
Lawrence, Sally	4:29:21 (17,071)	
Lawrence, Saskia	5:18:03 (26,617)	
Lawrence, Susan	4:56:38 (23,294)	
Lawrence, Vanessa	6:35:58 (31,472)	
Lawrence, Wendy	4:27:21 (16,561)	
Lawrenson, Anna	5:20:13 (26,917)	
Lawrenson, Helen	6:25:39 (31,187)	
Lawrie, Tamara	5:50:52 (29,774)	
Laws, Jane	3:16:29 (2,374)	
Lawson, Karen	6:24:35 (31,149)	
Lawson, Louise	5:45:56 (29,436)	
Lawson, Vanessa	4:15:28 (13,631)	
Lawton, Janet	4:35:20 (18,479)	
Lawton, Suzette	3:58:26 (9,818)	
Lazarova, Lepa	4:39:36 (19,459)	
Lazenby, Caroline	5:50:46 (29,770)	
Le, Tess	5:23:55 (27,397)	
Le Brazidec, Jacqueline	4:48:39 (21,561)	
Le Brazidec, Marie-Christine	4:49:28 (21,743)	
Le Callonec, Claudine	4:46:49 (21,150)	
Le Grange, Desiree	4:38:40 (19,245)	
Le Poidevin, Emily	4:01:38 (10,566)	
Le Roy, Karen	6:52:18 (31,765)	
Le Vey, Nicola	5:49:01 (29,640)	
Leach, Catherine	5:06:46 (25,069)	
Leach, Joanne	3:53:15 (8,487)	
Leach, Susan	4:22:09 (15,276)	
Leahy, Jacqueline	5:05:40 (24,912)	
Learmonth, Anna	5:10:28 (25,619)	
Leary, Joanne	5:38:40 (28,873)	
Leask, Mary	4:09:52 (12,315)	
Leather, Jane	3:36:03 (5,073)	
Leavey, Mary	7:10:29 (31,994)	
Leaviss, Isobel	4:57:38 (23,511)	
Leck, Michelle	4:55:43 (23,083)	
Ledgister, Vaniah	6:10:27 (30,659)	
Ledochowski, Margarita	4:31:43 (17,674)	
Lee, Alison	4:18:56 (14,492)	
Lee, Carolyn	4:17:20 (14,064)	
Lee, Emma	3:59:51 (10,187)	
Lee, Gillian	4:50:17 (21,919)	
Lee, Joe	4:38:01 (19,093)	
Lee, Michelle	2:43:41 (213)	
Lee, Rachel	3:42:53 (6,337)	
Lee, Sarah	4:03:14 (10,891)	
Lee, Tess	3:45:35 (6,846)	
Lee-Potter, Charlie	4:42:15 (20,039)	
Leese, Sally	4:55:22 (22,994)	
Leeson, Yvonne	3:44:25 (6,624)	
Leetham, Colette	4:32:19 (17,795)	
Le-Faye, Jolanne	5:43:02 (29,238)	
Lefebvre, Sandy	4:21:30 (15,113)	
Lefevre, Sarah	5:17:24 (26,527)	
Legassick, Margaret	4:53:23 (22,591)	
Legge, Maureen	6:25:11 (31,165)	
Leguel, Nadia	5:22:43 (27,239)	
Leigh, Caroline	5:38:40 (28,873)	
Leigh, Donna	5:38:40 (28,873)	
Leigh, Vanessa	4:24:18 (15,820)	
Leishman, Kirsty	3:43:11 (6,407)	
Leising, Mary	3:32:19 (4,510)	
Leleu, Roselyne	3:44:39 (6,658)	
Lemasurier, Katreena	4:34:46 (18,341)	
Lemettre, Isabelle	4:43:39 (20,417)	
Lemon, Kathleen	4:29:13 (17,044)	
Lemon, Morag	6:40:25 (31,546)	
Le-Mons, Dominique	3:32:25 (4,518)	
Lenaghan, Moira	4:11:02 (12,546)	
Lenihan, Helen	4:51:59 (22,305)	
Lenman, Nicky	4:33:38 (18,080)	
Lennon, Camilla	4:16:03 (13,750)	
Lennon, Caroline	4:23:40 (15,662)	
Lenz, Frances	4:30:19 (17,312)	
Leonard, Clare	6:49:29 (31,706)	
Leonard, Fiona	7:08:02 (31,973)	
Leonard, Kirsten	3:41:44 (6,097)	
Leong, Esther	4:46:28 (21,085)	
Lepetit, Florence	4:11:13 (12,581)	
Lernelius, Paula	4:05:54 (11,483)	
Lester, Carole	6:31:19 (31,356)	
Letham, Janet	5:07:32 (25,192)	
Letherby, Margaret	2:58:09 (780)	
Letts, Zandra	4:40:44 (19,690)	
Lever, Christine	6:13:25 (30,780)	
Levett, Clare	4:21:08 (15,014)	
Levy, Susan	5:27:06 (27,789)	
Lewellin, Susan	5:47:08 (29,498)	
Lewin, Judy	4:31:06 (17,525)	
Lewington, Anne	4:27:27 (16,581)	
Lewis, Barbara	6:12:14 (30,740)	
Lewis, Caroline	5:00:06 (23,994)	
Lewis, Cathryn	5:47:53 (29,566)	
Lewis, Clare	5:33:36 (28,430)	
Lewis, Hannah	4:52:37 (22,417)	
Lewis, Helen	7:52:42 (32,238)	
Lewis, Jodie	5:07:36 (25,201)	
Lewis, Josie	5:22:15 (27,178)	
Lewis, Karen	7:16:56 (32,051)	
Lewis, Kim	4:47:20 (21,254)	
Lewis, Melanie	4:35:58 (18,642)	
Lewis, Sally-Anne	4:33:56 (18,149)	
Lewis, Sherry	6:19:06 (30,978)	
Lewis, Susan	5:38:48 (28,882)	
Lewis, Terri	4:52:35 (22,411)	
Lewis, Tracey	4:14:51 (13,466)	
Lewis, Valerie	6:49:26 (31,700)	
Lewis, Verity	5:40:22 (29,024)	
Lewitt, Melanie	4:03:41 (10,982)	
Lewthwaite, Joanne	5:08:46 (25,367)	
Leyden, Maria	5:06:59 (25,103)	
Lezala, Anne	6:50:12 (31,727)	
Li, Karen	5:15:19 (26,293)	
Lichty-Engmann, Laurel	4:45:43 (20,889)	
Liddicoat, Donna	5:41:17 (29,100)	
Liddington, Rosalind	5:21:45 (27,122)	
Liddle, Pauline	5:11:20 (25,739)	
Lieberman, Jessica	4:21:06 (15,014)	
Lightfoot, Nicola	4:55:27 (23,015)	
Li-Kwai-Cheung, Anne-Marie	3:50:43 (7,890)	
Lilley, Genevieve	4:48:38 (21,558)	
Lilley, Miriam	5:38:18 (28,837)	
Lim, Audrey	4:49:34 (21,766)	
Limouzin, Elizabeth	4:32:11 (17,770)	
Lind, Mette	4:21:47 (15,180)	
Linden, Oonagh	5:29:01 (27,992)	
Lindsay, Caroline	4:57:02 (23,389)	
Lindsay, Gina	3:51:52 (8,169)	
Lindsay, Karin	4:09:34 (12,244)	
Lindsay, Melanie	4:35:33 (18,527)	
Lindsey, Karen	4:20:31 (14,873)	
Lindsey, Valerie	4:27:52 (16,687)	
Lindskog, Ylva	4:28:59 (16,986)	
Lines, Janet	6:47:14 (31,657)	
Lingenfelder, Angela	4:28:21 (16,807)	
Linklater, Emily	4:24:51 (15,962)	
Linnell, Suzanne	5:10:25 (25,611)	
Linzell, Laraine	4:44:28 (20,608)	
Linzenmeier, Isabel	4:30:14 (17,295)	
Lipede, Kehinde	3:54:59 (8,917)	
Lipinski, Ania	5:42:35 (29,215)	
Lippett, Karen	4:09:55 (12,329)	
Lipscomb, Emma	4:20:26 (14,854)	
Lipscombe, Emma	6:35:08 (31,450)	

Lipscombe, Kira 5:11:06 (25,707)
Liptrot, Julia 4:59:45 (23,933)
Litchfield, Hayley 5:58:54 (30,200)
Litherland, Trixie 5:10:05 (25,565)
Littell, Sarah 4:02:42 (10,781)
Little, Denise 5:14:33 (26,185)
Little, Georgina 4:26:46 (16,421)
Little, Gina 4:19:31 (14,619)
Little, Joanne 4:37:29 (18,981)
Little, Kate 3:33:13 (4,635)
Little, Lorraine 4:41:23 (19,844)
Little, Louise 3:32:25 (4,518)
Little, Maureen 3:51:33 (8,092)
Little, Rosalind 5:12:29 (25,895)
Littler, Jane 3:33:33 (4,687)
Littler, Jean 4:20:13 (14,798)
Liu, Geeho 4:43:15 (20,303)
Livermore, Oonagh 4:36:42 (18,809)
Livesey-Haworth, Elizabeth 5:30:46 (28,173)
Livingstone, Lorraine 5:45:18 (29,389)
Livingstone, Tracy 3:28:55 (3,991)
Llewellyn, Judith 3:34:38 (4,860)
Llewellyn, Katherine 4:47:45 (21,361)
Lloyd, Annette 5:36:39 (28,703)
Lloyd, Claire 3:58:20 (9,793)
Lloyd, Emma 5:14:26 (26,164)
Lloyd, Harriet 4:13:53 (13,226)
Lloyd, Lucy 4:47:06 (21,203)
Lloyd, Philippa 5:14:12 (26,120)
Lloyd, Stephanie 4:21:25 (15,095)
Loach, Kate 4:08:19 (11,963)
Loader, Carole 4:16:20 (13,815)
Lock, Philippa 4:26:33 (16,366)
Lockett, Jennifer 4:21:01 (14,983)
Lockwood, Anne 4:44:34 (20,626)
Lodge, Sophie 4:42:06 (20,009)
Lomax, Rachel 6:41:23 (31,557)
Lombard, Joanne 3:42:15 (6,194)
Lombardi, Patricia 3:48:57 (7,503)
Long, Alison 4:51:29 (22,206)
Long, Caroline 5:24:42 (27,498)
Long, Helen 4:12:46 (12,953)
Long, Janet 4:32:42 (17,879)
Long, Jennifer 4:43:51 (20,470)
Long, Joanne 4:25:24 (16,117)
Long, Justine 4:05:57 (11,497)
Long, Kimberley 4:28:46 (16,928)
Long, Sara 5:08:29 (25,333)
Long, Susan 4:59:06 (23,824)
Longley, Zira 4:05:00 (11,289)
Longworth, Jeannette 7:29:06 (32,146)
Loomes, Lynda 5:58:54 (30,200)
Loopstra, Ellen 4:36:20 (18,722)
Lopez, Karen 6:40:15 (31,541)
Lord, Alyson 5:28:10 (27,914)
Lord, Joanne 4:27:41 (16,643)
Lord, Ursula 6:21:21 (31,057)
Lord, Victoria 6:06:47 (30,521)
Lorentzen, Lise 4:04:09 (11,105)
Lott, Marion 5:56:14 (30,063)
Lotti, Gianna 5:40:43 (29,057)
Lotti, Stefania 5:40:43 (29,057)
Loureiro, Catherine 5:24:57 (27,529)
Lousada, Alison 5:04:42 (24,733)
Lovatt, Clare 5:29:56 (28,077)
Love, Francine 5:43:55 (29,302)
Love, Helen 7:16:13 (32,044)
Loveday, Kirsty 4:57:22 (23,453)
Lovegrove, Dianne 5:14:14 (26,132)
Lovell, Sally 3:43:39 (6,478)
Lovelock, Sally 4:38:11 (19,127)
Lovett, Joanna 6:00:48 (30,287)
Lowe, Caroline 5:48:58 (29,636)
Lowe, Elizabeth 5:29:04 (27,995)
Lowe, Kaitlyn 3:34:18 (4,795)
Lowe, Katharine 4:51:25 (22,182)
Lowe, Laura-Rose 4:38:39 (19,238)
Lowe, Lesley 5:56:10 (30,060)
Lowe, Vicki 4:19:09 (14,541)
Lowe, Wendy 5:20:13 (26,917)
Lowes, Kim 4:24:07 (15,781)
Lowndes, Valerie 5:43:07 (29,251)
Lowndes, Victoria 4:54:46 (22,879)
Lowson, Maureen 4:05:13 (11,333)
Lowther, Helen 6:02:14 (30,348)
Lowther, Julia 7:00:48 (31,900)
Lowther, Mariesha 4:37:19 (18,952)
Loxton, Helen 4:18:16 (14,294)
Loy, Francesca 4:58:25 (23,679)
Lua, Suet 4:41:38 (19,896)
Lucarotti, Anna 4:18:21 (14,316)
Luckett, Tracy 5:41:46 (29,142)
Luckman, Dolores 5:43:54 (29,299)
Luddington, Amanda 5:38:19 (28,841)
Lueders, Susanne 5:08:59 (25,401)
Luke, Anne 3:13:01 (1,992)
Lukha, Mona 4:47:22 (21,261)
Lumber, Liz 3:11:15 (1,779)
Lundkvist, Tina 4:14:55 (13,482)
Lunn, Gemma 4:36:36 (18,789)
Lunn, Victoria 3:52:32 (8,317)
Lusted, Margaret 6:35:20 (31,455)
Lusty, Karen 4:43:30 (20,375)
Luxton, Anita 3:43:44 (6,497)
Luxton, Jenny 5:17:03 (26,486)
Luxton, Susie 4:49:57 (21,851)
Lydon, Carole 3:46:16 (6,988)
Lynch, Jennifer 6:33:13 (31,404)
Lynch, Joanna 5:51:49 (29,822)
Lynch-Warden, Rachel 4:51:21 (22,167)
Lyndhurst, Virginia 6:23:24 (31,117)
Lynn, Caroline 5:33:26 (28,416)
Lyon, Hannah 5:22:52 (27,264)
Lyons, Andrea 4:43:37 (20,407)
Lyons, Denise 6:05:37 (30,485)
Lysons, Alison 4:54:22 (22,786)
Lytle, Lisa 4:14:54 (13,479)
Lytle, Lynn 4:14:55 (13,482)
Maber, Patricia 4:38:52 (19,295)
Mabert, Angela 5:03:50 (24,602)
Maby, Julie 7:12:52 (32,022)
Maca, Viktoria 4:36:02 (18,659)
MacArthy, Alison 4:50:59 (22,065)
Macaulay, Pauline 7:35:51 (32,188)
Macaulay, Sheila 5:08:58 (25,395)
Macauley, Siobhan 5:15:40 (26,336)
Macbeth, Deanne 4:32:51 (17,913)
MacCallum, Elizabeth 3:57:15 (9,517)
Maccariello, Bettina 3:58:24 (9,810)
Macdairmid, Veronica 4:30:58 (17,485)
Macdonald, Erika 4:58:52 (23,773)
Macdonald, Johanna 4:29:49 (17,199)
Macdonald, Lucie 3:51:46 (8,138)
Macdonald, Meriel 4:20:49 (14,931)
Macey, Teresa 6:18:08 (30,939)
Macfarlane, Fiona 6:36:06 (31,479)
MacGowan, Fiona 5:36:27 (28,680)
MacGregor, Jeanette 4:30:41 (17,414)
MacGregor, Sonja 5:11:57 (25,823)
MacGregor, Sylvia 6:32:18 (31,388)
MacInnes, Louise 4:34:46 (18,341)
MacInnes, Maureen 3:58:32 (9,844)
Macintosh, Julie-Ann 4:39:49 (19,504)
Macintyre, Megan 4:00:09 (10,260)
Mackay, Celia 6:20:52 (31,044)
Mackay, Sally 3:28:44 (3,952)
MacKemsley, Donna 7:12:48 (32,021)
Macken-Dunne, Irene 5:13:32 (26,049)
Mackenzie, Amanda 3:50:18 (7,801)
Mackenzie, Janet 5:12:04 (25,836)
Mackenzie, Kaeti 3:41:51 (6,123)
Mackenzie, Lesley 4:42:19 (20,059)
Mackenzie, Louisa 4:45:16 (20,788)
Mackenzie, Shona 5:04:59 (24,791)
Mackey, Jill 6:17:55 (30,928)
Mackey, Molly 4:04:22 (11,150)
Mackie, Charlotte 4:32:29 (17,830)
Mackinnon, Henrietta 3:43:05 (6,383)
Mackinnon, Paula 4:25:05 (16,021)
Mackley, Veronica 3:50:06 (7,752)
MacLaran, Philippa 4:26:48 (16,430)
Maclean, Alexandra 4:28:31 (16,861)
MacLellan-Smith, Rebecca 5:29:17 (28,016)
Macleod, Eliza 3:57:39 (9,607)
Macleod, Rebecca 4:22:40 (15,412)
Macleod, Susie 4:55:47 (23,107)
MacMaster, Jennifer 3:02:09 (1,066)
Macrae, Helen 4:20:43 (14,907)
Macrae, Rosemary 5:09:32 (25,481)
MacWhannell, Camilla 4:16:01 (13,746)
Maddern, Gill 5:03:06 (24,475)
Maddock, Suzanne 5:22:34 (27,222)
Madge, Mary 4:39:30 (19,439)
Madge, Suzy 4:47:34 (21,310)
Madgwick, Sarah 4:50:28 (21,956)
Madsen, Kirsten 4:17:21 (14,072)
Maeland, Anne Berit 4:11:42 (12,696)
Magdics, Claudia 4:42:56 (20,213)
Maggs, Denise 4:28:18 (16,789)
Maggs, Lisa 4:54:54 (22,903)
Magill, Jennifer 6:14:29 (30,810)
Magro, Anna Maria 4:10:23 (12,438)
Maguire, Frederica 6:49:27 (31,703)
Maguire, Maureen 6:28:39 (31,294)
Maguire, Sarah 3:32:10 (4,491)
Mahdavi, Maryam 4:04:33 (11,188)
Maher, Tracey 4:34:46 (18,341)
Mahon, Philippa 5:28:27 (27,938)
Mahwkopi, Katja 4:52:10 (22,333)
Maison, Margaret 4:36:19 (18,717)
Maitland, Fiona 5:33:48 (28,452)
Maitland, Louise 4:51:19 (22,159)
Major, Lucy 4:10:11 (12,389)
Major, Michelle 4:59:36 (23,903)
Malcolm, Judith 4:17:22 (14,074)
Malecki, Kathryn 4:58:09 (23,617)
Malek, Sonia 3:52:17 (8,263)
Maleney, Catherine 4:18:59 (14,504)
Malik, Farzana 5:58:17 (30,172)
Malkin, Alayne 3:48:23 (7,389)
Malkinson, Caroline 4:40:41 (19,680)
Mallace, Rosemary 5:38:12 (28,829)
Mallach, Denise 7:32:24 (32,169)
Mallach, Joy 7:32:24 (32,169)
Mallard, Jacqueline 4:24:40 (15,906)
Malley, Joyce 4:58:58 (23,792)
Mallinder, Susie 4:30:43 (17,422)
Mallon, Judith 4:38:24 (19,185)
Malone, Julie 4:18:24 (14,330)
Maltby, Emma 3:56:40 (9,365)
Maltby, Joanne 5:51:07 (29,790)
Mancuso, Lucia 4:05:09 (11,321)
Mandefro, Mehret 5:05:04 (24,806)
Manfield, Nicci 4:40:06 (19,556)
Manitta da Cruz, Emma 5:09:23 (25,461)
Manley, Angela 4:32:42 (17,879)
Manley, Lindsay 5:09:51 (25,521)
Manly, Rita 3:29:16 (4,036)
Mann, Amanda 4:27:27 (16,581)
Mann, Dawn 4:35:24 (18,495)
Mann, Dawn 5:22:23 (27,198)
Mann, Rosalind 4:13:53 (13,226)
Manners, Deborah 4:16:05 (13,762)
Manning, Karen 4:05:55 (11,487)
Mannion, Michelle 4:20:10 (14,788)
Mansbridge, Sue 4:26:42 (16,403)
Mansfield, Lynn 3:57:51 (9,663)
Mansley, Anna 5:56:21 (30,074)
Manson, Danielle 4:20:00 (14,743)
Mantell, Deborah 4:08:19 (11,963)
Manz, Michele 4:43:23 (20,347)
Maranzano, Rosemary 4:59:36 (23,903)
Marcer, Jane 5:07:10 (25,128)
Marchant, Alison 4:42:18 (20,053)
Marchant, Heather 6:50:04 (31,720)
Marchant, Judy 3:52:16 (8,262)
Marchant, Zina 3:16:39 (2,390)
Maree, Jeanne-Louise 5:30:34 (28,147)
Margetts, Laura 4:53:57 (22,705)
Markland, Kate 4:16:07 (13,766)
Markowicz, Naja 3:26:56 (3,665)
Marks, Karen 4:48:55 (21,618)
Markwick, Louise 3:56:47 (9,393)
Markwick, Selena 5:32:41 (28,345)
Marot, Véronique 2:55:01 (595)
Marotta, Deborah 4:09:53 (12,318)
Marriott, Catherine 3:59:37 (10,125)
Marriott, Diane 4:01:17 (10,491)
Marsden, Debbie 3:57:49 (9,650)

Marsden, Katie	5:05:24 (24,857)	
Marsh, Carla	6:02:28 (30,358)	
Marsh, Karen	4:27:08 (16,506)	
Marsh, Lucy	5:10:53 (25,670)	
Marsh, Sara	3:50:47 (7,905)	
Marshall, Andrea	4:07:05 (11,705)	
Marshall, Anne	4:07:34 (11,824)	
Marshall, Fiona	5:14:56 (26,239)	
Marshall, Kate	4:29:10 (17,031)	
Marshall, Laura	4:30:17 (17,305)	
Marshall, Rebecca	4:01:50 (10,607)	
Marshall, Ruth	5:29:33 (28,045)	
Marshall, Susan	4:52:13 (22,344)	
Marsterson, Lisa	5:45:02 (29,371)	
Marston, Jackie	3:45:18 (6,788)	
Martell, Sandra	4:31:36 (17,639)	
Martin, Alix	6:14:52 (30,825)	
Martin, Anna	5:30:15 (28,106)	
Martin, Annabel	5:44:50 (29,348)	
Martin, Beverley	5:06:37 (25,036)	
Martin, Carole	4:01:18 (10,495)	
Martin, Cathleen	4:32:46 (17,893)	
Martin, Elizabeth	4:46:06 (20,992)	
Martin, Emma	5:43:30 (29,270)	
Martin, Estelle	4:03:47 (11,007)	
Martin, Esther	5:04:54 (24,779)	
Martin, Heidi	3:25:10 (3,420)	
Martin, Helen	5:24:09 (27,427)	
Martin, Julie	4:52:12 (22,340)	
Martin, Kedge	6:14:35 (30,812)	
Martin, Loraine	5:55:48 (30,030)	
Martin, Maria	4:19:59 (14,737)	
Martin, Michelle	4:44:14 (20,554)	
Martin, Natalie	3:56:17 (9,268)	
Martin, Sarah	5:21:22 (27,068)	
Martin, Susan	4:35:46 (18,588)	
Martin, Teresa	5:36:15 (28,659)	
Martin, Victoria	4:39:17 (19,391)	
Martin-Clarke, Susan	3:16:53 (2,416)	
Martindale, Sandra	4:04:42 (11,225)	
Martinelli, Sara	6:23:44 (31,131)	
Martinez, Leticia	5:59:49 (30,250)	
Martins, Sylvaine	5:33:30 (28,421)	
Martinson, Svea	5:09:21 (25,456)	
Martle, Elana	6:11:00 (30,693)	
Martyn, Victoria	4:26:35 (16,375)	
Marzaioli, Sarah	4:12:31 (12,892)	
Mascitti, Rita	3:34:21 (4,805)	
Maskell, Anne	3:16:27 (2,371)	
Masnavi, Nerseh	4:45:33 (20,858)	
Mason, Camilla	4:32:44 (17,888)	
Mason, Claire	4:03:00 (10,839)	
Mason, Dawn	4:18:42 (14,423)	
Mason, Laila	5:21:43 (27,112)	
Mason, Wendy	4:54:15 (22,758)	
Massey, Annabel	5:05:42 (24,921)	
Massey, Laura	4:37:00 (18,878)	
Massey, Michelle	5:36:14 (28,657)	
Masson, Kim	3:16:15 (2,354)	
Massue, Valeska	5:49:41 (29,696)	
Masterton, Kathryn	3:45:56 (6,919)	
Masterton, Lorna	3:57:57 (9,694)	
Mateunas, Claire	5:07:01 (25,111)	
Mathen, Lucy	3:58:08 (9,739)	
Mather, Carla	5:11:23 (25,751)	
Mather, Caroline	5:54:13 (29,944)	
Mathers, Jo-Anne	4:31:06 (17,525)	
Matheson, Patricia	3:07:06 (1,416)	
Mathews, Annik	4:13:13 (13,055)	
Mathieson, Susan	4:35:59 (18,646)	
Mathys, Margrit	4:34:04 (18,186)	
Matiz, Ana	4:28:29 (16,850)	
Matthew, Alison	5:05:18 (24,840)	
Matthew, Jane	4:28:31 (16,861)	
Matthew, Karen	5:56:03 (30,051)	
Matthews, Imy	4:42:50 (20,192)	
Matthews, Jennifer	5:02:43 (24,422)	
Matthews, Karen	4:51:35 (22,223)	
Matthews, Karen	5:26:08 (27,693)	
Matthews, Kate	6:37:16 (31,493)	
Matthews, Kay	5:22:59 (27,284)	
Matthews, Linda	4:41:02 (19,763)	
Matthews, Lindsey	5:00:36 (24,090)	
Matthews, Lisa	4:51:43 (22,247)	
Matthews, Rebecca	3:59:38 (10,130)	
Matthews, Sophie	3:55:57 (9,165)	
Matthews, Suzie	6:07:18 (30,544)	
Matthews, Tanya	5:36:19 (28,665)	
Mattick, Theresa	4:48:59 (21,627)	
Maudsley, Barbara	5:37:09 (28,750)	
Mauk, Anne	5:36:26 (28,679)	
Mawdsley, Suzannah	5:17:47 (26,577)	
Mawer, Jane	4:15:05 (13,536)	
Maxwell, Dawn	4:47:21 (21,259)	
Maxwell, Gill	5:36:32 (28,689)	
May, Barry	5:33:46 (28,447)	
May, Helen	4:25:20 (16,096)	
May, Julia	5:20:36 (26,973)	
May, Philippa	3:55:16 (8,983)	
May, Stephanie	7:49:22 (32,230)	
Mayaud, Francine	4:23:28 (15,607)	
Mayers, Kirsty	5:29:45 (28,065)	
Mayland, Paula	5:18:15 (26,664)	
Maynard, Clare	5:40:16 (29,014)	
Maynard, Colette	3:21:39 (2,946)	
Maynard, Linda	4:27:06 (16,497)	
Mayne, Nicola	4:33:53 (18,138)	
Mayor, Marie	4:14:57 (13,492)	
Maytham, Vanessa	3:57:51 (9,663)	
Mayze, Karen	4:05:55 (11,487)	
Mbeki, Tracy	7:22:24 (32,087)	
Mburu, Philomena	4:03:43 (10,987)	
McAdam, Julia	5:46:26 (29,463)	
McAllister, Donna	4:35:50 (18,608)	
McAllister, Lynne	4:33:13 (17,987)	
McArthur, Genevieve	3:52:13 (8,247)	
McBain, Kirsty	6:25:36 (31,183)	
McBeal, Sylvia	5:04:56 (24,785)	
McBeath, Jacqueline	4:12:42 (12,937)	
McCabe, Julia	6:17:46 (30,916)	
McCabe, Katharine	5:24:39 (27,496)	
McCahill, Gabrielle	4:29:23 (17,084)	
McCahon, Mary	4:06:09 (11,526)	
McCall, Catherine	4:28:29 (16,850)	
McCallin, Hennie	7:33:23 (32,174)	
McCallum, Michaela	2:41:57 (178)	
McCandless, Louise	7:28:05 (32,144)	
McCarten, Paula	6:40:55 (31,552)	
McCarthy, Clair	5:44:21 (29,327)	
McCarthy, Helen	4:56:26 (23,245)	
McCarthy, Julie	4:14:46 (13,437)	
McCarthy, Katherine	4:59:03 (23,812)	
McCarthy, Kelly	4:50:11 (21,900)	
McCarthy, Philippa	4:07:33 (11,822)	
McCarthy, Su	4:35:33 (18,527)	
McCartney, Sarah	3:51:57 (8,182)	
McCaw, Eileen	5:24:45 (27,501)	
McChord, Marie	3:36:31 (5,146)	
McClarnon, Anna	6:03:31 (30,395)	
McClintock, Katrina	4:34:00 (18,168)	
McCluskey, Karyn	4:51:57 (22,301)	
McColl, Helen	4:57:04 (23,394)	
McColl, Sheena	4:54:56 (22,908)	
McConnell, Suzanne	4:57:07 (23,404)	
McCormick, Joanne	6:22:35 (31,089)	
McCormick, Michelle	4:05:09 (11,321)	
McCourt, Barbara	5:31:19 (28,231)	
McCracken, Catriona	4:14:29 (13,377)	
McCreery, Claire	3:25:41 (3,491)	
McCullock, Rachel	5:44:13 (29,318)	
McCutcheon, Madeleine	3:47:58 (7,311)	
McDonald, Anna	3:34:28 (4,833)	
McDonald, Janet	4:17:32 (14,125)	
McDonald, Jennie	4:58:23 (23,667)	
McDonald, Joanne	4:22:40 (15,412)	
McDonald, Julie	3:35:41 (5,025)	
McDonald, Linda	4:06:59 (11,684)	
McDonald, Sarah	4:13:45 (13,189)	
McDonald, Susan	4:16:46 (13,927)	
McDougal, Patricia	3:33:18 (4,645)	
McDougall, Leanne	4:40:02 (19,546)	
McDowell, Sarah	5:41:26 (29,109)	
McEvilly, Elaine	4:34:58 (18,388)	
McEvoy, Susan	4:48:16 (21,489)	
McFarlane, Davinia	4:41:34 (19,885)	
McFeggan, Tammy	6:55:26 (31,840)	
McGarrick, Tracey	5:48:30 (29,608)	
McGarry, Pauline	4:56:08 (23,177)	
McGarvie, Moira	4:00:01 (10,226)	
McGavigan, Claire	3:52:50 (8,377)	
McGill, Patricia	6:43:21 (31,598)	
McGill, Susan	4:56:42 (23,316)	
McGilloway, Paula	3:56:04 (9,198)	
McGough, Sally	5:05:40 (24,912)	
McGovern, Audrey	3:55:37 (9,081)	
McGowan, Lisa	7:22:52 (32,092)	
McGowan, Lorraine	7:34:40 (32,182)	
McGrath, Jane	3:58:36 (9,857)	
McGrath, Nikola	3:56:34 (9,338)	
McGregor, Jane	5:28:07 (27,902)	
McGregor, Kirsten	6:44:38 (31,614)	
McGregor, Lauren	4:15:32 (13,646)	
McGregor, Nicki	4:43:05 (20,256)	
McGuigan, Emma	4:09:05 (12,150)	
McGuinness, Maria	4:35:01 (18,402)	
McHardy, Irma	5:44:58 (29,364)	
McHendry, Sharon	4:49:33 (21,761)	
McHugh, Elizabeth	4:18:54 (14,479)	
McHugh, Emma	5:35:06 (28,563)	
McHugh, Sharon	3:30:44 (4,287)	
McIlroy, Louise	4:26:07 (16,280)	
McIndoe, Caroline	3:27:37 (3,756)	
McInnes, Suzanne	5:20:22 (26,933)	
McInnes-Raffan, Heather	4:04:15 (11,120)	
McIntosh, Jennie	6:53:06 (31,786)	
McIntosh, Joyce	7:26:12 (32,115)	
McIntyre, Sue	5:06:36 (25,033)	
McKaige, Kirsten	4:59:03 (23,812)	
McKay, Deborah	4:00:23 (10,310)	
McKay, Elke	5:08:07 (25,282)	
McKay, Fiona	4:27:17 (16,546)	
McKay, Jacqueline	3:26:48 (3,644)	
McKay, Meryl	4:41:18 (19,825)	
McKay, Nola	4:13:53 (13,226)	
McKearney, Sonia	7:26:56 (32,129)	
McKee, Christy	4:38:18 (19,161)	
McKeever, Susan Kellee	4:34:08 (18,198)	
McKenna, Christine	4:51:51 (22,278)	
McKenna, Lisa	5:42:24 (29,198)	
McKenzie, Claudia	4:37:41 (19,016)	
McKenzie, Denise	6:26:05 (31,208)	
McKeown, Mary	4:14:49 (13,458)	
McKillop, Jaqueline	4:09:17 (12,190)	
McKinney, Anne	5:48:08 (29,586)	
McKinney, Heather	5:00:40 (24,101)	
McKnight, Diana	6:22:53 (31,099)	
McLaren, Jill	6:13:19 (30,777)	
McLaren, Melody	5:15:02 (26,252)	
McLaren, Valerie	5:23:13 (27,314)	
McLaughlin, Frances	3:16:55 (2,422)	
McLaughlin, Frances	5:21:52 (27,132)	
McLean, Laura	5:33:49 (28,455)	
McLean, Pamela	5:54:39 (29,975)	
McLeod, Juliet	5:03:04 (24,467)	
McLindon, Laura	3:37:57 (5,405)	
McLoughlin, Anne	4:35:55 (18,625)	
McLoughlin, Sarah	3:17:18 (2,460)	
McMahon, Patricia	6:18:24 (30,956)	
McMaster, Joanne	4:16:50 (13,941)	
McMaster, Melanie	5:31:29 (28,243)	
McMillan, Paula	6:16:21 (30,869)	
McMillan, Sue	4:24:49 (15,954)	
McMullan, Lucinda	6:13:14 (30,773)	
McNabb, Laura	4:40:31 (19,654)	
McNally, Michelle	6:51:45 (31,760)	
McNally, Sharon	4:15:19 (13,599)	
McNamara, Helen	4:00:08 (10,257)	
McNaney, Sarah	3:59:22 (10,060)	
McNaughton, Angela	3:33:06 (4,614)	
McNeillie, Janice	4:39:09 (19,360)	
McNeilly, Angela	4:21:18 (15,060)	
McParland, Corrin	3:53:44 (8,598)	
McPheat, Julie	3:59:13 (10,007)	
McPherson-Kelly, Katrine	4:15:44 (13,679)	
McQueeney, Stacy	4:36:10 (18,682)	
McRae, Isla	4:35:38 (18,545)	
McSpadden, Lisa	3:45:02 (6,738)	
McSweeney, Kellie	4:22:22 (15,331)	
McTigue, Eunice	5:48:29 (29,605)	

McWilliam, Elizabeth....4:11:41 (12,687)
McWilliam, Helen....5:51:01 (29,787)
Meacham, Orla....7:58:59 (32,254)
Mead, Angela....5:11:21 (25,743)
Mead, Colette....4:39:00 (19,325)
Mead, Sherrie....5:06:41 (25,049)
Meadows, Patricia....5:38:25 (28,852)
Meakins, Teresa....7:10:02 (31,988)
Mearns, Kate....4:59:22 (23,868)
Mears, Hazel....4:06:57 (11,677)
Mears, Sarah....4:28:10 (16,756)
Mebride, Leanna....5:20:39 (26,979)
Medina, Amanda....5:56:16 (30,068)
Medlam, Amanda....5:41:54 (29,152)
Medley, Victoria....5:17:40 (26,567)
Meechan, Amanda....3:35:26 (4,984)
Meeds, Sandra....5:09:01 (25,411)
Meek, Rebecca....4:25:27 (16,130)
Meeke, Alicia....4:51:00 (22,070)
Meekins, Karen....4:19:03 (14,517)
Meeks, Sam....5:08:46 (25,367)
Meenan, Yvonne....5:11:11 (25,719)
Meering, Julia....5:28:39 (27,954)
Mehta, Jignasa....4:50:31 (21,972)
Melhuish, Molly....5:05:26 (24,865)
Mellersh, Denise....4:13:54 (13,233)
Mellis, Susan....4:44:47 (20,678)
Mellodew, Anita....2:53:54 (529)
Mellon, Elizabeth....4:34:18 (18,241)
Mellor, Juliet....5:22:14 (27,171)
Mellor, Rosemary....5:34:15 (28,500)
Mellors, Ruth....4:19:13 (14,555)
Melody, Rhonda....6:43:26 (31,599)
Melvin, Louise....4:14:53 (13,475)
Menaul, Rachel....4:07:22 (11,772)
Mendoza, Bonnie....4:46:27 (21,081)
Menin, Veronica....5:08:29 (25,333)
Mensah, Wendie....5:37:23 (28,766)
Menzies, Lynn....5:01:52 (24,293)
Mercer, Claudine....4:11:38 (12,671)
Mercer, Susan....5:52:37 (29,863)
Merchant, Samantha....5:12:54 (25,962)
Meredith, Audrey....5:23:38 (27,362)
Meredith, Clare....5:28:14 (27,920)
Meredith, Jean....4:31:07 (17,533)
Meredith, Rachel....5:07:02 (25,112)
Merley, Jean....4:13:33 (13,141)
Merrick, Elisabeth....4:39:23 (19,418)
Merrick, Julie....3:52:26 (8,296)
Merrill, Amy....4:32:23 (17,813)
Merrill, Carol....3:52:18 (8,267)
Merrills, Sharon....4:09:46 (12,291)
Messenger, Barbara....4:50:35 (21,987)
Messum, Joanne....6:00:59 (30,294)
Metais, Martine....3:47:14 (7,161)
Metcalf, Hannah....4:51:34 (22,217)
Metcalf, Valerie....4:16:10 (13,781)
Metcalfe, Charlotte....4:26:59 (16,465)
Metcalfe, Danae....4:58:43 (23,737)
Metcalfe, Emily....5:47:47 (29,558)
Metcalfe, Margaret....3:53:07 (8,453)
Metherell, Phillipa....4:35:09 (18,431)
Metz, Yvette....5:33:43 (28,438)
Metz, Zoe....4:38:21 (19,175)
Meyerhoff, Jill....5:59:53 (30,253)
Meyers, Sarah....4:30:56 (17,476)
Michael, Katie....4:11:59 (12,756)
Michaels, Helen....4:50:17 (21,919)
Michalski, Amanda....4:20:27 (14,860)
Michels, Phillipa....4:46:14 (21,026)
Middle, Georgina....4:51:03 (22,083)
Middleditch, Barbara....6:04:07 (30,413)
Middlehurst, Susan....4:27:26 (16,578)
Middlemast, Lynda....6:34:16 (31,431)
Middlemiss, Christine....5:06:11 (24,981)
Middlemiss, Julie....4:43:08 (20,270)
Middleton, Julie....5:58:36 (30,185)
Middleton, Linda....5:20:34 (26,965)
Middleton, Marion....4:29:35 (17,134)
Middleton, Sally....3:58:53 (9,939)
Middleton, Sarah....5:22:54 (27,267)
Midgley, Emma....4:57:01 (23,384)
Miki, Fumiko....5:43:06 (29,248)
Milbourn, Helen....5:36:08 (28,649)
Milburn, Susan....5:19:52 (26,868)
Mildren, Kerry....5:22:13 (27,168)
Mildwater, Lucy....4:47:48 (21,375)
Miles, Amy....4:43:18 (20,322)
Miles, Wendy....5:24:48 (27,508)
Milewski, Julie....5:58:30 (30,179)
Millar, Gillian....4:12:29 (12,880)
Millard, Lynette....4:57:07 (23,404)
Milledge, Ellie....4:18:36 (14,392)
Miller, Anne....4:20:43 (14,907)
Miller, Carol....3:24:30 (3,329)
Miller, Catherine....5:31:48 (28,262)
Miller, Catherine....5:53:36 (29,913)
Miller, Denise....5:17:07 (26,493)
Miller, Diane....6:42:41 (31,585)
Miller, Helen....3:45:21 (6,797)
Miller, Helene....4:26:36 (16,383)
Miller, Karen....5:30:06 (28,094)
Miller, Rowan....4:18:35 (14,387)
Miller, Susan....5:05:55 (24,946)
Millington, Eleanor....4:03:02 (10,850)
Millington, Hazel....4:53:51 (22,690)
Mills, Ann....7:13:16 (32,023)
Mills, Charlotte....4:55:59 (23,144)
Mills, Debra....4:50:28 (21,956)
Mills, Diana....4:06:13 (11,539)
Mills, Inge....5:31:07 (28,208)
Mills, Joanna....5:41:43 (29,138)
Mills, Julia....4:23:38 (15,654)
Mills, Karen....5:36:31 (28,685)
Mills, Pauline....4:42:55 (20,210)
Mills, Sandie....4:42:59 (20,229)
Milne, Claire....4:43:18 (20,322)
Milne, Lynda....4:04:15 (11,120)
Milo, Julie....4:57:56 (23,568)
Milton, Alison....3:30:44 (4,287)
Milton, Angie....5:03:10 (24,485)
Milton, Lucy....4:00:34 (10,340)
Milton, Philippa....4:48:22 (21,512)
Mimeles, Stephanie....4:13:37 (13,156)
Minas, Argyro....4:28:48 (16,935)
Minas, Christalla....4:11:53 (12,735)
Minford, Anne....4:16:36 (13,876)
Minhas, Gursharan....4:35:01 (18,402)
Minton, Zoe....5:44:52 (29,353)
Minty, Joan....4:12:26 (12,867)
Mireylees, Stephanie....5:01:14 (24,191)
Mirza, Shabana....5:36:13 (28,655)
Mistry, Bhavna....4:35:11 (18,438)
Mistry, Megan....5:21:37 (27,100)
Mitchell, Avril....4:46:01 (20,964)
Mitchell, Caroline....4:26:43 (16,405)
Mitchell, Catherine....5:09:48 (25,520)
Mitchell, Elaine....5:01:54 (24,294)
Mitchell, Helen....4:46:02 (20,971)
Mitchell, Jackie....4:27:54 (16,689)
Mitchell, Joanna....4:03:49 (11,017)
Mitchell, Karen....4:40:23 (19,626)
Mitchell, Katherine....4:11:53 (12,735)
Mitchell, Kerry....4:56:21 (23,230)
Mitchell, Lorraine....5:45:25 (29,398)
Mitchell, Mary....4:24:24 (15,841)
Mitchell, Monica....6:08:27 (30,589)
Mitchell, Pamela....5:00:45 (24,119)
Mitchell, Pauline....4:46:06 (20,992)
Mitchell, Sarah....4:26:55 (16,453)
Mitchell, Terry....4:22:05 (15,261)
Mithcell, Heather....3:57:21 (9,542)
Mitnacht-Kraus, Rita....4:11:37 (12,668)
Mitton, Desiree....4:15:50 (13,713)
Miyamae, Yoko....5:30:35 (28,150)
Mizzi, Valerie....4:24:43 (15,924)
Moakes, Clare....4:48:18 (21,496)
Moffat, Pauline....5:17:59 (26,607)
Moffatt, Petra....3:12:57 (1,981)
Moffitt, Marie....5:54:05 (29,936)
Mogridge, Wendy....5:07:41 (25,221)
Mohr-Kombach, Birgit....4:00:06 (10,244)
Moir, Karen....4:49:02 (21,640)
Mojcik, Jo....3:54:51 (8,879)
Moloney, Donna....4:06:14 (11,544)
Moloney, Jenny....3:52:08 (8,230)
Moloney, Paul....3:13:01 (1,992)
Molton, Emma....5:29:22 (28,025)
Molumby, Pauline....7:40:32 (32,206)
Molyneaux, Jo....4:10:40 (12,493)
Moncaster, Rachel....4:01:52 (10,613)
Money, Vanessa....3:49:40 (7,672)
Monks, Helen....5:42:35 (29,215)
Monro, Margaret....5:38:58 (28,896)
Monroe, Sarah....4:40:25 (19,635)
Montagu, Clare....6:51:41 (31,755)
Montford, Tracey....4:48:50 (21,598)
Moody, Alison....5:44:59 (29,367)
Moody, Dianne....4:36:01 (18,654)
Moody, Jill....6:46:02 (31,645)
Moody, Pat....5:06:39 (25,044)
Mooney, Carole....3:39:10 (5,623)
Mooney, Nicola....3:47:37 (7,241)
Moore, Amanda....4:54:09 (22,736)
Moore, Anjali....6:22:55 (31,101)
Moore, Anne....5:02:34 (24,400)
Moore, Bridgeen....3:56:06 (9,206)
Moore, Carolyn....3:51:04 (7,971)
Moore, Catherine....6:49:16 (31,697)
Moore, Diane....6:09:44 (30,630)
Moore, Karen....5:39:22 (28,929)
Moore, Kate....3:50:23 (7,822)
Moore, Muriel....5:12:59 (25,972)
Moore, Paula....4:39:09 (19,360)
Moore, Rachael....3:25:23 (3,452)
Moore, Sandra....6:25:00 (31,161)
Moore, Sue....4:29:29 (17,112)
Moores, Catherine....6:07:53 (30,563)
Moraiti, Marina....4:22:48 (15,442)
Moran, Sharon....5:33:12 (28,391)
Morcos, Wendy....4:40:07 (19,561)
Mordrick, Nicola....5:17:55 (26,600)
More, Nicola....5:43:46 (29,288)
Morehen, Katie....4:57:30 (23,482)
Moreno Fernandez, Antonia....3:27:48 (3,780)
Moreton, Penny....5:07:45 (25,235)
Moreton, Sue....4:21:44 (15,166)
Moretti-Adimari, Marianne....4:25:12 (16,056)
Morey, Susan....4:53:25 (22,599)
Morgan, Alison....3:40:59 (5,953)
Morgan, Alison....6:10:37 (30,667)
Morgan, Cathy....5:13:44 (26,072)
Morgan, Clare....4:16:03 (13,750)
Morgan, Denise....5:13:13 (26,002)
Morgan, Elizabeth....4:58:43 (23,737)
Morgan, Emma....3:46:43 (7,069)
Morgan, Helen....3:58:12 (9,755)
Morgan, Jacky....5:16:24 (26,414)
Morgan, Karen....4:35:26 (18,506)
Morgan, Karen....5:11:34 (25,770)
Morgan, Katherine....4:18:21 (14,316)
Morgan, Kirsten....5:28:57 (27,981)
Morgan, Lesley....5:24:36 (27,489)
Morgan, Louise....5:27:42 (27,857)
Morgan, Margaret....4:33:50 (18,123)
Morgan, Nichola....7:27:50 (32,141)
Morgan, Samantha....5:11:14 (25,727)
Morgan, Sandra....5:00:42 (24,106)
Morgan, Shan....3:17:44 (2,522)
Morgan, Stephanie....4:29:01 (16,994)
Morgan, Susan....4:55:46 (23,103)
Morgan, Tracey....5:23:51 (27,390)
Morgans, Dawn....6:40:28 (31,548)
Morimoto, Risa....5:52:11 (29,839)
Morley, Lesa....4:13:45 (13,189)
Morley, Susan....4:53:50 (22,686)
Morling, Gael....5:54:44 (29,983)
Mornzee, Nicola....4:19:24 (14,594)
Morris, Abigail....3:53:29 (8,536)
Morris, Andrea....4:11:29 (12,643)
Morris, Claire....5:01:05 (24,163)
Morris, Eleanor....5:05:50 (24,938)
Morris, Esther....4:54:15 (22,758)
Morris, Helen....6:14:52 (30,825)
Morris, Jan....3:59:21 (10,053)
Morris, Janet....4:46:00 (20,959)
Morris, Karen....5:20:15 (26,921)
Morris, Kelly....6:42:26 (31,580)
Morris, Margaret....4:23:46 (15,688)

Morris, Marianne 4:44:10 (20,533)
Morris, Mercy 4:38:17 (19,156)
Morris, Michelle 5:52:10 (29,837)
Morris, Miranda 5:48:57 (29,634)
Morris, Patricia 5:46:37 (29,472)
Morris, Phillippa 3:35:51 (5,049)
Morris, Rebecca 5:18:13 (26,657)
Morris, Rose 4:38:56 (19,311)
Morris, Sandra 6:30:08 (31,332)
Morris, Sharon 5:38:46 (28,879)
Morris, Susan 4:41:22 (19,839)
Morrish, Rosemary 5:14:36 (26,189)
Morrison, Carole 4:09:55 (12,329)
Morrison, Claire 5:32:16 (28,312)
Morrison, Lynne 7:29:18 (32,148)
Morrison, Sheila 4:30:30 (17,366)
Morrison, Theresa 5:30:54 (28,185)
Morrissey, Martina 5:17:24 (26,527)
Morrissey, Mitsuye 5:08:07 (25,282)
Morrow, Karen 4:28:33 (16,874)
Morse, Marie 4:21:34 (15,123)
Mort, Leah 5:12:32 (25,901)
Mortime, Sandra 4:29:54 (17,220)
Mortimer, Hilary 4:35:46 (18,588)
Mortimer, Rachel 5:09:43 (25,510)
Mortleman, Sally 3:51:47 (8,144)
Morton, Catherine 3:51:56 (8,180)
Morton, Rosemary 7:11:11 (32,002)
Morton, Sarah 4:07:10 (11,731)
Morton, Susanne 3:21:35 (2,939)
Mosedale, Amber 5:25:13 (27,578)
Moser, Wendy 5:39:33 (28,953)
Mosimann, Susanna 4:27:32 (16,610)
Moss, Anita 5:51:44 (29,820)
Moss, Carina 4:11:41 (12,687)
Moss, Caroline 3:14:19 (2,165)
Moss, Joanne 4:49:27 (21,737)
Moss, Karen 6:52:23 (31,767)
Moss, Kim 3:49:09 (7,548)
Mottram, Joanne 4:41:08 (19,783)
Mottram, Virginia 3:58:45 (9,901)
Mouat, Deborah 5:10:12 (25,582)
Moulden, Adeline 4:16:50 (13,941)
Mounsey, Pippa 4:06:44 (11,637)
Mourant, Libby 4:24:26 (15,850)
Mowatt, Natasha 3:12:33 (1,938)
Mower, Julie 5:56:29 (30,080)
Moyle, Avril 4:56:27 (23,248)
Mueller, Elske 3:53:11 (8,470)
Mueller, Sabine 4:45:36 (20,867)
Muge, Catherine 4:33:30 (18,060)
Muggridge, Mandy 4:05:25 (11,379)
Muir, Lindsay 4:10:12 (12,399)
Mularczyk, Noelle 6:38:25 (31,511)
Mulhern, Lisa 5:12:03 (25,833)
Mulholland, Karen 4:08:58 (12,124)
Muller, Gillian 5:27:52 (27,875)
Muller, Sonja 4:00:30 (10,327)
Mullins, Lyn 4:56:58 (23,371)
Mulvihill, Catherine 6:30:38 (31,343)
Mumby, Karen 4:44:38 (20,644)
Mumford, Jayne 3:41:49 (6,118)
Muncey, Lynn 4:26:19 (16,317)
Munday, Rosalind 5:07:00 (25,107)
Mundell, Katie 4:40:32 (19,657)
Munden, Ann 6:50:33 (31,733)
Munden, Olivia 5:17:56 (26,603)
Mundy, Claire 4:43:35 (20,396)
Mundy, Rachael 5:35:32 (28,598)
Mun-Gavin, Claire 4:55:30 (23,028)
Munke, Susan 6:47:47 (31,670)
Munns, Sharon 4:15:32 (13,646)
Munoz, Rosario 3:47:15 (7,171)
Munro, Fiona 4:46:35 (21,104)
Munro, Julie 4:48:46 (21,580)
Munro, Karen 4:23:32 (15,625)
Munro, Michele 5:39:22 (28,929)
Munt, Sarah 4:29:56 (17,227)
Munton, Louise 4:20:54 (14,954)
Murakami, Yuriko 6:57:49 (31,870)
Murch, Lisa 6:53:03 (31,782)
Murdin, Margaret 4:44:32 (20,620)
Murie, Barbara 6:13:40 (30,787)
Murphy, Alison 4:05:07 (11,315)
Murphy, Annette 3:52:47 (8,371)
Murphy, Bridget 4:51:54 (22,291)
Murphy, Carol 5:03:07 (24,477)
Murphy, Chris 5:51:53 (29,824)
Murphy, Christine 6:31:36 (31,367)
Murphy, Debbie 5:01:25 (24,224)
Murphy, Elizabeth 6:28:00 (31,266)
Murphy, Fiona 3:58:01 (9,712)
Murphy, Hannah 4:59:36 (23,903)
Murphy, Judith 5:56:31 (30,082)
Murphy, Julie 4:38:35 (19,221)
Murphy, Julie 6:28:04 (31,269)
Murphy, Kate 4:39:09 (19,360)
Murphy, Kathleen 3:56:49 (9,405)
Murphy, Kristen 4:08:43 (12,068)
Murphy, Marcia 4:47:50 (21,385)
Murphy, Mary 4:39:52 (19,514)
Murphy, Melissa 4:45:38 (20,876)
Murphy, Patricia 4:55:32 (23,035)
Murphy, Penny 4:42:45 (20,169)
Murphy, Ruth 4:36:23 (18,740)
Murphy, Stacey 4:42:37 (20,136)
Murray, Alyson 4:24:24 (15,841)
Murray, Annette 4:09:07 (12,156)
Murray, Emma 4:26:39 (16,391)
Murray, Jenny 3:28:44 (3,952)
Murray, Judy 4:41:17 (19,819)
Murray, Kay 4:04:53 (11,268)
Murray, Kerriann 5:54:43 (29,981)
Murray, Lindsay 4:33:03 (17,963)
Murray, Lyn 6:47:00 (31,655)
Murray, Marla 4:38:55 (19,308)
Murray, Natasha 6:25:25 (31,176)
Murray, Sandra 4:50:57 (22,059)
Murray, Shirley 5:18:10 (26,647)
Murray, Susie 5:42:18 (29,193)
Murray, Valerie 5:24:04 (27,419)
Murtagh, Joanne 6:26:19 (31,216)
Musgrave, Heather 4:29:21 (17,071)
Musgrave, Maureen 5:05:02 (24,796)
Musique, Marie 4:23:14 (15,554)
Musson, Sally 3:04:25 (1,206)
Muston, Rosemary 3:32:02 (4,476)
Muxworthy, Anja 3:54:52 (8,885)
Naden, Clare 3:51:13 (8,014)
Naga, Nalini 5:18:59 (26,754)
Naismith, Gemma 5:27:46 (27,867)
Najurally, Narisa 3:14:38 (2,202)
Nalder, Bree 4:17:24 (14,090)
Nanhoo-Robinson, Amanda 5:22:55 (27,271)
Nankivell, Cathryn 3:40:39 (5,891)
Nanthakumaran, Vanesa 6:30:46 (31,344)
Napper, Elizabeth 5:50:27 (29,745)
Nash, Alison 5:20:53 (27,006)
Nash, Deborah 5:44:55 (29,357)
Nash, Diana 4:27:39 (16,638)
Nash, Nicola 4:54:22 (22,786)
Navarrini, Fiorella 4:51:34 (22,217)
Naylor, Alison 4:25:54 (16,231)
Naylor, Christine 3:19:38 (2,715)
Naylor, Joanne 6:12:35 (30,752)
Naylor, Mary 4:05:31 (11,403)
Ndereba, Catherine 2:19:55 (24)
Neal, Belinda 6:18:10 (30,941)
Neale, Tamsin 3:30:42 (4,277)
Neave, Alice 5:41:31 (29,117)
Nee, Denise 3:50:49 (7,912)
Neely, Diana 4:38:58 (19,318)
Neethling, Tania 3:40:00 (5,788)
Neidhart, Jana 4:14:46 (13,437)
Neilson, Christine 3:44:27 (6,628)
Neilson, Julie 4:49:07 (21,652)
Nel, Georgina 5:00:29 (24,065)
Nelson, Chloe 3:34:42 (4,868)
Nelson, Claire 7:09:10 (31,982)
Nelson, Kim 3:34:34 (4,847)
Nelson, Laura 4:52:00 (22,308)
Nelson, Rosemary 4:36:18 (18,713)
Nelson, Sharon 4:19:55 (14,717)
Nelson, Valerie 5:40:08 (29,006)
Neocleous, Anna 4:35:28 (18,510)
Neocleous, Susan 4:55:25 (23,008)
Nequest, Anne 3:56:16 (9,263)
Nesbitt, Sarah 5:37:21 (28,763)
Nesdale, Eileen 5:19:45 (26,855)
Netherwood, Lisa 4:53:55 (22,699)
Nettleton, Michelle 4:51:45 (22,252)
Nevill, Ibby 4:16:46 (13,927)
Nevill, Louise 4:17:57 (14,241)
Nevill, Michelle 4:45:11 (20,767)
Nevill, Simone 4:44:04 (20,513)
Neville, Elizabeth 3:32:36 (4,540)
Neville, Samantha 5:36:51 (28,719)
Newall, Frances 5:43:30 (29,270)
Newbegin, Claudia 5:09:36 (25,491)
Newbery, Nichola 7:27:16 (32,132)
Newcombe, Fiona 4:08:54 (12,108)
Newell, Daryl 4:39:19 (19,403)
Newell, Georgina 4:42:31 (20,116)
Newell, Rebecca 4:00:27 (10,321)
Newell, Shirley 5:13:08 (25,993)
Newill, Karen 6:06:50 (30,524)
Newlove, Julia 4:34:12 (18,213)
Newman, Annette 4:52:11 (22,335)
Newman, Chloe 7:25:30 (32,113)
Newman, Gill 3:57:01 (9,461)
Newman, Jenny 6:47:34 (31,664)
Newman, Kim 4:51:50 (22,275)
Newman, Sheila 5:01:42 (24,257)
Newmann, Edwina 5:50:03 (29,719)
Newsholme, Caroline 4:41:38 (19,896)
Newton, Andrea 3:56:13 (9,249)
Newton, Catherine 5:54:21 (29,961)
Newton, Emma 4:13:01 (13,008)
Newton, Jo 4:16:23 (13,829)
Newton, Julia 4:04:51 (11,257)
Newton, Rachel 5:19:15 (26,795)
Newton, Sarah 3:10:28 (1,716)
Neyer, Katja 4:41:00 (19,752)
Neyra, Berengere 4:31:08 (17,538)
Ng, Chin Chin 5:49:11 (29,652)
Nguyen, Du 4:22:45 (15,429)
Nguyen, Quynh 6:13:32 (30,782)
Ni Eidhin, Mairead 5:18:55 (26,746)
Nichol, Melanie 3:57:29 (9,576)
Nichol, Sarah 4:15:06 (13,539)
Nicholas, Anna 4:51:32 (22,214)
Nicholls, Alison 3:31:26 (4,395)
Nicholls, Christine 4:01:59 (10,630)
Nicholls, Clair 5:27:43 (27,861)
Nicholls, Janet 3:52:28 (8,300)
Nicholls, Sarah 3:04:10 (1,194)
Nicholls, Sarah 5:17:54 (26,596)
Nichols, Bridget 6:35:43 (31,466)
Nichols, Claire 6:52:31 (31,770)
Nichols, Evelyn 4:20:53 (14,950)
Nichols, Louise 4:00:16 (10,283)
Nicholson, Gabriella 5:50:43 (29,766)
Nicholson, Hannah 4:19:23 (14,589)
Nicholson, Jennifer 5:19:13 (26,783)
Nicholson, Joanne 5:54:19 (29,958)
Nickson, Nathalie 4:08:40 (12,055)
Nicol, Diane 4:41:45 (19,931)
Nicol, Eileen 3:42:22 (6,214)
Nicol, Jessica 5:54:22 (29,962)
Nicoll, Rona 4:54:21 (22,779)
Nicolson, Marion 4:02:02 (10,642)
Nightingale, Louise 5:02:11 (24,347)
Nisbet, Heather 4:21:11 (15,030)
Nixon, Sarah 3:04:17 (1,200)
Njoroge-Mgbokwere, Wanjeri 5:27:18 (27,809)
Noake, Alyson 3:22:10 (3,004)
Nobbs, Catherine 4:09:10 (12,167)
Noble, Eileen 5:19:00 (26,757)
Noble, Emma 5:10:00 (25,547)
Noble, Karen 3:22:44 (3,075)
Noble, Monica 5:01:42 (24,257)
Noble, Pam 6:26:56 (31,228)
Nobles, Margaret 4:41:56 (19,979)
Nock, Tracey 4:29:35 (17,134)
Noher, Angelique 4:40:22 (19,623)
Noke, Dawn 6:28:34 (31,287)
Nolan, Alison 4:12:31 (12,892)
Nolan, Sarah 4:14:47 (13,445)
Nolan, Susan 3:29:12 (4,026)

Nolan, Victoria	4:39:19 (19,403)	
Noll, Julie	4:25:58 (16,242)	
Noll, Mechthild	4:06:05 (11,512)	
Nolte, Elizma	5:07:34 (25,197)	
Noonan, Helen	5:17:26 (26,531)	
Noppenberger, Trudi	3:26:47 (3,641)	
Norbury, Roaslie	5:13:53 (26,089)	
Nordin, Breege	3:22:27 (3,044)	
Norkett, Joan	5:59:11 (30,221)	
Norman, Mary	3:32:59 (4,596)	
Norman, Susan	4:57:31 (23,486)	
Norman, Tanya	6:59:44 (31,884)	
Norman, Vashti	4:47:56 (21,408)	
Norquay, Megan	3:53:11 (8,470)	
Norris, Angela	3:51:09 (7,995)	
Norris, Joan	5:50:14 (29,736)	
Norris, Tracy	5:22:55 (27,271)	
North, Lisa	3:33:46 (4,714)	
North, Sonya	5:53:14 (29,889)	
North, Tracey	6:01:52 (30,335)	
Northey, Sara	6:08:48 (30,598)	
Nothard, Julie	4:19:36 (14,639)	
Nothard, Rachel	4:19:36 (14,639)	
Nottle, Emily	5:08:58 (25,395)	
Noury, Ana	3:17:20 (2,464)	
Novak, Zuzana	5:01:19 (24,209)	
Nower, Jane	4:33:17 (18,001)	
Nowicka, Helen	4:14:19 (13,333)	
Nuir, Maureen	3:44:14 (6,589)	
Nunn, Rachel	5:25:06 (27,553)	
Nutt, Jane	4:51:45 (22,252)	
Nuttall, Portia	4:55:43 (23,083)	
Nuttall, Sue	6:18:19 (30,949)	
Nutton, Susan	7:53:37 (32,242)	
Nyman, Britt	4:10:25 (12,449)	
Nystrom, Marie	3:38:30 (5,494)	
Oakes, Anne	4:16:22 (13,823)	
Oakham, Shelley	7:05:47 (31,937)	
Oakley, Lindsay	6:01:11 (30,310)	
Oakley, Sacha	6:32:09 (31,384)	
Oakley, Suzan	5:38:33 (28,860)	
Oates, Emma	4:33:31 (18,064)	
Oates, Stephanie	5:16:09 (26,392)	
Oatham, Eleanor	4:46:01 (20,964)	
Oats, Elisabeth	4:34:58 (18,388)	
O'Brien, Ivana	4:32:18 (17,792)	
O'Brien, Jo	3:31:50 (4,452)	
O'Brien, Joanne	4:29:46 (17,188)	
O'Brien, Lorraine	7:18:20 (32,059)	
O'Brien, Mary	4:37:39 (19,009)	
Ochiltree, Elaine	4:03:15 (10,899)	
Ochong, Idalina	6:37:12 (31,491)	
O'Connell, Pamela	5:30:22 (28,128)	
O'Connell, Valerie	5:48:28 (29,603)	
O'Connor, Gill	3:05:47 (1,304)	
Oddie, Elaine	4:56:10 (23,189)	
O'Dell, Wendy	4:14:29 (13,377)	
O'Donnell, Christine	3:29:39 (4,118)	
O'Donnell, Patricia	5:27:05 (27,785)	
O'Donnell, Tracey	4:16:03 (13,750)	
O'Donovan, Bernie	3:42:33 (6,265)	
O'Dwyer, Valerie	5:20:35 (26,971)	
Offord, Kelsey	3:58:44 (9,892)	
Offredi, Doreen	6:27:29 (31,247)	
Ogden, Sharon	5:10:35 (25,633)	
Ogilvie, Charlotte	6:05:27 (30,474)	
Ogilvie, Felicity	3:43:09 (6,396)	
O'Gorman, Aimée	5:36:25 (28,675)	
O'Gorman, Gillian	3:58:31 (9,839)	
O'Grady, Lucy	3:28:30 (3,903)	
Ogungbesan, Pat	4:59:07 (23,830)	
O'Hagan, Collette	5:29:35 (28,049)	
O'Hanlon, Denise	3:56:50 (9,407)	
O'Hara, Monica	3:33:13 (4,635)	
Okane, Karen	4:09:52 (12,315)	
Oke, Liz	5:28:47 (27,966)	
O'Keefe, Patricia	3:33:51 (4,724)	
O'Keefe, Sally	6:08:12 (30,574)	
O'Keeffe, Alice	3:48:13 (7,362)	
Okoth, Kyra	4:57:43 (23,524)	
Oldfield, Chris	5:38:53 (28,888)	
Oldfield, Julie	5:15:13 (26,279)	
Oldham, Evelyn	4:49:45 (21,815)	
Oldman, Kathryn	3:55:09 (8,951)	
Olds, Denise	4:29:36 (17,139)	
Oldwood, Charlotte	7:01:03 (31,901)	
O'Leary, Emma	5:27:50 (27,872)	
O'Leary, Sarah	5:42:58 (29,235)	
Olise, Jennifer	6:45:15 (31,624)	
Oliver, Amanda	4:58:55 (23,784)	
Oliver, Kathleen	3:46:32 (7,041)	
Oliver, Linda	4:38:39 (19,238)	
Oliver, Lynn	5:33:25 (28,414)	
Oliver, Victoria	5:46:35 (29,467)	
Olliffe, Stephanie	3:22:50 (3,089)	
O'Meara, Annemarie	3:43:37 (6,469)	
Onaran, Melia	5:40:24 (29,029)	
O'Neill, Bridget	5:35:34 (28,600)	
O'Neill, Eilis	4:28:00 (16,706)	
O'Neill, Helen	4:52:46 (22,452)	
O'Neill, Hope	7:12:04 (32,012)	
Oosterhuis, Henriette	4:46:11 (21,012)	
Opute, Anne	4:34:50 (18,355)	
Orban, Mary	3:58:40 (9,877)	
Orchard, Cathlyn	4:32:02 (17,740)	
Orchard, Nicola	5:43:13 (29,256)	
O'Regan, Alexis	6:28:01 (31,267)	
O'Regan, Catherine	4:13:32 (13,134)	
O'Reilly, Sharron	6:23:58 (31,133)	
Orme, Rachel	4:18:42 (14,423)	
O'Rourke, Claire	5:05:31 (24,885)	
O'Rourke, Vera	3:51:36 (8,105)	
Orpilla, Jennifer	4:42:10 (20,022)	
Orr, Amanda	5:02:52 (24,440)	
Orrell, Jaye	5:53:48 (29,922)	
Orridge, Sharon	3:10:31 (1,719)	
Orth, Barbara	3:37:24 (5,311)	
Ortiz, Yolanda	4:52:31 (22,399)	
Orton, Olivia	4:45:50 (20,923)	
Osborne, Anna	4:52:51 (22,470)	
Osborne, Clare	4:28:21 (16,807)	
Osborne, Fiona	4:56:03 (23,158)	
Osborne, Janette	4:22:53 (15,466)	
Osborne, Lauren	5:37:23 (28,766)	
Osborne, Louise	4:36:43 (18,812)	
Osgerby, Sophie	4:32:33 (17,846)	
O'Shaughnessy, Teresa	4:49:34 (21,766)	
Osowska, Francesca	3:23:07 (3,129)	
O'Sullivan, Marie	3:43:40 (6,480)	
O'Sullivan, Maureen	5:21:30 (27,081)	
O'Sullivan, Nichola	5:56:01 (30,044)	
Oswald, Amanda	6:23:17 (31,111)	
Oswald, Claudia	3:54:36 (8,817)	
Ottaway, Julia	5:59:33 (30,242)	
Otten, Marianne	5:53:45 (29,918)	
Otto, Petra	4:49:49 (21,827)	
Ovens, Jan	3:55:13 (8,969)	
Overton, Anne	6:12:09 (30,734)	
Overton, Sam	6:42:19 (31,575)	
Ovett, Rachel	5:34:05 (28,485)	
Ovington, Debra	4:21:44 (15,166)	
Oween, Helen	4:42:59 (20,229)	
Owen, Carol	5:26:09 (27,696)	
Owen, Carys	4:13:25 (13,100)	
Owen, Dianne	4:55:24 (23,003)	
Owen, Josephine	5:19:23 (26,812)	
Owen, Kate	5:17:27 (26,536)	
Owen, Laura Jane	4:26:33 (16,366)	
Owen, Linda	4:01:07 (10,451)	
Owen, Mary	3:22:45 (3,077)	
Owen, Ruth	4:15:50 (13,713)	
Owens, Caron	4:41:08 (19,783)	
Owens, Leonie	7:07:35 (31,971)	
Oxby, Sara	4:36:55 (18,858)	
Oxley-Green, Emily	6:16:34 (30,880)	
Ozier, Patricia	4:50:29 (21,963)	
Paananen, Johanna	4:00:36 (10,345)	
Packman, Alison	4:40:23 (19,626)	
Padden, Mary	6:40:15 (31,541)	
Padfield, Rebecca	7:20:59 (32,074)	
Padfield, Sarah	4:44:15 (20,557)	
Pagan, Carol	3:22:43 (3,071)	
Pagdin, Linda	7:27:18 (32,133)	
Page, Alison	4:31:10 (17,543)	
Page, Allyson	5:32:51 (28,365)	
Page, Amanda	4:43:32 (20,388)	
Page, Andrea	4:55:55 (23,135)	
Page, Anna	4:57:26 (23,463)	
Page, Anna	5:45:14 (29,385)	
Page, Karen	4:55:52 (23,122)	
Page, Natalie	4:38:41 (19,250)	
Page, Romy	4:41:32 (19,874)	
Page, Ruth	4:37:56 (19,071)	
Page, Sarah	4:20:20 (14,824)	
Page, Sarah	5:43:15 (29,258)	
Page, Susan	5:32:06 (28,298)	
Page-Feuz, Maya	3:41:03 (5,968)	
Paget, Janice	5:38:57 (28,894)	
Paige, Carron	5:18:15 (26,664)	
Paine, Doreen	4:45:33 (20,858)	
Paisley, Christine	4:15:22 (13,607)	
Pakenham-Walsh, Jenny	6:10:11 (30,650)	
Palios, Julia	7:18:27 (32,060)	
Pallipet, Victoria	4:29:59 (17,239)	
Pallister, Valerie	4:27:17 (16,546)	
Palmer, Alison	4:00:06 (10,244)	
Palmer, Carol	4:15:47 (13,697)	
Palmer, Helen	4:41:20 (19,833)	
Palmer, Janice	3:19:32 (2,703)	
Palmer, Jennifer	5:56:03 (30,051)	
Palmer, Jocelyn	5:50:02 (29,716)	
Palmer, Julia	3:25:33 (3,468)	
Palmer, Lucy	5:30:58 (28,191)	
Palmer, Rachel	4:34:25 (18,271)	
Palmer, Vanessa	6:43:41 (31,607)	
Palmer, Zoe	5:30:58 (28,191)	
Pamplin, Diane	3:45:32 (6,837)	
Panella, Consuelo	5:22:57 (27,278)	
Panetta, Thérèse	4:25:44 (16,186)	
Papathomas, Nicola	5:34:18 (28,506)	
Pape, Emma	5:11:25 (25,755)	
Papoughnot, Sophie	5:00:58 (24,148)	
Papworth, Annette	4:47:53 (21,394)	
Paradine, Sarah	4:34:17 (18,234)	
Pardellans-Twite, Jane	4:52:59 (22,502)	
Parfitt, Sarah	4:11:26 (12,627)	
Parford, Karen	3:54:47 (8,863)	
Parise, Federica	5:41:07 (29,086)	
Parish, Jennie	4:35:03 (18,407)	
Parizel, Christine	4:09:03 (12,147)	
Park, Karen	4:41:10 (19,790)	
Parker, Alison	4:19:11 (14,548)	
Parker, Amanda	6:27:45 (31,258)	
Parker, Annette	4:51:25 (22,182)	
Parker, Audrey	4:43:35 (20,396)	
Parker, Carmel	4:17:24 (14,090)	
Parker, Eleanor	4:22:09 (15,276)	
Parker, Katherine	4:54:21 (22,779)	
Parker, Kristina	5:13:49 (26,083)	
Parker, Nicola	6:57:19 (31,863)	
Parker, Patricia	3:32:58 (4,591)	
Parker, Sarah	5:48:37 (29,612)	
Parker, Sheila	4:05:55 (11,487)	
Parker, Simone	5:23:17 (27,322)	
Parker, Sue	6:09:04 (30,607)	
Parker, Susan	4:22:29 (15,359)	
Parker, Susan	5:12:24 (25,881)	
Parker, Valerie	7:41:41 (32,214)	
Parker-Leehane, Freda	5:01:46 (24,274)	
Parkhouse, Chloe	4:53:32 (22,625)	
Parkin, Katherine	4:22:19 (15,321)	
Parkin, Paula	6:01:13 (30,311)	
Parkinson, Lucy	5:19:17 (26,798)	
Parnell, Lindsey	4:35:22 (18,486)	
Parr, Lyn	4:51:43 (22,247)	
Parr, Rachel	5:10:23 (25,606)	
Parris, Eva	3:06:07 (1,330)	
Parrott, Jayne	3:31:00 (4,327)	
Parrott, Sue	4:27:51 (16,680)	
Parry, Amanda	6:09:37 (30,622)	
Parry, Anna	4:20:01 (14,748)	
Parry, Anne	4:29:34 (17,127)	
Parry, Clare	4:01:08 (10,457)	
Parry, Fiona	4:56:08 (23,177)	
Parry, Heather	4:48:30 (21,534)	
Parry, Helen	5:21:55 (27,140)	
Parry, Julie	4:47:23 (21,269)	
Parry, Veronica	5:28:09 (27,908)	
Parry, Victoria	4:46:00 (20,959)	

Parry, Victoria..........5:58:17 (30,172)	Pender, Nicola..........5:12:11 (25,851)	Piercey, Julie..........5:49:14 (29,655)
Parsison, Julie..........6:45:26 (31,628)	Penfold, Suzanne..........4:55:39 (23,065)	Pierece, Susan..........5:04:20 (24,682)
Parsons, Abigail..........6:57:46 (31,869)	Penn, Claire..........4:41:08 (19,783)	Pierson, Jeanette..........3:41:25 (6,047)
Parsons, Connie..........5:45:59 (29,439)	Penn, Helen..........6:04:36 (30,437)	Pieterse, Wendy..........5:12:57 (25,969)
Parsons, Elizabeth..........4:47:36 (21,319)	Penn, Natasha..........4:07:38 (11,841)	Pigott, Suzanne..........5:56:14 (30,063)
Parsons, Helen..........4:14:11 (13,302)	Pennell, Brenda..........3:25:35 (3,473)	Pike, Helen..........5:40:48 (29,062)
Parsons, Jackie..........4:18:10 (14,283)	Pennell, Christine..........4:22:31 (15,369)	Pike, Rachel..........5:22:43 (27,239)
Parsons, Karen..........4:51:07 (22,108)	Penney, Carole..........7:39:49 (32,201)	Pike, Trudi..........3:36:36 (5,160)
Parsons, Pamela..........4:34:01 (18,170)	Penny, Hilary..........5:26:23 (27,722)	Pike, Zoe..........3:00:54 (995)
Parsons, Shauna..........5:32:32 (28,336)	Penny, Kate..........4:53:02 (22,509)	Pilarski, Marilyn..........4:33:59 (18,162)
Partridge, Isobel..........3:07:05 (1,410)	Penri, Llio..........4:29:40 (17,153)	Pilling, Angela..........4:47:37 (21,322)
Partridge, Patricia..........4:09:31 (12,230)	Pentland, Debbie..........5:32:49 (28,359)	Pim, Deborah..........5:08:15 (25,306)
Parvin, Rosemary..........5:25:07 (27,557)	Penycuick, Rachel..........4:35:35 (18,536)	Pim, Sophie..........4:11:17 (12,594)
Pascall, Jennifer..........5:01:13 (24,189)	Peppiatt, Barbara..........4:46:04 (20,982)	Pinder, Sandra..........4:21:44 (15,166)
Pascal-Mousselard, Aude..........4:15:22 (13,607)	Peppiatt, Jenny..........3:22:25 (3,039)	Pini, Daniella..........5:00:16 (24,031)
Pascoe, Margaret..........4:27:28 (16,593)	Percival, Sarah-Jane..........4:28:21 (16,807)	Pinner, Audrey..........6:26:34 (31,219)
Pascoe, Susanna..........5:02:41 (24,415)	Percy, Sharon..........3:48:12 (7,359)	Pinney, Gina..........6:04:53 (30,451)
Pasquinelli, Veronika..........4:19:27 (14,605)	Perfect, Maureen..........4:15:22 (13,607)	Pinniger, Emma..........6:52:42 (31,776)
Pass, Rachel..........3:54:45 (8,850)	Perkin, Anna..........5:14:20 (26,143)	Pipe, Marietta..........4:27:53 (16,688)
Passey, Elizabeth..........5:14:48 (26,217)	Perkin, Lynn..........3:57:46 (9,638)	Piper, Esme..........5:32:09 (28,303)
Passfield, Allie..........6:51:15 (31,747)	Perkins, Anne-Marie..........4:41:37 (19,894)	Piper, Nicola..........4:05:44 (11,440)
Patching, Katrina..........5:16:57 (26,474)	Perkins, Kerry..........6:50:29 (31,732)	Pirie, Karen..........4:36:26 (18,753)
Pate, Karen..........4:00:12 (10,271)	Perkins, Tracy..........5:22:50 (27,258)	Pitcher, Lorraine..........4:41:44 (19,928)
Patel, Chantal..........4:39:23 (19,418)	Perks, Deborah..........4:26:03 (16,264)	Pitchley, Karen..........5:45:20 (29,393)
Patel, Hansa..........5:25:17 (27,589)	Perks, Laura..........5:15:09 (26,271)	Pitman, Sarah..........4:34:03 (18,176)
Patel, Jayshree..........4:44:38 (20,644)	Pern, Sophy..........4:32:38 (17,859)	Pitt, Maresa..........3:41:05 (5,974)
Patel, Mrinal..........5:09:30 (25,474)	Perrott, Susan..........6:30:25 (31,339)	Pittman, Katy..........5:13:53 (26,089)
Patel, Mudrika..........4:52:35 (22,411)	Perry, Catherine..........3:48:09 (7,351)	Pittson, Judith..........4:27:44 (16,660)
Patel, Parul..........4:02:53 (10,824)	Perry, Karen..........5:35:22 (28,586)	Plant, Christine..........4:40:19 (19,614)
Patel, Priti..........4:38:32 (19,206)	Perry, Karin..........4:25:12 (16,056)	Plant, Grace..........3:54:54 (8,893)
Paterson, Lorraine..........3:38:49 (5,561)	Perry, Kyrsten..........5:13:34 (26,052)	Plant, Jayne..........4:40:44 (19,690)
Patterson, Christine..........5:38:46 (28,879)	Perry, Mandy..........4:18:20 (14,309)	Plant, Linda..........4:26:47 (16,427)
Patterson, Jillian..........4:25:44 (16,186)	Perry, Margaret..........5:47:46 (29,555)	Plater, Alison..........3:41:14 (5,996)
Patterson, Nicola..........5:41:14 (29,095)	Perry, Victoria..........2:58:40 (817)	Plater, Clare..........5:05:58 (24,948)
Pattison, Catherine..........6:15:06 (30,830)	Perryman, Anne..........6:00:40 (30,280)	Platt, Cheryl..........4:54:11 (22,744)
Pattison, Marian..........4:35:22 (18,486)	Persaud, Marcia..........5:19:06 (26,770)	Platt, Dawn..........3:54:49 (8,870)
Paul, Carol..........3:46:51 (7,093)	Pertusati, Darcel..........5:29:10 (28,002)	Platt, Eve..........4:41:04 (19,770)
Paul, Caroline..........3:44:50 (6,694)	Peters, Caroline..........5:26:00 (27,672)	Platt, Jayne..........4:02:26 (10,727)
Paul, Jaswinder..........5:38:18 (28,837)	Peters, Christina..........3:36:57 (5,223)	Platt, Sarah..........5:07:54 (25,250)
Paul, Sally..........4:43:56 (20,483)	Peters, Katie..........4:24:50 (15,959)	Platts, Emma..........4:14:23 (13,353)
Paul, Suzanna..........5:43:28 (29,267)	Petersen, Anke..........3:39:45 (5,738)	Pleasance, Andrea..........4:43:40 (20,423)
Pautard, Marlene..........3:42:44 (6,306)	Petersen, Grethe..........3:33:54 (4,734)	Pletts, Catherine..........5:16:25 (26,418)
Pavlovic, Ellen..........4:26:34 (16,370)	Petherick, Anna..........5:35:21 (28,584)	Pleydell-Bouverie, Camilla..........5:13:42 (26,067)
Pavlovich, Biserka..........4:33:41 (18,094)	Petoud, Ophelie..........6:35:29 (31,461)	Plummer, Faye..........5:34:03 (28,482)
Payne, Daphne..........4:52:57 (22,494)	Petropoulos, Julia..........4:12:53 (12,978)	Pobedonostzeff, Natalia..........4:55:52 (23,122)
Payne, Joanne..........4:37:27 (18,972)	Petrova, Ludmila..........2:23:14 (32)	Poett, Katy..........5:25:57 (27,659)
Payne, Julie..........5:51:10 (29,793)	Pettit, Paula..........5:08:59 (25,401)	Pogson, Linda..........5:29:15 (28,012)
Payne, Kim..........5:38:37 (28,869)	Pettitt, Jenny..........7:11:41 (32,009)	Poke, Celia..........4:50:04 (21,876)
Payne, Nina..........3:55:07 (8,944)	Pfersich, Andrea..........4:59:34 (23,897)	Pollard, Carol..........4:14:06 (13,282)
Payne, Sarah..........3:53:13 (8,479)	Phelps, Clare..........5:27:35 (27,845)	Pollard, Fiona..........6:08:32 (30,593)
Peace, Lesley..........6:49:59 (31,718)	Philippon-McGuinn, Sophie..........4:10:11 (12,389)	Pollard, Lesley..........4:18:58 (14,498)
Peachey, Martine..........5:32:46 (28,353)	Philip-Rafferty, Sandra..........5:29:16 (28,015)	Pollatos, Evonne..........5:14:24 (26,159)
Peacock, Julie..........4:41:25 (19,853)	Philips, Joanne..........4:35:56 (18,633)	Pollen, Isabel..........4:41:53 (19,971)
Peacock, Marcia..........4:13:15 (13,063)	Phillips, Cheryl..........6:55:18 (31,836)	Pompermaier, Rosie..........5:15:14 (26,282)
Peacock, Rebecca..........5:18:24 (26,683)	Phillips, Clare..........3:14:20 (2,169)	Ponder, Rosamund..........3:58:38 (9,867)
Pearce, Dory..........4:51:19 (22,159)	Phillips, Diana..........4:42:12 (20,029)	Ponte, Karen..........4:55:39 (23,065)
Pearce, Emma..........3:56:07 (9,214)	Phillips, Diane..........5:43:06 (29,248)	Pontefract, Elaine..........4:41:19 (19,797)
Pearce, Janie..........3:38:37 (5,521)	Phillips, Fiona..........5:10:07 (25,569)	Poole, Felicity..........6:16:28 (30,875)
Pearce, Lyn..........6:49:54 (31,717)	Phillips, Helen..........5:27:05 (27,785)	Poole, Margaret..........5:45:46 (29,425)
Pearce, Nerys..........5:31:12 (28,217)	Phillips, Keeley..........5:00:04 (23,991)	Poole, Valerie..........3:56:18 (9,271)
Pearce, Shannon..........4:56:30 (23,263)	Phillips, Lesley..........7:08:08 (31,975)	Poon, Louisa..........4:15:32 (13,646)
Pearce, Sheila..........5:57:17 (30,119)	Phillips, Rebecca..........4:31:38 (17,652)	Poon, Marilee..........3:33:05 (4,611)
Pearman, Georgina..........4:58:34 (23,711)	Phillips, Samantha..........4:56:51 (23,352)	Poonian, Tarsem..........6:15:48 (30,851)
Pearse, Joanne..........5:39:55 (28,983)	Phillips, Sara..........4:25:59 (16,248)	Poore, Nichola..........6:29:26 (31,312)
Pearson, Emma..........5:06:46 (25,069)	Phillips, Sonia..........3:33:12 (4,629)	Pope, Anne..........5:21:42 (27,108)
Pearson, Georgina..........4:59:51 (23,959)	Phillips, Tracey..........5:23:44 (27,375)	Pope, Helen..........4:15:17 (13,585)
Pearson, Helen..........6:15:38 (30,844)	Phillips, Tracy..........4:12:20 (12,845)	Pope, Nikki..........4:53:15 (22,556)
Pearson, Karin..........6:31:24 (31,358)	Phillis, Victoria..........5:31:29 (28,243)	Pope, Suzanne..........6:27:45 (31,258)
Pearson, Patricia..........4:56:38 (23,294)	Philpott, Victoria..........5:02:25 (24,376)	Popham, Julia..........6:01:28 (30,320)
Pearson, Samantha..........6:40:27 (31,547)	Phipps, Deborah..........4:34:44 (18,335)	Porjes, Jacqueline..........5:01:55 (24,300)
Pease, Merope..........5:21:38 (27,104)	Phipps, Elaine..........3:15:10 (2,257)	Porter, Charlotte..........3:41:41 (6,090)
Peck, Jane..........4:11:17 (12,594)	Phipps, Susan..........4:20:21 (14,829)	Porter, Dessie..........4:46:08 (21,003)
Peck, Rita..........4:02:20 (10,703)	Phoenix, Carolyn..........4:54:24 (22,795)	Porter, Gertrud..........4:37:50 (19,050)
Peddle, Samantha..........4:49:37 (21,784)	Piana, Marie-Laure..........4:16:35 (13,872)	Porter, Hazel..........3:14:48 (2,216)
Pedersen, Elin..........5:38:20 (28,843)	Picering, Jane..........4:04:39 (11,210)	Porter, Karen..........3:21:45 (2,959)
Pedro, Nusi..........4:36:48 (18,835)	Pickering, Anna..........4:06:53 (11,667)	Porter, Karen..........4:35:13 (18,449)
Peek, Kerry..........5:26:23 (27,722)	Pickering, Denise..........4:28:19 (16,794)	Porter, Lucy..........4:37:26 (18,971)
Peel, Erica..........4:47:42 (21,346)	Pickersgill, Penelope..........6:19:38 (31,001)	Porter, Sarah..........5:11:48 (25,801)
Peel, Marion..........5:22:20 (27,193)	Pickett, Helen..........3:55:12 (8,966)	Postill, Emily..........4:40:18 (19,608)
Peeters, Claire..........4:38:44 (19,263)	Pickles, Grace..........5:13:44 (26,072)	Potgieter, Lori..........4:03:32 (10,953)
Pelham, Fiona..........5:25:57 (27,659)	Pickup, Claire..........5:10:35 (25,633)	Potter, Jean..........5:08:20 (25,316)
Pelletier, Véronique..........4:30:23 (17,336)	Picton, Pauline..........4:49:53 (21,842)	Potticary, Lynda..........3:35:37 (5,015)
Pellin, Tara..........4:54:40 (22,857)	Pierce, Joanne..........6:17:12 (30,896)	Potts, Elaine..........5:25:47 (27,638)

Pouchkina, Rimma.......2:38:00 (132)
Poulter, Jennifer.......3:34:09 (4,768)
Poulter, Mandy.......3:50:12 (7,777)
Poulton, Deborah.......4:32:57 (17,935)
Powell, Carol.......5:38:58 (28,896)
Powell, Carolyn.......5:28:09 (27,908)
Powell, Julia.......4:31:19 (17,570)
Powell, Melissa.......6:02:59 (30,372)
Powell, Rebecca.......4:45:26 (20,829)
Powell, Rosie.......5:28:39 (27,954)
Powell, Samantha.......5:38:58 (28,896)
Power, Rebecca.......4:56:16 (23,214)
Powl, Joanna.......5:01:15 (24,194)
Pownall, Amanda.......4:23:33 (15,630)
Pownall, Loll.......5:53:46 (29,919)
Powrie, Catherine.......4:02:52 (10,819)
Pragnell, Charlotte.......4:28:09 (16,752)
Prance, Carole.......3:39:16 (5,647)
Pratt, Hazel.......6:10:36 (30,666)
Pratt, Mary.......4:28:29 (16,850)
Prechtl, Helga.......4:09:43 (12,277)
Preiner, Heidi.......5:12:25 (25,883)
Prendergast, Sharon.......4:08:27 (11,995)
Presas, Danielle.......4:31:00 (17,498)
Prestegar, Jane.......5:24:11 (27,435)
Prestegar, Kathleen.......5:27:18 (27,809)
Prestegar, Lynne.......3:44:11 (6,577)
Preston, Amanda.......4:39:08 (19,353)
Preston, Ann.......7:30:39 (32,158)
Preston, Joanne.......5:00:16 (24,031)
Preston, Laura.......4:14:57 (13,492)
Preston, Leigh.......5:04:05 (24,649)
Pretorius, Karen.......4:21:34 (15,123)
Preugschat, Susan.......4:35:20 (18,479)
Price, Diane.......5:39:18 (28,925)
Price, Filippa.......4:55:52 (23,122)
Price, Jacquelyn.......4:01:24 (10,519)
Price, Joanne.......4:09:15 (12,184)
Price, Kirsten.......5:24:32 (27,481)
Price, Liz.......4:28:23 (16,817)
Price, Nicola.......3:50:22 (7,817)
Price, Sally.......5:06:22 (25,004)
Price, Sally.......6:41:38 (31,559)
Price, Susannah.......3:34:04 (4,756)
Price, Vanessa.......5:16:37 (26,439)
Prideaux, Lesley.......3:51:22 (8,044)
Prideaux, Louise.......4:15:32 (13,646)
Priestley, Kahn.......6:23:17 (31,111)
Prifti, Sarah.......4:23:31 (15,619)
Prince, Louise.......4:13:53 (13,226)
Pringle, Donna.......5:28:11 (27,916)
Prior, Gaynor.......4:12:11 (12,813)
Prior, Ruth.......3:49:26 (7,616)
Prior, Tracey.......3:52:52 (8,386)
Pritchard, Claire.......5:11:12 (25,722)
Pritchard, Helen.......7:00:47 (31,899)
Pritchard, Karen.......5:54:58 (29,996)
Procter, Susanna.......4:52:31 (22,399)
Procter, Susannah.......4:59:51 (23,959)
Proffitt, Diana.......5:14:13 (26,129)
Prokocuka, Jelena.......2:24:01 (36)
Prosser, Carolyn.......3:54:17 (8,728)
Prudames, Caroline.......4:58:01 (23,583)
Prudenziati, Caroline.......4:14:14 (13,312)
Prudhommme, Magali.......4:45:09 (20,757)
Prue, Penelope.......4:57:58 (23,576)
Pryce, Caroline.......4:45:46 (20,905)
Pryce, Deborah.......4:46:13 (21,022)
Pryden, Ann.......3:37:35 (5,342)
Pryke, Gail.......3:13:54 (2,115)
Pryke, Sara.......5:43:09 (29,253)
Pryor, Shona.......4:40:49 (19,706)
Pucan, Sanja.......5:20:23 (26,937)
Puckeridge, Jayne.......3:50:06 (7,752)
Puech, Brenda.......4:45:45 (20,899)
Pugh, Amanda.......4:01:07 (10,451)
Pugh, Beth.......5:06:20 (24,998)
Pugh, Daphne.......5:03:48 (24,592)
Pugh, Gillian.......3:24:30 (3,329)
Pugh, Jane.......4:09:28 (12,219)
Pugsley, Gillian.......4:35:12 (18,442)
Pullar, Sally.......4:02:25 (10,723)
Pullen, Joanne.......4:54:51 (22,891)
Pullin, Natalie.......4:25:49 (16,205)
Pullum, Julie.......3:57:19 (9,533)
Pummell, Stephanie.......7:38:59 (32,197)
Purdham, Allison.......4:13:44 (13,184)
Purslow, Chris.......4:31:15 (17,558)
Purzer, Penny.......4:03:19 (10,916)
Putnam, Sarah.......5:21:00 (27,021)
Putzolu, Gabriella.......5:05:02 (24,796)
Pycroft, Ella.......5:54:56 (29,993)
Pycroft, Joy.......5:54:56 (29,993)
Pyle, Joanne.......5:56:52 (30,098)
Pyle, Michelle.......5:15:47 (26,357)
Pyper, Jennifer.......3:37:15 (5,282)
Qin, Duo.......5:24:44 (27,499)
Quantrill, Jane.......4:34:17 (18,234)
Quarrie, Joyce.......6:19:38 (31,001)
Queally, Gemma.......3:52:12 (8,243)
Quigley, Joanne.......4:46:33 (21,098)
Quill, Maura.......4:47:40 (21,339)
Quilter, Jenifer.......4:17:54 (14,230)
Quinn, Anne.......6:14:25 (30,806)
Quinn, Bernadette.......4:59:54 (23,967)
Quinn, Brigid.......4:03:45 (10,997)
Quinn, Emma.......4:25:40 (16,174)
Quinn, Laura.......4:47:56 (21,408)
Quinsey, Teresa.......6:42:21 (31,578)
Quirk, Deborah.......4:19:59 (14,737)
Rabbett, Kim.......6:56:38 (31,853)
Rabouhans, Marie-Louise.......5:12:00 (25,826)
Raby, Beth.......5:44:51 (29,349)
Raby, Nicola.......5:30:54 (28,185)

Radcliffe, Paula.......2:15:25 (16)

Radford, Susan.......3:43:15 (6,414)
Rae, Suzanne.......6:17:27 (30,905)
Raikes, Sophia.......5:34:13 (28,497)
Rainbird, Caroline.......4:40:35 (19,664)
Rainbird, Katy.......4:34:39 (18,321)
Rainger, Lesley.......3:42:31 (6,255)
Rait, Caroline.......4:56:40 (23,306)
Rajah, Najma.......3:59:00 (9,966)
Raley, Helen.......6:47:35 (31,667)
Ralleigh, Gita.......5:09:29 (25,472)
Ralph, Barbara.......3:17:26 (2,482)
Ralph, Caroline.......4:17:55 (14,235)
Ramalingam, Mahes.......4:58:24 (23,676)
Ramelli, Rosa.......4:57:02 (23,389)
Ramsay, Hilda.......4:51:45 (22,252)
Ramsay, Paula.......5:27:38 (27,853)
Ramsey, Paula.......3:52:17 (8,263)
Ramshaw, Sara.......4:31:36 (17,639)
Rance, Bunty.......4:14:48 (13,453)
Randall, Patricia.......4:19:36 (14,639)
Randle, Sally.......5:52:53 (29,874)
Randle, Wendy.......6:05:38 (30,486)
Randle-Bissell, Bev.......5:36:33 (28,694)
Ranshaw, Claire.......4:31:28 (17,607)
Rapley, Jean.......4:57:11 (23,426)
Rapson, Nicola.......4:57:33 (23,490)
Ratcliff, Nikki.......4:59:19 (23,859)
Ratcliffe, Allison.......4:00:57 (10,419)
Rau, Angela.......4:19:15 (14,568)
Rauch, Elizabeth.......4:09:37 (12,253)
Raven, Susanna.......4:58:42 (23,734)
Rawdon-Mogg, Alice.......6:02:16 (30,351)
Rawlings, Simone.......4:56:29 (23,255)
Rawson, Leanne.......6:10:33 (30,664)
Ray, Marcia.......6:11:19 (30,702)
Ray, Stephanie.......6:21:56 (31,073)
Rayman, Linda.......4:34:54 (18,372)
Raynard, Celeste.......7:53:12 (32,241)
Rayner, Marion.......3:18:05 (2,561)
Raynes, Deborah.......3:32:38 (4,547)
Rea, Jacqueline.......4:24:42 (15,915)
Read, Alison.......5:38:28 (28,854)
Read, Anna.......4:45:26 (20,829)
Read, Dawn.......4:11:10 (12,567)
Read, Kathrine.......4:49:15 (21,689)
Read, Philippa.......4:48:49 (21,595)
Read, Lucinda.......4:22:46 (15,434)
Reader, Carole.......4:30:24 (17,344)
Reader, Gillian.......5:08:51 (25,385)
Reader, Jacqui.......5:38:14 (28,832)
Reading, Barbara.......4:27:32 (16,610)
Real, Caroline.......4:09:35 (12,246)
Reale, Diane.......5:41:23 (29,106)
Reason, Lita.......4:40:19 (19,614)
Reasons, Fiona.......4:46:00 (20,959)
Rebello, Cindy.......3:34:40 (4,863)
Redden, Kirsty.......4:49:15 (21,689)
Reddy, Avshandrie.......4:40:10 (19,575)
Reddy, Joanne.......5:36:32 (28,689)
Redfern, Sally.......3:36:51 (5,204)
Redfern, Vicki.......2:53:28 (506)
Redgrave, Elizabeth-Ann.......5:03:11 (24,488)
Redhead, Diane.......5:33:56 (28,474)
Redmond, Anna.......5:32:07 (28,299)
Redpath, Janet.......3:51:51 (8,165)
Redwood, Kathryn.......5:48:47 (29,620)
Reed, Brenda.......7:34:06 (32,179)
Reed, Katharine.......5:03:31 (24,532)
Reed, Sandra.......7:22:31 (32,091)
Reenie, Katherine.......3:49:29 (7,629)
Rees, Deborah.......5:25:57 (27,659)
Rees, Elizabeth.......6:24:51 (31,157)
Rees, Jacqueline.......4:10:19 (12,419)
Rees, Juliana.......5:08:11 (25,295)
Rees, Ruth.......5:05:21 (24,849)
Rees, Sandra.......5:02:36 (24,409)
Rees, Sharon.......5:46:43 (29,477)
Reeves, Emma.......3:56:06 (9,206)
Regan, Paulette.......5:32:38 (28,342)
Regan, Rachelle.......4:07:57 (11,895)
Regan, Sarah-Jane.......3:48:46 (7,457)
Reid, Britt.......4:07:37 (11,838)
Reid, Carol.......3:34:24 (4,819)
Reid, Christine.......3:52:38 (8,338)
Reid, Jacqueline.......5:24:09 (27,427)
Reid, Kendra.......5:01:39 (24,252)
Reid, Morven.......3:37:22 (5,300)
Reid, Sarah.......3:53:57 (8,661)
Reid, Sheridan.......4:42:55 (20,210)
Reid, Zoe.......6:19:38 (31,001)
Reilly, Cynthia.......5:38:05 (28,818)
Rein, Sue.......3:44:43 (6,674)
Reissner, Louise.......5:41:01 (29,078)
Remond, Denise.......4:30:38 (17,399)
Renfree, Joann.......4:05:18 (11,351)
Renmant, Beverley.......3:47:33 (7,223)
Renton, Julia.......4:35:08 (18,427)
Renyard, Lauren.......5:40:00 (28,992)
Reston, Viveca.......3:34:19 (4,797)
Retigan, Jackie.......7:41:15 (32,212)
Reynolds, Abigail.......4:49:51 (21,838)
Reynolds, Alexandra.......4:19:14 (14,559)
Reynolds, Alison.......4:17:20 (14,064)
Reynolds, Joanne.......5:17:39 (26,566)
Reynolds, Kathy.......5:45:05 (29,376)
Reynolds, Lee.......5:14:55 (26,236)
Rhodes, Christine.......5:12:43 (25,934)
Rhodes, Deborah.......3:50:33 (7,854)
Rhodes, Helen.......6:20:11 (31,022)
Rhule, Suzanne.......5:07:56 (25,255)
Rhymes, Natasha.......3:40:07 (5,816)
Rice, Jacquie.......4:46:08 (21,003)

Rice, Melissa 5:48:04 (29,585)
Rice, Sheila 5:36:34 (28,697)
Rice-Tucker, Sandie..............5:08:37 (25,350)
Rich, Joanne 4:33:25 (18,036)
Rich, Judy 4:43:09 (20,273)
Richards, Christine 4:04:41 (11,222)
Richards, Denise 4:30:41 (17,414)
Richards, Donna 6:19:14 (30,980)
Richards, Emma 3:32:29 (4,528)
Richards, Helen 5:47:57 (29,571)
Richards, Jacqueline 5:00:08 (23,998)
Richards, Kim 3:45:40 (6,863)
Richards, Leonie 4:29:00 (16,991)
Richards, Linda 5:59:17 (30,226)
Richards, Sally 4:44:08 (20,525)
Richardson, Claire 4:49:48 (21,823)
Richardson, Dawn.................2:58:45 (828)
Richardson, Elizabeth 4:05:25 (11,379)
Richardson, Janet 4:31:30 (17,616)
Richardson, Jill 4:34:28 (18,281)
Richardson, Melanie 7:02:57 (31,911)
Richardson, Susan 4:54:49 (22,885)
Richardson-Wright, Rachel....4:48:43 (21,574)
Richings, Kim 4:13:27 (13,111)
Richmond, Alexandra............3:24:46 (3,367)
Richmond, Billy...................5:07:35 (25,199)
Richmond, Jacqueline 5:28:24 (27,932)
Richrdson, Lesley................3:17:56 (2,541)
Richter, Verena...................3:49:29 (7,629)
Rickaby, Emma....................5:01:59 (24,311)
Rickard, Alison 4:00:41 (10,361)
Rickhuss, Joanne.................4:50:29 (21,963)
Rickus, Tess.......................5:51:37 (29,812)
Rida, Samia 5:00:12 (24,016)
Rideout, Lesley...................4:44:45 (20,672)
Rider, Kathryn 4:39:46 (19,490)
Ridgway, Debra...................4:36:20 (18,722)
Ridgway, Frances 3:58:32 (9,844)
Ridgway, Hayley 4:28:13 (16,773)
Riding, Jayne 5:00:14 (24,022)
Riding, Joanna 4:21:09 (15,020)
Ridings, Tracy 4:21:41 (15,152)
Ridler, Samantha 4:06:18 (11,555)
Ridley, Sarah 4:39:17 (19,391)
Ridpath, Emma 5:32:11 (28,307)
Riedmuller, Ute...................4:03:34 (10,962)
Rieley, Elizabeth 4:24:36 (15,888)
Ries-Lentz, Simone 4:45:12 (20,772)
Rigby, Emma 4:43:42 (20,431)
Riggs, Amanda 4:34:11 (18,209)
Riggs, Carole 4:33:07 (17,973)
Riggs, Samantha 4:26:29 (16,351)
Righetti, Maria 4:51:51 (22,278)
Rigney, Lorna 5:50:08 (29,728)
Riley, Betty 5:15:54 (26,361)
Riley, Caroline 4:15:04 (13,529)
Riley, Jayne 4:32:56 (17,932)
Riley, Joanne 4:00:03 (10,233)
Riley, Rachel 4:33:00 (17,952)
Rimmer, Dawn 4:42:26 (20,093)
Rimmer, Helen 3:53:08 (8,457)
Rimmington, Donna..............4:20:53 (14,950)
Ringer, Samantha.................6:48:36 (31,684)
Ringham, Elizabeth...............3:51:35 (8,100)
Ripper, Georgina 3:59:10 (9,997)
Riseley, Julie 6:19:35 (30,997)
Riss, Rebecca 5:00:23 (24,048)
Ritchie, Deborah..................4:35:40 (18,555)
Ritchie, Sarah 5:57:57 (30,161)
Ritchie-Ingram, Nicola 4:54:27 (22,803)
Rithner, Line 3:51:02 (7,963)
Rivas, Paula 3:25:14 (3,432)
Rivers, Valerie 4:29:09 (17,026)
Rivett, Pam........................4:49:09 (21,662)
Rivett, Suzanne...................5:15:41 (26,339)
Roach, Danielle 3:59:50 (10,184)
Roake, Carly 4:33:53 (18,138)
Roake, Claire 4:28:07 (16,740)
Robatel, Helen 3:37:03 (5,241)
Robb, Carol 6:32:18 (31,388)
Robb, Rebecca....................3:38:27 (5,485)
Robbins, Carolyn.................3:31:32 (4,417)
Robbins, Donna...................3:42:29 (6,243)

Pace yourself

Anyone who is running the London Marathon should look out for 'pacers'. They are supplied by the magazine *Runner's World* and carry a sign on a stick, giving their target finish time. The groups vary from a sub-3-hour pace to a 'Get You Round' jogging option, with a one-minute walk break after every five minutes. These 'pacers' are invariably followed by large groups of runners who find that even-pacing is the best way to run the distance. The 'Get You Round' option, a method of combining running and walking, was popularised by former US Olympic athlete Jeff Galloway. He asserts that taking brief walk breaks long before your legs get tired can often improve your finishing time.

Robbins, Sarah 4:20:50 (14,938)
Robert, Vanessa...................4:27:16 (16,539)
Roberts, Carolyn 4:58:13 (23,629)
Roberts, Deborah.................4:32:04 (17,746)
Roberts, Diane 6:48:49 (31,690)
Roberts, Donna 6:26:43 (31,223)
Roberts, first name unknown 6:25:53 (31,199)
Roberts, Hayley 4:54:37 (22,841)
Roberts, Iona 4:11:35 (12,663)
Roberts, Jane 4:39:50 (19,508)
Roberts, Jean 7:40:17 (32,204)
Roberts, Jennifer 6:59:41 (31,881)
Roberts, Julie 4:18:44 (14,432)
Roberts, Katherine 4:56:20 (23,228)
Roberts, Kathryn 3:29:37 (4,114)
Roberts, Kathryn 3:50:00 (7,734)
Roberts, Katie 4:23:43 (15,676)
Roberts, Lorraine 3:58:15 (9,773)
Roberts, Margaret 7:14:10 (32,033)
Roberts, Pam 4:20:01 (14,748)
Roberts, Pennie 7:12:10 (32,013)
Roberts, Rachel 4:17:13 (14,036)
Roberts, Sylvia 3:40:00 (5,788)
Roberts, Teresa...................5:37:03 (28,743)
Roberts, Tracy.....................5:24:03 (27,415)
Roberts Jones, Bethan 4:47:31 (21,302)
Robertshaw, Kathleen 3:43:42 (6,489)
Robertson, Bridget................3:52:24 (8,288)
Robertson, Clare 4:05:25 (11,379)
Robertson, Isabel 5:00:59 (24,150)
Robertson, Jan 5:02:30 (24,386)
Robertson, Karen 5:19:02 (26,759)
Robertson, Kate 4:02:03 (10,647)
Robertson, Louise 6:03:31 (30,395)
Robertson, Michelle...............5:15:34 (26,327)
Robertson, Penelope 7:52:05 (32,236)
Robertson, Susan 3:39:34 (5,706)
Robins, Rachel 4:42:09 (20,019)
Robinson, Avril....................6:14:47 (30,821)
Robinson, Camilla.................5:00:59 (24,150)
Robinson, Catherine..............3:17:18 (2,460)
Robinson, Chantal 4:32:15 (17,784)
Robinson, Gemma 6:20:04 (31,018)
Robinson, Heather................3:08:33 (1,552)
Robinson, Jane 4:01:01 (10,435)
Robinson, Karen 3:56:46 (9,388)
Robinson, Leanne 5:48:44 (29,616)
Robinson, Liz......................3:44:00 (6,544)
Robinson, Marie 5:31:41 (28,255)
Robinson, Mary....................7:08:31 (31,976)
Robinson, Melinda................5:21:37 (27,100)

Robinson, Michelle 4:44:26 (20,602)
Robinson, Monique 5:33:47 (28,450)
Robinson, Nicola..................4:17:31 (14,115)
Robinson, Nicola..................4:54:02 (22,716)
Robinson, Paula 4:23:35 (15,635)
Robinson, Philippa 3:56:24 (9,294)
Robjohns, Karen 4:33:08 (17,976)
Roblin-Smith, Sarah 4:26:51 (16,439)
Robson, Adrienne 5:12:11 (25,851)
Robson, Dawn 3:58:04 (9,725)
Robson, Deborah 5:46:17 (29,453)
Robson, Lucy......................5:32:02 (28,294)
Robson, Nicola 4:47:49 (21,380)
Robson, Patricia 5:19:24 (26,818)
Roche, Alison 5:34:58 (28,550)
Roche, Jane 5:41:12 (29,091)
Roche, Kendra 4:31:29 (17,612)
Roche, Lucy 3:31:40 (4,429)
Rockliffe, Jacqueline 3:22:13 (3,013)
Rodber, Caroline..................4:44:27 (20,606)
Roderick, Hilary 3:53:43 (8,593)
Rodger, Miranda 5:39:17 (28,924)
Rodney, Melanie 6:27:23 (31,236)
Rodrigues, Carla...................6:14:01 (30,797)
Rodrigues Culshaw, Janice......3:31:22 (4,388)
Rodriguez, Sonia 3:57:42 (9,617)
Rodriguez-Minowitz, Victoria....3:54:21 (8,738)
Roe, Kate 5:09:22 (25,459)
Roe, Roma 4:57:07 (23,404)
Roesch, Sandra 5:06:47 (25,073)
Roffey, Susan 4:42:21 (20,067)
Rogan, Louise 4:34:47 (18,348)
Rogan, Michelle 4:43:41 (20,429)
Rogdeberg, Anniken 5:20:04 (26,896)
Rogers, Alexandra.................3:29:16 (4,036)
Rogers, Anne 4:25:33 (16,147)
Rogers, Caroline 4:25:46 (16,190)
Rogers, Deborah 6:24:09 (31,138)
Rogers, Denise 5:35:15 (28,576)
Rogers, Elizabeth 6:01:29 (30,321)
Rogers, Jamie 4:03:18 (10,913)
Rogers, Jeanette 5:30:20 (28,121)
Rogers, Kathryne 5:29:18 (28,019)
Rogers, Laura 4:12:24 (12,858)
Rogers, Marie 5:49:15 (29,658)
Rogerson, Cheryl 6:57:15 (31,862)
Rolfe, Helen 4:29:34 (17,127)
Rolland, Brigitte 4:47:03 (21,190)
Rollings, Emma 3:36:39 (5,170)
Rolls, Joanne 5:42:31 (29,210)
Rolph, Paula 5:41:54 (29,152)
Ronan-Heath, Carol...............5:47:28 (29,529)
Roper, Lucy 4:02:52 (10,819)
Rose, Christine 5:19:14 (26,789)
Rose, Eve 6:51:43 (31,758)
Rose, Joanne 5:10:20 (25,597)
Rose, Lorraine 5:02:03 (24,320)
Rose, Lucy.........................3:40:11 (5,829)
Rose, Sara 5:03:35 (24,545)
Rose, Sharon 4:41:23 (19,844)
Rose, Yasmine 4:54:24 (22,795)
Rosemergy, Nicola................4:02:15 (10,686)
Rosen-Nash, Ilkay 4:40:23 (19,626)
Rosenstiel, Regina 3:29:52 (4,151)
Rose-Quirie, Alison 3:38:00 (5,413)
Ross, Meg..........................4:51:15 (22,144)
Ross, Nicola 6:16:05 (30,861)
Ross, Rebecca 6:07:48 (30,561)
Ross, Wendy 4:01:01 (10,435)
Ross Russell, Fiona 3:22:46 (3,081)
Rossel, Olivio 4:04:12 (11,112)
Rossiter, Christina 5:22:42 (27,235)
Rossiter, Sally 4:33:28 (18,051)
Rossner, Meredith 3:37:24 (5,311)
Rostern, Shwezin 6:02:10 (30,347)
Rotheram, Clare...................4:45:44 (20,893)
Rotheram, Jo 5:04:02 (24,640)
Rotherham, Joanne 5:17:34 (26,556)
Rough, Francine 5:04:24 (24,692)
Rouncefield, Susan 3:59:16 (10,027)
Round-Ball, Catherine 4:50:35 (21,987)
Rouse, Judy 3:34:13 (4,783)
Rouse, Lucilla 4:11:09 (12,561)

Roussel, Kay....7:56:16 (32,248)
Rout, Patricia....4:07:07 (11,713)
Routledge, Joanne....4:03:46 (11,002)
Routley-Driver, Elizabeth....3:42:24 (6,219)
Rouy, Helene....4:14:24 (13,361)
Rowbotham, Tina....5:51:00 (29,785)
Rowe, Margaret....3:22:19 (3,023)
Rowe, Patricia....5:15:40 (26,336)
Rowe, Tarryn....6:22:05 (31,077)
Rowell, Vicky....5:05:27 (24,867)
Rowett, Peggy....6:27:25 (31,238)
Rowland, Patricia....5:16:17 (26,400)
Rowlands, Angela....4:40:46 (19,696)
Rowley-Williams, Sally....4:51:08 (22,115)
Rowlinson, Helen....4:38:44 (19,263)
Rowntree, Karen....4:12:32 (12,894)
Rowson, Lucie....5:36:39 (28,703)
Rowswell, Kathryn....4:39:49 (19,504)
Ruane, Carmel....4:55:34 (23,042)
Ruane, Jean....5:20:02 (26,894)
Rudaz, Katie....3:30:47 (4,294)
Rudd, Belinda....4:31:56 (17,716)
Rudge, Samantha....5:03:04 (24,467)
Rudrum, Martyn....5:00:33 (24,078)
Ruedisueli-Kools, Carla....3:58:11 (9,748)
Ruescher, Sabine....4:24:51 (15,962)
Ruess, André....3:37:09 (5,264)
Ruff, Rebecca....4:28:23 (16,817)
Ruffer, Dily....4:56:43 (23,320)
Ruggles, Wanda....7:30:06 (32,152)
Ruickbie, Liz....3:57:39 (9,607)
Rulens, Françoise....3:56:49 (9,405)
Rumbelow, Joanna....4:41:10 (19,790)
Rundle, Alison....4:40:35 (19,664)
Rundle, Nicole....5:44:06 (29,308)
Rungarara-Keenan, Margareth...6:01:15 (30,313)
Ruocco, Elizabeth....5:25:15 (27,585)
Ruocco, Frances....4:28:07 (16,740)
Ruscombe-King, Sarah....4:50:30 (21,968)
Rush, Penelope....4:30:54 (17,468)
Rush, Stephanie....6:11:34 (30,712)
Rushby, Maia....3:38:34 (5,507)
Rushton, Catherine....6:43:03 (31,593)
Rusling, Barbara....3:40:32 (5,871)
Russ, Katheleen....4:45:45 (20,899)
Russell, Abigail....6:16:32 (30,877)
Russell, Alison....4:06:13 (11,539)
Russell, Dorothea....4:46:32 (21,096)
Russell, Jacqueline....5:46:18 (29,454)
Russell, Judith....4:24:12 (15,797)
Russell, Julie....4:22:54 (15,471)
Russell, Margaret....4:39:56 (19,524)
Russell, Rebecca....6:18:18 (30,947)
Russell, Sally....4:30:58 (17,485)
Rust, Lindsay....4:02:36 (10,756)
Rust, Nicholas....4:04:06 (11,090)
Rutter, Amanda....4:58:50 (23,771)
Rutty, Karen....5:23:13 (27,314)
Rutz-Milicevic, Sandra....6:13:23 (30,779)
Ryan, Angela....5:36:28 (28,681)
Ryan, Catherine....4:35:27 (18,507)
Ryan, Jo-Anne....5:29:13 (28,009)
Ryan, Kerry....4:02:39 (10,769)
Ryan, Lisbeth....4:41:59 (19,987)
Ryan, Margaret....4:42:48 (20,180)
Ryan, Marian....4:13:36 (13,153)
Ryan, Mary....3:14:39 (2,203)
Ryan, Victoria....5:14:57 (26,241)
Ryden, Catherine....5:05:36 (24,900)
Ryder, Sarah....4:08:28 (12,002)
Ryder, Sophie....4:38:19 (19,167)
Ryles, Elizabeth....5:05:25 (24,863)
Saba, Nadia....4:56:36 (23,287)
Sabharwal, Laura....3:30:18 (4,219)
Sablan, Maria....4:30:22 (17,328)
Sabo, Cassandra....4:28:12 (16,766)
Sabrosa, Etelvina....4:58:08 (23,612)
Sada, Lucia....4:54:29 (22,810)
Saddington, Anne....5:38:12 (28,829)
Sadler, Fiona....5:46:25 (29,461)
Sadler, Lindsay....4:57:53 (23,557)
Saii, Azadeh....4:03:56 (11,044)
Sail, Annette....5:28:58 (27,983)
Saiman, Nathalie....4:19:49 (14,695)
Saini, Harpreet....4:51:02 (22,079)
Sainsbury, Noelene....5:15:22 (26,300)
Saint, Debbie....4:03:50 (11,021)
Saker, Sharon....5:36:51 (28,719)
Salazar, Juliet....5:34:05 (28,485)
Salley, Joanne....3:51:35 (8,100)
Salmon, Victoria....5:08:13 (25,302)
Salt, Adela....3:25:07 (3,411)
Salt, Sally Anne....5:18:09 (26,642)
Samms, Lisa....6:44:43 (31,616)
Sammut, Elizabeth....4:37:00 (18,878)
Samper, Ghislaine....4:25:35 (16,153)
Sampson, Felicity....5:27:32 (27,834)
Sams, Maddy....4:47:43 (21,351)
Samuel, Natasha....5:18:51 (26,739)
Samuel, Sarah....4:48:37 (21,554)
Samuels, Anne....5:02:33 (24,397)
Samuels, Jane....5:22:53 (27,266)
Samwell, Debra....5:17:10 (26,500)
Sanchez, Maria....7:21:28 (32,081)
Sanchez de Muniain, Sol....5:11:55 (25,816)
Sanchez-Clavero, Esmeralda....5:40:35 (29,041)
Sandberg, Rhona....3:31:32 (4,417)
Sanders, Andrea....6:18:53 (30,969)
Sanders, Barbara....3:53:39 (8,579)
Sanderson, Jean....3:40:47 (5,922)
Sanderson, Julie....5:00:31 (24,073)
Sandford, Cathie....4:55:02 (22,928)
Sandman, Victoria....4:17:23 (14,082)
Sands, Helen....3:58:19 (9,788)
Sands, Rebecca....5:08:02 (25,271)
Sargeant, Donna....4:57:33 (23,490)
Sargeant, Wendy....4:04:08 (11,098)
Sarif, Anouchka....5:07:52 (25,244)
Sarkin, Kiran....6:48:13 (31,680)
Sarosi, Mia....5:20:01 (26,890)
Sartori, Monica....5:05:26 (24,865)
Sarup, Louise....4:54:58 (22,913)
Satlmarsh, Amber....5:37:11 (28,751)
Satterly, Olga....5:02:54 (24,444)
Sault, Debbie....4:18:05 (14,269)
Saunders, Beryl....5:59:32 (30,240)
Saunders, Eve....5:21:40 (27,107)
Saunders, Kathryn....4:37:13 (18,925)
Saunders, Linda....6:28:35 (31,290)
Saunders, Sharon....5:26:23 (27,722)
Saunter, Kim....3:45:05 (6,754)
Savage, Claire....6:11:14 (30,700)
Savin, Jane....6:19:38 (31,001)
Savio, Itala....5:32:19 (28,321)
Savory, Linzi....6:15:38 (30,844)
Sawczak, Aneta....4:13:23 (13,091)
Sawtell, Clair....4:59:12 (23,843)
Sawyer, Victoria....7:12:11 (32,014)
Saxby, Sheila....6:20:49 (31,042)
Scales, Angie....5:28:47 (27,966)
Scammell, Kerry....5:04:33 (24,714)
Scarano, Christine....4:33:17 (18,001)
Scard, Victoria....4:43:43 (20,435)
Scarfe, Jacqueline....3:42:11 (6,187)
Scarr, Antonia....4:13:12 (13,049)
Scarr-Hall, Rachael....4:57:26 (23,463)
Scarth, Gillian....4:03:07 (10,870)
Schaerer, Patricia....3:48:08 (7,345)
Schaller, Etta....6:20:00 (31,017)
Scheepbouwer-Smeenk, Ineke....3:59:12 (10,004)
Schermer, Hendrika....6:07:23 (30,549)
Schiettecatte, Anne....5:09:41 (25,504)
Schipperijn, Jantien....5:03:36 (24,550)
Schipper-Van Hoek, Emily....4:17:40 (14,165)
Schmidders, Roswitha....3:51:31 (8,080)
Schmidt, Herta....5:12:56 (25,967)
Schmidt, Karina....5:52:37 (29,863)
Schmidt-Uili, Epirosa....4:30:23 (17,336)
Schneiderman, Frances....5:40:07 (29,005)
Schocke, Ulrike....3:28:16 (3,860)
Schoeman, Petra....4:46:20 (21,054)
Schoen, Chris....5:20:52 (27,005)
Schofield, Colette....4:38:15 (19,143)
Schofield, Fiona....3:40:24 (5,857)
Schofield, Jennifer....4:25:53 (16,224)
Scholey, Helen....5:07:36 (25,201)
Schooling, Tracey....3:45:08 (6,762)
Schrager-Powell, Vivien....5:48:55 (29,632)
Schrode, Jo....7:31:38 (32,165)
Schubert, Cecile....3:38:01 (5,419)
Schultz, Melody....3:15:03 (2,243)
Schumann, Heidi....4:22:52 (15,458)
Schwarz, Natalie....5:48:47 (29,620)
Schweitzer, Sonja....4:18:03 (14,260)
Schwenderman, Susan....4:23:28 (15,607)
Scoggins, Sally Ann....3:59:46 (10,167)
Scothern, Helen....6:07:17 (30,540)
Scotland, first name unknown....5:23:17 (27,322)
Scott, Amanda....5:14:59 (26,245)
Scott, Anne....4:38:39 (19,238)
Scott, Catherine....4:51:36 (22,225)
Scott, Emma....4:57:00 (23,382)
Scott, Emma....5:57:36 (30,144)
Scott, Jane....5:04:31 (24,708)
Scott, Katy....6:05:06 (30,455)
Scott, Lindsey....4:46:16 (21,035)
Scott, Maralyn....5:09:05 (25,419)
Scott, Nicola....5:57:52 (30,159)
Scott, Sandra....4:36:35 (18,785)
Scott, Serena....4:01:04 (10,446)
Scott, Sophie....4:06:01 (11,503)
Scott, Suzanne....6:16:17 (30,865)
Scott, Wendy....3:07:19 (1,440)
Scott Steer, Janet....4:19:44 (14,679)
Scott-Tomlin, Lynda....5:23:22 (27,335)
Scudamore, Ellie....5:05:28 (24,874)
Scudder, Sharon....6:24:46 (31,152)
Scudellaro, Kate....6:12:22 (30,748)
Scully, Lindsay....3:59:14 (10,014)
Scully, Teresa....3:08:55 (1,580)
Seabright, Laura....6:08:20 (30,579)
Seabrook, Patricia....4:30:08 (17,267)
Seago, Ann-Louise....4:37:35 (19,005)
Seagrave, Charlotte....3:54:32 (8,793)
Searle, Clare....4:32:32 (17,840)
Searle, Jill....3:51:58 (8,186)
Sebba, Henrietta....4:28:48 (16,935)
Sebire, Jacqueline....4:31:06 (17,525)
Sebti, Soraya....5:18:02 (26,614)
Secker, Catherine....4:31:39 (17,658)
Seddon, Elizabeth....5:17:04 (26,490)
Seddon, Serena....4:19:34 (14,631)
Sedgwick, Elizabeth....5:21:34 (27,093)
Sedman, Alison....3:09:01 (1,587)
Seelinger, Lisa....5:16:42 (26,451)
Seery, Nicola....7:27:18 (32,133)
Sefton, Amanda....4:42:26 (20,093)
Sefton, Denise....4:42:26 (20,093)
Segrue, Dawn....5:29:00 (27,990)
Sekkat, Nadia....3:24:43 (3,360)
Sekkat, Samiya....5:31:21 (28,235)
Selby, Andrea....4:56:09 (23,182)
Selby, Jenny....4:51:40 (22,241)
Sellars, Sinclair....5:42:10 (29,183)
Sellek, Yoko....4:09:31 (12,230)
Semenova, Zinaid....2:32:37 (78)
Sendall, Susan....4:56:40 (23,306)
Sendlhofer, Britta....4:06:18 (11,555)
Senior, Gill....3:39:55 (5,771)
Senior, Glencora....4:15:18 (13,592)
Senior, Jane....3:42:04 (6,162)
Sennitt, Alison....4:15:55 (13,725)
Sercombe, Vikki....3:11:31 (1,805)
Seth Smith, Carolina....3:40:10 (5,826)
Settle, Clare....3:32:50 (4,572)
Settle, Dianne....4:56:15 (23,212)
Sewell, Alison....5:04:14 (24,668)
Sewell, Lucy....5:24:36 (27,489)
Sewell, Teresa....4:21:57 (15,224)
Seymour, Zoe....5:15:57 (26,369)
Shabaya, Rose....6:04:59 (30,454)
Shabbas, Celine....4:47:42 (21,346)
Shadbolt, Veronica....3:29:59 (4,163)
Shah, Frisha....6:01:01 (30,299)
Shah, Rashmita....5:06:41 (25,049)
Shamlian, Natalie....5:10:08 (25,571)
Shams, Farnaz....3:27:49 (3,787)
Shanklyn, Caroline....4:20:06 (14,770)
Shannon, Clare....4:20:36 (14,888)

Suttle, Haley	3:51:52	(8,169)
Suttle, Selina	6:16:46	(30,889)
Sutton, Beverley	4:12:33	(12,902)
Sutton, Claire	6:10:31	(30,661)
Sutton, Clare	4:19:07	(14,534)
Sutton, Kate	4:11:58	(12,754)
Suzuki, Yoko	5:06:29	(25,014)
Swadling, Claire	5:50:53	(29,777)
Swadling, Jane	6:35:22	(31,457)
Swain, Emma	4:23:06	(15,512)
Swaine, Tessa	4:43:20	(20,328)
Swan, Eileen	4:30:24	(17,344)
Swan, Elaine	5:13:24	(26,025)
Swanberg, Eileen	6:25:11	(31,165)
Swann, Trudi	4:14:12	(13,308)
Swatman, Alison	3:50:57	(7,933)
Sweeney, Joanne	5:36:17	(28,662)
Sweeting, Karen	4:38:32	(19,206)
Swift, Jaine	3:25:34	(3,471)
Swift, Susan	5:54:03	(29,934)
Swithenby, Margaret	3:27:56	(3,807)
Sydenham, Carol	4:40:51	(19,716)
Syed, Huma	6:54:53	(31,831)
Syers, Lucy	4:51:38	(22,231)
Sykes, Jodie	5:43:36	(29,277)
Sykes, Louise	7:17:30	(32,054)
Sylvester, Jacqueline	4:23:10	(15,537)
Sylvester, Ruth	4:43:31	(20,382)
Symes, Natalie	4:39:15	(19,386)
Symes, Sylvia	6:12:17	(30,744)
Symonds, Karen	4:31:30	(17,616)
Szabo, Catherine	5:17:31	(26,547)
Sziler, Irene	4:51:26	(22,188)
Tabenor, Patricia	5:22:57	(27,278)
Tabor, Rosalind	3:15:06	(2,248)
Tadd, Sarah	5:50:12	(29,734)
Taddonio, Karin	6:28:06	(31,271)
Tadecicco, Louise	5:21:53	(27,136)
Tafel-Selman, Monique	4:40:05	(19,554)
Taggart, Emma	5:36:16	(28,661)
Tait, Deidre	4:47:01	(21,187)
Tait, Gillian	3:08:32	(1,551)
Tait, Samantha	7:02:58	(31,913)
Taiwo, Dele	4:34:22	(18,256)
Takaoka, Akemi	3:49:30	(7,634)
Takaoka, Matsumi	4:46:24	(21,070)
Takenami, Yoko	5:33:24	(28,411)
Talbot, Julie	4:56:39	(23,303)
Talbot, Lynn	5:03:33	(24,539)
Talbot, Nora	5:40:16	(29,014)
Talbot-Standen, Melissa	4:19:13	(14,555)
Tamsett, Nicola	5:20:41	(26,984)
Tan, Cecillia	7:15:03	(32,038)
Tan, Gien	3:14:33	(2,190)
Tang, Pin-Nee	7:31:36	(32,163)
Tanimoto, Eriko	4:13:19	(13,078)
Tanner, Louise	4:06:44	(11,637)
Tanser, Rose	5:20:53	(27,006)
Tapley, Julie	4:13:35	(13,146)
Tarrant, Teresa	5:20:30	(26,957)
Tarrant, Veronica	6:05:29	(30,476)
Tasker, Helen	4:40:18	(19,608)
Tasker, Lisa	5:10:44	(25,652)
Tawney, Anne	5:10:04	(25,561)
Taylor, Abigail	5:17:45	(26,571)
Taylor, Alison	3:53:02	(8,433)
Taylor, Andrea	4:38:03	(19,105)
Taylor, Barb	4:33:56	(18,149)
Taylor, Ceri	5:22:32	(27,219)
Taylor, Charlotte	4:35:54	(18,620)
Taylor, Cheryl	6:19:21	(30,986)
Taylor, Corinna	5:34:33	(28,526)
Taylor, Elizabeth	6:28:49	(31,298)
Taylor, Gail	3:57:35	(9,591)
Taylor, Gillian	6:17:53	(30,926)
Taylor, Guilaine	6:08:03	(30,567)
Taylor, Hannah	5:35:43	(28,614)
Taylor, Heather	4:51:22	(22,173)
Taylor, Jacqueline	6:20:57	(31,048)
Taylor, Jane	6:00:22	(30,268)
Taylor, Janet	5:06:14	(24,993)
Taylor, Janis	5:17:46	(26,574)
Taylor, Jean	3:54:19	(8,732)
Taylor, Jennifer	6:46:05	(31,647)
Taylor, Jill	5:28:59	(27,988)
Taylor, Joan	4:19:06	(14,530)
Taylor, Julie	5:08:44	(25,360)
Taylor, Karen	3:30:43	(4,282)
Taylor, Karen	5:27:27	(27,825)
Taylor, Kate	4:32:55	(17,928)
Taylor, Katharine	4:34:14	(18,220)
Taylor, Kim	4:13:25	(13,100)
Taylor, Lee	4:44:52	(20,689)
Taylor, Leila	4:21:18	(15,060)
Taylor, Lorna	4:43:14	(20,296)
Taylor, Lynda	4:41:10	(19,790)
Taylor, Lyndsey	6:35:55	(31,471)
Taylor, Mary	8:00:31	(32,256)
Taylor, Myfanwy	4:07:47	(11,867)
Taylor, Paula	5:19:13	(26,783)
Taylor, Rachel	5:15:11	(26,277)
Taylor, Rebecca	4:24:42	(15,915)
Taylor, Samantha	5:59:38	(30,247)
Taylor, Sheila	4:29:21	(17,071)
Taylor, Sophie	4:13:28	(13,116)
Taylor, Sue	5:39:25	(28,938)
Taylor, Susan	4:24:20	(15,829)
Taylor, Susan	4:54:49	(22,885)
Taylor, Susan	5:14:54	(26,232)
Taylor, Susan	6:13:33	(30,783)
Taylor, Suzy	6:12:02	(30,727)
Taylor, Tracey	5:35:40	(28,609)
Taylor-Barber, Gail	6:05:40	(30,487)
Taylor-Jones, Andrea	4:45:26	(20,829)
Teague, Celina	4:50:19	(21,926)
Teague, Peta-Ann	6:50:49	(31,740)
Teal, Sarah	4:59:51	(23,959)
Tebboth, Louise	5:17:30	(26,544)
Tedder, Karen	5:53:21	(29,897)
Tee, Sarah	5:13:25	(26,026)
Teenan, Elizabeth	5:49:31	(29,680)
Teggert, Rebecca	4:41:24	(19,848)
Telford, Katherine	5:13:58	(26,096)
Temperton, Carol	4:04:40	(11,216)
Temple, Angela	6:14:47	(30,821)
Temple, Anna	6:52:37	(31,773)
Temple, Eleanor	5:14:28	(26,170)
Templeman, Clare	4:19:56	(14,723)
Templeton, Louise	5:08:59	(25,401)
Tennant, Andrea	4:35:01	(18,402)
Tennant, Maggie	4:39:47	(19,497)
Tennant, Sarah	4:12:08	(12,795)
Terblanche, Cecilia	3:50:44	(7,894)
Terjesen, Siri	3:10:05	(1,683)
Terris, Jane	5:33:44	(28,440)
Tetley, Julia	5:36:08	(28,649)
Teunissen, Jenni	5:15:13	(26,279)
Thacker, Joanne	5:05:46	(24,930)
Thackray, Jacqueline	4:15:53	(13,722)
Thaler, Helene	4:02:10	(10,671)
Tham, Penelope	5:53:50	(29,923)
Thatcher, Janet	4:55:18	(22,977)
Thaxter, Gillian	6:25:04	(31,162)
Thaxter, Julie	6:54:47	(31,828)
Thaysen, Birgit	3:52:19	(8,271)
Theophanides, Kerry	5:31:56	(28,285)
Theron, Michelle	4:49:08	(21,655)
Thevenet-Smith, Ramona	3:14:31	(2,186)
Thistleton, Heather	4:38:03	(19,105)
Thom, Susan	4:35:23	(18,492)
Thoma Hinderling, Gabriela	4:40:08	(19,565)
Thomas, Annette	4:24:58	(15,990)
Thomas, Antoinette	3:33:45	(4,713)
Thomas, Bernadette	4:40:15	(19,591)
Thomas, Beryl	5:30:20	(28,121)
Thomas, Beverley	4:35:55	(18,625)
Thomas, Carole	5:08:11	(25,295)
Thomas, Dee	6:37:06	(31,489)
Thomas, Gail	5:25:51	(27,649)
Thomas, Gemma	4:50:27	(21,952)
Thomas, Geraldine	5:24:55	(27,524)
Thomas, Jacqueline	5:19:03	(26,763)
Thomas, Jane	4:15:28	(13,631)
Thomas, Janet	4:50:15	(21,909)
Thomas, Jeanette	3:48:44	(7,448)
Thomas, Joanne	7:13:17	(32,025)
Thomas, Julie	7:09:22	(31,985)
Thomas, Karen	6:52:19	(31,766)
Thomas, Kate	3:59:33	(10,105)
Thomas, Linda	5:14:08	(26,112)
Thomas, Liz	4:36:24	(18,744)
Thomas, Lorna	6:04:34	(30,432)
Thomas, Lucette	3:56:36	(9,346)
Thomas, Margaret	7:09:21	(31,984)
Thomas, Maxine	5:21:11	(27,047)
Thomas, Nunette	5:37:50	(28,799)
Thomas, Paula	5:44:14	(29,320)
Thomas, Selena	5:12:11	(25,851)
Thomas, Shan	4:54:35	(22,833)
Thomas, Sian	4:29:54	(17,220)
Thomas, Siobhan	4:43:05	(20,256)
Thomas, Sonia	5:20:18	(26,927)
Thomas, Sonia	6:55:15	(31,834)
Thomas, Susan	5:20:56	(27,015)
Thomas, Trudy	4:36:47	(18,833)
Thomas, Wendy	6:26:55	(31,227)
Thomas-McCormick, Susan	4:58:14	(23,633)
Thomi, Muriel	3:49:10	(7,555)
Thompson, Angela	4:14:01	(13,264)
Thompson, Anna	4:32:48	(17,898)
Thompson, Barbara	4:19:36	(14,639)
Thompson, Barbara	4:57:07	(23,404)
Thompson, Catriona	5:28:09	(27,908)
Thompson, Gillian	3:58:37	(9,862)
Thompson, Jane	3:20:20	(2,807)
Thompson, Jean	4:59:43	(23,927)
Thompson, Leslie	5:19:28	(26,827)
Thompson, Lisa	4:43:48	(20,453)
Thompson, Lorraine	4:24:34	(15,879)
Thompson, Louise	5:25:09	(27,561)
Thompson, Margaret	5:04:55	(24,782)
Thompson, Ruth	5:24:25	(27,461)
Thompson, Sharon	4:05:25	(11,379)
Thompson, Stephanie	6:52:30	(31,769)
Thompson, Vanda	4:51:04	(22,091)
Thompson, Vicky	4:55:59	(23,144)
Thompson, Victoria	4:49:25	(21,726)
Thompstone, Carol	7:33:23	(32,174)
Thomsen, Erna	5:28:11	(27,916)
Thomson, Amanda	6:31:45	(31,372)
Thomson, Catherine	6:09:45	(30,632)
Thomson, Ellen	4:16:13	(13,787)
Thomson, Jayne	7:02:05	(31,905)
Thomson, Julie	4:04:05	(11,084)
Thomson, Melanie	5:02:09	(24,335)
Thorn, Julia	3:46:51	(7,093)
Thorn, Penny	3:39:50	(5,754)
Thornburgh, Zoe	3:57:26	(9,564)
Thorne, Brenda	4:19:08	(14,538)
Thorne, Catherine	5:27:09	(27,797)
Thorne, Felicity	4:39:28	(19,434)
Thorne, Julia	5:51:15	(29,796)
Thorner, Sophie	5:33:09	(28,385)
Thornton, Avril	3:57:01	(9,461)
Thornton, Beth	4:50:34	(21,979)
Thornton, Rebecca	4:30:39	(17,402)
Thorogood, Jane	5:46:37	(29,472)
Thorogood, Wendy	5:14:17	(26,138)
Thorp, Amanda	5:22:43	(27,239)
Thorp, Carole	5:49:36	(29,689)
Thorp, Catherine	4:33:46	(18,108)
Thorrout, Françoise	3:20:34	(2,834)
Thubron, Julia	4:26:36	(16,383)
Thurlow, Lisa	4:19:05	(14,525)
Thurlow, Marcelle	6:04:19	(30,424)
Thurman, Alison	3:47:46	(7,274)
Thurnham, Rawewan	5:09:27	(25,468)
Thurston, Lorraine	4:16:31	(13,860)
Thurston, Nikki	4:28:19	(16,794)
Tibbott, Catherine	5:23:39	(27,364)
Tidey, Paula	4:08:31	(12,014)
Tier, Lindsey	5:05:18	(24,840)
Tighe, Julie	5:20:27	(26,947)
Tilbury, Margaret	4:59:28	(23,880)
Tiley, Michelle	3:48:46	(7,457)
Tiley-Phillips, Shirl	4:13:25	(13,100)
Tilley, Elaine	4:27:39	(16,638)
Tilley, Lisa	5:20:51	(27,004)
Tillotson, Eleanor	3:58:12	(9,755)

Von Fintel, Nichola	4:13:01	(13,008)
Von Werne, Elizabeth	6:38:45	(31,518)
Vonderhagen, Ute	4:57:57	(23,571)
Vonk-Verkerk, Margreet	3:43:28	(6,448)
Voss, Barbara	7:24:58	(32,108)
Vyas, Seema	4:27:06	(16,497)
Wacey, Ruth	5:23:51	(27,390)
Waddell, Susan	4:49:10	(21,667)
Wade, Angela	3:43:20	(6,431)
Wade, Claire	4:30:16	(17,302)
Wade, Jane	5:00:44	(24,113)
Wade, Kristine	4:12:39	(12,929)
Wade, Susan	6:30:09	(31,333)
Wadforth, Catherine	3:42:38	(6,280)
Wagjiani, Geeta	5:09:54	(25,527)
Wagner, Dawn	3:55:19	(8,999)
Wagner, Priya	4:36:10	(18,682)
Wagstaff, Nina	4:08:21	(11,969)
Wain, Barbara	6:46:06	(31,648)
Wainnan, Antonia	4:34:33	(18,296)
Wait, Debra	4:06:42	(11,625)
Waite, Debra	4:38:30	(19,198)
Waite, Nicola	5:10:15	(25,590)
Wakamura, Mineko	5:43:05	(29,246)
Wake, Nina	4:31:44	(17,676)
Wakefield, Dorothy	7:06:38	(31,952)
Wakelam, Julie	5:16:59	(26,478)
Wakelin, Emma	6:26:41	(31,222)
Wakelin, Sonia	4:36:59	(18,872)
Wakeling, Maureen	4:54:57	(22,910)
Wakely, Christine	6:43:01	(31,591)
Waldman, Louise	3:19:47	(2,733)
Waldram, Louise	4:14:58	(13,500)
Waldschmidt, Susanne	5:43:10	(29,254)
Walgate, Hannah	4:42:36	(20,134)
Walker, Alison	3:46:59	(7,121)
Walker, Allison	4:46:06	(20,992)
Walker, Angela	3:11:49	(1,838)
Walker, Corinna	4:48:26	(21,524)
Walker, Dale	4:56:35	(23,283)
Walker, Denise	4:00:05	(10,240)
Walker, Donna	5:49:49	(29,701)
Walker, Hilary	3:22:23	(3,034)
Walker, Jean	4:37:39	(19,009)
Walker, Jeanette	4:40:50	(19,712)
Walker, Jenny	4:05:38	(11,423)
Walker, Julia	3:57:55	(9,685)
Walker, Julie	6:31:51	(31,376)
Walker, Katherine	5:35:26	(28,590)
Walker, Margaret	5:58:18	(30,176)
Walker, Martina	4:08:51	(12,098)
Walker, Michelle	6:43:09	(31,596)
Walker, Naomi	3:50:44	(7,894)
Walker, Pauline	4:55:39	(23,065)
Walker, Rachel	6:13:01	(30,769)
Walker, Susan	4:47:00	(21,184)
Walker, Tracey	3:28:47	(3,966)
Walklate, Anna	4:13:04	(13,019)
Wall, Eileen	4:41:42	(19,919)
Wall, Gillian	6:20:21	(31,026)
Wall, Michala	4:34:11	(18,209)
Wallace, Donna	5:31:48	(28,262)
Wallace, Joanne	5:03:47	(24,589)
Wallace, Sally	4:04:22	(11,150)
Waller, Ciara	4:56:29	(23,255)
Waller, Kathleen	4:32:32	(17,840)
Waller, Teresa	5:47:30	(29,534)
Walls, Elizabeth	3:13:51	(2,107)
Walmsley, Elsie	5:03:09	(24,483)
Walmsley, Suzie	4:37:13	(18,925)
Walpole, Mary	4:52:14	(22,348)
Walsh, Brigid	3:58:20	(9,793)
Walsh, Eleanor	4:50:27	(21,952)
Walsh, Jacqueline	6:11:19	(30,702)
Walsh, Rebecca	4:47:02	(21,189)
Walsh, Victoria	5:25:10	(27,566)
Walter, Geraldine	4:58:20	(23,656)
Walter, Louise	4:50:37	(21,995)
Walters, Abigail	4:47:32	(21,304)
Walters, Gail	3:31:18	(4,381)
Walters, Jennifer	3:48:45	(7,453)
Walton, Deborah	7:12:38	(32,019)
Walton, Hilary	4:54:18	(22,770)
Walton, Iona	4:03:02	(10,850)
Walton, Laura	4:34:13	(18,216)
Walton, Sara	5:30:15	(28,106)
Wan, Sue-Yen	4:01:16	(10,486)
Wanzek, Hildegard	4:56:02	(23,152)
Waple, Karen	3:56:54	(9,422)
Warboys, Nickie	4:47:47	(21,368)
Ward, Alexandra	6:19:46	(31,008)
Ward, Annette	3:41:12	(5,988)
Ward, Charlotte	4:54:39	(22,849)
Ward, Christine	6:07:13	(30,537)
Ward, Elizabeth	3:56:29	(9,313)
Ward, Gayle	6:23:41	(31,127)
Ward, Helen	5:40:32	(29,036)
Ward, Jane	3:34:50	(4,883)
Ward, Katie	5:24:54	(27,520)
Ward, Lydia	5:54:54	(29,991)
Ward, Mandy	4:35:58	(18,642)
Ward, Maria	5:19:56	(26,877)
Ward, Maxine	4:09:43	(12,277)
Ward, Nicola	4:21:02	(14,988)
Ward, Stella	4:11:53	(12,735)
Ward, Susan	4:34:25	(18,271)
Ward, Yolanda	4:22:53	(15,466)
Warden, Jacqueline	6:30:03	(31,329)
Wardle, Andrea	3:25:41	(3,491)
Ward-Rotherham, Julie	5:33:24	(28,411)
Ward-Wyatt, Anne	6:49:53	(31,716)
Waring, Gabrielle	3:17:06	(2,438)
Waring, Janet	5:06:34	(25,028)
Warman, Kirsty	5:28:09	(27,908)
Warmino, Annette	3:54:45	(8,850)
Warne, Sharon	4:05:22	(11,366)
Warner, Anne	4:51:56	(22,297)
Warner, Julie	3:30:10	(4,196)
Warner, Pauline	4:00:37	(10,348)
Warrell, Althea	6:04:46	(30,445)
Warren, Andrea	4:51:03	(22,083)
Warren, Gillian	4:47:37	(21,322)
Warren, Julie	5:40:43	(29,057)
Warren, Karen	6:10:59	(30,690)
Warren, Kate	4:14:39	(13,413)
Warren, Tracey	5:29:28	(28,033)
Warrick, Stephanie	4:40:27	(19,643)
Warrington, Frances	4:22:30	(15,367)
Warville, Colleen	6:19:23	(30,987)
Wash, Zoe	5:25:53	(27,651)
Wassell, Julie	4:00:54	(10,407)
Watari, Harumi	5:06:13	(24,988)
Watchorn-Rice, Ruth	3:17:57	(2,543)
Waterfield, Julie	7:08:38	(31,978)
Waters, Bel	3:23:19	(3,150)
Waters, Esther	4:26:46	(16,421)
Wates, Melanie	4:03:14	(10,891)
Watkin, Karen	3:22:47	(3,085)
Watkins, Isobel	4:54:44	(22,872)
Watkins, Jill	6:19:37	(31,000)
Watkinson, Kenneth	4:42:41	(20,154)
Watling, Andrea	3:39:50	(5,754)
Watling, Azar	4:24:26	(15,850)
Watson, Alicia	3:51:17	(8,025)
Watson, Claire	4:29:41	(17,159)
Watson, Gill	4:33:24	(18,032)
Watson, Gytha	4:56:34	(23,280)
Watson, Heather	4:56:09	(23,182)
Watson, Irene	5:39:22	(28,929)
Watson, Jacqui	3:19:36	(2,710)
Watson, Jane	5:11:54	(25,812)
Watson, Jane	6:04:15	(30,420)
Watson, Lindsey	6:58:31	(31,876)
Watson, Louise	2:48:11	(340)
Watson, Lucy	3:35:34	(5,007)
Watson, Melanie	4:25:58	(16,242)
Watson, Pilar	5:32:46	(28,353)
Watson, Stephanie	4:35:07	(18,417)
Watson, Sue	4:17:44	(14,189)
Watson, Susan	7:07:07	(31,958)
Watson, Tracey	5:31:55	(28,281)
Watt, Caroline	3:51:07	(7,981)
Watt, Jacqueline	3:37:45	(5,376)
Watt, Janet	4:40:31	(19,654)
Watt, Louise	5:33:22	(28,408)
Watterson, Amanda	5:04:46	(24,752)
Watts, Gemma	3:50:48	(7,908)
Watts, Joanne	7:51:08	(32,234)
Waugh, Dawn	3:43:33	(6,455)
Way, Camilla	4:31:01	(17,502)
Way, Kate	4:26:44	(16,413)
Waylen, Kate	3:45:18	(6,788)
Weald, Caroline	5:18:26	(26,687)
Webb, Clair	4:33:23	(18,028)
Webb, Rose	4:26:10	(16,289)
Webb, Samantha	5:10:48	(25,663)
Webb, Sarah	8:07:16	(32,264)
Webb, Susan	4:55:29	(23,027)
Webber, Margaret	6:45:52	(31,643)
Webber, Michelle	5:45:00	(29,369)
Webster, Elizabeth	4:21:39	(15,143)
Webster, Evelyn	3:24:09	(3,273)
Webster, Katy	3:36:18	(5,115)
Webster, Lucinda	5:34:18	(28,506)
Webster, Sally	3:57:34	(9,590)
Webster, Serena	3:28:14	(3,854)
Weck, Anne	5:33:09	(28,385)
Weddell, Sally	5:47:58	(29,572)
Weeden, Samantha	4:57:56	(23,568)
Weekes, Donna	5:26:23	(27,722)
Weekes, Lisa	4:53:35	(22,635)
Weeks, Angela	5:30:31	(28,140)
Wegrzynski, Christina	5:22:59	(27,284)
Weinstein, Gail	6:56:47	(31,855)
Weir, Tracy	5:06:20	(24,998)
Weis, Jutta	4:03:47	(11,007)
Weisberg, Gerri	6:31:35	(31,366)
Weiss, Victoria	4:41:33	(19,882)
Welbourne, Jacqueline	5:02:10	(24,341)
Welch, Claire	4:55:23	(22,999)
Welch, Emma	3:18:52	(2,643)
Welch, Lucy	3:24:25	(3,320)
Welch, Margaret	7:07:20	(31,968)
Welford, Thérèse	6:08:00	(30,566)
Wells, Jackie	4:04:54	(11,270)
Wells, Jane	4:55:44	(23,091)
Wells, Jane	5:49:01	(29,640)
Wells, Naomi	5:53:09	(29,885)
Wells, Patricia	4:49:10	(21,667)
Wellsman, Jennifer	5:29:29	(28,036)
Welsby, Gillian	7:20:39	(32,071)
Welsh, Ann	4:51:26	(22,188)
Wemyss, Sarah	4:46:30	(21,094)
Wemyss, Sarah	5:41:39	(29,132)
Wenman, Debbie	3:25:46	(3,504)
Wersant, Marianne	4:44:37	(20,637)
Wescombe, Lisa	5:29:12	(28,005)
Wesley-Smith, Jayne	5:27:51	(27,873)
Wessar, Miriam	4:06:53	(11,667)
West, Catherine	4:39:43	(19,481)
West, Maureen	5:49:31	(29,680)
West, Nikki	5:24:22	(27,457)
Westbrook, Karen	4:50:38	(21,997)
Westcott, Nicola	5:09:57	(25,532)
Westhorp, Carol	5:08:15	(25,306)
Westlake, Samantha	3:27:41	(3,767)
Weston, Denise	4:08:13	(11,942)
Weston, Kathleen	5:06:22	(25,004)
Wetherall, Suzanne	4:41:45	(19,931)
Wetton, Adrienne	4:02:20	(10,703)
Wetzler, Andrea	4:08:34	(12,029)
Wharmby, Sally	3:42:01	(6,153)
Whatling, Kerry	4:14:22	(13,349)
Wheatley, Andrée	4:06:27	(11,583)
Wheatley, Angela	4:14:47	(13,445)
Wheatley, Kathryn	4:34:24	(18,266)
Wheeler, Adelle	5:05:17	(24,836)
Wheeler, Jennifer	5:03:48	(24,592)
Wheeler, Joanne	5:13:55	(26,092)
Wherry, Sharon	4:15:40	(13,668)
Whetton, Lydia	3:44:41	(6,664)
Whiley, Lesley	3:04:03	(1,186)
Whinney, Christine	4:27:07	(16,502)
Whitaker, Amelia	5:24:17	(27,449)
Whitaker, Jo	6:06:51	(30,525)
White, Alison	3:39:11	(5,626)
White, Angela	3:29:29	(4,090)
White, Carole	4:28:57	(16,982)
White, Caroline	3:30:22	(4,226)

White, Christine	5:02:10 (24,341)	
White, Elaine	5:02:42 (24,419)	
White, Elspeth	5:37:06 (28,746)	
White, Emily	5:10:32 (25,626)	
White, Hannah	6:08:49 (30,599)	
White, Helen	3:20:18 (2,803)	
White, Jeanette	4:25:44 (16,186)	
White, Jenny	4:32:22 (17,807)	
White, Joan	4:47:16 (21,237)	
White, Joanna	6:14:20 (30,804)	
White, Johanna	4:20:47 (14,923)	
White, Kate	4:45:06 (20,743)	
White, Katy	6:20:52 (31,044)	
White, Kirsty	6:09:57 (30,637)	
White, Natalie	4:40:17 (19,599)	
White, Nicola	6:26:19 (31,216)	
White, Nuala	4:03:15 (10,899)	
White, Pamela	4:36:35 (18,785)	
White, Pauline	3:49:10 (7,555)	
White, Ruth	3:51:09 (7,995)	
White, Sarah	4:13:28 (13,116)	
White, Sarah	5:36:30 (28,683)	
White, Suzanne	3:34:59 (4,908)	
White, Suzanne	4:51:07 (22,108)	
White, Una	5:13:07 (25,988)	
Whitefield, Lynda	5:29:17 (28,016)	
Whitehouse, Danielle	5:00:21 (24,044)	
Whitelegg, Linda	3:39:10 (5,623)	
Whiteley, Jill	3:24:40 (3,354)	
Whiteman, Victoria	4:30:44 (17,429)	
Whiter, Linda	4:40:55 (19,732)	
Whiteside, Helen	4:25:58 (16,242)	
Whitfield, Christine	3:19:15 (2,676)	
Whitley, Patricia	4:22:06 (15,265)	
Whitney, Carmen	6:49:05 (31,696)	
Whitney, Linda	5:07:23 (25,156)	
Whittaker, Geraldine	4:58:29 (23,696)	
Whittaker, Rachel	4:55:30 (23,028)	
Whittaker, Rosemary	4:52:16 (22,352)	
Whittaker, Susan	6:01:00 (30,295)	
Whittall, Chris	7:33:22 (32,173)	
Whittall, Liz	6:17:43 (30,911)	
Whittenbury, Alison	4:34:14 (18,220)	
Whittingham, Debra	4:10:31 (12,468)	
Whittington, Ruth	4:26:11 (16,293)	
Whittle, Sarah	5:48:22 (29,596)	
Whittle, Tracy	5:51:18 (29,799)	
Whitworth, Sarah	5:33:46 (28,447)	
Whyment, Martin	4:05:33 (11,410)	
Whyte, Geraldine	5:10:24 (25,608)	
Whyte, Sarah	4:58:17 (23,645)	
Wickenden, Ann	4:31:14 (17,553)	
Wickens, Sally	5:13:05 (25,984)	
Wicklow, Tania	4:09:59 (12,349)	
Wicks, Shirley	5:04:38 (24,721)	
Wiggett, Nicola	4:46:18 (21,045)	
Wiggins, Tamara	3:55:33 (9,062)	
Wigglesworth, Patricia	5:27:51 (27,873)	
Wigley, Bibiana	5:20:27 (26,947)	
Wilcock, Joanna	4:49:47 (21,820)	
Wilcock, Marie	5:22:05 (27,150)	
Wilcock, Sarah	5:33:30 (28,421)	
Wild, Elizabeth	3:56:42 (9,375)	
Wild, Jane	3:58:40 (9,877)	
Wild, Lisa	5:25:06 (27,553)	
Wild, Meg	3:45:13 (6,777)	
Wild, Sarah	4:38:37 (19,233)	
Wild, Stephanie	3:56:09 (9,225)	
Wiles, Juliette	4:38:31 (19,200)	
Wiliams, Ceri	6:39:14 (31,527)	
Wiliams, Joanna	4:05:58 (11,498)	
Wiliams, Julie	4:24:01 (15,756)	
Wilkes, Gay	5:43:43 (29,284)	
Wilkes, Victorian	4:24:00 (15,751)	
Wilkins, Carolyn	4:49:16 (21,694)	
Wilkinson, Carolyn	3:39:35 (5,713)	
Wilkinson, Dawn	4:13:40 (13,167)	
Wilkinson, Joy	3:40:02 (5,793)	
Wilkinson, Kristy	4:47:37 (21,322)	
Wilkinson, Lisa	3:40:24 (5,857)	
Wilkinson, Philip	4:27:22 (16,563)	
Willcox, Rebecca	4:35:28 (18,510)	
Willett, Annie	4:09:48 (12,301)	

Willett, Victoria	4:45:21 (20,809)	
Willetts, Stephanie	7:45:36 (32,225)	
Willfratt, Louise	5:04:19 (24,680)	
Williams, Alice	4:52:52 (22,477)	
Williams, Amber	3:36:50 (5,199)	
Williams, Andrea	5:49:50 (29,703)	
Williams, Angharad	6:45:25 (31,627)	
Williams, Annette	5:48:24 (29,600)	
Williams, Catherine	4:05:18 (11,351)	
Williams, Cecelia	5:03:03 (24,464)	
Williams, Cherry	4:54:37 (22,841)	
Williams, Debbie	5:48:53 (29,628)	
Williams, Diana	4:46:28 (21,085)	
Williams, Ellie	5:06:47 (25,073)	
Williams, Esta	3:50:57 (7,933)	
Williams, Esther	3:34:17 (4,791)	
Williams, Frances	3:33:44 (4,710)	
Williams, Gwenllian	5:08:17 (25,310)	
Williams, Gwenndolyn	5:45:23 (29,396)	
Williams, Helen	4:32:00 (17,730)	
Williams, Hilary	4:38:47 (19,278)	
Williams, Jackie	3:41:45 (6,101)	
Williams, Jacqueline	4:12:11 (12,813)	
Williams, Jane	4:31:40 (17,663)	
Williams, Jennifer	4:47:30 (21,298)	
Williams, Jenny	5:42:04 (29,171)	
Williams, Jo	4:35:09 (18,431)	
Williams, Karen	5:27:36 (27,849)	
Williams, Kate	5:59:23 (30,232)	
Williams, Laura	6:24:25 (31,143)	
Williams, Linda	5:34:25 (28,519)	
Williams, Madeleine	4:44:36 (20,633)	
Williams, Nicki	5:04:05 (24,649)	
Williams, Nina	4:49:28 (21,743)	
Williams, Olwen	5:22:05 (27,150)	
Williams, Paula	5:23:37 (27,360)	
Williams, Pauline	6:15:43 (30,849)	
Williams, Rachel	4:34:03 (18,176)	
Williams, Rachel	6:04:00 (30,410)	
Williams, Rochelle	4:09:24 (12,208)	
Williams, Sally	5:28:20 (27,924)	
Williams, Sarah	3:08:56 (1,581)	
Williams, Sarah	5:20:22 (26,933)	
Williams, Sarah	6:12:00 (30,726)	
Williams, Shirley	5:05:14 (24,832)	
Williams, Sian	5:48:47 (29,620)	
Williams, Stella	4:26:45 (16,417)	
Williams, Teresa	3:38:37 (5,521)	
Williams, Tracey	4:08:33 (12,024)	
Williams, Trudi	5:52:32 (29,854)	
Williams, Victoria	5:05:28 (24,874)	
Williams, Wendy	6:12:37 (30,754)	
Williamson, Anna	4:28:38 (16,894)	
Williamson, Hazel	4:35:58 (18,642)	
Williamson, Julia	5:27:54 (27,883)	
Williamson, Justine	4:23:04 (15,506)	
Williamson, Kate	3:38:16 (5,456)	
Williamson, Maria	5:13:30 (26,042)	
Williamson, Paula	4:45:53 (20,934)	
Williamson, Verleta	4:57:23 (23,456)	
Williamson-North, Hayley	4:29:50 (17,203)	
Williams-Royal, Deborah	5:10:32 (25,626)	
Willis, Christine	4:40:37 (19,670)	
Willis, Dawn	3:53:04 (8,442)	
Willis, Elizabeth	3:53:41 (8,586)	
Willis, Elizabeth	5:32:59 (28,373)	
Willis, Elizabeth	8:11:10 (32,268)	
Willis, Harriet	4:17:15 (14,045)	
Willis, Katherine	4:20:31 (14,873)	
Willis, Kay	4:39:50 (19,508)	
Willis, Linda	5:58:47 (30,190)	
Willmore, Maureen	6:43:03 (31,593)	
Willmott, Denise	4:57:28 (23,474)	
Willott, Carys	4:19:12 (14,551)	
Wills, Belinda	6:44:51 (31,618)	
Wills, Romilly	3:38:02 (5,421)	
Wills, Ruth	5:34:17 (28,505)	
Willson, Caroline	4:03:57 (11,048)	
Willson, Penny	3:09:01 (1,587)	
Wilson, Amy	6:33:06 (31,401)	
Wilson, Anita	4:50:46 (22,025)	
Wilson, Anne	3:33:13 (4,635)	
Wilson, Beverley	3:29:23 (4,062)	

Wilson, Carli	5:31:32 (28,247)	
Wilson, Danniele	5:41:51 (29,147)	
Wilson, Denise	6:49:26 (31,700)	
Wilson, Faye	4:05:01 (11,294)	
Wilson, Freda	4:37:23 (18,962)	
Wilson, Hazel	5:53:36 (29,913)	
Wilson, Heidi	3:23:31 (3,181)	
Wilson, Heidi	5:52:43 (29,870)	
Wilson, Helen	5:52:29 (29,852)	
Wilson, Irene	5:45:23 (29,396)	
Wilson, Katie	4:00:49 (10,390)	
Wilson, Lucinda	4:00:38 (10,355)	
Wilson, Mandy	4:15:02 (13,520)	
Wilson, Margaret	5:18:56 (26,748)	
Wilson, Mary	5:28:58 (27,983)	
Wilson, Michelle	4:55:24 (23,003)	
Wilson, Nicola	5:15:46 (26,352)	
Wilson, Rachel	5:23:08 (27,305)	
Wilson, Susan	5:48:46 (29,618)	
Wilson, Tabitha	6:25:11 (31,165)	
Wilson, Tanya	7:05:54 (31,938)	
Wilson, Thea	4:10:59 (12,539)	
Wilson, Tina	3:46:54 (7,103)	
Wilton, Jenny	4:16:42 (13,905)	
Wilyman, Lisa	3:01:34 (1,028)	
Wimble, Jane	4:37:11 (18,919)	
Winder, Clare	5:55:09 (30,009)	
Winder, Rachel	4:13:57 (13,244)	
Winders, Catherine	4:28:27 (16,839)	
Windsor, Claire	5:36:12 (28,654)	
Winfield, Alyson	5:12:37 (25,923)	
Wing, Julie	5:07:07 (25,122)	
Wing, Rebecca	4:14:19 (13,333)	
Wingate, Katherine	5:48:55 (29,632)	
Wingfield, Joan	3:28:42 (3,943)	
Winhede, Janne	7:00:25 (31,894)	
Winkworth, Louise	5:00:44 (24,113)	
Winn, Kate	4:52:28 (22,390)	
Winslow, Helen	4:51:03 (22,083)	
Winstanley, Chantelle	3:37:01 (5,235)	
Winstanley, Hazel	5:47:01 (29,492)	
Winstanley, Julie	5:23:50 (27,388)	
Winter, Henriette	4:57:33 (23,490)	
Winter, Julie	4:54:21 (22,779)	
Winter, Maureen	5:18:27 (26,692)	
Winter, Sara-Jane	5:47:48 (29,562)	
Winter, Suzanne	5:31:14 (28,218)	
Winterburn, Ann	4:47:58 (21,419)	
Winterhalder, Fiona	3:55:35 (9,070)	
Winterstein, Nadia	4:45:33 (20,858)	
Winton, Laura	5:38:35 (28,864)	
Wirk, Ravinder	4:31:24 (17,592)	
Wirth, Louise	4:25:56 (16,238)	
Wiscombe, Rebecca	3:58:45 (9,901)	
Wise, Anne	5:26:11 (27,698)	
Wise, Jan	6:36:35 (31,485)	
Wise, Kirstie	4:36:24 (18,744)	
Witham, Helen	3:39:01 (5,603)	
Witherden, Louise	4:43:27 (20,363)	
Withers, Alison	4:38:11 (19,127)	
Withers, Wendy	6:19:10 (30,979)	
Withey, Sarah	4:33:41 (18,094)	
Withill, Rachel	6:10:56 (30,685)	
Witty, Rebecca	4:58:40 (23,727)	
Wixley, Judith	3:37:37 (5,349)	
Woffinden, Janet	5:20:13 (26,917)	
Wold, Ellen	4:49:09 (21,662)	
Wolf, Christine	4:32:54 (17,924)	
Wolf, Nicola	5:32:16 (28,312)	
Wolfe, Vicky	4:45:21 (20,809)	
Wollett, Susan	5:39:25 (28,938)	
Wolter, Emma	5:25:15 (27,585)	
Wolverson, Alexandra	7:00:06 (31,890)	
Wong, Elaine	3:49:27 (7,621)	
Wong-Boutcher, Lin	5:08:19 (25,315)	
Wonnacott, Ann	4:56:50 (23,347)	
Wood, Amanda	4:19:28 (14,609)	
Wood, Joanna	5:00:35 (24,083)	
Wood, Kathryn	6:50:56 (31,742)	
Wood, Lucy	4:33:57 (18,153)	
Wood, Marlene	5:14:40 (26,199)	
Wood, Maryon	6:42:20 (31,577)	
Wood, Nicola	3:56:41 (9,372)	

Wood, Patricia 5:20:44 (26,990)
Wood, Pauline 5:09:18 (25,446)
Wood, Polly.................... 4:56:43 (23,320)
Wood, Rachel 4:16:08 (13,772)
Wood, Rebecca 4:37:05 (18,899)
Wood, Ruth 3:50:03 (7,743)
Wood, Sally 3:46:11 (6,969)
Wood, Sarah 4:46:03 (20,977)
Wood, Sarah 6:16:45 (30,887)
Wood, Sonia 5:30:53 (28,183)
Wood, Wendy 4:26:35 (16,375)
Woodbridge, Barbara.................... 5:55:38 (30,024)
Woodbridge, Caroline 4:28:07 (16,740)
Woodcock, Davina 4:36:38 (18,793)
Woodcock, Diane 6:27:28 (31,244)
Woodcock, Lynnette 4:39:03 (19,331)
Woodcock, Rachel.................... 3:42:10 (6,182)
Woodham, Helene 5:04:31 (24,708)
Woodham, Karen 7:16:58 (32,052)
Woodhams, Emma 4:13:09 (13,037)
Woodhouse, Jenny 4:45:40 (20,882)
Woodhouse, Wendy 3:46:33 (7,045)
Woodruff, Jane 6:16:56 (30,891)
Woods, Natalie 5:21:50 (27,129)
Woods, Pauline 3:54:28 (8,771)
Woods, Tracy 4:44:24 (20,596)
Woodward, Barbara 4:47:34 (21,310)
Woodward, Clare 4:37:27 (18,972)
Woodward, Genevieve.................... 4:48:26 (21,524)
Woodward, Marion 5:44:12 (29,315)
Woodward, Monica 4:23:35 (15,635)
Woodward, Patricia 5:43:07 (29,251)
Woodward, Zoe 3:31:55 (4,460)
Woolford, Elizabeth 5:14:41 (26,200)
Wooller, Diane.................... 3:57:56 (9,690)
Woolley, Gillian 3:36:29 (5,139)
Woolsey, Amy 5:20:34 (26,965)
Wootton, Jody.................... 3:58:18 (9,782)
Wootton, Zoe.................... 4:43:13 (20,292)
Worden, Wendy 5:23:14 (27,316)
Worf, Helen 5:54:53 (29,990)
Workman, Hayley.................... 4:58:27 (23,687)
Worley, Charlotte 4:48:40 (21,568)
Worley, Joanne.................... 4:34:56 (18,380)
Worrall, Shirley.................... 3:59:53 (10,197)
Worrall, Vivienne 4:05:42 (11,433)
Worrell, Lisa 5:42:48 (29,229)
Worth, Maria 4:07:12 (11,737)
Worthy, Diana.................... 4:06:12 (11,537)
Worts, Sarah 4:54:33 (22,823)
Wray, Antonia 4:46:04 (20,982)
Wray, Frances.................... 4:30:22 (17,328)
Wrench, Carol 7:27:13 (32,131)
Wright, Adele 4:28:10 (16,756)
Wright, Alexandra.................... 4:09:55 (12,329)
Wright, Charlotte 4:44:09 (20,527)
Wright, Esther 4:54:59 (22,917)
Wright, Francesca.................... 4:31:06 (17,525)
Wright, Geraldine 4:51:02 (22,079)
Wright, Hayley.................... 5:07:12 (25,130)
Wright, Helen.................... 4:05:49 (11,461)
Wright, Helen.................... 4:36:25 (18,750)
Wright, Helen.................... 4:47:57 (21,412)
Wright, Katie 4:43:15 (20,303)
Wright, Laura 4:29:42 (17,162)
Wright, Laura 5:13:56 (26,093)
Wright, Linda 4:25:14 (16,067)
Wright, Linda 6:28:45 (31,296)
Wright, Lisa 5:37:55 (28,804)
Wright, Sandra 5:56:50 (30,091)
Wright, Sandy 6:04:11 (30,416)
Wright, Suzanne.................... 4:32:39 (17,868)
Wright, Tracey 4:56:46 (23,329)
Wright, Vanessa 5:09:57 (25,532)
Wyatt, Helen.................... 5:17:59 (26,607)
Wyatt, Victoria.................... 4:05:14 (11,339)
Wykes-Dart, Carole.................... 4:24:38 (15,897)
Wylie, Linda 4:03:33 (10,957)
Wylie, Penny 3:38:12 (5,442)
Wyllie, Denise 5:02:59 (24,454)
Wyllie, Susan.................... 4:58:13 (23,629)
Wyngard, Clare.................... 3:24:41 (3,356)
Wyn-Jones, Ellen 5:44:08 (29,312)

Wynn, Greer.................... 4:07:50 (11,879)
Wynne, Anna.................... 4:11:14 (12,584)
Wynne, Catherine 5:03:34 (24,543)
Yallop, Julie.................... 4:04:38 (11,207)
Yamashita, Minobu.................... 5:42:19 (29,194)
Yarrow, Carol 3:33:49 (4,720)
Yarrow, Joanna.................... 4:55:15 (22,965)
Yarworth, Philippa 4:52:24 (22,376)
Yate, Gina 4:23:22 (15,583)
Yates, Alyson 4:44:38 (20,644)
Yates, Dorothea 4:55:41 (23,074)
Yates, Gill 4:29:03 (17,004)
Yates, Susan.................... 6:20:55 (31,047)
Yates, Vihara 5:31:34 (28,248)
Yearley, Annette 4:18:34 (14,380)
Yeates, Julie.................... 3:19:59 (2,758)
Yee, Orlena 4:28:01 (16,708)
Yendley, Susan 3:34:36 (4,852)
Yeoman, Helen 4:54:50 (22,890)
Yeomans, Debra.................... 4:18:40 (14,412)
Yeomans, Melanie 5:34:10 (28,495)
Yerby, Emma 5:01:18 (24,205)
Yerkey, Alison.................... 5:00:37 (24,097)
Yerkey, Jennifer 5:00:37 (24,097)
Yeung, Yuet 4:35:43 (18,565)
Yevko, Nicola 3:13:53 (2,114)
Yong, Gladys 3:52:04 (8,213)
York, Marie 3:43:48 (6,506)
Youds, Sarah 4:19:12 (14,551)
Youle, Joanne.................... 4:46:13 (21,022)
Young, Alan 4:14:40 (13,416)
Young, Angela 4:45:31 (20,851)
Young, Helen.................... 6:10:40 (30,672)
Young, Jane.................... 3:41:16 (6,000)
Young, Joanna.................... 5:00:11 (24,009)
Young, Lorna 4:44:14 (20,554)
Young, Lucy 4:03:44 (10,992)
Young, Melanie.................... 5:40:42 (29,056)
Young, Sarah.................... 4:01:50 (10,607)
Young, Sinead.................... 5:34:43 (28,531)
Young, Stephanie 5:13:16 (26,009)
Young, Sue.................... 6:04:13 (30,417)
Young, Yvonne.................... 5:28:28 (27,939)
Younie, Louise.................... 4:52:39 (22,431)
Yoxall, Karen 4:21:02 (14,988)
Yuen, Bo.................... 4:18:36 (14,392)
Yuill, Chris 4:20:39 (14,897)
Yule, Helen 2:59:37 (911)
Yull, Kerry 4:48:23 (21,515)
Zamparo, Doretta.................... 4:35:21 (18,483)
Zandigiacomo, Margherita.................... 4:37:41 (19,016)
Zanetti, Lara 4:04:46 (11,243)
Zeeck, Jennifer 4:12:55 (12,987)
Zeller, Ilse 4:16:19 (13,809)
Zeolla, Antonina 4:43:16 (20,309)
Zielinski, Lori 4:31:46 (17,682)
Zimmermann, Ursula 4:58:58 (23,792)
Zitman, Norma.................... 5:14:12 (26,120)
Zolliner, Antonia 4:00:38 (10,355)
Zona, Eleonora.................... 4:25:49 (16,205)
Zouppas, Margarite.................... 4:52:34 (22,407)
Zousko, Larissa.................... 2:28:05 (52)
Zuber, Julita.................... 5:06:41 (25,049)
Zulver, Allyn.................... 3:51:17 (8,025)
Zweekhorst-Ijdo, Wilma.................... 3:58:14 (9,764)

WHEELCHAIR ENTRANTS

Abrutat, David 2:46:55 (36)
Allen, Geoff 2:22:15 (32)
Andrews, Steve 3:07:57 (40)
Armstrong, Martin 2:49:13 (37)
Blichfeldt, Ebbe 1:52:40 (10)
Brennan, Deborah 2:17:32 (29)
Brogan, Chris 3:18:27 (42)
Cassell, Ric 3:07:24 (39)
Cheek, Andrew.................... 2:03:52 (16)
Craig, Paula 2:06:54 (24)
Derwin, Steve.................... 3:03:01 (38)
Erwin, Darrell.................... 2:19:32 (30)
Forde, Jerry.................... 3:15:44 (41)
Grey-Thompson, Tanni.................... 2:04:54 (19)
Hallam, James 2:15:18 (26)
Hanks, John 2:06:39 (22)

Herriot, Kenny 1:45:01 (7)
Holding, David.................... 1:46:20 (8)
Hunt, Paul 2:06:37 (21)
Hussain, Iftakhar.................... 2:31:17 (34)
Janthon, Ekkachai.................... 2:02:24 (15)

Jeannot, Joel.................... 1:32:02 (1)

Joel Jeannot is a French athlete (born 23 September 1965) in Martinique. In the 2004 Summer Paralympics, in Athens, he took gold in the 10,000m race and silver in the 4 × 400m relay. Four years earlier, at the 2000 Paralympics in Sydney he won a gold medal in the 4 × 400m relay. He was involved in an accident at the age of 25; a truck broke his back and paralysed him from the waist down. He decided that sport would help his rehabilitation. In 2003 Joel Jeannot beat David Weir for the London title and took three minutes off the course record, winning in 1:32:02 – just one week after he had won the Paris Marathon.

Le Gouic, Philippe 1:59:21 (11)
Lemeunier, Denis.................... 1:34:50 (3)
Leray, Gregory.................... 2:00:48 (12)
Nunnari, Paul 1:43:07 (6)
O'Connor, Gerald 2:06:46 (23)
Papworth, Kevin 1:46:49 (9)
Patel, Tushar.................... 1:42:56 (5)
Pierre, François 2:04:56 (20)

Porcellato, Francesca 2:04:21 (18)

Francesca Porcellato from Italy (born 5 September 1970) is famous as the only person to have won four London Marathon titles in a row (2003–2006). Her spinal cord was badly injured by a truck at the age of 18 months. Porcellato has taken part in wheelchair racing at every Summer Paralympic Games from 1988 to 2008, and in 2006 participated in the Winter Paralympics in Turin in cross-country sit-skiing. She has won a total of two gold (in Seoul in 1988) three silver, and five bronze medals, all in athletics. She is a prolific marathon racer and has taken part in almost one hundred such events, winning the majority of them.

Potter, Rachel 2:12:16 (25)
Powell, Richie.................... 2:01:06 (13)
Rea, Paul 2:16:13 (27)
Riggs, Stuart 2:20:16 (31)
Tan, William 2:30:07 (33)
Tolle, Charles 1:41:17 (4)
Turner, Jonathan 2:45:05 (35)
Watson, Wally 3:37:07 (43)
Weir, David 1:34:48 (2)
Williamson, Steve 2:04:10 (17)
Worrell, Wesley 2:16:18 (28)
Zanotti, Davide.................... 2:02:06 (14)

Francesca Porcellato and Joel Jeannot

InterContinental Hotels Group

2004

The 2004 London Marathon

The 2004 London Marathon was notable for the breakthrough of an 'unknown' and unheralded British woman.

London Marathon race director Dave Bedford is fond of saying that in a marathon crazy things can happen. 'We give as much respect to the chicken as we do to the winner,' he says. 'And there's a millionth of a percent chance that someone dressed as a chicken will run a blinder.'

Fuelled by a heady cocktail of hope, fear and adrenaline, that fairytale came good on a wet and blustery day in April 2004 when a 36-year-old unknown from Leeds, Tracey Morris, finished an amazing 10th in the women's race.

She finished top British woman in a time of 2:33:52, inside the Olympic qualifying standard. And it meant that the contact lens optician would line up alongside Paula Radcliffe in the Olympic Games in Athens.

'I can hardly believe it,' said Tracey after the race. 'I will now have to speak to my bosses and see if I can get the time off work.' Morris had only completed one London Marathon previously, going around in over three-and-a-half hours six years before. She had returned to serious running for just eighteen months when her talent had been spotted by top endurance coach Bud Baldaro, who encouraged her to try her second marathon.

'Nobody was more surprised than me,' she said. 'I never thought I would get anywhere near the Olympic qualifying time and my biggest fear was hitting the wall.' In a 10km race in Salford the week before the London Marathon she had won the princely sum of £50. So it must have come as a delight to her that the following weekend she

won £2,000 and found her name and her face plastered all over the papers.

In the men's race there was drama of a different kind when Evans Rutto from Kenya survived a slithering fall on the cobbles near the Tower of London. With blood still dripping from his cut knees, he went on to win his first London Marathon.

Rutto, who became the fastest debutant in marathon history in Chicago last year, broke away at 23 miles to finish in 2:06:18. His countryman, Sammy Korir, who ran alongside Rutto step-for-step until the Embankment, held on for second place, with world champion Jaouad Gharib from Morocco in third. Jon Brown was the first Briton home in 2:13:39. He was just 14 seconds ahead of the second Briton Dan Robinson. Both athletes achieved Olympic qualifying times.

It was a Kenyan double when Kenya's Margaret Okayo won her race after a tough battle with Romania's Constantina Dita. Ludmila Petrova from Russia snatched second late on from a tiring Constantina Dita. Okayo, a tiny figure standing just 4ft 11in, seemed to be buffeted by the wind in the middle of the race as the Romanian, Dita, built up a substantial lead. But in the final quarter of the race Okayo showed fine pace judgement and swept easily past the Romanian to win in 2:22:35.

In the men's wheelchair race, Saul Mendoza from Mexico marked his first London appearance by adding to his record of more than 200 wheelchair victories, winning in 1:36:56, almost 6 minutes clear of David Weir. Frenchman Alain Fuss was third in 1:45:25, while Tushar Patel suffered a puncture at 21 miles when in bronze position.

In the women's wheelchair race Italy's Francesca Porcellato triumphed once again in

2:04:58. Paula Craig was second in 2:07:52, saying afterwards she was delighted to beat pre-race favourite Gunilla Wallengren of Sweden who finished in 2:14:13.

Lord Archer, the novelist and former Conservative MP Jeffrey Archer, tackled his first marathon at the age of 64 in a bid to raise over a million pounds for charity. He struggled to the finish in 5 hours 26 minutes and was overtaken by a camel, a phone-box and a girl walking. He vowed that 'never again' would he go near the marathon.

One who didn't overtake him was Fauja Singh, who at the age of 93 became the oldest athlete to compete in the London Marathon so far. Running for the charity BLISS, he finished in an age-group record of 6:07:13.

Explanation of placing system

Each London Marathon year in this register is divided up into four categories: first, a summary of the **Elite Athletes**, containing names (last, first) and times (hours : minutes : seconds) of the top 50 male runners, top 50 female runners, top 3 male and top 2 female wheelchair entrants; then **Male Runners**, **Female Runners** and **Wheelchair Entrants**. These last three sections display the individual names and times of *every* entrant, including elite athletes, alphabetically and with their overall finishing position in that year's Marathon displayed in brackets alongside.

Some entrants have chosen to enhance past London Marathon entries with photos and recollections online at **www.aubreybooks.com**. Please visit the website to find out more about appearing in future editions.

ELITE ATHLETES

Top 50 male runners

Rutto, Evans	2:06:18
Korir, Sammy	2:06:48
Gharib, Jaouad	2:07:02
Baldini, Stefano	2:08:37
Tola, Tesfaye	2:09:07
Zwierzchiewski, Benoit	2:09:35
El Mouaziz, Abdelkader	2:09:42
Troop, Lee	2:09:58
Yuda, John	2:10:13
Kadon, Joseph	2:11:30
Ngolepus, Joseph	2:12:02
Kiplagat, William	2:12:04
Bezebeh, Sisay	2:12:05
Westcott, Scott A	2:13:30
Brown, Jon	2:13:39
Robinson, Dan	2:13:53
Pollias, Nikolaos	2:15:02
Cariss, Chris	2:15:08
Lobb, Hugh	2:15:49
Hudspith, Mark	2:16:15
Burns, Billy	2:16:18
Winton, Scott	2:17:40
McFarlane, John	2:17:53
Green, Michael S	2:18:11
Deacon, Bruce	2:18:30
Kirui, Philip	2:18:43
Hall, Stuart	2:18:45
Raven, Gareth J	2:18:49
Hoiom, Runar	2:18:52
Norman, Dave	2:18:53
Mitchinson, Dave	2:18:58
Bannister, Dominic	2:19:10
Zaragas, Lambros	2:19:21
McCloughlin, Cian	2:20:45
Sardella, Vito	2:20:51
Fisher, Ian T	2:21:04

Vega, Teodoro	2:21:11
Kokkotos, Gerasimos	2:21:19
Crossan, Gary	2:21:48
Marriott, Adrian	2:21:51
Smith, Matt	2:21:53
Brignone, Valerio	2:22:15
McKinney, Pauric	2:22:16
Birchall, Chris	2:22:23
Newport, Spencer	2:22:31
Proudlove, Michael J	2:22:40
Gougousis, Konstantinos	2:22:47
Altmann, Nick A	2:23:13
Croasdale, Mark	2:23:24
Lawler, James T	2:24:46

Top 50 female runners

Okayo, Margaret	2:22:35
Petrova, Ludmila	2:26:02
Dita, Constantina	2:26:52
Ivanova, Albina	2:27:25
Chepchumba, Joyce	2:28:01
Zakharova, Svetlana	2:28:10
Yingjie, Sun	2:28:32
Ivanova, Alina	2:28:48
Demidenko, Svetlana	2:33:06
Morris, Tracey A	2:33:52
Dagne, Birhan	2:34:45
Gallagher, Jackie	2:34:48
Lodge, Jo	2:34:49
Lee, Michelle	2:35:51
Harrison, Sue C	2:38:20
McCullum, Michaela	2:39:10
Yamauchi, Mara R	2:39:16
Souma, Spyridoula	2:40:34
Young, Valerie	2:41:32
Partridge, Susan	2:41:44
Moore, Rebecca V	2:43:50

Gratsani, Paraskevi	2:44:35
Moon, Melissa	2:44:41
Karimali, Magdalini	2:46:01
Koskei, Jane	2:46:16
Fletcher, Alison K	2:47:27
Vaughan, Valerie	2:47:56
Yff, Barbara T	2:48:10
Stiles, Amy M	2:50:33
Saina, Esther	2:50:56
Deasy, Margaret A	2:52:00
Ellis, Melanie J	2:52:01
Clark, Megan F	2:52:24
Wood, Kerrie J	2:54:52
Cooper, Louise J	2:54:58
Minniti, Antionette M	2:55:00
Dennison, Andrea M	2:55:08
Lavigne, Christine	2:56:05
Armstrong, Julia H	2:56:25
Heyes, Lisa	2:56:47
Richardson, Dawn P	2:57:13
Bruce, Susan A	2:57:15
Hoogerbrugge, Marianne	2:57:25
Wood, Sophie	2:57:25
Sly, Helen J	2:57:36
Murray, Jenny D	2:57:52
Nilmini, Sujeewa	2:58:14
Cox, Emma L	2:58:23
O'Connor, Gill	2:58:23
Felix, Jamie H	2:58:33

Top 3 male and top 2 female wheelchair entrants

Mendoza, Saul	1:36:56
Weir, David	1:42:50
Fuss, Alain	1:45:25
Porcellato, Francesca	2:04:58
Craig, Paula	2:07:52

MALE RUNNERS

Abaya, Edwin P 4:48:26 (22,765)
Abbey, Joseph 5:54:19 (30,162)
Abbey, Nick J 3:53:25 (9,361)
Abbey, Thomas O 6:04:52 (30,591)
Abbott, Colin 6:16:59 (30,933)
Abbott, David G 3:53:21 (9,351)
Abbott, Ian C 3:29:05 (4,431)
Abbott, Jon S 4:06:21 (12,748)
Abbott, Peter G 4:40:30 (21,028)
Abbott, Simon 4:47:05 (22,470)
Abbott, Trevor J 4:24:55 (17,288)
Abdulla, Darren P 4:26:45 (17,763)
Abel, James W 4:53:08 (23,639)
Abel, Lawrence J 2:58:42 (1,044)
Abel, Matthew R 5:20:31 (27,634)
Abell, John R 4:38:44 (20,649)
Abell, Keith 4:55:17 (24,059)
Abell, Richard A 3:36:10 (5,637)
Ab-Elwyn, Rhys 2:52:09 (597)
Abercrombie, Kevin 4:22:41 (16,746)
Abernethy, Peter G 4:28:51 (18,314)
Abernethy, Rob 4:14:05 (14,582)
Ablett, Ann P 5:07:39 (26,068)
Ablett, Justin P 4:25:43 (17,481)
Abnett, Terry D 4:04:11 (12,239)
Abraha, Asmelash 2:58:49 (1,058)
Abraham, Brian P 4:59:12 (24,828)
Abraham, Daran 5:40:43 (29,397)
Abraham, Nardos 3:51:44 (8,951)
Abraham, Philip I 3:16:23 (2,683)
Abraham, Zach 4:22:46 (16,764)
Abrahams, Adam R 4:17:57 (15,546)
Abrahams, Gary 5:54:39 (30,182)
Abrahams, Gary R 3:58:52 (10,963)
Abrahams, Gerald J 4:03:14 (12,010)
Abrahams, Ian D 3:40:17 (6,352)
Abrahams, Mark S 5:53:44 (30,141)
Abrahamson, Mark A 3:09:03 (1,905)
Abrams, Adam D 4:11:35 (13,994)
Abrines, Benjamin J 4:50:11 (23,107)
Abueg, Mel D 5:42:04 (29,487)
Abu-Kishek, Rabee A 4:50:37 (23,202)
Aby, Robert D 4:07:23 (12,982)
Acford, Bryan J 2:54:54 (747)
Ackerman, Dean A 6:43:25 (31,410)
Ackerman, Riaan 5:37:23 (29,145)
Ackers, Chris J 3:56:22 (10,202)
Ackroyd, Paul S 4:13:50 (14,528)
Acton, Dustin J 4:34:50 (19,784)
Adams, Adrian M 3:55:10 (9,839)
Adams, Allister A 3:15:57 (2,643)
Adams, Andrew C 3:25:30 (3,770)
Adams, Andrew D 3:44:35 (7,208)
Adams, Andrew K 3:58:08 (10,728)
Adams, Antony 5:39:22 (29,297)
Adams, Clayton J 3:54:14 (9,572)
Adams, David C 3:53:15 (9,324)
Adams, David J 4:17:36 (15,452)
Adams, Edward C 4:05:58 (12,653)
Adams, Glenn 4:43:05 (21,578)
Adams, Hugo J 3:50:42 (8,682)
Adams, Ian 4:58:00 (24,593)
Adams, James R 3:57:49 (10,622)
Adams, Jeff 5:38:15 (29,204)
Adams, Keith J 3:24:16 (3,601)
Adams, Leslie 4:34:46 (19,770)
Adams, Martin L 5:10:36 (26,451)
Adams, Michael C 4:46:40 (22,386)
Adams, Neil D 3:10:40 (2,068)
Adams, Neil V 3:31:56 (4,913)
Adams, Oliver L 4:29:27 (18,470)
Adams, Paul A 4:55:25 (24,088)
Adams, Paul A 4:56:27 (24,293)
Adams, Paul N 3:23:34 (3,508)
Adams, Peter F 4:54:12 (23,839)
Adams, Phil 3:01:05 (1,244)
Adams, Phillip 4:16:54 (15,282)
Adams, Robert J 4:01:15 (11,553)
Adams, Roger 4:54:35 (23,920)
Adams, Ronald E 2:28:22 (72)
Adams, Russell 4:22:17 (16,631)
Adams, Steve 2:53:15 (658)
Adams, Steve J 5:07:28 (26,042)
Adams, Steven M 3:46:41 (7,679)
Adams, Steven P 3:50:18 (8,574)
Adams, Wayne B 4:17:35 (15,450)
Adamson, Harry 4:26:47 (17,770)
Adamson, Kenneth J 4:24:01 (17,064)
Adamson, Richard A 5:12:17 (26,666)
Adamson, Robert H 4:48:00 (22,672)
Adderley, Mark C 5:15:36 (27,089)
Addis, Peter J 5:05:00 (25,693)
Addison, Paul 3:09:15 (1,924)
Addy, David 5:10:20 (26,418)
Addy, Paul G 3:30:42 (4,724)
Adekoya, Anthony D 3:19:28 (3,016)
Adelizzi, Stephano A 4:44:25 (21,894)
Adelsberg, Steven G 3:11:38 (2,152)
Adeluwoye, Ade 4:28:28 (18,220)
Adeosun, Olumide A 4:52:30 (23,532)
Adkin, Ian 3:05:54 (1,600)
Adkin, Roy M 4:17:22 (15,387)
Adkins, David D 3:18:02 (2,853)
Adkins, Peter J 3:36:13 (5,646)
Adlan-Merini, Mehdi 3:24:52 (3,672)
Adlard, Simon C 3:10:27 (2,050)
Adnitt, Gary A 3:07:32 (1,757)
Adnitt, Robert I 3:42:27 (6,730)
Adriaensen, Mil 3:22:43 (3,406)
Adshead, Lee 4:02:20 (11,823)
Adshead, Warren 4:37:36 (20,356)
Adu, Stephen 4:37:56 (20,449)
Aeberhard, Jonathan O 4:12:52 (14,292)
Aedy, Graham J 4:51:26 (23,335)
Afford, Mark 4:31:43 (19,033)
Afshar, Dan 3:15:42 (2,622)
Afzal, Rasub 4:56:57 (24,394)
Afzal, Sultan 6:52:39 (31,536)
Agard, Lionel 3:24:52 (3,672)
Agbo, Celestine O 3:37:12 (5,816)
Agent, Mark 4:32:43 (19,294)
Aggar, Martin R 4:19:00 (15,779)
Agnew, Colin J 4:22:51 (16,786)
Ah Leung, Gerard 6:05:40 (30,608)
Aherne, Daniel T 3:52:32 (9,136)
Ahir, Anil 4:18:47 (15,734)
Ahmad, Rafat 3:51:14 (8,813)
Ahmed, Afzal 5:17:27 (27,299)
Ahmed, Ben 4:31:53 (19,072)
Ahmed, Iftikhar 4:11:41 (14,021)
Ahmed, Naeem 3:48:27 (8,106)
Ahmed, Shoib 4:22:22 (16,660)
Ahmet, Mustafa 3:50:39 (8,671)
Ahrendt, Trevor M 4:33:48 (19,534)
Aidroos, Fred 3:23:50 (3,550)
Aiello, Enrico 4:00:31 (11,403)
Aiken, Alastair 5:46:11 (29,759)
Aiken, Scott 3:08:05 (1,811)
Aimable, Brian P 4:21:19 (16,337)
Aincey, Laurence M 4:30:09 (18,666)
Aindow, Colin J 3:57:59 (10,667)
Ainscie, Scott 5:15:57 (27,125)
Ainscough, William F 5:10:43 (26,469)
Ainsile, Timothy W 3:41:57 (6,633)
Ainslie, Paul 3:10:28 (2,053)
Ainsworth, Peter J 3:59:39 (11,206)
Aird, Haydn 4:04:42 (12,351)
Airey, John 4:41:39 (21,271)
Airey, John C 5:05:54 (25,823)
Airey, Timothy 3:44:18 (7,138)
Airoia, Mika O 4:38:20 (20,554)
Aitken, Fergis R 4:29:05 (18,370)
Aitken, Gordon M 3:29:05 (4,431)
Aitken, Jamie M 4:06:16 (12,727)
Aitken, Mark E 3:56:42 (10,302)
Aitkins, Donald 4:02:32 (11,864)
Akan, Yuksel D 5:44:27 (29,652)
Aked, Peter A 2:45:58 (356)
Akenhead, David 5:36:34 (29,066)
Akerman, Paul 5:52:41 (30,108)
Akeroyd, Philip F 3:56:24 (10,213)
Akers, Shawn R 5:02:47 (25,416)
Akhurst, John W 4:43:57 (21,786)
Alabaf-Sabaghi, Hassan 5:08:53 (26,219)
Alaka, Aderemi 3:07:25 (1,738)
Alam, Shah R 4:27:50 (18,050)
Alavi, Khurram G 4:03:21 (12,046)
Al-Azzawi, Ali 5:45:43 (29,737)
Alba, Stefano 4:47:42 (22,616)
Albar, Daniel 3:43:22 (6,930)
Albert, Doninique A 3:39:07 (6,150)
Albertelli, Gene M 4:29:13 (18,406)
Albertoni, Danilo 3:04:20 (1,479)
Albou, Stephane 4:07:46 (13,062)
Albrecht, Heiner 4:25:42 (17,477)
Albrighton, Matthew 4:42:19 (21,418)
Albuery, Bradley 5:26:57 (28,295)
Alden, William J 4:41:02 (21,131)
Alder, Jonathan M 5:00:49 (25,116)
Alder, Tristan R 6:03:46 (30,558)
Alderson, Michael J 4:17:52 (15,526)
Alderson, Richard 4:36:38 (20,162)
Alderson, Steven A 4:03:18 (12,032)
Alderton, George D 5:00:39 (25,086)
Aldhous, Peter 4:19:08 (15,812)
Aldis, Roger 3:00:56 (1,231)
Aldous, Mark R 3:58:12 (10,758)
Aldridge, Russell G 3:15:04 (2,561)
Aldridge, Tom F 3:46:09 (7,559)
Alexander, Barry 6:24:36 (31,122)
Alexander, Brian M 6:07:25 (30,661)
Alexander, Charles E 4:29:05 (18,370)
Alexander, Daniel L 3:24:11 (3,585)
Alexander, Gareth 4:50:35 (23,193)
Alexander, James R 4:49:22 (22,955)
Alexander, Mark I 4:03:35 (12,099)
Alexander, Mark J 3:04:54 (1,514)
Alexander, Nicholas 4:56:54 (24,384)
Alexander, Scott 4:24:08 (17,102)
Alexander, Scott J 4:34:36 (19,733)
Alexander, Stephen J 4:15:31 (14,931)
Aley, Anthony J 4:47:25 (22,546)
Alfonso, Joaquin 4:52:45 (23,577)
Alford, Graham M 3:32:02 (4,931)
Alford, Stephen 5:23:29 (27,916)
Alford, Stuart 4:33:59 (19,583)
Algacs, Dezso 7:42:29 (31,898)
Algar, Jacob S 4:51:35 (23,358)
Ali, Erol 3:34:26 (5,331)
Ali, Umit 6:30:01 (31,204)
Alibone, Mark F 3:31:26 (4,837)
Alija-Perez, Pedro 3:56:59 (10,385)
Alimonti, Daniele P 4:05:15 (12,472)
Alitonou, Charles 4:39:29 (20,822)
Alix, Eric 3:56:41 (10,298)
Alker, James D 3:33:58 (5,265)
Allan, David G 4:13:41 (14,491)
Allan, Douglas E 3:36:59 (5,766)
Allan, James 3:35:37 (5,544)
Allan, John 5:04:57 (25,686)
Allan, Jonathan 3:27:37 (4,150)
Allan, Marcus J 4:50:55 (23,258)
Allan, Nathan R 3:46:18 (7,602)
Allan, Peter C 4:37:47 (20,403)
Allan, Richard K 4:30:23 (18,724)
Allan, Richard W 4:53:10 (23,647)
Allan, Rob M 3:56:05 (10,109)
Allan, Ross C 4:23:58 (17,053)
Allard, Charles J Jnr 3:03:28 (1,406)
Allchorne, Conway N 5:06:01 (25,845)
Alldrread, Michael 3:49:29 (8,370)
Alledon, Toby D 4:37:58 (20,459)
Allen, Alexander M 4:52:08 (23,471)
Allen, Andrew J 4:25:03 (17,318)
Allen, Andrew J 4:45:29 (22,136)
Allen, Andrew P 3:17:40 (2,817)
Allen, Antony 6:51:26 (31,521)
Allen, Brian R 3:36:08 (5,631)
Allen, Charles A 3:48:34 (8,139)
Allen, Charles L 3:57:39 (10,581)
Allen, Charles R 3:26:43 (3,964)
Allen, Chris M 3:38:58 (6,126)
Allen, Christopher D 4:27:06 (17,864)
Allen, Daren P 3:43:57 (7,054)
Allen, Darryl J 4:01:55 (11,695)
Allen, David 3:50:10 (8,541)
Allen, David J 4:36:56 (20,236)
Allen, David K 3:21:19 (3,233)

Allen, David R 4:40:45 (21,075)
Allen, Dean A 4:37:04 (20,266)
Allen, Dean L 4:24:39 (17,218)
Allen, Donald R 4:38:01 (20,475)
Allen, Gavin 3:29:40 (4,528)
Allen, Greg 5:06:10 (25,869)
Allen, James A 4:58:44 (24,759)
Allen, James N 3:08:32 (1,854)
Allen, John 6:10:26 (30,739)
Allen, Jonathan D 3:52:35 (9,149)
Allen, Jonathan D 4:09:16 (13,446)
Allen, Jonathan P 3:58:11 (10,750)
Allen, Julian M 3:38:33 (6,056)
Allen, Kevin 3:09:32 (1,951)
Allen, Larry 5:13:40 (26,851)
Allen, Lee M 5:09:04 (26,247)
Allen, Lester 3:51:43 (8,945)
Allen, Marcus A 4:18:17 (15,603)
Allen, Martin C 3:42:40 (6,780)
Allen, Martin S 4:13:28 (14,442)
Allen, Matthew J 3:51:40 (8,930)
Allen, Michael E 5:58:06 (30,331)
Allen, Nicholas 4:59:51 (24,965)
Allen, Paul 3:29:41 (4,529)
Allen, Paul 4:31:17 (18,916)
Allen, Paul 5:11:51 (26,610)
Allen, Peter 4:31:40 (19,014)
Allen, Simon G 4:10:54 (13,848)
Allen, Stephen R 3:32:55 (5,085)
Allen, Steve P 3:33:19 (5,164)
Allen, Terry C 5:18:47 (27,447)
Allen, Ulick G 4:11:17 (13,926)
Allerstorfer, Gerhard 3:39:31 (6,220)
Allerton, Gavin N 4:19:15 (15,846)
Allin, Scott 5:01:01 (25,146)
Allingham, Richard 5:01:25 (25,211)
Allison, Christopher J 4:19:15 (15,846)
Allison, Craig M 3:30:15 (4,645)
Allison, Gordon A 3:22:22 (3,354)
Allison, Julian J 3:50:20 (8,589)
Allison, Marc W 3:59:49 (11,242)
Allison, Robert W 3:48:50 (8,222)
Allison, Stuart R 4:00:28 (11,390)
Alliston, Andrew J 4:57:57 (24,582)
Allitt, Matthew C 4:26:59 (17,836)
Allman, Andrew 5:20:46 (27,661)
Allott, Timothy 4:35:46 (19,977)
Allouah, Abdellatip P 4:53:04 (23,624)
Allouard, Herve 2:47:51 (415)
Alloway, Darren 4:21:04 (16,293)
Allpass, Samuel R 3:24:46 (3,657)
Allport, Trevor A 3:08:04 (1,809)
Allsop, Andrew 3:45:12 (7,348)
Allsop, David S 3:03:26 (1,401)
Allsop, Gordon A 2:57:04 (883)
Allsop, Paul 4:17:38 (15,461)
Allsop, Timothy K 2:50:24 (522)
Allsopp, Craig 2:59:17 (1,101)
Allsopp, Jamie 3:47:18 (7,831)
Allton, Kevin A 4:08:46 (13,311)
Alman, Ian P 5:35:30 (29,001)
Almond, Steve J 2:52:13 (601)
Alsford, Jonathan 4:44:34 (21,928)
Alsford, Richard C 3:57:02 (10,397)
Alsop, Rory M 4:35:09 (19,855)
Alsos, Bjorn 3:19:01 (2,954)
Alston, Richard 3:52:56 (9,235)
Alsworth, Michael D 4:35:46 (19,977)
Altmann, Nick A 2:23:13 (49)
Altree, Paul J 3:32:32 (5,009)
Alty, Robert 5:20:50 (27,666)
Alun-Jones, Paul 4:13:42 (14,496)
Alvarez Meijide, José Luis 3:39:44 (6,262)
Alvellos, Joao 4:09:34 (13,516)
Alwan, Tarek 4:57:01 (24,406)
Alwash, Craig 3:21:34 (3,266)
Amadi, Paul 4:33:03 (19,367)
Ambler, Ashley 5:21:12 (27,699)
Ambler, Iain D 3:45:31 (7,414)
Ambler, Robin G 4:18:42 (15,710)
Ambros, Jerome 2:57:53 (954)
Ambrose, Rob M 4:29:27 (18,470)
Ameer, Sam 5:20:12 (27,595)

The water of life

In the week before the Marathon, most runners boost their carbohydrate intake. Some try to avoid hitting 'The Wall' by carrying extra carbohydrate in the form of sports drinks, gels, and sports bars. Others go for pasta loading. Drinking the right amount of water or a glucose-based sports drink is essential, particularly on hot and humid days. Many run into problems at the crowded water stops. Don't go near the first couple of water stop tables, that's usually where all the first-timers break. Once you've grabbed your drink, get out into the middle of the road and walk to avoid getting jostled. At the start of the London Marathon in 1981, many drinks stations were makeshift affairs. One such, in London's East End, was resplendent with half a dozen girls attired in basques and fishnet stockings, dancing and offering drinks. Above them was a huge banner. It read irresistibly: GET YOUR KISS OF LIFE HERE.

Amendola, Antonio 4:07:06 (12,917)
Amendola, John P 5:45:33 (29,730)
Ames, Brian E 5:34:01 (28,891)
Ames, Tim M 3:58:57 (10,991)
Amesbauer, Karl 4:02:03 (11,730)
Amies, John B 4:43:08 (21,587)
Amla, Ismail 4:26:27 (17,684)
Amohia, Sohan S 5:26:26 (28,246)
Amorim, Pedro P 3:23:26 (3,491)
Amory, Stu R 4:55:17 (24,059)
Amos, John 4:20:24 (16,131)
Amos, Mark D 3:26:53 (3,999)
Amy, Marcus C 3:57:41 (10,589)
Amyes, Nigel 3:58:37 (10,891)
An, Pierre 4:16:50 (15,263)
Anam, Simon 5:08:00 (26,115)
Anand, Sanjay K 4:09:44 (13,563)
Anaya, Charles 4:05:38 (12,580)
Andel, Jan 4:09:13 (13,428)
Andersen, Jackrob H 5:12:01 (26,635)
Andersen, Jonny 3:30:54 (4,761)
Andersen, Kjell 4:35:43 (19,963)
Andersen, Morten 4:23:18 (16,894)
Andersen, Stein K 3:08:46 (1,873)
Anderson, Alan T 4:11:06 (13,889)
Anderson, Brian 3:52:59 (9,252)
Anderson, David 4:11:35 (13,994)
Anderson, David R 4:58:36 (24,736)
Anderson, Evan 4:54:22 (23,872)
Anderson, Garreth W 5:20:35 (27,641)
Anderson, Glynn L 4:16:24 (15,148)
Anderson, Graham 3:27:39 (4,156)
Anderson, Graham 3:32:20 (4,976)
Anderson, Ian P 3:57:09 (10,433)
Anderson, Ian S 2:44:23 (299)
Anderson, James H 4:00:18 (11,358)
Anderson, Keith 4:17:52 (15,526)
Anderson, Lewis 3:14:42 (2,525)
Anderson, Lindsay 3:35:55 (5,591)
Anderson, Mark 4:44:06 (21,815)
Anderson, Michael 4:51:59 (23,436)
Anderson, Nicholas W 3:21:18 (3,230)

Anderson, Nick 5:50:00 (29,965)
Anderson, Richard P 4:27:37 (17,996)
Anderson, Robert 3:45:34 (7,428)
Anderson, Stuart 2:54:47 (733)
Anderssen, Knut 4:22:42 (16,749)
Andersson, Leif A 6:49:03 (31,484)
Anderton, Daniel J 4:01:10 (11,542)
Andreas, Schoo 4:04:04 (12,200)
Andreini, Emmanuel 3:20:06 (3,078)
Andreou, Andy 3:47:47 (7,942)
Andrew, Clive 3:38:08 (5,983)
Andrew, Ian L 3:38:15 (6,004)
Andrew, James 5:16:05 (27,137)
Andrew, Kevin J 3:38:08 (5,983)
Andrew, Martin J 3:12:27 (2,246)
Andrew, Paul 3:22:40 (3,398)
Andrew, Paul W 3:21:53 (3,298)
Andrew, Sam M 3:06:22 (1,641)
Andrew, Stuart 3:56:37 (10,285)
Andrews, David 3:20:01 (3,069)
Andrews, Dorrien 5:07:17 (26,006)
Andrews, Ian A 5:29:10 (28,504)
Andrews, James L 3:15:35 (2,608)
Andrews, James P 3:55:50 (10,028)
Andrews, John 3:51:36 (8,916)
Andrews, John 5:21:19 (27,710)
Andrews, Julian R 4:08:56 (13,358)
Andrews, Mark 4:19:38 (15,934)
Andrews, Mark 4:49:13 (22,920)
Andrews, Mark 4:56:41 (24,340)
Andrews, Mark V 3:21:35 (3,267)
Andrews, Matthew 3:40:10 (6,335)
Andrews, Michael C 3:26:30 (3,917)
Andrews, Paul 3:39:59 (6,302)
Andrews, Ray 5:03:24 (25,500)
Andrews, Ricky 4:39:27 (20,817)
Andrews, Robert J 3:38:12 (5,995)
Andrews, Roger 4:47:54 (22,654)
Andrews, Simon G 4:31:43 (19,033)
Andrews, Simon K 4:13:33 (14,464)
Andrews, Timothy A 4:23:16 (16,885)
Andrews, Timothy A 4:35:13 (19,868)
Andrzejewski, Jan R 4:37:56 (20,449)
Andrzejewski, Stanley M 5:00:58 (25,139)
Anelay, Lance E 4:56:12 (24,247)
Angel, Jonathan A 4:50:05 (23,088)
Angel, Steven 4:35:20 (19,893)
Angelaki-King, Darren W 4:40:55 (21,109)
Angell, Keith E 5:32:29 (28,772)
Angenot, Pierre 4:09:17 (13,450)
Anglin, Morris A 5:10:44 (26,473)
Angus, Stephen 3:33:30 (5,189)
Angus, Steve 2:36:09 (137)
Anichkin, Alexander 3:59:25 (11,117)
Anker, Mark 4:34:26 (19,696)
Ankers, Stephen A 3:46:13 (7,585)
Annett, Michael 3:29:23 (4,482)
Annetts, David M 4:33:00 (19,359)
Annetts, Martyn 3:33:34 (5,197)
Annison, Mark S 4:39:04 (20,743)
Anniss, Duncan 4:18:53 (15,756)
Anscomb, Clive N 4:41:56 (21,332)
Ansell, John P 4:50:36 (23,198)
Anson, Malcolm 3:10:57 (2,096)
Anstead, Matthew J 3:32:50 (5,066)
Anstee, Nick J 3:55:07 (9,821)
Anstis, Richard S 5:19:51 (27,543)
Antcliff, Andrew J 3:04:58 (1,523)
Antcliffe, Jim 3:42:50 (6,818)
Antcliffe, Richard W 3:53:20 (9,348)
Anthoine, Pascal 3:23:55 (3,555)
Anthony, James K 4:21:52 (16,495)
Anthony, Paul 6:09:39 (30,719)
Antoine, Lallier 3:11:55 (2,183)
Antoni, Gergely 4:55:37 (24,122)
Anton-Morell, Emilio L 4:57:24 (24,473)
Antrobus, Daniel P 3:55:57 (10,067)
Aoiom, Mans 2:25:42 (54)
Apel, Wojciech A 5:57:42 (30,316)
Apicella, Laurence G 7:36:57 (31,883)
Applebee, John B 3:58:09 (10,729)
Appleby, Anthony 4:26:05 (17,600)
Appleby, David 3:10:09 (2,016)

Appleby, Glenn M 4:28:16 (18,162)
Appleby, Luke P 4:02:35 (11,872)
Appleby, Rodney J 3:46:30 (7,638)
Applelby, Paul 3:35:13 (5,462)
Appleton, Andrew D 3:17:49 (2,830)
Appleton, Andrew M 4:32:21 (19,199)
Appleton, Brian 4:29:38 (18,537)
Appleton, Mark A 3:02:24 (1,334)
Appleton, Mark R 3:12:29 (2,253)
Appleton, Robert J 4:11:12 (13,911)
Appleton, Steven R 4:11:12 (13,911)
Appleyard, Ben 4:17:18 (15,368)
Applin, Geoffrey S 4:30:19 (18,708)
Apthorp, Rupert J 3:53:05 (9,275)
Aram, Jim W 5:43:30 (29,590)
Aranguren, Aritz 4:37:51 (20,416)
Arbuthnott, Nicholas C 4:38:49 (20,670)
Archbold, Martin D 3:54:56 (9,763)
Archer, Andrew N 3:27:44 (4,174)
Archer, Charles 4:50:38 (23,204)

Archer, Jeffrey 5:26:24 (28,240)

Archer, Paul 4:43:45 (21,736)
Archer, Raymond 5:06:36 (25,929)
Archer, Richard 5:23:08 (27,885)
Archer, Robert E 3:51:24 (8,857)
Archer, Thomas J 3:33:12 (5,136)
Archer, William H 4:22:15 (16,623)
Archibald, William S 5:04:18 (25,602)
Archikov, Peter D 5:39:06 (29,272)
Ardouin, Cyril 4:33:27 (19,457)
Ardron, Philip 3:49:12 (8,309)
Aregger, Arthur 2:37:06 (155)
Argent, Adam M 4:28:22 (18,181)
Argent, James W 3:44:11 (7,113)
Argent, Simon P 4:56:19 (24,266)
Argent, Stephen 5:53:55 (30,149)
Argent, Timothy S 4:34:01 (19,594)
Argyle, Neil A 3:47:54 (7,975)
Aris, Greg J 3:54:44 (9,704)
Aristotelous, Andreas D 3:47:21 (7,844)
Aristotelous, Panos S 3:47:22 (7,847)
Ark, Bahadar S 4:10:26 (13,740)
Arkill, Lloyd A 4:51:52 (23,414)
Arlett, Neil A 4:30:49 (18,818)
Armani, Marco 3:14:37 (2,514)
Armellini, Armando A 4:50:39 (23,207)
Armer, Paul 4:12:50 (14,286)
Armist, Ronald 4:06:20 (12,742)
Armistead, Brent 4:40:46 (21,076)
Armit, Tim W 4:33:09 (19,391)
Armitage, James S 4:45:45 (22,199)
Armitage, Mark E 4:02:48 (11,927)
Armitage, Michael 4:17:08 (15,337)
Armitage, Michael R 4:18:23 (15,627)
Armitage, Neil 3:34:21 (5,318)
Armitage, Philip J 5:46:22 (29,774)
Armitage, Stuart D 4:47:25 (22,546)
Armitage, William J 3:33:25 (5,178)
Armitt, Robert 5:27:03 (28,304)
Armsden, Richard S 4:25:28 (17,418)
Armstrong, Benjamin J 3:22:49 (3,421)
Armstrong, David E 4:40:03 (20,931)
Armstrong, Drew C 3:53:51 (9,459)
Armstrong, Eric C 3:29:34 (4,512)
Armstrong, Glenn K 3:21:22 (3,240)
Armstrong, Ian 3:22:32 (3,383)
Armstrong, James W 5:27:50 (28,387)
Armstrong, John 4:14:53 (14,783)
Armstrong, John 4:55:50 (24,160)
Armstrong, John B 4:17:18 (15,368)
Armstrong, Mark A 2:39:33 (198)
Armstrong, Neil J 3:56:43 (10,308)
Armstrong, Nigel J 2:58:24 (1,006)
Armstrong, Paul 4:33:47 (19,531)
Armstrong, Thomas 4:35:05 (19,839)
Armstrong, Tim P 3:45:43 (7,465)
Arneil, Stephen 3:45:54 (7,507)
Arnel, Chris N 4:16:04 (15,065)
Arnel, Philip R 3:57:20 (10,492)
Arnell, Doug J 3:52:56 (9,235)
Arnell, Geoff I 3:03:34 (1,412)
Arnell, Robert 4:52:04 (23,458)
Arnold, Andrew 4:07:38 (13,040)
Arnold, Daniel B 3:50:41 (8,679)
Arnold, David P 3:53:51 (9,459)
Arnold, Ian 5:14:46 (26,999)
Arnold, James N 3:27:40 (4,162)
Arnold, Jonathan M 5:53:29 (30,135)
Arnold, Martin R 4:12:08 (14,122)
Arnold, Michael L 3:54:45 (9,711)
Arnold, Philip J 3:57:02 (10,397)
Arnold, Richard E 3:40:59 (6,472)
Arnold, Simon P 4:12:38 (14,242)
Arnold, Stephen G 3:22:49 (3,421)
Arnold, Stephen K 3:15:49 (2,634)
Arnold, Steve C 5:40:02 (29,340)
Arnold, Stuart 4:38:30 (20,596)
Arnott, Francis J 4:38:04 (20,488)
Arnott, Michael S 4:02:18 (11,805)
Arranto, Arno J 4:07:54 (13,090)
Arranto, Christian 3:16:28 (2,696)
Arrenberg, William F 4:09:15 (13,438)
Artaud, Didier 2:59:58 (1,154)
Arthur, Gary J 4:47:53 (22,651)
Arthur, Nigel A 3:43:10 (6,884)
Arthur, William G 4:30:14 (18,687)
Arthurton, Anthony W 4:11:03 (13,882)
Artuso, Gabriele 3:31:30 (4,850)
Arundel, Stuart T 4:25:05 (17,331)
Asbury, Andrew J 4:22:40 (16,740)
Asghar, Adam K 3:23:48 (3,544)
Ash, John H 4:57:29 (24,492)
Ash, Peter D 3:49:13 (8,312)
Ash, Roger G 4:09:24 (13,475)
Ashburn, Rob 6:02:36 (30,515)
Ashburner, Alan 3:14:09 (2,459)
Ashby, Gerald 4:26:47 (17,770)
Ashby, Jon 4:44:08 (21,825)
Ashby, Mark 2:57:18 (900)
Ashby, Martin L 4:44:25 (21,894)
Ashby, Nick C 3:55:02 (9,798)
Ashcombe, James T 4:30:09 (18,666)
Ashcroft, Anthony G 4:32:29 (19,235)
Ashcroft, Derek 3:03:57 (1,447)
Ashcroft, James M 4:07:05 (12,915)
Ashcroft, Paul S 4:18:35 (15,681)
Asher, Stephen A 4:37:58 (20,459)
Ashford, Brian C 5:38:14 (29,199)
Ashleigh-Morris, Damian T 4:02:03 (11,730)
Ashley, David A 6:27:42 (31,170)
Ashley, James 5:55:22 (30,217)
Ashley, John 3:25:09 (3,713)
Ashley, Jonathan H 3:02:18 (1,326)
Ashley, Michael A 4:43:20 (21,649)
Ashley, Stephen 4:52:31 (23,536)
Ashman, Jon M 3:58:09 (10,729)
Ashman, Jonathan 5:23:47 (27,952)
Ashman, Rod J 4:03:28 (12,072)
Ashmore, Philip 4:00:05 (11,311)
Ashton, Christopher 4:21:10 (16,302)
Ashton, Craig N 3:59:26 (11,121)
Ashton, David 4:58:32 (24,723)
Ashton, David A 3:57:07 (10,418)
Ashton, Gavin J 4:07:21 (12,970)
Ashton, James J 4:36:42 (20,183)
Ashton, Jamie 4:52:03 (23,457)
Ashton, Matthew A 3:50:40 (8,676)
Ashton, Owen J 4:10:48 (13,828)
Ashton, Paul 4:31:54 (19,080)
Ashton, Timothy C 3:57:42 (10,592)
Ashton-Jones, George J 4:06:13 (12,716)
Ashwell, Benjamin P 5:14:38 (26,985)
Ashworth, Michael W 5:29:59 (28,581)
Ashworth, Tom W 5:29:59 (28,581)
Asiedu, Eric 3:48:55 (8,233)
Askew, David M 3:32:15 (4,961)
Askew, Phil M 3:58:19 (10,795)
Askin, Daron G 4:10:25 (13,737)
Aslett, Robert W 4:07:37 (13,037)
Asopa, Vipin 3:46:57 (7,737)
Aspden, Kester 4:10:57 (13,858)
Aspel, Edward 4:20:45 (16,223)
Aspin, Chris J 4:44:47 (21,974)
Aspinall, Aaron J 3:15:33 (2,600)
Aspinall, Michael D 2:34:26 (114)
Aspinall, Nathan 3:15:33 (2,600)
Aspinall, Paul 4:52:22 (23,516)
Aspland, Richard I 4:08:44 (13,301)
Assollant, Gilles 3:37:23 (5,854)
Astbury, Tony 4:38:31 (20,598)
Astle, Thomas W 2:59:32 (1,125)
Aston, Andrew 2:48:54 (454)
Aston, Gary 4:08:07 (13,135)
Aston, Jeffrey R 3:20:02 (3,071)
Aston, Paul 3:18:06 (2,858)
Astridge, Brian P 4:39:21 (20,802)
Asumadu-Sakyi, Steve 4:47:37 (22,598)
Athawes, Jon 3:43:36 (6,979)
Atherton, Asa 4:28:39 (18,270)
Atherton, Mark E 3:49:13 (8,312)
Atherton, Philip J 2:39:13 (192)
Athey, Christopher P 3:36:07 (5,629)
Atkin, Antony C 3:45:22 (7,378)
Atkin, Stephen J 4:02:42 (11,899)
Atkin, Thomas C 4:44:16 (21,850)
Atkins, Andrew K 3:21:54 (3,299)
Atkins, Charles 3:51:34 (8,909)
Atkins, Christopher D 3:09:12 (1,917)
Atkins, Gareth D 5:24:37 (28,037)
Atkins, Gary J 5:11:25 (26,567)
Atkins, John P 5:06:05 (25,856)
Atkins, Lee J 3:30:36 (4,707)
Atkins, Paul K 2:59:16 (1,099)
Atkins, Richard 3:05:14 (1,549)
Atkins, Ted R 4:29:43 (18,557)
Atkinson, Brian G 6:17:53 (30,948)
Atkinson, Chris H 5:09:27 (26,299)
Atkinson, Chris J 3:33:07 (5,122)
Atkinson, Christopher N 5:30:31 (28,628)
Atkinson, David 2:48:18 (435)
Atkinson, David S 3:11:50 (2,174)
Atkinson, George 4:46:25 (22,344)
Atkinson, George B 4:01:33 (11,610)
Atkinson, Ian J 4:10:14 (13,688)
Atkinson, James 2:52:00 (590)
Atkinson, James S 4:33:07 (19,384)
Atkinson, Jason 3:44:32 (7,195)
Atkinson, John 2:55:01 (756)
Atkinson, John J 4:29:46 (18,573)
Atkinson, John K 5:09:34 (26,317)
Atkinson, Michael J 5:10:39 (26,460)
Atkinson, Michael R 3:54:04 (9,524)
Atkinson, Neil 4:00:38 (11,412)
Atkinson, Philip 4:41:57 (21,337)
Atkinson, Richard 5:26:25 (28,243)

Atkinson, Richard T	4:17:14 (15,354)
Atkinson, Robert I	3:31:04 (4,785)
Atkinson, Stuart D	4:05:46 (12,610)
Attard, Kevin L	3:52:07 (9,042)
Attard, Martin J	5:07:40 (26,071)
Attar-Zadeh, Darush	5:15:38 (27,093)
Atterbury, David	4:55:54 (24,183)
Atterbury, David C	3:40:29 (6,396)
Attewell, John H	4:27:22 (17,932)
Attridge, Simon	4:05:39 (12,583)
Attwater, Guy J	3:52:07 (9,042)
Attwell, Steve J	3:17:01 (2,749)
Attwood, Mark J	4:41:42 (21,283)
Attwood, Mark R	4:47:40 (22,608)
Attwood, Martin R	4:58:05 (24,617)
Attwood, Shaun J	4:24:49 (17,255)
Attwood-Smith, Nicholas W	3:31:47 (4,886)
Atwal, Dalwinder S	4:02:12 (11,780)
Atyeo, Darren	3:49:12 (8,309)
Auclair, Thierry M	3:27:35 (4,141)
Audas, Allen J	3:25:59 (3,846)
Audenshaw, Tony	3:00:04 (1,163)
Audino, Nazzareno	3:32:43 (5,045)
Audry, Doninique	2:57:04 (883)
Augo, Ochieng	3:19:53 (3,057)
Augustine, Anto K	4:31:33 (18,990)
Augustyn, Deon	3:40:26 (6,386)
Auinger, Juergen	3:43:41 (6,994)
Auld, Christopher W	3:31:09 (4,799)
Auricoste, Charles	6:03:45 (30,556)
Austen, Christopher P	4:40:22 (21,003)
Austen, Graham L	4:05:53 (12,634)
Austen, Thomas C	4:26:51 (17,785)
Austin, Alan	4:27:34 (17,982)
Austin, Anthony	4:53:45 (23,756)
Austin, Barry E	5:35:50 (29,021)
Austin, Christopher W	3:27:45 (4,179)
Austin, Daniel R	4:24:17 (17,141)
Austin, Dave N	3:35:48 (5,572)
Austin, David A	4:19:28 (15,905)
Austin, David J	3:59:16 (11,077)
Austin, Derek G	3:47:48 (7,946)
Austin, Huw R	4:09:53 (13,603)
Austin, Jon	3:56:13 (10,148)
Austin, Kevin A	4:24:04 (17,076)
Austin, Michael	5:03:09 (25,466)
Austin, Patrick B	3:56:46 (10,318)
Auston, Oliver	4:22:25 (16,671)
Avanzato, Roberto	2:56:26 (848)
Avanzi, Maurizio	4:24:10 (17,113)
Avenell, Garry	2:48:58 (459)
Avery, Edward A	4:54:50 (23,968)
Avery, Joe A	3:35:17 (5,477)
Avery, Marc J	3:59:38 (11,198)
Avery, Phil	3:33:46 (5,229)
Avery, Russell P	4:19:20 (15,866)
Aves, Clayton	3:06:27 (1,650)
Avey, Terry J	4:03:10 (11,997)
Aveyard, Jason G	3:46:40 (7,673)
Avinain, Claude	4:00:26 (11,386)
Aviss, Timothy H	5:02:36 (25,388)
Avital, David	4:29:55 (18,614)
Awcock, Colin S	3:50:14 (8,555)
Axton, Matthew D	2:39:58 (209)
Aylieff, Paul	4:25:58 (17,561)
Ayling, John V	5:54:33 (30,173)
Aylmer, Kerry W	5:05:16 (25,719)
Aylott, Jason M	3:50:48 (8,706)
Aylott, Stuart	3:57:29 (10,533)
Ayre, Ted	3:49:06 (8,281)
Ayres, Arthur J	3:58:04 (10,696)
Ayres, Christopher E	3:32:43 (5,045)
Ayres, Garry L	5:57:30 (30,310)
Ayres, Roger M	4:20:13 (16,069)
Babbedge, Norman	5:16:45 (27,225)
Babbs, Christian	4:22:07 (16,576)
Babington, Nick	3:43:08 (6,877)
Babu, Chandra	5:33:05 (28,814)
Bach, Freddy	4:17:05 (15,321)
Bach, Murray D	4:54:22 (23,872)
Bache, Christopher A	3:46:06 (7,547)
Bache, John	3:57:33 (10,555)
Bachmann, Marco	3:54:53 (9,748)
Baci, Arber	2:43:05 (269)
Back, Nicholas J	5:03:27 (25,512)
Back, Ray	4:55:34 (24,114)
Backstrom, Roger	3:34:33 (5,349)
Bacmaga, Jacek	2:57:21 (902)
Bacon, Ellis J	3:42:30 (6,746)
Bacon, Ian D	4:15:56 (15,037)
Bacon, Michael	3:51:14 (8,813)
Bacon, Steve J	3:09:44 (1,973)
Bacon, Steven	4:17:05 (15,321)
Bacon, Walter	5:00:57 (25,136)
Badenhurst, Heinrich	3:25:39 (3,792)
Bader, Brett S	5:57:56 (30,326)
Bader, Heinz	3:25:24 (3,747)
Badger, Jonathan	3:35:43 (5,559)
Badgery, Stephen P	3:21:22 (3,240)
Badhan, Parminder	3:20:28 (3,120)
Badillo, José	4:09:35 (13,520)
Badr, Ishmail	3:00:43 (1,209)
Bage, Steven	3:59:55 (11,273)
Bagenal, John	3:52:01 (9,016)
Baggaley, Clive R	3:33:01 (5,105)
Baggaley, Richard J	4:45:24 (22,117)
Baggs, David M	4:26:24 (17,675)
Baginski, Henning	3:31:23 (4,830)
Bagnall, Mark S	5:45:40 (29,733)
Bagnall, Stephen J	4:31:18 (18,922)
Bagshaw, Andrew	4:52:17 (23,499)
Baguley, Paul A	3:46:04 (7,539)
Bagwell, Matthew J	4:48:41 (22,812)
Bahra, Gurjeet S	5:29:14 (28,511)
Baigent, Derek	2:58:59 (1,072)
Bailey, Andrew J	5:47:38 (29,848)
Bailey, Andy N	3:55:10 (9,839)
Bailey, Anthony E	4:00:45 (11,434)
Bailey, Anton	4:57:32 (24,500)
Bailey, Bart J	3:41:43 (6,586)
Bailey, Chris J	4:40:41 (21,062)
Bailey, Clive V	5:18:35 (27,421)
Bailey, Daniel	3:29:54 (4,572)
Bailey, David C	3:43:26 (6,946)
Bailey, David M	4:13:06 (14,352)
Bailey, Howard	3:57:51 (10,632)
Bailey, John	3:46:16 (7,593)
Bailey, Kevin	7:23:04 (31,800)
Bailey, Mark J	3:50:36 (8,656)
Bailey, Neal A	3:36:57 (5,761)
Bailey, Neil A	5:28:20 (28,424)
Bailey, Neil J	4:30:43 (18,803)
Bailey, Paul	6:19:54 (31,011)
Bailey, Paul M	4:59:13 (24,833)
Bailey, Peter J	5:02:12 (25,320)
Bailey, Philip D	3:06:25 (1,648)
Bailey, Richard C	4:09:26 (13,486)
Bailey, Steven E	6:03:17 (30,538)
Bailey, Stewart A	4:12:30 (14,200)
Bailey, Stewart C	6:06:01 (30,620)
Bailey, Tom W	4:20:11 (16,059)
Bailey, Trevor	4:58:22 (24,679)
Baillest, Laurent	3:30:37 (4,713)
Baillie, Darren A	3:18:28 (2,893)
Baillie, Douglas A	4:38:51 (20,683)
Baillie, Murray A	4:38:52 (20,688)
Baillieul, Julien	3:54:38 (9,677)
Baily, Alexander M	3:16:09 (2,658)
Baily, Charlie	2:45:06 (328)
Bain, Alan	4:43:48 (21,749)
Bain, Andrew G	3:50:59 (8,746)
Bain, Douglas	4:11:41 (14,021)
Bain, William G	4:54:44 (23,947)
Bainbridge, Michael J	2:45:46 (352)
Baines, Joe A	4:21:14 (16,319)
Baines, Jonathan	3:57:57 (10,662)
Baines, Paul J	4:04:25 (12,288)
Baines, Steven R	4:10:58 (13,864)
Bainger, Graham E	3:15:08 (2,572)
Baird, Gordon J	3:18:15 (2,876)
Baird, John	3:15:12 (2,577)
Baird, John E	3:57:07 (10,418)
Baird, Timothy R	2:44:33 (304)
Bairwal, Don R	4:08:20 (13,186)
Baixauli, José B	4:50:20 (23,129)
Bajaj, Bobby	3:55:28 (9,921)
Baker, Andrew R	3:01:22 (1,270)
Baker, Antony W	4:20:28 (16,151)
Baker, Carl	2:55:47 (801)
Baker, Christopher	4:23:56 (17,046)
Baker, Clifford D	4:08:55 (13,355)
Baker, Clive A	2:57:26 (913)
Baker, David E	4:19:59 (16,029)
Baker, David J	3:58:00 (10,671)
Baker, David W	4:53:04 (23,624)
Baker, Duncan	2:57:05 (886)
Baker, Ed	8:30:34 (31,965)
Baker, Ged P	5:38:20 (29,216)
Baker, Graham	3:08:38 (1,861)
Baker, Ian D	4:14:07 (14,590)
Baker, James J	5:54:53 (30,193)
Baker, Jof	5:22:23 (27,819)
Baker, Jonathan R	4:12:57 (14,318)
Baker, Julian D	2:28:12 (70)
Baker, Leslie M	4:27:56 (18,074)
Baker, Mark D	4:58:11 (24,636)
Baker, Mark H	3:49:57 (8,489)
Baker, Mark J	3:46:47 (7,700)
Baker, Martin R	3:26:18 (3,889)
Baker, Matthew D	4:50:45 (23,225)
Baker, Michael D	4:26:03 (17,585)
Baker, Neil A	4:57:57 (24,582)
Baker, Nick M	2:48:52 (453)
Baker, Paul O	6:24:09 (31,113)
Baker, Philip J	4:50:45 (23,225)
Baker, Richard F	4:50:20 (23,129)
Baker, Richard J	3:43:54 (7,038)
Baker, Richard K	4:04:05 (12,208)
Baker, Roger E	3:56:56 (10,376)
Baker, Ross D	3:53:27 (9,366)
Baker, Sean P	4:14:13 (14,612)
Baker, Simon	3:26:27 (3,910)
Baker, Stephen T	5:22:43 (27,850)
Baker, Steve P	3:58:16 (10,780)
Baker, William J	6:55:17 (31,563)
Balakrishnan, Venkatesh	4:51:05 (23,288)
Balcazar, Guillermo	4:23:06 (16,842)
Balch, Bo O	3:45:40 (7,446)
Balch, Charles W	4:15:31 (14,931)
Balch, David R	3:41:00 (6,474)
Balcombe, Andrew	4:03:18 (12,032)
Baldey, Richard C	5:45:51 (29,745)
Baldini, Stefano	2:08:37 (4)
Baldock, Neil S	4:30:49 (18,818)
Baldock, Richard P	3:34:06 (5,284)
Baldwin, Christopher R	4:50:26 (23,167)
Baldwin, Elwyn	3:04:31 (1,490)
Baldwin, Gavin	4:58:23 (24,687)
Baldwin, Peter S	4:45:13 (22,085)
Bale, Mons	2:37:48 (168)
Bale, Simon M	2:54:46 (731)
Balfour, Geoffrey W	6:14:04 (30,847)
Balfour, Scott	2:53:11 (655)
Balgun, Tobi	7:01:51 (31,641)
Ball, Andrew	2:59:19 (1,104)
Ball, Andrew R	3:41:12 (6,513)
Ball, Anthony M	4:25:03 (17,318)
Ball, Benjamin G	3:28:06 (4,240)
Ball, David M	3:47:34 (7,898)
Ball, John	5:49:59 (29,964)
Ball, John D	3:37:39 (5,899)
Ball, Laurence J	5:37:34 (29,155)
Ball, Martin J	3:51:26 (8,868)
Ball, Michael A	4:16:15 (15,107)
Ball, Michael C	4:29:28 (18,481)
Ball, Peter	3:47:24 (7,854)
Ball, Richard	3:11:52 (2,177)
Ball, Richard L	4:21:52 (16,495)
Ball, Ronnie	3:38:21 (6,023)
Ball, Simon H	4:32:28 (19,231)
Ball, Stephen	4:30:24 (18,733)
Ball, Steve A	5:39:11 (29,284)
Ball, Stuart	4:54:00 (23,794)
Ball, Tim	4:59:08 (24,818)
Ballaam, Steve	4:23:01 (16,815)
Ballam, Paul A	3:56:25 (10,222)
Ballantyne, Andrew	4:08:25 (13,206)
Ballantyne, Barrie J	4:46:54 (22,424)
Ballantyne, David	3:39:08 (6,155)

Ballard, Lee M.....4:30:22 (18,720)	Barfoot, Anthony I.....4:10:29 (13,752)	Barnes, Simon P.....3:11:13 (2,116)
Ballard, Neil.....3:20:18 (3,099)	Barford, Julian P.....4:19:34 (15,925)	Barnes, Trevor.....3:21:20 (3,236)
Ballard, Nicolas.....4:00:51 (11,461)	Barg, Marco.....4:33:02 (19,364)	Barnett, Brian A.....3:46:17 (7,598)
Ballard, Richard.....6:09:25 (30,712)	Barge, Alistair D.....4:23:00 (16,812)	Barnett, Dave.....4:56:07 (24,232)
Ballett, Leighton C.....3:25:44 (3,804)	Barham, Andrew R.....7:07:03 (31,682)	Barnett, Graeme E.....3:34:51 (5,398)
Balls, Lee A.....4:06:58 (12,882)	Barham, David L.....3:46:07 (7,550)	Barnett, John M.....4:15:54 (15,029)
Balmer, David W.....3:22:51 (3,426)	Barham, Jeff P.....4:28:04 (18,115)	Barnett, Paul.....3:37:15 (5,822)
Balmer, Malcolm.....3:18:21 (2,882)	Barham, Paul.....3:57:37 (10,573)	Barnett, Paul M.....3:03:47 (1,430)
Balmer, William R.....4:24:40 (17,223)	Baring, Thomas.....3:47:04 (7,770)	Barnett, Simon J.....3:24:25 (3,618)
Bamber, Lee E.....4:33:48 (19,534)	Barkat, Gulzar.....5:29:38 (28,549)	Barnett, Simon J.....6:51:13 (31,515)
Bamford, Carl M.....3:41:05 (6,491)	Barke, Norman D.....5:11:55 (26,622)	Barney, Stephen D.....3:52:33 (9,139)
Bamford, David.....2:53:29 (668)	Barker, Christopher D.....3:57:13 (10,451)	Barnfield, Jonathan D.....4:07:57 (13,104)
Bamford, David R.....4:21:37 (16,425)	Barker, Christopher H.....4:55:32 (24,105)	Barningham, Richard A.....4:30:02 (18,639)
Bamford, George.....5:02:17 (25,336)	Barker, David R.....4:03:24 (12,057)	Barns, Timothy A.....3:41:59 (6,643)
Bamford, John.....3:16:26 (2,693)	Barker, Jim C.....5:38:59 (29,263)	Barnshaw, Daniel T.....3:12:26 (2,243)
Bammer, Reinhold.....2:58:45 (1,052)	Barker, John W.....2:51:51 (586)	Barnsley, Andrew.....3:16:52 (2,735)
Banahan, David.....5:32:29 (28,772)	Barker, Jon.....3:31:29 (4,847)	Barnsley, Frank A.....4:49:26 (22,961)
Banbrook, Anthony D.....3:33:55 (5,258)	Barker, Matthew J.....4:56:29 (24,305)	Barnwell, Mark A.....4:29:54 (18,610)
Bance, Elliott J.....4:38:52 (20,688)	Barker, Michael.....3:46:57 (7,737)	Baron, Peter R.....4:08:21 (13,191)
Bancroft, John E.....5:08:30 (26,182)	Barker, Michael J.....4:27:16 (17,916)	Barr, David.....3:26:16 (3,883)
Bandini, Fabio.....3:20:55 (3,192)	Barker, Michael J.....4:40:47 (21,081)	Barraclough, Ian D.....4:22:52 (16,788)
Banerjee, Somen R.....5:40:10 (29,349)	Barker, Michael M.....4:53:43 (23,753)	Barraclough, John A.....3:30:23 (4,669)
Banfield, Philip.....3:40:08 (6,330)	Barker, Nathan.....4:24:58 (17,300)	Barraclough, Timothy M.....3:39:42 (6,256)
Bangert, Alexander.....3:08:06 (1,814)	Barker, Nicholas A.....4:22:30 (16,701)	Barraclough, William W.....4:48:06 (22,698)
Banks, David.....3:46:10 (7,565)	Barker, Nick M.....4:21:18 (16,333)	Barrass, Anthony S.....5:20:47 (27,663)
Banks, Derek J.....5:53:45 (30,142)	Barker, Nigel C.....3:33:58 (5,265)	Barrass, Barnaby J.....3:01:16 (1,263)
Banks, Ian L.....3:57:21 (10,498)	Barker, Paul.....4:33:33 (19,477)	Barratt, Clinton D.....3:50:22 (8,597)
Banks, Jeremy Z.....4:54:06 (23,819)	Barker, Paul A.....4:20:55 (16,267)	Barren, Mark.....3:57:39 (10,581)
Banks, John.....3:57:18 (10,481)	Barker, Paul A.....4:51:51 (23,408)	Barrett, Andrew P.....4:15:37 (14,962)
Banks, Kevin J.....3:21:44 (3,284)	Barker, Paul H.....4:24:13 (17,127)	Barrett, Barrie G.....3:26:48 (3,988)
Banks, Martin P.....4:37:52 (20,422)	Barker, Philip.....4:32:43 (19,294)	Barrett, Daniel J.....4:07:29 (13,005)
Banks, Paul D.....3:48:01 (8,001)	Barker, Rob J.....4:56:41 (24,340)	Barrett, Dominic.....3:29:28 (4,498)
Banks, Peter J.....3:55:23 (9,901)	Barker, Simon J.....4:40:47 (21,081)	Barrett, Edward J.....4:54:27 (23,885)
Banks, Philip S.....4:43:27 (21,673)	Barker, Simon J.....4:56:24 (24,280)	Barrett, Gordon D.....3:00:56 (1,231)
Banks, Richard G.....3:50:33 (8,639)	Barker, Toby J.....4:43:46 (21,741)	Barrett, Jermaine.....6:30:57 (31,224)
Banks, Stephen.....3:24:38 (3,644)	Barker, Vernon I.....3:53:08 (9,291)	Barrett, Michael.....4:03:04 (11,970)
Banks, Tim D.....3:41:42 (6,582)	Barker, Victor E.....4:39:10 (20,764)	Barrett, Michael J.....4:33:29 (19,467)
Bankston, Bobby J.....3:44:26 (7,168)	Barker, Will A.....2:55:23 (778)	Barrett, Patrick A.....4:34:02 (19,599)
Banner, Tyr M.....4:21:51 (16,493)	Barker, William W.....3:20:08 (3,082)	Barrett, Paul N.....3:40:23 (6,377)
Bannerman, Ian.....3:32:49 (5,063)	Barksby, Keith.....5:20:49 (27,664)	Barrett, Philip J.....3:46:34 (7,653)
Bannerman, James S.....5:36:22 (29,050)	Barkway, Michael D.....3:12:06 (2,202)	Barrett, Roger K.....3:56:02 (10,094)
Bannerman, William M.....4:37:38 (20,370)	Barley, Allan C.....5:41:51 (29,478)	Barrett, Shaun K.....4:14:01 (14,572)
Bannister, Dominic.....2:19:10 (32)	Barley, Gary P.....4:39:00 (20,729)	Barrett, Simon J.....2:57:53 (954)
Bannister, John.....3:54:44 (9,704)	Barlow, Anthony C.....3:51:04 (8,758)	Barrett, Stephen.....3:07:23 (1,737)
Bannister, Jon.....4:16:06 (15,079)	Barlow, Charlie W.....3:47:49 (7,950)	Barretto, Dominic J.....4:06:01 (12,663)
Bannister, Mark H.....5:03:00 (25,520)	Barlow, Dave J.....4:53:33 (23,710)	Barrettt, Craig A.....3:37:43 (5,905)
Bannister, Peter J.....4:59:52 (24,968)	Barlow, Jason.....2:43:04 (268)	Barrie, William E.....4:36:32 (20,142)
Bannister, Stuart.....2:53:09 (651)	Barlow, Jonathan.....3:26:57 (4,008)	Barril, Patrick.....3:46:52 (7,719)
Bansal, Tarlok Singh.....6:14:51 (30,881)	Barlow, Lee.....3:12:57 (2,307)	Barrington, Adrian J.....4:22:26 (16,677)
Bantick, Mark.....3:30:16 (4,647)	Barltrop, Verne.....3:48:58 (8,245)	Barron, John.....5:30:34 (28,629)
Banton, CJ.....6:37:14 (31,324)	Barmby, Mark I.....3:37:33 (5,879)	Barron, Karl R.....3:11:49 (2,170)
Banton, Colin.....5:40:19 (29,357)	Barnaby, Harold M.....5:19:06 (27,477)	Barron, Michael E.....4:59:01 (24,798)
Banton, Jonathan D.....3:47:15 (7,817)	Barnard, Adam J.....3:58:34 (10,879)	Barron, Shaun M.....3:13:41 (2,396)
Barba, Robert.....5:02:43 (25,404)	Barnard, Gerald S.....4:51:29 (23,342)	Barrow, Paul.....5:26:58 (28,297)
Barbarinde, Olakunle A.....5:36:12 (29,040)	Barnard, Matthew J.....4:27:56 (18,074)	Barrow, Simon T.....4:33:29 (19,467)
Barbat, Anthony L.....3:20:11 (3,088)	Barnard, Michael.....3:11:11 (2,111)	Barrow, Stephen.....4:54:18 (23,855)
Barber, Allan J.....4:09:15 (13,438)	Barnard, Richard D.....5:00:29 (25,065)	Barrowman, Michael S.....3:53:57 (9,489)
Barber, David H.....4:10:28 (13,749)	Barnard, Trevor J.....4:40:05 (20,936)	Barrs, Gary E.....4:39:33 (20,833)
Barber, Eugene P.....4:08:19 (13,183)	Barne, Charles.....3:56:49 (10,337)	Barry, Chris.....4:54:54 (23,977)
Barber, Gareth C.....4:09:19 (13,455)	Barnes, Adam C.....4:21:24 (16,363)	Barry, Damien.....3:37:58 (5,955)
Barber, Gareth R.....4:42:28 (21,444)	Barnes, Andrew C.....4:36:40 (20,172)	Barry, Ian.....4:26:44 (17,755)
Barber, Gary K.....5:15:25 (27,068)	Barnes, Andy N.....3:39:23 (6,197)	Barry, James A.....4:11:23 (13,948)
Barber, Ian B.....3:15:11 (2,576)	Barnes, Antony.....5:42:43 (29,528)	Barry, Jason.....3:08:18 (1,832)
Barber, Jon.....4:22:15 (16,623)	Barnes, Calvin.....5:36:51 (29,094)	Barry, John D.....5:20:27 (27,623)
Barber, Kyle G.....3:17:19 (2,787)	Barnes, Darren M.....4:35:32 (19,936)	Barry, Julian A.....2:57:42 (933)
Barber, Martin P.....4:10:37 (13,786)	Barnes, David.....4:11:12 (13,911)	Bartell, Matthew J.....3:59:40 (11,212)
Barber, Nigel.....4:52:11 (23,479)	Barnes, David G.....3:05:57 (1,606)	Barteluk, Steve J.....5:03:15 (25,482)
Barber, Stephen J.....5:26:10 (28,208)	Barnes, David K.....4:02:19 (11,814)	Barter, James T.....4:55:23 (24,081)
Barbour, Hamish M.....3:43:03 (6,859)	Barnes, Gary J.....3:20:25 (3,110)	Barthel, Stephan.....3:47:04 (7,770)
Barbour, Leon A.....4:57:28 (24,490)	Barnes, James D.....5:10:40 (26,462)	Bartholomew, David P.....4:00:12 (11,343)
Barclay, David.....3:42:19 (6,700)	Barnes, James R.....3:37:55 (5,940)	Bartholomew, Scott.....5:24:12 (27,991)
Barclay, Jeffrey.....3:29:18 (4,471)	Barnes, John.....4:51:56 (23,431)	Bartle, Gary.....5:23:32 (27,929)
Barclay, Lucas W.....4:31:07 (18,880)	Barnes, John P.....5:40:50 (29,402)	Bartleet, Steve.....4:02:32 (11,864)
Barclay, Neil.....4:38:35 (20,615)	Barnes, Kevin L.....3:47:52 (7,963)	Bartlett, Bill.....4:23:58 (17,053)
Barclay, Paul C.....3:19:15 (2,992)	Barnes, Michael.....3:40:10 (6,335)	Bartlett, Christopher P.....4:35:17 (19,882)
Barclay, Richard D.....3:28:09 (4,254)	Barnes, Michael F.....3:15:46 (2,631)	Bartlett, Dave.....4:42:50 (21,530)
Bardelk, Graham P.....3:37:55 (5,940)	Barnes, Michael J.....4:53:05 (23,630)	Bartlett, David P.....4:24:26 (17,172)
Bardell, Ken G.....3:35:01 (5,429)	Barnes, Nicholas W.....4:37:03 (20,261)	Bartlett, Edwin H.....4:37:40 (20,375)
Bardell, Stephen J.....4:36:59 (20,249)	Barnes, Paul.....2:54:18 (708)	Bartlett, Gareth D.....4:17:07 (15,334)
Barden, Roy.....3:25:46 (3,810)	Barnes, Philip J.....6:08:28 (30,686)	Bartlett, Ian.....5:03:45 (25,548)
Bardsley, David W.....3:56:35 (10,274)	Barnes, Richard J.....4:02:49 (11,932)	Bartlett, James A.....5:23:29 (27,916)
Barends, Ronald.....4:24:49 (17,255)	Barnes, Richard W.....3:52:14 (9,064)	Bartlett, Keith B.....5:00:49 (25,116)
Barette, Paul.....5:32:12 (28,749)	Barnes, Roy J.....3:22:30 (3,375)	Bartlett, Malcolm J.....4:03:42 (12,125)

Bartlett, Martin B 4:06:20 (12,742)
Bartlett, Paul M 4:50:45 (23,225)
Bartlett, Richard W 3:14:24 (2,488)
Bartlett, Ross M 3:20:21 (3,104)
Bartley, David J 3:47:31 (7,883)
Barton, Henry P 3:44:28 (7,175)
Barton, Matthew C 4:23:01 (16,815)
Barton, Michael 4:41:25 (21,222)
Barton, Richard J 5:30:22 (28,613)
Barton, Rob M 3:47:40 (7,920)
Barton, Roger 3:28:07 (4,246)
Barton, Shaun 4:33:53 (19,556)
Barton, Tom E 3:36:03 (5,618)
Bartosik, James 4:34:33 (19,723)
Bartram, Kevin S 3:14:00 (2,432)
Bartram, Matt 3:30:51 (4,751)
Bartrip, Lee 4:31:57 (19,096)
Basham, Leslie J 4:16:27 (15,163)
Basham, Mark A 4:26:35 (17,723)
Basham, Paul 5:20:17 (27,605)
Bashford, Bryan E 4:20:44 (16,221)
Bashford, Guy C 3:05:06 (1,537)
Bashford, Kevin P 4:09:06 (13,399)
Bashir, Saqib J 5:37:09 (29,119)
Basili, Maurizio 2:57:40 (928)
Basini, Justin S 4:27:57 (18,082)
Basler, Marcel 3:11:03 (2,100)
Basler, Peter 2:40:34 (219)
Baslington, Robert M 4:39:42 (20,862)
Bass, Andrew 3:15:50 (2,635)
Bass, Simon N 4:10:06 (13,656)
Bassan, Gwynn 3:44:21 (7,146)
Bassani, Walter 4:38:49 (20,670)
Bassett, Christopher S 4:46:42 (22,393)
Bassett, Edward J 4:58:28 (24,711)
Bassett, John L 4:00:38 (11,412)
Bassett, Laurence J 4:58:28 (24,711)
Bassett, Lyndon G 4:58:30 (24,719)
Bassett, Nicholas D 3:58:29 (10,845)
Basso, Antonino 3:22:36 (3,390)
Basson, David H 4:23:10 (16,858)
Bastien, Olivier 4:31:05 (18,876)
Basu, Subhashis 3:30:29 (4,688)
Batchelor, Gary 3:37:16 (5,829)
Batchelor, Keith 4:06:06 (12,683)
Batchelor, Paul S 4:15:45 (14,988)
Batchelor, Philip 5:07:20 (26,022)
Bate, Michael J 5:46:22 (29,774)
Bateman, Andrew R 5:00:05 (25,006)
Bateman, Brian 4:09:19 (13,455)
Bateman, Daniel J 3:49:43 (8,428)
Bateman, David A 4:32:51 (19,322)
Bateman, Edward D 3:36:43 (5,728)
Bateman, Jeremy D 2:41:52 (241)
Bater, Bernie 3:08:08 (1,818)
Bates, Adam S 5:50:45 (30,002)
Bates, Grant J 4:01:02 (11,510)
Bates, Ian 4:59:14 (24,834)
Bates, Ian D 6:41:16 (31,378)
Bates, James E 4:01:02 (11,510)
Bates, Michael D 5:12:49 (26,734)
Bates, Peter C 5:26:39 (28,266)
Bates, Timothy 4:33:56 (19,573)
Bates, Wilfred A 5:55:11 (30,211)
Bathmaker, Robert J 4:15:49 (15,006)
Batley, Lloyd E 4:29:27 (18,470)
Batlle Rius, Enric 4:42:17 (21,408)
Batt, Marcus D 3:49:47 (8,447)
Batten, Algy 3:56:30 (10,250)
Batten, Andrew G 3:20:29 (3,124)
Batterham, Graham J 4:52:00 (23,438)
Batterham, Richard J 3:11:24 (2,134)
Battersby, Anthony K 3:05:04 (1,530)
Battersby, Nicholas P 4:02:30 (11,855)
Battersby, William L 3:57:02 (10,397)
Battershall, Tim J 2:57:49 (947)
Batterton, Daniel T 3:59:28 (11,140)
Batterton, David J 4:48:13 (22,723)
Battle, Clive D 3:59:32 (11,171)
Battle, Richard J 3:55:13 (9,854)
Batty, Christopher D 3:40:19 (6,359)
Batty, Ian L 3:50:36 (8,656)
Batty, Kevin 5:09:59 (26,375)
Batty, Philip 5:09:59 (26,375)
Baudat, Jean-Luc 4:06:13 (12,716)
Baughan, James D 3:57:42 (10,592)
Bauhs, Henrik 3:43:00 (6,850)
Baulch, Stuart L 3:07:22 (1,736)
Baum, John H 4:35:38 (19,950)
Baumann, Heinz 3:33:47 (5,233)
Baunach, Gerhard 3:28:40 (4,346)
Bausch, Thomas 4:20:00 (16,034)
Bawden, Phillip U 3:49:34 (8,396)
Bawden, Simon N 4:38:29 (20,594)
Baxendale, Samuel G 3:39:16 (6,172)
Baxendale, Toby O 3:27:51 (4,197)
Baxendell, Peter M 4:21:26 (16,373)
Baxter, Gary 4:41:22 (21,210)
Baxter, James A 4:41:44 (21,290)
Baxter, James N 4:41:42 (21,283)
Baxter, Justin S 4:26:31 (17,706)
Baxter, Michael D 3:57:17 (10,473)
Baxter, Neil 4:45:49 (22,213)
Baxter, Paul A 4:50:45 (23,225)
Baxter, Simon 3:21:07 (3,213)
Baxter, Simon C 4:05:01 (12,437)
Baxter, Simon S 3:53:23 (9,358)
Baxter-Warman, Rudi 4:28:01 (18,102)
Bayer, Malcolm 2:42:55 (265)
Bayes, Graham P 3:58:01 (10,681)
Baygual, Guillermo 3:38:38 (6,075)
Bayley, Derrick 4:59:22 (24,871)
Bayley, Geoffrey 4:54:34 (23,914)
Bayley-Dainton, Stuart J 3:34:00 (5,272)
Baylis, Andrew D 4:42:56 (21,553)
Bayliss, Garry 5:01:43 (25,261)
Bayliss, Michael C 3:57:35 (10,566)
Bayne, Tom J 4:05:19 (12,489)
Baynes, Andy C 5:22:28 (27,829)
Baynes, Charles B 3:54:13 (9,567)
Baynes, Chris P 3:40:30 (6,403)
Baynham, Anthony D 5:21:37 (27,742)
Baynham, Mark T 4:24:12 (17,122)
Baynham, Owen E 5:24:38 (28,039)
Bayon, Anthony P 4:27:08 (17,874)
Bazeley, Gary R 3:56:20 (10,190)
Bazzi, Gabriele 3:26:59 (4,018)
Beacock, John P 3:50:16 (8,567)
Beacroft, Richard J 5:33:57 (28,889)
Beadell, Conrad V 4:11:38 (14,011)
Beadell, Ray W 4:11:40 (14,020)
Beadle, David 3:11:22 (2,129)
Beadle, Michael S 3:38:19 (6,015)
Beagley, Anton 5:11:13 (26,543)
Beaken, Christopher G 4:22:58 (16,807)
Beal, Craig D 4:24:55 (17,288)
Beale, Nicholas 4:11:56 (14,072)
Beales, James B 5:14:37 (26,982)
Beaman, David G 5:19:36 (27,508)
Beamond, Jeffery 4:21:55 (16,505)
Bear, Hammerby 3:27:39 (4,156)
Beard, Daniel 3:43:24 (6,937)
Beard, Lloyd 4:38:57 (20,706)
Beard, Michael C 3:39:02 (6,139)
Beard, Nigel M 4:01:06 (11,528)
Beard, Paul R 4:04:47 (12,372)
Beard, Simon P 4:45:47 (22,207)
Beard, Stephen A 3:05:37 (1,577)
Beardmore, Mark H 4:30:52 (18,833)
Beardshall, Alan 3:52:09 (9,047)
Beardsmore, Keith J 2:53:53 (689)
Beardsworth, Stuart L 4:17:44 (15,489)
Bearman, Marc 2:57:34 (918)
Bearn, Hugh W 3:48:26 (8,102)
Bearn, John C 5:14:35 (26,976)
Beasley, Adam O 3:55:28 (9,921)
Beasley, Anthony 7:50:24 (31,915)
Beasley, Scott 3:40:36 (6,417)
Beasty, James S 3:43:52 (7,031)
Beatham, Matthew G 5:09:26 (26,295)
Beathe, Carl J 3:00:59 (1,236)
Beaton, Michael S 2:56:12 (831)
Beats, Kenny 3:58:58 (10,996)
Beattie, Brian W 3:35:27 (5,511)
Beattie, Kevin A 2:43:08 (272)
Beattie, Michael J 2:55:13 (768)
Beattie, Paul A 4:49:42 (23,014)
Beattie, Paul J 4:23:55 (17,043)
Beauchamp, Mark R 3:47:02 (7,763)
Beauchamp, Vernon 4:32:51 (19,322)
Beaumont, Charles H 4:27:41 (18,013)
Beaumont, Mark 3:03:58 (1,449)
Beaumont, Mark J 3:49:53 (8,469)
Beaumont, Richard 2:50:24 (522)
Beaumont, Richard 3:46:11 (7,573)
Beaumont, Scott 5:04:38 (25,643)
Beaver, Andrew I 3:30:01 (4,591)
Beaves, Chris G 4:55:48 (24,151)
Beazer, Derek G 5:33:55 (28,888)
Beazer, Philip J 3:15:23 (2,587)
Bebell, Richard H 4:41:38 (21,270)
Beck, Gary R 4:03:42 (12,125)
Beck, Ian F 4:34:25 (19,693)
Beck, Jeff 2:53:56 (693)
Beck, Michael G 4:18:24 (15,632)
Beck, Peter T 4:12:21 (14,158)
Beck, Tom J 5:20:38 (27,649)
Beckenlehner, Erich 3:47:27 (7,869)
Becker, Frank 3:18:17 (2,878)
Becker, Jeremy J 5:01:15 (25,175)
Becker, Ulrich 3:23:13 (3,464)
Beckett, Darren M 4:00:11 (11,337)
Beckett, Graham F 4:42:37 (21,476)
Beckett, John R 4:39:32 (20,829)
Beckingsale, John B 3:23:37 (3,519)
Beckwith, Piers 3:58:10 (10,745)
Beckwith, Simon R 6:21:29 (31,042)
Bedard, Chad I 3:20:33 (3,140)
Beddard, Richard M 5:10:25 (26,432)
Bedford, Graham J 4:23:13 (16,877)
Bedford, Jonathan C 4:20:37 (16,191)
Bedford, Peter 4:19:14 (15,841)
Bedford, Rupert W 4:54:47 (23,956)
Bedford, Samuel M 3:37:24 (5,860)
Bedford, Terence L 4:28:24 (18,193)
Bedggood, Dean V 3:53:45 (9,427)
Bedi, Manjit S 3:45:29 (7,403)
Bednall, Michael 4:22:54 (16,795)
Bedwell, Peter R 4:15:21 (14,889)
Bedwell, Tim 4:23:44 (16,996)
Bedworth, John R 3:55:32 (9,942)
Bee, Graham 4:26:25 (17,677)
Beech, David C 4:01:39 (11,633)
Beech, Graham W 5:07:57 (26,107)
Beech, James L 2:52:32 (617)
Beech, Ross M 5:37:12 (29,124)
Beecham, George E 5:50:48 (30,007)
Beeching, Gareth 3:50:53 (8,730)
Beecroft, Robbie H 3:50:32 (8,634)
Beeforth, Niel 3:59:54 (11,268)
Beeken, Tom G 4:05:17 (12,482)
Beeley, Will T 3:42:10 (6,674)
Beer, Craig A 5:19:59 (27,561)
Beer, Michael R 4:18:53 (15,756)
Beer, Simon 4:19:12 (15,834)
Beesley, Christopher 4:27:45 (18,026)
Beesley, Christopher A 4:04:07 (12,214)
Beesley, Ian S 3:38:29 (6,043)
Beeson, Benjamin N 2:47:32 (405)
Beeson, Luke C 3:54:55 (9,756)
Beeston, Tim R 3:55:50 (10,028)
Beet, Andrew J 4:29:53 (18,607)
Beetham, Stephen 4:24:10 (17,113)
Beeton, Alan P 3:39:39 (6,244)
Beeton, Andrew J 3:35:48 (5,572)
Beevers, Andrew R 3:53:36 (9,401)
Begg, Graham J 4:02:06 (11,746)
Beggs, William K 4:55:06 (24,013)
Begley, Damion J 3:13:28 (2,365)
Begley, Kenneth 2:39:48 (207)
Begley, Martin H 3:55:09 (9,837)
Begley, Simon G 4:20:54 (16,261)
Behan, Damien 3:43:50 (7,021)
Behan, Kenneth J 3:28:28 (4,316)
Behr, Hang Ulrich 4:28:59 (18,344)
Behrens, Robert 5:45:13 (29,706)
Beilfuss, James V 5:57:43 (30,317)
Beirne, Gerard 4:54:15 (23,844)
Beja, Eilon 3:47:00 (7,751)

LONDON MARATHON, 2004: MALE RUNNERS 399

Bek, Liam 3:03:37 (1,416)
Beketov, Andrei 3:44:02 (7,077)
Belcher, Paul F 3:09:30 (1,945)
Belcher, Peter A 2:43:38 (284)
Belcourt, Paul L 4:29:33 (18,505)
Beldom, Walter J 4:03:38 (12,110)
Beldon, Richard G 4:07:23 (12,982)
Belet, Regis 4:20:56 (16,271)
Beleyur, Ravindra 4:45:20 (22,104)
Belfort, Clive R 4:18:24 (15,632)
Belkin, Paul G 3:37:34 (5,884)
Bell, Andrew M 5:19:58 (27,557)
Bell, Andrew P 3:05:02 (1,527)
Bell, Duncan C 2:51:10 (550)
Bell, Graham 2:58:21 (999)
Bell, Graham A 3:46:08 (7,552)
Bell, Ian M 4:11:19 (13,933)
Bell, James 3:59:26 (11,121)
Bell, Joh D 3:04:51 (1,511)
Bell, Julian H 4:03:14 (12,010)
Bell, Justin R 4:26:59 (17,836)
Bell, Martin G 4:02:09 (11,764)
Bell, Mike 3:21:14 (3,225)
Bell, Nick 6:21:31 (31,045)
Bell, Nick G 4:05:58 (12,653)
Bell, Peter W 4:57:56 (24,576)
Bell, Richard J 3:11:44 (2,160)
Bell, Robert 4:20:24 (16,131)
Bell, Royce M 3:51:11 (8,798)
Bell, Simon P 4:41:12 (21,157)
Bell, Stephen K 3:34:05 (5,282)
Bell, Stuart J 3:35:49 (5,575)
Bell, Wayne P 2:59:31 (1,124)
Bellacosa, Maurizio 3:58:27 (10,834)
Bellamy, Darren 4:49:50 (23,049)
Bellamy, Edward J 3:27:46 (4,182)
Bellamy, Jean-Marie 3:29:36 (4,518)
Bellamy, Jonathan 3:38:14 (6,000)
Bellerby, Steven T 4:30:18 (18,703)
Belleville, Paul C 3:26:59 (4,018)
Bellido Verdu, Ezequiel 2:53:49 (685)
Bellis, James H 3:26:57 (4,008)
Bellmon, William S 6:12:34 (30,797)
Bello, Aurelio 4:15:43 (14,980)
Bellocchio, Giuseppe 3:30:01 (4,591)
Bellows, Guy A 4:27:07 (17,871)
Bell-Scott, Antony 3:44:34 (7,207)
Bellwood, Simon 3:27:25 (4,108)
Belton, Antony F 5:33:32 (28,854)
Belton, Chris C 3:00:49 (1,218)
Belton, Robert B 3:29:06 (4,434)
Belz, Valentin 2:50:14 (514)
Ben Mohamed, Kader 2:56:10 (825)
Benbow, Edward A 3:56:49 (10,337)
Bence, David E 5:24:36 (28,033)
Bence-Trower, Nicholas A 4:55:51 (24,162)
Bench, Kenneth J 4:04:21 (12,272)
Bendall, Matthew J 5:20:02 (27,571)
Bendle, Stephen A 3:47:00 (7,751)
Benedini, Luca 3:28:46 (4,367)
Bengue, John P 4:48:42 (22,820)
Bengue, Marc 4:17:33 (15,439)
Ben-Halim, Amr M 4:46:35 (22,371)
Benham, Kevin D 3:42:10 (6,674)
Benicio Junior, Benedicto C 3:44:38 (7,220)
Benito, Andrew 4:24:47 (17,246)
Benjamin, Stephen G 4:11:00 (13,873)
Benmore, Michael 4:40:59 (21,119)
Ben-Nathan, Marc I 4:12:40 (14,254)
Bennell, Kevin J 3:50:06 (8,528)
Bennett, Andrew 4:55:30 (24,099)
Bennett, Andrew D 4:05:52 (12,629)
Bennett, Barry J 4:07:15 (12,955)
Bennett, Ben D 2:52:10 (599)
Bennett, Bernard T 3:56:52 (10,354)
Bennett, David 4:06:01 (12,663)
Bennett, David G 4:27:45 (18,026)
Bennett, David J 3:18:23 (2,884)
Bennett, David M 4:34:35 (19,730)
Bennett, Duncan P 3:12:46 (2,282)
Bennett, Giles E 3:22:57 (3,435)
Bennett, Gordon S 4:28:46 (18,292)
Bennett, Graham N 4:47:06 (22,474)

Bennett, Harold R 5:32:01 (28,733)
Bennett, James 4:15:47 (15,000)
Bennett, James R 5:28:28 (28,433)
Bennett, Jeremy S 4:21:10 (16,302)
Bennett, Jon A 3:57:41 (10,589)
Bennett, Kevin M 3:07:52 (1,792)
Bennett, Lee B 3:51:25 (8,862)
Bennett, Lee M 5:46:31 (29,790)
Bennett, Mark 4:57:43 (24,538)
Bennett, Mark R 4:06:24 (12,761)
Bennett, Matthew 4:40:01 (20,924)
Bennett, Peter 4:27:58 (18,091)
Bennett, Peter J 3:56:03 (10,099)
Bennett, Peter L 3:40:02 (6,309)
Bennett, Philip E 4:47:48 (22,634)
Bennett, Richard 4:34:44 (19,765)
Bennett, Robin R 5:10:05 (26,386)
Bennett, Roger 2:56:14 (833)
Bennett, Sean R 3:03:12 (1,382)
Bennett, Sean W 3:54:43 (9,696)
Bennett, Simon L 5:18:10 (27,386)
Bennett, Steven A 3:04:18 (1,474)
Bennett, Stuart M 3:35:41 (5,552)
Bennett-Coles, Tarquin V 4:08:07 (13,135)
Bennett-King, Peter F 5:08:15 (26,150)
Benney, Simon F 4:27:59 (18,094)
Bennion, Philip E 6:21:45 (31,055)
Bennison, John 4:04:21 (12,272)
Benoist, Didier 3:55:31 (9,935)
Benoits, Claude 3:21:40 (3,273)
Benskin, Ian D 2:58:45 (1,052)
Benson, Bob F 3:10:17 (2,028)
Benson, David J 3:58:46 (10,939)
Benson, Ian C 3:46:52 (7,719)
Benson, Joel W 3:51:55 (8,995)
Benson, Stephen G 3:34:17 (5,309)
Benson, Stuart P 5:22:32 (27,836)
Benstead, Ian M 4:02:12 (11,780)
Benstead, Mark C 4:06:55 (12,867)
Bensusan, John T 6:04:02 (30,566)
Bent, Alan 3:39:36 (6,238)
Bentham, Mark A 5:14:25 (26,953)
Bentley, Adam M 4:45:04 (22,053)
Bentley, Chris 4:27:28 (17,948)
Bentley, Mark 3:10:23 (2,037)
Bentley, Michael E 4:04:16 (12,257)
Bentley, Richard M 4:17:02 (15,312)
Bentley, Robin J 2:34:37 (118)
Bentley, Simon 4:02:12 (11,780)
Bentley, Simon 4:47:57 (22,662)
Bentley, Stephen M 3:34:53 (5,405)
Benton, Andy 4:28:04 (18,115)
Benton, Daren R 4:29:19 (18,442)
Benton, Philip J 3:34:52 (5,400)
Benton, Russell 5:36:52 (29,098)
Bentzen, Tor Olan 3:48:32 (8,129)
Beouardi, Pierre 3:21:03 (3,206)
Berard, François D 3:32:25 (4,990)
Berdon, Michael J 3:32:48 (5,060)
Bereket, Ruphael 3:37:00 (5,768)
Berends, Dieter 4:52:41 (23,567)
Beresford, Jeff A 3:57:55 (10,651)
Beresford, Richard J 4:45:39 (22,177)
Berg, Reuben 4:44:09 (21,827)
Berg, Roger 3:48:30 (8,118)
Berg, Stephen E 4:32:19 (19,192)
Berger, Jean L 3:03:18 (1,389)
Berger, Joerg 4:12:28 (14,187)
Berger, Robert 3:54:25 (9,617)
Bergstrom, Per 5:07:14 (25,999)
Beriard, Laurent 4:07:48 (13,069)
Berka, Thorsten 3:44:25 (7,163)
Berlyn, Paul P 4:05:38 (12,580)
Berman, Gavin B 4:24:25 (17,167)
Bermuske, Michael 3:30:57 (4,771)

Bernard, Peter 6:07:19 (30,658)
Bernard, Ralph M 4:44:31 (21,913)
Bernard, Rascal-Paul 3:48:59 (8,251)
Bernardini, Mario 5:40:02 (29,340)
Bernaudeau, Eric J 4:02:23 (11,835)
Bernhard, Hans-Peter 3:59:34 (11,177)
Bernstein, Richard 2:58:31 (1,012)
Berntsen Vagen, Frode 4:34:35 (19,730)
Berridge, David H 3:45:04 (7,314)
Berry, Andrew 3:48:24 (8,098)
Berry, Chris W 6:28:00 (31,177)
Berry, Clifford 3:19:12 (2,983)
Berry, Darren J 4:34:18 (19,669)
Berry, David A 3:55:12 (9,848)
Berry, Dominic G 6:07:01 (30,648)
Berry, Gavin R 3:21:37 (3,271)
Berry, Leon 4:22:28 (16,690)
Berry, Michael P 4:29:39 (18,542)
Berry, Mike A 5:43:01 (29,567)
Berry, Mike P 3:04:21 (1,482)
Berry, Paul M 3:42:02 (6,659)
Berry, Paul M 3:45:31 (7,414)
Berry, Paul R 3:12:41 (2,269)
Berry, Richard T 5:16:46 (27,229)
Berry, Simon 4:22:45 (16,760)
Berry, Stephen F 5:32:48 (28,796)
Berstrom, Anders 3:31:04 (4,785)
Bertagne, Michael G 3:49:27 (8,365)
Bertolini, Gabriele 3:50:33 (8,639)
Bertolini, Gianfranco 3:21:28 (3,251)
Bertram, Roger 5:44:47 (29,677)
Berzosa-Feito, Miguel A 4:44:12 (21,837)
Besemer, Laurence P 5:00:21 (25,045)
Besly, Jonathan 5:26:57 (28,295)
Best, Andrew J 4:06:25 (12,765)
Best, Barry 5:16:41 (27,220)
Best, James F 5:19:33 (27,503)
Best, Keith J 5:17:38 (27,320)
Best, Nigel C 3:57:33 (10,555)
Best, Richard L 4:06:50 (12,844)
Best, Stephen R 3:43:25 (6,940)
Besutti, Vanni 3:56:49 (10,337)
Bethel, Simon 4:50:36 (23,198)
Bett, Kevin A 3:10:16 (2,024)
Bett, Tim M 3:28:27 (4,310)
Betteley, Andrew D 4:48:34 (22,786)
Bettella, Mario 4:50:00 (23,073)
Betteridge, Paul A 3:58:09 (10,729)
Betteridge, Shaun D 3:54:39 (9,684)
Bettis, Carl 3:42:37 (6,769)
Bettles, Kevin H 3:31:42 (4,874)
Betts, Mark P 3:10:23 (2,037)
Betts, Peter K 5:22:33 (27,839)
Betts, Simon 5:20:19 (27,610)
Betty, Stefan P 3:50:11 (8,545)
Bevan, Andrew C 3:57:57 (10,662)
Bevan, Andy G 3:26:23 (3,902)
Bevan, Jonathan 4:34:21 (19,678)
Bevan, Martyn W 5:24:06 (27,979)
Bevan, Steve 3:41:44 (6,592)
Beveridge, David 4:16:02 (15,057)
Beverley, David W 3:30:02 (4,597)
Beverly, Michael 4:14:50 (14,770)
Bevis, Malcolm 4:02:34 (11,870)
Bewers, Paul 5:18:44 (27,439)
Bewsy, Robin M 3:50:16 (8,567)
Bey, Nikki 3:53:00 (9,257)
Beyeler, Daniel 4:20:31 (16,164)
Beynon, Robert 4:56:18 (24,261)
Bezdel, Sebastian J 3:34:48 (5,389)
Bezebeh, Sisay 2:12:05 (13)
Bezodis, Mark 4:38:26 (20,581)
Bhakar, Bobby S 4:45:16 (22,091)
Bhakar, Jagmohan S 5:35:18 (28,980)
Bhakar, Surinder S 4:29:52 (18,599)
Bhalla, Ravinder 7:17:24 (31,767)
Bhalla, Surjit S 7:17:23 (31,766)
Bhambra, Gurpal S 5:06:43 (25,942)
Bharwana, Abu-Turab 3:20:48 (3,177)
Bhelay, Jasmeet 5:32:22 (28,764)
Bhinder, Hamdeep S 4:45:16 (22,091)
Bhogal, Amreek 4:00:08 (11,323)
Bhoja, Narshi 4:25:40 (17,469)

Bhumber, Satbinder S.....6:02:00 (30,487)
Bialik, Leigh E.....5:28:56 (28,476)
Bianchetti, Alfredo.....3:46:23 (7,617)
Biau, David.....3:01:39 (1,283)
Biau, Lionel.....3:13:15 (2,334)
Bickerton, Dennis.....4:13:04 (14,347)
Bickham, Darren R.....6:29:02 (31,188)
Bicknell, Luke J.....3:23:45 (3,538)
Biddle, David G.....4:34:33 (19,723)
Bidnell, David R.....3:46:37 (7,666)
Biederman, Carlos.....3:17:11 (2,770)
Bienkowski, Steve.....3:40:49 (6,441)
Bier, Nicholas A.....5:00:43 (25,100)
Bieris, Stan.....3:54:04 (9,524)
Biggar, Graeme H.....3:45:30 (7,409)
Biggin, Guy.....5:19:46 (27,530)
Biggs, Anthony S.....3:51:38 (8,926)
Biggs, Clive.....4:22:30 (16,701)
Biggs, Geoff D.....3:59:49 (11,242)
Biggs, Gerard M.....4:49:15 (22,927)
Biggs, Roger.....3:42:13 (6,686)
Biggs, Trevor F.....4:30:12 (18,679)
Biggs-Hayes, Thomas.....5:16:14 (27,159)
Bigland, Phil J.....5:10:32 (26,445)
Bigley, Alastair J.....3:42:06 (6,668)
Bigley, Matthew R.....2:45:14 (332)
Bignell, Michael I.....4:47:47 (22,630)
Bignell, Richard B.....5:13:00 (26,762)
Bigorre, Bernard.....3:44:41 (7,236)
Bildstein, Laurent.....3:08:52 (1,884)
Bilham, John I.....4:02:39 (11,886)
Biller, Andrew.....3:36:45 (5,734)
Billingham, Ian E.....4:28:03 (18,107)
Billinghurst, Keith.....3:50:05 (8,521)
Billingsley, Andrew J.....3:49:29 (8,370)
Billington, Jonathan R.....4:57:54 (24,568)
Billington, Mark.....3:46:57 (7,737)
Billson, Matthew B.....4:35:25 (19,914)
Biltcliffe, Andrew M.....4:45:03 (22,045)
Bilton, Darran E.....2:25:52 (56)
Bilton, Martin T.....4:13:48 (14,517)
Bilton, Matthew D.....3:39:52 (6,284)
Bimson, Kevin J.....4:03:10 (11,997)
Binder, Richard J.....4:23:05 (16,837)
Bindloss, Simon H.....3:25:01 (3,697)
Bindloss Gibb, Edward J.....4:57:27 (24,486)
Bindra, Amrit P.....5:41:31 (29,449)
Binggell, Markus.....3:19:08 (2,967)
Bingham, Hugh.....2:54:30 (720)
Bingham, John.....5:41:22 (29,434)
Bingham, Jonathan M.....4:14:31 (14,682)
Bingham, Roger C.....5:26:18 (28,224)
Bingham, Stuart J.....4:13:36 (14,480)
Bingley, Kenneth.....3:49:53 (8,469)
Binks, Graham.....4:35:23 (19,905)
Binks, Richard A.....3:44:03 (7,082)
Binnersley, Nigel J.....4:48:05 (22,694)
Binning, Richard J.....4:13:16 (14,395)
Binns, Adrian D.....4:07:25 (12,991)
Binns, Charles J.....6:35:16 (31,293)
Binns, Daniel J.....4:43:52 (21,766)
Binse, Nicolas.....3:49:23 (8,352)
Binse, Olivier M.....3:49:22 (8,344)
Binson, Benoit.....2:46:31 (370)
Bintein, Bruno.....4:07:32 (13,017)
Bioly, Matthias.....3:29:28 (4,498)
Biondi, Stefano.....4:31:54 (19,080)
Birch, David.....3:07:10 (1,718)
Birch, Graeme.....4:27:39 (18,004)
Birch, James J.....3:49:05 (8,277)
Birch, Michael.....4:28:26 (18,206)
Birch, Nigel P.....4:32:43 (19,294)
Birch, Robin M.....3:47:52 (7,963)
Birch, Tom.....4:44:03 (21,805)
Birch, Trevor I.....4:23:22 (16,905)
Birchall, Chris.....2:22:23 (44)
Birchall, Philip S.....4:19:36 (15,929)
Bird, Alan R.....3:14:22 (2,486)
Bird, Anthony L.....4:25:43 (17,481)
Bird, Danny.....2:46:58 (387)
Bird, David J.....3:17:15 (2,780)
Bird, Gavin D.....2:59:29 (1,119)
Bird, Graham M.....4:27:43 (18,019)
Bird, James A.....6:03:30 (30,546)
Bird, Jamie E.....3:00:35 (1,198)
Bird, Jonathan A.....3:35:50 (5,578)
Bird, Mark D.....3:22:08 (3,321)
Bird, Melvyn.....4:04:28 (12,306)
Bird, Nigel C.....4:28:31 (18,235)
Bird, Paul R.....5:27:15 (28,330)
Bird, Philip J.....3:56:47 (10,323)
Birkens, John B.....3:32:33 (5,013)
Birkett, Stephen M.....3:47:51 (7,958)
Birkinshaw, Timothy R.....3:14:30 (2,503)
Birks, David L.....3:30:16 (4,647)
Birnie, Kevin M.....5:13:32 (26,831)
Birse, Neil W.....3:55:49 (10,022)
Birstein, Edwin.....2:45:24 (337)
Birt, Dean A.....4:12:19 (14,151)
Birtwhistle, Jeff P.....5:30:50 (28,650)
Birtwistle, Andrew.....4:15:19 (14,884)
Bisang, Martin.....3:25:45 (3,806)
Bisby, Paul R.....3:24:05 (3,576)
Bischoff, Marcel R.....3:25:39 (3,792)
Biscomb, Geoffrey C.....3:26:53 (3,999)
Bishenden, Alan.....3:50:00 (8,506)
Bishop, Calvin.....3:45:46 (7,477)
Bishop, Daniel T.....2:53:01 (645)
Bishop, David A.....3:43:51 (7,028)
Bishop, David J.....5:28:25 (28,430)
Bishop, David L.....4:02:01 (11,723)
Bishop, Graham M.....4:03:02 (11,960)
Bishop, James O.....4:13:33 (14,464)
Bishop, Joseph D.....3:23:56 (3,558)
Bishop, Mark.....5:28:29 (28,436)
Bishop, Michael.....4:47:02 (22,456)
Bishop, Simon R.....3:54:46 (9,715)
Bishop, Stevie.....5:24:35 (28,030)
Bishop, Timothy S.....3:05:03 (1,528)
Bisla, Navtej S.....5:10:09 (26,394)
Bissell, Simon P.....4:21:45 (16,465)
Bissenden, Thomas J.....4:03:34 (12,092)
Bisset, Gordon.....6:03:40 (30,552)
Bisset, Trevor C.....3:26:43 (3,964)
Bissett, Richard.....4:09:22 (13,466)
Bisson, Henry R.....4:51:40 (23,371)
Bistrong, Richard.....4:16:35 (15,194)
Biswas, Anup.....6:02:55 (30,527)
Bixley, Russell A.....4:56:44 (24,349)
Bizby, David C.....4:37:28 (20,333)
Bjerregaard, Bo.....2:58:49 (1,058)
Bjorklund, Magnus.....3:58:21 (10,804)
Bjornermark, Thomas.....3:37:56 (5,951)
Bjurdalen, Anders.....4:05:33 (12,555)
Black, Alistair M.....4:05:32 (12,550)
Black, Barnaby D.....4:58:25 (24,698)
Black, Charles.....3:31:46 (4,882)
Black, David A.....4:05:37 (12,575)
Black, Hadley J.....4:05:33 (12,555)
Black, Ian M.....4:02:50 (11,934)
Black, Ian P.....3:44:22 (7,149)
Black, James D.....5:15:17 (27,054)
Black, John W.....5:13:07 (26,784)
Black, Martin J.....3:44:28 (7,175)
Black, Peter A.....5:00:58 (25,139)
Black, Richard.....4:28:26 (18,206)
Black, Stephen R.....4:29:34 (18,511)
Blackburn, Colin A.....5:11:29 (26,576)
Blackburn, Duncan W.....3:50:06 (8,528)
Blackburn, Martin.....4:31:19 (18,924)
Blackburn, Michael.....3:10:12 (2,020)
Blackburn, Sam P.....3:41:56 (6,627)
Blackburn, Simon A.....2:54:33 (722)
Blackburn, Stephen T.....5:57:28 (30,309)
Blackett, Daniel L.....5:14:22 (26,943)
Blackford, Colin H.....3:35:19 (5,487)
Blackhall, Mark.....6:16:12 (30,913)
Blackhurst, Jonathan.....4:25:45 (17,496)
Blackley, David.....2:55:38 (793)
Blackman, James E.....3:54:30 (9,635)
Blackman, Leslie K.....4:38:31 (20,598)
Blackman, Robert.....3:59:42 (11,222)
Blackman, Scott A.....3:36:42 (5,725)
Blackmore, Carl A.....4:09:58 (13,631)
Blackmore, Peter B.....4:46:48 (22,409)
Blackwell, Brett J.....3:52:01 (9,016)
Blackwell, Mark.....4:56:32 (24,321)
Blackwell, Nicholas A.....2:57:22 (904)
Blackwell, Paul A.....4:19:37 (15,931)
Blackwell, Phlip N.....3:30:23 (4,669)
Blackwell, Will S.....4:08:38 (13,268)
Blackwood, Christopher A.....3:50:14 (8,555)
Blacoe, Mathew R.....2:56:17 (837)
Bladel Van, Cees.....3:48:06 (8,023)
Bladen, Alan J.....4:47:39 (22,606)
Blades, Richard J.....2:57:12 (893)
Blades, Terry W.....5:06:20 (25,892)
Blain, Perry J.....5:56:03 (30,249)
Blaine, John S.....3:21:26 (3,249)
Blair, Alan J.....3:13:24 (2,357)
Blair, Andrew M.....4:08:23 (13,196)
Blair, David T.....4:17:32 (15,433)
Blair, James P.....4:18:35 (15,681)
Blair, Jonathan J.....4:08:34 (13,252)
Blair, Magnus.....4:27:58 (18,091)
Blair, Mark A.....5:22:52 (27,865)
Blair, Nigel J.....3:45:10 (7,339)
Blair, Simon B.....4:34:06 (19,625)
Blair III, Edward.....3:26:14 (3,875)
Blake, Adrian.....3:42:26 (6,727)
Blake, Christopher P.....3:42:10 (6,674)
Blake, Edward A.....3:45:20 (7,372)
Blake, Geoffrey M.....3:49:00 (8,254)
Blake, Keith.....5:22:49 (27,859)
Blake, Kevin M.....4:08:25 (13,206)
Blake, Peter.....3:37:13 (5,817)
Blake, Peter L.....3:45:59 (7,523)
Blake, Richard A.....2:57:56 (960)
Blake, Simon A.....4:46:22 (22,333)
Blake, Steven J.....4:58:22 (24,679)
Blakeman, Brian J.....5:37:50 (29,169)
Blakeman, Robert H.....5:23:08 (27,885)
Blakemore, Dominic W.....4:44:35 (21,932)
Blakemore, John P.....5:05:38 (25,779)
Blakemore, Rob J.....4:18:54 (15,758)
Blakey, David M.....4:32:39 (19,276)
Blanche, Michael A.....5:22:51 (27,862)
Bland, David S.....4:45:25 (22,120)
Bland, Matthew J.....4:34:41 (19,753)
Blandford, Ron G.....5:54:26 (30,167)
Blane, Tony J.....5:08:14 (26,147)
Blaney, Geoffrey.....3:48:39 (8,168)
Blanford, William.....4:25:23 (17,401)
Blankson, Samuel A.....5:24:47 (28,054)
Blanks-Price, Thomas A.....3:55:56 (10,062)
Blantern, Matt R.....4:29:24 (18,466)
Blantz, Andrew.....4:34:09 (19,635)
Blasé, Phillip I.....3:31:54 (4,901)
Blaskett, Neil.....3:53:05 (9,275)
Blatt, Andreas.....3:02:18 (1,326)
Blauensteiner, Horst.....2:53:56 (693)
Blazquez, Diego D.....3:00:57 (1,233)
Bleaken, Daniel G.....4:48:23 (22,756)
Bleakman, Frederick A.....3:28:44 (4,359)
Bleasdale, Mark W.....3:58:37 (10,891)
Blencowe, Rupert D.....4:56:16 (24,255)
Blenkinsop, Craig.....3:40:37 (6,418)
Bligh, William A.....6:21:18 (31,038)
Bliss, Arthur.....4:34:08 (19,632)
Bliss, Paul R.....4:39:15 (20,783)
Bliss, Robert G.....4:51:03 (23,282)
Bliszko, Ferenc S.....5:02:02 (25,303)
Blizzard, Gareth D.....2:57:58 (963)
Bloemen Daal, Gerrit.....5:30:28 (28,619)
Blofeld, Roger J.....4:48:04 (22,688)
Blofeld, Stephen V.....4:11:34 (13,988)
Blogg, Edward H.....5:09:33 (26,313)
Blois, Richard.....6:11:40 (30,776)
Blok, André.....3:18:23 (2,884)
Blokland, Koos.....5:25:48 (28,175)
Blom, Glenn.....3:56:13 (10,148)
Blomeley, Nicholas.....4:44:09 (21,827)
Blomfield, David.....4:29:48 (18,583)
Blommaert, Edward.....4:08:28 (13,221)
Bloom, Peter J.....4:54:54 (23,977)
Bloomfield, Clive W.....7:28:46 (31,839)
Bloomfield, Graham C.....4:13:09 (14,365)
Bloomfield, John B.....4:41:47 (21,304)
Bloomfield, Philip A.....4:39:03 (20,739)

Bloomfield, Stephen M.....5:12:44 (26,718)	Bond, Stephen D.....4:29:06 (18,377)	Bottomley, Edward A.....6:05:27 (30,602)
Blore, Geoffrey.....7:01:09 (31,635)	Bone, Drummond.....3:37:03 (5,783)	Bottoms, Dave.....4:28:03 (18,107)
Blount, David J.....4:28:18 (18,170)	Bone, Garry.....3:53:28 (9,373)	Boucher, Frank.....3:44:05 (7,092)
Blow, Peter J.....4:03:17 (12,025)	Bonella, Ricardo.....4:29:30 (18,492)	Boucher, Michael B.....2:33:29 (102)
Blower, Jonathan L.....4:20:13 (16,069)	Bonera, Steven R.....4:52:30 (23,532)	Boucher, Stuart C.....5:01:13 (25,173)
Blower, Lee.....4:07:00 (12,891)	Bongiorno, Carlo.....4:42:00 (21,344)	Bouchet, Jean-Louis.....2:59:30 (1,121)
Blowers, Marcus E.....5:08:59 (26,236)	Bonham, Andrew P.....7:19:20 (31,784)	Boucquey, Pascal.....4:10:25 (13,737)
Bloxham, Roy W.....4:15:06 (14,828)	Bonham, Jonathan J.....4:23:45 (17,002)	Boulby, Paul.....6:56:47 (31,582)
Bloye, Graham J.....5:18:26 (27,405)	Bonnafoux, Bernard.....5:19:14 (27,481)	Boulding, Paul A.....3:33:37 (5,208)
Blundell, Kevin H.....5:20:55 (27,674)	Bonnard, Stephen J.....4:48:04 (22,688)	Boulding, Scott A.....4:09:58 (13,631)
Blundell, Mark.....4:30:49 (18,818)	Bonnefous, Bernard.....3:25:03 (3,699)	Boulding, Simon P.....5:05:47 (25,797)
Blundell, Steve A.....5:51:24 (30,032)	Bonner, Dannie J.....4:19:54 (15,997)	Boullier, Alain.....4:09:49 (13,585)
Blundell, Tom.....4:13:24 (14,432)	Bonner, David T.....4:42:13 (21,388)	Boullier, Yvan.....4:06:16 (12,727)
Blunsten, Stephen M.....4:13:54 (14,543)	Bonner, Paul E.....4:19:54 (15,997)	Bouloy, Martial.....2:54:41 (725)
Blunt, Richard L.....3:57:02 (10,397)	Bonnet, Emmanuel.....3:54:35 (9,660)	Boultbee, Paul T.....3:38:59 (6,132)
Blyth, Andrew C.....4:59:27 (24,894)	Bonnet, Franck.....4:24:26 (17,172)	Boulter, Graham D.....4:55:49 (24,157)
Blyth, Kenneth S.....3:41:56 (6,627)	Bonnet, Pierre-Michel.....4:34:17 (19,666)	Boulton, Andrew W.....5:11:52 (26,613)
Blyth, Paul.....4:48:04 (22,688)	Bonnet, Xavier.....4:00:08 (11,323)	Boulton, Chris.....3:48:10 (8,039)
Blyth, Stephen L.....5:20:31 (27,634)	Bonnett, Curtis D.....3:26:48 (3,988)	Boulton, Leigh R.....4:36:51 (20,217)
Blythe, Scott.....4:41:57 (21,337)	Bonnett, James M.....4:21:11 (16,307)	Boulton, Paul A.....3:38:13 (5,998)
Blythe, Trevor J.....4:01:25 (11,581)	Bonthrone, Steven A.....3:26:55 (4,003)	Bourdeau, Guillaume.....3:19:23 (3,004)
Boadle, Jeremy T.....4:25:46 (17,503)	Bontoft, Alan.....2:55:34 (790)	Bourgeais, Pascal.....3:40:22 (6,373)
Boakes, Richard J.....5:14:32 (26,964)	Bontoft, Bernie A.....3:19:11 (2,980)	Bourke, Colin F.....5:08:10 (26,138)
Boal, John M.....3:49:10 (8,302)	Booer, Paul R.....5:34:24 (28,917)	Bourke, Daniel J.....3:58:29 (10,845)
Boam, Adrian J.....4:47:45 (22,624)	Bookallil, Matthew J.....2:57:46 (942)	Bourne, Darren A.....3:17:24 (2,795)
Board, Jonathan M.....4:18:54 (15,758)	Booker, Paul T.....4:16:48 (15,251)	Bourne, Frank.....6:09:04 (30,700)
Board, Nigel E.....4:13:47 (14,513)	Boole, Barry.....3:13:18 (2,343)	Bourne, Jonathan E.....4:38:12 (20,520)
Boardley, Ian.....3:10:25 (2,047)	Boomer, Andrew M.....4:28:59 (18,344)	Bourner, Graham A.....5:29:40 (28,551)
Boardley, Neal J.....3:24:51 (3,671)	Boon, David R.....3:48:05 (8,020)	Boutcher, Kelly.....5:52:23 (30,091)
Boardman, Keith.....2:56:31 (853)	Boon, Richard.....3:43:04 (6,864)	Boutenel, Joel.....3:58:14 (10,766)
Boardman, Martin J.....4:24:04 (17,076)	Boon, Robert.....3:00:00 (1,156)	Bouvier-Masson, Pascal.....3:07:37 (1,767)
Boardman, Tim.....7:17:14 (31,765)	Boons, Roger.....3:20:35 (3,148)	Boux, Jonathan A.....4:11:24 (13,951)
Boardman, Wayne J.....4:57:32 (24,500)	Boonstra, Daniel R.....4:52:21 (23,514)	Bovaird, Chris.....4:29:27 (18,470)
Boas, Jason.....4:10:07 (13,662)	Booth, Alistair J.....4:35:40 (19,956)	Bovill, Peter J.....3:28:48 (4,373)
Boast, Mark T.....4:35:51 (19,990)	Booth, Andrew J.....4:31:01 (18,861)	Boville, Matt A.....3:43:55 (7,043)
Boatwright, Toby R.....5:02:30 (25,374)	Booth, Anthony D.....3:50:26 (8,614)	Bovington, Jason.....4:39:18 (20,792)
Boddice, Christopher S.....6:31:12 (31,230)	Booth, Ashley J.....4:03:31 (12,082)	Bowcher, Adrian P.....3:59:40 (11,212)
Boddington, Christopher C.....5:11:17 (26,552)	Booth, David R.....3:20:40 (3,157)	Bowd, Ryan M.....3:12:40 (2,266)
Boden, Lazloe.....2:58:29 (1,011)	Booth, Mark A.....4:14:06 (14,587)	Bowden, Jeremy.....5:17:09 (27,268)
Boden, Marc I.....4:08:03 (13,124)	Booth, Peter R.....4:55:27 (24,092)	Bowden, Paul.....3:14:37 (2,514)
Boden, Mark A.....4:38:40 (20,632)	Booth, Roger.....2:55:19 (774)	Bowden, Peter A.....3:35:17 (5,477)
Boden, Sean.....4:42:19 (21,418)	Booth, Simon V.....3:31:09 (4,799)	Bowden, Phillip K.....5:29:27 (28,525)
Bodenhausen, Johannes B.....4:59:17 (24,846)	Booth, Vincent A.....3:14:09 (2,459)	Bowden, Raymond F.....3:55:34 (9,954)
Bodevin, Pierrew.....3:17:23 (2,794)	Boothby, Chris S.....4:10:27 (13,743)	Bowden, Simon J.....4:01:04 (11,523)
Bodily, John D.....4:12:27 (14,184)	Boothman, Ian J.....3:26:46 (3,980)	Bowden-Brown, Brian L.....5:23:26 (27,909)
Bodley, Matthew.....5:18:34 (27,417)	Boothman, Michael J.....5:17:39 (27,322)	Bowder, Jonathan.....3:36:09 (5,634)
Bodnarsky, Paul M.....5:06:39 (25,933)	Boothroyd, Jonathan.....3:55:24 (9,907)	Bowditch, Wayne P.....5:39:24 (29,300)
Boeck, Franz.....3:26:30 (3,917)	Boothroyd, Paul.....3:45:44 (7,468)	Bowdler, Ian R.....5:34:46 (28,941)
Boerresen, Oeyvino.....4:47:54 (22,654)	Boothroyd, Richard A.....3:09:13 (1,920)	Bowdler, Richard H.....2:59:42 (1,136)
Boes, Remco.....4:10:19 (13,708)	Bootman, Martin D.....4:53:20 (23,674)	Bowe, Garry R.....3:20:22 (3,107)
Boggis, Mark A.....3:58:31 (10,860)	Bootton, Gary.....3:44:33 (7,201)	Bowell, John D.....5:01:17 (25,181)
Bogocz, Axel.....4:28:34 (18,248)	Bordese, Francesco.....3:56:36 (10,280)	Bowell, Mark J.....3:51:34 (8,909)
Bogue, James Y.....3:16:45 (2,724)	Bordingnon, Daniele.....2:40:57 (226)	Bowen, Andrew D.....3:28:44 (4,359)
Bohan, Colin D.....4:54:02 (23,800)	Boreel, Jacob J.....4:41:27 (21,230)	Bowen, Chris E.....4:07:01 (12,896)
Bohl, Markus.....2:51:18 (556)	Boreham, Harry L.....4:51:50 (23,406)	Bowen, David A.....4:16:23 (15,142)
Boiston, Justin D.....3:57:49 (10,622)	Boreham, Paul J.....4:12:54 (14,302)	Bowen, James K.....3:42:59 (6,846)
Boland, Robert P.....3:23:11 (3,462)	Borgelt, Hans W.....3:33:29 (5,187)	Bowen, Keith J.....3:23:15 (3,471)
Boles, Kevin M.....4:18:36 (15,686)	Borgers, Peter P.....5:35:32 (29,002)	Bowen, Laurence J.....4:19:40 (15,943)
Boley, Michael L.....4:22:18 (16,637)	Borgne, Ulrich.....4:45:42 (22,190)	Bowen, Paul D.....3:46:46 (7,697)
Boley, Stephen D.....3:48:13 (8,055)	Borgstrom, Marcus.....4:50:15 (23,113)	Bowen, Sean.....2:54:54 (747)
Boll, Hans Werner.....3:48:36 (8,150)	Borgstrom, Yngve.....5:09:06 (26,254)	Bowen, Simon J.....3:19:23 (3,004)
Bolliger, Adolf.....6:50:46 (31,507)	Borgund, Ole J.....3:56:10 (10,128)	Bowen, Spencer J.....4:15:51 (15,015)
Bollington, Simon J.....4:25:08 (17,347)	Borland, David.....3:39:50 (6,280)	Bowen, Stuart D.....4:22:24 (16,666)
Bolster, Eric G.....3:39:55 (6,292)	Borley, David C.....4:54:02 (23,800)	Bowen-Morris, Ian D.....4:03:04 (11,970)
Bolster, Ian J.....3:58:27 (10,834)	Borley, Harry W.....4:54:01 (23,796)	Bower, Brian.....3:12:09 (2,208)
Bolt, Sean W.....4:03:21 (12,046)	Borstel, Howard R.....5:19:48 (27,532)	Bower, John S.....3:15:04 (2,561)
Bolton, Alexander.....4:16:35 (15,194)	Borton, Simon A.....3:14:28 (2,496)	Bower, Matthew J.....3:20:44 (3,164)
Bolton, David J.....5:01:17 (25,181)	Bosch, Ulf.....2:57:51 (949)	Bowerman, Paddy E.....4:22:25 (16,671)
Bolton, Richard P.....4:59:31 (24,906)	Bosher, Thomas A.....3:06:49 (1,687)	Bowers, Jared C.....4:58:20 (24,672)
Bolton, Ross.....4:19:17 (15,854)	Bosson, Paul J.....2:51:46 (582)	Bowes, Christopher D.....3:24:48 (3,660)
Bolton, Steve.....2:57:53 (954)	Bost, Claude.....5:12:18 (26,669)	Bowker, David.....4:23:11 (16,869)
Bolton, Wayne L.....4:06:33 (12,793)	Bostock, Derek.....3:43:19 (6,922)	Bowker, Richard H.....2:52:34 (621)
Bomford, Andrew P.....3:17:40 (2,817)	Bostock, Malcolm S.....3:35:48 (5,572)	Bowles, Alan.....5:20:05 (27,577)
Bonas, John.....6:10:04 (30,727)	Bostock, Marc.....4:28:23 (18,187)	Bowles, Brian C.....5:23:31 (27,924)
Bond, Allan J.....4:30:38 (18,788)	Boston, David J.....4:06:43 (12,821)	Bowles, Graham P.....4:54:25 (23,881)
Bond, Daniel M.....5:25:51 (28,181)	Boswell, Adam M.....4:38:46 (20,659)	Bowles, Keith D.....3:53:49 (9,448)
Bond, David.....4:14:46 (14,745)	Boswell, Bob.....5:00:59 (25,142)	Bowles, Matthew J.....4:11:49 (14,048)
Bond, Evan B.....2:37:59 (170)	Boswell, David M.....4:38:46 (20,659)	Bowman, Angus M.....3:44:45 (7,249)
Bond, Martin.....4:19:18 (15,857)	Bosworth, Jim E.....3:30:31 (4,692)	Bowman, Dave R.....3:48:22 (8,093)
Bond, Matthew J.....2:51:30 (569)	Botha, Louis T.....3:51:27 (8,875)	Bowman, John.....5:01:31 (25,224)
Bond, Michael J.....2:41:49 (239)	Botha, Paul.....4:47:33 (22,580)	Bowman, Nicholas D.....4:03:47 (12,144)
Bond, Peter A.....4:19:33 (15,921)	Bott, Matthew J.....3:55:12 (9,848)	Bowman, Philip A.....3:34:52 (5,400)
Bond, Richard.....3:20:01 (3,069)	Bottaro, Davide.....3:28:57 (4,407)	Bown, Nicholas V.....4:07:16 (12,960)

Bowron, Michael 3:25:18 (3,735)
Bowsher, Andrew C 3:44:39 (7,224)
Bowyer, Darren P 5:02:17 (25,336)
Bowyer, Malcolm J 3:00:17 (1,178)
Box, John K 6:40:49 (31,368)
Box, Matthew 3:35:52 (5,584)
Boxall, Andrew F 3:59:51 (11,253)
Boxall, Gordon W 3:56:14 (10,161)
Boxall, John E 4:39:53 (20,891)
Boxall, Steven M 6:14:56 (30,882)
Boxer, Richard B 4:07:25 (12,991)
Boy, Graeme I 4:02:45 (11,914)
Boyall, Timothy J 3:19:38 (3,034)
Boyce, Adam J 8:31:56 (31,967)
Boyce, Daniel M 4:56:39 (24,338)
Boyce, Gavin A 6:37:24 (31,331)
Boyce, Lawrence J 4:19:11 (15,825)
Boyd, Adrian J 4:38:33 (20,606)
Boyd, Andrew 4:28:43 (18,281)
Boyd, Andrew J 4:43:55 (21,778)
Boyd, Christopher S 4:48:31 (22,779)
Boyd, Daniel W 4:32:13 (19,172)
Boyd, David R 4:17:45 (15,494)
Boyd, James 3:45:40 (7,446)
Boyd, Norman 4:35:07 (19,844)
Boyd, Philip J 3:37:03 (5,783)
Boyd, Stephen P 4:59:21 (24,865)
Boyd, William 5:18:38 (27,427)
Boyde, Steven 4:10:24 (13,734)
Boyden, Matt 3:43:34 (6,974)
Boyden, Scott A 3:59:30 (11,157)
Boyeldieu, Edmond H 3:43:25 (6,940)
Boyes, Ian J 6:27:43 (31,171)
Boyes, John 3:30:03 (4,601)
Boyle, Andrew I 4:51:24 (23,330)
Boyle, Colin D 3:35:11 (5,456)
Boyle, David A 3:51:49 (8,972)
Boyle, Glen A 4:10:13 (13,681)
Boyle, Gordon R 4:16:16 (15,111)
Boyle, James A 6:07:00 (30,647)
Boyle, Mark C 4:03:25 (12,062)
Boyle, Martin J 3:44:44 (7,245)
Boys, Ian D 5:47:44 (29,856)
Boyton-Salts, Mark 2:55:27 (782)
Bozeat, Luke B 4:23:52 (17,030)
Brabyn, Matthew P 4:14:54 (14,786)
Bracamontes, Miguel A 4:34:15 (19,653)
Brace, Christopher J 3:50:01 (8,510)
Bracegirdle, Craig J 4:32:09 (19,152)
Bracey, Nick 3:47:51 (7,958)
Bracey, Paul R 4:12:36 (14,237)
Bracken, Edward J 4:22:14 (16,619)
Brackstone, Richard A 4:01:03 (11,516)
Bradbury, Alan K 3:19:00 (2,949)
Bradbury, David M 4:10:17 (13,697)
Bradbury, Gary J 3:40:20 (6,364)
Bradbury, Richard A 4:31:22 (18,945)
Bradbury, Thomas J 4:03:56 (12,176)
Brader, Phillip 4:22:07 (16,576)
Bradfield, Kevin 5:02:36 (25,388)
Bradford, Adam P 3:38:33 (6,056)
Bradford, Andrew E 5:35:25 (28,996)
Bradford, Andrew J 4:20:56 (16,271)
Bradley, Adam 3:33:02 (5,106)
Bradley, Barrington J 3:56:02 (10,094)
Bradley, John A 5:15:28 (27,074)
Bradley, Jonathan R 5:24:19 (28,005)
Bradley, Kyran G 4:00:53 (11,475)
Bradley, Lloyd 5:11:00 (26,505)
Bradley, Luke B 3:50:46 (8,698)
Bradley, Mark D 4:26:02 (17,579)
Bradley, Mark N 4:24:03 (17,072)
Bradley, Michael J 4:25:09 (17,351)
Bradley, Nicholas 3:55:34 (9,954)
Bradley, Paul R 3:28:22 (4,293)
Bradley, Terence J 5:43:30 (29,590)
Bradley, Tony J 4:25:15 (17,370)
Bradshaw, David R 4:00:09 (11,329)
Bradshaw, Grahame S 4:06:48 (12,836)
Bradshaw, John W 7:16:09 (31,759)
Bradshaw, Lyndon 3:39:20 (6,191)
Bradshaw, Shaun A 3:49:31 (8,380)
Bradshaw, Simon R 5:23:03 (27,874)
Bradshaw, Steve 4:29:27 (18,470)
Brady, Anthony 4:10:35 (13,774)
Brady, Dominic 4:47:49 (22,639)
Brady, Harold J 5:26:15 (28,216)
Brady, John C 3:38:21 (6,023)
Brady, Kieran J 4:33:23 (19,445)
Brady, Michael P 3:30:34 (4,703)
Brady, Paul A 3:22:48 (3,419)
Brady, Sean E 3:26:10 (3,870)
Brady, Shaun 3:59:52 (11,258)
Braham, Geoffrey E 3:48:07 (8,027)
Braid, Gordon 4:34:34 (19,726)
Braid-Lewis, Deane 4:46:37 (22,376)
Braidwood, Billy G 3:33:44 (5,223)
Brailey, Steven J 3:54:36 (9,666)
Brailsford, Owen J 4:43:14 (21,617)
Brain, Jaime N 3:25:54 (3,827)
Brain, Paul 4:22:25 (16,671)
Brain, Robert E 3:51:10 (8,789)
Braithwaite, Michael E 3:27:41 (4,164)
Braithwaite, Peter J 4:28:37 (18,259)
Braithwaite, Richard E 5:22:31 (27,834)
Braithwaite, Stephen A 5:10:41 (26,464)
Braithwaite, Steven 3:57:48 (10,618)
Braker, Robert C 4:14:09 (14,599)
Bramhall, Ewan 4:39:55 (20,901)
Bramhall, Philip 4:29:12 (18,402)
Bramley, Christopher R 4:17:59 (15,550)
Bramwell, Nicholas C 3:32:02 (4,931)
Branch, Alan D 4:01:01 (11,507)
Branch, Stuart 4:26:45 (17,763)
Branco, Miguel A 2:59:38 (1,131)
Brand, Leon P 3:17:08 (2,764)
Brand, Neal J 4:04:55 (12,411)
Brand, Philip 4:20:25 (16,136)
Brand, Roger J 3:49:51 (8,461)
Brand, Simon 4:30:01 (18,634)
Brandani, Alberto 5:17:14 (27,278)
Brandish, Stephen E 3:45:56 (7,514)
Brandom, Mark 4:53:40 (23,740)
Brandon Trye, Christopher P 3:20:46 (3,171)
Brandreth, Stephen 5:01:52 (25,280)
Brandt, David A 3:18:52 (2,938)
Brandt, Patrik 5:20:18 (27,609)
Branford, Olivier A 3:37:02 (5,776)
Brann, Phil M 4:34:27 (19,699)
Brannan, Paul F 4:27:10 (17,885)
Brannelly, John 3:26:19 (3,892)
Brannigan, Damien T 2:49:57 (501)
Brannigan, Malachy 3:37:53 (5,936)
Bransfield, Robert 5:01:24 (25,207)
Branson, Jonathan 3:56:17 (10,178)
Branston, Stephen M 4:26:25 (17,677)
Bratley, Richard 4:09:28 (13,490)
Bratton, Tim J 3:51:54 (8,989)
Braud, Francis R 3:52:48 (9,195)
Braude, Jeremy S 7:08:02 (31,693)
Braude, Jonathan H 4:37:46 (20,398)
Braun, Dominique H 2:47:10 (393)
Braun, Manfred 4:27:52 (18,059)
Brauns, Simon R 5:35:07 (28,966)
Braunton, David 2:46:08 (362)
Braunton, David W 4:25:35 (17,450)
Brauss, Michael S 3:44:42 (7,242)
Bray, Alan 3:56:57 (10,379)
Bray, Francis J 3:38:14 (6,000)
Bray, John E 4:05:40 (12,588)
Bray, Marcus 4:01:13 (11,547)
Bray, Nicholas J 4:34:51 (19,791)
Bray, Oliver D 4:58:11 (24,636)
Bray, Richard S 4:06:56 (12,871)
Bray, Robert 5:49:51 (29,955)
Bray, Thomas M 4:33:22 (19,441)
Bray, Vivian F 3:55:34 (9,954)
Braybrooke, David J 4:22:22 (16,660)
Brayne, Martin S 4:18:50 (15,748)
Brayshaw, Peter 4:15:21 (14,889)
Brayshaw, Simon M 3:27:39 (4,156)
Brazendale, David A 4:05:24 (12,510)
Brazier, Bill S 4:57:36 (24,513)
Brazier, Timothy R 4:46:53 (22,421)
Breaker, Ben 3:38:21 (6,023)
Brearley, Michael 3:09:43 (1,970)
Brearley, Stephen 4:30:49 (18,818)
Brecht, Philip T 4:13:29 (14,448)
Breen, Christopher C 3:44:37 (7,217)
Breen, John J 3:47:35 (7,903)
Breese, Ian C 4:09:51 (13,593)
Breese, Philip M 4:15:46 (14,993)
Bregman, Ben 5:14:07 (26,914)
Brehier, Pierre Y 3:24:24 (3,616)
Breinlinger, Jorn 4:52:34 (23,545)
Bremer, Henrik 4:15:27 (14,916)
Bremner-Smith, Julian P 6:02:51 (30,524)
Brennan, Joseph C 4:39:22 (20,805)
Brennan, Paul V 3:37:37 (5,895)
Brennan, Pete J 4:22:24 (16,666)
Brennan, Simon 3:54:15 (9,577)
Bresh, Steven E 4:10:16 (13,693)
Bresland, Noel P 3:45:59 (7,523)
Breslin, Declan 4:06:35 (12,801)
Breslin, Matthew 3:57:54 (10,649)
Breslin, William 4:10:16 (13,693)
Bretherick, Andy J 3:07:45 (1,784)
Brett, Christopher J 4:09:54 (13,607)
Brett, Colin M 3:56:58 (10,382)
Brett, Gavin 3:38:14 (6,000)
Brett, John T 4:11:48 (14,044)
Brett, Robert 4:56:56 (24,391)
Brett, Stephen 3:02:31 (1,341)
Brettell, John M 4:21:43 (16,457)
Brew, Patrick S 3:18:05 (2,857)
Brew, Stefan K 3:30:39 (4,718)
Brewer, Andrew 4:02:59 (11,950)
Brewer, John 3:34:01 (5,274)
Brewer, Jonathan A 3:27:12 (4,064)
Brewin, Nicholas 5:24:52 (28,064)
Brewster, Terry R 4:38:59 (20,721)
Breydin, Patrick 4:46:07 (22,272)
Bria Mas, Alejandro 4:26:05 (17,600)
Briars, Simon P 4:34:26 (19,696)
Brice, Ian R 4:24:53 (17,278)
Brickell, Adam P 3:35:15 (5,472)
Bridge, Kevin J 3:32:28 (4,998)
Bridgeford, Ross G 4:33:11 (19,399)
Bridgeman, Gary A 3:28:18 (4,282)
Bridger, Andrew J 4:35:32 (19,936)
Bridger, David W 4:40:48 (21,089)
Bridger, Matt L 4:00:29 (11,395)
Bridges, Anthony M 2:46:33 (372)
Bridges, Douglas J 3:50:16 (8,567)
Bridges, Ian G 3:41:55 (6,624)
Bridges, Keith A 4:40:21 (20,996)
Bridgewater, Andrew 5:09:10 (26,264)
Bridgman, Mark 4:25:37 (17,456)
Bridgwater, Christopher 4:41:09 (21,149)
Brier, Anthony J 4:39:00 (20,729)
Brier, Christopher A 4:01:58 (11,707)
Brierley, Andy 6:19:53 (31,010)
Brierley, Peter 4:47:27 (22,557)
Briers Danks, Rick L 3:54:54 (9,753)
Briffett, Stephen 4:06:31 (12,781)
Briggs, Jonathan M 3:33:18 (5,160)
Briggs, Michael E 5:09:30 (26,305)
Briggs, Michael J 5:15:15 (27,050)
Briggs, Peter I 3:44:30 (7,185)
Briggs, Simon 6:41:33 (31,382)
Briggs, Stephen 3:39:47 (6,271)
Briggs, Steven A 2:58:44 (1,049)
Briggs, Tony J 5:33:58 (28,890)
Bright, Duncan J 3:31:07 (4,792)
Bright, Jeremy 3:57:34 (10,563)
Bright, Neil 5:40:22 (29,364)
Bright, Philip D 5:24:41 (28,044)
Brighton, Michael J 5:00:56 (25,132)
Brightwell, Simon L 4:01:36 (11,622)
Brignoli, Sergio 4:19:03 (15,786)
Brignone, Valerio 2:22:15 (42)
Brigstock, Jamie R 4:18:19 (15,611)
Briguglio, Claudio 4:02:25 (11,842)
Brimmell, Robert J 4:59:53 (24,971)
Brindle, Peter 4:11:32 (13,978)
Brinklow, David A 5:40:31 (29,383)
Brinton, Nick J 4:09:56 (13,622)
Briscoe, Jonathan J 6:11:45 (30,779)
Brissenden, Phillip 4:11:17 (13,926)

Bristow, Ian C	4:02:26 (11,845)	
Britchford, Langley M	5:14:33 (26,969)	
Brito, Matt	3:34:23 (5,323)	
Brito, Sidney F	4:25:20 (17,389)	
Britt, Anthony J	4:44:06 (21,815)	
Brittain, Paul	3:53:44 (9,420)	
Britten, Alan D	4:41:30 (21,245)	
Britten, Tony R	3:22:07 (3,317)	
Britton, Charles T	4:16:28 (15,166)	
Britton, Gregory	3:34:32 (5,346)	
Britton, Jonathan E	5:32:47 (28,794)	
Britton, Nick	5:14:22 (26,943)	
Britton, Robert G	3:33:59 (5,268)	
Britton, Robin N	3:13:26 (2,363)	
Britton, Stuart J	4:24:21 (17,153)	
Broad, John F	4:16:19 (15,122)	
Broad, Jonathan P	4:44:52 (21,991)	
Broad, Matthew T	4:35:17 (19,882)	
Broad, Nigel M	5:17:52 (27,349)	
Broadbent, Christopher J	3:48:42 (8,185)	
Broadbent, Clive	5:48:39 (29,891)	
Broadbent, Steven S	4:21:44 (16,464)	
Broadfield, Andrew D	3:35:55 (5,591)	
Broadfoot, Peter	4:16:15 (15,107)	
Broadhead, Nicholas	5:15:43 (27,098)	
Broadhurst, Bruce	4:35:33 (19,939)	
Broadhurst, Carl	3:33:03 (5,109)	
Broadhurst, Christopher	4:38:49 (20,670)	
Broadhurst, Jack F	3:09:32 (1,951)	
Broadley, Kenneth J	4:47:40 (22,608)	
Broadstock, David C	6:04:39 (30,584)	
Broadstock, Robert E	4:08:06 (13,131)	
Broadwell, Daniel I	4:33:27 (19,457)	
Brock, Carsten	3:53:09 (9,297)	
Brock, David J	4:15:26 (14,909)	
Brock, Kevin H	3:57:03 (10,404)	
Brock, Neil M	2:53:10 (653)	
Brockenhurst, Aaron	3:50:48 (8,706)	
Brockington, Martin J	3:49:57 (8,489)	
Brocklehurst, Christopher J	3:25:46 (3,810)	
Brocklesby, Steve J	3:31:08 (4,797)	
Brockman, Michael J	4:18:27 (15,655)	
Brockway, Richard G	4:21:41 (16,443)	
Brockwell, John W	4:35:40 (19,956)	
Brod, Ralf	3:20:44 (3,164)	
Broderick, Patrick	3:58:23 (10,813)	
Broderick, Terence P	4:14:47 (14,752)	
Broderick, Wayne J	4:54:34 (23,914)	
Brodie, Andrew J	3:38:34 (6,063)	
Brodie, Paul A	4:39:12 (20,774)	
Brogan, Christopher J	2:49:27 (476)	
Brogan, David M	3:01:01 (1,238)	
Brogden, Richard A	3:28:56 (4,404)	
Brokenshaw, Michael J	4:30:44 (18,806)	
Bromage, Dan I	3:51:23 (8,853)	
Bromley, James D	7:28:12 (31,834)	
Bromley, Nigel G	3:46:36 (7,662)	
Brons, Jelle	3:59:15 (11,070)	
Brook, John	3:56:09 (10,121)	
Brook, John B	6:01:03 (30,453)	
Brook, Jonathan	3:40:56 (6,462)	
Brooke, Craig D	3:08:48 (1,880)	
Brooke, David A	5:57:21 (30,304)	
Brooke, David J	3:28:45 (4,364)	
Brooke, James M	4:55:43 (24,135)	
Brooke, Jeremy M	3:48:54 (8,230)	
Brooke, Lynne	4:27:57 (18,082)	
Brooke, Michael H	4:55:43 (24,135)	
Brooke, Nick J	3:12:47 (2,284)	
Brooker, Colin J	5:36:35 (29,067)	
Brooker, John J	3:58:07 (10,715)	
Brooker, Simon P	4:47:11 (22,497)	
Brooker-Tormey, Andy A	5:43:37 (29,601)	
Brookes, Chris G	3:09:31 (1,948)	
Brookes, David I	5:41:30 (29,446)	
Brookes, John L	5:24:21 (28,008)	
Brookes, Nigel A	3:11:58 (2,191)	
Brookes, Paul	3:25:06 (3,704)	
Brookes, Steven	4:19:21 (15,871)	
Brookes, Steven R	2:49:10 (466)	
Brookes, Wayne N	3:42:40 (6,780)	
Brooking, Ian D	5:50:17 (29,979)	
Brooks, Adrian	4:04:16 (12,257)	
Brooks, Andrew P	4:23:53 (17,034)	
Brooks, Christopher	4:26:51 (17,785)	
Brooks, David J	4:04:53 (12,402)	
Brooks, Duncan G	4:49:42 (23,014)	
Brooks, Gary	3:14:30 (2,503)	
Brooks, James	3:28:24 (4,301)	
Brooks, Kevin F	5:24:21 (28,008)	
Brooks, Marcus J	3:11:36 (2,149)	
Brooks, Mark E	3:23:10 (3,461)	
Brooks, Mark E	3:24:32 (3,627)	
Brooks, Mark P	4:24:34 (17,199)	
Brooks, Mike	3:04:22 (1,483)	
Brooks, Patrick J	4:53:54 (23,778)	
Brooks, Paul	4:33:35 (19,482)	
Brooks, Paul A	4:03:03 (11,965)	
Brooks, Paul H	4:03:23 (12,055)	
Brooks, Paul K	3:54:27 (9,627)	
Brooks, Peter N	4:43:28 (21,678)	
Brooks, Richard A	4:02:44 (11,910)	
Brooks, Roger M	4:11:52 (14,056)	
Brooks, Simon P	3:49:59 (8,501)	
Brooks, Stephen	5:14:16 (26,930)	
Brooks, Steve	3:52:00 (9,012)	
Brooks, Wayne	4:26:46 (17,766)	
Brooksbank, George S	3:18:20 (2,880)	
Brookwell, Chris	4:24:55 (17,288)	
Broom, Jack J	3:42:41 (6,785)	
Broom, John	2:42:35 (255)	
Broom, Neil W	4:36:53 (20,223)	
Broom, Peter	3:58:57 (10,991)	
Broomberg, Jonathan	3:31:23 (4,830)	
Broomfield, Jeremy R	4:04:25 (12,288)	
Broomfield, Mark T	3:57:12 (10,444)	
Brosnan, Michael F	5:01:35 (25,238)	
Brosnan, Patrick W	3:29:13 (4,455)	
Broster, Paul A	4:48:32 (22,781)	
Brotherston, Ken	4:09:24 (13,475)	
Brotherton, Anthony C	3:50:17 (8,572)	
Brouard, Martin P	5:13:08 (26,785)	
Brouchoud, Fernand	3:57:28 (10,527)	
Brougham, Jeremy R	3:42:40 (6,780)	
Broughton, Bob C	4:00:48 (11,444)	
Broughton, Gordon F	5:43:38 (29,603)	
Brouner, James W	3:26:42 (3,957)	
Browell, Robert I	4:13:21 (14,419)	
Brown, Adrian C	4:04:41 (12,345)	
Brown, Alan J	4:55:26 (24,090)	
Brown, Alan M	2:58:15 (990)	
Brown, Alastair M	3:58:58 (10,996)	
Brown, Alistair J	2:54:06 (700)	
Brown, Allan G	4:25:39 (17,465)	
Brown, Allan M	6:37:12 (31,322)	
Brown, Andrew	3:52:24 (9,111)	
Brown, Andrew C	5:42:52 (29,539)	
Brown, Andrew D	4:03:27 (12,067)	
Brown, Andrew J	4:08:15 (13,159)	
Brown, Andrew J	4:11:32 (13,978)	
Brown, Andrew J	4:12:29 (14,194)	
Brown, Andrew J	4:36:39 (20,167)	
Brown, Andrew P	4:15:52 (15,021)	
Brown, Andy C	6:13:00 (30,817)	
Brown, Andy J	3:28:01 (4,230)	
Brown, Anthony	4:13:05 (14,349)	
Brown, Barry M	5:12:02 (26,638)	
Brown, Chris P	3:58:16 (10,780)	
Brown, Christopher	3:39:52 (6,284)	
Brown, Christopher F	4:02:24 (11,839)	
Brown, Christopher T	3:48:35 (8,144)	
Brown, Cliff	3:29:42 (4,533)	
Brown, Colin	4:58:29 (24,718)	
Brown, Colin D	5:35:15 (28,976)	
Brown, Colin S	5:06:16 (25,885)	
Brown, Craig	4:33:28 (19,463)	
Brown, Darren P	3:55:42 (9,989)	
Brown, David	3:58:21 (10,804)	
Brown, David B	6:26:42 (31,152)	
Brown, David C	5:04:59 (25,690)	
Brown, David E	4:23:04 (16,830)	
Brown, David H	4:49:02 (22,883)	
Brown, David J	4:02:42 (11,899)	
Brown, David M	2:57:44 (936)	
Brown, David M	5:09:38 (26,325)	
Brown, Dean	4:28:48 (18,298)	
Brown, Dean C	4:46:47 (22,406)	
Brown, Derek	2:56:51 (873)	
Brown, Derek	4:37:16 (20,310)	
Brown, Derek A	4:31:49 (19,053)	
Brown, Dominic A	3:16:23 (2,683)	
Brown, Donald F	4:59:55 (24,976)	
Brown, Edward B	6:00:16 (30,423)	
Brown, Gavin A	5:37:03 (29,110)	
Brown, Geoffrey C	5:37:42 (29,161)	
Brown, Gordon	3:36:33 (5,703)	
Brown, Gordon	5:16:59 (27,258)	
Brown, Graeme H	4:01:17 (11,559)	
Brown, Graeme J	3:36:56 (5,756)	
Brown, Graham A	4:37:04 (20,266)	
Brown, Graham D	4:18:41 (15,707)	
Brown, Graham T	5:20:56 (27,676)	
Brown, Hamish R	4:24:21 (17,153)	
Brown, Iain P	4:31:49 (19,053)	
Brown, Ian	3:15:51 (2,637)	
Brown, Ian	4:29:42 (18,555)	
Brown, Ian M	4:29:43 (18,557)	
Brown, James H	3:05:04 (1,530)	
Brown, James M	4:34:16 (19,657)	
Brown, James R	3:36:30 (5,696)	
Brown, Jeremy	4:36:34 (20,147)	
Brown, Jim	4:11:45 (14,032)	
Brown, John W	4:19:48 (15,975)	
Brown, Jon	2:13:39 (15)	
Brown, Jonathan M	4:03:04 (11,970)	
Brown, Julian L	3:47:31 (7,883)	
Brown, Keith	3:24:15 (3,595)	
Brown, Keith	4:35:23 (19,905)	
Brown, Kenneth J	4:02:03 (11,730)	
Brown, Kevin	4:18:01 (15,557)	
Brown, Kevin G	3:17:35 (2,810)	
Brown, Lee	5:28:19 (28,422)	
Brown, Lee E	4:19:15 (15,846)	
Brown, Malcolm	5:30:55 (28,655)	
Brown, Mark	3:58:50 (10,954)	
Brown, Martin J	3:59:05 (11,024)	
Brown, Martin P	4:06:54 (12,862)	
Brown, Martin S	4:05:27 (12,523)	
Brown, Michael	4:37:05 (20,270)	
Brown, Michael J	3:44:46 (7,254)	
Brown, Michael J	3:50:26 (8,614)	
Brown, Michael J	4:45:51 (22,219)	
Brown, Michael P	4:15:55 (15,031)	
Brown, Mike T	3:29:42 (4,533)	
Brown, Neale F	4:55:55 (24,186)	
Brown, Neil W	4:45:50 (22,217)	
Brown, Nicholas M	5:12:47 (26,726)	
Brown, Nicholas P	4:27:33 (17,977)	
Brown, Nick	5:50:02 (29,968)	
Brown, Oliver J	4:58:24 (24,694)	
Brown, Patrick	4:30:22 (18,720)	
Brown, Paul	4:10:44 (13,806)	
Brown, Peter	4:44:57 (22,020)	
Brown, Peter G	4:10:32 (13,762)	
Brown, Peter N	5:35:37 (29,008)	
Brown, Peter T	4:34:03 (19,606)	
Brown, Ray D	4:22:06 (16,571)	
Brown, Reginald G	7:26:57 (31,825)	
Brown, Richard	4:04:42 (12,351)	
Brown, Richard	4:42:32 (21,460)	
Brown, Richard T	4:16:17 (15,114)	
Brown, Robert	4:38:18 (20,548)	
Brown, Robert H	4:32:25 (19,217)	
Brown, Rodney	4:24:22 (17,156)	
Brown, Roger A	5:11:39 (26,586)	
Brown, Roger J	4:56:13 (24,248)	
Brown, Ross R	5:03:29 (25,517)	
Brown, Russell L	4:10:42 (13,800)	
Brown, Shane P	3:46:16 (7,593)	
Brown, Simon W	3:58:07 (10,715)	
Brown, Stephen A	3:27:33 (4,138)	
Brown, Stephen J	4:58:25 (24,698)	
Brown, Steven A	3:51:59 (9,008)	
Brown, Stuart	4:20:33 (16,172)	
Brown, Stuart J	4:23:53 (17,034)	
Brown, Stuart P	3:29:04 (4,425)	
Brown, Stuart S	5:55:46 (30,234)	
Brown, Timothy S	2:53:20 (663)	

Brown, Timothy S	4:03:15 (12,017)
Brown, Tony	3:39:57 (6,295)
Brown, William	5:10:10 (26,396)
Brownbill, Paul D	3:48:35 (8,144)
Browne, Brian P	5:38:48 (29,246)
Browne, Christopher A	3:45:19 (7,367)
Browne, Christopher G	3:20:10 (3,086)
Browne, Mark A	5:09:59 (26,375)
Browne, Michael P	4:08:18 (13,177)
Browne, Nathan J	4:28:14 (18,153)
Browne, Nick	4:53:24 (23,687)
Browne, Simon P	4:42:15 (21,397)
Browne, Steve S	3:42:45 (6,801)
Brownhill, George	4:08:39 (13,272)
Browning, David	4:01:08 (11,534)
Browning, David E	4:51:08 (23,294)
Browning, Jeremy L	5:19:41 (27,520)
Browning, Keith S	4:11:48 (14,044)
Browning, Neil R	3:27:54 (4,211)
Browning, Paul	3:25:29 (3,767)
Browning, Riki A	4:16:32 (15,179)
Browning, Roger L	4:11:30 (13,968)
Brownlee, David F	3:36:25 (5,684)
Brownlee, Robert	4:16:54 (15,282)
Brownlie, Allan	3:37:17 (5,832)
Brownlie, Frank	4:39:40 (20,855)
Brownlie, Kent	4:58:42 (24,757)
Brownsword, Nigel P	4:58:41 (24,754)
Broxis, Paul	5:22:00 (27,772)
Bruccoleri, Donato	2:57:53 (954)
Bruce, Andrew K	3:15:08 (2,572)
Bruce, Andrew W	5:10:17 (26,412)
Bruce, Ian M	5:25:51 (28,181)
Bruce, Nigel C	4:17:33 (15,439)
Bruce, Paul R	6:07:34 (30,666)
Bruce, Perry C	3:41:37 (6,568)
Bruce, Richard J	4:04:23 (12,279)
Bruce, Sandy	5:56:53 (30,283)
Bruens, Ben C	3:09:45 (1,976)
Brule, Gerard	4:41:41 (21,276)
Brummitt, John A	4:00:15 (11,349)
Brundle, Paul R	3:28:52 (4,392)
Brunet, Frederic	2:32:25 (96)
Bruni, Roberto	3:25:37 (3,790)
Bruning, Ludger	3:27:02 (4,031)
Brunner, Simon P	4:16:56 (15,292)
Brunning, James J	3:34:50 (5,395)
Bruno, Hans	4:57:37 (24,518)
Brunskill, Iain R	4:27:06 (17,864)
Brunt, Dominic	4:17:25 (15,403)
Brunton, Graham S	4:23:56 (17,046)
Brunton, Guthrie W	3:18:15 (2,876)
Brunton, William R	4:27:40 (18,010)
Brusau, Bernard	4:44:20 (21,869)
Bruton, Peter J	5:08:17 (26,158)
Bruyninckx, Rudy	2:52:31 (616)
Bruzon, Nick K	5:01:40 (25,252)
Bryan, Adrian C	4:07:42 (13,056)
Bryan, Anthony P	5:41:50 (29,477)
Bryan, John B	6:57:46 (31,593)
Bryan, Jonathan G	4:36:55 (20,233)
Bryan, Peter W	3:56:11 (10,134)
Bryan, Stuart E	4:40:07 (20,943)
Bryant, Alex	4:56:19 (24,266)
Bryant, Dudley	4:08:57 (13,364)
Bryant, Jamie	4:18:54 (15,758)
Bryant, John	5:26:24 (28,240)
Bryant, John M	4:14:43 (14,732)
Bryant, Kevin J	4:52:25 (23,522)
Bryant, Mark J	2:49:56 (497)
Bryant, Mark N	3:17:22 (2,792)
Bryant, Paul J	4:07:50 (13,076)
Bryant, Richard H	5:12:47 (26,726)
Bryce, Murray	3:21:04 (3,208)
Brylow, Scott M	4:09:16 (13,446)
Bryon, Richard	3:34:20 (5,315)
Bryson, Patrick	3:19:14 (2,991)
Bubb, Nick J	3:46:54 (7,723)
Bubb, Philip G	3:58:09 (10,729)
Bucaille, Edourd	3:48:10 (8,039)
Buchan, Kevin A	5:40:24 (29,369)
Buchan, Philip A	3:57:50 (10,627)
Buchan, Stuart	2:38:43 (180)
Buchanan, Andrew	4:48:03 (22,682)
Buchanan, Iain D	3:54:14 (9,572)
Buchanan, James	4:36:25 (20,110)
Buchanan, Jim	4:36:04 (20,045)
Buchanan, Jonathan	3:39:24 (6,204)
Buchanan, Stephen C	4:43:40 (21,714)
Bucher, William	5:04:12 (25,597)
Buck, Simon A	4:45:25 (22,120)
Buckberry, Adam J	5:51:59 (30,063)
Buckberry, Alan	4:09:56 (13,622)
Buckenham, Clive G	4:11:38 (14,011)
Buckett, Daniel C	5:05:45 (25,792)
Buckingham, Donald	5:11:19 (26,557)
Buckingham, Graham L	3:27:50 (4,193)
Buckingham, Philip C	4:04:24 (12,282)
Buckland, Adam S	3:27:29 (4,124)
Buckland, Carl G	4:34:33 (19,723)
Buckland, Charles R	4:28:13 (18,151)
Buckland, Richard G	6:50:49 (31,509)
Buckley, Bernard A	3:57:40 (10,586)
Buckley, Brian W	3:08:21 (1,836)
Buckley, Edward F	3:18:37 (2,913)
Buckley, Glyn	3:58:34 (10,879)
Buckley, Ian M	4:29:46 (18,573)
Buckley, Michael J	4:39:39 (20,852)
Buckley, Paul A	2:43:53 (287)
Buckley, Robert A	3:50:02 (8,511)
Buckley, Robert N	4:43:05 (21,578)
Buckley, Stephen J	4:29:52 (18,599)
Bucknall, Alan J	4:28:10 (18,140)
Bucknell, Chris C	5:12:40 (26,708)
Buckthorp, Justin N	3:35:53 (5,587)
Budd, Graeme R	4:32:09 (19,152)
Budd, Ian	4:23:33 (16,953)
Buerger, Michael	4:19:14 (15,841)
Buerli, Roger A	4:08:56 (13,358)
Bugby, Anthony R	5:03:07 (25,461)
Bugeja, John A	3:20:14 (3,092)
Bugg, Ivan J	3:38:58 (6,126)
Buggins, Ian M	5:17:51 (27,346)
Buglass, Mark A	3:36:00 (5,612)
Buick, Jim	2:56:10 (825)
Buitendag, David	3:21:36 (3,269)
Bulaitis, Peter A	3:19:20 (2,999)
Buley, Mark	3:35:46 (5,567)
Bull, David R	4:19:44 (15,959)
Bull, Graham M	3:49:13 (8,312)
Bull, James R	3:44:45 (7,249)
Bull, Kevin J	5:21:23 (27,719)
Bull, Martyn G	6:57:59 (31,597)
Bull, Matthew W	4:23:22 (16,905)
Bull, Michael D	3:45:02 (7,311)
Bull, Michael J	3:32:50 (5,066)
Bull, Peter B	3:47:20 (7,837)
Bull, Ross	7:09:41 (31,706)
Bull, Steve	4:32:36 (19,261)
Bull, Tim	3:34:54 (5,411)
Bullard, Stuart J	4:23:31 (16,947)
Bullas, Jonathan M	5:37:24 (29,148)
Bullen, Kerry A	4:29:17 (18,422)
Bullen, Mark A	4:59:21 (24,865)
Buller, Robert S	7:12:53 (31,731)
Bulley, Jason	3:24:57 (3,684)
Bullions, Peter J	4:13:13 (14,385)
Bullmore, Joshua	4:48:18 (22,739)
Bullmore, Simon T	4:04:12 (12,240)
Bullock, Brian	4:16:20 (15,126)
Bullock, Paul D	2:59:13 (1,095)
Bullock, Peter K	4:49:45 (23,027)
Bullough, Duncan S	4:37:44 (20,387)
Bulmer, Hugo E	4:46:56 (22,430)
Bulmer, Steven M	5:22:12 (27,793)
Bulmer-Thomas, Victor	4:40:37 (21,043)
Bulthuis, Wildrik	3:42:44 (6,797)
Bumstead, Mark	2:49:58 (503)
Bumstead, Stephen S	2:55:14 (769)
Bunbury, Anthony G	3:58:05 (10,705)
Bunce, Nicholas H	4:36:34 (20,147)
Bunce, Philip R	4:15:53 (15,026)
Bunce, Stephen A	3:44:12 (7,114)
Bunch, Trevor I	3:54:10 (9,548)
Bundey, Paul	3:37:48 (5,922)
Bundy, Terry J	3:44:53 (7,283)
Bungay, Alan M	4:57:23 (24,471)
Bunn, Brian H	5:09:33 (26,313)
Bunn, David A	3:08:29 (1,848)
Bunn, Thomas	3:29:29 (4,501)
Bunner, Robert J	4:16:25 (15,152)
Bunting, Alistair J	3:12:55 (2,302)
Bunting, Peter A	4:24:31 (17,188)
Bunting, Timothy C	6:10:18 (30,735)
Bunting, William	4:47:31 (22,570)
Bunyan, Robert G	3:37:10 (5,808)
Bunyard, Peter R	4:39:21 (20,802)
Buono, Gerard	3:57:46 (10,609)
Burbanks, Magnus	2:56:58 (879)
Burbidge, Reginald	5:51:59 (30,063)
Burborough, Peter F	4:10:27 (13,743)
Burch, Jonathan W	3:57:59 (10,667)
Burch, Matthew I	4:24:41 (17,227)
Burch, Peter A	4:01:32 (11,605)
Burch, Philip J	4:58:14 (24,646)
Burchell, Simon	4:20:36 (16,187)
Burchett, David	5:35:09 (28,972)
Burchett, Gary P	3:26:50 (3,992)
Burchett, Rainer H	4:06:11 (12,708)
Burchill, Peter	4:12:49 (14,283)
Burcombe, Gary C	4:40:40 (21,059)
Burdeau, Ishmael H	2:48:05 (425)
Burdekin, Phil J	5:07:46 (26,089)
Burden, Robert	5:22:51 (27,862)
Burden, Stephen M	4:05:28 (12,529)
Burden, Stuart C	4:22:53 (16,791)
Burdett, Daniel P	3:39:19 (6,188)
Burdett, Jeremy R	4:33:33 (19,477)
Burditt, Gary A	3:42:35 (6,760)
Burdon, Michael A	4:54:33 (23,911)
Burfitt, David J	5:19:45 (27,528)
Burford, Colin J	3:42:29 (6,742)
Burford, Colin R	5:24:54 (28,069)
Burford, Lawrence C	4:36:01 (20,029)
Burford, Philip	4:34:21 (19,678)
Burge, Paul	5:43:38 (29,603)
Burger, Rob A	4:47:16 (22,514)
Burgess, Dean R	4:06:13 (12,716)
Burgess, John F	4:25:53 (17,536)
Burgess, John G	4:38:22 (20,564)
Burgess, John L	5:22:47 (27,858)
Burgess, Joshua L	4:00:30 (11,399)
Burgess, Rhodri O	5:32:06 (28,738)
Burgess, Timothy J	4:21:29 (16,385)
Burgess, Tom C	3:07:17 (1,726)
Burgess, Tom J	4:54:54 (23,977)
Burgh, Nigel	4:57:57 (24,582)
Burgin, Brian	3:47:30 (7,879)
Burgin, Graham	4:14:36 (14,706)
Burgin, Neil D	3:44:39 (7,224)
Burke, Adam J	3:54:00 (9,505)
Burke, Austin	5:07:33 (26,050)
Burke, Iain A	3:35:24 (5,502)
Burke, John G	4:54:54 (23,977)
Burke, Jonathan F	5:47:16 (29,826)
Burke, Kevin	3:09:19 (1,930)
Burke, Martin J	4:36:41 (20,179)
Burke, Paul H	3:17:36 (2,814)
Burke, Paul M	3:42:19 (6,700)
Burke, Paul S	3:58:28 (10,843)
Burke, Phillip J	5:07:02 (25,974)
Burke, Simon D	7:00:13 (31,628)
Burke, Thomas E	2:37:47 (167)
Burkhill, John H	6:52:27 (31,535)
Burl, Duncan J	4:05:17 (12,482)
Burleigh, Phil J	3:19:26 (3,013)
Burley, David A	4:43:00 (21,564)
Burley, Dennis F	4:17:01 (15,307)
Burley, John M	4:01:33 (11,610)
Burlinson, George	4:39:10 (20,764)
Burman, Kenneth H	4:34:41 (19,753)
Burn, David A	4:21:37 (16,425)
Burn, James D	3:06:58 (1,702)
Burnage, Andrew J	5:12:58 (26,755)
Burnage, Steven P	5:02:44 (25,408)
Burnett, Andrew	3:59:41 (11,218)
Burnett, Bryan	2:52:40 (624)
Burnett, Christopher	4:05:51 (12,627)
Burnett, Nigel	3:35:18 (5,483)

Burnham, Alan	5:47:38 (29,848)	
Burnhope, Stephen J	4:46:51 (22,415)	
Burningham, Leo	2:54:22 (711)	
Burns, Alastair	4:30:06 (18,655)	
Burns, Andrew J	4:31:40 (19,014)	
Burns, Andrew M	4:22:31 (16,703)	
Burns, Andrew R	5:10:47 (26,480)	
Burns, Billy	2:16:18 (21)	
Burns, David	5:22:33 (27,839)	
Burns, David H	5:36:36 (29,071)	
Burns, Graham	5:49:12 (29,917)	
Burns, Kenneth	3:14:12 (2,467)	
Burns, Paul M	3:06:40 (1,672)	
Burns, Peter G	4:07:25 (12,991)	
Burns, Robert J	3:14:40 (2,520)	
Burns, Simon J	5:16:21 (27,176)	
Burnside, Martin	4:36:35 (20,150)	
Burr, Mike	3:51:29 (8,880)	
Burr, Roland D	4:33:48 (19,534)	
Burr, Stephen C	5:20:01 (27,567)	
Burr, William J	3:38:18 (6,010)	
Burrell, Alan R	4:38:27 (20,584)	
Burrell, David A	3:17:12 (2,773)	
Burrell, John F	4:19:59 (16,029)	
Burrell, Jonathan W	4:18:57 (15,771)	
Burrell, Simon	3:47:29 (7,876)	
Burridge, Mark V	4:11:44 (14,029)	
Burridge, Peter J	5:14:39 (26,986)	
Burrows, Geoff C	5:08:16 (26,152)	
Burrows, John M	3:51:25 (8,862)	
Burrows, Jon E	4:26:41 (17,749)	
Burrows, Matthew H	4:45:23 (22,115)	
Burrows, Paul S	4:03:17 (12,025)	
Burrows, Simon J	3:55:08 (9,831)	
Burrows, Stuart N	4:01:20 (11,569)	
Burston, Jonathan C	5:53:52 (30,146)	
Burt, Alan M	3:45:42 (7,461)	
Burt, Cameron	2:49:37 (483)	
Burt, David W	5:23:55 (27,964)	
Burt, Peter E	3:51:26 (8,868)	
Burt, William A	4:07:50 (13,076)	
Burton, Adam R	3:34:35 (5,354)	
Burton, Andrew J	3:29:48 (4,553)	
Burton, Barnaby L	3:39:36 (6,238)	
Burton, Christopher R	5:36:12 (29,040)	
Burton, David	2:58:51 (1,061)	
Burton, David K	3:09:52 (1,989)	
Burton, Derek	4:38:11 (20,517)	
Burton, James C	4:22:01 (16,544)	
Burton, Jamie N	4:22:09 (16,588)	
Burton, Jeff D	3:05:53 (1,597)	
Burton, John	4:31:24 (18,950)	
Burton, John L	3:38:52 (6,111)	
Burton, Keith A	6:39:16 (31,351)	
Burton, Mark	3:01:01 (1,238)	
Burton, Nicholas E	3:23:47 (3,543)	
Burton, Robert	3:22:16 (3,338)	
Burton, Robert	4:56:09 (24,237)	
Burton, Terence C	4:32:54 (19,335)	
Burton, Toby L	3:57:33 (10,555)	
Burton, Wesley J	4:45:27 (22,129)	
Burtscher, Ingo M	3:54:41 (9,691)	
Burvill, David M	5:44:03 (29,627)	
Bury, Robert D	3:56:50 (10,348)	
Busa, Antonino	3:08:30 (1,850)	
Busby, Dominic P	4:03:16 (12,021)	
Busby, Stuart M	4:09:54 (13,607)	
Busby, William R	3:49:30 (8,376)	
Buscena, Bruno	3:31:00 (4,778)	
Busch, Graham	3:10:34 (2,061)	
Bush, Adam J	3:05:05 (1,533)	
Bush, Gary T	4:19:48 (15,975)	
Bush, Kevin M	3:07:35 (1,762)	
Bush, Martin R	5:19:14 (27,481)	
Bushby, Ray	3:02:45 (1,357)	
Bushell, Philip E	3:52:17 (9,079)	
Bushwell, Andrew J	4:24:38 (17,215)	
Bustard, Ian	5:36:55 (29,100)	
Buswell, Andy M	3:28:25 (4,305)	
Buswell, James A	3:56:48 (10,330)	
Buswell, Stephen M	3:00:50 (1,223)	
Butcher, Alan R	4:44:30 (21,912)	
Butcher, Alexander G	6:34:24 (31,280)	
Butcher, Barry	5:02:28 (25,367)	
Butcher, Christopher D	3:08:05 (1,811)	
Butcher, Gary	2:50:13 (513)	
Butcher, John N	4:03:40 (12,120)	
Butcher, Mark	5:58:14 (30,336)	
Butcher, Martin E	4:21:15 (16,323)	
Butcher, Philip J	3:48:36 (8,150)	
Butcher, Robert K	4:51:39 (23,369)	
Butelli, Cesare	3:36:22 (5,672)	
Buthelezi, Simon M	5:24:51 (28,062)	
Butland, Jonty	4:32:43 (19,294)	
Butler, Anthony J	3:07:37 (1,767)	
Butler, Benjamin J	3:57:22 (10,505)	
Butler, Bruce K	3:37:10 (5,808)	
Butler, Bryan	4:17:24 (15,399)	
Butler, Cavan L	4:38:33 (20,606)	
Butler, Christopher A	3:42:53 (6,830)	
Butler, Darren	5:02:00 (25,298)	
Butler, James P	4:15:52 (15,021)	
Butler, John	4:43:01 (21,566)	
Butler, John D	3:48:17 (8,074)	
Butler, Kenneth J	4:20:52 (16,250)	
Butler, Michael P	3:27:14 (4,070)	
Butler, Patrick T	2:58:32 (1,015)	
Butler, Philip J	3:34:33 (5,349)	
Butler, Robert J	4:07:15 (12,955)	
Butler, Roger G	5:57:01 (30,289)	
Butler, Sam	4:34:37 (19,738)	
Butler, Simon	3:40:30 (6,403)	
Butler, Stephen D	3:11:57 (2,188)	
Butler, Stephen J	5:07:25 (26,032)	
Butlin, Graeme N	4:01:07 (11,533)	
Butlin, Paul J	4:54:18 (23,855)	
Butson, Geoff H	3:38:33 (6,056)	
Butt, Andrew D	4:22:39 (16,737)	
Butt, David C	4:06:36 (12,807)	
Buttar, Satvinder S	4:31:48 (19,050)	
Butterfield, Karl M	5:27:55 (28,389)	
Butterfield, Pete J	4:05:35 (12,568)	
Butterfield, Richard	3:02:37 (1,346)	
Butterworth, James K	4:00:06 (11,316)	
Butterworth, Peter	2:49:43 (487)	
Butterworth, Philip R	3:17:02 (2,751)	
Button, Christopher J	4:53:04 (23,624)	
Buttress, Mark A	4:57:06 (24,420)	
Butts, Steven E	4:18:26 (15,647)	
Buwalda, Andrew D	3:44:25 (7,163)	
Buxton, Kevin	2:44:47 (318)	
Buxton, Stuart D	3:18:44 (2,924)	
Buxton, Thomas	3:14:04 (2,445)	
Byansi, Malachi	2:51:44 (580)	
Byarugaba, Richard P	5:24:10 (27,988)	
Bye, Alan F	3:22:57 (3,435)	
Bye, Benjamin W	4:08:08 (13,139)	
Byford, Graham A	3:37:20 (5,846)	
Byford, Mason J	4:19:24 (15,883)	
Byford, Matthew E	5:34:51 (28,946)	
Byford, Steven C	3:56:21 (10,196)	
Bygrave, Andrew	4:18:34 (15,680)	
Byres, Kelvin J	3:42:00 (6,646)	
Byrne, Anthony W	4:39:41 (20,859)	
Byrne, Charles	3:46:31 (7,689)	
Byrne, David A	2:45:15 (334)	
Byrne, James N	3:56:08 (10,117)	
Byrne, John	4:18:44 (15,717)	
Byrne, Kevin	3:26:05 (3,860)	
Byrne, Mark J	3:14:19 (2,480)	
Byrne, Mark P	5:21:00 (27,681)	
Byrne, Martin J	3:59:58 (11,284)	
Byrne, Patrick A	4:02:03 (11,730)	
Byrne, Rory	2:29:49 (80)	
Byrne, Sean P	3:46:43 (7,684)	
Byrne, Susan F	5:12:38 (26,704)	
Byrom, Chris	4:47:22 (22,533)	
Bytheway, Simon N	4:14:36 (14,706)	
Bywater-Lees, Ralph T	4:11:28 (13,962)	
Bywell, Robert	3:37:08 (5,800)	
Cable, Stephen J	3:08:56 (1,892)	
Cabrita, Mark J	2:58:52 (1,062)	
Cadavid Ospina, Walter	4:27:04 (17,859)	
Cadden, Paul D	5:03:09 (25,466)	
Caddy, David J	2:50:38 (532)	
Caddy, Ian P	4:02:39 (11,886)	
Cadene, Gislain	3:50:37 (8,662)	
Cadenhead, Neil	3:55:13 (9,854)	
Cadman, Alex I	4:29:29 (18,490)	
Cadman, Matthew A	4:18:31 (15,665)	
Cadman, Milton	4:15:39 (14,965)	
Cadman, Phil R	4:19:04 (15,792)	
Cadman, Stephen R	3:27:21 (4,094)	
Cahalarn, Spencer	5:02:14 (25,324)	
Caher, Charles F	5:15:18 (27,056)	
Cahill, Barry J	4:31:04 (18,870)	
Cahill, David E	5:01:33 (25,229)	
Cahill, Mike J	3:25:39 (3,792)	
Cahillane, Steven A	3:29:17 (4,469)	
Caillot, Alain	3:08:32 (1,854)	
Cain, Christopher W	2:57:11 (892)	
Cain, Francis	3:24:07 (3,578)	
Caine, Robert	4:19:26 (15,894)	
Cairns, Adam	3:54:02 (9,514)	
Cairns, Andrew N	5:07:37 (26,059)	
Cairns, Graham	4:51:48 (23,397)	
Cairns, Ian	4:16:32 (15,179)	
Cairns, Oliver W	3:49:24 (8,356)	
Cakebread, George H	8:08:41 (31,951)	
Cakebread, John G	3:06:45 (1,677)	
Calandro, Aldo	3:56:26 (10,228)	
Calaz, Kevin J	4:30:16 (18,694)	
Calcutt, Colin N	4:33:37 (19,492)	
Calcutt, Keith P	3:14:48 (2,537)	
Calcutt, Roy V	3:33:06 (5,116)	
Calder, Philip A	4:43:32 (21,692)	
Caldermead, William G	3:13:06 (2,317)	
Calderwood, Colin	3:46:46 (7,697)	
Caldicot, Peter J	2:55:55 (807)	
Caldwell, Craig	5:50:02 (29,968)	
Caldwell, Martin A	4:38:55 (20,699)	
Caldwell, Ronald	5:57:43 (30,317)	
Caldwell, Tobias	5:29:14 (28,511)	
Caldwell, William R	3:56:13 (10,148)	
Cali, Vittorio	3:05:42 (1,583)	
Calice, Clemens	3:37:10 (5,808)	
Callachan, David	3:50:17 (8,572)	
Callaghan, Colin T	4:50:11 (23,107)	
Callaghan, Eugene F	3:56:23 (10,204)	
Callaghan, Robert F	3:43:52 (7,031)	
Callaghan, Steve	4:01:36 (11,622)	
Callaghan, Timothy A	3:08:21 (1,836)	
Callagher, Damien J	3:30:06 (4,614)	
Callan, Maurice S	4:18:29 (15,661)	
Callanan, Peter	3:56:11 (10,134)	
Callard, Andrew M	3:54:50 (9,732)	
Callary, Lawrence P	4:07:12 (12,939)	
Caller, Mark J	4:28:27 (18,215)	
Callini, Franco	3:50:51 (8,720)	
Callister, Ian D	3:52:13 (9,061)	
Callow, James S	3:30:46 (4,735)	
Callow, Leo J	3:51:29 (8,880)	
Calnan, Neville M	4:44:03 (21,805)	
Calo, Armando	3:29:29 (4,501)	
Calthrop, Ben C	4:45:38 (22,171)	
Calvert, Craig L	3:08:54 (1,890)	
Calvert, Gerald M	3:34:39 (5,360)	
Calvert, Howard L	3:30:17 (4,652)	
Calvert, Jonathan R	3:28:24 (4,301)	
Cambe, Eric	3:32:26 (4,993)	
Cambiano, Dario	3:21:06 (3,212)	
Cambridge, Ross H	3:24:29 (3,624)	
Cameron, Andrew D	3:29:32 (4,507)	
Cameron, Colin	4:53:31 (23,704)	
Cameron, David J	2:45:38 (347)	
Cameron, Duncan	4:30:05 (18,650)	
Cameron, Ewen R	3:58:09 (10,729)	
Cameron, Pyers	3:50:24 (8,605)	
Cameron, Ronald A	5:24:40 (28,042)	
Cameron, Stuart J	3:31:48 (4,889)	
Camfield, Bryan	3:19:28 (3,016)	
Camilleri, Marco A	3:32:57 (5,090)	
Camisasca, Claudio	3:42:33 (6,754)	
Cammell, Jon T	4:03:24 (12,057)	
Camp, Brian	6:45:20 (31,445)	
Camp, Gary	4:10:35 (13,774)	
Campbell, Aaron J	5:14:14 (26,929)	
Campbell, Adam C	4:38:19 (20,551)	
Campbell, Allan B	5:00:44 (25,101)	

Campbell, Andrew M 4:29:32 (18,503)
Campbell, Andy 4:49:01 (22,878)
Campbell, Benedict 4:30:21 (18,716)
Campbell, Benjamin J 3:56:11 (10,134)
Campbell, Brian A 3:35:34 (5,535)
Campbell, Danny 3:59:39 (11,206)
Campbell, David 2:55:52 (803)
Campbell, David A 4:30:43 (18,803)
Campbell, Donald J 4:20:41 (16,206)
Campbell, Eric M 4:06:29 (12,775)
Campbell, Fergus 5:04:27 (25,622)
Campbell, Gary P 3:04:04 (1,455)
Campbell, Graeme 6:30:41 (31,217)
Campbell, Iain A 3:45:36 (7,441)
Campbell, Ian G 4:39:07 (20,751)
Campbell, Lee 3:06:21 (1,640)
Campbell, Malcolm 2:25:14 (53)
Campbell, Martin A 3:51:43 (8,945)
Campbell, Michael D 5:08:58 (26,231)
Campbell, Michael M 4:07:48 (13,069)
Campbell, Murray D 4:35:38 (19,950)
Campbell, Neil 3:57:46 (10,609)
Campbell, Neil D 3:57:29 (10,533)
Campbell, Niall P 3:23:27 (3,494)
Campbell, Nicholas D 4:07:02 (12,903)
Campbell, Paul F 4:25:38 (17,462)
Campbell, Richard 3:40:28 (6,393)
Campbell, Richard A 5:11:09 (26,527)
Campbell, Robin A 4:35:42 (19,961)
Campbell, Simon A 3:50:46 (8,698)
Campbell, Stuart K 4:29:00 (18,349)
Campbell, William 4:59:24 (24,883)
Campbell Clause, William R 4:43:28 (21,678)
Campbell-Barnard, James R 3:02:15 (1,321)
Campion, Mark A 3:22:19 (3,345)
Campion, Stephen W 3:13:10 (2,324)
Campling, Andrew 3:53:19 (9,342)
Campodonic, Mark J 4:03:04 (11,970)
Campos-Gomez, José F 2:54:54 (747)
Cane, Marc S 3:42:46 (6,803)
Caney, Mark W 4:24:41 (17,227)
Canham, Hugh G 3:27:49 (4,188)
Canham, Mark C 4:00:40 (11,418)
Canham, Ray D 4:57:13 (24,442)
Canham, Roger T 3:25:59 (3,846)
Cann, Andrew 4:57:16 (24,456)
Cann, Nicholas C 7:16:06 (31,755)
Canner, Leigh E 5:29:53 (28,572)
Canning, Tom J 4:10:30 (13,756)
Cannings, David 4:34:52 (19,796)
Cannings, Neil D 4:14:23 (14,648)
Cannon, Colin 3:31:26 (4,837)
Cannon, Gary 3:58:33 (10,874)
Cannon, Martin G 4:04:37 (12,333)
Cannon, Paul A 5:24:25 (28,019)
Canovas-Ruiz, Victor 3:12:42 (2,273)
Cant, Christopher R 2:58:12 (986)
Cant, Rob D 4:18:20 (15,616)
Cantwell, Matthew D 3:26:44 (3,969)
Cany, Frederic 3:12:20 (2,233)
Capel, Alan C 3:58:37 (10,891)
Capel, David 3:46:34 (7,653)
Capell, Martyn A 4:31:40 (19,014)
Capes, Christopher J 4:54:11 (23,835)
Capes, Ian P 3:50:52 (8,723)
Capetti, Giacomo 2:54:29 (717)
Caple, Kevin J 3:59:30 (11,157)
Caplen, Stephen G 3:53:09 (9,297)
Capocci, Paul M 4:11:04 (13,883)
Capon, Ian H 4:24:48 (17,251)
Caporali, Francesco 3:48:16 (8,069)
Capper, Graham 3:40:21 (6,368)
Capps, Christopher S 4:01:25 (11,581)
Caquet, Emanuel 3:07:39 (1,774)
Caquineau, Jean-Paul 4:43:25 (21,667)
Carabott, Francis A 4:25:38 (17,462)
Caramatti, Niccolo L 4:13:22 (14,423)
Carbin, Ian 3:41:19 (6,525)
Carbonnel, Jean-Marc 5:02:20 (25,351)
Carbury, Paul A 4:47:16 (22,514)
Carder, Anthony A 4:08:00 (13,115)
Carder, Christopher D 4:24:00 (17,062)
Cardiff, Patrick J 5:52:15 (30,080)
Cardoso, Abel 3:52:02 (9,021)
Cardy, Nicholas 4:33:05 (19,378)
Carey, Andrew J 5:13:15 (26,799)
Carey, Eddie 3:27:33 (4,138)
Carey, Mark J 3:46:56 (7,730)
Carey, Moray W 4:13:19 (14,411)
Carey, Patrick 4:24:54 (17,284)
Carey, Philip A 4:52:52 (23,593)
Cariello, Pietro 5:39:03 (29,270)
Cariou, Philippe 3:14:01 (2,437)
Cariss, Chris 2:15:08 (18)
Carlile, Paul 4:49:55 (23,062)
Carlile, Paul J 4:33:11 (19,399)
Carlin, Bob 3:49:27 (8,365)
Carlin, Brian E 2:54:23 (712)
Carlin, Christopher J 3:48:40 (8,176)
Carlin, Paul M 3:23:24 (3,489)
Carlino, Jacques D 5:02:01 (25,299)
Carlo, Matthew J 4:29:46 (18,573)
Carlson, Andrew I 5:24:06 (27,979)
Carmichael, Christopher P 4:49:21 (22,951)
Carmichael, David J 3:45:40 (7,446)
Carmichael, Duncan H 3:58:30 (10,856)
Carmichael, Stuart J 4:01:36 (11,622)
Carmody, James R 4:15:14 (14,863)
Carnegie, Malcolm 4:20:06 (16,047)
Carnell-Holdaway, Paul P 3:48:53 (8,227)
Carnet, Michel 6:00:16 (30,423)
Carney, Michael 4:22:59 (16,809)
Caroe, Chris 4:29:18 (18,431)
Caroe, Timothy D 4:29:18 (18,431)
Carolan, Christopher D 5:39:37 (29,312)
Carolan, Peter V 5:37:16 (29,133)
Carolan, Thomas J 5:34:27 (28,923)
Carpenter, Colin B 5:34:22 (28,913)
Carpenter, David L 5:29:42 (28,557)
Carpenter, Michael J 4:34:04 (19,614)
Carpenter, Neil 4:05:22 (12,501)
Carpenter, Trevor A 5:46:55 (29,807)
Carpentieri, Vincenzo 5:17:52 (27,349)
Carr, Adrian N 3:44:08 (7,102)
Carr, Damian 4:29:03 (18,360)
Carr, David 4:16:43 (15,231)
Carr, David 4:45:03 (22,045)
Carr, Graham E 4:23:26 (16,929)
Carr, Ian 4:45:36 (22,167)
Carr, James 3:43:09 (6,878)
Carr, James B 3:52:17 (9,079)
Carr, John 2:48:44 (448)
Carr, John D 4:04:03 (12,195)
Carr, Malcolm A 3:34:11 (5,296)
Carr, Mike J 4:06:33 (12,793)
Carr, Philip J 5:00:48 (25,112)
Carr, Tim D 3:37:34 (5,884)
Carrick, Alan A 4:33:06 (19,381)
Carrick, Martin 3:24:12 (3,589)
Carrier, Richard M 3:00:37 (1,201)
Carritt, Sean 3:30:27 (4,682)
Carrivick, Daniel M 3:14:49 (2,538)
Carroll, Alexander N 3:28:52 (4,392)
Carroll, D'Arcy 4:17:20 (15,383)
Carroll, Douglas 4:25:56 (17,551)
Carroll, John P 4:22:54 (16,795)
Carroll, Kevin 3:27:34 (4,140)
Carroll, Marty 3:27:43 (4,171)
Carroll, Michael J 4:20:28 (16,151)
Carroll, Michael J 4:48:52 (22,847)
Carroll, Paul L 3:29:11 (4,446)
Carroll, Philip S 3:43:58 (7,057)
Carroll, Raymond L 4:32:36 (19,261)
Carroll, Scott 4:23:30 (16,942)
Carroll, Sean J 4:03:37 (12,105)
Carroll, Simon J 4:22:29 (16,697)
Carroll, Steven D 4:21:51 (16,493)
Carroll, Vincent 2:48:10 (429)
Carron, Valery 3:56:54 (10,366)
Carsdale, Kenneth S 4:42:18 (21,414)
Carson, Tom J 3:45:25 (7,390)
Carss, James 4:41:23 (21,215)
Cartailler, Mathias 2:47:55 (419)
Cartawick, Paul A 4:48:10 (22,713)
Carter, Adam 5:28:13 (28,413)
Carter, Andrew 4:20:19 (16,106)
Carter, Andrew S 4:09:25 (13,482)
Carter, Anthony J 5:03:30 (25,520)
Carter, Dave A 2:36:50 (147)
Carter, David F 5:44:03 (29,627)
Carter, Dominic J 5:07:18 (26,020)
Carter, Eric J 4:03:17 (12,025)
Carter, Graeme P 4:35:00 (19,819)
Carter, James I 3:58:14 (10,766)
Carter, Lee D 4:49:14 (22,924)
Carter, Les P 4:15:59 (15,046)
Carter, Martin J 3:55:38 (9,974)
Carter, Martin J 4:18:24 (15,632)
Carter, Matt J 4:01:29 (11,592)
Carter, Michael 4:12:29 (14,194)
Carter, Michael J 3:48:16 (8,069)
Carter, Paul 4:31:14 (18,903)
Carter, Paul A 3:35:51 (5,580)
Carter, Paul J 4:08:41 (13,283)
Carter, Simon J 4:10:06 (13,656)
Carter, Stephen 4:45:26 (22,125)
Carter, Stephen J 3:41:31 (6,546)
Carter, Steven 5:08:55 (26,228)
Carter, Stuart 4:54:14 (23,842)
Carter-White, Timothy J 4:20:39 (16,198)
Carthy, Daniel M 2:38:10 (175)
Carton, Andy D 3:14:06 (2,449)
Cartwright, Daniel 4:37:43 (20,385)
Cartwright, Michael 5:12:22 (26,676)
Cartwright, Paul T 4:28:26 (18,206)
Cartwright, Robert G 3:39:57 (6,295)
Cartwright, Simon 4:04:31 (12,318)
Carty, Nick J 4:08:42 (13,291)
Carvalho, Agnelo 5:00:51 (25,123)
Carvalho, José A 3:49:32 (8,388)
Carvell, Andrew P 4:33:07 (19,384)
Carver, Gordon 3:52:04 (9,027)
Carver, Ronald J 4:56:31 (24,314)
Carwardine, Peter 4:55:55 (24,186)
Cary, Paul M 4:38:01 (20,475)
Casado, Pierre-François 4:33:21 (19,437)
Casallas, Hugo 4:07:56 (13,100)
Casati, Michele 3:49:48 (8,451)
Cascia, Luciano 4:18:24 (15,632)
Case, Anthony V 6:23:08 (31,083)
Case, Christopher 5:22:24 (27,822)
Case, Clive A 4:09:22 (13,466)
Case, Lee C 5:09:48 (26,358)
Casely, Bruce G 3:42:01 (6,654)
Casement, William R 3:37:01 (5,772)
Casey, Anthony D 2:52:59 (641)
Casey, Marc 3:50:06 (8,528)
Casey, Martin M 3:20:07 (3,079)
Casey, Paul D 3:25:18 (3,735)
Casey, Paul D 4:10:57 (13,858)
Cash, Adam J 3:41:57 (6,633)
Cash, Mark A 5:03:56 (25,570)
Cash, Mel 3:56:10 (10,128)
Cashman, James 4:05:16 (12,475)
Cashmore, Jeremy D 5:03:10 (25,472)
Cashmore, Marc J 3:05:53 (1,597)
Cason, Christopher J 4:17:28 (15,415)
Cass, John W 3:38:05 (5,973)
Casse, Colin J 5:05:23 (25,736)
Cassell, John S 3:26:43 (3,964)
Cassere, Peter J 5:38:15 (29,204)
Casserley, Kevin M 4:33:31 (19,473)
Casserley, Tom M 3:09:38 (1,964)
Cassidy, Bernard 3:26:07 (3,861)
Cassidy, James J 4:50:06 (23,091)
Cassidy, Martin N 4:20:14 (16,073)
Cassidy, Simon 4:54:08 (23,825)
Cassie, Paul 4:01:03 (11,516)
Cassim, James 3:46:11 (7,573)
Castagnola, Barry 4:10:45 (13,811)
Castellani, Stephane 3:37:15 (5,822)
Castle, Alan L 4:52:43 (23,571)
Castle, David J 4:39:32 (20,829)
Castle, John A 2:36:28 (141)
Castle, Matthew D 5:37:22 (29,143)
Castle, Nick 4:20:43 (16,217)
Castle, Robert E 3:56:47 (10,323)
Castle, Toby 3:24:22 (3,611)
Castrey, Gary 2:46:43 (382)

Caswell, Stephen L......3:50:28 (8,625)
Catalano, Michael......3:27:15 (4,075)
Cataldo, Anton......4:12:09 (14,125)
Catalod, Michel H......3:57:46 (10,609)
Catchelor, Steven R......5:28:39 (28,457)
Catchpole, Charles F......3:48:07 (8,027)
Catchpole, Nick J......4:57:56 (24,576)
Catchpole, Phil......3:46:10 (7,565)
Cates, Michael J......2:40:00 (210)
Catherall, Michael......5:10:39 (26,460)
Catlow, George W......4:24:15 (17,133)
Catmull, Julian A......3:08:23 (1,839)
Catt, Christopher......3:48:41 (8,183)
Cattaneo, Andrea......3:41:12 (6,513)
Catterall, Don......4:31:08 (18,885)
Cattermole, Alexander J......5:29:04 (28,489)
Cattermole, Peter A......4:30:57 (18,846)
Catton, Christopher G......3:38:00 (5,961)
Catton, Rodney......4:39:57 (20,904)
Caul, James P......3:57:06 (10,415)
Caulder, Graham A......3:14:15 (2,472)
Caulkett, Justin M......3:38:19 (6,015)
Caunce, Peter......3:54:36 (9,666)
Cavanagh, Mark T......4:40:38 (21,050)
Cavanagh, Scott J......5:25:54 (28,186)
Cavanagh, Sean A......3:49:20 (8,336)
Cavanagh, Timothy......5:16:57 (27,251)
Cavanna, Jean-Michel......4:55:06 (24,013)
Cave, Richard P......3:43:07 (6,875)
Cave, Stephen R......4:42:33 (21,462)
Caveney, Terence J......3:09:20 (1,932)
Caves, Craig M......4:52:04 (23,458)
Cavin, Stuart......4:41:41 (21,276)
Cawley, John W......3:38:23 (6,031)
Cawley, Mark C......4:14:28 (14,674)
Cawte, David......3:48:55 (8,233)
Cawthorne, Timothy J......5:45:21 (29,719)
Caygill, James R......5:48:11 (29,872)
Cayley, Gavin C......4:37:33 (20,346)
Cayton, Neil H......2:34:41 (120)
Cazenove, George D......3:57:23 (10,512)
Ceasar, Steven A......4:54:31 (23,899)
Cechi, Alessio......3:42:32 (6,751)
Ceely, Ian P......3:26:50 (3,992)
Celerier, Pascal......2:47:42 (408)
Cemon, François......2:58:36 (1,026)
Centofanti, Flavio......4:45:59 (22,245)
Cerutti, Daniele......4:03:20 (12,044)
Cevalte, Didier......3:45:45 (7,471)
Cevat, Martin......3:56:26 (10,228)
Chabalian, Philippe......4:14:49 (14,767)
Chabeli, Michael......5:46:08 (29,757)
Chadwick, Adam C......3:38:14 (6,000)
Chadwick, David J......4:29:27 (18,470)
Chadwick, Gavin......3:29:23 (4,482)
Chadwick, Nick R......3:34:30 (5,339)
Chadwick, Paul A......5:01:35 (25,238)
Chadwick, Peter J......4:56:31 (24,314)
Chadwick, Simon......4:10:18 (13,705)
Chadwick, Simon J......5:07:02 (25,974)
Chadwick, Stephen C......3:58:55 (10,979)
Chaffaut, Olivier......3:27:03 (4,036)
Chaffe, Gary A......4:32:13 (19,172)
Chaffe, Richard W......3:12:08 (2,206)
Chaffer, Paul......4:23:12 (16,873)
Chaffin, John R......5:18:10 (27,386)
Chaiken, Barry P......4:34:02 (19,599)
Chainey, Andrew S......3:17:45 (2,824)
Chaitel, Steven......5:11:00 (26,505)
Chakraborty, Aabir......4:10:39 (13,792)
Chalk, Ian......4:43:20 (21,649)
Chalk, John I......4:54:36 (23,923)
Chalkley, Duane......5:25:25 (28,131)
Challenger, Robert......3:49:45 (8,437)
Challis, Ben G......3:50:28 (8,625)
Challis, Peter......3:50:35 (8,651)
Challis, Raymond......3:42:52 (6,827)
Challoner, Michael......4:57:15 (24,450)
Chalmers, Alexander J......4:27:09 (17,880)
Chalmers, Daniel......4:06:44 (12,823)
Chalmers, David C......3:26:16 (3,883)
Chalmers, Mark A......5:08:05 (26,125)
Chalmers, William D......3:41:35 (6,561)

Chambellant, Yves......4:37:31 (20,342)
Chamberlain, Brian......4:23:06 (16,842)
Chamberlain, Gary B......3:52:24 (9,111)
Chamberlain, Mark......4:43:24 (21,662)
Chamberlain, Paul......3:28:17 (4,279)
Chambers, Alistair......2:57:15 (898)
Chambers, Alvin......4:56:00 (24,206)
Chambers, Brian D......4:27:39 (18,004)
Chambers, Christopher M......3:49:08 (8,291)
Chambers, Joseph......3:57:00 (10,390)
Chambers, Lee......3:41:57 (6,633)
Chambers, Neil A......3:18:56 (2,945)
Chambers, Paul J......5:45:16 (29,709)
Chambers, Simon R......4:30:19 (18,708)
Chambers, Steve......4:49:19 (22,942)
Chambers, Warrick A......5:31:47 (28,722)
Champalimaud, Lopo L......5:12:29 (26,690)
Champion, Charles W......4:33:22 (19,441)
Chan, Aaron......4:46:11 (22,293)
Chan, Danny......3:39:27 (6,209)
Chan, Kallp T......5:20:03 (27,573)
Chan, Peter......5:13:16 (26,801)
Chan, Sern J......4:12:30 (14,200)
Chana, Jaswant S......4:11:32 (13,978)
Chana, Piara S......4:35:34 (19,943)
Chance, Rickey A......4:22:12 (16,608)
Chancellor, Henry......3:33:27 (5,182)
Chandler, Gary W......2:45:12 (330)
Chandler, Jim A......3:29:51 (4,564)
Chandler, Mathew R......4:20:01 (16,037)
Chandler, Michael......4:19:28 (15,905)
Chandler, Peter J......3:40:15 (6,343)
Chandler, Simon D......3:29:17 (4,469)
Chandley, Paul J......4:23:00 (16,812)
Chandolia, Ajay K......6:55:27 (31,568)
Changer, David J......4:49:16 (22,932)
Channon, David......4:56:25 (24,283)
Channon, Mark G......4:24:47 (17,246)
Chant, Ian R......3:41:34 (6,553)
Chant, Ryan L......4:16:35 (15,194)
Chanter, Keith......5:31:35 (28,707)
Chantrey, David F......5:10:55 (26,498)
Chant-Sempill, Ian......4:34:05 (19,619)
Chapman, Alan......4:41:23 (21,215)
Chapman, Andrew J......4:26:35 (17,723)
Chapman, Andy J......4:46:44 (22,397)
Chapman, Christopher P......4:22:36 (16,728)
Chapman, David J......3:42:12 (6,681)
Chapman, David R......4:50:44 (23,219)
Chapman, Doninic A......5:11:45 (26,601)
Chapman, Gary I......2:58:24 (1,006)
Chapman, Glen M......4:04:24 (12,282)
Chapman, Graham S......4:21:47 (16,475)
Chapman, Jody C......3:40:27 (6,388)
Chapman, John......3:07:50 (1,789)
Chapman, John......3:45:10 (7,339)
Chapman, Leslie G......3:08:37 (1,858)
Chapman, Mark......3:13:40 (2,395)
Chapman, Neil......5:25:56 (28,189)
Chapman, Neil A......3:07:21 (1,733)
Chapman, Neil C......2:49:17 (469)
Chapman, Neil P......5:13:58 (26,890)
Chapman, Nigel......5:01:31 (25,224)
Chapman, Paul D......3:06:07 (1,622)
Chapman, Paul F......4:04:07 (12,214)
Chapman, Paul J......4:44:49 (21,980)
Chapman, Paul R......4:12:35 (14,228)
Chapman, Peter J......4:50:22 (23,142)
Chapman, Peter J......4:50:46 (23,231)
Chapman, Reg M......3:14:41 (2,524)
Chapman, Richard......4:37:19 (20,321)
Chapman, Robert D......4:24:33 (17,196)
Chapman, Simon......4:02:02 (11,726)
Chapman, Spencer W......5:02:47 (25,416)
Chapman, Steven P......3:50:32 (8,634)
Chapman, Toby......3:07:01 (1,705)
Chapman, Torquil I......4:05:22 (12,501)
Chapman, Wayne P......4:48:35 (22,790)
Chappell, Terry......4:34:19 (19,674)
Charalambous, Andreas......5:07:43 (26,081)
Charbon, Christian......3:25:49 (3,817)
Chard, Ken R......3:10:28 (2,053)
Chard, Stephen......3:44:18 (7,138)

Charles, Jonathan S......4:44:06 (21,815)
Charles, Mark R......5:22:00 (27,772)
Charles, Paul J......3:10:56 (2,094)
Charleston, Andy......3:54:15 (9,577)
Charleston, Derek F......3:26:24 (3,904)
Charlesworth, Gavin......4:27:23 (17,934)
Charlesworth, Richard J......3:13:56 (2,428)
Charlesworth, Stephen M......5:15:11 (27,037)
Charlton, Adam R......3:39:17 (6,180)
Charlton, David M......4:45:28 (22,134)
Charlton, Ian......4:23:37 (16,968)
Charlton, Russell......4:18:01 (15,557)
Charlton, Steven W......4:09:05 (13,398)
Charlwood, Richard S......4:29:21 (18,451)
Charman, David......6:49:09 (31,485)
Charman, Stephen J......6:43:03 (31,407)
Charnley, James R......3:28:51 (4,387)
Charnley, Lee W......3:45:06 (7,320)
Charnock, Graham......4:52:14 (23,491)
Charrondiere, Philippe......4:08:32 (13,239)
Charry, Jean-Michel......3:06:40 (1,672)
Chart, Malcolm......3:07:20 (1,732)
Chart, Robert J......3:18:20 (2,880)
Charters, Paul W......3:48:36 (8,150)
Chastan, Pascal......3:30:02 (4,597)
Chastellain, Olivier......4:51:59 (23,436)
Chatfield, Lance T......4:13:50 (14,528)
Chatfield, Mark......4:30:18 (18,703)
Chatfield, Michael F......5:39:07 (29,277)
Chatfield, Neil......3:19:04 (2,961)
Chatten, Simon......3:38:36 (6,069)
Chatterjee, Simon......4:01:16 (11,554)
Chatterton, Thomas R......4:35:51 (19,990)
Chatwin, Andrew J......4:06:02 (12,670)
Chauhan, Rajat......3:54:52 (9,741)
Chauhan, Sanjay......5:17:59 (27,364)
Chaukar, Milind A......4:52:30 (23,532)
Chauman, Abhishek......4:14:41 (14,725)
Chavda, Harish......7:00:11 (31,626)
Chawla, Raghav......2:53:49 (685)
Chawner, Colin L......4:12:41 (14,260)
Cheadle, Simon D......4:24:09 (17,105)
Cheah, Siew Yin......4:58:56 (24,785)
Cheal, Ben J......5:02:26 (25,363)
Chebouki, Karim......3:00:00 (1,156)
Checcacci, Lorenzo......2:28:16 (71)
Chedzey, Paul D......5:26:16 (28,220)
Cheesebrough, Timothy L......3:55:11 (9,845)
Cheesman, Charles......4:57:13 (24,442)
Cheetham, Ralph......6:11:21 (30,766)
Chelelgo, Elijah......2:28:08 (68)
Chell, Philip......4:38:24 (20,570)
Chemet, Jacques......4:00:11 (11,337)
Cheneviere, Giles......2:49:28 (479)
Cheney, Les......4:18:19 (15,611)
Cheney, Michael J......4:21:25 (16,367)
Chenu, Guy......3:36:40 (5,718)
Chepkwony, Haggai K......2:35:15 (127)
Chequer, James R......4:19:11 (15,825)
Chequer, Jon P......4:14:56 (14,792)
Cheroux, Claude......3:12:26 (2,243)
Cherruault, Lionel R......5:35:05 (28,965)
Cherry, Robert J......3:37:41 (5,902)
Cheshire, Geoffrey M......2:51:00 (543)
Cheshire, Nick J......4:12:09 (14,125)
Chesney, Jon P......5:45:18 (29,711)
Chester, Colin H......5:01:44 (25,265)
Chester, Martin B......3:46:27 (7,628)
Chester-Master, Benedict J......4:54:33 (23,911)
Chesterton, Colin A......4:48:52 (22,847)
Chestney, Jon S......3:10:54 (2,090)
Chesworth, Nicholas P......7:26:41 (31,823)
Chetwood, Jonathan D......5:02:04 (25,306)
Chetwood, Timothy J......4:14:40 (14,721)
Cheval, Thierry H......3:35:12 (5,458)
Cheyne, Brian......5:20:03 (27,573)
Chiapusso, Raffaele......3:29:35 (4,516)
Chiaranda, Gianfraneo......3:51:44 (8,951)
Chick, Jonathan B......3:56:06 (10,111)
Chico, Dan A......4:37:55 (20,444)
Chikhliwala, Kamlesh......6:08:38 (30,689)
Chikira, Hiroshi......4:29:14 (18,410)
Child, Colin W......4:21:29 (16,385)

Child, Keith R	3:52:43 (9,176)	
Child, Thomas P	3:35:51 (5,580)	
Child, Tim J	4:09:53 (13,603)	
Childe, Michael	4:06:34 (12,798)	
Childs, Andrew R	4:01:46 (11,664)	
Childs, David J	5:08:41 (26,200)	
Childs, Gary D	4:15:23 (14,897)	
Childs, John P	4:31:08 (18,885)	
Childs, Nicholas J	4:28:15 (18,158)	
Childs, Paul A	3:06:54 (1,694)	
Childs, Robert G	4:46:29 (22,354)	
Childs, Shaun E	3:38:53 (6,113)	
Chiles, Andrew D	3:48:38 (8,164)	
Chiles, Lawrence	3:33:11 (5,133)	
Chiles, Matthew	3:33:10 (5,129)	
Chillery, Richard F	3:19:15 (2,992)	
Chisholm, Jamie A	4:50:04 (23,085)	
Chislett, David W	3:48:28 (8,113)	
Chittell, Christopher	4:04:24 (12,282)	
Chittem, David J	3:31:42 (4,874)	
Chittenden, Tim	4:36:33 (20,144)	
Chitty, Ian R	3:44:57 (7,296)	
Chiu, Ambrose C	4:45:55 (22,232)	
Chivers, Michael P	4:27:46 (18,031)	
Chivers, Richard	4:12:33 (14,218)	
Chivers, Roger J	4:47:11 (22,497)	
Chodzko-Zajko, Piotr A	3:34:52 (5,400)	
Chopra, Raj K	4:37:47 (20,403)	
Chopra, Shiv K	4:44:50 (21,983)	
Chorley, Robert J	5:35:58 (29,026)	
Chorlton, Matthew R	3:14:07 (2,452)	
Chou, Alfred Y	3:05:56 (1,603)	
Choudhury, Ghazi S	5:46:30 (29,788)	
Choules, Cameron F	3:35:28 (5,519)	
Choules, David	3:13:38 (2,390)	
Chow, Gary	3:59:28 (11,140)	
Chow, Richard J	5:19:49 (27,535)	
Chowdhury, Muhibbur R	4:31:35 (18,998)	
Chown, Kevin F	4:12:57 (14,318)	
Chrisp, Paul	4:00:29 (11,395)	
Christensen, Adam J	5:41:40 (29,464)	
Christensen, Anders	5:25:43 (28,162)	
Christensen, Bjarne	3:55:29 (9,926)	
Christensen, Finn S	4:26:23 (17,672)	
Christensen, Keld	2:56:46 (867)	
Christian, Brian	5:16:38 (27,215)	
Christian, Marc	3:09:56 (1,996)	
Christie, David	3:45:29 (7,403)	
Christie, Guy M	4:30:05 (18,650)	
Christie, Rory	4:42:49 (21,524)	
Christie, Roy G	3:36:22 (5,672)	
Christie, Rupert V	3:58:18 (10,791)	
Christie, Sandy	3:18:41 (2,917)	
Christmas, David L	3:53:52 (9,469)	
Christodoulou, Harry	5:07:40 (26,071)	
Christofedou, Freddy	4:37:10 (20,284)	
Christofiders, Louis	4:48:37 (22,797)	
Christophe, Laurent	3:39:16 (6,172)	
Christopher, Adam T	4:23:28 (16,935)	
Christopher, John F	3:33:00 (5,099)	
Christopher, Leonard A	2:55:24 (780)	
Christopher, Martin J	3:51:47 (8,967)	
Christou, Petros	5:18:47 (27,447)	
Chrysafi, Peter A	4:32:33 (19,248)	
Chrystie, Ian P	5:13:02 (26,768)	
Chumber, Susheel	3:59:27 (11,132)	
Chung, Alex	4:24:30 (17,182)	
Church, Colin W	4:07:56 (13,100)	
Church, Ian S	3:40:26 (6,386)	
Church, John W	4:15:57 (15,041)	
Church, Richard J	6:56:17 (31,575)	
Church, Timothy J	4:11:02 (13,881)	
Churcher, Paul I	4:02:55 (11,942)	
Churchouse, Martin P	5:23:54 (27,961)	
Churchus, David B	4:05:44 (12,600)	
Churchyard, Michael J	4:32:17 (19,184)	
Cicalese, Luca	5:17:51 (27,346)	
Ciccariello, Antonio	3:29:32 (4,507)	
Cicero, Mimmo	4:50:00 (23,073)	
Cichosz, George	4:40:47 (21,081)	
Cicognola, Enzo	3:43:12 (6,894)	
Cicone, Stephen W	5:16:06 (27,140)	
Cinnamond, Marc	4:20:34 (16,177)	

Cinque, Giulio A	3:07:25 (1,738)	
Cinque, Giuseppe	4:32:56 (19,343)	
Cipollina, Giovanni	3:54:43 (9,696)	
Ciriq, Alberto	3:18:19 (2,879)	
Ciucci, Giueppe	5:04:19 (25,607)	
Ciudiskis, Graham R	5:18:22 (27,404)	
Clack, Geoffrey N	3:47:05 (7,776)	
Claeys, Koen	4:30:25 (18,736)	
Clafton, Edmund J	4:47:14 (22,504)	
Clancy, James	3:16:54 (2,740)	
Clancy, Kevin T	4:35:00 (19,819)	
Clanfield, Ian P	4:29:39 (18,542)	
Clapham, Jeremy A	3:15:19 (2,584)	
Clapham, Jeremy A	3:47:07 (7,784)	
Clapham, Mark J	4:15:51 (15,015)	
Clapperton, Robert C	3:41:58 (6,639)	
Clapson, Martin R	4:32:31 (19,240)	
Clapson, Victor J	4:20:22 (16,120)	
Clapton, Roland A	4:15:09 (14,846)	
Clare, Danny	3:35:00 (5,427)	
Clare, Matthew A	3:54:49 (9,726)	
Clare, Sean	2:59:49 (1,143)	
Clargo, John P	4:57:51 (24,557)	
Clark, Adrian C	2:56:15 (834)	
Clark, Alan L	4:36:11 (20,068)	
Clark, Allan	4:06:57 (12,879)	
Clark, Antony S	3:58:46 (10,939)	
Clark, Brian R	4:21:45 (16,465)	
Clark, Christopher	3:29:47 (4,550)	
Clark, Christopher J	3:45:34 (7,428)	
Clark, Darren G	3:50:31 (8,631)	
Clark, David	3:50:41 (8,679)	
Clark, David	4:14:34 (14,698)	
Clark, Edward D	4:12:56 (14,314)	
Clark, Fraser	4:07:34 (13,027)	
Clark, Geoff	3:48:39 (8,168)	
Clark, Geoffrey M	4:58:23 (24,687)	
Clark, Graham	4:51:33 (23,351)	
Clark, Hamish I	3:23:27 (3,494)	
Clark, Harry	4:59:47 (24,954)	
Clark, James S	3:39:36 (6,238)	
Clark, Jeremy S	3:49:45 (8,437)	
Clark, John	3:30:25 (4,677)	
Clark, John R	4:11:17 (13,926)	
Clark, Jonathan F	4:36:28 (20,123)	
Clark, Keiron P	4:29:09 (18,393)	
Clark, Kevin	4:14:28 (14,674)	
Clark, Mark A	3:07:35 (1,762)	
Clark, Mark D	4:04:39 (12,340)	
Clark, Matthew J	3:13:42 (2,399)	
Clark, Michael A	3:51:46 (8,962)	
Clark, Nicolas J	3:55:40 (9,976)	
Clark, Nigel J	4:42:18 (21,414)	
Clark, Paul D	3:07:13 (1,720)	
Clark, Peter H	3:27:11 (4,061)	
Clark, Peter J	3:55:56 (10,062)	
Clark, Peter J	4:11:29 (13,966)	
Clark, Peter J	4:26:37 (17,730)	
Clark, Philip J	4:34:11 (19,640)	
Clark, Richard G	4:36:30 (20,135)	
Clark, Robert G	3:38:25 (6,035)	
Clark, Robert J	4:50:17 (23,119)	
Clark, Robert P	3:33:15 (5,148)	
Clark, Rod S	4:49:01 (22,878)	
Clark, Sam R	5:05:47 (25,797)	
Clark, Samuel	4:50:35 (23,193)	
Clark, Simon P	3:58:32 (10,869)	
Clark, Stephen L	3:49:58 (8,497)	
Clarke, Alistair	3:45:30 (7,409)	
Clarke, Barry	3:57:44 (10,600)	
Clarke, Bruce D	3:07:56 (1,799)	
Clarke, Christopher	4:08:19 (13,183)	
Clarke, Christopher P	4:32:12 (19,165)	
Clarke, Craig C	4:07:12 (12,939)	
Clarke, Dale M	3:48:08 (8,034)	
Clarke, Dave E	3:57:06 (10,415)	
Clarke, David A	4:16:09 (15,093)	
Clarke, David A	5:44:03 (29,627)	
Clarke, Derrick	3:35:39 (5,548)	
Clarke, Gary J	5:32:05 (28,736)	
Clarke, Gordon M	4:04:24 (12,282)	
Clarke, Graham	4:19:45 (15,965)	
Clarke, Gregory J	3:28:17 (4,279)	

Clarke, Ian D	4:56:38 (24,337)	
Clarke, James A	3:56:02 (10,094)	
Clarke, James D	3:17:37 (2,815)	
Clarke, James M	4:21:21 (16,350)	
Clarke, Jeremy	5:15:25 (27,068)	
Clarke, John G	3:30:04 (4,608)	
Clarke, John J	4:18:56 (15,768)	
Clarke, John J	4:29:37 (18,527)	
Clarke, John M	5:09:52 (26,363)	
Clarke, John P	2:43:12 (273)	
Clarke, Julian P	3:15:31 (2,595)	
Clarke, Kenneth C	4:03:21 (12,046)	
Clarke, Liston	5:05:32 (25,769)	
Clarke, Martin I	4:00:23 (11,377)	
Clarke, Martin P	5:31:03 (28,663)	
Clarke, Michael D	3:31:15 (4,813)	
Clarke, Nicholas A	5:05:26 (25,743)	
Clarke, Nicholas J	3:18:28 (2,893)	
Clarke, Nicholas J	4:25:20 (17,389)	
Clarke, Paul A	4:10:06 (13,656)	
Clarke, Paul D	3:02:15 (1,321)	
Clarke, Paul T	4:45:57 (22,238)	
Clarke, Peter B	4:20:31 (16,164)	
Clarke, Peter C	3:50:22 (8,597)	
Clarke, Peter T	5:39:35 (29,309)	
Clarke, Philip	3:15:31 (2,595)	
Clarke, Richard M	4:26:52 (17,798)	
Clarke, Richard W	3:57:25 (10,516)	
Clarke, Rick A	3:58:23 (10,813)	
Clarke, Robert A	4:35:33 (19,939)	
Clarke, Robert G	3:58:16 (10,780)	
Clarke, Robin J	4:47:36 (22,591)	
Clarke, Roger S	3:50:48 (8,706)	
Clarke, Roy	4:12:47 (14,276)	
Clarke, Russell J	2:57:59 (966)	
Clarke, Samuel J	6:04:47 (30,588)	
Clarke, Simon P	3:44:12 (7,114)	
Clarke, Stephen	4:32:37 (19,266)	
Clarke, Tim S	4:38:39 (20,627)	
Clarke, Timothy	3:09:15 (1,924)	
Clarke, Vaughan C	4:39:30 (20,825)	
Clarke, William H	3:41:13 (6,516)	
Clarkson, Craig W	3:35:19 (5,487)	
Clarkson, Graham	3:14:12 (2,467)	
Clarkson, Richard J	4:06:16 (12,727)	
Clarkson, Simon D	4:14:52 (14,779)	
Clarrasso, Janot J	3:06:03 (1,615)	
Clasby, Jason T	3:12:13 (2,219)	
Clasper, Simon M	4:13:16 (14,395)	
Clatworthy, Graham P	5:16:34 (27,201)	
Clavel, Guillaume	3:53:51 (9,459)	
Clavey, David G	6:23:13 (31,085)	
Clawson, David R	2:59:01 (1,073)	
Clay, Richard	4:37:11 (20,293)	
Clay, Stephen J	4:25:06 (17,333)	
Clayden, Robert A	5:13:51 (26,879)	
Claydon, Mark C	4:39:58 (20,910)	
Claydon, Nicholas F	5:34:43 (28,940)	
Claydon, Paul	4:29:41 (18,550)	
Clayton, Bill	5:16:44 (27,223)	
Clayton, Christopher	4:46:44 (22,397)	
Clayton, David A	3:20:00 (3,066)	
Clayton, Dennis W	3:48:53 (8,227)	
Clayton, Ian	2:42:44 (261)	
Clayton, Ian	4:19:55 (16,003)	
Clayton, Luke B	4:38:16 (20,541)	
Clayton, Peter L	4:59:23 (24,880)	
Clayton, Simon J	3:05:08 (1,538)	
Clayton, Stephen F	3:55:07 (9,821)	
Clazey, Graeme	3:23:07 (3,453)	
Cleall, Leonard	5:10:00 (26,380)	
Cleary, Andrew M	3:17:57 (2,843)	
Cleary, John M	3:26:02 (3,852)	
Cleary, Michael J	4:52:16 (23,497)	
Cleary, Stephen	3:56:31 (10,258)	
Cleaver, James P	3:50:46 (8,698)	
Cleaver, James S	4:14:26 (14,659)	
Cleaver, Neil S	4:37:10 (20,284)	
Cleaver, Simon W	4:58:22 (24,679)	
Cleaver, Terence E	3:49:55 (8,477)	
Clegg, Gavin J	2:48:17 (434)	
Clegg, Geoff F	3:58:46 (10,939)	
Clegg, Mark	5:49:51 (29,955)	

Clegg, Peter J 3:31:55 (4,907)
Cleland, Stuart H 3:47:02 (7,763)
Clemence, Matt E 4:59:48 (24,960)
Clement, Paul 4:01:51 (11,682)
Clements, Andrew C 2:39:18 (194)
Clements, Andrew P 5:41:42 (29,468)
Clements, John K 4:23:35 (16,963)
Clements, Mark J 4:55:50 (24,160)
Clements, Peter 3:57:51 (10,632)
Clements, Philip 4:41:20 (21,201)
Clements, Richard J 6:46:11 (31,454)
Clements, Simon A 4:48:26 (22,765)
Clements, Thomas R 4:44:27 (21,899)
Clements, Trevor W 3:17:13 (2,775)
Clemons, Richard H 4:35:19 (19,889)
Clemson, Jonathan B 3:19:50 (3,050)
Clemson, Matt 4:25:52 (17,529)
Clench, James A 3:58:06 (10,710)
Clerc, Laurent A 3:23:36 (3,514)
Clery, Ed 4:58:27 (24,707)
Cleugh, Andrew 4:43:10 (21,595)
Cleugh, Tony 4:59:31 (24,906)
Cleverton, Marcus E 4:52:32 (23,538)
Cleves, Andrew J 2:50:22 (519)
Clewley, Anthony J 7:29:13 (31,841)
Clews, William M 3:12:52 (2,296)
Cliff, Nigel 3:54:55 (9,756)
Cliff, Thomas R 3:37:36 (5,890)
Cliffe, Shane L 3:25:26 (3,756)
Clifford, David C 4:37:37 (20,361)
Clifford, James H 4:30:05 (18,650)
Clifford, Les 3:44:16 (7,128)
Clifford, Peter P 3:42:54 (6,835)
Clifford, Robin C 4:01:57 (11,704)
Clifford, Sam A 4:54:07 (23,821)
Clifford, Stephen W 3:38:06 (5,979)
Clift, Ian M 4:02:11 (11,774)
Clifton, Dennis S 5:04:43 (25,653)
Clifton, Michael 3:11:55 (2,183)
Climie, David N 5:04:55 (25,681)
Clinch, Nick J 6:49:21 (31,490)
Clinnick, Stephen C 3:47:50 (7,954)
Clinton, Barrie J 4:38:25 (20,575)
Clinton, Dennis 4:37:53 (20,429)
Clinton, Niall P 4:41:04 (21,138)
Clipston, Michael I 4:36:14 (20,078)
Clish, Simon R 4:46:29 (22,354)
Cloke, Ian 5:16:58 (27,255)
Close, Edward 4:36:57 (20,243)
Close, Steven A 5:14:19 (26,936)
Clough, Jack 4:41:44 (21,290)
Clough, Julian S 3:12:11 (2,212)
Clough, Mark S 4:36:17 (20,086)
Clough, Nick N 5:36:21 (29,049)
Clough, Paul J 4:03:25 (12,062)
Clouston, Svein E 4:10:41 (13,796)
Clow, Daniel D 4:46:24 (22,340)
Clubb, Gary E 6:44:51 (31,433)
Clubb, Stuart A 5:16:31 (27,192)
Clubb, Stuart W 3:50:05 (8,521)
Clubley, Steve R 4:01:40 (11,640)
Clucas, Paul 5:39:07 (29,277)
Cluley, David 4:25:47 (17,509)
Clunan, Ronny 5:15:32 (27,084)
Clusker, Dean 4:01:54 (11,688)
Coade, David 3:20:17 (3,096)
Coales, David 2:56:11 (828)
Coates, Alan P 5:37:23 (29,145)
Coates, Brian W 3:10:24 (2,043)
Coates, David G 3:06:12 (1,627)
Coates, David R 6:00:42 (30,435)
Coates, Geoffrey E 3:59:38 (11,198)
Coates, James A 2:56:59 (881)
Coates, Nigel J 2:52:09 (597)
Coates, Richard 3:38:02 (5,968)
Coats, Brian G 6:44:32 (31,427)
Coats, Stan A 4:14:38 (14,716)
Cobb, Lee J 4:24:34 (17,199)
Cobb, Peter J 3:28:08 (4,251)
Cobbett, Peter L 4:27:47 (18,036)
Cobbett, Shaun W 4:45:34 (22,154)
Cobbold, Chris P 3:36:12 (5,644)
Cobby, Ian J 4:30:06 (18,655)

Cobill, Sebastian C 3:20:18 (3,099)
Cobley, Lee W 4:33:17 (19,422)
Coburn Davis, Terry G 3:51:14 (8,813)
Cochrane, Robert W 4:31:24 (18,950)
Cochrane, Warren 5:26:14 (28,214)
Cockayne, Andrew A 3:29:12 (4,449)
Cockayne, Nick J 5:12:49 (26,734)
Cockbain, Neil 3:09:23 (1,935)
Cockburn, 4:23:10 (16,858)
Cockburn, Ian W 3:37:18 (5,839)
Cocker, Mark G 6:50:11 (31,500)
Cockerell, William 2:27:18 (62)
Cockerton, Neil F 4:25:55 (17,545)
Cockx, Jeroen P 2:45:03 (327)
Codd, Philip J 4:22:18 (16,637)
Code, Peter 3:44:38 (7,220)
Codling, John C 4:15:31 (14,931)
Codling, Reginald I 4:44:32 (21,917)
Cody, Julian M 3:58:40 (10,913)
Coe, Matthew J 4:18:03 (15,565)
Coe, Robert J 4:03:50 (12,155)
Coen, Liam G 6:15:07 (30,888)
Coeshall, David C 4:03:34 (12,092)
Coffey, Ray P 4:35:29 (19,924)
Coghlan, Guy P 4:28:19 (18,173)
Coghlan, Ian 4:32:06 (19,133)
Coglan, Julian J 4:53:04 (23,624)
Cogman, David 3:53:43 (9,417)
Cohen, Adam P 3:35:12 (5,458)
Cohen, Andrew L 6:44:59 (31,436)
Cohen, Eilon A 6:50:55 (31,512)
Cohen, Howard 3:13:29 (2,369)
Cohen, Leon 3:33:35 (5,200)
Cohen, Malcolm S 5:06:21 (25,895)
Cohen, Michael S 3:46:37 (7,666)
Cohen, Richard 4:52:18 (23,503)
Cohen, Scott N 5:25:35 (28,146)
Cohen, Stephen M 4:47:44 (22,623)
Cohen, Stuart T 4:31:51 (19,061)
Coint, Philippe 4:09:32 (13,507)
Coker, David A 3:48:19 (8,081)
Coker, Thomas F 4:31:40 (19,014)
Colbourne, Richard S 3:55:47 (10,013)
Colbourne, Steve J 2:59:10 (1,088)
Colby, Andrew P 5:35:02 (28,959)
Cole, Alan 3:24:57 (3,684)
Cole, Brian 4:37:00 (20,252)
Cole, Brian J 2:29:23 (76)
Cole, Charles A 5:49:41 (29,942)
Cole, Christopher A 6:49:33 (31,493)
Cole, David R 5:52:25 (30,094)
Cole, Franklin T 3:10:47 (2,082)
Cole, Jeremy M 3:51:53 (8,985)
Cole, Jeremy N 3:21:58 (3,304)
Cole, Jonathan M 4:39:58 (20,910)
Cole, Kevin D 2:58:36 (1,026)
Cole, Martin 4:20:58 (16,276)
Cole, Paul 4:26:27 (17,684)
Cole, Paul B 5:02:01 (25,299)
Cole, Peter J 4:36:53 (20,223)
Cole, Ray 2:45:28 (341)
Cole, Richard 4:07:38 (13,040)
Cole, Simon R 4:21:31 (16,393)
Cole, Stephen H 3:23:57 (3,559)
Cole, Stephen H 3:53:16 (9,329)
Cole, Terry M 3:35:17 (5,477)
Cole, Tony 3:14:44 (2,531)
Coleby, William 3:55:04 (9,811)
Colegate, Andrew 3:43:06 (6,872)
Coleman, Colin R 5:19:36 (27,508)
Coleman, Gavin R 6:31:10 (31,228)
Coleman, Glenn R 5:07:26 (26,035)
Coleman, Ian M 6:31:10 (31,228)
Coleman, James 5:53:52 (30,146)
Coleman, James C 4:34:07 (19,631)
Coleman, James R 3:39:49 (6,275)
Coleman, John P 6:33:05 (31,266)
Coleman, Jonathan 3:35:19 (5,487)
Coleman, Kevin R 5:07:26 (26,035)
Coleman, Mark A 4:38:54 (20,693)
Coleman, Peter D 4:04:10 (12,234)
Coleman, Richard 4:34:29 (19,710)
Coleman, Richard J 3:54:19 (9,591)

Coleman, Rory J 5:03:57 (25,572)
Coleman, Stephen 4:21:01 (16,284)
Coleman, Thomas R 5:36:45 (29,083)
Coleman, Tony A 5:56:13 (30,258)
Coleman, William T 5:52:31 (30,096)
Colenutt, Martin 4:20:05 (16,046)
Coles, Alan 4:07:40 (13,048)
Coles, Christopher W 5:00:22 (25,047)
Coles, Daryl J 3:52:37 (9,154)
Coles, David R 3:04:04 (1,455)
Coles, Mark S 4:15:08 (14,840)
Coles, Matthew H 3:39:45 (6,265)
Coles, Matthew T 5:52:15 (30,080)
Coles, Phil K 3:29:08 (4,438)
Coles, Stuart M 3:51:31 (8,891)
Coley, Giles A 4:56:02 (24,217)
Coley, Philip F 4:20:25 (16,136)
Colfer, Eoghan D 3:51:25 (8,862)
Colfer, James J 3:30:03 (4,601)
Colhin-Carter, Jason R 6:25:52 (31,139)
Colin, Bruno 4:22:14 (16,619)
Colin, Etenne 2:56:38 (859)
Collard, Dominic P 4:00:51 (11,461)
Colledge, Ian A 4:05:40 (12,588)
Collender, Guy 5:23:29 (27,916)
Collenette, John P 4:18:13 (15,591)
Collerton, Liam 3:48:46 (8,200)
Collet, Christian F 4:06:43 (12,821)
Collett, Chris A 3:55:37 (9,966)
Collett, Les 3:55:02 (9,798)
Collett, Ray C 5:53:35 (30,136)
Colley, Frederick S 4:13:12 (14,376)
Colley, Ian R 4:15:55 (15,031)
Colley, James 3:44:54 (7,286)
Colley, John W 4:06:27 (12,769)
Collier, Andrew D 3:28:32 (4,326)
Collier, Andrew H 3:48:39 (8,168)
Collier, Andrew R 5:03:09 (25,466)
Collier, David S 2:49:07 (464)
Collier, John S 4:42:57 (21,555)
Collier, Paul D 4:47:34 (22,585)
Collier, Simon 5:35:33 (29,004)
Collin, Frederick S 4:51:02 (23,277)
Collin, Guillaume 3:26:14 (3,875)
Collin, Oliver R 3:43:29 (6,956)
Collinelli, Marco 3:11:24 (2,134)
Colling, Ian M 5:45:37 (29,732)
Collingbourne, Robert J 3:52:39 (9,162)
Collinge, Andrew 2:46:23 (367)
Collings, Chris C 4:38:49 (20,670)
Collings, Derek J 5:44:05 (29,630)
Collingwood, Neil 3:53:49 (9,448)
Collingwood, Paul S 3:12:41 (2,269)
Collino, Percy E 3:56:54 (10,366)
Collins, Adrian R 5:32:13 (28,751)
Collins, Barry J 3:10:42 (2,071)
Collins, Ben L 3:29:26 (4,493)
Collins, Brian P 5:40:01 (29,338)
Collins, Charles E 3:59:27 (11,132)
Collins, Duncan 2:54:04 (697)
Collins, Gilbert 4:18:08 (15,579)
Collins, Glen 3:58:35 (10,884)
Collins, Graham 2:59:47 (1,140)
Collins, Iain R 4:35:15 (19,875)
Collins, Jason L 4:25:03 (17,318)
Collins, John 3:13:30 (2,374)
Collins, Jonathan G 2:57:09 (891)
Collins, Lee 4:43:30 (21,685)
Collins, Lee J 4:16:51 (15,268)
Collins, Liam 4:19:25 (15,887)
Collins, Malcolm 3:20:14 (3,092)
Collins, Mark 4:13:53 (14,540)
Collins, Mark B 5:29:46 (28,565)
Collins, Mark G 4:14:48 (14,758)
Collins, Michael 3:36:49 (5,745)
Collins, Michael 4:37:28 (20,333)
Collins, Michael J 4:33:33 (19,477)
Collins, Michael J 5:16:17 (27,166)
Collins, Michael J 5:45:12 (29,705)
Collins, Mike 6:47:49 (31,472)
Collins, Neil P 4:11:23 (13,948)
Collins, Nigel 4:54:09 (23,830)
Collins, Patrick J 4:08:17 (13,170)

Collins, Peter	3:05:42 (1,583)	
Collins, Phillip T	3:27:36 (4,144)	
Collins, Richard P	4:36:10 (20,065)	
Collins, Robert A	4:46:24 (22,340)	
Collins, Sean	3:34:25 (5,327)	
Collins, Sean	4:01:21 (11,572)	
Collins, Simon P	5:56:26 (30,270)	
Collins, Simon R	4:27:36 (17,990)	
Collins, Tim J	4:48:26 (22,765)	
Collins, William S	3:32:00 (4,927)	
Collinson, Andrew J	2:56:44 (865)	
Collinson, Nick	3:36:29 (5,694)	
Collison, Nigel	3:46:28 (7,634)	
Collonnier, Vincent	3:28:22 (4,293)	
Collyer, Iain D	5:02:43 (25,404)	
Collyer, Richard	3:32:33 (5,013)	
Colmagro, Christian	4:36:24 (20,104)	
Colman, Graham R	3:35:56 (5,598)	
Colman, Ivan N	4:58:10 (24,633)	
Colman, Paul	3:44:28 (7,175)	
Colman, Thomas J	4:53:12 (23,654)	
Colnel, François	2:41:29 (231)	
Colome-Somoza, Josep	4:09:21 (13,462)	
Colton, Jason P	5:11:07 (26,524)	
Colverson, Nigel B	4:43:23 (21,659)	
Colville, Hugh	5:09:48 (26,358)	
Colyer, Sam	4:54:39 (23,932)	
Coman, Raphael A	3:57:51 (10,632)	
Combat, Michel	4:03:15 (12,017)	
Combes, George	5:17:28 (27,304)	
Comerford, Sean	5:11:24 (26,564)	
Comette, Allan J	5:09:17 (26,274)	
Comi, Sergio	4:02:48 (11,927)	
Comninos, Michael	3:04:23 (1,484)	
Comper, Paul	3:25:53 (3,825)	
Compton, Fred L	5:15:51 (27,114)	
Compton, Patrick J	4:25:46 (17,503)	
Compton, Stephen C	3:53:58 (9,493)	
Conaghan, James	4:02:44 (11,910)	
Concannon, Andrew	4:16:31 (15,177)	
Conder, Steven J	3:53:18 (9,340)	
Condon, Derek A	4:36:50 (20,214)	
Condon, Matthew P	5:29:06 (28,493)	
Coniglio, Tony	4:19:32 (15,917)	
Conley, Richard D	4:10:13 (13,681)	
Conlin, Geoffrey M	3:12:03 (2,199)	
Conlin, Jonathan G	4:35:43 (19,963)	
Conlin, Steve J	4:01:02 (11,510)	
Conlon, Toby J	3:09:27 (1,942)	
Connan, Brian	4:43:03 (21,574)	
Conneely, Ruriri	4:43:52 (21,766)	
Connell, Anthony	4:16:21 (15,131)	
Connell, Brian	5:10:24 (26,427)	
Connell, Brian A	3:56:30 (10,250)	
Connell, Christopher	3:42:53 (6,830)	
Connell, Diarmuid	4:56:29 (24,305)	
Connell, Gary A	4:30:23 (18,724)	
Connell, Martin J	4:39:53 (20,891)	
Connell, Russell F	4:56:28 (24,298)	
Connelley, Matthew J	3:42:48 (6,810)	
Connelly, David M	3:28:22 (4,293)	
Connelly, Robert A	4:35:34 (19,943)	
Connery, Neil E	4:16:36 (15,200)	
Connochie, Andrew R	3:24:09 (3,581)	
Connolly, Christopher J	5:34:34 (28,926)	
Connolly, Damian R	3:07:59 (1,804)	
Connolly, Daniel P	3:59:08 (11,040)	
Connolly, David	4:05:01 (12,437)	
Connolly, Dermot F	2:57:08 (890)	
Connolly, Edward J	3:59:28 (11,140)	
Connolly, Hugh J	3:01:02 (1,241)	
Connolly, James	6:02:36 (30,515)	
Connolly, James R	4:51:26 (23,335)	
Connolly, Michael	3:51:41 (8,936)	
Connolly, Michael R	6:41:06 (31,373)	
Connolly, Nathan N	4:17:08 (15,337)	
Connolly, Wayne L	3:06:15 (1,634)	
Connop, David W	3:36:42 (5,725)	
Connor, Dennis	3:16:32 (2,703)	
Connor, James M	4:31:33 (18,990)	
Connor, Robert A	4:18:48 (15,740)	
Connor, Roger G	3:51:45 (8,955)	
Connor, Shaun S	3:28:36 (4,335)	
Connors, Ronald	5:18:10 (27,386)	
Connor-Stead, Philip	4:09:45 (13,568)	
Conquest, Johnny	3:46:48 (7,702)	
Conradie, Arno	3:59:50 (11,249)	
Conroy, Adrian	4:26:37 (17,730)	
Conroy, Gerard	6:21:56 (31,059)	
Conroy, Ian M	4:58:04 (24,613)	
Conseil, Michel	4:00:48 (11,444)	
Constable, Derek J	4:30:08 (18,664)	
Constable, Ian	3:31:11 (4,808)	
Constant, Ludo A	3:50:18 (8,574)	
Constant, Simon N	5:29:03 (28,488)	
Contiero, Angelo	4:10:49 (13,830)	
Contractor, Bhadresh	4:44:27 (21,899)	
Convery, John J	2:35:03 (125)	
Conway, David	5:47:20 (29,829)	
Conway, David J	3:03:31 (1,408)	
Conway, Paul	4:25:45 (17,496)	
Conway, Stuart	3:25:06 (3,704)	
Conyers-Silverthorn, Rex M	4:31:31 (18,987)	
Coode, Richard W	5:58:13 (30,334)	
Cook, Adrian	4:01:40 (11,640)	
Cook, Alistair T	4:38:59 (20,721)	
Cook, Andrew M	3:05:24 (1,563)	
Cook, Andrew M	3:44:35 (7,208)	
Cook, Barry	5:31:13 (28,678)	
Cook, Chris M	3:50:58 (8,743)	
Cook, Cristian J	4:15:21 (14,889)	
Cook, Danny M	5:11:44 (26,596)	
Cook, David V	4:18:35 (15,681)	
Cook, Hugh J	3:20:17 (3,096)	
Cook, Jason S	3:25:50 (3,820)	
Cook, John W	4:40:06 (20,942)	
Cook, Jonathan J	3:47:26 (7,864)	
Cook, Martin A	4:29:39 (18,542)	
Cook, Michael J	4:06:28 (12,772)	
Cook, Nicholas D	4:47:49 (22,639)	
Cook, Nicholas G	4:27:39 (18,004)	
Cook, Nigel W	2:54:42 (727)	
Cook, Njkalas	3:27:29 (4,124)	
Cook, Paul R	3:49:19 (8,331)	
Cook, Peter D	4:09:52 (13,598)	
Cook, Peter G	4:01:39 (11,633)	
Cook, Peter R	4:48:09 (22,707)	
Cook, Richard A	4:25:18 (17,380)	
Cook, Robin H	3:50:31 (8,631)	
Cook, Simon A	4:22:18 (16,637)	
Cook, Stephen	4:13:10 (14,369)	
Cook, Stephen E	4:43:36 (21,701)	
Cook, Stephen G	3:31:56 (4,913)	
Cook, Steven A	5:44:14 (29,641)	
Cook, Timothy H	2:52:24 (608)	
Cook, Timothy P	3:32:26 (4,993)	
Cook, Tony W	4:45:30 (22,142)	
Cooke, Asa J	5:29:08 (28,498)	
Cooke, Barry J	3:51:41 (8,936)	
Cooke, Brian H	4:49:13 (22,920)	
Cooke, Bryan S	4:07:02 (12,903)	
Cooke, David J	4:37:44 (20,387)	
Cooke, Edward J	4:09:07 (13,402)	
Cooke, Gary J	3:40:49 (6,441)	
Cooke, James H	5:12:43 (26,715)	
Cooke, Jason L	2:56:26 (848)	
Cooke, Mitchell A	3:55:34 (9,954)	
Cooke, Patrick R	4:09:07 (13,402)	
Cooke, Paul	4:44:58 (22,027)	
Cooke, Paul	5:43:00 (29,562)	
Cooke, Peter T	3:59:19 (11,092)	
Cooke, Tim J	3:52:10 (9,053)	
Cookham, John	3:38:05 (5,973)	
Cook-Radmore, Adrian	4:24:58 (17,300)	
Cooksey, Andrew P	4:11:07 (13,895)	
Cookson, Noel	3:56:51 (10,285)	
Cookson, Peter G	4:06:52 (12,855)	
Cooley, Anthony G	3:46:17 (7,598)	
Cooley, Brian C	4:48:27 (22,772)	
Cooley, Neil A	3:36:41 (5,722)	
Coolican, David	3:52:41 (9,169)	
Coombes, Simon	2:49:32 (480)	
Coombs, Matias	3:40:19 (6,359)	
Coomer, Darren P	4:40:13 (20,965)	
Cooney, Jonathan	4:50:20 (23,129)	
Cooney, Kevin A	3:23:09 (3,460)	
Cooney, Richard L	3:51:16 (8,824)	
Coop, Harvey W	4:16:55 (15,288)	
Cooper, Alan	5:46:06 (29,755)	
Cooper, Alan P	5:03:15 (25,482)	
Cooper, Allan	3:56:53 (10,362)	
Cooper, Andrew B	4:11:34 (13,988)	
Cooper, Andrew J	4:49:41 (23,012)	
Cooper, Andrew W	5:08:51 (26,216)	
Cooper, Anthony J	4:19:18 (15,857)	
Cooper, Benjamin C	4:09:07 (13,402)	
Cooper, Carl J	2:58:32 (1,015)	
Cooper, Clive	4:08:42 (13,291)	
Cooper, David A	2:55:33 (788)	
Cooper, Gary G	5:03:28 (25,515)	
Cooper, Gary R	3:57:42 (10,592)	
Cooper, George	5:29:24 (28,524)	
Cooper, Giles S	5:42:46 (29,532)	
Cooper, Ian R	3:14:28 (2,496)	
Cooper, Ian T	4:22:23 (16,663)	
Cooper, James J	5:06:29 (25,908)	
Cooper, Jay W	4:31:20 (18,930)	
Cooper, John	4:38:25 (20,575)	
Cooper, John M	3:47:34 (7,898)	
Cooper, John M	3:54:17 (9,583)	
Cooper, Julian	4:27:51 (18,055)	
Cooper, Lee	5:50:05 (29,970)	
Cooper, Lee J	4:56:37 (24,333)	
Cooper, Lee N	4:39:56 (20,903)	
Cooper, Mark C	4:14:12 (14,611)	
Cooper, Mark R	4:58:37 (24,741)	
Cooper, Neil W	4:09:17 (13,450)	
Cooper, Nicholas G	3:24:37 (3,639)	
Cooper, Nigel	4:34:48 (19,778)	
Cooper, Paul A	4:28:23 (18,187)	
Cooper, Paul G	4:05:09 (12,456)	
Cooper, Paul G	5:03:17 (25,488)	
Cooper, Raymond W	4:19:59 (16,029)	
Cooper, Richard A	5:26:56 (28,294)	
Cooper, Richard C	4:44:23 (21,885)	
Cooper, Robert	5:36:40 (29,078)	
Cooper, Robert H	4:16:13 (15,104)	
Cooper, Robert J	4:04:03 (12,195)	
Cooper, Rodney C	3:50:02 (8,511)	
Cooper, Roger N	3:49:51 (8,461)	
Cooper, Roy	4:25:39 (17,465)	
Cooper, Stefan	4:48:04 (22,688)	
Cooper, Stephen J	4:04:03 (12,195)	
Cooper, Stephen J	5:24:46 (28,051)	
Cooper, Vincent	5:27:11 (28,322)	
Coopman, Christopher D	5:02:31 (25,379)	
Cope, David	4:16:54 (15,282)	
Cope, David S	5:47:56 (29,864)	
Cope, Trevor A	4:13:23 (14,430)	
Copestick, Robin J	2:36:52 (149)	
Copnall, Philip I	4:48:03 (22,682)	
Copp, Peter	4:32:14 (19,176)	
Coppack, Ian F	4:23:10 (16,858)	
Coppard, David J	4:27:29 (17,951)	
Coppeard, Patrick D	5:44:42 (29,669)	
Coppen, Dean	4:12:30 (14,200)	
Coppersmith, Laurie E	5:02:17 (25,336)	
Coppinger, Eugene	2:48:19 (437)	
Coppock, Mick	4:19:08 (15,812)	
Copsey, Paul	5:33:16 (28,831)	
Copus, Christopher D	3:06:15 (1,634)	
Copus, John W	5:36:47 (29,086)	
Copus, Martin R	3:44:03 (7,082)	
Corbarien, Alain	4:51:29 (23,342)	
Corbarieu, Thierry	3:31:20 (4,823)	
Corbet Owen, Peter D	4:03:26 (12,065)	
Corbett, Iain	4:32:49 (19,314)	
Corbett, James R	5:42:59 (29,559)	
Corbett, Jonathan C	3:37:52 (5,934)	
Corbett, Neil M	3:42:14 (6,691)	
Corbett, Paul J	4:15:42 (14,978)	
Corbett, Richard C	4:38:00 (20,466)	
Corbett, Ronald	4:05:58 (12,653)	
Corbould, Jason P	4:36:17 (20,086)	
Corbould, Leigh M	4:24:26 (17,172)	
Corby, Nicholas C	4:08:54 (13,348)	
Corcoran, Alan J	5:27:51 (28,388)	
Corcoran, Steve	3:44:05 (7,092)	
Cordery, Nicholas P	5:13:27 (26,819)	

Cordle, Sidney C 3:32:15 (4,961)
Cordrey, Christopher E 5:16:45 (27,225)
Cordwell, James P 2:49:39 (484)
Cordwell, Julian C 3:45:51 (7,492)
Corena, Mario 6:32:08 (31,246)
Corfield, Michael H 3:22:33 (3,387)
Cork, John 4:19:48 (15,975)
Corker, Eric W 4:36:43 (20,186)
Corker, John 3:57:36 (10,568)
Corkin, Simon J 3:25:49 (3,817)
Corless, David 4:15:55 (15,031)
Corlett, Ben A 3:35:40 (5,549)
Corlett, Brian J 4:49:35 (22,992)
Corlett, Michael W 4:14:42 (14,728)
Cormack, Stephen M 4:19:45 (15,965)
Cormell, Richard C 5:38:14 (29,199)
Cornali, Aldo 3:38:50 (6,105)
Cornall, Anthony J 4:18:26 (15,647)
Cornell, Chris M 3:44:30 (7,185)
Corner, Richard A 4:18:22 (15,623)
Cornford, Adrian W 3:14:46 (2,533)
Cornford, Richard J 4:26:40 (17,746)
Cornish, Lee D 4:29:46 (18,573)
Cornish, Nathan 3:57:05 (10,411)
Cornock, Andrew J 4:10:21 (13,716)
Cornwall, John B 4:40:24 (21,008)
Cornwall, Leslie J 4:27:20 (17,925)
Cornwall, Michael D 4:14:19 (14,626)
Cornwell, James K 5:07:44 (26,085)
Corper, Simon J 3:47:11 (7,801)
Corpez, Karl E 2:44:40 (311)
Corps, Daryl J 4:28:15 (18,158)
Corr, John P 3:38:09 (5,986)
Corr, Ronan 5:24:51 (28,062)
Corradini, Maurizio 3:54:38 (9,677)
Corrie, Malcolm B 4:34:18 (19,669)
Corrigan, John J 4:39:42 (20,862)
Corrigan, Kevin J 4:41:27 (21,230)
Corrigan, Kieron P 4:35:24 (19,912)
Corrigan, Patrik J 3:36:33 (5,703)
Corrigan, Stephen L 4:44:54 (22,002)
Corten, Paul J 4:39:54 (20,898)
Corton, James 5:25:43 (28,162)
Cosgrave, David P 4:30:23 (18,724)
Cosgrove, Stephen J 4:25:56 (17,551)
Cossington, Scott A 4:37:28 (20,333)
Costa, José Carlos 4:11:07 (13,895)
Costa, Michele 3:35:05 (5,442)
Costa, Pedro H 3:53:19 (9,342)
Costabile, Michele 4:22:42 (16,749)
Costain, Michael G 3:35:37 (5,544)
Costas, Paraskeva B 3:04:38 (1,501)
Costello, Aaron F 3:44:51 (7,273)
Costello, Daniel R 4:46:26 (22,347)
Costello, Kevin J 3:16:47 (2,728)
Costello, William M 5:18:36 (27,423)
Costidell, Peter A 3:52:35 (9,149)
Costiff, Nigel L 3:43:56 (7,047)
Coston, Max P 4:30:49 (18,818)
Coter, Mario 3:00:15 (1,174)
Cotta, David J 5:19:59 (27,561)
Cottam, Brian 4:57:22 (24,467)
Cotter, Trevor J 3:25:24 (3,747)
Cotterell, Joe F 4:09:10 (13,411)
Cotterell, Owen M 3:45:32 (7,420)
Cotterill, Mark A 3:06:46 (1,681)
Cottingham, Mark I 5:12:28 (26,688)
Cottis, Roy A 4:02:42 (11,899)
Cottle, Benjamin C 3:36:46 (5,738)
Cottle, Michael D 5:11:43 (26,592)
Cottle, Simon 3:52:14 (9,064)
Cotton, Andrew M 3:50:26 (8,614)
Cotton, Anthony E 3:41:33 (6,549)
Cotton, Chris 4:13:31 (14,456)
Cotton, Jason 4:19:25 (15,887)
Cotton, Jeremy D 5:09:45 (26,345)
Cotton, Roger B 4:34:10 (19,638)
Cotton, Stewart K 3:25:55 (3,832)
Cottrell, Brendan M 3:10:29 (2,056)
Cottrell, Dale L 3:42:48 (6,810)
Cottrell, David F 5:09:27 (26,299)
Cottrell, Jeffrey R 3:29:35 (4,516)
Cottrell, Tom 5:10:25 (26,432)

LONDON MARATHON

Cottrill, Philip G 4:08:29 (13,224)
Couch, Darren G 3:40:14 (6,341)
Couchman, Paul 4:26:43 (17,753)
Couchman, Simon P 3:53:31 (9,380)
Coughlan, Alan P 4:19:32 (15,917)
Coughlan, Edward G 7:43:29 (31,901)
Coughlin, John L 4:42:03 (21,362)
Coulam, Gary 2:56:21 (844)
Couldridge, David C 4:49:10 (22,912)
Coull, Paul D 3:44:32 (7,195)
Coulson, Arran 5:00:32 (25,069)
Coulson, Mark A 3:30:04 (4,608)
Coulson, Matthew J 4:46:05 (22,266)
Coulson, Stephen 3:44:54 (7,286)
Coulson, Steve 4:34:03 (19,606)
Coultas, Stephen R 4:06:10 (12,705)
Coulter, Peter R 3:54:44 (9,704)
Coumbe, Anthony P 3:32:35 (5,024)
Coupe, Andrew J 4:29:33 (18,505)
Coupe, Benjamin J 7:15:21 (31,748)
Coupe, Matthew R 3:34:07 (5,286)
Coupe, Simon 3:32:54 (5,083)
Cournane, Brendan 3:44:23 (7,150)
Court, Alan R 3:09:02 (1,903)
Court, Jamie 4:17:02 (15,312)
Court, Kenneth J 4:48:39 (22,803)
Court, Michael C 3:27:14 (4,070)
Court, Robert J 4:50:51 (23,243)
Courtenay, Matthew G 3:44:13 (7,120)
Courthiau, Daniel 4:36:24 (20,104)
Court-Johnston, Niel 5:09:51 (26,362)
Courtman, Simon P 4:26:30 (17,703)
Courtman-Stock, Paul S 3:38:57 (6,121)
Courtney, Chris G 3:43:46 (7,005)
Courtney, John 5:39:00 (29,265)
Courtney, Kevin S 3:03:21 (1,395)
Courtney, Trevor A 5:29:11 (28,506)
Cousens, Charles L 4:47:23 (22,540)
Cousens, Michael 5:28:01 (28,397)
Cousens, Simon J 4:49:07 (22,898)
Cousins, David P 5:18:01 (27,372)
Cousins, Ian R 4:22:55 (16,799)
Cousins, Paul 3:00:21 (1,181)
Cousins, Peter J 3:47:47 (7,942)
Cousins, Roger N 5:04:25 (25,620)
Cousins, Stephen 3:36:16 (5,655)
Coutant, Pascal 3:06:34 (1,662)
Couturier, Thierry C 5:14:24 (26,950)
Couzens, Michael W 3:55:56 (10,062)
Covelo-Lopez, Francisco J 3:22:22 (3,354)
Coveney, Andrew R 6:05:43 (30,611)
Covington, Neil J 2:49:59 (504)
Cowan, Christopher J 5:06:37 (25,931)
Cowan, David 4:44:11 (21,835)
Cowan, David J 7:07:08 (31,683)
Cowan, Harry 5:43:38 (29,603)
Cowan, Michael R 4:00:24 (11,380)
Cowan, Paul S 3:54:48 (9,722)
Cowan, Robert G 5:10:52 (26,492)
Coward, Allen E 3:55:43 (9,997)
Coward, Andrew D 3:34:59 (5,424)
Coward, David W 3:54:30 (9,635)
Coward, Jeremy 2:45:43 (350)
Cowdrey, Matthew R 3:46:22 (7,614)
Cowell, Antony J 3:24:58 (3,688)
Cowen, Stephen W 4:40:18 (20,984)
Cowhig, Philip J 4:13:12 (14,376)
Cowie, Malcom A 3:52:37 (9,154)
Cowin, Alan 3:28:18 (4,282)
Cowin, Malcolm I 4:14:41 (14,725)
Cowin, Timothy 4:20:36 (16,187)
Cowland, Dan 4:43:23 (21,659)
Cowley, Andrew 4:29:06 (18,377)
Cowley, Keith 3:02:36 (1,345)
Cowley, Nigel M 3:06:38 (1,666)

Cowley, Richard J 6:34:43 (31,284)
Cowling, Jeff 3:43:13 (6,899)
Cowper, Jonathan 3:49:32 (8,388)
Cowper-Smith, Adam 3:09:43 (1,970)
Cox, Alan 3:35:30 (5,525)
Cox, Andrew D 3:30:21 (4,663)
Cox, Barnaby 5:19:44 (27,527)
Cox, Chris 5:47:31 (29,840)
Cox, Craig A 3:47:26 (7,864)
Cox, Daniel R 3:34:59 (5,424)
Cox, Darren J 3:39:39 (6,244)
Cox, David 3:56:47 (10,323)
Cox, David I 3:37:48 (5,922)
Cox, Gary M 3:40:52 (6,448)
Cox, Ian A 3:52:04 (9,027)
Cox, John 4:44:01 (21,801)
Cox, Jonathan P 4:17:55 (15,538)
Cox, Justin A 3:04:10 (1,462)
Cox, Lee M 4:47:26 (22,552)
Cox, Martin 4:46:08 (22,275)
Cox, Michael R 4:32:08 (19,146)
Cox, Richard 4:03:24 (12,057)
Cox, Richard 5:25:01 (28,085)
Cox, Richard G 4:42:54 (21,541)
Cox, Simon J 5:43:05 (29,572)
Cox, Stephen J 2:56:20 (842)
Cox, Steve C 3:14:15 (2,472)
Cox, Steve M 4:53:16 (23,669)
Cox, Stewart R 5:01:37 (25,241)
Cox, William J 4:32:10 (19,158)
Coxhead, Ian S 2:51:49 (583)
Coxon, Gary 3:20:41 (3,160)
Coy, Martin J 5:32:06 (28,738)
Coyle, Alasdair J 3:22:28 (3,370)
Coyle, John J 4:00:44 (11,433)
Coyle, Kieran P 3:29:03 (4,422)
Coyle, Maurice P 3:41:27 (6,540)
Coyle, Terence P 2:52:59 (641)
Coyne, Michael J 4:05:16 (12,475)
Coyne, Stephen K 4:35:39 (19,954)
Cozens, Graham P 5:45:22 (29,720)
Crabb, Graham 3:38:33 (6,056)
Crabtree, John W 3:58:18 (10,791)
Crabtree, Mark A 2:58:45 (1,052)
Crabtree, Stewart 4:55:12 (24,037)
Cracknell, David J 4:26:39 (17,744)
Cradden, Brendan P 3:26:39 (3,942)
Craddock, Peter M 3:29:27 (4,497)
Crader, Michael 3:59:28 (11,140)
Crafer, Gary 4:10:11 (13,675)
Crager, John A 5:46:13 (29,762)
Cragg, Stephen 4:10:34 (13,773)
Cragg, Stuart J 2:50:41 (534)
Craggs, Douglas 3:44:38 (7,220)
Craig, Adam D 3:59:53 (11,261)
Craig, Alan R 4:50:35 (23,193)
Craig, Angus W 3:54:52 (9,741)
Craig, Gerard 2:53:24 (664)
Craig, Ian W 4:06:46 (12,832)
Craig, Richard T 5:26:34 (28,256)
Craig, Robert 5:00:33 (25,072)
Craig, Robert D 3:12:36 (2,263)
Craig, Scott 3:56:30 (10,266)
Craig, Sean 3:49:47 (8,447)
Craigen, Gregory J 4:33:19 (19,429)
Craig-McFeely, Richard B 3:38:51 (6,109)
Craig-McFeely, Simon J 4:15:14 (14,863)
Craik, Nicholas J 3:58:38 (10,899)
Cramphorn, John M 4:16:30 (15,174)
Crampton, Ian 2:30:54 (85)
Cran, Alexander N 3:25:24 (3,747)
Crane, Andrew J 4:35:59 (20,025)
Crane, Andrew R 5:18:26 (27,405)
Crane, Jeremy S 4:58:01 (24,597)
Crane, Michael W 3:44:01 (7,075)
Crane, Robert 4:29:18 (18,431)
Crane, Rosemary 4:59:18 (24,849)
Crane, Terence V 4:43:45 (21,736)
Crane, Tim 3:50:48 (8,706)
Crane, William T 3:15:05 (2,565)
Cranham, Nicholas 3:27:01 (4,027)
Cranson, Derek 6:02:46 (30,521)
Cranston, Mark J 4:25:55 (17,545)

Cranston, Nicholas J 3:58:22 (10,811)
Cratchley, Neil 3:59:49 (11,242)
Cravagan, Joe B 5:49:51 (29,955)
Craven, Paul A 3:59:49 (11,242)
Craven, Paul V 5:21:03 (27,685)
Craven, Shane A 5:11:02 (26,508)
Craven, Thomas H 5:14:45 (26,997)
Crawford, Andrew P 5:11:25 (26,567)
Crawford, David J 4:55:30 (24,099)
Crawford, Ian C 4:55:59 (24,204)
Crawford, Jason 3:33:13 (5,141)
Crawford, Lawson J 3:48:26 (8,102)
Crawford, Mark D 6:45:02 (31,439)
Crawford, Matthew J 5:30:24 (28,616)
Crawford, Richard H 3:20:25 (3,110)
Crawley, Samuel P 3:31:33 (4,859)
Crawley, Steven K 3:20:54 (3,191)
Crawshaw, Drew 3:30:08 (4,622)
Crawte, Antony M 4:58:27 (24,707)
Cray, Stephen 3:39:50 (6,280)
Crayston, David 3:06:02 (1,613)
Crayston, Gavin E 4:57:18 (24,461)
Creak, Jonathan B 2:36:36 (143)
Creak, Will H 4:59:39 (24,930)
Creamer, Hugh L 3:22:40 (3,398)
Crean, Adrian P 3:50:34 (8,645)
Creane, John E 2:39:39 (203)
Creaney, Edward 4:59:42 (24,940)
Crease, Gregory B 3:25:59 (3,846)
Creasey, Andy A 3:48:43 (8,189)
Creasey, Dan M 3:51:50 (8,976)
Creasy, James G 3:47:31 (7,883)
Creber, Jim E 3:44:30 (7,185)
Creer, Dean D 3:00:43 (1,209)
Crees, Stuart E 3:27:27 (4,115)
Creighton, Andrew J 4:33:48 (19,534)
Creighton, Peter 4:51:10 (23,300)
Creighton, Stephen W 4:45:57 (22,238)
Crema, Simone 3:24:36 (3,636)
Cremen, Vincent P 4:51:00 (23,270)
Crenol, Kevin N 2:35:59 (135)
Cresswell, Brent A 3:19:28 (3,016)
Cresswell, Jamie 4:24:46 (17,243)
Cresswell, Roy P 4:59:22 (24,871)
Cresswell-Hibbert, Charles E 3:48:21 (8,091)
Creus, Paul A 5:09:44 (26,342)
Crew, Danny E 3:35:24 (5,502)
Crew, Kevin E 3:03:35 (1,413)
Crew, Paul P 4:44:55 (22,015)
Crew, Steven J 4:22:27 (16,681)
Crewe, David 4:55:13 (24,044)
Cribier, Guillaume J 2:40:13 (217)
Crichton, Oliver P 4:36:48 (20,202)
Cridland, Barry J 4:59:10 (24,825)
Cridland, Lucas 4:19:18 (15,857)
Crighton, Andrew S 3:59:13 (11,064)
Crighton, Matthew D 3:31:16 (4,815)
Crimp, Benjamin A 3:37:11 (5,814)
Cripps, Jason K 4:12:29 (14,194)
Cripps, Kevin A 4:28:56 (18,334)
Cripps, Paul M 4:24:43 (17,233)
Criqui, Jean C 3:32:13 (4,957)
Crisman, Bill 4:40:28 (21,021)
Crisp, Clive 3:02:42 (1,353)
Crisp, Lloyd T 4:28:41 (18,276)
Crisp, Nicholas 4:42:11 (21,382)
Crispini, Marco 5:57:19 (30,303)
Cristin, Giuseppe 3:17:40 (2,817)
Critchard, Jonathan P 5:12:55 (26,751)
Critchfield, John 3:52:22 (9,103)
Critchley, Neil J 3:35:55 (5,591)
Critchlow, Alex M 4:57:50 (24,555)
Critchlow, Martin P 3:06:38 (1,666)
Critoph, Neville A 3:43:00 (6,850)
Crittenden, Robert J 3:35:09 (5,454)
Croal, Jeremy 4:14:34 (14,698)
Croasdale, Mark 2:23:24 (50)
Crocker, Matthew J 3:58:10 (10,745)
Crocker, Robert W 3:35:34 (5,535)
Crockford, John G 2:48:50 (449)
Croft, Anthony J 3:05:26 (1,565)
Croft, Anthony J 3:09:18 (1,929)
Croft, David 4:06:14 (12,722)
Croft, Dominic G 2:33:19 (101)
Croft, Jared A 3:31:58 (4,918)
Croft, Malcolm 4:17:03 (15,318)
Croft, Quentin 4:13:46 (14,508)
Croft, Stephen J 4:12:49 (14,283)
Crofts, Joe N 4:33:15 (19,417)
Croke, Simon J 4:56:58 (24,396)
Croll, Stephen J 5:31:08 (28,670)
Crols, Bart 3:36:36 (5,709)
Crombie, Alexander 3:39:49 (6,275)
Crome, Paul 4:29:34 (18,511)
Cromey, Simon A 4:57:51 (24,557)
Crompton, John 5:37:20 (29,137)
Crompton, Neil 2:36:56 (150)
Crompton, Peter 3:08:33 (1,856)
Crone, Colin F 4:13:02 (14,337)
Cronin, Alfred 2:59:01 (1,073)
Cronin, Geoff M 4:09:21 (13,462)
Cronin, Nick T 4:21:57 (16,516)
Cronin, Paul 3:34:53 (5,405)
Crook, Graham P 4:47:27 (22,557)
Crook, Michael J 3:58:59 (10,999)
Crook, Paul D 6:41:36 (31,384)
Croom, Andy R 7:05:15 (31,672)
Cropley, Nigel V 3:42:00 (6,646)
Cropper, David 4:08:08 (13,139)
Crosbie, Benjamin W 3:40:38 (6,423)
Crosbie, Raymond W 4:54:46 (23,954)
Crosby, John M 6:12:42 (30,804)
Crosby, Niel 4:21:46 (16,472)
Crosby, Paul R 3:43:49 (7,017)
Crosby, Stephen P 4:42:11 (21,382)
Crosby, Williams 3:45:18 (7,364)
Cross, Alex J 3:48:12 (8,047)
Cross, Anthony 4:59:03 (24,803)
Cross, Carl 5:00:02 (24,995)
Cross, Colin R 5:38:30 (29,230)
Cross, Fenton E 3:47:27 (7,869)
Cross, Howard 3:35:16 (5,474)
Cross, Ian N 4:50:08 (23,095)
Cross, Jeremy S 3:22:37 (3,394)
Cross, Mark A 5:21:07 (27,692)
Cross, Max D 4:26:22 (17,669)
Cross, Michael 5:22:29 (27,830)
Cross, Paul S 3:46:58 (7,741)
Cross, Peter 4:58:34 (24,729)
Cross, Peter H 5:12:09 (26,649)
Cross, Peter R 3:38:36 (6,069)
Cross, Roger J 3:55:10 (9,839)
Cross, Simon J 4:29:43 (18,557)
Cross, Stephen J 4:03:57 (12,179)
Cross, Terry P 3:50:43 (8,688)
Crossan, Gary 2:21:48 (39)
Crosse, Carl C 3:58:35 (10,884)
Crosse, Matthew P 3:12:20 (2,233)
Crossfield, Mark A 4:07:55 (13,094)
Crossingham, Rowan 3:45:26 (7,395)
Crossley, John 4:10:22 (13,723)
Crossley, Maxwell J 3:23:57 (3,559)
Crossley, Patrick D 4:05:43 (12,598)
Crossley, Peter J 3:55:15 (9,863)
Crosswell, Christopher W 3:42:11 (6,678)
Crotty, Andrew D 4:34:06 (19,625)
Crouch, Alan 4:16:22 (15,137)
Crouch, Bruce A 4:44:52 (21,991)
Crouch, Michael J 3:57:25 (10,516)
Crouch-Chivers, Paul R 4:11:39 (14,015)
Croucher, Antony R 4:30:52 (18,833)
Croucher, Gordon 3:07:25 (1,738)
Crow, Benjamin J 5:42:10 (29,493)
Crow, Gregory D 4:23:51 (17,025)
Crow, Mike 6:43:41 (31,414)
Crow, Peter 3:45:17 (7,361)
Crowe, David B 3:51:21 (8,846)
Crowe, Douglas J 5:12:25 (26,684)
Crowe, Michael A 3:36:22 (5,672)
Crowe, Robert 3:34:12 (5,298)
Crowe, Wayne 4:31:15 (18,909)
Crowell, Peter J 3:56:09 (10,121)
Crowell, Timothy P 3:25:50 (3,820)
Crowhurst, David S 5:42:52 (29,539)
Crowley, David M 3:47:00 (7,751)
Crowley, John 3:31:46 (4,882)
Crowley, Julian F 3:36:03 (5,618)
Crowley, Richard J 6:11:22 (30,768)
Crowley, Vincent P 3:02:44 (1,355)
Crowther, Ben 3:41:04 (6,486)
Croxford, Gary A 4:49:30 (22,980)
Croxson, Oliver J 3:36:23 (5,678)
Crudgington, James W 4:08:36 (13,260)
Cruickshank, Andrew 2:52:46 (630)
Cruickshank, Mike 3:11:37 (2,151)
Cruickshank, Sandy 3:38:16 (6,006)
Crummack, Ian J 4:11:05 (13,886)
Crummett, Stephen P 4:05:34 (12,563)
Crummey, Terence C 4:18:13 (15,591)
Crump, Jason 4:51:57 (23,432)
Crump, Jonathon H 4:55:09 (24,026)
Cruse, Mark C 3:27:22 (4,095)
Cruse, Peter 2:51:37 (575)
Crush, David P 3:50:49 (8,712)
Crutchfield, Donovan 4:31:58 (19,104)
Crutwell, G 5:24:40 (28,042)
Cruz, Arman 5:44:12 (29,635)
Cryne, Andrew R 4:29:51 (18,593)
Cubban, Tony 3:28:44 (4,359)
Cubbon, Andrew K 4:43:38 (21,707)
Cucchiara, Nicolo 3:41:54 (6,618)
Cucciniello, Carlo 3:59:05 (11,024)
Cucht, Matthew J 3:18:46 (2,927)
Cuddihy, Marc S 3:25:24 (3,747)
Cuddon, Kevin D 3:28:55 (4,402)
Cudmore, Miles A 3:20:14 (3,092)
Cuff, Shaun M 4:32:04 (19,124)
Cuffe, Jamie N 4:38:41 (20,637)
Cuffe, John G 6:02:35 (30,513)
Cuisenier, François 3:36:57 (5,761)
Cull-Dodd, Mick E 5:43:38 (29,603)
Cullen, Andrew 3:22:36 (3,390)
Cullen, Andrew J 5:17:57 (27,360)
Cullen, Brian 4:34:28 (19,704)
Cullen, Christian M 6:20:50 (31,029)
Cullen, David J 4:27:50 (18,050)
Cullen, Eamonn M 4:05:57 (12,650)
Cullen, Jim 5:12:48 (26,731)
Cullen, John J 5:12:47 (26,726)
Cullen, Mark T 3:54:23 (9,604)
Cullen, Martin J 4:10:15 (13,690)
Cullen, Patrick E 5:12:48 (26,731)
Cullen, Paul A 5:12:49 (26,734)
Cullen, Robert G 4:30:01 (18,634)
Cullen, Tony 5:17:57 (27,360)
Cullern, Doug A 4:16:28 (15,166)
Cullern, Doug A 4:16:28 (15,166)
Culley, David R 4:15:13 (14,859)
Culley, Simon 4:37:24 (20,328)
Culley, Simon J 3:34:04 (5,280)
Culley, Spencer 3:38:00 (5,961)
Cullingworth, Ian 3:14:21 (2,485)
Cullwick, Michael J 4:04:50 (12,385)
Culpan, Charlie J 4:56:04 (24,223)
Culver, Edward J 4:33:28 (19,463)
Culwin, Fintan 4:07:21 (12,970)
Cuming, Nick P 4:16:23 (15,142)
Cumiskey, Kenneth V 4:56:36 (24,329)
Cumming, Tom 5:41:02 (29,410)
Cummings, Glenworth E 5:35:43 (29,012)
Cummings, John M 6:06:05 (30,623)
Cummins, Kevin P 4:58:18 (24,666)
Cummins, Mark C 3:43:54 (7,038)
Cummins, Timothy 4:53:35 (23,718)
Cummins, Vernon L 4:59:15 (24,839)
Cumper, Stephen M 3:52:55 (9,231)
Cumpsty, Brian 3:17:06 (2,759)
Cundy, Andrew P 3:30:09 (4,626)
Cunliffe, David R 4:41:31 (21,248)
Cunliffe, Graham A 3:00:53 (1,229)
Cunliffe, Luke 3:57:12 (10,444)
Cunliffe, Ross A 6:01:25 (30,462)
Cunnane, Andrew T 4:39:19 (20,796)
Cunningham, David 5:06:02 (25,848)
Cunningham, David J 4:37:46 (20,398)
Cunningham, Fraser K 5:04:24 (25,614)
Cunningham, Julian P 4:41:00 (21,122)
Cunningham, Michael R 3:13:35 (2,382)
Cunningham, Ross 4:50:27 (23,173)

Cunningham, Ryan 3:47:09 (7,795)
Cunningham, Simon 4:01:34 (11,613)
Cunningham, Steve 2:51:21 (558)
Cunningham, Terence C 5:46:14 (29,764)
Curati, Peter 3:54:33 (9,651)
Curcher, Martin J 4:18:37 (15,691)
Curless, Brent 3:40:11 (6,337)
Curley, Stephen P 4:37:25 (20,332)
Curnow, Stuart L 6:27:53 (31,176)
Curphey, Paul T 2:51:01 (544)
Curran, Enda 3:26:18 (3,889)
Curran, Gary P 4:09:51 (13,593)
Curran, Richard J 3:50:12 (8,547)
Curran, Shaun M 4:17:14 (15,354)
Currell, Geoffrey 4:12:03 (14,105)
Currie, David S 3:47:55 (7,977)
Currie, Douglas Q 4:29:06 (18,377)
Currie, John 3:31:00 (4,778)
Currie, Lyndon 3:27:13 (4,066)
Curry, Andrew J 4:41:01 (21,126)
Curry, Joe H 3:24:33 (3,630)
Curry, John C 4:20:51 (16,244)
Curson, Ben E 3:43:40 (6,992)
Curtin, John J 3:18:25 (2,888)
Curtis, Andrew D 3:35:31 (5,527)
Curtis, Anthony S 4:33:45 (19,517)
Curtis, Dan 5:44:12 (29,635)
Curtis, Lee A 4:40:09 (20,951)
Curtis, Nicholas J 3:48:27 (8,106)
Curtis, Ray P 5:24:25 (28,019)
Curtis, Richard G 4:21:56 (16,512)
Curtis, Robert B 3:45:54 (7,507)
Curtis, Sean W 3:58:23 (10,813)
Curtis, Simon D 4:21:56 (16,512)
Curtis, Stephen 3:51:46 (8,962)
Curwin, Jeremy E 4:14:48 (14,758)
Cusse, Patrick 5:17:58 (27,363)
Custard, Curt 3:49:02 (8,263)
Cuthbert, Allan R 4:04:53 (12,402)
Cutler, Mark D 4:41:33 (21,254)
Cutt, Neil 3:17:21 (2,790)
Cutting, Keith C 3:54:10 (9,548)
Cutting, Robin 4:26:28 (17,691)
Cutting, Stephen J 4:56:28 (24,298)
Cuxac, Jean-Charles 3:33:40 (5,214)
Cuypers, Philip 3:58:15 (10,773)
Czarnocki, Chris 3:56:45 (10,311)
Czech, Albin 4:30:35 (18,777)
Czernuszka, Edward A 4:27:25 (17,941)
Czerwinski, David A 4:13:39 (14,487)
Czupalla, Juergen 3:52:47 (9,188)
Da Silva, Carlos 4:17:51 (15,523)
Da Silva, Panta 4:01:49 (11,672)
Daban, Bernard 4:58:35 (24,732)
Dable, Paul 3:51:46 (8,962)
Dable, Thomas J 4:39:17 (20,788)
Dabrowski, Barry 3:27:03 (4,036)
Dack, Paul J 4:19:56 (16,008)
Dackermann, Roman 4:35:23 (19,905)
Dacruz, Paul 4:29:59 (18,626)
Dadd, Tony 2:54:53 (743)
Dade, Michael R 4:04:19 (12,269)
Dagger, Guy W 4:15:05 (14,821)
Dagwell, Andrew S 6:20:12 (31,019)
Dahdouh, Fadi 4:18:35 (15,681)
Daines, Alan M 4:16:45 (15,237)
Dainty, Andrew H 4:23:48 (17,014)
Dainty, Robert L 4:49:55 (23,062)
Daish, Stephen R 3:53:51 (9,459)
Dajda, Richard 5:01:08 (25,165)
Dakin, Keith 3:42:56 (6,840)
Daking, Nicholas P 4:45:51 (22,219)
Dalan-Merini, Patrick 3:35:06 (5,445)
Dalby, Kevin 4:20:42 (16,211)
Dalby, Matthew J 3:04:45 (1,507)
Dale, Adrian B 3:03:20 (1,392)
Dale, Jonnie C 3:45:20 (7,372)
Dale, Jonny 3:48:15 (8,065)
Daley, James G 3:10:50 (2,085)
Daley, John R 3:16:19 (2,674)
Daley, Philip A 5:03:37 (25,534)
Daley, Trevor 5:16:24 (27,180)
Dall, Torsten 3:24:48 (3,660)
Dallas, David 4:30:45 (18,807)
Dallas, Gordon C 3:47:33 (7,894)
Dalrymple, Len 7:13:04 (31,733)
Dalton, Ian T 4:44:54 (22,002)
Dalton, Keith P 4:59:47 (24,954)
Dalton, Mark S 2:53:09 (651)
Dalton, William A 3:08:53 (1,889)
Daly, Fergus A 4:27:36 (17,990)
Daly, Hugh D 4:27:31 (17,965)
Daly, Kevin R 4:35:47 (19,981)
Daly, Michael JJ 4:55:33 (24,108)
Daly, Neil R 5:10:01 (26,382)
Daly, Sean E 6:06:15 (30,631)
Daly, Stephen 3:25:21 (3,741)
Dalziel, Julian A 3:04:15 (1,469)
Damamme, Emmanuel 3:34:33 (5,349)
D'Ambrogio, Victor J 5:17:32 (27,312)
D'Ambrosio, Gino S 4:42:26 (21,439)
Dames, Wayne 5:09:18 (26,277)
D'Amico, Claudio 3:54:40 (9,686)
Damle, Sameer D 4:28:03 (18,107)
Damon, Alex C 4:36:11 (20,068)
Damon, Peter 2:45:25 (338)
Danciger, Simon L 2:44:42 (317)
Dancy, Paul A 3:10:47 (2,082)
Dane, David T 4:13:01 (14,332)
Danelli, Paolo 4:15:22 (14,894)
Danemar, Erik C 3:54:11 (9,555)
D'Angelo, Luigi 3:39:32 (6,221)
Dangerfield, Paul R 3:36:10 (5,637)
Dangoor, Daniel E 3:28:32 (4,326)
Daniel, David 3:30:14 (4,641)
Daniel, Jeremy N 4:52:16 (23,497)
Daniel, Yves 4:02:10 (11,769)
Daniell, Roy W 2:34:38 (119)
Danielou, Yannick 3:21:05 (3,211)
Daniels, Adrian P 5:37:22 (29,143)
Daniels, Alan 4:40:13 (20,965)
Daniels, Andrew J 4:17:36 (15,452)
Daniels, Clive M 4:16:45 (15,237)
Daniels, Glynn M 3:30:09 (4,626)
Daniels, Henry 4:05:40 (12,588)
Daniels, James 3:50:52 (8,723)
Daniels, Mark 4:47:00 (22,449)
Daniels, Matthew D 5:48:35 (29,885)
Daniels, Michael 2:58:55 (1,067)
Daniels, Michael J 3:44:26 (7,168)
Daniels, Terence P 5:48:36 (29,886)
Daniels, Timothy W 4:58:33 (24,727)
Daniels, Zachary L 4:30:22 (18,720)
Danielsen, Staale 3:06:54 (1,694)
Danks, Simon J 3:23:40 (3,524)
Dann, Michael E 3:26:25 (3,906)
Dann, Neil R 3:18:49 (2,930)
Dann, Peter 4:18:36 (15,686)
Dann, Philip P 3:56:35 (10,274)
Dannan, Stephen 4:16:41 (15,228)
Danskin, Ian A 3:06:20 (1,639)
Danton, Mark H 3:52:15 (9,072)
Danvers, Simon G 4:18:31 (15,665)
Daoud, Elias 4:39:31 (20,826)
Darby, Ian L 3:43:29 (6,956)
Darby, Ian S 4:21:55 (16,505)
Darby, John A 4:29:54 (18,610)
Darby, Paul A 4:21:57 (16,516)
Darby, Paul S 4:18:46 (15,728)
Darbyshire, Malcolm 3:12:05 (2,201)
Darch, Gary 5:09:27 (26,299)
Darcy, Adrian K 3:27:59 (4,225)
Darcy, Kevin 3:02:14 (1,320)
D'Arcy, Lee P 3:57:38 (10,578)
D'Arcy, Luke J 3:00:29 (1,190)
D'Arcy, Michael P 4:14:36 (14,706)
Darderes, Mickael 4:10:11 (13,675)
Dargue, Kevin R 4:15:31 (14,931)
Dark, Andrew J 5:18:56 (27,457)
Dark, Jason P 3:40:53 (6,451)
Dark, Michael B 4:03:19 (12,036)
Darkins, Peter S 4:11:57 (14,077)
Darlaston, Guy W 4:34:45 (19,768)
Darling, Christopher T 4:04:09 (12,228)
Darlow, John R 5:02:53 (25,433)
Darnell, Marcus R 4:03:43 (12,132)
Darney, Bryan R 4:47:45 (22,624)
Dartington, Timothy C 5:14:29 (26,957)
Darvill, Neil J 4:19:53 (15,992)
Das, Devapriyo 4:27:01 (17,846)
Da-Silva, Antonio 2:49:59 (504)
Da-Silva, François 3:59:02 (11,012)
Dastych, Josef 3:11:32 (2,146)
Datta, Sanjib K 4:03:33 (12,089)
Dattani, Dilip 3:24:08 (3,579)
Daubney, Alisdair J 4:34:29 (19,710)
Daubney, Mark 5:31:12 (28,674)
Daugherty, Brian 3:40:47 (6,439)
Daugherty, Duane W 3:22:26 (3,365)
Dauncey, Chris 3:25:03 (3,699)
Davanzo, Luca 5:36:17 (29,046)
Davase, Thierry 3:34:23 (5,323)
Dave, Bhavesh 4:45:09 (22,070)
Davenhill, Jason C 2:58:34 (1,023)
Davenport, George H 5:04:01 (25,582)
Davenport, Michael S 4:43:14 (21,617)
Davenpotr, Roy 4:41:45 (21,296)
Davey, Alan K 3:56:00 (10,084)
Davey, Brian J 5:06:09 (25,866)
Davey, Edward 6:04:43 (30,587)
Davey, James 4:50:01 (23,077)
Davey, Kevin G 4:50:01 (23,077)
Davey, Lee 3:54:40 (9,686)
Davey, Mark R 4:02:19 (11,814)
Davey, Patrick W 4:27:00 (17,840)
Davey, Robert S 4:14:22 (14,641)
Davey, Trevor M 5:08:04 (26,124)
David, Carr 4:17:38 (15,461)
David, Gareth 3:57:26 (10,522)
David, Olivier 3:27:29 (4,124)
Davids, Anthony M 3:23:16 (3,474)
Davidson, Gary M 4:07:43 (13,059)
Davidson, Githui M 5:16:56 (27,249)
Davidson, Gordon I 4:49:03 (22,888)
Davidson, Graham E 3:57:56 (10,658)
Davidson, Iain 4:01:29 (11,592)
Davidson, James 4:14:31 (14,682)
Davidson, Ken 3:54:45 (9,711)
Davidson, Kenneth G 3:17:01 (2,749)
Davidson, Michael D 5:00:46 (25,108)
Davidson, Miles R 3:15:23 (2,587)
Davidson, Quintin 5:01:44 (25,265)
Davidson, Roy 3:30:53 (4,759)
Davidson, Thomas P 4:17:34 (15,448)
Davie, Barry 3:17:18 (2,784)
Davies, Adrian H 3:59:09 (11,047)
Davies, Adrian J 5:16:04 (27,136)
Davies, Andrew 4:48:22 (22,752)
Davies, Andrew C 4:32:07 (19,139)
Davies, Andrew J 3:38:43 (6,087)
Davies, Andrew K 2:52:11 (600)
Davies, Andrew L 3:43:20 (6,927)
Davies, Barry J 4:47:38 (22,603)
Davies, Benedikt C 3:07:28 (1,749)
Davies, Brian C 3:49:16 (8,323)
Davies, Bryn 5:24:12 (27,991)
Davies, Charles A 3:55:46 (10,010)
Davies, Christopher 4:58:51 (24,771)
Davies, Christopher J 5:08:33 (26,188)
Davies, Colin A 3:24:49 (3,665)
Davies, Colin H 3:04:43 (1,505)
Davies, Darhyl N 4:00:11 (11,337)
Davies, David 4:54:22 (23,872)
Davies, David A 4:06:01 (12,663)
Davies, David G 4:13:27 (14,440)
Davies, Dilwyn E 5:22:30 (27,831)
Davies, Gareth E 3:53:49 (9,448)
Davies, Gareth H 4:16:38 (15,217)
Davies, Gareth M 3:59:15 (11,070)
Davies, Gareth M 4:40:46 (21,076)
Davies, Gareth R 3:42:01 (6,654)
Davies, Gareth S 3:16:35 (2,707)
Davies, Gawain P 3:26:26 (3,909)
Davies, Geoff 3:40:27 (6,388)
Davies, Glyn E 5:14:47 (27,002)
Davies, Graham D 6:38:17 (31,343)
Davies, Graham M 3:59:35 (11,183)
Davies, Haydn 4:47:32 (22,574)
Davies, Haydn 5:36:38 (29,074)

Davies, Howard J	4:12:06 (14,115)	
Davies, Huw M	3:58:51 (10,960)	
Davies, Ivor J	4:38:00 (20,466)	
Davies, John M	5:08:07 (26,130)	
Davies, John R	4:18:40 (15,702)	
Davies, Jon	6:22:29 (31,073)	
Davies, Jonathan	3:17:06 (2,759)	
Davies, Keith J	2:53:14 (657)	
Davies, Kenneth A	4:44:24 (21,889)	
Davies, Kevin M	4:59:01 (24,798)	
Davies, Laurie D	3:53:16 (9,329)	
Davies, Lee	4:31:43 (19,033)	
Davies, Len C	3:56:37 (10,285)	
Davies, Mark R	3:53:19 (9,342)	
Davies, Mark R	4:59:20 (24,858)	
Davies, Martin W	3:58:24 (10,819)	
Davies, Matthew	4:06:31 (12,781)	
Davies, Michael	3:13:21 (2,350)	
Davies, Michael J	3:36:24 (5,682)	
Davies, Michael J	4:14:26 (14,659)	
Davies, Mikey J	4:46:22 (22,333)	
Davies, Neil	4:15:15 (14,870)	
Davies, Neil A	3:30:54 (4,761)	
Davies, Nicholas	3:33:00 (5,099)	
Davies, Nicholas F	2:58:36 (1,026)	
Davies, Owain H	3:56:32 (10,260)	
Davies, Paul A	3:06:34 (1,662)	
Davies, Paul D	3:29:08 (4,438)	
Davies, Peter A	4:21:16 (16,325)	
Davies, Phil G	4:39:04 (20,743)	
Davies, Philip B	4:56:52 (24,377)	
Davies, Rhys	4:39:45 (20,868)	
Davies, Richard D	3:23:05 (3,449)	
Davies, Richard L	3:02:37 (1,346)	
Davies, Richard W	4:32:11 (19,162)	
Davies, Robert T	3:55:05 (9,814)	
Davies, Roger L	3:48:47 (8,208)	
Davies, Rupert A	4:08:46 (13,311)	
Davies, Samuel J	3:48:14 (8,061)	
Davies, Scott	5:51:59 (30,035)	
Davies, Sean	5:13:29 (26,822)	
Davies, Stephen C	2:44:16 (295)	
Davies, Stephen J	3:16:52 (2,735)	
Davies, Steve I	4:38:04 (20,488)	
Davies, Steven	3:16:29 (2,698)	
Davies, Stuart M	4:16:24 (15,148)	
Davies, Terry	4:03:48 (12,150)	
Davies, Thomas G	3:23:07 (3,453)	
Davies, Timothy J	3:42:27 (6,730)	
Davies, Timothy J	4:33:25 (19,452)	
Davies, Trevor J	3:09:52 (1,989)	
Davies, Vernon J	4:15:40 (14,968)	
Davies, William G	4:20:38 (16,195)	
Davies MBE, Christopher	4:24:31 (17,188)	
Davies-Holmes, Robin	3:45:59 (7,523)	
Davis, Alan	4:48:09 (22,707)	
Davis, Andrew M	3:51:49 (8,972)	
Davis, Andy	3:12:03 (2,199)	
Davis, Anthony D	3:12:50 (2,291)	
Davis, Anthony P	3:20:00 (3,066)	
Davis, Brian	3:30:59 (4,775)	
Davis, Chris	3:46:08 (7,552)	
Davis, Danny	3:55:01 (9,794)	
Davis, Frank L	4:01:16 (11,554)	
Davis, George	5:23:46 (27,950)	
Davis, Glen	3:39:23 (6,197)	
Davis, James B	3:59:07 (11,035)	
Davis, John E	4:42:13 (21,388)	
Davis, John R	4:58:03 (24,609)	
Davis, Jonathan M	4:33:12 (19,405)	
Davis, Jonathan P	3:58:06 (10,710)	
Davis, Kevin	3:41:54 (6,618)	
Davis, Lee	3:53:44 (9,420)	
Davis, Marcus C	6:58:32 (31,603)	
Davis, Mark R	3:04:14 (1,467)	
Davis, Martin	3:56:01 (10,090)	
Davis, Martin B	3:00:31 (1,193)	
Davis, Martin J	2:53:13 (656)	
Davis, Matthew P	6:00:54 (30,443)	
Davis, Michael E	4:23:07 (16,847)	
Davis, Michael J	4:10:56 (13,856)	
Davis, Nicholas G	2:58:41 (1,039)	
Davis, Pascal	4:19:46 (15,969)	

Davis, Paul M	4:44:54 (22,002)	
Davis, Peter A	4:43:16 (21,627)	
Davis, Peter J	4:46:06 (22,270)	
Davis, Philip M	3:19:25 (3,008)	
Davis, Philip M	5:10:38 (26,456)	
Davis, Richard J	3:43:16 (6,911)	
Davis, Richard M	3:46:12 (7,578)	
Davis, Robert A	3:57:00 (10,390)	
Davis, Roger C	3:59:55 (11,273)	
Davis, Simon G	4:30:25 (18,736)	
Davis, Simon J	3:19:34 (3,025)	
Davis, Simon J	4:29:52 (18,599)	
Davis, Tim	3:53:54 (9,476)	
Davis, Timothy	4:27:23 (17,934)	
Davis, Timothy G	3:22:45 (3,410)	
Davis, Todd	3:55:33 (9,947)	
Davis, Wayne A	4:09:35 (13,520)	
Davison, Alan	3:38:20 (6,020)	
Davison, Guy D	4:57:25 (24,482)	
Davison, Paul	3:22:55 (3,432)	
Davison, Peter	4:30:57 (18,846)	
Davison, Robin A	5:24:54 (28,069)	
Davison, Scott H	3:47:36 (7,906)	
Davison, Stuart	5:10:50 (26,487)	
Davison, Trevor J	5:00:00 (24,991)	
Davy, James H	4:25:52 (17,529)	
Dawber, Andrew J	4:51:44 (23,387)	
Dawber, Nigel	3:32:05 (4,937)	
Dawe, Steve T	4:21:22 (16,352)	
Dawes, Duncan I	3:22:11 (3,325)	
Dawes, Matthew G	4:42:16 (21,402)	
Dawes, Steve P	4:20:07 (16,049)	
Dawkins, Jonathan P	4:58:36 (24,736)	
Dawkins, Steve J	3:59:09 (11,047)	
Dawn, Jason	4:05:55 (12,643)	
Dawney, Kevin R	5:08:16 (26,152)	
Daws, Neil R	5:55:49 (30,235)	
Daws, Peter M	3:13:36 (2,385)	
Dawson, Adam	3:53:36 (9,401)	
Dawson, Andrew P	3:37:48 (5,922)	
Dawson, Angus E	3:52:49 (9,204)	
Dawson, Carl	4:26:04 (17,593)	
Dawson, Gordon	4:44:23 (21,885)	
Dawson, Graham Neal	3:57:30 (10,538)	
Dawson, Grant	6:31:26 (31,235)	
Dawson, James A	4:26:52 (17,798)	
Dawson, Jamie C	4:21:55 (16,505)	
Dawson, John	4:57:23 (24,471)	
Dawson, Lee A	4:38:09 (20,508)	
Dawson, Lee A	4:50:45 (23,225)	
Dawson, Neil	5:43:47 (29,614)	
Dawson, Nigel J	3:34:18 (5,311)	
Dawson, Philip R	4:25:15 (17,370)	
Dawson, Roland J	5:07:17 (26,006)	
Dawson, Ryan	3:59:41 (11,218)	
Dawson, Tony	4:01:02 (11,510)	
Dawson, Vincent M	4:40:00 (20,919)	
Day, David A	3:26:45 (3,973)	
Day, David C	3:28:51 (4,387)	
Day, Garry M	4:28:33 (18,246)	
Day, Gavin P	4:29:00 (18,349)	
Day, Graham	4:04:51 (12,392)	
Day, Grant J	3:32:33 (5,013)	
Day, Ian N	3:55:29 (9,926)	
Day, Michael P	3:54:06 (9,530)	
Day, Patrick	4:27:22 (17,932)	
Day, Patrick I	3:23:49 (3,547)	
Day, Peter H	6:23:52 (31,103)	
Day, Richard	4:17:29 (15,419)	
Day, Rod	3:47:30 (7,879)	
Day, Thomas F	5:51:57 (30,059)	
Day, Tim M	3:55:55 (10,057)	
Day, Tom	4:59:39 (24,930)	
Daykin, Eric K	5:41:28 (29,443)	
D'Costa, David S	5:08:22 (26,170)	
De Belder, Daniel L	3:39:16 (6,172)	
De Billot, Philippe R	4:28:25 (18,198)	
De Clerk, Jason	4:45:40 (22,182)	
De Giorgi, Rodolfo	3:45:35 (7,435)	
De Grauwe, Peter	3:49:51 (8,461)	
De Groot, Ben A	4:04:33 (12,327)	
De Haan, Piet W	4:53:37 (23,730)	
De Jonge, Martin	3:37:46 (5,911)	

De Kegel, Dimitri Y	3:50:59 (8,746)	
De Ketelaere, Christophe	2:46:25 (368)	
De Ketelaere, Peter	2:47:03 (389)	
De La Bedoyere, Nick M	4:03:38 (12,110)	
De La Fage, Philippe	4:19:16 (15,851)	
De La Torre-Garcia, José A	3:24:11 (3,585)	
De Laszlo, Robert D	3:31:38 (4,865)	
De Luca, Paolo A	3:14:33 (2,509)	
De Luz-De La Fuente, Fidel A	4:50:04 (23,085)	
De Massey, David	4:39:46 (20,870)	
De Mello, Ambrose A	6:31:24 (31,233)	
De Melo, Luis Nuno	2:48:05 (425)	
De Mendoza, Consalvo	6:31:10 (31,226)	
De Paepe, Philippe	4:21:38 (16,430)	
De Plaen, Alain G	3:49:43 (8,428)	
De Renzy-Martin, Edward J	3:43:09 (6,878)	
De Silva, Ranith J	4:02:38 (11,881)	
De Sousa, Armenio	3:48:33 (8,135)	
De Souza, Mark V	4:34:22 (19,390)	
De Staelen, Serge	3:07:27 (1,748)	
De Swardt, Frans	3:56:06 (10,111)	
De Tommasi, Alessandro J	5:23:27 (27,912)	
De Toney, Etienne J	3:49:38 (8,410)	
De Turckheim, Eric C	4:15:21 (14,889)	
De Villiers, Michael	3:47:20 (7,837)	
De Weert, John D	4:22:44 (16,755)	
Deacon, Bruce	2:18:30 (25)	
Deacon, Guy H	4:38:55 (20,699)	
Deadman, Sean	4:02:08 (11,757)	
Deal, Martin R	4:13:35 (14,476)	
Deamer, Stuart D	4:41:52 (21,321)	
Dean, Alan J	3:16:24 (2,687)	
Dean, Fraser D	2:48:39 (442)	
Dean, Gary J	2:47:27 (399)	
Dean, Gavin	5:50:15 (29,977)	
Dean, Jason D	4:02:26 (11,845)	
Dean, Ken	4:04:06 (12,211)	
Dean, Mark R	5:13:32 (26,831)	
Dean, Matthew	5:10:09 (26,394)	
Dean, Matthew C	4:04:18 (12,263)	
Dean, Michael	3:24:44 (3,654)	
Dean, Philip A	4:14:00 (14,561)	
Dean, Robert J	4:41:25 (21,222)	
Dean, Simon J	4:40:16 (20,976)	
Dean, Simon M	4:55:30 (24,099)	
Dean, Toby	4:11:46 (14,036)	
Deane, Andrew J	3:29:30 (4,504)	
Deane, Finbarr J	5:09:26 (26,295)	
Deane, Kevin D	3:49:46 (8,444)	
Deane, Marcus J	7:17:13 (31,764)	
Dear, Richard A	3:42:01 (6,654)	
Dear, Will J	4:04:16 (12,257)	
Dearden, Alan R	3:47:14 (7,808)	
Deardon, Raymond R	7:08:39 (31,699)	
Dearing, Jonathan	4:11:37 (14,005)	
Dearlove, Melvyn W	4:33:08 (19,388)	
Dearsley, James A	5:01:41 (25,254)	
Dearsley, Mark	3:20:45 (3,168)	
Dearsley, Steven J	4:44:54 (22,002)	
Dearsley-Hitchcock, Giles L	4:33:38 (6,985)	
Deasy, John F	3:05:42 (1,583)	
De-Ath, Peter	3:52:46 (9,185)	
Debaghi, Hassan	3:23:08 (3,458)	
Debeurme, Leven	3:13:50 (2,412)	
Debortoli, Jean	2:48:51 (451)	
Decker, Jonathan D	4:25:30 (17,429)	
Decoffre, Bernard	3:44:49 (7,266)	
Decourcy, Graham	3:14:07 (2,452)	
Dector-Vega, German	4:36:16 (20,084)	
Deegan, Kevin A	3:58:29 (10,845)	
Deehan, John P	4:57:24 (24,473)	
Deeley, Michael J	4:59:51 (24,965)	
Deeley, Roger A	5:09:29 (26,303)	
Deely, Owen J	5:12:05 (26,643)	
Deen, Alvin	4:38:47 (20,664)	
Deeny, Simon	3:53:06 (9,282)	
Deering, Ross H	4:32:07 (19,139)	
Deery, Mark D	3:17:13 (2,775)	
Deftereos, Phillip	5:44:31 (29,657)	
Dehavilland, Andrew P	5:55:11 (30,211)	
Deht, Alan	2:49:19 (471)	
Deith, Matthew	4:38:36 (20,617)	
Dejoie, Regis	3:21:59 (3,305)	

Dejong, Albert	4:29:17 (18,422)
Del La Simone, François J	4:27:00 (17,840)
Delaire, Philippe	3:32:38 (5,037)
Delamain, Paul	3:55:41 (9,982)
Delaney, Anthony	4:02:18 (11,805)
Delaney, George R	4:15:29 (14,922)
Delaney, James	3:21:57 (3,302)
Delaney, John	4:55:29 (24,097)
Delaney, Mark P	3:53:59 (9,499)
Delany, John F	3:20:52 (3,186)
Delany, Michael	3:19:01 (2,954)
Delap, Martin R	3:37:46 (5,911)
Delatouche, David P	4:55:38 (24,125)
Delderfield, Kevin	3:30:49 (4,746)
Delea, Marc S	3:04:20 (1,479)
Delesclefs, James T	3:44:41 (7,236)
Delgrange, Jerome F	3:46:14 (7,589)
Delgrange, Roland	3:41:35 (6,561)
Deliquet, Stephane	4:40:13 (20,965)
Dell, Graeme J	4:30:11 (18,676)
Dell, Gregory J	2:42:28 (251)
Del-La Osa-Martinez, Juan S	3:25:00 (3,693)
Della-Porta, Louis A	4:23:43 (16,993)
Deller, Stephen A	6:06:06 (30,627)
Dell'Oro, Dean	2:52:15 (602)
Delpierre, Jean P	4:05:13 (12,466)
Deluca, Peter	4:35:51 (19,990)
Demain-Griffiths, Richard J	3:36:23 (5,678)
Demarco, Edward V	3:21:29 (3,254)
Demaret, Jean M	3:54:07 (9,532)
Demetz, Bertrand	4:42:00 (21,344)
Demilew, Daniel Y	5:14:47 (27,002)
Demmery, Christopher J	4:43:14 (21,617)
Dempsey, Robert L	5:35:49 (29,018)
Demuth, Matthias	3:33:51 (5,244)
Denley, Mark E	4:13:59 (14,559)
Denman, Stephen	6:27:35 (31,167)
Denmead, Matthew J	3:28:34 (4,331)
Dennett, Paul J	5:47:40 (29,852)
Dennett, Peter A	3:24:00 (3,564)
Denning, Gary	3:51:36 (8,916)
Denning, James	5:32:36 (28,783)
Denning, Paul R	4:29:21 (18,451)
Dennis, Allan J	4:01:19 (11,565)
Dennis, Geoff A	4:53:35 (23,718)
Dennis, Paul J	3:38:19 (6,015)
Dennis, Paul M	6:02:35 (30,513)
Dennis-Jones, Richard	3:27:51 (4,197)
Dennison, Paul	5:26:16 (28,220)
Denny, Colin A	4:48:47 (22,832)
Denny, William	4:28:00 (18,098)
Denoma, Michael B	4:27:15 (17,908)
Dent, Adrian	5:45:42 (29,735)
Dent, Garreth J	5:02:28 (25,367)
Dent, Nicholas J	6:06:54 (30,642)
Denton, Alistair J	4:44:32 (21,917)
Denton, Andrew W	3:44:03 (7,082)
Denton, David B	4:14:26 (14,659)
Denton, Gary	3:44:26 (7,168)
Denyer, Billy	3:08:22 (1,838)
Denyer, James E	3:49:23 (8,352)
Depala, Chetan	5:15:26 (27,070)
Depala, Ritesh	5:15:28 (27,074)
Depluverez, Paul	4:21:55 (16,505)
Depper, Geoff A	3:22:11 (3,325)
Depre, Luc	4:05:20 (12,494)
Derbyshire, Justin J	3:52:53 (9,218)
Derbyshire, Mark K	4:38:31 (20,598)
Derenoncourt, Pierre	4:28:56 (18,334)
Derks, Jan Win	3:30:12 (4,634)
Derrett, Joseph E	4:37:12 (20,298)
Derrick, Ian M	3:37:55 (5,940)
Derrick, Tony	4:17:30 (15,423)
Derrington, Richard	3:45:46 (7,477)
Derry, Ian S	4:59:14 (24,834)
Dervish, Haldun E	5:37:56 (29,175)
Desai, Coolin B	4:54:09 (23,830)
Desaleux, Barry R	5:18:47 (27,447)
Deschamps, Jean C	3:54:26 (9,622)
D'Escrivan, Julio C	3:42:23 (6,717)
Deslage, Mathieu M	3:58:50 (10,954)
Desmond, James	2:51:49 (583)
Desroches, Remy	3:33:29 (5,187)

De-Stael, Arnaud	3:11:48 (2,169)
Devall, John	3:21:55 (3,300)
Devaux, Jonathan J	3:28:41 (4,349)
Deveney, John M	4:56:30 (24,310)
Deveney, Liam M	3:59:13 (11,064)
Devenish, James	5:06:29 (25,908)
Devenish, Malcolm P	4:23:23 (16,914)
Devenney, Will	5:25:27 (28,132)
Devereux, James W	4:21:22 (16,352)
Devereux, Karl A	3:54:20 (9,596)
Devey, Dennis	4:34:27 (19,699)
Devico, Joseph G	3:12:27 (2,246)
Devine, Anthony F	6:10:18 (30,735)
Devine, Michael F	4:39:14 (20,781)
Devine, William	4:50:22 (23,142)
Devitt, Martin R	3:28:14 (4,273)
Devitt, Russell E	3:43:03 (6,859)
Devlin, Brian J	3:39:44 (6,262)
Devlin, Paul D	4:47:47 (22,630)
Devlin, Robert	4:18:31 (15,665)
Devoldere, Andrés A	4:31:14 (18,903)
Devonport, Karl J	4:04:07 (12,214)
Dew, John J	5:34:03 (28,892)
Dewaele, Steven A	2:41:11 (227)
Dewar, Alasdair C	4:07:43 (13,059)
Dewar, David H	3:32:06 (4,938)
Dewart, David R	3:36:44 (5,730)
Dewhurst, Brian	2:35:56 (134)
Dewhurst, Nigel C	3:33:52 (5,251)
Dewhurst, Phillip M	3:44:54 (7,286)
Dewings, Philip M	4:09:39 (13,542)
Dewsbery, Simon D	4:20:45 (16,223)
Dewsbury, Glyn R	4:20:21 (16,117)
Dewson, Gary N	4:48:35 (22,790)
Dexter, Adam P	4:32:25 (19,217)
Dexter, Colin G	5:18:44 (27,439)
D'Hulst, Jereon	3:37:02 (5,776)
Di Caro, Carlo	4:02:12 (11,780)
Di Fabio, Sergio	4:02:35 (11,872)
Di Fabrizio, Paolo G	3:58:01 (10,681)
Di Felice, Franco	4:58:37 (24,741)
Di Graci, Silvio	4:45:46 (22,204)
Di Gregorio, Pierangelo	4:09:12 (13,422)
Di Marco, Domenico	4:19:41 (15,947)
Di Mario, Carlo	4:51:34 (23,356)
Di Molfetta, Pasquale	3:56:23 (10,204)
Di Stasi, Salvatore	5:20:00 (27,563)
Diaglio, Paulo	2:53:10 (653)
Diamond, Gavin R	3:19:19 (2,997)
Diamond, Russell M	3:39:30 (6,216)
Diamond, Samuel P	3:32:09 (4,943)
Diana, Ernesto	3:36:36 (5,709)
Dias, Luis M	3:42:44 (6,797)
Diaz, Alvaro	4:19:24 (15,883)
Dibben, Martin	4:21:59 (16,530)
Dibble, Harley	3:52:18 (9,085)
Dick, Alistair	3:16:57 (2,742)
Dick, Andrew J	3:49:36 (8,403)
Dick, Michael	4:06:20 (12,742)
Dick, Michael J	3:15:16 (2,582)
Dickens, Paul A	3:40:03 (6,317)
Dickens, Robin C	4:16:50 (15,263)
Dickenson, Robert	3:03:25 (1,399)
Dickinson, David J	4:37:14 (20,304)
Dickinson, Ian W	4:24:58 (17,300)
Dickinson, John	3:54:20 (9,596)
Dickinson, Martin P	3:54:20 (9,596)
Dickinson, Norman	5:06:52 (25,955)
Dickinson, Philip H	3:40:43 (6,433)
Dickinson, Ralph	3:49:08 (8,291)
Dickinson, Simon M	4:08:37 (13,261)
Dickman, Andrew	4:12:35 (14,228)
Dickson, Alan R	3:29:55 (4,574)
Dickson, Charles J	4:06:32 (12,784)
Dickson, Colin L	3:22:22 (3,354)
Dickson, Darren	4:15:50 (15,010)
Dickson, David	3:20:02 (3,071)
Dickson, David R	3:56:47 (10,323)
Dickson, Neil S	4:49:16 (22,932)
Dickson, Nicholas	3:25:14 (3,725)
Dickson, Robert	3:13:35 (2,382)
Dickson, Stuart W	5:14:34 (26,971)
Dickson, William N	4:43:32 (21,692)

Diclemente, Alan	3:47:40 (7,920)
Didier, Gaetan	4:09:27 (13,488)
Didwell, Greg	5:28:46 (28,465)
Dieltiens, Nick	3:36:36 (5,709)
Dietch, Daniel	4:08:16 (13,165)
Digby, Adrian J	4:49:20 (22,947)
Digby, Karl J	4:32:17 (19,184)
Digby, Mark R	4:05:12 (12,462)
Digby-Baker, Hugh J	4:14:28 (14,674)
Diggines, Jonathan M	4:32:26 (19,220)
Dikken, Herbert	4:39:10 (20,764)
Dillane, Stephen M	3:40:07 (6,326)
Dillard, Dean A	3:54:44 (9,704)
Dilley, Stephen J	3:36:56 (5,756)
Dillin, Jason P	3:43:25 (6,940)
Dillon, James A	4:26:22 (17,669)
Dillon, Max D	3:05:11 (1,543)
Dillon, Oliver W	4:36:11 (20,068)
Dillon, Stewart I	4:46:30 (22,360)
Dillon, Thomas H	4:49:15 (22,927)
Dilworth, Joseph R	5:07:15 (26,004)
Dimarco, Kevin M	3:40:51 (6,445)
Dimbleby, Andy T	3:27:59 (4,225)
Dimech, John A	4:08:26 (13,211)
Dimelow, Geoffrey	3:54:23 (9,604)
Dimitriadis, Klistenis	5:00:59 (25,142)
Dimmer, Matthew R	4:59:10 (24,825)
Dimond, Steven A	3:39:39 (6,244)
Din, Abid Y	4:23:07 (16,847)
Din, Mudasar Y	3:51:44 (8,951)
Dineley, Mark	3:49:06 (8,281)
Dines, Ross P	4:17:36 (15,452)
Dingley, Graham J	3:07:05 (1,711)
Dinning, Robert P	4:33:32 (19,475)
Dinsdale, Jason C	3:40:30 (6,403)
Dinsmore, David	3:44:08 (7,102)
Dinsmore, Edward A	4:31:56 (19,093)
Dinwiddy, Mark P	3:30:03 (4,601)
Dipple, Stephen R	4:16:00 (15,050)
Dirks, Lee	5:40:22 (29,364)
Disney, Daniel J	5:13:09 (26,786)
Disney, Gary A	5:25:04 (28,095)
Diston, David	8:23:15 (31,961)
Ditri, Tony D	3:54:11 (9,555)
Diwell, Glyn	4:18:46 (15,728)
Dixon, Alistair R	3:57:55 (10,651)
Dixon, Clem	2:52:53 (636)
Dixon, Edward A	4:06:55 (12,867)
Dixon, Edward J	4:10:42 (13,800)
Dixon, Gary	4:29:07 (18,381)
Dixon, Gordon M	2:37:11 (158)
Dixon, Graeme M	3:21:43 (3,280)
Dixon, Ian H	4:24:12 (17,122)
Dixon, John	4:50:28 (23,178)
Dixon, Joseph G	4:10:59 (13,866)
Dixon, Mike	3:02:35 (1,343)
Dixon, Paul A	4:07:40 (13,048)
Dixon, Robert R	4:36:46 (20,194)
Dixon, Thomas P	4:02:21 (11,829)
Dixon-Savage, Paul	5:25:04 (28,095)
Dixson, Mark S	3:52:48 (9,195)
Dlhopolcek, Frantisek	4:05:41 (12,591)
Dobberstein, Ulf	4:57:51 (24,557)
Dobbs, Andrew R	3:57:22 (10,505)
Dobbs, Patrick A	3:11:06 (2,104)
Dobbs, Paul M	4:00:42 (11,429)
Dobby, Brett N	3:58:03 (10,689)
Dobedoe, Richard S	2:51:13 (551)
Dobie, Ronald	4:14:40 (14,721)
Doble, Robin T	3:12:06 (2,202)
Dobson, Alastair S	4:18:25 (15,642)
Dobson, Andrew J	4:08:41 (13,283)
Dobson, Brian	3:49:07 (8,286)
Dobson, David	3:16:38 (2,714)
Dobson, Dean C	3:44:39 (7,224)
Dobson, John A	5:17:46 (27,336)
Dobson, John W	4:34:34 (19,726)
Dobson, Michael	2:57:58 (963)
Dobson, Paul M	4:22:21 (16,654)
Dobson, Robin	3:27:41 (4,164)
Docekal, Alexander	3:06:47 (1,684)
Docherty, John H	5:48:11 (29,872)
Docherty, Paul	4:12:42 (14,263)

Docherty, William....4:12:30 (14,200)
Dockney, Ian A....3:45:50 (7,488)
Dodanis, Christos....2:59:56 (1,151)
Dodd, Alan N....4:14:47 (14,752)
Dodd, Clive C....4:19:25 (15,887)
Dodd, Jason....4:36:50 (20,214)
Dodd, Paul L....4:21:35 (16,409)
Dodd, Ray C....6:18:32 (30,972)
Dodd, Stephen J....4:54:33 (23,911)
Dodds, Andrew J....6:18:33 (30,973)
Dodds, Malcolm P....4:01:50 (11,675)
Dodds, Richard M....3:59:10 (11,049)
Dodds, Rupert....3:20:43 (3,161)
Dodge, Alan J....4:30:03 (18,646)
Dodge, Christopher G....4:12:06 (14,115)
Dodge, Richard M....4:25:39 (17,465)
Dodgson, Scott A....5:26:47 (28,277)
Dodridge, Nicholas J....4:11:53 (14,057)
Dodridge, Richard G....3:49:26 (8,363)
Dodson, Martin D....5:14:16 (26,930)
Dodwell, James S....3:34:14 (5,302)
Dodwell, Mark D....4:44:50 (21,983)
Doe, James....3:48:57 (8,241)
Doegl, Josef....4:22:43 (16,753)
Doerner, Wolfram....4:36:29 (20,131)
Doggett, Andrew M....3:39:35 (6,231)
Doherty, Alan....4:01:14 (11,550)
Doherty, Christopher....4:05:54 (12,640)
Doherty, Christopher J....3:55:00 (9,782)
Doherty, Damian P....4:38:44 (20,649)
Doherty, David....4:30:08 (18,664)
Doherty, Hugh M....4:45:29 (22,136)
Doherty, Ian R....2:59:28 (1,118)
Doherty, Jackie....3:13:28 (2,365)
Doherty, Jason P....4:22:21 (16,654)
Doherty, Kieran....4:38:44 (20,649)
Doherty, Paul J....3:55:20 (9,890)
Doig, Gavin A....4:26:31 (17,706)
Doktor, Bernd....4:22:46 (16,764)
Dolan, Aidan....4:29:22 (18,457)
Dolan, Robert....3:12:06 (2,202)
Dolan, Tim....4:54:27 (23,885)
Dolbel, Aaron P....3:52:44 (9,180)
Dolby, Stuart....5:02:16 (25,331)
Dolding, Philip J....5:13:11 (26,793)
Dolman, Antony R....4:33:46 (19,527)
Dolphin, Christopher C....3:57:11 (10,440)
Dolphin, James H....3:18:42 (2,922)
Dolton, Peter J....4:20:52 (16,250)
Domenicali, Nello....2:31:34 (92)
Domine, Marco....3:26:58 (4,013)
Dominelli, Damiano....3:05:36 (1,576)
Dommett, Mark....3:55:31 (9,935)
Dommett, Robert A....6:20:31 (31,025)
Domoney, Christopher J....4:05:48 (12,616)
Don, Russell....4:35:52 (19,997)
Donabie, Jeremy J....3:53:34 (9,395)
Donagh, Jason G....4:11:33 (13,985)
Donagh, Jerome G....4:06:30 (12,778)
Donaghue, Richard B....4:50:33 (23,191)
Donald, Andrew J....3:34:58 (5,419)
Donald, Christopher....4:39:08 (20,756)
Donald, Ed R....5:16:28 (27,185)
Donald, John T....4:15:01 (14,808)
Donaldson, Alex B....5:06:53 (25,959)
Donaldson, Andrew....3:59:29 (11,151)
Donaldson, Eric....3:03:27 (1,405)
Donaldson, Grant W....3:02:58 (1,365)
Donaldson, Patrick....3:32:59 (5,095)
Donaldson, Tom....4:32:49 (19,314)
Donaldson, William M....4:04:04 (12,200)
Donegan, Paul....3:44:40 (7,230)
Donn, Robert A....3:43:26 (6,946)
Donnan, Graeme E....3:24:23 (3,613)
Donnelly, Colm....3:45:04 (7,314)
Donnelly, John....3:13:52 (2,420)
Donnelly, John....3:40:57 (6,466)
Donnelly, Patrick....3:31:17 (4,818)
Donnelly, Robert J....5:00:59 (25,142)
Donoghue, Aidan E....4:26:44 (17,755)
Donoghue, Anthony O....7:13:17 (31,735)
Donoghue, Chris....2:47:59 (423)
Donoghue, Stephen....3:24:32 (3,627)
Donoghue, Stephen F....3:26:36 (3,932)
Donohoe, Bernard....4:54:14 (23,842)
Donohoe, Francis B....5:17:59 (27,364)
Donohue, Kevin....4:13:57 (14,553)
Donovan, Daniel J....5:48:36 (29,886)
Donovan, John....4:29:01 (18,356)
Donovan, Peter J....4:43:39 (21,711)
Donovan, Roy J....4:16:48 (15,251)
Dooley, John P....3:58:04 (10,696)
Dooley, Joseph....4:30:31 (18,764)
Dooley, Sean F....4:21:30 (16,389)
Dooling, Colin M....4:04:26 (12,294)
Doran, Patrick....6:38:06 (31,341)
Doran, Stuart....5:33:04 (28,813)
Dormenval, Remy....5:07:39 (26,068)
Dornan, Mark A....3:21:04 (3,208)
Dorr, Glenn B....4:21:56 (16,512)
Dossett, Andrew....4:19:27 (15,903)
Doswell, Stephen....4:26:55 (17,816)
Double, Matthew M....5:23:26 (27,909)
Douch, Julian....4:20:15 (16,077)
Douch, Leon....4:20:15 (16,077)
Douch, Martin....5:50:10 (29,974)
Dougall, Anthony L....4:20:52 (16,250)
Dougan, Michael J....3:40:52 (6,448)
Dougherty, Andrew....4:34:56 (19,807)
Dougherty, Hugh....3:49:06 (8,281)
Dougherty, John P....5:11:06 (26,517)
Doughty, Martin D....3:26:35 (3,930)
Douglas, Andrew G....7:45:53 (31,907)
Douglas, Martin R....3:36:13 (5,646)
Douglas, Neil....2:42:25 (250)
Douglas, Paul....2:55:39 (794)
Douglas, Peter J....4:58:14 (24,646)
Douglas, Stuart J....4:16:09 (15,093)
Doukhan, Assaf A....3:29:14 (4,461)
Douse, Richard M....4:25:28 (17,418)
Dousset, Nicolas P....3:46:46 (7,697)
Doust, Peter R....4:38:42 (20,643)
Dovaston, Ian T....3:21:23 (3,242)
Dove, Christopher W....4:34:51 (19,791)
Dover, Gary W....3:08:45 (1,870)
Dover, Ian....5:15:35 (27,088)
Dover, Terry....4:25:27 (17,413)
Dovey, James R....4:36:24 (20,104)
Dovey, Sam C....3:15:35 (2,608)
Doward, Neil L....3:25:55 (3,832)
Dowbiggin, Kevin J....4:51:44 (23,387)
Dowd, Charlie....4:20:07 (16,049)
Dowd, Christopher P....5:11:57 (26,624)
Dowd, David P....2:54:46 (731)
Dowdall, Kevin R....4:13:03 (14,343)
Dowdall, William J....7:02:44 (31,646)
Dowdeswell, Andrew N....3:42:23 (6,717)
Dowdy, Michael T....3:54:11 (9,555)
Dowdy, Richard L....6:57:26 (31,589)
Dowell, Paul....4:07:30 (13,010)
Dowers, Alan L....4:04:57 (12,422)
Dowler, Nicolas R....5:10:17 (26,412)
Dowling, Michael G....3:28:23 (4,300)
Dowling, Pete....3:58:02 (10,684)
Dowling, Sean P....3:54:09 (9,542)
Down, Malcolm....3:36:00 (5,612)
Downer, Conrad....4:26:33 (17,714)
Downes, Henry J....3:33:50 (5,240)
Downes, Paul J....3:42:25 (6,723)
Downes, Richard G....4:52:57 (23,606)
Downes, Steven L....5:42:57 (29,552)
Downes, Thomas....4:06:39 (12,815)
Downey, Gary A....4:20:23 (16,126)
Downey, Kevin....5:42:03 (29,486)
Downham, John J....3:27:50 (4,193)
Downham, Michael J....5:05:24 (25,739)
Downing, Mark D....4:32:15 (19,177)
Downing, Oliver J....3:26:37 (3,936)
Downing, Terry R....4:11:58 (14,083)
Downton, Brian T....3:27:44 (4,174)
Dowse, Robert....6:00:39 (30,432)
Dowse, Stephen....4:06:21 (12,748)
Dowsett, Frederick J....3:29:52 (4,565)
Dowsett, Kevin R....4:07:57 (13,104)
Dowsett, Mark....4:50:41 (23,215)
Dowsett, Peter C....3:15:43 (2,626)
Dowson, Andrew M....3:35:27 (5,511)
Dowson, Jason L....2:47:27 (399)
Dowthwaite, Neil J....3:43:47 (7,009)
Doxaran, David P....3:58:26 (10,832)
Doyle, Alastair K....3:07:53 (1,794)
Doyle, Christopher J....4:22:35 (16,719)
Doyle, Coleman C....4:34:31 (19,717)
Doyle, Eugene J....4:09:52 (13,598)
Doyle, Ian P....3:54:27 (9,627)
Doyle, Mark J....3:12:15 (2,225)
Doyle, Michael....3:38:39 (6,080)
Doyle, Pete....3:14:07 (2,452)
Doyle, Phil....2:59:56 (1,151)
Doyle, Russell W....4:10:03 (13,647)
Doyle, Shaun J....3:30:28 (4,687)
Doyle, Terence....3:17:45 (2,824)
Doyle, Tim J....4:44:21 (21,871)
D'Oyly, Timothy J....3:26:40 (3,946)
Drace-Francis, James....4:27:06 (17,864)
Drager, Henning....3:51:22 (8,849)
Drake, Jeffrey T....4:12:28 (14,187)
Drake, Justin....4:06:33 (12,793)
Drake, Steven....4:07:10 (12,931)
Drakeley, Graham....5:16:09 (27,147)
Drapeau, Jean M....3:38:18 (6,010)
Draper, Jason D....3:10:20 (2,032)
Draper, Joe D....4:58:30 (24,719)
Draper, Martin D....4:10:59 (13,866)
Draper, Peter A....4:20:59 (16,281)
Draper, Tom C....3:23:14 (3,467)
Dray, Alan G....4:49:09 (22,907)
Draycott, Mark S....5:39:06 (29,272)
Drayton, John S....3:21:12 (3,221)
Drea, Richard S....5:05:26 (25,743)
Dreiager, Kenneth....3:25:34 (3,777)
Dreiser, Timo....3:20:55 (3,192)
Dresen, Martijn T....4:22:51 (16,786)
Drew, David R....4:20:22 (16,120)
Drew, Edward....4:59:43 (24,942)
Drew, Ian....2:56:02 (812)
Drew, Keith J....4:11:31 (13,976)
Drew, Mark G....3:44:40 (7,230)
Drew, Philip....4:55:55 (24,186)
Drexel, Reinhard....4:09:46 (13,570)
Dreyer, Charles W....3:55:02 (9,798)
Driffill, Timothy J....3:51:15 (8,819)
Drinkwater, Samuel J....4:32:04 (19,124)
Driscoll, James P....5:19:31 (27,500)
Driscoll, Martin J....3:26:43 (3,964)
Driscoll, Patrick A....4:37:07 (20,278)
Driver, Ronnie A....3:52:53 (9,218)
Driver, Simon N....4:42:45 (21,506)
Drmesher, David C....5:20:38 (27,649)
Droegemueller, Ian....4:19:14 (15,841)
Drone, Ronak....5:00:29 (25,065)
Drouin, Didier....3:45:07 (7,322)
Drowley, Steve....4:11:30 (13,968)
Drozario, Lance....3:55:18 (9,880)
Drozario, Warren F....3:31:31 (4,853)
Druce, Ian C....3:07:50 (1,789)
Drugge, Jonas....3:22:27 (3,368)
Druker, Barry....6:19:10 (30,995)
Drummond, Blair M....3:59:43 (11,229)
Drummond, Duncan A....4:22:17 (16,631)
Drummond, James....5:14:11 (26,919)
Drummond, John A....5:02:25 (25,358)
Drury, David....4:38:51 (20,683)
Drury, John L....4:56:15 (24,252)
Dry, Peter F....3:27:27 (4,115)
Dryden, Colin M....4:25:11 (17,356)
Dryden, Steven....3:55:09 (9,837)
Drysdale, Keith G....4:50:52 (23,246)
Drzymalski, Nick....4:47:50 (22,644)
D'Silva, Vernon J....4:38:50 (20,677)
D'Souza, Clement O....4:38:47 (20,664)
D'Souza, Derrick R....4:02:41 (11,894)
D'Souza, Marcus N....4:37:47 (20,403)
Du Pisanic, Almero L....4:23:46 (17,008)
Du Plessis, David P....4:29:35 (18,517)
Du Toit, Anton....5:40:19 (29,357)
Dubay, William A....5:07:53 (26,098)
Dubois, Cor....4:31:29 (18,969)
Dubois, Eric....2:57:50 (948)

Dubow, Benjamin D	3:51:14 (8,813)	
Duckham, Edward C	4:28:46 (18,292)	
Duckworth, Kevin	2:45:50 (354)	
Duckworth, Paul A	4:13:34 (14,471)	
Ducros, Adrian P	4:09:51 (13,593)	
Dudack, Lee J	5:04:53 (25,675)	
Dudbridge, Frank	3:07:38 (1,771)	
Duddridge, Mark F	4:21:36 (16,420)	
Duddy, Gerard	2:57:41 (930)	
Dude, Viesturs	2:49:23 (473)	
Dudley, David A	4:09:02 (13,386)	
Dudley, Dennis C	3:51:27 (8,875)	
Dudman, Richard J	4:05:01 (12,437)	
Duerr, Richard N	4:56:37 (24,333)	
Dufetre, Claude	4:45:35 (22,162)	
Duff, Andrew	5:18:09 (27,380)	
Duff, Harry S	4:01:26 (11,584)	
Duffell, John A	3:17:58 (2,845)	
Duffey, Chris	4:22:59 (16,809)	
Duffield, Andrew	4:57:41 (24,535)	
Duffin, Michael J	4:58:00 (24,593)	
Duffin, Paul	5:35:10 (28,973)	
Duffitt, James A	3:59:47 (11,236)	
Duffus, Andrew G	4:08:27 (13,214)	
Duffy, Andrew D	3:06:24 (1,645)	
Duffy, Andrew M	4:08:39 (13,272)	
Duffy, Anthony P	3:56:39 (10,292)	
Duffy, Brian W	3:52:20 (9,096)	
Duffy, Eugene	5:03:58 (25,575)	
Duffy, Gerard	3:55:06 (9,818)	
Duffy, James	4:18:32 (15,670)	
Duffy, Liam J	3:14:07 (2,452)	
Duffy, Michael J	3:40:24 (6,380)	
Duffy, Philip	4:04:50 (12,385)	
Duffy, Richard L	4:02:31 (11,858)	
Dufosse, Laurent	3:19:59 (3,064)	
Dugan, Andrew P	5:07:07 (25,986)	
Duggan, Neil S	4:55:48 (24,151)	
Duggan, Patrick M	3:46:58 (7,741)	
Duggleby, Mark R	3:30:12 (4,634)	
Duggua, Rodney	5:32:48 (28,796)	
Duguid, David A	2:58:04 (977)	
Duhaney, Dennis	5:33:11 (28,821)	
Duke, Trevor	5:42:16 (29,500)	
Dulai, Gurjit S	3:55:18 (9,880)	
Dullehan, Michael F	4:12:24 (14,167)	
Dulson, Mark	4:00:42 (11,429)	
Duly, Paddy W	3:22:25 (3,363)	
Dumbrill, Douglas	4:53:09 (23,643)	
Dummer, Henry C	4:59:43 (24,942)	
Dumont, Pierre A	3:56:12 (10,142)	
Dunand, Bruno	3:34:39 (5,360)	
Dunbavand, Andrew	3:26:51 (3,996)	
Duncan, Andrew R	3:53:02 (9,265)	
Duncan, Brett	5:48:07 (29,871)	
Duncan, Edward R	3:08:05 (1,811)	
Duncan, Geoff	4:21:35 (16,409)	
Duncan, George B	4:43:10 (21,595)	
Duncan, Mark G	3:35:17 (5,477)	
Duncan, Mark R	4:10:17 (13,697)	
Duncan Smith, Iain	4:46:18 (22,317)	
Dunckley, Chris	3:33:54 (5,256)	
Duncombe, James M	6:13:08 (30,819)	
Duncton, Ross E	4:45:54 (22,229)	
Dundon, Steven	3:53:40 (9,413)	
Dunford, Andrew C	4:50:30 (23,179)	
Dungey, Kevin M	5:11:24 (26,564)	
Dunglinson, Matthew I	4:12:43 (14,270)	
Dunham, James A	4:11:33 (13,985)	
Dunham, Michael A	3:45:57 (7,517)	
Dunham, Paul A	4:12:42 (14,263)	
Dunk, Kieron S	4:26:10 (17,621)	
Dunk, Scott M	4:21:32 (16,398)	
Dunkerley, Andrew J	4:32:30 (19,237)	
Dunkerley, John A	4:03:45 (12,137)	
Dunkley, Timothy A	3:55:53 (10,045)	
Dunlea, Brian	4:27:05 (17,862)	
Dunleavy, James A	4:58:48 (24,765)	
Dunleavy, Mark	4:22:29 (16,697)	
Dunleavy, Michael J	4:43:52 (21,766)	
Dunlop, Andrew	4:15:13 (14,859)	
Dunlop, Craig M	4:31:38 (19,006)	
Dunlop, Ian S	3:50:36 (8,656)	
Dunlop, Wayne A	5:11:15 (26,550)	
Dunn, Anthony G	5:06:45 (25,943)	
Dunn, Barrie	3:20:29 (3,124)	
Dunn, Chris	4:20:18 (16,101)	
Dunn, Christopher A	5:13:22 (26,813)	
Dunn, Gary	4:06:32 (12,784)	
Dunn, Jeremy J	3:47:55 (7,977)	
Dunn, Norman F	4:37:06 (20,274)	
Dunn, Paul D	4:42:01 (21,348)	
Dunn, Peter H	3:37:23 (5,854)	
Dunn, Phillip M	5:30:29 (28,622)	
Dunn, Roger W	3:48:00 (7,995)	
Dunne, Ciaran A	4:00:54 (11,479)	
Dunne, Daire T	3:57:18 (10,481)	
Dunne, Dana P	5:27:46 (28,382)	
Dunne, Mark P	4:14:11 (14,607)	
Dunnett, Keith	4:25:24 (17,403)	
Dunning, Guy	3:55:58 (9,831)	
Dunning, Jamie	4:31:14 (18,903)	
Dunning, Thomas W	4:16:57 (15,294)	
Dunnington, Gary	4:01:54 (11,688)	
Dunstan, Richard E	4:46:09 (22,279)	
Dunwoody, Guy	4:23:31 (16,947)	
Dunwoody, Richard	3:17:50 (2,832)	
Dupain, Christopher N	4:06:23 (12,758)	
Dupain, Nigel C	4:35:50 (19,987)	
Dupee, Edward T	4:02:41 (11,894)	
Dupont, Jean M	4:28:08 (18,135)	
Dupont, Michel M	3:26:41 (3,951)	
Dupoy, Gavin S	3:31:05 (4,787)	
Duran, Rafael	4:24:48 (17,251)	
Durance, Richard	3:28:42 (4,353)	
Durand, Olivier	4:27:56 (18,074)	
Duranson, Roger	4:01:56 (11,701)	
Durant, Andrew	3:54:23 (9,604)	
Durden, Gary J	4:03:19 (12,036)	
Durden, Richard	5:20:54 (27,672)	
Durham, Michael C	5:02:43 (25,404)	
Durkan, Gregory M	5:25:09 (28,102)	
Durrani, Amer J	4:57:39 (24,521)	
Durrant, Barnaby G	4:34:38 (19,743)	
Durrant, Ian P	2:54:15 (705)	
Durrant, Mark J	3:58:27 (10,834)	
Durrant, Robin J	5:13:28 (26,820)	
Dursley, Paul	3:36:21 (5,667)	
Durston, Richard W	3:42:33 (6,754)	
Dusing, Arndt	3:53:21 (9,351)	
Dutch, James	4:43:39 (21,711)	
Duthie, Alex L	4:04:55 (12,411)	
Duthie, James	3:37:03 (5,783)	
Dutton, David	3:32:52 (5,075)	
Dutton, Gavin M	5:05:27 (25,747)	
Dutton, Kevin J	3:23:26 (3,491)	
Dutton, Paul J	3:55:40 (9,976)	
Dutton, Richard W	4:52:56 (23,605)	
Dutton, Stephen	3:24:01 (3,568)	
Dutton, Timothy E	4:50:44 (23,219)	
Duval, Andrew L	3:44:58 (7,301)	
Duval, Olivier	2:58:18 (995)	
Dux, Timothy A	3:24:36 (3,636)	
Duxbury, Paul C	4:07:25 (12,991)	
Dwivedi, Rahul	8:18:22 (31,957)	
Dwyer, Andrew	3:33:49 (5,237)	
Dwyer, David J	3:56:47 (10,323)	
Dwyer, James	4:40:27 (21,017)	
Dwyer, Nicholas M	3:23:14 (3,467)	
Dwyer, Sean	5:13:52 (26,880)	
Dwyer, Stuart J	5:08:56 (26,230)	
Dyckes, John J	3:05:12 (1,547)	
Dye, Mark J	4:28:50 (18,309)	
Dye, Timothy G	3:27:28 (4,122)	
Dyer, Dan	4:32:26 (19,220)	
Dyer, David A	3:59:30 (11,157)	
Dyer, Glen L	7:07:24 (31,686)	
Dyer, Graham J	5:49:09 (29,916)	
Dyer, Jonathan S	4:34:16 (19,657)	
Dyer, Mark J	4:41:00 (21,122)	
Dyer, Matthew	4:56:56 (24,391)	
Dyer, Matthew D	3:23:08 (3,458)	
Dyer, Rod	4:03:07 (11,983)	
Dyer, Tim	4:18:58 (15,773)	
Dyett, Terry D	4:44:36 (21,935)	
Dyke, Alan J	5:29:45 (28,562)	
Dyke, George M	4:59:18 (24,849)	
Dyson, Andrew I	3:53:35 (9,398)	
Dyson, Greg A	4:37:23 (20,326)	
Dyson, Philip M	4:48:43 (22,824)	
Dyson, Robert	3:28:12 (4,264)	
Dziubak, Stefan J	4:36:48 (20,202)	
Eades, Paul D	3:55:50 (10,028)	
Eadie, James A	3:36:26 (5,685)	
Eadon, David C	4:25:45 (17,496)	
Eady, Steven P	4:49:37 (22,999)	
Eager, Matthew E	4:19:43 (15,955)	
Eagles, Angus J	4:57:54 (24,568)	
Eagles, John G	7:03:16 (31,654)	
Eagles, Thomas R	3:42:20 (6,705)	
Eaglestone, William	3:58:33 (10,874)	
Ealing, Stuart W	4:29:31 (18,499)	
Eames, Andrew S	4:12:28 (14,187)	
Eardley, Matthew T	4:15:06 (14,828)	
Eardley-Taylor, Paul S	3:50:09 (8,538)	
Earl, David W	4:02:19 (11,814)	
Earl, Derek W	3:48:48 (8,211)	
Earl, Toby F	4:27:15 (17,908)	
Earle, Jonathan F	5:12:31 (26,694)	
Earle, Rupert L	3:41:39 (6,577)	
Earley, Gordon	3:48:42 (8,185)	
Earlham, Paul A	6:23:02 (31,078)	
Early, Adrian M	4:59:41 (24,936)	
Earp, Blieu W	4:34:50 (19,784)	
Earthy, Mark	6:29:28 (31,194)	
Easerbrook, Mark R	4:58:18 (24,666)	
Easey, Colin J	4:52:43 (23,571)	
Easey, Paul	3:49:33 (8,390)	
East, Edward J	3:46:20 (7,610)	
East, Tony J	4:25:44 (17,488)	
East, Trevor S	3:28:02 (4,232)	
Easter, Andrew A	5:33:52 (28,880)	
Easter, Andrew H	5:24:55 (28,072)	
Easter, Paul L	4:12:54 (14,302)	
Eastham, Barry R	3:09:25 (1,938)	
Eastham, Fred	4:35:05 (19,839)	
Eastham, Keith W	3:43:49 (7,017)	
Eastham, Robert E	4:16:52 (15,274)	
Easto, Simon P	3:24:44 (3,654)	
Easton, Daniel T	3:49:54 (8,473)	
Easton, Mark A	4:21:05 (16,295)	
Eastwood, Clive	3:36:51 (5,748)	
Eastwood, Hywel D	5:09:30 (26,305)	
Eastwood, Robert J	4:02:09 (11,764)	
Eaton, Paul M	5:32:35 (28,780)	
Eaton, Philip A	3:30:25 (4,417)	
Eaton, Stephen	4:36:04 (20,045)	
Eatslake, Simon F	3:18:49 (2,930)	
Ebsworth, David	5:13:25 (26,816)	
Eccles, Chris A	4:26:51 (17,785)	
Eccles, Michael	6:33:29 (31,273)	
Eccles, Michael D	5:51:12 (30,023)	
Eckhardt, Rupert H	5:15:24 (27,066)	
Eckley, Dominic A	3:44:03 (7,082)	
Eckman, Harry	5:36:13 (29,043)	
Eddes, Remko J	4:44:54 (22,002)	
Eddie, Gordon	4:25:43 (17,481)	
Eddison, Mark	3:37:24 (5,860)	
Ede, Philip A	3:35:08 (5,453)	
Edelsten, David M	4:42:08 (21,378)	
Eden, Michael	5:21:24 (27,720)	
Eden, Michael L	4:47:46 (22,629)	
Eden, Reg J	3:14:40 (2,520)	
Edensor, Ray	5:37:47 (29,164)	
Edge, Austen	4:38:45 (20,658)	
Edge, Michael	4:21:42 (16,449)	
Edge, Shane D	3:08:47 (1,876)	
Edgecliffe-Johnson, Robin R	3:52:03 (9,025)	
Ediker, Simon C	4:39:42 (20,862)	
Edkins, James D	3:57:07 (10,418)	
Edmands, Alan D	3:35:52 (5,584)	
Edmands, Simon F	5:38:14 (29,199)	
Edmead, Paul J	4:45:59 (22,245)	
Edmiston, James S	4:40:04 (20,934)	
Edmond, Kevin J	5:35:55 (29,022)	
Edmonds, Colin J	3:52:59 (9,252)	
Edmonds, Gary N	3:48:36 (8,150)	
Edmonds, Mark	4:28:03 (18,107)	
Edmonds, Yogi of Esher	3:55:05 (9,814)	

Etter, Niklaus 4:03:03 (11,965)
Ettlinger, Anthony C 4:38:09 (20,508)
Ettridge, Robert C 3:57:43 (10,597)
Euden, Martin J 3:56:36 (10,280)
Eul-Barker, Nick I 5:37:10 (29,122)
Euskirchen, Uwe 4:25:25 (17,405)
Eustace, Andrew 4:15:06 (14,828)
Eustace, John 4:15:33 (14,942)
Euving, Egbert 4:14:36 (14,706)
Evangelou, Costakis C 5:15:18 (27,056)
Evans, Aled M 3:25:27 (3,761)
Evans, Alexander J 5:13:03 (26,771)
Evans, Andrew J 5:13:32 (26,831)
Evans, Antony F 4:51:49 (23,402)
Evans, Barrie J 3:46:28 (7,634)
Evans, Barry G 3:53:36 (9,401)
Evans, Brent L 4:06:26 (12,767)
Evans, Brian N 3:42:51 (6,821)
Evans, Christian B 4:17:23 (15,392)
Evans, Christopher 5:03:31 (25,524)
Evans, Christopher J 5:10:05 (26,386)
Evans, Christopher J 6:19:30 (31,003)
Evans, Cliff N 3:54:12 (9,564)
Evans, Colin 4:11:28 (13,962)
Evans, Daniel 2:46:00 (358)
Evans, Daniel 3:58:59 (10,999)
Evans, Daniel M 5:27:08 (28,315)
Evans, Daren J 4:14:37 (14,713)
Evans, Darren T 6:10:22 (30,737)
Evans, Dave 3:47:36 (7,906)
Evans, David 4:23:05 (16,837)
Evans, David A 5:07:30 (26,046)
Evans, David J 4:36:04 (20,045)
Evans, David M 4:43:10 (21,595)
Evans, David M 4:52:00 (23,438)
Evans, David M 5:44:18 (29,644)
Evans, Dominic S 5:04:50 (25,668)
Evans, Edwin 3:12:14 (2,222)
Evans, Elfyn W 4:13:09 (14,365)
Evans, Eric D 5:17:02 (27,260)
Evans, Frank C 4:07:41 (13,053)
Evans, Gareth C 3:29:49 (4,558)
Evans, Gareth C 4:32:25 (19,217)
Evans, Gareth J 5:06:59 (25,966)
Evans, Gareth J 5:49:51 (29,955)
Evans, Gavin 3:02:07 (1,308)
Evans, Geraint 5:11:52 (26,613)
Evans, Geraint D 3:43:50 (7,021)
Evans, Geraint K 3:29:14 (4,461)
Evans, Glynn M 3:48:27 (8,106)
Evans, Graham A 2:46:50 (384)
Evans, Ian E 3:08:44 (1,868)
Evans, Ian L 3:45:29 (7,403)
Evans, Jamie D 4:30:57 (18,846)
Evans, Jason L 3:46:51 (7,713)
Evans, Jeffrey K 4:37:35 (20,352)
Evans, John B 3:07:12 (1,719)
Evans, John D 4:21:47 (16,475)
Evans, John D 4:30:03 (18,646)
Evans, John E 5:32:24 (28,767)
Evans, John V 3:39:25 (6,205)
Evans, Jonathan E 3:02:12 (1,317)
Evans, Jonathan G 5:08:51 (26,216)
Evans, J-Stewart G 3:37:17 (5,832)
Evans, Kalvin L 5:12:34 (26,700)
Evans, Kenneth V 4:07:57 (13,104)
Evans, Kevin J 3:59:48 (11,240)
Evans, Larry G 5:10:38 (26,456)
Evans, Lee A 4:21:59 (16,530)
Evans, Marc 2:44:57 (324)
Evans, Mark 3:58:53 (10,967)
Evans, Mark G 3:42:31 (6,749)
Evans, Martin 3:31:58 (4,918)
Evans, Matthew 3:30:39 (4,718)
Evans, Michael A 2:38:40 (179)
Evans, Michael J 4:09:36 (13,524)
Evans, Michael J 4:50:19 (23,126)
Evans, Michael S 5:50:25 (29,989)
Evans, Mike 3:58:09 (10,729)
Evans, Neil A 4:40:59 (21,119)
Evans, Nicholas 4:25:16 (17,376)
Evans, Nick A 4:37:31 (20,342)
Evans, Nick D 4:06:04 (12,675)
Evans, Nigel J 3:46:18 (7,602)
Evans, Noel B 3:49:29 (8,370)
Evans, Pascal J 2:59:16 (1,099)
Evans, Paul 7:35:34 (31,876)
Evans, Paul M 4:51:44 (23,387)
Evans, Peter 5:27:26 (28,350)
Evans, Peter M 4:11:16 (13,922)
Evans, Peter R 4:05:18 (12,487)
Evans, Philip R 5:19:37 (27,513)
Evans, Rhys D 3:46:51 (7,713)
Evans, Richard P 5:03:45 (25,548)
Evans, Robert A 4:43:54 (21,775)
Evans, Robert Z 4:41:15 (21,169)
Evans, Simon 3:21:25 (3,246)
Evans, Simon L 3:54:54 (9,753)
Evans, Stefan G 6:12:32 (30,795)
Evans, Stephen P 5:13:16 (26,801)
Evans, Stuart M 4:52:33 (23,539)
Evans, Thomas D 3:46:44 (7,686)
Evans, William 3:05:00 (1,524)
Evans MBE, Richard G 8:07:19 (31,949)
Evason, David 5:10:03 (26,383)
Eveleigh, Melvin R 4:58:28 (24,711)
Eveleigh, Paul M 3:32:43 (5,045)
Everard, Graeme I 3:58:37 (10,891)
Everest, Mark I 4:31:03 (18,866)
Everest, Terry J 3:12:33 (2,259)
Everett, Barry 4:43:16 (21,627)
Everett, Grahame 4:15:08 (14,840)
Everitt, Christopher J 5:02:09 (25,313)
Everitt, Geof 3:48:46 (8,200)
Eversden, Michael J 3:51:40 (8,930)
Everson, David 3:55:41 (9,982)
Everson, Desmond 3:27:52 (4,203)
Eves, Michael B 4:50:54 (23,251)
Eves, Peter J 3:46:34 (7,653)
Eves-Brown, Andrew C 4:20:41 (16,206)
Eveson, Jonathan 4:36:07 (20,059)
Ewbank, David C 4:55:33 (24,108)
Ewen, George M 4:34:11 (19,640)
Ewins, Oliver J 6:51:53 (31,527)
Exarchos, Nicholas A 4:29:03 (18,360)
Exley, Jonathan N 3:19:44 (3,043)
Exley, Martin J 2:50:55 (540)
Exley, Richard 7:04:17 (31,663)
Exworth, Matthew R 3:08:56 (1,892)
Eyles, George P 4:30:20 (18,711)
Eyles, Raymond A 4:51:04 (23,285)
Eyre, Martin J 4:18:51 (15,751)
Eyre-Brook, David G 3:45:12 (7,348)
Fabbri, Antonio 4:31:36 (18,999)
Fabian, Spencer 5:05:17 (25,721)
Fadiora, George E 3:42:28 (6,735)
Fagan, Daragh P 3:40:20 (6,364)
Fahmy, Fahmy F 4:30:13 (18,685)
Fahrenheim, Robert M 4:01:40 (11,640)
Fahy, Dominic M 5:08:31 (26,184)
Fahy, Martin J 5:21:20 (27,712)
Faiers, Gray 4:09:56 (13,622)
Faill, Jonathan M 4:52:06 (23,466)
Faint, Keith M 3:38:12 (5,995)
Fairbairn, Michael J 6:43:07 (31,408)
Fairbairn, Scott H 4:25:37 (17,456)
Fairbrass, Andrew J 3:56:04 (10,105)
Fairbrass, Keith 3:56:26 (10,228)
Fairbrother, Alex 4:15:08 (14,840)
Fairbrother, Paul J 4:10:36 (13,782)
Fairburn, Martin J 4:11:39 (14,015)
Fairclough, David 5:23:51 (27,956)
Fairfull, Gary 5:37:05 (29,112)
Fairhead, John M 5:16:09 (27,147)
Fairhurst, Wayne 2:58:04 (977)
Fairlie, Kenneth W 4:11:36 (13,999)
Fairs, Jon P 2:44:48 (319)
Fairweather, Andrew E 4:21:45 (16,465)
Faithfull, Paul 4:41:37 (21,262)
Falcao, Terry A 4:21:35 (16,409)
Falco, Jean B 4:57:36 (24,513)
Falconer, Gordon 3:15:39 (2,615)
Falconer, James R 4:02:05 (11,739)
Falk, Joshua J 5:59:02 (30,365)
Falkenberg, Erik 3:42:55 (6,838)
Fallmann, Ian P 3:48:15 (8,065)
Fallon, Alastair M 3:56:00 (10,084)
Fallon, Carl R 3:28:29 (4,319)
Fallon, Gary M 2:59:30 (1,121)
Fallon, Michael 5:33:28 (28,846)
Fallon, Thomas 3:23:11 (3,462)
Fallows, Rob S 5:43:36 (29,600)
Falquero, Edward A 3:41:33 (6,549)
Fanden, Roger C 4:09:46 (13,570)
Fane, George A 5:13:45 (26,859)
Fane, Patrick H 5:13:45 (26,859)
Fanning, Alastair S 3:13:43 (2,402)
Fanning, Ian M 3:37:59 (5,958)
Fanning, Jerome B 2:54:48 (734)
Fantuzzi, Alessandro 4:09:10 (13,411)
Fanuzzi, Gianpiero 3:24:54 (3,681)
Faraday, Michael J 5:27:10 (28,320)
Farag, Ben 3:19:31 (3,023)
Faratro, Filippo 4:04:21 (12,272)
Farazi, Dilawer J 5:41:29 (29,444)
Farebrother, Terry D 4:39:20 (20,799)
Fargnoli, Paolo D 3:52:22 (9,103)
Farina, Richard A 4:16:04 (15,065)
Farley, Darrell 4:24:50 (17,260)
Farlow, Andrew C 3:33:07 (5,122)
Farmer, Michael D 3:07:58 (1,802)
Farmer, Steven 3:42:35 (6,760)
Farndale, Martin D 3:58:43 (10,923)
Farndale, Nigel 5:10:30 (26,442)
Farnell, Mark A 2:39:04 (186)
Farnes, Jack 3:32:33 (5,013)
Farnham, Malcolm R 4:22:00 (16,537)
Farnsworth, Graham R 2:59:24 (1,113)
Farquharson, Rob 5:03:24 (25,500)
Farr, Graham C 3:40:27 (6,388)
Farran, Martin J 2:33:50 (105)
Farrant, Paul R 4:05:56 (12,648)
Farrar, Alasdair J 4:19:06 (15,803)
Farrar, Andrew J 3:15:37 (2,613)
Farrar, Gareth 3:55:52 (10,037)
Farrar, Malcolm H 4:19:06 (15,803)
Farrar, Richard 6:08:56 (30,694)
Farrell, Bernard W 4:08:39 (13,272)
Farrell, David 4:45:28 (22,134)
Farrell, Gary S 5:13:32 (26,831)
Farrell, Mark J 4:35:31 (19,929)
Farrell, Oliver 5:17:29 (27,306)
Farrell, Robert 5:29:27 (28,525)
Farrimond, Jonathan 6:33:59 (31,277)
Farrin, Dennis D 5:51:04 (30,018)
Farrington, Derek 3:27:29 (4,124)
Farrow, Andrew D 5:12:26 (26,686)
Farrow, Edward T 3:43:23 (6,933)
Farrow, John 4:55:34 (24,114)
Farrow, Mark A 4:39:31 (20,826)
Farrow, Robert R 4:31:43 (19,033)
Fasola, Pierfranco 3:55:48 (10,016)
Fas-Segarra, Vicente J 3:24:13 (3,592)
Fateh, Mohammed 7:05:51 (31,675)
Faulkner, David O 5:10:42 (26,466)
Faulkner, John 3:32:28 (4,998)
Faulkner, Kevin J 4:11:11 (13,909)
Faulkner, Kevin J 4:42:21 (21,425)
Faulkner, Richard A 5:48:52 (29,901)
Faulkner, Roger W 4:18:13 (15,591)
Faure, René 3:30:42 (4,724)
Faure, Wynton M 3:13:58 (2,429)
Faury, Jean M 3:07:31 (1,755)
Favre-Petit-Mermet, Serge 2:57:13 (895)
Favresse, Gael 4:07:42 (13,056)
Fawcett, Derrick 4:12:28 (14,187)
Fawcett, Douglas J 4:42:11 (21,382)
Fawcett, Malcolm S 4:42:54 (21,541)
Fawcett, Michael 3:45:08 (7,330)
Fawcett, Paul 3:45:09 (7,334)
Fawcett, Peter E 4:34:47 (19,774)
Fawcett, Steven P 3:44:30 (7,185)
Fay, Christopher D 4:00:41 (11,422)
Fay, James 5:29:17 (28,517)
Fay, Stephen M 3:33:51 (5,244)
Fazackerley, Darren J 3:38:43 (6,087)
Fazakerley, Mark 3:39:29 (6,214)
Feane, Kevin 4:15:44 (14,984)
Fearn, Neil W 4:15:01 (14,808)

Fearn, Steve R 4:45:09 (22,070)
Fearnhead, Mark A 3:29:01 (4,416)
Fearnhough, Thomas R 5:33:50 (28,874)
Fearnley, Martin G 4:38:54 (20,693)
Fearns, Donald P 5:06:36 (25,929)
Fearnyough, Paul 4:11:54 (14,063)
Feasey, Christopher J 3:42:40 (6,780)
Featherston, Samuel J 3:58:07 (10,715)
Featherstone, Chris P 3:40:42 (6,431)
Featherstone, Mark L 5:13:58 (26,890)
Featherstone, Walter 3:22:45 (3,410)
Featley, Colin E 4:29:14 (18,410)
Feaver, John N 3:55:17 (9,876)
Febvre, Luc 4:41:51 (21,317)
Fechter, Martin 3:00:29 (1,190)
Fedi, Daniele 3:49:33 (8,390)
Fedieu, Raymond 3:49:38 (8,410)
Feeney, Scott J 3:39:40 (6,252)
Fehsenfeld, Burkhard J 3:13:12 (2,329)
Feldman, Brian R 4:27:30 (17,957)
Feldman, Leonard 4:40:12 (20,963)
Felgueroso Villa, Pablo De Tars 5:22:18 (27,805)
Felipe, Robert 3:58:27 (10,834)
Fell, Andrew T 3:42:37 (6,769)
Fell, Mark M 5:22:54 (27,868)
Fell, Samuel J 3:34:44 (5,377)
Fell, Simon J 3:45:22 (7,378)
Fellowes-Freeman, Malcolm S 4:17:38 (15,461)
Fellows, Ben S 3:53:47 (9,436)
Fellows, John 3:49:05 (8,277)
Fellows, Keith J 3:20:39 (3,155)
Fellows, Matthew J 4:53:08 (23,639)
Fellows, Stephen E 5:16:45 (27,225)
Felstead, James M 3:37:41 (5,902)
Felstead, Mark T 5:40:18 (29,356)
Feltham, Barry 4:47:19 (22,523)
Feltham-White, Antony J 4:23:09 (16,854)
Felton, David J 3:20:30 (3,131)
Fender, Tom 5:16:50 (27,240)
Fenech, Jonathan L 4:56:36 (24,329)
Fenech, Michael 5:19:56 (27,551)
Fenkel, Frank 4:23:50 (17,023)
Fenn, Joel M 4:40:43 (21,068)
Fenn, Richard A 3:45:38 (7,443)
Fenn, Russell K 4:53:07 (23,636)
Fennell, Alexander 4:25:03 (17,318)
Fennell, Donald B 6:45:30 (31,447)
Fennell, Paul 4:19:45 (15,965)
Fenster, Jim C 5:06:26 (25,902)
Fent, Michael 4:55:39 (24,130)
Fenton, David J 4:02:19 (11,814)
Fenton, David N 4:14:43 (14,732)
Fenton, Gordon W 5:11:50 (26,609)
Fenton, Jeffrey A 4:11:30 (13,968)
Fenton, Les 3:25:35 (3,785)
Fenton, Terry A 4:13:36 (14,480)
Fenwick, Paul K 4:17:48 (15,507)
Fenwick, Peter R 4:01:38 (11,629)
Ferchichi, Maurice 3:17:18 (2,784)
Ferdinando, Martin J 6:50:03 (31,499)
Ferebee, David S 4:14:46 (14,745)
Fereday, David H 3:47:29 (7,876)
Ferguson, Cameron T 3:10:00 (2,001)
Ferguson, Carl A 3:30:48 (4,744)
Ferguson, David 4:09:54 (13,607)
Ferguson, David N 5:46:37 (29,796)
Ferguson, James R 3:58:44 (10,925)
Ferguson, Kenneth 4:54:15 (23,844)
Ferguson, Paul 6:11:31 (30,773)
Ferguson, William D 4:48:22 (22,752)
Fergusson, Eric 4:28:49 (18,304)
Fermi, Giuseppe 3:42:12 (6,681)
Fernandes, Fui M 4:09:41 (13,549)
Fernandez, Emmanuel 3:05:51 (1,595)
Fernandez, Marcos 4:12:33 (14,218)
Fernandez-Bedmar, Jesus 3:15:39 (2,615)
Fernandez-Galvez, Jesus 2:53:18 (662)
Fernee, Ronald N 4:01:19 (11,565)
Fernley, David 5:18:44 (27,439)
Ferns, Ged V 4:28:49 (18,304)
Ferrao, Carlos Alberto 2:39:03 (185)
Ferrar, Ian 4:54:31 (23,899)
Ferrar, Jonathan A 4:15:12 (14,856)
Ferraro, Julian 2:59:37 (1,128)
Ferreira, Adriano 4:15:35 (14,949)
Ferreira Dinis, Rui Nelson 4:28:25 (18,198)
Ferreira Do Carmo, Norberto J 4:14:42 (14,728)
Ferrelly, Neil A 3:40:00 (6,304)
Ferres, Peter J 3:15:45 (2,629)
Ferreux, Frederic 3:40:04 (6,320)
Ferriday, Ernest J 4:46:44 (22,397)
Ferrie, John T 5:35:35 (29,005)
Ferrier, Andrew J 4:26:58 (17,830)
Ferries, Brian A 4:02:24 (11,839)
Ferris, Peter A 3:44:05 (7,092)
Ferris, Steven A 2:56:49 (871)
Ferris MBE, Peter J 5:03:02 (25,450)
Fether, Harold R 4:03:45 (12,137)
Fetherstone, Michael J 4:45:11 (22,078)
Fetzer, Hans Martin 3:53:12 (9,318)
Fewster, David H 5:34:06 (28,895)
Fewtrell, Malcolm 5:15:51 (27,114)
Fey, Keith R 4:03:49 (12,152)
Fiaz, Artisham 3:55:42 (9,989)
Fichard, Gilbert 4:29:20 (18,444)
Fiddes, Alan G 3:53:47 (9,436)
Fiddes, Michael J 4:56:18 (24,261)
Field, Alan C 3:42:26 (6,727)
Field, Andrew E 3:07:36 (1,765)
Field, Andrew P 5:36:05 (29,033)
Field, Anthony 4:10:49 (13,830)
Field, David 4:21:49 (16,484)
Field, David A 4:17:30 (15,423)
Field, Donald A 3:04:26 (1,486)
Field, John 5:02:13 (25,321)
Field, John E 5:00:57 (25,136)
Field, Stephen P 3:25:46 (3,810)
Field, Steve 3:18:53 (2,940)
Field, Terry C 3:47:32 (7,893)
Field, Tim 6:15:53 (30,906)
Fielder, James R 3:55:28 (9,921)
Fieldhouse, David 3:11:27 (2,140)
Fieldhouse, Philip 5:18:41 (27,433)
Fielding, Paul 2:56:08 (824)
Fielding-Smith, Peter R 2:54:11 (704)
Fieldsend, Brian 2:35:41 (130)
Fielitz, Carsten 5:04:01 (25,582)
Fiennes, Ranulph 3:43:09 (6,878)
Fietkau, Mark 3:39:44 (6,262)
Figgins, Ian J 4:56:45 (24,352)
Figl, Anton 3:58:05 (10,705)
Figueiredo, Ricardo O 3:46:40 (7,673)
Filkins, Martin 6:03:15 (30,536)
Filler, Andrew E 5:30:41 (28,637)
Filler, Paul F 5:06:26 (25,902)
Filmer, Greg P 4:32:29 (19,235)
Filnambu, Jacques 3:08:23 (1,839)
Finbow, Robert 5:14:00 (26,899)
Finch, Craig A 5:31:21 (28,694)
Finch, George 4:19:07 (15,810)
Finch, Leslie V 4:37:36 (20,356)
Finch, Peter 3:28:34 (4,331)
Finch, Simon 3:41:15 (6,521)
Fincham, Andrew J 3:30:36 (4,707)
Fincham, Daron A 3:46:15 (7,591)
Findlay, Alistair M 5:12:16 (26,664)
Findley, Michael A 4:44:57 (22,020)
Fine, Howie 4:30:09 (18,666)
Fine, Martin H 3:45:14 (7,358)
Fineman, Simon 4:07:53 (13,085)
Finer, Red 4:03:16 (12,021)
Finer, Roland R 4:03:17 (12,025)
Finestone, Philip 3:09:20 (1,932)
Finill, Chris T 2:44:10 (291)
Fink, Ralf 2:49:27 (476)
Finlay, Jack A 3:51:26 (8,868)
Finlayson, John J 4:04:08 (12,223)
Finn, Andy W 3:51:55 (8,995)
Finn, Craig A 5:05:10 (25,710)
Finn, Graham R 5:12:13 (26,657)
Finn, Julian A 4:17:15 (15,357)
Finn, Paul E 3:56:31 (10,258)
Finn, Stephen 5:24:47 (28,054)
Finn, Terence H 4:51:55 (23,426)
Finnegan, Peter J 3:21:38 (3,272)
Finnemore, Chris 5:52:36 (30,105)
Finnerty, Andrew T 4:04:14 (12,249)
Finney, Colin J 3:16:31 (2,701)
Finney, Kelvin J 3:49:29 (8,370)
Finney, Kevin M 3:01:55 (1,296)
Finnigan, Martin 3:31:44 (4,877)
Fioravanti, Lorenzo 4:18:19 (15,611)
Fiorillo, Lorenzo 4:26:54 (17,812)
Firmin, Michael P 2:52:24 (608)
Firmin, Paul R 3:13:36 (2,385)
Firth, Adrian A 5:59:30 (30,391)
Firth, Colin 3:54:43 (9,696)
Firth, Daniel J 4:12:03 (14,105)
Firth, Darren J 3:38:33 (6,056)
Firth, Dominic M 4:17:06 (15,327)
Firth, Justin P 4:08:33 (13,251)
Firth, Malcolm R 4:07:06 (12,917)
Fischer, Alan 3:30:29 (4,688)
Fischer, Sylvain 3:36:57 (5,761)
Fischer-Beards, Mark A 4:07:12 (12,939)
Fish, Adam B 5:17:41 (27,326)
Fish, Andrew S 3:45:09 (7,334)
Fish, Bradley 4:32:40 (19,283)
Fish, Gary E 4:56:37 (24,333)
Fish, Mark A 5:09:32 (26,308)
Fish, Ralph G 5:09:32 (26,308)
Fish, Robin C 4:46:08 (22,275)
Fisher, Charles 3:43:56 (7,047)
Fisher, Daniel 4:27:03 (17,856)
Fisher, Dean 3:40:22 (6,373)
Fisher, Derek 5:43:30 (29,590)
Fisher, Gary A 4:10:32 (13,762)
Fisher, Geoff J 3:26:53 (3,999)
Fisher, Ian A 4:49:39 (23,008)
Fisher, Ian T 2:21:04 (36)
Fisher, John D 4:37:22 (20,325)
Fisher, Martin J 3:44:36 (7,213)
Fisher, Matthew R 3:22:14 (3,332)
Fisher, Michael 5:09:09 (26,260)
Fisher, Neil R 6:13:10 (30,820)
Fisher, Nigel A 3:43:46 (7,005)
Fisher, Paul K 4:57:15 (24,450)
Fisher, Ray J 5:04:02 (25,585)
Fisher, Robert P 4:55:45 (24,145)
Fisher, Rod N 4:43:11 (21,602)
Fisher, Roderick M 3:55:46 (10,010)
Fisher, Sam Y 4:42:41 (21,486)
Fisher, Steven 6:22:48 (31,076)
Fisher, Toney R 5:38:36 (29,240)
Fishpool, Sean 3:46:13 (7,585)
Fishwick, Ian N 5:03:35 (25,532)
Fishwick, Peter J 6:13:28 (30,831)
Fisk, Kristofor D 5:16:26 (27,184)
Fitch, Gavin H 4:27:57 (18,082)
Fitch-Peyton, David 3:13:19 (2,345)
Fittes, Andrew C 4:48:12 (22,721)
Fitts, Benjamin H 2:48:02 (424)
Fitz, Colin D 4:27:46 (18,031)
Fitzakerly, Anthony R 4:05:29 (12,532)
Fitzgerald, Anthony A 5:13:50 (26,878)
Fitzgerald, Brian 4:20:43 (16,217)
Fitzgerald, Gareth M 4:14:01 (14,572)
Fitzgerald, Harry L 4:01:36 (11,622)
Fitzgerald, Ian N 4:48:10 (22,713)
Fitzgerald, Mark J 3:56:45 (10,311)
Fitzgibbon, John F 4:37:46 (20,398)
Fitzhenry, Ray J 3:34:42 (5,370)
Fitzpatrick, Leland C 6:50:53 (31,511)
Fitzpatrick, Mark J 4:50:22 (23,142)
Fitzpatrick, Paul A 4:53:55 (23,780)
Fjeldheim, Trygue A 4:34:04 (19,614)
Flach, Jolan G 4:16:39 (15,220)
Flack, Alan K 7:11:18 (31,717)
Flack, Barry J 4:07:21 (12,970)
Flack, Nicholas 5:28:29 (28,436)
Flack, Paul T 4:29:03 (18,360)
Flack-Hill, Eliot 4:33:59 (19,583)
Flaherty, Brian J 7:59:20 (31,931)
Flaherty, David 8:00:01 (31,942)
Flaherty, Dennis 7:59:28 (31,934)
Flaherty, Festus G 5:54:38 (30,179)
Flaherty, Gerrard 7:59:26 (31,933)
Flaherty, Kevin 7:59:32 (31,937)
Flaherty, Michael 7:59:36 (31,940)

LONDON MARATHON

Fox, Adam	4:33:52 (19,549)
Fox, Andrew	4:31:32 (18,989)
Fox, Andy W	4:33:59 (19,583)
Fox, Barrie	3:30:40 (4,721)
Fox, Grant B	4:08:20 (13,186)
Fox, Grenville F	5:44:47 (29,677)
Fox, James	3:33:13 (5,141)
Fox, Jonathan L	4:23:56 (17,046)
Fox, Kevin J	4:21:33 (16,400)
Fox, Malcolm F	5:27:05 (28,310)
Fox, Martin	4:11:28 (13,962)
Fox, Martin R	3:49:19 (8,331)
Fox, Matthew P	4:11:04 (13,883)
Fox, Mike	5:20:15 (27,599)
Fox, Neil B	4:05:20 (12,494)
Fox, Paul F	3:29:52 (4,565)
Fox, Peter J	5:04:42 (25,650)
Fox, Philip G	2:53:51 (687)
Fox, Simon	5:49:01 (29,908)
Fox, Thomas W	5:26:14 (28,214)
Fox, Tim C	2:57:51 (949)
Fox, Vivian E	4:10:23 (13,729)
Fox, William S	3:23:41 (3,526)
Foxall, Peter L	3:09:47 (1,978)
Foxley, Nick C	3:54:08 (9,536)
Foxley, Timothy J	3:45:47 (7,480)
Fox-Robinson, William R	4:08:16 (13,165)
Foxwell, James R	3:40:02 (6,309)
Foxwell, Simon O	4:00:51 (11,461)
Frackowiak, Tom A	3:43:11 (6,890)
Fradley, Alan W	3:54:43 (9,696)
Frame, Michael J	4:26:27 (17,684)
Franca, José V	4:08:28 (13,221)
Francaud, Jean Jacque	4:43:20 (21,649)
France, Colin	3:29:46 (4,548)
Franceries, Axel	4:53:14 (23,663)
Frances, David G	4:14:08 (14,593)
Francey, Kenneth G	4:54:02 (23,800)
Francis, Donald K	3:45:22 (7,378)
Francis, Glyn	4:01:30 (11,600)
Francis, Hugh R	6:15:45 (30,904)
Francis, John P	8:37:25 (31,973)
Francis, Kevin R	2:57:47 (943)
Francis, Lee	3:32:39 (5,039)
Francis, Mark A	3:22:50 (3,424)
Francis, Matthew R	5:30:20 (28,609)
Francis, Raymond S	3:09:48 (1,979)
Francis, Richard J	3:36:15 (5,650)
Francis, Richard W	3:12:45 (2,281)
Francis, Stephen	3:42:36 (6,763)
Francis-Smith, Christopher D	3:59:08 (11,040)
Franck, Maccarrone	4:18:28 (15,659)
Franco, Roman	4:48:33 (22,783)
Frandsen, Finn	4:05:36 (12,573)
Frankie, Labiaux	2:52:40 (624)
Frankland, Anthony D	6:32:49 (31,260)
Franklin, John K	3:13:07 (2,319)
Franklin, John P	4:18:54 (15,758)
Franklin, Matthew J	4:56:52 (24,377)
Franklin, Paul R	4:23:23 (16,914)
Franklin, Raymond V	5:58:44 (30,359)
Franklin, Robert C	3:32:10 (4,947)
Franks, Adam S	4:45:57 (22,238)
Franks, Carl R	5:16:15 (27,162)
Franks, David N	5:22:53 (27,867)
Franks, Jason E	4:02:06 (11,746)
Franks, John H	5:24:38 (28,039)
Franks, Keith	3:35:29 (5,521)
Franks, Simon R	4:30:30 (18,760)
Franks, Tim H	3:56:46 (10,318)
Frankum, Martin J	4:17:36 (15,452)
Franz, Jonathon	5:29:18 (28,519)
Fraquelli, Andrea	3:41:11 (6,509)
Fraser, Alec D	4:09:51 (13,593)
Fraser, Derek	2:59:35 (1,127)
Fraser, Douglas	4:24:01 (17,064)
Fraser, Edward	4:11:00 (13,873)
Fraser, George	4:31:17 (18,916)
Fraser, Grant S	3:49:04 (8,268)
Fraser, Keith	3:25:35 (3,785)
Fraser, Kevin	3:18:30 (2,897)
Fraser, Mark E	3:38:12 (5,995)
Fraser, Martin	3:52:52 (9,216)
Fraser, Matthew	4:54:18 (23,855)
Fraser, Paul J	3:33:03 (5,109)
Fraser, Steven P	4:35:01 (19,825)
Fratamico, Nino	6:07:57 (30,673)
Frazer, Arnold R	5:16:40 (27,217)
Frazer, Robin H	5:08:16 (26,152)
Frearson, Paul C	4:12:07 (14,120)
Free, Alex M	5:35:12 (28,974)
Freear, Matthew R	3:28:10 (4,256)
Freedman, Clive	6:19:47 (31,009)
Freedman, Oliver S	4:52:06 (23,466)
Freedman, Simon D	3:26:14 (3,875)
Freegard, Mark D	6:05:07 (30,595)
Freel, Chris J	3:38:32 (6,051)
Freeman, Ben C	3:27:43 (4,171)
Freeman, Christopher J	4:47:57 (22,662)
Freeman, David J	2:45:58 (356)
Freeman, Donald A	5:17:27 (27,299)
Freeman, Julian P	4:18:12 (15,587)
Freeman, Mark E	4:57:24 (24,473)
Freeman, Neil D	4:49:41 (23,012)
Freeman, Peter	4:18:27 (15,655)
Freeman, Peter G	4:25:44 (17,488)
Freeman, Samuel	4:08:53 (13,342)
Freeman, Stephen	3:22:19 (3,345)
Freeman, Vaughan N	4:31:42 (19,029)
Freeston, Michael	3:41:38 (6,574)
Freeston, Andrew	5:44:37 (29,665)
Freestone, Tom J	5:49:43 (29,946)
Freeth, Len	6:25:40 (31,134)
Freke, Nick R	3:56:29 (10,248)
Freke, Thomas S	5:04:57 (25,686)
Frelich, Martin	2:36:01 (136)
French, Alan R	4:36:19 (20,090)
French, Brian	4:41:21 (21,206)
French, Kevin R	4:13:21 (14,419)
French, Michael J	4:04:48 (12,377)
French, Michael R	3:50:49 (8,712)
French, Neil	3:59:26 (11,121)
French, Nick H	4:20:51 (16,244)
French, Peter M	3:28:06 (4,240)
French, Raymond G	4:06:44 (12,823)
French, Sean	3:46:44 (7,686)
Fresch, Mark B	4:36:41 (20,179)
Fretwell, Philip J	4:31:26 (18,956)
Fretwell, Richard A	4:22:09 (16,588)
Freudenfeld, Anthony	4:30:35 (18,777)
Frew, Colin J	3:17:14 (2,778)
Frewer, Jeremy E	4:25:12 (17,362)
Frewer, Martyn A	4:15:46 (14,993)
Fribbins, Michael G	4:32:22 (19,206)
Friday, John H	3:47:16 (7,822)
Friday, Patrick	3:47:16 (7,822)
Friedman, Roy	5:46:22 (29,774)
Friedrich, Dieter	3:59:00 (11,007)
Friedrich, James K	3:08:17 (1,830)
Friel, Patrick E	3:49:22 (8,344)
Friel, Robert H	5:00:42 (25,095)
Friery, Andy M	5:11:25 (26,567)
Frigerio, Roberto	4:07:28 (13,001)
Frils, Klaus L	3:34:40 (5,362)
Frisby, Andrew W	4:08:29 (13,224)
Frisby, Peter M	4:09:11 (13,415)
Frischknecht, Harry	3:21:24 (3,243)
Frith, Stuart J	4:38:15 (20,533)
Frizzel, Peter A	3:38:49 (6,150)
Froehlke, Victor	3:09:40 (1,967)
Froese, Dirk	3:56:25 (10,222)
Froese, Helmut	4:16:36 (15,200)
Froggatt, Paul D	5:24:47 (28,054)
Frohnsdorff, David	4:57:46 (24,550)
Frolov, Yeugeny	5:49:40 (29,940)
Fromme, Dieter	4:13:44 (14,500)
Frondella, Luigi	2:53:36 (672)
Frosdick, Roland J	4:41:37 (21,262)
Frost, Andrew B	6:13:18 (30,822)
Frost, Colin	4:52:14 (23,491)
Frost, Grant	4:30:27 (18,745)
Frost, Jonathan G	3:30:54 (4,761)
Frost, Mark P	3:52:40 (9,165)
Frost, Martin A	4:13:41 (14,491)
Frost, Paul	4:26:28 (17,691)
Frost, Paul I	5:39:26 (29,304)
Frost, Paul L	4:58:02 (24,604)
Frost, Raymond	4:09:50 (13,591)
Frost, Richard M	5:27:15 (28,330)
Frost, Simon	4:08:13 (13,152)
Frost, Stephen R	5:38:39 (29,242)
Frost, Steven C	4:23:05 (16,837)
Frostig, Ronnie M	4:38:36 (20,617)
Froud, Michael	4:20:38 (16,195)
Frowein, Maarten	4:09:16 (13,446)
Frowen, Nigel G	5:02:17 (25,336)
Froy, Steve J	5:16:50 (27,240)
Fruhwuerth, Richard	3:59:26 (11,121)
Fruin, David J	5:26:32 (28,251)
Fry, Christopher M	3:39:32 (6,221)
Fry, Edward	4:35:44 (19,966)
Fry, Edward J	4:32:59 (19,354)
Fry, Henry R	3:14:05 (2,446)
Fry, Kevin P	4:36:30 (20,135)
Fry, Malcolm M	4:17:38 (15,461)
Fry, Matthew J	4:14:03 (14,577)
Fry, Tim C	4:17:19 (15,374)
Fryer, Alexander	3:36:09 (5,634)
Fryer, Laurence	4:07:41 (13,053)
Fryer, Tim	4:24:59 (17,307)
Fudge, Malcolm A	4:27:34 (17,982)
Fuentes, Antonio	3:58:19 (10,795)
Fuge, Christopher J	4:56:19 (24,266)
Fujii, Akira	3:49:57 (8,489)
Fujimoto, Takeshi	4:38:20 (20,554)
Fulcher, Frank A	3:19:04 (2,961)
Fulford-Brown, Chris M	4:12:53 (14,299)
Fullagar, Terry P	5:34:12 (28,903)
Fullbrook, Richard	3:50:52 (8,723)
Fuller, Adrian	2:57:43 (935)
Fuller, David M	5:27:18 (28,335)
Fuller, Luke D	4:32:16 (19,181)
Fuller, Martin G	3:09:01 (1,900)
Fuller, Richard	3:09:50 (1,984)
Fullerton, Angus N	4:29:32 (18,503)
Fullman, James P	4:24:05 (17,086)
Fundela, Peter T	4:54:09 (23,830)
Funke, Jost	5:02:57 (25,440)
Funnell, Nicholas C	6:03:40 (30,552)
Furber, Jeremy D	4:33:43 (19,508)
Furey, James D	4:01:29 (11,592)
Furghieri, Bernardo	3:03:38 (1,420)
Furhoff, Bjorn	3:09:50 (1,984)
Furlong, Gafyn W	4:13:36 (14,480)
Furlong, Michael J	4:01:52 (11,685)
Furness, Brian	4:36:56 (20,236)
Furness, Paul R	3:08:33 (1,856)
Furness, Tom	4:20:15 (16,077)
Furniss, Henry W	2:50:09 (511)
Furniss, Malcolm E	3:55:56 (10,062)
Fursey, Karl R	3:49:46 (8,444)
Fursey, Robert G	2:59:20 (1,105)
Furze, Jim R	3:42:50 (8,018)
Fussey, Adam J	4:14:46 (14,745)
Fustok, Salah	4:08:34 (13,252)
Futrell, Rod	3:35:57 (5,602)
Fyfe, Gregory R	3:55:15 (9,863)
Gabbert, Uwe	4:13:49 (14,521)
Gabbott, Jeremy A	4:27:15 (17,908)
Gable, Jeff	4:04:53 (12,402)
Gabrael, Admon	5:15:50 (27,112)
Gabriel, Michael C	4:48:53 (22,855)
Gabriel, Miles E	3:49:59 (8,501)
Gabriel, Simon C	3:43:18 (6,918)
Gabriel, Yvon	3:57:08 (10,429)
Gaches, Anton M	3:58:49 (10,948)
Gacon, Norbert	3:56:53 (10,362)
Gadd, Ronald	4:15:09 (14,846)
Gaddes, Jimmy	5:11:11 (26,535)
Gadgil, Devendra V	5:56:12 (30,255)
Gaffiney, Christopher M	4:20:25 (16,136)

Gaffney, John A	6:16:33 (30,923)	
Gage, John A	4:08:42 (13,291)	
Gaherty, Richard	4:19:20 (15,866)	
Gahir, Paul	5:23:31 (27,924)	
Gailer, Giles	3:22:56 (3,434)	
Gaines, Tony N	4:59:45 (24,949)	
Gainham, Justin C	5:54:38 (30,179)	
Gainlet, Patrick	3:49:41 (8,419)	
Gair, Christopher C	5:37:35 (29,156)	
Gair, Geoff K	5:11:28 (26,574)	
Gaitskell, Laurence G	4:20:31 (16,164)	
Gajadhar, Howard W	4:00:19 (11,363)	
Gajbutowicz, Andrzej	4:16:26 (15,157)	
Gale, Christopher D	4:51:38 (23,367)	
Gale, Matthew T	3:46:49 (7,707)	
Galea, Ian	4:46:18 (22,317)	
Galera-Valera, José M	4:26:05 (17,600)	
Galica, Mark P	5:25:36 (28,148)	
Gall, Robert	3:53:00 (9,257)	
Gallacher, Russell	3:46:40 (7,673)	
Gallacher, Scott J	4:14:36 (14,706)	
Gallagher, Christian J	4:38:28 (20,587)	
Gallagher, Kevin J	3:55:11 (9,845)	
Gallagher, Leslie J	4:55:02 (24,002)	
Gallagher, Mark	5:07:33 (26,050)	
Gallagher, Mark N	5:59:09 (30,371)	
Gallagher, Michael	4:31:07 (18,880)	
Gallagher, Richard	4:42:15 (21,397)	
Gallard, Richard J	3:26:04 (3,856)	
Gallazzi-Ralph, Charles	4:16:09 (15,093)	
Galley, André G	3:25:23 (3,745)	
Galley, Junior	2:56:46 (867)	
Galleymore, John	4:41:17 (21,181)	
Galliford, Miles	4:35:38 (19,950)	
Gallimore, Adam	3:24:58 (3,688)	
Galling, John R	3:06:05 (1,618)	
Gallivan, John F	6:32:03 (31,245)	
Gallo, Simon J	5:07:56 (26,103)	
Galloway, David R	3:09:10 (1,913)	
Galloway, George E	5:32:40 (28,788)	
Galloway, Gregory A	6:30:50 (31,219)	
Galloway, Shane D	5:32:25 (28,768)	
Galloway, Steve J	4:37:53 (20,429)	
Galloway, Thomas J	4:41:47 (21,304)	
Galpin, Matthew D	4:29:06 (18,377)	
Galpin, Vic A	3:53:41 (9,415)	
Gambelli, Michael J	3:58:45 (10,930)	
Gamble, Karl	4:57:27 (24,486)	
Gamble, Richard S	5:29:09 (28,499)	
Gamble, Rob G	3:43:43 (6,998)	
Gambrill, Michael C	4:25:29 (17,424)	
Gammage, Richard	3:18:37 (2,913)	
Gammon, Vincent J	3:35:01 (5,429)	
Gamston, Paul S	3:06:31 (1,655)	
Gamwells, Thomas O	5:30:09 (28,596)	
Gandhi, Raghav	4:18:25 (15,642)	
Gandon, Andrew J	3:19:37 (3,029)	
Gandy, Anthony P	4:29:34 (18,511)	
Gane, Jeremy C	4:14:43 (14,732)	
Ganesh, Jonathan	6:32:56 (31,261)	
Ganne, Jean M	3:06:54 (1,694)	
Gannicliffe, Christopher M	4:13:17 (14,399)	
Gannon, James W	3:58:39 (10,909)	
Gannon, Martin J	3:37:17 (5,832)	
Gannon, Peter J	4:26:52 (17,798)	
Gantley, Stephen O	3:59:10 (11,049)	
Garatti, Emiliano	4:03:21 (12,046)	
Garbett, Anthony	4:42:57 (21,555)	
Garbutt, Keith	2:44:27 (301)	
Garcha, Jas	4:38:57 (20,706)	
Garcha, Parvinder	5:37:14 (29,128)	
Garcia, Gustavo M	4:04:06 (12,211)	
Garcia, Patrick	3:42:54 (6,835)	
Garcia Eickelberg, Jorge	3:55:44 (10,001)	
Garcia-Martinez, Vicente	2:40:56 (225)	
Gard, Philip D	3:54:57 (9,768)	
Gardam, Matthew R	5:39:25 (29,303)	
Gardener, Chris	4:35:00 (19,819)	
Gardham, Tony	3:53:11 (9,310)	
Gardham, Lee J	4:42:53 (21,538)	
Gardiner, David	2:36:29 (142)	
Gardiner, Graham J	4:45:36 (22,167)	
Gardiner, John P	3:20:49 (3,181)	
Gardiner, Kevin L	3:53:21 (9,351)	
Gardiner, Paul J	5:49:42 (29,944)	
Gardiner, Philip J	3:17:47 (2,828)	
Gardiner, Richard H	2:26:08 (58)	
Gardiner, Willard D	4:11:45 (14,032)	
Gardner, Adrian	3:27:06 (4,043)	
Gardner, Dean J	4:27:52 (18,059)	
Gardner, Dean R	3:37:28 (5,870)	
Gardner, Duncan J	3:54:14 (9,572)	
Gardner, Ian F	3:20:51 (3,184)	
Gardner, Jai R	3:43:33 (6,968)	
Gardner, Jim	3:47:20 (7,837)	
Gardner, Keith D	4:32:37 (19,266)	
Gardner, Nicholas J	3:48:50 (8,222)	
Gardner, Nicholas J	4:25:45 (17,496)	
Gardner, Nigel D	4:29:22 (18,457)	
Gardner, Richard C	3:59:13 (11,064)	
Gardner, Robert J	3:44:52 (7,277)	
Gardner, Stuart	3:53:50 (9,453)	
Gardner, Timothy R	3:51:36 (8,916)	
Gardner, Toby C	3:51:14 (8,813)	
Garfield-Bennett, Edward C	5:48:30 (29,882)	
Gargallo, Henri	3:32:02 (4,931)	
Gargan, Nicholas J	4:22:44 (16,755)	
Gargaro, Vincent	3:58:27 (10,834)	
Gargiulo, Carlo	3:50:19 (8,581)	
Garland, Martin P	6:52:03 (31,531)	
Garland, Matthew J	4:56:22 (24,276)	
Garland, Michael	3:27:09 (4,053)	
Garland, Michael J	3:58:11 (10,750)	
Garland, Neil E	3:50:57 (8,741)	
Garlick, Peter A	4:34:59 (19,817)	
Garlick, Richard E	5:38:26 (29,224)	
Garlinge, Terry J	3:25:53 (3,825)	
Garman, John P	4:46:29 (22,354)	
Garmany, David H	4:18:13 (15,591)	
Garmson, John	2:53:04 (647)	
Garner, Joe P	4:19:51 (15,987)	
Garner, Les	4:56:45 (24,352)	
Garner, Michael	4:17:01 (15,307)	
Garner, Richard S	3:53:20 (9,348)	
Garnett, Howard K	4:22:01 (16,544)	
Garnier, Gerard	3:46:09 (7,559)	
Garnish, Jeffrey	4:08:01 (13,117)	
Garnsworthy, Duncan C	4:44:06 (21,815)	
Garrad-Cole, John W	3:27:49 (4,188)	
Garrard, Boyd C	3:19:39 (3,038)	
Garrard, Robert C	3:43:03 (6,859)	
Garratt, David J	4:27:15 (17,908)	
Garratt, Mark	2:56:04 (815)	
Garrett, Anthony P	4:08:54 (13,348)	
Garrett, Michael A	2:53:43 (675)	
Garrett, Philip A	4:54:03 (23,806)	
Garrett, William	4:05:27 (12,523)	
Garrity, Sam T	3:46:44 (7,686)	
Garrity, Terry	3:33:35 (5,200)	
Garrod, Adrian L	4:01:35 (11,620)	
Garrod, Steven	4:07:17 (12,962)	
Garside, Daniel S	5:34:03 (28,892)	
Garside, Duncan	5:00:58 (25,139)	
Garside, Paul	3:53:29 (9,376)	
Garside, Simon D	3:13:17 (2,340)	
Garstka, Sebastian	4:53:36 (23,725)	
Garvey, Chris J	4:10:12 (13,680)	
Garwood, Barry J	4:39:32 (20,829)	
Garwood, Nigel R	4:21:40 (16,439)	
Garwood, Robert M	5:23:25 (27,908)	
Garzia, Carmine	3:53:27 (9,366)	
Gascoigne, Mark Thomas T	3:27:12 (4,064)	
Gascoigne-Pees, Edward	5:05:57 (25,837)	
Gashe, Terence A	3:47:01 (7,756)	
Gaskarth, Andrew	3:00:36 (1,200)	
Gaskell, Anthony J	4:09:33 (13,512)	
Gaskell, Robert W	5:15:22 (27,062)	
Gasparini, Ivo	4:17:50 (15,517)	
Gasparroni, Max	3:35:49 (5,575)	
Gasper, Matthew	4:43:18 (21,636)	
Gasser, Timothy P	4:29:48 (18,583)	
Gasson, Brian E	4:19:03 (15,786)	
Gasson, Clive D	5:46:38 (29,797)	
Gasson, William J	6:18:26 (30,968)	
Gaston, Mathew R	4:23:46 (17,008)	
Gaston, Paul	4:16:18 (15,118)	
Gate, Andrew M	4:00:18 (11,358)	
Gatens, John R	3:48:10 (8,039)	
Gathercole, Darren T	5:02:28 (25,367)	
Gatiss, Ian W	5:20:21 (27,614)	
Gatley, James A	6:24:13 (31,116)	
Gatward, Jonathan	4:21:01 (16,284)	
Gaudon, Philippe	3:53:00 (9,257)	
Gaudreau, Robert	4:40:01 (20,924)	
Gauld, Sid	3:47:30 (7,879)	
Gaulder, Nicholas R	3:17:21 (2,790)	
Gaume, Marcelo	3:18:00 (2,849)	
Gaunt, Alistair J	4:59:24 (24,883)	
Gaunt, Martin	2:50:03 (507)	
Gaunt, Mike	4:38:51 (20,683)	
Gaunt-Edwards, Stephen	3:57:36 (10,568)	
Gaut, Gary P	4:16:54 (15,282)	
Gautama, Amit	4:38:17 (20,544)	
Gauthier, James D	3:11:14 (2,117)	
Gavin, Robert P	5:16:20 (27,175)	
Gawler, Keith R	4:25:14 (17,366)	
Gawn, Richard A	4:47:36 (22,591)	
Gay, Andrew J	5:06:04 (25,852)	
Gay, John R	4:11:14 (13,919)	
Gay, Richard	3:14:05 (2,446)	
Gaygan, Rob D	3:32:53 (5,079)	
Gayler, Duncan R	4:54:49 (23,962)	
Gaylord, Richard	4:58:52 (24,774)	
Gaymer, Adam T	4:41:30 (21,245)	
Gaymer, John G	5:08:54 (26,223)	
Gaymer, Nigel A	4:41:27 (21,230)	
Gayton, Alna C	4:44:20 (21,869)	
Gaytten, James	4:12:55 (14,307)	
Gaze, Robert A	5:49:51 (29,955)	
Gaze, Stevie T	4:36:40 (20,172)	
Gazeley, Simon	4:29:13 (18,406)	
Gazzard, Neil C	3:51:19 (8,836)	
Geach, Antony D	3:45:19 (19,889)	
Geal, Tim P	3:59:17 (11,083)	
Geaney, John S	4:04:40 (12,344)	
Geaney, Michael	3:24:52 (3,672)	
Gearing, Alan P	3:46:49 (7,707)	
Gearing, Daniel L	3:18:49 (2,930)	
Geary, Martin	3:55:53 (10,045)	
Geary, Vivian	4:51:28 (23,341)	
Gebbie, Paul	4:36:44 (20,188)	
Geddes, Fraser H	5:17:53 (27,253)	
Geddes, Ian	4:19:48 (15,975)	
Geddes, Tom A	4:25:20 (17,389)	
Gedin, Mats R	2:54:07 (701)	
Gedye, David K	4:45:40 (22,182)	
Gee, Christopher K	4:34:05 (19,603)	
Gee, Michael N	7:28:52 (31,840)	
Gee, Raymond	3:51:19 (8,836)	
Gee, Shaun	4:32:44 (19,300)	
Geen, Peter R	4:19:10 (15,822)	
Geenevasen, Lowie	3:29:26 (4,493)	
Geeson, Andrew L	3:51:54 (8,989)	
Geeson, Mark R	4:09:32 (13,507)	
Geisler, Lars	3:24:15 (3,595)	
Geitner, Joseph J	3:16:51 (2,733)	
Geldart, Jonathan C	5:14:57 (27,022)	
Gelder, Philip	4:36:48 (20,202)	
Gell, Colin	2:54:51 (738)	
Geller, Jon D	3:10:06 (2,011)	
Gelling, Stuart J	4:41:41 (21,276)	
Gemmell, Gordon D	3:53:26 (9,363)	
Generali, Gabriele	3:56:36 (10,280)	
Genevaz, Dominique	4:28:54 (18,327)	
Gentilhomme, Jean Luc E	3:59:11 (11,054)	
Gentle, Christopher R	3:23:35 (3,511)	
Geoghegan, Craig	3:31:40 (4,869)	
Geoghegan, Michael J	2:47:23 (397)	
George, Daryl R	5:18:40 (27,430)	
George, David J	4:08:41 (13,283)	
George, Graeme N	5:28:27 (28,432)	
George, James M	4:03:31 (12,082)	
George, Michael E	4:08:31 (13,236)	
George, Rayner C	4:12:26 (14,179)	
George, Richard	3:01:16 (1,263)	
George, Simon B	4:12:26 (14,179)	
Georgeson, Ian L	4:06:33 (12,793)	
Georgi, Thomas	3:59:08 (11,040)	
Georgiades, Dimos	3:58:48 (10,945)	

Georgiou, Chris	3:48:39	(8,168)
Geraghty, Keith	4:35:55	(20,006)
Geraghty, Roger C	2:55:10	(766)
Gerard, Philip B	3:27:38	(4,154)
Gerard, Tiennault	3:28:45	(4,364)
Gerber, Bernd	5:37:55	(29,173)
Gereke, Carsten	3:07:45	(1,784)
Gerges, Andy M	4:20:53	(16,256)
Gerhard, Flesch	4:45:34	(22,154)
Gerhard, Rolf	3:09:48	(1,979)
Gerrard, Colin J	4:13:13	(14,385)
Gerrard, Nick J	4:13:22	(14,423)
Gerrard, Simon C	4:06:52	(12,855)
Gerschner, Joerg	4:11:26	(13,956)
Gershilick, Anthony H	4:34:58	(19,813)
Gerundini, Richard	3:13:46	(2,404)
Gething, Fraser	3:22:50	(3,424)
Gething, Julian	3:55:43	(9,997)
Gething Lewis, Patrick J	4:11:38	(14,011)
Getvoldsen, Benjamin R	4:43:01	(21,566)
Geut, Jeroen C	3:55:45	(10,005)
Gevertz, Damian J	3:45:58	(7,521)
Geyser, Verster J	4:23:23	(16,914)
Ghalley, Jitmangat S	4:59:02	(24,801)
Gharbi, Babak	4:44:53	(21,995)
Gharib, Jaouad	2:07:02	(3)
Ghattaura, Sukhbeer S	4:55:10	(24,031)
Gheeraert, Frederic	3:59:19	(11,092)
Ghitti, Adalberto	4:55:21	(24,073)
Ghotra, Gurpal S	5:15:56	(27,122)
Ghrous, Nassir	4:30:29	(18,754)
Giacche, Robert	5:40:13	(29,351)
Giacomini, Fabrizio	3:05:50	(1,591)
Giambiasi, Philippe	4:24:04	(17,076)
Giannerini, Paolo	4:49:26	(22,961)
Giaretta, Ben	4:43:02	(21,570)
Gibb, Andy L	3:41:43	(6,586)
Gibb, Kenneth D	4:16:06	(15,079)
Gibbbs, Scott A	3:29:01	(4,416)
Gibbens, Richard B	3:44:28	(7,175)
Gibbins, Alex N	3:01:23	(1,271)
Gibbins, Andrew J	4:05:39	(12,583)
Gibbins, Martin J	4:58:01	(24,597)
Gibbon, Anthony D	4:06:17	(12,733)
Gibbon, Mark A	4:33:44	(19,511)
Gibbon, Phil M	4:16:04	(15,065)
Gibbons, Alan M	5:22:01	(27,775)
Gibbons, Andrew P	4:05:33	(12,555)
Gibbons, Brian	4:50:23	(23,153)
Gibbons, Duncan A	4:23:16	(16,885)
Gibbons, John	4:12:32	(14,214)
Gibbons, Kevin M	3:58:37	(10,891)
Gibbons, Michael P	3:26:17	(3,885)
Gibbons, Paul	3:45:48	(7,484)
Gibbons, Robert C	4:26:57	(17,825)
Gibbons, Ron	4:44:08	(21,825)
Gibbs, Ben	4:10:18	(13,705)
Gibbs, David W	4:13:44	(14,500)
Gibbs, Jamie S	5:06:34	(25,920)
Gibbs, Jonathan	5:46:16	(29,768)
Gibbs, Michael	3:57:29	(10,533)
Gibbs, Neil	4:44:22	(21,876)
Gibbs, Robert M	4:28:28	(18,220)
Gibbs, Stephen P	4:44:14	(21,844)
Gibbs, Stuart P	5:33:45	(28,866)
Gibbs, Tony	5:05:55	(25,828)
Giboreau, Henri	4:00:39	(11,416)
Gibson, Alan	4:50:51	(23,243)
Gibson, Andrew	3:45:22	(7,378)
Gibson, Chris M	4:44:56	(22,017)
Gibson, Daniel S	5:24:28	(28,023)
Gibson, Darryn S	4:17:32	(15,433)
Gibson, David	2:58:32	(1,015)
Gibson, David	3:12:43	(2,275)
Gibson, David N	5:25:37	(28,151)
Gibson, Dewi B	4:11:24	(13,951)
Gibson, George A	3:37:38	(5,897)
Gibson, Jamie W	4:03:54	(12,169)
Gibson, Jason K	4:40:11	(20,959)
Gibson, John D	4:08:18	(13,177)
Gibson, Mark	3:50:00	(8,506)
Gibson, Nigel P	3:52:33	(9,139)
Gibson, Paul	4:32:52	(19,327)

Gibson, Peter G	3:53:07	(9,287)
Gibson, Steve	4:24:57	(17,294)
Gibson-Robinson, Richard	3:32:35	(5,024)
Gicquel, Pascal	3:05:12	(1,547)
Giele, Henk P	5:32:06	(28,738)
Giersten, Bjoern	4:38:54	(20,693)
Gifford, Ryan L	4:34:50	(19,784)
Giggins, Neil R	3:24:25	(3,618)
Gigot, Jacques	3:14:08	(2,457)
Gilad, Roey	4:04:32	(12,323)
Gilbert, Andy M	3:52:14	(9,064)
Gilbert, Christopher P	3:08:37	(1,858)
Gilbert, Daniel M	4:36:03	(20,043)
Gilbert, Drummond A	3:48:05	(8,020)
Gilbert, Ian J	4:33:07	(19,384)
Gilbert, Jonathan P	3:44:55	(7,292)
Gilbert, Jonny D	3:49:19	(8,331)
Gilbert, Justin C	4:43:05	(21,578)
Gilbert, Kenneth T	7:56:39	(31,929)
Gilbert, Max	4:02:06	(11,746)
Gilbert, Pascal	3:13:54	(2,424)
Gilbert, Peter J	3:52:23	(9,108)
Gilbert, Ralph R	3:23:34	(3,508)
Gilbert, Richard G	3:26:00	(3,850)
Gilbert, Robert J	3:55:22	(9,897)
Gilbert, Tim J	4:23:25	(16,926)
Gilbert, Will R	3:48:44	(8,195)
Gilbertson, Mark A	2:43:33	(279)
Gilby, Pete R	4:15:11	(14,855)
Gilchrist, Tyrone	5:13:52	(26,880)
Gildea, James M	3:52:56	(9,235)
Gilder, James	4:00:00	(11,296)
Gilderdale, Andrew	4:17:33	(15,439)
Giles, Andrew D	5:26:11	(28,211)
Giles, Christopher A	3:49:00	(8,254)
Giles, Edward	3:54:40	(9,686)
Giles, Mark A	4:09:43	(13,562)
Giles, Mark I	4:50:55	(23,258)
Giles, Matt J	2:43:54	(288)
Giles, Steve P	3:03:53	(1,440)
Giles, Stuart J	3:50:58	(8,743)
Gilkes, James W	3:45:43	(7,465)
Gill, Amarjit Singh	6:02:13	(30,492)
Gill, Anthony	3:19:10	(2,975)
Gill, Christopher B	4:55:04	(24,007)
Gill, Colin	4:06:06	(12,683)
Gill, Darren C	4:54:30	(23,896)
Gill, David	3:58:31	(10,860)
Gill, David K	3:45:09	(7,334)
Gill, Gary N	3:22:30	(3,375)
Gill, Gavin G	4:26:51	(17,785)
Gill, James S	3:24:32	(3,627)
Gill, Jonathan	3:38:26	(6,036)
Gill, Jonathan R	4:44:31	(21,913)
Gill, Oliver W	3:27:24	(4,103)
Gill, Ray	4:36:48	(20,202)
Gill, Shami	5:04:46	(25,659)
Gill, Tim C	3:49:04	(8,268)
Gillam, Stephen	4:35:36	(19,947)
Gillan, Lee	3:28:41	(4,349)
Gillard, Andrew	4:02:16	(11,800)
Gillen, Timothy	3:23:20	(3,481)
Gillespie, Michael R	3:08:04	(1,809)
Gillespie, Neil D	5:27:38	(28,364)
Gillespie, Peter	4:17:19	(15,374)
Gillett, Daniel J	2:57:59	(966)
Gillett, Simon P	3:37:45	(5,910)
Gillick, Kieran P	3:09:53	(1,994)
Gillick, Matthew	3:39:12	(6,163)
Gillies, Grant P	4:34:30	(19,712)
Gillies, Robert	3:45:28	(7,400)
Gillies, Stewart D	4:51:48	(23,397)
Gillies, Stuart	4:41:25	(21,222)
Gilliland, David	4:25:37	(17,456)
Gillingham, John M	4:14:49	(14,767)
Gillitt, Richard J	3:30:43	(4,729)
Gilliver, Andy D	4:22:07	(16,576)
Gillman, Clive R	3:34:28	(5,335)
Gillott, Martin	4:12:35	(14,228)
Gillott, Sebastian D	4:03:07	(11,983)
Gillson, Stephen P	3:07:52	(1,792)
Gilman, Christopher E	3:35:24	(5,502)
Gilmore, Aaron	3:33:30	(5,189)

Gilmore, Alexander T	3:23:43	(3,530)
Gilmore, David E	4:26:42	(17,750)
Gilmour, Patrick	4:59:15	(24,839)
Gilroy, Francis J	3:07:54	(1,795)
Gilroy, William	4:55:55	(24,186)
Gil-Torregrosa, Bartholome	3:51:35	(8,913)
Giltrow, Mark J	4:52:51	(23,592)
Gimson, Ashley M	2:58:08	(981)
Ginley, Christopher	3:13:21	(2,350)
Ginty, Mark	4:00:53	(11,475)
Girard, Thierry	3:51:45	(8,955)
Girardelli, Adrian O	3:49:16	(8,323)
Girardet, Daniel	3:47:31	(7,883)
Giraudon, Marc G	6:18:19	(30,965)
Girlanda, Raffaele	3:22:43	(3,406)
Girling, Simon N	3:45:34	(7,428)
Girling, Stephen M	3:56:42	(10,302)
Gittoes, Robert J	3:29:59	(4,585)
Glackin, Brian	3:27:19	(4,084)
Gladwell, Nathan	4:29:14	(18,410)
Gladwin, Robert P	4:35:20	(19,893)
Glancy, Paul	3:28:51	(4,387)
Glancy, Steven R	5:10:43	(26,469)
Glanfield, Jon O	4:46:27	(22,349)
Glanville, Matthew	5:05:05	(25,700)
Glanville, Michael	4:19:40	(15,943)
Glanville, Richard	4:18:01	(15,557)
Glasby, Liam D	3:44:10	(7,110)
Glasgow, Andrew P	5:56:12	(30,255)
Glass, Stephen	4:19:41	(15,947)
Glassey, Ian	4:39:18	(20,792)
Glasson, Jamie	5:55:42	(30,231)
Glaves, Guy R	3:41:45	(6,597)
Glaysher, Rhys G	4:52:25	(23,522)
Glazebrook, Martin	4:58:21	(24,676)
Glazier, Darren	5:00:44	(25,101)
Glen, Andrew	3:27:31	(4,131)
Glen, Sandy	4:38:03	(20,484)
Glencross, Ian	4:41:41	(21,276)
Glencross, Philip S	4:28:56	(18,334)
Glendinning, Paul A	3:05:34	(1,575)
Glenister, James P	3:55:00	(9,782)
Glenn, Simon P	3:50:12	(8,547)
Glennie, Paul D	2:47:21	(396)
Glennon, Liam A	4:07:32	(13,017)
Glibbery, Adam J	4:25:27	(17,413)
Glisson, Michael J	5:10:26	(26,414)
Glover, Adrian D	4:17:11	(15,346)
Glover, James R	4:45:06	(22,064)
Glover, Lee A	4:07:33	(13,024)
Glover, Mark A	5:39:38	(29,313)
Glover, Matthew W	4:04:51	(12,392)
Gluning, Mark	4:06:11	(12,708)
Glynn, Alan	3:40:56	(6,462)
Glynn, John T	3:59:28	(11,140)
Glynn, Matthew E	3:27:16	(4,077)
Glynn, Paul F	4:20:16	(16,085)
Goad, Ben C	4:41:53	(21,323)
Goby, Howard E	3:43:59	(7,063)
Godbee, Peter J	4:11:24	(13,951)
Godber, David A	5:21:46	(27,755)
Godber, Rupert	4:25:45	(17,496)
Godbold, Matthew K	3:37:13	(5,817)
Godbold, Paul	3:51:55	(8,995)
Goddard, Barry	4:12:18	(14,149)
Goddard, Brian	4:40:09	(20,951)
Goddard, George	4:37:07	(20,278)
Goddard, Jeremy P	3:55:50	(10,028)
Goddard, John S	5:56:56	(30,285)
Goddard, Mark S	3:24:50	(3,667)
Goddard, Paul	3:57:18	(10,481)
Goddard, Steve	4:25:46	(17,503)
Goddard, Trevor E	3:33:35	(5,200)
Godden, Daniel A	4:20:19	(16,106)
Godden, Neil G	4:53:24	(23,687)
Godfray, Tim	4:59:26	(24,689)
Godfrey, Christopher N	4:22:13	(16,613)
Godfrey, Darren	7:12:22	(31,727)
Godfrey, Keir	4:47:58	(22,666)
Godfrey, Malcolm	3:29:01	(4,416)
Godfrey, Oliver C	3:13:10	(2,324)
Godot, Florian	3:15:23	(2,587)
Godrey, Andrew	4:28:56	(18,334)

Godsiff, Anthony A 3:36:14 (5,648)
Godwin, Philip R 3:57:49 (10,622)
Goeman, Wim J 5:05:17 (25,721)
Goertz, Frank 3:11:40 (2,154)
Goessweiner, Herwig C 4:26:25 (17,677)
Goff, Matthew P 3:55:33 (9,947)
Goffee, Robert 4:26:44 (17,755)
Goffredi, Remo 3:16:15 (2,666)
Goglio, Piero 4:23:55 (17,043)
Goguen, Michael 3:45:42 (7,461)
Gohil, Navnit L 6:13:28 (30,831)
Gohil, Vijay 4:53:49 (23,769)
Golby, Robert A 5:05:18 (25,726)
Gold, Adam J 5:01:26 (25,214)
Gold, Damian 3:24:41 (3,650)
Gold, David A 3:51:52 (8,981)
Gold, James A 4:25:19 (17,384)
Gold, Joel A 4:03:06 (11,979)
Gold, Jonathan 6:59:35 (31,618)
Gold, Paul A 4:01:38 (11,629)
Goldberg, Robert D 3:48:46 (8,200)
Golden, Brian C 2:52:44 (628)
Goldhill, Warren 4:24:50 (17,260)
Goldie, Johnny 3:29:16 (4,464)
Golding, John F 3:48:43 (8,189)
Golding, Neil D 3:34:12 (5,298)
Golding, Richard D 5:01:06 (25,160)
Goldman, Darren P 3:43:32 (6,965)
Goldman, James S 3:29:42 (4,533)
Goldsbrough, James 4:42:05 (21,366)
Goldsmith, Barry R 5:01:25 (25,211)
Goldsmith, Brian J 3:57:29 (10,533)
Goldsmith, Ian C 4:25:15 (17,370)
Goldsmith, Paul 4:54:55 (23,983)
Goldsmith, Paul R 3:33:19 (5,164)
Goldsmith, Simon A 3:43:14 (6,902)
Goldsmith, Stuart G 4:03:42 (12,125)
Goldsmith, Tim 4:14:58 (14,798)
Goldstein, Steven N 4:45:53 (22,225)
Goldsworthy, Gary L 4:35:31 (19,929)
Goldthorp, Alan 4:07:24 (12,989)
Goldthorp, Ian M 4:19:57 (16,013)
Goldup, Nick C 4:23:49 (17,017)
Golledge, Alex J 4:38:01 (20,475)
Gollings, Christopher K 3:49:15 (8,319)
Gomery, Simon A 4:38:21 (20,558)
Gomez, Carlos M 3:58:38 (10,899)
Gomez, Luis F 3:14:00 (2,432)
Gomez-Martinez, Miguel A 3:33:05 (5,112)
Gompertz, Gary G 5:26:02 (28,200)
Gondeck, Matthias 3:40:31 (6,408)
Gonsalves, Victor 4:04:30 (12,316)
Gonzalez, Jorge E 3:33:51 (5,244)
Gonzalez Jimenez, César L 4:03:02 (11,960)
Gooch, Graham A 4:23:29 (16,937)
Good, Christopher R 3:24:33 (3,630)
Good, Duncan G 4:31:04 (18,870)
Good, Michael E 4:00:25 (11,385)
Goodall, Francis J 3:36:05 (5,625)
Goodall, Ian 3:45:26 (7,395)
Goodall, James A 4:44:24 (21,889)
Goodall, Malcolm 3:40:40 (6,427)
Goodall, Martin J 4:12:21 (14,158)
Goodall, Peter W 4:09:24 (13,475)
Goodbun, Mark J 3:58:07 (10,715)
Goodchild, Nicholas J 4:01:48 (11,668)
Goode, James E 3:12:22 (2,236)
Goode, Paul J 3:54:44 (9,704)
Goode, Philip 2:55:05 (760)
Goode, Scott D 3:41:39 (6,577)
Gooden, Graham J 4:14:00 (14,561)
Gooden, Peter J 5:31:14 (28,680)
Gooderham, Maurice A 6:11:23 (30,769)
Goodeve, Luke C 4:28:12 (18,148)
Goodey, David J 4:29:20 (18,444)
Goodfellow, David R 4:47:04 (22,468)
Goodge, Doug J 3:48:36 (8,150)
Goodger, Gary 3:34:25 (5,327)
Goodier, Philip J 3:19:15 (2,992)
Gooding, Russell 4:18:05 (15,572)
Gooding, Simon P 4:28:26 (18,206)
Goodlet, Wade H 3:59:36 (11,188)
Goodman, Alan J 3:59:31 (11,166)
Goodman, James A 4:40:43 (21,068)
Goodman, James A 5:12:24 (26,680)
Goodman, Patrick J 4:01:36 (11,622)
Goodman, William A 5:13:15 (26,799)
Goodrich, Luke M 3:32:49 (5,063)
Goodrich, Mark A 4:41:51 (21,317)
Goodrich, Mark B 4:09:55 (13,615)
Goodrich, Steven G 5:16:15 (27,162)
Goodridge, Christopher M 2:29:42 (79)
Goodrum, Paul J 3:46:45 (7,695)
Goodrum, Russell 3:55:49 (10,022)
Goodsall, James A 3:28:05 (4,239)
Goodwill, Tony 4:12:10 (14,130)
Goodwin, Andrew W 5:17:39 (27,322)
Goodwin, David A 3:51:31 (8,891)
Goodwin, David J 4:31:51 (19,061)
Goodwin, Ian 3:44:42 (7,242)
Goodwin, Justin S 4:29:08 (18,389)
Goodwin, Martin D 4:52:58 (23,610)
Goodwin, Nicholas 5:26:00 (28,197)
Goodwin, Nigel J 4:38:09 (20,508)
Goodwin, Richard S 3:20:44 (3,164)
Goodwin, Stephen H 3:13:50 (2,412)
Goodwin, Syd C 4:41:22 (21,210)
Goodworth, David J 3:40:46 (6,438)
Goody, Chris A 4:53:48 (23,766)
Goody, Kevin G 7:03:44 (31,659)
Goody, Mark J 4:08:43 (13,298)
Goodyear, Paul A 3:34:48 (5,389)
Goodyer, Martin S 4:07:23 (12,982)
Goosey, Neil A 4:28:57 (18,342)
Goowin, William D 3:30:48 (4,744)
Gopal, Daniel 4:56:14 (24,249)
Gorasia, Dinesh N 5:41:31 (29,449)
Gorasia, Jayesh G 5:04:59 (25,690)
Gord, Paul M 3:53:08 (9,291)
Gordine, Alan R 5:06:04 (25,852)
Gordon, Andrew A 3:27:54 (4,211)
Gordon, Andrew J 4:40:16 (20,976)
Gordon, Barry 5:01:52 (25,280)
Gordon, Chris I 4:15:15 (14,870)
Gordon, Christoper R 4:51:51 (23,408)
Gordon, Christopher H 4:14:21 (14,636)
Gordon, Glenn M 3:42:04 (6,666)
Gordon, Jeffrey 3:58:38 (10,899)
Gordon, Johnathan N 3:47:04 (7,770)
Gordon, Jonathan S 4:45:19 (22,101)
Gordon, Ron M 4:44:51 (21,988)
Gordon Clark, Matthew 4:55:36 (24,118)
Gordon-Watson, Charles P 6:59:31 (31,617)
Gore, Michael N 2:43:37 (281)
Gorman, David 4:01:29 (11,592)
Gort, Thomas B 4:13:01 (14,332)
Gorton, Mark A 4:19:37 (15,931)
Gosling, Christopher P 5:39:51 (29,324)
Gosling, Raymond J 6:18:44 (30,986)
Gosling, Steven 5:24:26 (28,022)
Goslinga, Cees 4:15:32 (14,936)
Gosney, Paul 3:26:50 (3,992)
Goswell, Philip 4:19:34 (15,925)
Gottberg, Thomas 4:27:23 (17,934)
Gottelier, Patrick G 4:49:26 (22,961)
Gotts, Mark D 4:17:19 (15,374)
Goucher, Dave L 5:41:24 (29,438)
Goudie, Andrew J 3:35:55 (5,591)
Goudie, Chris 7:06:58 (31,679)
Gough, Charles A 5:03:16 (25,485)
Gough, Geoffrey D 4:24:55 (17,288)
Gough, James D 4:20:25 (16,136)
Gough, James G 5:25:50 (28,179)
Gough, Kevin 4:06:41 (12,817)
Gough, Paul 3:46:04 (7,539)
Gougousis, Konstantinos 2:22:47 (48)
Gouin, Pierre 3:22:24 (3,361)
Goulbourne, Patrick W 4:05:55 (12,643)
Gould, Daniel 3:59:34 (11,177)
Gould, John 4:32:07 (19,139)
Gould, Norman 5:27:31 (28,357)
Gould, Paul S 3:49:29 (8,370)
Gould, Peter A 3:56:46 (10,318)
Gould, Richard W 3:57:30 (10,538)
Gould, Simon J 4:20:53 (16,256)
Gould, Thomas 3:47:58 (7,988)
Gould, Timothy J 5:40:41 (29,394)
Gould, William A 4:30:24 (18,733)
Gouldburn, Sean 4:09:21 (13,462)
Goulding, John A 4:29:33 (18,505)
Goundry, Andrew C 3:34:27 (5,333)
Goundry, William R 3:28:10 (4,256)
Goupille, Philippe 3:28:27 (4,310)
Gourhant, Yvon 4:02:10 (11,769)
Gouriet, Richard J 5:38:13 (29,197)
Gourmez, Lucien 4:18:59 (15,775)
Gouwy, Pascal 3:29:42 (4,533)
Govoni, Riccardo 3:43:37 (6,984)
Gow, Bryn A 4:57:03 (24,413)
Gow, Chris 4:03:10 (11,997)
Gowans, Neill M 3:46:20 (7,610)
Gowans, Robert B 5:32:09 (28,746)
Goward, Robert J 4:45:20 (22,104)
Gower, Matt R 2:58:01 (972)
Gowing, Nigel P 4:38:04 (20,488)
Gowthorpe, Clive G 4:01:12 (11,546)
Goy, William 4:35:56 (20,009)
Goyheneix, Philippe 3:05:16 (1,553)
Grace, Ian F 3:30:08 (4,622)
Grace, John 4:57:33 (24,503)
Grace, Stuart 5:03:59 (25,579)
Gracie, Nick J 3:05:00 (1,524)
Grad, Werner 4:11:18 (13,932)
Grady, John N 3:52:19 (9,091)
Graefe, Hagen 3:43:51 (7,028)
Grafton, Mathew J 4:14:19 (14,626)
Graham, Alan 4:00:24 (11,380)
Graham, Alastair E 4:40:16 (20,976)
Graham, Alphonso R 6:41:28 (31,380)
Graham, Andrew N 3:34:23 (5,323)
Graham, Bill 2:53:53 (689)
Graham, Carroll 3:42:14 (6,691)
Graham, Charles 3:58:03 (10,689)
Graham, Charles F 3:25:59 (3,846)
Graham, Dominic A 3:57:05 (10,411)
Graham, Dominic E 4:15:50 (15,010)
Graham, Hugh 4:14:06 (14,587)
Graham, James M 4:23:41 (16,980)
Graham, Jeremy 4:21:41 (16,443)
Graham, Jim E 4:49:52 (23,057)
Graham, John 3:08:06 (1,814)
Graham, John 5:15:26 (27,070)
Graham, Lee A 4:06:18 (12,736)
Graham, Mark R 3:05:39 (1,579)
Graham, Martin J 5:39:19 (29,294)
Graham, Michael J 3:54:55 (9,756)
Graham, Peter 4:00:06 (11,316)
Graham, Ray K 4:14:10 (14,601)
Graham, Richard 4:05:07 (12,454)
Graham, Stephen T 5:13:32 (26,831)
Graham, Warren V 4:24:59 (17,307)
Graham Smith, Nicholas D 5:05:54 (25,823)
Grainge, Duncan R 5:07:18 (26,020)
Grainger, David J 4:21:41 (16,443)
Grainger, Luke 5:46:11 (29,759)
Grainger, Nick R 4:47:48 (22,634)
Grainger, Simon J 3:46:51 (7,713)
Grainger, Steve 3:27:11 (4,061)
Gramegna, Angelo 4:18:24 (15,632)
Gran, Ulf G 4:18:09 (15,584)
Granby, Mark L 3:48:26 (8,102)
Grandison, Rowen D 3:34:05 (5,282)
Grandmougin, Patrick 3:19:28 (3,016)
Grange, Andrew 4:09:23 (13,470)
Granger, Derek J 3:50:15 (8,563)
Granges, Thierry 3:00:49 (1,218)
Granier, Jean Pierre 4:18:03 (15,565)
Granigg, Raimund 4:21:40 (16,439)
Granstrom, James 4:02:47 (11,921)
Grant, Allan J 4:32:35 (19,254)
Grant, Allen 3:35:53 (5,587)
Grant, Andrew 5:38:55 (29,256)
Grant, Antonio B 2:53:08 (650)
Grant, Carl A 3:27:47 (4,185)
Grant, Clive 4:05:08 (12,455)
Grant, David B 3:28:14 (4,273)
Grant, David R 4:05:55 (12,643)
Grant, Frank 4:08:29 (13,224)
Grant, Ian R 6:03:58 (30,564)

Grant, John 5:06:32 (25,914)
Grant, Joubert 4:05:19 (12,489)
Grant, Ken P 3:58:34 (10,879)
Grant, Kevin 4:45:14 (22,087)
Grant, Matthew 3:33:06 (5,116)
Grant, Michael J 3:26:34 (3,926)
Grant, Michael J 3:30:38 (4,716)
Grant, Neil C 5:09:07 (26,256)
Grant, Patrick E 3:53:31 (9,380)
Grant, Patrick J 3:48:33 (8,135)
Grant, Peter 4:24:05 (17,086)
Grant, Peter J 3:58:14 (10,766)
Grant, Stuart J 5:28:14 (28,414)
Grant-Peterkin, Hugh D 3:49:07 (8,286)
Grass, Richard J 4:56:02 (24,217)
Grasset, Chris 4:29:59 (18,626)
Grattan, Patrick 4:10:05 (13,653)
Grave, Andrew J 5:40:24 (29,369)
Graves, Adam J 4:47:41 (22,614)
Graves, John 3:52:06 (9,036)
Graves, Matthew A 3:32:34 (5,019)
Graville, Jonathan R 4:47:24 (22,542)
Gravis, Craig B 4:13:18 (14,403)
Gray, Anthony D 3:12:32 (2,256)
Gray, Brian A 5:27:48 (28,384)
Gray, Christopher J 3:42:20 (6,705)
Gray, Denis K 4:46:44 (22,397)
Gray, Dennis 4:45:07 (22,067)
Gray, Ian 5:24:32 (28,029)
Gray, James 3:45:40 (7,446)
Gray, John B 3:50:31 (8,631)
Gray, Leon 4:58:45 (24,760)
Gray, Malcolm J 5:37:21 (29,138)
Gray, Mark J 3:49:22 (8,344)
Gray, Matthew B 4:24:40 (17,223)
Gray, Michael D 4:50:32 (23,188)
Gray, Myles R 4:24:20 (17,150)
Gray, Nigel 4:48:49 (22,841)
Gray, Paul 3:54:50 (9,732)
Gray, Paul 5:49:28 (29,928)
Gray, Paul R 3:30:22 (4,665)
Gray, Paul W 3:28:19 (4,285)
Gray, Rob 3:58:19 (10,795)
Gray, Robin D 3:57:17 (10,473)
Gray, Seamas 4:17:05 (15,321)
Gray, Simon T 4:32:28 (19,231)
Gray, Stefan N 3:59:13 (11,064)
Gray, Steven J 5:09:16 (26,272)
Gray, Thomas D 4:08:04 (13,128)
Gray, Todd C 3:31:24 (4,833)
Graybrook, Richard H 3:35:04 (5,436)
Graylen, Philip A 3:55:48 (10,016)
Grayson, Richard W 5:08:41 (26,200)
Greagsby, David J 4:17:36 (15,452)
Greany, Donald J 4:25:53 (17,536)
Greatrex, Robert J 4:15:56 (15,037)
Greaves, Andrew J 4:45:33 (22,148)
Greaves, Anthony B 4:08:32 (13,239)
Greaves, Barry J 4:54:20 (23,866)
Greaves, Gerard 4:01:27 (11,588)
Greaves, James C 3:58:03 (10,689)
Greaves, Jonathan M 3:07:19 (1,730)
Greaves, Martyn J 3:57:32 (10,550)
Greaves, Simon H 4:21:09 (16,300)
Grebowiec, Marek 3:48:40 (8,176)
Grech, Fabio 4:25:42 (17,477)
Greco, Aniello 2:49:04 (462)
Green, Adrian E 4:05:37 (12,575)
Green, Alan D 3:17:15 (2,780)
Green, Andrew 5:36:51 (29,094)
Green, Andrew D 4:24:31 (17,188)
Green, Andrew L 4:16:18 (15,118)
Green, Andrew M 3:30:45 (4,733)
Green, Andrew W 4:55:55 (24,186)
Green, Anthony G 4:04:25 (12,288)
Green, Benjamin R 4:42:55 (21,548)
Green, Brian R 4:20:46 (16,225)
Green, Bryan F 5:25:33 (28,143)
Green, Charles R 2:57:48 (946)
Green, Clive A 3:57:17 (10,473)
Green, Clive R 5:24:49 (28,060)
Green, Daniel R 5:23:29 (27,916)
Green, Darrin J 5:24:50 (28,061)
Green, David E 4:40:24 (21,008)
Green, David J 3:12:24 (2,240)
Green, David J 3:29:59 (4,585)
Green, David P 3:26:07 (3,861)
Green, David R 4:26:52 (17,798)
Green, Ed N 3:59:30 (11,157)
Green, Eric 3:37:47 (5,916)
Green, Gareth J 3:33:44 (5,223)
Green, John 3:00:03 (1,161)
Green, John 3:55:03 (9,806)
Green, John W 3:56:28 (10,241)
Green, Jono W 4:26:38 (17,736)
Green, Laurence 3:03:30 (1,407)
Green, Matt J 4:51:06 (23,293)
Green, Matthew J 4:23:22 (16,905)
Green, Matthew R 3:38:56 (6,119)
Green, Michael 4:19:07 (15,810)
Green, Michael D 4:41:10 (21,150)
Green, Michael J 3:58:17 (10,785)
Green, Michael J 4:31:39 (19,011)
Green, Michael R 3:21:30 (3,257)
Green, Michael R 3:37:36 (5,890)
Green, Michael S 2:18:11 (24)
Green, Mick 3:08:18 (1,832)
Green, Mike A 5:48:43 (29,896)
Green, Nick E 3:51:13 (8,810)
Green, Norman J 3:49:31 (8,380)
Green, Paul 3:27:26 (4,113)
Green, Peter W 4:23:22 (16,905)
Green, Philip J 5:13:35 (26,842)
Green, Roger B 3:19:00 (2,949)
Green, Rupert J 4:53:56 (23,785)
Green, Sean S 5:05:30 (25,760)
Green, Steven L 3:19:50 (3,050)
Green, Stuart A 3:56:08 (10,117)
Green, Terry D 4:08:37 (13,261)
Greenall, John E 4:24:55 (17,288)
Greenall, Thomas L 5:23:18 (27,897)
Greenaway, Christopher J 4:51:55 (23,426)
Greenaway, Matthew J 4:52:09 (23,474)
Greene, Brendan 2:50:58 (542)
Greene, Brendan F 4:09:29 (13,494)
Greene, David A 5:51:21 (30,028)
Greene, Gavin R 3:54:11 (9,555)
Greene, Martin E 5:27:41 (28,370)
Greene, Mike T 4:20:15 (16,077)
Greene, Paul W 4:37:12 (20,298)
Greenfield, Andrew W 5:56:20 (30,265)
Greenhalgh, Andrew F 3:51:07 (8,769)
Greenhalgh, Andrew S 4:48:41 (22,812)
Greenhalgh, John D 3:56:16 (10,171)
Greenhalgh, Mike G 3:49:16 (8,323)
Greenhalgh, Steven D 6:44:40 (31,430)
Greenham, David H 3:45:17 (7,361)
Greenland, Edward C 3:44:14 (7,124)
Greenleaf, Andrew H 2:40:40 (221)
Greenslade, Heath 4:45:08 (22,068)
Greensmith, Geoff C 4:13:46 (14,508)
Greensmith, John W 3:43:44 (7,001)
Greenstein, David 3:59:10 (11,049)
Greenway, Kevin 6:05:25 (30,601)
Greenwell, James 3:11:52 (2,177)
Greenwood, Andrew J 4:38:28 (20,587)
Greenwood, Andrew M 4:38:49 (20,670)
Greenwood, Ben 4:40:38 (21,050)
Greenwood, Charles 4:32:03 (19,121)
Greenwood, Clive T 3:25:14 (3,725)
Greenwood, Harry 4:29:44 (18,564)
Greenwood, James E 4:09:29 (13,494)
Greenwood, Paul 4:30:29 (18,754)
Greenwood, Richard R 4:49:14 (22,924)
Greenwood, Roy J 5:09:45 (26,345)
Greenwood, Tom F 4:12:44 (14,273)
Greer, Stephen R 5:23:31 (27,924)
Greer, Steven A 5:43:49 (29,618)
Greeves, Jerry J 2:48:23 (440)
Greevy, John 3:45:24 (7,387)
Gregg, Jason L 5:02:44 (25,408)
Gregg, Martin A 4:40:09 (20,951)
Gregg, Sean A 3:34:56 (5,415)
Gregg, Stephen P 3:44:02 (7,077)
Gregg, William S 3:35:34 (5,535)
Gregor, Zdenek J 3:51:11 (8,798)
Gregory, Adrian 4:02:11 (11,774)
Gregory, Craig 4:52:26 (23,525)
Gregory, David 4:48:59 (22,871)
Gregory, James 3:56:07 (10,115)
Gregory, Jeff P 3:48:22 (8,093)
Gregory, Kevin 4:17:23 (15,392)
Gregory, Lee T 5:43:19 (29,582)
Gregory, Mark 4:01:41 (11,647)
Gregory, Mark J 3:31:32 (4,856)
Gregory, Nicholas A 3:13:11 (2,327)
Gregory, Paul R 3:46:10 (7,565)
Gregory, Pete J 4:02:14 (11,789)
Gregory, Richard J 4:58:37 (24,741)
Gregory, Timothy J 4:34:30 (19,712)
Grehan, Peter 3:27:22 (4,095)
Greminger, Paul 3:09:04 (1,906)
Gremo, Adam D 5:20:10 (27,591)
Gremo, Chris S 4:38:58 (20,715)
Gresley, Stephen J 5:54:36 (30,178)
Greswell, Michael 5:23:29 (27,916)
Gretton, Stephen J 5:50:27 (29,992)
Gretton, Victor B 4:58:16 (24,659)
Grew, Adam D 4:14:35 (14,703)
Grewal, Varinder S 3:50:52 (8,723)
Grey, Paul 4:24:05 (17,086)
Grey, Stephen 4:19:58 (16,022)
Grice, Andrew 4:05:00 (12,429)
Gridley, David P 3:52:57 (9,242)
Grier, Duncan R 4:25:48 (17,515)
Grierson, James R 4:17:49 (15,512)
Grieve, Graham D 3:36:03 (5,618)
Grieves-Smith, Peter M 4:36:47 (20,198)
Griffen, Richard D 4:37:58 (20,459)
Griffin, Andrew J 4:21:35 (16,409)
Griffin, Christopher P 3:22:43 (3,406)
Griffin, Gareth R 3:42:24 (6,720)
Griffin, Paul A 4:47:54 (22,654)
Griffin, Richard F 3:57:21 (10,498)
Griffin, Richard M 4:21:58 (16,524)
Griffin, Robert E 4:03:14 (12,010)
Griffin, Stephen J 3:23:23 (3,485)
Griffin, William A 3:45:25 (7,390)
Griffith, Geoffrey 4:43:10 (21,595)
Griffith, Simon P 3:44:30 (7,185)
Griffiths, Allen R 5:09:44 (26,342)
Griffiths, Brian F 3:44:24 (7,161)
Griffiths, Bryn R 3:51:31 (8,891)
Griffiths, Daniel 4:53:25 (23,689)
Griffiths, Dave 4:05:48 (12,616)
Griffiths, David J 4:12:53 (14,299)
Griffiths, David M 3:52:50 (9,209)
Griffiths, Derek A 2:57:44 (936)
Griffiths, Frank 4:22:42 (16,749)
Griffiths, Jason N 4:45:42 (22,190)
Griffiths, John S 3:52:51 (9,213)
Griffiths, John W 3:52:59 (9,252)
Griffiths, Jon R 3:50:00 (8,506)
Griffiths, Jonathan M 5:30:26 (28,617)
Griffiths, Malcolm D 4:55:20 (24,071)
Griffiths, Mark A 4:00:28 (11,390)
Griffiths, Mike J 4:00:22 (11,372)
Griffiths, Neil T 4:35:13 (19,868)
Griffiths, Nick 4:14:27 (14,665)
Griffiths, Owain 4:09:15 (13,438)
Griffiths, Paul D 3:03:03 (1,369)
Griffiths, Paul W 3:21:47 (3,289)
Griffiths, Peter 3:13:37 (2,388)
Griffiths, Peter A 5:07:17 (26,006)
Griffiths, Robert E 3:53:51 (9,459)
Griffiths, Simon E 4:05:36 (12,573)
Griffiths, Simon N 2:53:00 (643)
Griffiths, Stephen J 5:00:51 (25,123)
Griffiths, William W 4:25:11 (17,356)
Grifiths, Neville 3:13:37 (2,388)
Grigg, Jeremy S 3:47:19 (7,834)
Grigg, John H 6:08:13 (30,680)
Griggs, David W 5:45:09 (29,700)
Griggs, Justin H 3:30:09 (4,626)
Grimaldi, Alexander C 4:10:50 (13,837)
Grimes, Anthony J 3:53:21 (9,351)
Grimes, Matthew I 3:46:25 (7,624)
Grimes, Philip 2:47:53 (417)
Grimmer, Ashley A 4:12:40 (14,254)

Grimmette, John A.	4:29:38 (18,537)	
Grimsdale, Paul D	3:23:28 (3,497)	
Grimsey, Wiliam	3:55:58 (10,074)	
Grimshaw, Allan R	4:07:22 (12,978)	
Grimshaw, Clive A	4:28:10 (18,140)	
Grimwood, Graham A	5:17:23 (27,293)	
Grimwood, Mark A	4:00:17 (11,355)	
Grindle, Richard G	3:31:31 (4,853)	
Grindu, Louis	3:57:18 (10,481)	
Grisa, Giuseppe	3:29:38 (4,524)	
Grist, Kevin	3:03:39 (1,421)	
Gristwood, Andrew T	3:21:24 (3,243)	
Grobler, Gerrie P	3:26:56 (4,005)	
Grocott, Ian F	3:27:55 (4,216)	
Groenestein, Paul A	4:44:02 (21,802)	
Groening, Daniel	3:49:08 (8,291)	
Groening, Wolfgang	3:29:33 (4,511)	
Grogan, Damian P	4:01:54 (11,688)	
Grogan, Ian J	4:17:28 (15,415)	
Grondona, Pietro	2:58:31 (1,012)	
Gronow, Richard M	3:46:31 (7,639)	
Groom, Paul A	4:24:28 (17,179)	
Groom, Steven D	3:39:42 (6,256)	
Groombridge, Julian	4:36:48 (20,202)	
Groombridge, Paul	4:00:22 (11,372)	
Groombridge, Stephen P	2:59:23 (1,111)	
Groome, Thomas J	4:18:00 (15,553)	
Groppe, Markus H	4:11:36 (13,999)	
Grose, Tim J	2:38:27 (177)	
Gross, Andreas	3:47:25 (7,856)	
Gross, Axel	3:57:13 (10,451)	
Gross, Helge	4:09:29 (13,494)	
Grossman, Ben	4:10:52 (13,844)	
Grossman, David B	5:03:45 (25,548)	
Grostate, Ian M	4:48:41 (22,812)	
Grosvenor, John-Barry	5:40:28 (29,377)	
Grosvenor, Michael	4:37:44 (20,387)	
Grote, Andreas	3:42:42 (6,790)	
Groth, Teit	3:39:10 (6,157)	
Groult, Jeanluc G	4:19:15 (15,846)	
Groundsell, Charles B	5:28:59 (28,484)	
Grove, Alex J	4:45:19 (22,101)	
Grove, Andrew P	3:00:58 (1,234)	
Grove, Christopher J	3:51:57 (9,003)	
Grove, Darren	3:53:50 (9,453)	
Grove, Manuel	7:41:17 (31,892)	
Grove, Shaun D	4:36:28 (20,123)	
Grover, John M	3:41:20 (6,528)	
Groves, Benjamin J	3:27:22 (4,095)	
Groves, Carl A	3:00:44 (1,213)	
Groves, David J	5:17:55 (27,355)	
Groves, Glen	2:37:12 (159)	
Groves, Nick T	3:01:01 (1,238)	
Groves, Paul S	5:52:55 (30,123)	
Gruat, Jerry	3:43:13 (6,899)	
Grubb, Martyn	2:58:41 (1,039)	
Gruber, Christian	4:42:19 (21,418)	
Grummitt, Sam M	3:56:07 (10,115)	
Grundei, Simon	5:21:33 (27,731)	
Grundy, Andrew S	4:01:14 (11,550)	
Grundy, David A	4:28:37 (18,259)	
Grundy, James	3:58:09 (10,729)	
Grunnill, Wayne E	5:24:21 (28,008)	
Gruszka, Marian	3:19:13 (2,987)	
Grzelec, Jaroslaw	3:04:27 (1,487)	
Guan, Ong E	4:02:31 (11,858)	
Gudhka, Nirav	4:32:59 (19,354)	
Gudino Penalver, Juan J	3:57:32 (10,550)	
Gudka, Piyush	3:42:59 (6,846)	
Guedj, Jonathan	5:40:57 (29,408)	
Gueffet, Maurice	3:48:37 (8,157)	
Guerra Zubiaga, David A	4:30:27 (18,745)	
Guest, Benjamin J	3:15:56 (2,641)	
Guest, David	3:47:36 (7,906)	
Guest, David W	4:47:28 (22,564)	
Guest, John S	4:12:52 (14,292)	
Guest, Robert J	3:02:15 (1,321)	
Guglielmi, Thomas A	5:19:29 (27,498)	
Guicciardi, Alberigo	5:17:16 (27,281)	
Guillabert, André	4:26:51 (17,785)	
Guillabert, Edouard	4:40:24 (21,008)	
Guillon, Jacques	3:14:30 (2,503)	
Guinan, Paul E	2:48:57 (457)	

Guinane, Simon J	4:21:57 (16,516)	
Guinee, Paul M	7:10:52 (31,714)	
Guiney, Daniel J	6:26:32 (31,150)	
Guinness, Jon H	4:30:07 (18,660)	
Guiseley, Andrew	3:33:19 (5,164)	
Guiter, Christian	4:35:02 (19,828)	
Gulde, Jurgen	4:33:10 (19,396)	
Gullis, Mike	3:27:40 (4,162)	
Gulliver, Bill A	5:23:10 (27,890)	
Gumbley, Roger	4:19:04 (15,792)	
Gummer, Paul D	4:04:28 (12,306)	
Gumpl, Thomas	3:43:12 (6,894)	
Gunn, Conor J	4:04:59 (12,426)	
Gunn, David	4:42:33 (21,462)	
Gunn, David E	4:39:00 (20,729)	
Gunn, Graham	4:17:30 (15,423)	
Gunn, John A	4:20:22 (16,120)	
Gunn, Marcus C	4:11:45 (14,032)	
Gunn, Mark L	4:17:30 (15,423)	
Gunn, Stuart J	4:49:22 (22,955)	
Gunnell, Jonathan A	4:20:20 (16,115)	
Gunning, Brinsley J	5:14:07 (26,914)	
Gunning, John	5:35:22 (28,990)	
Gunning, Simon M	3:46:27 (7,628)	
Gunningham, Robert P	3:24:20 (3,607)	
Gunter-Rees, Phillip J	3:57:22 (10,505)	
Gunther, David	6:12:51 (30,810)	
Gunton, Gary	3:31:01 (4,782)	
Gunton, Paul	3:57:37 (10,573)	
Guntrip, Peter A	5:18:34 (27,417)	
Guppy, Simon	5:06:09 (25,866)	
Gupta, Sanjeev	4:09:33 (13,512)	
Gupta, Sunil	5:10:27 (26,438)	
Gupta, Yogesh	5:21:30 (27,727)	
Guram, Charanjit S	4:22:44 (16,755)	
Gurd, Richard	3:05:55 (1,601)	
Gurney, Jon E	3:30:26 (4,680)	
Gurney, Nigel J	4:35:13 (19,868)	
Gurr, Alexander J	4:29:31 (18,499)	
Gurr, Stuart	3:22:18 (3,341)	
Gurrey, Mark C	4:36:35 (20,150)	
Gurung, Ishwor P	4:27:08 (17,874)	
Gurung, Raj K	4:31:12 (18,897)	
Gusenbauer, Andreas	4:20:35 (16,181)	
Gustard, Derek J	4:18:39 (15,700)	
Gustavsson, Henrik	3:47:00 (7,751)	
Gustavsson, Ulf	3:50:44 (8,692)	
Guth, Raphael	3:10:20 (2,032)	
Guthrie, David R	3:59:01 (11,010)	
Guthrie, Greg	5:45:48 (29,740)	
Guthrie, Jonathan J	4:32:32 (19,245)	
Guthrie, Mathew J	3:27:31 (4,131)	
Gutierrez, Carlos A	4:17:57 (15,546)	
Guy, Fred	4:55:32 (24,105)	
Guy, Geoffrey R	5:54:54 (30,194)	
Guy, John A	4:55:47 (24,149)	
Guy, Matthew S	3:23:19 (3,478)	
Guy, Richard M	4:03:50 (12,155)	
Guy, Robin W	3:46:58 (7,741)	
Gwillam, Andy M	2:50:07 (508)	
Gwilliam, Paul A	3:11:49 (2,170)	
Gwillim, Craig	3:52:04 (9,027)	
Gwillim, John A	3:34:59 (5,424)	
Gwilt, Mark A	3:34:22 (5,321)	
Gwizdala, Peter	4:39:24 (20,809)	
Gwynne, David	5:29:11 (28,506)	
Gwynne, David A	5:10:35 (26,449)	
Gyles, Paul S	4:40:15 (20,972)	
Gyte, Barry G	3:02:03 (1,305)	
Haarer, Peter S	2:31:30 (91)	
Haas, Jens	4:43:19 (21,642)	
Haase, Wolfgang	3:08:28 (1,847)	
Habershon, Stephen C	3:53:17 (9,335)	
Habieda, Lucjan	2:56:13 (832)	
Hacker, Paul	3:28:29 (4,319)	
Hacker, Peter J	3:46:04 (7,539)	
Hacker, Terry M	3:30:47 (4,738)	
Hackett, John	4:42:47 (21,515)	
Hackl, Rupert	3:42:31 (6,749)	
Hadden, Alex	5:09:02 (26,244)	
Haddon, Mark J	4:13:28 (14,442)	
Haddon, Matthew R	5:33:10 (28,820)	
Haddon, Paul L	4:29:28 (18,481)	

Haddon, Peter A	5:23:08 (27,885)	
Haddow, Scott	3:44:03 (7,082)	
Haddrell, Duncan J	5:23:52 (27,957)	
Haden, Stuart T	4:30:28 (18,750)	
Hadfield, Andrew M	4:33:52 (19,549)	
Hadfield, Graham	5:55:16 (30,214)	
Hadfield, Hugh W	3:57:44 (10,600)	
Hadfield, Stefan	4:03:35 (12,099)	
Hadfield, Tom D	2:33:31 (103)	
Hadjioannou, Panny	4:26:57 (17,825)	
Hadley, Graham	7:34:07 (31,868)	
Hadley, Jason P	5:09:08 (26,257)	
Hadley, Peter E	3:19:55 (3,059)	
Hadley, Robin P	4:34:50 (19,784)	
Hadley, William G	4:22:34 (16,716)	
Haederle, Jan M	3:09:10 (1,913)	
Haegeman, Wim	2:52:27 (615)	
Haetta, Nils I	3:09:33 (1,956)	
Haffenden, Gary A	4:22:38 (16,733)	
Hafner, Manfred	3:52:48 (9,195)	
Hagelin, Bernt	4:00:05 (11,311)	
Hagenbucher, Carsten	4:24:57 (17,294)	
Haggarty, Scot I	3:50:39 (8,671)	
Haggas, Neil R	2:52:44 (628)	
Haggerty, Steven J	3:13:15 (2,334)	
Haggett, Stephen P	4:36:40 (20,172)	
Hague, Peter	4:01:02 (11,510)	
Hague, Stephen J	3:27:24 (4,103)	
Hague-Holmes, Gerard M	4:27:09 (17,880)	
Hahn, Michael J	4:05:21 (12,498)	
Hahn, Ottmar	4:19:57 (16,013)	
Haig, Christiaan J	4:44:50 (21,983)	
Haig, Jim I	3:35:06 (5,445)	
Haigh, Andrew D	5:19:52 (27,544)	
Haigh, James D	3:31:21 (4,826)	
Haigh, Martin J	3:59:54 (11,268)	
Haigh, Michael D	4:38:05 (20,493)	
Haile, Paul M	5:12:30 (26,692)	
Hailes, Ian J	3:28:13 (4,266)	
Hailes, Roger J	3:21:24 (3,243)	
Hails, Stephen	3:17:09 (2,767)	
Hain, John	3:47:55 (7,977)	
Haines, Andrew	4:14:25 (14,465)	
Haines, Andrew J	4:16:29 (15,171)	
Haines, Ian	3:37:15 (5,822)	
Haines, Jonathan N	3:52:45 (9,183)	
Haines, Shaun T	3:31:20 (4,823)	
Haines, Stephen	3:20:25 (3,110)	
Haines, Timothy C	4:13:44 (14,500)	
Hainsworth, Paul J	3:07:35 (1,762)	
Haire, Geoffrey R	4:11:56 (14,072)	
Haire, Nick A	3:37:38 (5,897)	
Haith, Kenneth	3:39:04 (6,144)	
Haith, Peter	3:59:42 (11,222)	
Hajdu, Nicolas P	5:17:44 (27,331)	
Hajioff, Gideon	4:46:01 (22,255)	
Hajjaj, Mustapha	3:18:32 (2,902)	
Hake, Gary	4:38:44 (20,649)	
Hake, Robert G	4:10:50 (13,837)	
Hakhamaneshi, Bahram D	4:33:49 (19,545)	
Haldane, Richard E	5:00:42 (25,095)	
Hale, Alan M	5:55:35 (30,229)	
Hale, Anthony G	3:49:28 (8,368)	
Hale, Jamie L	4:18:26 (15,647)	
Hale, John R	4:41:50 (21,315)	
Hale, Robert C	4:54:02 (23,800)	
Hale, Robert J	4:31:54 (19,080)	
Hale, Terry	5:38:23 (29,221)	
Hales, Colin S	4:08:44 (13,301)	
Hales, Daniel S	4:31:54 (19,080)	
Hales, Darren J	3:48:02 (8,004)	
Hales, Jonathan H	4:12:31 (14,208)	
Hales, Matthew	4:01:37 (11,628)	
Halford, Daniel R	3:55:07 (9,821)	
Halford, David A	3:53:11 (9,310)	
Halford, Peter P	3:25:21 (3,741)	
Halgunset, Joerund	4:19:57 (16,013)	
Halgunset, Joralf	4:19:56 (16,008)	
Hall, Adrian J	4:50:30 (23,179)	
Hall, Alan	4:11:22 (13,945)	
Hall, Alan N	3:36:55 (5,755)	
Hall, Alex	3:19:36 (3,027)	
Hall, Alexander	4:58:02 (24,604)	

Hall, Andrew 3:26:30 (3,917)
Hall, Andy L 4:54:48 (23,961)
Hall, Anthony J 4:26:46 (17,766)
Hall, Anthony W 3:26:19 (3,892)
Hall, Arnold 6:30:12 (31,209)
Hall, Beverley J 4:41:32 (21,252)
Hall, Bruce J 3:04:37 (1,498)
Hall, Christopher J 3:35:55 (5,591)
Hall, Christopher J 3:57:10 (10,438)
Hall, Christopher M 3:29:56 (4,577)
Hall, Colin R 4:53:50 (23,772)
Hall, David 2:57:44 (936)
Hall, David A 3:08:16 (1,826)
Hall, David M 3:33:07 (5,122)
Hall, David R 4:00:06 (11,316)
Hall, David T 4:52:50 (23,590)
Hall, Derek J 4:03:05 (11,975)
Hall, Dominic J 4:09:38 (13,536)
Hall, Douglas O 4:07:23 (12,982)
Hall, Duane R 5:26:48 (28,280)
Hall, Edward W 5:40:22 (29,364)
Hall, Gareth 4:10:15 (13,690)
Hall, Gareth 4:24:04 (17,076)
Hall, Gary F 4:34:45 (19,768)
Hall, Geoffrey 5:01:40 (25,252)
Hall, Geoffrey A 4:24:37 (17,210)
Hall, Graeme A 2:49:57 (501)
Hall, Ian D 3:25:35 (3,785)
Hall, James 4:23:10 (16,858)
Hall, James A 4:55:37 (24,122)
Hall, James A 5:41:06 (29,416)
Hall, James C 3:32:13 (4,957)
Hall, James L 4:12:33 (14,218)
Hall, James W 6:40:54 (31,370)
Hall, Jerry-Lee 7:13:14 (31,734)
Hall, John 3:27:06 (4,043)
Hall, John 5:28:49 (28,471)
Hall, John M 3:40:16 (6,345)
Hall, Jonathan D 3:08:07 (1,817)
Hall, Julian L 4:01:03 (11,516)
Hall, Ken 4:43:18 (21,636)
Hall, Leo C 4:33:32 (19,475)
Hall, Leslie 4:53:45 (23,756)
Hall, Martin C 3:21:28 (3,251)
Hall, Martin D 3:27:44 (4,174)
Hall, Martin T 4:21:13 (16,315)
Hall, Matthew W 3:03:31 (1,408)
Hall, Michael 3:55:19 (9,887)
Hall, Michael R 4:40:43 (21,068)
Hall, Neil J 4:37:37 (20,361)
Hall, Nicky 3:03:45 (1,426)
Hall, Patrick D 2:52:02 (594)
Hall, Peter 5:20:17 (27,605)
Hall, Peter R 4:10:41 (13,796)
Hall, Philip S 3:46:49 (7,707)
Hall, Ray W 5:41:06 (29,416)
Hall, Raymond 3:04:54 (1,514)
Hall, Richard 3:53:18 (9,340)
Hall, Richard A 3:25:10 (3,716)
Hall, Richard J 4:42:34 (21,465)
Hall, Rob 2:45:42 (349)
Hall, Robert 4:55:35 (24,117)
Hall, Robert 4:55:46 (24,147)
Hall, Robert A 3:18:36 (2,909)
Hall, Robert W 3:36:08 (5,631)
Hall, Simon 2:54:50 (737)
Hall, Simon K 3:57:37 (10,573)
Hall, Simon R 2:46:35 (373)
Hall, Steven A 4:59:07 (24,814)
Hall, Stuart 2:18:45 (27)
Hall, Stuart T 3:58:04 (10,696)
Hall, Tim G 2:58:23 (1,003)
Hall, Tony 3:57:28 (10,527)
Hall, Wayne 5:45:18 (29,711)
Hall, William L 4:00:51 (11,461)
Hallam, Christopher 4:33:45 (19,517)
Hallam, Geoffrey 4:57:53 (24,564)
Hallam, Oliver J 4:27:39 (18,004)
Haller, Andrew 5:14:58 (27,024)
Hallett, Colin 3:20:44 (3,164)
Halliday, Andrew C 5:27:31 (28,357)
Halliday, John N 4:37:04 (20,266)
Halliday, Michael P 5:42:20 (29,506)
Halliday, Neil 3:59:11 (11,054)
Halliday, Roy 3:54:59 (9,778)
Halligan, Edward 4:52:45 (23,577)
Halliwell, John K 3:17:35 (2,810)
Halls, John A 3:11:09 (2,107)
Halls, Tim E 4:08:13 (13,152)
Halpenny, Samuel 4:26:04 (17,593)
Halsall, Philip 4:06:44 (12,823)
Halsall, Stephen 4:06:54 (12,862)
Halse, Tarquin E 4:20:56 (16,271)
Halsey, Michael W 5:24:24 (28,015)
Halsey, Robert N 4:15:30 (14,925)
Halson, Adrian M 4:30:18 (18,703)
Halton, Clifford R 4:23:48 (17,014)
Halvatzis, Nicos A 3:02:03 (1,305)
Halvey, Martin 2:48:41 (445)
Haly, Grant S 3:30:22 (4,665)
Ham, Clive R 3:52:26 (9,120)
Hamadi, Abelmounhim 3:07:44 (1,781)
Hamblen, Jonathan M 2:34:28 (115)
Hambleton, Stephen W 4:09:13 (13,428)
Hamblett, Trevor W 3:27:42 (4,168)
Hamblin, Brian J 4:48:35 (22,790)
Hamblin, Paul M 3:52:58 (9,248)
Hamblin, Roddy A 4:32:35 (19,254)
Hambly, Stephen M 5:04:19 (25,607)
Hambridge, Paul 3:29:47 (4,550)
Hamer, Chip 3:01:26 (1,273)
Hamer, David C 3:24:31 (3,626)
Hamer, Johannes P 4:52:12 (23,482)
Hamer, Steve 3:45:28 (7,400)
Hamer-Hodges, Gareth W 3:51:36 (8,916)
Hames, Chris 4:46:39 (22,383)
Hamill, Robert P 4:43:09 (21,591)
Hamilton, Alasdair N 4:01:09 (11,538)
Hamilton, Alastair L 3:57:04 (10,409)
Hamilton, Allan 3:16:47 (2,728)
Hamilton, Anthony P 3:56:49 (10,337)
Hamilton, Derek J 3:56:53 (10,362)
Hamilton, Douglas J 3:09:36 (1,961)
Hamilton, Edward S 3:13:38 (2,390)
Hamilton, George E 4:31:52 (19,066)
Hamilton, Gordon D 4:09:35 (13,520)
Hamilton, Graham M 3:00:52 (1,228)
Hamilton, James R 3:40:44 (6,436)
Hamilton, Jonathan B 3:47:31 (7,883)
Hamilton, Liam 3:33:12 (5,136)
Hamilton, Neil 4:42:39 (21,482)
Hamilton, Neil J 4:00:10 (11,331)
Hamilton, Nicholas 4:17:06 (15,327)
Hamilton, Robert D 7:14:39 (31,742)
Hamilton, Robert J 4:28:50 (18,309)
Hamilton, Rod 3:40:51 (6,445)
Hamilton, Steve J 3:21:09 (3,214)
Hamilton, Stuart 4:50:38 (23,204)
Hamilton-Brown, Robert V 5:45:30 (29,726)
Hamlet, Colin 3:36:22 (5,672)
Hamling, Mark 3:48:59 (8,251)
Hamling, Neil T 5:21:22 (27,713)
Hamling, Peter 4:21:27 (16,376)
Hammer, Matthias L 5:09:05 (26,250)
Hammersley, Mark A 4:19:40 (15,943)
Hammett, Rohan J 3:43:58 (7,057)
Hammond, Anthony J 4:08:49 (13,329)
Hammond, David J 3:47:07 (7,784)
Hammond, John K 3:43:29 (6,956)
Hammond, John M 3:50:54 (8,735)
Hammond, Mark P 3:14:02 (2,441)
Hammond, Mark S 5:04:37 (25,641)
Hammond, Neil 5:00:39 (25,086)
Hammond, Patrick 4:40:39 (21,054)
Hammond, Paul R 3:51:24 (8,857)
Hammond, Peter 6:46:30 (31,459)
Hammond, Robert C 4:33:14 (19,414)
Hammond, Robert J 4:04:43 (12,355)
Hammond, Stephen B 3:28:07 (4,246)
Hammonds, Stephen 5:48:58 (29,906)
Hamon, Patrick 3:32:31 (5,007)
Hampshire, Ben 4:09:55 (13,615)
Hampshire, James J 4:09:54 (13,607)
Hampshire, Neil C 3:58:38 (10,899)
Hampshire, Stephen J 4:55:17 (24,059)
Hampson, Frank A 4:18:10 (15,586)
Hampton, Anthony N 3:37:14 (5,820)
Hampton, Chris D 3:50:12 (8,547)
Hampton, Desmond M 4:01:44 (11,656)
Hampton, Edward T 3:49:25 (8,359)
Hampton, James E 3:50:12 (8,547)
Hampton, Jonathan C 4:45:33 (22,148)
Hampton, Ray 3:22:58 (3,438)
Hamsher, Mark W 4:43:27 (21,673)
Hamson, Peter J 4:01:22 (11,574)
Hanagan, Stuart D 3:56:09 (10,121)
Hanbergen, Richard 5:22:24 (27,822)
Hanberry, Matt 5:12:52 (26,742)
Hance, Connor C 5:42:07 (29,490)
Hancock, Anthony 3:13:50 (2,412)
Hancock, Jason 3:37:43 (5,905)
Hancock, Thomas 4:42:47 (21,515)
Hancocks, Matthew 4:10:32 (13,762)
Hancox, Grenville R 4:10:11 (13,675)
Hancox, Matthew J 3:58:20 (10,799)
Hancox, Philip G 4:48:47 (22,832)
Hancox, Robert G 3:17:32 (2,803)
Hand, Michael 3:03:06 (1,374)
Hand, Michael P 4:53:59 (23,791)
Hand, Rob W 2:55:50 (802)
Handley, Graham 4:33:17 (19,422)
Handley, Mark S 4:39:02 (20,735)
Handley, Tim D 4:08:55 (13,355)
Handy, Dexter R 6:19:04 (30,991)
Haneef, Mohammed 4:52:35 (23,549)
Hanga, Tibor Istvan 4:01:49 (11,672)
Haniver, William A 6:05:58 (30,619)
Hankel, Ruediger 4:02:48 (11,927)
Hankins, Timothy J 3:42:41 (6,785)
Hanks, Daniel 4:33:19 (19,429)
Hanks, Lee A 3:56:08 (10,117)
Hanlon, Alan G 3:44:21 (7,146)
Hanlon, Francis W 4:43:26 (21,671)
Hanlon, John J 4:05:53 (12,634)
Hanmer, Barry D 3:37:55 (5,940)
Hanna, Phil 3:48:48 (8,211)
Hannaford, Charles E 4:35:01 (19,825)
Hannah, David 4:04:51 (12,392)
Hannan, Neil 4:32:21 (19,199)
Hanner, Kevin 4:00:05 (11,311)
Hanney, Chris 4:24:57 (17,294)
Hanney, David P 3:28:13 (4,266)
Hannington, Warren 3:23:33 (3,504)
Hannon, Paul B 4:22:28 (16,690)
Hannon, Pete J 4:12:09 (14,125)
Hannon, Robert M 4:57:02 (24,410)
Hannon, Thomas M 3:39:19 (6,188)
Hanrahan, Sean N 3:33:24 (5,174)
Hanscomb, John W 4:24:36 (17,205)
Hansell, Edward S 4:34:28 (19,704)
Hansell, Jason W 4:53:23 (23,684)
Hansen, Daniel I 5:20:25 (27,620)
Hansen, Gregory J 3:43:00 (6,850)
Hansen, Mark C 5:00:04 (25,003)
Hansen, Michael P 3:47:17 (7,829)
Hansen, Ove M 3:57:50 (10,627)
Hansen, Paul 3:24:24 (3,616)
Hansen, Peter L 4:17:47 (15,503)
Hansford, Jerry 3:56:03 (10,099)
Hansler, Neil W 4:43:38 (21,707)
Hanslip, David 4:38:24 (20,570)
Hanson, Carl 4:14:32 (14,690)
Hanson, Carl 4:52:10 (23,476)
Hanson, Christopher P 3:54:51 (9,738)
Hanson, David A 3:53:45 (9,427)
Hanson, David J 3:17:04 (2,755)
Hanson, Edward A 3:27:06 (4,043)
Hanson, John 4:58:37 (24,741)
Hanson, Luke 3:50:20 (8,589)
Hanson, Nicholas 3:45:50 (7,488)
Hanson, Nicholas 4:57:59 (24,590)
Hanson, Nick J 4:12:25 (14,170)
Hanson, Paul 3:55:00 (9,782)
Hanson, Peter C 3:46:28 (7,634)
Hansson, Lennart 4:02:55 (11,942)
Hanvey, Tony 4:18:36 (15,686)
Haq, Naeem U 4:24:05 (17,086)
Harada, Nobuo 4:57:13 (24,442)
Haragan, Scott 4:09:36 (13,524)

Harb, Colin M 4:08:09 (13,146)
Harb, Jonathan A 3:37:10 (5,808)
Harbach, James 4:03:25 (12,062)
Harbach, Paul 5:18:18 (27,400)
Harbour, Jason V 3:01:11 (1,251)
Harbour, Joseph 4:24:41 (17,227)
Harcus, Graham 4:09:41 (13,549)
Hardaker, Christopher D 3:55:32 (9,942)
Hardcastle, Paul T 4:23:58 (17,053)
Hardiman, Russell A 3:11:11 (2,111)
Harding, Brian D 3:58:07 (10,715)
Harding, Brian H 4:19:37 (15,931)
Harding, Gary 3:31:01 (4,782)
Harding, Ian G 3:36:44 (5,730)
Harding, James C 3:26:03 (3,854)
Harding, Jason 3:41:49 (6,608)
Harding, Jeffrey K 2:54:45 (729)
Harding, John D 4:18:31 (15,665)
Harding, Mark D 3:39:16 (6,172)
Hardman, Eric 5:12:04 (26,641)
Hards, Neil A 4:38:07 (20,499)
Hardstone, Roger G 3:41:57 (6,633)
Hardwick, Andy 5:51:49 (30,051)
Hardwick, David 4:23:16 (16,885)
Hardwick, Matthew R 2:58:40 (1,037)
Hardy, Benajmin 4:00:56 (11,488)
Hardy, Graham 3:23:15 (3,471)
Hardy, Jan E 3:32:02 (4,931)
Hardy, John P 4:40:21 (20,996)
Hardy, Paul J 3:49:30 (8,376)
Hardy, Shane 4:54:41 (23,938)
Hardyman, Christopher J 4:57:22 (24,467)
Hare, Darrell 5:18:44 (27,439)
Hare, David E 5:10:25 (26,432)
Hare, Ian M 3:36:15 (5,650)
Hare, Nicholas A 3:59:16 (11,077)
Hare, Paul J 3:46:45 (7,695)
Harel, Noaz 3:20:11 (3,088)
Harfield, Patrick D 6:14:31 (30,863)
Harfield, Stephen P 6:14:32 (30,864)
Harfoot, James 3:59:18 (11,087)
Hargis, Brian 5:49:20 (29,924)
Hargrave, Peter J 3:01:41 (1,286)
Hargreaves, Craig 3:53:31 (9,380)
Hargreaves, Eric 6:44:33 (31,428)
Hargreaves, John S 3:04:34 (1,495)
Hargreaves, Mark R 2:24:59 (52)
Hargreaves, Michael S 5:21:32 (27,730)
Hargreaves, Richard N 4:44:28 (21,903)
Hargreaves, Stephen J 3:56:59 (10,385)
Hargreaves, Stuart 5:34:10 (28,901)
Harker, Alexander R 3:17:18 (2,784)
Harkin, Anthony J 4:41:33 (21,254)
Harkin, Max 4:55:02 (24,002)
Harkus, Gavin M 2:53:48 (681)
Harland, David W 3:51:18 (8,834)
Harland, Paul K 3:34:12 (5,298)
Harley, Brendan 4:28:39 (18,270)
Harley, Nigel 4:27:48 (18,039)
Harley, Tim Y 4:08:24 (13,199)
Harlow, Dan 3:46:35 (7,660)
Harlow, Derek 4:06:55 (12,867)
Harlow, Gary 3:56:48 (10,330)
Harman, Anthony P 4:16:39 (15,220)
Harman, Anthony R 4:11:46 (14,036)
Harman, Gary R 3:31:44 (4,877)
Harman, Keir D 3:45:13 (7,354)
Harman, Simon A 4:27:37 (17,996)
Harmer, Jon 3:08:19 (1,834)
Harmer, Simon E 4:58:14 (24,646)
Harmon, Jimmy B 5:40:42 (29,396)
Harms, Geert 3:56:19 (10,183)
Harms, Wim A 4:38:41 (20,637)
Harne, Jason M 3:34:27 (5,333)
Harnett, Dennis 3:32:26 (4,993)
Harnett, Jem C 4:08:05 (13,129)
Harnetty, John F 6:10:40 (30,747)
Harnisch, Thomas 4:56:29 (24,305)
Harper, David 5:14:32 (26,964)
Harper, Iain W 6:00:08 (30,414)
Harper, John M 3:27:44 (4,174)
Harper, Kenneth J 4:17:40 (15,473)
Harper, Matthew T 3:36:21 (5,667)
Harper, Robin S 4:27:00 (17,840)
Harper, Simon R 4:24:25 (17,167)
Harper, Steven P 3:40:14 (6,341)
Harpur, Brian J 5:31:12 (28,674)
Harr, Eric 3:17:09 (2,767)
Harran, James P 4:46:58 (22,439)
Harreld, Trevor J 4:30:48 (18,814)
Harridence, Darren M 4:10:01 (13,642)
Harries, Geraint R 4:37:49 (20,409)
Harrild, Benjamin H 5:01:24 (25,207)
Harrington, Harvie J 4:02:59 (11,950)
Harrington, Peter D 5:01:55 (25,289)
Harris, Adam C 4:07:54 (13,090)
Harris, Adrian C 4:02:32 (11,864)
Harris, Adrian J 4:50:55 (23,258)
Harris, Alan 3:50:14 (8,555)
Harris, Alan R 3:54:10 (9,548)
Harris, Alexander J 4:25:35 (17,450)
Harris, Andrew P 4:38:25 (20,575)
Harris, Andy W 3:51:57 (9,003)
Harris, Barry G 4:37:35 (20,352)
Harris, Benjamin G 4:16:23 (15,142)
Harris, Carl 3:00:09 (1,167)
Harris, Charles E 4:09:23 (13,470)
Harris, Chris J 4:17:35 (15,450)
Harris, Daniel J 4:21:19 (16,337)
Harris, David J 4:16:15 (15,107)
Harris, David J 4:31:58 (19,104)
Harris, David J 5:24:09 (27,984)
Harris, David L 4:28:24 (18,193)
Harris, Dominic 3:23:36 (3,514)
Harris, Garry E 3:02:25 (1,335)
Harris, Geoffrey 5:50:42 (30,000)
Harris, Howard A 5:09:59 (26,375)
Harris, Jamie R 3:40:16 (6,345)
Harris, Jeffery J 3:58:32 (10,869)
Harris, Jon 5:21:16 (27,705)
Harris, Jon G 3:17:22 (2,792)
Harris, Jonathan K 4:37:55 (20,444)
Harris, Kevin J 4:48:16 (22,731)
Harris, Lawrence I 4:27:10 (17,885)
Harris, Mark 2:59:06 (1,083)
Harris, Mark 4:25:21 (17,392)
Harris, Matthew C 3:23:49 (3,547)
Harris, Matthew J 4:45:48 (22,210)
Harris, Michael J 5:55:06 (30,204)
Harris, Nick E 4:22:20 (16,650)
Harris, Nigel J 3:44:15 (7,126)
Harris, Owen S 4:19:08 (15,812)
Harris, Paul F 5:38:55 (29,256)
Harris, Paul J 4:14:31 (14,682)
Harris, Paul M 4:10:59 (13,866)
Harris, Peter 5:15:28 (27,074)
Harris, Peter J 6:17:56 (30,951)
Harris, Peter L 3:47:14 (7,808)
Harris, Peter M 4:55:27 (24,092)
Harris, Raymond A 3:39:52 (6,284)
Harris, Robert E 4:02:17 (11,801)
Harris, Robert J 2:59:07 (1,085)
Harris, Robert M 4:02:30 (11,855)
Harris, Robin 4:23:24 (16,921)
Harris, Scott D 2:56:56 (877)
Harris, Stephen 3:33:13 (5,141)
Harris, Stephen R 3:51:10 (8,789)
Harris, Terry D 4:00:51 (11,461)
Harris, Tim E 3:55:54 (10,051)
Harris, Tim P 2:52:50 (633)
Harris, Timothy E 4:40:46 (21,076)
Harris, Trevor 4:37:55 (20,444)
Harris, William R 4:02:38 (11,881)
Harrison, Andrew J 2:54:23 (712)
Harrison, Andrew J 4:11:57 (14,077)
Harrison, Ben 3:55:33 (9,947)
Harrison, Charlie D 4:14:22 (14,641)
Harrison, Daniel 4:48:03 (22,682)
Harrison, Daniel N 3:53:19 (9,342)
Harrison, David A 3:43:34 (6,974)
Harrison, David A 4:37:08 (20,281)
Harrison, David J 5:26:33 (28,254)
Harrison, David P 4:42:24 (21,434)
Harrison, Dennis 5:18:30 (27,412)
Harrison, Derek J 3:17:35 (2,810)
Harrison, Geoffrey P 4:15:40 (14,968)
Harrison, Ian D 4:10:17 (13,697)
Harrison, James A 4:59:42 (24,940)
Harrison, Jamie A 5:38:22 (29,218)
Harrison, Jayson 4:44:12 (21,837)
Harrison, John 4:15:08 (14,840)
Harrison, John F 5:28:32 (28,442)
Harrison, Mark C 5:15:50 (27,112)
Harrison, Michael 3:28:20 (4,289)
Harrison, Michael W 4:15:34 (14,946)
Harrison, Mike G 4:05:02 (12,444)
Harrison, Nigel P 4:37:37 (20,361)
Harrison, Peter R 3:28:50 (4,383)
Harrison, Phillip D 4:57:40 (24,529)
Harrison, Piers G 4:45:35 (22,162)
Harrison, Simon 3:10:40 (2,068)
Harrison, Simon A 3:46:11 (7,573)
Harrison, Timothy 4:56:49 (24,367)
Harrison, Toby 5:03:02 (25,450)
Harrison, Tom 4:39:11 (20,772)
Harrison, Tom C 4:13:13 (14,385)
Harris-St John, Jeremy M 5:14:04 (26,911)
Harrop, Mark D 5:12:13 (26,657)
Harrop, Mark J 4:26:12 (17,631)
Harrop, Richard D 3:55:16 (9,868)
Harrop, Simon M 3:48:57 (8,241)
Harrow, Adrian 4:06:16 (12,727)
Harry, Michael P 5:19:14 (27,481)
Hart, Andrew 2:47:54 (418)
Hart, Andrew J 3:01:40 (1,285)
Hart, Andy D 4:59:47 (24,954)
Hart, Ben 5:06:08 (25,862)
Hart, Christopher A 3:41:37 (6,568)
Hart, Colin A 3:25:16 (3,729)
Hart, Craig A 4:11:43 (14,024)
Hart, Daniel A 3:24:27 (3,620)
Hart, David T 3:49:04 (8,268)
Hart, James W 3:40:15 (6,343)
Hart, Jon R 6:27:19 (31,161)
Hart, Mark E 4:22:02 (16,548)
Hart, Mathew 5:27:40 (28,369)
Hart, Nigel G 4:05:01 (12,437)
Hart, Oliver R 4:31:53 (19,072)
Hart, Patrick A 5:02:16 (25,331)
Hart, Richard J 3:33:55 (5,258)
Hart, Simon P 3:57:35 (10,566)
Hart, Stephen T 3:32:17 (4,965)
Hart, Trevor K 5:42:32 (29,517)
Harte, James B 4:15:40 (14,968)
Harte, John P 3:56:10 (10,128)
Harte, Michael W 4:07:36 (13,034)
Harte, Paul A 2:55:02 (757)
Hartell, Kevin P 6:09:11 (30,705)
Harten-Ash, Vernon J 4:05:14 (12,468)
Hartigan, Martin P 4:23:34 (16,961)
Hartin, Paul E 4:26:03 (17,585)
Hartkamp, Joerg 5:14:30 (26,959)
Hartland, Christopher C 3:55:16 (9,868)
Hartle, David C 5:08:42 (26,203)
Hartle, Rodney 4:20:16 (16,085)
Hartley, Alex J 4:21:23 (16,358)
Hartley, Andrew 3:08:17 (1,830)
Hartley, Andrew 4:55:41 (24,133)
Hartley, Carl D 6:53:59 (31,547)
Hartley, Chris I 5:39:34 (29,308)
Hartley, David A 4:52:53 (23,595)
Hartley, James L 4:32:26 (19,220)
Hartley, Jeremy W 4:08:24 (13,199)
Hartley, Kevin J 3:38:58 (6,126)
Hartley, Richard O 3:46:03 (7,534)
Hartley, Steve 4:38:17 (20,544)
Hartley, Tobias D 3:42:28 (6,735)
Hartner, Guenter 5:40:26 (29,375)
Hartnett, Ronan J 2:51:36 (573)
Hartshorn, Arthur T 5:50:45 (30,002)
Hartwell, Robert 4:42:46 (21,509)
Harvey, Adrian J 5:05:49 (25,808)
Harvey, Alan K 4:27:23 (17,934)
Harvey, Alex 3:17:08 (2,764)
Harvey, Andrew 4:57:11 (24,432)
Harvey, Andrew W 3:15:59 (2,648)
Harvey, Andy N 4:50:51 (23,243)
Harvey, Edward R 4:14:51 (14,773)
Harvey, Gary P 4:17:53 (15,532)

Hedges, Philip 3:50:05 (8,521)
Hedgley, Adrian W 4:59:08 (24,818)
Hedley, David P 4:35:20 (19,893)
Hedley, Nicholas G 3:28:35 (4,334)
Hedmann, Lindsay M 3:29:04 (4,425)
Heeb, Hans 3:08:57 (1,894)
Heeks, Steve J 3:24:11 (3,585)
Heelas, Jeremy N 4:41:37 (21,262)
Heeley, David 3:34:10 (5,293)
Heeley, Paul 2:58:37 (1,031)
Heeney, Roy A 3:44:44 (7,245)
Hefferman, Terry 4:45:29 (22,136)
Heg, James T 4:51:58 (23,433)
Hegarty, Declan 3:55:54 (10,051)
Hegarty, Sean A 4:28:59 (18,344)
Hegarty, Simon D 4:13:16 (14,395)
Hegerty, Paul B 3:58:30 (10,856)
Hehir, Andrew P 3:51:24 (8,857)
Heidinger, Wolfram 4:21:36 (16,420)
Heidman, Thomas R 4:03:06 (11,979)
Heighway, Mark C 4:40:00 (20,919)
Heilbock, Juergen A 3:07:36 (1,765)
Heimsath, Darren E 4:19:11 (15,825)
Heindel, Joachin 5:03:05 (25,458)
Heinel, Hans 3:07:07 (1,715)
Heinz, Werner 3:55:00 (9,782)
Heir, Jon Marius 4:17:20 (15,383)
Helbert, Guy 3:47:50 (7,954)
Helfenberger, Jean-Claude 4:08:53 (13,342)
Helfrich, Gerhard 3:38:32 (6,051)
Helgesson, Joakim H 4:35:36 (19,947)
Hell, Konrad 4:23:06 (16,842)
Hellawell, Peter J 3:21:28 (3,251)
Heller, Peter M 3:53:47 (9,436)
Hellewell, Matthew 3:41:15 (6,521)
Hellewell, William N 3:58:39 (10,909)
Hellin, Jon J 3:44:28 (7,175)
Hellings, Simon J 4:25:08 (17,347)
Helliwell, Peter 4:04:29 (12,312)
Hellyar, Jonathan A 4:32:15 (19,177)
Hellyer, Matthew C 3:51:08 (8,774)
Helm, David R 4:33:03 (19,367)
Helme, Michael A 3:15:31 (2,595)
Helmore, Jeffrey W 3:20:28 (3,120)
Helps, John 3:58:32 (10,869)
Helps, Michael W 4:15:35 (14,949)
Helyar, Robert 4:39:21 (20,802)
Heming, Martin 3:26:38 (3,940)
Hemingway, James R 4:16:32 (15,179)
Hemish, Stewart A 4:08:09 (13,146)
Hemming, Eddie 6:48:47 (31,481)
Hemming, James E 5:17:23 (27,293)
Hemmings, Andrew P 4:20:53 (16,256)
Hemmings, Kenneth W 4:48:52 (22,847)
Hemmings, Lance R 3:07:54 (1,795)
Hemms, Paul 4:22:28 (16,690)
Hemp, Kevin B 4:29:44 (18,564)
Hempsall, Rob 4:55:15 (24,052)
Hempstead, Charlie 4:13:09 (14,365)
Hemsley, Jason C 2:51:02 (546)
Hemsley, Nigel A 3:26:43 (3,964)
Hemsley, Richard M 3:46:19 (7,605)
Hemsworth, Kieran 4:35:53 (20,000)
Henchoz, Philip E 3:27:25 (4,108)
Henderson, Christopher R 3:10:02 (2,004)
Henderson, Craig J 2:38:45 (181)
Henderson, David W 3:28:02 (4,232)
Henderson, Derek J 3:56:40 (10,296)
Henderson, Gareth J 3:36:06 (5,628)
Henderson, Giles A 3:31:06 (4,788)
Henderson, Giles D 5:18:10 (27,386)
Henderson, Ian 3:40:02 (6,309)
Henderson, Ian N 4:16:55 (15,288)
Henderson, Malcolm I 4:25:54 (17,543)
Henderson, Michael A 4:25:38 (17,462)
Henderson, Shaun 5:48:52 (29,901)
Henderson, Simon A 4:01:55 (11,695)
Henderson, Wesley M 4:38:01 (20,475)
Henderson, William T 4:24:49 (17,255)
Henderson Slater, David 4:56:26 (24,289)
Hendley, Darren P 5:25:00 (28,082)
Hendley, Jon P 5:14:45 (26,997)
Hendon, Bruce S 3:49:13 (8,312)
Hendrick, Carl 4:48:59 (22,871)
Hendrie, Clifford J 4:07:46 (13,062)
Hendry, Stephen 4:39:10 (20,764)
Hendy, Brian K 4:42:48 (21,520)
Hendy, Paul M 3:52:26 (9,120)
Hendy, Peter M 3:54:24 (9,612)
Heneghan, Patrick M 3:52:57 (9,242)
Heneghan, Philip J 3:52:57 (9,242)
Heney, Kenneth J 2:56:11 (828)
Hengeler, Alois 3:59:35 (11,183)
Henn, Joseph 4:28:07 (18,126)
Hennebry, Michael C 4:48:34 (22,786)
Henness, Mark F 4:15:45 (14,988)
Hennessey, Brian 2:44:40 (311)
Hennigan, Paul F 3:57:13 (10,451)
Hennis, Gordon 4:56:40 (24,339)
Henriksen, Svein N 4:29:05 (18,370)
Henry, Derek 3:57:18 (10,481)
Henry, Matthew L 6:39:24 (31,353)
Henry, Michael 3:23:34 (3,508)
Henry, Sean M 4:46:16 (22,311)
Hensby, Gary 3:32:32 (5,009)
Hensey, Thomas B 4:53:13 (23,656)
Henshaw, John A 3:50:34 (8,645)
Henson, Dean 4:20:24 (16,131)
Henson, Stuart A 5:00:35 (25,073)
Henwood, Andrew J 4:37:42 (20,382)
Hepburn, Daniel R 5:40:40 (29,393)
Heppell, Andrew B 4:53:13 (23,656)
Heppenstall, Robert A 3:42:21 (6,709)
Herald, Frazer 5:21:51 (27,758)
Herat, Victor P 4:33:37 (19,492)
Herbert, Christopher I 3:27:19 (4,084)
Herbert, Ian 3:29:36 (4,518)
Herbert, James R 3:58:57 (10,991)
Herbert, Neil A 3:12:56 (2,305)
Herbert, Raymond L 5:05:00 (25,693)
Herbertson, Paul C 5:44:33 (29,661)
Herbette, Guillaume 4:08:26 (13,211)
Herbst, Lorenz 3:57:59 (10,667)
Herd, David 5:30:52 (28,654)
Herd, Jonathan J 5:30:50 (28,650)
Herd, William A 4:28:22 (18,181)
Herincx, David J 4:12:35 (14,228)
Heritage, Robert 4:42:42 (21,493)
Herman, Christopher R 3:30:27 (4,682)
Herman, Stephen M 5:30:58 (28,658)
Hernandez, Terry 3:46:03 (7,534)
Heron, Alan 4:32:12 (19,165)
Heron, Benjamin 3:45:50 (7,488)
Heron, David J 4:10:35 (13,774)
Heron, Keith 4:50:24 (23,158)
Herrada, Patrice 3:43:09 (6,878)
Herrick, Barry M 5:54:33 (30,173)
Herrick, Simon E 3:55:00 (9,782)
Herring, Ben 3:36:22 (5,672)
Herring, Richard K 4:17:50 (15,517)
Herring, Robert J 3:57:56 (10,658)
Herrington, Andrew 4:19:57 (16,013)
Herriott, Bryan P 4:44:12 (21,837)
Herrmann, Kenneth J 2:42:02 (243)
Hersee, Peter A 4:13:12 (14,376)
Herzic, Philipp D 3:36:40 (5,718)
Hescott, Guy B 4:08:40 (13,278)
Heselton, John 3:22:48 (3,419)
Hesk, Mark A 3:53:55 (9,481)
Hesketh, Benjamin H 4:08:50 (13,331)
Hesketh, David 3:49:04 (8,268)
Hesketh, Ian M 4:35:55 (20,006)
Hesketh-Roberts, Russell D 4:29:30 (18,492)
Heslehurst, Craig 3:15:07 (2,570)
Hesler, Ian W 3:17:24 (2,795)
Heslop, Neil M 4:02:33 (11,868)
Hester, David F 3:53:31 (9,380)
Hester, Ian 4:42:58 (21,559)
Hester, Liam K 3:28:10 (4,256)
Hester, Richard C 4:36:16 (20,084)
Hester, Toby J 5:35:25 (28,996)
Hetherington, David 6:06:56 (30,643)
Hetherington, Julian M 4:06:24 (12,761)
Hetherington, Mark S 3:30:05 (4,611)
Hettinger, Walter 3:46:25 (7,624)
Heusser, Urs 5:49:39 (29,939)
Hewes, Colin 4:43:39 (21,711)
Hewett, James E 4:09:26 (13,486)
Hewett, Kelvin E 4:12:25 (14,170)
Hewett, Tim J 3:49:30 (8,376)
Hewitt, Bryan J 5:02:37 (25,392)
Hewitt, David L 4:11:06 (13,889)
Hewitt, Dennis 5:26:46 (28,274)
Hewitt, Lee 6:00:49 (30,441)
Hewitt, Lee S 5:15:00 (27,026)
Hewitt, Martyn 3:24:12 (3,589)
Hewitt, Michael 3:26:36 (3,932)
Hewitt, Neville B 4:15:36 (14,955)
Hewitt, Paul 3:48:28 (8,113)
Hewitt, Roger P 3:43:14 (6,902)
Hewitt, Simon 3:12:11 (2,212)
Hewlett, Chris C 4:53:35 (23,718)
Hewlett, Erik L 4:57:52 (24,561)
Hewlett, John A 4:57:49 (24,553)
Hewson, Anthony J 3:33:00 (5,099)
Hewson, Duncan I 3:22:16 (3,338)
Hewson, Guy 5:14:31 (26,961)
Hewson, Julian D 4:49:36 (22,996)
Hewson, Tony 4:26:20 (17,663)
Heybrook, Francis 3:43:54 (7,038)
Heyburn, Geoffrey J 4:48:28 (22,774)
Heycock, Robert W 4:45:03 (22,045)
Heyden, Andrew P 2:45:46 (352)
Heyes, Richard C 4:22:53 (16,791)
Heyes, Steven 3:56:19 (10,183)
Heyman, Eric A 6:20:32 (31,026)
Heyn, Roland 3:15:31 (2,595)
Heys, Jez R 4:40:32 (21,034)
Heys, Simon R 3:16:48 (2,731)
Heywood, Andrew M 4:13:00 (14,329)
Heywood, Paul A 4:21:25 (16,367)
Hiatt, David A 3:34:30 (5,339)
Hibberd, Christopher 5:03:37 (25,534)
Hibberd, David J 3:28:19 (4,285)
Hibberd, Roy G 4:15:33 (14,942)
Hibberd, Stuart A 5:00:14 (25,031)
Hibbins, Andrew W 3:53:02 (9,265)
Hibbins, Matthew J 3:59:16 (11,077)
Hichens, Robert D 5:22:14 (27,798)
Hickley, Matthew E 3:58:09 (10,729)
Hickling, John A 3:24:48 (3,660)
Hickman, Graham K 5:14:30 (26,959)
Hickman, Mark 3:50:43 (8,688)
Hickman, Michael J 3:51:17 (8,828)
Hickman, Paul 3:34:48 (5,389)
Hickman, Stephen P 3:57:52 (10,639)
Hicks, Adam J 5:25:16 (28,114)
Hicks, Christopher A 4:31:29 (18,969)
Hicks, Fred W 5:02:15 (25,326)
Hicks, Joel M 3:59:32 (11,171)
Hicks, Neil D 4:27:19 (17,924)
Hicks, Paul 3:55:56 (10,062)
Hicks, Robert C 3:43:19 (6,922)
Hicks, Stephen J 3:04:32 (1,491)
Hicks, Stephen R 4:12:25 (14,170)
Hickson, John R 5:04:24 (25,614)
Hidalgo-Ibanez, Adolfo 3:18:28 (2,893)
Hidayat, Rahmat 7:19:42 (31,789)
Hidden, Philippe 5:21:34 (27,734)
Hide, George 2:40:10 (215)
Hider, David 4:01:34 (11,613)
Hides, Nick B 2:44:50 (320)
Hieber, Benedikt G 2:53:16 (660)
Hiecke, Jorg 3:21:30 (3,257)
Hietala, Veijo 3:43:21 (6,928)
Higdon, Simon M 3:22:29 (3,371)
Higgins, Alastair D 3:33:50 (5,240)
Higgins, Andrew J 4:07:53 (13,085)
Higgins, Edward R 3:53:59 (9,499)
Higgins, John 3:31:49 (4,892)
Higgins, Mark S 5:06:20 (25,892)
Higgins, Maurice G 4:11:22 (13,945)
Higgins, Noel T 6:21:57 (31,060)
Higgins, Pat 6:06:57 (30,645)
Higgins, Richard J 3:05:41 (1,581)
Higgins, Robert D 3:10:45 (2,077)
Higginson, Guy E 5:13:10 (26,790)
Higginson, Ross W 4:35:02 (19,828)
Higgitt, Martin G 3:28:21 (4,291)

Higgs, Mark W.	3:14:10	(2,464)
Highams, Paul M.	3:16:37	(2,712)
Highfield, Colin R.	3:06:33	(1,659)
Highfield, Mark	3:22:40	(3,398)
Hight, Christopher M	4:44:57	(22,020)
Hignell, Stephen P	4:18:19	(15,611)
Hilbery, Graham J	3:46:37	(7,666)
Hilbery, Oliver J.	4:01:39	(11,633)
Hilborne, Mike	4:31:15	(18,909)
Hilder, Ian J	3:44:51	(7,273)
Hilditch, Steven J	2:51:43	(578)
Hildore, Keith T	4:33:11	(19,399)
Hildreth, Jan H	5:28:35	(28,448)
Hildreth, Keith J	4:38:23	(20,566)
Hildyard, Michael L	3:22:05	(3,312)
Hiley, Keith M.	3:44:23	(7,150)
Hilkowitz, Robby	4:57:56	(24,576)
Hill, Adrian	3:47:05	(7,776)
Hill, Alex I	4:30:55	(18,844)
Hill, Amos R	6:23:19	(31,092)
Hill, Andrew M	4:59:28	(24,896)
Hill, Andrew W	5:47:10	(29,820)
Hill, Barry	5:12:28	(26,688)
Hill, David J	4:56:26	(24,289)
Hill, Edward C	3:32:50	(5,066)
Hill, Frank J	7:03:49	(31,660)
Hill, Gareth D.	3:39:05	(6,145)
Hill, Graham A	3:59:58	(11,284)
Hill, Gregory R	3:43:30	(6,962)
Hill, Ian H	3:23:57	(3,559)
Hill, Ivor	7:10:11	(31,711)
Hill, James D.	5:27:38	(28,364)
Hill, James E	4:01:48	(11,668)
Hill, James J	3:56:42	(10,302)
Hill, James S	4:17:38	(15,461)
Hill, John	5:23:52	(27,957)
Hill, Joseph	4:55:08	(24,022)
Hill, Justin B	3:10:03	(2,006)
Hill, Kenneth	3:03:35	(1,413)
Hill, Martin J	4:11:59	(14,088)
Hill, Martyn C.	4:30:34	(18,773)
Hill, Matthew	4:34:38	(19,743)
Hill, Matthew J	4:14:42	(14,728)
Hill, Matthew S.	5:32:52	(28,800)
Hill, Michael	5:19:58	(27,557)
Hill, Michael J	4:21:23	(16,358)
Hill, Paul C	6:17:32	(30,937)
Hill, Raymond	2:58:41	(1,039)
Hill, Richard W	5:31:18	(28,684)
Hill, Robert	3:44:23	(7,150)
Hill, Robert D.	3:31:30	(4,850)
Hill, Robert D.	6:20:04	(31,013)
Hill, Roger L.	3:15:29	(2,593)
Hill, Stephen	4:08:40	(13,278)
Hill, Stephen C.	3:59:30	(11,157)
Hill, Steven	4:33:23	(19,445)
Hill, Thomas G.	5:38:25	(29,223)
Hill, Thomas L.	5:40:29	(29,378)
Hill, Tim	3:50:00	(8,506)
Hill, Walter J.	3:01:19	(1,265)
Hillebrecht, Frank.	3:55:03	(9,806)
Hiller, Martin W	4:25:53	(17,536)
Hilliard, David J.	4:49:43	(23,021)
Hillier, Thomas N	3:24:52	(3,672)
Hillier, Tony.	5:23:28	(27,913)
Hillis, Tom J.	4:34:20	(19,676)
Hillman, Peter.	3:32:50	(5,066)
Hill-Wood, Charles D	4:20:50	(16,235)
Hilton, David	3:16:41	(2,718)
Hilton, Martin J	2:25:49	(55)
Hilton-Dennis, Matthew G.	4:05:49	(12,620)
Hiluta, Joe.	4:17:10	(15,343)
Hinchcliffe, Paul G	5:16:12	(27,155)
Hinchcliffe, Simon	3:29:04	(4,425)
Hinchcliffe, Steven W	5:16:12	(27,155)
Hinchliffe, Steven	4:46:14	(22,306)
Hind, Robert D	3:29:45	(4,544)
Hind, Stephen J.	3:51:06	(8,765)
Hinde, Stephen	4:37:49	(20,409)
Hindlett, Alan G.	5:42:17	(29,501)
Hinds, Alan K	4:20:27	(16,149)
Hinds, Barry	6:03:18	(30,539)
Hinds, Carlos R	5:30:11	(28,601)

Hine, Adrian J	4:23:34	(16,961)
Hine, Andrew C	3:45:35	(7,435)
Hine, Christopher S	3:18:50	(2,934)
Hine, Ian	4:21:20	(16,345)
Hinn, Achim	3:51:33	(8,905)
Hinson, Robert	4:28:56	(18,334)
Hinton, Alex J	3:32:17	(4,965)
Hinton, Jeremy J	4:08:41	(13,283)
Hinton, Ritchie P	4:41:48	(21,309)
Hinton, Robert J	3:32:11	(4,949)
Hinton, Thomas H	4:47:15	(22,509)
Hipshon, David	5:03:03	(25,453)
Hirani, Surendra D	5:55:32	(30,228)
Hirano, Shoetsu	4:34:43	(19,761)
Hird, Frank W	3:28:43	(4,358)
Hirsch, Donald B	3:36:59	(5,766)
Hirschavge, Menachem	5:03:06	(25,459)
Hirschield, Norbert.	3:59:10	(11,049)
Hirst, Jamie	4:11:12	(13,911)
Hirst, John	5:12:54	(26,749)
Hirst, Kevin A	4:50:32	(23,188)
Hirst, Matthew D.	3:46:11	(7,573)
Hirst, Michael A	3:58:38	(10,899)
Hirst, Richard D	3:59:36	(11,188)
Hirst, Russell J	5:33:13	(28,822)
Hirst, Simon T.	5:19:58	(27,557)
Hiscock, Jonathan N	2:54:45	(729)
Hiscock, Martin	3:36:28	(5,691)
Hiscox, John	3:35:41	(5,552)
Histe, Daniel.	4:20:50	(16,235)
Histon, John	5:21:57	(27,766)
Hita-Hita, Luis M.	3:15:03	(2,560)
Hitchcock, Ben.	3:34:33	(5,349)
Hitchcock, Gary	3:46:42	(7,682)
Hitchcock, Paul R	4:53:30	(23,702)
Hitchen, Patrick C	5:12:39	(26,706)
Hitchens, Richard J	4:30:42	(18,800)
Hitchin, John A	4:11:17	(13,926)
Hitman, Graham A	5:09:47	(26,355)
Hitman, Oliver B.	4:06:41	(12,817)
Hizzett, Brian	4:02:39	(11,886)
Ho, Ricky	3:56:16	(10,171)
Hoadley, James W	4:06:27	(12,769)
Hoadley, Raymond A	3:48:42	(8,185)
Hoang, Huong N	4:34:14	(19,649)
Hoare, Andrew P.	4:34:00	(19,587)
Hoare, Chris	3:56:19	(10,183)
Hoare, David	5:00:48	(25,112)
Hoare, Ian P	3:13:30	(2,374)
Hoare, Mark	4:06:05	(12,680)
Hoare, Michael V	5:09:46	(26,351)
Hoare, Paul D.	4:52:53	(23,595)
Hoare, Raymond	3:57:07	(10,418)
Hoatson, Alec W.	4:37:01	(20,254)
Hobbs, Benjamin J.	5:13:13	(26,798)
Hobbs, Daniel P	4:25:31	(17,434)
Hobbs, Ian D	4:51:00	(23,270)
Hobbs, Matthew D	5:03:16	(25,485)
Hobbs, Neil.	4:27:08	(17,874)
Hobbs, Philip	4:15:41	(14,973)
Hobbs, Richard	4:59:02	(24,801)
Hobbs, Robert P.	3:30:52	(4,756)
Hobbs, Roger M	4:21:10	(16,302)
Hobday, Nick J.	6:02:32	(30,510)
Hobman, David A	5:26:33	(28,254)
Hobman, Ian A.	5:54:52	(30,192)
Hobson, Gary K	4:22:31	(16,703)
Hobson, Simon A	5:08:25	(26,175)
Hochreiter, Werner.	2:44:28	(302)
Hockey, Paul H.	3:27:51	(4,197)
Hockings-Thompson, Steve B	2:59:01	(1,073)
Hockley, Tom	5:42:47	(29,533)
Hockney, Dennis	4:16:52	(15,274)
Hoda, Feroz	3:52:53	(9,218)
Hoddell, David	2:57:35	(919)
Hoddell, Mike	4:18:06	(15,574)
Hodder, Rupert J.	5:14:17	(26,934)
Hodey, Matthew R.	3:27:50	(4,193)
Hodge, Brian M	5:10:12	(26,398)
Hodge, Hugo R	4:04:41	(12,345)
Hodge, Paul J	5:55:22	(30,217)
Hodge, Tony G.	3:25:09	(3,713)
Hodges, Darren P	3:53:09	(9,297)

Hodges, Dave	4:14:47	(14,752)
Hodges, Jonathan D	4:30:14	(18,687)
Hodges, Kevan	3:57:20	(10,492)
Hodges, Kevin L.	5:17:19	(27,285)
Hodges, Michael D	3:44:58	(7,301)
Hodges, Nick	3:19:00	(2,949)
Hodges, Philip J	5:00:49	(25,116)
Hodges, Simon G	3:43:50	(7,021)
Hodgett, Matthew C.	4:36:20	(20,096)
Hodgetts, Peter	4:58:38	(24,745)
Hodgetts, Stephen J	3:10:37	(2,063)
Hodgkinson, David H	3:57:59	(10,667)
Hodgkinson, Peter.	3:22:47	(3,418)
Hodgkiss, William	3:17:26	(2,797)
Hodgson, Allan	3:01:03	(1,242)
Hodgson, Charles	3:58:11	(10,750)
Hodgson, Christopher L	2:48:54	(454)
Hodgson, David	4:01:30	(11,600)
Hodgson, David.	4:02:05	(11,739)
Hodgson, Duncan	4:07:35	(13,031)
Hodgson, Garreth S	4:06:12	(12,711)
Hodgson, Kenneth	4:06:13	(12,716)
Hodgson, Kieran M.	2:49:50	(492)
Hodgson, Matthew	3:31:55	(4,907)
Hodgson, Stuart P	5:48:53	(29,903)
Hodgson, Thomas A	3:08:45	(1,870)
Hodgson, Tony	3:11:04	(2,101)
Hodkin, Nigel B	4:02:20	(11,823)
Hodson, Adrian	5:06:49	(25,946)
Hodson, David.	3:20:40	(3,157)
Hodson, Richard C	4:10:36	(13,782)
Hoe, Michael W	3:26:21	(3,897)
Hoe, Simon G.	3:33:02	(5,106)
Hoedl, Wolfgang	3:55:53	(10,045)
Hoehn, Frank	4:48:39	(22,803)
Hoenicke, Klaus	3:33:07	(5,122)
Hoff, Svein Olau.	4:37:37	(20,361)
Hoffman, Mick J	4:13:12	(14,376)
Hoffmann, Juergen	3:42:52	(6,827)
Hofmann, Heribert.	3:17:02	(2,751)
Hofmann, Holm.	3:18:31	(2,898)
Hofmann, Mathias	3:30:46	(4,735)
Hogan, Andrew	4:39:10	(20,764)
Hogan, James	5:20:20	(27,613)
Hogan, Stephen	5:27:26	(28,350)
Hogan, Tony A	4:31:57	(19,096)
Hogarth, Ian	4:53:33	(23,710)
Hogarth, Martin	4:16:08	(15,089)
Hogarth, Stephen	4:10:11	(13,675)
Hogbin, Patrick R	4:56:53	(24,380)
Hogg, Andrew J	4:53:02	(23,619)
Hogg, Anthony J	3:45:50	(7,488)
Hogg, Chris S	3:28:48	(4,373)
Hogg, Edward T	4:13:57	(14,553)
Hogg, Johnny	3:52:53	(9,218)
Hogg, Keith A.	4:28:20	(18,174)
Hogg, Martin P.	4:08:26	(13,211)
Hogg, Paul R	4:08:27	(13,214)
Hogg, Quintin	4:34:49	(19,781)
Hogg, Richard G	4:41:18	(21,187)
Hogg, Richard J.	3:20:38	(3,152)
Hoggan, Brent C	3:00:58	(1,234)
Hoggett, Paul	4:08:14	(13,157)
Hohenfeld, Michael	3:27:24	(4,103)
Hohenschild, Oliver	3:29:16	(4,464)
Hoinka, Dieter	3:30:33	(4,699)
Hoiom, Runar	2:18:52	(29)
Holbrook, Andrew T	3:29:31	(4,506)
Holbrook, Philip P	3:44:05	(7,092)
Holbrough, Richard C	3:37:31	(5,877)
Holby, David J	4:51:11	(23,302)
Holdaway, Les B	4:23:49	(17,017)
Holdcroft, Dean	3:00:26	(1,188)
Holden, Adrian	4:54:54	(23,977)
Holden, Andrew P	3:14:25	(2,490)
Holden, Andrew W	4:29:36	(18,523)
Holden, David	4:28:23	(18,187)
Holden, Frank	5:26:20	(28,248)
Holden, Geoff	4:14:58	(14,798)
Holden, Grant D	4:40:51	(21,098)
Holden, Kevin T	5:49:46	(29,948)
Holden, Marcus.	4:16:35	(15,194)
Holden, Mick A	4:26:10	(17,621)

Holden, Patrick 4:44:27 (21,899)
Holden, Philip J 3:48:40 (8,176)
Holden, Stephen J 3:42:42 (6,790)
Holden Merris, Andrew 3:42:00 (6,646)
Holder, Benjamin W 4:05:42 (12,595)
Holder, John M 3:42:56 (6,840)
Holder, Julian T 4:04:52 (12,396)
Holder, Steven W 3:49:42 (8,424)
Holding, Neil H 3:00:32 (1,196)
Holding, Peter F 3:52:42 (9,174)
Holditch, Karl 4:04:14 (12,249)
Holdrick, Paul D 5:58:30 (30,349)
Holdsworth, Antony R 5:25:30 (28,137)
Holdsworth, Daniel M 3:23:45 (3,538)
Holdsworth, David C 4:44:36 (21,935)
Holdsworth, John 4:28:28 (18,220)
Hole, Gordon 4:15:04 (14,818)
Hole, James 4:07:26 (12,997)
Holgate, Paul 4:38:25 (20,575)
Holian, James S 3:31:22 (4,828)
Holian, John P 3:26:10 (3,870)
Holl, Robert C 5:01:20 (25,191)
Holland, Alex J 3:35:43 (5,559)
Holland, Ian K 4:55:52 (24,169)
Holland, John 4:03:37 (12,105)
Holland, John 4:15:50 (15,010)
Holland, John D 3:16:35 (2,707)
Holland, Mark A 4:14:08 (14,593)
Holland, Neil F 3:59:56 (11,279)
Holland, Paul E 3:54:43 (9,696)
Holland, Richard E 3:43:11 (6,890)
Holland, Rob M 5:09:36 (26,323)
Holland, Tom E 3:53:02 (9,265)
Hollanders, Roland 4:19:39 (15,940)
Hollands, James 5:33:14 (28,825)
Hollands, John R 3:47:09 (7,795)
Hollands, Mark T 3:23:27 (3,494)
Hollands, Mark W 3:58:29 (10,845)
Hollas, Andrew 3:44:17 (7,133)
Hollaus, Josef 3:36:33 (5,703)
Holleran, Martin 4:45:03 (22,045)
Holley, Marc 7:14:45 (31,744)
Holleyman, Steven 4:03:57 (12,179)
Holliday, Paul W 4:24:11 (17,117)
Holliday, Tom H 3:51:06 (8,765)
Hollier, Stephen H 2:45:26 (340)
Hollinggon, Allan 4:37:42 (20,382)
Hollingsworth, Alan P 3:52:47 (9,188)
Hollinshead, Christopher D 2:58:48 (1,057)
Hollinshead, Mark 4:54:17 (23,851)
Hollis, Iain D 4:18:55 (15,764)
Hollis, Kenneth J 3:34:08 (5,288)
Hollis, Sam J 3:12:48 (2,286)
Hollis, Stephen P 4:16:30 (15,174)
Hollis, Zachary M 3:24:44 (3,654)
Hollobone, Martin B 3:56:01 (10,090)
Hollow, Martin 6:06:27 (30,633)
Holloway, Benjamin J 4:34:36 (19,733)
Holloway, Matthew J 3:53:23 (9,358)
Holloway, Melvyn J 3:10:04 (2,008)
Holloway, Nick 4:12:08 (14,122)
Holloway, Richard B 3:58:26 (10,832)
Holloway, Robert M 3:18:41 (2,917)
Hollowood, Adam J 3:50:32 (8,634)
Hollyoak, Chris D 4:37:38 (20,370)
Hollywood, Bernie P 5:22:18 (27,805)
Hollywood, David W 3:34:55 (5,414)
Holman, Dave P 4:33:53 (19,556)
Holman, David 4:34:08 (19,632)
Holman, Paul S 3:37:26 (5,868)
Holman, Richard H 3:42:35 (6,760)
Holmberg, David J 3:57:19 (10,488)
Holme, Robert J 5:10:43 (26,469)
Holmes, Albert C 4:39:53 (20,891)
Holmes, Charles 3:50:51 (8,720)
Holmes, Darren 4:55:43 (24,135)
Holmes, Darren R 4:46:00 (22,250)
Holmes, Gary 3:12:08 (2,206)
Holmes, Jamie A 3:27:44 (4,174)
Holmes, John 3:56:04 (10,105)
Holmes, Leigh 4:39:41 (20,859)
Holmes, Mark D 4:45:34 (22,154)
Holmes, Nathan P 4:43:38 (21,707)

LONDON MARATHON

Holmes, Nicholas M 2:58:41 (1,039)
Holmes, Paul 5:03:56 (25,570)
Holmes, Paul D 6:14:41 (30,871)
Holmes, Paul J 4:07:39 (13,044)
Holmes, Peter H 4:04:04 (12,200)
Holmes, Richard A 3:10:23 (2,037)
Holmes, Robin 3:39:58 (6,298)
Holmes, Stephen P 4:44:11 (21,835)
Holmes, Thomas 5:27:18 (28,335)
Holmes, Thomas J 4:03:12 (12,007)
Holmes, Tim 3:48:10 (8,039)
Holmes, Tim R 3:52:17 (9,079)
Hols, Per E 4:32:46 (19,306)
Holt, Alan W 4:27:52 (18,059)
Holt, Andrew 3:46:05 (7,544)
Holt, Andrew D 7:15:59 (31,754)
Holt, Andrew J 2:37:14 (160)
Holt, Darrel I 3:49:31 (8,380)
Holt, Michael J 3:49:08 (8,291)
Holt, Nicholas M 3:49:05 (8,277)
Holt, Nick 4:54:45 (23,951)
Holt, Simon 3:05:38 (1,578)
Holt, Simon J 4:49:01 (22,878)
Holt, Tim C 5:10:15 (26,407)
Holt, Tony J 5:06:41 (25,937)
Holton, David R 4:13:22 (14,423)
Holy, Kristian J 5:04:42 (25,650)
Holyman, Ian 2:53:58 (695)
Holzer, Elmar 6:56:29 (31,579)
Holzhauer, Karl-Heinz 4:05:45 (12,606)
Holzweiler, Rainer 3:33:52 (5,251)
Homden, David R 4:16:26 (15,157)
Home, Steven 2:48:39 (442)
Homer, Barrie D 6:41:08 (31,376)
Homer, John G 3:45:08 (7,330)
Homer, Mark R 3:04:05 (1,458)
Homes, Simon P 3:56:55 (10,371)
Homewood, Gordon A 4:08:15 (13,159)
Homfray, Russell G 4:15:53 (15,026)
Hone, Dennis V 4:13:48 (14,517)
Hone, Michael S 4:15:05 (14,821)
Honey, Matthew J 4:22:41 (16,746)
Honeyman, David 5:59:52 (30,405)
Honeywill, Martin 5:35:44 (29,013)
Honeywood, Ian 4:24:03 (17,072)
Hong, Darryl K 4:46:08 (22,275)
Honnor, Ian C 3:53:27 (9,366)
Honour, Mark A 4:20:34 (16,177)
Hood, Andrew 3:47:33 (7,894)
Hood, Andrew M 3:43:30 (6,962)
Hood, Graeme 4:18:38 (15,695)
Hood, Philip K 3:45:52 (7,498)
Hoogeterp, Jaap 3:14:50 (2,542)
Hook, David A 3:38:59 (6,132)
Hook, John C 3:50:20 (8,589)
Hook, Philip F 3:37:03 (5,783)
Hook, Trevor L 4:05:25 (12,515)
Hooker, Michael D 3:38:07 (5,981)
Hookham, Paul A 4:23:55 (17,043)
Hoole, Philip A 2:51:23 (560)
Hooley, Andrew P 3:13:38 (2,390)
Hooper, Daniel 4:37:40 (20,375)
Hooper, David J 3:35:12 (5,458)
Hooper, Gavin M 4:02:05 (11,739)
Hooper, Graham 5:20:40 (27,655)
Hooper, James 4:31:52 (19,066)
Hooper, James L 3:28:56 (4,404)
Hooper, Louise A 4:13:52 (14,536)
Hooper, Marcus P 3:47:16 (7,822)
Hooper, Martin 3:45:23 (7,384)
Hooper, Martin R 4:57:11 (24,432)
Hooper, Nicholas J 4:06:34 (12,798)
Hooper, Patrick D 6:16:55 (30,929)
Hooper, Paul A 3:48:35 (8,144)

Hooper, Shaun I 4:41:14 (21,163)
Hooper, Steven C 3:50:07 (8,534)
Hope, Daniel R 6:09:11 (30,705)
Hope, Geoffrey A 5:07:13 (25,996)
Hope, Lee C 6:11:26 (30,771)
Hope, Max 5:21:07 (27,692)
Hope, Robert E 3:56:00 (10,084)
Hopegood, James 4:42:28 (21,444)
Hopes, Ben 3:54:26 (9,622)
Hopgood, Martin A 3:53:30 (9,378)
Hopkins, Andrew J 5:22:25 (27,826)
Hopkins, Brian 4:20:00 (16,034)
Hopkins, Chris 4:34:21 (19,678)
Hopkins, David M 4:36:54 (20,227)
Hopkins, Doug 6:18:36 (30,977)
Hopkins, Gary A 3:49:33 (8,390)
Hopkins, Graham A 3:51:54 (8,989)
Hopkins, Greg 3:44:25 (7,163)
Hopkins, John C 3:49:40 (8,416)
Hopkins, Marlon J 4:20:07 (16,049)
Hopkins, Martin J 4:32:03 (19,121)
Hopkins, Paul A 4:09:00 (13,380)
Hopkins, Peter R 5:28:15 (28,415)
Hopkins, Philip J 4:35:45 (19,971)
Hopkins, Rhys W 4:49:31 (22,981)
Hopkins, Simon J 3:52:24 (9,111)
Hopkins, Stuart D 3:43:47 (7,009)
Hopkinson, Neil D 3:07:33 (1,759)
Hopper, Andrew 4:16:20 (15,126)
Hopper, Ian 3:41:02 (6,480)
Hopper, Julian F 3:54:08 (9,536)
Hopper, Nicholas J 3:52:14 (9,064)
Hopper, Peter 3:07:34 (1,761)
Hopps, David J 4:18:18 (15,607)
Hopps, Peter W 3:13:52 (2,420)
Horak, Christian 3:43:15 (6,907)
Horan, William J 5:16:34 (27,201)
Horgan, John A 5:05:15 (25,718)
Horgan, Michael A 3:53:47 (9,436)
Horler, Martin 4:01:59 (11,712)
Horlock, Wayn E 4:26:11 (17,626)
Horn, Andrew 4:48:14 (22,725)
Horn, Derek J 3:04:16 (1,470)
Horn, Neil C 5:17:55 (27,355)
Horn, Oliver 3:52:54 (9,227)
Horn, Steven M 5:13:04 (26,780)
Horn, Stuart C 4:35:15 (19,875)
Horn, Svante P 5:24:00 (27,973)
Horn, Wylie 4:28:00 (18,098)
Hornbruch, Wolfgang 3:40:02 (6,309)
Hornby, Simon A 3:25:39 (3,792)
Horncastle, Kevin C 4:10:46 (13,816)
Horne, Andrew J 3:02:50 (1,359)
Horne, Chad M 3:25:36 (3,789)
Horne, Dale K 4:04:32 (12,323)
Horne, David R 3:29:12 (4,449)
Horne, Martin R 3:56:28 (10,241)
Horne, Matthew 3:38:00 (5,961)
Horne, Matthew L 4:42:54 (21,541)
Horner, David J 5:31:38 (28,710)
Horner, Geoffrey A 4:30:49 (18,818)
Horner, Michael 3:13:13 (2,331)
Horner, Richard E 2:58:36 (1,026)
Hornsby, Jack G 5:45:59 (29,749)
Hornsey, Phil J 4:26:06 (17,608)
Horridge, Chris 4:46:09 (22,279)
Horrocks, Charles 4:53:29 (23,699)
Horry, Geoff A 3:50:15 (8,563)
Horscroft, Paul R 5:25:21 (28,125)
Horseman, Jeff C 3:37:00 (5,768)
Horsfield, Terry M 3:49:37 (8,409)
Horsley, Graham M 3:10:39 (2,067)
Horsley, Simon A 3:06:04 (1,617)
Horsman, Jonathan 3:03:55 (1,443)
Horsman, Joseph 3:40:20 (6,364)
Horsman, Richard 5:40:00 (29,334)
Horst, Peter 4:29:48 (18,583)
Horton, Clive 3:43:07 (6,875)
Horton, Colin N 3:35:04 (5,436)
Horton, David L 4:18:43 (15,712)
Horton, Leigh S 3:56:24 (10,213)
Horton, Martyn T 4:47:18 (22,517)
Horton, Michael E 3:41:26 (6,537)

Horton, Peter H 3:35:00 (5,427)
Horton, Richard 4:03:17 (12,025)
Horton, Rob 4:40:05 (20,936)
Horton, Simon 3:36:15 (5,650)
Horwich, Lee M 4:17:16 (15,360)
Horwitch-Smith, Oliver E 4:21:18 (16,333)
Horwood, Mike J 3:26:59 (4,018)
Hosey, Richard P 3:37:17 (5,832)
Hosie, Euan A 3:31:10 (4,801)
Hosie, John J 3:11:45 (2,164)
Hosie, Nicol M 3:39:07 (6,150)
Hoskin, David M 2:52:00 (590)
Hosking, Andrew P 3:38:32 (6,051)
Hosking, Mark L 5:09:15 (26,271)
Hosking, Peter 3:53:52 (9,469)
Hosking, Tom 4:21:19 (16,337)
Hoskins, Stephen P 5:41:19 (29,433)
Hoskyn, John 4:46:57 (22,436)
Hossack, John 4:08:54 (13,348)
Hostetler, Thomas A 3:23:01 (3,442)
Hostler, Nick J 4:39:06 (20,748)
Hosue, David W 3:49:09 (8,297)
Hotchkiss, Andrew T 3:38:56 (6,119)
Hough, Andrew 3:22:07 (3,317)
Hough, Andrew F 3:55:37 (9,966)
Hough, Dermot P 3:50:10 (8,541)
Hough, Eliot N 4:21:17 (16,328)
Hough, Jason 3:50:36 (8,656)
Hough, Martin G 3:14:58 (2,557)
Hough, Oliver G 5:03:52 (25,562)
Houghton, Kevin T 4:01:54 (11,688)
Houghton, Nigel 3:46:22 (7,614)
Houghton, Philip D 4:29:22 (18,457)
Houghton, Ricky J 4:33:19 (19,429)
Houghton, Stephen J 3:25:15 (3,728)
Houghton, Toby J 3:28:13 (4,266)
Houlden, Grant P 4:29:16 (18,418)
Houlder, Peter J 4:09:07 (13,402)
Houlgrave, Paul 4:27:20 (17,925)
Houliston, Stuart D 3:29:48 (4,553)
Hoult, Michael J 3:47:25 (7,856)
Hoult, Nigel S 3:48:13 (8,055)
Hoult, Tim D 5:10:23 (26,425)
Houlton, Matthew 3:53:45 (9,427)
Houlton, Nicholas J 2:43:25 (275)
Hounsell, David C 3:55:45 (10,005)
Hounslow, Jon R 6:22:44 (31,075)
Hourigan, Christopher S 5:07:37 (26,059)
Hourquebie, Damian 5:08:20 (26,164)
Hourquebie, Philip A 5:08:21 (26,167)
House, Adam D 4:48:11 (22,718)
House, Jim 5:09:47 (26,355)
House, Kevin C 4:02:39 (11,886)
House, Mark S 3:49:09 (8,297)
House, Matt J 3:45:49 (7,485)
House, Richard A 4:46:05 (22,266)
Houwen, Sietze 4:14:31 (14,682)
Hovinga, Jelco 3:50:26 (8,614)
Hovinga, Wiebe 5:00:32 (25,069)
How, Chris 3:54:31 (9,641)
How, Jonathan A 3:16:31 (2,701)
Howard, Andrew M 4:54:02 (23,800)
Howard, Andy W 4:24:30 (17,182)
Howard, Chris L 4:24:12 (17,122)
Howard, David N 5:13:30 (26,825)
Howard, Denis 4:50:49 (23,239)
Howard, Gavin 3:51:10 (8,789)
Howard, Gavin E 5:16:51 (27,242)
Howard, Ivor J 3:04:45 (1,507)
Howard, Jason A 3:14:30 (2,503)
Howard, John P 4:05:53 (12,634)
Howard, Marc 3:03:37 (1,416)
Howard, Michael P 4:01:18 (11,562)
Howard, Nigel L 5:14:46 (26,999)
Howard, Paul J 4:28:35 (18,251)
Howard, Phillip 3:13:08 (2,321)
Howard, Richard P 4:48:02 (22,678)
Howard, Roger J 4:04:09 (12,228)
Howard, Stephen 3:27:39 (4,156)
Howarth, Alex J 4:33:53 (19,556)
Howarth, John 4:52:08 (23,471)
Howarth, John A 3:50:21 (8,595)
Howarth, Paul A 4:23:43 (16,993)
Howarth, Raymond P 2:58:40 (1,037)
Howarth, Richard J 2:54:51 (738)
Howarth, Roger M 5:07:40 (26,071)
Howarth, Stephen J 4:36:32 (20,142)
Howcroft, Thomas D 4:14:32 (14,690)
Howden, Alexander G 4:37:45 (20,391)
Howden, Peter 4:25:04 (17,327)
Howe, Andrew D 3:39:05 (6,145)
Howe, Gary 3:17:50 (2,832)
Howe, Mark 4:45:30 (22,142)
Howe, Martin 3:39:21 (6,192)
Howe, Richard C 3:25:08 (3,709)
Howe, Robert L 3:32:49 (5,063)
Howe, Simon C 4:23:51 (17,025)
Howe, Stewart L 4:29:55 (18,614)
Howell, Christopher E 6:39:30 (31,355)
Howell, Christopher J 3:41:23 (6,533)
Howell, David 3:53:37 (9,407)
Howell, Duncan 3:35:06 (5,445)
Howell, John 4:00:37 (11,411)
Howell, Mark 8:28:27 (31,964)
Howell, Mark E 5:13:00 (26,762)
Howell, Matthew J 3:58:09 (10,729)
Howell, Neil E 5:13:48 (26,872)
Howell, Ryan L 5:39:18 (29,290)
Howell, Scott 3:02:13 (1,318)
Howells, David S 3:30:36 (4,707)
Howells, Denis M 3:55:08 (9,831)
Howells, Malcolm 3:06:12 (1,627)
Howells, Robert D 3:37:53 (5,936)
Howells, Shaun D 3:49:28 (8,368)
Howes, Geoff E 4:33:03 (19,367)
Howes, Sean 3:57:07 (10,418)
Howett, Ian R 3:23:48 (3,544)
Howgego, James 3:59:55 (11,273)
Howie, John M 4:25:00 (17,311)
Howitt, Stuart B 4:26:07 (17,613)
Howladar, Farid 4:23:30 (16,942)
Howle, Clifford H 6:08:11 (30,679)
Howlett, David 5:15:38 (27,093)
Howlett, Kevin M 4:28:04 (18,115)
Howlett, Matthew M 4:38:19 (20,551)
Howlett, Stephen P 5:16:25 (27,181)
Howley, Vincent I 3:30:35 (4,705)
Howlorth, John 4:12:34 (14,225)
Howson, Stephen J 4:04:41 (12,345)
Hoyes, Joseph 4:28:54 (18,327)
Hoyland, Jack T 5:37:24 (29,148)
Hoyland, Richard J 3:41:09 (6,504)
Hoyle, Adrian D 3:22:36 (3,390)
Hoyle, Michael G 3:58:57 (10,991)
Hoyle, Nick M 3:57:19 (10,488)
Hoyle, Raymond J 6:52:43 (31,538)
Hoyles, James 3:48:30 (8,118)
Hu, Benjamin 4:32:26 (19,220)
Hubbard, Peter C 5:50:01 (29,966)
Hubbard, Richard B 4:25:52 (17,529)
Hubbard, Simon A 6:10:39 (30,746)
Hubber, Tim M 4:19:24 (15,883)
Hubble, Nick 4:15:59 (15,046)
Hubble, Peter L 4:09:04 (13,394)
Huber, Christian 2:59:12 (1,093)
Huck, Dave 2:53:01 (645)
Huck, Ernest F 3:09:34 (1,957)
Hucknall, Jonathan 4:49:06 (22,895)
Hudd, David J 4:26:07 (17,613)
Huddleston, Benjamin J 3:58:20 (10,799)
Hudgell, Ian R 4:16:34 (15,189)
Hudner, Brian J 4:11:30 (13,968)
Hudson, Adam D 4:00:50 (11,454)
Hudson, Alan 3:05:08 (1,538)
Hudson, Alistair G 4:57:15 (24,450)
Hudson, Bradley 3:42:03 (6,661)
Hudson, Chris 3:38:51 (6,109)
Hudson, Damian R 3:57:07 (10,418)
Hudson, Gary 4:03:17 (12,025)
Hudson, Guy 4:38:21 (20,558)
Hudson, Jason D 3:59:04 (11,019)
Hudson, John W 4:31:51 (19,061)
Hudson, Kenneth 3:37:02 (5,776)
Hudson, Kevin A 4:08:42 (13,291)
Hudson, Leslie 3:11:45 (2,164)
Hudson, Matthew J 4:18:15 (15,598)
Hudson, Michael J 4:42:54 (21,541)
Hudson, Paul R 3:50:29 (8,629)
Hudson, Paul W 4:33:48 (19,534)
Hudson, Piers J 4:48:47 (22,832)
Hudson, Richard A 3:09:14 (1,922)
Hudson, Ronald J 5:20:06 (27,581)
Hudson, Tony C 3:05:11 (1,543)
Hudspith, John E 2:56:34 (857)
Hudspith, Mark 2:16:15 (20)
Hueller, Emilio 3:56:21 (10,196)
Hufschmid, Walter M 3:53:33 (9,391)
Hugenroth, Florian C 3:41:00 (6,474)
Huggan, Paul 5:26:53 (28,290)
Huggett, Matthew 6:00:03 (30,410)
Huggon, Douglas 3:34:26 (5,331)
Hughes, Brian J 3:25:00 (3,693)
Hughes, Ceri 4:23:42 (16,989)
Hughes, Damian B 4:38:00 (20,466)
Hughes, Dave A 3:22:18 (3,341)
Hughes, David A 3:56:23 (10,204)
Hughes, David A 3:58:53 (10,967)
Hughes, David G 6:10:12 (30,732)
Hughes, David J 5:17:12 (27,272)
Hughes, David R 3:32:18 (4,970)
Hughes, David W 4:31:53 (19,072)
Hughes, Dean A 4:05:37 (12,575)
Hughes, Frank D 3:30:57 (4,771)
Hughes, Frederick J 3:53:09 (9,297)
Hughes, Gareth L 3:42:17 (6,697)
Hughes, Gareth P 4:10:00 (13,639)
Hughes, Gary 3:33:55 (5,258)
Hughes, Geraint 2:56:22 (845)
Hughes, Gregory R 4:00:05 (11,311)
Hughes, Hefin L 4:06:18 (12,736)
Hughes, Ian 3:11:12 (2,114)
Hughes, Ian J 4:00:54 (11,479)
Hughes, James 5:39:01 (29,267)
Hughes, James L 4:10:01 (13,642)
Hughes, Jay J 4:11:17 (13,926)
Hughes, Jeremy 4:59:54 (24,975)
Hughes, John K 5:00:11 (25,021)
Hughes, John M 5:24:30 (28,026)
Hughes, Jonathan D 5:32:02 (28,735)
Hughes, Kevin A 4:32:46 (19,306)
Hughes, Marc A 3:58:45 (10,930)
Hughes, Mark A 4:11:37 (14,005)
Hughes, Mark C 3:27:27 (4,115)
Hughes, Martin A 5:14:19 (26,936)
Hughes, Maurice 5:03:38 (25,539)
Hughes, Nicholas I 5:09:09 (26,260)
Hughes, Paul B 4:44:57 (22,020)
Hughes, Paul J 5:40:13 (29,351)
Hughes, Peter 4:19:11 (15,825)
Hughes, Peter D 4:44:23 (21,885)
Hughes, Peter J 3:02:37 (1,346)
Hughes, Philip G 4:12:11 (14,131)
Hughes, Richard J 4:44:57 (22,020)
Hughes, Richard J 4:45:49 (22,213)
Hughes, Robin D 5:11:57 (26,624)
Hughes, Rodger J 3:05:55 (1,601)
Hughes, Sean P 4:57:06 (24,420)
Hughes, Simon 3:29:59 (4,585)
Hughes, Simon D 4:04:50 (12,385)
Hughes, Stephen 4:07:55 (13,094)
Hughes, Stephen G 5:06:20 (25,892)
Hughes, Steven C 3:27:49 (4,188)
Hughes, Wayne A 4:10:51 (13,842)
Hughes MBE, Ifan R 3:36:43 (5,728)
Hughson, David C 3:58:55 (10,979)
Hugill, Gary W 3:19:56 (3,061)
Huhnholt, Theo 3:33:16 (5,153)
Huijsman, Rob 4:20:12 (16,064)
Huitric, Jean Yves 3:58:10 (10,745)
Huitson, Leslie A 3:34:16 (5,306)
Hulcoop, Brian M 5:07:12 (25,992)
Hulcoop, Stephen 4:41:28 (21,236)
Hull, Andrew 4:43:55 (21,778)
Hull, Andrew M 6:43:50 (31,415)
Hull, David J 5:10:29 (26,440)
Hulley, Michael S 3:17:15 (2,780)
Hulme, Anthony T 5:49:08 (29,915)
Hulme, Michael J 4:24:11 (17,117)
Hulme, Stephen C 4:56:20 (24,272)

Hulse, Christopher T	3:52:30 (9,134)	
Hulse, Mike J	3:39:35 (6,231)	
Hulse, Robin T	6:44:14 (31,420)	
Humber, Steven J	3:39:35 (6,231)	
Humberstone, Ian D	4:20:59 (16,281)	
Humble, Anthony J	5:47:45 (29,857)	
Humble, Brian	3:12:53 (2,299)	
Humblot, Pierre	4:21:14 (16,319)	
Humby, Mark A	4:40:17 (20,983)	
Hume, Lawrence C	3:53:47 (9,436)	
Hume, Marc	4:52:41 (23,567)	
Humm, David G	5:16:47 (27,230)	
Hummel, Martin H	3:54:37 (9,673)	
Humphrey, Andrew C	4:48:02 (22,678)	
Humphrey, Paul	4:24:00 (17,062)	
Humphrey, Robert M	3:53:57 (9,489)	
Humphreys, Gareth	4:16:44 (15,234)	
Humphreys, Kevin N	4:36:46 (20,194)	
Humphreys, Ray E	3:32:48 (5,060)	
Humphreys, Richard S	4:38:39 (20,627)	
Humphreys, Steve	3:12:22 (2,236)	
Humphreys Evans, Giles W	3:19:54 (3,058)	
Humphries, John J	3:56:45 (10,311)	
Humphries, Paul	3:26:45 (3,973)	
Humphries, Paul	4:55:53 (24,177)	
Humphries, Stephen A	4:13:57 (14,553)	
Hunnisett, Stephen M	3:30:06 (4,614)	
Hunt, Andrew J	3:14:10 (2,464)	
Hunt, Andrew R	3:28:57 (4,407)	
Hunt, Anthony	3:56:41 (10,298)	
Hunt, Christopher P	3:00:23 (1,186)	
Hunt, Darren R	4:53:22 (23,681)	
Hunt, David P	4:06:35 (12,801)	
Hunt, Gary	4:02:41 (11,894)	
Hunt, James A	4:27:06 (17,864)	
Hunt, James C	4:03:50 (12,155)	
Hunt, John D	4:14:34 (14,698)	
Hunt, Justin R	5:11:05 (26,514)	
Hunt, Mark	3:34:53 (5,405)	
Hunt, Matthew F	4:42:48 (21,520)	
Hunt, Matthew V	4:54:47 (23,956)	
Hunt, Richard J	5:06:42 (25,939)	
Hunt, Richard M	4:28:37 (18,259)	
Hunt, Robert I	3:24:37 (3,639)	
Hunt, Ross A	3:17:34 (2,808)	
Hunt, Simon M	2:51:05 (547)	
Hunt, Steve P	3:00:03 (1,161)	
Hunt, Thomas F	3:28:39 (4,343)	
Hunte, Christopher B	5:20:27 (27,623)	
Hunter, Craig R	3:44:01 (7,075)	
Hunter, Darren P	5:17:52 (27,349)	
Hunter, Donald	3:45:19 (7,367)	
Hunter, Harry W	3:42:13 (6,686)	
Hunter, James D	5:07:06 (25,982)	
Hunter, John J	4:12:45 (14,274)	
Hunter, Mark	4:29:44 (18,564)	
Hunter, Mark J	3:06:58 (1,702)	
Hunter, Michael L	5:31:29 (28,702)	
Hunter, Paul S	5:11:11 (26,535)	
Hunter, Pete J	4:38:15 (20,533)	
Hunter, Richard A	2:55:32 (786)	
Hunter, Richard S	3:54:20 (9,596)	
Hunting, Andrew M	6:26:21 (31,148)	
Hunting, Rupert A	4:21:11 (16,307)	
Huntingford, Stephen A	4:47:18 (22,517)	
Huntley, Graham	4:04:54 (12,409)	
Huntley, Noah	3:58:38 (10,899)	
Huntley, Stephen	4:43:40 (21,714)	
Hurcomb, Robert J	3:25:27 (3,761)	
Hurd, Andrew R	4:09:30 (13,501)	
Hurd, James M	3:20:57 (3,195)	
Hurford, Michael J	3:25:10 (3,716)	
Hurley, Michael	3:03:26 (1,401)	
Hurn, Anthony	3:09:59 (1,999)	
Hurp, David P	4:24:14 (17,129)	
Hurst, Alan	4:35:07 (19,844)	
Hurst, Ciaran	4:19:53 (15,992)	
Hurst, Geoff	4:43:02 (21,570)	
Hurst, John C	3:03:37 (1,416)	
Hurst, Philip E	4:50:25 (23,162)	
Hurst, Ron J	4:30:16 (18,694)	
Hurt, Andrew J	5:26:15 (28,216)	
Hurt, Paul F	4:47:22 (22,533)	
Hurtley, Charles	4:40:11 (20,959)	
Hurtley, Duncan A	6:35:29 (31,297)	
Husband, Eryl J	2:51:01 (544)	
Huser, Thomas M	3:45:14 (7,358)	
Husk, Gary J	3:31:20 (4,823)	
Hussain, Delwar	5:17:24 (27,296)	
Hussain, Faris	3:46:31 (7,639)	
Hussain, Haroon	5:06:26 (25,902)	
Hussain, Sarfraz	6:05:30 (30,605)	
Hussey, Alex D	3:00:02 (1,160)	
Hussey, William K	3:31:40 (4,869)	
Hutcheson, Adam J	4:16:39 (15,220)	
Hutcheson, Christopher	4:16:39 (15,220)	
Hutchings, David	4:21:42 (16,449)	
Hutchings, Jonathan C	3:57:00 (10,390)	
Hutchings, Mark A	3:49:50 (8,457)	
Hutchings, Richard G	4:24:20 (17,150)	
Hutchings, Terence R	7:54:24 (31,924)	
Hutchins, Michael	5:04:52 (25,672)	
Hutchinson, Alan K	3:00:53 (1,229)	
Hutchinson, Brett G	2:51:27 (565)	
Hutchinson, Ian	5:23:29 (27,916)	
Hutchinson, James	3:18:01 (2,850)	
Hutchinson, James P	3:43:38 (6,985)	
Hutchinson, James W	4:30:20 (18,711)	
Hutchinson, Justin J	3:55:25 (9,910)	
Hutchinson, Lloyd	5:29:07 (28,495)	
Hutchinson, Michael	3:37:16 (5,829)	
Hutchinson, Miles P	4:18:20 (15,616)	
Hutchinson, Neil G	5:10:14 (26,402)	
Hutchinson, Paul A	5:10:14 (26,402)	
Hutchinson, Richard S	4:15:58 (15,044)	
Hutchinson, Stephen	3:45:47 (7,480)	
Hutchinson, Thomas E	4:18:47 (15,734)	
Hutchion, Michael B	4:46:05 (22,266)	
Hutchison, Robert B	4:06:12 (12,711)	
Hutchison, Ross P	4:56:45 (24,352)	
Hutchison, Tom P	3:09:31 (1,948)	
Hutchon, Grant	3:53:04 (9,271)	
Huteson, Alwyn	5:28:10 (28,409)	
Hutten Czapski, Estanislao	4:14:19 (14,626)	
Hutton, Jeff	4:00:21 (11,369)	
Hutton, Paul	4:56:50 (24,371)	
Hutton, Peter G	3:46:56 (7,730)	
Hutton, Simon M	4:20:55 (16,267)	
Hutton, Steven A	3:19:01 (2,954)	
Huws, Llion D	3:21:42 (3,276)	
Huxstep, Charles W	3:40:09 (6,332)	
Huxtable, Richard F	3:33:43 (5,218)	
Huyton, Stephen J	3:16:32 (2,703)	
Hyams, David	4:20:17 (16,095)	
Hyatt, Gary F	3:23:16 (3,474)	
Hyde, Andrew L	5:33:31 (28,852)	
Hyde, Anthony P	6:30:04 (31,206)	
Hyde, Douglas J	3:19:08 (2,967)	
Hyde, Gordon E	5:36:24 (29,053)	
Hyde, Matthew D	6:29:54 (31,201)	
Hyde, Michael R	5:52:48 (30,116)	
Hyde, Nick P	3:55:40 (9,976)	
Hyde, Richard S	4:23:14 (16,879)	
Hyde, Steven M	4:33:36 (19,486)	
Hyde, Tim	2:41:40 (235)	
Hyder, Jonathan P	4:45:03 (22,045)	
Hyer, Jonathan N	4:22:24 (16,666)	
Hyer, Stephen L	3:55:07 (9,821)	
Hyland, Edward T	3:50:26 (8,614)	
Hyland, Martin	4:07:04 (12,911)	
Hyland, Michael R	3:36:35 (5,707)	
Hyland, Stephen J	4:48:03 (22,682)	
Hyland, Terence	3:15:27 (2,592)	
Hylla, Helmut	4:27:13 (17,897)	
Hyman, Samuel A	4:44:21 (21,871)	
Hymans, Michael H	3:49:55 (8,477)	
Hynes, Alan W	3:40:34 (6,413)	
Hynes, James V	4:25:32 (17,438)	
Hynes, John B	3:36:21 (5,667)	
Iannantuoni, Michele	3:32:40 (5,040)	
I'Anson, Andrew J	4:15:34 (14,946)	
I'Anson, Colin S	3:54:38 (9,677)	
Ibbott, Andrew P	4:22:08 (16,582)	
Ibbott, Chris P	4:22:08 (16,582)	
Ibbott, Paul	4:21:42 (16,449)	
Ibbs, Robert J	3:00:30 (1,192)	
Ibinson, Rod	3:58:30 (10,856)	
Ibrahim, Sharief	3:37:06 (5,796)	
Iceton, Ben	3:44:59 (7,305)	
Iceton, Glen S	4:42:30 (21,450)	
Ide, Philip J	3:13:28 (2,365)	
Idowu, Fidelis	4:00:46 (11,439)	
Iglehon, Uwa	4:57:20 (24,464)	
Igo, Gareth	3:55:20 (9,890)	
Igoe, Dermot J	5:13:48 (26,872)	
Ii, Yasushi	5:02:24 (25,356)	
Ikegami, Koji	3:00:31 (1,193)	
Iles, Chris G	4:43:34 (21,695)	
Iles, Robert J	4:08:02 (13,121)	
Ilett, Dan A	5:48:13 (29,874)	
Iliffe, Edward	4:08:02 (13,121)	
Illing, Paul	2:56:16 (835)	
Illingworth, Colin J	5:16:05 (27,137)	
Illman, Bradley W	3:26:15 (3,879)	
Illman, Keith J	3:26:15 (3,879)	
Ilsley, Charles D	5:35:44 (29,013)	
Ilsley, Mark D	4:19:32 (15,917)	
Imeson, Ian	3:23:44 (3,535)	
Impey, John C	4:17:40 (15,473)	
Impleton, Darren A	5:28:18 (28,418)	
Imrie, Colin	4:24:22 (17,156)	
Imrie, Gavin A	4:33:12 (19,405)	
Ince, Mark G	4:27:28 (17,948)	
Ince, Paul A	5:52:46 (30,113)	
Ince, Philip A	3:50:14 (8,555)	
Ing, John L	3:32:34 (5,019)	
Ingall, Alastair H	4:29:12 (18,402)	
Ingall-Tombs, Stuart M	3:24:16 (3,601)	
Ingham, Gareth M	4:01:11 (11,544)	
Ingham, James P	4:03:23 (12,055)	
Ingham, Mark R	4:36:56 (20,203)	
Ingham, Paul J	3:50:26 (8,614)	
Ingle, Sanjiv	4:24:53 (17,278)	
Ingleden, Neil	3:35:25 (5,507)	
Inglefield, Charlie	5:06:07 (25,860)	
Inglis, Alan	4:37:58 (20,459)	
Inglis, Gary	3:59:23 (11,111)	
Inglis, Gordon	7:15:47 (31,753)	
Inglis, Jon	4:29:44 (18,564)	
Inglis, Magnus J	3:30:14 (4,641)	
Inglis, Robert A	5:19:37 (27,513)	
Ingram, Charles W	6:09:39 (30,719)	
Ingram, Michael J	3:50:34 (8,645)	
Ingram, Tommy	3:25:26 (3,756)	
Ingrams, Lance E	4:42:07 (21,372)	
Ing-Simmons, Christopher H	3:31:33 (4,859)	
Inkeles, David M	6:32:25 (31,253)	
Inkeles, John J	4:47:24 (22,542)	
Inman, Gary J	4:03:17 (12,025)	
Inman, Mark	4:10:32 (13,762)	
Inman, Paul	4:04:38 (12,336)	
Inns, Neil J	3:44:38 (7,220)	
Insausti, Eider	5:29:09 (28,499)	
Inskip, Michael A	3:59:27 (11,132)	
Insley, Danny A	4:50:17 (23,119)	
Intveld, Ian W	3:04:08 (1,461)	
Inwards, Clive M	4:30:17 (18,700)	
Ionascu, Howard J	4:03:50 (12,155)	
Ipino, Alessandro	2:40:10 (215)	
Ipstone, Alan J	4:45:38 (22,171)	
Ireland, John P	6:09:38 (30,717)	
Ireland, Peter J	3:45:29 (7,403)	
Irine, Stuart D	3:18:06 (2,858)	
Irisarri-Nunez, José M	4:12:32 (14,214)	
Irons, Simon T	4:49:09 (22,907)	
Irvine, Andy	4:15:46 (14,993)	
Irvine, Angus D	4:47:27 (22,557)	
Irvine, Dougall	4:58:04 (24,613)	
Irvine, Keith R	3:34:30 (5,339)	
Irvine, Steven	3:53:05 (9,275)	
Irving, Colin	4:32:18 (19,188)	
Irving, Peter J	3:36:24 (5,682)	
Irwin, David S	3:33:11 (5,133)	
Irwin, Paul M	4:13:08 (14,362)	
Isaac, Meirion E	4:17:22 (15,387)	
Isaac, Nicholas	2:49:47 (490)	
Isaac, Raymond	3:57:58 (10,665)	
Isaac, Tim M	4:28:35 (18,251)	
Isaacs, Andrew J	4:09:11 (13,415)	

Name	Time (Position)
Isaksson, Jonny P	4:21:45 (16,465)
Isaksson, Mats E	3:27:02 (4,031)
Iseke, Hans	3:35:51 (5,580)
Isgren, Carl	4:19:06 (15,803)
Isherwood, Luke	3:12:38 (2,265)
Ishii, Kaoru	4:07:22 (12,978)
Ishimori, Yoshio	4:27:39 (18,004)
Islam, Mohammad F	5:11:11 (26,535)
Ismail, Mohamed S	5:01:18 (25,186)
Ismail, Sharif I	6:51:21 (31,518)
Israel, Yannick	3:27:13 (4,066)
Issa, Mousin	3:32:51 (5,072)
Isted, Christopher P	5:29:50 (28,570)
Isted, Darren	3:56:27 (10,235)
Isted, Steven W	5:29:54 (28,574)
Istvan, Galos	4:55:51 (24,162)
Ito, Yoshiyuki	4:59:28 (24,896)
Ittonen, Nils	5:50:18 (29,981)
Iturria, Joseba	4:34:01 (19,594)
Ive, Martin J	3:11:52 (2,177)
Ivens, Martin	4:07:07 (12,920)
Ivers, John G	4:40:21 (20,996)
Iversen, Gunnar	4:31:17 (18,916)
Ives, Gareth	4:16:00 (15,050)
Ives, Kevin R	4:25:34 (17,444)
Ives, Matthew	5:09:12 (26,268)
Ives, Stephen A	4:44:12 (21,837)
Ives, Stephen J	4:10:46 (13,816)
Iveson, John	7:00:09 (31,625)
Ivey, Chris	4:58:26 (24,703)
Ivins, John P	4:30:51 (18,829)
Ivory, Anthony M	3:45:49 (7,485)
Izaac, Jean J	4:19:09 (15,818)
Izart, Philippe	4:47:37 (22,598)
Jack, Ben	5:20:09 (27,588)
Jack, Chris D	3:45:25 (7,390)
Jack, Michael	3:57:31 (10,546)
Jack, Michael J	3:43:09 (6,878)
Jackman, Dominic J	4:24:34 (17,199)
Jackman, Keith M	5:06:28 (25,906)
Jackson, Andrew	2:39:11 (191)
Jackson, Andrew L	4:42:05 (21,366)
Jackson, Andrew S	3:13:31 (2,377)
Jackson, Andrew W	3:57:21 (10,498)
Jackson, Angus J	3:27:27 (4,115)
Jackson, Anthony	5:03:45 (25,548)
Jackson, Anthony C	4:07:15 (12,955)
Jackson, Ben E	4:31:54 (19,080)
Jackson, Christopher L	3:14:19 (2,480)
Jackson, Cliff G	4:20:22 (16,120)
Jackson, Colin	3:13:36 (2,385)
Jackson, Damian J	4:41:17 (21,181)
Jackson, Damon R	5:17:59 (27,364)
Jackson, Darren A	3:50:42 (8,682)
Jackson, David	3:41:19 (6,525)
Jackson, David G	4:06:08 (12,698)
Jackson, David R	4:57:09 (24,427)
Jackson, Dominic	3:48:04 (8,015)
Jackson, Fred A	5:50:23 (29,987)
Jackson, Gary J	5:23:45 (27,949)
Jackson, Gavin R	3:54:06 (9,530)
Jackson, George D	3:03:11 (1,381)
Jackson, John A	3:01:12 (1,254)
Jackson, Kevin J	3:22:05 (3,312)
Jackson, Kevyn L	3:53:31 (9,380)
Jackson, Leslie	4:07:15 (12,955)
Jackson, Malcolm	4:11:58 (14,083)
Jackson, Mark A	4:23:14 (16,879)
Jackson, Mark A	4:24:36 (17,205)
Jackson, Martin A	3:58:07 (10,715)
Jackson, Martin B	4:06:25 (12,765)
Jackson, Martyn R	4:01:50 (11,675)
Jackson, Matthew	3:35:15 (5,472)
Jackson, Neil	2:57:31 (916)
Jackson, Nicholas B	4:33:48 (19,534)
Jackson, Nigel	2:53:48 (681)
Jackson, Nigel J	4:08:29 (13,224)
Jackson, Paul A	4:08:20 (13,186)
Jackson, Paul B	3:14:43 (2,528)
Jackson, Peter H	4:00:56 (11,488)
Jackson, Peter T	4:46:56 (22,430)
Jackson, Philip	3:32:12 (4,952)
Jackson, Philip A	4:04:43 (12,355)
Jackson, Ross	3:29:29 (4,501)
Jackson, Simon L	5:17:44 (27,331)
Jackson, Stephen	5:03:40 (25,543)
Jackson, Steve	4:50:20 (23,129)
Jackson, Steve D	3:47:04 (7,770)
Jackson, Steve J	3:09:44 (1,973)
Jackson, Steven H	3:52:53 (9,218)
Jackson, Stewart W	5:42:49 (29,534)
Jackson, Tim	4:10:56 (13,856)
Jackson, Tony D	3:53:05 (9,275)
Jackson, Trevor J	3:47:45 (7,937)
Jackson, William E	4:11:30 (13,968)
Jacob, James	4:33:19 (19,429)
Jacob, Phillip A	3:30:03 (4,601)
Jacob, Simon P	5:17:20 (27,287)
Jacob, William J	3:59:22 (11,105)
Jacobs, Toby	3:22:45 (3,410)
Jacques, Ian	4:12:35 (14,228)
Jacqz, Maxime	5:01:38 (25,245)
Jaenicke, Bernd	3:16:42 (2,721)
Jaffe, Peter S	3:22:06 (3,315)
Jagdev, Kirpal S	4:58:30 (24,719)
Jaggard, Jamie R	4:24:36 (17,205)
Jagger, Duncan	5:59:45 (30,401)
Jagger, Martin A	3:55:42 (9,989)
Jaggers, Ben	5:26:35 (28,260)
Jago, Simon	4:10:23 (13,729)
Jahans, Stephen J	7:25:49 (31,816)
Jakoby, Martin W	5:14:24 (26,950)
Jalloh, Amadu A	3:04:46 (1,509)
Jalloh, Ibrahim	3:19:16 (2,995)
James, Adam T	5:41:39 (29,461)
James, Alwyn D	3:59:38 (11,198)
James, Andrew	4:25:41 (17,474)
James, Andrew W	2:37:23 (163)
James, Anton E	6:01:45 (30,475)
James, Christopher	5:27:04 (28,306)
James, Darren L	4:26:17 (17,653)
James, David	3:36:19 (5,662)
James, David R	3:50:59 (8,746)
James, Douglas	4:10:21 (13,716)
James, Hylton H	3:20:34 (3,145)
James, Ian F	2:57:24 (905)
James, Jim	4:51:53 (23,418)
James, Jon	4:39:18 (20,792)
James, Keith	5:25:54 (28,186)
James, Kevin D	3:29:48 (4,553)
James, Luke H	4:14:47 (14,752)
James, Mark R	3:59:27 (11,132)
James, Matt	3:44:35 (7,208)
James, Murray K	4:28:44 (18,288)
James, Neil P	3:48:40 (8,176)
James, Nick A	3:19:44 (3,043)
James, Paul J	4:57:31 (24,496)
James, Pete	4:07:24 (12,989)
James, Philip	4:11:33 (13,985)
James, Philip	6:50:20 (31,503)
James, Philip S	4:34:36 (19,733)
James, Russell M	4:43:50 (21,753)
James, Simon L	4:29:55 (18,614)
James, Simon W	4:05:01 (12,437)
James, Steve A	3:14:02 (2,441)
James, Stuart A	7:30:06 (31,846)
James, Tom	3:18:10 (2,868)
James, Wendell	4:04:28 (12,306)
James, William G	3:55:00 (9,782)
Jameson, Andrew D	4:28:13 (18,151)
Jameson, Dennis	4:31:04 (18,870)
Jameson-Till, Toby A	5:52:33 (30,099)
Jamieson, Andrew	4:05:33 (12,555)
Jamieson, Christopher J	4:44:06 (21,815)
Jamieson, George A	3:20:37 (3,151)
Jamieson, Ian D	3:47:34 (7,898)
Jamieson, Robin L	5:08:42 (26,203)
Jamieson, Stuart M	4:56:22 (24,276)
Jamil, Muhayman	4:16:06 (15,079)
Janas, Peter	6:14:09 (30,850)
Janaway, Richard G	5:10:30 (26,442)
Jandu, Dhanwant	5:51:37 (30,042)
Jandu, Sandeep	5:51:39 (30,043)
Jane, Stewart C	5:07:52 (26,096)
Janes, Graham C	3:54:23 (9,604)
Janes, Jeremy N	3:08:37 (1,858)
Janes, Keith	3:55:00 (9,782)
Janjuha, Sohail	4:00:29 (11,395)
Jannusch, Uwe	4:04:22 (12,275)
Jans, Ruud	4:14:51 (14,773)
Jansen, Chris T	4:28:08 (18,135)
Jansen, Jan	4:35:57 (20,016)
Jansen, Terence E	4:29:37 (18,527)
Janssens, Jacky H	3:49:17 (8,327)
Janssens, Jean-Marie	3:59:22 (11,105)
Jaques, Robert	5:09:08 (26,257)
Jaquin, Paul A	4:01:57 (11,704)
Jardin, David J	3:33:23 (5,173)
Jardine, Bret T	3:23:19 (3,478)
Jardine, Howard W	3:20:58 (3,197)
Jardine, Stephen J	3:48:01 (8,001)
Jarman, Charles K	4:04:13 (12,245)
Jarman, Danny L	5:02:16 (25,331)
Jarman, Michael C	6:52:07 (31,532)
Jarman, Russell A	4:54:31 (23,899)
Jarrett, Carl	4:47:35 (22,589)
Jarvis, Adrian S	4:48:29 (22,776)
Jarvis, Anthony D	4:40:27 (21,017)
Jarvis, Anthony S	4:53:46 (23,761)
Jarvis, Elliot R	4:11:46 (14,036)
Jarvis, Eric V	6:03:10 (30,534)
Jarvis, James L	3:15:19 (2,584)
Jarvis, John S	3:42:03 (6,661)
Jarvis, Joseph R	4:12:51 (14,289)
Jarvis, Lee W	4:41:03 (21,135)
Jarvis, Luke D	3:36:53 (5,751)
Jarvis, Philip Q	3:52:24 (9,111)
Jarvis, Tim A	4:10:05 (13,653)
Jary, Christian	4:10:06 (13,656)
Jasinski, Larry	4:18:41 (15,707)
Jasnoch, Paul	3:04:03 (1,454)
Jason, Niarchos	4:01:06 (11,528)
Jason, Robert J	3:38:27 (6,039)
Jasper, Andrew	4:17:57 (15,546)
Jasper, Mark A	6:10:33 (30,742)
Jauhola, Henrik M	4:23:45 (17,002)
Javid, Basit	4:15:32 (14,936)
Jay, Tim M	3:57:40 (10,586)
Jeacock, Paul A	4:06:22 (12,752)
Jeal, Paul A	4:10:22 (13,723)
Jeal, Steve	3:51:56 (9,001)
Jeanmonod, David	4:21:17 (16,328)
Jeanne, Eric	4:17:47 (15,503)
Jeans, Nicholas K	4:17:34 (15,448)
Jeary, Kevin	3:14:00 (2,432)
Jeeves, Stephen A	3:35:33 (5,533)
Jefedjian, Tony A	5:59:02 (30,365)
Jefferies, Jason D	4:39:52 (20,886)
Jefferies, Mark A	5:53:47 (30,143)
Jefferies, Mark J	3:22:39 (3,396)
Jefferies, Paul	4:02:06 (11,746)
Jefferies, Terence E	4:27:01 (17,846)
Jefferies, Tim	4:10:23 (13,729)
Jefferis, Alan D	6:55:24 (31,566)
Jeffers, Cameron M	3:51:47 (8,967)
Jefferson, Alan R	4:21:13 (16,315)
Jefferson, Paul S	3:44:23 (7,150)
Jefferson, Thomas L	4:55:38 (24,125)
Jeffery, Craig N	2:39:37 (200)
Jeffery, David	3:43:04 (6,864)
Jeffery, David L	3:00:23 (1,186)
Jeffery, Mark K	4:10:36 (13,782)
Jeffery, Michael D	5:26:49 (28,281)
Jeffery, Robert S	4:02:04 (11,735)
Jeffery, Simon M	4:44:49 (21,980)
Jeffies, Stacey	3:14:57 (2,554)
Jefford, Mark	2:58:34 (1,023)
Jeffrey, Allister	4:00:40 (11,418)
Jeffrey, Chris	5:36:49 (29,092)
Jeffrey, Colin S	4:47:12 (22,499)
Jeffrey, Gordon C	4:12:34 (14,225)
Jeffrey, Malcolm D	4:46:05 (22,266)
Jeffrey, Stephen P	2:55:24 (790)
Jeffrey, Tom	3:59:54 (11,268)
Jeffreys, Matthew D	6:54:23 (31,553)
Jeffries, Antony	4:09:58 (13,631)
Jeffries, Kevin J	3:27:18 (4,080)
Jeffries, Lee A	3:13:42 (2,399)
Jegeni, Adrian	4:26:50 (17,784)

Jelley, David 4:28:10 (18,140)
Jellicoe, David J 3:12:12 (2,216)
Jellis, David 3:54:59 (9,778)
Jemison, Gavin M 3:13:19 (2,345)
Jenart, Christopher 3:52:19 (9,091)
Jenkin, Huw D 2:50:08 (510)
Jenkins, Allyn 5:25:01 (28,085)
Jenkins, Andrew J 3:12:53 (2,299)
Jenkins, David 3:49:50 (8,457)
Jenkins, Gareth W 4:15:05 (14,821)
Jenkins, Jonathan 4:02:39 (11,886)
Jenkins, Lee 3:24:53 (3,679)
Jenkins, Paul R 4:05:44 (12,600)
Jenkins, Phil B 3:48:02 (8,004)
Jenkins, Philip H 3:39:18 (6,184)
Jenkins, Richard J 5:19:32 (27,502)
Jenkins, Richard M 4:20:50 (16,235)
Jenkins, Robert E 4:33:22 (19,441)
Jenkins, Timothy A 3:46:03 (7,534)
Jenkins, William H 4:58:58 (24,791)
Jenkinson, Christopher 4:08:58 (13,369)
Jenkinson, Colin R 4:58:36 (24,736)
Jenkinson, Gary J 3:50:47 (8,704)
Jenkinson, Neil 4:52:34 (23,545)
Jenkinson, Peter J 4:31:29 (18,969)
Jenks, John W 4:05:24 (12,510)
Jennens, Andrew P 4:15:55 (15,031)
Jenner, Marc E 4:33:47 (19,531)
Jennings, Barre 3:59:19 (11,092)
Jennings, David J 4:29:11 (18,400)
Jennings, David M 4:03:50 (12,155)
Jennings, James F 3:05:21 (1,557)
Jennings, John F 3:50:25 (8,611)
Jennings, Kevin 4:16:16 (15,111)
Jennings, Mark 5:16:34 (27,201)
Jennings, Mathew 3:52:26 (9,120)
Jennings, Murray J 4:02:14 (11,789)
Jennings, Neil R 3:37:57 (5,953)
Jennings, Nik G 5:43:38 (29,603)
Jennings, Odran J 3:49:39 (8,413)
Jennings, Richard S 4:01:29 (11,592)
Jennings, Ricky G 5:43:39 (29,609)
Jennings, Roy S 4:42:17 (21,408)
Jennings, Simon P 4:32:19 (19,192)
Jennings, Terry J 4:44:22 (21,876)
Jennings, Thomas J 3:52:56 (9,235)
Jennison, Phillip R 4:53:17 (23,670)
Jensen, Christian 4:15:20 (14,886)
Jensen, Ib 4:23:04 (16,830)
Jensen, Jan E 3:59:41 (11,218)
Jensen, Per M 4:08:46 (13,311)
Jensen, Stian 3:41:54 (6,618)
Jeoffroy, Matthew D 2:57:04 (883)
Jeppesen, Arne M 4:40:20 (20,991)
Jeppesen, Glenn 3:58:17 (10,785)
Jepson, Leigh 3:37:55 (5,940)
Jepsow, Liam R 3:39:12 (6,163)
Jerams, Steven 4:33:36 (19,486)
Jercic, Vasja 3:27:37 (4,150)
Jeremiah, Christopher D 3:59:10 (11,049)
Jeremy, Edward J 3:19:33 (3,024)
Jerram, Alan D 6:47:33 (31,471)
Jervis, Ben 4:20:54 (16,261)
Jervis, Mark E 4:34:36 (19,733)
Jerzak, Mark 3:10:11 (2,019)
Jesse, Kenji E 5:41:46 (29,474)
Jessop, Andrew D 3:43:58 (7,057)
Jessop, Julian H 4:18:25 (15,642)
Jessop, Neil A 4:20:30 (16,159)
Jest, Andrew N 3:37:17 (5,832)
Jew, Jason M 5:29:41 (28,555)
Jew, Nicholas J 3:58:04 (10,696)
Jewell, Andrew R 3:13:46 (2,404)
Jewell, Ian M 5:00:12 (25,023)
Jewell, Neville 3:11:23 (2,132)
Jewett, Barry W 5:02:48 (25,422)
Jewhurst, Espen 3:58:31 (10,860)
Jewkes, Richard J 3:46:25 (7,624)
Jex, Andrew 3:35:45 (5,565)
Jeyes, Andrew T 3:18:53 (2,940)
Jezzard, Ian 4:37:37 (20,361)
Jiggins, Ian A 5:55:22 (30,217)
Jimenez Buendia, José J 4:15:55 (15,031)
Jinks, Dominic J 4:26:26 (17,681)
Jinks, Graham 4:40:48 (21,089)
Job, Richard 4:26:06 (17,608)
Jobe, Matthew 3:27:20 (4,091)
Jobling, Christopher J 4:23:17 (16,891)
Jobling, David I 3:58:51 (10,960)
Jobling, Paul 4:40:46 (21,076)
Jobson, Stephen 4:17:54 (15,537)
Jocelyn, Nicholas V 4:22:07 (16,576)
Joffre, Dominque 3:12:00 (2,194)
Jogi, Narottam 5:44:50 (29,680)
Johann-Berkel, Kip M 4:05:18 (12,487)
Johansen, Baard 4:34:04 (19,614)
Johansson, Goran 3:40:54 (6,455)
Johansson, Kent 3:53:44 (9,420)
Johansson, Per-Olof E 4:09:01 (13,384)
Johansson, Sture 5:12:17 (26,666)
Johansson, Thomas P 5:06:34 (25,920)
John, Anthony D 4:36:59 (20,249)
John, Antony G 4:09:23 (13,470)
John, Colin D 6:35:00 (31,288)
John, Gareth M 4:47:37 (22,598)
John, Gary N 3:38:33 (6,056)
John, Gilbert G 3:44:18 (7,138)
Johnes, Christopher I 4:25:03 (17,318)
Johns, Dominic P 4:34:27 (19,699)
Johns, Julian E 3:50:15 (8,563)
Johns, Paul 4:00:01 (11,300)
Johnson, Adam W 4:35:51 (19,990)
Johnson, Alan W 4:26:38 (17,736)
Johnson, Andy J 5:24:58 (28,079)
Johnson, Anthony G 3:05:11 (1,543)
Johnson, Ben 4:40:18 (20,984)
Johnson, Ben J 4:14:24 (14,652)
Johnson, Brian 5:08:00 (26,115)
Johnson, Carter C 4:15:26 (14,909)
Johnson, Christopher 5:03:58 (25,575)
Johnson, Clive I 5:25:18 (28,122)
Johnson, Colin 5:47:10 (29,820)
Johnson, Daren J 3:51:56 (9,001)
Johnson, Darren W 3:11:25 (2,136)
Johnson, David 5:00:37 (25,080)
Johnson, David 5:10:38 (26,456)
Johnson, David B 4:08:32 (13,239)
Johnson, David B 4:28:30 (18,230)
Johnson, David N 3:56:32 (10,260)
Johnson, David P 4:01:18 (11,562)
Johnson, David R 4:15:06 (14,828)
Johnson, David T 4:32:31 (19,240)
Johnson, Edward M 5:40:39 (29,392)
Johnson, Eustace 4:43:30 (21,685)
Johnson, Gary 5:16:34 (27,201)
Johnson, Geoff 5:12:14 (26,660)
Johnson, Glen 3:14:56 (2,552)
Johnson, Graham A 3:48:13 (8,055)
Johnson, Guy A 4:56:21 (24,274)
Johnson, Henry T 4:16:20 (15,126)
Johnson, Hugh 4:46:10 (22,289)
Johnson, John A 3:12:40 (2,266)
Johnson, John L 3:53:17 (9,335)
Johnson, John S 4:41:55 (21,330)
Johnson, Karl A 3:34:51 (5,398)
Johnson, Kenny 3:39:35 (6,231)
Johnson, Kevin 3:49:54 (8,473)
Johnson, Kevin 4:36:02 (20,036)
Johnson, Kevin C 5:55:04 (30,203)
Johnson, Kevin I 3:17:43 (2,821)
Johnson, Kevin P 4:45:34 (22,154)
Johnson, Kirk J 4:32:50 (19,319)
Johnson, Lee 3:03:33 (1,410)
Johnson, Lee H 3:50:42 (8,682)
Johnson, Leo K 4:16:36 (15,200)
Johnson, Malcolm 3:46:18 (7,602)
Johnson, Mark C 5:07:53 (26,098)
Johnson, Mark S 3:54:47 (9,719)
Johnson, Mark S 4:26:44 (17,755)
Johnson, Matthew 4:38:23 (20,566)
Johnson, Mike 3:42:49 (6,813)
Johnson, Neil D 3:48:44 (8,195)
Johnson, Neil G 4:28:00 (18,098)
Johnson, Paul D 3:40:37 (6,418)
Johnson, Paul D 5:10:49 (26,486)
Johnson, Paul S 6:47:03 (31,466)
Johnson, Paul W 3:23:32 (3,503)
Johnson, Pete T 2:44:15 (294)
Johnson, Phillip R 6:34:35 (31,282)
Johnson, Ray D 3:48:40 (8,176)
Johnson, Raymond 4:43:23 (21,659)
Johnson, Richard 4:57:39 (24,521)
Johnson, Richard M 3:06:01 (1,612)
Johnson, Richard S 5:16:30 (27,187)
Johnson, Robert D 4:47:07 (22,481)
Johnson, Robert G 4:20:44 (16,221)
Johnson, Robert P 2:59:04 (1,078)
Johnson, Russell J 5:00:51 (25,123)
Johnson, Scott D 4:43:12 (21,605)
Johnson, Stephen 4:09:38 (13,536)
Johnson, Stephen C 4:41:55 (21,330)
Johnson, Stuart J 4:20:14 (16,073)
Johnson, Thomas 5:07:03 (25,976)
Johnson, Thomas W 4:14:03 (14,577)
Johnson, Tom R 3:47:50 (7,954)
Johnson, Tunde 5:07:00 (25,970)
Johnson, Walter D 5:34:38 (28,929)
Johnston, Adam 3:23:14 (3,467)
Johnston, Andrew P 4:35:45 (19,971)
Johnston, David J 4:45:59 (22,245)
Johnston, David R 3:27:25 (4,108)
Johnston, Ewan D 3:49:34 (8,396)
Johnston, Geoffrey I 3:49:31 (8,380)
Johnston, George 4:15:36 (14,955)
Johnston, Graham W 4:21:25 (16,367)
Johnston, Ivor W 3:34:52 (5,400)
Johnston, Jeremy J 3:56:34 (10,271)
Johnston, John A 4:07:26 (12,997)
Johnston, Mark 2:40:02 (212)
Johnston, Oliver W 3:25:42 (3,798)
Johnston, Sandy M 2:53:38 (673)
Johnston, Steven J 4:58:08 (24,624)
Johnston, Timothy P 3:41:22 (6,530)
Johnstone, Alan J 6:24:08 (31,111)
Johnstone, Grahame M 4:07:12 (12,939)
Johnstone, Ivor D 3:55:02 (9,798)
Joice, James M 4:07:02 (12,903)
Jokat, Brian 3:54:02 (9,514)
Jolley, Tim J 3:52:35 (9,149)
Jolliffe, Dave V 5:15:49 (27,109)
Jolliffe, Steven P 4:36:37 (20,159)
Jolly, John W 4:58:57 (24,789)
Jolly, Michael S 3:50:46 (8,698)
Jolly, Pete 4:28:25 (18,198)
Jolly, Raymond T 5:30:44 (28,638)
Jolly, Robert J 4:07:41 (13,053)
Jolly, Stephen G 4:10:45 (13,811)
Jolly, Stephen J 4:42:41 (21,486)
Joly, Olivier 3:46:37 (7,666)
Joly, Philippe 3:05:46 (1,588)
Joly, Rob B 3:44:23 (7,150)
Jonas, Jon M 5:44:32 (29,658)
Jones, Alan 4:21:50 (16,487)
Jones, Alan L 5:18:27 (27,410)
Jones, Alexander A 6:26:48 (31,154)
Jones, Alister R 2:52:43 (627)
Jones, Allen D 2:48:12 (432)
Jones, Andrew F 4:59:17 (24,846)
Jones, Andrew P 4:53:05 (23,630)
Jones, Andrew P 5:11:21 (26,560)
Jones, Andy D 2:51:27 (565)
Jones, Anthony 4:47:19 (22,523)
Jones, Anthony R 5:24:41 (28,044)
Jones, Arwel 3:18:13 (2,874)
Jones, Arwel W 3:10:01 (2,003)
Jones, Barry J 4:56:07 (24,232)
Jones, Bryn G 5:30:30 (28,625)
Jones, Charlie 3:26:07 (3,861)
Jones, Chris 4:10:58 (13,864)
Jones, Chris P 3:55:16 (9,868)
Jones, Chris P 4:56:22 (24,276)
Jones, Christopher 4:40:39 (21,054)
Jones, Christopher E 4:05:16 (12,475)
Jones, Christopher L 4:47:55 (22,658)
Jones, Christopher T 4:45:10 (22,075)
Jones, Craig 3:28:27 (4,310)
Jones, Daniel G 4:59:40 (24,934)
Jones, Daniel R 4:48:33 (22,783)
Jones, Darren H 3:58:17 (10,785)

Jones, Darren J	5:00:05 (25,006)	
Jones, Darren M	4:53:10 (23,647)	
Jones, David	3:34:11 (5,296)	
Jones, David	3:56:13 (10,148)	
Jones, David	4:18:13 (15,591)	
Jones, David A	3:15:51 (2,637)	
Jones, David A	3:25:56 (3,835)	
Jones, David A	4:27:10 (17,885)	
Jones, David A	4:48:25 (22,763)	
Jones, David B	3:40:25 (6,383)	
Jones, David G	4:28:15 (18,158)	
Jones, David J	4:28:40 (18,274)	
Jones, David M	4:36:05 (20,052)	
Jones, David O	3:47:16 (7,822)	
Jones, David R	2:43:00 (266)	
Jones, Dennis R	5:05:50 (25,812)	
Jones, Derek A	4:35:31 (19,929)	
Jones, Derwyn H	3:59:22 (11,105)	
Jones, Dewi E	3:16:28 (2,696)	
Jones, Dorian A	3:40:22 (6,373)	
Jones, Edward L	4:06:51 (12,849)	
Jones, Gareth	3:30:50 (4,747)	
Jones, Gareth	4:50:22 (23,142)	
Jones, Gareth A	4:29:39 (18,542)	
Jones, Gareth D	3:33:14 (5,146)	
Jones, Gareth E	3:49:24 (8,356)	
Jones, Gareth O	4:10:10 (13,668)	
Jones, Gareth R	4:18:01 (15,557)	
Jones, Gareth W	4:07:03 (12,909)	
Jones, Garry D	4:01:20 (11,569)	
Jones, Gary	4:05:27 (12,523)	
Jones, Gary D	3:59:33 (11,173)	
Jones, Gary P	4:01:29 (11,592)	
Jones, George C	4:51:09 (23,295)	
Jones, George R	4:15:33 (14,942)	
Jones, Gregory	6:14:21 (30,856)	
Jones, Gregory E	4:33:15 (19,417)	
Jones, Haydn R	5:08:02 (26,121)	
Jones, Howard N	3:55:48 (10,016)	
Jones, Hywel S	3:13:16 (2,337)	
Jones, Ian	3:36:26 (5,685)	
Jones, Ian C	6:15:07 (30,888)	
Jones, Ian E	4:17:30 (15,423)	
Jones, Ian F	4:46:12 (22,296)	
Jones, Ian G	2:59:25 (1,114)	
Jones, Ian J	4:27:10 (17,885)	
Jones, Ian R	3:38:05 (5,973)	
Jones, Irfon	3:51:22 (8,849)	
Jones, James C	3:56:48 (10,330)	
Jones, James P	4:54:00 (23,794)	
Jones, Jim	3:59:40 (11,212)	
Jones, John	4:05:19 (12,489)	
Jones, John E	6:10:17 (30,734)	
Jones, John K	4:37:05 (20,270)	
Jones, Justin L	4:47:58 (22,666)	
Jones, Kelvyn	3:05:42 (1,583)	
Jones, Ken L	5:19:04 (27,471)	
Jones, Kenneth I	4:34:01 (19,594)	
Jones, Kevin	4:29:05 (18,370)	
Jones, Kevin G	4:02:13 (11,786)	
Jones, Kevin P	4:58:18 (24,666)	
Jones, Kevin R	5:15:11 (27,037)	
Jones, Lawrence G	3:00:00 (1,156)	
Jones, Lee G	4:02:17 (11,801)	
Jones, Mark	4:39:29 (20,822)	
Jones, Martin	4:05:50 (12,625)	
Jones, Martin L	4:30:51 (18,829)	
Jones, Martyn R	4:26:13 (17,639)	
Jones, Matthew B	4:15:10 (14,850)	
Jones, Matthew E	4:19:26 (15,894)	
Jones, Michael A	4:12:38 (14,242)	
Jones, Michael D	3:09:48 (1,979)	
Jones, Michael D	5:06:10 (25,869)	
Jones, Michael J	5:31:12 (28,674)	
Jones, Michael R	5:02:52 (25,429)	
Jones, Michael V	5:09:06 (26,254)	
Jones, Michael W	3:28:26 (4,308)	
Jones, Milton P	4:43:57 (21,786)	
Jones, Neil	3:24:03 (3,571)	
Jones, Neil	3:47:56 (7,982)	
Jones, Neil A	4:16:48 (15,251)	
Jones, Neil O	3:51:31 (8,891)	
Jones, Nick	5:05:07 (25,705)	
Jones, Nick D	6:01:00 (30,448)	
Jones, Owen D	3:46:56 (7,730)	
Jones, Paul	4:24:33 (17,196)	
Jones, Paul D	4:12:02 (14,101)	
Jones, Paul M	4:02:00 (11,717)	
Jones, Perry	5:07:29 (26,045)	
Jones, Peter	3:10:53 (2,089)	
Jones, Peter	4:25:25 (17,405)	
Jones, Peter	4:29:37 (18,527)	
Jones, Peter D	5:58:25 (30,343)	
Jones, Peter K	4:28:42 (18,279)	
Jones, Peter R	3:43:59 (7,063)	
Jones, Phil C	3:45:04 (7,314)	
Jones, Philip A	5:20:22 (27,616)	
Jones, Piers	2:50:26 (524)	
Jones, Raymond A	4:07:48 (13,069)	
Jones, Raymond E	5:33:39 (28,862)	
Jones, Raymond T	6:09:27 (30,714)	
Jones, Rhydian	4:55:55 (24,186)	
Jones, Richie	4:20:15 (16,077)	
Jones, Robert J	4:29:48 (18,583)	
Jones, Rodri	2:30:49 (84)	
Jones, Ronald T	6:16:12 (30,913)	
Jones, Rowland W	4:08:27 (13,214)	
Jones, Russell	3:21:33 (3,264)	
Jones, Sam	5:01:30 (25,221)	
Jones, Sam D	5:16:23 (27,179)	
Jones, Samuel	4:03:59 (12,191)	
Jones, Sean K	5:00:00 (24,991)	
Jones, Shelby R	4:39:48 (20,876)	
Jones, Simon	3:04:04 (1,455)	
Jones, Simon A	3:55:58 (10,074)	
Jones, Simon M	4:04:20 (12,271)	
Jones, Stephen	3:29:39 (4,525)	
Jones, Stephen	3:49:48 (8,451)	
Jones, Stephen	4:10:19 (13,708)	
Jones, Stephen	5:21:55 (27,763)	
Jones, Stephen A	3:24:23 (3,613)	
Jones, Stephen D	3:42:14 (6,691)	
Jones, Stephen J	3:56:09 (10,121)	
Jones, Stephen N	2:50:07 (508)	
Jones, Stephen P	3:55:16 (9,868)	
Jones, Steven G	4:37:24 (20,328)	
Jones, Terence M	4:28:10 (18,140)	
Jones, Timothy A	4:48:12 (22,721)	
Jones, Timothy D	3:35:13 (5,462)	
Jones, Tudur D	3:55:02 (9,798)	
Jones, Vernon	4:23:08 (16,851)	
Jones, William	4:36:40 (20,172)	
Jones, Wyn	4:41:24 (21,220)	
Jones Parry, Paul S	6:00:35 (30,430)	
Jones-Davies, Richard A	4:11:06 (13,889)	
Jonkers, Marco	3:26:47 (3,983)	
Jonsson, Janake	4:42:50 (21,530)	
Joppin, Christian	3:59:03 (11,016)	
Jordan, Anthony M	3:35:34 (5,535)	
Jordan, Frenny	4:04:04 (12,200)	
Jordan, John J	4:43:52 (21,766)	
Jordan, John W	4:10:03 (13,647)	
Jordan, Nick H	3:27:10 (4,057)	
Jordan, Paul W	4:39:47 (20,873)	
Jordan, Peter A	3:46:09 (7,559)	
Jordan, Peter D	4:16:38 (15,217)	
Jordan, Philip J	4:08:17 (13,170)	
Jordan, Pieter R	4:24:32 (17,192)	
Jordan, Tom C	4:39:19 (20,796)	
Jose, Jemy	3:47:53 (7,969)	
Joseph, Nicholas M	4:14:13 (14,612)	
Joseph, Ronnie	4:30:34 (18,773)	
Josephs, David S	3:27:32 (4,137)	
Josephs, Merrick L	3:50:08 (8,536)	
Jost, Robert W	3:03:22 (1,396)	
Jotangia, Neil	3:08:30 (1,850)	
Jouandet, Denis	2:46:35 (373)	
Joubert, Anton D	4:23:41 (16,980)	
Jouglas, Jean-Jacques	3:08:30 (1,850)	
Joules, Keith	2:54:48 (734)	
Jourdain, Jacques	3:31:08 (4,797)	
Jowers, John	4:57:40 (24,529)	
Jowitt, Andrew	4:54:52 (23,971)	
Joy, Matthew R	3:49:04 (8,268)	
Joy, Stephen	5:11:06 (26,517)	
Joyce, Alan D	4:11:39 (14,015)	
Joyce, Daniel	4:30:21 (18,716)	
Joyce, Jim	4:14:46 (14,745)	
Joyce, Jonathan M	4:19:57 (16,013)	
Joyce, Michael	3:54:30 (9,635)	
Joyce, Michael J	4:28:05 (18,123)	
Joyce, Michael S	3:59:48 (11,240)	
Joyce, Paul W	3:19:37 (3,029)	
Joyner, Matt W	5:36:28 (29,058)	
Joynson, Mark	3:14:00 (2,432)	
Joynson, Mike A	4:11:23 (13,948)	
Judd, Nicholas O	4:19:19 (15,860)	
Judd, Peter J	4:41:21 (21,206)	
Judd, Steven A	3:57:14 (10,600)	
Judge, Bruce G	2:39:09 (189)	
Judge, David	3:58:00 (10,671)	
Judge, Greg	3:36:08 (5,631)	
Judge, James C	4:19:56 (16,008)	
Judge, Sean P	3:48:04 (8,015)	
Jugg, Trevor D	4:36:09 (20,063)	
Jukes, Paul F	5:58:10 (30,332)	
Julian, Ben	3:29:09 (4,440)	
Julian, Kevin A	3:00:48 (1,217)	
Julian, Matt R	6:55:21 (31,565)	
Julien, James W	6:07:30 (30,662)	
Julyan, Michael	4:38:34 (20,611)	
Jummon, Arnold	4:02:06 (11,746)	
Jump, Graham A	4:49:01 (22,878)	
Jump, Nathen L	4:28:29 (18,227)	
Jung, Norbert	3:02:01 (1,301)	
Juniper, Adam	3:05:29 (1,569)	
Jupp, Ian D	4:10:35 (13,774)	
Jupp, Michael A	3:58:05 (10,705)	
Jurgens, Mark J	3:11:14 (2,117)	
Jurgens, Werner	3:58:29 (10,845)	
Jury, Stephen	4:25:04 (17,327)	
Jutte, Stephan	4:26:21 (17,667)	
Juxon, Robert P	4:16:55 (15,288)	
Kaczmarek, Pawel A	4:18:47 (15,734)	
Kadon, Joseph	2:11:30 (10)	
Kaemena, Neil D	4:41:11 (21,153)	
Kaempif, Hartmut	5:01:21 (25,194)	
Kahlow, Edward J	3:41:54 (6,618)	
Kain, William S	5:42:25 (29,511)	
Kainz, Michael	3:58:59 (10,999)	
Kakembo, Adam T	4:19:29 (15,908)	
Kalair, Daljit K	7:30:04 (31,845)	
Kalee, Mathus J	4:02:41 (11,894)	
Kalidoski, Steven	5:28:29 (28,436)	
Kalinsky, Sydney M	7:01:39 (31,638)	
Kalle, Anti	3:56:08 (10,117)	
Kam, Elias	4:51:44 (23,387)	
Kamaluddin, Jonathan D	5:06:59 (25,966)	
Kamen, Steven R	3:16:41 (2,718)	
Kaminsky, Roy	5:02:08 (25,310)	
Kandrac, Martin	4:52:57 (23,606)	
Kane, Andrew	3:47:41 (7,925)	
Kane, John	3:22:52 (3,429)	
Kane, Jonathan J	3:30:42 (4,724)	
Kane, Kenneth E	4:10:07 (13,662)	
Kane, Nicholas M	3:12:44 (2,279)	
Kane, Paul M	7:13:39 (31,738)	
Kane, Tony	3:48:03 (8,008)	
Kang, Gurpreet	6:40:59 (31,371)	
Kang, Kamaljit	4:34:21 (19,678)	
Kanisch, Holger	3:15:02 (2,559)	
Kansagra, Rishi R	4:37:11 (20,293)	
Kany, Jean	3:28:17 (4,279)	
Kaplan, Jeffrey A	4:02:09 (11,764)	
Kapoor, Neil	2:56:54 (876)	
Kapur, Reginald	3:51:59 (9,008)	
Kara, Ajay	5:25:08 (28,100)	
Kara, Zaahid Z	3:56:54 (10,366)	
Karavadra, Ranjeet B	4:53:15 (23,668)	
Karbani, Faizal A	5:03:38 (25,539)	
Karlas, Richard M	4:08:27 (13,214)	
Karlberg, Johan P	4:21:25 (16,367)	
Karlsson, Mats	3:38:05 (5,973)	
Karlsson, Robert	3:35:14 (5,467)	
Karn, James	4:18:22 (15,623)	
Kasprzak, Mark	4:12:59 (14,328)	
Kassis, Jean-Louis	8:13:00 (31,954)	
Kaszvbowski, Anton N	3:38:34 (6,063)	
Kat, Gregory	3:11:14 (2,117)	

Katagiri, Taichi 3:56:49 (10,337)
Katechia, Bhagesh C 3:22:39 (3,396)
Katkou, Gennady 3:57:46 (10,609)
Katsiaounis, Adonis 5:46:01 (29,750)
Katz, Jonathan 3:22:23 (3,358)
Katz, Mark 5:23:55 (27,964)
Katzinger, Josef 3:04:32 (1,491)
Kaufmann, Norbert 4:10:19 (13,708)
Kaushik, Vivek 6:13:18 (30,822)
Kavanagh, Kevin S 4:09:52 (13,598)
Kavanagh, Martin J 3:49:03 (8,264)
Kavanagh, Terry 5:00:35 (25,073)
Kavanagh, Terry F 4:08:48 (13,325)
Kawasaki, Makoto 3:38:41 (6,083)
Kay, Benjamin J 3:49:54 (8,473)
Kay, Danny 3:29:03 (4,422)
Kay, Francis N 4:21:38 (16,430)
Kay, Graeme E 6:14:22 (30,858)
Kay, Martin T 3:58:56 (10,987)
Kay, Matthew S 2:59:22 (1,109)
Kay, Peter A 5:09:41 (26,336)
Kay, Peter J 4:52:39 (23,557)
Kay, Tim 4:45:34 (22,154)
Kay, William G 4:18:14 (15,597)
Kaye, Ian 6:28:30 (31,181)
Kayes, Oliver J 3:58:45 (10,930)
Kayley, Mike 3:35:35 (5,541)
Kazalbash, Imran M 3:56:35 (10,274)
Kazalbash, Kamran 4:30:37 (18,784)
Kazikin, Stanislav A 3:41:42 (6,582)
Kean, Alasdair A 2:44:41 (313)
Kean, Martin 4:21:17 (16,328)
Keane, Glenn B 6:37:50 (31,336)
Keaney, Dominic 4:13:24 (14,432)
Kear, Neil 3:32:56 (5,086)
Kearney, Peter D 4:43:43 (21,726)
Kearney, Tony 3:29:04 (4,425)
Kearns, Adrian 3:44:46 (7,254)
Kearns, Brian 3:53:23 (9,358)
Kearns, Eamon J 4:56:18 (24,261)
Kearsley, Matthew B 4:20:14 (16,073)
Keat, Paul M 5:52:44 (30,112)
Keates, Garry 4:55:43 (24,135)
Keates, Matthew E 3:45:21 (7,376)
Keating, Dermot J 4:35:31 (19,929)
Keating, Niall J 4:00:21 (11,369)
Keating, Nicholas M 3:55:54 (10,051)
Keating, Rory B 4:47:04 (22,468)
Keayes, Donald N 4:32:35 (19,254)
Keayes, Spencer R 5:03:27 (25,512)
Kedar, John D 4:20:36 (16,187)
Keddilty, Anthony J 4:45:05 (22,059)
Kedney, Gary J 3:35:55 (5,591)
Keeble, Ian R 2:55:16 (770)
Keeble, John R 4:54:17 (23,851)
Keech, Donald E 5:11:09 (26,527)
Keech, Leonard R 4:55:53 (24,177)
Keech, Tony 3:21:03 (3,206)
Keegan, Arthur M 5:36:37 (29,072)
Keel, David C 3:42:33 (6,754)
Keeler, Andy T 3:19:11 (2,980)
Keeling, Adam R 4:32:17 (19,184)
Keeling, Christopher D 4:20:35 (16,181)
Keely, Tom 3:41:10 (6,507)
Keen, Howard S 4:35:48 (19,982)
Keen, Robert J 4:37:52 (20,422)
Keen, William 4:07:18 (12,963)
Keenan, Frank E 3:59:55 (11,273)
Keenan, Wayne J 5:03:34 (25,530)
Keene, Huw M 3:36:11 (5,639)
Keenleyside, Piers B 3:57:48 (10,618)
Keep, David J 4:15:07 (14,834)
Keep, Robert P 4:12:49 (14,283)
Keep, Trevor 3:31:07 (4,792)
Keepence, Stephen L 4:04:13 (12,245)
Keevil, Raymond J 4:07:31 (13,012)
Kefford, Andrew J 4:18:59 (15,775)
Kehoe, Peter E 5:15:45 (27,100)
Kehoe, Robert F 4:21:42 (16,449)
Keighery, John P 6:01:46 (30,478)
Keighley, Charles J 3:45:41 (7,455)
Keilloh, Richard J 5:22:07 (27,784)
Keilty, Sean C 4:47:55 (22,658)
Keir, Derek B 4:23:24 (16,921)
Keirs, Neil 3:33:56 (5,262)
Keith, Tony J 3:19:35 (3,026)
Keith, William H 3:31:16 (4,815)
Kekewich, Colin I 3:20:29 (3,124)
Kelf, David L 3:46:54 (7,723)
Kelham, Christopher S 3:56:11 (10,134)
Kelland, Peter J 3:10:33 (2,059)
Kelland, Scott D 4:25:56 (17,551)
Kellaway, Andrew D 2:57:59 (966)
Kellaway, Roy R 3:12:09 (2,208)
Kelleher, Cornelius 3:02:54 (1,362)
Keller, Thomas 3:33:34 (5,197)
Kellett, Gary K 3:12:49 (2,290)
Kelley, Christopher M 4:33:02 (19,364)
Kelley, Kevin H 4:40:37 (21,043)
Kellogg, Michael K 5:00:04 (25,003)
Kelly, Andrew J 4:55:19 (24,067)
Kelly, Chris 4:09:19 (13,455)
Kelly, Christopher J 3:26:27 (3,910)
Kelly, Christopher S 4:43:47 (21,746)
Kelly, Ciaran P 4:27:09 (17,880)
Kelly, Colin S 5:30:45 (28,640)
Kelly, Daniel P 4:24:06 (17,092)
Kelly, David B 5:13:32 (26,831)
Kelly, David P 3:46:58 (7,741)
Kelly, Dean 5:29:53 (28,572)
Kelly, Dean L 4:21:58 (16,524)
Kelly, Dermot J 3:55:41 (9,982)
Kelly, Gareth O 5:34:59 (28,955)
Kelly, Jason P 6:13:19 (30,826)
Kelly, John 3:32:41 (5,041)
Kelly, John M 3:50:49 (8,712)
Kelly, Jon 4:22:50 (16,783)
Kelly, Joseph P 4:38:04 (20,488)
Kelly, Keith D 3:26:58 (4,013)
Kelly, Kevin P 4:22:37 (16,731)
Kelly, Liam G 4:21:23 (16,358)
Kelly, Mark F 3:56:25 (10,222)
Kelly, Michael 3:25:00 (3,693)
Kelly, Michael A 5:43:48 (29,616)
Kelly, Oisin S 3:53:56 (9,484)
Kelly, Paul M 3:26:17 (3,885)
Kelly, Paul P 3:42:49 (6,813)
Kelly, Peter D 4:17:43 (15,485)
Kelly, Sean 3:05:30 (1,572)
Kelly, Stephen 3:17:53 (2,838)
Kelly, Stephen 3:24:15 (3,595)
Kelly, Stephen C 4:48:40 (22,807)
Kelly, Stephen P 5:58:41 (30,356)
Kelly, Terence 4:08:30 (13,231)
Kelly, Thomas G 8:26:41 (31,962)
Kelly, Tim C 3:01:44 (1,288)
Kelly, William 5:01:49 (25,275)
Kelsall, Mike 5:15:14 (27,046)
Kelsey, Peter J 4:34:19 (19,674)
Kelso, Barnaby 6:14:49 (30,878)
Kelso, William 4:05:12 (12,462)
Kelting, John R 4:13:19 (14,411)
Kember, Julian J 4:13:10 (14,369)
Kemlo, Mike I 4:55:57 (24,200)
Kemmerling, Thomas J 4:18:47 (15,734)
Kemp, Albert L 3:44:23 (7,150)
Kemp, Benjamin J 3:05:26 (1,565)
Kemp, James 4:36:02 (20,036)
Kemp, Jason R 5:11:14 (26,547)
Kemp, Jon M 2:58:22 (1,002)
Kemp, Jonathan P 3:53:44 (9,420)
Kemp, Martyn 3:51:20 (8,842)
Kemp, Peter J 6:01:01 (30,449)
Kemp, Philip A 3:43:33 (6,968)
Kemp, Robert G 4:25:51 (17,526)
Kemp, Stephen 5:22:16 (27,802)
Kemp, Stewart J 3:30:01 (4,591)
Kempgens, Arnot 4:00:57 (11,494)
Kempthorne, Mark R 5:23:28 (27,913)
Kenchington, Chris J 2:58:44 (1,049)
Kenchington, Nicholas S 2:47:30 (404)
Kendall, Ian D 4:44:37 (21,943)
Kendall, Jason P 4:08:39 (13,272)
Kendall, Stuart J 3:59:11 (11,054)
Kendrick, Alastair 4:56:16 (24,255)
Kendrick, Philip 2:46:07 (361)
Kendrick, Shane C 5:10:45 (26,476)
Kendrick, Stuart A 3:52:46 (9,185)
Kenna, Michael M 4:18:29 (15,661)
Kennan, David R 3:54:43 (9,696)
Kennan, Robert M 4:23:45 (17,002)
Kenndey, Ian D 4:32:54 (19,335)
Kennedy, Adam J 3:49:09 (8,297)
Kennedy, Alan J 4:07:53 (13,085)
Kennedy, Andrew D 5:00:32 (25,069)
Kennedy, Andrew J 4:40:59 (21,119)
Kennedy, Anthony R 3:45:20 (7,372)
Kennedy, Chris 3:20:29 (3,124)
Kennedy, Craig P 3:20:35 (3,148)
Kennedy, Donald E 2:58:17 (994)
Kennedy, Dougie 3:46:27 (7,628)
Kennedy, George 3:32:46 (5,056)
Kennedy, George R 4:08:58 (13,369)
Kennedy, Graham R 3:18:21 (2,882)
Kennedy, Ian 4:06:53 (12,860)
Kennedy, James P 3:32:06 (4,938)
Kennedy, Les 3:24:02 (3,569)
Kennedy, Mark 4:09:10 (13,411)
Kennedy, Mick 3:56:09 (10,121)
Kennedy, Paul J 4:42:58 (21,559)
Kennedy, Peter D 3:54:01 (9,510)
Kennedy, Philip A 4:24:15 (17,133)
Kennedy, Richard D 3:02:56 (1,363)
Kennedy, Richard W 3:43:19 (6,922)
Kennedy, Rodger A 3:48:53 (8,227)
Kennedy, Rory 4:11:53 (14,057)
Kennedy, Scott H 2:49:40 (485)
Kennerley, Dominic M 3:58:42 (10,919)
Kenneth, Robert J 3:43:55 (7,043)
Kennett, Steffan A 2:59:21 (1,108)
Kenney, Alexander C 5:05:50 (25,812)
Kenny, Chris 3:41:46 (6,599)
Kenny, Jack 3:47:03 (7,768)
Kenny, John C 4:37:06 (20,274)
Kenny, Liam J 5:15:29 (27,079)
Kenny, Triss P 3:16:13 (2,663)
Kenrick, Dom 4:12:55 (14,307)
Kensett, Martin J 3:37:46 (5,911)
Kent, Ashley H 4:36:47 (20,198)
Kent, Bryan H 4:59:23 (24,880)
Kent, Christopher J 4:25:34 (17,444)
Kent, Gary M 3:53:27 (9,366)
Kent, Joss A 3:55:42 (9,989)
Kent, Mark T 5:06:08 (25,862)
Kent, Michael J 4:24:18 (17,142)
Kent, Nigel A 4:12:56 (14,314)
Kent, Paul S 2:57:54 (959)
Kent, Richard 4:03:39 (12,118)
Kent, Sam G 4:43:30 (21,685)
Kent, Steven 6:51:23 (31,520)
Kent, Steven J 5:39:02 (29,268)
Kent, Tony 5:09:04 (26,247)
Kent, Walter J 4:18:07 (15,576)
Kenton, Benjamin C 3:34:43 (5,371)
Kenward, David J 3:53:40 (9,413)
Kenwright, Michael J 3:37:09 (5,804)
Kenwright, Paul N 5:01:16 (25,178)
Kenyon, Ronald J 4:15:51 (15,015)
Kenyon, Stephen 3:14:36 (2,513)
Kenzo, Banno 5:14:03 (26,909)
Keogh, David J 4:18:42 (15,710)
Keogh, Martin E 4:17:41 (15,479)
Keogh, Steven 4:59:53 (24,971)
Kerins, Scott 4:38:13 (20,524)
Kerley, Stuart J 5:09:43 (26,339)
Kerr, Alastair 3:56:57 (10,379)
Kerr, Benjamin J 4:11:05 (13,886)
Kerr, Cameron D 4:26:15 (17,648)
Kerr, Clive 6:37:29 (31,333)
Kerr, Duncan P 3:36:16 (5,655)
Kerr, Ian D 4:05:59 (12,657)
Kerr, James C 5:01:20 (25,191)
Kerr, James D 3:45:11 (7,342)
Kerr, Jim 3:39:56 (6,294)
Kerr, Malcolm J 3:41:17 (6,523)
Kerr, Phillip J 4:38:53 (20,691)
Kerr, Richard S 4:10:17 (13,697)
Kerr, Stephen 4:17:45 (15,494)
Kerr, Tim J 5:31:48 (28,723)

Kerridge, Dave....4:38:00 (20,466)
Kerridge, Donald L....3:00:13 (1,171)
Kerrigan, Charles P....4:24:57 (17,294)
Kerry, David G....4:11:39 (14,015)
Kershaw, Christopher R....4:42:46 (21,509)
Kershaw, Steven P....5:10:07 (26,393)
Kershaw, Wayne J....3:42:27 (6,730)
Kerslake, Ian M....3:51:23 (8,853)
Kersley, William....5:29:15 (28,513)
Kerswell, Peter L....3:41:37 (6,568)
Kerton, Christopher....5:13:16 (26,801)
Keruevant, Alain....3:53:59 (9,499)
Kesby, Phillip D....4:43:56 (21,785)
Kessler, Peter....4:46:14 (22,306)
Kester, Philip....5:00:14 (25,031)
Kestle, Michael J....3:07:55 (1,798)
Kestner, Eric T....4:23:26 (16,929)
Ketenci, Giray....5:13:58 (26,890)
Kett, Brian F....4:23:02 (16,820)
Ketteridge, Sean R....2:57:38 (926)
Kettlewell, Jonathan P....4:02:35 (11,872)
Kewley, David M....3:57:49 (10,622)
Kewley, Steven....4:44:53 (21,995)
Keya, Alexander....4:06:44 (12,823)
Keymer, Stefan J....3:46:24 (7,620)
Keys, Ivor G....5:16:30 (27,187)
Keys, John F....3:40:57 (6,466)
Keyworth, Andrew....4:59:12 (24,828)
Keyworth, Antony J....3:30:33 (4,699)
Khabiri, Bijan....4:54:27 (23,885)
Khaboka, Bandubuila A....5:01:18 (25,186)
Khadga, Kabindra....3:40:00 (6,304)
Khampha, Azwinndini....4:02:53 (11,936)
Khan, Ahmed....4:26:08 (17,620)
Khan, Ashraff....2:55:46 (798)
Khan, Rivhu....4:46:42 (22,393)
Khan, Sascha A....5:22:20 (27,808)
Khan, Shafiq A....4:31:21 (18,935)
Khan, Shakeel I....4:44:17 (21,855)
Khan, Zia U....4:30:53 (18,837)
Khangura, Bobby....6:00:12 (30,421)
Khanna, Shaman....3:59:17 (11,083)
Khella, Kalvinder S....6:30:27 (31,212)
Khorsi, Aymen....4:40:55 (21,109)
Khouri, Dudley....5:07:17 (26,006)
Khushal, Pretesh....5:09:21 (26,285)
Kibble, James J....3:45:41 (7,455)
Kibblewhite, Gary....5:22:21 (27,812)
Kibblewhite, Michael....4:27:49 (18,044)
Kidby, Peter A....8:43:26 (31,975)
Kidd, Darren T....4:39:02 (20,735)
Kidd, David W....3:54:35 (9,660)
Kiddle, Rick T....2:46:15 (363)
Kidner, Elliot K....5:04:56 (25,685)
Kiefer, Simon....4:18:01 (15,557)
Kiely, Marc....4:27:20 (17,925)
Kiely, Paul M....4:12:00 (14,095)
Kiemel, Hans....2:58:25 (1,008)
Kiener, Hanspeter....4:08:03 (13,124)
Kiernan, Patrick....3:06:07 (1,622)
Kight, John....2:52:54 (637)
Kiladis, Matthew J....5:17:39 (27,322)
Kilbane, Conor C....3:40:29 (6,396)
Kilburn, Nigel D....4:11:30 (13,968)
Kilby, Andrew N....3:55:50 (10,028)
Kilgour, Robert J....3:57:28 (10,527)
Kilkenny, Kevin J....3:58:43 (10,923)
Killeen, Matthew A....6:23:55 (31,105)
Killeen, Michael A....3:44:58 (7,301)
Killer-Ginzky, Paul S....3:47:14 (7,808)
Killington, Lee R....5:26:54 (28,291)
Kilmister, Steve J....4:42:48 (21,520)
Kilpatrick, Jeremy....4:28:07 (18,126)
Kiltie, David R....3:45:44 (7,468)
Kimber, Adrian....4:11:58 (14,083)
Kimber, Gary A....3:58:51 (10,960)
Kimber, Jim....4:13:18 (14,403)
Kimber, John....3:48:08 (8,034)
Kimber, John F....5:20:11 (27,593)
Kimber, Nicholas....4:09:52 (13,598)
Kimber, Phil....3:30:58 (4,774)
Kimber, Ted A....4:06:00 (12,662)
Kimberley, William P....4:36:37 (20,159)
Kimble, Mark P....5:05:56 (25,834)
Kimble, Peter J....4:39:07 (20,751)
Kimmins, Simon....4:16:16 (15,111)
Kinch, Graham S....4:41:51 (21,317)
Kinch, Henry W....3:50:08 (8,536)
Kinchington, Richard G....5:22:20 (27,808)
Kind, Scott W....5:06:33 (25,917)
Kindell, Matthew C....4:04:45 (12,367)
King, Alan J....4:49:46 (23,033)
King, Andrew J....3:54:55 (9,756)
King, Andrew J....5:07:06 (25,982)
King, Bryan T....3:42:12 (6,681)
King, Charles F....4:14:48 (14,758)
King, Charles W....4:46:14 (22,306)
King, Dave....3:19:12 (2,983)
King, David J....5:03:13 (25,478)
King, David M....3:16:15 (2,666)
King, David S....4:26:53 (17,808)
King, Dennis....4:13:12 (14,376)
King, Douglas J....4:54:07 (23,821)
King, Garry O....4:44:28 (21,903)
King, Gerry S....3:07:37 (1,767)
King, Graham....4:55:06 (24,013)
King, Ian....2:56:05 (818)
King, Ian T....4:09:02 (13,386)
King, James F....4:03:42 (12,125)
King, Jonny A....5:41:59 (29,482)
King, Julian G....2:58:37 (1,031)
King, Justin W....3:48:07 (8,027)
King, Kevin L....7:29:44 (31,843)
King, Len J....4:28:59 (18,344)
King, Leslie....3:45:52 (7,498)
King, Lewis B....4:07:01 (12,896)
King, Malcolm S....3:51:46 (8,962)
King, Martin....3:14:18 (2,477)
King, Mathew....4:27:45 (18,026)
King, Matthew J....4:08:47 (13,317)
King, Nigel....4:26:29 (17,696)
King, Paul A....3:54:35 (9,660)
King, Paul A....4:00:41 (11,422)
King, Paul J....3:29:48 (4,553)
King, Paul T....4:48:41 (22,812)
King, Peter M....5:52:18 (30,087)
King, Philip J....3:54:45 (9,711)
King, Richard J....3:51:31 (8,891)
King, Ricky....4:58:15 (24,653)
King, Robert A....3:41:40 (6,579)
King, Robert A....4:46:11 (22,293)
King, Robert M....5:07:14 (25,999)
King, Scott D....4:14:14 (14,615)
King, Stephen R....4:14:08 (14,593)
Kingdon, Adam L....5:42:24 (29,509)
Kingdon, Steve L....4:17:11 (15,346)
Kinggett, Steven J....4:10:13 (13,681)
Kingstad, Richard C....2:42:49 (263)
Kingston, Adrian S....4:37:28 (20,333)
Kingston, Carl J....4:19:22 (15,874)
Kingston, Daniel J....4:03:12 (12,007)
Kingston, Matthew....3:17:12 (2,773)
Kingston, Patrick W....4:27:55 (18,067)
Kingston, Peter S....4:21:27 (16,376)
Kingswood, Phillip....5:52:31 (30,096)
Kingswood, Stephen P....3:19:24 (3,007)
Kinight, Kevin M....4:05:09 (12,456)
Kinloch, Charles....4:14:27 (14,665)
Kinneer, Richard W....3:52:09 (9,047)
Kinnersley, Ian....4:05:48 (12,616)
Kinninmonth, Andrew....3:46:16 (7,593)
Kinsella, David A....4:46:18 (22,317)
Kinsella, Sean P....6:23:16 (31,087)
Kinsey, Nicholas J....2:41:26 (229)
Kinsey, William G....5:16:40 (27,217)
Kinsley, Graham....4:22:52 (16,788)
Kinson, Trevor R....4:17:52 (15,526)
Kiplagat, William....2:12:04 (12)
Kipling, Gerard A....4:10:17 (13,697)
Kirby, Andrew....4:26:30 (17,703)
Kirby, Andrew J....4:51:09 (23,295)
Kirby, Colin....3:45:35 (7,435)
Kirby, Jason L....3:53:09 (9,297)
Kirby, Lee J....4:50:17 (23,119)
Kirby, Martin B....3:20:27 (3,115)
Kirby, Richard....3:44:23 (7,150)
Kirby, Scott R....5:33:52 (28,880)
Kirby, Simon J....4:50:17 (23,119)
Kirby, Steven....5:42:57 (29,552)
Kirby, Steven E....3:16:07 (2,655)
Kirk, Alexei J....4:55:13 (24,044)
Kirk, Alvin J....5:36:49 (29,092)
Kirk, Andrew C....5:05:47 (25,797)
Kirk, Andrew P....3:59:07 (11,035)
Kirk, Matthew....4:35:53 (20,000)
Kirk, Michael J....5:10:14 (26,402)
Kirk, Neil....2:51:22 (559)
Kirk, Richard G....4:21:20 (16,345)
Kirkbride, Allen J....3:35:18 (5,483)
Kirkby, Leonard....3:58:21 (10,804)
Kirkdale, Brian K....3:12:32 (2,256)
Kirke-Smith, Douglas....4:44:36 (21,935)
Kirkham, Christopher....3:30:36 (4,707)
Kirkland, Jim P....4:25:43 (17,481)
Kirkman, David E....3:44:16 (7,128)
Kirkpatrick, Mark....4:32:01 (19,116)
Kirkum, Michael J....5:52:00 (30,066)
Kirkwood, Gareth R....4:11:10 (13,904)
Kirkwood, James E....5:51:22 (30,030)
Kirkwood, Robert L....4:00:17 (11,355)
Kirlew, Lance....2:48:20 (438)
Kirsop, Neil....4:02:08 (11,757)
Kirsopp, Grahame N....4:40:22 (21,003)
Kirton, John P....3:47:07 (7,784)
Kirui, Philip....2:18:43 (26)
Kirwan, Ian M....3:43:32 (6,965)
Kirwan, Stephen A....4:50:40 (23,210)
Kirwin, Philip A....2:37:21 (162)
Kisbee, Murray P....3:14:09 (2,459)
Kissane, John E....4:47:05 (22,470)
Kist, Fred....5:08:00 (26,115)
Kitchen, Andrew M....3:31:58 (4,918)
Kitchen, Anthony J....3:37:36 (5,890)
Kitchen, Christopher R....3:54:53 (9,748)
Kitchen, Neil D....3:50:39 (8,671)
Kitchen, Nick R....3:39:36 (6,238)
Kitcher, Ray P....4:56:46 (24,358)
Kitchin, Paul....5:17:52 (27,349)
Kitching, Barrie....4:29:11 (18,400)
Kitching, Ian D....2:47:27 (399)
Kitching, Peter A....4:38:00 (20,466)
Kite, Edward R....3:34:41 (5,366)
Kiteley, Mark....5:01:02 (25,150)
Kitteridge, Shayne R....4:59:46 (24,952)
Kittle, Ian D....3:39:13 (6,166)
Kittler, Robert L....4:56:01 (24,211)
Kittoe, Edmund W....3:19:25 (3,008)
Kittrell, Charles R....4:29:42 (18,555)
Kjaerulf, Flemming....3:03:49 (1,433)
Kjelleras, Jesper....4:19:25 (15,887)
Klabe, Neil E....3:09:09 (1,911)
Klamminger, Hans....5:21:17 (27,707)
Klawitter, Lutz....4:25:13 (17,363)
Kleibrink, Luuk....4:05:17 (12,482)
Klein, Klaus....3:19:06 (2,964)
Klein, Michel....2:58:20 (998)
Klein, Stanley....5:06:11 (25,872)
Kleinknecht, Guenter....3:12:59 (2,309)
Kleinman, Martin....4:59:43 (24,942)
Klenerman, Paul....3:59:31 (11,166)
Klesser, Dean G....4:36:49 (20,211)
Klooster, Thomas....3:51:07 (8,769)
Kluth, David C....4:27:04 (17,859)
Klym, Steven P....5:10:18 (26,416)
Knapp, John A....2:55:33 (788)
Knapp, Neil....3:42:10 (6,674)
Knauder, Robert....3:23:13 (3,464)
Knibbs, Alec V....5:39:00 (29,265)
Knight, Adam J....4:47:06 (22,474)
Knight, Alan R....4:22:21 (16,654)
Knight, Andrew D....4:47:26 (22,552)
Knight, Andrew J....3:42:08 (6,672)
Knight, Anthony D....3:51:17 (8,828)
Knight, Charles C....3:54:31 (9,641)
Knight, Chris....3:51:25 (8,862)
Knight, Darren J....4:11:43 (14,024)
Knight, Darren R....4:29:45 (18,571)
Knight, Dave L....3:47:25 (7,856)
Knight, David A....3:55:26 (9,914)

Knight, David M 4:03:19 (12,036)
Knight, James A 3:27:37 (4,150)
Knight, Jason 4:02:47 (11,921)
Knight, Joshua P 3:34:57 (5,418)
Knight, Kenneth 3:55:31 (9,935)
Knight, Kevin 4:02:03 (11,730)
Knight, Kevin L 4:14:56 (14,792)
Knight, Lee R 4:06:28 (12,772)
Knight, Matthew D 5:28:47 (28,469)
Knight, Paul J 3:24:04 (3,574)
Knight, Peter 4:00:04 (11,308)
Knight, Richard P 8:33:43 (31,972)
Knight, Richard W 5:12:58 (26,755)
Knight, Robert 4:20:18 (16,101)
Knight, Roger M 4:47:45 (22,624)
Knight, Sam 4:47:42 (22,616)
Knight, Stefan A 4:08:15 (13,159)
Knight, Stuart J 3:59:28 (11,140)
Knight, Terry R 5:46:18 (29,770)
Knight-Baker, Martin R 4:00:48 (11,444)
Knights, Jim 4:49:37 (22,999)
Knock, Michael J 4:38:49 (20,670)
Knoll, Herbert 3:58:04 (10,696)
Knott, Crawford A 6:04:24 (30,579)
Knott, Paul J 4:36:33 (20,144)
Knowles, John 3:28:52 (4,392)
Knowles, Martin R 3:43:44 (7,001)
Knowles, Nigel P 3:38:46 (6,093)
Knowles, Peter J 4:43:38 (21,707)
Knowles, Peter K 3:58:00 (10,671)
Knowles, Simon F 3:36:18 (5,659)
Knox, Darren 6:02:26 (30,503)
Knox, Jonathan D 4:50:44 (23,219)
Knox, Tom 4:14:18 (14,623)
Knudsen, Earl 3:46:48 (7,702)
Knudsen, Knud Erik 2:53:24 (664)
Kobayashi, Masanori 4:48:57 (22,865)
Kobayashi, Yoshikazu 4:32:18 (19,188)
Kobler, Alfred 3:33:13 (5,141)
Koch, Peter R 3:29:00 (4,413)
Koch, Roger G 4:35:45 (19,971)
Koczian, Markus 4:59:24 (24,883)
Koe, Digby M 4:11:01 (13,875)
Koehler, Werner 3:58:25 (10,824)
Koelewijn, Jan 4:00:09 (11,329)
Koffler, Adam M 3:57:07 (10,418)
Kogel, Holger 4:24:54 (17,284)
Kogler, Nikolaus 3:20:29 (3,124)
Kohler, Armin 3:31:00 (4,778)
Koini, Andreas 3:46:57 (7,737)
Kokkotos, Gerasimos 2:21:19 (38)
Kolind, Jesper 3:25:46 (3,810)
Kolling, Ralph 4:05:46 (12,610)
Kolter, Giles A 5:25:20 (28,123)
Konradt, Stephan 5:04:24 (25,614)
Kooger, Pieter J 3:47:48 (7,946)
Kooten, Arno V 3:54:11 (9,555)
Kopec, Christopher J 5:20:19 (27,610)
Kopetzky, Matthias 4:19:11 (15,825)
Koppel, Herwig 2:48:39 (442)
Kor, Michael C 4:32:06 (19,133)
Kordowski, Nicholas 4:38:31 (20,598)
Korir, Sammy 2:06:48 (2)
Korn, Abner P 4:20:11 (16,059)
Koroscik, Karl 4:50:52 (23,246)
Korten, Christopher J 4:08:59 (13,377)
Korten, Robert 4:23:11 (16,869)
Kos, Marc 3:38:38 (6,075)
Koshy, Sam G 5:05:39 (25,780)
Kosin, Volker 4:17:43 (15,485)
Koski, Matti T 5:09:38 (26,325)
Kossoff, Simon 4:21:27 (16,376)
Kovats, Steven L 2:55:57 (809)
Kozel, Thomas 4:23:06 (16,842)
Koziarski, Paul 4:00:59 (11,504)
Kozlikin, Vitali 4:23:08 (16,851)
Kramer, Alexander 4:52:01 (23,447)
Kramer, Dani 4:59:52 (24,968)
Kramer, Daniel 4:44:28 (21,903)
Kramer, Steve 4:31:06 (18,879)
Krause, John C 3:45:10 (7,339)
Kreiner, Claus 3:17:11 (2,770)
Kreuzmair, Karl 3:21:55 (3,300)
Krismer, Peter M 4:15:48 (15,003)
Kristensen, Kaj O 3:23:07 (3,453)
Kroenke, Klaus M 3:06:47 (1,684)
Krook, Sven 5:22:39 (27,846)
Kruger, Alex M 5:15:49 (27,109)
Kruger, Riaan 4:04:49 (12,379)
Kruppa, Robert 4:52:59 (23,614)
Ktorides, Andrew 4:35:26 (19,919)
Kubheka, Simo S 4:21:30 (16,389)
Kudar, Graham M 4:02:21 (11,829)
Kudera, Michael 4:21:58 (16,524)
Kueberuwa, Gray I 3:06:34 (1,662)
Kuhn, Alexander D 3:21:11 (3,220)
Kuhn, Heiko 3:22:20 (3,348)
Kuhn, Michael E 3:43:34 (6,974)
Kumar, Pardeep 4:58:49 (24,766)
Kumar, Vijay 6:42:51 (31,405)
Kumarasingham, Selvakumar 7:40:37 (31,891)
Kuronen, Mikko K 2:49:26 (475)
Kurth, Peter 4:18:02 (15,564)
Kurz, Michael 3:20:09 (3,084)
Kusmierek, Mariusz 6:00:03 (30,410)
Kwisthout, Johan H 4:27:57 (18,082)
Kyle, Peter 4:02:38 (11,881)
Kyne, David M 3:14:38 (2,516)
Kynoch, Michael A 4:07:58 (13,110)
Kyritsis, Neoclis 4:37:40 (20,375)
Kyte, Peter D 5:14:07 (26,914)
Kyte, Peter J 3:55:55 (10,057)
Laad, Hiten P 5:42:17 (29,501)
Laban, James 4:19:03 (15,786)
Labandeira, José A 2:54:54 (747)
Labarr, Winston J 4:44:44 (21,961)
Labouysse, Marc 3:08:41 (1,866)
Labudzki, Jacek 2:52:51 (635)
Labuschagne, Timothy 3:46:23 (7,617)
Lacarcel Wandosell, José 3:38:55 (6,115)
Lacey, Alex 4:26:19 (17,658)
Lacey, Charles P 6:29:42 (31,198)
Lacey, Ian 4:37:35 (20,352)
Lacey, Ian N 3:53:10 (9,303)
Lacey, Joe M 3:21:16 (3,227)
Lacey, Mark D 2:49:55 (495)
Lacey, Peter T 4:08:32 (13,239)
Lacey, Sean P 5:05:28 (25,751)
Lacey, Simon D 3:49:21 (8,338)
Lachance, David 5:15:56 (27,122)
Lack, Andy J 3:25:08 (3,709)
Lacombe, Regis 2:29:50 (81)
Lacome, Jean-Luc 5:56:23 (30,267)
Lacy, David 4:43:35 (21,696)
Lad, Mahesh 5:37:02 (29,108)
Lad, Nishit 5:26:46 (28,274)
Lad, Pravine 6:52:39 (31,536)
Ladd, Joe 3:29:13 (4,455)
Ladd, Paul 6:02:30 (30,507)
Ladner, Kevin F 4:21:59 (16,530)
Ladocha, David 3:17:49 (2,830)
Ladron De Guevara, Carlos A 3:27:27 (4,115)
Ladron De Guevara, José T 3:24:56 (3,683)
Ladwa, Dayalal D 4:37:45 (20,391)
Laenens, Francis 4:15:28 (14,920)
Lafay, Raymond 3:38:11 (5,992)
Lafleche, Trevor A 5:15:14 (27,046)
Laflin, Michael J 5:12:03 (26,640)
Lafond, Frederic 4:40:08 (20,947)
Laforge, François 3:51:05 (8,762)
Lafronza, Mauro 3:16:18 (2,670)
Lagarde, Patrice 4:07:38 (13,040)
Lagerstedt, Christian 4:32:46 (19,306)
Lagnado, Lawrence A 4:35:58 (20,021)
Lagnado, Max 3:29:49 (4,558)
Lai, Lip 4:00:41 (11,422)
Lai, Simon 4:14:59 (14,801)
Laidler, Stephen T 2:58:32 (1,015)
Laine, Alexander 4:28:02 (18,105)
Laing, George 3:33:05 (5,112)
Laing, Richard A 4:01:08 (11,534)
Laing, William 3:23:43 (3,530)
Lainsbury, Raymond J 4:24:57 (17,294)
Laird, Ewan S 3:52:22 (9,103)
Laird, Gordon L 5:00:55 (25,130)
Laird, Ian S 4:34:44 (19,765)
Laird, James A 3:53:11 (9,310)
Laird, John M 4:54:36 (23,923)
Laishley, Andrew J 5:34:56 (28,952)
Lait, Gavin 4:55:01 (23,999)
Laithwaite, Marc 2:59:47 (1,140)
Laitinen, Jussi 4:15:29 (14,922)
Lake, Andrew S 5:02:39 (25,396)
Lake, Danny 3:02:13 (1,318)
Lake, Jamie A 3:49:48 (8,451)
Lake, Philip N 3:59:40 (11,212)
Lake, Richard 4:08:13 (13,152)
Lake, Stewart R 3:33:24 (5,174)
Laker, Andrew 3:25:16 (3,729)
Lakey, Daniel J 4:00:17 (11,355)
Lakhani, Raj B 4:33:33 (19,477)
Lakin, Keith J 5:10:41 (26,464)
Lalani, Shiraz D 5:21:42 (27,750)
Lally, John G 4:28:55 (18,331)
Lalor, Peter R 4:51:01 (23,274)
Lam, Marcus 6:59:28 (31,614)
Lamb, Brent J 3:19:27 (3,014)
Lamb, Duncan J 4:59:44 (24,948)
Lamb, Ian 3:13:16 (2,337)
Lamb, James W 3:59:28 (11,140)
Lamb, Jonathan D 4:12:58 (14,321)
Lamb, Keith S 4:34:23 (19,689)
Lamb, Ken D 3:47:38 (7,914)
Lamb, Malcolm N 4:06:04 (12,675)
Lamb, Nicholas B 3:57:17 (10,473)
Lamb, Philip R 4:11:20 (13,938)
Lamb, Robert G 3:33:06 (5,116)
Lamb, Simon 5:25:38 (28,156)
Lambard, Lee 4:08:38 (13,268)
Lambert, Andrew 3:37:49 (5,926)
Lambert, Heath J 3:58:11 (10,750)
Lambert, Jacques 3:32:33 (5,013)
Lambert, Jonathan P 4:31:07 (18,880)
Lambert, Martin J 4:10:27 (13,743)
Lambert, Nigel K 4:26:23 (17,672)
Lambourn, David J 4:36:50 (20,214)
Lambourn, Nigel 4:16:57 (15,294)
Lambourn, Peter N 3:02:29 (1,339)
Lambourne, Martin G 4:30:21 (18,716)
Lambton, Nigel W 4:47:49 (22,639)
Lammali, Aziouz 2:52:19 (604)
Lammas, Edward 3:38:34 (6,063)
Lammas, Scott A 5:18:57 (27,459)
Lamond, Alastair C 4:11:41 (14,021)
Lamont, Christopher P 2:55:21 (776)
Lamont, Clinton H 3:50:40 (8,676)
Lamont, Jason D 6:27:41 (31,169)
Lamprecht, Tertius 4:10:26 (13,740)
Lamza, Ernie W 3:09:02 (1,903)
Lancaster, Craig 4:45:02 (22,040)
Lancaster, David J 5:56:28 (30,272)
Lancaster, Gregory 5:17:40 (27,325)
Lancaster, Ian J 5:24:36 (28,033)
Lancaster, Jonathan 4:20:52 (16,250)
Lancaster, Kenneth A 6:16:30 (30,920)
Lancaster, Simon 3:32:22 (4,981)
Lancaster, Steven J 5:19:03 (27,470)
Lanckham, Kevin T 3:02:17 (1,325)
Landais, Christian 3:45:07 (7,322)
Landau, David 6:09:18 (30,710)
Landegren, Peter 3:23:23 (3,485)
Landells, Stephen H 3:19:10 (2,975)
Lander, Chris M 4:54:20 (23,866)
Lander, Eric T 3:27:10 (4,057)
Landers, Nicholas M 3:54:13 (9,567)
Landrock, Christian 3:39:47 (6,271)
Lane, Alan R 4:17:50 (15,517)
Lane, Andrew 2:58:45 (1,052)
Lane, Barnard R 4:35:17 (19,882)
Lane, Gary S 5:06:52 (25,955)
Lane, Graham J 5:08:07 (26,130)
Lane, James K 4:46:59 (22,444)
Lane, Jonathan M 4:59:23 (24,880)
Lane, Justin G 3:11:55 (2,183)
Lane, Malcolm R 4:27:09 (17,880)
Lane, Matt F 3:54:25 (9,617)
Lane, Michael C 3:50:54 (8,735)
Lane, Mick 5:14:41 (26,990)
Lane, Pete J 4:49:42 (23,014)

LONDON MARATHON

Lane, Ronald F	3:15:40 (2,618)
Lane, Stephen	4:42:26 (21,439)
Lane, Tony A	4:43:21 (21,654)
Lang, Fabrice	3:19:38 (3,034)
Lang, Guy	3:48:03 (8,008)
Lang, John	4:01:18 (11,562)
Langan, Dale T	4:15:24 (14,899)
Langdon, Miles D	4:09:07 (13,402)
Lange, Alexander	4:20:21 (16,117)
Langham, Anthony R	4:28:43 (18,281)
Langham, Garry	4:15:48 (15,003)
Langlands, Fraser J	4:22:44 (16,755)
Langlet, Thierry	3:53:20 (9,348)
Langley, Alex	5:05:52 (25,818)
Langley, Colin	2:47:43 (410)
Langley, Lawrence K	3:49:01 (8,258)
Langley, Nick J	4:44:29 (21,908)
Langley, Nigel A	4:44:12 (21,837)
Langley, Peter G	4:03:54 (12,169)
Langley, Robert F	4:34:53 (19,800)
Langley, Thomas J	4:23:31 (16,947)
Langlois, Marcus J	4:13:59 (14,559)
Langrish, Trevor M	4:09:10 (13,411)
Langsdale, Philip R	5:54:49 (30,188)
Langston, Kevin M	4:51:40 (23,371)
Langthorne, Chris	4:19:57 (16,013)
Langton, Duma D	4:22:03 (16,556)
Langton, Michael S	5:44:33 (29,661)
Lanham, James P	3:49:57 (8,489)
Lanigan, Sean	5:38:15 (29,204)
Lankenau, Karl T	4:13:24 (14,432)
Lanning, Robert	4:43:35 (21,696)
Lannon, Martin G	3:44:28 (7,175)
Lannon, Peter J	5:21:10 (27,697)
Lansdell, Alan	7:26:36 (31,821)
Lantsbery, David	3:40:48 (6,440)
Lanzafame, Gaetano M	4:05:50 (12,625)
Lappin, Brian	4:59:55 (24,976)
Lappin, James R	4:02:01 (11,723)
Larby, Paul M	5:44:27 (29,652)
Large, David L	5:56:03 (30,249)
Large, Phillip H	3:03:47 (1,430)
Large, Richard	3:11:47 (2,167)
Large, Steven G	3:06:23 (1,643)
Largeron, Bertrand	3:48:51 (8,226)
Lari, Francesco	3:27:51 (4,197)
Larive, Ian E	3:39:23 (6,197)
Lark, Shaun A	3:32:07 (4,942)
Larkin, Kevin M	4:51:16 (23,312)
Larmour, Andrew G	3:49:49 (8,455)
Larner, Daniel	4:51:46 (23,393)
Larner, Ian	4:37:36 (20,356)
Laroche, Cyril	2:53:15 (658)
Laroche, Dominique	3:52:23 (9,108)
Larsen, Claus	3:49:15 (8,319)
Larsen, Jonhard	2:54:20 (710)
Larsen, Per	4:04:25 (12,288)
Larser, Preber	3:43:09 (6,878)
Larsson, Charles A	4:21:38 (16,430)
Larter, Stewart	3:59:01 (11,010)
Lartey, Lawrence	4:47:03 (22,463)
Lascelles, Martin C	3:12:43 (2,275)
Lashmar, Anthony	2:43:40 (285)
Last, Martin R	4:34:31 (19,717)
Latala, Timothy G	4:47:49 (22,639)
Latchford, Thomas	3:35:52 (5,584)
Latham, Andrew S	4:22:24 (16,666)
Latham, Philip M	4:49:07 (22,898)
Latham, Russell	6:30:32 (31,214)
Latham, Thomas R	5:33:52 (28,880)
Lathwell, Simon G	3:06:33 (1,659)
Latin, David M	4:41:43 (21,286)
Lattanzio, Theodore A	4:55:13 (24,044)
Latteman, Mark R	3:42:19 (6,700)
Latter, John I	3:10:52 (2,087)
Latter, Oliver L	5:32:18 (28,760)
Latter, Patrick N	4:08:39 (13,272)
Latty, Shane	3:53:17 (9,335)
Laubis, Hans P	4:33:59 (19,583)
Laudato, Laudato Adriano	3:50:42 (8,682)
Lauga, Philippe	3:19:08 (2,967)
Laughton, Robbie G	4:24:44 (17,238)
Laukkanen, Jukka	5:16:35 (27,207)

Laurence, Garry E	4:22:20 (16,650)
Lauriault, François E	4:54:19 (23,863)
Laurie, Graham D	3:29:18 (4,471)
Lautenbacher, Gerg	3:46:09 (7,559)
Laux, Henning	4:55:15 (24,052)
Lavender, Tony	4:34:06 (19,625)
Lavery, Adrian C	3:17:52 (2,836)
Lavery, Alan J	3:06:45 (1,677)
Lavery, Richard C	4:39:08 (20,756)
Lavin, Gerard M	3:56:41 (10,298)
Lavin, Paul	3:45:12 (7,348)
Lavin, Stuart J	4:25:11 (17,356)
Lavy, Jeremy	3:49:53 (8,469)
Law, Alan S	4:17:38 (15,461)
Law, Albert H	3:47:16 (7,822)
Law, Andrew	4:02:21 (11,829)
Law, Andrew M	4:15:19 (14,884)
Law, Chris J	3:56:16 (10,171)
Law, David	4:33:17 (19,422)
Law, Gareth O	4:49:27 (22,969)
Law, Graham M	3:38:50 (6,105)
Law, Matthew A	3:21:29 (3,254)
Law, Matthew F	3:41:37 (6,568)
Law, Maxwell R	4:29:17 (18,422)
Law, Nicholas R	3:43:14 (6,902)
Law, Nigel L	4:20:25 (16,136)
Law, Peter W	4:15:36 (14,955)
Law, Richard	3:24:57 (3,684)
Law, Simon N	2:59:20 (1,105)
Law, Steven	4:14:28 (14,674)
Lawes, Timothy G	2:44:37 (309)
Lawler, James T	2:24:46 (51)
Lawless, Gareth	5:16:57 (27,251)
Lawless, Kev P	3:55:57 (10,067)
Lawley, Rob	4:11:35 (13,994)
Lawlor, Anthony J	2:54:57 (751)
Lawlor, Kevin J	4:46:25 (22,344)
Lawlor, Sean	3:35:51 (5,580)
Lawlor, Simon G	4:19:41 (15,947)
Lawne, James J	3:26:41 (3,951)
Lawrence, Antony R	4:50:20 (23,129)
Lawrence, Bernard	7:13:28 (31,736)
Lawrence, David J	3:12:56 (2,305)
Lawrence, Francis S	4:29:17 (18,422)
Lawrence, Graham	5:52:47 (30,114)
Lawrence, Ian P	4:04:55 (12,411)
Lawrence, Jimmy	4:18:40 (15,702)
Lawrence, Kenneth R	4:24:12 (17,122)
Lawrence, Mark D	4:23:32 (16,950)
Lawrence, Martin	4:09:54 (13,607)
Lawrence, Paul D	4:34:46 (19,770)
Lawrence, Peter	6:38:44 (31,347)
Lawrence, Philip I	3:33:24 (5,174)
Lawrence, Richard C	4:53:21 (23,676)
Lawrence, Richard G	3:44:26 (7,168)
Lawrence, Richard N	4:06:44 (12,823)
Lawrence, Simon A	3:16:34 (2,706)
Lawrence, Stephen J	3:58:44 (10,925)
Lawrence, Tyrone P	3:04:32 (1,491)
Lawrie, David M	3:41:47 (6,603)
Lawrie, Denis M	5:02:58 (25,444)
Lawrie, Robert D	3:57:20 (10,492)
Laws, David J	4:24:23 (17,162)
Lawson, David A	4:22:27 (16,681)
Lawson, James	3:20:56 (3,194)
Lawson, James	3:47:49 (7,950)
Lawson, Mark R	2:50:37 (531)
Lawson, Martin	4:09:40 (13,546)
Lawson, Phillip D	4:28:34 (18,248)
Lawson, Stephen	4:53:13 (23,656)
Lawson, Stuart I	5:11:53 (26,617)
Lawson, William P	3:27:36 (4,144)
Lawther, Dennis	4:58:15 (24,653)
Lawton, Alasdair R	4:05:43 (12,598)

Lawton, Brian	4:45:06 (22,064)
Lawton, Bryan W	3:09:45 (1,976)
Lawton, Daniel P	4:14:16 (14,620)
Lawton, Mark	6:15:01 (30,887)
Lawton, Peter J	3:27:01 (4,027)
Lawton, Richard	4:01:34 (11,613)
Lawton, Timothy W	5:01:03 (25,152)
Lay, John L	4:14:49 (14,767)
Lay, Uwe	4:11:37 (14,005)
Laycock, Andrew	3:51:59 (9,008)
Laycock, Grant	3:40:58 (6,469)
Laycock, Philip T	4:25:18 (17,380)
Laycock, Richard P	4:28:27 (18,215)
Layton, James R	3:51:24 (8,857)
Lazaruk, Simon J	4:29:25 (18,469)
Lazell, Martin E	4:42:11 (21,382)
Lazzaro, Vito	6:15:36 (30,897)
Le Barch, Gabriel	2:41:28 (230)
Le Borgne, Michel	4:08:31 (13,236)
Le Cocq, Nick J	3:39:14 (6,168)
Le Guevel, Yvon	3:44:29 (7,181)
Le Huray, Mathew P	3:59:26 (11,121)
Le Leu, Seth J	4:37:43 (20,385)
Le Mestre, Bernard	3:20:58 (3,197)
Le Nardou, Christian	3:57:08 (10,429)
Le Sech, Denis	3:43:33 (6,968)
Le Sueur, Guy	5:28:02 (28,399)
Lea, Michael R	4:06:38 (12,811)
Lea, Peter J	5:41:24 (29,438)
Leach, Benjamin J	3:00:20 (1,180)
Leach, Chris M	5:34:07 (28,897)
Leach, Darren	3:37:44 (5,908)
Leach, David J	3:35:06 (5,445)
Leach, Graham	4:09:30 (13,501)
Leach, Matthew J	4:28:52 (18,317)
Leach, Paul J	3:36:51 (5,748)
Leach, Simon J	3:55:50 (10,028)
Leadbetter, Simon A	4:10:52 (13,844)
Leadbetter, Stephen J	5:49:01 (29,908)
Leader, David A	3:26:58 (4,013)
Leader, Tom	4:20:15 (16,077)
Lea-Gerrard, Andrew	4:15:27 (14,916)
Leahy, Andrew M	5:55:57 (30,241)
Leahy, Justin P	3:25:33 (3,776)
Leak, Andrew S	5:45:25 (29,721)
Leak, Christopher S	4:22:10 (16,596)
Leal, Juan M	4:21:40 (16,439)
Learoyd, Stewart E	4:08:02 (13,121)
Leary, James A	3:23:43 (3,530)
Leathard, Matthew J	3:32:25 (4,990)
Leaute, Etienne	3:09:39 (1,965)
Leaver, Andrew	5:10:47 (26,480)
Leaver, Christopher J	5:31:41 (28,715)
Leaver, Marcus E	5:17:49 (27,339)
Leavy, Oran	4:08:32 (13,239)
Lebarbenchon, Vincent	4:09:24 (13,475)
Leber, Patrice	3:55:34 (9,954)
Leber, Thierry	3:25:12 (3,721)
Leblanc, Joel R	4:28:14 (18,153)
Lebon, Richard S	4:13:20 (14,414)
Lechlein, Peter	4:54:47 (23,956)
Leciaguecahar, Stephane J	3:46:12 (7,578)
Leclair, John A	4:29:40 (18,548)
Leclercq, Alexandre	3:47:11 (7,801)
Lecomte, Guy	3:21:10 (3,218)
Lecomte, Patrick	4:08:43 (13,298)
Lecroix, Gerard	3:58:23 (10,813)
Ledger, Dan	4:02:31 (11,858)
Ledgerton, Andrew J	3:58:11 (10,750)
Ledsom, Gregg S	4:32:15 (19,177)
Ledwaba-Chapman, Tony	3:34:49 (5,393)
Lee, Aaron	5:33:14 (28,825)
Lee, Adrian	4:29:20 (18,444)
Lee, Aidan J	4:58:47 (24,762)
Lee, Alan	4:31:07 (18,880)
Lee, Alec	5:08:10 (26,138)
Lee, Andrew G	3:47:23 (7,848)
Lee, Andy	4:51:46 (23,393)
Lee, Antony	5:42:50 (29,535)
Lee, Billy N	4:32:10 (19,158)
Lee, Brian M	4:42:59 (21,561)
Lee, Bryan	4:36:00 (20,027)
Lee, Charlie G	3:55:37 (9,966)

Lee, Daniel....3:56:27 (10,235)
Lee, Daniel....4:00:16 (11,353)
Lee, Daren M....3:30:53 (4,759)
Lee, David....3:22:20 (3,348)
Lee, David F....6:05:44 (30,614)
Lee, David P....3:52:43 (9,176)
Lee, Dennis C....4:50:49 (23,239)
Lee, Dennis K....4:59:21 (24,865)
Lee, Geoffrey C....2:59:51 (1,146)
Lee, James P....3:24:04 (3,574)
Lee, Jayson....3:40:16 (6,345)
Lee, John....3:43:18 (6,918)
Lee, Jonathan....4:24:03 (17,072)
Lee, Kevin P....4:14:03 (14,577)
Lee, Kin Hong....4:24:06 (17,092)
Lee, Martin....2:54:17 (707)
Lee, Matthew....5:00:15 (25,033)
Lee, Matthew C....4:20:16 (16,085)
Lee, Michael D....3:07:49 (1,787)
Lee, Nick T....4:26:04 (17,593)
Lee, Nigel....3:09:26 (1,940)
Lee, Patrick T....4:21:58 (16,524)
Lee, Paul A....3:50:45 (8,694)
Lee, Philip J....3:19:02 (2,958)
Lee, Philip M....4:25:11 (17,356)
Lee, Richard G....3:08:40 (1,864)
Lee, Ronald G....6:17:40 (30,943)
Lee, Royston A....2:58:13 (987)
Lee, Stephen A....4:47:21 (22,530)
Lee, Wei Liang J....4:12:26 (14,179)
Lee, William T....4:11:54 (14,063)
Leech, David S....3:47:15 (7,817)
Leech, Jason R....3:41:35 (6,561)
Leeds, Colin M....4:24:16 (17,136)
Leeke, Josh J....4:15:51 (15,015)
Leeke, Thomas G....4:06:51 (12,849)
Leeks, David R....4:08:01 (13,117)
Lee-Majors, Chrstian....6:07:13 (30,653)
Leering, Robert....4:01:19 (11,565)
Lees, George....3:20:29 (3,124)
Lees, Jason....4:32:52 (19,327)
Lees, Peter C....5:22:06 (27,783)
Lees, Robin....4:54:37 (23,926)
Lees, Wayne M....3:45:51 (7,492)
Lefebvre, Roland P....3:26:42 (3,957)
Lefelre, J....4:32:26 (19,220)
Lefever, James S....4:06:59 (12,889)
Leff, Adam....4:54:52 (23,971)
Lefrancq, Remi....3:32:37 (5,033)
Legard, Jonathan....4:46:38 (22,382)
Legassick, David T....4:44:47 (21,974)
Legate, Roger A....6:50:22 (31,504)
Leger, Francis....4:52:24 (23,517)
Leggate, Bill T....3:34:10 (5,293)
Leggate, Jody R....4:13:49 (14,521)
Legge, Alex J....3:27:02 (4,031)
Legge, David....3:47:28 (7,873)
Legge, Joe H....4:28:04 (18,115)
Legge, Justin S....4:47:03 (22,463)
Leggett, John N....3:58:55 (10,979)
Leggett, Stephen W....5:21:31 (27,728)
Leggott, Richard J....4:11:47 (14,041)
Leguay, Martin....5:04:34 (25,634)
Lehrer, Alex....3:48:58 (8,245)
Leigh, Alex....3:42:13 (6,686)
Leigh, Christopher W....4:43:21 (21,654)
Leigh, David Ronald....5:19:10 (27,480)
Leigh, Edward D....4:33:03 (19,367)
Leigh, Michael R....4:35:29 (19,924)
Leigh, Robert D....4:03:51 (12,162)
Leigh, Roger J....5:12:21 (26,675)
Leigh, Samuel J....3:59:59 (11,291)
Leigh, Ya'agov....4:55:12 (24,037)
Leighfield, Stephen P....3:16:21 (2,679)
Leigh-Smith, Simon....3:33:46 (5,229)
Leighton, Martin J....4:32:00 (19,113)
Leighton, Nigel....2:53:54 (691)
Leijdekker, Olaf....3:54:10 (9,548)
Leinster, Robert W....3:49:56 (8,482)
Leiper, James S....4:41:39 (21,271)
Leiserach, Joseph S....5:06:12 (25,874)
Leitch, David N....4:15:28 (14,920)
Lelievre, Robert F....3:40:18 (6,357)
Lemass, Frank....4:17:51 (15,523)
Lembke, Peter....5:27:19 (28,340)
Lemoine, Serge....3:25:37 (3,790)
Lenderyou, Timothy V....4:58:22 (24,679)
Lendon, Jason M....3:17:54 (2,841)
Lenehan, Philip P....3:58:00 (10,671)
Lenglos, Patrick....3:47:25 (7,856)
Lennock, Ian C....4:35:07 (19,844)
Lennon, James G....3:22:57 (3,435)
Lennox, Adam P....4:53:55 (23,780)
Lennox, Brendan A....5:32:08 (28,743)
Lennox, Gordon J....3:10:44 (2,075)
Lennox, Mark....4:41:18 (21,187)
Lenti, Marcelo C....3:52:26 (9,120)
Lenting, Jerden....4:39:59 (20,917)
Lenton, Steven M....4:06:11 (12,708)
Leonard, Christian D....4:47:08 (22,487)
Leonard, Daniel....4:43:03 (21,574)
Leonard, John B....3:42:12 (6,681)
Leonard, Michael D....4:29:04 (18,366)
Leonard, Nicholas J....3:58:14 (10,766)
Leonard, Paul....3:57:51 (10,632)
Leonard, Paul G....3:59:59 (11,291)
Leonard, Simon....3:34:17 (5,309)
Leon-Benitez, Manuel....3:23:03 (3,446)
Le-Picard, Loic....3:31:59 (4,922)
Lepidi, Jean-Pierre....4:20:26 (16,146)
Lepidi, Pierre....4:18:12 (15,587)
Lepine, Brent....5:46:14 (29,764)
Lepore, James....3:46:32 (7,644)
Leppard, Robert K....5:33:27 (28,845)
Lepper, Ben S....3:07:57 (1,800)
Lepperdinger, Hubert....3:48:31 (8,124)
Lepperdinger, Urs....4:25:16 (17,376)
Lerner, Jonathan A....3:52:08 (9,044)
Leschner, Ralf....3:57:15 (10,463)
Lesley, David J....4:15:34 (14,946)
Leslie, Anthony D....5:25:48 (28,175)
Leslie, David M....3:56:33 (10,266)
Leslie, Max A....4:02:26 (11,845)
Leslie Melville, Jake....4:40:25 (21,012)
Lesser, Daniel....3:55:57 (10,067)
Lessware, Edward P....4:12:27 (14,184)
Lester, Stephen J....3:53:16 (9,329)
Lester, Stuart....5:10:44 (26,473)
Letford, John....3:05:05 (1,533)
Le-Tiec, Pascal....4:16:17 (15,114)
Le-Tort, Jean-François....4:28:48 (18,298)
Letting, Ian J....5:17:37 (27,319)
Letton, David....4:11:59 (14,088)
Letts, Adam C....4:46:12 (22,296)
Leung, Victor M....5:58:54 (30,361)
Leung, William....4:06:44 (12,823)
Leuw, Peter J....3:51:07 (8,769)
Levan, Andrew J....5:13:03 (26,771)
Levan, David....3:53:57 (9,489)
Levassort, Thierry....3:50:18 (8,574)
Lever, Adrian M....4:21:01 (16,284)
Lever, Ian C....4:37:53 (20,429)
Leverett, Steve G....5:28:47 (28,469)
Leverton, Jack....3:15:57 (2,643)
Levesley, James....4:17:46 (15,499)
Levett, Dan J....4:09:48 (13,577)
Levick, Paul E....2:57:25 (908)
Levin, Didi....4:27:47 (18,036)
Levine, Luke H....3:35:40 (5,549)
Levison, John....3:01:14 (1,259)
Levitt, Martyn J....4:37:37 (20,361)
Levy, Daniel W....4:37:01 (20,254)
Levy, Danny....3:42:37 (6,769)
Levy, Frederic E....3:55:33 (9,947)
Levy, Jason....4:59:12 (24,828)
Levy, Martin R....4:25:33 (17,440)
Levy, Tomer....4:52:06 (23,466)
Lewin, Robert M....4:08:15 (13,159)
Lewington, Simon D....5:17:45 (27,333)
Lewis, Adrian J....3:18:06 (2,858)
Lewis, Andrew D....3:48:38 (8,164)
Lewis, Andrew D....5:02:24 (25,356)
Lewis, Andy....4:07:42 (13,056)
Lewis, Andy J....4:41:25 (21,222)
Lewis, Ceri....4:52:50 (23,590)
Lewis, Christopher P....3:23:41 (3,526)
Lewis, David....5:35:04 (28,963)
Lewis, David B....5:49:31 (29,931)
Lewis, David G....4:20:15 (16,077)
Lewis, David J....3:53:53 (9,474)
Lewis, David M....4:30:48 (18,814)
Lewis, Dennis J....4:23:56 (17,046)
Lewis, Gareth H....3:57:09 (10,433)
Lewis, Gerald G....5:20:39 (27,653)
Lewis, Graham M....3:03:08 (1,378)
Lewis, Ian F....4:29:37 (18,527)
Lewis, John D....3:40:02 (6,309)
Lewis, John W....4:31:41 (19,022)
Lewis, Jonathan....3:45:06 (7,320)
Lewis, Jonathan P....4:56:01 (24,211)
Lewis, Julian P....3:26:27 (3,910)
Lewis, Lee....4:19:42 (15,953)
Lewis, Lee....5:21:48 (27,757)
Lewis, Mark....4:57:34 (24,508)
Lewis, Mark J....2:48:18 (435)
Lewis, Matthew....3:50:24 (8,605)
Lewis, Nathaniel T....4:25:22 (17,396)
Lewis, Neil....3:30:31 (4,692)
Lewis, Nick H....4:02:31 (11,858)
Lewis, Paul J....3:59:13 (11,064)
Lewis, Paul X....4:50:15 (23,113)
Lewis, Peter J....4:44:18 (21,858)
Lewis, Peter J....6:35:42 (31,302)
Lewis, Peter M....3:31:54 (4,901)
Lewis, Peter N....4:27:56 (18,074)
Lewis, Phillip G....4:58:21 (24,676)
Lewis, Richard J....5:17:22 (27,290)
Lewis, Robert J....5:42:32 (29,517)
Lewis, Robert N....3:55:51 (10,036)
Lewis, Roy....4:22:16 (16,628)
Lewis, Seth....3:45:05 (7,318)
Lewis, Simon....3:32:20 (4,976)
Lewis, Simon....4:41:18 (21,187)
Lewis, Simon D....4:08:24 (13,199)
Lewis, Simon E....3:48:18 (8,077)
Lewis, Stephen B....3:11:09 (2,107)
Lewis, Steven J....3:22:32 (3,383)
Lewis, Steven J....3:47:27 (7,869)
Lewis, Timothy R....4:39:38 (20,847)
Lewis, Trevor A....3:17:30 (2,801)
Lewis, Trevor G....4:48:29 (22,776)
Lewis, Wesley J....4:17:15 (15,357)
Lewis-Brown, Christopher....4:32:42 (19,291)
Lewis-Head, Lewis....5:58:10 (30,332)
Lewith, Tom F....4:06:06 (12,683)
Ley, Edward....3:37:30 (5,873)
Leyenda, Manuel....3:27:27 (4,115)
Leyens, Adam B....4:43:50 (21,753)
Leyens, Oliver....4:42:03 (21,362)
Leyshon, Dave....5:09:18 (26,277)
Leyton, Erik....3:33:57 (5,263)
Lfofstadt, Alexander D....4:12:02 (14,101)
Liang, Michael....4:10:46 (13,816)
Liaume, François....3:24:21 (3,609)
Lichtenstern, Albert....4:22:19 (16,647)
Licourt, Patrick....3:24:09 (3,581)
Liddell, Andrew R....3:11:07 (2,105)
Liddell, Anthony B....3:59:39 (11,206)
Liddell, Colin....3:48:10 (8,039)
Liddle, Alan....4:13:25 (14,437)
Liddle, Alexander B....3:19:08 (2,967)
Liddle, Andrew J....4:28:30 (18,230)
Liddle, Andy A....3:21:18 (3,230)
Liddle, Robert A....4:57:39 (24,521)
Liddle, Robert H....3:04:19 (1,476)
Lidgett, Steven A....4:51:03 (23,282)
Lidster, Jonathan L....4:42:21 (21,425)
Liduena, Jean-Marc F....3:53:59 (9,499)
Liechti, Yves....3:42:59 (6,846)
Liedtke, Wilfried....5:20:10 (27,591)
Liepok, Michael....3:27:07 (4,047)
Lifford, Dean W....5:34:51 (28,946)
Liggins, William J....4:22:00 (16,537)
Light, Matt....4:56:06 (24,231)
Light, Timothy H....4:32:54 (19,335)
Lightfoot, Nigel O....4:21:41 (16,443)
Lightfoot, Philip A....3:41:32 (6,547)
Lightning, David W....4:21:52 (16,495)
Lightwood, Barry....5:32:32 (28,778)

Likeman, Peter R 5:27:56 (28,393)
Lilley, Joseph N 3:49:55 (8,477)
Lilley, Stephen D 4:44:18 (21,858)
Lillie, Mark T 3:54:08 (9,536)
Lillie, Roger A 4:45:01 (22,032)
Lilly, Gordon M 4:16:18 (15,118)
Lillywhite, Dominic L 4:44:32 (21,917)
Lim, Adrian B 4:47:29 (22,566)
Lim, Eng B 4:31:57 (19,096)
Lima, Eduardo M 3:42:19 (6,700)
Limb, Patrick F 4:20:02 (16,039)
Linares, Charles A 5:57:05 (30,290)
Linares-Linares, Juan J 4:18:00 (15,553)
Linassi, Luigi 4:53:36 (23,725)
Linbourne, Mark P 2:43:06 (271)
Linbourne, Matthew J 2:36:15 (138)
Lincoln, Aaron S 3:37:04 (5,790)
Lincoln, Nick 4:39:46 (20,870)
Lindell, Robert M 4:18:08 (15,579)
Linden, Roy S 3:56:33 (10,266)
Lindner, Sam P 4:35:45 (19,971)
Lindop, Robert 5:28:34 (28,446)
Lindqvist, Claes C 5:00:17 (25,035)
Lindsay, Donald 3:26:53 (3,999)
Lindsay, Raymond N 4:41:48 (21,309)
Lindsay, William R 4:27:48 (18,039)
Lindsey, Dean M 3:45:32 (7,420)
Lindsey, Paul D 4:26:58 (17,830)
Lindsley, Charles R 4:56:11 (24,242)
Lindvall, Johan I 4:48:09 (22,707)
Line, Geoffrey K 4:49:02 (22,883)
Line, Matthew J 3:52:22 (9,103)
Linegar, Clive R 4:17:53 (15,532)
Linehan, Kevin P 3:13:31 (2,377)
Lines, Dave H 5:45:04 (29,695)
Lines, Derek C 2:40:01 (211)
Lines, Nicholas C 4:34:34 (19,726)
Ling, Anders 3:59:33 (11,173)
Ling, Daniel P 3:03:15 (1,385)
Ling, Darren T 4:54:17 (23,851)
Ling, Jonathan G 3:31:19 (4,822)
Ling, Terry M 6:35:21 (31,294)
Lingard, Alex L 3:37:23 (5,854)
Lingard, Christpher J 3:35:56 (5,598)
Lingard, John 3:32:34 (5,019)
Lingard, Robert J 3:40:21 (6,368)
Link, Simon J 2:44:16 (295)
Linning, Frankie J 4:50:27 (23,173)
Linstead, Andrew R 3:55:52 (10,037)
Linstead, Michael D 5:03:45 (25,548)
Lintern, Marc A 3:21:12 (3,221)
Lintern, Richard D 4:42:40 (21,484)
Linton, John 4:35:02 (19,828)
Linton, Martin 4:37:03 (20,261)
Liossis, Roger 7:09:47 (31,707)
Lipczynski, Nicholas J 5:12:59 (26,759)
Lippett, Heath 4:10:41 (13,796)
Lippiett, Adam J 3:10:15 (2,022)
Lipscombe, Roger G 3:55:17 (9,876)
Lipshitz, Daniel 5:04:35 (25,636)
Lipsitz, Jonathan W 3:59:30 (11,157)
Lister, Andrew 3:46:27 (7,628)
Lister, Ewart G 3:24:47 (3,658)
Lister, Matthew D 3:53:56 (9,484)
Lister, Matthew J 3:56:49 (10,337)
Litchfield, Steven 4:30:28 (18,750)
Litrenta, Louis 3:23:01 (3,442)
Little, Allan 4:46:17 (22,314)
Little, Anthony N 3:54:32 (9,648)
Little, Chris J 4:43:47 (21,746)
Little, David 3:22:32 (3,383)
Little, David W 4:40:26 (21,016)
Little, George 3:44:57 (7,296)
Little, George R 2:57:41 (930)
Little, Marc 3:33:08 (5,127)
Little, Paul A 4:31:08 (18,885)
Little, Peter 4:04:26 (12,294)
Little, Ronald J 4:22:11 (16,598)
Little, Steven R 5:25:29 (28,135)
Little, Steven T 4:37:04 (20,266)
Little, Tony 4:54:53 (23,974)
Littlechild, Nigel P 4:12:50 (14,286)
Littlefair, Lyndon B 3:53:39 (9,411)
Littleproud, James 4:08:12 (13,151)
Littler, Darren M 6:01:44 (30,473)
Littler, David 3:36:31 (5,699)
Littler, David J 3:25:08 (3,709)
Littler, Steve T 2:27:36 (65)
Littleton, David 5:22:32 (27,836)
Littleton, Jamie 6:03:57 (30,563)
Littlewood, Richard S 3:15:39 (2,615)
Littlewood, Simon J 4:01:24 (11,579)
Littlewood, Stephen J 3:08:46 (1,873)
Litton, Thomas 5:14:42 (26,992)
Litvin, Norman P 2:58:05 (979)
Liu, Danny M 4:36:25 (20,110)
Liu, David 3:37:14 (5,820)
Lively, Brennan 3:04:20 (1,479)
Livingston, James E 3:25:20 (3,739)
Livingstone, Adrian J 4:47:55 (22,658)
Livingstone, Paul J 4:13:18 (14,403)
Llanos-Madrigal, José L 3:52:41 (9,169)
Llewellyn, Clive 4:42:59 (21,561)
Llewellyn, Laurence 3:35:22 (5,497)
Llewellyn, Mark N 4:45:29 (22,136)
Llewellyn, Mark W 4:06:22 (12,752)
Llewellyn, Peter 3:51:43 (8,945)
Llewellyn, William L 5:30:23 (28,615)
Llewellyn Jones, Tristram C 5:36:10 (29,036)
Llewelyn, Rhodri W 3:01:44 (1,288)
Llewelyn, Robert W 4:25:48 (17,515)
Lloyd, Adrian C 4:09:58 (13,631)
Lloyd, Andrew 3:39:48 (6,274)
Lloyd, Andrew J 3:56:54 (10,366)
Lloyd, Andrew J 4:13:24 (14,432)
Lloyd, Benjamin J 3:06:46 (1,681)
Lloyd, Chris P 4:17:22 (15,387)
Lloyd, David G 3:45:55 (7,510)
Lloyd, Gareth 4:43:17 (21,634)
Lloyd, Ian J 4:38:10 (20,513)
Lloyd, Jim J 4:08:13 (13,152)
Lloyd, Luke 3:53:07 (9,287)
Lloyd, Mark 4:02:02 (11,726)
Lloyd, Martin P 3:03:40 (1,423)
Lloyd, Nigel P 5:21:39 (27,746)
Lloyd, Paul 5:26:15 (28,216)
Lloyd, Peter A 3:33:45 (5,227)
Lloyd, Shawn 5:16:41 (27,220)
Lloyd, Simon B 3:39:54 (6,290)
Lloyd, Simon T 3:37:41 (5,902)
Lloyd, Thomas P 5:24:16 (28,000)
Lloyd, Tim A 5:07:49 (26,092)
Lloyd, Tony A 5:56:15 (30,261)
Lloyd Owen, Harry D 4:43:13 (21,610)
Lloyd-Game, Jonathan 4:32:35 (19,254)
Llywelyn, Gareth 5:40:08 (29,347)
Loakes, Martin S 4:35:20 (19,893)
Lobb, Hugh 2:15:49 (19)
Lobb, Matthew R 3:36:46 (5,738)
Lobel, Mark D 4:20:32 (16,171)
Lobina, Angelo 2:54:41 (725)
Lobo, Alric G 4:26:29 (17,696)
Lock, Andrew S 4:46:53 (22,421)
Lock, Ben 5:17:59 (27,364)
Lock, David S 4:27:30 (17,957)
Lock, David S 7:28:08 (31,833)
Lock, Graham W 2:59:51 (1,146)
Lock, Martin P 3:30:31 (4,692)
Locke, Kevin 6:35:27 (31,296)
Locke, Terry 5:26:17 (28,223)
Locker, Steven G 3:09:07 (1,910)
Lockett, John 4:03:47 (12,144)
Lockett, Patrick 3:19:00 (2,949)
Lockey, Alistair J 3:11:42 (2,159)
Lockhart, Charles D 5:40:37 (29,388)
Lockwood, Paul R 4:12:39 (14,247)
Lockwood, Richard 4:53:28 (23,696)
Lockwood, Simon R 4:40:58 (21,117)
Lockwood, Stephen A 4:01:31 (11,604)
Lockyer, Derek 2:51:14 (552)
Lockyer, Jeremy 3:46:55 (7,726)
Loder-Symonds, James R 4:53:28 (23,696)
Lodge, Alain V 3:57:33 (10,555)
Lodge, Stuart 3:43:59 (7,063)
Lodge, Tom 4:22:46 (16,764)
Loeber, Peter J 3:43:19 (6,922)
Loersch, Heiko 3:43:11 (6,890)
Loerzer, Michael 5:01:20 (25,191)
Loferski, Todd G 3:37:10 (5,808)
Loftus, James 5:10:47 (26,480)
Logan, Paul 5:05:44 (25,787)
Logan, Peter W 3:50:19 (8,581)
Loglisci, Corrado 4:06:05 (12,680)
Logue, John C 5:02:30 (25,374)
Lohle, Victor 4:06:06 (12,683)
Lokitari Lotam, Mark 2:36:37 (144)
Lomaglio, Carlo 3:04:30 (1,489)
Lomas, Adrian 4:32:41 (19,288)
Lomas, Barry J 3:40:17 (6,352)
Lomas, Stephen D 3:43:41 (6,994)
Lomas-Brown, Richard E 2:59:22 (1,109)
Lomax, Michael 3:43:59 (7,063)
Lombard, Deon 5:08:54 (26,223)
Lommaert, Filip R 5:26:32 (28,251)
Lon, Daniel 4:51:58 (23,433)
Londesborough, James 3:11:00 (2,099)
Lonergan, John W 3:25:30 (3,770)
Lonergan, Sean 6:00:42 (30,435)
Loney, Jon M 4:50:33 (23,191)
Lonfat, Jean L 4:54:19 (23,863)
Lonfat, Pierre M 2:51:14 (552)
Long, Andrew 3:47:52 (7,963)
Long, Andrew J 4:04:52 (12,396)
Long, Chris 3:54:30 (9,635)
Long, David J 3:18:27 (2,890)
Long, Jonathan 4:28:27 (18,215)
Long, Keith E 3:33:15 (5,148)
Long, Malcolm 4:23:23 (16,914)
Long, Mark B 3:35:37 (5,544)
Long, Martin K 5:20:07 (27,583)
Long, Neal L 5:20:08 (27,586)
Long, Owen 4:43:25 (21,667)
Long, Simon A 3:55:35 (9,963)
Long, Simon A 4:32:35 (19,254)
Long, Stephen T 3:30:17 (4,652)
Longdon, Justin 5:02:54 (25,435)
Longhurst, Martin 3:11:17 (2,123)
Longhurst, Paul R 3:42:39 (6,775)
Longhurst, Philip J 3:43:38 (6,985)
Longman, Adrian P 5:57:33 (30,313)
Longstaff, Martyn W 4:21:50 (16,487)
Longstaff, Tony 4:09:38 (13,536)
Lonsdale, David J 3:45:40 (7,446)
Lonsdale, Guy A 4:00:50 (11,454)
Lonsdale, Richard I 5:19:31 (27,500)
Looker, David 3:57:07 (10,418)
Looker, Jeff 3:18:54 (2,943)
Looker, Robert 3:25:25 (3,753)
Loom, Jason 4:59:35 (24,918)
Loong, Hing Tong 5:46:22 (29,774)
Loose, D 3:10:54 (2,090)
Loosli, Pteer O 3:17:50 (2,832)
Loots, Gerrit 3:54:35 (9,660)
Lopes Cardozo, Vladimir 3:31:28 (4,842)
Lopez, Gerard J 5:54:33 (30,173)
Lopez, José 3:50:40 (8,676)
Lopez, Thierry M 5:55:59 (30,244)
Lopez De Arroyabe, Tim 3:49:03 (8,264)
Lopez-Caballero, Alberto 3:11:40 (2,154)
Lord, Chris J 3:51:20 (8,842)
Lord, Cliff C 4:38:46 (20,659)
Lord, James A 4:28:50 (18,309)
Lord, Mark R 3:43:10 (6,884)
Lord, Paul D 6:37:20 (31,329)
Lord, Steven T 2:54:29 (717)
Lorente Esteban, Andrés 3:48:30 (8,118)
Lorenzo, Antonio 4:54:39 (23,932)
Lorient, David 3:58:53 (10,967)
Loriggio, Ian H 3:00:09 (1,167)
Lorimer, Graeme C 4:18:00 (15,553)
Lorkin, James P 5:39:52 (29,325)
Lormans, Eric A 4:34:04 (19,614)
Lorrain, Pierre J 4:32:44 (19,300)
Lorriman-Hughes, Mark D 4:27:01 (17,846)
Losada-Narra, José 2:59:11 (1,092)
Lothian, Andrew 6:09:33 (30,715)
Lothian, Paul 4:21:26 (16,373)
Lotter, Grant 7:41:38 (31,893)
Lottey, Andrew N 5:14:21 (26,939)

Lotti, Daniele 4:11:43 (14,024)
Loubes, Gerard 4:11:15 (13,921)
Louden, Paul T 4:51:40 (23,371)
Loughins, Peter 3:21:48 (3,290)
Loughlin, David Noel 4:07:21 (12,970)
Loughrey, Neil C 3:00:45 (1,215)
Louis, Dominique 3:45:40 (7,446)
Lourtie, José 4:45:34 (22,154)
Louw, Andrew 3:34:03 (5,278)
Lovatt, Philip A 4:44:33 (21,925)
Love, Danny J 4:23:33 (16,953)
Love, Nikolay A 3:58:18 (10,791)
Lovegrove, Melvyn R 5:17:36 (27,318)
Lovegrove, Paul R 4:57:52 (24,561)
Lovell, John D 3:52:54 (9,227)
Lovell, Joseph F 4:29:27 (18,470)
Lovell, Matthew 4:45:18 (22,096)
Lovell, Nick 3:33:38 (5,209)
Lovell, Peter 3:33:25 (5,178)
Lovell, Stephen F 3:52:18 (9,085)
Loveridge, David R 4:03:33 (12,089)
Lovesey, William R 3:21:48 (3,290)
Lovett, Brian J 3:30:17 (4,652)
Lovett, Ferdinand 3:44:23 (7,150)
Lovett, Stephen C 3:12:42 (2,273)
Lovett, Terence J 3:25:16 (3,729)
Lovewell, Peter 5:11:30 (26,577)
Lovidge, Leslie J 3:44:37 (7,217)
Low, Alex G 3:27:31 (4,131)
Low, Nicholas M 4:07:13 (12,945)
Low, Roger L 3:38:18 (6,010)
Low, Stephen A 2:58:26 (1,009)
Lowe, Aaron C 3:38:32 (6,051)
Lowe, Alexander V 3:51:23 (8,853)
Lowe, Alistair J 3:33:17 (5,156)
Lowe, Ben 4:36:19 (20,090)
Lowe, Christopher 4:35:52 (19,997)
Lowe, Christopher N 4:08:00 (13,115)
Lowe, Craig M 4:31:45 (19,041)
Lowe, Eamonn A 6:14:10 (30,851)
Lowe, Graham P 4:46:04 (22,264)
Lowe, Ian R 4:39:02 (20,735)
Lowe, James A 4:28:41 (18,276)
Lowe, Jeremy J 3:53:27 (9,366)
Lowe, Michael R 5:07:40 (26,071)
Lowe, Patrick J 3:08:20 (1,835)
Lowe, Paul 4:50:00 (23,073)
Lowe, Paul A 3:38:04 (5,971)
Lowe, Simon J 4:41:31 (21,248)
Lowe, Terry S 4:45:12 (22,081)
Lowe, Timothy R 4:54:59 (23,991)
Lower, Rob W 4:28:04 (18,115)
Lowers, Marc R 4:16:05 (15,072)
Lowes, Andrew 3:10:28 (2,053)
Lowes, Ronald D 4:39:38 (20,847)
Lowings, Graham 4:56:31 (24,314)
Lowish, David M 3:33:50 (5,240)
Lowndes, Charly A 4:50:31 (23,183)
Lownie, Mark 4:42:26 (21,439)
Lownsbrough, Richard 4:27:48 (18,039)
Lowson, Richard 3:38:46 (6,093)
Lowthorpe, Alan M 4:15:13 (14,859)
Loxton, Paul A 3:10:09 (2,016)
Loy, Martin 3:01:43 (1,287)
Loydall, Jonathan P 4:34:14 (19,649)
Loyer, Christian R 5:55:01 (30,197)
Luangpraseuth, Somdeth 3:37:26 (5,868)
Lubi, Viljar 3:44:52 (7,277)
Luby, Michael 6:27:26 (31,162)
Lucarotti, John R 4:20:25 (16,136)
Lucas, Alan 3:48:49 (8,219)
Lucas, Antoine 4:44:43 (21,958)
Lucas, Daryl 4:44:33 (21,925)
Lucas, Dean 4:53:07 (23,636)
Lucas, Ian A 6:00:05 (30,413)
Lucas, Matthew B 5:06:34 (25,920)
Lucas, Mike 4:36:26 (20,116)
Lucas, Simon 4:28:08 (18,135)
Lucazeau, Olivier 4:18:04 (15,568)
Luck, Jamie D 3:18:51 (2,935)
Luck, Stephen J 5:46:13 (29,762)
Lucker, Alan 3:36:45 (5,734)
Luckhurst, Michael R 5:35:20 (28,983)
Luckhurst, Simon 4:07:55 (13,094)
Lucking, David G 3:21:49 (3,293)
Lucor, Patrick 4:23:04 (16,830)
Luddington, Martin J 4:35:00 (19,819)
Ludlow, Stephen 4:15:13 (14,859)
Ludorf, Franz 3:45:11 (7,342)
Luesley, Christopher J 3:49:57 (8,489)
Luevano-Martinez, Guillermo 5:30:37 (28,631)
Luff, Bradley I 4:59:53 (24,971)
Luff, Christoph 4:54:16 (23,849)
Luisi, Vito 4:10:30 (13,756)
Luizy, Hubert 4:42:16 (21,402)
Luke, Iain 4:39:41 (20,859)
Lumby, David K 5:26:16 (28,220)
Lumsden, William 4:36:19 (20,090)
Lunberg, Adam B 4:32:45 (19,303)
Lund, Geoff F 4:04:28 (12,306)
Lund, Karl-Yngve 4:21:56 (16,512)
Lund, Peter D 4:19:04 (15,792)
Lund, Simon 2:46:40 (375)
Lundblad, Christian 3:43:15 (6,907)
Lund-Conlon, Philip 4:00:18 (11,358)
Lundie, Alex J 3:36:02 (5,615)
Lundie, Blair A 4:54:25 (23,881)
Lundie Sadd, Richard J 4:07:34 (13,027)
Lundovist, Thomas 3:59:25 (11,117)
Lundy, Andrew P 3:47:50 (7,954)
Lundy, Mark T 4:38:01 (20,475)
Lunn, Chris J 3:35:58 (5,606)
Lunn, Robert 4:00:23 (11,377)
Lunn, Robert M 5:03:24 (25,500)
Lunt, Brian 4:50:40 (23,210)
Lunt, David W 5:33:25 (28,843)
Lupton, Anthony 5:12:54 (26,749)
Lupton, David W 4:00:42 (11,429)
Lupton, Malcolm 4:20:42 (16,211)
Luth, Jan H 4:36:43 (20,186)
Luxton, Paul J 3:58:27 (10,834)
Luxton, Phillip H 5:03:10 (25,472)
Lyall, Graham 3:12:41 (2,269)
Lyall, Thomas 3:54:01 (9,510)
Lycett, Michael 5:59:31 (30,392)
Lycett Green, John 5:37:06 (29,113)
Lyddon, Robin P 3:33:35 (5,200)
Lyle, David 3:48:44 (8,195)
Lynam, Robert G 3:13:17 (2,340)
Lynas, Stewart W 3:02:26 (1,336)
Lynch, Andrew J 2:36:58 (152)
Lynch, Barry J 5:44:45 (29,675)
Lynch, Benjamin J 3:57:30 (10,538)
Lynch, Conor 5:14:48 (27,005)
Lynch, Kevin D 5:19:30 (27,499)
Lynch, Mark V 4:01:55 (11,695)
Lynch, Paul A 4:51:30 (23,345)
Lynch, Rob 5:27:49 (28,386)
Lynch, Robert M 5:33:00 (28,808)
Lynch, Roger D 4:38:05 (20,493)
Lynch, Warren M 2:35:10 (126)
Lynch-Brown, Adam J 4:51:47 (23,395)
Lynch-Brown, Mark P 6:08:13 (30,680)
Lynch-Warden, John D 5:19:20 (27,493)
Lyne, Denis 4:32:53 (19,332)
Lyne, Eliot 2:39:53 (208)
Lynn, David J 5:20:09 (27,588)
Lynn, Jeff 3:40:59 (6,472)
Lynn, Michael A 3:56:23 (10,204)
Lynn, Trevor F 5:31:01 (28,660)
Lynock, Mark 4:20:48 (16,230)
Lynton, Paul R 4:18:46 (15,728)
Lyon, Ben B 4:50:49 (23,239)
Lyon, Fred 4:45:42 (22,190)
Lyon, James D 3:42:21 (6,709)
Lyon, Nick A 4:07:28 (13,001)
Lyon, Paul C 4:06:57 (12,879)
Lyon, Richard 4:35:26 (19,919)
Lyons, Carl 4:06:32 (12,784)
Lyons, Dale R 4:19:55 (16,003)
Lyons, Frank J 3:48:15 (8,065)
Lyons, James M 4:01:53 (11,687)
Lyons, Kevin O 4:10:32 (13,762)
Lyons, Mark D 4:19:03 (15,786)
Lyons, Michael J 4:27:10 (17,885)
Lysons, Michael K 5:31:11 (28,671)
Lythgoe, Nicholas G 4:42:12 (21,386)
Lyttle, Paddy 4:02:54 (11,940)
Maan, Zafar 4:26:01 (17,571)
Mabbitt, Andrew 5:20:50 (27,666)
Mabey, Andrew 4:33:41 (19,502)
Mabey, Peter F 3:14:27 (2,493)
MacAlister, Gary S 3:50:22 (8,597)
Macann, Benjamin M 3:35:42 (5,557)
Macarthur, John L 5:03:16 (25,485)
Macarthur, Trevor J 3:00:12 (1,170)
Macartney, Andrew J 6:01:53 (30,482)
MacAskill, Andy K 2:42:45 (262)
Macaulay, Allan 3:25:18 (3,735)
Macaulay, Ludwig V 5:07:14 (25,999)
Macauley, Alan D 3:26:21 (3,897)
Macauley, Philip J 4:06:06 (12,683)
Macbeth, Kenneth D 3:02:16 (1,324)
Maccario, Marco 4:02:29 (11,852)
MacCarthy, Vernon 3:43:17 (6,914)
MacCurrach, Edward 3:34:13 (5,301)
Macdonald, Andrew K 4:02:40 (11,892)
Macdonald, Andrew M 4:45:12 (22,081)
Macdonald, Andrew P 3:56:22 (10,202)
Macdonald, Craig 4:38:39 (20,627)
Macdonald, Craig W 3:40:19 (6,359)
Macdonald, Dominic R 4:02:57 (11,946)
Macdonald, Euan 3:39:27 (6,209)
Macdonald, George A 4:37:11 (20,293)
Macdonald, Gordon W 4:22:33 (16,713)
Macdonald, Ian J 2:41:12 (228)
Macdonald, James M 4:58:35 (24,732)
Macdonald, James V 4:36:04 (20,045)
Macdonald, John A 4:40:00 (20,919)
Macdonald, Kevin N 3:26:09 (3,868)
Macdonald, Malcolm C 4:38:28 (20,587)
Macdonald, Roderick C 4:13:19 (14,411)
Macdonald, Simon T 3:29:00 (4,413)
Macdonald, Steve G 4:45:10 (22,075)
Macdonald, Stewart F 2:29:24 (77)
MacDougall, Colin R 5:32:35 (28,780)
MacDowall, Simon C 4:49:51 (23,052)
Mace, Robert 4:56:55 (24,387)
Macey, Mark 4:57:28 (24,490)
Macey, Richard M 5:07:23 (26,027)
Macey, Terence J 3:50:10 (8,541)
Macfarlane, Fraser B 4:33:45 (19,517)
MacGarrow, Kevin G 4:24:14 (17,129)
MacGillivray, John B 3:40:17 (6,352)
MacGregor, Calum D 4:20:49 (16,233)
MacGregor, David J 5:06:40 (25,935)
MacGregor, Graeme S 3:23:59 (3,563)
MacGregor, Jim K 3:05:22 (1,559)
MacGregor, John C 3:14:56 (2,552)
MacGregor, Martin G 3:27:49 (4,188)
MacGregor, Philip R 3:35:34 (5,535)
Machell, Ben R 3:59:21 (11,101)
Machin, Niall C 3:52:01 (9,016)
Machnik, Daniel L 5:05:03 (25,697)
Machray, Simon M 3:20:59 (3,200)
Macias, Carlos J 2:52:50 (633)
MacInnes, Roddy P 4:02:43 (11,906)
Macintosh, George A 4:00:15 (11,349)
Macintyre, Ivan G 6:01:40 (30,470)
Mack, Darren R 3:02:35 (1,343)
Mack, Martin W 3:16:46 (2,725)
Mackay, Colin D 3:02:53 (1,361)
Mackay, Jason S 4:45:40 (22,182)
Mackay, John 3:30:19 (4,659)
Mackay, Matthew R 4:35:56 (20,009)
Mackay, Michael 3:24:43 (3,653)
Mackay, Mike 4:30:33 (18,769)
Mackay, Neil S 3:14:03 (2,444)
Mackay, Steve 5:35:36 (29,006)
Mackay, William J 4:01:23 (11,576)
Mackelden, Stephen P 4:48:26 (22,765)
Mackenzie, Chris S 3:58:49 (10,948)
Mackenzie, Christopher J 4:59:01 (24,798)
Mackenzie, James 3:40:32 (6,409)
Mackenzie, John D 4:11:46 (14,036)
Mackenzie, Kenneth J 3:40:54 (6,455)
Mackenzie, Morris 3:30:36 (4,707)
Mackenzie, Richard 6:21:42 (31,052)
Mackenzie, Robert E 3:42:25 (6,723)

Mackey, Brian R 3:20:18 (3,099)
Mackey, Paul E 3:38:47 (6,096)
Mackie, James M 4:34:48 (19,778)
Mackie, Richard C 3:47:53 (7,969)
Mackinnon, Angus 4:51:55 (23,426)
Mackinnon, Neil 5:07:04 (25,978)
Mackintosh, Jamie S 3:56:27 (10,235)
Mackintosh, Keith P 5:47:15 (29,824)
Mackintosh, Nicholas I 3:41:49 (6,608)
Maclaren, Edward J 5:35:37 (29,008)
Maclean, Adam C 4:26:04 (17,593)
Maclean, Angus C 3:28:11 (4,261)
Maclean, David 3:58:53 (10,967)
Maclean, Fergus R 2:37:38 (165)
MacLennan, Kenneth 4:05:23 (12,503)
Macleod, Andrew 3:35:09 (5,454)
Macleod, Douglas G 4:48:00 (22,672)
Macleod, Kenneth L 5:19:53 (27,546)
Macleod-Miller, Leslie W 3:52:53 (9,218)
MacManus, Dominic C 4:02:07 (11,755)
MacMaster, Glen 3:59:20 (11,096)
Macmillan, Douglas T 5:07:34 (26,053)
Macmillan, Hamish W 3:38:11 (5,992)
Macmillan, Mark 6:05:50 (30,617)
MacNaughton, Iain S 3:42:14 (6,691)
MacNeill, Stewart 4:12:52 (14,292)
Macpherson, James R 3:48:00 (7,995)
Macpherson, William N 4:36:26 (20,116)
MacQueen, Anthony N 2:55:45 (797)
MacQueen, Ian M 3:53:31 (9,380)
MacQueen, Robert M 4:14:32 (14,690)
Macrae, Christopher 4:00:47 (11,441)
Macrae, Donald F 3:46:33 (7,648)
Macrae, Mark 5:27:08 (28,315)
Macrae, Ross J 4:32:33 (19,248)
MacSephney, Scott A 3:00:19 (1,179)
Maddams, Derek 6:42:13 (31,394)
Maddams, Russell 2:31:39 (93)
Madden, Andrew T 4:54:40 (23,935)
Madden, Daniel T 5:21:09 (27,695)
Madden, Michael T 5:06:12 (25,874)
Maddison, Peter J 3:29:13 (4,455)
Maddock, Richard T 3:57:03 (10,404)
Maddocks, Terry 4:50:54 (23,251)
Madeley, Sean D 4:40:39 (21,054)
Madge, Jolyon P 4:22:40 (16,740)
Madlani, Vivek D 5:04:44 (25,656)
Maffey, Daryl A 4:12:17 (14,147)
Maffon, Alain 4:14:26 (14,659)
Magee, Nicholas P 4:53:39 (23,737)
Magee, Peter T 4:41:36 (21,261)
Magee, Richard P 5:16:17 (27,166)
Magee, Robert D 5:05:13 (25,713)
Mager, Karl-Heinz 3:58:47 (10,943)
Maggs, Adrian 2:58:52 (1,062)
Maggs, Paul V 4:34:25 (19,693)
Maggs, Simon D 3:56:52 (10,354)
Magin, Thierry 3:26:07 (3,861)
Magni, David J 4:50:54 (23,251)
Magnus, Daniel S 4:32:56 (19,343)
Magnusson, Per-Ake 5:52:43 (30,110)
Magron, Bernard 3:25:34 (3,777)
Maguire, Alex C 4:12:22 (14,162)
Maguire, Gerard J 4:20:58 (16,276)
Maguire, Graham 3:17:31 (2,802)
Maguire, John P 3:55:52 (10,037)
Maguire, Michael J 4:22:13 (16,613)
Maguire, Roger H 4:18:41 (15,707)
Maguire, Samuel D 4:23:23 (16,914)
Maguire, Terence J 6:00:54 (30,443)
Mahadeo, Robin R 5:04:09 (25,591)
Mahaffey, Simon H 4:40:21 (20,996)
Maharaj, Vijay 4:43:07 (21,585)
Mahe, Stephen D 4:58:04 (24,613)
Maher, Derek P 3:48:16 (8,069)
Maher, Julian S 6:04:20 (30,573)
Maher, Kevin M 4:58:08 (24,624)
Maher, Martin J 4:16:03 (15,059)
Maher, Thomas 3:53:10 (9,303)
Mahmud, Shamsul Z 5:25:43 (28,162)
Mahon, Michael 3:43:10 (6,884)
Mahoney, James 4:14:27 (14,665)
Mahoney, Mark 4:48:23 (22,756)
Mahoney, Paul 4:42:41 (21,486)
Mahoney, Terry M 4:16:24 (15,148)
Mahony, Dominic J 3:18:54 (2,943)
Mahoungou, Guy-Ernest 3:47:06 (7,779)
Mai, Wolf Dieter 4:42:18 (21,414)
Maidens, Neil 4:03:22 (12,054)
Maidment, Christian B 3:39:19 (6,188)
Maidment, Jeffrey C 5:01:42 (25,257)
Maidment, Michael 3:51:21 (8,846)
Mailich, Rob A 4:47:06 (22,474)
Maillard, Edmund D 4:58:08 (24,624)
Maille, Jean-Luc 3:47:07 (7,784)
Main, Peter 3:44:12 (7,114)
Maini, Raj 3:06:54 (1,694)
Mainwaring, Mike R 3:43:15 (6,907)
Mair, Johann 2:44:07 (290)
Mair, Robert 3:08:29 (1,848)
Mair, Robert 6:27:27 (31,164)
Maire, Philippe 3:05:23 (1,562)
Mairet, Marcel 3:33:36 (5,205)
Maironis, Darren 2:56:00 (811)
Maisbitt, Stephen W 4:17:38 (15,461)
Maisey, Colin J 4:16:06 (15,079)
Maitland, David L 4:59:15 (24,839)
Maitland, Lewis 3:55:08 (9,831)
Majer, Peter E 3:31:53 (4,898)
Majerski, Allan J 4:38:36 (20,617)
Majithia, Shailen S 3:52:41 (9,169)
Major, Gavin 4:42:23 (21,432)
Major, Martin 4:08:32 (13,239)
Major, Paul L 3:49:33 (8,390)
Major, Steven 3:37:43 (5,905)
Major, William G 3:18:06 (2,858)
Mak, Kenneth 5:52:58 (30,127)
Makin, Frank H 3:44:48 (7,261)
Makkar, Avneesh 6:04:20 (30,573)
Makwana, Milan 5:43:28 (29,589)
Mal, Firouz 4:03:44 (12,134)
Malcolm, Ian B 2:58:35 (1,025)
Malcolm, Solomon A 4:34:03 (19,606)
Malcolm, Thomas E 3:22:53 (3,430)
Male, Tony 4:41:28 (21,236)
Males, Anthony R 3:20:52 (3,186)
Males, Stuart G 3:05:14 (1,549)
Malhi, Gurminder S 5:19:37 (27,513)
Maling, Giles A 3:20:22 (3,107)
Malinge, David S 4:05:20 (12,494)
Malins, Anthony E 5:02:07 (25,309)
Malkin, Steve M 4:13:20 (14,414)
Mallaby, David J 3:59:40 (11,212)
Mallace, John S 3:58:40 (10,913)
Mallach, Michael 7:11:13 (31,716)
Mallalieu, Pete T 4:45:53 (22,225)
Mallen, Garry C 4:05:14 (12,468)
Malley, Michael A 3:54:36 (9,666)
Malliff, James A 5:45:14 (29,708)
Mallinder, James P 4:18:27 (15,655)
Mallinder, Jason J 3:26:12 (3,872)
Mallison, Peter G 2:42:40 (257)
Malloch, Timothy 4:05:00 (12,429)
Mallon, Timothy J 4:12:39 (14,247)
Mallow, Olaf 4:54:43 (23,944)
Malloy, Colin J 3:55:22 (9,897)
Malone, Anthony 6:18:34 (30,974)
Malone, Jamie 5:29:09 (28,499)
Malone, Lawrence J 3:27:36 (4,144)
Malone, Martin J 3:52:09 (9,047)
Malone, Sean 5:20:28 (27,628)
Malone, Timothy J 3:20:39 (3,155)
Maloney, Liam E 3:03:57 (1,447)
Maloney, Michael 3:22:08 (3,321)
Malou, Jean-Claude 4:42:46 (21,509)
Malpass, Christopher J 4:11:13 (13,916)
Maltby, Adam C 5:04:51 (25,670)
Maltby, Daniel P 5:42:07 (29,490)
Malton, Russell J 4:22:34 (16,716)
Malynn, Nicholas 2:51:37 (575)
Malyon, Carole L 5:52:55 (30,123)
Mammatt, Guy R 4:14:28 (14,674)
Mancinelli, Domenico 3:31:15 (4,813)
Mandalia, Mirren R 4:22:27 (16,681)
Mander, Peter V 3:59:34 (11,177)
Mandeville, Robin J 4:03:31 (12,082)
Mandier, Bernard 3:05:11 (1,543)
Manek, Krishna 5:09:56 (26,370)
Mangas De Arriba, José A 4:52:17 (23,499)
Mangat, Jasdip S 2:49:56 (497)
Mangeot, Andrew 3:43:59 (7,063)
Mangin, Eric 3:38:26 (6,036)
Mangin, Pascal 3:42:22 (6,714)
Mangold, Hanspeter 4:23:10 (16,858)
Maniam, Stephen 3:07:57 (1,800)
Manington, David 3:47:25 (7,856)
Manley, David C 4:15:20 (14,886)
Manley, Martin J 4:43:01 (21,566)
Manley, Stephen J 3:31:10 (4,801)
Mann, Alan S 3:17:47 (2,828)
Mann, Bradley J 3:55:47 (10,013)
Mann, Chris B 4:57:59 (24,590)
Mann, Dave K 2:59:46 (1,138)
Mann, David G 4:06:56 (12,871)
Mann, Edward B 4:23:10 (16,858)
Mann, Greg D 4:37:49 (20,409)
Mann, Paul A 3:09:32 (1,951)
Mann, Raj 3:30:38 (4,716)
Mann, Simon E 4:48:55 (22,857)
Mann, Stuart H 3:19:51 (3,054)
Mann, Stuart J 4:32:39 (19,276)
Manners, Richard W 3:32:52 (5,075)
Mann-Heatley, Martin L 4:17:40 (15,473)
Mannick, Suren 4:11:16 (13,922)
Manning, Andrew M 4:15:16 (14,876)
Manning, David 5:20:56 (27,676)
Manning, David R 4:58:53 (24,778)
Manning, Duncan 3:10:37 (2,063)
Manning, Greg A 4:02:15 (11,796)
Manning, Jason 3:16:06 (2,654)
Manning, John 3:38:19 (6,015)
Manning, Julian H 2:56:26 (848)
Manning, Paul C 3:48:54 (8,230)
Manning, Richard J 3:55:58 (10,074)
Manning, Rodger A 3:06:19 (1,638)
Manning, Wayne A 3:46:21 (7,612)
Mannion, John R 4:31:33 (18,990)
Mannion, Michael 4:36:46 (20,194)
Mannion, Nicholas J 2:52:57 (639)
Mansell, Doug 5:06:53 (25,959)
Mansell, Peter R 5:31:05 (28,665)
Mansell, Richard S 4:59:49 (24,961)
Manser, Darren N 3:21:29 (3,254)
Mansfield, Andrew 3:23:00 (3,439)
Mansfield, Angus 4:29:18 (18,431)
Mansfield, Daniel N 2:48:50 (449)
Mansfield, Stephen P 4:02:08 (11,757)
Mansfield, Tim 4:24:16 (17,136)
Manship, Philip A 4:19:44 (15,959)
Mansi, Andrew J 3:02:22 (1,332)
Manske, Wilfried 3:20:32 (3,139)
Manson, David 4:05:54 (12,640)
Manuel, Silas 6:01:43 (30,472)
Manzi, Daniel 4:11:53 (14,057)
Mapp, Christopher 4:40:05 (20,936)
Mapperley, Carl P 3:40:58 (6,469)
Maraia, Antonio 3:14:01 (2,437)
Marais, Piers F 4:27:41 (18,013)
Maraldo, Maxime 4:24:51 (17,268)
Maranta, Michael G 3:56:39 (10,292)
Marcal, Daniel R 4:06:06 (12,683)
March, Steve P 3:08:08 (1,818)
Marchant, Damon 5:17:59 (27,364)
Marchant, Gary J 7:32:19 (31,861)
Marchant, Peter J 4:58:16 (24,659)
Marchant, Roy 4:43:40 (21,714)
Marchegiani, Gaetano 4:30:06 (18,655)
Marchione, Angelo 3:42:58 (6,843)
Marcinowicz, Adam L 4:00:26 (11,386)
Marcos, Jean M 4:01:14 (11,550)
Marcus, Ian 4:39:12 (20,774)
Marenghi, Marcel 5:12:53 (26,746)
Margalith, Raziel 3:53:51 (9,459)
Margaria, Franco 3:28:22 (4,293)
Margereson, Matthew P 3:31:16 (4,815)
Margerison, James J 4:08:29 (13,224)
Margham, Thomas H 3:49:22 (8,344)
Margolis, Geoffrey A 4:18:38 (15,695)
Margulies, Daniel A 3:18:04 (2,854)

Margutti, Enrico 4:16:21 (15,131)
Mariner, Timothy C 3:39:03 (6,140)
Maris, Ian J 3:23:33 (3,504)
Marjoribanks, James B 3:58:37 (10,891)
Marjot, Christopher 4:51:02 (23,277)
Marke, Neil T 3:14:43 (2,528)
Markham, Dean 4:02:57 (11,946)
Markham, Roger 5:10:24 (26,427)
Marklew, Steve 2:44:20 (297)
Markley, Nicholas D 4:03:08 (11,990)
Marklund, Tony 3:07:30 (1,753)
Markowicz, Stephen 3:43:25 (6,940)
Marks, Brian 3:00:40 (1,205)
Marks, John H 4:26:24 (17,675)
Marks, Owen R 3:34:00 (5,272)
Marks, Peter J 4:47:20 (22,526)
Marks, Richard 3:52:58 (9,248)
Marks, Roger 4:31:29 (18,969)
Marks, Stuart A 3:24:47 (3,658)
Marland, Edward J 3:35:27 (5,511)
Marley, Graham W 4:06:34 (12,798)
Marley-Shaw, Edward W 4:05:03 (12,446)
Marlow, Paul C 4:27:33 (17,977)
Marlow, Paul G 3:26:45 (3,973)
Marlow, Shaun 4:49:10 (22,912)
Marpole, Andrew J 4:24:32 (17,192)
Marquis-Jones, Peter H 4:37:20 (20,322)
Marr, Peter C 2:57:47 (943)
Marrero, Jorge L 4:39:53 (20,891)
Marrie, Thierry 3:12:27 (2,246)
Marriott, Adrian 2:21:51 (40)
Marriott, David S 4:45:24 (22,117)
Marriott, Glen G 3:49:59 (8,501)
Marriott, Jason P 5:15:31 (27,082)
Marriott, Jeff R 4:04:28 (12,306)
Marriott, Robert G 6:13:19 (30,826)
Marriott, Robert J 4:22:26 (16,677)
Marriott, Roger J 3:37:17 (5,832)
Marriott, Simon C 4:42:13 (21,388)
Marriott, Steven G 5:26:21 (28,234)
Marriott-Reynolds, Anthony E 3:49:00 (8,254)
Marron, David J 3:57:56 (10,658)
Marron, Stephen E 4:54:47 (23,956)
Marrone, Marco 4:27:33 (17,977)
Marsden, Andrew N 3:33:13 (5,141)
Marsden, John 4:52:12 (23,482)
Marsden, Justin R 3:37:00 (5,768)
Marsden, Owen L 4:45:18 (22,096)
Marsden, Paul W 3:18:01 (2,850)
Marsden, Richard H 4:53:21 (23,676)
Marsden, Stuart W 4:03:11 (12,003)
Marseglia, Pasquale 2:45:25 (338)
Marsh, Alan D 4:09:02 (13,386)
Marsh, David 3:59:31 (11,166)
Marsh, Gary J 4:39:33 (20,833)
Marsh, Gary L 4:06:54 (12,862)
Marsh, Geoff R 4:30:12 (18,679)
Marsh, Geoffrey H 4:20:04 (16,044)
Marsh, Pete 3:44:03 (7,082)
Marsh, Richard J 3:57:16 (10,466)
Marsh, Rob J 4:29:13 (18,406)
Marsh, Stephen R 5:06:57 (25,964)
Marsh, Steve P 5:28:58 (28,481)
Marsh, Terry P 5:38:58 (29,262)
Marshall, Andrew J 3:16:19 (2,674)
Marshall, Andrew R 4:41:34 (21,258)
Marshall, Andrew W 3:54:12 (9,564)
Marshall, Anthony 4:30:18 (18,703)
Marshall, Ben 4:00:24 (11,380)
Marshall, Craig P 3:55:23 (9,901)
Marshall, Dan 4:48:24 (22,759)
Marshall, David E 4:10:18 (13,705)
Marshall, David J 4:55:48 (24,151)
Marshall, Dean L 5:26:37 (28,262)
Marshall, George 5:09:39 (26,328)
Marshall, Ian 3:10:52 (2,087)
Marshall, Ian R 3:58:25 (10,824)
Marshall, Ian T 3:06:49 (1,687)
Marshall, James 4:21:40 (16,439)
Marshall, James J 4:11:51 (14,053)
Marshall, Jason 5:30:44 (28,638)
Marshall, Jonathan P 3:12:14 (2,222)
Marshall, Kevin A 5:36:44 (29,081)
Marshall, Lloyd H 2:38:54 (183)
Marshall, Nicholas A 4:46:00 (22,250)
Marshall, Oliver 2:56:23 (846)
Marshall, Paul 3:42:49 (6,813)
Marshall, Paul R 4:14:27 (14,665)
Marshall, Peter 3:40:17 (6,352)
Marshall, Richard L 3:33:45 (5,227)
Marshall, Robert 6:16:03 (30,909)
Marshall, Robert 6:46:58 (31,464)
Marshall, Robert D 4:33:46 (19,527)
Marshall, Robert E 3:31:01 (4,782)
Marshall, Simon A 3:52:56 (9,235)
Marshall, Simon O 3:54:10 (9,548)
Marshall, Stephen 2:46:47 (383)
Marshall, Steven 3:51:51 (8,977)
Marshall, Thomas C 3:37:30 (5,873)
Marshall, Thomas J 3:14:07 (2,452)
Marshall, Tom 3:57:45 (10,605)
Marshall, William C 4:40:51 (21,098)
Marshman, Adrian J 4:00:33 (11,405)
Marson, Peter P 4:39:57 (20,904)
Marson, Yves 3:18:08 (2,865)
Marston, Andrew D 4:14:26 (14,659)
Marston, Glyn A 3:22:27 (3,368)
Martel, Brian 5:29:30 (28,532)
Martell, Nevin 4:42:15 (21,397)
Martell, Paul M 3:55:11 (9,845)
Martin, Andrew J 4:19:06 (15,803)
Martin, Andrew T 4:15:35 (14,949)
Martin, Bob 3:14:09 (2,459)
Martin, Brett 3:54:35 (9,660)
Martin, Charles W 3:59:37 (11,195)
Martin, Christopher K 7:26:35 (31,820)
Martin, Cliff P 3:44:47 (7,259)
Martin, Danny 3:44:30 (7,185)
Martin, David C 4:45:23 (22,115)
Martin, David C 4:50:22 (23,142)
Martin, David E 4:09:29 (13,494)
Martin, David W 4:51:36 (23,362)
Martin, Dean P 4:31:31 (18,987)
Martin, Don M 6:28:13 (31,178)
Martin, Georges 4:36:24 (20,104)
Martin, Gerard 4:12:11 (14,131)
Martin, Ian 5:20:46 (27,661)
Martin, Jean 4:47:58 (22,666)
Martin, Jim 4:32:20 (19,195)
Martin, John C 6:24:08 (31,111)
Martin, Neil C 3:52:49 (9,204)
Martin, Nicholas 3:57:28 (10,527)
Martin, Nicholas J 3:46:44 (7,686)
Martin, Paul G 3:55:15 (9,863)
Martin, Paul J 3:27:13 (4,066)
Martin, Philip 3:39:57 (6,295)
Martin, Richard P 4:08:52 (13,338)
Martin, Rob A 3:56:12 (10,142)
Martin, Scott 4:54:40 (23,935)
Martin, Simon D 4:22:48 (16,771)
Martin, Stephen 4:50:21 (23,138)
Martin, Stephen 5:07:26 (26,035)
Martin, Stephen L 4:49:52 (23,057)
Martin, Thomas M 4:42:38 (21,477)
Martin, Tim A 3:36:41 (5,722)
Martin, Trevor 3:03:20 (1,392)
Martindale, Tim 3:30:24 (4,674)
Martinetti, Fabrizio 2:51:31 (570)
Martinez Gomez, Diego 3:47:23 (7,848)
Martin-Garrido, José M 3:43:53 (7,034)
Martins, Antonio M 3:13:51 (2,417)
Martin-Smith, Kollyn P 3:03:37 (1,416)
Martiradonna, Marcello 3:23:23 (3,485)
Maruziva, Leslie R 4:48:07 (22,699)
Marven, Roger 4:26:25 (17,677)
Marvin, Richard J 4:34:12 (19,644)
Marwood, Tim 5:30:48 (28,646)
Maryan, Richard 4:43:02 (21,570)
Marzal-Lopez, Enrique 3:37:08 (5,800)
Mascall, Bruce 4:25:33 (17,440)
Mascarenhas, Nigel A 4:41:57 (21,337)
Mascialino, Claudio 3:42:43 (6,795)
Masding, James E 5:50:58 (30,014)
Masetti-Zannini, Alberto 5:14:02 (26,906)
Masey, John 5:57:33 (30,313)
Mash, Raymond E 6:14:59 (30,884)
Masi, Massimiliano 3:59:02 (11,012)
Maskell, Paul N 4:05:30 (12,539)
Maskell, Simon 4:03:11 (12,003)
Maskery, Ryan D 4:39:25 (20,811)
Maslen, Andy M 4:06:22 (12,752)
Maslinski, Julian M 3:30:51 (4,751)
Mason, Alan 4:47:22 (22,533)
Mason, Andrew 4:47:14 (22,504)
Mason, Anthony D 4:53:14 (23,663)
Mason, Brendon L 4:24:50 (17,260)
Mason, Christopher J 2:55:29 (784)
Mason, David R 3:47:14 (7,808)
Mason, Edward C 4:15:56 (15,037)
Mason, Finlay J 5:16:58 (27,255)
Mason, James E 4:13:43 (14,498)
Mason, Jeremy M 4:32:37 (19,266)
Mason, John E 5:04:45 (25,657)
Mason, Jon E 4:59:41 (24,936)
Mason, Leslie J 3:42:47 (6,807)
Mason, Malcolm E 4:38:25 (20,575)
Mason, Marc 3:13:19 (2,345)
Mason, Martin A 4:13:21 (14,419)
Mason, Michael C 4:02:47 (11,921)
Mason, Michael J 3:46:59 (7,750)
Mason, Neil A 4:46:07 (22,272)
Mason, Paul 4:09:34 (13,516)
Mason, Peter J 3:40:24 (6,380)
Mason, Peter J 3:58:57 (10,991)
Mason, Peter J 4:20:50 (16,235)
Mason, Simon J 5:18:45 (27,445)
Mason, Trevor 2:47:20 (395)
Mason, Will T 3:25:40 (3,796)
Masotti, Giorgio 4:04:59 (12,426)
Massardi, Paolo 3:34:50 (5,395)
Massera, Aldo 4:04:55 (12,411)
Massey, Adrian P 3:10:06 (2,011)
Massey, Andrew R 4:16:12 (15,103)
Massey, Ian 3:46:12 (7,578)
Massey, Julian P 4:30:16 (18,694)
Massey, Nick 4:40:46 (21,076)
Massey, Raymond C 4:00:47 (11,441)
Massiah, Michael 4:55:09 (24,026)
Massingham, Paul J 2:51:33 (572)
Masso, Maurizio 3:42:20 (6,705)
Massy, Paul R 4:11:08 (13,897)
Master, Moosa 4:03:46 (12,140)
Masterman, Darren 5:57:07 (30,292)
Masters, Adam 3:32:06 (4,938)
Masters, Craig D 4:04:14 (12,249)
Masters, Gary 3:19:06 (2,964)
Masters, Michael S 5:05:50 (25,812)
Masterson, Michael J 3:26:37 (3,936)
Masterton, Brian 5:26:34 (28,256)
Masting, Danny F 4:43:59 (21,791)
Maston, Francis 3:55:49 (10,022)
Masuch, Marcel 4:00:33 (11,405)
Masui, Shin 5:08:08 (26,132)
Masumura, Masaaki 4:55:49 (24,157)
Matchett, David 4:43:35 (21,696)
Mateev, Milen 3:49:31 (8,380)
Mateo Martos, José 3:53:48 (9,444)
Mathai, Oliver 3:58:38 (10,899)
Mathebula, Ndumiso G 5:08:11 (26,142)
Mather, Antony 4:25:58 (17,561)
Mather, Colin 4:34:31 (19,717)
Mather, Nigel 4:21:50 (16,487)
Matheron, Gerrard 4:23:03 (16,825)
Mathers, Frank G 3:48:22 (8,093)
Mathers, George E 4:09:55 (13,615)
Matheson, Andrew J 4:01:13 (11,547)
Mathew, Malcolm C 3:27:24 (4,103)
Mathias, Andrew B 4:29:41 (18,550)
Mathieson, Paul S 3:26:42 (3,957)
Mathieu, Thomas 3:52:34 (9,144)
Mathys, Markus 3:48:06 (8,023)
Matijuk, Stephen M 5:33:19 (28,834)
Matson, Alistair G 3:19:48 (3,049)
Matsubara, Shunji 2:53:51 (687)
Matsuoka, Toshiyuki 7:26:14 (31,818)
Mattens, Gunther 3:00:49 (1,218)
Matthams, David J 4:37:11 (20,293)
Matthews, Alan L 3:23:00 (3,439)
Matthews, Christopher J 3:48:08 (8,034)

Matthews, David 3:45:27 (7,397)
Matthews, Eric G 6:56:38 (31,581)
Matthews, Gary R 3:38:06 (5,979)
Matthews, Gerry A 5:08:06 (26,129)
Matthews, Hamilton I 3:33:17 (5,156)
Matthews, John 5:19:47 (27,531)
Matthews, John R 3:28:07 (4,246)
Matthews, Julian S 3:56:11 (10,134)
Matthews, Karl 4:50:02 (23,083)
Matthews, Mark P 3:58:29 (10,845)
Matthews, Nick W 4:51:41 (23,378)
Matthews, Peter C 4:46:30 (22,360)
Matthews, Philip M 4:35:08 (19,851)
Matthews, Philip N 4:12:16 (14,142)
Matthews, Richard A 4:55:57 (24,200)
Matthews, Richard J 4:54:23 (23,875)
Matthews, Ricky 5:08:05 (26,125)
Matthews, Ron M 7:04:55 (31,669)
Matthews, Stephen P 4:11:34 (13,988)
Mattison, Michael J 3:12:55 (2,302)
Matts, Charles J 4:17:08 (15,337)
Matzen, Michael 4:04:52 (12,396)
Matzinger, Mario 3:34:54 (5,411)
Mauclair, Laurent 3:27:06 (4,043)
Maudsley, Martin R 4:57:05 (24,417)
Maughan, David B 3:10:44 (2,075)
Maughan, Simon T 3:48:58 (8,245)
Mauldon, Kenneth P 4:04:49 (12,379)
Maull, Stephen M 4:20:03 (16,042)
Maume, Michael D 3:38:07 (5,981)
Maund, William S 3:54:10 (9,548)
Maunders, Dave J 5:52:10 (30,074)
Maura, Valter 4:49:28 (22,975)
Maura-Cooper, Carl 5:00:44 (25,101)
Maurice-Jones, Mark N 3:51:26 (8,868)
Maury, Neil 3:26:24 (3,904)
Maw, Richard G 3:25:56 (3,835)
Mawby, Andrew 4:33:17 (19,422)
Mawdsley, Paul A 4:51:05 (23,288)
Mawer, Roger 4:18:07 (15,576)
Mawson, Julian D 2:33:57 (108)
Maxwell, Alistair G 4:31:28 (18,966)
Maxwell, Allan H 4:57:45 (24,545)
Maxwell, Andrew D 6:09:04 (30,700)
Maxwell, Christopher K 4:53:54 (23,778)
Maxwell, Iain F 3:59:29 (11,151)
Maxwell, Rory N 3:57:39 (10,581)
Maxwell, Stephen R 3:33:44 (5,223)
May, Albert S 4:20:26 (16,146)
May, Anthony J 5:01:58 (25,296)
May, Colin 4:53:42 (23,749)
May, Gavin R 2:44:56 (323)
May, Giles J 3:12:23 (2,239)
May, John P 5:33:49 (28,872)
May, Kevin 3:06:45 (1,677)
May, Mike 4:20:26 (16,146)
May, Richard A 4:10:43 (13,804)
May, Robin A 3:45:31 (7,414)
May, Stephen P 4:38:08 (20,505)
May, Steven E 5:00:53 (25,126)
May, Terry J 4:44:21 (21,871)
May, Tom 2:54:09 (703)
Maybury, Andrew L 4:01:29 (11,592)
Mayers, Jamie 3:30:22 (4,665)
Mayers, Nick 2:44:57 (324)
Mayers, Stuart W 3:54:34 (9,655)
Mayes, Matthew E 4:16:58 (15,296)
Mayes, Phil 5:43:06 (29,573)
Mayes, Stephen G 4:23:04 (16,830)
Mayfield, Mark 3:49:39 (8,413)
Mayhall, Tony 3:42:03 (6,661)
Maynard, Andrew T 3:29:57 (4,580)
Maynard, Geoff J 5:44:50 (29,680)
Maynard, Graham L 3:04:56 (1,518)
Mayne, Jonathan N 4:46:59 (22,444)
Mayne, Richard D 5:08:43 (26,205)
Mayo, Paul R 4:17:17 (15,365)
Mayo, Philip I 3:21:46 (3,285)
Mayo, Robert 4:22:29 (16,697)
Mayo, Santiago 4:51:44 (23,387)
Mayson, Paul 3:51:48 (8,970)
Maywood, Paul C 6:46:59 (31,465)
Mazey, Rosstan 4:09:04 (13,394)
Mazumder, Sandeep 3:50:45 (8,694)
Mazur, first name unknown 4:01:49 (11,672)
Mazzei, Roberto 4:46:09 (22,279)
Mbuyi, Joseph 3:26:42 (3,957)
McAdam, Stuart 4:40:19 (20,989)
McAdden, James F 4:02:43 (11,906)
McAinsh, Andy I 4:21:41 (16,443)
McAleer, Richard 5:01:39 (25,247)
McAleese, Aaron M 3:55:31 (9,935)
McAlister, Graham 4:33:57 (19,580)
McAllister, Darren J 2:47:00 (388)
McAllister, Ian 3:56:19 (10,183)
McAllister, Malachy 3:02:27 (1,337)
McAllister, Mark J 3:57:02 (10,397)
McAllister, Robin J 4:31:02 (18,864)
McAllister, William A 3:37:47 (5,916)
McAllister-Williams, Richard H 3:09:34 (1,957)
McAlonan, Thomas W 5:40:24 (29,369)
McAnaney, Sammy 2:43:14 (274)
McAndrew, Douglas A 4:14:51 (14,773)
McAndrew, Seamus J 3:40:58 (6,469)
McAnea, Thomas C 3:59:17 (11,083)
McArdle, Edward 3:47:14 (7,808)
McAslan, Alastair R 4:24:11 (17,117)
McAvoy, Nigel J 4:43:37 (21,705)
McBain, Alastair 3:40:19 (6,359)
McBeath, Stuart T 4:48:01 (22,677)
McBride, Geoff H 4:40:15 (20,972)
McBride, Hugh A 6:32:56 (31,261)
McBride, James S 5:27:08 (28,315)
McCabe, Adnrew 5:44:28 (29,654)
McCabe, Alan 4:17:02 (15,312)
McCabe, Andy G 4:15:24 (14,899)
McCabe, Edward J 3:23:26 (3,491)
McCabe, Michael E 3:14:01 (2,437)
McCabe, Peadar J 5:08:39 (26,197)
McCaffrey, Robert J 3:14:43 (2,528)
McCall, Colin W 5:11:04 (26,512)
McCall, Steve D 4:10:35 (13,774)
McCallion, Seamus M 3:05:52 (1,596)
McCallum, Angus C 4:06:23 (12,758)
McCallum, Hamish E 5:00:02 (24,995)
McCann, Colin J 4:42:24 (21,434)
McCann, Craig D 4:56:25 (24,283)
McCann, Gerard J 3:00:35 (1,198)
McCann, Joe 2:51:25 (563)
McCann, John D 3:46:08 (7,552)
McCann, John G 4:37:54 (20,437)
McCann, Matt J 4:56:09 (24,237)
McCann, Philip 4:31:26 (18,956)
McCann, Simon 4:20:40 (16,200)
McCarley, Stuart J 4:08:20 (13,186)
McCarrick, Derek 6:14:34 (30,865)
McCartan, Stephen 4:15:43 (14,980)
McCarter, Dominic 2:42:20 (248)
McCarthy, Brian P 4:04:24 (12,282)
McCarthy, Chris P 4:05:23 (12,503)
McCarthy, Christian J 4:07:26 (12,997)
McCarthy, Gerard F 4:09:32 (13,507)
McCarthy, Ian 4:41:16 (21,179)
McCarthy, John 3:49:33 (8,390)
McCarthy, Keith D 4:30:47 (18,812)
McCarthy, Keith R 4:06:52 (12,855)
McCarthy, Martin 4:11:25 (13,954)
McCarthy, Neil D 4:35:07 (19,844)
McCarthy, Philip R 4:33:17 (19,422)
McCartney, Sean R 3:06:05 (1,618)
McCashey, Ian R 3:45:02 (7,311)
McCauley, Brian T 4:54:06 (23,819)
McCauley, Eamonn 5:48:15 (29,876)
McCauley, Edward 5:16:36 (27,210)
McCausland, Keith 4:26:52 (17,798)
McCaw, Gordon J 3:44:54 (7,286)
McClelland, Paul B 2:50:32 (526)
McClory, John 4:35:00 (19,819)
McCloskey, Peter 4:26:43 (17,753)
McCloughlin, Cian 2:20:45 (34)
McCloy, Neil 4:19:57 (16,013)
McClumpha, Neil D 3:27:35 (4,141)
McClune, Stephen R 4:42:20 (21,423)
McClure, Charles C 3:38:43 (6,087)
McClure, Greg M 3:24:34 (3,632)
McCoig, Mac 4:21:22 (16,352)
McConaghie, Martin G 3:44:13 (7,120)
McConalogue, Ian R 6:21:31 (31,045)
McConnell, Anthony P 3:38:33 (6,056)
McConnell, Euan F 3:09:12 (1,917)
McConnell, John O 5:02:18 (25,345)
McConville, Cathal 4:44:02 (21,802)
McConville, John P 2:51:53 (588)
McConville, Kevin 3:58:24 (10,819)
McConville, Ray 4:44:02 (21,802)
McCool, Peter J 4:37:41 (20,379)
McCord, Andrew 4:19:59 (16,029)
McCord, Jonathan M 4:39:57 (20,904)
McCord, Peter N 4:15:07 (14,834)
McCorkell, Michael C 3:28:48 (4,373)
McCormack, Donall J 4:24:33 (17,196)
McCormack, Graham 4:50:55 (23,258)
McCormack, John J 4:51:20 (23,323)
McCormack, Tom 4:38:00 (20,466)
McCormick, Andrew B 3:13:51 (2,417)
McCormick, Andrew D 4:12:51 (14,289)
McCormick, Graham 3:55:01 (9,794)
McCosker, Cathal 4:42:54 (21,541)
McCosker-Smith, James 4:17:25 (15,403)
McCover, Neil 3:08:01 (1,807)
McCoy, Andrew J 2:45:09 (329)
McCoy, David T 3:06:46 (1,681)
McCoy, Philip J 2:51:24 (561)
McCoy, Robin E 3:11:27 (2,140)
McCracken, Alistair J 3:47:28 (7,873)
McCracken, Shaun W 3:36:12 (5,644)
McCrae, John 5:39:50 (29,322)
McCrorie, William M 4:16:06 (15,079)
McCrossin, Paul A 3:12:30 (2,254)
McCubbing, Mark R 4:38:20 (20,554)
McCubbins, Phillip W 3:11:22 (2,129)
McCullagh, Nicholas J 4:20:41 (16,206)
McCullagh, Oliver J 3:42:30 (6,746)
McCullagh, Philip W 4:55:17 (24,059)
McCullie, Alec 4:23:57 (17,052)
McCulloch, David C 4:10:27 (13,743)
McCulloch, Stephen J 4:17:53 (15,532)
McCullough, John 3:25:26 (3,756)
McCune, Joseph M 4:42:32 (21,460)
McCurry, Stephen 3:33:41 (5,217)
McDaid, Anthony M 3:33:40 (5,214)
McDaid, Gerard 3:31:26 (4,837)
McDavitt, Robert H 5:28:40 (28,458)
McDermott, Cristian 4:56:33 (24,322)
McDermott, Gary 3:58:31 (10,860)
McDermott, Ian 4:23:41 (16,980)
McDermott, Ian M 4:50:58 (23,266)
McDermott, James H 5:18:09 (27,380)
McDermott, Paul A 3:18:27 (2,890)
McDiarmid, Archie H 5:04:52 (25,672)
McDonagh, Michael A 4:04:10 (12,234)
McDonagh, Robert A 3:57:30 (10,538)
McDonagh, Wayne A 4:31:29 (18,969)
McDonald, Andy J 4:50:40 (23,210)
McDonald, Brian J 2:52:17 (603)
McDonald, David S 4:09:33 (13,512)
McDonald, Jamie T 3:28:42 (4,353)
McDonald, Lars T 3:55:27 (9,916)
McDonald, Michael J 3:50:22 (8,597)
McDonald, Neil 3:59:51 (11,253)
McDonald, Peter 3:09:27 (1,942)
McDonald, Robert 3:02:08 (1,310)
McDonald, Stanley R 4:24:20 (17,150)
McDonald, Stephen 4:58:54 (24,780)
McDonald, Steven 5:45:02 (29,694)
McDonald-Liggins, Anthony N 3:28:27 (4,310)
McDonnell, Fergal 3:26:31 (3,922)
McDonnell, Ian D 5:18:43 (27,434)
McDonnell, James M 2:52:26 (612)
McDonnell, Kevin P 5:46:48 (29,805)
McDonnell, Sean J 4:55:47 (24,149)
McDonnell, Terence 4:45:38 (22,171)
McDonough, Alister M 4:49:38 (23,004)
McDonough, Keith W 4:25:30 (17,429)
McDonough, Martin T 3:43:53 (7,034)
McDougle, Tim 4:25:06 (17,333)
McEachen, Angus 3:07:44 (1,781)
McElhinney, David 4:24:43 (17,233)
McElwaine, Barry H 3:42:40 (6,780)

McErlain, Phil 5:41:34 (29,453)
McEvilly, Stuart-Paul 5:45:28 (29,725)
McEvoy, Gavin P 5:25:59 (28,195)
McEvoy, Michael S 4:28:03 (18,107)
McEvoy, Sean P 4:14:18 (14,623)
McEwan, Andrew 3:59:08 (11,040)
McEwan, Duncan B 5:07:01 (25,972)
McEwan, James W 3:40:07 (6,326)
McEwan, Robert 3:13:20 (2,348)
McFadden, Joe T 4:34:23 (19,689)
McFadden, Thomas G 4:37:53 (20,429)
McFadyen, James G 4:53:09 (23,643)
McFadyen, Kevin J 4:59:25 (24,887)
McFadzean, William A 4:25:48 (17,515)
McFarland, Richard E 5:11:18 (26,556)
McFarlane, Andrew N 2:58:26 (1,009)
McFarlane, John 2:17:53 (23)
McFarlane, Winston R 4:37:54 (20,437)
McFarthing, Paul C 4:03:38 (12,110)
McGaffin, Phil 4:02:47 (11,921)
McGannity, Paul R 3:44:12 (7,114)
McGarahan, Kevin-Francis 4:57:55 (24,572)
McGargle, Ian B 5:06:15 (25,882)
McGee, Brian K 4:19:55 (16,003)
McGee, David 3:50:50 (8,717)
McGee, Seamus G 3:49:21 (8,338)
McGeever, Mark 4:17:27 (15,412)
McGeoch, Mick 2:41:56 (242)
McGhee, John 5:20:00 (27,563)
McGibbon, Michael P 3:22:25 (3,363)
McGill, Clive D 4:19:56 (16,008)
McGill, Colin A 3:23:52 (3,552)
McGill, James G 3:55:20 (9,890)
McGill, Paul 4:47:06 (22,474)
McGillan, Brian 4:31:15 (18,909)
McGillan, David 4:42:43 (21,499)
McGinley, Mark D 4:00:11 (11,337)
McGinty, Gary H 4:52:31 (23,536)
McGivern, James K 4:16:08 (15,089)
McGivern, Robert 4:10:03 (13,647)
McGivney, James 4:54:34 (23,914)
McGlashan, Andrew J 5:19:18 (27,489)
McGlashan, Nick 4:16:06 (15,079)
McGlennon, David L 2:59:39 (1,132)
McGlynn, Antony 4:24:57 (17,294)
McGlynn, Peter 4:39:09 (20,762)
McGlynn, Stuart E 4:45:56 (22,235)
McGoldrick, Michael J 3:16:52 (2,735)
McGough, Kevin S 3:44:15 (7,126)
McGovern, James G 3:55:27 (9,916)
McGovern, James P 6:30:39 (31,216)
McGovern, Michael J 4:48:55 (22,857)
McGovern, Plunkett 4:28:11 (18,146)
McGowan, Peter 4:03:10 (11,997)
McGowan, Robbie G 6:06:05 (30,623)
McGowan, Ruairi B 4:43:43 (21,726)
McGrane, Ian M 4:05:34 (12,563)
McGrath, Colin 4:48:20 (22,747)
McGrath, Daniel R 3:22:04 (3,310)
McGrath, Darren M 4:03:45 (12,137)
McGrath, Darren P 4:08:25 (13,206)
McGrath, David 3:16:21 (2,679)
McGrath, Kevin P 3:35:21 (5,496)
McGrath, Liam S 4:32:54 (19,335)
McGrath, Michael J 3:16:22 (2,682)
McGregor, Campbell 3:31:31 (4,853)
McGregor, David K 2:31:21 (90)
McGregor, Peter 3:52:06 (9,036)
McGregor, Scott A 3:01:36 (1,280)
McGroarty, Patrick 3:50:41 (8,679)
McGuigan, Philip M 3:24:49 (3,665)
McGuigan, Robert J 4:44:45 (21,967)
McGuinness, Andrew J 4:22:19 (16,647)
McGuinness, George 3:51:29 (8,880)
McGuinness, Harold 3:53:13 (9,320)
McGuinness, Kristin 3:14:19 (2,480)
McGuire, Colum 4:42:38 (21,477)
McGuire, Danny 5:08:58 (26,231)
McGuire, John 3:40:51 (6,445)
McGuire, Jonathan D 4:34:03 (19,606)
McGuirk, Andrew 3:58:50 (10,954)
McGuirk, Richard B 3:01:15 (1,261)
McGuirk, Stephen J 5:01:32 (25,227)
McGurk, David 3:51:10 (8,789)
McHale, Robert E 3:31:54 (4,901)
McHenry, Joseph W 3:56:32 (10,260)
McHugh, Cathal 3:37:30 (5,873)
McHugh, Michael J 4:55:18 (24,066)
McHugh, Sean P 4:55:17 (24,059)
McHugh, Shaun 3:51:43 (8,945)
McIlhargey, Neil D 3:03:09 (1,380)
McInerney, Michael A 2:57:41 (930)
McInerney, Michael K 3:50:02 (8,511)
McInnes, Duncan H 5:12:59 (26,759)
McIntosh, Andy 3:29:47 (4,550)
McIntosh, Christopher G 3:19:58 (3,063)
McIntosh, Graeme 4:30:00 (18,633)
McIntosh, Graham 4:34:05 (19,619)
McIntosh, James 5:42:19 (29,503)
McIntyre, Kevin A 3:40:41 (6,429)
McIntyre, Ruairdh B 3:34:22 (5,321)
McIntyre, Tim 3:12:58 (2,308)
McIver, Duncan J 3:09:57 (1,998)
McIver, Gary P 5:13:53 (26,885)
McIver, Russell J 4:15:27 (14,916)
McKane, Christopher H 4:48:52 (22,847)
McKay, Andrew P 4:44:34 (21,928)
McKay, Colin G 5:25:37 (28,151)
McKay, Hamish 4:40:21 (20,996)
McKay, Keith J 3:14:49 (2,538)
McKay, Peter 4:14:26 (14,659)
McKay, Robert 3:06:40 (1,672)
McKay, Sinclair 3:33:36 (5,205)
McKay, Stephen G 3:10:25 (2,047)
McKay, Tom J 3:15:33 (2,600)
McKechnie, James D 4:35:01 (19,825)
McKee, Brian A 5:54:50 (30,190)
McKee, Scott 4:48:26 (22,765)
McKeever, Gareth J 3:17:20 (2,788)
McKeith, Ronald S 5:07:13 (25,996)
McKell, Laurence E 4:08:22 (13,193)
McKellar, James 4:12:02 (14,101)
McKellar, Robert 4:21:43 (16,457)
McKelvey, Allan 3:48:20 (8,087)
McKenna, Eugene P 3:56:00 (10,084)
McKenna, Gary P 3:04:37 (1,498)
McKenna, Graham M 3:42:51 (6,821)
McKenna, Jason 4:11:06 (13,889)
McKenna, John F 3:57:54 (10,649)
McKenna, Patrick J 4:52:24 (23,517)
McKenna, Paul 4:37:10 (20,284)
McKenna, Wesley J 3:41:34 (6,553)
McKenning, Matthew J 4:27:46 (18,031)
McKenzie, Andrew D 5:09:38 (26,325)
McKenzie, Darren 4:14:36 (14,706)
McKenzie, Gavin 4:32:09 (19,152)
McKenzie, Kenneth 3:25:34 (3,777)
McKenzie, Kenneth A 4:31:43 (19,033)
McKenzie, Mark S 4:39:28 (20,820)
McKenzie, Rob S 4:45:08 (22,068)
McKeown, Benedict C 4:54:20 (23,866)
McKeown, Kenneth J 3:42:41 (6,785)
McKeown, Mark J 4:33:53 (19,556)
McKeown, Thomas P 3:47:40 (7,920)
McKevitt, Simon 2:34:19 (111)
McKibbin, Stephen P 3:34:53 (5,405)
McKillop, Robert M 4:53:05 (23,630)
McKinlay, Jason P 4:52:06 (23,466)
McKinley, John 3:27:14 (4,070)
McKinney, Pauric 2:22:16 (43)
McKnight, Alex 4:11:09 (13,903)
McKnight, Lenny 4:51:40 (23,371)
McLachlan, Robert L 4:32:36 (19,261)
McLaren, Lawrence 5:07:13 (25,996)
McLaughlan, Christopher A 5:13:02 (26,768)
McLaughlin, Brian 4:01:57 (11,704)
McLaughlin, Daniel 2:56:38 (859)
McLaughlin, Declan 3:47:52 (7,963)
McLaughlin, Gavin J 3:10:16 (2,024)
McLaughlin, Ian R 4:49:22 (22,955)
McLaughlin, Martin 3:33:24 (5,174)
McLaughlin, Michael 3:37:55 (5,940)
McLaughlin, Philip 5:26:42 (28,271)
McLean, Alastair J 4:16:48 (15,251)
McLean, Angus 3:46:16 (7,593)
McLean, Charles F 6:57:47 (31,595)
McLean, Craig R 3:29:42 (4,533)
McLean, Daniel O 5:15:07 (27,034)
McLean, Dave G 5:26:59 (28,299)
McLean, Julian S 3:50:18 (8,574)
McLean, Simon D 5:15:11 (27,037)
McLean, Stephen A 4:02:19 (11,814)
McLean, Stuart 4:56:35 (24,326)
McLean, Wayne R 5:26:35 (28,260)
McLean-Kerr, Owen 7:18:16 (31,774)
McLeish, Bruce J 4:40:37 (21,043)
McLelland, Steve 3:46:44 (7,686)
McLennan, Daniel J 3:23:15 (3,471)
McLennan, Norman S 2:55:46 (798)
McLeod, Daniel J 5:16:08 (27,143)
McLeod, Ian 4:22:12 (16,608)
McLeod, Ian P 4:25:28 (17,418)
McLeod, John 4:09:11 (13,415)
McLoughlin, Stephen 4:13:55 (14,547)
McLuckie, Russ J 4:06:17 (12,733)
McLundie, William M 5:16:21 (27,176)
McMahon, James H 4:09:09 (13,408)
McMahon, John R 4:21:15 (16,323)
McMahon, Neil 3:37:05 (5,793)
McMahon, Nicholas J 4:02:23 (11,835)
McManamon, John G 3:51:03 (8,755)
McManus, James 4:41:07 (21,146)
McManus, Kevin A 3:20:11 (3,088)
McManus, William F 4:38:36 (20,617)
McMaster, Philip J 3:25:47 (3,814)
McMillan, Craig D 2:37:07 (156)
McMillan, Darren 4:54:58 (23,989)
McMillan, David W 4:27:41 (18,013)
McMillan, Fraser 4:12:55 (14,307)
McMonagle, Jamie J 2:51:38 (577)
McMonagle, Noel 5:06:42 (25,939)
McMorrow, Kevin V 4:23:15 (16,884)
McMullen, Alexander B 4:11:59 (14,088)
McMurray, Graeme I 4:09:11 (13,415)
McMyler, Sean A 2:49:55 (495)
McNally, Anthony P 4:16:06 (15,079)
McNally, Brian L 5:58:41 (30,356)
McNally, John 3:58:11 (10,750)
McNally, John R 3:10:30 (2,058)
McNamara, Peter J 4:28:43 (18,281)
McNaught, Keith 4:05:00 (12,429)
McNaughton, Gavin A 4:55:16 (24,056)
McNaull, Allisdhair T 3:36:52 (5,750)
McNealy, Steven 4:24:37 (17,210)
McNeela, Damian 5:01:42 (25,257)
McNeill, Andrew J 6:10:53 (30,754)
McNeill, Andrew S 3:18:38 (2,915)
McNeill, Gary P 3:49:44 (8,434)
McNeill, Ian 3:28:47 (4,368)
McNelis, Robin N 2:58:32 (1,015)
McNelliey, John J 3:47:53 (7,969)
McNicholas, Marius J 4:26:58 (17,830)
McNulty, Chris 5:52:54 (30,120)
McNulty, Paul 3:59:49 (11,242)
McOugall, Dean 3:33:15 (5,148)
McParland, Gerard 2:52:33 (619)
McParland, John E 3:26:29 (3,915)
McPhail, Colin A 4:09:09 (13,408)
McPheat, Martin D 3:18:36 (2,909)
McPherson, George A 2:59:07 (1,085)
McPherson, Kemp M 4:06:50 (12,844)
McPherson, Richard G 3:11:51 (2,176)
McPhie, Cameron S 3:48:19 (8,081)
McPhillips, Luke M 4:31:04 (18,870)
McQuaid, Patrick G 4:49:59 (23,071)
McQueen, Mark P 4:33:53 (19,556)
McQuillan, Andrew 4:16:04 (15,065)
McQuillen-Wright, Chris C 2:48:59 (460)
McQuire, Nicholas 3:10:45 (2,077)
McReynolds, David 4:34:13 (19,646)
McRoberts, Dermot J 4:02:45 (11,914)
McShane, Jonathan 4:16:05 (15,072)
McShane, Marc E 4:23:51 (17,025)
McShane, Michael E 4:04:00 (12,193)
McSharry, Alex J 3:50:06 (8,528)
McSharry, James P 5:31:02 (28,662)
McSharry, Philip 4:17:28 (15,415)
McSkimming, John F 3:23:49 (3,547)
McSparron, Paul D 3:44:49 (7,266)

McSweeney, Brian G 4:31:44 (19,039)
McSweeney, Christopher P..........4:01:58 (11,707)
McSweeney, Rod..........................6:15:38 (30,899)
McTurk, James R..........................4:29:51 (18,593)
McVeigh, Allan J..........................4:36:03 (20,043)
McWilliam, Alan J 4:00:22 (11,372)
McWilliam, Alasdair J...................5:10:05 (26,386)
McWilliam, Thomas.....................2:57:45 (939)
Meachen, John C 4:07:46 (13,062)
Meacock, David J.........................6:21:29 (31,042)
Mead, Adrian...............................3:08:38 (1,861)
Mead, Andrew D 3:42:42 (6,790)
Mead, Colin A 4:55:00 (23,995)
Mead, Paul J 3:55:50 (10,028)
Mead, Raymond 4:41:54 (21,326)
Meade, Ian D................................3:48:17 (8,074)
Meade, James R............................4:25:15 (17,370)
Meadows, Daniel E.......................3:26:46 (3,980)
Meadows, James C........................4:06:01 (12,663)
Meadows, John D 4:52:39 (23,557)
Meadows, Terry D 4:25:52 (17,529)
Meadows, Tom.............................4:03:11 (12,003)
Meads, Jason R 4:50:14 (23,111)

Meagor, David R...........................3:19:09 (2,972)

My third entry in London after running with brother Lucas in 2002 and on my own a year later, I bettered my time again, beating the 3:20 mark and achieving my personal best. I ran New York with Lucas the same year and we raised £6,000 for NCH (now Action for Children). It was a wet race, which helped as we stayed cool. I started separately to my brother so we didn't know how each other fared until then end! The crowds were great and having my children watch for the first time was encouraging too. It was my Marathon peak, as my return in 2007, after an injury delayed me a year, was in the record hot year and my time reflected it too. Great event though and greatly organised!

Meagor, Lucas 4:04:16 (12,257)

I'd run 2001 and 2002 and then rested! I ran with my brother, David Meagor, in both London and New York and we raised £6,000 for NCH (now Action for Children). Dave did his best ever time whilst I failed to make it under 4 hours still and have never since bettered him! But I'd be back in 2006!

Meakin, Paul R.............................4:02:43 (11,906)
Meakin, William A.........................3:51:13 (8,810)
Meakins, Chris..............................5:37:09 (29,119)
Meaning, David J...........................5:21:36 (27,739)
Meanwell, David...........................3:25:42 (3,798)
Mearns, Trevor P 5:13:25 (26,816)
Mears, Ian 4:29:30 (18,492)
Mears, Kristian P 4:51:14 (23,310)
Mears, Richard A..........................3:23:00 (3,439)
Mears, Steven 5:53:04 (30,130)
Medcraft, Kenneth R 3:32:25 (4,990)
Medcraft, Peter.............................4:43:12 (21,605)
Medhurst, Steve J 3:47:19 (7,834)
Medlen, Stuart A...........................4:31:20 (18,930)
Medley, Malcolm G.......................4:21:33 (16,400)
Medley, Ray S................................3:48:27 (8,106)
Medling, William D.......................4:35:57 (20,016)
Medlock, Andrew..........................5:13:34 (26,841)
Medlock, Warren...........................5:07:38 (26,066)
Medway, Kevin L...........................6:21:39 (31,051)
Meech, Victor D 4:12:04 (14,108)
Meegan, Robin G 3:45:57 (7,517)
Meehan, John P.............................3:36:03 (5,618)
Meehan, Tony................................4:12:19 (14,151)
Meeke, Simon J 4:06:51 (12,849)
Meekley, James J 4:35:29 (19,924)
Meeran, Hanif...............................3:48:38 (8,164)
Mehat, Raminder 4:32:00 (19,113)
Mehr, Amir S 5:06:50 (25,951)
Mei, Christian...............................3:10:27 (2,050)
Meier, Thomas 3:44:35 (7,208)
Meighan, Jamie R..........................4:14:51 (14,773)
Meimel, Mario...............................3:00:05 (1,165)
Mein, Trevor J...............................3:30:17 (4,652)
Meinderts, Aad J............................3:52:27 (9,126)
Meinderts, Wim A.........................3:35:47 (5,569)
Meir, Martin J 3:50:42 (8,682)
Meirion-Williams, Richard J 4:14:31 (14,682)
Meisel, Kevin 4:54:51 (23,969)
Melander, Per-Erik 4:08:15 (13,159)
Melby, Brage.................................3:19:02 (2,958)
Meldrum, Alan C 7:07:18 (31,685)
Meldrum, Patrick K.......................3:45:35 (7,435)
Melhuish, Paul 4:50:32 (23,188)
Melia, Anthony..............................4:07:09 (12,927)
Melik, Richard G...........................4:31:25 (18,952)
Melindo, Giuseppe........................4:58:03 (24,609)
Mellanby, James R 3:19:28 (3,016)
Mellem, Ola...................................2:59:06 (1,083)
Melleney, Michael 5:01:15 (25,175)
Melloh, Joachim 3:50:32 (8,634)
Mellon, James................................5:15:18 (27,056)
Mellon, Mark L 3:15:50 (2,635)
Mellor, Andrew J 4:29:38 (18,537)
Mellor, Chris R 4:03:14 (12,010)
Mellor, Clive P 3:51:52 (8,981)
Mellor, Dennis...............................4:53:39 (23,737)
Mellor, Keith A 3:11:09 (2,107)
Mellor, Mike 3:52:10 (9,053)
Mellor, Tom 3:04:02 (1,452)
Mellors, Benjamin T 3:52:28 (9,128)
Mellors, Nick 4:53:36 (23,725)
Mellows, Jonathan P......................3:47:59 (7,991)
Mellows, Steve 4:17:42 (15,480)
Melmoth, Oliver J 4:48:58 (22,868)
Melott, Daniel 5:02:48 (25,422)
Melrose, Alexander H...................4:52:39 (23,557)
Melrose, Jonathan.........................3:45:57 (7,517)
Melton, Ben...................................4:38:46 (20,659)
Meltzer, Martin..............................4:44:54 (22,002)
Melville, Christopher P.................4:44:32 (21,917)
Melville, Iain B 4:28:36 (18,256)
Melvin, John N 4:06:06 (12,683)
Melvin, Rob 3:53:54 (9,476)
Menage, Christophe 3:53:54 (9,476)
Menage, Rupert C..........................4:37:31 (20,342)
Mendelsson, David M 4:27:24 (17,940)
Mendes, Manuel.............................3:57:58 (10,665)
Mendez, Omar 5:06:52 (25,955)
Menezes, Martim...........................3:12:52 (2,296)
Menhinick, Robert C 4:26:51 (17,785)
Menken, Lars..................................3:59:08 (11,040)
Menon, David A 3:58:45 (10,930)
Menon, Dhruv................................4:49:47 (23,036)
Menozzi, Guido 2:45:33 (344)
Mensley, Peter W..........................3:02:30 (1,340)
Menyweather, Craig 4:36:57 (20,243)
Menzies, Alexander G...................3:34:58 (5,419)
Menzies, Jamie D...........................3:44:29 (7,181)
Mepham, Derek C..........................4:01:20 (11,569)
Mercadal, Christian........................3:43:39 (6,989)
Mercer, Anthony 5:34:38 (28,929)
Mercer, Christian 4:06:32 (12,784)
Mercer, David 3:36:44 (5,730)
Mercer, Peter A 6:12:49 (30,807)
Mercer, Philip L 3:49:06 (8,281)
Mercer, Samuel 5:31:45 (28,721)
Mercurio, Salvatore.......................5:33:32 (28,854)
Meredith, Adrian H 3:50:45 (8,694)
Meredith, Duncan..........................5:47:57 (29,865)
Meredith, Matthew C....................3:58:45 (10,930)
Meredith, Philip W 4:19:44 (15,959)
Meredith, Roy................................3:48:24 (8,098)
Meredith, Sean T 4:04:30 (12,316)
Meredith, Simon S........................2:39:20 (195)
Meredith, Tim D 3:52:04 (9,027)
Merfield, Gordon S.......................3:46:52 (7,719)
Mergler, Michael A........................3:27:00 (4,024)
Meriot, François 4:01:45 (11,659)
Merkel, Cyril..................................3:42:29 (6,742)
Merlino, Albert..............................3:49:18 (8,329)
Mermier, Vincent 3:04:25 (1,485)
Merrall, Grant 3:15:42 (2,622)
Merrett, Anthony S 3:30:32 (4,697)
Merrick, Brian 4:25:02 (17,314)
Merrick, Jason L............................5:03:20 (25,493)
Merriden, Trevor K.......................4:25:02 (17,314)
Merrifield, Jeffrey A 4:31:21 (18,935)
Merriman, Andrew.........................4:02:01 (11,723)
Merriman, Andrew.........................5:10:36 (26,451)
Merriman, David W.......................4:21:19 (16,337)
Merritt, Andrew G.........................4:52:47 (23,581)
Merritt, Anthony E........................4:25:18 (17,380)
Merritt, Simon...............................3:20:47 (3,173)
Merriweather, Richard J...............4:55:48 (24,151)
Merron, Bernard J..........................3:25:54 (3,827)
Merry, Paul D................................3:48:48 (8,211)
Merry, Richard A...........................3:32:09 (4,943)
Mertens, Leo 3:24:00 (3,564)
Mesnard, Laurent 4:21:50 (16,487)
Messiant, Frederic..........................3:10:35 (2,062)
Messinger, William T 3:58:05 (10,705)
Metcalf, Alan E..............................2:45:44 (351)
Metcalf, Graham 5:19:25 (27,496)
Metcalf, Julian 4:11:34 (13,988)
Metcalf, Michael............................5:37:38 (29,160)
Metcalf, Peter 3:59:15 (11,070)
Metcalf, Peter J 4:19:57 (16,013)
Metcalf, Richard C 3:43:28 (6,955)
Metcalfe, Alan W 3:08:06 (1,814)
Metcalfe, Barry 3:16:35 (2,707)
Metcalfe, Brian..............................4:09:03 (13,390)
Metcalfe, Christopher...................4:53:21 (23,676)
Metcalfe, Christopher J.................4:00:03 (11,306)
Metcalfe, David C..........................3:29:52 (4,565)
Metcalfe, Len.................................3:53:32 (9,390)
Metcalfe-Gibson, James E 3:36:07 (5,629)
Metson, Leslie P 5:08:55 (26,228)
Metters, Ryan.................................4:01:03 (11,516)
Mettler, Laurent.............................3:32:31 (5,007)
Mew, Simon J.................................3:52:29 (9,130)
Mewes, Stephen.............................5:22:14 (27,798)
Meyer, Karsten..............................4:08:58 (13,369)
Meyer, Michael W.........................5:24:45 (28,048)
Meyer, Oliver N 4:02:12 (11,780)
Meyer, Philippe 4:24:43 (17,233)
Meyer, Tobie A 3:32:35 (5,024)
Meyler, Chris 3:59:22 (11,105)
Meyrick, Daniel J..........................4:01:56 (11,701)
Meyrick, Ian R 4:56:17 (24,260)
Mgloin, Barry P 4:32:18 (19,188)
Miah, S..4:36:28 (20,123)
Micallef, Charles 3:37:28 (5,870)
Michael, Christopher P.................2:47:47 (413)
Michael, Dennis 3:49:42 (8,424)
Michalak, Richard S......................4:03:36 (12,103)
Michalski, Pierre 4:13:01 (14,332)
Michel, Gerard 4:23:53 (17,034)
Michelon, Christophe....................3:32:56 (5,086)
Michie, James R.............................3:14:50 (2,542)
Mickelburgh, Mark E 4:18:54 (15,758)
Micklewright, David 3:54:38 (9,677)
Middlebrook, James E 5:35:28 (28,998)
Middlebrook, Scott J 4:41:56 (21,332)
Middleditch, Andrew P..................4:05:29 (12,532)
Middlemas, Mark R........................4:29:38 (18,537)
Middleton, Andrew G....................6:18:04 (30,960)

Middleton, Brian....3:16:23 (2,683)
Middleton, Clive....3:12:48 (2,286)
Middleton, Colin A....3:42:41 (6,785)
Middleton, George T....2:50:51 (538)
Middleton, Kevan....3:50:35 (8,651)
Middleton, Nicholas E....5:23:34 (27,932)
Middleton, Paul....5:13:19 (26,807)
Middleton, Simon P....5:08:41 (26,200)
Middleton, Thomas F....3:06:00 (1,610)
Middleton, William S....3:51:24 (8,857)
Middlewick, Andrew R....4:45:39 (22,177)
Middlewood, Damian J....4:31:45 (19,041)
Midgley, David....4:37:05 (20,270)
Midgley, Keith....3:32:44 (5,049)
Midgley, Martin N....3:00:41 (1,206)
Midgley, Richard....3:52:54 (9,227)
Midha, Sanjiv....3:56:13 (10,148)
Mifsud, Daniel J....4:15:35 (14,949)
Miget, Leland C....4:01:39 (11,633)
Migne, Claude....3:47:10 (7,797)
Mignon, Sebastien....6:02:26 (30,503)
Mihdidin, Yashraj....3:05:57 (1,606)
Mikalsen, Andreas....4:20:23 (16,126)
Mikkelsen, Morten....3:56:47 (10,323)
Milan, Simon B....4:59:38 (24,925)
Milburn, Ian W....3:39:52 (6,284)
Milburn, Lee....3:41:11 (6,509)
Milburn, Mark W....4:33:46 (19,527)
Milde, Volker....4:47:08 (22,487)
Miles, Christopher T....4:47:34 (22,585)
Miles, David....3:05:29 (1,569)
Miles, David....3:52:28 (9,128)
Miles, Larry C....5:21:52 (27,759)
Miles, Philip B....4:01:56 (11,701)
Miles, Phillip....3:53:52 (9,469)
Miles, Stanley G....6:03:16 (30,537)
Miles, Stephen T....4:13:30 (14,452)
Miles, Tony....3:38:37 (6,073)
Millar, Gordon N....4:23:18 (16,894)
Millar, Julian D....4:44:46 (21,971)
Millar, Michael....5:06:22 (25,896)
Millar, Nicholas J....3:07:18 (1,729)
Millar, Philip E....3:57:01 (10,394)
Millar, Robin J....5:20:00 (27,563)
Millard, Duncan....3:33:21 (5,169)
Millard, Iain....4:57:57 (24,582)
Millard, Paul J....5:01:48 (25,274)
Miller, Andrew....3:48:29 (8,116)
Miller, Andrew W....4:05:44 (12,600)
Miller, Brendon B....4:32:58 (19,351)
Miller, Christopher J....3:47:21 (7,844)
Miller, Christopher J....5:34:05 (28,894)
Miller, Christopher R....5:10:16 (26,409)
Miller, Clifton....6:16:25 (30,918)
Miller, David J....2:37:49 (169)
Miller, David M....3:32:10 (4,947)
Miller, Davide P....6:02:36 (30,515)
Miller, Frank....3:29:45 (4,544)
Miller, Graeme....3:03:51 (1,437)
Miller, Graham L....3:47:53 (7,969)
Miller, Hugh F....3:49:43 (8,428)
Miller, James E....3:40:11 (6,337)
Miller, James F....3:36:18 (5,659)
Miller, Jamie....5:06:08 (25,862)
Miller, Jeremy S....5:34:06 (28,895)
Miller, Jonny L....3:25:08 (3,709)
Miller, Keigh A....4:45:15 (22,088)
Miller, Kenneth....4:15:39 (14,965)
Miller, Kevin R....4:49:50 (23,049)
Miller, Les D....5:33:49 (28,872)
Miller, Malcolm D....4:52:40 (23,564)
Miller, Mark I....4:31:36 (18,999)
Miller, Matthew....4:41:25 (21,222)
Miller, Nick M....3:50:46 (8,698)
Miller, Paul....3:25:29 (3,767)
Miller, Peter....3:11:40 (2,154)
Miller, Robert J....4:40:09 (20,951)
Miller, Scott R....3:43:36 (6,979)
Miller, Simon C....4:17:44 (15,489)
Miller, Stephen....6:02:42 (30,520)
Miller, Stephen P....5:08:00 (26,115)
Miller, Steven....2:49:36 (482)
Miller, Tom....3:31:25 (4,835)
Miller, Tony....4:25:19 (17,384)
Miller-Jones, Charles E....3:23:28 (3,497)
Millership, Andrew M....4:13:46 (14,508)
Millership, Anthony J....3:37:24 (5,860)
Millership, Stephen J....4:41:48 (21,309)
Millet, Jean....3:48:12 (8,047)
Milliam, James A....5:32:15 (28,755)
Millichap, Simon R....3:18:36 (2,909)
Milligan, Keith M....4:02:10 (11,769)
Milligan, Mark A....3:34:21 (5,318)
Milligan, Michael I....3:38:38 (6,075)
Milligan, Phillip....5:45:18 (29,711)
Milligan, Robert A....3:14:38 (2,516)
Milliken, Robert M....4:59:17 (24,846)
Milliner, Christopher L....2:59:49 (1,143)
Millington, Dan....4:00:58 (11,498)
Millington, Eddie C....5:13:10 (26,790)
Millington, John W....4:39:26 (20,814)
Millington, Mike G....4:45:01 (22,032)
Millington, Peter....4:28:32 (18,240)
Millington, Simon A....4:05:27 (12,523)
Millman, Geoffrey S....5:31:40 (28,711)
Millot, Claude....4:25:36 (17,453)
Mills, Andrew....4:59:12 (24,828)
Mills, Anthony....4:23:04 (16,830)
Mills, Conrad S....5:08:10 (26,138)
Mills, David....3:45:55 (7,510)
Mills, David J....3:58:59 (10,999)
Mills, David J....4:51:30 (23,345)
Mills, Edward....3:53:13 (9,320)
Mills, Eric S....3:58:00 (10,671)
Mills, Gavin R....3:05:26 (1,565)
Mills, Gerald D....5:22:21 (27,812)
Mills, Graham C....5:31:50 (28,726)
Mills, James R....5:40:02 (29,340)
Mills, Michael P....4:27:36 (17,990)
Mills, Peter R....5:26:41 (28,270)
Mills, Robert....4:01:26 (11,584)
Mills, Robert W....4:11:37 (14,005)
Mills, Simon....4:39:16 (20,786)
Mills, Stephen J....3:38:16 (6,006)
Mills, Stephen M....3:59:58 (11,284)
Mills, Steven J....3:18:08 (2,865)
Mills, Stuart A....3:11:14 (2,117)
Mills, Stuart M....3:28:36 (4,335)
Millward, Graham E....3:54:50 (9,732)
Millward, Ian D....4:29:28 (18,481)
Millward, Paul....4:15:25 (14,904)
Milne, Ian J....3:32:23 (4,985)
Milne, John F....2:48:09 (428)
Milne, Robert B....5:32:35 (28,780)
Milne, Stephen R....3:54:30 (9,635)
Milner, David N....3:24:10 (3,584)
Milner, Donald G....5:23:40 (27,942)
Milner, Hartley J....3:47:41 (7,925)
Milner, Jason J....4:21:57 (16,516)
Milner, Nigel F....4:33:45 (19,517)
Milner, Nigel K....4:31:36 (18,999)
Milner, Paul....5:29:05 (28,490)
Milnes, Alistair L....4:05:19 (12,489)
Milone, Michael....4:27:05 (17,862)
Milsom, Chris M....5:17:14 (27,278)
Milsom, Peter R....7:24:55 (31,811)
Milsom, Stephen J....4:17:42 (15,480)
Milson, Charlie....4:29:30 (18,492)
Milton, Graham A....3:33:15 (5,148)
Milton, Jason J....3:39:33 (6,224)
Milton, Leslie G....4:59:00 (24,793)
Milton, Raymond J....4:53:08 (23,639)
Milton, Robert....3:27:02 (4,031)
Milton-White, Andrew R....4:40:28 (21,021)
Mimnagh, William R....5:23:01 (27,871)
Minards, Richard A....3:56:23 (10,204)
Minder, Patrik....5:16:17 (27,166)
Mineo, Lorenzo....4:11:59 (14,088)
Miners, Neil....4:49:34 (22,990)
Miners, Roger P....3:55:52 (10,037)
Mines, Ben M....3:47:27 (7,869)
Miness, Timothy M....4:43:55 (21,778)
Minge, John C....4:40:38 (21,050)
Minhall, Martin P....4:18:56 (15,768)
Minhas, Pardip S....4:34:23 (19,689)
Minne, Bertil....3:44:41 (7,236)
Minnis, Mark....5:02:28 (25,367)
Minns, Stephen....3:55:52 (10,037)
Minshull, Ian....3:54:20 (9,596)
Minsky, Bernard S....4:16:43 (15,231)
Minto, Robert W....4:55:55 (24,186)
Minty, Kevin J....2:52:46 (630)
Mintz, Henry G....4:24:42 (17,231)
Miralles-Atar, Juan M....4:51:19 (23,320)
Misra, Prakash....7:09:11 (31,701)
Misselbrook, Neil G....4:19:55 (16,003)
Misseldine, Mark....4:37:54 (20,437)
Missions, David W....4:55:12 (24,037)
Mistry, Alpesh K....4:54:37 (23,926)
Mistry, Elesh C....6:03:50 (30,560)
Mistry, Hitesh S....3:09:00 (1,898)
Mistry, Janek K....3:56:52 (10,354)
Mistry, Jayanti....4:41:46 (21,301)
Mistry, Narindra A....3:29:55 (4,574)
Mistry, Satish....6:18:25 (30,967)
Mitcham, Phil B....5:01:53 (25,284)
Mitchell, Andy K....3:16:05 (2,652)
Mitchell, Anthony B....4:14:00 (14,561)
Mitchell, Craig G....4:04:47 (12,372)
Mitchell, Dean W....4:14:00 (14,561)
Mitchell, Edward P....3:21:43 (3,280)
Mitchell, George....2:52:56 (638)
Mitchell, Gordon D....4:21:16 (16,325)
Mitchell, Gordon H....5:38:05 (29,187)
Mitchell, Gordon R....3:42:22 (6,714)
Mitchell, Ian G....4:54:49 (23,962)
Mitchell, James....4:35:28 (19,922)
Mitchell, James E....4:57:53 (24,564)
Mitchell, Jess T....6:03:51 (30,561)
Mitchell, Lee....6:05:14 (30,598)
Mitchell, Michael J....3:35:01 (5,429)
Mitchell, Nicholas L....3:28:44 (4,359)
Mitchell, Patrick....3:30:09 (4,626)
Mitchell, Paul....5:38:16 (29,209)
Mitchell, Paul R....2:52:34 (621)
Mitchell, Peter A....4:00:05 (11,311)
Mitchell, Peter J....6:16:56 (30,931)
Mitchell, Philip H....4:02:04 (11,735)
Mitchell, Richard H....4:11:37 (14,005)
Mitchell, Sean....3:26:34 (3,926)
Mitchell, Simon J....3:48:07 (8,027)
Mitchell, Steven....4:17:51 (15,523)
Mitchell, Stuart R....3:59:23 (11,111)
Mitchell, Trevor J....4:53:21 (23,676)
Mitchell, William J....3:30:03 (4,601)
Mitchell, William K....5:24:54 (28,069)
Mitchem, Andrew L....5:23:35 (27,935)
Mitchener, Paul J....3:40:01 (6,306)
Mitchinson, Dave....2:18:58 (31)
Mitella, Costakis....5:09:40 (26,331)
Mittal, Aditya....5:22:24 (27,822)
Mittman, Jerome J....3:56:10 (10,128)
Mitty, Leslie....4:50:16 (23,115)
Miura, Takamichi....3:52:57 (9,242)
Miyajima, Isamu....3:40:23 (6,377)
Mizen, Alexander E....6:08:42 (30,692)
Mizen, Barrie D....6:01:55 (30,486)
Mizen, Geoff P....4:01:22 (11,574)
Mizura, Jerzy....4:14:20 (14,632)
Moaven, Amir....4:11:35 (13,994)
Moberly, James....3:57:15 (10,463)
Mockett, Lee P....4:24:19 (17,148)
Mockford, David....4:53:04 (23,624)
Modaher, Jasvir....6:05:42 (30,610)
Modi, Chetan S....3:58:45 (10,930)
Moehle, Andreas....4:47:08 (22,487)
Moerkved, Erik....3:48:32 (8,129)
Moffat, Graeme J....4:19:50 (15,983)
Moffatt, Jason....4:31:40 (19,014)
Moffatt, Kevin B....4:00:33 (11,405)
Moffatt, Nigel A....4:45:05 (22,059)
Moffett, David J....3:14:27 (2,493)
Mogan, Robert A....3:16:14 (2,665)
Mogford, Michael P....4:14:54 (14,786)
Mogg, David K....4:44:16 (21,850)
Mogg, Helmut....5:17:45 (27,333)
Moggia, Gianni....2:54:53 (743)
Mogridge, Chris....3:28:59 (4,411)
Mogridge, Clifford....6:23:33 (31,100)

Mohagen, Sverre T.	2:48:22 (439)
Mohamed, Abdelsalam E.	4:20:53 (16,256)
Mohamed, Salim	3:43:49 (7,017)
Mohamed, Yassin	5:08:32 (26,186)
Mohammed, Tarek	4:47:50 (22,644)
Mohan, Bernard P	4:19:21 (15,871)
Mohanlal, Hitesh A	5:22:38 (27,845)
Mohr, Johannes	5:28:36 (28,450)
Moi, Nikolai	5:11:31 (26,580)
Moine, Frederic	3:46:34 (7,653)
Moir, Richard D	4:18:48 (15,740)
Moita, Paulo J	5:21:38 (27,744)
Molas, Jacques	3:34:50 (5,395)
Mole, Daniel L	5:41:25 (29,440)
Moles, David W	4:51:17 (23,315)
Molesworth, Tony	4:00:08 (11,323)
Molinaro, Alfie M	5:46:22 (29,774)
Mollart, Nick E	3:37:49 (5,926)
Molley, Alan J	4:06:56 (12,871)
Mollison, Ardian J	4:13:07 (14,359)
Molloy, Andrew N	5:59:12 (30,373)
Molloy, Anthony P	4:09:38 (13,536)
Molloy, Benjamin M	3:27:41 (4,164)
Molloy, Lee P	5:04:08 (25,590)
Molloy, Michael	4:22:27 (16,681)
Molyneaux, Ryan J	3:47:42 (7,933)
Molyneux, David	5:28:18 (28,418)
Molyneux, John	6:22:12 (31,064)
Molyneux, Paul M	2:49:27 (476)
Molyneux, Sidney A	4:23:17 (16,891)
Momoniat, Nazim	4:47:54 (22,654)
Monaghan, Kevin T	3:44:07 (7,097)
Monaghan, Raymund F	3:43:34 (6,974)
Monahan, Barry T	4:44:29 (21,908)
Moncaster, Christopher J	3:18:35 (2,907)
Money, Antony H	4:41:47 (21,304)
Money, Jonathan M	4:09:29 (13,494)
Money, Stephen	2:34:31 (116)
Moneypenny, Colin	5:19:08 (27,479)
Monger, Desmond L	4:09:40 (13,546)
Monk, Phillip D	3:28:52 (4,392)
Monkhouse, Andrew L	4:17:09 (15,341)
Monkley, Robert P	4:03:05 (11,975)
Monks, Christopher S	4:45:55 (22,232)
Monks, David T	4:49:27 (22,969)
Monks, Gavin S	3:03:51 (1,437)
Monksfield, Peter A	4:07:18 (12,963)
Monkton, Michael C	4:54:18 (23,855)
Montague, Peter	6:21:27 (31,041)
Montanaro, Charles G	4:36:48 (20,202)
Montaque, Peter	5:15:14 (27,046)
Monteilus, Fabien	5:02:31 (25,379)
Monteird, José Edvardo	2:50:44 (536)
Montgomerie, James	4:24:48 (17,251)
Montgomerie, James	4:56:27 (24,293)
Montgomery, Alan	5:29:09 (28,499)
Montgomery, Mark J	4:20:29 (16,157)
Montgomery, Michael J	3:46:32 (7,644)
Montgomery, Richard R	4:31:30 (18,982)
Montgomery, Scott	5:33:34 (28,856)
Montgomery, Steve	3:44:56 (7,293)
Montgomery, Tony M	4:23:07 (16,847)
Montoya, Francis	4:32:43 (19,294)
Mood, Mike J	3:06:16 (1,636)
Moodie, Richard P	4:46:12 (22,296)
Moody, Andrew B	4:03:38 (12,110)
Moody, Ben	3:56:29 (10,248)
Moody, Colin	3:06:07 (1,622)
Moody, Douglas G	3:11:04 (2,101)
Moody, Simon C	4:04:38 (12,336)
Moolman, William W	6:00:33 (30,428)
Moon, Chris	5:06:06 (25,859)
Moon, Christopher M	4:27:21 (17,931)
Moon, Lee M	6:45:37 (31,448)
Moon, Stephen A	4:19:47 (15,973)
Mooney, Christopher G	4:04:52 (12,396)
Moor, Dominic J	5:24:24 (28,015)
Moorby, Vinny	3:58:45 (10,930)
Moore, Aaron B	3:59:03 (11,016)
Moore, Adrian	4:06:59 (12,889)
Moore, Andrew	3:54:48 (9,722)
Moore, Andrew J	4:57:13 (24,442)
Moore, Andrew P	5:13:52 (26,880)

Moore, Anthony C	4:32:08 (19,146)
Moore, Benjamin H	3:52:21 (9,099)
Moore, Brett	3:18:06 (2,858)
Moore, Brian	3:08:52 (1,884)
Moore, Brian	5:22:15 (27,801)
Moore, Christopher J	4:47:34 (22,585)
Moore, David M	4:30:12 (18,679)
Moore, David R	4:42:24 (21,434)
Moore, Dominic J	6:54:53 (31,559)
Moore, Douglas A	4:12:24 (14,167)
Moore, Edward J	4:11:49 (14,048)
Moore, Gerry	3:48:12 (8,047)
Moore, Giles R	5:02:08 (25,310)
Moore, Graham S	2:55:34 (790)
Moore, Ian N	4:02:38 (11,881)
Moore, Jim I	4:31:08 (18,885)
Moore, Jimmy C	4:26:14 (17,644)
Moore, John P	4:05:00 (12,429)
Moore, John S	4:46:56 (22,430)
Moore, Joseph I	4:36:29 (20,131)
Moore, Justin M	4:44:26 (21,897)
Moore, Kevin J	3:10:29 (2,056)
Moore, Melwyn J	4:08:52 (13,338)
Moore, Michael F	2:41:47 (238)
Moore, Nicholas J	5:08:53 (26,219)
Moore, Nick R	4:06:41 (12,817)
Moore, Peter R	4:30:31 (18,764)
Moore, Peter W	4:29:54 (18,610)
Moore, Phillip C	5:21:33 (27,731)
Moore, Ralph N	3:43:05 (6,868)
Moore, Richard J	3:04:16 (1,470)
Moore, Richard J	3:24:12 (3,589)
Moore, Roger K	3:24:13 (3,592)
Moore, Roger W	4:40:54 (21,107)
Moore, Simon A	4:13:29 (14,448)
Moore, Stephen A	4:50:10 (23,103)
Moore, Stephen D	4:31:38 (19,006)
Moore, Trevor A	3:00:04 (1,163)
Moore, William	4:04:19 (12,269)
Moore-Gillon, John C	3:58:31 (10,860)
Moorhouse, Adrian	3:55:43 (9,997)
Moorhouse, Nicholas	5:57:22 (30,305)
Moorsom, David M	4:16:42 (15,229)
Moos, Christopher J	3:56:55 (10,371)
Moraghan, John	5:19:04 (27,471)
Morales Ingles, Francisco	3:37:03 (5,783)
Moran, Beano	3:50:26 (8,614)
Moran, Craig	3:26:59 (4,018)
Moran, David	3:28:40 (4,346)
Moran, Dennis	3:29:24 (4,488)
Moran, Fraser	3:55:10 (9,839)
Moran, John B	3:39:22 (6,195)
Moran, Michael M	3:51:53 (8,985)
Moran, Paschal P	3:25:56 (3,835)
Moran, Patrick A	3:34:20 (5,315)
Moran, Paul	3:28:13 (4,266)
Morbey, Alastair A	4:31:29 (18,969)
Morbin, Greg	4:39:54 (20,898)
Moreau, Pascal	3:55:55 (10,057)
Morel, Pierre L	4:01:23 (11,576)
Morelli, Massimo F	4:11:01 (13,875)
More-Molyneux, Michael G	5:23:22 (27,901)
Morenas, Ransley	3:45:30 (7,409)
Moreton, Joshua T	3:46:27 (7,628)
Moreton, Lee	3:55:02 (9,798)
Moreton, Lloyd	6:23:22 (31,094)
Moretti, William	3:25:57 (3,841)
Morfey, Piers A	3:38:57 (6,121)
Morgan, Andrew	3:55:07 (9,821)
Morgan, Andrew D	6:33:00 (31,263)
Morgan, Anthony T	4:22:08 (16,582)
Morgan, Bill	3:25:48 (3,815)
Morgan, Charles N	4:00:50 (11,454)
Morgan, Christopher J	4:22:09 (16,588)
Morgan, Christopher J	4:32:16 (19,181)
Morgan, Christopher V	4:35:31 (19,929)
Morgan, Colin	4:20:42 (16,211)
Morgan, David K	4:01:52 (11,685)
Morgan, David R	4:24:39 (17,218)
Morgan, Dewi	4:15:07 (14,834)
Morgan, Hugh J	5:57:22 (30,305)
Morgan, Jason	4:56:54 (24,384)
Morgan, John	5:03:47 (25,554)

Morgan, John V	4:52:58 (23,610)
Morgan, Jonathan D	4:37:56 (20,449)
Morgan, Jonathan G	3:18:36 (2,909)
Morgan, Joseph J	4:40:15 (20,972)
Morgan, Kenneth L	4:44:09 (21,827)
Morgan, Laurence A	3:39:33 (6,224)
Morgan, Martyn P	4:17:01 (15,307)
Morgan, Oliver G	4:54:35 (23,920)
Morgan, Phil J	5:43:15 (29,579)
Morgan, Rhodri	3:29:59 (4,585)
Morgan, Rhodri T	4:48:32 (22,781)
Morgan, Richard	4:14:38 (14,716)
Morgan, Richard A	3:51:37 (8,922)
Morgan, Richard J	3:35:22 (5,497)
Morgan, Richard P	6:10:05 (30,729)
Morgan, Robert D	4:43:13 (21,610)
Morgan, Robert W	3:20:34 (3,145)
Morgan, Roger	3:48:45 (8,198)
Morgan, Russell J	4:38:28 (20,587)
Morgan, Simon A	4:04:56 (12,418)
Morgan, Stephen J	4:18:22 (15,623)
Morgan, Steven G	5:37:10 (29,122)
Morgan, Thomas J	5:32:34 (28,779)
Morgan, Timothy S	4:21:33 (16,400)
Morgans, David G	4:28:50 (18,309)
Morgenstern, Fano	3:29:11 (4,446)
Mori, Fabio	3:43:25 (6,940)
Moriarty, Michael F	3:52:48 (9,195)
Morin, Denis P	3:26:08 (3,867)
Morison, Ian J	3:39:11 (6,161)
Morland, Peter	5:31:48 (28,723)
Morley, Adam K	3:49:30 (8,376)
Morley, Andy S	4:22:15 (16,623)
Morley, Christopher	4:00:38 (11,412)
Morley, Phil A	2:53:44 (678)
Morley, Richard	4:31:27 (18,963)
Morley, Simon	4:50:56 (23,264)
Morling, Craig L	4:21:55 (16,505)
Morling, Matt J	4:16:09 (15,093)
Mornet, Roland	3:38:08 (5,983)
Morpuss, Guy	4:02:23 (11,835)
Morrell, Gregory S	3:28:39 (4,343)
Morrell, Thomas R	3:51:08 (8,774)
Morrey, John	4:00:32 (11,404)
Morrice, Stanley W	5:16:55 (27,248)
Morrin, Keiran J	4:22:16 (16,628)
Morris, Ashley G	3:28:03 (4,234)
Morris, Barry	4:24:07 (17,097)
Morris, Ben J	5:24:13 (27,994)
Morris, Christoher J	3:26:44 (3,969)
Morris, David	3:46:40 (7,673)
Morris, David A	5:01:21 (25,194)
Morris, Doug P	4:14:46 (14,745)
Morris, Garth	3:14:17 (2,475)
Morris, Graham C	3:59:45 (11,233)
Morris, John	4:44:21 (21,871)
Morris, John D	3:11:14 (2,117)
Morris, Keith H	3:58:14 (10,766)
Morris, Lionel E	5:34:17 (28,911)
Morris, Mark	2:58:33 (1,021)
Morris, Meirion L	5:52:42 (30,109)
Morris, Michael	4:49:45 (23,027)
Morris, Neil	4:54:28 (23,891)
Morris, Neil G	5:14:22 (26,943)
Morris, Philip	2:58:09 (982)
Morris, Philip J	5:00:21 (25,045)
Morris, Pual	4:46:01 (22,255)
Morris, Robert	4:35:07 (19,844)
Morris, Robert P	3:58:00 (10,671)
Morris, Simon C	5:45:10 (29,701)
Morris, Stephen P	4:51:42 (23,382)
Morris, Thomas A	3:20:33 (3,140)
Morrish, James W	5:21:22 (27,713)
Morrison, Alastair	3:02:22 (1,332)
Morrison, Alastair J	4:18:04 (15,568)
Morrison, Christopher F	2:47:37 (407)
Morrison, Darren R	5:01:58 (25,296)
Morrison, Derek J	3:34:37 (5,355)
Morrison, James H	4:12:58 (14,231)
Morrison, James M	3:57:31 (10,546)
Morrison, Joseph R	3:22:14 (3,332)
Morrison, Keith	4:57:29 (24,492)
Morrison, Paul	3:59:46 (11,235)

Morrison, Sid 3:29:25 (4,490)
Morrissey, Matthew C 3:58:20 (10,799)
Morrow, Cathal 4:10:24 (13,734)
Morrow, David P 6:08:13 (30,680)
Morrow, Peter A 3:55:18 (9,880)
Morse, Lee R 4:03:12 (12,007)
Morse, Martin L 4:55:24 (24,084)
Morse, Nathan J 4:42:24 (21,434)
Morsley, John H 3:36:22 (5,672)
Mort, Stuart G 5:08:22 (26,170)
Mortazavi, Shad 4:17:39 (15,470)
Mortensen, David 3:00:31 (1,193)
Mortensen, Michael C 3:46:40 (7,673)
Mortimer, Andrew P 4:26:52 (17,798)
Mortimer, Andrew P 5:00:15 (25,033)
Mortimer, Daniel R 3:39:58 (6,298)
Mortimer, Daniel S 4:17:22 (15,387)
Mortimer, John G 4:13:31 (14,456)
Mortimore, Andrew J 3:30:56 (4,769)
Morton, Alan 5:55:50 (30,236)
Morton, Andrew 4:17:47 (15,503)
Morton, Andrew D 6:24:00 (31,108)
Morton, Andrew R 4:14:43 (14,732)
Morton, Brian G 4:44:51 (21,988)
Morton, Clive R 3:35:14 (5,467)
Morton, Colin 6:06:05 (30,623)
Morton, Colin B 6:07:32 (30,664)
Morton, David J 3:45:31 (7,414)
Morton, Gary 3:45:32 (7,420)
Morton, Jamie E 4:24:30 (17,182)
Morton, Mark N 4:24:53 (17,278)
Morton, Paul N 4:05:49 (12,620)
Morton, Philip J 4:43:41 (21,718)
Morton, Simon 5:59:42 (30,400)
Morton, Stephen J 4:46:27 (22,349)
Morton, Stuart 4:53:38 (23,733)
Morton-Holmes, Gavin J 5:42:56 (29,547)
Morton-Jack, Richard 4:36:45 (20,191)
Morum, Gregory J 3:38:46 (6,093)
Morvan, Eric 2:38:56 (184)
Morwood, Ian 4:19:49 (15,981)
Moseley, Andrew J 3:56:44 (10,310)
Moseley, David J 3:45:32 (7,420)
Moseley, Simon 3:18:45 (2,926)
Moser, Gary 3:51:12 (8,806)
Moses, Ephraim J 7:12:44 (31,728)
Mosley, Andrew J 3:32:15 (4,961)
Mosley, Ian 3:49:19 (8,331)
Mosley, Paul G 5:21:41 (27,748)
Mosobbir, Misbah U 4:17:29 (15,419)
Moss, Andrew 4:08:40 (13,278)
Moss, Andrew J 4:29:52 (18,599)
Moss, Charles H 4:50:06 (23,091)
Moss, David T 6:19:33 (31,005)
Moss, Grant 3:49:46 (8,444)
Moss, Jeremy 4:06:38 (12,811)
Moss, Moddy J 3:51:52 (8,981)
Moss, Patrick 3:37:49 (5,926)
Moss, Peter L 5:18:26 (27,405)
Moss, Stephen J 4:34:36 (19,733)
Mostafid, Hugh 4:45:16 (22,091)
Mostarda, Mario 3:14:13 (2,470)
Moth, Steven W 3:58:55 (10,979)
Motson, Nicholas E 4:09:36 (13,524)
Mott, Philip E 3:56:49 (10,337)
Mott, Shane 3:24:42 (3,651)
Mottershead, Gary 3:29:42 (4,533)
Mottram, Gareth 3:48:47 (8,208)
Mottram, Philip J 6:08:02 (30,674)
Moughtin, Ross 4:42:30 (21,450)
Mould, Alan T 2:57:42 (933)
Mould, John R 4:27:37 (17,996)
Moulder, David R 3:27:38 (4,154)
Moulding, Craig 3:29:50 (4,562)
Moulding, Paul M 4:48:40 (22,807)
Moulson, John P 4:09:24 (13,475)
Mouncey, David J 3:35:13 (5,462)
Mount, Andy 4:11:59 (14,088)
Mount, James G 5:59:08 (30,369)
Mount, Steven P 3:55:14 (9,860)
Mountain, Richard J 3:45:51 (7,492)
Mountfield, Steven J 4:56:24 (24,280)
Mountford, Ali 3:45:33 (7,425)

Mountford, Paul J 2:33:57 (108)
Mountford, Philip F 3:44:41 (7,236)
Mourlon, Didier 4:08:54 (13,348)
Mousset, Jean-Patrick 4:03:27 (12,067)
Moutou, Eddy 5:56:22 (30,266)
Mouzer, Robert 3:17:34 (2,808)
Movini, Giancarlo 3:24:00 (3,564)
Mowat, Raymond J 4:34:27 (19,699)
Mowatt, James F 4:50:20 (23,129)
Mowbray, Christian M 5:45:32 (29,729)
Mowle, Lee C 3:05:22 (1,559)
Moxon, David S 3:53:31 (9,380)
Moyes, Peter D 4:19:31 (15,913)
Moylan-Jones, Michael 4:08:47 (13,317)
Moynes, Kevin A 5:27:30 (28,355)
Moyniham, Carl 4:01:35 (11,620)
Moyse, Graham A 2:56:32 (855)
Mozuelos, Thierry 3:16:46 (2,725)
Mrashani, Simon 2:37:59 (170)
Mreches, Carlo 3:13:08 (2,321)
Muboro, Edward 4:04:45 (12,367)
Muchamore, Luke A 4:14:01 (14,572)
Muck, Klaus 3:50:48 (8,706)
Muddle, Richard J 5:44:33 (29,661)
Mudge, Ian 3:19:39 (3,038)
Mudie, Andrew J 4:56:04 (24,223)
Mudie, Christopher M 4:08:23 (13,196)
Mueller, Bernd 4:25:47 (17,509)
Mueller, Markus 3:15:58 (2,647)
Mueller, Sebastian 3:58:59 (10,999)
Muggleton, Neil G 3:49:09 (8,297)
Mughal, Muntzer 4:17:18 (15,368)
Muhammad, Darren 4:27:30 (17,957)
Muir, Graham 3:42:03 (6,661)
Muir, Malcolm J 2:47:36 (406)
Muir, Roger C 5:22:20 (27,808)
Muirhead, Graeme A 3:36:05 (5,625)
Muirhead-Smith, Andrew W 3:48:46 (8,200)
Mujtaba, Peter 4:18:38 (15,695)
Mulcahy, Peter W 4:01:28 (11,591)
Mulcahy, Tim J 3:53:51 (9,459)
Muldowney, William M 5:00:38 (25,082)
Mules, Alistair 5:12:55 (26,751)
Mules, Burnard L 5:12:51 (26,740)
Mulhearn, Ben 4:00:58 (11,498)
Mulholland, David J 3:59:28 (11,140)
Mulholland, Jim P 4:41:54 (21,326)
Mulholland, Mark 3:59:57 (11,280)
Mulholland, Terence M 4:20:10 (16,057)
Mulindwa, Steve 5:18:44 (27,439)
Mullaly, John J 5:13:52 (26,880)
Mullaney, Desmond M 5:29:59 (28,581)
Mullarkey, Peter J 3:13:22 (2,353)
Mullem, Stephen 6:08:58 (30,697)
Mullen, Jim O 3:15:13 (2,578)
Mullens, Stephen B 3:53:58 (9,493)
Muller, Anton M 3:29:52 (4,565)
Mullery, Peter J 3:09:40 (1,967)
Mulley, Peter J 3:29:23 (4,482)
Mulligan, John 4:16:34 (15,189)
Mullin, Mark J 4:37:48 (20,406)
Mullins, Andrew P 4:57:40 (24,529)
Mullins, Jinnie 6:17:36 (30,940)
Mulliss, Rowan J 3:48:48 (8,211)
Mumford, Mark 4:09:15 (13,438)
Mummery, Michael S 4:14:46 (14,745)
Munasinghe, Indumina C 4:07:53 (13,085)
Munday, Bryan A 3:45:30 (7,409)
Munden, Tony 3:55:41 (9,982)
Mundy, Bob 4:28:11 (18,146)
Mundy, James 3:55:27 (9,916)
Mundy, Stuart C 4:23:49 (17,017)
Munford, Andrew J 3:58:00 (10,671)
Munn, Philip E 3:55:05 (9,814)

Munns, Brian 3:10:58 (2,097)
Munns, Gary J 4:57:36 (24,513)
Munro, Adam 4:11:10 (13,904)
Munro, Dafydd R 3:23:19 (3,478)
Munro, Neil F 4:27:23 (17,934)
Munro, Phillip 3:04:56 (1,518)
Munroe, Andy J 3:21:40 (3,273)
Munsch, Pierre 4:23:05 (16,837)
Munson, John P 5:00:01 (24,993)
Munson, William B 5:34:38 (28,929)
Munt, Derek P 3:41:13 (6,516)
Munton, Steve C 6:02:47 (30,522)
Murchison, Andrew 3:23:21 (3,483)
Murday, James E 4:42:05 (21,366)
Murden, Philip J 6:14:41 (30,871)
Murdoch, Graeme A 3:06:02 (1,613)
Murdoch, Grant 3:47:07 (7,784)
Murdoch, Ian E 5:08:17 (26,158)
Murdoch, Steven J 3:56:55 (10,371)
Mures, Luis 4:49:28 (22,975)
Murfin, Grant E 3:05:03 (1,528)
Murfitt, Darren N 3:09:48 (1,979)
Murison, Kevin 3:12:27 (2,246)
Murkin, Steven D 4:28:52 (18,317)
Murnane, Steven M 4:59:29 (24,901)
Murphy, Aidan G 3:46:58 (7,741)
Murphy, Alan J 5:32:19 (28,761)
Murphy, Andrew D 3:49:15 (8,319)
Murphy, Bernard 2:31:11 (88)
Murphy, Brendan 4:13:41 (14,491)
Murphy, Daniel M 4:33:51 (19,547)
Murphy, Dennis J 4:56:49 (24,367)
Murphy, Eddie T 5:57:18 (30,301)
Murphy, Emmet F 6:16:33 (30,923)
Murphy, Francis G 3:53:22 (9,356)
Murphy, Gary R 4:52:00 (23,438)
Murphy, Gerald A 4:04:49 (12,379)
Murphy, Gerry 3:59:12 (11,060)
Murphy, Ian H 4:38:40 (20,632)
Murphy, Jeff 4:13:12 (14,376)
Murphy, John D 4:15:07 (14,834)
Murphy, John F 3:13:16 (2,337)
Murphy, John M 3:51:45 (8,955)
Murphy, Kevin J 2:53:43 (675)
Murphy, Lee W 4:02:19 (11,814)
Murphy, Martin 2:57:35 (919)
Murphy, Michael D 3:53:06 (9,282)
Murphy, Patrick B 5:23:41 (27,943)
Murphy, Peter 5:14:35 (26,976)
Murphy, Peter J 3:16:18 (2,670)
Murphy, Philip J 3:37:50 (5,931)
Murphy, Russ S 4:36:41 (20,179)
Murphy, Ryan 4:51:04 (23,285)
Murphy, Stephen 5:33:36 (28,858)
Murphy, Stuart N 3:51:40 (8,930)
Murphy, Thomas A 5:42:19 (29,503)
Murphy, William 4:20:40 (16,200)
Murphy, William J 2:58:03 (976)
Murray, Andrew 3:15:43 (2,626)
Murray, Andrew 4:14:34 (14,698)
Murray, Barrie E 4:47:09 (22,491)
Murray, David J 4:04:56 (12,418)
Murray, Finlay J 3:50:09 (8,538)
Murray, Francis 4:19:26 (15,894)
Murray, Graeme 4:11:51 (14,053)
Murray, Hugh 3:27:10 (4,057)
Murray, Iain 2:56:32 (855)
Murray, Iain D 4:26:38 (17,736)
Murray, Ian 4:44:50 (21,983)
Murray, Ian S 5:02:54 (25,435)
Murray, James B 4:30:06 (18,655)
Murray, James I 3:09:39 (1,965)
Murray, Jamie 2:47:56 (420)
Murray, Joe 4:12:54 (14,302)
Murray, John H 7:12:11 (31,723)
Murray, Ken 5:10:57 (26,501)
Murray, Kevin P 3:34:47 (5,385)
Murray, Mark 3:55:45 (10,005)
Murray, Paul 4:06:12 (12,711)
Murray, Paul 4:45:53 (22,225)
Murray, Paul A 3:56:59 (10,385)
Murray, Paul J 4:34:11 (19,640)
Murray, Robert D 3:53:07 (9,287)

Murray, Rory	3:34:20	(5,315)
Murray, Seamus	7:18:30	(31,775)
Murray, Shane M	3:53:49	(9,448)
Murray, Stephen	3:42:58	(6,843)
Murray, Stephen M	4:12:31	(14,208)
Murray, Stephen P	4:51:09	(23,295)
Murray, Terry G	5:02:45	(25,411)
Murray, Thomas C	5:20:51	(27,669)
Murray, Tim	4:05:39	(12,583)
Murrell, Alistair I	4:17:04	(15,319)
Murrell, Mark A	5:12:52	(26,742)
Murrell, Nick	3:50:27	(8,623)
Murrells, Ben	5:10:54	(26,496)
Murtagh, Matthew	4:55:44	(24,143)
Murtagh, Peter M	2:33:03	(98)
Murtagh, Tim J	5:16:33	(27,198)
Murton, Perry	4:52:58	(23,610)
Murumets, Chris A	4:38:08	(20,505)
Musa, Olawole G	5:33:19	(28,834)
Musgrave, Richard G	5:33:16	(28,831)
Musgrove, Brandon P	4:00:15	(11,349)
Musk, Martin S	4:25:31	(17,434)
Muskett, Alan P	3:29:34	(4,512)
Mussett, Adrian	2:42:32	(252)
Mussi, Dean	4:31:57	(19,096)
Musson, Julian P	4:57:31	(24,496)
Mutch, Graeme P	3:16:36	(2,710)
Mutch, Joseph N	4:11:08	(13,897)
Mutimer, Ian V	4:48:14	(22,725)
Mutini, Lorenzo	3:01:46	(1,290)
Mutter, David W	3:42:30	(6,746)
Muzzell, James D	4:57:02	(24,410)
Mwaka, Martin	3:20:04	(3,076)
Mwanza, Phil	4:21:42	(16,449)
Myatt, Phillip D	4:49:56	(23,065)
Mycock, Stuart I	4:30:58	(18,852)
Myers, Ian P	4:16:51	(15,268)
Myers, Jonathan R	4:20:09	(16,055)
Myers, Nicholas S	4:05:02	(12,444)
Myers, William M	4:28:31	(18,235)
Myerscough, Robert S	3:49:36	(8,403)
Myhill, Andrew	2:59:55	(1,150)
Myhill, Ben W	3:46:19	(7,605)
Myners, Peter D	3:43:48	(7,013)
Mytton, Steven S	3:40:16	(6,345)
Nadin, Bruce D	4:29:47	(18,580)
Nagamine, Sellchiro	3:38:42	(6,086)
Nagel, David C	4:46:18	(22,317)
Nagel, Trevor J	3:27:09	(4,053)
Nagl, Phil J	5:09:18	(26,277)
Nagle, Stephen A	4:17:42	(15,480)
Nagra, Bhovinder S	4:26:54	(17,812)
Nagra, Jaswinder S	6:44:37	(31,429)
Naidoo, Kebsi R	5:23:55	(27,964)
Naidoo, Thavendra	4:12:28	(14,187)
Nalton, Andrew B	2:40:32	(218)
Naman, Colin	5:10:24	(26,427)
Nandha, Jadvinder S	3:56:56	(10,376)
Nannini, Giancarlo	5:11:17	(26,552)
Nanson, Andrew J	4:24:40	(17,223)
Nanton, Kingsley	2:54:24	(714)
Napier, Charles J	4:12:16	(14,142)
Napier, James W	4:11:54	(14,063)
Napier, Stafford B	4:30:22	(18,720)
Napper, Nick	3:35:11	(5,456)
Narey, Peter	4:29:27	(18,470)
Nash, James A	4:30:41	(18,797)
Nash, Paul D	3:54:53	(9,748)
Nash, Paul S	3:37:04	(5,790)
Nash, Philip J	3:08:47	(1,876)
Nash, Robin	2:35:19	(128)
Nash, Seven R	3:52:48	(9,195)
Nash, Shaun J	5:38:22	(29,218)
Nash, Stephen T	5:48:37	(29,889)
Nash, Steven	4:28:14	(18,153)
Nash, William H	4:10:57	(13,858)
Nashir, Tooran	5:29:32	(28,537)
Natali, Bruno	4:56:30	(24,310)
Natali, Paul E	3:56:30	(10,250)
Nathan, Sacha G	6:50:17	(31,502)
Nathwani, Rajen V	4:13:27	(14,440)
Natt, Stephen G	3:44:17	(7,133)
Naughton, Christopher J	5:03:48	(25,556)

Navarro-Guillamon, Tomas	5:41:05	(29,413)
Naves, Yves	4:43:16	(21,627)
Navesey, Ged	4:06:12	(12,711)
Navrady, Jeremy L	3:28:00	(4,227)
Naylor, Andrew M	3:57:01	(10,394)
Naylor, Dave G	3:12:53	(2,299)
Naylor, Mark S	5:39:45	(29,317)
Naylor, Michael J	5:09:40	(26,331)
Naylor, Thomas H	4:58:17	(24,663)
Naylor, Zach J	3:23:35	(3,511)
Nayton, Mark S	5:27:55	(28,389)
Nazar, Shabir	5:14:52	(27,013)
Nazzaro, Francesco	4:17:13	(15,351)
Ndiritu, James	3:30:03	(4,601)
Ndlovu, Mandla	3:45:07	(7,322)
Neads, Kevin M	3:30:52	(4,756)
Neal, Gregory G	4:20:39	(16,198)
Neal, Kevin G	4:47:10	(22,493)
Neal, Richard J	6:03:28	(30,545)
Neal, Tom D	5:25:02	(28,089)
Neal, Trevor J	4:24:37	(17,210)
Neale, Daniel P	4:54:59	(23,991)
Neale, Mark G	3:54:07	(9,532)
Neale, Paul J	3:46:41	(7,679)
Neale, Paul W	4:42:50	(21,530)
Neale, Rayment S	5:34:24	(28,917)
Neale, Robert J	4:24:52	(17,274)
Neall, Alexander J	4:43:53	(21,774)
Neary, Aiden	4:39:58	(20,910)
Neaves, Antony B	4:21:12	(16,311)
Nebb, Andrew L	4:23:52	(17,030)
Need, Paul	4:41:46	(21,301)
Needham, Paul	4:10:14	(13,688)
Neglia, Alessandro	4:33:00	(19,359)
Negro, Marco	3:11:44	(2,160)
Negyal, Omar R	5:25:42	(28,159)
Neill, John J	4:40:15	(20,972)
Neill, Michael	4:02:15	(11,796)
Neill, Paul A	4:19:04	(15,792)
Neill, Peter	4:36:52	(20,222)
Neill, Richard H	4:39:00	(20,729)
Neill, Thomas J	3:34:52	(5,400)
Neilsen, Karl E	4:12:37	(14,239)
Neilson, John M	4:16:50	(15,263)
Neilson, Oliver S	4:56:53	(24,380)
Neimantas, Paul A	4:07:02	(12,903)
Nel, Paul	5:00:38	(25,082)
Nelhams, Michael	3:07:01	(1,705)
Nellins, Christopher T	3:03:46	(1,427)
Nellis, Joseph G	4:40:07	(20,943)
Nelson, Alan J	3:35:06	(5,445)
Nelson, Andrew S	2:57:57	(962)
Nelson, Carl	4:23:02	(16,820)
Nelson, Chris	3:49:58	(8,497)
Nelson, Christopher	4:41:43	(21,286)
Nelson, Darren	3:43:45	(7,003)
Nelson, Dennis	4:17:23	(15,392)
Nelson, Paul J	3:58:07	(10,715)
Nelson, Shaun J	5:58:05	(30,330)
Nelson, Stephen P	4:35:04	(19,835)
Nelson-Barnes, Russell C	4:16:22	(15,137)
Nesbitt, Andrew D	4:36:56	(20,236)
Nesbitt, John R	5:25:21	(28,125)
Nesbitt, Nicholas	5:03:26	(25,507)
Nesden, Patrick	5:24:41	(28,044)
Nesson, Patrick J	4:15:26	(14,909)
Nester, Christopher J	7:21:41	(31,798)
Nethercott, Craig M	4:16:52	(15,274)
Nettleton, Andrew	4:08:53	(13,342)
Nettuno, Tommy	2:52:21	(606)
Neubeck, Scott C	4:08:17	(13,170)
Neugarten, Steven	4:57:38	(24,520)
Neumann, Stephen R	5:06:46	(25,944)
Neumayer, Thomas	4:39:43	(20,866)
Nevett, Paul	4:00:29	(11,395)
Nevill, Dominic	4:45:22	(22,112)
Nevill, Peter C	3:33:57	(5,263)
Nevill, Peter J	4:29:48	(18,583)
Neville, Chris	5:02:46	(25,415)
Neville, Kevin P	5:02:17	(25,336)
Neville, Simon G	3:09:04	(1,906)
Neville, Stephen T	4:12:48	(14,279)
Nevin, Frank G	4:35:05	(19,839)

New, Barry G	4:28:39	(18,270)
New, Stephen B	3:44:53	(7,283)
Newall, Oliver	4:14:33	(14,694)
Newbold, Jason D	3:49:01	(8,258)
Newbold, Mark J	5:54:05	(30,154)
Newbould, Paul B	3:58:22	(10,811)
Newbury, Andrew W	3:25:16	(3,729)
Newbury, Steve J	5:07:21	(26,024)
Newcombe, Colin R	4:16:45	(15,237)
Newcombe, Frank F	3:38:50	(6,105)
Newell, Dion E	4:13:52	(14,536)
Newell, Guy R	3:33:17	(5,156)
Newell, Jonathan	4:57:20	(24,464)
Newell, Julian A	2:47:03	(389)
Newell, Mark S	3:45:58	(7,521)
Newell, Michael A	4:50:05	(23,088)
Newell, Peter J	3:39:26	(6,207)
Newell, Terry	5:30:49	(28,648)
Newhill, Lewis S	4:19:58	(16,022)
Newing, Michael A	4:35:52	(19,997)
Newitt, Dale J	5:11:59	(26,630)
Newland, Alan J	5:04:22	(25,613)
Newland, John	4:41:53	(21,323)
Newlands, Alistair R	3:41:00	(6,474)
Newman, Adam	4:21:11	(16,307)
Newman, Andrew	3:27:15	(4,075)
Newman, Andrew J	4:21:43	(16,457)
Newman, Brian T	3:23:36	(3,514)
Newman, Christian G	4:40:29	(21,027)
Newman, Christopher G	3:45:59	(7,523)
Newman, Darren B	3:28:31	(4,323)
Newman, David W	5:52:07	(30,070)
Newman, Edward	4:48:04	(22,688)
Newman, Gavin J	4:08:37	(13,261)
Newman, Graeme R	4:13:18	(14,403)
Newman, Karl	3:55:19	(9,887)
Newman, Martin C	3:38:13	(5,998)
Newman, Maurice T	3:50:09	(8,538)
Newman, Neville J	4:36:39	(20,167)
Newman, Patrick J	4:17:32	(15,433)
Newman, Paul	3:35:57	(5,602)
Newman, Paul A	3:54:37	(9,673)
Newman, Paul J	6:39:44	(31,358)
Newman, Paul L	4:43:18	(21,636)
Newman, Paul S	3:05:42	(1,583)
Newman, Philip D	4:08:13	(13,152)
Newman, Philip G	4:55:56	(24,198)
Newman, Robbie	4:06:02	(12,670)
Newman, Ron	3:46:44	(7,686)
Newman, Wayne C	6:52:19	(31,534)
Newnes, Keith	4:49:16	(22,932)
Newport, Spencer	2:22:31	(45)
Newrick, Ian A	4:15:03	(14,814)
Newsome, Christopher G	4:01:51	(11,682)
Newsome, Paul T	3:50:36	(8,656)
Newsome, Rory J	4:21:11	(16,307)
Newsome, Simon J	5:03:48	(25,556)
Newstead, Paul R	3:59:11	(11,054)
Newstone, Simon A	3:23:40	(3,524)
Newton, Alan	4:05:12	(12,462)
Newton, David J	5:17:22	(27,290)
Newton, Garth T	3:24:52	(3,672)
Newton, Gavin J	3:33:15	(5,148)
Newton, Glyn W	3:38:22	(6,028)
Newton, Jonathan A	4:07:31	(13,012)
Newton, Kevin M	4:37:41	(20,379)
Newton, Philip S	4:37:41	(20,379)
Newton, Phillip E	5:36:33	(29,064)
Newton, Robert P	4:23:46	(17,008)
Newton, Ross	3:59:25	(11,117)
Newton, Simon J	3:12:50	(2,291)
Newton, Simon P	2:46:03	(360)
Newton, William G	4:03:43	(12,132)
Neylan, Anthony J	3:31:28	(4,842)
Neylan, Michael J	3:25:27	(3,761)
Neyland, Daniel R	4:16:34	(15,189)
Ng, Anthony	3:47:54	(7,975)
Ng, Chun Wee	4:06:46	(12,832)
Ng, Chun-Wing	3:59:20	(11,096)
Ngan, Siong-Kin	4:28:26	(18,583)
Ngcikhwe, Xolani	3:01:14	(1,259)
Ngcongo, Phumlani	3:31:59	(4,922)
Ngo, Hung H	4:52:48	(23,585)

Ngolepus, Joseph	2:12:02 (11)
Nguimfack, Alain C.	2:55:32 (786)
Niaudot, Jean-Louis	3:42:12 (6,681)
Nice, Andy	4:00:57 (11,494)
Nicholas, Simon J.	3:40:55 (6,459)
Nicholl, James A.	4:32:58 (19,351)
Nicholl, Matthew	5:14:21 (26,939)
Nicholl, Tony	5:13:43 (26,857)
Nicholls, Adrian	4:38:38 (20,622)
Nicholls, Andrew S.	3:08:48 (1,880)
Nicholls, Gary	4:19:13 (15,839)
Nicholls, Gary R.	5:13:46 (26,864)
Nicholls, Jeremy J.	3:59:39 (11,206)
Nicholls, Jimmy	5:09:20 (26,282)
Nicholls, Jonathan	4:36:48 (20,202)
Nicholls, Kevin C.	5:05:55 (25,828)
Nicholls, Mark	4:39:54 (20,898)
Nicholls, Martin	6:19:09 (30,993)
Nicholls, Matthew W.	4:36:48 (20,202)
Nicholls, Paul	3:46:40 (7,673)
Nicholls, Philip J.	4:12:01 (14,097)
Nicholls, Simon G.	4:01:55 (11,695)
Nichols, Alistair M.	5:00:42 (25,095)
Nichols, Carl	4:28:26 (18,206)
Nichols, Charles E.	4:10:49 (13,830)
Nichols, Geoff S.	4:04:09 (12,228)
Nichols, Paul A.	4:01:54 (11,688)
Nichols, Tom A.	4:00:18 (11,358)
Nichols, William	5:40:01 (29,338)
Nicholson, Alan D.	6:20:28 (31,023)
Nicholson, Andrew	4:23:18 (16,894)
Nicholson, Brian G.	4:01:46 (11,664)
Nicholson, Jonathan	4:59:26 (24,889)
Nicholson, Patrick	4:22:04 (16,561)
Nicholson, Paul J.	3:23:21 (3,483)
Nicholson, Phil H.	3:25:35 (3,785)
Nicholson, Philip D.	4:23:49 (17,017)
Nickau, Hanno	3:10:17 (2,028)
Nickerson, Damion P.	6:04:06 (30,567)
Nicklette, Trevor M.	5:10:54 (26,496)
Nicklin, Garry S.	3:43:06 (6,872)
Nicklin, Paul J.	4:20:35 (16,181)
Nicklin, Richard M.	4:28:20 (18,174)
Nicklin, Tim	4:03:08 (11,990)
Nickson, Stephen J.	4:36:54 (20,227)
Nicol, Derek W.	5:11:09 (26,527)
Nicol, John R.	4:04:43 (12,355)
Nicol, Jonathan C.	3:56:15 (10,166)
Nicolaci, Giovanni	2:56:41 (862)
Nicolas, Jean	3:48:03 (8,008)
Nicoll, Chris	2:51:29 (568)
Nicoll, Mark A.	5:33:07 (28,817)
Nicoll, Michael S.	4:31:19 (18,924)
Nicoll, Rona	4:25:36 (17,453)
Nicoll, Simon H.	3:20:33 (3,140)
Niduaza, Don A.	5:45:25 (29,721)
Niebelschutz, Gerd Peter	3:13:25 (2,361)
Niedermaier-Reed, Robert A.	5:15:13 (27,043)
Niehoff, Carsten	5:50:34 (29,996)
Niehoff, Hennig	5:50:33 (29,995)
Nield, Carl	4:37:29 (20,339)
Nielsen, Gynther B.	3:52:13 (9,061)
Nielsen, Klaus	4:58:13 (24,643)
Nielsen, Rolf	3:45:45 (7,471)
Nielsen, Soren W.	3:51:55 (8,995)
Nielsen-Mazewski, Paul S.	3:15:08 (2,572)
Niemeyer, Manuel	4:29:34 (18,511)
Niemi, Jukka	4:43:45 (21,736)
Niessen, Rob B.	4:26:28 (17,691)
Nieto Tabernero, Juan C.	3:32:44 (5,049)
Nieuwenboom, Erik	3:51:00 (8,749)
Nightingale, Keith P.	4:49:31 (22,981)
Nightingale, Mark J.	3:35:23 (5,499)
Nightingale, Paul C.	4:46:02 (22,259)
Niida, Akira	4:15:03 (14,814)
Nijhawan, Anil	6:35:38 (31,301)
Nikiforov, Petar O.	3:28:48 (4,373)
Niklasson, Nicholas J.	4:22:04 (16,561)
Nilsson, Magnus	3:28:48 (4,373)
Nimmegeers, Johan	3:14:55 (2,549)
Nimmo, Steven G.	3:34:40 (5,362)
Niro La Torretta, Marco	3:56:57 (10,379)
Nisbet, Jonathan	4:22:17 (16,631)

Nisbet, Peter G.	3:56:28 (10,241)
Nisbet, Richmond	3:15:26 (2,591)
Nisbet, Robert N.	4:47:08 (22,487)
Niscola, Terenzio	4:19:02 (15,782)
Nishiura, Shoichi	6:35:32 (31,299)
Nissen, Tom B.	4:00:24 (11,380)
Nisslein, Karl	4:06:56 (12,871)
Niven, Andrew C.	5:18:03 (27,374)
Niven, Martin J.	4:00:10 (11,331)
Nixon, Andrew	4:46:39 (22,383)
Nixon, David P.	6:35:29 (31,297)
Nixon, Fionn T.	4:24:40 (17,223)
Nixon, Philip R.	3:40:08 (6,330)
Njagi, Hammond M.	4:10:45 (13,811)
Njeje, Cawe	2:54:25 (715)
Njoroge, Mungara	4:26:38 (17,736)
Noad, Ian D.	3:00:51 (1,225)
Noah, Lewis	4:07:20 (12,969)
Noakes, Colin B.	4:41:47 (21,304)
Noakes, Gary	3:37:47 (5,916)
Nobbs, Jonathan P.	4:45:46 (22,204)
Nobbs, Peter J.	6:36:54 (31,318)
Noble, Benjamin G.	5:12:15 (26,662)
Noble, Don	5:21:25 (27,722)
Noble, Gerrard G.	4:16:35 (15,194)
Noble, James A.	5:18:47 (27,447)
Noble, Jamie	3:57:14 (10,458)
Noble, Jeff	3:40:02 (6,309)
Noble, Mark	5:25:13 (28,108)
Noble, Mark A.	5:28:54 (28,473)
Noble, Mike J.	3:49:25 (8,359)
Noble, Paul G.	4:13:04 (14,347)
Nock, Graham S.	3:06:44 (1,676)
Nodeland, Ole Gerhard	3:49:57 (8,489)
Noebauer, Klaus	3:57:01 (10,394)
Noffki, Gavin W.	3:59:06 (11,030)
Noisaen, Sunthorn	4:41:07 (21,146)
Nolan, Andrew	4:25:50 (17,522)
Nolan, Andrew R.	4:48:27 (22,772)
Nolan, Brian	2:53:43 (675)
Nolan, Christopher W.	5:06:02 (25,848)
Nolan, Francis S.	5:38:34 (29,234)
Nolan, Keith	3:22:51 (3,426)
Nolan, Marlon B.	5:17:12 (27,272)
Nolan, Michael D.	3:57:14 (10,458)
Noller, Mark C.	4:27:06 (17,864)
Noone, Andrew J.	5:00:25 (25,054)
Noone, Jason L.	4:48:19 (22,742)
Noone, Richard	4:23:44 (16,996)
Norbury, David L.	4:40:03 (20,931)
Norbury, Ray	5:15:09 (27,035)
Norden, Mark	4:26:06 (17,608)
Nordin, Abdurauf	5:13:58 (26,890)
Nordstrand, Mauritz	5:35:56 (29,023)
Norgate, Tom	5:59:29 (30,390)
Norgett, Gary D.	4:34:38 (19,743)
Norley, Lyndon E.	3:22:54 (3,431)
Norman, Alastair S.	4:32:37 (19,266)
Norman, Dave	2:18:53 (30)
Norman, George	3:48:46 (8,200)
Norman, Michael	4:52:49 (23,588)
Norman, Nigel	4:09:44 (13,563)
Norman, Terry	5:31:25 (28,697)
Normand, Ivor W.	3:01:19 (1,265)
Normanton, Adrian	6:07:33 (30,665)
Norridge, Christopher	4:07:44 (13,061)
Norris, Chris	4:26:34 (17,718)
Norris, David S.	5:00:47 (25,110)
Norris, John F.	3:30:06 (4,614)
Norris, Mark J.	4:47:43 (22,618)
Norris, Philip M.	4:51:05 (23,288)
Norris, Richard A.	2:50:18 (518)
Norris, Robert A.	4:07:11 (12,936)
Norris-Jones, Simon R.	5:13:02 (26,768)
North, John S.	3:29:05 (4,431)
North, Shaun R.	2:44:39 (310)
Northall, Luke A.	2:53:48 (681)
Northcott, Adrian P.	3:29:22 (4,478)
Northey, Michael R.	3:25:57 (3,841)
Northfield, Paul C.	6:23:18 (31,091)
Northwood, Mark S.	5:13:48 (26,872)
Norton, Andrew R.	4:29:38 (18,537)
Norton, Bernard J.	5:19:01 (27,466)

Norton, Carl	4:18:23 (15,627)
Norton, Kieron G.	4:22:13 (16,613)
Norton, Mark D.	4:09:41 (13,549)
Norton, Nick	3:52:11 (9,057)
Norton, Paul F.	5:09:52 (26,363)
Norton, Roger J.	5:29:46 (28,565)
Norton, Steve	4:09:06 (13,399)
Nostrand, Michael	4:36:25 (20,110)
Nota, Bernd	3:59:22 (11,105)
Notman, Michael I.	3:48:18 (8,077)
Nott, Christopher P.	3:27:36 (4,144)
Nott, James C.	4:10:47 (13,824)
Nottingham, Duncan	3:27:54 (4,211)
Notton, Simon P.	5:07:24 (26,028)
Noulis, René	3:41:55 (6,624)
Nourse, Robert J.	3:39:05 (6,145)
Nowacki, Wies	2:54:18 (708)
Nozari, Darioush	4:08:37 (13,261)
Nuell, Richard F.	4:57:01 (24,406)
Nugent, Ross I.	2:59:37 (1,128)
Nuijten, Mark J.	4:38:32 (20,603)
Nunes, Andrew	3:34:31 (5,344)
Nunn, David P.	4:21:38 (16,430)
Nunn, David P.	4:30:05 (18,650)
Nunn, Jason D.	4:32:21 (19,199)
Nunn, John	5:37:08 (29,116)
Nunn, John M.	3:47:44 (7,934)
Nunn, Robert P.	4:54:29 (23,894)
Nunn, Simon C.	3:46:22 (7,614)
Nunnerley, Philip H.	4:31:08 (18,885)
Nuriddin, Mammedly N.	3:32:17 (4,965)
Nurse, Marcus R.	4:25:10 (17,355)
Nurse, Roger J.	5:07:05 (25,979)
Nurtman, Mickey S.	4:16:59 (15,301)
Nutbeem, Roy S.	3:41:17 (6,523)
Nutley, Gary D.	4:38:59 (20,721)
Nutt, Matthew R.	3:07:03 (1,708)
Nuttall, Chris	5:37:00 (29,107)
Nuttall, John S.	6:02:54 (30,526)
Nuttall, Martin C.	3:41:44 (6,592)
Nutter, Eric	3:55:07 (9,821)
Nuttycombe, William D.	4:47:21 (22,530)
Nuzzo, Giuseppe	4:13:07 (14,359)
Nyamu, Maxwell M.	2:46:40 (375)
Nyarko, Michael E.	4:38:56 (20,702)
Nyberg, Stefan	4:22:57 (16,804)
Nye, Alan D.	3:58:27 (10,834)
Nye, John	5:14:44 (26,994)
Nykolyszyn, Roman M.	3:49:35 (8,401)
Nyunt, Uo T.	5:08:54 (26,223)
Oakes, Anthony G.	4:38:42 (20,643)
Oakes, Harold W.	5:04:36 (25,638)
Oakes, Mark W.	2:59:18 (1,102)
Oakes, Michael C.	3:18:56 (2,945)
Oakhill, Jon S.	4:47:29 (22,566)
Oakhill, Nicholas C.	4:47:27 (22,557)
Oakland, Simon N.	3:57:36 (10,568)
Oakley, Andrew	3:33:43 (5,218)
Oakley, Brian J.	5:10:17 (26,412)
Oakley, Christopher	4:22:09 (16,588)
Oakley, Ricky	4:12:02 (14,101)
Oakley, Trevor	3:44:48 (7,261)
Oakwell, Paul D.	4:02:02 (11,726)
Oates, David	4:13:33 (14,464)
Oates, Kevin M.	3:09:36 (1,961)
Oatham, Phil	3:14:31 (2,508)
O'Beirne, Andrew M.	2:51:32 (571)
Oberholzer, Willem A.	3:41:27 (6,540)
Oberndoerfer, Martin	3:38:05 (5,973)
Oborski, Andrzej I.	4:05:41 (12,591)
O'Brien, Anthony M.	3:41:09 (6,504)
O'Brien, Bernie J.	4:11:49 (14,048)
O'Brien, David P.	3:12:48 (2,286)
O'Brien, Ian	4:35:48 (19,982)
O'Brien, John F.	3:56:55 (10,371)
O'Brien, John I.	4:37:59 (20,464)
O'Brien, John J.	4:04:07 (12,214)
O'Brien, Kevin F.	4:49:51 (23,052)
O'Brien, Kevin P.	3:39:15 (6,171)
O'Brien, Lee	4:54:03 (23,806)
O'Brien, Michael D.	3:37:59 (5,958)
O'Brien, Michael S.	4:38:40 (20,632)
O'Brien, Noel J.	3:52:57 (9,242)

O'Brien, Paraic....4:50:08 (23,095)
O'Brien, Richard T....3:42:33 (6,754)
O'Brien, Robin E....3:48:43 (8,189)
O'Brien, Shane....3:43:33 (6,968)
O'Brien, Steven....3:38:27 (6,039)
O'Brien, Steven M....3:48:58 (8,245)
O'Brien, Wesley J....4:16:28 (15,166)
O'Brien-Brackenburey, Brendan....5:16:13 (27,157)
O'Byrne, Andrew....4:50:36 (23,198)
O'Carroll, Ronan J....4:15:30 (14,925)
Ochse, Darryl A....3:13:52 (2,420)
Ockwell, Chris....5:01:17 (25,181)
Ocleppo, Franco....3:49:31 (8,380)
O'Connell, Daniel....3:18:04 (2,854)
O'Connell, Eoin....2:39:05 (188)
O'Connell, Gareth T....3:25:28 (3,765)
O'Connell, James J....5:15:44 (27,099)
O'Connell, James N....3:45:33 (7,425)
O'Connell, Martin G....3:59:38 (11,198)
O'Connell, Maurice A....3:23:25 (3,490)
O'Connell, Michael J....4:56:48 (24,361)
O'Connell, Peter J....4:18:03 (15,565)
O'Connor, Barnabas J....5:16:21 (27,176)
O'Connor, Darren N....3:54:19 (9,591)
O'Connor, David A....4:05:41 (12,591)
O'Connor, Edward J....4:23:42 (16,989)
O'Connor, Hubert M....4:51:36 (23,362)
O'Connor, Ian J....4:45:53 (22,225)
O'Connor, John F....5:41:02 (29,410)
O'Connor, Maurice....4:06:57 (12,879)
O'Connor, Michael D....5:15:11 (27,037)
O'Connor, Paul....3:54:49 (9,726)
O'Connor, Ray....3:56:21 (10,196)
O'Connor, Tim P....3:11:55 (2,183)
O'Connor, William J....3:49:35 (8,401)
Octave, Michael....3:32:09 (4,943)
Oddy, Huw M....5:14:54 (27,016)
Oddy, Jonathan W....4:04:09 (12,228)
O'Dea, Stephen J....3:40:30 (6,403)
Odehnal, Thomas....4:18:55 (15,764)
Odell, Mark J....3:53:33 (9,391)
Odeniyi, Ade....4:58:28 (24,711)
Odey, Loyd J....3:50:19 (8,581)
Odhiambo, Wasiema J....2:27:37 (66)
Odihiri, Rusty E....6:37:17 (31,326)
O'Donnell, Deryck G....5:27:21 (28,347)
O'Donnell, Gary J....3:34:56 (5,415)
O'Donnell, Gus....6:46:19 (31,457)
O'Donnell, Kevin....4:02:20 (11,823)
O'Donnell, Kieron....3:14:28 (2,496)
O'Donnell, Matthew J....4:09:28 (13,490)
O'Donnell, Nick M....5:42:24 (29,509)
O'Donnellan, Edin H....4:14:48 (14,758)
O'Donnoghue, Raghnall....3:41:28 (6,542)
O'Donoghue, James J....3:57:52 (10,639)
O'Donoghue, Thomas....3:14:00 (2,432)
O'Donovan, Chris....4:03:24 (12,057)
O'Donovan, Colin....4:20:56 (16,271)
O'Donovan, Timothy....3:30:46 (4,735)
O'Driscoll, Barry....4:29:14 (18,410)
Odurny, Allan....3:34:53 (5,405)
O'Dwyer, Cornelius J....6:32:13 (31,250)
O'Dwyer, Daragh H....3:57:10 (10,438)
O'Dwyer, Garry P....4:47:00 (22,449)
O'Dwyer, Luke....3:55:00 (9,782)
O'Dwyer, Paul J....3:48:14 (8,061)
Oehen, Beat....3:06:29 (1,652)
Oesch, Jean-Didier....2:38:46 (182)
Oestberg, Bjarki....3:09:44 (1,973)
Oestberg, Eirik....4:39:33 (20,833)
Oestberg, Geir....3:45:19 (7,367)
Oestland, Torbjoern....3:57:34 (10,563)
Offei, Sean M....6:43:26 (31,411)
Offer, Clive....5:54:30 (30,171)
Offer, Malcolm J....4:36:51 (20,217)
Offord, Karl....4:56:35 (24,326)
O'Flaherty, Paul....4:07:48 (13,069)
Ogan, Graham K....5:25:45 (28,170)
O'Gara, Carlos P....4:42:52 (21,535)
Ogborn, Steve D....2:45:01 (326)
Ogden, David M....2:51:44 (580)
Ogden, Neil J....3:26:17 (3,885)
Ogden, Paul J....4:19:05 (15,799)
Ogden, Peter J....4:34:00 (19,587)
Ogg, Stevie C....2:47:56 (420)
Ogierman, Andrew....4:58:26 (24,703)
Ogilvy, Peter....4:04:27 (12,300)
Oglesby, Mark C....3:18:44 (2,924)
O'Gorman, James P....5:01:33 (25,229)
O'Gorman, Keith P....4:44:35 (21,932)
O'Gorman, Neil A....3:44:02 (7,077)
O'Grady, Daniel J....3:47:48 (7,946)
O'Grady, Eugene P....5:51:04 (30,018)
O'Grady, John C....3:17:11 (2,770)
O'Grady, Stephen T....3:40:32 (6,409)
Ogunniake, Michael A....4:56:31 (24,314)
Ogunyemi, Jackson....4:42:31 (21,455)
O'Hagan, Terence....4:29:55 (18,614)
O'Hara, Shane....3:43:47 (7,009)
O'Hare, Niall M....4:55:00 (23,995)
Ohlson, Stefan G....4:32:46 (19,306)
O'Hooley, Dominic B....3:08:13 (1,820)
Oka, Suehiro....5:19:23 (27,495)
O'Kane, Brian J....2:45:13 (331)
O'Kane, Philip C....3:53:05 (9,275)
Okantey, Edward....4:24:30 (17,182)
O'Keefe, Steven....8:44:26 (31,976)
O'Keeffe, Gerald J....5:06:42 (25,939)
O'Keeffe, Jeremiah J....3:47:08 (7,790)
O'Keeffe, Justin R....3:28:30 (4,321)
O'Keeffe, Terence G....3:54:57 (9,768)
Okeleke Nezianya, Vincent I....4:40:32 (21,034)
O'Kelly, Steven D....3:32:44 (5,049)
Okon, Ernest....6:17:43 (30,945)
Oladimeji, Anthony....5:11:44 (26,596)
Olaribigbe, Robert M....4:09:29 (13,494)
Old, Neil T....4:40:20 (20,991)
Oldfield, Christopher M....3:30:29 (4,688)
Oldham, Peter M....3:45:52 (7,498)
Oldroyd, Francis W....4:26:51 (17,785)
Oldroyd, Mark A....3:25:41 (3,797)
Olds, Jack L....5:25:17 (28,117)
O'Leary, Andrew R....5:23:20 (27,899)
O'Leary, Christopher T....4:31:20 (18,930)
O'Leary, James A....4:11:08 (13,897)
O'Leary, Kevin....5:26:05 (28,203)
Olejak, Bernd R....4:13:51 (14,532)
Olesen, René F....3:54:39 (9,684)
Olgiati, Andrea....3:54:01 (9,510)
Oliff, Grainger....5:26:26 (28,246)
Oliphant, Graham R....5:20:59 (27,680)
Oliphant, Robert A....4:48:24 (22,759)
Oliveira, Carlos A....4:40:02 (20,928)
Oliveira, Silvi....4:40:02 (20,928)
Oliver, Brian D....4:26:31 (17,706)
Oliver, Damian P....5:02:47 (25,416)
Oliver, Daniel S....4:51:09 (23,295)
Oliver, Kevein W....3:55:13 (9,854)
Oliver, Peter H....4:19:43 (15,955)
Oliver, Richard T....4:05:25 (12,515)
Oliver, Steve....3:59:38 (11,198)
Oliver, Steven....4:32:20 (19,195)
Oliver, William....4:04:47 (12,372)
Oliver-Bellasis, Richard C....4:12:39 (14,247)
Olivier, Jean-Michel....4:03:07 (11,983)
Olivo, Octavio....3:43:29 (6,956)
Olley, Justin....4:37:55 (20,444)
Olley, Leon S....4:01:01 (11,507)
Olmedo, Pablo....2:31:13 (89)
Olney, Paul J....4:44:00 (21,794)
Olney, Robert A....4:02:42 (11,899)
Olofsson, Leif....6:02:06 (30,490)
Olsen, David A....3:30:45 (4,733)
Olsen, David J....4:33:38 (19,496)
Olsen, Kurt....3:30:14 (4,641)
Olson, Philip A....3:58:49 (10,948)
Olsson, Kent....4:52:47 (23,581)
Olsthoorn, Johannes P....3:55:07 (9,821)
Olubaji, Abdul....5:02:47 (25,416)
Oludimu, Babatunde O....8:20:00 (31,959)
Olukoya, Rod G....5:16:34 (27,201)
Olusanya, Olusegun O....4:31:20 (18,930)
O'Mahony, Hugues....3:45:05 (7,318)
O'Mahony, John A....3:30:52 (4,756)
O'Malley, Kiaran J....4:30:01 (18,634)
O'Malley, Sean....4:20:17 (16,095)
O'Maonaigh-Lennon, Neil P....3:48:00 (7,995)
O'Mara, Gerald....4:32:54 (19,335)
Omari, Saad I....3:15:42 (2,622)
Omderwater, Petrus S....4:59:50 (24,964)
O'Muchu, Daithi....3:51:29 (8,880)
O'Neil, Christopher J....4:35:22 (19,903)
O'Neil, Stephen....3:30:18 (4,657)
O'Neil, Wiliam P....3:08:52 (1,884)
O'Neill, Adam A....4:20:12 (16,064)
O'Neill, Charles....5:05:29 (25,756)
O'Neill, Douglas....3:41:04 (6,486)
O'Neill, Eamonn....4:11:25 (13,954)
O'Neill, Gerand....6:24:21 (31,118)
O'Neill, James A....5:05:29 (25,756)
O'Neill, Joseph....5:13:12 (26,795)
O'Neill, Kieran....3:45:45 (7,471)
O'Neill, Ian R....3:06:32 (1,657)
O'Neill, Patrick....4:19:34 (15,925)
Ong, Juling....4:57:39 (24,521)
Ong, Wei Hiam....4:41:37 (21,262)
Ongaro, Mauro....2:36:18 (139)
Ongers, Russell....5:33:29 (28,849)
Onions, Darren....4:27:18 (17,920)
Onions, Terry....3:56:16 (10,171)
Onslow, Richard E....3:47:59 (7,991)
Onwere, Chuks....4:56:52 (24,377)
Ooi, Adrian S....3:54:49 (9,726)
Oon, Zhihao....6:03:20 (30,540)
Oosterbaan, Rob C....3:50:24 (8,605)
Oosthizen, Gabriel H....3:55:03 (9,806)
Opperman, Christoff H....3:41:56 (6,627)
Or Kam Fat, Patricks N....4:40:18 (20,984)
Oram, David H....4:38:39 (20,627)
Orange, Jon....2:31:05 (87)
Orchard, Gerald....3:29:32 (4,507)
Orchard, Lawrence D....3:05:29 (1,569)
Ord, Douglas A....3:29:53 (4,569)
Orde, Hugh S....3:53:15 (9,324)
O'Regan, David....4:14:52 (14,779)
O'Reilly, Eddy J....3:31:35 (4,861)
O'Reilly, John....4:33:14 (19,414)
O'Reilly, Shane....3:47:08 (7,790)
Organ, Christopher D....4:41:19 (21,194)
Orgaz-Casero, Jenaro....3:38:10 (5,989)
Orhiuny, Wilson E....5:14:12 (26,923)
Oria, Gerald....6:11:13 (30,760)
Orlandi, Dario....3:11:39 (2,153)
Orledge, Kevin J....4:03:08 (11,990)
Orloff, James A....4:33:56 (19,573)
Orme, Jonathan N....3:20:48 (3,177)
Orme, Robert....6:03:43 (30,554)
Ormerod, David....5:07:45 (26,086)
Ormond, Paul A....3:29:56 (4,577)
Ormrod, Chris....4:22:36 (16,728)
Ormrod, David J....4:37:46 (20,398)
Ormston, Jeff R....4:18:08 (15,579)
Orodea, Miguel A....3:32:01 (4,930)
O'Rourke, Alan....3:01:11 (1,251)
O'Rourke, Martin D....4:35:16 (19,880)
Orr, Billy....2:55:39 (794)
Orr, David....3:50:36 (8,656)
Orr, Jim....4:13:40 (14,489)
Orrell, Geoffrey S....4:37:01 (20,254)
Orrell, Stewart....3:57:17 (10,473)
Orridge, Christian....3:26:41 (3,951)
Orriss, Mike G....5:11:47 (26,603)
Orsing, Hans O....6:40:14 (31,362)
Ortega-Serrano, Antonio....4:03:38 (12,110)
Ortner, Gerhard....4:43:08 (21,587)
Ortoli, Jean-Marc....3:29:39 (4,525)
Orton, John R....3:35:04 (5,436)
Orton, Nick....3:50:42 (8,682)
Orus-Sampietro, José A....3:33:52 (5,251)
Osborn, Colin H....4:51:30 (23,345)
Osborn, James P....3:25:44 (3,804)
Osborn, Kevan....4:27:17 (17,918)
Osborn, Mark E....3:53:38 (9,410)
Osborn, Roger....3:35:44 (5,563)
Osborne, Ian....3:10:51 (2,086)
Osborne, Jarrod S....3:25:51 (3,824)
Osborne, Julian A....3:56:39 (10,292)
Osborne, Matthew C....4:22:25 (16,671)
Osborne, Nicky....4:47:22 (22,533)

Osborne, Nigel K	3:36:02 (5,615)	
Osborne, Nigel M	4:27:38 (18,000)	
Osborne, Peter M	3:26:09 (3,868)	
Osborne, Ryan H	5:41:42 (29,468)	
Osborne, Simon M	3:38:29 (6,043)	
Osborne, Timothy J	6:07:23 (30,659)	
Osen, Adam N	3:58:45 (10,930)	
Osgathorpe, Andy F	4:42:46 (21,509)	
O'Shea, Denis F	3:58:44 (10,925)	
O'Shea, Dermot P	5:16:58 (27,255)	
O'Shea, John	4:39:15 (20,783)	
O'Shea, John A	3:45:37 (7,442)	
O'Shea, John P	4:29:52 (18,599)	
O'Shea, Paul J	5:25:32 (28,141)	
O'Shea, Sean O	4:17:28 (15,415)	
Osibote, John	4:31:02 (18,864)	
Osinowo, Remi	3:54:16 (9,581)	
Osman, Jon	3:12:43 (2,275)	
Osment, Andrew T	2:50:22 (519)	
Osmond, James	5:37:13 (29,126)	
Ossitt, Simon D	4:09:39 (13,542)	
Ostler, David B	4:04:49 (12,379)	
Ostlund, Anders F	3:49:08 (8,291)	
Ostrowski, Francis J	4:54:09 (23,830)	
O'Sullivan, Brendon J	5:02:26 (25,363)	
O'Sullivan, Chris	7:27:25 (31,827)	
O'Sullivan, John E	4:21:27 (16,376)	
O'Sullivan, Michael C	4:42:46 (21,509)	
O'Sullivan, Michael P	3:00:51 (1,225)	
O'Sullivan, Sean P	5:02:26 (25,363)	
Oswald, Richard A	3:45:11 (7,342)	
Oswald MVO, Christopher J	3:58:16 (10,780)	
Otake, Takeshi	5:11:13 (26,543)	
O'Toole, Gregory A	4:03:32 (12,088)	
Ott, Keith T	4:58:51 (24,771)	
Otten, Rainer	4:11:38 (14,011)	
Ottey, David L	4:44:00 (21,794)	
Ottey, Martin	4:13:30 (14,452)	
Otto, Kevin	3:35:24 (5,502)	
Otto, Robert C	5:37:55 (29,173)	
Oude Kamphuis, Richard B	4:06:35 (12,801)	
Oudet, Eric	3:09:28 (1,944)	
Outhwaite, Jef	3:20:47 (3,173)	
Outka, Mike	4:29:53 (18,607)	
Ovenden, David M	5:26:27 (28,249)	
Overstall, Antony M	5:23:23 (27,904)	
Overstall, Gerald D	4:27:09 (17,880)	
Overstall, Richard C	3:43:58 (7,057)	
Overton, Paul	5:04:11 (25,595)	
Owen, Adrian R	4:10:21 (13,716)	
Owen, Aled	4:10:57 (13,858)	
Owen, Andrew L	4:40:28 (21,021)	
Owen, Brett R	4:39:53 (20,891)	
Owen, Bryan A	4:15:16 (14,876)	
Owen, Bryan V	4:32:52 (19,327)	
Owen, Craig S	4:55:55 (24,186)	
Owen, David J	3:45:13 (7,354)	
Owen, David S	5:29:57 (28,579)	
Owen, Ed P	4:59:22 (24,871)	
Owen, Eugene	3:32:43 (5,045)	
Owen, Gareth	5:37:47 (29,164)	
Owen, Gary M	4:18:27 (15,655)	
Owen, John D	3:38:55 (6,115)	
Owen, Jonathan D	3:44:33 (7,201)	
Owen, Keith F	4:11:47 (14,041)	
Owen, Kevin	3:04:13 (1,466)	
Owen, Mark C	3:28:50 (4,383)	
Owen, Mark J	3:48:13 (8,055)	
Owen, Martin J	4:16:48 (15,251)	
Owen, Mei J	4:25:51 (17,526)	
Owen, Michael J	3:47:55 (7,977)	
Owen, Mike D	5:22:23 (27,819)	
Owen, Paul G	4:44:15 (21,847)	
Owen, Paul L	4:04:15 (12,254)	
Owen, Rhys L	4:00:21 (11,369)	
Owen, Richard	4:52:08 (23,471)	
Owen, Richard J	2:49:46 (489)	
Owen, Robert	3:46:51 (7,713)	
Owen, Shaun	4:04:55 (12,411)	
Owen, Shaun W	3:52:08 (9,044)	
Owen, Simon	3:35:19 (5,487)	
Owen, Simon D	4:42:16 (21,402)	
Owen, Stanley E	4:28:36 (18,256)	
Owen, Stephen G	3:47:40 (7,920)	
Owen, Steven	3:41:04 (6,486)	
Owen-Jones, Roger W	4:30:14 (18,687)	
Owens, Christopher S	3:51:45 (8,955)	
Owens, Christopher W	4:06:03 (12,674)	
Owens, David H	3:20:43 (3,161)	
Owens, Ivor	8:05:37 (31,948)	
Owens, Nicholas J	4:26:42 (17,750)	
Owens, Robert C	4:32:32 (19,245)	
Owens, Stuart I	4:45:11 (22,078)	
Owens, Terry M	5:02:31 (25,379)	
Owens, Thomas M	2:42:37 (256)	
Owers, David	3:45:46 (7,477)	
Owers, Terry W	6:45:06 (31,440)	
Owles, Brian B	4:03:00 (11,954)	
Owst, Malcolm	5:06:58 (25,965)	
Oxby, Martyn	4:35:09 (19,855)	
Oxford, Kevin	3:48:41 (8,183)	
Oxley, Chris	4:06:09 (12,700)	
Oxley, David	5:14:44 (26,994)	
Oxley, Mark S	3:53:57 (9,489)	
Oxley, Pierre J	4:06:58 (12,882)	
Oxley, Robert A	3:57:30 (10,538)	
Oyeyinka, Samuel D	4:08:51 (13,334)	
Oza, Pranav J	4:34:13 (19,646)	
Pabla, Jagdees S	5:59:21 (30,379)	
Pacaud, Christopher M	4:51:48 (23,397)	
Pacey, Darren M	3:20:31 (3,135)	
Pack, Mark A	4:08:58 (13,369)	
Packer, Leigh J	3:11:31 (2,145)	
Packer, Malcolm	2:43:30 (277)	
Packwood, Keith	4:29:18 (18,431)	
Paddison, Henry J	4:15:30 (14,925)	
Paddison, Jonathan C	5:16:10 (27,151)	
Paddon, Neil A	3:21:13 (3,224)	
Padgett, Marc	3:55:00 (9,782)	
Padilla, Ray	3:44:57 (7,296)	
Paez, Mario H	3:42:25 (6,723)	
Page, Aaron J	3:55:34 (9,954)	
Page, Andrew C	3:56:59 (10,385)	
Page, Anthony W	6:37:59 (31,340)	
Page, Ashley C	3:37:13 (5,817)	
Page, Ben W	4:44:32 (21,917)	
Page, Colin	4:57:27 (24,486)	
Page, Colin T	5:11:00 (26,505)	
Page, David	5:13:31 (26,828)	
Page, Derek J	2:59:41 (1,133)	
Page, Edmund J	5:22:03 (27,777)	
Page, Gary A	5:07:30 (26,046)	
Page, Gary M	4:33:13 (19,411)	
Page, Ian W	5:29:19 (28,520)	
Page, Martyn A	5:35:07 (28,966)	
Page, Michael K	3:53:59 (9,499)	
Page, Michael L	3:56:19 (10,183)	
Page, Michael R	3:03:05 (1,372)	
Page, Mick	2:46:15 (363)	
Page, Robert	3:35:31 (5,527)	
Page, Robert E	4:16:51 (15,268)	
Page, Robert G	5:15:15 (27,050)	
Page, Robin	3:35:27 (5,511)	
Page, Stephen R	4:20:17 (16,095)	
Page, Warren	4:26:48 (17,775)	
Pagels, Lutz	3:42:38 (6,773)	
Paget, Martin J	4:44:13 (21,842)	
Pagett, Richard M	4:21:32 (16,398)	
Paige, Nicholas D	5:06:09 (25,866)	
Paine, Alan R	4:10:10 (13,668)	
Paine, William A	6:05:30 (30,605)	
Painter, Mark	5:50:47 (30,006)	
Pajak, Lee R	3:35:04 (5,436)	
Pakenham, Tom J	4:55:06 (24,013)	
Pakey, John A	3:56:28 (10,241)	
Palframan, Lewis O	6:02:22 (30,499)	
Palfrey, Daryl B	3:07:31 (1,755)	
Palfrey, Malcolm D	4:12:22 (14,162)	
Palfreyman, Samuel H	6:05:01 (30,593)	
Palij, Andrew M	4:02:48 (11,927)	
Palin-Bell, Richard J	4:15:49 (15,006)	
Pallant, Robert A	4:30:42 (18,800)	
Pallister, Andrew	4:14:00 (14,561)	
Pallister, Stephen P	3:31:45 (4,881)	
Pallot, Steve T	2:58:21 (999)	
Palluotto, Anthony	5:10:26 (26,436)	
Palmer, Andrew J	4:38:44 (20,649)	
Palmer, Andrew R	3:33:10 (5,129)	
Palmer, Arthur M	4:02:18 (11,805)	
Palmer, David R	2:47:29 (403)	
Palmer, Earl D	5:29:12 (28,509)	
Palmer, Eric E	3:03:41 (1,424)	
Palmer, James R	3:47:17 (7,829)	
Palmer, Jeff E	3:46:44 (7,686)	
Palmer, Joe S	4:12:13 (14,135)	
Palmer, Jonathan K	4:23:10 (16,858)	
Palmer, Jonathon T	4:17:26 (15,406)	
Palmer, Mark	5:00:07 (25,013)	
Palmer, Mark J	5:06:23 (25,899)	
Palmer, Max	5:14:51 (27,011)	
Palmer, Mervyn G	4:12:35 (14,228)	
Palmer, Michael J	3:35:58 (5,606)	
Palmer, Roy N	2:34:23 (113)	
Palmer, Simon T	4:56:04 (24,223)	
Palmer, Stephen	4:49:17 (22,937)	
Palmer, Steven F	3:54:09 (9,542)	
Palmer, Stuart C	4:54:01 (23,796)	
Palmer, Thomas G	3:43:23 (6,933)	
Palombella, Andrew N	3:07:59 (1,804)	
Palombo, Sandro	3:16:50 (2,732)	
Palomo Sevilla, Juan	3:18:59 (2,948)	
Palser, Graham V	3:33:30 (5,189)	
Palser, Tristan S	4:17:38 (15,461)	
Pamment, Richard	4:34:58 (19,813)	
Pampanini, Sebastian G	4:46:35 (22,371)	
Pamplin, Asa R	5:23:43 (27,946)	
Pampling, Lynton J	4:29:40 (18,548)	
Panarisi, Giovanni	4:19:26 (15,894)	
Panayiotou, Marios	3:15:16 (2,582)	
Pandini, Giulio	3:48:13 (8,055)	
Panesar, Harpal	3:51:32 (8,899)	
Pang, Brian	3:40:44 (6,436)	
Pang, Philip K	5:21:13 (27,701)	
Pankhania, Mahendra M	6:25:52 (31,139)	
Pankhurst, Benjamin D	4:47:00 (22,449)	
Pankhurst, Stephen	4:58:54 (24,780)	
Panne, Jaskaran S	4:11:30 (13,968)	
Pannell, Ralph H	3:25:17 (3,733)	
Pannu, Trip	4:59:33 (24,914)	
Panter, John A	5:03:59 (25,579)	
Panter, Kevin A	4:42:16 (21,402)	
Panting, Robert J	4:07:37 (13,037)	
Pantlin, Andrew W	3:59:02 (11,012)	
Papa, Dominic	4:40:22 (21,003)	
Parachout, Alain	5:12:30 (26,692)	
Paradise, Matthew B	4:45:48 (22,210)	
Paramor, Jon	3:33:11 (5,133)	
Paramore, Ian	2:49:48 (491)	
Parashar, Anuraag	3:55:18 (9,880)	
Pardon, Andrew	4:24:45 (17,241)	
Parekh, Bhupesh	6:24:28 (31,119)	
Parekh, Dhruv	5:20:29 (27,631)	
Pares, John E	2:55:54 (805)	
Parfitt, Colin E	3:51:45 (8,955)	
Parfitt, Kevin R	3:16:29 (2,698)	
Parfitt, Mark	3:46:58 (7,741)	
Pargiter, David R	4:22:49 (16,777)	
Parish, George W	4:33:41 (19,502)	
Park, David J	4:10:10 (13,668)	
Park, Gregor J	3:37:17 (5,832)	
Park, Iain F	3:55:12 (9,848)	
Park, John A	3:45:24 (7,387)	
Park, Michael J	4:21:24 (16,363)	
Park, Mungo	3:54:30 (9,635)	
Parke, Kevin D	3:30:54 (4,761)	
Parker, Adam R	3:29:25 (4,490)	
Parker, Alan J	5:16:31 (27,192)	
Parker, Alun G	4:37:10 (20,284)	
Parker, Brian H	3:56:25 (10,222)	
Parker, Christopher	4:16:33 (15,186)	
Parker, Colin B	3:49:51 (8,461)	
Parker, David G	4:45:09 (22,070)	
Parker, Dirk E	5:27:36 (28,361)	
Parker, Edward H	4:02:27 (11,850)	
Parker, Gareth	5:01:06 (25,160)	
Parker, Geoffrey B	3:34:02 (5,276)	
Parker, Ian J	3:19:23 (3,004)	
Parker, James L	4:42:55 (21,548)	
Parker, Jason D	5:40:46 (29,401)	

Parker, Matthew 4:52:57 (23,606)
Parker, Mel T 2:53:33 (671)
Parker, Michael G...................5:03:25 (25,506)
Parker, Neil R 4:29:15 (18,416)
Parker, Nicholas A..................5:51:23 (30,031)
Parker, Paul A.........................3:20:59 (3,200)
Parker, Peter E........................4:28:33 (18,246)
Parker, Richard 3:08:47 (1,876)
Parker, Richard M 4:31:29 (18,969)
Parker, Robert B......................3:52:58 (9,248)
Parker, Robert B......................4:13:29 (14,448)
Parker, Roger W 4:56:25 (24,283)
Parker, Russ J 3:43:56 (7,047)
Parker, Stephen R 4:09:00 (13,380)
Parker, Terence T....................4:43:46 (21,741)
Parker-Varty, Martin D 5:55:22 (30,217)
Parkes, Benjamin 3:43:05 (6,868)
Parkes, David A 3:45:57 (7,517)
Parkes, Graham.......................4:16:32 (15,179)
Parkes, Keith S........................3:51:45 (8,955)
Parkes, Matthew W..................4:09:35 (13,520)
Parkes, Nigel J 3:51:33 (8,905)
Parkes, Simon 4:26:12 (17,631)
Parkes, Tim 5:40:37 (29,388)
Parkin, Keith 2:52:42 (626)
Parkin, Thomas B....................5:01:39 (25,247)
Parkins, Derek 3:13:28 (2,365)
Parkinson, Alastair 5:06:17 (25,886)
Parkinson, Brendan 3:43:14 (6,902)
Parkinson, Colin S 4:50:02 (23,083)
Parkinson, Henry M.................3:40:29 (6,396)
Parkinson, Neil F.....................4:02:22 (11,832)
Parkinson, Paul D 2:56:02 (812)
Parks, Raymund B 6:00:47 (30,439)
Parmar, Nilesh R 5:59:18 (30,378)
Parmley, Andrew C..................5:25:03 (28,093)
Parnell, Philip J 4:33:04 (19,372)
Parnell, Robert C 3:30:13 (4,637)
Parodi, Enrico 4:17:22 (15,387)
Parr, Richard D........................5:49:58 (29,962)
Parr, Robert A.........................4:55:28 (24,095)
Parrett, Martyn R.....................5:09:01 (26,240)
Parris, Stephen 3:50:46 (8,698)
Parrish, Jack...........................4:34:49 (19,781)
Parrott, Nicholas L..................4:19:04 (15,792)
Parry, Alister R........................3:39:18 (6,184)
Parry, Brian 4:28:15 (18,158)
Parry, Christopher J 3:12:22 (2,236)
Parry, David J 3:08:52 (1,884)
Parry, David J 5:15:11 (27,037)
Parry, Ian 4:47:40 (22,608)
Parry, Jonathan 5:38:17 (29,210)
Parry, Lee K 5:54:01 (30,151)
Parry, Malcolm 3:56:51 (10,351)
Parry, Mark R..........................5:50:56 (30,010)
Parry, Martyn K.......................4:16:23 (15,142)
Parry, Richard.........................3:16:47 (2,728)
Parry, Walter K........................5:30:18 (28,606)
Parry-Jones, Jonathan D..........3:27:10 (4,057)
Parsley, Elvis I.........................2:48:57 (457)
Parslow, Stephen P 3:41:41 (6,580)
Parsons, Adam P.....................4:14:48 (14,758)
Parsons, Andrew A 5:01:29 (25,219)
Parsons, Gary.........................3:29:22 (4,478)
Parsons, Graham D 5:18:37 (27,424)
Parsons, Ian G 3:48:47 (8,208)
Parsons, James R 4:08:16 (13,165)
Parsons, Jeffrey G 3:55:12 (9,848)
Parsons, Martin N 4:21:34 (16,405)
Parsons, Martyn L 5:47:30 (29,838)
Parsons, Michael D 5:01:33 (25,229)
Parsons, Michael G 5:11:20 (26,558)
Parsons, Michael J 4:25:32 (17,438)
Parsons, Michael W.................4:59:06 (24,811)
Parsons, Phil 3:03:55 (1,443)
Parsons, Robert F 6:54:27 (31,554)
Parsons, Simon P....................4:43:51 (21,761)
Parsons, Stephen B 4:53:35 (23,718)
Partington, Jamie E.................4:18:55 (15,764)
Parton, Adam M 3:12:46 (2,282)
Parton, Terence 3:14:52 (2,547)
Partridge, Alan R.....................4:02:46 (11,920)
Partridge, Anthony W 3:58:48 (10,945)

Partridge, David A....................4:38:40 (20,632)

This was our first marathon and while we were filled with anticipation and excitement, we were also very nervous – would we get to the end?! After running the first 10 miles with my friend Richard I forged ahead. Turning the corner onto Tower Bridge was the most uplifting experience and will stay with me forever. Miles 17 to 20 were the toughest but the crowds kept me going and the last 6 miles were truly wonderful running along Embankment and up The Mall. Incredible organisation, supportive fellow runners and amazing public support – proud to be British! An amazing day but 'never again' – a phrase I have repeated during and after each of my four subsequent London Marathons!

Partridge, Gary A 4:57:13 (24,442)
Partridge, Nicholas A...............3:51:21 (8,846)
Partridge, Philip 6:30:09 (31,208)
Partridge, Ted..........................2:39:28 (196)
Paschke, Frank 3:23:14 (3,467)
Pascoe, Barry 3:30:11 (4,633)
Pascoe, Matthew J 3:25:45 (3,806)
Pascoe, Nicholas L 3:40:33 (6,411)
Pascoe, Wayne A....................3:48:20 (8,087)
Pask, John L 3:43:22 (6,930)
Pask, Martyn A........................6:17:21 (30,935)
Pasquet, Adrian S 4:28:23 (18,187)
Pasquinelli, Claudio 4:04:22 (12,275)
Pass, Christopher N 6:15:49 (30,905)
Pass, Terry M 3:47:02 (7,763)
Passe, Michel A.......................3:59:58 (11,284)
Passer, Andrew.......................3:58:15 (10,773)
Passey, Adrian 2:35:27 (129)
Passier, Pierre 3:57:33 (10,555)
Passway, Norman D 3:37:33 (5,879)
Pastor, David J.........................3:00:06 (1,166)

Patching, Andrew J 4:31:17 (18,916)
Patching, Russell B..................7:24:27 (31,803)
Pate, Thomas..........................3:44:30 (7,185)
Patel, Amit 5:11:09 (26,527)
Patel, Bhavesh 5:37:57 (29,177)
Patel, Bhavesh T.....................4:30:12 (18,679)
Patel, Bhupendra 5:12:31 (26,694)
Patel, Cookie 5:00:19 (25,042)
Patel, Ghansham D 4:08:35 (13,256)
Patel, Haroon 5:10:25 (26,432)
Patel, Hitesh 4:58:27 (24,707)
Patel, Kalpesh 3:29:09 (4,440)
Patel, Kalpesh 5:45:31 (29,728)
Patel, Kash 5:22:09 (27,790)
Patel, Ketan J 4:47:13 (22,503)
Patel, Mahendra K...................3:49:04 (8,268)
Patel, Mayank B......................4:23:14 (16,879)
Patel, Narendra 4:02:45 (11,914)
Patel, Omar L 5:16:17 (27,166)
Patel, Raj B 3:22:41 (3,401)
Patel, Rashik C........................4:44:24 (21,889)
Patel, Sanjai V.........................5:31:40 (28,711)
Patel, Sanjay K........................5:11:52 (26,613)
Patel, Shivlal H 4:08:35 (13,256)
Patel, Siraj...............................4:05:24 (12,510)
Patel, Vinai 5:25:02 (28,089)
Patel, Zuber I 4:42:53 (21,538)
Paterson, Andrew....................4:25:22 (17,396)
Paterson, Anthony...................5:07:46 (26,089)
Paterson, Anthony L................4:39:31 (20,826)
Paterson, David J.....................4:17:56 (15,540)
Paterson, David J.....................6:12:02 (30,785)
Paterson, James A...................3:30:59 (4,775)
Paterson, James A...................4:16:56 (15,292)
Paterson, James T....................3:59:28 (11,140)
Paterson, Keith 3:13:33 (2,380)
Paterson, Rory 4:00:55 (11,483)
Paterson, Stephen 6:42:11 (31,393)
Patmore, Michael J..................3:43:03 (6,859)
Patmore-Hill, David J...............4:10:45 (13,811)
Patnick, Simon L......................5:50:30 (29,994)
Paton, Alastair 4:32:04 (19,124)
Paton, Colin G.........................2:42:06 (244)
Paton, Damian 4:16:46 (15,242)
Paton, Kevin 4:59:22 (24,871)
Paton, Malcolm 4:01:17 (11,559)
Paton, Philip S 3:39:18 (6,184)
Patrick, Glen A 4:19:41 (15,947)
Patroni, James 5:41:39 (29,461)
Patten, Craig P........................5:20:08 (27,586)
Patten, Kevin A........................4:21:20 (16,345)
Patterson, Alexander R............4:54:15 (23,844)
Patterson, Brian G...................3:35:18 (5,483)
Patterson, Christopher E..........3:22:20 (3,348)
Patterson, David J....................5:23:42 (27,944)
Patterson, Dean K...................3:45:11 (7,342)
Patterson, Iain S 4:06:49 (12,842)
Patterson, John.......................4:23:10 (16,858)
Patterson, Lee J 5:51:52 (30,054)
Patterson, Malcolm W..............4:06:35 (12,801)
Patterson, Oliver J 4:31:13 (18,899)
Patterson, Stephen A...............4:00:57 (11,494)
Pattinama, Jacobis M...............3:44:18 (7,138)
Pattinson, Jonathan K..............4:46:31 (22,365)
Pattinson, Neill........................3:03:05 (1,372)
Pattison, Michael E 6:37:03 (31,320)
Pattison, Robert J 5:16:49 (27,232)
Pattni, Sharad B......................5:46:09 (29,758)
Patton, William 4:08:38 (13,268)
Paul, Adrian M 4:09:38 (13,536)
Paul, Bob 5:22:31 (27,834)
Paul, David A..........................3:48:48 (8,211)
Paul, Douglas W 4:27:17 (17,918)
Paul, Gavin L 4:32:02 (19,119)
Paul, Ken V 4:20:19 (16,106)
Paul, Lee S 3:14:09 (2,459)
Paul, Leslie 3:58:09 (10,729)
Paul, Robert............................4:30:28 (18,750)
Paul, Simon P 4:11:10 (13,904)
Paul, Varun 4:24:18 (17,142)
Pauley, George D 3:16:38 (2,714)
Paulsen, Jan E.........................3:37:02 (5,776)
Paulsen, Michael 3:19:29 (3,021)

Paveley, John E 6:59:28 (31,614)
Pawson, Chris W 3:58:50 (10,954)
Pawson, Mark 6:39:43 (31,357)
Pay, Keri A 4:37:38 (20,370)
Payg, Anthony G 4:47:27 (22,557)
Payn, John E 5:13:36 (26,845)
Payne, Alastair W 2:56:42 (863)
Payne, Andy 5:20:37 (27,647)
Payne, Anthony 3:11:30 (2,144)
Payne, Anthony C 4:06:07 (12,693)
Payne, Colin A 3:35:06 (5,445)
Payne, Dave R 3:17:41 (2,820)
Payne, David A 3:53:56 (9,484)
Payne, Gary F 4:57:27 (24,486)
Payne, George W 3:47:04 (7,770)
Payne, Ian 4:32:28 (19,231)
Payne, Ian F 4:34:37 (19,738)
Payne, James N 4:32:34 (19,251)
Payne, John J 4:32:56 (19,343)
Payne, John P 4:48:56 (22,862)
Payne, Jonathan N 4:20:46 (16,225)
Payne, Mark A 4:30:07 (18,660)
Payne, Matthew R 3:22:12 (3,328)
Payne, Neville R 5:17:13 (27,275)
Payne, Philip C 4:36:29 (20,131)
Payne, Philip L 5:20:34 (27,639)
Payne, Simon W 4:00:13 (11,346)
Payne, Steve 2:31:51 (95)
Payne, Steven M 4:57:33 (24,503)
Payne, Stuart B 3:49:54 (8,473)
Paynter, Stephen D 3:53:29 (9,376)
Payton, Tim 4:48:36 (22,795)
Paz, Belkis 5:27:38 (28,364)
Paz-Suarez, José A 2:40:40 (221)
Pazzaglia, Paolo 4:05:41 (12,591)
Peace, Chris M 3:45:34 (7,428)
Peace, Kevin M 4:47:43 (22,618)
Peace, Michael S 3:25:43 (3,801)
Peacher, Mark S 4:53:23 (23,684)
Peachey, David A 4:29:13 (18,406)
Peachey, Michael 3:12:07 (2,205)
Peacock, Christopher J 4:26:38 (17,736)
Peacock, Darren 4:21:39 (16,435)
Peacock, Kieron J 3:53:51 (9,459)
Peacock, Kim C 5:59:24 (30,382)
Peacock, Richard W 4:39:27 (20,817)
Peacock, Stephen 2:42:49 (263)
Pead, Mark S 3:14:40 (2,520)
Peagam, Duncan 5:13:46 (26,864)
Peake, Andrew J 3:44:23 (7,150)
Peaple, Derek J 2:56:10 (825)
Peaple, Nicholas 3:29:10 (4,443)
Pearce, Andrew 3:18:48 (2,928)
Pearce, Andrew P 3:55:54 (10,051)
Pearce, Andrew R 4:36:38 (20,162)
Pearce, Anthony P 4:17:56 (15,540)
Pearce, Antony 4:07:47 (13,066)
Pearce, Christopher H 4:01:04 (11,523)
Pearce, Christopher M 3:49:36 (8,403)
Pearce, Clive 4:24:35 (17,203)
Pearce, Darren K 4:31:21 (18,935)
Pearce, David 2:44:22 (298)
Pearce, David M 3:43:43 (6,998)
Pearce, Gareth 4:01:30 (11,600)
Pearce, Glenn S 4:25:04 (17,327)
Pearce, Glyn 5:37:26 (29,150)
Pearce, Kelvin 4:01:03 (11,516)
Pearce, Matthew G 4:30:53 (18,837)
Pearce, Matthew R 3:07:54 (1,795)
Pearce, Paul G 5:18:45 (27,445)
Pearce, Raymond 2:44:50 (320)
Pearce, Richard A 6:53:35 (31,544)
Pearce, Robert 2:58:18 (995)
Pearce, Robert L 3:17:03 (2,754)
Pearce, Steve 4:31:29 (18,969)
Pearce, William 4:07:29 (13,005)
Pearcey, Edward R 5:43:57 (29,624)
Pearcey, Joshua 4:44:16 (21,850)
Pearcy, Russell D 6:44:48 (31,432)
Pearman, David J 4:46:58 (22,439)
Pearrson, Don 3:13:02 (2,312)
Pears, Richard 4:10:21 (13,716)
Pears, Thomas M 3:47:01 (7,756)
Pearse, Gary 3:29:42 (4,533)
Pearse, Scott A 5:50:54 (30,008)
Pearson, Alexander 5:13:03 (26,771)
Pearson, Andrew 4:05:16 (12,475)
Pearson, Andrew J 4:06:52 (12,855)
Pearson, Anthony 3:49:50 (8,457)
Pearson, Brian 6:18:59 (30,988)
Pearson, Charles J 4:56:10 (24,240)
Pearson, Edward J 4:42:42 (21,493)
Pearson, Hugh A 3:39:46 (6,268)
Pearson, Mark R 3:40:38 (6,423)
Pearson, Matthew L 4:19:33 (15,921)
Pearson, Michael 3:09:16 (1,927)
Pearson, Philip 5:01:50 (25,278)
Pearson, Richard P 4:27:56 (18,074)
Pearson, Russell J 4:12:58 (14,321)
Pearson, Stephen R 3:22:31 (3,380)
Pearson, Toby 3:08:51 (1,883)
Pearson, Toby C 4:14:02 (14,576)
Peart, Clinton B 4:18:06 (15,574)
Peasgood, Andrew D 4:23:53 (17,034)
Peat, Geoff 3:35:05 (5,442)
Peat, Simon B 4:44:57 (22,020)
Peaty, Matt 3:30:44 (4,732)
Pebrett, Renato 3:34:04 (5,280)
Peck, Andrew M 4:12:50 (14,286)
Peck, David A 4:55:24 (24,084)
Peck, Graham 5:29:52 (28,571)
Peck, Ian J 5:04:14 (25,598)
Peck, Martin 3:26:49 (3,991)
Pecoraro, Antonio 2:54:59 (754)
Pecorella, Creste 4:52:18 (23,503)
Pedder, Alan C 4:37:08 (20,281)
Pedder, Malcolm J 3:12:02 (2,196)
Peddie, Alexander S 2:57:53 (954)
Pedersen, Egil T 4:49:31 (22,981)
Pedersen, Erling 4:48:22 (22,752)
Pedersen, Kenneth 5:25:48 (28,175)
Pedersen, Morten T 3:54:32 (9,648)
Pedlar, Charlie 3:01:07 (1,247)
Pedley, Robert S 5:32:57 (28,804)
Pedlow, Martin 3:20:50 (3,182)
Pedrick, Leslie 3:52:13 (9,061)
Pedro, Michael 4:34:52 (19,796)
Peel, Edward 4:43:13 (21,610)
Peel, Mike 3:46:51 (7,713)
Peers, Jonathan J 3:38:24 (6,032)
Peet, Andrew G 3:08:30 (1,850)
Peet, Michael 4:16:05 (15,072)
Peet, Robert J 3:35:57 (5,602)
Pegden, Jeffrey V 4:16:46 (15,242)
Pegg, Jonathan C 4:13:17 (14,399)
Pegram, Kevin J 3:43:50 (7,021)
Peleszok, Matthew J 4:38:51 (20,683)
Pelizza, Stefano 4:27:45 (18,026)
Pellegrino, Domenico 3:27:36 (4,144)
Pellegrino, Pietro 2:59:41 (1,133)
Pelley, Andy J 5:24:56 (28,075)
Pelley, Mark C 4:19:22 (15,874)
Pelling, Clifford J 3:55:23 (9,901)
Pellow, Mathew J 2:56:36 (858)
Pells, Colin G 3:53:56 (9,484)
Pemberton, Gareth J 3:10:43 (2,073)
Pemberton, Jack 5:25:57 (28,193)
Pemble, Colin I 3:08:45 (1,870)
Pena-Iglesias, Juan J 3:40:01 (6,306)
Pendle, David 3:36:09 (5,634)
Pendleton, Peter M 4:32:32 (19,245)
Pendrick, Graham R 3:29:16 (4,464)
Pendrill, Geoff R 3:58:06 (10,710)
Penfold, Daniel B 4:27:56 (18,074)
Penfold, Garry L 5:03:30 (25,520)
Penfold, Jon M 3:47:16 (7,822)
Penfold, Robert A 4:48:38 (22,801)
Pengelly, Adrian 3:51:02 (8,753)
Pengelly, Andrew 4:47:36 (22,591)
Pengelly, Andrew J 3:24:30 (3,625)
Pengelly, Gary P 4:28:28 (18,220)
Pengilley, Robert J 4:42:19 (21,418)
Penhale, Bruce 3:07:26 (1,742)
Penland, Peter R 4:16:47 (15,247)
Penn, Matthew W 5:15:34 (27,085)
Penn, Nicholas J 3:22:46 (3,416)
Penney, Andrew D 3:18:01 (2,850)
Penney, Simon 2:49:42 (486)
Pennicott, Derek J 3:39:51 (6,283)
Pennington, Brian 3:42:46 (6,803)
Pennington, Graham C 4:39:52 (20,886)
Pennington, Michael 3:40:25 (6,383)
Penniston, Alex J 4:09:52 (13,598)
Penniston, Chris 4:26:27 (17,684)
Penny, Andrew W 3:47:56 (7,982)
Penny, Nicholas M 3:14:05 (2,446)
Penny, Stephen R 5:01:34 (25,235)
Pennycook, Dave 4:47:07 (22,481)
Penprase, Jason M 4:23:01 (16,815)
Penry, Craig 6:13:44 (30,839)
Pensivy, Stephane 4:02:10 (11,769)
Penska, Richard 5:40:22 (29,364)
Pentecost, Beau 4:00:55 (11,483)
Penther, Martin 5:25:10 (28,104)
Pentin, Richard P 3:06:31 (1,655)
Pentith, Mark 5:04:55 (25,681)
Pentland, Bob 3:05:31 (1,573)
Pentzin, Viking 5:50:17 (29,979)
Penz, Ronald 4:03:28 (12,072)
Pepin, Nick 2:49:13 (468)
Pepper, Matthew J 5:23:06 (27,879)
Pepper, Peter R 5:46:16 (29,768)
Pepper, Richard M 4:53:25 (23,689)
Pepperrell, Mark J 4:54:49 (23,962)
Peralta, Paul C 4:59:06 (24,811)
Peraltha, Jorge 4:14:40 (14,721)
Perarnau Grau, Juan 4:41:13 (21,160)
Perchat, Denis 3:36:56 (5,756)
Percival, Keith 4:32:56 (19,343)
Percival, Martin E 3:18:52 (2,938)
Percival, Paul A 4:21:26 (16,373)
Percival, Richard 3:41:34 (6,553)
Percy, Robin J 4:24:19 (17,148)
Pereira, Gavin D 4:48:16 (22,731)
Pereira, Victor Manuel 3:07:41 (1,778)
Pereira Cerqueiro, Paulino 4:25:17 (17,379)
Peretti, Gianfranco 3:24:36 (3,636)
Perez, Manuel A 3:33:17 (5,156)
Perfect, Andrew 3:03:47 (1,430)
Perham, Simon E 3:06:45 (1,677)
Perkin, Simon L 3:44:07 (7,097)
Perkins, Andrew F 4:07:13 (12,945)
Perkins, David 4:08:43 (13,298)
Perkins, John D 4:41:12 (21,157)
Perkins, John E 4:36:53 (20,223)
Perkins, Martyn 3:16:13 (2,663)
Perkins, Scott J 5:09:21 (26,285)
Perkins, Tony H 6:49:49 (31,497)
Perks, David R 5:43:34 (29,597)
Perman, Tim 4:35:23 (19,905)
Peron, Alain 5:00:50 (25,121)
Perot, Neil S 5:11:06 (26,517)
Perren, Peter J 5:22:03 (27,777)
Perrier, Ludovic 3:32:28 (4,998)
Perrier, Raymond A 4:05:42 (12,595)
Perrig, Jean-Christophe 3:26:40 (3,946)
Perrin, Stephen R 2:55:36 (792)
Perris, Richard H 4:08:09 (13,146)
Perry, Andrew 3:52:02 (9,021)
Perry, Bryan W 4:59:18 (24,849)
Perry, Christopher E 4:19:19 (15,860)
Perry, Christopher M 3:29:23 (4,482)
Perry, David 3:30:39 (4,718)
Perry, David N 3:42:37 (6,769)
Perry, Ian D 4:24:04 (17,076)
Perry, Kevin C 3:15:33 (2,600)
Perry, Mark R 5:03:37 (25,534)
Perry, Matt L 3:06:39 (1,669)
Perry, Simon D 4:58:23 (24,687)
Perry, Stephen 3:09:26 (1,940)
Perry, Steve 4:02:00 (11,717)
Persch, Peter Roman 2:58:55 (1,067)
Pescott, Kiley J 3:30:20 (4,661)
Pesquero, Gary D 3:05:40 (1,580)
Petch, Christopher J 3:16:52 (2,735)
Petek, Werner 3:12:25 (2,242)
Peter, Christopher F 3:56:14 (10,161)
Peter, Edwin 4:54:02 (23,800)
Peterges, Udo 2:54:15 (705)

Peterka, Gerhard J 4:03:19 (12,036)
Peters, Edward G....................3:56:13 (10,148)
Peters, Jason I....................4:23:58 (17,053)
Peters, Mark A....................3:44:29 (7,181)
Peters, Martin....................4:42:17 (21,408)
Peters, Rich M....................4:13:34 (14,471)
Peters, Sam W....................3:49:36 (8,403)
Peters, Winfried....................3:37:05 (5,793)
Peterson, Gene C....................4:50:30 (23,179)
Petignat, Romain J....................4:15:46 (14,993)
Petit, Jeremy R....................5:22:08 (27,785)
Petite, Joseph M....................4:19:04 (15,792)
Petitgenet, Michael....................2:54:04 (697)
Petrazzini, Giuseppe....................4:16:46 (15,242)
Petreni, Enzo G....................5:05:54 (25,823)
Petrides, John G....................5:52:32 (30,098)
Petrie, James C....................5:46:39 (29,798)
Petrie, Trevor C....................6:03:47 (30,559)
Petrou, Peter....................4:52:57 (23,606)
Petrovic, Darko....................4:15:10 (14,850)
Pettengell, Geoff R....................4:28:43 (18,281)
Petters, William C....................5:04:18 (25,602)
Pettersen, Morten....................4:59:37 (24,923)
Pettersson, Torbjorn....................4:04:42 (12,351)
Pettifer, Robert M....................4:17:39 (15,470)
Pettifor, Jon A....................3:43:05 (6,868)
Pettit, Neil....................3:53:07 (9,287)
Pettitt, Alan....................3:55:04 (9,811)
Pettitt, Martin J....................4:29:58 (18,624)
Pettitt, Martin J....................4:57:45 (24,545)
Pettitt, Nigel M....................3:41:50 (6,612)
Pettitt, Tim....................3:53:49 (9,448)
Petts, Phil J....................5:38:11 (29,195)
Petty, Adrian A....................4:09:14 (13,432)
Petty, Christopher A....................3:55:44 (10,001)
Petty, Richard J....................2:43:03 (267)
Petty-Mayor, Mark E....................3:36:01 (5,614)
Pewer, Michael....................4:09:02 (13,386)
Pez, Frank L....................5:29:49 (28,569)
Pfaff, Marcus....................3:44:04 (7,090)
Pfeiffer, Andrew....................3:22:08 (3,321)
Pfeiffer, Michael J....................5:48:38 (29,890)
Pflanz, Tobias....................5:13:38 (26,849)
Phan Van Phi, Pierre....................4:14:54 (14,786)
Pharaoh, Keith I....................4:41:15 (21,169)
Pharoah, Peter....................3:39:06 (6,148)
Phee, William....................5:27:09 (28,319)
Phelan, Chris....................2:54:05 (699)
Phelan, Declan R....................3:20:33 (3,140)
Phelan, Stephen....................4:19:25 (15,887)
Phelps, Brian J....................3:30:16 (4,647)
Phelps, Mark A....................3:38:16 (6,006)
Phelps, Stephen E....................3:56:19 (10,183)
Phenis, Wayne P....................3:56:30 (10,250)
Phibbs, James M....................3:21:51 (3,295)
Philip, Jacques....................3:51:58 (9,006)
Philip, John D....................3:39:33 (6,224)
Philippe, Jean-François....................3:10:23 (2,037)
Philippides, Philip....................3:48:27 (8,106)
Philips, John D....................4:12:29 (14,194)
Phillips, Andrew....................2:52:22 (607)
Phillips, Andrew....................4:24:46 (17,243)
Phillips, Andrew B....................5:22:57 (27,869)
Phillips, Andrew M....................3:52:06 (9,036)
Phillips, Andy D....................3:51:16 (8,824)
Phillips, Anthony J....................4:48:43 (22,824)
Phillips, Anthony P....................3:38:50 (6,105)
Phillips, Ben....................4:43:30 (21,685)
Phillips, Ben J....................4:02:13 (11,786)
Phillips, Charles....................3:55:30 (9,929)
Phillips, Chris L....................4:03:08 (11,990)
Phillips, Chris M....................4:34:58 (19,813)
Phillips, Daniel....................3:59:57 (11,280)
Phillips, Darren....................4:55:29 (24,097)
Phillips, David H....................3:54:44 (9,704)
Phillips, David M....................4:47:12 (22,499)
Phillips, David R....................3:57:25 (10,516)
Phillips, David S....................3:53:35 (9,398)
Phillips, Dean R....................4:23:29 (16,937)
Phillips, Don G....................6:20:11 (31,017)
Phillips, Duncan C....................5:44:06 (29,631)
Phillips, Gary V....................3:57:25 (10,516)
Phillips, George W....................5:26:52 (28,287)
Phillips, Hamish D....................4:43:27 (21,673)
Phillips, James E....................4:37:51 (20,416)
Phillips, James H....................4:50:52 (23,246)
Phillips, Jesse B....................3:37:39 (5,899)
Phillips, John N....................4:20:25 (16,136)
Phillips, Jonathan R....................5:46:26 (29,781)
Phillips, Jonny....................3:42:00 (6,646)
Phillips, Leonard J....................3:52:59 (9,252)
Phillips, Mark....................3:40:21 (6,368)
Phillips, Martin C....................3:45:22 (7,378)
Phillips, Matthew N....................6:22:12 (31,064)
Phillips, Mervyn R....................3:21:57 (3,302)
Phillips, Michael H....................5:53:21 (30,133)
Phillips, Monty J....................3:19:10 (2,975)
Phillips, Nicholas....................4:54:05 (23,812)
Phillips, Nicholas D....................5:50:16 (29,978)
Phillips, Nick A....................3:34:43 (5,371)
Phillips, Patrick J....................3:28:42 (4,353)
Phillips, Paul....................4:19:36 (15,929)
Phillips, Paul....................4:23:26 (16,929)
Phillips, Paul D....................4:08:19 (13,183)
Phillips, Peter....................4:12:12 (14,133)
Phillips, Rhodri M....................3:46:09 (7,559)
Phillips, Richard J....................3:22:46 (3,416)
Phillips, Robert A....................5:27:29 (28,354)
Phillips, Robert K....................3:19:11 (2,980)
Phillips, Roger....................4:19:19 (15,860)
Phillips, Simon A....................5:17:16 (27,281)
Phillips, Simon C....................4:26:49 (17,777)
Phillips, Simon E....................6:49:23 (31,491)
Phillips, Simon R....................3:50:06 (8,528)
Phillips, Stephen M....................4:08:42 (13,291)
Phillips, Steve J....................3:28:03 (4,234)
Phillips, Steven J....................5:44:42 (29,669)
Phillips, Steven N....................6:22:12 (31,064)
Phillips, Stuart E....................3:40:53 (6,451)
Phillips, Toby L....................4:03:29 (12,075)
Phillipson, Jamie....................4:53:13 (23,656)
Phillis, Jason M....................4:29:08 (18,389)
Phillis, Richard G....................3:47:00 (7,751)
Phillpot, Timothy S....................4:17:30 (15,423)
Philoux, Albert....................3:32:35 (5,024)
Philp, Andrew J....................3:55:22 (9,897)
Philp, Russell P....................3:56:25 (10,222)
Philp, Stephen....................3:59:58 (11,284)
Philpot, Saul T....................4:14:52 (14,779)
Philpott, Andy J....................4:31:41 (19,022)
Philpott, Ian G....................5:21:45 (27,753)
Philpott, John C....................2:58:09 (982)
Philpotts, Dennis L....................4:35:59 (20,025)
Phipps, Andrew J....................3:45:07 (7,322)
Phipps, Kevin M....................4:15:45 (14,988)
Phipps, Patrick....................3:56:35 (10,274)
Phipson, Peter....................3:48:43 (8,189)
Phoenix, Mike....................4:38:13 (20,524)
Phoenix, Tobias J....................4:26:51 (17,785)
Pichler, Cletus....................4:37:14 (20,304)
Pichler, Johann....................3:39:30 (6,216)
Pick, Robert M....................3:20:27 (3,115)
Pickard, Michael L....................5:52:03 (30,067)
Picker, Christian D....................2:57:51 (949)
Picker, Martin N....................3:40:43 (6,433)
Pickering, David C....................2:54:25 (715)
Pickering, David C....................4:18:26 (15,647)
Pickering, Deano R....................4:03:07 (11,983)
Pickering, Derrick J....................5:10:40 (26,462)
Pickering, Richard....................3:10:54 (2,090)
Pickering, Steven....................3:14:34 (2,511)
Pickett, Brian W....................5:26:39 (28,266)
Pickett, Ian A....................3:40:33 (6,411)
Pickett, Ian J....................5:11:43 (26,592)
Pickford, Stuart....................3:55:47 (10,013)
Pickles, John S....................3:57:09 (10,433)
Pickthall, Chris....................4:32:49 (19,314)
Pickthall, Stephen R....................3:48:32 (8,129)
Pickton, Barry J....................5:33:37 (28,860)
Pickup, Jeffrey....................3:12:27 (2,246)
Pickup, Mark G....................5:11:44 (26,596)
Pickup, Richard....................3:56:10 (10,128)
Picot, Michael J....................4:24:22 (17,156)
Picou, Jean-Pierre....................3:23:51 (3,551)
Picton, Nicholas W....................5:14:56 (27,020)
Pierce, James....................5:14:51 (27,011)
Piercy, Desmond....................3:40:02 (6,309)
Piercy, Neil R....................4:29:31 (18,499)
Pierini, Piero....................4:20:17 (16,095)
Pierpoint, Richard....................4:43:52 (21,766)
Piersall, Anthony C....................4:41:05 (21,139)
Pierson, Edward G....................3:55:44 (10,001)
Pietquin, Jean-Jierre....................4:18:46 (15,728)
Piggott, Adrian....................4:12:06 (14,115)
Piggott, Richard T....................3:00:16 (1,175)
Pigott-Smith, Tom E....................4:29:52 (18,599)
Pihl, Johan....................3:46:49 (7,707)
Pike, Andrew R....................3:17:07 (2,762)
Pike, Andrew S....................5:56:14 (30,259)
Pike, Damian J....................4:08:32 (13,239)
Pike, Daniel P....................4:16:20 (15,126)
Pike, David....................2:58:07 (980)
Pike, David....................3:56:36 (10,280)
Pike, David J....................3:40:53 (6,451)
Pike, Graham J....................4:13:46 (14,508)
Pike, John....................4:27:47 (18,036)
Pike, Jon E....................3:05:05 (1,533)
Pike, Jonathan C....................4:51:52 (23,414)
Pike, Martyn....................5:06:19 (25,890)
Pike, Will....................4:31:33 (18,990)
Pilch, Richard....................3:57:51 (10,632)
Pilcher, Ian M....................4:16:23 (15,142)
Pilcher, Martin E....................5:15:45 (27,100)
Pile, Ian J....................3:43:17 (6,914)
Pilette, Alain....................4:25:43 (17,481)
Pilfold, Mike E....................5:24:53 (28,065)
Pilkington, Mark....................4:05:09 (12,456)
Pilkington, Michael S....................5:14:02 (26,906)
Pill, Stephen J....................3:03:22 (1,396)
Pillar, David A....................4:06:47 (12,834)
Piller, Clive R....................4:29:30 (18,492)
Pilley, Daniel M....................5:26:13 (28,212)
Pilling, Kristian J....................4:04:31 (12,318)
Pilling, Mark....................4:18:55 (15,764)
Pilling, Paul M....................3:47:59 (7,991)
Pillinger, Gregory S....................4:25:08 (17,347)
Pimm, Christopher....................4:39:42 (20,862)
Pinches, Joss....................3:07:15 (1,722)
Pinder, David A....................3:44:59 (7,305)
Pinder, George....................3:27:01 (4,027)
Pine, Roger S....................3:24:18 (3,603)
Pinel, Damian J....................4:41:15 (21,169)
Pinhal, Alfredo....................4:14:24 (14,652)
Pink, Jonathan A....................4:37:06 (20,274)
Pink, Robert L....................4:28:35 (18,251)
Pink, Simon J....................3:57:17 (10,473)
Pinkerton, Andrew....................5:51:44 (30,047)
Pinkerton, Andrew R....................4:26:23 (17,672)
Pinkham, Matthew R....................5:14:34 (26,971)
Pinkham, Zachary J....................4:55:48 (24,151)
Pinkney, Rupert A....................4:38:39 (20,627)
Pinna, Pietro....................2:35:53 (133)
Pinner, Mark J....................4:30:27 (18,745)
Pinnick, David....................4:07:40 (13,048)
Pinniger, Anthony R....................4:25:53 (17,536)
Pinson, Anthony W....................4:57:47 (24,551)
Piotrowski, Henryk B....................2:46:41 (377)
Piotrowski, Martek....................3:49:21 (8,338)
Piovanacci, Daniel J....................3:37:37 (5,895)
Piovesana, Martin....................3:56:02 (10,094)
Piper, Chris....................2:59:03 (1,077)
Piper, Christopher C....................3:53:03 (9,270)
Piper, Christopher J....................5:24:13 (27,994)
Piper, Colin....................3:53:17 (9,335)
Piper, Daniel F....................5:24:24 (28,015)
Piper, David J....................4:18:51 (15,751)
Piper, Harold N....................4:51:45 (23,392)
Piper, Jon....................4:54:44 (23,947)
Piper, Laurence J....................4:42:35 (21,470)
Pippard, David A....................4:06:26 (12,767)
Pires, Artur F....................2:53:45 (679)
Pires, Daniel L....................3:48:40 (8,176)
Pires, Luis S....................3:12:48 (2,286)
Pirozzolo, Mario G....................4:44:59 (22,029)
Pitchell, Ian....................3:37:52 (5,934)
Pitcher, Albert G....................5:36:38 (29,074)
Pitcher, Derek G....................3:07:26 (1,742)
Pitcher, Gordon....................4:50:53 (23,249)
Piterzak, John....................4:23:38 (16,971)

Pitkin, Brian H	4:05:06 (12,448)	
Pitman, Michael	3:30:47 (4,738)	
Pitman, Stuart E	4:56:44 (24,349)	
Pitt, Alexander J	3:28:10 (4,256)	
Pitt, Alexander J	7:24:27 (31,803)	
Pitt, Clement D	4:44:40 (21,952)	
Pitt, Darren K	5:45:11 (29,704)	
Pitt, Edmund	4:33:43 (19,508)	
Pitt, Graham J	3:58:52 (10,963)	
Pitt, Richard W	2:53:16 (660)	
Pitt, Stephen C	4:31:54 (19,080)	
Pitt, Stewart	3:57:44 (10,600)	
Pittaway, Ian J	3:40:02 (6,309)	
Pittet, Dominique	2:57:27 (914)	
Pittilloni, Dominique	3:32:06 (4,938)	
Pitts, Malcolm N	4:54:03 (23,806)	
Pitts, Robert E	4:27:08 (17,874)	
Pitts, Simon M	3:37:02 (5,776)	
Pitts, Stephen	4:02:05 (11,739)	
Pixberg, Martin	3:33:12 (5,136)	
Pizzato, Reny	4:02:13 (11,786)	
Place, Kevin B	4:22:56 (16,802)	
Planner, Donald	5:59:51 (30,404)	
Plant, Gareth A	3:06:25 (1,648)	
Plant, James K	5:13:18 (26,805)	
Plant, Nathan J	4:11:39 (14,015)	
Plant, Stephen P	4:23:35 (16,963)	
Planton, Serge	2:43:31 (278)	
Platt, David	5:34:15 (28,908)	
Platt, David N	4:23:47 (17,013)	
Platt, Gary A	3:38:28 (6,042)	
Platt, Geoffrey A	5:17:14 (27,278)	
Platt, Nigel	4:18:45 (15,723)	
Platt, Raymond E	4:06:07 (12,693)	
Platt, Robert	4:03:46 (12,140)	
Platt, Terry M	3:47:56 (7,982)	
Platte, David M	3:51:12 (8,806)	
Platts, Rob	2:54:33 (722)	
Playdon, Vincent	3:59:47 (11,236)	
Player, Mark R	4:23:02 (16,820)	
Playford-Smith, Terry	4:52:37 (23,553)	
Playle, Spencer J	4:19:23 (15,878)	
Plaza, Luis A	5:17:51 (27,346)	
Plaza Lastras, Pablo	2:47:43 (410)	
Pleasance, Neal G	4:15:51 (15,015)	
Pledger, Shane A	4:30:32 (18,767)	
Plews, Andrew	3:59:15 (11,070)	
Plimmer, Peter S	3:21:32 (3,261)	
Plimsaul, Ray G	5:38:08 (29,191)	
Plint, Michael J	2:58:21 (999)	
Ploner, Luigi	3:40:27 (6,388)	
Plowman, Dean	4:21:19 (16,337)	
Plowman, Ian A	5:16:57 (27,251)	
Plowman, Peter F	3:13:21 (2,350)	
Plowman, Robin	4:32:08 (19,146)	
Pluck, Mark	3:11:09 (2,107)	
Plumb, Steven J	4:22:46 (16,764)	
Plumbly, Greg M	4:05:30 (12,539)	
Plummer, Alan E	3:51:18 (8,834)	
Plummer, Martin	5:07:33 (26,050)	
Plump, Brent	3:52:49 (9,204)	
Plumridge, Maurice J	3:30:54 (4,761)	
Plumstead, Pat	3:01:57 (1,297)	
Plumstead, Stephen M	3:31:10 (4,801)	
Plunkett, Mark D	3:48:49 (8,219)	
Pocock, Andrew	4:41:01 (21,126)	
Pocock, Frank	3:43:40 (6,992)	
Pocock, Jeremy D	4:32:38 (19,273)	
Pocock, John W	3:22:10 (3,324)	
Pocock, Martin	4:07:36 (13,034)	
Pocock, Victor J	4:28:54 (18,327)	
Podbery, Adrian	3:19:52 (3,056)	
Poeham, Nikolaus	4:05:28 (12,529)	
Poelman, Antonius	3:19:50 (3,050)	
Poels, Martien	4:38:32 (20,603)	
Poesinger, Edwin	4:06:16 (12,727)	
Poeting, Klaus	4:09:22 (13,466)	
Pogoriutschnig, Walter	3:11:36 (2,149)	
Pohl, Dieter	4:48:13 (22,723)	
Pohling, Andreas	4:06:49 (12,842)	
Pohling, Ulf	4:13:06 (14,352)	
Poingdestre, Marc J	4:24:04 (17,076)	
Pointer, Daniel M	4:41:56 (21,332)	
Pointing, Andrew R	3:44:33 (7,201)	
Poiret, Pierre	4:00:49 (11,449)	
Pokolski, Lee A	4:27:49 (18,044)	
Pol, Chrisjan	4:55:04 (24,007)	
Polaine, Neal	4:05:21 (12,498)	
Polden, Robert J	4:04:55 (12,411)	
Pole, Christopher P	5:45:50 (29,743)	
Pole-Baker, Michael J	5:02:28 (25,367)	
Poli, Roberto	3:26:19 (3,892)	
Politi, Domenico	3:32:58 (5,092)	
Poljanc, Hannes	3:36:17 (5,658)	
Pollard, Andrew B	5:08:12 (26,143)	
Pollard, Glenn A	5:14:50 (27,007)	
Pollard, Ian F	3:04:54 (1,514)	
Pollard, James A	4:07:13 (12,945)	
Pollard, Michael G	5:24:53 (28,065)	
Pollard, Philip M	3:48:50 (8,222)	
Pollard, Simon R	4:52:14 (23,491)	
Pollen, Richard J	3:35:47 (5,569)	
Pollen, Samuel	5:05:00 (25,693)	
Polley, Ian R	4:47:07 (22,481)	
Polley, Keith A	4:42:54 (21,541)	
Pollias, Nikolaos	2:15:02 (17)	
Pollington, Graham B	4:32:49 (19,314)	
Pollington, Sebastian T	4:45:40 (22,182)	
Pollitt, Richard J	3:59:36 (11,188)	
Pollock, Andrew J	4:58:16 (24,659)	
Pollock, Austin G	4:33:27 (19,457)	
Pollock, David J	3:25:07 (3,707)	
Pollock, Robert A	3:03:18 (1,389)	
Pollock, William	5:19:42 (27,523)	
Polsinelli, Carmine	3:02:20 (1,329)	
Polzer, Harald	4:44:53 (21,995)	
Pomario, Sean R	3:47:49 (7,950)	
Pomerance, Alex R	4:29:59 (18,626)	
Pomeroy, Richard T	3:41:58 (6,639)	
Pomfret, Robert M	3:53:31 (9,380)	
Pomfret, Sean J	4:56:45 (24,352)	
Pomposo-Galbarriartu, Pedro	3:25:22 (3,744)	
Pomroy, Jonaathan A	4:22:18 (16,637)	
Pond, Chris	4:17:13 (15,351)	
Pond, Christopher M	3:48:03 (8,008)	
Pond, Jeff	3:51:03 (8,755)	
Ponder, William A	3:31:57 (4,916)	
Poneskis, John	5:50:09 (29,973)	
Ponnau, Mikael	3:09:56 (1,996)	
Ponsford, Henry J	3:42:18 (6,699)	
Pool, Robert C	5:14:01 (26,904)	
Poole, Alan D	4:18:29 (15,661)	
Poole, Brian C	3:53:16 (9,329)	
Poole, David J	4:00:30 (11,399)	
Poole, David N	3:39:39 (6,244)	
Poole, Derek J	3:21:42 (3,276)	
Poole, Mark R	4:20:16 (16,085)	
Poole, Robert W	4:14:22 (14,641)	
Poole, Stephen M	3:10:24 (2,043)	
Poole-Wilson, William	4:57:14 (24,447)	
Popadynec, Max	5:12:29 (26,690)	
Pope, Alan G	3:31:53 (4,898)	
Pope, Andrew J	4:49:07 (22,898)	
Pope, Charles A	3:28:54 (4,400)	
Pope, Christopher S	4:08:35 (13,256)	
Pope, Duane	5:59:14 (30,375)	
Pope, Graham M	5:14:02 (26,906)	
Pope, Mark E	3:26:23 (3,902)	
Pope, Richard M	3:53:36 (9,401)	
Pope, Robert J	3:42:33 (6,754)	
Pope, Roger	5:57:14 (30,296)	
Pope, Stephen A	2:45:35 (346)	
Popham, Andrew H	3:49:40 (8,416)	
Popov, Mikhail	3:00:16 (1,175)	
Popper, David G	5:04:52 (25,672)	
Popplestone, Alan	3:21:16 (3,227)	
Popplewell, Alex H	4:45:02 (22,040)	
Porcer, Gregory G	4:41:28 (21,236)	
Pors, Berg	4:06:48 (12,836)	
Porte, David	5:56:05 (30,252)	
Porteous, Andrew	2:47:52 (416)	
Porteous, Henry J	3:12:02 (2,196)	
Porter, Alex J	3:30:32 (4,697)	
Porter, Barry	4:07:04 (12,911)	
Porter, Danny M	4:35:10 (19,858)	
Porter, Graham	4:00:46 (11,439)	
Porter, John	5:39:50 (29,322)	
Porter, Keith D	4:43:40 (21,714)	
Porter, Patrick W	4:01:54 (11,688)	
Porter, Roger	3:03:55 (1,443)	
Porter, Sean J	4:29:14 (18,410)	
Porter, Simon	5:08:53 (26,219)	
Portier, Pascal	4:00:51 (11,461)	
Portmann, Damien	3:42:41 (6,785)	
Porto, Edjon D	3:37:33 (5,879)	
Porto, Santiago	3:02:56 (1,363)	
Portsmouth, Barry R	4:28:03 (18,107)	
Portus, James O	4:56:48 (24,361)	
Posgate, David A	4:11:27 (13,959)	
Poskitt, Matthew R	3:48:35 (8,144)	
Possing, Romain	2:40:08 (213)	
Possnett, Jason P	5:51:01 (30,016)	
Posso, Carlos A	4:54:57 (23,987)	
Postlethwaite, Alan V	3:06:39 (1,669)	
Poston, John	5:46:05 (29,753)	
Potelle, Michel	3:20:02 (3,071)	
Potter, Alan W	4:09:33 (13,512)	
Potter, Andrew V	3:56:28 (10,241)	
Potter, David	3:33:05 (5,112)	
Potter, David L	3:19:09 (2,972)	
Potter, Francis C	4:49:45 (23,027)	
Potter, Ian D	3:46:25 (7,624)	
Potter, Jonathan I	4:24:31 (17,188)	
Potter, Malcolm	4:40:09 (20,951)	
Potter, Martin R	5:23:37 (27,936)	
Potter, Michael	4:35:02 (19,828)	
Potter, Michael J	4:45:03 (22,045)	
Potter, Nicholas	4:13:49 (14,521)	
Potter, Richard G	4:20:50 (16,235)	
Potter, Robert	4:44:27 (21,899)	
Potter, Stephen D	4:17:31 (15,429)	
Potter, Vincent F	4:26:37 (17,730)	
Pottinger, Gavin J	4:59:38 (24,925)	
Potts, Colin I	2:56:18 (838)	
Potts, Jeff R	5:06:34 (25,920)	
Potts, Jonathan R	4:52:01 (23,447)	
Potts, Martin O	4:12:43 (14,270)	
Potts, Paul L	4:20:08 (16,053)	
Potts, Tony	4:56:43 (24,346)	
Poulain, Guy	3:37:36 (5,890)	
Poulier, Sean S	4:55:08 (24,022)	
Poulin, Frederic	4:10:49 (13,830)	
Pouls, Mathieu	5:05:07 (25,705)	
Poulsom, Thomas J	4:27:02 (17,853)	
Poulson, Michael W	4:24:52 (17,274)	
Poulter, Chris	5:00:36 (25,076)	
Poulton, Stephen J	5:12:48 (26,731)	
Poulton, Zachary N	3:54:26 (9,622)	
Pound, Stephen	5:00:54 (25,127)	
Pounder, Michael J	2:40:45 (223)	
Pounder, Nick J	3:42:39 (6,775)	
Pounder, Ron	3:57:48 (10,618)	
Pountain-Holes, Tim P	3:51:27 (8,875)	
Poutout, Philippe	2:58:19 (997)	
Powell, Adam C	3:55:13 (9,854)	
Powell, Adrian D	3:13:54 (2,424)	
Powell, Andrew L	3:50:25 (8,611)	
Powell, Christopher C	5:09:55 (26,368)	
Powell, Danny R	4:49:23 (22,958)	
Powell, Derren J	5:23:32 (27,929)	
Powell, Dorian A	5:27:20 (28,344)	
Powell, Eliot J	3:25:02 (3,698)	
Powell, Ian J	4:08:34 (13,252)	
Powell, Jason D	3:29:48 (4,553)	
Powell, Jeremy S	5:00:02 (24,995)	
Powell, John	4:49:38 (23,004)	
Powell, John E	4:45:55 (22,232)	
Powell, Jonathan M	4:17:06 (15,327)	
Powell, Jonathan R	5:18:11 (27,391)	
Powell, Mark	4:12:16 (14,142)	
Powell, Martin J	2:49:11 (467)	
Powell, Paul	3:59:20 (11,096)	
Powell, Ray A	3:35:19 (5,487)	
Powell, Richard A	5:07:24 (26,028)	
Powell, Richard W	5:13:40 (26,851)	
Powell, Scott J	5:34:12 (28,903)	
Powell, Stephan J	3:25:11 (3,718)	
Powell, Stephen M	3:55:08 (9,831)	
Powell, Steven	4:48:33 (22,783)	

Powell, Steven G	3:06:51 (1,692)
Power, Andy J	2:56:02 (812)
Power, Henry C	4:32:50 (19,319)
Power, Niall T	4:52:13 (23,488)
Power, Richard	4:03:30 (12,078)
Power, Robert	3:58:07 (10,715)
Power, Sean T	4:52:05 (23,461)
Power, Simon	3:55:37 (9,966)
Power, Tony	4:34:43 (19,761)
Powers, Gary R	4:10:33 (13,770)
Powis, Gary M	4:51:20 (23,323)
Powling, Mark	4:29:41 (18,550)
Pownall, Paul D	4:37:38 (20,370)
Powrie, Duncan J	5:07:08 (25,987)
Powys, Rhys	4:18:28 (15,659)
Poyser, Andrew R	4:07:48 (13,069)
Pozo, Anton R	4:17:07 (15,334)
Pozza, Vinicio	3:07:17 (1,726)
Praastrup, Leif	3:40:21 (6,368)
Prabhakar, Sajiv	5:32:57 (28,804)
Praher, Peter	3:49:09 (8,297)
Prat, Robert	4:00:06 (11,316)
Prathalingam, Nilendran S	3:07:44 (1,781)
Pratt, Alan J	3:51:15 (8,819)
Pratt, Ben T	3:57:33 (10,555)
Pratt, David	3:51:09 (8,781)
Pratt, Garry T	5:05:28 (25,751)
Pratt, Kevin M	4:07:11 (12,936)
Pratten, Benjamin C	4:51:52 (23,414)
Pre, Mickael	3:42:21 (6,709)
Preater, Adrian C	5:22:12 (27,793)
Prebble, John	3:41:41 (6,580)
Precchiazzi, Matteo	2:54:33 (722)
Precious, John N	3:47:53 (7,969)
Precious, Stephen M	3:45:00 (7,309)
Preece, Brian	5:12:24 (26,680)
Preece, David J	3:14:55 (2,549)
Preece, Richard J	4:00:55 (11,483)
Preedy, Daniel T	4:51:43 (23,385)
Prendergast, Thomas F	3:50:39 (8,671)
Prentis, Charlie P	3:24:52 (3,672)
Prescott, Marcus J	5:06:32 (25,914)
Prescott, Robert	5:56:56 (30,285)
Press, James	3:08:40 (1,864)
Preston, Adrian P	3:20:08 (3,082)
Preston, Andrew N	3:20:10 (3,086)
Preston, Bamber R	3:15:41 (2,620)
Preston, David N	3:59:26 (11,121)
Preston, Gareth J	2:59:18 (1,102)
Preston, Garry D	4:42:22 (21,429)
Preston, Gary M	3:41:56 (6,627)
Preston, Graham R	4:15:01 (14,808)
Preston, Jim E	4:12:40 (14,254)
Preston, Joe M	4:14:51 (14,773)
Preston, Kevin	3:44:00 (7,071)
Preston, Kevin B	5:11:14 (26,547)
Preston, Leigh P	4:30:10 (18,672)
Preston, Marc A	5:05:48 (25,804)
Preston, Mark A	3:48:31 (8,124)
Preston, Mark S	4:01:36 (11,622)
Preston, Martin G	4:46:12 (22,296)
Preston, Paul	3:29:36 (4,518)
Preston, Robert J	4:56:25 (24,283)
Preston, Ross	4:48:48 (22,838)
Preston, Stephen	3:16:07 (2,655)
Preston, Terry	3:47:07 (7,784)
Prestwood, Mark A	2:36:59 (153)
Pretorius, Carel	5:40:27 (29,376)
Prevost, Alain	2:46:26 (369)
Prevost, Ivan J	4:58:20 (24,672)
Prevost, Jason	4:12:31 (14,208)
Price, Aaron P	4:40:43 (21,068)
Price, Andrew J	3:51:40 (8,930)
Price, Benjamin D	3:48:12 (8,047)
Price, Brian S	4:30:34 (18,773)
Price, Colin	4:10:35 (13,774)
Price, Colin A	5:16:31 (27,192)
Price, Colin M	4:11:08 (13,897)
Price, Darren E	4:06:32 (12,784)
Price, Dave J	3:03:54 (1,442)
Price, David A	3:48:30 (8,118)
Price, David P	4:23:56 (17,046)
Price, David W	5:17:27 (27,299)

Price, Gareth	4:46:53 (22,421)
Price, Gareth D	4:08:37 (13,261)
Price, George	5:28:35 (28,448)
Price, Glyn D	4:01:24 (11,579)
Price, Howard P	3:15:57 (2,643)
Price, Ian	2:59:04 (1,078)
Price, Ian M	3:09:11 (1,915)
Price, Ian R	3:09:59 (1,999)
Price, James	3:04:40 (1,504)
Price, Jamie	4:07:00 (12,891)
Price, Jason M	4:33:25 (19,452)
Price, Jeremy C	4:52:01 (23,447)
Price, Jeremy P	4:49:12 (22,918)
Price, Jim R	4:30:35 (18,777)
Price, Jonathan	4:06:56 (12,871)
Price, Jonathan	5:41:05 (29,413)
Price, Kenneth J	4:59:20 (24,858)
Price, Kingsley R	4:36:18 (20,088)
Price, Luke J	4:22:39 (16,737)
Price, Lynn	4:30:25 (18,736)
Price, Malcolm	3:45:56 (7,514)
Price, Mark S	4:18:32 (15,670)
Price, Martin D	4:54:56 (23,985)
Price, Martin R	3:31:55 (4,907)
Price, Neil J	4:01:17 (11,559)
Price, Nicholas H	4:46:35 (22,371)
Price, Paul E	5:41:05 (29,413)
Price, Paul T	3:24:59 (3,691)
Price, Richard P	3:56:48 (10,330)
Price, Robert A	6:10:06 (30,731)
Price, Rodger	4:29:35 (18,517)
Price, Rodney G	4:06:36 (12,807)
Price, Scott A	4:51:51 (23,408)
Price, Sean C	3:49:07 (8,286)
Price, Simon H	5:10:20 (26,418)
Price, Simon J	5:00:28 (25,060)
Price, Stephen	5:47:33 (29,843)
Price, Stephen J	2:59:20 (1,105)
Price, Stephen J	4:42:42 (21,493)
Price, Tim G	4:01:44 (11,656)
Price, Timothy C	4:27:13 (17,897)
Price Stephens, David G	2:53:47 (680)
Prideaux, Ian R	4:20:50 (16,235)
Prieels, Frank R	4:34:28 (19,704)
Priekulis, Bernie	3:13:15 (2,334)
Prieler, Albrecht	2:58:36 (1,026)
Priest, Andrew C	3:51:28 (8,879)
Priestley, Andrew P	4:29:48 (18,583)
Priestley, Jamie J	3:40:03 (6,317)
Priestley, Spencer D	3:49:45 (8,437)
Prieto, José	2:56:47 (869)
Prifti, Andrew J	3:46:44 (7,686)
Prigg, James R	4:34:41 (19,753)
Primas, Christian	2:43:37 (281)
Primavesi, Adrian J	3:22:45 (3,410)
Prime, David	4:16:49 (15,259)
Primrose, Noel	3:48:11 (8,044)
Prin, Jean-Louis	4:12:33 (14,218)
Prince, Colin J	4:45:17 (22,095)
Pringle, Andrew A	3:16:37 (2,712)
Pringle, Kevin A	4:06:32 (12,784)
Pringle, Lee P	3:47:01 (7,756)
Pringle, Robert	4:06:21 (12,748)
Prior, Stephen	4:28:44 (18,288)
Prior, Tony	4:34:58 (19,813)
Prisk, James S	5:09:23 (26,292)
Priston, Andrew P	3:51:35 (8,913)
Pritchard, Andrew J	3:30:31 (4,692)
Pritchard, David	5:55:55 (30,240)
Pritchard, Gary D	5:54:33 (30,173)
Pritchard, Ian G	5:21:11 (27,698)
Pritchard, James	3:22:41 (3,401)
Pritchard, Jim A	4:24:29 (17,180)
Pritchard, John R	3:53:52 (9,469)
Pritchard, Mark	3:48:31 (8,124)
Pritchard, Mark	3:54:31 (9,641)
Pritchard, Matt P	3:06:38 (1,666)
Pritchard, Peter J	6:00:11 (30,420)
Pritchard, Rory T	3:11:18 (2,126)
Pritchard, Simon G	3:05:56 (1,603)
Pritchett, Michael D	5:09:21 (26,285)
Probert, Simon J	3:19:22 (3,001)
Probst, Tom R	4:38:59 (20,721)

Procter, Kent	3:49:00 (8,254)
Procter, Scott D	3:37:23 (5,854)
Proctor, Mathieu Y	4:07:47 (13,066)
Proctor, Simon J	3:36:28 (5,691)
Proger, William	3:46:43 (7,684)
Proietti, Roberto F	4:18:19 (15,611)
Prole, Nicholas M	4:29:35 (18,517)
Prosser, David	3:32:28 (4,998)
Prosser, Jeffrey J	5:15:02 (27,029)
Prosser, Mark C	4:00:40 (11,418)
Prosser, Steven J	3:13:39 (2,393)
Protano, Joseph	4:17:37 (15,458)
Prothero, Jonathan	4:37:30 (20,340)
Prothero, Robert A	2:48:06 (427)
Protheroe, Mark	4:27:29 (17,951)
Proud, David	4:52:43 (23,571)
Proudfoot, Trevor A	4:51:04 (23,285)
Proudley, Gavin	2:54:51 (738)
Proudlove, Michael J	2:22:40 (47)
Provoost, Johan	3:59:29 (11,151)
Prudham, Joseph P	3:44:12 (7,114)
Prunbauer, Lucas A	3:56:23 (10,204)
Pryce, Jonathan C	4:50:40 (23,210)
Pryce, Mike R	4:22:28 (16,690)
Pryce, Paul	5:08:31 (26,184)
Prydderch, Geoffrey E	4:28:00 (18,098)
Pryde, Graham	4:04:27 (12,300)
Pryde, Mark R	4:56:01 (24,211)
Prydon, John	3:35:30 (5,525)
Pryor, Dave	3:28:07 (4,246)
Ptches, Stuart	3:35:18 (5,483)
Puccini, Luigi	3:05:50 (1,591)
Puchala, Lee D	4:44:57 (22,020)
Puddick, Julian U	3:40:01 (6,306)
Pudney, David G	4:57:47 (24,551)
Pudsey, David J	3:16:18 (2,670)
Pugh, Adrian E	3:27:19 (4,084)
Pugh, Andrew	5:45:53 (29,747)
Pugh, Eddie	4:11:01 (13,875)
Pugh, Harvey	4:18:17 (15,603)
Pugh, Martyn S	4:32:40 (19,283)
Pugh, Nicholas	4:02:14 (11,789)
Pugh, Patrick F	3:18:56 (2,945)
Pugh, Roderick M	3:10:03 (2,006)
Pugliese, Francesco	2:59:10 (1,088)
Pugsley, Richard C	3:41:44 (6,592)
Pugsley, Steven A	5:09:05 (26,250)
Puitgmal, Gilbert	3:42:36 (6,763)
Pulfer, Anthony C	4:12:22 (14,162)
Pulford, Andy J	4:29:51 (18,593)
Pulford, Gary	4:15:05 (14,821)
Pulford, Tom G	5:43:26 (29,588)
Puliatti, Carmelo	3:38:30 (6,048)
Pull, Matthew R	4:57:10 (24,429)
Pullan, John K	3:45:29 (7,403)
Pullen, Andrew J	4:21:30 (16,389)
Pullen, Graham	3:52:06 (9,036)
Pullen, Gregory R	4:35:21 (19,898)
Pullen, Leslie C	4:26:29 (17,696)
Pullen, Matthew T	3:15:01 (2,558)
Pulley, Mark R	3:54:49 (9,726)
Pullinger, Jeremy	3:50:35 (8,651)
Pullinger, Stephen J	3:28:59 (4,411)
Pullman, David	3:49:25 (8,359)
Pulman, Darren J	5:21:22 (27,713)
Pulsford, John R	4:04:47 (12,372)
Pumfrey, Andrew M	5:17:38 (27,320)
Pumfrey, Jon P	4:03:01 (11,957)
Pummell, Michael A	4:17:48 (15,507)
Punyer, Clive	5:29:02 (28,485)
Pupo, Carlos A	3:31:28 (4,842)
Purcell, Darren D	4:43:24 (21,662)
Purcell, Sean A	4:34:17 (19,666)
Purchase, Malcolm M	3:53:55 (9,481)
Purdon, Jason Thomas	3:10:37 (2,063)
Purdy, Justin	4:08:45 (13,307)
Purdy, Vincent H	3:30:19 (4,659)
Puri, Aman	4:57:36 (24,513)
Puricelli, John A	4:26:11 (17,626)
Purkiss, Christopher R	4:10:03 (13,647)
Purland, Richard K	3:57:47 (10,615)
Purnell, Raymond	3:50:34 (8,645)
Purser, Antony G	5:01:12 (25,172)

Purser, Matt G 4:48:07 (22,699)
Purser, Michael J 4:29:30 (18,492)
Purser, Nicholas J 3:38:01 (5,967)
Pursey, Adam J 5:32:39 (28,786)
Pursey, Len 5:10:12 (26,398)
Purvis, Darren M 2:50:35 (529)
Purvis, Stanley S 5:36:22 (29,050)
Pushkar, Piyush 3:43:26 (6,946)
Pussard, Marc L 4:41:18 (21,187)
Putnam, Alexander J 3:04:02 (1,452)
Putz, Juergen W 4:36:04 (20,045)
Puuncett, Ian M 4:48:19 (22,742)
Pybis, Mark 5:29:44 (28,560)
Pye, Adam J 4:43:51 (21,761)
Pye, Alan E 3:00:44 (1,213)
Pye, Roy F 3:47:14 (7,808)
Pyke, Stephen H 2:37:09 (157)
Pyle, Lee J 5:10:24 (26,427)
Pyner, Michael J 6:12:24 (30,790)
Pyper, Robin S 3:38:40 (6,082)
Quacqvarelli, Nunzio 4:07:32 (13,017)
Quaile, Deric R 4:33:40 (19,500)
Quantrill, Philip 2:58:57 (1,070)
Quarry, Jamie 3:14:29 (2,501)
Quayle, John 3:32:47 (5,058)
Queenan, John A 3:10:25 (2,047)
Quelch, Steven 4:56:21 (24,274)
Quennell, Richard G 2:56:11 (828)
Querstret, John P 3:19:57 (3,062)
Quickenden, David W 5:36:51 (29,094)
Quilliam, Graham A 3:20:28 (3,120)
Quinn, Andrew C 3:41:10 (6,507)
Quinn, Anthony 3:30:02 (4,597)
Quinn, Bob C 4:53:30 (23,702)
Quinn, Colin I 3:20:25 (3,110)
Quinn, Dennis F 4:39:52 (20,886)
Quinn, Eamonn 5:49:47 (29,951)
Quinn, Ian 6:02:00 (30,487)
Quinn, James R 4:32:22 (19,206)
Quinn, John P 3:53:56 (9,484)
Quinn, John V 5:01:14 (25,174)
Quinn, Keiran A 5:35:13 (28,975)
Quinn, Mark 3:55:33 (9,947)
Quinn, Mark J 4:39:47 (20,873)
Quinn, Patrick M 6:25:03 (31,126)
Quinn, Ray 4:21:48 (16,480)
Quinn, Sean P 4:06:55 (12,867)
Quinn, Simon D 7:45:52 (31,906)
Quinn, Stephen D 4:22:17 (16,631)
Quinn, Tony 4:27:31 (17,965)
Quint, Guy A 3:53:46 (9,435)
Quinten, Chris 5:25:03 (28,093)
Quintin, Pascal 2:46:41 (377)
Quinton, Matthew 3:51:04 (8,758)
Quittelier, Michel W 4:47:25 (22,546)
Quoirin, Sebastien 2:56:42 (863)
Quraishi, Ayaz 4:42:19 (21,418)
Quy, Kevin P 4:00:40 (11,418)
Raban-Williams, Robin A 4:43:24 (21,662)
Rabbetts, Mark A 2:54:53 (743)
Rabe, Kai 5:11:48 (26,604)
Rabe, Mark K 3:56:49 (10,337)
Rabey, Derrick A 3:13:06 (2,317)
Rabiller, Gerard 3:18:42 (2,922)
Rabjohns, Peter 2:56:18 (838)
Raboldt, Marco 4:33:48 (19,534)
Rackley, Benjamin J 3:46:01 (7,529)
Radcliffe, Martin 4:57:11 (24,432)
Radcliffe, Martin W 4:55:40 (24,132)
Radcliffe, Nicholas J 5:02:54 (25,435)
Radcliffe, Tobias A 2:53:32 (669)
Radeloff, Wilm 4:08:41 (13,283)
Radford, Max A 3:42:01 (6,654)
Radford, Warren D 4:02:59 (11,950)
Radia, Shyam S 4:35:35 (19,945)
Radomir, Michael 3:35:31 (5,527)
Rae, Geoff H 4:03:38 (12,110)
Rae, Neil 3:46:03 (7,534)
Rafferty, Mark D 4:25:26 (17,408)
Rafferty, Neil 4:16:08 (15,089)
Raffill, Jason P 3:41:52 (6,615)
Rafiee, Sep 3:26:59 (4,018)
Rahim, Anwar 4:32:59 (19,354)
Rahman, Arshadur 5:16:30 (27,187)
Rai, Bharat 3:40:24 (6,380)
Rai, Gurpreet 3:56:27 (10,235)
Raife, Lee 4:16:32 (15,179)
Raimondo, René P 4:23:25 (16,926)
Rainbird, Derek W 3:57:03 (10,404)
Raine, Simon E 5:00:45 (25,105)
Rainer-Seath, Ian C 6:02:18 (30,496)
Rainey, Jason 4:24:16 (17,136)
Rains, John G 4:25:07 (17,337)
Rajani, Kamlesh 5:01:15 (25,175)
Rajendram, Alexander H 6:37:18 (31,328)
Rajkumar, Vellore J 6:29:13 (31,191)
Ralph, John 4:38:12 (20,520)
Ralph, John H 4:13:33 (14,464)
Ralph-Bowman, Josh N 4:03:55 (12,173)
Rama, Amit H 4:19:40 (15,943)
Ramakrishna, Suresha 5:49:02 (29,910)
Raman, Manoj 4:30:29 (18,754)
Ramana, Hailey 4:20:54 (16,261)
Ramchurn, Jason 3:30:47 (4,738)
Ramon, Ray E 4:05:12 (12,462)
Ramos, Pedro S 4:01:40 (11,640)
Rampling, Colin F 4:48:57 (22,865)
Rampling, Peter A 3:59:59 (11,291)
Ramsay, Douglas V 3:41:05 (6,491)
Ramsay, Gordon J 3:30:37 (4,713)
Ramsay, Grant M 2:42:40 (257)
Ramsay, Kevin R 3:55:30 (9,929)
Ramsay, Malcolm C 4:38:21 (20,558)
Ramsay, Neil A 3:49:18 (8,329)
Ramsay, Peter 4:58:16 (24,659)
Ramsay, Steven A 3:29:57 (4,580)
Ramsden, Adrian P 6:32:02 (31,244)
Ramsden, Ben C 4:40:48 (21,089)
Ramsden, James 6:33:20 (31,270)
Ramsden, Mark J 5:27:43 (28,374)
Ramsden, Matthew 5:40:03 (29,344)
Ramsden, Nigel A 2:49:56 (497)
Ramsden, Paul 4:57:32 (24,500)
Ramsden, Peter D 3:41:43 (6,586)
Ramsden, Richard M 5:11:54 (26,620)
Ramsell, Christopher D 2:52:07 (595)
Ramsey, John W 3:12:36 (2,263)
Ramsey, Mark W 3:35:05 (5,442)
Ramsey, Timothy J 3:42:26 (6,727)
Ramzan, Nadin 4:27:55 (18,067)
Rana, Sampurna 5:55:11 (30,211)
Rance, Keith J 3:59:44 (11,231)
Rance, Mark C 4:55:24 (24,084)
Rance, Matt P 4:55:23 (24,081)
Rance, Phillip B 4:49:29 (22,978)
Rand, Keith W 3:44:21 (7,146)
Randall, Christopher N 4:27:00 (17,840)
Randall, David A 5:10:32 (26,445)
Randall, David W 4:09:12 (13,422)
Randall, Gary P 4:08:27 (13,214)
Randall, Michael J 4:26:03 (17,585)
Randall, Stewart 3:58:04 (10,696)
Randall, Timothy S 4:32:43 (19,294)
Randhawa, Inderjit S 4:59:39 (24,930)
Randle, Paul M 3:57:17 (10,473)
Randle, Richard J 3:11:16 (2,122)
Randles, Stephen 3:56:45 (10,311)
Rands, Duncan 4:13:24 (14,432)
Randtoul, Stephen J 5:07:57 (26,107)
Ranger, Terry E 4:28:02 (18,105)
Rankin, Ben C 4:02:06 (11,746)
Rankin, David J 4:36:51 (20,217)
Rankin, Eeyin A 3:30:07 (4,619)
Rankin, Tom D 4:02:06 (11,746)
Rankine, David A 5:03:13 (25,478)
Rankine, James 5:02:25 (25,358)
Ransom, Richard W 4:17:19 (15,374)
Ransome, Alan F 3:55:42 (9,989)
Raper, Raymond J 3:20:17 (3,096)
Raphael, Derek N 5:04:54 (25,678)
Rapley, Nicholas 3:49:21 (8,338)
Rappel, Christian 4:56:16 (24,255)
Rashid, Mohsin 4:05:33 (12,555)
Rasmussen, Bent E 4:32:48 (19,312)
Raspaud, Christian 3:39:07 (6,150)
Raspin, Paul G 3:23:33 (3,504)
Ratcliff, Chris 4:26:15 (17,648)
Ratcliff, Mark A 5:23:01 (27,871)
Ratcliffe, Nigel S 4:05:01 (12,437)
Ratcliffe, Paul 5:22:24 (27,822)
Ratcliffe, Peter E 3:20:07 (3,079)
Ratcliffe, Robert A 3:26:56 (4,005)
Rathbone, Dan J 2:46:57 (386)
Rathbone, Mark A 3:13:41 (2,396)
Rathe, Austin G 4:15:26 (14,909)
Ratnasuriya, Vishanka 4:29:52 (18,599)
Rau, Philippe 4:45:47 (22,207)
Raugei, Paolo 3:33:22 (5,171)
Raull, Jamie 3:56:32 (10,260)
Rauscher, Thomas 3:42:28 (6,735)
Raven, Gareth J 2:18:49 (28)
Raven, Philip M 3:38:48 (6,098)
Raw, Ed C 5:26:10 (28,208)
Raw, Richard M 4:17:05 (15,321)
Rawes, Carl B 3:55:48 (10,016)
Rawes, Neil J 5:09:32 (26,308)
Rawling, James 5:42:54 (29,545)
Rawlings, Jeremy D 3:57:46 (10,609)
Rawlings, Kevin D 3:24:38 (3,644)
Rawlings, Matthew R 4:31:19 (18,924)
Rawlings, Richard M 4:30:11 (18,676)
Rawlins, Jody C 3:44:48 (7,261)
Rawlinson, Brian F 4:22:04 (16,561)
Rawlinson, Francis 5:47:20 (29,829)
Rawlinson, John 3:13:29 (2,369)
Rawlinson, Lee 5:37:28 (29,151)
Rawlinson, Paul 3:54:24 (9,612)
Rawlinson, Robert J 4:35:33 (19,939)
Rawlinson, Toby J 3:57:18 (10,481)
Rawlinson, Tony 3:58:49 (10,948)
Rawson, Stephen 5:12:22 (26,676)
Rawson, Trevor 5:22:22 (27,817)
Ray, Graham 6:11:57 (30,782)
Ray, Sanjit 4:41:05 (21,139)
Ray, Scott E 4:11:27 (13,959)
Ray, Stephen 5:18:19 (27,402)
Raybould, Ed 3:47:51 (7,958)
Raybould, Frank 4:25:15 (17,370)
Raybould, Trevor D 4:57:22 (24,467)
Raybould, Will 3:34:53 (5,405)
Rayden, William H 3:44:51 (7,273)
Rayfield, David W 2:57:25 (908)
Rayfield, Gavin B 5:13:06 (26,781)
Raymakers, Hans 4:48:49 (22,841)
Rayment, Adrian 4:29:52 (18,599)
Rayment, Paul 5:10:57 (26,501)
Raymond, Byron J 3:02:52 (1,360)
Raymond, Joshua 3:56:35 (10,274)
Rayne, Damian R 4:58:57 (24,789)
Rayner, Jeremy C 3:45:59 (7,523)
Rayner, Julian A 3:34:40 (5,362)
Rayner, Kevin 5:05:23 (25,736)
Rayner, Martin J 3:48:19 (8,081)
Rayner, Paul J 4:58:34 (24,729)
Rayner, Paul M 3:48:37 (8,157)
Rayner, Wayne A 5:37:28 (29,151)
Raynor, Andrew P 4:30:54 (18,842)
Raynor, David A 3:54:02 (9,514)
Raynor, John D 4:05:15 (12,472)
Raynor, Leonard A 3:19:46 (3,045)
Raynor, Tony 3:54:23 (9,604)
Raynor, Trevor D 3:25:30 (3,770)
Rayson, Chris 4:00:12 (11,343)
Rayson, Gregor E 4:33:05 (19,378)
Rayson, Paul W 3:54:19 (9,591)
Re, Alfredo 4:52:18 (23,503)
Rea, Andrew S 4:59:26 (24,889)
Rea, Martin 2:44:26 (300)
Rea, Paul A 3:20:00 (3,066)
Read, Chris M 6:15:44 (30,902)
Read, John 3:56:12 (10,142)
Read, Malcolm W 3:32:30 (5,004)
Read, Matthew J 6:36:54 (31,318)
Read, Mike W 3:41:44 (6,592)
Read, Nicholas J 3:47:31 (7,883)
Read, Richard A 5:41:53 (29,481)
Read, Sean M 3:27:57 (4,222)
Read, Stephen C 5:18:37 (27,424)
Read, Tom E 3:57:19 (10,488)

Reade, Daniel J....4:54:23 (23,875)
Reade, Timothy....3:54:48 (9,722)
Reader, Frank R....6:08:06 (30,676)
Reader, Jonathan D....4:09:36 (13,524)
Reader, Malcolm F....5:23:30 (27,923)
Reader, Philip....6:14:15 (30,854)
Reader, Rob....4:21:57 (16,516)
Reader, Simon W....3:44:53 (7,283)
Reader, Steve G....6:06:06 (30,627)
Reading, David....3:42:46 (6,803)
Reading, Gary B....4:52:06 (23,466)
Readman, Ben G....3:35:56 (5,598)
Readman, John....3:52:16 (9,076)
Realff, Justin N....3:07:21 (1,733)
Reay, Jonathan S....3:51:10 (8,789)
Reayer, Garrath R....3:57:21 (10,498)
Rebelo, Adlino S....5:14:37 (26,982)
Recalcati, Sergio....3:08:52 (1,884)
Redcliffe, Warren B....4:29:05 (18,370)
Redden, Phil....2:49:22 (472)
Reddicliffe, Alexander....3:45:12 (7,348)
Redding, Chris....4:33:00 (19,359)
Redelucq, Julien....3:31:36 (4,862)
Redern, James A....4:06:38 (12,811)
Redfearn, Simon W....4:26:34 (17,718)
Redfern, Michael G....4:28:44 (18,288)
Redford, Phillip W....4:00:04 (11,308)
Redford, Roy....6:41:03 (31,372)
Redgrave, David E....4:56:07 (24,232)
Redgrove, Nicholas....3:44:08 (7,102)
Redhouse, David....2:58:52 (1,062)
Redman, Carl A....4:58:21 (24,676)
Redman, Nevil....4:23:37 (16,968)
Redmayne, William G....4:00:13 (11,346)
Redmond, Alasdair I....3:52:55 (9,231)
Redmond, Darren....4:08:24 (13,199)
Redmond, Ian M....4:37:15 (20,306)
Redpath, David W....3:46:17 (7,598)
Redshaw, Peter J....3:59:26 (11,121)
Redston, Joe....4:21:25 (16,367)
Redwood, Leslie W....3:21:42 (3,276)
Reece, Christopher A....4:00:28 (11,390)
Reece, Philip J....3:41:48 (6,605)
Reed, Alan....3:03:51 (1,437)
Reed, Gareth H....5:25:07 (28,099)
Reed, James....3:56:45 (10,311)
Reed, Peter A....5:36:58 (29,105)
Reed, Samuel....5:22:34 (27,841)
Reed, Simon J....3:28:13 (4,266)
Reed, Simon J....4:58:38 (24,745)
Reed, Stephen....4:31:07 (18,880)
Reed, Stewart....3:56:20 (10,190)
Reed, William J....3:59:07 (11,035)
Reeday, Philip M....4:05:45 (12,606)
Reeder, Roy W....2:37:00 (154)
Reedman, Malcolm....5:00:26 (25,058)
Rees, Adrian....4:12:39 (14,247)
Rees, Alan C....4:23:41 (16,980)
Rees, Alun....3:59:12 (11,060)
Rees, Andy J....4:13:05 (14,349)
Rees, Christopher O....4:02:17 (11,801)
Rees, Colin J....3:02:40 (1,350)
Rees, Damon M....4:45:13 (22,085)
Rees, Dorian P....4:12:09 (14,125)
Rees, Edward J....4:35:44 (19,966)
Rees, Gareth....3:48:14 (8,061)
Rees, Huw....3:55:40 (9,976)
Rees, James C....4:58:52 (24,774)
Rees, James E....4:03:33 (12,089)
Rees, John N....4:53:45 (23,756)
Rees, Larry....3:52:24 (9,111)
Rees, Mark E....4:25:13 (17,363)
Rees, Michael....4:22:55 (16,799)
Rees, Michael A....5:04:46 (25,659)
Rees, Paul....3:53:42 (9,416)
Rees, Richard B....4:03:09 (11,996)
Rees, Timothy....5:02:11 (25,318)
Reetz, Wolfgang....3:07:05 (1,711)
Reeve, David M....4:24:30 (17,182)
Reeve, Graham P....4:44:36 (21,935)
Reeve, Peter J....4:47:58 (22,666)
Reeve, Robert....5:15:30 (27,081)
Reeve, Robin B....3:43:12 (6,894)
Reeves, Alan M....5:25:20 (28,123)
Reeves, Gavin J....4:49:26 (22,961)
Reeves, Jason M....5:09:31 (26,307)
Reeves, Lawrence S....7:01:38 (31,637)
Reeves, Robb....4:16:47 (15,247)
Reeves, Stephen J....5:14:32 (26,964)
Regan, James W....4:12:00 (14,095)
Regan, Patrick C....3:45:30 (7,409)
Regan, Phillip....6:07:15 (30,655)
Rehn, Lars....3:47:18 (7,831)
Rehwinkel, Johann P....3:34:30 (5,339)
Reid, Alistair C....4:19:58 (16,022)
Reid, Brendon J....4:41:56 (21,332)
Reid, Brian D....4:28:26 (18,206)
Reid, Charles R....4:08:50 (13,331)
Reid, Chris....3:37:50 (5,931)
Reid, Clive S....3:11:58 (2,191)
Reid, Colin....4:10:29 (13,752)
Reid, David A....3:40:34 (6,413)
Reid, David I....4:28:07 (18,126)
Reid, Douglas....3:19:16 (2,995)
Reid, Edward....3:22:51 (3,426)
Reid, Garrick R....5:28:05 (28,402)
Reid, Gordon....2:52:33 (619)
Reid, Hamish....5:26:07 (28,206)
Reid, Ian....4:46:23 (22,338)
Reid, Ian A....6:54:09 (31,550)
Reid, Ian D....2:57:36 (922)
Reid, James....3:40:22 (6,373)
Reid, James....4:06:54 (12,862)
Reid, Mark A....3:16:59 (2,746)
Reid, Michael J....4:05:23 (12,503)
Reid, Nevill A....3:58:36 (10,888)
Reid, Peter B....3:11:34 (2,147)
Reid, Richard N....4:11:08 (13,897)
Reid, Stuart....5:59:35 (30,396)
Reid, William G....3:43:26 (6,946)
Reidy, Noel....4:20:25 (16,136)
Reilly, David J....4:45:31 (22,144)
Reilly, Gerard....3:25:25 (3,753)
Reilly, Michael W....4:00:03 (11,306)
Reilly, Ronan J....3:52:11 (9,057)
Reinhardt, Pierre....4:36:15 (20,082)
Reining, Robert....3:53:13 (9,320)
Reiter, Anton....4:51:18 (23,316)
Rej, Edward R....3:52:50 (9,209)
Relf, Carlton....5:15:37 (27,091)
Remy, Thierry....4:27:20 (17,925)
Renak, Leigh M....5:21:03 (27,685)
Rendall, Julian I....2:39:37 (200)
Renders, Keith S....4:40:37 (21,043)
Rennie, Les....3:44:13 (7,120)
Rennie, Nigel....3:54:11 (9,555)
Rennie, Stephen R....2:39:47 (206)
Renshaw, Arthur W....3:48:37 (8,157)
Renshaw, Benedict....4:35:35 (19,945)
Renshaw, Peter....4:38:07 (20,499)
Rentner, Mattias....3:56:04 (10,105)
Renton, Neil A....2:54:53 (743)
Renu, Martti....4:52:12 (23,482)
Renwick, David....3:40:13 (6,340)
Rescorla, Philip L....4:22:13 (16,613)
Reseigh, Jonathan K....3:49:06 (8,281)
Resta, Carlo....3:21:40 (3,273)
Reston, Rhydian H....3:23:55 (3,555)
Reveiz, Carlos....3:42:01 (6,654)
Reveiz, Luis F....3:54:10 (9,548)
Revelant, Arnold....4:13:13 (14,385)
Revell, Colin H....4:02:44 (11,910)
Revell, Craig J....4:59:22 (24,871)
Revell, John C....4:21:19 (16,337)
Revell, Kevin J....2:44:55 (322)
Revess, John A....4:46:52 (22,419)
Revill, Jason....3:28:36 (4,335)
Revis, David....5:03:52 (25,562)
Rew, Ben P....3:31:50 (4,894)
Rew, John....3:43:10 (6,884)
Rexed, Henrik....3:51:05 (8,762)
Rey, Claude....5:33:20 (28,837)
Rey, Michel....4:42:50 (21,530)
Reynaert, Peter....4:22:46 (16,764)
Reynolds, Adrian C....3:59:33 (11,173)
Reynolds, Andrew W....4:24:26 (17,172)
Reynolds, Anthony....3:47:19 (7,834)
Reynolds, Benjamin L....3:58:03 (10,689)
Reynolds, Douglas A....4:39:08 (20,756)
Reynolds, Gary....4:09:48 (13,577)
Reynolds, Gavin J....3:26:40 (3,946)
Reynolds, Graham H....3:47:36 (7,906)
Reynolds, Guy J....4:59:29 (24,901)
Reynolds, James C....4:16:39 (15,220)
Reynolds, James W....4:45:35 (22,162)
Reynolds, John....3:07:49 (1,787)
Reynolds, Jon....3:48:02 (8,004)
Reynolds, Lee....2:52:24 (608)
Reynolds, Martin....3:43:05 (6,868)
Reynolds, Matthew J....4:06:32 (12,784)
Reynolds, Matthew J....4:42:35 (21,470)
Reynolds, Nigel....3:38:38 (6,075)
Reynolds, Paul....2:53:06 (649)
Reynolds, Paul P....4:13:33 (14,464)
Reynolds, Philip J....3:48:37 (8,157)
Reynolds, Piero P....2:59:58 (1,154)
Reynolds, Richard....5:19:40 (27,519)
Reynolds, Richard G....4:16:11 (15,099)
Reynolds, Steve....5:47:52 (29,859)
Reynolds, Steven J....5:42:39 (29,523)
Reynolds-Jones, Robert....3:23:38 (3,522)
Rhimes, Godfrey H....2:41:41 (236)
Rhodes, Andrew....4:31:58 (19,104)
Rhodes, Andrew D....3:38:57 (6,121)
Rhodes, Christopher P....3:46:55 (7,726)
Rhodes, David L....3:36:30 (5,696)
Rhodes, Graeme P....4:33:54 (19,566)
Rhodes, James D....3:33:38 (5,209)
Rhodes, Jonathan R....4:41:34 (21,258)
Rhodes, Lee A....4:12:54 (14,302)
Rhodes, Malcolm S....4:10:27 (13,743)
Rhodes, Robert D....3:38:19 (6,015)
Rhodes, Stuart M....3:58:13 (10,763)
Rhodes, Toby M....4:22:33 (16,713)
Rhule, Desmond....3:32:35 (5,024)
Riat, Amerdeep S....4:32:31 (19,240)
Ribeiro, Abilio J....2:59:05 (1,081)
Riccardi, Roberto M....3:01:50 (1,293)
Ricci, Lorenzo....3:06:23 (1,643)
Rice, Adrian....4:26:29 (17,696)
Rice, Denis A....3:42:13 (6,686)
Rice, James....4:23:43 (16,993)
Rice, James E....4:14:47 (14,752)
Rice, Mark D....3:31:10 (4,801)
Rice, Martin J....3:23:13 (3,464)
Rice, Reagan....3:31:57 (4,916)
Rice, Stuart R....3:46:12 (7,578)
Rice, Tim....5:18:10 (27,386)
Rice, Wayne....4:04:57 (12,422)
Rich, Alvin A....2:50:30 (525)
Rich, Andreas N....3:28:31 (4,323)
Rich, Andrew J....5:42:45 (29,531)
Rich, Anthony M....4:30:03 (18,646)
Rich, Geoff....3:14:38 (2,516)
Rich, Michael D....3:45:29 (7,403)
Rich, Stephen J....3:43:16 (6,911)
Richard, Gilles....3:16:30 (2,700)
Richard, Lucien....4:58:51 (24,771)
Richard, Philippe....3:54:40 (9,686)
Richard, Thomas....3:10:04 (2,008)
Richard, Victor....4:24:41 (17,227)
Richards, Alan S....5:18:59 (27,462)
Richards, Andrew R....4:01:45 (11,659)
Richards, Barry....4:08:47 (13,317)
Richards, Chris....3:45:23 (7,384)
Richards, Doug A....4:55:59 (24,204)
Richards, Gavin P....3:35:50 (5,578)
Richards, Gordon....2:57:05 (886)
Richards, Gwilym....4:38:09 (20,508)
Richards, Hywel G....4:43:10 (21,595)
Richards, Ian G....3:04:14 (1,467)
Richards, James A....3:54:57 (9,768)
Richards, Jim D....4:17:59 (15,550)
Richards, Jonathon M....4:39:55 (20,901)
Richards, Kevin J....4:27:43 (18,019)
Richards, Kevin S....3:48:58 (8,245)
Richards, Mark....3:27:23 (4,100)
Richards, Mark....5:10:36 (26,451)
Richards, Mark L....2:59:50 (1,145)

Richards, Martin L	4:26:19 (17,658)	
Richards, Paul S	3:22:04 (3,310)	
Richards, Robert E	4:44:04 (21,810)	
Richards, Simon J	4:00:39 (11,416)	
Richards, Stephen	5:25:17 (28,117)	
Richards, Thomas G	4:54:34 (23,914)	
Richards, Toby	4:07:08 (12,923)	
Richardson, Alan J	3:52:47 (9,188)	
Richardson, Andrew M	4:25:48 (17,515)	
Richardson, Andrew S	5:45:20 (29,715)	
Richardson, Brian	3:29:53 (4,569)	
Richardson, Colin	2:58:32 (1,015)	
Richardson, Eamonn	3:49:24 (8,356)	
Richardson, Gary	4:58:19 (24,670)	
Richardson, Gary J	5:05:03 (25,697)	
Richardson, Graham E	4:12:24 (14,167)	
Richardson, Heinz B	4:17:00 (15,304)	
Richardson, Ian A	3:28:33 (4,330)	
Richardson, James	4:33:09 (19,391)	
Richardson, James G	4:25:11 (17,356)	
Richardson, Jason	6:31:36 (31,237)	
Richardson, Jonathan P	4:09:12 (13,422)	
Richardson, Justin P	5:57:10 (30,294)	
Richardson, Kevin	4:13:14 (14,390)	
Richardson, Kevin J	4:28:04 (18,115)	
Richardson, Kevin R	4:38:08 (20,505)	
Richardson, Neil G	5:01:03 (25,152)	
Richardson, Nick	3:27:03 (4,036)	
Richardson, Nigel G	3:45:51 (7,492)	
Richardson, Paul	4:07:12 (12,939)	
Richardson, Paul W	5:07:11 (25,991)	
Richardson, Peter	4:25:26 (17,408)	
Richardson, Philip D	4:41:54 (21,326)	
Richardson, Robin J	4:32:20 (19,195)	
Richardson, Stuart G	4:40:41 (21,062)	
Richardson, Thomas E	4:37:03 (20,261)	
Richer, Adrian C	4:28:46 (18,292)	
Riches, Andy N	5:07:37 (26,059)	
Riches, Ian A	4:04:32 (12,323)	
Riches, Mark	3:37:16 (5,829)	
Riches, Mark J	5:47:22 (29,832)	
Riches, Timothy J	3:20:53 (3,189)	
Riches, Wayne P	3:51:20 (8,842)	
Richman, Aryeh	5:37:32 (29,153)	
Richmond, David J	3:53:53 (9,474)	
Richmond, Joyn	3:56:45 (10,311)	
Richmond, Karn	4:37:40 (20,375)	
Rickard, John A	3:43:36 (6,979)	
Rickard, Lee M	4:36:41 (20,179)	
Rickards, Leslie D	4:14:24 (14,652)	
Rickenberg, Darren	4:57:11 (24,432)	
Rickers, Stuart J	4:42:45 (21,506)	
Ricketson, Patrick E	3:38:41 (6,083)	
Rickett, Peter	4:41:11 (21,153)	
Ricketts, David M	4:02:36 (11,879)	
Ricketts, Derek J	3:39:14 (6,168)	
Ricketts, Graham S	4:26:02 (17,579)	
Ricketts, Richard A	2:57:59 (966)	
Ricketts, Theo R	3:15:54 (2,640)	
Ricketts, Toby	6:06:10 (30,630)	
Rickson, Tim	4:23:29 (16,937)	
Rickwood, Simon L	4:38:42 (20,643)	
Riconda, Roberto	5:09:08 (26,257)	
Riddell, Drew	4:36:00 (20,027)	
Riddell, Gary J	3:06:03 (1,615)	
Ridd-Jones, Stuart B	4:00:53 (11,475)	
Riddle, Roddy	2:44:34 (307)	
Rideout, James S	3:14:47 (2,535)	
Rider, Andrew	5:17:57 (27,360)	
Rider, Mark R	3:49:39 (8,413)	
Rider, Tim	3:31:46 (4,882)	
Ridge, Wynn C	5:11:09 (26,527)	
Ridger, Matthew C	3:32:23 (4,985)	
Ridgers, Stephen T	4:38:51 (20,683)	
Ridgeway, Paul	2:59:44 (1,137)	
Ridgway, Mark	3:18:24 (2,887)	
Riding, Geoff I	4:20:19 (16,106)	
Riding, George	3:37:55 (5,940)	
Ridley, Bill E	2:59:12 (1,093)	
Ridley, David W	5:15:10 (27,036)	
Ridley, Michael T	3:50:53 (8,730)	
Ridley, Simon N	4:18:49 (15,744)	
Ridout, John P	3:10:06 (2,011)	

Rielander, Ian	5:52:13 (30,077)	
Rieu, Denis	6:17:58 (30,952)	
Rieux, Stephane	3:58:24 (10,819)	
Rigamonti, Michele	3:27:18 (4,080)	
Rigby, Alan D	5:23:58 (27,970)	
Rigby, Bill	5:23:32 (27,929)	
Rigby, Carl	4:19:58 (16,022)	
Rigby, David N	3:42:36 (6,763)	
Rigby, Neil A	4:23:38 (16,971)	
Rigby, Shaun N	4:27:12 (17,892)	
Rigden, Andrew D	4:27:52 (18,059)	
Riggs, Nicholas S	3:29:06 (4,434)	
Rijna, Herman	4:09:48 (13,577)	
Riley, Christopher J	5:07:34 (26,053)	
Riley, Gerard	4:47:43 (22,618)	
Riley, James M	4:57:34 (24,508)	
Riley, Jamie D	5:27:43 (28,374)	
Riley, Lee J	3:54:41 (9,691)	
Riley, Mark	5:51:56 (30,058)	
Riley, Nick	3:53:48 (9,444)	
Riley, Peter J	4:15:49 (15,006)	
Riley, Shawn D	3:28:06 (4,240)	
Riley, Steven A	3:59:20 (11,096)	
Riley, Trevor I	4:05:27 (12,523)	
Riley, Warren N	4:05:58 (12,653)	
Rimmer, Paul A	4:16:06 (15,079)	
Rimmer, Paul W	4:34:32 (19,722)	
Rimmington, Paul	4:35:20 (19,893)	
Rimoldi, Umberto	4:07:40 (13,048)	
Rindlisbacher, Daniel	3:06:24 (1,645)	
Ringstrom, Daniel T	4:24:24 (17,164)	
Riordan, Joseph G	6:22:14 (31,069)	
Rippon, William A	3:47:18 (7,831)	
Rishworth, Stephen P	3:48:23 (8,097)	
Rist, Mark B	4:31:18 (18,922)	
Rist, Soren	3:39:39 (6,244)	
Ritchie, Jonathan	4:26:49 (17,777)	
Ritchie, Keith D	3:15:51 (2,637)	
Ritchie, Paul	3:49:05 (8,277)	
Ritchie, William R	3:50:04 (8,517)	
Ritstier, Wouter	3:58:29 (10,845)	
Riva, Roberto	3:56:30 (10,250)	
Rivers, Brian	3:30:15 (4,645)	
Rivers, Terry M	3:25:56 (3,835)	
Rix, Ian J	4:35:57 (20,016)	
Rix, Jeremy G	5:23:26 (27,909)	
Rix, Michael W	3:59:50 (11,249)	
Rixon, Christopher G	4:37:56 (20,449)	
Rixon, David M	3:31:51 (4,895)	
Rixon, Edward J	3:52:38 (9,159)	
Roach, Greg	3:01:04 (1,243)	
Roach, William P	4:40:27 (21,017)	
Robb, Andrew J	3:56:52 (10,354)	
Robb, Graham	4:44:22 (21,876)	
Robbertse, Jake P	4:37:37 (20,361)	
Robbertse, Marthinus J	4:38:57 (20,706)	
Robbie, Hamish	4:16:01 (15,053)	
Robbins, Keith G	4:14:53 (14,783)	
Robbins, Kevin A	3:55:06 (9,818)	
Robbins, Michael J	4:22:06 (16,571)	
Robe, Alec	5:12:17 (26,666)	
Robershaw, Simon	4:47:45 (22,624)	
Roberson, Adam	4:20:19 (16,106)	
Robert, Iain A	2:49:02 (461)	
Robert, Paul C	5:24:46 (28,051)	
Roberts, Adam	4:34:06 (19,625)	
Roberts, Alan	3:28:49 (4,381)	
Roberts, Andrew	4:49:21 (22,951)	
Roberts, Andrew M	3:37:01 (5,772)	
Roberts, Anthony	5:02:19 (25,346)	
Roberts, Austin P	3:47:29 (7,876)	
Roberts, Barry J	4:37:35 (20,352)	
Roberts, Barry W	4:35:48 (19,982)	
Roberts, Christopher I	6:15:42 (30,901)	
Roberts, Coyle M	3:23:04 (3,448)	
Roberts, David	3:44:59 (7,305)	
Roberts, David	4:27:46 (18,031)	
Roberts, David B	4:32:12 (19,165)	
Roberts, David L	4:31:58 (19,104)	
Roberts, David W	5:07:41 (26,079)	
Roberts, Gareth D	4:00:48 (11,444)	
Roberts, Gareth P	4:19:00 (15,779)	
Roberts, Glyn C	4:03:54 (12,169)	

Roberts, Harry	4:35:36 (19,947)	
Roberts, Haydn	4:10:10 (13,668)	
Roberts, Ian D	3:18:23 (2,884)	
Roberts, Ian W	3:14:14 (2,471)	
Roberts, Ifor	5:30:18 (28,606)	
Roberts, Ioan W	4:10:09 (13,666)	
Roberts, James A	4:50:05 (23,088)	
Roberts, Jeff L	4:52:19 (23,509)	
Roberts, Jeremy	5:06:14 (25,881)	
Roberts, John C	3:40:29 (6,396)	
Roberts, Jonathan C	4:44:07 (21,823)	
Roberts, Justin J	4:26:17 (17,653)	
Roberts, Kerry J	2:59:07 (1,085)	
Roberts, Malcolm	2:58:15 (990)	
Roberts, Matt A	4:25:19 (17,384)	
Roberts, Matt J	4:54:31 (23,899)	
Roberts, Matthew E	4:08:57 (13,364)	
Roberts, Matthew I	4:34:51 (19,791)	
Roberts, Matthew J	4:58:10 (24,633)	
Roberts, Nicholas A	4:03:14 (12,010)	
Roberts, Paul	4:53:00 (23,617)	
Roberts, Phil T	4:09:57 (13,625)	
Roberts, Philip T	3:53:12 (9,318)	
Roberts, Simon J	3:12:28 (2,251)	
Roberts, Stephen A	4:51:18 (23,316)	
Roberts, Stephen J	3:26:40 (3,946)	
Roberts, Stephen M	3:56:48 (10,330)	
Roberts, Steve J	3:40:17 (6,352)	
Roberts, Tim	3:51:10 (8,789)	
Roberts, Toby D	4:28:27 (18,215)	
Roberts, William J	4:39:23 (20,808)	
Robertshaw, Jason S	3:30:08 (4,622)	
Robertshaw, Leslie E	4:28:22 (18,181)	
Robertshaw, Tom	3:03:18 (1,389)	
Robertson, Alan I	3:04:36 (1,496)	
Robertson, Andrew C	3:43:26 (6,946)	
Robertson, David A	4:39:20 (20,799)	
Robertson, David P	4:55:43 (24,135)	
Robertson, George A	4:47:09 (22,491)	
Robertson, Gordon	4:43:57 (21,786)	
Robertson, Ian M	3:41:46 (6,599)	
Robertson, James	3:45:45 (7,471)	
Robertson, James	4:13:44 (14,500)	
Robertson, John P	3:54:15 (9,577)	
Robertson, Lex	4:00:56 (11,488)	
Robertson, Matthew A	4:05:29 (12,532)	
Robertson, Peter C	4:14:34 (14,698)	
Robertson, Scott	3:49:17 (8,327)	
Robertson, Stephen T	4:40:58 (21,117)	
Robertson, Stewart D	3:25:56 (3,835)	
Robertson, Stuart J	3:44:44 (7,245)	
Robertson, Thomas H	4:08:46 (13,311)	
Robertson, William	5:20:41 (27,656)	
Robins, Andrew J	3:20:45 (3,168)	
Robins, Martin	3:58:19 (10,795)	
Robins, William	4:45:41 (22,186)	
Robinson, Alex	3:12:59 (2,309)	
Robinson, Alex	4:21:35 (16,409)	
Robinson, Anthony W	3:53:16 (9,329)	
Robinson, Brendan T	3:48:15 (8,065)	
Robinson, Chris	5:15:52 (27,117)	
Robinson, Damian N	4:09:04 (13,394)	
Robinson, Dan	2:13:53 (16)	
Robinson, Daniel	4:26:47 (17,770)	
Robinson, Darryl W	4:29:00 (18,349)	
Robinson, David	3:32:23 (4,985)	
Robinson, David K	3:56:28 (10,241)	
Robinson, Duncan A	3:50:16 (8,567)	
Robinson, Gary M	5:17:28 (27,304)	
Robinson, Geoffrey L	5:05:49 (25,849)	
Robinson, George H	5:11:07 (26,524)	
Robinson, Graham	4:09:34 (13,516)	
Robinson, Iain	5:23:01 (27,871)	
Robinson, Ian	3:30:30 (4,691)	
Robinson, John P	3:38:27 (6,039)	
Robinson, Jonathan A	5:12:55 (26,751)	
Robinson, Jonathan H	2:55:56 (808)	
Robinson, Jonathan M	4:19:38 (15,934)	
Robinson, Kenneth E	3:07:07 (1,715)	
Robinson, Kevin J	5:10:48 (26,483)	
Robinson, Mark	3:35:27 (5,511)	
Robinson, Michael A	3:51:07 (8,769)	
Robinson, Michael E	3:55:13 (9,854)	

Robinson, Michael E....4:31:26 (18,956)
Robinson, Nathan S....4:32:09 (19,152)
Robinson, Neil....5:09:34 (26,317)
Robinson, Neil J....5:17:06 (27,264)
Robinson, Neil S....5:05:40 (25,783)
Robinson, Nigel K....3:49:19 (8,331)
Robinson, Paul J....5:46:15 (29,766)
Robinson, Peter J....4:45:39 (22,177)
Robinson, Peter L....4:48:56 (22,862)
Robinson, Peter M....4:46:20 (22,323)
Robinson, Peter M....5:22:21 (27,812)
Robinson, Philip W....4:54:13 (23,840)
Robinson, Phillip G....3:28:04 (4,237)
Robinson, Robert....3:52:38 (9,159)
Robinson, Robert....5:05:44 (25,787)
Robinson, Simon....4:48:09 (22,707)
Robinson, Simon A....4:24:29 (17,180)
Robinson, Simon D....4:22:45 (16,760)
Robinson, Stephen....5:29:31 (28,535)
Robinson, Stephen D....4:12:04 (14,108)
Robinson, Stephen F....5:33:36 (28,858)
Robinson, Steven....4:15:00 (14,803)
Robinson, Stuart D....4:42:49 (21,524)
Robinson, Thomas D....3:53:25 (9,361)
Robinson, Timothy L....3:45:04 (7,314)
Robinson, Tom D....5:26:02 (28,200)
Robinson, Victor C....4:48:40 (22,807)
Robinson, Victor R....5:21:25 (27,722)
Robson, Darren P....5:04:33 (25,633)
Robson, Fred T....4:44:54 (22,002)
Robson, Philip J....2:52:48 (632)
Robson, Philip J....3:51:51 (8,977)
Robson, Ryan....5:21:38 (27,744)
Robson, Terry R....3:38:03 (5,970)
Rocha, Dominique L....4:15:57 (15,041)
Rocha, Marco A....4:28:56 (18,334)
Roche, Barry T....4:00:02 (11,305)
Roche, Brendan J....3:51:29 (8,880)
Roche, Geoffrey F....4:08:47 (13,317)
Roche, James A....5:36:01 (29,031)
Roche, Philip B....4:30:21 (18,716)
Roche, Richard A....4:00:24 (11,380)
Roche, Richard J....4:32:53 (19,332)
Rochester, Paul J....6:07:18 (30,657)
Rochester, Tom S....3:43:02 (6,855)
Rockliffe, Richard J....4:04:53 (12,402)
Rodda, John K....3:55:50 (10,028)
Rodda, Philip F....3:28:41 (4,349)
Rodda, Robert C....3:37:55 (5,940)
Roddis, Matthew J....4:34:37 (19,738)
Roden, Dominic R....4:51:13 (23,306)
Roden, John....5:22:45 (27,852)
Roden, Michael....4:06:14 (12,722)
Rodger, Edward....3:42:44 (6,797)
Rodger, Jody S....3:16:18 (2,670)
Rodger, John D....4:07:15 (12,955)
Rodger, Peter S....3:16:03 (2,650)
Rodgers, Ian G....3:54:13 (9,567)
Rodgers, Paul J....4:02:19 (11,814)
Rodgers, Simon J....4:16:09 (15,093)
Rodgers, Tim J....4:59:16 (24,845)
Rodi, Christopher M....5:51:25 (30,033)
Rodier, Jean Pierre....4:02:08 (11,757)
Rodin, Peter A....3:59:33 (11,173)
Rodney, Anthony G....3:46:56 (7,730)
Rodon, Philippe....4:16:58 (15,296)
Rodriguez-Alba, Antonio M....4:27:32 (17,973)
Rodriguez-Garcia, Francisco J....3:01:26 (1,273)
Roe, Chris J....4:07:50 (13,076)
Roe, David C....3:34:06 (5,284)
Roe, John W....4:17:26 (15,406)
Roe, Nigel....4:11:32 (13,978)
Roe, Peter....4:41:28 (21,236)
Roe, Terence R....5:28:09 (28,406)
Roebuck, Tony....3:45:41 (7,455)
Roelandt, Michel....5:04:47 (25,662)
Roessler, Ralf....4:02:35 (11,872)
Roffey, David....4:18:47 (15,734)
Rogan, Gary P....4:57:34 (24,508)
Rogan, Josh....4:47:40 (22,608)
Rogbeer, Shan K....5:08:21 (26,167)
Rogers, Adam S....3:51:17 (8,828)
Rogers, Adrian G....4:39:17 (20,788)
Rogers, Andrew G....4:48:42 (22,820)
Rogers, Ben....4:09:41 (13,549)
Rogers, Benjamin....3:55:58 (10,074)
Rogers, Benjamin D....4:43:12 (21,605)
Rogers, Chris....4:50:25 (23,162)
Rogers, Christopher M....5:35:41 (29,011)
Rogers, Dave M....3:34:19 (5,313)
Rogers, David O....4:16:02 (15,057)
Rogers, Edward J....5:44:23 (29,649)
Rogers, James R....4:00:27 (11,388)
Rogers, John....4:07:10 (12,931)
Rogers, Julian R....4:23:39 (16,977)
Rogers, Lee....4:04:44 (12,364)
Rogers, Lee D....4:35:21 (19,898)
Rogers, Nigel....4:43:54 (21,775)
Rogers, Nigel J....5:31:43 (28,717)
Rogers, Paul....4:36:30 (20,135)
Rogers, Paul A....4:05:24 (12,510)
Rogers, Philip D....3:21:35 (3,267)
Rogers, Raymond J....4:11:21 (13,939)
Rogers, Sean G....4:56:58 (24,396)
Rogers, Timothy M....5:05:18 (25,726)
Rogers, William E....3:53:06 (9,282)
Rogerson, Alan....4:52:18 (23,503)
Rogerson, Robert J....2:56:19 (841)
Rogowski, John T....4:29:03 (18,360)
Rohloff, Lewis G....4:16:11 (15,099)
Rold, Christopher P....3:32:13 (4,957)
Roleston, Norman E....3:45:18 (7,364)
Rolfe, Christopher W....4:26:07 (17,613)
Rolfe, Les....4:15:05 (14,821)
Rolfe, Michael A....3:31:25 (4,835)
Rollier, Dominique....3:04:38 (1,501)
Rolling, Bruno....3:34:58 (5,419)
Rollings, Chris J....4:26:38 (17,736)
Rollings, Nicholas J....4:41:44 (21,290)
Rolls, Mark D....4:28:40 (18,274)
Rolph, Bruce....6:09:40 (30,722)
Roma, Paul....4:59:47 (24,954)
Romain, Alex....3:32:21 (4,979)
Romanholi, José C....3:26:40 (3,946)
Romecin, Thomas J....3:39:49 (6,275)
Romero, Claudio F....3:03:06 (1,374)
Romero, Thomas....3:55:45 (10,005)
Ronayne, Ian....3:17:10 (2,769)
Rondou, Michel....4:01:43 (11,652)
Rongier, Bruno....3:59:04 (11,019)
Roniger, Timothy S....3:16:17 (2,669)
Ronnan, Andrew....5:13:25 (26,816)
Rons, Herve....3:04:36 (1,496)
Ronsisvalle, Luca....3:28:24 (4,301)
Roofe, Jason....3:36:26 (5,685)
Rook, John....3:51:31 (8,891)
Rook, Spencer....3:07:01 (1,705)
Roots, Charles A....4:48:29 (22,776)
Roper, Andy D....4:42:57 (21,555)
Roper, Luke J....3:41:11 (6,509)
Roper, Martin J....4:15:23 (14,897)
Roper, Nigel D....3:48:03 (8,008)
Roper, Stephen C....4:14:37 (14,713)
Rosbrook, Simon J....4:04:56 (12,418)
Roscoe, Gareth P....3:40:18 (6,357)
Rose, Andrew....5:05:55 (25,828)
Rose, Andrew D....5:55:02 (30,200)
Rose, Andrew L....3:46:13 (7,585)
Rose, Andrew M....3:07:40 (1,776)
Rose, Andrew M....4:38:11 (20,517)
Rose, Christopher....4:00:49 (11,449)
Rose, Daniel....7:04:28 (31,665)
Rose, Daniel G....4:39:06 (20,748)
Rose, Darren M....5:00:10 (25,018)
Rose, David E....3:32:35 (5,024)
Rose, David M....3:58:15 (10,773)
Rose, Edward S....3:52:19 (9,091)
Rose, Gary....3:55:30 (9,929)
Rose, Guy J....4:11:51 (14,053)
Rose, James S....3:31:55 (4,907)
Rose, Mark A....4:05:35 (12,568)
Rose, Martin....3:33:22 (5,171)
Rose, Paul A....3:11:04 (2,101)
Rose, Sean A....2:58:02 (974)
Rose, Tom J....5:02:25 (25,358)
Rose, Tony....5:13:23 (26,815)
Rosenberg, Michael C....3:59:04 (11,019)
Rosenberg, Richard B....4:39:12 (20,774)
Rosendahl, Gerald....3:38:44 (6,090)
Rosenfeld, David J....4:36:39 (20,167)
Rosie, John....4:10:55 (13,850)
Rosini, Don T....4:11:36 (13,999)
Ross, Alastair W....4:12:48 (14,279)
Ross, Andrew....4:54:04 (23,810)
Ross, Christopher J....3:16:26 (2,693)
Ross, David W....3:49:57 (8,489)
Ross, George J....4:26:35 (17,723)
Ross, Graeme R....3:16:57 (2,742)
Ross, Gregor....4:22:23 (16,663)
Ross, James A....5:33:47 (28,868)
Ross, Julian T....5:14:10 (26,918)
Ross, Michael C....4:05:46 (12,610)
Ross, Rick P....4:33:29 (19,467)
Ross, Thomas N....3:45:08 (7,330)
Ross Martyn, Philip....5:55:25 (30,225)
Rosser, Simon J....3:59:02 (11,012)
Rossi, Giuseppe....7:09:25 (31,702)
Rossiter, Martyn....3:46:34 (7,653)
Rossiter, Robert J....4:50:22 (23,142)
Ross-McNairn, Jonathon E....4:21:49 (16,484)
Rossor, Matthew....3:59:16 (11,077)
Rossow, William C....4:37:06 (20,274)
Rostad, Hans A....3:35:31 (5,527)
Rostern, Paul....4:12:30 (14,200)
Roth, Carel W....4:01:55 (11,695)
Roth, Christian G....5:09:49 (26,360)
Rother, Andreas....3:38:16 (6,006)
Rothera, David J....5:17:29 (27,306)
Rotheram, Mark J....3:52:17 (9,079)
Rothery, Mark....4:43:45 (21,736)
Rothin, Keigh W....4:06:45 (12,830)
Rothon, Walter M....3:59:59 (11,291)
Rothwell, Alan....4:01:59 (11,712)
Rothwell, Alex C....3:50:37 (8,662)
Rothwell, Simon J....3:09:50 (1,984)
Roudil, Gilbert....3:42:51 (6,821)
Rougeron, Gilles....3:11:22 (2,129)
Roughan, Michael....6:36:38 (31,316)
Roughsedge, Peter J....4:51:13 (23,306)
Roulstone, Colin J....5:41:44 (29,471)
Roulstone, Ges A....5:22:17 (27,803)
Rounce, Phil....6:25:27 (31,131)
Rouquet, Patrice....3:48:25 (8,100)
Rourke, James P....4:47:51 (22,648)
Rourke, Nick D....3:55:02 (9,798)
Rourke, Simon M....3:39:30 (6,216)
Rouse, Adam....2:46:31 (370)
Rouse, Stephen....3:14:18 (2,477)
Rout, Russell M....3:33:51 (5,244)
Routledge, George....6:10:05 (30,729)
Roux, Michel....3:34:07 (5,286)
Roux, Nicholas J....3:55:17 (9,876)
Rowan, Matthew S....3:41:33 (6,549)
Rowe, Clifford G....5:29:19 (28,520)
Rowe, David W....3:04:06 (1,459)
Rowe, Davied L....5:31:27 (28,701)
Rowe, Gregory....5:06:40 (25,935)
Rowe, Ian W....4:26:06 (17,608)
Rowe, John A....3:34:47 (5,385)
Rowe, Jonathan C....4:13:23 (14,430)
Rowe, Martin....4:21:07 (16,296)
Rowe, Philip J....6:11:42 (30,778)
Rowe, Richard T....4:12:07 (14,120)
Rowe, Steven....4:05:46 (12,610)
Rowe, Steven I....4:58:52 (24,774)
Rowe, Timothy M....3:17:00 (2,748)
Rowell, Barry M....4:44:39 (21,947)
Rowell, Ben....3:53:15 (9,324)
Rowies, Wim....3:46:42 (7,682)
Rowland, Andrew J....2:53:28 (667)
Rowland, Christopher M....5:38:09 (29,193)
Rowland, Daniel J....4:20:46 (16,225)
Rowland, Edward....5:22:50 (27,860)
Rowland, Graham....3:48:00 (7,995)
Rowland, Ian....2:47:42 (408)
Rowland, Matt F....4:13:28 (14,442)
Rowland, Michael J....5:35:17 (28,978)
Rowland, Robert....4:09:15 (13,438)
Rowlands, Charles E....3:41:49 (6,608)

Rowlands, Peter 4:49:19 (22,942)
Rowley, Chris R 3:52:57 (9,242)
Rowley, David J 4:10:21 (13,716)
Rowley, John 3:51:08 (8,774)
Rowley, Stephen J 5:50:25 (29,989)
Rowling, Mark L 3:00:50 (1,223)
Rowntree, Justin G 4:31:53 (19,072)
Rowson, David R 4:19:03 (15,786)
Roxborough, Michael J 4:17:25 (15,403)
Roy, Steve M 4:51:58 (23,433)
Royal, Christopher J 3:43:56 (7,047)
Royce, John 3:33:03 (5,109)
Royden, Barry 2:34:35 (117)
Royden, Mark 4:01:09 (11,538)
Royston, Christian 4:29:49 (18,589)
Rozier, Edward C 4:23:22 (16,905)
Ruane, Anthony J 4:23:22 (16,905)
Ruault, James 3:44:32 (7,195)
Rubenstein, Brian 4:50:31 (23,183)
Rubio Perez, José F 3:50:28 (8,625)
Rubira, Alexandre 3:34:08 (5,288)
Ruby, Clive M 5:04:07 (25,588)
Ruby, Elliot 4:06:04 (12,675)
Rudd, Christopher S 4:25:21 (17,392)
Rudd, Darren J 3:56:04 (10,105)
Rudd, Jacob 6:18:00 (30,957)
Rudd, Keith 3:04:44 (1,506)
Rudd, Stephen J 4:46:37 (22,376)
Ruddock, Len J 5:14:54 (27,016)
Rudge, Colin 5:41:22 (29,434)
Rudgyard, Iain D 4:40:01 (20,924)
Rudiferia, Ferdinando 4:18:49 (15,744)
Rudkin, Brian J 3:47:20 (7,837)
Rudkin, Marcus A 4:30:39 (18,791)
Rudman, Luke 4:19:03 (15,786)
Rudrum, Martyn I 5:28:09 (28,406)
Ruehmele, Mark 3:39:23 (6,197)
Ruffell, Graham A 5:00:18 (25,039)
Ruffell, Mark 5:33:52 (28,880)
Ruhen, Pete M 4:09:13 (13,428)
Ruia, Alok 3:49:03 (8,264)
Ruiz, Leon F 4:03:35 (12,099)
Ruiz-Martin, José A 3:20:53 (3,189)
Rule, Rob 3:13:10 (2,324)
Rumble, John 4:10:10 (13,668)
Rumbles, Christopher R 4:27:55 (18,067)
Rumbold, Anthony D 4:43:17 (21,634)
Rumbold, Keith E 4:30:33 (18,769)
Rumney, Darren M 3:01:06 (1,246)
Runacres, Mark J 3:33:00 (5,099)
Rundle, Kevin D 3:55:23 (9,901)
Rundle, Michael 3:34:38 (5,358)
Rundstrom, Nigel D 3:58:31 (10,860)
Runyard, Steven 3:35:55 (5,591)
Ruppert, Charles 4:13:21 (14,419)
Ruscoe, Steven G 5:09:21 (26,285)
Rusell, David 4:59:05 (24,808)
Rush, Antony J 3:30:34 (4,703)
Rushby, Philip J 3:57:45 (10,605)
Rushmer, Gary 3:04:01 (1,451)
Rushmer, Martin 4:11:21 (13,939)
Rushton, Matthew J 4:34:55 (19,804)
Rushton, Sam P 4:48:16 (22,731)
Rushworth, Paul D 3:11:54 (2,181)
Russ, Mark 4:12:25 (14,170)
Russell, Adrian S 3:40:20 (6,364)
Russell, Alastair J 4:39:39 (20,852)
Russell, Alexander 4:23:16 (16,885)
Russell, Barry M 4:54:05 (23,812)
Russell, Ben J 4:34:51 (19,791)
Russell, Ben J 4:44:15 (21,847)
Russell, Christopher J 5:20:16 (27,602)
Russell, Daniel J 3:58:21 (10,804)
Russell, David C 4:57:12 (24,438)
Russell, Duncan J 3:50:43 (8,688)
Russell, Gavin P 4:12:39 (14,247)
Russell, John G 4:24:30 (17,182)
Russell, John J 3:46:31 (7,639)
Russell, John R 3:12:24 (2,240)
Russell, Joseph G 4:43:06 (21,582)
Russell, Justin N 4:15:29 (14,922)
Russell, Kelvin D 2:58:00 (971)
Russell, Michael I 3:55:55 (10,057)
Russell, Nigel D 2:54:49 (736)
Russell, Phillip 3:11:46 (2,166)
Russell, Shaune D 3:07:40 (1,776)
Russell, Stephen F 3:14:16 (2,474)
Russell, Stephen M 4:19:54 (15,997)
Russell, Steven D 4:31:26 (18,956)
Russell Oulds, Graham 5:11:59 (26,630)
Russo, Jean-Marc T 3:29:32 (4,507)
Russo, Raymond J 5:38:54 (29,253)
Russo, Vito 4:07:31 (13,012)
Ruston, Keith J 4:35:19 (19,889)
Rutherford, Craig N 4:14:57 (14,795)
Rutherford, David 3:39:39 (6,244)
Rutherford, Ian 3:25:31 (3,773)
Rutherford, Ian 3:45:31 (7,414)
Rutherford, Jan N 3:34:46 (5,383)
Rutherford, Kevin 3:44:09 (7,109)
Rutherford, Simon J 3:24:42 (3,651)
Rutherford, Tim J 4:12:47 (14,276)
Rutledge, Benjamin P 4:01:50 (11,675)
Rutsatz, Martin 4:29:07 (18,381)
Rutt, Carl J 4:00:00 (11,296)
Rutten, Jan J 4:57:36 (24,513)
Rutter, Neil B 5:07:24 (26,028)
Rutter, Neil E 4:11:45 (14,032)
Rutter, Tom D 5:25:15 (28,112)
Rutterford, Alan 3:26:45 (3,973)
Ruttle, David A 3:55:16 (9,868)

Rutto, Evans 2:06:18 (1)

Evans Rutto (born 8 April 1978 in Marakwet District) is a Kenyan long-distance runner. He made the fastest ever debut marathon, winning the 2003 Chicago Marathon in 2:05:50 – at that point in time the fourth fastest marathon ever recorded (after Paul Tergat, Sammy Korir and Khalid Khannouchi). Rutto was an underdog coming into the 2003 Chicago Marathon. His longest distance prior to his debut was the half-marathon. But the Chicago race director, Carey Pinkowski, spotted his amazing potential. Rutto ran the eighth fastest 10,000m in the world in June 2000, and in October 2001 he covered the Bristol half-marathon in 1:00:43. Rutto won the 2004 London Marathon title in 2:06:18, beating Sammy Korir to the finish by half a minute, and took a second title in Chicago in 2004 in 2:06:16. The following year, a series of illnesses and injuries hit Rutto. He was fourth in the 2005 Chicago Marathon, and 10th in London. In 2006, he was again 10th in London. While training for the 2008 London Marathon, Rutto fell foul of the Kenyan presidential elections and the resulting violence. Rutto is married with three children. His father was an athlete, Kilimo Yano, who had a personal best in the 10,000m of 29 minutes.

Ruxton, David S 4:08:24 (13,199)
Ruzewicz, Raymond 4:16:50 (15,263)
Ryall, Daniel K 7:02:19 (31,645)
Ryalls, Terry 3:28:39 (4,343)
Ryament, Alan E 7:35:31 (31,874)
Ryan, Andrew G 4:05:30 (12,539)
Ryan, Barry J 3:34:16 (5,306)
Ryan, Bill 5:07:58 (26,111)
Ryan, Chris P 4:30:01 (18,634)
Ryan, Martin J 4:03:27 (12,067)
Ryan, Michael J 3:55:07 (9,821)
Ryan, Neil T 4:37:38 (20,370)
Ryan, Paul 4:19:52 (15,990)
Ryan, Paul A 3:58:42 (10,919)
Ryan, Paul W 3:55:33 (9,947)
Ryan, Peter G 6:25:15 (31,128)
Ryan, Sean M 5:25:33 (28,143)
Ryan, Shane A 4:38:47 (20,664)
Ryan, Tony 4:34:59 (19,817)
Ryan, William P 4:34:56 (19,807)
Rybka, Karsten 3:00:01 (1,159)
Rycroft, Frank E 4:36:39 (20,167)
Ryder, Alastair 5:29:45 (28,562)
Ryder, Clive S 3:34:58 (5,419)
Ryder, Colin 3:54:03 (9,518)
Ryder, David A 3:28:06 (4,240)
Ryder, Dele 4:26:05 (17,600)
Ryder, Kevin 3:54:04 (9,524)
Ryder, Paul D 4:03:18 (12,032)
Ryder, Steven W 4:12:35 (14,228)
Rye, Jonathan P 4:37:54 (20,437)
Rye, Joseph M 2:43:37 (281)
Ryffel, Markus 2:58:54 (1,066)
Rykens, Alasdair E 3:26:52 (3,997)
Rylance, Tom 4:31:59 (19,111)
Ryland, John L 5:10:06 (26,389)
Rylett, Carl M 3:58:58 (10,996)
Ryman, Paul J 4:41:29 (21,243)
Rynn, Stephen 4:14:48 (14,758)
Ryntjes, Simon D 3:32:23 (4,985)
Rytter, Jens 4:19:50 (15,983)
Saary, Alexander M 3:24:50 (3,667)
Sachdeva, Manoj K 3:20:28 (3,120)
Sacks, Daniel 2:51:43 (578)
Sacks, Gary H 4:49:23 (22,958)
Saddington, Craig J 4:47:48 (22,634)
Sadiq, Michael W 4:19:14 (15,841)
Sadler, Chris J 5:00:23 (25,051)
Sadler, David 5:02:45 (25,411)
Sadler, Jonathan P 3:55:37 (9,966)
Sadler, Richard 4:34:50 (19,784)
Saer, Angus A 3:44:08 (7,102)
Sa'feio, Simon W 3:50:53 (8,730)
Safford, Bob J 4:28:56 (18,334)
Sage, Bernard 3:36:18 (5,659)
Sahans, Gurmukh S 4:55:05 (24,011)
Sahu, Jonathan 3:24:03 (3,571)
Saihan, Zubin 4:18:25 (15,642)
Sailer, Frank 3:47:38 (7,914)
Saill, Anthony D 3:40:29 (6,396)
Saint, Alastair J 4:22:05 (16,565)
Sainty, Christopher D 5:33:05 (28,814)
Sainty, Martin 4:11:04 (13,883)
Saker, Andrew M 4:13:50 (14,528)
Saker, Matthew C 3:19:10 (2,975)
Salama, Alan D 3:46:34 (7,653)
Salamin, Michel 3:15:22 (2,586)
Sale, Murray 4:11:37 (14,005)
Sale, Sean R 5:12:58 (26,755)
Sales, Roger J 3:56:24 (10,213)
Saliba, Themis 5:12:43 (26,715)
Salisbury, Colin 6:46:26 (31,458)
Salisbury, David P 3:28:11 (4,261)
Salisbury, Mark 3:31:39 (4,867)
Salisbury, Martin 3:48:04 (8,015)
Salkeld, Bill 3:36:28 (5,691)

Sall, Ian P.........3:39:34 (6,228)
Salmon, Clarence A.........3:52:41 (9,169)
Salmon, Geoffrey.........5:09:29 (26,303)
Salmon, Keith M.........5:05:35 (25,777)
Salmon, Stefan R.........4:46:30 (22,360)
Salt, Jonathan A.........4:53:49 (23,769)
Salt, Jonathan T.........4:00:07 (11,320)
Salt, Neil.........3:36:37 (5,714)
Salt, Peter W.........5:13:03 (26,771)
Salt, Phillip P.........4:16:05 (15,072)
Salt, Stephen B.........3:54:52 (9,741)
Salt, Tim.........3:48:39 (8,168)
Salter, Karl A.........3:48:11 (8,044)
Salter, Kevin.........4:58:25 (24,698)
Salter, Neil G.........3:13:35 (2,382)
Salti, Sam.........4:36:42 (20,183)
Saltmarsh, Douglas J.........5:56:57 (30,287)
Salton, Matthew.........4:43:49 (21,751)
Saltrick, Christopher J.........3:39:16 (6,172)
Salvesen, Duncan J.........3:46:27 (7,628)
Salvesen, Hal D.........4:01:08 (11,534)
Salvesen, Tom M.........4:08:56 (13,358)
Salvetti, Giorgio.........4:14:19 (14,626)
Salvin, Pete R.........4:00:58 (11,498)
Salway, Evan W.........5:23:31 (27,924)
Sambhi, Davinder S.........3:55:48 (10,016)
Sambhi, Sarwjit.........4:00:22 (11,372)
Sambridge, Ron.........4:46:44 (22,397)
Sambrook, Gregory.........4:33:12 (19,405)
Samek, Vlado.........3:58:45 (10,930)
Samele, Thierry.........3:52:16 (9,076)
Samler, Charles T.........3:57:02 (10,397)
Samme, Matthew J.........3:32:32 (5,009)
Sammons, Michael J.........4:49:21 (22,951)
Sammons, Robert F.........4:14:25 (14,655)
Sampayo, Christopher M.........5:24:37 (28,037)
Sampayo, David M.........4:10:40 (13,793)
Sampol, Juan.........4:40:08 (20,947)
Sampson, Phil H.........4:57:57 (24,582)
Samra, Harjap S.........3:50:57 (8,741)
Sams, Kevin J.........3:26:42 (3,957)
Samuel, Japhet F.........3:24:27 (3,620)
Samuel, Nicolas M.........3:35:16 (5,474)
Samuel-Lajeunesse, Rafael.........4:28:10 (18,140)
Samuelsson, Stig H.........4:53:14 (23,663)
Sanchez Espejo, Daniel.........3:26:58 (4,013)
Sandall, Philip G.........4:02:23 (11,835)
Sandalls, Stephen J.........3:32:59 (5,095)
Sandells, Charlie K.........3:48:26 (8,102)
Sandeman, Donald.........3:29:16 (4,464)
Sander, Axel.........4:43:16 (21,627)
Sandercombe, Robert.........3:23:43 (3,530)
Sanders, Dave M.........4:18:24 (15,632)
Sanders, Gerald K.........3:51:01 (8,752)
Sanders, Graeme T.........3:38:57 (6,121)
Sanders, John B.........4:49:38 (23,004)
Sanders, Lee T.........4:24:50 (17,260)
Sanders, Martin.........2:42:22 (249)
Sanders, Neil J.........5:08:58 (26,231)
Sanders, Noel C.........5:55:51 (30,237)
Sanders, Paul.........4:40:30 (21,028)
Sanders, Paul C.........4:23:58 (17,053)
Sanders, Shane C.........3:44:52 (7,277)
Sanders, Tim J.........5:45:13 (29,706)
Sanderson, Brian J.........3:42:42 (6,790)
Sanderson, Gareth L.........3:20:59 (3,200)
Sanderson, Kenneth.........3:12:14 (2,222)
Sanderson, Michael.........2:59:14 (1,097)
Sanderson, Neil.........3:57:52 (10,639)
Sandersson, Johan.........4:38:25 (20,575)
Sandford, Andrew D.........5:14:11 (26,919)
Sandford, Mark H.........3:30:17 (4,652)
Sandford, Richard P.........4:45:25 (22,120)
Sandhu, Amanjeet.........4:43:01 (21,566)
Sandhu, David.........4:59:20 (24,858)
Sandhu, John.........5:07:31 (26,049)
Sandhu, Sundeep S.........4:46:00 (22,250)
Sandhu, Surinder P.........3:29:37 (4,522)
Sandhu, Tal.........5:43:50 (29,619)
Sandison, David J.........3:49:40 (8,416)
Sandison, Will I.........4:30:16 (18,694)
Sandrey, Mark J.........4:46:22 (22,333)
Sandrin, Andrea.........4:42:22 (21,429)
Sands, Richard J.........4:10:46 (13,816)
Sandwith, Mark.........3:59:00 (11,007)
Sanford, Gary M.........4:50:48 (23,235)
Sanger, Philip B.........2:45:41 (348)
Sanghera, Gurjinder S.........5:11:21 (26,560)
Sanghera, Kirn K.........4:02:29 (11,852)
Sanghera, Lember.........5:59:12 (30,373)
Sanghvi, Ajay M.........5:02:13 (25,321)
Sanham, Robert A.........4:27:14 (17,904)
Sankey, Jeremy C.........4:33:49 (19,545)
Sankey, Stuart C.........5:59:26 (30,388)
Sanmartin, Manuel.........3:40:09 (6,332)
Sanna, Ruzeru.........4:45:47 (22,207)
Sansom, Adam C.........5:06:50 (25,951)
Sansom, Andrew.........7:18:08 (31,773)
Sansom, Chris J.........3:27:45 (4,179)
Sansome, Gary.........3:51:42 (8,940)
Sanson, Luigi.........3:48:08 (8,034)
Sant, Peter.........4:44:18 (21,858)
Santamaria, Carlos.........3:34:25 (5,327)
Santana, Dominic.........4:20:16 (16,085)
Santer, Christopher J.........4:52:19 (23,509)
Santucci, Marcelo S.........3:58:00 (10,671)
Saouli, Mohammed.........4:46:31 (22,365)
Sapp, Robert M.........5:10:13 (26,400)
Sarai Singh, Surinder.........4:20:58 (16,276)
Saraiva, Narciso M.........2:57:52 (952)
Sarallo, Antonio.........5:14:24 (26,950)
Sardella, Enrico.........4:42:31 (21,455)
Sardella, Vito.........2:20:51 (35)
Sargeant, Malcolm C.........4:36:02 (20,036)
Sargeant, Scott A.........3:45:27 (7,397)
Sargeaunt, Philip B.........3:38:57 (6,121)
Sargood, John P.........5:29:40 (28,551)
Sargood, Richard H.........4:25:34 (17,444)
Sari, Abdulkadir.........3:46:10 (7,565)
Sarkies, Adrian.........4:09:36 (13,524)
Sarson, Peter.........3:29:04 (4,425)
Sartain, Adrian T.........4:49:13 (22,920)
Sartain, John R.........3:57:22 (10,505)
Sarti, Piero L.........6:30:50 (31,219)
Sarwa, Stefan E.........4:26:49 (17,777)
Sass, Peter A.........6:06:57 (30,645)
Satchwill, David A.........3:58:12 (10,758)
Sato, Kiyoshi.........4:06:02 (12,670)
Sattentau, Quentin J.........3:29:18 (4,471)
Satterthwaite, Christopher J.........4:26:44 (17,755)
Satterthwaite, Derek W.........5:45:40 (29,733)
Satterthwaite, John B.........4:53:18 (23,671)
Sauer, Beiner.........5:02:10 (25,316)
Sauer, Ulrich.........3:21:48 (3,290)
Saugeot, Cedric.........3:37:22 (5,851)
Saunders, Andrew T.........4:21:47 (16,475)
Saunders, Christopher C.........3:26:30 (3,917)
Saunders, Colin.........4:19:25 (15,887)
Saunders, David A.........4:12:31 (14,208)
Saunders, Gary.........4:35:17 (19,882)
Saunders, Gavin N.........5:14:00 (26,899)
Saunders, Jason W.........4:22:32 (16,709)
Saunders, John C.........3:24:15 (3,595)
Saunders, Julian A.........4:27:44 (18,023)
Saunders, Kevin J.........4:14:00 (14,561)
Saunders, Martin P.........4:07:58 (13,110)
Saunders, Peter J.........3:52:39 (9,162)
Saunders, Peter J.........3:59:25 (11,117)
Saunders, Rowan G.........4:19:08 (15,812)
Saunders, Simon P.........5:19:00 (27,464)
Saunders, Stephen.........3:50:26 (8,614)
Saunders, Steve.........3:25:13 (3,722)
Saunderson, Mark.........3:22:30 (3,375)
Saunderson, Paul R.........4:37:10 (20,284)
Saundes, Raymond R.........4:14:51 (14,773)
Sauniere, Jerome.........4:12:20 (14,156)
Saupin, Alexis.........3:47:03 (7,768)
Sautereau, Carl.........4:46:12 (22,296)
Savage, Andrew J.........6:42:31 (31,398)
Savage, Graham.........5:19:56 (27,551)
Savage, Jeffery M.........4:51:33 (23,351)
Savage, Leonard.........5:38:59 (29,263)
Savage, Luke.........5:01:47 (25,271)
Savage, Rob P.........5:12:46 (26,723)
Savage, Sean P.........4:03:11 (12,003)
Savage, Steven D.........3:41:04 (6,486)
Savage, Terry D.........3:46:53 (7,722)
Savill, David C.........4:02:40 (11,892)
Savill, Mathew.........4:03:07 (11,983)
Savill, Shayne J.........5:07:27 (26,040)
Saville, Philip.........4:17:24 (15,399)
Savin, Guy.........4:54:05 (23,812)
Savino, Jim.........4:04:04 (12,200)
Savino, Salvatore.........4:04:39 (12,340)
Savopoulos, Peter.........4:33:17 (19,422)
Sawayama, Shigero.........4:47:49 (22,639)
Sawdon, Neville J.........3:13:39 (2,393)
Sawford, Paul M.........3:38:59 (6,132)
Sawyer, John D.........3:32:32 (5,009)
Sawyer, Jonathan M.........4:55:00 (23,995)
Sawyer, Richard.........4:26:35 (17,723)
Saxton, Michael J.........4:37:18 (20,315)
Sayburn, Ronan J.........4:14:36 (14,706)
Sayer, Gabriel L.........3:55:18 (9,880)
Sayers, Brian A.........4:34:15 (19,653)
Sayers, Johnny J.........5:33:54 (28,886)
Sayers, Steve J.........3:21:02 (3,205)
Sayers, Victor R.........3:19:50 (3,050)
Sayle, Mark.........4:38:04 (20,488)
Sayle, Roger B.........4:28:20 (18,174)
Scahill, Aidan J.........5:46:54 (29,806)
Scaife, Michael.........4:21:22 (16,352)
Scaldini, Daniele.........4:34:05 (19,619)
Scales, Joseph A.........5:10:55 (26,498)
Scales, Martyn R.........3:57:00 (10,390)
Scaneider, Marcel.........3:53:58 (9,493)
Scanlon, Jeremiah J.........4:16:25 (15,152)
Scanlon, John P.........3:38:22 (6,028)
Scanlon, Maurice J.........5:20:35 (27,641)
Scanlon, Peter J.........4:26:07 (17,613)
Scannell, Howard B.........3:59:36 (11,188)
Scarborough, Derek.........2:42:14 (246)
Scarborough, Linton J.........3:08:16 (1,826)
Scarfe, Geoff M.........4:04:55 (12,411)
Scarinci, Gianluca.........3:38:59 (6,132)
Scarinci, Marco.........3:30:33 (4,699)
Scarlett, Mervyn S.........3:36:53 (5,751)
Scarpellini, Nello.........3:53:10 (9,303)
Scarrott, Ian J.........4:51:14 (23,310)
Scarsi, Giovanni.........3:32:58 (5,092)
Scase, Douglas W.........4:59:41 (24,936)
Schaerer, Juerg.........4:13:02 (14,337)
Schafer, Christian.........3:42:53 (6,830)
Schafer, Wolfgang.........3:27:49 (4,188)
Schaller, Hermann.........4:17:12 (15,349)
Scharfe, Nico.........3:54:46 (9,715)
Scharinger, Markus.........2:53:48 (681)
Scherer, Wolfgang.........4:11:21 (13,939)
Scheunemann, Dirk P.........3:46:03 (7,534)
Schindler, Joseph.........3:58:16 (10,780)
Schlanker, Andrew D.........4:26:45 (17,763)
Schledde, Raimund.........3:12:43 (2,275)
Schlegl, Ulrich.........3:17:28 (2,799)
Schlender, Marten.........3:42:19 (6,700)
Schlorff, Max.........3:14:46 (2,533)
Schlosser, Darren J.........4:16:05 (15,072)
Schmalohr, Rolf.........4:29:22 (18,457)
Schmid, Andreas.........2:36:51 (148)
Schmidhammer, Arno.........4:20:20 (16,115)
Schmidt, Carsten.........4:49:48 (23,044)
Schmidt, Daniel B.........4:09:25 (13,482)
Schmidt-Soltau, Nils S.........4:33:01 (19,363)
Schmidt-Soltau, Peer.........3:54:57 (9,768)
Schmit, Jean Paul.........3:34:47 (5,385)
Schmitt, Ernesto.........3:48:58 (8,245)
Schmitt, Patrice.........3:41:42 (6,582)
Schneider, Michael F.........4:08:40 (13,278)
Schneider, Pierre.........3:39:41 (6,253)
Schnell, Norbert.........3:27:52 (4,203)
Schoene, Michael.........3:01:27 (1,275)
Schoenfelder, Thilo.........3:43:10 (6,884)
Schofield, Alan.........3:53:30 (9,378)
Schofield, Darren M.........4:28:17 (18,165)
Schofield, David.........4:39:29 (20,822)
Schofield, Gerard A.........4:13:07 (14,359)
Schofield, Graham.........3:37:23 (5,854)
Schofield, James.........2:54:58 (752)
Schofield, John P.........5:31:03 (28,663)
Schofield, Michael.........4:55:28 (24,095)

Schofield, Michael R....................3:20:09 (3,084)
Schofield, Nigel L 3:37:11 (5,814)
Schofield, Paul N 3:49:56 (8,482)
Schofield, William R....................5:05:34 (25,774)
Schogger, Rudi D 5:09:03 (26,245)
Scholer, Roy S..............................4:01:19 (11,565)
Scholes, Anthony 3:41:35 (6,561)
Scholes, Damien A 2:49:59 (504)
Scholey, Nigel R 4:22:54 (16,795)
Scholten, Johannes P 6:23:54 (31,104)
Schonnemann, Soren T...............4:15:06 (14,828)
Schoofs, William R......................3:25:09 (3,713)
Schramm, Yigal 3:36:32 (5,702)
Schreiber, Andreas......................4:44:26 (21,897)
Schrenk, Georg 3:13:05 (2,316)
Schroder, Kevin 4:15:04 (14,818)
Schroeder, Gerhard 3:46:34 (7,653)
Schroeter, Detlef 3:32:17 (4,965)
Schroter, Karl-Heinz 3:31:55 (4,907)
Schubert, Peter A 3:40:40 (6,427)
Schultz Zehden, Wolfgang 4:36:04 (20,045)
Schulz, Peter...............................3:47:45 (7,937)
Schulze, Ralph.............................3:30:18 (4,657)
Schumann, Paul 2:57:59 (966)
Schumann, Ronald 3:43:36 (6,979)
Schumann, Thomas 3:24:37 (3,639)
Schuster, David A 5:44:44 (29,672)
Schutrumpf, Armin 3:43:01 (6,854)
Schutte, Andrew C 4:14:17 (14,622)
Schutte, Jonathan J 4:52:44 (23,574)
Schwarz, David R 6:22:07 (31,062)
Schwarz, Geoff C.........................6:22:06 (31,061)
Schwarz, Infgolf S........................3:50:54 (8,735)
Schwarzenbach, Guy E................3:37:54 (5,938)
Schweifer, Reinhard 3:43:59 (7,063)
Sciotti, Valentino.........................3:11:55 (2,183)
Scoffham, Peter N 3:40:41 (6,429)
Scorer, Robert 4:39:49 (20,879)
Scot, George 3:23:46 (3,542)
Scotcher, David J 3:31:44 (4,877)
Scotney, Paul A 5:08:52 (26,218)
Scott, Adrian J 4:36:23 (20,103)
Scott, Alan L 4:48:48 (22,838)
Scott, Alexander J 5:04:19 (25,607)
Scott, Andy C 6:08:58 (30,697)
Scott, Anthony N 3:44:30 (7,185)
Scott, Chris 4:23:52 (17,030)
Scott, Chris 5:10:28 (26,439)
Scott, Christopher J.....................4:19:50 (15,983)
Scott, Christopher R 4:36:47 (20,198)
Scott, Daniel D 4:01:11 (11,544)
Scott, Danny A 2:56:18 (838)
Scott, David S..............................4:22:32 (16,709)
Scott, David W 3:12:52 (2,296)
Scott, Grae M...............................3:07:41 (1,778)
Scott, Hugo D 3:26:37 (3,936)
Scott, Ian 3:03:42 (1,425)
Scott, Ian R 4:19:19 (15,860)
Scott, Ian T 3:56:53 (10,362)
Scott, Jason 4:22:55 (16,799)
Scott, John 4:12:29 (14,194)
Scott, Justin 5:47:13 (29,823)
Scott, Kevin 3:50:19 (8,581)
Scott, Kevin N 4:58:34 (24,729)
Scott, Lee R 3:01:58 (1,299)
Scott, Martin 3:02:10 (1,313)
Scott, Neil 3:48:43 (8,189)
Scott, Patrick D 4:07:18 (12,963)
Scott, Peter G 3:48:11 (8,044)
Scott, Richard 4:20:16 (16,085)
Scott, Richard A 4:01:16 (11,554)
Scott, Richard J 3:52:06 (9,036)
Scott, Robert J 5:20:37 (27,647)
Scott, Robin H 3:11:17 (2,123)
Scott, Samuel 4:25:47 (17,509)
Scott, Stephen A 4:23:13 (16,877)
Scott, Steve 4:15:25 (14,904)
Scott, Steven J 3:07:25 (1,738)
Scott, Ty 4:14:43 (14,732)
Scott, William N 5:15:15 (27,050)
Scott Knight, Ben J.......................3:39:42 (6,256)
Scott-Cook, Maxwell A................4:55:15 (24,052)
Scott-Jones, Peter D 3:29:13 (4,455)

Scottow, Adrian P 4:15:35 (14,949)
Scott-Ralphs, David M................3:41:44 (6,592)
Scott-Sawyer, Desmond F............4:35:18 (19,888)
Scott-Tomlin, Oliver....................6:12:34 (30,797)
Scowcroft, Andrew K...................3:32:46 (5,056)
Scozzese, Felice 3:38:49 (6,102)
Scriven, David A 4:42:49 (21,524)
Scriven, Harvey W 4:01:39 (11,633)
Scriven, Thomas H.......................5:03:28 (25,515)
Scrivener, Chris 3:09:52 (1,989)
Scullard, Jonathan P 3:28:08 (4,251)
Scully, David A 4:07:37 (13,037)
Scully, Kevin J 4:32:20 (19,195)
Scully, Michael............................4:06:45 (12,830)
Scutt, Michael S...........................3:44:10 (7,110)
Scyner, Mark A 3:58:29 (10,845)
Seabrook, Richard 3:44:46 (7,254)
Seager, Daniel D 4:14:33 (14,694)
Seager, Richard J 5:41:37 (29,459)
Seagrave, James 3:40:27 (6,388)
Seal, Daniel M 4:41:01 (21,126)
Seal, Peter J 4:22:05 (16,565)
Sealey, Robert M.........................5:30:00 (28,584)
Sealy, David.................................3:55:37 (9,966)
Seamark, David J..........................5:03:38 (25,539)
Searil, David 3:40:43 (6,433)
Searl, Nick P 4:16:44 (15,234)
Searle, Ken B 4:55:55 (24,186)
Searle, Mick 4:30:16 (18,694)
Sears, Andrew J............................4:44:18 (21,858)
Sears, Derek J 4:07:52 (13,082)
Seaton, Mark I.............................4:34:15 (19,653)
Seaton, Steven 4:23:23 (16,914)
Seaward, Martin V 4:36:26 (20,116)
Sebastiano, Pica...........................3:38:18 (6,010)
Sebire, Jonathan R 4:17:13 (15,351)
Sebley, Benjamin W 3:12:19 (2,228)
Sebley, Nicholas D 3:23:45 (3,538)
Seddon, Andrew H.......................2:57:24 (905)
Seddon, Dwaine P 4:09:36 (13,524)
Seddon, Jeff 3:10:22 (2,035)
Seddon, Russell W 5:13:33 (26,839)
Sedge, Martyn J 3:08:16 (1,826)
Sedgfield, Alex B..........................5:07:56 (26,103)
Sedgley, Trevor 5:36:20 (29,048)
Sedgmond, Andrew M 3:57:31 (10,546)
Sedgwick, Glenn C 5:05:22 (25,734)
Sedgwick, Stephen 3:44:07 (7,097)
Sedgwick, Stephen J.....................3:57:16 (10,466)
Sedman, John M 4:17:45 (15,494)
Seekings, Harry E........................4:28:29 (18,227)
Seeley, Benjamin R 4:42:01 (21,348)
Sefton, Paul S 3:27:31 (4,131)
Segal, Oliver P 4:22:31 (16,703)
Segall, Alan M 4:02:31 (11,858)
Segovia, Claudio E 5:35:00 (28,956)
Seidel, Dale L 4:45:19 (22,101)
Seignobosc, Christian 3:27:48 (4,187)
Seitz, Theodor E 3:59:34 (11,177)
Seitz, Theodor-Cyrus B 4:05:51 (12,627)
Sejlitz, Gunnar............................3:56:48 (10,330)
Sekhon, Gurdeep S 3:47:55 (7,977)
Selby, Jason D 5:30:10 (28,599)
Selby, Martin 5:15:57 (27,125)
Selby, Paul...................................5:15:57 (27,125)
Selke, Christoph 3:35:35 (5,541)
Sell, Richard E.............................4:30:12 (18,679)
Sellers, Andrew J 4:05:45 (12,606)
Sellers, David A 4:09:11 (13,415)
Sellick, James 4:30:35 (18,777)
Sellick, Robert A 3:46:10 (7,565)
Sellwood, Jonathan H 4:09:48 (13,577)
Sellwood, Michael J.....................3:59:36 (11,188)
Selmes, Ian P 3:23:03 (3,446)
Selway, Richard J 4:26:04 (17,593)

Selwyn, Raymond A.....................3:20:47 (3,173)
Sema, Enio 4:57:00 (24,404)
Semmens, Philip 4:34:38 (19,743)
Semmo, Nasser............................4:04:47 (12,372)
Sempill, Colin D 3:47:37 (7,910)
Semple, Ian 4:19:46 (15,969)
Sen, Paul A 4:49:48 (23,044)
Sena, Richard A 3:26:20 (3,896)
Senior, Gregory A 4:48:19 (22,742)
Senior, Mark D 4:23:58 (17,053)
Senkiw, Walter 4:32:44 (19,300)
Septier, Eric 4:10:02 (13,644)
Serani, Gabriele 3:52:05 (9,033)
Sergeant, David C.........................3:29:09 (4,440)
Sergeant, Jamie C.........................3:55:30 (9,929)
Series, Grant 4:17:09 (15,341)
Serrano, Henrik 3:18:29 (2,896)
Serrano-Vera, Luis M 3:28:52 (4,392)
Servaes, Michael J........................4:58:25 (24,698)
Setchell, Norman W 7:59:19 (31,930)
Setford, John A.............................4:02:14 (11,789)
Sethard-Wright, Matthew G.........5:23:44 (27,948)
Severn, Gary F 4:33:55 (19,569)
Sewell, Andrew P 3:07:29 (1,751)
Sewell, Michael C 3:44:19 (7,142)
Sewell, Peter F 5:10:43 (26,469)
Sewell, William P 4:05:32 (12,550)
Sexton, Patrick J 5:00:24 (25,052)
Sexty, Roger G 3:22:07 (3,317)
Seymour, Christopher J 3:59:06 (11,030)
Seymour, Christopher S 4:32:39 (19,276)
Seymour, David A 3:17:14 (2,778)
Seymour, Mark 5:09:41 (26,336)
Seymour, Michael J 5:29:41 (28,555)
Seymour, Richard D 6:25:48 (31,137)
Seymour, Thomas J 3:44:33 (7,201)
Shackleford, Paul M 4:11:54 (14,063)
Shadwell, Scott 4:29:39 (18,542)
Shafee, Rex 4:57:43 (24,538)
Shafier, Lawrence E 3:09:36 (1,961)
Shah, Amit A 4:19:13 (15,839)
Shah, Anuj 5:34:10 (28,901)
Shah, Hamel M 4:39:57 (20,904)
Shah, Harish R 4:36:13 (20,076)
Shah, Kaushik 3:50:52 (8,723)
Shah, Neerav 4:22:05 (16,565)
Shah, Neil 4:19:44 (15,959)
Shah, Nicholas 4:24:06 (17,092)
Shah, Rasiklal L 5:32:05 (28,736)
Shah, Romal 4:55:19 (24,067)
Shah, Sailesh G 5:52:10 (30,074)
Shah, Sanjay 5:37:35 (29,156)
Shah, Sunil 4:21:13 (16,315)
Shah, Vishal M 4:51:47 (23,395)
Shaikh, Shakil A 4:27:57 (18,082)
Shakeshaft, Andrew B 3:06:30 (1,653)
Shakeshaft, John 4:22:40 (16,740)
Shakespeare, Stephen J 4:19:11 (15,825)
Shallice, Andy..............................4:04:35 (12,330)
Shalom, Dan................................3:38:00 (5,961)
Shamsavanpour, Ali.....................5:11:17 (26,552)
Shanahan, Matthew J 5:36:11 (29,037)
Shankland, Tony D.......................5:59:59 (30,408)
Shanks, Andrew D 4:23:05 (16,837)
Shanks, Roderick A 3:23:37 (3,519)
Shann, Tommy 4:38:54 (20,693)
Shannahan, Tony P 5:26:37 (28,262)
Shannon, Martin W 4:51:33 (23,351)
Shannon, Michael W 3:55:57 (10,067)
Share, Michael P 4:21:54 (16,500)
Sharkey, Mark 4:34:54 (19,802)
Sharland, Michael J......................3:33:06 (5,116)
Sharma, Amit..............................4:21:48 (16,480)
Sharma, Kishore K 3:55:52 (10,037)
Sharma, Manish 5:30:15 (28,604)
Sharma, Sanjai.............................3:07:16 (1,725)
Sharma, Viv 5:14:33 (26,969)
Sharman, David P.........................3:55:32 (9,942)
Sharman, Richard 4:25:02 (17,314)
Sharon, Lionel H 4:28:31 (18,235)
Sharp, Andrew D 3:46:15 (7,591)
Sharp, Christopher B 3:40:16 (6,345)
Sharp, Ian 4:17:18 (15,368)

Sharp, Ian 4:49:55 (23,062)
Sharp, Jeremy F 3:14:28 (2,496)
Sharp, Jeremy G 4:20:30 (16,159)
Sharp, Michael 5:05:07 (25,705)
Sharp, Michael D 3:29:12 (4,449)
Sharp, Paul W 5:24:21 (28,008)
Sharp, Pete A 6:36:37 (31,315)
Sharp, Steve 4:40:53 (21,105)
Sharp, Stuart R 4:09:36 (13,524)
Sharp, Thomas K 4:33:40 (19,500)
Sharpe, Andrew J 4:54:41 (23,938)
Sharpe, Anthony C 4:26:53 (17,808)
Sharpe, Danny P 5:38:50 (29,249)
Sharpe, David W 5:42:05 (29,488)
Sharpe, Justin R 3:46:32 (7,644)
Sharpe, Michael 6:02:16 (30,493)
Sharples, Stephen R 3:54:07 (9,532)
Sharpley, Robert D 4:40:43 (21,068)
Sharratt, Leo 4:50:54 (23,251)
Sharrock, Gavin J 5:11:11 (26,535)
Shatford, Jeremy M 4:46:34 (22,368)
Shaw, Adam 5:43:08 (29,575)
Shaw, Andrew 3:59:55 (11,273)
Shaw, Andy 4:40:22 (21,003)
Shaw, Anthony J 3:47:20 (7,837)
Shaw, Ben M 3:30:21 (4,663)
Shaw, Chris G 4:44:45 (21,967)
Shaw, Colin E 4:48:28 (22,774)
Shaw, Darren P 4:10:28 (13,749)
Shaw, Dave B 4:15:26 (14,909)
Shaw, David A 2:56:26 (848)
Shaw, David N 3:27:28 (4,122)
Shaw, David N 4:20:18 (16,101)
Shaw, Dean P 4:49:02 (22,883)
Shaw, Duncan 4:32:52 (19,327)
Shaw, Gary J 3:19:38 (3,034)
Shaw, Gerry 3:07:37 (1,767)
Shaw, Graham L 3:43:30 (6,962)
Shaw, Graham W 3:24:52 (3,672)
Shaw, James 3:43:55 (7,043)
Shaw, James C 3:23:45 (3,538)
Shaw, Jeremy D 4:46:10 (22,289)
Shaw, Jonathan P 3:58:21 (10,804)
Shaw, Leslie J 5:11:44 (26,596)
Shaw, Michael R 4:08:53 (13,342)
Shaw, Mike 4:43:21 (21,654)
Shaw, Neil M 3:05:08 (1,538)
Shaw, Paul A 3:58:03 (10,689)
Shaw, Paul S 3:24:02 (3,569)
Shaw, Peter E 3:05:48 (1,589)
Shaw, Philip E 3:38:18 (6,010)
Shaw, Robert A 4:18:45 (15,723)
Shaw, Robert J 3:27:14 (4,070)
Shaw, Robert M 4:04:02 (12,194)
Shaw, Simon A 4:38:15 (20,533)
Shaw, Stephen D 4:08:22 (13,193)
Shaw, Stuart A 3:21:09 (3,214)
Shaw, Stuart K 4:10:13 (13,681)
Shayers, Timothy P 3:38:15 (6,004)
Shean, John R 3:42:20 (6,705)
Sheard, Nicholas A 3:14:29 (2,501)
Sheard, Steven 3:10:42 (2,071)
Shearer, Colin J 4:33:28 (19,463)
Shearer, Craig 4:54:42 (23,940)
Shearer, Richard J 2:36:24 (140)
Shearman, Cliff P 3:47:45 (7,937)
Shearman, Robert W 4:53:09 (23,643)
Sheedy, Ben P 4:25:41 (17,474)
Sheehan, Brendan M 4:47:02 (22,456)
Sheehan, Jonathan A 3:59:22 (11,105)
Sheehan, Martin 3:20:38 (3,152)
Sheehan, Michael J 3:43:38 (6,985)
Sheehan, Michael J 3:43:56 (7,047)
Sheehy, Patrick T 3:51:17 (8,828)
Sheen, Philip 3:48:19 (8,081)
Sheibani, Mohammad 4:27:00 (17,840)
Sheikh, Aref 5:19:15 (27,486)
Sheikh, Omar F 4:28:03 (18,107)
Sheldon, Anthony J 3:05:08 (1,538)
Sheldon, Mark 3:34:45 (5,381)
Sheldrake, Jonathan G 3:32:29 (5,003)
Sheldrick, Russell S 3:56:03 (10,099)
Shellard, Michael G 4:04:26 (12,294)
Shelley, Alan W 6:18:59 (30,988)
Shelley, Alastair L 5:01:27 (25,217)
Shelley, Desmond R 4:18:40 (15,702)
Shelly, Simon 4:36:28 (20,123)
Shelton, Andrew 2:56:04 (815)
Shelton, Michael R 3:19:37 (3,029)
Shelton, Nicholas 4:19:26 (15,894)
Shelton, Richard C 4:03:53 (12,166)
Shennan, John M 3:34:09 (5,291)
Shenton, Paul J 4:46:51 (22,415)
Shenton, Peter G 4:17:32 (15,433)
Shepard, Ian 5:28:58 (28,481)
Shephard, Mark S 4:09:03 (13,390)
Shephard, Simon A 4:34:41 (19,753)
Shepheard, Nicholas S 3:07:08 (1,717)
Shepheard, Peter E 4:29:21 (18,451)
Shepherd, Adam R 5:55:01 (30,197)
Shepherd, André T 3:09:00 (1,898)
Shepherd, Ben 3:30:05 (4,611)
Shepherd, Chris R 4:14:54 (14,786)
Shepherd, Joe 3:55:40 (9,976)
Shepherd, Laurie 5:03:23 (25,497)
Shepherd, Paul A 3:55:16 (9,868)
Shepherd, Simon P 4:30:35 (18,777)
Shepherd, Terence K 3:34:58 (5,419)
Shepley, Sebastian A 2:36:39 (145)
Sheppard, Adrian J 4:39:16 (20,786)
Sheppard, Andrew 3:41:34 (6,553)
Sheppard, Jonathan 4:33:41 (19,502)
Sheppard, Michael T 4:17:46 (15,499)
Sheppard, Nicholas 5:20:09 (27,588)
Sheppard, Phil 4:55:57 (24,200)
Sheppard, Simon 4:12:28 (14,187)
Shepperd, Nicholas J 3:30:33 (4,699)
Sheridan, Andrew 4:39:17 (20,788)
Sheridan, David 4:07:16 (12,960)
Sheridan, Mark 3:47:26 (7,864)
Sheriff, Philip M 3:29:24 (4,488)
Shering, Chris J 3:17:07 (2,762)
Sherlock, Gareth 3:41:43 (6,586)
Sherlock, Peter J 3:38:10 (5,989)
Sherlock, Richard G 3:58:34 (10,879)
Sherman, Robin 5:12:02 (26,638)
Sherratt, Ian C 4:08:56 (13,358)
Sherriff, Michael J 3:58:55 (10,979)
Sherrocks, John F 3:54:17 (9,583)
Sherwood, Edwin R 5:24:05 (27,978)
Sherwood, Paul E 4:26:39 (17,744)
Sherwood, Ronnie 3:46:10 (7,565)
Shew, Peter 4:54:42 (23,940)
Shibli, Simon A 3:43:43 (6,998)
Shiel, Danny J 5:19:45 (27,528)
Shiel, Stephen W 3:53:11 (9,310)
Shiel, Terence J 4:57:45 (24,545)
Shield, Ian W 3:59:12 (11,060)
Shields, John A 3:32:12 (4,952)
Shields, Peter 3:10:22 (2,035)
Shillito, James R 4:08:18 (13,177)
Shimada, Susumu 3:52:02 (9,021)
Shimada, Yoshihiro 4:02:47 (11,921)
Shimizu, Tadanori 4:15:45 (14,988)
Shingfield, Jonathan A 4:39:40 (20,855)
Shipley, David H 6:40:20 (31,365)
Shipman, Jim M 3:42:47 (6,807)
Shipp, Martin W 3:30:50 (4,747)
Shipton, Daniel 4:21:17 (16,328)
Shipton, James R 3:42:54 (6,835)
Shipton, Mark W 3:33:27 (5,182)
Shipway, David J 3:50:05 (8,521)
Shiraki, Shinichiro 4:31:30 (18,982)
Shirley, Andrew 3:37:25 (5,864)
Shirley, David 3:22:15 (3,335)
Shirley, Peter J 2:55:18 (772)
Shoesmith, Tony D 4:39:18 (20,792)
Sholl, William H 3:51:02 (8,753)
Shone, Grahame P 3:00:22 (1,184)
Shore, Ben 4:10:36 (13,782)
Shore, Martin P 2:29:30 (78)
Shore, Richard E 3:39:39 (6,244)
Shore, Richard I 4:04:27 (12,300)
Shoreland, James A 4:07:39 (13,044)
Shorey, Tim J 4:19:02 (15,782)
Shorney, Richard H 4:47:20 (22,526)
Shorrock, Daniel J 4:28:28 (18,220)
Short, Duncan R 3:48:30 (8,118)
Short, Garry J 3:00:51 (1,225)
Short, Gary J 4:40:30 (21,028)
Short, Robert 6:10:52 (30,753)
Short, Tony 4:43:51 (21,761)
Shorters, Alex F 3:57:45 (10,605)
Shortman, Philip J 4:23:45 (17,002)
Shosanya, Sam O 4:23:40 (16,978)
Shoults, Will C 3:20:40 (3,157)
Shrager, Tom M 5:40:38 (29,390)
Shreeve, Phil 3:28:49 (4,381)
Shrimplin, Stephen 4:18:32 (15,670)
Shrubsole, Dean M 4:41:37 (21,262)
Shubber, Salim 6:32:10 (31,247)
Shuck, Steve P 2:59:23 (1,111)
Shulman, Brad M 4:42:04 (21,364)
Shurrock, Stephen J 5:03:26 (25,507)
Shute, Kevin E 4:09:37 (13,534)
Shuttleworth, Chris B 4:40:25 (21,012)
Shuttleworth, David 4:33:03 (19,367)
Shuttleworth, Keith 5:42:30 (29,514)
Shyjka, Michael G 3:51:43 (8,945)
Sibbald, Lee 4:21:23 (16,358)
Sibley, Neil 4:20:37 (16,191)
Sibson, Andrew D 4:44:54 (22,002)
Sica Amaduzzi, Aldo 3:46:24 (7,620)
Sicaud, Jean-Louis 3:31:10 (4,801)
Sidaway, Stephen H 3:21:18 (3,230)
Siddall, Stuart J 4:24:45 (17,241)
Siddens, John A 2:39:30 (197)
Sidders, Andrew J 4:07:02 (12,903)
Sidders, Stuart J 4:40:41 (21,062)
Siddiqi, Shahab A 3:34:41 (5,366)
Siddle, Graham M 5:19:05 (27,474)
Siddons, Barrie J 4:22:09 (16,588)
Siddy, Martin B 4:40:20 (20,991)
Sidebotham, John P 2:55:27 (782)
Sidhu, Jagir 5:12:12 (26,654)
Sidi-Moussa, Abdelkader K 3:36:57 (5,761)
Sidwick, Bob 3:30:01 (4,591)
Siebra, Clauirton A 5:24:18 (28,003)
Siefert, Michael T 4:52:18 (23,503)
Siegieniuk, Valdomiro 3:24:09 (3,581)
Siegrist, Robert B 4:32:26 (19,220)
Sieni, Alberto 4:22:02 (16,548)
Siers, Brian A 4:38:57 (20,706)
Siffert, Thierry 3:07:38 (1,771)
Siggers, Aidan F 3:52:37 (9,154)
Siggers, Andrew J 3:29:49 (4,558)
Silberstein, Jorge 4:38:35 (20,615)
Silby, Philip F 5:28:04 (28,401)
Silcock, Graham 4:27:12 (17,892)
Silcock, Richard C 4:26:32 (17,710)
Silk, Jonathan C 4:31:53 (19,072)
Silk, Peter J 4:22:11 (16,598)
Silkstone, Edwin B 5:23:46 (27,950)
Sillers, Jonathan A 4:42:51 (21,534)
Sillett, Craig 4:12:31 (14,208)
Sills, Brian W 5:55:23 (30,224)
Sills, Colin S 4:38:23 (20,566)
Sills, Matthew R 4:42:49 (21,524)
Silva, Claudio 3:11:57 (2,188)
Silva, Timothy M 4:24:04 (17,076)
Silver, Michael I 4:40:55 (21,109)
Silverman, Brian 5:54:29 (30,169)
Silverman, Zach B 5:28:21 (28,426)
Silvers, Rod M 4:41:23 (21,215)
Silverstein, Justin 5:37:32 (29,153)
Silverthorn, Kevin R 3:36:42 (5,725)
Silverton, Ross L 4:26:19 (17,658)
Silvester, Jonathan D 3:52:40 (9,165)
Silvey, Adrian 4:09:57 (13,625)
Sim, Craig 4:31:08 (18,885)
Sim, Li B 4:54:44 (23,947)
Sim, Richard A 4:25:26 (17,408)
Simcock, Greg 3:44:41 (7,236)
Simcox, John A 3:51:06 (8,765)
Sime, Andrew J 4:49:26 (22,961)
Simkins, Paul J 4:04:50 (12,385)
Simmonds, Alistair D 4:30:15 (18,691)
Simmonds, Andrew J 4:23:24 (16,921)
Simmonds, Gavin W 3:49:36 (8,403)

Old timers

In 2004, 93-year-old Fauja Singh clocked 6:7:13. He promptly retired but said he might be tempted back to be the first finisher over 100. The oldest woman to complete the marathon was Jenny Allen who completed the London at the age of 90 in 2002. She finished in 11:34:00.

Simmons, James S 4:31:40 (19,014)
Simmons, Keith P....................6:19:17 (30,997)
Simmons, Martin 5:27:07 (28,312)
Simmons, Paul D......................4:29:59 (18,626)
Simmons, Peter 3:51:30 (8,888)
Simmons, Tim 3:54:16 (9,581)
Simmons, Trevor H..................5:12:01 (26,635)
Simms, Jonathan J....................4:56:19 (24,266)
Simms, William M 3:50:43 (8,688)
Simo, Ricard P 5:28:06 (28,405)
Simon, Paul F...........................4:17:58 (15,549)
Simons, Alastair V....................5:23:07 (27,882)
Simons, Paul H.........................3:58:25 (10,824)
Simons, Roger A.......................5:07:40 (26,071)
Simpkin, Andrew P 4:57:15 (24,450)
Simpson, Andrew D 4:04:44 (12,364)
Simpson, Antony T 4:31:14 (18,903)
Simpson, Colin L 3:15:48 (2,633)
Simpson, Daniel Z....................3:52:32 (9,136)
Simpson, Danny L.....................4:17:23 (15,392)
Simpson, Darryl F 4:24:49 (17,255)
Simpson, David 3:18:10 (2,868)
Simpson, David A......................5:19:18 (27,489)
Simpson, David D......................5:07:17 (26,006)
Simpson, David E......................3:44:48 (7,261)
Simpson, Edward 4:44:06 (21,815)
Simpson, Gareth 3:52:26 (9,120)
Simpson, Gareth S 3:07:43 (1,780)
Simpson, Gerry M 4:12:32 (14,214)
Simpson, Iain 3:45:56 (7,514)
Simpson, Ian S.........................3:42:58 (6,843)
Simpson, John 4:25:09 (17,351)
Simpson, John R 5:39:58 (29,332)
Simpson, Jonathan D 4:17:26 (15,406)
Simpson, Keith A 3:12:09 (2,208)
Simpson, Kenneth J 4:24:44 (17,238)
Simpson, Mark E 5:41:23 (29,437)
Simpson, Matt S 3:53:10 (9,303)
Simpson, Paul 6:30:56 (31,223)
Simpson, Peter B 3:55:32 (9,942)
Simpson, Richard H..................3:56:47 (10,323)
Simpson, Richard J 3:20:36 (3,150)
Simpson, Robert J 3:53:48 (9,444)
Simpson, Russell J 5:56:27 (30,271)
Simpson, Steven E.....................2:47:44 (412)
Simpson, Stuart R 6:04:51 (30,590)
Simpson, Tony..........................7:35:31 (31,874)
Sims, Andy D 4:02:31 (11,858)
Sims, Antony G.........................4:39:38 (20,847)
Sims, Lee..................................4:08:08 (13,139)
Sims, Matthew C.......................3:14:57 (2,554)
Sims, Michael 5:32:19 (28,761)
Sims, Paul M 3:50:38 (8,670)
Sinar, Kevin J 3:54:00 (9,505)
Sinclair, Ashley J.....................3:31:58 (4,918)
Sinclair, David A......................3:41:09 (6,504)
Sinclair, Hamish W...................5:16:00 (27,132)
Sinclair, Ian M 5:13:12 (26,795)
Sinclair, James D......................4:22:18 (16,637)
Sinclair, Kevin 3:31:53 (4,898)
Sinclair, Malcolm.....................3:44:08 (7,102)
Sinclair, Mark P 5:04:28 (25,623)
Sinclair, Nigel J........................3:21:19 (3,233)
Sinclair, Paul J 3:46:29 (7,637)
Sinclair, Richard H...................4:33:06 (19,381)
Sinclair, Terence F....................2:56:30 (852)
Sinden, Matthew 5:09:19 (26,280)

Singer, Christopher....................4:40:05 (20,936)
Singer, Colin G..........................3:38:10 (5,989)
Singer, Florian C 3:34:37 (5,355)
Singer, Humphrey S...................3:51:08 (8,774)
Singer, Stuart 3:53:31 (9,380)
Singh, Ajit 5:49:32 (29,933)
Singh, Amarprit.........................4:22:56 (16,802)
Singh, Amrik.............................5:49:32 (29,933)
Singh, Anil K.............................4:14:27 (14,665)
Singh, Avtar 4:37:24 (20,328)
Singh, Bhupender.......................2:55:54 (805)

Singh, Fauja 6:07:13 (30,653)

Singh, George G.........................4:07:23 (12,982)
Singh, Graham A........................5:02:27 (25,366)
Singh, Harbhag 4:13:53 (14,540)
Singh, Harjinder 4:41:26 (21,228)
Singh, Harjit 4:18:58 (15,773)
Singh, Harmander......................6:07:11 (30,652)
Singh, Inderjit 5:11:23 (26,563)
Singh, Jagjit J............................5:08:27 (26,177)
Singh, Manjit 4:36:20 (20,096)
Singh, Pavandip 5:03:11 (25,475)
Singh, Sheeraz M 4:10:28 (13,749)
Singh, Steve 5:32:31 (28,777)
Singh Badyal, Jaspal 5:26:22 (28,237)
Sirett, Darren B 4:20:58 (16,276)
Sirett, Giles R............................4:07:13 (12,945)
Sirett, Mike D............................3:42:23 (6,717)
Sirignano, Arnalod.....................5:13:58 (26,890)
Siriwardana, Nimatha K.............4:30:23 (18,724)
Sissons, Guy R...........................4:53:40 (23,740)
Sisto, Egidio..............................5:59:25 (30,383)
Sitruk, Thierry 4:01:34 (11,613)
Siu, Alan Y 3:20:59 (3,200)
Siu, Simon T 3:43:10 (6,884)
Sivyer, Stephen 4:58:15 (24,653)
S'jacob, Oliver P.........................3:31:30 (4,850)
Sjogren, Heinz...........................3:10:10 (2,018)
Sjostrand, Ulf............................6:29:32 (31,195)
Skaaden, Tore............................3:31:47 (4,886)
Skaja, Joseph M 3:57:22 (10,505)
Skaper, George 3:30:13 (4,637)
Skedgell, Steven P 4:19:20 (15,866)
Skeene, Andrew N 5:08:28 (26,180)
Skeggs, James D.........................5:13:09 (26,786)
Skelly, Martin 4:13:28 (14,442)
Skelly, Tim J 4:56:31 (24,314)

Skelt, Christopher 4:59:26 (24,889)
Skelton, Chris............................3:19:25 (3,008)
Skelton, Mark A.........................4:41:19 (21,194)
Skelton, Nick.............................5:36:05 (29,033)
Skelton, Stephen D 4:26:10 (17,621)
Skelton, Travis J........................3:51:36 (8,916)
Skerm, Paul A............................3:36:15 (5,650)
Skerrett, Robert M 4:57:10 (24,429)
Skidmore, Jonathan 2:58:02 (974)
Skidmore, Paul 4:05:25 (12,515)
Skilbeck, Paul 4:45:26 (22,125)
Skilbeck, Richard 3:33:32 (5,194)
Skingley, Ian D 3:10:41 (2,070)
Skinner, Dale M 5:12:18 (26,669)
Skinner, George 6:08:40 (30,690)
Skinner, Kevin L........................2:51:27 (565)
Skinner, Martin 3:55:32 (9,942)
Skinner, Martyn P 4:00:01 (11,300)
Skinner, Michael 3:46:48 (7,702)
Skinner, Raymond A 3:54:09 (9,542)
Skinner, Stephen N 3:47:08 (7,790)
Skipp, Paul G.............................3:02:27 (1,337)
Skipper, Barry M 4:39:11 (20,772)
Skipper, Edward D 4:16:48 (15,251)
Skivington, Ian J........................5:08:30 (26,182)
Skov, Henrik 2:59:13 (1,095)
Skrabania, Dean R 3:55:26 (9,914)
Skrine, Alexander M 3:59:19 (11,092)
Skyrme, Stephen 5:24:53 (28,065)
Slack, Gordon E.........................3:55:19 (9,887)
Slack, William A 3:49:41 (8,419)
Slade, Darren 3:26:14 (3,875)
Slade, Nick D.............................4:04:56 (12,418)
Slade, Rob M 4:21:48 (16,480)
Slade, Stephen G 4:19:15 (15,846)
Slane, Richard G 3:50:21 (8,595)
Slape, Robert W.........................4:09:48 (13,577)
Slater, Alan 4:29:55 (18,614)
Slater, Alfred C 4:07:14 (12,952)
Slater, Bryan C 5:08:58 (26,231)
Slater, Charles P 3:49:56 (8,482)
Slater, David W..........................3:52:59 (9,252)
Slater, Gavin 4:07:28 (13,001)
Slater, Graham R 4:43:35 (21,696)
Slater, Jeff M 4:08:58 (13,369)
Slater, Mark A............................3:52:29 (9,130)
Slater, Martin F..........................5:20:05 (27,577)
Slater, Michael 4:34:28 (19,704)
Slater, Paul N.............................3:14:06 (2,449)
Slater, Peter J 3:25:54 (3,827)
Slater, Philip H...........................3:49:11 (8,306)
Slater, Richard J.........................3:13:46 (2,404)
Slater, Richard V 4:36:24 (20,104)
Slater, Stephen F 4:55:44 (24,143)
Slator, Clive 4:16:37 (15,211)
Slayne, Andrew R 5:25:51 (28,181)
Slee, Ian S 4:26:03 (17,585)
Slee, Robert 3:08:59 (1,896)
Sleep, Anthony R 4:41:24 (21,220)
Sleep, Christopher J...................4:10:47 (13,824)
Sleight, Andrew K 3:21:59 (3,305)
Slinger, John A 3:07:03 (1,708)
Slinger, Robert A 3:33:07 (5,122)
Slingsby, Dominic S...................4:42:45 (21,506)
Slingsby, Mark 3:02:34 (1,342)
Slinn, Gregory J.........................5:09:34 (26,317)
Sloan, Jonathan A 4:08:48 (13,325)
Sloan, Matthew W 4:10:42 (13,800)
Sloley, Robert J 3:00:13 (1,171)
Sloman, Gary 4:02:18 (11,805)
Sloman, Hywel 4:20:37 (16,191)
Slot, Peter G..............................4:20:11 (16,059)
Slowly, Daniel 3:50:51 (8,720)
Sluis, Frank 2:51:25 (563)
Sluman, Jon D 4:50:26 (23,167)
Slutter, Benjamin R 4:34:38 (19,743)
Sly, Michael J 5:42:52 (29,539)
Smale, Chris P 4:04:07 (12,214)
Smale, Don C 4:33:56 (19,573)
Small, Iain R 6:00:08 (30,414)
Small, Stephen 4:49:10 (22,912)
Smallbone, Craig.......................3:27:54 (4,211)
Smalldridge, Danny 4:53:53 (23,774)

Name	Time	Name	Time	Name	Time
Smalley, Alan C	3:59:11 (11,054)	Smith, David K	5:29:05 (28,490)	Smith, Mark	5:05:40 (25,783)
Smalley, David J	6:49:16 (31,488)	Smith, David M	2:56:06 (820)	Smith, Mark A	3:59:49 (11,242)
Smallman, Darryl	4:57:57 (24,582)	Smith, David M	3:40:55 (6,459)	Smith, Mark A	5:05:05 (25,700)
Smalls, Allen	2:40:08 (213)	Smith, David N	3:51:33 (8,905)	Smith, Mark C	4:27:38 (18,000)
Smallwood, Andrew C	3:46:10 (7,565)	Smith, David P	3:44:36 (7,213)	Smith, Mark D	4:42:07 (21,372)
Smallwood, Mark	4:36:12 (20,072)	Smith, David S	6:02:37 (30,519)	Smith, Mark G	4:07:28 (13,001)
Smart, Andy I	4:08:17 (13,170)	Smith, David W	4:17:55 (15,538)	Smith, Martin E	4:10:50 (13,837)
Smart, Anthony D	3:32:52 (5,075)	Smith, Dean A	4:43:43 (21,726)	Smith, Martin J	3:07:29 (1,751)
Smart, Jeremy C	4:56:59 (24,400)	Smith, Dean G	4:36:58 (20,247)	Smith, Martin J	4:57:43 (24,538)
Smeddle, Jeremy H	3:55:27 (9,916)	Smith, Derek N	5:01:55 (25,289)	Smith, Martin R	4:20:10 (16,057)
Smee, Tim	3:50:02 (8,511)	Smith, Derek P	5:37:15 (29,130)	Smith, Martyn D	4:52:42 (23,570)
Smethurst, Christopher F	4:31:55 (19,088)	Smith, Derek R	5:38:26 (29,224)	Smith, Martyn P	3:27:17 (4,078)
Smethurst, Mike	3:17:53 (2,838)	Smith, Dominic A	4:08:27 (13,214)	Smith, Mathew	4:15:09 (14,846)
Smiles, Peter A	4:47:02 (22,456)	Smith, Donal E	3:41:43 (6,586)	Smith, Matt	2:21:53 (41)
Smillie, Andrew	3:51:54 (8,989)	Smith, Donald H	4:20:40 (16,200)	Smith, Matt C	3:39:29 (6,214)
Smit, François J	5:00:13 (25,027)	Smith, Douglas R	6:31:24 (31,233)	Smith, Matthew	3:39:27 (6,209)
Smit, Stephan B	4:22:08 (16,582)	Smith, Duane B	6:48:05 (31,476)	Smith, Matthew	4:07:52 (13,082)
Smith, Adam B	4:28:06 (18,125)	Smith, Duncan I	3:04:52 (1,512)	Smith, Matthew	5:00:54 (25,127)
Smith, Adam P	4:13:10 (14,369)	Smith, Edwin J	3:35:07 (5,452)	Smith, Matthew D	5:15:36 (27,089)
Smith, Adrian A	3:45:27 (7,397)	Smith, Erik K	2:57:12 (893)	Smith, Matthew G	4:10:38 (13,789)
Smith, Adrian P	4:12:30 (14,200)	Smith, Fred	6:46:18 (31,456)	Smith, Michael J	3:12:00 (2,194)
Smith, Alan H	3:35:01 (5,429)	Smith, Garry N	5:05:31 (25,766)	Smith, Michael J	3:44:40 (7,230)
Smith, Alan J	4:00:00 (11,296)	Smith, Gary	3:57:19 (10,488)	Smith, Michael J	4:28:37 (18,259)
Smith, Alasdair J	4:23:33 (16,953)	Smith, Gary	4:31:09 (18,892)	Smith, Michael J	5:02:03 (25,304)
Smith, Alexander J	4:38:54 (20,693)	Smith, Gary	4:33:11 (19,399)	Smith, Mike	3:13:24 (2,357)
Smith, Allan	5:12:09 (26,649)	Smith, Gary S	4:05:10 (12,459)	Smith, Mike P	4:08:18 (13,177)
Smith, Alun	3:32:58 (5,092)	Smith, Geoffrey B	3:48:31 (8,124)	Smith, Neal A	3:49:07 (8,286)
Smith, Andrew	3:55:49 (10,022)	Smith, George G	4:49:31 (22,981)	Smith, Neil A	4:31:10 (18,895)
Smith, Andrew	4:36:35 (20,150)	Smith, Gerry C	2:49:56 (497)	Smith, Neil C	4:09:57 (13,625)
Smith, Andrew C	3:21:04 (3,208)	Smith, Glynn R	3:46:23 (7,617)	Smith, Neil R	4:26:58 (17,830)
Smith, Andrew G	3:16:25 (2,690)	Smith, Graeme D	5:14:34 (26,971)	Smith, Nicholas J	2:57:58 (963)
Smith, Andrew G	4:04:34 (12,329)	Smith, Graham A	5:43:45 (29,613)	Smith, Nicholas P	3:50:53 (8,730)
Smith, Andrew J	2:53:04 (647)	Smith, Graham D	3:59:20 (11,096)	Smith, Nicholas S	3:24:37 (3,639)
Smith, Andrew J	3:21:25 (3,246)	Smith, Grant A	4:12:37 (14,239)	Smith, Nigel	5:33:51 (28,878)
Smith, Andrew J	3:49:36 (8,403)	Smith, Gray	4:28:46 (18,292)	Smith, Patrick G	4:31:47 (19,049)
Smith, Andrew J	4:08:57 (13,364)	Smith, Greg	3:42:28 (6,735)	Smith, Paul	3:45:07 (7,322)
Smith, Andrew J	4:47:01 (22,453)	Smith, Guy	3:47:41 (7,925)	Smith, Paul A	3:33:47 (5,233)
Smith, Andrew P	4:39:05 (20,747)	Smith, Harry J	5:32:40 (28,788)	Smith, Paul A	4:37:12 (20,298)
Smith, Andrew R	4:18:44 (15,717)	Smith, Howard J	4:44:19 (21,865)	Smith, Paul A	4:37:45 (20,391)
Smith, Andy M	3:33:08 (5,127)	Smith, Howard T	5:28:54 (28,473)	Smith, Paul D	4:28:45 (18,291)
Smith, Andy M	4:38:54 (20,693)	Smith, Iain M	3:46:21 (7,612)	Smith, Paul E	4:52:00 (23,438)
Smith, Anthony G	5:24:00 (27,973)	Smith, Ian G	3:13:25 (2,361)	Smith, Paul M	3:37:03 (5,783)
Smith, Anthony K	3:59:35 (11,183)	Smith, Ian M	3:31:00 (4,778)	Smith, Peter	2:57:18 (900)
Smith, Anthony R	3:51:13 (8,810)	Smith, Ian R	7:51:15 (31,917)	Smith, Peter A	3:09:11 (1,915)
Smith, Anthony W	4:54:03 (23,806)	Smith, James	3:45:07 (7,322)	Smith, Peter A	3:48:00 (7,995)
Smith, Antony J	3:24:08 (3,579)	Smith, James D	3:51:29 (8,880)	Smith, Peter D	4:11:50 (14,052)
Smith, Ashley M	3:53:11 (9,310)	Smith, James J	3:09:43 (1,970)	Smith, Peter L	4:22:35 (16,719)
Smith, Ashley M	4:27:06 (17,864)	Smith, James L	6:35:21 (31,294)	Smith, Peter M	3:58:33 (10,874)
Smith, Austin D	3:35:29 (5,521)	Smith, Jamie A	4:07:53 (13,085)	Smith, Peter V	3:58:34 (10,879)
Smith, Barrie	6:42:24 (31,397)	Smith, Jamie J	4:14:48 (14,758)	Smith, Philip	3:32:44 (5,049)
Smith, Ben J	3:48:40 (8,176)	Smith, Jamie T	4:26:56 (17,821)	Smith, Philip A	4:02:25 (11,842)
Smith, Benjamin J	5:18:47 (27,447)	Smith, Jason	4:06:31 (12,781)	Smith, Philip R	5:33:50 (28,874)
Smith, Bernhard	4:49:37 (22,999)	Smith, Jason	6:32:12 (31,249)	Smith, Philip W	4:34:12 (19,644)
Smith, Bradford T	4:05:45 (12,606)	Smith, Jason N	4:12:48 (14,279)	Smith, Phillip	6:59:12 (31,609)
Smith, Brett	5:33:50 (28,874)	Smith, Jeremy R	3:42:44 (6,797)	Smith, Raymond A	4:25:23 (17,401)
Smith, Brian R	3:22:05 (3,312)	Smith, John	4:18:21 (15,618)	Smith, Richard	3:45:51 (7,492)
Smith, Campbell B	3:36:45 (5,734)	Smith, John D	5:16:25 (27,181)	Smith, Richard A	4:05:31 (12,547)
Smith, Carl D	4:47:05 (22,470)	Smith, John G	5:42:50 (29,535)	Smith, Richard C	3:27:55 (4,216)
Smith, Carl J	4:29:04 (18,366)	Smith, John M	4:08:21 (13,191)	Smith, Richard D	6:58:59 (31,606)
Smith, Carl P	3:28:26 (4,308)	Smith, John M	4:56:53 (24,380)	Smith, Richard J	3:59:04 (11,019)
Smith, Chris	4:47:14 (22,504)	Smith, John P	4:04:39 (12,340)	Smith, Richard W	5:04:29 (25,624)
Smith, Chris C	4:35:12 (19,866)	Smith, John R	4:04:12 (12,240)	Smith, Robert	5:15:02 (27,029)
Smith, Christopher A	3:46:02 (7,532)	Smith, Jonathan A	4:29:29 (18,490)	Smith, Robert	8:31:03 (31,966)
Smith, Christopher C	3:55:18 (9,880)	Smith, Jonathan J	3:55:13 (9,854)	Smith, Robert A	3:01:21 (1,269)
Smith, Christopher J	4:00:11 (11,337)	Smith, Jonathan P	4:09:00 (13,380)	Smith, Robert D	3:24:15 (3,595)
Smith, Christopher R	5:03:40 (25,543)	Smith, Jonathan P	4:24:47 (17,246)	Smith, Robert H	5:40:25 (29,373)
Smith, Clifford	4:31:13 (18,899)	Smith, Jonathan P	5:23:22 (27,901)	Smith, Robert J	3:54:50 (9,732)
Smith, Clive	4:23:50 (17,023)	Smith, Jonathon P	4:55:07 (24,019)	Smith, Robert M	4:06:58 (12,882)
Smith, Clive S	3:31:55 (4,907)	Smith, Julian A	3:56:49 (10,337)	Smith, Robert M	4:58:58 (24,791)
Smith, Colin J	3:38:37 (6,073)	Smith, Kai J	3:54:32 (9,648)	Smith, Robin A	4:55:32 (24,105)
Smith, Colin N	3:57:14 (10,458)	Smith, Keith	3:25:31 (3,773)	Smith, Robin M	3:37:23 (5,854)
Smith, Craig	3:49:31 (8,380)	Smith, Keith	4:23:22 (16,905)	Smith, Roderick G	4:20:11 (16,059)
Smith, Craig	6:51:59 (31,529)	Smith, Keith A	3:09:14 (1,922)	Smith, Roger A	3:40:39 (6,426)
Smith, Craig J	4:15:24 (14,899)	Smith, Kempley M	3:27:03 (4,036)	Smith, Roger M	3:49:15 (8,319)
Smith, Daniel J	4:08:58 (13,369)	Smith, Kevin J	3:49:58 (8,497)	Smith, Ronald J	4:56:27 (24,293)
Smith, Darren F	5:04:34 (25,634)	Smith, Kevin J	4:28:14 (18,153)	Smith, Roy C	3:35:45 (5,565)
Smith, Darren P	5:01:39 (25,247)	Smith, Kevin W	2:45:54 (355)	Smith, Royston	3:35:46 (5,567)
Smith, Darren R	4:22:49 (16,777)	Smith, Les	5:01:41 (25,254)	Smith, Russell D	3:58:07 (10,715)
Smith, David	4:10:46 (13,816)	Smith, Lyndon	3:41:03 (6,483)	Smith, Russell H	3:57:08 (10,429)
Smith, David A	3:24:34 (3,632)	Smith, Malcolm	3:51:26 (8,868)	Smith, Russell J	4:19:32 (15,917)
Smith, David A	3:49:07 (8,286)	Smith, Malcolm D	4:20:40 (16,200)	Smith, Russell J	4:44:15 (21,847)
Smith, David J	4:12:23 (14,165)	Smith, Mark	4:01:00 (11,506)	Smith, Sean D	3:55:52 (10,037)
Smith, David J	4:44:49 (21,980)	Smith, Mark	4:39:57 (20,904)	Smith, Sean G	3:41:07 (6,501)

Smith, Simon A 2:38:04 (173)
Smith, Simon G 3:23:36 (3,514)
Smith, Stanley P 3:55:06 (9,818)
Smith, Stephen 2:37:44 (166)
Smith, Stephen 3:53:15 (9,324)
Smith, Stephen 4:58:35 (24,732)
Smith, Stephen 5:01:01 (25,146)
Smith, Stephen J 4:41:25 (21,222)
Smith, Stephen M 4:33:52 (19,549)
Smith, Stephen R 5:09:32 (26,308)
Smith, Steve 4:40:09 (20,951)
Smith, Steve R 3:11:50 (2,174)
Smith, Steven 3:37:25 (5,864)
Smith, Steven D 4:49:07 (22,898)
Smith, Steven K 4:28:37 (18,259)
Smith, Stuart D 4:17:59 (15,550)
Smith, Stuart L 3:32:17 (4,965)
Smith, Terence 4:45:45 (22,199)
Smith, Terrance 3:47:14 (7,808)
Smith, Terry M 4:39:51 (20,882)
Smith, Thomas 3:20:25 (3,110)
Smith, Thomas C 3:52:11 (9,057)
Smith, Tim 4:02:11 (11,774)
Smith, Tim D 4:45:56 (22,235)
Smith, Timothy 3:28:18 (4,282)
Smith, Tom H 4:27:32 (17,973)
Smith, Tony 4:44:52 (21,991)
Smith, Tony D 4:57:30 (24,494)
Smith, Tony F 5:12:58 (26,755)
Smith, Trevor C 6:07:53 (30,668)
Smith, Wayne 3:27:13 (4,066)
Smith, Wesley P 4:02:05 (11,739)
Smith, William G 3:41:06 (6,498)
Smithers, Paul 4:11:59 (14,088)
Smithson, Alasdair T 3:42:22 (6,714)
Smout, Grahame D 6:16:22 (30,916)
Smy, Jamie E 4:05:59 (12,657)
Smyth, Cecil W 3:13:49 (2,411)
Smyth, David A 3:49:57 (8,489)
Smyth, Keith J 3:51:32 (8,899)
Smyth, Michael D 4:26:17 (17,653)
Smyth, Patrick E 5:08:27 (26,177)
Smyth, Stephen 4:04:53 (12,402)
Smyth, Thomas R 4:31:34 (18,995)
Smyth, Trevor I 6:28:38 (31,184)
Smythe, Stephen 3:01:13 (1,256)
Snaith, Darren G 4:10:08 (13,664)
Snaith, Philip R 4:42:02 (21,355)
Snape, Carl 3:55:21 (9,894)
Snead, Martin P 4:06:14 (12,722)
Sneary, Lawrence W 5:27:56 (28,393)
Snee, Jon P 4:19:46 (15,969)
Snelgrove, William R 3:23:02 (3,444)
Snell, Mark J 5:01:27 (25,217)
Snelling, Andrew G 4:22:57 (16,804)
Sneyd, Brian J 5:19:56 (27,551)
Snizek, Stephen 5:12:10 (26,651)
Snode, Chris 4:38:16 (20,541)
Snook, Daniel G 3:26:50 (3,992)
Snook, Glenn R 4:19:08 (15,812)
Snook, Matt 4:20:35 (16,181)
Snook, Peter L 5:21:35 (27,736)
Snook, Steven R 3:24:06 (3,577)
Snow, Andrew L 3:49:44 (8,434)
Snow, Michael 3:51:46 (8,962)
Snow, Simon G 4:55:16 (24,056)
Snow, Stephen P 4:14:46 (14,745)
Snowden, Matthew D 4:42:41 (21,486)
Snowdon, James P 3:18:25 (2,888)
Snyman, Michael 5:00:41 (25,092)
Soames, Brian 4:44:34 (21,928)
Soar, Andy M 4:10:50 (13,837)
Sobek, George P 3:32:34 (5,019)
Sobey, Kieron J 4:16:00 (15,050)
Sodeinde, Opeoluwa 5:16:59 (27,258)
Soden, Christopher 3:45:20 (7,372)
Soderquist, Martin G 4:56:05 (24,229)
Soerensen, Steen 3:07:15 (1,722)
Sohi, John S 5:18:49 (27,453)
Solanki, Sanjay 5:14:12 (26,923)
Soldic, Marian 4:08:07 (13,135)
Sole, Jason A 4:00:50 (11,454)
Solender, Neil D 4:07:19 (12,968)
Soler, Jean-Luc 3:10:46 (2,079)
Solomon, Anthony 5:38:17 (29,210)
Solomon, Dvid B 4:43:32 (21,692)
Solomon, Trevor B 5:44:50 (29,680)
Solomons, Alan S 3:42:42 (6,790)
Solomons, Alex 4:36:12 (20,072)
Somers, John P 4:42:05 (21,366)
Somers, Vincent 4:19:20 (15,866)
Somerville, Anthony F 5:06:29 (25,908)
Somerville, Hamish 5:17:33 (27,314)
Somerville-Cotton, Justin C 4:55:13 (24,044)
Sommer, Henderikus J 4:13:51 (14,532)
Sommerville, Ian P 4:37:01 (20,254)
Sommerville, William 4:18:26 (15,647)
Sondh, Javaher S 5:25:28 (28,134)
Sondrall, Steven A 3:21:12 (3,221)
Sonner, Desmond O 4:22:50 (16,783)
Sonqvist, Nils 4:04:12 (12,240)
Sontan, Richard 6:12:54 (30,813)
Sood, Nishant 4:24:05 (17,086)
Soole, Brian P 3:26:18 (3,889)
Soper, Desmond P 4:53:29 (23,699)
Soper, John M 5:06:51 (25,954)
Soppelsa, Jean-Frederic 4:13:22 (14,423)
Sorensen, Johnny K 3:35:42 (5,557)
Sorensen, Torben 4:04:43 (12,355)
Sorenti, Chris J 4:34:50 (19,784)
Sorg, Sebastian 3:44:50 (7,270)
Sotheran, Gavin J 3:56:16 (10,171)
Sothisrihari, Saranga R 4:48:10 (22,713)
Soto, Christophe 4:16:17 (15,114)
Sottovia, Paolo 3:02:11 (1,316)
Soubrillard, Alain 3:48:49 (8,219)
Souden, Alex J 3:37:20 (5,846)
Soufleris, John 5:21:45 (27,753)
Soulan, Alain 3:01:11 (1,251)
Souquet, Michel 3:14:42 (2,525)
Sousa, José Afonso 3:05:24 (1,563)
Souter, Gary W 4:30:15 (18,691)
South, Michael J 4:25:37 (17,456)
South, Richard P 4:54:09 (23,830)
Southall, Roger 4:30:54 (18,842)
Southam, Christopher 2:47:24 (398)
Southern, Steven A 4:27:49 (18,044)
Southerton, Clive M 3:48:27 (8,106)
Southgate, Anthony C 4:58:52 (24,774)
Southgate, Duncan A 3:53:19 (9,342)
Southon, Patrick J 4:13:49 (14,521)
Southward, William D 4:50:01 (23,077)
Southwell, Geoffrey C 5:42:06 (29,489)
Southwell, Philip 4:10:00 (13,639)
Sowler, Jonathan G 4:26:55 (17,816)
Sowton, Chris R 6:18:26 (30,968)
Spackman, David J 3:20:48 (3,177)
Spalton, Mark A 3:43:02 (6,855)
Spamer, Kay 3:27:58 (4,224)
Spampatti, Mirko 4:20:06 (16,047)
Spampinato, Daniel H 4:03:58 (12,184)
Spang, Gerd 4:42:39 (21,482)
Spanier, Toby J 6:23:47 (31,102)
Sparkes, Stephen 4:44:36 (21,935)
Sparks, Jason L 5:12:32 (26,696)
Sparks, Steven 4:07:01 (12,896)
Sparks, Tony W 4:09:04 (13,394)
Sparling, Gari 4:28:38 (18,267)
Sparrey, Graham M 3:45:31 (7,414)
Sparrow, Clive 3:35:35 (5,541)
Sparrow, Matthew S 3:20:58 (3,197)
Sparrow, Philip W 3:56:26 (10,228)
Sparrow, Roger L 3:57:50 (10,627)
Sparrow, Tim A 4:11:57 (14,077)
Spataro, Roberto 3:32:50 (5,066)
Speake, Malcolm D 4:16:52 (15,274)
Speake, Peter G 2:42:40 (257)
Speake, William J 2:42:41 (260)
Spear, David W 4:04:23 (12,279)
Spears, Julian P 4:19:28 (15,905)
Spears, Paul 3:48:48 (8,211)
Specht, Dominique 3:31:12 (4,809)
Spedding, Robert 4:24:26 (17,172)
Speed, Christopher A 3:40:29 (6,396)
Speed, David P 4:27:32 (17,973)
Speed, Mark F 4:02:18 (11,805)
Speedy, James 4:21:52 (16,495)
Speer, Ben 5:20:02 (27,571)
Spelling, Paul M 3:20:29 (3,124)
Spelman, Daryl 3:47:14 (7,808)
Spelman, Peter J 3:42:06 (6,668)
Spence, Alan 4:43:45 (21,736)
Spence, David A 3:16:11 (2,661)
Spence, Ian E 5:29:56 (28,577)
Spence, James M 6:01:53 (30,482)
Spence, Simon J 4:08:16 (13,165)
Spenceley, Matthew A 3:47:41 (7,925)
Spencer, Andrew M 3:03:07 (1,377)
Spencer, Andy P 3:36:41 (5,722)
Spencer, Anthony W 3:58:09 (10,729)
Spencer, Christian E 5:49:53 (29,961)
Spencer, Colin D 3:33:14 (5,146)
Spencer, David 3:30:50 (4,747)
Spencer, Dennis 4:40:16 (20,976)
Spencer, Eric 3:44:23 (7,150)
Spencer, Ian 3:15:33 (2,600)
Spencer, Ian H 3:21:32 (3,261)
Spencer, James P 4:55:15 (24,052)
Spencer, Jeremy H 3:02:09 (1,312)
Spencer, John A 5:32:26 (28,771)
Spencer, Kevin 4:22:40 (16,740)
Spencer, Lucien F 3:39:10 (6,157)
Spencer, Matthew 3:56:24 (10,213)
Spencer, Paul A 4:43:16 (21,627)
Spencer, Robert 4:38:29 (20,594)
Spencer, Ryan M 3:53:11 (9,310)
Spencer, Steven J 5:39:56 (29,328)
Spencer, Stuart P 3:40:34 (6,413)
Spencer, William 4:01:54 (11,688)
Spender, David E 4:26:11 (17,626)
Spiceley, Paul D 3:19:55 (3,059)
Spicer, Robert 3:39:35 (6,231)
Spicer, Thomas 4:15:59 (15,046)
Spiers, Adam 3:27:00 (4,024)
Spiers, Robert D 5:49:14 (29,919)
Spillane, John 3:35:25 (5,507)
Spilsbury, Ian R 2:58:11 (985)
Spinelli, Giansenio 4:17:44 (15,489)
Spink, Andrew J 3:57:55 (10,651)
Spink, Chris J 3:49:16 (8,323)
Spink, Peter J 4:43:36 (21,701)
Spinks, Timothy R 4:31:25 (18,952)
Spissu, Antonio 4:47:33 (22,580)
Spoerer, Peter A 5:13:49 (26,877)
Spolander, Brandon G 3:43:02 (6,855)
Spooner, Michael J 5:42:56 (29,547)
Spooner, Paul S 4:21:19 (16,337)
Spotswood, Richard 3:25:26 (3,756)
Spouse, Andrew D 4:36:26 (20,116)
Spouse, Iain 3:07:26 (1,742)
Spowart, Jeffrey D 4:22:26 (16,677)
Spratley, Ken G 3:47:01 (7,756)
Spratt, Norman S 3:08:13 (1,820)
Sprigings, Grant G 5:16:07 (27,142)
Springer, Marcellus A 3:31:12 (4,809)
Springer, Olaf B 3:14:12 (2,467)
Springett, Adrian 3:40:35 (6,416)
Spruit, Peter C 3:28:52 (4,392)
Spruzs, Michael 3:53:01 (9,261)
Spurling, Scott E 3:42:32 (6,751)
Spurr, James C 4:42:55 (21,548)
Squier, Will 4:33:05 (19,378)
Squillino, Anton 5:18:40 (27,430)
Squire, Anthony 3:10:27 (2,050)
Squires, Gary R 3:28:28 (4,316)
Squires, Stuart J 4:18:38 (15,695)
Sreeves, John C 3:30:13 (4,637)
Srikandakumar, Anton 5:27:24 (28,349)
Srikandan, Eric 5:47:31 (29,840)
Srikantha, Thurairajah 5:20:43 (27,658)
Sroka, Marek P 5:02:03 (25,304)
St Clair Roberts, John 4:02:53 (11,936)
St Croix, Dennis 4:05:57 (12,650)
St John, Anthony T 4:12:20 (14,156)
St John, Mick 3:51:41 (8,936)
St John Webster, Alexander 3:59:58 (11,284)
St John-Heath, Gavin 5:47:01 (29,811)
Stabbins, Richard A 4:24:07 (17,097)
Stacey, Gary J 4:47:07 (22,481)

Stickland, Richard A 4:36:45 (20,191)
Stickley, John F 6:25:41 (31,135)
Stidwill, Ricky 5:32:47 (28,794)
Stiff, Matthew 4:36:38 (20,162)
Stiff, Michael 2:55:22 (777)
Stiles, Andrew D 3:01:08 (1,248)
Stiles, Andrew N 2:52:37 (623)
Still, Stuart J 3:54:58 (9,772)
Stillet, Dan 4:59:39 (24,930)
Stillwell, David 4:16:35 (15,194)
Stimming, Juergen 3:13:50 (2,412)
Stimpson, Glenn C 3:44:02 (7,077)
Stimpson, Ian J 4:54:40 (23,935)
Stimpson, Tom V 6:43:58 (31,417)
Stimson, Derrick J 3:58:49 (10,948)
Stirling, Iain G 4:36:14 (20,078)
Stirling, Warren C 3:53:48 (9,444)
Stitt, Paul D 2:54:00 (696)
Stoakes, Paul 4:31:56 (19,093)
Stoate, Howard G 3:51:32 (8,899)
Stobbeleir, Erik 3:26:42 (3,957)
Stobie, William J 3:49:44 (8,434)
Stock, Andrew N 3:26:04 (3,856)
Stockdale, Mark R 4:58:27 (24,707)
Stockdale, Peter C 3:38:47 (6,096)
Stocker, Robin I 3:44:39 (7,224)
Stockford, Ivor 4:15:22 (14,894)
Stocks, Richard L 5:07:59 (26,113)
Stoddart, Keith W 4:36:01 (20,029)
Stogaard, Bent 2:58:14 (988)
Stok, Jaqmes 4:06:32 (12,784)
Stoker, Daniel C 4:45:39 (22,177)
Stoker, Gary 4:00:30 (11,399)
Stoker, Michael 3:18:49 (2,930)
Stokes, David 4:36:02 (20,036)
Stokes, David C 3:48:20 (8,087)
Stokes, Gavin J 3:45:55 (7,510)
Stokes, Jamie L 4:35:08 (19,851)
Stokes, John M 6:21:30 (31,044)
Stokes, Paul A 4:21:31 (16,393)
Stokes, Russell J 2:44:13 (293)
Stokes, Steve 4:55:12 (24,037)
Stokes, Wayne I 3:30:40 (4,721)
Stoll, Eddie S 7:36:38 (31,881)
Stolte, Flip 4:11:30 (13,968)
Stone, Andrew 3:54:51 (9,738)
Stone, Barry 3:56:18 (10,181)
Stone, Chris J 4:29:27 (18,470)
Stone, David M 2:42:17 (247)
Stone, Derek C 2:59:04 (1,078)
Stone, Ian A 4:26:55 (17,816)
Stone, Jonathan D 4:40:25 (21,012)
Stone, Jonathan P 4:29:18 (18,431)
Stone, Kevin J 3:45:45 (7,471)
Stone, Lee 4:56:04 (24,223)
Stone, Manuel S 4:33:19 (19,429)
Stone, Nigel J 3:14:08 (2,457)
Stone, Philip 6:31:03 (31,225)
Stone, Timothy J 4:30:48 (18,814)
Stonebridge, David G 4:05:15 (12,472)
Stoneham, Christian W 4:12:21 (14,158)
Stoneham, Scott D 3:56:49 (10,337)
Stonehouse, Gerald 4:39:36 (20,840)
Stonehouse, Michael R 5:47:30 (29,838)
Stonehouse, Sebastien M 4:33:12 (19,405)
Stoneley, Andrew M 4:00:58 (11,498)
Stoneley, Paul A 3:31:39 (4,867)
Stoneman, Christopher J 3:53:54 (9,476)
Stoneman, James B 4:46:28 (22,352)
Stoneman-Merret, Jonathan A 3:52:10 (9,053)
Stones, Leslie 7:00:30 (31,632)
Stonier, Chris D 3:32:59 (5,095)
Stoodley, Grant E 4:13:54 (14,543)
Storer, Graham N 3:51:26 (8,868)
Storey, John 3:15:40 (2,618)
Storey, John 5:51:04 (30,018)
Storey, Kenneth 3:18:10 (2,868)
Storey, Philip 4:30:27 (18,745)
Storey, Russ 4:20:01 (16,037)
Storey, Stephen 5:14:31 (26,961)
Stork, Robert F 3:56:26 (10,228)
Storm, James C 4:24:09 (17,105)
Storrie, Martin J 3:52:37 (9,154)
Story, Thomas E 4:00:01 (11,300)
Stothard, David 3:53:50 (9,453)
Stott, Charles S 5:13:09 (26,786)
Stott, Chris 4:34:18 (19,669)
Stott, Douglas P 3:37:18 (5,839)
Stott, Matthew J 4:16:31 (15,177)
Stott, Nic 4:27:02 (17,853)
Stoves, Nigel G 4:03:58 (12,184)
Stowe, Jonathan D 4:15:14 (14,863)
Stowe, Paul 4:27:14 (17,904)
Stowell, David 4:54:39 (23,932)
Stowell, Mark 5:14:58 (27,024)
Strachan, Deborah R 4:28:48 (18,298)
Strachan, Russell K 6:36:02 (31,307)
Stradiotto, Michel G 3:46:50 (7,711)
Stradling, Richard C 3:57:55 (10,651)
Straffi, Giacomo 3:17:29 (2,800)
Stragier, Koenraad 2:50:43 (535)
Stragier, Lieven 3:00:42 (1,208)
Strain, Ian 3:29:45 (4,544)
Strain, John H 4:35:10 (19,858)
Strain, Mark A 4:26:49 (17,777)
Straker, Simon J 4:16:22 (15,137)
Straker, Thomas M 6:55:29 (31,569)
Strandkvist, Jorgen 4:28:52 (18,317)
Strang, Andrew 4:45:38 (22,171)
Strange, Adam 4:59:31 (24,906)
Strange, Peter D 3:51:40 (8,930)
Strange, Peter J 4:31:13 (18,899)
Stratford, Gary C 3:14:34 (2,511)
Stratford, Lawrie D 4:41:27 (21,230)
Stratford, Matthew J 2:52:26 (612)
Straton, Josh 4:06:51 (12,849)
Stratton, Matthew A 4:17:18 (15,368)
Straubinger, Christina 4:20:03 (16,042)
Straughan, Ross E 3:48:21 (8,091)
Strauswald, Richard K 3:25:43 (3,801)
Straw, Kevin 2:53:32 (669)
Strawbridge, Ian D 3:57:51 (10,632)
Strawson, John D 4:08:48 (13,325)
Streather, Chris 3:26:28 (3,914)
Streek, Gary 3:53:50 (9,453)
Streek, Simon R 4:06:09 (12,700)
Street, Neil A 5:05:57 (25,837)
Street, William 3:53:16 (9,329)
Street, William M 3:48:39 (8,168)
Streeter, Andrew C 4:57:56 (24,576)
Streeter, Jonathon C 6:02:34 (30,512)
Streitmayer, Juergen 3:55:53 (10,045)
Stret, John 5:11:11 (26,535)
Stretch, Keith C 3:39:21 (6,192)
Stretton, Neil W 3:42:14 (6,691)
Streuff, Herbert 3:53:34 (9,395)
Strickland, Andrew I 3:54:11 (9,555)
Strickland, Steve W 3:56:14 (10,161)
Stringer, David A 3:27:53 (4,206)
Stringer, Gary J 3:56:32 (10,260)
Stringer, Thomas H 4:44:22 (21,876)
Stripp, Matthew S 4:34:06 (19,625)
Stritter, Josef 4:19:44 (15,959)
Strivens, Martin R 4:13:22 (14,423)
Stroeno, Olav 3:53:58 (9,493)
Stromsmoe, Ian 3:21:42 (3,276)
Stromsoe, Michael 3:39:17 (6,180)
Strong, David 4:16:34 (15,189)
Stroud, Mike 3:52:15 (9,072)
Stroud, Steve A 4:44:53 (21,995)
Stroud, Steven A 4:06:01 (12,663)
Stroud, Steven P 4:22:28 (16,690)
Strouts, Paul R 4:19:22 (15,874)
Strowbridge, Christopher 4:15:41 (14,973)
Stryke, John S 6:10:57 (30,757)
Stuart, Michael J 4:06:38 (12,811)
Stuart, Roy A 3:43:48 (7,013)
Stuart-Grant, Alan J 3:41:48 (6,605)
Stubbs, David A 2:59:46 (1,138)
Stubbs, Gareth W 3:11:49 (2,170)
Stubbs, George 4:08:30 (13,231)
Stubbs, James L 4:17:49 (15,512)
Stubbs, Jason E 4:47:36 (22,591)
Stubbs, Michael D 3:54:18 (9,589)
Stubbs, Richard 4:25:57 (17,555)
Stuchbury, James H 4:29:08 (18,389)
Stuckey, John 4:38:00 (20,466)
Studley, John G 3:58:04 (10,696)
Stuebing, Kurt 4:39:14 (20,781)
Sturdy, Greg J 3:32:53 (5,079)
Sturgeon, Ian J 5:08:09 (26,135)
Sturges, David A 4:31:03 (18,866)
Sturgess, Matthew J 4:10:44 (13,806)
Sturgess, Philip J 4:06:56 (12,871)
Sturla, Timothy S 3:33:31 (5,192)
Sturley, John 5:00:18 (25,039)
Sturt, Brian C 4:42:01 (21,348)
Styles, Geoff 4:32:26 (19,220)
Subervie, Jean 4:27:25 (17,941)
Such, Nicholas J 4:10:55 (13,850)
Suchaire, Yannick 4:57:33 (24,503)
Suckling, Adam 3:44:12 (7,114)
Suckling, Anthony J 4:02:53 (11,936)
Sueke, Henri 3:35:41 (5,552)
Sugar, John D 3:59:18 (11,087)
Sugars, Clive J 4:26:57 (17,825)
Sugden, George T 4:53:05 (23,630)
Sulley, Andrew R 5:03:54 (25,565)
Sullivan, Daniel J 3:12:19 (2,228)
Sullivan, Dieter L 5:19:53 (27,546)
Sullivan, Gordon P 4:28:22 (18,181)
Sullivan, Liam A 4:08:24 (13,199)
Sullivan, Michael G 4:40:39 (21,054)
Sullivan, Neil C 4:44:56 (22,017)
Sullivan, Paul D 3:09:05 (1,908)
Sullivan, Peter G 4:28:21 (18,178)
Sullivan, Robert L 5:01:03 (25,152)
Sullivan, Ross A 4:43:20 (21,649)
Sullivan, Sam A 3:19:13 (2,987)
Sullivan, Sean 3:42:29 (6,742)
Sullivan, Stephen M 4:08:06 (13,131)
Sullivan, Stuart C 5:33:14 (28,825)
Summerhill, Stephen J 4:38:46 (20,659)
Summers, Christopher 5:40:29 (29,378)
Summers, Daniel J 3:53:26 (9,363)
Summers, Darrell J 4:59:43 (24,942)
Summers, David A 4:26:49 (17,777)
Summers, David L 4:23:33 (16,953)
Summers, Derek G 3:52:14 (9,064)
Summers, Jonathan W 4:55:08 (24,022)
Summers, Kevin 3:54:55 (9,756)
Summers, Mark 3:41:57 (6,633)
Summers, Martin 3:00:34 (1,197)
Summers, Paul D 3:46:08 (7,552)
Summers, Peter 3:13:02 (2,312)
Summers, Russell A 4:13:06 (14,352)
Summers, Shaun A 4:03:37 (12,105)
Sumner, Andrew P 4:12:19 (14,151)
Sumner, Gary S 5:37:57 (29,177)
Sund, Malkit S 4:13:47 (14,513)
Sundvik, Harri H 3:33:43 (5,218)
Sunner, Joe 4:56:36 (24,329)
Sunner, Pavitar 4:42:13 (21,388)
Surey, Ross 4:03:01 (11,957)
Suri, Naveen 4:41:57 (21,337)
Surrey, Sam M 3:28:53 (4,398)
Sutcliffe, David A 4:56:55 (24,387)
Sutcliffe, David P 3:32:37 (5,033)
Sutcliffe, Jonathan R 3:46:08 (7,552)
Sutcliffe, Mark J 5:35:21 (28,986)
Suter, Hans 4:47:34 (22,585)
Sutherland, Alasdair R 4:21:43 (16,457)
Sutherland, Alister G 6:04:15 (30,571)
Sutherland, Andrew D 4:46:46 (22,404)
Sutherland, Cameron 5:14:26 (26,954)
Sutherland, Christopher 5:21:59 (27,770)
Sutherland, Christopher J 3:57:06 (10,415)
Sutherland, David J 4:19:10 (15,822)
Sutherland, Graeme 4:24:32 (17,192)
Sutherland, Hugh 4:41:22 (21,210)
Sutherland, Leslie 4:55:21 (24,073)
Suttle, Richard J 3:06:14 (1,631)
Suttle, Stephen D 3:19:27 (3,014)
Sutton, Alan J 5:37:09 (29,119)
Sutton, Andy K 4:49:37 (22,999)
Sutton, Antony P 5:02:17 (25,336)
Sutton, Darren 3:42:28 (6,735)
Sutton, Darren C 3:46:44 (7,686)
Sutton, David R 4:34:17 (19,666)

Sutton, Errol R 5:57:16 (30,298)
Sutton, Gareth L 5:21:24 (27,720)
Sutton, Jeremy P....4:05:00 (12,429)
Sutton, John E....4:49:18 (22,939)
Sutton, Malcolm J 4:24:02 (17,068)
Sutton, Mark A....3:54:37 (9,673)
Sutton, Mark C....3:33:51 (5,244)
Sutton, Nigel D....4:44:59 (22,029)
Sutton, Philip M....3:45:40 (7,446)
Sutton, Richard C 3:39:39 (6,244)
Sutton, Tom M 3:49:13 (8,312)
Sutton-Gibbs, Peter A 4:00:45 (11,434)
Suzuki, Satoshi 4:14:23 (14,648)
Svanfeldt, Fredrik....2:27:35 (64)
Svendsen, Klaus....3:43:45 (7,003)
Svenilson, Peter....4:35:23 (19,905)
Svensson, Goran....4:14:25 (14,655)
Swaby, Adam....4:57:05 (24,417)
Swain, Michael J 3:54:09 (9,542)
Swainson, Mike J 5:03:55 (25,566)
Swales, John S....3:52:47 (9,188)
Swales, Philip P....4:07:02 (12,903)
Swallow, David C....4:33:08 (19,388)
Swallow, Ian M....3:23:17 (3,477)
Swallow, Matthew F 4:26:03 (17,585)
Swallow, Nigel....6:26:25 (31,149)
Swan, Andrew C 6:28:46 (31,186)
Swan, Jonathan E 3:50:54 (8,735)
Swan, Kim R 3:32:52 (5,075)
Swan, Michael R....4:57:52 (24,561)
Swankie, Troy D....3:17:57 (2,843)
Swann, Andrew D....5:30:09 (28,596)
Swann, Garry R....4:05:01 (12,437)
Swann, Graham....4:15:48 (15,003)
Swanton, Ian P 4:28:37 (18,259)
Swanton, John 5:51:00 (30,015)
Swarbrick, Matthew J 3:14:40 (2,520)
Swart, André....3:45:19 (7,367)
Swash, Andrew J 4:22:40 (16,740)
Swatton, Duncan....4:55:53 (24,177)
Swatton, Greg....4:09:55 (13,615)
Swatton, Neville R....4:09:55 (13,615)
Sweeney, Anthony J....4:03:55 (12,173)
Sweeney, Anthony M....5:00:50 (25,121)
Sweeney, Hugh G....5:57:49 (30,324)
Sweeney, John P 5:33:25 (28,843)
Sweeney, Mark E....2:56:58 (879)
Sweeney, Michael P....3:57:15 (10,463)
Sweet, Richard A....3:13:51 (2,417)
Sweet, Roger J....4:49:58 (23,070)
Sweeting, Paul 4:29:34 (18,511)
Sweetland, Philip B 3:55:57 (10,067)
Swift, Christopher T....4:32:09 (19,152)
Swift, James M 5:11:06 (26,517)
Swift, Simon....3:49:43 (8,428)
Swilinski, Michael....3:46:38 (7,670)
Swindells, Adam C 4:49:31 (22,981)
Swingler, David P....3:25:24 (3,747)
Swingler, Jonathan D 5:05:54 (25,823)
Swisher, Michael A 4:14:55 (14,790)
Swit, Jason....4:48:26 (22,765)
Sycamore, Paul C 6:03:08 (30,530)
Sykes, Christopher A....4:29:35 (18,517)
Sykes, Christopher M....3:25:42 (3,798)
Sykes, Christopher P 4:20:16 (16,085)
Sykes, Ian C 3:30:37 (4,713)
Sykes, Justin....3:39:01 (6,137)
Sykes, Toby G....3:10:56 (2,094)
Sylvester, Martin T....5:21:43 (27,751)
Sylvester, Nigel C....4:12:01 (14,097)
Symeou, Nicos....5:02:30 (25,374)
Symes, Martyn D....4:13:41 (14,491)
Symington, Ian....3:04:54 (1,514)
Symonds, Andrew M 2:37:33 (164)
Symonds, Duncan J....4:42:17 (21,408)
Symonds, Ian T 4:45:36 (22,167)
Symonds, Laurence....4:50:47 (23,233)
Symonds, Stephen D....3:24:35 (3,635)
Symons, David S 2:34:10 (110)
Syner, Paul....4:13:02 (14,337)
Syradd, Ray A....4:10:06 (13,656)
Syred, Mark 3:21:51 (3,295)
Sysum, Mark C....3:15:15 (2,581)
Taaffe, Nigel A....4:00:07 (11,320)
Tabb, Stephen R....5:01:23 (25,201)
Tabenor, Peter F....3:46:55 (7,726)
Tabiner, Ben 4:28:49 (18,304)
Tabor, Frank R....4:08:44 (13,301)
Tabor, Paul A....3:35:58 (5,606)
Tack, Ian R....3:01:05 (1,244)
Tackley, Stephen J 4:07:26 (12,997)
Tadie, Alexis J....3:00:16 (1,175)
Taelman, Marc J 3:26:57 (4,008)
Taggart, James....4:07:09 (12,927)
Tagney, Gregory P 3:28:08 (4,251)
Taheri, Mehran 3:38:35 (6,067)
Tait, Alan S 3:20:03 (3,074)
Tajima, Tomio 3:56:13 (10,148)
Takagi, Kenichi....3:53:31 (9,380)
Takamura, Takehito....6:30:50 (31,219)
Takano, Hideo....4:34:25 (19,693)
Takano, Satoshi 3:27:23 (4,100)
Takle, Andrew K....4:16:26 (15,157)
Talbot, Andrew E....3:25:34 (3,777)
Talbot, David B....4:52:12 (23,482)
Talbot, Mark B....4:21:16 (16,325)
Talbot, Michael A....4:10:20 (13,713)
Talbot, Nicholas M....4:10:02 (13,644)
Talbot, Sean V 4:09:37 (13,534)
Talbot, Wayne D 4:04:27 (12,300)
Talbot-Jones, Ian 4:04:09 (12,228)
Talbott, Mark T 4:41:15 (21,169)
Talliss, Richard J....4:10:17 (13,697)
Tambini, Gino B....3:51:19 (8,836)
Tambyraja, Rabin 5:16:02 (27,134)
Tamer, Attila A....3:51:11 (8,798)
Tammas-Hastings, Daniel J....3:33:00 (5,099)
Tampkins, Neil D 3:57:52 (10,639)
Tampling, Stephen J 4:29:59 (18,626)
Tan, Joon Y....4:38:12 (20,520)
Tancos, Tim....2:48:35 (441)
Tanda, Amarjit K....5:12:50 (26,738)
Tandy, Ian J....4:46:09 (22,279)
Tang, Johnny C....4:33:27 (19,457)
Taniguchi, Takahiro....4:56:42 (24,345)
Tanker, Peter N 3:38:09 (5,986)
Tanner, Adrian G 2:43:29 (276)
Tanner, Griff P....3:47:57 (7,985)
Tanner, Jean-Paul....4:50:46 (23,231)
Tanner, Ross W....5:12:46 (26,723)
Tannett, Simon J 4:14:42 (14,728)
Tannian, Mark....5:47:15 (29,824)
Tansey, Michael P....3:27:27 (4,115)
Tapley, Peter D 4:11:06 (13,889)
Taplin, Derek R....4:44:44 (21,961)
Tappenden, Christopher P....4:11:13 (13,916)
Tappin, Roy K....4:16:51 (15,268)
Tapping, David A....4:26:29 (17,696)
Tapsfield, Andrew 3:57:11 (10,440)
Taranik, Dan....5:17:04 (27,263)
Tarkanyi, John L....3:00:21 (1,181)
Tarleton, Michael P....5:17:21 (27,288)
Taroni, Henry J....4:21:54 (16,500)
Tarquinio, Catello....3:15:29 (2,593)
Tarring, Keith....4:11:16 (13,922)
Tarry, Simon C....3:43:33 (6,968)
Tarver, Andrew D 3:57:33 (10,555)
Tarzey, Robert J 4:09:11 (13,415)
Tasker, Adam D 4:40:25 (21,012)
Tasker, Grahame D....3:26:36 (3,932)
Tasker, John....3:30:09 (4,626)
Tasker, John J....3:47:48 (7,946)
Tasker, Mark J....4:22:00 (16,537)
Tasker, Niall C....4:41:14 (21,163)
Tasker, Simon P....4:08:37 (13,261)
Tassell, Guy H....4:12:13 (14,135)
Tate, Alexander J....2:51:14 (552)
Tate, Andrew 3:31:18 (4,819)
Tate, Andrew C....4:27:59 (18,094)
Tate, Andrew J....5:53:37 (30,137)
Tate, Chris N....3:04:00 (1,450)
Tate, Doug J....4:54:32 (23,906)
Tate, Jeffrey M 4:59:30 (24,905)
Tate, Stephen R....5:00:42 (25,095)
Tatham, Alasdair G 2:43:05 (269)
Tatham, Charles....4:04:44 (12,364)
Tatlow, Nick 4:09:49 (13,585)
Tattersall, Toby....3:38:44 (6,090)
Tattershall, Darren M....4:03:15 (12,017)
Tattum, Paul M....3:56:09 (10,121)
Tatum, Steven J 4:39:08 (20,756)
Taub, Robert J 7:18:07 (31,772)
Tavare, Jim....3:31:52 (4,897)
Tavatgis, Koster....3:41:07 (6,501)
Tavecchiu, Claudio....6:02:48 (30,523)
Tavenor, Jack T....4:27:43 (18,019)
Tawse, Alister W....3:46:33 (7,648)
Tayar, Michael A....4:40:57 (21,115)
Taylar, Robert B....4:14:00 (14,561)
Taylor, Adrian M....3:55:01 (9,794)
Taylor, Andrew 4:18:51 (15,751)
Taylor, Andrew J....4:04:51 (12,392)
Taylor, Andrew J....4:46:03 (22,261)
Taylor, Anthony G 3:45:13 (7,354)
Taylor, Benjamin 3:28:24 (4,301)
Taylor, Benjamin M....4:08:29 (13,224)
Taylor, Bernard F....6:03:54 (30,562)
Taylor, Brant....3:10:19 (2,030)
Taylor, Brent....3:59:21 (11,101)
Taylor, Brian 5:22:08 (27,785)
Taylor, Bryon A....5:18:14 (27,394)
Taylor, Chris S....5:01:26 (25,214)
Taylor, Christopher J....4:22:39 (16,737)
Taylor, Colin D 3:57:32 (10,550)
Taylor, Colin J....4:30:13 (18,685)
Taylor, Craig 3:52:34 (9,144)
Taylor, Darren L....4:05:06 (12,448)
Taylor, David A 4:30:52 (18,833)
Taylor, David E 3:22:18 (3,341)
Taylor, David E 4:32:01 (19,116)
Taylor, Derek A....4:49:32 (22,989)
Taylor, Desmond 3:41:06 (6,498)
Taylor, Drew....2:57:40 (928)
Taylor, Eric....3:09:52 (1,989)
Taylor, George K....2:50:36 (530)
Taylor, Glen 4:16:15 (15,107)
Taylor, Graham....5:05:30 (25,760)
Taylor, Graham A 3:32:03 (4,935)
Taylor, Graham A 4:16:01 (15,053)
Taylor, Graham C....3:04:33 (1,494)
Taylor, Guy A 3:42:02 (6,659)
Taylor, Ian D 4:32:17 (19,184)
Taylor, Ian R 3:58:17 (10,785)
Taylor, James....4:22:41 (16,746)
Taylor, James M 4:06:54 (12,862)
Taylor, James P 3:35:28 (5,519)
Taylor, James S....5:05:12 (25,712)
Taylor, James W....5:03:57 (25,572)
Taylor, Jim A 5:31:06 (28,667)
Taylor, John 3:52:41 (9,169)
Taylor, John 3:58:20 (10,799)
Taylor, John 4:43:51 (21,761)
Taylor, John C....3:09:51 (1,987)
Taylor, John L....5:10:48 (26,483)
Taylor, John W....3:28:37 (4,338)
Taylor, Jonathan P....4:55:56 (24,198)
Taylor, Keith 4:36:14 (20,078)
Taylor, Keith R....4:01:05 (11,526)
Taylor, Kenneth M....4:28:07 (18,126)
Taylor, Kevin 4:24:54 (17,284)
Taylor, Kevin J....3:42:47 (6,807)
Taylor, Lance 3:35:56 (5,598)
Taylor, Laurence S....5:23:07 (27,882)
Taylor, Lee 3:54:34 (9,655)
Taylor, Lee 4:58:35 (24,732)
Taylor, Les R 4:14:47 (14,752)
Taylor, Lewis J....4:51:35 (23,358)
Taylor, Malcolm C 4:44:40 (21,952)
Taylor, Mark....3:33:54 (5,256)
Taylor, Mark....4:48:42 (22,820)
Taylor, Mark A 4:12:18 (14,149)
Taylor, Mark B 3:50:19 (8,581)
Taylor, Mark B 4:44:42 (21,956)
Taylor, Mark J 3:01:13 (1,256)
Taylor, Mark J 3:19:05 (2,963)
Taylor, Mark S....5:00:05 (25,006)
Taylor, Martin R....5:39:18 (29,290)
Taylor, Martin S 3:33:06 (5,116)
Taylor, Martin T....4:04:18 (12,263)

Taylor, Martyn G	8:42:50	(31,974)
Taylor, Matthew J	3:03:14	(1,384)
Taylor, Matthew J	4:25:48	(17,515)
Taylor, Michael	4:49:53	(23,059)
Taylor, Michael A	3:50:19	(8,581)
Taylor, Michael A	4:20:33	(16,172)
Taylor, Neil A	3:27:08	(4,050)
Taylor, Neil G	3:24:39	(3,647)
Taylor, Neil R	4:29:07	(18,381)
Taylor, Nicholas	3:55:49	(10,022)
Taylor, Nicholas J	3:17:33	(2,807)
Taylor, Nichols C	3:27:04	(4,041)
Taylor, Nick R	4:27:02	(17,853)
Taylor, Nigel K	4:11:54	(14,063)
Taylor, Nigel R	3:22:01	(3,307)
Taylor, Norman G	4:41:13	(21,160)
Taylor, Paul	4:30:19	(18,708)
Taylor, Paul A	4:25:31	(17,434)
Taylor, Paul F	3:53:45	(9,427)
Taylor, Paul M	3:29:13	(4,455)
Taylor, Paul R	4:22:34	(16,716)
Taylor, Paul S	4:32:47	(19,311)
Taylor, Paul S	5:08:38	(26,194)
Taylor, Peter	3:30:13	(4,637)
Taylor, Peter M	4:47:50	(22,644)
Taylor, Philip	2:48:56	(456)
Taylor, Philip C	4:42:49	(21,524)
Taylor, Philip G	4:16:49	(15,259)
Taylor, Phillip G	2:45:18	(335)
Taylor, Richard J	4:49:07	(22,898)
Taylor, Richard M	3:44:56	(7,293)
Taylor, Richard P	6:36:07	(31,309)
Taylor, Richard T	4:54:42	(23,940)
Taylor, Richard W	4:23:53	(17,034)
Taylor, Richard W	5:09:01	(26,240)
Taylor, Robert	3:48:04	(8,015)
Taylor, Robert	5:29:11	(28,506)
Taylor, Robert C	4:49:00	(22,875)
Taylor, Robert M	4:36:22	(20,100)
Taylor, Rory	3:33:28	(5,185)
Taylor, Ross S	4:30:16	(18,694)
Taylor, Russell	3:53:54	(9,476)
Taylor, Saul M	4:03:54	(12,169)
Taylor, Scott G	6:01:01	(30,449)
Taylor, Scott I	4:11:58	(14,083)
Taylor, Shaun I	4:35:07	(19,844)
Taylor, Simeon	4:43:19	(21,642)
Taylor, Stephen P	3:48:48	(8,211)
Taylor, Stephen P	4:25:42	(17,477)
Taylor, Stuart	4:49:09	(22,907)
Taylor, Stuart M	4:20:52	(16,250)
Taylor, Trevor B	4:38:11	(20,517)
Taylor, Trevor W	4:03:44	(12,134)
Taylor, Wilfrid R	3:10:16	(2,024)
Taylor, William J	3:49:59	(8,501)
Taylor-Page, Robert J	4:11:19	(13,933)
Taylor-Sabine, Jonathan L	5:40:54	(29,405)
Taylor-Schofield, Nigel C	5:39:30	(29,306)
Taylorson, Simon L	3:58:38	(10,899)
Taylor-Wilkin, Nigel D	3:58:00	(10,671)
Teagle, Paul M	5:38:39	(29,242)
Teague, Neil J	4:09:32	(13,507)
Teague, William	3:21:30	(3,257)
Teare, Ivan	3:27:42	(4,168)
Teasdale, David I	5:48:41	(29,893)
Teasdale, Mike J	5:08:02	(26,121)
Tebbutt, Alex	4:18:38	(15,695)
Tedcastle, Robert J	4:45:27	(22,129)
Tedd, Michael J	3:16:58	(2,744)
Tedder, Julian L	3:29:23	(4,482)
Tee, Paul K	2:56:04	(815)
Teece, Alan J	5:49:48	(29,952)
Teer, Ryan	3:30:24	(4,674)
Teigny, Philippe	3:41:32	(6,547)
Tejos, Christian A	3:58:49	(10,948)
Telford, Andrew D	3:35:43	(5,559)
Telford, Ross	3:37:02	(5,776)
Tempest, Philip G	3:58:23	(10,813)
Templeman, Paul	4:14:57	(14,795)
Tench, Nigel F	3:11:25	(2,136)
Tennant, David M	5:22:04	(27,781)
Tennant, Edward I	4:44:44	(21,961)
Tennant, John	3:14:49	(2,538)

Tennant, Mark A	3:41:28	(6,542)
Tennent, Trevor B	4:57:06	(24,420)
Tennyson, Mark	2:41:31	(232)
Terblanche, Etienne	4:58:01	(24,597)
Terol, Salvador	3:03:06	(1,374)
Terpstra, Robert	4:12:36	(14,237)
Terrey, Andy	5:04:48	(25,663)
Terrill, Chris F	4:24:07	(17,097)
Terrington, Nigel P	3:54:04	(9,524)
Terris, David A	4:19:58	(16,022)
Terry, Andrew	5:06:05	(25,856)
Terry, Christopher C	5:29:36	(28,545)
Terry, Graham	4:13:32	(14,462)
Terry, Ian	4:38:50	(20,677)
Terry, Stephen	4:40:20	(20,991)
Teschner Steinhardt, Rainer	4:23:38	(16,971)
Testar, Stuart J	4:01:50	(11,675)
Tester, Eric J	6:05:17	(30,600)
Tetley, Christopher J	4:14:08	(14,593)
Tetlow, Hamish S	4:04:32	(12,323)
Tetrel, Gilbert	4:00:19	(11,363)
Tetstall, Peter A	4:13:17	(14,399)
Teverson, Mark L	5:38:04	(29,186)
Thackray, Andrew	4:36:11	(20,068)
Thackray, Charles A	4:03:58	(12,184)
Thackwray, Michael R	4:22:03	(16,556)
Thackwray, Timothy	3:59:53	(11,261)
Thake, Andrew J	2:29:15	(75)
Thand, Mandip S	4:22:04	(16,561)
Thassim, Niel	4:59:12	(24,828)
Thatcher, Gary A	5:02:13	(25,321)
Thatcher, Jeremy J	8:00:59	(31,943)
Thaw, George	5:48:03	(29,869)
Thayre, Gary A	3:24:15	(3,595)
Theaker, Damien J	3:13:26	(2,363)
Thein, Tobias	3:47:01	(7,756)
Thelu, Charlie	4:42:31	(21,455)
Thelwall-Jones, Simon	3:40:23	(6,377)
Theobald, Alex D	5:52:36	(30,105)
Theophani, Fanos	4:53:03	(23,622)
Thepenier, Pierre	3:45:54	(7,507)
Theron, Frederik J	4:31:53	(19,072)
Thevenard, Jean-Christian	3:35:13	(5,462)
Thickett, Keith	3:34:29	(5,338)
Thickett, Maxwell D	4:52:14	(23,491)
Thin, Andrew	3:00:49	(1,218)
Thing, James E	3:32:53	(5,079)
Thirkettle, James R	4:11:36	(13,999)
Thirlwell, Jonathan C	4:46:50	(22,411)
Thiruchelvam, Paul	3:59:38	(11,198)
Thistleton, Terry	5:11:56	(26,623)
Thodesen, David R	4:31:57	(19,096)
Thodesen, Michael J	4:31:57	(19,096)
Thom, James D	4:23:28	(16,935)
Thoma, Nigel C	5:06:33	(25,917)
Thomas, Adrian	4:52:40	(23,564)
Thomas, Adrian M	5:11:08	(26,526)
Thomas, Alan	3:01:39	(1,283)
Thomas, Alan	4:22:53	(16,791)
Thomas, Alan E	3:34:15	(5,305)
Thomas, Alex	4:56:01	(24,211)
Thomas, Allan	3:47:53	(7,969)
Thomas, Andrew	4:57:24	(24,473)
Thomas, Andrew G	4:33:20	(19,434)
Thomas, Andrew P	4:39:58	(20,910)
Thomas, Andrew R	3:16:03	(2,650)
Thomas, Andrew R	4:17:17	(15,365)
Thomas, Anthony	3:55:03	(9,806)
Thomas, Austen J	3:10:24	(2,043)
Thomas, Barry	4:26:58	(17,830)
Thomas, Bobby A	5:01:19	(25,189)
Thomas, Christophe	4:13:48	(14,517)
Thomas, Christopher D	5:32:12	(28,749)
Thomas, Danny	4:26:51	(17,785)
Thomas, David A	3:53:17	(9,335)
Thomas, David A	6:22:17	(31,070)
Thomas, David I	3:51:54	(8,989)
Thomas, David P	3:37:19	(5,844)
Thomas, Dean R	3:58:13	(10,763)
Thomas, Delpeuche	4:07:29	(13,005)
Thomas, Derek C	3:46:47	(7,700)
Thomas, Des G	4:32:06	(19,133)
Thomas, Dylan O	5:08:36	(26,192)

Thomas, Eric J	3:07:39	(1,774)
Thomas, Evan	4:36:55	(20,233)
Thomas, Gareth	2:45:14	(332)
Thomas, Gareth R	2:39:34	(199)
Thomas, Gavin	4:00:12	(11,343)
Thomas, Geoff J	3:50:18	(8,574)
Thomas, Gerald A	4:32:07	(19,139)
Thomas, Graham	2:55:44	(796)
Thomas, Graham C	4:38:18	(20,548)
Thomas, Henry J	3:43:17	(6,914)
Thomas, Hew B	5:07:51	(26,095)
Thomas, Ian E	3:33:59	(5,268)
Thomas, Ian J	4:07:39	(13,044)
Thomas, Ian K	4:25:13	(17,363)
Thomas, Ian M	4:26:47	(17,770)
Thomas, Ian P	3:51:19	(8,836)
Thomas, Ian W	3:37:19	(5,844)
Thomas, Iestyn	3:49:01	(8,258)
Thomas, Jerome	3:39:08	(6,155)
Thomas, John P	4:13:50	(14,528)
Thomas, Justin	3:27:50	(4,193)
Thomas, Leighton N	3:25:27	(3,761)
Thomas, Lenny	3:08:46	(1,873)
Thomas, Mark	4:25:57	(17,555)
Thomas, Martin	3:19:13	(2,987)
Thomas, Matthew R	4:16:27	(15,163)
Thomas, Michael L	3:33:51	(5,244)
Thomas, Neil D	3:55:03	(9,806)
Thomas, Neil D	3:58:31	(10,860)
Thomas, Nicholas V	3:47:33	(7,894)
Thomas, Patrick J	4:51:27	(23,338)
Thomas, Paul	3:42:52	(6,827)
Thomas, Paul	5:01:17	(25,181)
Thomas, Paul B	4:49:04	(22,889)
Thomas, Paul D	3:41:46	(6,599)
Thomas, Paul S	3:46:58	(7,741)
Thomas, Peter	3:19:22	(3,001)
Thomas, Peter	4:46:15	(22,310)
Thomas, Raymond F	4:29:43	(18,557)
Thomas, Richard	3:54:25	(9,617)
Thomas, Robert	4:13:45	(14,505)
Thomas, Robert J	5:20:38	(27,649)
Thomas, Robert M	3:31:14	(4,812)
Thomas, Russell	3:13:07	(2,319)
Thomas, Russell	4:22:02	(16,548)
Thomas, Simon A	4:11:06	(13,889)
Thomas, Simon H	5:02:10	(25,316)
Thomas, Simon R	3:04:19	(1,476)
Thomas, Stephen B	5:01:19	(25,189)
Thomas, Stephen G	4:59:28	(24,896)
Thomas, Wayne	2:36:46	(146)
Thomas, William K	2:56:06	(820)
Thomas MBE, Mike J	5:10:37	(26,454)
Thomason, Francis L	3:44:40	(7,230)
Thomlinson, Alan	4:54:30	(23,896)
Thompson, Aaron	4:40:34	(21,039)
Thompson, Adrian L	3:22:22	(3,354)
Thompson, Alan C	4:28:50	(18,309)
Thompson, Alan J	4:52:14	(23,491)
Thompson, Allan D	4:15:15	(14,870)
Thompson, Andrew D	2:50:15	(516)
Thompson, Andrew G	3:51:00	(8,749)
Thompson, Andrew J	3:54:33	(9,651)
Thompson, Andy	3:47:10	(7,797)
Thompson, Barry S	3:08:16	(1,826)
Thompson, Brian J	5:22:23	(27,819)
Thompson, Christopher G	5:01:23	(25,201)
Thompson, Christopher J	3:20:19	(3,102)
Thompson, Christopher J	4:14:41	(14,725)
Thompson, Colin D	3:13:41	(2,396)
Thompson, Damion	3:39:50	(6,280)
Thompson, Darren J	3:55:17	(9,876)
Thompson, David J	4:21:18	(16,333)
Thompson, David John	3:04:17	(1,472)
Thompson, David M	3:13:23	(2,356)
Thompson, David P	3:30:47	(4,738)
Thompson, David S	4:37:10	(20,284)
Thompson, Frank W	4:43:19	(21,642)
Thompson, Gary A	5:41:11	(29,423)
Thompson, Gavin S	4:32:33	(19,248)
Thompson, George	4:51:54	(23,423)
Thompson, Iain C	3:24:19	(3,604)
Thompson, Ian J	4:08:44	(13,301)

Thompson, James	3:19:41 (3,040)	
Thompson, James A	5:30:38 (28,634)	
Thompson, John	5:38:54 (29,253)	
Thompson, John A	5:04:30 (25,627)	
Thompson, John S	3:01:00 (1,237)	
Thompson, Jonathan A	4:20:02 (16,039)	
Thompson, Kevin	4:18:16 (15,600)	
Thompson, Laurence	3:26:44 (3,969)	
Thompson, Mark E	3:48:20 (8,087)	
Thompson, Martin	3:25:55 (3,832)	
Thompson, Mathew I	3:56:26 (10,228)	
Thompson, Matthew T	3:47:57 (7,985)	
Thompson, Melvyn R	4:18:15 (15,598)	
Thompson, Michael	3:56:51 (10,351)	
Thompson, Michael P	3:26:47 (3,983)	
Thompson, Mike	5:26:20 (28,228)	
Thompson, Nicholas	4:57:37 (24,518)	
Thompson, Nigel	4:40:34 (21,039)	
Thompson, Nigel P	3:20:03 (3,074)	
Thompson, Paul	3:26:07 (3,861)	
Thompson, Paul	3:51:55 (8,995)	
Thompson, Paul D	3:29:10 (4,443)	
Thompson, Peter A	4:59:25 (24,887)	
Thompson, Peter C	5:12:32 (26,696)	
Thompson, Peter D	2:58:01 (972)	
Thompson, Peter J	7:03:13 (31,653)	
Thompson, Phillip D	5:38:56 (29,259)	
Thompson, Robert E	3:24:27 (3,620)	
Thompson, Robert J	3:52:19 (9,091)	
Thompson, Robert P	4:30:30 (18,760)	
Thompson, Simon P	4:40:02 (20,928)	
Thompson, Stephen N	4:02:35 (11,872)	
Thompson, Stuart M	4:52:13 (23,488)	
Thompson, Toby	3:47:20 (7,837)	
Thompson, Tracey	4:26:26 (17,681)	
Thompson, Victor M	3:47:01 (7,756)	
Thoms, Holger	3:35:31 (5,527)	
Thomsen, Jan	3:18:31 (2,898)	
Thomsett, Sam	4:40:47 (21,081)	
Thomson, Adam F	3:16:23 (2,683)	
Thomson, Alan R	4:03:41 (12,122)	
Thomson, Andrew J	3:07:32 (1,757)	
Thomson, Andy	5:45:26 (29,723)	
Thomson, David G	4:33:26 (19,454)	
Thomson, David I	5:00:12 (25,023)	
Thomson, David P	4:40:05 (20,936)	
Thomson, Fraser	4:54:01 (23,796)	
Thomson, Gary	5:01:44 (25,265)	
Thomson, Graeme A	4:14:07 (14,590)	
Thomson, Grant S	5:59:41 (30,399)	
Thomson, Mark A	4:44:54 (22,002)	
Thomson, Michael A	3:06:14 (1,631)	
Thomson, Mike J	3:35:14 (5,467)	
Thomson, Noel D	4:27:57 (18,082)	
Thomson, Paul A	3:06:40 (1,672)	
Thomson, Richard	3:28:47 (4,368)	
Thomson, Robin C	4:22:54 (16,795)	
Thomson, Stephen	3:12:02 (2,196)	
Thorburn, Peter	4:06:51 (12,849)	
Thorn, Mike A	3:28:20 (4,289)	
Thorn, Richard I	2:58:37 (1,031)	
Thornby, David G	3:20:38 (3,152)	
Thorndyke, Trevor	3:52:14 (9,064)	
Thorne, Colin	5:03:00 (25,446)	
Thorne, Darren T	4:36:49 (20,211)	
Thorne, John	5:00:04 (25,003)	
Thorne, Samuel J	4:03:14 (12,010)	
Thorne, Samuel S	4:51:43 (23,385)	
Thorne, Timothy M	3:59:31 (11,166)	
Thorne, William A	3:44:33 (7,201)	
Thornely, Ronnie L	4:40:55 (21,109)	
Thorner, Roddy B	4:15:01 (14,808)	
Thornett, Raymond G	3:46:24 (7,620)	
Thorneycroft, Martin P	3:27:09 (4,053)	
Thornley, Allan W	4:31:00 (18,858)	
Thornley, Jeremy G	3:40:56 (6,462)	
Thornton, Clive S	3:53:05 (9,275)	
Thornton, Dean A	3:09:22 (1,934)	
Thornton, James P	4:05:23 (12,503)	
Thornton, Keith J	3:24:19 (3,604)	
Thornton, Kevin J	3:23:31 (3,502)	
Thornton, Paul	3:54:52 (9,741)	
Thornton, Peter J	5:25:32 (28,141)	

Thornton, Philip J	3:34:43 (5,371)	
Thornton, Robert J	4:04:38 (12,336)	
Thornton, Stanley	4:52:11 (23,479)	
Thorogood, Keith S	4:25:14 (17,366)	
Thorp, Nick J	5:04:21 (25,611)	
Thorp, Rupert W	4:26:02 (17,579)	
Thorpe, John M	3:02:59 (1,366)	
Thorpe, Jon E	3:03:17 (1,387)	
Thorpe, Martin	4:34:01 (19,594)	
Thorpe, Richard J	4:22:40 (16,740)	
Thorpe, Steve A	4:31:54 (19,080)	
Thorpe, Steven J	4:32:05 (19,131)	
Thorvaldsen, Vestein	3:00:39 (1,203)	
Thouvenin, Thierry	2:57:45 (939)	
Thraves, Jonathan M	3:31:49 (4,892)	
Threlfall, Mark J	3:34:44 (5,377)	
Thubron, David	4:41:54 (21,326)	
Thubron, Neil A	3:01:34 (1,279)	
Thuillier, Wilfrid	3:47:57 (7,985)	
Thunberg, Sten H	3:15:06 (2,567)	
Thurgood, Hugh A	3:46:38 (7,670)	
Thurgood, Marc	3:47:46 (7,940)	
Thurgood, Mark	3:33:43 (5,218)	
Thurgood, Peter S	5:40:25 (29,373)	
Thurley, Adam	4:37:24 (20,328)	
Thurlow, James	3:48:35 (8,144)	
Thurman, Ian J	5:30:03 (28,588)	
Thursby-Pelham, Brian	5:22:04 (27,781)	
Thurston, Philip R	4:22:26 (16,677)	
Thurtle, Gary D	5:52:06 (30,068)	
Thurtle, Ian C	4:08:22 (13,193)	
Tiago, Dionisio	3:37:22 (5,851)	
Tibaldi, Justin	4:10:32 (13,762)	
Tibbetts, Graham M	3:22:49 (3,421)	
Tibenderana, James	4:03:30 (12,078)	
Tickle, Andrew B	6:21:42 (31,052)	
Tickle, Mark S	3:30:56 (4,769)	
Tidey, Ian	4:14:15 (14,619)	
Tidiman, Steve	2:58:16 (993)	
Tidnam, Matthew P	4:46:37 (22,376)	
Tidon, Erwin S	7:00:45 (31,634)	
Tierney, Trevor D	3:43:41 (6,994)	
Tietz, Joachim	3:39:27 (6,209)	
Tietz, Karl	3:10:00 (2,001)	
Tighe, Raymond J	4:48:24 (22,759)	
Tilke, Warren	3:16:09 (2,658)	
Till, Stephen M	3:36:30 (5,696)	
Tillbrooke, Tony	4:42:21 (21,425)	
Tiller, Nicholas B	3:33:18 (5,160)	
Tiller, Raymond T	4:16:54 (15,282)	
Tiller, Robert	4:22:52 (16,788)	
Tillery, Andrew J	2:52:08 (596)	
Tillett, Ian M	3:20:51 (3,184)	
Tillett, Sean	4:12:40 (14,254)	
Tilley, David	3:19:02 (2,958)	
Tilley, Ian R	4:31:26 (18,956)	
Tilley, Jason A	2:51:59 (589)	
Tilley, Kevin	2:46:42 (380)	
Tilley, Richard I	4:31:26 (18,956)	
Tilling, Mark W	5:26:00 (28,197)	
Tillott, Neil D	4:06:56 (12,871)	
Tillott, Nigel G	3:34:40 (5,362)	
Tilly, Ross	4:11:54 (14,063)	
Tilson, Adam J	6:18:31 (30,971)	
Tilson, Scott A	3:55:48 (10,016)	
Tilstone, David	4:42:14 (21,395)	
Tilstone, Jules D	5:09:57 (26,372)	
Tilstone, Paul J	5:09:59 (26,375)	
Timbers, Ben	4:23:01 (16,815)	
Timbers, David A	3:43:47 (7,009)	
Timlin, Shane M	4:12:14 (14,139)	
Timm, Dominic	4:03:29 (12,075)	
Timmins, Colin W	3:16:24 (2,687)	
Timmis, Jonathan P	3:50:25 (8,611)	
Timmis, William	4:07:18 (12,963)	
Timms, Giles M	2:48:51 (451)	
Timms, Paul T	3:58:37 (10,891)	
Timms, Richard V	5:22:37 (27,843)	
Timpson, Anthony E	4:06:18 (12,736)	
Tims, Mike	4:24:39 (17,218)	
Timson, Albert W	5:10:06 (26,389)	
Timson, Andrew	4:31:30 (18,982)	
Timson, Brian A	4:49:47 (23,036)	

Timson, Mark	4:49:47 (23,036)	
Tindall, David	4:41:51 (21,317)	
Tindall, Mark A	3:29:01 (4,416)	
Tiney, Paul E	5:25:43 (28,162)	
Tingley, Mark B	5:53:00 (30,128)	
Tinham, Andrew L	4:15:49 (15,006)	
Tini, Gianluca	2:38:00 (172)	
Tinkler, Antony A	4:22:27 (16,681)	
Tinkler, Alan P	5:30:11 (28,601)	
Tinkler, Andrew J	4:04:10 (12,234)	
Tinline, David P	3:51:34 (8,909)	
Tinline, Robert J	3:51:35 (8,913)	
Tinsley, David	3:39:07 (6,150)	
Tinsley, Sid	3:30:07 (4,619)	
Tiozzo, Angelo	4:02:10 (11,769)	
Tiplady, David R	4:03:21 (12,046)	
Tiplady, Simon J	4:00:50 (11,454)	
Tipper, Tom P	3:45:22 (7,378)	
Tiraboschi, Osvaldo	3:37:47 (5,916)	
Tischer, Claus	3:10:13 (2,021)	
Tischer, Horst	3:01:58 (1,299)	
Tisdall, Ben	6:17:35 (30,939)	
Tisi, Simon J	3:38:36 (6,069)	
Tislevoll, Steinar	4:54:05 (23,812)	
Tisor, Andrew J	4:08:32 (13,239)	
Titchener, Frank	4:55:07 (24,019)	
Titherly, Mark D	5:12:33 (26,699)	
Titley, Andy	3:22:24 (3,361)	
Titov, Alexander S	3:45:39 (7,445)	
Tittley, Stephen A	5:11:44 (26,596)	
Toal, James	3:47:31 (7,883)	
Tobin, James A	5:51:33 (30,041)	
Tobin, Shaun E	3:49:12 (8,309)	
Toby, Jackson	3:17:51 (2,835)	
Tod, Simon J	4:12:40 (14,254)	
Todd, Alexander J	4:35:40 (19,956)	
Todd, Andrew M	3:37:01 (5,715)	
Todd, David	3:38:58 (6,126)	
Todd, Keith I	3:57:21 (10,498)	
Todd, Kenneth C	6:35:37 (31,300)	
Todd, Michael	5:26:44 (28,273)	
Todd, Paul	2:37:20 (161)	
Todd, Richard	3:01:12 (1,254)	
Todd, Rory D	4:04:42 (12,351)	
Todd, William	3:31:21 (4,826)	
Toet, Arie C	4:31:46 (19,044)	
Toft, Dave	4:14:25 (14,655)	
Toft, Michael D	3:42:55 (6,838)	
Togtema, Hans	4:20:19 (16,106)	
Tohani, Sanjay	5:41:39 (29,461)	
Tojeiro, Rob	2:44:05 (289)	
Tola, Tesfaye	2:09:07 (5)	
Tolentina, Laberne P	5:50:11 (29,975)	
Tollfree, John	4:36:53 (20,223)	
Tollner, Martin E	4:08:53 (13,342)	
Tomassi, Nick	3:50:37 (8,662)	
Tombling, Anthony	4:40:31 (21,031)	
Tombs, Jonathan M	3:39:34 (6,228)	
Tomin, Valentine T	4:14:13 (14,612)	
Tomkins, Paul J	4:18:14 (15,717)	
Tomkinson, Andrew D	4:30:03 (18,646)	
Tomkinson-Hill, Nicholas M	3:34:43 (5,371)	
Tomlin, Alan C	3:31:48 (4,889)	
Tomlin, David L	2:50:14 (514)	
Tomlin, Neil K	3:56:17 (10,178)	
Tomlin, Stephen	7:30:47 (31,851)	
Tomlinson, Christopher	4:51:10 (23,300)	
Tomlinson, Daniel H	3:58:33 (10,874)	
Tomlinson, Dean L	4:31:36 (18,999)	
Tomlinson, Fred	7:03:01 (31,649)	
Tomlinson, Ian M	4:11:32 (13,978)	
Tomlinson, Mark W	2:50:53 (539)	
Tomlinson, Matthew J	3:25:54 (3,827)	
Tomlinson, Michael	6:56:25 (31,578)	
Tomlinson, Ryan	3:31:06 (4,788)	
Tomlinson, William	3:32:22 (4,981)	
Tommassoni, Francesco	4:36:08 (20,062)	
Tommis, David	6:29:56 (31,202)	
Tompsett, Matt T	5:05:17 (25,721)	
Toms, David A	4:04:04 (12,200)	
Toms, Graham C	4:07:47 (13,066)	
Toms, Neil	4:22:49 (16,777)	
Toms, Simon P	4:22:24 (16,666)	

Tomsa, David	4:55:43 (24,135)	
Tomsett, John M	3:50:33 (8,639)	
Tomson, Paul H	5:25:08 (28,100)	
Ton That, Peter	5:24:59 (28,080)	
Tondeleir, Pierre	3:10:46 (2,079)	
Tong, Andrew D	3:29:04 (4,425)	
Tonge, Peter D	2:51:49 (583)	
Tonkin, Brendan K	4:51:02 (23,277)	
Tonkin, Craig	3:47:41 (7,925)	
Tonkinson, Paul R	3:09:19 (1,930)	
Tonner, Benjamin	3:49:42 (8,424)	
Tonzani, Antonio	3:28:45 (4,364)	
Toogood, Michael W	4:41:39 (21,271)	
Toogood, Paul J	6:14:39 (30,869)	
Tooke, Richard	5:04:45 (25,657)	
Tooley, Mark A	4:09:36 (13,524)	
Toomey, Christopher I	4:02:41 (11,894)	
Toomey, Iain M	3:27:19 (4,084)	
Toon, Andrew R	4:14:10 (14,601)	
Toone, James T	3:30:51 (4,751)	
Toone, Richard S	3:33:05 (5,112)	
Toonen, Hans	5:26:21 (28,234)	
Toop, Keith	2:59:26 (1,116)	
Tooze, Matthew D	3:23:48 (3,544)	
Topham, Nigel R	4:17:45 (15,494)	
Tordoff, Mark	3:34:32 (5,346)	
Torok, Oliver	5:35:20 (28,983)	
Torp, Morten	4:42:47 (21,515)	
Torrance, Duncan A	5:43:48 (29,616)	
Torrens, Pip	4:02:43 (11,906)	
Torry, Hugh J	2:54:52 (741)	
Torstensen, Asgeir	4:07:57 (13,104)	
Torsti, Esko	5:12:23 (26,679)	
Tosh, Ian D	4:50:42 (23,218)	
Tostevin, Craig	5:02:15 (25,326)	
Toth, Miklos	3:20:24 (3,109)	
Totterdell, Graham W	4:52:53 (23,595)	
Touches, Norbert	3:04:57 (1,522)	
Toudic, Gerald M	3:13:32 (2,379)	
Toulson, Michael	5:49:58 (29,962)	
Toumazis, Tom C	5:00:28 (25,060)	
Touret, Marc G	3:41:35 (6,561)	
Tovey, Norman E	7:11:12 (31,715)	
Tovey, Simon J	4:09:14 (13,432)	
Towell, Christopher C	3:58:55 (10,979)	
Towell, Shaun A	5:02:09 (25,313)	
Town, James N	4:09:58 (13,631)	
Towner, John R	4:43:13 (21,610)	
Townley, Mike D	2:54:29 (717)	
Townsend, Edward	4:28:18 (18,170)	
Townsend, Graham J	3:17:45 (2,824)	
Townsend, John L	3:26:44 (3,969)	
Townsend, John T	4:44:19 (21,865)	
Townsend, Martin	3:13:17 (2,340)	
Townsend, Philip S	2:59:14 (1,097)	
Townsend, Stuart	5:09:21 (26,285)	
Townsend, Victor J	6:41:06 (31,373)	
Townsend-Handscomb, Darren	4:23:03 (16,825)	
Townsley, Scott J	4:32:09 (19,152)	
Townsley, Steven J	3:59:26 (11,121)	
Toye, Anthony	3:20:31 (3,135)	
Toye, David A	4:09:41 (13,549)	
Tozer, Don P	5:34:55 (28,951)	
Tozer, Ross W	3:12:13 (2,219)	
Trabanino, Herbert	3:19:25 (3,008)	
Tracey, Francis J	3:03:49 (1,433)	
Tracy, David L	5:22:08 (27,785)	
Train, Terence S	4:32:59 (19,354)	
Trainer, Craig P	3:42:36 (6,763)	
Trainor, Gareth	5:38:56 (29,259)	
Tran, Van N	3:57:29 (10,533)	
Trant, Andrew W	4:17:50 (15,517)	
Tranter, Ian K	4:50:22 (23,142)	
Tranter, Jim	4:56:18 (24,261)	
Tranter, Paul	3:09:23 (1,935)	
Tranter, Robin	5:22:37 (27,843)	
Trask, Roger	4:55:31 (24,102)	
Travers, Andrew R	4:41:14 (21,163)	
Travers, Guy	3:57:28 (10,527)	
Travers, Tim	3:53:44 (9,420)	
Travi, Lee C	3:59:42 (11,222)	
Travis, Jason E	5:31:56 (28,730)	
Traynor, Darrell B	3:52:17 (9,079)	
Traynor, Harry	3:41:47 (6,603)	
Traynor, John	4:15:07 (14,834)	
Traynor, Mark W	2:53:27 (666)	
Traynor, Patrick	5:20:19 (27,610)	
Treadwell, Brian	4:50:08 (23,095)	
Treadwell, Mark S	4:26:03 (17,585)	
Treadwell, Robert W	4:07:33 (13,024)	
Treagust, Daniel J	4:23:11 (16,869)	
Trebilcock, Mark C	4:09:27 (13,488)	
Tredget, Laurence E	4:39:07 (20,751)	
Tredget, Steven J	3:34:32 (5,346)	
Treen, Danny J	5:28:17 (28,417)	
Tregubov, Victor	3:08:27 (1,846)	
Treherne, Dave	3:27:51 (4,197)	
Treherne, Jonathan S	4:26:57 (17,825)	
Tremble, Philip J	3:37:22 (5,851)	
Trendall, David C	4:30:29 (18,754)	
Treneman, Brian P	4:13:30 (14,452)	
Trenga, Laurent F	7:11:18 (31,717)	
Trent, Miles N	4:17:16 (15,360)	
Tresca, Arnaud	3:20:27 (3,115)	
Trethewey, Martin P	4:23:56 (17,046)	
Trett, James E	4:42:26 (21,439)	
Trevor, Anthony R	4:36:24 (20,104)	
Trewinnard, Philip J	5:13:41 (26,854)	
Trianni, Massimo	3:38:26 (6,036)	
Tribley, Russell	4:04:13 (12,245)	
Trice, Cyril L	6:37:04 (31,321)	
Trick, Robert C	4:29:07 (18,381)	
Trickett, Joel D	4:40:14 (20,970)	
Trickett, Philip J	4:17:01 (15,307)	
Trigger, Mark E	3:43:46 (7,005)	
Trigger, Matthew W	4:14:43 (14,732)	
Trill, Gerard A	4:02:05 (11,739)	
Trimble, Chris	5:02:42 (25,403)	
Trimble, Sean D	3:41:25 (6,535)	
Trincado-Perez, Alberto	3:44:46 (7,254)	
Tripp, Daniel	3:54:34 (9,655)	
Triptree, Tim G	4:42:44 (21,505)	
Tristram, Andrew G	4:28:05 (18,123)	
Trivedi, Amit M	5:57:30 (30,310)	
Trivedi, Deven	5:22:45 (27,852)	
Trodd, Ron C	4:26:00 (17,568)	
Trodden, John E	4:36:56 (20,236)	
Trollope, Richard	3:55:14 (9,860)	
Trollope, Stephen C	3:54:34 (9,655)	
Troman, Stephen C	3:54:44 (9,704)	
Tromans, Stuart J	3:10:38 (2,066)	
Troop, Lee	2:09:58 (8)	
Trory, John A	3:47:38 (7,914)	
Trost, Manfred	4:02:06 (11,746)	
Trotman, Benjamin P	4:28:25 (18,198)	
Trotman, Michael J	4:02:38 (11,881)	
Trotman, Paul A	4:28:25 (18,198)	
Trotman, William J	4:22:09 (16,588)	
Trott, Martin N	3:55:18 (9,868)	
Trotter, Michael A	3:18:41 (2,917)	
Troughton, Mick	4:02:36 (11,879)	
Troup, Michael G	3:14:54 (2,548)	
Trout, Alan J	5:52:54 (30,120)	
Trout, Gordon	3:40:57 (6,466)	
Trowles, Colin A	4:38:27 (20,584)	
Trowsdale, John	4:37:54 (20,437)	
Truan, Steven	4:27:48 (18,039)	
Truderung, Sven	3:48:33 (8,135)	
Trudgill, Graham J	3:35:27 (5,511)	
Truelove, Joseph T	4:23:41 (16,980)	
Truman, Andrew W	3:28:47 (4,368)	
Truman, Daniel J	3:18:11 (2,871)	
Truman, Ian	3:51:42 (8,940)	
Trump, Stephen C	3:43:52 (7,031)	
Trumper, David	4:14:20 (14,632)	
Trundle, Gary	3:39:25 (6,205)	
Truscott, Chris G	2:34:56 (124)	
Trussell, Stephen M	3:04:18 (1,474)	
Trussler, Mark J	3:53:47 (9,436)	
Try, Chris E	2:51:08 (548)	
Tsavliris, Alex	4:44:39 (21,947)	
Tsavliris, George A	5:31:50 (28,726)	
Tschudi, Fritz	2:57:56 (960)	
Tschvertz, Michael	4:40:14 (20,970)	
Tse, Kenny	3:58:50 (10,954)	
Tsignora, Alan T	4:53:53 (23,774)	
Tsoi, Andy C	3:43:06 (6,872)	
Tsun, Ah Boon	4:29:36 (18,523)	
Tu, Hai M	4:50:37 (23,202)	
Tubb, Anthony A	5:07:37 (26,059)	
Tubb, Gerald	4:20:23 (16,126)	
Tubbs, Trevor D	3:51:11 (8,798)	
Tubman, Neil	5:11:48 (26,604)	
Tucker, Alastair J	4:52:48 (23,585)	
Tucker, Allan J	5:18:11 (27,391)	
Tucker, Andrew J	4:36:35 (20,150)	
Tucker, Andrew M	4:58:55 (24,783)	
Tucker, Colin	4:47:06 (22,474)	
Tucker, David K	3:15:42 (2,622)	
Tucker, Edward J	4:45:04 (22,053)	
Tucker, Graham J	3:09:30 (1,945)	
Tucker, Guy	3:12:26 (2,243)	
Tucker, Jeremy A	3:01:28 (1,277)	
Tucker, Paul	4:32:27 (19,229)	
Tucker, Richard J	5:18:47 (27,447)	
Tucker, Robert J	5:02:11 (25,318)	
Tucker, Russell P	4:28:32 (18,240)	
Tucker, Stephen J	3:13:29 (2,369)	
Tuckett, Mark A	3:14:51 (2,546)	
Tudor, Jonathan D	3:56:27 (10,235)	
Tudor, Simon C	5:57:47 (30,322)	
Tueter, Trygve K	3:08:15 (1,824)	
Tuffnell, Shaun	3:48:02 (8,004)	
Tufnell, Michael H	3:57:55 (10,651)	
Tufton, Grant	5:18:34 (27,417)	
Tufton, Richard E	5:18:00 (27,371)	
Tugwell, Peter M	5:40:06 (29,345)	
Tulett, Dominic J	5:39:24 (29,300)	
Tull, David	3:28:15 (4,277)	
Tulley, Colin J	6:53:59 (31,547)	
Tulley, Jonathan C	4:36:57 (20,243)	
Tulloch, Andy	4:42:38 (21,477)	
Tulloch, James A	5:26:55 (28,293)	
Tulloch, Jim M	4:29:17 (18,422)	
Tulloch, Kevin J	2:46:51 (385)	
Tully, John	4:49:16 (22,932)	
Tully, Simon J	4:53:13 (23,656)	
Tully, Stephen P	6:06:44 (30,698)	
Tunaley, John	4:29:18 (18,431)	
Tunn, Martin	4:47:25 (22,546)	
Tunstall, Glenn J	4:26:33 (17,714)	
Tunstall, Paul	3:55:16 (9,868)	
Tunstall-Pedoe, Hugh D	4:47:32 (22,574)	
Tunvor, Raj	4:31:41 (19,022)	
Tuplin, Lee J	3:53:45 (9,427)	
Tupling, Steve	5:31:58 (28,732)	
Tura, Sylvio	5:11:04 (26,512)	
Turcan, Thierry	4:38:47 (20,664)	
Turci, Mario	5:27:44 (28,377)	
Turek, Jeremy	5:00:30 (25,067)	
Turkington, Richard	2:32:38 (97)	
Turkoglu, Bahattin	4:04:43 (12,323)	
Turley, Stuart	4:03:58 (12,184)	
Turnbull, Colin H	5:05:14 (25,717)	
Turnbull, David R	3:41:28 (6,542)	
Turnbull, John R	3:44:45 (7,249)	
Turnbull, Keith	4:50:04 (23,085)	
Turnbull, Martin	4:01:32 (11,605)	
Turnbull, Nicholas C	3:29:54 (4,572)	
Turnbull, Patrick M	4:43:25 (21,667)	
Turner, Alan T	5:09:39 (26,328)	
Turner, Alex	4:24:51 (17,268)	
Turner, Alex J	3:54:55 (9,756)	
Turner, Andrew J	2:55:46 (798)	
Turner, Andrew M	4:53:32 (23,707)	
Turner, Barry J	8:01:58 (31,944)	
Turner, Brian R	4:23:41 (16,980)	
Turner, Chris D	3:54:55 (9,756)	
Turner, Chris L	4:40:49 (21,093)	
Turner, Christopher	4:09:28 (13,490)	
Turner, Christopher J	4:51:13 (23,306)	
Turner, Craig S	3:56:27 (10,235)	
Turner, Dean	4:35:57 (20,016)	
Turner, Graham N	5:04:24 (25,614)	
Turner, Hugh	5:27:12 (28,323)	
Turner, Ian A	4:25:00 (17,311)	
Turner, Ian G	4:17:32 (15,433)	
Turner, Ian M	4:47:24 (22,542)	

Turner, Ian N.	3:40:04 (6,320)
Turner, James	4:00:52 (11,468)
Turner, Jason R.	3:14:17 (2,475)
Turner, Jimmie J.	5:05:21 (25,732)
Turner, John E.	3:24:27 (3,620)
Turner, Jonathan C	3:48:37 (8,157)
Turner, Joseph	3:52:47 (9,188)
Turner, Julian P	3:29:01 (4,416)
Turner, Lee	4:58:17 (24,663)
Turner, Luke P	3:34:09 (5,291)
Turner, Mark	4:22:18 (16,637)
Turner, Mark	4:34:31 (19,717)
Turner, Mark	6:38:12 (31,342)
Turner, Mark G.	5:00:41 (25,092)
Turner, Mark J.	5:28:05 (28,402)
Turner, Matthew C	3:05:08 (1,538)
Turner, Michael S.	3:49:47 (8,447)
Turner, Neil	3:34:41 (5,366)
Turner, Nicholas S.	2:58:39 (1,035)
Turner, Paul	4:25:25 (17,405)
Turner, Paul	4:26:10 (17,621)
Turner, Peter A.	4:24:07 (17,097)
Turner, Peter J.	2:49:18 (470)
Turner, Richard	5:19:50 (27,540)
Turner, Richard D.	4:17:46 (15,499)
Turner, Shaun A.	4:17:49 (15,512)
Turney, Gary E.	4:48:56 (22,862)
Turney, Jonathan M	4:03:28 (12,072)
Turnpenny, Lee	4:06:53 (12,860)
Turpin, Jamie M	4:29:18 (18,431)
Turrell, Craig A	3:27:23 (4,100)
Turrell, Giles M	4:48:41 (22,812)
Turrell, Peter F	2:43:34 (280)
Turton, Les J.	3:10:06 (2,011)
Turvey, Stephen K	4:54:18 (23,855)
Tusler, Fraser K.	3:34:08 (5,288)
Tustin, Bayley J	3:41:03 (6,483)
Tusting, Richard J.	4:46:22 (22,333)
Tutt, Cedric L.	4:18:16 (15,600)
Tutt, Conrad	4:59:47 (24,954)
Tutt, Mark J.	4:23:29 (16,937)
Tutton, Robert D.	4:19:19 (15,860)
Tutty, Robin	4:22:59 (16,809)
Twaddle, Ian	4:22:09 (16,588)
Twani, Siya	6:13:31 (30,834)
Tweddle, David J.	4:32:58 (19,351)
Tweddle, Norman W	4:46:50 (22,411)
Tweddle, Richard J.	2:55:09 (765)
Tweed, Daniel C	4:27:39 (18,004)
Tweedie, Ronald M	5:25:22 (28,127)
Twigg, Martin J	5:58:30 (30,349)
Twine, James L	2:57:36 (922)
Twinn, Jason G	5:51:32 (30,038)
Twitchett, Gary G	5:19:33 (27,503)
Twizell, David W	4:21:07 (16,296)
Twomey, Barry M	4:25:19 (17,384)
Twomey, Eamonn	3:08:26 (1,843)
Twomey, Humphrey	2:45:28 (341)
Twose, Gary R	5:47:29 (29,836)
Tyas, Adrian J	4:23:52 (17,030)
Tyas, Keith	4:02:19 (11,814)
Tyas, William J	4:23:51 (17,025)
Tye, Stuart E	3:41:56 (6,627)
Tyldesley, Heath S	4:59:45 (24,949)
Tyldesley, Mark J.	4:18:44 (15,717)
Tyler, David J.	4:57:42 (24,537)
Tyler, John	2:57:47 (943)
Tyler, Keith	5:16:13 (27,157)
Tyler, Kevin	3:07:47 (1,786)
Tyler, Mark P	4:14:28 (14,674)
Tyler, Stephen	4:48:07 (22,699)
Tymon, Oscar	5:14:50 (27,007)
Tyrrell, Chris	5:05:51 (25,815)
Tyrrell, Michael	4:43:11 (21,602)
Tyrrell, Philip G	4:58:40 (24,750)
Tyrrell, Steven M	4:39:08 (20,756)
Tyrrell, William J	3:24:50 (3,667)
Tyson, Roy F	4:10:23 (13,729)
Tyszkiewicz, John Z	4:20:11 (16,059)
Tyzack, David J.	4:56:11 (24,242)
Ubsdell, Simon	2:55:06 (763)
Uchida, Ikuo	5:45:51 (29,745)
Uden, Michael	3:57:32 (10,550)
Udugampola, Vernon	6:18:39 (30,979)
Uebelgunne, Deltef R	4:06:48 (12,836)
Ueckermann, Marius J	2:48:41 (445)
Uff, Frederick	4:20:37 (16,191)
Uglow, Simon N	4:27:30 (17,957)
Ultich, Kai-Uwe	3:23:35 (3,511)
Umney, James D	3:19:37 (3,029)
Underdown, Kevin C	3:25:57 (3,841)
Underhill, Gareth R	4:23:10 (16,858)
Underhill, Keith W.	4:59:55 (24,976)
Underwood, James W	3:51:58 (9,006)
Underwood, Stuart M	2:49:54 (494)
Unerman, Alan S	6:12:35 (30,802)
Unerman, David B	5:55:01 (30,197)
Unerman, Martin H	6:12:34 (30,797)
Ung, Hy C	4:06:14 (12,722)
Ungi, Thomas	4:54:31 (23,899)
Ungi, Thomas E	4:24:32 (17,192)
Ungoed-Thomas, Mark L	4:41:45 (21,296)
Unitt, Andrew V	3:13:20 (2,348)
Unsted, Paul S	3:52:14 (9,064)
Unwin, Barry N	4:07:31 (13,012)
Unwin, Will	3:20:27 (3,115)
Upfield, Malcolm	4:45:02 (22,040)
Upton, James A	3:46:01 (7,529)
Ural, Jon	4:54:05 (23,812)
Urch, David M	3:49:48 (8,451)
Ure, Alan M	3:32:30 (5,004)
Urmston, Michael J	3:22:30 (3,375)
Urne, John S.	2:36:57 (151)
Urron, Geoffrey	4:22:49 (16,777)
Ursell, Jonathan M	4:01:59 (11,712)
Urwin, Roger C	4:33:38 (19,496)
Usborne, Gary D	3:43:48 (7,013)
Usero Lopez, Angel	4:14:44 (14,740)
Usher, John	4:30:52 (18,833)
Utley, Crispin B	4:20:41 (16,206)
Utley, Jonathan J	4:43:27 (21,673)
Utteridge, Glenn R	3:35:38 (5,547)
Utterson, Paul	2:58:42 (1,044)
Utting, Simon J	6:37:25 (31,332)
Utting, Stephen D	4:20:15 (16,077)
Utton, Damian N	3:04:28 (1,488)
Utz, Pascal	3:27:41 (4,164)
Vaccaro, Daniel P	3:46:05 (7,544)
Vachell, David A	5:20:16 (27,602)
Vagliasindi, Riccaardo	3:36:02 (5,615)
Vail, Vince	4:57:15 (24,450)
Valder, Alexander J	4:59:29 (24,901)
Vale, Christopher A	4:48:41 (22,812)
Vale, Paul A	4:38:57 (20,706)
Valentine, Alan A	3:45:33 (7,425)
Valentine, David	4:21:35 (16,409)
Valentine, Mark C	4:42:57 (21,555)
Valkenburg, Martin P	4:37:18 (20,315)
Vallance, Roger W	3:09:35 (1,959)
Vallance, Stephen M	4:56:01 (24,211)
Vallario, Anthony G	4:25:34 (17,444)
Valler, Garry	5:02:47 (25,416)
Vallis, John H.	3:29:22 (4,478)
Vallis, Keith D	2:51:24 (561)
Vamben, Eric S	2:44:12 (292)
Van Alderwegen, Damian E	3:26:31 (3,922)
Van Alderwegen, Frank S	4:31:56 (19,093)
Van Asbeck, Edward J	3:52:51 (9,213)
Van Bergen, Theo	3:36:31 (5,699)
Van Bockstael, Peter	3:47:31 (7,883)
Van Brussel, Georges	3:57:30 (10,538)
Van De Gruiter, Karel	4:26:49 (17,777)
Van Den Berg, Piet	4:28:07 (18,126)
Van Den Broeck, Herman	3:16:59 (2,746)
Van Der Bijl, Jan	3:55:30 (9,929)
Van Der Bunt, Ronald	3:58:25 (10,824)
Van Der Linden, Gary O	4:03:19 (12,036)
Van Der Merwe, Willem C	4:07:01 (12,896)
Van Der Sluis, Adri	3:31:22 (4,828)
Van Der Wal, Machiel J	4:16:18 (15,118)
Van Der Wateren, Arthur J	4:49:57 (23,067)
Van Doninck, Francis W	4:03:50 (12,155)
Van Dongelen, Jeroen P	4:38:37 (20,621)
Van Egeraat, Walfried	3:48:36 (8,150)
Van Eijk, Frank	3:07:30 (1,753)
Van Elkan, Dean	3:58:09 (10,729)
Van Gelder, Jacobus D	4:00:52 (11,468)
Van Hecke, Geoges	3:12:50 (2,291)
Van Heerden, Jaco	6:18:10 (30,961)
Van Heiningen, Andrew	3:55:02 (9,798)
Van Heusden, Johan	3:44:07 (7,097)
Van Heysbroeck, Frederik	3:41:51 (6,614)
Van Hilst, Rudolf	3:31:28 (4,842)
Van Hoey, José A	5:15:22 (27,062)
Van Hoorebeke, Willy	3:26:45 (3,973)
Van Keirsbilck, Marmix R	3:01:38 (1,282)
Van Kessel, Erwin	5:44:42 (29,669)
Van Leest, Arno	4:57:54 (24,568)
Van Maurik, Gerardus J	4:28:37 (18,259)
Van Niekerk, Eitenne	3:10:08 (2,015)
Van Paasschen, Fritts	3:41:45 (6,597)
Van Roon, Peter	5:24:00 (27,973)
Van Santen, Dick	4:27:01 (17,846)
Van Sikkelerus, Stephanus H	4:26:27 (17,684)
Van Tebberen, Gary	7:15:32 (31,751)
Van Til, Hans	4:31:50 (19,056)
Van Vuuren, Johan	4:43:50 (21,753)
Van Weesep, Jeroen	3:06:39 (1,669)
Van Wieringen, Simon	5:01:25 (25,211)
Van Woerkom, Alfons B	4:28:04 (18,115)
Van Wonderen, Jan J	3:13:04 (2,315)
Van Wyk, Derek D	4:47:03 (22,463)
Van Wyk, Rian	3:38:48 (6,098)
Van Zanen, Ronald	6:02:27 (30,506)
Vandeghinste, Frans	2:44:33 (304)
Vanderschommen, Luk F	5:45:26 (29,723)
Van-Orden, Simon B	3:04:11 (1,464)
Vanschagen, Mark	5:30:57 (28,656)
Vanstone, Martin	4:42:01 (21,348)
Vanstone, Neil A.	5:08:22 (26,170)
Varadinek-Skelton, John	3:54:56 (9,763)
Varah, Paul	4:07:03 (12,909)
Varcin, Baris	3:18:41 (2,917)
Varden, Mark G	2:56:31 (853)
Vardy, Antony J	3:50:19 (8,581)
Varga, Laszlo	3:12:34 (2,260)
Varghese, Bobin	5:11:53 (26,617)
Varia, Luv V	5:15:42 (27,097)
Varley, David J	3:31:44 (4,877)
Varley, James	3:24:11 (3,585)
Varndell, Andrew J	5:34:28 (28,924)
Varndell, Peter J	3:44:14 (7,124)
Varney, Ken M	4:34:48 (19,778)
Varney, Kevin E.	3:27:24 (4,103)
Varwig, David L	3:25:17 (3,733)
Vasco, Antonio	3:56:21 (10,196)
Vasko, Richard W	5:33:42 (28,864)
Vassie, Christopher J	4:20:16 (16,085)
Vassie, Gary D	5:21:26 (27,724)
Vassiliades, Steven	2:56:20 (842)
Vassiliou, Vasso	4:27:50 (18,050)
Vaughan, Alex F	3:05:50 (1,591)
Vaughan, Anthony	4:38:58 (20,715)
Vaughan, Bryan	2:39:42 (205)
Vaughan, Bryan J.	3:34:10 (5,293)
Vaughan, Daniel	2:48:43 (447)
Vaughan, David	3:27:53 (4,206)
Vaughan, Duncan A	5:01:54 (25,287)
Vaughan, Gareth L.	4:29:02 (18,358)
Vaughan, Gareth M	5:15:34 (27,085)
Veal, Clive L.	4:02:05 (11,739)
Veale, James	3:20:27 (3,115)
Veale, Nicolas J	4:11:43 (14,024)
Veasey, Dominick J	3:38:21 (6,023)
Veats, William J	4:04:38 (12,336)
Vecchiotti, Mauro	3:47:47 (7,942)
Veckert, Werner	5:49:40 (29,940)
Veevers, Michael	5:00:48 (25,112)
Vega, Teodoro	2:21:11 (37)
Vegro, Symon	4:26:52 (17,798)
Veiga, Jaime P	3:47:05 (7,776)
Veitch, Jamie S	4:00:41 (11,422)
Vekaria, Balu	6:15:30 (30,895)
Vekic, John	4:15:10 (14,850)
Velasco, David G	3:12:51 (2,294)
Veldman, Hans	3:43:27 (6,951)
Velhas, Ismael J.	4:02:20 (11,823)
Velinor, Tony	5:11:17 (26,552)
Vellieux, Bertrand	4:11:44 (14,029)

Velody, Nicholas 4:22:07 (16,576)
Veloso, Manuel 3:33:59 (5,268)
Venables, Alan 4:25:26 (17,408)
Venafro, Marcello 2:34:22 (112)
Venafro, Roberto 2:39:04 (186)
Veni, Simon R 5:10:15 (26,407)
Venning, Jonathan C 3:32:11 (4,949)
Venters, John V 4:21:07 (16,296)
Ventimiglia, Antonio 4:08:52 (13,338)
Venus, Mark T 5:41:37 (29,459)
Venuti, Luca 3:39:06 (6,148)
Verberkt, Bart 3:06:30 (1,653)
Vercauteren, Filip 3:46:33 (7,648)
Verchain, Michel 3:51:17 (8,828)
Vercoe, Rik 3:49:21 (8,338)
Vere, Derek 5:22:02 (27,776)
Vergerson, Timothy J 6:47:56 (31,473)
Verhage, Wim 3:50:50 (8,717)
Verhulst, Georges 3:34:19 (5,313)
Verita, Mario 4:09:34 (13,516)
Verity, Lee 4:10:44 (13,806)
Vermoter, Roger A 4:04:43 (12,355)
Vernedal, Patrick 4:19:31 (15,913)
Vernon, Darren 3:45:53 (7,503)
Vernon, Mike 4:53:27 (23,694)
Vernon, Paul A 3:15:33 (2,600)
Vernon, Richard D 3:55:59 (10,081)
Vernon, Vicenzo 4:36:40 (20,172)
Vero, Alexander J 3:35:14 (5,467)
Verpalen, Hans 4:49:34 (22,990)
Verpoest, Frederik M 3:58:27 (10,834)
Vesely, Michael 3:38:34 (6,063)
Vester, Tommy 3:26:39 (3,942)
Vialls, Terry 5:08:08 (26,132)
Vian, Andrew S 3:09:30 (1,945)
Vicente, Carlos 3:41:20 (6,528)
Vickers, Bernard 2:55:23 (778)
Vickers, Graham M 4:02:27 (11,850)
Vickers, Simon 4:52:05 (23,461)
Vickery, James R 4:53:34 (23,715)
Vickery, Nicholas T 3:59:18 (11,087)
Victor, Darnell 4:31:55 (19,088)
Victor, Doug 4:49:20 (22,947)
Vidal, Paulo 4:09:41 (13,549)
Vidal, Richard M 4:09:21 (13,462)
Vieten, Holger R 3:41:38 (6,574)
Vig, Neil 3:51:09 (8,781)
Viggars, Scott A 5:44:57 (29,691)
Vijay, Amarjit 4:41:19 (21,194)
Vilana-Riera, David 2:53:54 (691)
Vile, Martin J 3:02:01 (1,301)
Villet, Monet 4:06:22 (12,752)
Villette, Jean Miche 3:02:10 (1,313)
Vince, Ian F 5:54:58 (30,195)
Vincent, Daniel 3:23:07 (3,453)
Vincent, Edward M 3:36:23 (5,678)
Vincent, Gregory K 4:30:05 (18,650)
Vincent, Robin 3:27:56 (4,220)
Vincent, Roger J 4:38:15 (20,533)
Vincent, Stephen J 4:47:35 (22,589)
Vincent, Wayne A 3:01:19 (1,265)
Vine, Ray H 5:10:21 (26,421)
Vine, Terry 4:17:36 (15,452)
Viney, Peter 5:36:17 (29,046)
Vingerhoets, Jan 3:49:41 (8,419)
Vinnai, Balazs Janos 4:09:40 (13,546)
Vinten, Stephen R 3:02:04 (1,307)
Vio, Carlo 3:03:50 (1,436)
Vitali, Mauro 3:03:17 (1,387)
Vitucci, Michele 3:20:47 (3,173)
Vizard, Ian 4:45:29 (22,136)
Vlasblom, Alexander 3:20:45 (3,168)
Vlootman, Marius 3:14:50 (2,542)
Vodoz, Yvan 4:42:05 (21,366)
Vogel, Herb 4:08:39 (13,272)
Vogt, Jim 3:57:07 (10,418)
Vohra, Sachdev K 4:23:46 (17,008)
Voice, Andrew 3:56:01 (10,090)
Voldsatov, Andrei 5:35:03 (28,962)
Vollentine, Brian 3:29:10 (4,443)
Voller, Kevin D 4:14:14 (14,615)
Vollmar, Eduard 4:54:59 (23,991)
Vollmer, Karsten 3:48:34 (8,139)
Volpato, Sebastiano 3:48:03 (8,008)
Volpi, Alberto 3:34:25 (5,327)
Von Bonsdorff, Claus M 3:43:33 (6,968)
Von Delius, Nico 4:20:48 (16,230)
Von Delwig, Mikael 5:12:55 (26,751)
Von Hurter, Max 4:07:14 (12,952)
Vonlanthen, Gilbert 3:07:05 (1,711)
Vorres, Dimitri 2:57:27 (914)
Vos, Berend J 4:39:00 (20,729)
Vos, Graham P 4:52:17 (23,499)
Vos, Samuel 4:28:16 (18,162)
Vosper, Andy J 4:17:40 (15,473)
Voss, Dave R 4:27:43 (18,019)
Voss, Lothar 4:55:48 (24,151)
Vouillamoz, Jean M 2:56:06 (820)
Vout, Tony R 3:13:29 (2,369)
Vowles, Gareth 4:51:51 (23,408)
Vowles, Lee 6:04:49 (30,589)
Vromman, Steven 3:58:06 (10,710)
Vuadens, Jerome 3:48:37 (8,157)
Vuidart, Marc 2:45:33 (344)
Vye, Donan A 3:38:11 (5,992)
Waby, Paul 2:49:52 (493)
Waddell, James 4:50:10 (23,103)
Waddington, Andrew 5:03:48 (25,556)
Waddup, Peter 3:55:25 (9,910)
Waddup, Phillip A 4:57:45 (24,545)
Wade, Andrew M 4:30:47 (18,812)
Wade, Antony A 4:01:42 (11,650)
Wade, Bruce 4:46:14 (22,306)
Wade, Charles 3:46:39 (7,672)
Wade, Christopher M 3:53:36 (9,401)
Wade, Guy S 4:18:24 (15,632)
Wade, Ian 4:09:20 (13,460)
Wade, Jeff 4:53:45 (23,756)
Wade, Patrick 4:17:26 (15,406)
Wade, Peter 4:17:44 (15,489)
Wade, Peter J 3:39:26 (6,207)
Wade, Russell C 4:46:24 (22,340)
Wade, William M 4:06:29 (12,775)
Wadey, Robert M 4:31:37 (19,005)
Wadham, James J 5:05:24 (25,739)
Wadher, Yogesh 4:49:31 (22,981)
Wadley, Mark R 3:13:24 (2,357)
Wadsworth, Adrian M 2:57:07 (889)
Wadsworth, Alan S 4:08:44 (13,301)
Waffner, Jurgen 5:12:45 (26,720)
Waffner, Volker 4:29:28 (18,481)
Wagener, Dieter 5:01:32 (25,227)
Wagenheim, Mark 3:33:35 (5,200)
Wager, Christopher R 6:16:01 (30,908)
Waggett, Philip R 4:18:44 (15,717)
Waghorn, Arthur M 4:09:42 (13,560)
Wagner, Guy 3:26:02 (3,852)
Wagner, Martima 4:45:49 (22,213)
Wagner, Richard P 4:52:46 (23,580)
Wagstaff, Neil 3:47:38 (7,914)
Wahlmueller, Gerhard 3:45:40 (7,446)
Waibel, Peter 4:36:22 (20,100)
Wain, Gary A 3:56:52 (10,354)
Wainewright, David M 7:06:06 (31,677)
Wainwright, Gareth A 3:01:10 (1,250)
Wainwright, Michael 4:42:34 (21,465)
Wainwright, Simon D 3:31:32 (4,856)
Waite, Colin R 4:37:45 (20,391)
Waite, Marcus 4:26:52 (17,798)
Waite, Mark 3:35:16 (5,474)
Waite, Michael A 4:04:04 (12,200)
Waite, Paul F 5:28:32 (28,442)
Wakefield, Christopher P 3:21:46 (3,285)
Wakefield, Mark A 4:21:02 (16,290)
Wakefield, Paul J 4:20:13 (16,069)
Wakeford, Ben G 4:20:23 (16,126)
Wakeford, Stephen 3:22:26 (3,365)
Wakeling, Hayden C 5:28:55 (28,475)
Wakerley, Nick 4:39:38 (20,847)
Wakley, Eric S 4:18:43 (15,712)
Wakonig, Peter 3:23:39 (3,523)
Walbank, Andrew D 5:18:49 (27,453)
Walbank, Mark J 3:18:09 (2,867)
Walburn, Stephen R 4:43:55 (21,778)
Walby, Oliver J 3:33:02 (5,106)
Walden, Darren A 4:14:37 (14,713)
Walden, James A 5:27:20 (28,344)
Walden, Mark 3:37:46 (5,911)
Walder, Kieran J 4:39:45 (20,868)
Waldie, Brian 3:23:33 (3,504)
Waldman, Stuart 4:38:33 (20,606)
Waldron, David J 3:15:33 (2,600)
Walduck, Jason A 3:56:58 (10,382)
Wales, David I 4:15:16 (14,876)
Walford, James N 3:22:15 (3,335)
Walford, Lawrence 4:26:05 (17,600)
Walford, Peter N 5:03:26 (25,507)
Walisko, Robert J 5:23:10 (27,890)
Walker, Adam 5:27:08 (28,315)
Walker, Alan R 3:32:44 (5,049)
Walker, Alan W 6:19:42 (31,008)
Walker, Andrew K 4:09:57 (13,625)
Walker, Angus C 3:31:59 (4,922)
Walker, Bruce 3:40:12 (6,339)
Walker, Carl J 4:07:58 (13,110)
Walker, Christopher J 3:59:57 (11,280)
Walker, Christopher S 3:58:06 (10,710)
Walker, Darren J 4:34:02 (19,599)
Walker, Dave 3:51:10 (8,789)
Walker, David 4:38:07 (20,499)
Walker, David F 4:30:10 (18,672)
Walker, David G 3:33:51 (5,244)
Walker, Derek A 2:49:08 (465)
Walker, Gareth G 4:47:01 (22,453)
Walker, Gary 4:07:55 (13,094)
Walker, Gary A 3:00:39 (1,203)
Walker, Geof 4:09:18 (13,453)
Walker, Gordon J 4:10:30 (13,756)
Walker, Joseph A 3:15:14 (2,580)
Walker, Kevin R 3:35:14 (5,467)
Walker, Lee S 4:27:29 (17,951)
Walker, Marc 3:35:06 (5,445)
Walker, Mark 2:51:51 (586)
Walker, Martin J 3:16:27 (2,695)
Walker, Martyn J 4:54:19 (23,863)
Walker, Michael 4:24:47 (17,246)
Walker, Michael I 3:05:53 (1,597)
Walker, Michael J 3:59:17 (11,083)
Walker, Michael T 4:02:25 (11,842)
Walker, Mike 2:58:15 (990)
Walker, Neil 4:18:26 (15,647)
Walker, Neil A 4:26:58 (17,830)
Walker, Oliver 4:38:33 (20,606)
Walker, Owen D 3:35:23 (5,499)
Walker, Peter J 3:56:24 (10,213)
Walker, Phil 2:38:06 (174)
Walker, Robert 3:51:15 (8,819)
Walker, Robert J 3:08:44 (1,868)
Walker, Robert J 4:27:34 (17,982)
Walker, Robert S 4:22:01 (16,544)
Walker, Russell P 4:11:32 (13,978)
Walker, Simon 4:14:40 (14,721)
Walker, Simon K 4:32:21 (19,199)
Walker, Stephen 3:22:19 (3,345)
Walker, Stephen 5:36:57 (29,104)
Walker, Stephen A 4:13:52 (14,536)
Walker, Steven J 5:07:01 (25,972)
Walker, Steven W 2:59:10 (1,088)
Walker, Stuart D 2:55:30 (785)
Walker, Tony J 4:23:14 (16,879)
Walker-Buckton, Tristan 5:05:57 (25,837)
Walkey, Grant S 3:54:00 (9,505)
Walklett, Philip D 4:22:45 (16,760)
Wall, Michael J 3:47:52 (7,963)
Wall, Terry 2:30:19 (82)
Wallace, Andrew 3:55:23 (9,901)
Wallace, Anthony S 3:46:19 (7,605)
Wallace, Darren A 3:55:31 (9,935)
Wallace, David E 4:49:51 (23,052)
Wallace, Doug 3:54:24 (9,612)
Wallace, Gary J 3:52:43 (9,176)
Wallace, Greg S 4:15:05 (14,821)
Wallace, Jim 2:55:17 (771)
Wallace, John F 5:14:01 (26,904)
Wallace, John R 3:38:21 (6,023)
Wallace, John W 5:53:48 (30,144)
Wallace, Melvin 3:41:58 (6,639)
Wallace, Paul 4:26:44 (17,755)
Wallace, Peter W 3:50:05 (8,521)

LONDON MARATHON

Wallace, Sam	4:31:19 (18,924)
Wallace, Spencer	3:43:15 (6,907)
Wallace, Steve	4:51:18 (23,316)
Wallace, Steven I	3:51:52 (8,981)
Wallace, Stuart	3:58:09 (10,729)
Wallace, Tony S	4:54:23 (23,875)
Wallace, Westlee J	4:37:13 (20,301)
Walland, John	5:03:14 (25,480)
Waller, Edward A	3:54:41 (9,691)
Waller, Gary	4:34:30 (19,712)
Waller, James	3:54:03 (9,518)
Waller, Justin	4:01:47 (11,667)
Waller, Patrick J	3:55:59 (10,081)
Waller, Tom	3:33:36 (5,205)
Walliker, Alexander C	3:35:59 (5,610)
Wallington, Darren J	4:37:51 (20,416)
Wallington, James I	3:07:28 (1,749)
Wallis, Andrew M	3:18:31 (2,898)
Wallis, Gary	5:03:26 (25,507)
Wallis, Gordon W	5:00:35 (25,073)
Wallis, Ian M	3:59:51 (11,253)
Wallis, John	2:57:21 (902)
Wallis, Neil	4:42:43 (21,499)
Wallis, Patrick B	3:55:12 (9,848)
Wallis, Peter J	3:42:36 (6,763)
Wallis, Philip J	3:41:11 (6,509)
Wallis, Scott D	4:25:14 (17,366)
Wallman, James A	4:27:58 (18,091)
Wallsgrove, Ian C	4:06:40 (12,816)
Wallwork, Daniel	4:06:44 (12,823)
Wallwork, David M	4:59:56 (24,981)
Walmsley, David	4:24:09 (17,105)
Walmsley, Graham	5:10:50 (26,487)
Walmsley, Michael	4:29:46 (18,573)
Walmsley, Paul G	4:41:15 (21,169)
Walmsley, Shaun	4:27:41 (18,013)
Walsh, Andrew J	4:21:55 (16,505)
Walsh, Brendan J	3:46:19 (7,605)
Walsh, Carl P	3:29:13 (4,455)
Walsh, Chris	4:43:42 (21,723)
Walsh, Colin J	3:54:40 (9,686)
Walsh, Daniel M	4:11:36 (13,999)
Walsh, David	3:50:26 (8,614)
Walsh, David A	2:41:34 (234)
Walsh, Fred W	5:02:15 (25,326)
Walsh, Garry	3:42:16 (6,696)
Walsh, George L	4:51:20 (23,323)
Walsh, Ian L	3:41:34 (6,553)
Walsh, Jonathan W	4:35:11 (19,861)
Walsh, Michael I	3:11:17 (2,123)
Walsh, Patrick J	5:09:40 (26,331)
Walsh, Peter J	3:22:16 (3,338)
Walsh, Steve R	3:28:38 (4,340)
Walsh, Timothy P	3:57:04 (10,409)
Walsh, Tony	5:00:46 (25,108)
Walsham, James	2:59:01 (1,073)
Walshaw, John B	5:10:04 (26,385)
Walshe, Tony	3:36:58 (5,765)
Walter, Klaus	4:41:27 (21,230)
Walter, Michael D	3:28:51 (4,387)
Walters, Adrian	3:50:05 (8,521)
Walters, Alan	2:56:07 (823)
Walters, Edward S	3:58:46 (10,939)
Walters, Humphrey J	4:36:55 (20,233)
Walters, Karl	4:19:52 (15,990)
Walters, Matthew M	4:58:28 (24,711)
Walters, Paul	3:55:57 (10,067)
Walters, Philip J	4:52:10 (23,476)
Walthall, Barry	5:56:12 (30,255)
Walthall, Jonathan M	4:57:05 (24,417)
Walthan, Robert	5:08:40 (26,199)
Waltho, Jonathan G	4:45:59 (22,245)
Waltoln, Stuart	4:58:15 (24,653)
Walton, Christopher R	4:41:17 (21,181)
Walton, Colin S	4:25:45 (17,496)
Walton, David J	4:09:53 (13,615)
Walton, David S	3:53:33 (9,391)
Walton, Ewan T	3:22:23 (3,358)
Walton, Frank	5:50:56 (30,010)
Walton, Gary P	4:18:26 (15,647)
Walton, Gary S	4:29:16 (18,418)
Walton, James M	4:30:37 (18,784)
Walton, Jim P	4:53:55 (23,780)

Walton, Mark S	5:35:23 (28,991)
Walton, Michael	3:25:25 (3,753)
Walton, Peter M	4:39:33 (20,833)
Walton, Philip L	4:48:44 (22,827)
Walton, Tim A	5:17:42 (27,329)
Walton, Toby	3:54:43 (9,696)
Wan, Peter S	4:34:20 (19,676)
Wann, Robert	6:08:56 (30,964)
Warburton, James P	4:08:57 (13,364)
Warburton, Lee D	5:01:56 (25,293)
Warburton, Paul	5:02:55 (25,439)
Warburton, Peter	3:05:16 (1,553)
Ward, Adam J	4:26:03 (17,585)
Ward, Alan	3:47:15 (7,817)
Ward, Alexander	3:47:41 (7,925)
Ward, Andrew	5:22:14 (27,798)
Ward, Andrew D	2:59:41 (1,133)
Ward, Anthony	4:21:29 (16,385)
Ward, Ashley K	5:22:08 (27,785)
Ward, Benjamin D	4:01:34 (11,613)
Ward, Christopher E	3:59:08 (11,040)
Ward, Christopher J	4:53:46 (23,761)
Ward, Colin	3:22:45 (3,410)
Ward, Colin	3:53:04 (9,271)
Ward, Colin	5:16:54 (27,246)
Ward, Daniel	3:22:03 (3,308)
Ward, David	5:31:15 (28,682)
Ward, David J	3:30:16 (4,647)
Ward, Gary	4:43:11 (21,602)
Ward, Gerard D	5:03:58 (25,575)
Ward, Ian J	3:06:09 (1,625)
Ward, James R	3:08:55 (1,891)
Ward, Jason J	6:02:23 (30,501)
Ward, John	4:22:49 (16,777)
Ward, John A	2:55:02 (757)
Ward, John J	4:38:48 (20,668)
Ward, John R	6:09:58 (30,726)
Ward, Joseph	4:05:25 (12,515)
Ward, Kevin B	4:25:07 (17,337)
Ward, Lawrence R	4:50:26 (23,167)
Ward, Mark	3:25:48 (3,815)
Ward, Martin S	4:15:02 (14,812)
Ward, Mathew B	4:51:50 (23,406)
Ward, Matt	5:28:31 (28,439)
Ward, Michael	6:55:36 (31,570)
Ward, Mick	3:24:13 (3,592)
Ward, Nicholas J	4:43:16 (21,627)
Ward, Paul A	4:16:51 (15,268)
Ward, Paul B	4:05:31 (12,547)
Ward, Paul G	4:46:37 (22,376)
Ward, Paul G	5:35:04 (28,963)
Ward, Paul J	4:22:10 (16,596)
Ward, Peter J	4:50:12 (23,109)
Ward, Peter M	3:26:04 (3,856)
Ward, Peter M	4:29:09 (18,393)
Ward, Richard C	4:33:29 (19,467)
Ward, Seth	3:52:53 (9,218)
Ward, Simon	5:43:00 (29,562)
Ward, Simon J	4:01:32 (11,605)
Ward, Thomas J	4:27:30 (17,957)
Ward, William	3:39:14 (6,168)
Wardale, Terry J	3:17:05 (2,758)
Wardell, Chris	3:39:34 (6,228)
Wardell, Geoffrey M	5:33:20 (28,837)
Warden, Martin J	5:47:04 (29,814)
Warden, Paul R	4:16:37 (15,211)
Ward-Horner, Dominic M	4:07:30 (13,010)
Wardlan, Steven J	4:33:10 (19,396)
Wardlaw, Robert G	3:12:51 (2,294)
Wardle, Kim	4:02:55 (11,942)
Wardle, Mark R	4:35:08 (19,851)
Wardle, Timothy J	4:09:46 (13,570)
Wardman, Steve	4:32:19 (19,192)
Wardrope, David	3:50:48 (8,706)
Ward-Smith, Wayland J	4:11:46 (14,036)

Ware, Colin S	4:21:37 (16,425)
Ware, Graham H	4:46:27 (22,349)
Ware, Nicholas A	3:54:38 (9,677)
Ware, Nigel J	4:15:40 (14,968)
Ware, Steven T	5:56:00 (30,246)
Wareham, Michael P	2:58:42 (1,044)
Wareing, Brian	3:05:28 (1,568)
Wareing, Brian J	5:09:40 (26,331)
Wareing, James N	5:00:36 (25,076)
Wareing, Nathan J	4:38:58 (20,715)
Wareing, Simon	4:20:08 (16,053)
Waring, Carl P	3:50:15 (8,563)
Waring, Marc P	3:46:31 (7,639)
Warmer, Tony D	3:19:47 (3,048)
Warmington, Paul A	4:21:13 (16,315)
Warn, Francis T	5:34:47 (28,943)
Warn, Timothy J	3:17:06 (2,759)
Warne, Andrew A	4:24:42 (17,231)
Warne, Richard P	4:43:50 (21,753)
Warner, Barton J	4:21:01 (16,284)
Warner, Benjamin J	4:00:01 (11,300)
Warner, Edmond W	3:27:53 (4,206)
Warner, Gary	3:43:16 (6,911)
Warner, Jonathan S	5:15:16 (27,053)
Warner, Keith	5:10:06 (26,389)
Warner, Kim	3:19:13 (2,987)
Warner, Lance S	4:11:53 (14,057)
Warner, Michael	4:26:40 (17,746)
Warner, Michael B	3:22:38 (3,395)
Warner, Michael F	5:49:15 (29,920)
Warner, Richard A	4:29:24 (18,466)
Warner, Simon P	3:54:03 (9,518)
Warner, Timothy J	3:40:53 (6,451)
Warnes, Adam W	5:17:13 (27,275)
Warnes, Michael C	3:42:36 (6,763)
Warnock, Jim	4:32:54 (19,335)
Warnock, Michael J	4:17:56 (15,540)
Warnock, Peter I	3:51:11 (8,798)
Warr, Timothy S	4:37:57 (20,454)
Warren, Gary S	3:44:47 (7,259)
Warren, George P	4:19:48 (15,975)
Warren, Huw	3:27:18 (4,080)
Warren, Martin R	5:29:32 (28,537)
Warren, Matthew	3:13:24 (2,357)
Warren, Michael C	5:00:12 (25,023)
Warren, Michael S	4:49:59 (23,071)
Warren, Peter L	4:38:28 (20,587)
Warren, Richard	3:56:21 (10,196)
Warren, Robert Y	3:37:09 (5,804)
Warren, Stephen P	4:00:41 (11,422)
Warren, Toby S	4:36:56 (20,236)
Warrick, Michael J	3:03:26 (1,401)
Warrilow, Paul A	4:27:01 (17,846)
Warriner, Ben	4:32:39 (19,276)
Warriner, Keith	4:13:13 (14,385)
Warrington, Nigel J	4:21:46 (16,472)
Warwick, Gary A	3:59:37 (11,195)
Warwick, Lee J	4:58:15 (24,653)
Warwick, Paul I	4:22:12 (16,608)
Warwick, Rupert E	4:49:13 (22,920)
Washbrook, David T	3:54:37 (9,673)
Washington, John R	4:18:31 (15,665)
Wasley, Matt J	4:19:38 (15,934)
Waslidge, Neil B	2:55:19 (774)
Watchorn, Stephen P	3:44:46 (7,254)
Waterfall, Sam	3:49:34 (8,396)
Waterhouse, Andrew S	3:20:57 (3,195)
Waterhouse, Peter	3:26:25 (3,906)
Wateridge, Justin	4:19:06 (15,803)
Wateridge, Matthew R	3:45:16 (7,360)
Waterlow, Roy G	3:05:31 (1,573)
Waterman, Alan	5:27:19 (28,340)
Waterman, David J	3:13:52 (2,420)
Waterman, Kevin	3:58:47 (10,943)
Waterman, Ryan R	3:02:10 (1,313)
Waterman, Steven J	4:14:57 (14,795)
Waters, Andrew S	3:54:31 (9,641)
Waters, Donald J	4:33:45 (19,517)
Waters, Graham S	5:13:20 (26,809)
Waters, John I	7:00:31 (31,633)
Waters, Matthew S	5:13:32 (26,831)
Waters, Phil P	3:51:15 (8,819)
Waters, Robert L	5:03:07 (25,461)

Waters, Stephen A....3:14:33 (2,509)
Waters, William J....3:51:09 (8,781)
Waterton, Joseph A....4:31:21 (18,935)
Waterton, Richard J....5:22:18 (27,805)
Waterworth, Phillip A....4:03:34 (12,092)
Waterworth, Stephen G....5:55:07 (30,206)
Watherston, Sam R....4:07:50 (13,076)
Watine, Eric....4:25:27 (17,413)
Watkin, Andrew R....4:18:32 (15,670)
Watkin, Nigel....3:11:40 (2,154)
Watkins, Dean....3:39:10 (6,157)
Watkins, Gene A....5:28:01 (28,397)
Watkins, James L....3:13:29 (2,369)
Watkins, John F....4:54:20 (23,866)
Watkins, John K....3:52:54 (9,227)
Watkins, Mark T....5:20:14 (27,598)
Watkins, Martin A....4:37:11 (20,293)
Watkins, Michael D....4:42:28 (21,444)
Watkins, Philip....4:03:52 (12,163)
Watkins, Philip D....4:40:47 (21,081)
Watkins, Simon....4:22:31 (16,703)
Watkins, Simon D....4:21:45 (16,465)
Watkinson, James....4:24:16 (17,136)
Watkinson, Peter G....3:13:42 (2,399)
Watkinson, Robert J....3:35:57 (5,602)
Watling, Carl A....4:21:09 (16,300)
Watling, Kenneth A....5:37:12 (29,124)
Watson, Alastair....4:12:38 (14,242)
Watson, Andrew J....5:11:20 (26,558)
Watson, Andrew L....3:29:34 (4,512)
Watson, Andrew P....4:18:21 (15,618)
Watson, Ashley J....3:52:27 (9,126)
Watson, Bryan R....3:14:50 (2,542)
Watson, Chris J....3:26:42 (3,957)
Watson, David....3:16:32 (2,703)
Watson, David....3:22:31 (3,380)
Watson, David F....2:31:02 (86)
Watson, David J....3:07:04 (1,710)
Watson, David M....5:49:02 (29,910)
Watson, Derek M....4:17:01 (15,307)
Watson, Derek S....3:53:36 (9,401)
Watson, Graham A....4:19:30 (15,911)
Watson, Iain R....4:49:29 (22,978)
Watson, Ian G....4:31:52 (19,066)
Watson, Ian P....4:35:16 (19,880)
Watson, Ian W....3:44:36 (7,213)
Watson, James....4:05:17 (12,482)
Watson, Keith....4:27:10 (17,885)
Watson, Kent....3:23:06 (3,450)
Watson, Lester W....4:12:08 (14,122)
Watson, Luke....4:28:32 (18,240)
Watson, Mark....4:33:27 (19,457)
Watson, Matthew J....4:34:42 (19,759)
Watson, Michael W....4:20:07 (16,049)
Watson, Murray M....4:45:58 (22,244)
Watson, Paul....3:31:38 (4,865)
Watson, Paul M....3:07:26 (1,742)
Watson, Peter D....3:15:46 (2,631)
Watson, Philip D....5:19:37 (27,513)
Watson, Philip J....2:50:17 (517)
Watson, Roy A....4:49:47 (23,036)
Watson, Steve R....4:51:54 (23,423)
Watson, Stuart....2:56:57 (878)
Watson, Timothy M....5:28:02 (28,399)
Watson-Steward, Duncan M....4:10:31 (13,759)
Watt, Andrew....5:16:18 (27,173)
Watt, Brian J....4:13:44 (14,500)
Watt, Errol....3:59:53 (11,261)
Watt, Gareth J....3:40:06 (6,322)
Watt, Graeme D....4:38:00 (20,466)
Watt, Michael....4:10:55 (13,850)
Watt, Simon D....3:09:25 (1,938)
Watt, Simon J....4:24:44 (17,238)
Wattam, Andrew D....3:39:11 (6,161)
Watters, John....4:46:13 (22,304)
Watton, Michael....3:45:55 (7,510)
Watts, Allen E....6:33:06 (31,267)
Watts, Andrew J....3:10:16 (2,024)
Watts, Charles....4:24:09 (17,105)
Watts, Chris....4:28:34 (18,248)
Watts, Damon G....3:31:29 (4,847)
Watts, David M....3:22:07 (3,317)
Watts, John....5:24:35 (28,030)
Watts, Joseph W....5:52:52 (30,119)
Watts, Karl....3:33:26 (5,181)
Watts, Lee....4:16:03 (15,059)
Watts, Matthew J....5:07:14 (25,999)
Watts, Matthew L....4:10:17 (13,697)
Watts, Nathan S....3:28:07 (4,246)
Watts, Neil....4:57:41 (24,535)
Watts, Paul A....4:52:59 (23,614)
Watts, Paul J....4:03:34 (12,092)
Watts, Paul R....4:03:10 (11,997)
Watts, Peter....3:36:11 (5,639)
Watts, Robert....3:02:20 (1,329)
Watts, Roy J....5:02:15 (25,326)
Watts, Simon J....3:52:29 (9,130)
Watts, Stephen H....4:34:21 (19,678)
Watts, Steve L....4:45:29 (22,136)
Waudby, Trevor W....4:44:37 (21,943)
Waugh, David I....4:16:04 (15,065)
Waugh, Gary....4:40:07 (20,943)
Waugh, Steven C....4:05:39 (12,583)
Waughman, Gary E....4:05:33 (12,555)
Way, Lawrence C....4:09:03 (13,390)
Way, Pete....3:57:26 (10,522)
Wayatt, Robert G....4:15:50 (15,010)
Wayland, John W....4:16:49 (15,259)
Wayne, David H....4:07:55 (13,094)
Wazir, Aly....5:14:22 (26,943)
Weatherley, Paul....4:53:36 (23,725)
Weatherstone, Barry....5:07:36 (26,057)
Weaver, John....6:23:27 (31,095)
Weaver, John M....3:27:42 (4,168)
Weaver, Scot S....3:42:28 (6,735)
Weavers, Keith C....4:17:19 (15,374)
Weavers, Terry P....3:03:26 (1,401)
Weaving, Matthew P....5:01:24 (25,207)
Weaving, Peter G....3:14:25 (2,490)
Weavis, Andrew G....5:02:45 (25,411)
Webb, Adam....3:52:24 (9,111)
Webb, Adrian J....3:50:20 (8,589)
Webb, Alan D....4:46:21 (22,326)
Webb, Alex....2:57:35 (919)
Webb, Colin R....4:04:22 (12,275)
Webb, Daniel J....4:21:59 (16,530)
Webb, David J....3:21:09 (3,214)
Webb, David M....4:34:49 (19,781)
Webb, David P....3:25:45 (3,806)
Webb, Harvey J....3:20:16 (3,095)
Webb, Jason A....4:23:03 (16,825)
Webb, Joe P....3:28:21 (4,291)
Webb, Jonathan P....3:54:24 (9,612)
Webb, Mark B....5:02:16 (25,331)
Webb, Nicholas A....3:46:04 (7,539)
Webb, Nigel....4:01:46 (11,664)
Webb, Richard....4:56:48 (24,361)
Webb, Richard H....4:30:59 (18,855)
Webb, Robert G....4:22:33 (16,713)
Webb, Robert J....3:54:00 (9,505)
Webb, Simon P....3:18:12 (2,873)
Webb, Stuart G....3:31:27 (4,841)
Webb, Trevor....4:38:34 (20,611)
Webbe, Richard A....4:42:49 (21,524)
Webber, Antony M....3:31:51 (4,895)
Webber, Dominic G....3:47:26 (7,864)
Webber, Ian C....4:00:49 (11,449)
Webber, James....3:56:15 (10,166)
Webber, Kevin J....3:50:16 (8,567)
Webborn, Martin J....3:14:20 (2,484)
Weber, Elmar....4:44:24 (21,889)
Weber, Rolf....4:45:18 (22,096)
Webley, Ian N....4:41:14 (21,163)
Webster, Adam....4:08:45 (13,307)
Webster, Andrew....3:57:18 (10,481)
Webster, Andrew....4:47:25 (22,546)
Webster, Andrew E....4:09:19 (13,455)
Webster, Christopher R....6:31:09 (31,226)
Webster, Craig S....3:52:18 (9,085)
Webster, Daryl J....4:41:28 (21,236)
Webster, Dave J....4:39:37 (20,843)
Webster, David T....5:01:34 (25,235)
Webster, Edward J....4:45:24 (22,117)
Webster, Gilbert....5:03:09 (25,466)
Webster, Jim R....3:25:11 (3,718)
Webster, Jon....3:34:44 (5,377)
Webster, Lee A....4:29:44 (18,564)
Webster, Mark....5:05:33 (25,771)
Webster, Martyn....4:26:51 (17,785)
Webster, Neil G....4:46:20 (22,323)
Webster, Paul A....4:24:01 (17,064)
Webster, Richard....3:02:40 (1,350)
Webster, Roland M....3:54:35 (9,660)
Webster, Stuart....3:59:44 (11,231)
Webster, Terry M....3:52:08 (9,044)
Weckmann, Timo....3:31:47 (4,886)
Weckwerth, Martin....2:59:57 (1,153)
Wedge, Iain D....2:51:36 (573)
Wedge, Marcus J....4:07:31 (13,012)
Wedlake, Paul J....6:26:03 (31,145)
Wedlock, Keith R....4:41:41 (21,276)
Weedon, Max R....5:28:37 (28,453)
Weeks, David J....3:56:55 (10,371)
Weeks, Joseph P....5:30:00 (28,584)
Weeks, Steven....3:59:36 (11,188)
Weetman, Darren....6:27:31 (31,166)
Wegerhoff, Sean....3:26:59 (4,018)
Wegg, Terry J....3:16:44 (2,723)
Wehner, Oliver....4:14:56 (14,792)
Wehr, Gerhard....3:28:54 (4,400)
Wehrle, Stephen R....4:08:08 (13,139)
Weight, Patrick F....3:59:23 (11,111)
Weightman, Mark J....5:31:57 (28,731)
Weilguni, Guenter R....3:59:26 (11,121)
Weinberg, Jonathan....4:34:39 (19,750)
Weinger, Neil A....5:04:07 (25,588)
Weippert, Hans....3:58:15 (10,773)
Weir, Andrew P....2:27:14 (61)
Weir, Antony M....4:46:40 (22,386)
Weir, Barry J....3:13:55 (2,427)
Weir, Carl A....5:00:09 (25,016)
Weir, Colin....5:58:33 (30,352)
Weir, Paul....4:25:29 (17,424)
Weir, Robert J....3:45:42 (7,461)
Weir, Thomas....4:10:33 (13,770)
Weirig, Nico....3:09:01 (1,900)
Weiss, Dominik J....4:34:03 (19,606)
Weitzel, Stefan H....3:43:17 (6,914)
Welbourn, Richard....3:14:57 (2,554)
Welby, Alexander J....4:58:41 (24,754)
Welch, Christopher P....4:58:08 (24,624)
Welch, David M....6:06:04 (30,621)
Welch, Dick....5:37:48 (29,167)
Welch, Graham J....4:29:09 (18,393)
Welch, Ian R....3:48:12 (8,047)
Welch, Michael J....3:23:30 (3,500)
Welch, Paul M....4:16:39 (15,220)
Welham, Grant P....3:28:25 (4,305)
Wellburn, Richard S....4:53:52 (23,773)
Weller, Martin C....3:46:04 (7,539)
Weller, Paul L....3:39:16 (6,172)
Weller, Tom C....3:32:00 (4,927)
Wellings, Keith B....4:40:38 (21,050)
Wellington, Allen....5:58:56 (30,362)
Wellman, Timothy S....3:16:46 (2,725)
Wells, Alan M....4:12:58 (14,321)
Wells, Andrew J....4:51:53 (23,418)
Wells, Brian R....4:55:26 (24,090)
Wells, Colin....5:00:22 (25,047)
Wells, Craig L....4:14:21 (14,636)
Wells, Daniel P....3:06:12 (1,627)
Wells, David J....4:32:24 (19,215)
Wells, Keith W....3:28:32 (4,326)
Wells, Lloyd J....4:15:36 (14,955)
Wells, Matthew J....4:19:12 (15,834)
Wells, Nathan P....4:45:41 (22,186)
Wells, Nigel....4:56:00 (24,206)
Wells, Paul....3:06:50 (1,690)
Wells, Rob C....3:44:54 (7,286)
Wells, Simon M....4:17:24 (15,399)
Wells, Stephen C....4:20:40 (16,200)
Wells-Cole, Mark C....3:50:55 (8,739)
Welsh, Berny M....4:05:14 (12,468)
Welsh, Brian....5:31:19 (28,685)
Welsh, Darryn P....3:39:23 (6,197)
Welsh, Mike....5:11:35 (26,583)
Welsh, Paul....5:31:19 (28,685)
Welsh, Shaun L....4:03:05 (11,975)
Welton, Peter M....3:59:27 (11,132)

Wemhoener, Frank 3:56:20 (10,190)
Wemmel, Jan 4:59:36 (24,922)
Wenmouth, Richard J 4:46:04 (22,264)
Wentworth, Alfred 4:12:26 (14,179)
Werder, Gary J 7:21:08 (31,793)
Wermter, Peter 5:33:54 (28,886)
Wescomb, Christopher P 3:12:47 (2,284)
Wescott, Miles J 4:36:20 (20,096)
Wesson, David M 4:30:02 (18,639)
Wesson, Lee G 5:02:22 (25,353)
West, Andrew W 4:32:46 (19,306)
West, Clive 4:08:14 (13,157)
West, Colin 2:53:00 (643)
West, Colin J 5:33:48 (28,870)
West, Gareth S 4:12:13 (14,135)
West, Graeme P 4:22:28 (16,690)
West, Ian A 4:04:26 (12,294)
West, Ian P 4:37:54 (20,437)
West, Jeremy C 5:46:15 (29,766)
West, Kevin M 2:48:10 (429)
West, Martyn 4:25:21 (17,392)
West, Matthew P 3:27:30 (4,128)
West, Matthew S 5:15:55 (27,119)
West, Neil A 4:59:09 (24,822)
West, Neil P 5:19:01 (27,466)
West, Robert J 3:42:45 (6,801)
West, Stephen 4:17:46 (15,499)
West, Stephen A 3:44:48 (7,261)
Westaway, Julian C 3:51:10 (8,789)
Westbrook, Jon L 4:03:47 (12,144)
Westbrook, Richard 3:50:37 (8,662)
Westbury, Patrick J 5:15:52 (27,117)
Westbury, Tony J 3:37:25 (5,864)
Westcott, Christopher 4:46:58 (22,439)
Westcott, Scott A 2:13:30 (14)
Westcott, Tarne 4:11:58 (14,083)
Westerlund, Marcel S 4:02:51 (11,935)
Westerman, Mick A 3:42:27 (6,730)
Western, Phillip 3:19:09 (2,972)
Westgate, Mark A 5:07:12 (25,992)
Westgate, Nicholas R 3:53:04 (9,271)
Westgate, Richard C 3:47:24 (7,854)
Westhead, Sam J 2:40:46 (224)
Westholm, Niclas 5:54:41 (30,184)
Westlake, Andrew 4:34:16 (19,657)
Westlake, Graham E 3:48:25 (8,100)
Westlake, Mark L 4:32:30 (19,237)
Westlake, Peter 3:07:15 (1,722)
Westlake, Steven T 3:17:54 (2,841)
Westlake, Trevor A 4:29:57 (18,623)
Westman, Sven-Eric 5:00:12 (25,023)
Westmore, Jeremy 3:34:47 (5,385)
Weston, Gerald E 4:26:37 (17,730)
Weston, Guy W 3:40:06 (6,322)
Weston, Jeff K 3:50:27 (8,623)
Weston, Martin N 4:34:44 (19,765)
Weston, Mikail J 4:24:09 (17,105)
Weston, Robert P 5:13:37 (26,847)
Westpfel, Ashley J 4:25:52 (17,529)
Westwater, Neil 3:58:50 (10,954)
West-Watson, David 4:10:20 (13,713)
Westwood, Jamie 3:19:59 (3,064)
Wetherilt, Timothy N 3:55:44 (10,001)
Wetton, James A 4:05:27 (12,523)
Weyell, Christopher S 3:33:18 (5,160)
Weyell, Peter W 4:36:18 (20,088)
Whale, David J 3:20:04 (3,076)
Whall, Lee 5:07:56 (26,103)
Whalley, Adrian 3:14:06 (2,449)
Whalley, Darren P 6:35:42 (31,302)
Wharram, Mark 3:57:05 (10,411)
Wharton, Andrew J 3:36:15 (5,650)
Wharton, Anthony J 3:59:54 (11,268)
Whatford, Howard M 4:20:43 (16,217)
Whatley, David K 4:53:28 (23,696)
Whatmore, Gary A 3:58:33 (10,874)
Whatton, Ian 3:32:12 (4,952)
Wheat, Alan E 3:24:53 (3,679)
Wheatley, David G 4:20:51 (16,244)
Wheatley, Mark A 3:57:55 (10,651)
Wheatley, Timothy J 4:26:52 (17,798)
Wheaton, Mark 5:16:53 (27,245)
Wheeler, Alan A 3:37:54 (5,938)
Wheeler, André 5:16:29 (27,186)
Wheeler, Andrew 7:08:37 (31,698)
Wheeler, Andrew W 4:06:36 (12,807)
Wheeler, Brendon J 4:33:56 (19,573)
Wheeler, Dean 4:19:54 (15,997)
Wheeler, John G 4:01:44 (11,656)
Wheeler, Martyn S 4:52:24 (23,517)
Wheeler, Matthew B 4:05:52 (12,629)
Wheeler, Michael A 3:49:04 (8,268)
Wheeler, Michalis R 6:14:40 (30,870)
Wheeler, Paul E 4:25:26 (17,408)
Wheeler, Paul M 3:44:41 (7,236)
Wheeler, Ralph H 4:20:09 (16,055)
Wheeler, Robert 4:55:51 (24,162)
Wheeler, Simon 4:59:28 (24,896)
Wheeler, Sydney J 3:54:58 (9,772)
Whelan, Alan P 4:44:45 (21,967)
Whelan, Nick 4:50:09 (23,101)
Whellams, Dominic A 5:02:36 (25,388)
Wheller, Robert J 4:01:40 (11,640)
Wheller, Stephen 5:26:20 (28,228)
Whibley, Ben P 4:42:48 (21,520)
Whiffin, Eric M 4:48:39 (22,803)
Whiffin, James L 3:26:22 (3,900)
Whillier, Roy T 4:16:29 (15,171)
Whitaker, Charles A 3:15:09 (2,575)
Whitaker, Edward 3:59:27 (11,132)
Whitaker, Keith H 3:36:36 (5,709)
Whitby, John 4:26:49 (17,777)
Whitcomb, John P 4:49:35 (22,992)
White, Andrew R 3:48:13 (8,055)
White, Andrew R 3:54:54 (9,753)
White, Andrew R 4:54:13 (23,840)
White, Anthoney S 4:23:26 (16,929)
White, Anthony P 4:58:23 (24,687)
White, Ben T 5:00:45 (25,105)
White, Brian 4:53:38 (23,733)
White, Brian P 5:32:40 (28,788)
White, Colin 3:34:28 (5,335)
White, Damian P 4:29:37 (18,527)
White, Daniel 4:14:16 (14,620)
White, Daniel E 4:18:21 (15,618)
White, David 5:29:29 (28,530)
White, David C 4:27:03 (17,856)
White, David G 4:59:57 (24,983)
White, Dean 3:41:34 (6,553)
White, Dean A 3:53:44 (9,420)
White, Derek F 3:19:42 (3,042)
White, Douglas A 5:05:28 (25,751)
White, Douglas M 5:46:23 (29,779)
White, Gary G 4:00:15 (11,349)
White, Greg 4:05:21 (12,498)
White, Grenville 4:05:04 (12,447)
White, Ian 5:51:58 (30,060)
White, Ian R 2:47:48 (414)
White, James M 3:06:16 (1,636)
White, James M 3:50:52 (8,723)
White, Jeremy M 4:02:32 (11,864)
White, John 4:29:44 (18,564)
White, John M 5:11:16 (26,551)
White, Josh 3:58:59 (10,999)
White, Keith R 4:21:48 (16,480)
White, Kevin M 5:27:04 (28,306)
White, Liam A 4:46:50 (22,411)
White, Mark 3:03:25 (1,399)
White, Martin 4:19:41 (15,947)
White, Martin D 4:01:06 (11,528)
White, Martin J 4:16:45 (15,237)
White, Michael 3:48:55 (8,233)
White, Mike P 2:58:10 (984)
White, Neil A 4:38:09 (20,508)
White, Nick A 5:00:49 (25,116)
White, Paul J 4:37:55 (20,444)
White, Paul J 5:05:20 (25,731)
White, Peter 4:43:46 (21,741)
White, Peter M 5:06:05 (25,856)
White, Philip D 5:09:13 (26,269)
White, Robert P 4:34:57 (19,810)
White, Ronald J 3:45:53 (7,503)
White, Roy W 4:05:10 (12,459)
White, Scott D 5:51:59 (30,063)
White, Shane 6:12:34 (30,797)
White, Simon D 5:34:08 (28,899)
White, Simon J 4:23:33 (16,953)
White, Stephen J 4:43:09 (21,591)
White, Stephen R 3:43:04 (6,864)
White, Steve M 3:26:35 (3,930)
White, Terence 4:46:17 (22,314)
White, Thomas C 3:47:15 (7,817)
White, Tony 3:56:15 (10,166)
White, Trevor F 4:11:10 (13,904)
White, William P 5:24:39 (28,041)
White Doyle, James W 4:44:22 (21,876)
Whiteaker, James H 5:20:29 (27,631)
White-Doyle, Jonathan 4:30:29 (18,754)
Whitefield, Christopher P 5:01:16 (25,178)
Whitefield, Rupert H 4:21:31 (16,393)
Whitehead, Andrew S 3:58:21 (10,804)
Whitehead, David 3:52:49 (9,204)
Whitehead, David 4:08:53 (13,342)
Whitehead, David A 4:36:26 (20,116)
Whitehead, David E 4:26:59 (17,836)
Whitehead, Ian 5:02:19 (25,346)
Whitehead, Ian D 3:26:13 (3,874)
Whitehead, John D 3:48:05 (8,020)
Whitehead, Michael R 3:16:53 (2,739)
Whitehead, Nigel J 4:45:11 (22,078)
Whitehead, Reno A 4:25:44 (17,488)
Whitehead, Yuri S 5:48:03 (29,869)
Whitehorn, Robert J 3:52:05 (9,033)
Whitehouse, Andrew J 4:49:07 (22,898)
Whitehouse, Dean B 3:38:54 (6,114)
Whitehouse, Ian R 3:05:56 (1,603)
Whitehouse, Neil R 3:47:38 (7,914)
Whitehouse, Nicholas 5:25:42 (28,159)
Whitelam, Richard 3:42:29 (6,742)
Whitelaw, Martin L 4:23:10 (16,858)
Whitelegg, Richard 2:45:22 (336)
Whiteley, Andrew 3:45:00 (7,309)
Whiteley, Nigel P 4:55:54 (24,183)
Whiteley, Stephen P 4:22:16 (16,628)
Whitelock, James 3:56:06 (10,111)
Whitelock, Mark 3:17:13 (2,775)
Whitelock, Neil P 3:37:36 (5,890)
Whitelock, Stephen J 3:27:09 (4,053)
Whiteman, Richard J 4:01:59 (11,712)
Whiteman, Simon P 3:51:07 (8,769)
Whiter, George A 5:04:06 (25,586)
Whiteside, Mark N 4:27:13 (17,897)
Whitesmith, Michael B 4:06:19 (12,740)
Whitfield, Richard C 4:45:20 (22,104)
Whitford, Frank K 3:14:01 (2,437)
Whiting, Andrew C 4:57:09 (24,427)
Whiting, Marshall D 6:57:23 (31,588)
Whiting, Michael D 4:14:21 (14,636)
Whiting, Richard 4:54:07 (23,821)
Whiting, Simeon L 4:38:58 (20,715)
Whitley, David C 4:12:04 (14,108)
Whitley, Ian D 3:59:45 (11,233)
Whitley, John S 5:30:22 (28,613)
Whitley, Paul R 4:05:35 (12,568)
Whitlock, Tony R 3:29:45 (4,544)
Whitlock-James, Nigel 4:48:42 (22,820)
Whitman, Anthony C 3:30:27 (4,682)
Whitmarsh, Tobias G 3:32:12 (4,952)
Whitmarsh-Knight, Simon J 4:31:19 (18,924)
Whitmore, Alex J 4:48:47 (22,832)
Whitmore, David K 4:53:40 (23,740)
Whitmore, Ivon E 2:57:38 (926)
Whitmore, Paul T 4:54:18 (23,855)
Whittaker, Ben 4:05:30 (12,539)
Whittaker, John 3:51:09 (8,781)
Whittaker, Mark 4:02:26 (11,845)
Whittaker, Nicolas P 3:59:42 (11,222)
Whittaker, Paul 4:28:23 (18,187)
Whittaker, Paul K 5:27:55 (28,389)
Whittaker, Stuart M 3:55:31 (9,935)
Whittell, Brian 4:17:00 (15,304)
Whittingham, Conrad A 5:03:09 (25,466)
Whittingham, David A 4:56:36 (24,329)
Whittingham, Iain M 3:49:45 (8,437)
Whittingham, Jacob 4:05:38 (12,580)
Whittington, Darren 4:29:39 (18,542)
Whittington, David H 5:40:53 (29,404)
Whittington, Robert 6:01:45 (30,475)
Whittington, Russell 3:26:32 (3,924)

Whittle, Roger A....4:23:02 (16,820)
Whittle, Stuart I....4:49:44 (23,025)
Whitworth, David....3:31:48 (4,889)
Whitworth, David C....3:41:12 (6,513)
Whitworth, Mark....4:08:47 (13,317)
Whitworth, William J....3:59:16 (11,077)
Whoriskey, Niall F....3:26:55 (4,003)
Whybrow, Nikki....5:03:10 (25,472)
Whybrow, Peter B....5:06:01 (25,845)
Whyman, Len M....5:07:21 (26,024)
Whyman, Mark W....4:57:16 (24,456)
Whyman, Matt A....4:52:54 (23,603)
Whyte, Angus M....4:29:35 (18,517)
Whyte, Gregory....3:11:52 (2,177)
Whyte, Lawrence A....4:38:42 (20,643)
Wibberley, Brian....3:33:43 (5,218)
Wibberley, Michael S....4:32:30 (19,237)
Wichman, Carl C....3:31:41 (4,871)
Wichtermann, Jurg....3:54:58 (9,772)
Wickenden, Lee C....4:50:23 (23,153)
Wickenden, Richard J....4:31:09 (18,892)
Wickenden, Stephen....3:59:04 (11,019)
Wickerson, David S....5:21:53 (27,761)
Wickett, Guy R....4:38:07 (20,499)
Wickham, David W....4:22:47 (16,769)
Wickham, Stephen P....3:25:32 (3,775)
Wicks, James....3:37:01 (5,772)
Wicks, Pete L....3:21:27 (3,250)
Wicks, Timothy L....4:37:10 (20,284)
Widdick, Dorian....3:27:22 (4,095)
Widdowson, James A....3:59:05 (11,024)
Widdrington, Ian H....3:02:43 (1,354)
Widener, Floyd M....3:38:29 (6,043)
Widmann, Christoph....2:49:45 (488)
Wieczorek, Stefan....4:55:58 (24,203)
Wiekhusen, Michael....4:33:35 (19,482)
Wield, Christopher....4:49:26 (22,961)
Wiendick, Markus....3:42:00 (6,646)
Wiesbauer, Clive F....4:39:37 (20,843)
Wiesner, Werner....3:46:06 (7,547)
Wigforss, David....4:32:03 (19,121)
Wiggall, Adam R....3:11:23 (2,132)
Wiggins, Colin L....4:49:06 (22,895)
Wigginton, Richard....3:48:06 (8,023)
Wigglesworth, Ben....4:37:58 (20,459)
Wigley, Gavin J....3:45:25 (7,390)
Wigley, Timothy J....2:51:08 (548)
Wignall, Andrew P....4:49:25 (22,960)
Wignall, Derek D....3:44:05 (7,092)
Wignell, Marcus J....3:46:56 (7,730)
Wijeyekoon, Sanjaya....5:33:13 (28,822)
Wijnia, Martin J....3:50:23 (8,602)
Wiklander, Tomas N....4:50:48 (23,235)
Wilbraham, Glen P....4:26:55 (17,816)
Wilbur, Duncan....4:29:59 (18,626)
Wilby, Guy D....3:48:00 (7,995)
Wilcock, Andy....4:45:04 (22,053)
Wilcock, Martin....2:54:44 (728)
Wilcock, Martin....2:56:53 (874)
Wilcock, Paul....3:50:07 (8,534)
Wilcock, Paul R....3:30:01 (4,591)
Wilcox, Alan F....4:00:55 (11,483)
Wilcox, Jeremy....3:58:44 (10,925)
Wilcox, Mark K....5:42:57 (29,552)
Wilcox, Michael....3:13:58 (2,429)
Wild, Andrew J....6:44:22 (31,424)
Wild, Keith....2:59:10 (1,088)
Wild, Kirk A....5:09:10 (26,264)
Wild, Reginald....3:20:43 (3,161)
Wild, Trevor....3:15:56 (2,641)
Wildbore, David C....3:41:35 (6,561)
Wilde, Anthony....4:47:26 (22,552)
Wilde, Ben P....6:01:25 (30,462)
Wilde, Osamu....4:03:42 (12,125)
Wilde, Stephen P....5:01:55 (25,289)
Wilden, Terry D....5:16:30 (27,187)
Wilder, Paul....4:43:15 (21,620)
Wildey, Lee D....3:54:09 (9,542)
Wildhaber, Christoph....3:28:40 (4,346)
Wilding, Keith....4:39:24 (20,809)
Wildman, Christopher M....4:48:48 (22,838)
Wildman, Martin J....4:26:15 (17,648)
Wiles, Andrew J....4:17:33 (15,439)
Wiles, Jonathan H....4:53:38 (23,733)
Wiles, Richard....3:33:31 (5,192)
Wilhelm, Andreas....3:45:45 (7,471)
Wilhelm, Martin....3:17:43 (2,821)
Wiliams, James D....5:45:33 (29,730)
Wiliams, Jason M....6:01:14 (30,457)
Wilikinson, Mark J....4:40:00 (20,919)
Wilkerson, David....3:52:33 (9,139)
Wilkes, Jeffrey W....4:20:29 (16,157)
Wilkes, Patrick G....3:57:43 (10,597)
Wilkes, Roger J....4:06:19 (12,740)
Wilkey, Michael A....4:09:23 (13,470)
Wilkie, Stuart H....5:23:19 (27,898)
Wilkie, Thomas A....5:22:51 (27,862)
Wilkins, Bruce G....4:07:01 (12,896)
Wilkins, Dan P....5:19:36 (27,508)
Wilkins, Michael....4:29:36 (18,523)
Wilkins, Olly J....4:17:40 (15,473)
Wilkinson, Andrew W....3:33:34 (5,197)
Wilkinson, Ben L....3:28:58 (4,409)
Wilkinson, Dirk....4:00:22 (11,372)
Wilkinson, Edward F....3:54:17 (9,583)
Wilkinson, Garth....4:05:26 (12,521)
Wilkinson, Graham....2:42:34 (254)
Wilkinson, Ian D....4:30:41 (18,797)
Wilkinson, Ian J....3:41:49 (6,608)
Wilkinson, Ian R....4:53:42 (23,749)
Wilkinson, James M....5:07:55 (26,102)
Wilkinson, John....3:52:09 (9,047)
Wilkinson, Jonathan R....4:14:50 (14,770)
Wilkinson, Mark....4:15:25 (14,904)
Wilkinson, Mark....4:19:26 (15,894)
Wilkinson, Mark A....3:50:04 (8,517)
Wilkinson, Martin J....3:13:44 (2,403)
Wilkinson, Matthew J....4:44:10 (21,831)
Wilkinson, Matthew P....4:04:18 (12,263)
Wilkinson, Michael....5:19:05 (27,474)
Wilkinson, Michael B....4:23:21 (16,903)
Wilkinson, Oliver R....4:04:17 (12,262)
Wilkinson, Rob A....4:16:25 (15,152)
Wilkinson, Stephen R....5:33:43 (28,865)
Wilkinson, Tim R....4:11:56 (14,072)
Wilks, Thomas M....5:20:28 (27,628)
Willard, Adam C....3:44:40 (7,230)
Willatgamuwa, Don S....5:05:46 (25,795)
Willerton, Andy....3:52:09 (9,047)
Willett, Michael F....3:18:27 (2,890)
Willett, Raymond A....3:50:04 (8,517)
Willetts, Jimnah D....4:06:07 (12,693)
Willetts, John M....4:47:31 (22,570)
Willetts, Martin J....3:13:01 (2,311)
Willgrass, Elvin....6:36:40 (31,317)
Williams, Alan P....4:28:49 (18,304)
Williams, Alan R....4:08:16 (13,165)
Williams, Alex....4:26:14 (17,644)
Williams, Alun....3:22:44 (3,409)
Williams, Alun....5:12:06 (26,645)
Williams, Andrew....4:10:59 (13,866)
Williams, Andrew....5:34:39 (28,935)
Williams, Andrew H....4:45:34 (22,154)
Williams, Andrew L....4:20:19 (16,106)
Williams, Andrew P....3:12:28 (2,251)
Williams, Ayo....4:14:11 (14,607)
Williams, Ben....3:53:22 (9,356)
Williams, Benjamin....5:00:25 (25,054)
Williams, Benjamin....5:04:49 (25,666)
Williams, Byron J....4:03:04 (11,970)
Williams, Charles R....3:47:51 (7,958)
Williams, Chris....5:03:32 (25,527)
Williams, Chris J....3:59:49 (11,242)
Williams, Chris W....3:29:43 (4,543)
Williams, Christopher....3:25:13 (3,722)
Williams, Christopher M....4:08:25 (13,206)
Williams, Christopher R....4:05:59 (12,657)
Williams, Colin....3:41:34 (6,553)
Williams, Daniel J....4:09:14 (13,432)
Williams, Daniel J....4:54:45 (23,951)
Williams, David....4:40:13 (20,965)
Williams, David....4:48:45 (22,828)
Williams, David G....5:20:03 (27,573)
Williams, David H....3:56:26 (10,228)
Williams, David J....2:31:48 (94)
Williams, David J....5:15:49 (27,109)
Williams, David R....4:16:03 (15,059)
Williams, David S....5:05:37 (25,778)
Williams, David W....3:44:43 (7,244)
Williams, Dennis S....3:20:12 (3,091)
Williams, Edward I....4:07:33 (13,024)
Williams, Eric L....5:16:49 (27,232)
Williams, Gareth....2:59:27 (1,117)
Williams, Gareth....5:32:08 (28,743)
Williams, Gareth C....3:44:19 (7,142)
Williams, Gareth E....3:47:51 (7,958)
Williams, Gareth I....4:22:06 (16,571)
Williams, Gareth J....2:26:15 (59)
Williams, Gary....5:03:29 (25,517)
Williams, Graham A....4:41:44 (21,290)
Williams, Graham P....4:46:09 (22,279)
Williams, Gregory F....4:54:18 (23,855)
Williams, Gwyn T....3:48:07 (8,027)
Williams, Ian....4:17:06 (15,327)
Williams, James A....3:57:08 (10,429)
Williams, James C....4:53:48 (23,766)
Williams, Jamie....5:06:52 (25,955)
Williams, Jason M....2:51:19 (557)
Williams, John....3:31:43 (4,876)
Williams, John....4:34:02 (19,599)
Williams, John D....4:22:48 (16,771)
Williams, John E....4:23:19 (16,898)
Williams, John P....3:47:23 (7,848)
Williams, Jon A....4:02:11 (11,774)
Williams, Jonathan D....3:12:34 (2,260)
Williams, Jonathan D....3:53:21 (9,351)
Williams, Jonathan L....4:07:49 (13,074)
Williams, Keith....4:29:27 (18,470)
Williams, Keith....5:08:54 (26,223)
Williams, Ken....3:53:58 (9,493)
Williams, Kevin....4:53:23 (23,684)
Williams, Kevin P....4:14:35 (14,703)
Williams, Kevin S....3:50:33 (8,639)
Williams, Les....3:26:57 (4,008)
Williams, Leslie....4:04:18 (12,263)
Williams, Lindsay R....3:47:04 (7,770)
Williams, Luke B....4:03:30 (12,078)
Williams, Mark....3:33:53 (5,255)
Williams, Mark A....4:25:11 (17,356)
Williams, Mark E....4:11:01 (13,875)
Williams, Mark H....4:53:58 (23,790)
Williams, Mark J....4:14:10 (14,601)
Williams, Mark K....3:09:51 (1,987)
Williams, Mark L....3:33:49 (5,237)
Williams, Martin....4:19:41 (15,947)
Williams, Martin J....2:58:39 (1,035)
Williams, Martin P....4:57:01 (24,406)
Williams, Matthew J....5:26:42 (28,271)
Williams, Michael....3:52:21 (9,099)
Williams, Michael....4:07:35 (13,031)
Williams, Michael E....2:55:57 (809)
Williams, Nefyn....3:52:48 (9,195)
Williams, Neville K....4:14:09 (14,599)
Williams, Nicholas J....3:52:00 (9,012)
Williams, Nicholas J....4:31:39 (19,011)
Williams, Nick....5:12:24 (26,680)
Williams, Nick J....3:51:04 (8,758)
Williams, Nigel D....4:23:22 (16,905)
Williams, Nigel S....4:26:22 (17,669)
Williams, Owen J....3:16:20 (2,677)
Williams, Paul....3:58:07 (10,715)
Williams, Paul....4:15:52 (15,021)
Williams, Paul....4:18:18 (15,607)
Williams, Paul....4:19:11 (15,825)
Williams, Paul D....3:20:59 (3,200)
Williams, Paul D....3:32:37 (5,033)
Williams, Paul D....3:35:04 (5,436)
Williams, Paul D....4:07:32 (13,017)
Williams, Paul M....3:42:38 (6,773)
Williams, Paul R....4:19:23 (15,878)
Williams, Peter....4:23:58 (17,053)
Williams, Peter D....3:24:48 (3,660)
Williams, Peter M....5:59:55 (30,407)
Williams, Rhys....4:34:52 (19,796)
Williams, Richard....4:02:39 (11,886)
Williams, Richard C....3:41:25 (6,535)
Williams, Richard J....4:14:48 (14,758)
Williams, Richard W....3:35:25 (5,507)
Williams, Roger....4:19:31 (15,913)

Williams, Ronald 3:24:22 (3,611)
Williams, Ross J 4:56:48 (24,361)
Williams, Royston D 4:37:54 (20,437)
Williams, Ryan D 4:40:24 (21,008)
Williams, Samuel G 3:27:47 (4,185)
Williams, Scott G 3:51:25 (8,862)
Williams, Scott R 4:17:53 (15,532)
Williams, Sebastian 3:22:34 (3,388)
Williams, Shaun I 5:05:27 (25,747)
Williams, Simon 4:34:02 (19,599)
Williams, Simon C 3:50:10 (8,541)
Williams, Simon K 4:41:30 (21,245)
Williams, Simon P 3:41:22 (6,530)
Williams, Stephen A 4:05:19 (12,489)
Williams, Stephen D 3:59:29 (11,151)
Williams, Stephen P 4:16:04 (15,065)
Williams, Steve J 4:53:29 (23,699)
Williams, Thomas A 3:00:21 (1,181)
Williams, Thomas A 5:06:22 (25,896)
Williams, Timothy 4:45:33 (22,148)
Williams, Tom 4:33:38 (19,496)
Williams, Wynford S 3:45:13 (7,354)
Williamson, Alex M 4:26:12 (17,631)
Williamson, Andrew J 3:36:34 (5,706)
Williamson, Anthony M 4:33:07 (19,384)
Williamson, Chris 3:20:30 (3,131)
Williamson, Chris M 4:04:25 (12,288)
Williamson, Colin J 3:29:56 (4,577)
Williamson, Craig 3:10:46 (2,079)
Williamson, Darren A 3:50:14 (8,555)
Williamson, David F 3:56:11 (10,134)
Williamson, Gillian A 4:18:57 (15,771)
Williamson, Gordon D 6:02:08 (30,491)
Williamson, Guy B 4:23:40 (16,978)
Williamson, Malcolm R 5:07:40 (26,071)
Williamson, Mark 3:49:52 (8,466)
Williamson, Martin 3:49:21 (8,338)
Williamson, Michael 7:43:55 (31,904)
Williamson, Neil G 4:27:37 (17,996)
Williamson, Nick J 4:07:01 (12,896)
Williamson, Paul 3:46:32 (7,644)
Williamson, Peter K 4:34:38 (19,743)
Williamson, Stephen W 3:01:20 (1,268)
Willis, Andy J 4:31:46 (19,044)
Willis, David 5:34:19 (28,912)
Willis, Gary S 3:37:03 (5,783)
Willis, James A 5:26:22 (28,237)
Willis, James M 4:35:14 (19,873)
Willis, Matthew 4:14:10 (14,601)
Willis, Matthew J 3:04:11 (1,464)
Willis, Michael A 3:47:37 (7,910)
Willis, Peter J 3:31:06 (4,788)
Willis, Stephen 4:05:23 (12,503)
Willis, Stephen M 3:27:56 (4,220)
Willis, Tim J 4:32:01 (19,116)
Willmitt, William J 2:57:36 (922)
Willmott, Greg G 4:28:16 (18,162)
Willmott, Ian 4:01:09 (11,538)
Willmott, Martin G 3:44:26 (7,168)
Willmott, William T 5:13:56 (26,889)
Willoughby, Gary K 3:35:41 (5,552)
Willoughby, Rae 4:46:56 (22,430)
Willoughby, Shane 4:19:10 (15,822)
Willoughby, Trevor 4:46:55 (22,425)
Willows, Peter B 4:22:53 (16,791)
Wills, Bernard W 4:22:35 (16,719)
Wills, Mark R 3:46:36 (7,662)
Willsher, Adam P 4:38:24 (20,570)
Willson, Anthony J 4:31:14 (18,903)
Willson, Kevin 4:26:13 (17,639)
Willson, Robert J 3:45:47 (7,480)
Wilmot, Andrew H 3:11:49 (2,170)
Wilmot, Patrick A 3:49:56 (8,482)
Wilmott, Peter 3:17:32 (2,803)
Wilmshurst, Andrew P 2:50:10 (512)
Wilner, Joseph 5:25:56 (28,189)
Wilshaw, John T 5:38:05 (29,187)
Wilsmore, Paul H 3:08:14 (1,822)
Wilson, Andrew B 3:57:45 (10,605)
Wilson, Andrew P 3:56:52 (10,354)
Wilson, Anthony 3:48:22 (8,093)
Wilson, Barry 2:49:35 (481)
Wilson, Ben A 3:36:27 (5,688)
Wilson, Benjamin J 4:04:27 (12,300)
Wilson, Caley 3:37:18 (5,839)
Wilson, Charles M 4:02:58 (11,948)
Wilson, Charlie E 4:18:33 (15,677)
Wilson, Christopher L 3:32:51 (5,072)
Wilson, Clive C 5:34:24 (28,917)
Wilson, Craig A 3:47:31 (7,883)
Wilson, Daniel J 6:30:19 (31,210)
Wilson, David 4:23:03 (16,825)
Wilson, David H 3:32:19 (4,973)
Wilson, David J 3:54:31 (9,641)
Wilson, David P 4:36:04 (20,045)
Wilson, Donough 6:04:25 (30,580)
Wilson, Duncan M 4:59:49 (24,961)
Wilson, Dylan J 3:24:03 (3,571)
Wilson, Eoin J 5:46:35 (29,795)
Wilson, Eric J 2:48:12 (432)
Wilson, Errol 4:36:46 (20,194)
Wilson, Geoffrey K 4:48:08 (22,703)
Wilson, Gordon A 3:11:11 (2,111)
Wilson, Gordon H 5:54:19 (30,162)
Wilson, Gordon R 3:57:43 (10,597)
Wilson, Greg 4:09:22 (13,466)
Wilson, Gregory J 5:21:36 (27,739)
Wilson, Ian R 5:44:37 (29,665)
Wilson, James 3:49:08 (8,291)
Wilson, Jim B 3:54:52 (9,741)
Wilson, John A 5:06:18 (25,888)
Wilson, John C 3:44:58 (7,301)
Wilson, John C 4:49:02 (22,883)
Wilson, John P 4:00:01 (11,300)
Wilson, Jon D 3:55:49 (10,022)
Wilson, Kenneth 3:27:31 (4,131)
Wilson, Mark A 3:35:53 (5,587)
Wilson, Mark H 3:53:08 (9,291)
Wilson, Mark R 3:36:44 (5,730)
Wilson, Mathew 4:25:28 (17,418)
Wilson, Matthew R 4:32:04 (19,124)
Wilson, Michael 3:55:25 (9,910)
Wilson, Michael G 3:35:20 (5,493)
Wilson, Neil A 4:58:22 (24,679)
Wilson, Nicholas M 3:30:24 (4,674)
Wilson, Nick 3:13:14 (2,332)
Wilson, Oliver 5:38:07 (29,190)
Wilson, Oliver E 4:11:53 (14,057)
Wilson, Oliver J 3:38:48 (6,098)
Wilson, Peter J 3:40:37 (6,418)
Wilson, Phillip 4:36:31 (20,139)
Wilson, Ramon D 3:55:58 (10,074)
Wilson, Rhydderch 4:21:20 (16,345)
Wilson, Richard 4:55:07 (24,019)
Wilson, Richard A 6:01:13 (30,456)
Wilson, Robert 2:44:41 (313)
Wilson, Robert D 5:33:39 (28,862)
Wilson, Robin 4:51:02 (23,277)
Wilson, Robin H 4:34:09 (19,635)
Wilson, Simon R 5:20:39 (27,653)
Wilson, Steven I 4:08:48 (13,325)
Wilson, Stuart J 4:53:55 (23,780)
Wilson, Terry R 4:12:15 (14,140)
Wilson, Tony 3:23:55 (3,555)
Wilson, Trevor R 3:23:52 (3,552)
Wilson-Ward, Martin L 4:53:35 (23,718)
Wilton, David 3:52:21 (9,099)
Wilton, Graham G 3:01:09 (1,249)
Wilton, John F 4:21:34 (16,405)
Wilton, Julian C 4:08:30 (13,231)
Wilton, Philip J 4:09:41 (13,549)
Wilton, Steven W 5:12:46 (26,723)
Wiltshire, Ian 4:55:06 (24,013)
Wiltshire, Jonathan I 4:29:10 (18,398)
Wiltshire, Richard 5:44:25 (29,651)
Wimble, Christopher E 3:15:05 (2,565)
Wimble, Nathan E 4:31:14 (18,903)
Winch, Bryan D 4:24:24 (17,164)
Winchester, Terry 3:58:44 (10,925)
Winckler, Joachim 4:26:30 (17,703)
Wind, Kevan I 3:19:01 (2,954)
Windebank, Ian 4:54:45 (23,951)
Windebank, Mark R 3:27:07 (4,047)
Winder, Asa D 2:55:02 (757)
Winder, John 4:29:07 (18,381)
Winder, Robert W 6:23:06 (31,081)
Windham-Wright, Thor 5:25:47 (28,173)
Windle, Lee T 4:26:44 (17,755)
Windover, Jonathan M 5:13:45 (26,859)
Windsor, Nicholas P 4:47:39 (22,606)
Winfield, David J 3:39:46 (6,268)
Winfield, Jason 3:58:20 (10,799)
Winfield, Nicholas 3:48:38 (8,164)
Winfield, Stephen J 3:27:19 (4,084)
Wing, John S 3:55:21 (9,894)
Wing, Kevin F 5:54:21 (30,164)
Wingate, Thomas M 5:25:05 (28,097)
Wingfield, Matt C 4:24:58 (17,300)
Wingfield, Michael N 3:43:48 (7,013)
Wingrove, Gary P 4:42:42 (21,493)
Winning, Glen 2:56:50 (872)
Winsbury, Mark W 3:58:03 (10,689)
Winslade, James C 4:49:51 (23,052)
Winslow, Michael P 3:41:13 (6,516)
Winston, Nick 3:32:00 (4,927)
Winston, Roger F 3:42:11 (6,678)
Winter, Alan J 6:34:45 (31,286)
Winter, Darren 5:26:37 (28,262)
Winter, John 3:59:30 (11,157)
Winter, Leigh J 5:21:36 (27,739)
Winter, Martin 4:00:47 (11,441)
Winter, Michael 4:05:48 (12,616)
Winterbone, Edward J 4:21:57 (16,516)
Winterbottom, Lawrence J 3:27:55 (4,216)
Winterflood, Mark 3:18:39 (2,916)
Winters, John T 4:12:52 (14,292)
Winters, Stephen 4:15:10 (14,850)
Wintle, David A 2:59:32 (1,125)
Wintle, George 4:16:04 (15,065)
Winton, Scott 2:17:40 (22)
Wintrip, Clive 2:56:44 (865)
Wiper, Gerard V 4:25:48 (17,515)
Wisbey, Gavin L 4:46:37 (22,376)
Wisdom, Martin 3:34:01 (5,274)
Wisdom, Richard J 5:08:35 (26,190)
Wise, Andrew S 4:35:54 (20,003)
Wise, Chris A 3:27:08 (4,050)
Wise, David E 6:24:32 (31,121)
Wise, John 3:06:05 (1,618)
Wise, Peter G 5:03:43 (25,547)
Wise, Richard J 4:48:22 (22,752)
Wise, Stephen 3:41:38 (6,574)
Wiseman, Christian D 4:18:17 (15,603)
Wiseman, John H 4:44:48 (21,979)
Wiseman, Sqot 3:14:18 (2,477)
Wiseman, Timothy R 4:18:49 (15,744)
Wiskin, Anthony E 3:36:46 (5,738)
Wistow, Richard A 4:05:17 (12,482)
Witcombe, Paul C 3:06:11 (1,626)
Withecombe, Mark W 4:30:58 (18,852)
Witherick, Roger A 3:16:42 (2,721)
Withers, Bill 3:55:42 (9,989)
Withers, David G 4:13:25 (14,437)
Withers, Dominic P 4:32:49 (19,314)
Withers, Julian J 4:15:17 (14,879)
Withers, Paul J 3:42:51 (6,821)
Withers, Scott D 3:28:22 (4,293)
Withers, Stephen R 3:39:22 (6,195)
Withey, Fraser J 3:39:27 (6,209)
Withy, Jake 4:39:37 (20,843)
Witt, Robert 5:10:10 (26,396)
Wittek, Rudiger 3:58:56 (10,987)
Witten, Mark L 3:39:49 (6,275)
Wittenberg, Olivier 4:03:31 (12,082)
Wittering, Mark A 2:52:26 (612)
Witts, Jamie 4:04:29 (12,312)
Witts, Jonathan R 4:14:10 (14,601)
Wodu, Uche C 6:32:19 (31,251)
Wohlmann, Harald 3:23:44 (3,535)
Wohrer, Erich 4:26:14 (17,644)
Wojo, Toshitaka 4:18:29 (15,661)
Wolf, Joachim 2:38:35 (178)
Wolfe, Shaun J 5:06:39 (25,933)
Wolfendale, Stewart 3:51:39 (8,928)
Wolff, Steven R 4:22:17 (16,631)
Wollebaek, Dag 3:52:50 (9,209)
Wollebaek, Jens 4:34:21 (19,678)
Wollerton, Terry 3:28:37 (4,338)
Wolovitz, Lionel 3:18:35 (2,907)

Wolstencroft, John A. 4:01:39 (11,633)
Wolton, Peter H 4:23:04 (16,830)
Wong, Terence 4:25:36 (17,453)
Wonnacott, Ian M 5:40:45 (29,398)
Wood, Alan D 6:41:07 (31,375)
Wood, Anthony H 3:57:24 (10,514)
Wood, Ashley 4:37:52 (20,422)
Wood, Brad 4:24:02 (17,068)
Wood, Brian D 6:19:35 (31,006)
Wood, Chris A 4:46:55 (22,425)
Wood, Christopher D 4:21:20 (16,345)
Wood, Dan 4:13:11 (14,373)
Wood, Daniel J 4:32:55 (19,342)
Wood, David 4:06:50 (12,844)
Wood, David M 4:17:56 (15,540)
Wood, David R 4:21:35 (16,409)
Wood, David T 4:20:40 (16,200)
Wood, Gareth D 3:07:50 (1,789)
Wood, Gary R 4:05:06 (12,448)
Wood, Gavin B 3:54:08 (9,536)
Wood, Graham 3:57:16 (10,466)
Wood, Graham R 3:38:30 (6,048)
Wood, Halvor H 4:04:48 (12,377)
Wood, Haydn C 4:05:14 (12,468)
Wood, Ian D 3:31:06 (4,788)
Wood, Ian G 5:14:18 (26,935)
Wood, Ian M 4:55:55 (24,186)
Wood, Ian S 5:01:30 (25,221)
Wood, Jeffrey A 4:26:34 (17,718)
Wood, Jeremy R 3:47:59 (7,991)
Wood, Joe D 4:00:55 (11,483)
Wood, John D 4:07:23 (12,982)
Wood, John P 3:56:17 (10,178)
Wood, Jonathan 4:32:35 (19,254)
Wood, Jonathan A 3:26:41 (3,951)
Wood, Julian R 4:20:31 (16,164)
Wood, Kevin G 4:06:06 (12,683)
Wood, Malcolm G 3:29:30 (4,504)
Wood, Marc E 4:10:46 (13,816)
Wood, Matthew S 4:27:31 (17,965)
Wood, Michael 3:29:46 (4,548)
Wood, Michael 4:14:31 (14,682)
Wood, Neil D 4:07:46 (13,062)
Wood, Neil G 5:13:29 (26,822)
Wood, Nicholas C 2:55:05 (760)
Wood, Nicholas D 3:58:41 (10,915)
Wood, Nick K 3:42:03 (6,661)
Wood, Paul G 4:52:29 (23,530)
Wood, Paul K 4:36:01 (20,029)
Wood, Peter A 4:52:33 (23,539)
Wood, Peter J 3:16:15 (2,666)
Wood, Philip M 3:54:51 (9,738)
Wood, Samuel C 4:17:33 (15,439)
Wood, Simon A 4:22:47 (16,769)
Wood, Stephen M 3:58:41 (10,915)
Wood, Stephen P 3:23:57 (3,559)
Wood, Steve W 3:18:11 (2,871)
Wood, Steven C 4:15:27 (14,916)
Wood, Stuart J 4:30:02 (18,639)
Wood, Terry 3:31:54 (4,901)
Wood, Thomas J 4:12:55 (14,307)
Wood, Tim F 3:32:57 (5,090)
Wood, Timothy S 3:29:12 (4,449)
Wood, Trevor C 3:36:45 (5,734)
Woodall, Brian E 4:18:46 (15,728)
Woodard, Richard D 4:04:24 (12,282)
Woodbridge, Jamie 3:44:03 (7,082)
Woodburn, Peter J 2:49:25 (474)
Woodcock, Clive A 3:59:30 (11,157)
Woodcock, Stephen 4:23:08 (16,851)
Woodcock, Timothy D 4:13:18 (14,403)
Wooden, Matthew C 3:29:41 (4,529)
Wooden, Simon W 4:16:34 (15,189)
Woodeson, James M 3:16:38 (2,714)
Woodfine, John D 4:56:11 (24,242)
Woodfine, Stephen R 4:25:02 (17,314)
Woodford, Bruce M 5:12:40 (26,708)
Woodford, Philip 5:05:47 (25,797)
Woodgate, Christopher E 6:27:14 (31,160)
Woodha,, Neil J 3:39:46 (6,268)
Woodhead, Jonathon A 3:50:53 (8,730)
Woodhead, Mark A 4:39:44 (20,867)
Woodhouse, David G 3:23:41 (3,526)
Woodhouse, Tim 5:27:42 (28,371)
Woodley, Alan 4:44:00 (21,794)
Woodley, David W 4:17:31 (15,429)
Woodley, Gregory K 4:52:02 (23,453)
Woodley, James R 4:13:06 (14,352)
Woodley, Timothy C 5:35:23 (28,991)
Woodlock, Michael 3:56:11 (10,134)
Woodman, John M 4:46:55 (22,425)
Woodman, Mark J 2:39:37 (200)
Woodman, Tom 3:33:27 (5,182)
Woodroof, Alan R 4:12:38 (14,242)
Woodroofe, Paul 3:49:22 (8,344)
Woodrow, Alex 4:56:03 (24,221)
Woodrow, Andrew C 5:04:46 (25,659)
Woodrow, Simon D 5:22:03 (27,777)
Woodrow, William J 4:56:03 (24,221)
Woodruff, Raymond 3:15:06 (2,567)
Woods, Colin 3:44:17 (7,133)
Woods, Dennis L 4:30:59 (18,855)
Woods, Garry 3:16:25 (2,690)
Woods, George H 4:03:47 (12,144)
Woods, Ian B 3:46:13 (7,585)
Woods, Martin J 4:06:10 (12,705)
Woods, Robert G 4:27:50 (18,050)
Woods, Roland S 3:42:43 (6,795)
Woods, Timothy J 3:44:32 (7,195)
Woodward, Barry M 6:14:59 (30,884)
Woodward, Chad 5:29:30 (28,532)
Woodward, Keith 3:42:53 (6,830)
Woodward, Mark 3:39:01 (6,137)
Woodward, Mark 5:25:02 (28,089)
Woodward, Mark 5:30:47 (28,645)
Woodward, Michael 4:57:55 (24,572)
Woodward, Paul G 4:30:50 (18,825)
Woodward, Paul N 3:22:18 (3,341)
Woodward, Paul T 4:06:50 (12,844)
Woodward, Robert 4:08:15 (13,159)
Woodward, Spencer B 4:44:45 (21,967)
Woodward, William P 4:50:18 (23,124)
Woodwards, Nicholas M 4:35:11 (19,861)
Woodworth, James P 4:16:58 (15,296)
Wookey, Nigel 4:25:04 (17,327)
Wool, Simon 4:15:17 (14,879)
Woolcock, Anthony 3:49:45 (8,437)
Woolcock, Mark A 6:39:09 (31,350)
Woolf, Ben D 4:07:25 (12,991)
Woolfall, Martyn P 5:15:19 (27,059)
Woolgrove, David R 5:14:26 (26,954)
Woolhouse, Michael G 3:32:27 (4,996)
Wooliscroft, Neil 5:22:17 (27,803)
Woollard, Duncan R 5:37:18 (29,136)
Woollard, Steven 3:20:34 (3,145)
Woolley, Jason A 3:56:24 (10,213)
Woolley, Martin 2:57:32 (917)
Woolley, Ricky 3:25:50 (3,820)
Woollon, Andy 3:41:58 (6,639)
Woolnough, Shaun R 5:46:19 (29,772)
Woon, Jayson M 3:58:29 (10,845)
Wootton, Gary N 3:51:22 (8,849)
Wootton, Terence E 4:17:29 (15,419)
Worgan, Lee 6:37:21 (31,330)
Worgan, Russell J 4:24:58 (17,300)
World, Paul 3:54:19 (9,591)
Wormald, Derek 3:49:13 (8,312)
Worman, Philip J 5:23:17 (27,896)
Wormull, Daniel S 5:20:13 (27,596)
Worrall, Anthony G 4:15:57 (15,041)
Worsfold, Davy T 4:25:47 (17,509)
Worsfold, Lee 4:24:58 (17,300)
Worsfold, Philip 4:30:27 (18,745)
Worsfold, Richard A 3:39:42 (6,256)
Worsfold, Robert A 4:47:53 (22,651)
Worsley, Martin S 3:36:20 (5,664)
Worsnip, James C 5:31:20 (28,688)
Worswick, Neil D 3:00:41 (1,206)
Wort, Steven S 3:19:08 (2,967)
Worth, Andrew G 5:52:34 (30,100)
Worth, Paul A 3:39:36 (6,238)
Worthing, Shane 4:24:59 (17,307)
Wortley, Andrew J 4:13:36 (14,480)
Wortley, Phil 4:45:50 (22,217)
Wortman, Lawrence D 4:44:53 (21,995)
Wotton, Sean 3:56:30 (10,250)
Wouters, Toon 4:31:42 (19,029)
Wrake, Kevin S 3:30:00 (4,590)
Wrangles, Andrew S 5:04:55 (25,681)
Wrapson, Chip 4:11:19 (13,933)
Wrapson, Nigel C 3:52:18 (9,085)
Wrather, Andy M 3:58:07 (10,715)
Wray, Gary J 5:54:24 (30,166)
Wray, Michael 5:07:17 (26,006)
Wray, Paul G 4:56:41 (24,340)
Wray, Peter D 4:24:52 (17,274)
Wray, Peter J 3:59:05 (11,024)
Wray, Robert M 3:02:18 (1,326)
Wren, David P 3:28:19 (4,285)
Wren, Geoffrey S 3:52:06 (9,036)
Wren, James A 4:45:54 (22,229)
Wrench, Robin P 3:14:39 (2,519)
Wrenn, Nick 3:36:23 (5,678)
Wrenn, Simon A 4:28:07 (18,126)
Wressell, Mark W 3:58:09 (10,729)
Wretham, Craig M 4:30:58 (18,852)
Wride, Justin R 4:10:22 (13,723)
Wright, Alexander D 4:36:56 (20,236)
Wright, Alexander E 5:00:40 (25,089)
Wright, Andrew 4:30:34 (18,773)
Wright, Andrew L 3:02:37 (1,346)
Wright, Andrew N 3:58:24 (10,819)
Wright, Andy 5:20:56 (27,676)
Wright, Anthony J 4:12:25 (14,170)
Wright, Benjamin N 3:55:35 (9,963)
Wright, Bernard A 3:45:41 (7,455)
Wright, Brian A 5:07:47 (26,091)
Wright, Christopher J 4:46:21 (22,326)
Wright, Christopher P 4:52:40 (23,564)
Wright, Daniel J 3:34:16 (5,306)
Wright, Daniel M 3:22:34 (3,388)
Wright, Darren P 4:25:06 (17,333)
Wright, David G 2:50:39 (533)
Wright, David J 3:47:38 (7,914)
Wright, David J 4:16:33 (15,186)
Wright, David J 4:50:10 (23,103)
Wright, Dennis A 5:21:26 (27,724)
Wright, Derek 3:23:07 (3,453)
Wright, Derek F 3:29:36 (4,518)
Wright, Derek M 4:17:49 (15,512)
Wright, Edward A 4:21:35 (16,409)
Wright, Edwin D 4:21:34 (16,405)
Wright, Gary J 4:15:55 (15,031)
Wright, Graeme 4:49:49 (23,046)
Wright, Graeme D 4:15:36 (14,955)
Wright, Ian 4:03:06 (11,979)
Wright, John 4:27:35 (17,989)
Wright, John E 4:22:18 (16,637)
Wright, John J 3:59:21 (11,101)
Wright, Ken 5:52:07 (30,070)
Wright, Kenneth M 4:53:11 (23,651)
Wright, Kevin C 5:34:07 (28,897)
Wright, Laurence D 3:29:26 (4,493)
Wright, Matt S 5:05:16 (25,719)
Wright, Michael P 5:00:20 (25,043)
Wright, Nick J 3:55:59 (10,081)
Wright, Nigel 4:44:52 (21,991)
Wright, Oliver G 3:14:10 (2,464)
Wright, Paul E 5:00:25 (25,054)
Wright, Paul S 4:28:28 (18,220)
Wright, Paul W 3:16:11 (2,661)
Wright, Peter T 3:18:13 (2,874)
Wright, Philip E 4:31:58 (19,104)
Wright, Philip S 4:28:31 (18,235)
Wright, Phillip T 5:31:40 (28,711)
Wright, Rob J 5:09:32 (26,308)
Wright, Robert A 5:23:34 (27,932)
Wright, Robert C 4:09:12 (13,422)
Wright, Robert L 4:05:26 (12,521)
Wright, Rollo A 4:08:42 (13,291)
Wright, Simon C 3:58:59 (10,999)
Wright, Stephen 4:16:26 (15,157)
Wright, Stephen 4:29:18 (18,431)
Wright, Stephen A 4:35:46 (19,977)
Wright, Steven P 4:16:22 (15,137)
Wright, Stuart L 3:53:50 (9,453)
Wright, Thomas D 5:27:18 (28,335)
Wright, Timothy 3:46:55 (7,726)
Wright, Tom D 3:51:09 (8,781)

Wright, William S 4:20:22 (16,120)
Wrightham, Leslie 4:53:04 (23,624)
Writer, Jeremy D 4:46:34 (22,368)
Wrobel, Peter A 3:51:32 (8,899)
Wroblewski, Steven J 3:12:40 (2,266)
Wroe, Stephen A 3:52:30 (9,134)
Wrottesley, Mike G 3:26:41 (3,951)
Wrout, Andrew P 3:28:14 (4,273)
Wrublick, Bernhard 3:08:15 (1,824)
Wuernli, Sam 3:15:07 (2,570)
Wurth, Hans 4:37:51 (20,416)
Wurzer, Markus 3:15:35 (2,608)
Wurzer, Roman 3:08:26 (1,843)
Wyatt, Andrew A 4:47:10 (22,493)
Wyatt, Chris L 3:58:54 (10,974)
Wyatt, Darren 3:38:29 (6,043)
Wyatt, Esmond J 3:49:11 (8,306)
Wyatt, James R 3:12:17 (2,227)
Wyatt, Jeremy N 4:17:02 (15,312)
Wyatt, Jonathan G 4:13:06 (14,352)
Wycocki-Jones, Simon J 4:18:18 (15,607)
Wyke, Justin A 3:37:59 (5,958)
Wykeham, Philip H 3:44:49 (7,266)
Wyldes, Mark E 3:55:43 (9,997)
Wyler, Peter 3:41:37 (6,568)
Wyles, Andrew G 4:30:57 (18,846)
Wyles, Chris 3:10:21 (2,034)
Wyles, Matthew P 4:02:45 (11,914)
Wyles, Peter 3:11:58 (2,191)
Wylie, Alistair 4:56:43 (24,346)
Wylie, Pete T 3:29:06 (4,434)
Wyllie, Alan T 3:27:53 (4,206)
Wynands, Ian M 3:58:48 (10,945)
Wynant, Paul A 4:03:57 (12,179)
Wynburne, John P 5:00:39 (25,086)
Wynn, Edward L 3:51:26 (8,868)
Wynne, Corin 4:14:35 (14,703)
Wynne, Daniel M 3:47:35 (7,903)
Wynne, Philip G 3:50:23 (8,602)
Wynne, Rob H 2:46:17 (366)
Wynne Davies, David 3:34:03 (5,278)
Wyse, Andrew R 4:54:27 (23,885)
Xaba, Josias 3:13:22 (2,353)
Xerri, Richard 3:27:30 (4,128)
Yadave, Rush L 4:11:21 (13,939)
Yam, Kenny 3:49:22 (8,344)
Yamaura, Tomoomi 4:01:50 (11,675)
Yan, Henry 4:28:28 (18,220)
Yapp, Ian N 4:12:57 (14,318)
Yardley, Christopher M 4:08:57 (13,364)
Yarr, Roddy 3:37:15 (5,822)
Yarrow, Andrew J 3:34:02 (5,276)
Yarrow, David C 5:00:13 (25,027)
Yarrow, Thomas J 3:56:11 (10,134)
Yarwood, Clive D 4:17:27 (15,412)
Yates, Adrian E 3:04:17 (1,472)
Yates, Alexander 4:33:27 (19,457)
Yates, Anthony J 4:11:22 (13,945)
Yates, Anthony J 5:01:45 (25,268)
Yates, Chris J 3:51:51 (8,977)
Yates, Clifford R 5:16:33 (27,198)
Yates, Eric W 4:50:48 (23,235)
Yates, Kevin R 5:27:44 (28,377)
Yates, Malcolm 5:15:56 (27,122)
Yates, Neil A 5:54:07 (30,155)
Yates, Philip A 4:38:50 (20,677)
Yates, Rich N 3:29:02 (4,421)
Yates, Robert 3:34:18 (5,311)
Yates, Robert J 5:37:16 (29,133)
Yates, Stephen T 5:10:45 (26,476)
Yazaki, Etsuro 3:11:57 (2,188)
Yazdabadi, Alan A 3:58:02 (10,684)
Yeabsley, David C 4:56:35 (24,326)
Yeadon, Andrew 5:48:36 (29,886)
Yeaman, Neil 5:41:07 (29,419)
Yeates, Matthew D 4:23:02 (16,820)
Yeo, Christopher J 4:25:05 (17,331)
Yeoman, Mark 3:12:41 (2,269)
Yeomans, Mark J 3:32:28 (4,998)
Yeomans, Martin C 3:25:20 (3,739)
Yeomans, Phillip 3:48:57 (8,241)
Yerby, Brett 5:36:44 (29,081)
Yerby, Patrick 4:40:13 (20,965)
Yetts, Trevor P 5:52:43 (30,110)
Yianni, Christopher 3:52:44 (9,180)
Yianni, Nick 4:08:40 (13,278)
Yianni, Yiannakis 6:24:04 (31,109)
Yildiz, Nevil 4:09:00 (13,380)
Yiu, Joseph M 4:10:50 (13,837)
Yobera, Cyprian G 3:53:19 (9,342)
Yoder, Peter N 3:44:31 (7,193)
Yoe, Chris M 3:50:13 (8,552)
York, Martin A 4:38:00 (20,466)
Yorke, Matthew P 3:31:07 (4,792)
Yorke, Peter E 4:41:08 (21,148)
Yoshida, Tamotsu 4:09:48 (13,577)
Yost, Shaun K 4:45:02 (22,040)
Youlden, James A 4:55:19 (24,067)
Young, Alexander W 4:35:26 (19,919)
Young, Andrew T 4:52:36 (23,551)
Young, Barry P 3:24:50 (3,667)
Young, Charles 3:56:03 (10,099)
Young, Clinton J 3:52:24 (9,111)
Young, Colin L 3:44:39 (7,224)
Young, Colin S 4:44:29 (21,908)
Young, Dan O 4:27:32 (17,973)
Young, Denis 3:58:15 (10,773)
Young, Geoffrey 5:01:31 (25,224)
Young, Glenn T 3:17:52 (2,836)
Young, Gregory P 4:25:55 (17,545)
Young, Ian 3:29:16 (4,464)
Young, Ian W 3:55:27 (9,916)
Young, James 4:57:11 (24,432)
Young, James R 2:56:53 (874)
Young, Jason R 5:11:48 (26,604)
Young, John A 4:26:26 (17,681)
Young, John H 5:24:09 (27,984)
Young, Justin P 4:11:57 (14,077)
Young, Kenneth W 4:47:32 (22,574)
Young, Lester J 5:13:46 (26,864)
Young, Mark R 4:50:14 (23,111)
Young, Martin A 4:19:20 (15,866)
Young, Matthew J 3:48:12 (8,047)
Young, Nigel 4:38:59 (20,721)
Young, Patrick A 4:49:43 (23,021)
Young, Peter M 3:52:52 (9,216)
Young, Richard 5:39:21 (29,295)
Young, Robert H 4:25:24 (17,403)
Young, Robert J 3:54:59 (9,778)
Young, Roderick J 4:45:03 (22,045)
Young, Roy 3:53:45 (9,427)
Young, Simon D 3:33:25 (5,178)
Young, Terence 5:25:39 (28,157)
Young, Timothy I 4:47:01 (22,453)
Young, Timothy P 3:01:15 (1,261)
Young, Tom 3:58:52 (10,963)
Young, Warren 4:02:06 (11,746)
Young, William G 7:24:02 (31,802)
Younger, Kenneth W 5:24:10 (27,988)
Younis, Omar S 4:14:44 (14,740)
Yoxall, Bill 3:10:59 (2,098)
Yu, James 4:24:09 (17,105)
Yuda, John 2:10:13 (9)
Yuen, Leonard H 3:50:29 (8,629)
Yuill, Edward 4:09:49 (13,585)
Yuill, Ian G 3:01:25 (1,272)
Yuill, Peter 3:46:16 (7,593)
Yuille, Alec J 4:31:29 (18,969)
Yuille, Andrew J 4:31:29 (18,969)
Yuravlivker, Dror 4:38:48 (20,668)
Zaccagnino, Raffaele 3:30:04 (4,608)
Zahedieh, Ahmad 3:45:59 (7,523)
Zahn, Ruediger 4:47:06 (22,474)
Zahora, Manfred 3:29:20 (4,475)
Zalewski, Robert G 4:09:06 (13,399)
Zander, Joerg W 4:01:43 (11,652)
Zanelli, Gary N 3:35:43 (5,559)
Zaninotto, Luca 3:50:11 (8,545)
Zanon, Alessandro 3:15:13 (2,578)
Zapf, Aaron 4:14:08 (14,593)
Zappelini, Alain 3:43:29 (6,956)
Zappia, Domenico 3:12:30 (2,254)
Zaragas, Lambros 2:19:21 (33)
Zarkadas, Lambros 2:30:29 (83)
Zarri, John 4:55:22 (24,078)
Zaveri, Rishi 5:09:55 (26,368)
Zavoli, Primo 4:15:54 (15,029)
Zazzi, Michael 4:03:10 (11,997)
Zeising, Michael 4:00:53 (11,475)
Zerbel, Ulf 3:55:55 (10,057)
Zerny, Adam M 3:21:52 (3,297)
Zevadya, Wodage 2:33:05 (99)
Zeyssolff, Olivier 2:57:00 (882)
Zhang, Yi 5:07:41 (26,079)
Zibell, Matias 4:44:54 (22,002)
Ziebell, Heiko 4:07:36 (13,034)
Zieger, Achim 5:15:20 (27,060)
Ziehli, Jean Luc 4:44:36 (21,935)
Zielinski, Jeremy V 3:01:47 (1,291)
Ziepe, Colin W 5:52:36 (30,105)
Zimmer, Martin H 3:43:24 (6,937)
Zimmermann, Danilo 3:53:01 (9,261)
Zingarett, Stefano 3:53:47 (9,436)
Zinni, Vincenzo 4:43:42 (21,723)
Zipfell, Stephen 3:47:10 (7,797)
Zirovnik, Juergen 4:40:07 (20,943)
Zoller, Gary J 3:35:19 (5,487)
Zorn, Guenther 3:50:28 (8,625)
Zuccotto, Giancarlo 4:12:25 (14,170)
Zugic, Richard 3:09:55 (1,995)
Zuidgeest, Michel 3:26:07 (3,861)
Zur Eich, Adam W 2:52:58 (640)
Zwierzanski, Michael 4:45:39 (22,177)
Zwierzchiewski, Benoit 2:09:35 (6)

FEMALE RUNNERS

Abbey, Juliette L 5:26:25 (28,243)
Abdon Jones, Caroline H 4:25:44 (17,488)
Abel, Julia F 5:07:00 (25,970)
Abokhair, Laura F 5:41:13 (29,425)
Abraham, Faye A 4:33:24 (19,447)
Abraham, Maria 4:18:48 (15,740)
Abraham, Rebecca A 5:19:42 (27,523)
Abrahams, Nicola J 3:38:58 (6,126)
Abramson, Sarah E 4:23:30 (16,942)
Ace, Paula 4:11:57 (14,077)
Ackland, Sacha M 4:04:03 (12,195)
Acroyd, Helen L 3:54:41 (9,691)
Adams, Amanda J 5:25:14 (28,109)
Adams, Angela J 4:32:22 (19,206)
Adams, Barbara L 5:16:48 (27,231)
Adams, Celestine A 4:43:52 (21,766)
Adams, Charmaine C 4:25:09 (17,351)
Adams, Deirdre 5:59:21 (30,379)
Adams, Diane L 6:48:19 (31,477)
Adams, Helen I 5:12:16 (26,664)
Adams, Jacqueline M 3:52:42 (9,174)
Adams, Jennifer L 4:43:55 (21,778)
Adams, Julie C 5:32:25 (28,768)
Adams, Kate 4:34:15 (19,653)
Adams, Linda 4:37:37 (20,361)
Adams, Susan P 4:57:58 (24,588)
Adams, Tara D 3:59:21 (11,101)
Adams, Tracy 3:51:59 (9,008)
Adams, Victoria J 4:13:00 (14,329)
Adams, Wendy F 6:45:53 (31,450)
Adamson, Alison 4:45:43 (22,194)
Adamson, Julia 4:56:27 (24,293)
Adcock, Miriam V 4:19:16 (15,851)
Addy, Vivian 4:54:26 (23,883)
Adlan-Merini, Chistel 4:24:27 (17,178)
Adler, Kalindi K 4:56:30 (24,310)
Adler, Michael 4:13:01 (14,332)
Adlum, Jane 5:07:45 (26,086)
Adole, Corinne 3:28:48 (4,373)
Aedy, Megan E 5:15:12 (27,042)
Afrifa, Ayowa O 4:47:00 (22,449)
Agatha Neita, Pauline 6:41:46 (31,386)
Agnew, Rebecca E 4:19:39 (15,940)
Aguiar, Noela C 7:25:57 (31,817)
Aguilar, Maria A 4:29:50 (18,591)
Aguilera, Gloria P 6:30:23 (31,211)
Ahearn, Ginette 5:11:46 (26,602)
Ahmad, Sharon A 5:06:04 (25,852)
Ahmed, Azi 5:27:15 (28,330)
Ahmed, Hannah 5:14:40 (26,988)
Aigbirhio, Az A 7:07:28 (31,688)
Aiken, Alison M 4:22:00 (16,537)
Ainsworth, Pat 5:08:10 (26,138)

Aird, Lucy J....6:32:35 (31,255)
Aitchison, Kathryn T....5:12:53 (26,746)
Aitchison, Lorraine....5:27:26 (28,350)
Aitchison, Pauline A....3:41:26 (6,537)
Ajibode, Margaret....4:28:29 (18,227)
Akala, Janet....6:46:32 (31,460)
Akehurst, Christine A....3:55:05 (9,814)
Akeroyd, Suzanne....3:24:40 (3,648)
Akers, Penny M....4:18:23 (15,627)
Akers, Sharon C....7:07:39 (31,690)
Akrill, Kate E....5:01:11 (25,171)
Akyuz, Gun....4:44:31 (21,913)
Alder, Ettie-Ann....5:48:42 (29,894)
Alderson, Tracy C....4:51:12 (23,304)
Alderton, Jacqueline....4:17:44 (15,489)
Aldous, Jacqueline A....3:30:03 (4,601)
Aldridge, Kirsten....5:39:49 (29,320)
Aldridge, Wendy J....4:23:44 (16,996)
Alexander, Eve F....5:05:34 (25,774)
Alexander, Geraldine J....4:06:01 (12,663)
Alexander, Rosalyn L....2:59:48 (1,142)
Alexander, Rosemarie....5:30:07 (28,593)
Alexander, Susannah M....4:49:21 (22,951)
Alford, Rebecca J....4:06:14 (12,722)
Alfsen, Gunvor....5:04:50 (25,668)
Algeo, Lucy C....4:26:20 (17,663)
Al-Homoud, Samar J....7:37:26 (31,887)
Ali, Beverley A....4:58:11 (24,636)
Alker, Kathryn....3:36:37 (5,714)
Allamby, Lorraine G....4:08:38 (13,268)
Allan, Deshara Queen....6:57:09 (31,583)
Allan, Justine....5:58:27 (30,346)
Allaway, Caroline....3:45:34 (7,428)
Allaway, Rachel H....5:00:45 (25,105)
Allbutt, Lynne Y....5:50:20 (29,985)
Alldred, Janet....6:00:04 (30,412)
Allen, Ashley H....5:47:55 (29,861)
Allen, Charlotte E....5:11:31 (26,580)
Allen, Eithne....3:58:18 (10,791)
Allen, Elisabeth J....4:26:01 (17,571)
Allen, Heather....3:46:58 (7,741)
Allen, Helen E....5:00:56 (25,132)
Allen, Joanna L....4:21:46 (16,472)
Allen, Kelly....4:01:41 (11,647)
Allen, Louise M....4:57:08 (24,424)
Allen, Meghan....4:52:19 (23,509)
Allen, Michele A....3:49:43 (8,428)
Allen, Samantha F....5:41:40 (29,464)
Allen, Tracey....4:35:10 (19,858)
Allen, Yvonne A....5:36:40 (29,078)
Allgood, Angela....4:15:44 (14,984)
Allingan, June....5:30:21 (28,611)
Allison, Julie....4:03:02 (11,960)
Allwood, Jacinda L....5:02:59 (25,445)
Al-Maif, Janice....4:04:08 (12,223)
Alp, Oguz....6:12:33 (30,796)
Alverson, Clare F....4:33:56 (19,573)
Alvis, Katherine S....6:04:21 (30,575)
Amas, Helen J....4:53:46 (23,761)
Ambler, Gaynor....3:57:53 (10,646)
Ambler, Helen C....5:20:38 (27,649)
Ambrose, Jane S....4:54:42 (23,940)
Amigo, Caroline S....4:15:38 (14,964)
Amos, Tina S....5:24:13 (27,994)
Amvrosiou, Maria....5:30:34 (28,629)
Amy, Chris....4:50:31 (23,183)
Andersen, Tone....4:50:22 (23,142)
Anderson, Glenda A....3:53:10 (9,303)
Anderson, Irene....3:52:16 (9,076)
Anderson, Jackie A....3:50:14 (8,555)
Anderson, Jean....4:21:12 (16,311)
Anderson, Julie S....4:38:53 (20,691)
Anderson, Kelda....3:47:25 (7,856)
Anderson, Lucy A....4:54:31 (23,899)
Anderson, Lydia M....6:18:56 (30,987)
Anderson, Rose M....4:30:50 (18,825)
Anderson, Sarah M....4:30:43 (18,803)
Andersson, Liselott....3:58:12 (10,758)
Anderton, Tracy L....4:30:10 (18,672)
Andreu, Maite....5:30:01 (28,587)
Andrew, Barbara....6:46:33 (31,462)
Andrew, Florence....6:52:49 (31,539)
Andrew, Melissa C....5:40:30 (29,382)
Andrews, Amanda J....4:22:20 (16,650)
Andrews, Annalisa....4:44:00 (21,794)
Andrews, Carol A....4:41:19 (21,194)
Andrews, Heidi....4:13:33 (14,464)
Andrews, Lisa D....5:51:53 (30,056)
Angel, Laura S....5:15:23 (27,065)
Angel, Melanie R....4:41:01 (21,126)
Angell, Anila....5:27:56 (28,393)
Anglier, Rebecca A....4:44:18 (21,858)
Anguenot, Joelle....4:09:17 (13,450)
Angullia, Freida E....5:09:26 (26,295)
Angus, Kelly....4:09:11 (13,415)
Ankers, Elaine J....5:18:09 (27,380)
Annesley, Carol A....4:24:22 (17,156)
Anstee, Jessica....5:45:56 (29,748)
Anthony, Julie A....4:44:22 (21,876)
Antonius, Jackie A....6:59:27 (31,612)
Anzelon, Kathleen M....6:43:35 (31,413)
Apenteng, Kate....4:39:33 (20,833)
Aplin, Amie J....5:33:00 (28,808)
Appel Lipsius, Linda B....3:36:40 (5,718)
Apperley, Mavis I....4:18:07 (15,576)
Applegate, Nadia E....4:36:07 (20,059)
April, Merrill....3:38:36 (6,069)
Arber, Helen F....5:46:19 (29,772)
Arbery, Bethany C....4:34:13 (19,646)
Arbon, Fay B....4:37:28 (20,333)
Arcangelo, Helena M....5:02:45 (25,411)
Archer, Margaret Y....7:19:30 (31,786)
Archer, Nicole....3:30:23 (4,669)
Archer, Sian H....5:39:18 (29,290)
Arden, Zoe....4:41:11 (21,153)
Ardron, Susie Y....3:49:11 (8,306)
Argyle, Kirsty A....4:57:24 (24,473)
Arkell, Katherine J....5:11:13 (26,543)
Arkinstall, Melissa J....3:09:49 (1,983)
Armitt, Joanna....5:27:03 (28,304)
Armstrong, Anne....5:47:07 (29,817)
Armstrong, Julia H....2:56:25 (847)
Armstrong, Julianne D....4:07:54 (13,090)
Armstrong, Mary....5:30:50 (28,650)
Armstrong, Rosemary F....3:57:03 (10,404)
Armstrong, Sarah J....4:30:10 (18,672)
Armstrong-Ball, Melanie A....4:50:20 (23,129)
Armstrong-Janes, Caroline N....6:22:25 (31,072)
Arnold, Kate L....3:59:43 (11,229)
Arnold, Louise E....6:33:58 (31,276)
Arpaia, Gabriel....4:26:32 (17,710)
Arscott, Ann M....4:47:50 (22,644)
Arscott, Penelope A....4:09:50 (13,591)
Arumbakkam, Abhirami....5:34:50 (28,944)
Arundale, Lisa J....3:08:59 (1,896)
Asbury, Lesley....7:29:38 (31,842)
Ascher, Pascale I....5:20:16 (27,602)
Asghar, Anita....5:14:41 (26,990)
Ash, Hayley E....4:44:31 (21,913)
Ash, Nicola K....5:27:38 (28,364)
Ashby, Susan J....5:31:06 (28,667)
Ashcroft, Cynthia....4:24:37 (17,210)
Ashcroft, Joanna....5:35:02 (28,959)
Ashcroft, Naomi K....3:41:29 (6,545)
Ashdown, Cheryl D....4:23:04 (16,830)
Ashdown, Sophie R....4:09:41 (13,549)
Ashdown, Vanessa A....4:03:56 (12,176)
Ashford, Claire E....4:54:08 (23,825)
Ashford, Kathy H....4:17:27 (15,412)
Ashford, Nicola....4:47:43 (22,618)
Ashley, Lisa J....4:02:20 (11,823)
Ashley, Susan E....3:28:13 (4,266)
Ashmead, Caroline....4:30:25 (18,736)
Ashraf, Yasmin A....4:36:54 (20,227)
Ashton, Jennifer....4:45:01 (22,032)
Ashurst, Teresa....4:13:35 (14,476)
Ashworth, Sarah J....3:50:18 (8,574)
Askew, Clare J....4:57:58 (24,588)
Askew, Sharon G....4:18:48 (15,740)
Askew, Zena L....6:15:21 (30,894)
Askwith, Celia....5:33:13 (28,822)
Asplin, Sharon R....4:32:04 (19,124)
Assmus, Heike E....4:30:46 (18,809)
Assoun, Marie T....4:36:15 (20,082)
Aston, Jennifer....4:50:27 (23,173)
Aston, Julie....5:13:53 (26,885)
Astridge, Helen M....4:45:18 (22,096)
Atheldt, Susanne....3:51:31 (8,891)
Atherfold, Karen....6:04:21 (30,575)
Atherton, Emily L....5:05:09 (25,708)
Atherton, Gisele....4:59:20 (24,858)
Atherton, Sereca L....3:25:13 (3,722)
Atkins, Anna L....4:29:00 (18,349)
Atkins, Jennifer L....4:53:32 (23,707)
Atkins, Julie M....3:56:51 (10,351)
Atkins, Michelle....5:30:18 (28,606)
Atkins, Nicola....5:48:21 (29,878)
Atkinson, Christina A....6:17:52 (30,947)
Atkinson, Claire E....4:29:31 (18,499)
Atkinson, Helen R....4:59:58 (24,986)
Atkinson, Jan M....5:38:23 (29,221)
Atkinson, Joanna R....4:49:40 (23,009)
Atkinson, Margaret J....5:09:01 (26,240)
Atkinson, Wendy J....4:42:13 (21,388)
Attenburrow, Ralda C....4:37:49 (20,409)
Atwal, Karen....5:08:29 (26,181)
Atwal, Ranjit Kaur K....5:52:34 (30,100)
Aucott, Gemma L....5:18:43 (27,434)
Augis, Mona....3:46:33 (7,648)
Augur, Zanne T....4:24:54 (17,284)
Auld, Jennifer L....5:28:28 (28,433)
Aussenberg, Glenda J....7:34:41 (31,870)
Austin, Barbara A....6:03:22 (30,542)
Austin, Carol L....3:49:23 (8,352)
Austin, Joanna....4:39:15 (20,783)
Austin, Julie....5:33:00 (28,808)
Austin, Lynda J....4:58:01 (24,597)
Austin, Sarah L....4:00:08 (11,323)
Austin, Victoria L....5:24:45 (28,048)
Auton, Rachael C....4:13:32 (14,462)
Avery, Helen A....5:03:31 (25,524)
Aves, Susan M....3:38:55 (6,115)
Avitabile, Silvia....3:45:25 (7,390)
Awal, Lani....4:33:00 (19,359)
Ayers, Karen Q....4:56:04 (24,223)
Ayers, Samantha J....3:22:31 (3,380)
Ayling, Caroline J....5:54:33 (30,173)
Ayodeji, Kim A....4:36:01 (20,029)
Ayres, Natalie V....6:14:42 (30,874)
Baber, Louise A....4:12:31 (14,208)
Babington, Amanda J....5:20:27 (27,623)
Backhouse, Bonita F....5:18:58 (27,461)
Bacon, Gill....3:04:53 (1,513)
Badcock, Janine....5:00:05 (25,006)
Badenoch, Emma C....3:58:35 (10,884)
Baerselman, Tessa A....3:59:11 (11,054)
Bagnall, Bridget C....4:09:31 (13,504)
Bagnall, Helen....5:17:08 (27,266)
Bailey, Claire H....5:44:51 (29,683)
Bailey, Corrine M....5:34:40 (28,936)
Bailey, Eileen....4:41:48 (21,309)
Bailey, Gemma L....4:29:28 (18,481)
Bailey, Leanne....4:58:38 (24,745)
Bailey, Lisa J....4:43:08 (21,587)
Bailey, Lisa J....5:22:20 (27,808)
Bailey, Margaret A....5:02:19 (25,346)
Bailey, Nikki....5:55:03 (30,202)
Bailey, Rosie A....5:55:44 (30,232)
Bailey, Sharon M....5:00:36 (25,076)
Bailey, Veronica J....4:49:47 (23,036)
Bailey, Victoria....4:15:00 (14,803)
Baily, Katherine E....6:42:15 (31,396)
Bain, Judy A....5:42:10 (29,493)
Bain, Karen A....3:44:00 (7,071)
Bainbridge, Laura A....4:21:14 (16,319)
Bainbridge, Wendy E....5:06:25 (25,901)
Bainsfair, Victoria A....4:52:28 (23,528)
Bairstow, Elaine C....4:46:40 (22,386)
Baker, Carole A....6:14:42 (30,874)
Baker, Deana E....3:33:16 (5,153)
Baker, Dominique L....4:34:09 (19,635)
Baker, Elizabeth C....4:33:04 (19,372)
Baker, Joanne L....4:10:13 (13,681)
Baker, Louise C....5:04:41 (25,649)
Baker, Patsy....3:59:24 (11,115)
Baker, Sally H....3:06:22 (1,641)
Baker, Sara F....5:01:08 (25,165)
Baker, Sarah A....5:28:32 (28,442)
Baker, Susan C....5:31:20 (28,688)

Baker, Trish A	7:28:23 (31,835)	
Balafas, Anna	4:34:43 (19,761)	
Balazova, Martina	4:55:39 (24,130)	
Balazs, Jane T	5:31:23 (28,696)	
Balcazar, Leticia	5:23:29 (27,916)	
Baldacchino, Patricia	3:06:05 (1,618)	
Baldino, Maria	5:27:12 (28,323)	
Baldo, Martine	4:03:38 (12,110)	
Baldwin, Debra Jane	4:32:34 (19,251)	
Baldwin, Jenny J	7:18:57 (31,776)	
Bale, Nichola C	6:28:37 (31,183)	
Bales, Vicki	3:30:25 (4,677)	
Balgera, Arianna	4:34:26 (19,696)	
Ball, Ann	4:36:54 (20,227)	
Ball, Fiona C	3:47:11 (7,801)	
Ball, Janet E	3:51:19 (8,836)	
Ball, Susan C	6:31:54 (31,242)	
Ballantyne, Rachel	4:26:03 (17,585)	
Balsdon, Claire H	4:45:33 (22,148)	
Balshaw, Harriet S	5:42:12 (29,495)	
Baltrop, Julia	3:18:32 (2,902)	
Balzuweit, Stefanie	5:04:15 (25,599)	
Bamford, Janet	4:58:23 (24,687)	
Bancroft, Trish	3:44:25 (7,163)	
Bane, Deony	4:52:58 (23,610)	
Banger, Amy L	4:09:44 (13,563)	
Banham, Karen J	3:52:29 (9,130)	
Banks, Angela L	3:41:50 (6,612)	
Banks, Christine M	4:22:58 (16,807)	
Banks, Faye Marie	3:09:12 (1,917)	
Bannatyne, Lucy E	4:04:31 (12,318)	
Banwait, Jasbinder K	6:09:06 (30,703)	
Baranowski, Kirsty E	4:53:31 (23,704)	
Barber, Judy H	4:59:43 (24,942)	
Barber, Lyn K	5:28:57 (28,479)	
Barber, Rita C	5:24:48 (28,058)	
Barber, Sue	4:10:08 (13,664)	
Barboni, Gloria	4:43:43 (21,726)	
Barbour, Debra A	3:57:38 (10,578)	
Barcham, Anna	4:56:25 (24,283)	
Barclay, Linda A	3:57:57 (10,662)	
Bardeleben, Liria N	4:53:46 (23,761)	
Barg, Claudia	4:33:04 (19,372)	
Bargetto, Vanya	4:58:11 (24,636)	
Bark, Caroline S	4:14:31 (14,682)	
Barker, Ann L	3:18:41 (2,917)	
Barker, Carrie A	5:17:16 (27,281)	
Barker, Claire S	4:17:10 (15,343)	
Barker, Fiona	5:12:18 (26,669)	
Barker, Jackie S	3:27:46 (4,182)	
Barker, Janet L	4:12:17 (14,147)	
Barker, Jasmine R	5:10:52 (26,492)	
Barker, Susan	4:32:50 (19,319)	
Barkway, Hilary J	5:38:21 (29,217)	
Barlass, Emily R	4:06:09 (12,700)	
Barley, Julie A	3:12:19 (2,228)	
Barley, Sharon I	4:38:59 (20,721)	
Barlow, Melanie L	4:49:17 (22,937)	
Barnbrook, Tamasin L	5:24:30 (28,026)	
Barnes, Hayley	3:06:50 (1,690)	
Barnes, Heather J	5:38:41 (29,244)	
Barnes, Jackie C	4:52:05 (23,461)	
Barnes, Jacqueline A	4:12:35 (14,228)	
Barnes, Jane M	4:05:06 (12,448)	
Barnes, Jill	5:07:20 (26,022)	
Barnes, Patricia M	5:06:17 (25,886)	
Barnes, Sue E	3:34:48 (5,389)	
Barnes, Wendy A	3:30:27 (4,682)	
Barnett, Gillian	5:30:03 (28,588)	
Barnett, Marion H	7:51:18 (31,918)	
Barnett, Sarah	4:53:11 (23,651)	
Barnett, Tracy D	4:33:31 (19,473)	
Barnfather, Gina C	5:42:51 (29,538)	
Barnham, Kate M	5:20:23 (27,618)	
Barnwell, Jessica L	6:23:01 (31,077)	
Baron, Julie A	6:03:04 (30,529)	
Baron, Lorraine A	3:39:59 (6,302)	
Barons, Julie M	4:52:25 (23,522)	
Barr, Ellen	4:09:46 (13,570)	
Barr, Iva B	6:26:43 (31,153)	
Barr, Jackie A	5:03:21 (25,494)	
Barr, Janice E	5:05:13 (25,713)	
Barrass, Sandra	5:12:53 (26,746)	

Barrat, Sally J	4:54:43 (23,944)	
Barrett, Anita J	3:54:15 (9,577)	
Barrett, Ann	4:38:57 (20,706)	
Barrett, Caroline	4:10:40 (13,793)	
Barrett, Caroline	5:48:30 (29,882)	
Barrett, Gillian M	4:03:46 (12,140)	
Barrett, Jane E	4:45:33 (22,148)	
Barrett, Victoria	3:02:21 (1,331)	
Barritt, Christine E	7:51:26 (31,919)	
Barron, Hayley	4:01:43 (11,652)	
Barrow-Green, June E	3:35:49 (5,575)	
Barry, Elizabeth J	4:40:52 (21,102)	
Barson, Angela M	5:36:24 (29,053)	
Barstow, Jacqueline K	6:44:04 (31,418)	
Barter, Emma E	4:55:23 (24,081)	
Barter, Patricia A	4:12:42 (14,263)	
Bartholomew, Anna L	4:44:44 (21,961)	
Bartimote, Joan A	4:16:47 (15,247)	
Bartlett, Victoria L	4:22:12 (16,608)	
Barton, Kelly Jane	5:49:42 (29,944)	
Barton, Lin A	4:06:56 (12,871)	
Barton, Vicky	5:27:18 (28,335)	
Bart-Williams, Ruth A	5:28:46 (28,465)	
Bashford, Ann C	6:14:05 (30,848)	
Bass, Irenie R	4:03:16 (12,021)	
Bassett-Hall, Sarah K	4:59:08 (24,818)	
Bassi, Tanya	4:24:06 (17,092)	
Bate, Mary B	3:55:10 (9,839)	
Bate, Samantha J	3:35:40 (5,549)	
Bateman, Evelyn I	4:32:31 (19,240)	
Bateman, Victoria A	5:08:05 (26,125)	
Bates, Gillian M	4:12:40 (14,254)	
Bates, Janet S	6:09:36 (30,716)	
Bates, Patricia M	5:39:10 (29,282)	
Bath, Ann	3:53:43 (9,417)	
Bath, Doreen A	4:09:47 (13,575)	
Batho, Emma L	4:10:35 (13,774)	
Batstone, Jennifer	4:49:54 (23,060)	
Battersby, Judith A	4:47:36 (22,591)	
Battersby, Susan C	4:57:33 (24,503)	
Battle, Nicola J	4:34:22 (19,685)	
Battson, Elaine C	3:43:04 (6,864)	
Batty, Karen M	4:06:12 (12,711)	
Baudin, Claire	4:26:38 (17,736)	
Bauer, Vanda S	5:37:03 (29,110)	
Baugher, Elizabeth A	5:30:06 (28,592)	
Baumgartner, Rebecca J	4:38:24 (20,570)	
Baxter, Anne L	5:02:51 (25,426)	
Baxter, Carol A	4:26:05 (17,600)	
Baxter, Jane	5:40:07 (29,346)	
Baxter, Jane L	6:51:15 (31,516)	
Baxter, Kay F	7:19:03 (31,778)	
Baxter, Wendy S	4:31:41 (19,022)	
Bayne, Kristin	5:59:17 (30,376)	
Baynes, Marion	6:24:16 (31,117)	
Baynham, Jessica	4:26:56 (17,821)	
Beadle, Deborah J	5:25:29 (28,135)	
Bealey, Nicola M	4:16:03 (15,059)	
Beament, Claire	4:38:57 (20,706)	
Bear, Angie	3:55:42 (9,989)	
Bearder, Deborah J	5:00:40 (25,089)	
Beardmore, Donna M	4:39:03 (20,739)	
Beardmore, Lisa J	4:30:53 (18,837)	
Beardsworth, Vikki S	5:53:43 (30,140)	
Bearman-Hayes, Sherrie-Ann	4:46:12 (22,296)	
Beasley, Mandy	7:50:23 (31,914)	
Beattie, Julie	3:55:15 (9,863)	
Beattie, Victoria S	5:11:25 (26,567)	
Beauchamp, Debbie E	4:51:16 (23,312)	
Beaumont, Lucy	3:45:09 (7,334)	
Beauvillain Dellery, Marie A	5:35:45 (29,017)	
Beaver, Genie	3:14:23 (2,487)	
Bebb, Kate E	3:39:53 (6,289)	
Beck, Emma J	5:20:36 (27,645)	
Beck, Sue J	4:44:21 (21,871)	
Becker, Andrea	4:14:52 (14,779)	
Becker, Liza	5:47:57 (29,865)	
Beckett, Kate	5:08:53 (26,219)	
Beckett, Sandra M	5:17:50 (27,341)	
Beckley, Cynthia M	5:39:23 (29,299)	
Beckwith, Julie L	4:05:31 (12,547)	
Beckwith, Yvonne	4:02:00 (11,717)	
Beddis, Gail D	3:57:05 (10,411)	

Bedford, Anita A	7:04:42 (31,666)	
Bedford, Suzanna J	3:39:03 (6,140)	
Beecham, Helen C	4:19:17 (15,854)	
Beechinor, Georgina A	5:48:51 (29,900)	
Beek Van, Coby	4:49:20 (22,947)	
Beeke, Sarah G	6:51:38 (31,523)	
Beesley, Caroline L	4:55:17 (24,059)	
Beeston, Jayne A	6:01:38 (30,468)	
Beeston, Shelley A	3:57:49 (10,622)	
Beilfuss, Donna K	4:59:26 (24,889)	
Beke, Yvon	4:56:15 (24,252)	
Belbin, Ruth E	3:32:56 (5,086)	
Belcham, Kay E	4:53:59 (23,791)	
Belet, Pascale	4:37:18 (20,315)	
Belk, Doreen S	5:55:44 (30,232)	
Bell, Alice	4:22:14 (16,619)	
Bell, Angela	5:15:05 (27,032)	
Bell, Ann E	3:22:36 (3,390)	
Bell, Louise	3:50:04 (8,517)	
Bell, Rachael S	4:13:54 (14,543)	
Bell, Sarah J	6:21:31 (31,045)	
Bell Macdonald, Minette A	3:56:23 (10,204)	
Bellamy, Ellen	4:39:02 (20,735)	
Bellamy, Rachel	3:59:39 (11,206)	
Bellingham, Kylie	4:11:11 (13,909)	
Bellmon, Sharon D	6:12:34 (30,797)	
Bello, Rashidat K	4:51:34 (23,356)	
Bendall, Sarah J	4:38:50 (20,677)	
Benfield, Alison	4:23:53 (17,034)	
Benfield, Dianne M	5:40:12 (29,350)	
Benford, Johanna A	6:25:58 (31,143)	
Benjamin, Floella	4:52:53 (23,595)	
Benjamin, Sarah E	4:11:56 (14,072)	
Bennett, Bridie R	5:24:55 (28,072)	
Bennett, Christine	4:54:49 (23,962)	
Bennett, Deanne E	3:58:25 (10,824)	
Bennett, Elettra T	5:00:05 (25,006)	
Bennett, Gillian C	5:00:57 (25,136)	
Bennett, Hazel	5:30:46 (28,642)	
Bennett, Nicola L	4:46:47 (22,406)	
Bennett, Paula G	4:38:03 (20,484)	
Bennett, Ruth H	4:38:38 (20,622)	
Bennett, Sally A	4:47:31 (22,570)	
Bennett, Sara L	4:30:02 (18,639)	
Bennett, Tessa J	3:39:32 (6,221)	
Bennett-Hornsey, Lindsay	3:48:35 (8,144)	
Bennetts, Sarah H	3:32:20 (4,976)	
Benson, Catherine E	4:37:20 (20,322)	
Benson, Gaynor	3:37:44 (5,908)	
Benson, Marianne	6:41:55 (31,390)	
Benson, Mary M	4:27:12 (17,892)	
Benstead, Amanda M	3:44:50 (7,270)	
Bentley, Karen	5:17:54 (27,354)	
Bentley, Laura J	4:06:16 (12,727)	
Benton, Jenny	4:11:16 (13,922)	
Benton-Smith, Lucy	6:36:24 (31,313)	
Bentz, Caroline S	3:50:18 (8,574)	
Benzimra, Ruth E	5:41:13 (29,425)	
Beresford, Carly T	5:43:30 (29,590)	
Bernays, Juliet V	4:25:42 (17,477)	
Berriman, Lindsey K	3:25:34 (3,777)	
Berrington, Krystyna M	4:09:29 (13,494)	
Berry, Amy M	5:18:57 (27,459)	
Berry, Angela C	4:26:15 (17,648)	
Berry, Anjie J	4:38:23 (20,566)	
Berry, Cheryle J	6:40:41 (31,367)	
Berry, Fiona E	4:16:55 (15,288)	
Berry, Janet E	5:19:18 (27,489)	
Berry, Kathryn M	3:59:53 (11,261)	
Berry, Nicola A	4:02:18 (11,805)	
Berry, Olivia M	3:24:59 (3,691)	
Berry, Sara L	3:30:06 (4,614)	
Berry, Sheila L	4:29:22 (18,457)	
Berry, Stephanie P	4:44:00 (21,794)	
Berry, Victoria C	3:51:37 (8,922)	
Berryman, Caroline	4:17:16 (15,360)	
Bertero, Alice	2:59:51 (1,146)	
Berthier, Véronique	4:26:37 (17,730)	
Bertoli, Natalina	4:33:24 (19,447)	
Berwick, Helen	4:47:14 (22,504)	
Besson, Lesley	4:27:08 (17,874)	
Best, Laura	4:45:04 (22,053)	
Best, Paula M	4:25:47 (17,509)	

Best, Vivienne M	6:07:07 (30,650)	
Bethune, Deirdre	3:58:56 (10,987)	
Bett, Dionne J	5:16:08 (27,143)	
Betts, Carol A	3:33:47 (5,233)	
Betts, Fiona H	3:31:24 (4,833)	
Beukes, Elizabeth C	3:40:06 (6,322)	
Bevan, Jackie H	5:22:21 (27,812)	
Beveridge, Harriet D	4:35:43 (19,963)	
Beverley, Dena	4:33:51 (19,547)	
Beverley, Lucy J	4:24:22 (17,156)	
Beverley, Wendy	5:19:35 (27,507)	
Bexon, Hazel E	6:07:08 (30,651)	
Bezuijen-Boonstra, Sandra	4:31:49 (19,053)	
Bhakar, Rajwant	6:20:23 (31,022)	
Bhoja, Indira	4:45:22 (22,112)	
Bickers, Maura L	5:37:35 (29,156)	
Bickers, Sarah V	4:34:30 (19,712)	
Bickerstaffe, Kate	4:05:00 (12,429)	
Bickford, Kate	5:09:45 (26,345)	
Bicknell, Elizabeth	3:37:21 (5,850)	
Biddle, Katharine	3:59:00 (11,007)	
Biddle, Laura	4:14:04 (14,581)	
Bide, Carol	5:54:31 (30,172)	
Bidston, Joanna H	3:32:12 (4,952)	
Biermanski, Brigitta	4:09:30 (13,501)	
Biggs, Suzette L	5:40:22 (29,364)	
Biggs-Hayes, Rachel L	5:00:06 (25,012)	
Billingham, Anne E	4:07:04 (12,911)	
Billingham, Kim	6:01:49 (30,480)	
Billingham, Lauren A	6:58:39 (31,604)	
Bingham, Rosie J	4:33:18 (19,428)	
Binns, Clare	4:33:21 (19,437)	
Binns, Sally H	4:29:21 (18,451)	
Bioly, Birgitt	3:50:20 (8,589)	
Bir, Sukhjinder	6:21:16 (31,037)	
Birakos, Jane	5:21:22 (27,713)	
Birch, Annie M	3:53:37 (9,407)	
Birch, Bridget	4:30:26 (18,742)	
Birch, Hayley	4:04:16 (12,257)	
Birchall, Amanda J	5:38:53 (29,251)	
Birchall, Elizabeth A	3:50:49 (8,712)	
Bircher, Carolyn S	4:43:19 (21,642)	
Bird, Penelope R	5:41:30 (29,446)	
Bird, Sarah A	5:01:33 (25,229)	
Birdsall, Trish	6:57:12 (31,584)	
Birkett, Catherine	4:58:50 (24,768)	
Birks, Louise S	4:53:10 (23,647)	
Birrell, Joanne	4:59:10 (24,825)	
Bishop, Jill M	3:57:13 (10,451)	
Bishop, Katie M	5:49:02 (29,910)	
Bishop, Louise M	5:20:25 (27,620)	
Bishop, Pauline B	3:52:23 (9,108)	
Bishop, Rachel M	4:42:07 (21,372)	
Bishopp, Helen	5:11:06 (26,517)	
Bishopp, Sara A	3:03:00 (1,367)	
Bixley, Lynda R	6:09:16 (30,709)	
Black, Nancy R	5:06:41 (25,937)	
Black, Sue M	3:23:06 (3,450)	
Blackburn, Kathleen	4:20:51 (16,244)	
Blackburn, Ruth	4:03:48 (12,150)	
Blackburn, Tania	4:36:07 (20,059)	
Blackburn, Tracy J	8:15:10 (31,955)	
Blackley, Aileen M	5:22:39 (27,846)	
Blackman, Melinda L	5:17:32 (27,312)	
Blackmore, Elisa	5:42:54 (29,545)	
Blackshaw, Victoria J	3:53:00 (9,257)	
Blackwell, Lesley A	5:23:13 (27,893)	
Blackwell, Victoria K	6:03:43 (30,554)	
Blackwood-Murray, Jessica	4:21:59 (16,530)	
Blair, Janet	5:16:11 (27,166)	
Blair, Julie A	4:04:49 (12,379)	
Blake, Ann-Maree T	3:54:02 (9,514)	
Blake, Elizabeth	4:22:35 (16,719)	
Blake, Janine P	5:46:29 (29,785)	
Blake, Lorraine M	4:53:37 (23,730)	
Blake, Stephanie	4:16:17 (15,114)	
Blakemore, Susan R	3:41:06 (6,498)	
Blakey, Debbie	6:11:59 (30,783)	
Blakey, Hannah J	4:35:13 (19,868)	
Blakiston, Vikki J	5:01:24 (25,207)	
Blamey, Margaret M	7:59:22 (31,932)	
Blamires, Joanna	4:54:11 (23,835)	
Blanch, Amy-Rose M	4:21:31 (16,393)	
Bland, Victoria	4:52:12 (23,482)	
Bland, Yvonne C	4:23:19 (16,898)	
Blasby, Anne F	4:21:43 (16,457)	
Blee, Sarah L	5:33:28 (28,846)	
Blethyn, Brenda	6:57:46 (31,593)	
Blomley, Rachel L	5:01:47 (25,271)	
Bloore, Jane	4:23:42 (16,989)	
Blore Mitchell, Carolyn A	3:52:40 (9,165)	
Blott, Natasha L	4:59:58 (24,986)	
Blythe, Dawn M	4:57:40 (24,529)	
Blythe, Lucy R	5:39:02 (29,268)	
Boal, Wendy A	4:28:54 (18,327)	
Board, Frances J	4:06:30 (12,778)	
Board, Helen M	4:06:27 (12,769)	
Boardman, Lynda J	6:14:37 (30,867)	
Boardman, Tanya S	4:17:07 (15,334)	
Boast, Cathryn J	4:32:57 (19,349)	
Boatman, Lesley	5:13:01 (26,765)	
Boden, Lesley S	4:33:08 (19,388)	
Boden, Patricia A	3:45:24 (7,387)	
Bodiam, Claire A	4:38:13 (20,524)	
Bogie, Alison	3:40:49 (6,441)	
Bogue, Mary T	4:59:38 (24,925)	
Bohmer-Laubis, Jacqueline C	4:37:18 (20,315)	
Bolan, Nicola	5:06:03 (25,850)	
Bolla, Jaskamal K	3:43:12 (6,894)	
Bolland, Marie Louise	6:14:14 (30,853)	
Bolsover, Jacquie A	4:16:59 (15,301)	
Bolton, Claire M	5:13:40 (26,851)	
Bolton, Katrina H	5:14:07 (26,914)	
Bolton, Marianne	4:02:11 (11,774)	
Bonas, Daryl M	6:10:04 (30,727)	
Bond, Charlotte E	4:46:17 (22,314)	
Bond, Robyn S	5:01:26 (25,214)	
Bond, Susan A	4:35:30 (19,927)	
Bonham, Miki S	7:19:17 (31,782)	
Bonner, Joanna	3:32:37 (5,033)	
Bonner, Joanne M	4:28:17 (18,165)	
Bonninga, Shelagh M	5:51:50 (30,052)	
Boodhoo, Cecilia	4:24:37 (17,210)	
Booker, Janet	4:43:47 (21,746)	
Boon, Jennifer A	4:35:41 (19,959)	
Boon Von Ochessee, Catharina H	4:23:45 (17,002)	
Booth, Charlotte M	4:11:29 (13,966)	
Booth, Donna A	6:14:34 (30,865)	
Booth, Fiona J	5:51:03 (30,017)	
Booth, Melanie J	4:20:59 (16,281)	
Bootle, Jo	4:41:19 (21,194)	
Booty, Cassandra S	4:45:32 (22,146)	
Borgars, Natasha R	5:25:17 (28,117)	
Boriello, Elena	3:30:47 (4,738)	
Borrell, Ellie	4:31:43 (19,033)	
Borrill, Jenny A	4:44:28 (21,903)	
Borrill, Rachel E	4:23:41 (16,980)	
Bortoli Gnych, Rosanna M	5:13:53 (26,885)	
Bosher, Alison	4:29:17 (18,422)	
Boshier, Aliette F	5:08:05 (26,125)	
Boss, Alexandra M	3:51:55 (8,995)	
Bossy, Jeanine	4:36:12 (20,072)	
Bost, Christine	5:12:19 (26,673)	
Bostick, Sharon L	5:34:38 (28,929)	
Boswell, Carol	6:27:43 (31,171)	
Boswell, Laura	5:13:28 (26,820)	
Botello, Michelle C	4:25:47 (17,509)	
Bott, Alison	4:31:29 (18,969)	
Bott, Elizabeth A	4:29:00 (18,349)	
Bott, Joy A	5:22:34 (27,841)	
Boulcott, Nicola H	4:15:30 (14,925)	
Boulger, Anne E	4:28:04 (18,115)	
Boulle, Josiane	2:59:05 (1,081)	
Bourke, Marie A	4:48:41 (22,812)	
Bourne, Suzanne	5:36:45 (29,083)	
Bourne, Tamsin R	5:17:47 (27,338)	
Boutcher, Sherry D	4:47:33 (22,580)	
Boutenel, Véronique	3:50:32 (8,634)	
Bowditch, Lucy	3:18:51 (2,935)	
Bowdler, Sarah M	4:42:00 (21,344)	
Bowen, Samantha	4:28:35 (18,251)	
Bowen, Samantha J	6:37:13 (31,323)	
Bowen, Sioned	6:30:32 (31,214)	
Bower, Helen A	5:32:15 (28,755)	
Bower, Hilary	5:31:42 (28,716)	
Bower, Marie A	4:48:03 (22,682)	
Bowers, Pauline A	5:18:43 (27,434)	
Bowes, Elizabeth J	4:14:28 (14,674)	
Bowes, Helen	4:49:11 (22,916)	
Bowker, Carol M	3:15:04 (2,561)	
Bowler, Wendy K	5:07:25 (26,032)	
Bowles, Ann	3:52:03 (9,025)	
Bowles, Liza A	3:42:51 (6,821)	
Bowles, Niki S	4:07:00 (12,891)	
Bowman, Jean W	5:20:33 (27,637)	
Bown, Rachel H	3:13:47 (2,408)	
Bowsher, Judi S	3:41:05 (6,491)	
Bowyer, Amy L	4:51:33 (23,351)	
Bowyer, Lucy F	4:08:08 (13,139)	
Box, Carol A	5:50:01 (29,966)	
Boyall, Elizabeth M	4:58:55 (24,783)	
Boyce, Bronwen	4:23:58 (17,053)	
Boyce, Cliona E	4:22:28 (16,690)	
Boyko, Lara A	8:09:11 (31,952)	
Boyle, Abigail L	6:02:21 (30,498)	
Boyle, Brenda M	5:41:08 (29,421)	
Boyle, Carole A	5:00:02 (24,995)	
Bradbury, Emma J	4:10:16 (13,693)	
Bradbury, Taryn K	4:15:41 (14,973)	
Bradfield, Kerry	4:56:28 (24,298)	
Bradford, Cheryl	6:29:46 (31,199)	
Bradford, Katie J	4:47:02 (22,456)	
Bradley, Deborah A	4:24:03 (17,072)	
Bradley, Jayne M	4:18:56 (15,768)	
Bradley, Julie	6:05:44 (30,614)	
Bradley, Karen	3:12:19 (2,228)	
Bradley, Melanie J	3:56:09 (10,121)	
Bradley, Samantha J	4:44:55 (22,015)	
Bradshaw, Elanor	4:27:11 (17,891)	
Bradshaw, Judith E	4:26:04 (17,593)	
Bradshaw, Kate D	6:41:13 (31,377)	
Bradshaw, Philippa E	4:37:45 (20,391)	
Bradwell, Carol L	4:46:23 (22,338)	
Brady, Deborah L	5:02:01 (25,299)	
Brady, Sandra C	4:45:05 (22,059)	
Brady, Theresa	3:17:59 (2,847)	
Brady, Tina A	4:58:15 (24,653)	
Braes, Linda A	4:57:24 (24,473)	
Braggins, Lucy C	4:22:27 (16,681)	
Braidwood, Phillippa	5:49:21 (29,925)	
Brailsford, Victoria A	4:47:47 (22,630)	
Braithwaite, June F	5:04:58 (25,689)	
Braker, Julie L	4:40:48 (21,089)	
Branch, Diane M	4:27:36 (17,990)	
Branchett, Emma E	4:26:19 (17,658)	
Brand, Alison J	4:50:41 (23,215)	
Brand, Felicity J	4:43:07 (21,585)	
Brand, Rosemary	4:25:41 (17,474)	
Brand, Veronica C	5:09:16 (26,272)	
Brandel, Kimberly A	5:00:01 (24,993)	
Brandt, Hanna	4:50:01 (23,077)	
Brasier, Katherine D	3:45:41 (7,455)	
Brasnett, Laura E	4:53:41 (23,747)	
Brassfield, Emily M	3:45:09 (7,334)	
Bratby, Katie J	4:05:55 (12,643)	
Bray, Brydie D	3:52:26 (9,120)	
Bray, Sarah	4:10:13 (13,681)	
Brayford, Donna J	5:59:45 (30,401)	
Brayford, Lucy	3:11:29 (2,143)	
Brazier, Enid D	6:55:24 (31,566)	
Breach, Nicola J	3:49:55 (8,477)	
Breckon, Katherine E	6:13:49 (30,841)	
Bredenkamp, Lorett E	7:13:42 (31,739)	
Breen, Michelle	6:17:33 (30,938)	
Brennan, Anna M	5:44:47 (29,677)	
Brennan, Jackie M	4:58:53 (24,778)	
Brennan, Rebecca J	4:03:44 (12,134)	
Brennan Green, Julie M	3:51:15 (8,819)	
Brenner, first name unknown	3:51:51 (8,977)	
Brentnall, Claire L	3:28:50 (4,383)	
Bresher, Alison D	5:29:44 (28,560)	
Breslin, Elaine M	5:24:24 (28,015)	
Brett, Emma	5:59:07 (30,368)	
Brett, Jennifer A	6:31:45 (31,240)	
Brett, Lucinda J	4:44:47 (21,974)	
Brett, Sandra Y	3:13:30 (2,374)	
Brett, Vanessa A	5:18:04 (27,376)	
Brewer, Heather J	5:12:10 (26,651)	
Brewis, Linda M	3:37:07 (5,799)	

Brewster, Elaine	5:35:00 (28,956)
Brewster, Victoria L	3:48:46 (8,200)
Brice, Katie H	4:39:58 (20,910)
Brice, Margaret C	5:18:16 (27,397)
Brice, Sharon J	4:18:18 (15,607)
Brickland, Patricia	4:26:12 (17,631)
Brickwood, Elizabeth R	4:42:34 (21,465)
Bridge, Rachael E	5:51:29 (30,035)
Bridgeman, Jo	6:41:33 (31,382)
Bridgen, Elizabeth V	3:57:52 (10,639)
Bridgman, Jean	4:59:04 (24,806)
Bridgstock, Virginia M	5:07:17 (26,006)
Briefel, Terri M	4:04:31 (12,318)
Briggs, Christine A	4:24:36 (17,205)
Briggs, Emma L	3:59:42 (11,222)
Briggs, Gail E	4:25:58 (17,561)
Briggs, Joanna K	4:09:25 (13,482)
Briggs, Julie L	3:06:32 (1,657)
Briggs, Kathryn	4:34:16 (19,657)
Briggs, Lisa	5:02:22 (25,353)
Briggs, Susan D	5:17:55 (27,355)
Bright, Kirsteen E	4:15:25 (14,904)
Brighton, Susan L	3:39:03 (6,140)
Brightwell, Emma	5:22:13 (27,796)
Brightwell, Julia A	5:19:49 (27,535)
Brightwell, Natalie A	4:41:43 (21,286)
Brimmer, Christy J	6:10:53 (30,754)
Brind, Joanne H	4:27:20 (17,925)
Brine, Denise A	4:49:35 (22,992)
Bringlow, Véronique	3:06:33 (1,659)
Brinklow, Patricia M	5:40:31 (29,383)
Bristow, Mary	4:51:32 (23,349)
Bristow Tyler, Linda	5:16:14 (27,159)
Britt, Jane L	4:32:57 (19,349)
Britton, Heather D	4:53:33 (23,710)
Britton, Rosemary A	4:01:26 (11,584)
Britton, Toni	3:37:09 (5,804)
Brixton-Lee, Aimée S	4:11:47 (14,041)
Broadbent, Catherine J	3:54:33 (9,651)
Broadfoot, Belinda J	3:13:47 (2,408)
Broadhead, Jennifer	4:29:21 (18,451)
Broadhurst, Maria L	4:33:53 (19,556)
Broadley, Patricia M	4:47:40 (22,608)
Brock, Colette	6:54:15 (31,551)
Brock, Rebecca L	5:29:56 (28,577)
Brockwell, Emma L	5:02:29 (25,373)
Brockwell, Kirstie A	4:18:04 (15,568)
Broda, Krysia B	3:56:15 (10,166)
Brodbin, Allison J	5:02:34 (25,384)
Broderick, Annaliese	3:54:12 (9,564)
Brodie, Roisin B	4:39:12 (20,774)
Broekhof, Mary	4:03:53 (12,166)
Brog, Annabel L	4:06:29 (12,775)
Brokenshaw, Shirley J	3:44:08 (7,102)
Brokenshire, Ethel I	3:36:20 (5,664)
Bromley, Gina J	4:54:18 (23,855)
Bromley, Michaela G	3:20:07 (3,079)
Bromley, Sarah	5:38:14 (29,199)
Bronneberg, Elisabeth S	4:09:41 (13,549)
Bronner, Stephanie	3:44:52 (7,277)
Bronson, Vivian	5:11:31 (26,580)
Brook, Christine E	4:03:57 (12,179)
Brook, Jennie L	4:49:00 (22,875)
Brook, Lina M	4:44:03 (21,805)
Brook, Lindsey C	4:41:19 (21,194)
Brook, Maxine L	4:57:35 (24,512)
Brookbanks, Adele	4:00:52 (11,468)
Brooker, Janet S	5:44:12 (29,635)
Brooker, Lisa J	4:49:36 (22,996)
Brookes, Celia	4:19:57 (16,013)
Brooks, Bonni	4:31:10 (18,895)
Brooks, Charlie	5:23:38 (27,938)
Brooks, Christine M	4:27:18 (17,920)
Brooks, Claire H	3:57:13 (10,451)
Brooks, Kate A	5:05:52 (25,818)
Brooks, Lindsey J	4:50:27 (23,173)
Brooks, Lucy J	3:03:46 (1,427)
Brooks, Peggy A	5:06:27 (25,905)
Brooks, Sarah R	4:55:34 (24,114)
Brooks, Vicki J	5:13:11 (26,793)
Broom, Linda J	3:54:56 (9,763)
Broomfield, Debby M	5:19:00 (27,464)
Brosch, Emma F	3:47:13 (7,807)

Brosnan, Julie M	3:58:42 (10,919)
Brothwell, Anne	4:46:44 (22,397)
Brough, Kirsty J	5:17:10 (27,269)
Broughton, Andrea C	4:21:04 (16,293)
Broughton, Melissa H	5:55:10 (30,210)
Brown, Aileen S	3:05:58 (1,609)
Brown, Amanda J	6:39:18 (31,352)
Brown, Angela	5:00:41 (25,092)
Brown, Ann E	4:33:42 (19,507)
Brown, Anne M	5:32:51 (28,798)
Brown, April S	5:20:23 (27,618)
Brown, Carol A	5:06:34 (25,920)
Brown, Catherine	4:43:22 (21,658)
Brown, Charlotte L	4:39:10 (20,764)
Brown, Esther J	5:17:21 (27,288)
Brown, Fiona M	3:59:03 (11,016)
Brown, Hayley L	4:50:35 (23,193)
Brown, Helen E	4:23:26 (16,929)
Brown, Jacqueline H	6:10:41 (30,748)
Brown, Johanna E	4:05:53 (12,634)
Brown, Julie	4:00:00 (11,296)
Brown, Julie	4:32:23 (19,213)
Brown, Karen M	4:30:57 (18,846)
Brown, Kerry	4:37:28 (20,333)
Brown, Lindsey	5:29:07 (28,495)
Brown, Madalaine S	3:52:15 (9,072)
Brown, Monica	6:16:32 (30,921)
Brown, Nicola L	7:26:36 (31,821)
Brown, Patricia	4:30:49 (18,818)
Brown, Rhona M	4:25:49 (17,521)
Brown, Sally P	5:43:37 (29,601)
Brown, Samantha	4:55:36 (24,118)
Brown, Sheila	5:00:22 (25,047)
Brown, Valerie	4:18:24 (15,632)
Brown, Yvonne J	4:58:10 (24,633)
Browne, Deborah J	5:06:59 (25,966)
Browne, Gabrielle	3:47:31 (7,883)
Browne, Helena	7:21:39 (31,797)
Browne, Marion	5:09:58 (26,374)
Browne, Susan M	4:13:20 (14,414)
Brownhill, Anne	4:29:31 (14,553)
Browning, Angela	7:50:41 (31,916)
Browning, Elisabeth	6:04:21 (30,575)
Brownlie, Julie A	4:19:26 (15,894)
Brozicevic, Sonja	4:44:04 (21,810)
Bruce, Claire L	4:22:38 (16,733)
Bruce, Erika L	4:36:54 (20,227)
Bruce, Susan A	2:57:15 (898)
Bruhl, Sabine	4:39:17 (20,788)
Bruland, Susan E	6:35:53 (31,304)
Brumby, Tandy J	5:02:17 (25,336)
Brunton, Helen	4:28:36 (18,256)
Brunton, Suzanna Y	3:26:46 (3,980)
Brusheim, Margareta B	3:54:56 (9,763)
Brussels, Linzi M	4:11:01 (13,875)
Bryan, Delyth W	4:08:49 (13,329)
Bryan, Lorraine	5:21:35 (27,736)
Bryan, Nicola A	3:21:46 (3,285)
Bryan, Sheila	6:32:29 (31,254)
Bryant, Beverley J	4:17:19 (15,374)
Bryant, Carol	4:50:31 (23,183)
Bryant, Ceri E	5:46:30 (29,788)
Bryant, Jennifer A	4:08:20 (13,186)
Bryant, Joanna	3:55:41 (9,982)
Bryant, Julie C	5:20:21 (27,614)
Bryant, Katherine E	3:59:15 (11,070)
Bryant, Lynn D	4:59:09 (24,822)
Bryant, Sian E	4:52:26 (23,525)
Bryant, Sophie E	5:08:18 (26,161)
Buce, Sarah J	4:48:02 (22,678)
Buchan, Isabel L	4:21:35 (16,409)
Buchanan, Arabella P	4:55:51 (24,162)
Bucher, Annabel J	4:16:32 (15,179)
Buchholz, Molly E	3:41:03 (6,483)
Buck, Grete	4:34:54 (19,802)
Buck, Jane F	3:50:13 (8,552)
Buck, Susan K	5:42:09 (29,492)
Buckby, Lucy E	4:39:13 (20,779)
Buckland, Carol	3:54:34 (9,655)
Buckland, Caroline J	6:23:10 (31,084)
Buckle, Julie	5:50:56 (30,010)
Buckle, Pauline	5:20:36 (27,645)
Buckledee, Christine A	6:14:27 (30,860)

Buckley, Diane	4:10:33 (13,770)
Buckley, Joan	4:55:11 (24,034)
Buckley, Lena	5:58:24 (30,340)
Buckley, Myra C	4:19:46 (15,969)
Buckley, Nikola J	3:25:04 (3,703)
Buckley, Sally E	6:02:22 (30,499)
Budd, Katy L	4:48:39 (22,803)
Budd, Vivien K	5:11:28 (26,574)
Budenberg, Anne E	3:42:33 (6,754)
Budgen, Sarah L	5:45:04 (29,695)
Buffini, Lauren	4:00:08 (11,323)
Bugler, Sarah M	5:48:39 (29,891)
Buick, Catriona J	3:48:08 (8,034)
Buist, Alexandra E	5:28:31 (28,439)
Buitendag, Emma L	4:43:05 (21,578)
Bull, Elizabeth K	4:24:04 (17,076)
Bull, Mary T	3:55:00 (9,782)
Bull, Michelle B	4:18:51 (15,751)
Bull, Natasha W	4:37:01 (20,254)
Bullen, Helen L	5:20:07 (27,583)
Buller, Sarah K	4:50:06 (23,091)
Bullivant, Ina	4:30:20 (18,711)
Bullock, Jane L	5:21:18 (27,708)
Bullock, Jenny M	5:04:39 (25,645)
Bullock, Pamela A	4:46:20 (22,323)
Bullock, Rachel	4:41:50 (21,315)
Bulow, Kathryn J	3:36:27 (5,688)
Bunce, Denise	5:32:08 (28,743)
Bundy, Sabrina A	7:26:18 (31,819)
Bunt, Deb	4:30:57 (18,846)
Bunten, Susan	3:38:02 (5,968)
Bunting, Paula J	5:24:19 (28,005)
Burch, Stella M	4:13:37 (14,484)
Burchett, Judith S	4:14:22 (14,641)
Burchfield, Joanne	4:06:30 (12,778)
Burgess, Alison R	4:57:14 (24,447)
Burgess, Helen	4:14:00 (14,561)
Burgess, Kathryn E	4:22:32 (16,709)
Burgess, Maxine M	3:53:15 (9,324)
Burgess, Zoe J	4:07:54 (13,090)
Burghardt, Iris	4:33:04 (19,372)
Burke, Alison E	4:41:20 (21,201)
Burke, Birgit	4:09:09 (13,408)
Burke, Catherine E	4:36:40 (20,172)
Burke, Deborah E	4:38:43 (20,648)
Burke, Frances B	4:16:59 (15,301)
Burke, Jacqui	4:28:52 (18,317)
Burke, Janet	5:24:57 (28,076)
Burke, Mary R	6:17:22 (30,936)
Burke, Morag	4:45:15 (22,088)
Burke, Polly A	4:32:02 (19,119)
Burke, Samantha J	7:00:14 (31,630)
Burley, Caroline L	4:35:56 (20,009)
Burlingham, Maxine J	5:44:52 (29,685)
Burn, Tina H	5:17:59 (27,364)
Burnard, Marcia A	5:34:14 (28,905)
Burnell, Linda R	5:52:35 (30,104)
Burnell, Sally	5:05:49 (25,808)
Burness Todd, Lindsey H	5:19:53 (27,546)
Burnett, Anita	4:21:29 (16,385)
Burnett, Lucy M	3:38:32 (6,051)
Burnett, Sally A	6:00:59 (30,447)
Burnett-Wells, Claire E	4:13:20 (14,414)
Burns, Claire E	4:31:59 (19,111)
Burns, Pamela J	5:50:57 (30,013)
Burns, Tamsin T	5:26:31 (28,250)
Burrell, Alexandra N	4:46:28 (22,352)
Burridge, Deborah J	3:11:27 (2,140)
Burrow, Rachel	4:22:21 (16,654)
Burrows, Allison J	5:22:21 (27,812)
Burston, Helen J	3:59:58 (11,284)
Burton, Christine J	4:19:33 (15,921)
Burton, Claire A	3:49:20 (8,336)
Burton, Linda M	6:31:12 (31,230)
Burton, Nicky A	6:14:41 (30,871)
Bury, Alison J	5:07:05 (25,979)
Bushell, Kelly V	4:54:38 (23,930)
Bushell, Lucy A	5:09:10 (26,264)
Bushnell, Margaret C	4:33:53 (19,556)
Buslova, Natalia B	4:42:17 (21,408)
Bussell, Fiona A	3:51:17 (8,828)
Bussey, Amanda C	3:36:53 (5,751)
Busst, Clare	4:41:29 (21,243)

Butcher, Ceri E.	5:38:17 (29,210)	
Butcher, Emily J.	4:48:18 (22,739)	
Butcher, Joanne L.	5:02:28 (25,367)	
Butcher, Rebecca J.	7:18:57 (31,776)	
Butcher, Susan E.	5:58:13 (30,334)	
Butler, Bridget S.	3:49:42 (8,424)	
Butler, Fran	4:56:59 (24,400)	
Butler, Gail C.	4:33:24 (19,447)	
Butler, Georgina T.	5:12:19 (26,673)	
Butler, Helen J.	3:45:47 (7,480)	
Butler, Jane E.	5:09:19 (26,280)	
Butler, Jane	4:10:32 (13,762)	
Butler, Lotte E.	4:06:13 (12,716)	
Butler, Nicole	5:11:30 (26,577)	
Butler, Sandra J.	5:14:28 (26,956)	
Butler, Sharlene	4:10:32 (13,762)	
Butler, Vanessa L.	3:43:32 (6,965)	
Butt, Laura H.	4:02:15 (11,796)	
Butterfield, Caroline A.	6:49:10 (31,487)	
Butterfield, Katharine L.	3:35:24 (5,502)	
Butterill, Carol	4:14:07 (14,590)	
Butters, Shelley	4:12:52 (14,292)	
Butterworth, Elizabeth M.	4:56:28 (24,298)	
Buttle, Deborah A.	4:36:34 (20,147)	
Buxton, Jane L.	4:00:59 (11,504)	
Buxton, Meriel L.	4:17:48 (15,507)	
Bye, Amanda J.	5:49:38 (29,937)	
Byram, Ellie	5:28:16 (28,416)	
Byrne, Linda	7:10:01 (31,709)	
Byrne, Louise	4:31:29 (18,969)	
Byrom, Jenny M.	4:38:56 (20,702)	
Caccavo, Lisa	4:53:55 (23,780)	
Caddeo, Anna	4:17:23 (15,392)	
Cadger, Katrina	3:58:36 (10,888)	
Cadman, Ket	4:50:25 (23,162)	
Cahn, Julie L.	4:10:22 (13,723)	
Cain, Joanne L.	4:38:38 (20,622)	
Cainelli, Sue	3:47:02 (7,763)	
Cakebread, Sarah L.	4:41:35 (21,260)	
Caldicott, Lucy W.	5:25:09 (28,102)	
Caldwell, Gillian M.	5:57:43 (30,317)	
Caldwell, Julia	6:18:40 (30,980)	
Caldwell, Kathleen	7:59:32 (31,937)	
Caley, Kathy M.	4:25:44 (17,488)	
Callaghan, Lynne E.	3:47:21 (7,844)	
Callaghan, Rosaline F.	5:47:57 (29,865)	
Callan, Doreen	4:19:45 (15,965)	
Callan, Janna R.	5:42:50 (29,535)	
Callan, Julia H.	4:27:56 (18,074)	
Callery, Paula E.	4:09:59 (13,637)	
Callingham, Kathy J.	4:53:02 (23,619)	
Callingham-Lello, Sandra G.	4:23:33 (16,953)	
Calliste, Gillian L.	4:27:31 (17,965)	
Callow, Joanne E.	4:34:11 (19,640)	
Calnan, Ann R.	4:32:04 (19,124)	
Calver, Jennifer C.	3:37:56 (5,951)	
Calverley, Amanda J.	4:03:02 (11,960)	
Calvert, Gail	3:14:28 (2,496)	
Calvin, Zita	4:40:39 (21,054)	
Cameron, Joan	7:03:05 (31,650)	
Cameron, Laura S.	5:59:25 (30,383)	
Cameron, Olivia F.	3:26:52 (3,997)	
Cameron-Mowat, Victoria H.	5:37:15 (29,130)	
Camm, Karen D.	4:19:09 (15,818)	
Camp, Debbie J.	4:50:44 (23,219)	
Campbell, Annette	5:36:56 (29,102)	
Campbell, Celia J.	5:11:11 (26,535)	
Campbell, Claire A.	6:16:07 (30,910)	
Campbell, Georgina J.	4:01:05 (11,526)	
Campbell, Gill	3:44:45 (7,249)	
Campbell, Ilidia N.	3:47:23 (7,848)	
Campbell, Joanne E.	3:43:53 (7,034)	
Campbell, Laura	5:04:17 (25,600)	
Campbell, Lisa J.	4:54:36 (23,923)	
Campbell, Marion E.	6:01:21 (30,459)	
Campbell, Rosie E.	3:52:38 (9,159)	
Campbell, Sheila H.	4:29:33 (18,505)	
Campbell, Sony E.	4:36:44 (20,188)	
Campbell-Wood, Jan S.	5:20:43 (27,658)	
Campion, Caroline	6:44:08 (31,419)	
Campofiore, Gial G.	5:26:50 (28,282)	
Candy, Rachel H.	4:55:09 (24,026)	
Canham, Rachael A.	5:26:06 (28,205)	
Cann, Claire M.	3:15:33 (2,600)	
Cann, Lee-Anne M.	3:28:47 (4,368)	
Cann, Sarah L.	5:00:17 (25,035)	
Cannan, Heather D.	4:53:09 (23,643)	
Cannell, Linda C.	6:24:50 (31,125)	
Canning, Claire	5:06:34 (25,920)	
Canning, Tali	4:24:46 (17,243)	
Cantlay, Kaye L.	3:54:17 (9,583)	
Cantwell, Sally	5:25:46 (28,171)	
Capel, Jill H.	4:27:33 (17,977)	
Capelo, Gillian	4:34:50 (19,784)	
Capes, Wendy L.	5:40:00 (29,334)	
Capobianco, Pasqualina	7:24:53 (31,810)	
Capoferri, Monica	6:07:23 (30,659)	
Caporaso, Julie	5:18:43 (27,434)	
Car, Minka R.	5:00:28 (25,060)	
Carder, Judith L.	4:52:49 (23,588)	
Carew-Robinson, Katie D.	4:29:00 (18,349)	
Cariss, Helen L.	5:42:53 (29,544)	
Cariss, Sue M.	3:10:04 (2,008)	
Carleton, Meghan A.	3:11:47 (2,167)	
Carlin, Annette K.	3:25:23 (3,745)	
Carlin, Lynne	5:12:10 (26,651)	
Carline, Susan	5:41:16 (29,427)	
Carloss, Anna	5:40:00 (29,334)	
Carlson, Sheila A.	5:54:59 (30,196)	
Carlton, Rebecca	4:55:11 (24,034)	
Carmichael, Barbara J.	5:44:02 (29,626)	
Carmichael, Linda J.	4:40:28 (21,021)	
Carmona, Francisca	4:18:24 (15,632)	
Carnaghan, Jane	5:44:32 (29,658)	
Carnall, Karen G.	5:04:09 (25,591)	
Carnicelli, Eileen M.	5:21:37 (27,742)	
Carpenter, Lisa	4:49:07 (22,898)	
Carr, Barbara A.	4:39:10 (20,764)	
Carr, Michelle L.	3:52:19 (9,091)	
Carroll, Anne-Marie	5:14:40 (26,988)	
Carse, Dawn C.	3:56:06 (10,111)	
Carter, Angela	6:30:05 (31,207)	
Carter, Anne M.	4:56:11 (24,242)	
Carter, Carol A.	3:59:42 (11,222)	
Carter, Diane R.	4:55:12 (24,037)	
Carter, Fiona	4:31:48 (19,050)	
Carter, Gill	4:10:16 (13,693)	
Carter, Gillian	5:34:24 (28,917)	
Carter, Helen S.	5:01:54 (25,287)	
Carter, Jackie	4:30:38 (18,788)	
Carter, Naomi S.	4:57:26 (24,485)	
Carter, Nicola	4:00:19 (11,363)	
Carter, Rebecca J.	4:45:33 (22,148)	
Carter, Ruth P.	4:28:22 (18,181)	
Carter, Sarah E.	5:55:08 (30,208)	
Carter, Siobhan A.	4:54:46 (23,954)	
Carter, Trish	5:55:02 (30,200)	
Cartmell, Caroline M.	4:03:37 (12,105)	
Cartmell, Terri M.	4:04:46 (12,370)	
Carver, Alison J.	4:26:05 (17,600)	
Carver, Helen L.	4:53:42 (23,749)	
Carver, Marie L.	6:14:25 (30,859)	
Carwardine, Amy J.	4:55:55 (24,186)	
Cary, Catherine J.	4:24:49 (17,255)	
Casal, Eva	6:18:34 (30,974)	
Case, Carolyn J.	5:19:48 (27,532)	
Casey, Angela M.	7:04:43 (31,667)	
Casey, Sarah L.	3:46:56 (7,730)	
Cason, Julie	4:28:38 (18,267)	
Casserly, Francesca L.	5:44:13 (29,638)	
Cassidy, Donna L.	7:24:30 (31,808)	
Cassie, Sarah J.	4:13:31 (14,456)	
Cassin-Hunt, Jodie C.	4:25:55 (17,545)	
Casson, Michelle M.	6:01:06 (30,454)	
Castle, Emily J.	6:06:40 (30,636)	
Castle, Emma M.	3:13:46 (2,404)	
Castle, Rosemary A.	4:51:01 (23,274)	
Castleton, Joanne E.	4:59:38 (24,925)	
Cater, Sharon D.	5:11:43 (26,592)	
Cathrea, Shelley D.	4:48:16 (22,731)	
Catley, Hannah L.	4:06:48 (12,836)	
Cattell, Kate E.	3:53:35 (9,398)	
Catterson, Christine A.	4:04:31 (12,318)	
Catterwell, Nadia V.	3:54:56 (9,763)	
Catton, Gurwant K.	6:23:55 (31,105)	
Catton, Michelle T.	5:16:10 (27,151)	
Caulfield, Susan M.	4:21:53 (16,499)	
Causer, Linda S.	5:16:54 (27,246)	
Cave, Hazel J.	6:55:08 (31,561)	
Caven, Alexandra J.	3:30:43 (4,729)	
Caveney, Sandra M.	4:27:07 (17,871)	
Cawte, Pamela J.	7:12:20 (31,725)	
Cawthorne, Helen	2:58:37 (1,031)	
Cefferty, Margaret R.	5:32:51 (28,798)	
Celenza, Elaine M.	6:00:48 (30,440)	
Cerutti, Christina	5:39:17 (29,287)	
Chadwick, Claire E.	4:04:05 (12,208)	
Chadwick, Jemma A.	4:49:14 (22,924)	
Chadwick, Rebecca J.	4:38:21 (20,558)	
Chaffe, Caroline A.	7:30:27 (31,849)	
Chalkley, Sara	5:55:22 (30,217)	
Challis, Maria I.	4:03:19 (12,036)	
Challis, Vicki J.	6:45:39 (31,449)	
Chalmers, Katie	5:34:15 (28,908)	
Chamberlain, Claire L.	4:55:21 (24,073)	
Chamberlain, Diane L.	5:13:03 (26,771)	
Chamberlain, Laura M.	4:26:12 (17,631)	
Chambers, Jean	4:31:36 (18,999)	
Chambers, Lorraine	4:27:01 (17,846)	
Champion, Julie E.	6:12:21 (30,788)	
Champion, Karly A.	3:56:33 (10,266)	
Champion, Rachel J.	4:16:03 (15,059)	
Chan, Harriet	4:26:19 (17,658)	
Chan, San Mei	4:48:05 (22,694)	
Chandler, Helen D.	5:32:22 (28,764)	
Chandler, Trudi	6:45:55 (31,451)	
Chang, Ailsa W.	3:40:29 (6,396)	
Chaple, Lucy M.	4:32:08 (19,146)	
Chapman, Alison C.	4:46:21 (22,326)	
Chapman, Alison J.	5:11:05 (26,514)	
Chapman, Catherine M.	4:28:09 (18,139)	
Chapman, Clare	4:09:15 (13,438)	
Chapman, Clare H.	6:38:27 (31,344)	
Chapman, Corinne W.	4:41:20 (21,201)	
Chapman, Cynthia M.	4:10:05 (13,653)	
Chapman, Helen J.	4:01:48 (11,668)	
Chapman, Kathryn L.	4:37:03 (20,261)	
Chapman, Lesley	3:27:52 (4,203)	
Chapman, Nicola A.	5:18:56 (27,457)	
Chapman, Pamela K.	4:13:18 (14,403)	
Chapman, Sally A.	3:49:34 (8,396)	
Chapman, Stephanie	5:59:39 (30,397)	
Chapman, Tracey A.	4:27:54 (18,065)	
Chapple, Alice G.	3:45:40 (7,446)	
Charles, Patricia	4:40:40 (21,059)	
Charlesworth, Marian J.	6:13:01 (30,818)	
Charlesworth, Susan M.	4:03:05 (11,975)	
Charlett, Pauline A.	5:17:49 (27,339)	
Charlton, Emma D.	4:50:16 (23,115)	
Charman, Alison M.	6:16:57 (30,932)	
Charnock, Miranda	5:50:25 (29,989)	
Chater, Ann Marie	4:14:03 (14,577)	
Chatoo, Ayn	5:44:38 (29,668)	
Chattington, Charlene T.	5:05:56 (25,834)	
Chauhan, Jyoti	5:12:39 (26,706)	
Chaves, Loren H.	4:45:41 (22,186)	
Chawner, Kay S.	4:12:42 (14,263)	
Cheal, Linda E.	5:13:44 (26,858)	
Cheal, Suzanne A.	4:52:47 (23,581)	
Cheatle, Kathleen M.	6:02:16 (30,493)	
Cheese, Fiona C.	4:56:15 (24,252)	
Cheetham, Lesley	4:16:09 (15,093)	
Cheetham, Sophie C.	4:55:21 (24,073)	
Chenhall, Joanne M.	5:05:47 (25,797)	
Chepchumba, Joyce	2:28:01 (67)	
Cherrier, Helene	3:15:57 (2,643)	
Cherry, Anne J.	4:15:32 (14,936)	
Cherry, Cynthia L.	5:54:29 (30,169)	
Cherry, Elaine	4:45:03 (22,045)	
Cheshire, Sarah	4:43:51 (21,761)	
Chester-Walsh, Vikki D.	6:25:58 (31,143)	
Chestnutt, Sarah	3:42:07 (6,670)	
Chesworth, Janice	4:45:27 (22,129)	
Chesworth, Katie	4:38:56 (20,702)	
Chetwynd, Helen J.	5:51:40 (30,044)	
Cheung, Lynn S.	5:31:05 (28,665)	
Cheung, Vanessa	4:43:24 (21,662)	
Chew, Ai-Lean	5:37:08 (29,116)	
Chibout, Myriam	4:05:49 (12,620)	
Chidaushe, Dorothy	4:41:33 (21,254)	

Child, Anne E 4:14:43 (14,732)
Child, Charlotte E 5:39:35 (29,309)
Child, Jillian D 3:55:04 (9,811)
Child, Michelle C 4:56:02 (24,217)
Childerhouse, Anna C 4:04:10 (12,234)
Chipkin, Laura 3:23:20 (3,481)
Chipperfield, Christine E 5:05:03 (25,697)
Chisholm, Clare 4:28:53 (18,325)
Chisholm, Gina 5:32:30 (28,774)
Chissim, Clare T 4:32:12 (19,165)
Chiswick, Samantha J 3:59:47 (11,236)
Chittenden, Thea 6:04:39 (30,584)
Chopra, Sunita 4:37:48 (20,406)
Chorley, Fiona C 5:33:22 (28,839)
Chote, Andrea M 4:33:45 (19,517)
Christensen, Karen 5:58:42 (30,358)
Christensen-Barton, Alfreda 6:36:25 (31,314)
Christie, Erica M 3:13:18 (2,343)
Christie, Megan R 5:24:21 (28,008)
Christie, Nathalie 3:16:21 (2,679)
Christie, Tina D 3:56:16 (10,171)
Christophers, Irene 3:56:13 (10,148)
Christophorou, Penelope J 4:18:59 (15,775)
Chu, Patricia 7:19:35 (31,787)
Chua, Cheng T 3:58:14 (10,766)
Chubb, Jacqueline R 4:23:49 (17,017)
Chupkina, Valentina F 5:18:26 (27,405)
Church, Moya A 4:19:58 (16,022)
Churchill, Danielle 5:27:42 (28,371)
Cicmanec, Jan 4:05:25 (12,515)
Cicone, Lou 6:09:25 (30,712)
Ciuffardi, Nina R 4:37:52 (20,422)
Claessens, Martine M 5:15:22 (27,062)
Clague, Jennie T 6:57:14 (31,586)
Clague, Louise 4:33:44 (19,511)
Clamp, Joanne 3:27:37 (4,150)
Clampett, Linda S 3:55:53 (10,045)
Clapham, Penelope E 4:32:10 (19,158)
Clare, June T 4:43:50 (21,753)
Clare, Sam J 5:53:28 (30,134)
Claridge, Althea 5:56:01 (30,248)
Clark, Elspeth S 4:52:52 (23,593)
Clark, Janet 5:59:31 (30,392)
Clark, Jean E 4:43:44 (21,732)
Clark, Joanne K 4:24:11 (17,117)
Clark, Justine L 4:38:15 (20,533)
Clark, Karina A 5:26:18 (28,224)
Clark, Lisa A 7:19:04 (31,779)
Clark, Megan F 2:52:24 (608)
Clark, Sandra 4:08:03 (13,124)
Clark, Sarah K 3:58:09 (10,729)
Clark, Susanna V 5:04:35 (25,636)
Clark, Teresa A 3:42:32 (6,751)
Clarke, Alison J 5:09:53 (26,366)
Clarke, Annette J 3:32:41 (5,041)
Clarke, Caroline 5:16:35 (27,207)
Clarke, Charmaine S 4:48:00 (22,672)
Clarke, Geraldine 4:55:12 (24,037)
Clarke, Irene M 6:55:14 (31,562)
Clarke, Jackie 4:53:00 (23,617)
Clarke, Joanne E 5:20:50 (27,666)
Clarke, Karen 4:02:08 (11,757)
Clarke, Katie E 4:46:57 (22,436)
Clarke, Leslie C 4:39:20 (20,799)
Clarke, Louise M 4:27:41 (18,013)
Clarke, Una 6:49:59 (31,498)
Clarke, Victoria 3:08:03 (1,808)
Clarke-Noble, Désirée A 3:50:34 (8,645)
Clarkson, Eva Maria 4:38:15 (20,533)
Clarkson, Helen L 7:27:35 (31,829)
Clarkson, Linda P 3:00:43 (1,209)
Clawson, Julie 4:08:18 (13,177)
Clayton, Brenda E 4:45:26 (22,125)
Clayton, Kellimarie 8:02:34 (31,945)
Cleatherd, Louise M 3:49:38 (8,410)
Cleathero, Claire 3:07:06 (1,714)
Clegg, Jane E 4:01:41 (11,647)
Cleland, Georgia L 3:59:52 (11,258)
Clelland, Eleanor J 4:59:14 (24,834)
Clemens, Linda A 3:31:59 (4,922)
Clement, Deedee 4:46:37 (22,376)
Clement, Janice 4:16:28 (15,166)
Clements, Mary E 4:23:11 (16,869)
Clements, Rosemary A 6:49:33 (31,493)
Clements, Susan M 3:57:51 (10,632)
Clements, Vicky 4:26:20 (17,663)
Clemo, Sarah E 3:28:38 (4,340)
Cleverly, Elizabeth H 5:36:35 (29,067)
Clifford, Lizzie 3:33:52 (5,251)
Clift, Marianne N 4:27:40 (18,010)
Clinch, Georgina 4:10:26 (13,740)
Clinton, Jane 4:05:16 (12,475)
Clipsham, Patricia 6:37:32 (31,334)
Clode, Emma L 4:44:03 (21,805)
Close, Joanna A 4:28:48 (18,298)
Close, Julia H 3:14:25 (2,490)
Clothier, Esther T 4:37:52 (20,422)
Clouder, Samantha P 4:49:42 (23,014)
Clouston, Jennifer M 4:04:07 (12,214)
Clowes, Sophie 3:48:04 (8,015)
Clubb, Barbara F 5:16:30 (27,187)
Clutterbuck, Julia A 4:02:53 (11,936)
Clutton, Diana L 4:44:59 (22,029)
Coates, Catherine L 4:01:34 (11,613)
Coates, Paula 5:33:23 (28,841)
Coatsworth, Emma 3:52:39 (9,162)
Cobby, Janet A 4:30:09 (18,666)
Cobby, Jennifer M 5:42:19 (29,503)
Cochran, Teri Jo 5:52:49 (30,118)
Cochrane, Angela L 4:44:47 (21,974)
Cockcroft, Rachel A 4:27:49 (18,044)
Cocker, Sophie L 4:24:35 (17,203)
Cockman, Philippa J 4:34:55 (19,804)
Cocksedge, Ann 4:47:02 (22,456)
Codogno, Elena 4:51:54 (23,423)
Coetzee, Elizabeth B 4:04:09 (12,228)
Coghill, Samantha J 4:01:02 (11,510)
Cohen, Donna M 6:14:11 (30,852)
Cohen, Ellana 4:23:44 (16,996)
Cohen, Nicola J 4:44:18 (21,858)
Cohen, Rachel J 4:16:33 (15,186)
Cohen, Wendy P 6:44:59 (31,436)
Colclough, Jane E 4:00:54 (11,479)
Cole, Helen E 5:15:24 (27,066)
Cole, Jill E 6:49:32 (31,492)
Cole, Joanne S 4:10:38 (13,789)
Cole, Kathryn 4:31:09 (18,892)
Cole, Rachel A 4:48:36 (22,795)
Cole, Sue 4:13:31 (14,456)
Coleman, Heather 7:32:44 (31,863)
Coleman, Helen M 7:01:44 (31,640)
Coleman, Michelle A 3:43:25 (6,940)
Coleman, Patricia J 4:13:02 (14,337)
Coleman, Sarah 5:03:57 (25,572)
Colenutt, Margaret 5:49:19 (29,923)
Coles, Jane E 3:26:57 (4,008)
Coles, Lynsey A 5:00:22 (25,047)
Colin-Jones, Victoria 4:57:30 (24,494)
Colinswood, Karen H 4:38:02 (20,483)
Coll, Nuala P 7:28:02 (31,832)
Collard-Odle, Tamara L 5:22:26 (27,827)
Collet, Marie M 4:33:26 (19,454)
Colleypriest, Catherine C 5:55:57 (30,241)
Collier, Katie J 5:26:47 (28,277)
Collinge, Maddy 3:32:14 (4,960)
Collings, Glenys 4:23:24 (16,921)
Collins, Angela M 4:53:45 (23,756)
Collins, Claire 5:47:25 (29,833)
Collins, Emma L 4:34:46 (19,770)
Collins, Hilary A 3:51:27 (8,875)
Collins, Jeanette A 4:38:21 (20,558)
Collins, Julia V 5:25:01 (28,085)
Collins, Kate E 4:13:14 (14,390)
Collins, Kim N 4:42:42 (21,493)
Collins, Louise J 4:38:01 (20,475)
Collins, Michelle A 4:00:45 (11,434)
Collins, Sarah L 4:51:24 (23,330)
Collins, Sharon K 4:16:51 (15,268)
Collins, Tina 5:19:17 (27,488)
Collins, Virginia 4:09:45 (13,568)
Collinson, Audrey 5:37:53 (29,171)
Collinson, Caroline 3:49:10 (8,302)
Collison, Linda 4:32:51 (19,322)
Collison, Sarah J 5:14:50 (27,007)
Collonnier, Françoise 4:19:27 (15,903)
Colman, Kathleen V 4:25:16 (17,376)
Colman, Norman 5:02:37 (25,392)
Colman, Rachel L 6:11:46 (30,780)
Colosio, Marinella 4:43:59 (21,791)
Colquhoun, Shirley J 3:28:06 (4,240)
Colville, Rachel A 4:08:59 (13,377)
Colwell, Fiona L 5:57:56 (30,326)
Colwell, Sally 4:13:33 (14,464)
Colyer, Sophie E 4:13:34 (14,471)
Combe, Elisabeth 5:03:08 (25,463)
Comben, Elizabeth A 4:42:41 (21,486)
Combrink, Jane 4:23:14 (16,879)
Comerford, Anna 4:58:47 (24,762)
Compton, Madeline 5:59:00 (30,364)
Compton-Cook, Emma L 5:54:11 (30,157)
Conbe, Marianne 4:32:37 (19,266)
Coney, Debbie C 3:35:29 (5,521)
Coney, Diane J 3:42:04 (6,666)
Conley, Julie 4:45:59 (22,245)
Conneely, Vivienne 2:58:46 (1,056)
Connelly, Helen R 3:44:49 (7,266)
Connolly, Gemma L 4:20:52 (16,250)
Connolly, Kirsty-Ann 5:34:42 (28,939)
Connolly, Leann 4:38:14 (20,530)
Connolly, Sally M 5:44:29 (29,655)
Connolly, Sian M 5:10:16 (26,409)
Connolly, Tessa M 4:53:41 (23,747)
Connor, Janet 4:26:56 (17,821)
Consolver, Kay E 5:14:52 (27,013)
Convert, Raffaelle J 5:03:06 (25,459)
Conway, Claire A 5:02:51 (25,426)
Conway, Claire G 4:12:25 (14,170)
Conway, Dianne K 7:28:42 (31,837)
Conway, Susan A 4:24:23 (17,162)
Cooil, Jan M 4:24:02 (17,068)
Cook, Allison 3:59:18 (11,087)
Cook, Cory F 5:32:37 (28,784)
Cook, Elaine J 4:35:32 (19,936)
Cook, Helen J 6:46:34 (31,463)
Cook, Helen S 3:52:32 (9,136)
Cook, Jennie 7:55:55 (31,927)
Cook, Julia H 4:24:07 (17,097)
Cook, Louise 4:14:05 (14,582)
Cook, Paula F 5:25:11 (28,105)
Cook, Samantha J 3:57:23 (10,512)
Cook, Sandra 4:43:36 (21,701)
Cook, Sara J 4:35:02 (19,828)
Cook, Shirley K 4:56:05 (24,229)
Cook, Susan M 4:42:56 (21,553)
Cook, Vanessa 4:41:41 (21,276)
Cooke, Camille F 3:57:20 (10,492)
Cooke, Michelle V 4:10:47 (13,824)
Cooke-Simmons, Julia K 3:40:28 (6,393)
Coombe, Susan R 5:59:40 (30,398)
Coombs, Megan 5:41:12 (29,424)
Coombs, Sarah-Jane 5:51:32 (30,038)
Coonan, Donna L 5:33:31 (28,852)
Cooney, Maire K 4:03:40 (12,120)
Cooney, Siobhan M 4:31:12 (18,897)
Coop, Andrea T 4:37:53 (20,429)
Coope, Margaret 4:48:47 (22,832)
Cooper, Anne M 5:13:01 (26,765)
Cooper, Clare D 4:49:06 (22,895)
Cooper, Fiona K 5:27:13 (28,326)
Cooper, Jane E 5:50:45 (30,002)
Cooper, Katherine J 5:24:46 (28,051)
Cooper, Louise J 2:54:58 (752)
Cooper, Lynne S 4:03:29 (12,075)
Cooper, Patience A 4:07:01 (12,896)
Cooper, Sarah E 5:08:39 (26,197)
Cooper, Valerie J 4:46:09 (22,279)
Cooper, Verena J 4:52:27 (23,527)
Cooper, Wendy A 5:05:28 (25,751)
Cooper-Clark, Rosemary E 4:19:50 (15,983)
Coote, Tracey L 5:45:20 (29,715)
Coppens, An 5:44:51 (29,683)
Copus, Suzanne M 4:03:42 (12,125)
Corbett, Nicola J 3:51:42 (8,940)
Corbey, Eleonora B 4:53:27 (23,694)
Corbishley, Yvonne 4:46:40 (22,386)
Corby, Clare E 4:50:16 (23,115)
Corcoran, Brigid G 3:59:28 (11,140)
Corcoran, Caroline B 6:29:10 (31,189)
Cord, Susan M 3:35:41 (5,552)

Cording, Penny S	4:48:08 (22,703)	
Cordingly, Beth	4:42:13 (21,388)	
Cordon, Anne-Françoise	4:16:47 (15,247)	
Corfield, Samantha J	4:00:10 (11,331)	
Corless, Brigid	4:24:51 (17,268)	
Corley, Nancy J	5:00:40 (25,089)	
Cornelis, Ikkelien	3:54:26 (9,622)	
Cornell, Carol A	4:31:19 (18,924)	
Cornforth, Carolyn J	4:10:17 (13,697)	
Cornish, Aldona	5:04:30 (25,627)	
Cornwell, Catherine E	4:15:32 (14,936)	
Corrall, Karen A	5:43:52 (29,620)	
Correa, Carmen F	4:47:56 (22,661)	
Correia, Dorita M	3:56:45 (10,311)	
Corrie, Jeannette S	3:47:46 (7,940)	
Corrigan, Jennifer L	3:50:03 (8,515)	
Corry, Annette F	6:12:00 (30,784)	
Corten, Clare A	4:39:53 (20,891)	
Cortizo, Kath	4:05:42 (12,595)	
Cosbert, Lavern	5:39:18 (29,290)	
Cosby, Beckie	4:42:02 (21,355)	
Cosh, Nicola	7:14:45 (31,744)	
Costello, Elizabeth J	4:22:00 (16,537)	
Coster, Debbie A	3:50:47 (8,704)	
Costiff, Christine	3:13:14 (2,332)	
Cottam, Jude	5:35:17 (28,978)	
Cotter, Lucy C	4:49:37 (22,999)	
Cottereau, Thérèse	4:24:06 (17,092)	
Cotterell, Sally	3:49:13 (8,312)	
Cotterell, Fiona	4:34:53 (19,800)	
Cottiss, Michele	5:02:52 (25,429)	
Cotton, Lesley C	4:35:22 (19,903)	
Cotton, Nicola J	4:21:36 (16,420)	
Cottrell, Maureen J	5:23:48 (27,953)	
Cottrill, Nicola J	4:50:24 (23,158)	
Couchman, Katherine E	5:44:18 (29,644)	
Coughlan, Gerry F	3:26:37 (3,936)	
Coull, Gemma E	3:51:00 (8,749)	
Coulson, Vicki B	5:09:52 (26,363)	
Coulter, Dawn	4:40:09 (20,951)	
Coulter, Suzie	3:51:14 (8,813)	
Couper, Suzanne E	3:51:41 (8,936)	
Coupland, Tracey	4:31:57 (19,096)	
Courier, Victoria L	4:10:19 (13,708)	
Court, Jilly	4:51:35 (23,358)	
Courtman, Jeanette J	5:30:10 (28,599)	
Courtman, Louise E	3:59:05 (11,024)	
Courtney, Alexandra M	4:03:03 (11,965)	
Courtney, Jenny J	5:05:30 (25,760)	
Cousen, Sharon L	3:56:38 (10,289)	
Cousin, Kate J	4:29:58 (18,624)	
Cousins, Kirstie	4:40:21 (20,996)	
Coventry, Nerys	5:21:02 (27,682)	
Coward, Sophie L	6:01:44 (30,473)	
Coward, Susan M	6:01:45 (30,475)	
Cowell, Eleanor	4:04:07 (12,214)	
Cowie, Alexis M	5:36:39 (29,077)	
Cowley, Laura J	3:09:01 (1,900)	
Cowling, Gert T	3:49:50 (8,457)	
Cox, Amy	5:25:56 (28,189)	
Cox, Camilla M	3:39:23 (6,197)	
Cox, Christine	5:43:30 (29,590)	
Cox, Deborah C	5:52:20 (30,088)	
Cox, Emma L	2:58:23 (1,003)	
Cox, Fawne	6:16:27 (30,919)	
Cox, Jenny	4:12:30 (14,200)	
Cox, Katy	6:44:27 (31,426)	
Cox, Lorraine M	5:33:47 (28,868)	
Cox, Patricia	7:59:34 (31,939)	
Cox, Rachel E	4:16:07 (15,088)	
Cox, Rosalind J	4:17:40 (15,473)	
Cox, Sarah E	5:35:49 (29,018)	
Cox, Sarah V	4:49:31 (22,981)	
Coxon, Victoria	5:50:36 (29,999)	
Coyle, Colette E	4:48:15 (22,727)	
Coyne, Glenis V	4:30:09 (18,666)	
Coyne, Julie	5:58:29 (30,348)	
Crabb, Claire L	4:39:52 (20,886)	
Crabb, Mary	4:22:15 (16,623)	
Cracknell, Louise J	4:04:23 (12,279)	
Craddock, Simone A	3:37:15 (5,822)	
Cradock, Carol A	6:59:56 (31,620)	
Craggs, Marilyn C	4:01:45 (11,659)	

Craggs, Rosalind M	5:19:49 (27,535)	
Craine, Lorraine E	5:43:59 (29,625)	
Crane, Alison K	3:30:35 (4,705)	
Crane, Denise	4:58:26 (24,703)	
Crane, Gemma L	5:43:31 (29,595)	
Crane, Gill	4:53:53 (23,774)	
Crane, Victoria	3:41:34 (6,553)	
Cranmer, Catherine	4:35:55 (20,006)	
Crann, Geraldine	4:19:51 (15,987)	
Craven, Dorothy A	6:57:43 (31,591)	
Craven, Emily E	7:17:44 (31,769)	
Crawford, Abigail L	6:45:01 (31,438)	
Crawford, Emma J	4:11:55 (14,071)	
Crawford, Helene	8:32:26 (31,969)	
Crawford, Mandy	4:49:15 (22,927)	
Crawford, Terry	4:51:41 (23,378)	
Crawley, Linda M	4:43:44 (21,732)	
Craythorn, Janine	3:47:10 (7,797)	
Cream, Tania J	3:48:07 (8,027)	
Creasy, Laurie A	4:47:38 (22,603)	
Creech, Jane K	5:56:38 (30,276)	
Creighton, Elizabeth C	4:45:57 (22,238)	
Cremen, Sandra	4:52:02 (23,453)	
Crew, Eugenia	4:36:05 (20,052)	
Crichton, Wendy A	6:13:28 (30,831)	
Cringle, Hanine M	4:14:33 (14,694)	
Crisp, Rebecca E	3:27:45 (4,179)	
Crisp, Sarah M	4:17:06 (15,327)	
Crocker, Jennifer H	5:46:07 (29,756)	
Crocker, Joanna K	4:45:31 (22,144)	
Crocker, Louise	4:51:26 (23,335)	
Crocker, Rosemarie J	4:16:43 (15,231)	
Crockett, Kim J	4:31:21 (18,935)	
Crocombe, Anne-Marie	4:27:34 (17,982)	
Croft, Elaine D	5:16:49 (27,232)	
Crofts, Amanda J	4:45:44 (22,195)	
Crome, Debra J	4:14:05 (14,582)	
Cronin-Jones, Susan	4:30:31 (18,764)	
Crook, Helen S	4:12:26 (14,179)	
Crook, Jill L	4:21:24 (16,363)	
Crookes, Diane M	4:37:18 (20,315)	
Croome, Lorraine	3:37:09 (5,804)	
Crosby, Laura E	5:02:15 (25,326)	
Cross, Catherine	5:40:33 (29,386)	
Cross, Charlotte L	4:20:36 (16,187)	
Cross, Fiona M	4:13:02 (14,337)	
Cross, Helen C	4:38:30 (20,596)	
Cross, Laura A	5:38:30 (29,230)	
Cross, Nerys P	4:58:33 (24,727)	
Cross, Rebekah S	4:42:47 (21,515)	
Cross, Stefanie	5:17:25 (27,298)	
Cross, Valerie	5:28:57 (28,479)	
Crossfield, Sophie C	4:57:15 (24,450)	
Crossley, Elaine S	3:46:12 (7,578)	
Crossley, Susan A	4:23:17 (16,891)	
Crosswell, Avril J	7:28:01 (31,831)	
Crosswell, Fiona	5:20:07 (27,583)	
Crosswell, Margaret E	4:23:16 (16,885)	
Crotch-Harvey, Ali L	5:21:13 (27,701)	
Crothall, Philippa M	5:14:11 (26,919)	
Crouch, Fiona E	4:44:53 (21,995)	
Crowe, Margaret E	4:03:58 (12,184)	
Crowe, Melanie	5:00:10 (25,018)	
Crowhurst, Maureen	6:00:37 (30,431)	
Crowhurst, Paula L	5:00:56 (25,132)	
Crowle, Revis	2:58:49 (1,058)	
Crowley, Maria E	3:41:02 (6,480)	
Crowley, Sharon	4:20:53 (16,256)	
Croxford, Tracie	3:18:32 (2,902)	
Cruickshank, Katrina	4:09:20 (13,460)	
Cruickshank, Wendy M	3:32:45 (5,055)	
Crump, Malika	5:39:42 (29,315)	
Cruse, Julie	3:29:49 (4,558)	
Cryan, Karen T	5:31:14 (28,680)	
Cualfield, Vanda	3:53:45 (9,427)	
Cudahy, Karen M	4:50:47 (23,233)	
Cudok, Charlotte M	4:55:49 (24,157)	
Cudworth, Jennifer J	6:20:07 (31,015)	
Culbert, Amy L	4:42:28 (21,444)	
Culican, Nichola J	3:33:12 (5,136)	
Culin-Moir, Linda	4:04:53 (12,402)	
Cullen, Alison C	4:08:55 (13,355)	
Cullen, Ginny A	5:23:03 (27,874)	

Cullen, Jennie	4:27:38 (18,000)	
Cullen, Judith	7:16:20 (31,761)	
Cullen, Stephanie J	4:38:17 (20,544)	
Cullimore, Jeanette A	5:15:45 (27,100)	
Cullum, Gail P	3:59:06 (11,030)	
Cully, Christine H	3:49:58 (8,497)	
Cuming, Amanda J	4:16:24 (15,148)	
Cumming, Jade B	4:17:33 (15,439)	
Cumming, Susan	5:46:33 (29,794)	
Cummings, Emma L	4:27:25 (17,941)	
Cummins, Fiona S	3:24:57 (3,684)	
Cummins, Hannah M	5:38:27 (29,226)	
Cunliffe, Elizabeth S	5:11:42 (26,588)	
Cunningham, Carol A	4:32:27 (19,229)	
Cunningham, Helen M	4:57:56 (24,576)	
Cunningham, Pamela M	4:19:49 (15,981)	
Cunningham, Veronica A	5:05:56 (25,834)	
Curd, Anglea M	4:03:42 (12,125)	
Curl, Carmel A	4:27:52 (18,059)	
Curran, Fiona	5:33:05 (28,814)	
Curran, Jane S	4:28:26 (18,206)	
Curran, Pauline S	5:54:51 (30,191)	
Currie, Alexandra V	4:53:22 (23,681)	
Currie, Francine	5:44:24 (29,650)	
Currie, Gail E	4:51:22 (23,328)	
Currimjee, Nadine	4:31:30 (18,982)	
Curry, Allison J	4:22:11 (16,598)	
Curtin, Helen M	3:39:47 (6,271)	
Curtin, Shelley	5:17:08 (27,266)	
Curtis, Caroline P	3:47:40 (7,920)	
Curtis, Eleanor F	4:24:36 (17,205)	
Curtis, Lois A	3:32:34 (5,019)	
Curtis, Madeleine A	5:39:15 (29,286)	
Curtis, Tina S	5:35:07 (28,966)	
Custard, Emily	5:13:00 (26,762)	
Custis, Kate E	3:36:38 (5,717)	
Cuthell, Emma E	4:53:06 (23,635)	
Cutler, Sarah	3:49:10 (8,302)	
Cutmore, Michaela J	4:33:35 (19,482)	
Cutter, Jacqueline A	4:48:35 (22,790)	
Cutting, Helen E	5:56:15 (30,261)	
Czaplinski Treadwell, Anne	3:51:37 (8,922)	
Czyron, Vera	5:03:18 (25,491)	
Dagley, Jeanette	4:44:50 (21,983)	
Dagne, Birhan	2:34:45 (121)	
Dakers, Caroline	4:49:27 (22,969)	
Dale, Alison V	5:19:52 (27,544)	
Dale, Andrea P	5:34:52 (28,948)	
Dale, Chrissie	3:46:09 (7,559)	
Dale, Nicola I	4:10:32 (13,762)	
Dale, Sue I	3:47:58 (7,988)	
Daley, Alyssa M	4:16:53 (15,279)	
Daley, Susan	7:17:56 (31,770)	
Dalingwater, Jeanette M	3:35:23 (5,499)	
Daly, Jacqueline	5:27:37 (28,363)	
Daly, Ruby M	5:04:37 (25,641)	
Daly, Vanessa	5:33:14 (28,825)	
Dalzell, Julie	3:42:00 (6,646)	
Dalziel, Anne C	4:57:20 (24,464)	
Damato, Frankanne	4:27:55 (18,067)	
Damen, Janet M	4:04:18 (12,263)	
Dana, Emily	4:19:02 (15,782)	
Dance, Helen	4:42:36 (21,472)	
Dancy, Georgina N	5:06:54 (25,961)	
Dane, Nicole	4:48:05 (22,694)	
Dangelo, Erica J	4:36:51 (20,217)	
Daniel, Dusanka	5:02:30 (25,374)	
Daniels, Caireen M	4:10:21 (13,716)	
Daniels, Naomi	4:50:21 (23,138)	
Dann, Lisa A	6:12:56 (30,815)	
Danning, Sarah C	4:16:30 (15,174)	
Danvers, Natalie S	4:42:52 (21,535)	
Darby, Jenny L	5:05:34 (25,774)	
Dardel, Estela	3:43:50 (7,021)	
Darke, Tracy A	3:11:44 (2,160)	
Darroch, Liza Q	4:28:01 (18,102)	
Darsley, Anne L	4:28:07 (18,126)	
Dart, Charity	3:49:59 (8,501)	
Dattani, Cara M	5:39:07 (29,277)	
Daughters, Neslee R	3:50:06 (8,528)	
Davenport, Elaine M	5:57:05 (30,290)	
Davenport, Nicola A	5:47:55 (29,861)	
Davey, Elizabeth	4:43:52 (21,766)	

Davey, Helen F..............4:01:09 (11,538)
Davey, Jean..................3:47:52 (7,963)
Davey, Madeleine 4:41:22 (21,210)
David, Anna.................3:30:51 (4,751)
David, Karen E..............4:40:50 (21,095)
Davidson, Ann...............4:21:27 (16,376)
Davidson, Carolyn J.........4:34:03 (19,606)
Davidson, Cressida A........5:08:44 (26,207)
Davidson, Lisa..............5:59:25 (30,383)
Davidson, Sarah J...........5:30:37 (28,631)
Davidson, Sharon G..........5:23:53 (27,960)
Davidson, Violet............4:36:40 (20,172)
Davies, Annie M.............5:07:40 (26,071)
Davies, Caroline L..........5:05:05 (25,700)
Davies, Claire J............4:52:34 (23,545)
Davies, Debra M.............4:54:15 (23,844)
Davies, Donna E.............7:10:20 (31,712)
Davies, Elizabeth...........6:05:10 (30,596)
Davies, Emma................4:20:34 (16,177)
Davies, Emma Jane...........4:39:35 (20,839)
Davies, Erica...............5:08:58 (26,231)
Davies, Hazel M.............3:58:39 (10,909)
Davies, Helen A.............3:55:34 (9,954)
Davies, Jan.................4:28:52 (18,317)
Davies, Jan W...............4:13:08 (14,362)
Davies, Jean................4:16:26 (15,157)
Davies, Joanne..............4:31:58 (19,104)
Davies, Julie A.............5:21:43 (27,751)
Davies, Linda...............4:40:08 (20,947)
Davies, Lisa J..............4:29:55 (18,614)
Davies, Lisa M..............6:04:01 (30,565)
Davies, Liz.................5:35:24 (28,995)
Davies, Lorraine H..........4:37:23 (20,326)
Davies, Lyn A...............4:36:12 (20,072)
Davies, Marina L............3:55:15 (9,863)
Davies, Nia.................4:32:39 (19,276)
Davies, Olivia E............4:43:41 (21,718)
Davies, Pam.................3:35:26 (5,510)
Davies, Rachel..............4:25:59 (17,565)
Davies, Rebecca J...........4:04:54 (12,409)
Davies, Rita................4:25:21 (17,392)
Davies, Rowena L............4:45:32 (22,146)
Davies, Ruth................5:42:42 (29,527)
Davies, Ruth A..............4:47:32 (22,574)
Davies, Samantha J..........5:06:13 (25,876)
Davies, Sandra C............5:06:13 (25,876)
Davies, Sara J..............3:45:12 (7,348)
Davies, Sarah...............6:00:19 (30,425)
Davies, Shan F..............5:07:54 (26,100)
Davies, Susan J.............5:51:43 (30,046)
Davies, Suzannah J..........4:20:12 (16,064)
Davies, Suzanne.............3:47:08 (7,790)
Davies, Tina A..............4:35:42 (19,961)
Davies, Yvonne M............3:37:24 (5,860)
Davis, Beth.................3:38:05 (5,973)
Davis, Brenda...............5:26:01 (28,199)
Davis, Carly................4:47:19 (22,523)
Davis, Caroline E...........4:08:07 (13,135)
Davis, Charlotte A..........4:18:37 (15,691)
Davis, Clare L..............4:41:14 (21,163)
Davis, Esther...............4:48:24 (22,759)
Davis, Hannah...............4:56:55 (24,387)
Davis, Hazel C..............4:06:07 (12,693)
Davis, Janet................4:03:03 (11,965)
Davis, Karen P..............4:13:51 (14,532)
Davis, Kate.................5:29:36 (28,545)
Davis, Katherine A..........3:17:53 (2,838)
Davis, Katherine A..........5:06:04 (25,852)
Davis, Katrina A............3:57:50 (10,627)
Davis, Kelly................5:34:36 (28,927)
Davis, Laura J..............3:54:33 (9,651)
Davis, Melisaa J............5:06:31 (25,912)
Davis, Samantha M...........4:31:41 (19,022)
Davis, Tara M...............6:34:23 (31,279)
Davis, Tina.................4:27:23 (17,934)
Davis, Vikki J..............4:38:21 (20,558)
Davison, Victoria C.........6:33:16 (31,269)
Davy, Rosemary J............4:57:39 (24,521)
Dawber, Emma E..............3:59:39 (11,206)
Dawe, Barbara A.............5:17:33 (27,314)
Dawes, Lucy.................4:09:54 (13,607)
Dawkins, Pauline D..........5:13:22 (26,813)
Dawson, Anne B..............6:35:08 (31,290)

Dawson, Christine R.........3:35:13 (5,462)
Dawson, Diane...............4:47:23 (22,540)
Dawson, Emily A.............5:05:17 (25,721)
Dawson, Emma M..............5:31:33 (28,703)
Dawson, Kirsty J............3:57:44 (10,600)
Dawson, Zoe A...............4:08:54 (13,348)
Day, Anita J................4:29:43 (18,557)
Day, Johanna M..............3:56:01 (10,090)
Day, Julie A................5:50:19 (29,984)
Day, Karen..................4:57:45 (24,545)
Day, Lesley C...............3:22:14 (3,332)
Day, Nicola J...............5:18:40 (27,430)
Day, Tanya E................4:32:40 (19,283)
Day, Theresa A..............4:58:39 (24,749)
De Backer, Jacqueline.......4:36:31 (20,139)
De Groot, Mhorag............3:36:49 (5,745)
De Haast, Laura.............4:17:43 (15,485)
De Jong, Stephanie..........4:59:32 (24,909)
De Klerk, Joan..............5:02:16 (25,331)
De Luca-O'Neil, Antonella...4:00:45 (11,434)
De Rojas, Jacqueline........4:24:16 (17,136)
De Siun, Giselle S..........5:42:59 (29,559)
De Stefani, Loretta.........4:42:25 (21,438)
De Swart, Louis.............4:46:41 (22,391)
De Villiers, Marilize.......4:19:23 (15,878)
De Wulf, Kristien M.........5:29:15 (28,513)
Deacon, Alexandra F.........4:38:58 (20,715)
Deacon, Claire E............4:52:09 (23,474)
Deakin, Lindsay C...........4:36:45 (20,191)
Dean, Emma K................5:46:05 (29,753)
Dean, Julie A...............4:53:44 (23,755)
Deane, Rachel...............3:57:33 (10,555)
Dearie, Cindy L.............6:06:41 (30,637)
Dearing, Annabel L..........5:09:45 (26,345)
Deasy, Margaret A...........2:52:00 (590)
Debere, Stephanie J.........4:26:29 (17,696)
Decamp, Isabelle............3:57:36 (10,568)
Decristofaro, Antonietta....5:58:33 (30,352)
Dedman, Kirstin J...........4:57:10 (24,429)
Dee, Nicky A................3:26:58 (4,013)
Deehan, Martha..............7:31:33 (31,855)
Deeley, Elizabeth A.........4:49:35 (22,992)
Deering, Georgiana M........5:32:53 (28,802)
Deering, Lisa M.............5:08:19 (26,162)
Deery, Anne C...............5:53:02 (30,129)
Deffarges, Claudine.........4:24:26 (17,172)
Deherty, Ann T..............4:49:05 (22,892)
Deighton, Sheila J..........6:42:36 (31,399)
Dekker, Marika..............7:00:08 (31,624)
Delahoy, Fiona J............5:00:17 (25,035)
Delaney, Martina R..........5:26:32 (28,251)
Delbo, Tunde................4:43:57 (21,786)
Delhanty, Anna M............5:00:48 (25,112)
De-Liege, Fay...............5:09:46 (26,351)
Demidenko, Svetlana.........2:33:06 (100)
Den Hartog-Melis, Maria.....4:08:45 (13,307)
Denbury, Joan...............4:13:58 (14,558)
Denley, Louise D............3:32:18 (4,970)
Denne, Linda J..............6:18:11 (30,963)
Denning, Sally M............4:29:20 (18,444)
Dennis, Beth A..............4:43:36 (21,701)
Dennison, Andrea M..........2:55:08 (764)
Dennison, Jane M............5:17:45 (27,333)
Dennison, Joanne............4:03:52 (12,163)
Dennison, Patricia M........3:45:34 (7,428)
Denny, Karen K..............4:47:26 (22,552)
Denotti, Lena M.............4:43:30 (21,685)
Denston, Sharon.............7:48:30 (31,912)
Dent, Catherine.............4:16:26 (15,157)
Denyer, Brigitte............4:52:17 (23,499)
Denyer, Lucy................4:15:17 (14,879)
Derenoncourt, Edith.........4:11:32 (13,978)
Dering, Jo..................3:05:21 (1,557)
Dervish, Sheree.............6:35:57 (31,306)
Desborough, Katrina.........5:35:44 (29,013)
Desmond, Martha G...........5:15:34 (27,085)
Despretz, Paula.............5:00:20 (25,043)
Dessert, Patricia C.........4:20:50 (16,235)
Devenish, Lucinda K.........5:46:32 (29,792)
Devine, Cathy L.............4:21:27 (16,376)
Devine, Elaine..............5:03:02 (25,450)
Devlin, Anne................4:46:08 (22,275)
Devlin, Karen...............4:11:53 (14,057)

Devlin, Paula R.............4:59:22 (24,871)
Devonport, Kirsty L.........4:44:16 (21,850)
Dewar, Angela G.............4:03:55 (12,173)
Dewar, Joanna C.............5:31:44 (28,720)
Dey, Bridgett...............4:51:27 (23,338)
Dey, Hannah L...............5:12:38 (26,704)
Dhanota-Jones, Teena S......4:56:14 (24,249)
Dhillon, Rupi...............5:20:55 (27,674)
Diamond, Mica B.............5:20:05 (27,577)
Diaz, Sarah A...............4:38:27 (20,584)
Dick, Patricia A............3:29:42 (4,533)
Dicker, Amanda..............5:01:37 (25,241)
Dickie, Gillian N...........4:26:20 (17,663)
Dickinson, Barbara J........4:20:21 (16,117)
Dickinson, Charlotte L......4:25:50 (17,522)
Dickinson, Emma.............3:54:46 (9,715)
Dickinson, Lucy A...........4:40:11 (20,959)
Dickinson, Maxine...........4:19:47 (15,973)
Dickson, Adwoa-Shanti.......6:24:10 (31,114)
Dickson, Georgina M.........5:08:44 (26,207)
Dickson, Kim M..............5:04:30 (25,627)
Dickson, Sally..............4:31:38 (19,006)
Diegutis, Liz M.............4:51:19 (23,320)
Diesch, Jutta...............3:47:44 (7,934)
Digby, Helen F..............3:43:58 (7,057)
Dillon, Sara J..............5:25:43 (28,162)
Dillon, Ursula C............4:55:12 (24,037)
Diprose, Caroline L.........4:12:33 (14,218)
Disbury, Rebecca............4:00:07 (11,320)
Disley, Kate E..............3:28:41 (4,349)
Disney, Glennys.............3:11:12 (2,114)
Dita, Constantina...........2:26:52 (60)
Divine, Suzanna J...........4:46:09 (22,279)
Dix, Antonia M..............4:37:15 (20,306)
Dixon, Emma H...............5:40:56 (29,407)
Dixon, Lyn..................4:39:36 (20,840)
Dixon, Michelle A...........4:20:55 (16,267)
Dizadji, Tala S.............5:58:24 (30,340)
D'Mello, Kerry L............5:23:07 (27,882)
Doak, Jennifer..............5:52:48 (30,116)
Dobson, Lesley..............3:26:34 (3,926)
Docherty, Caroline B........5:02:17 (25,336)
Dodd, Katharine A...........5:52:16 (30,082)
Dodd, Sue P.................4:32:11 (19,162)
Dodd, Tracy.................4:21:17 (16,328)
Doddington, Denise A........3:39:43 (6,260)
Dodds, Vanessa J............4:20:31 (16,164)
Dodin, Kelsang D............4:54:23 (23,875)
Dods, Verity K..............5:32:25 (28,768)
Dodsworht, Karen M..........4:38:56 (20,702)
Doel, Susan E...............6:20:14 (31,021)
Doherty, Hayley M...........4:44:00 (21,794)
Doherty, Madeleine S........4:29:21 (18,451)
Doherty, Marie C............4:22:21 (16,654)
Dolman, Alison M............5:36:16 (29,045)
Dolman, Patricia............7:07:01 (31,681)
Domoney, Sarah L............5:12:15 (26,662)
Donadieu, Emma-Lynn.........4:31:15 (18,909)
Donald, Christine S.........7:03:36 (31,656)
Donaldson, Gillian E........6:21:51 (31,057)
Donaldson, Judith L.........4:12:38 (14,242)
Donaldson, Lesley A.........7:33:06 (31,865)
Donaldson, Susan J..........3:35:53 (5,587)
Doneman, Jane C.............3:56:52 (10,354)
Donneger, Karin C...........3:57:27 (10,525)
Donnell, Caroline W.........5:21:15 (27,704)
Donnelly, Bernadette........5:35:21 (28,986)
Donnelly, Elaine M..........4:32:06 (19,133)
Donnelly, Jayne.............7:07:36 (31,689)
Donnelly, Nicola J..........4:36:31 (20,139)
Donoghue, Eileen............4:10:44 (13,806)
Donoghue, Paula J...........4:32:06 (19,133)
Donoghue, Suzi E............3:35:32 (5,532)
Donovan, Ceri...............4:06:24 (12,761)
Donovan, Laura J............4:27:51 (18,055)
Doolan, Frances B...........5:03:24 (25,500)
Dopson, Sarah L.............4:27:55 (18,067)
Doran, Maxine...............5:50:18 (29,981)
Dormer, Julie A.............3:30:05 (4,611)
Dorrell, Patricia A.........4:01:26 (11,538)
Dougall, Annie K............4:22:49 (16,777)
Doughty, Caroline J.........5:31:33 (28,703)
Doughty, Sara L.............4:08:58 (13,369)

LONDON MARATHON

Douglas, Gaye I	4:58:08	(24,624)
Douglas, Gill	4:11:36	(13,999)
Douglas, Natalie	3:52:18	(9,085)
Douglas, Sue	4:09:16	(13,446)
Douglas, Wendy P	5:04:17	(25,600)
Douguet, Odile	3:54:26	(9,622)
Dove, Emma	5:12:00	(26,633)
Dovey, Katy	5:27:15	(28,330)
Dow, Michelle A	4:55:33	(24,108)
Dowden, Lesley A	5:52:13	(30,077)
Dowding, Claire H	4:42:38	(21,477)
Dowding, Janina L	4:51:09	(23,295)
Dowding, Rachel	3:58:15	(10,773)
Dowell, Melissa J	3:19:00	(2,949)
Down, Dominique	4:21:10	(16,302)
Downes, Anna	4:34:31	(19,717)
Downes, Joanna C	4:02:59	(11,950)
Downes, Tamarisk F	4:27:30	(17,957)
Downey, Aileen P	3:59:57	(11,280)
Downing, Anne	4:51:40	(23,371)
Downing, Fiona W	5:42:15	(29,498)
Downing, Sarah	5:26:51	(28,284)
Downs, Ursula	5:03:19	(25,492)
Dowsett, Anna F	5:01:21	(25,194)
Doyle, Katrina H	4:28:39	(18,270)
Doyle, Shirley P	4:45:45	(22,199)
Drage, Debbie	5:29:16	(28,515)
Drake, Kathryn M	4:56:59	(24,400)
Drane, Michele E	6:04:19	(30,572)
Draper, Eleanor	4:19:51	(15,987)
Draper, Jane A	4:20:28	(16,151)
Drapkin, Jane R	3:58:54	(10,974)
Dray, Carol S	4:33:21	(19,437)
Dray, Jodie C	3:41:05	(6,491)
Drenth, Hermie	3:09:32	(1,951)
Drew, Jackie V	4:40:18	(20,984)
Drexel, Gertrud	4:09:44	(13,563)
Driffield, Jill	5:29:57	(28,579)
Driscoll, Catherine A	4:50:08	(23,095)
Driscoll, Jean M	5:12:41	(26,712)
Driscoll, Sue J	4:42:14	(21,395)
Driscoll, Susie C	4:48:58	(22,868)
Driver, Carole D	4:43:41	(21,718)
Drnasin, Stephanie C	3:45:12	(7,348)
Droog, Sarah J	4:48:52	(22,847)
Drummond, Clara	4:24:25	(17,167)
Drummond, Helen F	5:50:34	(29,996)
Druvaskalns, Lina	5:03:45	(25,548)
Dryden, Catriona	4:17:23	(15,392)
Drysdale, Catriona L	4:00:54	(11,479)
Du Plessis, Tania	5:40:55	(29,406)
Dubini, Ludovica	4:46:26	(22,347)
Dubois, Véronique	3:51:22	(8,849)
Duce, Lisa A	4:57:43	(24,538)
Duchenne, Claire	4:42:15	(21,397)
Duck, Bobbie	6:25:23	(31,130)
Duckworth, Laura M	4:05:35	(12,568)
Dudley, Emer B	3:25:56	(3,835)
Duerden, Joanna E	4:47:18	(22,517)
Duerden, Kate F	4:24:09	(17,105)
Duff, Jenny B	4:27:15	(17,908)
Duffield, Helen	4:40:51	(21,098)
Duffy, Fiona M	3:32:19	(4,973)
Duffy, Jo	4:50:26	(23,167)
Duffy, Therezia	3:48:32	(8,129)
Dufty, Carol	5:18:09	(27,380)
Duggan, Andrea	5:03:34	(25,530)
Duggan, Julia F	4:30:29	(18,754)
Duguid, Susan A	6:47:28	(31,470)
Duke, Michelle L	5:47:08	(29,819)
Dullroy, Bronnie	4:13:00	(14,329)
Dummer, Sophie J	5:11:42	(26,588)
Dunbar, Julia M	5:07:37	(26,059)
Dunbar, Susan M	7:16:52	(31,763)
Duncan, Gillian	4:54:52	(23,971)
Duncan, Margaret	4:07:29	(13,005)
Dundas, Ruth	4:47:31	(22,570)
Dunderdale, Trina E	6:40:18	(31,364)
Dundon, Jo	4:36:22	(20,100)
Dungate, Stephanie	4:47:38	(22,603)
Dunkin, Tina	4:58:00	(24,593)
Dunlop, Caroline A	5:51:21	(30,028)
Dunn, Emma L	5:26:47	(28,277)

Dunn, Jenny A	4:56:00	(24,206)
Dunn, Sally J	4:20:58	(16,276)
Dunne, Kathryn A	4:51:18	(23,316)
Dunne, Orla M	5:29:13	(28,510)
Dunne, Sheena P	4:16:46	(15,242)
Dunne, Shelia M	3:26:39	(3,942)
Dunning, Michelle	4:05:06	(12,448)
Dunnk, Susan J	5:11:09	(26,527)
Dunsire, Isobel M	5:44:37	(29,665)
Dunster, Bernadette	4:31:26	(18,956)
Dupain, Emma L	4:35:50	(19,987)
Durbin, Julia	4:57:31	(24,496)
Durrant, Charlotte J	4:34:35	(19,730)
Durston, Alison C	5:23:54	(27,961)
Duthie, Tracy L	4:38:13	(20,524)
Duval-Macsporran, Dawn J	5:02:31	(25,379)
Dyble, Yvonne F	6:03:30	(30,546)
Dyer, Abigail R	3:34:44	(5,377)
Dyer, Caroline F	4:32:40	(19,283)
Dyett, Audrey A	4:03:16	(12,021)
Dyke, Carole	3:49:31	(8,380)
Dykes, Rita	4:25:54	(17,543)
Dymond, Penni C	3:46:01	(7,529)
Dymore-Brown, Linda S	3:54:25	(9,617)
Dzialdow, Resi G	4:13:12	(14,376)
Eager, Caroline T	4:42:41	(21,486)
Eagle, Lynda	4:10:57	(13,858)
Eaglen, Yvonne E	4:52:37	(23,553)
Ealham, Elizabeth R	6:23:02	(31,078)
Earl, Annmarie	6:44:14	(31,420)
Earl, Monika P	5:04:39	(25,645)
Earthy, Marianne	5:15:05	(27,032)
Easson, Jayne K	4:25:08	(17,347)
Eastham, Nicola C	7:29:46	(31,844)
Easton, Joanne C	6:18:00	(30,957)
Eastwood, Kathryn J	3:29:11	(4,446)
Eastwood, Susan	4:46:01	(22,255)
Eaton, Debbie	4:06:48	(12,836)
Eaton, Helen E	4:38:34	(20,611)
Ebanks, Alison C	5:31:20	(28,688)
Ebden, Diane J	6:40:02	(31,359)
Ebdon, Alison	4:36:29	(20,131)
Eccles, Heather	6:33:29	(31,273)
Eckhardt, Wendy S	4:21:35	(16,409)
Edbrooke, Tessa L	5:00:03	(25,001)
Eddleston, Susan P	5:28:19	(28,422)
Eden, Pam E	4:41:17	(21,181)
Edenbrow, Tamsin J	4:58:01	(24,597)
Edgell, Julie	3:46:08	(7,552)
Edleston, Teresa L	4:07:57	(13,104)
Edmonds, Rebecca M	4:45:02	(22,040)
Edmondson, Deborah A	3:24:19	(3,604)
Edmondson, Shona A	6:08:34	(30,687)
Edmunds, Sally M	5:05:30	(25,760)
Edmunds, Samuel	5:16:35	(27,207)
Edridge, Karen	4:29:20	(18,444)
Edwards, Anna M	5:44:55	(29,687)
Edwards, Catrin F	4:12:32	(14,214)
Edwards, Christine E	7:22:33	(31,799)
Edwards, Clare R	4:41:31	(21,248)
Edwards, Emma L	5:02:43	(25,404)
Edwards, Fizzy G	5:34:22	(28,913)
Edwards, Janice C	5:24:47	(28,054)
Edwards, Julie	5:10:06	(26,389)
Edwards, Mary-Louise	5:03:55	(25,566)
Edwards, Melanie	4:49:31	(22,981)
Edwards, Nuala M	7:04:03	(31,661)
Edwards, Penny J	3:19:19	(2,997)
Edwards, Rachel J	4:04:58	(12,424)
Edwards, Rachel J	4:36:39	(20,167)
Edwards, Rosalind A	7:21:17	(31,794)
Edwards, Sally P	4:13:28	(14,442)
Edwards, Sandra M	5:33:30	(28,850)
Edwards, Sharon L	5:41:06	(29,416)
Edwards, Sian	5:57:56	(30,326)

Edwards, Traci	3:54:03	(9,518)
Edwards, Valerie C	5:39:58	(29,332)
Edwards, Wendy M	3:19:12	(2,983)
Edwards, Yvonne	4:42:23	(21,432)
Edwell, Lisa C	4:14:18	(14,623)
Egan, Sharon	4:55:21	(24,073)
Eggl, Waltrand	5:04:38	(25,643)
Ehrenberg, Margaret	3:27:19	(4,084)
Eisele, Michelle	3:44:50	(7,270)
Eiseman, Alexis A	5:44:58	(29,692)
Ekanger, Morag	4:32:07	(19,139)
Eke, Tina H	4:23:06	(16,842)
Elaute, Marie F	4:27:49	(18,044)
Elcome, Lorraine L	5:42:01	(29,485)
Elden, Rachel	4:48:55	(22,857)
Elder, Rachel	5:01:51	(25,279)
Elderfield, Helen L	5:13:30	(26,825)
Eley, Joanna L	5:47:35	(29,846)
Eley, Kerry A	4:21:33	(16,400)
Elford, Sophie L	4:22:11	(16,598)
Elkington, Jill A	6:12:30	(30,794)
Elkington, Ruth I	4:08:01	(13,117)
Ellacott, Suzy J	4:55:16	(24,056)
Elliman, Judith	4:27:18	(17,920)
Elliot, Marie A	3:03:16	(1,386)
Elliott, Annie J	7:39:40	(31,890)
Elliott, Catherine J	4:22:08	(16,582)
Elliott, Dawn	5:15:27	(27,073)
Elliott, Demelza C	5:34:25	(28,921)
Elliott, Ellie	3:56:12	(10,142)
Elliott, Gillian C	4:07:18	(12,963)
Elliott, Gillian L	5:01:39	(25,247)
Elliott, Joanne L	4:14:14	(14,615)
Elliott, Katharine F	3:57:12	(10,444)
Elliott, Michelle C	4:53:40	(23,740)
Elliott, Nicola M	5:06:34	(25,920)
Elliott, Patricia A	4:22:03	(16,556)
Elliott, Rachel L	4:01:38	(11,629)
Elliott, Vanessa	4:46:57	(22,436)
Elliott, Victoria M	7:07:39	(31,690)
Ellis, Amanda J	4:44:51	(21,988)
Ellis, Bridgid K	3:47:28	(7,873)
Ellis, Charlotte C	3:58:09	(10,729)
Ellis, Jane D	6:38:59	(31,349)
Ellis, Janine E	3:59:53	(11,261)
Ellis, Jennifer	4:58:07	(24,624)
Ellis, Julie	4:46:47	(22,406)
Ellis, Melanie J	2:52:01	(593)
Ellis, Melissa S	6:27:36	(31,168)
Ellis, Michelle A	4:47:14	(22,504)
Ellis, Nicola J	4:49:56	(23,065)
Ellis, Tracey	4:03:41	(12,122)
Ellison, Annette	3:48:55	(8,233)
Ellsmore, Katie	5:44:13	(29,638)
Ellsmore, Rebecca	7:24:27	(31,803)
Elmes, Kellie	5:17:12	(27,272)
El-Safty, Suzanne E	3:44:20	(7,145)
Else, Michelle M	5:05:06	(25,704)
Elsmore, Katherine L	4:37:15	(20,306)
Elstub, Tracy	4:14:23	(14,648)
Elvin, Sarah L	5:19:58	(27,557)
Emerson, Patricia C	6:41:40	(31,385)
Emery, Holly	4:53:11	(23,651)
Emes, Alison J	4:35:49	(19,985)
Emsden, Suzanne L	5:55:08	(30,208)
Eneman, Arlene	7:00:13	(31,628)
Engel, Barbara	4:27:13	(17,897)
Engert, Clare H	4:30:59	(18,855)
England, Susan P	4:57:03	(24,413)
Engledew, Catherine J	5:18:14	(27,394)
Englefield, Shakira L	4:46:52	(22,419)
English, Caroline L	4:22:03	(16,556)
English, Teresa J	3:39:49	(6,275)
Ennenbach, Petra	3:21:25	(3,246)
Enwright, Marthese	5:12:32	(26,696)
Epp, Nadine P	4:12:54	(14,302)
Erculiani, Katayoun	5:05:53	(25,821)
Erdal, Sarah J	4:03:56	(12,167)
Ergueta, Maria P	6:17:53	(30,948)
Ergueta, Paula A	6:55:18	(31,564)
Ergueta, Tamara M	7:24:28	(31,806)
Ernst, Christine M	4:57:40	(24,529)
Ernst, Elise	6:25:55	(31,141)

Ernst, Nicolette M	4:46:09 (22,279)	
Esposito, Lauren E	3:15:25 (2,590)	
Etheridge, Helen D	4:12:16 (14,142)	
Etheridge, Joanne L	5:49:46 (29,948)	
Etheridge, Kate N	4:41:23 (21,215)	
Etter, Ann C	7:39:01 (31,889)	
Eustice, Stacey A	7:07:24 (31,686)	
Evangelista, Elizabeth C	4:23:42 (16,989)	
Evans, Alice	3:05:50 (1,591)	
Evans, Angela M	5:19:37 (27,513)	
Evans, Anna J	4:13:47 (14,513)	
Evans, Betty	7:17:34 (31,768)	
Evans, Carol A	3:02:02 (1,304)	
Evans, Carrie E	4:03:49 (12,152)	
Evans, Christina J	3:12:11 (2,212)	
Evans, Corinne P	7:24:28 (31,806)	
Evans, Debbie	4:33:09 (19,391)	
Evans, Denise A	4:08:41 (13,283)	
Evans, Diane E	3:58:12 (10,758)	
Evans, Eiri	4:22:21 (16,654)	
Evans, Elizabeth	4:19:53 (15,992)	
Evans, Gillian M	4:22:27 (16,681)	
Evans, Helen E	3:15:06 (2,567)	
Evans, Julia A	5:13:03 (26,771)	
Evans, Kathryn D	4:36:30 (20,135)	
Evans, Maria	4:32:40 (19,283)	
Evans, Marian W	4:38:01 (20,475)	
Evans, Maureen T	5:46:56 (29,808)	
Evans, Ruth E	5:03:31 (25,524)	
Evans, Samantha L	4:56:45 (24,352)	
Evans, Sandra D	3:44:57 (7,296)	
Evans, Sarah R	5:17:19 (27,285)	
Evans, Siobhan A	3:23:02 (3,444)	
Evason, Cheryl A	4:27:33 (17,977)	
Eveleigh, Hannah K	3:28:11 (4,261)	
Everatt, Joann L	3:31:37 (4,863)	
Everett, Anna M	5:26:51 (28,284)	
Everingham, Deborah L	4:59:53 (24,971)	
Everitt, Marie T	4:17:20 (15,383)	
Everitt, Patricia A	5:26:40 (28,268)	
Ewing, Jenny L	4:45:52 (22,222)	
Ewins, Sharon L	5:01:05 (25,159)	
Eynon, Deirdre P	3:44:57 (7,296)	
Eyre, Annabelle C	4:46:56 (22,430)	
Eyres, Rachel N	4:54:08 (23,825)	
Ezeta, Ana Paula	3:41:43 (6,586)	
Ezzaldin, Kathryn L	4:52:20 (23,513)	
Faahan-Smith, Kristen P	4:53:40 (23,740)	
Faben, Jennifer	3:37:35 (5,888)	
Faichen, Shirley	4:55:53 (24,177)	
Fairclough, Sue	4:48:49 (22,841)	
Fairhurst, Louise E	4:22:09 (16,588)	
Fairley, Nicola M	5:26:52 (28,287)	
Fairlie, Alice L	4:25:43 (17,481)	
Fairweather, Carol	4:12:29 (14,194)	
Falla, Nicola A	4:02:30 (11,855)	
Fallon, Bethan	3:34:14 (5,302)	
Fane, Heloise A	5:13:45 (26,859)	
Farebrother, Alice J	5:27:44 (28,377)	
Farey, Jane	5:30:30 (28,625)	
Farley, Angela J	4:15:30 (14,925)	
Farley, Beverley P	3:33:50 (5,240)	
Farman, Michelle C	3:24:21 (3,609)	
Farmer, Alice	4:59:07 (24,814)	
Farmer, Alice M	5:01:23 (25,201)	
Farmer, Elizabeth A	5:18:16 (27,397)	
Farmer, Joanna M	3:38:31 (6,050)	
Farmer, Juliet V	4:59:45 (24,949)	
Farnell, Sarah J	4:34:47 (19,774)	
Farney, Sarah L	4:08:51 (13,334)	
Farrall, Ali	3:35:34 (5,535)	
Farrant, Annabelle L	4:35:05 (19,839)	
Farrar, Ian	4:54:01 (23,796)	
Farrar, Julie	5:42:35 (29,522)	
Farrar, Julie	6:47:24 (31,468)	
Farrell, Ellen M	5:38:51 (29,250)	
Farrow, Diane E	4:41:19 (21,194)	
Farrow, Jane L	4:19:19 (15,860)	
Farrow, Pam W	5:00:31 (25,068)	
Fasal, Mary	5:25:50 (28,179)	
Faulkner, Judy M	5:19:06 (27,477)	
Faulkner, Phillippa	4:49:15 (22,927)	
Faust, Nicola E	4:00:52 (11,468)	

Favier, Emmanuelle	4:24:51 (17,268)	
Fawcett, Claude G	6:58:57 (31,605)	
Fawcett, Trudy J	3:22:55 (3,432)	
Fawcus, Abi A	3:54:23 (9,604)	
Fearn, Katrina D	5:11:03 (26,510)	
Fears, Melody	4:56:41 (24,340)	
Feather, Lisa J	4:48:43 (22,824)	
Featherstone, Mychelle K	5:23:39 (27,940)	
Fee, Monica	4:04:12 (12,240)	
Feeley, Alison B	6:05:13 (30,597)	
Feld, Joanne	5:05:48 (25,804)	
Felden-Funke, Bettina	5:02:57 (25,440)	
Feldman, Kristine L	4:30:53 (18,837)	
Felix, Jamie H	2:58:33 (1,021)	
Fellows, Joanne E	4:13:35 (14,476)	
Fellows, Lisa M	5:43:00 (29,562)	
Fellows, Sarah K	4:42:17 (21,408)	
Fenech, Jacqueline N	4:39:36 (20,840)	
Fenelon, Patsy E	3:43:36 (6,979)	
Fenn, Margaret L	3:55:21 (9,894)	
Fentiman, Judy V	6:35:07 (31,289)	
Fenton, Ann H	3:57:39 (10,581)	
Fenton, Catherine T	5:10:52 (26,492)	
Fenton, Selina	4:08:23 (13,196)	
Fenwick, Caron L	4:34:22 (19,685)	
Fenwick, Ruth A	4:51:11 (23,302)	
Ferguson, Christine	3:30:12 (4,634)	
Ferguson, Elizabeth	3:28:28 (4,316)	
Ferguson, Lucy A	3:55:16 (9,868)	
Ferguson, Sarah V	8:32:01 (31,968)	
Ferguson, Vandana	4:02:42 (11,899)	
Fermor, Julia	4:40:52 (21,102)	
Fernandez, Claire P	5:03:01 (25,448)	
Fernandez, Corinne	3:33:46 (5,229)	
Fernandez, Isabel	3:48:01 (8,001)	
Ferns, Geraldine	4:59:20 (24,858)	
Ferrari, Anita C	7:00:02 (31,622)	
Ferrari Ellis, Caroline D	5:32:42 (28,791)	
Ferreira, Elizka D	3:28:13 (4,266)	
Ferreira, Erica K	4:58:30 (24,719)	
Fetti, Amanda	6:10:23 (30,738)	
Feuchter, Petra	4:26:28 (17,691)	
Fiddament-Harris, Heather M	3:41:55 (6,624)	
Fidge, Ann E	4:24:25 (17,167)	
Fidgett, Serena K	4:49:36 (22,996)	
Field, Antonia L	4:24:43 (17,233)	
Field, Sarah A	4:38:15 (20,533)	
Field, Susan L	4:33:41 (19,502)	
Fielden, Margie P	5:23:43 (27,946)	
Fielder, Sarah	5:24:06 (27,979)	
Fieldhouse, Tracey M	5:25:41 (28,158)	
File, Hayley C	4:39:04 (20,743)	
Filer, Sara-Marie	4:49:27 (22,969)	
Filkins, Terri	4:37:57 (20,454)	
Findlay, Celia A	3:25:19 (3,738)	
Findley, Helen I	5:10:21 (26,421)	
Fines, Helen R	3:04:56 (1,518)	
Fingerhut, Margaret R	5:10:14 (26,402)	
Finn, Deirdre F	3:31:07 (4,792)	
Finnegan, Claire P	4:36:28 (20,123)	
Finney, Helen E	5:31:07 (28,669)	
Finney, Louise K	4:37:52 (20,422)	
Fionda, Charlotte E	4:16:20 (15,126)	
Firmin, Sharon M	5:05:49 (25,808)	
Firth, Gemma	4:50:20 (23,129)	
Firth, Mellissa	4:41:31 (21,248)	
Firth, Sue J	5:41:00 (29,409)	
Firth, Veronica J	5:54:42 (30,185)	
Fischer, Carmen	4:23:54 (17,041)	
Fischer, Catherine J	4:30:39 (18,791)	
Fischer, Marie- Anne	3:42:11 (6,678)	
Fischer, Noele	5:08:19 (26,162)	
Fisher, Denise	5:59:26 (30,388)	
Fisher, Emma	5:31:21 (28,694)	
Fisher, Karen L	4:59:22 (24,871)	
Fisher, Katherine M	4:07:21 (12,970)	
Fisher, Sarah	5:20:15 (27,599)	
Fisher, Sarah A	6:31:41 (31,238)	
Fishpool, Jayne E	5:08:27 (26,177)	
Fitch, Wendy J	4:42:55 (21,548)	
Fitch-Roy, Gina M	4:10:06 (13,656)	
Fitton, Emma R	4:30:46 (18,809)	
Fitzgerald, Sara	4:07:08 (12,923)	

Fitzgerald-Davies, Denise	4:10:37 (13,786)	
Fitzmaurice-Cotton, Heather	3:17:08 (2,764)	
Flack, Margaret R	7:11:18 (31,717)	
Flanagan, Colette M	5:25:02 (28,089)	
Flanagan, Marie-Louise	5:19:14 (27,481)	
Flann, Kathy E	4:03:47 (12,144)	
Flay, Alexandra J	3:37:20 (5,846)	
Fleetwood, Lisa M	5:11:12 (26,541)	
Fleming, Jemima H	5:21:40 (27,747)	
Fleming, Nicola A	3:39:45 (6,265)	
Fleming, RV	5:30:58 (28,658)	
Fletcher, Alison K	2:47:27 (399)	
Fletcher, Johanna	3:31:13 (4,811)	
Fletcher, Julie A	7:03:36 (31,656)	
Fletcher, Margaret	5:20:04 (27,576)	
Fletcher, Maria	4:11:54 (14,063)	
Fletcher, Monica J	3:59:29 (11,151)	
Fletcher, Susan J	7:03:36 (31,656)	
Fletcher, Vivienne A	6:10:33 (30,742)	
Fletcher, Zoe H	3:51:16 (8,824)	
Fletcher-Smith, Gemma T	5:06:37 (25,931)	
Flett, Nadine L	4:47:37 (22,598)	
Flewitt, Sue A	4:57:17 (24,459)	
Fligg, Jayne A	5:39:27 (29,305)	
Flint, Debbie A	5:36:33 (29,064)	
Flint, Michelle E	3:43:50 (7,021)	
Flint, Penny L	4:59:14 (24,834)	
Flittner, Christine M	3:58:35 (10,884)	
Flood, Jane L	5:24:18 (28,003)	
Flook, Jacqueline A	5:13:19 (26,807)	
Flores-Laird, Dorina	4:58:47 (24,762)	
Flounders, Linda A	5:32:30 (28,774)	
Flynn, Helen M	5:03:55 (25,566)	
Foley, Niamh A	5:15:55 (27,119)	
Foley, Nicola P	5:15:55 (27,119)	
Foley, Penelope D	4:30:06 (18,655)	
Foley, Ruth E	4:35:11 (19,861)	
Folkard, Heidi C	3:52:35 (9,149)	
Follan, Anne	3:35:01 (5,429)	
Folliard, Suzanne D	4:27:36 (17,990)	
Fontaine, Marie C	4:01:03 (11,516)	
Fookes, Anita J	3:59:30 (11,157)	
Foord, Pauline E	4:20:18 (16,101)	
Forbes, Charlie N	5:36:35 (29,067)	
Forbes, Johanna E	4:11:17 (13,926)	
Ford, Debbie	5:38:30 (29,230)	
Ford, Jane E	4:02:20 (11,823)	
Ford, Katherine A	3:54:58 (9,772)	
Ford, Lesley M	4:05:32 (12,550)	
Ford, Liz	4:57:00 (24,404)	
Ford, Pamela	6:51:41 (31,525)	
Fordham, Krista A	5:13:46 (26,864)	
Foreman, Karen M	4:29:33 (18,505)	
Foreman, Wendy M	5:08:38 (26,194)	
Forkin, Natalie E	3:24:37 (3,639)	
Forman, Catriona M	3:47:02 (7,763)	
Formella, Samantha L	4:58:02 (24,604)	
Formon, Sally A	3:48:50 (8,222)	
Forrest, Sophie C	3:37:35 (5,888)	
Forrester, Claire	7:43:07 (31,900)	
Forrester, Karen J	5:52:16 (30,082)	
Forseth, Kelley A	4:50:24 (23,158)	
Forster, Antonia F	5:14:37 (26,982)	
Forster, Erica K	5:44:22 (29,646)	
Forster, Karen E	5:25:23 (28,128)	
Forster, Katherine E	4:44:10 (21,831)	
Forster, Kim	4:26:52 (17,798)	
Forster, Michaela	7:31:21 (31,853)	
Forsyth, Anne	6:13:47 (30,840)	
Forsythe, Anna K	4:19:14 (15,837)	
Fortes Mayer, Gail E	3:21:33 (3,264)	
Fortune, Ashley	6:42:48 (31,403)	
Forward, Claire P	4:15:41 (14,973)	
Foss, Angela J	3:57:17 (10,473)	
Fossey, Alison	4:05:00 (12,429)	
Foster, Becky M	8:27:40 (31,963)	
Foster, Dilys H	7:07:54 (31,692)	
Foster, Heather A	4:02:11 (11,774)	
Foster, Helen C	4:56:33 (24,322)	
Foster, Julie A	4:46:59 (22,444)	
Foster, Laura A	4:14:50 (14,770)	
Foster, Linda	4:25:40 (17,469)	
Foster, Lisa	4:42:02 (21,355)	

Foster, Melanie J	5:00:24 (25,052)
Foster, Nicola	3:52:01 (9,016)
Foster, Rosalind C	3:34:46 (5,383)
Foster, Rosey	5:50:29 (29,993)
Foster, Sonja A	3:45:11 (7,342)
Foster, Susan M	4:46:25 (22,344)
Fotheringham, Lisa S	4:48:18 (22,739)
Foudy, Michele L	5:56:47 (30,281)
Fourrier, Babette	3:52:40 (9,165)
Fovargue, Kathryn L	4:06:35 (12,801)
Fowler, Claire	3:16:05 (2,652)
Fowler, Hannah J	5:12:14 (26,660)
Fowler, Jackie R	4:26:00 (17,568)
Fowler, Kay	3:34:28 (5,335)
Fowler, Mouveta A	4:09:12 (13,422)
Fowler, Nicola J	4:09:12 (13,422)
Fox, Annette K	4:26:06 (17,608)
Fox, Barbara A	4:41:56 (21,332)
Fox, Janine A	4:27:46 (18,031)
Fox, Penelope J	4:55:38 (24,125)
Fox, Sabine	4:07:12 (12,939)
Foyster, Mandy L	3:28:31 (4,323)
Fraczek, Linda M	5:35:08 (28,971)
Frame, Melissa J	4:27:36 (17,990)
Frampton, Lynn	5:08:20 (26,164)
France, Jacqueline R	3:05:05 (1,533)
Francis, Amy C	3:56:43 (10,308)
Francis, Christina V	5:01:39 (25,247)
Francis, Janine M	3:08:14 (1,822)
Francis, Patricia	5:19:57 (27,556)
Francisco, Maria E	4:22:35 (16,719)
Francombe, Heather	4:41:21 (21,206)
Frank, Flora	6:05:43 (30,611)
Frankcom, Marie	5:03:42 (25,546)
Frankish, Sally	4:21:25 (16,367)
Franklin, Jenny A	4:07:10 (12,931)
Franklin, Jessica S	3:36:56 (5,756)
Franklin, Kay E	4:51:42 (23,382)
Franklin, Rachael	4:04:59 (12,426)
Franks, June	3:50:37 (8,662)
Franz, Wolfgang	4:10:00 (13,639)
Fraser, Jane	4:36:35 (20,150)
Fraser, Samantha	4:22:11 (16,598)
Fraser, Victoria J	4:22:20 (16,650)
Frater, Emma R	4:52:47 (23,581)
Fravalo, Sylvie	4:19:48 (15,975)
Frederick, Delores	7:16:35 (31,762)
Frederick, Natasha N	4:44:19 (21,865)
Freebody, Amy C	5:42:15 (29,498)
Freebody, Claire L	3:58:27 (10,834)
Freed, June A	5:06:32 (25,914)
Freed, Lindsa J	3:55:22 (9,897)
Freegard, Emilia	5:03:37 (25,534)
Freeman, Caroline D	4:17:53 (15,532)
Freeman, Clare L	3:30:59 (4,775)
Freer, Emma J	4:43:54 (21,775)
Freestone, Elizabeth	5:49:44 (29,947)
French, Gaynor T	4:22:11 (16,598)
French, Gillian E	5:21:04 (27,687)
French, Julie Y	4:43:10 (21,595)
French, Louise M	4:35:02 (19,828)
French, Rosemarie E	4:37:49 (20,409)
French, Suzanne E	4:07:56 (13,100)
French, Yvonne A	3:55:20 (9,890)
Frewin, Elaine D	4:26:56 (17,821)
Freyne, Susan	3:54:49 (9,726)
Friedman, Lesley	6:36:19 (31,312)
Friis, Deb	3:55:40 (9,976)
Frith, June	4:19:05 (15,799)
Froggatt, Cindy J	4:29:04 (18,366)
Frost, Alison	4:40:42 (21,066)
Frost, Beverley J	5:14:22 (26,943)
Frost, Kirsty S	6:52:10 (31,533)
Frost, Sammy	5:43:07 (29,574)
Frost, Sarah J	3:38:55 (6,115)
Fry, Debra L	4:42:40 (21,484)
Fry, Emma L	4:21:02 (16,290)
Fry, Gillian E	5:57:56 (30,326)
Fryer, Natalie L	3:31:26 (4,837)
Fuchs, Martha	4:19:30 (15,911)
Fuhri, Tessa J	4:29:34 (18,511)
Fukazawa, Yasuko	5:56:41 (30,278)
Fulenwider, Erika L	4:45:42 (22,190)

Fulford-Brown, Danielle M	4:58:41 (24,754)
Fullard, Brenda	4:10:10 (13,668)
Fuller, Dianne J	5:01:42 (25,257)
Fuller, Ruth E	4:34:39 (19,750)
Funk, Collene A	5:11:06 (26,517)
Furbank, Valerie A	5:04:21 (25,611)
Furlong-Walker, Jazz	6:09:55 (30,725)
Furner, Sue M	4:10:11 (13,675)
Furness, Pat A	5:50:35 (29,998)
Furse, Jeni A	6:32:40 (31,259)
Furzeland, Julie A	5:27:32 (28,359)
Fyvie-Rae, Sarah C	4:35:56 (20,009)
Gabbert, Barbara	4:13:49 (14,521)
Gable, Sonia K	4:35:58 (20,021)
Gabriel, Susie J	4:49:27 (22,969)
Gabrys, Alexandra	3:30:20 (4,661)
Gadd, Catherine L	4:31:46 (19,044)
Gadd, Sarah J	3:57:16 (10,466)
Gadsby, Claire	4:44:00 (21,794)
Gaffey, Jane E	4:39:48 (20,876)
Gahagan, Marie	4:50:09 (23,101)
Gahan, Lucy J	4:52:36 (23,551)
Gaimster, Lorraine	4:10:25 (13,737)
Gainham, Andrea C	5:54:38 (30,179)
Gaj, Hayley M	6:35:14 (31,291)
Gajic, Javorka V	4:51:03 (23,282)
Gale, Nuala J	4:47:47 (22,630)
Galeozzie, Emma R	4:38:41 (20,637)
Galindo Salmeron, Carmen	4:23:38 (16,971)
Gallagher, Emer	5:30:40 (28,635)
Gallagher, Jackie	2:34:48 (122)
Gallagher, Katherine A	6:02:51 (30,524)
Gallagher, Margaret A	6:16:39 (30,927)
Gallagher, Michelle J	5:45:48 (29,740)
Gallagher, Tania J	6:10:50 (30,750)
Galligan, Angela C	4:56:14 (24,249)
Galloway, Fiona K	6:30:50 (31,219)
Galloway, Julie A	5:24:17 (28,002)
Galvin, Basha	4:58:46 (24,761)
Gamble, Lisa J	3:57:16 (10,466)
Gamblin, Judith C	3:30:16 (4,647)
Game, Fiona	4:34:28 (19,704)
Gammeter, Monika	3:30:47 (4,738)
Gammon, Mair	5:19:04 (27,471)
Gane, Clare E	5:52:27 (30,095)
Gapp, Joanna I	3:29:12 (4,449)
Gapper, Stephanie J	4:16:05 (15,072)
Gappy, Tina L	3:28:56 (4,404)
Gappy, Tracy J	3:28:55 (4,402)
Gardener, Sue E	4:05:52 (12,629)
Gardiner, Cherie M	4:22:48 (16,771)
Gardiner, Christel W	5:00:28 (25,060)
Gardiner, Helen	4:59:34 (24,916)
Gardiner, Victoria	3:30:23 (4,669)
Gardner, Julie R	6:19:32 (31,004)
Gardner, Kim J	4:36:19 (20,090)
Gardner, Lucy J	5:52:17 (30,085)
Gardner, Nicola M	4:33:30 (19,472)
Gardner, Rachel	4:08:03 (13,124)
Gardner, Trish	5:14:54 (27,016)
Gardner-Hall, Sarah J	3:39:13 (6,166)
Gargya, Amy	4:19:02 (15,782)
Garner, Claire L	4:26:27 (17,684)
Garner, Rachel J	4:32:45 (19,303)
Garner, Stephanie J	4:55:53 (24,177)
Garner Jones, Annetta	3:44:45 (7,249)
Garnett, Emma C	7:36:49 (31,882)
Garnett, Kathleen	4:42:01 (21,348)
Garnsworthy, Kate	6:47:57 (31,474)
Garrard, Anna E	4:04:07 (12,214)
Garratt, Anna M	4:51:36 (23,362)
Garratt, Jeanette Y	4:17:33 (15,439)
Garraway, Kate	4:23:19 (16,888)
Garrett, Sarah L	3:57:16 (10,466)
Garrod, Beverley J	5:57:39 (30,315)
Garrod, Susan A	4:06:24 (12,761)
Garvey, Julie C	5:23:42 (27,944)
Garwood, Kate L	6:13:19 (30,826)
Gascoigne, Emma J	4:56:08 (24,235)
Gaskill, Joanna D	3:49:53 (8,469)
Gaskin, Diane	4:32:23 (19,213)
Gaskin, Leila	3:21:14 (3,225)
Gater, Nicola	5:03:58 (25,575)

Gates, Dominique	5:49:07 (29,914)
Gates, Nicol L	4:50:27 (23,173)
Gattlen, Djazira	4:38:41 (20,637)
Gattward, Sandra M	4:57:19 (24,463)
Gatward, Sara	4:13:18 (14,403)
Gaunt, Traci L	5:24:57 (28,076)
Gautier, Sue	4:09:13 (13,428)
Gauvin, Sarah J	3:50:52 (8,723)
Gauzan, Elisabeth	5:20:54 (27,672)
Gay, Carina A	4:11:49 (14,048)
Gaymer, Anna L	5:08:54 (26,223)
Gaymer, Annamarie D	5:46:29 (29,785)
Gaymer, Kirstin A	4:05:55 (12,643)
Geddes, Sarah	3:42:49 (6,813)
Gellett, Anne E	4:13:51 (14,532)
Gemmell, Eileen	5:03:17 (25,488)
Genevaz, Claudine	3:46:12 (7,578)
Gent, Joanne C	3:49:25 (8,359)
Geoghegan, Dawn C	4:18:44 (15,717)
Geoghegan, Emma M	4:44:46 (21,971)
George, Alison L	4:10:41 (13,796)
George, Anne B	4:29:51 (18,593)
George, Jane D	3:41:46 (6,599)
Georghiou, Dorothy J	3:25:34 (3,777)
Gera, Nisha	5:27:19 (28,340)
Geraghty, Faith R	4:02:18 (11,805)
Gerard Leigh, Emily R	4:31:28 (18,966)
Gerber, Rosalie H	4:30:15 (18,691)
Gerlach, Angelika	3:57:36 (10,568)
German, Gemma	4:52:24 (23,517)
Gharbi, Waida	4:35:31 (19,929)
Gheera, Manjit	5:23:37 (27,936)
Ghio, Emily J	5:37:07 (29,115)
Ghiorse, Victoria L	4:56:00 (24,206)
Giannios, Despina	3:34:45 (5,381)
Gibb, Fiona	5:41:41 (29,466)
Gibbons, Cheryl E	4:24:18 (17,142)
Gibbons, Helen	4:20:24 (16,131)
Gibbons, Kate M	4:26:46 (17,766)
Gibbs, Elaine R	3:57:47 (10,615)
Gibbs, Julia C	4:17:06 (15,327)
Gibling, Stella M	4:22:06 (16,571)
Gibson, Beverley-Jane	3:17:32 (2,803)
Gibson, Claudine	4:09:32 (13,507)
Gibson, Daryl A	4:01:13 (11,547)
Gibson, Deborah C	4:30:26 (18,742)
Gibson, Donna M	5:13:01 (26,765)
Gibson, Helena J	5:25:37 (28,151)
Gibson, Mandy	5:14:54 (27,016)
Gibson, Nicola L	4:53:10 (23,647)
Gibson, Shirley R	4:08:59 (13,377)
Gibson, Tammy	7:35:17 (31,873)
Gicquel, Claire	3:26:12 (3,872)
Giddings, Helen M	3:46:11 (7,573)
Giehl, Andrea	4:05:46 (12,610)
Gilbert, Christine	4:04:08 (12,223)
Gilbert, Gina A	4:22:14 (16,619)
Gilbert, Jennifer M	4:55:31 (24,102)
Gilbert, Lisha F	5:38:29 (29,229)
Gilbert, Pamela	4:40:11 (20,959)
Gilbert, Tracey A	5:38:28 (29,228)
Gilbey, Laura	5:39:06 (29,272)
Gilbey, Lynette	4:13:31 (14,456)
Gilby, Sue N	3:42:09 (6,673)
Gilchrist, Kerry A	5:42:56 (29,547)
Giles, Jeannette L	5:02:05 (25,308)
Giles, Karen A	4:32:48 (19,312)
Giles, Karla A	5:11:12 (26,541)
Giles, Penny A	4:41:45 (21,296)
Gill, Gillan	4:49:45 (23,027)
Gill, Jo K	4:36:47 (20,198)
Gill, Joan E	5:44:35 (29,664)
Gillan, Hayley C	5:42:41 (29,526)
Gillani, Clare M	6:09:46 (30,723)
Gillespie, Jennifer M	5:32:07 (28,741)
Gillett, Michaela J	4:37:49 (20,409)
Gillie, Sheila J	4:01:50 (11,675)
Gillies, Sarah	4:54:28 (23,891)
Gilmour, Caroline A	5:14:00 (26,899)
Gilpin, Jasmine E	5:56:00 (30,246)
Gilroy, Poppy R	5:07:56 (26,103)
Gilsenan, Charlotte M	4:09:41 (13,549)
Gilshaw, Deborah E	4:49:42 (23,014)

Gimblett, Sian	5:30:30 (28,625)
Giordanengo, Rebecca L	4:50:19 (23,126)
Gipp, Diana M	3:13:02 (2,312)
Girking, Kate L	6:03:21 (30,541)
Gisborne, Sally A	3:54:14 (9,572)
Gjerlov, Charlotte	4:58:20 (24,672)
Glazebrook, Clare L	3:15:36 (2,611)
Glazebrook, Jacqueline J	6:00:57 (30,446)
Gleave, Sarah L	4:51:21 (23,326)
Glencross, Amy	4:43:09 (21,591)
Glenister, Clare	5:18:11 (27,391)
Glenn, Sian	7:12:50 (31,730)
Glibbery, Sarah Jane	5:33:48 (28,870)
Gloor, Barbara	4:45:12 (22,081)
Gloster, Louise	4:35:30 (19,927)
Glover, Beryl A	4:11:26 (13,956)
Glover, Di R	5:24:10 (27,988)
Glover, Rebecca	3:55:37 (9,966)
Gluck, Gill T	5:07:17 (26,006)
Glyde, Hilary M	5:20:57 (27,679)
Glynternick, Nadine C	5:09:01 (26,240)
Godard, Kimberly L	6:01:22 (30,461)
Goddard, Lesley E	5:41:35 (29,456)
Goddard, Thelma M	4:46:48 (22,409)
Godfrey, Joanne E	4:51:02 (23,277)
Godfrey, Laura	7:12:20 (31,725)
Godfrey, Lesley C	4:22:57 (16,804)
Godson, Suzi	4:54:57 (23,987)
Godwin, Lorraine A	7:30:07 (31,847)
Goebel, Katja	4:22:05 (16,565)
Goeman, Ank M	5:05:17 (25,721)
Gohil, Sarah C	3:37:06 (5,796)
Gold, Lorna	5:33:15 (28,830)
Goldhill, Sophie H	4:19:21 (15,871)
Goldie, Clare	4:57:54 (24,568)
Goldie, Martha E	4:12:34 (14,225)
Goldie, Samantha	5:31:20 (28,688)
Goldin, Nicole	5:31:43 (28,717)
Golding, Beth A	4:42:41 (21,486)
Goldman, Robyn L	4:31:00 (18,858)
Goldsmith, Fiona V	4:43:28 (21,678)
Goldsmith, Nicky M	5:01:21 (25,194)
Goldsworthy, Emma L	5:00:49 (25,116)
Goldwin, Eleanor K	4:46:03 (22,261)
Golightly, Jennie A	5:13:35 (26,842)
Golsby, Carol J	3:53:27 (9,366)
Gomez, Katia	4:29:07 (18,381)
Goncalves, Anna	4:53:22 (23,681)
Gonzalez, Susana	4:16:25 (15,152)
Gonzalez, Teodora	7:27:47 (31,830)
Good, Jessica	5:37:15 (29,130)
Good, Joy	5:14:56 (27,020)
Goodall, Karen I	4:42:21 (21,425)
Goodall, Suzanne R	4:24:43 (17,233)
Goodchild, Alice M	4:31:38 (19,006)
Goodchild, Heidi	4:26:04 (17,593)
Goodchild, Sarah R	4:56:04 (24,223)
Goode, Andrea	3:27:05 (4,042)
Goode, Valerie J	4:04:06 (12,211)
Gooderham, Jean M	6:13:37 (30,835)
Goodhop, Victoria W	5:52:47 (30,114)
Goodman, Madeline	4:21:36 (16,420)
Goodman, Sophie V	5:24:36 (28,033)
Goodson, Lenore T	6:37:33 (31,335)
Goodwin, Jean	4:26:59 (17,836)
Goodwin, Samantha A	4:10:23 (13,729)
Goodwin, Vivien C	3:51:53 (8,985)
Goorney, Joanna M	3:39:45 (6,265)
Gordon, Claire F	3:08:31 (1,853)
Gordon, Elizabeth J	4:51:51 (23,408)
Gordon, Gillian A	4:51:01 (23,274)
Gordon, Karen	4:06:04 (12,675)
Gordon Clark, Lucy F	4:55:36 (24,118)
Gorge, Angela L	4:50:01 (23,077)
Gorman, Barbara	5:06:11 (25,872)
Gosling, Nina E	5:03:32 (25,527)
Goslinga, Rosita B	4:27:20 (17,925)
Gotts, Jenna	6:56:20 (31,576)
Goudie, Angela M	6:32:20 (31,252)
Gough, Bridget I	4:42:22 (21,429)
Gough, Lucie J	4:41:37 (21,262)
Gough, Teresa	4:58:24 (24,694)
Goul Wheerer, Françoise	4:09:23 (13,470)
Goulbourne, Victoria D	4:19:26 (15,894)
Gould, Keith	3:49:10 (8,302)
Gould, Lucinda J	4:40:52 (21,102)
Gould, Sarah L	4:49:28 (22,975)
Goulding, Alison E	5:31:37 (28,709)
Goulding, Debbie A	5:56:11 (30,254)
Goulty, Wendover	5:10:46 (26,479)
Gower, Susan J	5:38:01 (29,183)
Gowland, Kate M	4:55:46 (24,147)
Gow-Smith, Julia K	3:25:11 (3,718)
Goya-Perez, Louise	4:42:33 (21,462)
Grady, Carol A	3:43:21 (6,928)
Graeben, Asta	6:42:50 (31,404)
Graefe, Edda	3:35:20 (5,493)
Graf, Caroline	5:19:54 (27,549)
Graham, Christiane	4:53:25 (23,689)
Graham, Elaine M	4:26:53 (17,808)
Graham, Eleanor M	4:17:48 (15,507)
Graham, Elizabeth H	4:20:00 (16,034)
Graham, Janet E	4:25:56 (17,551)
Graham, Janice A	3:50:58 (8,743)
Graham, Joan M	4:47:22 (22,533)
Graham, Susan E	3:54:09 (9,542)
Graham-Palmer, Annabelle R	4:05:54 (12,640)
Grahamslaw, Margaret	4:26:38 (17,736)
Grandy, Sarah A	4:08:01 (13,117)
Grange, Anna	4:24:13 (17,127)
Grange, Elizabeth J	4:06:17 (12,733)
Grange, Francine	4:56:23 (24,279)
Granger, Julie A	5:37:58 (29,180)
Granger, Rachel L	3:42:13 (6,686)
Granigg, Gabrielle M	4:21:42 (16,449)
Gransby, Clare	3:51:03 (8,755)
Grant, Andrea L	3:58:41 (10,915)
Grant, Colleen R	5:29:05 (28,490)
Grant, Jacqueline M	5:23:23 (27,904)
Grant, Kate J	4:41:41 (21,276)
Grant, Maria	5:05:23 (25,736)
Grant, Marilyn S	3:26:21 (3,897)
Grant, Naomi H	3:42:53 (6,830)
Grant, Pamela C	3:46:33 (7,648)
Grant, Sheila	5:03:21 (25,494)
Grantham, Julia	5:40:02 (29,340)
Grant-Ives, Bonnie	4:05:23 (12,503)
Gratsani, Paraskevi	2:44:35 (308)
Grave, Linda M	3:41:00 (6,474)
Graver, Joanne L	6:49:34 (31,495)
Graves, Emily	4:12:25 (14,170)
Graves, Jeanette S	4:58:32 (24,723)
Gravestock, Rebecca J	4:38:22 (20,564)
Graville, Sandra L	3:33:58 (5,265)
Gray, Charlotte	4:26:48 (17,775)
Gray, Christine D	4:12:13 (14,135)
Gray, Elaine	4:45:57 (22,238)
Gray, Frances	5:06:00 (25,844)
Gray, Jacqui M	5:21:56 (27,764)
Gray, Jenny S	4:46:12 (22,296)
Gray, Julia C	5:06:03 (25,850)
Gray, Louise J	3:40:07 (6,326)
Gray, Marian B	4:25:33 (17,440)
Gray, Michelle	4:06:20 (12,742)
Gray, Michelle L	4:55:52 (24,169)
Gray, Morven E	5:37:13 (29,126)
Gray, Rachel M	4:17:32 (15,433)
Gray, Rebecca L	4:20:17 (16,095)
Gray, Rosaire P	3:48:34 (8,139)
Graybrook, Karen L	4:25:22 (17,396)
Gray-Conchar, Nicole	5:41:32 (29,452)
Grayson, Penny A	3:58:32 (10,869)
Greany, Helen M	4:25:52 (17,529)
Greasley, Cathie	4:29:49 (18,589)
Greatorex, Jacqueline	4:40:36 (21,042)
Greaves, Debbie L	4:19:06 (15,803)
Greaves, Tracey	4:33:33 (19,477)
Greeff, Sunette	6:12:29 (30,793)
Green, Alexis M	4:48:58 (22,868)
Green, Becky J	5:12:52 (26,742)
Green, Carole A	4:09:57 (13,625)
Green, Caroline J	6:32:39 (31,257)
Green, Coral	5:51:19 (30,026)
Green, Diana M	5:48:48 (29,897)
Green, Fiona	4:13:57 (14,553)
Green, Helen S	4:34:42 (19,759)
Green, Jackie A	4:35:15 (19,875)
Green, Joanne L	4:01:32 (11,605)
Green, Josephine	4:59:40 (24,934)
Green, Karen E	3:59:14 (11,069)
Green, Lucy A	4:46:16 (22,311)
Green, Mandy	4:39:26 (20,814)
Green, Michelle C	6:09:21 (30,711)
Green, Nichola K	3:47:49 (7,950)
Green, Ruth	5:32:10 (28,748)
Green, Sarah R	5:31:25 (28,697)
Green, Theodosia	4:14:11 (14,607)
Green, Trudi	3:29:59 (4,585)
Green, Zoe	5:33:24 (28,842)
Greenall, Frances M	5:41:41 (29,466)
Greenall, Vicki A	3:09:13 (1,920)
Greenbank, Deborah	4:55:36 (24,118)
Green-Davis, Elizabeth A	4:59:04 (24,806)
Greene, Janet	5:01:07 (25,163)
Greene, Rosemary A	5:51:20 (30,027)
Greenfield, Jane E	4:42:10 (21,380)
Greenfield, Joanna D	5:03:08 (25,463)
Greening, Christine	6:04:35 (30,583)
Greentree, Prudence A	4:52:15 (23,496)
Greenwood, Celia	3:46:12 (7,578)
Greenwood, Clare M	4:25:46 (17,503)
Greenwood, Eliazbeth J	4:36:49 (20,211)
Greenwood, Kathryn E	4:48:17 (22,735)
Greenwood, Marilyn	4:28:20 (18,174)
Gregg, Lisa M	4:40:20 (20,991)
Gregori, Barbara M	4:36:13 (20,076)
Gregory, Allison K	4:59:57 (24,983)
Gregory, Donna L	4:31:44 (19,039)
Gregory, Kate	4:46:02 (22,259)
Gregory, Marie	4:51:37 (23,366)
Gregory, Sarah L	3:45:52 (7,498)
Gregory, Suzanne K	4:07:13 (12,945)
Gregson, Deborah A	4:17:52 (15,526)
Gregurec, Julia	4:28:30 (18,230)
Gremillion, Ledsha R	8:10:00 (31,953)
Gremo, Charley L	5:20:11 (27,593)
Grewenig, Heike	5:15:28 (27,074)
Grice, Clare A	3:10:02 (2,004)
Grierson-Jackson, Jean	3:43:35 (6,978)
Grieve, Kat	3:51:20 (8,842)
Grieveson, Jane	4:37:10 (20,284)
Griffin, Colette M	5:31:19 (28,685)
Griffin, Jennie	4:11:28 (13,962)
Griffin, Lorne	5:41:22 (29,434)
Griffin, Mandy	4:14:23 (14,648)
Griffin, Patricia	5:25:23 (28,128)
Griffiths, Alison C	3:33:48 (5,236)
Griffiths, Amanda	4:37:37 (20,361)
Griffiths, Angela M	3:33:49 (5,237)
Griffiths, Bianca	5:46:56 (29,808)
Griffiths, Coleen	4:52:39 (23,557)
Griffiths, Elizabeth J	5:51:45 (30,049)
Griffiths, Helen C	5:47:28 (29,834)
Griffiths, Joy L	3:36:11 (5,639)
Griffiths, Karen E	5:16:41 (27,220)
Griffiths, Kelly J	5:12:42 (26,714)
Griffiths, Kelly R	4:59:29 (24,901)
Griffiths, Patricia A	5:35:16 (28,977)
Griffiths, Rebekah A	3:33:32 (5,194)
Grimes, Claire M	4:53:13 (23,616)
Grimes, Michele	5:33:01 (28,811)
Grimes, Samantha	3:56:40 (10,296)
Grimsey, Jan L	6:56:12 (31,574)
Grimshaw, Caroline A	4:47:53 (22,651)
Grindell, Julia P	4:25:53 (17,536)
Grindu, Christiane	4:12:58 (14,321)
Gringer, Domenica	4:47:20 (22,526)
Gristwood, Julia M	3:46:51 (7,713)
Gromett, Samantha J	3:42:51 (6,821)
Gronne, Margit Irene I	4:58:11 (24,636)
Grooby, Janis A	5:54:13 (30,159)
Groombridge, Ruth P	4:46:01 (22,255)
Groombrigde, Carrie A	5:57:43 (30,317)
Grothier, Lucy D	5:22:50 (27,860)
Grove, Dawn L	5:27:14 (28,328)
Grover, Jennifer J	7:25:23 (31,814)
Groves, Brigitte	4:56:50 (24,371)
Groves, Helen J	5:57:00 (30,288)
Groves-Raines, Heidi M	3:49:43 (8,428)

Name	Time (Position)
Grubb, Sarah L	3:53:08 (9,291)
Grum, Catherine I	4:55:11 (24,034)
Grundy, Celia	4:51:42 (23,382)
Grzyb, Malgorzata A	4:46:43 (22,395)
Guard, Maureen	4:24:39 (17,218)
Guerroumi, Massera	3:54:58 (9,772)
Guesnon, Ghislaine	3:44:23 (7,150)
Guest, Kate E	4:56:50 (24,371)
Guidera, Rachel	5:54:18 (30,160)
Guignard, Lise	4:11:34 (13,988)
Guillien-André, Marie G	3:57:38 (10,578)
Guinard, Marie Pascal J	5:27:00 (28,301)
Guiney, Barbara J	5:05:22 (25,734)
Gulland, Sarah J	3:26:25 (3,906)
Gulliver, Claire T	3:44:02 (7,077)
Gundry, Jacqueline A	3:59:15 (11,070)
Gunn, Yvonne	5:18:29 (27,411)
Gunner, Lisa M	4:50:25 (23,162)
Gunter, Lorraine	5:21:58 (27,767)
Gupta, Sumeena	4:49:00 (22,875)
Gurney, Cathryn	4:47:36 (22,591)
Gurney, Ruth	6:44:53 (31,434)
Gutcher, Lianne	3:58:25 (10,824)
Guttenberger, Sharon K	4:15:25 (14,904)
Guy, Janet M	6:11:16 (30,763)
Guy, Rosemary	4:47:58 (22,666)
Guy, Samantha	3:38:29 (6,043)
Guynan, Justine S	6:19:23 (31,001)
Guyver, Lisa J	4:09:49 (13,585)
Gwaderi, Razia	6:34:58 (31,287)
Haber, Christine J	3:37:15 (5,822)
Habgood, Sarah L	3:39:58 (6,298)
Hackathorn, Teri M	5:20:42 (27,657)
Hackett, Ruth A	5:21:58 (27,767)
Hackett, Susie	4:29:04 (18,366)
Hackworth, Sarah J	4:03:34 (12,092)
Haddon, Natalie A	4:46:22 (22,333)
Hadfield, Janet	4:44:32 (21,917)
Hadley, Margaret A	4:58:24 (24,694)
Hadley, Marilyn	4:46:50 (22,411)
Hadley, Nicola J	4:32:22 (19,206)
Hagan, Grace M	5:24:07 (27,982)
Hagen, Jean L	4:47:18 (22,517)
Haggar, Tracy K	4:56:33 (24,322)
Hagger, Faye	4:46:56 (22,430)
Hagon, Tracey	4:13:26 (14,439)
Hahnel, Ilona	4:33:35 (19,482)
Haig-Ferguson, Ruth M	4:33:16 (19,419)
Haigh, Helen L	5:34:40 (28,936)
Haigh, Tarnya	5:43:38 (29,603)
Haile, Emma	4:15:08 (14,840)
Hailey, Dee	4:02:34 (11,870)
Haillay, Emma J	3:41:56 (6,627)
Haine, Alice L	5:41:35 (29,456)
Haines, Caroline J	5:26:38 (28,265)
Haines, Lesley L	3:16:41 (2,718)
Haines, Liliana	4:06:10 (12,705)
Haining, Rachel J	3:15:44 (2,628)
Hairsine, Janet E	3:25:57 (3,841)
Halberda, Ruth M	4:45:38 (22,171)
Hale, Carole	5:21:08 (27,694)
Hale, Caroline J	3:24:23 (3,613)
Hale, Griselda F	6:33:10 (31,268)
Hale, Irene S	4:53:24 (23,769)
Hale, Isla R	4:14:59 (14,801)
Hale, Katharine M	4:33:29 (19,467)
Hale, Sue	5:05:29 (25,756)
Hale, Vanessa J	4:04:52 (12,396)
Hales, Diane C	4:40:32 (21,034)
Hales, Elizabeth S	3:06:59 (1,704)
Halfhead, Harriet L	4:26:54 (17,812)
Halifax, Amanda I	6:27:48 (31,175)
Hall, Alison E	4:32:22 (19,206)
Hall, Amanda J	4:53:49 (23,769)
Hall, Cathy	4:23:36 (16,966)
Hall, Christine	4:40:22 (21,003)
Hall, Deborah A	4:16:36 (15,200)
Hall, Gillian M	4:00:48 (11,444)
Hall, Jennifer J	5:00:27 (25,059)
Hall, Kate	5:16:37 (27,213)
Hall, Kate M	6:12:49 (30,807)
Hall, Kathryn C	4:56:00 (24,206)
Hall, Ladan	5:28:28 (28,433)
Hall, Linda J	4:10:54 (13,848)
Hall, Louise J	4:22:22 (16,660)
Hall, Martha A	3:28:09 (4,254)
Hall, Melissa R	4:09:54 (13,607)
Hall, Moira	5:01:41 (25,254)
Hall, Pauline N	3:45:02 (7,311)
Hall, Stephanie K	4:13:09 (14,365)
Hall, Tracey	4:37:50 (20,415)
Hall, Wendy M	5:26:18 (28,224)
Hallam, Denise	4:24:58 (17,300)
Hallam, Jane S	4:19:26 (15,894)
Hallam, Tracey	4:33:45 (19,517)
Hallecker, Andrea	3:50:12 (8,547)
Hallett, Sandra	3:43:57 (7,054)
Halliburton, Sharon	3:48:54 (8,230)
Halliday, Sarah L	6:04:22 (30,578)
Halligan, Sarah J	4:38:50 (20,677)
Halliwell, Gemma L	4:15:44 (14,984)
Hallsworth, Anna K	4:15:09 (14,846)
Hall-Thompson, Beth R	3:45:53 (7,503)
Halsey, Barbara	6:08:20 (30,685)
Halsey, Sevren M	5:54:11 (30,157)
Halstead, Tracey L	3:45:18 (7,364)
Hamblin, Clare S	4:44:06 (21,815)
Hamer, Janice R	5:34:50 (28,944)
Hamer-Davies, Elizabeth A	6:12:25 (30,791)
Hamilton, Christine	3:33:38 (5,209)
Hamilton, Deborah N	3:28:38 (4,340)
Hamilton, Erni	3:15:04 (2,561)
Hamilton, Hilary	3:16:36 (2,710)
Hamilton, Margaret E	5:25:58 (28,194)
Hamlin, Katy C	4:38:20 (20,554)
Hammer, Katherine A	5:09:05 (26,250)
Hammer, Susan	4:29:55 (18,614)
Hammersley, Elizabeth M	4:42:01 (21,348)
Hammerton, Louise S	3:39:12 (6,163)
Hammerton, Miriam L	4:17:37 (15,458)
Hammond, Lesley M	4:25:37 (17,456)
Hammond, Lisa	4:48:00 (22,672)
Hammond, Petra A	8:22:47 (31,960)
Hampson, Anna	3:57:30 (10,538)
Hampton, Jane M	5:21:46 (27,755)
Hanakova, Jarka	4:45:34 (22,154)
Hancock, Emma L	4:52:04 (23,458)
Hancock, Lucy K	4:19:38 (15,934)
Hancock, Marie-Claire G	4:22:29 (16,697)
Hancock, Melissa	4:04:41 (12,345)
Hancox, Caroline	4:42:08 (21,378)
Hancox, Rona Dee	7:36:08 (31,879)
Hand, Claudia L	4:48:57 (22,865)
Handford, Sarah J	5:27:32 (28,359)
Haney, Gerri	4:20:25 (16,136)
Hanlon, Rogeria N	5:09:21 (26,285)
Hanna, Catherine R	3:29:03 (4,422)
Hannaford, Liz J	5:42:31 (29,515)
Hannah, Linda C	5:19:41 (27,520)
Hannant, Fiona	5:47:01 (29,811)
Hannigan, Ann	5:54:04 (30,153)
Hansell, Clare L	5:04:51 (25,670)
Hansell, Naomi I	4:35:41 (19,959)
Hansen, Alison	4:23:00 (16,812)
Hansen, Brooke	4:22:38 (16,733)
Hansen, Claire	4:18:36 (15,686)
Hansen, Darcy	4:42:04 (21,364)
Hansen, Gro Haarklou	4:34:52 (19,796)
Hansford, Joanna	5:36:00 (29,029)
Hanshaw, Geraldine T	5:13:52 (26,880)
Hanson, Claire L	4:00:56 (11,488)
Hanson, Emma	4:42:39 (19,276)
Hanson, Michele A	4:26:11 (17,626)
Hapke, Michelle A	6:33:21 (31,271)
Happs, Gillian S	4:47:48 (22,634)
Harbach, Elizabeth	4:03:27 (12,067)
Harber, Sandra A	5:24:04 (27,977)
Harbige, Tina C	4:57:50 (24,555)
Hardcastle, Stephanie J	5:18:49 (27,453)
Hardegger, Monica T	3:51:49 (8,972)
Harden, Alexis	5:44:56 (29,688)
Hardey, Jennifer E	6:54:46 (31,556)
Harding, Alexandra E	4:26:34 (17,718)
Harding, Anita L	3:53:58 (9,493)
Harding, Belinda	4:31:21 (18,935)
Harding, Emma L	5:26:25 (28,243)
Harding, Jane S	4:31:15 (18,909)
Hardman, Dianne C	5:15:31 (27,082)
Hardman, Pamela M	5:10:48 (26,483)
Hards, Sarah E	5:43:12 (29,577)
Hardy, Alicia K	5:03:23 (25,497)
Hardy, Caroline J	4:50:53 (23,249)
Hardy, Karen M	3:57:53 (10,646)
Hardy, Lisa M	5:01:45 (25,268)
Hardy, Lorraine	3:05:16 (1,553)
Hare, Darcy	4:31:13 (18,899)
Hare, Rachel H	4:54:55 (23,983)
Hargie, Patricia G	4:43:12 (21,605)
Hargrave, Louise S	4:36:59 (10,385)
Harison, Rachel C	4:43:29 (21,682)
Harker, Kay M	4:40:56 (21,113)
Harland, Rachel C	4:02:45 (11,914)
Harlow, Jane A	4:31:30 (18,982)
Harman, Claire E	6:11:55 (30,781)
Harman, Maria P	5:53:53 (30,148)
Harne, Vicky R	4:03:06 (11,979)
Harnisch, Sybille	4:56:29 (24,305)
Harper, Alison C	5:38:01 (29,183)
Harper, Kathleen A	5:03:47 (25,554)
Harper, Sarah	6:44:53 (31,434)
Harris, Abi	4:06:41 (12,817)
Harris, Anita J	4:43:50 (21,753)
Harris, Caroline A	6:14:45 (30,876)
Harris, Carolyn	4:09:25 (13,482)
Harris, Dee	6:10:29 (30,741)
Harris, Donna J	3:56:20 (10,190)
Harris, Emma J	5:03:35 (25,529)
Harris, Emma J	5:50:42 (30,000)
Harris, Jane E	3:54:58 (9,772)
Harris, Linda	3:05:00 (1,524)
Harris, Nicola C	4:13:31 (14,456)
Harris, Nicola J	4:20:28 (16,151)
Harris, Nicola J	4:28:30 (18,230)
Harris, Nicola L	5:05:30 (25,760)
Harris, Rachel C	6:02:26 (30,503)
Harris, Sandra	5:07:43 (26,081)
Harris, Sarah A	4:58:56 (24,785)
Harris, Sarah E	4:36:38 (20,162)
Harris, Sharalie M	4:31:34 (18,995)
Harris, Tammie A	5:16:49 (27,232)
Harris, Vanessa J	5:30:20 (28,609)
Harris, Victoria E	4:15:46 (14,993)
Harrison, Elizabeth J	5:35:44 (29,013)
Harrison, Gill M	3:29:22 (4,478)
Harrison, Jennifer M	4:54:32 (23,906)
Harrison, Judith	5:01:22 (25,198)
Harrison, Julie M	5:01:22 (25,198)
Harrison, Karen	3:30:07 (4,619)
Harrison, Louise J	4:15:14 (14,863)
Harrison, Ruth C	4:31:50 (19,056)
Harrison, Sarah D	6:22:07 (31,062)
Harrison, Sonja	5:13:53 (26,885)
Harrison, Sue C	2:38:20 (176)
Harrison, Susan T	4:31:39 (19,011)
Harrison, Susanna J	3:12:16 (2,226)
Harrison, Tania Y	5:05:44 (25,787)
Harrison, Vikki K	3:31:54 (4,901)
Harrison, Wendy E	4:22:35 (16,719)
Harrop, Bernadette L	3:29:25 (4,490)
Harrow, Alison J	3:34:14 (5,302)
Harsent, Jill E	4:45:21 (22,109)
Hart, Alice G	3:59:52 (11,258)
Hart, Barbara-Ann	5:41:43 (29,470)
Hart, Caroline F	4:31:54 (19,080)
Hart, Caroline J	3:34:41 (5,366)
Hart, Cherie-Anne C	3:51:30 (8,888)
Hart, Denece	5:27:39 (28,368)
Hart, Gail	5:08:47 (26,213)
Hart, Hazel A	5:09:17 (26,267)
Hart, Linda R	4:41:58 (21,342)
Hart, Rachel E	4:17:21 (15,386)
Hart, Sarah E	6:20:30 (31,024)
Hart, Victoria	4:25:40 (17,469)
Harte, Barbara A	3:48:48 (8,211)
Hartigan, Beverley M	3:03:03 (1,369)
Hartland, Jasmine	4:22:27 (16,681)
Hartland, Wendy L	4:43:16 (21,627)
Hartless, Pauline Q	5:50:06 (29,971)
Hartley, Dawn K	4:24:22 (17,156)

Hoch, Anna 4:41:42 (21,283)
Hockedy, Sally I 5:34:14 (28,905)
Hockings, Kim T 5:57:43 (30,317)
Hockley, Marie 3:48:56 (8,238)
Hodge, Jacqueline E 6:11:11 (30,759)
Hodge, Jodi T 4:38:01 (20,475)
Hodge, Lesley 4:14:39 (14,718)
Hodges, Natalie J 5:36:47 (29,086)
Hodgkin, Louise 6:09:54 (30,724)
Hodgkins, Amanda 4:32:59 (19,354)
Hodgson, Jane L 4:02:00 (11,717)
Hodgson, Shelley 4:25:31 (17,434)
Hodson, Laura J 5:05:31 (25,766)
Hodson, Nicola J 4:27:18 (17,920)
Hoe, Anita J 6:15:38 (30,899)
Hoffen, Kate V 4:18:21 (15,618)
Hoffman, Patricia A 5:05:18 (25,726)
Hofland, Justine M 6:12:50 (30,809)
Hofmann, Stephanie 4:32:36 (19,261)
Hofstotter, Petra 4:43:10 (21,595)
Hogan, Susan A 4:07:40 (13,048)
Hogarth, Lynn 5:31:12 (28,674)
Hogarth, Margaret E 4:53:33 (23,710)
Hogben, Carolyn A 4:20:30 (16,159)
Hogg, Gillian D 5:26:24 (28,240)
Hogg, Katherine L 5:38:55 (29,256)
Hogg, Natalie M 5:12:01 (26,635)
Hogkin, Sarah J 6:18:35 (30,976)
Hogsden, Juliet E 5:15:17 (27,054)
Hoines, Tracey A 4:27:25 (17,941)
Holbrook, Katie M 5:35:49 (29,018)
Holdcroft, Clare L 3:48:19 (8,081)
Holden, Claire 6:41:16 (31,378)
Holden, Dorothy 4:58:00 (24,593)
Holden, Heather J 4:15:03 (14,814)
Holden, Janet 4:34:22 (19,685)
Holden, Rachael E 5:26:21 (28,234)
Holden, Sandra M 5:05:39 (25,780)
Holden, Tracey 4:22:11 (16,598)
Holder, Desonta 5:45:30 (29,726)
Holland, Angela 5:52:55 (30,123)
Holland, Claire L 4:19:29 (15,908)
Holland, Vicky E 6:00:01 (30,409)
Hollands, Michelle K 3:58:28 (10,843)
Holliday, Clare R 4:21:27 (16,376)
Holliday, Jill 4:35:04 (19,835)
Holliday, Kim 4:00:08 (11,323)
Holliday, Susan M 3:41:54 (6,618)
Hollidge, Heather A 6:43:52 (31,416)
Holling, Lene 4:15:04 (14,818)
Hollingshead, Ruth E 7:15:05 (31,746)
Hollingsworth, Clare E 5:25:51 (28,181)
Hollins, Annick 5:01:00 (25,145)
Hollins, Claire L 4:42:43 (21,499)
Hollinshead, Monique G 3:04:48 (1,510)
Hollis, Claire A 3:59:47 (11,236)
Hollomby, Jane E 4:58:08 (24,624)
Holloway, Catherine J 3:17:58 (2,845)
Holly, Kim 5:03:03 (25,453)
Hollyman, Anna M 3:51:45 (8,955)
Holmes, Alison M 4:06:04 (12,675)
Holmes, Deborah L 3:58:39 (10,909)
Holmes, Fiona J 6:32:36 (31,256)
Holmes, Gillian M 5:35:29 (28,999)
Holmes, Laura A 4:48:55 (22,857)
Holmes, Laura S 3:26:45 (3,973)
Holmes, Lesley 3:53:05 (9,275)
Holmes, Linda C 4:29:35 (18,517)
Holmes, Samantha L 4:28:17 (18,165)
Holmes, Sandra D 3:04:19 (1,476)
Holmes, Susan J 6:23:59 (31,107)
Holmes, Susan N 4:33:10 (19,396)
Holohan, Caroline A 6:21:08 (31,035)
Holroyd, Annette B 4:38:44 (20,649)
Holt, Christine E 6:28:54 (31,187)
Holt, Genevieve C 6:04:56 (30,592)
Holt, Julia A 5:05:33 (25,771)
Holt, Suzanne 4:57:34 (24,508)
Holt, Tina 5:08:35 (26,190)
Holt, Veronica A 4:46:09 (22,279)
Holzhauer, Elisabeth 4:27:51 (18,055)
Homer, Britta 3:23:06 (3,450)
Homersham, Nicola 6:21:25 (31,040)
Homfray, Mel J 5:23:31 (27,924)
Honeybourne, Julie R 4:53:43 (23,753)
Honeywill, Jenna R 4:33:54 (19,566)
Hoogerbrugge, Marianne 2:57:25 (908)
Hoogeveen, Marielle 3:54:17 (9,583)
Hoogveld, Maike 4:28:18 (18,170)
Hooke, Amanda 5:45:16 (29,709)
Hooker, Kelly A 6:17:59 (30,954)
Hooper, Janet E 4:09:36 (13,524)
Hooper, Julie S 4:38:10 (20,513)
Hooper, Karen T 5:40:21 (29,361)
Hooper, Martha 5:39:55 (29,327)
Hooton, Mary 5:11:54 (26,620)
Hope, Alison 4:27:50 (18,050)
Hope, Lisa C 5:30:17 (28,605)
Hope, Sarah L 4:30:39 (18,791)
Hopkins, Alison C 3:47:06 (7,779)
Hopkins, Clare M 4:39:00 (20,729)
Hopkins, Lynn 5:44:06 (29,631)
Hopkins, Philippa 4:27:03 (17,856)
Hopper, Jennifer M 5:07:06 (25,982)
Hopwood, Joanna 5:38:14 (29,199)
Horan, Jennifer S 3:51:19 (8,836)
Horkins, Candis S 7:37:04 (31,885)
Horn, Fiona E 4:03:21 (12,046)
Horne, Joanne C 5:17:22 (27,290)
Horner, Lucy V 5:11:26 (26,572)
Hornsby, Gillian L 3:52:49 (9,204)
Hornschuh, Renée 5:28:58 (28,481)
Horobin, Louise 4:48:37 (22,797)
Horohan, Sarah L 4:20:17 (16,095)
Horsford, Sara A 6:48:59 (31,482)
Horton, Janet E 5:30:46 (28,642)
Horton, Sarah J 4:20:35 (16,181)
Horwich, Zoe A 4:17:16 (15,360)
Hosburn, Emma J 4:13:55 (14,547)
Hosking, Heather E 4:39:49 (20,879)
Hosking, Mimi 4:18:04 (15,568)
Hossack, Susan L 4:10:10 (13,668)
Hostetler, Carmen M 4:11:26 (13,956)
Hotchkiss, Pauline 4:28:01 (18,102)
Hough, Jane S 4:22:05 (16,565)
Houghton, Kristina D 4:55:33 (24,108)
Houghton, Sandra 4:01:42 (11,650)
Houlden, Nicola J 4:55:01 (23,999)
Hounsell, Joanne P 4:15:02 (14,812)
Hourd, Tricia 4:46:58 (22,439)
Hourston, Fiona J 4:40:28 (21,021)
Housden, Tess S 4:34:01 (19,594)
House, Rachel L 4:58:01 (24,597)
Househam, Elizabeth A 4:22:48 (16,771)
Houston, Sharon A 5:35:57 (29,025)
Houwen Holwerda, Frida 5:25:30 (28,137)
How, Alison L 3:53:08 (9,291)
Howard, Caroline L 3:27:25 (4,108)
Howard, Geraldine A 4:16:21 (15,131)
Howard, Hazel 3:56:12 (10,142)
Howard, Jacqueline I 5:30:09 (28,596)
Howard, Juliet A 5:27:30 (28,355)
Howard, Lisa J 4:58:56 (24,785)
Howard, Lynn 4:51:51 (23,408)
Howard, Sarah P 5:47:38 (29,848)
Howard, Sue 5:03:01 (25,448)
Howat, Michelle Y 3:57:41 (10,589)
Howdle, Sally 4:46:29 (22,354)
Howe, Angela D 2:59:30 (1,121)
Howe, Anne L 3:53:51 (9,459)
Howe, Hilary A 4:52:05 (23,461)
Howe, Natalie M 4:28:55 (18,331)
Howell, Anushka 4:37:17 (20,313)
Howell, Jude 4:25:53 (17,536)
Howell, Katrina E 4:58:11 (24,636)
Howell, Katy 4:08:51 (13,334)
Howell, Nicola S 5:05:45 (25,792)
Howell, Pamela I 4:39:04 (20,743)
Howell, Zoe L 5:01:43 (25,261)
Howells, Charlotte A 5:06:13 (25,876)
Howick, Geraldine 5:44:22 (29,646)
Howitt, Judith 6:07:31 (30,663)
Howle, Eleanor J 6:08:09 (30,677)
Howlett, Dena L 6:23:04 (31,080)
Howlett, Melissa J 5:58:16 (30,337)
Howlett, Midge E 3:48:34 (8,139)
Hoy, Diane T 5:21:13 (27,701)
Hoyland, Joanne M 3:28:16 (4,278)
Hribal, Lucie 5:05:01 (25,696)
Htomson, Jane E 4:09:01 (13,384)
Hubbard, Penelope 4:31:55 (19,088)
Huckle, Lita M 5:29:42 (28,557)
Huckle, Sarah L 4:54:11 (23,835)
Huckle, Susan A 5:14:46 (26,999)
Hudders, Yvonne M 5:03:14 (25,480)
Hudson, Catherine 4:26:33 (17,714)
Hudson, Elizabeth M 5:31:36 (28,708)
Hudson, Gill M 4:31:42 (19,029)
Hudson, Janice L 4:16:54 (15,282)
Hudson, Leila A 3:47:41 (7,925)
Hudson, Lindsay 5:05:31 (25,766)
Hudson, Nicky 3:11:54 (2,181)
Hudson, Nicola M 3:47:44 (7,934)
Hudson, Suzi J 4:41:52 (21,321)
Hudson, Vanessa H 4:28:30 (18,230)
Hudson, Victoria 5:43:01 (29,567)
Huey, Suzanne S 4:54:58 (23,989)
Huffer, Debbie K 4:01:29 (11,592)
Huggett, Bridget M 5:53:57 (30,150)
Huggett, Sylvia A 3:45:07 (7,322)
Hughes, Amanda 5:39:10 (29,282)
Hughes, Becky 6:44:14 (31,420)
Hughes, Catherine 4:11:01 (13,875)
Hughes, Clare L 3:45:53 (7,503)
Hughes, Diane L 4:12:05 (14,113)
Hughes, Elaine A 7:26:41 (31,823)
Hughes, Gail P 4:44:33 (21,925)
Hughes, Jane E 6:35:14 (31,291)
Hughes, Janice M 4:25:58 (17,561)
Hughes, Lucy 5:31:20 (28,688)
Hughes, Maggie A 2:58:43 (1,048)
Hughes, Mandy J 4:59:59 (24,989)
Hughes, Marion J 7:03:20 (31,655)
Hughes, Meg Y 4:14:27 (14,665)
Hughes, Nicola J 4:42:00 (21,344)
Hughes, Pauline 4:06:58 (12,882)
Hughes, Rachel L 6:42:36 (31,399)
Hughes, Ruth 4:31:29 (18,969)
Hughes, Ruth M 5:04:57 (25,686)
Hughes, Sarah C 5:42:59 (29,559)
Hughes, Shelley 4:25:09 (17,351)
Hughes, Shirley M 4:10:43 (13,804)
Hughes, Sylvia M 6:51:08 (31,513)
Hullcoop, Jane 6:08:40 (30,690)
Humberstone, Josephine C 3:52:55 (9,231)
Hume, Emmy 3:48:39 (8,168)
Hume, Shirley 3:37:18 (5,839)
Hume, Sophie C 4:52:41 (23,567)
Humphrey, Sonia N 3:26:03 (3,854)
Humphreys Elvis, Rebecca 4:52:30 (23,532)
Humphreys, Susan L 5:55:17 (30,215)
Humphries, Mary M 4:35:06 (19,843)
Humphries, Sharon T 5:05:59 (25,842)
Humphry, Charlotte 5:36:12 (29,040)
Hun Ter, Christine H 6:08:37 (30,688)
Hunt, Christine V 4:15:58 (15,044)
Hunt, Joanna 3:58:00 (10,671)
Hunt, Kathrine 5:26:58 (28,297)
Hunt, Linda 3:54:46 (9,715)
Hunt, Sarah 5:12:43 (26,715)
Hunter, Angela N 4:59:20 (24,858)
Hunter, Anne 4:33:53 (19,556)
Hunter, Emma L 3:24:40 (3,648)
Hunter, Jackie A 5:24:07 (27,982)
Hunter, Juliet A 4:26:32 (17,710)
Hunter, Susanne 3:44:51 (7,273)
Huntington, Lucy C 4:25:40 (17,469)
Huntley, Susan J 5:00:44 (25,101)
Hurd, Paula B 3:52:51 (9,213)
Hurrell, Kirsten 5:15:58 (27,130)
Hurrell, Ruth 4:31:04 (18,870)
Hurst, Julie E 4:21:28 (16,384)
Hurt, Hazel 6:01:54 (30,485)
Huss, Keeley L 4:58:40 (24,750)
Hussain, Nazeya 4:55:38 (24,125)
Hussain, Sally-Ann 4:39:40 (20,855)
Husted, Carole A 6:28:39 (31,185)
Huszar, Maria 7:05:33 (31,674)
Hutchings, Sally 5:36:47 (29,086)

Jones, Melinda J	3:47:16 (7,822)
Jones, Melissa D	4:41:47 (21,304)
Jones, Michaela	4:31:23 (18,946)
Jones, Nicky D	3:19:21 (3,000)
Jones, Nina L	4:03:08 (11,990)
Jones, Paddy I	5:30:05 (28,591)
Jones, Penny	4:07:21 (12,970)
Jones, Penny A	4:30:50 (18,825)
Jones, Rachel E	5:30:40 (28,635)
Jones, Rebecca F	4:43:44 (21,732)
Jones, Rebecca M	3:41:04 (6,486)
Jones, Rebekah	5:58:24 (30,340)
Jones, Rhian E	4:15:41 (14,973)
Jones, Rhona S	4:43:27 (21,673)
Jones, Rosemary A	4:26:07 (17,613)
Jones, Ruth E	5:21:02 (27,682)
Jones, Samantha A	5:17:23 (27,293)
Jones, Samantha J	6:13:58 (30,843)
Jones, Sandra L	4:16:21 (15,131)
Jones, Sarah	5:57:14 (30,296)
Jones, Sarah J	4:45:01 (22,032)
Jones, Sarah J	6:09:06 (30,703)
Jones, Sarah V	5:02:08 (25,310)
Jones, Saran C	4:04:07 (12,214)
Jones, Sharon	3:58:11 (10,750)
Jones, Shelley E	6:33:00 (31,263)
Jones, Sian M	5:18:02 (27,373)
Jones, Tina	4:59:51 (24,965)
Jones, Tina L	4:23:29 (16,937)
Jones, Tracey C	5:43:15 (29,579)
Jones, Vanessa D	5:24:59 (28,080)
Jones, Victoria H	5:02:53 (25,433)
Jones, Victoria J	5:37:56 (29,175)
Jones, Victoria L	6:49:09 (31,485)
Jones, Wendy	3:09:06 (1,909)
Jones, Yvonne I	3:31:56 (4,913)
Jones, Yvonne T	5:01:35 (25,238)
Jones, Zoe H	3:37:57 (5,953)
Jordan, Eileen M	5:02:57 (25,440)
Jordan, Rosie J	4:55:00 (23,995)
Jorth, Susan	5:22:59 (27,870)
Joslin, Alison	4:44:04 (21,810)
Joubel, Gwenola	3:25:07 (3,707)
Jouslin, Marianne	3:42:07 (6,670)
Jowett, Faye L	4:33:46 (19,527)
Joyce, Amelia A	5:32:13 (28,751)
Joyce, Ann	5:06:50 (25,951)
Joyce, Catherine	6:59:17 (31,611)
Joyce, Maria	5:22:52 (27,865)
Joyce, Marion F	5:04:39 (25,645)
Joyner, Lesley J	4:49:26 (22,961)
Juckett, Stacy M	4:15:46 (14,993)
Judd, Diana M	5:15:45 (27,100)
Judd, Laura	4:24:59 (17,307)
Judd, Zoe	7:04:14 (31,662)
Judge, Belinda J	4:21:55 (16,505)
Judson, Jill Y	4:41:05 (21,139)
Jukes, Philippa	6:30:27 (31,212)
Junghans, Antje	4:56:16 (24,255)
Jupp, Gail	3:56:33 (10,266)
Jupp, Helen E	4:08:46 (13,311)
Jurd, Jasmine A	4:55:10 (24,031)
Jury, Martina M	4:29:02 (18,358)
Jutte, Taryn J	4:45:44 (22,195)
Kaempif, Ina	4:50:54 (23,251)
Kail, Dorian J	4:03:08 (11,990)
Kail, Nancy R	5:14:05 (26,912)
Kakehashi, Suzy	4:58:06 (24,620)
Kalinik, Eve	4:01:27 (11,588)
Kalymnios, Triada I	4:46:06 (22,270)
Kamijo, Yumiko	7:55:16 (31,925)
Kanegaonkar, Rita	5:11:58 (26,627)
Kantor, Amanda	4:34:00 (19,587)
Karg, Karin	4:26:28 (17,691)
Karimali, Magdalini	2:46:01 (359)
Karlsson, Ulrika C	4:31:08 (18,885)
Karooz, Julia M	5:07:12 (25,992)
Karvonen, Lissa E	4:18:37 (15,691)
Kary, Nicola	4:25:39 (17,465)
Kasapi, Eleni	4:38:07 (20,499)
Katz, Joanna	4:21:10 (16,302)
Kaur, Kamaljit	7:19:28 (31,785)
Kavanagh, Jan	4:45:52 (22,222)

Kavde, Karen J	4:56:46 (24,358)
Kay, Clare J	5:01:55 (25,289)
Kay, Zoe I	3:26:22 (3,900)
Keal, Verity	4:25:34 (17,444)
Keane, Susie M	5:39:47 (29,318)
Kearley, Vivienne T	5:25:27 (28,132)
Kearney, Melanie J	5:25:47 (28,173)
Kearns, Nicola	5:00:42 (25,095)
Keasley, Jacqueline	3:37:28 (5,870)
Keating, Siobhan M	4:28:07 (18,126)
Keay, Jeanne K	4:55:02 (24,002)
Kedney, Carol M	4:25:43 (17,481)
Keeble, Vivienne M	4:48:46 (22,830)
Keefe, Jenny A	5:31:50 (28,726)
Keenan, Margareth	5:31:11 (28,671)
Keenan, Nicki J	5:00:36 (25,076)
Keenan, Rachel M	5:07:30 (26,046)
Keene, Alison T	5:03:00 (25,446)
Keenleyside, Kathryn S	4:35:11 (19,861)
Keenoy, Andrea J	4:07:00 (12,891)
Keeping, Sarah L	7:15:05 (31,746)
Keet-Marsh, Lorayne M	3:56:02 (10,094)
Kefford-Watson, Angela F	3:16:20 (2,677)
Keh, Joanna	4:17:16 (15,360)
Keighley, Sally A	4:30:36 (18,782)
Keith, Caroline M	4:46:55 (22,425)
Keith, Catherine	4:15:17 (14,879)
Kelleher, Susanne M	5:04:59 (25,690)
Keller, Kerstin	4:53:48 (23,766)
Kelly, Angela	4:46:13 (22,304)
Kelly, Anne-Louise	3:28:27 (4,310)
Kelly, Bethan N	4:51:16 (23,312)
Kelly, Diane	3:22:03 (3,308)
Kelly, Maire	4:55:38 (24,125)
Kelly, Peg	4:06:07 (12,693)
Kelly, Simone	5:11:51 (26,610)
Kelly, Sue E	4:36:02 (20,036)
Kelly, Tara	6:36:12 (31,310)
Kemp, Andrea N	4:58:13 (24,643)
Kemp, Gail L	5:13:21 (26,811)
Kemp, Hilary D	4:00:57 (11,494)
Kemp, Kira G	3:36:46 (5,738)
Kemp, Robyn	4:57:01 (24,406)
Kempster, Jackie	4:54:27 (23,885)
Kempton, Catherine J	4:31:21 (18,935)
Kendall, Jeanette	3:32:22 (4,981)
Kenden, Fran	3:30:55 (4,767)
Kendrick, Gayle	4:35:38 (19,950)
Kennan, Louise E	4:18:37 (15,691)
Kennard, Amber S	4:45:10 (22,075)
Kennard, Lisa	4:47:52 (22,649)
Kenneally, Tanya	4:05:30 (12,539)
Kennedy, Donna L	4:01:39 (11,633)
Kennedy, Emma	5:56:40 (30,277)
Kennedy, Jane A	4:01:40 (11,640)
Kennedy, Julie	5:12:08 (26,646)
Kennedy, Kathryn D	4:08:05 (13,129)
Kennedy, Linda	4:06:48 (12,836)
Kennedy, Lorna A	5:35:58 (29,026)
Kennedy, Lorna E	3:55:14 (9,860)
Kennedy, Noreen	5:49:41 (29,942)
Kennedy, Ruth A	4:27:52 (18,059)
Kennedy, Sinead	4:41:02 (21,131)
Kennerson, Emma M	4:43:15 (21,620)
Kennett, Deborah S	5:13:37 (26,847)
Kennett, Elizabeth J	3:32:41 (5,041)
Kennett, Mia R	4:15:15 (14,870)
Kent, Alma	5:34:22 (28,913)
Kent, Nicki	4:33:22 (19,441)
Kent, Rachael L	5:45:20 (29,715)
Kent, Ruth M	4:27:29 (17,951)
Kent, Tiffany J	4:01:45 (11,659)
Keough, Julie	4:02:14 (11,789)
Keppel, Henny A	4:41:18 (21,187)
Kernahan, Emma C	6:08:57 (30,696)
Kernan, Emma J	4:25:57 (17,555)
Kerner, Caroll	3:37:33 (5,879)
Kerr, Angela	4:37:57 (20,454)
Kerr, Jill C	7:09:50 (31,708)
Kerr, Linza	4:32:37 (19,266)
Kerr, Marie E	5:38:57 (29,261)
Kerr, Marion H	5:21:26 (27,724)
Kerr, Mary	4:03:34 (12,092)

Kerr, Val	3:30:14 (4,641)
Kerridge, Victoria L	4:26:13 (17,639)
Kerrigan, Christine A	4:10:24 (13,734)
Kerschl, Heidi G	5:05:45 (25,786)
Kestseven, Joanna C	5:04:43 (25,653)
Kettle, Anthea J	3:59:38 (11,198)
Kewley, Lucy R	4:44:54 (22,002)
Key, Kathryn A	5:06:34 (25,920)
Keys, Diane J	5:16:31 (27,192)
Khadoi, Laura H	3:49:23 (8,352)
Khalique, Nageena	4:01:33 (11,610)
Khan, Balquees Y	4:29:12 (18,402)
Khan, Cheryl M	5:40:08 (29,347)
Khan, Saira	4:33:36 (19,486)
Khan, Shanaz	5:39:47 (29,318)
Khetani, Heidi J	6:53:02 (31,542)
Khouri, Carla L	5:07:17 (26,006)
Kibble, Carol A	6:21:42 (31,052)
Kibble, Mary J	4:52:02 (23,453)
Kibble, Sally E	4:40:57 (21,115)
Kidby, Christine H	7:47:02 (31,910)
Kidney, Roseanne M	4:33:16 (19,419)
Kieran, Gwen M	3:13:54 (2,424)
Kiesling, Jutta	4:43:12 (21,605)
Kift, Joanne	5:01:01 (25,146)
Kilay, Betsy	4:59:15 (24,839)
Kilgour, Vivien Y	3:52:20 (9,096)
Killean, Elizabeth J	5:39:38 (29,313)
Killick, Nina	4:26:12 (17,631)
Killington, Lorraine D	5:26:50 (28,282)
Kim, Young H	4:59:41 (24,936)
Kimber, Helen L	4:23:49 (17,017)
Kimber-Smith, Esther R	4:41:26 (21,228)
Kimlim, Juliet	4:56:27 (24,293)
Kimmitt, Jackie M	5:20:17 (27,605)
Kimpe, Kathleen	4:48:21 (22,750)
Kinder, MA	4:16:46 (15,242)
King, Alison M	4:42:13 (21,388)
King, Andrea M	4:14:48 (14,758)
King, Anne E	5:04:54 (25,678)
King, Annette S	4:55:06 (24,013)
King, April L	4:52:53 (23,595)
King, Caroline E	5:18:26 (27,405)
King, Catherine J	5:17:24 (27,296)
King, Clair-Annette	4:15:59 (15,046)
King, Claire L	4:27:29 (17,951)
King, Deborah	3:34:37 (5,355)
King, Elizabeth M	4:30:53 (18,837)
King, Frances E	4:26:01 (17,571)
King, Hayley	4:48:19 (22,742)
King, Jane	5:05:46 (25,795)
King, Janine M	4:43:25 (21,667)
King, Laura Y	4:19:56 (16,008)
King, Lindsay H	5:29:34 (28,541)
King, Melissa	5:51:50 (30,052)
King, Natalie S	5:02:35 (25,387)
King, Sarah A	5:19:26 (27,497)
King, Sarah G	4:16:42 (15,229)
King, Sharon D	4:52:00 (23,438)
King, Susan A	4:59:19 (24,852)
King, Teresa R	3:03:49 (1,433)
King, Tina S	5:13:29 (26,822)
King, Tracey E	5:09:04 (26,247)
King, Virginia	4:25:46 (17,503)
King, Yvonne	4:03:15 (12,017)
Kingdon, Paula	4:16:44 (15,234)
Kingsley, Anna	4:54:53 (23,974)
Kingston, Amy-Rose	4:29:55 (18,454)
Kingston, Deborah	4:30:01 (18,634)
Kingston, Elizabeth L	4:54:04 (23,810)
Kinnaman, Jennifer S	5:29:32 (28,537)
Kinsella, Lisa	6:23:16 (31,087)
Kinsey, Caroline B	4:15:40 (14,968)
Kinsey, Catherine S	4:47:03 (22,463)
Kirby, Fiona	4:49:40 (23,009)
Kirby, Joanna	4:55:54 (24,183)
Kirby, Maria A	4:50:41 (23,215)
Kirby, Maureen	4:20:12 (16,064)
Kirby, Paula E	5:04:54 (25,678)
Kirby, Sayula G	3:35:17 (5,477)
Kirby, Zoe A	4:57:08 (24,424)
Kirk, Elizabeth S	5:36:48 (29,090)
Kirk, Lesley S	3:21:19 (3,233)

Kirk, Marianne 4:21:47 (16,475)
Kirk, Rachel 5:18:04 (27,376)
Kirkby, Rachel 4:14:22 (14,641)
Kirkcaldy, Helen L 4:46:19 (22,322)
Kirkhouse, Sally 4:41:18 (21,187)
Kirkpatrick, Katherine A 4:42:12 (21,386)
Kirkwood-Lowe, Sue M 5:09:46 (26,351)
Kirsch, Anna F 4:21:45 (16,465)
Kirston, Maria M 5:19:01 (27,466)
Kirwan, Elaine T 4:26:55 (17,816)
Kishver, Shahida 5:43:56 (29,623)
Kissane, Corrin E 5:17:29 (27,306)
Kitchen, Charlotte A 4:13:48 (14,517)
Kitchen, Julie A 4:05:57 (12,650)
Kitchen, Stephanie 7:53:04 (31,923)
Kitchine, Janette M 4:30:41 (18,797)
Kitching, Sally A 4:43:46 (21,741)
Kitching Dilima, Anna E 3:33:18 (5,160)
Kittilsen, Kristina R 3:51:12 (8,806)
Klaassen, Jessica J 5:10:50 (26,487)
Klein, Keely 4:52:00 (23,438)
Klein, Miriam X 4:48:17 (22,735)
Klein, Shanie 4:52:00 (23,438)
Klemedtson, Elna 4:46:59 (22,444)
Knee, Wendy E 5:06:34 (25,920)
Kneen, Suzanne M 4:49:50 (23,049)
Kneller, Sarah L 7:55:49 (31,926)
Knight, Ann E 5:21:33 (27,731)
Knight, Carol L 3:29:55 (4,574)
Knight, Caroline S 5:19:19 (27,492)
Knight, Catherine E 4:20:23 (16,126)
Knight, Claire D 3:29:58 (4,583)
Knight, Emily C 5:42:57 (29,552)
Knight, Jenny L 5:46:18 (29,770)
Knight, Julie 4:49:46 (23,033)
Knight, Kate 6:08:54 (30,693)
Knight, Margaret I 4:29:07 (18,381)
Knight, Rosie C 4:30:12 (18,679)
Knights, Lisa J 2:58:56 (1,069)
Knill, Pamela J 7:37:03 (31,884)
Knopp, Rosalind J 3:29:07 (4,437)
Knott, Angela 4:05:13 (12,466)
Knott, Bertha C 5:21:31 (27,728)
Knowlden, Tina M 4:35:09 (19,855)
Knowles, Emma J 4:11:43 (14,024)
Knowles, Joanne 5:14:57 (27,022)
Knowles, Laura P 4:03:58 (12,184)
Knox, Isobel 3:19:37 (3,029)
Koelewijn-Scheper, Hillichje 4:00:10 (11,331)
Kogan, Helen 6:00:15 (30,422)
Kol, Deborah A 3:45:35 (7,435)
Komp, Claudia 4:10:59 (13,866)
Konradt, Beate 5:04:25 (25,620)
Koppang, Deborah A 5:01:23 (25,201)
Koskei, Jane 2:46:16 (365)
Kostoris, Sarah V 4:55:51 (24,162)
Kotarba, Anna M 5:46:46 (29,803)
Koufou, Angela K 5:14:29 (26,957)
Kraftaite, Asta 4:20:51 (16,244)
Krawczyk, Danusia P 4:45:45 (22,199)
Krill, Allison P 3:27:20 (4,091)
Krishnan, Priya T 6:56:36 (31,580)
Kristensen, Kitty 3:23:37 (3,519)
Kroese, Rebecca L 4:12:39 (14,247)
Krollig, Sharon J 4:16:29 (15,171)
Krueger, Sousan 4:47:15 (22,509)
Krumm, Kimiko 3:27:00 (4,024)
Kruse, Jennifer A 3:28:00 (4,227)
Kuczaj, Daria 4:24:47 (17,246)
Kuhn, Trudy 3:29:23 (4,482)
Kullar, Richenda M 4:12:23 (14,165)
Kumar, Kathleen 4:55:09 (24,026)
Kunz, Beatrice 4:06:47 (12,834)
Kuper, Hannah E 4:29:51 (18,593)
Kuritko, Christina P 4:38:49 (20,670)
Kurz, Hazel L 4:57:49 (24,553)
Kussmaul, Sabine 4:29:55 (18,614)
Kwon Tilby, Young Hae 5:23:03 (27,874)
Lacey, Karen 5:15:13 (27,043)
Lack, Vicky M 3:58:21 (10,804)
Lackey, Sian P 5:36:32 (29,061)
Ladds, Katie 6:16:09 (30,912)
Lafferty, June M 5:28:33 (28,445)

Lagan, Gemma A 5:01:33 (25,229)
Lagomarsino, Laura 3:12:20 (2,233)
Lai, Alicia 4:35:21 (19,898)
Laidlaw, Linda 4:29:07 (18,381)
Laidler, Leonore 6:40:49 (31,368)
Laing, Lucy E 5:27:26 (28,350)
Laing, Victoria I 4:42:02 (21,355)
Lainsbury, Kelly-Anne 4:20:54 (16,261)
Lake, Debra C 4:14:44 (14,740)
Lakeland, Janine L 4:08:17 (13,170)
Lamb, Robyn 5:33:37 (28,860)
Lambe, Jennifer 5:38:33 (29,233)
Lambert, Daphne 6:23:29 (31,097)
Lambert, Jennie L 4:34:02 (19,599)
Lambert, Kim V 3:54:36 (9,666)
Lambert, Nathalie J 5:05:59 (25,842)
Lambert, Shannon 4:52:10 (23,476)
Lambert, Sue Q 3:36:21 (5,667)
Lambrechts, Patsy 5:03:24 (25,500)
Lamey, Josie V 3:59:50 (11,249)
Lander, Tracey J 4:36:05 (20,052)
Landing, Sarah 6:18:43 (30,982)
Lane, Alison J 3:14:02 (2,441)
Lane, Christine M 4:01:21 (11,572)
Lane, Debbie A 4:53:18 (23,671)
Lane, Helen J 4:48:17 (22,735)
Lane, Kellie M 4:07:39 (13,044)
Lane, Linda M 4:55:37 (24,122)
Lane, Sam L 4:13:34 (14,471)
Lane, Samantha 5:09:05 (26,250)
Lang, Fiona C 3:38:04 (5,971)
Lang, Melanie J 4:11:19 (13,933)
Lang, Nicola L 5:30:46 (28,642)
Langdale, Joanne 4:30:23 (18,724)
Langdon, Kaite J 4:50:13 (23,110)
Langensiepen, Julia 4:00:49 (11,449)
Langham, Victoria R 4:08:35 (13,256)
Langley, Faye 4:57:51 (24,557)
Langley, Heather J 5:51:41 (30,045)
Langley, Jill K 4:24:50 (17,260)
Langley, Joyce K 5:39:56 (29,328)
Langley, Lisa C 5:05:18 (25,726)
Langley-Hobbs, Joanna M 4:32:51 (19,322)
Langston, Caroline S 4:31:23 (18,946)
Lanham, Jennifer A 4:42:18 (21,414)
Lanigan, Sue 4:13:01 (14,332)
Lankenau, Naomi 4:48:51 (22,845)
Lankester, Anna 3:14:42 (2,525)
Lannon, Fiona J 4:54:15 (23,844)
Lansbury, Tracey J 7:02:07 (31,644)
Lapointe, Nathalie M 3:44:29 (7,181)
Larham, Pamela 3:59:40 (11,212)
Larkin, Mary 3:31:59 (4,922)
Larner, Barbara M 6:37:16 (31,325)
Larner, Catherine 6:04:11 (30,568)
Larner, Jaz 4:59:37 (24,923)
Larner, Sara-Jane 4:42:01 (21,348)
Larsen, Kira L 3:54:24 (9,612)
Larsen, Rikke 3:26:27 (3,910)
Laske, Bettina 5:14:16 (26,930)
Lasta, Antonella 6:09:13 (30,707)
Laudin, Jenny J 4:58:03 (24,609)
Lavender, Vanessa S 5:33:08 (28,818)
Lavers, Ann I 4:29:37 (18,527)
Lavigne, Christine 2:56:05 (818)
Lavin, Valerie 6:23:06 (31,081)
Lavis, Libby A 4:02:14 (11,789)
Law, Barbara D 4:10:19 (13,708)
Law, Caroline L 6:13:41 (30,838)
Law, Nicola A 5:26:20 (28,228)
Law, Tia G 5:13:20 (26,809)
Lawless, Kate S 4:12:35 (14,228)
Lawrence, Carianne S 5:24:53 (28,065)
Lawrence, Janet R 4:37:03 (20,261)
Lawrence, Joy 6:23:28 (31,096)
Lawrence, Susan C 4:43:26 (21,671)
Lawrence, Suzi 4:08:51 (13,334)
Lawrie, Eula G 4:57:24 (24,473)
Lawson, Clare M 3:56:34 (10,271)
Lawson, Jane L 4:54:32 (23,906)
Lawson, Janice P 4:54:32 (23,906)
Lawton, Jacqueline A 5:05:45 (25,792)
Lawton, Michelle 5:08:47 (26,213)

Lawton, Suzette M 3:49:56 (8,482)
Lay, Deborah 5:14:42 (26,992)
Lazare, Jacqueline I 5:16:15 (27,162)
Lazarova, Lepa 4:32:38 (19,273)
Le Bihan, Françoise 4:04:45 (12,367)
Le Bihan, Katrina 4:59:47 (24,954)
Le Couilliard, Christine E 4:30:32 (18,767)
Le Garnec, Regine 4:38:17 (20,544)
Le Narquand, Wendy J 5:13:42 (26,855)
Lea, Heidi J 4:09:24 (13,475)
Lea, Janet M 5:46:45 (29,802)
Leach, Anne E 4:56:08 (24,235)
Leach, Carrie A 4:13:08 (14,362)
Leach, Joanne 4:28:52 (18,317)
Leach, Lindsey K 5:28:09 (28,406)
Leach, Susan M 5:35:19 (28,981)
Leader, Elizabeth 3:12:19 (2,228)
Leah, Candice L 3:12:55 (2,302)
Leahy, Jacqueline A 6:05:33 (30,607)
Leal-Santos, Alicia 3:13:47 (2,408)
Leaver, Judith M 7:35:37 (31,877)
Le-Dain, Claude 5:02:57 (25,440)
Ledsham, Jo 4:41:21 (21,206)
Lee, Alison 5:39:08 (29,281)
Lee, Annette 5:25:44 (28,167)
Lee, Carolyn 4:01:06 (11,528)
Lee, Diane 4:29:14 (18,410)
Lee, Erma E 5:37:21 (29,138)
Lee, Gillian 4:27:48 (18,039)
Lee, Joanne M 4:22:13 (16,613)
Lee, Michelle 2:35:51 (132)
Lee, Michelle 4:17:43 (15,485)
Lee, Rebecca E 4:20:48 (16,230)
Lee, Rebecca L 4:45:16 (22,091)
Lee, Sandra L 4:13:46 (14,508)
Lee, Sarah R 3:43:02 (6,855)
Lee, Shufo 5:18:03 (27,374)
Lee, Tess 3:26:41 (3,951)
Lee, Tracey D 5:10:22 (26,424)
Lee-Anderson, Jude C 4:18:59 (15,775)
Leeke, Charlotte A 5:38:22 (29,218)
Leeson, Yvonne 3:44:27 (7,173)
Lefebvre, Sandy L 4:42:07 (21,372)
Legard, Jane 4:53:03 (23,622)
Legeron, Isabelle M 4:56:01 (24,211)
Leggett, Anne 3:37:20 (5,846)
Leggett, Janet D 3:39:52 (6,284)
Leggett, Michelle 4:03:27 (12,067)
Leguay, Françoise 3:27:02 (4,031)
Leigh, Anne R 6:31:53 (31,241)
Leighton, Michelle J 4:03:46 (12,140)
Leighton, Susan 4:49:47 (23,036)
Leimberger, Margarete 3:44:40 (7,230)
Leiw, Anita 3:53:08 (9,291)
Leleu, Roselyn 3:38:39 (6,080)
Leleux, Sarah J 5:13:45 (26,859)
Lembke, Ulla M 5:27:19 (28,340)
Lemke, Erika 4:40:04 (20,934)
Lemor, Christiane 3:51:29 (8,880)
Lenaghan, Moira 3:57:32 (10,550)
Lendak, Andrea 4:03:35 (12,099)
Leng, Jude R 5:29:29 (28,530)
Lennon, Susan H 3:41:00 (6,474)
Lenton, Jeanette 4:59:55 (24,976)
Leonard, Anastasia M 6:12:23 (30,789)
Leonard, Angela J 3:44:17 (7,133)
Leonard, Catherine 3:30:42 (4,724)
Leonard, Kirsten A 3:41:59 (6,643)
Leonard, Sue C 5:33:02 (28,812)
Lepore, Yvonne 4:03:19 (12,036)
Leppard, Julie D 5:33:28 (28,846)
Lerner, Julie M 6:15:56 (30,907)
Lesar, Eleonora L 5:19:05 (27,474)
Lesh, Lynn A 5:44:30 (29,656)
Lesley, Georgina 5:50:55 (30,009)
Leslie, Kirsten A 4:35:14 (19,873)
Letts, Rachel J 4:15:14 (14,863)
Letts, Zandra G 4:20:31 (16,164)
Levene, Susan L 4:31:34 (18,995)
Leventhal, Sara 4:41:17 (21,181)
Lever, Joan M 5:18:09 (27,380)
Lever, Phillipa J 5:56:32 (30,274)
Leverett, Ann E 4:18:47 (15,734)

Levett, Clare L 4:10:59 (13,866)
Levi, Laura 5:01:34 (25,235)
Levine, Tessa 4:42:02 (21,355)
Levitt, Julie M 5:11:25 (26,567)
Lewendon, Christina G 5:01:47 (25,271)
Lewin, Judy 4:13:06 (14,352)
Lewinbuk, Elana M 5:55:26 (30,226)
Lewis, Anne J 4:56:33 (24,322)
Lewis, Catherine 5:27:20 (28,344)
Lewis, Elizabeth A 5:41:31 (29,449)
Lewis, Fran 4:31:57 (19,096)
Lewis, Georgia A 5:55:17 (30,215)
Lewis, Helen 5:50:20 (29,985)
Lewis, Joanna 4:47:37 (22,598)
Lewis, Julie 3:33:00 (5,099)
Lewis, Kathy 3:56:19 (10,183)
Lewis, Laleh 7:12:19 (31,724)
Lewis, Lynne 4:10:03 (13,647)
Lewis, Melanie 8:08:00 (31,950)
Lewis, Nia K 5:02:21 (25,352)
Lewis, Rachel 4:29:59 (18,626)
Lewis, Rebecca A 4:08:54 (13,348)
Lewis, Sally-Anne 4:41:11 (21,153)
Lewis, Sarah 3:57:12 (10,444)
Lewis, Sarah V 6:42:07 (31,391)
Lewis, Suzy 4:52:33 (23,539)
Lewis-Brown, Melaine S 4:36:05 (20,052)
Lewtas, Susanne A 4:17:33 (15,439)
Ley, Jacqueline 5:07:35 (26,056)
Leyland, Linda A 3:40:03 (6,317)
Li, Ka Yee 6:53:48 (31,545)
Li, May-Fay J 3:26:04 (3,856)
Li, Rita S 4:15:00 (14,803)
Liberty, Darrelyn J 4:48:52 (22,847)
Lidbury, Hilary M 5:26:59 (28,299)
Liesenfeld, Winnie 4:24:39 (17,218)
Lightbody, Ellinore D 4:54:37 (23,926)
Li-Kwai-Cheung, Anne M 3:38:58 (6,126)
Lilley, Helen C 3:48:43 (8,189)
Lillie, Lisa M 4:52:44 (23,574)
Lillingston-Price, Jane 4:15:14 (14,863)
Lillistone, Christine 4:27:57 (18,082)
Lim, Audrey 4:01:27 (11,588)
Lim, Pai Choo 6:14:50 (30,879)
Lind, Emma 3:59:12 (11,060)
Lindenberg, Sue 4:36:25 (20,110)
Lindley, Denise 4:30:45 (18,807)
Lindores, Sharon A 4:04:14 (12,249)
Lindsay, Jackie A 3:32:42 (5,044)
Lindsay, Kathleen C 4:52:28 (23,528)
Lindsey, Valerie A 4:25:30 (17,429)
Lindsley, Sarah J 4:56:11 (24,242)
Lindstrom, Lina 5:59:08 (30,369)
Linford, Liz 6:39:26 (31,354)
Linnard, Rachid 5:01:53 (25,284)
Linney, Catherine E 4:06:22 (12,752)
Lintott, Catherine M 4:12:55 (14,307)
Lintott, Sally 5:03:40 (25,543)
Linzell, Laraine A 4:43:43 (21,726)
Lion, Charlotte E 4:20:14 (16,073)
Lip, Geraldine E 4:13:11 (14,373)
Lipede, Kehinde F 4:09:03 (13,390)
Lippitt, Jennifer M 4:21:54 (16,500)
Lis, Emily C 3:37:06 (5,796)
Lishman, Gill 4:40:31 (21,031)
Lissenden, Rosemary A 4:14:31 (14,682)
Lister, Claire 3:57:37 (10,573)
Litchfield, Linda M 4:51:12 (23,304)
Litterick, Emma C 3:32:35 (5,024)
Little, Catherine J 5:08:44 (26,207)
Little, Georgina 4:00:28 (11,390)
Little, Gina M 3:58:56 (10,987)
Little, Paula J 3:43:00 (6,850)
Little, Sarah 5:36:26 (29,056)
Littler, Jan 3:29:20 (4,475)
Littlewood, Annette 5:39:53 (29,326)
Littlewood, Karen A 5:12:08 (26,646)
Liversidge, Christine 4:51:41 (23,378)
Livesey, Alison A 4:28:25 (18,198)
Livingstone, Harriet A 5:14:12 (26,923)
Livingstone, Helen J 3:10:54 (2,090)
Livingstone, Lisa 3:41:22 (6,530)
Ljubojevic, Angelica 4:25:22 (17,396)
Llewellyn, Catherine 4:39:58 (20,910)
Llewellyn, Charlotte M 5:24:22 (28,014)
Llewellyn, Karen 5:05:53 (25,821)
Lloyd, Catrin 5:11:52 (26,613)
Lloyd, Emma J 4:35:39 (19,954)
Lloyd, Helen A 3:57:20 (10,492)
Lloyd, Isabella 4:47:02 (22,456)
Lloyd, Kim J 4:46:03 (22,261)
Lloyd, Linda 4:24:21 (17,153)
Lloyd, Mia 7:37:20 (31,886)
Lloyd, Nicola W 4:00:16 (11,353)
Lloyd, Philippa R 6:37:57 (31,339)
Lloyd-Williams, Leonie C 5:52:06 (30,068)
Lo, Carrie A 4:31:27 (18,963)
Loach, Kate E 3:44:17 (7,133)
Loader, Carole A 4:23:44 (16,996)
Loader, Leonie 5:49:50 (29,954)
Loane, Sarah 4:14:53 (14,783)
Local, Michelle T 5:16:51 (27,242)
Locher Ulrich, Beatrice R 4:16:53 (15,279)
Lockie, Joanne L 3:48:03 (8,008)
Lockwood, Charlotte E 6:06:50 (30,641)
Lockwood, Linda A 4:12:41 (14,260)
Loczenski, Barbara 4:22:35 (16,719)
Lodge, Jo 2:34:49 (123)
Lodwig, Clare E 3:50:23 (8,602)
Lofts, Fiona J 5:14:53 (27,015)
Loftus, Eileen 5:51:15 (30,024)
Loftus, Susanne C 4:41:22 (21,210)
Lombard, Joanne E 5:06:07 (25,860)
London, Joanna 4:11:57 (14,077)
Long, Amy 5:06:15 (25,882)
Long, Charlotte L 3:47:34 (7,898)
Long, Janet N 4:29:41 (18,550)
Long, Justine S 3:52:43 (9,176)
Long, Lynn P 4:48:51 (22,845)
Long, Rachael E 5:48:42 (29,894)
Long, Rebecca L 3:58:54 (10,974)
Long, Sandra J 4:16:25 (15,152)
Long, Vanessa K 5:14:00 (26,899)
Loomes, Lynda A 6:10:34 (30,744)
Loose, Phillippa A 4:33:45 (19,517)
Lopata, Rachel A 5:03:29 (25,517)
Lopez, Eva M 4:41:06 (21,142)
Lopez, Hazel 5:11:51 (26,610)
Lord, Carol A 4:43:08 (21,587)
Lord, Mary T 4:55:53 (24,177)
Lord, Victoria G 5:42:57 (29,552)
Lothian, Elizabeth M 4:48:52 (22,847)
Lotz, Petro 4:40:51 (21,098)
Lou, Xin Xin 4:59:19 (24,852)
Louch, Karen 4:52:53 (23,595)
Loughran, Jill M 4:44:07 (21,823)
Loughrey, Elizabeth E 5:21:56 (27,764)
Louw, Elsie 4:05:44 (12,600)
Lovastikova, Milena 4:11:14 (13,919)
Love, Christine A 5:18:55 (27,456)
Love, Nicola J 4:35:56 (20,009)
Love, Robi D 5:48:55 (29,904)
Lovegrove, Amanda E 3:44:08 (7,102)
Lovegrove, Amy J 5:39:49 (29,320)
Lovegrove, Deborah 4:45:44 (22,195)
Lovelace, Clare S 5:29:36 (28,545)
Loveless, Denise 3:42:56 (6,840)
Lovell, Fiona M 4:21:35 (16,409)
Lovell, Joanne S 5:09:39 (26,328)
Lovell, Sally J 3:29:41 (4,529)
Lovesey, Jennifer 3:52:48 (9,195)
Lovett, Kelly J 4:59:19 (24,852)
Lovett, Tamsin V 4:59:19 (24,852)
Loveys, Lara F 4:45:54 (22,229)
Lowe, Freda J 4:54:16 (23,849)
Lowe, Keryn E 4:25:52 (17,529)
Lowe, Paula A 4:44:32 (21,917)
Lowe, Rochelle M 4:36:33 (20,144)
Lowes, Kim 4:00:19 (11,363)
Lowry, Sarah J 4:47:15 (22,509)
Lowther, Tracey D 5:08:15 (26,150)
Loy, Francesca 4:48:34 (22,786)
Lucas, Elizabeth H 5:24:20 (28,007)
Lucas, Isabelle 4:58:36 (24,736)
Lucas, Naomi S 4:53:37 (23,730)
Lucas, Pauline A 3:56:42 (10,302)
Lucas, Susan 3:52:45 (9,183)
Lucas-Storrie, Anne 5:13:31 (26,828)
Luckin, Jennifer D 5:32:09 (28,746)
Luckman, Marion R 5:28:38 (28,454)
Ludman, Wendy B 6:14:50 (30,879)
Ludtke, Karin 4:50:49 (23,239)
Luebkeman, Laurel A 4:37:10 (20,284)
Lugton, Helen J 3:58:17 (10,785)
Lumb, Eve 5:07:57 (26,107)
Lumber, Liz 3:13:22 (2,353)
Lundell, Stephanie A 5:11:59 (26,630)
Lundy, Caroline B 3:56:00 (10,084)
Lunn, Lynn 4:41:46 (21,301)
Lunn, Stephanie J 4:45:18 (22,096)
Lunney, Joanna D 6:34:43 (31,284)
Lunney, Nichola C 5:58:28 (30,347)
Lunnon, Emma C 4:58:28 (24,711)
Lupson, Lorna 6:51:38 (31,523)
Lupton, Lesley-Anne 5:57:08 (30,293)
Lupton, Marianne 4:20:51 (16,244)
Lusty, Elizabeth R 3:33:59 (5,268)
Luth, Grietje T 5:25:30 (28,137)
Luton, Sophie M 4:38:13 (20,524)
Luxford, Katherine G 3:55:07 (9,821)
Lyden, Catherine A 4:52:11 (23,479)
Lygo, Pauline E 3:57:09 (10,433)
Lyle, Susan V 3:58:25 (10,824)
Lyman, Ella T 3:57:37 (10,573)
Lymath, Sara D 7:31:35 (31,856)
Lynch, Debbie C 5:07:17 (26,006)
Lynch, Jane 5:01:53 (25,284)
Lynch, Mary M 4:14:06 (14,587)
Lynch, Rita M 4:39:08 (20,756)
Lynch, Robyn M 5:29:40 (28,551)
Lynch-Aird, Jeanne E 4:38:26 (20,581)
Lynch-Warden, Rachel J 5:28:38 (28,454)
Lyne, Clare R 4:36:59 (20,249)
Lyne, Olivia M 4:36:58 (20,247)
Lynn, Michaela M 4:21:59 (16,530)
Lyon, Lynn 4:28:51 (18,314)
Lyons, Alison M 4:28:24 (18,193)
Lyons, Julia F 4:27:55 (18,067)
Lysne, Kristin S 3:54:52 (9,741)
Lysons, Alison J 5:31:11 (28,671)
Lythell, Jennifer A 6:19:19 (30,999)
Maby, Julie 7:20:10 (31,790)
Macaulay, Sheila M 4:35:21 (19,898)
Macbeth, Deanne V 4:17:00 (15,304)
Maccariello, Bettina 4:01:43 (11,652)
MacConachie, Kirsty I 5:13:09 (26,786)
Macdonald, Alison 3:27:54 (4,211)
Macdonald, Geraldine 6:17:53 (30,948)
Macdonald, Lucie E 3:37:04 (5,790)
Macdonald, Natalie 3:57:31 (10,546)
Macdonald, Ros F 3:40:28 (6,393)
Macdonald, Vanessa 5:11:53 (26,617)
Macdonald, Vivienne 4:38:10 (20,513)
Macfarlane, Fiona M 5:11:42 (26,588)
MacFie, Alison 5:20:33 (27,637)
MacGregor, Katherine E 4:45:09 (22,070)
MacGregor, Sue M 3:36:47 (5,742)
Machell, Ingrid J 3:34:38 (5,358)
MacInnes, Maureen 4:02:42 (11,899)
Macintosh, Fiona 3:39:35 (6,231)
Macintyre, Elizabeth J 5:37:08 (29,116)
Mackay, Deborah 4:08:08 (13,139)
Mackay, Jennifer S 5:20:05 (27,577)
Mackay, Kirstine S 7:11:28 (31,720)
Mackay, Lucy S 4:02:18 (11,805)
Mackay, Sharon 5:05:44 (25,787)
Mackay, Theresa C 6:13:18 (30,822)
Mackellar, Claire 4:13:12 (14,376)
Mackenzie, Donna 6:30:03 (31,205)
Mackenzie, Janet M 4:56:58 (24,396)
Mackenzie, Joanna C 3:45:21 (7,376)
Mackenzie, Kaeti A 3:19:36 (3,027)
Mackenzie, Katherine E 3:43:03 (6,859)
Mackie, Hazel G 4:15:47 (15,000)
Mackinlay, Catherine A 4:16:36 (15,200)
Mackinnon, Henrietta J 3:20:30 (3,131)
Mackworth, Octavia F 5:09:37 (26,324)
Maclean, Fiona 7:18:01 (31,771)
Maclean, Mairi T 4:43:02 (21,570)

Maclean, Rachel F........................4:39:22 (20,805)
MacLeary, Rebekah......................4:44:22 (21,876)
MacLehose, Polly..........................3:29:42 (4,533)
MacLennan, Miriam L.................4:20:25 (16,136)
Macleod, Katy M...........................3:48:36 (8,150)
MacMaster, Jennifer H.................3:06:52 (1,693)
MacNaughtan, Jane S.................4:34:00 (19,587)
Maconaghie, Diane E...................5:14:12 (26,923)
MacPhee, Margaret L.................4:38:05 (20,493)
Macpherson, Caroline A.............4:19:44 (15,959)
Macpherson, Susie......................4:55:52 (24,169)
Macrae, Christine D....................5:47:20 (29,829)
Maddams, Angela M...................6:42:08 (31,392)
Madden, Anya K...........................4:10:49 (13,830)
Madden, Oonagh M....................4:41:16 (21,179)
Maddock, Rachael J....................4:13:20 (14,414)
Maddocks, Jennifer H..................3:28:42 (4,353)
Maddox, Debrah A........................4:16:36 (15,200)
Madeira, Allison..........................5:47:38 (29,848)
Madell, Soraya E..........................4:09:53 (13,603)
Madge, Carole C..........................5:52:17 (30,085)
Maeda, Taeko..............................4:10:55 (13,850)
Magee, Suzanna M......................5:09:34 (26,317)
Mageean, Anne............................4:18:32 (15,670)
Maguire, Anne.............................6:08:15 (30,684)
Maguire, Megan J.........................4:25:03 (17,318)
Maguire, Paula.............................6:57:53 (31,596)
Maguire, Sarah.............................3:21:21 (3,239)
Mahal, Anita.................................4:49:47 (23,036)
Maher, Laura M.............................4:08:47 (13,317)
Mahmoud, Sonia E.......................4:23:54 (17,041)
Mahoney, Karen...........................4:59:19 (24,852)
Mahy, Helena...............................5:01:03 (25,152)
Mai, Hannelore.............................5:28:22 (28,428)
Maidment, Marilyn F....................3:34:21 (5,318)
Maidment, Nicola L......................6:29:56 (31,202)
Maillet, Catherine.........................5:21:34 (27,734)
Mair, Tracy A................................5:02:19 (25,346)
Maisey, Margaret.........................4:51:21 (23,326)
Maison, Margaret C......................4:11:59 (14,088)
Maitland Walker, Lucy J...............5:40:45 (29,398)
Major, Michelle............................5:32:19 (28,761)
Major, Sally..................................4:32:13 (19,172)
Makcin, Mary.................................3:32:11 (4,949)
Male, Jennie.................................4:18:16 (15,600)
Male, Samantha J.........................5:26:10 (28,208)
Male, Teresa M.............................4:27:15 (17,908)
Malek, Sonia L...............................3:52:05 (9,033)
Maletzki, Antje.............................4:13:55 (14,547)
Malik, Maryum..............................4:30:46 (18,809)
Malin, Frances C...........................3:31:41 (4,871)
Malizio, Marguerite L...................5:45:08 (29,699)
Maljaars, Johanna E.....................4:41:02 (21,131)
Mallery, Lynne..............................6:21:31 (31,045)
Mallett, Sally L..............................5:25:30 (28,137)
Mallory, Penny D...........................4:54:49 (23,962)
Malone, Helen..............................5:29:09 (28,499)
Malone, Rachel.............................5:20:27 (27,623)
Maltby, Hannah K.........................5:03:39 (25,542)
Malyon, Claire L............................4:09:53 (13,603)
Man, Teresa T...............................4:21:24 (16,363)
Mancell, Sara K.............................3:42:39 (6,775)
Mancini, Keely L...........................4:32:28 (19,231)
Mancini, Phillipa...........................5:17:13 (27,275)
Manders, Tracey...........................4:54:29 (23,894)
Manera, Claudia...........................3:58:24 (10,819)
Mangham, Jacqueline E...............4:40:41 (21,062)
Mani, Shobana..............................6:02:36 (30,515)
Manley, Anne M............................5:37:47 (29,164)
Manly, Rita....................................3:28:01 (4,230)
Mann, Shelley A............................5:45:18 (29,711)
Manning, Mo M.............................3:44:32 (7,195)
Manning, Nicola S.........................5:19:50 (27,540)
Mannion, Eileen C.........................3:06:28 (1,651)
Manocha, Sarah............................4:53:14 (23,663)
Manock, Kirsty..............................4:25:53 (17,536)
Mansbridge, Rebecca M...............5:08:32 (26,186)
Mansell-Moullin, Jenny M............3:36:04 (5,624)
Manser, Jackie H..........................5:26:34 (28,256)
Mansfield, Julie.............................5:22:03 (27,777)
Mansfield, Lynn S..........................4:05:35 (12,568)
Mansfield, Syreeta M....................4:18:43 (15,712)
Mansford, Clare F..........................3:45:44 (7,468)

Manson, Chantell M....................5:14:39 (26,986)
Manvell, Aimée L.........................4:03:03 (11,965)
Mapala, Grace..............................6:48:26 (31,478)
Marals, Nadine.............................3:57:12 (10,444)
Marcenaro, Janina........................7:05:55 (31,676)
Marchant, Jane E..........................4:55:05 (24,011)
Marchant, Judy C..........................3:44:19 (7,142)
Marchant, Zina D..........................3:19:38 (3,034)
Marchini, Marisa..........................4:10:29 (13,752)
Marcucci, Jo..................................7:31:25 (31,854)
Marcus, Sarah E............................4:38:59 (20,721)
Margerrrison, Victoria.................6:13:19 (30,826)
Marginson, Lesley.........................5:32:39 (28,786)
Mark, Catherine A........................4:09:48 (13,577)
Markham, Ann O...........................6:53:56 (31,546)
Markham, Anna M.........................5:29:17 (28,517)
Marks, Elizabeth J.........................4:37:34 (20,349)
Marks, Gudrun G..........................5:56:34 (30,275)
Marks, Helen.................................4:59:21 (24,865)
Marks, Sherryl A...........................4:03:18 (12,032)
Marley, Karen...............................5:45:20 (29,715)
Marlow, Melissa A........................4:55:22 (24,078)
Marnell, Sheila..............................5:02:25 (25,358)
Marr, Leanne V.............................4:40:32 (21,034)
Marriott, Dawn.............................6:45:18 (31,441)
Marriott-Dodington, Sandra M...4:01:58 (11,707)
Marriott-Reynolds, Lynne...........5:37:42 (29,161)
Marsden, Debbie A........................3:37:50 (5,931)
Marsden, Joanne...........................4:29:12 (18,402)
Marsh, Sara E...............................3:51:12 (8,806)
Marshall, Angela S........................5:39:11 (29,284)
Marshall, Catriona J......................3:56:18 (10,181)
Marshall, Claire L..........................3:36:54 (5,754)
Marshall, Dawn K..........................3:40:52 (6,448)
Marshall, Gillian............................4:16:19 (15,122)
Marshall, Janet M..........................4:08:42 (13,291)
Marshall, Judith R.........................4:09:31 (13,504)
Marshall, Julie K...........................4:38:14 (20,530)
Marshall, Pat M.............................5:06:23 (25,899)
Marshall, Patricia J........................6:46:12 (31,455)
Marshall, Sarah E..........................4:15:12 (14,856)
Marshall, Sheila M.........................4:16:22 (15,137)
Marshall, Susan.............................5:00:38 (25,082)
Marshall, Susan E..........................3:30:23 (4,669)
Marston, Joanna O.........................4:59:32 (24,909)
Martel, Rhiannon M.......................5:29:30 (28,532)
Martens, Hannah...........................4:52:53 (23,595)
Martin, Adelle...............................5:39:06 (29,272)
Martin, Alicja.................................6:58:00 (31,598)
Martin, Amanda J..........................3:35:27 (5,511)
Martin, Anna L...............................5:16:06 (27,140)
Martin, Carol A..............................3:44:37 (7,217)
Martin, Colette M..........................4:46:24 (22,340)
Martin, Debbie..............................4:25:51 (17,526)
Martin, Debbie J............................4:33:14 (19,414)
Martin, Elizabeth A........................3:58:42 (10,919)
Martin, Frances G..........................4:55:17 (24,059)
Martin, Jane V...............................5:02:19 (25,346)
Martin, Jill E..................................4:49:11 (22,916)
Martin, Joanna..............................5:11:22 (26,562)
Martin, Julie A...............................5:04:24 (25,614)
Martin, Kara..................................5:36:53 (29,099)
Martin, Kerry A.............................5:34:56 (28,952)
Martin, Kim F.................................3:28:27 (4,310)
Martin, Lisa....................................5:42:20 (29,506)
Martin, Lynn..................................5:37:51 (29,170)
Martin, Natalie A...........................3:41:54 (6,618)
Martin, Penelope...........................6:23:38 (31,101)
Martin, Sarah E..............................3:48:07 (8,027)
Martin, Sharmon L.........................4:12:42 (14,263)
Martin, Stephanie J........................3:14:19 (2,480)
Martin, Susan G.............................4:25:07 (17,337)
Martin, Teresa M...........................5:20:49 (27,664)
Martinali, Lorna H.........................6:20:02 (31,012)
Martins, Faye B..............................5:40:21 (29,361)
Martins, Marketa...........................5:04:48 (25,663)
Martin-Smith, Mandy.....................4:21:43 (16,457)
Maruyama, Chieko.........................5:01:22 (25,198)
Marval, Anitia L.............................4:07:58 (13,110)
Maskell, Shelly A...........................5:37:44 (29,163)
Mason, Adele K..............................6:17:41 (30,944)
Mason, Angharad E........................3:25:00 (3,693)
Mason, Jenny F...............................5:25:14 (28,109)

Mason, Sara...................................4:14:39 (14,718)
Massey, Francesca L......................5:58:26 (30,345)
Massey, Jacqueline A.....................3:19:41 (3,040)
Massey, Nikki J...............................4:55:10 (24,031)
Massie, Kirsti A..............................4:41:15 (21,169)
Masson, Kerry J..............................4:38:18 (20,548)
Masson, Kim C................................3:08:26 (1,843)
Masters, Joanne.............................4:32:04 (19,124)
Masters, Wendy E..........................4:57:55 (24,572)
Masterson, Rachel J........................5:30:21 (28,611)
Mathers, Sue..................................5:35:23 (28,991)
Matheson, Joanna...........................4:36:09 (20,063)
Matheson, Patricia E.......................3:09:16 (1,927)
Mathew, Alys..................................4:06:35 (12,801)
Mathieson, Kirstie J........................4:46:34 (22,368)
Mathys, Margrit..............................5:00:09 (25,016)
Matijuk, Jill I..................................5:33:22 (28,839)
Matshaba, Lethepu.........................4:31:28 (18,966)
Matsuoka, Akie...............................4:17:38 (15,461)
Matthews, Dawn E..........................5:05:55 (25,828)
Matthews, Denise...........................4:23:30 (16,942)
Matthews, Jane E............................4:56:16 (24,255)
Matthews, Jennifer J........................5:10:16 (26,409)
Matthews, Rosemary M...................5:07:24 (26,028)
Matthews, Sarah A...........................3:49:26 (8,363)
Matthews, Sophia F.........................5:20:31 (27,634)
Matthews, Susan R..........................5:58:32 (30,351)
Mattinson, Karen A.........................4:34:55 (19,804)
Maude, Heather L............................5:45:50 (29,743)
Mauldon, Glynis..............................4:29:28 (18,481)
Maule, Lisa C...................................4:16:40 (15,226)
Maver, Julie.....................................4:44:46 (21,971)
Maw, Victoria E...............................5:31:13 (28,678)
Mawer, Tracy D...............................4:27:15 (17,908)
Maxey, Jane P..................................5:29:19 (28,520)
May, Holly G....................................3:06:34 (1,662)
May, Marion K.................................4:16:58 (15,296)
May, Sophie.....................................6:12:59 (30,816)
Maycock, Zoe E...............................4:52:19 (23,509)
Mayhew, Kathryn.............................5:22:30 (27,831)
Maynard, Annastazia-Jo..................6:06:37 (30,635)
Mayne, Caroline E............................4:46:59 (22,444)
Mayo, Caroline J...............................5:24:55 (28,072)
Mazzuca, Marzia...............................3:44:16 (7,128)
McAleese, Susannah L.....................4:27:13 (17,897)
McAllen, Nikoletta P........................3:58:02 (10,684)

McAndrew, Nell...............................3:22:29 (3,371)

McAteer, Kirsten N..........................5:08:59 (26,236)
McAuliffe, Sheila.............................5:44:56 (29,688)
McBain, Kirsty..................................6:11:06 (30,758)
McBride, Claire C.............................3:49:52 (8,466)
McCafferty, Sheree J........................4:42:06 (21,371)
McCallum, Marina............................3:59:31 (11,166)
McCallum, Susan P...........................4:14:10 (14,601)

McCammick, Linda.....7:20:29 (31,791)
McCance-Price, Louise P.....4:40:47 (21,081)
McCann, Mary.....5:17:27 (27,299)
McCarthy, Christine.....3:08:00 (1,806)
McCarthy, Elizabeth J.....5:12:05 (26,643)
McCarthy, Katy J.....5:13:36 (26,845)
McCarthy, Victoria J.....4:08:29 (13,224)
McCay, Jackie F.....7:31:38 (31,857)
McConaghy, Yvonne.....4:49:01 (22,878)
McConnell, Anita R.....5:34:38 (28,929)
McConnell, Claire E.....4:41:49 (21,313)
McConville, Catherine.....6:01:47 (30,479)
McConville, Julie.....6:54:51 (31,557)
McCord, Mimi.....4:44:43 (21,958)
McCormick, Ruth.....4:12:25 (14,170)
McCoy, Sylvia H.....5:56:14 (30,259)
McCracken, Catriona.....3:28:42 (4,353)
McCreery, Claire E.....3:32:27 (4,996)
McCrindle, Paula J.....3:26:39 (3,942)
McCubbins, Baiju.....3:47:26 (7,864)
McCullum, Michaela.....2:39:10 (190)
McCunn, Fiona J.....4:37:36 (20,356)
McCutcheon, Madeleine C.....3:50:20 (8,589)
McDaid, Rebecca L.....5:09:45 (26,345)
McDermott, Carol A.....6:27:26 (31,162)
McDermott, Janice M.....5:27:45 (28,380)
McDermott, Karen E.....4:31:27 (18,963)
McDermott, Kerry L.....6:27:27 (31,164)
McDonagh, Lorraine M.....3:44:54 (7,286)
McDonald, Alison.....4:31:50 (19,056)
McDonald, Anna.....3:31:28 (4,842)
McDonald, Candice R.....3:20:31 (3,135)
McDonald, Dawn K.....4:00:51 (11,461)
McDonald, Deborah J.....5:47:07 (29,817)
McDonald, Jennifer.....5:08:14 (26,147)
McDonald, Joanne M.....4:00:58 (11,498)
McDonald, Kristal.....4:04:13 (12,245)
McDonald, Tracy L.....4:32:21 (19,199)
McDonnell, Melissa J.....3:39:30 (6,216)
McDougle, Alison M.....4:25:06 (17,333)
McElligott, Helen V.....6:40:17 (31,363)
McEwan, Jeannette.....5:17:30 (27,309)
McEwen, Laura J.....4:44:54 (22,002)
McFadzean, Clare E.....4:17:29 (15,419)
McFall, Josie.....6:50:52 (31,510)
McFarlane, Isabel.....4:37:46 (20,398)
McGachie, Amanda L.....5:38:12 (29,196)
McGann, Geraldine.....4:33:48 (19,534)
McGann, Sandra.....4:22:02 (16,548)
McGarrick, Tracey.....5:31:43 (28,717)
McGarry, Jacqueline.....5:29:27 (28,525)
McGavin, Tina.....5:02:14 (25,324)
McGhee, Angela.....5:47:41 (29,853)
McGhie, Cathy F.....6:23:13 (31,085)
McGimpsey, Rita J.....3:44:16 (7,128)
McGinley, Linda J.....4:32:21 (19,199)
McGinnis, Samantha M.....6:34:33 (31,281)
McGinty, Jane.....5:38:49 (29,247)
McGivney, Tracy.....4:54:34 (23,914)
McGlynn, Jenna.....4:32:05 (19,131)
McGowan, Marianne.....5:28:05 (28,402)
McGregor-Macdonald, Brigette J.7:03:06 (31,651)
McGrogan, Patricia.....4:29:16 (18,418)
McGuinness, Angela.....4:35:07 (19,844)
McHarry-Holt, Helen J.....4:22:12 (16,608)
McKay, Alison M.....4:31:17 (18,916)
McKay, Anne.....5:08:03 (26,123)
McKay, Maggie.....4:25:55 (17,545)
McKay, Nola E.....3:49:41 (8,419)
McKay, Ronni.....5:10:42 (26,466)
McKay, Vicky.....4:40:21 (20,996)
McKeating, Sarah H.....3:26:56 (4,005)
McKee, Christy T.....4:27:38 (18,000)
McKee, Sarah Amy.....5:54:49 (30,188)
McKenna, Ann P.....5:33:50 (28,874)
McKenna, Bronwyn.....4:50:31 (23,183)
McKenna, Julie.....4:40:37 (21,043)
McKenzie, Anne.....4:14:14 (14,615)
McKenzie, Jane C.....4:12:58 (14,321)
McKenzie, Janet V.....3:28:06 (4,240)
McKenzie, Maureen A.....3:40:42 (6,431)
McKerrow, Joan E.....7:00:11 (31,626)
McKey, Katharine L.....5:25:44 (28,167)
McKibbin, Donna C.....4:35:02 (19,828)
McKie, Suzanne E.....4:25:03 (17,318)
McKinley, Hilda.....4:25:35 (17,450)
McKinnon, Amanda J.....4:52:37 (23,553)
McKinnon, Fiona.....5:10:44 (26,473)
McKinnon, Suzanne M.....3:51:34 (8,909)
McLafferty, Beth.....3:58:53 (10,967)
McLauchlan, Clare.....4:24:18 (17,142)
McLaughlin, Ann.....3:37:55 (5,940)
McLaughlin, Anna M.....3:26:00 (3,850)
McLaughlin, Claire.....4:10:57 (13,858)
McLay, Natalie K.....3:53:28 (9,373)
McLean, Alison.....4:48:23 (22,756)
McLean, Arlene.....5:40:19 (29,357)
McLean, Fiona G.....4:14:28 (14,674)
McLean, Virginia.....5:40:00 (29,334)
McLeman, Jane L.....4:10:55 (13,850)
McLennan, Miranda C.....3:15:31 (2,595)
McLennan, Sharron L.....4:48:07 (22,699)
McLindon, Laura.....3:30:51 (4,751)
McLoughlin, Eileen P.....4:41:15 (21,169)
McLoughlin, Helen J.....4:13:56 (14,552)
McLoughlin, Mary.....4:28:49 (18,304)
McMahon, Debbie.....3:39:55 (6,292)
McManus, Susannah.....4:07:13 (12,945)
McMinn, Anita J.....4:45:51 (22,219)
McMurdock, Fiona M.....4:35:23 (19,905)
McNair, Helen-Marie.....6:08:10 (30,678)
McNally, Jane M.....3:57:14 (10,458)
McNamara, Hayley.....5:26:03 (28,202)
McNeilly, Yvonne J.....6:11:32 (30,774)
McNelis, Julie L.....4:44:24 (21,889)
McNicholas, Brenda.....4:36:01 (20,029)
McNicholas, Catherine M.....4:30:25 (18,736)
McNicol, Catriona M.....5:42:26 (29,512)
McNutt, Helen C.....3:58:10 (10,745)
McPartlan, Veronica M.....5:02:54 (25,435)
McPaul, Carol A.....4:31:01 (18,861)
McPhedran, Moira H.....4:55:04 (24,007)
McPhee, Catherine J.....3:43:57 (7,054)
McQuie, Holly L.....4:17:12 (15,349)
McSporran, Loraine A.....4:31:51 (19,061)
McSwain, Catherine E.....4:50:21 (23,138)
McSwiney, Sarah.....4:42:43 (21,499)
McTaggart, Vicky L.....3:40:37 (6,418)
McTurk, Sophie J.....4:42:43 (21,499)
McWeeney, Mary.....4:26:27 (17,684)
McWilliam, Kate H.....3:55:45 (10,005)
McWilliams, Francesca.....4:27:14 (17,904)
Meaburn, Emma L.....4:30:07 (18,660)
Mead, Ann.....5:52:34 (30,100)
Mead, Kealy L.....6:29:53 (31,200)
Meador, Chrys.....3:58:54 (10,974)
Meadows, Anne.....4:27:44 (18,023)
Meadows, Dawn E.....4:52:39 (23,557)
Meakin, Kathryn A.....4:21:39 (16,435)
Meakings, Lisa A.....5:06:28 (25,906)
Measor, Karen.....5:05:48 (25,804)
Medina, Nicola J.....4:45:48 (22,210)
Meehan, Heidi L.....3:22:15 (3,335)
Mehta, Susan.....4:44:23 (21,885)
Meijer, Martha.....4:52:48 (23,585)
Meikle, Angela M.....4:43:15 (21,620)
Meiners, Susan.....4:34:18 (19,669)
Mellis, Susan.....5:19:33 (27,503)
Mellor, Carol G.....4:53:35 (23,718)
Meltzer, Taylor J.....4:51:23 (23,329)
Mendell, Amy C.....4:12:43 (14,270)
Mendelsohn, Vanesa E.....4:28:41 (18,276)
Mendoza, Helen M.....6:14:00 (30,844)
Meneses Cornea, Sandra V.....4:45:49 (22,213)
Menzies-Gow, Megan.....4:51:38 (23,367)
Mercer, Gillian M.....6:12:16 (30,786)
Mercer, Julie M.....3:51:09 (8,781)
Mercer-Rees, Alix.....3:56:52 (10,354)
Merchant, Nicola C.....5:36:37 (29,072)
Mercy, Jane E.....4:36:37 (20,159)
Meredith, Jean.....4:44:36 (21,935)
Meredith, Olivia C.....5:17:55 (27,355)
Merley, Jean A.....3:43:18 (6,918)
Merrick, Nancy E.....4:46:51 (22,415)
Merrill, Amy.....4:49:26 (22,961)
Merrill, Carol E.....4:19:43 (15,955)
Merrill, Rebecca.....4:49:27 (22,969)
Merriman, Holly M.....4:55:13 (24,044)
Merritt, Diane P.....4:31:52 (19,066)
Merz, Caroline.....4:15:35 (14,949)
Messinger, Kim M.....5:26:05 (28,203)
Meston, Niki.....3:39:41 (6,253)
Mestre, Paula.....4:39:57 (20,904)
Mesure, Helen.....8:05:35 (31,947)
Metcalf, Tracey.....4:14:01 (14,572)
Metcalfe, Alison M.....4:27:14 (17,904)
Metcalfe, Caroline D.....5:03:17 (25,488)
Metcalfe, Margaret R.....3:50:45 (8,694)
Metcalfe, Suzanne.....4:33:16 (19,419)
Mexted, Jackie M.....3:16:51 (2,733)
Meyer, Natalie K.....5:14:34 (26,971)
Meyers, Sarah E.....4:33:12 (19,405)
Michael, Anne E.....5:39:56 (29,328)
Michael, Jessica L.....4:15:05 (14,821)
Michalak, Dorothy N.....3:48:17 (8,074)
Michelet, Claire E.....4:45:41 (22,186)
Middlehurst, Ann-Marie M.....5:06:56 (25,963)
Middlehurst, Sue E.....4:26:12 (17,631)
Middlemass, Helen.....4:58:07 (24,622)
Middlemost, Shirley.....3:53:01 (9,261)
Middleton, Anna L.....3:51:08 (8,774)
Middleton, Caroline J.....6:22:20 (31,071)
Middleton, Heather M.....6:39:42 (31,356)
Middleton, Heidi E.....3:54:18 (9,589)
Middleton, Joanne L.....4:49:51 (23,052)
Middleton, Linda M.....4:00:41 (11,422)
Middleton, Marion R.....3:53:10 (9,303)
Middleton, Sarah.....5:03:15 (25,482)
Middleton, Victoria L.....4:55:45 (24,145)
Midgley, Linda.....3:52:04 (9,027)
Miki, Yurina.....4:46:36 (22,374)
Mikkelsen, Kirsten.....4:50:01 (23,077)
Mikuska, Eva.....4:30:02 (18,639)
Mileham, Claire E.....4:18:17 (15,603)
Milek, Celia R.....4:27:44 (18,023)
Miles, Joanna.....4:59:32 (24,909)
Miles, Katherine S.....4:19:54 (15,997)
Milford, Sarah L.....7:31:11 (31,852)
Mill, Martha L.....4:33:48 (19,534)
Millar, Gillian M.....3:37:49 (5,926)
Millar, Jayne F.....4:41:15 (21,169)
Millard, Beth.....4:08:32 (13,239)
Millard, Fiona J.....4:48:09 (22,707)
Miller, Barbara.....4:10:46 (13,816)
Miller, Carol A.....5:29:47 (28,567)
Miller, Claire R.....4:36:25 (20,110)
Miller, Irene J.....4:17:56 (15,540)
Miller, Jane.....3:46:50 (7,711)
Miller, Joanna L.....4:03:59 (12,191)
Miller, Katrina.....5:57:17 (30,300)
Miller, Lisa M.....4:56:30 (24,310)
Miller, Mandy C.....4:07:56 (13,100)
Miller, Valerie A.....5:44:32 (29,658)
Milles, Philippa C.....4:44:34 (21,928)
Millican, Amanda J.....4:47:43 (22,618)
Millichip, Jane A.....4:22:38 (16,733)
Milligan, Gabrielle J.....4:14:08 (14,593)
Millington, Eleanor J.....4:12:21 (14,158)
Millington, Hazel E.....6:20:04 (31,013)
Mills, Charlotte S.....5:04:30 (25,627)
Mills, Clare.....5:41:51 (29,478)
Mills, Debbie.....5:12:45 (26,720)
Mills, Francesca L.....5:11:06 (26,517)
Mills, Melanie J.....4:42:53 (21,538)
Mills, Patsy.....5:02:44 (25,408)
Mills, Victoria M.....4:33:53 (19,556)
Mills, Yasmin.....7:33:25 (31,867)
Millward, Jane E.....6:35:55 (31,305)
Millward, Margaret F.....4:50:59 (23,268)
Miln, Davinia.....7:12:45 (31,729)
Milne, Fiona.....4:35:23 (19,905)
Milne, Lucy M.....4:45:04 (22,053)
Milne, Nicola E.....6:59:27 (31,612)
Milne, Sarah E.....4:08:27 (13,214)
Milsom, Elizabeth V.....4:41:15 (21,169)
Milton, Angie.....4:59:00 (24,793)
Mindelsohn, Katie A.....4:41:44 (21,290)
Mingay, Christine B.....5:30:07 (28,593)
Minge, Jackie A.....4:05:53 (12,634)

Minney, Christine D.....5:24:13 (27,994)
Minniti, Antionette M.....2:55:00 (755)
Minton, Jacqueline L.....5:59:25 (30,383)
Misson, Susanna C.....4:25:45 (17,496)
Mistry, Kumud.....5:27:04 (28,306)
Mitas, Jenifer.....4:39:49 (20,879)
Mitchell, Annie.....6:16:55 (30,929)
Mitchell, Dale A.....5:36:25 (29,055)
Mitchell, Donna L.....4:18:33 (15,677)
Mitchell, Heather M.....4:11:56 (14,072)
Mitchell, Judi A.....7:42:02 (31,894)
Mitchell, Kate R.....5:10:29 (26,440)
Mitchell, Laura J.....4:42:34 (21,465)
Mitchell, Libby A.....3:58:37 (10,891)
Mitchell, Lisa.....3:39:16 (6,172)
Mitchell, Pauline A.....4:41:10 (21,150)
Mitchelson, Janet.....4:43:42 (21,723)
Mitra, Rohini.....4:23:45 (17,002)
Miura, Hiroko.....6:28:35 (31,182)
Miwa, Satomi.....3:17:38 (2,816)
Mizen, Angela.....4:21:49 (16,484)
Mockridge, Nicki J.....3:18:06 (2,858)
Mocock, Katherine J.....4:52:13 (23,488)
Moffat, Jeannie L.....4:16:50 (15,263)
Moffatt, Helen R.....4:45:05 (22,059)
Mohammad, Ayesha.....4:28:24 (18,193)
Moir, Karen.....4:01:40 (11,640)
Moiser, Suzanne J.....4:17:18 (15,368)
Molas-Ardichen, Christine.....3:57:30 (10,538)
Mole De Cano, Rebecca A.....4:46:58 (22,439)
Moller, Maaike I.....3:59:28 (11,140)
Monaghan, Elizabeth C.....5:09:46 (26,351)
Monckton, Kirsty L.....4:41:18 (21,187)
Moncrieff, Jane.....4:06:58 (12,882)
Moncur, Fiona A.....4:37:18 (20,315)
Mondo, Sandra.....5:09:24 (26,294)
Money, Jean.....5:35:02 (28,959)
Money, Vanessa E.....3:47:12 (7,805)
Monk, Jacqueline E.....3:55:46 (10,010)
Monroe, Ruth.....4:37:01 (20,254)
Montgomery, Lis J.....5:28:46 (28,465)
Montgomery, Sarah L.....4:47:07 (22,481)
Moodie, Lynne M.....6:06:18 (30,632)
Moody, Grainne.....4:25:34 (17,444)
Moon, Clare J.....4:27:55 (18,067)
Moon, Melissa.....2:44:41 (313)
Moon, Paula J.....4:16:19 (15,122)
Moore, Alison J.....3:54:28 (9,630)
Moore, Cathie.....5:30:28 (28,619)
Moore, Christine S.....4:29:51 (18,593)
Moore, Dawn.....5:28:51 (28,472)
Moore, Emily J.....5:08:09 (26,135)
Moore, Joanna.....4:33:52 (19,549)
Moore, Joanne L.....5:17:50 (27,341)
Moore, Julie A.....5:48:14 (29,875)
Moore, Kate.....4:08:09 (13,146)
Moore, Lynda R.....4:43:35 (21,696)
Moore, Molly S.....4:28:46 (18,292)
Moore, Natasha A.....5:49:26 (29,926)
Moore, Nicole M.....5:16:17 (27,166)
Moore, Rebecca V.....2:43:50 (286)
Moore, Sally A.....5:26:51 (28,284)
Moore, Tiffany J.....5:32:54 (28,803)
Moore, Tracey.....5:27:05 (28,310)
Morales, Madeline I.....4:20:49 (16,233)
Morcos, Wendy.....4:34:27 (19,699)
Mordecai, Jeannie C.....4:34:05 (19,619)
Morecroft, Katherine E.....4:05:53 (12,634)
Moreton, Melanie J.....4:38:06 (20,498)
Morgan, Amanda-Jane.....4:25:03 (17,318)
Morgan, Carol A.....4:43:20 (21,649)
Morgan, Ceri N.....6:00:42 (30,435)
Morgan, Claire E.....4:50:16 (23,115)
Morgan, Deborah M.....5:55:53 (30,238)
Morgan, Denise.....7:13:38 (31,737)
Morgan, Judith A.....5:42:12 (29,495)
Morgan, Julian E.....4:18:45 (15,723)
Morgan, Karen A.....4:55:13 (24,044)
Morgan, Lesley J.....5:24:48 (28,058)
Morgan, Lisa J.....5:12:00 (26,633)
Morgan, Lowri E.....3:22:29 (3,371)
Morgan, Maggie.....5:51:15 (30,024)
Morgan, Michelle P.....6:16:22 (30,916)
Morgan, Nicola K.....3:29:42 (4,533)
Morgan, Philippa J.....4:45:46 (22,204)
Morgan, Shan.....3:09:15 (1,924)
Morgan, Susan L.....4:26:01 (17,571)
Morgans, Kathryn L.....4:28:53 (18,325)
Morley, Emma J.....4:10:22 (13,723)
Morley, Kate E.....4:33:44 (19,511)
Mornet, Françoise.....5:17:31 (27,311)
Morral, Bertha E.....5:45:10 (29,701)
Morris, Adele C.....3:48:42 (8,185)
Morris, Andrea.....3:55:36 (9,965)
Morris, Anne F.....4:39:51 (20,882)
Morris, Debbie G.....6:26:11 (31,147)
Morris, Elzabeth A.....5:24:12 (27,991)
Morris, Fiona.....4:12:01 (14,097)
Morris, Harriet J.....5:03:52 (25,562)
Morris, Helen B.....5:48:20 (29,877)
Morris, Johanne S.....5:36:38 (29,074)
Morris, Julie.....5:09:43 (26,339)
Morris, June M.....5:15:28 (27,074)
Morris, Katy H.....4:32:00 (19,113)
Morris, Marianne L.....5:01:16 (25,178)
Morris, Michelle J.....5:35:19 (28,981)
Morris, Susan P.....5:41:08 (29,421)
Morris, Tracey A.....2:33:52 (107)
Morrison, Laurie L.....4:32:37 (19,266)
Mort, Helen.....4:34:03 (19,606)
Mortimer, Hilary.....4:25:07 (17,337)
Mortley, Bev J.....7:23:25 (31,801)
Mortlock, Brenda.....5:37:49 (29,168)
Morton, Alison J.....4:48:26 (22,765)
Morton, Carol L.....4:44:36 (21,935)
Morton, Marie K.....3:51:54 (8,989)
Morton, Rebecca H.....6:06:05 (30,623)
Mosby, Linda K.....5:07:08 (25,987)
Moscoso, Susana.....5:46:47 (29,804)
Mosley, Helen G.....5:21:41 (27,748)
Mosman, Amy C.....7:28:43 (31,838)
Moss, Anita C.....5:45:47 (29,739)
Moss, Jean.....6:20:07 (31,015)
Moss, Kerry A.....4:39:32 (20,829)
Moss, Kim E.....3:54:31 (9,641)
Moss, Natalie C.....4:39:10 (20,764)
Moss, Rebecca C.....5:42:31 (29,515)
Moss, Sophie.....5:29:02 (28,485)
Mostyn, Chloe.....4:35:45 (19,971)
Mostyn, Melissa B.....5:13:30 (26,825)
Motley, Michaeleen D.....4:18:32 (15,670)
Mott, Jacqui A.....5:05:51 (25,815)
Motta, Simonetta.....4:19:59 (16,029)
Mottershead, Emily.....6:09:14 (30,708)
Mouat, Christine M.....3:40:21 (6,368)
Mouat, Rachel E.....4:45:35 (22,162)
Mould, Frances J.....6:03:26 (30,544)
Mould, Natasha A.....3:36:56 (5,756)
Moule, Victoria.....4:33:09 (19,391)
Moullin, Alison.....7:16:18 (31,760)
Mountford, Tanya.....4:40:37 (21,043)
Mowatt, Kate.....4:50:19 (23,126)
Moyle, Avril J.....4:55:19 (24,067)
Moynihan, Clare L.....4:15:39 (14,965)
Mueller, Carmen.....4:23:24 (16,921)
Mueller, Kerstin.....4:18:23 (15,627)
Muir, Denise.....3:09:23 (1,935)
Muir, Joanne L.....4:29:09 (18,393)
Muir, Katie A.....6:24:11 (31,115)
Muir, Shelagh R.....4:09:15 (13,438)
Mulford, Kay S.....4:58:49 (24,766)
Mulhall, Sarah L.....3:48:16 (8,069)
Mulhern, Lisa M.....4:47:59 (22,671)
Mulholland, Louise J.....4:25:28 (17,418)
Mulholland, Vanessa.....3:22:20 (3,348)
Mullan, Fiona S.....4:39:26 (20,814)
Mullenger, Clare.....3:59:55 (11,273)
Mullett, Kay P.....5:43:23 (29,584)
Mullett, Rachel T.....5:10:59 (26,504)
Mulligan, Jennifer C.....4:52:44 (23,574)
Mulligan, Lindsay.....5:56:07 (30,253)
Mulligan, Paula M.....5:14:03 (26,909)
Mullins, Nora C.....6:17:39 (30,942)
Mulvihill, Catherine.....5:09:35 (26,322)
Munday, Eileen J.....5:42:52 (29,539)
Munday, Tara.....5:41:30 (29,446)
Munde, Janis C.....4:47:32 (22,574)
Munn, Stacy D.....3:56:39 (10,292)
Munnings, Sarah J.....4:29:16 (18,418)
Munro, Julie.....5:13:59 (26,897)
Munro, Karen T.....4:21:37 (16,425)
Munton, Deborah S.....3:48:29 (8,116)
Murdoch, Elizabeth J.....4:40:03 (20,931)
Murnan, Katherine.....4:15:26 (14,909)
Murphy, Ann C.....4:09:59 (13,637)
Murphy, Anne Elaine.....7:14:28 (31,741)
Murphy, Brenda M.....5:27:04 (28,306)
Murphy, Clare F.....5:22:46 (27,854)
Murphy, Fiona.....4:01:23 (11,576)
Murphy, Karen E.....3:10:24 (2,043)
Murphy, Melissa M.....4:13:52 (14,536)
Murphy, Michelle J.....4:08:17 (13,170)
Murphy, Nicola A.....6:25:44 (31,136)
Murphy, Nicola T.....4:38:40 (20,632)
Murphy, Patricia.....4:23:32 (16,950)
Murphy, Penny E.....5:53:38 (30,138)
Murphy, Roisin M.....5:06:59 (25,966)
Murphy, Samantha A.....3:33:28 (5,185)
Murphy, Sharon P.....3:54:53 (9,748)
Murphy, Stacey.....4:33:56 (19,573)
Murphy, Susan C.....4:36:06 (20,056)
Murphy, Teresa.....3:28:10 (4,256)
Murphy, Teresa L.....4:55:09 (24,026)
Murray, Anne.....4:47:33 (22,580)
Murray, Beverley A.....4:02:55 (11,942)
Murray, Christine V.....4:59:22 (24,871)
Murray, Clare A.....4:29:17 (18,422)
Murray, Deborah.....4:36:42 (20,183)
Murray, Helen F.....5:20:51 (27,669)
Murray, Jenny D.....2:57:52 (952)
Murray, Katherine M.....4:49:57 (23,067)
Murray-Walker, Claire.....5:16:36 (27,210)
Mursell, Andrea.....4:21:54 (16,500)
Murtagh, Natalie M.....5:18:31 (27,413)
Murzell, Janet.....5:14:22 (26,943)
Musrat, Aterah.....4:39:37 (20,843)
Mussett, Annette D.....3:27:08 (4,050)
Musson, Sally M.....3:00:22 (1,184)
Mwamuye, Betty U.....5:08:25 (26,175)
Myatt, Melissa J.....4:17:19 (15,374)
Myers, Helen J.....6:45:19 (31,443)
Myles, Alexsandra.....4:40:31 (21,031)
Myles, Fiona.....4:16:21 (15,131)
Nadin, Louise.....4:29:47 (18,580)
Nagra, Rashpal K.....6:19:12 (30,996)
Nairn, Fionn.....3:20:46 (3,171)
Najurally, Narisa.....3:15:45 (2,629)
Nallaiah, Sobana.....5:26:40 (28,268)
Nampanga, Juma.....4:09:48 (13,577)
Nandra, Kirat K.....4:22:13 (16,613)
Nanhoo-Robinson, Amanda.....5:41:04 (29,412)
Nash, Alison.....4:55:55 (24,186)
Nash, Beverley J.....4:53:07 (23,636)
Nash, Sharon L.....4:29:09 (18,393)
Nasir, Clare L.....6:23:21 (31,093)
Nathan, Jane C.....4:43:09 (21,591)
Naude, Karen P.....3:25:29 (3,767)
Naughton, Caroline P.....5:03:49 (25,559)
Naylor, Sarah J.....4:34:21 (19,678)
Naylor, Sarah J.....6:58:03 (31,599)
Naylor, Wendy J.....5:41:59 (29,482)
Naylor-Maury, Jane H.....4:13:55 (14,547)
Naysmith, Fiona M.....4:58:28 (24,711)
Neacy, Bridget C.....4:19:53 (15,992)
Neal, Kelli J.....4:59:58 (24,986)
Neal, Sarah E.....4:36:25 (20,110)
Neal, Susan E.....6:38:29 (31,345)
Neale, Caroline L.....4:28:42 (18,279)
Neale, Kerry.....5:27:12 (28,323)
Neale, Mandy J.....4:18:45 (15,723)
Nee, Mary T.....6:36:13 (31,311)
Needleman, Hilary C.....3:54:36 (9,666)
Neenan, Jacqueline.....4:35:25 (19,914)
Neeson, Elmear.....4:19:05 (15,799)
Negussie, Mahlet T.....4:54:38 (23,930)
Nehra, Bharti.....4:37:53 (20,429)
Neighbour, Helen.....5:15:47 (27,106)
Neighbour, Sarah L.....5:56:03 (30,249)
Neil, Caroline.....4:43:29 (21,682)

Neil, Fiona H	4:29:19	(18,442)
Neil, Lucy A	4:29:27	(18,470)
Neill, Ashley	7:00:22	(31,631)
Neilsen, Britt K	4:00:04	(11,308)
Neilson, Carrie M	4:24:48	(17,251)
Neita, Annette	6:41:46	(31,386)
Neita, Kathleen A	6:41:46	(31,386)
Neita, Sarah L	6:14:08	(30,849)
Nejaime, Loraine	6:16:32	(30,921)
Nelson, Jacqueline E	4:43:50	(21,753)
Nelson, Jaime M	4:49:42	(23,014)
Nelson, Kim F	3:33:10	(5,129)
Nelson, Lesley A	4:18:21	(15,618)
Nelson, Marion C	4:40:28	(21,021)
Nelson, Paula	4:36:20	(20,096)
Nelson, Sally E	5:06:13	(25,876)
Neo, Amy	3:51:23	(8,853)
Nesfield, Sarah L	4:31:46	(19,044)
Nester, Katharine M	3:54:49	(9,726)
Nethisinghe, Chandima	4:06:28	(12,772)
Netttleton, Michelle L	4:40:42	(21,066)
Neumann, Ana M	4:16:05	(15,072)
Nevill, Abigail R	6:03:33	(30,551)
Nevill, Ibby	3:37:58	(5,955)
Neville, Elizabeth	3:39:21	(6,192)
Neville, Louise S	3:54:52	(9,741)
Neville, Sharon L	4:03:14	(12,010)
Nevin, Joanna	4:39:51	(20,882)
Newark, Lindsay A	5:28:41	(28,459)
Newbigging, Caroline J	4:56:28	(24,298)
Newcombe, Helen	4:03:07	(11,983)
Newcombe, Litini S	4:41:58	(21,342)
Newell, Alison	5:52:07	(30,070)
Newell, Angela	3:43:27	(6,951)
Newell, Sharon	4:14:11	(14,607)
Newington, Laura	4:55:20	(24,071)
Newington, Samantha J	3:53:47	(9,436)
Newington-Bridges, Lucinda M	4:33:37	(19,492)
Newland, Anita M	4:44:44	(21,961)
Newland, Marie	4:41:53	(21,323)
Newman, Gill	3:47:06	(7,779)
Newman, Janet M	5:54:23	(30,165)
Newman, Kate P	4:23:26	(16,929)
Newman, Ledra	4:56:18	(24,261)
Newman, Mary	5:13:35	(26,842)
Newman, Sarah A	4:03:57	(12,179)
Newman, Tacey	4:42:31	(21,455)
Newport, Belinda	4:05:00	(12,429)
Newport, Samantha L	4:41:12	(21,157)
Newson, Emma H	4:34:24	(19,692)
Newstead, An Ya V	6:50:48	(31,508)
Newton, Christine	5:28:22	(28,428)
Newton, Julie A	5:17:27	(27,299)
Newton, Lois H	5:24:15	(27,999)
Newton-Dunn, Tracey	6:20:58	(31,030)
Ney, Katrina	6:17:49	(30,946)
Ni Eidain, Mairead A	5:28:56	(28,476)
Ni Mhochain, Seosaimhin S	6:18:43	(30,982)
Nichetti, Maria	5:23:14	(27,894)
Nichls, Alison	3:24:20	(3,607)
Nicholas, Brenda	6:10:26	(30,739)
Nicholas, Charlotte R	4:03:30	(12,078)
Nicholettos, Louise M	4:28:32	(18,240)
Nicholl, Grace J	5:14:22	(26,943)
Nicholls, Frances S	5:04:18	(25,602)
Nicholls, Sarah J	4:57:43	(24,538)
Nicholls, Sarah L	4:54:59	(23,991)
Nicholls, Stephanie C	4:59:03	(24,803)
Nicholls, Yvonne	3:37:10	(5,808)
Nichols, Karen J	5:03:36	(25,533)
Nichols, Louise A	4:09:15	(13,438)
Nichols, Lyn S	4:30:20	(18,711)
Nichols, Margaret J	4:14:00	(14,561)
Nichols, Suzanne M	4:57:53	(24,564)
Nickolay-Kell, Aledandra P	5:20:06	(27,581)
Nicol, Eileen N	3:32:48	(5,060)
Nicol, Moira	3:57:46	(10,609)
Nicol, Suzanne E	4:46:46	(22,404)
Nieschmidt, Elke J	4:27:34	(17,982)
Nightingale, Michelle	5:25:48	(28,175)
Nightingale, Nicola J	5:13:06	(26,781)
Nijenhuis, Carole T	6:07:56	(30,672)
Nilmini, Sujeewa	2:58:14	(988)
Nilsson, Malin	3:56:03	(10,099)
Nishikawa, Kanako	4:12:16	(14,142)
Nishiura, Kinuko	6:23:30	(31,099)
Nisslein, Doris	4:25:15	(17,370)
Nitsch, Isene	6:57:12	(31,584)
Nitsch, Jo M	3:50:33	(8,639)
Niven, Stephanie	4:35:11	(19,861)
Noakes, Deborah A	4:30:51	(18,829)
Noble, Elizabeth M	4:50:10	(23,103)
Nobles, Margaret	4:31:50	(19,056)
Nodder, Jane C	4:28:38	(18,267)
Noel, Jacqueline D	5:11:58	(26,627)
Nolan, Kerry J	4:54:56	(23,985)
Nolan, Liz S	5:38:35	(29,237)
Nolan, Tina	4:16:23	(15,142)
Noller, Deborah L	3:32:36	(5,031)
Nordin, Breege J	3:20:31	(3,135)
Noresi, Cinzia	3:36:03	(5,618)
Norman, Alison L	5:18:38	(27,427)
Norman, Heidi L	5:39:17	(29,287)
Norman, Laura	4:48:59	(22,871)
Norman, Mary	3:40:06	(6,322)
Normand, Ainsley M	3:20:52	(3,186)
Norquay, Megan J	3:37:58	(5,955)
Norris, Ellen	5:49:52	(29,960)
Norris, Jennifer M	3:14:49	(2,538)
Norris, Shirley A	5:33:09	(28,819)
North, Alison	4:12:33	(14,218)
North, Heather J	3:55:57	(10,067)
Northam, Julie A	5:07:49	(26,092)
Northey, Victoria J	5:01:04	(25,157)
Norton, Julie A	3:44:56	(7,293)
Norton, Karena C	4:12:37	(14,239)
Norton, Sarah J	5:09:53	(26,366)
Notley, Joanna M	4:28:26	(18,206)
Nottage, Barbara J	7:28:40	(31,836)
Nottra, Rawinder K	4:01:50	(11,675)
Nouraud, Mandelle	3:28:47	(4,368)
Nowakowski, Maria	5:14:35	(26,976)
Nowell, Lucille M	6:23:17	(31,089)
Noyce, Jemima L	4:43:49	(21,751)
Noye, Jayne M	7:20:29	(31,791)
Nugent, Ann M	6:21:01	(31,032)
Nunn, Caroline L	4:09:38	(13,536)
Nunn, Elizabeth	4:27:04	(17,859)
Nunn, Gillian D	4:54:30	(23,896)
Nutley, Mary E	4:47:02	(22,456)
Nutting, Judy A	3:33:06	(5,116)
Nutting, Julie A	4:55:42	(24,134)
Nyqvist, Marie	3:28:22	(4,293)
Oakes, Anne	4:16:21	(15,131)
Oakes, Fiona L	2:59:25	(1,114)
Oakley, Carol M	4:13:39	(14,487)
Oakley, Carole L	5:13:59	(26,897)
Oakley, Claire M	4:26:02	(17,579)
Oakley, Kate E	6:03:10	(30,534)
Oakley, Sacha J	5:10:17	(26,412)
Oakley, Sarah E	6:00:34	(30,429)
Oakley, Suzan E	4:54:43	(23,944)
Oatts, Elizabeth G	3:56:14	(10,161)
Oberer, Marnie	3:21:43	(3,280)
O'Brien, Bernadette	3:34:49	(5,393)
O'Brien, Helen L	4:48:52	(22,847)
O'Brien, Jane L	6:01:15	(30,458)
O'Brien, Johanna C	3:49:03	(8,264)
O'Brien, Maria A	5:56:43	(30,280)
O'Brien, Tracy A	7:15:24	(31,750)
O'Brien, Victoria M	5:49:38	(29,937)
Ochiltree, Elaine E	4:37:34	(20,349)
Ochsner, Christina	3:57:52	(10,639)
O'Connell, Emily	3:36:11	(5,639)
O'Connell, Pamela J	4:47:45	(22,624)
O'Connor, Aoife H	3:36:48	(5,743)
O'Connor, Brenda P	5:00:28	(25,060)
O'Connor, Gill	2:58:23	(1,003)
O'Connor, Naomi	6:20:38	(31,027)
O'Connor, Sandra M	5:36:00	(29,029)
Odams, Suzanne E	5:41:36	(29,458)
Oddy, Suzannah J	3:52:55	(9,231)
O'Dea, Susan J	4:31:33	(18,990)
O'Donnell, Anne M	4:01:45	(11,659)
O'Donnell, Catherine F	5:41:47	(29,476)
O'Donnell, Jo R	3:46:19	(7,605)
O'Donnell, Patricia K	5:07:06	(25,982)
O'Donnell, Sharon	8:02:34	(31,945)
O'Donoghue, Gussie A	7:34:48	(31,871)
O'Donovan, Bernie	3:30:43	(4,729)
O'Donovan, Jean P	4:22:23	(16,663)
O'Farrell, Jayne M	5:47:05	(29,816)
O'Farrell, Suzanne	4:33:55	(19,569)
Offedi, Doreen	6:12:17	(30,787)
Offer, Caroline V	4:56:41	(24,340)
Ogier, Angela R	4:50:23	(23,153)
Ogilvie, Debra	3:55:41	(9,982)
Ogley, Julia A	5:51:31	(30,037)
O'Gorman-Harte, Miriam M	4:34:57	(19,810)
O'Groman, Carmel	5:34:53	(28,949)
Ogungbesan, Pat O	5:02:31	(25,379)
O'Hagan, Colette M	4:44:10	(21,831)
O'Hagan, Denise M	5:01:03	(25,152)
O'Hanlon, Tracy	7:52:27	(31,920)
O'Hara, Pauline J	5:01:02	(25,150)
O'Hare, Carol	4:26:17	(17,653)
O'Hare, Susan J	3:56:50	(10,348)
O'Hooley, Rebecca A	4:07:22	(12,978)
Okamoto, Hideko	4:54:32	(23,906)

Okayo, Margaret 2:22:35 (46)

Margaret Okayo from Kenya (born 30 May 1976) started running while at primary school. She was recruited by Kenya Prisons Service, home to the country's top women marathon runners. At the 1998 Commonwealth Games she finished fifth in 10,000m. She finished 13th at the 1999 IAAF World Half Marathon Championships. Among her most successful races are wins at the 2001 and 2003 New York Marathon, the 2002 Boston Marathon and the 2004 London Marathon. She held the course records at the New York Marathon and the Boston Marathon. She represented her native Kenya in the 2004 Olympic Games in Athens but did not finish the marathon. She spends three months a year training in Brescia, Italy. Okayo is of the Gusii tribe. She is managed by Federico Rosa and coached by Gabriele Rosa. She is just 152cm tall and weighs 43kg. She is the fifth of nine children from the third of her father's three wives. She donated part of the $160,000 she made by winning the 2003 New York Marathon to a fund for Kenyan orphans.

O'Keefe, Avena	4:08:32	(13,239)
O'Keefe, Collette L	4:28:25	(18,198)
O'Keefe, Lisa A	5:17:41	(27,326)
Okoturo, Nnenna A	5:46:39	(29,798)
Oldfield, Helen M	3:26:38	(3,940)
Oldfield, Julie C	5:49:27	(29,927)
Oldfield, Lisa J	3:48:59	(8,251)
Oldman, Joanna	5:08:00	(26,115)
Oleary, Amanda J	3:20:21	(3,104)

Oliphant, Anne S	4:12:51 (14,289)	
Oliver, Jacqueline	4:44:22 (21,876)	
Oliver, Joanna K	5:06:18 (25,888)	
Oliver, Lynn M	4:12:12 (14,133)	
Oliver, Mary-Louise	5:21:22 (27,713)	
Oliver, Sue S	5:47:28 (29,834)	
Olkowski, Kristina E	4:58:22 (24,679)	
Olley, Michelle	5:08:12 (26,143)	
Olney, Yvonne	4:48:20 (22,747)	
Olson, Mandy F	5:12:44 (26,718)	
O'Mahoney, Jane M	5:12:45 (26,720)	
Omar, Gillian M	5:49:31 (29,931)	
Ombler, Sharon L	3:45:41 (7,455)	
Omogehin, Oluwole	5:54:08 (30,156)	
Omoregbee, Anthea D	5:59:46 (30,403)	
O'Neill, Deirdre M	3:46:14 (7,589)	
O'Neill, Heike K	4:58:36 (24,736)	
O'Neill, Lisa	7:08:57 (31,700)	
O'Neill, Loraine J	4:55:52 (24,169)	
O'Neill, Patricia A	3:56:13 (10,148)	
O'Neill, Rachel C	3:51:38 (8,926)	
Ong, Clara	4:31:41 (19,022)	
Oosthuizen, Vicki H	4:33:28 (19,463)	
Oram, Claire M	5:36:47 (29,086)	
Orange, Elizabeth A	5:40:45 (29,398)	
Orban, Mariybridget	4:26:35 (17,723)	
Ordidge, Lisa J	5:24:45 (28,048)	
O'Regan, Catherine P	4:03:49 (12,152)	
O'Reilly, Siobhan	4:06:06 (12,683)	
Oria, Ann	6:11:13 (30,760)	
Oriaikhi, Eghosa	7:11:28 (31,720)	
Orme, Jacqueline A	4:12:45 (14,274)	
Ormerod, Jean F	7:15:22 (31,749)	
Ormsby, Emma M	5:25:52 (28,185)	
Orr, Roslyn D	5:38:15 (29,204)	
Orr, Suzanne L	5:38:15 (29,204)	
Orridge, Harriet G	5:18:04 (27,376)	
Orridge, Sharon I	2:58:44 (1,049)	
Orth, Barbara	3:29:58 (4,583)	
Orton, Paula L	4:53:31 (23,704)	
Orvieto, Eleonora	3:49:56 (8,482)	
Osborn, Janice	5:41:44 (29,471)	
Osborne, Anna B	5:53:12 (30,131)	
Osborne, Fiona M	5:20:22 (27,616)	
Osborne, Janette C	4:28:52 (18,317)	
Osborne, Lisa J	4:43:29 (21,682)	
Osborne, Michelle H	4:38:57 (20,706)	
Osbourn, Tracey	5:14:13 (26,928)	
Oscroft, Susie V	4:44:39 (21,947)	
Osei-Gyamfi, Vera	5:41:46 (29,474)	
O'Shaughnessy, Siobhan M	5:08:20 (26,164)	
Oslar, Samantha J	5:16:00 (27,132)	
Osmand, Kerry L	5:18:35 (27,421)	
Osowska, Francesca	3:21:20 (3,236)	
O'Sullivan, Fiona M	5:09:33 (26,313)	
O'Sullivan, Kerry A	7:27:24 (31,826)	
O'Sullivan, Maureen N	5:10:33 (26,447)	
O'Sullivan, Niamh L	6:03:09 (30,533)	
Otley, Deborah	3:53:09 (9,297)	
Ott, Kathy S	4:23:41 (16,980)	
Ottaway, Andrew M	5:07:57 (26,107)	
Ottaway, Julia Y	5:12:40 (26,708)	
Ottewill, Brend	5:24:16 (28,000)	
Otto, Silvia	4:47:15 (22,509)	
Otton, Norma	4:39:09 (20,762)	
Oughton, Emma C	4:09:14 (13,432)	
Outten, Candy M	4:29:36 (18,523)	
Ovens, Jan	3:44:10 (7,110)	
Ovstedal, Jenny L	4:19:54 (15,997)	
Owen, Dianne B	5:37:23 (29,145)	
Owen, Helen M	5:38:13 (29,197)	
Owen, Josephine	4:15:00 (14,803)	
Owen, Juliet	4:13:42 (14,496)	
Owen, Lisa M	6:32:39 (31,257)	
Owen, Mary	3:23:41 (3,526)	
Owen, Sarah J	4:28:56 (18,334)	
Owen, Sharon	6:18:24 (30,966)	
Owen, Victoria J	4:58:56 (24,785)	
Owens, Elizabeth M	5:22:43 (27,850)	
Owens, Josie	4:04:58 (12,424)	
Owens, Karen M	5:07:34 (26,053)	
Owens, Sally A	4:31:52 (19,066)	
Owens, Shirley	4:31:52 (19,066)	
Owst, Jennie R	4:45:56 (22,235)	
Paananen, Johanna M	3:57:56 (10,658)	
Pacaud, Sam	4:51:49 (23,402)	
Packer, Clare	4:52:24 (23,517)	
Packer, Samantha	5:01:01 (25,146)	
Packman, Alison J	4:33:44 (19,511)	
Paddock, Sarah	4:59:52 (24,968)	
Padgham, Melanie A	3:36:37 (5,714)	
Padmore, Susan	4:47:10 (22,493)	
Page, Andrea L	4:20:12 (16,064)	
Page, Clare V	3:27:17 (4,078)	
Page, Jane M	5:48:59 (29,907)	
Page, Janice	5:13:32 (26,831)	
Page, Karen E	4:59:15 (24,839)	
Page, Lorna J	5:09:14 (26,270)	
Page, Melissa C	4:43:06 (21,582)	
Page, Tonia	5:00:56 (25,132)	
Page, Victoria	5:41:34 (29,453)	
Paget, Yvonne M	4:44:13 (21,842)	
Pagnamenta, Rachel C	4:44:17 (21,855)	
Pairoux, Chantal	4:49:07 (22,898)	
Palacios, Andrea	4:57:18 (24,461)	
Palfreyman, Anna E	5:06:10 (25,869)	
Paling, Judith E	4:24:15 (17,133)	
Pall, Linda	7:52:27 (31,920)	
Palles, Claire L	4:10:55 (13,850)	
Pallett, Suzy C	4:18:01 (15,557)	
Palmer, Camilla F	6:15:12 (30,891)	
Palmer, Carol L	4:27:40 (18,010)	
Palmer, Debbie A	5:00:07 (25,013)	
Palmer, Deborah	4:23:12 (16,873)	
Palmer, Elaine A	4:17:50 (15,517)	
Palmer, Emma R	3:53:52 (9,469)	
Palmer, Heidi A	4:38:50 (20,677)	
Palmer, Janet	5:31:33 (28,703)	
Palmer, Jocelyn W	5:24:35 (28,030)	
Palmer, Julia	3:16:19 (2,674)	
Palmer, Michelle D	5:08:13 (26,145)	
Palmer, Rachel A	4:20:30 (16,159)	
Palmer, Sarah A	5:17:02 (27,260)	
Palmer, Sarah J	5:16:15 (27,162)	
Panay, Claire A	5:08:16 (26,152)	
Panayides, Louise-Ann K	5:44:10 (29,634)	
Panayis, Tania E	5:10:42 (26,466)	
Panayotopoulos, Electra	5:07:16 (26,005)	
Pang, Jin	4:20:38 (16,195)	
Panigirakis, Sophie	5:17:55 (27,355)	
Panizza, Amanda K	3:35:17 (5,477)	
Pannell, Maria	4:15:15 (14,870)	
Papaioannou, Joanna	6:38:53 (31,348)	
Papworth, Annette E	4:18:23 (15,627)	
Parchment, Marion	4:08:58 (13,369)	
Pardo, Miren	4:34:00 (19,587)	
Pare, Mona C	4:11:27 (13,959)	
Parfitt, Pauline	3:51:42 (8,940)	
Parfitt, Sarah	4:04:14 (12,249)	
Park, Debbie	4:55:04 (24,007)	
Park, Hattie A	4:13:03 (14,343)	
Park, Lilian E	5:08:44 (26,207)	
Parker, Alyssa B	3:17:02 (2,751)	
Parker, Annette	4:30:30 (18,760)	
Parker, Bonnie R	3:59:05 (11,024)	
Parker, Cathy	6:37:55 (31,338)	
Parker, Claire	4:51:19 (23,320)	
Parker, Debbie L	5:28:36 (28,450)	
Parker, Debra J	4:25:07 (17,337)	
Parker, Felicity J	5:28:36 (28,450)	
Parker, Helen E	4:49:19 (22,942)	
Parker, Helen M	4:52:00 (23,438)	
Parker, Juliet	4:53:13 (23,656)	
Parker, Kim S	4:21:34 (16,405)	
Parker, Lise J	4:43:13 (21,610)	
Parker, Louise E	4:13:30 (14,452)	
Parker, Michaela D	4:50:44 (23,219)	
Parker, Nicola A	5:49:46 (29,948)	
Parker, Patricia A	4:26:10 (17,621)	
Parker, Patsy	5:16:32 (27,196)	
Parker, Rachel L	4:28:31 (18,235)	
Parker, Sandra	4:34:41 (19,753)	
Parker, Sarah E	3:59:35 (11,183)	
Parker, Susy A	3:55:30 (9,929)	
Parker-Varty, Dawn W	5:55:22 (30,217)	
Parkes, Caroline M	4:38:38 (20,622)	
Parkes, Helen K	4:21:59 (16,530)	
Parkes, Sally M	5:20:35 (27,641)	
Parkes, Tamara J	5:28:43 (28,461)	
Parkin, Kirsteen L	4:50:59 (23,268)	
Parkinson, Jill E	4:26:51 (17,785)	
Parkinson, Sylvie	5:02:09 (25,313)	
Parle, Shirley Y	3:51:42 (8,940)	
Parmar, Dipa	5:25:56 (28,189)	
Parnell, Aimée L	4:17:23 (15,392)	
Parnham, Gayle R	5:39:44 (29,316)	
Parr, Emily	5:28:34 (28,446)	
Parr, Sarah J	4:08:32 (13,239)	
Parr, Susan J	5:07:38 (26,066)	
Parrella, Gilda	5:42:56 (29,547)	
Parrott, Margaret A	5:13:06 (26,781)	
Parry, Clare H	3:57:42 (10,592)	
Parry, Emma C	3:01:32 (1,278)	
Parry, Helen	5:37:53 (29,171)	
Parry, Jan E	4:48:25 (22,763)	
Parry, Jane H	4:18:43 (15,712)	
Parry, Rebekah J	5:17:50 (27,341)	
Parry, Tracey A	5:43:25 (29,586)	
Parry-Jones, Sara L	3:33:46 (5,229)	
Parsons, Elizabeth J	4:23:16 (16,885)	
Parsons, Heather E	4:22:02 (16,548)	
Parsons, Nikki J	5:14:20 (26,938)	
Parsons, Pamela A	4:05:30 (12,539)	
Parsons, Tina P	5:01:33 (25,229)	
Partington, Fiona A	4:10:20 (13,713)	
Parton, Lynne E	4:33:53 (19,556)	
Partridge, Diane L	4:59:20 (24,858)	
Partridge, Gill M	4:54:34 (23,914)	
Partridge, Isobel	2:59:37 (1,128)	
Partridge, Susan	2:41:44 (237)	
Pascal, Claudine	5:13:42 (26,855)	
Pashley, Anne	4:39:22 (20,805)	
Pasquinelli, Veronika	4:04:22 (12,275)	
Pass, Donna M	4:48:00 (22,672)	
Passanisi, Paola	3:37:46 (5,911)	
Passmore, Alison W	6:14:27 (30,860)	
Passway, Tracey J	3:37:33 (5,879)	
Pastor-Rodes, Maria A	4:57:22 (24,467)	
Patchava, Anushka	6:49:17 (31,489)	
Patching, Katrina J	4:35:49 (19,985)	
Patel, Hansa T	5:42:43 (29,528)	
Patel, Jaimi R	5:42:13 (29,497)	
Patel, Minaxi	4:52:00 (23,438)	
Patel, Mona	5:08:09 (26,135)	
Patel, Neeshe	3:50:35 (8,651)	
Patel, Nisha	6:52:50 (31,541)	
Patel, Pravina	4:58:25 (24,698)	
Patel, Shaila	6:37:17 (31,516)	
Patel, Sushila	5:22:22 (27,817)	
Patel, Trupti	7:02:05 (31,643)	
Pateman, Felicity M	5:09:09 (26,260)	
Paterson, Angela J	6:46:32 (31,460)	
Paterson, Claire G	3:56:24 (10,213)	
Paterson, Helen C	4:04:29 (12,312)	
Paterson, Sarah C	3:54:17 (9,583)	
Pathe, Louise A	4:56:44 (24,349)	
Patil, Mangala L	4:55:25 (24,088)	
Paton, Paddy S	4:33:56 (19,573)	
Patterson, Christine	4:22:06 (16,571)	
Patterson, Claire E	6:06:56 (30,643)	
Patterson, Kelly J	5:06:49 (25,946)	
Patterson, Nicole	4:44:43 (21,958)	
Patterson, Sarah	5:51:52 (30,054)	
Pattison, Marian V	5:16:49 (27,232)	
Paul, Carol	4:18:22 (15,623)	
Pauler, Angela	5:15:02 (27,029)	
Pavey, Patricia J	5:01:10 (25,170)	
Pavlikova, Ivana	3:53:11 (9,310)	
Paxton, Colin J	4:05:52 (12,629)	
Paxton, Elizabeth M	4:32:12 (19,165)	
Paxton, Pamela J	4:05:52 (12,629)	
Payne, Daphne	5:02:39 (25,396)	
Payne, Debbie	6:06:33 (30,634)	
Payne, Julie E	4:42:02 (21,355)	
Payne, Kim A	5:08:22 (26,170)	
Payne, Lisa	4:15:00 (14,803)	
Payne, Louise M	4:38:58 (20,715)	
Payne, Shona C	5:07:28 (26,042)	
Paynter, Karin K	5:05:18 (25,726)	

Pringle, Dawn L....4:27:34 (17,982)
Pritchard, Pamela M....5:55:54 (30,239)
Pritchett, Jennifer A....4:50:39 (23,207)
Pritchett, Julie....5:20:01 (27,567)
Pritemps, Helene....4:40:50 (21,095)
Procter, Sarah F....3:49:01 (8,258)
Prosser, Phyllis D....5:28:44 (28,464)
Proud, Lucy A....4:12:53 (14,299)
Prue, Penelope A....5:08:45 (26,212)
Pryke, Gail B....3:14:55 (2,549)
Ptacek, Alison C....5:02:48 (25,422)
Puech, Brenda....4:18:01 (15,557)
Pugh, Daphne W....5:42:40 (29,524)
Pugh, Jessica C....4:37:07 (20,278)
Pugh, Lisa J....5:07:26 (26,035)
Pullar, Rosemary E....3:51:49 (8,972)
Pumphrey, Kate E....3:43:54 (7,038)
Punch, Rachel L....3:57:03 (10,404)
Pupin, Emilie....3:31:07 (4,792)
Puplett, Gemma....4:22:19 (16,647)
Purcell, Laura M....3:52:15 (9,072)
Purdie, Andrea J....4:20:50 (16,235)
Purdie, Sarah J....4:19:39 (15,940)
Purkis, Sue....4:58:19 (24,670)
Purnell, Jacqueline M....4:41:20 (21,201)
Purshouse, Sharon....4:56:19 (24,266)
Purslow, Christine M....4:26:02 (17,579)
Purvis, Jacqueline....4:56:57 (24,394)
Putland, Ann E....5:32:59 (28,807)
Putris, Samira H....5:51:58 (30,060)
Pye, Catherine....3:57:09 (10,433)
Pye, Deborah J....3:56:38 (10,289)
Pye, Lisa M....4:02:48 (11,927)
Pyne, Janet L....5:09:17 (26,274)
Pyper, Jennifer L....3:19:10 (2,975)
Quainoo, Mary A....6:59:07 (31,608)
Qualtrough, Kath....3:56:14 (10,161)
Quartermain, Emma....5:42:22 (29,508)
Quartermaine, Amanda J....4:57:11 (24,432)
Quayle, Anna M....4:32:31 (19,240)
Quayle, Marina C....4:35:08 (19,851)
Quenby, Elizabeth J....4:57:44 (24,544)
Querfurth, Keren....4:22:07 (16,576)
Quicke, Emma A....4:35:53 (20,000)
Quigg, Deirdre....3:33:12 (5,136)
Quinn, Anne C....6:03:45 (30,556)
Quinn, Brigid....4:05:44 (12,600)
Quinn, Cora....4:48:40 (22,807)
Quinn, Emma-Jane....3:49:22 (8,344)
Quinn, Jamie E....3:39:33 (6,224)
Quinsee, Deborah J....4:52:45 (23,577)
Quinton, Catherine F....3:21:17 (3,229)
Quittner, Joanne....5:03:22 (25,496)
Raban-Williams, Catherine M....4:43:24 (21,662)
Rabbitt, Alison....4:31:17 (18,916)
Rabson, Katharine I....4:28:32 (18,240)
Rackey, Carolyn J....4:44:58 (22,027)
Radford, Anna H....4:32:15 (19,177)
Radford, Jane....3:52:44 (9,180)
Radford, Susan A....3:42:39 (6,775)
Rafferty, Elizabeth....4:16:08 (15,089)
Rafferty, Liz J....5:32:42 (28,791)
Rahou, Sarah....3:49:22 (8,344)
Rai, Harinder K....6:11:19 (30,764)
Rai, Kulbir K....6:11:19 (30,764)
Rainbird, Dorothy....6:52:49 (31,539)
Rainbird, Katy A....4:52:33 (23,539)
Raine, Kate H....4:44:44 (21,961)
Raine, Katherine L....6:18:27 (30,970)
Rainer, Margit....5:37:17 (29,135)
Rainger, Lesley....3:26:19 (3,892)
Rainsford, Sally A....6:01:53 (30,482)
Ralph, Barbara....3:22:11 (3,325)
Ralph, Karen....4:33:36 (19,486)
Ram, Karen Z....6:16:36 (30,926)
Ram, Vidya....4:51:25 (23,333)
Rambridge, Janice M....5:43:03 (29,570)
Ramm, Ruth V....4:56:48 (24,361)
Ramsay, Tana....3:55:25 (9,910)
Ramsbottom, Katie L....4:30:23 (18,724)
Ramsden, Jane....4:39:53 (20,891)
Ramsden, Lesley....5:31:26 (28,700)
Ramsey, Pamela M....5:32:30 (28,774)
Ramsey, Paula....3:43:12 (6,894)
Rana, Naheed....4:15:20 (14,886)
Rand, Emma D....4:14:19 (14,626)
Randall, Cheryl L....4:55:01 (23,999)
Randall, Helen....4:36:54 (20,227)
Randall, Helen C....5:47:02 (29,813)
Rankin, Janice....4:55:33 (24,108)
Ransley, Melanie R....4:17:31 (15,429)
Ranson, Pauline F....4:02:44 (11,910)
Rapley, Elizabeth A....5:04:43 (25,653)
Ratcliffe, Alli....3:51:30 (8,888)
Rathke, Irit....5:36:32 (29,061)
Rathore, Rita....4:31:55 (19,088)
Raval, Deepa....5:09:57 (26,372)
Ravenscroft, Tracey L....4:05:16 (12,475)
Rawat, Amina....5:01:29 (25,219)
Rawlins, Sally J....4:03:00 (11,954)
Rawlinson, Linda D....4:32:12 (19,165)
Rawson, Angela....3:55:28 (9,921)
Rawson, Pamela F....4:46:10 (22,289)
Rayif, Frances....5:37:58 (29,180)
Raynel, Natasha E....3:50:49 (8,712)
Rayner, Daryl....4:39:12 (20,774)
Rayner, Elizabeth....4:10:31 (13,759)
Rayner, Marion R....3:09:42 (1,969)
Rea, Isobel....5:00:38 (25,082)
Rea, Maureen....4:36:19 (20,090)
Read, Anna K....4:56:49 (24,367)
Read, Charlotte A....4:04:05 (12,208)
Read, Dawn....3:41:42 (6,582)
Read, Susan D....5:18:37 (27,424)
Reade, Steve....5:07:05 (25,979)
Reader, Lesley....6:14:16 (30,855)
Reading, Avril....5:35:00 (28,956)
Reading, Jill E....4:15:30 (14,925)
Ready, Deborah J....4:20:46 (16,225)
Reale, Diane....5:06:49 (25,946)
Realmuto, Sarah L....3:43:19 (6,922)
Reay, Lynne....5:25:15 (28,112)
Redd, Amanda A....4:48:47 (22,832)
Reddin, Ainslie J....4:28:25 (18,198)
Redfern, Kathy F....4:04:41 (12,345)
Redford, Nathalie....4:42:38 (21,477)
Redpath, Charlotte M....5:24:31 (28,028)
Redpath, Janet M....3:52:36 (9,153)
Reed, Adele J....7:36:25 (31,880)
Reed, Barbara A....4:56:58 (24,396)
Reed, Brenda....7:03:06 (31,651)
Reed, Catherine A....3:46:58 (7,741)
Reed, Gwyneth M....4:36:28 (20,123)
Reed, Katharine R....4:50:23 (23,153)
Reeds, Jane....4:47:22 (22,533)
Rees, Caroline S....4:30:30 (18,760)
Rees, Elizabeth A....5:51:08 (30,022)
Rees, Jacqui....5:07:08 (25,987)
Rees, Lisa E....4:27:51 (18,055)
Reeve, Nadine....5:23:49 (27,955)
Reeves, Angela....4:28:51 (18,314)
Reeves, Emma E....5:14:35 (26,976)
Reeves, Jennifer L....5:00:07 (25,013)
Reeves, Julie A....4:20:54 (16,261)
Reeves, Stella J....5:04:18 (25,602)
Regan, Lara J....3:59:24 (11,115)
Regan, Maxine J....6:06:07 (30,629)
Regan, Paulette L....4:51:29 (23,342)
Reich, Kate....5:25:35 (28,146)
Reid, Amanda J....4:06:23 (12,758)
Reid, Anna L....4:40:37 (21,043)
Reid, Carol A....3:29:20 (4,475)
Reid, Jacqueline E....4:16:37 (15,211)
Reid, Jan....4:21:58 (16,524)
Reid, Penny E....3:58:07 (10,715)
Reid, Stephanie F....5:40:17 (29,355)
Reid, Yvonne M....4:55:02 (24,002)
Reid-Smith, Gaynor J....3:59:34 (11,177)
Reilly, Cynthia A....5:34:38 (28,929)
Reindorf, Veronica F....6:59:59 (31,621)
Reinhardt, Linda S....4:25:37 (17,456)
Reintsema, Anne-Margo....4:54:37 (23,926)
Rengifo, Andrea....7:11:55 (31,722)
Rennie, Anita....3:46:08 (7,552)
Rennolls, Sarah M....5:46:43 (29,801)
Renton, Karen G....4:18:45 (15,723)
Renwick, Dawne....3:32:21 (4,979)
Renyard, Lauren E....3:57:22 (10,505)
Renzetti, Marta....5:54:44 (30,186)
Resnick, Debra I....3:39:54 (6,290)
Revell, Kim E....4:47:52 (22,649)
Reynolds, Abigail M....4:35:54 (20,003)
Reynolds, Andrea....4:19:23 (15,878)
Reynolds, Barbara....5:26:19 (28,227)
Reynolds, Cathleen....4:11:48 (14,044)
Reynolds, Catriona M....4:41:00 (21,122)
Reynolds, Donna J....4:45:35 (22,162)
Reynolds, Ruth....7:14:44 (31,743)
Reynolds, Sarah....3:41:01 (6,479)
Rhodes, Lindsay A....4:56:31 (24,314)
Riach, Christine....5:22:30 (27,831)
Riachi, Marie-Christine....5:12:25 (26,684)
Rice, Liz....4:08:08 (13,139)
Richards, Alison J....4:54:53 (23,974)
Richards, Claire....4:44:22 (21,876)
Richards, Donna M....6:17:36 (30,940)
Richards, Emma V....3:28:32 (4,326)
Richards, Gillian....4:35:51 (19,990)
Richards, Julie A....4:03:53 (12,166)
Richards, Karen....4:07:35 (13,031)
Richards, Leisha G....7:08:33 (31,697)
Richards, Lindsey A....6:16:53 (30,928)
Richards, Lise E....4:30:24 (18,733)
Richards, Natalie M....4:08:30 (13,231)
Richards, Pauline G....3:30:57 (4,771)
Richards, Ruth G....4:19:17 (15,854)
Richards, Sarah J....4:41:06 (21,142)
Richards, Sarah J....4:53:42 (23,749)
Richards, Tara....4:57:39 (24,521)
Richardson, Alexandra....3:20:20 (3,103)
Richardson, Dawn P....2:57:13 (895)
Richardson, Jane....4:10:31 (13,759)
Richardson, Jen....4:10:48 (13,828)
Richardson, Joanne H....5:59:21 (30,379)
Richardson, Lesley C....3:21:09 (3,214)
Richardson, Linda K....4:22:35 (16,719)
Richardson, Lucinda....4:33:21 (19,437)
Richardson, Natalie S....5:14:12 (26,923)
Richardson, Susan P....5:04:32 (25,631)
Richardson, Theresa A....4:59:33 (24,914)
Riches, Jackie F....7:01:43 (31,639)
Richmond, Denise....4:52:21 (23,514)
Rickard, Donna....4:22:01 (16,544)
Rickard, Karin....3:55:33 (9,947)
Rickett, Jane....4:35:04 (19,835)
Riddell, Claire E....4:05:34 (12,563)
Rider, Sharon A....4:49:15 (22,927)
Ridgard, Nicola J....5:21:59 (27,770)
Ridge, Paula M....5:11:09 (26,527)
Ridge, Sheila J....4:31:03 (18,866)
Ridger, Christine A....5:41:51 (29,478)
Ridgley, Julie R....3:44:24 (7,161)
Ridgway, Denise....4:38:57 (20,706)
Riding, Liona....4:30:42 (18,800)
Ridler, Amy G....5:02:34 (25,384)
Ridler, Rebecca J....4:34:04 (19,614)
Ridley, Sarah E....5:11:05 (26,514)
Ridley-Smith, Sophie....6:32:11 (31,248)
Rigby, Jessica C....4:51:24 (23,330)
Riggs, Samantha....4:58:50 (24,768)
Riley, Helen E....6:45:19 (31,443)
Riley, Joanne L....3:56:36 (10,280)
Riley, Kathrine E....5:18:21 (27,403)
Riley, Rachel L....3:30:01 (4,591)
Rimmer, Beverley A....4:08:52 (13,338)
Ringham, Liz J....3:20:30 (3,131)
Risby, Kay E....3:51:16 (8,824)
Ritchie, Amanda J....3:54:05 (9,528)
Ritchie, Anna....5:07:40 (26,071)
Ritchie, Kirsty-Jane....4:03:31 (12,082)

Ritchie, Sarah B	5:25:37 (28,151)	
Rivans, Paula V	5:13:21 (26,811)	
Rivas, Paula	3:27:19 (4,084)	
Rive, Christine M	5:09:56 (26,370)	
Rive, Leanne	4:23:37 (16,968)	
Rivers, Anna J	5:49:12 (29,917)	
Rizvi, Yasmin	7:25:09 (31,812)	
Roach, Denise V	3:43:29 (6,956)	
Roads, Annette	4:04:41 (12,345)	
Roads, Emily J	5:13:10 (26,790)	
Roake, Claire E	3:52:00 (9,012)	
Robbins, Diane E	4:28:59 (18,344)	
Robbins, Joanna L	3:58:10 (10,745)	
Roberson, Jane C	6:10:43 (30,749)	
Roberson, Julia H	4:21:12 (16,311)	
Roberts, Annette	4:02:42 (11,899)	
Roberts, Bethan	4:25:07 (17,337)	
Roberts, Carole M	3:39:10 (6,157)	
Roberts, Christine E	4:13:49 (14,521)	
Roberts, Claire	5:03:55 (25,566)	
Roberts, Emma	5:39:22 (29,297)	
Roberts, Erin	4:34:03 (19,606)	
Roberts, Fiona G	5:02:41 (25,400)	
Roberts, Gillian L	4:21:31 (16,393)	
Roberts, Helen	4:04:49 (12,379)	
Roberts, Jennifer A	4:55:52 (24,169)	
Roberts, Laura J	5:52:20 (30,088)	
Roberts, Maryjane	5:59:33 (30,395)	
Roberts, Michele J	5:16:37 (27,213)	
Roberts, Rachel E	6:04:14 (30,569)	
Roberts, Rebecca M	4:57:04 (24,415)	
Roberts, Sharon N	4:27:25 (17,941)	
Roberts, Sylvia	3:32:54 (5,083)	
Roberts, Ursula G	5:29:42 (28,557)	
Roberts, Valerie A	5:33:46 (28,867)	
Robertshaw, Alex J	4:49:49 (23,046)	
Robertson, Abbie	3:45:49 (7,485)	
Robertson, Lee M	5:51:32 (30,038)	
Robertson, Louise A	3:47:12 (7,805)	
Robertson, Louise M	4:27:01 (17,846)	
Robertson, Naomi	4:47:57 (22,662)	
Robertson, Nicola C	4:00:49 (11,449)	
Robertson, Susan	5:39:06 (29,272)	
Robertson, Tarryn	4:05:39 (12,583)	
Robertson, Tracey	4:37:48 (20,406)	
Robertson, Victoria K	4:38:12 (20,520)	
Robey, Jeanette L	4:50:30 (23,179)	
Robins, Alison J	5:23:28 (27,913)	
Robinson, Annamaria	4:38:59 (20,721)	
Robinson, Carol E	6:55:40 (31,572)	
Robinson, Daniele S	4:57:24 (24,473)	
Robinson, Deborah	3:49:55 (8,477)	
Robinson, Elizabeth L	5:43:41 (29,610)	
Robinson, Emily H	4:16:19 (15,122)	
Robinson, Emma	5:02:39 (25,396)	
Robinson, Emma T	4:21:39 (16,435)	
Robinson, Helen J	5:57:18 (30,301)	
Robinson, Jane	4:17:26 (15,406)	
Robinson, Lynda	4:17:37 (15,458)	
Robinson, Margaret M	4:52:01 (23,447)	
Robinson, Pippa M	4:43:03 (21,574)	
Robinson, Rebecca A	4:53:57 (23,788)	
Robinson, Sally B	4:38:44 (20,649)	
Robinson, Samantha J	4:25:46 (17,503)	
Robinson, Sarah J	3:57:25 (10,516)	
Robirosa, Susannah R	4:10:02 (13,644)	
Robjohns, Karen	4:25:44 (17,488)	
Robson, Dany L	3:28:48 (4,373)	
Robson, Glenda	4:47:12 (22,499)	
Robson, Hannah E	6:51:31 (31,522)	
Robson, Jacqueline A	3:27:43 (4,171)	
Robson, Jane D	5:19:41 (27,520)	
Robson, Juliet E	4:24:08 (17,102)	
Rochester, Catherine J	7:08:18 (31,695)	
Rochez, Hazel M	4:27:57 (18,082)	
Rocks-Engelman, Rachel A	4:51:53 (23,418)	
Rode, Charlotte F	5:13:38 (26,849)	
Roden, Dorothy	5:03:30 (25,520)	
Roden, Susan M	5:47:42 (29,854)	
Rodriguez-Riveiro, Maria J	4:59:06 (24,811)	
Rodwell, Elizabeth L	4:44:25 (21,894)	
Roe, Elizabeth M	4:55:43 (24,135)	
Roffey, Emma	6:19:25 (31,002)	
Roffey, Susan D	4:06:32 (12,784)	
Rogan, Claire L	4:53:56 (23,785)	
Rogan, Marion G	4:17:56 (15,540)	
Rogers, Alexandra J	3:28:58 (4,409)	
Rogers, Claire E	5:17:50 (27,341)	
Rogers, Clare M	5:14:05 (26,912)	
Rogers, Helen K	5:04:09 (25,591)	
Rogers, Kate J	4:40:10 (20,958)	
Rogers, Maxine J	5:07:43 (26,081)	
Rogers, Natalie	5:33:34 (28,856)	
Rogers, Victoria J	5:05:47 (25,797)	
Rogerson, Jean	4:30:17 (18,700)	
Rohellec, Edith	4:19:11 (15,825)	
Roland, Kara E	4:45:36 (22,167)	
Rolfe, Janet	5:27:56 (28,393)	
Rolfe, Lorraine	5:07:12 (25,992)	
Rolinson, Sarah E	5:43:00 (29,562)	
Roll, Yvonne	3:45:19 (7,367)	
Rollason, Clare R	5:55:59 (30,244)	
Rollings, Ann B	3:53:02 (9,265)	
Rollins, Laura J	4:01:16 (11,554)	
Rollinson, Kerry A	6:17:11 (30,934)	
Rolls, Antonia	5:54:03 (30,152)	
Rolls, Leanne	6:04:42 (30,586)	
Rolt, Georgina A	3:43:42 (6,997)	
Romaine, Kimberly	3:51:31 (8,891)	
Roman, Danielle J	4:22:37 (16,731)	
Romecin, Lindsay H	3:44:31 (7,193)	
Ronalds, Belinda	4:24:53 (17,278)	
Ronaldson, Joanne	3:00:11 (1,169)	
Ronaldson, Leah C	7:59:42 (31,941)	
Ronzoni, Nicoletta	3:51:37 (8,922)	
Rooney, Sharron D	5:36:03 (29,032)	
Rootes, Anna J	5:31:25 (28,697)	
Roots, Marian P	5:46:23 (29,779)	
Roper, Amaryllis K	3:41:05 (6,491)	
Roper, Lucy B	5:23:09 (27,889)	
Rosatelli, Martina	3:39:58 (6,298)	
Rose, Abigail S	5:04:49 (25,666)	
Rose, Amy E	5:47:49 (29,858)	
Rose, Chris V	4:16:38 (15,217)	
Rose, Eileen M	5:15:48 (27,108)	
Rose, Joanne	4:37:16 (20,310)	
Rose, Julie	4:56:20 (24,272)	
Rose, Karen	6:21:55 (31,058)	
Rose, Vivienne M	4:21:42 (16,449)	
Rosenbaum, Michele E	3:48:46 (8,200)	
Rosen-Nash, Ilkay	4:57:33 (24,503)	
Roslyn, Kate A	5:26:26 (28,246)	
Ross, Alison J	3:51:32 (8,899)	
Ross, Caroline A	5:57:32 (30,312)	
Ross, Suzann	5:39:24 (29,300)	
Ross Williams, Laura M	4:35:44 (19,966)	
Rossall, Sue	6:36:03 (31,308)	
Rothwell, Natalie	4:33:37 (19,492)	
Rouard, Magali	4:13:11 (14,373)	
Roulstone, Suzanne	5:44:13 (29,638)	
Rounce, Jane P	6:25:30 (31,132)	
Rounsefell, Naomi M	3:27:18 (4,080)	
Rouse, Judy H	3:34:23 (5,323)	
Routledge, Alison M	4:48:37 (22,797)	
Routledge, Eleanor	4:59:32 (24,909)	
Routledge, Joanne	3:54:13 (9,567)	
Rowe, Margaret A	3:30:10 (4,632)	
Rowe, Shirley A	5:25:05 (28,097)	
Rowett, Ann	4:53:08 (23,639)	
Rowland, Ameeta J	5:28:25 (28,430)	
Rowland, Lisa J	5:38:09 (29,193)	
Rowland, Teresa C	4:13:45 (14,505)	
Rowlands, Angela	4:27:31 (17,965)	
Rowlerson, Sarah L	4:11:12 (13,911)	
Rowley, Sarah E	3:58:59 (10,999)	
Rowling, Rachel	6:47:24 (31,468)	
Rowntree, Karen	4:24:05 (17,086)	
Roworth, Wendy L	4:52:53 (23,595)	
Rowson, Meriel C	4:07:29 (13,005)	
Roxburgh, Jan	3:02:07 (1,308)	
Roxby, Angela	3:59:27 (11,132)	
Roy, Christine	3:42:00 (6,646)	
Royan, Rachel J	5:30:45 (28,640)	
Rubio-Lago, Martha	4:09:39 (13,542)	
Ruddock, Kathryn L	5:43:00 (29,562)	
Ruder, Birga	5:24:09 (27,984)	
Rudge, Christine	6:01:08 (30,455)	
Rudkin-Wilson, Natasha	4:21:21 (16,350)	
Rudrum, Stefanie A	5:28:10 (28,409)	
Ruggles, Nicola L	5:47:12 (29,822)	
Ruggles, Wanda B	7:49:55 (31,913)	
Ruhmann, Elke	5:29:35 (28,544)	
Rule, Lorraine	4:05:37 (12,575)	
Runyard, Abigail	4:03:01 (11,957)	
Rushby, Sonia M	3:52:18 (9,085)	
Rushworth, Karen Y	5:32:17 (28,758)	
Rusinowski, Karen L	6:02:57 (30,528)	
Russell, Angie J	5:58:25 (30,343)	
Russell, Debbie L	3:29:41 (4,529)	
Russell, Katie V	4:38:33 (20,606)	
Russell, Sally C	6:01:02 (30,452)	
Russell, Sarah J	3:40:19 (6,359)	
Russell, Victoria J	4:27:15 (17,908)	
Russell-Stracey, Polly	5:00:02 (24,995)	
Russo, Debra A	4:54:28 (23,891)	
Rust, Lindsay	4:58:23 (24,687)	
Ruth, Katharine M	5:09:49 (26,360)	
Rutkoske, Lisa A	4:56:25 (24,283)	
Rutter, Helen K	4:22:02 (16,548)	
Rutterford-Adams, Angela J	4:28:12 (18,148)	
Ruxton, Ellie A	4:57:59 (24,590)	
Ryan, Angela	3:52:10 (9,053)	
Ryan, Anne	6:49:44 (31,496)	
Ryan, Claire	5:26:46 (28,274)	
Ryan, Helen J	4:30:37 (18,784)	
Ryan, Jennifer H	5:05:52 (25,818)	
Ryan, Marian P	3:49:52 (8,466)	
Ryan, Michelle L	3:54:53 (9,748)	
Ryan, Nancy T	4:34:56 (19,807)	
Ryan, Natasha	6:25:18 (31,129)	
Rycroft, Sarah E	4:59:09 (24,822)	
Ryder, Helen S	4:32:24 (19,215)	
Ryder, Meg C	4:35:04 (19,835)	
Ryder, Samantha J	4:21:39 (16,435)	
Ryecart, Mariella	3:56:35 (10,274)	
Rylance, Emma S	5:14:21 (26,939)	
Ryland, Nicky M	5:09:03 (26,245)	
Sacchetti, Alessandra	3:48:06 (8,023)	
Sadgrove, Philippa T	5:05:40 (25,783)	
Sadler, Angela S	3:07:38 (1,771)	
Sadler, Janet	5:14:48 (27,005)	
Sadler, Maxine F	4:25:29 (17,424)	
Sadler, Penny C	4:26:16 (17,652)	
Saggers, Jane C	4:12:56 (14,314)	
Sagoo, Ravinder K	4:33:04 (19,372)	
Sail, Annette	5:09:27 (26,299)	
Saiman, Nathalie J	4:47:18 (22,517)	
Saina, Esther	2:50:56 (541)	
Saint, Debbie M	3:52:17 (9,079)	
Saise, Shannon K	6:47:16 (31,467)	
Salaam, Saira	5:06:33 (25,917)	
Salathiel, Charlotte L	4:51:53 (23,418)	
Sale, Emily	4:58:23 (24,687)	
Sales, Charlene M	4:48:09 (22,707)	
Sales, Eleanor M	5:05:27 (25,747)	
Salisbury, Helen R	4:54:27 (23,885)	
Sallis, Caroline J	4:05:32 (12,550)	
Salmon, Paulette M	4:35:33 (19,939)	
Salome-Bentley, Nicola J	5:33:19 (28,834)	
Salt, Adele M	3:09:09 (1,911)	
Salt, Sally Anne	4:43:37 (21,705)	
Salter, Jennifer A	3:43:56 (7,047)	
Sammes, Rachel	3:55:34 (9,954)	
Sammons, Jean E	5:36:59 (29,106)	
Sample, Jessica L	4:50:21 (23,138)	
Sampson, Katharine E	5:54:46 (30,187)	
Sampson, Natasha J	5:21:05 (27,809)	
Sams, Maddy	4:09:57 (13,625)	
Samson, Rachel	5:12:49 (26,734)	
Samuel, Anna C	4:07:00 (12,891)	
Samuel, Gill	5:51:45 (30,049)	
Samuel, Kate	3:59:29 (11,161)	
Samuel, Katie L	5:40:29 (29,378)	
Sandberg, Rhona M C	3:42:21 (6,709)	
Sandberg, Ruth M	4:02:00 (11,717)	
Sandeman, Margaret	4:05:16 (12,475)	
Sanders, Barbara E	3:31:29 (4,847)	
Sanders, Francesca L	4:33:54 (19,566)	
Sanders, Lynda B	5:47:55 (29,861)	

Sanders, Melanie A 4:32:21 (19,199)
Sanders, Sarah M 4:03:41 (12,122)
Sanders, Susie H 4:37:51 (20,416)
Sanders, Tracey A 4:51:32 (23,349)
Sanders, Trudy C 5:39:03 (29,270)
Sanderson, Olivia A 3:22:13 (3,329)
Sanderson, Sylvia E 5:23:24 (27,906)
Sandhu, Polly 4:36:10 (20,065)
Sandhu, Pushpinder 6:01:39 (30,469)
Sandrawich, Laura K 6:18:02 (30,959)
Sang, Stephanie A 7:30:30 (31,850)
Sanganee, Krisi M 4:53:53 (23,774)
Sansom, Brenda 6:15:08 (30,890)
Sansom, Carole A 6:01:40 (30,470)
Sansom, Sarah J 4:39:48 (20,876)
Santos, Christina A 4:59:05 (24,808)
Santos, Maria 3:25:50 (3,820)
Sargeant, Bina 4:25:57 (17,555)
Sargeant, Helen S 4:51:55 (23,426)
Sargeant, Pauline 3:59:26 (11,121)
Sargent, Clare 6:03:08 (30,530)
Sargent, Joanna 3:57:53 (10,646)
Sarker, Gopa 4:34:14 (19,649)
Sarkies, Amy 3:32:22 (4,981)
Sarti, Daniela E 5:07:43 (26,081)
Sarvari, Diana C 3:31:10 (4,801)
Satchwell, Susan 4:45:38 (22,171)
Saund, Debra 5:57:16 (30,298)
Saunders, Donna 4:55:43 (24,135)
Saunders, Jane T 5:46:41 (29,800)
Saunders, Juliet E 5:39:21 (29,295)
Saunders, Kathryn R 4:32:16 (19,181)
Saunders, Lisa Jane 4:44:42 (21,956)
Saunders, Nina C 4:52:34 (23,545)
Saunter, Kim S 3:45:17 (7,361)
Savill, Anna K 3:30:09 (4,626)
Savopoulos, Kirstin L 4:08:30 (13,231)
Sawhney, Aarti E 4:26:42 (17,750)
Sawyer, Carolyn B 5:02:04 (25,306)
Saxon, Joan E 4:08:32 (13,239)
Sayer, Alison E 5:08:17 (26,158)
Sayer, Avan P 4:33:48 (19,534)
Sayer, Christine S 5:05:58 (25,841)
Sayers, Judith A 4:24:18 (17,142)
Sayes, Alison 4:32:22 (19,206)
Saywell, Lynne J 5:50:45 (30,002)
Scahill, Helen L 5:38:35 (29,237)
Scales, Wendy 5:00:37 (25,080)
Scanlon, Emer A 3:19:51 (3,054)
Scantlebury, Hannah R 4:50:58 (23,266)
Scarborough, Karen L 5:00:54 (25,127)
Scarcelli, Valeria 5:38:45 (29,245)
Scarfe, Jacqueline K 3:40:54 (6,455)
Scarisbrick, Jane 4:26:53 (17,808)
Scarlett, Rhiannon C 4:58:14 (24,646)
Scarr, Nikki K 4:37:56 (20,449)
Schaerer, Patricia 3:54:25 (9,617)
Schaffer, Janie 5:43:08 (29,575)
Scheller-Kieburg, Kerstin 4:39:39 (20,852)
Schermuly, Allegra C 5:46:04 (29,752)
Scherpenisse, Inge 3:48:28 (8,113)
Scheuer, Johanna A 4:37:13 (20,301)
Schmidhammer, Ingrid 4:20:19 (16,106)
Schmidt, Mari 5:23:24 (27,906)
Schmiedel, Lauren A 4:25:55 (17,545)
Schoeman, Vera 4:27:45 (18,026)
Schofield, Ruth V 3:10:33 (2,059)
Schofield, Sheila R 3:48:33 (8,135)
Scholes, Lisa 3:56:13 (10,148)
Scholey, Helen M 4:53:59 (23,791)
Scholey, Julie A 3:22:30 (3,375)
Scholey, Lindsay J 3:37:55 (5,940)
Scholten, Arleen 3:35:44 (5,563)
Schrager-Powell, Vivien J 5:18:15 (27,396)
Schuetz, Patricia A 4:30:38 (18,788)
Schulz, Hedda 4:34:16 (19,657)
Schulz, Monika 2:58:42 (1,044)
Schulze, Claudia L 3:54:50 (9,732)
Schulze, Monika 4:37:31 (20,342)
Schwartz, Tracie L 4:13:02 (14,337)
Schwarzer, Ursula 4:45:05 (22,059)
Schweiger, Jenny 4:19:16 (15,851)
Schweitzer, Nicole 5:30:50 (28,650)
Scicluna, Kim J 5:27:15 (28,330)
Scotchford, Janet 3:54:14 (9,572)
Scotland, Christina E 4:12:47 (14,276)
Scotland-Judd, Beverley 4:59:24 (24,883)
Scott, Amanda J 7:16:08 (31,756)
Scott, Dawn 4:59:59 (24,989)
Scott, Deborah A 5:34:14 (28,905)
Scott, Elizabeth A 4:30:18 (18,703)
Scott, Emma L 5:26:07 (28,206)
Scott, Helena V 3:57:12 (10,444)
Scott, Hilary 6:05:55 (30,618)
Scott, Kathryn A 4:06:33 (12,793)
Scott, Katie Jane 4:27:54 (18,065)
Scott, Lorraine 4:40:12 (20,963)
Scott, Lucy D 4:34:14 (19,649)
Scott, May 5:30:48 (28,646)
Scott, Sallie J 5:26:52 (28,287)
Scott, Sarah R 4:17:45 (15,494)
Scott, Tracy A 6:13:18 (30,822)
Scott Tomlin, Lynda 5:32:22 (28,764)
Scrivener, Sarah 3:18:34 (2,906)
Scroggs, Josephine 4:34:06 (19,625)
Scudellaro, Kate 5:12:59 (26,759)
Scullard, Helen H 5:09:41 (26,336)
Seabrook, Patricia H 4:45:25 (22,120)
Seabrook, Sandra J 5:08:49 (26,215)
Seago, Amanda J 4:26:32 (17,710)
Seagrave, Charlotte J 3:41:02 (6,480)
Sealy, Wendy L 3:58:55 (10,979)
Searle, Deirdre 5:38:18 (29,213)
Searle, Jane C 4:01:34 (11,613)
Searle, Lisa J 4:05:37 (12,575)
Seary, Eleanor K 6:29:27 (31,193)
Seath, Patricia M 5:16:49 (27,232)
Seaton, Katharine S 5:14:35 (26,976)
Sebire, Joanne M 4:32:07 (19,139)
Secker, Tracey M 6:42:52 (31,406)
Seed, Kris 6:58:59 (31,606)
Seers, Kate 5:29:40 (28,551)
Segala, Françoise 4:57:06 (24,420)
Segar, Justine M 4:43:18 (21,636)
Segers, Greet A 4:34:05 (19,619)
Seignobosc, Corinne 4:45:44 (22,195)
Seiler, Heidi 3:48:16 (8,069)
Sekhon, Mohina L 5:06:19 (25,890)
Sela, Nadav 4:43:43 (21,726)
Selby, Jenny 5:28:43 (28,461)
Selby, Linda 4:16:14 (15,106)
Self, Charlotte L 4:00:30 (11,399)
Self, Julia L 5:02:41 (25,400)
Selig, Helen E 6:18:12 (30,964)
Seller, Susan 4:12:27 (14,184)
Sellick, Claire 5:09:26 (26,295)
Sellick, Dawn M 6:19:18 (30,998)
Sellings, Janet M 6:44:25 (31,425)
Semple, Marie 4:08:54 (13,348)
Sen Gupta, Riya 5:17:33 (27,314)
Senior, Gill V 3:36:11 (5,639)
Senior, Jacqueline 4:42:43 (21,499)
Senior, Jane E 3:44:25 (7,163)
Sepede, Clare E 5:19:56 (27,551)
Sercombe, Karen A 4:56:24 (24,280)
Sercombe, Vikki A 3:06:55 (1,699)
Servante, Naomi A 5:42:44 (29,530)
Sessions, Clare A 4:27:00 (17,840)
Setter, Katy I 3:42:00 (6,646)
Severn, Eileen M 4:17:17 (15,365)
Seward, Hannah E 5:43:03 (29,570)
Sexauer, Ann M 4:26:11 (17,626)
Sexton, Dawn A 5:04:00 (25,581)
Seymour, Allison 5:06:01 (25,845)
Seymour, Catherine V 4:37:34 (20,349)
Seymour, Christine 5:01:18 (25,186)
Seymour, Gemma 4:59:21 (24,865)
Seymour, Jennifer A 5:32:13 (28,751)
Seymour, Meg 4:29:22 (18,457)
Seymour, Samantha L 5:20:26 (27,622)
Seymour, Zoe C 4:32:39 (19,276)
Shadbolt, Veronica M 3:36:31 (5,699)
Shah, Jayshree 4:51:33 (23,351)
Shah, Meera M 6:07:53 (30,668)
Shah, Sujita 4:29:18 (18,431)
Shams, Fari 3:22:42 (3,404)
Shanks, Jackie A 3:21:32 (3,261)
Shannon, Debbie 4:56:19 (24,266)
Shannon, Jennifer J 7:07:10 (31,684)
Shapiro, Karen E 5:20:28 (27,628)
Shapton, Natalie 6:27:47 (31,174)
Sharland, Joanne 4:03:36 (12,103)
Sharp, Claire J 5:29:32 (28,537)
Sharp, Fiona 5:38:34 (29,234)
Sharp, Fiona B 3:28:25 (4,305)
Sharp, Jacqueline A 3:49:56 (8,482)
Sharp, Rebecca 4:28:17 (18,165)
Sharp, Samantha M 4:29:10 (18,398)
Sharp, Susan A 3:04:37 (1,498)
Sharpe, Jane H 6:02:31 (30,508)
Sharpe, Lindsey N 4:13:18 (14,403)
Sharpe, Philippa 4:47:25 (22,546)
Sharples, Vikki L 5:37:02 (29,108)
Shaw, Anthea L 6:11:38 (30,775)
Shaw, Carol A 3:57:52 (10,639)
Shaw, Caroline A 4:42:07 (21,372)
Shaw, Catherine 4:38:28 (20,587)
Shaw, Chriselda 4:43:48 (21,749)
Shaw, Donna M 3:58:03 (10,689)
Shaw, Esther 4:32:42 (19,291)
Shaw, Heidi L 4:40:19 (20,989)
Shaw, Helen L 4:37:00 (20,252)
Shaw, Hester E 5:43:41 (29,610)
Shaw, Julie A 5:02:40 (25,399)
Shaw, Kay 5:12:37 (26,703)
Shaw, Lisa J 3:57:40 (10,586)
Shaw, Michelle 5:23:59 (27,972)
Shaw, Nadine L 4:58:32 (24,723)
Shayne, Kim E 4:03:39 (12,118)
Shearer, Joanna M 4:44:19 (21,865)
Sheehan, Claire R 4:30:02 (18,639)
Sheehan, Jo 5:50:23 (29,987)
Sheehan, Sheila M 5:34:46 (28,941)
Sheen, Amy J 3:50:13 (8,552)
Sheeran, Jane 4:45:27 (22,129)
Sheers, Linda 6:27:04 (31,156)
Sheldon, Karen A 4:46:16 (22,311)
Sheldrick, Heulwen L 4:40:44 (21,073)
Shelfer, Lisa A 4:57:12 (24,438)
Shelley, Catherine J 3:40:16 (6,345)
Shelley, Sarah A 5:28:20 (28,424)
Shelton, Katie J 4:30:33 (18,769)
Shenstone, Jayne 5:16:09 (27,147)
Shenton, Fiona C 3:15:38 (2,614)
Shenton, Rachel C 5:34:16 (28,910)
Shephard, Alex T 4:17:10 (15,343)
Shephard, Carolyn 5:45:42 (29,735)
Shepherd, Bethan L 4:19:35 (15,928)
Shepherd, Jennfer M 4:12:56 (14,314)
Shepherd, Jet Jon J 3:21:30 (3,257)
Shepherd, Karen S 6:14:46 (30,877)
Shepherd, Katie E 4:00:28 (11,390)
Sheppard, Carol A 5:36:11 (29,037)
Shepstone, Julie A 6:19:01 (30,990)
Sherab, Claire H 4:19:09 (15,818)
Sheridan, Alison J 4:25:44 (17,488)
Sheriff, Lisa J 5:16:38 (27,215)
Sherlock, Amanda J 4:31:25 (18,952)
Sherriff, Hollie J 5:59:09 (30,371)
Sherwood, Patricia A 5:24:02 (27,976)
Sherwood, Sarah 4:55:22 (24,078)
Shewell, Sarah J 3:47:14 (7,808)
Shields, Joanna M 4:21:18 (16,333)
Shields, Rebecca C 3:52:01 (9,016)
Shillington, Clare 5:10:57 (26,501)
Shinners, Kathryn 4:43:59 (21,791)
Shipley, Adele V 4:21:01 (16,284)
Shipp, Catherine G 4:21:12 (16,311)
Shone, Jennie 5:08:13 (26,145)
Shopoff Rooff, Karen 3:44:44 (7,245)
Shore, Anne 6:27:43 (31,171)
Short, Caroline 5:13:58 (26,890)
Short, Elizabeth A 4:15:36 (14,955)
Short, Pat 6:24:39 (31,124)
Short, Rachel M 3:26:29 (3,915)
Shorter, Tracey C 4:44:56 (22,017)
Shorthouse, Kirsty A 4:46:29 (22,354)
Shorthouse, Susan 4:10:04 (13,652)
Shotbolt, Andrea J 4:50:00 (23,073)

Shotton, Angie C.	5:30:29 (28,622)	
Shotton, Bryanie S	4:30:09 (18,666)	
Shotton, Terri	5:41:34 (29,453)	
Shtenko, Lucy	5:25:46 (28,171)	
Shuker, Heather	4:01:03 (11,516)	
Shyjka, Susan H	3:56:28 (10,241)	
Sida, Samantha	3:45:34 (7,428)	
Siddle, Jennifer C	7:03:00 (31,648)	
Siegel, Jill G	5:48:55 (29,904)	
Siers, Beckie	3:59:18 (11,087)	
Siggers, Louise P	5:02:38 (25,395)	
Sigu, Véronique	4:00:45 (11,434)	
Sikora, Emma E	4:44:03 (21,805)	
Sikorska, Ann	4:11:10 (13,904)	
Silk, Ceri R	4:52:38 (23,556)	
Sills, Ruth M	3:28:00 (4,227)	
Silverman, Joanne R	7:32:11 (31,860)	
Silverman, Myriam D	5:03:12 (25,477)	
Sim, Grace E	4:39:07 (20,751)	
Simek, Zoe C	4:44:14 (21,844)	
Simkin, Elizabeth R	4:39:03 (20,739)	
Simlinger, Waltrand	3:42:28 (6,735)	
Simmons, Angela L	5:27:07 (28,312)	
Simmons, Ann E	4:32:51 (19,322)	
Simmons, Emma L	4:31:40 (19,014)	
Simmons, Lyn	4:31:25 (18,952)	
Simmons, Melanie J	4:53:34 (23,715)	
Simmons, Sarah	3:12:34 (2,260)	
Simms, Jane K	4:33:55 (19,569)	
Simms, Jennifer S	4:59:35 (24,918)	
Simon, Joann T	4:17:42 (15,480)	
Simon, Kate A	4:33:55 (19,569)	
Simon OBE, Josette	6:38:30 (31,346)	
Simons, Joanna L	5:10:34 (26,448)	
Simpson, Belinda	3:59:27 (11,132)	
Simpson, Claire E	4:12:39 (14,247)	
Simpson, Elizabeth A	5:17:06 (27,264)	
Simpson, Fiona C	4:08:47 (13,317)	
Simpson, Joanna	4:57:17 (24,459)	
Simpson, Joanna E	3:36:03 (5,618)	
Simpson, Katie S	3:46:05 (7,544)	
Simpson, Liz	4:13:54 (14,543)	
Simpson, Louise	5:46:58 (29,810)	
Simpson, Louise C	4:06:09 (12,700)	
Simpson, Patricia M	4:18:40 (15,702)	
Sims, Ann C	4:49:46 (23,033)	
Sinclair, Nina K	3:50:37 (8,662)	
Singh, Sandra D	4:59:19 (24,852)	
Singleton, Helen A	4:42:31 (21,455)	
Singleton, Michelle	2:58:57 (1,070)	
Singleton, Veronica C	3:25:14 (3,725)	
Siret, Tracey L	5:42:33 (29,519)	
Sitlani, Sophie A	5:44:58 (29,692)	
Sjoo, Solweig	4:47:18 (22,517)	
Skelly, Christina L	5:38:53 (29,251)	
Skelton, Vicky G	3:13:34 (2,381)	
Skidmore, Julia S	3:59:16 (11,077)	
Skilbeck, Patricia	4:45:26 (22,125)	
Skiner, Catherine J	3:54:22 (9,602)	
Skingle, Maria C	4:39:07 (20,751)	
Skinner, Deborah N	5:10:50 (26,487)	
Skinner, Sally J	4:35:19 (19,889)	
Skyrme, Zoe	6:31:41 (31,238)	
Slack, Debbie A	3:51:29 (8,880)	
Slack, Natalie	4:57:40 (24,529)	
Slade, Catherine	4:20:13 (16,069)	
Slade, Debbie J	4:51:36 (23,362)	
Slade, Katharine E	5:03:51 (25,561)	
Slamon, Lynne	4:03:24 (12,057)	
Slane, Lise A	5:18:38 (27,427)	
Slater, Jane T	4:57:53 (24,564)	
Slatford, Karen	5:29:07 (28,495)	
Sledge, Charlotte E	3:51:08 (8,774)	
Slingsby, Fiona	4:31:21 (18,935)	
Sloan, Anna M	3:15:41 (2,620)	
Sloan, Jacqueline E	5:03:08 (25,463)	
Sloan, Laura J	7:09:27 (31,703)	
Sloan, Lesley	4:18:50 (15,748)	
Sloan, Vanessa	3:57:07 (10,418)	
Sly, Helen J	2:57:36 (922)	
Sly, Sharon	5:42:52 (29,539)	
Small, Annika	5:41:18 (29,432)	
Small, Christina	4:25:19 (17,384)	

Small, Elizabeth A	5:21:09 (27,695)	
Small, Lorna J	6:00:09 (30,419)	
Smallwood, Sylvia	4:44:16 (21,850)	
Smart, Chris J	4:38:15 (20,533)	
Smart, Christianne F	5:00:03 (25,001)	
Smart, Rachael D	6:07:54 (30,670)	
Smart, Sally	4:45:01 (22,032)	
Smedley, Harriet	4:54:05 (23,812)	
Smelt-Webb, Caroline R	4:00:20 (11,368)	
Smethurst, Charlotte P	3:52:53 (9,218)	
Smethurst, Helen E	3:11:41 (2,158)	
Smiley, Laura	3:37:55 (5,940)	
Smith, Alexandra	4:29:22 (18,457)	
Smith, Alexandra L	4:39:52 (20,886)	
Smith, Ali C	6:48:30 (31,479)	
Smith, Alison B	5:06:31 (25,912)	
Smith, Amy L	4:10:40 (13,793)	
Smith, Angela	5:05:30 (25,760)	
Smith, Anna M	6:08:13 (30,680)	
Smith, Bernadette M	4:13:47 (14,513)	
Smith, Brenda	5:37:21 (29,138)	
Smith, Bryony H	4:48:19 (22,742)	
Smith, Catherine H	4:13:10 (14,369)	
Smith, Catherine M	4:02:14 (11,789)	
Smith, Christine A	4:40:49 (21,093)	
Smith, Christy L	5:04:29 (25,624)	
Smith, Claire K	5:24:21 (28,008)	
Smith, Debbie	3:58:53 (10,967)	
Smith, Debbie	4:32:18 (19,188)	
Smith, Deborah E	4:49:07 (22,898)	
Smith, Demelza M	5:13:16 (26,801)	
Smith, Elaine	6:51:51 (31,526)	
Smith, Elaine G	4:28:22 (18,181)	
Smith, Eleanor R	4:34:37 (19,738)	
Smith, Esra	4:25:30 (17,429)	
Smith, Fiona H	4:49:45 (23,027)	
Smith, Gillian S	4:06:58 (12,882)	
Smith, Gillian S	6:51:09 (31,514)	
Smith, Hannah S	5:01:37 (25,241)	
Smith, Helen	5:31:20 (28,688)	
Smith, Helen F	3:56:10 (10,128)	
Smith, Helen T	5:28:11 (28,411)	
Smith, Jacqueline	4:29:53 (18,607)	
Smith, Jacqueline D	3:28:30 (4,321)	
Smith, Jacqueline L	4:18:05 (15,572)	
Smith, Jane	4:49:20 (22,947)	
Smith, Jane E	4:40:16 (20,976)	
Smith, Jane E	5:52:12 (30,076)	
Smith, Jennie L	4:49:05 (22,892)	
Smith, Jennifer A	5:25:24 (28,130)	
Smith, Jennifer J	4:57:25 (24,482)	
Smith, Joyce D	6:22:12 (31,064)	
Smith, Julia A	6:01:34 (30,465)	
Smith, Julie A	6:14:37 (30,867)	
Smith, Julie B	5:52:13 (30,077)	
Smith, June	4:46:43 (22,395)	
Smith, Karen E	4:44:47 (21,974)	
Smith, Karen J	4:04:37 (12,333)	
Smith, Kate J	4:18:43 (15,712)	
Smith, Kathleen F	5:47:57 (29,865)	
Smith, Kathryne	6:34:00 (31,278)	
Smith, Laura	4:24:04 (17,076)	
Smith, Lesley	4:59:27 (24,894)	
Smith, Linda P	3:57:21 (10,498)	
Smith, Lindsey R	4:50:40 (23,210)	
Smith, Lynn T	6:06:04 (30,621)	
Smith, Madeleine L	5:26:23 (28,239)	
Smith, Margaret	4:05:33 (12,555)	
Smith, Maria	4:19:12 (15,834)	
Smith, Maria L	5:33:51 (28,878)	
Smith, Melanie	3:51:33 (8,905)	
Smith, Michelle J	5:28:12 (28,412)	
Smith, Natasha R	4:33:48 (19,534)	
Smith, Norma F	3:52:02 (9,021)	
Smith, Patricia A	5:01:49 (25,275)	
Smith, Pauline R	5:43:34 (29,597)	
Smith, Rebecca L	3:30:31 (4,692)	
Smith, Rowena H	4:51:52 (23,414)	
Smith, Samantha J	3:44:00 (7,071)	
Smith, Samantha J	4:45:25 (22,120)	
Smith, Sandra K	4:23:32 (16,950)	
Smith, Sarah A	6:10:51 (30,752)	
Smith, Sharon	4:47:05 (22,470)	

Smith, Sharon H	3:24:38 (3,644)	
Smith, Sheena E	4:44:28 (21,903)	
Smith, Sheila	5:16:19 (27,174)	
Smith, Sheila D	5:22:40 (27,848)	
Smith, Sian	5:24:28 (28,023)	
Smith, Sian	6:15:14 (30,892)	
Smith, Simon C	6:48:04 (31,475)	
Smith, Valerie D	4:25:14 (17,366)	
Smith, Victoria L	4:23:22 (16,905)	
Smithers, Bebba E	5:34:40 (28,936)	
Smits, Engelina	4:29:50 (18,591)	
Smyth, Anne E	3:58:02 (10,684)	
Smyth, Cara	5:15:59 (27,131)	
Smyth, Fiona A	4:31:42 (19,029)	
Smyth, Jessica R	5:18:44 (27,439)	
Smyth, Kate A	4:58:03 (24,609)	
Smythe, Nicole J	4:31:04 (18,870)	
Snaith, Susan	3:50:37 (8,662)	
Snape, Chloe R	4:01:58 (11,707)	
Snape, Kathleen M	4:48:20 (22,747)	
Sneddon, Hazel G	3:59:36 (11,188)	
Snee, Julia A	5:59:32 (30,394)	
Snelders, Charlotte J	4:17:02 (15,312)	
Snelling, Emma K	3:49:49 (8,455)	
Snelling, Jean E	5:16:25 (27,181)	
Snook, Davina N	4:50:22 (23,142)	
Snook, Suzanne E	4:08:47 (13,317)	
Snow, Barbara A	7:16:08 (31,756)	
Snow, Tracey	4:58:24 (24,694)	
Soar, Susan R	4:16:01 (15,053)	
Sokal, Rachel	3:48:12 (8,047)	
Soltysiak, Beverley J	6:17:59 (30,954)	
Somerville, Ann	4:42:47 (21,515)	
Somerville, Emma H	4:34:10 (19,638)	
Sommers, Rhian	3:38:09 (5,986)	
Sommerville, Lorna	4:23:07 (16,847)	
Sorensen, Lotte H	4:09:51 (13,593)	
Souma, Spyridoula	2:40:34 (219)	
Soure, Sylvie	4:54:31 (23,899)	
Southern, Cassie	4:24:50 (17,260)	
Sowter, Elizabeth M	3:18:31 (2,898)	
Spahn, Christina U	4:54:05 (23,812)	
Spalton, Anne	5:16:40 (27,217)	
Sparham, Michele D	5:41:07 (29,419)	
Spark, Linda A	5:16:09 (27,147)	
Sparks, Katharine	3:56:25 (10,222)	
Speake, Celia	3:59:26 (11,121)	
Speake, Rachel A	4:16:52 (15,274)	
Spear, Wendy K	4:04:18 (12,263)	
Spechley, Melanie	5:40:16 (29,354)	
Speed, Louise J	4:29:33 (18,505)	
Speers, Rebecca J	3:42:24 (6,720)	
Spence, Irena J	4:52:35 (23,549)	
Spence, Lynne	6:12:42 (30,804)	
Spenceley, Leanne T	3:52:22 (9,103)	
Spencer, Claire	5:39:56 (29,328)	
Spencer, Sharon T	7:21:24 (31,795)	
Spencer, Tamieka N	5:29:10 (28,504)	
Spencer, Trudy A	4:37:21 (20,324)	
Spencer-Smith, Pamela E	5:30:26 (28,617)	
Spiller, Josephine R	3:46:48 (7,702)	
Spinatsch, Jmelda	3:55:23 (9,901)	
Spinks, Gillian C	6:13:40 (30,837)	
Spittlehouse, Karen L	5:24:57 (28,076)	
Spong, Carole	3:38:52 (6,111)	
Spooner, Jayne B	5:42:56 (29,547)	
Spooner, Karen	4:10:59 (13,866)	
Spooner, Sharon	5:05:05 (25,700)	
Spray, Michelle L	5:23:58 (27,970)	
Spriggs, Lisa J	5:37:59 (29,182)	
Spruyt, Maryn L	4:04:10 (12,234)	
Spurgeon, Debbie J	5:06:46 (25,944)	
Squires, Rose M	6:16:08 (30,911)	
Stacey, Helen D	6:16:15 (30,915)	
Stacey, Verity	3:08:47 (1,876)	
Stack, Maria E	7:44:45 (31,905)	
Stack, Natalie	5:26:54 (28,291)	
Staerck, Eleanor J	4:48:08 (22,703)	
Staffelot, Kristine	4:59:00 (24,793)	
Stafford, Diane	4:07:04 (12,911)	
Stafford, Julie	3:52:00 (9,012)	
Stafford, Melanie J	3:48:31 (8,124)	
Stafford, Roberta S	4:32:26 (19,220)	

Stafford, Sandra A........7:19:35 (31,787)
Stainer, Judith........4:07:34 (13,027)
Stairs, Tracy J........5:15:57 (27,125)
Stalker, Sherry........4:21:50 (16,487)
Stalley, Jessica I........4:20:18 (16,101)
Stalmans, Tine........3:21:46 (3,285)
Stammers, Faye L........4:43:41 (21,718)
Stamp, Helen M........4:59:38 (24,925)
Stamper, June E........5:45:49 (29,742)
Stanbridge, Carol D........5:04:32 (25,631)
Stanbridge, Katharin J........6:04:14 (30,569)
Standing, Helen S........4:16:58 (15,296)
Stanford, Zoe........4:46:18 (22,317)
Stanley, Elizabeth A........6:53:12 (31,543)
Stanley, Emma........4:56:54 (24,384)
Stanley, Glenda M........4:15:56 (15,037)
Stanley, Helen........4:47:17 (22,516)
Stannett, Kate F........4:06:09 (12,700)
Stansfield, Rebecca........4:55:02 (24,002)
Stanton, Josephine........6:05:28 (30,604)
Stapleton, Claire H........4:15:33 (14,942)
Stares, Diane B........3:52:56 (9,235)
Startin, Naomi........4:37:17 (20,313)
Statton, Sarah A........4:00:50 (11,454)
Staud, Daniela........4:51:00 (23,270)
Staynor, Chris A........7:05:00 (31,670)
Ste Marie, Kathleen R........6:25:55 (31,141)
Stead, Karen M........5:15:14 (27,046)
Stead, Ruth........4:35:31 (19,929)
Steadman, Mandy L........5:05:47 (25,797)
Stearns, Annabelle V........3:18:33 (2,905)
Stebbing, Paula A........4:42:36 (21,472)
Stedman, Eleanor J........5:08:33 (26,188)
Stedman, Susi........4:52:01 (23,447)
Steel, Margaret P........4:33:36 (19,486)
Steele, Adele L........5:12:18 (26,669)
Steele, Barbara J........5:33:14 (28,825)
Steele, Jeanette M........6:11:15 (30,762)
Steele, Julia A........3:37:34 (5,884)
Steele, Morag........5:47:19 (29,828)
Steenbergen, Alida........3:56:30 (10,250)
Steer, Deborah A........3:01:49 (1,292)
Steer, Eeny........3:56:13 (10,148)
Steer, Sylvia........4:42:36 (21,472)
Steere, Shannon L........4:33:20 (19,434)
Steeves, Elizabeth........4:04:36 (12,331)
Steffensmeier, Kristie L........4:08:25 (13,206)
Steidinger, Silke M........6:50:41 (31,506)
Stein, Angelica S........4:46:09 (22,279)
Steinbergs, Sally........7:14:02 (31,740)
Steinbrecher, Irene M........5:12:51 (26,740)
Stenhouse, Sheila E........4:58:08 (24,624)
Stephens, Anne M........4:38:03 (20,484)
Stephens, Bronwen L........4:28:21 (18,178)
Stephens, Catherine J........3:53:28 (9,373)
Stephens, Jane........3:17:46 (2,827)
Stephens, Jessica........4:55:14 (24,050)
Stephens, Joanna K........4:34:38 (19,743)
Stephens, Joanne........5:36:56 (29,102)
Stephens, Lucy........5:53:39 (30,139)
Stephens, Rachel J........5:19:36 (27,508)
Stephens, Sonya........4:00:18 (11,358)
Stephenson, Elizabeth G........4:32:41 (19,288)
Stephenson, Jaine J........3:29:12 (4,449)
Stephenson, Kim........3:06:55 (1,699)
Stepp, Victoria........4:25:27 (17,413)
Sterling, Julie K........4:43:21 (21,654)
Stevens, Alison L........5:41:26 (29,442)
Stevens, Caron L........4:02:54 (11,940)
Stevens, Claire M........3:57:22 (10,505)
Stevens, Emma........5:25:11 (28,105)
Stevens, Erin M........4:10:47 (13,824)
Stevens, Faye G........4:55:51 (24,162)
Stevens, Gillian........3:38:00 (5,961)
Stevens, Gillian........5:52:21 (30,090)
Stevens, Heather........3:51:57 (9,003)
Stevens, Jacqueline........4:30:48 (18,814)
Stevens, Margit........6:31:59 (31,243)
Stevens, Meliora E........3:57:26 (10,522)
Stevens, Michele K........4:50:24 (23,158)
Stevens, Patricia A........3:59:07 (11,035)
Stevens, Theresa H........5:01:06 (25,160)
Stevens, Tina R........5:01:57 (25,295)
Stevenson, Deborah........6:14:58 (30,883)
Stevenson, Emma L........4:20:34 (16,177)
Stevenson, Faye E........4:23:33 (16,953)
Stevenson, Gillian A........3:17:35 (2,810)
Stevenson, Helen R........4:47:41 (22,614)
Stevenson, Michelle........3:52:04 (9,027)
Stevenson, Nicola........4:36:06 (20,056)
Steward, Claire E........3:29:50 (4,562)
Steward, Ruth........4:24:50 (17,260)
Stewart, Diana J........5:46:12 (29,761)
Stewart, Helen C........6:15:00 (30,886)
Stewart, Jacqueline M........5:43:15 (29,579)
Stewart, Katrina A........4:33:26 (19,454)
Stewart, Lynda M........7:04:50 (31,668)
Stewart, Nicola M........5:22:09 (27,790)
Steyn, Wendy L........5:16:33 (27,198)
Stickings, Ruth E........4:11:05 (13,886)
Stiles, Amy M........2:50:33 (527)
Stiles, Heather J........4:38:44 (20,649)
Stiles, Tracy D........5:25:17 (28,117)
Stock, Manfred........4:48:54 (22,856)
Stockbridge, Louise M........6:00:20 (30,426)
Stocker, Emma M........4:43:06 (21,582)
Stockwell, Mia........4:44:54 (22,002)
Stoddard, Amy S........4:08:17 (13,170)
Stoker, Deborah J........5:10:00 (26,380)
Stollberg, Dorte........3:54:29 (9,632)
Stone, Gina........4:05:28 (12,529)
Stone, Jodie........5:13:03 (26,771)
Stone, Marie L........5:15:57 (27,125)
Stone, Pat A........6:21:01 (31,032)
Stone, Veronica A........4:20:31 (16,164)
Stoneham, Lucy A........4:10:53 (13,847)
Stonely, Jayne A........4:54:17 (23,851)
Stonham, Samantha L........7:09:27 (31,703)
Stonley Collins, Suzanne........4:17:11 (15,346)
Stopforth, Karen N........5:59:25 (30,383)
Storey, Anne-Marie L........4:36:02 (20,036)
Storey, Caroline J........3:58:13 (10,763)
Storey, Katherine........3:53:55 (9,481)
Storey, Pamela........5:53:48 (30,144)
Stott, Leanne........5:07:37 (26,059)
Stott, Natalie J........5:07:39 (26,068)
Stott, Rachel L........6:24:06 (31,110)
Stott, Vita M........5:03:04 (25,456)
Stout, Carys G........6:29:36 (31,196)
Stovell, Samantha J........4:48:08 (22,703)
Stowell, Christine M........3:39:23 (6,197)
Stradling, Sarah L........3:22:32 (3,383)
Strange, Fiona J........3:19:12 (2,983)
Strange, Tracy A........5:20:00 (27,563)
Stratford, Sarah J........3:42:27 (6,730)
Stratton, Rachel L........5:53:13 (30,132)
Strawbridge, Kay........4:07:34 (13,027)
Streatfield, Katie M........5:17:46 (27,336)
Street, Jennifer A........5:17:59 (27,364)
Streeter, Pam A........5:56:42 (30,279)
Strickalnd, Susan M........4:31:36 (18,999)
Stringer, Lynda K........6:44:46 (31,431)
Strong, Claire........3:56:23 (10,204)
Strudwick, Sandi E........3:55:12 (9,848)
Struzyna, Katherine L........4:39:27 (20,817)
Stuart, Fiona........5:00:18 (25,039)
Stuart, Pamela L........4:01:16 (11,554)
Stuart-Smith, Julien R........4:43:50 (21,753)
Stubbins, Amanda E........4:00:10 (11,331)
Stubbs, Helen J........3:36:40 (5,718)
Stubbs, Sally J........3:36:20 (5,664)
Sturgeon, Tina........5:08:08 (26,132)
Sturges, Dawn L........4:19:58 (16,022)
Sturgess, Michele........6:02:33 (30,511)
Sturgis, Niki........5:10:53 (26,495)
Stutely, Francesca B........4:42:29 (21,449)
Stuttard, Rosalind........5:03:26 (25,507)
Stychinsky, Kim T........3:54:48 (9,722)
Styles, Claire L........4:31:40 (19,014)
Such, Emma M........4:39:58 (20,910)
Sugden, Ingrid........4:51:31 (23,348)
Sugg, Tracey E........4:22:05 (16,565)
Sullivan, Cindy........3:05:19 (1,556)
Sullivan, Deborah........4:48:11 (22,718)
Sullivan, Jo M........4:17:08 (15,337)
Sullivan, Laura........4:33:04 (19,372)
Sully, Catherine J........3:35:12 (5,458)
Sultana, Rebeka........7:34:29 (31,869)
Summerfield, Alison F........4:14:05 (14,582)
Summers, Carol........5:01:08 (25,165)
Summers, Deborah J........4:03:37 (12,105)
Summers, Elizabeth T........4:55:14 (24,050)
Summerton, Jenny L........5:12:35 (26,702)
Sumner, Diana M........3:49:47 (8,447)
Sumner, Eileen D........4:01:32 (11,605)
Sumner, Julie A........4:36:26 (20,116)
Sumner, Linda........5:37:57 (29,177)
Surridge, Lucy E........5:01:52 (25,280)
Sutcliff, Emma L........3:53:59 (9,499)
Sutherland, Isabel M........3:37:15 (5,822)
Sutton, Nicola........4:25:57 (17,555)
Sutton, Sarah E........3:55:31 (9,935)
Swainson, Ann M........5:19:54 (27,549)
Swallow, Jayne A........6:40:08 (31,360)
Swan, Eileen M........4:41:28 (21,236)
Swann, Trudi........3:53:04 (9,271)
Swarbrick, Heather J........4:14:27 (14,665)
Swarbrick, Jacqui G........5:40:13 (29,351)
Swardstrom, Meghan C........4:47:57 (22,662)
Swatman, Alison M........4:35:54 (20,003)
Swaysland, Sarah L........3:39:17 (6,180)
Sweeney, Michele........4:57:31 (24,496)
Swift, Amanda A........5:26:20 (28,228)
Swift, Rachel H........4:35:45 (19,971)
Swinnerton, Shelagh A........4:23:19 (16,898)
Swinton, Julie D........7:25:23 (31,814)
Sworn, Carol........4:13:17 (14,399)
Sydenham, Jeanette A........4:36:36 (20,156)
Syed, Rebecca J........4:00:13 (11,346)
Sykes, Branwen E........5:56:23 (30,267)
Sykes, Catherine........5:35:21 (28,986)
Sykes, Christine A........4:50:17 (23,119)
Sykes, Julie C........4:52:55 (23,604)
Sylvester, Susan E........4:31:15 (18,909)
Syme, Alison J........5:38:01 (29,183)
Symonds, Claire B........4:00:27 (11,388)
Symons, Kate........3:38:44 (6,090)
Szostak, Teresa T........4:51:25 (23,333)
Szpak, Lynn........5:05:11 (25,711)
Szymczak, Monika........4:44:37 (21,943)
Taane, Ginny V........4:20:27 (16,149)
Tabor, Ros........3:09:35 (1,959)
Tagliente, Faola........6:15:37 (30,898)
Tahon, Isabelle J........5:40:21 (29,361)
Tait, Marie-Jo........6:49:01 (31,483)
Takaki, Jennifer T........4:28:14 (18,153)
Takala, Hanna L........5:28:46 (28,465)
Talbot, Jane L........7:42:07 (31,895)
Talbot, Katie J........5:27:48 (28,384)
Taleb, Carole........4:26:35 (17,723)
Tall, Lousia E........5:16:11 (27,153)
Tall, Vanessa R........4:09:36 (13,524)
Talukder, D Soraya........7:45:55 (31,908)
Tam, Judy........4:51:39 (23,369)
Tame, Catherine H........5:58:45 (30,360)
Tancray, Maryvonne........4:37:16 (20,310)
Tang, Dawn W........4:32:56 (19,343)
Tankard, Melanie J........3:56:15 (10,166)
Tanner, Lynn C........3:31:23 (4,830)
Tanner, Trudy E........4:05:49 (12,620)
Tapper, Lynne D........6:48:42 (31,480)
Tasker, Catherine S........4:15:31 (14,931)
Tatam, Margaret........5:57:27 (30,308)
Tatchley, Maria........4:07:25 (12,991)
Tate, Janet........4:18:33 (15,677)
Tate, Michelle Y........5:25:36 (28,148)
Tatum, Hayley L........4:33:09 (19,391)
Tavakoli, Leila........4:31:46 (19,044)
Taylor, Alison J........4:40:50 (21,095)
Taylor, Alison J........4:41:45 (21,296)
Taylor, Bridgeen M........5:30:49 (28,648)
Taylor, Caroline O........5:14:34 (26,971)
Taylor, Catherine S........4:20:33 (16,172)
Taylor, Corinna........5:47:16 (29,826)
Taylor, Dawn J........5:09:00 (26,239)
Taylor, Deborah C........3:57:21 (10,498)
Taylor, Diana M........5:10:14 (26,402)
Taylor, Eleanor N........3:56:13 (10,148)
Taylor, Emma L........4:41:13 (21,160)

Taylor, Fiona L.....................4:57:39 (24,521)
Taylor, Heidi.........................4:56:28 (24,298)
Taylor, Helen........................6:34:42 (31,283)
Taylor, Helen P.....................3:47:23 (7,848)
Taylor, Jacqueline F..............5:54:26 (30,167)
Taylor, Jacqueline S..............4:26:13 (17,639)
Taylor, Jeanette....................5:29:48 (28,568)
Taylor, Jennifer D.................5:14:32 (26,964)
Taylor, Johanna....................3:50:14 (8,555)
Taylor, Judy.........................4:58:12 (24,642)
Taylor, Karen........................5:49:17 (29,922)
Taylor, Karen P.....................3:36:29 (5,694)
Taylor, Kate E.......................3:57:34 (10,563)
Taylor, Katherine M...............4:05:49 (12,620)
Taylor, Leila.........................4:13:22 (14,423)
Taylor, Lesley P....................4:43:03 (21,574)
Taylor, Lorna........................4:06:52 (12,855)
Taylor, Lynda........................4:21:36 (16,420)
Taylor, Margaret....................5:12:12 (26,654)
Taylor, Natalie.......................3:54:27 (9,627)
Taylor, Natalie.......................4:18:50 (15,748)
Taylor, Nicola J.....................4:41:14 (21,163)
Taylor, Patricia M..................3:39:17 (6,180)
Taylor, Polly J.......................4:15:24 (14,899)
Taylor, Rachel.......................4:41:49 (21,313)
Taylor, Rebecca L..................4:44:37 (21,943)
Taylor, Rhian W....................5:30:14 (28,603)
Taylor, Rosalind E.................4:56:51 (24,375)
Taylor, Sally.........................4:08:37 (13,261)
Taylor, Sandra M...................5:56:55 (30,284)
Taylor, Sheila A.....................4:13:34 (14,471)
Taylor, Shirley A....................5:25:11 (28,105)
Taylor, Stephanie E...............4:22:11 (16,598)
Taylor, Susan A.....................5:23:48 (27,953)
Taylor, Susan M....................4:07:21 (12,970)
Taylor, Tabitha J....................5:20:13 (27,596)
Taylor, Tricia A......................4:33:20 (19,434)
Taylor-Jones, Andrea J..........4:25:07 (17,337)
Teague, Mary........................6:05:43 (30,611)
Teal, Sarah...........................4:49:09 (22,907)
Teasdale, Jane......................3:56:16 (10,171)
Teasdale, Jennifer.................4:00:10 (11,331)
Teasel, Michelle....................3:24:55 (3,682)
Tebbutt, Zoe E......................4:49:44 (23,025)
Tees, Judith J........................4:54:47 (23,956)
Teeuwen, Willeke..................4:29:47 (18,580)
Teixiera, Yvonne...................3:53:01 (9,261)
Telfer, Shona S.....................3:54:22 (9,602)
Telford, Claire M...................5:43:20 (29,583)
Telling, Nicola C...................4:02:35 (11,872)
Temperton, Carol L...............4:16:40 (15,226)
Temple, Katy A......................4:55:52 (24,169)
Temple, Rebecca...................5:05:48 (25,804)
Templeman, Sharon R............4:15:32 (14,936)
Tennant, Maggie B.................4:45:21 (22,109)
Tennant, Pippa J....................4:43:28 (21,678)
Terblanche, Margott...............4:58:01 (24,597)
Teresa, Emilio.......................5:28:21 (28,426)
Terjesen, Siri........................3:12:13 (2,219)
Terris, Catherine J.................4:23:46 (17,008)
Terry, Carolyn A....................5:13:03 (26,771)
Testo, Sue............................3:57:20 (10,492)
Thacker, Jacqueline S............6:28:28 (31,180)
Thaysen, Birgit......................3:36:35 (5,707)
Theadon, Jane I.....................5:07:37 (26,059)
Theedom, Jacqueline F..........4:56:59 (24,400)
Thepenier, Chantal................4:06:21 (12,748)
Thevenet-Smith, Ramona E.......3:14:45 (2,532)
Thibaud, Ewa E.....................4:42:10 (21,380)
Thick, Jacqui........................4:04:33 (12,327)
Thistleton, Heather J.............4:48:55 (22,857)
Thliard, Anna S......................4:02:09 (11,764)
Thom, Susan E......................4:15:47 (15,000)
Thomas, Angela B..................4:33:47 (19,531)
Thomas, Ann.........................3:08:38 (1,861)
Thomas, Annette P.................4:26:05 (17,600)
Thomas, Antoinette L.............3:43:39 (6,989)
Thomas, Beverley..................4:32:36 (19,261)
Thomas, Caroline...................5:13:47 (26,869)
Thomas, Catherine D..............3:46:07 (7,550)
Thomas, Clare V....................5:32:14 (28,754)
Thomas, Dawn A....................4:17:06 (15,327)
Thomas, Debbie H..................3:08:23 (1,839)

LONDON MARATHON

Thomas, Denise G..................4:36:10 (20,065)
Thomas, Diana L....................5:01:09 (25,169)
Thomas, Elena W...................5:21:35 (27,736)
Thomas, Elizabeth H..............4:40:44 (21,073)
Thomas, Elizabeth J...............4:38:10 (20,513)
Thomas, Hannah M.................4:18:08 (15,579)
Thomas, Janine L...................4:22:15 (16,623)
Thomas, Jeanette...................3:39:35 (6,231)
Thomas, John........................6:51:19 (31,517)
Thomas, Josine E...................4:21:14 (16,319)
Thomas, Judith A...................3:54:00 (9,505)
Thomas, Karen E....................4:34:43 (19,761)
Thomas, Laura E....................6:59:13 (31,610)
Thomas, Linda M....................3:51:25 (8,862)
Thomas, Lucy M.....................4:58:06 (24,620)
Thomas, Mollie C...................3:50:50 (8,717)
Thomas, Olga........................4:15:42 (14,978)
Thomas, Sally E.....................5:14:44 (26,994)
Thomas, Sarah J.....................5:27:14 (28,328)
Thomas, Sian.........................4:42:46 (21,509)
Thomas, Sophie C...................4:56:43 (24,346)
Thomas, Sue J........................4:28:24 (18,193)
Thomas, Wendy......................7:05:05 (31,671)
Thompson, Alison...................3:48:14 (8,061)
Thompson, Angela M..............3:58:11 (10,750)
Thompson, Charlotte J............7:32:27 (31,862)
Thompson, Claire M................5:41:17 (29,429)
Thompson, Francine H.............5:29:16 (28,515)
Thompson, Geraldine D...........5:07:03 (25,976)
Thompson, Hilary A.................3:58:29 (10,845)
Thompson, Jean E...................4:52:05 (23,461)
Thompson, Karin M.................4:56:31 (24,314)
Thompson, Lisa J....................4:34:16 (19,657)
Thompson, Lorna E.................5:01:07 (25,163)
Thompson, Margaret...............4:44:09 (21,827)
Thompson, Maria L.................5:04:36 (25,638)
Thompson, Paul......................4:34:00 (19,587)
Thompson, Rosie J..................4:22:42 (16,749)
Thompson, Sara.....................5:38:54 (29,253)
Thompson, Sarah L.................4:05:56 (12,648)
Thompson, Susan...................4:35:25 (19,914)
Thompson, Victoria I...............6:22:41 (31,074)
Thomson, Amy.......................3:57:24 (10,514)
Thomson, Delia L....................6:05:14 (30,598)
Thomson, Janet F...................5:52:57 (30,126)
Thomson, Margaret A..............4:09:55 (13,615)
Thomson, Sandra...................4:31:41 (19,022)
Thomson, Sarah J...................3:47:15 (7,817)
Thomson, Valerie A.................5:16:49 (27,232)
Thore-Rabut, Fabienne............4:16:36 (15,200)
Thorn, Penny J.......................3:27:20 (4,091)
Thorne, Helen........................5:28:38 (28,454)
Thorne, Sarah L.....................5:12:34 (26,700)
Thornes, Sheila M...................4:33:43 (19,508)
Thornewill, Fiona S.................3:47:06 (7,779)
Thornton, Deirdre...................4:45:01 (22,032)
Thornton, Jayne L...................5:21:52 (27,759)
Thorogood, Adrienne M...........5:58:59 (30,363)
Thorpe, Andrea M...................4:33:52 (19,549)
Thorpe, Beverley....................4:43:18 (21,636)
Thorpe, Rosemary M...............4:49:05 (22,892)
Thorpe, Sarah L.....................4:05:29 (12,532)
Thorpe, Shirley A....................4:31:00 (18,858)
Thorvaldsen, Paula................4:34:08 (19,632)
Thrower, Julie A.....................3:59:37 (11,195)
Thrower, Michelle...................4:53:02 (23,619)
Thulien, Jann........................4:09:44 (13,563)
Thurlow, Julie A.....................4:32:53 (19,332)
Thurlow, Lisa.........................3:48:32 (8,129)
Tibbs, Denise........................3:27:39 (4,156)
Tiedtke, Brenda......................3:52:48 (9,195)
Tieghi, Chiara........................4:01:10 (11,542)
Tier, Grace Y..........................4:00:42 (11,429)
Tigar, Karen..........................5:21:16 (27,705)

Till, Eileen M.........................5:03:03 (25,453)
Tillett, Ella............................4:45:06 (22,064)
Tilt, Carole A.........................4:50:35 (23,193)
Timlin, Elaine........................5:17:16 (27,281)
Timmins, Elizabeth................5:04:10 (25,594)
Timothy, Camille D.................5:33:18 (28,833)
Timothy, Nicola L...................4:04:43 (12,355)
Tims, Caroline.......................3:55:58 (10,074)
Tin, Lwin..............................5:36:31 (29,060)
Tincknell, Geraldine...............3:55:54 (10,051)
Tindale, Gemma.....................4:55:27 (24,092)
Tingstad, Elin Maaleng...........3:51:39 (8,928)
Tinker, Julie K.......................3:58:04 (10,696)
Tinnirello, Guiseppina............4:41:27 (21,230)
Tinsley, Judith C....................3:39:07 (6,150)
Tissington, Amanda J.............5:55:22 (30,217)
Titchener, Lorraine A..............4:44:35 (21,932)
Tiwana, Tarnjit.......................4:35:12 (19,866)
Tkinson, Irene.......................3:48:19 (8,081)
Tobon, Jeniffer......................5:22:08 (27,785)
Toby, Julia K..........................4:49:47 (23,036)
Todd, Libby J.........................4:20:46 (16,225)
Todd, Rachel C......................5:16:17 (27,166)
Todd, Yvette E.......................4:40:32 (21,034)
Todd Uhres, Christine............5:52:24 (30,092)
Toder, Elizabeth A..................4:31:55 (19,088)
Toley, Philippa S....................4:19:38 (15,934)
Tolfrey, Lilian C.....................4:48:03 (22,682)
Toller, Katie L........................5:12:27 (26,687)
Tolley, Kim A..........................6:01:28 (30,464)
Tollit, Julie L..........................5:07:58 (26,111)
Tomas, Lisa...........................4:23:09 (16,854)
Tombs, Amanda J...................4:26:54 (17,812)
Tombs, Gail...........................3:52:50 (9,209)
Tomkins, Gill.........................4:41:37 (21,262)
Tomkinson-Hill, Louise A........4:08:46 (13,311)
Tomlin, Tina..........................4:29:18 (18,431)
Tomlinson, Claire...................4:29:37 (18,527)
Tomlinson, Debbie.................4:31:23 (18,946)
Tomlinson, Jane E..................6:56:23 (31,577)
Tomlinson, Paula E.................5:38:49 (29,247)
Tompkins, Claire E.................5:25:00 (28,082)
Toms, Melanie.......................4:00:52 (11,468)
Toms, Michele........................4:21:23 (16,358)
Tomsett, Ruth........................4:00:11 (11,337)
Tomter, Edel..........................4:33:11 (19,399)
Tomter, Henriette...................4:25:59 (17,565)
Toner, Julie F.........................4:06:58 (12,882)
Tongue, Jo............................4:58:18 (24,666)
Tonkin, Jane E.......................4:40:47 (21,081)
Tonkin, Lisa V........................4:30:50 (18,825)
Tonkin, Tracy.........................4:44:10 (21,831)
Toone, Alison R......................5:16:11 (27,153)
Topham, Rosemary E..............8:32:26 (31,969)
Tophill, Samantha J................3:05:04 (1,530)
Topliss, Brenda J....................3:54:38 (9,677)
Topp, Kathryn........................5:08:00 (26,115)
Tori, Tiziana...........................5:05:55 (25,828)
Torosyan-Compton, Silva........6:11:25 (30,770)
Torr, Jacqueline.....................5:02:49 (25,425)
Tossounian, Charlotte M.........3:48:37 (8,157)
Toulson, Heather J.................5:21:12 (27,699)
Toulson, Helen.......................4:49:57 (23,067)
Tournier, Yasmina..................4:23:30 (16,942)
Tournijand, Laure...................4:45:20 (22,104)
Townend, Corrina L................4:29:37 (18,527)
Townend, Karen J...................4:43:44 (21,732)
Townes, Suzanne M................4:14:43 (14,732)
Towns, Jill M..........................5:27:46 (28,382)
Townsend, Karen A.................4:29:37 (18,527)
Townsend, Katie.....................5:03:24 (25,500)
Townsend, Laura J..................4:49:19 (22,942)
Tracey, June..........................4:16:11 (15,099)
Treacher, Helen E...................4:02:04 (11,735)
Treacy, Susan M.....................3:41:59 (6,643)
Treadwell, Julie......................3:58:23 (10,813)
Treadwell, Rosalind A.............4:05:11 (12,461)
Treanor, Jayne A.....................3:54:01 (9,510)
Trebilcock, Lucy C..................4:27:07 (17,871)
Tregaskis, Nicola S.................5:30:28 (28,619)
Treleaven, Kate E...................5:07:54 (26,100)
Trembath, Elianne M...............4:15:52 (15,021)
Tremlett, Caroline M................4:13:22 (14,423)

Tresler, Gabrielle M 4:19:12 (15,834)
Trett, Ann D 5:34:23 (28,916)
Trickey, Kay P 4:07:10 (12,931)
Triegaarot, Jeanette E 3:38:38 (6,075)
Trim, Gemma L 4:17:52 (15,526)
Trim, Madeleine L 3:51:11 (8,798)
Tripp, Lisa A 5:15:00 (27,026)
Troger, Michaela 4:05:47 (12,615)
Troisi, Sarah 4:22:02 (16,548)
Tropeano, Mandy A 4:19:42 (15,953)
Troy, Niamh 4:14:21 (14,636)
Trubridge, Leila P 5:54:39 (30,182)
Trump, Amanda J 4:16:36 (15,200)
Trundle, Samantha 4:02:22 (11,832)
Truscott, Ella 4:36:36 (20,156)
Trustram, Paula 4:54:07 (23,821)
Tse, Tania 5:27:36 (28,361)
Tubb, Rachel 5:40:29 (29,378)
Tucker, D 3:32:33 (5,013)
Tucker, Gillian 4:52:33 (23,539)
Tucker, Hazel 6:02:17 (30,495)
Tucker, Rachel C 4:52:33 (23,539)
Tudball, Sarah L 3:56:41 (10,298)
Tuffin, Angela J 6:26:03 (31,145)
Tulett, Joan 4:42:59 (21,561)
Tulloch, Sarah L 5:52:34 (30,100)
Tully, Susan A 6:06:44 (30,638)
Tummons, Sharon L 4:37:53 (20,429)
Tunbridge, Annabel K 4:37:44 (20,387)
Tunney, Jane L 7:16:08 (31,756)
Turkington, Helen R 4:42:42 (21,493)
Turle, Sara E 4:43:46 (21,741)
Turley, Christine E 4:31:38 (19,006)
Turnbull, Jean 5:57:10 (30,294)
Turnell, Amber A 6:02:18 (30,496)
Turner, Clare 4:52:02 (23,453)
Turner, Clare S 4:49:43 (23,021)
Turner, Erika J 4:12:19 (14,151)
Turner, Geraldine S 5:17:50 (27,341)
Turner, Helen 4:34:16 (19,657)
Turner, Jane L 5:27:45 (28,380)
Turner, Janet A 6:29:19 (31,192)
Turner, Jennifer C 6:11:21 (30,766)
Turner, Kate 4:24:51 (17,268)
Turner, Lara C 3:57:02 (10,397)
Turner, Natalie 4:03:02 (11,960)
Turner, Rosslyn A 6:19:09 (30,993)
Turner, Sue J 5:12:52 (26,742)
Turnley, Jayne 4:27:31 (17,965)
Turton, Helen 3:35:04 (5,436)
Turulyte, Dovile 4:31:03 (18,866)
Tutin, Angela M 4:41:23 (21,215)
Tutin, Joanna M 4:46:39 (22,383)
Tuton, Maria 4:32:06 (19,133)
Tweed, Janice 4:32:54 (19,335)
Tweedie, Rachel A 3:41:13 (6,516)
Twelftree, Gillian E 4:40:16 (20,976)
Twelvetree, Yvonne 3:50:24 (8,605)
Twigg, Lynda 4:21:54 (16,500)
Twigg, Natalie C 5:49:48 (29,952)
Twyman, Lucy M 4:49:12 (22,918)
Tyler, Deborah J 5:25:59 (28,195)
Tyler, Imogen J 4:34:46 (19,770)
Tyler, Linda 4:46:40 (22,386)
Tyrrell, Jill P 4:42:16 (21,402)
Tyson, Deborah M 5:28:42 (28,460)
Tyson, Linda A 4:56:45 (24,352)
Tytler, Kathryn M 4:26:12 (17,631)
Ubierna-Diez, Marisa 3:07:26 (1,742)
Ugwu, Tania 4:14:22 (14,641)
Ultich, Katrin 4:46:21 (22,326)
Umunna, Chinwe F 3:48:45 (8,198)
Underwood, Claire 4:36:48 (20,202)
Underwood, Lorraine H 4:31:53 (19,072)
Unger-Schwiebacher, Birgitt 4:32:11 (19,162)
Unwin, Susannah 3:43:59 (7,063)
Uren, Lisa C 3:48:30 (8,118)
Urquhart, Lauren 3:56:37 (10,285)
Urry, Jeanette 5:56:28 (30,272)
Usher, Christine 4:11:13 (13,916)
Usher, Karen D 5:15:45 (27,100)
Usher, Tanya I 4:03:38 (12,110)
Usherwood, Louisa K 5:33:52 (28,880)
Utting, Susan A 3:29:37 (4,522)
Vaid, Helen 5:29:23 (28,523)
Vail, Teresa G 4:57:16 (24,456)
Valapinee, Anick M 3:17:04 (2,755)
Valdes-Fernandez, Ana Maria 4:37:45 (20,391)
Valenti, Cinzia 5:09:40 (26,331)
Valiente-Salas, Gracia 3:07:26 (1,742)
Vamadeva, Sarita V 4:28:37 (18,259)
Van Der Merwe, Susara 4:47:36 (22,591)
Van Der Merwe, Yvette 4:04:26 (12,294)
Van Der Sluis, Marja 4:23:23 (16,914)
Van Der Veldt, Helen 5:40:41 (29,394)
Van Dijk, Suzan M 4:47:06 (22,474)
Van Elk, Marjon M 4:47:27 (22,557)
Van Helden, Charmaine 3:53:10 (9,303)
Van Herel, Aleida A 3:53:06 (9,282)
Van Leengoed, Rosemarie 3:42:49 (6,813)
Van Loen, Belinda C 4:32:07 (19,139)
Van Tebberen, Gillian A 7:15:32 (31,751)
Van Winden, Lidy 4:08:28 (13,221)
Vanhatalo, Anni T 3:31:18 (4,819)
Vanhatalo, Emmi M 3:34:31 (5,344)
Vanhoutte, Victoria J 5:27:00 (28,301)
Van-Orden, Elaine V 4:23:09 (16,854)
Varecka, Molly M 4:58:42 (24,757)
Varndell-Dawes, Paula 4:57:39 (24,521)
Varnish, Helen C 4:25:07 (17,337)
Vaughan, Diane E 4:02:17 (11,801)
Vaughan, Valerie 2:47:56 (420)
Vautier, Beverly C 5:28:31 (28,439)
Veenhuizen, Susan 4:35:57 (20,016)
Veliz, Julana K 4:48:15 (22,727)
Velleman, Karyn H 3:51:44 (8,951)
Velzeboer, Anya 4:49:40 (23,009)
Venables, Holly K 4:37:59 (20,464)
Venn, Kerry J 3:52:24 (9,111)
Verdier, Pascale 4:49:18 (22,939)
Verhoeven, Vreni 3:22:21 (3,353)
Vermeersch, Heidi 4:24:10 (17,113)
Verney, Eugenie 4:22:02 (16,548)
Vernis, Helene C 3:48:46 (8,200)
Vervant, Daniele 4:08:41 (13,283)
Vick, Sarah 4:11:44 (14,029)
Vickers, Ann 5:13:48 (26,872)
Vickery, Shirley A 3:58:29 (10,845)
Victor, Christina R 4:04:46 (12,370)
Viel, Dominique 3:54:07 (9,532)
Vilmshurst, Kim L 3:29:53 (4,569)
Vincent, Ellie 4:05:33 (12,555)
Vincent, Jan 4:09:47 (13,575)
Vincent, Louise N 4:28:10 (18,140)
Vines, Andrea J 3:57:47 (10,615)
Vines, Katherine M 5:04:53 (25,675)
Vinnicombe, Helen G 3:27:25 (4,108)
Vinter, Carol 5:24:09 (27,984)
Vinton, Linda A 4:14:55 (14,790)
Virdi, Tamsin R 5:24:28 (28,023)
Virgo, Tamsin E 4:06:08 (12,698)
Visagie, Peta M 4:20:33 (16,172)
Vitale-Cumper, Giulietta 3:32:30 (5,004)
Vivian, Christina 3:38:20 (6,020)
Voinot, Alison 5:19:49 (27,535)
Vollaro, Tracy 5:57:48 (30,323)
Voller, Karin 3:40:30 (6,403)
Von Gerard, Elizabeth 5:12:13 (26,657)
Vote, Michelle 3:54:47 (9,719)
Vozza, Maria 3:32:19 (4,973)
Vuagniaux, Alison M 3:13:09 (2,323)
Vynnycky, Emilia 3:52:11 (9,057)
Wachter Vinzens, Karla 5:25:14 (28,109)
Waddell, Jacqui A 4:17:48 (15,507)
Wade, Anderley C 4:20:28 (16,151)
Wade, Claire V 4:21:27 (16,376)
Wade, Heather 4:48:40 (22,807)
Wade, Jane M 4:20:16 (16,085)
Wadey, Susan C 4:57:55 (24,572)
Wadley, Sue 4:41:33 (21,254)
Wagh, Claire U 3:43:53 (7,034)
Wagman, Debra 4:26:37 (17,730)
Wagner, Ellen 4:57:14 (24,447)
Wagstaff, Emma 5:04:42 (25,650)
Wagstaff, Lesley J 4:52:29 (23,530)
Wain, Natalie E 4:45:27 (22,129)
Wainewright, Joanne T 7:06:06 (31,677)
Wait, Debra E 3:29:14 (4,461)
Waite, Amanda J 4:50:39 (23,207)
Waite, Claire I 7:56:05 (31,928)
Waite, Sheila J 3:29:39 (4,525)
Waite, Sophie A 3:40:09 (6,332)
Wake, Gillian 6:14:01 (30,846)
Wake, Nina A 4:04:39 (12,340)
Wakefield, Gillian E 4:18:39 (15,700)
Wakefield, Lucy J 4:16:36 (15,200)
Wakelin, Elizabeth M 4:21:50 (16,487)
Wakeling, Maureen M 3:52:47 (9,188)
Walberg, Vicki 5:02:41 (25,400)
Waldman, Louise J 3:16:07 (2,655)
Waldron, Denise D 4:41:10 (21,150)
Wale, Siv 6:13:10 (30,820)
Walford, Anne P 5:07:21 (26,024)
Walford, Jennifer 4:37:05 (20,270)
Walisko, Elizabeth A 5:23:08 (27,885)
Walker, Anne W 5:14:16 (26,930)
Walker, Cindy P 6:40:23 (31,366)
Walker, Donna 4:30:17 (18,700)
Walker, Donna M 5:11:57 (26,624)
Walker, Elaine 7:06:59 (31,680)
Walker, Henrietta S 5:14:47 (27,002)
Walker, Hilary 3:42:48 (6,810)
Walker, Janet 3:57:13 (10,451)
Walker, Jennifer L 4:35:00 (19,819)
Walker, Julie 3:52:58 (9,248)
Walker, Kate E 6:09:05 (30,702)
Walker, Lisa 6:54:57 (31,560)
Walker, Lou 4:39:38 (20,847)
Walker, Margaret 4:59:00 (24,793)
Walker, Michelle 3:26:32 (3,924)
Walker, Rebecca 4:53:40 (23,740)
Walker, Rosemary I 5:23:57 (27,969)
Walker, Susan A 4:13:03 (14,343)
Walker, Susan E 4:09:28 (13,490)
Walker, Tracey A 4:40:54 (21,107)
Wall, Wendy 4:32:13 (19,172)
Wallace, Jacqui 4:41:20 (21,201)
Wallace, Jennie A 3:50:24 (8,605)
Wallace, Jennifer J 3:55:10 (9,839)
Wallace, Lindsey H 6:12:53 (30,811)
Wallace, Lucy J 4:38:52 (20,688)
Wallace, Sara A 3:47:35 (7,903)
Wallbridge, Clare L 5:45:45 (29,738)
Waller, Ciara A 4:27:12 (17,892)
Waller, Irene 5:31:01 (28,660)
Waller, José E 6:57:45 (31,592)
Wallman, Tanya 4:49:19 (22,942)
Walls, Elizabeth V 3:16:09 (2,658)
Wallwork, Sally A 4:59:56 (24,981)
Walmsley, Kathryn J 4:04:43 (12,355)
Walmsley, Kerry A 6:26:57 (31,155)
Walpole, Jan 3:51:47 (8,967)
Walsh, Adrienne E 4:14:58 (14,798)
Walsh, Amanda J 5:39:33 (29,307)
Walsh, Cathryn A 4:19:00 (15,779)
Walsh, Christine M 7:19:09 (31,781)
Walsh, Denise C 5:16:14 (27,159)
Walsh, Kathleen M 4:17:26 (15,406)
Walsh, Linda J 4:02:12 (11,780)
Walsh, Rosemary 3:59:59 (11,291)
Walsh, Siobhan E 4:59:43 (24,942)
Walsham, Bernice M 3:56:46 (10,318)
Walter, Angela J 4:53:47 (23,765)
Walter, Geraldine M 4:21:37 (16,425)
Walters, Carol 4:49:02 (22,883)
Walters, Caroline P 5:05:29 (25,756)
Walters, Dawn C 5:36:26 (29,056)
Walters, Karen G 4:43:15 (21,620)
Walters, Natalie W 4:34:16 (19,657)
Walton, Hilary J 4:50:26 (23,167)
Walton, Lucy J 4:59:35 (24,918)
Walton, Petra B 5:17:33 (27,314)
Wann, Maura 7:08:20 (31,696)
Ward, Amanda 4:35:25 (19,914)
Ward, Annette E 3:55:29 (9,926)
Ward, Caroline 4:44:18 (21,858)
Ward, Elizabeth A 3:53:27 (9,366)
Ward, Felicity 3:53:37 (9,407)
Ward, Helen 3:56:23 (10,204)

Ward, Helen 4:45:20 (22,104)
Ward, Helen C 4:07:32 (13,017)
Ward, Joanna M 5:01:38 (25,245)
Ward, Joanne 6:02:24 (30,502)
Ward, Katie 5:27:43 (28,374)
Ward, Kirstyn 4:17:14 (15,354)
Ward, Linda 4:03:26 (12,065)
Ward, Lorraine 5:22:13 (27,796)
Ward, Meryl 4:51:49 (23,402)
Ward, Mina L 5:46:26 (29,781)
Ward, Sara J 3:53:06 (9,282)
Ward, Stella 4:01:06 (11,528)
Ward, Susan M 4:07:23 (12,982)
Ward, Zoe M 4:23:36 (16,966)
Ward-Booth, Sara 4:44:29 (21,908)
Warden, Claire 4:15:43 (14,980)
Warden, Jacqueline L 5:47:04 (29,814)
Warden, Yvonne G 3:37:00 (5,768)
Wardropper, Tina 4:04:26 (12,294)
Ward-Rotherham, Julie 4:53:05 (23,630)
Wargent, Julie C 4:21:41 (16,443)
Wark, Mary K 3:50:44 (8,692)
Warman, Tanya 4:22:11 (16,598)
Warner, Denise C 4:22:32 (16,709)
Warner, Gail L 3:59:50 (11,249)
Warner, Jane 5:14:35 (26,976)
Warner, Julie 3:27:11 (4,061)
Warner, Marita 4:08:06 (13,131)
Warner, Naomi 3:10:15 (2,022)
Warner, Pat L 3:59:51 (11,253)
Warrell, Althea 6:12:42 (30,804)
Warren, Natalie 4:03:52 (12,163)
Warrender, Helen L 5:23:54 (27,961)
Warrener, Tracey M 4:36:28 (20,123)
Warrick, Stephanie 4:29:28 (18,481)
Warrington, Catherine L 5:47:33 (29,843)
Wasch, Josephine 4:55:51 (24,162)
Wateridge, Katrina L 4:23:48 (17,014)
Waters, Bel A 3:18:04 (2,854)
Waters, Esther 4:16:49 (15,259)
Waters, Julie 4:12:04 (14,108)
Waters, Marianne 5:09:09 (26,260)
Wates, Amanda 4:21:43 (16,457)
Watkins, Anna C 5:30:37 (28,631)
Watkins, Rachel 4:19:12 (15,834)
Watkins, Shirley J 6:01:01 (30,449)
Watkins, Yvonne M 5:36:23 (29,052)
Watkinson, Ali R 3:51:10 (8,789)
Watkinson, Lynne L 3:26:17 (3,885)
Watling, Jo 4:59:55 (24,976)
Watson, Alex E 6:20:58 (31,030)
Watson, Anna-Marie 3:58:55 (10,979)
Watson, Camilla 5:25:36 (28,148)
Watson, Carol A 4:22:27 (16,681)
Watson, Caroline S 5:02:22 (25,353)
Watson, Christina M 4:45:15 (22,088)
Watson, Deborah J 5:12:50 (26,738)
Watson, Emma L 5:05:55 (25,828)
Watson, Jacqui 3:05:41 (1,581)
Watson, Jane E 5:12:47 (26,726)
Watson, Janet S 4:37:57 (20,454)
Watson, Jennifer A 4:16:13 (15,104)
Watson, Karen L 3:22:45 (3,410)
Watson, Laura 5:34:58 (28,954)
Watson, Nichola R 5:23:06 (27,879)
Watson, Nicola J 6:12:28 (30,792)
Watson, Sally D 5:15:47 (27,106)
Watson, Sarah E 5:49:02 (29,910)
Watson, Sarah J 4:22:25 (16,671)
Watson, Sue 4:24:14 (17,129)
Watson, Susan J 3:33:40 (5,214)
Watson, Tanya C 6:58:11 (31,600)
Watt, Jacqueline M 3:37:02 (5,776)
Watt, Kerry B 4:07:09 (12,927)
Watton, Shirley A 5:35:32 (29,002)
Watts, Heather E 4:17:47 (15,503)
Watts, Jennifer A 5:01:42 (25,257)
Watts, Kelly L 5:22:46 (27,854)
Watts, Nicola A 4:07:11 (12,936)
Watts, Paula 3:58:02 (10,684)
Watts, Ruth E 4:48:38 (22,801)
Watts, Vanessa L 5:10:50 (26,487)
Watts, Vivienne A 5:13:18 (26,805)

Waugh, Carol M 4:56:51 (24,375)
Waugh, Dawn E 3:32:38 (5,037)
Way, Nicky J 3:31:10 (4,801)
Way, Philippa K 4:24:09 (17,105)
Way, Sally E 3:57:48 (10,618)
Wayne, Samantha 4:39:28 (20,820)
Wearn, Donna 5:14:11 (26,919)
Weaver, Clair 4:17:04 (15,319)
Webb, Judith 4:21:01 (16,284)
Webb, Julia A 5:06:29 (25,908)
Webb, Lizzie A 4:41:39 (21,271)
Webb, Sally 3:44:52 (7,277)
Webber, Clare 4:12:48 (14,279)
Webber, Elizabeth J 5:18:06 (27,379)
Webber, Hilary 7:32:44 (31,863)
Webber, Katie M 5:05:51 (25,815)
Webbs, Amy 3:44:27 (7,173)
Weber, Bernadette H 4:37:57 (20,454)
Webster, Anne M 4:34:28 (19,704)
Webster, Catherine A 4:53:18 (23,671)
Webster, Katy M 3:08:43 (1,867)
Webster, Lynne 4:50:54 (23,251)
Webster, Paula S 4:22:44 (16,755)
Weddell, Paula L 4:44:17 (21,855)
Wedrychowski, Barbara M 6:04:25 (30,580)
Weedon, Linda 4:59:22 (24,871)
Weekes, Jenna K 4:26:29 (17,696)
Weeks, Gail 6:11:40 (30,776)
Wegrzynski, Christina 5:09:44 (26,342)
Wehl, Robin L 4:56:29 (24,305)
Weibold, Gerlinde 4:38:14 (20,530)
Weichert, Heike 4:46:32 (22,367)
Weight, Georgina 6:37:53 (31,337)
Weinberger, Josephine S 4:03:58 (12,184)
Weir, Lorraine 4:38:41 (20,637)
Weir, Susan E 4:43:19 (21,642)
Weiser, Karen 5:38:27 (29,226)
Welbourne, Jacqueline 4:49:54 (23,060)
Welch, Emily L 5:11:38 (26,585)
Welch, Emma V 3:12:10 (2,211)
Welch, Louise 3:59:06 (11,030)
Welch, Lucy C 3:12:11 (2,212)
Welch, Margaret A 4:20:43 (16,217)
Weldon, Georgina M 5:05:54 (25,823)
Welling, Hannah J 5:42:33 (29,519)
Wellings, Linda M 5:04:29 (25,624)
Wells, Ali J 4:30:40 (18,794)
Wells, Diane L 4:42:16 (21,402)
Wells, Heather O 4:12:05 (14,113)
Wells, Jacqueline E 5:44:44 (29,672)
Wells, Julia C 4:05:06 (12,448)
Wells, Lorraine 4:31:45 (19,041)
Wells, Lorraine E 4:58:13 (24,643)
Wells, Patricia M 4:18:26 (15,647)
Wenborne, Sheila A 6:05:44 (30,614)
Werne, Elizabeth T 6:43:31 (31,412)
Wertli, Beatrice 3:19:22 (3,001)
Wescott, Sandra A 3:43:50 (7,021)
Wesel, Inge 5:31:52 (28,729)
Wesley, Belinda 6:10:54 (30,756)
West, Diane B 6:06:49 (30,640)
West, Julie 4:04:37 (12,333)
West, Nicola 4:43:15 (21,620)
West, Sara J 5:03:09 (25,466)
West, Tracey J 3:06:00 (1,610)
West, Victoria L 5:08:59 (26,236)
West, Zoe 3:36:14 (5,648)
Westby, Tina 5:11:27 (26,573)
Westgarth, Susan C 4:24:52 (17,274)
Westgate, Jacqueline L 4:58:40 (24,750)
Westgate, Pamela H 4:10:49 (13,830)
Westhead, Jessica R 4:37:42 (20,382)
Weston, Denise 3:53:14 (9,323)
Weston, Judith C 4:02:08 (11,757)
Weston, Natasha T 4:36:14 (20,078)
Westwick, Jolene K 4:35:46 (19,977)
Wetherall, Suzanne 4:30:14 (18,687)
Wettone, Jennifer C 5:04:48 (25,663)
Wharmby, Sally J 3:47:34 (7,898)
Whatmore, Dana M 4:27:59 (18,094)
Wheatley, Mary E 6:40:12 (31,361)
Wheatstone, Sarah E 4:53:14 (23,663)
Wheeler, Donna E 4:04:03 (12,195)

Wheeler, Kim 4:00:56 (11,488)
Wheeler, Naomi 4:59:28 (24,896)
Wheeler, Sarah N 4:04:29 (12,312)
Wheeler, Sarah R 4:33:36 (19,486)
Whelan, Christine M 5:21:04 (27,687)
Whelan, Clare 7:36:05 (31,878)
Whelan, Louise 4:50:08 (23,095)
Whidburn, Amy G 4:09:42 (13,560)
Whiley, Lesley 3:00:43 (1,209)
Whitcombe, Lisa J 4:58:26 (24,703)
White, Alison L 3:43:11 (6,890)
White, Amanda J 4:48:37 (22,797)
White, Ashleigh 4:05:20 (12,494)
White, Caroline S 3:41:23 (6,533)
White, Christine A 7:43:48 (31,902)
White, Elizabeth M 4:33:06 (19,381)
White, Emma C 5:43:35 (29,599)
White, Hilary J 4:28:57 (18,342)
White, Jenette A 5:07:17 (26,006)
White, Jessica R 3:44:00 (7,071)
White, Kate 4:58:05 (24,617)
White, Kate J 4:37:53 (20,429)
White, Lois A 4:07:49 (13,074)
White, Lucy 3:45:23 (7,384)
White, Lucy J 5:09:11 (26,267)
White, Lynsey M 5:35:07 (28,966)
White, Natalie C 4:32:26 (19,220)
White, Pamela L 3:59:53 (11,261)
White, Philly D 4:43:41 (21,718)
White, Rebecca E 5:04:36 (25,638)
White, Sally A 4:58:14 (24,646)
White, Sarah J 4:35:56 (20,009)
White, Sylvia 3:52:56 (9,235)
White, Tiffany C 5:34:08 (28,899)
Whitefield, Lynda 5:44:22 (29,646)
Whitehead, Brenda A 5:12:41 (26,712)
Whitehead, Claire 4:38:44 (20,649)
Whitehead, Fiona E 4:08:24 (13,199)
Whitehead, Michelle L 3:42:21 (6,709)
Whitehead, Sarah 3:17:32 (2,803)
Whitehead, Sharon A 4:35:44 (19,966)
Whitehouse, Anna C 5:05:26 (25,743)
Whitehouse, Emily 5:39:36 (29,311)
Whitehurst, Louise M 4:18:54 (15,758)
Whitley, Jane 4:02:49 (11,932)
Whitlock, Carman 6:51:21 (31,518)
Whitmore, Pippa L 5:29:27 (28,525)
Whitnall, Lynn K 4:48:34 (22,786)
Whittaker, Joanne L 5:01:43 (25,261)
Whittaker, Sarah L 5:27:55 (28,389)
Whittaker, Susan 6:21:06 (31,034)
Whittaker, Vicky C 4:24:53 (17,278)
Whitten, Erica J 7:43:48 (31,902)
Whitten, Selina I 3:34:43 (5,371)
Whitters, Caralea 4:53:36 (23,725)
Whitting, Polly K 6:33:24 (31,272)
Whittle, Debbie 5:31:33 (28,703)
Whitwell, Penelope J 3:58:12 (10,758)
Whitworth, Elizabeth A 5:06:15 (25,882)
Whitworth, Gemma R 4:33:13 (19,411)
Whitworth, Katie H 5:26:20 (28,228)
Why, Christina J 4:09:08 (13,407)
Whybrow, Andrea 4:39:25 (20,811)
Whyte, Heather L 5:30:29 (28,622)
Whyte, Jennifer L 4:45:01 (22,032)
Whytefield, Collette 5:32:15 (28,755)
Wick, Barbara A 4:28:48 (18,298)
Wicke, Dorothy M 4:04:15 (12,254)
Wickee, Marilyn J 5:11:58 (26,627)
Widdowson, Rachael 5:29:38 (28,549)
Widmer, Monika 3:11:20 (2,128)
Wigg, Alison H 4:40:47 (21,081)
Wiggans, Elizabeth N 5:29:02 (28,485)
Wigley, Julia C 5:20:17 (27,605)
Wilcookson, Emma 5:52:16 (30,082)
Wilcox, Joanna S 4:35:17 (19,882)
Wilcox, Julie K 5:09:47 (26,355)
Wild, Clare E 5:04:11 (25,595)
Wild, Denise J 6:51:56 (31,528)
Wilde, Kelly W 5:50:18 (29,981)
Wilde, Nicola 3:21:49 (3,293)
Wilde, Sarah J 4:46:44 (22,397)
Wildhaber, Dorothea 4:10:49 (13,830)

Wilding, Jacqueline 5:08:16 (26,152)
Wilding, Judith 5:28:18 (28,418)
Wiles, Nicola S 4:49:18 (22,939)
Wilford, Louise M 4:54:23 (23,875)
Wilkens, Kim B 4:43:19 (21,642)
Wilkes, Vivien 4:56:26 (24,289)
Wilkie, Gillian M 4:41:03 (21,135)
Wilkie, Rose 3:37:30 (5,873)
Wilkinson, Angela 5:46:28 (29,784)
Wilkinson, Dorothy A 3:29:00 (4,413)
Wilkinson, Francine M 4:37:36 (20,356)
Wilkinson, Helen L 3:59:23 (11,111)
Wilkinson, Jo M 4:39:47 (20,873)
Wilkinson, Joy L 3:52:14 (9,064)
Wilkinson, Kate M 4:32:10 (19,158)
Wilkinson, Lisa 3:44:35 (7,208)
Wilkinson, Maria 5:55:07 (30,206)
Wilkinson, Maxine G 4:47:28 (22,564)
Willans, Sandra 5:25:37 (28,151)
Willcock, Louise E 5:38:18 (29,213)
Willdigg, Jane 3:59:41 (11,218)
Willetts, Stephanie 7:27:29 (31,828)
Williams, Alexandra E 4:14:22 (14,641)
Williams, Ann 5:35:29 (28,999)
Williams, Beverley A 4:58:17 (24,663)
Williams, Carol A 4:26:01 (17,571)
Williams, Caroline L 6:45:58 (31,452)
Williams, Deborah 5:05:26 (25,743)
Williams, Deborah A 6:01:35 (30,467)
Williams, Donna L 4:38:38 (20,622)
Williams, Emilie J 4:36:51 (20,217)
Williams, Emily J 4:09:54 (13,607)
Williams, Geraldine 5:06:13 (25,876)
Williams, Helen S 5:06:22 (25,896)
Williams, Iona W 4:48:02 (22,678)
Williams, Isobel 4:34:41 (19,753)
Williams, Jackie M 3:51:40 (8,930)
Williams, Jacqueline R 4:24:12 (17,122)
Williams, Jane M 4:15:15 (14,870)
Williams, Jennefer A 4:57:25 (24,482)
Williams, Joy 3:37:18 (5,839)
Williams, Kate M 4:59:21 (24,865)
Williams, Katie 7:19:07 (31,780)
Williams, Lisa K 4:53:12 (23,654)
Williams, Louise 3:52:33 (9,139)
Williams, Lynwen 5:41:44 (29,471)
Williams, Madeleine M 5:15:13 (27,043)
Williams, Margaret 3:52:48 (9,195)
Williams, Megan M 4:09:14 (13,432)
Williams, Michelle L 4:29:17 (18,422)
Williams, Nicola A 6:42:47 (31,402)
Williams, Paula M 5:34:33 (28,925)
Williams, Pauline 6:04:28 (30,582)
Williams, Rachael E 4:10:29 (13,752)
Williams, Rebecca J 4:56:26 (24,289)
Williams, Rebecca L 4:30:11 (18,676)
Williams, Safina 4:36:36 (20,156)
Williams, Sally E 4:50:38 (23,204)
Williams, Sarah A 3:03:53 (1,440)
Williams, Sharon 3:43:24 (6,937)
Williams, Sharon 5:30:00 (28,584)
Williams, Shirley A 4:53:32 (23,707)
Williams, Silifa 4:22:25 (16,671)
Williams, Susan 5:17:41 (27,326)
Williams, Teresa K 3:22:13 (3,329)
Williams, Wendy J 5:43:47 (29,614)
Williamson, Deborah A 4:50:36 (23,198)
Williamson, Kelly 6:00:08 (30,414)
Williamson, Michelle 6:00:08 (30,414)
Willington, Louise M 3:37:08 (5,800)
Willis, Carol J 4:24:08 (17,102)
Willis, Charlotte E 5:09:21 (26,285)
Willis, Elizabeth J 4:03:34 (12,092)
Willis, Janet A 5:25:44 (28,167)
Willis, Jo 4:53:25 (23,689)
Willis, Lisa C 4:47:27 (22,557)
Willis, Sarah L 5:11:43 (26,592)
Willmott, Denise C 4:37:52 (20,422)
Willoughby, Emma L 4:20:28 (16,151)
Willson, Emma 5:20:35 (27,641)
Wilshaw, Lynda J 5:38:05 (29,187)
Wilsher, Rachael M 3:34:56 (5,415)
Wilshin, Sarah V 4:48:10 (22,713)
Wilson, Amanda J 5:04:55 (25,681)
Wilson, Angela 4:02:58 (11,948)
Wilson, Beverley J 3:02:44 (1,355)
Wilson, Cathy S 4:16:01 (15,053)
Wilson, Debbie L 4:15:36 (14,955)
Wilson, Emma A 4:12:06 (14,115)
Wilson, Emma L 5:01:08 (25,165)
Wilson, Freda 4:51:05 (23,288)
Wilson, Heidi J 3:13:58 (2,429)
Wilson, Helen 5:33:52 (28,880)
Wilson, Irene M 6:00:23 (30,427)
Wilson, J 4:30:33 (18,769)
Wilson, Jane 3:04:39 (1,503)
Wilson, Jane O 4:47:22 (22,533)
Wilson, Jessica 4:46:11 (22,293)
Wilson, Joanne C 3:25:34 (3,777)
Wilson, Julia D 4:01:55 (11,695)
Wilson, Karen J 3:39:41 (6,253)
Wilson, Kerry A 4:18:32 (15,670)
Wilson, Lauren H 5:47:31 (29,840)
Wilson, Linda J 4:11:21 (13,939)
Wilson, Lorraine E 3:43:27 (6,951)
Wilson, Lynne M 5:41:16 (29,427)
Wilson, Nathalie 6:07:03 (30,649)
Wilson, Nicola A 3:28:34 (4,331)
Wilson, Nicola C 4:14:33 (14,694)
Wilson, Peta J 5:22:46 (27,854)
Wilson, Rebecca 4:30:23 (18,724)
Wilson, Rosemary E 3:26:36 (3,932)
Wilson, Ruth J 4:42:02 (21,355)
Wilson, Sara J 7:31:54 (31,858)
Wilson, Simone C 3:25:43 (3,801)
Wilson, Stephanie J 4:07:38 (13,040)
Wilson, Sue 3:45:38 (7,443)
Wilson, Sue L 5:15:51 (27,114)
Wilson, Tanya C 4:29:00 (18,349)
Wilson, Veronica G 5:44:44 (29,672)
Wilson, Wendy E 6:57:17 (31,587)
Wiltshire, Brenda I 5:25:42 (28,159)
Wing, Julie A 4:48:15 (22,727)
Wingate, Katherine M 6:16:33 (30,923)
Wingfield, Joan 3:19:46 (3,045)
Wingfield, Zoe E 4:44:39 (21,947)
Winkworth, Jessica J 5:47:29 (29,836)
Winship, Pippa L 6:02:31 (30,508)
Winstanley, Abigail 4:20:24 (16,131)
Winter, Annelis 5:16:52 (27,244)
Winter, Claire 4:10:52 (13,844)
Winter, Dagmar 4:48:46 (22,830)
Winter, Kirsty D 4:12:52 (14,292)
Winter, Miriam 6:00:49 (30,441)
Winterburn, Sarah A 6:18:42 (30,981)
Winterson, Victoria A 3:54:08 (9,536)
Winterton, Sue M 4:44:53 (21,995)
Wiscombe, Rebecca A 3:55:24 (9,907)
Wisdom, Carole J 5:12:40 (26,708)
Wise, Paula M 4:39:03 (20,739)
Wiseman, Marianne 5:15:26 (27,070)
Witham, Helen M 3:49:41 (8,419)
Witham, Marion 5:46:27 (29,783)
Witherden, Louise 4:21:38 (16,430)
Witherick, Claire D 4:47:10 (22,493)
Withers, Barbara A 6:25:33 (31,133)
Withers, Pamela R 3:52:53 (9,218)
Withers, Rachel J 4:26:01 (17,571)
Withnall, Anna 4:28:27 (18,215)
Withrington, Ann M 5:03:04 (25,456)
Wixon, Rebecca L 4:14:21 (14,636)
Wohanka, Oonafh 3:26:15 (3,879)
Wohlers, Regima 3:54:36 (9,666)
Wold, Ellen S 4:16:11 (15,099)
Wolfberg, Rachel A 5:36:48 (29,090)
Wolfe, Paula H 5:56:50 (30,282)
Wolfendale, Vivienne 4:02:15 (11,796)
Womersley, Lynne 3:58:38 (10,899)
Wong, Margaret L 5:40:35 (29,387)
Wong, Nicole 6:05:27 (30,602)
Wong, Patsy 4:38:07 (20,499)
Wood, Amanda J 4:14:27 (14,665)
Wood, Angela M 4:31:23 (18,946)
Wood, Barbara J 3:43:23 (6,933)
Wood, Deborah A 4:27:16 (17,916)
Wood, Eleanor M 3:47:25 (7,856)
Wood, Elizabeth A 4:57:12 (24,438)
Wood, Jackie 3:43:49 (7,017)
Wood, Jodie A 3:30:36 (4,707)
Wood, Kerrie J 2:54:52 (741)
Wood, Rachel J 4:17:42 (15,480)
Wood, Rebekah L 3:51:36 (8,916)
Wood, Ruth 3:43:58 (7,057)
Wood, Sophie 2:57:25 (908)
Wood, Tabatha E 4:18:40 (15,702)
Wood, Tana R 4:22:00 (16,537)
Wood, Tricia L 5:30:08 (28,595)
Woodard, Suzanne 5:09:20 (26,282)
Woodburn, Jane L 4:05:59 (12,657)
Wooder, Stella 5:13:33 (26,839)
Woodford, Helen E 7:33:15 (31,866)
Woodgate, Vivienne F 4:20:54 (16,261)
Woodham, Sari H 3:31:32 (4,856)
Woodhams, Emma L 3:51:32 (8,899)
Woodhead, Jane L 5:01:52 (25,280)
Woodhouse, Elaine 4:17:31 (15,429)
Woodhouse, Kate F 4:17:05 (15,321)
Woodhouse, Katy E 3:58:07 (10,715)
Woodhouse, Wendy J 3:42:46 (6,803)
Woodley, Helen M 3:09:52 (1,989)
Woodley, Jayne 4:51:53 (23,418)
Woodman, Cathy A 4:40:56 (21,113)
Woodman, Pauline M 5:00:25 (25,054)
Woodman, Rebecca E 3:40:07 (6,326)
Woodroff, Nicola J 5:14:00 (26,899)
Woodrow, Joyce 5:57:24 (30,307)
Woodrow, Roberta K 6:00:55 (30,445)
Woodrow, Rosalyn L 4:54:26 (23,883)
Woods, Isla A 4:24:11 (17,117)
Woods, Laurie J 5:18:33 (27,415)
Woodward, Amanda L 6:15:44 (30,902)
Woodward, Hazel R 4:29:24 (18,466)
Woodward, Lesley 3:46:36 (7,662)
Woodward, Lisa J 6:03:08 (30,530)
Wooldridge, Kate R 4:06:51 (12,849)
Woolgar, Lorrie 4:03:20 (12,044)
Wooller, Diane E 3:48:56 (8,238)
Woolley, Allison 6:07:40 (30,667)
Woolley, Catherine A 4:45:01 (22,032)
Woolley, Sue E 5:28:56 (28,476)
Woolley, Theresa 3:51:09 (8,781)
Woolliscroft, Rachel L 4:34:16 (19,657)
Woolnough, Jennifer L 5:20:27 (27,623)
Woolnough, Sarah 4:35:51 (19,990)
Woolsey, Amy C 5:24:36 (28,033)
Wooltorton, Rebecca E 4:46:36 (22,374)
Woolven, Maire B 6:20:44 (31,028)
Woor, Nicola J 5:17:10 (27,269)
Wooster, Yvonne M 3:42:50 (6,818)
Wootten, Frances 4:48:10 (22,713)
Wootton, Joanna 4:49:04 (22,889)
Wootton, Kim J 4:54:23 (23,875)
Worboys, Caroline 4:37:15 (20,306)
Worden, Anne-Marie 6:26:32 (31,150)
Worland, Suzanne C 5:42:40 (29,524)
Wormald, Philippa F 4:57:56 (24,576)
Worrall, Caroline J 4:22:00 (16,537)
Worrell-Jude, Elizabeth Y 6:30:43 (31,218)
Worsfold, Shirley A 3:35:33 (5,533)
Worth, Jenny J 5:11:10 (26,534)
Worth, Katie 4:15:03 (14,814)
Worthington, Jeanie C 4:58:38 (24,745)
Worthy, Diana C 3:56:30 (10,250)
Wotton, Dawn 4:48:49 (22,841)
Wotton, Deborah 4:33:58 (19,581)
Wotton, Lisa S 3:47:11 (7,801)
Wreglesworth, Hayley 4:24:10 (17,113)
Wretham, Zoe 6:08:59 (30,699)
Wright, Eleanor 4:24:18 (17,142)
Wright, Jacqui 4:50:54 (23,251)
Wright, Joanna 4:19:22 (15,874)
Wright, Joanna 5:16:03 (27,135)
Wright, Joanne 3:57:14 (10,458)
Wright, Joanne L 4:47:32 (22,574)
Wright, Josie A 6:03:32 (30,549)
Wright, Judy M 4:51:48 (23,397)
Wright, Juliana H 4:33:02 (19,364)
Wright, Karena 4:32:38 (19,273)
Wright, Laura J 3:27:53 (4,206)

Wright, Linda A 4:46:21 (22,326)
Wright, Louisa J 4:05:34 (12,563)
Wright, Maggie M 5:08:43 (26,205)
Wright, Mandy 3:04:07 (1,460)
Wright, Maureen A 3:56:32 (10,260)
Wright, Nadine A 5:10:45 (26,476)
Wright, Rosemary V 5:52:07 (30,070)
Wright, Sandra G 7:48:15 (31,911)
Wright, Sarah 4:57:04 (24,415)
Wright, Sharon L 4:25:03 (17,318)
Wright, Suzanne 4:15:14 (14,863)
Wright, Theresa A 4:21:45 (16,465)
Wring, Jill 4:21:42 (16,449)
Wurth, Gertrud 4:39:19 (20,796)
Wyatt, Sara J 4:13:28 (14,442)
Wykes-Dart, Carole A 4:13:12 (14,376)
Wylie, Jayne L 4:32:34 (19,251)
Wylie, Susan 5:00:17 (25,035)
Wyngard, Clare E 3:40:37 (6,418)
Wynn, Carol F 6:11:28 (30,772)
Wynn, Greer M 3:41:53 (6,617)
Wynne, Catherine S 4:34:00 (19,587)
Wynne, Theresa A 3:45:43 (7,465)
Wynter, Lorna 4:30:51 (18,829)
Xehia, Jehan 5:23:52 (27,957)
Yakubu, Catherine N 4:56:09 (24,237)
Yamauchi, Mara R 2:39:16 (193)
Yarrow, Carol S 3:28:12 (4,264)
Yarrow, Nicola L 4:08:41 (13,283)
Yarwood, Katherine A 3:47:37 (7,910)
Yates, Alison M 4:22:45 (16,760)
Yates, Lois 3:49:04 (8,268)
Yates, Susie 5:21:05 (27,689)
Yazbek, Elizabeth G 4:26:14 (17,644)
Yearley, Lesley C 4:23:33 (16,953)
Yeld, Rophina 4:04:27 (12,300)
Yeldham, Anne E 5:31:49 (28,725)
Yellappa, Vandana 4:40:18 (20,984)
Yendell, Zoe L 4:22:50 (16,783)
Yendley, Susan E 3:45:08 (7,330)
Yeomans, Stephen 3:39:03 (6,140)
Yerby, Emma 4:39:46 (20,870)
Yevko, Nicola 3:05:22 (1,559)
Yff, Barbara T 2:48:10 (429)
Yingjie, Sun 2:28:32 (73)
Ynez-Tulsen, Elizabeth 5:47:36 (29,847)
Yochum, Laura A 5:06:49 (25,946)
York, Elizabeth R 4:48:35 (22,790)
York, Sarah C 5:29:31 (28,535)
Yost, Alison J 3:49:01 (8,258)
Yost, Marielle 3:11:44 (2,160)
Young, Christine A 4:06:13 (12,716)
Young, Fiona D 4:51:41 (23,378)
Young, Helen L 4:51:13 (23,306)
Young, Helen M 7:21:24 (31,795)
Young, Hilary 3:55:39 (9,975)
Young, Hilary J 5:27:01 (28,303)
Young, Lynn L 4:23:03 (16,825)
Young, Nicola D 5:43:01 (29,567)
Young, Polly E 3:41:35 (6,561)
Young, Sarah 3:57:12 (10,444)
Young, Teresa E 5:35:07 (28,966)
Young, Valerie 2:41:32 (233)
Yoxall, Karen 3:53:44 (9,420)
Yuill, Chris 3:52:34 (9,144)
Yule, Helen J 2:58:41 (1,039)
Zahora, Sabine 5:05:32 (25,769)
Zajkowska, Katarzyna 4:40:01 (20,924)
Zak, Susan K 4:15:07 (14,834)
Zakharova, Svetlana 2:28:10 (69)
Zammit, Ellen F 6:25:03 (31,126)
Zawadski, Simone 4:25:01 (17,313)
Zdanowicz, Lisa M 4:48:21 (22,750)
Zeytin, Simone 3:55:34 (9,954)
Zoe, Stewart 5:16:05 (27,137)
Zona, Eleonora 3:57:39 (10,581)
Zuckerman, Rachel 3:37:25 (5,864)

WHEELCHAIR ENTRANTS

Adams, Jeff 1:59:07 (5)
Allen, Geof 2:21:44 (13)
Carruthers, Peter 3:09:43 (26)
Cassell, Ric 3:42:36 (29)

Cheek, Andrew 2:03:31 (7)
Craig, Paula 2:07:52 (10)
Delaey, Jean 2:22:04 (14)
Derwin, Steve 3:25:15 (28)
Downing, Peter 3:01:27 (24)
Fuss, Alain 1:45:25 (3)
Gajdiciar, Vladimir 2:25:05 (15)
Hallam, James 2:33:45 (20)
Hanley, Chris 2:42:39 (23)
Kukla, Daniel 2:05:02 (9)
Lewis, Michelle 2:32:28 (19)

Mendoza, Saul 1:36:56 (1)

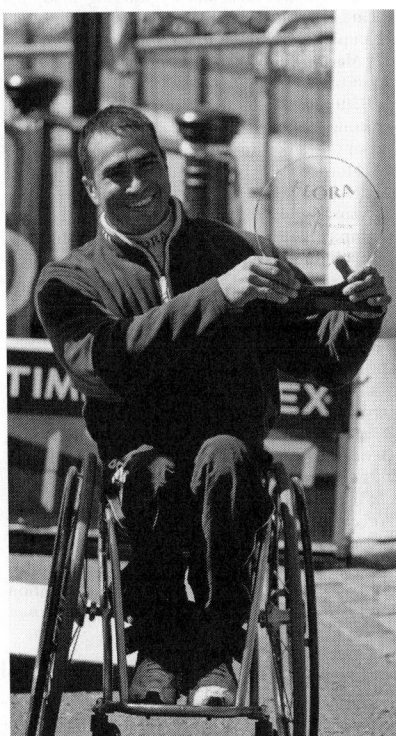

Saul Mendoza, from Mexico, (born 6 January 1967) was the men's wheelchair winner of the 2004 and 2005 London Marathon. He won six medals in different athletics events at the Paralympic Games – two gold, one silver and three bronze – in a career that spanned from Seoul 1988 to Beijing 2008. He was the flag-bearer for the Mexican team in the Sydney 2000 and Beijing 2008 Paralympic Games. In training he is alleged to tot up 200 miles a week. Mendoza contracted polio in an epidemic in Mexico that affected thousands of babies in the late 1960s. At that time Mendoza was less than a year old but he has always loved sports. He has won more than 200 road races during his long career and became Mexican Athlete of the Twentieth Century. Mendoza is also competitive at kayaking and horseback riding and his potential as an athlete was spotted while playing basketball.

Patel, Tushar 1:51:03 (4)
Porcellato, Francesca 2:04:58 (8)
Rea, Paul 2:38:04 (21)
Richards, Jason 2:00:11 (6)
Richardson, Lee 2:39:52 (22)
Smith, Robert 3:06:02 (25)
Vingerder, Stephane 2:28:23 (17)
Wallengren, Gunilla 2:14:13 (11)
Weir, David 1:42:50 (2)
Williamson, Steve 2:18:44 (12)
Wimpress, Ron 3:13:05 (27)
Worrell, Wesley 2:28:19 (16)
Zanotti, Davide 2:30:02 (18)

When Marathon Day dawns hot and warm, spare a thought for those who will later swelter in fancy dress – the rhinos, the camels, the pantomime horses. Billy Wilson, founder of the Tough Guy Race in the Midlands, recorded his fastest time in the London Marathon while running as a pantomime horse. When the other part of the double-act pulled out with cramp and exhaustion, Wilson enlisted a substitute from the crowd and carried on regardless. Before the finish the horse performed an extravagant equine curtsey outside the gates of Buckingham Palace 'as a mark of respect for the Queen'.

The 2005 London Marathon

Paula Radcliffe's disappointment in the Olympic Games of 2004, where she failed to finish, meant that the thousands who watched her race in the 2005 London Marathon did so with a mixture of hope and fear.

But Paula's performance in 2005 was every bit as triumphant as her previous two runs in London, scattering any lingering doubts about her fine ability. Her time of 2:17:42 was the third fastest ever for a woman runner, and a world record for a women's-only race.

But, bizarrely, the race will be remembered by many because Paula Radcliffe had to squat by the side of the road at the 22-mile mark after her stomach reacted to her pre-race meal.

'When I'm racing I'm totally focused on winning the race and running as fast as possible,' she said later. 'I was losing time because I was having stomach cramps and I thought *I just need to go and I'll be fine.*' She added: 'I want to apologise to the nation. I didn't really want to resort to that in front of hundreds of thousands of people.'

Race organisers may have believed that the 950 toilets lining the route should have prevented such embarrassment. But Radcliffe had other ideas. 'I would have had to go through the barriers and the crowd and then probably sign three autographs when I came out,' she said.

Radcliffe took control of the race after seven miles and went on to win her third London and fifth major international marathon title. Two years previously she set the world record of 2:15:25 when she ran with the men, but in this 2005 race she insisted victory, rather than records, was her main goal. She beat second-placed Romanian Constantina Dita by more than 5 minutes. Susan Chepkemei, who ran Radcliffe so close in New

York the previous November, finished over 6 minutes behind in third in 2:24:00. Last year's winner Okayo was fourth in 2:25:22 while Ireland's Sonia O'Sullivan posted a personal best of 2:29:01 in finishing eighth.

It was one of the toughest London Marathons as temperatures soared on a warm spring day. Hundreds suffered from dehydration and a 59-year-old man from Cambridgeshire collapsed on the course and subsequently died in hospital.

The men's race had a glittering field that included the current Olympic and world champions and the world record holder.

Martin Lel of Kenya came home in 2:07:26, 23 seconds in front of Moroccan Jaouad Gharib in 2:07:49 with the South African Hendrick Ramaala crossing the line 43 seconds later. It was Lel's first major title since he won in New York in 2003.

Morocco's two-time London winner Abdelkader El Mouaziz picked off the fading Kenyans to take fourth spot in 2:09:03. The 2004 Olympic champion, Stefano Baldini, Italy, finished fifth and the first British runner, Jon Brown, set a personal best of 2:09:31, finishing sixth to move him up to twelfth on the British all-time list.

In the men's wheelchair race Mexican Saul Mendoza retained his title in 1:35:51 after sprinting ahead of a pack of seven in Birdcage Walk with just 800 metres to go. Only 13 seconds separated the top seven and Mendoza finished 3 seconds ahead of Canadian Jeff Adams. Briton David Weir finished in third in 1:36:03, narrowly ahead of training partner Tushar Patel.

In the women's wheelchair race Francesca Porcellato of Italy completed the first hat-trick of victories since Kay MacShane won three London titles between 1984 and 1986. Britain's 18-year-old rising star Shelly Woods stayed in contention until the last 400 metres when Porcellato used

her experience to pull away for victory in 1:56:59. Tanni Grey-Thompson lost contact after about 15 miles, and finished third in 2:02:39.

Sir Steve Redgrave, five-time Olympic rowing gold medallist, clocked 4:21. 'As long as I can break my personal best of 4:52 then I'll be happy just to shuffle along,' he said. 'The next day, I was out on the water by 10am rowing in a charity event with Matthew Pinsent. Getting into the boat was difficult, the rowing was fine but then getting out again was quite awkward.'

Explanation of placing system

Each London Marathon year in this register is divided up into four categories: first, a summary of the **Elite Athletes**, containing names (last, first) and times (hours : minutes : seconds) of the top 50 male runners, top 50 female runners, top 3 male and top 2 female wheelchair entrants; then **Male Runners**, **Female Runners** and **Wheelchair Entrants**. These last three sections display the individual names and times of *every* entrant, including elite athletes, alphabetically and with their overall finishing position in that year's Marathon displayed in brackets alongside.

Some entrants have chosen to enhance past London Marathon entries with photos and recollections online at www.aubreybooks.com. Please visit the website to find out more about appearing in future editions.

— ELITE ATHLETES —

Top 50 male runners

Lel, Martin	2:07:26
Gharib, Jaouad	2:07:49
Ramaala, Hendrick	2:08:32
El Mouaziz, Abdelkader	2:09:03
Baldini, Stefano	2:09:25
Brown, Jon	2:09:31
Suwa, Toshinari	2:10:23
Tergat, Paul	2:11:38
Korir, Sammy	2:12:36
Rutto, Evans	2:12:49
Cherono, Fredrick	2:13:58
Pena, Antonio	2:14:31
Lobb, Huw	2:14:33
Tadesse, Kassa	2:15:09
Njenga, Daniel	2:15:25
Smith, Matt	2:16:23
Kibet, Luke	2:16:40
Winton, Scott	2:17:01
Green, Michael	2:18:31
Norman, Dave	2:18:34
Sandstad, Henrik	2:18:36
Taylor, David W	2:18:47
Jones, Andi	2:18:53
Achmueller, Hermann	2:18:56
Coleman, Mike	2:19:42
Raven, Gareth	2:20:00
Cooray, Anuradah	2:20:16
McFarlane, John	2:20:54
Lambert, Toby	2:21:24
Szalkai, Anders	2:21:27
Fisher, Ian	2:21:40
Wilkinson, Neil	2:22:12
Leighton, Nigel	2:22:23
Birchall, Chris	2:22:24
Peigne, Vincent	2:23:17
Mitchinson, Dave	2:24:01

Proudlove, Michael J	2:24:02
Harkness, Ian R	2:24:10
Weir, Andrew P	2:24:21
Altmann, Nick A	2:24:38
Muir, AC	2:24:53
Rees-Jones, Steve M	2:25:07
Shaw, Matt	2:25:12
Hamidi, Said	2:25:17
Vedrine, David	2:25:25
Macdonald, Stewart F	2:26:21
Le-Borgne, Nicolas	2:26:22
Van Zyl, Anton	2:26:23
Baker, Julian D	2:26:42
Moroncini, Fauzio	2:26:52

Top 50 female runners

Radcliffe, Paula	2:17:42
Dita, Constantina	2:22:50
Chepkemei, Susan	2:24:00
Okayo, Margaret	2:25:22
Petrova, Lyudmila	2:26:29
Johnson, Benita	2:26:32
Chepchumba, Joyce	2:27:01
O'Sullivan, Sonia	2:29:01
Seboka, Mulu	2:30:54
Yamauchi, Mara	2:31:52
Loroupe, Tegla	2:34:42
Haining, Hayley	2:35:23
Mason, Debbie	2:36:59
Yelling, Liz	2:37:42
Partridge, Sue	2:37:50
Hassell, Lucy	2:39:20
Stiles, Amy	2:39:37
Harrison, Sue	2:39:54
Morris, Sharon	2:40:18
Clague, Jenny	2:41:21
Shelley, Lauren K	2:41:42

Yingjie, Sun	2:42:05
Appleton, Deborah J	2:42:24
Powell, Pauline P	2:43:26
Keddie, Gill	2:44:17
Braham, Alice R	2:45:06
Watson, Louise C	2:47:00
Mercado, Yolanda	2:47:47
May, Holly G	2:48:47
Murray, Jenny D	2:49:01
Oakes, Fiona L	2:49:56
Webster, Katy M	2:50:46
Archer, Emma J	2:51:36
Stott, Jamie H	2:52:24
Hartney, Liz E	2:52:30
Briggs, Julie L	2:52:45
Deasy, Margaret A	2:53:23
McIntosh, Toni	2:53:39
Fiddes, Gemma B	2:53:44
Cowley, Laura J	2:53:47
Crowle, Revis	2:53:57
Salt, Adela M	2:53:59
Bird, Nicola E	2:54:10
Le Good, Nicola J	2:54:30
Thornburgh, Zoe K	2:54:56
Wood, Sophie M	2:54:57
Myers, Malindi E	2:55:30
Hazlitt, Karen	2:55:44
Murphy, Christine	2:55:53
Naylor, Christine M	2:55:54

Top 3 male and top 2 female wheelchair entrants

Mendoza, Saul	1:35:51
Adams, Jeff	1:35:54
Weir, David	1:36:03
Porcellato, Francesca	1:56:59
Woods, Shelly	1:57:03

MALE RUNNERS

Abado, Michel ... 4:13:02 (13,888)
Abbas Syed, Isaura M ... 5:14:24 (28,245)
Abbassi-Ghadi, Behrouz ... 6:16:22 (33,799)
Abbey, Nick J ... 4:12:24 (13,726)
Abbot, Brian ... 5:39:11 (31,332)
Abbott, Bruce J ... 4:25:37 (17,321)
Abbott, Colin J ... 6:37:50 (34,453)
Abbott, Craig ... 4:42:21 (21,705)
Abbott, Gyles ... 3:42:39 (6,492)
Abbott, John L ... 5:25:14 (29,774)
Abbott, Jon S ... 4:45:01 (22,333)
Abbott, Jonathan P ... 3:15:43 (2,542)
Abbott, Julian C ... 3:15:44 (2,544)
Abbott, Paul ... 4:02:32 (11,283)
Abbott, Peter G ... 4:15:48 (14,660)
Abbott, Peter G ... 4:29:56 (18,573)
Abel, Lawrence J ... 3:06:20 (1,579)
Ab-Elwyn, Rhys ... 2:54:59 (740)
Abercrombie, Graham L ... 4:13:16 (13,955)
Ablett, Alan ... 4:21:33 (16,217)
Ablett, Richard A ... 7:15:37 (35,039)
Ablewhite, Jonathan D ... 4:43:09 (21,902)
Abley, Bev J ... 5:18:40 (28,900)
Aboulfaraj, Hani A ... 4:11:50 (13,570)
Abousselam, Michael ... 3:23:49 (3,423)
Abraham, Doninic ... 4:30:45 (18,784)
Abraham, Philip I ... 3:39:31 (5,917)
Abraham, Richard J ... 4:21:57 (16,317)
Abrahams, Michael S ... 3:37:48 (5,618)
Abrahams, Trevor R ... 4:49:32 (23,365)
Abrahim, Harold S ... 3:59:06 (10,469)
Abram, Barry E ... 3:05:45 (1,535)
Abram, Ron R ... 4:45:04 (22,342)
Abreu, Ivair R ... 4:48:35 (23,143)
Abrey, Russell J ... 3:41:03 (6,192)
Absous, Olivier ... 3:44:50 (6,919)
Achatz, Frank ... 4:46:03 (22,562)
Acheson, Alan D ... 5:15:04 (28,345)
Acheson, Marc ... 4:57:56 (25,307)
Acheson, Timothy I ... 3:33:21 (4,938)
Achmueller, Hermann ... 2:18:56 (25)
Ackers, Chris J ... 3:45:18 (7,005)
Acton, Christy J ... 3:59:43 (10,635)
Acton, Robert P ... 3:21:23 (3,121)
Adair, Lucas B ... 4:47:27 (22,875)
Adam, David ... 3:35:11 (5,208)
Adams, Andrew C ... 3:24:52 (3,564)
Adams, Anthony K ... 4:00:32 (10,843)
Adams, Ben W ... 4:41:08 (21,428)
Adams, Chris J ... 4:43:14 (21,919)
Adams, Christopher D ... 3:40:39 (6,111)
Adams, Christopher J ... 3:13:20 (2,276)
Adams, Christopher J ... 3:30:21 (4,498)
Adams, Christopher P ... 3:53:50 (8,942)
Adams, David ... 4:53:42 (24,353)
Adams, David ... 5:38:57 (31,303)
Adams, David C ... 3:55:39 (9,411)
Adams, Douglas V ... 4:15:36 (14,607)
Adams, Guy R ... 3:45:05 (6,969)
Adams, Ian ... 4:38:52 (20,844)
Adams, Jack ... 5:10:35 (27,588)
Adams, John ... 4:39:14 (20,942)
Adams, John E ... 4:18:46 (15,452)
Adams, John H ... 4:12:55 (13,862)
Adams, John R ... 3:14:38 (2,433)
Adams, Mark ... 4:08:19 (12,645)
Adams, Mark J ... 4:58:59 (25,557)
Adams, Matthew H ... 4:45:59 (22,549)
Adams, Matthew J ... 3:51:55 (8,466)
Adams, Miguel C ... 3:55:32 (9,376)
Adams, Neil G ... 5:06:53 (27,039)
Adams, Paul A ... 4:45:25 (22,419)
Adams, Paul A ... 5:07:41 (27,172)
Adams, Peter F ... 5:02:42 (26,274)
Adams, Peter W ... 4:28:49 (18,254)
Adams, Phil ... 3:38:34 (5,735)
Adams, Scott S ... 6:59:16 (34,858)
Adams, Simon Q ... 5:38:57 (31,303)
Adams, Stephen J ... 4:27:14 (17,813)
Adams, Steve ... 2:53:58 (683)
Adams, Stuart L ... 4:40:28 (21,251)
Adams, Thomas J ... 2:52:55 (631)
Adams, Tom ... 5:07:06 (27,076)
Adams, Tony ... 5:50:34 (32,308)
Adams, William F ... 3:59:43 (10,635)
Adamson, James R ... 3:53:54 (8,953)
Adamson, Paul D ... 5:15:54 (28,466)
Adamson, Stuart ... 5:26:06 (29,883)
Adcock, Tony ... 3:59:20 (10,527)
Addington-Smith, James ... 4:33:20 (19,395)
Addison, Chris J ... 3:35:37 (5,285)
Addison, Guy C ... 3:48:17 (7,652)
Addison, Paul ... 3:10:07 (1,938)
Addison, Thomas E ... 5:00:03 (25,782)
Addy, David I ... 5:28:38 (30,202)
Addy, John B ... 3:08:10 (1,730)
Addy, Paul G ... 3:38:10 (5,677)
Ade Ondjobi, Peter ... 5:03:48 (26,484)
Adekoya, Anthony D ... 3:23:04 (3,308)
Adeleye, Michael ... 5:19:35 (29,048)
Adeline, Regis ... 3:33:40 (4,985)
Adelizzi, Stephano A ... 5:01:50 (26,114)
Adey, Matt ... 3:28:11 (4,141)
Adey, Matthew J ... 3:56:22 (9,623)
Adeyemo, Tony ... 4:37:08 (20,399)
Adibe, Chuck O ... 5:33:30 (30,725)
Adkin, Carl F ... 5:05:02 (26,690)
Adkins, David D ... 3:07:01 (1,637)
Adkins, Simon ... 3:44:02 (6,749)
Adkins, Tony F ... 4:09:56 (13,079)
Adlam, Chris ... 3:29:34 (4,367)
Adlam, David P ... 4:45:06 (22,354)
Adlam, Hugh ... 3:53:47 (8,930)
Adlam, Michael J ... 4:23:49 (16,808)
Adlard, Simon C ... 3:14:31 (2,420)
Adler, Thomas J ... 4:09:04 (12,846)
Admoni, Assaf ... 4:16:45 (14,902)
Adriaanse, Johannes G ... 4:42:12 (21,676)
Adshead, Colin T ... 4:26:44 (17,672)
Adu, Stephen ... 5:23:28 (29,538)
Aenderkerk, Wilfried ... 2:53:32 (661)
Aerschmann, Joseph ... 4:54:32 (24,559)
Affleck, Michael V ... 3:36:52 (5,473)
Afshar, Dan ... 3:28:00 (4,104)
Agar, Thomas P ... 4:29:12 (18,365)
Agates, Alan R ... 4:38:16 (20,689)
Agbamu, Alexander O ... 3:53:00 (8,717)
Ager, Gary W ... 6:04:40 (33,252)
Ageros, Benjamin ... 3:11:21 (2,067)
Aggett, Neil R ... 3:38:45 (5,765)
Aghanian, Raffi ... 4:31:08 (18,862)
Agnew, Douglas J ... 4:22:19 (16,425)
Agrawal, David N ... 3:23:02 (3,304)
Agrawal, Deepak ... 5:10:39 (27,597)
Agui, Taro ... 2:43:21 (277)
Ahern, David J ... 4:30:21 (18,690)
Ahir, Anil ... 3:54:21 (9,062)
Ahlin, Joakim N ... 5:10:34 (27,582)
Ahmed, Ismael ... 5:33:39 (30,745)
Ahmed, Maher ... 4:19:42 (15,721)
Ahmed, Sheeraz ... 4:20:32 (15,943)
Ahmed, Waleed ... 5:28:19 (30,170)
Ahmet, Sol ... 3:46:42 (7,284)
Ahmetoglu, Mehmet ... 4:16:37 (14,866)
Ah-Mouck, Gilbert ... 4:42:38 (21,781)
Ahrling, Christian ... 4:08:25 (12,675)
Ahuja, Anand S ... 5:32:59 (30,671)
Ahumada, Jorge ... 4:03:45 (11,559)
Aiken, Scott M ... 3:22:54 (3,283)
Aillet, Luc ... 4:03:14 (11,440)
Aimable, Michael ... 6:30:13 (34,261)
Ainscow, Edward K ... 3:22:07 (3,202)
Ainslie, Paul ... 3:19:23 (2,921)
Ainsworth, Martin S ... 3:14:13 (2,383)
Ainsworth, Peter J ... 3:28:06 (4,126)
Ainsworth, Richard C ... 5:21:36 (29,300)
Ainsworth, Timothy G ... 6:46:40 (34,648)
Aird, Tim R ... 4:56:34 (25,029)
Aitchison, John ... 5:58:18 (32,861)
Aitken, Mark E ... 3:35:47 (5,308)
Aitken, Mike A ... 3:35:14 (5,213)
Aitken, Raymond C ... 3:33:57 (5,036)
Aitken, Willam ... 3:49:09 (7,854)
Aitkinson, Duncan J ... 4:16:57 (14,944)
Akast, Tim ... 4:54:13 (24,479)
Akbar, Gul ... 4:05:36 (12,006)
Aked, Matthew J ... 4:45:02 (22,337)
Aked, Peter A ... 2:54:26 (707)
Aked, Terry B ... 6:06:31 (33,362)
Akenhead, David ... 6:04:47 (33,256)
Akerman, Paul R ... 4:57:25 (25,215)
Akers, Neil ... 4:02:39 (11,303)
Akhtar, Mohammed Z ... 4:08:45 (12,755)
Akhtar, Raihan ... 4:36:10 (20,122)
Akhurst, Graeme A ... 3:53:39 (8,896)
Akhurst, Iain ... 2:48:54 (463)
Akindolie, Akintunde O ... 7:29:08 (35,120)
Akinkugbe, Olugbenga ... 4:57:06 (25,154)
Akinluyi, Timothy O ... 5:41:48 (31,578)
Aksland, Sverre ... 2:48:32 (441)
Alaka, Aderemi M ... 5:08:04 (27,229)
Albers, Hartmut ... 3:23:16 (3,345)
Albon, Christopher J ... 4:57:14 (25,181)
Albrecht, Chris ... 4:15:21 (14,537)
Alcock, David ... 3:13:23 (2,289)
Alcock, Michael ... 4:51:01 (23,736)
Alcon, John ... 5:21:46 (29,323)
Alcraft, Nicholas J ... 3:52:09 (8,517)
Alden, Gareth J ... 5:00:15 (25,831)
Alden, Jonathan S ... 4:39:01 (20,885)
Alden, Stephen R ... 3:24:39 (3,533)
Alderson, David ... 4:16:02 (14,724)
Alderson, David ... 5:01:24 (26,044)
Alderson, Paul ... 4:02:51 (11,352)
Alderton, Colin N ... 5:00:43 (25,920)
Aldrich, Gary ... 5:34:38 (30,868)
Aldridge, David R ... 4:40:57 (21,375)
Aldridge, Michael J ... 4:43:55 (22,077)
Aldunate, Patricio ... 5:17:27 (28,705)
Aldus, Daniel ... 4:10:12 (13,140)
Aldwinckle, John C ... 2:56:02 (808)
Aldworth, David ... 4:14:20 (14,251)
Alexander, Anthony M ... 3:49:55 (8,021)
Alexander, Brian M ... 5:34:15 (30,813)
Alexander, Christopher I ... 4:07:20 (12,427)
Alexander, David W ... 4:47:58 (22,997)
Alexander, John S ... 3:46:37 (7,266)
Alexander, Mark I ... 4:32:58 (19,307)
Alexander, Mark K ... 3:24:39 (3,533)
Alexander, Philip J ... 6:16:52 (33,818)
Alexander, Scott J ... 4:39:30 (21,013)
Alexander, Stephen J ... 3:47:02 (7,357)
Alexander, Thomas G ... 5:01:23 (26,039)
Alford, Carl M ... 4:51:32 (23,841)
Alford, Mark J ... 4:34:51 (19,804)
Alford, Paul F ... 3:51:00 (8,257)
Alford, Robert L ... 4:49:48 (23,449)
Algacs, Dezso J ... 9:13:51 (35,255)
Algar, Neil J ... 5:33:12 (30,689)
Algra, James ... 5:57:35 (32,810)
Ali, Altan H ... 4:15:44 (14,647)
Ali, Aziz I ... 5:24:41 (29,708)
Ali, Liton ... 5:46:36 (31,989)
Ali, Majid ... 4:25:55 (17,404)
Ali, Sharafat ... 4:38:33 (20,764)
Alim, Omar ... 4:34:37 (19,740)
Al-Janabi, Laith I ... 4:52:26 (24,037)
Alkins, John S ... 5:43:58 (31,759)
Allam, Keith ... 3:24:17 (3,480)
Allan, Alistair G ... 3:02:27 (1,294)
Allan, Ash R ... 3:57:12 (9,891)
Allan, Graham D ... 3:30:09 (4,470)
Allan, Marcus J ... 5:12:56 (27,988)
Allan, Peter D ... 3:35:35 (5,276)
Allan, Robert W ... 5:27:21 (30,021)
Allan, Thomas S ... 5:36:00 (30,992)
Allan, Tony ... 4:43:59 (22,094)
Allan, William ... 2:59:31 (1,090)
Allard, David ... 6:22:16 (34,001)
Allard, Paul ... 5:20:08 (29,120)
Allard, Charles J Jnr ... 3:04:38 (1,439)
Allaway, Dennis ... 4:08:21 (12,659)
Allbones, Stephen D ... 3:21:55 (3,174)
Allcock, Chris N ... 4:08:08 (12,598)
Allder, Colin R ... 4:11:53 (13,581)
Allegretti, Francesco F ... 3:29:16 (4,324)
Allegris, Christophe ... 5:21:09 (29,255)
Allen, Andrew J ... 4:09:39 (12,999)

Allen, Andrew J 4:16:18 (14,793)
Allen, Bradley J..........3:51:41 (8,408)
Allen, Brian 4:37:32 (20,502)
Allen, Charlie 4:06:32 (12,221)
Allen, Christopher 4:23:14 (16,661)
Allen, Daren P..........3:44:39 (6,868)
Allen, David J..........2:46:25 (358)
Allen, Derek 5:10:34 (27,582)
Allen, Derek J..........4:25:56 (17,409)
Allen, Gavin P..........3:31:40 (4,703)
Allen, Gavin R 3:26:57 (3,921)
Allen, George 5:13:06 (28,013)
Allen, Hugh N..........3:21:39 (3,144)
Allen, Ian..........4:11:31 (13,486)
Allen, James N..........3:06:50 (1,622)
Allen, Jimmy R 4:24:15 (16,915)
Allen, Jon C..........5:42:37 (31,639)
Allen, Jonathan P 5:04:24 (26,583)
Allen, Jonathan R..........3:30:49 (4,581)
Allen, Julian..........3:57:29 (9,973)
Allen, Julian..........4:38:20 (20,704)
Allen, Kai 4:32:00 (19,087)
Allen, Keith W..........5:02:16 (26,194)
Allen, Kevin 3:06:55 (1,629)
Allen, Kevin 4:22:01 (16,343)
Allen, Lee M..........6:06:37 (33,363)
Allen, Luke..........4:32:00 (19,087)
Allen, Malcolm G 3:45:24 (7,030)
Allen, Mark I 3:08:14 (1,736)
Allen, Martin S 3:33:34 (4,966)
Allen, Matt..........2:48:53 (461)
Allen, Matthew J..........4:14:09 (14,194)
Allen, Michael E..........6:20:56 (33,951)
Allen, Patrick R 5:29:27 (30,302)
Allen, Patrick T 4:11:11 (13,402)
Allen, Peter A..........3:43:45 (6,693)
Allen, Philip..........3:50:55 (8,239)
Allen, Philip J 5:06:30 (26,964)
Allen, Philip R..........4:13:00 (13,878)
Allen, Richard D 6:22:59 (34,020)
Allen, Stephen R..........3:35:23 (5,237)
Allen, Stephen T..........4:48:09 (23,042)
Allen, Steve..........3:37:57 (5,638)
Allen, Steven R..........5:22:20 (29,388)
Allen, Stuart E..........4:00:56 (10,935)
Allen, Wayne R..........4:12:01 (13,628)
Allender, Karl A..........3:41:33 (6,287)
Allenway, Matthew J 4:49:02 (23,246)
Allen-Wielebnowski, Tobi O 4:22:43 (16,540)
Allers, Johann..........4:06:02 (12,102)
Allerton, David C 5:56:30 (32,732)
Allerton, Josh..........2:56:35 (849)
Alleyne, Christopher M 5:16:27 (28,540)
Allford, Simon J..........3:22:21 (3,231)
Allingham, Richard..........4:48:44 (23,175)
Allison, Gordon A 3:24:23 (3,504)
Allison, Nicholas 3:41:59 (6,372)
Allison, Robert M..........4:19:25 (15,643)
Allison, Stuart R 4:16:40 (14,881)
Alliston, Andrew J 5:26:52 (29,959)
Allmark, Terence V..........4:52:10 (23,979)
Allnutt, Hans 5:36:26 (31,043)
Allovard, Herve 2:48:48 (458)
Allport, Jeremy C 4:52:55 (24,153)
Allport, Trevor A 3:00:52 (1,183)
Allsop, Timothy..........3:43:18 (6,620)
Allsopp, Brian..........5:19:42 (29,060)
Allsopp, Craig..........3:03:47 (1,388)
Allsopp, Tim D 4:11:29 (13,482)
Allum, Peter A..........4:30:58 (18,829)
Almashan, Leon 4:46:32 (22,675)
Almeida, Paulo I..........4:15:49 (14,669)
Almeida, Salvador 3:52:44 (8,670)
Almey, Richard B..........4:01:31 (11,052)
Almgren, Tor..........2:48:33 (442)
Almond, Steve J..........2:48:55 (464)
Alongi, Luca 4:10:16 (13,160)
Alovisi, Julian..........3:38:34 (5,735)
Alpendre, Miguel 3:44:05 (6,756)
Alqassar, Laith 5:49:04 (32,189)
Al-Salim, Atheer..........4:10:04 (13,106)
Alsbury, Simon F 5:34:33 (30,850)
Alston, Richard A..........3:32:08 (4,764)
Alstowe, David J..........4:36:11 (20,125)
Altmann, Nick A..........2:24:38 (43)
Alty, Robert..........5:56:35 (32,738)
Alwash, Craig..........2:53:11 (643)
Alzaga, Raul E..........4:06:49 (12,288)
Amans, John D 3:41:49 (6,341)
Amarjit, Singh Gill 5:53:42 (32,546)
Amatt, Robert..........3:30:14 (4,483)
Ambler, David G..........4:18:46 (15,452)
Ambler, Richard J..........6:12:45 (33,653)
Ambler, Robin G 4:13:01 (13,886)
Ambler, Stuart P 6:47:46 (34,672)
Ambrosio, Carlos..........4:23:17 (16,683)
Amendola, Antonio 4:35:14 (19,895)
Amery, Leigh P..........5:10:43 (27,604)
Amery, Nathan G..........3:59:07 (10,473)
Ames, Mark L 3:39:42 (5,951)
Ames, Matthew D 4:49:54 (23,473)
Amin, Saj 4:58:48 (25,510)
Amjid, Imtiaz..........5:23:08 (29,497)
Amla, Ismail..........3:58:13 (10,199)
Ammon, Donald W..........4:34:52 (19,811)
Amoils, Matthew..........2:57:27 (919)
Amoo, Paul J..........3:27:46 (4,071)
Amos, Anthony P 4:21:41 (16,252)
Amos, James B..........4:40:28 (21,251)
Amoss, Andy..........4:26:09 (17,492)
Amphlett, Neil R 4:21:33 (16,217)
Amusan, Kunle..........5:30:59 (30,467)
Anders, Garry..........5:20:03 (29,107)
Andersen, Bjarne 4:11:11 (13,402)
Anderson, Alan 5:27:14 (30,004)
Anderson, Alan T..........4:36:12 (20,127)
Anderson, Brian M..........4:09:43 (13,016)
Anderson, Brian P..........3:25:02 (3,589)
Anderson, Daniel J..........2:32:02 (86)
Anderson, Garreth W 4:02:46 (11,335)
Anderson, Gavin S 4:26:49 (17,692)
Anderson, Ian D..........4:34:26 (19,699)
Anderson, Ian D..........6:46:31 (34,643)
Anderson, James D..........3:34:07 (5,063)
Anderson, James H 3:53:42 (8,909)
Anderson, Mark 4:20:42 (15,991)
Anderson, Mark R..........3:06:21 (1,580)
Anderson, Michael R 3:01:28 (1,214)
Anderson, Neil J..........3:58:11 (10,184)
Anderson, Paul S..........4:33:51 (19,533)
Anderson, Robert C..........4:12:36 (13,774)
Anderson, Rory 4:16:15 (14,781)
Anderson, Roy..........5:37:28 (31,138)
Anderson, Scott L 3:54:05 (8,992)
Anderson, Scott M 4:27:42 (17,951)
Anderson, Stephen J..........4:12:14 (13,679)
Anderson, Stephen J..........5:10:05 (27,518)
Anderson, Steven R..........5:12:33 (27,919)
Anderson, Stuart S 3:54:46 (9,176)
Anderson, Tony..........5:11:20 (27,712)
Anderson, Warwick A..........3:53:57 (8,964)
Anderson-Cole, Adam D..........4:47:05 (22,790)
Anderssen, Knut..........4:07:53 (12,550)
Andersson, Johnny..........5:37:19 (31,118)
Andersson, Mattias..........3:26:29 (3,844)
Andrea, Grant K..........4:14:02 (14,158)
Andreassen, John-Arild..........4:05:03 (11,878)
Andrés-Arranz, Rafael..........3:23:41 (3,398)
Andreson, Lindsay 3:31:22 (4,662)
Andrew, Christian W..........4:33:35 (19,459)
Andrew, Clive..........3:49:17 (7,887)
Andrew, Darren M 3:54:37 (9,126)
Andrew, Duncan..........4:56:59 (25,126)
Andrew, Kevin J..........3:49:17 (7,887)
Andrew, Michael 4:22:01 (16,343)
Andrew, Sam M 2:58:02 (958)
Andrew, Stuart..........3:57:31 (9,988)
Andrews, Damian S 4:29:00 (18,306)
Andrews, Daniel P..........5:11:12 (27,687)
Andrews, David..........3:13:12 (2,267)
Andrews, David J 3:55:52 (9,480)
Andrews, Dean R..........4:00:26 (10,813)
Andrews, James 3:53:55 (8,958)
Andrews, James 5:13:52 (28,144)
Andrews, John I..........4:27:21 (17,838)
Andrews, John J..........6:05:53 (33,323)
Andrews, Jonathan J..........6:07:18 (33,405)
Andrews, Julian R..........4:05:32 (11,996)
Andrews, Marin J..........2:54:05 (691)
Andrews, Mark 5:09:03 (27,359)
Andrews, Mark J 3:40:51 (6,157)
Andrews, Mark V..........3:22:33 (3,249)
Andrews, Martin N..........4:33:39 (19,473)
Andrews, Matthew..........3:34:52 (5,166)
Andrews, Michael..........4:01:23 (11,020)
Andrews, Neil K..........4:49:18 (23,306)
Andrews, Nicholas L 3:41:23 (6,255)
Andrews, Nicolas H..........4:41:52 (21,602)
Andrews, Paul A 5:49:16 (32,208)
Andrews, Peter R..........3:21:09 (3,100)
Andrews, Roger D 4:46:08 (22,585)
Andrews, Simon G 5:14:37 (28,283)
Andrews, Simon K..........3:51:50 (8,449)
Andrews, Timothy A 5:39:50 (31,400)
Andrzesewski, Stanley M..........5:22:59 (29,486)
Angel, Andrew R 5:04:30 (26,599)
Angel, Anthony L..........4:28:29 (18,162)
Angel, Martin 4:00:53 (10,927)
Angell, Keith E 5:48:04 (32,099)
Angioletti, Paolo Severino..........3:48:46 (7,777)
Angol, Michael 5:20:25 (29,165)
Angold, Christopher F..........4:57:55 (25,304)
Angus, Gerald..........3:38:51 (5,784)
Angus, Stephen A..........5:59:28 (32,944)
Angus, Stuart J..........7:04:56 (34,924)
Angus, Thomas..........5:45:11 (31,867)
Angus, Wayne M..........5:58:26 (32,868)
Anibaba, Ade..........4:31:12 (18,884)
Anibaba, Deji..........5:47:26 (32,054)
Aniello, Roberto..........3:35:49 (5,310)
Annals, Marc J 3:40:43 (6,123)
Annett, Alex C..........5:19:33 (29,042)
Annette, Colin S..........5:26:22 (29,907)
Annis, Mark J..........4:02:20 (11,226)
Anrude, Edward W..........4:13:25 (13,993)
Ansari, Asif..........5:52:26 (32,456)
Anscombe, Matthew H 4:09:47 (13,035)
Ansell, Martin J..........4:21:28 (16,195)
Ansell, Richard P..........2:51:18 (550)
Anstee, Nick J..........3:57:35 (10,007)
Antcliffe, Mark J..........3:11:09 (2,045)
Anthony, Gabriel S..........3:38:03 (5,656)
Anthony, Thomas..........4:59:17 (25,623)
Anthun, Bjoern..........5:00:51 (25,946)
Antoine, Jean-Stephane..........4:31:26 (18,951)
Antonoff, Nicolas..........4:53:22 (24,265)
Antony, Murray S..........3:16:45 (2,656)
Antony, Scott G 2:53:18 (650)
Anttila, Petri J..........4:18:48 (15,464)
Antwis, Mark R 5:44:40 (31,816)
Anwar, Aresh J 4:26:06 (17,475)
Anyon, Michael S 7:13:00 (35,016)
Ap Gwilym, Llywelyn..........4:17:40 (15,130)
Aponte, Carlos J 4:32:06 (19,109)
Appavoo, Soondra M..........5:01:01 (25,978)
Appel, Peter..........3:07:28 (1,674)
Apperley, Ian 3:47:11 (7,386)
Apperley, Ian J..........3:14:39 (2,437)
Appiah, Louis L..........5:34:16 (30,815)
Applebee, John 3:58:44 (10,363)
Appleby, Glenn M 4:43:49 (22,058)
Appleby, Paul H..........4:12:44 (13,811)
Appleby, Paul R..........4:12:45 (13,817)
Appleby, Rodney J..........3:26:08 (3,783)
Applegate, Philip S..........3:54:41 (9,149)
Appleing, David N..........4:00:35 (10,865)
Appleton, Brian..........4:52:18 (24,014)
Appleton, Ian 3:58:18 (10,227)
Appleton, Paul A..........5:16:58 (28,642)
Appleyard, Andrew D 5:54:41 (32,611)
Apps, Michael J 6:23:21 (34,033)
Aprahamian, Miran W..........3:38:34 (5,735)
Apte, Shirish M..........4:53:30 (24,300)
Apthorp, Miles Q 4:34:52 (19,811)
Apthorp, Rupert J 4:05:37 (12,008)
Arakaki, Yoshinori..........3:53:30 (8,855)
Arbery, Giles R..........5:17:10 (28,671)
Arbib, Benjamin G..........4:14:03 (14,164)
Arch, Alex J..........4:10:18 (13,169)

Archer, Andrew N 3:59:45 (10,649)
Archer, Anthony W 3:09:31 (1,858)
Archer, Paul 4:34:32 (19,722)
Archer, Raymond 5:46:20 (31,966)
Archer, Steven W 4:39:06 (20,901)
Archer, Thomas J 5:26:01 (29,869)
Archer, Tim J 4:37:16 (20,433)
Archibald, Andrew D 4:36:22 (20,188)
Archibald, Paul G 3:26:07 (3,781)
Archman, Philip A 3:41:19 (6,238)
Argent, Alan W 4:46:20 (22,629)
Argent, Dean J 4:37:07 (20,391)
Argyle, Paul G 5:10:53 (27,634)
Arimaldi, Marco 3:21:08 (3,097)
Ariolli, Giovanni 3:14:53 (2,470)
Arkill, Lloyd A 4:22:21 (16,435)
Arlette, Mica J 3:50:25 (8,131)
Arlott, Mick C 4:27:52 (18,005)
Armist, Ronald 3:49:35 (7,948)
Armistead, Hugo W 4:00:41 (10,883)
Armit, Tim 3:54:05 (8,992)
Armitage, Alan C 5:00:26 (25,868)
Armitage, Dave J 4:29:32 (18,476)
Armitage, John W 4:41:24 (21,498)
Armitage, Mark E 3:55:30 (9,368)
Armitage, Mark R 4:41:23 (21,489)
Armitage, Neil 3:34:14 (5,086)
Armour, Stuart 5:14:18 (28,231)
Armstrong, Chris R 4:34:16 (19,654)
Armstrong, Christopher J 5:32:57 (30,666)
Armstrong, Damian M 3:46:07 (7,164)
Armstrong, David J 3:04:26 (1,422)
Armstrong, David P 3:58:19 (10,232)
Armstrong, George 3:36:42 (5,454)
Armstrong, Ian 3:26:43 (3,887)
Armstrong, James 5:43:33 (31,724)
Armstrong, James L 7:29:44 (35,125)
Armstrong, John 3:56:07 (9,543)
Armstrong, Lee 5:40:32 (31,472)
Armstrong, Mark A 4:01:02 (10,954)
Armstrong, Neil A 4:56:18 (24,965)
Armstrong, Nigel J 2:53:20 (652)
Armstrong, Paul G 4:53:00 (24,174)
Armstrong, Peter H 3:09:49 (1,899)
Armstrong, Robert 5:26:23 (29,908)
Armstrong, Robert J 3:08:33 (1,762)
Armstrong, Robert J 3:16:31 (2,636)
Arnaud, Luc 4:41:53 (21,603)
Arnaud, Paul 4:18:31 (15,364)
Arnefalk, Roger 4:33:44 (19,499)
Arnel, Philip R 4:44:09 (22,129)
Arnel, Richard J 4:44:09 (22,129)
Arnell, Daniel S 3:54:28 (9,093)
Arney, Robert J 5:45:50 (31,925)
Arnold, Andrew 4:13:52 (14,105)
Arnold, Andrew T 5:16:41 (28,573)
Arnold, Daryl L 3:16:59 (2,674)
Arnold, Dave 3:10:29 (1,977)
Arnold, David M 4:28:18 (18,111)
Arnold, James M 4:15:53 (14,682)
Arnold, Martin R 3:44:33 (6,848)
Arnold, Matthew B 3:56:33 (9,675)
Arnold, Nicholas J 5:04:51 (26,658)
Arnold, Richard D 4:55:42 (24,818)
Arnold, Richard G 6:43:58 (34,600)
Arnold, Simon E 5:08:51 (27,331)
Arnold, Simon P 3:48:31 (7,715)
Arnold, Stephen 6:27:04 (34,162)
Arnold, Stephen C 5:27:04 (29,982)
Arnold, Terence A 4:14:10 (14,201)
Arondel, Bruno 3:21:19 (3,117)
Arrowsmith, James 4:08:43 (12,743)
Arrowsmith, Timothy J 4:15:42 (14,636)
Arteaga, Rafael 4:41:00 (21,395)
Arthey, Chris 3:12:14 (2,168)
Arthur, Antony 4:00:21 (10,794)
Arthur, Luke 3:44:30 (6,836)
Arthur, Paul D 4:53:39 (24,344)
Arthurton, Anthony W 4:02:02 (11,167)
Arvasli, Alf R 4:53:57 (24,411)
Asberg, Stig 3:36:21 (5,401)
Aschwanden, Rolf 4:21:26 (16,188)
Asensio, José M 3:59:41 (10,627)
Asfaha, Amaniel A 4:40:32 (21,267)
Asgeirsson, Sveinn 2:56:38 (854)
Ash, David 4:28:47 (18,241)
Ash, David G 5:00:13 (25,823)
Ash, Jason J 4:21:17 (16,140)
Ash, Phillip J 4:44:56 (22,307)
Ashbolt, David W 4:48:34 (23,135)
Ashburn, Justin P 3:53:17 (8,792)
Ashburn, Rob 4:41:29 (21,518)
Ashburner, Alan 3:14:36 (2,430)
Ashby, Charles E 3:18:48 (2,861)
Ashby, Derren J 4:46:21 (22,635)
Ashby, Gerald 4:58:27 (25,429)
Ashby, James S 4:03:14 (11,440)
Ashby, Jonathan 4:32:35 (19,225)
Ashby, Mark 3:10:24 (1,967)
Ashby, Mark 3:30:56 (4,595)
Ashby, Mark R 4:19:43 (15,727)
Ashby, Nick C 3:51:42 (8,412)
Ashby, Paul 3:23:10 (3,326)
Ashby, Thomas S 4:22:55 (16,585)
Ashcombe, Mark G 3:26:45 (3,894)
Ashcroft, Anthony G 4:52:45 (24,114)
Ashcroft, Christopher 4:11:25 (13,458)
Ashcroft, Paul S 4:10:59 (13,345)
Ashelford, Tim J 2:58:58 (1,031)
Ashenden, Simon V 4:56:08 (24,925)
Ashforth, Alan 3:09:56 (1,912)
Ashley, Paul M 3:27:03 (3,936)
Ashley, Richard C 4:53:08 (24,205)
Ashley, Simon W 4:36:57 (20,343)
Ashman, Rod J 4:24:45 (17,059)
Ashmore, Philip M 4:39:52 (21,101)
Ashpool, Gavin D 4:09:18 (12,908)
Ashraf, Muhammad 4:33:41 (19,485)
Ashraf, Shahbaz 4:31:33 (18,986)
Ashton, Alan 3:30:12 (4,476)
Ashton, Antony R 3:28:02 (4,109)
Ashton, Jeffrey 3:37:52 (5,629)
Ashton, Jonathan 4:28:54 (18,274)
Ashton, Neil G 4:18:05 (15,231)
Ashton, Stephen M 5:10:54 (27,638)
Ashurst, Bernard 4:33:04 (19,330)
Ashurst, Simon P 4:32:27 (19,196)
Ashwell, Benjamin P 5:02:16 (26,194)
Ashwell, Mark 3:16:06 (2,590)
Ashwell, Simon M 4:18:46 (15,452)
Ashwood, Keith E 4:14:15 (14,229)
Ashwood, Roger 3:45:01 (6,958)
Ashworth, Chris 3:18:47 (2,858)
Ashworth, Henry T 5:33:33 (30,732)
Ashworth, James R 4:34:30 (19,711)
Ashworth, John 3:57:35 (10,007)
Ashworth, Jonathan D 3:13:43 (2,328)
Ashworth, Luke C 4:20:37 (15,968)
Ashworth, Tim 4:20:27 (15,929)
Asiedu, Eric 4:07:43 (12,503)
Askew, Heath 3:33:51 (5,023)
Askew, Jason M 4:34:31 (19,721)
Askew, Phil M 3:54:08 (9,005)
Askew, Simeon M 3:47:50 (7,533)
Askin, Ciaran G 4:20:19 (15,892)
Aspden, Stephen 3:58:54 (10,408)
Aspel, Edward 4:52:36 (24,074)
Aspengren, Henrik C 4:53:32 (24,310)
Aspin, Christopher J 4:33:23 (19,403)
Aspin, James Gideon 3:55:44 (9,443)
Aspinall, Aaron J 3:38:37 (5,741)
Aspinall, Nathan E 2:59:23 (1,081)
Aspinall, Steven 5:43:55 (31,754)
Aspinall, Steven W 5:48:41 (32,150)
Aspinell, Mathew J 4:52:01 (23,939)
Asplen, David J 4:27:53 (18,007)
Asselin, Olivier 4:15:03 (14,464)
Asser, Gregory V 3:30:04 (4,463)
Assheton, David N 5:49:31 (32,226)
Assomull, Ravi G 5:11:47 (27,784)
Astin, David J 4:38:22 (20,718)
Astle, Ross L 4:09:06 (12,860)
Astle, Thomas W 3:22:35 (3,251)
Astles, Peter M 4:06:29 (12,209)
Aston, Andrew 2:50:21 (508)
Aston, Christopher 3:43:37 (6,672)
Aston, Edgar 3:57:55 (10,116)
Aston, Jeffrey R 3:47:02 (7,357)
Aston, John 3:10:36 (1,988)
Astruc, Olivier 3:49:51 (8,007)
Atfield, Paul E 4:23:53 (16,822)
Atherton, Graham 4:58:29 (25,438)
Atherton, John A 4:27:04 (17,765)
Atherton, Joseph G 4:00:20 (10,792)
Atherton, Mark J 4:14:58 (14,430)
Atherton, Myles D 3:38:15 (5,689)
Athey, Christopher A 3:45:01 (6,958)
Atkin, Alex P 3:37:01 (5,500)
Atkin, Oliver J 5:07:02 (27,061)
Atkin, Philip L 5:56:44 (32,752)
Atkin, Rob 4:25:10 (17,172)
Atkins, Gary J 4:34:45 (19,777)
Atkins, Ian 4:52:00 (23,936)
Atkins, John P 3:19:21 (2,915)
Atkins, Paul K 2:53:59 (686)
Atkins, Richard D 3:31:35 (4,690)
Atkins, Sean E 4:27:51 (17,998)
Atkins, Simon E 4:44:32 (22,217)
Atkins, Timothy 3:47:41 (7,496)
Atkins-Linnell, Steve A 4:18:16 (15,283)
Atkinson, Chris J 3:27:10 (3,951)
Atkinson, Christopher M 4:23:59 (16,844)
Atkinson, David 3:16:47 (2,662)
Atkinson, Dougal 4:14:10 (14,201)
Atkinson, Ian J 3:49:23 (7,908)
Atkinson, Michael J 5:38:28 (31,248)
Atkinson, Paul J 3:27:40 (4,054)
Atkinson, Robert J 5:01:42 (26,092)
Atkinson, Stephen R 3:37:59 (5,644)
Atkinson, Timothy 5:08:35 (27,296)
Atkinson Cox, Martin J 3:58:59 (10,427)
Atonen, Meelis 3:19:56 (2,989)
Attanasio, Andrea 3:54:23 (9,073)
Attewell, Clifford S 3:49:02 (7,831)
Attewell, Gary 3:27:18 (3,978)
Attlewell, John H 4:09:22 (12,926)
Attridge, Stephen A 3:54:54 (9,215)
Attwood, Alexander G 5:00:35 (25,893)
Attwood, Keith A 4:19:51 (15,764)
Attwood, Mark J 4:33:56 (19,554)
Attwood Smith, Nicholas W 3:24:46 (3,552)
Attwooll, Jolyon 2:54:41 (725)
Atwal, Sarvjit S 4:33:25 (19,409)
Au, Tobias 4:11:02 (13,361)
Auber, Daniel J 3:34:01 (5,051)
Aubry, Patrick 4:24:12 (16,901)
Audenshaw, Tony 3:03:07 (1,339)
Auger, Martin J 3:18:11 (2,802)
Augusto, Armellin 3:29:11 (4,311)
Auld, Nick 5:30:19 (30,397)
Auroy, Gerard 3:30:57 (4,598)
Austen, William S 3:56:14 (9,583)
Austin, Anthony 4:34:34 (19,732)
Austin, Barry E 5:28:07 (30,126)
Austin, Christopher W 3:24:28 (3,514)
Austin, Clive 3:53:09 (8,756)
Austin, Craig 2:56:46 (868)
Austin, David A 3:58:46 (10,375)
Austin, David J 4:30:27 (18,712)
Austin, Huw R 3:50:17 (8,099)
Austin, Jon 4:25:21 (17,227)
Austin, Mark S 4:58:48 (25,510)
Austin, Matthew J 5:48:52 (32,170)
Austin, Nicholas J 3:39:18 (5,868)
Austin, Peter K 4:22:14 (16,402)
Austin, Robert C 4:49:35 (23,381)
Austin, Robert W 5:35:56 (30,985)
Austin, Simon B 4:20:47 (16,017)
Austin, Simon J 4:24:00 (16,851)
Austin, Will R 4:00:24 (10,804)
Austin-Vautier, Harvey 4:26:33 (17,616)
Austin-White, David 5:21:35 (29,298)
Avar, Diethar 3:42:58 (6,537)
Averley, Richard F 4:53:30 (24,300)
Avery, Benjamin T 5:22:36 (29,440)
Avery, David S 4:24:00 (16,851)
Avery, Joe A 3:13:38 (2,319)
Avery, Lawrence J 4:43:03 (21,881)
Avery, Peter D 4:48:48 (23,192)

Avery, Peter N.	4:03:47 (11,569)	
Avery, Philip N.	5:04:49 (26,653)	
Avery, Steven J.	6:13:47 (33,691)	
Aves, Clayton A.	3:18:39 (2,843)	
Avey, John	4:58:37 (25,472)	
Avrili, Walter A.	4:25:25 (17,257)	
Awuah, Darren R.	5:48:39 (32,148)	
Axam, Gary L.	3:49:16 (7,883)	
Axelsen, Richard	4:32:33 (19,219)	
Axon, Edward	4:01:52 (11,119)	
Ayala-Angear, Edward E.	4:06:42 (12,266)	
Aycock, Russell J.	4:17:47 (15,154)	
Ayers, Robert J.	4:00:50 (10,910)	
Aylen, Gary D	5:02:51 (26,307)	
Ayles, Anthony	3:35:32 (5,267)	
Ayling, Colin J	4:04:57 (11,849)	
Ayling, John V	5:10:36 (27,592)	
Ayling, Terry J.	4:13:59 (14,141)	
Aylmer, Richard J	5:23:53 (29,601)	
Aylmore, James R	2:53:29 (660)	
Aylmore, Mark	4:57:42 (25,263)	
Aylott, Jason M	4:04:02 (11,646)	
Aylward, Robin A.	4:09:50 (13,049)	
Ayres, Laurie H	4:46:34 (22,684)	
Ayres, Lawrence	3:20:42 (3,062)	
Ayres, Max	3:46:37 (7,266)	
Ayres, Roger M	3:55:44 (9,443)	
Ayres, Terry B	4:04:59 (11,856)	
Ayton, Robert J	4:24:27 (16,977)	
Babb, Steve M.	2:59:33 (1,094)	
Baber, Duncan S.	5:22:49 (29,463)	
Babonau, David	5:05:46 (26,837)	
Bacchus, Tyrone	6:00:03 (32,984)	
Bach, Claude	4:00:32 (10,843)	
Bache, John	3:51:31 (8,373)	
Bachu, Abdalla	5:09:06 (27,370)	
Baci, Arber	2:43:21 (277)	
Back, Leon J	5:30:46 (30,439)	
Back, Nicholas J.	5:15:15 (28,378)	
Backhouse, Ian	5:14:10 (28,204)	
Backhurst, Tony	4:44:14 (22,152)	
Bacon, Clive	4:19:17 (15,604)	
Bacon, Gary	4:17:57 (15,189)	
Bacon, Paul A	4:56:09 (24,929)	
Bacon, Robert A.	4:53:38 (24,338)	
Bacon, Simon A.	5:26:56 (29,968)	
Bacon, Simon D	4:18:52 (15,479)	
Bacon, Steven	4:50:05 (23,508)	
Badger, Kenneth I.	4:17:16 (15,029)	
Badgery, Andrew	5:08:53 (27,337)	
Badgery, Stephen	3:13:02 (2,249)	
Badham, Neil A.	3:54:34 (9,116)	
Badillo, José	4:15:54 (14,683)	
Baer, Philip L.	3:25:13 (3,627)	
Baga, Satvinder	5:39:18 (31,351)	
Bagehot, Alex S	4:43:11 (21,911)	
Baggaley, David	5:26:17 (29,901)	
Baggaley, Geoffrey	3:37:25 (5,559)	
Baggaley, Henry W	4:17:15 (15,021)	
Baggaley, Oliver J	4:03:30 (11,498)	
Baggaley, Simon C.	5:14:04 (28,180)	
Baggs, Len	4:52:04 (23,954)	
Bagguley, Simon D	4:09:22 (12,926)	
Bagnall, Scott A.	4:31:02 (18,843)	
Bagshaw, Andrew	4:51:37 (23,855)	
Baid, Subodh	4:56:55 (25,117)	
Baigent, Mark J.	4:08:23 (12,664)	
Bailey, Adam D	4:10:03 (13,101)	
Bailey, Alan V.	5:04:06 (26,538)	
Bailey, Andrew I	4:56:26 (24,996)	
Bailey, Andy N	4:07:34 (12,467)	
Bailey, Barry	5:59:41 (32,958)	
Bailey, Chris J.	5:59:22 (32,937)	
Bailey, Christian N.	4:01:46 (11,104)	
Bailey, Colin	4:48:50 (23,195)	
Bailey, Curtis R	2:54:03 (688)	
Bailey, David A.	3:43:09 (6,581)	
Bailey, David D	4:39:16 (20,957)	
Bailey, David J	3:13:28 (2,296)	
Bailey, Duncan W	4:43:42 (22,033)	
Bailey, Frank J.	3:44:04 (6,751)	
Bailey, Graham J	4:47:00 (22,772)	
Bailey, Ian A.	4:43:29 (21,974)	

Bailey, Kevin	3:55:58 (9,508)	
Bailey, Kevin D.	5:41:13 (31,529)	
Bailey, Lee	3:16:18 (2,618)	
Bailey, Marcus P	4:24:30 (16,994)	
Bailey, Mark A.	4:27:38 (17,934)	
Bailey, Mark J.	4:11:29 (13,482)	
Bailey, Mark S	5:04:06 (26,538)	
Bailey, Michael J.	5:30:32 (30,415)	
Bailey, Nicholas	4:15:29 (14,573)	
Bailey, Nicholas G	5:37:51 (31,175)	
Bailey, Peter S.	4:11:59 (13,619)	
Bailey, Philip D	3:56:48 (9,753)	
Bailey, Richard	5:07:35 (27,156)	
Bailey, Richard A.	4:45:51 (22,510)	
Bailey, Richard C.	3:58:57 (10,417)	
Bailey, Richard N.	3:54:52 (9,202)	
Bailey, Robin C.	3:52:58 (8,712)	
Bailey, Shane	3:34:18 (5,096)	
Bailey, Steven E	5:32:42 (30,636)	
Bailey, Stuart E	4:42:39 (21,786)	
Bailey, Thomas J	4:53:16 (24,239)	
Bailey, Thomas W	5:52:49 (32,484)	
Bailey, Toby M	3:55:16 (9,298)	
Baillie, Angus R	3:57:17 (9,915)	
Baillie, Michael J	2:53:02 (638)	
Bain, Alan	4:48:51 (23,199)	
Bain, Ian	5:22:32 (29,427)	
Bain, Robert W	3:46:11 (7,176)	
Bainbridge, Adam G	5:44:02 (31,761)	
Bainbridge, Peter D	4:22:17 (16,416)	
Baines, Ian	5:31:45 (30,537)	
Baines, Jonathan N	4:02:51 (11,352)	
Baines, Lee A.	4:40:59 (21,385)	
Baines, Mark A	5:09:46 (27,480)	
Baines, Simon D	2:37:39 (148)	
Baines, Stephen J	4:58:15 (25,384)	
Bains, Narinder S	4:13:54 (14,112)	
Baird, Danny	4:21:41 (16,252)	
Baird, John E	4:07:35 (12,472)	
Bairner, Douglas I	3:30:38 (4,549)	
Baisden, Kevin J.	5:08:58 (27,350)	
Bajwa, Jasdeep S	5:30:02 (30,366)	
Bak, Hans	3:30:20 (4,494)	
Baker, Adam	3:47:17 (7,411)	
Baker, Andrew	2:57:01 (885)	
Baker, Andrew J	5:12:44 (27,958)	
Baker, Barry M	4:09:11 (12,882)	
Baker, Brendan P	4:00:12 (10,766)	
Baker, Carl	2:55:29 (765)	
Baker, Charlie N.	3:55:37 (9,406)	
Baker, Christopher	3:52:49 (8,686)	
Baker, Christopher C	3:28:23 (4,175)	
Baker, Clive A	2:58:05 (961)	
Baker, David A.	5:12:31 (27,913)	
Baker, David J	3:55:24 (9,337)	
Baker, Gavin T	4:52:57 (24,158)	
Baker, Gordon R	5:29:53 (30,347)	
Baker, Graham	3:10:06 (1,933)	
Baker, Henry P	5:18:21 (28,843)	
Baker, Hurburt	4:50:29 (23,623)	
Baker, Ian D.	3:51:37 (8,392)	
Baker, James	5:56:46 (32,760)	
Baker, John W	4:46:11 (22,600)	
Baker, Jolyon	4:08:40 (12,733)	
Baker, Julian D	2:26:42 (55)	
Baker, Kevin L	5:25:52 (29,849)	
Baker, Kevin R	3:50:33 (8,158)	
Baker, Mark D	4:34:16 (19,654)	
Baker, Mark D	4:55:28 (24,766)	
Baker, Mark H	3:52:39 (8,646)	
Baker, Mark J	3:53:49 (8,938)	
Baker, Mark S	3:19:40 (2,961)	
Baker, Martin G	4:33:17 (19,377)	
Baker, Matthew	4:08:03 (12,583)	
Baker, Matthew G	4:05:02 (11,871)	
Baker, Michael	5:23:57 (29,614)	
Baker, Michael P	5:02:47 (26,292)	
Baker, Neville	2:52:01 (591)	
Baker, Nick	3:59:26 (10,552)	
Baker, Paul E	4:52:08 (23,972)	
Baker, Robert	3:58:48 (10,390)	
Baker, Stephen R.	4:02:28 (11,262)	
Baker, Steve	6:07:26 (33,417)	

Baker, Steven M	4:01:52 (11,119)	
Baker, Stuart	5:38:06 (31,205)	
Baker, Stuart A	5:52:31 (32,465)	
Baker, Thomas A	4:12:02 (13,630)	
Baker, Tim J	4:11:32 (13,489)	
Baker, Trevor	4:03:52 (11,598)	
Bakewell, Andrew P	3:52:28 (8,596)	
Bakewell, Jon M	5:41:33 (31,561)	
Baki, Adam	5:00:22 (25,861)	
Bakker, John	4:44:32 (22,217)	
Bakshi, Rajan S	5:10:58 (27,648)	
Balacco, Francesco	3:25:10 (3,615)	
Balakrishnan, Venkatesh	5:06:18 (26,919)	
Balavoine, Fabrice M	3:01:39 (1,236)	
Balbi, John A	5:51:03 (32,341)	
Balcer, Matthew A	4:25:04 (17,142)	
Baldassari, Giovanni	4:23:07 (16,636)	
Balderson, Simon W	3:56:49 (9,757)	
Baldini, Gianluca	3:23:04 (3,308)	
Baldini, Stefano	2:09:25 (5)	
Baldock, Anthony J	3:29:51 (4,428)	
Baldock, Michael J	3:21:32 (3,135)	
Baldock, Nick P	4:29:44 (18,530)	
Baldock, Richard P	3:53:03 (8,731)	
Baldock, Robert J	4:02:39 (11,303)	
Baldwin, David S	3:12:06 (2,154)	
Baldwin, John D	5:53:03 (32,502)	
Baldwin, Kelvin J	4:22:32 (16,482)	
Baldwin, Mark S	4:29:06 (18,344)	
Baldwin, Matthew J	5:06:45 (27,008)	
Baldwin, Michael	3:58:24 (10,261)	
Baldwin, Steven C	3:57:11 (9,887)	
Baldwinson, Benjamin M	3:40:52 (6,161)	
Bale, Alan	4:06:09 (12,133)	
Bale, Ian R	5:26:23 (29,908)	
Bale, James	4:52:12 (23,985)	
Bale, Matthew	5:14:34 (28,273)	
Bale, Mons	2:36:37 (128)	
Bale, Simon M	3:10:19 (1,961)	
Balestrieri, Ermanno	5:09:13 (27,392)	
Balfe, Stephen J	3:26:34 (3,859)	
Balivo, Niocola	4:32:06 (19,109)	
Balivo, Raffaele	3:57:31 (9,988)	
Ball, Adrian P	2:50:41 (525)	
Ball, Andrew	3:09:50 (1,900)	
Ball, Andrew J	3:36:28 (5,420)	
Ball, Andrew R	4:04:31 (11,749)	
Ball, Benjamin T	4:57:33 (25,239)	
Ball, David	4:08:23 (12,664)	
Ball, Douglas	4:39:14 (20,942)	
Ball, Garry P	4:12:54 (13,857)	
Ball, Graham	2:56:21 (831)	
Ball, Ian C	4:05:10 (11,916)	
Ball, James D	4:36:14 (20,141)	
Ball, Kevin	4:24:40 (17,032)	
Ball, Kevin J	4:25:43 (17,351)	
Ball, Mark J	5:00:15 (25,831)	
Ball, Martin C	4:32:55 (19,295)	
Ball, Martin J	3:25:52 (3,734)	
Ball, Richard J	4:02:43 (11,323)	
Ball, Richard L	3:41:02 (6,186)	
Ball, Simon J	5:21:48 (29,327)	
Ball, Simon R	4:33:30 (19,433)	
Ball, Stephen A	8:00:10 (35,230)	
Ball, Steven	4:46:54 (22,753)	
Ball, Wayne G	4:03:56 (11,612)	
Ballagher, Bruce	4:37:27 (20,482)	
Ballantine, Ewan	3:23:07 (3,320)	
Ballantine, Robert	4:18:17 (15,290)	
Ballantyne, Andrew B	4:05:56 (12,080)	
Ballantyne, Stuart	5:04:16 (26,566)	
Ballard, David E	4:51:11 (23,769)	
Ballard, David J	4:42:29 (21,739)	
Ballard, David W	4:28:36 (18,195)	
Ballard, Martin D	5:01:23 (26,039)	
Ballard, William F	4:55:29 (24,769)	
Ballentyne, Thomas H	5:01:15 (26,016)	
Ballett, Leighton C.	3:19:55 (2,986)	
Balling, Louis	3:23:19 (3,353)	
Ballinger, Wayne	5:07:09 (27,086)	
Balmer, Malcolm	3:32:12 (4,773)	
Balshaw, Martin J	5:03:55 (26,506)	
Balsiger, Daniel	3:23:00 (3,294)	

Balson, Jonathan	4:31:58	(19,078)
Balzarini, Dimitri	4:55:50	(24,856)
Bamber, Neil S.	5:30:53	(30,451)
Bamber, Richard W.	4:36:21	(20,177)
Bambrick, Michael J.	5:03:09	(26,376)
Bambrick, Stephen	3:30:12	(4,476)
Bamelis, Tim	3:30:31	(4,532)
Bamford, Alistair P.	4:17:04	(14,973)
Bamford, George	5:14:26	(28,252)
Bamford, Karl R.	4:24:32	(17,001)
Bampfylde, Simon A.	4:02:38	(11,298)
Bamsey, Philip L.	3:38:49	(5,779)
Banarsee, Neil P.	6:27:31	(34,181)
Banbrook, Stuart	3:30:28	(4,518)
Banbury, Neil	4:59:30	(25,663)
Bance, Elliott J.	3:56:27	(9,652)
Bancroft, Anthony D.	3:25:58	(3,748)
Bancroft, David	5:08:36	(27,298)
Bancroft, David R.	3:54:38	(9,135)
Bandy, Chris P.	3:47:13	(7,395)
Bandy, Ian C.	4:07:08	(12,379)
Banfi, Michael J.	3:21:37	(3,142)
Banfield, Luke A.	5:24:37	(29,698)
Banfield, Mark R.	4:31:09	(18,866)
Bangash, Haider	5:26:32	(29,927)
Bangert, Alexander	3:54:37	(9,126)
Banham, Mark A.	4:18:59	(15,507)
Banham, Mark R.	5:12:05	(27,839)
Banham, Paul D.	5:26:01	(29,869)
Banister, Nigel E.	4:41:27	(21,511)
Banjo, Chris	6:07:57	(33,440)
Banks, Christopher J.	4:09:11	(12,882)
Banks, Paul D.	3:33:15	(4,919)
Banks, Peter G.	2:41:42	(233)
Banks, Timothy D.	3:30:05	(4,466)
Banner, Oliver J.	3:55:53	(9,484)
Bannister, Michael	3:09:32	(1,861)
Bannister, Peter J.	5:10:26	(27,560)
Bannister, Stuart	2:59:01	(1,036)
Banno, Giancarlo	4:27:43	(17,955)
Bannon, Alan D.	5:13:29	(28,082)
Bansal, Amarjit S.	6:11:43	(33,600)
Bansal, Tavinder	4:35:25	(19,955)
Bansal, Vikrant	3:29:44	(4,401)
Bant, Phil J.	4:15:28	(14,566)
Banyard, John	3:31:37	(4,697)
Bara, James O.	3:28:43	(4,226)
Barankay, Iwan	4:35:51	(20,055)
Baraud, Patrick	3:49:53	(8,014)
Barber, Andrew W.	4:27:57	(18,022)
Barber, Gary K.	5:24:27	(29,678)
Barber, Jeremy	4:08:33	(12,702)
Barber, Jon	4:21:25	(16,179)
Barber, Jon	4:21:25	(16,179)
Barber, Kyle G.	3:02:07	(1,270)
Barber, Michael S.	3:08:48	(1,790)
Barber, Nigel	4:41:42	(21,564)
Barber, Phil A.	3:52:42	(8,661)
Barber, Tristan J.	4:21:14	(16,124)
Barber, Wayne	6:17:58	(33,851)
Barbert, Kenneth G.	3:35:43	(5,299)
Barbet, Andy J.	5:42:49	(31,666)
Barbour, Laurence J.	4:29:23	(18,428)
Barbour, Richard	4:45:05	(22,347)
Barbour, Walter	4:31:32	(18,978)
Barchetti, Martin P.	4:39:14	(20,942)
Barclay, Andrew D.	4:37:40	(20,539)
Barclay, Anthony	4:05:21	(11,957)
Barclay, Rodney G.	3:46:17	(7,199)
Barclay, Rupert D.	3:29:45	(4,408)
Bardell, Michael D.	4:29:19	(18,409)
Barden, Joseph C.	4:25:25	(17,257)
Bardeschi, Antonio	3:40:42	(6,117)
Bardsley, Adam	3:07:00	(1,634)
Bardsley, Mark E.	4:08:38	(12,722)
Barfield, Richard A.	6:12:39	(33,648)
Barfoot, Anthony I.	3:49:09	(7,854)
Barfoot, David R.	5:59:46	(32,965)
Bargatzki, Achim	4:54:07	(24,454)
Bargh, Donald M.	4:20:09	(15,840)
Bargrove, Anthony L.	5:18:34	(28,877)
Barham, Lee C.	6:33:19	(34,339)
Barham, Mark	4:44:18	(22,169)
Barham, Paul	3:56:42	(9,726)
Bariselli, Roberto	4:02:16	(11,217)
Barker, Adam G.	3:28:41	(4,221)
Barker, Alister J.	4:50:16	(23,551)
Barker, Andrew F.	4:12:17	(13,692)
Barker, Andrew M.	4:59:11	(25,600)
Barker, Charles	3:57:30	(9,979)
Barker, Christopher E.	4:14:01	(14,152)
Barker, Craig J.	3:57:30	(9,979)
Barker, Daniel J.	5:32:36	(30,625)
Barker, David A.	4:16:30	(14,836)
Barker, David R.	3:58:00	(10,142)
Barker, David S.	4:04:11	(11,678)
Barker, Graeme B.	5:24:58	(29,741)
Barker, Ian B.	3:20:25	(3,037)
Barker, Ian E.	4:33:43	(19,492)
Barker, James	4:20:48	(16,022)
Barker, John	4:25:17	(17,211)
Barker, John D.	4:08:49	(12,773)
Barker, John M.	5:01:04	(25,988)
Barker, John W.	3:19:22	(2,919)
Barker, Jonathan M.	4:43:39	(22,025)
Barker, Mark S.	4:47:49	(22,967)
Barker, Michael B.	5:30:19	(30,397)
Barker, Nick M.	2:39:48	(200)
Barker, Nigel C.	3:40:11	(6,038)
Barker, Paul A.	4:55:33	(24,782)
Barker, Paul E.	5:12:41	(27,940)
Barker, Paul J.	4:26:19	(17,542)
Barker, Paul W.	4:40:44	(21,315)
Barker, Ryan	2:56:32	(845)
Barker, Steve	5:00:50	(25,942)
Barker, Stuart C.	4:03:48	(11,576)
Barker, Toby J.	5:15:52	(28,463)
Barklam, Anthony C.	4:16:57	(14,944)
Barley, Allan C.	5:34:25	(30,837)
Barley, Paul J.	5:38:18	(31,229)
Barley, Phillip L.	4:49:20	(23,320)
Barlow, Alexander P.	3:35:16	(5,217)
Barlow, Anthony	6:38:35	(34,472)
Barlow, Carl	3:47:52	(7,541)
Barlow, Chris	3:56:49	(9,757)
Barlow, Daniel W.	4:19:05	(15,544)
Barlow, David	6:10:52	(33,569)
Barlow, David J.	3:55:15	(9,292)
Barlow, Gary M.	4:51:29	(23,828)
Barlow, George R.	4:34:47	(19,786)
Barlow, Howard	3:43:21	(6,630)
Barlow, Michael R.	3:59:29	(10,567)
Barlow, Neil	3:59:32	(10,582)
Barlow, Nicholas K.	4:30:35	(18,745)
Barlow, Paul M.	3:25:54	(3,743)
Barlow, Simon A.	4:38:25	(20,732)
Barlow, Thomas P.	3:16:16	(2,615)
Barlow, William M.	4:01:49	(11,114)
Barnacle, Adiran M.	4:31:17	(18,913)
Barnard, John S.	4:51:03	(23,746)
Barnard, Mark J.	4:44:43	(22,253)
Barnard, Stephen A.	4:40:39	(21,296)
Barnard-Richardson, John	4:36:13	(20,135)
Barnes, Adam	5:38:59	(31,308)
Barnes, Adam L.	3:26:42	(3,885)
Barnes, Alan D.	3:45:39	(7,071)
Barnes, Andrew C.	4:19:58	(15,792)
Barnes, Brandon	5:08:48	(27,319)
Barnes, Brian W.	4:03:15	(11,447)
Barnes, Clifford S.	4:22:41	(16,532)
Barnes, Clinton C.	4:20:16	(15,879)
Barnes, Darren	3:52:28	(8,596)
Barnes, Darren	4:14:04	(14,173)
Barnes, David	4:34:25	(19,695)
Barnes, David G.	3:01:16	(1,204)
Barnes, Ellis J.	4:53:24	(24,275)
Barnes, Garry	5:08:48	(27,319)
Barnes, Gary R.	3:49:51	(8,007)
Barnes, Howard J.	4:21:19	(16,147)
Barnes, Keith A.	5:33:38	(30,743)
Barnes, Michael	4:20:51	(16,035)
Barnes, Mick	3:27:09	(3,950)
Barnes, Nigel	3:12:49	(2,229)
Barnes, Richard A.	5:00:10	(25,808)
Barnes, Richard C.	4:24:39	(17,026)
Barnes, Richard W.	3:45:03	(6,963)
Barnes, Roy J.	3:35:29	(5,260)
Barnes, Simon P.	3:17:31	(2,736)
Barnes, Steven J.	5:43:02	(31,679)
Barnes, Terry J.	4:58:10	(25,364)
Barnes, Trevor	3:28:29	(4,194)
Barnes, William J.	4:44:57	(22,313)
Barnes-Smith, Martin J.	3:24:28	(3,514)
Barnett, Daniel A.	4:09:01	(12,831)
Barnett, Graeme E.	4:13:30	(14,017)
Barnett, John E.	5:35:05	(30,913)
Barnett, Kevin	4:59:43	(25,717)
Barnett, Lee D.	4:59:37	(25,692)
Barnett, Mathew P.	4:34:18	(19,665)
Barnett, Paul D.	5:26:29	(29,920)
Barnett, Paul John B.	5:35:08	(30,922)
Barnett, Philip	3:26:40	(3,881)
Barney, Steve	3:41:21	(6,248)
Barningham, Richard A.	4:31:13	(18,888)
Barnshw, Daniel T.	3:28:28	(4,192)
Barnwell, Peter G.	5:00:17	(25,841)
Baron, Tom	4:17:19	(15,042)
Barone, William S.	4:51:18	(23,793)
Barr, Clive R.	4:00:35	(10,865)
Barr, David	3:28:07	(4,131)
Barr, Jonathan P.	3:29:03	(4,282)
Barr, Roger M.	2:59:43	(1,104)
Barr, Sam	4:01:13	(10,985)
Barr, Simon J.	4:56:15	(24,950)
Barraclough, Richard	5:01:17	(26,025)
Barraclough, Timothy M.	3:47:27	(7,447)
Barraclough, Wiliam W.	4:38:21	(20,709)
Barrance, Barry J.	5:11:14	(27,695)
Barratt, Chris M.	5:41:34	(31,562)
Barratt, Nick	5:16:53	(28,620)
Barre, Didier	4:09:44	(13,022)
Barre, Seb D.	4:26:09	(17,492)
Barrell, Stuart	4:26:27	(17,585)
Barrett, Barrie G.	3:24:53	(3,568)
Barrett, Brian M.	3:57:14	(9,902)
Barrett, Chris	3:06:13	(1,569)
Barrett, Daren	4:31:29	(18,965)
Barrett, Darren S.	5:33:55	(30,768)
Barrett, David	2:44:05	(297)
Barrett, David R.	4:21:19	(16,147)
Barrett, Giles P.	3:47:50	(7,533)
Barrett, Gordon D.	3:09:46	(1,892)
Barrett, Graham D.	3:40:19	(6,052)
Barrett, John C.	5:06:20	(26,926)
Barrett, John E.	4:11:54	(13,590)
Barrett, Lee	4:03:53	(11,602)
Barrett, Mark A.	5:40:08	(31,432)
Barrett, Mark A.	5:56:37	(32,743)
Barrett, Mark J.	4:56:47	(25,090)
Barrett, Michael J.	5:06:21	(26,931)
Barrett, Nicholas	3:46:22	(7,216)
Barrett, Paul	4:34:02	(19,575)
Barrett, Seanie	3:18:47	(2,858)
Barrett, Simon J.	2:32:31	(88)
Barrett, Simon T.	4:41:40	(21,558)
Barrett, Stephen J.	3:03:26	(1,358)
Barrett, Toby C.	5:00:32	(25,881)
Barrick, Marcus	4:36:17	(20,156)
Barrie, Martin J.	4:29:07	(18,345)
Barrio, César	3:54:32	(9,056)
Barritt, Robert J.	4:03:30	(11,498)
Barron, Nathan	4:12:27	(13,737)
Barrons, Anthony	5:49:11	(32,199)
Barrow, Christopher	4:53:54	(24,395)
Barrow, Keith	5:20:01	(29,098)
Barrows, Matthew	4:05:46	(12,041)
Barrs, Gary E.	4:45:24	(22,414)
Barry, Brendan	7:02:20	(34,894)
Barry, Giles D.	4:19:38	(15,705)
Barry, James D.	3:44:32	(6,845)
Barry, Jason	2:58:02	(958)
Barry, John P.	2:57:11	(898)
Barry, Julian A.	2:56:17	(828)
Barry, Michael J.	4:02:15	(11,212)
Barry, Steven	3:26:25	(3,831)
Barry, William A.	4:53:21	(24,263)
Barsby, David R.	3:44:50	(6,919)
Barstad, John O.	3:43:14	(6,595)
Barteczko, Igor	3:42:02	(6,385)

Bartel, Gerard....3:48:01 (7,587)
Barter, Nigel D....4:04:56 (11,847)
Bartholomew, David....4:32:32 (19,217)
Bartholomew, David....4:40:37 (21,289)
Bartholomew, John....8:06:02 (35,238)
Barthorpe, Carl A....5:15:56 (28,472)
Bartlett, Andrew W....5:08:01 (27,222)
Bartlett, Christopher....4:17:51 (15,170)
Bartlett, David P....3:54:17 (9,043)
Bartlett, David R....4:59:03 (25,574)
Bartlett, Edwin H....4:51:50 (23,896)
Bartlett, Gareth D....4:28:10 (18,078)
Bartlett, Ian M....4:19:57 (15,788)
Bartlett, Mike J....4:10:34 (13,237)
Bartlett, Paul R....4:15:55 (14,693)
Bartlett, Simon E....3:46:35 (7,258)
Bartley, Lee A....4:26:30 (17,600)
Bartley, Michael G....3:47:54 (7,548)
Bartolini, Valter....3:53:47 (8,930)
Barton, Alan J....4:16:07 (14,747)
Barton, Bob....4:47:11 (22,818)
Barton, Chris D....5:15:54 (28,466)
Barton, Craig A....4:42:03 (21,634)
Barton, David....4:48:21 (23,088)
Barton, David....5:35:52 (30,982)
Barton, Des P....4:20:49 (16,026)
Barton, John....5:15:52 (28,463)
Barton, Ken G....4:10:28 (13,218)
Barton, Michael....4:10:46 (13,276)
Barton, Michael J....3:34:24 (5,110)
Barton, Nicholas C....5:26:35 (29,931)
Barton, Patrick J....3:55:43 (9,435)
Barton, Richard J....5:06:09 (26,902)
Barton, Roger J....6:03:21 (33,181)
Barton, Stephen....4:35:45 (20,033)
Barton, Warren....4:02:47 (11,339)
Bartram, Mark E....3:29:44 (4,401)
Bartram, Matt....3:48:20 (7,664)
Bartram, Paul M....5:34:27 (30,843)
Bartrip, Lee....4:13:51 (14,103)
Bartrum, Tim J....3:17:17 (2,714)
Bartup, Ross J....3:33:52 (5,024)
Bartz, Joerg....3:12:01 (2,142)
Barwick, Paul....6:07:48 (33,430)
Barwin, Lee....5:16:33 (28,556)
Barzey, Aaron D....5:30:55 (30,457)
Basalo, Carlos V....3:04:48 (1,451)
Basey, Andrew G....3:23:08 (3,321)
Basford, Peter J....4:08:37 (12,718)
Basger, Oliver....5:06:46 (27,014)
Basham, Chris M....6:53:18 (34,776)
Basham, Leslie J....4:10:58 (13,339)
Basham, Oliver C....4:39:01 (20,885)
Bashford, David J....3:43:54 (6,720)
Bashford, Graham....6:11:45 (33,601)
Bashford, Guy C....2:55:53 (801)
Bashford, James....4:58:04 (25,343)
Basi, Peter....3:22:13 (3,217)
Bason, Andrew G....3:47:36 (7,474)
Bass, Andrew P....3:00:33 (1,158)
Bass, Anthony W....6:05:48 (33,313)
Bass, Norman D....5:02:51 (26,307)
Bass, Richard....2:54:07 (694)
Bass, Shaf D....4:01:23 (11,020)
Bass, William R....4:53:34 (24,318)
Bassan, Gwynn....3:28:02 (4,109)
Bassei, Fabio....3:16:52 (2,665)
Bassett, Adrian....4:36:08 (20,113)
Bassett, Andrew L....3:30:22 (4,503)
Bassett, Cliff S....5:16:13 (28,509)
Bassett, Neville....4:58:06 (25,351)
Bassett-Cross, James F....3:55:57 (9,501)
Bassi, Paul J....5:17:05 (28,662)
Bassu, Piero....4:23:16 (16,675)
Bastian, Kevin C....3:46:24 (7,222)
Bastian, Marc S....3:57:45 (10,051)
Bastian, Marco....3:22:06 (3,199)
Bastier, Jean-Paul....5:45:24 (31,889)
Basu, Subhashis....3:18:19 (2,814)
Batchelar, Nicholas J....3:22:05 (3,196)
Batchelor, Keith....4:27:35 (17,915)
Batchelor, Nick J....3:26:16 (3,803)
Bate, Andrew....4:28:40 (18,206)
Bate, Roman C....3:59:17 (10,515)
Bateman, Brian J....5:56:11 (32,717)
Bateman, Edward D....4:37:04 (20,372)
Bateman, Jeremy D....2:50:06 (502)
Bateman, John C....4:19:55 (15,779)
Bateman, Jonathan S....2:29:10 (64)
Bateman, Jonathan S....3:02:32 (1,299)
Bateman, Robert R....4:33:40 (19,477)
Bates, Adam S....5:30:58 (30,465)
Bates, Alex V....4:31:36 (18,997)
Bates, Andrew P....4:13:54 (14,112)
Bates, Ben J....5:09:54 (27,498)
Bates, Daniel C....5:08:52 (27,334)
Bates, David A....3:46:57 (7,338)
Bates, Ian....5:06:30 (26,964)
Bates, Kevin P....3:54:20 (9,053)
Bates, Richard T....5:42:19 (31,613)
Bates, Simon....4:33:58 (19,560)
Bates, Stephen J....4:12:51 (13,844)
Bates, Steven....5:16:16 (28,513)
Bateson, Ashley E....4:47:26 (22,868)
Bateson, Garry....3:44:04 (6,751)
Bateson, Mark W....5:57:39 (32,814)
Bateson, Nick....2:57:25 (917)
Bath, Gareth....4:31:57 (19,073)
Batham, Norman L....5:10:40 (27,601)
Bathgate, Andrew J....4:05:02 (11,871)
Bathmaker, Robert J....4:22:21 (16,435)
Batrick, Lee....4:30:24 (18,702)
Batson, Adam J....4:50:50 (23,699)
Batson, Paul J....4:22:24 (16,445)
Batstone, Michael....4:00:23 (10,799)
Battaglia, Giuliano....3:24:50 (3,556)
Battell, Kevin....3:28:43 (4,226)
Batten, Andrew G....3:32:53 (4,868)
Batten, Matthew E....4:11:05 (13,375)
Batterbee, Ian R....6:35:42 (34,403)
Batterbury, Clive E....3:40:21 (6,064)
Batterbury, Mark....3:56:22 (9,623)
Battersby, John M....4:07:10 (12,387)
Battersby, Nicholas P....3:25:58 (3,748)
Battershall, Tim J....2:56:41 (859)
Battison, Andrew....4:42:36 (21,769)
Battisti, Renato....3:26:52 (3,904)
Battle, Richard J....4:12:30 (13,747)
Battrick, Thomas C....4:15:17 (14,524)
Batty, David H....3:48:37 (7,745)
Batty, Graham W....4:36:24 (20,195)
Batty, Richard....3:32:06 (4,763)
Battye, John R....4:18:08 (15,242)
Baty, Adrian J....3:58:38 (10,318)
Baty, Richard J....4:22:03 (16,356)
Baucher, Gerald M....5:22:32 (29,427)
Baucutt, Graham M....5:35:08 (30,922)
Bauer, Christoph....3:55:53 (9,484)
Bauer, Christophe....3:15:59 (2,570)
Bauhs, Henrik....3:51:27 (8,365)
Baulk, Geoffrey D....6:33:45 (34,348)
Baulk, Stuart J....4:51:51 (23,900)
Baur, Horst....4:16:12 (14,765)
Bausor, Matthew J....3:35:57 (5,331)
Bavington, Michael....3:40:01 (5,998)
Bawden, Benjamin T....3:35:33 (5,269)
Bawden, Mike....5:00:10 (25,808)
Bax, Trevor....3:53:55 (8,958)
Baxendale, Peter....5:20:27 (29,171)
Baxendale, Samuel G....3:52:40 (8,651)
Baxter, Alan....4:43:10 (21,905)
Baxter, Andrew C....3:38:30 (5,724)
Baxter, Charlie J....3:10:11 (1,947)
Baxter, Colin R....5:20:17 (29,139)
Baxter, David C....5:00:20 (25,852)
Baxter, Eric....3:27:47 (4,073)
Baxter, Gary....4:49:22 (23,332)
Baxter, Gordon S....3:10:08 (1,940)
Baxter, Gregory D....2:50:28 (512)
Baxter, John G....2:48:14 (424)
Baxter, Justin S....5:13:19 (28,046)
Baxter, Mark A....5:35:02 (30,910)
Baxter, Mark J....4:18:16 (15,283)
Baxter-Warren, Rudi....4:49:37 (23,402)
Bay, Martin J....4:08:06 (12,590)
Bayer, Malcolm....3:43:36 (6,670)
Bayes, Graham P....4:00:46 (10,902)
Bayes, Matthew J....4:55:44 (24,827)
Bayes, Toby A....4:27:44 (17,963)
Bayley, Mark A....4:09:10 (12,878)
Baylis, David S....4:34:09 (19,608)
Baylis, Matthew....4:05:01 (11,864)
Bayliss, Andrew J....4:40:45 (21,320)
Bayliss, Stephen J....2:55:02 (744)
Bayly, Chris E....4:38:36 (20,777)
Bayly, Marc....3:52:44 (8,670)
Bayly, Robin M....5:30:48 (30,443)
Bayman, Robert....3:13:02 (2,249)
Bayne, Thomas J....4:16:00 (14,715)
Baynes, Charles B....3:19:14 (2,903)
Baynham, Anthony D....5:58:55 (32,905)
Baynhan, Karl S....4:29:40 (18,510)
Bayon, Tony....4:16:58 (14,948)
Baysal, Ugur....4:51:57 (23,919)
Bazalgette, Guy R....3:53:45 (8,922)
Bazior, Philippe W....3:31:39 (4,701)
Bazley, Peter G....3:29:37 (4,376)
Beadell, Conrad....3:37:21 (5,548)
Beadle, Michael....3:56:42 (9,726)
Beadle, Mike S....5:00:27 (25,873)
Beadle, Stephen P....4:08:00 (12,571)
Beadsmoore, Jonathan E....3:57:58 (10,135)
Beagley, Mark A....3:14:42 (2,445)
Beal, Jean-Philippe F....4:29:32 (18,476)
Beale, Darren....7:07:21 (34,953)
Beales, Robert D....7:00:16 (34,873)
Beall, Richard B....4:17:33 (15,102)
Beamish, Ian C....4:11:47 (13,559)
Beany, Captain....5:18:12 (28,818)
Beard, John M....6:43:31 (34,582)
Beard, Lloyd....4:57:57 (25,314)
Beard, Michael C....3:15:51 (2,552)
Beardmore, Paul....4:06:33 (12,225)
Beardsley, Charles S....4:30:48 (18,793)
Beardsmore, Keith J....2:59:32 (1,091)
Beardsworth, Stuart L....4:11:50 (13,570)
Bearman, Jamie R....4:23:24 (16,712)
Bearn, Hugh W....4:22:06 (16,367)
Bearn, Phil....4:21:15 (16,129)
Bearne, Joseph E....5:02:04 (26,160)
Beasant, Campbell A....4:01:11 (10,977)
Beasley, Andrew R....5:22:27 (29,411)
Beasley, Christopher A....4:50:12 (23,534)
Beasley, Glen....3:53:17 (8,792)
Beasley, Thomas N....5:38:07 (31,208)
Beathe, Carl J....3:07:25 (1,667)
Beatie, Ian....5:14:06 (28,189)
Beaton, Finlay K....5:07:15 (27,109)
Beaton, Michael F....3:04:16 (1,413)
Beats, Kenneth....4:53:14 (24,231)
Beattie, Adrian J....4:20:54 (16,051)
Beattie, Brian W....3:25:47 (3,715)
Beattie, David....2:55:06 (747)
Beattie, Garth C....4:38:57 (20,860)
Beattie, Ian J....3:15:28 (2,523)
Beattie, Kevin A....2:43:07 (272)
Beattie, Michael J....2:57:25 (917)
Beattie, Patrick E....4:10:14 (13,147)
Beatty, Clive....5:02:40 (26,268)
Beatty, Nick C....6:07:24 (33,415)
Beauchamp, Dominic P....3:55:04 (9,251)
Beauchamp, Keith M....3:32:05 (4,759)
Beaumont, Craig S....4:32:27 (19,196)
Beaumont, Ged S....4:09:44 (13,022)
Beaumont, Stuart D....5:01:04 (25,988)
Beaumont, Thomas M....4:31:40 (19,011)
Beavan, Carl A....6:09:45 (33,524)
Beaven, Phillip J....3:52:23 (8,574)
Beavis, Julian....4:44:16 (22,160)
Beazeley, Chris D....3:46:13 (7,182)
Beazer, Philip J....3:00:34 (1,161)
Beck, Andrew J....3:40:49 (6,142)
Beck, Anthony R....4:31:06 (18,853)
Beck, David M....3:48:04 (7,606)
Beck, Ian F....4:33:58 (19,560)
Beck, Shaun S....5:00:10 (25,808)
Beckers, Volker....4:49:43 (23,429)
Beckett, Dean A....5:05:01 (26,687)
Beckett, Stephen J....3:53:54 (8,953)

Beckett, Stephen P.	4:36:22 (20,188)	
Beckwith, Mark A.	3:52:33 (8,615)	
Beckwith, Stephen B.	4:22:06 (16,367)	
Bedbrook, Michael W.	4:22:50 (16,565)	
Beddard, Roger S.	4:56:53 (25,110)	
Bedder, Stephen R.	3:32:19 (4,790)	
Beddows, Rob A.	4:27:04 (17,765)	
Bedeschi, Carlo	5:05:20 (26,756)	
Bedford, David J.	4:08:34 (12,705)	
Bedford, Gary J.	3:24:00 (3,446)	
Bedford, Graham J.	4:02:14 (11,210)	
Bedford, Jonathan C.	4:29:02 (18,320)	
Bedford, Peter	4:43:42 (22,033)	
Bedia, Bharat	3:42:10 (6,413)	
Bednall, Michael	4:13:22 (13,982)	
Bednash, Graham	4:48:06 (23,031)	
Bedwell, Andrew	3:49:31 (7,938)	
Bedwell, Peter R.	4:22:21 (16,435)	
Bee, Paul	5:34:42 (30,874)	
Bee, Tony	4:14:07 (14,184)	
Beech, James E.	3:28:11 (4,141)	
Beech, Ken	4:15:15 (14,515)	
Beech, Ross M.	5:22:29 (29,418)	
Beech, Stephen J.	3:39:18 (5,868)	
Beecham, George E.	5:58:30 (32,880)	
Beeching, Mark A.	6:03:11 (33,155)	
Beedell, Mark T.	4:55:48 (24,841)	
Beeks, Darren C.	5:58:56 (32,908)	
Beeks, Ramon A.	5:58:56 (32,908)	
Beeks, Stephen J.	5:58:55 (32,905)	
Beeley, Adam E.	4:31:43 (19,024)	
Beer, Nigel E.	3:47:35 (7,469)	
Beer, Peter G.	2:59:00 (1,033)	
Bees, William	4:04:57 (11,849)	
Beesley, Ian S.	3:38:27 (5,718)	
Beesley, Jonathan D.	4:51:43 (23,877)	
Beesley, Mark J.	4:56:53 (25,026)	
Beeston, Tim R.	3:59:15 (10,510)	
Beet, Simon T.	4:40:19 (21,212)	
Beeton, Andrew J.	3:43:17 (6,613)	
Beeton, James F.	3:33:28 (4,956)	
Beever, Matthew P.	4:18:13 (15,269)	
Beevers, Al R.	3:28:28 (4,192)	
Beggs, Kenneth W.	4:39:24 (20,989)	
Begley, Kenneth	3:09:55 (1,911)	
Behagg, David J.	4:11:14 (13,413)	
Behaghel, Eric	4:39:09 (20,911)	
Behl, Edward J.	4:56:47 (25,090)	
Behn, Klaus	3:49:58 (8,031)	
Behncke, Burghard	4:31:07 (18,858)	
Behrens, Gordon G.	5:01:02 (25,983)	
Bein, Timmo	4:08:14 (12,622)	
Beirne, Christopher J.	5:23:34 (29,553)	
Beja, Eilon	4:21:39 (16,244)	
Belbin, Simon J.	4:50:57 (23,719)	
Belcher, Gordon	5:18:11 (28,815)	
Belcher, James R.	5:19:00 (28,945)	
Belcher, John A.	5:05:28 (26,789)	
Belcher, Simon A.	3:25:51 (3,730)	
Beldon, Richard	4:11:03 (13,368)	
Belfield, David C.	5:33:38 (30,743)	
Belfort, Clive	3:44:37 (6,864)	
Belhomme, Ross	5:21:11 (29,262)	
Bell, Alistair J.	5:11:00 (27,653)	
Bell, Andrew M.	3:31:13 (4,634)	
Bell, Anthony C.	4:02:01 (11,161)	
Bell, Dave	4:43:55 (22,077)	
Bell, David J.	3:58:45 (10,366)	
Bell, David M.	2:58:18 (973)	
Bell, Duncan	4:58:07 (25,353)	
Bell, Edward	2:59:37 (1,099)	
Bell, Geoffrey D.	4:41:09 (21,432)	
Bell, Jason	4:54:08 (24,456)	
Bell, John D.	3:04:28 (1,424)	
Bell, Martin A.	4:38:44 (20,809)	
Bell, Martin G.	3:50:10 (8,077)	
Bell, Matthew J.	2:37:40 (149)	
Bell, Michael W.	3:14:11 (2,378)	
Bell, Nicholas J.	3:45:26 (7,040)	
Bell, Nick G.	3:36:08 (5,360)	
Bell, Paul	2:52:02 (593)	
Bell, Paul C.	4:50:34 (23,645)	
Bell, Peter J.	4:58:19 (25,395)	
Bell, Philip	3:45:39 (7,071)	
Bell, Richard C.	5:19:46 (29,073)	
Bell, Robert A.	3:20:32 (3,048)	
Bell, Robert G.	3:41:31 (6,276)	
Bell, Robert I.	4:46:48 (22,734)	
Bell, Roger E.	4:03:56 (11,612)	
Bell, Scot T.	4:51:50 (23,896)	
Bell, Sean E.	6:43:50 (34,593)	
Bell, Terence S.	3:13:15 (2,271)	
Bell, William	4:47:49 (22,967)	
Bell Hutt, Alan D.	3:37:10 (5,521)	
Bellacosa, Maurizio	3:45:46 (7,088)	
Bellamy, Darren W.	5:34:58 (30,900)	
Bellars, Stephen B.	4:18:27 (15,350)	
Bellenger, Regis	3:30:33 (4,538)	
Bellettini, Ermanno	4:09:47 (13,035)	
Belleville, Paul C.	2:58:13 (969)	
Bellido Gonzalez, Juan Carlos	3:14:45 (2,453)	
Bellini, Rolando	5:35:14 (30,928)	
Bellis, Stephen	3:33:14 (4,915)	
Bellis, Tom C.	4:15:45 (14,650)	
Bello, Aurelio M.	4:17:52 (15,174)	
Belloni, Raffaele	3:00:33 (1,158)	
Bellwood, Tom	5:52:23 (32,446)	
Belmar, Steve	6:09:04 (33,492)	
Belsey, Peter J.	3:34:05 (5,058)	
Belton, Tony	6:11:42 (33,599)	
Beminga, Holger	4:54:22 (24,518)	
Benaine, Errol	4:32:46 (19,264)	
Benayad, Reda	4:06:06 (12,121)	
Bence, Ashley	4:50:08 (23,523)	
Bence-Trower, Nicholas A.	4:35:56 (20,070)	
Bendall, Chris C.	4:27:44 (17,963)	
Bending, Michael R.	6:40:43 (34,519)	
Bendle, Simon J.	3:58:48 (10,390)	
Bendle, Stephen A.	3:37:46 (5,612)	
Benedict, Jerome	6:54:57 (34,798)	
Benerjee, Somen R.	4:59:34 (25,675)	
Benetti, Gianluca	4:55:02 (24,683)	
Benger, Nicholas	3:30:20 (4,494)	
Bengue, Marc	4:31:43 (19,024)	
Benham, Jason S.	3:26:34 (3,859)	
Beniston, Paul	4:09:03 (12,838)	
Benke, Graham N.	4:38:03 (20,632)	
Benn, William	5:40:20 (31,447)	
Ben-Nathan, Marc I.	4:26:45 (17,678)	
Bennell, Kevin J.	4:11:19 (13,434)	
Bennell, Martin P.	5:14:01 (28,175)	
Bennet, John E.	3:46:27 (7,232)	
Bennett, Andrew S.	6:03:47 (33,210)	
Bennett, Bernard T.	3:56:15 (9,585)	
Bennett, Brian	5:06:59 (27,053)	
Bennett, Daniel A.	4:03:09 (11,421)	
Bennett, Daniel R.	5:44:46 (31,825)	
Bennett, David	3:55:05 (9,253)	
Bennett, David H.	3:10:33 (1,983)	
Bennett, David J.	4:31:16 (18,904)	
Bennett, David M.	4:30:57 (18,826)	
Bennett, David M.	4:49:51 (23,461)	
Bennett, Douglas J.	5:40:43 (31,481)	
Bennett, Gary P.	7:52:19 (35,217)	
Bennett, Graham J.	5:45:18 (31,879)	
Bennett, Gregory W.	4:57:57 (25,314)	
Bennett, Jamie K.	5:46:13 (31,957)	
Bennett, Jason S.	6:19:46 (33,909)	
Bennett, John	3:22:46 (3,270)	
Bennett, John J.	4:09:47 (13,035)	
Bennett, Jon A.	3:42:45 (6,505)	
Bennett, Jonathan R.	4:29:16 (18,390)	
Bennett, Julian F.	4:41:13 (21,451)	
Bennett, Mark	4:47:20 (22,840)	
Bennett, Mark T.	3:27:05 (3,940)	
Bennett, Martin J.	4:15:28 (14,566)	
Bennett, Martin P.	5:27:15 (30,008)	
Bennett, Nick W.	4:08:36 (12,716)	
Bennett, Raymond	4:15:31 (14,588)	
Bennett, Richard	5:11:20 (27,712)	
Bennett, Richard C.	3:56:16 (9,589)	
Bennett, Richard M.	3:35:24 (5,241)	
Bennett, Roger	2:55:52 (798)	
Bennett, Sean R.	3:02:22 (1,290)	
Bennett, Sean W.	3:46:58 (7,343)	
Bennett, Simon P.	4:52:28 (24,045)	
Bennett, Steven A.	3:02:54 (1,325)	
Bennett, Tom	3:39:09 (5,841)	
Bennett, Warren O.	5:24:51 (29,729)	
Bennetts, Colin	3:40:50 (6,148)	
Bennetts, Philip	3:51:25 (8,359)	
Bennetts, Steve	3:58:18 (10,227)	
Bennie, Alexander S.	3:40:32 (6,089)	
Bennion, Bernard E.	4:13:03 (13,894)	
Bennion, Kerry R.	4:57:24 (25,208)	
Bennison, Mark B.	4:11:38 (13,518)	
Benoit, Markus	3:29:18 (4,325)	
Benoist, Didier	3:29:06 (4,296)	
Benoit, Christopher S.	4:30:32 (18,735)	
Benson, Daniel L.	3:55:23 (9,332)	
Benson, Ian	2:59:17 (1,067)	
Benson, Ian E.	3:36:58 (5,495)	
Benson, James	2:39:24 (184)	
Benson, Richard J.	5:00:04 (25,787)	
Benson, Rodney D.	5:36:16 (31,022)	
Benson, Tim	4:14:23 (14,267)	
Benson, Tristan	3:33:53 (5,026)	
Benstead, Neal D.	6:04:05 (33,224)	
Bent, Edward R.	4:43:35 (22,003)	
Bentley, Anthony C.	2:54:31 (715)	
Bentley, Christopher W.	4:22:00 (16,335)	
Bentley, Ian R.	4:56:12 (24,940)	
Bentley, James A.	6:38:21 (34,465)	
Bentley, James M.	4:38:21 (20,709)	
Bentley, James R.	3:00:26 (1,154)	
Bentley, John S.	4:14:59 (14,437)	
Bentley, Mark	3:12:48 (2,226)	
Bentley, Robin J.	2:36:50 (132)	
Bentley, Sefton	4:21:59 (16,326)	
Bentley-Smith, Aidan J.	3:51:23 (8,348)	
Benton, Andy	3:55:14 (9,284)	
Benton, Brian A.	4:46:31 (22,671)	
Benton, David C.	5:59:09 (32,920)	
Benton, Tom A.	3:59:55 (10,701)	
Ben-Yehuda, Niv	4:20:50 (16,030)	
Benzie, Andrew A.	4:25:36 (17,315)	
Beoggood, Dean	4:13:00 (13,878)	
Berardelli, Claudio	3:31:56 (4,736)	
Bereds, Dieter	4:51:30 (23,829)	
Berens, Craig	5:21:41 (29,309)	
Beresfod, Christopher R.	3:41:07 (6,204)	
Beresford, Nick J.	2:55:44 (788)	
Beresford, Patrick M.	4:50:12 (23,534)	
Beresford, Trevor J.	6:53:16 (34,775)	
Berg, Ian R.	4:17:50 (15,168)	
Berg, Stephen E.	4:45:58 (22,544)	
Berg, Ty R.	2:37:59 (159)	
Berger, Daniel	3:31:11 (4,625)	
Berger, David	5:54:29 (32,599)	
Bergerat, Frederic	3:33:59 (5,045)	
Bergqvist, Philip E.	4:15:46 (14,651)	
Berkerey, Gavin M.	4:52:28 (24,045)	
Berknov, Kim	4:34:16 (19,654)	
Berland, Dominique H.	3:10:47 (2,006)	
Berleen, Abdi-Karim	3:15:23 (2,512)	
Berlie, Adrian J.	3:52:50 (8,688)	
Bernal, Carlos P.	4:14:47 (14,372)	
Bernard, David	5:19:13 (28,976)	
Bernard, Ralph M.	4:40:19 (21,212)	
Bernard, Sam G.	5:02:33 (26,237)	
Bernardini, Raymond M.	3:14:22 (2,401)	
Bernardo, Fernando	4:40:47 (21,332)	
Bernhardson, Brian K.	3:33:07 (4,901)	
Bernini, Andrea	4:05:52 (12,063)	
Bernstein, Richard P.	2:57:13 (903)	
Berridge, Matthew J.	4:45:14 (22,379)	
Berridge, Richard N.	4:57:06 (25,154)	
Berridge, Robert W.	5:01:26 (26,047)	
Berrie, Jonathan A.	4:42:57 (21,860)	
Berriman, Roger J.	4:06:52 (12,303)	
Berry, Anthony J.	4:02:04 (11,175)	
Berry, David F.	4:39:56 (21,122)	
Berry, Gavin R.	4:19:03 (15,527)	
Berry, George	4:19:19 (15,616)	
Berry, Glynn D.	5:44:10 (31,777)	
Berry, Graeme H.	3:50:01 (8,042)	
Berry, Jonathan D.	4:56:51 (25,101)	
Berry, Keith P.	5:10:54 (27,638)	
Berry, Mark S.	4:48:53 (23,205)	

Blair, Simon 3:50:24 (8,122)
Blaize, Matt 5:29:13 (30,265)
Blake, Adam R 3:54:23 (9,073)
Blake, Geoffrey M 3:51:54 (8,461)
Blake, John R 3:52:54 (8,700)
Blake, Matthew J 5:47:05 (32,026)
Blake, Michael C 5:00:09 (25,803)
Blake, Steve 4:27:58 (18,025)
Blake, Tim E 4:24:14 (16,912)
Blake, Tom 3:30:21 (4,498)
Blakeman, Robert H 4:36:35 (20,243)
Blakemore, Stephen J 3:26:14 (3,799)
Blakeney, Simon W 4:42:41 (21,795)
Blakesbrough, Simon K 3:54:22 (9,070)
Blakey, Kevin M 3:51:42 (8,412)
Blakey, Paul E 4:03:58 (11,624)
Blakey, Raymond W 6:06:04 (33,332)
Blanc, Jean-Luc 3:42:29 (6,468)
Bland, Andrew M 4:45:31 (22,434)
Bland, David J 6:03:50 (33,213)
Bland, Ian 4:36:34 (20,238)
Bland, Matthew D 2:56:11 (819)
Bland, Philip A 4:12:13 (13,670)
Blandford, Stephen M 4:48:10 (23,045)
Blaney, Fergal 4:18:08 (15,242)
Blanford, Richard M 4:16:27 (14,828)
Blanks, Doug T 5:20:01 (29,098)
Blann, Andrew 4:46:45 (22,719)
Blantz, Andrew 4:48:50 (23,195)
Blatcher, James R 4:53:56 (24,402)
Blatchford, Charles R 4:54:55 (24,641)
Blatchford, Tony 4:34:05 (19,587)
Blaydon, Matthew T 3:32:15 (4,781)
Blaylock, Steve L 3:26:00 (3,757)
Blaymires, Gary R 4:23:29 (16,726)
Blazeby, Simon 5:07:24 (27,131)
Blazier, Darren J 2:55:16 (751)
Bleaken, Daniel G 5:07:12 (27,103)
Bleakley, Mansell R 5:30:27 (30,410)
Bleasdale, Craig P 3:36:23 (5,403)
Bleeck, Peter J 4:12:39 (13,790)
Blewett, Lee 3:58:38 (10,318)
Blewett, Myles J 4:35:48 (20,042)
Blight, Stephen 4:58:22 (25,406)
Blincoe, Andrew M 4:29:09 (18,354)
Bliss, David 5:29:25 (30,293)
Bliss, Howard 5:03:56 (26,507)
Blissett, Luther L 5:47:03 (32,022)
Block, Martin L 4:32:48 (19,270)
Bloemendaal, Gerrit 6:28:54 (34,214)
Blofield, David J 4:41:13 (21,451)
Blogg, Kieran M 3:46:02 (7,144)
Blois, Richard 6:57:46 (34,839)
Blok, Dirk J 4:31:11 (18,879)
Blokland, Koos 5:44:57 (31,845)
Blom, Dirk P 5:23:18 (29,517)
Bloodworth, Timothy 3:14:33 (2,424)
Bloomfield, Barry F 3:31:37 (4,697)
Bloomfield, Colin 3:54:51 (9,198)
Bloor, Charles D 3:43:04 (6,565)
Blossier, Patrick 3:25:57 (3,746)
Blount, David J 4:48:24 (23,104)
Blount, Warren M 3:58:13 (10,199)
Blow, Clay 6:33:58 (34,352)
Blower, Lee 3:59:02 (10,443)
Blowers, Lee J 4:00:34 (10,857)
Bloxham, Clive 5:31:48 (30,545)
Bloxham, Roy W 4:06:53 (12,311)
Blue, Neil A 4:50:06 (23,514)
Blundell, Steve G 6:15:01 (33,735)
Blunden, Martin W 3:20:45 (3,070)
Blunt, Gareth D 5:30:15 (30,391)
Bly, Jude 3:06:13 (1,569)
Blyth, Kenny S 3:37:46 (5,612)
Blythe, Nicholas S 5:27:38 (30,059)
Blythe, Tom S 3:38:50 (5,781)
Blythen, Timothy R 3:25:41 (3,702)
Boa, Philip 5:36:29 (31,053)
Boam, Ady J 5:02:45 (26,284)
Board, Terry J 5:05:23 (26,771)
Boardman, Adam R 4:25:47 (17,373)
Boardman, Andrew D 3:13:58 (2,355)
Boardman, Christopher 3:57:24 (9,949)
Boardman, Wayne J 4:08:18 (12,636)
Boarer, Samuel T 5:49:58 (32,259)
Bock, Eberhard 4:55:03 (24,687)
Bocock, Stephen 5:01:06 (25,996)
Boddington, Peter D 3:58:44 (10,363)
Boddy, Clifford 3:25:10 (3,615)
Boddy, Michael J 3:25:05 (3,602)
Boddy, Simon 3:04:40 (1,442)
Boden, Gerald N 4:55:12 (24,719)
Boden, Lazloe 3:39:23 (5,891)
Boden, Mark A 4:54:01 (24,433)
Bodenburg, Rainer 3:34:35 (5,134)
Bodenhausen, Johannes B 5:07:06 (27,076)
Bodycomb, Russell J 6:01:15 (33,038)
Bodzek, Josef 3:49:40 (7,972)
Boehmer, Heiner K 4:05:16 (11,936)
Boelstler, Robert 4:04:40 (11,786)
Bogaire, Ori 3:57:38 (10,024)
Bogert, Anthony R 5:28:44 (30,211)
Bogert, John 4:53:39 (24,344)
Bogg, Charles H 3:49:07 (7,850)
Boggia, Les P 5:47:01 (32,020)
Boggis, Mark A 3:51:45 (8,425)
Bogush, Jeremy H 4:18:45 (15,444)
Bohli, Rudolf E 3:35:28 (5,255)
Bohr, Werner H 3:03:08 (1,341)
Boikwei, Emmanuel E 5:20:23 (29,158)
Boland, Mark J 4:45:13 (22,374)
Boler, Richard 4:19:27 (15,649)
Boles, Kevin M 4:31:31 (18,974)
Bolger, Brian D 4:42:27 (21,732)
Boling, Steve H 4:55:04 (24,693)
Bolton, Andrew 5:07:36 (27,159)
Bolton, Darren J 3:55:50 (9,472)
Bolton, David J 4:50:35 (23,647)
Bolton, Ian J 4:56:35 (25,035)
Bolton, Ross E 4:13:59 (14,141)
Bolton, Steve J 2:55:54 (803)
Bolton, Wayne L 4:28:54 (18,274)
Bonanno, Antonio 3:26:55 (3,914)
Bonarrigo, Marco 3:26:18 (3,810)
Bond, Adrian D 5:02:39 (26,263)
Bond, Andrew W 4:28:29 (18,162)
Bond, Craig A 4:47:28 (22,880)
Bond, Evan B 2:35:20 (115)
Bond, Glynn 4:06:33 (12,225)
Bond, Julian R 4:18:03 (15,220)
Bond, Leslie H 4:45:30 (22,432)
Bond, Michael C 4:59:00 (25,559)
Bond, Michael J 2:44:09 (300)
Bond, Paul A 3:37:15 (5,532)
Bond, Philip J 3:11:31 (2,079)
Bond, Raymond M 7:03:00 (34,904)
Bone, David 3:29:41 (4,390)
Bone, Jonathan P 4:45:01 (22,333)
Bone, Kenneth G 5:58:26 (32,868)
Bone, Michael A 4:56:10 (24,932)
Bone, Patrick 3:59:19 (10,522)
Bonelli, Anthony S 5:03:25 (26,420)
Boner, Dennis M 5:13:29 (28,082)
Bonera, Steven R 5:10:02 (27,515)
Bones, Colin G 4:02:50 (11,348)
Boney, Oliver C 3:29:26 (4,344)
Bongaerts, Roy J 3:53:04 (8,733)
Bonifacious, Barry 3:56:57 (9,798)
Bonnavion, Jean 4:55:47 (24,837)
Bonner, Nick D 3:54:20 (9,053)
Bonner, Richard E 3:30:04 (4,463)
Bonner, Timothy M 3:53:12 (8,770)
Bonner-Davies, Tobias A 4:37:40 (20,539)
Bonnett, Glenn S 3:33:45 (4,998)
Bonno, Yann 3:41:57 (6,368)
Bonometti, Giorgio 5:00:38 (25,906)
Bonson, Philippe 3:20:02 (3,001)
Bonthrone, Steven A 3:39:58 (5,991)
Bontoft, Alan 2:54:28 (709)
Boobbyer, Mark 4:23:34 (16,746)
Booker, Colin D 7:18:34 (35,067)
Booker, James W 4:13:45 (14,077)
Booker, Johnny 7:18:34 (35,067)
Booker, Steve R 3:08:54 (1,801)
Bookham, Colin 3:48:02 (7,592)
Bookham, Kevin 3:48:02 (7,592)
Boom, Kent F 5:05:43 (26,829)
Boon, Clive A 4:59:11 (25,600)
Boon, Dominic R 3:38:45 (5,765)
Boon, Matthew E 4:36:18 (20,164)
Boon, Robert 2:59:52 (1,119)
Boon, Tim 4:28:59 (18,304)
Boone, Scott D 3:56:15 (9,585)
Boorer, Craig E 4:32:29 (19,207)
Boorman, Nickolas 4:22:34 (16,492)
Boorman, William K 5:24:14 (29,650)
Booter, Joel 5:32:21 (30,595)
Booth, Adam S 3:26:51 (3,903)
Booth, Allan 5:55:20 (32,669)
Booth, Andrew A 3:56:58 (9,803)
Booth, Andrew J 4:50:16 (23,551)
Booth, Ashley D 4:08:51 (12,787)
Booth, Colin M 4:50:55 (23,715)
Booth, David 4:18:38 (15,408)
Booth, Gary M 4:15:40 (14,624)
Booth, Geoffrey N 3:27:06 (3,943)
Booth, Julian 4:19:42 (15,721)
Booth, Levi J 3:16:09 (2,597)
Booth, Richard 3:47:19 (7,419)
Booth, Robin 4:47:10 (22,813)
Booth, Roger 4:01:17 (11,000)
Booth, Terence 5:02:56 (26,327)
Booth, Vincent A 2:55:43 (786)
Booty, Craig L 4:55:43 (24,822)
Bor, Joseph S 4:22:51 (16,568)
Boranga, Mario 3:56:12 (9,575)
Bordley, Simon 5:25:12 (29,771)
Boreel, Jacob 4:05:16 (11,936)
Boreham, Paul J 4:01:28 (11,041)
Boreham, Samuel J 4:15:18 (14,527)
Borghese, Gilbert J 3:24:32 (3,521)
Borghi, Graziano 4:58:33 (25,455)
Borgman, Paul 3:51:06 (8,283)
Borgund, Ole J 4:02:00 (11,155)
Borland, Douglas J 4:48:26 (23,111)
Borley, David C 4:44:31 (22,215)
Bormann, Stefan-Christian 4:11:54 (13,590)
Born, John 4:03:12 (11,432)
Borrego, Cristobal 4:38:28 (20,749)
Borrero, José L 3:38:51 (5,784)
Borret, Wim 5:06:30 (26,964)
Bortoft, Arron P 3:40:31 (6,086)
Borzone, Ugo 3:25:58 (3,748)
Bosanko, Steven G 4:34:41 (19,762)
Bosch, Ulf 2:56:41 (859)
Boschetti, Paul L 4:12:25 (13,730)
Boschi, Stefano 3:59:56 (10,705)
Boseley, Richard S 3:48:58 (7,815)
Boserup, Soren 4:20:45 (16,007)
Bosgraaf, Jan-Jaap 3:52:41 (8,657)
Bosley, Graham J 5:13:22 (28,053)
Bosley, Philip M 4:21:01 (16,078)
Bosson, Paul J 2:51:54 (582)
Bostock, Lee A 3:49:01 (7,826)
Bostock, Malcolm S 2:59:03 (1,041)
Boston, David T 4:30:01 (18,591)
Boston, Nasser 4:01:20 (11,007)
Boswell, Mel 4:08:59 (12,823)
Boswell, Robert 5:41:45 (31,571)
Boswell, Stuart N 3:14:44 (2,451)
Bosworth, Paul D 4:54:17 (24,496)
Bosworth, Philip C 4:21:50 (16,292)
Botes, Juan 3:53:36 (8,883)
Botfield, Glyn J 3:53:38 (8,892)
Botha, Louis T 3:54:39 (9,139)
Botha, Peter 3:56:52 (9,775)
Botham, Stephen 3:42:07 (6,406)
Bothner, Frieder 3:50:29 (8,147)
Bothorel, Alain 3:28:32 (4,203)
Bott, Adam J 6:10:01 (33,533)
Bott, Thomas C 3:54:51 (9,198)
Bottell, Mark 5:13:37 (28,103)
Bottomley, Ian F 4:14:47 (14,372)
Bottoms, Dave 4:59:15 (25,615)
Bottrill, Darren J 3:25:11 (3,618)
Boucault, Darren S 4:01:34 (11,062)
Boucher, Michael B 2:30:31 (72)
Boucher, Raymond P 4:25:37 (17,321)
Boucher, William J 3:36:45 (5,458)

Bougeard, Christophe	4:47:33 (22,891)
Boughton, Brian S	5:15:43 (28,445)
Boughton, Ellis J	4:27:12 (17,802)
Boughton, Jeremy	3:41:24 (6,259)
Boughton, Neil C	5:04:38 (26,618)
Bouhours, Gilles	3:59:44 (10,641)
Boulby, Kenneth A	3:59:51 (10,682)
Bould, Paul G	4:24:09 (16,890)
Boult, Stephen W	4:04:02 (11,646)
Boulter, David	3:58:46 (10,375)
Boulton, Andrew W	3:57:29 (9,973)
Boulton, Richard C	4:21:29 (16,200)
Boulton, Richard H	5:09:28 (27,432)
Boulton, Robert	5:00:45 (25,926)
Boundy, Stuart R	4:07:19 (12,423)
Bourde, Marc P	5:57:57 (32,831)
Bourdillon, Patrick C	4:26:01 (17,441)
Bourget, Darren M	4:09:20 (12,917)
Bourke, Daniel J	4:47:27 (22,875)
Bourke, Jim F	5:05:57 (26,862)
Bourke, Mark A	3:43:58 (6,736)
Bourne, Chris	4:40:41 (21,303)
Bourne, Frank F	6:07:56 (33,439)
Bourne, Matthew C	5:11:59 (27,819)
Bourne, Richard L	4:23:22 (16,706)
Bourne, Stanley B	5:20:37 (29,201)
Bourquin, Marc B	3:01:45 (1,243)
Boursicot, Laurent	4:21:16 (16,135)
Boutall, Christopher D	4:55:03 (24,687)
Boutcher, Kelly	5:52:23 (32,446)
Boutilier, James R	4:20:08 (15,838)
Bouzon, Daniel	2:59:55 (1,121)
Bovaird, Christopher J	3:49:09 (7,854)
Bovey, Adrian	5:03:57 (26,509)
Bovill, Chris	4:10:26 (13,215)
Boville, Matt A	3:43:21 (6,630)
Bowal, Paul	4:14:50 (14,390)
Bowden, Martin R	3:57:29 (9,973)
Bowden, Paul	4:04:07 (11,665)
Bowditch, Mark	3:07:36 (1,687)
Bowell, Clive R.	4:38:21 (20,709)
Bowell, Mark J	4:29:10 (18,359)
Bowen, Baron A	3:54:51 (9,198)
Bowen, Brian M	4:46:04 (22,566)
Bowen, Chris H	7:07:14 (34,952)
Bowen, Gary	4:42:21 (21,705)
Bowen, James A	5:09:03 (27,359)
Bowen, Kevin A	6:24:52 (34,091)
Bowen, Leslie A	5:03:12 (26,385)
Bowen, Marcus T	4:17:40 (15,130)
Bowen, Mathew	4:58:23 (25,412)
Bowen, Paul	5:34:22 (30,824)
Bowen, Paul D	3:52:43 (8,664)
Bowen, Simon J	4:15:52 (14,678)
Bowen, William	4:07:24 (12,438)
Bower, Adrian K	4:01:28 (11,041)
Bower, Brian	3:12:01 (2,142)
Bower, Rick P	4:17:45 (15,149)
Bower, Will	4:39:54 (21,112)
Bowerman, Paddy E	4:05:44 (12,036)
Bowers, David J	4:47:53 (22,985)
Bowers, Nick	4:05:42 (12,026)
Bowers, Paul A	3:58:42 (10,347)
Bowers, Philip D	3:51:27 (8,365)
Bowery, Richard P	4:22:26 (16,453)
Bowes, David	4:32:40 (19,244)
Bowie, David A	4:50:13 (23,539)
Bowie, Stephen B	4:22:00 (16,335)
Bowie, William B	4:22:00 (16,335)
Bowker, John R	3:05:05 (1,473)
Bowker, Robert J	4:04:08 (11,670)
Bowkett, Andrew	4:24:48 (17,071)
Bowkett, Nick J	5:30:40 (30,431)
Bowler, Neil A	4:22:52 (16,574)
Bowler, Robert S	4:34:13 (19,634)
Bowles, Andrew M	4:12:14 (13,679)
Bowles, Darren D	5:44:53 (31,838)
Bowles, Mark J	4:12:44 (13,811)
Bowles, Paul J	3:31:13 (4,634)
Bowley, Michael D	5:51:55 (32,407)
Bowling, Christopher J	3:59:59 (10,724)
Bowling, Shane P	3:55:15 (9,292)
Bowlzer, Nicholas M	3:33:08 (4,904)

Bowman, David R	3:39:33 (5,923)
Bowman, Jeremy D	4:58:43 (25,489)
Bowman, Mark O	4:02:52 (11,357)
Bowman, Michael T	5:19:07 (28,958)
Bowman, Nicholas D	3:56:54 (9,785)
Bown, Alan C	6:23:55 (34,058)
Bownes, George H	3:19:06 (2,890)
Bowring, Guy A	5:04:05 (26,527)
Bowsher, Edward J	5:31:24 (30,508)
Bowyer, Gary A	3:56:55 (9,787)
Bowyer, Malcolm J	3:02:12 (1,278)
Box, Ian	3:29:10 (4,306)
Box, Matthew	3:40:49 (6,142)
Box, Peter J	4:26:22 (17,555)
Boxall, Ben J	4:40:33 (21,273)
Boxall, Richard J	4:29:13 (18,372)
Boyall, Timothy J	3:40:17 (6,048)
Boyce, Hugo M	3:50:51 (8,224)
Boyce, Richard E	3:26:59 (3,927)
Boyd, David	4:24:29 (16,984)
Boyd, Derek A	6:41:28 (34,533)
Boyd, Eric	5:22:26 (29,404)
Boyd, Fergus M	3:44:55 (6,940)
Boyd, Robert P	3:56:27 (9,652)
Boyd-Rochford, Josh	5:21:08 (29,253)
Boyer, Gilles	4:00:12 (10,766)
Boyer, Stephan	4:13:03 (13,894)
Boyes, Ricky J	4:48:10 (23,045)
Boyle, Anthony J	5:12:41 (27,940)
Boyle, Henry R	4:01:15 (10,995)
Boyle, James	3:57:14 (9,902)
Boyle, James J	4:39:57 (21,127)
Boyle, Malachy E	4:18:55 (15,489)
Boyle, Martin J	3:53:32 (8,866)
Boyter, Gavin	3:16:14 (2,607)
Braackstone, Lawrence C	4:35:58 (20,078)
Brabant, Valery	4:02:53 (11,359)
Brace, Christopher P	4:55:48 (24,841)
Bracegirdle, Ian	5:04:42 (26,631)
Bracegirdle, Paul A	5:54:04 (32,572)
Bracewell, Richard A	3:59:48 (10,666)
Bracey, Nick	3:44:04 (6,751)
Brachet, Remy	3:39:30 (5,913)
Bracken, Neil	4:21:34 (16,221)
Brackenbury, Colin D	4:53:21 (24,263)
Brackett, Damian M	3:46:44 (7,290)
Brackstone, Mark A	4:28:55 (18,279)
Bradbeer, Keiran D	4:39:29 (21,008)
Bradbury, Alan K	3:20:35 (3,054)
Bradbury, Kelvin E	3:54:15 (9,034)
Bradbury, Matthew	4:03:02 (11,396)
Bradbury, Scott	5:01:29 (26,061)
Bradbury, Simon P	4:53:18 (24,251)
Bradbury, Thomas J	4:20:14 (15,866)
Braddock, David A	5:11:38 (27,760)
Brader, Phillip	4:07:07 (12,376)
Bradfield, Kevin	4:41:50 (21,597)
Bradfield, Richard J	3:53:10 (8,762)
Bradfield, Tim M	5:27:36 (30,054)
Bradford, Malcolm J	6:56:36 (34,824)
Bradford, Matt	3:40:32 (6,089)
Bradford, Nick	3:42:06 (6,401)
Bradley, Barrington J	3:56:06 (9,538)
Bradley, Christian J	4:47:29 (22,883)
Bradley, David L	4:32:09 (19,127)
Bradley, Dean M	4:41:24 (21,498)
Bradley, Harvey	3:48:00 (7,581)
Bradley, James A	3:52:59 (8,713)
Bradley, Justin M	4:11:38 (13,518)
Bradley, Leslie J	4:47:44 (22,949)
Bradley, Malcolm	3:31:20 (4,656)
Bradley, Mark	4:06:40 (12,257)
Bradley, Matthew J	4:13:57 (14,131)
Bradley, Michael	3:56:37 (9,696)
Bradley, Neil S	4:13:16 (13,955)
Bradley, Richard J	3:29:36 (4,370)
Bradley, Tony J	4:33:21 (19,396)
Bradley, William A	4:10:46 (13,276)
Bradnam, Stephen E	3:14:22 (2,401)
Bradnock, Stephen J	3:30:59 (4,601)
Bradshaw, Brian S	5:27:23 (30,028)
Bradshaw, Dean	5:19:29 (29,029)
Bradshaw, Gary	4:14:24 (14,273)

Bradshaw, John V	5:21:45 (29,320)
Bradshaw, Nigel T	4:50:22 (23,585)
Bradshaw, Stephen	4:03:45 (11,559)
Bradwell, Andrew D	5:01:11 (26,007)
Brady, Anthony	4:17:42 (15,140)
Brady, Bryan	4:15:00 (14,448)
Brady, Carl	4:18:13 (15,269)
Brady, Gerry J	6:24:54 (34,095)
Brady, John C	3:33:57 (5,036)
Brady, Joseph M	2:56:57 (882)
Brady, Matthew	3:39:40 (5,945)
Brady, Michael	3:38:25 (5,712)
Brady, Peter F	5:21:09 (29,255)
Bragg, Stephen J	3:35:02 (5,189)
Bragg, Thomas W	4:35:20 (19,919)
Brahams, Nigel R	4:05:37 (12,008)
Brain, Alun L	4:13:14 (13,948)
Brain, Robert E	3:38:42 (5,754)
Braithwaite, Andrew J	6:31:57 (34,304)
Braithwaite, Lee A	4:52:52 (24,143)
Braithwaite, Michael	4:36:05 (20,104)
Braithwaite, Peter W	4:13:32 (14,024)
Brake, Martin J	4:58:53 (25,530)
Brakes, William R	5:24:19 (29,660)
Bramble, George A	3:30:29 (4,523)
Brame, Tony	5:04:03 (26,522)
Brameld, Mervyn	4:06:41 (12,260)
Bramhall, Chris	5:02:43 (26,278)
Bramhall, Paul J	3:39:13 (5,854)
Bramley, Matthew	3:59:01 (10,439)
Bramley, Wayne	2:56:36 (851)
Bramwell, Nicholas J	5:15:13 (28,374)
Branca, Andrea	2:59:59 (1,128)
Branch, Alan D	4:10:59 (13,345)
Branch, Mark P	4:56:09 (24,929)
Brand, Julian A	3:19:40 (2,961)
Brand, Mark	4:08:29 (12,690)
Brand, Martin	4:38:16 (20,689)
Brand, Peter A	4:58:56 (25,541)
Brand, Philip	4:12:25 (13,730)
Brand, Richard	4:09:41 (13,007)
Brand, Roger J	3:42:22 (6,445)
Brand, Stephen D	5:29:21 (30,285)
Brandon, Chris	4:48:17 (23,073)
Brandon, Dirk	2:52:23 (607)
Brandon, Graham T	4:50:07 (23,518)
Brandt, Daniel G	4:38:45 (20,814)
Brandt, Henrik L	5:22:37 (29,444)
Brandt, Paul	3:34:29 (5,122)
Braniff, Ian J	3:29:25 (4,341)
Brannagan, Malcolm	4:22:06 (16,367)
Brannelly, John	3:35:09 (5,203)
Brannigan, Damien T	2:52:04 (595)
Brannigan, Malatuy	4:23:53 (16,822)
Brannock, John W	4:02:07 (11,186)
Brans, Cornelis J	4:17:13 (15,015)
Bransgrove, Jamie C	5:52:33 (32,469)
Bransom, Kenneth A	4:29:25 (18,439)
Branson, Benjamin J	4:36:53 (20,328)
Branson, Jonathan	3:56:12 (9,575)
Branson, Martin C	4:33:31 (19,440)
Branston, Rob J	4:11:52 (13,574)
Brant, Bruce	3:49:13 (7,866)
Brantjes, Willem P	5:45:50 (31,925)
Brasher, Martin L	3:56:01 (9,517)
Brassington, Andrew R	4:49:34 (23,379)
Bratherton, Michael	4:48:13 (23,056)
Bratten, Alistair	3:36:03 (5,346)
Braunton, David W	4:41:29 (21,518)
Braverman, Terry P	5:03:42 (26,461)
Bray, Alan	3:47:22 (7,430)
Bray, David M	5:24:40 (29,705)
Bray, Edward W	3:48:17 (7,652)
Bray, Jonathan	4:10:57 (13,333)
Bray, Michael G	4:02:25 (11,250)
Bray, Oliver D	4:38:40 (20,792)
Bray, Richard S	3:46:54 (7,330)
Bray, Robert A	3:58:31 (10,293)
Bray, Vivian F	3:54:56 (9,226)
Braybrook, Colin A	3:23:30 (3,374)
Braybrook, James W	5:09:03 (27,359)
Braybrook, Mark H	4:43:17 (21,930)
Brazier, Bill S	4:26:24 (17,570)

Brazil, Mick J	3:59:45 (10,649)
Breaden, Andrew J	3:57:38 (10,024)
Brear, Stephen E	5:00:50 (25,942)
Brearley, Kenneth R	4:29:20 (18,412)
Brearley, Michael	3:07:55 (1,706)
Brecht, Philip T	4:01:23 (11,020)
Breen, Martin J	5:16:35 (28,561)
Breese, Ian C	4:18:20 (15,307)
Breitmoser, Frank	4:44:05 (22,113)
Brench, Darren E	3:35:23 (5,237)
Brenchley, Simon P	5:35:18 (30,932)
Brencic, Alexej	3:49:19 (7,897)
Brennan, Dave	6:50:01 (34,709)
Brennan, Ian H	3:51:47 (8,433)
Brennan, John F	4:19:13 (15,582)
Brennan, Mark	5:09:26 (27,427)
Brennan, Neill	3:52:47 (8,682)
Brennan, Paul M	3:47:13 (7,395)
Brennan, Seamus	5:46:50 (32,002)
Brennan, Steven P	5:19:31 (29,035)
Brennan, Thaddeus P	4:53:32 (24,310)
Brennan, Tim J	5:46:49 (32,001)
Brennan, Timothy R	3:46:29 (7,241)
Brennand, Thomas C	4:46:54 (22,753)
Brenner, Bruce	5:02:00 (26,143)
Brenner, Walter H	3:42:20 (6,438)
Brent, Tim J	4:29:07 (18,345)
Brentnall, Mark N	3:36:25 (5,412)
Brereton, Allan A	4:35:21 (19,931)
Bresadola, Fabrizio	4:27:27 (17,869)
Bresland, Noel P	3:50:49 (8,211)
Breslin, Beau	4:17:24 (15,068)
Breslin, Edward D	4:15:28 (14,566)
Breslin, Matthew	3:46:27 (7,232)
Breslin, Peter R	3:38:14 (5,684)
Brett, Barry J	4:34:39 (19,748)
Brett, Ian D	3:54:07 (8,999)
Brett, Marc A	6:42:35 (34,558)
Brett, Stephen	3:15:59 (2,570)
Breuer, John P	3:07:27 (1,672)
Breuling, Thomas A	4:19:43 (15,727)
Brew, Patrick	3:07:34 (1,682)
Brewer, Adam	4:10:53 (13,310)
Brewer, Andrew	3:34:45 (5,151)
Brewer, John	3:56:39 (9,710)
Brewer, John R	3:41:01 (6,182)
Brewer, Steven W	3:09:25 (1,853)
Brewitt, Jonathan K	3:41:02 (6,186)
Brewster, David C	4:45:48 (22,498)
Brewster, Graham J	4:41:05 (21,412)
Brian, Thomas J	5:25:42 (29,823)
Briars, Mark S	4:15:58 (14,707)
Brice, Paddy	3:17:00 (2,676)
Brichet, David	4:10:54 (13,317)
Bridge, James	4:13:56 (14,125)
Bridge, Peter E	5:58:23 (32,867)
Bridger, Darren J	3:56:34 (9,681)
Bridger, James F	3:55:00 (9,238)
Bridges, Anthony M	2:52:32 (612)
Bridges, Jonathan	4:09:21 (12,921)
Bridges, Paul H	3:56:10 (9,562)
Bridgland, Neil P	5:11:34 (27,752)
Bridgman, Rob O	4:28:54 (18,274)
Bridgwood, Richard J	4:37:28 (20,489)
Bridle, David	3:27:54 (4,091)
Bridson, Mark A	3:41:32 (6,282)
Briens, Jean-Marc G	3:18:31 (2,834)
Brier, Anthony J	4:53:17 (24,243)
Brier, Chris A	4:03:25 (11,485)
Brierley, Alexander	4:16:46 (14,907)
Brierley, Michael A	6:01:07 (33,031)
Briffett, Stephen	4:32:25 (19,190)
Briggs, Andrew M	6:37:07 (34,435)
Briggs, Daniel R	5:06:07 (26,894)
Briggs, David J	4:34:09 (19,608)
Briggs, Gary	4:10:53 (13,310)
Briggs, Michael J	4:07:10 (12,387)
Briggs, Michael P	4:47:11 (22,818)
Briggs, Peter I	3:37:26 (5,564)
Briggs, Robert	5:01:19 (26,031)
Bright, Barry	3:47:54 (7,548)
Bright, Jeremy	3:52:06 (8,504)
Bright, John	4:51:36 (23,853)

Bright, Kevin J	3:54:27 (9,088)
Bright, Mark	4:12:27 (13,737)
Brightman, Patrick J	4:43:32 (21,990)
Brightwell, Jonathan J	4:23:02 (16,607)
Brightwell, Terry G	3:16:44 (2,651)
Brignoli, Marco	5:16:47 (28,597)
Briley, Colin J	4:24:20 (16,938)
Briley, Gary	4:55:40 (24,804)
Briley, Stephen J	4:55:37 (24,795)
Brimblecombe, David M	5:11:55 (27,807)
Brimson, Jason H	5:02:15 (26,190)
Brind, Adam J	4:47:33 (22,891)
Brine, Alan C	4:07:28 (12,452)
Brine, Jonathan P	3:11:02 (2,037)
Bringloe, Scott W	4:36:48 (20,306)
Brinklow, David A	6:04:43 (33,254)
Brinkschulte, Holger	4:02:00 (11,155)
Brisco, Douglas A	2:54:49 (733)
Brisco, John	4:40:32 (21,267)
Briscoe, Leigh S	5:13:36 (28,101)
Briscoe, Philip A	4:54:26 (24,534)
Brislen, Christopher	4:57:14 (25,181)
Bristow, Ian C	4:21:16 (16,135)
Bristow, Simon P	4:51:25 (23,816)
Briswalter, Jean-Luc	2:48:44 (450)
Brito, Matt J	3:52:32 (8,612)
Britten, Darryl P	6:01:22 (33,042)
Brittleton, Peter C	3:15:58 (2,567)
Britton, Alan R	3:39:58 (5,991)
Britton, Russell	4:53:09 (24,210)
Brixey, Barry	4:54:37 (24,578)
Broad, Carl W	4:25:13 (17,189)
Broad, Matthew J	3:50:55 (8,239)
Broad, Nigel P	3:38:16 (5,693)
Broad, Robert J	4:24:39 (17,026)
Broadbent, Alex	4:45:28 (22,425)
Broadbent, Christopher J	4:06:52 (12,303)
Broadbent, Steven S	3:40:19 (6,052)
Broadhurst, Bruce	4:36:44 (20,289)
Broadley, Anthony P	4:41:21 (21,479)
Broadway, Matthew E	4:15:27 (14,563)
Brock, Peter	4:01:18 (11,001)
Brockhurst, Daniel	4:01:53 (11,124)
Brocklehurst, Alexander J	4:11:44 (13,548)
Brocklehurst, Christopher	4:40:33 (21,273)
Brocklehurst, Matthew E	4:13:32 (14,024)
Brocklehurst, Richard H	3:47:38 (7,482)
Brocklesby, Christopher W	5:09:24 (27,422)
Brockman, Michael J	3:59:02 (10,443)
Brockwell, Darren J	5:01:52 (26,118)
Broder, Philip	4:51:59 (23,932)
Broderick, Derek	7:05:39 (34,935)
Brodie, Alexander	4:50:18 (23,564)
Brodie, Andy J	4:22:35 (16,497)
Brody, Keith	3:05:01 (1,468)
Brody, Martin	3:42:15 (6,425)
Brogden, Richard A	3:06:37 (1,603)
Brogini, Marco	3:57:44 (10,045)
Bromley, Elliott M	5:03:06 (26,362)
Bromley, Martin	3:47:59 (7,573)
Bromley, Michael A	4:39:08 (20,907)
Bromley, Nigel G	4:21:30 (16,207)
Bromwich, Neil P	3:47:12 (7,391)
Brons, David	5:21:20 (29,279)
Brook, Giles T	3:48:13 (7,636)
Brook, John	5:49:10 (32,195)
Brook, Stephen W	3:47:31 (7,460)
Brookbanks, Kevin	4:38:41 (20,794)
Brooke, Anthony D	3:07:53 (1,704)
Brooke, David J	3:26:48 (3,900)
Brooke, Nick J	3:26:00 (3,757)
Brooke-Little, Leo J	3:50:22 (8,118)
Brooker, John S	3:41:52 (6,348)
Brooker, Keith P	5:22:30 (29,419)
Brooker, Matthew J	4:14:15 (14,229)
Brooker, Robert C	5:12:00 (27,822)
Brooker, Vince R	4:31:31 (18,974)
Brookes, Alan R	4:21:32 (16,213)
Brookes, David R	4:57:34 (25,242)
Brookes, Gareth	4:29:33 (18,482)
Brookes, James P	3:56:29 (9,659)
Brookes, James W	3:55:44 (9,443)
Brookes, John L	5:31:55 (30,551)

Brookes, Neil	4:15:52 (14,678)
Brookes, Nigel A	3:13:21 (2,281)
Brookes, Steven R	2:48:06 (421)
Brookes, Thomas	4:19:45 (15,740)
Brookfield, Anthony J	5:19:09 (28,963)
Brooking, Timothy J	3:53:43 (8,917)
Brooks, Andrew J	3:43:54 (6,720)
Brooks, Anthony D	5:52:24 (32,451)
Brooks, Christopher	4:12:38 (13,788)
Brooks, Colin	5:33:08 (30,683)
Brooks, Darren N	5:31:20 (30,495)
Brooks, Dave A	3:33:46 (5,003)
Brooks, Edward E	4:58:24 (25,416)
Brooks, Graham L	4:29:33 (18,482)
Brooks, Graham L	5:06:11 (26,905)
Brooks, James	3:51:54 (8,461)
Brooks, Joshua J	5:17:33 (28,726)
Brooks, Michael	3:16:06 (2,590)
Brooks, Nick	4:13:17 (13,964)
Brooks, Patrick J	5:58:07 (32,849)
Brooks, Paul G	4:40:11 (21,182)
Brooks, Paul K	3:23:49 (3,423)
Brooks, Paul S	3:54:52 (9,202)
Brooks, Richard A	3:57:49 (10,080)
Brooks, Simon J	4:50:39 (23,662)
Brooks, Simon P	3:30:53 (4,588)
Brooks, Steve P	6:50:06 (34,725)
Brooks, Stuart M	5:54:11 (32,582)
Brooks, Tim	3:47:23 (7,434)
Brookshaw, Ben I	3:34:21 (5,101)
Broom, David M	4:41:25 (21,502)
Broom, Jack J	4:01:15 (10,995)
Broom, John	2:51:08 (542)
Broomberg, Jonathan	3:52:00 (8,485)
Broome, George B	5:59:28 (32,944)
Broomfield, Martyn R	4:10:15 (13,153)
Broomhall, Ian P	5:10:11 (27,525)
Brophy, John	4:56:37 (25,045)
Brosi, Henry	4:34:02 (19,575)
Broster, Carl R	4:04:02 (11,646)
Broster, Richard B	4:07:46 (12,523)
Brotherton, Anthony C	3:49:08 (7,851)
Brotherton, Guy C	5:36:35 (31,066)
Brouard, Arnaud	4:00:24 (10,804)
Brough, Jon R	3:12:17 (2,172)
Brougham, Sam M	5:30:08 (30,375)
Broughton, Alan	2:44:42 (312)
Broughton, David	4:26:57 (17,737)
Broughton, Graham R	4:09:56 (13,079)
Broughton, Nicholas C	3:14:17 (2,391)
Broughton, Robert C	4:04:27 (11,734)
Browes, Christopher J	4:47:46 (22,960)
Brown, Adam J	4:30:14 (18,662)
Brown, Adrian P	4:44:44 (22,255)
Brown, Aidan	4:58:18 (25,393)
Brown, Alan	7:07:04 (34,949)
Brown, Alan R	4:25:58 (17,423)
Brown, Alastair I	4:29:04 (18,330)
Brown, Alastair M	3:54:18 (9,046)
Brown, Alexander	4:34:30 (19,711)
Brown, Alexander J	4:47:09 (22,806)
Brown, Allan	4:28:47 (18,241)
Brown, Andrew	4:26:06 (17,475)
Brown, Andrew J	3:52:39 (8,646)
Brown, Andrew J	4:30:30 (18,731)
Brown, Andrew K	3:46:32 (7,247)
Brown, Andrew N	4:52:57 (24,158)
Brown, Andrew R	5:21:42 (29,312)
Brown, Andy J	3:34:36 (5,135)
Brown, Anthony D	5:43:18 (31,702)
Brown, Anthony J	3:54:55 (9,221)
Brown, Chris	5:16:48 (28,601)
Brown, Chris N	4:19:06 (15,547)
Brown, Christopher D	5:05:48 (26,844)
Brown, Clifford	3:03:01 (1,331)
Brown, Colin	4:05:35 (12,003)
Brown, Daniel M	3:45:22 (7,023)
Brown, Daniel S	4:44:50 (22,281)
Brown, Darran	4:37:29 (20,494)
Brown, David	4:33:56 (19,554)
Brown, David C	6:51:42 (34,748)
Brown, David H	2:58:43 (1,006)
Brown, David I	4:38:43 (20,803)

Brown, David J	3:47:43 (7,509)	
Brown, David M	4:47:55 (22,992)	
Brown, David R	5:00:07 (25,798)	
Brown, David R	5:46:45 (31,996)	
Brown, David W	3:58:23 (10,255)	
Brown, Dean C	4:27:50 (17,992)	
Brown, Derek	2:55:41 (784)	
Brown, Donald F	5:13:56 (28,156)	
Brown, Duncan H	3:40:53 (6,165)	
Brown, Duncan J	4:36:47 (20,298)	
Brown, Eivind	4:27:54 (18,015)	
Brown, Gary R	4:17:32 (15,097)	
Brown, Gavin D	4:37:14 (20,423)	
Brown, Gavin W	4:29:54 (18,567)	
Brown, Geoffrey H	5:13:47 (28,130)	
Brown, Godfrey L	3:59:42 (10,630)	
Brown, Gordon	3:33:26 (4,951)	
Brown, Henry C	2:32:56 (93)	
Brown, Ian	3:09:18 (1,842)	
Brown, Ian C	4:41:06 (21,422)	
Brown, Ian J	4:51:34 (23,846)	
Brown, Ian M	2:58:43 (1,006)	
Brown, Ian V	5:47:47 (32,079)	
Brown, James	3:51:19 (8,333)	
Brown, James C	4:39:00 (20,879)	
Brown, James H	3:06:40 (1,607)	
Brown, James H	4:35:13 (19,887)	
Brown, James M	3:52:40 (8,651)	
Brown, James R	3:34:23 (5,107)	
Brown, Jamie L	4:19:10 (15,567)	
Brown, Jeff M	4:13:46 (14,083)	
Brown, Jeffrey M	4:12:00 (13,625)	
Brown, Jeremy C	4:05:19 (11,952)	
Brown, Joe	4:57:09 (25,164)	
Brown, John A	5:53:36 (32,539)	
Brown, John G	4:50:38 (23,658)	
Brown, John M	5:42:29 (31,625)	
Brown, John R	3:51:14 (8,309)	
Brown, Jon	2:09:31 (6)	
Brown, Joseph	4:44:23 (22,188)	
Brown, Kale	4:26:12 (17,508)	
Brown, Keith W	3:27:28 (4,012)	
Brown, Lawrence K	4:05:25 (11,971)	
Brown, Malcolm A	5:26:16 (29,898)	
Brown, Martin	4:02:14 (11,210)	
Brown, Martin J	3:35:52 (5,317)	
Brown, Matthew J	3:59:17 (10,515)	
Brown, Matthew S	4:04:27 (11,734)	
Brown, Michael J	3:34:15 (5,091)	
Brown, Michael M	4:21:50 (16,292)	
Brown, Michael N	5:09:04 (27,362)	
Brown, Michael P	5:01:10 (26,002)	
Brown, Neil G	3:48:47 (7,780)	
Brown, Nicholas E	4:10:55 (13,323)	
Brown, Patrick	4:57:10 (25,169)	
Brown, Paul A	4:00:30 (10,832)	
Brown, Paul D	4:22:02 (16,350)	
Brown, Paul R	4:54:34 (24,573)	
Brown, Raymond	5:43:53 (31,751)	
Brown, Richard A	5:16:41 (28,573)	
Brown, Richard C	4:38:12 (20,670)	
Brown, Richard H	6:42:34 (34,557)	
Brown, Richard M	4:53:58 (24,415)	
Brown, Richard S	3:41:13 (6,218)	
Brown, Rob	4:27:10 (17,792)	
Brown, Robert	4:33:46 (19,513)	
Brown, Robert A	3:50:12 (8,084)	
Brown, Robert G	4:07:17 (12,413)	
Brown, Robert J	4:12:32 (13,752)	
Brown, Roger J	5:13:37 (28,103)	
Brown, Roger L	5:29:34 (30,314)	
Brown, Roger M	4:03:53 (11,602)	
Brown, Roger S	2:55:21 (757)	
Brown, Roger T	4:31:29 (18,965)	
Brown, Roy G	4:55:14 (24,726)	
Brown, Shaun	3:04:32 (1,431)	
Brown, Simon	3:20:25 (3,037)	
Brown, Simon J	3:07:59 (1,714)	
Brown, Simon J	4:48:52 (23,202)	
Brown, Steen H	3:55:28 (9,358)	
Brown, Stephen	4:30:20 (18,687)	
Brown, Stephen J	3:08:19 (1,746)	
Brown, Steve R	4:54:10 (24,463)	
Brown, Terence G	3:57:07 (9,864)	
Brown, Terry R	4:06:56 (12,324)	
Brown, Thomas W	3:39:03 (5,830)	
Brown, Timothy P	3:57:09 (9,875)	
Brown, Timothy S	2:43:03 (267)	
Brown, William E	4:29:22 (18,420)	
Brown, William J	5:58:29 (32,877)	
Brown, William R	4:39:07 (20,904)	
Brown, Zach R	4:46:20 (22,629)	
Brownbill, Philip	4:16:48 (14,913)	
Brownbill, Roger L	5:18:34 (28,877)	
Browne, Christopher	4:20:16 (15,879)	
Browne, Daryl S	4:41:55 (21,607)	
Browne, Russell F	4:27:35 (17,915)	
Browne, Shaun	4:38:41 (20,794)	
Browne, Simon M	4:56:58 (25,124)	
Brownie, Francis	4:24:08 (16,886)	
Brownigg, Matthew Haydon	3:41:26 (6,266)	
Browning, Allen J	5:02:20 (26,207)	
Browning, Brian J	6:22:17 (34,003)	
Browning, David C	4:11:01 (13,354)	
Browning, John K	4:08:18 (12,636)	
Browning, Matthew	5:41:26 (31,546)	
Browning, Paul	3:20:58 (3,084)	
Browning, Peter C	4:14:21 (14,257)	
Browning, Roger L	4:10:12 (13,140)	
Browning, Terry	3:29:32 (4,361)	
Brownlie, Alan R	4:08:01 (12,574)	
Brownlie, James M	6:12:02 (33,618)	
Brownlie, Peter R	4:06:19 (12,171)	
Brownlow, Peter R	5:01:59 (26,142)	
Brownson, Glen	4:29:14 (18,375)	
Broxton, Gareth M	4:46:01 (22,554)	
Broxton, Mark D	3:49:06 (7,847)	
Bruce, Andrew K	3:13:23 (2,289)	
Bruce, Charles D	4:01:06 (10,962)	
Bruce, Sandy	4:45:29 (22,429)	
Bruce-Williams, James A	4:42:55 (21,855)	
Brudenell, Guy J	5:25:06 (29,760)	
Bruggheman, Denis	3:04:43 (1,443)	
Brugts, Peter	3:37:21 (5,548)	
Brumby, Ged	4:27:36 (17,921)	
Brun, Daniel	3:18:12 (2,804)	
Brun, Gerard	4:01:44 (11,097)	
Brun, Jean-Louis M	4:41:05 (21,412)	
Brunclik, Martin	4:00:13 (10,771)	
Brundle, Michael F	4:13:58 (14,135)	
Bruneau, Doninic	3:51:15 (8,316)	
Bruner, Paul L	3:54:45 (9,171)	
Bruni, Gianpaulo	3:12:39 (2,210)	
Bruni, Roberto	3:27:39 (4,047)	
Bruniges, Colin D	4:03:44 (11,554)	
Brunngartner, Fanz	4:07:55 (12,557)	
Brunskill, Simon N	3:47:13 (7,395)	
Brunton, Guthrie W	3:13:08 (2,261)	
Brunton, Keith A	4:41:37 (21,549)	
Brushett, Adam K	3:36:58 (5,495)	
Brushett, Matthew J	4:15:33 (14,593)	
Bruton, Richard W	4:38:52 (20,844)	
Bruton, Russell F	4:46:11 (22,600)	
Bruyneel, Hendrik	2:43:05 (268)	
Bruyns, François	3:14:44 (2,451)	
Bruzek, Karl	3:50:48 (8,208)	
Bryan, Andrew P	4:35:31 (19,981)	
Bryan, Anthony P	5:34:23 (30,828)	
Bryan, Benedict J	4:32:37 (19,231)	
Bryan, John B	6:36:22 (34,418)	
Bryan, Maxwell C	4:25:40 (17,337)	
Bryan, Peter	4:00:30 (10,832)	
Bryan, Philip E	4:16:08 (14,751)	
Bryan, Stephen	4:00:23 (10,799)	
Bryant, Adam L	3:53:14 (8,778)	
Bryant, Andrew D	3:16:07 (2,593)	
Bryant, Gavin J	4:17:59 (15,201)	
Bryant, John M	3:57:47 (10,070)	
Bryant, John W	4:50:06 (23,514)	
Bryant, Keith A	3:53:48 (8,934)	
Bryant, Michael R	5:00:25 (25,866)	
Bryant, Peter S	4:57:56 (25,307)	
Bryant, Robert E	4:17:59 (15,201)	
Bryant, Stewart R	3:41:53 (6,351)	
Bryant, William G	5:00:16 (25,838)	
Bryanton, Paul	5:58:32 (32,882)	
Bryer, Steven M	3:49:51 (8,007)	
Bryngelsson, Anders M	3:44:56 (6,946)	
Bryson, Daniel B	4:10:09 (13,127)	
Btitton, Matthew C	3:45:20 (7,012)	
Bubb, Nick J	4:15:11 (14,498)	
Bublitz, Gerhard	4:42:37 (21,776)	
Buchan, Fraser J	5:14:14 (28,214)	
Buchan, Rob	3:52:33 (8,615)	
Buchan, Stuart	2:42:52 (261)	
Buchanan, Jason C	4:07:34 (12,467)	
Buchanan, Mark	4:25:00 (17,125)	
Buchanan, Michael J	4:18:32 (15,368)	
Buchanan, Nigel B	4:40:18 (21,209)	
Bucher, Mark	2:55:44 (788)	
Buck, Colin M	5:11:35 (27,754)	
Buck, Gerald	4:13:10 (13,928)	
Buck, Jonathan	4:18:10 (15,253)	
Bucke, Colin J	4:03:53 (11,602)	
Buckell, Gary A	5:28:45 (30,214)	
Buckenham, Peter J	4:25:06 (17,152)	
Buckhurst, William W	4:18:42 (15,433)	
Buckingham, Christopher	4:33:30 (19,433)	
Buckingham, Mark A	5:09:25 (27,426)	
Buckingham, Pete	3:27:44 (4,064)	
Buckingham, Peter J	3:25:32 (3,680)	
Buckley, Allan L	4:04:29 (11,741)	
Buckley, Andrew	4:05:59 (12,090)	
Buckley, Andrew L	6:39:26 (34,491)	
Buckley, Brian W	3:51:27 (8,365)	
Buckley, Darryl	3:52:29 (8,599)	
Buckley, David M	3:58:02 (10,152)	
Buckley, Dawson	5:15:32 (28,422)	
Buckley, James A	4:14:57 (14,425)	
Buckley, James D	4:10:03 (13,101)	
Buckley, James E	3:58:02 (10,152)	
Buckley, Jonathan E	3:13:06 (2,257)	
Buckley, Peter	4:40:56 (21,371)	
Buckley, Robert A	3:38:26 (5,714)	
Buckley, Stephen J	4:32:54 (19,289)	
Buckley, Stephen M	5:44:07 (31,771)	
Buckley, Steven W	4:02:01 (11,161)	
Buckley, Trevor J	4:46:45 (22,719)	
Buckroyd, Andrew D	3:52:06 (8,504)	
Budd, Craig W	5:27:58 (30,097)	
Budd, Ian	4:28:40 (18,206)	
Budd, Joseph A	5:43:35 (31,727)	
Budd, Simon K	4:49:35 (23,381)	
Budd, Stephen A	5:16:14 (28,511)	
Budden, Patrick A	4:51:49 (23,894)	
Budge, Kurt R	4:08:34 (12,705)	
Budgett, Charles E	5:08:03 (27,226)	
Bugby, Antony	5:34:43 (30,879)	
Bugg, Ivan J	3:45:31 (7,050)	
Buglass, Mark A	3:39:57 (5,986)	
Buglass, Thomas	7:03:11 (34,907)	
Buick, Jason	5:02:38 (26,256)	
Buick, Jim	2:58:28 (988)	
Buitendag, David	4:58:35 (25,463)	
Bukhari, Aamir R	5:36:14 (31,018)	
Bull, Adrian S	4:40:57 (21,375)	
Bull, David I	3:55:23 (9,332)	
Bull, Graham M	3:20:33 (3,051)	
Bull, John M	3:22:44 (3,265)	
Bull, Jonathan C	4:14:08 (14,189)	
Bull, Kevin R	4:33:29 (19,425)	
Bull, Martyn G	7:06:29 (34,944)	
Bull, Michael D	3:54:54 (9,215)	
Bull, Nicholas F	3:28:42 (4,224)	
Bull, Nicholas J	5:07:26 (27,135)	
Bull, Peter B	3:43:00 (6,549)	
Bull, Ross	7:19:44 (35,072)	
Bull, Steve	3:28:54 (4,259)	
Bull, Tim	3:24:27 (3,512)	
Bulleid, Dean C	4:24:29 (16,984)	
Bullen, Paul	3:23:58 (3,443)	
Bullen, Samuel D	3:57:31 (9,988)	
Buller, Jamie	3:30:47 (4,578)	
Bulley, Dvid A	3:39:38 (5,935)	
Bulley, Rick	5:44:15 (31,784)	
Bulloch, Nick J	3:52:09 (8,517)	
Bullock, Andrew J	3:20:35 (3,054)	
Bullock, George	4:47:46 (22,960)	
Bullock, Jeremy P	5:11:13 (27,690)	

Bullock, Myles S 3:35:27 (5,249)
Bullock, Nicholas C 4:07:28 (12,452)
Bullock, Paul D 3:07:33 (1,679)
Bullock, Paul G 5:07:54 (27,201)
Bullock, Phillip J 4:13:16 (13,955)
Bullock, Terry 2:54:59 (740)
Bulpitt, Barry J 3:45:12 (6,991)
Bumford, Gavin 3:34:49 (5,161)
Bumpstead, Neil A 4:59:46 (25,730)
Bumstead, Mark 2:56:44 (865)
Bunce, Anthony C 5:39:36 (31,382)
Bunce, Craig 5:26:35 (29,931)
Bunce, Gary J 4:28:39 (18,203)
Bunce, Robin A 4:04:00 (11,633)
Bunch, Andrew D 3:47:57 (7,560)
Bunclark, Nick J 4:00:05 (10,748)
Buncombe, Mark 5:00:45 (25,926)
Bunn, Graem N 3:52:24 (8,578)
Bunney, Tim 3:42:37 (6,486)
Bunschuch, Uwe Klaus 5:50:22 (32,291)
Bunston, Michael J 3:22:42 (3,263)
Bunt, Andrew D 2:51:55 (584)
Bunting, Simon J 4:59:00 (25,559)
Bunting, William 4:51:55 (23,915)
Bunyan, James G 4:41:20 (21,474)
Bunyan, Robet G 3:07:54 (1,705)
Burbante, Marcello 3:12:45 (2,220)
Burbidge, Reginald 6:33:18 (34,337)
Burborough, Peter F 3:53:47 (8,930)
Burch, Ben J 4:20:58 (16,070)
Burch, Dominic 4:27:37 (17,926)
Burch, Matthew I 3:53:54 (8,953)
Burchett, Rainer H 4:19:28 (15,654)
Burden, John P 4:21:34 (16,221)
Burden, Stuart C 3:50:34 (8,162)
Burdett, Daniel P 4:15:22 (14,540)
Burdett, John W 5:40:38 (31,479)
Burdett, Steve J 4:45:24 (22,414)
Burdis, Kevin J 3:53:02 (8,727)
Burditt, Gary A 4:07:30 (12,460)
Burdock, Matthew 4:33:48 (19,518)
Burdon, Brian 5:36:13 (31,014)
Burdon, Michael S 3:32:42 (4,844)
Bureau, Thierry 4:41:27 (21,511)
Burford, Peter 3:18:59 (2,879)
Burford, Rhys A 3:44:43 (6,885)
Burgan, Simon M 5:01:04 (25,988)
Burge, Raymond L 4:58:35 (25,463)
Burge, Richard B 3:59:40 (10,620)
Burge, Stephen N 3:53:33 (8,871)
Burger, Carl 5:47:45 (32,076)
Burger, Derick 4:53:24 (24,275)
Burger, Rudolf 3:57:49 (10,080)
Burgess, Adam J 5:03:53 (26,500)
Burgess, Andrew R 4:02:48 (11,342)
Burgess, Chris J 6:22:05 (33,994)
Burgess, Daniel H 4:03:49 (11,584)
Burgess, Henry H 4:23:58 (16,840)
Burgess, Ian J 4:10:55 (13,323)
Burgess, Ian R 4:10:50 (13,298)
Burgess, John 4:29:22 (18,420)
Burgess, John A 3:03:36 (1,373)
Burgess, John F 3:45:46 (7,088)
Burgess, John G 4:41:05 (21,412)
Burgess, Matthew H 4:27:53 (18,007)
Burgess, Michael 3:28:49 (4,247)
Burgess, Quentin J 4:23:36 (16,754)
Burgess, Rae J 4:27:43 (17,955)
Burgess, Tom C 3:34:14 (5,086)
Burghall, Anthony R 3:40:10 (6,031)
Burgin, Graham 3:59:39 (10,615)
Burgin, Philip R 5:08:39 (27,303)
Burgoyne, Paul A 4:50:28 (23,618)
Burgoyne, William L 4:35:02 (19,860)
Burhouse, Ben J 3:59:28 (10,560)
Burin, Christopher A 4:17:41 (15,134)
Burin, Nigel T 4:14:48 (14,379)
Burke, James 4:14:44 (14,358)
Burke, John M 4:30:00 (18,584)
Burke, Kevin 2:57:43 (932)
Burke, Martin 5:05:08 (26,710)
Burke, Martin J 3:41:17 (6,228)
Burke, Michael 2:59:20 (1,073)
Burke, Michael 3:25:26 (3,659)
Burke, Russ 4:16:43 (14,893)
Burke, Shaun P 4:54:30 (24,551)
Burke, Simon D 4:36:26 (20,209)
Burke, Thomas 4:30:49 (18,799)
Burke, Thomas E 2:59:46 (1,108)
Burke, Thomas J 4:14:51 (14,396)
Burke, Tom D 5:37:01 (31,101)
Burkhill, John H 6:58:30 (34,843)
Burkinshaw, Jeremy P 4:15:05 (14,473)
Burle, Michael G 4:26:18 (17,538)
Burley, Neil F 5:16:44 (28,586)
Burley, Simon J 3:21:40 (3,148)
Burlinson, George 5:00:35 (25,893)
Burman, Kenneth 4:49:44 (23,435)
Burn, Andrew R 4:31:23 (18,940)
Burnage, Andrew 6:05:00 (33,268)
Burnell, Henry F 5:59:47 (32,966)
Burness, Keith 4:31:50 (19,049)
Burnet, John F 4:10:33 (13,232)
Burnett, Bryan 2:59:48 (1,112)
Burnett, Christopher 4:37:10 (20,405)
Burnett, Colin E 4:53:19 (24,257)
Burnett, Desmond 5:01:00 (25,975)
Burnett, Michael 4:29:46 (18,537)
Burnham, Chris J 3:56:55 (9,787)
Burnham, John C 5:29:16 (30,268)
Burnham, Malcolm J 4:58:33 (25,455)
Burnip, Glenn K 4:14:16 (14,239)
Burns, Alastair 4:15:59 (14,710)
Burns, Conor G 4:20:07 (15,836)
Burns, Cullen K 4:42:49 (21,823)
Burns, Francis 5:23:42 (29,575)
Burns, James A 3:27:46 (4,071)
Burns, John 5:12:00 (27,822)
Burns, Lee 4:51:37 (23,855)
Burns, Paul M 3:30:39 (4,552)
Burns, Robert 5:27:29 (30,041)
Burns, Robert J 3:19:32 (2,946)
Burnside, Martin T 3:52:40 (8,651)
Burr, Paul D 5:18:08 (28,806)
Burr, Richard 4:38:54 (20,849)
Burrage, James R 6:06:58 (33,387)
Burras, Damian J 3:25:49 (3,721)
Burras, Stephen J 3:53:54 (8,953)
Burraway, Peter J 5:06:29 (26,959)
Burrell, Aleck 6:08:27 (33,462)
Burrell, Harry P 4:22:24 (16,445)
Burrell, John F 4:11:57 (13,608)
Burrell, Jonathan W 4:48:52 (23,202)
Burrell, Kevin 4:14:56 (14,419)
Burrell, Steven J 7:04:53 (34,923)
Burridge, Matthew A 5:23:56 (29,609)
Burrow, Craig P 3:49:27 (7,924)
Burrows, Alan 4:29:15 (18,379)
Burrows, Brian 5:08:17 (27,257)
Burrows, David G 4:06:19 (12,171)
Burrows, Jonathan M 5:13:28 (28,076)
Burrows, Lee J 5:38:33 (31,259)
Burrows, Mark J 3:52:11 (8,523)
Burrows, Mark J 4:02:16 (11,217)
Burrows, Tim J 5:10:06 (27,519)
Burstow, Clive A 4:14:43 (14,352)
Burt, Adam W 4:30:02 (18,600)
Burt, Alex 3:13:34 (2,310)
Burt, Anthony J 3:32:19 (4,790)
Burt, James S 3:49:21 (7,903)
Burt, John C 3:14:39 (2,437)
Burt, Mike 4:48:38 (23,158)
Burt, Nicholas J 5:59:55 (32,978)
Burt, Nigel F 4:55:56 (24,884)
Burt, Peter 4:30:26 (18,709)
Burt, Ray 4:49:41 (23,424)
Burtenshaw, Ronald O 4:54:51 (24,630)
Burthen, Stephen 2:59:49 (1,115)
Burton, Andrew M 4:17:19 (15,042)
Burton, Ben 3:37:33 (5,586)
Burton, Christopher R 5:26:17 (29,901)
Burton, Cliff C 4:17:05 (14,977)
Burton, Colin L 5:24:11 (29,642)
Burton, David 3:01:47 (1,246)
Burton, David B 5:17:51 (28,765)
Burton, David K 3:31:21 (4,658)
Burton, Denys 3:50:27 (8,138)
Burton, James C 4:22:38 (16,518)
Burton, James W 3:13:39 (2,322)
Burton, Jeff D 3:57:50 (10,089)
Burton, John L 3:23:28 (3,370)
Burton, Jon P 4:15:00 (14,448)
Burton, Paul A 3:39:18 (5,868)
Burton, Robert 4:08:10 (12,605)
Burton, Robert J 2:48:13 (423)
Burtt, William R 5:41:13 (31,529)
Burwood, Christopher M 3:51:24 (8,353)
Busby, David 5:02:34 (26,241)
Busch, Daniel J 3:05:20 (1,500)
Busch, Graham 3:21:16 (3,110)
Busche, Michael L 4:55:51 (24,862)
Busciala, Bartolomeo 4:10:47 (13,281)
Busetto, Simone 2:31:38 (84)
Bush, Daniel R 4:34:11 (19,617)
Bush, James 4:05:54 (12,073)
Bush, John R 5:18:22 (28,846)
Bush, Kevin M 3:11:56 (2,133)
Bush, Mark A 3:17:52 (2,777)
Bush, Michael R 3:42:42 (6,498)
Bush, Simeon 4:34:32 (19,722)
Bush, Timothy J 3:53:50 (8,942)
Bushby, Lee 3:47:58 (7,568)
Bushby, Ray 3:19:41 (2,964)
Bushell, Colin A 7:05:07 (34,925)
Bushell, David 3:56:10 (9,562)
Bushell, Jeremy 3:38:55 (5,798)
Bushell, Matthew J 3:36:13 (5,374)
Businger, Mark 4:44:39 (22,236)
Buskell, Paul J 4:57:41 (25,260)
Buss, Kenneth 4:48:23 (23,100)
Buss, Michael H 4:29:25 (18,439)
Bussol, Jacques 3:36:13 (5,374)
Bustard, Ian 3:33:33 (4,962)
Buswell, Andy M 4:19:23 (15,632)
Buswell, Roger H 4:40:28 (21,251)
Butcher, Alexander G 6:19:49 (33,911)
Butcher, Gary 2:46:20 (357)
Butcher, James 4:53:45 (24,366)
Butcher, John N 5:31:41 (30,531)
Butcher, Thomas M 3:52:24 (8,578)
Butcher, Tom P 3:38:54 (5,793)
Butcher, Vince L 5:14:16 (28,221)
Butcher, Wesley J 3:41:47 (6,333)
Butchers, Stuart J 3:59:56 (10,705)
Butland, Jonathan 4:09:20 (12,917)
Butler, Alan D 4:26:22 (17,555)
Butler, Benjamin J 3:24:52 (3,564)
Butler, Brett B 7:48:23 (35,201)
Butler, Brian 3:04:00 (1,400)
Butler, Brian W 3:51:14 (8,309)
Butler, Daniel P 4:55:16 (24,731)
Butler, David 3:51:14 (8,309)
Butler, David K 3:15:59 (2,570)
Butler, David R 4:07:52 (12,547)
Butler, David R 4:20:49 (16,026)
Butler, Frank 5:06:50 (27,026)
Butler, Gerard P 4:33:05 (19,340)
Butler, Jason P 3:59:25 (10,548)
Butler, Jeffrey 3:02:20 (1,288)
Butler, John D 3:58:27 (10,272)
Butler, Kenneth J 5:03:41 (26,458)
Butler, Mark 4:31:25 (18,947)
Butler, Martin S 3:29:32 (4,361)
Butler, Matthew A 3:29:45 (4,408)
Butler, Matthew S 3:27:11 (3,958)
Butler, Patrick T 3:02:42 (1,316)
Butler, Peter P 4:01:18 (11,001)
Butler, Robert J 4:55:36 (24,789)
Butler, Robin 3:46:10 (7,174)
Butler, Ryan W 3:58:27 (10,272)
Butler, Scott R 4:49:36 (23,388)
Butler, Sean P 5:52:05 (32,418)
Butler, Simon W 4:33:52 (19,538)
Butler, Steve J 4:33:18 (19,385)
Butt, Dan 5:07:00 (27,057)
Butt, Najam 5:24:40 (29,705)
Butterfield, Charles J 5:54:43 (32,614)
Butterfield, Gary 4:34:36 (19,738)
Butterfield, Karl M 5:14:17 (28,225)

Name	Time	Number
Butterfield, Pete J	4:08:34	(12,705)
Butters, Peter J	4:10:48	(13,289)
Butterworth, Peter	2:49:42	(489)
Buttery, Paul A	3:43:05	(6,570)
Button, Christopher E	4:16:13	(14,771)
Button, Phillip D	3:15:54	(2,557)
Buxani, Dipak	5:08:48	(27,319)
Buxton, Kevin	2:46:56	(369)
Buxton, Michael D	4:25:32	(17,296)
Buxton, Nigel M	4:40:35	(21,280)
Buxton, Thomas	3:10:57	(2,026)
Buzwell, Tim	5:42:19	(31,613)
Bxgott Webb, Benjamin	4:57:23	(25,203)
Byard, David B	4:50:50	(23,699)
Byard, James A	4:19:44	(15,733)
Bye, Alan F	3:20:19	(3,028)
Bye, Barry J	3:29:56	(4,444)
Bye, Benjamin G	3:58:36	(10,310)
Bye, Roger	4:22:29	(16,467)
Byer, Victor E	4:09:04	(12,846)
Byers, Richard J	2:55:43	(786)
Byfield, Richard S	4:25:29	(17,280)
Byfleet, Jeremy A	3:32:21	(4,798)
Bygrave, Michael	6:17:08	(33,829)
Byrne, Chris	5:04:53	(26,666)
Byrne, David	4:07:36	(12,479)
Byrne, David A	2:41:31	(230)
Byrne, David J	5:08:49	(27,324)
Byrne, Duncan J	3:33:09	(4,906)
Byrne, Francis	4:08:52	(12,792)
Byrne, Gerry J	3:26:01	(3,764)
Byrne, John	4:15:59	(14,710)
Byrne, John	4:30:11	(18,652)
Byrne, Kenneth	3:16:07	(2,593)
Byrne, Kevin C	3:25:12	(3,624)
Byrne, Mark V	4:14:11	(14,207)
Byrne, Matthew	4:24:29	(16,984)
Byrne, Russell J	3:52:11	(8,523)
Byrne, Shaun	4:04:47	(11,811)
Byrom, Andrew E	4:33:54	(19,546)
Byrom, Christopher E	4:31:51	(19,052)
Byrom, Jamie C	5:34:59	(30,902)
Byrom, Matthew W	3:22:49	(3,276)
Caballero, José	3:30:22	(4,503)
Cabaret, Denis	4:03:09	(11,421)
Cable, Stephen D	4:22:41	(16,532)
Cable, Tim N	4:23:18	(16,690)
Caborn, Richard	4:51:31	(23,836)
Cabot, Tristan J	5:05:30	(26,797)
Cabrelli, Paolo	5:24:40	(29,705)
Cackett, Geoffrey	5:59:59	(32,948)
Cadd, Robert D	4:36:03	(20,093)
Cadden, Paul D	5:29:56	(30,355)
Caddy, Chris M	4:25:51	(17,387)
Caddy, David J	3:02:33	(1,301)
Cade, Graham J	4:25:45	(17,365)
Cadge, Paul S	5:33:07	(30,679)
Cadigan, Thomas P	5:33:36	(30,736)
Cadman, James M	5:18:18	(28,837)
Cadman, John H	4:34:41	(19,762)
Cadman, Karl	3:56:02	(9,518)
Cadman, Peter M	5:59:39	(32,957)
Cadman, Phil R	4:58:37	(25,472)
Cadness, Garrath A	4:25:23	(17,241)
Cadogan, Lee C	4:31:12	(18,884)
Cady, Chris	5:30:17	(30,395)
Cager, Russell I	4:24:43	(17,047)
Cagney, Christopher J	5:54:50	(32,626)
Cahill, Barry J	3:29:10	(4,306)
Cahill, David W	3:54:40	(9,144)
Cahillane, John M	3:55:20	(9,315)
Cain, Charles	3:57:49	(10,080)
Cain, Christopher E	3:35:27	(5,249)
Cain, David T	4:13:06	(13,910)
Cain, Robert	4:08:29	(12,690)
Cain, Scott	3:27:59	(4,102)
Cain, Stephen D	4:46:30	(22,668)
Cain, Steven E	3:51:47	(8,433)
Cainer, Geoff	3:50:17	(8,099)
Cain-Jones, Ellis	5:01:32	(26,073)
Cairnie, Peter E	3:43:21	(6,630)
Cairns, John L	5:40:53	(31,493)
Cairns, Paul	4:48:20	(23,083)
Cairns, Steve	2:31:03	(79)
Caisley, Alastair G	4:16:14	(14,775)
Cakebread, John G	2:54:29	(711)
Cakebread, Paul J	5:32:07	(30,565)
Calabro, Anthony J	5:20:22	(29,154)
Calaminus, Simon D	4:16:36	(14,862)
Calamote, Armand	3:15:24	(2,513)
Calcagno, Christiano	3:45:05	(6,969)
Calder, Thomas A	4:10:41	(13,261)
Caldicott, Peter J	2:49:47	(492)
Caldwell, Christopher C	5:17:44	(28,745)
Caldwell, Gareth J	4:03:13	(11,435)
Caley, Steven J	4:23:30	(16,728)
Califano, Salvatore	3:31:41	(4,705)
Calla, Mats O	3:53:45	(8,922)
Callachan, David	3:35:21	(5,232)
Calladine, Paul	5:32:40	(30,634)
Calladine, Paul G	4:43:54	(22,070)
Callaghan, Peter J	4:10:19	(13,176)
Callaghan, Timothy A	2:59:16	(1,064)
Callan, Mark J	3:37:26	(5,564)
Calland, Gary J	5:35:57	(30,987)
Callander, David J	3:14:41	(2,443)
Calleja, Miguel A	3:42:27	(6,464)
Calleja, Raymond	4:58:58	(25,552)
Callenfels, Otto G	3:43:46	(6,698)
Caller, Mark J	4:56:44	(25,078)
Callister, David I	4:07:09	(12,382)
Callow, James	3:36:28	(5,420)
Callow, Leo J	4:11:59	(13,619)
Callow, Mark	5:20:22	(29,154)
Calluaud, Thierry	4:57:00	(25,128)
Calmonson, Byron	4:06:46	(12,277)
Calner, Matthew P	3:54:52	(9,202)
Calo, Armando	3:09:22	(1,850)
Calow, Neil K	4:34:51	(19,804)
Calrke, Richard	3:34:24	(5,110)
Calrke, Tom W	4:59:03	(25,574)
Calthrop, Ben C	3:47:55	(7,553)
Calverley, Robert	4:28:14	(18,095)
Calverley, Thomas P	5:04:15	(26,561)
Calvert, Ewan	4:12:56	(13,865)
Calvert, John	3:29:43	(4,397)
Calvert, Jonathan R	3:30:00	(4,454)
Calvert, Mark A	3:42:29	(6,468)
Calvert, Philip	4:18:00	(15,210)
Camber, Tom B	4:55:48	(24,841)
Cambridge, Gary	4:09:57	(13,082)
Cameron, Andrew D	3:22:28	(3,238)
Cameron, Angus J	4:47:12	(22,821)
Cameron, Colin	4:35:23	(19,947)
Cameron, Derek A	3:51:39	(8,400)
Cameron, Duncan A	4:47:10	(22,813)
Cameron, Ewan	3:48:01	(7,587)
Cameron, Ewen R	4:03:55	(11,608)
Cameron, Jeremy W	5:06:18	(26,919)
Cameron, John A	3:16:36	(2,641)
Cameron-Wood, Robert A	3:19:58	(2,993)
Camfield, Bryan	2:58:57	(1,028)
Cammidge, Chris Y	4:28:29	(18,162)
Camp, Gareth R	3:38:18	(5,699)
Camp, Paul	3:48:15	(7,645)
Campagna, Massimiliano	4:11:28	(13,477)
Campbell, Aidan	3:20:20	(3,029)
Campbell, Andrew M	4:03:34	(11,519)
Campbell, Barrie S	5:35:31	(30,957)
Campbell, Brian	3:56:55	(9,787)
Campbell, Brian A	3:42:58	(6,537)
Campbell, Chris J	2:58:52	(1,020)
Campbell, Colin	4:33:09	(19,352)
Campbell, Craig	3:40:21	(6,064)
Campbell, David	3:56:49	(9,757)
Campbell, Donal	5:11:43	(27,775)
Campbell, Eric	4:08:19	(12,645)
Campbell, Gary P	2:59:43	(1,104)
Campbell, Geoff	3:01:00	(1,191)
Campbell, Jason S	3:38:05	(5,664)
Campbell, Jeremy W	5:08:06	(27,236)
Campbell, John	4:57:58	(25,319)
Campbell, Lee	3:10:58	(2,029)
Campbell, Leroy	3:32:36	(4,833)
Campbell, Lorne N	3:55:10	(9,268)
Campbell, Malcolm S	4:06:36	(12,241)
Campbell, Mark	4:35:08	(19,879)
Campbell, Neville J	4:37:35	(20,520)
Campbell, Paul A	5:48:50	(32,168)
Campbell, Robert O	4:33:47	(19,516)
Campbell, Ryan J	5:30:13	(30,385)
Campbell, Scott P	3:44:52	(6,993)
Campbell, Stephen A	4:27:47	(17,980)
Campbell, Steven	3:56:55	(9,787)
Campbell, Thomas D	4:49:32	(23,365)
Campbell-Clause, James C	5:06:30	(26,964)
Campedelli, Guido	4:14:31	(14,299)
Campion, Mark A	3:03:29	(1,363)
Campion, Stephen W	3:11:38	(2,093)
Campion, Timothy C	3:59:10	(10,488)
Campione, Francesco	4:33:29	(19,425)
Camplisson, Kevin G	4:35:56	(20,070)
Campos, José F	2:52:06	(599)
Canale, Andrew J	4:38:59	(20,871)
Canavan, Peter	4:52:15	(24,004)
Cane, Philip E	5:16:18	(28,521)
Canella, Davide	3:30:17	(4,486)
Canham, Paul A	3:50:49	(8,211)
Canham, Ray D	4:37:32	(20,502)
Canizares, Francisco	3:27:06	(3,943)
Cankett, Mark C	4:08:17	(12,632)
Cann, Andrew	5:02:42	(26,274)
Cann, Graeme	4:56:24	(24,990)
Canner, Barrie	6:54:12	(34,787)
Canning, Chris R	4:29:09	(18,354)
Cannon, Michael E	5:18:41	(28,903)
Cansdale, Gavin	4:20:09	(15,840)
Cansfield, Christopher C	6:34:39	(34,369)
Cant, Christopher P	5:31:05	(30,478)
Cantle, Steven D	3:35:19	(5,226)
Canton, Geoffrey J	5:37:01	(31,101)
Cantrill, Lee N	4:00:32	(10,843)
Cantwell, Alan J	3:58:41	(10,341)
Caparini, Davide	3:44:57	(6,949)
Capel, David	4:30:42	(18,769)
Capes, Christopher J	4:28:51	(18,262)
Capetta, Diego	3:08:49	(1,792)
Capetti, Giacomo	3:29:14	(4,317)
Capezio, Frank V	5:20:41	(29,205)
Caplen, Stephen G	3:56:29	(9,659)
Capon, Ian H	4:40:10	(21,175)
Capon, Malcolm K	4:04:46	(11,807)
Capp, Alastair C	3:59:28	(10,560)
Cappelletti, Pierre	4:04:06	(11,661)
Capper, Paul A	4:52:11	(23,981)
Cappiello, Paolo	4:13:32	(14,024)
Cappucci, Vincenzo	3:53:09	(8,756)
Capstick, John L	3:57:46	(10,058)
Caramatti, Niccolo L	3:03:50	(1,391)
Carassai, Ermanno	4:03:31	(11,504)
Carbonaro, Sauveur	3:31:11	(4,625)
Carbone, Nick	6:06:25	(33,355)
Carbonell, Jean-Marc	4:29:52	(18,555)
Carbosiero, Lino C	6:17:58	(33,851)
Carbury, Giles B	5:11:32	(27,745)
Card, Neil A	5:02:30	(26,232)
Cardenas, Gustavo	3:29:41	(4,390)
Carder, Anthony E	4:24:06	(16,876)
Carder, Shane P	4:52:12	(23,985)
Cardnell, Gary	4:01:05	(10,960)
Cardon, Clive R	3:58:58	(10,419)
Cardy, Ian M	3:31:26	(4,668)
Care, Jeffrey	3:26:34	(3,859)
Carew, Stephen	5:24:37	(29,698)
Carew Pole, Johnny A	3:06:04	(1,556)
Carey, Allan	4:22:09	(16,385)
Carey, John F	4:54:10	(24,463)
Carless, Darren M	4:16:20	(14,805)
Carley, Ian P	3:58:32	(10,296)
Carlin, Brian E	2:59:49	(1,115)
Carlos, Lozano Quijada	3:05:06	(1,474)
Carloz, Didier	3:48:42	(7,763)
Carlsen, Finn	4:39:34	(21,032)
Carmichael, Jeremy R	3:36:13	(5,374)
Carmichael, Stuart J	4:53:11	(24,217)
Carmo, Diogo	4:24:49	(17,075)
Carnall, Simon J	4:14:23	(14,267)
Carne, Andrew C	4:37:13	(20,416)

Carne, Simon B 4:50:16 (23,551)
Carnes, John M 4:37:05 (20,377)
Carnet, Michel 4:28:49 (18,254)
Carnevale, Nicolas J 4:06:24 (12,192)
Carney, Michael 4:07:06 (12,372)
Carney, Michael D 4:25:32 (17,296)
Carnochan, Graeme I 5:04:10 (26,548)
Carolan, Thomas J 4:25:59 (17,429)
Caron, Thierry A 3:21:46 (3,159)
Carpenter, Andrew 4:27:49 (17,987)
Carpenter, Julian 3:40:04 (6,010)
Carpenter, Mark R 3:07:20 (1,654)
Carpenter, Trevor A 3:59:51 (10,682)
Carr, Adam G 4:45:42 (22,480)
Carr, Adrian N 4:01:27 (11,038)
Carr, Brian M 4:25:24 (17,246)
Carr, David 4:26:26 (17,580)
Carr, David G 4:55:36 (24,789)
Carr, Ian 3:38:17 (5,695)
Carr, Ian 4:33:52 (19,538)
Carr, Ian J 4:17:11 (15,007)
Carr, James B 3:47:17 (7,411)
Carr, Jeremy D 4:57:12 (25,173)
Carr, John 2:42:44 (258)
Carr, Kenneth 5:48:08 (32,106)
Carr, Malcolm A 3:31:13 (4,634)
Carr, Mike J 4:21:56 (16,312)
Carr, Mikey 4:59:44 (25,719)
Carr, Oliver 4:53:48 (24,383)
Carr, Paul B 4:47:16 (22,831)
Carr, Peter J 5:02:35 (26,245)
Carr, Robert 3:50:34 (8,162)
Carr, Stephen 5:05:58 (26,864)
Carr, Stephen P 3:58:59 (10,427)
Carrera, Jean-Louis 3:42:21 (6,441)
Carretta, Renato 3:23:49 (3,423)
Carriage, Ian P 3:53:06 (8,743)
Carrier, David M 4:32:22 (19,179)
Carrigan, David 6:26:55 (34,158)
Carrigan, Paul 4:18:35 (15,388)
Carrillo, Oscar M 3:39:52 (5,977)
Carrivick, Luke 3:51:11 (8,297)
Carroll, Bernard J 4:17:01 (14,962)
Carroll, Brett 4:04:26 (11,731)
Carroll, Gerard 3:40:08 (6,023)
Carroll, John 3:38:52 (5,789)
Carroll, John P 4:35:29 (19,972)
Carroll, Justin 4:15:16 (14,520)
Carroll, Michael A 4:25:41 (17,341)
Carroll, Pat 6:31:00 (34,274)
Carroll, Raymond M 5:08:14 (27,253)
Carroll, Vincent 2:49:24 (480)
Carson, Graham H 4:32:00 (19,087)
Carson, Jasper P 4:23:57 (16,837)
Carson, Jon Grieve G 3:25:17 (3,641)
Carstens, Theunis H 3:46:53 (7,326)
Carswell, Derek M 4:52:36 (24,074)
Carter, Andrew S 3:09:48 (1,897)
Carter, Andrew S 3:23:55 (3,439)
Carter, Andrew S 5:06:28 (26,958)
Carter, Anthony 3:21:29 (3,131)
Carter, Christopher D 4:42:01 (21,631)
Carter, Darryl 3:11:36 (2,087)
Carter, Dave 2:37:57 (158)
Carter, David 3:00:01 (1,131)
Carter, David C 5:10:10 (27,524)
Carter, David L 3:26:13 (3,797)
Carter, Graeme P 4:50:18 (23,564)
Carter, Graham M 4:19:15 (15,595)
Carter, Graham S 3:31:00 (4,608)
Carter, Jason L 5:17:39 (28,738)
Carter, Jonathan A 4:25:25 (17,257)
Carter, Les P 3:46:38 (7,270)
Carter, Mark 3:29:28 (4,350)
Carter, Michael L 3:55:12 (9,276)
Carter, Norman J 4:01:44 (11,097)
Carter, Patrick M 4:40:54 (21,361)
Carter, Paul 4:04:19 (11,705)
Carter, Paul A 3:28:55 (4,263)
Carter, Paul J 4:19:03 (15,527)
Carter, Philip 3:03:03 (1,332)
Carter, Philip E 3:43:35 (6,665)
Carter, Randolph H 4:40:17 (21,203)
Carter, Robert S 4:04:11 (11,678)
Carter, Simon L 4:58:21 (25,402)
Carter, Steven V 3:19:49 (2,979)
Carter, Timothy I 3:05:10 (1,481)
Carter Lee, Andrew R 4:09:38 (12,991)
Carter-Griffiths, Ben C 4:17:57 (15,189)
Cartledge, Raymond 4:59:02 (25,569)
Cartlidge, Peter A 3:32:27 (4,811)
Cartman, Richard 3:27:41 (4,057)
Cartolano, Emilio 4:42:04 (21,640)
Carton, Andy D 3:08:33 (1,762)
Carton, Keith S 4:10:57 (13,333)
Cartwright, David F 2:53:40 (666)
Cartwright, Edward 2:53:26 (656)
Cartwright, John M 4:37:13 (20,416)
Cartwright, Kevin 4:36:21 (20,177)
Cartwright, Kieron 3:59:00 (10,430)
Cartwright, Matthew 3:45:48 (7,095)
Cartwright, Matthew W 4:19:13 (15,582)
Cartwright, Michael J 5:09:35 (27,451)
Cartwright, Peter J 4:55:47 (24,837)
Cartwright, Stephen J 5:49:57 (32,258)
Carty, Damien 5:16:52 (28,617)
Carty, Peter 5:34:58 (30,900)
Caruana, John A 5:14:30 (28,261)
Carvalho, Jorge 4:23:16 (16,675)
Carvalho, Tiago 4:15:55 (14,693)
Carvell, Andrew P 4:36:09 (20,117)
Carver, Ricki A 4:33:32 (19,444)
Carver, Rowan V 4:37:14 (20,423)
Carvill-Biggs, Simon P 4:37:46 (20,571)
Cary, Clive S 3:47:46 (7,517)
Casadevall, Miguel 3:28:59 (4,269)
Casanovas, Federico 4:34:02 (19,575)
Cascarini, James A 2:54:37 (721)
Case, Barry J 4:05:01 (11,864)
Caseley, Richard J 4:49:36 (23,388)
Casely, Gordon 4:26:45 (17,678)
Caseman, Richard 5:37:00 (31,099)
Casement, William R 4:15:59 (14,710)
Casey, Anthony D 2:48:29 (437)
Casey, Daniel 4:22:47 (16,553)
Casey, Daniel J 6:31:14 (34,286)
Casey, Michael P 3:21:57 (3,180)
Casfikis, Marcus W 4:06:13 (12,144)
Cash, Simon R 4:06:52 (12,303)
Cashmore, Nicholas 3:48:06 (7,618)
Caskey, Robert C 4:11:17 (13,424)
Cason, Christopher J 3:41:37 (6,302)
Casper, Brian S 6:26:49 (34,151)
Casquinho, Pedro C 4:23:16 (16,675)
Cass, David R 4:19:11 (15,575)
Cass, John J 5:15:03 (28,344)
Cassell, David J 4:07:54 (12,553)
Cassell, John S 3:18:52 (2,868)
Cassells, Stephen E 3:29:54 (4,438)
Casserley, Tom M 2:56:49 (874)
Cassidy, Frederick M 4:34:40 (19,753)
Cassidy, Gary 2:59:15 (1,062)
Cassidy, Gerard W 4:58:57 (25,544)
Cassidy, James J 4:50:24 (23,596)
Cassidy, Jonathan M 3:55:54 (9,488)
Cassidy, Joseph M 3:56:13 (9,578)
Cassidy, Robin 5:17:31 (28,719)
Cassley, Kevan 5:53:49 (32,552)
Castavheiaa, Nuno 3:59:05 (10,462)
Castces-Greene, Terence M 3:59:03 (10,451)
Castel, Dominique 5:05:45 (26,833)
Castell, Phil A 3:48:00 (7,581)
Castell, William T 4:12:57 (13,869)
Castilho, Paulo 4:45:00 (22,325)
Castle, John A 2:36:56 (136)
Castle, Robert E 3:52:12 (8,526)
Castle, Steven J 5:28:13 (30,147)
Castle, Toby 3:34:08 (5,066)
Castle, Willy 3:47:44 (7,512)
Castree, Stephen 4:47:50 (22,974)
Castresana, José 3:29:33 (4,364)
Caswell, Ian P 7:04:42 (34,922)
Catchpole, Austin 3:52:02 (8,490)
Catchpole, Charles F 4:10:56 (13,329)
Catchpole, Christopher R 3:17:48 (2,768)
Catchpole, Daniel P 4:45:55 (22,534)
Catchpool, Alan 4:21:27 (16,190)
Cates, Andrew 4:34:10 (19,615)
Cation, James N 5:15:19 (28,389)
Catita, José M 3:30:06 (4,467)
Catling, Richard J 4:14:43 (14,352)
Catlow, Ian J 3:56:24 (9,636)
Catmull, Jeremy J 3:22:15 (3,223)
Catmull, Julian 3:17:31 (2,736)
Caton, Nicholas 4:45:45 (22,486)
Catt, Christopher 3:32:27 (4,811)
Cattaneo, Dean 4:42:50 (21,830)
Cattaneo, Paolo 4:22:22 (16,438)
Cattell, Michael J 6:18:14 (33,861)
Catterall, William P 5:00:51 (25,946)
Catterill, Richard E 4:33:18 (19,385)
Catto, John 3:14:45 (2,453)
Catton, Rodney E 4:53:30 (24,300)
Caulder, Graham A 3:07:09 (1,646)
Caulfield, Alan 4:51:26 (23,821)
Caunce, Paul S 5:57:58 (32,832)
Caunce, Peter 4:34:09 (19,608)
Caunt, John E 4:07:29 (12,455)
Caunter, Gary C 4:26:57 (17,737)
Causey, Mark J 3:51:44 (8,418)
Causon, Roger A 5:04:31 (26,602)
Cautick, Ravi M 3:49:47 (7,996)
Cavalla, Paul 3:56:16 (9,589)
Cavalli, Mark A 5:20:46 (29,211)
Cavanagh, Andy 3:09:38 (1,876)
Cavanagh, Sean A 3:47:54 (7,548)
Cavannagh, Lance C 3:47:38 (7,482)
Cave, Oliver J 5:12:42 (27,949)
Cave, Steven 5:07:54 (27,201)
Cave, William K 4:07:23 (12,432)
Cavill, Stuart R 3:56:40 (9,714)
Cawkwell, Pat 3:53:25 (8,835)
Cawley, David 5:22:05 (29,364)
Cawood, Andrew M 3:24:22 (3,502)
Cayley, Gavin C 3:27:28 (4,012)
Cayton, Neil H 2:31:12 (81)
Cazenove, George D 3:57:31 (9,988)
Cazorla, Frederic A 3:54:10 (9,019)
Cecchetti, Claudio 3:28:06 (4,126)
Cecil, Michael J 4:14:18 (14,245)
Centenaro, Luigino 4:28:03 (18,043)
Cepeda, Jimmy 4:06:41 (12,260)
Cera Costa, Amado 3:36:17 (5,387)
Cerveau, Jacques 3:32:23 (4,803)
Cervenka, John M 4:33:04 (19,330)
Cerzosimo, Fabrizio 7:11:25 (34,996)
Cesari, Franco 4:36:40 (20,273)
Cessford, James 3:56:09 (9,552)
Chaar, Fida'a 3:30:44 (4,565)
Chabeli, Michael 6:06:49 (33,379)
Chadaway, Paul R 3:23:34 (3,385)
Chadburn, Michael 4:10:57 (13,333)
Chadwick, Craig 4:04:48 (11,817)
Chadwick, Nick R 3:44:42 (6,880)
Chadwick, Peter J 5:04:38 (26,618)
Chadwick, Richard A 5:47:56 (32,095)
Chaffe, Gary A 5:16:17 (28,515)
Chaffe, Richard W 3:23:25 (3,364)
Chainey, Ross A 3:44:45 (6,889)
Chaix, Bruno 5:01:37 (26,083)
Chakaborty, Aabir 4:46:16 (22,615)
Chakraborty, Jaydeep 4:06:49 (12,288)
Chalberlain, Martin H 4:33:27 (19,417)
Chalk, Anthony W 3:40:16 (6,044)
Chalke, Steve J 4:27:50 (17,992)
Chalker, James 5:04:32 (26,606)
Chalker, Wayne 5:31:45 (30,537)
Chalkley, John W 4:25:36 (17,315)
Challis, Jason D 4:19:34 (15,684)
Challis, Ross J 6:18:34 (33,876)
Challis, Simon A 5:17:11 (28,673)
Challis, Steven 6:22:52 (34,017)
Challis, Steven E 5:07:02 (27,061)
Challoner, Robert 3:50:12 (8,084)
Chalmers, Adrian B 4:55:50 (24,856)
Chalmers, Alexander J 4:24:32 (17,001)
Chalmers, Douglas S 4:57:52 (25,293)
Chalmers, John E 4:05:59 (12,090)
Chamberlain, Darren C 3:57:09 (9,875)

Chamberlain, Gary B....3:49:00 (7,821)
Chamberlain, John....3:57:49 (10,080)
Chamberlain, Mark J....2:40:20 (208)
Chamberlain, Neil I....3:44:11 (6,784)
Chamberlain, Paul E....3:49:49 (8,000)
Chamberlain, Robert J....4:47:50 (22,974)
Chamberlain, Stephen P....3:01:25 (1,210)
Chamberlin, Simon J....4:19:13 (15,582)
Chambers, Carl A....4:16:09 (14,755)
Chambers, David L....4:14:22 (14,263)
Chambers, Dominic....5:11:07 (27,670)
Chambers, Ian G....5:22:45 (29,458)
Chambers, Keith....3:23:30 (3,374)
Chambers, Lindley W....3:25:52 (3,734)
Chambers, Mark....4:38:26 (20,736)
Chambers, Mark A....4:02:23 (11,246)
Chambers, Mark R....4:21:49 (16,287)
Chambers, Noel....3:02:52 (1,324)
Chambers, Peter J....5:18:32 (28,869)
Chambers, Philip D....3:49:57 (8,026)
Chambers, Richard H....3:38:38 (5,744)
Chambers, Richard J....5:53:28 (32,533)
Chambers, Stephen J....5:47:12 (32,033)
Champ, Lee....5:41:36 (31,565)
Champbell-Barnard, James R....5:28:04 (30,111)
Champion, Dylan....4:55:30 (24,771)
Champion, Mark S....3:20:10 (3,016)
Champion, Ross J....3:56:47 (9,749)
Champness, Paul....4:00:59 (10,945)
Chan, Cedric C....5:32:50 (30,657)
Chan, Shun-On....3:55:10 (9,268)
Chana, Amardeep S....4:14:46 (14,369)
Chana, Ravi S....4:19:31 (15,668)
Chance, Jonathan S....7:22:17 (35,086)
Chandak, Akhil....4:29:14 (18,375)
Chandler, Gary W....2:36:41 (130)
Chandler, Huw M....4:39:10 (20,916)
Chandler, James....4:41:40 (21,558)
Chandler, James H....3:43:09 (6,581)
Chandler, Michael....4:33:25 (19,409)
Chandler, Paul....4:14:21 (14,257)
Chandler, Paul....5:03:26 (26,425)
Chandler, Ross A....3:57:28 (9,969)
Chandler, Stephen J....5:12:48 (27,969)
Chandley, Paul J....4:15:15 (14,515)
Chandley, Peter....3:23:51 (3,430)
Chanet, Benjamin....4:11:05 (13,375)
Chang, Joseph E....3:40:47 (6,136)
Channer, Dan S....4:00:10 (10,759)
Chant, Doug R....3:24:39 (3,533)
Chantreau, Benoit....3:28:22 (4,169)
Chantry, John W....4:29:09 (18,354)
Chant-Sempill, Ian....4:38:23 (20,724)
Chaplin, Neil J....4:11:35 (13,500)
Chaplin, Robert L....7:34:51 (35,158)
Chaplin, Tony R....3:59:45 (10,649)
Chapman, Anthony C....4:59:19 (25,632)
Chapman, Bruce G....7:19:29 (35,071)
Chapman, Christoph A....6:00:48 (33,015)
Chapman, Christopher P....4:41:15 (21,460)
Chapman, Christopher S....4:33:45 (19,506)
Chapman, Colin....4:05:12 (11,921)
Chapman, Colin F....5:24:55 (29,734)
Chapman, David....4:07:26 (12,444)
Chapman, David J....3:51:44 (8,418)
Chapman, David P....3:58:57 (10,417)
Chapman, Derek....5:12:22 (27,874)
Chapman, Edward P....4:19:03 (15,527)
Chapman, Gary I....3:33:23 (4,944)
Chapman, Howard R....5:02:33 (26,237)
Chapman, Iain T....5:31:21 (30,501)
Chapman, Ian M....4:13:34 (14,036)
Chapman, John....4:00:52 (10,922)
Chapman, John....4:44:16 (22,160)
Chapman, Leslie G....2:58:47 (1,014)
Chapman, Leslie R....9:00:06 (35,252)
Chapman, Mark....2:56:40 (858)
Chapman, Matthew....4:32:59 (19,314)
Chapman, Neil A....3:47:20 (7,425)
Chapman, Nick J....4:59:40 (25,705)
Chapman, Nigel....3:22:45 (3,267)
Chapman, Nigel....4:40:00 (21,142)
Chapman, Paul F....4:21:43 (16,259)
Chapman, Paul R....5:11:13 (27,690)
Chapman, Peter D....5:31:15 (30,490)
Chapman, Peter J....4:05:09 (11,914)
Chapman, Peter J....4:59:35 (25,682)
Chapman, Richard....3:51:37 (8,392)
Chapman, Richard....4:09:43 (13,016)
Chapman, Richard A....3:57:52 (10,102)
Chapman, Richard M....3:47:53 (7,545)
Chapman, Roy....5:03:58 (26,514)
Chapman, Simon....3:57:21 (9,933)
Chapman, Stewart M....4:28:14 (18,095)
Chapman, Vernon L....3:57:18 (9,920)
Chappell, Anthony D....4:27:21 (17,838)
Chappell, Darren J....4:28:17 (18,110)
Chappell, David....5:05:59 (26,868)
Chappell, Mark G....4:08:57 (12,813)
Chappell, Paul....4:42:19 (21,702)
Charalambous, Kiri....4:26:47 (17,687)
Chard, Ken R....3:18:42 (2,849)
Chard, Ricky D....4:16:20 (14,805)
Charles, Andrew J....4:03:30 (11,498)
Charles, Henry W....4:26:02 (17,447)
Charles, Nicholas L....3:42:58 (6,537)
Charles, Paul J....3:07:10 (1,647)
Charles-Edwards, James L....5:24:16 (29,657)
Charleston, Rod J....4:05:15 (11,929)
Charlesworth, Graham J....4:46:15 (22,611)
Charlton, David A....6:13:32 (33,682)
Charlton, Roger J....4:45:51 (22,510)
Charlwood, Andrew S....4:14:32 (14,300)
Charlwood, Martyn....4:19:07 (15,553)
Charman, Nigel R....3:18:16 (2,811)
Charman, Philip G....4:25:16 (17,206)
Charnaud, Giles S....5:07:46 (27,185)
Charnock, Bill....3:28:11 (4,141)
Chart, Mike C....4:56:17 (24,962)
Charters, Mark E....4:52:39 (24,091)
Charters, Paul W....4:12:13 (13,670)
Chase, Daniel J....4:37:05 (20,377)
Chase, James W....5:58:46 (32,893)
Chatburn, Dean P....5:00:00 (25,776)
Chater, Andrew N....4:18:29 (15,359)
Chater, Paul....4:23:05 (16,625)
Chatterjee, Subhra....5:25:17 (29,780)
Chatterton, Andy J....3:48:22 (7,677)
Chatwin, Paul M....4:20:40 (15,981)
Chauhan, Rajat....3:13:33 (2,308)
Chaumet, Didier M....3:35:45 (5,305)
Chaundler, Christopher D....4:13:35 (14,037)
Chauveau, Patrice....3:03:04 (1,334)
Chavda, Harish....5:51:35 (32,380)
Cheal, Ben J....3:53:14 (8,778)
Cheal, Nicholas....5:14:28 (28,258)
Cheal, Stephen H....4:28:22 (18,129)
Checa, Miguel....3:36:21 (5,401)
Checchi, Renzo....3:39:21 (5,879)
Checkley, Darren R....5:13:02 (28,003)
Cheema, Kirandeep S....7:13:59 (35,025)
Cheeseman, Mark A....4:57:08 (25,161)
Cheeseman, Terry L....5:12:43 (27,953)
Cheesman, Charles....5:16:01 (28,482)
Cheetham, Andrew J....3:51:20 (8,336)
Cheetham, Christopher J....4:00:13 (10,771)
Cheetham, John D....5:32:25 (30,607)
Cheetham, John G....5:12:22 (27,874)
Cheetham, Thomas R....4:05:31 (11,991)
Chell, David....3:45:04 (6,966)
Chell, Philip....4:38:59 (20,871)
Chelton, Hugo R....3:36:58 (5,495)
Cheng, David....4:58:53 (25,530)
Cherchi, Giuseppe....4:19:10 (15,567)
Cherif, Christian M....4:26:02 (17,447)
Cherono, Fredrick....2:13:58 (11)
Cherrill, James L....4:25:40 (17,337)
Cherry, Mark....4:58:57 (25,544)
Cherry, Nicholas W....3:54:05 (8,992)
Cherry, Robert J....3:31:40 (4,703)
Cherry, Steven....3:53:12 (8,770)
Chesby, Colin P....4:08:53 (12,797)
Cheshire, Geoffrey M....3:09:57 (1,917)
Chesmore, Rupert N....4:19:30 (15,665)
Chessell, Austin W....7:20:39 (35,079)
Chester, Christopher P....5:38:25 (31,238)
Chester, Ian G....4:21:02 (16,083)
Chester, Martin G....3:16:53 (2,668)
Chesters, David T....4:24:36 (17,016)
Chesterton, Peter B....4:48:48 (23,192)
Chestney, Christopher P....3:56:33 (9,675)
Chestney, Jon....3:03:19 (1,349)
Chetty, Karthigeyan....5:41:02 (31,517)
Cheung, Hin....4:22:35 (16,497)
Cheung, Matthew....3:37:49 (5,620)
Cheung, Simon....4:42:26 (21,725)
Cheung, Yiu-Cheung....4:44:40 (22,240)
Chhibber, Vineet....5:32:04 (30,563)
Chiaramonte, Ivan A....3:48:14 (7,641)
Chick, David A....5:14:33 (28,268)
Chick, Joseph E....4:21:45 (16,271)
Chidgey, Marcus M....5:30:13 (30,385)
Chidwick, Ian M....3:15:46 (2,545)
Chilcott, Pete....5:33:25 (30,708)
Childs, Duncan J....4:25:09 (17,169)
Childs, Kevin J....4:56:16 (24,955)
Childs, Michael J....5:35:26 (30,949)
Childs, Paul A....3:02:36 (1,304)
Childs, Paul A....5:11:51 (27,795)
Childs, Peter J....4:02:54 (11,367)
Childs, Peter J....4:40:42 (21,310)
Childs, Peter J....5:14:19 (28,233)
Childs, Shaun E....3:55:27 (9,353)
Chilelli, Fabrizio....3:53:42 (8,909)
Chiles, Adrian....4:33:56 (19,554)
Chiles, Andrew D....4:31:59 (19,083)
Chilton, John P....4:26:25 (17,578)
Chilton, Simon G....4:09:04 (12,846)
Chilvers, Paul M....4:00:09 (10,756)
Chin, Yit-Kwong....4:02:46 (11,335)
Chippendale, Mark....3:03:34 (1,371)
Chippendale, Neil F....2:59:01 (1,036)
Chisholm, Barry J....3:17:22 (2,720)
Chisholm, David....5:14:16 (28,221)
Chisholm, Paul R....3:51:47 (8,433)
Chislett, Mark W....4:23:09 (16,644)
Chisnall, Clive J....4:22:15 (16,407)
Chiswell, Gary....6:08:03 (33,447)
Chittell, Chris....4:40:18 (21,209)
Chittem, David J....4:23:02 (16,607)
Chitty, Bryan A....4:17:29 (15,090)
Chivers, Adam P....5:31:39 (30,527)
Chivers, Gareth R....3:22:23 (3,232)
Chivers, Ian....3:48:45 (7,775)
Chivers, John T....6:33:02 (34,330)
Chiverton, Graham M....5:15:17 (28,386)
Chllice, Michael A....4:53:46 (24,374)
Chodock, Marc....4:38:19 (20,702)
Chodzko-Zajko, Piotr A....4:03:23 (11,476)
Choi, Dong C....4:29:16 (18,390)
Choi, Kom Yuu....3:50:07 (8,064)
Choi, Wai-Lun....4:24:55 (17,096)
Choi, Yan....3:56:25 (9,637)
Chorlton, Gordon C....4:23:06 (16,631)
Chorlton, Rodney S....4:15:01 (14,457)
Chouglay, Anwar....4:42:41 (21,795)
Choules, David....3:05:43 (1,531)
Chow, Kar-Fai....5:35:23 (30,945)
Chowdhury, Minto....4:08:37 (12,718)
Chrimes, John M....4:16:15 (14,781)
Christensen, Allan....4:48:44 (23,175)
Christensen, Daniel P....4:44:08 (22,126)
Christensen, Mike....3:25:44 (3,708)
Christie, Alan D....4:20:34 (15,954)
Christie, Andrew....6:15:34 (33,763)
Christie, Callum D....4:55:16 (24,731)
Christie, David....3:10:37 (1,992)
Christie, David....3:43:20 (6,626)
Christie, Delroy....4:53:51 (24,390)
Christie, Graeme I....4:01:36 (11,066)
Christie, Justin P....3:54:25 (9,081)
Christie, Rupert V....4:11:50 (13,570)
Christie, Sandy....3:15:51 (2,552)
Christie, Simon....4:10:51 (13,303)
Christie, Stephen J....3:55:38 (9,408)
Christmas, Lee....2:47:48 (402)
Christodoulou, Harry....4:58:58 (25,552)
Christopher, Robert J....4:02:22 (11,240)
Chrysanthou, Viannis....5:03:19 (26,407)

Chrystal, John 3:30:47 (4,578)
Chu, Francis 4:04:31 (11,749)
Chubb, Kevin D 4:55:43 (24,822)
Chubb, Richard A 3:48:50 (7,796)
Chubb, William J 5:47:13 (32,035)
Chudley, John E 4:47:46 (22,960)
Chung, Kinming 5:08:29 (27,285)
Church, Alistair M 3:45:50 (7,101)
Church, Fraser D 5:14:51 (28,320)
Church, Jerome H 4:44:14 (22,152)
Church, Martin 3:42:25 (6,457)
Church, Timothy M 3:53:28 (8,851)
Church, William J 3:32:40 (4,839)
Churchard, Neil P 4:05:03 (11,878)
Churcher, David 3:11:11 (2,049)
Churcher, Matthew J 4:20:43 (15,995)
Churchill, George M 4:04:34 (11,761)
Churchill, Henry C 3:39:02 (5,823)
Churchill, Paul S 5:12:49 (27,975)
Churchman, Nigel M 5:32:18 (30,590)
Churney, Benjamin T 4:18:35 (15,388)
Cian Chon Carraige, Caoilf 3:59:34 (10,593)
Cibardo, Ricky F 6:23:59 (34,064)
Ciccarelli, Vincenzo 4:39:38 (21,053)
Cid, Manuel E 3:42:00 (6,376)
Cieslik, Benoit J 3:15:40 (2,537)
Cieslik, John A 4:19:28 (15,654)
Cioffi, Attikio 4:23:35 (16,752)
Ciucci, Giuseppe G 3:49:33 (7,944)
Civita, Giovanni 3:34:54 (5,168)
Clack, Paul A 3:14:52 (2,468)
Clack, Tom M 3:50:01 (8,042)
Clairdge, Neal K 5:47:45 (32,076)
Clancy, Andrew 3:02:12 (1,278)
Clancy, Gerald 3:46:00 (7,133)
Clancy, Paul F 4:07:19 (12,423)
Clanet, Jean Claude 3:44:10 (6,779)
Clanford, Piers M 3:46:25 (7,226)
Clapham, Jeremy A 3:55:18 (9,310)
Clappen, Nicholas S 5:40:14 (31,442)
Clapperton, Robert C 4:09:38 (12,991)
Clapson, Barrie 4:06:05 (12,117)
Clapson, Victor J 4:41:25 (21,502)
Clapton, Daniel 4:11:18 (13,428)
Clarabut, Raymond A 3:48:35 (7,736)
Clare, Danny 3:47:35 (7,469)
Clare, Jonathan R 3:03:40 (1,381)
Clare, Leigh P 4:56:53 (25,110)
Clarehugh, Mark 2:39:38 (192)
Claridge, Robert A 4:44:00 (22,099)
Claridge, Stephen W 6:23:57 (34,060)
Clark, Andrew B 4:45:25 (22,419)
Clark, Andrew P 4:23:44 (16,788)
Clark, Andy 3:51:26 (8,362)
Clark, Benjamin J 4:21:06 (16,093)
Clark, Charles 5:34:49 (30,889)
Clark, Charles A 3:19:03 (2,885)
Clark, Colin E 4:29:45 (18,533)
Clark, Daniel E 5:32:36 (30,625)
Clark, Daniel J 3:57:45 (10,051)
Clark, David 4:42:36 (21,769)
Clark, David 4:54:53 (24,637)
Clark, David A 3:30:10 (4,473)
Clark, David L 3:33:50 (5,018)
Clark, Derek 5:25:04 (29,754)
Clark, Fraser M 4:03:38 (11,530)
Clark, Geoff 4:37:39 (20,529)
Clark, George 4:13:57 (14,131)
Clark, Graham A 5:03:52 (26,498)
Clark, Iain L 3:57:14 (9,902)
Clark, Ian K 5:33:06 (30,678)
Clark, Jason L 3:39:10 (5,843)
Clark, John 4:58:28 (25,436)
Clark, John B 4:52:08 (23,972)
Clark, John R 4:23:10 (16,647)
Clark, Jon R 4:28:12 (18,085)
Clark, Joseph J 3:37:56 (5,636)
Clark, Kevin J 4:37:01 (20,360)
Clark, Kevin P 4:01:20 (11,007)
Clark, Martin J 4:58:59 (25,557)
Clark, Michael 3:57:32 (9,997)
Clark, Neil J 3:52:15 (8,542)
Clark, Neil R 4:00:27 (10,818)
Clark, Neil R 4:39:26 (20,996)
Clark, Nigel J 3:58:28 (10,278)
Clark, Oliver G 3:59:44 (10,641)
Clark, Philip D 5:16:38 (28,566)
Clark, Raymond C 4:09:41 (13,007)
Clark, Richard H 3:14:13 (2,383)
Clark, Richard J 3:57:32 (9,997)
Clark, Richard N 4:52:40 (24,096)
Clark, Robert 4:21:59 (16,326)
Clark, Robert M 4:02:53 (11,359)
Clark, Rodney 4:16:21 (14,811)
Clark, Sam R 4:31:09 (18,866)
Clark, Simon 3:29:43 (4,397)
Clark, Steve R 4:20:53 (16,043)
Clark, Steven 4:07:50 (12,537)
Clark, Steven P 4:40:14 (21,196)
Clark, Steven V 4:31:02 (18,843)
Clark, Stuart W 4:11:05 (13,375)
Clark, Tom 3:15:49 (2,550)
Clark, Will A 3:57:15 (9,905)
Clarke, Adam S 3:47:39 (7,492)
Clarke, Andrew 5:00:49 (25,940)
Clarke, Andrew M 4:04:06 (11,661)
Clarke, Andy 3:54:13 (9,025)
Clarke, Andy D 4:33:15 (19,370)
Clarke, Anthony 4:07:05 (12,368)
Clarke, Avid J 3:03:25 (1,356)
Clarke, Chris 4:09:01 (12,831)
Clarke, Christopher D 3:30:27 (4,515)
Clarke, Conor B 6:38:27 (34,469)
Clarke, David 5:13:31 (28,087)
Clarke, Fintan J 6:12:13 (33,626)
Clarke, Fraser 4:57:52 (25,293)
Clarke, Gareth J 3:47:38 (7,482)
Clarke, Garry P 3:38:01 (5,650)
Clarke, Glenn 4:01:26 (11,032)
Clarke, Gordon G 5:02:51 (26,307)
Clarke, Gordon M 4:00:53 (10,927)
Clarke, Graham R 4:53:17 (24,243)
Clarke, Gregory J 3:40:39 (6,111)
Clarke, Ian 3:30:10 (4,473)
Clarke, Jack A 4:27:10 (17,792)
Clarke, John 3:34:40 (5,144)
Clarke, John A 3:51:14 (8,309)
Clarke, John B 5:06:57 (27,051)
Clarke, John G 3:42:22 (6,445)
Clarke, John J 4:05:15 (11,929)
Clarke, Joseph C 4:27:39 (17,937)
Clarke, Martin H 3:05:51 (1,541)
Clarke, Michael 5:06:49 (27,020)
Clarke, Michael A 4:25:43 (17,351)
Clarke, Michael E 3:47:05 (7,369)
Clarke, Michael F 3:43:57 (6,732)
Clarke, Neil S 4:38:15 (20,683)
Clarke, Nicholas J 4:54:28 (24,548)
Clarke, Nicholas P 4:00:28 (10,822)
Clarke, Nigel A 4:04:47 (11,811)
Clarke, Paul A 4:54:45 (24,610)
Clarke, Paul A 5:00:19 (25,851)
Clarke, Peter C 3:39:14 (5,858)
Clarke, Philip 4:26:13 (17,511)
Clarke, Philip R 4:28:18 (18,111)
Clarke, Richard F 4:17:57 (15,189)
Clarke, Robert A 5:00:48 (25,935)
Clarke, Robert J 3:38:27 (5,718)
Clarke, Robert M 6:12:08 (33,623)
Clarke, Robert V 3:51:49 (8,445)
Clarke, Roger 3:44:46 (6,898)
Clarke, Roger D 5:28:51 (30,223)
Clarke, Roy M 5:48:45 (32,156)
Clarke, Russell J 2:54:25 (705)
Clarke, Russell P 4:47:48 (22,965)
Clarke, Sam J 3:57:10 (9,880)
Clarke, Samuel J 4:20:53 (16,043)
Clarke, Scott A 3:34:02 (5,053)
Clarke, Simon 3:35:33 (5,269)
Clarke, Simon R 3:45:53 (7,114)
Clarke, Sion 5:04:44 (26,636)
Clarke, Stephen J 4:42:59 (21,871)
Clarke, Steven C 4:43:00 (21,876)
Clarke, Steven P 7:32:22 (35,146)
Clarke, Thomas 4:14:38 (14,325)
Clarke, Thomas N 5:03:06 (26,362)
Clarke, Tim A 5:03:37 (26,448)
Clarkson, Alan 3:12:14 (2,168)
Clarkson, Graham 3:08:53 (1,800)
Clarkson, Nigel A 5:09:20 (27,411)
Clarkson, Richard J 4:02:32 (11,283)
Classen, Alex 3:25:26 (3,659)
Classey, Stephen 3:58:43 (10,354)
Clatworth, Michael D 4:11:33 (13,494)
Clatworthy, Timothy J 2:57:54 (950)
Claus, Frank A 5:14:57 (28,332)
Clausen, Jake 4:46:38 (22,696)
Claveau, Mathias A 4:06:34 (12,232)
Clawson, Mark 5:04:10 (26,548)
Clay, Charlie J 4:14:04 (14,173)
Clay, Christopher 3:55:23 (9,332)
Clay, Nigel R 5:22:07 (29,368)
Clay, Paul 4:09:25 (12,936)
Clayden, Robert A 4:30:39 (18,760)
Claydon, Paul 4:34:12 (19,624)
Clayson, Ben 3:33:33 (4,962)
Clayton, Andrew 4:02:26 (11,255)
Clayton, Bill 5:00:47 (25,932)
Clayton, Christopher P 3:28:41 (4,221)
Clayton, David P 4:07:09 (12,382)
Clayton, Ian 2:42:53 (262)
Clayton, Mark 3:06:19 (1,576)
Clayton, Mark 4:49:20 (23,320)
Clayton, Richard B 5:27:24 (30,030)
Clayworth, Darryl L 4:51:53 (23,905)
Cleak, James D 4:53:45 (24,366)
Cleall, Leonard 5:05:46 (26,837)
Cleary, Michael D 4:20:07 (15,836)
Cleary, Michael J 4:36:52 (20,324)
Cleary, Thomas 5:46:01 (31,937)
Clease, Edward C 3:22:16 (3,225)
Cleaver, Jim 4:38:34 (20,767)
Cleaver, Neil S 4:55:14 (24,726)
Cleaver, Paul D 4:02:22 (11,240)
Clegg, Steven J 4:09:22 (12,926)
Clemens, John B 3:12:29 (2,194)
Clement, Colin 5:07:42 (27,176)
Clement, Gael M 4:55:05 (24,697)
Clement, Patrick 2:45:17 (329)
Clement, Tim 3:58:54 (10,408)
Clements, Andrew C 2:30:42 (73)
Clements, Edward 4:33:38 (19,470)
Clements, Jon A 4:49:39 (23,411)
Clements, Mark I 4:25:57 (17,413)
Clements, Martin 3:20:06 (3,011)
Clements, Nick B 3:43:46 (6,698)
Clements, Paul 4:42:18 (21,699)
Clements, Paul J 4:47:10 (22,813)
Clements, Robert J 4:00:23 (10,799)
Clements, Thomas R 4:26:00 (17,435)
Clery, Ciaran 5:22:32 (29,427)
Cleveland, Paul F 4:21:37 (16,234)
Cleveland, Richard R 4:09:21 (12,921)
Clevely, Rupert 4:38:03 (20,632)
Cleverly, Mark 4:10:16 (13,160)
Clevett, Alan G 5:18:23 (28,849)
Clevett, Neil D 5:41:00 (31,511)
Clewlow, Melvin T 3:19:50 (2,980)
Cliff, Christopher 4:28:33 (18,181)
Cliff, Simon 4:54:42 (24,594)
Clifford, Gavin 4:13:56 (14,125)
Clifford, Gordon D 4:18:59 (15,507)
Clifford, James A 5:29:18 (30,273)
Clifford, Paul J 5:30:59 (30,467)
Clifford, Stephen W 3:33:57 (5,036)
Clifford-Smith, Jon L 4:25:45 (17,365)
Clifton, Luke S 4:14:14 (14,220)
Clifton, Michael 3:10:28 (1,974)
Clissold, Cole 3:38:53 (5,792)
Cloak, David P 4:12:50 (13,840)
Cloete, Albert P 5:59:37 (32,953)
Cloherty, Patrick 5:11:02 (27,661)
Clohessy, Martin A 4:11:36 (13,506)
Cloke, Michael A 5:04:05 (26,527)
Clokey, John 4:07:54 (12,553)
Cloonan, Peter G 4:27:33 (17,906)
Close, Daniel J 3:20:16 (3,022)
Close, David S 4:31:32 (18,978)
Close, Edward 3:45:34 (7,059)

Close, Matthew J	4:28:01 (18,034)	
Close, Steven A	5:39:26 (31,368)	
Clothier, Ian E	4:31:49 (19,048)	
Clothier, Thomas J	4:29:10 (18,359)	
Clough, Paul J	3:28:05 (4,120)	
Clough, Trevor	3:27:32 (4,028)	
Clougherty, Anthony P	4:58:22 (25,406)	
Clowes, Jason W	5:17:59 (28,779)	
Clune, David	5:23:51 (29,593)	
Clusker, Dean	3:58:39 (10,323)	
Clutterbuck, Andrew M	4:02:28 (11,262)	
Clutterbuck, Stephen A	4:58:33 (25,455)	
Clutton, Andy E	4:13:04 (13,904)	
Clyne, Dave J	4:57:41 (25,260)	
Clynes, Declan P	2:50:07 (503)	
Clynes, Patrick	4:07:47 (12,529)	
Coade, David	3:24:37 (3,529)	
Coales, David	2:56:07 (814)	
Coates, Andrew P	3:57:44 (10,045)	
Coates, Brian W	3:20:30 (3,045)	
Coates, Chris J	4:00:11 (10,762)	
Coates, Christopher J	3:39:04 (5,832)	
Coates, David H	4:04:00 (11,633)	
Coates, Geoffrey E	4:02:20 (11,226)	
Coates, Graeme D	3:12:20 (2,179)	
Coates, Nigel J	2:52:55 (631)	
Coates, Phillip A	4:04:25 (11,724)	
Coates, Steven J	3:54:09 (9,013)	
Coats, Peter H	4:05:52 (12,063)	
Cobb, Darrin S	6:38:28 (34,471)	
Cobb, James	4:30:50 (18,805)	
Cobb, John	4:24:29 (16,984)	
Cobb, Parrish	4:48:38 (23,158)	
Cobban, Dave A	4:16:06 (14,738)	
Cobbett, Peter L	5:14:05 (28,182)	
Cobbold, James	5:17:39 (28,738)	
Cobbold, Matthew N	3:46:28 (7,236)	
Cochou, Pierre	3:28:37 (4,215)	
Cochran, Mark C	4:19:30 (15,665)	
Cochrane, Jason I	3:55:43 (9,435)	
Cochrane, Robert W	3:54:15 (9,034)	
Cockayne, Nicholas J	3:28:20 (4,164)	
Cockburn, Martin J	4:49:29 (23,355)	
Cockell, Terry J	4:25:43 (17,351)	
Cocker, Simon A	3:57:46 (10,058)	
Cockerell, Barney J	3:34:12 (5,078)	
Cockerton, Neil F	4:58:29 (25,438)	
Cockrell, Nigel B	3:54:49 (9,187)	
Cocks, Dean C	4:07:45 (12,516)	
Codastefano, Giuseppe	3:24:55 (3,570)	
Codd, Raoul J	4:41:09 (21,432)	
Code, Peter	4:30:54 (18,819)	
Coden, Danilo	3:01:55 (1,253)	
Codrai, Andrew O	3:54:23 (9,073)	
Cody, Eddie	5:26:24 (29,912)	
Cody, Luke F	5:00:31 (25,880)	
Coe, Christopher S	6:18:25 (33,867)	
Coe, Neil A	2:48:04 (419)	
Coe, Nigel A	4:09:08 (12,870)	
Coe, William D	4:43:36 (22,007)	
Coetzer, Cornelius	6:41:03 (34,526)	
Coffey, Raymond	5:37:40 (31,157)	
Coffey, Robert N	3:53:41 (8,904)	
Coffin, Malcolm	4:51:16 (23,786)	
Coffin, Tim G	3:53:49 (8,938)	
Coghlan, Ian	4:32:16 (19,152)	
Coglan, Julian J	4:14:18 (14,245)	
Cohen, Howard	3:10:00 (1,923)	
Cohen, Joel	4:06:28 (12,204)	
Cohen, Lewis A	4:46:30 (22,668)	
Cohen, Robert P	4:49:39 (23,411)	
Cohen, Shimshon	4:55:20 (24,745)	
Cohen-Price, Daniel L	5:51:57 (32,410)	
Cokelaere, Johan R	4:03:44 (11,554)	
Coker, Rob T	3:42:59 (6,545)	
Colbeck, John F	3:28:20 (4,164)	
Colbeck, Mark	5:37:38 (31,154)	
Colborne, Graham	4:28:12 (18,085)	
Colbourne, George T	4:33:08 (19,347)	
Colbourne, Jonathan D	4:20:20 (15,896)	
Colbourne, Paul N	4:14:53 (14,406)	
Colbourne, Steve J	3:07:01 (1,637)	
Colbridge, Ian	5:33:37 (30,738)	
Cole, Alan	3:31:19 (4,654)	
Cole, Brian	4:40:11 (21,182)	
Cole, Brian J	2:36:53 (135)	
Cole, David R	4:30:53 (18,815)	
Cole, Kevin D	3:17:10 (2,697)	
Cole, Michael G	4:52:38 (24,088)	
Cole, Ray	2:41:25 (229)	
Cole, Richard E	5:25:16 (29,775)	
Cole, Richard J	4:25:05 (17,146)	
Cole, Samuel A	4:28:10 (18,078)	
Cole, Simon C	5:29:00 (30,245)	
Cole, Stephen D	3:56:39 (9,710)	
Cole, Stephen H	4:18:23 (15,319)	
Cole, Stephen M	3:03:55 (1,395)	
Cole, Stephen P	5:12:41 (27,940)	
Cole, Steven J	4:54:03 (24,439)	
Cole, Tony	3:14:08 (2,371)	
Colebeck, Graham W	4:53:16 (24,239)	
Colegrave, John B	3:48:49 (7,792)	
Coleman, Daniel S	5:42:14 (31,605)	
Coleman, David W	5:37:46 (31,164)	
Coleman, Glen	2:50:28 (512)	
Coleman, Glenn R	5:56:32 (32,734)	
Coleman, Jamie C	4:15:46 (14,651)	
Coleman, John P	6:38:17 (34,463)	
Coleman, Justin D	4:03:49 (11,584)	
Coleman, Mark	4:20:52 (16,039)	
Coleman, Mark K	4:26:17 (17,527)	
Coleman, Martin R	5:45:32 (31,899)	
Coleman, Matt R	5:05:47 (26,841)	
Coleman, Mike	2:19:42 (26)	
Coleman, Neil M	3:26:32 (3,854)	
Coleman, Paul A	5:29:45 (30,335)	
Coleman, Phillip M	5:07:11 (27,096)	
Coleman, Richard	4:57:34 (25,242)	
Coleman, Robert J	3:48:38 (7,749)	
Coleman, Rory J	5:28:15 (30,158)	
Coleman, Stuart R	3:36:47 (5,465)	
Coleman, William A	5:43:32 (31,722)	
Coles, Chris L	3:15:25 (2,518)	
Coles, Ian R	4:47:38 (22,922)	
Coles, Jason N	4:35:19 (19,911)	
Coles, Kim	4:17:09 (15,001)	
Coles, Paul	3:17:47 (2,764)	
Coles, Richard A	5:08:04 (27,229)	
Coles, Sam F	3:55:21 (9,321)	
Coles, Samuel	4:52:28 (24,045)	
Coles, Scott	3:46:09 (7,170)	
Coles, Simon G	4:12:08 (13,648)	
Coles, Terence G	3:41:19 (6,238)	
Coleshill, Paul G	5:48:14 (32,116)	
Coley, Christopher M	4:16:00 (14,715)	
Colfer, James J	3:47:08 (7,380)	
Colgan, Richard W	4:21:40 (16,247)	
Colgate, Lee M	6:03:28 (33,187)	
Colhoun, Colm	5:33:30 (30,725)	
Collado-Torres, Francisco	4:05:56 (12,080)	
Collenette, John P	4:15:06 (14,476)	
Coller, Jonny C	4:11:59 (13,619)	
Collerton, Liam	3:36:09 (5,365)	
Collett, Chris A	4:08:43 (12,743)	
Collett, Les	3:54:18 (9,046)	
Collett, Matthew R	3:39:17 (5,864)	
Collett, Ray C	5:58:05 (32,844)	
Colley, Frederick S	5:06:14 (26,909)	
Colley, John W	4:28:56 (18,286)	
Collier, Christopher J	4:10:46 (13,276)	
Collier, Darren W	3:42:09 (6,411)	
Collier, David S	2:48:45 (452)	
Collier, Ian R	5:40:21 (31,452)	
Collier, James	5:23:11 (29,502)	
Collier, Jeffrey E	3:51:16 (8,321)	
Collier, John S	5:01:43 (26,095)	
Collier, Paul D	3:53:12 (8,770)	
Collin, Kevin W	4:55:53 (24,871)	
Colling, Kevan	3:57:55 (10,116)	
Colling, Steven C	3:48:43 (7,766)	
Collingbourne, Robert J	4:19:20 (15,619)	
Collinge, Andrew	2:39:10 (178)	
Collinge, Dave A	4:46:12 (22,604)	
Collingham, Steven R	4:27:51 (17,998)	
Collings, Derek J	5:15:28 (28,415)	
Collingwood, Mark A	3:28:51 (4,253)	
Collingwood, Neil	3:59:04 (10,456)	
Collins, Adrian R	4:30:14 (18,662)	
Collins, Alan J	3:50:56 (8,245)	
Collins, Alan J	4:22:36 (16,503)	
Collins, Andrew C	3:56:50 (9,766)	
Collins, Andrew D	4:53:02 (24,183)	
Collins, Andy	3:07:40 (1,691)	
Collins, Anthony	6:00:13 (32,987)	
Collins, Barry J	3:09:59 (1,918)	
Collins, Benjamin J	4:28:21 (18,122)	
Collins, Darren R	6:07:48 (33,430)	
Collins, Duncan	2:54:04 (689)	
Collins, Gary M	6:46:18 (34,632)	
Collins, Gilbert H	5:17:58 (28,776)	
Collins, Graham	3:44:48 (6,904)	
Collins, Iain M	6:13:19 (33,671)	
Collins, James A	3:53:20 (8,813)	
Collins, James A	5:10:29 (27,569)	
Collins, Jason	5:00:18 (25,845)	
Collins, Jonathan G	2:46:01 (349)	
Collins, Justin W	4:21:11 (16,105)	
Collins, Kevin J	3:30:50 (4,583)	
Collins, Liam C	4:31:58 (19,078)	
Collins, Matt	4:15:36 (14,607)	
Collins, Michael	3:37:38 (5,592)	
Collins, Michael J	4:56:21 (24,977)	
Collins, Paul M	3:44:18 (6,796)	
Collins, Philip	3:52:44 (8,670)	
Collins, Robert A	5:21:00 (29,236)	
Collins, Stephen	5:02:34 (26,241)	
Collins, Steve P	4:39:43 (21,070)	
Collins, Steven S	3:28:10 (4,138)	
Collinson, Andrew J	3:13:55 (2,241)	
Collinson, Daniel P	4:14:14 (14,220)	
Collinson, Mark W	3:09:17 (1,840)	
Collis, Guy W	3:36:52 (5,473)	
Collis, James G	3:41:22 (6,251)	
Collis, Matt	4:35:41 (20,016)	
Collyer, William L	4:55:09 (24,713)	
Colman, Jesse M	4:13:13 (13,944)	
Colmer, Douglas J	4:12:38 (13,788)	
Colovos, Philippe	3:40:43 (6,123)	
Colquhoun, Richard	5:00:46 (25,929)	
Colton, Eric	5:15:16 (28,383)	
Colton, Kevin	5:15:17 (28,386)	
Colverd, Christien J	4:24:24 (16,956)	
Colwell, Shane A	5:09:19 (27,407)	
Colyer, Nigel J	4:54:09 (24,460)	
Comber, Clifford C	3:27:38 (4,042)	
Comber, David R	5:02:51 (26,307)	
Combes, George	5:13:25 (28,063)	
Comer, Nick V	4:37:09 (20,404)	
Comette, Allan J	4:49:29 (23,355)	
Cominetti, Bertrand	3:53:25 (8,835)	
Commander, Richard A	3:43:46 (6,698)	
Comninos, Michael	3:02:34 (1,303)	
Compton, Aram M	5:29:30 (30,308)	
Compton, Derek K	5:18:34 (28,877)	
Compton, Robert A	3:27:27 (4,008)	
Comte, Xavier	3:26:42 (3,885)	
Concannon, Peter J	4:25:09 (17,169)	
Condell, John	3:10:42 (2,000)	
Condie, William G	4:17:16 (15,029)	
Condon, Dave T	4:26:54 (17,718)	
Condon, Michael J	5:02:05 (26,167)	
Conduit-Smith, Luke B	4:13:59 (14,141)	
Condulmari, Gianmaria	3:29:42 (4,395)	
Condulmari, Roberto	3:29:44 (4,401)	
Conen, Jean	4:19:18 (15,611)	
Coney, Richard I	3:10:06 (1,933)	
Confetti, Carla V	4:22:50 (16,565)	
Conheady, Brian	6:57:02 (34,830)	
Coningham-Rolls, John S	4:47:19 (22,838)	
Conley, Neil M	4:22:51 (16,568)	
Conlon, David G	3:44:05 (6,756)	
Conlon, John J	6:39:32 (34,495)	
Conlon, Kevin G	2:51:32 (565)	
Conlon, Michael P	3:24:50 (3,556)	
Conlon, Paul M	4:26:57 (17,737)	
Connan, Neil P	4:50:12 (23,534)	
Connearn, Dale	3:41:50 (6,343)	
Connell, Christopher	3:50:07 (8,064)	
Connell, John L	5:03:08 (26,369)	

Connell, Michael	5:01:15 (26,016)	
Connell, Michael	6:53:21 (34,777)	
Conners, Kevin D	3:27:29 (4,017)	
Connery, Neil E	4:02:53 (11,359)	
Connolly, Arthur G	5:01:49 (26,109)	
Connolly, David M	3:36:55 (5,484)	
Connolly, Dermot F	2:51:22 (554)	
Connolly, Gabriel P	3:52:56 (8,705)	
Connolly, Gary	3:49:19 (7,897)	
Connolly, James	3:39:40 (5,945)	
Connolly, James	4:29:13 (18,372)	
Connolly, James	6:14:18 (33,709)	
Connolly, John	4:09:05 (12,853)	
Connolly, John C	5:05:59 (26,868)	
Connolly, Kevin	4:37:21 (20,457)	
Connolly, Mark W	4:34:14 (19,646)	
Connolly, Matthew J	4:55:21 (24,747)	
Connolly, Sean F	4:51:11 (23,769)	
Connolly, Shane R	2:57:03 (886)	
Connop, David W	4:01:59 (11,150)	
Connor, David P	2:41:15 (224)	
Connor, Eddie	5:41:50 (31,583)	
Connor, Jerome T	3:54:27 (9,088)	
Connor, Paul M	4:34:13 (19,634)	
Connor, Paul W	4:13:16 (13,955)	
Connor, Shaun S	3:21:57 (3,180)	
Connors, Andrew A	3:29:27 (4,347)	
Connors, Robert J	3:42:21 (6,441)	
Connor-Stead, Philip	4:19:06 (15,547)	
Conrad, Tom	5:39:03 (31,314)	
Conradson, David J	3:29:09 (4,305)	
Conroy, Lee	4:39:11 (20,923)	
Conroy, Stuart	4:26:36 (17,631)	
Constant, Christopher C	5:19:43 (29,064)	
Constantinou, Andreas	5:54:00 (32,564)	
Contini, Colin	4:48:53 (23,205)	
Convery, John J	2:36:59 (138)	
Convy, Paul M	5:11:20 (27,712)	
Conway, David J	3:04:44 (1,447)	
Conway, Liam P	3:10:07 (1,938)	
Conway, Matthew	4:39:19 (20,967)	
Conway, Michael	3:46:43 (7,287)	
Conway, Michael G	6:38:44 (34,479)	
Conway, Neil P	3:58:33 (10,303)	
Conway, Paul E	4:48:58 (23,227)	
Conway, Stephen J	4:05:28 (11,982)	
Conway, Stuart	3:51:37 (8,392)	
Conway, Wayne	6:15:32 (33,759)	
Coogan, Adam C	4:16:14 (14,775)	
Cook, Alan	3:10:36 (1,988)	
Cook, Allan	6:03:49 (33,212)	
Cook, Andrew	4:18:11 (15,261)	
Cook, Andrew D	4:55:38 (24,799)	
Cook, Andy J	4:29:20 (18,412)	
Cook, Barry T	3:10:04 (1,928)	
Cook, Ben W	4:14:29 (14,290)	
Cook, Chris M	3:50:10 (8,077)	
Cook, Christopher J	5:13:46 (28,126)	
Cook, Colin A	4:53:58 (24,415)	
Cook, Darren	3:29:25 (4,341)	
Cook, Darren J	4:19:56 (15,782)	
Cook, David J	4:04:23 (11,718)	
Cook, David J	4:12:45 (13,817)	
Cook, David V	4:24:23 (16,949)	
Cook, Geoffrey	3:53:55 (8,958)	
Cook, Graham P	4:46:02 (22,557)	
Cook, Ian J	4:10:47 (13,281)	
Cook, Jason S	3:19:51 (2,981)	
Cook, John A	4:17:15 (15,021)	
Cook, Keith A	3:59:53 (10,694)	
Cook, Kristopher M	4:02:38 (11,298)	
Cook, Martyn R	4:57:31 (25,230)	
Cook, Matthew T	5:29:38 (30,323)	
Cook, Nathan M	4:58:50 (25,521)	
Cook, Neil J	3:30:54 (4,590)	
Cook, Nigel W	2:57:30 (924)	
Cook, Paul	6:06:30 (33,357)	
Cook, Paul A	4:51:12 (23,777)	
Cook, Peter D	4:22:39 (16,523)	
Cook, Peter M	4:30:01 (18,591)	
Cook, Phil J	2:40:31 (211)	
Cook, Philip M	5:22:26 (29,409)	
Cook, Richard	4:41:44 (21,573)	
Cook, Richard I	3:28:17 (4,155)	
Cook, Simon	4:19:17 (15,604)	
Cook, Stephen	3:42:42 (6,498)	
Cook, Stephen J	4:18:48 (15,464)	
Cook, Timothy H	2:46:52 (367)	
Cook, Timothy J	3:52:33 (8,615)	
Cook, Vincent O	6:18:12 (33,860)	
Cooke, Bradley J	4:03:08 (11,416)	
Cooke, Christopher R	3:55:40 (9,416)	
Cooke, David	4:15:26 (14,558)	
Cooke, Jason L	6:10:14 (33,541)	
Cooke, Jonathan D	4:13:22 (13,982)	
Cooke, Justin	3:31:32 (4,685)	
Cooke, Michael A	3:13:40 (2,325)	
Cooke, Richard D	3:58:20 (10,237)	
Cooke, Robert E	3:04:08 (1,405)	
Cooke, Tim	3:30:52 (4,587)	
Cookman, Graham R	3:26:21 (3,820)	
Cooksey, Andrew P	4:18:10 (15,253)	
Cookson, Jim	4:16:40 (14,881)	
Cookson, Mark A	3:27:30 (4,020)	
Cookson, Noel	4:22:20 (16,429)	
Coolen, Hans	3:58:08 (10,176)	
Cooley, Anthony G	3:26:34 (3,859)	
Coomber, Mark R	5:30:56 (30,461)	
Coomber, Steve J	4:16:37 (14,866)	
Coombes, Gary P	3:43:11 (6,588)	
Coombs, Chris K	3:48:51 (7,800)	
Coombs, Henri M	3:01:01 (1,192)	
Coombs, Roger R	5:13:23 (28,055)	
Coomer, Darren P	4:27:33 (17,906)	
Cooney, Andrew S	3:12:38 (2,207)	
Cooney, John J	4:25:05 (17,146)	
Cooney, Shaun K	4:54:56 (24,648)	
Cooney, Timothy	5:35:41 (30,966)	
Cooper, Adam	3:17:15 (2,709)	
Cooper, Adam R	3:51:59 (8,483)	
Cooper, Alan W	6:22:52 (34,017)	
Cooper, Andrew J	5:02:46 (26,290)	
Cooper, Benjamin J	3:50:49 (8,211)	
Cooper, Brian	4:01:55 (11,134)	
Cooper, Clive	4:52:27 (24,041)	
Cooper, David	3:45:10 (6,984)	
Cooper, David	4:50:47 (23,690)	
Cooper, David J	4:56:10 (24,932)	
Cooper, Douglas N	3:39:50 (5,971)	
Cooper, Gary	5:19:49 (29,078)	
Cooper, Gary G	5:49:54 (32,253)	
Cooper, Ian	4:18:26 (15,345)	
Cooper, Ian R	3:25:36 (3,686)	
Cooper, James N	4:26:21 (17,548)	
Cooper, John F	4:01:31 (11,052)	
Cooper, John M	4:03:43 (11,548)	
Cooper, Jonathan M	3:33:04 (4,896)	
Cooper, Kenneth C	3:25:51 (3,730)	
Cooper, Kevin P	6:05:52 (33,320)	
Cooper, Larry F	6:28:05 (34,196)	
Cooper, Mark C	4:56:19 (24,967)	
Cooper, Matthew D	4:30:59 (18,831)	
Cooper, Michael J	3:28:50 (4,249)	
Cooper, Neil V	3:21:47 (3,165)	
Cooper, Paul	5:18:28 (28,854)	
Cooper, Paul C	4:27:22 (17,845)	
Cooper, Paul J	3:53:34 (8,875)	
Cooper, Paul R	4:55:45 (24,831)	
Cooper, Philip A	4:21:54 (16,306)	
Cooper, Philip J	3:05:28 (1,515)	
Cooper, Richard D	4:55:48 (24,841)	
Cooper, Richard J	4:07:20 (12,427)	
Cooper, Robert H	4:26:17 (17,527)	
Cooper, Robert W	4:24:28 (16,982)	
Cooper, Russell J	3:41:02 (6,186)	
Cooper, Scott A	4:59:24 (25,641)	
Cooper, Stephen	4:03:43 (11,548)	
Cooper, Stephen J	3:38:06 (5,667)	
Cooray, Anuradah	2:20:16 (28)	
Cooray, Benedict	4:23:03 (16,612)	
Coote, Mark R	4:16:07 (14,747)	
Coote, Patrick S	3:41:16 (6,225)	
Cope, Trevor A	4:27:42 (17,951)	
Copeland, Alexander	3:48:12 (7,634)	
Copeland, Gary E	2:57:16 (906)	
Copeland, Gideon M	5:26:56 (29,968)	
Copland, Andy	3:54:42 (9,154)	
Copley, Andrew J	5:14:06 (28,189)	
Copley, Ben	2:56:08 (816)	
Coppen, Dean	4:05:04 (11,882)	
Coppin, François	4:30:11 (18,652)	
Coppock, James A	3:10:21 (1,965)	
Coppock, Mick	4:12:33 (13,760)	
Coppola, Rosario	4:06:33 (12,225)	
Copsey, Ben	6:33:19 (34,339)	
Copus, Christopher D	3:11:19 (2,061)	
Copus, Martin R	3:27:52 (4,087)	
Corbersmith, Steven L	5:20:16 (29,136)	
Corbett, Colin F	5:40:43 (31,481)	
Corbett, David T	3:56:53 (9,781)	
Corbett, Gary A	4:03:05 (11,406)	
Corbett, Jo	2:44:00 (295)	
Corbett, Jonathan J	3:40:43 (6,123)	
Corbett, Richard C	4:41:23 (21,489)	
Corbett, Rupert T	4:37:46 (20,571)	
Corbin, Dexter L	5:14:43 (28,306)	
Corbin, Giles	4:01:40 (11,082)	
Corbould, Percy R	7:44:32 (35,192)	
Corby, Michael J	4:59:27 (25,653)	
Corby, Nick C	4:49:58 (23,488)	
Corcoles, Antonio D	4:46:22 (22,639)	
Corcoran, Chris	3:14:06 (2,367)	
Corcoran, Cornelius L	3:53:42 (8,909)	
Corcoran, Dermot	5:09:36 (27,456)	
Corcoran, John	4:43:17 (21,930)	
Corcuff, Claude P	4:41:58 (21,617)	
Corcuff, Didier P	4:41:57 (21,615)	
Corden, Dougal M	3:55:25 (9,342)	
Corden, James M	3:17:02 (2,680)	
Cordery, John P	4:48:09 (23,042)	
Cordery, Lee F	4:45:00 (22,325)	
Cordle, Ben S	4:18:50 (15,473)	
Corfield, Brian L	3:36:29 (5,425)	
Corfield, Michael H	3:32:15 (4,781)	
Corke, Richard C	5:18:07 (28,805)	
Corke, Rod G	5:13:50 (28,138)	
Corkindale, Timothy	4:00:21 (10,794)	
Corkrey, Larry	5:03:39 (26,453)	
Corless, Michael J	3:38:25 (5,712)	
Corlett, Ben	3:19:56 (2,989)	
Corlett, John B	4:26:53 (17,714)	
Corley, Steven M	3:23:14 (3,339)	
Cormano, Donato	5:19:09 (28,963)	
Cornelius, Neil D	5:20:10 (29,127)	
Cornell, Mark K	3:25:48 (3,716)	
Cornell, Matthew J	4:39:11 (20,923)	
Cornell, Steven A	4:14:43 (14,352)	
Corner, John W	4:31:14 (18,894)	
Corner, Marc	3:18:51 (2,866)	
Corney, Rupert J	4:07:37 (12,483)	
Cornfield, Geoffrey	4:15:30 (14,582)	
Cornford, Adrian W	3:07:48 (1,699)	
Cornick, Neil	3:39:45 (5,958)	
Cornish, Alan G	3:41:47 (6,333)	
Cornish, Darren J	3:51:36 (8,388)	
Cornish, David P	4:38:51 (20,840)	
Cornish, Iain	3:55:14 (9,284)	
Cornish, Nathan	3:59:25 (10,548)	
Cornwall, Dale M	4:18:56 (15,494)	
Cornwall, John B	5:05:07 (26,707)	
Cornwell, Nick	3:52:03 (8,493)	
Corps, Daryl J	4:44:01 (22,105)	
Corr, Eugene C	4:18:40 (15,420)	
Correia De Barros, Ricardo	3:42:31 (6,471)	
Corrie, Andrew I	3:52:59 (8,713)	
Corriente Sanchez, Manuel E	3:41:33 (6,287)	
Corrigan, John J	4:35:24 (19,951)	
Corrigan, Patrik J	3:29:07 (4,300)	
Corsini, Russell G	3:09:34 (1,865)	
Cortese, Guiseppe	4:43:32 (21,990)	
Corti, Dominic F	4:30:22 (18,693)	
Corton, James	5:24:02 (29,627)	
Cory, Ben L	4:30:08 (18,636)	
Cory, Lee	4:35:23 (19,947)	
Coscia, Frederic	3:46:14 (7,188)	
Cosgrave, Andrew	4:00:39 (10,877)	
Cosgrave, James	3:25:00 (3,583)	
Cosgriff, Andrew P	4:26:30 (17,600)	
Cosgrove, Ian	5:03:29 (26,431)	

Costa, Cesare	2:31:10 (80)	
Costa, Costas A	3:59:44 (10,641)	
Costa, Erico C	3:47:22 (7,430)	
Costain, Michael G	4:10:08 (13,123)	
Costanza, Kevin S	4:26:54 (17,718)	
Costard, Martin D	4:52:21 (24,026)	
Costas, Barry	3:16:37 (2,642)	
Costas, Paul	3:10:20 (1,963)	
Costel, Cater	4:47:36 (22,907)	
Costello, Christopher M	4:31:23 (18,940)	
Costelloe, Paul	4:18:17 (15,290)	
Coster, Malcolm	3:09:14 (1,834)	
Costiff, Nigel L	3:53:51 (8,947)	
Costley, Benjamin R	4:52:03 (23,948)	
Costley, Edward	4:50:32 (23,636)	
Cotam, Nick J	4:01:28 (11,041)	
Cotillard, Paul R	4:01:19 (11,005)	
Cotin, Arnaud	4:04:47 (11,811)	
Cottam, Christopher	4:09:18 (12,908)	
Cottam, Mark W	3:36:43 (5,455)	
Cottam, Richard	5:02:50 (26,301)	
Cottee, Tony R	5:18:28 (28,854)	
Cotterill, Andrew J	5:19:58 (29,091)	
Cotterill, Mark A	3:15:15 (2,499)	
Cottey, Tony	3:53:36 (8,883)	
Cotti, Marco	3:54:41 (9,149)	
Cottier, Andrew C	2:47:06 (376)	
Cottingham, Paul S	3:56:17 (9,599)	
Cottis, John D	3:03:41 (1,383)	
Cottis, Roy A	3:53:01 (8,720)	
Cottle, Benjamin C	3:21:43 (3,156)	
Cotton, Anthony E	3:30:19 (4,490)	
Cotton, Chris	4:03:43 (11,548)	
Cotton, John C	4:18:37 (15,399)	
Cotton, Mark H	5:25:34 (29,813)	
Cotton, Rod N	3:31:07 (4,620)	
Cottrell, Andrew W	4:31:26 (18,951)	
Cottrill, Gary P	3:56:55 (9,787)	
Cottrill, Philip G	5:09:05 (27,365)	
Cotzias, Constantin M	3:16:45 (2,656)	
Couch, John R	4:53:14 (24,231)	
Coughlan, Brian J	4:11:02 (13,361)	
Coughlan, James G	4:18:50 (15,473)	
Coughlan, Jeremy C	4:13:24 (13,990)	
Coughlan, Kevin G	6:00:11 (32,986)	
Coughlan, Matthew L	3:42:08 (6,408)	
Coughlan, Simon D	3:44:44 (6,888)	
Coughlin, Richard D	4:38:11 (20,667)	
Couillard, Marc	3:09:45 (1,891)	
Coulibaly, Bougary	3:55:30 (9,368)	
Coulson, Jeffrey	4:34:43 (19,772)	
Coulson, Paul R	5:24:32 (29,687)	
Coulson, Peter	3:46:30 (7,243)	
Coulson, Phillip W	5:05:47 (26,841)	
Coulson, Stephen	4:20:24 (15,912)	
Coulston, Mark	4:39:45 (21,081)	
Coulter, Joseph	4:39:04 (20,896)	
Coulter, Peter E	4:34:24 (19,693)	
Coulthard, Julian N	4:37:34 (20,515)	
Coulthard, Matthew W	6:02:03 (33,086)	
Coultrup, Timothy J	3:45:42 (7,076)	
Coupe, Benjamin	5:52:31 (32,465)	
Coupe, Paul	4:35:34 (19,988)	
Coupes, Dominic J	4:17:15 (15,021)	
Courage, Mark	4:23:48 (16,804)	
Course, Dominic A	3:40:33 (6,094)	
Court, Alan R	3:10:55 (2,023)	
Court, James	4:37:33 (20,509)	
Court, Jeremy J	4:37:01 (20,360)	
Court, John W	4:09:52 (13,059)	
Court, Michael C	3:09:17 (1,840)	
Court, Philip A	3:57:39 (10,027)	
Court, Robert I	3:49:37 (7,958)	
Courtier, Robert S	5:15:32 (28,422)	
Courtman-Stock, Paul S	3:29:00 (4,273)	
Courtney, Denise	4:36:36 (20,253)	
Courtney, John	5:22:35 (29,436)	
Courtney, Kevin S	2:59:18 (1,069)	
Courtney, Peter	4:53:46 (24,374)	
Courtney, Trevor A	5:15:22 (28,396)	
Cousens, Charles L	5:01:03 (25,986)	
Cousens, Michael D	4:51:46 (23,884)	
Cousens, Simon J	5:34:19 (30,821)	
Cousins, Darren G	4:15:13 (14,508)	
Cousins, Patrick C	3:21:49 (3,167)	
Cousins, Roger N	4:47:24 (22,856)	
Cousins, Stuart	4:26:50 (17,694)	
Coutts, David	4:25:34 (17,307)	
Couzy, François	3:59:14 (10,503)	
Coverdale, Philip A	4:06:30 (12,213)	
Covington, Neil J	2:52:41 (620)	
Covus, Steven D	5:07:09 (27,086)	
Cowan, Alan R	6:03:10 (33,152)	
Cowan, Christopher	4:54:59 (24,668)	
Cowan, Harry	5:43:27 (31,714)	
Cowan, Nicholas E	4:45:49 (22,504)	
Cowap, Donald H	4:55:51 (24,862)	
Coward, Andrew C	3:27:24 (3,996)	
Coward, Jeremy	3:09:51 (1,903)	
Cowdry, Jon M	4:48:36 (23,147)	
Cowell, Courtney J	4:23:38 (16,761)	
Cowell, Justin K	4:10:17 (13,164)	
Cowell, Richard J	3:11:49 (2,119)	
Cowen, Daniel S	4:15:48 (14,660)	
Cowen, Stephen W	4:39:39 (21,057)	
Cowland, Jeffrey	5:41:48 (31,578)	
Cowley, Brian M	5:01:50 (26,114)	
Cowley, John	4:17:07 (14,991)	
Cowley, Nigel M	3:15:21 (2,509)	
Cowley, Tim J	3:36:00 (5,342)	
Cowlin, Jonathan	4:18:58 (15,502)	
Cowling, Jeff	3:20:45 (3,070)	
Cowling, Michael A	4:07:27 (12,448)	
Cowling, Michael L	4:51:53 (23,905)	
Cowls, Stephen J	4:16:02 (14,724)	
Cowper, Ian P	3:50:49 (8,211)	
Cowper-Coles, John P	4:52:58 (24,166)	
Cox, Adrian J	3:34:32 (5,127)	
Cox, Alan	3:20:41 (3,060)	
Cox, Andrew	4:15:29 (14,573)	
Cox, Barnaby	4:34:06 (19,591)	
Cox, Barny T	4:24:23 (16,949)	
Cox, Benjamin G	3:59:50 (10,676)	
Cox, Bob J	5:45:39 (31,905)	
Cox, Brett M	4:44:36 (22,227)	
Cox, Brian A	5:33:17 (30,698)	
Cox, Christopher B	5:00:11 (25,813)	
Cox, Darren J	3:24:23 (3,504)	
Cox, David	5:02:39 (26,263)	
Cox, David A	4:43:52 (22,064)	
Cox, Dean E	5:06:52 (27,036)	
Cox, Edward W	4:07:01 (12,350)	
Cox, Jonathan R	3:34:30 (5,124)	
Cox, Justin A	2:59:21 (1,077)	
Cox, Mark	4:34:57 (19,842)	
Cox, Mark A	3:25:40 (3,699)	
Cox, Mark M	3:26:26 (3,839)	
Cox, Matthew D	4:38:23 (20,724)	
Cox, Michael P	5:06:02 (26,881)	
Cox, Paul	2:50:26 (511)	
Cox, Paul A	7:10:00 (34,978)	
Cox, Peter	4:40:27 (21,243)	
Cox, Philip J	4:40:24 (21,231)	
Cox, Richard	5:22:19 (29,386)	
Cox, Richard W	4:27:40 (17,942)	
Cox, Rory W	4:23:46 (16,794)	
Cox, Simon J	4:06:04 (12,114)	
Cox, Spencer C	3:46:08 (7,167)	
Cox, Stephen J	2:46:34 (360)	
Cox, Steven M	5:19:50 (29,080)	
Cox, William J	4:57:01 (25,135)	
Coxhead, Dean	4:13:00 (13,878)	
Coxhead, Ian S	2:51:35 (569)	
Coxhill, Benny A	4:02:58 (11,383)	
Coxhill, Neil	4:45:29 (22,429)	
Coxon, Gary	3:25:55 (3,745)	
Coxon, Luke S	3:11:55 (2,130)	
Coy, Adrian J	4:35:30 (19,975)	
Coyle, Jimmy M	5:08:06 (27,236)	
Coyle, John	4:18:48 (15,464)	
Coyle, Louis	4:05:24 (11,967)	
Coyle, Michael J	5:17:03 (28,656)	
Coyle, Terence P	2:50:47 (532)	
Coyle, William J	3:08:48 (1,790)	
Coyne, A J	5:13:01 (28,000)	
Coyne, Michael J	4:29:00 (18,306)	
Coyne, Owen A	4:58:29 (25,438)	
Coyne, Paul D	3:57:47 (10,070)	
Crabtree, Graham J	3:51:55 (8,466)	
Crabtree, Mark A	3:28:01 (4,107)	
Crabtree, Nicholas A	4:34:12 (19,624)	
Cracknell, David J	4:42:40 (21,793)	
Cracknell, Shaun	4:45:24 (22,414)	
Cradden, Brendan P	3:32:24 (4,806)	
Craddock, Peter M	3:38:47 (5,774)	
Crafer, Gary	4:11:43 (13,543)	
Craft, Alan P	4:26:51 (17,703)	
Craft, David C	4:08:40 (12,733)	
Craft, Jake	4:38:56 (20,857)	
Cragg, Stephen	5:02:55 (26,325)	
Cragg, Stuart J	2:45:43 (340)	
Craig, Adam	3:38:46 (5,772)	
Craig, Alan R	5:03:13 (26,387)	
Craig, Aubrey	4:36:02 (20,091)	
Craig, Christopher	3:38:44 (5,759)	
Craig, Gavin M	4:26:38 (17,643)	
Craig, Gerard	2:54:42 (726)	
Craig, Matthew	4:19:42 (15,721)	
Craig, Matthew A	4:05:51 (12,057)	
Craig, Michael	2:54:42 (726)	
Craig, Michael	3:50:51 (8,224)	
Craig, Oliver	3:54:55 (9,221)	
Craig, Robert C	4:32:19 (19,170)	
Craig, Scott	3:36:18 (5,392)	
Craigie, David G	3:38:06 (5,667)	
Craine, Gary A	4:49:21 (23,326)	
Craine, Nigel M	4:39:28 (21,001)	
Craker, Jason F	5:05:27 (26,786)	
Cramp, Harvey E	3:21:32 (3,135)	
Crampey, James M	2:48:11 (422)	
Crampton, James	3:57:24 (9,949)	
Cran, Alexander N	3:17:03 (2,684)	
Crane, Andrew J	4:18:41 (15,427)	
Crane, Howard	4:04:02 (11,646)	
Crane, Lee	5:48:27 (32,133)	
Crane, Michael J	4:50:22 (23,585)	
Crane, Peter J	3:19:32 (2,946)	
Crane, Stephen D	4:10:05 (13,109)	
Crane, William T	3:12:42 (2,216)	
Cranidge, Stuart	5:42:44 (31,654)	
Crank, David W	4:46:16 (22,615)	
Cranstoun, Mark J	4:50:19 (23,572)	
Cranwell, Mark A	3:06:40 (1,607)	
Craven, Mark J	5:12:23 (27,882)	
Craven, Paul A	4:28:48 (18,250)	
Craven, Paul V	4:27:46 (17,973)	
Craven, Philip D	6:15:28 (33,753)	
Craven, William H	5:34:37 (30,863)	
Crawford, Andrew P	6:08:16 (33,457)	
Crawford, Blake L	3:44:11 (6,784)	
Crawford, Darran A	5:21:14 (29,265)	
Crawford, David	3:56:29 (9,693)	
Crawford, Gary A	4:53:30 (24,300)	
Crawford, John	4:24:42 (17,043)	
Crawford, Mark	3:46:51 (7,316)	
Crawford, Mark D	5:08:53 (27,337)	
Crawford, Rick P	3:17:14 (2,706)	
Crawford, Robert K	4:50:45 (23,683)	
Crawford, Scott C	4:14:45 (14,363)	
Crawford, Victor S	4:07:14 (12,399)	
Crawley, Mike	4:18:09 (15,249)	
Crawshaw, Andrew P	3:27:38 (4,042)	
Crawshaw, Braddan J	4:03:57 (11,617)	
Crawshaw, John S	4:28:31 (18,173)	
Crawshaw, Michael J	3:25:43 (3,704)	
Crawshaw, Paul A	4:52:23 (24,031)	
Crawte, Tony	4:05:15 (11,929)	
Cray, John M	4:11:43 (13,543)	
Creamer, Patrick D	4:24:01 (16,857)	
Crease, Gregory D	3:36:26 (5,415)	
Creasey, James E	3:27:55 (4,093)	
Creasey, Paul D	4:12:44 (13,811)	
Creasy, Ian A	4:18:43 (15,438)	
Creed, Anthony E	5:32:23 (30,603)	
Creed, Ben B	3:48:04 (7,606)	
Creed, Hugh M	3:49:54 (8,017)	
Creedon, Stephen M	5:02:33 (26,237)	
Creevy, Scott	4:27:19 (17,829)	
Creigh, David	3:43:01 (6,553)	

Cremer, Arne 3:55:40 (9,416)
Cremin, Ciaran 4:45:22 (22,406)
Cremor, Robert J 7:17:55 (35,061)
Crerie, Vincent R 4:55:41 (24,815)
Cresey, Andy A 4:06:46 (12,277)
Cresswell, Wayne 4:11:01 (13,354)
Cretton, Gary L 4:35:46 (20,036)
Crew, Mark 4:36:29 (20,223)
Crewe, Alan 3:43:11 (6,588)
Cribb, Stephen T 4:27:07 (17,780)
Crichton, Andrew K 4:00:33 (10,852)
Crichton-Sharp, Christopher 4:59:58 (25,771)
Crick, Steve J 5:09:54 (27,498)
Cridland, Andrew P 4:00:03 (10,741)
Crimp, Alastair R 4:19:32 (15,674)
Crinson, Andy C 4:51:58 (23,925)
Crippa, Alexander 4:11:08 (13,388)
Cripps, Graham C 4:07:00 (12,343)
Criscuolo, Ciro 5:45:35 (31,900)
Criso, John P 4:28:40 (18,206)
Crisp, Clive 3:18:25 (2,822)
Crisp, John R 3:37:26 (5,564)
Crispie, Gerard T 2:58:45 (1,010)
Crispin, Andrew D 5:32:14 (30,581)
Crispin, Stuart J 6:09:45 (33,524)
Criss, Richard 4:23:20 (16,701)
Critchfield, John 4:02:56 (11,378)
Critchley, Gavin 4:35:13 (19,887)
Critchley, Lee 6:15:45 (33,773)
Critchlow, Guy C 4:11:33 (13,494)
Croal, Jeremy 4:18:04 (15,226)
Crocker, Bernard 6:51:47 (34,749)
Crocker, Jeremy D 4:37:20 (20,456)
Crocker, Matthew 3:54:00 (8,977)
Crocker, Nick M 4:05:16 (11,936)
Crocket, Graham D 5:13:59 (28,168)
Crockford, John G 2:48:43 (447)
Crockford, Tom L 4:33:43 (19,492)
Croft, Anthony J 3:01:37 (1,233)
Croft, Christopher R 4:06:01 (12,096)
Croft, David A 4:46:50 (22,741)
Croft, James D 3:46:57 (7,338)
Croft, Nigel D 3:49:13 (7,866)
Croft, Philip D 4:55:00 (24,674)
Croft, Tony W 4:05:30 (11,985)
Crofts, Darren 4:27:45 (17,968)
Crofts, Darren A 4:21:44 (16,266)
Crofts, Joe N 4:55:40 (24,804)
Crofts-Barnes, Anthony J 4:50:48 (23,694)
Crole-Rees, Matthew J 5:03:09 (26,376)
Croll, Stewart 4:03:23 (11,476)
Crollick, David L 4:37:58 (20,610)
Cromby, Michael 3:48:43 (7,766)
Cromey, Simon A 4:44:54 (22,298)
Crompton, Duncan 3:50:41 (8,184)
Crompton, Neil W 2:48:56 (465)
Crompton, Nicholas W 3:41:34 (6,290)
Crone, Paul G 5:43:08 (31,691)
Cronen, David 4:08:35 (12,711)
Cronin, Alfred 3:15:56 (2,560)
Cronin, Barry A 5:20:03 (29,107)
Cronin, Patrick 4:21:13 (16,113)
Crook, Christopher S 4:39:15 (20,953)
Crook, David 4:01:11 (10,977)
Crook, Ed P 4:29:54 (18,567)
Crook, Mark 4:27:22 (17,845)
Crook, Michael R 4:39:15 (20,953)
Crook, Paul A 4:34:35 (19,736)
Crook, Richard B 4:54:08 (24,456)
Crook, Simon M 4:19:49 (15,756)
Crookall, Jonathan 4:17:25 (15,078)
Crooks, Alistair J 3:59:15 (10,510)
Crooks, David R 4:20:47 (16,017)
Crooks, Robert 5:46:58 (32,014)
Crooks, Samuel 5:03:13 (26,387)
Crooms, Neil A 4:04:11 (11,678)
Crosbie, Donald E 4:30:07 (18,630)
Crosby, Trevor A 3:56:51 (9,769)
Crosher, Andrew D 5:57:31 (32,805)
Crosland, David 3:21:14 (3,108)
Cross, Alex J 3:24:50 (3,556)
Cross, Anthony W 3:04:37 (1,437)
Cross, Gerard B 5:36:06 (31,004)
Cross, Graham 5:58:17 (32,860)
Cross, Howard W 3:45:31 (7,050)
Cross, Jeremy A 4:50:35 (23,647)
Cross, Kevin J 3:56:42 (9,726)
Cross, Mark 3:11:01 (2,034)
Cross, Neil 4:54:44 (24,603)
Cross, Peter 5:22:05 (29,364)
Cross, Peter H 5:11:05 (27,668)
Cross, Peter R 3:19:35 (2,953)
Cross, Philip J 3:06:54 (1,627)
Cross, Stephen A 3:16:27 (2,630)
Cross, Stephen D 3:55:08 (9,258)
Cross, Stephen J 4:04:50 (11,822)
Cross, Terence A 4:51:06 (23,751)
Crossfield, Richard 4:27:46 (17,973)
Crossingham, Rowan 3:24:05 (3,456)
Crossland, Timothy J 2:39:14 (180)
Crosslands, Alan 4:31:51 (19,052)
Crossley, Dominic F 3:51:19 (8,333)
Crossley, Patrick D 4:33:41 (19,485)
Crossley, Peter J 3:56:26 (9,645)
Crossley, Robert J 5:06:12 (26,906)
Crossman, Tim J 4:03:47 (11,569)
Crothers, Alastair C 5:26:35 (29,931)
Crotty, Andrew D 4:12:57 (13,869)
Croucher, Graham J 4:12:40 (13,794)
Crow, George 4:20:09 (15,840)
Crow, Peter 3:20:28 (3,043)
Crowcombe, Matthew D 5:01:34 (26,076)
Crowder, David 6:11:55 (33,609)
Crowder, Spencer J 4:45:16 (22,384)
Crowe, Douglas J 4:54:00 (24,428)
Crowe, Neal H 3:25:49 (3,721)
Crowe, Philip D 4:33:15 (19,370)
Crowell, Peter J 3:51:05 (8,278)
Crowhurst, Daniel G 3:36:35 (5,442)
Crowhurst, Keith A 3:59:33 (10,590)
Crowley, Nick 5:22:17 (29,385)
Crowley, Richard J 7:04:10 (34,911)
Crowley, Vincent P 3:28:14 (4,149)
Crowther, Julian G 2:51:41 (573)
Croxford, Michael J 4:42:26 (21,725)
Croxford, Stuart G 4:46:41 (22,704)
Croy, Elden 5:19:11 (28,970)
Crozier, Andrew R 5:32:21 (30,595)
Crozier, Michael J 4:17:56 (15,184)
Crozier, Peter 3:12:34 (2,200)
Crudgington, James W 3:53:09 (8,756)
Cruickshank, George A 4:48:18 (23,075)
Cruickshank, James M 7:17:04 (35,053)
Cruickshank, Sandy 3:32:13 (4,777)
Cruise, James A 5:43:15 (31,697)
Crumpler, Matthew P 4:05:04 (11,882)
Crumpler, Simon R 3:59:49 (10,667)
Crundwell, Malcolm C 4:16:52 (14,929)
Cruse-Drew, Timothy J 3:37:52 (5,629)
Crussell, Nick 5:27:29 (30,041)
Cruz, Efren P 3:41:17 (6,228)
Cruz Cintron, Bienvenido 4:01:38 (11,075)
Csapo, Adam 3:02:27 (1,294)
Cubbage, Kevin J 4:46:13 (22,606)
Cubitt, David 5:04:18 (26,570)
Cuddigan, Troy J 5:16:04 (28,487)
Cuddon, Kevin D 4:28:50 (18,258)
Cudmore, Miles A 3:13:39 (2,322)
Cuff, Paul E 2:55:22 (758)
Cuffe, James M 3:22:08 (3,204)
Cuffe, John G 5:37:26 (31,133)
Cukerman, Albert 5:03:40 (26,456)
Culie, Marc 3:12:46 (2,222)
Cullen, Christopher P 4:01:13 (10,985)
Cullen, David E 5:30:35 (30,421)
Cullen, Martin J 4:18:45 (15,444)
Cullen, Rodney P 4:54:35 (24,576)
Cullen, Rory C 6:58:14 (34,841)
Cullens, James A 5:26:36 (29,935)
Cullern, Doug 4:21:25 (16,179)
Culley, Kirk S 4:03:13 (11,435)
Cullinane, John 3:31:12 (4,631)
Culliney, Kevin 4:27:28 (17,875)
Culliney, Kristian 4:17:07 (14,991)
Culling, Gary 4:55:30 (24,771)
Culling, Stephen C 3:56:20 (9,614)
Cullington, Paul W 5:03:06 (26,362)
Cullom, Jonathan M 2:46:42 (365)
Cullwick, Michael J 4:42:38 (21,781)
Culpan, Charlie J 4:13:10 (13,928)
Culpan, Philip S 2:43:36 (284)
Culwin, Fintan 4:15:01 (14,457)
Cumber, Geoffrey 2:59:34 (1,096)
Cumberbatch, Lee 5:25:13 (29,772)
Cumberlege, Jonathan C 4:30:43 (18,772)
Cuming, Matthew 3:11:47 (2,116)
Cumiskey, Thomas P 4:31:27 (18,957)
Cumming, Andrew M 3:55:46 (9,455)
Cummings, John A 4:16:11 (14,762)
Cummings, John F 4:19:50 (15,763)
Cummings, John M 5:38:17 (31,228)
Cummings, Trevor 3:32:20 (4,793)
Cummins, Denis 5:22:20 (29,388)
Cummins, James 3:05:27 (1,513)
Cummins, Mark C 3:46:57 (7,338)
Cummins, Nicholas J 4:53:09 (24,210)
Cummins, Timothy D 4:49:39 (23,411)
Cundell, Ian 4:10:33 (13,232)
Cunliffe, Drew 3:50:00 (8,038)
Cunliffe, Graham A 2:56:25 (836)
Cunliffe, Ross 4:09:21 (12,921)
Cunnew, David A 5:22:51 (29,465)
Cunningham, David 5:05:26 (26,785)
Cunningham, David A 5:00:06 (25,795)
Cunningham, Graeme 4:56:35 (25,035)
Cunningham, Iain W 4:12:45 (13,817)
Cunningham, Jim D 4:17:48 (15,158)
Cunningham, John 4:52:12 (23,985)
Cunningham, John P 4:14:58 (14,430)
Cunningham, Lindsay R 2:51:59 (589)
Cunningham, Michael R 3:10:28 (1,974)
Cunningham, Philip P 3:10:05 (1,932)
Cunningham, Ross 4:38:39 (20,786)
Cunningham, Steve 2:47:20 (381)
Cunningham, Stuart J 2:54:30 (713)
Cunningham, Thomas E 5:13:33 (28,091)
Cunningham, Wayne S 4:16:38 (14,871)
Cunnington, Philip M 3:30:28 (4,518)
Curan, Tony 3:41:18 (6,236)
Curcher, Martin J 5:15:25 (28,408)
Curd, Paul A 3:28:33 (4,206)
Curless, Brent 3:27:54 (4,091)
Curlew, Simon 5:04:56 (26,677)
Curmak, Cem 3:53:53 (8,950)
Curnin, Andrew D 3:28:33 (4,206)
Curnow, Neville R 4:24:25 (16,965)
Curphey, Paul T 2:55:40 (783)
Curran, Dominic T 4:46:07 (22,584)
Curran, Liam 5:24:26 (29,674)
Curran, Patrick L 2:34:28 (108)
Currie, Alaster P 4:15:00 (14,448)
Currie, Kenneth M 4:51:49 (23,894)
Currie, Patrick J 4:08:41 (12,739)
Currington, Darren L 3:47:02 (7,357)
Curry, Dave E 3:48:27 (7,692)
Curry, John C 4:11:59 (13,619)
Curry, Peter 4:48:26 (23,111)
Cursiter, Paul 3:45:16 (7,000)
Curson, Benjamin E 3:33:13 (4,911)
Curtis, Graham R 5:40:51 (31,489)
Curtis, Matthew J 5:41:28 (31,549)
Curtis, Neil B 3:40:38 (6,108)
Curtis, Peter S 3:44:54 (6,937)
Curtis, Ray P 5:32:44 (30,641)
Curtis, Robert B 3:23:40 (3,396)
Curtis, Stephen 5:06:32 (26,972)
Curtis, Steven A 2:55:49 (794)
Curtis, Stuart K 3:46:18 (7,202)
Curtis, Thomas S 4:38:24 (20,727)
Curtis, Tony I 4:02:53 (11,359)
Curzon, Scott L 6:25:02 (34,098)
Cusack, Jake 3:46:28 (7,236)
Cusack, Seamus 5:06:06 (26,890)
Cushing, Spencer 4:08:03 (12,583)
Cushley, David 5:31:25 (30,510)
Cuthbert, Kevin R 4:13:02 (13,888)
Cuthbert, Philip D 3:14:36 (2,430)
Cuthbert, Simon 5:11:19 (27,708)
Cutler, Colin J 5:33:41 (30,746)

Cutler, John L	4:18:04 (15,226)	Dancy, Ben	4:07:05 (12,368)	Davey, Matthew	4:56:14 (24,946)
Cutler, John M	3:51:44 (8,418)	Daniel, Andrew R	3:26:52 (3,904)	Davey, Nicholas A	4:08:18 (12,636)
Cutler, Michael C	4:08:24 (12,667)	Daniel, David M	3:35:43 (5,299)	Davey, Oliver	3:52:03 (8,493)
Cutler, Neil A	3:52:14 (8,537)	Daniel, Jeremy P	4:12:54 (13,857)	Davey, Peter R	4:37:14 (20,423)
Cutler, Paul	4:27:33 (17,906)	Daniel, Richard W	4:21:50 (16,292)	Davey, Ralph	4:40:13 (21,191)
Cutter, Gordon L	4:36:29 (20,223)	Daniel, Stephen	3:30:38 (4,549)	David, Marc	5:08:17 (27,257)
Cutts, Nigel P	4:36:13 (20,135)	Daniells, Brian R	3:46:52 (7,318)	Davidow, Jake A	3:56:02 (9,518)
Cuviello, Stephen P	5:33:28 (30,719)	Daniells, Michael J	5:49:56 (32,257)	Davidson, Alistair S	5:39:13 (31,336)
Czaja, Jean-Claude	3:43:42 (6,684)	Daniels, Alan J	4:38:04 (20,638)	Davidson, Andrew L	5:49:49 (32,246)
Czernin, Peter J	4:37:28 (20,489)	Daniels, Clive	4:10:59 (13,345)	Davidson, Andy W	3:52:01 (8,488)
Czernuszka, Edward A	4:25:02 (17,133)	Daniels, Clive M	4:19:37 (15,699)	Davidson, Colin I	2:53:28 (658)
Czerwinski, David A	4:13:55 (14,122)	Daniels, David P	5:53:14 (32,518)	Davidson, Crawford	4:22:13 (16,399)
Czub, Zenon	3:19:47 (2,977)	Daniels, Gary	5:13:28 (28,076)	Davidson, Gary J	4:29:39 (18,506)
Da Costa, Jorge	6:01:24 (33,044)	Daniels, Martyn I	5:32:13 (30,579)	Davidson, George F	3:33:15 (4,919)
Da Silva, Carlos	2:42:59 (265)	Daniels, Michael	3:09:34 (1,865)	Davidson, Gordon	4:11:49 (13,568)
Da Silva, Deolor	5:05:16 (26,741)	Daniels, Michael J	3:44:31 (6,839)	Davidson, Ian	4:17:00 (14,955)
Da Silva, Panta	3:56:13 (9,578)	Daniels, Paul	3:26:38 (3,876)	Davidson, James	5:57:31 (32,812)
Da Silva, Pedro	4:18:41 (15,427)	Daniels, Paul	4:29:27 (18,448)	Davidson, Keith S	5:15:20 (28,390)
Dabbs, Jonathan M	2:48:05 (420)	Daniels, Peter D	4:18:48 (15,464)	Davidson, Miles R	3:14:09 (2,375)
Dable, Thomas J	4:43:27 (21,964)	Daniels, Steve G	5:04:45 (26,638)	Davidson, Neil A	4:54:42 (24,594)
Daborn, David R	4:05:50 (12,055)	Danks, Colin F	5:12:39 (27,937)	Davidson, Robert R	5:13:10 (28,017)
Dabrowski, Barry	3:27:16 (3,971)	Danks, Peter R	5:19:00 (28,945)	Davidson, Robin	3:32:16 (4,786)
Dacampo, Michele	3:27:23 (3,988)	Dann, Peter	4:20:10 (15,846)	Davidson, Roy	3:30:50 (4,583)
Dadds, Aaron J	4:06:37 (12,247)	Dann, Tim J	5:33:55 (30,768)	Davidson, Stuart I	3:27:44 (4,064)
Dade, Richard C	3:57:26 (9,961)	Danskin, Ian A	3:06:10 (1,565)	Davies, Adam E	4:54:14 (24,486)
Dady, Stephen M	4:31:14 (18,894)	D'Antona, Giovanni	4:19:02 (15,523)	Davies, Adrian H	4:56:26 (24,996)
Daelemans, Ronald	3:55:14 (9,284)	Danvers, Benjamin	2:52:21 (606)	Davies, Adrian J	4:09:17 (12,903)
Dagger, Richard J	3:51:23 (8,348)	Danyluk, Marek J	4:30:38 (18,755)	Davies, Alan	3:54:37 (9,126)
D'Agostino, Luca	3:48:36 (7,741)	Daplyn, Peter	3:59:59 (10,724)	Davies, Alexander J	3:44:48 (6,904)
Dahdouh, Fadi	4:30:05 (18,615)	Darby, Iain M	2:48:43 (447)	Davies, Alexander T	4:24:28 (16,982)
Daines, Andrew P	4:12:10 (13,657)	Darby, John A	4:18:25 (15,334)	Davies, Andrew K	2:44:06 (299)
Dainton, Stephen B	4:12:19 (13,699)	Darby, Mark R	4:12:48 (13,833)	Davies, Andrew L	3:50:57 (8,248)
Daish, Lee J	3:51:45 (8,425)	Darby, Matthew J	4:22:07 (16,375)	Davies, Andrew M	3:59:12 (10,496)
Dakin, Anthony J	5:17:59 (28,779)	Darby, Paul A	4:39:59 (21,136)	Davies, Andrew Q	4:35:25 (19,955)
Dakin, Brian R	3:19:22 (2,919)	Darbyshire, Malcolm	3:05:47 (1,539)	Davies, Andrew T	3:22:30 (3,242)
Dalby, Anthony B	5:00:36 (25,898)	Darbyshire, Peter	4:32:45 (19,258)	Davies, Ben	4:50:36 (23,649)
Dale, Adrian B	3:08:55 (1,802)	D'Arcy, Lee P	3:47:48 (7,525)	Davies, Brian C	3:56:46 (9,740)
Dale, Christopher	4:50:08 (23,523)	Dardalis, Nick	4:14:20 (14,251)	Davies, Carwyn	4:03:47 (11,569)
Dale, Derrick R	3:41:25 (6,261)	Dardis, Colm J	3:45:32 (7,054)	Davies, Christopher	3:31:16 (4,647)
Dale, James	4:06:06 (12,121)	Dark, Anthony G	4:44:29 (22,210)	Davies, Christopher B	3:46:13 (7,182)
Dale, James R	3:57:59 (10,138)	Dark, Stuart	5:45:24 (31,889)	Davies, Clive T	3:06:11 (1,566)
Dale, Jeffrey	4:31:46 (19,038)	Darke, Adam	4:45:05 (22,347)	Davies, Conrad C	3:44:28 (6,827)
Dale, Michael J	4:55:03 (24,687)	Darke, Christopher J	3:59:23 (10,541)	Davies, Craig	5:53:40 (32,544)
Dale, Paul	4:12:34 (13,765)	Darkins, Peter S	3:54:28 (9,093)	Davies, Daniel	5:00:57 (25,969)
Daley, John R	4:34:41 (19,762)	Darley, Dan	2:54:49 (733)	Davies, David	4:51:25 (23,816)
Daley, Justin M	5:14:56 (28,331)	Darley, Edward P	5:07:42 (27,176)	Davies, Gareth H	3:50:25 (8,131)
Dalgarno, Stuart G	4:16:44 (14,898)	Darling, Michael R	3:47:38 (7,482)	Davies, Gareth H	4:21:19 (16,147)
Dalla Bona, Giorgio	3:44:09 (6,774)	Darling, Richard J	2:53:37 (664)	Davies, Gareth J	4:30:06 (18,621)
Dallas, Gordon C	3:44:14 (6,789)	Darlington, William R	4:32:43 (19,250)	Davies, Gareth M	4:55:12 (24,719)
Dallas, Ian A	3:33:18 (4,928)	Darnbrook, Bob	5:03:27 (26,427)	Davies, Gareth R	3:59:49 (10,667)
Dallas, James R	4:33:39 (19,473)	Darroch, Robert	4:51:34 (23,846)	Davies, Gavin R	2:45:50 (343)
Dallas, Robert S	4:43:17 (21,930)	Darton, Peter J	3:35:16 (5,217)	Davies, Gavin S	4:16:49 (14,918)
Dalley, Robert J	4:05:44 (12,036)	Darvell, Jack A	5:10:49 (27,620)	Davies, Geoffrey	5:41:45 (31,571)
Dalling, Kevin	3:47:21 (7,428)	Darvill, Nicholas R	5:35:29 (30,953)	Davies, Glyn R	6:26:45 (34,148)
Dalloz, Vincent	3:52:35 (8,625)	D'Asero, Carmelo	4:03:38 (11,530)	Davies, Gordon	4:57:30 (25,228)
Dally, James R	4:41:48 (21,590)	Dasgupta, Ranjit K	4:56:08 (24,925)	Davies, Graham M	3:41:50 (6,343)
Dalton, Andrew J	3:28:22 (4,169)	Dasgupta, Steven N	5:08:11 (27,246)	Davies, Haydn	5:32:47 (30,651)
Dalton, Andrew M	4:10:19 (13,196)	Datta, Julian N	4:46:28 (22,661)	Davies, Huw	3:40:19 (6,052)
Dalton, Anthony J	4:28:32 (18,176)	Dattani, Dilip	3:10:10 (1,945)	Davies, Huw	4:03:57 (11,617)
Dalton, Mark S	2:53:18 (650)	Dattani, Kunal R	6:12:25 (33,636)	Davies, Hywel J	4:47:58 (22,997)
Dalton, Nick H	3:15:51 (2,552)	Daube, Philippe F	4:08:52 (12,792)	Davies, Ian	4:19:28 (15,654)
Dalton, Ralph J	4:49:43 (23,429)	Daubney, Alisdair J	4:48:37 (23,154)	Davies, Ian J	3:30:00 (4,454)
Dalton, William A	3:12:14 (2,168)	Daughtrey, Michael J	5:37:20 (31,121)	Davies, Iwan T	3:52:47 (8,682)
D'Alton, Anthony J	4:26:21 (17,548)	Dauncey, Chris	3:27:20 (3,983)	Davies, James E	5:16:47 (28,597)
Daly, Edmund	6:47:22 (34,663)	Dauncey, Timothy M	3:17:34 (2,744)	Davies, James S	4:14:03 (14,164)
Daly, Fergus A	4:21:45 (16,271)	Daut, Burkhard	5:40:01 (31,418)	Davies, Jeffrey	3:20:56 (3,083)
Daly, Hugh D	3:55:18 (9,310)	Davenport, David P	3:59:11 (10,493)	Davies, Jerry M	4:03:01 (11,393)
Daly, John D	3:28:23 (4,175)	Davenport, Graham J	4:49:19 (23,315)	Davies, John A	4:03:52 (11,598)
Daly, Kevin R	4:19:44 (15,733)	Davenport, James E	4:00:27 (10,818)	Davies, John E	3:52:08 (8,512)
Daly, Martin C	4:33:17 (19,377)	Davenport, Matt	3:58:23 (10,255)	Davies, John G	4:25:04 (17,142)
Daly, Shaun M	3:51:43 (8,416)	Davenport, Michael S	4:16:11 (14,762)	Davies, John R	4:18:47 (15,460)
Daly, Stephen J	4:09:07 (12,865)	Davenport, Robert A	4:22:48 (16,558)	Davies, Jonathan C	3:31:30 (4,680)
Dalzel-Job, Malcolm J	3:14:48 (2,460)	Daversa, Romano	4:02:28 (11,262)	Davies, Julian	5:05:40 (26,817)
Damant, Chris J	5:00:09 (25,803)	Davey, Anthony J	4:51:02 (23,741)	Davies, Justin J	5:59:26 (32,942)
D'Ambrosio, Gino	4:40:13 (21,191)	Davey, Christopher	5:54:33 (32,606)	Davies, Keith J	2:57:49 (942)
Damian, José Luis	4:12:20 (13,707)	Davey, Craig	2:48:27 (435)	Davies, Kenneth M	6:02:44 (33,123)
Damm, Matthias	4:37:35 (20,520)	Davey, Edward	7:13:00 (35,016)	Davies, Kevin	4:21:36 (16,229)
Dampney, Hugh T	4:19:24 (15,636)	Davey, Ian G	5:12:41 (27,940)	Davies, Kevin M	3:57:07 (9,864)
Danaci, Erdogan	5:00:07 (25,798)	Davey, Keiron	3:42:48 (6,511)	Davies, Kevin R	3:57:33 (9,999)
Danbury, Richard J	4:50:36 (23,649)	Davey, Kevin G	3:16:44 (2,651)	Davies, Lawrence F	3:58:08 (10,176)
Dance, Matthew L	5:33:37 (30,738)	Davey, Mark	4:39:35 (21,037)	Davies, Lee T	4:10:24 (13,204)
Dance, Richard	3:12:01 (2,142)	Davey, Martin C	4:14:56 (14,419)	Davies, Leighton E	3:51:26 (8,362)
Danciger, Simon L	2:49:06 (472)		Davies, Marc B	3:58:19 (10,232)

Davies, Marc H	4:49:21	(23,326)
Davies, Mark M	3:22:30	(3,242)
Davies, Mark O	4:23:42	(16,776)
Davies, Mark R	5:36:28	(31,048)
Davies, Martin L	4:00:25	(10,808)
Davies, Martin W	4:38:55	(20,853)
Davies, Martyn W	4:06:36	(12,241)
Davies, Mathew	3:52:43	(8,664)
Davies, Matthew A	5:15:46	(28,453)
Davies, Michael	5:05:23	(26,771)
Davies, Michael	5:40:56	(31,498)
Davies, Michael G	5:52:17	(32,438)
Davies, Michael H	3:20:45	(3,070)
Davies, Michael J	4:14:45	(14,363)
Davies, Michael J	4:38:04	(20,638)
Davies, Michael J	6:02:03	(33,086)
Davies, Mike	3:04:43	(1,443)
Davies, Neale	4:42:07	(21,657)
Davies, Neil A	3:40:44	(6,126)
Davies, Neville	4:38:45	(20,814)
Davies, Nicholas F	3:05:18	(1,496)
Davies, Nicholas J	5:02:18	(26,202)
Davies, Nick	4:01:36	(11,066)
Davies, Nigel	3:35:38	(5,289)
Davies, Oliver J	3:59:36	(10,599)
Davies, Patrick C	5:50:09	(32,273)
Davies, Paul	5:08:32	(27,289)
Davies, Paul A	2:53:27	(657)
Davies, Paul A	4:03:31	(11,504)
Davies, Paul E	4:55:35	(24,786)
Davies, Paul G	4:56:46	(25,089)
Davies, Paul M	3:42:10	(6,413)
Davies, Pete H	3:50:14	(8,095)
Davies, Peter M	5:15:59	(28,476)
Davies, Phil J	3:27:52	(4,087)
Davies, Phillip E	5:38:52	(31,295)
Davies, Richard J	3:47:47	(7,521)
Davies, Richard J	4:14:09	(14,194)
Davies, Robert	5:40:14	(31,442)
Davies, Robert G	5:20:00	(29,095)
Davies, Ross G	4:48:31	(23,125)
Davies, Roy	4:54:25	(24,528)
Davies, Ryan	6:50:01	(34,709)
Davies, Samuel S	3:49:30	(7,933)
Davies, Simon	3:08:16	(1,739)
Davies, Simon	5:01:00	(25,975)
Davies, Stephen C	2:44:37	(310)
Davies, Stephen J	3:58:52	(10,402)
Davies, Stephen K	5:28:37	(30,200)
Davies, Steve	3:23:46	(3,411)
Davies, Stewart T	5:55:42	(32,694)
Davies, Stuart M	5:23:36	(29,560)
Davies, Thomas	4:01:07	(10,965)
Davies, Thomas E	3:33:47	(5,006)
Davies, Thomas G	3:12:16	(2,171)
Davies, Timothy C	4:31:45	(19,032)
Davies, Tom W	4:22:04	(16,360)
Davies, Tony L	3:24:55	(3,570)
Davies, Trevor J	4:26:42	(17,658)
Davies, Warren B	4:33:37	(19,468)
Davies, Will	5:12:37	(27,929)
Davis, Adrian J	5:05:37	(26,808)
Davis, Andrew R	3:19:32	(2,946)
Davis, Anthony	3:01:30	(1,221)
Davis, Anthony J	4:26:25	(17,578)
Davis, Christopher	5:06:37	(26,986)
Davis, Darren J	4:17:21	(15,050)
Davis, David B	3:54:53	(9,212)
Davis, Frank	4:30:49	(18,799)
Davis, Jim	3:34:14	(5,086)
Davis, Joe A	3:49:00	(7,821)
Davis, John E	4:09:54	(13,071)
Davis, John W	4:34:57	(19,842)
Davis, Justin	4:41:48	(21,590)
Davis, Kevin	5:42:17	(31,609)
Davis, Kevin J	3:09:46	(1,892)
Davis, Lee A	6:16:06	(33,786)
Davis, Mark	2:56:36	(851)
Davis, Mark	3:56:03	(9,522)
Davis, Mark	4:26:21	(17,548)
Davis, Mark A	3:50:36	(8,170)
Davis, Martin	3:14:38	(2,433)
Davis, Martin J	2:58:06	(963)

Davis, Neil L	4:40:11	(21,182)
Davis, Nicholas G	3:00:04	(1,133)
Davis, Paul	4:06:31	(12,218)
Davis, Paul A	4:18:19	(15,301)
Davis, Paul A	5:23:21	(29,522)
Davis, Paul J	6:09:07	(33,495)
Davis, Peter	3:57:23	(9,945)
Davis, Peter	5:39:38	(31,386)
Davis, Peter B	3:50:03	(8,051)
Davis, Peter D	4:56:16	(24,955)
Davis, Philip	3:07:39	(1,690)
Davis, Phillip J	4:29:10	(18,359)
Davis, Richard M	3:08:59	(1,809)
Davis, Simon J	4:56:15	(24,950)
Davis, Stephen J	5:20:02	(29,102)
Davis, Steve G	3:18:25	(2,822)
Davis, Tim R	4:19:31	(15,668)
Davison, Neil A	2:37:00	(140)
Davison, Paul R	3:54:39	(9,139)
Davison, Scott H	4:03:07	(11,414)
Davison, Trevor J	5:12:22	(27,874)
Davitt, Patrick W	4:39:13	(20,937)
Davius, Russell S	4:31:32	(18,978)
Davoren, Peter J	5:07:59	(27,215)
Davy, Jason M	4:52:57	(24,158)
Davy, Martin S	5:13:52	(28,144)
Davy, Stephen P	3:36:31	(5,430)
Daw, John C	4:53:10	(24,213)
Daw, Stuart J	4:10:53	(13,310)
Dawber, Nigel	3:08:52	(1,797)
Dawber, Steven	5:06:38	(26,990)
Dawe, Alexander J	4:33:43	(19,492)
Dawe, Andy J	4:18:59	(15,507)
Dawe, James	4:52:40	(24,096)
Dawe, Jamie	5:26:25	(29,914)
Dawe, Jeffrey P	4:10:51	(13,303)
Dawe, Quentin R	4:58:49	(25,515)
Dawes, Graham A	5:42:20	(31,615)
Dawes, Ian P	4:26:54	(17,718)
Dawes, Paul	4:21:54	(16,306)
Dawes, Paul W	3:10:26	(1,973)
Dawes, Stephen	4:31:34	(18,989)
Dawkins, Ian H	6:16:52	(33,818)
Dawnay, Nicolas S	3:44:48	(6,904)
Dawney, Kevin R	5:33:17	(30,698)
Dawrant, Robert A	4:54:10	(24,463)
Daws, Peter M	3:00:07	(1,137)
Dawson, Allen J	4:51:44	(23,879)
Dawson, Andrew S	3:48:30	(7,709)
Dawson, Ben P	4:17:22	(15,055)
Dawson, David J	4:44:36	(22,227)
Dawson, Gordon	4:45:08	(22,363)
Dawson, Howard J	3:25:11	(3,618)
Dawson, Jason L	3:27:13	(3,964)
Dawson, John	4:44:49	(22,276)
Dawson, John E	4:28:24	(18,142)
Dawson, John J	3:51:06	(8,283)
Dawson, John J	3:59:41	(10,627)
Dawson, Kenneth A	5:40:43	(31,481)
Dawson, Neil A	4:40:46	(21,327)
Dawson, Nigel J	3:28:50	(4,249)
Dawson, Paul	6:50:02	(34,718)
Dawson, Peter M	4:59:56	(25,764)
Dawson, Richard L	3:42:26	(6,460)
Dawson, Robert E	5:23:34	(29,553)
Dawson, Steve	2:59:57	(1,125)
Dawson, Stephen	3:17:28	(2,730)
Dawson, Timothy M	5:36:02	(30,998)
Dawsonm, Ian L	5:42:56	(31,674)
Day, Barnaby	3:35:34	(5,272)
Day, David A	3:19:55	(2,986)
Day, Ian J	4:19:59	(15,797)
Day, Kyle	5:16:31	(28,550)
Day, Marc	4:49:21	(23,326)
Day, Martyn P	4:38:58	(20,868)
Day, Matthew J	4:49:00	(23,235)
Day, Paul	3:39:06	(5,834)
Day, Paul W	4:15:02	(14,462)
Day, Peter	4:53:28	(24,294)
Day, Rob R	4:15:03	(14,464)
Day, Simon	5:07:29	(27,143)
Day, Thomas F	4:15:22	(14,540)
Dayment, Paul	5:21:55	(29,339)

D'Castro, Lloyd G	4:06:23	(12,186)
D'Cruz, Jude	4:34:11	(19,617)
D'Cruze, Anna M	5:34:10	(30,803)
De Beer, Russell E	5:34:02	(30,786)
De Beer, Zach J	5:25:01	(29,748)
De Boer, Peter	3:19:10	(2,896)
De Bruijn, Ian	3:58:45	(10,366)
De Castro, Antonio	4:35:18	(19,908)
De Charentenay, Ghislain B	3:56:16	(9,589)
De Chateaufort, François-Xavier	3:57:37	(10,020)
De Clerk, Jason	5:45:09	(31,862)
De Freyne, Stuart P	3:49:43	(7,981)
De Gidlow, Robert	3:55:40	(9,416)
De Jong, Bert	3:40:49	(6,142)
De Keyser, Gust	4:07:56	(12,561)
De La Haye, Mark R	3:26:11	(3,791)
De La Hoz, Guillermo	6:33:43	(34,347)
De La Pena, Isaias	4:10:41	(13,261)
De Luc, Tristan A	4:05:53	(12,068)
De Marillac, Martin	5:22:55	(29,473)
De Mori, Pietro	5:34:07	(30,791)
De Rafael-Topfer, Bernardo	3:40:52	(6,161)
De Ridder, Robert J	4:50:33	(23,642)
De Roeck, Danny	5:02:05	(26,167)
De Rosee, Max T	3:52:30	(8,605)
De Rus-Mendoza, Ignacio	4:39:15	(20,953)
De Santos-Sau, Josep	3:48:25	(7,686)
De Sensi, Matteo	2:40:46	(215)
De Silva, Kasun I	4:46:48	(22,734)
De Souza, Douglas	3:56:59	(9,809)
De Tomi, Siro	5:28:08	(30,130)
De Val, Thomas E	4:06:11	(12,137)
De Villiers, Philip M	3:10:58	(2,029)
De Vries, Egbert J	4:14:27	(14,285)
De Vrind, Hans J	6:09:31	(33,518)
Deacon, Greg	4:21:38	(16,238)
Deacy, Anthony J	3:29:49	(4,423)
Deadman, Peter J	4:06:36	(12,241)
Deadman, Sean A	4:06:33	(12,225)
Deagle, Peter A	3:36:56	(5,487)
Deakin, Barry	4:44:36	(22,227)
Deakin, Henry J	4:42:27	(21,732)
Deakin, Leon N	4:44:33	(22,221)
Deakin, Mark J	5:12:11	(27,854)
Deakin, Peter I	4:55:58	(24,892)
Dealey, Laurence A	4:30:41	(18,765)
Deamer, Steve	5:23:54	(29,602)
Dean, Alan M	4:54:56	(24,648)
Dean, Andrew P	5:54:50	(32,626)
Dean, Gary	4:50:00	(23,495)
Dean, Gary J	2:51:14	(548)
Dean, James	5:32:48	(30,652)
Dean, John	4:25:11	(17,182)
Dean, K	3:47:41	(7,496)
Dean, Ken	4:13:30	(14,017)
Dean, Kevin G	3:53:01	(8,720)
Dean, Mark J	3:25:45	(3,710)
Dean, Mark R	3:08:27	(1,753)
Dean, Paul	4:02:16	(11,217)
Dean, Peter J	4:23:22	(16,706)
Dean, Richard W	4:49:24	(23,334)
Dean, Robert M	3:51:31	(8,373)
Dean, Simon J	4:14:20	(14,251)
Dean, Trevor	4:15:36	(14,607)
Deane, Alan M	5:09:59	(27,509)
Deane, James	3:29:41	(4,390)
Deaner, Jonathan N	3:59:44	(10,641)
Deans, Keith A	5:17:56	(28,772)
Deans, Matthew W	4:31:13	(18,888)
Dear, Gary P	5:13:27	(28,071)
Dear, Peter L	5:13:27	(28,071)
Dear, Richard A	3:33:29	(4,957)
Dear, Stephen	4:17:38	(15,118)
Dearden, Mark	3:56:38	(9,707)
Dearing, Peter	4:16:54	(14,935)
Dearing, Thomas J	4:00:51	(10,913)
Dearlove, David J	4:45:34	(22,448)
Dearsley, Tony P	3:35:00	(5,182)
Dearson, Michael E	6:28:59	(34,218)
Deasy, John F	3:12:40	(2,212)
Deaton, Michael J	3:29:11	(4,311)
Deaville, Robert C	5:17:48	(28,760)
De-Bellefon, Vincent	4:34:55	(19,831)

Debnam, Andrew P 3:45:31 (7,050)
Debnam, Dave 3:34:20 (5,098)
Decamps, Didier 4:00:37 (10,871)
Decent, Michael L 4:48:21 (23,088)
Decesero, Luciano 2:52:20 (603)
Dector-Vega, German 4:41:33 (21,537)
Deddis, Jonathan 3:20:26 (3,040)
Dedionigi, Gianni 3:44:21 (6,805)
Deegan, Timothy W 3:50:05 (8,058)
Deeley, Philip 5:33:14 (30,694)
Deery, Francis E 5:03:09 (26,376)
Deery, William 4:50:36 (23,649)
Defauw, Michel 4:03:04 (11,402)
Deffay, Patrick 3:32:22 (4,800)
Defillion, Nicolas J 4:20:51 (16,035)
De-Fontenay, Stephane 3:56:47 (9,749)
Deftereos, Phillip 5:21:09 (29,255)
Dega, Raman K 5:51:33 (32,378)
Degenhardt, Oliver 4:17:36 (15,113)
Degia, Ilyas 5:41:34 (31,562)
Degraeve, Wouter 3:17:35 (2,746)
Deimling, Andreas 3:09:41 (1,877)
Dekzoppo, David K 4:56:52 (25,107)
Del Mar, Sigmund B 5:15:14 (28,375)
Del Porto, Paolo 3:28:44 (4,229)
Delafolie, Giles 3:10:36 (1,988)
Delahoy, Trevor R 4:08:05 (12,587)
Delaney, Andrew K 3:32:26 (4,808)
Delaney, Anthony 4:08:04 (12,585)
Delaney, Joe 5:27:49 (30,077)
Delaney, Paul A 4:30:08 (18,636)
Delaney, Russell J 5:07:20 (27,119)
Delany, John F 3:15:17 (2,502)
Delattre, Jean-Marie 4:21:27 (16,190)
De-Lattre, Guilhem 3:46:55 (7,333)
Delaunay, Yankel 5:25:35 (29,816)
Delb, Christian 4:54:26 (24,534)
Delbridge, Andrew 4:40:00 (21,142)
Delerin, Serge 3:42:48 (6,511)
Delew, Russell 3:50:13 (8,089)
Delf, Dominic C 5:38:55 (31,298)
Delhoy, Mark 4:32:23 (19,184)
Dell, Graeme J 3:56:05 (9,533)
Dell, Gregory J 2:45:43 (340)
Della Maestra, Darren J 4:34:38 (19,743)
Dellar, Peter R 2:58:49 (1,016)
Dellen, David C 3:14:02 (2,360)
Dellepiane, Emilio 5:06:25 (26,948)
Deller, Matthew F 4:46:25 (22,653)
Deller, Stephen A 6:17:57 (33,850)
Demery, Martin 7:39:33 (35,173)
Demmer, Holger 4:32:06 (19,109)
Dempsey, Jay P 6:44:28 (34,607)
Dempsey, Patrick J 3:49:24 (7,914)
Dench, Gary 2:58:04 (960)
Denham, Paul M 3:56:57 (9,798)
Denham, Terence N 4:55:21 (24,747)
Deniel, François 3:19:23 (2,921)
Denis, Vincent 5:14:49 (28,314)
Denison, Nicholas J 4:46:41 (22,704)
Dennehy, Brian B 4:21:17 (16,140)
Dennett, Peter A 4:10:07 (13,120)
Dennington, Barry A 5:18:29 (28,860)
Dennis, Anthony M 5:27:35 (30,053)
Dennis, Garry 6:17:59 (33,854)
Dennis, Geoffrey A 5:50:36 (32,310)
Dennis, Paul A 3:36:39 (5,448)
Dennis, Paul A 4:04:39 (11,784)
Dennis, Paul J 3:26:03 (3,773)
Dennis, Paul M 5:37:25 (31,130)
Dennis-Jones, Richard 3:10:14 (1,951)
Dennison, Paul J 4:45:58 (22,544)
Denny, Steven P 3:38:29 (5,723)
Dennyu, Paul 5:18:47 (28,917)
Dent, John B 3:51:21 (8,343)
Dent, John C 4:18:56 (15,494)
Dent, Michael J 5:23:46 (29,581)
Denton, Alistair J 4:43:33 (21,996)
Denton, Andrew W 3:34:51 (5,164)
Denton, David G 4:08:55 (12,806)
Denton, Jeremy P 5:39:28 (31,373)
Denton, Michael G 4:34:38 (19,743)
Denton, Paul 4:41:22 (21,484)
Denver, Paul 5:24:23 (29,670)
Denwood, Richard N 2:59:32 (1,091)
Denyer, Peter R 4:10:14 (13,147)
Depoortere, Ronny 3:57:20 (9,929)
Derbyshire, Nicholas J 4:20:44 (16,001)
Derbyshire, Robert 4:12:36 (13,774)
Derham, Richard O 4:07:55 (12,557)
Dermul, Patrick 3:25:39 (3,695)
Derriennic, Patrick 3:16:04 (2,584)
Derrington, Richard 3:53:05 (8,739)
Derry, Mark D 3:32:48 (4,858)
Dervish, Tolga 5:34:42 (30,874)
Desai, Khaleel M 4:21:40 (16,247)
Desai, Mukesh 6:01:24 (33,044)
Desborough, Paul 4:17:13 (15,015)
Desmond, Jim 2:47:48 (402)
Despeghel, Guy 4:30:08 (18,636)
Desplaces, Jean-Pascal M 4:11:35 (13,500)
De-Stael, Arnaud 3:13:26 (2,295)
De-Talhouet, Hugues 4:14:40 (14,341)
Detsiny, Michael 7:25:59 (35,107)
Devane, Timothy D 3:45:23 (7,026)
Devas, William 3:47:57 (7,560)
Deveney, Liam M 4:18:16 (15,283)
Devenish, Alistair A 5:31:38 (30,524)
Devenish, Malcolm P 4:32:59 (19,314)
Devenish, Peter E 5:31:38 (30,524)
Deves, Darren 5:14:37 (28,283)
Devine, Barry M 4:36:52 (20,324)
Devine, Michael M 3:22:36 (3,254)
Devine, Richard J 4:41:41 (21,561)
Devine, Ronald J 5:16:57 (28,637)
Devine, William 5:27:57 (30,095)
Devitt, Martin R 3:38:59 (5,812)
Devitt, Russell E 3:26:05 (3,779)
Devlin, Eamon 4:34:56 (19,836)
Devlin, Giles 3:45:15 (6,998)
Devlin, Paul D 4:29:55 (18,570)
Devlin, Robert 3:44:39 (6,868)
Devlin, Sean 3:59:59 (10,724)
Dew, Bev E 3:48:37 (7,745)
Dewar, Ian D 3:46:38 (7,270)
Dewey, Oliver M 4:43:15 (21,923)
Dewhurst, Benjamin T 4:38:59 (20,871)
Dewhurst, Brian J 2:37:17 (144)
Dewhurst, Stephen K 4:53:36 (24,329)
Dewsbury, Glyn R 4:31:40 (19,011)
Dewson, Neville R 4:26:10 (17,498)
Dexter, Colin G 5:35:07 (30,920)
Dexter, Jonathan R 4:42:13 (21,683)
Dey, Chris J 4:49:25 (23,342)
Dey, James 4:53:18 (24,251)
Dhaliwal, Jagdeep S 3:22:02 (3,191)
D'Helft, Gaetan 4:46:02 (22,557)
Dhillon, Gurminder S 5:14:10 (28,204)
Dhindsa, Sukhjinder S 5:14:17 (28,225)
Di Palma, Nicola 4:38:21 (20,709)
Di Trapani, Francesco 3:26:55 (3,914)
Diamond, Samuel P 3:39:54 (5,980)
Diamond, Stephen P 3:41:44 (6,322)
Dias, Brandon 3:28:22 (4,169)
Diaz, José A 5:19:26 (29,015)
Diaz, Miguel 3:56:56 (9,796)
Diaz-Gavier, Patricio 4:11:25 (13,458)
Dick, Andrew J 3:26:36 (3,870)
Dick, Michael J 3:33:33 (4,962)
Dick, William 6:34:32 (34,365)
Dicken, Aled 5:01:50 (26,114)
Dicken, Scott F 3:52:08 (8,512)
Dickens, Andrew W 4:28:30 (18,168)
Dickens, David S 4:38:41 (20,794)
Dickens, Jonathan 3:44:50 (6,919)
Dickens, Jonathan T 4:03:15 (11,447)
Dickens, Mark I 4:50:32 (23,636)
Dickens, Phillip M 2:47:39 (394)
Dickenson, Andrew 3:31:57 (4,739)
Dickenson, Darren M 7:45:08 (35,193)
Dickey, Daniel 5:25:43 (29,826)
Dickinson, Christopher R 5:18:49 (28,922)
Dickinson, David J 5:18:46 (28,915)
Dickinson, David M 6:22:02 (33,992)
Dickinson, Philip H 3:55:48 (9,461)
Dickinson, Ralph 3:37:06 (5,515)
Dickinson, Simon 6:24:40 (34,080)
Dickinson, Steve 5:29:34 (30,314)
Dickinson-Green, Christopher R 6:03:51 (33,214)
Dickman, Jeremy C 4:29:22 (18,420)
Dickson, Alan R 3:28:09 (4,135)
Dickson, Andrew 4:35:54 (20,065)
Dickson, David D 5:26:31 (29,925)
Dickson, David R 3:44:16 (6,794)
Dickson, Robert 3:25:21 (3,651)
Dickson, Simon M 3:32:13 (4,777)
Dickson, Stuart R 4:26:09 (17,492)
Di-Clemente, Alan 3:47:18 (7,417)
Diddams, Greg 2:57:47 (940)
Diddams, Paul 3:43:44 (6,690)
Dideron, Yves 4:39:59 (21,136)
Dieffenbacher, Joachim 4:21:53 (16,304)
Dietch, Daniel M 3:29:59 (4,451)
Dif, Philippe 3:49:10 (7,861)
Diffey, John G 3:05:13 (1,488)
Diffley, Mark G 4:00:01 (10,732)
Difranco, Mike D 3:32:12 (4,773)
Di-Gaudio, Giuseppe 4:32:10 (19,129)
Digby, Adrian J 4:10:37 (13,242)
Digby, Colin J 3:55:57 (9,501)
Digby, Peter H 4:09:33 (12,974)
Digby-Baker, Hugh J 4:27:28 (17,875)
Dignam, David A 5:34:22 (30,824)
Dignan, Robert M 6:16:43 (33,808)
Digweed, Danny 3:53:29 (8,853)
Dijkhuizen, Roelf S 3:18:38 (2,838)
Dijkstra, Jacob 4:16:09 (14,755)
Dilaver, Asim 6:23:35 (34,040)
Dilley, Brian J 4:24:44 (17,055)
Dilley, Paul S 4:14:53 (14,406)
Dillom, Oliver 4:05:39 (12,016)
Dillon, John E 4:27:28 (17,875)
Dillon, Kevin J 5:47:20 (32,043)
Dillon, Liam P 4:14:50 (14,390)
Dillon, Richard A 5:01:06 (25,996)
Dillon, Terence 5:21:43 (29,315)
Dillon, Thomas 4:41:32 (21,535)
Dilloway, Luke E 3:50:27 (8,138)
Dilnot, Noel 4:36:32 (20,235)
Dilnot, Peter G 3:41:08 (6,208)
Dilworth, Joseph R 5:15:23 (28,401)
Dimambro, Franco 6:44:19 (34,603)
Dimbleby, Nicholas J 3:16:30 (2,635)
Dimbleby, Peter J 2:51:16 (549)
Dimmick, Roy 4:15:01 (14,457)
Dimmock, Lee J 5:33:53 (30,763)
Dineen, Martin 4:48:02 (23,017)
Dines, Michael J 4:08:20 (12,655)
Dingwall, Basil 4:33:05 (19,340)
Dingwall, Gordon I 4:17:40 (15,130)
Dinkeldein, Jonathan M 3:45:49 (7,098)
Dinn, Anthony J 3:58:45 (10,366)
Diplock, Richard A 6:21:59 (33,987)
Dirkes, Charles E 4:30:47 (18,789)
Discombe, Chris N 2:48:03 (418)
Disley, Hugh 5:23:54 (29,602)
Disley, Jason J 4:07:04 (12,360)
Ditcham, Robert 6:17:04 (33,826)
Ditcher, Steven 4:21:07 (16,094)
Dittrich, Lee P 4:06:18 (12,166)
Divall, Andrew 3:58:11 (10,184)
Dives, Steven J 4:06:30 (12,213)
Dix, Christopher 3:47:35 (7,469)
Dix, Karl E 4:44:50 (22,281)
Dix, Neil 5:27:09 (29,992)
Dix, Nigel 4:56:20 (24,971)
Dixon, Ashley 4:20:01 (15,807)
Dixon, Chris 3:22:30 (3,242)
Dixon, Ciaran 6:18:25 (33,867)
Dixon, Clem 2:50:55 (537)
Dixon, Conrad B 3:39:23 (5,891)
Dixon, Craig L 4:44:19 (22,177)
Dixon, Cyril 3:56:07 (9,543)
Dixon, David J 4:34:52 (19,811)
Dixon, Ellis S 4:41:02 (21,402)
Dixon, Garrie P 4:01:52 (11,119)
Dixon, Gary J 2:41:40 (232)
Dixon, Gordon M 2:42:44 (258)
Dixon, Graeme M 3:11:36 (2,087)

Dixon, Ian H	4:15:08 (14,487)	
Dixon, James	5:59:34 (32,952)	
Dixon, James A	4:22:14 (16,402)	
Dixon, Jay	3:55:13 (9,280)	
Dixon, Kevin M	5:35:21 (30,940)	
Dixon, Leo S	4:30:44 (18,778)	
Dixon, Mark B	4:09:29 (12,955)	
Dixon, Peter R	5:44:26 (31,796)	
Dixon, Reginald	7:06:46 (34,948)	
Dixon, Richard J	3:34:10 (5,070)	
Dixon, Scott	4:08:55 (12,806)	
Dixon, Simon P	4:42:09 (21,664)	
Dixon, Stephen J	3:46:09 (7,170)	
Dixon, Timothy A	4:04:50 (11,822)	
Dixon-Box, Russell B	3:38:19 (5,702)	
Djidi, Kamel	3:10:51 (2,014)	
Dlhopolcek, Frantisek	4:05:32 (11,996)	
D'Mello, Kevin A	4:25:53 (17,396)	
Dobb, Patrick P	4:55:54 (24,874)	
Dobbie, Adam S	4:01:49 (11,114)	
Dobbie, Peter C	4:49:03 (23,250)	
Dobbs, Andrew R	3:26:57 (3,921)	
Dobbs, Douglas J	4:00:52 (10,922)	
Dobbs, Patrick A	3:28:11 (4,141)	
Dobbs, Simon V	4:21:56 (16,312)	
Dobie, George A	4:59:18 (25,628)	
Dobigeon, Christophe	4:02:23 (11,246)	
Doble, Robin T	4:02:16 (11,217)	
Dobson, Andrew C	5:19:08 (28,961)	
Dobson, Christopher M	4:40:35 (21,280)	
Dobson, Jeffrey J	4:55:49 (24,854)	
Dobson, John W	4:54:46 (24,614)	
Dobson, Jonathan	3:58:42 (10,347)	
Dobson, Michael	3:20:30 (3,045)	
Dobson, Robin	3:20:33 (3,051)	
Dobson, Rupert	3:08:35 (1,768)	
Dobson, Wayne C	5:43:05 (31,685)	
Docherty, Craig	4:24:27 (16,977)	
Docherty, Richard	3:16:58 (2,672)	
Docherty, Steven J	3:10:47 (2,006)	
Doczyminskyi, Roman M	4:26:22 (17,555)	
Dodd, Andrew M	4:16:18 (14,793)	
Dodd, Christopher P	4:47:13 (22,823)	
Dodd, Clive C	3:57:03 (9,837)	
Dodd, Darren M	5:15:38 (28,438)	
Dodd, Gavin R	4:51:20 (23,804)	
Dodd, Jason	5:09:48 (27,485)	
Dodd, John A	5:10:48 (27,617)	
Dodd, Philip W	5:33:52 (30,762)	
Dodd, Robert P	5:10:39 (27,597)	
Dodd, Robert W	5:27:39 (30,061)	
Dodd, Stephen J	4:19:38 (15,705)	
Dodds, Alastair	4:34:51 (19,804)	
Dodds, Chris	3:13:03 (2,251)	
Dodds, Neil J	4:28:34 (18,187)	
Dodgson, Matthew C	4:27:50 (17,992)	
Dodsley, Keith M	4:11:03 (13,368)	
Dodson, Edward C	3:35:45 (5,305)	
Dodson, Martin D	3:57:50 (10,089)	
Dodwell, Edward M	2:48:39 (444)	
Dodwell, Stephen C	4:04:13 (11,687)	
Doe, David W	5:57:03 (32,778)	
Doherty, Austin G	3:56:15 (9,585)	
Doherty, John J	3:35:41 (5,293)	
Doherty, Joseph A	7:17:05 (35,054)	
Doherty, Michael L	4:06:40 (12,257)	
Doherty, Peter J	4:58:27 (25,429)	
Doherty, Thomas M	4:21:24 (16,171)	
Dokic, Stevan	3:57:34 (10,003)	
Dolan, Andrew	4:58:15 (25,384)	
Dolan, Paul S	4:26:28 (17,590)	
Dolan, Robert M	3:15:06 (2,486)	
Dolan, Stanley W	4:25:59 (17,429)	
Dolby, David R	4:57:24 (25,208)	
Doleski, Mark W	2:57:11 (898)	
Dolley, Mark	4:10:14 (13,147)	
Dollin, Nathan L	5:42:17 (31,609)	
Dolman, Antony R	4:22:55 (16,585)	
Dolphin, Christopher C	3:40:36 (6,101)	
Dolton, Paul M	4:27:13 (17,806)	
Domaille, Mark	2:58:08 (966)	
Domercq, Pascal	4:22:07 (16,375)	
Dommett, Robert A	6:35:21 (34,388)	
Don, Russell	4:16:31 (14,840)	
Donachie, David	3:47:41 (7,496)	
Donaghey, David	5:16:08 (28,494)	
Donaghy, Simon P	3:20:02 (3,001)	
Donald, Andrew J	3:59:56 (10,705)	
Donaldson, Drew	2:54:43 (728)	
Donaldson, Eric	3:18:42 (2,849)	
Donaldson, Matthew C	5:52:23 (32,446)	
Donaldson, Richard J	4:16:05 (14,734)	
Donaldson, William	4:20:22 (15,903)	
Donat, Martin	3:33:09 (4,906)	
Donato, Lorenzo	3:16:44 (2,651)	
Donetti, Stephane	4:25:29 (17,280)	
Donga, Colman	5:13:38 (28,106)	
Donkers, Rob	3:48:20 (7,664)	
Donnachie, Craig D	4:20:53 (16,043)	
Donnan, Graeme E	3:14:32 (2,423)	
Donnelly, Anthony	3:56:17 (9,599)	
Donnelly, Arthur	3:02:10 (1,275)	
Donnelly, Eugene	4:57:12 (25,173)	
Donnelly, Leo	4:53:44 (24,363)	
Donnelly, Mark	3:43:57 (6,732)	
Donnelly, Martin J	5:08:55 (27,342)	
Donnelly, Michael	3:39:30 (5,913)	
Donnelly, Nigel W	5:28:05 (30,115)	
Donnelly, Patrick D	4:08:13 (12,619)	
Donnelly, Stephen P	3:57:58 (10,135)	
Donnier, Nicolas	3:24:09 (3,464)	
Donoghue, Gary J	3:26:53 (3,908)	
Donohue, Carl A	3:32:57 (4,882)	
Donovan, Alan E	4:23:40 (16,766)	
Donovan, Christopher	4:49:46 (23,440)	
Donovan, James	6:00:43 (33,012)	
Donovan, Richard A	3:59:52 (10,688)	
Donovan, Scott	6:50:21 (34,732)	
Donsberger, Michael	4:41:24 (21,498)	
Doolan, James E	4:10:05 (13,109)	
Dooley, Joseph M	5:26:08 (29,887)	
Dooley, Victor J	4:11:24 (13,453)	
Dooling, Graham C	4:09:39 (12,999)	
Doonan, D Brian	4:17:26 (15,081)	
Doran, John M	5:50:00 (32,264)	
Doran, Joseph R	4:40:57 (21,375)	
Dorey, Colin R	3:45:33 (7,057)	
Dorks, Mark E	4:54:22 (24,518)	
Dorman, Edgar K	4:05:59 (12,090)	
Dorn, Helmut	2:41:19 (225)	
Dorrington, Mark	4:15:15 (14,515)	
Dorrofield, Brian K	3:48:50 (7,796)	
Dorward, Neil L	3:08:15 (1,738)	
Dosanjh, Rupinder S	7:08:02 (34,958)	
Doshi, Rajen A	4:39:37 (21,050)	
Doster, Stephen	4:19:10 (15,567)	
Dougal, Andrew J	3:39:49 (5,967)	
Dougall, Scott	3:52:06 (8,504)	
Doughty, Garry	3:47:59 (7,573)	
Doughty, Jonathan M	5:51:15 (32,352)	
Doughty, Matthew	5:24:19 (29,660)	
Douglas, James	4:19:00 (15,517)	
Douglas, James M	6:06:50 (33,381)	
Douglas, Keith S	4:47:26 (22,868)	
Douglas, Michael P	3:22:07 (3,202)	
Douglas, Nicholas P	3:24:08 (3,462)	
Douglas, Paul	2:59:14 (1,059)	
Douglas, Paul R	4:21:01 (16,078)	
Douglas, Richard T	4:22:01 (16,343)	
Douglas, Stuart D	4:09:08 (12,870)	
Douglas, Stuart J	2:53:50 (673)	
Douglas, Timothy J	3:22:14 (3,219)	
Dourlen, Jean-Marie	3:04:30 (1,426)	
Doust, Peter R	4:22:36 (16,503)	
Douthwaite, Michael	4:33:22 (19,400)	
Douthwaite, Neil	3:35:05 (5,196)	
Dove, Chris	3:58:52 (10,402)	
Dove, John D	4:48:49 (23,194)	
Dovedi, Stephen S	4:29:23 (18,428)	
Dover, Gary W	3:06:42 (1,610)	
Dover, Terry A	3:27:58 (4,098)	
Dovey, Andrew M	4:41:16 (21,468)	
Dow, Paul R	3:41:54 (6,360)	
Dowber, Mark	4:05:11 (11,920)	
Dowd, Charlie	4:24:41 (17,039)	
Dowd, John J	4:40:00 (21,142)	
Dowd, Joseph	4:22:06 (16,367)	
Dowding, Andrew W	3:33:05 (4,898)	
Dowding, Michael	6:08:01 (33,446)	
Dowdy, John J	3:12:38 (2,207)	
Dowell, Paul	4:16:07 (14,747)	
Dower, Raju	4:36:37 (20,258)	
Dower, Stephen M	4:48:19 (23,077)	
Dowle, Peter J	3:57:26 (9,961)	
Dowling, Aaron F	3:34:56 (5,172)	
Dowling, David	4:28:20 (18,117)	
Dowling, John	5:56:29 (32,730)	
Dowling, Matthew J	4:26:56 (17,732)	
Dowling, Paul T	7:36:42 (35,163)	
Down, Calvin J	4:42:03 (21,634)	
Down, James C	4:11:37 (13,508)	
Down, Malcolm R	3:18:50 (2,864)	
Down, Stephen A	4:11:47 (13,559)	
Downes, Paul J	3:18:10 (2,797)	
Downey, James	5:54:30 (32,601)	
Downey, Kevin	5:42:16 (31,606)	
Downham, John J	3:27:23 (3,988)	
Downie, Timothy J	3:28:15 (4,150)	
Downing, Keith G	5:01:26 (26,047)	
Downing, Terence R	3:54:06 (8,996)	
Downs, James A	3:41:16 (6,225)	
Downs, Richard S	3:44:41 (6,876)	
Downton, Chuck P	3:46:11 (7,176)	
Dowrick, Michael J	3:55:14 (9,284)	
Dowse, Ray	4:25:27 (17,265)	
Dowsett, David J	5:56:35 (32,738)	
Dowsett, Guy	4:09:29 (12,955)	
Dowsett, Peter C	3:19:00 (2,881)	
Dowsey, Ben	4:44:53 (22,293)	
Dowson, John R	3:43:59 (6,737)	
Doyel, Philip	3:47:43 (7,509)	
Doyle, Alastair K	3:02:36 (1,304)	
Doyle, Andrew J	4:37:28 (20,489)	
Doyle, Edward F	3:20:25 (3,037)	
Doyle, Gerrard	4:40:21 (21,221)	
Doyle, Kevin J	3:57:22 (9,939)	
Doyle, Noel G	5:18:55 (28,933)	
Doyle, Paddy	6:29:37 (34,245)	
Doyle, Pete	3:22:54 (3,283)	
Dragazis, Dimitri	6:03:30 (33,190)	
Drage, Jonathan O	4:24:30 (16,994)	
Dragoni, Enzo	5:05:29 (26,793)	
Drain, Alec R	5:08:53 (27,337)	
Draisey, Michael P	4:53:36 (24,329)	
Drake, Alexander Y	4:02:30 (11,272)	
Drake, Barry M	4:10:09 (13,127)	
Drake, Brian J	4:12:53 (13,848)	
Drake, Chris	4:24:12 (16,901)	
Drake, Gary D	3:29:52 (4,433)	
Drake, Harold	5:29:22 (30,289)	
Drake, Jeffrey T	4:04:37 (11,774)	
Drake, Justin	4:09:05 (12,853)	
Drake, Nick M	4:40:39 (21,296)	
Drake, Oliver	4:14:50 (14,390)	
Drake, Steve R	4:30:29 (18,722)	
Dramburg, Michael	5:41:30 (31,552)	
Dramburg, Sebastian	5:18:11 (28,815)	
Drane, Adam	7:25:52 (35,104)	
Dransfield, Paul	4:20:26 (15,922)	
Drant, Antony P	4:17:20 (15,049)	
Draper, Dean	4:10:10 (13,133)	
Draper, Roger J	3:45:07 (6,974)	
Drathen, Jan H	4:39:17 (20,961)	
Dray, Matthew	3:55:33 (9,385)	
Draycott, Andrew L	4:38:44 (20,809)	
Draycott, Ray	3:46:22 (7,216)	
Drayton, Matthew D	4:10:50 (13,298)	
Drayton, Nigel N	3:34:42 (5,147)	
Drayton, Paul A	4:19:57 (15,788)	
Dreadon, Kent B	3:25:00 (3,583)	
Drecksler, Rolf	5:24:15 (29,653)	
Drejer, Jens	4:07:19 (12,423)	
Dresser, John A	3:27:50 (4,082)	
Drew, Ben D	3:53:05 (8,739)	
Drew, Chris A	5:09:16 (27,398)	
Drew, Ian	2:49:30 (484)	
Drew, Kieron	3:59:36 (10,599)	
Drew, Mark C	4:59:30 (25,663)	
Drew, Martin S	4:47:23 (22,851)	

Drew, Michael P 3:52:31 (8,609)
Drew, Miles 4:38:56 (20,857)
Drew, Redmond C 3:55:14 (9,284)
Drew, Richard E 4:54:56 (24,648)
Drew, William 4:18:26 (15,345)
Dring, Nathan M 6:41:41 (34,538)
Drinkwater, Nicholas G 5:07:59 (27,215)
Driscoll, Hugh J 4:19:42 (15,721)
Driscoll, Paul R 5:57:40 (32,817)
Driscoll, Sean P 3:25:28 (3,666)
Driver, Kevin M 5:02:15 (26,190)
Driver, Paul 4:23:07 (16,636)
Dronisio, Tiago 3:44:19 (6,799)
Droux, Daniel 3:25:28 (3,666)
Droux, Dominique 3:29:54 (4,438)
Druce, Edward C 3:59:04 (10,456)
Drummond, Alastair C 3:31:32 (4,685)
Drummond, Samuel 2:55:31 (771)
Drury, Colin L 4:38:08 (20,656)
Drury, James S 3:55:16 (9,298)
Drury, Peter J 4:24:47 (17,070)
Drutman, Bradley 3:59:00 (10,430)
Dryden, Colin M 4:26:06 (17,475)
Dryden, Piers A 3:44:33 (6,848)
Dryden, Steven 4:09:28 (12,950)
Dryhurst, Oliver B 4:10:01 (13,095)
Drysdale, Alex 3:46:28 (7,236)
Drysdale, James 5:22:54 (29,471)
D'Souza, Clement P 4:14:07 (14,184)
D'Souza, Derrick R 4:16:16 (14,786)
D'Souza, Mathew G 4:42:30 (21,742)
Du Feu, John E 3:26:38 (3,876)
Du Plessis, André M 4:36:53 (20,328)
Du Plessis, Michael O 4:21:09 (16,099)
Du Toit, Jannie 4:09:40 (13,006)
Du Toit, Pieter 4:40:06 (21,154)
Duarte-Diaz, José J 3:10:03 (1,926)
Dubery, Robert P 5:52:31 (32,465)
Dublish, Shashank 4:20:48 (16,022)
Dubourg, Gregory 3:00:00 (1,130)
Dubug, Thierry 3:26:08 (3,783)
Duby, Lior 3:40:04 (6,010)
Duche, Jerome 3:42:53 (6,523)
Duck, Philip 3:42:00 (6,376)
Duckering, Matthew P 3:39:24 (5,893)
Duckhouse, Paul 5:08:00 (27,220)
Duckworth, Archie 4:20:24 (15,912)
Duckworth, Christopher P 4:25:55 (17,404)
Duckworth, Kevin P 2:43:25 (279)
Ducout, Jacques 3:56:43 (9,732)
Dudas, Andrew 4:05:47 (12,047)
Dudbridge, Frank 2:47:42 (396)
Dudbridge, Freddie H 4:49:10 (23,277)
Duddell, Stephen J 2:48:29 (437)
Dudfield, Philip J 3:26:29 (3,844)
Dudhill, John 3:12:01 (2,142)
Dudley, George B 4:54:57 (24,658)
Dudman, Richard J 4:29:30 (18,467)
Dudney, Alan G 4:33:30 (19,433)
Dudok, John 3:44:28 (6,827)
Dudzinski, Krzysztof L 5:17:17 (28,685)
Duff, Andrew J 3:50:28 (8,142)
Duff, Howard 4:18:18 (15,296)
Duff, Stephen P 4:10:24 (13,204)
Duffield, Andrew 5:28:02 (30,107)
Duffield, Geoff 6:16:50 (33,815)
Duffield, Roger A 5:37:10 (31,114)
Duffill, Graham W 3:48:38 (7,749)
Duffy, Andrew D 3:02:18 (1,285)
Duffy, Bernard 4:28:38 (18,201)
Duffy, John T 5:51:12 (32,351)
Duffy, Kevin 4:09:48 (13,044)
Duffy, Liam J 3:10:52 (2,017)
Duffy, Michael 4:12:37 (13,781)
Duffy, Michael J 3:48:00 (7,581)
Duffy, Michael J 4:48:50 (23,195)
Duffy, Philip 4:11:52 (13,574)
Duffy, Sean 4:05:39 (12,016)
Duffy, Shane 4:12:12 (13,664)
Duffy, Steven J 4:11:49 (13,568)
Duffy, Terence 4:24:49 (17,075)
Duffy, Thomas J 3:14:26 (2,407)
Dufon, Olivier 3:58:20 (10,237)
Dugan, Wellington C 3:46:24 (7,222)
Dugdale, Mark A 4:06:23 (12,186)
Duggal, Dipak K 3:53:27 (8,848)
Duggal, Sunil K 4:13:49 (14,093)
Duggan, Ian C 3:34:13 (5,082)
Duggan, Neil S 4:28:06 (18,057)
Duggan, Nicholas D 4:45:45 (22,486)
Duggan, Sean P 4:41:14 (21,454)
Dugmore, Dorian L 4:51:31 (23,836)
Dugmore, Peter J 4:22:33 (16,486)
Duguid, William R 4:08:28 (12,687)
Duke, Bernie 3:57:03 (9,837)
Duke, Chris A 3:08:02 (1,718)
Dukes, Nicholas J 2:54:05 (691)
Dukes, Stephen J 4:52:33 (24,065)
Dulai, Gurjit S 4:28:43 (18,225)
Dullehan, Michael F 3:57:13 (9,898)
Duly, Paddy W 3:18:39 (2,843)
Dumas, Jean-Michel 3:39:04 (5,832)
Dumper, Alan J 2:59:52 (1,119)
Dun, Craig 4:35:26 (19,965)
Dunbar, Adrian M 4:39:59 (21,136)
Dunbar, Chris J 5:36:30 (31,057)
Duncalf, Christopher R 3:46:05 (7,158)
Duncan, Christopher S 4:39:24 (20,989)
Duncan, Edward R 3:04:21 (1,416)
Duncan, John E 4:36:58 (20,347)
Duncan, Mark S 3:50:49 (8,211)
Duncan, Robert J 3:52:46 (8,678)
Duncan, Roddy I 5:19:50 (29,080)
Duncan, Rory 4:31:13 (18,888)
Dunckley, Matthew G 4:01:58 (11,145)
Duncombe, Andrew 3:12:04 (2,148)
Dunford, Michael H 3:28:22 (4,169)
Dunford, Nicholas R 4:20:56 (16,061)
Dungate, Keith S 4:14:09 (14,194)
Dungay, Andrew S 4:36:48 (20,306)
Dungey, Kevin M 5:01:14 (26,013)
Dunham, Alan D 4:23:52 (16,818)
Dunkerley, Andrew 4:22:15 (16,407)
Dunkerley, Paul 3:00:24 (1,151)
Dunkley, Blake J 6:19:24 (33,901)
Dunkley, Paul 4:52:40 (24,096)
Dunlea, Brian 4:35:59 (20,081)
Dunlop, Paul 3:22:26 (3,236)
Dunlop, Shaun A 3:18:55 (2,875)
Dunlop, Wayne A 5:03:20 (26,409)
Dunn, Alexander R 4:16:59 (14,951)
Dunn, Andrew 4:54:11 (24,471)
Dunn, Andrew M 4:27:31 (17,894)
Dunn, Anthony A 4:06:07 (12,126)
Dunn, Barrie 3:12:00 (2,140)
Dunn, Chris 4:54:13 (24,479)
Dunn, Chris A 5:54:45 (32,619)
Dunn, Darren S 2:42:31 (253)
Dunn, David J 3:47:10 (7,384)
Dunn, Derek W 3:30:02 (4,459)
Dunn, George 3:23:52 (3,434)
Dunn, Graham J 4:10:47 (13,281)
Dunn, Ian R 4:29:21 (18,416)
Dunn, James A 4:44:09 (22,129)
Dunn, John C 6:19:50 (33,912)
Dunn, Jonathan M 5:19:06 (28,954)
Dunn, Mark S 4:14:56 (14,419)
Dunn, Matthew 4:00:50 (10,910)
Dunn, Mike 3:49:41 (7,976)
Dunn, Peter C 4:48:22 (23,095)
Dunn, Peter J 3:37:57 (5,638)
Dunn, Peter M 4:14:38 (14,325)
Dunn, Roger W 4:57:42 (25,263)
Dunn, Simon C 3:56:21 (9,620)
Dunn, Stephen 4:52:19 (24,018)
Dunnage, Edward 7:58:37 (35,226)
Dunne, Gerry A 3:40:49 (6,142)
Dunne, Jeff 3:14:10 (2,376)
Dunne, John 7:07:57 (34,956)
Dunne, Leigh J 4:19:53 (15,770)
Dunne, Mark P 4:46:09 (22,593)
Dunne, Michael N 4:28:30 (18,168)
Dunnett, James 4:33:27 (19,417)
Dunnett, Keith 5:05:37 (26,808)
Dunning, Peter A 5:17:12 (28,674)
Dunning, Richard J 5:43:18 (31,702)
Dunn-Morey, Thomas M 5:16:56 (28,634)
Dunsford, Paul J 4:41:23 (21,489)
Dunstone, Philip R 3:37:04 (5,507)
Dunton, John L 5:55:08 (32,648)
Duo, Dominic J 6:05:52 (33,320)
Dupain, Chris N 4:14:56 (14,419)
Du-Prat, Edward W 4:06:03 (12,107)
Duquemin, Oliver C 4:54:55 (24,641)
Durack, James E 3:59:35 (10,594)
Durand, John 4:58:30 (25,443)
Durannel, Benoit L 3:43:39 (6,679)
Durant, Andrew 3:32:12 (4,773)
Durant, Neil 5:23:45 (29,576)
Durber, Matthew A 3:37:57 (5,638)
Durdy, Steven 3:03:19 (1,349)
Durham, Michael C 4:27:19 (17,829)
Durham, Neil 5:25:27 (29,795)
Durham, Timothy S 4:18:18 (15,296)
During, Jeremond 5:05:41 (26,821)
Durkan, Gregory M 5:03:08 (26,369)
Durkin, Luke E 4:29:17 (18,396)
Durrani, Amer J 4:53:08 (24,205)
Durrant, Nick P 4:26:42 (17,658)
Dursley, Paul 3:38:15 (5,689)
Dutaret, Jean-Louis 4:34:29 (19,706)
Dutch, James 5:18:56 (28,934)
Dutch, Steffan M 3:53:20 (8,813)
Dutfield, Tim J 4:04:52 (11,829)
Dutnall, Kevin J 5:33:11 (30,686)
Dutton, Alex D 4:06:20 (12,177)
Dutton, Chris 5:20:59 (29,234)
Dutton, David 3:37:26 (5,564)
Dutton, Gavin M 4:13:36 (14,043)
Dutton, Jonathan M 4:24:49 (17,075)
Dutton, Paul A 3:55:05 (9,253)
Dutton, Richard J 4:45:24 (22,414)
Duzanson, Steve 2:57:40 (929)
Dwarakanath, Anandapuram D 4:36:58 (20,347)
Dwyer, Adam C 4:06:13 (12,144)
Dwyer, Christopher M 3:08:55 (1,802)
Dwyer, John B 3:28:31 (4,201)
Dwyer, John W 5:59:07 (32,919)
Dwyer, Kevin J 3:50:41 (8,184)
Dwyer, Liam G 5:25:58 (29,866)
Dybdahl, Geir 3:27:30 (4,020)
Dyble, Glen J 4:52:37 (24,080)
Dyble, Stephen 5:44:19 (31,790)
Dyde, Martin C 3:09:03 (1,816)
Dyer, Christopher J 4:55:30 (24,771)
Dyer, James E 5:37:28 (31,138)
Dyer, Jonathan S 4:16:40 (14,881)
Dyer, Peter E 3:24:06 (3,460)
Dyer, Richard S 4:11:26 (13,467)
Dyer, Stephen G 5:39:55 (31,404)
Dyet, Wiliam J 3:18:30 (2,832)
Dykes, Kenneth J 4:27:54 (18,015)
Dylla, Walter 5:42:38 (31,642)
Dymond, Stephen J 4:35:48 (20,042)
Dyson, David R 3:59:23 (10,541)
Dzavik, Richard A 4:08:24 (12,667)
Dziedzic, George J 4:30:13 (18,659)
Dziewulski, Peter 6:26:05 (34,129)
Dziubak, Stefan J 4:39:14 (20,942)
Eachus, Peter 5:17:01 (28,648)
Eade, Matthew J 4:13:57 (14,131)
Eaden, Ken 4:27:46 (17,973)
Eadie, Christopher 3:48:56 (7,811)
Eadie, Simon G 4:05:18 (11,948)
Eadon, David C 4:43:42 (22,033)
Eady, Robert W 4:19:56 (15,782)
Eagles, Graham R 4:22:08 (16,380)
Eagles, Thomas R 3:39:08 (5,839)
Eaglestone, Kevin D 3:04:55 (1,464)
Eagling, Nicholas R 5:32:08 (30,568)
Eakin, Terry J 3:18:38 (2,838)
Eakins, Alastair S 3:56:22 (9,623)
Eames, Richard J 5:05:49 (26,846)
Eamonson, Paul D 4:11:10 (13,397)
Eardley, Craig 4:43:51 (22,063)
Eardley-Taylor, Paul S 4:13:23 (13,987)
Earl, Cliff 3:45:21 (7,017)
Earl, Jared R 4:02:05 (11,181)
Earl, Martin J 4:26:55 (17,724)

Earl, Martyn B 3:49:18 (7,893)
Earl, Peter J 3:47:59 (7,573)
Earl, Thomas P 3:45:19 (7,009)
Early, Jonathan M 5:50:30 (32,300)
Earthy, Mark 5:47:13 (32,035)
Earthy, Paul S 4:22:59 (16,595)
Easingwood, Alan M 3:29:18 (4,325)
Eason, Adam D 3:52:02 (8,490)
East, David A 5:14:17 (28,225)
East, Lloyd J 4:31:54 (19,060)
East, Martyn 4:37:41 (20,547)
East, Michael B 3:33:37 (4,977)
East, Tony J 3:58:07 (10,171)
East, Trevor S 3:30:03 (4,460)
Eastabrook, Paul J 4:25:52 (17,392)
Eastaugh, Chris D 3:06:14 (1,573)
Easter, Stephen J 4:19:45 (15,740)
Eastham, Fred 4:52:57 (24,158)
Eastleigh, Ian J 5:28:13 (30,147)
Eastment, Neil G 5:13:58 (28,164)
Eastmond, Richard J 4:34:21 (19,676)
Easton, Charles E 4:17:55 (15,181)
Easton, Mark A 4:38:21 (20,709)
Eatherden, Robert J 4:17:47 (15,154)
Eaton, Antony J 6:08:07 (33,450)
Eaton, Malcolm 5:41:55 (31,595)
Eaton, Nick J 4:03:32 (11,510)
Eaudin, Jean-Baptiste 3:37:27 (5,570)
Eavers, Christopher J 3:26:41 (3,883)
Eavis, Benjamin J 5:21:05 (29,248)
Ebrahim, Richard 3:58:39 (10,323)
Ebrill, Bowie 3:56:06 (9,538)
Ebsworth, Jonathan 4:29:05 (18,334)
Eccles, Peter T 5:03:08 (26,369)
Eccleshare, William 3:52:05 (8,500)
Ecclestone, Dennis T 4:53:38 (24,338)
Echardt, Johan 3:15:07 (2,487)
Eddison, John M 3:24:03 (3,454)
Ede, David G 5:17:08 (28,669)
Edear, Robert 3:53:18 (8,801)
Edell, Samuel 4:37:32 (20,502)
Edelmann, Jesper S 5:38:54 (31,296)
Eden, Martin J 6:22:07 (33,996)
Eden, Matthew 4:36:25 (20,203)
Eden, Paul 4:57:21 (25,202)
Eden, Reg J 3:26:25 (3,831)
Edensor, Ray 5:20:22 (29,154)
Edgar, Jonathan M 4:39:35 (21,037)
Edgar, Paul 5:19:26 (29,015)
Edgar, Stephen 3:22:08 (3,204)
Edge, Chris 4:55:42 (24,818)
Edge, Michael 4:00:26 (10,813)
Edge, Shane D 2:59:23 (1,081)
Edge, Steven D 5:04:30 (26,599)
Edgecliffe-Johnson, Robin R 3:58:36 (10,310)
Edgeler, Del 4:27:40 (17,942)
Edgeley, Nick P 3:12:34 (2,200)
Edgell, Jonathan L 3:35:36 (5,279)
Edgell, Rhys 4:51:09 (23,761)
Edington, Peter J 4:07:46 (12,523)
Edlin, David A 4:59:44 (25,719)
Edmeades, Allan J 4:35:22 (19,940)
Edmonds, Benjamin 4:55:52 (24,868)
Edmonds, Chris R 5:59:06 (32,918)
Edmonds, Daniel P 3:59:46 (10,654)
Edmonds, Gavin 3:02:55 (1,327)
Edmonds, Michael 4:28:42 (18,219)
Edmonds, Neil R 4:30:33 (18,739)
Edmonds, Paul S 5:03:08 (26,369)
Edmonds, Roger W 4:09:44 (13,022)
Edmondson, Ian 3:44:57 (6,949)
Edmondson, Jamie 4:02:42 (11,315)
Edmondson, Stephen A 4:34:52 (19,811)
Edmondson, Stewart J 3:15:58 (2,567)
Edmondson-Jones, John P 4:48:34 (23,135)
Edmonson, Bryan R 4:37:19 (20,451)
Edmundson, Joe 3:51:14 (8,309)
Edney, Roger E 4:19:13 (15,582)
Edridge, Norman F 3:46:02 (7,144)
Edstrom, Johan 3:47:00 (7,350)
Edwards, Alan J 3:09:05 (1,819)
Edwards, Andrew N 4:39:43 (21,070)
Edwards, Andy I 5:13:47 (28,130)
Edwards, Chris J 3:05:39 (1,526)
Edwards, Chris J 5:08:18 (27,261)
Edwards, Colin 5:16:44 (28,586)
Edwards, Craig M 3:47:25 (7,440)
Edwards, Daniel A 3:55:10 (9,268)
Edwards, Darren P 3:58:22 (10,250)
Edwards, David 3:33:48 (5,008)
Edwards, David A 3:44:45 (6,889)
Edwards, Derek 5:29:47 (30,337)
Edwards, Duncan 4:37:13 (20,416)
Edwards, Duncan 6:02:26 (33,103)
Edwards, Gareth 3:41:17 (6,228)
Edwards, Gareth 3:46:37 (7,266)
Edwards, Gareth 5:06:40 (26,995)
Edwards, Gary 6:01:58 (33,078)
Edwards, George W 5:41:28 (31,549)
Edwards, Glyn P 4:30:50 (18,805)
Edwards, Huw L 4:35:42 (20,019)
Edwards, Ian 3:57:39 (10,027)
Edwards, Ian M 4:12:17 (13,692)
Edwards, Ian P 4:01:23 (11,020)
Edwards, Jamie 6:00:15 (32,988)
Edwards, Jeremy P 4:23:14 (16,661)
Edwards, Jim 3:34:24 (5,110)
Edwards, John W 4:44:55 (22,301)
Edwards, Jonathan M 4:37:39 (20,529)
Edwards, Justin P 3:50:08 (8,070)
Edwards, Keith R 4:53:56 (24,402)
Edwards, Kenneth D 4:36:21 (20,177)
Edwards, Kevin A 3:56:19 (9,609)
Edwards, Kevin J 3:58:39 (10,323)
Edwards, Lloyd 4:54:09 (24,460)
Edwards, Marcus J 3:55:56 (9,498)
Edwards, Mark 3:05:21 (1,502)
Edwards, Mark 3:53:20 (8,813)
Edwards, Mark 4:23:47 (16,796)
Edwards, Mark 4:54:12 (24,475)
Edwards, Mark 5:05:55 (26,855)
Edwards, Mark A 4:13:54 (14,112)
Edwards, Mark A 4:38:34 (20,767)
Edwards, Martin 3:40:06 (6,017)
Edwards, Matthew 3:46:13 (7,182)
Edwards, Matthew 4:23:07 (16,636)
Edwards, Matthew J 3:09:41 (1,877)
Edwards, Mike W 4:20:54 (16,051)
Edwards, Neil 3:01:32 (1,223)
Edwards, Neil I 3:50:43 (8,192)
Edwards, Nicholas C 4:15:12 (14,502)
Edwards, Orlando 2:36:51 (133)
Edwards, Paul 4:23:31 (16,732)
Edwards, Paul 4:26:03 (17,455)
Edwards, Paul A 4:50:05 (23,508)
Edwards, Peter F 3:22:30 (3,242)
Edwards, Peter J 4:11:17 (13,424)
Edwards, Philip J 4:39:32 (21,022)
Edwards, Richard M 3:44:43 (6,885)
Edwards, Robert J 3:00:22 (1,147)
Edwards, Robert J 3:06:27 (1,592)
Edwards, Robert J 3:47:19 (7,419)
Edwards, Robert S 2:56:22 (833)
Edwards, Robert T 4:39:45 (21,081)
Edwards, Robin A 4:50:18 (23,564)
Edwards, Roger T 4:37:48 (20,580)
Edwards, Ross 4:06:15 (12,154)
Edwards, Rowan W 3:38:05 (5,664)
Edwards, Ryan T 5:04:59 (26,683)
Edwards, Sam R 4:31:34 (18,989)
Edwards, Simon G 5:39:10 (31,328)
Edwards, Stephen J 3:59:03 (10,451)
Edwards, Steve 3:01:34 (1,230)
Edwards, Tom S 4:43:11 (21,911)
Edwards-Stuart, Luke 4:06:25 (12,193)
Edwin, Mark R 3:40:02 (6,002)
Eeles, Steven F 7:51:20 (35,210)
Eels, Stuart W 4:17:30 (15,092)
Egan, Anthony J 4:25:38 (17,330)
Egan, Fergus 3:53:59 (8,972)
Egan, John P 4:30:38 (18,755)
Egan, Timothy 4:19:47 (15,748)
Egbor, Michael 4:47:45 (22,953)
Egeland, Frode 2:59:00 (1,033)
Egelie, Edward C 3:05:09 (1,479)
Egerton, Charles 6:10:14 (33,541)
Eggboro, David 4:14:55 (14,417)
Eggert, Andreas 5:17:27 (28,705)
Eggleton, Bernard J 3:41:31 (6,276)
Egloff, Jean-Philippe 3:39:40 (5,945)
Ehren, Gary R 4:00:00 (10,728)
Eide, Eirik 3:59:07 (10,473)
Einarsson, Stefan O 3:49:32 (7,940)
Eisermann, Lorenz 4:53:29 (24,297)
Eke, Gary J 4:11:53 (13,581)
Ekers, Michael G 3:41:13 (6,218)
Ekestrow, Sven-Bertil 5:01:55 (26,129)
Ekins, Russell M 4:33:24 (19,407)
El Habbal, Magdi H 4:40:29 (21,257)
El Mouaziz, Abdelkader 2:09:03 (4)
El Sharkawy, Mohamed A 4:36:21 (20,177)
El Zein, Issam 4:08:36 (12,716)
Elbro, Matthew J 3:06:03 (1,553)
Elder, Charles 2:58:50 (1,019)
Elder, Jonathon 5:28:46 (30,215)
Elder, Roderick 4:08:19 (12,645)
Eldered, Jonathan M 3:44:42 (6,880)
Eldrett, Christian A 3:38:48 (5,776)
Elford, John N 7:36:20 (35,162)
Elgar, Timothy M 4:26:26 (17,580)
Elgie, Neil L 5:04:40 (26,623)
Elgood, Will R 5:08:09 (27,245)
Elia, Petros 5:24:48 (29,719)
Elias, George 4:59:42 (25,711)
Eliasson, Stefan A 2:48:47 (455)
Elikwu, Charles E 4:06:58 (12,333)
Elizondo, Alejandro 4:08:24 (12,667)
Elkan, Stephen J 4:23:14 (16,661)
El-Karaksy, Mohamed A 4:34:01 (19,569)
Elkhadraoui, Anouar 4:32:08 (19,122)
Elkhadraoui, Khalid 4:32:08 (19,122)
Elkington, Garry S 2:50:33 (518)
Elkington, Jason E 3:04:50 (1,454)
Elkins, George R 4:10:10 (13,133)
Ell, Jonathon 3:42:32 (6,472)
Ellens, David A 4:18:23 (15,319)
Ellens, Nigel A 4:18:23 (15,319)
Ellerby, Vincent R 3:00:37 (1,164)
Ellery, John K 3:48:03 (7,598)
Elles, Bertie 4:33:30 (19,433)
Elley, Duncan R 3:51:25 (8,359)
Elliiott, Jonathan 3:59:08 (10,479)
Elliman, Max 5:43:48 (31,747)
Elling, Mark 4:41:44 (21,573)
Ellingsrud, Bjorn 4:52:50 (24,134)
Elliot, James G 5:12:41 (27,940)
Elliot, Kevin 4:50:47 (23,690)
Elliot, Robin C 4:11:15 (13,416)
Elliott, Alexander 3:29:49 (4,423)
Elliott, Andrew J 4:43:12 (21,915)
Elliott, Andrew P 4:18:28 (15,354)
Elliott, Corin C 4:01:26 (11,032)
Elliott, Cy 5:05:13 (26,729)
Elliott, Daryl 4:54:56 (24,648)
Elliott, David W 4:28:10 (18,078)
Elliott, Desmond I 5:02:37 (26,255)
Elliott, Gavin B 3:47:18 (7,417)
Elliott, John 3:36:17 (5,387)
Elliott, Jonathan C 4:32:13 (19,141)
Elliott, Kenneth 4:16:48 (14,913)
Elliott, Michael 5:02:18 (26,202)
Elliott, Nickolas A 3:43:15 (6,605)
Elliott, Philip D 4:46:33 (22,679)
Elliott, Robert 3:24:09 (3,464)
Elliott, Stephen P 5:08:58 (27,350)
Elliott, Tony G 6:12:28 (33,639)
Ellis, Albert J 5:40:12 (31,437)
Ellis, Ben J 4:06:34 (12,232)
Ellis, Benjamin P 5:08:03 (27,226)
Ellis, Carl 3:09:46 (1,892)
Ellis, Darren J 3:06:52 (1,624)
Ellis, Eamonn K 5:48:54 (32,172)
Ellis, Edward G 3:57:26 (9,961)
Ellis, Garry E 4:41:07 (21,424)
Ellis, James D 4:19:35 (15,686)
Ellis, Jason A 4:20:16 (15,879)
Ellis, John W 3:34:14 (5,086)
Ellis, Jonathan M 4:54:16 (24,492)
Ellis, Keith 5:34:38 (30,868)

Ellis, Kevan P	3:26:11 (3,791)	
Ellis, Martin	6:23:31 (34,039)	
Ellis, Matthew C.	4:04:36 (11,768)	
Ellis, Michael D	3:21:27 (3,125)	
Ellis, Michael P	4:03:28 (11,490)	
Ellis, Richard J	4:29:49 (18,548)	
Ellis, Robert W	5:40:31 (31,469)	
Ellis, Stephen	4:38:44 (20,809)	
Ellis, Steven J	3:40:50 (6,148)	
Ellis, Thomas E.	4:04:36 (11,768)	
Ellis, Tim	2:49:40 (488)	
Ellis, Tim H	3:38:55 (5,798)	
Ellis, Tony	3:43:55 (6,725)	
Ellis, Trevor S.	4:27:53 (18,007)	
Ellis, Vince	3:17:17 (2,714)	
Ellis-Keeler, Christopher J	4:43:15 (21,923)	
Ellison, Mark W	3:00:26 (1,154)	
Ellison, Richard W	3:26:01 (3,764)	
Ellison, Robert G.	4:39:32 (21,022)	
Ellithorn, Mark R	3:01:28 (1,214)	
Ellson, Matthew J	3:35:14 (5,213)	
Ellson, Michael	5:16:59 (28,644)	
Ellwood, Guy F	3:24:26 (3,510)	
Elmore, Mark E	3:31:53 (4,730)	
Elms, Michael R	3:48:02 (7,592)	
Elofsson, Torgny	5:18:25 (28,852)	
Elphick, Andrew C	3:56:41 (9,722)	
Elrick, James E.	3:38:32 (5,731)	
Elsafty, Aymn	4:57:28 (25,222)	
Elsby, Dominic A	2:43:26 (280)	
Elsmere, Alan	2:58:40 (1,002)	
Elsmore, Steven	5:49:01 (32,184)	
Elson, Donald G	5:11:29 (27,735)	
Elson, Nigel C	3:05:52 (1,544)	
Elston-Green, Oliver N	4:22:47 (16,553)	
Elswood, Steve R	3:13:00 (2,246)	
Elsworth, Lester J	4:31:55 (19,064)	
Elsworthy, Mark	4:32:29 (19,207)	
Elton, Mark A	3:41:36 (6,298)	
Elton, Paul B.	4:00:43 (10,890)	
Elverd, Stephen C	3:48:30 (7,709)	
Elvin, Mark	4:19:07 (15,553)	
Elvin, Mark D	4:30:26 (18,709)	
Elvin, Steven J	2:55:58 (806)	
Elvins, Robert A.	5:48:36 (32,142)	
Elwell, David G	4:58:09 (25,359)	
Elwell, Kenneth J	4:58:30 (25,443)	
Elzinga, Jesse R	3:23:44 (3,408)	
Emanuele, Michele	4:31:22 (18,937)	
Embleton, Eddie T.	4:26:41 (17,656)	
Emerson, John E	4:13:39 (14,058)	
Emery, Andrew S	4:05:24 (11,967)	
Emery, Graham	4:49:57 (23,483)	
Emery, Pete N.	4:37:42 (20,554)	
Emery, Peter K.	3:08:00 (1,715)	
Emery, Trevor S.	3:58:18 (10,227)	
Emirali, Kenan	3:47:42 (7,506)	
Emm, Stephen D.	4:52:31 (24,058)	
Emmerson, Lloyd	4:45:37 (22,463)	
Emmet, Robert A	4:42:50 (21,830)	
Emmines, James R.	3:05:11 (1,483)	
Emmins, David J	4:56:28 (25,006)	
Emms, Tony D	4:18:14 (15,273)	
Emreton, Duncan A	6:20:43 (33,941)	
Emsley, Simon J	4:11:43 (13,543)	
Emsley-Martin, Paul S	4:35:53 (20,062)	
Enders, David J	4:21:19 (16,147)	
Endicott, James	5:31:32 (30,519)	
Engelmann, Paul M	4:10:07 (13,120)	
Engels, Andreas	3:04:35 (1,434)	
England, John R	4:56:41 (25,064)	
England, Michael	3:51:23 (8,348)	
England, Nicholas P	3:07:21 (1,656)	
English, Charles E	4:45:48 (22,498)	
English, David E	4:07:23 (12,432)	
English, Derek J	3:54:21 (9,062)	
English, Michael T	5:21:49 (29,329)	
English, Philip G	5:23:37 (29,562)	
English, Robert J	3:28:50 (4,249)	
English, Robert J	3:52:33 (8,615)	
English, Thomas G.	4:15:07 (14,478)	
Engstom, Bo	4:21:29 (16,200)	
Ennis, Stephen A	5:40:06 (31,427)	

Enright, Edward F	3:40:10 (6,031)	
Enright, Niall J	4:23:51 (16,816)	
Enrique, Oromendia	4:26:24 (17,570)	
Enstone, Howard P	7:47:05 (35,200)	
Enthoven, Richard F	4:04:46 (11,807)	
Entwistle, Peter R	2:48:00 (414)	
Ephgrave, Paul	4:14:27 (14,285)	
Epozdemir, Metin	4:11:54 (13,590)	
Epps, Terry A	3:04:33 (1,432)	
Epsom, Joseph	4:25:07 (17,159)	
Erdal, Helge M	4:27:29 (17,884)	
Erickson, Kevin	4:06:14 (12,149)	
Eriksson, Duncan	4:57:02 (25,138)	
Eriksson, Lars	4:27:28 (17,875)	
Erlund, Kai E	4:18:28 (15,354)	
Errington, Luke	4:31:55 (19,064)	
Erskine, Andrew K	3:21:39 (3,144)	
Erskine, Kevin A	3:26:54 (3,911)	
Erting, Niels	2:39:39 (193)	
Escott, Marcus	5:11:55 (27,807)	
Esperanza, Ruben N	4:37:02 (20,364)	
Espiritusanto, José A	4:22:29 (16,467)	
Esposito, Ciro	3:28:46 (4,238)	
Essex, Gavin C	3:50:52 (8,228)	
Essex, Matthew J	3:39:30 (5,913)	
Estall, Richard M	3:57:18 (9,920)	
Estbrook, Ernest W	4:17:04 (14,973)	
Esteban, Mark R	3:54:37 (9,126)	
Estick, Peter V	4:56:23 (24,986)	
Estrada, Diego	4:10:22 (13,186)	
Estreich, Steven	4:26:23 (17,561)	
Esvant, Jean-Yves	3:58:05 (10,164)	
Etchells, Matthew F	4:46:22 (22,639)	
Etchells, Simon J	4:29:12 (18,365)	
Ethelston, Andrew	5:30:06 (30,371)	
Etheredge, James O	4:05:42 (12,026)	
Etheridge, Paul	3:02:12 (1,278)	
Etherington, James D	3:46:15 (7,197)	
Etherington, Stephen P	4:09:29 (12,955)	
Ettinger, Damian J	7:06:02 (34,938)	
Ettlinger, Anthony C	4:59:22 (25,637)	
Euden, Martin J	3:33:48 (5,008)	
Eustace, Paul M	3:47:47 (7,521)	
Evangelisti, Deigo	4:17:36 (15,113)	
Evan-Hughes, Jonathan D	4:30:37 (18,750)	
Evans, Aled M	3:31:57 (4,739)	
Evans, Alexander J	5:31:22 (30,504)	
Evans, Alun T	3:11:37 (2,089)	
Evans, Andrew W	4:17:26 (15,081)	
Evans, Anthony F	5:26:42 (29,946)	
Evans, Barrie J	3:51:54 (8,461)	
Evans, Barry	4:56:41 (25,064)	
Evans, Ben P	4:19:28 (15,654)	
Evans, Bernard H	4:37:32 (20,502)	
Evans, Brandon J	6:19:58 (33,914)	
Evans, Brian D	4:29:36 (18,497)	
Evans, Carl	5:15:06 (28,351)	
Evans, Chris	4:41:12 (21,446)	
Evans, Christopher D	5:04:53 (26,666)	
Evans, Christopher R	4:56:23 (24,986)	
Evans, Clifford B	5:02:50 (26,301)	
Evans, Clive E	3:35:40 (5,292)	
Evans, Daniei	2:54:24 (703)	
Evans, Daniel M	4:15:41 (14,633)	
Evans, Daniel R	2:50:50 (533)	
Evans, David A	5:32:14 (30,581)	
Evans, Derian	4:55:51 (24,862)	
Evans, Des	4:18:41 (15,427)	
Evans, Dylan	4:24:58 (17,113)	
Evans, Dylan R	5:17:40 (28,741)	
Evans, Edwin	3:15:59 (2,570)	
Evans, Frank C	4:53:02 (24,183)	
Evans, Gareth W	4:24:22 (16,944)	
Evans, Gavin M	2:54:04 (689)	
Evans, Glyn D	7:32:11 (35,145)	
Evans, Glynn M	3:42:55 (6,528)	
Evans, Glynn R	5:12:58 (27,994)	
Evans, Graham R	4:04:38 (11,779)	
Evans, Harford	4:01:42 (11,091)	
Evans, Hywel G	3:27:10 (3,951)	
Evans, Ian E	3:10:18 (1,958)	
Evans, Ian K	4:44:59 (22,321)	
Evans, James N	3:09:10 (1,829)	

Evans, Jamie	3:41:29 (6,273)	
Evans, John E.	4:57:58 (25,319)	
Evans, John H	4:30:09 (18,646)	
Evans, John M	4:44:40 (22,240)	
Evans, John-Stewart G	3:49:55 (8,021)	
Evans, Leon	5:06:19 (26,922)	
Evans, Marc T	2:39:04 (175)	
Evans, Mark A	3:38:18 (5,699)	
Evans, Mark A	4:40:45 (21,320)	
Evans, Martin G	3:47:38 (7,482)	
Evans, Matthew C	5:28:05 (30,115)	
Evans, Michael	2:40:51 (216)	
Evans, Michael D	3:10:12 (1,949)	
Evans, Michael J	5:44:30 (31,763)	
Evans, Michael R	3:47:59 (7,573)	
Evans, Noel S	3:23:33 (3,381)	
Evans, Paul	4:06:18 (12,166)	
Evans, Paul G	4:02:22 (11,240)	
Evans, Peter D	4:49:14 (23,288)	
Evans, Philip	4:38:50 (20,836)	
Evans, Philippe	4:37:27 (20,482)	
Evans, Richard J	6:16:56 (33,822)	
Evans, Ricky J	4:00:23 (10,799)	
Evans, Robert J	4:52:46 (24,119)	
Evans, Robin S	3:43:18 (6,620)	
Evans, Russell	4:44:06 (22,117)	
Evans, Russell J	4:55:15 (24,728)	
Evans, Simon A	5:02:44 (26,281)	
Evans, Simon J	5:05:21 (26,764)	
Evans, Stuart J	4:41:42 (21,564)	
Evans, Stuart M	5:28:54 (30,235)	
Evans, Vaughan	3:35:20 (5,227)	
Evans, William J	4:53:05 (24,196)	
Eve, Clive	4:48:34 (23,135)	
Eve, James N	2:55:22 (758)	
Evea, Joseph O	3:18:34 (2,836)	
Eveleigh, Peter R	4:26:42 (17,658)	
Eveleigh, Rick	4:28:35 (18,191)	
Evennett-Watts, Steve M	3:26:00 (3,757)	
Evered, Jonathan F	3:14:49 (2,462)	
Everest, Terry J	3:03:10 (1,343)	
Everett, Christopher N	4:32:24 (19,188)	
Everett, Mike	4:13:35 (14,037)	
Everett, Paul J	4:35:04 (19,865)	
Everett, Philip F	3:39:12 (5,850)	
Everett, Thomas G	3:44:30 (6,836)	
Everitt, Darren	4:05:16 (11,936)	
Everitt, Jeffrey	3:49:03 (7,836)	
Everitt, Matthew R	6:42:30 (34,555)	
Everitt, Nick B	3:52:50 (8,688)	
Everitt, Robert M	3:40:45 (6,127)	
Evers, Randall	3:43:23 (6,633)	
Everton, Dave R	3:41:19 (6,238)	
Everton, David S	4:47:20 (22,840)	
Eves, Peter J	3:50:34 (8,162)	
Evzona, Andrew	4:40:07 (21,157)	
Ewer, Ian V	4:14:11 (14,207)	
Ewin, Alexander D	3:00:42 (1,173)	
Ewin, Mark J	4:09:46 (13,032)	
Ewing, Andrew G	4:13:09 (13,092)	
Ewing, Paul N	4:49:59 (23,492)	
Ewing, Tom	5:06:24 (26,946)	
Exall, Ian A	4:26:05 (17,469)	
Exley, David R	5:32:36 (30,625)	
Extence, Gary J	6:38:26 (34,467)	
Eydens, Jean-Christoph	3:39:55 (5,982)	
Eyes, Jonathan	4:16:50 (14,922)	
Eyles, George P	4:14:48 (14,379)	
Eynon, Mark A	4:43:26 (21,961)	
Eyre, Peter	3:51:50 (8,449)	
Eyre, Richard,	4:36:42 (20,279)	
Eyre, Torbjorn K	6:01:39 (33,060)	
Ezekiel, Laurent M	4:29:40 (18,510)	
Fabbri, Massimiliano	3:25:58 (3,748)	
Fackrell, Steve J	4:07:29 (12,455)	
Facon, Frederique	3:41:23 (6,255)	
Facon, Jean O	4:35:10 (19,883)	
Fagan, Chris	4:42:05 (21,645)	
Fagan, Joseph	3:31:11 (4,625)	
Fagg, Simon M	4:28:56 (18,286)	
Faherty, Aidan	4:22:34 (16,492)	
Fahey, Ernest B	5:06:05 (26,887)	
Fahey, William T	3:29:38 (4,381)	

Fahy, Peter M	3:12:07 (2,155)
Faill, Jonahtan M	3:36:56 (5,487)
Faint, Keith M	3:51:31 (8,373)
Fairbairn, James A	4:18:57 (15,499)
Fairbairn, Sam	3:47:50 (7,533)
Fairbairn, Scott H	4:00:45 (10,899)
Fairbourn, James M	3:02:41 (1,315)
Fairbrother, Paul J	4:18:09 (15,249)
Fairburn, Emyr H	4:55:19 (24,738)
Fairclough, Daniel R	3:24:55 (3,570)
Fairclough, Matthew W	3:14:43 (2,449)
Fairclough, Neil	5:13:03 (28,007)
Fairclough, Neil R	4:14:12 (14,213)
Fairclough, Thomas	3:45:53 (7,114)
Fairclough, Vincent W	5:30:28 (30,412)
Fairfax, Keith	4:42:32 (21,747)
Fairhurst, Charles B	4:47:04 (22,784)
Fairhurst, Wayne	2:53:51 (674)
Fairie, Andrew J	5:11:49 (27,791)
Fairlamb, Ian	3:32:31 (4,822)
Fairlie, Gordon H	3:28:47 (4,240)
Fairweather, Andy E	4:09:30 (12,963)
Faithfull, James	4:01:54 (11,128)
Faithfull, Kim T	4:05:43 (12,033)
Falco, Pietro	5:06:45 (27,008)
Falco, Raffaele	4:19:03 (15,527)
Falconer, Gordon	3:10:53 (2,021)
Falconio, Gennaro	3:46:49 (7,308)
Falcus, Brett H	4:26:39 (17,648)
Falk, Christopher	2:56:45 (867)
Falk, Roland	5:52:30 (32,464)
Falk, Seb L	3:48:08 (7,622)
Falk, Stephan	3:34:20 (5,098)
Falkenberg, Henrik B	3:44:48 (6,904)
Fall, Ian R	4:34:01 (19,569)
Fallmann, Ian P	3:50:47 (8,204)
Fallon, Gary M	3:00:54 (1,186)
Fallon, Michael C	5:21:09 (29,255)
Fallon, Michael J	4:45:16 (22,384)
Fallowfield, Jonathan A	3:19:27 (2,930)
Fallsjo, Niklas E	4:24:57 (17,107)
Falshaw, David S	4:44:56 (22,307)
Fancy, Peter R	3:25:53 (3,739)
Fanecco, Paolo	5:02:09 (26,174)
Fanning, Patrick	3:40:23 (6,073)
Farag, Ben U	3:16:10 (2,600)
Faragher, David L	4:15:26 (14,558)
Farinas, Pedro	3:16:47 (2,662)
Farley, Adam	4:32:04 (19,104)
Farley, Jonathan	4:17:41 (15,134)
Farley, Mark C	3:48:03 (7,598)
Farley, Nicholas J	3:43:54 (6,720)
Farman, Andrew J	4:22:35 (16,497)
Farmer, Anthony R	4:23:32 (16,735)
Farmer, Mark A	4:48:35 (23,143)
Farmer, Norman	6:40:49 (34,520)
Farmer, Tim	3:25:31 (3,677)
Farnell, Mark A	2:47:38 (393)
Farnell, Robert S	4:52:53 (24,146)
Farnsworth, Gary A	4:54:50 (24,628)
Farnsworth, Simon J	5:41:32 (31,556)
Farnworth, Andy	3:07:05 (1,641)
Faron, Henri	4:13:10 (13,928)
Farquhar, Graham R	5:16:24 (28,535)
Farquhar, Keith M	3:33:48 (5,008)
Farquharson, David	4:09:35 (12,978)
Farquharson, Stuart A	4:36:19 (20,168)
Farr, Antony P	4:30:14 (18,662)
Farr, David M	4:18:45 (15,444)
Farr, Paul R	4:30:56 (18,823)
Farr, Rob	4:49:17 (23,300)
Farrands, Adam P	5:59:01 (32,913)
Farrant, Paul	5:00:26 (25,868)
Farrell, Bernard W	4:02:54 (11,367)
Farrell, Jason E	5:12:25 (27,890)
Farrell, Mark	4:27:30 (17,891)
Farrell, Mark J	3:46:43 (7,287)
Farrell, Paul R	4:39:40 (21,060)
Farrell, Thomas A	4:27:56 (18,020)
Farrell, Trevor L	5:22:28 (29,415)
Farrer, Richard H	5:25:54 (29,854)
Farrer, Tyrone N	3:46:06 (7,161)
Farrimond, Jonathan M	6:48:13 (34,679)
Farrington, Doug G	5:04:30 (26,599)
Farris, Andrew S	6:04:48 (33,257)
Farrow, Jonathan M	4:29:17 (18,396)
Farrow, Nigel A	3:15:31 (2,526)
Farthing, Christopher M	4:26:12 (17,508)
Farthing, Jonathan M	4:19:49 (15,756)
Farthing, Nigel C	4:05:05 (11,889)
Fasoli, Massimo	3:30:59 (4,601)
Fattori, Livio	5:14:08 (28,198)
Faudot, Jacques	4:24:49 (17,075)
Faughnan, Mark J	3:00:37 (1,164)
Faulkner, Anthony T	4:49:03 (23,250)
Faulkner, James W	3:24:13 (3,474)
Faulkner, John	3:40:59 (6,177)
Faulkner, Kevin	3:54:40 (9,144)
Faulkner, Kevin J	4:07:57 (12,566)
Faulkner, Matthew	4:47:53 (22,985)
Faultless, Graham G	4:01:13 (10,985)
Favennec, Claude	3:56:13 (9,578)
Fawbert, Mark	4:04:33 (11,757)
Fawcett, Gregg P	4:16:44 (14,898)
Fawcett, Richard	4:22:28 (16,464)
Fawkes, Richard J	3:41:55 (6,364)
Fawn, Russell L	4:43:54 (22,070)
Fay, Andrew	3:09:42 (1,881)
Fay, Stewart J	4:57:46 (25,275)
Fayers, David S	5:43:33 (31,724)
Fearns, Donald P	5:18:53 (28,930)
Fearnyough, Paul	3:55:40 (9,416)
Featehrstone, Richard J	3:35:58 (5,337)
Fedden, Richard J	5:09:24 (27,422)
Feeley, Paul	4:27:31 (17,894)
Feeney, John R	6:40:23 (34,516)
Feeney, Kevin J	5:30:33 (30,416)
Feger, Andrewas	5:28:13 (30,147)
Feige, Thorsten	4:25:39 (17,335)
Feilder, Jamie R	5:32:12 (30,576)
Feist, Christopher	4:18:05 (15,231)
Feist, Phil	3:05:51 (1,541)
Feld, David	3:36:24 (5,405)
Feldman, Mark A	3:55:47 (9,457)
Felgate, Paul D	4:40:39 (21,296)
Fell, Joe	4:25:36 (17,315)
Fell, Nicholas J	5:01:47 (26,103)
Fell, Stephan P	5:49:20 (32,215)
Fell, Stephen C	3:05:46 (1,537)
Fellingham, Richard	4:21:59 (16,326)
Fellows, John S	3:45:51 (7,106)
Fellows, Keith J	3:55:01 (9,241)
Fells, Daniel J	5:55:04 (32,644)
Fels, Frans	5:29:57 (30,356)
Felstead, Alec I	4:00:57 (10,938)
Felstead, Ian R	4:07:03 (12,356)
Feltham, Ellis L	5:09:06 (27,370)
Feltham, Paul A	4:32:01 (19,093)
Felton, Paul M	5:15:12 (28,369)
Felton, Tim C	4:55:02 (24,683)
Fenn, Nigel R	3:43:07 (6,576)
Fenn, Richard J	4:28:21 (18,122)
Fennell, Jim	5:05:19 (26,753)
Fennelly, John D	5:28:54 (30,235)
Fenner, Simon J	3:29:30 (4,354)
Fenney, Steven	2:57:03 (886)
Fenosik, Steven J	4:20:11 (15,852)
Fenton, Adrian M	3:54:07 (8,999)
Fenton, Andrew P	4:36:26 (20,209)
Fenton, David J	3:48:02 (7,592)
Fenton, Jeffrey A	3:48:42 (7,763)
Fenton, Stewart	3:52:40 (8,651)
Fenwick, Gavin M	4:05:04 (11,882)
Fenwick, Paul I	4:44:03 (22,107)
Fenwick, Robert G	4:24:29 (16,984)
Ferante, Luigi	3:07:55 (1,706)
Ferdinando, Martin J	6:22:38 (34,015)
Fereday, David H	3:54:09 (9,013)
Ferguson, Adam	5:11:03 (27,664)
Ferguson, Andrew F	4:37:02 (20,364)
Ferguson, Andrew J	3:15:37 (2,533)
Ferguson, Carl A	3:58:20 (10,237)
Ferguson, David W	4:41:00 (21,395)
Ferguson, Gary	3:14:03 (2,362)
Ferguson, Jamie	5:05:13 (26,729)
Ferguson, Keith	4:21:58 (16,322)
Ferguson, Kenneth R	3:56:18 (9,605)
Ferguson, Paul J	4:52:08 (23,972)
Ferguson, Rick J	3:46:50 (7,314)
Ferguson, Robert A	5:03:51 (26,494)
Fergusson, Bruce	5:51:41 (32,387)
Fergusson, Duncan J	4:24:02 (16,863)
Fergusson, Euan R	3:08:59 (1,809)
Fergusson, James	4:56:44 (25,078)
Fergusson, Michael S	5:33:23 (30,704)
Fermbo, Tommy	4:22:08 (16,380)
Fernandez, John	5:20:00 (29,095)
Fernandez-Galvez, Jesus	2:50:28 (512)
Fernando, Pineda Gil	3:21:42 (3,154)
Fernee, Alan	5:44:39 (31,814)
Fernet, Alain	3:53:14 (8,778)
Ferneyhough, Rodney	3:53:06 (8,743)
Ferns, Gerard V	4:29:17 (18,396)
Ferrafiat, Christian	3:52:36 (8,629)
Ferrar, Ian	5:35:18 (30,932)
Ferrar, Mark	5:04:51 (26,658)
Ferrara, Tony	4:21:43 (16,259)
Ferrari, Matteo	4:01:59 (11,150)
Ferrario, Mark A	4:44:07 (22,122)
Ferraris, Luigi	4:26:46 (17,683)
Ferrer Fabregas, Josep A	5:17:44 (28,745)
Ferrett, Stephen J	4:59:32 (25,670)
Ferri, Ed J	4:11:03 (13,368)
Ferriday, Ernest J	4:42:33 (21,751)
Ferrier, Dave	5:28:01 (30,105)
Ferrington, John W	5:16:44 (28,586)
Ferris, Christopher	4:06:26 (12,197)
Ferris, James L	4:30:01 (18,591)
Ferris, Paul C	3:58:45 (10,366)
Ferris, Steven A	3:04:46 (1,448)
Ferris MBE, Peter J	3:27:32 (4,028)
Ferry, Cedric J	4:14:11 (14,207)
Ferry, Gareth E	4:18:25 (15,334)
Ferry, Martin J	4:18:25 (15,334)
Fery, Christophe	3:31:01 (4,611)
Fether, Harold R	4:22:10 (16,389)
Fetherston, Richard W	5:38:25 (31,238)
Fewtrell, Malcolm	5:22:36 (29,440)
Ffowcs-Williams, Gareth I	4:45:17 (22,390)
Fhima, Meyer	4:39:07 (20,904)
Fiander, Mark P	5:50:44 (32,322)
Fichelscher, Andreas	4:22:09 (16,385)
Fickel, Bob D	4:41:00 (21,395)
Fiddis, Richard	4:01:25 (11,028)
Field, Adam P	4:09:21 (12,921)
Field, Alan C	3:42:30 (6,470)
Field, Andrew	4:36:17 (20,156)
Field, Andrew E	3:17:25 (2,724)
Field, Ashleigh K	3:18:27 (2,828)
Field, Brian J	5:03:10 (26,381)
Field, David A	4:16:56 (14,939)
Field, David A	4:49:30 (23,359)
Field, Dean T	3:00:37 (1,164)
Field, Don J	5:35:06 (30,918)
Field, Gary	5:54:13 (32,583)
Field, Geoffrey	3:49:23 (7,908)
Field, Keith M	5:02:15 (26,190)
Field, Kevin J	3:42:01 (6,379)
Field, Nigel J	4:29:53 (18,561)
Field, Robert M	5:13:13 (28,025)
Field, Stephen A	5:33:59 (30,779)
Field, Steve	3:13:35 (2,314)
Fielder, Colin M	4:10:22 (13,186)
Fielder, David	4:12:32 (13,752)
Fielder, Rob J	5:14:23 (28,242)
Fielding, Alastair G	5:14:47 (28,310)
Fielding, Kevin J	4:39:53 (21,106)
Fielding, Michael	4:30:09 (18,646)
Fieldsend, Nicholas D	5:03:21 (26,410)
Fietze, Lutz	4:52:04 (23,954)
Fiford, Carl	4:04:41 (11,790)
Figgins, William A	4:11:43 (13,543)
Filmer, Greg P	4:06:44 (12,273)
Final, Peter L	5:38:06 (31,205)
Finch, Alex G	4:28:51 (18,262)
Finch, David	3:55:55 (9,495)
Finch, David	4:23:18 (16,690)
Finch, Howard J	4:11:35 (13,500)
Finch, Malcolm J	5:05:27 (26,786)

Finch, Paul J 3:57:04 (9,843)
Finch, Peter L 3:37:38 (5,592)
Finch, William A 5:10:35 (27,588)
Fincham, Daron A 3:50:20 (8,112)
Finck, Gregory A 2:57:44 (935)
Findlay, Alastair M 3:43:45 (6,693)
Findlay, Alexander J 3:28:49 (4,247)
Findlay, David G 4:44:26 (22,201)
Findlay, Samuel D 4:40:37 (21,289)
Fine, Martin H 3:57:56 (10,123)
Finegan, Steven D 5:22:05 (29,364)
Finill, Chris T 2:53:45 (669)
Finlay, Douglas K 3:53:46 (8,928)
Finlay, Grant A 4:33:04 (19,330)
Finlay, Samwel L 5:20:27 (29,171)
Finlayson, Andrew I 3:52:29 (8,599)
Finley, Duncan L 4:37:18 (20,445)
Finn, Alistair B 4:06:53 (12,311)
Finn, Allan G 5:17:18 (28,688)
Finn, Graham R 4:42:02 (21,633)
Finn, Julian A 4:32:17 (19,158)
Finn, Paul L 4:21:49 (16,287)
Finn, Steve P 4:55:31 (24,776)
Finnegan, Gary J 4:25:53 (17,396)
Finnegan, Neil 4:10:43 (13,271)
Finnemore, Charlie 3:55:40 (9,416)
Finnerty, Edward E 5:46:46 (31,997)
Finney, John R 3:57:13 (9,898)
Finney, Kevin M 3:00:45 (1,177)
Finney, Mark 3:53:36 (8,883)
Finnie, Kenneth J 4:05:47 (12,047)
Finnie, Steven 3:33:46 (5,003)
Fioravante, Melchiorre 3:42:27 (6,464)
Fiore, Bruno 2:55:34 (776)
Fiorotto, Gilies 3:13:38 (2,319)
Firking, Keith A 4:09:56 (13,079)
Firman, Marco 4:03:29 (11,493)
Firmin, Michael P 2:39:05 (176)
Firmin, Paul R 2:58:23 (983)
Firth, Alistair 3:26:36 (3,870)
Firth, Colin 4:13:08 (13,916)
Firth, David J 4:26:23 (17,561)
Firth, Edward 4:22:09 (16,385)
Firth, Justin P 4:19:01 (15,519)
Firth, Nick J 5:14:09 (28,202)
Firth, Victor 7:01:41 (34,890)
Fischer, Jochen 4:19:11 (15,575)
Fischer, Kai 2:36:14 (124)
Fischer, Klaus W 5:01:30 (26,064)
Fischer, Peter M 5:00:54 (25,962)
Fischer-Brocks, Dietrich 3:59:28 (10,560)
Fish, Andrew N 3:58:47 (10,382)
Fish, Bradley D 5:10:46 (27,610)
Fish, Simon J 4:56:21 (24,977)
Fishbourne, Magnus J 3:34:08 (5,066)
Fishel, Simon B 4:13:12 (13,942)
Fisher, Alex J 4:14:36 (14,318)
Fisher, Andrew 5:46:34 (31,985)
Fisher, Ben J 4:08:09 (12,604)
Fisher, Brian A 3:56:52 (9,775)
Fisher, Charles R 4:42:21 (21,705)
Fisher, David 4:07:23 (12,432)
Fisher, David P 4:15:55 (14,693)
Fisher, David R 4:32:12 (19,134)
Fisher, Edward J 3:49:42 (7,978)
Fisher, Elliott J 4:19:20 (15,619)
Fisher, George A 3:54:50 (9,193)
Fisher, Harry B 3:45:19 (7,009)
Fisher, Ian 2:21:40 (32)
Fisher, John D 5:04:58 (26,682)
Fisher, John T 5:03:31 (26,435)
Fisher, Mark G 5:24:24 (29,673)
Fisher, Mark T 4:18:30 (15,361)
Fisher, Michael 5:36:04 (31,002)
Fisher, Michael L 4:41:36 (21,548)
Fisher, Neil R 4:39:46 (21,084)
Fisher, Richard E 4:26:11 (17,503)
Fisher, Roderick M 4:06:53 (12,311)
Fisher, Roger G 5:16:56 (28,634)
Fisher, Rupert F 4:40:27 (21,243)
Fisher, Sam Y 5:01:53 (26,124)
Fisher, Scott A 4:07:03 (12,356)
Fisher, Simon 3:49:42 (7,978)
Fisher, Simon J 4:19:28 (15,654)
Fisher, Steve 6:31:55 (34,303)
Fisher, William E 4:14:02 (14,158)
Fishwick, David E 5:00:13 (25,823)
Fishwick, Nicholas G 4:17:19 (15,042)
Fiske Jackson, Andrew R 4:00:00 (10,728)
Fitch, Andrew 3:36:34 (5,441)
Fitch, Chris D 5:03:37 (26,448)
Fitch, Ian R 4:55:36 (24,789)
Fitchett, Matt 3:27:48 (4,077)
Fitness, Kelvin J 3:43:44 (6,690)
Fitsall, Trevor J 4:24:58 (17,113)
Fitt, John A 4:48:41 (23,165)
Fitt, Peter J 4:12:12 (13,664)
Fittock, Ian J 4:03:11 (11,427)
Fitts, Benjamin H 3:52:44 (8,670)
Fitzgerald, Gareth M 4:24:20 (16,938)
Fitzgerald, Kevin 4:04:41 (11,790)
Fitzgerald, Mark A 3:46:45 (7,297)
Fitzgerald, Mark J 4:03:56 (11,612)
Fitzgerald, Michael N 5:27:11 (29,995)
Fitzgerald, Richard N 4:35:35 (19,992)
Fitzgerald, Simon R 5:04:29 (26,595)
Fitzjohn, Daniel 3:25:20 (3,649)
Fitzjohn, Graeme E 3:47:05 (7,369)
Fitzpatrick, John A 4:06:13 (12,144)
Fitzpatrick, Martin H 3:47:02 (7,357)
Fitzpatrick, Robert 6:23:46 (34,049)
Fitzpatrick, Shane N 3:35:15 (5,216)
Flack, Alan A 5:16:56 (28,634)
Flack, Andrew J 4:26:11 (17,503)
Flack, Karl D 4:33:44 (19,499)
Flaherty, Finbar 4:46:47 (22,727)
Flaherty, Peter F 5:08:46 (27,316)
Flanagan, Adam M 4:37:17 (20,440)
Flanagan, Brian J 4:08:44 (12,749)
Flanagan, Martin 3:27:11 (3,958)
Flander, Jamie 4:25:43 (17,351)
Flannaghan, John P 5:14:06 (28,189)
Flannery, John J 3:36:55 (5,484)
Flannery, Michael B 5:10:11 (27,525)
Flashman, Keith 4:59:07 (25,588)
Flashman, Mark 5:53:25 (32,530)
Flaum, Anthony D 5:21:00 (29,236)
Flavell, Christopher J 2:47:15 (377)
Flavell, Julian A 3:50:18 (8,104)
Flavin, Paul 3:32:35 (4,832)
Flay, Darren A 4:09:27 (12,943)
Fleeman, Nicholas J 4:56:52 (25,107)
Fleet, John D 3:34:43 (5,148)
Fleet, Kevin E 4:37:24 (20,472)
Fleet, Robert 3:57:20 (9,929)
Fleming, Anthony 4:17:48 (15,158)
Fleming, Antony E 4:28:32 (18,176)
Fleming, Brendan 5:03:41 (26,458)
Fleming, Ian J 5:29:20 (30,279)
Fleming, Ian M 4:27:32 (17,900)
Fleming, Lee 4:24:00 (16,851)
Fleming, Mark H 3:32:39 (4,836)
Fleming, Peter J 3:29:48 (4,417)
Fleming, Scott 4:19:39 (15,709)
Fleming, Simon L 4:43:23 (21,954)
Flemming, Keith 4:26:42 (17,658)
Flesher, Roy 2:58:27 (985)
Fletcher, Alan J 4:21:36 (16,229)
Fletcher, Andrew D 3:07:02 (1,639)
Fletcher, Cedric J 2:50:39 (523)
Fletcher, Chris 2:59:48 (1,112)
Fletcher, Chris D 2:56:16 (827)
Fletcher, Colin S 6:05:29 (33,294)
Fletcher, David P 4:20:28 (15,933)
Fletcher, Kevin 4:14:39 (14,337)
Fletcher, Mark J 3:47:49 (7,531)
Fletcher, Paul D 3:30:40 (4,556)
Fletcher, Richard M 3:52:01 (8,488)
Fletcher, Robert T 3:48:56 (7,811)
Fletcher, Robert W 4:38:21 (20,709)
Fletcher, Roger C 5:27:06 (29,988)
Fletcher, Simon M 4:25:28 (17,273)
Fletcher, Tristan S 4:40:08 (21,164)
Fletcher, Wayne G 4:40:45 (21,320)
Flett, Andrew M 4:21:43 (16,259)
Flint, John W 3:42:04 (6,391)
Flinton, Scott 3:20:55 (3,082)
Flitton, Matthew 5:15:22 (28,396)
Flockhart, Kevin R 5:04:46 (26,642)
Flood, Darryn J 2:59:20 (1,073)
Florida-James, Michael D 3:10:46 (2,005)
Flounders, Duncan 5:44:29 (31,801)
Flowe, Curtis G 3:17:30 (2,735)
Flower, Giles S 3:59:21 (10,533)
Flower, Martyn R 2:56:46 (868)
Flower, Michael J 4:02:09 (11,195)
Flower, Richard W 4:33:42 (19,488)
Flowers, Mike J 3:41:12 (6,215)
Flowers, Roy 4:41:16 (21,468)
Floyd, Robert J 3:16:44 (2,651)
Floyd, Warren 4:21:59 (16,326)
Flynn, Anthony 4:03:45 (11,559)
Flynn, David M 3:54:52 (9,202)
Flynn, Graham 7:51:14 (35,208)
Flynn, John M 5:12:32 (27,915)
Flynn, Kevin 5:47:47 (32,079)
Flynn, Martin J 4:47:33 (22,891)
Flynn, Matthew R 4:54:17 (24,496)
Flynn, Paul 3:58:09 (10,178)
Flynn, Simon J 4:34:49 (19,797)
Foddering, Ian J 4:14:40 (14,341)
Foddy, Matthew D 3:17:52 (2,777)
Fogell, Jonatham A 4:18:19 (15,301)
Fogelman, David J 4:40:06 (21,154)
Fogg, Brian 4:30:57 (18,826)
Fogg, William 4:31:44 (19,029)
Folan, Chris 3:06:07 (1,561)
Folb, Peter 5:18:21 (28,843)
Foley, David M 3:46:00 (7,133)
Foley, Kieran G 4:16:46 (14,907)
Foley, Matthew C 3:17:56 (2,782)
Foley, Steven K 2:58:27 (985)
Folkard, David M 4:21:17 (16,140)
Folkerd, David R 5:28:38 (30,202)
Folkesson, Erik A 3:31:27 (4,671)
Follett, Saul 4:57:28 (25,222)
Folley, Stuart J 3:14:40 (2,440)
Folta, Tomas 4:34:23 (19,689)
Fondrillon, Jean-Claude 3:48:32 (7,724)
Fonseca, Fernando 4:47:39 (22,927)
Font Gomez, David 4:11:16 (13,419)
Fontaine, Paul 5:18:19 (28,840)
Foo, Kim A 3:05:00 (1,467)
Foody, Peter M 2:39:32 (189)
Foord, Jeremy J 4:12:31 (13,751)
Foort, Mark 6:16:47 (33,812)
Forbes, Emile P 3:56:58 (9,803)
Forbes, Hamish C 3:48:33 (7,727)
Forbes, Justin 4:49:03 (23,250)
Forbes, Mike G 4:27:12 (17,802)
Forbes, Stephen W 2:46:38 (363)
Forcadette, Paul 4:12:10 (13,657)
Forcer, Iain 4:23:14 (16,661)
Forcer, Stephen M 3:26:15 (3,801)
Ford, Adrian M 4:35:56 (20,070)
Ford, Andrew D 4:56:41 (25,064)
Ford, Chris 4:59:05 (25,582)
Ford, Christopher G 4:23:05 (16,625)
Ford, Christopher T 4:31:57 (19,073)
Ford, David J 5:52:11 (32,423)
Ford, David R 3:52:33 (8,615)
Ford, Gary J 3:57:24 (9,949)
Ford, Greg V 5:19:16 (28,988)
Ford, John B 3:25:49 (3,721)
Ford, Kevan S 3:33:45 (4,998)
Ford, Martin C 3:03:26 (1,358)
Ford, Matt D 3:44:45 (6,889)
Ford, Matthew J 3:20:48 (3,075)
Ford, Matthew J 5:36:37 (31,070)
Ford, Mike J 4:12:56 (13,865)
Ford, Nick H 4:45:34 (22,448)
Ford, Paul G 3:45:57 (7,124)
Ford, Paul J 3:45:42 (7,076)
Ford, Richard 6:02:12 (33,092)
Ford, Richard L 4:20:21 (15,898)
Ford, Robert A 4:13:32 (14,024)
Ford, Robert E 5:00:01 (25,778)
Forde, Gearoid M 3:57:51 (10,094)
Fordham, Paul 3:30:21 (4,498)

Fordyce, Bruce 3:49:36 (7,956)
Forecast, Tony 5:00:14 (25,828)
Foreman, Timothy F 3:23:15 (3,343)
Forgan, Jamie A 5:12:34 (27,921)
Forgione, Luigi 6:03:20 (33,178)
Forrest, Nicholas D 3:24:58 (3,581)
Forrest, Roy A 5:39:01 (31,312)
Forrest, Stuart G 5:20:17 (29,139)
Forrester, Ian W 4:10:01 (13,095)
Forrester, Paul 5:31:23 (30,505)
Forrester, Stuart R 3:50:42 (8,189)
Forsdike, Karl L 6:10:28 (33,549)
Forsdyke, David S 4:34:24 (19,693)
Forshaw, Robert J 3:56:58 (9,803)
Forshaw, Steven J 4:20:05 (15,826)
Forshew, Jeremy 3:53:57 (8,964)
Forster, Adrian J 4:04:30 (11,746)
Forster, David M 4:42:58 (21,867)
Forster, Guy W 3:43:04 (6,565)
Forster, James 5:38:09 (31,213)
Forster, Richard 3:41:25 (6,261)
Forster, Steve 4:14:13 (14,217)
Forster Brown, Chris M 3:39:21 (5,879)
Forster-Jones, Paul L 3:41:22 (6,251)
Forsyth, John R 5:49:50 (32,249)
Forte, Phil 3:09:32 (1,861)
Fortey, Richard J 5:20:59 (29,234)
Fortuna, Wayne F 3:46:49 (7,308)
Fortune, Henry J 5:15:14 (28,375)
Forty, Peter J 3:12:26 (2,189)
Fosker, Steven P 4:47:26 (22,868)
Fossat, Eric 3:25:58 (3,748)
Fossett, James J 3:11:18 (2,060)
Fossey, Damon 4:35:23 (19,947)
Foster, Andrew J 4:26:38 (17,643)
Foster, Bob B 5:43:52 (31,750)
Foster, Colm C 3:59:01 (10,439)
Foster, David 4:30:05 (18,615)
Foster, David A 3:35:59 (5,340)
Foster, David J 4:14:50 (14,390)
Foster, David M 4:58:08 (25,355)
Foster, Donald 3:34:26 (5,116)
Foster, Gregory K 5:19:16 (28,988)
Foster, Jason T 4:33:06 (19,343)
Foster, Karl 4:08:18 (12,636)
Foster, Kevin 3:48:54 (7,802)
Foster, Kevin P 3:29:02 (4,277)
Foster, Lee T 5:32:43 (30,639)
Foster, Leon 3:11:01 (2,034)
Foster, Mark L 4:44:59 (22,321)
Foster, Martin J 3:52:29 (8,599)
Foster, Paul S 4:03:37 (11,528)
Foster, Philip A 3:49:08 (7,851)
Foster, Quentin S 2:33:10 (96)
Foster, Scott E 4:51:51 (23,900)
Foster, Stephen J 5:21:02 (29,243)
Foster, Steven 5:02:09 (26,174)
Foster, Terence E 3:44:22 (6,811)
Foster, Timothy R 4:30:26 (18,709)
Foster, Trevor 4:25:32 (17,296)
Fotherby, Andrew W 4:24:24 (16,956)
Fotherby, Kenneth J 2:51:54 (582)
Foulkes, Carl J 3:26:57 (3,921)
Fountain, Alan L 5:47:54 (32,092)
Fountain, Colin A 4:01:20 (11,007)
Fouques, Michel 4:10:28 (13,218)
Fovargue, Ian 4:11:04 (13,373)
Fowkes, Gary 4:24:44 (17,055)
Fowler, Charlie N 4:11:22 (13,444)
Fowler, Craig A 3:23:06 (3,315)
Fowler, David 3:48:12 (7,634)
Fowler, George E 3:46:02 (7,144)
Fowler, Ian J 5:33:27 (30,718)
Fowler, Jeffrey F 3:39:21 (5,879)
Fowler, Kevin 3:01:30 (1,221)
Fowler, Mark C 4:19:33 (15,680)
Fowler, Nathan S 5:13:29 (28,082)
Fowler, Nick S 5:02:10 (26,181)
Fowler, Simon 3:39:16 (5,862)
Fowler, Stephen P 3:59:11 (10,493)
Fowler, Steven 4:17:15 (15,021)
Fowles, Stephen W 3:29:11 (4,311)
Fox, Adam 4:18:35 (15,388)
Fox, Andrew 4:09:46 (13,032)
Fox, Anthony M 4:20:30 (15,937)
Fox, Christopher M 4:31:16 (18,904)
Fox, George W 4:00:25 (10,808)
Fox, Ian R 5:19:10 (28,969)
Fox, Jason 4:30:32 (18,735)
Fox, John 5:36:04 (31,002)
Fox, Jonathan D 5:49:35 (32,230)
Fox, Killian 4:39:02 (20,890)
Fox, Matthew J 3:57:12 (9,891)
Fox, Matthew J 4:54:26 (24,534)
Fox, Michael A 4:59:16 (25,620)
Fox, Neil 4:56:17 (24,962)
Fox, Nicholas 4:22:20 (16,429)
Fox, Paul R 3:49:35 (7,948)
Fox, Paul S 4:41:42 (21,564)
Fox, Thomas W 6:05:18 (33,288)
Foxall, Peter L 3:04:50 (1,454)
Foxley, Tim J 3:38:00 (5,648)
Foxwell, Matt 4:51:21 (23,809)
Foy, James S 3:49:39 (7,965)
Foy, Will J 4:24:26 (16,970)
Fragniere, Roger 5:01:01 (25,978)
Fraimout, Jean-Marc 3:32:18 (4,787)
Frain, Gregory 3:58:23 (10,255)
Frame, Doug G 7:40:52 (35,176)
Framnes, Kjell E 3:39:59 (5,995)
Frampton, Bruce S 4:25:36 (17,315)
Frampton, Oliver 5:00:52 (25,953)
Francalanci, Renato 3:09:20 (1,846)
France, Colin 4:32:05 (19,107)
Franceschini, Pietro D 4:13:20 (13,975)
Franchetta, Matteo 4:07:48 (12,533)
Franchini, Davide 3:05:25 (1,511)
Francilien, Paul 4:45:18 (22,395)
Francillia, Gary 4:06:23 (12,186)
Francini, Sergio 4:13:13 (13,944)
Francis, Alistair L 3:40:08 (6,023)
Francis, James S 4:07:28 (12,452)
Francis, John 4:20:14 (15,866)
Francis, Lee T 3:47:56 (7,557)
Francis, Michael J 3:53:25 (8,835)
Francis, Michael J 4:01:24 (11,024)
Francis, Nicholas J 4:43:18 (21,935)
Francis, Peter 5:19:45 (29,071)
Francis, Richard C 4:08:43 (12,743)
Francis, Richard W 3:26:21 (3,820)
Francis, Simon M 4:26:52 (17,706)
Francis, Stephen 3:54:35 (9,119)
Francis, Stuart 4:14:45 (14,363)
Francis, Tim M 3:30:34 (4,541)
Francisco Javier, Avellana 4:11:15 (13,416)
Francke, Brynmor 4:49:22 (23,332)
Franco, Luca 3:51:42 (8,412)
François, Jean Jacques 3:47:21 (7,428)
Francome, Peter C 4:45:01 (22,333)
Frangoullides, Tasos G 3:38:07 (5,669)
Franke, Christian 3:27:55 (4,093)
Franke, Mike 4:12:23 (13,721)
Franke, Uwe 3:27:56 (4,096)
Frankis, Richard 5:36:37 (31,070)
Frankish, Mark L 3:53:10 (8,762)
Frankland, Anthony D 5:54:48 (32,622)
Franklin, Alan J 5:19:26 (29,015)
Franklin, David P 4:21:29 (16,200)
Franklin, Henry G 4:36:31 (20,231)
Franklin, John 6:11:56 (33,610)
Franklin, Martin A 4:32:27 (19,196)
Franklin, Matthew E 4:19:36 (15,692)
Franklin, Richard G 4:15:06 (14,476)
Franklin, Richard J 3:47:29 (7,454)
Franklin, Stephen M 3:57:54 (10,110)
Franklin, Tim 3:20:23 (3,035)
Frankopan, Nicholas 3:52:12 (8,526)
Franks, David A 3:28:47 (4,240)
Franks, John H 5:50:00 (32,264)
Frankum, Martin J 4:12:44 (13,811)
Frary, Dale R 4:34:53 (19,819)
Fraser, Alexander A 5:12:59 (27,996)
Fraser, Andrew J 4:29:26 (18,442)
Fraser, Daniel G 5:05:43 (26,829)
Fraser, David A 3:54:07 (8,999)
Fraser, Derek 3:13:32 (2,307)
Fraser, Derek A 4:18:33 (15,373)
Fraser, Douglas J 4:23:52 (16,818)
Fraser, Graeme A 4:32:12 (19,134)
Fraser, Martin 4:12:45 (13,817)
Fraser, Martin S 3:55:26 (9,347)
Fraser, Michael 4:33:43 (19,492)
Fraser, Simon C 4:50:07 (23,518)
Fraser, Stephen 4:14:03 (14,164)
Fraser, Steven P 4:52:45 (24,114)
Fraser, William 3:56:03 (9,522)
Frawley, Aidan C 5:49:33 (32,227)
Frawley, David A 4:25:42 (17,345)
Frazer, Christopher D 4:14:07 (14,184)
Frazer, Mark 4:36:31 (20,231)
Frazer, Ricky B 3:23:41 (3,398)
Frearson, Paul C 4:38:22 (20,718)
Fredriksen, Ben 4:28:02 (18,036)
Freedman, Clive 4:40:47 (21,332)
Freedman, Paul 6:00:17 (32,991)
Freel, Christopher J 3:36:28 (5,420)
Freeman, Ashley R 6:02:59 (33,143)
Freeman, Brett A 4:47:38 (22,922)
Freeman, Colin 4:41:30 (21,523)
Freeman, Darren 4:08:06 (12,590)
Freeman, David J 2:43:33 (283)
Freeman, Glenn R 4:54:48 (24,622)
Freeman, James T 3:08:10 (1,730)
Freeman, Jonathan R 3:59:21 (10,533)
Freeman, Kirk G 5:20:11 (29,129)
Freeman, Paul 2:56:12 (822)
Freeman, Paul D 3:04:54 (1,462)
Freeman, Peter 4:02:44 (11,329)
Freeman, Peter G 4:41:34 (21,542)
Freeman, Roy H 3:40:01 (5,998)
Freeman, Samuel E 3:49:38 (7,962)
Freeman, Stuart B 4:41:50 (21,597)
Freer, Nicholas D 3:05:30 (1,518)
Freer, Robert I 4:23:04 (16,619)
Freeston, Paul 3:53:50 (8,942)
Frei, Helmut 2:49:46 (491)
Freitag, Joachim 3:20:11 (3,019)
French, Anthony T 4:14:59 (14,437)
French, Freddie 5:00:04 (25,787)
French, Gareth R 4:27:32 (17,900)
French, Graham A 4:10:46 (13,276)
French, Mark 4:34:13 (19,634)
French, Michael B 4:04:01 (11,640)
French, Peter S 3:43:35 (6,665)
French, Richard A 3:11:03 (2,038)
French, Sean 3:58:50 (10,397)
Frenette, Spencer C 5:20:30 (29,180)
Fresnais, Jean-Pierre 6:05:55 (33,328)
Fresson, Nick 4:41:16 (21,468)
Fretwell, Philip J 4:14:42 (14,346)
Frew, Colin J 3:06:48 (1,617)
Frewer, Martyn A 3:54:50 (9,193)
Frewin, John A 5:56:51 (32,763)
Frewin, Richard 3:57:59 (10,138)
Frewin, Steven W 5:44:02 (31,761)
Frey, Michael 5:47:10 (32,031)
Frey, Peter 4:10:58 (13,339)
Fribbens, Mark I 4:17:12 (15,011)
Fribbins, Michael G 4:57:59 (25,324)
Fricker, Colin W 3:24:19 (3,493)
Friedrich, Karsten 3:14:18 (2,392)
Friel, Robert H 4:29:46 (18,537)
Friend, Andrew S 5:13:02 (28,003)
Friend, Gordon C 4:01:25 (11,028)
Friezo, David C 4:29:12 (18,365)
Frigerio, Emanuele 3:56:22 (9,623)
Frisby, Billy 4:51:40 (23,863)
Frisby, Brian 4:02:33 (11,287)
Frisby, Craig P 4:12:42 (13,805)
Frisby, Peter M 3:54:54 (9,215)
Frisneda, Pedro R 3:13:28 (2,296)
Frith, Andrew J 3:58:28 (10,278)
Frith, Barry S 4:40:09 (21,171)
Frith, Michael C 5:54:04 (32,572)
Frith, Robert 4:41:55 (21,607)
Frizzell, Euan A 5:05:18 (26,749)
Frode-Jensen, Niels 3:47:41 (7,496)
Froggatt, Richard 4:25:07 (17,159)
Fromme, Paul 2:49:15 (476)

Garrity, Roger P....4:34:33 (19,727)
Garrod, James W....5:34:56 (30,897)
Garrod, Neil....3:41:35 (6,294)
Garrod, Simon A....3:51:58 (8,476)
Garrood, Richard....4:48:59 (23,231)
Garry, Dean....3:17:47 (2,764)
Garside, Duncan....5:10:01 (27,513)
Garside, Jamie....3:57:57 (10,127)
Garside, Simon D....3:23:03 (3,307)
Garstang, Malcolm D....5:06:49 (27,020)
Garvey, Clement J....3:47:36 (7,474)
Garvey, Steve....3:22:51 (3,278)
Garvey, William F....4:52:22 (24,027)
Garwood, Alan P....4:02:24 (11,248)
Gaschni, Fred....3:38:39 (5,745)
Gascoigne-Pees, Edward....5:30:07 (30,372)
Gashe, Terry A....3:40:34 (6,097)
Gaskarth, Andrew....2:54:44 (730)
Gaskell, David R....3:27:31 (4,025)
Gaskell, Marcus A....4:05:05 (11,889)
Gaskell, Nicholas B....4:49:17 (23,300)
Gaskill, Eddy A....4:10:21 (13,182)
Gaskin, Gary....4:20:31 (15,939)
Gaskin, James E....5:14:34 (28,273)
Gaskin, Martin J....4:36:08 (20,113)
Gaskins, Scott....4:13:23 (13,987)
Gasque, Kenneth S....5:23:32 (29,547)
Gateau, Vincent....4:07:26 (12,444)
Gately, John....3:51:15 (8,316)
Gaterell, Paul A....4:22:39 (16,523)
Gates, Anthony B....5:18:15 (28,828)
Gates, Michael....5:33:51 (30,759)
Gates, Terry R....5:01:44 (26,096)
Gathmann, Graeme P....4:50:14 (23,545)
Gatley, James A....7:00:32 (34,877)
Gatrad, Raazik....4:48:23 (23,100)
Gatson, Kenneth C....4:45:33 (22,445)
Gaude, Ludovic....4:00:58 (10,941)
Gauge, Nathan A....5:09:43 (27,473)
Gaughy, David....5:40:12 (31,437)
Gaul, Richard....4:40:07 (21,157)
Gauld, Sid....3:29:03 (4,282)
Gaulder, Nicholas R....3:29:51 (4,428)
Gaume, Marcelo J....3:12:13 (2,167)
Gaunt, Martin....2:48:26 (430)
Gaunt, Mike....5:42:45 (31,657)
Gauntlett, Nicholas C....5:20:32 (29,187)
Gauteux, Bruno....3:57:26 (9,961)
Gautheret, Pierre....4:38:14 (20,678)
Gauthier, James D....3:16:41 (2,646)
Gautier, Frederic....3:41:24 (6,259)
Gavin, Dominic M....4:55:48 (24,841)
Gavin, Michael P....3:23:49 (3,423)
Gavin, Smith....3:26:12 (3,794)
Gavin, Wayne....4:28:20 (18,117)
Gay, Andrew J....4:55:03 (24,687)
Gay, Antony J....6:22:13 (33,999)
Gay, Christopher D....4:03:21 (11,473)
Gay, Edward J....4:45:45 (22,486)
Gayer, David J....3:46:11 (7,176)
Gayle, Terry....3:33:21 (4,938)
Gaylor, Neal R....4:01:39 (11,078)
Gayner, Ronald G....3:58:47 (10,382)
Gaze, Barry I....3:01:16 (1,204)
Gaze, Peter J....4:17:49 (15,163)
Gaze, Stevie T....5:36:26 (31,043)
Geale, David B....6:12:54 (33,657)
Gear, Alistair B....4:03:06 (11,411)
Gearing, Daniel L....3:30:29 (4,523)
Geary, Darin....5:07:11 (27,096)
Geatrell, Keir J....3:21:41 (3,151)
Geddes, Fraser H....5:06:09 (26,902)
Gedin, Mats R....2:47:24 (385)
Gee, Anthony D....4:52:23 (24,031)
Gee, Christopher....4:41:22 (21,484)
Gee, Craig P....4:21:56 (16,312)
Gee, David W....3:29:19 (4,328)
Gee, Michael B....3:42:02 (6,385)
Gee, Raymond....4:13:20 (13,975)
Geen, Peter R....4:51:07 (23,754)
Geeson, Andrew L....4:40:32 (21,267)
Gehr, Walter....4:11:37 (13,508)
Geither, Joseph....3:04:21 (1,416)
Gelardi, Peter....4:36:24 (20,195)
Gelb, Sivan....4:53:47 (24,379)
Geldard, Timothy J....5:34:09 (30,801)
Geller, Laurence....4:48:27 (23,114)
Gemmell, Brian F....4:26:55 (17,724)
Gemmell, James E....5:29:18 (30,273)
Gendai, Koichi....4:42:12 (21,676)
Gendu, Pritpal S....5:39:55 (31,404)
Generalis, Sotos C....4:37:18 (20,445)
Genes, Christopher M....3:09:59 (1,918)
Genn, Andrew....5:11:09 (27,679)
Gennery, Michael J....5:00:36 (25,898)
Genoud, Patrick....2:52:40 (618)
Gent, Andy P....4:14:59 (14,437)
Gentili, Stephen J....3:25:53 (3,739)
Gentle, Christopher R....3:33:15 (4,919)
Gentle, John F....4:42:47 (21,819)
Gentle, Kevin E....5:37:30 (31,142)
Gentle, Matthew T....5:23:28 (29,538)
Geoghegan, Craig A....3:28:34 (4,211)
George, Bernard D....5:22:02 (29,352)
George, Craig A....4:15:08 (14,487)
George, Gavin D....6:13:54 (33,701)
George, George J....3:46:56 (7,336)
George, Iain P....5:11:52 (27,798)
George, Ian R....3:14:49 (2,462)
George, Kevin L....3:42:37 (6,486)
George, Martin....4:33:30 (19,433)
George, Michael J....4:11:08 (13,388)
George, Robert M....4:29:35 (18,491)
George, Simon....4:02:24 (11,248)
George, Steve D....3:36:45 (5,458)
George, Stuart C....6:16:34 (33,802)
Georgiou, George....6:29:55 (34,252)
Ger, Larry....4:36:57 (20,343)
Geraghty, Jason W....4:45:50 (22,509)
Geraghty, Roger C....3:09:07 (1,823)
Gerard, Frederique....3:40:36 (6,101)
Gerbel, Yvon....4:06:08 (12,130)
Gerdts, Florian....3:52:51 (8,695)
Gerloni, Robert....3:30:47 (4,578)
Germain, Yves....3:05:13 (1,488)
German, Paul....5:40:17 (31,445)
Germeney, Phillip N....4:09:24 (12,933)
Gerrard, Andrew M....4:31:52 (19,057)
Gerrard, Jerome....3:43:59 (6,737)
Gerrard, Timothy W....3:26:55 (3,914)
Gerundini, Anthony R....3:01:53 (1,251)
Geschiere, Leen....5:13:35 (28,099)
Gething, Julian....4:09:12 (12,890)
Ghag, Rajinder....6:31:09 (34,280)
Gharib, Jaouad....2:07:49 (2)
Ghattaura, Sukhbeer S....4:39:00 (20,879)
Gherardi, Bernard....2:56:20 (830)
Gheri, Marco....4:52:38 (24,088)
Ghermaoui, Jamel....2:53:11 (643)
Ghermezian, Romano R....2:50:53 (535)
Gialanella, Tony....5:17:17 (28,685)
Giammona, Matteo....2:52:55 (631)
Gianfranceschi, Gianluca....4:39:40 (21,060)
Gianni, Stefano....2:54:35 (719)
Gianvito, Ottomano....3:15:57 (2,565)
Gibb, Darren W....5:00:18 (25,845)
Gibb, Nick....5:15:33 (28,429)
Gibbard, Adrian B....3:06:25 (1,585)
Gibbins, Alex N....2:47:57 (411)
Gibbon, Adrian C....3:43:08 (6,579)
Gibbons, Alastair....3:07:23 (1,662)
Gibbons, Linford M....2:57:57 (951)
Gibbons, Michael....5:59:10 (32,923)
Gibbons, Neil P....4:18:56 (15,494)
Gibbons, Paul A....6:18:04 (33,855)
Gibbons, Simon I....4:26:34 (17,623)
Gibbons, Steve....3:31:39 (4,701)
Gibbs, Ben L....3:28:25 (4,185)
Gibbs, Brian T....3:55:34 (9,394)
Gibbs, Colin....6:52:51 (34,767)
Gibbs, Colin J....5:05:45 (26,833)
Gibbs, Hugh T....3:17:47 (2,764)
Gibbs, Ian D....4:46:20 (22,629)
Gibbs, Jason....4:33:54 (19,546)
Gibbs, Mark A....4:22:15 (16,407)
Gibbs, Paul A....4:56:37 (25,045)
Gibbs, Robert M....4:36:27 (20,216)
Gibbs, Ronald E....5:14:52 (28,323)
Gibbs, Stephen P....3:50:04 (8,055)
Gibbs, Timothy....3:28:13 (4,147)
Gibbs, Tony S....6:30:54 (34,270)
Gibby, Robert H....3:39:16 (5,862)
Giblin, Ted P....5:16:45 (28,589)
Gibosn, Ewen M....4:25:53 (17,396)
Gibson, Alan....5:22:59 (29,486)
Gibson, Andrew....4:00:49 (10,907)
Gibson, Brett....5:46:24 (31,973)
Gibson, Colin....3:41:05 (6,199)
Gibson, Daniel J....6:41:35 (34,534)
Gibson, David M....4:20:37 (15,968)
Gibson, David S....4:13:27 (14,003)
Gibson, Dean....3:00:40 (1,171)
Gibson, John D....4:14:23 (14,267)
Gibson, Matthew J....3:57:07 (9,864)
Gibson, Oliver....3:19:16 (2,908)
Gibson, Peter L....4:15:40 (14,624)
Gibson, Robert E....3:55:38 (9,408)
Gibson, Robin....4:57:09 (25,164)
Gibson, Stephen J....4:25:38 (17,330)
Gibson, Stuart....3:26:58 (3,925)
Gibson, Stuart....5:13:52 (28,144)
Giddens, Philip J....5:47:26 (32,054)
Giddins, Stephen J....5:22:38 (29,449)
Gidman, Paul A....6:26:43 (34,147)
Gidus, Stephen D....3:29:49 (4,423)
Gierberg, Wolfgang....4:03:39 (11,534)
Gifford, Andrew P....3:57:43 (10,044)
Gifford, Roger F....3:46:25 (7,226)
Gifford-Pike, Ross S....4:34:28 (19,704)
Giglioli, Arlo....6:07:10 (33,399)
Gilbart-Smith, Peter....3:54:27 (9,088)
Gilbert, Alexander L....3:52:10 (8,520)
Gilbert, Andrew....3:42:27 (6,464)
Gilbert, Andrew J....3:54:25 (9,081)
Gilbert, Andy....3:18:18 (2,813)
Gilbert, Damian L....5:11:42 (27,769)
Gilbert, Jonathan P....4:07:10 (12,387)
Gilbert, Marcus W....4:07:14 (12,399)
Gilbert, Mark....4:21:05 (16,089)
Gilbert, Martin....6:22:22 (34,004)
Gilbert, Phillip S....5:02:42 (26,274)
Gilbert-Smith, Dougal J....5:12:26 (27,895)
Gilbody, Keith....4:53:59 (24,424)
Gilbride, Darren T....5:08:19 (27,262)
Gilchrist, Francis J....4:10:15 (13,153)
Gilchrist, Kieran E....6:29:56 (34,253)
Gilchrist, Robert D....5:34:48 (30,884)
Gilchrist, Tyrone....5:34:40 (30,870)
Gildea, Paul A....3:18:00 (2,787)
Gildersleve, David....5:38:07 (31,208)
Giles, Antony C....4:33:35 (19,459)
Giles, Duncan....3:59:46 (10,654)
Giles, Graeme N....4:02:00 (11,155)
Giles, Martin R....2:51:32 (565)
Giles, Nick....4:41:33 (21,537)
Giles, Robin C....7:30:12 (35,129)
Giles, Spencer....3:07:24 (1,664)
Gilham, Barry J....4:31:43 (19,024)
Gill, Adrian S....3:10:03 (1,926)
Gill, Alan W....5:24:28 (29,679)
Gill, Andy D....5:04:42 (26,631)
Gill, Colin....4:28:48 (18,250)
Gill, David J....4:23:49 (16,808)
Gill, Jagdeep....5:46:09 (31,946)
Gill, Lakhbir S....4:58:57 (25,544)
Gill, Mark J....3:52:56 (8,705)
Gill, Michael P....4:53:58 (24,415)
Gill, Paul....4:31:08 (18,862)
Gill, Peter....4:46:24 (22,648)
Gill, Ray....4:34:17 (19,660)
Gill, Richard....3:35:03 (5,191)
Gill, Rickey S....4:34:40 (19,753)
Gill, Robert W....4:41:01 (21,400)
Gill, Roy P....5:03:21 (26,410)
Gill, Simon....4:16:52 (14,929)
Gill, Thomas J....3:56:05 (9,533)
Gill, Timothy C....3:38:22 (5,705)
Gillam, Stephen....4:36:06 (20,108)
Gillan, Alistair....3:11:11 (2,049)

Gillard, Claude	3:32:27	(4,811)
Gillard, Vernon M	3:37:38	(5,592)
Gillatt, Stephen M	4:57:09	(25,164)
Gilles, Dean H	4:03:16	(11,449)
Gillespie, Andrew J	4:08:42	(12,740)
Gillespie, Frank G	4:06:13	(12,144)
Gillespie, James R	4:15:40	(14,624)
Gillespie, Neil D	4:05:06	(11,897)
Gillespie, Stuart T	4:04:23	(11,718)
Gillett, Daniel J	2:53:17	(649)
Gillett, Dean H	4:16:00	(14,715)
Gillett, Simon P	3:28:18	(4,160)
Gillette, Tony	5:19:56	(29,087)
Gillick, Kieran P	2:54:38	(723)
Gillies, Anthony J	4:34:09	(19,608)
Gillies, Stuart	4:29:41	(18,516)
Gilligan, Barry	3:46:20	(7,209)
Gilligan, Edward J	3:06:58	(1,632)
Gilling, Jonathan C	2:42:59	(265)
Gilling, Ralph	4:26:49	(17,692)
Gillingham, Mark	5:17:43	(28,743)
Gillings, Stephen W	6:35:16	(34,385)
Gilliver, Ian	5:15:16	(28,383)
Gillman, Chris	4:51:27	(23,824)
Gillman, Clive R	4:18:33	(15,373)
Gillooly, Jamie	6:17:06	(33,828)
Gillot, Leslie	4:45:47	(22,491)
Gillott, Peter W	4:21:41	(16,252)
Gillott, Stuart J	4:39:59	(21,136)
Gillson, Stephen P	3:13:14	(2,268)
Gilmartin, Mark P	5:33:07	(30,679)
Gilmore, Alexander T	3:23:17	(3,348)
Gilmour, Brian J	5:02:50	(26,301)
Gilmour, Marc	5:04:31	(26,602)
Gilmour, Paul R	4:06:18	(12,166)
Gilmour, Rory C	4:21:28	(16,195)
Gilmour, Stephen	3:16:59	(2,674)
Gilmour, Stewart	4:08:34	(12,705)
Gilroy, Francis J	3:11:19	(2,061)
Gilroy, Robert	2:30:15	(71)
Gilroy, Robson M	4:34:22	(19,684)
Gilson, Steven E	4:49:12	(23,282)
Gilson, Thomas D	3:53:01	(8,720)
Gimber, Andreas	4:11:02	(13,361)
Gimber, Martin	4:11:02	(13,361)
Gimeno Santolaria, Alvaro	2:45:09	(323)
Gimpel, Mo J	4:38:18	(20,697)
Gimson, Ashley M	3:01:14	(1,202)
Gingell, Stephen B	4:12:36	(13,774)
Ginman, Anthony	5:42:48	(31,662)
Ginn, Alan J	3:26:16	(3,803)
Giora, Francesco	5:47:22	(32,046)
Giordano, Robert	4:26:23	(17,561)
Giovannoni, Gavin	2:55:51	(797)
Giovino, Alberto	3:27:29	(4,017)
Gipp, Peter R	3:18:10	(2,797)
Gir, Tim	5:46:05	(31,940)
Girard, Robert	4:46:42	(22,709)
Giraud, Christian	3:59:57	(10,713)
Giraud, Vincent	4:42:09	(21,664)
Girdlestone, Paul	4:34:39	(19,748)
Girdlestone, Stephen	3:58:27	(10,272)
Girling, Alan	4:52:40	(24,096)
Gitau Macharia, David	2:36:27	(115)
Githui, Davidson M	4:25:29	(17,280)
Gitkin, Charles L	5:07:11	(27,096)
Gittdes, Jonathan M	4:46:49	(22,738)
Gittins, Ian E	4:07:17	(12,413)
Gittoes, Robert J	3:37:57	(5,638)
Giuseppe, Gallarotti	4:13:55	(14,122)
Gladding, Edward J	4:01:59	(11,150)
Gladwell, Ian D	3:06:06	(1,559)
Gladwell, Nathan	3:48:31	(7,715)
Glaister, Grant E	3:48:41	(7,757)
Glanagan, Tadhg J	3:39:18	(5,868)
Glancy, Ryan P	4:29:55	(18,570)
Glanville, Matthew F	4:22:51	(16,568)
Glass, John C	4:52:17	(24,010)
Glassett, Paul A	4:35:44	(20,026)
Glassock, Christopher P	4:52:24	(24,033)
Glassock, Stephen M	5:28:31	(30,188)
Glasspool, Jonathan M	4:41:22	(21,484)
Glaudel, Pascal	3:05:41	(1,529)

Glave, Junior	3:59:28	(10,560)
Glazier, David M	4:00:40	(10,879)
Gleadall, Owen	4:51:41	(23,869)
Gleadall, Stephen	3:40:20	(6,060)
Gledhill, Liam F	4:11:10	(13,397)
Gleeson, Michael A	5:53:50	(32,554)
Gleeson, Michael J	4:31:21	(18,934)
Gleig, Sean	4:20:50	(16,030)
Glen, Andrew	3:30:51	(4,585)
Glendenning, David	3:28:03	(4,113)
Glendining, Daniel	3:48:50	(7,796)
Glendinning, Andrew E	3:24:48	(3,553)
Glendinning, Thomas B	3:46:23	(7,219)
Glenister, Graham	4:03:39	(11,534)
Glenister, Kevin A	4:16:39	(14,876)
Glenn, Martin R	3:54:57	(9,228)
Glenn, Robert	4:53:37	(24,333)
Glenville, David	4:58:33	(25,455)
Glenville, Simon	3:33:58	(5,041)
Glew, Peter D	4:29:07	(18,345)
Glock, Hans J	3:12:28	(2,192)
Glock, Mike C	5:27:52	(30,084)
Glogg, James J	4:21:57	(16,317)
Glossop, Peter	4:33:39	(19,473)
Gloudemans, Kyle M	5:05:18	(26,749)
Glover, Adrian D	5:17:50	(28,763)
Glover, Adrian P	4:45:19	(22,397)
Glover, Bryan	4:38:18	(20,697)
Glover, Davey I	7:13:06	(35,018)
Glover, Michael E	4:48:34	(23,135)
Glover, Simon M	4:03:57	(11,617)
Glover, Stuart	4:35:22	(19,940)
Glyn, Patrick	3:50:49	(8,211)
Glynn, Chris D	4:53:37	(24,333)
Glynn, Jack T	3:57:39	(10,027)
Glynn, Keith M	4:24:43	(17,047)
Glynn, Peter G	3:58:27	(10,272)
Goatly, Michael J	5:13:47	(28,130)
Gobbato, Stefano	3:32:33	(4,826)
Gobbett, Richard J	3:06:50	(1,622)
Gobert, Christophe	3:57:49	(10,080)
Godbee, Peter J	3:59:19	(10,522)
Godber, Neil A	4:12:37	(13,781)
Godbold, Brian	4:08:53	(12,797)
Goddard, Alex B	4:26:08	(17,487)
Goddard, Barry	4:00:37	(10,871)
Goddard, Kevin J	3:19:12	(2,899)
Goddard, Paul	4:00:12	(10,766)
Goddard, Stephen A	3:35:14	(5,213)
Goddard, Trevor E	3:25:05	(3,602)
Godden, Ian D	2:57:51	(948)
Godeau, Gregory	4:09:00	(12,826)
Godfree, Ian J	3:49:01	(7,826)
Godfrey, Christopher J	4:03:25	(11,485)
Godfrey, Malcolm	3:26:25	(3,831)
Godfrey, Mark J	4:12:58	(13,874)
Godfrey, Paul S	5:29:58	(30,358)
Godfrey, Richard	6:26:46	(34,150)
Godinho, Jorge	3:31:09	(4,621)
Godwin, Daniel	3:55:49	(9,467)
Godwin, David J	4:20:19	(15,892)
Godwin, Dean	6:15:09	(33,741)
Godwin, William B	4:21:57	(16,317)
Godzik, Kyle J	4:01:25	(11,028)
Goenka, Anupam	5:37:56	(31,189)
Goertz, Thomas	4:42:30	(21,742)
Goessweiner, Herwig C	3:55:45	(9,450)
Goff, Chris R	3:59:24	(10,546)
Goff, Matthew P	4:06:22	(12,184)
Goff, Robert S	4:18:11	(15,261)
Goffe, Oliver A	4:15:35	(14,603)
Goggin, Chris C	5:03:11	(26,382)
Goggin, James	5:32:33	(30,621)
Goguen, Michael	3:46:44	(7,290)
Golaszewski, Jan	5:22:02	(29,352)
Gold, David A	4:02:01	(11,161)
Gold, James A	4:39:10	(20,916)
Goldberg, Mark	3:55:26	(9,347)
Golden, Michael	4:40:49	(21,340)
Goldenberg, Mark P	5:07:56	(27,207)
Golder, Richard C	4:23:43	(16,781)
Goldfinch, Dean	4:07:43	(12,503)
Golding, Ian A	4:45:00	(22,325)

Golding, John F	3:45:20	(7,012)
Golding, Kenneth I	4:09:04	(12,846)
Golding, Richard N	3:59:30	(10,571)
Goldman, Garry R	4:50:28	(23,618)
Goldring, Rob	5:00:03	(25,782)
Goldsmith, Howard	3:32:51	(4,863)
Goldsmith, Paul	5:17:36	(28,733)
Goldsmith, Simon A	3:28:09	(4,135)
Goldsmith, Stuart G	4:23:18	(16,690)
Goldspink, Phil	5:15:54	(28,466)
Goldstein, Mark	3:13:51	(2,342)
Goldstein, Steven N	4:37:06	(20,386)
Goldstone, Philip	5:15:34	(28,430)
Goldthorpe, Ian M	4:41:31	(21,529)
Goldup, Matthew	5:24:00	(29,618)
Goldup, Rob J	5:24:00	(29,618)
Gomez, Hernan	4:41:45	(21,578)
Gomez Gonzalez, Antonio	4:07:45	(12,516)
Gomez-Chinchon, Carlos	3:57:53	(10,107)
Gomez-Raggio, José A	5:03:28	(26,428)
Gomm, Christopher D	4:01:57	(11,138)
Gompertz, Simon	4:19:46	(15,743)
Goncalves, Eridio K	3:40:35	(6,100)
Goncalves, Norbert	3:16:34	(2,640)
Goncalves, Vitor M	4:23:17	(16,683)
Gong, Michael	4:50:04	(23,505)
Gonzalez, José M	3:36:16	(5,386)
Gonzalez, Manuel T	3:46:01	(7,140)
Gonzalez, Victor	3:35:44	(5,303)
Gooch, Adrian L	6:07:20	(33,410)
Gooch, Alan	5:28:14	(30,155)
Gooch, Christopher A	4:27:37	(17,926)
Goodacre, James P	4:55:26	(24,764)
Goodall, Colin R	5:08:21	(27,266)
Goodall, David P	3:40:19	(6,052)
Goodall, Graham B	4:56:35	(25,035)
Goodall, James N	5:28:48	(30,219)
Goodall, John	2:54:23	(702)
Goodall, Malcolm	3:43:47	(6,703)
Goodall, William K	5:05:10	(26,718)
Gooday, Tom O	4:10:29	(13,224)
Goodayle, Robert J	4:44:58	(22,316)
Goodburn, Ben	3:40:49	(6,142)
Goodchild, James P	5:21:06	(29,249)
Goodchild, Leslie G	4:40:19	(21,212)
Goodchild, Robert C	4:11:19	(13,434)
Goodchild, William H	4:28:10	(18,078)
Gooddy, John F	3:57:18	(9,920)
Goode, Andrew A	4:55:12	(24,719)
Goode, Darren	4:31:21	(18,934)
Goode, James E	2:58:32	(996)
Goode, Philip	2:57:50	(945)
Goode, Tom	5:36:54	(31,092)
Gooden, Steven	5:48:55	(32,175)
Goodeve, Andrew	4:41:46	(21,584)
Goodey, James	4:34:21	(19,676)
Goodfellow, Charles M	4:24:38	(17,025)
Goodhew, Robert C	6:49:52	(34,705)
Goodier, Alistair J	4:18:19	(15,301)
Goodings, Kevin R	5:34:03	(30,788)
Goodkind, Marc G	3:56:09	(9,552)
Goodman, Adam R	4:16:36	(14,862)
Goodman, Andrew J	4:13:42	(14,068)
Goodman, Paul J	3:51:33	(8,382)
Goodman, Roy	3:59:40	(10,620)
Goodreid, Ian C	3:40:46	(6,132)
Goodridge, Andrew M	5:32:20	(30,594)
Goodrum, Martin C	4:25:21	(17,227)
Goodsell, Mark R	5:00:04	(25,787)
Goodson, Alan R	4:22:14	(16,402)
Goodson, Mark	4:39:53	(21,106)
Goodwen, Peter J	3:41:23	(6,255)
Goodwin, Andrew M	4:20:59	(16,071)
Goodwin, Ashley	5:46:02	(31,938)
Goodwin, Barry	3:52:27	(8,593)
Goodwin, Daniel	6:16:03	(33,781)
Goodwin, David	3:18:15	(2,809)
Goodwin, David A	4:20:55	(16,055)
Goodwin, Frederick V	4:32:49	(19,274)
Goodwin, Ian V	3:38:39	(5,745)
Goodwin, John C	4:33:32	(19,444)
Goodwin, Julian	3:19:06	(2,890)
Goodwin, Mark I	3:27:37	(4,039)

Goodwin, Matthew	4:23:32 (16,735)	Gould, Keith	3:45:10 (6,984)
Goodwin, Michael	3:42:36 (6,481)	Gould, Martyn D	4:44:45 (22,262)
Goodwin, Peter D	4:43:30 (21,980)	Gould, Neil	3:48:26 (7,690)
Goodwin, Peter D	5:02:24 (26,218)	Gould, Timothy J	5:04:53 (26,666)
Goodwin, Sean	3:37:43 (5,605)	Gould, Will	6:00:16 (32,989)
Goodwin, Simon T	5:25:23 (29,787)	Goulding, Mark	3:52:28 (8,596)
Goodwin, Stephen H	3:01:45 (1,243)	Goulevant, Thierry	3:40:27 (6,080)
Goodwin, Stuart D	4:03:49 (11,584)	Goulis, James	2:33:05 (95)
Goodwin, Tim P	4:10:09 (13,127)	Gournay, Kevin J	3:47:42 (7,506)
Goody, Chris A	5:13:23 (28,055)	Gouveia, José R	5:39:13 (31,336)
Goodyear, Paul A	3:25:08 (3,612)	Govi, Gabriele	3:21:20 (3,119)
Goodyer, Stephen J	4:30:02 (18,600)	Gow, Chris	4:46:24 (22,648)
Gopalakrishnan, Kathiravelu	5:38:43 (31,279)	Gowdy, Stephen	4:25:26 (17,262)
Goppelt, Robert	3:19:03 (2,885)	Gower, Edward M	5:36:15 (31,020)
Goransson, Paul N	3:24:44 (3,544)	Goyvaerts, Eric	4:19:05 (15,544)
Gorasia, Dinesh N	5:45:03 (31,852)	Gozio, Dionigi	3:44:24 (6,820)
Gordine, Alan R	5:23:02 (29,491)	Grace, C	4:14:58 (14,430)
Gordon, Adam	5:21:09 (29,255)	Grace, Michael P	4:23:01 (16,604)
Gordon, Adrian T	3:57:05 (9,850)	Grace, Mike	3:35:30 (5,264)
Gordon, Allan	5:42:40 (31,649)	Grace, Stephen R	4:31:25 (18,947)
Gordon, Benjamin J	5:06:07 (26,894)	Gracie, Nick J	3:04:11 (1,406)
Gordon, Christopher R	5:02:01 (26,147)	Gradden, Craig W	4:29:17 (18,396)
Gordon, Darren D	3:22:55 (3,286)	Gradwell, Mark	4:08:19 (12,645)
Gordon, David A	4:27:11 (17,798)	Gradwell, Nicholas C	4:17:19 (15,042)
Gordon, Ewen J	4:22:22 (16,438)	Grady, David M	4:24:39 (17,026)
Gordon, Frank E	3:31:15 (4,643)	Grafe, Ingo	4:35:25 (19,955)
Gordon, Jeffrey	4:10:52 (13,307)	Grafton, Jonathan G	4:29:39 (18,506)
Gordon, John A	4:38:10 (20,664)	Gragy, Christian	2:52:49 (627)
Gordon, Jonathan N	3:08:19 (1,746)	Grah, Olivier	4:09:52 (13,059)
Gordon, Paul A	4:23:29 (16,726)	Graham, Alexander J	5:03:15 (26,392)
Gordon, Paul A	4:45:31 (22,434)	Graham, Andrew P	5:28:58 (30,242)
Gordon, Richard P	5:59:48 (32,969)	Graham, Antony P	3:51:05 (8,278)
Gordon, Robert M	4:52:29 (24,052)	Graham, Archibald	4:29:04 (18,330)
Gordon, Samuel J	4:05:56 (12,080)	Graham, Bill J	2:52:43 (621)
Gordon, Steven J	4:01:47 (11,109)	Graham, Charles F	4:08:57 (12,813)
Gordon, St-John	3:58:28 (10,278)	Graham, Christopher M	4:23:18 (16,690)
Gordon, Tony D	4:28:28 (18,156)	Graham, Christopher P	3:40:38 (6,108)
Gore, Andrew K	2:38:46 (171)	Graham, Hugh	3:44:18 (6,796)
Gore, Matthew	4:31:19 (18,923)	Graham, Iain A	4:15:30 (14,582)
Gore, Nigel S	4:01:11 (10,977)	Graham, Ian A	2:59:20 (1,073)
Gorges, Jean Claude	4:03:40 (11,538)	Graham, James M	4:39:54 (21,112)
Goring, Jonathan C	3:56:30 (9,663)	Graham, John C	5:07:30 (27,147)
Gorla, Roberto	2:45:01 (320)	Graham, John E	4:05:25 (11,971)
Gorman, David	4:24:30 (16,994)	Graham, Mark	3:37:27 (5,570)
Gorman, Frankie M	3:25:51 (3,730)	Graham, Mark A	3:58:16 (10,210)
Gorman, Stephen	4:54:32 (24,559)	Graham, Martin P	3:55:12 (9,276)
Gormley, Gerard A	3:15:46 (2,545)	Graham, Michael J	3:37:30 (5,582)
Gormley, John E	3:59:56 (10,705)	Graham, Neil	4:11:22 (13,444)
Gormley, Leslie R	4:44:51 (22,285)	Graham, Paul J	4:37:06 (20,386)
Gorn, Michael	4:50:30 (23,626)	Graham, Peter	4:13:41 (14,064)
Gornall, Les	6:33:07 (34,332)	Graham, Peter S	5:38:34 (31,262)
Gorrie, Thomas J	4:57:42 (25,263)	Graham, Simon	4:40:33 (21,273)
Gorski, Antoni	4:43:56 (22,081)	Graham, Stuart	3:48:21 (7,672)
Gorst, Richard	2:59:13 (1,057)	Graham, Thomas G	3:50:52 (8,228)
Gorton, Oliver W	3:45:44 (7,082)	Graham, Warren V	4:29:58 (18,577)
Gortz, Paul A	3:30:25 (4,508)	Grainger, Andrew	4:19:49 (15,756)
Gosling, Christopher P	4:47:58 (22,997)	Grainger, David A	6:41:36 (34,536)
Gosling, Mike	4:27:59 (18,029)	Grainger, John M	5:12:41 (27,940)
Gosling, Peter D	3:16:58 (2,672)	Grainger, Michael G	4:07:12 (12,393)
Gosmann, Norbert	3:09:10 (1,829)	Grainger, Nick R	5:30:49 (30,444)
Gosnell, Andy	3:14:49 (2,462)	Grainger, Richard J	3:29:10 (4,306)
Goss, Billy N	3:54:15 (9,034)	Grainger, Robert P	3:32:19 (4,790)
Goss, John D	4:57:40 (25,259)	Grainger, Steve	3:06:33 (1,598)
Goss, Malcolm P	4:18:24 (15,327)	Grammaticas, Antonios	5:12:52 (27,980)
Gossage, Michael J	4:58:43 (25,489)	Gramshammer, Florian	4:11:25 (13,458)
Gossett, Monique	4:48:09 (23,042)	Granata, Cesare	3:12:44 (2,218)
Gothard, Dominic	4:36:14 (20,141)	Granby, Mark L	3:56:46 (9,740)
Gotte, Richard	3:30:24 (4,506)	Grand, Adrian M	3:03:46 (1,387)
Gottlieb, Craig H	5:49:37 (32,235)	Grandet, Laurent	4:00:34 (10,857)
Gottlieb, Gabriel H	3:32:20 (4,793)	Graney, Barry M	3:07:17 (1,652)
Gotts, Mark	4:40:24 (21,231)	Grange, Michel	4:23:54 (16,827)
Gottschalk, Wolfgang	4:33:17 (19,377)	Granger, Andrew J	4:26:38 (17,643)
Goucher, Dave L	4:40:49 (21,340)	Granger, Derek J	3:41:45 (6,324)
Gouck, Duncan J	3:14:23 (2,404)	Grangier, Luc	3:14:42 (2,445)
Gough, James	5:05:06 (26,700)	Grant, Allan	4:04:08 (11,670)
Gough, Tim F	4:39:00 (20,879)	Grant, Allen	4:01:22 (11,017)
Goulbourne, Patrick W	4:35:04 (19,865)	Grant, Andrew	4:55:25 (24,762)
Gould, Alistair T	4:47:37 (22,915)	Grant, Andrew M	4:47:20 (22,840)
Gould, Andrew J	4:50:48 (23,694)	Grant, Andrew T	4:39:00 (20,879)
Gould, Antony J	3:08:27 (1,753)	Grant, Antonio B	2:32:08 (87)
Gould, Daniel	4:14:34 (14,311)	Grant, Ben N	3:47:01 (7,354)
Gould, Gwyn W	3:33:50 (5,018)	Grant, Daniel J	4:36:38 (20,263)
Gould, Jason S	3:16:16 (2,615)	Grant, David L	4:52:58 (24,166)

Grant, Douglas R	5:16:45 (28,589)
Grant, Frank	4:31:37 (19,001)
Grant, Ian L	4:20:59 (16,071)
Grant, Kevin	5:36:26 (31,043)
Grant, Liam	4:00:40 (10,879)
Grant, Matthew W	5:24:49 (29,721)
Grant, Peter	3:31:26 (4,668)
Grant, Peter	4:37:30 (20,498)
Grant, Peter	5:55:13 (32,660)
Grant, Peter J	5:02:48 (26,294)
Grant, Peter T	4:53:45 (24,366)
Grant, Stephen	5:36:25 (31,040)
Grant, Steven J	4:58:25 (25,422)
Grant, Stewart M	4:49:47 (23,444)
Grant, Tony	3:40:41 (6,115)
Grant, Wayne A	5:00:21 (25,856)
Grant, William E	2:34:59 (113)
Grassi, Ben D	5:34:28 (30,845)
Grassick, Mark R	5:06:26 (26,950)
Grassick, Richard K	5:06:27 (26,953)
Gratton, Kenneth S	4:25:56 (17,409)
Graves, Andrew	3:53:07 (8,748)
Graves, Paul G	4:08:40 (12,733)
Gravett, Paul F	5:45:48 (31,921)
Gravier, Eric	3:34:21 (5,101)
Gravis, Craig B	4:36:09 (20,117)
Gray, Adam D	4:02:49 (11,345)
Gray, Alan R	4:47:09 (22,806)
Gray, Anthony D	3:13:24 (2,291)
Gray, Bernard P	3:55:17 (9,307)
Gray, Brian A	4:31:27 (18,957)
Gray, Christopher J	3:12:40 (2,212)
Gray, Colin R	3:09:00 (1,812)
Gray, David C	3:23:48 (3,419)
Gray, Dennis	4:49:12 (23,282)
Gray, Eddie	4:19:16 (15,596)
Gray, Fraser	4:07:00 (12,343)
Gray, Geoffrey I	2:47:22 (384)
Gray, Ian	4:54:27 (24,543)
Gray, John A	4:26:52 (17,706)
Gray, Jonathan A	4:24:18 (16,924)
Gray, Kelvin D	3:46:36 (7,264)
Gray, Kevin N	5:21:24 (29,287)
Gray, Kieron L	5:18:43 (28,908)
Gray, Malcolm F	4:20:51 (16,035)
Gray, Malcolm J	6:07:09 (33,397)
Gray, Mark A	5:51:55 (32,407)
Gray, Martin P	3:30:13 (4,480)
Gray, Michael J	4:11:01 (13,354)
Gray, Neil	3:09:20 (1,846)
Gray, Nick	3:27:21 (3,987)
Gray, Nigel	5:08:15 (27,256)
Gray, Oliver	4:34:12 (19,624)
Gray, Patrick J	4:03:22 (11,474)
Gray, Paul	4:21:26 (16,188)
Gray, Paul R	3:48:18 (7,657)
Gray, Peter	2:59:12 (1,056)
Gray, Philip K	5:47:39 (32,070)
Gray, Scott R	5:36:58 (31,098)
Gray, Steven J	5:16:47 (28,597)
Gray, Stuart N	4:20:12 (15,854)
Grayling, Patrick H	5:15:49 (28,458)
Grazzini, Romeo	3:33:55 (5,030)
Grealy, Michael J	3:46:14 (7,188)
Greaney, Ronald P	5:18:29 (28,860)
Greaney, Stuart F	3:41:00 (6,180)
Greasby, Peter W	4:42:13 (21,683)
Greatorex, Chad N	4:34:05 (19,587)
Greaves, Daniel	5:09:29 (27,437)
Greaves, Paul M	3:03:38 (1,379)
Greeff, Gordon	5:49:43 (32,243)
Greeff, Johannes P	4:42:13 (21,683)
Greeffier, Christophe P	2:55:30 (767)
Green, Alexander L	4:02:00 (11,155)
Green, Alister	5:18:34 (28,877)
Green, Andrew	4:28:22 (18,129)
Green, Andrew	5:26:34 (29,929)
Green, Benjamin R	4:16:09 (14,755)
Green, Brett J	4:13:10 (13,928)
Green, Chris N	5:51:49 (32,397)
Green, Colin J	3:35:04 (5,194)
Green, Daniel	4:25:55 (17,404)
Green, David	3:05:03 (1,470)

Green, David	5:50:59 (32,332)	
Green, David A	4:41:47 (21,585)	
Green, David D	5:28:53 (30,233)	
Green, David J	3:09:05 (1,819)	
Green, David P	4:05:20 (11,955)	
Green, Francis A	4:39:08 (20,907)	
Green, James	4:46:53 (22,750)	
Green, Jeremy	6:56:41 (34,826)	
Green, Jim	5:02:03 (26,155)	
Green, Joe	4:58:18 (25,393)	
Green, John G	4:54:17 (24,496)	
Green, John J	4:26:14 (17,515)	
Green, John K	2:59:13 (1,057)	
Green, Jonathan P	3:49:30 (7,933)	
Green, Keith A	4:55:22 (24,751)	
Green, Keith D	3:28:41 (4,221)	
Green, Kevin R	4:16:33 (14,845)	
Green, Leo P	3:56:37 (9,696)	
Green, Mark G	3:50:29 (8,147)	
Green, Mark R	4:42:41 (21,795)	
Green, Matthew A	4:30:21 (18,690)	
Green, Matthew R	4:24:40 (17,032)	
Green, Michael	2:18:31 (20)	
Green, Michael	3:11:25 (2,073)	
Green, Michael D	3:31:15 (4,643)	
Green, Michael D	5:53:58 (32,561)	
Green, Michael S	3:51:18 (8,328)	
Green, Michael S	4:09:14 (12,897)	
Green, Michael T	5:08:27 (27,277)	
Green, Mick	3:06:03 (1,553)	
Green, Mike A	4:19:29 (15,662)	
Green, Nicholas	4:46:08 (22,585)	
Green, Nicholas E	4:18:33 (15,373)	
Green, Nigel	4:43:44 (22,043)	
Green, Norman J	3:48:08 (7,622)	
Green, Paul	3:58:41 (10,341)	
Green, Paul A	5:45:59 (31,933)	
Green, Peter	3:56:33 (9,675)	
Green, Peter W	3:45:11 (6,988)	
Green, Philip J	5:16:35 (28,561)	
Green, Richard W	4:38:38 (20,784)	
Green, Robin J	4:28:13 (18,091)	
Green, Shaun N	4:06:03 (12,107)	
Green, Stephen	4:36:29 (20,223)	
Green, Steven L	3:11:37 (2,089)	
Green, Stuart D	4:22:45 (16,546)	
Green, Thomas	5:59:49 (32,971)	
Green, Thomas C	3:11:16 (2,059)	
Green, Tony C	6:03:56 (33,219)	
Green, Tony J	3:44:28 (6,827)	
Green, Tony J	5:06:22 (26,936)	
Green, Trevor J	4:41:22 (21,484)	
Green, Wesley D	4:43:49 (22,058)	
Green, William H	4:51:30 (23,829)	
Greenacre, Neil R	3:14:22 (2,401)	
Greenaway, Jonathan M	4:49:35 (23,381)	
Greene, Alan	4:50:28 (23,618)	
Greene, Clive	6:48:07 (34,677)	
Greene, David A	6:08:36 (33,469)	
Greene, Harvey S	6:16:51 (33,816)	
Greene, Owen J	2:38:15 (166)	
Greener, John S	3:50:52 (8,228)	
Greenhaigh, Andrew	5:51:00 (32,334)	
Greenhalgh, Andrew F	4:14:51 (14,396)	
Greenhalgh, Clifford	4:48:39 (23,160)	
Greenhalgh, Ian F	3:55:33 (9,385)	
Greenhalgh, Jack	4:02:28 (11,262)	
Greenhalgh, Peter M	4:38:41 (20,794)	
Greenham, David H	4:16:18 (14,793)	
Greenhough, Anthony	3:43:27 (6,645)	
Greenland, James A	3:18:23 (2,820)	
Greenlaw, Raymond	3:02:38 (1,307)	
Greenleaf, Andrew H	2:33:56 (103)	
Greenley, Ben	5:16:23 (28,530)	
Greenough, Craig H	3:02:09 (1,274)	
Greenslade, Christopher W	4:27:51 (17,998)	
Greenslade, David M	4:08:46 (12,758)	
Greenslade, Oliver	3:53:07 (8,748)	
Greenway, Nick	5:14:37 (28,283)	
Greenway, Paul J	4:09:59 (13,086)	
Greenwell, James	3:10:19 (1,961)	
Greenwell, Robert N	5:35:45 (30,972)	
Greenwood, Andrew	4:07:56 (12,561)	
Greenwood, James	5:07:11 (27,096)	
Greenwood, Joel	4:50:22 (23,585)	
Greenwood, Jonathan R	4:03:10 (11,425)	
Greenwood, Matthew D	4:36:21 (20,177)	
Greenwood, Michael	5:18:37 (28,893)	
Greenwood, Peter A	3:53:45 (8,922)	
Greenwood, Tom	3:56:09 (9,552)	
Greer, David A	4:16:30 (14,836)	
Greer, James T	5:18:58 (28,940)	
Greeves, Jerry J	2:46:58 (370)	
Greevy, John	3:41:35 (6,294)	
Gregg, Stephen	4:05:07 (11,903)	
Gregg, William	5:33:56 (30,772)	
Gregg, William S	3:38:02 (5,653)	
Greggs, Jonathan W	3:51:31 (8,373)	
Gregory, Darren	5:13:47 (28,130)	
Gregory, David	4:24:18 (16,924)	
Gregory, David J	6:03:18 (33,168)	
Gregory, Edwin	3:27:10 (3,951)	
Gregory, John	6:01:42 (33,065)	
Gregory, Jonathan	4:47:16 (22,831)	
Gregory, Jonathan	5:34:35 (30,858)	
Gregory, Mark T	5:12:53 (27,982)	
Gregory, Michael J	4:10:21 (13,182)	
Gregory, Neil K	4:56:07 (24,920)	
Gregory, Nicholas A	3:09:34 (1,865)	
Gregory, Paul D	5:56:48 (32,761)	
Gregory, Paul F	2:48:56 (465)	
Gregory, Peter	4:53:20 (24,262)	
Gregory, Peter J	4:00:15 (10,778)	
Gregory, Robert P	3:07:28 (1,674)	
Gregory, Stephen P	5:09:07 (27,375)	
Gregory, Steven P	3:38:22 (5,705)	
Gregson, David	5:12:37 (27,929)	
Gregson, Dennis	4:18:28 (15,354)	
Gregson, Paul T	5:09:47 (27,482)	
Gregson, Warren A	3:44:36 (6,860)	
Grehan, Mark	4:37:30 (20,498)	
Grehan, Michael J	3:11:32 (2,081)	
Greig, Andrew J	4:18:54 (15,483)	
Greig, Edward S	3:20:03 (3,005)	
Greig, Jonathan M	3:14:08 (2,371)	
Greig, Lindsey C	5:46:48 (32,000)	
Greig, Paul H	5:52:48 (32,483)	
Gremo, Christopher S	4:33:05 (19,340)	
Gremo, Stuart N	5:40:02 (31,419)	
Gretton, Victor B	5:13:50 (28,138)	
Grevelius, Fredrik	3:25:49 (3,721)	
Grevendonk, Rik	3:11:51 (2,125)	
Greves, Daniel P	4:16:12 (14,765)	
Greville-Collins, Adam	4:11:53 (13,581)	
Grewal, Jeff	4:46:27 (22,657)	
Grey, Garry	3:39:19 (5,877)	
Grey, William M	3:24:19 (3,493)	
Greyling, Garth A	4:30:40 (18,764)	
Gribben, Lawrence D	4:07:42 (12,495)	
Grice, Andrew J	3:57:26 (9,961)	
Grice, Benjamin L	4:42:16 (21,693)	
Grice, Neil K	4:44:51 (22,285)	
Gridley, David P	3:50:52 (8,228)	
Grieco, Salvatore	4:46:27 (22,657)	
Grierson Rickford, Timothy	4:08:48 (12,769)	
Grieve, Andrew R	5:00:05 (25,792)	
Grieve, Graham D	3:16:16 (2,615)	
Grieve, Michael R	7:31:51 (35,142)	
Grieves-Smith, Peter M	4:52:44 (24,111)	
Griffault, Frederic	3:13:47 (2,337)	
Griffen, Richard D	4:45:54 (22,524)	
Griffin, Andrew P	4:13:46 (14,083)	
Griffin, Christopher M	5:16:17 (28,515)	
Griffin, Edward A	4:14:50 (14,390)	
Griffin, Mark	3:32:02 (4,753)	
Griffin, Mark S	3:39:21 (5,879)	
Griffin, Matthew J	5:37:57 (31,191)	
Griffin, Michael	4:51:58 (23,925)	
Griffin, Paul R	2:49:17 (477)	
Griffin, Paul S	6:38:05 (34,459)	
Griffith, John O	3:11:46 (2,114)	
Griffiths, Andrew	4:35:33 (19,986)	
Griffiths, Anthony E	3:29:06 (4,296)	
Griffiths, Bryn R	4:25:52 (17,392)	
Griffiths, David	3:54:47 (9,179)	
Griffiths, David J	4:28:09 (18,075)	
Griffiths, Emmet J	3:56:46 (9,740)	
Griffiths, Gareth J	5:43:54 (31,753)	
Griffiths, Geraint L	5:39:34 (31,380)	
Griffiths, Ian N	4:27:20 (17,833)	
Griffiths, Jackson E	4:48:54 (23,212)	
Griffiths, Johnathon	5:51:37 (32,382)	
Griffiths, Julian	3:34:46 (5,156)	
Griffiths, Justin J	3:33:52 (5,024)	
Griffiths, Keith D	4:35:02 (19,860)	
Griffiths, Mark	4:12:58 (13,874)	
Griffiths, Mark	5:30:25 (30,407)	
Griffiths, Mark A	3:13:57 (2,353)	
Griffiths, Mark B	4:03:26 (11,489)	
Griffiths, Mark D	4:02:46 (11,335)	
Griffiths, Mark J	4:37:44 (20,561)	
Griffiths, Martin D	3:58:47 (10,382)	
Griffiths, Michael	4:44:35 (22,225)	
Griffiths, Michael W	4:42:35 (21,765)	
Griffiths, Mike J	3:42:04 (6,391)	
Griffiths, Nicholas J	5:17:58 (28,776)	
Griffiths, Nigel E	3:42:56 (6,531)	
Griffiths, Nigel P	4:18:18 (15,296)	
Griffiths, Owen E	4:32:13 (19,141)	
Griffiths, Paul	4:21:24 (16,171)	
Griffiths, Paul A	5:19:48 (29,076)	
Griffiths, Paul W	3:10:04 (1,928)	
Griffiths, Thomas P	4:15:23 (14,547)	
Grifiths, Peter	3:25:08 (3,612)	
Griggs, John	4:23:43 (16,781)	
Griggs, Michael	5:42:31 (31,628)	
Grigson, David J	4:39:55 (21,117)	
Grilli, Stefano	3:01:49 (1,249)	
Grimault, Fabrice	3:43:49 (6,709)	
Grime, Christopher J	4:11:22 (13,444)	
Grimes, Christopher J	4:05:30 (11,985)	
Grimes, Ian P	3:45:38 (7,069)	
Grimes, Joseph G	5:57:01 (32,774)	
Grimes, Keith D	4:36:20 (20,172)	
Grimes, Norman S	4:46:51 (22,744)	
Grimes, Philip	2:50:11 (504)	
Grimmer, Harold	6:01:28 (33,052)	
Grimsdale, David J	3:28:40 (4,219)	
Grimsey, Mark	4:16:08 (14,751)	
Grimsey, William	3:36:54 (5,482)	
Grimshaw, David P	3:46:30 (7,243)	
Grimshaw, Grahame D	4:11:01 (13,354)	
Grimsley, Paul	6:12:55 (33,659)	
Grimwade, David J	6:12:13 (33,626)	
Grimwood, Graham A	4:31:51 (19,052)	
Grinbergs, Andris R	5:53:59 (32,562)	
Grindle, Stephen P	4:49:06 (23,267)	
Grindley, Samuel C	3:56:37 (9,696)	
Grindu, Louis	4:09:29 (12,955)	
Grinhaff, Philip D	4:39:38 (21,053)	
Grint, Lee S	5:46:50 (32,002)	
Grinter, Andrew B	4:29:52 (18,555)	
Grinter, Carl E	3:32:32 (4,825)	
Grist, Anthony P	5:02:59 (26,338)	
Grist, Stuart M	5:02:59 (26,338)	
Gristwood, Andrew T	3:12:09 (2,159)	
Gritton, Terence D	4:08:00 (12,571)	
Grivel, Jean-Louis	3:07:56 (1,708)	
Grocott, Tony E	3:55:42 (9,429)	
Grogan, Peter	5:00:58 (25,970)	
Groody, Vincent P	4:21:25 (16,179)	
Groom, Alex W	3:37:53 (5,631)	
Groom, Gary	3:32:27 (4,811)	
Groom, Jamie T	4:42:57 (21,860)	
Groom, Michael A	4:15:40 (14,624)	
Groom, Paul A	4:57:11 (25,171)	
Groombridge, Jason N	5:17:04 (28,660)	
Groombridge, Jeremy C	5:23:45 (29,576)	
Groombridge, Stephen P	2:45:49 (342)	
Groome, Desmond T	3:44:51 (6,928)	
Grose, Tim J	2:33:53 (102)	
Gross, Gary	4:18:42 (15,433)	
Gross, Karl	3:23:58 (3,443)	
Gross, Nicholas M	3:24:30 (3,516)	
Gross, Ray C	4:45:53 (22,516)	
Grosso, Giulio	3:54:06 (8,996)	
Grosvenor, Iain R	4:49:29 (23,355)	
Grosvenor, John B	4:56:36 (25,042)	
Grosvenor, Michael W	5:27:05 (29,985)	

Grosz, Harald	3:29:51 (4,428)
Grout, Andrew D	5:13:17 (28,040)
Grout, Steven R	3:35:58 (5,337)
Grove, Andrew P	3:21:51 (3,169)
Grove, Darren	3:58:17 (10,220)
Groves, Andrew D	3:51:14 (8,309)
Groves, Carl A	3:20:03 (3,005)
Groves, Glen	2:34:19 (106)
Groves, Ian J	5:26:24 (29,912)
Groves, Nick T	2:58:49 (1,016)
Groves, Patrick N	4:43:28 (21,969)
Groves, Ricky A	6:04:10 (33,229)
Groves, Rik G	3:44:39 (6,868)
Grubb, Andrew D	3:22:55 (3,286)
Grubb, Darren C	6:13:00 (33,664)
Grubb, Martyn P	3:16:28 (2,631)
Grubjerg, Andreas B	4:05:38 (12,012)
Gruenes, Walter D	4:15:07 (14,478)
Gruenewald, Arnd	3:11:56 (2,133)
Gruenig, Hans-Peter	4:58:28 (25,436)
Gruenzinger, Walter	3:16:12 (2,603)
Grundberg, Christopher O	4:05:23 (11,964)
Grundy, Ian M	3:42:24 (6,450)
Grundy, James	4:15:48 (14,660)
Grundy, Kieran J	3:44:01 (6,746)
Grunwaldt, Ryan T	4:38:39 (20,786)
Gryce, Andy	5:25:23 (29,787)
Grzesiczek, Stefan J	4:34:56 (19,836)
Guard, Martin J	3:58:42 (10,347)
Gubbins, Matthew J	5:13:03 (28,007)
Guck, Philip J	6:13:30 (33,680)
Gudka, Bobby	5:39:35 (31,381)
Gudka, Chandrakant R	5:22:57 (29,480)
Gudka, Piyush Z	3:51:46 (8,429)
Gudmundsson, Niels R	3:48:34 (7,730)
Gueguen, Christian	3:31:17 (4,649)
Guerin, James D	4:55:48 (24,841)
Guermellou, Abdel H	4:45:00 (22,325)
Guerrero, Pablo	4:13:45 (14,077)
Guerrier, Chris	3:00:27 (1,156)
Guerrieri, Mireno	4:16:20 (14,805)
Guest, Benjamin J	3:04:01 (1,402)
Guest, Henry	4:04:16 (11,698)
Guest, Ian	4:20:21 (15,898)
Guest, Martin N	5:34:52 (30,891)
Guest, Nicholas D	3:39:25 (5,896)
Guest, Robert J	3:11:20 (2,063)
Gueterbock, Tom F	3:43:32 (6,658)
Gueusquin, Philippe	3:39:31 (5,917)
Guichaoua, Alain	3:32:56 (4,880)
Guichot, Christian	3:57:10 (9,880)
Guichot, Guilhem	3:13:46 (2,335)
Guidi, Silvio	3:43:59 (6,737)
Guidobaldi, Franco	4:08:08 (12,598)
Guihen, Patrick C	5:13:44 (28,119)
Guillemain, Philippe	2:47:24 (385)
Guinness, Jon H	4:42:55 (21,855)
Guisasola, Inigo	4:21:22 (16,164)
Guise, Stephen R	4:18:26 (15,345)
Guiseley, Andrew	3:12:29 (2,194)
Gulaid, Abdirashid	6:24:45 (34,083)
Gullis, Peter K	3:37:06 (5,515)
Gulliver, John C	3:34:26 (5,116)
Gulliver, Keith P	5:35:11 (30,927)
Gumez, Patrick	3:58:37 (10,314)
Gummer, Matthew J	3:44:19 (6,799)
Gunatilake, Harish R	5:29:05 (30,258)
Gunby, Craig W	2:56:54 (880)
Gundersen, Erling	3:43:23 (6,633)
Guneri, Erol	6:22:37 (34,012)
Gunn, Adam D	4:44:11 (22,138)
Gunn, Graham	4:20:57 (16,067)
Gunn, John A	4:20:22 (15,903)
Gunn, Mark L	4:20:57 (16,067)
Gunn, Peter R	3:50:37 (8,173)
Gunnel, Peter R	5:33:03 (30,673)
Gunnell, Jonathan	4:31:19 (18,923)
Gunner, Mark J	5:26:36 (29,935)
Gunning, Derrick L	4:55:40 (24,804)
Gunson, Thomas H	3:52:15 (8,542)
Gunstensen, Paul J	4:49:33 (23,371)
Gunter, Martyn E	5:42:48 (31,662)
Gunther, Steven P	3:06:11 (1,566)
Gunz, Alexander J	3:23:14 (3,339)
Gupta, Puneet K	4:56:05 (24,912)
Gupta, Sanjeev	4:17:34 (15,106)
Gupta, Suman	3:27:48 (4,077)
Gurd, Richard	2:50:54 (536)
Gurria, Angel	4:16:27 (14,828)
Gurung, Posh B	7:08:33 (34,962)
Gurung, Raj	4:52:05 (23,961)
Guschmann, Michael	3:28:57 (4,266)
Gustafson, Michael J	3:20:45 (3,070)
Guszpit, Ireneusz	3:29:37 (4,376)
Gutheil, Joa Carlos T	3:59:19 (10,522)
Guthrie, Duncan	6:29:32 (34,242)
Guthrie, Peter C	4:52:53 (24,146)
Gutierrez, Donato A	3:54:13 (9,025)
Gutierrez, Oscar	3:54:33 (9,112)
Gutierrez Ribalagua, Gonzalo	4:52:00 (23,936)
Guy, Allister C	4:32:37 (19,231)
Guy, Bernard	4:22:26 (16,453)
Guy, Dave D	3:40:46 (6,132)
Guy, Fred	5:36:35 (31,066)
Guy, Philip A	5:07:47 (27,187)
Guyard, Fabrice	4:58:14 (25,380)
Gwiliam, Lee	4:25:17 (17,211)
Gwillam, Andy M	2:51:23 (557)
Gwilliam, David	3:41:52 (6,348)
Gwizdala, Peter	5:23:30 (29,543)
Gwynne, Alan J	4:36:21 (20,177)
Gylfason, Oddgeir	3:49:09 (7,854)
Gyte, Barry G	2:52:30 (609)
Haas, Otto	2:57:36 (925)
Haas, Roger	3:46:03 (7,147)
Haas, Vincent	4:09:44 (13,022)
Haase, Wolfgang	4:03:40 (11,538)
Habbestad, Olav	3:15:24 (2,513)
Habkirk, John F	6:32:52 (34,326)
Habrant, Arnaud	3:36:12 (5,371)
Hack, Raymond	3:41:34 (6,290)
Hack, Richard S	4:16:32 (14,842)
Hacker, Craig	4:17:22 (15,055)
Hackett, Adrian M	7:27:17 (35,114)
Hackman, Michael J	5:00:32 (25,881)
Hackney, Thomas	4:13:03 (13,894)
Hackwood, Colin R	4:29:29 (18,457)
Hadden, Nicholas D	3:56:16 (9,589)
Haddleton, Steven	3:19:36 (2,955)
Haddock, Paul	5:11:22 (27,719)
Haddow, Reid A	4:07:13 (12,395)
Haddow, Tristan H	4:14:38 (14,325)
Haden, Mark H	4:07:18 (12,421)
Hadfield, Graham	6:46:16 (34,630)
Hadfield, Hugh W	4:35:51 (20,055)
Hadfield, John B	5:16:40 (28,571)
Hadfield, Tom	2:38:43 (170)
Hadi, Benjamin	5:48:31 (32,136)
Hadjidakis, Dimitri	4:30:24 (18,702)
Hadjimichael, Stelios	3:51:24 (8,353)
Hadjioannou, Panny	4:25:48 (17,377)
Hadley, Greg R	3:24:08 (3,462)
Hadley, James A	4:37:27 (20,482)
Hadley, Ronald J	4:36:59 (20,350)
Hadwen, Tom	4:03:19 (11,465)
Haering, Markus	4:27:23 (17,853)
Haesaert, Ronny A	3:46:44 (7,290)
Haesli, Markus	3:17:32 (2,742)
Haffenden, Gary A	4:28:21 (18,122)
Hagen, Oeivind R	4:48:23 (23,100)
Hagenbucher, Carsten	3:46:32 (7,247)
Haggart, Robin J	3:51:19 (8,333)
Haggas, Neil R	2:55:30 (767)
Hagger, Andrew G	4:26:39 (17,648)
Haggert, Stephen P	4:54:43 (24,598)
Haggerty, Del P	4:37:39 (20,529)
Haggerty, Michael J	5:45:24 (31,889)
Haggett, Robert J	5:03:35 (26,440)
Hague, Stephen J	3:56:35 (9,687)
Hague-Holmes, Martin G	4:27:51 (17,998)
Hagues, Mark W	5:12:45 (27,959)
Hahn, Adam R	4:00:06 (10,752)
Hahn, Maik	5:19:13 (28,976)
Hahnel, James C	4:36:22 (20,188)
Haig, Derek W	3:59:12 (10,496)
Haigh, Gary K	5:11:44 (27,779)
Haigh, Jason	3:17:35 (2,746)
Haigh, Keith R	4:02:58 (11,383)
Haigh, Michael D	4:34:57 (19,842)
Haighton, Barry P	3:38:02 (5,653)
Haile, Anthony J	3:36:31 (5,430)
Haile, Paul M	5:23:59 (29,617)
Hain, John	4:23:34 (16,746)
Haines, Andrew	4:07:16 (12,409)
Haines, Ian J	3:21:59 (3,183)
Haines, Richard A	3:23:21 (3,358)
Haines, Stephen	3:17:10 (2,697)
Haines, Timothy C	4:00:42 (10,887)
Haines, Trevor	4:23:08 (16,640)
Haines, Trevor	6:35:09 (34,382)
Hainsworth, David	3:54:38 (9,135)
Hainsworth, Paul J	3:11:28 (2,076)
Hair, Simon P	4:08:43 (12,743)
Haire, Geoffrey R	4:22:45 (16,546)
Haire, Nick A	3:22:05 (3,196)
Hairsine, Richard M	4:13:15 (13,952)
Hakhamaneshi, Bahram	4:15:26 (14,558)
Haldane, Dan	3:50:26 (8,133)
Hale, Andrew	4:06:38 (12,250)
Hale, Brendon J	3:59:32 (10,582)
Hale, Bryan D	4:24:53 (17,090)
Hale, Jonathan D	4:37:41 (20,547)
Hales, Colin S	4:14:19 (14,248)
Hales, Daniel S	4:49:17 (23,300)
Hales, Jason	5:39:53 (31,403)
Halford, David	3:29:07 (4,300)
Halford, Matthew J	3:33:38 (4,979)
Halford, Peter P	3:12:27 (2,191)
Halgarth, Ben	3:59:31 (10,576)
Halkin, Cosh K	5:52:29 (32,463)
Hall, Alan W	4:54:02 (24,436)
Hall, Andrew J	3:46:13 (7,182)
Hall, Andrew K	3:57:54 (10,110)
Hall, Anthony W	3:56:50 (9,766)
Hall, Arnold W	6:37:11 (34,436)
Hall, Benjamin J	3:36:14 (5,378)
Hall, Brian D	4:52:51 (24,140)
Hall, Brian R	2:33:02 (94)
Hall, Chad K	3:47:33 (7,466)
Hall, Chas R	3:58:29 (10,288)
Hall, Chris J	5:04:22 (26,578)
Hall, Christopher J	3:33:39 (4,983)
Hall, Christopher J	3:57:00 (9,815)
Hall, Clive S	4:26:52 (17,706)
Hall, Colin R	4:11:38 (13,518)
Hall, Cormac A	4:09:01 (12,831)
Hall, Daniel J	4:20:23 (15,909)
Hall, David	2:56:04 (811)
Hall, David A	5:20:27 (29,171)
Hall, David J	2:50:24 (510)
Hall, Gary F	5:55:09 (32,649)
Hall, Geoffrey A	4:28:55 (18,293)
Hall, Giles J	3:57:05 (9,850)
Hall, Giles W	4:09:23 (12,930)
Hall, Glenn M	5:00:40 (25,915)
Hall, Greg J	5:05:59 (26,868)
Hall, Ian D	4:06:05 (12,117)
Hall, Ian N	5:40:58 (31,505)
Hall, James	6:50:01 (34,709)
Hall, James A	4:58:52 (25,527)
Hall, James F	4:28:13 (18,091)
Hall, Jamie	4:16:54 (14,935)
Hall, John C	3:22:41 (3,261)
Hall, John D	4:32:36 (19,228)
Hall, Jonathan	3:47:40 (7,494)
Hall, Keith	4:15:51 (14,677)
Hall, Kieran D	5:09:18 (27,403)
Hall, Kristian J	4:29:29 (18,457)
Hall, Leslie	4:47:39 (22,927)
Hall, Marcus G	4:03:16 (11,449)
Hall, Mark	4:03:44 (11,514)
Hall, Mark	4:18:16 (15,283)
Hall, Mark J	4:56:12 (24,940)
Hall, Mark W	5:13:45 (28,125)
Hall, Martin J	4:13:59 (14,141)
Hall, Martin K	2:46:03 (350)
Hall, Michael	4:01:57 (11,138)
Hall, Michael	4:42:57 (21,860)
Hall, Michael R	4:55:42 (24,818)

Hall, Mike A 5:54:01 (32,567)
Hall, Miles D 4:02:20 (11,226)
Hall, Patrick D 2:51:22 (554)
Hall, Peter 3:19:57 (2,992)
Hall, Peter 4:14:23 (14,267)
Hall, Peter 4:44:15 (22,155)
Hall, Peter C 5:26:09 (29,888)
Hall, Raymond 4:03:28 (11,490)
Hall, Richard 5:13:13 (28,025)
Hall, Richard A 3:28:34 (4,211)
Hall, Richard J 4:11:53 (13,581)
Hall, Richard W 3:17:05 (2,687)
Hall, Rob 2:44:39 (311)
Hall, Sam T 4:26:00 (17,435)
Hall, Simon C 4:11:13 (13,409)
Hall, Steve J 4:33:44 (19,499)
Hall, Stuart 4:22:59 (16,595)
Hall, Stuart 5:13:14 (28,029)
Hall, Tim 3:53:57 (8,964)
Hallam, Christopher 4:49:19 (23,315)
Hallam, Ian W 3:55:08 (9,258)
Hallam, Luke F 4:41:09 (21,432)
Hallam, Neil 4:28:41 (18,212)
Hallard, Richard J 3:54:04 (8,991)
Hallett, Martin J 6:03:19 (33,170)
Hallett, Steve 4:49:39 (23,411)
Halley, Simon J 3:25:21 (3,651)
Halliday, Ben D 4:23:40 (16,766)
Halliday, Chris 3:51:57 (8,473)
Halliday, Garry 5:24:10 (29,640)
Halliday, John N 5:09:17 (27,400)
Halliday, Karl J 3:48:33 (7,727)
Halliday, Patrick L 5:01:31 (26,069)
Hallifax, Ben G 3:33:13 (4,911)
Halling, Rod 3:55:42 (9,429)
Hallinon, Carl W 5:14:28 (28,258)
Hallion, Simon J 5:20:25 (29,165)
Hallitt, Andrew S 3:49:12 (7,863)
Halliwell, John K 3:08:42 (1,780)
Halls, Mark A 3:13:20 (2,276)
Halls, Terry 4:55:11 (24,717)
Halms, Jason M 5:34:02 (30,786)
Halpenny, Kieran P 4:17:46 (15,152)
Halpin, Liam J 4:09:37 (12,987)
Halpin, Michael J 4:12:44 (13,811)
Halsall, Alan 6:50:02 (34,718)
Halvey, James P 4:03:41 (11,542)
Halvey, Martin 2:56:50 (877)
Hamadi, Abdelmounhim 3:25:12 (3,624)
Hamblin, Steven H 4:11:01 (13,354)
Hamer, Carl A 4:07:17 (12,413)
Hamer, Chip 3:04:48 (1,451)
Hamer, David C 3:23:14 (3,339)
Hamer, David R 3:37:05 (5,512)
Hamer, Mark 2:54:29 (711)
Hamer, Michael A 5:34:47 (30,883)
Hames, Graham M 5:33:37 (30,738)
Hamidi, Said 2:25:17 (47)
Hamill, Eric P 4:15:02 (14,462)
Hamill, Gary 4:26:54 (17,718)
Hamill, Richard 5:17:29 (28,713)
Hamilton, Alistair 4:03:14 (11,440)
Hamilton, Allan D 3:23:30 (3,374)
Hamilton, Anthony P 4:23:53 (16,822)
Hamilton, Barry R 4:51:17 (23,789)
Hamilton, Bob 3:39:43 (5,954)
Hamilton, Brian 4:40:45 (21,320)
Hamilton, Brian R 3:30:19 (4,490)
Hamilton, Craig 3:38:17 (5,695)
Hamilton, Declan N 4:59:23 (25,639)
Hamilton, Duncan J 4:03:36 (11,526)
Hamilton, Edward S 3:09:25 (1,853)
Hamilton, Graeme 5:06:53 (27,039)
Hamilton, Graham R 4:18:34 (15,382)
Hamilton, Jeremy I 5:01:30 (26,064)
Hamilton, Kevin M 6:56:17 (34,817)
Hamilton, Mark R 4:47:21 (22,845)
Hamilton, Stephen G 5:35:39 (30,962)
Hamilton, William 3:36:46 (5,462)
Hamilton-Brown, Robert V 5:53:15 (32,520)
Hamke, Hans-Wilhelm 3:28:47 (4,240)
Hamlett, Mark A 4:52:54 (24,149)
Hamlett, Peter 4:47:13 (22,823)
Hamley, Jeremy F 3:10:14 (1,951)
Hamlin, Richard J 4:13:27 (14,003)
Hamman, Wessel J 4:56:55 (25,117)
Hammel, Matthew T 4:35:51 (20,055)
Hammer, Matthias L 4:58:04 (25,343)
Hammer, Robert H 3:56:55 (9,787)
Hammett, Rohan J 3:45:29 (7,047)
Hammond, Andrew P 3:56:59 (9,809)
Hammond, Brendan W 5:00:12 (25,820)
Hammond, Daniel J 3:11:14 (2,056)
Hammond, Gary D 5:13:14 (28,029)
Hammond, Gary M 3:47:11 (7,386)
Hammond, John A 3:41:46 (6,327)
Hammond, Lee 4:41:53 (21,603)
Hammond, Mark 3:46:40 (7,276)
Hammond, Miles 3:38:27 (5,718)
Hammond, Patrick M 3:50:47 (8,204)
Hammond, Stephen 6:21:45 (33,976)
Hamon, Jean-François 7:06:02 (34,938)
Hamon, Philippe 3:18:39 (2,843)
Hampden, Christopher S 5:00:33 (25,887)
Hampshire, Ben 3:47:36 (7,474)
Hampshire, Steve 4:35:22 (19,940)
Hampton, Edward T 4:13:14 (13,948)
Hampton, Neil G 4:25:18 (17,217)
Hampton, Ray 3:23:17 (3,348)
Hampton, Simon J 4:44:42 (22,249)
Hampton, Vincent 5:04:05 (26,527)
Hamshaw, David A 4:41:47 (21,585)
Hanafin, Thomas M 4:49:35 (23,381)
Hanbidge, John A 4:34:30 (19,711)
Hanbury, Martin A 3:54:57 (9,228)
Hancock, Anthony 3:38:51 (5,784)
Hancock, Dave 3:37:25 (5,559)
Hancock, Duncan W 4:41:07 (21,424)
Hancock, Keith G 5:01:57 (26,136)
Hancock, Peter L 4:12:24 (13,726)
Hancock, Rhys G 5:16:48 (28,601)
Hancock, Richard 4:32:06 (19,109)
Hancock, Robert S 4:31:51 (19,052)
Hancock, Wayne 4:45:56 (22,539)
Hancox, Duncan J 3:04:47 (1,449)
Hancox, Grenville R 4:27:12 (17,802)
Hancox, Michael J 4:12:23 (13,721)
Hancox, Robert G 3:25:04 (3,599)
Hand, Michael 3:24:42 (3,540)
Hand, Simon 4:14:14 (14,220)
Handel, Paul D 4:38:58 (20,868)
Handley, David I 3:49:44 (7,985)
Handley, Graham 4:17:42 (15,140)
Handley, Matthew D 5:11:18 (27,706)
Handley, Simon J 3:34:54 (5,168)
Handman, Luke 4:30:20 (18,687)
Hands, Richard S 3:59:38 (10,612)
Handy, Lionel P 3:22:57 (3,291)
Hanison, Darren 5:29:28 (30,303)
Hankinson, Gary 4:26:27 (17,585)
Hanley, Alan P 3:12:49 (2,229)
Hanley, Michael J 4:55:07 (24,707)
Hanley, Neil 5:29:28 (30,303)
Hanlon, Francis W 5:03:39 (26,453)
Hanly, Ray P 3:50:44 (8,194)
Hanman, Tim B 3:09:31 (1,858)
Hann, Jonathan H 4:50:57 (23,719)
Hanna, Thomas 3:51:02 (8,261)
Hannah, Dale R 5:15:30 (28,417)
Hannah, Gregor 3:56:37 (9,696)
Hannam, Scott 5:12:31 (27,913)
Hannan, Neil 4:22:01 (16,343)
Hannaway, Paul 4:47:42 (22,945)
Hannesbo, Morten 5:19:42 (29,060)
Hannigan, Andrew 4:25:41 (17,341)
Hannington, Nicholas R 6:01:27 (33,051)
Hannon, Myles T 4:21:34 (16,221)
Hanover, Nicholas 3:34:05 (5,058)
Hanscomb, John W 4:38:04 (20,638)
Hansen, Allan C 4:10:04 (13,106)
Hansen, Erwin 4:29:29 (18,457)
Hansen, Henrik R 4:11:52 (13,574)
Hansen, Jan Birger 2:43:16 (274)
Hansen, Joern 4:03:31 (11,504)
Hansen, Lars S 3:41:33 (6,287)
Hansen, Paul S 3:26:28 (3,843)
Hansler, Neil W 4:46:08 (22,585)
Hanson, Christopher 4:19:10 (15,567)
Hanson, David A 3:39:56 (5,985)
Hanson, David J 3:25:01 (3,588)
Hanson, David P 4:21:07 (16,094)
Hanson, Ian 7:26:02 (35,108)
Hanson, Paul 3:47:58 (7,568)
Hanson-Church, Steven A 4:29:05 (18,334)
Hanton, Glenn 5:58:18 (32,861)
Harber, Colin M 4:41:24 (21,498)
Harber, Kevin D 4:29:16 (18,390)
Harbinson, Christopher J 3:58:14 (10,203)
Harbinson, Michael A 3:58:13 (10,199)
Harbison, Iain S 4:49:16 (23,296)
Harbour, Jason V 2:50:41 (525)
Harbridge, Simon R 4:54:37 (24,578)
Hardacre, Stephen 4:48:56 (23,219)
Hardaker, Christopher D 3:43:30 (6,652)
Hardaker, Steve 3:14:33 (2,424)
Hardcastle, John K 3:48:18 (7,657)
Harden, Edward P 4:39:58 (21,129)
Hardick, John N 4:10:45 (13,275)
Hardicre, Steven T 5:40:21 (31,452)
Hardie, John 4:56:20 (24,971)
Hardie, Mark 5:03:45 (26,470)
Harding, Anthony 5:11:23 (27,723)
Harding, Ben 4:28:40 (18,206)
Harding, Chris J 4:44:32 (22,217)
Harding, Craig 3:56:51 (9,769)
Harding, George 5:06:55 (27,045)
Harding, Jason P 3:39:14 (5,858)
Harding, John D 4:48:58 (23,227)
Harding, Keith J 5:30:01 (30,363)
Harding, Mark 4:01:58 (11,145)
Harding, Neil C 5:28:13 (30,147)
Harding, Peter M 3:59:58 (10,717)
Harding, Philip L 3:18:56 (2,876)
Harding, Robert J 4:19:58 (15,792)
Harding, Terence P 5:09:13 (27,392)
Hardman, Arthur R 4:13:58 (14,135)
Hardman, Chris 5:29:34 (30,314)
Hardman, Damien M 4:56:58 (25,124)
Hardman, Graham L 6:49:26 (34,698)
Hardman, Michael J 4:15:44 (14,647)
Hardman, Philip D 4:18:29 (15,359)
Hardstaff, Ian N 3:22:08 (3,204)
Hardy, Graham 4:42:47 (21,819)
Hardy, Jim 4:01:58 (11,145)
Hardy, John C 3:29:21 (4,331)
Hardy, Jonathan C 4:00:18 (10,787)
Hardy, Philip J 4:58:31 (25,448)
Hardy, Sean 4:09:49 (13,045)
Hare, Mike J 3:59:10 (10,488)
Hare, Stephen 6:01:57 (33,074)
Haresnape, Charles W 4:15:54 (14,683)
Harfield, Patrick D 6:33:07 (34,332)
Harfield, Stephen P 6:33:05 (34,331)
Harfoot, Richard A 5:30:35 (30,421)
Harford, James A 4:10:07 (13,120)
Harford, Mark B 2:53:05 (639)
Harford, Richard 4:10:47 (13,281)
Hargedorn, Uwe 4:53:15 (24,237)
Hargreaves, Ian R 4:37:39 (20,529)
Hargreaves, James P 4:39:28 (21,001)
Hargreaves, John S 3:02:59 (1,330)
Hargreaves, Michael S 5:06:14 (26,909)
Hargreaves, Roger T 3:50:12 (8,084)
Hargreaves, Stephen J 4:11:19 (13,434)
Hargreves, Jonathan M 4:17:01 (14,962)
Hargreves, Tim 5:14:17 (28,225)
Hargroves, Robert E 4:59:09 (25,593)
Harji, Aswin 5:04:51 (26,658)
Harker, Alan L 3:44:53 (6,935)
Harker, Ian C 4:18:00 (15,210)
Harket, Chris 4:35:47 (20,039)
Harkin, Eamon J 4:39:03 (20,894)
Harkin, Ian 4:49:58 (23,488)
Harkins, Bernard J 4:57:14 (25,181)
Harkins, David 3:28:44 (4,229)
Harkness, Ian R 2:24:10 (41)
Harkness, John 4:37:33 (20,509)
Harkus, Gavin M 2:58:08 (966)
Harland, Alan 2:51:52 (580)

Harland, Derek L	4:17:48 (15,158)	
Harland, Garry	4:27:08 (17,785)	
Harley, Andrew K	4:53:19 (24,257)	
Harley, Colin P	3:16:13 (2,606)	
Harley, Richard A	5:12:41 (27,940)	
Harling, Andrew J	6:03:13 (33,161)	
Harlow, Carl S	4:12:51 (13,844)	
Harlow, David T	3:39:30 (5,913)	
Harlow, Derek	3:51:41 (8,408)	
Harlow, Gary D	3:49:27 (7,924)	
Harman, Alan	3:26:47 (3,897)	
Harman, Matthew P	3:57:10 (9,880)	
Harmer, Bob J	5:00:44 (25,923)	
Harmer, Charles R	5:13:08 (28,014)	
Harmer, William E	5:13:43 (28,116)	
Harmsworth, Michael D	4:35:19 (19,911)	
Harness, Ben D	4:01:54 (11,128)	
Harney, Brian	3:30:54 (4,590)	
Harnwell, Tony P	5:26:28 (29,918)	
Harper, Andrew J	4:55:27 (24,765)	
Harper, Andrew M	3:29:36 (4,370)	
Harper, Anthony	3:48:11 (7,631)	
Harper, Aubrey G	4:08:56 (12,809)	
Harper, Charles D	3:23:57 (3,441)	
Harper, Chris	3:47:04 (7,364)	
Harper, Giles E	4:37:47 (20,575)	
Harper, Graham	4:24:48 (17,071)	
Harper, Ian M	4:08:33 (12,702)	
Harper, John	4:44:34 (22,222)	
Harper, Nicholas P	4:11:24 (13,453)	
Harper, Paul W	2:34:09 (104)	
Harper, Robert A	4:57:20 (25,199)	
Harper, Robin A	3:55:32 (9,376)	
Harper, Steven	5:25:51 (29,847)	
Harper, Stuart J	4:51:16 (23,786)	
Harper, Tim F	4:17:27 (15,084)	
Harries, Paul J	4:40:55 (21,366)	
Harries, Richard	5:29:16 (30,268)	
Harries, Stuart P	3:39:57 (5,986)	
Harrill, George	4:23:16 (16,675)	
Harrington, Jonathon A	5:55:26 (32,673)	
Harrington, Malcolm F	3:58:39 (10,323)	
Harrington, Marcus G	4:06:31 (12,218)	
Harrington, Patrick	5:04:29 (26,595)	
Harrington, Steven G	3:53:36 (8,883)	
Harriott, Craig	5:28:41 (30,206)	
Harris, Alexander S	3:00:13 (1,141)	
Harris, Andrew D	5:16:00 (28,479)	
Harris, Andrew P	4:41:12 (21,446)	
Harris, Barry G	4:48:37 (23,154)	
Harris, Ben T	3:54:33 (9,112)	
Harris, Brian C	4:22:31 (16,476)	
Harris, Carl	3:02:01 (1,263)	
Harris, Colin D	4:53:24 (24,275)	
Harris, David M	4:52:57 (24,158)	
Harris, David P	4:05:01 (11,864)	
Harris, David P	4:09:05 (12,853)	
Harris, Garry	2:58:21 (977)	
Harris, Gary	2:44:04 (296)	
Harris, George P	4:50:05 (23,508)	
Harris, Giles	3:35:52 (5,317)	
Harris, Graham D	6:45:08 (34,621)	
Harris, Jack H	4:50:37 (23,655)	
Harris, James	4:49:38 (23,408)	
Harris, Jamie R	3:19:30 (2,937)	
Harris, Jason D	4:19:49 (15,756)	
Harris, Jeffrey D	5:12:24 (27,886)	
Harris, John	4:30:10 (18,648)	
Harris, Julian	4:51:41 (23,869)	
Harris, Kieran P	5:34:24 (30,833)	
Harris, Lawrence J	4:08:28 (12,687)	
Harris, Mark R	5:01:22 (26,036)	
Harris, Matt	4:48:53 (23,205)	
Harris, Matthew C	3:24:10 (3,468)	
Harris, Matthew I	5:01:03 (25,986)	
Harris, Michael T	3:40:21 (6,064)	
Harris, Neil	4:01:56 (11,136)	
Harris, Nigel	4:25:35 (17,310)	
Harris, Paul	4:12:23 (13,721)	
Harris, Paul D	3:51:25 (8,359)	
Harris, Paul D	4:38:27 (20,745)	
Harris, Paul F	6:23:46 (34,049)	
Harris, Peter J	4:11:08 (13,388)	
Harris, Peter J	4:37:47 (20,575)	
Harris, Peter J	7:06:17 (34,942)	
Harris, Peter N	5:19:22 (29,002)	
Harris, Phillip I	4:04:29 (11,741)	
Harris, Rhydwyn	3:36:03 (5,346)	
Harris, Richard J	4:08:24 (12,667)	
Harris, Richard J	4:10:23 (13,194)	
Harris, Richard J	4:44:44 (22,255)	
Harris, Robert J	2:50:36 (521)	
Harris, Robin S	4:15:34 (14,599)	
Harris, Rod	2:30:52 (76)	
Harris, Simon	5:22:07 (29,368)	
Harris, Simon	5:29:26 (30,297)	
Harris, Simon P	4:55:34 (24,783)	
Harris, Stephen	3:21:09 (3,100)	
Harris, Steve J	4:39:30 (21,013)	
Harris, Steven	6:39:43 (34,503)	
Harris, Steven P	4:53:44 (24,363)	
Harris, Steven R	4:30:47 (18,789)	
Harris, Tim E	4:07:35 (12,472)	
Harris, Tim P	3:14:29 (2,411)	
Harris, Timothy J	2:59:46 (1,108)	
Harris, William R	3:58:33 (10,303)	
Harrison, Adrian J	5:30:51 (30,445)	
Harrison, Andrew J	2:42:07 (245)	
Harrison, Brian	4:56:47 (25,090)	
Harrison, Chad A	6:01:33 (33,057)	
Harrison, David A	5:06:01 (26,876)	
Harrison, David J	4:15:33 (14,593)	
Harrison, Derek W	3:30:28 (4,518)	
Harrison, James	4:31:43 (19,024)	
Harrison, James A	4:45:32 (22,439)	
Harrison, John T	4:19:27 (15,649)	
Harrison, Jonathan C	3:50:13 (8,089)	
Harrison, Jude D	4:26:46 (17,683)	
Harrison, Julian S	5:13:11 (28,021)	
Harrison, Laurence O	3:29:33 (4,364)	
Harrison, Mark	4:11:05 (13,375)	
Harrison, Mark	4:27:22 (17,845)	
Harrison, Mark W	4:16:20 (14,805)	
Harrison, Martin	3:43:31 (6,654)	
Harrison, Martin J	5:32:24 (30,605)	
Harrison, Michael W	4:32:01 (19,093)	
Harrison, Nick A	4:16:06 (14,738)	
Harrison, Oliver	3:34:54 (5,168)	
Harrison, Paul	4:34:20 (19,671)	
Harrison, Paul B	4:10:28 (13,218)	
Harrison, Peter J	5:06:49 (27,020)	
Harrison, Richard	3:50:52 (8,228)	
Harrison, Richard P	3:08:33 (1,762)	
Harrison, Richard P	3:46:21 (7,211)	
Harrison, Robert J	3:49:13 (7,866)	
Harrison, Robert M	2:59:22 (1,078)	
Harrison, Scott D	3:52:20 (8,563)	
Harrison, Simon W	3:24:52 (3,564)	
Harrison, Stephen	4:03:45 (11,559)	
Harrison, Stephen J	4:36:14 (20,141)	
Harrison, Steve	3:09:53 (1,908)	
Harrison, Steve J	4:02:05 (11,181)	
Harrison, Tim J	4:53:01 (24,177)	
Harrison, Tom	4:18:16 (15,283)	
Harris-Watts, Chris P	4:11:16 (13,419)	
Harrold, Kevan	4:59:25 (25,647)	
Harrow, Martin D	3:24:44 (3,544)	
Harry, Chris	2:36:57 (137)	
Harry, Ian D	3:41:32 (6,282)	
Harston, Dale	3:56:44 (9,734)	
Hart, Al	2:31:23 (82)	
Hart, Andrew C	4:45:39 (22,472)	
Hart, Andrew D	2:51:31 (564)	
Hart, Andy D	4:59:27 (25,653)	
Hart, Anthony W	4:36:23 (20,194)	
Hart, Craig A	4:00:10 (10,759)	
Hart, David W	2:59:26 (1,084)	
Hart, Dominic	3:59:14 (10,503)	
Hart, James	3:44:18 (6,796)	
Hart, Malcolm	4:04:29 (11,741)	
Hart, Mark A	4:07:29 (12,455)	
Hart, Matthew	4:26:06 (17,475)	
Hart, Paul M	3:20:13 (3,020)	
Hart, Peter J	3:57:23 (9,945)	
Hart, Tony D	3:12:01 (2,142)	
Harte, David	4:53:01 (24,177)	
Harte, James	4:05:38 (12,012)	
Harte, Tony	3:31:27 (4,671)	
Hartland, Chris C	4:43:36 (22,007)	
Hartle, Joseph	5:10:51 (27,624)	
Hartle, Peter	5:10:51 (27,624)	
Hartley, Adrian J	4:37:38 (20,527)	
Hartley, Alexander C	4:14:04 (14,173)	
Hartley, Chris	3:23:28 (3,370)	
Hartley, David	4:49:01 (23,241)	
Hartley, Geoffrey H	5:13:33 (28,091)	
Hartley, Jay	4:27:51 (17,998)	
Hartley, Kevin J	3:39:07 (5,836)	
Hartley, Steve	4:15:10 (14,493)	
Hartley, Steve	4:25:40 (17,337)	
Hartley, Stuart D	5:25:16 (29,775)	
Hartnell, Matthew	4:26:44 (17,672)	
Hartnett, Michael	4:58:06 (25,351)	
Hartnett, Peter	5:22:43 (29,456)	
Hartop, Rob M	4:26:17 (17,527)	
Hartshorn, George B	3:58:32 (10,296)	
Hartt, Leslie B	4:10:18 (13,169)	
Hartung, Adam J	4:09:36 (12,983)	
Harvey, Adrian J	5:55:29 (32,679)	
Harvey, Alan P	4:24:30 (16,994)	
Harvey, Alex	3:11:39 (2,098)	
Harvey, Andrew J	5:50:41 (32,315)	
Harvey, Benjamin W	4:28:16 (18,105)	
Harvey, Christopher	4:09:49 (13,045)	
Harvey, Christopher	6:50:01 (34,709)	
Harvey, David G	4:19:53 (15,770)	
Harvey, Derek J	5:01:29 (26,061)	
Harvey, Edward G	5:35:21 (30,940)	
Harvey, Glen D	3:36:31 (5,430)	
Harvey, Ian D	3:23:05 (3,311)	
Harvey, Ian M	3:10:43 (2,002)	
Harvey, James B	2:42:19 (248)	
Harvey, John P	4:42:26 (21,725)	
Harvey, Neil B	4:12:23 (13,721)	
Harvey, Peter	5:09:35 (27,451)	
Harvey, Peter J	3:08:05 (1,722)	
Harvey, Philip J	4:25:35 (17,310)	
Harvey, Stephen R	3:43:38 (6,677)	
Harvey, Terry G	3:55:43 (9,435)	
Harvey, Timothy J	5:37:06 (31,110)	
Harvie, Gavin D	3:12:52 (2,238)	
Harwood, David J	4:48:58 (23,227)	
Harwood, Derek H	5:20:36 (29,197)	
Harwood, Paul	2:30:43 (74)	
Harwood, Paul	4:09:06 (12,860)	
Harwood, Richard J	4:18:49 (15,470)	
Harwood, Simon J	3:16:14 (2,607)	
Haselhan, Jason	3:39:36 (5,930)	
Hashim, Simon J	5:27:54 (30,091)	
Haskett, David M	6:02:16 (33,094)	
Hasler, Paul G	2:29:20 (65)	
Hasler, Ralph	4:59:11 (25,600)	
Hasler, Tom	3:33:45 (4,998)	
Haslett, Francis P	5:54:37 (32,609)	
Haslett, Matthew	4:29:26 (18,442)	
Hassall, Joseph P	4:18:42 (15,433)	
Hassan-Hicks, Tanner	4:27:16 (17,818)	
Hassan-Hicks, Turgay	4:05:51 (12,057)	
Hassett, Daragm J	3:15:41 (2,540)	
Hasslacher, James M	3:30:32 (4,533)	
Hasson, John D	3:30:58 (4,599)	
Hastie, Richard P	4:01:42 (11,091)	
Hastings, Derek	4:34:06 (19,591)	
Hastings, Matthew	4:24:40 (17,032)	
Hastings, Neil A	6:01:42 (33,065)	
Hatch, David M	5:08:34 (27,295)	
Hatch, Robert J	3:40:04 (6,010)	
Hatcher, Gary	3:44:42 (6,880)	
Hatcher, Kevin C	4:13:49 (14,093)	
Hateley, Paul A	4:15:24 (14,551)	
Hatfield, Alexander J	4:19:14 (15,589)	
Hatfield, Rob J	4:38:26 (20,736)	
Hathaway, Adrian J	4:44:57 (22,313)	
Hathaway, Carl A	4:30:33 (18,739)	
Hather, Sean A	4:08:38 (12,722)	
Hathway, Mark S	4:12:28 (13,741)	
Hatley, Mark S	3:45:22 (7,023)	
Hatton, David G	4:12:22 (13,716)	
Hatton, Mark	5:11:17 (27,701)	

Hatton, Michael	2:47:18 (378)	
Hatton, Stephen J	3:04:52 (1,459)	
Haub, Karl-Erivan W	3:58:21 (10,243)	
Haugen, Lars A	4:36:16 (20,149)	
Haughton, Colin T	3:29:05 (4,291)	
Hauksson, Bjorn A	3:42:42 (6,498)	
Hauptfleisch, Erich	3:23:46 (3,411)	
Hausweiler, Ralf	4:09:28 (12,950)	
Hauxwell, Will	5:22:13 (29,377)	
Havard, Andrew R	4:11:25 (13,458)	
Havard, Martin	5:23:30 (29,543)	
Havard, Tom	5:17:57 (28,773)	
Havelin, Fintan P	5:18:00 (28,784)	
Havelock, John	4:40:48 (21,338)	
Havenhand, David C	3:07:44 (1,695)	
Havers, Nick P	3:51:04 (8,274)	
Havill, Robert S	4:26:54 (17,718)	
Haw, Richard A	5:29:07 (30,260)	
Haward, Rob D	3:48:05 (7,614)	
Hawes, Bill R	2:57:18 (907)	
Hawes, David R	2:48:26 (430)	
Hawes, Nicholas P	3:56:11 (9,571)	
Hawes, Steven A	3:58:02 (10,152)	
Hawes, Wesley J	3:13:54 (2,345)	
Hawker, Simon R	2:50:55 (537)	
Hawkes, Colin A	3:45:41 (7,074)	
Hawkes, Keith S	3:07:49 (1,701)	
Hawkes, Sean	7:52:16 (35,215)	
Hawkey, Nigel P	3:59:27 (10,557)	
Hawkins, Andrew R	2:58:37 (998)	
Hawkins, Ben L	5:18:36 (28,892)	
Hawkins, Daniel	3:39:00 (5,817)	
Hawkins, Daniel M	4:37:11 (20,408)	
Hawkins, Darren C	5:30:33 (30,416)	
Hawkins, Edward D	3:44:55 (6,940)	
Hawkins, Graeme	3:04:13 (1,412)	
Hawkins, Ian S	6:23:46 (34,049)	
Hawkins, Ivor G	3:36:24 (5,405)	
Hawkins, James M	4:41:33 (21,537)	
Hawkins, John B	4:06:28 (12,204)	
Hawkins, Jonathan D	3:44:23 (6,815)	
Hawkins, Kenneth V	4:51:00 (23,734)	
Hawkins, Martin S	3:10:29 (1,977)	
Hawkins, Neil J	4:28:47 (18,241)	
Hawkins, Robert J	4:13:28 (14,011)	
Hawkins, Stephen	4:14:39 (14,337)	
Hawkins, Timothy J	2:56:23 (834)	
Hawksley, Andrew K	5:14:15 (28,217)	
Hawliczek, Edward J	3:45:25 (7,037)	
Hawlinlzek, Simon E	4:15:18 (14,527)	
Haworth, Daniel R	5:24:39 (29,701)	
Haworth, Ian M	4:15:27 (14,563)	
Haworth, Martin J	4:36:13 (20,135)	
Hay, Alastair P	3:35:39 (5,290)	
Hay, David G	3:59:40 (10,620)	
Hay, John R	3:46:52 (7,318)	
Hay, John R	5:43:09 (31,693)	
Hay, Richard A	5:47:03 (32,022)	
Hayashi, Masao	5:22:15 (29,381)	
Haycock, Christopher A	4:56:37 (25,045)	
Haycock, Edward G	4:57:07 (25,157)	
Haycock, Patrick M	5:35:09 (30,925)	
Hayday, Marcus A	4:54:08 (24,456)	
Hayday, Nick T	3:53:14 (8,778)	
Hayden, Barry E	4:40:59 (21,385)	
Hayden, Christopher J	5:06:21 (26,931)	
Hayden, Colin J	4:47:04 (22,784)	
Hayden, Glynn P	5:46:05 (31,940)	
Hayden, Mark E	4:10:23 (13,194)	
Hayden, Neil A	3:48:04 (7,606)	
Hayden, Peter H	5:16:24 (28,535)	
Hayden, Stuart	4:34:14 (19,646)	
Haydon, Dennis J	5:42:44 (31,654)	
Hayes, Andrew B	3:23:12 (3,331)	
Hayes, Anthony M	3:36:40 (5,449)	
Hayes, Brian	4:53:58 (24,415)	
Hayes, Chris J	6:14:40 (33,723)	
Hayes, Colin F	5:14:40 (28,296)	
Hayes, David	5:25:01 (29,748)	
Hayes, John P	3:52:36 (8,629)	
Hayes, Julian	4:06:26 (12,197)	
Hayes, Ken	4:55:38 (24,799)	
Hayes, Leigh C	3:56:25 (9,637)	
Hayes, Malcolm	6:28:50 (34,211)	
Hayes, Nicholas	3:58:20 (10,237)	
Hayes, Peter J	4:17:43 (15,145)	
Hayes, Peter R	4:55:09 (24,713)	
Hayes, Roger B	2:56:10 (818)	
Hayes, Stuart D	4:54:33 (24,566)	
Hayler, Ian C	3:45:56 (7,122)	
Hayler, Robert	4:36:38 (20,263)	
Hayles, Timothy J	3:52:43 (8,664)	
Hayman, Craig J	3:57:26 (9,961)	
Haymes, Anthony S	3:40:58 (6,173)	
Haynes, Alex J	3:24:02 (3,452)	
Haynes, Alexander I	3:52:19 (8,560)	
Haynes, Andrew L	3:49:39 (7,965)	
Haynes, Anton	5:00:35 (25,893)	
Haynes, David C	3:45:23 (7,026)	
Haynes, Glyn	5:16:00 (28,479)	
Haynes, James R	3:56:20 (9,614)	
Haynes, John E	4:54:26 (24,534)	
Haynes, Kevin C	3:02:39 (1,309)	
Haynes, Leslie	5:11:08 (27,675)	
Haynes, Mark S	4:56:55 (25,117)	
Haynes, Stewart	3:17:00 (2,676)	
Haynes-Coote, Michael R	4:00:19 (10,790)	
Hays, Anthony D	3:58:37 (10,314)	
Hays, Brian P	4:51:40 (23,863)	
Haythornthwaite, James I	4:39:33 (21,027)	
Hayton, David M	3:11:31 (2,079)	
Hayton, James A	4:18:55 (15,489)	
Hayues, Michael G	3:33:07 (4,901)	
Hayward, Christopher N	3:55:34 (9,394)	
Hayward, Colin	4:29:33 (18,482)	
Hayward, Gavin P	3:13:22 (2,286)	
Hayward, Lee F	4:54:27 (24,543)	
Hayward, Neil	3:55:14 (9,284)	
Hayward, Peter J	3:59:09 (10,485)	
Hayward, Richard D	4:11:27 (13,474)	
Hayward, Rupert C	4:35:52 (20,058)	
Haywood, Benedict N	4:59:56 (25,764)	
Haywood, Nick J	4:20:43 (15,995)	
Haywood, Roy	5:15:58 (28,475)	
Haze, Lee E	5:55:18 (32,666)	
Hazel, Neil C	5:06:38 (26,990)	
Hazeldon, David	5:19:20 (28,997)	
Hazell, Justin L	4:07:26 (12,444)	
Hazotte, Christian	4:04:31 (11,749)	
Head, Anthony	5:51:42 (32,388)	
Head, Ashley	4:06:20 (12,177)	
Head, Gary J	4:07:13 (12,395)	
Head, Julian P	3:44:07 (6,763)	
Head, Peter J	5:45:35 (31,900)	
Head, Robert C	5:04:22 (26,578)	
Head, Stephen P	3:53:04 (8,733)	
Headly, Nicholas I	4:49:03 (23,250)	
Headon, David L	2:55:30 (767)	
Headon, Robert J	5:46:11 (31,954)	
Heal, David S	4:21:46 (16,276)	
Healey, Ben A	3:32:55 (4,879)	
Healey, Clive R	3:48:48 (7,788)	
Healey, David J	5:49:14 (32,206)	
Healey, James T	5:02:32 (26,234)	
Healey, Mark B	3:36:44 (5,457)	
Healey, Stephen M	4:45:00 (22,325)	
Healy, Christopher	3:19:27 (2,930)	
Healy, Daniel	5:24:06 (29,629)	
Healy, Finbar	4:19:33 (15,680)	
Healy, Gareth P	3:20:34 (3,053)	
Healy, Lee J	3:36:06 (5,355)	
Healy, Paul R	3:55:53 (9,484)	
Heaney, David	5:11:07 (27,670)	
Heaney, Michael	4:26:38 (17,643)	
Heap, Michael A	3:05:14 (1,490)	
Heapy, Terence	4:04:40 (11,786)	
Heard, Nicholas D	6:49:18 (34,696)	
Hearn, Clive D	3:34:45 (5,151)	
Hearn, Jason	4:34:23 (19,689)	
Hearn, Thomas W	3:45:20 (7,012)	
Hearnden, Simon T	3:02:33 (1,301)	
Hearne, Matthew	3:53:00 (8,717)	
Hearsey, Stephen D	5:27:50 (30,081)	
Heary, Philip	5:12:09 (27,853)	
Heasman, Julian G	4:18:38 (15,408)	
Heath, Alexander	3:50:54 (8,237)	
Heath, Barry R	4:09:20 (12,917)	
Heath, Frederick C	4:16:05 (14,734)	
Heath, Les J	2:51:34 (568)	
Heath, Philip M	4:14:35 (14,315)	
Heath, Rob D	4:30:22 (18,693)	
Heath, Roger	4:37:02 (20,364)	
Heath, Tom P	5:01:26 (26,047)	
Heathcote, Alex	4:47:05 (22,790)	
Heathcote, John	4:23:01 (16,604)	
Heathcote, Paul	3:59:17 (10,515)	
Heather, Adam J	5:24:55 (29,734)	
Heatherington, Jason R	3:28:30 (4,198)	
Heaton, Stuart P	2:56:12 (822)	
Heaton-Armstrong, John W	3:19:00 (2,881)	
Heaven, Lloyd S	4:48:06 (23,031)	
Heaver, Dan	3:42:35 (6,477)	
Hebenstreit, Joachim	3:50:21 (8,116)	
Hechtkopf, Michael	5:11:44 (27,779)	
Hedderly, Nicholas J	3:49:22 (7,906)	
Hedderwick, Robert S	3:38:17 (5,695)	
Heddle, James A	3:59:43 (10,635)	
Heddon, Anthony P	5:36:21 (31,034)	
Hedger, Graham	2:54:26 (707)	
Hedges, Brian R	4:35:41 (20,016)	
Hedges, Clive V	3:10:10 (1,945)	
Hedges, David A	5:07:10 (27,091)	
Hedges, Paul	3:56:34 (9,681)	
Hedges, Richard	4:11:25 (13,458)	
Hedley, Thomas R	5:50:20 (32,289)	
Heeks, Steve J	3:29:54 (4,438)	
Heel, Robin J	4:18:14 (15,273)	
Heeley, David	3:31:13 (4,634)	
Heeley, Paul	3:09:31 (1,858)	
Heeson, Mark E	5:01:35 (26,079)	
Hefferan, Mike J	6:54:52 (34,797)	
Hefferan, Rob	4:03:13 (11,435)	
Hefferman, Terry	3:55:21 (9,321)	
Hefford, Nigel J	3:59:54 (10,698)	
Heffron, Peter H	5:00:15 (25,831)	
Hegarty, Sean A	4:35:55 (20,066)	
Hegerty, Paul B	4:02:43 (11,323)	
Hegesippe, Mickael	3:12:08 (2,156)	
Heggarty, Hugo	3:40:41 (6,115)	
Heggenes, Svein Erik	4:38:54 (20,849)	
Hegley, Marc	5:06:41 (26,998)	
Hehir, Gerry	3:29:01 (4,276)	
Hehir, Ron	5:09:31 (27,440)	
Hehir, Sam	3:31:27 (4,671)	
Heighley, Stephen T	5:20:09 (29,122)	
Heinpuu, Derek	4:28:06 (18,057)	
Heinskou, Torben	3:37:40 (5,599)	
Heir, Jon	3:54:42 (9,154)	
Heiron, Andrew G	4:25:24 (17,246)	
Helin, Vesa T	4:09:38 (12,991)	
Hellawell, Peter J	3:13:21 (2,281)	
Hellberg, Morten	4:09:55 (13,074)	
Hellen, Brian P	4:39:06 (20,901)	
Hellings, Chris J	4:15:12 (14,502)	
Helliwell, Peter	3:23:26 (3,367)	
Hellman, Bruce E	3:50:24 (8,122)	
Hellmers, Christopher L	3:17:12 (2,702)	
Hellyar, Jonathan A	4:47:19 (22,838)	
Helmer, Jamie	2:52:10 (600)	
Hemans, Matthew J	4:56:34 (25,029)	
Hember, Marcus J	4:37:44 (20,561)	
Hemming, Herbert R	5:05:10 (26,718)	
Hemming-Tayler, Dale J	5:24:01 (29,621)	
Hemms, Martin R	3:33:14 (4,915)	
Hemson, Robert A	5:44:32 (31,808)	
Hemsworth, Kieran A	4:20:46 (16,010)	
Hemsworth, Richard A	3:58:28 (10,278)	
Hemus, Clive G	4:17:27 (15,084)	
Hemy, Vaughan	2:51:47 (577)	
Henaghan, Thomas L	3:42:06 (6,401)	
Henchie, Richard W	4:25:37 (17,321)	
Henderson, Andrew T	6:50:01 (34,709)	
Henderson, Bernard	6:26:28 (34,141)	
Henderson, Brian S	4:11:14 (13,413)	
Henderson, David	5:34:08 (30,796)	
Henderson, Ed J	4:29:08 (18,350)	
Henderson, Iain A	5:05:22 (26,768)	
Henderson, Ian	4:09:51 (13,058)	
Henderson, Ian	5:34:07 (30,791)	

Henderson, Ian J 3:59:13 (10,500)
Henderson, James 4:23:54 (16,827)
Henderson, Jeremy G 3:35:39 (5,290)
Henderson, John 5:24:33 (29,693)
Henderson, Jon 4:51:18 (23,793)
Henderson, Malcolm I 4:57:07 (25,157)
Henderson, Mark T 4:51:18 (23,793)
Henderson, Michael A 4:46:48 (22,734)
Henderson, Neil D 5:19:07 (28,958)
Henderson, Peter W 3:51:03 (8,265)
Henderson, Simon A 4:32:02 (19,098)
Henderson, Stephen M 3:44:20 (6,802)
Henderson, Stuart J 4:40:55 (21,366)
Henderson, William J 3:21:06 (3,093)
Henderson-Slater, David 5:00:17 (25,841)
Hendicott, James R 4:37:45 (20,567)
Hendrey, Neil J 3:04:59 (1,466)
Hendrie, David E 5:00:39 (25,909)
Hendry, Ian P 5:14:53 (28,324)
Hendry, Robert S 3:18:22 (2,818)
Hendry, Russell I 4:10:02 (13,098)
Hendry, Will M 6:11:48 (33,604)
Hendy, Michael D 5:37:24 (31,127)
Heney, Kenneth J 3:06:18 (1,575)
Henly, Steve P 4:09:25 (12,936)
Hennell, Martin J 4:43:54 (22,070)
Hennessey, Brian 2:42:15 (247)
Hennessy, Philip 3:08:07 (1,725)
Henney, Scot M 5:11:52 (27,798)
Henningsen, Michael 3:25:43 (3,704)
Henry, Angelo 3:23:41 (3,398)
Henry, Derek 3:56:05 (9,533)
Henry, Gregory C 4:03:43 (11,548)
Hensby, Matthew 3:33:38 (4,979)
Hensby, Paul A 3:33:38 (4,979)
Hensey, Thomas B 4:35:28 (19,968)
Henshaw, John 3:39:28 (5,904)
Henshaw, Scott 3:46:31 (7,246)
Henshilwood, Guy 4:27:28 (17,875)
Henson, Dean 4:24:33 (17,007)
Henson, Neil J 3:57:00 (9,815)
Henton, Mark 4:11:54 (13,590)
Henwood, John J 4:55:45 (24,831)
Henwood, Peter J 6:38:27 (34,469)
Hepburn, Scott A 4:04:25 (11,724)
Hepburne-Scott, George J 4:18:39 (15,414)
Heppell, David 6:56:26 (34,820)
Hepple, Chris 4:50:37 (23,655)
Hepworth, Ian D 4:04:13 (11,687)
Herbage, Mark J 4:08:02 (12,579)
Herbert, Francis P 3:49:26 (7,917)
Herbert, James 5:34:34 (30,854)
Herbert, John P 4:10:48 (13,289)
Herbert, Jonathan N 3:56:10 (9,562)
Herbert, Neil A 3:39:47 (5,960)
Herbert, Raymond L 6:28:55 (34,216)
Herbert, Stephen G 4:31:56 (19,069)
Herd, Daniel N 5:08:58 (27,350)
Herd, Jonathan J 4:39:50 (21,096)
Herdman, Allan 3:28:58 (4,268)
Herman, Ron 5:20:36 (29,197)
Hermand, Jean-Christopher 4:53:39 (24,344)
Hermans, Carl R 3:33:37 (4,977)
Hernandez, Terry 3:55:21 (9,321)
Heron, David O 4:55:08 (24,711)
Heron, Keith 4:29:35 (18,491)
Herrera Carrillo, German 4:45:05 (22,347)
Herring, Adam J 4:00:57 (10,938)
Herring, Steven 2:37:56 (156)
Herrington, Andrew 3:58:28 (10,278)
Herrmann, Andrew T 3:15:11 (2,495)
Herrmann, Ken J 3:20:54 (3,080)
Herstad, Are 4:57:17 (25,189)
Hesel, Morten Heede 4:12:27 (13,737)
Hesketh, Benjamin H 4:08:25 (12,675)
Hesketh, David 3:40:03 (6,005)
Hesketh, James W 4:43:50 (22,061)
Hesketh, Mark R 3:41:36 (6,298)
Hesketh-Roberts, Russell D 4:49:53 (23,469)
Heskin, Paul F 4:53:02 (24,183)
Hesp, Robert J 3:18:59 (2,879)
Hesten, Paul 5:53:03 (32,502)
Hester, Liam K 3:22:09 (3,211)
Heterhington, Mark S 3:18:11 (2,802)
Hetherington, David 4:08:58 (12,817)
Hetherington, Michael E 4:57:51 (25,290)
Hettiaratchy, Shehan P 3:45:49 (7,098)
Heuff, Alexander C 4:43:29 (21,974)
Hewertson, Chris 3:57:36 (10,015)
Hewish, Mark C 4:20:53 (16,043)
Hewison, Michael J 4:02:47 (11,339)
Hewitt, Brian N 3:57:52 (10,102)
Hewitt, Damien F 4:34:12 (19,624)
Hewitt, Dennis 6:15:12 (33,745)
Hewitt, Phil 4:20:46 (16,010)
Hewitt, Roger P 3:59:57 (10,713)
Hewitt, Simon 3:17:55 (2,781)
Hewitt, Stephen R 4:04:51 (11,825)
Hewlett, David J 4:39:08 (20,907)
Hewlett, Martin J 3:39:32 (5,920)
Hewlett, Robert W 4:22:26 (16,453)
Hewson, Anthony J 3:23:23 (3,360)
Hewson, Geoffrey A 4:10:26 (13,215)
Hewson, Guy 5:58:04 (32,840)
Hewson, Julian D 4:30:17 (18,678)
Heyden, Andrew P 2:39:06 (177)
Heyer, Hubertus 2:51:11 (545)
Heyes, Richard C 4:05:16 (11,936)
Heys, John D 5:16:39 (28,569)
Heywood, Fraser R 6:11:19 (33,585)
Heywood, George J 4:38:27 (20,745)
Hibberd, Matthew D 3:03:15 (1,346)
Hibberd, Roy G 4:16:19 (14,799)
Hibbert, Stephen C 4:26:47 (17,687)
Hibbitt, Michael I 4:18:24 (15,327)
Hick, Martin C 5:04:46 (26,642)
Hickey, Christopher J 4:30:00 (18,584)
Hickey, Colm F 5:24:46 (29,717)
Hickey, James W 4:34:20 (19,671)
Hickling, Benjamin C 5:14:57 (28,332)
Hickling, Mark T 2:47:50 (404)
Hickling, Phillip J 4:51:53 (23,905)
Hickman, Ben M 5:12:14 (27,858)
Hickman, Mark 3:41:19 (6,238)
Hickman, Neil 4:14:54 (14,412)
Hickman, Paul 3:36:36 (5,445)
Hickman, Simon C 3:44:46 (6,898)
Hickman, Tom 5:30:59 (30,467)
Hickmott, Patrick E 4:22:02 (16,350)
Hickmott, Stephen R 4:02:26 (11,255)
Hicks, Adam J 5:01:47 (26,103)
Hicks, Alan 3:34:22 (5,105)
Hicks, Brian R 3:21:41 (3,151)
Hicks, Christopher A 5:23:49 (29,587)
Hicks, David 4:18:42 (15,433)
Hicks, Ian 4:00:52 (10,922)
Hicks, Karl D 3:47:06 (7,372)
Hicks, Marten W 4:24:27 (16,977)
Hicks, Michael J 2:58:18 (973)
Hicks, Paul 3:50:09 (8,073)
Hicks, Simon R 5:27:53 (30,086)
Hicks, Timothy W 3:17:16 (2,711)
Hicks, William J 4:31:02 (18,843)
Hickton, Neil C 6:23:58 (34,063)
Hides, Nick B 2:50:35 (520)
Hieber, Benedikt G 2:59:08 (1,048)
Higdon, Simon M 3:39:42 (5,951)
Higgins, Andrew 3:58:45 (10,366)
Higgins, Bernard 3:23:05 (3,311)
Higgins, Daniel J 2:49:26 (482)
Higgins, Eamon P 3:48:03 (7,598)
Higgins, Ian 4:59:37 (25,692)
Higgins, James W 4:00:51 (10,913)
Higgins, Peter J 3:21:08 (3,097)
Higgins, Richard J 2:46:05 (351)
Higgins, Robert D 2:58:28 (988)
Higgins, Robert W 4:19:30 (15,665)
Higgins, Steven G 4:04:59 (11,856)
Higgins, Timothy G 4:39:29 (21,008)
Higginsonson, Liam T 4:49:57 (23,483)
Higglesden, Matthew W 3:16:03 (2,580)
Higgs, Antony E 4:09:50 (13,049)
Higgs, David J 4:50:25 (23,603)
Higgs, David W 3:29:07 (4,300)
Higgs, Matthew 4:30:48 (18,793)
Higgs, Matthew J 5:07:22 (27,123)
Higham, Christopher W 4:46:52 (22,745)
Highfield, Colin R 3:28:03 (4,113)
Highfield, Mark 3:55:03 (9,245)
Highley, Robert C 3:49:14 (7,872)
Highmore, Martyn J 4:56:27 (25,001)
Hight, Christopher M 4:52:41 (24,101)
Higson, Andrew 3:15:35 (2,530)
Higson, Gary 4:34:41 (19,762)
Higton, Paul W 4:15:29 (14,573)
Hijkoop, Frans 4:09:17 (12,903)
Hilber, Klaus 5:21:49 (29,329)
Hilber, Markus 4:02:05 (11,181)
Hilbery, Graham J 3:46:36 (7,264)
Hilborn, Bradley R 4:43:07 (21,891)
Hilborne, Mike 5:40:29 (31,465)
Hilditch, Graeme R 3:29:24 (4,338)
Hildreth, Jan H 6:16:08 (33,790)
Hildreth, Keith J 4:51:31 (23,836)
Hildwein, Marc 3:43:49 (6,709)
Hilgers, Axel 3:47:04 (7,364)
Hill, Adrian 3:50:42 (8,189)
Hill, Adrian P 3:49:30 (7,933)
Hill, Andrew G 3:30:12 (4,476)
Hill, Brian 5:41:45 (31,571)
Hill, Christopher D 4:37:24 (20,472)
Hill, Christopher J 4:36:27 (20,216)
Hill, Clive J 5:58:49 (32,894)
Hill, Daniel B 5:17:43 (28,743)
Hill, Dave M 2:50:58 (540)
Hill, David J 4:51:58 (23,925)
Hill, Gregory R 3:26:01 (3,764)
Hill, Ian H 3:27:01 (3,931)
Hill, Ivor 8:01:08 (35,233)
Hill, James P 4:22:15 (16,407)
Hill, Jeremy J 7:04:10 (34,911)
Hill, Jeremy O 4:28:54 (18,274)
Hill, Joseph 4:24:46 (17,064)
Hill, Kenneth 3:13:01 (2,248)
Hill, Kevin I 5:01:58 (26,141)
Hill, Mark A 3:13:54 (2,345)
Hill, Mark I 5:09:37 (27,458)
Hill, Mark R 2:50:12 (505)
Hill, Martin F 4:26:34 (17,623)
Hill, Matthew 6:09:46 (33,526)
Hill, Matthew D 3:45:55 (7,120)
Hill, Michael 3:38:26 (5,714)
Hill, Miguel S 4:29:02 (18,320)
Hill, Nicholas 4:28:28 (18,156)
Hill, Olando 4:11:26 (13,467)
Hill, Paul W 3:16:12 (2,603)
Hill, Philip J 4:17:16 (15,029)
Hill, Raymond W 4:16:56 (14,939)
Hill, Richard 5:16:23 (28,530)
Hill, Richard A 3:29:03 (4,282)
Hill, Richard W 5:25:08 (29,766)
Hill, Robert D 5:14:23 (28,242)
Hill, Rod W 4:19:37 (15,699)
Hill, Shaun P 4:26:57 (17,737)
Hill, Simon B 3:04:31 (1,429)
Hill, Simon F 3:59:23 (10,541)
Hill, Simon M 4:43:38 (22,019)
Hill, Simon P 4:13:56 (14,125)
Hill, Stephen 3:58:13 (10,199)
Hill, Stephen 4:32:38 (19,235)
Hill, Stephen 5:48:49 (32,163)
Hill, Stephen R 3:58:18 (10,227)
Hill, Stuart C 4:20:09 (15,840)
Hill, Tommy J 4:10:38 (13,248)
Hill, Trevor J 4:37:00 (20,357)
Hill, Walter J 2:52:05 (597)
Hill, Will 3:24:48 (3,553)
Hilland, Colin 3:39:18 (5,868)
Hillery, Brian P 4:09:38 (12,991)
Hilliar, Darryl W 2:48:01 (415)
Hilliard, David J 5:01:52 (26,118)
Hillier, Luke 4:14:13 (14,217)
Hillier, Mark J 4:15:47 (14,656)
Hillier, Martin R 4:42:09 (21,664)
Hillier, Paul A 4:26:30 (17,600)
Hills, Richard 3:57:03 (9,837)
Hills, Stephen M 4:17:17 (15,034)
Hills, Zachary 3:29:02 (4,277)
Hilsenbek, Karl 2:57:58 (955)

Hollins, Jonathan D 4:32:50 (19,275)
Hollinson, Peter D 4:30:02 (18,600)
Hollis, Ashley S 2:56:28 (840)
Hollis, Jim M 4:57:09 (25,164)
Hollis, Jonathan S 4:24:59 (17,117)
Hollis, Luke 3:55:26 (9,347)
Hollis, Paul 4:36:52 (20,324)
Hollis, Peter J 4:49:36 (23,388)
Hollis, Stephen P 4:08:58 (12,817)
Holloway, Adam 3:58:42 (10,347)
Holloway, Andrew T 3:27:47 (4,073)
Holloway, Chris R 4:21:13 (16,113)
Holloway, Darren P 3:53:48 (8,934)
Holloway, Donald 3:40:04 (6,010)
Holloway, Nick 4:18:53 (15,481)
Holloway, Patrick J 5:23:54 (29,602)
Holloway, Paul G 4:24:13 (16,908)
Holloway, William C 4:53:56 (24,402)
Hollstein, Rolf Dieter 5:43:43 (31,738)
Hollwell, James 3:56:52 (9,775)
Holm, Jorn J 3:57:35 (10,007)
Holman, James C 3:59:33 (10,590)
Holman, James C 6:42:28 (34,554)
Holmberg, Henrik 3:49:08 (7,851)
Holme, Tom G 5:20:24 (29,161)
Holmes, Albert 5:05:23 (26,771)
Holmes, Darren 4:44:53 (22,293)
Holmes, Eric W 3:36:18 (5,392)
Holmes, Frank L 3:30:28 (4,518)
Holmes, Fraser 4:01:19 (11,005)
Holmes, Gary 3:12:30 (2,196)
Holmes, Geoff A 4:16:27 (14,828)
Holmes, Ian H 3:27:08 (3,948)
Holmes, Karl 5:06:01 (26,876)
Holmes, Keith 3:01:41 (1,239)
Holmes, Leigh D 4:33:50 (19,529)
Holmes, Marcus J 3:46:38 (7,270)
Holmes, Michael A 3:54:21 (9,062)
Holmes, Michael J 4:35:48 (20,042)
Holmes, Mike T 2:48:21 (425)
Holmes, Neil 4:53:04 (24,194)
Holmes, Nicholas M 2:51:56 (587)
Holmes, Richard A 3:13:00 (2,246)
Holmes, Robin 3:24:30 (3,516)
Holmes, Simon A 4:17:05 (14,977)
Holmes, Simon C 4:59:08 (25,591)
Holmes, Stephen P 4:45:40 (22,474)
Holmes, Steven 3:30:25 (4,508)
Holmes, Thomas 5:12:32 (27,915)
Holmsberg, Anders 3:28:21 (4,168)
Holness, Andrew C 4:42:58 (21,867)
Holroyd, Alan J 4:43:56 (22,081)
Holsten, Per E 3:43:59 (6,737)
Holt, Alan W 4:27:22 (17,845)
Holt, Andrew 3:38:09 (5,674)
Holt, Andrew J 2:49:22 (479)
Holt, Julian D 4:15:36 (14,607)
Holt, Mark A 5:13:47 (28,130)
Holt, Martin J 3:50:05 (8,058)
Holt, Philip 3:18:02 (2,789)
Holt, Philip 4:59:21 (25,635)
Holt, Stuart 4:52:01 (23,939)
Holt, Tim C 4:56:05 (24,912)
Holton, Pete A 2:52:55 (631)
Holzmann, Jonathan J 4:32:00 (19,087)
Homa, Peter A 4:27:10 (17,792)
Homan, Daniel 4:10:06 (13,115)
Home, Steven 2:43:43 (286)
Homer, James N 4:51:43 (23,877)
Homes, Bradley J 5:54:21 (32,593)
Homewood, Gary P 4:18:24 (15,327)
Hone, Dennis V 3:44:52 (6,933)
Honekamp, Wilfried 4:58:32 (25,452)
Honey, Damian J 3:42:07 (6,406)
Honey, Jason 4:55:45 (24,831)
Honeyball, David I 4:26:58 (17,745)
Honeyman, Neil J 3:59:32 (10,582)
Honney, John M 5:37:03 (31,104)
Honnor, Ian C 3:15:22 (2,510)
Hood, David I 3:35:23 (5,237)
Hood, Graeme 4:09:45 (13,029)
Hood, Graham R 3:44:29 (6,833)
Hoodless, Robert J 3:28:23 (4,175)

Last but not least

A bus, known as the 'Grim Sweeper', trails the London Marathon field at the speed of a seven-hour-runner. Officially, the roads are closed after five hours but the organizers seem to stretch this as long as they can. Runners might be asked to keep to the pavement, but the finish team will be there until the 7.30pm tail-enders have wobbled across the line to receive their medals.

Hoodless, Stephen P 6:19:03 (33,889)
Hook, David J 3:09:47 (1,895)
Hook, Laurence J 4:12:52 (13,847)
Hook, Martin C 5:02:34 (26,241)
Hook, Matthew S 3:02:18 (1,285)
Hook, Simon L 4:15:34 (14,599)
Hook, Trevor L 2:57:53 (949)
Hooker, Andrew N 4:28:05 (18,049)
Hooker, Bob J 3:56:51 (9,769)
Hooker, David D 6:42:09 (34,549)
Hooker, Gary F 4:44:44 (22,255)
Hooker, Michael D 3:36:12 (5,371)
Hooker, Philip J 3:43:14 (6,595)
Hooker, Richard 4:28:05 (18,049)
Hookinson, Joseph S 3:29:37 (4,376)
Hooks, Alan J 5:06:17 (26,917)
Hooks, Ian D 5:01:41 (26,091)
Hoole, Nathan L 4:08:15 (12,628)
Hooley, Andrew P 3:09:35 (1,870)
Hooley, Iain W 4:00:06 (10,752)
Hoon, Mark A 2:39:32 (189)
Hooper, Andrew 4:23:18 (16,690)
Hooper, Chris J 5:32:48 (30,652)
Hooper, James C 3:48:21 (7,672)
Hooper, Martin 3:33:01 (4,890)
Hooper, Martin R 4:16:23 (14,817)
Hooper, Matthew S 4:44:04 (22,108)
Hooper, Paul D 3:13:06 (2,257)
Hooper, Peter W 3:23:06 (3,315)
Hooper, Simon A 4:56:14 (24,946)
Hooper, Steve L 5:24:20 (29,666)
Hooton, Nigel J 3:50:02 (8,047)
Hope, Alex 2:51:12 (546)
Hope, Gary J 2:37:14 (143)
Hope, Geoffrey A 5:29:59 (30,361)
Hope, Lee C 6:16:10 (33,793)
Hope, Robert J 4:26:04 (17,462)
Hope, Stephen W 4:46:05 (22,571)
Hope-Gill, Thomas F 4:21:11 (16,105)
Hopegood, James 5:27:23 (30,028)
Hopewell, Peter 3:54:56 (9,226)
Hopewell, Philip R 4:45:03 (22,338)
Hopgood, Martin 3:55:32 (9,376)
Hopkins, Adam R 5:06:22 (26,936)
Hopkins, Darren M 4:57:34 (25,242)
Hopkins, David A 6:03:35 (33,193)
Hopkins, Douglas 5:50:22 (32,291)
Hopkins, Gabriel 3:43:02 (6,556)
Hopkins, Gareth E 5:13:43 (28,116)
Hopkins, Graham A 4:05:08 (11,907)
Hopkins, Greg 3:48:09 (7,627)
Hopkins, Howard L 4:06:21 (12,182)
Hopkins, Martin J 4:25:24 (17,246)
Hopkins, Michael 3:43:48 (6,706)
Hopkins, Michael 5:00:59 (25,973)
Hopkins, Owen J 5:40:04 (31,423)
Hopkins, Philip J 5:05:21 (26,764)
Hopkins, Rhys D 5:27:06 (29,988)
Hopkins, Ronnie 4:39:26 (20,996)
Hopkinson, Neil D 3:06:19 (1,576)
Hoppe, Ingo 6:56:29 (34,822)
Hopper, Andrew J 3:58:17 (10,220)
Hopper, John W 4:34:46 (19,781)
Hopper, Jon M 5:21:14 (29,265)
Hopper, Nicholas 3:51:08 (8,292)
Hopper, Peter 3:04:38 (1,439)
Hopper, Robert C 4:39:21 (20,977)
Hoppey, Neil J 4:19:14 (15,589)
Hopps, Peter W 3:11:33 (2,082)
Hopton, Paul 5:36:19 (31,031)
Hopton, Tim P 5:27:29 (30,041)
Hopwood, Craig A 4:18:24 (15,327)
Hopwood, Malcolm J 5:30:12 (30,383)
Horan, Philip C 4:09:46 (13,032)
Horder, Matthew B 5:18:40 (28,900)
Horgan, John 4:16:39 (14,876)
Horm, Steven M 5:12:14 (27,858)
Horn, Ian 4:07:06 (12,372)
Horn, Jeff 4:28:50 (18,258)
Hornby, Colin 4:07:55 (12,557)
Hornby, Fraser 4:40:53 (21,358)
Hornby, Steven 4:12:56 (13,865)
Horne, Barry 4:08:54 (12,802)
Horne, Barry 4:20:15 (15,875)
Horne, Kenderik T 3:50:05 (8,058)
Horne, Patrick 3:58:01 (10,148)
Horne, Richard 3:55:28 (9,358)
Horner, Andrew D 3:48:17 (7,652)
Horner, Gary A 4:15:17 (14,524)
Horner, Paul M 5:00:04 (25,787)
Horner, Richard E 3:03:59 (1,396)
Horner, Richard M 5:00:08 (25,800)
Hornsby, Charles P 4:46:43 (22,714)
Hornung, Chris 2:43:06 (270)
Horrell, Peter 3:59:10 (10,488)
Horridge, Chris R 4:43:58 (22,090)
Horridge, William A 4:29:02 (18,320)
Horrigan, Ian R 4:25:19 (17,221)
Horrocks, Andrew R 5:23:04 (29,493)
Horrocks, Brian F 5:18:17 (28,833)
Horrocks, Matthew 3:16:14 (2,607)
Horrocks, Stephen J 3:58:05 (10,164)
Horsburgh, James R 4:13:41 (14,064)
Horsewood, Stuart M 4:13:25 (13,993)
Horsfall, Andrew G 5:56:07 (32,713)
Horsfall, Chris 3:23:30 (3,374)
Horsfield, Terry M 3:20:35 (3,054)
Horsham, Randolph 5:28:00 (30,103)
Horsley, Graham M 3:04:22 (1,419)
Horsley, Simon A 3:05:07 (1,476)
Horsley, Simon J 6:14:19 (33,711)
Horsman, Gary J 3:39:13 (5,854)
Horsman, Joseph 3:25:57 (3,746)
Horstead, Graeme K 3:36:01 (5,344)
Horstmann, Michael 4:12:04 (13,636)
Horsup, Matthew R 4:50:17 (23,556)
Horton, Clive 3:26:43 (3,887)
Horton, David L 4:26:43 (17,667)
Horton, Leigh S 3:58:29 (10,288)
Horton, Leslie 3:11:52 (2,127)
Horton, Luke J 4:27:28 (17,875)
Horton, Michael E 3:28:33 (4,206)
Horton, Nicholas B 3:13:19 (2,275)
Horton, Patrick A 4:47:26 (22,868)
Horton, Peter H 3:13:06 (2,257)
Horton, Philip L 3:40:21 (6,064)
Horwood, Clive 5:36:17 (31,026)
Horwood, Geoffrey D 5:48:21 (32,129)
Horwood, Graham S 3:57:48 (10,076)
Horwood, Mike J 3:29:58 (4,448)
Horwood, Stephen N 6:07:21 (33,411)
Hosell, Simon 4:35:12 (19,885)
Hosier, Colin J 5:20:28 (29,177)
Hosier, Daniel 7:29:38 (35,123)
Hoskin, Howard O 2:56:53 (879)
Hoskin, Jeremy D 4:50:25 (23,603)
Hosking, Mark L 4:49:49 (23,454)
Hosking, Richard P 5:23:49 (29,587)
Hoskins, Julian M 6:17:43 (33,843)
Hoskuldsson, Gauti 2:50:46 (529)
Hoskyn, John D 4:57:17 (25,189)
Hossain, Syed 5:00:51 (25,946)
Hotchkies, Gary M 4:15:56 (14,696)
Hotten, David B 4:25:22 (17,235)
Houde, Joseph F 5:48:37 (32,145)
Hough, Richard I 3:57:39 (10,027)

Hougham, Paul R....4:20:53 (16,043)
Houghton, Chris A....3:56:11 (9,571)
Houghton, Greg....3:48:25 (7,686)
Houghton, John A....4:18:40 (15,420)
Houghton, Marc....5:01:33 (26,074)
Houghton, Mark P....5:48:37 (32,145)
Houghton, Philip D....4:07:15 (12,403)
Houghton, Toby J....3:35:29 (5,260)
Houlden, Chris....5:11:53 (27,802)
Houlder, Fraser....3:43:59 (6,737)
Houlihan, Denis....4:42:12 (21,676)
Houlton, Matthew....3:39:47 (5,960)
Houlton, Nicholas J....2:39:42 (196)
Housden, Duncan....5:35:16 (30,930)
House, David....3:57:42 (10,038)
House, Ed R....4:35:08 (19,879)
House, Marc P....4:06:41 (12,260)
House, Richard F....3:21:46 (3,159)
House, Richard T....3:54:20 (9,053)
Housham, Kevin J....4:18:46 (15,452)
Houston, Ian....4:30:43 (18,772)
Houston, Paul....4:44:16 (22,160)
Houston, Robert D....3:38:33 (5,732)
Houten, Brian G....4:09:39 (12,999)
Hovda, Allan....3:25:10 (3,615)
Hovden, Jon....3:29:31 (4,358)
Hovel, Bernard....3:43:03 (6,561)
How, Timothy....4:22:06 (16,367)
Howard, Allan D....4:24:57 (17,107)
Howard, Andrew P....4:20:13 (15,857)
Howard, Ben R....3:59:09 (10,485)
Howard, Brian J....5:42:22 (31,618)
Howard, Charles D....3:35:11 (5,208)
Howard, Clive....4:04:05 (11,657)
Howard, Conrad A....3:56:40 (9,714)
Howard, David....3:18:57 (2,877)
Howard, David J....4:54:34 (24,573)
Howard, Gary....4:08:11 (12,607)
Howard, Henry D....3:59:46 (10,654)
Howard, James A....3:47:53 (7,545)
Howard, Jason A....3:21:46 (3,159)
Howard, John N....4:01:33 (11,058)
Howard, Kenneth....3:10:06 (1,933)
Howard, Martin P....5:52:47 (32,482)
Howard, Nick A....4:38:18 (20,697)
Howard, Paul J....4:06:11 (12,137)
Howard, Philip E....3:31:56 (4,736)
Howard, Richard....3:56:58 (9,803)
Howard, Simon J....4:11:19 (13,434)
Howard, Simon M....4:47:59 (23,004)
Howard, Wayne....4:07:45 (12,516)
Howard Keyes, Alex....4:11:06 (13,381)
Howarth, Charlie R....4:32:07 (19,117)
Howarth, Chris....5:11:24 (27,725)
Howarth, Chris....5:16:17 (28,515)
Howarth, Ian M....4:35:19 (19,911)
Howarth, John R....2:38:30 (168)
Howarth, John R....4:06:28 (12,204)
Howarth, Kevin D....3:55:26 (9,347)
Howarth, Nigel....5:43:03 (31,681)
Howarth, Philip R....4:35:20 (19,919)
Howarth, Raymond....4:58:41 (25,482)
Howarth, Raymond P....3:09:43 (1,885)
Howarth, Steve....4:35:57 (20,075)
Howat, Brian R....6:03:33 (33,192)
Howath, Alex....4:19:03 (15,527)
Howe, Andrew D....3:45:21 (7,017)
Howe, Andrew G....5:45:08 (31,861)
Howe, Andrew J....3:49:19 (7,897)
Howe, Andrew K....4:27:40 (17,942)
Howe, Daryl....6:01:08 (33,032)
Howe, Grahame T....4:27:33 (17,906)
Howe, Jacob M....2:52:03 (594)
Howe, Michael....3:28:32 (4,203)
Howe, Russell....3:58:19 (10,232)
Howe, Simon J....4:49:12 (23,282)
Howe, Steven C....4:14:57 (14,425)
Howell, Andrew....5:10:24 (27,555)
Howell, Brian....4:04:36 (11,768)
Howell, Christopher E....7:15:45 (35,041)
Howell, David....5:39:14 (31,342)
Howell, John....3:42:55 (6,528)
Howell, Jonathan V....3:10:11 (1,947)
Howell, Mark....4:06:41 (12,260)
Howell, Neil E....5:48:57 (32,179)
Howell, Peter J....4:12:55 (13,862)
Howell, Roger M....5:49:18 (32,211)
Howell, Scott J....3:01:17 (1,207)
Howell, Sebastian E....3:23:33 (3,381)
Howells, Andrew C....4:20:12 (15,854)
Howells, David C....3:28:53 (4,258)
Howells, David G....3:48:47 (7,780)
Howells, Denis M....4:09:28 (12,950)
Howells, Gareth I....4:06:23 (12,186)
Howells, Gareth P....5:46:47 (31,998)
Howells, Gerwyn W....5:51:38 (32,384)
Howells, Mark D....4:53:45 (24,366)
Howes, Colin T....3:37:45 (5,609)
Howes, David....5:39:08 (31,325)
Howes, Geoff E....4:45:20 (22,400)
Howes, Robert....4:47:22 (22,847)
Howes, Tim....4:02:32 (11,283)
Howes, Toby C....4:54:51 (24,630)
Howes, William J....3:27:16 (3,971)
Howick, Lawrence L....3:56:52 (9,775)
Howick, Stuart R....3:44:00 (6,742)
Howie, Azon A....3:44:48 (6,904)
Howie, Douglas I....4:08:51 (12,787)
Howie, John M....4:22:41 (16,532)
Howitt, Alistair J....4:53:11 (24,217)
Howland, Kenneth....5:05:18 (26,749)
Howles, Martin P....3:36:29 (5,425)
Howlett, David S....4:37:56 (20,603)
Howley, David M....4:16:50 (14,922)
Howsom, Dominic J....4:50:56 (23,717)
Hoy, David J....4:55:37 (24,795)
Hoy, Simon J....4:48:11 (23,048)
Hoyle, Raymond I....6:28:01 (34,195)
Hoyles, Ashley....4:09:13 (12,895)
Hua, Binh....3:56:25 (9,637)
Huard, Patrick....4:01:45 (11,101)
Hubabrd, Daine....4:55:13 (24,722)
Hubbard, Jym....5:15:59 (28,476)
Hubbard, Peter C....5:44:30 (31,806)
Hubbard, Tony B....3:44:12 (6,787)
Hubbard, Trevor M....4:46:52 (22,745)
Hubble, Nick....4:05:55 (12,078)
Hubert, Xavier....3:54:27 (9,088)
Huck, Dave....2:55:17 (754)
Huck, Ernest F....3:13:47 (2,337)
Hucker, Peter I....5:15:05 (28,346)
Huddy, Hugh....4:42:36 (21,769)
Hudson, Alan....3:08:38 (1,771)
Hudson, Damian R....4:21:04 (16,088)
Hudson, Davie F....4:31:47 (19,042)
Hudson, Dean....4:43:42 (22,033)
Hudson, Geoffrey T....4:26:55 (17,724)
Hudson, James F....4:10:37 (13,242)
Hudson, Jason....5:14:47 (28,310)
Hudson, Justin M....5:00:43 (25,920)
Hudson, Kevin....5:51:11 (32,350)
Hudson, Kevin A....3:31:55 (4,733)
Hudson, Michael J....4:38:21 (20,709)
Hudson, Peter S....6:51:10 (34,742)
Hudson, Richard A....3:03:37 (1,377)
Hudson, Simon....3:08:11 (1,733)
Hudson, Thomas G....4:45:53 (22,516)
Hudspith, John E....2:58:33 (997)
Huebner, Fred....3:57:28 (9,969)
Huete-Allut, Antonio....2:50:31 (516)
Huettinger, Helmut....3:51:22 (8,346)
Hufler, Guntram....4:34:05 (19,587)
Hufler, Kurt....3:34:56 (5,172)
Hufnagl, Hansjorg....3:44:48 (6,904)
Huggett, Brian J....5:44:30 (31,806)
Huggett, Ronald....4:59:00 (25,559)
Huggins, Ben J....4:31:34 (18,989)
Huggins, Brian E....4:21:43 (16,259)
Huggins, Jason....4:14:03 (14,164)
Huggins, Mervyn....4:14:38 (14,325)
Huggins, Terence....5:19:57 (29,090)
Hughes, Anthony J....4:43:08 (21,895)
Hughes, Arthur....4:48:19 (23,077)
Hughes, Brian J....3:59:55 (10,701)
Hughes, Ceri....4:00:38 (10,876)
Hughes, Chris B....5:02:31 (26,233)
Hughes, Connie E....4:25:30 (17,286)
Hughes, Dafydd L....4:15:42 (14,636)
Hughes, Daniel J....4:42:54 (21,853)
Hughes, Darren....4:46:09 (22,593)
Hughes, David A....4:24:06 (16,876)
Hughes, David A....4:30:59 (18,831)
Hughes, David C....3:37:37 (5,590)
Hughes, David L....4:47:50 (22,974)
Hughes, Frank D....3:18:43 (2,852)
Hughes, Gareth L....3:47:24 (7,438)
Hughes, Gary D....5:14:33 (28,268)
Hughes, Gary J....4:35:53 (20,062)
Hughes, Gavin B....6:02:35 (33,112)
Hughes, Geoffrey....3:34:04 (5,055)
Hughes, Geraint....2:59:57 (1,125)
Hughes, Graham E....3:48:29 (7,702)
Hughes, Gregory R....3:54:07 (8,999)
Hughes, Hefin L....3:46:05 (7,158)
Hughes, Ian C....3:57:19 (9,925)
Hughes, Ifan R....3:40:46 (6,132)
Hughes, James....5:22:35 (29,436)
Hughes, James L....5:00:48 (25,935)
Hughes, James M....4:48:05 (23,029)
Hughes, Jonathan M....4:15:11 (14,498)
Hughes, Jonathan R....3:23:43 (3,405)
Hughes, Justin....5:34:48 (30,884)
Hughes, Justin M....3:57:22 (9,939)
Hughes, Karl A....5:57:34 (32,808)
Hughes, Kenneth W....4:30:28 (18,717)
Hughes, Kevin....5:00:37 (25,903)
Hughes, Kevin A....4:07:43 (12,503)
Hughes, Kris D....3:58:23 (10,255)
Hughes, Leslie....3:48:08 (7,622)
Hughes, Mark D....4:17:41 (15,134)
Hughes, Mark J....3:49:19 (7,897)
Hughes, Mark T....3:25:03 (3,597)
Hughes, Martin A....5:10:34 (27,582)
Hughes, Meirion P....4:08:15 (12,628)
Hughes, Michael....4:40:11 (21,182)
Hughes, Michael J....5:20:18 (29,142)
Hughes, Neil A....3:46:18 (7,202)
Hughes, Owen C....5:00:14 (25,828)
Hughes, Paul F....3:46:18 (7,202)
Hughes, Paul J....6:28:16 (34,205)
Hughes, Peter J....4:16:19 (14,799)
Hughes, Peter M....4:09:07 (12,865)
Hughes, Richard A....4:51:08 (23,759)
Hughes, Richard J....4:38:03 (20,632)
Hughes, Richard L....5:15:32 (28,422)
Hughes, Richard P....3:36:05 (5,354)
Hughes, Simon C....6:32:52 (34,326)
Hughes, Stephen....4:32:30 (19,212)
Hughes, Stephen F....3:17:31 (2,736)
Hughes, Stephen L....5:08:28 (27,281)
Hughes, Steven J....5:00:34 (25,890)
Hughes, Terry P....3:23:40 (3,396)
Hughes, Tim D....3:20:00 (2,996)
Hughes-Roberts, John....4:28:22 (18,129)
Hugkulstone, David A....3:42:51 (6,518)
Hugman, Michael J....4:35:30 (19,975)
Huille, Alexandre....3:54:44 (9,167)
Huille, Matthieu....3:35:37 (5,285)
Huke, Christopher W....3:52:17 (8,551)
Huke, Michael C....3:25:33 (3,683)
Hukins, Gary T....3:28:08 (4,133)
Hulcoop, Simon....4:41:44 (21,573)
Hulcoop, Stephen V....4:59:52 (25,750)
Hulgrew, Brendan....4:22:58 (16,592)
Hull, David J....5:31:00 (30,470)
Hull, Jonathan A....4:00:42 (10,887)
Hull, Richard....5:37:45 (31,163)
Hull, Simon C....3:09:41 (1,877)
Hulme, John P....4:03:33 (11,514)
Hulme, Robert C....5:33:54 (30,766)
Hulse, Christopher T....5:55:10 (32,652)
Hulse, Darren R....4:32:25 (19,190)
Hulse, Michael....6:03:15 (33,164)
Hulsmann, Daniel....4:31:28 (18,962)
Humber, David....3:59:00 (10,430)
Humble, Anthony J....4:52:16 (24,006)
Humble, Brian....3:31:52 (4,726)
Humblot, Pierre....4:26:36 (17,631)
Hume, Jon P....4:58:02 (25,335)

Irish, Bill	3:53:20	(8,813)
Irlam, James C	3:43:23	(6,633)
Irons, Graham	4:14:30	(14,297)
Irons, Nathan G	4:28:33	(18,181)
Ironside, Alexander	3:21:14	(3,108)
Irvine, Daniel T	3:22:51	(3,278)
Irvine, David W	5:14:39	(28,294)
Irvine, Mark	2:51:09	(543)
Irvine-Brown, Richard L	4:43:54	(22,070)
Irving, Leslie	4:31:39	(19,007)
Irving, Paul W	5:13:44	(28,119)
Irwin, Daniel	3:33:25	(4,948)
Irwin, Laurie E	3:42:37	(6,486)
Irwin, Paul M	4:12:09	(13,650)
Isaac, Chris W	4:53:02	(24,183)
Isaac, David T	4:48:21	(23,088)
Isaac, Robert J	5:18:04	(28,794)
Isaac, Vincent	3:28:10	(4,138)
Isaacs, David W	4:32:14	(19,146)
Isaacs, Graham K	4:16:38	(14,871)
Isaacs, Jason	3:34:29	(5,122)
Isam, Lloyd	4:28:13	(18,091)
Iseke, Hans	3:35:34	(5,272)
Isherwood, Paul R	3:03:15	(1,346)
Isherwood, Robert G	4:49:32	(23,365)
Isherwood, Roger D	5:39:17	(31,348)
Isherwood, Trevor S	3:14:35	(2,427)
Ishmael, Michael F	4:44:41	(22,245)
Islam, Sayeed Z	4:46:47	(22,727)
Isotalo, Erkka T	4:29:42	(18,520)
Israel, Alberto Rodrigue	3:59:20	(10,527)
Israel, Stephen J	4:47:36	(22,907)
Issa, Mohsin	3:25:19	(3,647)
Isted, Darren	4:57:56	(25,307)
Iturbe Usanda, Eduardo	3:23:47	(3,416)
Ive, Martin J	3:07:24	(1,664)
Ive, Scott A	4:10:02	(13,098)
Ivers, John G	3:56:48	(9,753)
Iversen, Benjamin R	4:14:33	(14,304)
Iverson, Wendell W	5:03:13	(26,387)
Ives, Kevin R	3:48:34	(7,730)
Ives, Philip A	6:32:33	(34,319)
Ives, Phillip E	5:11:08	(27,675)
Ives, Stuart S	3:20:02	(3,001)
Iveson, Gary J	3:56:49	(9,757)
Iveson, Paul D	4:07:31	(12,463)
Iveson, Richard P	3:55:50	(9,472)
Ivings, Greg	5:09:53	(27,493)
Ivory, Damien R	5:19:24	(29,009)
Iwama, Masahiro	4:15:57	(14,698)
Izard, John C	4:42:12	(21,676)
Iztueta, Joseba G	4:12:12	(13,664)
Izza, Michael D	5:29:40	(30,326)
Jaatten, Alf I	5:20:49	(29,219)
Jack, David	5:54:57	(32,638)
Jack, David A	5:44:56	(31,844)
Jack, Fergus R	4:26:21	(17,548)
Jack, Jonathan	3:54:20	(9,053)
Jackets, Gary R	3:51:37	(8,392)
Jacklin, William J	4:58:09	(25,359)
Jackman, Stephen P	3:46:06	(7,161)
Jacks, Daniel R	4:09:50	(13,049)
Jackson, Alan	3:21:46	(3,159)
Jackson, Alan	3:54:18	(9,046)
Jackson, Alan H	4:43:22	(21,949)
Jackson, Andrew	2:36:38	(129)
Jackson, Andrew	4:09:27	(12,943)
Jackson, Bob	3:13:03	(2,251)
Jackson, Colin J	5:20:14	(29,134)
Jackson, Darren	4:26:45	(17,678)
Jackson, David	4:04:42	(11,796)
Jackson, David A	3:49:11	(7,862)
Jackson, David R	4:58:14	(25,380)
Jackson, Dean	4:16:35	(14,854)
Jackson, Derek	3:15:52	(2,555)
Jackson, Dominic J	5:06:03	(26,885)
Jackson, Edward J	5:07:03	(27,068)
Jackson, George D	2:58:30	(992)
Jackson, Glynn	6:59:51	(34,865)
Jackson, Graham D	5:22:24	(29,404)
Jackson, Guy	4:24:39	(17,026)
Jackson, Iain P	4:03:06	(11,411)
Jackson, Jeremy T	5:06:02	(26,881)

Jackson, Kenneth P	4:45:36	(22,458)
Jackson, Lee R	3:05:52	(1,544)
Jackson, Mark H	4:59:01	(25,565)
Jackson, Martin P	5:08:03	(27,226)
Jackson, Martyn R	4:01:07	(10,965)
Jackson, Michael A	4:21:46	(16,276)
Jackson, Mick E	4:29:20	(18,412)
Jackson, Neil	2:59:00	(1,033)
Jackson, Nicholas	5:06:06	(26,890)
Jackson, Paul	6:31:57	(34,304)
Jackson, Peter	4:49:01	(23,241)
Jackson, Peter J	4:43:03	(21,881)
Jackson, Peter N	3:33:19	(4,931)
Jackson, Peter N	4:29:48	(18,545)
Jackson, Richard	3:40:48	(6,141)
Jackson, Robert D	4:14:26	(14,283)
Jackson, Russell K	5:03:23	(26,417)
Jackson, Sarah B	5:04:15	(26,561)
Jackson, Simon A	3:29:44	(4,401)
Jackson, Stan	5:02:45	(26,284)
Jackson, Stephen	3:44:00	(6,742)
Jackson, Stephen J	4:37:59	(20,616)
Jackson, Stephen R	4:05:05	(11,889)
Jackson, Steve J	2:59:43	(1,104)
Jackson, Stewart W	5:24:11	(29,642)
Jackson, Sydney I	4:01:59	(11,150)
Jackson, Timothy M	4:29:15	(18,379)
Jackson, Trevor J	3:56:00	(9,513)
Jacob, David	3:46:59	(7,346)
Jacob, James	4:21:16	(16,135)
Jacob, Kevin M	3:40:50	(6,148)
Jacob, Phillip A	2:58:22	(980)
Jacobs, Andrew P	3:00:38	(1,167)
Jacobs, David	3:35:21	(5,232)
Jacobs, Kenneth J	6:05:29	(33,294)
Jacobs, Michael U	5:48:49	(32,163)
Jacobs, Robert E	2:49:05	(471)
Jacobs, Stephen M	4:43:37	(22,015)
Jacobs, Steve	4:47:45	(22,953)
Jacobs, Terry R	4:14:20	(14,251)
Jacobson, Brian	3:17:49	(2,770)
Jacobson, Robert	2:57:58	(955)
Jacq, Germain	3:21:05	(3,092)
Jacques, Richard	5:29:17	(30,271)
Jacquiau, Philippe	3:49:01	(7,826)
Jaffe, Pete S	3:31:24	(4,663)
Jaffe, Steven H	6:24:11	(34,069)
Jagan, Chris	3:26:37	(3,872)
Jagger, Tom G	4:27:45	(17,968)
Jagpal, Kamaljit J	4:37:26	(20,481)
Jahans, Stephen D	4:40:01	(21,147)
Jakins, Brian	5:33:31	(30,729)
Jakl, Martin	4:28:29	(18,162)
Jakubowski, Juergen	5:25:22	(29,784)
Jallal, Craig	4:48:32	(23,130)
Jalloh, Abraham A	2:46:37	(362)
Jalloh, Ibrahim	3:11:05	(2,041)
Jamard, Douglas	4:04:55	(11,843)
James, Adrian J	3:56:30	(9,663)
James, Alan	5:11:19	(27,708)
James, Alexander H	3:31:05	(4,617)
James, Alistair M	5:14:29	(28,260)
James, Andrew C	5:44:49	(31,832)
James, Andrew W	2:36:04	(122)
James, Barry	5:40:55	(31,497)
James, Bruce	6:06:17	(33,347)
James, Charles J	4:25:13	(17,189)
James, Christopher S	3:45:21	(7,017)
James, Darren R	4:49:13	(23,286)
James, David	4:30:29	(18,722)
James, David R	3:54:20	(9,053)
James, Eric	3:19:21	(2,915)
James, Gwyn	4:10:24	(13,204)
James, Hywel M	3:30:44	(4,565)
James, Iain R	3:59:43	(10,635)
James, Ian F	2:43:51	(290)
James, Jonathan	4:26:15	(17,519)
James, Keith M	4:04:04	(11,654)
James, Laurence M	3:54:18	(9,046)
James, Mark D	3:46:01	(7,140)
James, Mark J	4:09:03	(12,838)
James, Matthew R	3:35:56	(5,327)
James, Matthew R	4:15:00	(14,448)

James, Michael F	5:10:06	(27,519)
James, Neil P	3:29:04	(4,286)
James, Nick	3:15:10	(2,492)
James, Peter	4:02:13	(11,206)
James, Philip	3:50:18	(8,104)
James, Philip	4:02:21	(11,234)
James, Philip N	4:39:02	(20,890)
James, Raymond O	4:05:06	(11,897)
James, Robert S	2:34:43	(110)
James, Russell M	5:19:32	(29,038)
James, Simon	4:04:14	(11,691)
James, Simon H	4:29:22	(18,420)
James, Simon L	4:59:57	(25,766)
James, Stephen C	6:01:58	(33,078)
James, Stephen P	5:02:57	(26,329)
James, Steve A	3:28:12	(4,146)
James, Timothy A	3:48:59	(7,818)
James, Wendell	4:29:31	(18,470)
James, William	5:28:18	(30,168)
James, William George	4:02:12	(11,204)
Jamieson, Christopher J	3:59:04	(10,456)
Jamieson, George A	3:17:29	(2,733)
Jamieson, Ryan	3:54:12	(9,023)
Jamieson, Simon J	3:41:23	(6,255)
Janaway, Mark R	4:58:04	(25,343)
Jandoli, Vincenzo	3:51:56	(8,470)
Jandu, Dhanwant	6:08:08	(33,452)
Jandu, Randeep	6:04:57	(33,267)
Jandu, Sandeep	6:28:06	(34,197)
Jandu, Sukhbindar	6:27:15	(34,174)
Jandu, Sulakhan Singh	4:34:58	(19,847)
Janec, Steve	4:22:26	(16,453)
Janes, Jeremy N	3:14:35	(2,427)
Janes, Richard G	3:44:35	(6,857)
Janikiewicz, Douglas	4:06:41	(12,260)
Janna, Ruzeri	5:03:31	(26,435)
Jans, Ruud	4:16:42	(14,891)
Janse Van Rensburg, Eduard	4:43:46	(22,053)
Jansen, Grant W	3:06:48	(1,617)
Jansen, Wiktor	4:02:38	(11,298)
Janssen, Marco E	4:11:57	(13,608)
Jaouen, Joel	4:19:29	(15,662)
Jappy, Stephen D	4:43:48	(22,057)
Jar, Steve T	3:16:04	(2,584)
Jardine, Howard W	3:13:31	(2,304)
Jarman, Alan W	4:59:39	(25,701)
Jarman, Alexander E	3:46:14	(7,188)
Jarman, Charles	4:45:54	(22,524)
Jarman, Roy F	6:02:56	(33,139)
Jarman, Shane M	5:30:16	(30,394)
Jarrard, Simon E	5:07:11	(27,096)
Jarratt, Timothy	3:53:30	(8,855)
Jarrett, Robert A	5:44:22	(31,792)
Jarrett, Robin D	5:28:05	(30,115)
Jarrey, Michael C	4:51:11	(23,769)
Jarrold, Darren M	3:35:56	(5,327)
Jarvie, Scott R	3:25:29	(3,668)
Jarvie, Willie	3:14:39	(2,437)
Jarvis, Bernard	3:06:49	(1,619)
Jarvis, Christopher C	3:39:14	(5,858)
Jarvis, James E	3:01:37	(1,233)
Jarvis, Johnathan R	4:57:28	(25,222)
Jarvis, Sam D	4:12:18	(13,698)
Jarvis, Simon J	3:45:44	(7,082)
Jarvis, Steve	5:13:31	(28,087)
Jarvis, Thomas M	4:13:29	(14,015)
Jarvus, Mark M	3:11:11	(2,049)
Jaspal, Singh	5:19:29	(29,029)
Jassal, Sunny	4:28:30	(18,168)
Jathar, Pankaj P	5:04:56	(26,677)
Javadi, Mustafa	4:56:02	(24,907)
Jay, Adam	3:46:18	(7,202)
Jayes, Timothy M	4:02:28	(11,262)
Jbornum, Jan C	4:35:49	(20,047)
Jeacock, Paul A	4:52:11	(23,981)
Jean-Paul, Desmond	4:17:27	(15,084)
Jeary, Kevin	3:12:10	(2,160)
Jefferies, David L	5:08:40	(27,305)
Jefferies, Michael G	4:17:00	(14,955)
Jefferies, Paul	3:36:55	(5,484)
Jefferies, Stephen P	4:06:58	(12,333)
Jefferis, Christopher J	4:13:31	(14,023)
Jeffers, Kenneth F	5:11:41	(27,766)

Jefferson, Sean	5:59:58 (32,979)	
Jeffery, Adam P	3:40:08 (6,023)	
Jeffery, Craig N	2:54:38 (723)	
Jeffery, David L	2:55:47 (792)	
Jeffery, Edward W	4:31:41 (19,016)	
Jeffery, Martin J	4:14:14 (14,220)	
Jeffery, Paul B	3:34:58 (5,180)	
Jeffery, Robert D	5:24:55 (29,734)	
Jeffery, Simon P	4:43:41 (22,028)	
Jeffery, Stephen P	2:48:57 (468)	
Jefferys, Luke D	4:50:38 (23,658)	
Jefford, Mark	3:14:20 (2,397)	
Jeffrey, Adam J	3:23:58 (3,443)	
Jeffrey, Gordon C	4:03:46 (11,567)	
Jeffrey, Keith J	3:42:36 (6,481)	
Jeffrey, Malcolm D	5:03:59 (26,515)	
Jeffrey, Tom	3:50:36 (8,170)	
Jeffreys, Adrian C	5:50:44 (32,322)	
Jeffreys, Karl R	3:14:10 (2,376)	
Jeffries, Antony	4:35:01 (19,855)	
Jeffries, Kevin J	3:10:02 (1,924)	
Jeffries, Marc	4:39:24 (20,989)	
Jelf, Simon E	5:55:44 (32,696)	
Jelley, David	2:57:41 (931)	
Jelley, Derek A	7:01:43 (34,891)	
Jelley, Peter J	5:50:13 (32,280)	
Jellicoe, George N	4:23:57 (16,837)	
Jellis, David P	3:45:47 (7,091)	
Jelliss, Stuart K	3:38:45 (5,765)	
Jelly, Harry J	4:43:13 (21,917)	
Jelstad, Rolf	5:34:23 (30,828)	
Jelu, Yanick	4:09:52 (13,059)	
Jenkin, Andrew B	5:39:09 (31,327)	
Jenkin, Daniel J	3:21:02 (3,088)	
Jenkins, Adam P	6:07:29 (33,418)	
Jenkins, Andrew	5:25:59 (29,867)	
Jenkins, Ben	3:59:40 (10,620)	
Jenkins, Carlyle	3:52:22 (8,569)	
Jenkins, Charlie	4:19:19 (15,616)	
Jenkins, Chris	4:37:16 (20,433)	
Jenkins, Clifford I	4:32:56 (19,303)	
Jenkins, Clive A	3:49:05 (7,843)	
Jenkins, Colin	4:12:13 (13,670)	
Jenkins, David E	5:14:22 (28,241)	
Jenkins, David R	3:50:46 (8,200)	
Jenkins, Dominic A	5:07:18 (27,116)	
Jenkins, Gareth A	4:07:35 (12,472)	
Jenkins, Geraint H	4:21:15 (16,129)	
Jenkins, Glyn J	4:18:59 (15,507)	
Jenkins, Jonathan	3:59:40 (10,620)	
Jenkins, Keith D	4:27:41 (17,947)	
Jenkins, Mark R	3:56:59 (9,809)	
Jenkins, Michael A	4:05:38 (12,012)	
Jenkins, Michael J	4:44:42 (22,249)	
Jenkins, Paul	7:30:08 (35,127)	
Jenkins, Paul J	3:16:29 (2,632)	
Jenkins, Peter	5:11:35 (27,754)	
Jenkins, Robert A	4:39:38 (21,053)	
Jenkins, Robert E	4:42:43 (21,804)	
Jenkins, Stephen E	5:22:02 (29,352)	
Jenkins, Steve M	3:56:09 (9,552)	
Jenkins MBE, Ian C	6:22:31 (34,010)	
Jenkinson, Brett	4:54:39 (24,583)	
Jenkinson, Lee	4:14:45 (14,363)	
Jenkinson, Paul M	4:59:13 (25,610)	
Jenks, John W	4:25:03 (17,137)	
Jenn, Dieter	4:49:01 (23,241)	
Jenn, Marc S	5:15:11 (28,365)	
Jenner, Christopher M	4:33:11 (19,360)	
Jenner, Marc E	4:28:27 (18,153)	
Jenner, Paul	4:16:03 (14,729)	
Jennings, Barry I	5:02:43 (26,278)	
Jennings, Dan W	4:53:57 (24,411)	
Jennings, David	4:48:36 (23,147)	
Jennings, Francis R	4:14:01 (14,152)	
Jennings, James A	3:34:30 (5,124)	
Jennings, John F	3:37:19 (5,539)	
Jennings, Kenneth G	4:35:06 (19,873)	
Jennings, Matthew S	4:15:42 (14,636)	
Jennings, Max E	4:19:37 (15,699)	
Jennings, Michael C	4:05:48 (12,052)	
Jennings, Nicholas M	4:07:24 (12,438)	
Jennings, Paul	3:19:13 (2,901)	
Jennings, Peter	3:11:01 (2,034)	
Jennings, Ross C	5:23:36 (29,560)	
Jennings, Shaun	4:53:31 (24,307)	
Jensen, Cameron R	3:56:39 (9,710)	
Jensen, Jann	4:34:10 (19,615)	
Jensen, Roy	4:39:58 (21,129)	
Jenson, Lars-Moller	4:02:41 (11,309)	
Jenzen, Dieter	5:39:47 (31,395)	
Jepps, Neil J	5:29:26 (30,297)	
Jepson, Christopher	3:13:05 (2,255)	
Jepson, Graham A	3:33:58 (5,041)	
Jepson, John C	4:02:28 (11,262)	
Jepson, Paul	4:23:15 (16,669)	
Jerams, Stephen	4:55:23 (24,754)	
Jercic, Vasja	3:29:15 (4,321)	
Jeremy, Edward J	3:04:12 (1,408)	
Jerrett, Nicholas A	4:03:59 (11,626)	
Jeske, Andrew	3:11:50 (2,122)	
Jessop, Mark	4:54:51 (24,630)	
Jessop, Toby G	4:49:52 (23,466)	
Jestico, Dan	3:46:52 (7,318)	
Jevons, Ben	5:31:58 (30,557)	
Jewell, Alan	3:32:54 (4,873)	
Jewell, Christopher R	4:46:28 (22,661)	
Jewell, Ian M	5:06:12 (26,906)	
Jex, Andrew	4:05:05 (11,889)	
Jhooti, Sarabjit J	4:23:32 (16,735)	
Jiggins, Dean E	4:47:33 (22,891)	
Jimenez-Hernandez, Santiago	5:09:35 (27,451)	
Jimenez-Ridruejo, Francisco J	4:24:10 (16,894)	
Jiwa, Shiraz	4:20:42 (15,991)	
Jobanputra, Rajesh	3:57:27 (9,968)	
Jobanputra, Shabir	5:11:36 (27,758)	
Joble, Mike J	4:13:06 (13,910)	
Jobling, Christopher J	5:04:47 (26,647)	
Jobling, Paul	5:04:50 (26,655)	
Jobson, Roger W	4:03:25 (11,485)	
Jocelyn, Steven M	3:58:43 (10,354)	
Joe, Toju	4:43:10 (21,905)	
Johan, Eugene	4:59:41 (25,708)	
Johannes, Michael	3:26:25 (3,831)	
Johannesen, Preben	3:29:05 (4,291)	
Johannessen, Marius	4:03:44 (11,554)	
Johans, Mike J	5:54:58 (32,639)	
Johansen, Einar O	4:29:29 (18,457)	
Johansen, Helge	3:48:18 (7,657)	
Johansen, Jesper B	4:19:24 (15,636)	
Johansen, Michael N	3:37:17 (5,534)	
Johansson, Kent	4:00:26 (10,813)	
Johansson, Tomas	5:32:49 (30,656)	
Johansson, Ulf G	4:38:26 (20,736)	
John, Andrew M	3:55:22 (9,329)	
John, Anthony D	4:05:29 (11,983)	
John, Antony G	4:18:49 (15,470)	
John, Barry R	4:17:24 (15,068)	
John, Caspar R	4:18:02 (15,218)	
John, Dean C	3:05:08 (1,477)	
John, Morris	4:16:34 (14,851)	
John, Steve	4:55:37 (24,795)	
John, Tim J	4:41:31 (21,529)	
Johnes, Michael G	5:28:47 (30,217)	
John-Lewis, Johnson	3:43:17 (6,613)	
Johnsen, Vegard	3:43:52 (6,715)	
Johnson, Andrew	3:55:43 (9,435)	
Johnson, Andrew	5:02:51 (26,307)	
Johnson, Andrew G	3:41:53 (6,351)	
Johnson, Andrew K	4:09:23 (12,930)	
Johnson, Andrew N	4:01:16 (10,998)	
Johnson, Andrew S	3:33:55 (5,030)	
Johnson, Andrew W	4:02:08 (11,190)	
Johnson, Anthony C	3:53:51 (8,947)	
Johnson, Anthony D	4:15:38 (14,617)	
Johnson, Ben	4:05:46 (12,041)	
Johnson, Brian	4:51:18 (23,793)	
Johnson, Christopher B	4:25:32 (17,296)	
Johnson, Christopher M	4:15:00 (14,448)	
Johnson, Clive F	5:11:21 (27,716)	
Johnson, Clive I	4:58:44 (25,493)	
Johnson, Darrell L	3:59:27 (10,557)	
Johnson, Darren J	4:55:34 (24,783)	
Johnson, David L	3:48:35 (7,736)	
Johnson, Dominic P	5:18:52 (28,927)	
Johnson, Garry B	5:23:21 (29,522)	
Johnson, Gary C	4:06:19 (12,171)	
Johnson, Gerald C	4:28:16 (18,105)	
Johnson, Graham D	3:55:02 (9,243)	
Johnson, Harvey	4:41:15 (21,460)	
Johnson, Iain A	4:02:06 (11,185)	
Johnson, Ian C	4:11:46 (13,555)	
Johnson, Ian D	4:12:34 (13,765)	
Johnson, Ian K	3:44:43 (6,885)	
Johnson, James I	5:21:57 (29,346)	
Johnson, Jason	4:43:41 (22,028)	
Johnson, Jay P	3:39:36 (5,930)	
Johnson, John R	2:59:30 (1,089)	
Johnson, Joseph R	4:57:39 (25,256)	
Johnson, Julian C	4:20:57 (16,067)	
Johnson, Lee	4:03:42 (11,545)	
Johnson, Lee	5:01:56 (26,132)	
Johnson, Luke M	3:59:16 (10,513)	
Johnson, Marc A	4:39:19 (20,967)	
Johnson, Mark A	5:28:08 (30,130)	
Johnson, Mark A	5:41:52 (31,587)	
Johnson, Mark S	4:36:50 (20,314)	
Johnson, Martyn G	3:53:18 (8,801)	
Johnson, Michael	5:07:17 (27,113)	
Johnson, Mickey	3:53:23 (8,826)	
Johnson, Mike	4:03:33 (11,514)	
Johnson, Myles G	4:07:35 (12,472)	
Johnson, Neale	4:49:38 (23,408)	
Johnson, Neil	3:47:03 (7,362)	
Johnson, Neil	5:13:57 (28,161)	
Johnson, Nigel K	4:27:49 (17,987)	
Johnson, Oliver R	3:44:51 (6,928)	
Johnson, Paul	6:04:52 (33,260)	
Johnson, Peter	4:05:23 (11,964)	
Johnson, Ray D	3:56:02 (9,518)	
Johnson, Raymond	5:19:29 (29,029)	
Johnson, Richard	5:00:43 (25,920)	
Johnson, Richard M	3:18:26 (2,826)	
Johnson, Robert G	4:44:16 (22,160)	
Johnson, Robert P	2:59:55 (1,121)	
Johnson, Rowland A	4:31:29 (18,965)	
Johnson, Simon	4:12:10 (13,657)	
Johnson, Simon C	3:19:46 (2,975)	
Johnson, Stephen H	4:32:54 (19,289)	
Johnson, Stephen H	4:41:23 (21,489)	
Johnson, Steve D	4:38:08 (20,656)	
Johnson, Steven D	5:25:26 (29,794)	
Johnson, Stuart	4:40:11 (21,182)	
Johnson, Thomas	5:36:23 (31,037)	
Johnson, Tunde	4:53:49 (24,387)	
Johnson, Wayne	6:15:33 (33,762)	
Johnson, William A	4:54:19 (24,508)	
Johnson, William F	3:19:14 (2,903)	
Johnston, Anthony C	5:23:11 (29,502)	
Johnston, Daren W	4:15:26 (14,558)	
Johnston, Gary S	5:35:30 (30,955)	
Johnston, Gordon J	4:06:26 (12,197)	
Johnston, Ian	3:57:06 (9,856)	
Johnston, Kevin	3:51:13 (8,305)	
Johnston, Lee J	4:23:17 (16,683)	
Johnston, Mark	2:46:38 (363)	
Johnston, Mark N	4:26:15 (17,519)	
Johnston, Peter M	4:41:03 (21,407)	
Johnston, Richard R	4:55:52 (24,868)	
Johnston, Steve P	3:39:48 (5,963)	
Johnstone, Allan D	4:22:29 (16,467)	
Johnstone, Douglas	3:27:39 (4,047)	
Johnstone, John F	4:48:36 (23,147)	
Johnstone, Mark J	5:05:40 (26,817)	
Johnstone, Michael	4:30:59 (18,831)	
Johnstone, Paul S	4:01:32 (11,055)	
Johnstone, Thomas F	5:35:21 (30,940)	
Johnstone-Robertson, Graeme	3:33:19 (4,931)	
Joiner, Andrew G	3:15:39 (2,535)	
Joinson, Leslie J	4:42:35 (21,765)	
Jokat, Brian A	4:07:45 (12,516)	
Jol, Onno	4:49:11 (23,280)	
Jolliffe, David T	4:47:37 (22,915)	
Jolliffe, Gary P	8:14:56 (35,242)	
Jolliffe, Tony	4:43:10 (21,905)	
Jolly, Andrew J	4:18:45 (15,444)	
Jolly, Derek V	3:45:58 (7,127)	
Jolly, Steve D	4:13:06 (13,910)	
Jolly, Timothy J	4:16:48 (14,913)	

Jones, Aaron S	3:11:39	(2,098)
Jones, Alan	3:59:35	(10,594)
Jones, Alan	5:28:01	(30,105)
Jones, Alan D	4:26:06	(17,475)
Jones, Alexander A	5:33:13	(30,691)
Jones, Allan N	4:11:46	(13,555)
Jones, Allen D	2:47:27	(387)
Jones, Alun R	5:13:25	(28,063)
Jones, Andi	2:18:53	(24)
Jones, Andrew	5:16:57	(28,637)
Jones, Andrew C	4:34:52	(19,811)
Jones, Andrew D	4:18:22	(15,315)
Jones, Andrew K	4:46:09	(22,593)
Jones, Andrew M	6:05:42	(33,307)
Jones, Anthony N	4:31:33	(18,986)
Jones, Anthony R	4:55:50	(24,856)
Jones, Arwyn L	5:24:01	(29,621)
Jones, Barrie J	3:21:02	(3,088)
Jones, Barry J	4:35:28	(19,968)
Jones, Ben	4:28:51	(18,262)
Jones, Benjamin G	5:18:32	(28,869)
Jones, Bernard	3:57:46	(10,058)
Jones, Brendon S	6:21:59	(33,987)
Jones, Brian	5:05:59	(26,868)
Jones, Brinley	5:07:19	(27,117)
Jones, Bruce A	3:22:29	(3,240)
Jones, Brynmor P	3:52:50	(8,688)
Jones, Chris	4:14:38	(14,325)
Jones, Chris S	4:08:32	(12,697)
Jones, Christopher J	5:42:16	(31,606)
Jones, Christopher L	4:29:37	(18,499)
Jones, Clifford	5:49:08	(32,192)
Jones, Colin	4:49:25	(23,342)
Jones, Colin W	4:37:21	(20,457)
Jones, Daniel C	3:58:16	(10,210)
Jones, Darren H	3:47:44	(7,512)
Jones, Darren J	2:47:53	(408)
Jones, Darren W	5:03:15	(26,392)
Jones, Dave	3:55:31	(9,373)
Jones, David A	3:37:19	(5,539)
Jones, David A	4:14:59	(14,437)
Jones, David C	3:18:23	(2,820)
Jones, David G	4:59:35	(25,682)
Jones, David J	4:33:02	(19,320)
Jones, David J	4:40:52	(21,352)
Jones, David J	5:16:51	(28,616)
Jones, David M	5:07:54	(27,201)
Jones, David P	4:09:35	(12,978)
Jones, David R	2:48:43	(447)
Jones, David R	4:14:51	(14,396)
Jones, David T	4:26:56	(17,732)
Jones, David W	3:36:15	(5,382)
Jones, Derek A	4:04:12	(11,684)
Jones, Derek A	5:40:46	(31,485)
Jones, Desi	4:10:18	(13,169)
Jones, Dewi E	3:20:10	(3,016)
Jones, Digby M	5:58:26	(32,868)
Jones, Dominic N	4:17:13	(15,015)
Jones, Douglas S	5:07:38	(27,166)
Jones, Francis A	4:44:57	(22,313)
Jones, Gareth	5:20:44	(29,207)
Jones, Gareth D	4:05:40	(12,019)
Jones, Gareth D	4:13:22	(13,982)
Jones, Gareth E	4:22:57	(16,590)
Jones, Gareth J	4:22:53	(16,576)
Jones, Gareth L	3:42:39	(6,492)
Jones, Gareth R	4:21:19	(16,147)
Jones, Gareth W	4:35:36	(19,998)
Jones, Gari	4:23:09	(16,644)
Jones, Gary	3:59:27	(10,557)
Jones, Gary M	3:41:46	(6,327)
Jones, George	4:41:39	(21,555)
Jones, George	5:57:30	(32,804)
Jones, George C	4:32:00	(19,087)
Jones, Geraint O	4:24:24	(16,956)
Jones, Graham G	4:06:18	(12,166)
Jones, Graham J	4:11:24	(13,453)
Jones, Hefin	5:38:25	(31,238)
Jones, Hugh W	5:24:30	(29,684)
Jones, Huw A	5:02:16	(26,194)
Jones, Huw E	3:57:30	(9,979)
Jones, Hywel W	5:14:19	(28,233)
Jones, Ian	4:09:53	(13,063)

Jones, Ian	5:36:32	(31,060)
Jones, Ian G	3:29:58	(4,448)
Jones, Ian H	3:54:09	(9,013)
Jones, Ian M	4:15:12	(14,502)
Jones, Jerome	4:46:47	(22,727)
Jones, John	5:13:01	(28,000)
Jones, John A	4:32:03	(19,102)
Jones, Keith	5:03:48	(26,484)
Jones, Keith A	3:59:14	(10,503)
Jones, Keith G	3:58:16	(10,210)
Jones, Ken L	5:18:06	(28,798)
Jones, Kenneth I	4:25:22	(17,235)
Jones, Kevin	4:52:12	(23,985)
Jones, Kevin F	4:41:56	(21,610)
Jones, Kevin M	5:35:49	(30,978)
Jones, Lawrence G	3:10:29	(1,977)
Jones, Lee M	4:25:05	(17,146)
Jones, Linda M	6:01:22	(33,042)
Jones, Malcolm J	5:48:44	(32,154)
Jones, Mark	4:50:32	(23,636)
Jones, Mark A	5:38:38	(31,271)
Jones, Martin D	4:25:47	(17,373)
Jones, Martin G	3:40:09	(6,028)
Jones, Martin L	4:19:12	(15,579)
Jones, Matthew E	4:01:33	(11,058)
Jones, Matthew P	2:39:57	(204)
Jones, Merrick A	4:51:24	(23,814)
Jones, Michael	5:03:38	(26,452)
Jones, Michael S	4:04:18	(11,701)
Jones, Michael W	3:37:51	(5,627)
Jones, Nathan D	3:14:30	(2,416)
Jones, Neil A	4:21:58	(16,322)
Jones, Neil A	5:03:46	(26,476)
Jones, Nicholas P	5:02:51	(26,307)
Jones, Nigel F	2:56:08	(816)
Jones, Oliver	2:56:26	(837)
Jones, Owen L	4:56:48	(25,095)
Jones, Patrick	4:12:36	(13,774)
Jones, Paul	4:35:50	(20,050)
Jones, Paul	4:47:53	(22,985)
Jones, Paul	4:54:58	(24,663)
Jones, Paul C	4:59:22	(25,637)
Jones, Paul M	4:13:10	(13,928)
Jones, Peter	3:28:51	(4,253)
Jones, Peter K	4:36:20	(20,172)
Jones, Peter L	3:37:24	(5,557)
Jones, Philip E	5:55:32	(32,683)
Jones, Piers	3:13:29	(2,300)
Jones, Ralph D	4:16:06	(14,738)
Jones, Ralph W	4:19:31	(15,668)
Jones, Raymond	5:12:03	(27,831)
Jones, Rex	4:17:23	(15,063)
Jones, Rhys	4:30:51	(18,810)
Jones, Rhys V	5:10:16	(27,534)
Jones, Richard A	4:50:15	(23,548)
Jones, Richard J	4:44:56	(22,307)
Jones, Richard M	3:25:20	(3,649)
Jones, Richard M	3:46:14	(7,188)
Jones, Rob	3:42:39	(6,492)
Jones, Robert A	4:53:03	(24,190)
Jones, Rodri	2:28:06	(59)
Jones, Russell	3:14:29	(2,411)
Jones, Sam	4:30:44	(18,778)
Jones, Sam G	5:01:28	(26,058)
Jones, Scott P	3:58:53	(10,406)
Jones, Sean W	4:47:33	(22,891)
Jones, Simon	2:38:33	(169)
Jones, Simon	3:19:43	(2,969)
Jones, Simon	4:11:47	(13,559)
Jones, Simon N	4:15:36	(14,607)
Jones, Stephen	3:08:03	(1,720)
Jones, Stephen	4:05:54	(12,073)
Jones, Stephen	5:02:12	(26,183)
Jones, Stephen	5:13:09	(28,015)
Jones, Stephen J	3:49:59	(8,033)
Jones, Stephen M	4:49:44	(23,435)
Jones, Stephen N	2:51:29	(562)
Jones, Stephen R	3:03:32	(1,366)
Jones, Stephen R	4:06:14	(12,149)
Jones, Steve	3:44:50	(6,919)
Jones, Steve K	3:53:32	(8,866)
Jones, Steven G	4:51:17	(23,789)
Jones, Steven I	2:40:24	(209)

Jones, Terry M	3:59:47	(10,661)
Jones, Terry W	3:49:32	(7,940)
Jones, Theodore L	3:57:01	(9,820)
Jones, Thomas H	3:37:09	(5,519)
Jones, Tim A	4:05:33	(12,000)
Jones, Tim J	4:12:05	(13,639)
Jones, Tim S	3:59:05	(10,462)
Jones, Trevor	4:58:52	(25,527)
Jones, Trevor B	4:01:21	(11,012)
Jones, Vincent M	4:12:35	(13,769)
Jones, Walter	5:27:33	(30,051)
Jones, William	4:35:43	(20,024)
Jones, William K	4:01:29	(11,047)
Jones-Davies, Aled L	5:03:15	(26,392)
Jopson, Terry I	4:14:37	(14,323)
Jordan, Anthony M	3:35:00	(5,182)
Jordan, Chris	5:20:53	(29,223)
Jordan, Christopher J	4:22:34	(16,492)
Jordan, Christopher M	4:48:46	(23,187)
Jordan, Dominic	4:16:48	(14,913)
Jordan, Mark	3:54:33	(9,112)
Jordan, Mark	4:21:22	(16,164)
Jordan, Mark A	3:52:14	(8,537)
Jordan, Mike	4:24:16	(16,918)
Jordan, Paul W	5:28:20	(30,173)
Jordan, Peter A	4:16:49	(14,918)
Jordan, Philip	3:57:35	(10,007)
Jordan, Roger W	6:22:59	(34,020)
Jordan, Shaun G	4:02:30	(11,272)
Jorgensen, Andrew C	3:48:08	(7,622)
Jorgensen, Max J	3:32:42	(4,844)
Jose, Jemy	3:44:45	(6,889)
Josefsburg, Alon	3:09:15	(1,836)
Joseph, Charles M	6:26:49	(34,151)
Joseph, Joer	5:19:09	(28,963)
Joseph, John D	5:38:33	(31,259)
Joseph, John P	6:26:49	(34,151)
Joseph, Jonathan G	4:24:53	(17,090)
Joseph-Edouard, Jean-Claude	3:33:23	(4,944)
Josephs, David S	3:43:33	(6,660)
Josephs, Merrick L	3:29:58	(4,448)
Joshi, Anil	4:21:45	(16,271)
Jospehs, Michael A	5:09:42	(27,470)
Joss, Norman J	4:33:45	(19,506)
Jost, Robert W	3:11:38	(2,093)
Jost, Werner	4:05:47	(12,047)
Joubert, Nick	4:59:50	(25,745)
Joules, Keith	2:49:33	(485)
Journaix, Dominique	3:42:45	(6,505)
Joy, Danny	4:50:17	(23,556)
Joyce, Alan D	4:03:23	(11,476)
Joyce, Simon R	5:12:42	(27,949)
Joyce, Tom A	3:53:13	(8,774)
Joyce-Hess, Jonathan K	3:20:27	(3,042)
Joynson, Mark	3:04:22	(1,419)
Jubault, Jean-Pierre	3:50:41	(8,184)
Juckes, Ian T	4:09:03	(12,838)
Judah, Nathan	6:36:52	(34,431)
Judd, Peter J	4:39:58	(21,129)
Jude, Dominic	3:33:49	(5,014)
Judelle, Bernard	3:58:16	(10,210)
Judge, Alastair D	2:57:57	(951)
Judge, Ciaran C	5:00:51	(25,946)
Judge, Dave J	4:36:41	(20,274)
Judge, David J	4:14:27	(14,285)
Judge, Sean P	3:54:32	(9,105)
Judges, Oliver P	6:08:57	(33,486)
Juergens, Mario	2:48:47	(455)
Jugg, Andrew L	4:55:53	(24,871)
Jukes, Andrew M	3:26:29	(3,844)
Julian, Raul J	3:40:10	(6,031)
Jung, Bernard	3:27:11	(3,958)
Jung, Hans-Juergen	4:13:07	(13,915)
Jupe, Nicholas P	4:54:45	(24,610)
Jupp, Anthony	3:50:09	(8,073)
Jupp, Peter R	4:23:22	(16,706)
Jurgens, Mark J	3:18:21	(2,817)
Jury, Tim	4:18:27	(15,350)
Justice, David R	3:52:50	(8,688)
Jutterstrom, Matts	4:23:18	(16,690)
Kabrick, Norman	3:59:05	(10,462)
Kadar, Sheik K	4:46:56	(22,757)
Kaempfer, Alexander	4:32:55	(19,295)

Kaempfer, Matthias 5:39:28 (31,373)
Kaess, Hermann 3:48:45 (7,775)
Kahlon, Gurjinder 5:06:15 (26,911)
Kain, Duncan J 6:11:45 (33,601)
Kain, Nicholas A 4:51:47 (23,888)
Kainth, Ranjiet 3:27:45 (4,067)
Kaiser, Ken 3:46:49 (7,308)
Kakkindiris, Stelios 4:33:54 (19,546)
Kakuda, Yoshihiro 4:02:15 (11,212)
Kalach, Hassan 3:19:01 (2,883)
Kalia, Roop N 4:31:16 (18,904)
Kaligotla, Sudhir 6:33:42 (34,346)
Kalke, Stefan 3:31:20 (4,656)
Kallumpram, Ashok A 4:52:19 (24,018)
Kalogianis, John L 4:15:33 (14,593)
Kalsey, Narinder S 6:04:27 (33,243)
Kaminski-Morrow, David J 4:47:53 (22,985)
Kane, Adrian 4:46:00 (22,551)
Kane, Anthony 4:06:49 (12,288)
Kane, Michael J 5:01:14 (26,013)
Kane, Nick M 3:02:51 (1,323)
Kania, Mike 4:30:01 (18,591)
Kanji, Mohamed 6:29:17 (34,235)
Kanthamoorthy, Kalavannan 6:09:24 (33,510)
Kantor, Gregg 6:35:59 (34,408)
Kanumilli, Naresh 4:19:58 (15,792)
Kanzig, Gerhard 3:42:24 (6,450)
Kaou, Samir N 3:44:56 (6,946)
Kaponi, Andrew 5:31:43 (30,533)
Kapoor, Neil 6:05:10 (33,282)
Kapoor, Sonny 4:41:02 (21,402)
Kapoor, Vikas 4:30:46 (18,786)
Kapp, Josef 3:40:32 (6,089)
Kappler, Markus 5:16:50 (28,612)
Kappus, Reinhard 5:15:36 (28,434)
Karalius, Paul 4:56:42 (25,072)
Karbani, Tim 3:56:25 (9,637)
Kareth, Thomas 3:20:09 (3,014)
Karlsen, Morten 4:38:42 (20,799)
Karlsson, Erik B 4:41:35 (21,544)
Karlsson, Krister 3:52:31 (8,609)
Karlsson, Mats 3:04:50 (1,454)
Karlsson, Mats 3:23:02 (3,304)
Karlsson, Patrik 2:57:24 (914)
Karlsson, Richard 3:47:20 (7,425)
Karolemeas, George A 3:54:30 (9,098)
Karpf, Alf G 3:30:13 (4,480)
Karunaratne, Rosh 4:08:56 (12,809)
Kasolowsky, Christophe 3:55:33 (9,385)
Kasper, Nicholas R 4:40:26 (21,241)
Kassam, Imranali 5:01:54 (26,128)
Katechia, Bhagesh C 3:21:55 (3,174)
Kates, Shaun A 5:25:48 (29,842)
Kato Tetlie, Sten K 4:12:53 (13,848)
Kaufmann, Markus 3:50:06 (8,062)
Kavanagh, David 5:00:40 (25,915)
Kavanagh, Ian K 3:50:24 (8,122)
Kavanagh, Joseph P 3:28:44 (4,229)
Kavanagh, Kevin S 3:54:30 (9,098)
Kavanagh, Peter 4:28:07 (18,064)
Kavanagh, Terence 5:06:07 (26,894)
Kavs, Miran 2:47:37 (392)
Kay, Danny 3:32:03 (4,756)
Kay, John H 2:59:27 (1,085)
Kay, Jonathan B 4:08:37 (12,718)
Kay, Matthew S 2:51:21 (553)
Kay, Paul B 4:49:18 (23,306)
Kay, Robert R 3:03:20 (1,351)
Kay, Samuel K 3:40:03 (6,005)
Kay, Thomas 5:27:44 (30,068)
Kaye, Alexis 5:12:35 (27,923)
Kaye, Martin 4:30:02 (18,600)
Kaye, Robert S 4:42:36 (21,769)
Kayley, Mike 4:07:56 (12,561)
Kay-Shuttleworth, William 3:44:31 (6,839)
Kazalbash, Imran M 4:04:58 (11,855)
Kazalbash, Kamran 4:34:30 (19,711)
Kazimierski, Michael 2:46:50 (366)
Keal, Adam P 4:21:24 (16,171)
Kean, Martin 3:31:31 (4,682)
Keane, Glen B 5:41:18 (31,538)
Keane, Glenn B 6:43:07 (34,572)
Keane, Mark 4:09:18 (12,908)
Keane, Padraig F 4:16:16 (14,786)
Keane, Patrick C 3:52:15 (8,542)
Keane, Paul J 5:20:00 (29,095)
Keane, Richard E 6:22:00 (33,989)
Keany, Anthony N 3:44:41 (6,876)
Kear, Alexander J 5:19:18 (28,991)
Kear, Neil 3:53:18 (8,801)
Kearley, Adrian H 3:44:04 (6,751)
Kearney, Patrick J 5:12:02 (27,826)
Kearney, Robert 3:21:16 (3,110)
Kearns, Brian 3:59:36 (10,599)
Kearns, Joe 3:47:24 (7,438)
Kearns, Kevin P 3:32:42 (4,844)
Kearsley, Graham S 4:53:38 (24,338)
Kearsley, Mark P 5:28:42 (30,207)
Keast, Robert E 4:52:41 (24,101)
Keates, Rob M 3:46:49 (7,308)
Keating, Dermot J 3:57:42 (10,038)
Keating, Mike J 4:52:26 (24,037)
Keating, Nicholas M 3:55:50 (9,472)
Keatley, Peter A 4:48:56 (23,219)
Keats, Gavin J 3:58:23 (10,255)
Keayes, Donald N 4:52:17 (24,010)
Keayes, Michael D 5:13:18 (28,043)
Keddy, Kevan C 5:14:38 (28,291)
Keeble, Ian R 2:53:48 (672)
Keeble, Tony R 4:58:57 (25,544)
Keech, Tony 3:35:08 (5,201)
Keefe, James C 5:20:20 (29,146)
Keegan, Dan A 4:28:13 (18,091)
Keegan, David J 4:12:06 (13,640)
Keegan, Malcolm 4:24:59 (17,117)
Keegan, Martin E 4:24:35 (17,010)
Keegan, Simon 5:12:25 (27,890)
Keelan, Peter 4:40:30 (21,259)
Keeler, Nicholas 3:30:49 (4,581)
Keeling, Albert G 5:09:17 (27,400)
Keeling, Colin L 3:53:34 (8,875)
Keeling, David J 5:05:34 (26,803)
Keeling, Geoff 4:55:43 (24,822)
Keeling, Neil 4:37:42 (20,554)
Keen, Howard S 4:37:47 (20,575)
Keen, Kevin I 4:06:02 (12,102)
Keen, Richard J 4:05:14 (11,926)
Keen, Steve 4:50:17 (23,556)
Keenaghan, Martin P 3:55:16 (9,298)
Keenaghan, Shaun N 3:55:16 (9,298)
Keenan, Brian 4:04:37 (11,774)
Keenan, Christopher J 6:09:01 (33,488)
Keenan, Dave 2:48:01 (415)
Keenan, David M 3:23:17 (3,348)
Keenan, Ian 4:04:27 (11,734)
Keenan, Richard P 4:36:06 (20,108)
Keenan, Simon J 3:50:55 (8,239)
Keene, Benjamin G 3:21:17 (3,112)
Keene, Graham S 4:01:35 (11,064)
Keene, Nick R 4:17:06 (14,982)
Keene, Robert A 4:18:18 (15,296)
Keenleyside, Piers B 3:39:38 (5,935)
Keeping, Lee M 6:50:20 (34,731)
Keet, Wayne L 3:16:09 (2,597)
Kehoe, David P 4:51:20 (23,804)
Kehoe, Michael J 5:01:01 (25,978)
Kehoe, Robert F 4:17:32 (15,097)
Keighley, Charles J 4:24:48 (17,071)
Keighley, Russell 4:22:05 (16,362)
Keilloh, Richard J 5:28:13 (30,147)
Keily, Nick J 5:17:01 (28,648)
Keirs, James N 3:57:29 (9,973)
Keith, Bruce R 5:07:03 (27,068)
Kelchtermans, Peter J 2:49:12 (474)
Kelf, Jason R 3:37:42 (5,604)
Kelf, Jon 3:56:07 (9,543)
Kelf, Paul D 4:52:39 (24,091)
Kelford, Colin D 4:47:26 (22,868)
Kell, Lee A 3:48:23 (7,681)
Kellas, Gary 4:55:01 (24,679)
Kellaway, Andrew D 3:09:59 (1,918)
Kellaway, Roy R 2:50:52 (534)
Kelleher, Peter A 3:54:07 (8,999)
Kellens, Willy 3:36:35 (5,442)
Kellert, Karlheinz 4:36:03 (20,093)
Kellet, Michael C 4:06:39 (12,252)
Kelley, Philip 3:39:26 (5,898)
Kelley, Simon T 5:18:45 (28,911)
Kellock, Robert O 4:39:35 (21,037)
Kellow, Wayne R 5:06:23 (26,942)
Kelly, Adam R 4:04:24 (11,721)
Kelly, Alan V 5:36:13 (31,014)
Kelly, Andrew 4:41:42 (21,564)
Kelly, Andrew R 3:34:26 (5,116)
Kelly, Ann S 5:51:32 (32,375)
Kelly, Anthony R 4:25:02 (17,133)
Kelly, Brian 4:14:38 (14,325)
Kelly, Chris 3:57:38 (10,024)
Kelly, Christopher 3:34:22 (5,105)
Kelly, Christopher J 3:39:07 (5,836)
Kelly, Christopher T 3:36:29 (5,425)
Kelly, Ciaran P 4:37:19 (20,451)
Kelly, Clive J 4:01:46 (11,104)
Kelly, Darren 5:20:45 (29,208)
Kelly, Derek E 4:16:12 (14,765)
Kelly, Douglas D 5:26:13 (29,894)
Kelly, Graham 3:52:38 (8,641)
Kelly, Graham C 3:41:19 (6,238)
Kelly, Greg P 5:00:18 (25,845)
Kelly, Hugh 3:05:19 (1,498)
Kelly, James 4:19:24 (15,636)
Kelly, John 3:21:36 (3,141)
Kelly, Jonathan H 4:37:19 (20,451)
Kelly, Kevin P 3:57:57 (10,127)
Kelly, Kimo 5:10:03 (27,517)
Kelly, Lawrence J 3:31:32 (4,685)
Kelly, Martin C 4:27:47 (17,980)
Kelly, Michael F 3:54:30 (9,098)
Kelly, Michael G 5:52:12 (32,427)
Kelly, Nick C 3:43:48 (6,706)
Kelly, Paul C 4:25:30 (17,286)
Kelly, Paul J 5:15:50 (28,459)
Kelly, Peter J 5:17:23 (28,695)
Kelly, Phillip A 5:06:35 (26,980)
Kelly, Richard J 4:11:20 (13,440)
Kelly, Robin N 4:15:48 (14,660)
Kelly, Robin P 5:12:35 (27,923)
Kelly, Russell G 3:55:32 (9,376)
Kelly, Stephen 4:24:35 (17,010)
Kelly, Stephen P 5:44:51 (31,836)
Kelly, Terence 4:29:26 (18,442)
Kelsall, Michael 4:10:37 (13,242)
Kelsey, Bruce S 5:03:41 (26,458)
Kelsey, Dan T 4:14:38 (14,325)
Kelsey, Martin H 3:48:41 (7,757)
Kelsey, Peter R 6:10:14 (33,541)
Kelsey, Russell C 4:28:26 (18,146)
Kelsey-Smith, Trevor B 4:30:05 (18,615)
Kelso, William 3:38:11 (5,678)
Kemmler, Daniel W 4:29:34 (18,486)
Kemp, Adrian J 4:35:44 (20,026)
Kemp, Albert L 3:39:21 (5,879)
Kemp, Jimmy A 5:39:49 (31,398)
Kemp, John A 4:41:41 (21,561)
Kemp, Jon M 2:58:55 (1,025)
Kemp, Jonathan C 3:49:25 (7,916)
Kemp, Mark A 5:06:33 (26,976)
Kemp, Martyn 4:42:17 (21,696)
Kemp, Michael T 5:22:27 (29,411)
Kemp, Simon A 3:29:27 (4,347)
Kemp, Stephen J 4:10:58 (13,339)
Kempen, Andrew W 3:42:01 (6,379)
Kempen, Stephen J 5:09:23 (27,417)
Kempf, Fred 4:09:09 (12,876)
Kempthorne, Mark R 4:38:20 (20,704)
Kench, Peter J 5:59:47 (32,966)
Kenchington, Christopher J 2:59:27 (1,085)
Kendal, Paul G 5:34:59 (30,902)
Kendall, Alex P 3:44:49 (6,915)
Kendall, Craig L 6:03:17 (33,165)
Kendall, Cuthbert W 4:09:32 (12,971)
Kendall, Danny 3:42:17 (6,431)
Kendall, Graham P 3:35:34 (5,272)
Kendall, Phillip A 4:32:12 (19,134)
Kendall, Rowland W 4:14:58 (14,430)
Kendrick, Alastair 4:19:18 (15,611)
Kendrick, Philip 2:45:02 (321)
Kenison, Robert C 3:48:21 (7,672)
Kenna, David 4:45:26 (22,423)

Kenna, Michael M 4:58:44 (25,493)
Kennard, Christopher A 3:08:31 (1,759)
Kennard, Stephen R 5:08:26 (27,275)
Kennealy, Gareth 4:27:36 (17,921)
Kennedy, Adam 4:09:26 (12,939)
Kennedy, Benedict 5:15:26 (28,410)
Kennedy, Graham R 3:16:38 (2,644)
Kennedy, Ian D 3:47:30 (7,459)
Kennedy, James M 4:39:23 (20,985)
Kennedy, Les 4:04:37 (11,774)
Kennedy, Mark A 4:55:03 (24,687)
Kennedy, Peter E 3:21:11 (3,104)
Kennedy, Richard J 4:44:41 (22,245)
Kennedy, Rory 4:20:35 (15,958)
Kennedy, Scott H 3:01:14 (1,202)
Kennedy, Thomas 3:53:44 (8,921)
Kennelly, Terence J 6:49:00 (34,690)
Kennerley, Philip R 3:47:46 (7,517)
Kenneth, Robert J 4:22:36 (16,503)
Kennett, Steffan A 2:50:05 (501)
Kenny, James H 4:03:59 (11,626)
Kenny, Jimmy A 6:02:54 (33,136)
Kenny, Neil A 4:28:05 (18,049)
Kenny, Noel J 4:57:27 (25,219)
Kenny, Peter F 3:53:16 (8,786)
Kenny, Triss P 2:59:27 (1,085)
Kent, Antony J 5:21:20 (29,279)
Kent, Benjamin D 4:02:38 (11,298)
Kent, Clark 6:29:12 (34,233)
Kent, Graham S 3:54:02 (8,983)
Kent, James 3:45:42 (7,076)
Kent, John 6:25:28 (34,110)
Kent, Mark A 4:20:55 (16,055)
Kent, Matthew 4:19:43 (15,727)
Kent, Steven 5:05:09 (26,713)
Kent, Walter J 4:20:30 (15,937)
Kenworthy, Lawrence J 3:28:00 (4,104)
Kenyon, Craig 4:38:04 (20,638)
Kenyon, Stephen 3:43:55 (6,725)
Kenyon Muir, Nick E 2:58:55 (1,025)
Keogh, Paul E 5:34:08 (30,796)
Keoghan, Joel 4:47:37 (22,915)
Keohane, Joe G 4:42:18 (21,699)
Kerfoot, Chris 4:59:45 (25,725)
Kerger, Danilo 3:59:02 (10,443)
Kerler, Richard 4:06:58 (12,333)
Kerleroux, Benjamin 4:18:21 (15,312)
Kermani, Faiz 5:22:33 (29,431)
Kern, Bernd 3:57:12 (9,891)
Kernagis, Ray 4:08:04 (12,585)
Kernohan, Michael J 4:25:08 (17,163)
Kerr, Alan R 4:55:49 (24,854)
Kerr, David J 4:28:30 (18,168)
Kerr, Gavin J 3:36:24 (5,405)
Kerr, John 4:15:47 (14,656)
Kerr, Roger J 3:45:52 (7,111)
Kerrigan, Brian F 5:20:24 (29,161)
Kerrigan, Charles P 3:31:13 (4,634)
Kerrison, Martin R 5:13:16 (28,036)
Kerry, David G 3:59:26 (10,552)
Kerry, Edward J 3:30:26 (4,511)
Kersey, Austin T 3:51:06 (8,283)
Kersey, David 4:33:48 (19,518)
Kershaw, Grenville R 4:24:22 (16,944)
Kershaw, James R 4:24:22 (16,944)
Kershaw, John N 3:51:17 (8,324)
Kershaw, Steven P 5:34:01 (30,783)
Kerslake, David J 4:05:54 (12,073)
Kerslake, William R 4:40:17 (21,203)
Kerton, Christopher 5:17:18 (28,688)
Kesby, William J 5:22:52 (29,467)
Kessens, Anders J 4:02:56 (11,378)
Kessler, Peter 4:46:11 (22,600)
Kesson, Roderick A 5:45:13 (31,873)
Kestle, Michael J 3:03:32 (1,366)
Ketchell, Robert I 3:58:54 (10,408)
Ketenci, Hukmu 4:58:46 (25,504)
Ketteridge, Sean R 2:58:15 (971)
Kettleborough, Ian 4:40:32 (21,267)
Key, Jonathan W 3:04:12 (1,408)
Keys, Nicholas 2:53:52 (677)
Keyte, James P 4:07:44 (12,510)
Keyworth, Antony J 3:20:48 (3,075)
Khan, Ali 4:00:19 (10,790)
Khan, Amyn 4:02:38 (11,298)
Khan, Ashraff 3:33:08 (4,904)
Khan, Shafiq A 3:52:37 (8,636)
Khan, Shakeel I 5:32:30 (30,615)
Khan, Tariq 3:55:54 (9,488)
Khandelwal, Ajay 4:31:13 (18,888)
Khanna, Graham D 5:21:35 (29,298)
Kibet, Luke 2:16:40 (17)
Kibunja Gachuhi, Joseph 2:32:51 (91)
Kidd, Alexander L 4:56:32 (25,022)
Kidd, Andrew G 4:20:36 (15,962)
Kidd, Darren T 4:53:10 (24,213)
Kidd, David 3:50:57 (8,248)
Kidd, Michael J 3:08:28 (1,756)
Kidd, Richie 3:54:21 (9,062)
Kidd, William 4:34:51 (19,804)
Kiddle, Steven J 3:51:17 (8,324)
Kidner, Elliot K 5:19:34 (29,044)
Kidson, Ian J 4:15:41 (14,633)
Kiely, Cornelius T 4:17:18 (15,036)
Kiersey, Neil D 4:43:13 (21,917)
Kiesel, Martin 3:39:27 (5,899)
Kightley, David B 4:20:25 (15,918)
Kilby, Philip A 6:25:42 (34,117)
Kilby, Robert E 4:37:55 (20,600)
Kilduff, Jason A 3:09:56 (1,912)
Kilgannon, John F 5:01:53 (26,124)
Kilgannon, Patrick 5:01:52 (26,118)
Kilkenny, Kevin J 4:41:19 (21,473)
Kilkenny, Mark J 4:16:33 (14,845)
Killian, Patrick 4:54:43 (24,598)
Killick, Ian L 4:24:24 (16,956)
Killingley, Ben 4:10:54 (13,317)
Kilner, James E 3:34:12 (5,078)
Kilner, John A 4:11:25 (13,458)
Kilner, John M 6:03:44 (33,202)
Kilpatrick, Thomas T 4:03:07 (11,414)
Kilpatrick, Tim F 4:52:01 (23,939)
Kilpin, Henry G 5:10:09 (27,522)
Kilsby, Gary P 5:03:34 (26,439)
Kilshaw, Brad 3:45:46 (7,088)
Kilshaw, Ian M 3:15:38 (2,534)
Kiltie, David R 3:53:37 (8,888)
Kim, Tae Wan 3:56:52 (9,775)
Kimbell, Jeff A 4:45:54 (22,524)
Kimber, Geoffrey J 4:41:56 (21,610)
Kimber, Jim 3:48:28 (7,699)
Kimber, John 4:54:10 (24,463)
Kimber, Nicholas 3:43:07 (6,576)
Kimber, Philip L 4:04:13 (11,687)
Kimberley, Simon 4:16:12 (14,765)
Kimble, Anthony J 4:27:17 (17,822)
Kimmins, Christopher P 4:21:00 (16,075)
Kind, John L 4:23:47 (16,796)
Kindell, Daniel J 4:58:49 (25,515)
Kindon, Noel B 2:34:23 (107)
King, Alan J 4:44:40 (22,240)
King, Alan S 4:21:23 (16,169)
King, Andrew B 4:16:53 (14,932)
King, Andrew J 4:25:10 (17,172)
King, Andrew M 4:56:36 (25,042)
King, Brian G 6:04:32 (33,248)
King, Chris C 4:25:45 (17,365)
King, Christopher A 7:46:10 (35,197)
King, Christopher J 4:20:21 (15,898)
King, Craig 4:28:41 (18,212)
King, Darragh J 3:04:35 (1,434)
King, David A 3:24:25 (3,508)
King, David G 4:19:13 (15,582)
King, David M 3:12:31 (2,197)
King, Dennis 3:59:53 (10,694)
King, Gary 4:54:57 (24,658)
King, Gerry S 3:11:42 (2,105)
King, Glenn 7:04:17 (34,914)
King, Graham K 2:54:34 (718)
King, Ian 3:09:53 (1,908)
King, Ian T 3:09:06 (1,821)
King, James 4:36:24 (20,195)
King, James F 3:33:13 (4,911)
King, James R 3:43:28 (6,647)
King, John G 7:48:44 (35,204)
King, Lamin A 5:40:25 (31,462)
King, Leonard J 5:04:34 (26,608)
King, Leslie 4:07:58 (12,568)
King, Mark A 5:26:02 (29,875)
King, Marwan T 4:20:14 (15,866)
King, Mathew 4:02:26 (11,255)
King, Matt 3:50:26 (8,133)
King, Matthew B 3:39:10 (5,843)
King, Matthew J 3:57:21 (9,933)
King, Nicholas J 3:47:04 (7,364)
King, Nicholas S 5:07:09 (27,086)
King, Peter M 5:52:28 (32,460)
King, Richard I 3:47:31 (7,460)
King, Richard J 4:13:56 (14,125)
King, Richard P 4:17:56 (15,184)
King, Robert A 4:37:06 (20,386)
King, Roger 6:42:44 (34,562)
King, Seth 4:08:25 (12,675)
King, Simon J 4:18:46 (15,452)
King, Stephen J 5:33:51 (30,759)
King, Stephen P 3:50:12 (8,084)
King, Thomas J 6:26:12 (34,133)
King, Tommy M 4:17:48 (15,158)
King, Tony R 5:41:02 (31,517)
King, Warwick A 5:11:14 (27,695)
Kingay, Adrian K 3:56:46 (9,740)
Kingdon, Adam F 3:51:20 (8,336)
Kingsford-Bere, Paul E 4:43:08 (21,895)
Kingstad, Richard C 2:47:50 (404)
Kingston, Aidan D 4:56:18 (24,965)
Kingston, Anthony P 3:57:24 (9,949)
Kingston, Danny W 4:20:50 (16,030)
Kingston, Gerry R 3:22:24 (3,233)
Kingston, Josh J 7:30:09 (35,128)
Kingston, Simon M 3:57:51 (10,094)
Kingston-Lee, Matthew F 3:07:52 (1,703)
Kingswood, Kevin B 4:09:17 (12,903)
Kingswood, Phillip A 5:44:06 (31,769)
Kini, Vidyuth U 6:08:51 (33,479)
Kinlen, Geoffrey J 3:24:14 (3,476)
Kinnaird, Phillip 5:09:34 (27,449)
Kinns, Derek P 5:03:26 (26,425)
Kinoshita, Shigeru 4:37:11 (20,408)
Kinsell, Paul B 4:43:45 (22,049)
Kinsella, Edward J 5:41:50 (31,583)
Kinsella, Matthew J 4:48:15 (23,065)
Kinsella, Paul J 2:41:46 (238)
Kinsella, William C 4:42:30 (21,742)
Kinsey, Nicholas J 2:41:42 (233)
Kipling, William T 4:39:10 (20,916)
Kipp, Charles 5:17:27 (28,705)
Kippax, Nigel T 4:03:09 (11,421)
Kirby, Andrew 3:53:16 (8,786)
Kirby, David A 4:08:24 (12,667)
Kirby, Jason L 3:57:11 (9,887)
Kirby, Michael A 4:00:30 (10,832)
Kirby, Michael J 7:52:52 (35,218)
Kirby, Neil A 4:02:13 (11,206)
Kirby, Robert A 4:25:24 (17,246)
Kirby, Roger M 4:25:43 (17,351)
Kirby, Sean S 4:24:22 (16,944)
Kirby, Simon 4:28:27 (18,153)
Kirby, Simon J 4:59:45 (25,725)
Kirby, Steven E 2:59:29 (1,088)
Kirchheimer, James A 4:01:29 (11,047)
Kirchner, Richard P 3:44:25 (6,823)
Kirk, Elliott 3:44:05 (6,756)
Kirk, John E 5:59:09 (32,920)
Kirk, John M 3:41:17 (6,228)
Kirk, Kevin J 3:44:33 (6,848)
Kirk, Mark S 3:10:37 (1,992)
Kirk, Micahel J 6:07:37 (33,422)
Kirk, Neil 2:51:25 (559)
Kirk, Nicholas S 4:45:59 (22,549)
Kirk, Richard M 6:59:26 (34,861)
Kirkby, Darron M 4:17:10 (15,004)
Kirkby, Jack P 7:31:39 (35,139)
Kirkby, John W 5:00:59 (25,973)
Kirkby, Simon 3:57:39 (10,027)
Kirkdale, Brian G 4:01:06 (10,962)
Kirke, Ross 3:48:18 (7,657)
Kirkham, Adrian J 4:44:55 (22,301)
Kirkham, Andrew S 5:21:23 (29,286)
Kirkham, David E 3:35:56 (5,327)

Kirkham, Michael S....4:40:37 (21,289)
Kirkham, Stan W....5:20:05 (29,115)
Kirkham Brown, Jody....4:55:36 (24,789)
Kirkland, David....4:30:29 (18,722)
Kirkland, John A....5:41:27 (31,547)
Kirkman, Colin D....4:18:37 (15,399)
Kirkpatrick, Neil S....4:11:20 (13,440)
Kirkwood, Cameron....3:49:58 (8,031)
Kirkwood, Gareth R....3:48:55 (7,809)
Kirkwood, Mark S....5:32:21 (30,595)
Kirrage, Stephen F....5:14:42 (28,303)
Kirsop, Dale....5:19:06 (28,954)
Kirsop, Neil W....4:20:04 (15,817)
Kiruthi, John....4:25:43 (17,351)
Kirwan, Robert E....4:14:39 (14,337)
Kisaka, Job Nelson....4:03:04 (11,402)
Kitchen, Neil D....3:44:40 (6,872)
Kitchen, Nick R....3:21:19 (3,117)
Kitchener, Peter J....5:48:49 (32,163)
Kitching, Barrie....4:26:42 (17,658)
Kitching, Russell E....4:27:13 (17,806)
Kitley, Richard H....3:46:21 (7,211)
Kitson, Paul....2:53:22 (653)
Kitson, Paul J....4:11:40 (13,525)
Kitson, Phil G....3:12:58 (2,243)
Kitson, Terry C....4:49:40 (23,422)
Kittle, Ian D....3:28:23 (4,175)
Kittle, Peter N....4:32:54 (19,289)
Kittler, Robert L....4:55:44 (24,827)
Kjellgren, Goran....4:23:07 (16,636)
Klein, Barry....4:24:59 (17,117)
Klein, David....3:57:07 (9,864)
Klein, Peter G....3:50:02 (8,047)
Klein, Richard B....5:30:55 (30,457)
Klein, Wolfgang....3:59:36 (10,599)
Kleinfeld-Fowell, Mark A....4:49:36 (23,388)
Kleinman, Martin....5:28:47 (30,217)
Kleinsteuber, Uli....4:25:32 (17,296)
Klenerman, Paul....3:55:20 (9,315)
Klesser, Dean G....3:32:43 (4,847)
Kliegl, Timothy J....3:49:04 (7,840)
Kling, Peter....5:23:20 (29,519)
Klintback, Mattias....4:27:32 (17,900)
Klos, Andreas....4:12:37 (13,781)
Klostergaard, Torben....3:45:59 (7,132)
Kluger, Jason L....4:31:20 (18,927)
Knapp, John A....2:46:10 (354)
Knapp, Keith W....4:54:56 (24,648)
Knapp, Martin A....4:02:20 (11,226)
Knapp, Robert J....4:16:30 (14,836)
Knapp, Russell D....4:42:32 (21,747)
Kneller, Philip C....5:13:24 (28,061)
Knibbs, Alex V....6:16:05 (33,785)
Knight, Alan R....5:11:35 (27,754)
Knight, Alastair....3:52:46 (8,678)
Knight, Andrew D....4:26:19 (17,542)
Knight, Andrew G....4:28:05 (18,049)
Knight, Anthony D....4:12:53 (13,848)
Knight, Barry M....4:30:47 (18,789)
Knight, Brian A....4:36:26 (20,209)
Knight, Brian P....6:04:17 (33,231)
Knight, Chris....4:24:51 (17,085)
Knight, Chris A....5:14:19 (28,233)
Knight, Chris R....5:43:35 (31,727)
Knight, Dave L....3:56:20 (9,614)
Knight, David A....2:35:32 (118)
Knight, David A....3:57:06 (9,856)
Knight, David M....4:28:15 (18,101)
Knight, Gordon L....3:31:06 (4,619)
Knight, James....5:16:01 (28,482)
Knight, James A....3:48:25 (7,686)
Knight, John D....5:27:53 (30,086)
Knight, John M....5:50:29 (32,297)
Knight, Jon P....4:15:57 (14,698)
Knight, Kevin L....4:21:51 (16,297)
Knight, Malcolm J....3:23:13 (3,334)
Knight, Peter E....4:16:24 (14,820)
Knight, Peter J....4:17:24 (15,068)
Knight, Richard W....5:29:20 (30,279)
Knight, Rob....3:44:21 (6,805)
Knight, Rob....4:57:00 (25,128)
Knight, Robin J....4:01:28 (11,041)
Knight, Roger I....4:47:36 (22,907)
Knight, Stefan A....3:42:53 (6,523)
Knight, Steven....5:18:00 (28,784)
Knight, Steven P....4:40:36 (21,285)
Knight, Stuart A....3:21:40 (3,148)
Knight, Stuart P....5:05:42 (26,827)
Knight, Thomas....3:21:54 (3,171)
Knight, Thomas J....4:15:54 (14,683)
Knightall, Adrian C....4:54:45 (24,610)
Knightley, John P....5:41:47 (31,576)
Knightley, Terence J....2:56:42 (861)
Knighton, Simon....3:43:23 (6,633)
Knights, Jim....5:12:16 (27,865)
Knill-Jones, Andrew D....4:43:31 (21,988)
Knoerig, Volker....5:08:50 (27,327)
Knopp, Darren K....4:39:10 (20,916)
Knott, Andrew C....5:55:30 (32,680)
Knott, David C....5:12:47 (27,966)
Knott, Emily J....4:41:02 (21,402)
Knott, John W....4:32:34 (19,223)
Knott, Laurence....3:25:41 (3,702)
Knott, Peter J....4:18:02 (15,218)
Knowland, Nicholas....5:54:26 (32,596)
Knowles, Adrian W....3:29:22 (4,333)
Knowles, Andrew M....3:43:04 (6,565)
Knowles, John W....4:07:11 (12,391)
Knowles, Michael A....3:43:37 (6,672)
Knowles, Mick P....5:27:59 (30,101)
Knowles, Patrick....5:19:16 (28,988)
Knowles, Paul M....3:06:32 (1,597)
Knowles, Simon F....3:40:46 (6,132)
Knowles, Stephen....3:56:28 (9,656)
Knox, Tom F....4:18:08 (15,242)
Kobbe, Clemens....3:49:46 (7,993)
Kober, Russell....2:57:57 (951)
Kobir, Abdul....4:53:58 (24,415)
Koch, Danny P....4:28:40 (18,206)
Koch, Hans....3:01:29 (1,218)
Koch, Horst D....3:42:58 (6,537)
Koch, Markus....3:19:44 (2,971)
Koch, Roger....4:49:36 (23,388)
Koe, Digby M....4:14:04 (14,173)
Koe, Richard....4:20:52 (16,039)
Koekoek, Luke J....4:25:23 (17,241)
Koessl, Manfred....3:16:05 (2,589)
Kofler, Simon....4:13:21 (13,978)
Koh, Thianpoh....5:32:31 (30,616)
Kojima, Giichi....5:43:16 (31,698)
Kokolay, Michael....6:34:39 (34,369)
Kolbe, Stefan....2:53:51 (674)
Kollen, John L....4:55:54 (24,874)
Koller, Denis....3:35:28 (5,255)
Kolling, Alan T....6:42:37 (34,559)
Kollnberger, Simon D....4:21:37 (16,234)
Kolthoff, Thomas....2:56:59 (884)
Konecsni, Peter....3:22:08 (3,204)
Konig, Hans A....4:38:04 (20,638)
Konir, Helmut J....3:32:11 (4,771)
Konstantinidis, Marios....4:44:15 (22,155)
Koopmeiners, Christoph....2:59:22 (1,078)
Kopiecki, Stefan J....6:02:41 (33,118)
Kopitsis, Nicolas P....4:37:19 (20,451)
Korir, Sammy....2:12:36 (9)
Kormornick, Lawrence M....4:15:14 (14,511)
Korsgen, Stephan....4:21:48 (16,284)
Kosciuczyk, Leon....4:39:40 (21,060)
Koshy, Sam G....5:24:09 (29,638)
Koskimies, Neikki T....5:28:02 (30,107)
Kosoko, Anthony....3:11:49 (2,119)
Koster, Johannes....5:16:09 (28,498)
Kostoris, William....4:11:30 (13,485)
Kosuge, Tsuneo....4:33:09 (19,352)
Kotecha, Pratish C....5:48:09 (32,108)
Kothari, Raj....4:18:10 (15,253)
Kovatchev, Alexander M....3:38:01 (5,650)
Kowalenko, Steven P....3:28:54 (4,259)
Kowenicki, Richard A....3:39:08 (5,839)
Kowolik, Thomas....5:17:28 (28,709)
Kraakman, Cor....3:36:46 (5,462)
Kragten, Ger W....2:50:57 (539)
Kratz, Philip R....5:54:19 (32,589)
Krause, Andreas....3:17:49 (2,770)
Krause, John C....3:41:17 (6,228)
Kreckeler, Kevin R....4:28:22 (18,129)
Kreindl, Oliver....3:24:37 (3,529)
Krelle, Jonathan D....4:05:25 (11,971)
Kreth, Reinhard....3:36:19 (5,397)
Kretsehmer, Olaf....3:24:25 (3,508)
Kreusler, Hans-Ernst....4:40:37 (21,289)
Kreuter, Eric A....4:53:14 (24,231)
Kristensen, Soren....4:09:03 (12,838)
Kristjansson, Johann....3:23:01 (3,300)
Krivonozka, Steve J....4:55:44 (24,827)
Kroll, Martin....3:56:40 (9,714)
Kronholm Hansen, Erik A....4:47:58 (22,997)
Kropfitsch, Urban....3:23:55 (3,439)
Kruger, Bernfried....4:42:49 (21,823)
Kruijer, Roelof....4:20:46 (16,010)
Krusche, Stefan....3:19:12 (2,899)
Kruse, Willem H....4:41:26 (21,506)
Kubasiak, Leszek....5:31:15 (30,490)
Kuepper, Lukas....3:01:28 (1,214)
Kuhn, Oliver G....4:11:09 (13,396)
Kuist, Lars A....4:01:53 (11,124)
Kulashe, Lungile....3:17:28 (2,730)
Kulick, Landon J....5:48:18 (32,126)
Kullar, Hardeep S....4:23:16 (16,675)
Kumar, Prarabdha....6:41:03 (34,526)
Kumar, Raj....4:38:01 (20,627)
Kumar, Vijay....6:20:40 (33,938)
Kunst, Alexander G....3:53:01 (8,720)
Kuntzer, Rolf....4:19:22 (15,629)
Kunz, Olivier....4:16:40 (14,881)
Kuper, Gordon I....3:25:02 (3,589)
Kurmanbayev, Mukhamed-Ali....4:12:33 (13,760)
Kuroiwa, Yu....3:07:41 (1,692)
Kuronen, Mikko K....2:39:30 (187)
Kurowski, Richard....5:36:18 (31,029)
Kurth, Norman....3:42:01 (6,379)
Kuru, Sidath....5:46:28 (31,975)
Kuster, Martin....2:49:24 (480)
Kutner, David B....4:25:35 (17,310)
Kuwamori, Shigetoshi....5:39:57 (31,409)
Kvamme, Ole M....3:44:00 (6,742)
Kwan, Timothy....5:14:07 (28,196)
Kyne, David M....3:16:23 (2,623)
Kyritsis, Nick....4:24:50 (17,081)
Kyte, Julian G....4:02:00 (11,155)
Kyte, Peter J....3:58:03 (10,159)
Labourel, Claude....3:24:11 (3,470)
Labuschagne, Peet I....3:23:37 (3,389)
Labuschagne, Timothy J....3:38:14 (5,684)
Lacarcel Wandosell, Alfonso....4:53:42 (24,353)
Lacchini, Angelo....3:28:33 (4,206)
Lacey, Alan....4:01:13 (10,985)
Lacey, Charles P....5:53:10 (32,513)
Lacey, Christopher W....4:00:32 (10,843)
Lacey, Desmond J....6:07:52 (33,437)
Lacey, Douglas N....4:11:40 (13,525)
Lacey, Ian....3:47:17 (7,411)
Lacey, Ian N....3:51:13 (8,305)
Lacey, Mark D....2:49:55 (496)
Lacey, Peter C....3:21:10 (3,102)
Lacey, Thomas....3:35:33 (5,269)
Lacey, Tom....7:48:28 (35,202)
Lack, Richard A....2:52:34 (614)
Lacy, Neal....3:34:04 (5,055)
Lad, Mahesh....5:38:56 (31,301)
Ladanowski, John....3:27:19 (3,980)
Ladbury, Patrick S....3:52:04 (8,498)
Ladd, Joe....3:24:51 (3,562)
Ladlow, Peter....4:25:10 (17,172)
Lafleche, Trevor A....4:56:43 (25,073)
Lafosse, Stephane B....4:38:30 (20,757)
Lafuente, Fernando....3:34:50 (5,162)
Lagedamont, Marcel....3:41:57 (6,368)
Lagemann, Godo....4:25:08 (17,163)
Laghi, Pierahgelo....4:09:18 (12,908)
Lagioia, Giovanni....3:25:49 (3,721)
Lagnado, Max....3:35:17 (5,222)
Lagreve, Jacques....3:39:12 (5,850)
Lagrou, Yves....2:51:40 (572)
Laher, Amir Y....5:35:30 (30,955)
Lai, Stephen K....6:16:39 (33,806)
Laidlaw, Colin....5:05:27 (26,786)
Laidlaw, Jonathan J....4:30:04 (18,611)
Laignel, Guy....4:40:35 (21,280)

Laine, Markko	3:43:15 (6,605)
Laing, Cameron D	4:26:33 (17,616)
Laing, Steven R	4:52:06 (23,966)
Laird, Allister	4:35:47 (20,039)
Laird, Jamie	3:30:15 (4,484)
Laird Craig, Robert J	4:53:25 (24,281)
Lake, Brian	5:39:00 (31,310)
Lake, Jon M	3:43:43 (6,686)
Lake, Paul T	4:32:43 (19,250)
Lake, Philip N	4:56:51 (25,101)
Lake, Robert J	4:14:41 (14,343)
Lakey, Daniel J	4:09:28 (12,950)
Lakins, John F	6:24:52 (34,091)
Lal, Archie	7:12:24 (35,010)
Lally, Chris	6:55:55 (34,810)
Lam, David C	4:50:31 (23,630)
Lamb, Andy	3:12:47 (2,223)
Lamb, Charles D	4:05:16 (11,936)
Lamb, Dave	5:12:47 (27,966)
Lamb, Gary	4:10:15 (13,153)
Lamb, Jamie A	4:31:17 (18,913)
Lamb, Jason F	4:44:10 (22,135)
Lamb, Ken D	3:56:45 (9,736)
Lamb, Mark I	3:44:55 (6,940)
Lamb, Michael J	4:55:58 (24,892)
Lamb, Nicholas B	3:51:07 (8,288)
Lamb, Nick P	5:32:36 (30,625)
Lamb, Philip R	4:02:20 (11,226)
Lamb, Terry P	4:16:19 (14,799)
Lambden, Murray M	2:43:06 (270)
Lambert, Andrew	5:26:36 (29,935)
Lambert, Craig	4:02:15 (11,212)
Lambert, David K	4:16:15 (14,781)
Lambert, Heath J	3:46:09 (7,170)
Lambert, John E	5:15:00 (28,340)
Lambert, Jonathan P	4:35:35 (19,992)
Lambert, Matthew K	4:53:54 (24,395)
Lambert, Noel M	6:03:19 (33,170)
Lambert, Roger	6:52:51 (34,767)
Lambert, Toby	2:21:24 (30)
Lambkin, Gary P	3:40:03 (6,005)
Lambley, Charles J	3:59:02 (10,443)
Lambourne, Seve	5:54:55 (32,634)
Lambrecht, Antoon M	4:43:33 (21,996)
Lambrou, Daniel	3:09:14 (1,834)
Lamburne, Thomas	4:09:05 (12,853)
Lammali, Azlouz	3:03:38 (1,379)
Lammas, Edward	3:46:42 (7,284)
Lammas, Scott A	4:49:48 (23,449)
Lamola, Angelo	3:55:24 (9,337)
Lamonby, Charles L	3:46:03 (7,147)
Lamont, Christopher P	2:55:04 (745)
Lamont, Christopher P	6:08:20 (33,459)
Lamont, Fraser	5:18:49 (28,922)
Lamont, Jason D	5:43:03 (31,681)
Lamplough, Andrew S	3:46:26 (7,228)
Lamy, Pascal A	4:07:38 (12,486)
Lamza, Ernie W	3:00:17 (1,146)
Lanahan, Paul C	5:05:04 (26,695)
Lanao, Jean-Jacques	2:44:32 (308)
Lancaster, Brian M	5:10:33 (27,579)
Lancaster, Kenneth A	6:40:32 (34,517)
Lancerin, Paolo	3:48:36 (7,741)
Lanckham, Kevin T	2:47:02 (375)
Lancucki, Tadeusz	4:57:53 (25,296)
Landa, Hardev S	5:52:45 (32,477)
Lander, Alan J	3:21:22 (3,120)
Lander, Christopher M	4:06:33 (12,225)
Lander, Eric T	3:39:50 (5,971)
Lander, Gregory R	4:25:48 (17,377)
Lander, Noel F	3:41:02 (6,186)
Landers, David G	4:08:56 (12,809)
Landers, Gary G	4:07:25 (12,442)
Landfried, Daniel	4:45:44 (22,483)
Landgren, Sven-Ake	4:33:32 (19,444)
Landmark, Gerhard J	4:21:13 (16,113)
Landolfi, Luigi	5:56:06 (32,712)
Landowski, Paul E	3:12:36 (2,203)
Landstad, Finn K	3:41:30 (6,275)
Lane, Alan R	4:09:42 (13,012)
Lane, Andrew G	2:56:54 (880)
Lane, Andrew J	4:38:47 (20,825)
Lane, Anthony W	3:15:58 (2,567)

Lane, Barnard R	5:51:23 (32,362)
Lane, Edward J	4:50:24 (23,596)
Lane, Gary R	4:13:49 (14,093)
Lane, Graham	4:27:14 (17,813)
Lane, Jason	4:21:28 (16,195)
Lane, Johnny N	4:19:44 (15,733)
Lane, Kevin R	4:24:26 (16,970)
Lane, Malcolm R	4:20:55 (16,055)
Lane, Matt	3:51:14 (8,309)
Lane, Michael	4:31:34 (18,989)
Lane, Nigel A	4:54:47 (24,621)
Lane, Peter A	4:50:08 (23,523)
Lane, Ronald F	3:24:20 (3,497)
Lane, Stephen J	5:00:53 (25,958)
Lane, Timothy J	4:41:14 (21,454)
Lang, Angus I	5:08:51 (27,331)
Lang, Ben	2:46:59 (372)
Lang, Bob	4:47:52 (22,982)
Lang, David J	4:10:25 (13,211)
Lang, John	4:31:09 (18,866)
Langan, Adrian	4:35:04 (19,865)
Langan, Stephen	3:39:12 (5,850)
Langbein, Jochen	4:36:35 (20,243)
Langdon, Ben	4:28:43 (18,225)
Langdon, Jack	4:41:41 (21,561)
Langdon, Miles D	4:19:07 (15,553)
Langer, Andreas	4:47:50 (22,974)
Langfield, Steven	5:20:20 (29,146)
Langford, Haydon	3:57:18 (9,920)
Langford, Karl	5:08:32 (27,289)
Langford, Martin P	5:16:48 (28,601)
Langford, Rob	6:36:46 (34,427)
Langham, Anthony R	4:17:07 (14,991)
Langham, Neil	3:18:29 (2,829)
Langham, Simon	4:15:41 (14,633)
Langhammer, Jens	3:57:51 (10,094)
Langhoff, Tobias	2:39:44 (197)
Langlais, Sylvain	3:59:39 (10,615)
Langley, Gregory	8:36:53 (35,248)
Langley, Jason C	4:07:47 (12,529)
Langley, Nicholas G	4:36:06 (20,108)
Langley, Paul	6:50:04 (34,722)
Langley, Peter G	4:00:51 (10,913)
Langley, Peter J	3:45:58 (7,127)
Langley, Philip M	4:18:33 (15,373)
Langley, Robert F	2:59:06 (1,046)
Langley, Thomas J	4:35:42 (20,019)
Langouroux, Gary	6:27:14 (34,173)
Langridge, Russel	4:37:07 (20,391)
Langrish, Ray J	5:13:47 (28,130)
Langsdale, Philip R	6:45:22 (34,624)
Langslow, David J	4:49:15 (23,293)
Langston, Brian	3:58:14 (10,203)
Langton, Michael S	5:39:29 (31,375)
Langton, William	3:29:19 (4,328)
Lanham, James P	3:53:49 (8,938)
Lanham, Mark R	4:51:38 (23,859)
Lanham, Stephen	5:20:33 (29,192)
Laniado, Benjamin	4:47:44 (22,949)
Lankenau, Karl T	4:30:53 (18,815)
Lannes, Gilles	4:12:34 (13,765)
Lannigan, Michael D	4:44:19 (22,177)
Lant, Keith	3:55:02 (9,243)
Lantree, Tom G	4:30:46 (18,786)
Lantsbury, Robert A	4:26:04 (17,462)
Lapenna, Roberto A	3:54:54 (9,215)
Lapierre, Patrice	4:04:25 (11,724)
Laporte, Philippe	3:51:57 (8,473)
Lapthorne, Nigel J	5:57:44 (32,822)
Lapworth, Kevin T	4:21:43 (16,259)
Larcarcel Wandosell, José	4:53:43 (24,358)
Lardner, Mark	4:18:51 (15,476)
Large, Ian R	5:29:13 (30,265)
Large, Richard M	2:58:53 (1,021)
Largey, Eamon	5:33:55 (30,768)
Larkin, Kevin M	4:23:51 (16,816)
Larking, David P	4:01:20 (11,007)
Larman, James P	3:30:59 (4,601)
Larner, Ian	4:59:06 (25,586)
Larocca, Tomas M	4:16:16 (14,786)
Larrington, Michael J	4:33:36 (19,465)
Larter, Simon H	5:10:47 (27,614)
Lascelles, Martin C	2:57:50 (945)

Lashmar, Ben	3:18:20 (2,816)
Lashmar, Tony	2:43:55 (291)
Lasseter, David N	4:17:01 (14,962)
Last, David J	4:18:25 (15,334)
Last, Jares S	5:10:30 (27,572)
Last, Jonathan S	3:28:43 (4,226)
Last, Martin R	5:30:07 (30,372)
Last, Philip K	5:20:04 (29,111)
Lasvergnas, Christian	3:55:15 (9,292)
Latcham, Anthony	4:44:51 (22,285)
Latcham, Samuel G	4:33:08 (19,347)
Lategan, Andries J	5:51:00 (32,334)
Lategan, François J	5:44:27 (31,798)
Latham, Steven G	3:56:38 (9,707)
Lathwell, Simon G	3:02:14 (1,282)
Latorre, Matthew	4:24:01 (16,857)
Latsis, John S	4:34:26 (19,699)
Latter, John I	3:18:06 (2,795)
Latter, Stuart P	3:28:32 (4,203)
Latto, Brian	4:46:16 (22,615)
Lau, Chung-Wai	4:44:41 (22,245)
Lau, Hing L	3:29:48 (4,417)
Lau, William	3:53:38 (8,892)
Laubis, Hans P	4:31:41 (19,016)
Lauchlan, Robert A	4:34:11 (19,617)
Lauder, Iain	4:56:05 (24,912)
Laughton, Michael J	3:48:57 (7,814)
Laughton, Philip C	3:58:39 (10,323)
Launay, Michel R	4:11:05 (13,375)
Laurans, Mickael	4:58:31 (25,448)
Laurence, Garry E	4:04:04 (11,654)
Lauriault, François E	4:25:17 (17,211)
Laurie, Steven	2:48:21 (425)
Laux, Reinhard	3:55:55 (9,495)
Lavan, Michael J	3:53:42 (8,909)
Lavelle, Peter	4:07:46 (12,523)
Lavender, Jack S	4:20:48 (16,022)
Lavender, James D	5:56:44 (32,752)
Laverty, Daniel J	5:19:22 (29,002)
Lavrijsen, Bart	3:20:42 (3,062)
Law, Alan	4:02:42 (11,315)
Law, Andrew P	4:48:07 (23,037)
Law, Christopher N	3:26:35 (3,866)
Law, David	5:04:01 (26,519)
Law, Graham M	3:21:59 (3,183)
Law, Gregory R	3:49:44 (7,985)
Law, Michael R	5:08:52 (27,334)
Law, Robert B	3:23:01 (3,300)
Law, Simon N	3:08:08 (1,727)
Law, Steven	4:37:34 (20,515)
Lawal-Rieley, Thomas C	5:13:54 (28,150)
Lawes, Nik	4:35:24 (19,951)
Lawler, Christopher P	4:05:16 (11,936)
Lawler, Nicholas K	3:40:49 (6,142)
Lawless, Philip	5:35:05 (30,913)
Lawless, Tom R	4:02:25 (11,250)
Lawley, Rob	3:59:49 (10,667)
Lawley, Steven G	3:56:39 (9,710)
Lawlon, Michael S	4:02:16 (11,217)
Lawlor, Anthony J	3:16:01 (2,577)
Lawlor, Paul A	3:13:16 (2,272)
Lawlor, Sean	3:25:26 (3,659)
Lawrance, Richard S	3:59:13 (10,500)
Lawrence, Alan	4:40:53 (21,358)
Lawrence, Allan	5:03:04 (26,352)
Lawrence, Chris R	3:34:17 (5,095)
Lawrence, Christer S	4:56:36 (25,042)
Lawrence, David J	3:48:58 (7,815)
Lawrence, David W	5:44:17 (31,789)
Lawrence, John	5:20:02 (29,102)
Lawrence, Kevin	4:28:35 (18,191)
Lawrence, Lee J	4:25:42 (17,345)
Lawrence, Martin D	4:46:31 (22,671)
Lawrence, Michael A	4:52:28 (24,045)
Lawrence, Michael C	4:54:44 (24,603)
Lawrence, Michael-John	3:25:04 (3,599)
Lawrence, Nicholas K	3:40:03 (6,005)
Lawrence, Richard A	3:55:03 (9,245)
Lawrence, Richard N	3:38:54 (5,793)
Lawrence, Robert	3:57:29 (9,973)
Lawrence, Ronnie J	3:50:29 (8,147)
Lawrence, Steve T	4:13:19 (13,968)
Lawrence, Thomas W	4:49:06 (23,267)

Lawrenson, Paul 5:33:56 (30,772)
Lawrenson, Simon E 4:20:51 (16,035)
Laws, David J 4:18:51 (15,476)
Laws, Derek W 4:06:49 (12,288)
Laws, Nicholas 4:44:35 (22,225)
Lawson, Andrew M 3:27:52 (4,087)
Lawson, Benjamin W 4:20:18 (15,889)
Lawson, Henry J 6:07:22 (33,412)
Lawson, Ian 3:05:45 (1,535)
Lawson, Ian M 5:28:04 (30,111)
Lawson, James A 4:00:36 (10,867)
Lawson, Jason C 4:01:55 (11,134)
Lawson, Laurence B 3:58:41 (10,341)
Lawson, Matthew J 3:44:41 (6,876)
Lawson, Philip 5:57:03 (32,778)
Lawson, Richard 5:07:36 (27,159)
Lawson, Steven A 4:33:09 (19,352)
Lawson-Cruttenden, Arthur T 5:36:48 (31,086)
Lawton, Bjorn 3:31:04 (4,614)
Lawton, Bryan W 3:19:31 (2,945)
Lawton, David 5:55:55 (32,704)
Lawton, James P 3:29:07 (4,300)
Lawuers, Bert L 3:50:51 (8,224)
Lax, James P 4:40:42 (21,310)
Lay, John L 4:07:44 (12,510)
Lay, Peter A 4:12:29 (13,742)
Laycock, Andrew J 3:55:11 (9,273)
Laycock, Christopher J 4:07:16 (12,409)
Laycock, Jeremy A 4:46:06 (22,578)
Laycock, Philip T 3:58:27 (10,272)
Laycock, Thomas W 4:11:19 (13,434)
Laydon, Richard J 3:50:30 (8,150)
Layley, Christopher D 5:34:24 (30,833)
Layton, Erik J 3:28:16 (4,154)
Layton, Gary R 4:35:19 (19,911)
Layton, William J 3:21:54 (3,171)
Lazell, Sebastian H 4:56:34 (25,029)
Lazier, Patrick 3:59:42 (10,630)
Lazzari, Giuseppe 5:03:11 (26,382)
Le Bihan, Jaques 4:31:30 (18,972)
Le Bon, Snoz 5:52:46 (32,479)
Le Breton, Stephane P 4:00:14 (10,774)
Le Breton, Tim 4:07:44 (12,510)
Le Brun, Frederic 4:50:03 (23,504)
Le Cocq, Nick J 3:06:33 (1,598)
Le Cue, John 6:19:41 (33,906)
Le Garrec, Fabrice 6:35:32 (34,397)
Le Goff, Gerard 3:55:37 (9,406)
Le Gresley, Edward M 3:34:40 (5,144)
Le Masurier, James 5:06:18 (26,919)
Le Tissier, Tim J 4:23:44 (16,788)
Le Velly, Michel 3:13:25 (2,293)
Lea, Alex P 3:56:26 (9,645)
Lea, Jeffrey H 3:59:14 (10,503)
Lea, Mark J 4:54:54 (24,640)
Leach, Arran S 4:13:10 (13,928)
Leach, Benjamin J 2:57:46 (938)
Leach, Colin 4:45:21 (22,401)
Leach, John D 3:33:18 (4,928)
Leach, Matthew E 4:26:18 (17,538)
Leach, Michael 5:17:37 (28,735)
Leach, Stuart M 4:20:04 (15,817)
Leadbeater, Kenneth M 5:55:34 (32,687)
Leadbeater, Richard P 3:52:36 (8,629)
Leadbetter, Daniel L 3:38:40 (5,749)
Leadbitter, Morgan 4:15:38 (14,617)
Leader, Gary R 3:43:56 (6,731)
Leader, Rob J 5:35:00 (30,907)
Leafe, Jonathan G 4:59:05 (25,582)
Leafe, Richard N 3:27:50 (4,082)
Leahy, Justin P 3:43:23 (6,633)
Leak, Christopher S 4:29:17 (18,396)
Leaper, John M 4:33:45 (19,506)
Lear, Rob E 4:05:23 (11,964)
Learad, Dennis 3:27:15 (3,968)
Learman, Simon J 3:56:04 (9,524)
Learoyd, John 4:48:34 (23,135)
Leary, Mark 3:34:45 (5,151)
Leary-Joyce, John 4:47:05 (22,790)
Leat, Ashley J 3:52:37 (8,636)
Leather, John 4:40:19 (21,212)
Leather, Michael T 3:43:17 (6,613)
Leather, Scott J 4:42:51 (21,833)
Leatherdale, Malcolm C 3:52:16 (8,547)
Leathers, Simon M 4:42:59 (21,871)
Leaver, David 4:09:27 (12,943)
Leaver, Stuart J 4:53:19 (24,257)
Leblond, Gerard 4:07:37 (12,483)
Le-Borgne, Nicolas 2:26:22 (51)
Le-Bras, Sebastien 3:42:59 (6,545)
Lebret, Alain 4:02:50 (11,348)
Lecapitaine, Daniel 4:33:10 (19,355)
Lecerf, Laurent 3:51:54 (8,461)
Leck, Andrew 2:41:46 (238)
Leckie, Bill 5:48:41 (32,150)
Leclerq, Didier 4:14:57 (14,425)
Lecoester, Guillaume 3:38:56 (5,802)
Ledder, Paul R 3:48:03 (7,598)
Lederman, Eli R 4:30:14 (18,662)
Ledesma, Agustin 4:56:16 (24,955)
Ledger, Bill M 4:54:17 (24,496)
Ledingham, Paul D 3:45:54 (7,118)
Ledwidge, Alan 4:00:43 (10,890)
Lee, Adrian C 3:24:19 (3,493)
Lee, Andrew 4:40:08 (21,164)
Lee, Andrew D 4:06:57 (12,329)
Lee, Andrew J 5:53:52 (32,555)
Lee, Andy 5:12:03 (27,831)
Lee, Aylmer 6:09:54 (33,531)
Lee, Charles G 4:06:21 (12,182)
Lee, Christian 7:02:23 (34,897)
Lee, Christopher 4:17:18 (15,036)
Lee, Christopher A 4:52:54 (24,149)
Lee, Christopher D 4:42:25 (21,722)
Lee, Christopher W 5:14:08 (28,198)
Lee, David J 4:19:22 (15,629)
Lee, David R 4:18:54 (15,483)
Lee, Duncan S 4:51:07 (23,754)
Lee, Eddie 3:50:37 (8,173)
Lee, Gareth J 4:17:24 (15,068)
Lee, James R 3:38:11 (5,678)
Lee, Jonathan 3:35:35 (5,276)
Lee, Kar Chun Basco 4:26:44 (17,672)
Lee, Kin-Hung A 4:15:29 (14,573)
Lee, Malcolm G 4:12:48 (13,833)
Lee, Marcus T 4:10:22 (13,186)
Lee, Martin 4:57:17 (25,189)
Lee, Matt 5:05:13 (26,729)
Lee, Michael M 3:46:44 (7,290)
Lee, Michael W 3:57:11 (9,887)
Lee, Neil 3:49:37 (7,958)
Lee, Nicholas 4:49:30 (23,359)
Lee, Nigel 3:05:24 (1,509)
Lee, Peter G 3:17:11 (2,701)
Lee, Philip M 4:16:42 (14,891)
Lee, Richard G 3:05:14 (1,490)
Lee, Ricky 4:41:45 (21,578)
Lee, Robert S 4:56:26 (24,996)
Lee, Roger D 4:37:57 (20,606)
Lee, Royston A 2:52:58 (635)
Lee, Simon 5:04:53 (26,666)
Lee, Simon J 4:57:03 (25,143)
Lee, William T 4:27:13 (17,806)
Leech, Bruce R 4:50:57 (23,719)
Leech, Lewis W 4:39:34 (21,032)
Lee-Harwood, Blake J 4:23:40 (16,766)
Leek, Peter J 2:54:28 (709)
Leek, Shawn J 4:58:02 (25,335)
Leeks, Clinton E 4:01:07 (10,965)
Leeks, David 4:47:24 (22,856)
Lee-Miller, Jonny 3:14:21 (2,400)
Leeper, Julian A 4:34:40 (19,753)
Leeper, Simon J 4:05:08 (11,907)
Lees, Ivan A 4:12:48 (13,833)
Leeson, Anthony R 3:54:24 (9,077)
Leete, Matthew A 4:45:07 (22,357)
Leeves, Paul I 3:51:56 (8,470)
Lefebvre, Loic 3:20:03 (3,005)
Lefort, Regis J 3:25:29 (3,668)
Lefteri, Donny 4:41:28 (21,516)
Le-Gallez, Richard S 4:33:49 (19,523)
Legassick, David T 3:16:43 (2,650)
Leger, Jonathan 4:48:31 (23,125)
Legg, Christopher J 4:46:03 (22,562)
Legg, Dominic J 2:59:56 (1,124)
Legg, Jonathan 4:03:57 (11,617)
Legge, Andrew R 4:21:31 (16,211)
Legge, Timothy 2:53:53 (679)
Leggett, Theo E 4:45:12 (22,371)
Leggott, Richard J 4:05:08 (11,907)
Legh-Smith, Mark 4:07:25 (12,442)
Lehmann, Martin A 3:48:10 (7,629)
Leigh, Christopher W 3:48:05 (7,614)
Leigh, Darren R 4:05:04 (11,882)
Leigh, David Ronald 5:15:07 (28,354)
Leigh, Ian 3:52:45 (8,676)
Leigh, Michael R 5:12:26 (27,895)
Leigh, Robert D 3:47:50 (7,533)
Leigh, Ya'acov 4:28:21 (18,122)
Leighton, David 3:30:38 (4,549)
Leighton, Martin 4:12:30 (13,747)
Leighton, Niel 3:57:49 (10,080)
Leighton, Nigel 2:22:23 (34)
Leinster, Robert W 5:01:02 (25,983)
Leiper, James G 4:44:18 (22,169)
Le-Jossec, Bruno 4:26:32 (17,612)

Lel, Martin 2:07:26 (1)

Martin Lel (born 29 October 1978 in Kapsabet) is a Kenyan long distance runner. He won the London Marathon in 2005, 2007, and 2008, the New York City Marathon in 2003 and 2007 and the Great North Run in 2007 and 2009. His personal best time, as of April 2008, is 2:05:15, which he ran in the 2008 London Marathon setting a course record. Lel is coached by Gabriele Rosa and lives and trains in Namibia after he fled Kenya to escape the tribal-political violence. He is the fifth child of six brothers and three sisters and was raised in the town of Kapsabet in the Rift Valley. His father was a preacher and a subsistence farmer. Lel has made good provision for his family. 'I have built a good house for them, whereby they have more space. I have built a house for me nearby. And my brothers and sisters live there too. I have given them land, and animals. So they are all comfortable,' he said.

Leland, Howard C 5:47:22 (32,046)
Lelliott, Stephen 3:01:04 (1,195)
Leman, Antoine 4:09:47 (13,035)
Lemke, Grant G 2:54:45 (731)
Lemmon, James J 7:05:52 (34,937)
Lemmon, Stephen 5:09:11 (27,385)
Lemoine, Gaetan 3:58:37 (10,314)
Lemon, Keith 4:33:25 (19,409)
Lemp, René 4:00:05 (10,748)
Lemunier, Arnaud 3:34:15 (5,091)
Lendon, Jason M 2:46:27 (359)
Lenehan, Kevin 4:05:46 (12,041)
Lengauer-Stockner, Peter 3:45:32 (7,054)

Lenihan, Kevin G 3:02:17 (1,284)
Lennard, Andrew 4:24:29 (16,984)
Lennon, Conor M 3:38:56 (5,802)
Lennon, James G. 3:11:27 (2,075)
Lennon, Roger S 4:13:11 (13,938)
Lennox, Adam P 4:14:38 (14,325)
Lennox, Brendan A 5:07:47 (27,187)
Lenon, Mark E 4:14:09 (14,194)
Lenton, Steven J 3:40:58 (6,173)
Leo, Thomas 4:04:35 (11,764)
Leon, Luis 3:26:03 (3,773)
Leon, Philippe 3:49:01 (7,826)
Leon De La Barra, Antonio 5:12:22 (27,874)
Leonard, Andrew J 4:44:42 (22,249)
Leonard, Charles R 5:04:27 (26,592)
Leonard, Paul 3:50:00 (8,038)
Leone, August J 4:44:15 (22,155)
Leonidas, Diogo 3:34:45 (5,151)
Leon-Villapalos, Jorge 6:26:05 (34,129)
Lepage, Christopher 2:39:23 (183)
Lepcha, Ashish A 3:55:13 (9,280)
Le-Pennec, Dominique 3:11:37 (2,089)
Lepine, Steven R 3:59:50 (10,676)
Lepinoit, Eric 3:47:52 (7,541)
Lepkowski, Thaddeus J 4:05:08 (11,907)
Leppard, James E 4:55:59 (24,898)
Lerisson, Patrice 4:39:44 (21,077)
Leroy, Bertrand 2:43:58 (292)
Lesage, Jocelyn 3:32:53 (4,868)
Lescott, Rupert A 3:09:47 (1,895)
Leshetz, Matthew 4:14:21 (14,257)
Lesley, Richard J 3:52:53 (8,697)
Leslie, Glen A 4:05:58 (12,087)
Leslie, Neil 5:04:35 (26,611)
Lester, Andrew C 4:07:00 (12,343)
Lester, Andrew M 5:02:00 (26,143)
Lester, John E 5:38:51 (31,293)
Lester, Mark A 4:13:40 (14,060)
Lester, Paul M 4:37:08 (20,399)
Lester, Peter S 3:47:29 (7,454)
Lester, Roy E 5:19:31 (29,035)
Lesurf, Mark D 4:58:15 (25,384)
Leterme, Marc 3:54:02 (8,983)
Letford, John 3:35:36 (5,279)
Leth, Bendtchresten 4:04:10 (11,894)
Lethaby, Raymond J 4:26:17 (17,527)
Letham, Rick P 3:05:02 (1,469)
Letton, David 3:27:06 (3,943)
Leung, Ken 5:23:19 (29,518)
Leung, Victor 4:00:17 (10,784)
Leung, Wan Hong 4:20:22 (15,903)
Leuschner, Helmut 2:43:59 (293)
Leuw, Peter J 3:39:38 (5,935)
Levene, Paul 3:56:37 (9,696)
Levens, Philip 3:16:45 (2,656)
Lever, John 5:42:49 (31,666)
Leveritt, Stephen R 4:00:30 (10,832)
Levett, Dan J 4:20:46 (16,010)
Levett, Geoffrey J 4:32:37 (19,231)
Levett, Peter D 4:38:59 (20,871)
Levi, Russel L 4:14:25 (14,280)
Levick, John W 3:12:26 (2,189)
Levine, Hugh A 4:21:25 (16,179)
Levine, Mark 3:08:14 (1,736)
Levinson, Thomas A 4:04:35 (11,764)
Levitt, Julian E 4:22:32 (16,482)
Levitt, Justin M 3:56:56 (9,796)
Levy, Dan 3:33:59 (5,045)
Levy, Daniel W 4:45:40 (22,474)
Levy, Kevin D 5:03:43 (26,466)
Levy, Simon J 3:15:24 (2,513)
Lewer, Aidan P 3:48:20 (7,664)
Lewiecki, John 6:14:19 (33,711)
Lewin, Michael 4:31:41 (19,016)
Lewis, Adrian 4:39:02 (20,890)
Lewis, Alex J 4:42:38 (21,781)
Lewis, Allan 4:17:19 (15,042)
Lewis, Andrew 4:17:18 (15,036)
Lewis, Andrew A 4:55:59 (24,898)
Lewis, Andrew J 5:18:17 (28,833)
Lewis, Andrew K 4:22:58 (16,592)
Lewis, Andy F 3:35:31 (5,265)
Lewis, Andy J 4:36:17 (20,156)

Lewis, Anton C 3:59:57 (10,713)
Lewis, Ben J 2:45:26 (334)
Lewis, Benjamin 5:32:36 (30,625)
Lewis, Brandon K 5:18:20 (28,841)
Lewis, Colin 3:26:26 (3,839)
Lewis, Daniel D 5:32:36 (30,625)
Lewis, Daniel J 4:01:12 (10,984)
Lewis, Darren J 3:07:31 (1,676)
Lewis, Darryll J 5:12:08 (27,852)
Lewis, David 3:57:51 (10,094)
Lewis, David 5:36:16 (31,022)
Lewis, David G 4:31:00 (18,837)
Lewis, David I 4:13:28 (14,011)
Lewis, David P 3:21:04 (3,090)
Lewis, Dennis J 4:19:18 (15,611)
Lewis, Dennis J 5:50:36 (32,310)
Lewis, David J 3:51:33 (8,382)
Lewis, Elliott J 6:32:35 (34,320)
Lewis, Gareth D 4:13:56 (14,125)
Lewis, Gareth H 3:39:35 (5,928)
Lewis, Gary R 4:27:19 (17,829)
Lewis, Gary S 3:54:40 (9,144)
Lewis, Gary S 4:19:16 (15,596)
Lewis, Graham 4:21:16 (16,135)
Lewis, Howard C 4:42:42 (21,800)
Lewis, Ian F 5:16:50 (28,612)
Lewis, Jake 3:59:46 (10,654)
Lewis, Jody 4:09:18 (12,908)
Lewis, John D 3:29:30 (4,354)
Lewis, John E 3:25:39 (3,695)
Lewis, John L 5:45:07 (31,856)
Lewis, Jonathan P 5:22:28 (29,415)
Lewis, Julian D 4:06:35 (12,238)
Lewis, Kieran J 4:36:51 (20,319)
Lewis, Mark 4:11:35 (13,500)
Lewis, Mark J 2:47:29 (388)
Lewis, Mark S 4:30:59 (18,831)
Lewis, Martin W 4:50:19 (23,572)
Lewis, Martyn R 3:52:36 (8,629)
Lewis, Matthew E 3:52:33 (8,615)
Lewis, Michael S 4:02:02 (11,167)
Lewis, Paul 5:33:28 (30,719)
Lewis, Paul A 4:24:23 (16,949)
Lewis, Paul C 3:45:14 (6,995)
Lewis, Paul G 4:45:51 (22,510)
Lewis, Paul J 4:45:54 (22,524)
Lewis, Paul R 3:30:20 (4,494)
Lewis, Peter 4:26:42 (17,658)
Lewis, Peter J 4:56:28 (25,006)
Lewis, Philip D 4:58:27 (25,429)
Lewis, Piers H 3:24:18 (3,486)
Lewis, Richard J 4:29:03 (18,326)
Lewis, Robert W 4:28:55 (18,279)
Lewis, Seth 3:30:30 (4,526)
Lewis, Simon 2:49:58 (499)
Lewis, Simon P 4:43:19 (21,940)
Lewis, Stephen B 3:30:44 (4,565)
Lewis, Stephen R 4:20:44 (16,001)
Lewis, Steve 3:40:20 (6,060)
Lewis, Steven 5:00:44 (25,923)
Lewis, Steven J 3:42:22 (6,445)
Lewsey, David G 5:06:59 (27,053)
Ley, Jonathan J 4:22:23 (16,444)
Leydecker, Mark E 3:50:32 (8,153)
Leyenda, Manuel 3:30:43 (4,561)
Leyk, Wolfgang 4:05:40 (12,019)
Leyland, Jim 6:22:37 (34,012)
Leyland, Ralph C 5:34:07 (30,791)
Leyland, Simon J 4:05:08 (11,907)
Leysner, John 3:51:24 (8,353)
Lherieau, Christophe 3:39:33 (5,923)
Lhon, William 3:23:43 (3,405)
Liaboeuf, Michel A 4:41:05 (21,412)
Lias, Steven L 4:59:00 (25,559)
Licata, Riccardo 4:52:32 (24,061)
Licciardi, Francis 4:32:18 (19,162)
Lichtsinn, Rainer 4:12:09 (13,650)
Lickfold, Kevin 4:36:51 (20,319)
Lida, Joshua 4:53:38 (24,338)
Liddell, Jamie 3:29:00 (4,273)
Liddle, Alan 4:01:00 (10,949)
Liddle, David A 3:24:21 (3,498)
Liddle, Elliot L 4:07:02 (12,355)

Liddle, Geroge 3:49:06 (7,847)
Liddle, Justin 5:05:19 (26,753)
Liddle, Robert H 3:22:19 (3,229)
Liesche, Andreas 3:47:58 (7,568)
Light, Duncan I 3:38:45 (5,765)
Light, Irwin 5:14:34 (28,273)
Light, Mark P 4:37:45 (20,567)
Light, Richard 4:23:20 (16,701)
Lightburn, Steve P 4:01:04 (10,958)
Lightfoot, Ian 5:51:32 (32,375)
Lightfoot, James R 4:04:00 (11,633)
Lightning, David W 3:58:36 (10,310)
Lightwood, Barry 5:12:16 (27,865)
Lijnen, Filip J 3:33:58 (5,041)
Like, Martin R 4:11:41 (13,534)
Lill, Nick 4:01:54 (11,128)
Lilley, Martin T 5:39:27 (31,371)
Lilley, Paul M 3:58:39 (10,323)
Lillico, Ronald G 4:12:26 (13,734)
Lillie, Frederick 4:52:41 (24,101)
Lillie, Mark T 3:35:20 (5,227)
Lillis, Wayne P 2:59:33 (1,094)
Lilly, Damian P 4:47:25 (22,861)
Lilly, Robert 4:41:33 (21,537)
Lim, Ming 4:44:06 (22,117)
Lima, Sigurd 3:26:50 (3,901)
Limb, Richard E 4:15:00 (14,448)
Linaker, David J 4:44:12 (22,142)
Linard, Adam D 4:44:00 (22,099)
Linathan, Julian 3:34:07 (5,063)
Lincoln, Christian P 5:28:59 (30,243)
Linden, Gary G 3:49:59 (8,033)
Lindenmuth, Thomas G 7:14:14 (35,028)
Linder, Thierry 3:36:41 (5,451)
Lindesay, Matthew W 5:21:49 (29,329)
Lindfield, David J 4:36:35 (20,243)
Linding, Thomas 4:01:41 (11,086)
Lindner, Sam P 5:21:06 (29,249)
Lindop, Matthew 3:56:49 (9,757)
Lindsay, James T 3:27:17 (3,973)
Lindsay, Mark A 4:30:16 (18,672)
Lindsay, Nigel M 3:59:40 (10,592)
Lindsay, Patrick A 4:25:02 (17,133)
Lindsay, Stuart A 4:39:50 (21,096)
Lindsay, William R 4:54:25 (24,528)
Line, Ian 3:53:18 (8,801)
Linehan, Kevin P 3:12:18 (2,175)
Lines, Lee R 4:24:52 (17,087)
Lines, Peter T 4:08:14 (12,622)
Liney, David J 4:29:47 (18,540)
Ling, Barry P 4:43:26 (21,961)
Ling, Jonathan G 3:18:29 (2,829)
Ling, Lee M 6:14:48 (33,727)
Lingard, Richard 4:11:33 (13,494)
Lingard, Scott O 4:07:03 (12,356)
Lings, Julian J 3:07:05 (1,641)
Linke, Michael 3:44:50 (6,919)
Linley, Craig 4:50:45 (23,683)
Linley, Paul 4:32:30 (19,212)
Linnell, Anthony J 4:19:13 (15,582)
Linning, Frankie J 4:29:54 (18,567)
Linssen, Ton 3:44:56 (6,946)
Linstead, Michael D 5:04:36 (26,612)
Lintern, Anthony E 3:49:15 (7,881)
Linton, Darren J 3:54:56 (5,172)
Linton, John 4:25:25 (17,257)
Linturn, Anthony J 3:59:52 (10,688)
Lipinski, Kai S 3:40:15 (6,043)
Lippiatt, Robert 4:23:01 (16,604)
Lipshitz, Daniel 4:53:47 (24,379)
Liptrot, Ian P 4:08:48 (12,769)
Liptrott, Mark 4:33:19 (19,390)
Liptrott, Simon W 3:45:58 (7,127)
Lirola-Maldonado, José A 3:21:17 (3,112)
Lisk, Alan T 4:37:41 (20,547)
Lisle, Richard A 3:32:21 (4,798)
Lisser, Michael 5:16:45 (28,589)
Lister, Andrew R 4:02:45 (11,332)
Lister, Daniel 3:53:40 (8,900)
Lister, James S 4:21:38 (16,238)
Lister, Joseph W 5:36:40 (31,074)
Lister, Nicholas P 3:30:30 (4,526)
Lister, Robert C 4:12:19 (13,699)

Lowson, Richard J 3:07:31 (1,676)
Lowther, Adrian 2:36:47 (131)
Lowther, Jason C 4:58:19 (25,395)
Lowther, Mark J 5:51:51 (32,401)
Loxton, David R 4:34:48 (19,789)
Loxton, Paul A 3:55:32 (9,376)
Lua, Suet 4:21:21 (16,159)
Luby, Michael A 5:43:43 (31,738)
Lucas, Adam 3:41:31 (6,276)
Lucas, Alan 3:48:59 (7,818)
Lucas, Bernard S 3:42:33 (6,474)
Lucas, Mark A 3:47:16 (7,405)
Lucas, Martin J 4:39:20 (20,975)
Lucas, Michael A 7:00:48 (34,885)
Lucas, Tim D 4:56:07 (24,920)
Lucchesi, Giovanni 5:06:23 (26,942)
Luce, John M 5:13:37 (28,103)
Lucey, Michael P 4:50:57 (23,719)
Lucht, Matt J 3:24:36 (3,527)
Lucignano, Giuseppe 5:15:35 (28,432)
Lucin, Alessandro 4:13:24 (13,990)
Luck, Jamie D 3:25:50 (3,728)
Luckett, Ben J 5:31:24 (30,508)
Luckett, Giles 6:20:18 (33,930)
Luckhurst, Anthony P 5:15:46 (28,453)
Luckhurst, Paul K 4:40:28 (21,251)
Lucy, John E 4:10:50 (13,298)
Ludiman, Mark 4:05:18 (11,948)
Ludlam, Chris D 4:01:02 (10,954)
Ludlow, Peter J 4:58:44 (25,493)
Ludlow-Palafox, Carlos 4:54:44 (24,603)
Ludwig, Juergen 4:05:46 (12,041)
Ludzker, Ben M 5:05:20 (26,756)
Lueger, Guenter 3:37:41 (5,602)
Luff, Bradley I 5:45:18 (31,879)
Luisi, Vito 4:07:04 (12,360)
Luke, Ian R 5:48:13 (32,113)
Luke, Richard I 3:53:09 (8,756)
Luke-Macauley, Ian N 5:45:31 (31,897)
Lukeman, James 5:35:55 (30,984)
Lukins, Colin I 3:27:08 (3,948)
Lumber, Ralph W 5:01:47 (26,103)
Lumley, Ben 5:27:00 (29,977)
Lumley, Paul 4:08:08 (12,598)
Lumsdon, Timothy W 4:26:30 (17,600)
Lund, Kelvin 5:00:24 (25,863)
Lund, Michael 5:57:10 (32,784)
Lund, Paul F 3:49:56 (8,024)
Lund, Simon 2:54:11 (698)
Lundie, Blair A 6:18:31 (33,872)
Lundsjo, Lars 2:55:05 (746)
Lundy, Richard P 4:42:36 (21,769)
Lunn, Anthony T 2:50:45 (528)
Lunn, Gary J 3:11:50 (2,122)
Lunn, Martin R 3:59:28 (10,560)
Lunn, Richard I 4:36:37 (20,258)
Lunn, Rob 5:09:53 (27,493)
Lunn, Robert M 4:50:18 (23,564)
Lunn, Robert W 4:28:41 (18,212)
Lunney, Adam 5:33:04 (30,675)
Lunt, David W 5:37:19 (31,118)
Lunt, Geoffrey 4:38:45 (20,814)
Lunt, Keith R 3:29:45 (4,408)
Lupson, David J 5:11:24 (27,725)
Lupton, David W 3:55:34 (9,394)
Lupton, John A 3:55:22 (9,329)
Lurcott, Richard P 4:42:59 (21,871)
Luscher, Gerard P 4:07:43 (12,503)
Luscombe, Mark R 4:54:01 (24,433)
Luscombe, Neil D 5:09:28 (27,432)
Lush, Mike 5:06:36 (26,982)
Lutje, Matthias 3:54:03 (8,986)
Lutman, Damien 4:08:52 (12,792)
Luton, Sam 2:56:47 (872)
Lutter, Joern 5:22:23 (29,400)
Luty, Clive M 3:44:25 (6,823)
Lutz, Thomas P 4:29:36 (18,497)
Luxton, Martin J 3:55:00 (9,238)
Lyall, Graham 3:23:32 (3,380)
Lyall, Gregor J 4:26:21 (17,548)
Lyas, Ashley D 4:27:31 (17,894)
Lyberg, Dag A 4:10:20 (13,179)
Lyden, Thomas R 4:48:53 (23,205)
Lydon, Peter J 4:46:58 (22,765)
Lymer, Peter J 4:39:30 (21,013)
Lynam, Robert G 3:30:42 (4,560)
Lynch, Andrew J 2:36:11 (123)
Lynch, Benjamin J 4:49:52 (23,466)
Lynch, Colm 5:06:19 (26,922)
Lynch, Conor 4:14:02 (14,158)
Lynch, Damian P 4:06:14 (12,149)
Lynch, Edward F 5:21:42 (29,312)
Lynch, Robert M 6:05:48 (33,313)
Lynch, Timothy 5:43:29 (31,715)
Lynch, Warren M 2:32:44 (90)
Lynds, Andrew J 4:26:16 (17,521)
Lyne, Andrew G 3:00:49 (1,181)
Lyness, Martin J 6:26:03 (34,126)
Lyness, Roy 5:16:13 (28,509)
Lynn, Justin 4:17:56 (15,184)
Lyon, Andrew D 3:25:17 (3,641)
Lyon, John 4:26:37 (17,636)
Lyon, Mark 4:54:43 (24,598)
Lyon, Mark 4:55:56 (24,884)
Lyon, Michael W 4:54:34 (24,573)
Lyon, Robert G 4:56:40 (25,061)
Lyon, Roger J 6:19:32 (33,905)
Lyons, Dale R 5:12:46 (27,963)
Lyons, David J 4:21:29 (16,200)
Lyons, James M 3:17:18 (2,717)
Lyons, James S 4:12:41 (13,798)
Lyons, Richard M 3:36:15 (5,382)
Lyons, Stephen E 5:09:56 (27,501)
Lyons Lowe, Damian J 4:00:30 (10,832)
Lyps, Emmanuel 3:30:43 (4,561)
Lyth, Gordon M 4:41:31 (21,529)
Maalim, Yusuf 4:15:00 (14,448)
Maasland, Tom C 4:19:09 (15,562)
Mabb, Philip A 5:24:21 (29,668)
Mabbs, Alan 6:42:38 (34,560)
Mabbutt, Martin C 3:37:25 (5,559)
Maben, James T 3:52:29 (8,599)
Mabey, Peter F 3:22:29 (3,240)
MacAllister, Colin 4:03:20 (11,469)
Macaluso, Paul J 5:26:25 (29,914)
Macarez, Florent 3:24:57 (3,578)
MacArthur, John D 4:28:57 (18,292)
MacArthur, John L 4:53:46 (24,374)
MacArthur, Trevor J 2:54:10 (696)
MacAskill, Andy 2:38:05 (163)
Macaulay, John R 4:00:48 (10,905)
Macaulay, Neil D 5:08:39 (27,303)
MacCarrick, Timothy 3:41:16 (6,225)
Maccarrone, Franck 4:15:48 (14,660)
Mac Conleitreac, Pel 6:10:42 (33,563)
Macdonald, Alasdair J 6:25:37 (34,115)
Macdonald, Alex J 4:45:32 (22,439)
Mac Donald, Alistair J 3:27:49 (4,079)
Macdonald, Brian A 4:30:10 (18,648)
Macdonald, Calum R 4:52:04 (23,954)
Macdonald, Gary 3:41:25 (6,261)
Macdonald, Gordon W 4:00:32 (10,843)
Macdonald, Graeme B 3:54:35 (9,119)
Macdonald, Hamish F 3:27:28 (4,012)
Macdonald, Ian J 2:40:11 (205)
Macdonald, James G 4:54:56 (24,648)
Macdonald, Jamie P 3:46:10 (7,174)
Macdonald, John A 5:10:20 (27,546)
Macdonald, John P 4:22:06 (16,367)
Macdonald, Kelvin 5:26:04 (29,879)
Macdonald, Neil A 4:51:07 (23,754)
Macdonald, Phillip R 3:46:53 (7,326)
Macdonald, Robert I 4:50:30 (23,626)
Macdonald, Robert J 6:05:48 (33,313)
Macdonald, Ross B 3:48:29 (7,702)
Macdonald, Stewart F 2:26:21 (50)
Macdonald, Stuart C 4:55:00 (24,674)
Macdonald Blyth, Eric 4:47:05 (22,790)
Macdonald-Spiers, Justin 4:50:21 (23,579)
MacDougald, Alexander 3:28:29 (4,194)
MacDougall, Roy C 5:40:47 (31,487)
Mace, Dominique 3:45:02 (6,962)
Mace, Jeremy R 4:21:28 (16,195)
MacEnhill, Damian P 3:10:34 (1,985)
Macey, David 4:11:00 (13,350)
Macey, Mark R 5:02:16 (26,194)
Macey, Terence J 3:44:20 (6,802)
MacFadyen, Brian 3:21:42 (3,154)
Macfarlane, Robert E 3:41:17 (6,228)
MacGibbon, Michael A 3:48:29 (7,702)
MacGregor, Calum D 4:00:45 (10,899)
MacGregor, Graeme S 3:25:07 (3,609)
MacGregor, Hugo 4:56:54 (25,116)
MacGregor, Jim K 3:38:03 (5,656)
MacGregor, John C 3:23:19 (3,353)
MacGregor, Stuart A 3:23:37 (3,389)
Machielse, Wilco M 4:08:11 (12,607)
Machin, Brian-Rocky R 4:44:04 (22,108)
Machin, Nigel O 4:36:26 (20,209)
Macias, Carlos J 3:02:14 (1,282)
MacInnes, Christopher 4:56:28 (25,006)
MacInnes, Roddy P 3:56:34 (9,681)
Mack, Antony 4:26:11 (17,503)
Mack, Darren R 2:47:56 (410)
Mackay, Alan R 4:13:11 (13,938)
Mackay, Alexander D 3:22:14 (3,219)
Mackay, Andrew J 3:44:24 (6,820)
Mackay, Duncan G 5:14:09 (28,202)
Mackay, Gary J 5:21:24 (29,287)
Mackay, Ian 2:56:43 (863)
Mackay, Ian 4:29:02 (18,320)
Mackay, James 4:21:10 (16,102)
Mackay, Jay 6:47:30 (34,668)
Mackay, John A 3:22:54 (3,283)
Mackay, Michael J 3:08:45 (1,786)
Mackay, Richard G 5:20:46 (29,211)
MacKeith, Samuel A 4:12:10 (13,657)
MacKenney, John F 3:54:43 (9,158)
Mackenzie, Graham A 3:35:49 (5,310)
Mackenzie, James R 3:43:34 (6,661)
Mackenzie, John D 4:20:56 (16,061)
Mackenzie, Ken R 3:35:57 (5,331)
Mackenzie, Kevin 3:26:24 (3,830)
Mackenzie, Michael A 4:24:24 (16,956)
Mackenzie, Robert E 3:59:55 (10,701)
Mackenzie, Roddy H 4:45:34 (22,448)
Mackenzie, Simon 4:20:55 (16,055)
Mackenzie, Stephen J 3:26:02 (3,770)
Mackenzie-Charrington, Patrick 4:06:49 (12,288)
Mackervoy, Stephen M 4:45:28 (22,425)
Mackey, Darren J 4:54:39 (24,583)
Mackey, Ian M 4:17:22 (15,055)
Mackie, Alistair J 4:24:08 (16,886)
Mackie, Brian 3:07:34 (1,682)
Mackie, David G 5:18:34 (28,877)
Mackie, James F 4:28:24 (18,142)
Mackie, Simon J 3:41:28 (6,271)
Mackie, Thomas R 3:37:22 (5,551)
Mackinnon, Neil A 5:05:54 (26,853)
Mackinnon, Robert A 3:44:23 (6,815)
Mackintosh, Jamie S 4:00:56 (10,935)
Mackintosh, Nicholas I 3:49:59 (8,033)
Mackley, Daniel J 4:23:34 (16,746)
Mackness, Anthony S 3:26:55 (3,914)
MacLachlan, Alastair J 2:56:32 (845)
MacLagan, Ross A 4:16:15 (14,781)
Maclaren, Charles 5:12:30 (27,910)
Maclaren, Edward J 4:59:44 (25,719)
Maclaren, Paul 3:01:38 (1,235)
Maclean, Charles C 4:29:14 (18,375)
Maclean, Christopher G 5:06:49 (27,020)
Maclean, Colin W 4:51:12 (23,777)
Maclean, Fergus R 3:43:46 (6,698)
Maclean, Matthew 5:10:36 (27,592)
Maclean, Richard A 4:34:50 (19,800)
Maclean, Richard G 4:29:15 (18,379)
Maclean, Thomas I 6:26:30 (34,142)
MacLennan, Colin N 4:04:51 (11,825)
MacLennan, Kenneth 4:59:39 (25,701)
Macleod, Alex 5:43:45 (31,742)
Macleod, Don I 4:25:06 (17,152)
Macleod, Douglas G 4:58:23 (25,412)
Macleod, Duncan R 4:06:27 (12,201)
Macleod, James A 5:19:21 (28,998)
Macleod, Mark 5:30:52 (30,448)
Macleod, Stuart 5:20:45 (29,208)
MacLure, Steven A 4:17:51 (15,170)
MacManus, Paul A 3:20:15 (3,021)
Mac Matheuna, Ultan M 5:05:12 (26,725)

Macmillan, John R 4:12:14 (13,679)
Macmillan, Mark 5:12:41 (27,940)
Macmillan, Philip P 2:57:07 (892)
Macon, Dominique 3:39:39 (5,941)
Macpherson, David 3:45:23 (7,026)
Macpherson, James R 3:33:41 (4,989)
Macpherson, Robin J 4:18:45 (15,444)
Macpherson, William R 4:29:08 (18,350)
MacQueen, Anthony N 3:00:47 (1,180)
MacQueen, Ian M 3:56:45 (9,736)
MacSporran, Kenneth G 4:22:15 (16,407)
MacSweeney, Conor A 5:47:49 (32,083)
MacTavish, Alasdair J 4:56:40 (25,061)
MacWhirter, James R 4:54:03 (24,439)
Maddams, Russell 2:29:59 (69)
Madden, Gary 4:11:53 (13,581)
Madder, Michael J 3:47:01 (7,354)
Madderson, Jonathan L 3:39:32 (5,920)
Maddison, Antony D 3:53:24 (8,831)
Maddison, Peter J 3:25:02 (3,589)
Maddison, Simon C 4:34:04 (19,583)
Maddison, Stephen 5:17:26 (28,701)
Maddock, Alan 5:12:24 (27,886)
Maddock, Andrew S 3:53:08 (8,753)
Maddock, Mark A 5:27:48 (30,075)
Maddock, Michael D 6:03:10 (33,152)
Maddock, Richard T 4:37:25 (20,478)
Maddocks, Jonathan R 4:05:42 (12,026)
Maden, David N 5:02:45 (26,284)
Madgwick, Tim P 4:03:20 (11,469)
Madin, Joseph 4:15:49 (14,669)
Madlmair, Friedrich 3:26:23 (3,824)
Madotto, Francesco 3:15:05 (2,484)
Madsen, Bjarne 3:42:51 (6,518)
Madsen, Harald 5:09:00 (27,357)
Madsen, Karl T 4:00:29 (10,828)
Maeno, Shoji 3:41:56 (6,366)
Maeswaran, Shanmuga S 5:12:32 (27,915)
Maffetti, Luca 4:25:14 (17,196)
Magan, Bryan A 4:44:54 (22,298)
Magee, Colin C 3:19:40 (2,961)
Magee, Paul M 5:07:33 (27,152)
Magee, Stephen T 5:50:47 (32,328)
Maggs, Nigel J 3:47:38 (7,482)
Magill, James N 4:39:00 (20,879)
Magill, John A 4:04:57 (11,849)
Magin, Thierry 3:20:49 (3,077)
Magistri, Alvaro 4:07:15 (12,403)
Magl, Phil J 4:55:41 (24,815)
Magnall, Philip M 3:31:29 (4,678)
Magness, Ian J 5:25:07 (29,763)
Magni, Roberto 4:31:47 (19,042)
Magnin, Jacques L 4:14:48 (14,379)
Magowan, Philip 4:53:17 (24,243)
Magri, Sergio 5:00:39 (25,909)
Magson, Clive 4:52:28 (24,045)
Maguire, Alex C 4:00:11 (10,762)
Maguire, Bob 3:53:01 (8,720)
Maguire, Joseph 5:15:11 (28,365)
Maguire, Paul 4:46:53 (22,750)
Maguire, Paul A 3:56:35 (9,687)
Maguire, Stephen F 4:49:58 (23,488)
Maguire, Terence J 5:54:00 (32,564)
Maguire, Tim J 3:57:00 (9,815)
Mahe, Jean-Michel 5:27:49 (30,077)
Maher, Christian M 4:59:51 (25,747)
Maher, Derek P 4:15:30 (14,582)
Maher, Leigh G 4:19:16 (15,596)
Maher, Patrick 4:07:15 (12,403)
Maheswaran, Tim 4:37:13 (20,416)
Maholam, Ian 3:32:52 (4,864)
Mahon, Michael 3:47:16 (7,405)
Mahon, Nicholas 3:34:24 (5,110)
Mahoney, Clive 4:29:38 (18,505)
Mahony, Gerard O 5:25:46 (29,837)
Mahot, Denis 3:10:32 (1,981)
Mahsoudi, Bruno 3:41:10 (6,212)
Mahuma, Kenneth B 3:45:55 (7,120)
Maiden, John A 4:14:00 (14,148)
Maidens, Geoff G 5:46:42 (31,994)
Maidment, Jem 4:43:52 (22,064)
Maidment, Neil E 4:53:55 (24,398)
Maier, Roland 3:59:36 (10,599)
Maile, John 5:28:16 (30,160)
Mailes, Ian R 4:57:00 (25,128)
Main, Vincent G 3:30:29 (4,523)
Maini, Samir 4:40:40 (21,301)
Mainwaring, Michael R 3:37:04 (5,507)
Mainwaring, Paul 4:32:58 (19,307)
Maiorana, Gaspare 2:43:43 (286)
Mair, Robert 6:19:25 (33,902)
Mair, Robin J 4:26:50 (17,694)
Maitland, Charles M 3:31:29 (4,678)
Majithia, Anil 5:40:06 (31,427)
Major, Paul L 2:36:31 (126)
Majors, Lee 7:02:22 (34,896)
Makepeace, Alan D 4:02:59 (11,389)
Makepeace, Daniel B 4:14:05 (14,181)
Makin, Frank H 3:54:58 (9,232)
Makino, Shigenobu 6:33:07 (34,332)
Mal, Firouz 3:32:03 (4,756)
Malassine, Didier E 2:45:39 (336)
Malavialle, Philippe 3:56:17 (9,599)
Malby, Anthony C 3:24:56 (3,576)
Malcolm, Andrew P 5:12:18 (27,870)
Malcolm, Ian B 2:46:06 (352)
Malcolm, Michael 4:08:45 (12,755)
Malcolm, Solomon A 4:11:08 (13,388)
Malcolm, Thomas E 3:23:13 (3,334)
Maldar, Alec 3:36:52 (5,473)
Malde, Sam 4:43:29 (21,974)
Maldonato, Gregorio 3:29:48 (4,417)
Male, Gavin L 5:47:28 (32,060)
Male, Tony K 5:07:58 (27,211)
Maley, Sean 3:01:03 (1,194)
Malherbe, Michael 3:35:49 (5,310)
Malhomme, Nicholas H 4:30:08 (18,636)
Malia, Vincent 5:25:31 (29,808)
Malik, Abdul 6:19:51 (33,913)
Malik, Alan 3:52:19 (8,560)
Malin, William F 3:49:26 (7,917)
Malizia, Richard C 5:10:48 (27,617)
Malkomess, Juergen 5:30:02 (30,366)
Mallery, Phillip P 3:10:38 (1,995)
Malleson, Nigel 5:10:38 (27,596)
Mallett, Anthony S 4:15:32 (14,589)
Mallett, Gary P 5:57:10 (32,784)
Malley, Adam 4:48:21 (23,088)
Malley, Michael A 3:53:26 (8,844)
Mallinder, James P 3:52:50 (8,688)
Mallinson, Frazer H 4:37:53 (20,594)
Mallinson, James R 3:27:47 (4,073)
Mallison, Peter G 2:43:48 (289)
Mallon, John 3:27:17 (3,973)
Malloth, Thomas N 3:53:26 (8,844)
Malmqvist, Tony 3:36:11 (5,369)
Malone, Alex 4:04:28 (11,740)
Malone, Brendan P 4:11:18 (13,428)
Malone, Fergus 3:50:35 (8,166)
Malone, Ryan M 6:02:45 (33,124)
Malone, Sean 5:37:51 (31,175)
Maloney, Craig 4:44:23 (22,188)
Maloney, Liam E 3:35:43 (5,299)
Maloney, Mark J 3:52:13 (8,532)
Maloy, Barry 4:20:53 (16,043)
Maloy, Graham 5:39:38 (31,386)
Malpas, Jamie J 4:42:58 (21,867)
Malson, Dominic M 3:44:28 (6,827)
Maltby, Nigel R 4:13:00 (13,878)
Malzacher, Frido 4:40:43 (21,314)
Mamer, Steve G 3:30:23 (4,505)
Mamet, Alex G 4:41:47 (21,585)
Man, Wai L 6:14:58 (33,732)
Mancel, Gregory 3:42:14 (6,422)
Mancer, Jez 2:41:42 (233)
Mancho, José 4:44:16 (22,160)
Mancini, Eric P 3:19:30 (2,937)
Mander, David 5:04:59 (26,683)
Mandry, James G 4:00:36 (10,867)
Mangaroo, Kelvin 5:05:20 (26,756)
Mangeolles, Paul S 5:07:41 (27,172)
Mangeot, Andrew R 3:48:56 (7,811)
Manley, Nick 3:33:42 (4,990)
Mann, Alan J 3:38:54 (5,793)
Mann, Christopher D 4:01:01 (10,952)
Mann, David 6:16:14 (33,796)
Mann, Dean 3:55:25 (9,342)
Mann, Jason P 4:15:34 (14,599)
Mann, Julian 2:39:45 (198)
Mann, Kenneth A 5:41:31 (31,553)
Mann, Kester A 3:24:34 (3,523)
Mann, Lee 5:56:34 (32,736)
Mann, Lee J 4:42:49 (21,823)
Mann, Nick P 3:48:05 (7,614)
Mann, Paul A 3:06:01 (1,552)
Mann, Peter C 2:48:31 (439)
Mann, Sodi 4:58:25 (25,422)
Mann, Stuart H 3:15:30 (2,525)
Mann, Sukhpal 4:34:13 (19,634)
Manners, Ian B 3:50:15 (8,097)
Manners, Jonathan E 5:37:39 (31,156)
Manning, Jason I 2:57:14 (905)
Manning, John R 3:28:34 (4,211)
Manning, Julian H 2:45:39 (336)
Manning, Justin 4:54:05 (24,447)
Manning, Neil J 4:54:05 (24,447)
Manning, Paul 4:16:43 (14,893)
Manning, Roger S 4:19:24 (15,636)
Mannion, Sean M 5:03:02 (26,349)
Mansell Lewis, Edward 4:17:22 (15,055)
Manser, Darren N 3:45:36 (7,065)
Manser, Jeff 4:03:49 (11,584)
Mansfield, Adrian 4:28:02 (18,036)
Mansfield, Andrew 3:48:26 (7,690)
Mansfield, Brian A 4:08:01 (12,574)
Mansfield, David 4:57:04 (25,146)
Mansfield, David A 3:35:10 (5,205)
Mansfield, David S 3:41:42 (6,316)
Mansfield, Simon A 3:57:05 (9,850)
Mansfield, Stephen P 3:59:22 (10,538)
Mansi, Andrew J 3:07:44 (1,695)
Mansi, Dominic A 4:08:37 (12,718)
Mansilla, Mario H 5:14:30 (28,261)
Manson, Charlie R 4:38:15 (20,683)
Manson, Christopher J 5:29:40 (30,326)
Manson, James 4:05:06 (11,897)
Manson, James W 6:49:30 (34,701)
Manson, John R 4:55:08 (24,711)
Manson, Peter 4:58:22 (25,406)
Mansour, Paul R 4:24:57 (17,107)
Mansukhani, Raoul 3:54:52 (9,202)
Mansur, Elan 4:44:13 (22,147)
Manteau, Jerome J 3:32:09 (4,769)
Mantle, David S 3:37:27 (5,570)
Manton, Roger P 3:18:52 (2,868)
Manuel Jesus, Gutierrez Gonza 3:57:35 (10,007)
Manville, Simon R 4:56:15 (24,950)
Manz, Rudi D 4:52:13 (23,995)
Manze, David P 5:05:20 (26,756)
Maout, Yann N 3:14:58 (2,477)
Mapp, Daniel P 4:46:04 (22,566)
Mapstone, Nicholas P 3:53:37 (8,888)
Maragall, Juan 4:19:41 (15,719)
Maraia, Antonio 2:54:37 (721)
Marais, Jacky 4:23:15 (16,669)
Maratos, Stephen P 3:46:47 (7,305)
Marcadier, Pascal 4:48:15 (23,065)
March, Michael 6:11:13 (33,583)
March, Richard P 3:41:58 (6,370)
March, Steve P 3:03:21 (1,353)
Marchand, Pierre 4:51:03 (23,746)
Marchant, Gary 7:34:33 (35,156)
Marchant, Peter R 4:16:19 (14,799)
Marchant, Stephane 4:35:29 (19,972)
Marchegiani, Gaetano 4:28:06 (18,057)
Marchetti, Emiliano 2:33:13 (97)
Marcolongo, Roberto 3:50:05 (8,058)
Marcussen, Kurt K 3:06:25 (1,585)
Marczinzik, Uwe 3:02:24 (1,291)
Margereson, Matthew P 3:24:05 (3,456)
Margetts, Jeremy D 4:47:29 (22,883)
Margetts, Robert J 4:56:04 (24,910)
Marginson, George W 4:30:38 (18,755)
Margolis, Geoffrey A 3:59:28 (10,560)
Maric, Peter 4:40:51 (21,348)
Marie, Spencer 4:33:55 (19,551)
Marigold, Robert V 3:58:34 (10,306)
Marini, Riccardo 3:41:31 (6,276)
Marinko, John 3:23:37 (3,389)

Marino, Giovanni 2:58:54 (1,024)
Marion, Terance S 4:22:27 (16,461)
Marjoram, Gareth K 4:43:33 (21,996)
Marjoram, Paul S 4:12:50 (13,840)
Marjot, Christopher 5:09:45 (27,477)
Mark, Andrew 4:55:35 (24,786)
Mark, Stephen P 6:37:33 (34,443)
Marke, Tom O 3:57:36 (10,015)
Markham, Neil 3:13:14 (2,268)
Markies, Jeroen 4:23:18 (16,690)
Marklew, Steve 2:47:42 (396)
Markley, Simon A 2:45:39 (336)
Marks, Alexander M 4:39:28 (21,001)
Marks, Brian K 3:20:43 (3,068)
Marks, John H 4:20:43 (15,995)
Marks, Jonathan G 3:59:51 (10,682)
Marks, Roger 4:45:09 (22,365)
Marks, Simon 4:19:14 (15,589)
Markson, Adam 5:14:26 (28,252)
Markusson, Fredrik 4:16:51 (14,927)
Markwell, Kevin M 4:34:21 (19,676)
Markwick, Carl A 4:53:45 (24,366)
Marler, Stephen 5:00:21 (25,856)
Marley, Ian 6:52:59 (34,771)
Marley-Shaw, Edward W 4:28:50 (18,258)
Marlow, Christopher G 4:22:29 (16,467)
Marner, Oliver J 4:25:49 (17,381)
Marques, Fernando M 4:12:32 (13,752)
Marques, Paulo S 4:25:51 (17,387)
Marques Da Silva, Elio A 3:44:20 (6,802)
Marr, Andrew M 5:22:16 (29,383)
Marriott, Gavin D 3:30:00 (4,454)
Marriott, Mark 3:58:57 (10,417)
Marris, Kevan P 4:39:38 (21,053)
Marris, Roger 4:25:50 (17,383)
Marroco, Vincent R 3:19:34 (2,951)
Marrs, Tony 5:16:12 (28,504)
Marsden, David 6:49:08 (34,694)
Marsden, Jason C 4:09:01 (12,831)
Marsden, Nicholas J 4:04:03 (11,650)
Marsden, Peter J 5:46:35 (31,988)
Marsden, Philip B 3:34:57 (5,177)
Marseglia, Pasquale 2:46:59 (372)
Marsh, Andrew J 5:29:34 (30,314)
Marsh, Billy J 4:42:53 (21,847)
Marsh, Brett 4:08:35 (12,711)
Marsh, Daniel J 3:22:41 (3,261)
Marsh, Kevin A 5:02:12 (26,183)
Marsh, Patrick C 4:15:11 (14,498)
Marsh, Pete 2:58:44 (1,009)
Marsh, Robert A 4:30:51 (18,810)
Marsh, Ronald J 3:55:14 (9,284)
Marsh, Terry 6:23:57 (34,060)
Marsh, Tyrone J 6:04:24 (33,237)
Marshall, Andrew 3:18:02 (2,789)
Marshall, Andrew J 3:50:41 (8,184)
Marshall, Ben C 3:58:29 (10,288)
Marshall, Christopher A 4:35:08 (19,879)
Marshall, Christopher J 4:10:12 (13,140)
Marshall, David P 4:48:46 (23,187)
Marshall, Gary 5:13:13 (28,025)
Marshall, Gerald B 3:48:18 (7,657)
Marshall, Graham 5:33:44 (30,751)
Marshall, Ian T 3:01:52 (1,250)
Marshall, James 4:02:25 (11,250)
Marshall, Jamie 4:49:28 (23,353)
Marshall, Jason A 4:45:49 (22,504)
Marshall, Jason J 5:59:14 (32,927)
Marshall, John F 3:11:39 (2,098)
Marshall, Lee H 3:49:21 (7,903)
Marshall, Lee S 3:59:38 (10,612)
Marshall, Nicholas J 3:33:17 (4,924)
Marshall, Paul 3:19:28 (2,932)
Marshall, Paul R 4:48:24 (23,104)
Marshall, Ray 3:01:59 (1,261)
Marshall, Steph 3:56:10 (9,562)
Marshall, Stephen 2:55:36 (778)
Marshall, Stephen A 3:58:32 (10,296)
Marshall, Steven 6:43:47 (34,590)
Marshall, Stuart 3:30:28 (4,518)
Marshall, Tim 3:50:28 (8,142)
Marsico, Maurizio 3:09:56 (1,912)
Marston, Andrew D 3:52:24 (8,578)
Marston, Glyn A 4:15:20 (14,534)
Martell, Paul 3:52:21 (8,566)
Martell, Robert A 4:22:12 (16,397)
Marten, James A 6:46:37 (34,647)
Martin, Andrew C 4:46:20 (22,629)
Martin, Andrew J 3:56:55 (9,787)
Martin, Andy 5:06:56 (27,049)
Martin, Anore C 2:41:13 (223)
Martin, Ben A 5:36:10 (31,011)
Martin, Brett 5:16:28 (28,544)
Martin, Carleton E 4:03:50 (11,590)
Martin, Charles E 4:17:51 (15,170)
Martin, Charles W 3:52:23 (8,574)
Martin, Chris D 3:40:40 (6,114)
Martin, Colin J 4:10:03 (13,101)
Martin, Daniel S 4:22:26 (16,453)
Martin, David N 4:24:36 (17,016)
Martin, David W 4:59:58 (25,771)
Martin, Don 6:39:08 (34,487)
Martin, Ian H 4:03:51 (11,595)
Martin, James 5:07:02 (27,061)
Martin, Jean-Pierre 3:53:40 (8,900)
Martin, Jeffrey M 4:29:31 (18,470)
Martin, Jim 4:31:09 (18,866)
Martin, Jonathan M 3:58:32 (10,296)
Martin, Lee M 3:37:13 (5,525)
Martin, Michael 3:37:02 (5,503)
Martin, Michael F 4:10:42 (13,267)
Martin, Michael V 5:36:15 (31,020)
Martin, Neil C 4:57:57 (25,314)
Martin, Nicholas C 5:04:42 (26,631)
Martin, Paul 4:17:07 (14,991)
Martin, Paul E 4:21:08 (16,097)
Martin, Peter C 5:43:25 (31,711)
Martin, Phil D 4:53:33 (24,313)
Martin, Philippe 4:24:30 (16,994)
Martin, Sean 3:51:30 (8,369)
Martin, Simon J 4:42:04 (21,640)
Martin, Stephen 4:21:32 (16,213)
Martin, Stephen L 3:33:20 (4,936)
Martin, Stephen P 4:30:18 (18,681)
Martin, Stewart 4:41:09 (21,432)
Martin, Thomas M 4:38:24 (20,727)
Martin, Thomas T 3:40:47 (6,136)
Martin, Timothy S 3:42:58 (6,537)
Martin Perez, Andrés 3:47:12 (7,391)
Martinet, Patrick 3:56:17 (9,599)
Martinez, Diego 4:13:06 (13,910)
Martinez, Xavier 4:13:08 (13,916)
Martinson, Travis R 5:30:10 (30,380)
Martland, Raymond J 3:46:12 (7,180)
Martorana, Lelio 3:24:34 (3,523)
Martyn, Nicholas A 2:28:14 (60)
Martyn, Simon W 4:12:33 (13,760)
Maruschka, Stefan 3:17:42 (2,754)
Marval, Jonathan S 3:40:51 (6,157)
Marven, Roger A 4:44:13 (22,147)
Mary, Gerard M 3:13:59 (2,359)
Marzano, Matthew 6:20:20 (33,931)
Marzi, Piergiovanni 5:18:47 (28,917)
Marzolini, Lorenzo 5:03:35 (26,440)
Mascetti, Angelo 4:30:10 (18,648)
Mascolo, Antonio 4:49:25 (23,342)
Mash, David 4:32:29 (19,207)
Mash, Raymond E 5:58:02 (32,836)
Maskell, Alan P 5:51:56 (32,409)
Maskell, Simon P 3:54:52 (9,202)
Maslen, Robert P 3:27:25 (4,000)
Maslinski, Julian M 3:27:35 (4,033)
Mason, Alan B 4:54:05 (24,447)
Mason, Andrew 4:50:30 (23,626)
Mason, Andrew G 3:31:38 (4,699)
Mason, Andrew J 4:49:33 (23,371)
Mason, Andy 5:00:22 (25,861)
Mason, Ben 3:57:01 (9,820)
Mason, Benjamin G 4:14:36 (14,318)
Mason, Carl F 4:49:08 (23,271)
Mason, Christopher J 3:07:32 (1,678)
Mason, David 3:19:35 (2,953)
Mason, David W 4:03:58 (11,624)
Mason, Duncan A 4:21:39 (16,244)
Mason, Ferdie J 5:58:33 (32,883)
Mason, Graham 4:04:14 (11,691)
Mason, Jack 3:13:55 (2,347)
Mason, James A 4:11:56 (13,602)
Mason, James E 4:29:28 (18,453)
Mason, Jonathan P 4:27:19 (17,829)
Mason, Malcolm E 4:43:09 (21,902)
Mason, Martin A 4:41:58 (21,617)
Mason, Martin G 4:23:02 (16,607)
Mason, Michael C 4:10:58 (13,339)
Mason, Michael J 4:18:41 (15,427)
Mason, Neil A 4:41:49 (21,592)
Mason, Nicholas B 4:10:24 (13,204)
Mason, Paul 3:53:24 (8,831)
Mason, Paul 4:36:56 (20,339)
Mason, Paul T 3:32:01 (4,751)
Mason, Peter 3:45:47 (7,091)
Mason, Peter J 3:55:45 (9,450)
Mason, Richard J 4:38:34 (20,767)
Mason, Simon 4:35:52 (20,058)
Mason, Simon D 4:14:36 (14,318)
Mason, Stephen 3:36:15 (5,382)
Mason, Timothy J 4:15:58 (14,707)
Mason, Timothy J 4:32:25 (19,190)
Mason, William P 3:19:01 (2,883)
Masraff, Charles M 4:38:13 (20,674)
Mass, James E 4:14:49 (14,385)
Massey, Adrian P 3:19:13 (2,901)
Massey, Ian J 5:46:10 (31,952)
Massey, Richard J 5:29:18 (30,273)
Massey, Stephen 3:26:20 (3,816)
Massey, Terry 4:25:10 (17,172)
Massow, Mark P 4:38:15 (20,683)
Mast, Robert J 3:06:24 (1,581)
Masterman, Andrew P 4:11:45 (13,552)
Masters, Christopher P 4:19:09 (15,562)
Masters, Daniel J 4:44:37 (22,231)
Masters, Dudley W 5:43:36 (31,730)
Masters, Harry E 3:53:02 (8,727)
Mastroianni, Alberto 4:10:23 (13,194)
Masuda, Kazuo 5:26:51 (29,956)
Matamoros, Alejandro 3:24:53 (3,568)
Matcham, Tim H 4:13:09 (13,922)
Matharu, Jagjivan S 5:07:34 (27,154)
Matharu, Ricky T 4:27:35 (17,915)
Mathe, Jean-Yves A 3:18:03 (2,791)
Matheiken, Sean 4:21:27 (16,190)
Mather, Alan 4:44:20 (22,181)
Mather, Christopher 4:24:43 (17,047)
Mather, Godfrey 3:52:37 (8,636)
Mathews, Steven 4:45:43 (22,482)
Mathias, Andrew D 4:25:32 (17,296)
Mathias, Huw 4:43:18 (21,935)
Mathias, Jason 5:10:28 (27,565)
Mathias, Thomas D 4:25:49 (17,381)
Mathieson, Philip J 4:08:58 (12,817)
Mathiesonh, Andrew D 4:58:33 (25,455)
Mathieu, Jean-Claude 5:04:41 (26,627)
Mathis, Tommy D 5:23:06 (29,495)
Mathurin, Mark A 4:47:33 (22,891)
Maton, Nicholas J 3:51:13 (8,305)
Matrau, Gerald 5:05:49 (26,846)
Matseke, Padi H 4:31:03 (18,847)
Matson, Alistair G 3:21:27 (3,125)
Matson, Andrew M 5:16:50 (28,612)
Mattacks, Peter D 3:37:53 (5,631)
Matten, Sean D 4:42:05 (21,645)
Matthai, Clarence C 4:51:20 (23,804)
Matthew, Graham 5:22:02 (29,352)
Matthew, Stuart J 4:45:54 (22,524)
Matthews, Alan 5:02:44 (26,281)
Matthews, Andrew J 5:07:56 (27,207)
Matthews, Barry A 8:15:13 (35,243)
Matthews, Benjamin W 5:03:01 (26,344)
Matthews, Brian 4:27:45 (17,968)
Matthews, Charles F 4:39:17 (20,961)
Matthews, Christopher P 3:58:02 (10,152)
Matthews, Dene J 4:06:57 (12,329)
Matthews, Gary M 2:42:54 (263)
Matthews, Hefin 3:19:26 (2,927)
Matthews, Ian R 3:37:54 (5,634)
Matthews, Jason B 3:55:57 (9,501)
Matthews, Jeff A 3:27:28 (4,012)
Matthews, Jonathan D 5:54:26 (32,596)
Matthews, Jonathan H 4:41:23 (21,489)

Matthews, Kevin P....4:19:38 (15,705)
Matthews, Paul....4:24:06 (16,876)
Matthews, Paul D....3:55:57 (9,501)
Matthews, Peter....3:49:57 (8,026)
Matthews, Roy....4:29:58 (18,577)
Matthews, Russell G....3:46:41 (7,279)
Matthews, Stephen J....6:05:54 (33,326)
Matthews, Tim J....5:46:30 (31,980)
Matthews-Jones, Paul G....4:50:13 (23,539)
Mattison, Michael J....3:04:54 (1,462)
Mattock, Robert A....4:32:55 (19,295)
Matts, Charles J....4:05:38 (12,012)
Mattson, Andy....4:52:48 (24,128)
Matula, André P....4:22:17 (16,416)
Matze, Heiko....3:14:20 (2,397)
Maude, Christian G....3:34:54 (5,168)
Maume, Michael D....3:59:19 (10,522)
Maun, James R....4:49:00 (23,235)
Maunder, Andrew J....4:00:08 (10,755)
Maung, Tun Z....5:14:46 (28,309)
Maura-Cooper, Carl....4:51:13 (23,781)
Maurattel, Egbert....4:32:26 (19,195)
Mauraza, Joseba....3:36:32 (5,437)
Maurer, Richard....3:16:41 (2,646)
Maurizi, Stephen J....4:39:43 (21,070)
Mauro, Eugenio....3:12:11 (2,163)
Mauro, Ferrarini....3:42:54 (6,526)
Mavin, Simon W....6:05:24 (33,292)
Mawer, Roger....4:16:39 (14,876)
Mawson, Julian D....2:37:11 (142)
Maxfield, Simon....4:38:21 (20,709)
Maxton, Drummond....4:54:14 (24,486)
Maxwell, Christopher K....4:49:09 (23,273)
Maxwell, Marius P....3:51:16 (8,321)
Maxwell, Paul A....3:57:45 (10,051)
Maxwell, Peter T....4:00:02 (10,736)
Maxwell, Richardo....7:19:23 (35,070)
May, Adrian....4:10:53 (13,310)
May, Andrew J....3:54:55 (9,221)
May, Colin....4:09:09 (12,876)
May, David J....5:05:09 (26,713)
May, Gavin R....2:57:10 (896)
May, Graham H....2:54:51 (737)
May, Howard A....4:13:21 (13,978)
May, John P....4:24:46 (17,064)
May, Kevin....4:06:54 (12,320)
May, Kieron R....5:11:42 (27,769)
May, Mike....4:25:08 (17,163)
May, Paul G....5:40:08 (31,432)
May, Peter....3:29:53 (4,435)
May, Stephen R....4:41:30 (21,523)
May, Toby M....5:23:51 (29,593)
Mayall, Robert C....3:41:38 (6,310)
Maydew, Jonathan R....4:26:04 (17,462)
Maye, Joe....6:05:43 (33,308)
Mayes, Jonathan W....3:48:47 (7,780)
Mayes, Robert....4:34:21 (19,676)
Mayhew, Daniel A....3:17:59 (2,786)
Mayhew, Gary L....4:19:53 (15,770)
Mayhew, Graham....5:19:21 (28,998)
Maylandt, Werner....4:28:56 (18,286)
Maynard, Fred N....4:30:08 (18,636)
Maynard, Graham L....3:20:53 (3,079)
Mayne, Christopher S....4:26:33 (17,616)
Mayne, Paul Z....4:26:39 (17,648)
Mayne, Rob....3:52:43 (8,664)
Mayne, Ryan....4:47:20 (22,840)
Mayne, Sam N....3:55:48 (9,461)
Mayo, Alistair B....5:28:36 (30,195)
Mayo, Andrew C....4:05:14 (11,926)
Mayo, Simon C....3:50:45 (8,198)
Mayo, Simon E....3:48:34 (7,730)
Mayson, Andy G....4:41:09 (21,432)
Mayson, Howard J....4:05:25 (11,971)
Maytham, Gary D....4:57:05 (25,151)
Maywood, Bryan J....5:17:26 (28,701)
Mazuel, Alain....5:04:16 (26,566)
Mazur, first name unknown....3:45:24 (7,030)
McAdam, Geoffrey....4:19:46 (15,743)
McAdams, Peter V....4:54:26 (24,534)
McAleer, Richard S....5:38:09 (31,213)
McAleese, Lyle....4:49:17 (23,300)
McAlister, Anthony L....4:57:55 (25,304)
McAllister, Brian....4:38:45 (20,814)
McAllister, James A....4:46:09 (22,593)
McAllister, Robert D....4:06:01 (12,096)
McAllister, William A....3:42:47 (6,509)
McAllister-Williams, Richard H....3:04:12 (1,408)
McAnaney, Michael J....3:44:01 (6,746)
McAndrew, Ian N....5:41:20 (31,539)
McAnea, Thomas C....4:01:58 (11,145)
McArdle, Aidan....3:30:45 (4,575)
McAree, William R....3:18:09 (2,796)
McArthur, Alexander D....4:57:23 (25,203)
McArthur, Kenneth....3:50:32 (8,153)
McArthur, Sean J....4:09:50 (13,049)
McAslan, Alastair....4:36:44 (20,289)
McAuley, Eugene....4:11:40 (13,525)
McAuliffe, Jason D....4:04:43 (11,798)
McBain, James....3:25:03 (3,597)
McBain, Neil....3:33:17 (4,924)
McBeath, Gavin R....4:00:17 (10,784)
McBriar, Martin P....4:52:09 (23,977)
McBride, Andrew....4:59:26 (25,651)
McBride, Hugh A....6:45:40 (34,625)
McBride, James....5:30:23 (30,402)
McBride, Martin G....3:26:07 (3,781)
McBroom, Alexander....4:46:44 (22,717)
McCabe, Andrew G....5:09:57 (27,505)
McCabe, Mark A....5:53:05 (32,506)
McCabe, Martin J....4:29:53 (18,561)
McCabe, Michael E....3:09:02 (1,815)
McCabe, Philip E....5:53:05 (32,506)
McCabe, Sean P....4:31:45 (19,032)
McCafferty, Thomas....3:57:41 (10,035)
McCaffery, Stephen A....3:29:19 (4,328)
McCaffory, Steve....5:29:18 (30,273)
McCaffrey, Ben....4:33:35 (19,459)
McCaffrey, John....3:37:20 (5,545)
McCaffrey, Jon P....5:06:59 (27,053)
McCaffrey, Mark....5:47:12 (32,033)
McCahey, Pat R....4:07:09 (12,382)
McCall, Robert....3:26:30 (3,849)
McCall, Steven D....3:49:39 (7,965)
McCallion, Seamus M....2:59:18 (1,069)
McCallum, Andrew J....3:18:53 (2,871)
McCallum, Angus C....4:02:43 (11,323)
McCallum, Glenn....4:34:01 (19,569)
McCallum, Iain E....4:44:31 (22,215)
McCallum, Naran K....4:45:23 (22,411)
McCalmont, Stewart H....5:39:05 (31,318)
McCamley, John M....5:05:56 (26,858)
McCann, Alec....3:36:32 (5,437)
McCann, Christopher J....4:19:24 (15,636)
McCann, Eamon M....4:04:39 (11,784)
McCann, Gerard J....3:13:29 (2,300)
McCann, Joe....2:54:24 (703)
McCann, John D....3:41:53 (6,351)
McCann, Niall J....4:29:45 (18,533)
McCann, Paul....3:49:40 (7,972)
McCann, Paul G....3:49:03 (7,836)
McCann, Robert....4:21:33 (16,217)
McCann, Sean....3:28:30 (4,198)
McCarley, Stuart J....4:38:15 (20,683)
McCarron, Timothy J....4:28:43 (18,225)
McCartan, Stephen....4:15:30 (14,582)
McCarter, Dominic....2:47:21 (382)
McCarthy, Andrew J....4:46:16 (22,615)
McCarthy, Bernard J....5:02:26 (26,226)
McCarthy, Brian....3:50:55 (8,239)
McCarthy, Ciaran....5:04:10 (26,548)
McCarthy, Craig M....4:39:14 (20,942)
McCarthy, David G....4:40:16 (21,200)
McCarthy, Glen E....4:14:58 (14,430)
McCarthy, John....4:01:41 (11,086)
McCarthy, John....4:12:09 (13,650)
McCarthy, John T....3:59:33 (10,590)
McCarthy, Keith D....5:05:17 (26,746)
McCarthy, Michael R....4:25:57 (17,413)
McCarthy, Paul....5:59:59 (32,982)
McCarthy, William....3:22:16 (3,225)
McCartney, Hugh....4:58:29 (25,438)
McCartney, Samuel....4:22:25 (16,449)
McCaugherty, Simon....3:05:54 (1,547)
McCaughin, Richard A....5:17:37 (28,735)
McCauley, Edward....5:45:09 (31,862)
McCausland, Daniel H....6:20:01 (33,917)
McCavley, David T....4:02:57 (11,381)
McClatchey, Andy....5:09:11 (27,385)
McClaughlin, Stuart E....4:20:26 (15,922)
McClave, James J....4:49:43 (23,429)
McClelland, Ian M....4:54:51 (24,630)
McClelland, James R....4:08:02 (12,579)
McCloskey, Peter....4:46:26 (22,655)
McCloud, Victor A....4:02:22 (11,240)
McClure, Gary....4:03:56 (11,612)
McClure, Greg M....3:12:17 (2,172)
McCole, Derek C....3:24:18 (3,486)
McCole, Nathan....4:55:54 (24,874)
McColgan, Martin P....3:41:13 (6,218)
McColl, Ewen M....3:12:01 (2,142)
McCombe, Paul R....4:04:57 (11,849)
McConchie, Damien R....4:13:05 (13,906)
McConnachy, Justin J....4:24:54 (17,094)
McConnell, Anthony P....3:43:05 (6,570)
McConnell, John J....4:58:30 (25,443)
McConnell-Wood, Steven....3:01:33 (1,229)
McConville, Alistair G....4:19:54 (15,775)
McConville, John P....2:57:09 (893)
McCord, Richard J....3:15:40 (2,537)
McCormack, Ben....4:21:46 (16,276)
McCormack, Graham....5:17:07 (28,666)
McCormack, Kyle A....5:06:08 (26,899)
McCormack, Patrick T....4:00:44 (10,893)
McCormack, Ralph W....5:34:32 (30,849)
McCormick, Andrew B....3:36:26 (5,415)
McCormick, Andrew D....6:32:20 (34,314)
McCormick, Duncan J....4:45:47 (22,491)
McCormick, Graham....3:44:30 (6,836)
McCormick, James....6:14:42 (33,724)
McCormick, Peter....3:52:00 (8,485)
McCosker, Luke C....4:06:10 (12,134)
McCoubrey, Robin....3:59:00 (10,430)
McCowatt, Arran J....5:10:25 (27,558)
McCoy, Andrew....2:41:54 (241)
McCoy, Nick S....4:42:38 (21,781)
McCoy, Robin E....3:08:58 (1,807)
McCracken, Julian....4:53:35 (24,323)
McCrea, Richard A....5:23:51 (29,593)
McCready, Ian G....5:30:09 (30,378)
McCready, Joseph A....2:35:29 (117)
McCreath, Colin F....3:52:36 (8,629)
McCrory, Martin P....5:08:07 (27,241)
McCrostie, Grant H....3:49:33 (7,944)
McCrystal, David....4:39:39 (21,057)
McCullagh, Nicholas J....4:12:19 (13,699)
McCullie, Alec....4:30:42 (18,769)
McCulloch, Howard J....3:36:28 (5,420)
McCullough, Alexander O....6:38:38 (34,478)
McCullough, John....3:27:25 (4,000)
McCullough, Stephen J....4:57:48 (25,281)
McCurry, Stephen....3:29:53 (4,435)
McCusker, Charles P....4:09:47 (13,035)
McCusker, Eamonn....3:49:35 (7,948)
McCutcheon, Neil M....4:55:32 (24,777)
McDaid, Gerard....3:58:07 (10,171)
McDermid, Andrew J....6:07:35 (33,421)
McDermott, Christopher....4:39:36 (21,047)
McDermott, Ciaran J....3:33:43 (4,993)
McDermott, John R....2:55:17 (754)
McDermott, Nigel....3:23:13 (3,334)
McDermott, Raymond A....4:34:48 (19,789)
McDermott, Russ....5:29:18 (30,273)
McDermott, Sean E....5:24:01 (29,621)
McDermottroe, Joseph....4:19:36 (15,692)
McDevitt, Peter R....3:12:39 (2,210)
McDonagh, Nicholas J....3:15:50 (2,551)
McDonald, Alan....2:59:40 (1,102)
McDonald, Alan....3:12:23 (2,183)
McDonald, Alan M....4:29:43 (18,525)
McDonald, Blair....4:23:56 (16,834)
McDonald, Charles A....6:50:03 (34,721)
McDonald, David A....4:57:59 (25,324)
McDonald, Duncan C....4:29:32 (18,476)
McDonald, Geoff....3:43:31 (6,654)
McDonald, Glynn W....3:23:47 (3,416)
McDonald, John D....5:08:59 (27,354)
McDonald, Lars....3:54:08 (9,005)
McDonald, Peter....3:06:13 (1,569)

McDonald, Philip F	3:51:37 (8,392)	
McDonald, Philip H	3:09:34 (1,865)	
McDonald, Robert	3:31:44 (4,708)	
McDonald, Rod W	3:44:33 (6,848)	
McDonald, Steven	6:15:44 (33,771)	
McDonald, Thomas P	3:57:46 (10,058)	
McDonald-Liggins, Anthony N	3:58:00 (10,142)	
McDoniel, Jack	6:07:48 (33,430)	
McDonnell, Christopher J	5:05:23 (26,771)	
McDonnell, Daren P	4:03:39 (11,534)	
McDonnell, Jeremy	4:22:35 (16,497)	
McDonnell, Paul A	3:54:43 (9,158)	
McDonnell, Rafael	3:27:25 (4,000)	
McDonnell, William A	4:10:23 (13,194)	
McDonough, Robert J	3:31:21 (4,658)	
McDougal, Richard J	3:54:37 (9,126)	
McDougall, Ian P	4:49:36 (23,388)	
McDougall, Kevin	4:59:29 (25,659)	
McEachen, Angus	3:42:02 (6,385)	
McElhinney, Andrew S	3:59:20 (10,527)	
McElhinney, Philip H	3:25:38 (3,692)	
McElroy, Darragh	4:23:00 (16,600)	
McEntagart, Gerry	3:40:13 (6,040)	
McEvilly, Ian	4:17:49 (15,163)	
McEwan, Gordon W	4:40:08 (21,164)	
McEwan, Joseph	3:39:22 (5,886)	
McEwan, Robert	3:04:02 (1,403)	
McFadzean, Christopher M	4:40:36 (21,285)	
McFadzean, Graeme S	4:38:42 (20,799)	
McFarlane, Ian	4:11:56 (13,602)	
McFarlane, John	2:20:54 (29)	
McFarlane, Roderick	5:03:05 (26,359)	
McFarnon, Gregory S	4:11:17 (13,424)	
McFaul, John M	4:40:56 (21,371)	
McGaffin, Phil	4:09:49 (13,045)	
McGahan, Brendan	5:45:29 (31,894)	
McGahan, Kevin	5:12:14 (27,858)	
McGarr, Gerry F	4:45:15 (22,381)	
McGarrigle, Mark J	4:00:03 (10,741)	
McGarry, Paul R	8:27:35 (35,245)	
McGarty, William	5:30:15 (30,391)	
McGavock, Philip R	3:09:50 (1,900)	
McGee, Peter J	4:32:20 (19,172)	
McGibbon, Tom B	4:36:14 (20,141)	
McGill, Alex	3:19:21 (2,915)	
McGill, Colin A	3:00:32 (1,157)	
McGillan, Andrew M	3:41:39 (6,313)	
McGillan, David P	5:57:11 (32,787)	
McGilligan, Hugh P	2:45:12 (324)	
McGilligan, Liam E	3:39:01 (5,821)	
McGilligan, Sean N	4:45:53 (22,516)	
McGilloway, Frederick C	5:15:50 (28,459)	
McGilloway, Justin J	4:00:58 (10,941)	
McGilloway, Paul J	2:53:15 (648)	
McGinley, Ciaran	4:49:39 (23,411)	
McGinley, Mark	3:57:16 (9,909)	
McGinley, Stephen P	4:49:00 (23,235)	
McGinley, Thomas	6:20:54 (33,950)	
McGinnity, Nigel M	5:20:32 (29,187)	
McGinty, Declan M	4:43:26 (21,961)	
McGinty, Martin P	3:38:30 (5,724)	
McGirr, Fergus J	2:51:33 (567)	
McGivern, Kieran	5:11:54 (27,805)	
McGlachie, Steven M	3:59:32 (10,582)	
McGlashan, Andrew J	3:48:59 (7,818)	
McGlashan, Nick	4:13:33 (14,032)	
McGlashen, Graham G	6:16:34 (33,802)	
McGlennon, David L	3:10:53 (1,983)	
McGlory, Neil J	3:59:00 (10,430)	
McGlynn, Alan	4:54:48 (24,622)	
McGlynn, Liam	3:28:54 (4,259)	
McGlynn, Peter	4:43:38 (22,019)	
McGonnell, James	4:02:50 (11,348)	
McGougan, Duncan H	3:02:03 (1,265)	
McGovern, Hugh P	4:30:16 (18,672)	
McGovern, Plunkett	5:11:23 (27,723)	
McGow, William	9:50:00 (35,256)	
McGowan, Gary	4:56:17 (24,962)	
McGowan, Steve	4:13:38 (14,053)	
McGown, John P	5:24:49 (29,721)	
McGrady, Alan P	5:12:35 (27,923)	
McGrail, Steven T	5:03:16 (26,397)	
McGranaghan, Roy P	4:41:37 (21,549)	

McGrane, Ian M	4:00:26 (10,813)	
McGrath, Alan	4:12:11 (13,662)	
McGrath, Chris	5:24:33 (29,693)	
McGrath, Chris G	4:56:44 (25,078)	
McGrath, Colin	5:03:42 (26,461)	
McGrath, David	3:10:55 (2,023)	
McGrath, Dennis J	3:25:24 (3,656)	
McGrath, Ged	3:51:20 (8,336)	
McGrath, Gregory	4:08:27 (12,684)	
McGrath, Jody	3:57:50 (10,089)	
McGrath, Michael J	3:17:52 (2,777)	
McGrath, Patrick S	3:13:29 (2,300)	
McGrath, Simon	4:47:06 (22,796)	
McGread, Michael P	3:26:43 (3,887)	
McGreevy, Stuart D	5:13:33 (28,091)	
McGregor, Alec	4:11:08 (13,388)	
McGregor, Campbell	3:37:38 (5,592)	
McGregor, Edward J	7:12:36 (35,012)	
McGregor, Ian D	3:58:07 (10,171)	
McGregor, Scott J	3:47:12 (7,391)	
McGroarty, Andrew P	3:35:07 (5,199)	
McGrory, Stephen M	2:50:20 (507)	
McGuffie, Andrew	3:28:27 (4,188)	
McGuigan, Brian	4:38:57 (20,860)	
McGuigan, David S	5:13:33 (28,091)	
McGuigan, Paul D	5:11:04 (27,665)	
McGuiness, Stephen M	3:05:43 (1,531)	
McGuinness, Patrick	6:04:40 (33,252)	
McGuire, John	4:08:06 (12,590)	
McGuire, Jonathan D	4:29:57 (18,576)	
McGuirk, Richard B	3:39:44 (5,956)	
McGurk, David	3:43:57 (6,732)	
McGurk, Jonathan J	5:25:42 (29,823)	
McGurth, Lawrence F	4:34:32 (19,722)	
McHale, Cameron	3:56:57 (9,798)	
McHardy, Barry	4:48:04 (23,024)	
McHugh, Cian	3:21:27 (3,125)	
McHugh, Greg J	4:29:27 (18,448)	
McHugh, Peter G	3:33:05 (4,898)	
McIlwaine, David E	4:05:34 (12,002)	
McInally, Ian A	5:20:32 (29,187)	
McInerney, David C	4:27:06 (17,775)	
McInerney, John J	5:42:47 (31,660)	
McInerney, Michael A	3:04:30 (1,426)	
McInerney, Michael C	3:59:57 (10,713)	
McInnes, Andrew R	3:38:49 (5,779)	
McInnes, Neil	4:51:10 (23,766)	
McInnes, Neil A	4:30:12 (18,655)	
McIntosh, Douglas L	5:00:32 (25,881)	
McIntosh, Graeme	4:32:23 (19,184)	
McIntosh, Peter J	5:09:22 (27,415)	
McIntyre, David J	3:06:44 (1,611)	
McIntyre, John P	7:12:23 (35,009)	
McIntyre, Rob	3:47:07 (7,377)	
McIntyre, Tim J	3:09:26 (1,855)	
McIver, Duncan J	3:27:49 (4,079)	
McIver, Gary P	5:10:21 (27,550)	
McKaine, Nigel J	4:19:04 (15,537)	
McKane, Christopher H	5:37:30 (31,142)	
McKay, Ewan W	3:10:40 (1,997)	
McKay, Fergus P	3:35:12 (5,211)	
McKay, Keith	4:13:16 (13,955)	
McKay, Robert	3:19:15 (2,906)	
McKay, Sinclair F	3:27:47 (4,073)	
McKay, Stuart	5:29:38 (30,323)	
McKeckney, Chris J	6:09:26 (33,514)	
McKee, Alexander	5:02:36 (26,250)	
McKee, Darren I	4:04:20 (11,710)	
McKee, John J	3:39:27 (5,899)	
McKee, Ray	4:27:04 (17,765)	
McKee, Stephen	4:46:05 (22,571)	
McKeeman, Andrew P	3:11:35 (2,085)	
McKell, Lawrence E	4:09:00 (12,826)	
McKellar, Gordon J	3:38:56 (5,802)	
McKellar, James R	4:16:08 (14,751)	
McKenlay, Jonathan	4:06:03 (12,107)	
McKenna, David	3:26:01 (3,764)	
McKenna, Gary P	3:08:06 (1,674)	
McKenna, Gerard F	4:12:22 (13,716)	
McKenna, Gerard H	3:56:26 (9,645)	
McKenna, Graham M	3:44:10 (6,779)	
McKenna, Hugh	4:14:10 (14,201)	
McKenna, Joseph	4:23:03 (16,612)	

McKenna, Michael G	4:00:28 (10,822)	
McKenna, Seamus T	4:10:25 (13,211)	
McKenna, Sean N	5:15:22 (28,396)	
McKenning, Matthew J	3:50:11 (8,081)	
McKenzie, Gordon S	4:38:16 (20,689)	
McKenzie, Ian R	3:51:50 (8,449)	
McKenzie, Rob S	5:02:28 (26,230)	
McKeon, Daniel T	3:53:25 (8,835)	
McKeown, Anthony D	4:36:00 (20,084)	
McKeown, Brendan	5:25:05 (29,757)	
McKeown, Damian	4:32:46 (19,264)	
McKeown, Des M	3:43:06 (6,573)	
McKeown, Kieran	3:28:24 (4,181)	
McKeown, Mark J	4:51:30 (23,849)	
McKeown, Philip J	5:08:05 (27,234)	
McKeown, Thomas P	4:54:27 (24,543)	
McKerral, Calum S	3:42:04 (6,391)	
McKevitt, Vincent D	4:14:08 (14,189)	
McKibbin, Ross J	5:12:23 (27,882)	
McKie, Richard J	3:58:43 (10,354)	
McKie, Russell A	4:19:20 (15,619)	
McKillion, Gary S	4:21:02 (16,083)	
McKinlay, Jason P	4:50:24 (23,596)	
McKinlay, John	3:59:51 (10,682)	
McKinlay, Sebastian M	4:00:51 (10,913)	
McKinley, John	4:08:49 (12,773)	
McKinley, Matthew J	6:13:28 (33,677)	
McKinnell, Colin	4:22:41 (16,532)	
McKinnell, Ian	4:19:08 (15,558)	
McKinnon, Gary	3:58:21 (10,243)	
McKinnon, Stewart J	5:19:34 (29,044)	
McKintosh, Kevin J	4:10:23 (13,194)	
McKnight, Robert A	7:20:16 (35,077)	
McLachlan, Robert L	5:24:14 (29,650)	
McLaren, Guy N	3:37:18 (5,536)	
McLaren, James C	3:51:48 (8,441)	
McLaren, Larry	5:09:57 (27,505)	
McLaren, Neil	4:31:58 (19,078)	
McLaughlan, Stuart J	5:11:19 (27,708)	
McLaughlin, Brian J	3:57:08 (9,870)	
McLaughlin, Daniel	4:12:25 (13,730)	
McLaughlin, Danny	3:07:49 (1,701)	
McLaughlin, Danny	5:31:32 (30,519)	
McLaughlin, Gerald	5:16:42 (28,578)	
McLaughlin, Iain J	4:41:08 (21,428)	
McLaughlin, James A	3:25:14 (3,631)	
McLaughlin, Joseph P	4:41:21 (21,479)	
McLaughlin, Mark A	4:45:05 (22,347)	
McLaughlin, Michael J	3:37:01 (5,500)	
McLaughlin, Philip	4:49:05 (23,265)	
McLaughlin, Robert I	5:05:39 (26,813)	
McLaughlin, Simon D	3:41:05 (6,199)	
McLaughlin, Stephen B	7:17:03 (35,050)	
McLean, David A	3:30:44 (4,565)	
McLean, Henry	4:05:42 (12,026)	
McLean, James F	4:17:45 (15,149)	
McLeary, Robert	5:36:19 (31,031)	
McLelland, David	2:51:44 (575)	
McLelland, Steve	3:50:55 (8,239)	
McLeman, Andrew C	3:25:26 (3,659)	
McLennan, Robert A	3:13:20 (2,276)	
McLeod, Alastair D	3:33:59 (5,045)	
McLeod, Andrew J	3:53:00 (8,717)	
McLeod, Gordon G	4:15:54 (14,683)	
McLeod, Ian D	4:34:22 (19,684)	
McLeod, John	4:08:06 (12,590)	
McLeod, Jonny P	4:01:43 (11,095)	
McLeod, Kirk	4:42:12 (21,676)	
McLeod, Roderick W	3:46:27 (7,232)	
McLeod-Hatch, James L	4:11:18 (13,428)	
McLinden, Andrew	2:46:18 (356)	
McLintock, Scott M	3:11:49 (2,119)	
McLoone, Thomas F	5:25:53 (29,850)	
McLoughlin, Antony G	4:09:02 (12,837)	
McLoughlin, Harold L	6:08:03 (33,447)	
McLoughlin, Ian J	5:59:48 (32,969)	
McLoughlin, Joseph	4:25:15 (17,203)	
McLoughlin, Mark T	3:56:19 (9,609)	
McLoughlin, Peter J	4:19:55 (15,779)	
McLoughlin, Rob E	3:58:25 (10,266)	
McLougholin, Adrian	4:49:02 (23,246)	
McMahon, Greg R	4:17:15 (15,021)	
McMahon, Joe	4:35:39 (20,005)	

McMahon, John P 3:10:47 (2,006)
McMahon, Nicholas J 4:04:35 (11,764)
McMahon, Peter L 4:45:13 (22,374)
McMahon, Sean J 5:13:23 (28,055)
McManmon, Pascal J 4:00:51 (10,913)
McManus, Gary 3:16:15 (2,611)
McManus, Graham F 4:25:52 (17,392)
McManus, John 4:18:01 (15,212)
McManus, Jonathan P 4:18:01 (15,212)
McManus, Kevin A 3:11:38 (2,093)
McManus, Luke 4:49:03 (23,250)
McManus, Michael 4:54:09 (24,460)
McManus, Peter D 3:28:13 (4,147)
McMeekin, Lee W 2:52:04 (595)
McMenamin, Thomas J 4:16:28 (14,834)
McMillan, Andrew 4:38:28 (20,749)
McMillan, Craig D 2:37:03 (141)
McMillan, David W 4:24:00 (16,851)
McMillan, James 3:52:29 (8,599)
McMonagle, Dennis P 4:10:03 (13,101)
McMonagle, Noel 3:25:30 (3,672)
McMullan, James 3:09:44 (1,887)
McMullan, Raymond J 5:40:58 (31,505)
McMullen, David 5:32:32 (30,618)
McMurdo, Alan C 3:59:42 (10,630)
McMurray, Graham A 5:10:31 (27,576)
McMurray, Tony 6:24:50 (34,089)
McMyler, Sean A 2:49:20 (478)
McNab, Tony D 5:32:48 (30,652)
McNair, Martin A 4:53:41 (24,350)
McNally, David J 5:03:51 (26,494)
McNally, John 4:10:22 (13,186)
McNally, John R 2:59:35 (1,098)
McNamara, Gary T 3:50:18 (8,104)
McNamara, Martin M 4:34:17 (19,660)
McNamara, Paul 4:18:54 (15,483)
McNamara, Robert 4:10:08 (13,123)
McNamara, Stephen C 3:52:30 (8,605)
McNamara, Timothy J 5:07:05 (27,075)
McNaught, Iain D 3:32:53 (4,868)
McNaull, Allisdhair T 3:37:02 (5,503)
McNeil, Fraser 4:09:01 (12,831)
McNeil, Martin R 5:06:53 (27,039)
McNeil, Matthew K 4:05:51 (12,057)
McNeil, Neil J 4:16:04 (14,730)
McNeill, Barry P 3:39:49 (5,967)
McNeill, Stuart 4:13:27 (14,003)
McNeish, Andrew J 3:53:16 (8,786)
McNelis, Michael J 3:23:06 (3,315)
McNelis, Robin N 3:10:40 (1,997)
McNicholas, Stephen J 3:12:45 (2,220)
McNulty, Henry B 4:02:15 (11,212)
McNulty, John 4:30:22 (18,693)
McNulty, Michael 4:38:28 (20,749)
McNulty, Mick P 4:25:20 (17,224)
McNulty, Myles F 3:32:38 (4,834)
McNutt, James 4:24:20 (16,938)
McPartlin, Andrew J 3:48:07 (7,619)
McPaul, Robert 5:29:21 (30,285)
McPhail, Thomas W 3:00:53 (1,185)
McPhee, Simon R 4:08:47 (12,764)
McPherson, George A 3:07:08 (1,643)
McPhillips, Luke M 4:03:42 (11,545)
McQueen, Jamie 4:36:51 (20,319)
McQueen, Mark P 4:36:24 (20,195)
McQuillan, Carl 5:57:56 (32,829)
McQuillen-Wright, Chris C 3:23:48 (3,419)
McQuin, Steve 3:27:24 (3,996)
McRae, David D 4:46:39 (22,698)
McRobbie, Andrew E 4:35:50 (20,050)
McShane, Dean K 4:15:46 (14,651)
McShane, Dessie C 3:11:35 (2,085)
McShane, James C 5:19:45 (29,071)
McShane, Michael A 4:01:21 (11,012)
McShea, Brian A 4:51:07 (23,754)
McSherry, Shaun J 4:09:04 (12,846)
McSpadden, Martin J 4:28:21 (18,122)
McSpadden, Tim T 3:33:25 (4,948)
McSteen, Andrew W 4:16:54 (14,935)
McSweeney, Aidan P 4:31:45 (19,032)
McSweeney, Brian G 4:24:43 (17,047)
McSweeney, Christopher P 3:47:57 (7,560)
McSweeney, James N 4:37:59 (20,616)
McSweeney, Mike P 5:02:25 (26,223)
McVeigh, Neil G 5:51:05 (32,345)
McVeigh, Philip A 4:50:42 (23,675)
McVennon, Keith C 6:07:05 (33,392)
McVey, Geoffrey P 3:52:59 (8,713)
McWade, Neil A 4:57:00 (25,128)
McWeeney, Brendan N 3:48:54 (7,802)
McWilliam, Eric 4:16:33 (14,845)
McWilliam, Robert G 3:26:38 (3,876)
Meachem, John A 3:59:07 (10,473)
Meachen, Graham M 3:48:04 (7,606)
Meacock, Peter 5:22:20 (29,388)
Mead, Adrian 3:05:17 (1,492)
Mead, Daniel P 4:52:17 (24,010)
Mead, Darrell K 5:01:30 (26,064)
Mead, David W 4:52:57 (24,158)
Mead, Edward S 4:18:09 (15,249)
Mead, John W 5:24:19 (29,660)
Mead, Paul J 4:00:21 (10,794)
Mead-Briggs, Richard J 4:19:41 (15,719)
Meade, Ian D 3:55:49 (9,467)
Meaden, Paul A 3:54:31 (9,103)
Meadmore, Robert 4:46:06 (22,578)
Meadows, Chris C 4:10:08 (13,123)
Meadows, Chris S 4:26:21 (17,548)
Meadows, David 4:48:23 (23,100)
Meadows, Ian 4:00:34 (10,857)
Meadows, John D 5:01:22 (26,036)
Meadows, John W 5:18:41 (28,903)
Meadows, Jonathan D 4:22:51 (16,568)
Meadows, Kristen P 5:18:37 (28,893)
Meadows, Terry D 4:09:28 (12,950)
Meads, Matthew D 3:43:54 (6,720)
Meakin, Alan J 6:17:14 (33,832)
Meakin, Paul R 4:19:01 (15,519)
Meakings, Andrew R 4:19:35 (15,686)
Meakins, Chris 5:56:59 (32,769)
Mean, Richard J 4:31:22 (18,937)
Meaney, John M 3:56:25 (9,637)
Mears, Mark W 4:59:47 (25,736)
Measham, Haydon H 4:38:10 (20,664)
Measures, Keith 4:44:44 (22,255)
Medcalf, Andrew A 4:41:15 (21,460)
Medcraft, Jonathan P 3:31:16 (4,647)
Medcraft, Paul W 4:55:09 (24,713)
Medd, Arton 4:09:29 (12,955)
Meddeman, Kevin J 3:53:33 (8,871)
Mee, Colin E 3:38:40 (5,749)
Mee, Simon J 5:17:23 (28,695)
Meehan, John P 4:49:26 (23,348)
Meek, Andrew J 4:47:52 (22,982)
Meek, Graham 4:28:16 (18,105)
Meeke, James S 4:29:05 (18,334)
Meenan, Christopher G 3:09:19 (1,844)
Megali, Aldo R 4:17:02 (14,967)
Meggiato, Michael P 3:56:40 (9,714)
Meggitt, Ryder 5:10:19 (27,543)
Meghjee, Ashif 3:12:05 (2,152)
Mehew, Bruce 4:38:24 (20,727)
Mehmed, Deniz 3:22:44 (3,265)
Mehmet, Haluk M 5:41:52 (31,587)
Mehrfar, Keyvan 4:24:06 (16,876)
Mehta, Saahil N 4:41:35 (21,544)
Meier, Peter 4:53:56 (24,402)
Meier, Robert P 3:44:21 (6,805)
Meier, Sean L 4:57:50 (25,286)
Meier, Stephen E 4:57:38 (25,254)
Meir, Barry J 3:48:13 (7,636)
Meisland, Oddvar 3:50:18 (8,104)
Melby, Brage 3:31:48 (4,718)
Melcher, Bernhard 3:54:20 (9,053)
Meldrum, James D 2:47:46 (398)
Meldrum, John M 3:34:23 (5,107)
Meldrum, Julian T 3:11:59 (2,138)
Melen, Thomas C 3:50:10 (8,077)
Melhuish, Stuart J 5:27:14 (30,004)
Melisi, Mauro 4:31:00 (18,837)
Mella, Mirio A 4:18:42 (15,433)
Meller, David 3:02:55 (1,327)
Melli, Mirko 3:59:51 (10,682)
Mellon, James 4:19:56 (15,782)
Mellon, James 6:29:47 (34,248)
Mellon, Mark L 3:23:29 (3,373)
Mellor, Adrian J 3:43:41 (6,683)
Mellor, Dennis 4:50:32 (23,636)
Mellor, Ian 3:43:50 (6,711)
Mellor, Michael I 4:21:54 (16,306)
Mellor, Tom 2:49:42 (489)
Mellows, Steve 4:17:59 (15,201)
Melrose, Graham R 3:08:12 (1,734)
Melville, Colin A 4:22:07 (16,375)
Melville, Neil C 3:25:43 (3,704)
Melville-Smith, John 5:25:51 (29,847)
Melvin, James H 4:22:10 (16,389)
Memmott, Neil 4:11:11 (13,402)
Memun, José 3:56:07 (9,543)
Menday, Stephen M 3:43:45 (6,693)
Mendelssohn, James C 5:19:07 (28,958)
Mendez, Edson O 5:03:07 (26,367)
Mendonca Dias, José F 4:19:32 (15,674)
Mendrys, Andy D 4:22:37 (16,514)
Menelaws, Steven P 4:47:09 (22,806)
Menendez, Juan C 4:27:16 (17,818)
Menezes, Nicholas S 4:30:15 (18,667)
Menezes, Timothy F 6:38:46 (34,480)
Menzinger, David A 5:33:21 (30,700)
Mepham, Derek C 4:11:26 (13,467)
Mepham, Stephen 3:56:46 (9,740)
Mercanti, Francesco 3:12:59 (2,244)
Mercer, Alastair 3:57:06 (9,856)
Mercer, Darren P 4:02:35 (11,291)
Mercer, Michael W 5:24:19 (29,660)
Mercer, Paul F 4:16:33 (14,845)
Mercer, Robert P 4:57:13 (25,179)
Mercer, Tom A 3:45:22 (7,023)
Mercereau, Remy 4:38:57 (20,860)
Merdith, Matthew C 3:48:34 (7,730)
Meredith, Adrian G 5:33:03 (30,673)
Meredith, Darren J 4:30:48 (18,793)
Meredith, Roy 3:47:26 (7,445)
Meredith, Tim D 3:56:54 (9,785)
Meredith, Will 4:32:58 (19,307)
Merley, Christian 4:04:01 (11,640)
Mernagh, Michael P 4:29:21 (18,416)
Merrell, Stephen P 4:07:36 (12,479)
Merrells, Jason 5:06:27 (26,953)
Merrett, Anthony S 3:28:54 (4,259)
Merrick, Clive A 3:41:29 (6,273)
Merrick, Graham C 5:21:27 (29,291)
Merrick, Ronan L 3:05:31 (1,520)
Merrison, Philip W 4:13:13 (13,944)
Merritt, Anthony E 4:53:07 (24,201)
Merritt, Darren M 4:13:45 (14,077)
Merritt, Jason M 4:15:42 (14,636)
Merritt, William J 3:13:28 (2,296)
Merron, Bernard J 3:10:45 (2,003)
Merry, Charles M 4:07:38 (12,486)
Merry, Graham J 5:45:44 (31,914)
Merry, Richard A 4:19:18 (15,611)
Merry, Russell A 5:31:40 (30,529)
Mertes, Christopher 3:53:59 (8,972)
Mesquita, Pedro M 3:46:35 (7,258)
Metcalf, Andrew S 3:58:16 (10,210)
Metcalf, Chris J 4:56:49 (25,098)
Metcalfe, Barry 3:13:34 (2,310)
Metcalfe, Christopher 5:13:51 (28,141)
Metcalfe, Lee 5:40:14 (31,442)
Metcalfe, Len 4:20:54 (16,051)
Metcalfe, Mark 4:18:01 (15,212)
Metcalfe, Tim C 5:07:41 (27,172)
Metherall, Michael J 4:24:12 (16,901)
Methley, David J 4:30:53 (18,815)
Meurice, Nicholas H 4:38:16 (20,689)
Meutsuri, Kazuyuki 3:16:52 (2,665)
Mews, Tobias A 3:27:23 (3,988)
Meyer, Christian 6:10:13 (33,539)
Meyer, Kevin 3:58:39 (10,323)
Meyer, Philippe 4:06:37 (12,247)
Meyruey, Olivier 3:40:37 (6,106)
Meziani, Fabrice 3:53:30 (8,855)
Miah, Akhtar 4:14:29 (14,290)
Miah, Harun 4:43:08 (21,895)
Miall, Benjamin S 3:57:13 (9,898)
Mian, Anees F 5:08:50 (27,327)
Mias, Peter 3:37:50 (5,623)
Michael, Andreas S 4:23:34 (16,746)

Michael, Desmond 2:50:46 (529)
Michael, Nick 3:54:44 (9,167)
Michaeloudis, Lee C 4:19:02 (15,523)
Michalas, Apostolos A 5:02:21 (26,210)
Michalos, Theodore 4:57:53 (25,296)
Miche, Jean-Jacques 4:04:48 (11,817)
Michell, Ian P 4:30:24 (18,702)
Michon, Jean-Pierre 3:17:42 (2,754)
Mickleburgh, Christopher 3:13:34 (2,310)
Mickleburgh, David C 4:59:15 (25,615)
Mickleburgh, Mark E 3:41:09 (6,209)
Mickleburgh, Trevor J 3:40:19 (6,052)
Micklethwaite, David A 4:23:11 (16,652)
Micklewright, David 3:27:01 (3,931)
Middlebrook, Alan 2:58:45 (1,010)
Middleditch, Stephen 5:11:42 (27,769)
Middlemas, Ian 4:08:19 (12,645)
Middlemass, Andrew 4:04:19 (11,705)
Middleton, Andrew 7:14:09 (35,027)
Middleton, Brian 3:13:28 (2,296)
Middleton, Clive 3:48:02 (7,592)
Middleton, Dan C 5:57:40 (32,817)
Middleton, George D 3:59:39 (10,615)
Middleton, Graham A 4:53:59 (24,424)
Middleton, Ian 6:10:29 (33,551)
Middleton, James R 5:19:59 (29,093)
Middleton, Michael J 5:54:04 (32,572)
Middleton, Neil M 3:25:02 (3,589)
Middleton, Patrick H 5:17:45 (28,750)
Middleton, Robin J 4:38:06 (20,648)
Middleton, Roger L 3:53:23 (8,826)
Middleton, Toby P 3:41:31 (6,276)
Middleton, William S 4:01:36 (11,066)
Middlewick, Ashley R 4:48:42 (23,168)
Midgley, David 5:05:09 (26,713)
Midgley, Martin N 3:09:07 (1,823)
Midgley, Richard 4:32:07 (19,117)
Midwinter, Lloyd T 4:04:31 (11,749)
Midwood, Howard 4:13:03 (13,894)
Midworth, Nick S 3:55:41 (9,423)
Mihdidin, Yashraj 3:08:39 (1,773)
Mikellides, Andreas 3:56:41 (9,722)
Milbradt, Udo 4:05:27 (11,980)
Milburn, Mark W 5:37:03 (31,104)
Milburn, Peter 3:03:13 (1,345)
Mild, Ron W 4:12:20 (13,707)
Mileham, Stephen 5:40:20 (31,447)
Miles, Albert J 4:40:33 (21,273)
Miles, Christian J 3:26:19 (3,814)
Miles, Christopher T 4:40:55 (21,366)
Miles, David 3:14:11 (2,378)
Miles, David M 4:54:26 (24,534)
Miles, Gregory 4:59:40 (25,705)
Miles, John C 4:10:47 (13,281)
Miles, Laurence 2:45:19 (330)
Miles, Malcolm D 6:00:51 (33,018)
Miles, Nick G 4:21:44 (16,266)
Miles, Noel R 2:55:52 (798)
Miles, Patrick W 4:15:10 (14,493)
Miles, Paul 4:16:00 (14,715)
Miles, Paul G 3:51:15 (8,316)
Miles, Paul J 4:42:21 (21,705)
Miles, Paul W 3:14:06 (2,367)
Miles, Phillip 2:59:57 (1,125)
Miles, Richard A 4:47:39 (22,927)
Miles, William 5:00:12 (25,820)
Milesi, Filippo 3:30:09 (4,470)
Milesi, Luca 5:39:24 (31,366)
Milkins, Stephen D 4:37:39 (20,529)
Millar, Craig 5:33:54 (30,766)
Millar, Gordon N 4:28:05 (18,049)
Millar, John M 3:52:23 (8,574)
Millar, Steve J 7:31:33 (35,138)
Millard, Duncan R 3:49:13 (7,866)
Millard, Iain 5:26:52 (29,959)
Millard, John B 5:32:26 (30,609)
Millard, Leigh A 3:20:32 (3,048)
Millard, Simon 3:44:21 (6,805)
Millatt, Jonathan R 5:26:06 (29,883)
Millbanks, Jon 4:38:24 (20,727)
Millen, Ross I 5:15:47 (28,455)
Miller, Adam M 5:48:36 (32,142)
Miller, Alan D 3:45:18 (7,005)
Miller, Andrew 4:31:37 (19,001)
Miller, Andrew 5:54:43 (32,614)
Miller, Andrew G 4:02:53 (11,359)
Miller, Anthony J 4:44:12 (22,142)
Miller, Christopher P 5:12:22 (27,874)
Miller, Daniel H 5:55:58 (32,706)
Miller, David A 5:52:14 (32,431)
Miller, David R 3:58:16 (10,210)
Miller, David W 3:51:51 (8,454)
Miller, Ed P 4:37:47 (20,575)
Miller, Gary 4:09:39 (12,999)
Miller, Grant 4:27:39 (17,937)
Miller, Jack W 2:55:41 (784)
Miller, Kenneth 4:08:44 (12,749)
Miller, Leon 5:37:25 (31,130)
Miller, Les D 5:19:09 (28,963)
Miller, Lewis P 5:49:24 (32,222)
Miller, Marc J 4:15:57 (14,698)
Miller, Martin 3:26:27 (3,842)
Miller, Martyn 5:15:08 (28,356)
Miller, Neil A 2:29:49 (68)
Miller, Neil O 4:25:29 (17,280)
Miller, Nicholas W 4:53:49 (24,387)
Miller, Nicholas W 5:05:20 (26,756)
Miller, Paul D 3:35:29 (5,260)
Miller, Peter 3:11:58 (2,137)
Miller, Peter J 3:48:27 (7,692)
Miller, Peter S 3:50:02 (8,047)
Miller, Roy C 5:40:53 (31,493)
Miller, Shaun W 4:32:38 (19,235)
Miller, Stephen 6:56:42 (34,827)
Miller, Stephen R 3:21:55 (3,174)
Miller, Steven 2:40:57 (218)
Miller, Steven J 5:38:45 (31,285)
Miller, Stuart C 4:21:40 (16,247)
Miller, Stuart E 5:47:35 (32,066)
Miller, Tom 3:51:34 (8,385)
Millershiop, Stephan J 4:37:33 (20,509)
Millet, Ronald F 4:27:41 (17,947)
Millett, Christopher 4:49:12 (23,282)
Millichope, Mark A 4:13:33 (14,032)
Milligan, Robert A 3:01:04 (1,195)
Millin Er, Chris L 2:54:32 (717)
Millington, Rob 3:51:01 (8,259)
Millington, Stuart J 5:28:42 (30,207)
Millman, Jeremy C 3:50:49 (8,211)
Millman, Robin 4:36:35 (20,243)
Mills, Aldam D 5:15:32 (28,422)
Mills, Christopher D 3:47:59 (7,573)
Mills, Christopher M 4:03:48 (11,576)
Mills, Christopher N 4:38:26 (20,736)
Mills, Craig 4:56:34 (25,029)
Mills, David S 4:14:56 (14,419)
Mills, Fred R 5:14:11 (28,208)
Mills, Gerald D 5:13:00 (27,998)
Mills, Glyn M 5:33:05 (30,677)
Mills, John 4:33:10 (19,355)
Mills, John P 4:30:04 (18,611)
Mills, Keith R 4:12:11 (13,662)
Mills, Malcolm 5:06:51 (27,029)
Mills, Nicholas D 4:39:37 (21,050)
Mills, Paul 4:21:02 (16,083)
Mills, Peter D 5:43:11 (31,695)
Mills, Robert A 3:29:02 (4,277)
Mills, Robert S 4:39:14 (20,942)
Mills, Roger C 4:37:59 (20,616)
Mills, Stephen J 3:29:24 (4,338)
Mills, Stephen M 3:47:09 (7,382)
Mills, Stuart 3:16:37 (2,642)
Millward, Graham E 3:46:22 (7,216)
Millward, Nicholas 4:46:06 (22,578)
Millward, Reuben T 4:52:34 (24,067)
Millward, Wayne 5:11:26 (27,729)
Millwood- Hargrave, Martyn F 4:22:31 (16,476)
Milne, Andrew P 4:58:12 (25,375)
Milne, Andrew S 4:24:42 (17,043)
Milne, Christopher E 5:06:04 (26,886)
Milne, Marc M 4:19:44 (15,733)
Milne, Michael D 5:14:05 (28,182)
Milne, Robert M 5:00:58 (25,970)
Milne, Ronald M 3:39:38 (5,935)
Milne, Stephen 3:08:35 (1,768)
Milner, Colin S 4:28:23 (18,137)
Milner, Ian 3:48:32 (7,724)
Milner, James S 4:01:51 (11,118)
Milner, Mark 4:20:43 (15,995)
Milner, Nigel F 3:47:51 (7,539)
Milner, Nigel K 4:30:15 (18,667)
Milner, Paul A 4:24:37 (17,022)
Milner, William N 3:44:55 (6,940)
Milnes, Luke A 3:54:01 (8,979)
Milone, Carmelo 3:37:59 (5,644)
Milotn, Michael R 4:28:48 (18,250)
Milton, John S 4:57:04 (25,146)
Milton, Mark J 4:28:47 (18,241)
Milton, Simon C 4:18:04 (15,226)
Milward, Colin 4:18:54 (15,483)
Milway, Jeremy 3:58:39 (10,323)
Min, Jungkee 4:29:30 (18,467)
Min, Tom 3:33:17 (4,924)
Miners, Anthony R 4:06:02 (12,102)
Minett, Terry 3:35:22 (5,236)
Mingay, Simon 3:15:10 (2,492)
Minhas, Raj S 4:43:43 (22,039)
Minikin, Paul 3:59:15 (10,510)
Minney, Les 5:12:26 (27,895)
Minnis, James R 4:56:10 (24,932)
Minns, Andrew J 3:58:05 (10,164)
Minns, Richard H 4:38:17 (20,695)
Minshall, Nicholas C 5:32:35 (30,623)
Minshull, Ian S 3:59:01 (10,439)
Minshull, Paul 3:39:55 (5,982)
Minsky, Bernard S 4:17:15 (15,021)
Mintram, Ian 3:42:00 (6,376)
Mir, Zlatan 4:09:59 (13,086)
Mirams, Philip D 4:57:54 (25,302)
Misje, Roar 3:12:04 (2,148)
Misselbrook, Allen K 3:59:46 (10,654)
Misson, Trev 3:26:56 (3,920)
Mistretta, Gaetano 4:37:12 (20,412)
Mistretta, Pietro 4:37:14 (20,423)
Mistry, Jayanti 4:10:55 (13,323)
Mistry, Mahendra 5:13:28 (28,076)
Mistry, Shashi M 6:42:27 (34,553)
Mistry, Shashikant V 5:39:38 (31,386)
Mistry, Surendra 4:53:42 (24,353)
Mitcehll, Daniel J 4:39:52 (21,101)
Mitchell, Aidan A 3:12:24 (2,185)
Mitchell, Andrew 3:43:52 (6,715)
Mitchell, Barry W 4:56:14 (24,946)
Mitchell, Bernard J 4:01:40 (11,082)
Mitchell, Charlie E 3:49:59 (8,033)
Mitchell, Christopher A 4:02:41 (11,309)
Mitchell, Christopher C 5:20:45 (29,208)
Mitchell, Christopher I 4:19:37 (15,699)
Mitchell, Colin 4:09:03 (12,838)
Mitchell, David 3:33:40 (4,985)
Mitchell, David A 4:30:25 (18,707)
Mitchell, Duncan P 3:55:29 (9,364)
Mitchell, Gary J 6:22:00 (33,989)
Mitchell, George 2:58:37 (998)
Mitchell, Gregory 5:43:42 (31,736)
Mitchell, Ian 5:59:16 (32,931)
Mitchell, James 4:27:32 (17,900)
Mitchell, James H 3:53:43 (8,917)
Mitchell, James K 3:50:57 (8,248)
Mitchell, James W 5:09:46 (27,480)
Mitchell, Kieron J 3:15:48 (2,549)
Mitchell, Matthew 4:51:50 (23,896)
Mitchell, Matthew J 4:00:14 (10,774)
Mitchell, Paul R 2:47:57 (411)
Mitchell, Peter A 3:46:33 (7,251)
Mitchell, Peter J 4:40:51 (21,348)
Mitchell, Peter J 6:38:46 (34,480)
Mitchell, Richard 3:59:58 (10,717)
Mitchell, Robert J 4:14:24 (14,273)
Mitchell, Shane E 4:17:54 (15,179)
Mitchell, Stephen J 4:14:44 (14,358)
Mitchell, Tom 4:25:41 (17,341)
Mitchell, William J 4:07:19 (12,423)
Mitchener, Paul J 3:38:42 (5,754)
Mitchinson, Dave 2:24:01 (39)
Mitjana, Philippe 3:50:48 (8,208)
Mitsumizo, Ken 3:05:20 (1,500)
Miura, Akio 4:22:07 (16,375)
Miwa, Shinichi 3:51:47 (8,433)

Miyamoto, Kazuo 4:25:35 (17,310)
Mo, Wupu 5:43:16 (31,698)
Moat, Colin E 4:38:00 (20,622)
Moat, Darren E 3:14:54 (2,474)
Moate, Toby J 4:13:49 (14,093)
Mobberley, Jonathan N 3:38:11 (5,678)
Mobbs, David A 5:09:33 (27,447)
Mobbs, David C 5:51:21 (32,358)
Mobbs, Philip 3:47:14 (7,398)
Mobbs, Steve 3:13:03 (2,251)
Moberly, James 4:29:23 (18,428)
Moberly, Thomas A 3:52:00 (8,485)
Mocharrafie, Bassam M 4:35:40 (20,010)
Modaher, Jasvir Singh 6:11:08 (33,580)
Modaher, Tejinder S 6:02:39 (33,117)
Modena, Luigi 3:43:11 (6,588)
Modlock, Matthew J 3:48:54 (7,802)
Moelbach, Lars 3:37:57 (5,638)
Moelwyn Williams, Daniel J 3:40:59 (6,177)
Moffat, Graeme J 3:48:17 (7,652)
Moffat, Graeme J 4:43:47 (22,055)
Moffat, Mark G 3:51:33 (8,382)
Moffatt, Matthew 4:18:24 (15,327)
Moffett, David J 3:32:08 (4,764)
Moffett, James S 4:09:36 (12,983)
Mogan, John E 4:12:16 (13,688)
Moggach, Stuart A 4:05:02 (11,871)
Mogridge, Chris 3:47:27 (7,447)
Mohamed, André 5:05:46 (26,837)
Mohamed, Salim 3:48:39 (7,753)
Mohan, Bernard P 4:25:06 (17,152)
Mohan, James D 3:36:24 (5,405)
Moi, Roberto 2:56:21 (831)
Moir, David R 3:27:35 (4,033)
Moir, Ray 4:49:00 (23,235)
Moir, Robert J 4:02:04 (11,175)
Moisan, David J 2:43:16 (274)
Moisley, David J 3:42:47 (6,509)
Moisson, Edward P 4:49:51 (23,461)
Moizan, Christian 2:59:02 (1,039)
Molada Lopez, Pablo 3:47:41 (7,496)
Molai, Gabriele 5:40:34 (31,475)
Mole, Andrew A 4:36:03 (20,093)
Mole, David J 4:12:53 (13,848)
Mole, Denis H 5:11:21 (27,716)
Mole, James 4:39:32 (21,022)
Moles, Chris M 4:48:08 (23,041)
Molin, Beat 3:54:41 (9,149)
Mollers, Frank 5:49:40 (32,241)
Molloy, Chris 6:13:05 (33,666)
Molloy, David A 6:01:58 (33,078)
Molloy, John M 3:37:58 (5,643)
Molloy, Malcolm 6:01:58 (33,078)
Molloy, Michael 4:52:35 (24,070)
Molloy, Steve J 5:28:06 (30,124)
Moloney, Adam P 4:44:12 (22,142)
Moloney, Der 3:37:26 (5,564)
Molony, James E 3:19:37 (2,957)
Molony, Neil 3:50:48 (8,208)
Molyneux, David P 4:39:21 (20,977)
Molyneux, Graham J 3:11:51 (2,125)
Molyneux, Paul 2:42:30 (252)
Molyneux, Sidney A 4:11:10 (13,397)
Momoniat, Nazim 4:36:14 (20,141)
Mompean, Cayetano 4:14:59 (14,437)
Moncrieff, Marc 3:52:35 (8,625)
Moncur, Iain M 5:30:13 (30,385)
Monday, John 4:47:17 (22,835)
Monegomery, William 5:56:04 (32,711)
Money, Antony H 5:37:27 (31,136)
Money, Mark W 4:44:10 (22,135)
Monger, Steven T 3:52:44 (8,670)
Monk, Chris J 3:51:02 (8,261)
Monk, Mike J 4:34:48 (19,789)
Monk, Paul 3:58:43 (10,354)
Monk, Rowland M 3:47:53 (7,545)
Monk, Sebastian P 3:25:14 (3,631)
Monk, Stephen D 5:22:10 (29,372)
Monkhouse, Chris R 5:05:58 (26,864)
Monks, Chris M 4:37:59 (20,616)
Monks, John F 4:12:13 (13,670)
Monks, Stuart 3:45:01 (6,958)
Monserez, Jean-François 3:41:48 (6,337)
Monsi, Simon 5:27:00 (29,977)
Montague, Ian L 3:49:03 (7,836)
Montague, Joe 5:00:46 (25,929)
Montague, Peter A 6:38:22 (34,466)
Montague, Sean D 4:52:50 (24,134)
Montan, Bengt 5:42:12 (31,604)
Monteiro, Paulo A 6:12:39 (33,648)
Monteith, Angus J 2:58:53 (1,021)
Monteith, Joseph S 5:31:20 (30,495)
Montero Morales, Diego 5:06:41 (26,998)
Monterubbiano, Giorgio 3:30:09 (4,470)
Monteverde, Miguel E 3:02:38 (1,307)
Montgomerie, James 6:18:42 (33,880)
Montgomerie, Nick P 4:29:45 (18,533)
Montgomery, Kevin J 4:15:30 (14,582)
Montgomery, Neil S 4:36:09 (20,117)
Montgomery, Paul 5:21:55 (29,339)
Montgomery, Paul M 4:58:14 (25,380)
Montgomery, Scott 5:33:50 (30,758)
Monton, Colin I 4:02:42 (11,315)
Monument, Simon J 4:44:11 (22,138)
Mood, Saouli 4:56:39 (25,056)
Moody, Adrian T 3:35:08 (5,201)
Moody, Andrew P 5:49:35 (32,230)
Moody, Colin A 3:03:36 (1,373)
Moody, Douglas G 3:08:17 (1,741)
Moody, James 5:01:16 (26,019)
Moody, Jonathan K 4:16:24 (14,820)
Moody, Mark A 3:31:33 (4,689)
Moody, Peter K 4:31:24 (18,945)
Moody, Tony S 6:12:22 (33,632)
Moohan, Michael J 5:17:33 (28,726)
Moon, Ashley J 4:55:11 (24,717)
Mooney, Austin F 2:59:22 (1,078)
Mooney, Paul 3:28:23 (4,175)
Mooney, Steve 4:57:51 (25,290)
Moorcroft, John 3:51:24 (8,353)
Moore, Alan 4:19:56 (15,782)
Moore, Andrew 3:54:21 (9,062)
Moore, Andrew C 5:01:36 (26,081)
Moore, Andrew K 3:43:15 (6,605)
Moore, Andrew M 3:09:06 (1,821)
Moore, Andrew P 3:39:50 (5,971)
Moore, Austen J 3:50:22 (8,118)
Moore, Brian 5:35:06 (30,918)
Moore, Brian C 3:31:48 (4,718)
Moore, Christopher D 5:54:56 (32,636)
Moore, Colin W 5:25:29 (29,803)
Moore, Darren J 5:07:10 (27,091)
Moore, David G 2:52:58 (635)
Moore, David W 3:45:17 (7,004)
Moore, Dominic O 3:43:09 (6,581)
Moore, Eric R 4:57:14 (25,181)
Moore, Galen T 5:36:32 (31,060)
Moore, Gary 5:28:36 (30,195)
Moore, Gary W 4:24:44 (17,055)
Moore, Giles R 4:10:10 (13,133)
Moore, Graham 4:17:23 (15,063)
Moore, Graham F 3:04:11 (1,406)
Moore, Graham P 3:59:25 (10,548)
Moore, Graham S 2:51:55 (584)
Moore, James S 4:22:11 (16,392)
Moore, Jimmy C 4:37:12 (20,412)
Moore, Leigh J 6:34:00 (34,353)
Moore, Mark J 4:04:59 (11,856)
Moore, Martin C 5:19:50 (29,080)
Moore, Melwyn J 4:29:37 (18,499)
Moore, Michael F 2:38:51 (172)
Moore, Mick J 3:23:27 (3,369)
Moore, Neil R 4:56:38 (25,050)
Moore, Nicholas S 4:59:44 (25,719)
Moore, Nigel T 3:37:31 (5,583)
Moore, Oliver G 3:44:45 (6,889)
Moore, Peter 4:20:27 (15,929)
Moore, Philip 3:41:49 (6,341)
Moore, Richard 4:24:44 (17,055)
Moore, Richard J 3:11:50 (2,122)
Moore, Sam 4:23:20 (16,701)
Moore, Stephen J 5:31:18 (30,492)
Moore, Stuart J 4:20:13 (15,857)
Moore, Thomas P 4:09:50 (13,049)
Moore, Tom W 3:55:31 (9,373)
Moore, William P 6:03:45 (33,204)
Moore-Barton, Tim C 3:36:50 (5,471)
Moorey, Guy R 4:36:49 (20,311)
Moorhouse, Graham L 3:18:45 (2,855)
Moorhouse, John B 3:40:52 (6,161)
Moquet, François-Xavier 3:28:26 (4,186)
Mora, Ricardo 3:38:43 (5,757)
Morais, Luis M 4:42:52 (21,838)
Morales, Alexandre J 3:48:11 (7,631)
Moran, Christopher 3:56:37 (9,696)
Moran, James C 6:36:38 (34,424)
Moran, Mark P 3:47:57 (7,560)
Moran, Michael M 3:48:38 (7,749)
Moran, Michael S 6:36:38 (34,424)
Moran, Paschal P 3:31:18 (4,651)
Moran, Peter V 3:42:46 (6,507)
Morant, William 4:32:07 (19,117)
More, Leo A 4:25:57 (17,413)
Moreau, Tony 3:41:19 (6,238)
Moreau Pascal, Dominique 4:53:39 (24,344)
More-Molyneux, Michael G 6:00:24 (32,997)
Moret, Fabio 3:50:00 (8,038)
Moreton, Darren 4:24:46 (17,064)
Moreton, Lloyd 6:50:54 (34,734)
Moretti, Giovanni M 3:30:15 (4,484)
Moretto, Gerardo 4:39:04 (20,896)
Morfey, Michael J 4:39:42 (21,067)
Morford, Richard J 3:53:18 (8,801)
Morgan, Alan 4:45:40 (22,474)
Morgan, Andrew J 4:16:21 (14,811)
Morgan, Andrew P 3:14:42 (2,445)
Morgan, Chris 4:19:32 (15,674)
Morgan, Daniel R 3:45:50 (7,101)
Morgan, David R 5:14:40 (28,296)
Morgan, Derek J 4:46:09 (22,593)
Morgan, Edward A 4:30:17 (18,678)
Morgan, Emyr W 3:07:56 (1,708)
Morgan, Gareth H 3:46:35 (7,258)
Morgan, Gene 5:14:37 (28,283)
Morgan, Ian W 3:23:46 (3,411)
Morgan, Jeremy A 4:21:11 (16,105)
Morgan, John V 4:35:27 (19,966)
Morgan, Mark J 5:31:49 (30,547)
Morgan, Martin L 3:55:28 (9,358)
Morgan, Nicholas D 3:54:57 (9,228)
Morgan, Nick J 3:08:42 (1,780)
Morgan, Nicola K 3:41:32 (6,282)
Morgan, Patrick J 4:06:46 (12,277)
Morgan, Peter A 4:43:27 (21,964)
Morgan, Philip 3:14:51 (2,466)
Morgan, Phillip N 4:23:59 (16,844)
Morgan, Raymond B 3:11:45 (2,113)
Morgan, Rhodri T 5:03:05 (26,359)
Morgan, Richard C 5:01:19 (26,031)
Morgan, Richard J 4:36:55 (20,335)
Morgan, Richard L 3:18:58 (2,878)
Morgan, Robert D 4:50:27 (23,612)
Morgan, Robert L 4:23:09 (16,644)
Morgan, Roger 3:40:50 (6,148)
Morgan, Sean 3:19:30 (2,937)
Morgan, Simon D 4:23:46 (16,794)
Morgan, Simon P 3:23:39 (3,394)
Morgan, Stacey J 2:59:05 (1,044)
Morgan, Stephen T 6:30:26 (34,263)
Morgan, Steven A 5:45:39 (31,905)
Morgan, Steven R 3:09:10 (1,829)
Morgan, Thomas J 5:25:54 (29,854)
Morgan, Timothy D 4:37:21 (20,457)
Morgan, Tom 4:40:27 (21,243)
Morgan, Wayne 4:06:13 (12,144)
Morin, Joel M 3:52:26 (8,591)
Morlacci, Patrizio 4:24:57 (17,107)
Morley, Chris D 4:39:31 (21,019)
Morley, Colin J 4:31:54 (19,060)
Morley, Michael J 3:27:40 (4,054)
Morley, Phil A 2:56:43 (863)
Morley, Shane C 5:39:55 (31,404)
Morley, Stephen J 4:36:21 (20,177)
Morley, Stewart J 4:47:42 (22,945)
Morley, Thomas J 3:55:40 (9,416)
Morley, Wayne 3:44:51 (6,928)
Moroncini, Fauzio 2:26:52 (56)
Morpuss, Guy 4:56:39 (25,056)
Morpuss, Simon 4:41:26 (21,506)

Morrans, Niel 3:54:16 (9,038)
Morrell, David 4:12:34 (13,765)
Morris, Alan J 3:48:27 (7,692)
Morris, Alan W 4:14:48 (14,379)
Morris, Andrew M 3:49:56 (8,024)
Morris, Andy W 3:51:43 (8,416)
Morris, Barry 4:28:28 (18,156)
Morris, Brian J 2:57:11 (898)
Morris, Chris J 3:11:37 (2,089)
Morris, David G 5:17:01 (28,648)
Morris, David L 4:11:08 (13,388)
Morris, David P 4:37:59 (20,616)
Morris, David R 5:21:20 (29,279)
Morris, Dean G 4:48:11 (23,048)
Morris, Edward 4:54:30 (24,551)
Morris, Gareth B 5:55:35 (32,688)
Morris, Geoffrey R 5:17:02 (28,652)
Morris, Glyn E 3:30:44 (4,565)
Morris, Guy 4:32:18 (19,162)
Morris, Iain D 3:12:23 (2,183)
Morris, James D 4:07:17 (12,413)
Morris, James P 3:25:52 (3,734)
Morris, James P 5:52:28 (32,460)
Morris, James S 3:05:41 (1,529)
Morris, John D 3:08:31 (1,759)
Morris, Keith H 4:13:46 (14,083)
Morris, Kevin M 3:27:15 (3,968)
Morris, Lee 4:29:40 (18,510)
Morris, Mark 3:02:36 (1,304)
Morris, Mark 3:42:38 (6,490)
Morris, Matthew 4:15:05 (14,473)
Morris, Paul 3:48:31 (7,715)
Morris, Paul 5:59:47 (32,966)
Morris, Paul A 4:19:49 (15,756)
Morris, Paul D 5:41:15 (31,532)
Morris, Paul M 3:16:22 (2,622)
Morris, Paul W 3:10:09 (1,942)
Morris, Peter T 4:57:26 (25,218)
Morris, Philip 2:55:37 (780)
Morris, Philip J 4:41:08 (21,428)
Morris, Philip S 4:03:47 (11,569)
Morris, Robert P 4:07:44 (12,510)
Morris, Robert P 4:55:58 (24,892)
Morris, Samuel A 5:40:09 (31,435)
Morris, Simon 3:25:39 (3,695)
Morris, Simon B 3:46:54 (7,330)
Morris, Stephen 4:58:54 (25,536)
Morris, Stephen 5:29:45 (30,335)
Morris, Stephen D 4:41:35 (21,544)
Morris, Terence D 4:24:46 (17,064)
Morris, Thomas A 3:08:31 (1,759)
Morris, Wayne N 5:36:48 (31,086)
Morrish, Jonathan P 4:03:16 (11,449)
Morrish, Richard F 4:41:07 (21,424)
Morrish, Stuart R 3:41:07 (6,204)
Morrison, Alastair 3:20:04 (3,009)
Morrison, Andrew 4:43:56 (22,081)
Morrison, Andrew C 3:53:28 (8,851)
Morrison, Dougal 4:39:13 (20,937)
Morrison, Edward S 5:27:05 (29,985)
Morrison, Ian 3:57:04 (9,843)
Morrison, Ian M 4:13:11 (13,938)
Morrison, James M 3:51:32 (8,379)
Morrison, Joe R 3:30:43 (4,561)
Morrison, John S 4:37:32 (20,502)
Morrison, Jonathan H 4:53:24 (24,275)
Morrison, Paul J 4:12:13 (13,670)
Morrison, Sid 3:31:09 (4,621)
Morrison, Simon C 3:59:54 (10,698)
Morrissey, Kevin W 4:55:19 (24,738)
Morrow, David G 3:52:24 (8,578)
Morrow, Kieran 3:23:26 (3,367)
Morrow, Paul 5:47:26 (32,054)
Morrow, Robert J 5:33:24 (30,706)
Mort, Allan D 4:30:37 (18,750)
Mort, Stephen 4:10:14 (13,147)
Mortazavi, Mahmood 3:56:07 (9,543)
Mortensen, James S 5:42:32 (31,630)
Mortensen, Lind 3:53:30 (8,855)
Mortensen, Michael C 3:43:57 (6,732)
Mortgat, Michel 4:49:59 (23,492)
Mortimer, Alan B 5:10:45 (27,608)
Mortimer, Alistair D 4:04:43 (11,798)
Mortimer, David G 3:47:41 (7,496)
Mortimer, Robert W 3:29:40 (4,389)
Mortimer, Simon T 2:53:58 (683)
Mortimore, Richard 3:50:17 (8,099)
Mortin, John 3:57:24 (9,949)
Mortlock, David A 4:42:16 (21,693)
Mortlock, Paul C 3:35:21 (5,232)
Morton, Alan C 6:36:27 (34,420)
Morton, Andrew D 4:04:07 (11,665)
Morton, Brian 4:56:29 (25,014)
Morton, Chris M 4:21:34 (16,221)
Morton, Christopher J 4:27:43 (17,955)
Morton, Colin 4:53:19 (24,257)
Morton, Colin S 7:31:08 (35,136)
Morton, Gary E 3:17:51 (2,776)
Morton, Glenn M 3:45:06 (6,972)
Morton, Iain 3:38:22 (5,705)
Morton, Iwan T 4:20:05 (15,826)
Morton, Scott 3:47:25 (7,440)
Morton, Simon R 4:35:19 (19,911)
Morton, Steven J 3:00:39 (1,169)
Morton, Tim J 3:45:21 (7,017)
Morwood, Ian R 4:41:15 (21,460)
Mosaid, Sarwat L 3:59:40 (10,620)
Moschettoni, Luigi 4:44:13 (22,147)
Moseley, Andrew 6:01:03 (33,028)
Moss, Anthony P 3:42:26 (6,460)
Moss, Barry O 4:13:19 (13,968)
Moss, David 3:53:32 (8,866)
Moss, George T 4:15:13 (14,508)
Moss, Grant 3:49:13 (7,866)
Moss, James B 5:34:35 (30,858)
Moss, Jeremy P 4:11:50 (13,570)
Moss, Keith 3:29:04 (4,286)
Moss, Moddy J 3:54:53 (9,212)
Moss, Nicholas C 4:18:36 (15,394)
Moss, Stephen D 4:09:06 (12,860)
Moss, Timothy 4:36:30 (20,228)
Mossavati, Kaveh 4:40:19 (21,212)
Mosscrop, Jon J 4:09:55 (13,074)
Motai, Futao F 4:17:06 (14,982)
Moth, Simon J 3:21:13 (3,105)
Moth, Steven W 3:43:14 (6,595)
Mothersole, Richard G 6:09:07 (33,495)
Motherwell, David 4:49:48 (23,449)
Motimer, James 4:42:37 (21,776)
Motley, Michael 4:57:24 (25,208)
Motson, Nicholas E 4:19:14 (15,589)
Mott, Shane 3:17:12 (2,702)
Mott, Stephen D 3:43:54 (6,720)
Mottahed, Timothy 4:08:54 (12,802)
Motte, Adrian 5:48:12 (32,111)
Motte, David W 3:43:47 (6,703)
Mottet, Richard 3:58:10 (10,181)
Mottram, Patrick G 4:22:19 (16,425)
Mottram, Paul J 3:06:16 (1,574)
Mouganie, Tarek 4:31:16 (18,904)
Mould, Alan T 3:08:59 (1,809)
Mould, David J 5:17:15 (28,682)
Mould, Michael R 4:18:25 (15,334)
Moulden, Andrew J 3:33:14 (4,915)
Moulden, Paul A 4:26:45 (17,678)
Moule, Jonathan D 4:13:42 (14,068)
Moulton, Benjamin G 5:40:51 (31,489)
Mound, David G 4:48:12 (23,054)
Mounsey, Glenn N 4:10:34 (13,237)
Mountain, Richard J 4:57:47 (25,278)
Mountbatten, Ivar A 4:18:18 (15,296)
Mountford, Ian 3:47:26 (7,445)
Mountford, Paul J 2:33:41 (99)
Mountney, Edward C 4:45:11 (22,369)
Mouquin, Franck 3:05:26 (1,512)
Mouret, Eric 4:28:35 (18,191)
Mousicos, Christopher 4:20:31 (15,939)
Mouton, Richard 3:54:24 (9,077)
Moutou, Jean-Charles 4:05:07 (11,903)
Mowat, Cameron M 5:41:49 (31,582)
Mowbray, Henry B 4:33:16 (19,375)
Moxham, Paul A 3:25:48 (3,716)
Moxon, David S 3:45:14 (6,995)
Moy, Michael 4:22:53 (16,576)
Moy, Paul E 4:23:26 (16,718)
Moyle, Lindsay H 5:03:30 (26,434)
Moyles, David 4:14:01 (14,152)
Moyns, Daniel 4:12:02 (13,630)
Moyo, Bhekitshe 3:00:06 (1,134)
Mozo, José Antonio De Pablo 2:39:31 (188)
Mrozek, Roman 3:26:02 (3,770)
Muchamore, Del R 4:00:18 (10,787)
Mucklan, Damian F 4:20:23 (15,909)
Muddimer, Dave C 4:24:13 (16,908)
Mudge, Paul K 4:14:29 (14,290)
Mudie, Rory A 4:29:17 (18,396)
Muecke-Franke, Hans-Jurgen 4:44:06 (22,117)
Mueller, Joerg-Peter 3:55:33 (9,385)
Mueller, Marcus B 2:52:45 (624)
Mueller, Uwe 5:20:36 (29,197)
Muers, Kevin R 5:03:00 (26,341)
Muetzel, Peter 3:51:50 (8,449)
Muganga, Isaac N 3:24:45 (3,548)
Mugford, John D 5:33:43 (30,747)
Mughal, Muntzer 4:40:51 (21,348)
Mughal, Shahid 3:45:08 (6,979)
Muhlmann, Michael 3:36:31 (5,430)
Muir, AC 2:24:53 (44)
Muir, Adrian 4:33:57 (19,557)
Muir, Jamie 4:46:00 (22,551)
Muir, Jonathan 5:37:04 (31,108)
Muir, Malcolm J 4:16:53 (14,932)
Mulcahy, Jonathan P 4:05:02 (11,871)
Mulchrone, Jonathan E 3:53:52 (8,949)
Mulcock, Antony 3:58:34 (10,306)
Muldoon, Kevin M 4:45:16 (22,384)
Mulero-Garcia, José 4:27:06 (17,775)
Mulgrew, Hugh 5:57:48 (32,823)
Mulheirn, Ian J 3:42:58 (6,537)
Mulholland, Al E 4:29:58 (18,577)
Mulholland, Mark 3:58:42 (10,347)
Mulindna, Steve 5:16:52 (28,617)
Mullan, Matthew J 4:49:31 (23,363)
Mullan, Paul 3:41:47 (6,333)
Mullaney, Christopher 5:14:58 (28,337)
Mullarkey, Peter J 3:12:24 (2,185)
Mullen, Antony 4:54:32 (24,559)
Mullen, Michael 4:23:08 (16,640)
Muller, Boudewijn M 4:13:59 (14,141)
Muller, Guy 3:45:24 (7,030)
Mullery, Peter J 3:13:22 (2,286)
Mullet, Lee 4:04:33 (11,757)
Mulligan, Martin 5:12:37 (27,929)
Mullinger, Tony 4:14:20 (14,251)
Mullins, Stephen G 5:22:08 (29,370)
Mullins, Stephen J 5:58:53 (32,904)
Mulraney, Anthony J 5:38:46 (31,287)
Mulrooney, Michael A 6:25:57 (34,122)
Mulvaney, Michael J 4:17:08 (14,997)
Mulvey, Graeme L 3:23:49 (3,423)
Mulvey, Scott P 5:23:40 (29,569)
Mumby, Roger 3:10:32 (1,981)
Mumford, Justin S 3:49:52 (8,011)
Mumford, Mark 4:12:44 (13,811)
Muncaster, Ian 4:01:53 (11,124)
Munday, Neil 5:43:50 (31,749)
Munday, Richard D 3:17:41 (2,753)
Munday, Rick 5:43:49 (31,748)
Munday, Simon E 4:33:49 (19,523)
Mundy, Bob 4:20:01 (15,807)
Mundy, James 3:51:17 (8,324)
Munford, Andrew 3:50:52 (8,228)
Munford, Paul M 4:53:33 (24,313)
Munford, Stephen L 6:39:37 (34,498)
Munn, James 5:25:04 (29,754)
Munnery, David N 3:36:28 (5,420)
Munnery, Samuel W 3:33:21 (4,938)
Munns, Brian 2:54:45 (731)
Munro, Andrew J 4:56:29 (25,014)
Munro, Colin T 3:08:10 (1,730)
Munro, Jason K 3:57:20 (9,929)
Munro, Mark S 4:11:18 (13,428)
Munro, Peter J 4:31:10 (18,876)
Munro, Stephen T 5:34:29 (30,847)
Munroe, Andy J 3:18:29 (2,829)
Munroe, Mike J 4:30:01 (18,591)
Munsamy, Stanley 4:42:26 (21,725)
Munslow, Graham J 4:21:35 (16,228)
Munt, Derek P 3:23:06 (3,315)

Munt, Roger G	3:29:06 (4,296)	Murtagh, Simon J	3:59:06 (10,469)	Natali, Paul E	3:54:24 (9,077)
Muona, Jukka	5:05:33 (26,802)	Musa, Wayne O	5:32:54 (30,659)	Nathan, Gopi	4:32:20 (19,172)
Murakoshi, Hiroyuki	3:51:30 (8,369)	Muschinski, Lothar	4:35:20 (19,919)	Nathan, Paul J	4:03:39 (11,534)
Murciano, Jean-Louis	3:43:37 (6,672)	Musgrove, Eric W	3:20:23 (3,035)	Nathan, Robert	5:00:18 (25,845)
Murdoch, Graeme A	3:07:00 (1,634)	Musgrove, Stephen	3:11:12 (2,054)	Nathan, Steven H	5:51:04 (32,343)
Murdoch, Ian A	4:01:15 (10,995)	Musk, John C	5:18:14 (28,824)	Nation, Richard	4:22:24 (16,445)
Murdoch, Steven J	2:47:55 (409)	Muskett, Alan P	3:54:57 (9,228)	Naughton, Geoffrey	4:02:28 (11,262)
Murdock, Gerard P	4:19:46 (15,743)	Muslu, Kenan	5:22:30 (29,419)	Naughton, Joe R.	5:30:40 (30,431)
Mures, José L	4:13:16 (13,955)	Mussa, Munir	8:07:41 (35,239)	Navalpotro, José	4:13:01 (13,886)
Murgatroyd, Lee J	4:30:15 (18,667)	Mussell, Nick	4:59:44 (25,719)	Navarro-Marin, Jorge	4:11:07 (13,384)
Murison, Kevin S	2:54:36 (720)	Musselwhite, James	3:28:03 (4,113)	Naviaux, Benoit	3:55:46 (9,455)
Murphy, Adrian	5:45:59 (31,933)	Mussner, Ivan	3:30:25 (4,508)	Navin, Michael D	4:11:40 (13,525)
Murphy, Aidan V	4:14:15 (14,229)	Musson, Julian P	4:38:06 (20,648)	Navrady, Jeremy L	3:33:13 (4,911)
Murphy, Alan J	5:22:38 (29,449)	Musson, Keith	3:23:46 (3,411)	Nawaz, Umar	5:05:23 (26,771)
Murphy, Andrew J	3:40:29 (6,083)	Musson, Michael S	4:31:23 (18,940)	Nayak, Amit	4:47:51 (22,979)
Murphy, Andrew J	4:56:08 (24,925)	Mustafa, Yusuf	6:00:35 (33,006)	Nayler, Mark J	3:52:13 (8,532)
Murphy, Anthony J	4:26:43 (17,667)	Mustonen, Leo	3:53:11 (8,768)	Naylor, Andrew J	3:46:58 (7,343)
Murphy, Christopher C	5:10:57 (27,645)	Mutch, Graeme P	3:02:26 (1,292)	Naylor, Dave G	3:10:09 (1,942)
Murphy, Christopher D	4:11:46 (13,555)	Mutch, Joseph N	3:51:58 (8,476)	Naylor, Jonathan R	3:31:32 (4,685)
Murphy, Cormac I	5:02:58 (26,335)	Mutini, Lorenzo	3:08:42 (1,780)	Naylor, Tim G	4:02:26 (11,255)
Murphy, Daniel P	3:44:31 (6,839)	Mutter, Dave W	3:45:19 (7,009)	Naylor-Leyland, John	3:47:08 (7,380)
Murphy, Danny	4:54:00 (24,428)	Muttett, David C	5:20:11 (29,129)	Nazir, Rizwan	4:14:00 (14,148)
Murphy, David	4:50:25 (23,603)	Mutton, Brian	4:57:50 (25,286)	Ndawula, Bobby	3:47:57 (7,560)
Murphy, David	5:33:59 (30,779)	Mutton, Colin T	4:27:43 (17,955)	Nduka, Nyeche E	7:02:21 (34,895)
Murphy, Donal F	3:24:55 (3,570)	Mutyaba, Robert	4:48:04 (23,024)	Neads, Kevin M	3:19:56 (2,989)
Murphy, Donal G	4:58:22 (25,406)	Mutz, Dieter	3:49:23 (7,908)	Neal, David C	3:21:31 (3,132)
Murphy, Dudley	5:58:22 (32,866)	Muxlow, Adam	3:36:57 (5,494)	Neal, Gregory G	4:37:12 (20,412)
Murphy, Gerry	3:54:45 (9,171)	Muyambo, Bray T	5:46:16 (31,963)	Neal, Robert G	4:30:58 (18,829)
Murphy, Jeff	4:25:11 (17,182)	Muzariri, Pius S	5:43:31 (31,718)	Neal, Tom D	5:14:01 (28,175)
Murphy, John C	3:59:45 (10,649)	Mvubu, Mispah D	4:49:19 (23,315)	Neal, Trevor J	5:19:24 (29,009)
Murphy, Jonathan P	3:47:12 (7,391)	Myers, Charles R	5:01:25 (26,045)	Neale, Andrew J	4:55:51 (24,862)
Murphy, Justin S	4:31:31 (18,974)	Myers, Gary W	4:44:46 (22,270)	Neale, Darren J	3:44:53 (6,935)
Murphy, Kevin J	4:24:18 (16,924)	Myers, Iain D	3:44:21 (6,805)	Neale, David A	4:09:32 (12,971)
Murphy, Les	4:35:44 (20,026)	Myers, Nicholas S	3:43:39 (6,679)	Neale, James	3:36:58 (5,495)
Murphy, Mark A	4:27:44 (17,963)	Myers, Roger F	3:27:10 (3,951)	Neale, James	3:41:14 (6,222)
Murphy, Mark F	4:23:41 (16,775)	Myerscough, Robert S	4:11:16 (13,419)	Neale, Paul J	3:32:44 (4,848)
Murphy, Martin F	5:06:31 (26,971)	Myerscough, Steve V	3:10:48 (2,011)	Neale, Stefan	3:25:14 (3,631)
Murphy, Michael G	4:36:44 (20,289)	Myhan, Jeremy F	6:28:18 (34,206)	Nealon, Nick M	3:27:26 (4,005)
Murphy, Mike D	3:46:13 (7,182)	Myhill, Andrew	3:14:38 (2,433)	Neary, Gary M	4:50:09 (23,528)
Murphy, Nathan J	4:42:34 (21,761)	Myhill, Ben W	3:37:14 (5,528)	Neary, Stephen A	4:46:37 (22,692)
Murphy, Niall	4:05:19 (11,952)	Myhre, Stephen J	4:08:46 (12,758)	Nebioglw, Erdal	4:59:03 (25,574)
Murphy, Patrick	4:24:50 (17,081)	Mylchreest, Peter A	4:00:37 (10,871)	Neczaj, Martin P	4:46:19 (22,626)
Murphy, Paul	3:42:01 (6,379)	Myles, David A	5:40:31 (31,469)	Needham, Christopher S	5:36:40 (31,074)
Murphy, Paul R	3:27:52 (4,087)	Mynard, Andrew B	3:02:29 (1,297)	Needham, Justin C	3:17:28 (2,730)
Murphy, Paul W	3:56:00 (9,513)	Mynors, Robert T	4:48:02 (23,017)	Needham, Michael R	5:44:48 (31,829)
Murphy, Peter A	3:31:12 (4,631)	Myres, Peter J	4:20:05 (15,826)	Needham, Trevor N	5:38:27 (31,245)
Murphy, Rory	5:41:39 (31,568)	Myyrylainen, Jouko	3:39:39 (5,941)	Needham, Wayne	3:53:36 (8,883)
Murphy, Sean	4:01:21 (11,012)	Nagaya, Hiroyuki	3:33:31 (4,960)	Neel, Christophe J	3:42:36 (6,481)
Murphy, Sean D	4:05:51 (12,057)	Nagel, Avid C	5:02:27 (26,228)	Neep, Roger W	5:04:47 (26,647)
Murphy, Simon J	4:33:42 (19,488)	Nagel, Marco	4:07:17 (12,413)	Neergaard, FP	3:58:46 (10,375)
Murphy, Steve	4:50:23 (23,592)	Nagler, Alex R	5:57:01 (32,774)	Neeson, Patrick J	4:02:03 (11,170)
Murphy, Thomas	5:02:22 (26,213)	Nagler, Stuart M	5:57:01 (32,774)	Nehk, Michael	3:33:25 (4,948)
Murphy, Tony	4:34:51 (19,804)	Naidoo, Udesh	4:27:54 (18,015)	Neidermaier-Reed, Robert A	5:05:03 (26,693)
Murphy, Vincent J	3:42:25 (6,457)	Naish, James R	4:12:20 (13,707)	Neill, Caspar	4:03:08 (11,416)
Murray, Alan S	4:25:28 (17,273)	Najada, Keiron	4:30:22 (18,693)	Neill, Lawrence J	3:00:07 (1,137)
Murray, Alasdair	3:23:54 (3,438)	Nake, Michael	3:51:23 (8,348)	Neill, Shaun M	5:03:21 (26,410)
Murray, Andrew	3:28:05 (4,120)	Nallapareddy, Venkareddy	5:31:18 (30,492)	Neill, Thomas J	3:24:34 (3,523)
Murray, Christopher H	5:31:20 (30,495)	Nalton, Andrew B.	2:37:55 (155)	Neilon, Christopher D	3:57:01 (9,820)
Murray, Christopher W	4:32:07 (19,117)	Nana, Parmanand V	6:30:00 (34,256)	Neilson, Andrew R	6:38:02 (34,455)
Murray, Ian	2:46:00 (348)	Nance, David J	3:40:55 (6,167)	Neilson, Darran A	3:54:22 (9,070)
Murray, James I	3:43:03 (6,561)	Nancekivell, Kevin	3:43:05 (6,570)	Neilson, Edward W	3:20:17 (3,023)
Murray, Jason S	5:24:32 (29,687)	Nanthan, Siva	6:14:02 (33,704)	Nelhams, Michael	3:29:36 (4,370)
Murray, Joe	4:43:10 (21,905)	Nanton, Kingsley	2:52:51 (629)	Neligan, Andrew J	3:42:19 (6,435)
Murray, John A	4:01:11 (10,977)	Napier, Gordon	4:35:42 (20,019)	Nell, Matthew A	3:15:25 (2,518)
Murray, Joseph P	5:06:19 (26,922)	Napier, Owen E	4:51:23 (23,813)	Nell, William J	5:01:40 (26,089)
Murray, Ken J	5:38:55 (31,298)	Napkins, Nicky	3:55:32 (9,376)	Nellis, Joseph G	4:56:32 (25,022)
Murray, Neil A	4:13:49 (14,093)	Napolitano, Vincenzo	3:27:04 (3,939)	Nelmes, Andrew A	5:38:56 (31,301)
Murray, Patrick	4:00:17 (10,784)	Napper, Harold G	5:28:55 (30,239)	Nelson, Anthony	4:48:40 (23,162)
Murray, Robert J	3:23:38 (3,392)	Nara, Norihiro	5:33:59 (30,779)	Nelson, Benjamin D	3:18:52 (2,868)
Murray, Roy J	4:49:24 (23,334)	Naraine, Guy M	4:17:11 (15,007)	Nelson, Carl	4:43:33 (21,996)
Murray, Stephen M	4:21:57 (16,317)	Nardini, Robert	3:02:43 (1,317)	Nelson, Colin R	4:21:19 (16,147)
Murray, Stuart	7:50:40 (35,207)	Narvaez, Manuel	3:41:55 (6,364)	Nelson, Dennis R	4:18:25 (15,334)
Murray, Terry	5:25:20 (29,783)	Naseer, Tahir	5:07:42 (27,176)	Nelson, Gary T	5:17:22 (28,692)
Murray, Tom	5:48:15 (32,117)	Nash, Adam J	4:30:28 (18,717)	Nelson, James J	4:11:45 (13,552)
Murray, William	4:08:52 (12,792)	Nash, James W	6:03:17 (33,165)	Nelson, Johnathan J	3:50:39 (8,180)
Murray, William	5:11:59 (27,819)	Nash, Jonathan	4:14:33 (14,304)	Nelson, Keith J	4:02:28 (11,262)
Murray, William F	3:30:37 (4,546)	Nash, Mike	4:19:03 (15,527)	Nelson, Lee	4:32:39 (19,238)
Murray, William N	4:21:58 (16,322)	Nash, Peter L	3:27:19 (3,980)	Nelson, Mark R	4:48:51 (23,199)
Murrell, Kevin	4:34:46 (19,781)	Nash, Simon P	5:03:28 (26,428)	Nelson, Matthew M	4:00:56 (10,935)
Murrell, Steven P	3:39:12 (5,850)	Nash, Steven	4:53:58 (24,415)	Nelson, Michael	4:09:11 (12,882)
Murrells, Stephen C	4:23:24 (16,712)	Nash, Tim C	4:27:29 (17,884)	Nelson, Peer C	4:47:04 (22,784)
Murrin, Thomas W	5:33:08 (30,683)	Nash, Tim N	3:27:36 (4,036)	Nelson, Richard D	3:25:16 (3,639)
Mursell, John W	3:28:17 (4,155)	Nass, Reinhard	4:25:54 (17,401)	Nelson, Stephen J	4:31:05 (18,850)

Nelson, Stuart A	3:54:43	(9,158)
Nelson, Stuart R	5:08:00	(27,220)
Neocleous, Richard R	4:56:22	(24,981)
Nesbit, John A	3:58:10	(10,181)
Nesbitt, Graeme	4:07:11	(12,391)
Nesden, Patrick	5:25:27	(29,795)
Ness, Patrick M	4:34:41	(19,762)
Nester, Michael J	2:43:09	(273)
Nestor, Tom W	4:29:33	(18,482)
Nethercleft, Mark	3:46:08	(7,167)
Nethercott, Thomas	4:37:43	(20,559)
Neto, Luis M	4:14:33	(14,304)
Nettleford, Clive	5:01:42	(26,092)
Nettuno, Tommy	2:50:17	(506)
Neudecker, Georg	4:21:48	(16,284)
Neugarten, Steven P	4:38:24	(20,727)
Neumann, Andreas	3:38:37	(5,741)
Neumann, Kai	5:12:41	(27,940)
Neumerzhtskiy, Vasiliy	2:54:49	(733)
Neveu, Michel	2:57:46	(938)
Nevill, Peter C	3:23:12	(3,331)
Nevill, Timothy J	4:54:17	(24,496)
Neville, Martin	4:36:57	(20,343)
Neville, Paul D	4:41:47	(21,585)
Neville, Simon G	3:11:20	(2,063)
Neville, Stephen T	4:06:17	(12,163)
Nevin, Frank G	4:04:40	(11,786)
Nevitt, James B	4:06:16	(12,159)
Nevola, Venturino R	2:52:51	(629)
New, Stephen B	4:19:51	(15,764)
Newall, John A	2:54:11	(698)
Newbould, Garry	4:29:19	(18,409)
Newbury, Christopher A	5:25:16	(29,775)
Newbury, Duncan J	3:18:40	(2,847)
Newbury, Richard A	4:01:30	(11,050)
Newbury, Steven J	6:03:46	(33,208)
Newby, David	5:21:03	(29,244)
Newby, Ray P	3:41:25	(6,261)
Newcombe, Ian	3:19:54	(2,985)
Newell, Frank A	6:11:19	(33,585)
Newell, Ian J	3:04:37	(1,437)
Newell, Jonathan	4:12:21	(13,713)
Newell, Julian A	2:54:18	(701)
Newell, Richard	6:29:01	(34,221)
Newell, Richard A	4:28:29	(18,162)
Newell, Russell T	4:32:03	(19,102)
Newell, Steve J	3:26:34	(3,859)
Newell, Terry	6:07:17	(33,403)
Newey, Andrew	4:46:17	(22,621)
Newhouse, Richard	3:37:45	(5,609)
Newing, Andrew P	3:37:03	(5,506)
Newland, Alan J	4:05:27	(11,980)
Newland, Darren M	4:13:37	(14,046)
Newman, Andrew	4:05:21	(11,957)
Newman, Bryan J	3:48:30	(7,709)
Newman, Carl S	4:21:41	(16,252)
Newman, Craig	4:47:15	(22,828)
Newman, Darren M	3:30:17	(4,486)
Newman, David A	4:09:27	(12,943)
Newman, David J	5:04:57	(26,680)
Newman, Gavin J	4:17:16	(15,029)
Newman, Geoffrey J	3:54:54	(9,215)
Newman, Ian	4:34:59	(19,851)
Newman, John L	3:39:09	(5,841)
Newman, Justin M	6:43:17	(34,576)
Newman, Mark	4:29:53	(18,561)
Newman, Neville J	4:23:13	(16,655)
Newman, Nick J	3:57:24	(9,949)
Newman, Paul	3:43:39	(6,679)
Newman, Paul G	4:33:04	(19,330)
Newman, Paul M	4:51:09	(23,761)
Newman, Philip	4:49:34	(23,379)
Newman, Ralph J	3:46:19	(7,207)
Newman, Ronald F	3:39:18	(5,868)
Newman, Sean	4:05:21	(11,957)
Newman, Simon D	4:09:27	(12,943)
Newmarch, Geoffrey W	4:53:22	(24,265)
Newmarch, Mark W	3:42:50	(6,514)
Newnham, Andrew M	4:25:23	(17,241)
Newrick, Paul G	3:24:24	(3,506)
Newsam, Michael T	5:51:19	(32,355)
Newsham, Lee R	4:13:04	(13,904)
Newton, Anthony V	5:05:06	(26,700)

Newton, Craig	5:12:04	(27,834)
Newton, Gavin J	3:19:18	(2,910)
Newton, Graham R	6:01:25	(33,046)
Newton, Harry J	4:38:35	(20,774)
Newton, Ian P	4:43:40	(22,026)
Newton, Jonathan A	4:02:11	(11,201)
Newton, Keith D	2:37:49	(151)
Newton, Mark	4:19:40	(15,714)
Newton, Peter J	2:58:22	(980)
Newton, Peter N	3:44:21	(6,805)
Newton, Philip J	4:00:30	(10,832)
Newton, Richard C	3:46:34	(7,254)
Newton, Rodger	6:11:23	(33,589)
Newton, Ronald A	4:23:37	(16,756)
Newton, Simon P	2:51:26	(560)
Neystre, Vincent	3:02:08	(1,273)
Ng, Anthony	3:46:52	(7,318)
Ng, Joe C	4:57:56	(25,307)
Ng, Ronald	4:48:28	(23,119)
Niblett, Eden P	5:07:27	(27,138)
Niblett, James D	5:15:05	(28,346)
Niblock, Peter	5:33:16	(30,697)
Nice, Alan L	6:12:04	(33,620)
Nicel, John M	3:58:59	(10,427)
Nichol, Ian J	4:14:24	(14,273)
Nicholas, David R	4:51:38	(23,859)
Nicholas, Dean T	3:01:57	(1,255)
Nicholas, Stephen R	4:24:27	(16,977)
Nicholl, Daniel J	6:30:06	(34,259)
Nicholl, David J	4:43:30	(21,980)
Nicholl, Matthew C	4:02:33	(11,287)
Nicholls, Alan J	4:19:03	(15,527)
Nicholls, Andrew P	4:38:09	(20,660)
Nicholls, Andrew P	6:04:28	(33,245)
Nicholls, Andrew S	3:03:20	(1,351)
Nicholls, Anthony R	3:16:56	(2,670)
Nicholls, Daniel	6:09:25	(33,512)
Nicholls, James R	3:59:53	(10,694)
Nicholls, Jonathan	4:43:02	(21,878)
Nicholls, Kenneth E	4:19:17	(15,604)
Nicholls, Michael J	4:10:49	(13,292)
Nicholls, Paul	4:26:24	(17,570)
Nicholls, Philip G	5:12:27	(27,901)
Nicholls, Ron C	3:22:57	(3,291)
Nicholls, Stephen	5:48:59	(32,181)
Nichols, Carl	4:43:58	(22,090)
Nichols, Carl A	3:49:15	(7,881)
Nichols, Gary R	4:24:23	(16,949)
Nichols, James E	3:17:23	(2,721)
Nichols, Joseph	4:46:58	(22,765)
Nichols, Oliver	3:52:56	(8,705)
Nichols, Peter	4:32:51	(19,276)
Nicholson, Bobby A	4:09:37	(12,987)
Nicholson, Brian G	4:05:59	(12,090)
Nicholson, Chris	4:15:48	(14,660)
Nicholson, David A	4:19:16	(15,596)
Nicholson, James	4:58:03	(25,338)
Nicholson, Jason M	4:02:21	(11,234)
Nicholson, John W	4:47:40	(22,936)
Nicholson, Martin P	3:42:56	(6,531)
Nicholson, Richard D	3:14:33	(2,424)
Nicholson, Roy D	3:52:24	(8,578)
Nicholson, Steven K	4:07:42	(12,495)
Nickau, Hanno L	3:07:33	(1,679)
Nickerson, Damion P	6:12:28	(33,639)
Nicol, David	3:47:06	(7,372)
Nicol, Graeme	4:27:27	(17,869)
Nicol, Simon P	3:42:42	(6,498)
Nicoll, Iain	4:23:26	(16,718)
Nicoll, Steve K	4:23:08	(16,640)
Nicoll, Steven	3:52:49	(8,686)
Niculescu, Liviy D	4:32:18	(19,162)
Niebelschutz, Gert	3:03:53	(1,393)
Niedner, Claude J	3:46:38	(7,270)
Niekerken, Uwe	3:47:46	(7,517)
Nielsen, Kasper R	3:48:00	(7,581)
Nielsen, Ole	4:04:45	(11,803)
Nielsen, Thomas B	3:19:15	(2,906)
Nielsen, Thomas Jarl O	3:16:03	(2,580)
Nielsen Mazewski, Paul S	3:17:26	(2,726)
Nighall, Alick G	3:44:40	(6,872)
Nightingale, David	3:23:13	(3,334)
Nightingale, Sandy R	3:37:32	(5,584)

Nihal, Navtesh	4:26:09	(17,492)
Nijhawan, Anil	6:35:35	(34,398)
Nijjar, Avtar S	4:19:23	(15,632)
Nikic, Sveto	4:03:57	(11,617)
Nilsen, Tor	3:39:11	(5,847)
Nimmo, Steven G	3:16:23	(2,623)
Nind, Richard D	3:31:19	(4,654)
Nisbet, Jack	3:06:12	(1,568)
Nisbet, Peter J	4:27:47	(17,980)
Nishimoto, Kenji	4:30:51	(18,810)
Nivelet, Dominique H	3:11:08	(2,044)
Niven, Martin J	5:25:30	(29,806)
Nivola, Gianpaolo	5:24:08	(29,635)
Nixon, Billy C	3:33:50	(5,018)
Nixon, David	4:24:10	(16,894)
Nixon, Simon P	5:28:27	(30,183)
Nixon, Stuart G	5:13:44	(28,119)
Njenga, Daniel	2:15:25	(15)
Nkonge, Eric M	4:42:11	(21,674)
Nkosi, Duma	5:09:28	(27,432)
Noad, Jonathan J	3:47:59	(7,573)
Noad, Peter J	3:31:46	(4,712)
Noah, Josh	4:00:49	(10,907)
Noakes, Ben A	4:17:12	(15,011)
Noakes, Colin B	4:39:17	(20,961)
Noble, Christopher J	4:11:22	(13,444)
Noble, Ian G	4:01:02	(10,954)
Noble, James M	4:09:42	(13,012)
Noble, Jeff	3:27:14	(3,965)
Noble, Paul M	4:08:06	(12,590)
Noble, Richard A	4:39:40	(21,060)
Noble, Robert V	5:23:26	(29,531)
Noble, Terry J	4:51:17	(23,789)
Noble Jones, Terence	5:50:14	(32,282)
Nock, Graham S	3:05:06	(1,474)
Nockles, Grant E	4:01:27	(11,038)
Noel, Vernon L	6:11:36	(33,597)
Nogues, Francis	3:47:31	(7,460)
Nogues, Jean	4:06:51	(12,301)
Noke, Ray D	3:57:10	(9,880)
Nokes, Kieran P	5:14:20	(28,236)
Nolan, Brian	2:55:22	(758)
Nolan, John A	3:57:06	(9,856)
Nolan, Nev	4:41:29	(21,518)
Nolan, Paul T	4:25:10	(17,172)
Nolan, Tony	3:46:17	(7,199)
Noomen, Cornerlis	4:07:51	(12,543)
Noon, John R	5:38:37	(31,268)
Noonan, Eamonn T	3:11:06	(2,043)
Noonan, John F	4:39:56	(21,122)
Noore, Nigel J	5:30:11	(30,381)
Norbury, Michael J	3:21:54	(3,171)
Norman, Alistair J	4:26:32	(17,612)
Norman, Ben E	3:33:03	(4,893)
Norman, Colin J	4:53:34	(24,318)
Norman, Dave	2:18:34	(21)
Norman, David	3:43:08	(6,579)
Norman, Drew J	4:50:59	(23,728)
Norman, Harry W	3:44:22	(6,811)
Norman, James R	5:22:00	(29,351)
Norman, Nigel B	4:30:28	(18,717)
Norman, Phillip E	4:59:16	(25,620)
Norman, Stephen A	4:09:22	(12,926)
Normoyle, Trevor F	3:52:25	(8,589)
Norridge, Christopher	4:14:00	(14,148)
Norris, Benedict J	4:20:44	(16,001)
Norris, Daniel	3:29:36	(4,370)
Norris, John F	3:28:15	(4,150)
Norris, Michael J	4:52:04	(23,954)
Norris, Peter	3:00:57	(1,189)
Norris, Philip J	3:57:51	(10,094)
Norris, Simon R	4:14:04	(14,173)
North, Anthony D	3:58:35	(10,308)
North, Ernest F	4:43:42	(22,033)
North, Glenn R	2:46:15	(355)
North, Ian	4:11:37	(13,508)
North, Jason	4:27:12	(17,802)
North, Mark G	5:32:03	(30,562)
North, Paul R	4:30:36	(18,747)
North, Philip G	4:42:43	(21,804)
North, Rhys J	4:11:20	(13,440)
North, Tom A	5:18:00	(28,784)
Northcott, Adrian P	3:26:45	(3,894)

Northeast, Graham P....4:25:37 (17,321)
Northern, Paul....3:32:44 (4,848)
Northfield, Ian R....4:31:38 (19,004)
Northmore, Andrew B....3:49:13 (7,866)
Northwood, Anthony J....4:32:45 (19,258)
Norton, Arthur L....4:31:47 (19,042)
Norton, Carl....3:40:03 (6,005)
Norton, David R....5:28:48 (30,219)
Norton, James A....3:52:07 (8,508)
Norton, Peter J....4:18:43 (15,438)
Norton, Roger J....5:19:28 (29,024)
Norval, Richard J....4:37:33 (20,509)
Noschese, Giuseppe....5:01:44 (26,096)
Nothnagel, Edgar....4:12:42 (13,805)
Notley, William H....4:09:45 (13,029)
Nott, Chris....3:45:24 (7,030)
Nottage, Clive A....4:55:41 (24,815)
Nottidge, Richard R....4:00:02 (10,736)
Nouillan, Bill....4:50:20 (23,576)
Nowacki, Wies....2:58:38 (1,000)
Nowosielski, Andrzej W....3:31:13 (4,634)
Nucera, Massimo....4:09:03 (12,838)
Nugent, James....4:32:14 (19,146)
Nugent, Paul....3:36:49 (5,469)
Nugus, Ian R....5:34:42 (30,874)
Nugus, John P....2:50:21 (508)
Nugus, John P....4:58:44 (25,493)
Nulder, Wesleigh M....3:56:32 (9,671)
Nullens, Stef....3:11:52 (2,127)
Nunez, José R....3:30:30 (4,526)
Nunn, Gregory F....4:15:40 (14,624)
Nunn, Stephen J....3:42:24 (6,450)
Nurit, Thierry....2:53:14 (646)
Nurse, John D....4:42:22 (21,714)
Nussbaum, David A....5:12:53 (27,982)
Nussey, Mark....3:37:05 (5,512)
Nute, Dominic L....4:58:50 (25,521)
Nuti, Mark G....6:48:16 (34,680)
Nutt, Alan E....4:40:52 (21,352)
Nutt, Anthony....4:34:33 (19,727)
Nuttall, Christopher....6:45:04 (34,616)
Nuttall, Nicholas M....4:23:32 (16,735)
Nuttall, Paul D....4:39:07 (20,904)
Nuttall, Peter E....4:31:41 (19,016)
Nutter, Eric....4:12:41 (13,798)
Nuttycombe, William D....4:50:39 (23,662)
Nye, Alex C....4:12:53 (13,848)
Nye, James V....4:07:35 (12,472)
Nye, John....5:21:45 (29,320)
Nye, Paul....4:26:37 (17,636)
Nye, Steven J....4:46:57 (22,761)
Nygards, Mattias....4:10:51 (13,303)
Nykolyszyn, Myron J....4:19:32 (15,674)
Nylund, Ulf....3:35:25 (5,243)
Nyunt, UT....4:21:24 (16,171)
Oak, Makarand K....5:20:20 (29,146)
Oakes, Dave J....4:47:29 (22,883)
Oakes, John D....4:36:42 (20,279)
Oakes, Michael....3:26:01 (3,764)
Oakes, Wally....4:55:44 (24,827)
Oakins, Matthew J....4:52:37 (24,080)
Oakley, Alan....4:42:23 (21,719)
Oakley, Andrew....3:59:08 (10,479)
Oakley, Richard....4:23:19 (16,700)
Oakshott, Angus W....3:56:16 (9,589)
Oakwell, Paul D....4:02:01 (11,161)
Oaten, Colin M....4:28:48 (18,250)
Oates, David A....4:22:17 (16,416)
Oates, Kevin M....3:14:31 (2,420)
Oates, Neil....5:47:06 (32,029)
Oates, Stephen M....3:49:39 (7,965)
Oates, Stephen M....4:57:18 (25,195)
Oatham, Philip W....3:10:17 (1,956)
Obee, Martin J....4:33:28 (19,421)
Oberndorfer, Wilhelm....3:46:59 (7,346)
Oborski, Andrzej I....4:15:04 (14,470)
O'Boyle, Fergus....5:40:23 (31,458)
O'Brien, Adrian G....3:42:11 (6,418)
O'Brien, Anthony S....3:23:05 (3,311)
O'Brien, Chris R....4:55:59 (24,898)
O'Brien, Christopher P....4:08:43 (12,743)
O'Brien, David J....4:43:43 (22,039)
O'Brien, David P....3:50:08 (8,070)
O'Brien, Frank....5:39:10 (31,328)
O'Brien, Frank....5:57:18 (32,795)
O'Brien, Ian....4:38:58 (20,868)
O'Brien, Jarlath P....4:12:30 (13,747)
O'Brien, Justin J....3:41:37 (6,302)
O'Brien, Kieran O....3:32:22 (4,800)
O'Brien, Martin I....5:22:27 (29,411)
O'Brien, Martin J....4:36:10 (20,122)
O'Brien, Neil J....4:59:25 (25,647)
O'Brien, Nigel D....4:48:42 (23,168)
O'Brien, Patrick J....5:39:07 (31,324)
O'Brien, Peter....4:11:40 (13,525)
O'Brien, Peter....5:50:48 (32,329)
O'Brien, Wesley J....5:40:57 (31,501)
O'Brien-Brackenburey, Brendan....5:22:27 (29,411)
O'Callaghan, Conrad E....5:23:50 (29,590)
O'Callaghan, Michael....5:12:27 (27,901)
O'Callaghan, Pat....4:39:36 (21,047)
O'Callaghan, Tyler K....3:44:24 (6,820)
Ockford, Simon....4:11:41 (13,534)
Ockwell, Chris....4:53:58 (24,415)
Ockwood, Paul R....4:16:22 (14,814)
O'Connell, Brian E....3:55:49 (9,467)
O'Connell, Eoin G....2:31:01 (78)
O'Connell, Gareth....3:23:41 (3,398)
O'Connell, Gerry N....5:31:46 (30,540)
O'Connell, James A....3:41:01 (6,182)
O'Connell, Michael....3:29:04 (4,286)
O'Connell, Neil....4:02:41 (11,309)
O'Connor, Andrew....3:14:15 (2,387)
O'Connor, Anthony....2:50:38 (522)
O'Connor, Chris....3:22:31 (3,248)
O'Connor, David A....6:16:00 (33,778)
O'Connor, Denis J....3:18:16 (2,811)
O'Connor, Dominic....3:42:52 (6,521)
O'Connor, Geoff....4:35:16 (19,900)
O'Connor, Ian J....4:54:18 (24,505)
O'Connor, James....5:52:39 (32,473)
O'Connor, John....3:46:49 (7,308)
O'Connor, John F....5:11:17 (27,701)
O'Connor, Lee A....4:58:20 (25,400)
O'Connor, Ray....3:48:23 (7,681)
O'Connor, Richard P....4:41:01 (21,400)
O'Connor, Rory....4:01:37 (11,072)
O'Connor, Ross A....3:07:22 (1,659)
O'Connor, Sean J....3:35:02 (5,189)
O'Connor, Sean M....5:57:39 (32,814)
O'Connor, Terence A....4:48:41 (23,165)
O'Connor, Tim....3:03:44 (1,385)
O'Connor, Trevor....3:18:48 (2,861)
O'Connor, William J....3:40:50 (6,148)
Oddie, James R....3:39:32 (5,920)
Oddie, William....4:02:18 (11,222)
Oddy, Richard J....4:40:53 (21,358)
O'Dea, Enda J....4:40:39 (21,296)
O'Dea, Stephen J....3:32:40 (4,839)
Odell, Graham A....4:35:25 (19,955)
Odendaal, Dolf P....4:36:18 (20,164)
Odgers, Ian....4:12:27 (13,737)
O'Donnell, Gus....6:46:22 (34,637)
O'Donnell, Mark....4:16:43 (14,893)
O'Donnell, Mark....5:08:40 (27,305)
O'Donnell, Michael T....5:01:52 (26,118)
O'Donnell, Paul V....3:05:17 (1,492)
O'Donnell, Thomas E....3:57:24 (9,949)
O'Donoghue, Robert....5:50:19 (32,288)
O'Donoghue, Thomas....3:04:29 (1,425)
O'Donovan, Chris....3:55:42 (9,429)
O'Donovan, Paul....5:24:33 (29,693)
O'Driscoll, Barry....3:19:04 (2,889)
O'Dwyer, Robert D....4:45:57 (22,543)
Oeen, Jan O....3:48:36 (7,741)
Oerlemans, Mari....3:42:57 (6,535)
Oeygard, Svein H....4:19:20 (15,619)
O'Farrell, Michael A....7:37:43 (35,165)
Offa, Christopher J....4:59:46 (25,730)
Offa, John....5:54:10 (32,581)
Offe, Mark....3:47:04 (7,364)
Offer, Malcolm J....5:04:22 (26,578)
Offord, Paul W....5:14:32 (28,266)
Offord, Richard J....4:11:53 (13,581)
O'Flaherty, Lee....3:49:43 (7,981)
O'Flanagan, Martin....4:26:33 (17,616)
O'Flynn, Nicholas A....3:26:47 (3,897)
Ogan, Graham K....5:13:14 (28,029)
Ogborn, Steve D....2:42:54 (263)
Ogden, David M....2:47:46 (398)
Ogden, Richard A....4:39:34 (21,032)
O'Gierman, Andrew....5:32:22 (30,600)
Ogoe, Bernard K....4:36:43 (20,286)
O'Gorman, Neil A....3:46:40 (7,276)
O'Grady, Geoff V....3:34:13 (5,082)
O'Grady, John C....3:03:59 (1,396)
Ogunnaike, Michael A....4:29:50 (18,550)
Ogunyemi, Jackson....5:36:16 (31,022)
O'Hagan, Malcolm E....3:30:59 (4,601)
O'Halloran, Danny M....4:01:11 (10,977)
O'Hanlon, Mark....4:11:32 (13,489)
O'Hanlon, Mike J....4:13:54 (14,112)
O'Hara, Daniel J....4:50:50 (23,699)
O'Hara, Peter....3:02:44 (1,319)
O'Hara, Stephen....4:43:42 (22,033)
O'Hare, Liam....2:48:44 (450)
O'Hare, Terrence S....4:18:21 (15,312)
Ohsiek, Alois....3:45:52 (7,111)
Oishi, Shigeshi....4:01:52 (11,119)
O'Kane, Finbarr M....3:30:36 (4,545)
O'Kane, Sean....4:49:02 (23,246)
O'Keeeffe, Terence G....4:13:45 (14,077)
O'Keefe, David....2:48:24 (429)
O'Keefe, Denis L....3:45:10 (6,984)
O'Keefe, Michael....3:37:14 (5,528)
O'Keefe, Steven....4:19:02 (15,523)
O'Keeffe, Kevin C....4:51:57 (23,919)
O'Keeffe, Neal....5:08:04 (27,229)
Okell, Tim J....5:41:16 (31,535)
Okpeh, Addison O....5:02:41 (26,270)
Oksanen, Risto....3:36:04 (5,350)
Olaso Vega, Magela J....3:05:22 (1,505)
Old, Tom O....4:33:32 (19,444)
Oldale, John....6:31:33 (34,291)
Oldbury, James E....4:46:06 (22,578)
Oldenkott, Hendrik H....3:53:55 (8,958)
Oldfield, Adam P....5:04:14 (26,558)
Oldfield, Christopher J....3:52:38 (8,641)
Oldfield, Richard....4:35:30 (19,975)
Oldfield, Richard....5:22:20 (29,388)
Oldham, Ryan....4:33:47 (19,516)
O'Learm, Patrick C....3:55:27 (9,353)
O'Leary, Benedict P....3:00:39 (1,169)
O'Leary, James A....4:20:48 (16,022)
O'Leary, Sean D....3:51:50 (8,449)
Oleksiewicz, Martin B....2:55:52 (798)
Oliphant, Antony D....4:12:57 (13,869)
Oliphant, Graham R....4:55:28 (24,766)
Olivant, Vernon J....3:20:58 (3,084)
Olive, Daniel....4:10:18 (13,169)
Oliveira, Antonio F....5:21:44 (29,318)
Oliver, Andrew J....4:29:05 (18,334)
Oliver, Danny....3:26:32 (3,854)
Oliver, Earl J....4:35:23 (19,947)
Oliver, John C....4:40:51 (21,348)
Oliver, Jonathan P....4:13:57 (14,131)
Oliver, Martin L....3:52:41 (8,657)
Oliver, Michael....5:45:02 (31,850)
Oliver, Michael F....3:21:18 (3,115)
Oliver, Phillip J....4:50:01 (23,500)
Oliver, Rafael....5:55:40 (32,691)
Oliver, Raymond A....3:46:23 (7,219)
Oliver, Richard T....4:19:12 (15,579)
Oliver, Russell P....4:10:24 (13,204)
Oliver, Steven....3:55:56 (9,498)
Oliver, Steven....5:00:11 (25,813)
Oliver, Stuart M....4:27:53 (18,007)
Oliver-Bellasis, Richard....4:33:25 (19,409)
Olivier, Darrel L....3:52:46 (8,678)
Olivieri, Marco....4:14:34 (14,311)
Ollerhead, Colin....6:47:27 (34,667)
Ollerhead, Richard J....4:14:10 (14,201)
Ollerton, David B....4:25:21 (17,227)
Olliff, Nigel J....5:04:15 (26,561)
Ollington, Jonathan....4:32:25 (19,190)
Ollis, Graham C....4:08:47 (12,764)
O'Loughlin, Paul D....4:18:48 (15,464)
O'Loughlin, Paul M....3:35:20 (5,227)
O'Loughlin, Tim P....3:25:35 (3,685)

Olsen, James T 4:47:07 (22,800)
Olsina, Jacques 3:54:43 (9,158)
Olsina, Michel 4:21:14 (16,124)
Olsson, Bjorn M 3:13:09 (2,263)
Olsson, Gunnar 3:55:03 (9,245)
Oluborode, Anthony 3:53:16 (8,786)
Olver, George W 4:10:14 (13,147)
O'Mahoney, Alan J 4:38:27 (20,745)
O'Mahoney, Patrick J 4:42:27 (21,732)
O'Mahony, James 4:31:06 (18,853)
O'Mahony, John A 3:09:30 (1,857)
O'Malley, Colin M 3:16:12 (2,603)
O'Malley, Jeff P 4:47:38 (22,922)
O'Malley, John R 4:45:37 (22,463)
O'Malley, Mark R 4:14:12 (14,213)
O'Meara, Philip 3:08:07 (1,725)
Omondi, John S 6:18:46 (33,882)
O'Neal, Jeremy S 4:12:22 (13,716)
O'Neil, John F 5:58:58 (32,911)
O'Neil, William 3:09:42 (1,881)
O'Neill, Andy E 3:12:18 (2,175)
O'Neill, David S 3:39:34 (5,927)
O'Neill, Edward F 3:38:57 (5,807)
O'Neill, Gary A 5:21:43 (29,315)
O'Neill, Gerard 3:43:35 (6,665)
O'Neill, Kevin J 3:22:56 (3,290)
O'Neill, Mark J 3:51:26 (8,362)
O'Neill, Michael M 4:23:10 (16,647)
O'Neill, Patrick 4:14:49 (14,385)
O'Neill, Patrick 4:42:37 (21,776)
O'Neill, Robert 4:08:18 (12,636)
O'Neill, Shaun 5:20:12 (29,132)
O'Neill, Spencer J 5:58:05 (32,844)
O'Neill, Stephen D 5:53:34 (32,538)
Ong, Wei Hiam 3:53:17 (8,792)
Onhaus, Thomas 4:26:57 (17,737)
Onions, Tom W 3:29:22 (4,333)
O'Nions, Darren 4:55:04 (24,693)
Onslow, Ian B 7:08:19 (34,960)
Oozeerally, Husein 3:50:01 (8,042)
Opdahl, Geir 3:53:25 (8,835)
Oppici, Filippo 3:40:07 (6,019)
Oppitz, Heinz 3:25:16 (3,639)
Or Kam Fat, Patrice N 4:56:27 (25,001)
Orange, Darren G 4:28:03 (18,043)
Orchard, Mark J 3:57:25 (9,958)
Orchard, Paul 6:15:45 (33,773)
O'Reilly, John P 4:31:35 (18,995)
O'Reilly, Martin N 3:49:09 (7,854)
O'Reilly, Richard A 4:50:59 (23,728)
Organ, Philip E 3:17:00 (2,676)
Orhiunu, Wilson 6:21:57 (33,986)
Oriani, Marco 3:59:36 (10,599)
O'Riordan, Michael 3:50:44 (8,194)
O'Riordan, Raymond D 4:09:54 (13,071)
Ormea, Gianbattista 3:35:53 (5,320)
Orme-Smith, James D 3:00:13 (1,141)
Ormisher, Richard 6:46:23 (34,641)
Ormond, John M 5:03:17 (26,400)
Ormond, Paul A 3:35:17 (5,222)
O'Rourke, Martin D 4:53:14 (24,231)
Orpen, James R 4:20:39 (15,978)
Orpwood, Peter S 4:38:41 (20,794)
Orr, Benjamin S 4:12:16 (13,688)
Orr, Billy 2:45:00 (318)
Orr, Danny 4:14:38 (14,325)
Orr, David 3:25:45 (3,710)
Orr, Graeme A 3:12:48 (2,226)
Orr, Jim P 4:19:39 (15,709)
Orr, Wesley 5:18:09 (28,808)
Orridge, David 3:39:02 (5,823)
Orrin, Martin 4:55:06 (24,700)
Orriss, Michael O 3:48:49 (7,792)
Orrock, Duncan J 3:53:53 (8,950)
Orton, Anthony D 4:40:27 (21,243)
Orton, Jamie L 3:48:29 (7,702)
Orton, Sebastian G 3:48:31 (7,715)
Orzechowski, Pawel 4:23:17 (16,683)
Osawe, Iyobosa 4:34:34 (19,732)
Osborn, Kevan 4:58:09 (25,359)
Osborn, Thomas 5:26:10 (29,890)
Osborne, Andrew J 3:26:43 (3,887)
Osborne, Craig A 4:23:26 (16,718)
Osborne, David 3:54:27 (9,088)
Osborne, Douglas 4:32:18 (19,162)
Osborne, Ian R 4:23:27 (16,723)
Osborne, Lee J 4:08:51 (12,787)
Osborne, Mark 5:08:14 (27,253)
Osborne, Martin J 3:27:03 (3,936)
Osborne, Matthew C 4:04:48 (11,817)
Osborne, Nigel K 3:55:34 (9,394)
Osborne, Peter C 3:52:16 (8,547)
Osborne, Peter M 3:20:10 (3,016)
Osborne, Scott S 5:30:54 (30,454)
Osborne, Simon D 3:57:24 (9,949)
Osbourne, Nigel S 4:01:26 (11,032)
Oscroft, Geoffrey A 7:17:07 (35,056)
O'Seaghdha, Diarmuid 2:37:19 (145)
Oseman, James H 3:43:24 (6,639)
Osepian, Franck 6:02:15 (33,093)
O'Shaughnessy, Peter 5:19:04 (28,949)
O'Shea, Gerard D 4:42:41 (21,795)
O'Shea, Peter 3:46:50 (7,314)
O'Shea, Tom G 4:18:10 (15,253)
Osinowo, Remi 4:19:21 (15,624)
Osler, Jon 4:46:58 (22,765)
Osman, Ismat N 5:29:50 (30,341)
Osman, Rick 4:37:46 (20,571)
Osmond, Paul J 4:42:35 (21,765)
Ospital, Jean-Louis 3:54:43 (9,158)
Ostblom, Andersostblom 5:19:43 (29,064)
Oster, Christoph 4:33:52 (19,538)
O'Sullivan, Anthony K 5:22:52 (29,467)
O'Sullivan, Damian 3:09:16 (1,838)
O'Sullivan, Donal G 4:11:14 (13,413)
O'Sullivan, Mark P 6:18:25 (33,867)
O'Sullivan, Peter W 2:45:00 (318)
O'Sullivan, Sonny T 5:21:12 (29,264)
Oswald, Robin J 4:11:59 (13,619)
Oswin, Michael A 3:51:09 (8,294)
Oswin, Raymond G 4:35:53 (20,062)
Otchie, Andrew 5:45:49 (31,924)
Otesanya, Femi 6:58:59 (34,850)
Otley, Robert O 4:30:01 (18,591)
O'Toole, Matthew S 4:09:11 (12,882)
O'Toole, Peter R 4:10:05 (13,109)
Ott, Wolfram 3:56:04 (9,524)
Ottaway, Sean 3:47:55 (7,553)
Otten, Frank T 4:23:59 (16,844)
Ottey, David L 4:52:31 (24,058)
Otto, Kevin 3:34:01 (5,051)
Otto, Wolfgang 5:08:22 (27,267)
Otwal, Mukhtiar S 4:35:22 (19,940)
Oughton, Ben P 5:48:50 (32,168)
Ould, Ben 5:23:57 (29,614)
Ounsley, Howard 3:47:15 (7,403)
Oury, Loren H 6:23:36 (34,042)
Outred, Philip J 3:53:45 (8,922)
Outten, Jonathan 5:10:53 (27,634)
Ovenden, David M 5:34:34 (30,854)
Overby, Martin D 5:06:01 (26,876)
Overman, Karl M 5:53:24 (32,528)
Overstall, Gerald D 3:54:39 (9,139)
Overstall, Richard C 3:45:36 (7,065)
Overton, David C 4:47:52 (22,982)
Overton, Paul R 4:15:54 (14,683)
Owen, Albert 6:17:47 (33,844)
Owen, Andrew 3:47:38 (7,482)
Owen, Andrew M 5:21:58 (29,349)
Owen, Andrew R 3:57:02 (9,828)
Owen, Andy J 4:47:21 (22,845)
Owen, Brennan 6:50:01 (34,709)
Owen, Chris 5:31:23 (30,505)
Owen, Chris A 3:35:55 (5,324)
Owen, Christopher 4:38:19 (20,702)
Owen, Craig 4:35:20 (19,919)
Owen, Daniel 3:48:21 (7,672)
Owen, David A 3:12:48 (2,226)
Owen, Dewi W 7:13:29 (35,020)
Owen, Eugene 3:49:14 (7,872)
Owen, Findlay 5:41:11 (31,527)
Owen, Garry P 6:19:14 (33,897)
Owen, Gary D 5:06:48 (27,017)
Owen, Gary J 4:02:04 (11,175)
Owen, John 6:16:56 (33,822)
Owen, John D 4:26:30 (17,600)
Owen, Kevin 2:48:23 (428)
Owen, Patrick 3:51:40 (8,405)
Owen, Paul C 3:36:27 (5,419)
Owen, Philip C 4:09:01 (12,831)
Owen, Shaun W 3:56:33 (9,675)
Owen, Stanhope 5:18:09 (28,808)
Owen, Stanley E 5:08:11 (27,246)
Owen, Steven D 3:55:11 (9,273)
Owen, Thomas H 3:24:11 (3,470)
Owen, Tim E 5:04:24 (26,583)
Owen, Timothy H 6:01:39 (33,060)
Owen, Wayne 3:33:07 (4,901)
Owen, Will H 5:27:27 (30,037)
Owen, William 4:54:15 (24,489)
Owens, David H 3:17:08 (2,694)
Owens, Desmond A 4:06:38 (12,250)
Owens, Nicholas J 4:20:03 (15,813)
Owens, Philip D 4:21:30 (16,207)
Owen-Smith, Gareth J 4:32:27 (19,196)
Owers, Ian H 5:29:57 (30,356)
Owers, Terry W 7:05:09 (34,926)
Owions, Darren 3:58:18 (10,227)
Ownsworth, Antony A 5:38:11 (31,218)
Oxberry, Paul 4:46:34 (22,684)
Oxley, Chris 3:43:14 (6,595)
Oxley, Philip M 4:29:53 (18,561)
Oyebode, Femi 5:09:55 (27,500)
Oza, Pranav J 5:04:39 (26,622)
Paas, Rainer 4:02:25 (11,250)
Pabi, Hubert 3:06:04 (1,556)
Pace, David A 4:41:28 (21,516)
Pace, Mark F 3:58:36 (10,310)
Pace, Richard 7:15:39 (35,040)
Pacey, Darren M 3:04:06 (1,404)
Pacey, Russell 3:45:11 (6,988)
Pack, Peter C 4:40:40 (21,301)
Pack, Simon E 4:56:10 (24,932)
Packard, Christopher J 4:26:19 (17,542)
Packe, Chris 4:27:31 (17,894)
Packer, Gary 5:38:02 (31,198)
Packer, Jon 4:23:54 (16,827)
Packer, Kerry 5:21:55 (29,339)
Packer, Leigh J 2:57:49 (942)
Packer, Malcolm P 2:44:12 (301)
Packham, David P 5:06:51 (27,029)
Padden, Thomas 3:21:33 (3,138)
Paddick, Phillip 4:26:40 (17,653)
Paddock, Lee S 4:20:35 (15,958)
Padfield, Roy S 4:51:47 (23,888)
Padgett, Marc 3:52:43 (8,664)
Page, Andrew J 3:33:03 (4,893)
Page, David 4:50:36 (23,649)
Page, Geoffrey W 5:26:54 (29,962)
Page, Graham J 5:21:16 (29,271)
Page, Ian W 4:57:47 (25,278)
Page, Jeremy L 3:59:55 (10,701)
Page, Neal S 2:57:43 (932)
Page, Neil G 5:36:17 (31,026)
Page, Nicholas W 4:37:13 (20,416)
Page, Nick V 2:55:22 (758)
Page, Stephen J 3:55:57 (9,501)
Page, Stephen R 4:29:52 (18,555)
Page, Steven D 3:49:38 (7,962)
Page Turner, Edward H 4:34:29 (19,706)
Page-Dove, Max J 4:13:27 (14,003)
Paget, Scott 4:53:47 (24,379)
Paget, Victor L 5:02:02 (26,152)
Pain, Jonathan R 4:45:23 (22,411)
Pain, Thomas J 4:16:39 (14,876)
Paine, Alan R 4:17:00 (14,955)
Paine, Andrew I 6:47:50 (34,674)
Paine, Malcolm A 3:10:17 (1,956)
Paine, Martin C 3:48:46 (7,777)
Painter, Mark D 5:05:53 (26,852)
Pairault, Fabrice 2:59:18 (1,069)
Pais, José R 3:49:17 (7,887)
Paiva, Carlos C 3:59:05 (10,462)
Paiva, Joao M 4:23:22 (16,706)
Pakey, John 4:02:55 (11,374)
Pal, Sukhdev S 4:16:06 (14,738)
Palacios, Emilio 3:19:41 (2,964)
Palchetti, Massimo 3:43:09 (6,581)
Palcic, Raymond 4:57:46 (25,275)

Palfrey, Daryl B 3:10:04 (1,928)
Palfrey, Richard 6:50:01 (34,709)
Palin, Edward J 5:28:51 (30,223)
Paliy, Alexey 3:52:22 (8,569)
Palkowits, Manfred 3:55:15 (9,292)
Pallister, Andrew 4:12:24 (13,726)
Pallister, Paul G 3:34:21 (5,101)
Palluotto, Anthony 5:11:32 (27,745)
Palmer, Andrew 4:44:53 (22,293)
Palmer, Andrew E 4:42:22 (21,714)
Palmer, Benjamin C 5:30:35 (30,421)
Palmer, David C 3:38:56 (5,802)
Palmer, Drew 3:46:01 (7,140)
Palmer, Graeme 5:00:21 (25,856)
Palmer, Graham F 4:06:26 (12,197)
Palmer, Ian R 3:53:22 (8,825)
Palmer, Jason M 2:53:28 (658)
Palmer, Karl 4:34:07 (19,601)
Palmer, Kelvin J 3:18:45 (2,855)
Palmer, Kenneth L 3:09:09 (1,828)
Palmer, Kevin N 4:09:30 (12,963)
Palmer, Lee 5:05:20 (26,756)
Palmer, Mervyn G 4:16:43 (14,893)
Palmer, Nicholas M 4:45:05 (22,347)
Palmer, Paul R 4:09:43 (13,016)
Palmer, Richard C 4:07:56 (12,561)
Palmer, Robert G 4:34:25 (19,695)
Palmer, Rod H 3:35:01 (5,186)
Palmer, Roy N 2:37:52 (154)
Palmer, Sandy G 4:26:01 (17,441)
Palmer, Stephen J 6:18:33 (33,875)
Palmer, Wayne A 5:20:23 (29,158)
Palser, Graham V 3:57:48 (10,076)
Pampel, Scott M 3:45:35 (7,063)
Pampellone, Wayne 5:48:22 (32,131)
Pamplin, John 4:36:32 (20,235)
Panayiotou, Savvas 3:13:07 (2,260)
Pandit, David 4:30:29 (18,722)
Pandit, Steph J 4:04:15 (11,696)
Panditharatna, Asi 5:18:28 (28,854)
Panesar, Harpal 3:57:54 (10,110)
Pang, David 4:21:25 (16,179)
Pang, Hang 4:00:34 (10,857)
Pankhania, Ashok 4:59:13 (25,610)
Pankhania, Mahendra M 7:32:25 (35,147)
Pannell, Stephen 3:37:10 (5,521)
Pansegrau, Erhard 4:36:56 (20,339)
Pantel, Sascha 3:06:59 (1,633)
Papasolomontos, Anastasios 4:15:54 (14,683)
Papay, Barnaby 4:50:15 (23,548)
Papi, Shaun P 5:30:56 (30,461)
Papworth, Alex J 4:39:58 (21,129)
Papworth, Jonathan R 5:09:32 (27,442)
Paramor, Jon 3:27:35 (4,033)
Paramore, Ian 2:46:06 (352)
Parashar, Anuraag 5:46:43 (31,995)
Parayre, Ludovic 4:34:57 (19,842)
Parazzoli, Carlo 3:08:17 (1,741)
Pardoe, Christopher 4:35:37 (20,002)
Parello, Salvatore 3:11:47 (2,116)
Parent, Serge J 3:55:08 (9,258)
Parfitt, Dean J 4:03:14 (11,440)
Parfrey, Robert T 3:32:20 (4,793)
Pargeter, Matthew J 4:53:00 (24,174)
Pargiter, David R 3:43:16 (6,610)
Parikh, Pranav 5:14:45 (28,308)
Paris, Christophe 3:30:59 (4,601)
Parish, David J 4:00:29 (10,828)
Parish, George W 4:34:55 (19,831)
Park, Alistair R 4:29:12 (18,365)
Park, Desmond 4:50:54 (23,711)
Park, Geoffrey 6:59:23 (34,859)
Park, Graham R 4:11:55 (13,597)
Park, Gregor J 3:25:12 (3,624)
Park, John 3:34:18 (5,096)
Park, Louise E 6:45:07 (34,619)
Park, Nicholas W 3:11:04 (2,040)
Parker, Andrew C 4:30:29 (18,722)
Parker, Brian W 3:43:06 (6,573)
Parker, Christian M 7:03:29 (34,909)
Parker, Christopher 4:38:44 (20,809)
Parker, Colin 5:45:30 (31,896)
Parker, Dave C 4:30:43 (18,772)
Parker, David 5:36:40 (31,074)
Parker, George 4:48:35 (23,143)
Parker, Graham 4:01:49 (11,114)
Parker, Harry B 4:06:53 (12,311)
Parker, James L 4:43:20 (21,943)
Parker, Jason R 4:38:50 (20,836)
Parker, John S 4:11:32 (13,489)
Parker, Jonathan 4:42:13 (21,683)
Parker, Kent A 3:39:52 (5,977)
Parker, Kevin R 4:05:26 (11,978)
Parker, Lee 4:10:42 (13,267)
Parker, Malcolm G 4:10:18 (13,169)
Parker, Matthew J 4:15:33 (14,593)
Parker, Michael A 3:23:45 (3,410)
Parker, Muir A 4:44:32 (22,217)
Parker, Nick A 4:12:42 (13,805)
Parker, Richard A 4:19:26 (15,647)
Parker, Richard D 3:53:58 (8,968)
Parker, Robert B 4:16:27 (14,828)
Parker, Robert J 3:53:25 (8,835)
Parker, Robin 4:14:52 (14,403)
Parker, Roger C 4:16:16 (14,786)
Parker, Roger W 5:19:32 (29,038)
Parker, Simon P 3:58:19 (10,232)
Parker, Stephen 3:16:14 (2,607)
Parker, Stuart M 4:07:01 (12,350)
Parker, Terence T 4:54:24 (24,525)
Parker-Seale, Neil 4:53:22 (24,265)
Parkes, Daniel J 4:52:36 (24,074)
Parkes, Dave A 3:37:29 (5,578)
Parkes, David J 4:01:28 (11,041)
Parkes, Jasprit S 4:40:07 (21,157)
Parkes, Matthew W 4:23:04 (16,619)
Parkes, Roy S 4:00:29 (10,828)
Parkes, Thomas R 4:20:37 (15,968)
Parkes, Tim J 4:49:36 (23,388)
Parkin, Andrew G 4:34:58 (19,847)
Parkin, Andrew J 5:24:23 (29,670)
Parkin, Geogre E 4:05:51 (12,057)
Parkin, Keith 2:56:44 (865)
Parkin, Paul 3:48:37 (7,745)
Parkin, Shaun M 3:15:47 (2,547)
Parkin, Thomas B 5:25:25 (29,793)
Parkin, Timothy 4:13:20 (13,975)
Parkington, David 2:45:25 (333)
Parkins, Colin 3:29:35 (4,369)
Parkinson, Fraser N 4:45:49 (22,504)
Parkinson, Gary R 4:20:00 (15,802)
Parkinson, Ian L 4:27:11 (17,798)
Parkinson, Simon R 3:30:07 (4,469)
Parks, Ian 5:33:15 (30,695)
Parks, Nicholas J 3:39:38 (5,935)
Parks, Robbie M 3:28:04 (4,118)
Parlato, Shane D 5:27:58 (30,097)
Parlour, Stephen 4:18:01 (15,212)
Parmenter, Robert A 5:03:01 (26,344)
Parmentier, Michel 4:45:53 (22,516)
Parmiter, Thomas M 4:48:20 (23,083)
Parnall, Matthew J 4:19:59 (15,797)
Parnell, Adam J 4:09:08 (12,870)
Parnell, Christopher J 4:23:37 (16,756)
Parnell, John L 3:38:18 (5,699)
Parnell, Robert M 4:26:37 (17,636)
Parnell, Stephen 4:30:50 (18,805)
Parr, Christopher G 3:56:21 (9,620)
Parr, Richard P 4:39:16 (20,957)
Parreno Penarubia, Vicente 3:51:38 (8,398)
Parr-Ferris, Len 4:28:54 (18,274)
Parris, Sebastian H 4:24:08 (16,886)
Parrish, Keith J 3:35:36 (5,279)
Parrish, Robin A 5:02:55 (26,325)
Parrott, Lee B 4:50:47 (23,690)
Parrott, Neil S 5:27:46 (30,072)
Parrott, Nicholas C 4:44:52 (22,291)
Parry, Ashley 2:45:39 (336)
Parry, Colin R 4:25:29 (17,280)
Parry, Duffy E 4:36:59 (20,350)
Parry, Haydn R 4:56:48 (25,095)
Parry, Ian G 4:46:19 (22,626)
Parry, Kenneth 4:54:56 (24,648)
Parry, Kevin S 3:21:13 (3,105)
Parry, Malcolm 3:48:27 (7,692)
Parry, Martyn K 4:08:18 (12,636)
Parry, Timothy 4:07:41 (12,493)
Parry, William 4:37:56 (20,603)
Parsell, Howard V 2:34:57 (112)
Parsison, Keith R 4:37:42 (20,554)
Parsley, Elvis I 2:50:40 (524)
Parson, Andrew F 4:29:16 (18,390)
Parson, Robert M 4:29:15 (18,379)
Parsons, Andrew 3:23:20 (3,355)
Parsons, Andy 4:28:06 (18,057)
Parsons, Ben 4:42:04 (21,640)
Parsons, David 3:53:31 (8,861)
Parsons, Edward D 4:20:19 (15,892)
Parsons, Glen A 4:20:34 (15,954)
Parsons, Graham T 4:31:42 (19,022)
Parsons, Ian G 3:23:00 (3,294)
Parsons, Larry 5:15:00 (28,340)
Parsons, Lee 5:51:01 (32,338)
Parsons, Marc R 4:52:27 (24,041)
Parsons, Michael E 5:05:39 (26,813)
Parsons, Oliver J 3:00:23 (1,149)
Parsons, Richard J 4:27:58 (18,025)
Parsons, Rick A 3:03:32 (1,366)
Parsons, Robert F 7:00:25 (34,875)
Parsons, Roger J 4:28:45 (18,234)
Parsons, Russell W 4:04:59 (11,856)
Parsons, William 5:16:53 (28,620)
Parton, Michael 5:10:51 (27,624)
Parton, Terence 3:48:04 (7,606)
Parton, Timothy D 5:22:22 (29,398)
Partridge, Christopher A 5:07:48 (27,189)
Partridge, David A 4:57:58 (25,319)
Partridge, Keith G 3:08:56 (1,806)
Partridge, Roland W 3:56:06 (9,538)
Partridge, Simon D 3:01:58 (1,260)
Partridge, Simon P 4:43:22 (21,949)
Partridge, Stephen L 3:50:00 (8,038)
Partridge, Timothy 4:28:09 (18,075)
Pascoe, Alexander 4:34:41 (19,762)
Pascoe, Chris J 5:20:54 (29,224)
Pascoe, John A 4:20:36 (15,962)
Pascoe, Matthew J 3:27:14 (3,965)
Pascoe, Simon P 4:18:27 (15,350)
Pascucci, Alessandro 3:00:02 (1,132)
Pask, Adrian J 4:18:06 (15,236)
Pask, Christopher D 4:24:43 (17,047)
Pask, Neil 4:38:47 (20,825)
Paskins, Paul N 3:38:50 (5,781)
Pasquale, Guerino 3:27:14 (3,965)
Pass, Ian J 3:33:49 (5,014)
Pass, Steve J 3:58:32 (10,296)
Passeri, Massimo 3:11:05 (2,041)
Passingham, Keith W 4:24:32 (17,001)
Pastorino, Fabio 3:37:19 (5,539)
Pastorino, Simone 4:17:28 (15,088)
Pataky, Joseph A 5:37:26 (31,133)
Patch, Martin R 4:54:30 (24,551)
Patchell, Thomas E 5:27:46 (30,072)
Patchett, Mark J 5:17:31 (28,719)
Pate, Thomas 4:14:59 (14,437)
Patel, Alpesh P 4:39:53 (21,106)
Patel, Anil 4:57:12 (25,173)
Patel, Arvind 4:52:25 (24,034)
Patel, Ashok K 4:16:21 (14,811)
Patel, Bejal K 4:49:36 (23,388)
Patel, Dee 3:06:25 (1,585)
Patel, Dee 5:58:10 (32,852)
Patel, Hinesh 7:00:08 (34,869)
Patel, Hitesh 4:14:42 (14,346)
Patel, Keiran A 4:16:28 (14,834)
Patel, Mahendra K 3:57:55 (10,116)
Patel, Mitesh T 3:59:21 (10,533)
Patel, Naren M 5:28:26 (30,180)
Patel, Praful A 4:51:52 (23,903)
Patel, Raj 3:41:19 (6,238)
Patel, Ramesh J 6:43:43 (34,588)
Patel, Sailesh 5:59:14 (32,927)
Patel, Sandip R 5:47:33 (32,063)
Patel, Sanjai V 4:48:11 (23,048)
Patel, Sasha 4:16:56 (14,939)
Patel, Vijay G 4:55:57 (24,888)
Patel, Yakub 5:33:44 (30,751)
Paterlini, Francesco 5:15:08 (28,356)
Paterson, Alastair R 3:05:03 (1,470)

Paterson, Douglas 2:58:49 (1,016)
Paterson, Duncan 5:30:13 (30,385)
Paterson, Keith 3:23:34 (3,385)
Paterson, Malcolm G 4:50:18 (23,564)
Paterson, Peter L 5:21:00 (29,236)
Paterson, Stephen J 2:57:45 (937)
Paterson, Stuart M 3:57:17 (9,915)
Patey, Daniel F 5:27:12 (29,999)
Patience, James 5:12:24 (27,886)
Patience, Kevin S 4:12:29 (13,742)
Patient, Philip R 5:51:35 (32,380)
Patissou, Patrick 3:56:20 (9,614)
Paton, Bruce M 3:41:58 (6,370)
Paton, Callum C 5:30:39 (30,427)
Paton, Colin 2:39:13 (179)
Paton, Douglas A 3:13:57 (2,353)
Paton, Philip S 3:44:50 (6,919)
Patrick, Andrew K 4:31:06 (18,853)
Patrick, Andy W 5:35:14 (30,928)
Patrick, Mark A 4:50:06 (23,514)
Patrick, Martin K 4:57:31 (25,230)
Patrick, Paul C 4:15:24 (14,551)
Patsalides, Tass 4:30:30 (18,731)
Pattani, Bhupendra 4:49:21 (23,326)
Patten, Paul G 5:46:56 (32,010)
Patten, William 4:25:41 (17,341)
Patterson, David 4:58:35 (25,463)
Patterson, Dean K 3:56:25 (9,637)
Patterson, Grant A 3:33:29 (4,957)
Patterson, Jay L 3:58:11 (10,184)
Patterson, John 3:48:30 (7,709)
Patterson, Richard E 4:56:45 (25,083)
Patterson, Stephen 6:29:09 (34,224)
Pattinson, Gary 4:24:43 (17,047)
Pattinson, Kent 5:14:05 (28,182)
Pattinson, Neill C 2:56:58 (883)
Pattison, Andrew 4:06:59 (12,340)
Pattison, Gary 5:42:22 (31,618)
Pattison, Mark 4:44:49 (22,276)
Pattman, Christian A 5:31:56 (30,553)
Pattni, Sharad B 6:20:22 (33,933)
Patton, Ben M 4:45:48 (22,498)
Patton, Robert W 4:46:36 (22,688)
Patwal, General S 6:11:54 (33,608)
Paul, Alastair J 4:06:39 (12,252)
Paul, Bob H 4:52:02 (23,944)
Paul, David W 4:25:45 (17,365)
Paul, Jonathan M 4:02:37 (11,296)
Paul, Ray J 4:46:01 (22,554)
Paul, Stuart S 3:25:29 (3,668)
Pauley, George D 3:06:38 (1,604)
Paulson, Michael R 5:18:29 (28,860)
Pauzers, Valdis I 3:13:11 (2,266)
Pavitt, Stuart 5:48:47 (32,161)
Pavlik, Ambroz 4:00:09 (10,756)
Pawar, Gurmej S 4:47:25 (22,861)
Pawlett, Mark 4:06:49 (12,288)
Pawlowski, Francis 4:41:57 (21,615)
Pawsey, Christian O 3:56:16 (9,589)
Pawson, Mark C 4:24:00 (16,851)
Pawson, Rob 3:42:35 (6,477)
Pay, Keri A 5:54:20 (32,591)
Payet-Gaspard, Timothee 4:02:03 (11,170)
Payn, John E 4:34:54 (19,825)
Payne, Andrew C 5:10:33 (27,579)
Payne, Andrew G 5:58:07 (32,849)
Payne, Andrew M 4:17:57 (15,189)
Payne, Anthony 3:07:56 (1,708)
Payne, Anthony C 3:50:33 (8,158)
Payne, Charles J 4:04:44 (11,801)
Payne, Dave R 3:24:18 (3,486)
Payne, David 4:09:31 (12,967)
Payne, Garry P 2:32:36 (89)
Payne, Gary 5:02:16 (26,194)
Payne, Gavin R 4:14:01 (14,152)
Payne, George E 5:58:49 (32,894)
Payne, Ian F 4:28:55 (18,279)
Payne, James N 5:08:13 (27,248)
Payne, Kevin J 4:10:23 (13,194)
Payne, Kevin L 4:39:10 (20,916)
Payne, Matthew 5:08:58 (27,350)
Payne, Michael J 4:49:36 (23,388)
Payne, Mike 4:16:34 (14,851)
Payne, Neil J 4:14:11 (14,207)
Payne, Neil T 4:08:05 (12,587)
Payne, Robert 3:56:30 (9,663)
Payne, Stephen R 5:11:42 (27,769)
Payne, Stephen T 3:46:07 (7,164)
Payne, Steve 2:33:42 (100)
Payne, Steven C 5:39:46 (31,393)
Peabody, Ian 4:05:40 (12,019)
Peace, Andrew G 5:26:27 (29,917)
Peace, Ian D 5:22:31 (29,423)
Peace, Kevin M 4:02:04 (11,175)
Peace, Michael S 3:10:37 (1,992)
Peach, Andrew 4:59:35 (25,682)
Peach, Jonathan R 3:31:09 (4,621)
Peach, Jonathan R 6:36:12 (34,413)
Peach, Tony M 3:25:48 (3,716)
Peachey, Ian J 4:50:34 (23,645)
Peachey, Michael 3:11:24 (2,069)
Peacock, David 3:59:00 (10,430)
Peacock, David M 4:11:23 (13,450)
Peacock, Jimmy K 6:31:26 (34,289)
Peacock, Oliver 3:46:05 (7,158)
Peacock, Paul M 5:44:28 (31,800)
Peacock, Robert J 3:28:05 (4,120)
Peacock, Simon 4:39:11 (20,923)
Peacock, Steven M 5:17:44 (28,745)
Peacock, Trevor 3:52:08 (8,512)
Pead, Jeffrey 5:45:16 (31,876)
Pead, Mark S 3:28:29 (4,194)
Peak, Daniel 4:12:07 (13,642)
Peake, Andrew J 3:50:20 (8,112)
Peaple, Derek J 2:57:37 (928)
Pearce, Adam 4:09:58 (13,085)
Pearce, Andrew I 3:40:57 (6,171)
Pearce, Andrew R 4:33:39 (19,473)
Pearce, Andrew R 4:57:02 (25,138)
Pearce, Ashley D 3:06:29 (1,594)
Pearce, Christopher J 4:30:39 (18,760)
Pearce, David 2:41:44 (237)
Pearce, David K 4:36:53 (20,328)
Pearce, David M 3:40:04 (6,010)
Pearce, Glyn 5:41:10 (31,525)
Pearce, Ian J 4:43:49 (22,058)
Pearce, James 3:51:04 (8,274)
Pearce, Lee M 3:16:10 (2,600)
Pearce, Michael D 4:37:23 (20,469)
Pearce, Paul 2:37:56 (156)
Pearce, Paul G 5:35:08 (30,922)
Pearce, Raymond 2:44:12 (301)
Pearce, Richard W 4:44:53 (22,293)
Pearce, Robert 3:25:14 (3,631)
Pearce, Stephen E 5:04:11 (26,554)
Pearce, Steve 4:01:52 (11,119)
Pearce, Tim W 3:46:39 (7,274)
Pearcey, David F 4:04:03 (11,650)
Pearch, Sam S 3:15:09 (2,491)
Peard, Kelvin M 4:56:07 (24,920)
Pearman, Glynn M 4:31:44 (19,029)
Pears, Bryan M 3:50:15 (8,097)
Pearsall, Quenten 4:20:43 (15,995)
Pearse, Michael R 6:20:46 (33,944)
Pearse, Morgan 5:47:41 (32,074)
Pearson, Andrew 4:23:15 (16,669)
Pearson, Andrew J 3:29:06 (4,296)
Pearson, Anthony 4:08:16 (12,631)
Pearson, Charlie P 3:24:12 (3,472)
Pearson, Christopher J 3:19:39 (2,960)
Pearson, Don 3:14:51 (2,466)
Pearson, Hugh A 3:14:19 (2,394)
Pearson, Ian 4:07:50 (12,537)
Pearson, James J 4:33:40 (19,477)
Pearson, James M 4:07:44 (12,510)
Pearson, Lewis N 5:30:01 (30,363)
Pearson, Martin J 3:35:28 (5,255)
Pearson, Michael D 4:31:56 (19,069)
Pearson, Michael W 4:14:42 (14,346)
Pearson, Peter E 4:55:32 (24,777)
Pearson, Simon G 6:55:55 (34,810)
Pearson, Toby S 2:55:07 (748)
Pearson, William E 4:51:02 (23,741)
Pease, Alastair K 3:43:31 (6,654)
Peasgood, David M 4:08:38 (12,722)
Peat, Dan 5:09:50 (27,489)
Peats, Michael D 4:22:36 (16,503)
Peberdy, Jon M 5:55:11 (32,654)
Peck, Adrian J 4:54:11 (24,471)
Peck, Adrian J 4:59:34 (25,675)
Peck, Andrew 5:41:50 (31,583)
Peck, Barry M 6:00:54 (33,025)
Peck, Simon G 5:55:13 (32,660)
Peckett, Graham N 5:44:25 (31,795)
Peckett, Jason M 5:42:06 (31,600)
Pecoraro, Antonio 2:49:04 (470)
Pedder-Smith, Stephen M 3:12:12 (2,166)
Pedgrift, Alexander A 4:48:15 (23,065)
Pedlar, Charlie 3:07:44 (1,695)
Pedler, Martin N 4:30:48 (18,793)
Pedrick, Bruce I 4:06:34 (12,232)
Pedrolli, Fabrizio 4:13:24 (13,990)
Peek, Steven J 5:35:37 (30,960)
Peel, Benjamin 4:59:04 (25,581)
Peel, Chris 3:55:48 (9,461)
Peel, Derrick K 5:06:41 (26,998)
Peel, Jonathan 5:25:43 (29,826)
Peel, Mike 4:36:09 (20,117)
Peer, André 3:02:06 (1,268)
Peers, Alan 3:56:04 (9,524)
Peers, Andrew G 4:54:30 (24,551)
Peers, Richard 3:50:12 (8,084)
Peers, Ryan A 4:53:22 (24,265)
Peers, Wayne V 4:58:39 (25,478)
Peerwala, Joy N 4:31:15 (18,898)
Peet, David J 5:28:17 (30,164)
Pegna, Robin 4:36:37 (20,258)
Peigne, Vincent 2:23:17 (37)
Peill, Charles 4:33:32 (19,444)
Peirce, Gary B 3:52:38 (8,641)
Peitzmann, Martin 3:28:02 (4,109)
Pekrul, Jorn 4:34:54 (19,825)
Peleszok, Matthew J 5:39:11 (31,332)
Peligra, Carmelo 3:54:15 (9,034)
Pell, David J 4:26:52 (17,706)
Pell, Gary 4:35:44 (20,026)
Pell, Ryden 5:31:00 (30,470)
Pells, Colin G 3:34:47 (5,159)
Peluso, Antonio 4:05:53 (12,068)
Pelzer, Horst 3:31:59 (4,744)
Pelzer, Thomas 4:41:34 (21,542)
Pemberton, Alan R 2:59:20 (1,073)
Pemberton, Anthony 5:33:55 (30,768)
Pemberton, Gareth J 3:05:43 (1,531)
Pemberton, Robin 3:43:35 (6,665)
Pena, Antonio 2:14:31 (12)
Pena, Dominique 4:33:18 (19,385)
Pena, Paulo A 4:57:59 (25,324)
Penaluna, Karl S 4:19:59 (15,797)
Pender, Jon R 3:46:06 (7,161)
Pender, Kieren P 5:07:08 (27,081)
Pendered, William M 3:35:45 (5,305)
Pendlebury, David S 4:59:09 (25,593)
Pendleton, David J 5:07:09 (27,086)
Pendred, Stuart G 6:10:57 (33,572)
Pendrill, Steven C 3:48:03 (7,598)
Penfold, Andrew P 3:30:30 (4,526)
Penfold, Colin M 5:48:06 (32,102)
Peng, Michael 4:06:50 (12,297)
Penger, Matthew J 4:12:09 (13,650)
Pengilly, Keith J 3:51:40 (8,405)
Penhale, Bruce 3:05:11 (1,483)
Peniche, Hector 4:43:08 (21,895)
Penkner, Johann 3:34:46 (5,156)
Penman, Andrew 4:41:51 (21,599)
Penman, Jeff D 4:40:10 (21,175)
Penman, Steve L 4:41:27 (21,511)
Penn, Chris A 3:14:50 (2,465)
Penn, John 4:25:17 (17,211)
Penn, Jon 4:15:36 (14,607)
Penn, Kevin A 5:02:36 (26,250)
Penn, Timothy J 3:55:36 (9,403)
Pennacchiotti, Marco 2:59:37 (1,099)
Pennells, Derek 4:59:53 (25,752)
Penney, Andrew D 2:57:48 (941)
Penney, Bob 4:08:06 (12,590)
Penney, Stuart A 4:57:12 (25,173)
Penneycard, Matthew J 5:19:18 (28,991)
Pennicott, Derek J 3:55:34 (9,394)

Pennie, Raymond G	4:32:06 (19,109)	
Pennington, Colin	3:57:33 (9,999)	
Pennington, Ian	4:51:41 (23,869)	
Pennington, Jason	4:03:18 (11,462)	
Pennington, Michael	3:50:44 (8,194)	
Pennington, Michael J	2:59:14 (1,059)	
Pennock, Richard	5:31:05 (30,478)	
Penny, Darryl G	4:29:15 (18,379)	
Penny, David A	3:46:37 (7,266)	
Penny, Keith I	4:58:29 (25,438)	
Penny, Mark J	3:44:46 (6,898)	
Pennycook, Dave	4:10:31 (13,230)	
Penrose, Noel R	4:30:49 (18,799)	
Pentin, Richard P	3:03:05 (1,335)	
Pentland, Bob	3:03:36 (1,373)	
Pepi, Valerio	4:44:55 (22,301)	
Pepin, Nick	4:17:59 (15,201)	
Pepper, Ian R	5:26:28 (29,918)	
Pepper, Matthew J	5:00:38 (25,906)	
Peppiatt, Daniel J	4:29:51 (18,551)	
Peppiatt, Malcolm W	5:03:53 (26,500)	
Peralta, Paul C	4:18:56 (15,494)	
Perathoner, Peter	3:05:52 (1,544)	
Perazzini, Fabio	2:35:00 (114)	
Percival, Glenn	6:29:00 (34,220)	
Percival, Mark N	4:21:44 (16,266)	
Percival, Richard	3:26:10 (3,790)	
Percival, Robert W	5:48:49 (32,163)	
Percival-Smith, Paul E	3:31:52 (4,726)	
Perera, Ruwan	5:12:54 (27,984)	
Perez, Allen J	4:56:41 (25,064)	
Perez, Eugenio	6:06:41 (33,367)	
Perez, Jorge M	3:37:59 (5,644)	
Perez, Rafael	5:14:14 (28,214)	
Perez, Rafael	5:14:24 (28,245)	
Perez De Herrasti, Andrés	4:58:21 (25,402)	
Perez Diaz, Kevin A	3:42:50 (6,514)	
Perez Gaspar, Carlos	3:43:13 (6,593)	
Perez-Gaspar, Carlos	2:58:13 (969)	
Perez-Rodriguez, Marcos	4:04:54 (11,839)	
Perin, Germano	3:27:39 (4,047)	
Perkin, Simon L	3:44:14 (6,789)	
Perkins, Christopher	4:13:30 (14,017)	
Perkins, Dominic G	4:41:55 (21,607)	
Perkins, Jeff J	4:23:48 (16,804)	
Perkins, Jeremy C	5:19:24 (29,009)	
Perkins, John D	5:04:45 (26,638)	
Perkins, John P	4:13:49 (14,093)	
Perkins, Martyn	2:55:26 (763)	
Perkins, Phil J	4:22:44 (16,544)	
Perkins, Philip	4:12:19 (13,699)	
Perkins, Simon C	3:59:30 (10,571)	
Perks, Jonathan E	3:38:57 (5,807)	
Perks, Wesley J	4:13:03 (13,894)	
Perret, Jean-Claude	4:25:21 (17,227)	
Perrett, Davydd L	4:54:11 (24,471)	
Perrett, John E	4:09:29 (12,955)	
Perrett, Richard	5:19:14 (28,982)	
Perrett, Royden W	3:31:45 (4,711)	
Perrier, Claude	3:54:40 (9,144)	
Perrin, Ian P	3:36:32 (5,437)	
Perrin, Jonathan A	3:17:21 (2,718)	
Perrin, Mark S	3:24:17 (3,480)	
Perrin, Stephen R	3:01:42 (1,240)	
Perrin, Thierry C	4:31:59 (19,083)	
Perron, Ben R	4:31:47 (19,042)	
Perry, Adrain	3:40:21 (6,064)	
Perry, Dan J	5:11:52 (27,798)	
Perry, David A	3:32:57 (4,882)	
Perry, Giles C	5:29:04 (30,253)	
Perry, Jason M	3:16:15 (2,611)	
Perry, John S	4:33:42 (19,488)	
Perry, Jonathan M	4:41:38 (21,552)	
Perry, Kenneth M	5:38:07 (31,208)	
Perry, Kevin	4:21:11 (16,105)	
Perry, Lee	4:29:31 (18,470)	
Perry, Luke B	5:29:04 (30,253)	
Perry, Mark A	3:35:55 (5,324)	
Perry, Mark T	4:40:46 (21,327)	
Perry, Mathew B	3:19:45 (2,972)	
Perry, Matthew	4:38:26 (20,736)	
Perry, Matthew J	4:09:04 (12,846)	
Perry, Neil J	3:28:06 (4,126)	
Perry, Neil S	3:37:38 (5,592)	
Perry, Robert J	3:06:49 (1,619)	
Perry, Simon D	3:26:37 (3,872)	
Perry, Simon W	3:49:37 (7,958)	
Perry, Stephen	3:12:36 (2,203)	
Perry, Steve	5:08:52 (27,334)	
Perry, Thomas J	4:52:04 (23,954)	
Perry, Tim M	4:11:32 (13,489)	
Perryman-Best, Nevil	4:13:41 (14,064)	
Pers, Barrie J	6:01:12 (33,035)	
Persson, Chris	5:12:42 (27,949)	
Peruzzo, Alberto	5:15:31 (28,421)	
Peruzzo, Rolf	4:39:27 (21,000)	
Peschke, Guido	3:14:08 (2,371)	
Pesenti, Jean-Claude M	3:55:20 (9,315)	
Pesquero, Gary D	3:08:34 (1,766)	
Petagna, Daniele	3:34:36 (5,135)	
Peterges, Udo E	2:50:31 (516)	
Peters, Dan	4:22:32 (16,482)	
Peters, Derren J	4:05:35 (12,003)	
Peters, Gary R	4:20:36 (15,962)	
Peters, John E	3:23:53 (3,437)	
Peters, Michael	4:04:08 (11,670)	
Peters, Nigel J	4:35:04 (19,865)	
Peters, Timothy M	4:58:45 (25,503)	
Petersen, Poul E	4:27:37 (17,926)	
Petersen, Uwe	4:00:04 (10,745)	
Petersen, William A	3:41:32 (6,282)	
Peterson, Calum H	3:41:05 (6,199)	
Peterson, Thomas F	4:26:50 (17,694)	
Petesch, Peter J	4:25:28 (17,273)	
Petherwick, Brian	4:32:42 (19,248)	
Petignat, Henri C	4:08:58 (12,817)	
Petit, Patrick	3:18:30 (2,832)	
Petite, Joe M	4:23:00 (16,600)	
Petk, Jerzy	4:43:56 (22,081)	
Petk, Zygmunt	4:34:49 (19,797)	
Petrides, John G	5:56:57 (32,766)	
Petrie, Al	4:05:25 (11,971)	
Petrie, Christopher C	4:22:36 (16,503)	
Petrie, Gavin R	4:17:22 (15,055)	
Petrou, Peter	4:58:33 (25,455)	
Petrounakos, George	4:12:46 (13,825)	
Petrovic, Darko	4:15:47 (14,656)	
Petruso, Tony	3:43:14 (6,595)	
Petschar, Andreas	2:48:27 (435)	
Pettersen, Mark	5:37:57 (31,191)	
Pettifer, Charles A	4:54:22 (24,518)	
Pettinelli, William	3:36:41 (5,451)	
Pettitt, Martin J	4:29:58 (18,577)	
Pettitt, Nigel M	3:37:24 (5,557)	
Petty-Mayor, Mark E	3:27:34 (4,031)	
Pfaller, Franco	4:23:25 (16,715)	
Pflugi, Andreas	2:58:07 (964)	
Phan-Van-Minh, Bernard	3:40:06 (6,017)	
Phelan, Chris	2:45:13 (325)	
Phelan, Robin	5:06:46 (27,014)	
Phelouzat, Dominique	3:37:23 (5,554)	
Phenis, Wayne P	5:56:44 (32,752)	
Philander, Robin	4:40:12 (21,188)	
Philip, Paul J	4:38:01 (20,627)	
Philippe, Didier	2:56:46 (868)	
Philipps, Edward R	4:00:41 (10,883)	
Philips, George A	7:04:19 (34,915)	
Phillimore, Nicholas P	3:26:11 (3,791)	
Phillips, Alec W	5:02:05 (26,167)	
Phillips, Andrew J	4:42:37 (21,776)	
Phillips, Anthony	4:20:33 (15,948)	
Phillips, Ben J	4:08:44 (12,749)	
Phillips, Chris A	6:00:16 (32,989)	
Phillips, Clifford J	4:07:34 (12,467)	
Phillips, Conor P	5:00:49 (25,940)	
Phillips, Darren	4:02:41 (11,309)	
Phillips, Darren J	4:38:42 (20,799)	
Phillips, Dave R	6:44:52 (34,614)	
Phillips, David	5:26:45 (29,952)	
Phillips, David J	5:21:28 (29,292)	
Phillips, David M	4:20:32 (15,943)	
Phillips, Dean R	4:30:44 (18,778)	
Phillips, Gary	3:21:26 (3,124)	
Phillips, Graeme C	5:14:47 (28,310)	
Phillips, Huw	4:23:18 (16,690)	
Phillips, Huw	4:59:28 (25,655)	
Phillips, Jeremy C	4:43:38 (22,019)	
Phillips, John S	3:26:18 (3,810)	
Phillips, Joshua A	6:00:17 (32,991)	
Phillips, Leonard J	3:33:50 (5,018)	
Phillips, Mark A	3:56:40 (9,714)	
Phillips, Mark A	5:29:00 (30,245)	
Phillips, Mark I	3:50:49 (8,211)	
Phillips, Mike	3:57:04 (9,843)	
Phillips, Paul	3:55:03 (9,245)	
Phillips, Paul D	4:02:31 (11,276)	
Phillips, Peter	3:58:49 (10,393)	
Phillips, Peter F	4:18:59 (15,507)	
Phillips, Richard J	4:28:47 (18,241)	
Phillips, Rob	3:01:11 (1,201)	
Phillips, Roger S	3:47:58 (7,568)	
Phillips, Rowland	7:17:03 (35,050)	
Phillips, Shaun P	3:06:24 (1,581)	
Phillips, Stephen	4:40:07 (21,157)	
Phillips, Steven J	6:00:18 (32,993)	
Phillips, Tom	4:00:34 (10,857)	
Phillips, Wilfred P	5:29:31 (30,310)	
Phillips, William A	4:27:18 (17,825)	
Phillis, Richard G	4:13:35 (14,037)	
Philp, Dean J	4:45:21 (22,401)	
Philpot, David S	3:01:32 (1,223)	
Philpot, Ian D	5:27:31 (30,049)	
Philpott, Garry	5:11:57 (27,814)	
Philpott, Neil	4:03:45 (11,559)	
Philpott, Paul	6:06:43 (33,372)	
Philpotts, Dennis L	4:31:04 (18,849)	
Phimister, Neil A	5:07:31 (27,149)	
Phipps, Andrew J	3:23:23 (3,360)	
Phipps, Daniel J	5:07:50 (27,196)	
Phipps, Kevin M	3:42:58 (6,537)	
Phipps, Matthew D	4:44:34 (22,222)	
Phipps, Richie J	4:13:38 (14,053)	
Phipps, William S	3:37:15 (5,532)	
Phoenix, Ian	4:52:22 (24,027)	
Phypers, David I	4:46:32 (22,675)	
Pianezzi, Xavier	5:06:07 (26,894)	
Picat, Jean M	3:48:22 (7,677)	
Picceni, Daniele	2:31:36 (83)	
Picchi, Guglielmo	3:23:39 (3,394)	
Piccinini, Antonio	3:35:41 (5,293)	
Pichler, Cletus	4:41:59 (21,623)	
Pichler, Maximilian	3:54:32 (9,105)	
Picillo, Gianfranco	4:46:14 (22,609)	
Pick, David	4:49:35 (23,381)	
Pick, David C	4:30:15 (18,667)	
Pick, Gavin M	5:10:58 (27,648)	
Pick, Malcolm E	3:59:56 (10,705)	
Pickard, Edward J	4:50:21 (23,579)	
Pickard, Gareth E	3:28:24 (4,181)	
Pickard, John	4:40:21 (21,221)	
Picker, Christian D	2:59:08 (1,048)	
Pickering, Anthony P	3:19:25 (2,926)	
Pickering, Clive J	3:58:40 (10,338)	
Pickering, David C	2:57:23 (912)	
Pickering, Derrick J	5:41:27 (31,547)	
Pickering, Jon	3:33:40 (4,985)	
Pickering, Joseph N	3:56:30 (9,663)	
Pickering, Richard	3:11:15 (2,058)	
Pickering, Steven	3:23:10 (3,326)	
Pickersgill, Alroy M	4:35:06 (19,873)	
Pickett, Dominique E	3:08:43 (1,784)	
Pickett, Paul E	5:30:33 (30,416)	
Pickford, Shaun R	3:43:00 (6,549)	
Pickin, Lee	5:09:47 (27,482)	
Pickles, Roger L	5:18:24 (28,850)	
Pickthall, Chris	3:52:30 (8,605)	
Pickup, Antony	3:25:43 (3,704)	
Pickup, Jeffrey	3:28:31 (4,201)	
Picozzi, Alberto	3:50:24 (8,122)	
Pidd, Harry B	3:32:40 (4,839)	
Pidgeon, Nick H	3:44:01 (6,746)	
Pierce, Dominic J	3:09:53 (1,908)	
Pierce, Matthew D	4:02:51 (11,352)	
Pierce, Stewart W	3:58:50 (10,397)	
Piercey, Gordon W	4:49:53 (23,469)	
Piercy, Michael P	4:27:50 (17,992)	
Piercy, Neil R	4:27:02 (17,755)	
Pieri, Paolo	4:34:52 (19,811)	
Pierru, Stephane	4:02:52 (11,357)	

Piggot, Gareth D	4:15:49 (14,669)	
Pignagnoli, Sergio	3:57:53 (10,107)	
Pignon, Didier M	3:21:13 (3,105)	
Pigott, Richard	3:55:09 (9,263)	
Pigram, Matthew D	5:40:51 (31,489)	
Piguillem, Simon F	3:00:11 (1,139)	
Pihlens, Mark	4:30:27 (18,712)	
Pike, Andy	6:38:37 (34,476)	
Pike, Christopher	5:11:43 (27,775)	
Pike, David W	2:57:28 (920)	
Pike, Iain R	4:18:57 (15,499)	
Pike, John	5:11:38 (27,760)	
Pike, John L	4:08:54 (12,802)	
Pike, Steven J	4:22:46 (16,550)	
Pikejko, Andy J	4:31:09 (18,866)	
Pilbeam, David M	5:11:32 (27,745)	
Pilch, Richard F	4:09:26 (12,939)	
Pilcher, Martin K	3:33:36 (4,974)	
Pilgrim, Michael J	6:33:20 (34,341)	
Pill, Stephen J	3:48:44 (7,770)	
Pillai, Perumal	4:03:48 (11,576)	
Pillar, David A	4:28:36 (18,195)	
Pilley, Daniel M	5:41:31 (31,553)	
Pilley, John R	5:25:54 (29,854)	
Pilliner, Mark	4:00:13 (10,771)	
Pilliner, Neil J	4:18:19 (15,301)	
Pillinger, Karl S	4:44:45 (22,262)	
Pilot, Colin	4:12:32 (13,752)	
Pilotti, Giuseppe	5:31:55 (30,551)	
Pimlott, Timothy J	4:11:52 (13,574)	
Pinchbeck, Carl J	4:25:00 (17,125)	
Pinches, Joss	3:05:09 (1,479)	
Pinckney, Simon	4:22:33 (16,486)	
Ping, Darren J	4:13:37 (14,046)	
Pink, Robert L	2:55:01 (743)	
Pinkham, Paul K	4:11:16 (13,419)	
Pinkney, Michael E	3:53:53 (8,950)	
Pinner, John	4:08:10 (12,605)	
Pinnick, David	4:13:51 (14,103)	
Pinniger, Anthony R	4:08:12 (12,615)	
Pinniger, David E	5:10:14 (27,531)	
Pinnion, Clive R	2:58:31 (993)	
Pinon, Philippe	3:39:10 (5,843)	
Pinto, Antonio	2:29:22 (66)	
Pinto, Jason C	3:57:15 (9,905)	
Pinto, Tomas	4:23:16 (16,675)	
Piontek, Ray	6:10:41 (33,560)	
Pipe, Tim	3:17:43 (2,759)	
Piper, Alan L	4:41:25 (21,502)	
Piper, Harold N	5:04:24 (26,583)	
Piper, Laurence J	5:46:32 (31,982)	
Piper, Michael	4:16:04 (14,730)	
Piper, Pete	4:38:07 (20,654)	
Piper, Russell W	5:34:26 (30,840)	
Piper, Thomas J	4:53:36 (24,329)	
Piper-Hunter, Allistair R	4:18:28 (15,354)	
Pippard, Mark	5:07:35 (27,156)	
Pires, Arthur F	2:59:18 (1,069)	
Pires, José L	3:53:38 (8,892)	
Pires, Owen E	5:54:26 (32,596)	
Pirie, Chriska M	4:59:17 (25,623)	
Pirozzolo, Mario G	5:06:22 (26,936)	
Pistilli, Stefano	3:17:10 (2,697)	
Pistis, Giovanni	3:08:17 (1,741)	
Pita, José	3:44:40 (6,872)	
Pitchell, Ian	3:28:04 (4,118)	
Pitcher, Alan C	4:06:03 (12,107)	
Pitcher, David J	5:45:31 (31,897)	
Pitcher, Gordon	5:19:26 (29,015)	
Pitcher, Stephen D	4:12:26 (13,734)	
Pitchford, Richard J	5:02:54 (26,320)	
Pitchley, Danny C	4:31:36 (18,997)	
Piterzak, John	4:12:45 (13,817)	
Pitman, Mark A	3:54:21 (9,062)	
Pitman, Rhys G	4:49:41 (23,424)	
Pitney, Simon	4:55:38 (24,799)	
Pitt, Alan	3:05:27 (1,513)	
Pitt, Oliver	4:47:08 (22,802)	
Pitt, Richard W	2:52:20 (603)	
Pitt, Timothy R	3:53:43 (8,917)	
Pitt, William	5:10:26 (27,560)	
Pittam, Daniel T	3:57:04 (9,843)	
Pittavino, Didier	3:43:14 (6,595)	

Pittaway, Mark	2:56:11 (819)	
Pitts, Colin P	2:42:43 (257)	
Pitts, James R	3:51:39 (8,400)	
Pitzalis, Giuseppe	4:21:54 (16,306)	
Pivert, Jean-Baptiste	2:58:31 (993)	
Plachta, Jean-Pierre	3:59:30 (10,571)	
Plank, Tony J	4:02:10 (11,199)	
Planner, Don	5:58:10 (32,852)	
Planner, Stuart	5:58:10 (32,852)	
Plant, Gareth A	3:10:42 (2,000)	
Plant, Lee A	4:22:20 (16,429)	
Plaschy, Stephan	3:51:18 (8,328)	
Plasett, Malcolm	5:13:38 (28,106)	
Plaskett, Gary R	4:52:03 (23,948)	
Plaskett, Warren P	3:57:12 (9,891)	
Plastow, Luke	7:56:29 (35,223)	
Platel, Paul J	4:30:54 (18,819)	
Plato, Anthony	3:57:21 (9,933)	
Platt, David N	4:33:59 (19,566)	
Platt, Gareth E	4:34:08 (19,604)	
Platt, Glen Q	5:38:40 (31,274)	
Platt, James S	4:12:49 (13,837)	
Platt, Philip J	5:43:38 (31,731)	
Platt, Raymond E	4:04:33 (11,757)	
Platts, Les M	4:37:17 (20,440)	
Platts, Oliver C	4:59:42 (25,711)	
Platts, Rob	2:59:03 (1,041)	
Platts, Steven B	3:27:27 (4,008)	
Platts, Tom N	3:41:54 (6,360)	
Playford, Alexander J	4:23:15 (16,669)	
Playford, Luke J	4:28:23 (18,137)	
Playford-Smith, Terry R	5:29:20 (30,279)	
Playle, David J	4:48:16 (23,070)	
Plaza, Sergio	3:30:24 (4,506)	
Plaza Fernandez, Francisco	4:25:40 (17,337)	
Pleasance, Barrie M	4:37:08 (20,399)	
Pleasance, Neal G	4:49:39 (23,411)	
Pledge, Alan D	3:38:41 (5,753)	
Pledger, Phil I	3:52:42 (8,661)	
Plenderleith, Scott M	3:50:57 (8,148)	
Pliego-Moreno, Ivan	4:20:01 (15,807)	
Plimmer, James M	4:28:47 (18,241)	
Plimmer, Peter S	3:17:42 (2,754)	
Plougoulm, Philippe	4:36:28 (20,220)	
Plowman, Barry	3:21:48 (3,166)	
Plowman, David A	5:23:32 (29,547)	
Plowman, Robin	5:02:57 (26,329)	
Pluck, Colin	4:14:12 (14,213)	
Pluckrose, Allan	3:55:34 (9,394)	
Plumb, Steven J	3:53:10 (8,762)	
Plumbley, Andrew I	4:41:03 (21,407)	
Plummer, Bradley C	3:20:21 (3,031)	
Plummer, Lee C	4:41:16 (21,468)	
Plummer, Martin	5:23:23 (29,526)	
Plummer, Matthew R	4:09:10 (12,878)	
Plummer, Simon R	3:49:57 (8,026)	
Plumstead, Mark K	3:05:35 (1,524)	
Plumtree, David K	4:11:55 (13,597)	
Plunkett, Douglas T	4:03:03 (11,398)	
Plunkett, Mark D	3:48:36 (7,741)	
Plush, Christopher	4:47:32 (22,889)	
Plutino, Sebastiano	4:48:30 (23,124)	
Plykker, Jakob M	4:05:53 (12,068)	
Plyte, Mark K	6:12:30 (33,643)	
Pocklington, Paul D	4:04:37 (11,774)	
Pocock, Francis C	5:28:52 (30,229)	
Pocock, Frank	4:48:11 (23,048)	
Pocock, John W	3:31:28 (4,675)	
Pocock, Michael J	3:30:46 (4,576)	
Pocock, Michael S	4:47:50 (22,974)	
Pocock, Toby	5:04:14 (26,558)	
Podbury, James	3:20:26 (3,040)	
Podini, Lorenzo	4:00:37 (10,871)	
Podmore, Anthony W	7:11:34 (34,997)	
Pogson, Andrew D	4:49:00 (23,235)	
Pohl, David M	6:50:10 (34,726)	
Pointon, Nicholas	5:02:35 (26,245)	
Poirier, Richard	3:44:10 (6,779)	
Poke, Victor	5:52:11 (32,423)	
Pol, Henk	3:34:07 (5,063)	
Pol, Jan	3:34:06 (5,061)	
Pollard, Darren P	3:54:50 (9,193)	
Pollard, Ian	4:25:33 (17,302)	

Pollard, Ian C	5:45:26 (31,892)	
Pollard, Michael R	4:55:50 (24,856)	
Pollard, Nicholas J	4:37:21 (20,457)	
Pollard, Robert J	4:37:45 (20,567)	
Pollard, Scott B	4:19:52 (15,767)	
Pollen, Samuel	3:31:21 (4,658)	
Pollett, Derek J	3:56:02 (9,518)	
Polley, Keith A	4:53:53 (24,394)	
Pollicelli, Giovanni	3:19:26 (2,927)	
Pollock, Austin G	4:35:32 (19,984)	
Pollock, David J	3:19:52 (2,983)	
Pollock, Jeremy R	2:51:28 (561)	
Pollock, Neil	2:48:22 (427)	
Pollock, Robert A	3:13:44 (2,330)	
Pollock, William M	5:17:29 (28,713)	
Pollok, Scott R	4:23:42 (16,776)	
Pomerance, Alex R	4:41:05 (21,412)	
Pommen, Wayne L	3:34:02 (5,053)	
Pommier, Georges V	5:15:43 (28,445)	
Ponce-Taylor, Daniel J	3:59:05 (10,462)	
Ponchelle, Jerome R	3:57:02 (9,828)	
Pond, Andrew J	4:15:08 (14,487)	
Pond, Chris	4:13:42 (14,068)	
Pond, Christopher M	3:25:31 (3,677)	
Pond, Shaun J	3:47:41 (7,496)	
Ponder, Geoffrey C	5:51:32 (32,375)	
Pontet, Christopher E	5:07:04 (27,072)	
Pook, Richard	4:05:22 (11,961)	
Pook, Simon	6:17:51 (33,846)	
Pool, Richard	3:26:04 (3,778)	
Poole, Grayson J	4:10:58 (13,339)	
Poole, John A	3:48:01 (7,587)	
Poole, Stephen G	4:10:27 (13,217)	
Pooley, Michael	4:56:55 (25,117)	
Poolman, Alexander I	3:24:45 (3,548)	
Popat, Vishal	5:38:58 (31,306)	
Pope, Alan G	3:25:39 (3,695)	
Pope, Bob	3:47:03 (7,362)	
Pope, Brian R	3:47:59 (7,573)	
Pope, Christopher S	4:40:52 (21,352)	
Pope, Robert P	4:34:30 (19,711)	
Pope, Stuart M	5:11:33 (27,749)	
Popham, Andrew H	3:56:42 (9,726)	
Popham, Brett	3:14:30 (2,416)	
Popplewell, Alex H	4:52:58 (24,166)	
Poptgieter, Rudolph	3:35:01 (5,186)	
Porada, Wolfgang	4:06:47 (12,283)	
Poree, Thierry	4:30:24 (18,702)	
Porre, Roland	4:11:41 (13,534)	
Porreca, Julian	4:30:06 (18,621)	
Porro, Riccardo	3:39:35 (5,928)	
Porteous, Henry J	3:10:39 (1,996)	
Porter, Allen D	4:46:45 (22,719)	
Porter, Barry	4:19:58 (15,792)	
Porter, Brian	4:03:20 (11,469)	
Porter, Daniel J	3:26:33 (3,857)	
Porter, Jonathan E	3:50:03 (8,051)	
Porter, Keith	4:51:21 (23,809)	
Porter, Liam C	3:41:47 (6,333)	
Porter, Mitchell	4:41:56 (21,610)	
Porter, Roger A	3:42:01 (6,379)	
Porter, Sean J	4:46:03 (22,562)	
Porter, Stanley V	4:20:32 (15,943)	
Porter, Stephen J	3:48:47 (7,780)	
Portmann, Zeno	2:56:13 (824)	
Portnoi, Josh S	4:04:36 (11,768)	
Portsmouth, Barry R	5:06:40 (26,995)	
Portsmouth, Stephen G	5:46:00 (31,936)	
Portus, James O	4:01:30 (11,050)	
Portz, James	5:21:51 (29,334)	
Post, Martin J	4:10:20 (13,179)	
Postance, Paul D	4:24:42 (17,043)	
Postings, Ian J	3:50:04 (8,055)	
Postler, Peter	4:14:17 (14,241)	
Postlethwaite, Alan V	3:07:56 (1,708)	
Postlethwaite, Kurt J	5:25:22 (29,784)	
Postma, Bernd	4:20:16 (15,879)	
Potter, Alan W	4:00:21 (10,794)	
Potter, Chris J	3:40:10 (6,031)	
Potter, Christopher D	6:09:14 (33,503)	
Potter, Craig J	5:16:21 (28,527)	
Potter, Darren	5:14:53 (28,324)	
Potter, Francis C	4:43:38 (22,019)	

Potter, Graham M 3:54:31 (9,103)
Potter, Guy R 4:54:32 (24,559)
Potter, James P 4:04:50 (11,822)
Potter, Jarrod M 6:27:28 (34,178)
Potter, Mark E 6:33:56 (34,351)
Potter, Mark J 4:00:01 (10,732)
Potter, Michael J 3:54:30 (9,098)
Potter, Richard T 5:51:28 (32,369)
Pottie, Hector M 3:52:05 (8,500)
Potts, Andrew D 4:21:10 (16,102)
Potts, Christopher G 4:45:54 (22,524)
Potts, Colin I 2:39:41 (195)
Potts, Edward W 4:51:37 (23,855)
Potts, Graham M 4:54:15 (24,489)
Potts, Jonathan R 4:23:49 (16,808)
Potts, Tony 5:00:10 (25,808)
Pouille, Philippe 4:43:32 (21,990)
Poulain, John 5:00:11 (25,813)
Poulter, David W 5:13:26 (28,067)
Poulton, Michael J 4:33:23 (19,403)
Poulton, Richard 5:09:08 (27,377)
Poulton, Tim J 3:57:16 (9,909)
Pound, Rhys 5:23:45 (29,576)
Pound, Stephen 5:08:50 (27,327)
Pounder, Anthony 4:09:29 (12,955)
Pounder, Michael J 3:06:44 (1,611)
Pounder, Nicholas J 3:44:07 (6,763)
Pountney, David J 4:43:15 (21,923)
Pourtau, Jean-François 3:23:01 (3,300)
Povey, Andy 4:04:37 (11,774)
Povey, Karl M 2:51:46 (576)
Povey, Kenneth G 4:23:06 (16,631)
Pow, Brian G 5:07:49 (27,192)
Pow, Simon J 5:07:49 (27,192)
Powell, Alan J 4:34:48 (19,789)
Powell, Andrew D 5:06:02 (26,881)
Powell, Craig A 7:37:49 (35,167)
Powell, David J 4:41:25 (21,502)
Powell, Eliot J 3:29:45 (4,408)
Powell, Gareth T 3:14:16 (2,388)
Powell, John C 4:22:15 (16,407)
Powell, John D 5:24:53 (29,732)
Powell, Martin J 3:45:18 (7,005)
Powell, Michael E 3:24:57 (3,578)
Powell, Nathan C 3:08:00 (1,715)
Powell, Neil 5:00:11 (25,813)
Powell, Neil 5:29:13 (30,265)
Powell, Rhys D 5:00:20 (25,852)
Powell, Richard A 4:51:16 (23,786)
Powell, Robert D 4:17:37 (15,115)
Powell, Russell 4:33:26 (19,415)
Powell, Simon C 3:04:17 (1,414)
Powell, Stephan J 3:21:25 (3,123)
Powell, Stephen D 4:23:40 (16,766)
Powell, Steve 5:38:33 (31,259)
Powell, Tarquin 3:59:17 (10,515)
Powell, William J 4:48:01 (23,014)
Power, Andrew J 3:39:17 (5,864)
Power, Gerald 4:34:30 (19,711)
Power, Greg C 4:51:58 (23,925)
Power, Michael 4:12:16 (13,688)
Power, Steven G 3:16:38 (2,644)
Powis, Gary M 4:50:00 (23,495)
Powles, James 3:59:14 (10,503)
Powles, Michael 3:56:35 (9,687)
Pownall, Lee J 4:03:35 (11,521)
Powney, Simon D 3:49:19 (7,897)
Poynton, Ian M 4:23:54 (16,827)
Poynton, Joe B 4:43:45 (22,049)
Pozzi, Francesco 3:57:06 (9,856)
Pracucci, Maurizio 3:03:08 (1,341)
Prada, Graziano A 3:56:22 (9,623)
Pradier, Lionnell 4:07:47 (12,529)
Pradillon, Jean-François 3:56:10 (9,562)
Prager, Ian 5:13:27 (28,071)
Pragnell, Scott W 4:26:05 (17,469)
Prangle, Dennis 5:10:29 (27,569)
Prangley, Michael C 4:19:26 (15,647)
Pratesi, Stefano 4:18:47 (15,460)
Pratiu, Bruno 4:13:13 (13,944)
Pratt, Derek R 3:13:35 (2,314)
Pratt, Grant B 4:49:46 (23,440)
Pratt, Michael I 4:26:59 (17,749)
Pratt, Steve 4:22:34 (16,492)
Pratt, William J 5:31:59 (30,560)
Pratten, Ben C 4:30:02 (18,600)
Pratten, Kenneth R 4:28:37 (18,200)
Pready, Nicholas S 6:23:44 (34,047)
Prebble, John 4:13:37 (14,046)
Prebost, Ivan J 5:39:56 (31,407)
Precious, Graeme 4:19:04 (15,537)
Preece, Anthony J 5:20:17 (29,139)
Preece, Clive L 5:01:04 (25,988)
Preece, Dave J 3:32:10 (4,770)
Preece, David J 3:08:41 (1,776)
Preece, Steven 4:41:00 (21,395)
Prendergast, John P 5:32:45 (30,643)
Prentice, Neil P 3:11:11 (2,049)
Prescott, Richard W 4:47:25 (22,861)
Presland, Geoff K 5:43:31 (31,718)
Presle, Alain F 3:47:36 (7,474)
Prest, Michael J 4:34:11 (19,617)
Presti, Giovanni 5:18:04 (28,794)
Preston, Andrew 4:12:17 (13,692)
Preston, Edmund F 4:07:45 (12,516)
Preston, Kevin B 4:42:11 (21,674)
Preston, Nick 6:47:06 (34,659)
Preston, Terry 3:55:29 (9,364)
Prestt, Charlie J 3:46:00 (7,133)
Pretsell, Barry C 4:56:22 (24,981)
Prewer, David M 4:48:50 (23,195)
Pribel, Frank 4:03:02 (11,396)
Price, Aaron P 5:21:54 (29,338)
Price, Alex D 3:55:20 (9,315)
Price, Ben I 6:23:15 (34,031)
Price, Benjamin D 3:19:52 (2,983)
Price, Craig G 5:27:06 (29,988)
Price, Dave J 2:58:38 (1,000)
Price, David 4:20:41 (15,986)
Price, David A 4:27:20 (17,833)
Price, David C 4:19:04 (15,537)
Price, David C 5:11:44 (27,779)
Price, David C 5:15:30 (28,417)
Price, David M 5:56:35 (32,738)
Price, Duncan N 5:02:41 (26,270)
Price, George 5:34:29 (30,847)
Price, Ian 3:09:42 (1,881)
Price, Ian R 3:10:41 (1,999)
Price, James 3:00:46 (1,179)
Price, Mark 4:58:47 (25,506)
Price, Mark E 5:16:09 (28,498)
Price, Martin G 2:50:29 (515)
Price, Matthew E 3:14:35 (2,427)
Price, Michael E 5:34:37 (30,863)
Price, Michael H 5:15:20 (28,390)
Price, Michael J 3:14:06 (2,367)
Price, Nigel M 4:57:00 (25,128)
Price, Paul E 3:51:58 (8,476)
Price, Richard 4:48:03 (23,022)
Price, Richard T 3:06:45 (1,614)
Price, Robert C 4:13:37 (14,046)
Price, Rupert J 3:25:54 (3,743)
Price, Russell G 4:41:33 (21,537)
Price, Simon R 3:44:38 (6,866)
Price, Simon R 4:54:40 (24,586)
Price, Stephen 3:28:17 (4,155)
Price, Stephen 5:19:59 (29,093)
Price, Stephen J 3:12:25 (2,187)
Price, Stephen J 4:20:16 (15,879)
Price, Wynne 4:46:47 (22,727)
Prickett, Andrew T 3:53:55 (8,958)
Prickett, Michael N 4:51:59 (23,932)
Priddes, Richard 5:08:27 (27,277)
Pridding, Simon C 3:36:56 (5,487)
Priddy, David P 3:35:24 (5,241)
Pride, Simon 3:02:40 (1,311)
Prideaux, Ian R 4:14:08 (14,189)
Prieg, Hans-Peter 3:41:42 (6,316)
Priest, Andrew C 3:50:13 (8,089)
Priest, David L 4:19:40 (15,714)
Priest, Jonny 4:57:39 (25,256)
Priestley, James N 5:37:53 (31,180)
Priestley, Lee I 4:30:13 (18,659)
Priestley, Malcolm 4:43:25 (21,956)
Priestley, Steve G 4:48:25 (23,107)
Prieto, José L 3:06:33 (1,598)
Prigmore, Sean A 4:03:10 (11,425)
Prime, David D 4:15:59 (14,710)
Primo, Giorgio 3:42:43 (6,503)
Primrose, Noel 4:06:19 (12,171)
Prince, Chris J 3:24:49 (3,555)
Prince, Kelvin M 4:02:12 (11,204)
Prince, Stefan 4:27:55 (18,019)
Pring, Richard A 4:53:59 (24,424)
Pringle, Alistair M 4:21:36 (16,229)
Pringle, Kevin A 3:37:41 (5,602)
Pringle, Nicholas C 3:34:46 (5,156)
Pringle, Stuart A 2:59:51 (1,117)
Prior, Barry E 4:58:38 (25,476)
Prior, Chris J 4:45:16 (22,384)
Prior, Daniel J 4:56:25 (24,995)
Prior, Dave M 4:40:25 (21,238)
Prior, David J 4:39:17 (20,961)
Prior, Leslie J 5:46:33 (31,983)
Prior, Oli 4:48:24 (23,104)
Prior, Paul W 5:21:45 (29,320)
Prior, Stephen J 4:35:46 (20,036)
Prior, Steven R 5:07:17 (27,113)
Priscott, Philip J 4:38:34 (20,767)
Priscott, Simon 5:16:36 (28,564)
Pritchard, Adrian R 4:09:18 (12,908)
Pritchard, Christopher 4:59:16 (25,620)
Pritchard, Dafydd G 5:08:59 (27,354)
Pritchard, David A 4:25:01 (17,130)
Pritchard, David S 3:49:03 (7,836)
Pritchard, Gary T 5:04:57 (26,680)
Pritchard, Hugh W 5:54:49 (32,624)
Pritchard, Keith M 3:01:44 (1,241)
Pritchard, Keith W 5:29:16 (30,268)
Pritchard, Nigel G 4:49:18 (23,306)
Pritchard, Nigel J 3:23:04 (3,308)
Pritchard, Rhodri J 4:52:07 (23,970)
Pritchard, Roy T 3:04:00 (1,400)
Pritchard, Spencer 4:36:14 (20,141)
Pritchard, Stephen R 4:12:29 (13,742)
Pritchard, William S 4:05:10 (11,916)
Pritchard-McLean, Kyle 3:36:10 (5,368)
Pritchett, Andrew N 5:11:24 (27,725)
Probert, Martyn R 4:34:59 (19,851)
Procter, Andrew J 4:52:05 (23,961)
Proctor, Dan A 4:00:01 (10,732)
Pro'homme, Nicolas 3:37:49 (5,620)
Proietti, Roberto F 4:18:11 (15,261)
Prosperino, Michael 3:55:12 (9,276)
Prosser, Robert C 3:39:21 (5,879)
Protais, Jean-Baptiste 2:44:22 (305)
Prothero, Jonathan 4:17:56 (15,184)
Prothero, Robert A 2:57:09 (893)
Proudfoot, Stuart A 4:58:53 (25,530)
Proudlove, Michael J 2:24:02 (40)
Pruden, John M 5:35:39 (30,962)
Prudham, Joseph P 3:51:05 (8,278)
Pryke, Andrew M 3:38:59 (5,812)
Pryor, Richard 5:32:05 (30,564)
Prytherch, David S 4:15:44 (14,647)
Psink, Eric J 3:44:48 (6,904)
Ptchelinseff, Johan 4:22:42 (16,538)
Puckey, Stephen J 4:25:48 (17,377)
Puddick, Julian U 3:24:27 (3,512)
Puddy, Christopher J 5:21:40 (29,307)
Pudsey, David J 3:08:46 (1,787)
Puettmann, Claus 5:15:09 (28,360)
Puffette, Kevin J 3:50:20 (8,112)
Pugh, Adrian E 3:35:11 (5,208)
Pugh, Brian 6:08:54 (33,482)
Pugh, Cliff 3:46:09 (7,170)
Pugh, Eddie 4:19:21 (15,624)
Pugh, Gareth J 5:11:11 (27,684)
Pugh, Giles J 5:09:08 (27,377)
Pugh, Graham K 3:19:08 (2,895)
Pugh, Mike R 4:06:39 (12,252)
Pugh, Nicholas 4:33:26 (19,415)
Pugh, Robert M 3:46:44 (7,290)
Pugh, Roderick M 3:10:31 (1,980)
Puig-Codes, Jordi 3:17:16 (2,711)
Pulford, Andy J 4:22:39 (16,523)
Pulford, Colin C 5:13:03 (28,007)
Pulford, Tom G 5:53:42 (32,546)
Pull, Howard C 4:11:35 (13,500)

Pullen, James C 4:51:41 (23,869)
Pullen, Leslie C 5:49:23 (32,220)
Pullen, Martin 4:59:03 (25,574)
Pullen, Robert F 4:29:31 (18,470)
Pulley, Nicholas R 4:15:50 (14,673)
Pullinger, Jeremy A 3:24:13 (3,474)
Pullman, Mark 5:27:55 (30,092)
Pulman, Willilam F 3:56:09 (9,552)
Puncher, Kevin P 4:07:51 (12,543)
Punja, Ali N 3:56:07 (9,543)
Purbrick, Andrew 5:11:24 (27,725)
Purbrick, Brendan J 4:09:00 (12,826)
Purbrick, Stuart 4:08:29 (12,690)
Purcell, Darren D 4:35:17 (19,907)
Purcell, Ian S 4:04:47 (11,811)
Purcell, Sean A 4:14:04 (14,173)
Purdey, Kevin J 4:32:58 (19,307)
Purdon, Jason T 3:11:54 (2,129)
Purdy, Alan T 4:17:39 (15,125)
Purdy, Philip 5:26:01 (29,869)
Puri, Aman 5:39:41 (31,390)
Purkiss, Mark C 3:49:50 (8,002)
Purkiss, Simon A 4:38:12 (20,670)
Purnal, Bart D 3:51:11 (8,297)
Purnell, Gareth J 4:17:00 (14,955)
Purr, Steven D 4:38:03 (20,632)
Purriss-McEndoo, Saun 3:01:01 (1,192)
Purse, Dean A 5:21:47 (29,324)
Pursell, Jim 4:29:47 (18,540)
Purser, Michael J 4:25:44 (17,359)
Pursglove, Mark D 3:39:43 (5,954)
Purslow, Philip 3:55:47 (9,457)
Purssord, Keith D 5:08:04 (27,229)
Purves, James 4:12:39 (13,790)
Purvis, Darrell A 5:44:29 (31,801)
Purvis, Darren 2:38:21 (167)
Purvis, Derek 3:47:07 (7,377)
Purvis, Duncan 3:48:49 (7,792)
Purvis, Malcolm 5:57:49 (32,824)
Purvis, Stewart 4:47:02 (22,777)
Pusch, Gerhard 4:52:52 (24,143)
Pusche, Michael 4:56:28 (25,006)
Putland, Dean S 4:28:55 (18,279)
Putley, Colin S 3:25:31 (3,677)
Puttick, Timothy 4:38:27 (20,745)
Puttock, Richard M 4:28:34 (18,187)
Putz, Rudolk 3:31:53 (4,730)
Pyatt, Alastair C 3:45:16 (7,000)
Pye, Alan E 2:59:32 (1,091)
Pye, Christopher D 4:39:44 (21,077)
Pye, Geoffrey M 4:23:39 (16,764)
Pye, Ian D 4:52:47 (24,123)
Pye, Shaw D 3:17:50 (2,774)
Pyemont, James 4:20:04 (15,817)
Pyne, David J 5:57:06 (32,783)
Pyne, Ross 4:11:03 (13,368)
Pyrke, Christopher 4:38:55 (20,853)
Pywell, Mark J 2:57:49 (942)
Quagliato, Christopher 3:48:54 (7,802)
Quagliotto, Roberto 3:20:35 (3,054)
Quaile, Deric R 5:25:09 (29,767)
Quantrill, Philip 2:56:36 (851)
Quarm, Derrick 5:11:47 (27,784)
Quarman, Nigel 4:06:52 (12,303)
Quartermaine, Richard A 3:57:17 (9,915)
Quartly, Leonard S 3:56:46 (9,740)
Quayle, Paul D 3:42:16 (6,430)
Quayle, Peter 4:59:53 (25,752)
Quayle, Stephen B 4:24:20 (16,938)
Quelch, Steven R 4:40:59 (21,385)
Quemard, Stefan C 6:28:59 (34,218)
Quennell, Richard G 2:56:42 (861)
Quesne, Eric R 4:22:54 (16,579)
Quest, Jonathan 3:03:05 (1,335)
Quested, Barry D 4:51:24 (23,814)
Quick, Andrew J 3:26:23 (3,824)
Quick, James H 2:58:53 (1,021)
Quick, Rob J 4:38:12 (20,670)
Quigley, Michael G 5:31:20 (30,495)
Quigley, Paul 5:29:44 (30,333)
Quigley, Thomas D 4:21:09 (16,099)
Quilitz, Horst-Peter 4:51:36 (23,853)
Quilter, Shane C 4:59:38 (25,697)
Quilter, Stuart J 4:29:35 (18,491)
Quin, Adrian A 6:31:11 (34,282)
Quince, Roger P 3:27:24 (3,996)
Quiney, Nial F 3:58:28 (10,278)
Quinn, Bob 5:42:48 (31,662)
Quinn, Brendan T 6:43:24 (34,580)
Quinn, Charles E 4:50:59 (23,728)
Quinn, David 3:27:28 (4,012)
Quinn, David 5:06:21 (26,931)
Quinn, Dennis F 4:41:20 (21,474)
Quinn, Eamonn 6:42:05 (34,548)
Quinn, Ewan J 4:04:59 (11,856)
Quinn, Greg 3:14:52 (2,468)
Quinn, Ian C 6:19:19 (33,898)
Quinn, Kenneth P 3:50:17 (8,099)
Quinn, Malcolm K 4:42:24 (21,720)
Quinn, Paul R 4:02:15 (11,212)
Quinn, Richard J 5:27:00 (29,977)
Quinn, Scott A 4:57:13 (25,179)
Quinn, Simon 4:46:31 (22,671)
Quinn, Stephen J 3:41:45 (6,324)
Quint, David P 6:17:33 (33,840)
Quintana, Guillermo 5:08:25 (27,272)
Quirk, Paul A 4:01:22 (11,017)
Quirke, Nicholas S 4:23:40 (16,766)
Qushair, Hani S 4:08:21 (12,659)
Quy, Andrew J 5:01:31 (26,069)
Rabbetts, Mark A 2:57:21 (909)
Rabett, Justin R 3:33:59 (5,045)
Rabin, Wayne D 4:59:25 (25,647)
Rabjohns, Peter 3:02:20 (1,288)
Raburaud, Vincent 4:06:42 (12,266)
Raby, John 4:27:59 (18,029)
Raby, Lee 3:51:51 (8,454)
Racineux, Pierre 3:33:32 (4,961)
Rackham, Andrew V 3:59:29 (10,567)
Rackham, Douglas N 2:48:34 (443)
Rackham, Simon J 4:21:00 (16,075)
Rackliffe, Robert A 4:10:37 (13,242)
Rackstraw, Stephen A 5:29:22 (30,289)
Radcliffe, Richard 3:14:02 (2,360)
Radford, David M 3:45:48 (7,095)
Radford, Nicholas L 3:40:45 (6,127)
Radjen, Stevo 3:43:02 (6,556)
Radkiewicz, Ted 6:43:54 (34,597)
Rae, Ewan G 4:30:06 (18,621)
Rae, Geoff H 4:14:39 (14,337)
Rae, Ian A 3:35:41 (5,293)
Rae, Neil 3:31:46 (4,712)
Raeburn, Hamish 3:31:57 (4,739)
Raffell, Roger G 4:36:42 (20,279)
Rafferty, Mark A 3:31:58 (4,742)
Rafferty, Nicholas J 4:07:53 (12,550)
Raftry, Andrew J 3:48:07 (7,619)
Ragg, Peter C 4:47:27 (22,875)
Ragot, Joel 3:22:04 (3,195)
Rahman, Emdad 5:52:46 (32,479)
Raife, Lee 4:14:27 (14,285)
Rainey, David 3:59:07 (10,473)
Rainey, Jackson 3:54:39 (9,139)
Rainford, Mark 4:41:20 (21,474)
Rainoldi, Eugenio 3:34:57 (5,177)
Raja, Ketan N 3:49:54 (8,017)
Raja, Rickey 6:18:52 (33,887)
Rakusen, Lloyd 4:27:56 (18,020)
Ralph, David R 5:07:49 (27,192)
Ramaala, Hendrick 2:08:32 (3)
Ramadorai, Tarun 5:09:22 (27,415)
Ramage, Alan 3:05:18 (1,496)
Ramakrishna, Suresha 5:52:05 (32,418)
Ramalhal, Rui M 3:37:55 (5,635)
Ramalingam, Shay 5:23:13 (29,505)
Raman, Mani A 6:03:20 (33,178)
Raman, Manoj 4:30:19 (18,683)
Ramanauskas, Stephen 4:48:54 (23,212)
Ramasubramanian, Srivatsan 5:57:36 (32,811)
Ramdeen, Krishna 5:08:24 (27,269)
Ramey, Mark A 6:04:03 (33,223)
Ramm, Ian D 5:08:28 (27,281)
Ramon, Franck 3:10:22 (1,966)
Ramos, Roberto E 5:23:29 (29,542)
Rampton, James J 6:33:39 (34,345)
Ramsay, Gordon 3:38:48 (5,776)
Ramsay, Grant M 2:38:10 (164)
Ramsay, Jonathan R 3:36:20 (5,399)
Ramsay, Norrie C 4:16:37 (14,866)
Ramsay, Steve A 3:25:06 (3,606)
Ramsbottom, John 4:37:54 (20,596)
Ramsbottom, Paul 4:00:05 (10,748)
Ramsden, Lee C 5:06:51 (27,029)
Ramsden, Simon O 3:39:48 (5,963)
Ramsden, Stephen C 4:34:06 (19,591)
Ramsell, Chris D 2:41:01 (220)
Ramsey, Nicholas G 4:50:20 (23,576)
Ramzan, Nadim 4:15:16 (14,520)
Rance, Anthony J 3:58:22 (10,250)
Rance, Keith J 4:14:59 (14,437)
Rancon, Pierre 4:26:04 (17,462)
Rand, Edward C 4:37:02 (20,364)
Randall, Andrew M 4:43:45 (22,049)
Randall, David S 4:47:45 (22,953)
Randall, Derek 4:56:38 (25,050)
Randall, Michael J 5:40:56 (31,498)
Randall, Paul R 5:34:27 (30,843)
Randall, Steve M 4:16:12 (14,765)
Randall, Trevor 4:38:15 (20,683)
Randerwala, Hemal A 4:59:47 (25,736)
Randle, Paul M 4:05:41 (12,023)
Randles, Stephen 4:12:17 (13,692)
Rands, Martin J 3:39:37 (5,933)
Ranger, Terry E 3:49:50 (8,002)
Rankin, Eeyin 4:05:32 (11,996)
Rankin, Geoffrey I 3:29:05 (4,291)
Rankin, Shane A 5:33:45 (30,754)
Rann, Stuart G 5:02:52 (26,313)
Rannard, David P 4:35:18 (19,908)
Ransay, Tristan M 4:47:07 (22,800)
Ransom, Alan F 3:46:52 (7,318)
Ransom, Jeremy C 2:59:55 (1,121)
Rantell, Dave A 2:55:39 (781)
Rao, Krishna C 7:51:44 (35,213)
Raper, Alistair J 5:25:39 (29,819)
Raper, Ray J 3:26:26 (3,839)
Rapet, Vincent 3:01:55 (1,253)
Raphael, Michael Jnr 5:45:48 (31,921)
Rapley, Nicholas 3:55:43 (9,435)
Rappolt, Jason P 4:08:50 (12,782)
Rash, Edward C 3:40:21 (6,064)
Rashid, Maqsood M 3:31:48 (4,718)
Ratchford, David L 3:54:16 (9,038)
Ratcliff, Steve M 3:43:01 (6,553)
Ratcliffe, Ian 5:00:41 (25,918)
Ratcliffe, Paul A 3:28:06 (4,126)
Ratcliffe, Paul J 5:28:18 (30,168)
Ratcliffe, Peter E 3:23:30 (3,374)
Rathbone, Colin E 3:12:11 (2,163)
Rattray, Ian S 4:07:53 (12,550)
Raveh, Doron 4:35:48 (20,042)
Raven, Gareth 2:20:00 (27)
Raven, James 4:49:09 (23,273)
Ravenscroft, Daniel S 4:30:04 (18,611)
Ravndal, Kjell M 3:32:49 (4,859)
Raw, Richard M 4:38:59 (20,871)
Rawes, James 4:30:07 (18,630)
Rawles, Jason 6:15:28 (33,753)
Rawling, James A 5:21:36 (29,300)
Rawlings, Charlie R 3:59:32 (10,582)
Rawlings, George I 4:13:12 (13,942)
Rawlings, Len 4:29:37 (18,499)
Rawlings, Stephen G 3:52:56 (8,705)
Rawlins, Andrew M 3:28:45 (4,234)
Rawlinson, Brian F 4:35:19 (19,911)
Rawlinson, Lee 5:36:13 (31,014)
Ray, Christopher P 5:32:29 (30,613)
Ray, Graeme 3:38:42 (5,754)
Ray, Kaushik 5:25:56 (29,859)
Ray, Pijush K 6:58:27 (34,842)
Ray, Simon J 4:15:03 (14,464)
Ray, Simon J 4:49:50 (23,458)
Rayfield, David W 3:04:51 (1,457)
Rayment, Ewan 4:49:05 (23,265)
Rayment, Paul 5:38:55 (31,298)
Raymond, Benn 4:27:26 (17,864)
Raymond, Byron J 2:51:30 (563)
Raymond, Joad 3:16:07 (2,593)
Raymond, Marcel 5:16:28 (28,544)

Raymond, Michael W 4:16:05 (14,734)
Raymond, Paul D 4:30:41 (18,765)
Rayner, Alastair J 3:40:04 (6,010)
Rayner, Andrew 5:13:19 (28,046)
Rayner, Andrew C 6:49:03 (34,691)
Rayner, Gary R 2:56:39 (855)
Rayner, Paul R 4:21:11 (16,105)
Raynor, Andrew P 4:57:43 (25,270)
Raynor, David A 4:16:00 (14,715)
Ray-Smith, Duncan K 4:27:36 (17,921)
Rayson, Christopher J 4:46:17 (22,621)
Rayson, Paul W 3:15:39 (2,535)
Re, Enrico 4:01:41 (11,086)
Rea, Anthony W 4:07:17 (12,413)
Rea, Fraser J 4:23:05 (16,625)
Read, Chris M 7:16:32 (35,044)
Read, Christopher K 3:29:14 (4,317)
Read, Gareth A 6:41:48 (34,542)
Read, Ian 3:28:47 (4,240)
Read, John V 4:03:31 (11,504)
Read, Jonathan M 4:10:01 (13,095)
Read, Jonathan R 4:14:17 (14,241)
Read, Keith A 3:26:25 (3,831)
Read, Malcolm W 4:20:36 (15,962)
Read, Nicholas J 3:54:54 (9,215)
Read, Norbert A 3:58:47 (10,382)
Read, Richard C 4:14:42 (14,346)
Read, Ronald S 3:13:24 (2,291)
Read, Simon A 3:58:22 (10,250)
Read, Tom E 3:38:03 (5,656)
Reade, Brian 3:34:05 (5,058)
Reade, John A 5:26:06 (29,883)
Reade, Martin K 5:59:45 (32,963)
Reader, Frank R 5:34:15 (30,813)
Reader, John 5:50:42 (32,316)
Reader, Mark 4:15:35 (14,603)
Readfern, Lee B 5:37:58 (31,193)
Reading, Laurence 5:37:00 (31,099)
Reading, Roderick N 4:26:42 (17,658)
Readings, Thomas 6:24:53 (34,093)
Readman, Ben G 3:39:54 (5,980)
Ready, Thomas N 4:14:19 (14,248)
Realmuto, Piero 4:58:46 (25,504)
Reames, Philip 4:16:34 (14,851)
Reardon, Tim 6:06:47 (33,377)
Reason, Chris H 3:36:18 (5,392)
Reason, Colin D 6:05:07 (33,274)
Reason, Simon D 3:56:37 (9,696)
Reay, Alasdair L 4:17:42 (15,140)
Reay, Jonathan R 3:39:00 (5,817)
Reay, Kenneth S 4:52:58 (24,166)
Reay, Timothy 4:52:16 (24,006)
Rebmann, Fredy 4:44:04 (22,108)
Rechenmann, Guy 3:32:45 (4,851)
Recio, Albert Caballero 2:48:45 (452)
Redden, Phil 4:13:33 (14,032)
Reddicliffe, Alexander 3:41:01 (6,182)
Redding, Chris 4:07:50 (12,537)
Redding, Colin 6:18:25 (33,867)
Redfern, Gary 4:58:57 (25,544)
Redford, Robert 3:34:26 (5,116)
Redford, Roy 6:53:07 (34,773)
Redgrave, Steve 4:21:36 (16,229)
Redman, Andy 3:08:05 (1,722)
Redman, Nevil 4:22:45 (16,546)
Redman, Timothy 3:44:08 (6,770)
Redmayne, Mark N 3:41:37 (6,302)
Redmond, Alasdair I 4:23:03 (16,612)
Redmond, Michael 4:40:30 (21,259)
Redpath, David W 3:46:39 (7,274)
Redpath, Neil A 4:48:28 (23,119)
Redwood, Derek S 4:57:55 (25,304)
Redwood, Simon 4:55:06 (24,700)
Reece, Philip J 3:36:40 (5,449)
Reed, Alan 3:12:22 (2,182)
Reed, Chris D 3:43:30 (6,652)
Reed, Christopher J 3:25:52 (3,734)
Reed, Darryl A 3:11:24 (2,069)
Reed, Duncan 4:12:42 (13,805)
Reed, Mark 2:54:06 (693)
Reed, Mark D 4:02:08 (11,190)
Reed, Michael J 4:36:24 (20,195)
Reed, Neal R 4:46:28 (22,661)
Reed, Paul S 5:10:19 (27,543)
Reed, Peter A 4:06:43 (12,270)
Reed, Peter A 4:12:08 (13,648)
Reed, Simon R 4:53:03 (24,190)
Reed, Stephen A 5:22:35 (29,436)
Reed, Stuart A 4:56:47 (25,090)
Reeder, Jim 4:32:29 (19,207)
Reekie, Grant J 3:43:38 (6,677)
Reeks, Kieren J 4:19:01 (15,519)
Re'em, Aaron M 3:22:52 (3,280)
Rees, Alan 4:41:51 (21,599)
Rees, Colin J 3:26:23 (3,824)
Rees, Dorian P 4:14:08 (14,189)
Rees, Gareth H 4:03:52 (11,598)
Rees, Graham G 5:06:13 (26,908)
Rees, Huw 4:01:16 (10,998)
Rees, John P 4:46:02 (22,557)
Rees, Martin 4:12:32 (13,752)
Rees, Nathan 4:57:23 (25,203)
Rees, Nigel K 6:42:40 (34,561)
Rees, Richard J 4:52:32 (24,061)
Rees, Stephen W 4:58:47 (25,506)
Rees, Steve 5:02:52 (26,313)
Rees, Stuart R 4:34:48 (19,789)
Rees-Jones, Steve M 2:25:07 (45)
Rees-Saunders, Mark A 4:10:49 (13,292)
Rees-Thomas, Paul I 4:52:30 (24,055)
Reeve, Bradley 4:47:14 (22,827)
Reeve, Damon A 3:20:07 (3,012)
Reeve, David M 4:24:49 (17,075)
Reeve, Jason 4:29:09 (18,354)
Reeve, Jason C 4:13:30 (14,017)
Reevell, John 3:30:41 (4,559)
Reeves, Alan C 4:13:27 (14,003)
Reeves, Andrew B 2:41:38 (231)
Reeves, Barry G 4:55:24 (24,758)
Reeves, Gavin J 4:29:13 (18,372)
Reeves, John P 5:20:56 (29,229)
Reeves, Jonathan J 3:34:15 (5,091)
Reeves, Paul D 4:02:09 (11,195)
Reeves, Peter P 4:53:58 (24,415)
Reeves, Robert J 4:55:54 (24,874)
Reeves, Scott D 3:10:47 (2,006)
Reeves, Steve R 3:50:52 (8,228)
Reeves, Stuart N 3:07:20 (1,654)
Reeves, Thomas G 4:32:45 (19,258)
Regan, Andy N 4:17:18 (15,036)
Regan, Maurice F 3:28:15 (4,150)
Regan, Patrick C 3:23:05 (3,311)
Rehberg, Dirk 3:58:39 (10,323)
Rehman, Maj 4:29:44 (18,530)
Rehner, Christoph 4:03:18 (11,462)
Reid, Adam P 4:02:55 (11,374)
Reid, Brian D 4:57:23 (25,203)
Reid, Clive S 3:14:29 (2,411)
Reid, Craig A 4:46:53 (22,750)
Reid, David A 3:54:21 (9,062)
Reid, Fraser M 3:23:25 (3,364)
Reid, Gavin 3:20:09 (3,014)
Reid, Guy J 3:13:31 (2,304)
Reid, Hamish L 4:22:00 (16,335)
Reid, Ian R 4:21:39 (16,244)
Reid, James A 4:15:10 (14,493)
Reid, James C 4:27:06 (17,775)
Reid, Jamie M 2:34:44 (111)
Reid, John 3:32:52 (4,864)
Reid, John F 3:27:45 (4,067)
Reid, Julian S 4:37:41 (20,547)
Reid, Kevin S 4:29:27 (18,448)
Reid, Matt E 4:35:29 (19,972)
Reid, Michael J 3:55:54 (9,488)
Reid, Nicholas I 3:00:23 (1,149)
Reid, Peter A 3:29:29 (4,351)
Reid, Peter K 3:02:02 (1,264)
Reid, Richard M 5:06:43 (27,004)
Reid, Toby G 5:10:46 (27,610)
Reidy, Noel F 4:12:30 (13,747)
Reihill, Tony 4:04:03 (11,650)
Reijs, Ian J 4:06:16 (12,159)
Reilly, Leonard J 2:35:48 (120)
Reilly, Lewis S 4:37:30 (20,498)
Reilly, Michael W 3:44:48 (6,904)
Reilly, Peter A 3:55:55 (9,495)
Reilly, Stephen J 3:20:03 (3,005)
Reilly, Stuart C 2:59:14 (1,059)
Reimann, Stefan 3:21:04 (3,090)
Reinelt, Ulrich 3:19:55 (2,986)
Reinhardt, Klaus 4:50:09 (23,528)
Reino, Ryan P 5:16:23 (28,530)
Reiss, Anthony J 4:29:05 (18,334)
Reiter, Anton 4:43:25 (21,956)
Relton, Richard R 3:46:03 (7,147)
Renals, Paul 5:12:51 (27,979)
Renard, Guy 3:24:01 (3,450)
Rendell, John G 5:24:44 (29,714)
Rennie, Gavin H 4:45:03 (22,338)
Rennie, George N 4:13:39 (14,058)
Rennie, James S 3:54:08 (9,005)
Rennie, Keith J 4:28:58 (18,297)
Rennison, David C 4:34:54 (19,825)
Rennow, Tor 4:36:04 (20,102)
Renny, Steven W 3:11:41 (2,102)
Renouard, Patrice 3:59:42 (10,630)
Renshaw, William B 3:18:46 (2,857)
Repschlaeger, Frank 4:54:00 (24,428)
Resta, Carlo 3:23:00 (3,294)
Reston, Rhydian H 3:35:53 (5,320)
Retalic, Ronald 4:07:47 (12,529)
Retallack, Guy G 5:15:27 (28,414)
Reukauf, Thomas 3:48:43 (7,766)
Reunbrouck, Frank 4:59:31 (25,668)
Reutenauer, Christopher 4:20:49 (16,026)
Reveley, Adam N 4:49:15 (23,293)
Revell, John C 4:06:39 (12,252)
Revere, Simon D 4:23:32 (16,735)
Revill, Jason 3:28:18 (4,160)
Revill, Justin 3:45:04 (6,966)
Revolvo, Tomas 3:13:08 (2,261)
Rew, Simon 3:56:09 (9,552)
Reyes, Axel 2:56:39 (855)
Reynolds, Andrew J 3:40:45 (6,127)
Reynolds, Andrew K 4:16:06 (14,738)
Reynolds, Anthony 3:46:26 (7,228)
Reynolds, Damian P 4:33:13 (19,363)
Reynolds, Dean 4:32:51 (19,276)
Reynolds, Edward M 3:43:14 (6,595)
Reynolds, Graham 3:40:55 (6,167)
Reynolds, Graham 4:01:14 (10,991)
Reynolds, Guy J 5:09:39 (27,463)
Reynolds, James G 2:57:28 (920)
Reynolds, John 5:05:22 (26,768)
Reynolds, John A 4:51:06 (23,751)
Reynolds, Lee M 4:00:04 (10,745)
Reynolds, Mark A 4:13:58 (14,135)
Reynolds, Markus 3:32:00 (4,748)
Reynolds, Neil A 4:19:47 (15,748)
Reynolds, Paul 2:55:55 (805)
Reynolds, Paul 4:33:41 (19,485)
Reynolds, Paul A 5:02:46 (26,290)
Reynolds, Peter W 4:59:32 (25,670)
Reynolds, Phil M 4:17:09 (15,001)
Reynolds, Philip 6:18:42 (33,880)
Reynolds, Philip J 3:40:45 (6,127)
Reynolds, Richard G 4:53:23 (24,270)
Reynolds, Stephen J 3:43:43 (6,686)
Reynolds, Steven 3:51:12 (8,303)
Reynolds, Thomas A 3:32:47 (4,854)
Rhan, Joseph J 4:14:14 (14,220)
Rhimes, Godfrey H 2:49:35 (486)
Rhodes, Andrew D 3:14:48 (2,460)
Rhodes, David 4:31:01 (18,840)
Rhodes, David L 3:34:23 (5,107)
Rhodes, Ian 3:02:40 (1,311)
Rhodes, John 5:15:08 (28,356)
Rhodes, Kevin 3:55:45 (9,450)
Rhodes, Paul G 5:22:05 (29,364)
Rhodes, Steve 4:28:14 (18,095)
Rhodes, Steven B 3:55:42 (9,429)
Rhodes, Timothy C 4:41:54 (21,605)
Rhys Davies, Stephen 4:31:06 (18,853)
Rial, David 4:09:55 (13,074)
Rians, John G 4:27:00 (17,752)
Riba Corrons, Carles 3:44:07 (6,763)
Riba Satonnas, Jordi 3:44:07 (6,763)
Ribbands, Derek 4:35:58 (20,078)
Ribeiro, David C 6:35:47 (34,404)

Ribeiro, Lucedino	4:46:33	(22,679)
Ribeiro, Raoul	3:57:44	(10,045)
Ricca, Philippe P	4:14:33	(14,304)
Ricci, Ezio	3:11:10	(2,046)
Ricci, Mario	3:27:03	(3,936)
Rice, Craig T	5:07:56	(27,207)
Rice, Gareth D	3:16:45	(2,656)
Rice, James B	6:26:04	(34,127)
Rice, James W	6:22:05	(33,994)
Rice, Mick	2:50:03	(500)
Rice, Nicholas G	5:14:12	(28,212)
Rice, Tim J	3:42:04	(6,391)
Rich, Andrew J	5:29:07	(30,260)
Rich, David R	4:41:12	(21,446)
Rich, Stephen J	3:53:57	(8,964)
Richards, Alan D	4:25:57	(17,413)
Richards, Alistair H	3:34:43	(5,148)
Richards, Andrew D	3:16:26	(2,629)
Richards, Andy D	4:05:52	(12,063)
Richards, Ben P	3:58:29	(10,288)
Richards, Christopher P	4:50:23	(23,592)
Richards, Craig	4:03:05	(11,406)
Richards, Dave J	3:09:56	(1,912)
Richards, Gary L	4:48:56	(23,219)
Richards, Gordon	3:05:19	(1,498)
Richards, James I	3:29:30	(4,354)
Richards, Jason	4:39:55	(21,117)
Richards, Keith S	3:50:40	(8,182)
Richards, Kenneth C	4:33:33	(19,453)
Richards, Lyn H	5:05:19	(26,753)
Richards, Mark L	3:04:43	(1,443)
Richards, Michael K	3:26:00	(3,757)
Richards, Nicholas	4:25:58	(17,423)
Richards, Paul	4:22:08	(16,380)
Richards, Paul A	3:30:00	(4,454)
Richards, Paul S	3:23:43	(3,405)
Richards, Philip H	3:41:59	(6,372)
Richards, Robert	4:40:54	(21,361)
Richards, Simon D	5:49:05	(32,191)
Richards, Toby	3:53:34	(8,875)
Richardson, Adam K	5:10:47	(27,614)
Richardson, Adam N	3:37:27	(5,570)
Richardson, Alan	4:17:46	(15,152)
Richardson, Alan J	4:04:52	(11,829)
Richardson, Andrew	4:55:40	(24,804)
Richardson, Andrew F	2:53:06	(640)
Richardson, Andrew J	6:11:11	(33,581)
Richardson, Andrew T	3:58:17	(10,220)
Richardson, Anthony K	3:23:13	(3,334)
Richardson, Bob	3:31:46	(4,712)
Richardson, Charlie H	4:58:40	(25,479)
Richardson, Christopher J	4:32:55	(19,295)
Richardson, Colin D	3:12:38	(2,207)
Richardson, Craig	3:43:28	(6,647)
Richardson, David	4:43:32	(21,990)
Richardson, David	4:47:54	(22,990)
Richardson, David	6:48:00	(34,676)
Richardson, Donald	3:45:28	(7,045)
Richardson, Duncan	4:25:27	(17,265)
Richardson, Eamonn P	3:42:14	(6,422)
Richardson, Garry J	5:12:02	(27,826)
Richardson, Glen	4:29:37	(18,499)
Richardson, Hilary L	4:14:46	(14,369)
Richardson, James L	5:05:48	(26,844)
Richardson, James O	4:33:35	(19,459)
Richardson, Jamie T	5:25:46	(29,837)
Richardson, John P	4:24:36	(17,016)
Richardson, John J	6:02:32	(33,107)
Richardson, Jonathan M	4:35:58	(20,078)
Richardson, Kenelm K	4:14:59	(14,437)
Richardson, Kevin J	5:00:33	(25,887)
Richardson, Kevin R	4:25:04	(17,142)
Richardson, Martin	4:10:21	(13,182)
Richardson, Neal A	4:02:25	(11,250)
Richardson, Neil	3:55:32	(9,376)
Richardson, Neil G	4:38:28	(20,749)
Richardson, Nigel	3:26:20	(3,816)
Richardson, Nigel G	3:57:51	(10,094)
Richardson, Paul	3:50:17	(8,099)
Richardson, Paul	4:29:34	(18,486)
Richardson, Paul W	4:37:29	(20,494)
Richardson, Philip J	3:46:24	(7,222)
Richardson, Scott	5:09:20	(27,411)

Richardson, Simon C	2:59:11	(1,055)
Richardson, Timothy R	7:40:26	(35,174)
Richardson, Toby C	4:49:59	(23,492)
Richardson, Trevor E	5:28:00	(30,103)
Riches, Christopher D	3:41:22	(6,251)
Riches, Kenneth	4:36:39	(20,270)
Riches, Mark C	2:53:11	(643)
Riches, Nicholas G	3:53:59	(8,972)
Richman, Aryeh	5:48:32	(32,137)
Richman, Paul J	4:27:24	(17,857)
Richmond, David F	3:14:47	(2,459)
Richmond, David J	4:13:58	(14,135)
Richmond, Kenny	2:45:27	(335)
Richmond, Mark K	4:29:31	(18,470)
Richmond, William	4:10:56	(13,329)
Rickard, Marcus J	5:11:57	(27,814)
Ricketts, David M	3:43:51	(6,713)
Rickwood, Trevor E	4:32:38	(19,235)
Riddell, Charlie P	4:30:46	(18,786)
Riddell, Lachlan	3:27:23	(3,988)
Riddick, Karl N	3:22:09	(3,211)
Riddle, Dean	3:59:23	(10,541)
Ride, Michael R	5:07:58	(27,211)
Ridehalgh, Ben P	4:49:27	(23,350)
Rider, Andy	5:09:30	(27,438)
Rider, Jerry	5:00:09	(25,803)
Rider, Simon	5:45:59	(31,933)
Rider, Steve	6:08:00	(33,445)
Ridge, Terry	4:11:28	(13,477)
Ridge, Tim J	4:34:12	(19,624)
Ridgeway, Paul B	2:58:19	(975)
Ridgewell, Ian S	5:16:50	(28,612)
Ridgway, Mark	3:58:11	(10,184)
Ridgway, Nicolas P	4:42:08	(21,661)
Ridgway, Simon A	4:07:00	(12,343)
Riding, Callum J	5:12:39	(27,937)
Ridler, Adam J	5:19:04	(28,949)
Ridley, Bill	2:59:51	(1,117)
Ridley, Joss T	4:10:38	(13,248)
Ridley, Matthew	3:54:38	(9,135)
Ridley, Peter F	3:35:10	(5,205)
Ridout, John P	3:08:43	(1,784)
Ridout, Simon J	4:07:13	(12,395)
Riedel, Stefan	3:46:00	(7,133)
Riedl, Norbert	3:33:49	(5,014)
Rielander, Ian R	4:36:43	(20,286)
Riesenmey, René	4:29:39	(18,506)
Riethmuller, Drew	3:48:43	(7,766)
Rievel, Arne	4:20:50	(16,030)
Rigby, Billy	5:20:01	(29,098)
Rigby, Carl	5:27:05	(29,985)
Rigby, Colin	2:30:09	(70)
Rigby, Neil A	4:24:53	(17,090)
Rigby, Richard P	3:36:18	(5,392)
Rigg, David C	3:07:23	(1,662)
Rigg, Nigel K	3:00:45	(1,177)
Riglar, Stephen M	4:04:36	(11,768)
Rigney, Noel C	4:33:52	(19,538)
Rijsenbrij, Ronald	4:05:12	(11,921)
Riley, Adam J	5:28:16	(30,160)
Riley, Andrew J	3:49:16	(7,883)
Riley, Andrew R	4:18:26	(15,345)
Riley, Christopher J	4:47:35	(22,906)
Riley, Colin A	5:40:34	(31,475)
Riley, Daiman John	4:15:43	(14,642)
Riley, Gerard	4:56:48	(25,095)
Riley, James M	4:02:31	(11,276)
Riley, Jamie D	4:46:57	(22,761)
Riley, Matthew C	4:17:03	(14,971)
Riley, Matthew R	5:57:14	(32,791)
Riley, Michael J	4:20:10	(15,846)
Riley, Patrick	2:57:43	(932)
Riley, Richard P	4:08:44	(12,749)
Riley, Simon J	3:02:28	(1,296)
Riley, Steve	3:32:49	(4,859)
Riley, Trevor I	3:59:06	(10,469)
Riley, Walter	5:39:45	(31,391)
Riley, William F	4:18:37	(15,399)
Riley-Jordan, Peter B	4:48:51	(23,199)
Rimmer, Anthony D	4:21:49	(16,287)
Rimmer, Paul	4:25:27	(17,265)
Rinderknecht, Paul	3:56:40	(9,714)
Ringham, Simon P	3:36:24	(5,405)

Ringshaw, Matt J	5:16:28	(28,544)
Riordan, Richard P	3:22:01	(3,189)
Riordan, Tim J	3:58:24	(10,261)
Ripley, Neil S	5:04:46	(26,642)
Ripman, Jamie J	3:53:40	(8,900)
Rippier, Oliver	3:30:19	(4,490)
Ripping, David P	5:03:35	(26,440)
Risk, John L	4:36:52	(20,324)
Ritchie, Daniel I	4:23:59	(16,844)
Ritchie, Kirk P	5:31:56	(30,553)
Ritchie, Michael	4:19:04	(15,537)
Ritchie, Ronald J	4:09:13	(12,895)
Ritchie, William P	4:15:12	(14,502)
Ritsema, Henk	5:00:20	(25,852)
Ritson, Gavin B	3:41:09	(6,209)
Ritson, Martin	5:02:20	(26,207)
Rivas May, Marco	3:44:23	(6,815)
Rivera, Juan H	3:52:30	(8,605)
Rivero, Jean-Louis F	5:05:02	(26,690)
Rivers, Roderick	4:37:34	(20,515)
Rivers, Stephen D	4:01:11	(10,977)
Rivers, Terry M	3:25:24	(3,656)
Rivett, Karl P	4:24:25	(16,965)
Riviere, Simon J	4:23:43	(16,781)
Rix, Jamie M	4:53:37	(24,333)
Rixen, Bruce P	5:03:43	(26,466)
Rixon, Edward J	3:58:17	(10,220)
Roach, Stephen M	3:35:26	(5,245)
Robb, Andrew J	3:26:02	(3,770)
Robb, David W	4:53:18	(24,251)
Robb, Paul A	4:53:45	(24,366)
Robbins, Brian	5:22:31	(29,423)
Robbins, Fred E	4:30:37	(18,750)
Robbins, Gordon C	3:32:05	(4,759)
Robbins, Grant B	4:38:36	(20,777)
Robbins, Jason C	3:06:26	(1,590)
Robbins, Keith A	3:24:33	(3,522)
Robbins, Keith G	4:13:43	(14,075)
Robbins, Martin	5:07:11	(27,096)
Robbins, Michael J	4:35:28	(19,968)
Robbins, Neil F	3:23:16	(3,345)
Robbs, Ian	6:21:41	(33,972)
Robe, Alec	5:44:49	(31,832)
Robert, Alan F	4:28:28	(18,156)
Robert, Iain A	2:45:56	(345)
Robert, Russell W	4:54:33	(24,566)
Roberts, Alan	3:48:27	(7,692)
Roberts, Alan	4:51:12	(23,777)
Roberts, Alan D	5:59:28	(32,944)
Roberts, Alex R	3:40:59	(6,177)
Roberts, Alfred C	3:24:00	(3,446)
Roberts, Andrew	3:49:53	(8,014)
Roberts, Andrew	5:23:02	(29,491)
Roberts, Andrew D	4:33:03	(19,327)
Roberts, Andrew J	3:32:05	(4,759)
Roberts, Andrew P	5:44:13	(31,783)
Roberts, Andy M	3:55:16	(9,298)
Roberts, Antony V	3:36:45	(5,458)
Roberts, Ashley M	3:58:21	(10,243)
Roberts, Benjamin J	4:20:22	(15,903)
Roberts, Bryan M	4:50:27	(23,612)
Roberts, Colin	4:30:34	(18,743)
Roberts, David	3:40:17	(6,048)
Roberts, David A	2:28:31	(62)
Roberts, David A	3:00:06	(1,134)
Roberts, David C	3:36:51	(5,472)
Roberts, David C	4:54:12	(24,475)
Roberts, David L	3:30:21	(4,498)
Roberts, Dean M	5:27:30	(30,046)
Roberts, Edward C	3:47:31	(7,460)
Roberts, Gareth P	4:34:55	(19,831)
Roberts, Gareth W	4:53:28	(24,294)
Roberts, Gary J	4:34:01	(19,560)
Roberts, Glenn M	4:45:35	(22,453)
Roberts, Glyn C	4:19:46	(15,743)
Roberts, Greg	4:34:03	(19,579)
Roberts, Ian W	3:21:07	(3,094)
Roberts, Ifor O	4:22:28	(16,464)
Roberts, Iorwerth	4:14:22	(14,263)
Roberts, Ivor L	4:52:26	(24,037)
Roberts, James E	4:20:37	(15,968)
Roberts, Jamie	3:00:25	(1,153)
Roberts, John A	4:31:22	(18,937)

Roberts, John E	5:18:08	(28,806)
Roberts, John R	2:52:39	(617)
Roberts, Julian T	4:23:43	(16,781)
Roberts, Kerry J	3:07:13	(1,649)
Roberts, Lee E	4:53:11	(24,217)
Roberts, Mark O	6:27:04	(34,162)
Roberts, Mark P	5:05:41	(26,821)
Roberts, Mark W	3:55:20	(9,315)
Roberts, Martin J	6:06:22	(33,350)
Roberts, Neville	4:03:00	(11,391)
Roberts, Nicholas	4:32:55	(19,295)
Roberts, Nicholas M	5:08:17	(27,257)
Roberts, Nick A	3:32:02	(4,753)
Roberts, Paul E	4:32:52	(19,279)
Roberts, Paul W	5:14:33	(28,268)
Roberts, Pete B	2:59:16	(1,064)
Roberts, Peter A	4:51:21	(23,809)
Roberts, Peter J	4:46:02	(22,557)
Roberts, Peter W	5:05:07	(26,707)
Roberts, Phil J	5:20:31	(29,182)
Roberts, Philip D	3:58:17	(10,220)
Roberts, Philip J	4:11:54	(13,590)
Roberts, Philip T	3:50:09	(8,073)
Roberts, Rhys	5:33:53	(30,763)
Roberts, Robin B	3:42:48	(6,511)
Roberts, Scott J	6:05:00	(33,268)
Roberts, Shaun G	4:51:01	(23,736)
Roberts, Simon A	3:00:12	(1,140)
Roberts, Simon J	3:06:00	(1,551)
Roberts, Simon M	4:51:53	(23,905)
Roberts, Stephen	4:29:19	(18,409)
Roberts, Stephen K	4:02:44	(11,329)
Roberts, Stephen M	3:43:50	(6,711)
Roberts, Stephen W	3:26:52	(3,904)
Roberts, Steve	3:36:53	(5,477)
Roberts, Steve J	3:23:14	(3,339)
Roberts, Steve L	4:37:39	(20,529)
Roberts, Tim	3:45:16	(7,000)
Roberts, Trevor J	4:13:29	(14,015)
Robertshaw, Simon	3:52:39	(8,646)
Robertshaw, Tom	3:09:50	(1,900)
Robertson, Allan M	4:35:36	(19,998)
Robertson, David	5:01:18	(26,029)
Robertson, Euan C	3:58:45	(10,366)
Robertson, Frazer	4:18:04	(15,226)
Robertson, Gordon	4:01:46	(11,104)
Robertson, Gregor D	5:22:52	(29,467)
Robertson, Ian H	3:28:52	(4,256)
Robertson, Ian M	3:20:42	(3,062)
Robertson, James A	4:15:54	(14,683)
Robertson, John M	3:51:11	(8,297)
Robertson, John P	3:40:31	(6,086)
Robertson, John R	3:36:23	(5,403)
Robertson, Joshua S	4:19:07	(15,553)
Robertson, Karl G	6:36:00	(34,410)
Robertson, Lex	4:10:29	(13,224)
Robertson, Mark S	5:05:41	(26,821)
Robertson, Michael I	4:21:59	(16,326)
Robertson, Mike J	3:57:15	(9,905)
Robertson, Noel	4:49:01	(23,241)
Robertson, Paul	3:04:21	(1,416)
Robertson, Paul J	3:32:29	(4,820)
Robertson, Peter	4:22:25	(16,449)
Robertson, Peter C	4:06:00	(12,094)
Robertson, Steven J	2:58:05	(961)
Robertson, Stewart D	3:15:05	(2,484)
Robertson, Stuart V	3:53:54	(8,953)
Robey, Christopher J	4:21:50	(16,292)
Robinne, Benoit	4:46:54	(22,753)
Robins, Paul	3:43:17	(6,613)
Robins, Stephen D	3:33:20	(4,936)
Robins, Steven J	3:29:57	(4,446)
Robinson, Aaron E	4:09:34	(12,977)
Robinson, Alex	3:26:03	(3,773)
Robinson, Andrew	3:40:10	(6,031)
Robinson, Andrew	5:24:16	(29,657)
Robinson, Andy P	3:19:45	(2,972)
Robinson, Anthony	3:25:36	(3,686)
Robinson, Barry J	4:43:19	(21,940)
Robinson, Benjamin E	4:16:32	(14,842)
Robinson, Christopher S	3:55:07	(9,257)
Robinson, Daniel	4:53:16	(24,239)
Robinson, Dave J	4:32:22	(19,179)

Robinson, David	4:10:18	(13,169)
Robinson, David A	5:07:12	(27,103)
Robinson, David J	3:11:20	(2,063)
Robinson, David K	3:19:06	(2,890)
Robinson, Fred D	3:41:14	(6,222)
Robinson, Gary A	4:36:03	(20,093)
Robinson, Geoffrey C	5:24:39	(29,701)
Robinson, George	3:04:47	(1,449)
Robinson, Gerald	5:11:17	(27,701)
Robinson, Glen J	5:09:32	(27,442)
Robinson, Gordon A	4:15:25	(14,555)
Robinson, Graham K	4:28:21	(18,122)
Robinson, Howard J	4:47:09	(22,806)
Robinson, Ian R	4:04:08	(11,670)
Robinson, James S	4:45:32	(22,439)
Robinson, John	4:08:14	(12,622)
Robinson, Jonathan C	4:10:08	(13,123)
Robinson, Jonathan E	4:22:20	(16,429)
Robinson, Kenneth E	3:20:01	(2,998)
Robinson, Kevin J	5:22:45	(29,458)
Robinson, Mark A	3:43:17	(6,613)
Robinson, Mark A	4:51:10	(23,766)
Robinson, Matthew W	3:56:13	(9,578)
Robinson, Meirion P	4:42:42	(21,800)
Robinson, Nigel T	4:37:07	(20,391)
Robinson, Oliver V	3:41:03	(6,192)
Robinson, Paul	4:25:03	(17,137)
Robinson, Peter A	4:42:03	(21,634)
Robinson, Phillip M	3:55:54	(9,488)
Robinson, Ronald H	4:06:56	(12,324)
Robinson, Simon	3:55:21	(9,321)
Robinson, Simon J	3:45:36	(7,065)
Robinson, Simon R	3:47:00	(7,350)
Robinson, Steven A	4:11:12	(13,406)
Robinson, Stuart G	2:38:04	(162)
Robinson, Terry A	5:31:27	(30,514)
Robinson, Thomas J	3:18:50	(2,864)
Robinson, Thomas S	4:15:14	(14,511)
Robinson, Timothy R	4:25:00	(17,125)
Robinson, Victor	4:39:29	(21,008)
Robinson, William A	4:04:00	(11,633)
Robl, Daniel	3:32:28	(4,819)
Robles, Martin Roy	5:08:25	(27,272)
Robottom, Charles E	4:42:56	(21,858)
Robshaw, Craig	2:57:28	(920)
Robson, David A	4:43:34	(22,002)
Robson, David W	4:05:06	(11,897)
Robson, Dean	4:28:34	(18,187)
Robson, Fred T	5:04:38	(26,618)
Robson, Graham D	3:25:15	(3,637)
Robson, Hugo J	4:42:07	(21,657)
Robson, Mark	3:47:25	(7,440)
Robson, Mark A	3:48:18	(7,657)
Robson, Paul D	5:59:49	(32,971)
Robson, Philip J	2:48:26	(430)
Robson, Simon	5:43:06	(31,686)
Robson, Terence	4:07:08	(12,379)
Robson, Terry	3:34:12	(5,078)
Robson, Wayne	3:58:00	(10,142)
Rocchi, Carlo	4:49:24	(23,334)
Rocha, Fernando T	3:15:55	(2,559)
Roche, Angus	3:48:14	(7,641)
Roche, Brendan J	4:12:09	(13,650)
Roche, Brendan M	3:33:12	(4,910)
Roche, David P	4:05:05	(11,889)
Roche, Michael P	6:04:29	(33,246)
Roche, Michel	3:31:18	(4,651)
Roche, Richard A	4:01:53	(11,124)
Roche, Stephen W	7:03:04	(34,905)
Rocher, Franck	3:34:41	(5,146)
Rocher, Graham P	3:38:07	(5,669)
Rochester, Matthew C	3:25:14	(3,631)
Rocheta, Patrick	3:58:56	(10,414)
Rochussen, Gavin M	3:47:38	(7,482)
Rockey, Alan J	3:08:49	(1,792)
Rockliffe, Albert E	3:57:56	(10,123)
Rockliffe, Richard J	4:06:51	(12,301)
Rodd, Owen J	3:35:57	(5,331)
Rodda, Alan P	4:14:16	(14,239)
Rodda, John K	3:50:56	(8,245)
Rodda, Robert C	3:31:25	(4,666)
Rode, Eckhard	3:56:20	(9,614)
Rodell, Michael	5:27:53	(30,086)

Roderick, Kevin	4:06:36	(12,241)
Rodewald, Mike	4:05:46	(12,041)
Rodger, James	4:54:12	(24,475)
Rodger, Jody S	3:28:17	(4,155)
Rodger, John D	4:34:33	(19,727)
Rodger, Tommy	5:14:20	(28,236)
Rodgers, James	3:21:46	(3,159)
Rodgers, Matthew R	4:08:19	(12,645)
Rodgers, Paul D	4:38:07	(20,654)
Rodgers, Paul J	4:15:42	(14,636)
Rodgers, Simon J	3:39:22	(5,886)
Rodgerson, Phillip J	4:48:44	(23,175)
Rodricks, Warren K	5:37:49	(31,169)
Rodrigues, Antonio	4:23:17	(16,683)
Rodrigues, Duarte H	5:29:41	(30,330)
Rodrigues, Mervyn A	3:14:20	(2,397)
Rodrigues, Stephen G	3:53:71	(8,792)
Rodriguez, Arturo	4:26:29	(17,593)
Rodriguez, Marcos A	4:25:39	(17,335)
Rodriguez, Xavier	3:53:31	(8,861)
Rodway, Charlie W	4:15:52	(14,678)
Rodwell, Maurice W	3:46:26	(7,228)
Rodwell, Michael A	5:46:23	(31,971)
Rodwell, Timothy	6:02:52	(33,134)
Roe, Alan M	4:40:20	(21,218)
Roe, John W	4:25:22	(17,235)
Roe, Terence R	5:08:42	(27,311)
Roe, William G	5:34:42	(30,874)
Roebuck, Martin P	4:24:10	(16,894)
Roebuck, Tony	3:38:57	(5,807)
Roedel, Timothy C	4:15:52	(14,678)
Roelofsz, Ian	4:40:25	(21,284)
Roeske, Ralf	3:11:34	(2,083)
Roets, Lourens	5:14:10	(28,204)
Roff, Neil A	4:27:27	(17,869)
Rogatzki, Hartmut	4:28:26	(18,146)
Rogers, Andrew N	5:29:17	(30,271)
Rogers, Dominic P	3:53:33	(8,871)
Rogers, James H	4:01:57	(11,138)
Rogers, James P	3:58:54	(10,408)
Rogers, Jamie P	3:46:07	(7,164)
Rogers, John A	2:51:12	(546)
Rogers, Mark E	4:11:46	(13,555)
Rogers, Mark R	3:53:46	(8,928)
Rogers, Martin T	4:58:53	(25,530)
Rogers, Michael R	3:53:19	(8,809)
Rogers, Michael S	4:35:42	(20,019)
Rogers, Nigel M	4:16:33	(14,845)
Rogers, Paul	3:53:15	(8,783)
Rogers, Paul S	3:29:02	(4,277)
Rogers, Philip	4:13:05	(13,906)
Rogers, Philip A	3:27:10	(3,951)
Rogers, Philip J	4:16:13	(14,771)
Rogers, Timothy M	4:16:54	(14,935)
Rogers, Timothy M	5:03:46	(26,476)
Rogerson, Neil L	4:33:17	(19,377)
Rogerson, Paul C	6:23:29	(34,037)
Rogowski, John T	4:03:49	(11,584)
Roguet, Jean-Michel	4:12:32	(13,752)
Roige-Tost, Joan M	3:57:02	(9,828)
Roland, Michael	3:52:17	(8,551)
Rolf, Kevin J	5:25:44	(29,829)
Rolfe, David N	5:59:02	(32,915)
Rolfe, Gerald A	3:45:54	(7,118)
Rolfe, John W	5:33:28	(30,719)
Rolfe, Les J	4:06:25	(12,193)
Rolfe, Matthew	4:19:17	(15,604)
Rolfe, Michael A	2:47:58	(413)
Rolling, Bruno	3:48:41	(7,757)
Rollings, Chris J	4:35:27	(19,966)
Rollings, Matt J	4:20:05	(15,826)
Rollinson, Simon R	5:55:59	(32,707)
Rollo, Derek R	4:20:06	(15,832)
Rolls, Dominic F	4:59:15	(25,615)
Romagnoli, Fabio	2:42:38	(255)
Romani, Gino	4:17:51	(15,170)
Romasanta, Nicolas	4:11:25	(13,458)
Rombouts, Ronald	4:34:19	(19,668)
Rome, Regis A	3:47:37	(7,480)
Romero-Blanco, José M	4:30:39	(18,760)
Ronan, Paul	4:13:55	(14,122)
Ronnan, Andrew	4:49:14	(23,288)
Rook, John	3:49:46	(7,993)

Rook, Jonathan 4:24:19 (16,932)
Rook, Spencer J 3:05:36 (1,525)
Rooke, Reg V 4:25:11 (17,182)
Rooke, Timothy J 3:56:41 (9,722)
Rookes, Jonathan M 5:17:35 (28,731)
Roome, Paul C 3:26:58 (3,925)
Roonan, Mark A 5:39:57 (31,409)
Rooney, Tom 4:35:16 (19,900)
Roos, Olle 3:27:06 (3,943)
Root, David J 4:28:06 (18,057)
Rootes, Bryan E 3:56:18 (9,605)
Roper, Chris B 3:28:18 (4,160)
Roper, Goy 2:51:53 (581)
Roper, Ian D 3:49:16 (7,883)
Roper, Luke J 3:49:39 (7,965)
Roper, Martin J 4:23:35 (16,752)
Roper, Simon 4:49:18 (23,306)
Roper, Tom 4:32:11 (19,131)
Roper, Tristan J 3:28:23 (4,175)
Ropson, Andrew C 4:34:08 (19,604)
Roptin, Serge 4:02:26 (11,255)
Rosbrook, Simon J 3:59:22 (10,538)
Rose, Alistair M 4:00:05 (10,748)
Rose, Andrew 6:05:20 (33,290)
Rose, Andrew D 5:47:43 (32,075)
Rose, Anthony 3:59:08 (10,479)
Rose, Ben R 5:05:50 (26,848)
Rose, Christopher 4:38:39 (20,786)
Rose, David 4:29:28 (18,453)
Rose, Derek 4:58:35 (25,463)
Rose, Edward J 4:59:23 (25,639)
Rose, Gary 4:09:44 (13,022)
Rose, Ian 4:47:22 (22,847)
Rose, John E 5:33:43 (30,747)
Rose, Johnathan W 3:44:05 (6,756)
Rose, Jonathan 4:26:24 (17,570)
Rose, Martin D 3:30:18 (4,489)
Rose, Michael 4:25:55 (17,404)
Rose, Michael 7:10:58 (34,985)
Rose, Nicholas J 5:20:15 (29,135)
Rose, Nigel M 5:03:05 (26,359)
Rose, Paul J 2:53:36 (663)
Rose, Richard I 6:03:17 (33,165)
Rose, Sean A 2:55:07 (748)
Rose, Stephen D 5:55:49 (32,699)
Rose, Stuart K 4:10:51 (13,303)
Rose, Tony 4:24:45 (17,059)
Rose, Tony I 3:28:45 (4,234)
Rosedale, Benjamin J 3:20:39 (3,059)
Rosell, Martin J 3:35:29 (5,260)
Rosello, Alex L 4:34:52 (19,811)
Rosemont, Jonathan D 4:40:59 (21,385)
Rosengren, Tomas M 4:13:22 (13,982)
Rosenthal, James P 5:04:52 (26,663)
Rosenthal, Tom 5:18:13 (28,820)
Roseveare, Blake 4:04:01 (11,640)
Rosin, Alexei J 4:34:04 (19,583)
Rospocher, Frederic 3:48:54 (7,802)
Ross, Adrian P 5:08:19 (27,262)
Ross, Allan 4:09:08 (12,870)
Ross, Andrew 4:55:22 (24,751)
Ross, Andrew M 4:23:10 (16,647)
Ross, Andrew T 4:15:57 (14,698)
Ross, Bruce J 4:09:53 (13,063)
Ross, Charlie 5:00:18 (25,845)
Ross, Christopher 4:15:33 (14,593)
Ross, Christopher J 3:11:24 (2,069)
Ross, Daniel M 5:31:05 (30,478)
Ross, David P 3:41:53 (6,351)
Ross, Duncan J 4:40:02 (21,149)
Ross, Ian F 5:03:12 (26,385)
Ross, Ian N 4:39:11 (20,923)
Ross, Kenneth 5:36:12 (31,013)
Ross, Matt J 4:24:03 (16,868)
Ross, Michael C 4:05:19 (11,952)
Ross Gower, Sam 4:15:15 (14,515)
Rossberg, Arnold 5:08:56 (27,345)
Rosser, Adam W 4:22:03 (16,356)
Rossetti, Fabio 4:24:12 (16,901)
Rossetti, Giacomo 4:27:24 (17,857)
Rossetti, Gilberto 4:46:42 (22,709)
Rossetti, Luca 4:12:57 (13,869)
Rossetti, Massimo 4:36:38 (20,263)

Rossi, Alex H 3:41:01 (6,182)
Rossi, Claudio 5:23:55 (29,607)
Rossi, Edward A 6:13:36 (33,685)
Rossi, Guiseppe 6:54:48 (34,795)
Rossignol, Alain P 3:53:39 (8,896)
Rossington, Paul 3:31:49 (4,722)
Rossiter, Garth M 4:48:05 (23,029)
Rossiter, Philippe R 5:21:28 (29,292)
Rost, Carl-Herik 2:55:36 (778)
Rothband, Nigel 5:38:02 (31,198)
Rothengast, Joachim 3:32:41 (4,842)
Rothera, Malcolm 3:38:12 (5,681)
Rothkopf, Robert 3:32:31 (4,822)
Rothwell, Colin 3:10:20 (1,963)
Roukin, Joseph M 4:08:59 (12,823)
Roulston, Greg 4:55:25 (24,762)
Rounce, Phil 4:40:09 (21,171)
Round, Steve 3:29:34 (4,367)
Rounding, Simon 5:51:00 (32,334)
Rourke, Anthony 4:38:59 (20,871)
Rouse, Adam 2:39:26 (185)
Rouse, Anthony L 4:00:42 (10,887)
Rouse, Nick Q 4:39:45 (21,081)
Rouse, Stephen 3:13:55 (2,347)
Rousell, Lee T 5:34:23 (30,828)
Rousselet, Serge 3:54:14 (9,029)
Routledge, Dale P 3:43:03 (6,561)
Routledge, Jonathan 5:17:03 (28,656)
Routley, Luke J 4:01:20 (11,007)

Roux, Michel A 3:18:00 (2,787)

Rovera, Roberto 5:16:04 (28,487)
Row, Paul M 3:12:10 (2,160)
Rowan, Sean 3:20:31 (3,047)
Rowat, Peter J 2:48:39 (444)
Rowbotham, Malcolm J 3:43:15 (6,605)
Rowbottom, Peter J 5:49:37 (32,235)
Rowe, Alan Y 5:21:26 (29,290)
Rowe, Andrew J 5:24:32 (29,687)
Rowe, Ben J 5:34:59 (30,902)
Rowe, Brian D 4:57:45 (25,272)
Rowe, Christopher S 4:30:02 (18,600)
Rowe, Dave 4:19:22 (15,629)
Rowe, John C 5:13:52 (28,144)
Rowe, Malcolm J 3:54:01 (8,979)
Rowe, Martin 4:24:20 (16,938)
Rowe, Michael J 4:39:53 (21,106)
Rowe, Neil 4:27:06 (17,775)

Rowe, Nicholas 3:50:22 (8,118)
Rowe, Philip 4:32:39 (19,238)
Rowe, Philip H 4:00:30 (10,832)
Rowe, Simon A 5:24:32 (29,687)
Rowe, Simon J 3:41:45 (6,324)
Rowe, Steven I 4:50:36 (23,649)
Rowell, Alan 4:43:17 (21,930)
Rowell, Barry M 4:24:04 (16,870)
Rowell, Ben 4:13:58 (14,135)
Rowland, Adam J 5:19:08 (28,961)
Rowland, Chris M 4:27:18 (17,825)
Rowland, George F 5:17:34 (28,730)
Rowland, Ian 2:48:02 (417)
Rowland, Mark 4:16:48 (14,913)
Rowland, Mark 5:58:59 (32,912)
Rowland, Michael J 5:37:03 (31,104)
Rowland, Michael W 4:02:53 (11,359)
Rowland, Robert D 5:46:08 (31,944)
Rowlands, Darren W 2:44:47 (313)
Rowlands, David 4:03:00 (11,391)
Rowlands, Peter 4:17:21 (15,050)
Rowley, Chris R 3:48:54 (7,802)
Rowley, David B 4:21:18 (16,145)
Rowley, David C 6:29:08 (34,223)
Rowley, David J 4:44:55 (22,301)
Rowley, James R 3:16:46 (2,660)
Rowley, Peter S 6:36:30 (34,421)
Rowley, Peter W 3:49:44 (7,985)
Rowlinson, Cliff J 4:56:35 (25,035)
Rowson, Neil J 3:59:07 (10,473)
Rowson, Tom 5:40:25 (31,462)
Roxborough, Andrew 3:55:23 (9,332)
Roxborough, Michael J 4:13:02 (13,888)
Roy, Jason G 3:27:38 (4,042)
Royce, Peter H 5:13:40 (28,112)
Royle, Neil F 4:24:07 (16,881)
Rozasty, Shane M 5:03:49 (26,489)
Rozet, Jean-Patrick J 3:36:06 (5,355)
Rozewicz, Leon M 4:38:45 (20,814)
Rozier, Kevin J 4:57:03 (25,143)
Rtuston, Stuart R 3:43:55 (6,725)
Ruane, Anthony J 4:17:53 (15,177)
Ruane, Patrick J 5:35:27 (30,952)
Rucklidge, Paul 5:37:26 (31,133)
Rudall, David C 3:17:27 (2,729)
Rudd, Arthur 4:32:06 (19,109)
Rudd, Derek A 5:52:15 (32,433)
Rudd, Greg 5:54:14 (32,586)
Rudd, James H 4:31:30 (18,972)
Rudd, Timothy J 4:14:44 (14,358)
Rudd-Clarke, Peter J 3:48:39 (7,753)
Ruddle, Paul D 3:08:47 (1,788)
Ruddy, Martin J 4:42:39 (21,786)
Rudge, Anthony L 4:00:32 (10,843)
Rudge, David P 4:36:17 (20,156)
Rudkin, Karl 4:09:36 (12,983)
Rudley, Gary 5:47:27 (32,058)
Rudnas, Per- Erik 4:46:36 (22,688)
Rudnick, Errol S 4:28:29 (18,162)
Rudolph, Jason J 4:13:09 (13,922)
Rud-Petersen, Lars 3:17:24 (2,723)
Rueda, Richard 3:55:43 (9,435)
Ruellan, Gregory I 4:27:20 (17,833)
Rueve, Hans-Joachim 2:57:04 (889)
Ruffell, Andrew 3:44:11 (6,784)
Ruffell, Richard H 3:10:25 (1,969)
Ruffhead, Peter J 3:46:21 (7,211)
Ruffle, Steve 5:32:26 (30,609)
Rugeroni, Andrew A 4:22:05 (16,362)
Rugg, Richard 4:14:38 (14,325)
Ruhen, Peter M 4:13:26 (13,998)
Rumbles, Chris R 4:26:31 (17,608)
Rummey, Ian 4:16:12 (14,765)
Rumsby, Mark J 5:27:37 (30,056)
Runkee, Timothy J 5:45:57 (31,928)
Rupp, Kurt 4:36:42 (20,279)
Rupp, Marcus 3:27:01 (3,931)
Ruscoe, Steven G 4:24:43 (17,047)
Rusenfeld, David 4:23:13 (16,655)
Rush, Stuart E 5:23:46 (29,581)
Rusha, Guy 5:07:01 (27,060)
Rushby, Ian J 4:02:55 (11,374)
Rushmer, Gary 3:12:40 (2,212)

Rushton, Peter R....4:47:39 (22,927)
Rushworth, Paul D....3:11:59 (2,138)
Russ, Lucian F....6:13:41 (33,687)
Russell, Anthony L....4:55:37 (24,795)
Russell, Barry M....5:18:06 (28,798)
Russell, Christopher J....4:29:55 (18,570)
Russell, Clive G....5:02:15 (26,190)
Russell, Dean....4:34:14 (19,646)
Russell, Dominic H....3:38:44 (5,759)
Russell, Ian D....3:03:40 (1,381)
Russell, Jack B....5:47:39 (32,070)
Russell, James....4:17:08 (14,997)
Russell, James A....4:36:12 (20,127)
Russell, James D....5:38:15 (31,226)
Russell, Jimmy W....3:54:08 (9,005)
Russell, John C....3:15:19 (2,506)
Russell, John R....3:06:34 (1,601)
Russell, Justin C....3:52:36 (8,629)
Russell, Mark J....4:41:14 (21,454)
Russell, Mike....4:42:38 (21,781)
Russell, Neill H....4:47:04 (22,784)
Russell, Peter J....2:44:54 (316)
Russell, Philip....3:19:30 (2,937)
Russell, Philip W....4:24:58 (17,113)
Russell, Phillip E....3:35:41 (5,293)
Russell, Richard J....5:22:24 (29,404)
Russell, Richard M....5:19:15 (28,986)
Russell, Richard P....3:59:08 (10,479)
Russell, Shaune D....3:03:24 (1,354)
Russell, Stephen F....3:13:17 (2,273)
Russell, Stephen J....4:31:13 (18,888)
Russell, Thomas....3:44:47 (6,901)
Russell, Timothy B....5:06:02 (26,881)
Russell, Trevor J....4:09:18 (12,908)
Russon, Christopher L....3:28:34 (4,211)
Russon, Nick C....4:54:04 (24,443)
Rust, James D....3:12:25 (2,187)
Rustad, Luke R....5:51:04 (32,343)
Rutherford, David A....3:54:34 (9,116)
Rutherford, Ian....3:22:08 (3,204)
Rutherford, Neil....3:34:36 (5,135)
Rutherford, Paul A....3:36:54 (5,482)
Rutherford, Simon J....2:40:51 (216)
Rutland, Graham R....4:38:18 (20,697)
Rutt, Carl J....3:45:07 (6,974)
Rutter, John....3:51:49 (8,445)
Rutter, Stuart....4:34:40 (19,753)
Ruttew, George....3:25:32 (3,680)
Rutto, Evans....2:12:49 (10)
Ryall, Barry J....5:09:10 (27,383)
Ryalls, Terrence....3:23:33 (3,381)
Ryan, Andrew P....4:39:30 (21,013)
Ryan, Chris M....5:50:43 (32,317)
Ryan, Ciaran....4:02:56 (11,378)
Ryan, Daniel J....5:11:59 (27,819)
Ryan, Edward....5:46:18 (31,964)
Ryan, John....4:07:50 (12,537)
Ryan, Jon....4:46:06 (22,578)
Ryan, Marc....4:27:21 (17,838)
Ryan, Martin N....7:57:07 (35,225)
Ryan, Patrick J....5:00:15 (25,831)
Ryan, Paul W....4:23:15 (16,669)
Ryan, Robert A....3:10:52 (2,017)
Ryan, Shane P....4:56:43 (25,073)
Ryan, Terence....4:47:59 (23,004)
Ryan, Tony....6:29:37 (34,245)
Ryan, Wayne M....3:28:00 (4,104)
Rybka, Karsten....3:00:33 (1,158)
Rycroft, Alan....5:26:20 (29,906)
Ryder, John....4:27:04 (17,765)
Ryder, John G....3:43:37 (6,672)
Ryder, Mark....6:13:26 (33,675)
Ryder, Simon....3:55:15 (9,292)
Rye, Andrew E....4:06:01 (12,096)
Rye, Joe M....2:44:05 (297)
Rye, Kim B....5:01:37 (26,083)
Ryeland, John....5:55:09 (32,649)
Saan, Ain....3:24:18 (3,486)
Sabel, Adrian G....4:03:12 (11,432)
Sabharwal, Ravi A....5:06:29 (26,959)
Sabin, Andrew....3:15:56 (2,560)
Sacks, Daniel....3:07:33 (1,679)
Saddington, William K....4:27:50 (17,992)
Sadek, Ahmed-Ramadan H....3:44:00 (6,742)
Sadler, Alan....5:38:37 (31,268)
Sadler, Brett A....5:21:37 (29,302)
Sadler, Clayton W....4:42:32 (21,747)
Sadnicki, Stefan M....3:34:13 (5,082)
Saer, Dylan O....4:43:35 (22,003)
Saether, Dagfinn....4:11:03 (13,368)
Sagar, Nicholas....3:25:34 (3,684)
Sage, Andrew J....4:32:23 (19,184)
Sage, Gary L....3:35:41 (5,293)
Sage, Roland J....4:43:54 (22,070)
Saggs, Mark....4:34:12 (19,624)
Saggu, Ranvir S....5:42:33 (31,634)
Saha, Soumen....5:19:14 (28,982)
Saha, Sujit K....5:17:32 (28,723)
Sahota, Harpreet....4:29:43 (18,525)
Saibeni, Paolo....4:03:49 (11,584)
Said, Craig T....5:52:13 (32,429)
Sailer, Lutz M....4:09:10 (12,878)
Sainty, Martin....4:13:45 (14,077)
Saito, Toshihiko....5:07:59 (27,215)
Saklow, Alex J....3:58:42 (10,347)
Sale, Dominic M....3:43:10 (6,586)
Sale, Matt R....3:26:03 (3,773)
Sale, Sean R....5:12:25 (27,890)
Sale, Stewart L....4:12:37 (13,781)
Salem, Jonathan M....5:06:39 (26,994)
Salem, Paul A....4:21:13 (16,113)
Sales, Alexander....3:47:45 (7,514)
Sales, Roger....3:59:20 (10,527)
Sali, Zakariyya....4:32:24 (19,188)
Saliba, Themis....5:07:22 (27,123)
Salinas, Manuel....4:28:14 (18,095)
Salisbury, James R....5:03:49 (26,489)
Salisbury, Jonathan M....4:37:25 (20,478)
Salisbury, Peter G....5:03:42 (26,461)
Sallaba, Milan....3:37:33 (5,586)
Salmon, Jon....4:06:19 (12,171)
Salmon, Richard....7:11:00 (34,987)
Salmon, Stefan R....4:26:13 (17,511)
Salonia, Paul J....5:32:40 (30,634)
Salt, Neil....3:29:14 (4,317)
Salt, Tim R....3:55:48 (9,461)
Salte, Rein Harald....4:17:06 (14,982)
Salter, Chris....3:27:42 (4,061)
Salter, Chris E....5:00:13 (25,823)
Salter, Julian G....3:11:14 (2,056)
Salter, Kevin....4:59:02 (25,569)
Salter, Neil H....5:36:08 (31,007)
Salter, Nigel J....4:12:46 (13,825)
Salter, Peter....3:46:18 (7,202)
Salters, Remy K....3:59:02 (10,443)
Saltrick, Christopher J....4:23:16 (16,675)
Sambells, Christopher S....3:29:04 (4,286)
Sambrook, Philip A....3:58:43 (10,354)
Sammes, Mark A....5:27:37 (30,056)
Sample, Ian R....4:08:12 (12,615)
Sampol, Juan....4:21:23 (16,169)
Sampson, Ceri D....4:13:10 (13,928)
Sampson, Kufreh....4:32:22 (19,179)
Sampson, Michael L....4:23:05 (16,625)
Sampson, Stuart....4:37:06 (20,386)
Samray, Daniel....4:34:38 (19,743)
Sams, Christopher R....5:39:48 (31,397)
Sams, Ron A....5:39:02 (31,313)
Samson, James R....3:43:04 (6,565)
Samson, Phil J....3:11:34 (2,083)
Samter, Mark G....4:37:27 (20,482)
Samuel, Graham J....6:21:36 (33,969)
Samuels, Bill R....4:43:14 (21,919)
Samways, Paul....4:41:29 (21,518)
Sanchez, Manuel....3:46:04 (7,153)
Sanchez Torres, Horacio....4:10:09 (13,127)
Sanchez-Burgos, Elisaroo....4:20:09 (15,840)
Sanchez-Migallon, Juan R....3:28:57 (4,266)
Sanctuary, Nigel L....4:46:56 (22,757)
Sandeman, Donald S....3:14:16 (2,388)
Sandercock, Graham M....4:39:23 (20,985)
Sandercombe, Robert....3:35:20 (5,227)
Sanders, David P....4:44:23 (22,188)
Sanders, Gerald K....3:44:40 (6,872)
Sanders, Graham R....5:47:54 (32,092)
Sanders, Justin L....4:32:52 (19,279)
Sanders, Kevin D....4:08:47 (12,764)
Sanders, Leslie W....4:09:44 (13,022)
Sanders, Martin B....2:39:26 (185)
Sanders, Neil J....5:38:08 (31,212)
Sanders, Paul R....4:14:21 (14,257)
Sanders, Richard....4:50:24 (23,596)
Sanders, Stephen W....4:32:42 (19,248)
Sanders, Steve P....4:24:03 (16,868)
Sanders, Thomas W....6:01:41 (33,064)
Sanderson, Andrew J....4:32:33 (19,219)
Sanderson, Brian....4:03:51 (11,595)
Sanderson, Craig....3:37:38 (5,592)
Sanderson, Kenneth....3:10:53 (2,021)
Sanderson, Mike....6:19:06 (33,891)
Sanderson, Paul J....2:51:42 (574)
Sanderson, Peter J....3:45:20 (7,012)
Sanderson, Terry M....4:17:48 (15,158)
Sanderson, Tom D....3:33:27 (4,954)
Sandham, Stephen....3:20:54 (3,080)
Sandhu, Dilbag Singh....4:54:16 (24,492)
Sandhu, John S....3:20:32 (3,048)
Sandhu, Ranjeet S....4:06:17 (12,163)
Sandilands, William....3:21:28 (3,129)
Sandmoe, Bjoern....4:15:50 (14,673)
Sands, Benjamin J....4:37:05 (20,377)
Sands, Daniel M....5:12:23 (27,882)
Sands, Martin J....4:02:31 (11,276)
Sandstad, Henrik....2:18:36 (22)
Sanford, Steve P....6:41:11 (34,530)
Sanford, Yenal E....4:48:25 (23,107)
Sangala, Nicholas C....4:34:03 (19,579)
Sanger, Philip B....2:44:56 (317)
Sanghera, Bal....3:51:02 (8,261)
Sanghera, Kirn K....4:56:38 (25,050)
Sanghera, Lember S....6:42:45 (34,565)
Sangster, Ben R....3:55:47 (9,457)
Sanhaie, Adam N....5:08:26 (27,275)
Sanham, Robert A....3:56:10 (9,562)
Sankey, Paul W....2:35:51 (121)
Sankey, Stuart C....6:27:06 (34,167)
Sanotra, Sumeet....5:55:33 (32,684)
Sansom, Chris J....3:30:37 (4,546)
Sansom, Derek T....3:22:55 (3,286)
Sansom, James C....5:07:02 (27,061)
Sansom, Matthew C....3:40:36 (6,101)
Sanson, Neil R....5:16:54 (28,624)
Sant, Paul M....3:44:19 (6,799)
Santamarta Banos, Carlos....3:26:00 (3,757)
Santiago, Antonio....3:19:18 (2,910)
Santiago, Joseph....3:26:30 (3,849)
Santini, Alex....4:39:48 (21,093)
Santoro, Francesco....4:13:54 (14,112)
Santos-Moreno, Juan A....3:05:10 (1,481)
Saoul, Daniel A....3:46:45 (7,297)
Sapsford, James....3:52:57 (8,711)
Sara, Richard J....5:13:17 (28,040)
Sarabia, Guillermo....5:09:01 (27,358)
Saracini, Giorgio....4:13:38 (14,053)
Sardar, Shahid....5:36:30 (31,057)
Sarfo-Kantanka, Mark E....5:34:16 (30,815)
Sargeant, Steven G....5:24:26 (29,674)
Sargent, David G....2:42:45 (260)
Sargent, Edward....4:06:30 (12,213)
Sargent, Matthew....3:41:27 (6,268)
Sargent, Paul....5:02:52 (26,313)
Sargent, Richard....4:06:29 (12,209)
Sargent, Richard....4:56:16 (24,955)
Sargent, Rob....3:21:18 (3,115)
Sargerson, Colin....4:26:40 (17,653)
Sarjeant, Michael A....5:17:12 (28,674)
Sarrand, Loic....2:56:18 (829)
Sarti, Gabriele....3:19:10 (2,896)
Sartin, Rob D....3:13:36 (2,318)
Sassone, Matthew....3:58:46 (10,375)
Sato, Kenji....2:48:56 (465)
Sato, Masayoshi....5:53:44 (32,548)
Sato, Takaaki....5:47:22 (32,046)
Satterthwaite, Christopher J....4:50:21 (23,579)
Sattler, Christoph....4:06:30 (12,213)
Satzinger, Rainer....4:49:18 (23,306)
Sauer, Glen J....3:09:52 (1,905)
Sauer, Reiner....5:53:02 (32,499)
Sauer, Ulrich....3:43:28 (6,647)

Saunders, Andrew C 4:45:13 (22,374)
Saunders, Andrew T....4:05:53 (12,068)
Saunders, Andy 4:58:44 (25,493)
Saunders, Ben 3:02:47 (1,320)
Saunders, Christian D....4:27:47 (17,980)
Saunders, Colin 4:12:09 (13,650)
Saunders, Jason W....4:40:20 (21,218)
Saunders, John P....4:20:24 (15,912)
Saunders, Karl 5:00:10 (25,808)
Saunders, Kevin J 3:57:00 (9,815)
Saunders, Mark J 4:04:30 (11,746)
Saunders, Neil 5:07:15 (27,109)
Saunders, Paul A 4:24:26 (16,970)
Saunders, Peter J 3:41:43 (6,319)
Saunders, Rhys 4:11:36 (13,506)
Saunders, Richard....3:59:14 (10,503)
Saunders, Richard R 4:01:14 (10,991)
Saunders, Robert J 4:33:32 (19,444)
Saunders, Rowan G....3:30:12 (4,476)
Saunders, Sarah J 4:38:51 (20,840)
Saunders, Stephen 3:30:56 (4,595)
Saunders, Thomas H 3:37:28 (5,575)
Saunderson, Eric M 4:52:02 (23,944)
Saunderson, Ian 4:08:40 (12,733)
Saunderson, William B 7:00:53 (34,886)
Saurin, Adrian T 3:56:16 (9,589)
Sauvary, Kelvyn 5:38:30 (31,250)
Sauveplane, Jean Marie E....3:26:00 (3,757)
Savage, Brian 3:29:29 (4,351)
Savage, Emma 4:27:51 (17,998)
Savage, James S....2:51:48 (579)
Savage, John 6:12:08 (33,623)
Savage, Mark....4:06:57 (12,329)
Savage, Mark T 3:38:14 (5,684)
Savage, Neil 5:51:49 (32,397)
Savage, Regan N....3:30:06 (4,467)
Savage, Toby 3:22:55 (3,286)
Savanelli, Filippo....5:28:52 (30,229)
Savastio, Andrea 3:26:29 (3,844)
Savery, Ernie J....5:27:21 (30,021)
Saville, Michael G....6:13:04 (33,665)
Saville, Rob D 5:20:54 (29,224)
Savino, Salvatore 4:08:49 (12,773)
Savoy, Hubert M....4:25:31 (17,290)
Savoy, William J 5:26:56 (29,968)
Savvitchev, Alexei 3:30:37 (4,546)
Sawers, Matthew R 6:32:23 (34,316)
Sawko, Peter W....4:06:50 (12,297)
Sawtell, Paul W 6:47:20 (34,662)
Sawyer, Robert F....4:58:51 (25,524)
Sawyers, Craig G....3:37:18 (5,536)
Saxby, Graham....6:00:30 (33,002)
Sayburn, Robert P 4:34:03 (19,579)
Sayburn, Ronan....4:30:21 (18,690)
Sayce, Jonathan R....3:28:37 (4,215)
Sayed, Jeff T....4:17:37 (15,115)
Sayer, Edward O 4:19:35 (15,686)
Sayers, Andrew J 4:21:47 (16,280)
Sayers, Brian A 4:24:18 (16,924)
Sayers, Nigel T....3:50:27 (8,138)
Sayle, Mark 4:48:55 (23,216)
Sayward, William J....4:56:19 (24,967)
Scales, Julian F....6:08:41 (33,474)
Scales, Robin 4:01:37 (11,072)
Scales, Simon 4:31:45 (19,032)
Scanlan, Bernard A....3:33:04 (4,896)
Scanlan, Timothy W....3:25:37 (3,689)
Scanlon, Bernard J 4:43:33 (21,996)
Scanlon, John P....3:48:03 (7,598)
Scanlon, Peter J 3:59:17 (10,515)
Scanlon, Sean....5:19:36 (29,050)
Scaramuzza, John....5:01:10 (26,002)
Scarborough, Derek....2:45:24 (332)
Scarfe, Geoff M 4:23:56 (16,834)
Scarratt, Alan J 5:36:29 (31,053)
Scarrow, Benjamin 5:10:24 (27,555)
Scarry, Mark D....4:08:12 (12,615)
Scase, Henry....5:46:58 (32,014)
Sceats, Christopher J....4:15:26 (14,558)
Sceats, Kevin J....6:18:32 (33,874)
Schad, Gunnar 2:56:02 (808)
Schaekel, Andrewas 3:28:59 (4,269)
Schaeppi, Jurg....4:06:28 (12,204)
Schafberger, Armin....3:49:17 (7,887)
Schafer, Christian....4:15:07 (14,478)
Schafer, Wolgang....3:40:29 (6,083)
Schaffner, Jean 4:25:27 (17,265)
Schaller, Walter 4:27:32 (17,900)
Schapira, Paul S....4:05:25 (11,971)
Scheinhutte, Gerd-Ingo....3:39:27 (5,899)
Schendel, Michael....4:13:16 (13,955)
Schenk, Kurt S....4:50:45 (23,683)
Schenk, Michael P....5:12:27 (27,901)
Scherz, Thomas....5:39:20 (31,358)
Schieda, Fabrizzio 4:23:14 (16,661)
Schiess, Lothar 3:49:26 (7,917)
Schiffer, Hans-Wilhelm....4:02:34 (11,290)
Schimmel, Nicholas P....5:57:01 (32,774)
Schiorlin, Antonio R....3:51:36 (8,388)
Schippel, John E 6:10:44 (33,566)
Schittone, Joe 3:40:19 (6,052)
Schlender, Marten....3:26:01 (3,764)
Schliemann, Henrik O 5:01:12 (26,008)
Schmassmann, Rolf....3:29:59 (4,451)
Schmidt, Caspar 3:33:19 (4,931)
Schmidt, Frank....4:15:25 (14,555)
Schmidt, Markus J....5:25:06 (29,760)
Schmidt, Ulrich....3:46:40 (7,276)
Schmierer, Ashley D....4:57:32 (25,234)
Schmitt, Mark K 4:37:04 (20,372)
Schmitz, Helmut 3:32:18 (4,787)
Schnaudigel, Christoph....3:56:29 (9,659)
Schneider, Daniel M 4:42:35 (21,765)
Schneider, Matthew J 5:07:08 (27,081)
Schneider, Michael F 3:45:51 (7,106)
Schnell, Stefan....3:09:41 (1,877)
Schoenfeld, Gary H....3:57:57 (10,127)
Schofield, Darren M 4:22:38 (16,518)
Schofield, Graham 3:25:26 (3,659)
Schofield, James....2:58:57 (1,028)
Schofield, John P 5:18:34 (28,877)
Schofield, Michael 4:42:27 (21,732)
Schofield, Paul N 4:43:56 (22,081)
Schofield, Paul P 4:55:40 (24,804)
Scholer, Roy S....3:48:13 (7,636)
Scholes, Jeff....4:33:21 (19,396)
Scholes, Robert D....5:06:47 (27,016)
Scholey, David C....4:22:15 (16,407)
Scholz, Karl R....5:04:26 (26,591)
Scholzhorn, Ulrich....2:51:57 (588)
School, Joan 2:51:10 (544)
Schooler, Andrew M....5:10:18 (27,541)
Schooling, Robert J....3:35:57 (5,331)
Schrader, Robert E....3:45:05 (6,969)
Schreiber, Bernard G....4:51:34 (23,846)
Schubach, Wolfgang 3:56:58 (9,803)
Schueler, Norbert....4:50:41 (23,672)
Schuitemaker, Jos....3:33:34 (4,966)
Schulpen, Laurens....5:49:38 (32,238)
Schultz, David H....6:43:53 (34,595)
Schulz, Christian 3:53:37 (8,888)
Schulze, Norbert....4:09:53 (13,063)
Schumann, Paul D 2:53:52 (677)
Schurmann, David 4:59:39 (25,701)
Schurmann, Jason 3:45:51 (7,106)
Schuster, Stephan....3:59:47 (10,661)
Schwandt, Volker 4:22:03 (16,356)
Schwartz, Eric....3:27:11 (3,958)
Schwarz, Eberhard....3:55:14 (9,284)
Schwarz, Stefan 3:14:30 (2,416)
Schwarzler, Ronald....3:40:10 (6,031)
Schweer, Marco 3:23:33 (3,381)
Schweiger, Andreas....3:51:04 (8,274)
Schweizer, Olaf....3:17:33 (2,743)
Scoffham, Alastair W....4:13:27 (14,003)
Scoines, Robert I....2:56:05 (812)
Scolaro, Giampiero....3:52:03 (8,493)
Scollick, Craig....4:05:17 (11,944)
Scordamaglia, Oliviero 2:49:47 (492)
Scoresby, Neil A....4:50:42 (23,675)
Scorey, Nick 5:05:05 (26,698)
Scotchford, Colin A 3:29:33 (4,364)
Scothern, Martin C 4:00:53 (10,927)
Scotney, Richie 4:12:19 (13,699)
Scott, Alan F 4:59:17 (25,623)
Scott, Alan L....4:31:08 (18,862)
Scott, Andrew....4:17:47 (15,154)
Scott, Andrew D 5:34:42 (30,874)
Scott, Anthony N....3:43:06 (6,573)
Scott, Barry W....4:27:03 (17,759)
Scott, Chris R....3:53:35 (8,879)
Scott, Christopher E 3:27:51 (4,085)
Scott, Christopher J....4:24:32 (17,001)
Scott, Colin....3:43:45 (6,693)
Scott, Crispin R 3:27:15 (3,968)
Scott, Danny A....2:59:47 (1,110)
Scott, David J 6:21:53 (33,984)
Scott, Dominic D....4:35:08 (19,879)
Scott, Douglas F....3:38:03 (5,656)
Scott, George....4:18:15 (15,280)
Scott, Glenn....4:41:43 (21,569)
Scott, Hugo D....3:28:40 (4,219)
Scott, Ian....3:04:26 (1,422)
Scott, Ian D....4:37:07 (20,391)
Scott, Ian S....3:46:53 (7,326)
Scott, Ian T....4:14:29 (14,290)
Scott, James 3:12:36 (2,203)
Scott, James 6:26:07 (34,131)
Scott, Jamie A....4:18:37 (15,399)
Scott, Jonathan P....6:02:42 (33,121)
Scott, Julian 3:45:43 (7,080)
Scott, Kevin....3:38:22 (5,705)
Scott, Lee....4:26:34 (17,623)
Scott, Lee R 3:01:57 (1,255)
Scott, Mark R....4:51:01 (23,736)
Scott, Neil 4:54:37 (24,578)
Scott, Norris....5:14:37 (28,283)
Scott, Paul....4:34:30 (19,711)
Scott, Paul....4:53:07 (24,201)
Scott, Paul A 4:12:57 (13,869)
Scott, Richard....4:06:50 (12,297)
Scott, Richard....4:52:22 (24,027)
Scott, Robert....3:18:38 (2,838)
Scott, Robert D....4:25:58 (17,423)
Scott, Stephen J....4:32:44 (19,256)
Scott, Steve D....6:03:23 (33,182)
Scott, Steven 4:20:25 (15,918)
Scott, Stewart....3:57:36 (10,015)
Scott, Stuart 3:17:23 (2,721)
Scott, Thomas C....3:44:49 (6,915)
Scott, Timothy J....5:38:48 (31,289)
Scott, Tom E 4:51:30 (23,829)
Scott, Warren D....4:20:12 (15,854)
Scott, William A....4:11:15 (13,416)
Scowcroft, Andrew K....3:28:56 (4,265)
Scrafton, Anthony T 4:30:13 (18,659)
Scrase, Andrew P....5:32:57 (30,666)
Scrase, Russell J 4:11:40 (13,525)
Scriven, Mark J 4:11:07 (13,384)
Scrivener, Chris 3:03:24 (1,354)
Scrivener, Keith A....4:18:32 (15,368)
Scruton, Neil 2:58:29 (990)
Scruton, Tim A....4:10:03 (13,101)
Scudder, Darren....4:52:19 (24,018)
Scullard, Jon P....3:25:48 (3,716)
Scully, Anthony....6:06:43 (33,372)
Scully, Kevin G....5:09:59 (27,509)
Scurr, Andrew P....3:42:55 (6,528)
Scuto, Franco 4:46:37 (22,692)
Seaberg, Alan 4:03:16 (11,449)
Seaborne MBE, Edward....4:57:35 (25,247)
Seabrook, Joe P 4:36:41 (20,274)
Seagrave, Adam....4:17:38 (15,118)
Seal, Richard 6:32:18 (34,313)
Sealey, Ian J....3:51:21 (8,343)
Sealey, Robert M....6:26:45 (34,148)
Sealy, David G....4:39:29 (21,008)
Seaman, Carl 5:31:20 (30,495)
Seaman, Geoff R 4:01:10 (10,973)
Seaman, Nigel D 4:29:17 (18,396)
Seamark, Jamie R....2:56:05 (812)
Sear, Paul....5:03:45 (26,470)
Searle, Greg....3:25:13 (3,627)
Searle, Ian R 4:32:17 (19,158)
Searle, Richard C 4:43:06 (21,889)
Seaton, Stephen 4:20:39 (15,978)
Sechiari, Paul J 4:19:24 (15,636)
Secrett, Jon 3:44:41 (6,876)
Secton, David H 3:08:38 (1,771)

Sedaghat, Kaywan M....5:16:38 (28,566)
Seddon, Alfred B....4:54:40 (24,586)
Seddon, Andrew H....2:54:59 (740)
Seddon, Dwaine P....4:36:16 (20,149)
Seddon, Jeff....2:57:04 (889)
Sedge, Ian....3:05:31 (1,520)
Sedge, Martyn J....2:57:13 (903)
Sedgebeer, Robert J....5:23:40 (29,569)
Sedgmond, Andrew M....3:42:24 (6,450)
Sedgwick, Alan....3:53:02 (8,727)
Sedgwick, Glenn C....4:38:12 (20,670)
Sedgwick, Stephan....4:10:17 (13,164)
Seed, David E....3:52:55 (8,704)
Seeds, Michael W....5:46:12 (31,956)
Seel, Tim R....3:51:47 (8,433)
Seelandt, Frank....3:31:44 (4,708)
Seex, Peter....5:28:07 (30,126)
Segall, Alan M....3:57:03 (9,837)
Segawa, Yoshimitsu....4:52:13 (23,995)
Seger, Andy M....5:58:00 (32,834)
Seguineau, Jean....4:41:59 (21,623)
Sehijpal, Harmesh K....3:53:41 (8,904)
Sehmi, Rashpal....5:51:20 (32,356)
Seiderer, Daniel....4:31:52 (19,057)
Seifert, Kristina I....4:25:08 (17,163)
Seiffert, Philip....3:43:12 (6,592)
Seitz, Donald K....4:10:25 (13,211)
Seivewright, Andrew....4:19:09 (15,562)
Sejourne, Yann....3:58:03 (10,159)
Sekine, Shigeru....5:12:27 (27,901)
Selby, Paul....4:53:19 (24,257)
Selby, Robin C....4:11:40 (13,525)
Self, David R....3:59:31 (10,576)
Selkirk, Simon....5:21:06 (29,249)
Sell, Andrew C....3:52:41 (8,657)
Sell, Richard E....4:28:57 (18,292)
Sellem, Thierry....3:45:34 (7,059)
Sellen, Gavin R....4:17:01 (14,962)
Sellick, Joe....3:57:17 (9,915)
Sellwood, Gavin P....4:26:18 (17,538)
Sellwood, Steven J....4:26:17 (17,527)
Selman, Christopher I....4:55:58 (24,892)
Selves, Stephen J....4:28:46 (18,237)
Selvey, James....6:06:58 (33,387)
Selway, Richard J....4:26:36 (17,631)
Semmelmann, Herman....5:17:02 (28,652)
Sen, Paul A....5:08:37 (27,302)
Senior, Stuart....5:26:59 (29,976)
Senkiw, Walter....4:39:15 (20,953)
Senneck, David....4:02:03 (11,170)
Sephton, David....4:22:01 (16,343)
Serafi, Ibrahim....5:30:33 (30,416)
Serano, Javier Lazaro....3:37:43 (5,605)
Sercombe, Stephen J....3:57:41 (10,035)
Seretis, Spiro....5:46:09 (31,946)
Sergeant, Jonathan C....4:29:23 (18,428)
Sergeant, Robert W....4:29:22 (18,420)
Sergeant, Stephen G....4:45:09 (22,365)
Sergio, Bianchi....3:01:09 (1,199)
Serigstad, Sven....3:51:03 (8,265)
Seris, Patrick....4:37:33 (20,509)
Serre, Olivier....3:23:42 (3,402)
Sesay, Abdul K....4:06:32 (12,221)
Sessions, Tim J....3:34:38 (5,140)
Setchell, Alexander M....4:37:52 (20,591)
Setford, John A....4:09:55 (13,074)
Settembrini, Francesco....3:25:49 (3,721)
Settle, Richard J....3:35:03 (5,191)
Seville, Kevin....3:44:54 (6,937)
Sevink, Berrie....4:03:48 (11,576)
Sevink, Eddie....4:03:48 (11,576)
Sevink, Marco....3:54:35 (9,119)
Sewart, Simon D....3:16:29 (2,632)
Sewell, Alan....4:37:25 (20,478)
Sewell, Andrew P....3:09:44 (1,887)
Sewell, Derek J....4:19:36 (15,692)
Sewell, Richard A....3:27:00 (3,929)
Sewell, Sean....5:02:10 (26,181)
Sewell, Toby H....3:48:16 (7,648)
Seymour, Julian P....4:47:08 (22,802)
Seymour, Mark A....4:17:14 (15,020)
Seymour, Matthew W....4:20:40 (15,981)
Seymour, Timothy R....3:39:29 (5,912)
Seymour, Tom J....3:58:49 (10,393)
Sforza, Claudio....3:14:45 (2,453)
Sgrilli, Stefano....4:15:57 (14,698)
Shackleton, Alexander D....4:40:24 (21,231)
Shackleton, Andy....4:07:54 (12,553)
Shackleton, David....3:29:52 (4,433)
Shackleton, Richard P....3:41:54 (6,360)
Shadbolt, Alan....4:43:44 (22,043)
Shaddock, Graham....4:10:29 (13,224)
Shafee, Rex....4:40:22 (21,225)
Shafier, Lawrence E....3:04:31 (1,429)
Shaftain, Neil....4:24:55 (17,096)
Shah, John F....5:13:15 (28,033)
Shah, Kaushik....3:28:24 (4,181)
Shah, Naresh....4:14:43 (14,352)
Shah, Neil N....6:36:44 (34,426)
Shah, Rasiklal L....5:42:50 (31,668)
Shah, Romal....4:27:53 (18,007)
Shah, Sunil P....4:43:28 (21,969)
Shakesby, Tim D....3:49:44 (7,985)
Shakeshaft, Andrew B....3:10:45 (2,003)
Shakespeare, Simon J....4:08:19 (12,645)
Shaldon, Chris S....5:12:06 (27,845)
Shambayati, Behdad....4:06:34 (12,232)
Shamdasani, Anil A....4:45:34 (22,448)
Shand, Alan J....4:20:14 (15,866)
Shand, Euan C....4:22:49 (16,562)
Shandley, Adrian P....4:20:37 (15,968)
Shankland, Matthew....4:10:37 (13,242)
Shanks, Thomas P....3:51:37 (8,392)
Shanley, David A....4:30:07 (18,630)
Shanley, Kevin....6:53:43 (34,779)
Shanley, William T....3:59:37 (10,608)
Shannon, Martin R....5:48:08 (32,106)
Shannon, Michael W....4:02:41 (11,309)
Shapiro, Eduardo....3:59:12 (10,496)
Shapland, Chris L....4:06:36 (12,241)
Share, Adrian W....4:27:13 (17,806)
Sharkey, Jonathan D....2:59:03 (1,041)
Sharkey, Jonathan G....3:57:35 (10,007)
Sharkey, Mark....4:02:18 (11,222)
Sharland, Richard J....3:27:41 (4,057)
Sharma, Asheesh....6:31:09 (34,280)
Sharma, Ashish....5:30:08 (30,375)
Sharma, Hari D....5:50:25 (32,293)
Sharma, Sanjai....3:21:34 (3,139)
Sharma, Vivek M....7:34:39 (35,157)
Sharman, Ben D....4:33:35 (19,459)
Sharman, Greig J....3:46:55 (7,333)
Sharnock, David R....4:46:05 (22,571)
Sharp, Anthony R....4:35:44 (20,026)
Sharp, Chris B....3:52:07 (8,508)
Sharp, Christopher W....4:52:03 (23,948)
Sharp, Colin W....4:42:46 (21,817)
Sharp, Daniel R....6:14:07 (33,707)
Sharp, Fabian A....4:32:46 (19,264)
Sharp, Jeremy....3:33:45 (4,998)
Sharp, Jeremy C....4:26:31 (17,608)
Sharp, John D....3:49:50 (8,002)
Sharp, Kenneth....4:24:55 (17,096)
Sharp, Martin A....4:34:36 (19,738)
Sharp, Michael J....4:07:42 (12,495)
Sharp, Noel R....5:56:58 (32,768)
Sharp, Stephen....4:29:29 (18,457)
Sharp, Steve M....4:16:50 (14,922)
Sharp, Stewart....4:28:10 (18,078)
Sharp, Stuart R....3:58:39 (10,323)
Sharp, Timothy J....3:17:03 (2,684)
Sharpe, Dave....5:09:05 (27,365)
Sharpe, David W....5:03:01 (26,344)
Sharpe, Garry J....4:28:18 (18,111)
Sharpe, Jack C....5:13:25 (28,063)
Sharpe, Jeremy E....3:42:34 (6,475)
Sharpe, Matthew L....4:53:51 (24,390)
Sharpe, Neil G....3:57:06 (9,856)
Sharpe, Richard A....4:53:51 (24,390)
Sharpe, Robert D....3:58:12 (10,193)
Sharples, Stephen R....4:32:57 (19,304)
Sharpley, Robert D....4:42:27 (21,732)
Sharratt, Leo....4:40:10 (21,175)
Shattock, Jamie K....5:11:10 (27,681)
Shaughnessy, John....3:41:42 (6,316)
Shaw, Alastair....3:55:54 (9,488)
Shaw, Andrew D....4:20:00 (15,802)
Shaw, Carl....4:40:45 (21,320)
Shaw, Christopher P....4:30:19 (18,683)
Shaw, Colin E....4:11:31 (13,486)
Shaw, Dale A....4:59:50 (25,745)
Shaw, Darren P....4:08:39 (12,728)
Shaw, David A....3:09:59 (1,918)
Shaw, David B....4:22:59 (16,595)
Shaw, Edward D....4:00:43 (10,890)
Shaw, Gary D....3:31:04 (4,614)
Shaw, Gerry A....3:01:46 (1,245)
Shaw, Jeremy....4:20:44 (16,001)
Shaw, John....5:09:53 (27,493)
Shaw, John E....4:38:48 (20,830)
Shaw, Jon D....5:11:55 (27,807)
Shaw, Mark T....4:37:17 (20,440)
Shaw, Martyn S....5:40:23 (31,458)
Shaw, Matt....2:25:12 (46)
Shaw, Mike....4:27:10 (17,792)
Shaw, Neil M....3:06:49 (1,619)
Shaw, Paul B....4:40:44 (21,315)
Shaw, Paul D....3:38:50 (5,781)
Shaw, Paul K....4:13:16 (13,955)
Shaw, Paul W....4:39:56 (21,122)
Shaw, Peter E....3:08:30 (1,757)
Shaw, Phillip R....6:15:38 (33,767)
Shaw, Rob C....4:06:58 (12,333)
Shawcroft, Graham P....3:39:24 (5,893)
Shawyer, Andrew D....3:22:16 (3,225)
Shaya, Darrin M....3:50:36 (8,170)
Shayler, Richard J....5:32:45 (30,643)
Shea, Nicholas J....3:27:43 (4,063)
Sheard, Bryan A....3:50:03 (8,051)
Shearer, Andrew J....3:48:07 (7,619)
Shearer, Colin....4:54:26 (24,534)
Shearer, Nic J....3:49:45 (7,990)
Shearer, Richard J....2:42:41 (256)
Shearing, Jonathan M....5:25:42 (29,823)
Shearing, Philip R....4:58:27 (25,429)
Sheedy, Ben P....3:32:00 (4,748)
Sheehan, Martin G....3:06:41 (1,609)
Sheehan, Thomas M....4:04:11 (11,678)
Sheen, Christopher L....5:49:01 (32,184)
Sheen, Geoffrey....5:29:54 (30,349)
Sheen, Graham....3:57:57 (10,127)
Sheikh, Omar F....4:35:50 (20,050)
Shek, Kim....5:45:41 (31,911)
Shekle, Raymond J....7:04:35 (34,919)
Sheldon, Tony J....2:46:34 (360)
Sheldrake, Kevin....4:28:30 (18,168)
Sheliker, John....4:45:21 (22,401)
Shelley, Neil J....5:20:02 (29,102)
Shelswell, Richard....4:21:52 (16,302)
Shelton, Michael J....4:37:40 (20,539)
Shelton, Michael R....3:11:30 (2,078)
Shemar, Raji L....3:36:24 (5,405)
Shephard, Mark....5:10:02 (27,515)
Shephard, Richard G....3:08:52 (1,797)
Shephard, Ryland C....5:04:33 (26,607)
Shepheard, Peter E....6:05:50 (33,317)
Shepherd, Adam....6:09:44 (33,523)
Shepherd, Andrew....4:24:50 (17,081)
Shepherd, Andrew G....3:33:34 (4,966)
Shepherd, Andrew P....6:11:01 (33,573)
Shepherd, Barry....5:59:09 (32,920)
Shepherd, Ben....3:51:04 (8,274)
Shepherd, Brian W....6:03:39 (33,196)
Shepherd, David H....4:51:44 (23,879)
Shepherd, David S....5:09:57 (27,505)
Shepherd, George M....4:24:19 (16,932)
Shepherd, Jack....3:25:07 (3,609)
Shepherd, Joe....4:22:22 (16,438)
Shepherd, Michael T....4:46:37 (22,692)
Shepherd, Neil B....4:19:03 (15,527)
Shepherd, Robert M....3:15:29 (2,524)
Shepherd, Samuel J....5:08:50 (27,327)
Shepherd, Steven J....5:06:55 (27,045)
Shepherd, Tom R....5:29:40 (30,326)
Shepherd, Trevor....4:08:53 (12,797)
Sheppard, Andrew....3:45:34 (7,059)
Sheppard, Dean C....3:12:17 (2,172)
Sheppard, Donald M....6:44:01 (34,601)
Sheppard, Jamie K....5:41:21 (31,541)

Sheppard, Jay W 4:42:26 (21,725)
Sheppard, John A 5:11:58 (27,817)
Sheppard, Matthew R 3:36:53 (5,477)
Sheppard, Philip 5:53:52 (32,555)
Shepperson, Malcolm C 4:01:02 (10,954)
Shepperson, Mark A 4:43:44 (22,043)
Sher, Julian 4:28:45 (18,234)
Sherard, Paul N 4:17:41 (15,134)
Shercliff, Hugh R 4:13:37 (14,046)
Sheridan, Andy J 4:34:38 (19,743)
Sheridan, David 5:36:56 (31,096)
Sheridan, Pat 4:44:50 (22,281)
Sheridan, Stephen 4:39:14 (20,942)
Sheriff, Daniel P 3:16:55 (2,669)
Shering, David J 4:27:51 (17,998)
Sherrell, Paul W 5:38:30 (31,250)
Sherriff, Michael J 4:33:34 (19,455)
Sherrocks, John F 3:53:21 (8,820)
Sherry, Padraig H 3:37:12 (5,524)
Shersby, Richard P 4:44:00 (22,099)
Sherwin, Geoff J 4:46:18 (22,625)
Sherwin, Paul 4:33:11 (19,360)
Sherwood, Mark P 4:04:29 (11,741)
Shevlin, John 3:48:01 (7,587)
Shew, Peter 4:27:05 (17,771)
Shibata, Akinori 4:07:36 (12,479)
Shield, Jeremy M 3:09:29 (1,856)
Shields, John A 3:16:41 (2,646)
Shields, Peter 3:17:25 (2,724)
Shiels, Andrew 4:22:36 (16,503)
Shillabeer, Edmund H 4:45:56 (22,539)
Shilleto, Joseph 5:08:24 (27,269)
Shilleto, Simon J 4:11:44 (13,548)
Shimmen, Alan T 4:54:55 (24,641)
Shimmen, Andrew M 4:14:02 (14,158)
Shimmen, Michael 6:41:36 (34,536)
Shimmin, Greg 4:03:23 (11,476)
Shimmin, Robert J 3:52:50 (8,688)
Shine, Keith P 4:35:30 (19,975)
Shingleton, Matt A 3:36:08 (5,360)
Shipley, David H 5:04:10 (26,548)
Shipman, John 5:29:26 (30,297)
Shipman, John P 5:25:23 (29,787)
Shipton, Paul G 4:59:55 (25,761)
Shipway, Rich M 2:52:05 (597)
Shiraki, Shinichiro 5:12:05 (27,839)
Shires, Neil A 3:06:30 (1,595)
Shirley, William 3:46:13 (7,182)
Shirt, Christopher J 5:33:21 (30,700)
Shockley, Bernard A 4:35:37 (20,002)
Shoemark, Ian W 3:58:12 (10,193)
Shone, Grahame P 4:00:25 (10,808)
Shone, Iain H 3:01:32 (1,223)
Shoobert, Mark 3:42:01 (6,379)
Shore, Andrew J 5:25:46 (29,837)
Shore, Ben 3:44:02 (6,749)
Shore, Glen S 3:57:51 (10,094)
Shore, Mathew D 5:17:59 (28,779)
Shore, Roger D 5:33:36 (30,736)
Shorrock, Adrain B 2:56:35 (849)
Short, Alan 5:27:14 (30,004)
Short, Alan J 5:08:49 (27,324)
Short, Andrew J 4:52:54 (24,149)
Short, Arthur 3:12:40 (2,212)
Short, Clive R 3:09:42 (1,881)
Short, Garry J 3:05:29 (1,516)
Short, Jonathan R 3:59:18 (10,520)
Short, Kevin 3:23:31 (3,379)
Short, Richard 4:19:25 (15,643)
Short, Robert W 3:47:04 (7,364)
Shortall, Anthony 4:55:48 (24,841)
Shotbolt, Adrian W 4:12:22 (13,716)
Shoults, Will C 3:17:03 (2,684)
Shout, Andy M 4:30:23 (18,698)
Shovelin, Philip 5:00:26 (25,868)
Shreeve, Simon J 4:01:54 (11,128)
Shrerry, Karl 3:08:47 (1,788)
Shrimplin, Stephen 4:11:59 (13,619)
Shrimpton, Benjamin J 3:13:41 (2,326)
Shropshire, Mark C 3:29:57 (4,446)
Shrubsole, Clive E 4:04:26 (11,731)
Shrubsole, Marc P 4:23:04 (16,619)
Shuck, Steve P 3:03:28 (1,361)

Shuker, Richard J 3:29:13 (4,316)
Shukla, Tarun C 5:44:45 (31,824)
Shute, Jack 4:21:15 (16,129)
Shute, Matthew T 4:35:57 (20,075)
Shutler, Lee H 3:33:27 (4,954)
Shuttlewood, Simon R 3:57:01 (9,820)
Shuttleworth, Chris 4:21:09 (16,099)
Siapatis, John 5:55:23 (32,671)
Sibille, Pierre 3:45:50 (7,101)
Sibley, Andrew K 4:54:41 (24,589)
Sibley, Neil 3:24:04 (3,455)
Sibson, Andrew D 5:03:42 (26,461)
Siciunas, Arunas 2:52:36 (616)
Sick, Horst 4:18:49 (15,470)
Sicura, Federico 4:33:40 (19,477)
Siddall, Chris 5:15:22 (28,396)
Siddall, Stuart J 4:11:23 (13,450)
Sidders, Andrew J 4:07:24 (12,438)
Sidders, Stuart J 5:02:32 (26,234)
Siddiqui, Parvez 6:06:46 (33,375)
Siddle, Paul 3:02:18 (1,285)
Siddons, Barrie J 4:00:00 (10,728)
Siderfin, Robert P 4:45:55 (22,534)
Sidney, Julian D 4:36:50 (20,314)
Sieben, Sven 4:11:10 (13,397)
Sigaud, Daniel M 4:55:40 (24,804)
Sigaud, Gregory 6:30:03 (34,258)
Signorato, Carlo A 3:29:05 (4,291)
Sigsworth, Richard L 4:16:37 (14,866)
Sigurdarson, Sigurdur H 3:39:13 (5,854)
Sihver, Ken G 4:10:52 (13,307)
Silcock, Richard C 4:26:01 (17,441)
Silk, Dominic J 5:10:17 (27,539)
Sillett, Craig 4:44:24 (22,193)
Silmon, Mark O 4:18:03 (15,220)
Silva, Edson C 5:25:45 (29,833)
Silva, Simon 3:59:13 (10,500)
Silver, Andrew 3:59:02 (10,443)
Silver, Andrew C 2:55:22 (758)
Silverberg, Antony N 4:00:49 (10,907)
Silverman, Paul C 4:36:47 (20,298)
Silvers, Andrew R 4:24:52 (17,087)
Silverthorn, Kevin R 3:53:43 (8,917)
Silverton, Ross L 4:06:11 (12,137)
Simcox, Alex D 3:43:34 (6,661)
Sime, Andrew 4:09:06 (12,860)
Simeoni, Alan J 4:47:49 (22,967)
Simgleton, Jim P 5:01:18 (26,029)
Simkins, Anthony P 4:43:36 (22,007)
Simkins, Paul F 4:34:45 (19,777)
Simkins, Paul J 3:48:20 (7,664)
Simkiss, Gary J 4:47:33 (22,891)
Simmonds, Andrew J 4:39:04 (20,896)
Simmonds, Guy 3:51:06 (8,283)
Simmonds, Jonathan A 4:29:23 (18,428)
Simmonds, Peter B 3:25:00 (3,583)
Simmons, Christopher A 3:53:39 (8,896)
Simmons, Dean A 5:03:04 (26,352)
Simmons, Eric 6:31:11 (34,282)
Simmons, Graham R 5:05:58 (26,864)
Simmons, James S 4:32:14 (19,146)
Simmons, Joseph J 6:17:04 (33,826)
Simmons, Keith H 6:23:03 (34,023)
Simmons, Neale J 4:45:53 (22,516)
Simmons, Robin M 4:26:17 (17,527)
Simmons, Sid 3:30:32 (4,533)
Simmons, Stephen 5:31:57 (30,556)
Simms, Adrian 5:42:05 (31,599)
Simms, Andrew D 4:06:39 (12,252)
Simms, Andrew W 6:04:49 (33,258)
Simms, Mark P 3:35:20 (5,227)
Simms, Michael A 4:45:35 (22,453)
Simms, Michael G 4:50:04 (23,505)
Simon, Alberto 3:33:44 (4,995)
Simon, Nicholas 5:30:43 (30,435)
Simon, Nik G 5:36:31 (31,059)
Simon, Paul F 4:35:45 (20,033)
Simon, Steven A 4:29:21 (18,416)
Simonds, Ronald 4:58:16 (25,388)
Simonin, Gerard C 3:31:13 (4,634)
Simons, Trevor J 4:58:24 (25,416)
Simonsen, Benny B 3:32:39 (4,836)
Simonsen, Mads 3:40:21 (6,064)

Simpkins, Richard A 4:32:54 (19,289)
Simpson, Brian J 6:05:08 (33,278)
Simpson, Colin J 3:12:33 (2,198)
Simpson, Dave 6:12:29 (33,641)
Simpson, David 3:31:50 (4,724)
Simpson, David S 3:15:56 (2,560)
Simpson, Donald A 3:49:09 (7,854)
Simpson, Duncan 5:03:49 (26,489)
Simpson, Eddie 2:29:35 (67)
Simpson, Gareth S 3:23:25 (3,364)
Simpson, Gerry M 4:07:46 (12,523)
Simpson, Ian 5:05:09 (26,713)
Simpson, Jamie A 5:01:01 (25,978)
Simpson, John 4:08:45 (12,755)
Simpson, John E 3:49:01 (7,826)
Simpson, John P 4:38:49 (20,833)
Simpson, Mark C 2:58:10 (968)
Simpson, Paul D 3:59:56 (10,705)
Simpson, Paul H 3:51:44 (8,418)
Simpson, Peter 6:19:29 (33,904)
Simpson, Richard G 4:47:17 (22,835)
Simpson, Richard H 4:26:04 (17,462)
Simpson, Richard J 3:15:07 (2,487)
Simpson, Richard J 4:58:07 (25,353)
Simpson, Robert D 4:47:29 (22,883)
Simpson, Robert J 3:58:16 (10,210)
Simpson, Russell J 4:19:54 (15,775)
Simpson, Stephen P 4:40:39 (21,296)
Simpson, Steven E 2:47:19 (380)
Simpson, Stuart C 5:05:28 (26,789)
Simpson, Stuart J 3:40:16 (6,044)
Simpson, Timothy D 5:32:07 (30,565)
Simpson, Tom P 3:54:52 (9,202)
Sims, David A 5:18:32 (28,869)
Sims, Gordon J 4:25:42 (17,345)
Sims, Mark P 3:26:03 (3,773)
Sinapius, Haymon G 3:40:58 (6,173)
Sinclair, Ashley J 3:33:50 (5,018)
Sinclair, Christopher I 3:58:48 (10,390)
Sinclair, Ian C 3:14:12 (2,382)
Sinclair, Ian M 4:42:51 (21,833)
Sinclair, Jamie G 4:10:06 (13,115)
Sinclair, Kevin 3:29:51 (4,428)
Sinclair, Malcolm 3:12:21 (2,181)
Sinclair, Mike J 4:36:58 (20,347)
Sinclair, Oliver J 3:47:05 (7,369)
Sinclair, Paul J 3:52:40 (8,651)
Sinclair, Robin J 5:31:10 (30,482)
Sinclair, Terence F 3:46:08 (7,167)
Sinfield, Jim R 5:05:07 (26,707)
Singell, Russell W 5:09:39 (27,463)
Singer, Alexander 5:39:15 (31,345)
Singer, Colin G 3:35:59 (5,340)
Singer, Gary F 4:15:07 (14,478)
Singer, Humphrey S 3:22:28 (3,238)
Singh, Amarprit 3:49:17 (7,887)
Singh, Charanjit 4:27:01 (17,754)
Singh, David 3:59:46 (10,654)
Singh, George G 4:28:20 (18,117)
Singh, Harjinder 4:57:24 (25,208)
Singh, Harmander 6:09:14 (33,503)
Singh, Makhan 5:14:20 (28,236)
Singh, Manjit 3:52:43 (8,664)
Singh, Manjit 4:59:53 (25,752)
Singh, Ravinder 4:14:09 (14,194)
Singh, Steven R 3:41:39 (6,313)
Singh, Tajinder 4:26:05 (17,469)
Singh Hear, Malkit 5:29:25 (30,293)
Single, Peter 3:24:21 (3,498)
Singleton, Brian N 4:34:01 (19,569)
Singleton, Jamie 4:32:41 (19,247)
Singleton, John 4:45:52 (22,513)
Singleton, Mark 5:29:32 (30,313)
Singleton, Michael 4:08:50 (12,782)
Singleton, Nicholas J 4:39:35 (21,037)
Singleton, Philip 4:15:43 (14,642)
Sinkinson, Richard C 4:39:13 (20,937)
Sinnott, Colin E 3:33:35 (4,970)
Sinnott, Vincent 4:32:31 (19,216)
Sinopoli, Antonello 2:45:14 (326)
Sinton-Hewitt, Paul P 3:24:35 (3,526)
Siosten, Bjorn 4:32:21 (19,176)
Sipling, Kevin 4:04:38 (11,779)

Sirdar, Michael	4:00:07 (10,754)	
Sirois, Kenneth E	4:11:37 (13,508)	
Sirrell, Brett	3:22:16 (3,225)	
Sirs, Nicholas	2:40:17 (206)	
Sisley, Roger C	4:20:45 (16,007)	
Sisodiya, Ranjit	4:06:47 (12,283)	
Sitaram, V	4:52:05 (23,961)	
Sitch, Aubrey J	5:29:20 (30,279)	
Sivelle, Philip M	5:50:09 (32,273)	
Sixsmith, Rob C	4:03:22 (11,474)	
Sizeland, Tim J	3:13:58 (2,355)	
Skaper, George	3:33:53 (5,026)	
Skeates, Tony	4:33:34 (19,455)	
Skeath, Matthew D	4:26:34 (17,623)	
Skeene, Andrew N	5:49:17 (32,210)	
Skellorn, Raymond	4:12:33 (13,760)	
Skelton, Aaron M	4:29:29 (18,457)	
Skelton, Martin J	5:19:41 (29,058)	
Skelton, Travis	3:32:15 (4,781)	
Skene, Robert G	5:43:31 (31,718)	
Skene, Stephen N	3:39:02 (5,823)	
Skentelbery, Neil	4:29:43 (18,525)	
Skerrett, Stephen A	4:37:04 (20,372)	
Skidmore, Gary M	5:24:02 (29,627)	
Skidmore, Nik E	4:17:31 (15,094)	
Skiff, David G	5:31:25 (30,510)	
Skilton, Hayden J	4:22:16 (16,415)	
Skingle, Michael R	5:28:10 (30,137)	
Skingley, Ian D	3:13:35 (2,314)	
Skinner, Brian C	5:22:54 (29,471)	
Skinner, David L	4:21:29 (16,200)	
Skinner, Graham M	5:14:06 (28,189)	
Skinner, John F.	4:35:35 (19,992)	
Skinner, John P	4:58:44 (25,493)	
Skinner, Peter R	4:46:52 (22,745)	
Skipp, Asa J	6:07:18 (33,405)	
Skipp, Paul A	3:47:57 (7,560)	
Skipper, Bjarni	3:38:44 (5,759)	
Skipper, Gavin D	4:04:01 (11,640)	
Skyrme, Jeremy M	4:20:13 (15,857)	
Skyrme, Stephen S	4:37:21 (20,457)	
Slade, Dean R	5:39:04 (31,316)	
Slade, Matthew J	5:07:13 (27,106)	
Slade, Rob M	3:49:05 (7,843)	
Slager, John	4:49:53 (23,469)	
Slaney, Aaron J	5:34:18 (30,818)	
Slate, Alfred	4:22:46 (16,550)	
Slate, David J	5:25:49 (29,844)	
Slater, Bryan C	5:06:33 (26,976)	
Slater, Daniel	3:41:53 (6,351)	
Slater, David	3:12:04 (2,148)	
Slater, Mark J	5:15:54 (28,466)	
Slater, Mark P	4:21:43 (16,259)	
Slater, Matthew P	4:24:46 (17,064)	
Slater, Paul A	4:59:57 (25,766)	
Slater, Paul N	3:01:40 (1,238)	
Slater, Paul W	4:33:21 (19,396)	
Slater, Philip H	3:45:52 (7,111)	
Slater, Richard	3:49:27 (7,924)	
Slater, Stephen	5:02:38 (26,256)	
Slater, Steve R	5:09:14 (27,395)	
Slatter, Mark	3:54:05 (8,992)	
Slattery, Roderick A	4:10:55 (13,323)	
Slavin, John	3:38:44 (5,759)	
Slavin, Joseph	5:18:52 (28,927)	
Sleat, Wesley	3:25:40 (3,699)	
Slee, Barrie	4:10:41 (13,261)	
Slee, Daniel J	4:10:41 (13,261)	
Slee, Robert	3:11:20 (2,063)	
Sleeth, Howard	4:16:44 (14,898)	
Slinn, Gregory J	4:53:47 (24,379)	
Sloan, Andrew N	4:37:16 (20,433)	
Sloan, Mark S	6:10:29 (33,551)	
Sloan, Seamus	4:21:37 (16,234)	
Sloane, Andrew J	4:11:40 (13,525)	
Sloley, Robert	3:12:49 (2,229)	
Sloman, Gary	3:54:45 (9,171)	
Sloss, Philip A	4:21:58 (16,322)	
Sloth, Mikael	5:20:10 (29,127)	
Sloth, Morten	4:30:37 (18,750)	
Slowik, Pawel	4:52:46 (24,119)	
Slyth, Stanley	5:20:21 (29,151)	
Smail, Kevin F	4:37:15 (20,431)	
Smailes, Brian G	4:10:47 (13,281)	
Smale, Jonathan	3:55:39 (9,411)	
Small, Brian M	4:43:11 (21,911)	
Small, Edward W	4:50:52 (23,706)	
Small, Matthew P	4:36:47 (20,298)	
Smallbone, Craig	3:05:46 (1,537)	
Smalley, Lee J	6:05:45 (33,310)	
Smalley, Neil D	5:05:41 (26,821)	
Smallman, Chris C	3:20:02 (3,001)	
Smallman, Darryl	5:23:13 (29,505)	
Smallman, Graham H	4:47:58 (22,997)	
Smalls, Allen	2:39:53 (202)	
Smart, Darren I	3:53:26 (8,844)	
Smart, David T	4:42:15 (21,689)	
Smart, George D	4:45:18 (22,395)	
Smart, Liam M	5:50:45 (32,326)	
Smart, Richard	4:42:30 (21,742)	
Smart, Roy M	4:48:37 (23,154)	
Smart, Trevor S	4:09:43 (13,016)	
Smart, William	5:07:24 (27,131)	
Smeddle, Jeremy H	3:52:15 (8,542)	
Smedley, Michael	6:07:18 (33,405)	
Smedley, William T	4:14:03 (14,164)	
Smedsrud, Kjell E	3:39:57 (5,986)	
Smee, Alistair G	5:03:48 (26,484)	
Smerdon, Andrew E	4:47:38 (22,922)	
Smethurst, Oliver T	4:35:34 (19,988)	
Smiles, Peter A	4:41:43 (21,569)	
Smit, Ben	4:58:55 (25,539)	
Smit, Jason	4:06:49 (12,288)	
Smitam, David L	3:53:08 (8,753)	
Smith, Adrian	5:15:14 (28,375)	
Smith, Adrian P	4:25:58 (17,423)	
Smith, Alan M	4:11:07 (13,384)	
Smith, Alan R	3:29:39 (4,386)	
Smith, Alan R	4:40:59 (21,385)	
Smith, Alex F	3:10:25 (1,969)	
Smith, André B	4:55:15 (24,728)	
Smith, Andrew	4:07:42 (12,495)	
Smith, Andrew	4:44:24 (22,193)	
Smith, Andrew	5:47:14 (32,037)	
Smith, Andrew A	6:54:38 (34,791)	
Smith, Andrew G	3:03:59 (1,396)	
Smith, Andrew G	3:51:39 (8,400)	
Smith, Andrew G	4:08:51 (12,787)	
Smith, Andrew J	3:17:06 (2,689)	
Smith, Andrew J	5:25:50 (29,845)	
Smith, Andrew K	3:35:49 (5,310)	
Smith, Andrew K	3:56:36 (9,695)	
Smith, Andrew M	3:24:42 (3,540)	
Smith, Andrew V	5:35:19 (30,935)	
Smith, Andy M	3:59:29 (10,567)	
Smith, Andy M	4:10:39 (13,254)	
Smith, Anthony J	4:52:18 (24,014)	
Smith, Anthony R	4:18:33 (15,373)	
Smith, Barry J	5:14:35 (28,278)	
Smith, Barry S	4:35:50 (20,050)	
Smith, Ben G	4:02:13 (11,206)	
Smith, Ben J	4:00:40 (10,879)	
Smith, Bernard	4:37:40 (20,539)	
Smith, Brian	5:04:05 (26,527)	
Smith, Brian A	5:54:47 (32,621)	
Smith, Bruce M	5:51:40 (32,385)	
Smith, Bryan S	4:49:04 (23,259)	
Smith, Carl	4:29:45 (18,533)	
Smith, Chris	5:08:28 (27,281)	
Smith, Chris A	3:17:58 (2,785)	
Smith, Chris R	5:18:38 (28,895)	
Smith, Christopher A	3:39:49 (5,967)	
Smith, Christopher A	7:05:33 (34,932)	
Smith, Christopher E	4:25:59 (17,429)	
Smith, Christopher J	4:05:08 (11,907)	
Smith, Christopher J	4:27:50 (17,992)	
Smith, Colin P	5:08:51 (27,331)	
Smith, Colin R	3:55:30 (9,368)	
Smith, Colin R	4:14:33 (14,304)	
Smith, Craig	6:21:49 (33,981)	
Smith, Craig D	5:04:22 (26,578)	
Smith, Damon J	4:56:30 (25,018)	
Smith, Dan J	3:10:36 (1,988)	
Smith, Daniel J	3:15:53 (2,556)	
Smith, Daniel J	4:07:38 (12,486)	
Smith, Darius J	4:18:07 (15,239)	
Smith, Darren K	4:10:12 (13,140)	
Smith, Darren L	8:00:15 (35,231)	
Smith, David A	6:30:01 (34,257)	
Smith, David F	3:36:04 (5,350)	
Smith, David G	3:40:50 (6,148)	
Smith, David G	7:18:01 (35,063)	
Smith, David J	3:45:42 (7,076)	
Smith, David J	4:59:35 (25,682)	
Smith, David M	2:49:56 (497)	
Smith, David M	4:09:33 (12,974)	
Smith, David R	4:38:52 (20,844)	
Smith, David W	4:23:55 (16,833)	
Smith, Derek R	4:03:05 (11,406)	
Smith, Derrick K	3:37:19 (5,539)	
Smith, Dominic G	4:33:45 (19,506)	
Smith, Duncan F	4:20:40 (15,981)	
Smith, Duncan H	4:38:09 (20,660)	
Smith, Ernest	6:10:28 (33,549)	
Smith, Frazer A	4:11:26 (13,460)	
Smith, Fred	6:46:22 (34,637)	
Smith, Garry A	5:15:30 (28,417)	
Smith, Gary	4:22:28 (16,464)	
Smith, Gary M	4:18:08 (15,242)	
Smith, Gavin C	5:03:07 (26,367)	
Smith, Geoff R	4:42:45 (21,811)	
Smith, George L	4:42:06 (21,653)	
Smith, Gerard	4:45:05 (22,347)	
Smith, Gerry C	2:53:06 (640)	
Smith, Glenn	4:10:33 (13,232)	
Smith, Gordon A	3:40:47 (6,136)	
Smith, Graham	4:45:23 (22,411)	
Smith, Graham	6:45:12 (34,622)	
Smith, Graham A	4:09:27 (12,943)	
Smith, Graham M	2:51:24 (558)	
Smith, Graham M	4:20:21 (15,898)	
Smith, Graham P	3:49:28 (7,928)	
Smith, Grant D	5:21:25 (29,289)	
Smith, Grant W	3:49:54 (8,017)	
Smith, Gregory C	3:39:24 (5,893)	
Smith, Gregory M	3:56:05 (9,533)	
Smith, Gruffydd H	4:00:20 (10,792)	
Smith, Guy O	3:55:04 (9,251)	
Smith, Guy O	4:03:24 (11,481)	
Smith, Harry	4:39:58 (21,129)	
Smith, Iain	4:42:33 (21,751)	
Smith, Iain M	3:39:51 (5,975)	
Smith, Iain M	5:25:43 (29,826)	
Smith, Ian	3:46:04 (7,153)	
Smith, Ian	4:18:16 (15,283)	
Smith, Ian	4:19:31 (15,668)	
Smith, Ian	5:30:26 (30,408)	
Smith, Ian A	4:29:29 (18,457)	
Smith, Ian G	4:21:20 (16,155)	
Smith, Ian J	2:42:25 (251)	
Smith, Ian M	3:45:57 (7,124)	
Smith, Ian S	4:01:57 (11,138)	
Smith, Jack M	4:15:22 (14,540)	
Smith, James	4:53:10 (24,213)	
Smith, James A	3:47:06 (7,372)	
Smith, James E	4:25:17 (17,211)	
Smith, James P	4:20:56 (16,061)	
Smith, James P	6:39:42 (34,502)	
Smith, James T	4:34:15 (19,649)	
Smith, James T	5:20:18 (29,142)	
Smith, James W	3:47:31 (7,460)	
Smith, Jamie L	3:43:10 (6,586)	
Smith, Jason C	3:50:19 (8,109)	
Smith, Jeff	5:55:14 (32,665)	
Smith, Jeffrey D	4:10:28 (13,218)	
Smith, Jeremy J	3:40:25 (6,075)	
Smith, Jeremy P	3:37:49 (5,620)	
Smith, Jeremy R	4:50:16 (23,551)	
Smith, Jim	3:38:21 (5,704)	
Smith, Jim A	4:40:59 (21,385)	
Smith, John	3:32:45 (4,851)	
Smith, John	4:05:03 (11,878)	
Smith, John L	4:21:41 (16,252)	
Smith, John M	3:56:22 (9,623)	
Smith, Jonathan D	4:43:28 (21,969)	
Smith, Jonathan M	5:02:45 (26,284)	
Smith, Jonathan M	5:10:23 (27,551)	
Smith, Jonathan P	4:18:06 (15,236)	
Smith, Joshua I	6:49:26 (34,698)	

Smith, Julian P 3:46:14 (7,188)
Smith, Keith A 3:16:57 (2,671)
Smith, Kelvin B 4:21:51 (16,297)
Smith, Kendall M 3:55:10 (9,268)

Smith, Kenneth D 5:36:27 (31,047)

Taking part in the London Marathon for me is a buzz. Running around the great landmarks and being cheered on by the mass crowds and bands playing really pushes you to another level. Each time I reach a famous landmark I get shivers down my spine, and running to the finish line leaves tears in my eyes.

Smith, Kevin D 4:06:10 (12,134)
Smith, Kevin D 5:14:24 (28,245)
Smith, Kevin G 6:00:41 (33,011)
Smith, Kevin J 4:43:06 (21,889)
Smith, Kevin M 2:51:55 (584)
Smith, Lawrence D 3:53:11 (8,768)
Smith, Lawrence G 5:12:30 (27,910)
Smith, Lee 3:48:31 (7,715)
Smith, Lee M 3:28:06 (4,126)
Smith, Les 5:12:59 (27,996)
Smith, Luke S 5:18:24 (28,850)
Smith, Malcolm 4:03:33 (11,514)
Smith, Malcolm 4:50:28 (23,618)
Smith, Malcolm P 3:34:11 (5,073)
Smith, Malcolm R 3:58:57 (10,417)
Smith, Mark 3:59:49 (10,667)
Smith, Mark 4:39:19 (20,967)
Smith, Mark 5:00:06 (25,795)
Smith, Mark 5:20:32 (29,187)
Smith, Mark A 3:24:45 (3,548)
Smith, Mark A 4:44:18 (22,169)
Smith, Mark B 4:29:43 (18,525)
Smith, Mark E 4:38:43 (20,803)
Smith, Mark G 4:57:34 (25,242)
Smith, Mark J 4:20:16 (15,879)
Smith, Mark S 4:08:46 (12,758)
Smith, Mark T 7:28:04 (35,118)
Smith, Martin A 3:44:47 (6,901)
Smith, Martin E 4:18:17 (15,290)
Smith, Martin G 3:24:52 (3,564)
Smith, Martin G 4:34:17 (19,660)
Smith, Martin J 2:56:30 (843)
Smith, Martin R 4:06:58 (12,333)
Smith, Martin S 3:38:04 (5,661)
Smith, Martyn 5:13:02 (28,003)
Smith, Martyn P 3:14:07 (2,370)
Smith, Matt 2:16:23 (16)
Smith, Matthew 5:03:25 (26,420)
Smith, Matthew D 3:33:21 (4,938)
Smith, Michael J 3:50:38 (8,178)
Smith, Michael J 4:51:05 (23,749)
Smith, Michael W 3:47:09 (7,382)
Smith, Mike 3:13:58 (2,355)
Smith, Neil 5:12:43 (27,953)
Smith, Neil A 4:50:45 (23,683)
Smith, Neil C 4:20:24 (15,912)
Smith, Neil F 3:12:54 (2,239)
Smith, Neil M 5:29:30 (30,308)
Smith, Niall J 4:51:37 (23,855)
Smith, Nicholas 5:38:43 (31,279)
Smith, Nick F 4:24:37 (17,022)
Smith, Nick P 5:36:01 (30,996)
Smith, Nigel A 3:14:55 (2,475)
Smith, Nigel J 3:55:41 (9,423)
Smith, Norman 4:06:35 (12,238)
Smith, Paul 3:52:25 (8,589)
Smith, Paul 4:29:18 (18,406)
Smith, Paul 5:34:34 (30,854)
Smith, Paul 5:34:50 (30,890)
Smith, Paul A 4:15:35 (14,603)
Smith, Paul A 5:37:58 (31,193)
Smith, Paul D 4:17:32 (15,097)
Smith, Paul D 4:46:20 (22,629)
Smith, Paul J 3:41:46 (6,327)
Smith, Peter 2:55:29 (765)
Smith, Peter A 3:06:04 (1,556)
Smith, Peter S 6:22:02 (33,992)
Smith, Philip 4:42:09 (21,664)
Smith, Raymond G 4:47:59 (23,004)
Smith, Richard 4:17:34 (15,106)
Smith, Richard D 4:42:10 (21,670)
Smith, Richard D 5:35:57 (30,987)
Smith, Richard G 3:50:24 (8,122)
Smith, Richard M 4:38:04 (20,638)
Smith, Ricky L 4:56:51 (25,101)
Smith, Rikki W 4:51:33 (23,842)
Smith, Robert A 4:02:54 (11,367)
Smith, Robert D 3:58:45 (10,366)
Smith, Robert D 4:57:01 (25,135)
Smith, Robert G 4:40:41 (21,303)
Smith, Robert J 3:44:31 (6,839)
Smith, Robert M 5:06:23 (26,942)
Smith, Robert S 3:15:59 (2,570)
Smith, Robert W 5:12:38 (27,934)
Smith, Robin 5:55:10 (32,652)
Smith, Ronald J 3:41:43 (6,319)
Smith, Roy C 3:25:05 (3,602)
Smith, Russell C 4:18:36 (15,394)
Smith, Russell D 3:10:52 (2,017)
Smith, Russell H 3:49:37 (7,958)
Smith, Russell J 4:32:16 (19,152)
Smith, Russell K 4:51:11 (23,769)
Smith, Scott M 4:12:17 (13,692)
Smith, Sean 2:54:43 (728)
Smith, Shaun J 4:48:02 (23,017)
Smith, Shaun R 4:19:12 (15,579)
Smith, Shaune W 5:26:19 (29,904)
Smith, Simon A 2:34:11 (105)
Smith, Simon D 5:28:53 (30,233)
Smith, Simon G 3:40:50 (6,148)
Smith, Simon P 5:19:44 (29,067)
Smith, Simon T 5:24:28 (29,679)
Smith, Stephen 3:40:33 (6,094)
Smith, Stephen 5:02:24 (26,218)
Smith, Stephen 5:06:30 (26,964)
Smith, Stephen F 4:40:47 (21,332)
Smith, Stephen G 4:04:12 (11,684)
Smith, Stephen J 4:39:19 (20,967)
Smith, Stephen R 3:10:08 (1,940)
Smith, Stephen R 4:23:33 (16,745)
Smith, Stephen R 5:22:04 (29,362)
Smith, Steve 4:40:31 (21,263)
Smith, Steve R 4:52:20 (24,021)
Smith, Steven 3:14:46 (2,458)
Smith, Steven G 5:19:14 (28,982)
Smith, Steven J 3:15:31 (2,526)
Smith, Stuart 3:27:19 (3,980)
Smith, Stuart J 4:35:55 (20,066)
Smith, Stuart M 5:57:51 (32,827)
Smith, Terence 5:39:19 (31,352)
Smith, Terry A 4:13:35 (14,037)
Smith, Thomas C 3:43:09 (6,581)
Smith, Thomas P 3:08:55 (1,802)
Smith, Tim 3:47:54 (7,548)
Smith, Tim P 4:42:12 (21,676)
Smith, Timothy 5:38:43 (31,279)
Smith, Timothy E 3:47:14 (7,398)
Smith, Timothy J 4:24:55 (17,096)
Smith, Timothy J 4:38:48 (20,830)
Smith, Tony 4:36:18 (20,164)
Smith, Tony C 4:07:05 (12,368)
Smith, Trevor S 4:43:37 (22,015)
Smith, Victor W 4:04:22 (11,717)
Smith, William E 4:17:32 (15,097)
Smith, William G 4:03:59 (11,626)
Smith, William R 3:29:41 (4,390)
Smitham, Thomas E 3:45:25 (7,037)
Smitherman, Charles W 6:08:55 (33,484)
Smithers, Charles E 4:32:23 (19,184)
Smithers, Chris S 4:17:06 (14,982)
Smith-Malvorsen, Paul J 5:09:39 (27,463)
Smithson, James 5:15:12 (28,369)
Smithson, Peter D 3:59:19 (10,522)
Smithson, Russell M 3:01:16 (1,204)
Smithwhite, Desmond 4:44:38 (22,233)
Smoult, Robin M 3:12:51 (2,236)
Smout, Grahame D 4:58:42 (25,483)
Smy, David J 4:23:31 (16,732)
Smyth, Ben A 4:06:42 (12,266)
Smyth, Calum P 3:56:32 (9,671)
Smyth, Cecil W 3:19:28 (2,932)
Smyth, James 4:06:01 (12,096)
Smyth, Jason 3:53:50 (8,942)
Smyth, John H 2:53:44 (667)
Smyth, Maurice T 5:59:18 (32,934)
Smyth, Michael S 3:26:37 (3,872)
Smyth, Patrick E 5:23:26 (29,531)
Smyth, Ray 3:32:47 (4,854)
Smyth, Troy A 4:35:12 (19,885)
Smythe, Stephen J 2:46:58 (370)
Smythe, Stephen J 3:05:12 (1,486)
Smythe, Todd B 3:53:38 (8,892)
Snaith, Darren G 4:27:08 (17,785)
Snead, Martin P 3:53:45 (8,922)
Sneddon, David M 4:27:45 (17,968)
Sneddon, Robert 3:56:23 (9,634)
Snelgrove, William R 2:57:03 (886)
Snell, David J 3:24:18 (3,486)
Snell, David J 3:28:18 (4,160)
Snell, Michael J 4:18:39 (15,414)
Snell, Richard 4:35:19 (19,911)
Snelling, David E 4:11:38 (13,518)
Snelling, Matthew J 5:01:49 (26,109)
Snelling, Michael 4:36:59 (20,350)
Snoddy, Paul 4:54:19 (24,508)
Snoeks, Jozef 3:04:53 (1,461)
Snook, Gareth 3:51:30 (8,369)
Snow, David R 3:56:49 (9,757)
Snow, Dean 4:37:58 (20,610)
Snow, Patrick R 4:02:42 (11,315)
Snow, Robert B 5:34:22 (30,824)
Snowball, Peter 4:10:06 (13,115)
Snowden, Craig I 5:17:29 (28,713)
Snowden, Kevin 4:44:55 (22,301)
Snyman, Russell B 4:59:24 (25,641)
Soar, Andrew M 4:27:21 (17,838)
Soares, Anibal 4:28:52 (18,268)
Sobek, George P 4:12:09 (13,650)
Sobenes, Juan R 4:12:14 (13,679)
Soberg, Chris 5:36:45 (31,084)
Sobrino, Adolfo 3:09:03 (1,816)
Soder, Philip D 5:52:42 (32,476)
Soderberg, Philip D 3:56:25 (9,637)
Soerensen, Bjarne 4:54:53 (24,637)
Soerensen, Steen 3:00:38 (1,167)
Sokhal, Satnam 5:36:43 (31,079)
Sola, Giampiero 6:18:49 (33,884)
Solanki, Baiju 4:49:31 (23,363)
Sole, Adrian T 3:58:05 (10,164)
Sole, Joe 4:42:01 (21,631)
Solender, Neil 3:32:08 (4,764)
Sollas, Vernon 3:49:21 (7,903)
Solly, John C 2:45:14 (326)
Soloman, Nicholas J 4:08:33 (12,702)
Solomon, Alexandru 5:00:27 (25,873)
Solomons, Daniel R 3:09:04 (1,818)
Solomons, Gary E 3:54:09 (9,013)
Solomou, Anthony 6:06:13 (33,342)
Solti, Joe A 4:46:08 (22,585)
Solti, Nicholas L 4:46:08 (22,585)
Solvang, Trygue M 3:30:59 (4,601)
Somerfield, Guy N 4:28:41 (18,212)
Somersall, David A 3:46:01 (7,140)
Somes-Charlton, Christopher H 4:39:09 (20,911)
Sommerville, William 4:15:07 (14,478)
Sones, John H 5:03:08 (26,369)
Sontan, Richard 5:56:29 (32,730)
Sood, Tej 3:48:55 (7,809)
Soper, John M 5:16:41 (28,573)
Soper, Mark 4:45:54 (22,524)
Soper, Paul 4:45:54 (22,524)
Soper, Thomas 3:39:39 (5,941)
Sorby, Robert C 3:39:36 (5,930)
Sorce, Vince 6:03:19 (33,170)
Sorensen, Claus L 4:47:33 (22,891)
Soto, José 4:11:53 (13,581)
Sotomayor, Alvaro E 5:16:41 (28,573)
Souen, Mauricio 2:56:29 (842)
Soulby, Brian C 3:54:55 (9,221)
Soulier, Gerard 3:17:09 (2,695)
Sousa, Edgar 4:42:52 (21,838)
South, Clifford R 4:19:04 (15,537)

South, Michael J	4:10:31 (13,230)	
South, Rob P	3:17:02 (2,680)	
Southall, John M	5:42:38 (31,642)	
Southall, Peter W	3:04:43 (1,443)	
Southam, Christopher	2:38:03 (161)	
Southern, Mark J	4:36:34 (20,238)	
Southey, Adrian B	4:29:26 (18,442)	
Southgate, Gary R	3:44:45 (6,889)	
Southin, Barney S	2:56:11 (819)	
Southwell, Chris M	4:17:58 (15,194)	
Southwell, David B	5:20:09 (29,122)	
Southwell, Gary T	5:14:05 (28,182)	
Southwell, Niall J	4:04:26 (11,731)	
Southwell, Philip	4:16:10 (14,759)	
Southworth, Nathaniel S	4:46:34 (22,684)	
Souza, Ney C	4:17:25 (15,078)	
Souza Lourgiro, Guilherme M	4:18:19 (15,301)	
Sovegjarto, Pete	3:57:46 (10,058)	
Sowerby, Andrew B	5:52:15 (32,433)	
Spackman, Paul	4:14:41 (14,343)	
Spagnoli, Alberto	3:24:55 (3,570)	
Spagnoli, Aldo	4:08:11 (12,607)	
Spain, David J	2:59:24 (1,083)	
Spalding, Daniel G	3:41:07 (6,204)	
Spalton, Mark	3:53:24 (8,831)	
Spano, Matthew	4:37:42 (20,554)	
Spanyol, Thomas A	4:00:52 (10,922)	
Sparano, Silvio	3:42:59 (6,545)	
Spare, Tracey P	3:36:26 (5,415)	
Sparkes, Andrew B	5:17:22 (28,692)	
Sparkes, Jon W	5:19:40 (29,056)	
Sparkes, Philip R	4:16:18 (14,793)	
Sparkes, Stefan C	4:56:43 (25,073)	
Sparkes, Steve	4:16:18 (14,793)	
Sparkman, Roger	4:49:24 (23,334)	
Sparks, David	3:29:36 (4,370)	
Sparrey, Graham M	3:11:24 (2,069)	
Sparrow, Alen J	3:44:29 (6,833)	
Sparrow, Matthew S	3:21:01 (3,087)	
Spaul, Graham	4:24:18 (16,924)	
Spayne, John	4:30:41 (18,765)	
Spayne, Nick J	4:30:43 (18,772)	
Speake, Malcolm D	3:40:28 (6,082)	
Speake, Peter G	2:47:34 (391)	
Speakman, Michael J	3:57:20 (9,929)	
Spear, Christoper B	3:59:00 (10,430)	
Spear, Philip M	5:39:21 (31,360)	
Spearing, Warwick S	3:57:30 (9,979)	
Specterman, David B	5:38:07 (31,208)	
Spedding, Simon D	2:57:36 (925)	
Speder, Manfred	3:52:20 (8,563)	
Speed, Christopher A	3:32:47 (4,854)	
Speed, Mark F	3:53:58 (8,968)	
Speed, Morley W	3:32:12 (4,773)	
Speer, Lester	3:51:58 (8,476)	
Speers, Paul A	6:20:17 (33,929)	
Speight, Chris	2:55:34 (776)	
Speke, Alexander E	5:14:21 (28,239)	
Speller, Ian F	5:30:54 (30,454)	
Spelling, Stewart P	4:55:36 (24,789)	
Spells, Roger P	3:55:05 (9,253)	
Spelman, Peter J	3:32:11 (4,771)	
Spelman, Robert M	3:29:05 (4,291)	
Speltens, Johan J	4:22:02 (16,350)	
Spence, Andrew D	6:50:10 (34,726)	
Spence, Darren	6:20:27 (33,935)	
Spence, James M	5:49:44 (32,244)	
Spence, Martin T	3:50:50 (8,219)	
Spencer, Andrew M	3:07:24 (1,664)	
Spencer, Andrew N	3:57:12 (9,891)	
Spencer, Anthony P	3:01:44 (1,241)	
Spencer, Brian	4:25:07 (17,159)	
Spencer, Colin D	3:25:53 (3,739)	
Spencer, David	3:36:00 (5,342)	
Spencer, David	4:56:30 (25,018)	
Spencer, David J	4:12:10 (13,657)	
Spencer, Ian	3:22:05 (3,196)	
Spencer, James P	4:27:45 (17,968)	
Spencer, Jeremy R	4:53:01 (24,177)	
Spencer, Julian T	3:01:57 (1,255)	
Spencer, Kevin P	3:09:07 (1,823)	
Spencer, Lucien F	3:13:21 (2,281)	
Spencer, Mark	3:52:12 (8,526)	

Spencer, Matthew	4:29:32 (18,476)	
Spencer, Matthew	4:35:47 (20,039)	
Spencer, Matthew A	4:01:26 (11,032)	
Spencer, Philip	3:51:41 (8,408)	
Spencer, Robert M	3:09:07 (1,823)	
Spencer, Ryan M	3:29:30 (4,354)	
Spencer, Stephen	5:00:48 (25,935)	
Spencer, Steven J	5:02:24 (26,218)	
Spencer, Steven R	5:05:39 (26,813)	
Spencer-Jones, Jonathan L	3:31:46 (4,712)	
Spencer-Smith, Angelo M	5:27:26 (30,034)	
Spensley, Martin J	4:33:29 (19,425)	
Sperber, Marcus	4:09:35 (12,978)	
Spicer, Andrew O	5:23:08 (29,497)	
Spicer, Robert	3:45:26 (7,040)	
Spier, Ben D	4:27:10 (17,792)	
Spierings, George J	3:58:43 (10,354)	
Spiers, Adam	3:27:20 (3,983)	
Spiers, Roger	3:46:45 (7,297)	
Spiller, Gerry W	4:57:07 (25,157)	
Spiller, Tatton L	4:37:02 (20,364)	
Spina, Romano	3:32:23 (4,803)	
Spindler, Andrew	4:21:51 (16,297)	
Spinetto, Mike	5:09:04 (27,362)	
Spink, Jonathan G	4:16:52 (14,929)	
Spinks, Roger E	4:30:48 (18,793)	
Spiteri, Thomas R	5:10:23 (27,551)	
Spittle, Andrew M	3:51:35 (8,386)	
Spitzer, Edward W	4:35:31 (19,981)	
Spivey, Garry M	4:02:59 (11,389)	
Spooner, Cliff D	4:53:01 (24,177)	
Spooner, Martin	5:02:38 (26,256)	
Spoor, Malcolm J	4:29:07 (18,345)	
Spotswood, Eric R	3:43:20 (6,626)	
Spouse, Iain K	3:10:28 (1,974)	
Spragg, Christian	5:09:30 (27,438)	
Spragg, Matthew J	4:41:10 (21,439)	
Spranklen, Brendan	5:49:13 (32,201)	
Spratt, Norman S	3:01:59 (1,261)	
Spray, David M	6:07:00 (33,390)	
Springall, Darryl P	3:47:11 (7,386)	
Springer, Marcellus A	3:05:08 (1,477)	
Springham, James	4:29:34 (18,486)	
Springthorpe, Nigel	4:29:42 (18,520)	
Sprules, Anthony J	3:13:38 (2,319)	
Sprules, Christopher F	3:08:23 (1,748)	
Spry, Doug	4:42:16 (21,693)	
Spry, Jason M	4:15:39 (14,621)	
Spurgeon, Jeremy C	4:56:06 (24,918)	
Spurgeon, Neil J	4:11:33 (13,494)	
Spurr, James C	4:43:02 (21,878)	
Spurrier, Mark	5:42:32 (31,630)	
Squeri, Francesco	3:11:10 (2,046)	
Squibb, Rick	5:17:35 (28,731)	
Squire, David F	4:42:45 (21,811)	
Srivastava, Avadh K	4:41:32 (21,535)	
St Clair Roberts, John	3:51:18 (8,328)	
St Croix, Dennis	4:05:17 (11,944)	
St John, Anthony T	4:19:39 (15,709)	
St John, Christopher M	4:18:22 (15,315)	
St John, Michael	3:44:08 (6,770)	
St Quintin, Daniel	4:53:24 (24,275)	
Stables, Dominic L	5:40:08 (31,432)	
Stables, Thomas W	4:12:46 (13,825)	
Stacey, Colin F	5:11:27 (27,731)	
Stacey, Robin	4:50:52 (23,706)	
Stacey, Steven	5:03:32 (26,438)	
Stack, Dave J	5:16:32 (28,554)	
Staddon, Simon C	4:35:35 (19,992)	
Staff, Granville	4:03:35 (11,521)	
Staffan, James M	5:04:59 (26,683)	
Stafford, John F	4:08:21 (12,659)	
Stafford, John F	4:43:28 (21,969)	
Stafford, Mick J	4:08:49 (12,773)	
Stafford, Paul A	3:23:35 (3,087)	
Stafford, Paul A	4:11:18 (13,428)	
Stafford, Thomas M	4:50:05 (23,508)	
Stagg, Christopher J	4:43:27 (21,964)	
Staggs, Robert J	3:51:06 (8,283)	
Stainbank, Warner D	4:05:05 (11,889)	
Stainer, Peter	2:43:30 (282)	
Staines, Michael R	3:47:47 (7,521)	
Stainthorpe, Andrew	5:16:27 (28,540)	

Staley, Richard D	4:02:43 (11,323)	
Stalker, Andrew J	4:30:44 (18,778)	
Stallard, Bruce	6:06:46 (33,375)	
Stallard, Paul	4:05:52 (12,063)	
Stalley, Andrew C	3:57:42 (10,038)	
Stamenic, Ivan	4:09:41 (13,007)	
Stamp, Gregory M	3:47:35 (7,469)	
Stamper, John T	4:11:33 (13,494)	
Stamper, Michael J	5:48:37 (32,145)	
Stanaway, Anthony D	5:43:57 (31,756)	
Stanbridge, Tony	4:19:32 (15,674)	
Stancliffe, Tom	4:10:50 (13,298)	
Stancombe, John M	4:08:14 (12,622)	
Stancombe, Mark R	4:52:26 (24,037)	
Standen, Gary D	3:40:09 (6,028)	
Standen, Matthew I	4:45:22 (22,406)	
Standen, Melvin L	3:36:35 (5,442)	
Standing, Andrew J	5:33:26 (30,714)	
Standing, David T	4:16:57 (14,944)	
Standing, Robert D	4:44:27 (22,205)	
Stanford, Andrew C	5:40:22 (31,457)	
Stanford, Paul R	3:31:00 (4,608)	
Stanford, Richard J	3:29:31 (4,358)	
Stanger, Mike J	4:18:14 (15,273)	
Stanhope, Christopher J	5:41:06 (31,521)	
Stanhope, Robert N	5:06:09 (26,902)	
Staniland, Anthony	3:39:21 (5,879)	
Staniland, Paul	4:00:03 (10,741)	
Stankard, Enda	2:53:23 (654)	
Stanley, David	5:41:07 (31,522)	
Stanley, David J	3:17:43 (2,759)	
Stanley, Dean D	4:42:44 (21,809)	
Stanley, Drew W	4:55:18 (24,735)	
Stanley, James D	4:02:29 (11,271)	
Stanley, Kevin R	3:47:55 (7,553)	
Stanley, Kieran S	5:56:19 (32,726)	
Stanley, Lloyd R	3:53:26 (8,844)	
Stanley, Mark W	5:26:46 (29,953)	
Stanley, Martin J	4:15:48 (14,660)	
Stannard, Alan	3:44:34 (6,854)	
Stannett, Charlie	5:03:22 (26,414)	
Stannett, Guy L	4:42:45 (21,811)	
Stansfield, Jonathan C	5:30:39 (30,427)	
Stansfield, Peter	3:29:27 (4,347)	
Stanton, Peter	3:57:35 (10,007)	
Stanton, Richard J	4:30:34 (18,743)	
Stanton, Ross P	3:40:26 (6,077)	
Stanton, Stephen A	4:20:13 (15,857)	
Stanway, Sean	5:45:07 (31,856)	
Staples, Francis A	6:13:51 (33,697)	
Staples, James F	4:08:50 (12,782)	
Stapleton, Danny M	4:27:22 (17,845)	
Stapleton, Julian	4:47:34 (22,902)	
Starbrook, Samuel J	5:01:09 (26,001)	
Starbuck, Rob D	4:18:59 (15,507)	
Starchan, Darren S	5:11:11 (27,684)	
Stares, David M	4:34:02 (19,575)	
Stark, Stephen	3:08:41 (1,776)	
Starkey, Andrew J	2:55:50 (796)	
Starkey, Jason P	5:38:03 (31,200)	
Starkey, Simon C	4:50:20 (23,576)	
Starks, Jack W	4:22:14 (16,402)	
Start, Graham P	4:13:19 (13,968)	
Statham, Malcolm J	3:23:08 (3,321)	
Staton, Mark	3:22:00 (3,186)	
Staton, Tim C	4:00:37 (10,871)	
Statter, Graham J	3:36:04 (5,350)	
Statter, Ian G	4:44:07 (22,122)	
Stead, David M	5:22:14 (29,379)	
Stead, Harry	4:11:42 (13,538)	
Steadman, Jake W	4:49:35 (23,381)	
Steadman, Mark R	3:47:54 (7,548)	
Steadman, Terry	3:31:11 (4,625)	
Stearman, Phillip R	6:50:01 (34,709)	
Stearn, Martyn K	4:21:14 (16,124)	
Stearn, Nick A	3:27:23 (3,988)	
Stearn, Thomas F	3:33:35 (4,970)	
Steatham, James	3:51:47 (8,433)	
Stebbings, Justin P	6:23:05 (34,024)	
Stebbins, Donald J	4:48:45 (23,182)	
Steed, Gareth	4:25:13 (17,189)	
Steegen, François	3:30:32 (4,533)	
Steel, Mark I	4:07:43 (12,503)	

Steel, William D	4:44:15 (22,155)	
Steele, Chris D	3:54:46 (9,176)	
Steele, Josh B	5:12:39 (27,937)	
Steele, Ross A	4:29:47 (18,540)	
Steeles, Simon P	3:39:11 (5,847)	
Steene, Mark S	4:32:25 (19,190)	
Steer, Barry	5:02:04 (26,160)	
Steer, Mark A	4:23:03 (16,612)	
Steers, Paul J	4:08:35 (12,711)	
Stefan, Martin D	5:00:03 (25,782)	
Steindl, Werner	2:53:47 (670)	
Steinke, Brad	4:17:38 (15,118)	
Steinmetz, Paul D	5:00:36 (25,898)	
Stella, Bernardo	6:23:43 (34,046)	
Stemp, Iain C	3:24:09 (3,464)	
Stenger, Ken A	3:39:57 (5,986)	
Stenson, Ged	6:54:12 (34,787)	
Stenson, Michael	5:16:49 (28,611)	
Stensrod, Knut	3:40:01 (5,998)	
Stent, Daniel J	4:37:48 (20,580)	
Stentiford, Mark N	4:34:33 (19,727)	
Stephen, Ian A	4:26:45 (17,678)	
Stephen, Keigh A	4:03:08 (11,416)	
Stephens, Alan	5:05:50 (26,848)	
Stephens, Arthur L	4:44:09 (22,129)	
Stephens, Brian	5:13:57 (28,161)	
Stephens, Craig P	5:04:45 (26,638)	
Stephens, David	3:10:25 (1,969)	
Stephens, David C	4:28:33 (18,181)	
Stephens, George H	2:53:14 (646)	
Stephens, Graham C	2:48:41 (446)	
Stephens, Josh	4:34:11 (19,617)	
Stephens, Neale G	3:06:09 (1,564)	
Stephens, Nicholas	2:49:28 (483)	
Stephens, Nigel G	3:26:17 (3,808)	
Stephens, Raymond	4:46:47 (22,727)	
Stephens, Tim	5:10:19 (27,543)	
Stephens, Tony	4:46:59 (22,770)	
Stephenson, Brian	6:23:37 (34,043)	
Stephenson, Charlie	4:17:02 (14,967)	
Stephenson, Jeffrey B	4:20:44 (16,001)	
Stephenson, Johnathon R	7:05:34 (34,933)	
Stephenson, Robin J	4:36:01 (20,087)	
Stephenson, Stuart A	3:56:17 (9,599)	
Stephinson, Peter W	4:50:31 (23,630)	
Stepien, Marek P	4:34:29 (19,706)	
Stepney, Dean	5:19:33 (29,042)	
Steppe, Steven A	4:24:19 (16,932)	
Steptoe, Colin F	2:39:51 (201)	
Sternkopf, Stefan	2:57:12 (902)	
Steven, Mike J	5:13:11 (28,021)	
Stevens, Andrew	4:23:17 (16,683)	
Stevens, Anthony	4:38:35 (20,774)	
Stevens, Benjamin J	4:39:24 (20,989)	
Stevens, Chris	4:38:50 (20,836)	
Stevens, Dave	5:32:22 (30,600)	
Stevens, Dean A	4:15:00 (14,448)	
Stevens, Gary	7:13:39 (35,022)	
Stevens, Graham J	3:29:23 (4,336)	
Stevens, Greg	2:47:21 (382)	
Stevens, Greg J	5:43:40 (31,733)	
Stevens, Gregory J	5:07:45 (27,181)	
Stevens, John P	4:08:11 (12,607)	
Stevens, Jonathan E	3:54:20 (9,053)	
Stevens, Kevin G	4:57:29 (25,226)	
Stevens, Paul D	5:59:28 (32,944)	
Stevens, Paul J	4:59:42 (25,711)	
Stevens, Peter J	4:22:27 (16,461)	
Stevens, Phil G	4:12:14 (13,679)	
Stevens, Robert J	4:06:06 (12,121)	
Stevens, Robert J	4:22:48 (16,558)	
Stevens, Thomas L	4:46:05 (22,571)	
Stevens, Trevor J	5:02:22 (26,213)	
Stevenson, Andrew G	5:07:58 (27,211)	
Stevenson, Chris S	4:26:02 (17,447)	
Stevenson, Derek	4:49:39 (23,411)	
Stevenson, Ian B	4:02:31 (11,276)	
Stevenson, John A	4:10:33 (13,232)	
Stevenson, Leslie	3:55:30 (9,368)	
Stevenson, Mark B	4:13:42 (14,068)	
Stevenson, Mark J	4:33:25 (19,409)	
Stevenson, Paul A	5:19:11 (28,970)	
Stevenson, Richard J	5:12:57 (27,991)	

Stevenson, Robert	4:39:47 (21,089)	
Stevenson, Robert W	4:01:22 (11,017)	
Stevenson, Simon	4:34:26 (19,699)	
Stevenson, Trevor	6:20:51 (33,947)	
Stevick, Joseph	3:41:15 (6,224)	
Stevlet, Benoit M	4:55:46 (24,835)	
Stevnson, Andrew J	3:09:51 (1,903)	
Steward, Geoffrey A	4:25:53 (17,396)	
Steward, Jonathan A	5:02:49 (26,297)	
Stewart, Andrew D	2:52:33 (613)	
Stewart, Brian	3:46:14 (7,188)	
Stewart, David G	6:11:47 (33,603)	
Stewart, Douglas	4:59:37 (25,692)	
Stewart, Gary M	4:02:49 (11,345)	
Stewart, Gavin	4:06:07 (12,126)	
Stewart, Iain	4:11:25 (13,458)	
Stewart, Ian D	4:40:28 (21,251)	
Stewart, James P	3:03:41 (1,383)	
Stewart, Lee	6:20:24 (33,934)	
Stewart, Matthew C	4:26:26 (17,580)	
Stewart, Michael A	3:01:57 (1,255)	
Stewart, Michael D	4:40:19 (21,212)	
Stewart, Nick	4:07:06 (12,372)	
Stewart, Oliver J	6:26:30 (34,142)	
Stewart, Owen P	3:57:08 (9,870)	
Stewart, Peter J	4:23:20 (16,701)	
Stewart, Robert A	3:39:02 (5,823)	
Stewart, Simon C	2:48:48 (458)	
Stewart, Steven J	5:02:09 (26,174)	
Stewart, William	4:14:47 (14,372)	
Stick, Carl R	4:03:04 (11,402)	
Stickland, David G	4:16:06 (14,738)	
Stickley, John F	6:23:12 (34,028)	
Stiff, Adam K	4:09:04 (12,846)	
Stiff, Kevin D	4:30:06 (18,621)	
Stiff, Michael	2:41:19 (225)	
Stiles, Andrew N	4:18:59 (15,507)	
Stiles, Lee A	4:32:27 (19,196)	
Stilgoe, Joseph R	4:02:36 (11,294)	
Still, Stuart	3:00:42 (1,173)	
Stillings, Peter W	6:01:25 (33,046)	
Stillman, Richard S	4:28:38 (18,201)	
Stillwell, Kevin M	4:28:46 (18,237)	
Stimpson, Owen W	5:02:24 (26,218)	
Stinchcombe, Nigel S	3:21:34 (3,139)	
Stinton, Howard R	3:52:07 (8,508)	
Stipic, Raphael	6:47:24 (34,665)	
Stirland, Barry R	4:26:06 (17,475)	
Stirlign, James I	3:23:50 (3,428)	
Stirling, Iain G	4:25:05 (17,146)	
Stirling, Kenneth A	3:47:16 (7,405)	
Stirling, Mark J	4:31:14 (18,894)	
Stirling, Tom	3:58:04 (10,161)	
Stoate, Howard G	3:59:41 (10,627)	
Stobart, Benjamin R	6:29:10 (34,226)	
Stock, Jon P	4:09:20 (12,917)	
Stock, Paul A	6:04:00 (33,221)	
Stockburn, Paul W	3:05:24 (1,509)	
Stockdale, Desmond H	4:46:44 (22,717)	
Stockdale, Peter C	3:17:49 (2,770)	
Stocker, Robin I	3:28:22 (4,169)	
Stockford, Ivor	4:00:55 (10,932)	
Stockings, Richard J	4:32:45 (19,258)	
Stocks, Michael A	3:28:48 (4,246)	
Stocks, Terry E	4:18:39 (15,414)	
Stockwell, Jonathan P	4:04:46 (11,807)	
Stoddart, Keith W	4:47:00 (22,772)	
Stoeks-Gipson, Daniel R	4:20:17 (15,888)	
Stoker, Michael	3:25:23 (3,654)	
Stokes, Craig M	4:52:13 (23,995)	
Stokes, David	5:01:55 (26,129)	
Stokes, David C	3:31:55 (4,733)	
Stokes, Derek	4:45:54 (22,524)	
Stokes, Michael	4:27:46 (17,973)	
Stokoe, Philip	4:57:08 (25,161)	
Stone, Damien	4:50:59 (23,728)	
Stone, Daniel	5:54:13 (32,583)	
Stone, David J	5:12:04 (27,834)	
Stone, David M	2:39:40 (194)	
Stone, Derek C	2:54:49 (733)	
Stone, Ethan E	3:40:05 (6,016)	
Stone, Gaby	5:25:53 (29,850)	
Stone, Greg	5:32:38 (30,632)	

Stone, Ian A	4:53:17 (24,243)	
Stone, Jonathan D	4:52:13 (23,995)	
Stone, Kevin W	5:12:05 (27,839)	
Stone, Mark	4:08:20 (12,655)	
Stone, Matthew T	4:00:15 (10,778)	
Stone, Neville M	6:52:23 (34,760)	
Stone, Nicholas	4:17:38 (15,118)	
Stone, Nigel J	3:08:18 (1,745)	
Stone, Nigel J	4:25:27 (17,265)	
Stone, Timothy J	4:51:47 (23,888)	
Stone, Tom J	6:55:17 (34,804)	
Stoneham, Andrew N	5:01:12 (26,008)	
Stoneham, Christian W	3:59:26 (10,552)	
Stoneley, Andrew M	3:44:45 (6,889)	
Stoneley, Jonathan R	3:23:51 (3,430)	
Stoneman-Roberts, Gareth J	4:43:22 (21,949)	
Stoner, Adrian	3:57:30 (9,979)	
Stopard, Nigel	3:23:50 (3,428)	
Stopher, Jed P	4:44:36 (22,227)	
Storch, Georg	4:07:23 (12,432)	
Storer, David A	4:18:55 (15,489)	
Storer, Graham N	3:43:11 (6,588)	
Storer, Iain M	3:53:40 (8,900)	
Storer, William	4:43:09 (21,902)	
Storey, Chris M	5:17:00 (28,645)	
Storey, Christopher M	4:21:47 (16,280)	
Storey, John	5:10:20 (27,546)	
Storey, Kenneth	3:53:30 (8,855)	
Storey, Miles	4:33:11 (19,360)	
Storey, Paulo	3:53:29 (8,853)	
Storey, Philip A	4:34:20 (19,671)	
Storey, Richard H	4:01:31 (11,052)	
Storey, Simon E	5:24:57 (29,739)	
Storms, John D	3:18:05 (2,794)	
Story, Anthony A	6:48:38 (34,686)	
Story, Richard C	4:17:52 (15,174)	
Stotesbury, Freddie M	3:45:18 (7,005)	
Stott, Charles S	3:49:23 (7,908)	
Stott, Charlie	4:02:35 (11,291)	
Stott, David	5:34:07 (30,791)	
Stott, Ian C	3:44:50 (6,919)	
Stott, Patrick	4:08:49 (12,773)	
Stott, Richard	4:16:02 (14,724)	
Stout, Brian R	3:01:48 (1,247)	
Stout, James D	3:36:31 (5,430)	
Stoute, Colin F	6:25:32 (34,113)	
Stow, Andrew	6:04:54 (33,264)	
Stowell, Matthew	3:54:16 (9,038)	
Stowell, Sam D	3:23:42 (3,402)	
Straffi, Giacomo	3:12:00 (2,140)	
Strafford, Anthony M	4:15:54 (14,683)	
Strain, David C	4:23:11 (16,652)	
Strain, Sean	4:15:30 (14,582)	
Strakeljahn, Juergen	4:08:13 (12,619)	
Straker, Timothy D	6:46:50 (34,653)	
Stramer, Brian M	2:59:34 (1,096)	
Strand, Alan	4:46:30 (22,668)	
Strange, Frank	4:45:58 (22,544)	
Strange, John	3:58:38 (10,318)	
Stranger-Jones, Anthony J	3:01:28 (1,214)	
Stratford, Gary C	3:03:37 (1,377)	
Stratford, Matthew J	2:58:46 (1,012)	
Stratton, Garry D	3:48:47 (7,780)	
Stratton, Jeremy	2:52:44 (623)	
Straughan, Ross E	4:03:33 (11,514)	
Straw, Mark A	4:06:01 (12,096)	
Strawbridge, James	5:04:52 (26,663)	
Streatfield, Frederick W	5:43:08 (31,691)	
Streep, Ton	3:40:31 (6,086)	
Street, Ian	4:13:27 (14,003)	
Street, Neil A	5:30:07 (30,372)	
Street, Paul A	2:45:14 (326)	
Street, René	4:37:45 (20,567)	
Street, Samuel D	3:54:44 (9,167)	
Street, William M	4:22:46 (16,550)	
Streeter, Jack	4:26:33 (17,616)	
Streits, Lawrence A	3:33:45 (4,998)	
Stretton, Malcolm W	5:04:46 (26,642)	
Stretton, Simon	5:11:07 (27,670)	
Streule, Michael J	4:25:33 (17,302)	
Strick, Alex	5:07:36 (27,159)	
Strickland, Steve W	4:30:44 (18,778)	
Stride, Fraser W	3:44:08 (6,770)	

Strike, Mal 4:30:23 (18,698)
Stringer, David 3:19:43 (2,969)
Stringer, James 4:30:33 (18,739)
Stringer, Robert A 7:12:19 (35,008)
Stringfellow, Dene W 3:51:51 (8,454)
Stringle, Julian 4:46:04 (22,566)
Stroffolino, Nicholas 6:53:45 (34,780)
Strom, Bryan T 3:36:01 (5,344)
Strong, Layne 5:53:29 (32,535)
Strother, Iain A 4:16:56 (14,939)
Stroud, Fraser W 4:57:47 (25,278)
Stroud, Mike A 4:55:07 (24,707)
Strowger, Alan L 4:15:36 (14,607)
Strutt, Barry J 5:03:50 (26,493)
Stuart, Darren C 4:43:07 (21,891)
Stuart, Paul D 4:26:02 (17,447)
Stuart, Stephen E 3:21:28 (3,129)
Stubbings, Andrew M 3:29:18 (4,325)
Stubbings, Ian M 4:51:41 (23,869)
Stubbings, Liam J 5:26:30 (29,922)
Stubbs, David A 3:08:17 (1,741)
Stubbs, Richard J 4:33:03 (19,327)
Stuberg, Michael J 4:10:56 (13,329)
Stuckey, John 4:46:39 (22,698)
Stuckey, Lee F 4:43:58 (22,090)
Studley, John G 3:51:52 (8,459)
Studley, Nigel K 4:47:40 (22,936)
Studwell, David 4:49:37 (23,402)
Stuffer, Stefano 3:30:17 (4,486)
Sturdy, Phil A 4:30:05 (18,615)
Sturges, Robert A 4:17:21 (15,050)
Sturla, Timothy S 3:28:10 (4,138)
Sturm, Alain 3:56:14 (9,583)
Sturton, Peter J 3:31:13 (4,634)
Sturtridge, Neil K 5:20:25 (29,165)
Styles, Andrew 4:58:42 (25,483)
Suarez, Michael R 4:32:08 (19,122)
Subbiani, Gary 3:57:49 (10,080)
Subbiani, Matthew J 4:46:46 (22,725)
Subbiano, Gary B 5:37:07 (31,111)
Such, Philip R 5:27:24 (30,030)
Suff, Maxwell P 3:44:06 (6,761)
Sugden, George T 6:32:54 (34,328)
Sugden, Peter H 3:10:06 (1,933)
Sugnot, Frederic 3:59:54 (10,698)
Sugrue, Lee 4:37:05 (20,377)
Sulik, Ladislav 4:42:14 (21,688)
Suller, Jason G 4:35:05 (19,871)
Sullivan, Alex P 3:54:36 (9,124)
Sullivan, Christopher J 6:13:49 (33,696)
Sullivan, Dieter L 5:39:47 (31,395)
Sullivan, Gary P 4:11:54 (13,590)
Sullivan, John J 4:55:28 (24,766)
Sullivan, Lee P 6:53:21 (34,777)
Sullivan, Mark J 4:22:18 (16,421)
Sullivan, Mark S 5:57:12 (32,788)
Sullivan, Peter 4:44:58 (22,316)
Sullivan, Phillip J 5:02:03 (26,155)
Sullivan, Richard T 3:28:07 (4,131)
Sullivan, Rob 5:34:24 (30,833)
Sullivan, Steven J 4:05:43 (12,033)
Sullivan, Tim 3:07:35 (1,684)
Sulonen, Pauli O 3:49:52 (8,011)
Summerfield, Anthony E 6:37:29 (34,441)
Summerfield, Daniel S 4:40:16 (21,200)
Summerfield, Neil P 4:41:45 (21,578)
Summers, Andrew 3:42:38 (6,490)
Summers, Darrell A 5:59:49 (32,971)
Summers, Derek G 4:25:16 (17,206)
Summers, Garry K 5:08:36 (27,298)
Summers, Lee 5:59:49 (32,971)
Summers, Peter 3:26:50 (3,901)
Summers, Russell A 3:49:12 (7,863)
Summerton, John 5:49:13 (32,201)
Summerton, Phillip A 4:21:11 (16,105)
Sumner, Alan 3:49:02 (7,831)
Sumner, Jason P 4:06:20 (12,177)
Sumners, Simon P 3:22:43 (3,264)
Sumpter, James P 2:47:40 (395)
Sunderland, Darren L 6:22:08 (33,997)
Sunderland, Oliver R 3:24:17 (3,480)
Sundsteigen, Nils D 3:44:28 (6,827)
Sunner, Pavitar 4:59:53 (25,752)
Suothwell, Alfred M 5:14:11 (28,208)
Supie, Philippe 3:45:53 (7,114)
Sura, Ruediger C 5:16:12 (28,504)
Surfield, Christopher 4:08:34 (12,705)
Surgeon, Matthew 4:44:39 (22,236)
Surman, David K 4:34:08 (19,604)
Surrage, Joseph P 4:40:31 (21,263)
Surrage, Richard S 3:38:39 (5,745)
Surrey, Samuel M 3:08:39 (1,773)
Sutcliffe, Barry 4:47:59 (23,004)
Sutcliffe, Chris D 7:14:49 (35,031)
Sutcliffe, David J 3:26:35 (3,866)
Suter, Martin 3:57:09 (9,875)
Suters, Glenn A 3:50:31 (8,152)
Sutherland, Alasdair R 3:58:49 (10,393)
Sutherland, Leslie 5:10:26 (27,560)
Sutherland, Michael 3:05:51 (1,541)
Sutherland, Paul F 4:54:04 (24,443)
Sutherland, Robert E 3:39:27 (5,899)
Sutherland, Thabian 3:24:43 (3,543)
Sutherland, William F 5:05:29 (26,793)
Sutman, Frank J 3:48:35 (7,736)
Sutter, David A 5:03:13 (26,387)
Sutton, David 5:25:13 (29,772)
Sutton, Jez P 4:31:19 (18,923)
Sutton, John E 4:37:23 (20,469)
Sutton, Lee D 4:53:15 (24,237)
Sutton, Malcolm J 4:01:39 (11,078)
Sutton, Paul R 6:23:35 (34,040)
Sutton, Philip N 4:52:05 (23,961)
Sutton, Phillip 4:05:33 (12,000)
Sutton, Steve L 6:53:56 (34,783)
Suwa, Toshinari 2:10:23 (7)
Svangtun, Martin 4:15:05 (14,473)
Svinos, Michael R 4:40:10 (21,175)
Swain, Austin B 3:27:55 (4,093)
Swain, Craig 4:42:19 (21,702)
Swain, Jonathan 4:42:19 (21,702)
Swaine, Peter 2:41:23 (228)
Swainson, Christopher G 4:08:59 (12,823)
Swainson, David J 3:59:58 (10,717)
Swainson, Mike J 4:56:51 (25,101)
Swales, Peter N 4:50:40 (23,669)
Swallow, Nigel 6:25:21 (34,104)
Swallow, Shaun 3:06:08 (1,563)
Swan, Alan 3:11:42 (2,105)
Swan, Jonathan E 3:57:31 (9,988)
Swan, Kim R 3:35:07 (5,199)
Swan, Martin C 3:17:47 (2,764)
Swanepoel, Anthony 3:35:26 (5,245)
Swanepoel, Trevor J 5:22:10 (29,372)
Swann, Graham A 4:58:09 (25,359)
Swann, James M 4:10:57 (13,333)
Swann, Richard 4:59:57 (25,766)
Swannell, Ian J 3:44:45 (6,889)
Swanson, Marcus 5:24:55 (29,734)
Swanston, Peter D 3:49:45 (7,990)
Swanton, Paul N 3:02:40 (1,311)
Swart, Adam I 5:07:10 (27,091)
Swatton, Neville R 3:32:15 (4,781)
Sweeney, Gerard 6:12:23 (33,633)
Sweeney, Paul T 4:28:58 (18,297)
Sweeney, Thomas E 3:28:46 (4,238)
Sweet, David P 3:28:09 (4,135)
Sweny, Paul A 4:21:29 (16,200)
Swery, Raphael A 3:53:58 (8,968)
Swift, Andrew 3:24:59 (3,582)
Swift, Brian R 3:33:35 (4,970)
Swift, Christopher P 3:25:40 (3,699)
Swift, Derrick J 3:01:32 (1,223)
Swift, James M 4:52:22 (24,027)
Swift, Peter D 5:17:05 (28,662)
Swindin, Robin T 3:47:48 (7,525)
Swingler, David G 4:26:35 (17,629)
Swinney, Alan D 5:07:08 (27,081)
Swinney, Gordon R 5:34:14 (30,811)
Swinney, Terry 6:00:01 (32,983)
Swycher, Stuart S 5:38:50 (31,292)
Sycamore, Paul C 5:57:16 (32,793)
Sydenham, Christopher R 4:19:56 (15,782)
Sydenham, Deric A 5:26:19 (29,904)
Syed, Zahid 4:07:59 (12,570)
Sykes, Christopher A 4:03:43 (11,548)
Sykes, Colin 4:13:59 (14,141)
Sykes, Peter P 4:38:39 (20,786)
Sykes, Toby G 3:07:04 (1,640)
Symeou, Nicos 4:42:58 (21,867)
Symes, Graham J 4:10:59 (13,345)
Symes, Robert 3:25:29 (3,668)
Symington, Ian 3:03:59 (1,396)
Symon, Witney D 5:46:52 (32,004)
Symonds, Barrie 3:22:20 (3,230)
Symonds, Mark A 4:26:55 (17,724)
Symonds, Paul 5:49:04 (32,189)
Symondson, Nick 6:35:12 (34,383)
Symons, David S 2:28:19 (61)
Symons, David W 4:25:45 (17,365)
Syrett, Jason 3:52:14 (8,537)
Szalkai, Anders 2:21:27 (31)
Szkwarok, Stefan 3:52:08 (8,512)
Szmierek, Keith 5:07:22 (27,123)
Szpot, Ireneusz 3:07:58 (1,713)
Sztarkman, Herve 3:08:58 (1,807)
Szulc, Clive 4:39:58 (21,129)
Szumilewicz, Paul 3:40:47 (6,136)
Szwinto, Henry 2:57:23 (912)
Szymanski, Mark R 4:02:13 (11,206)
Szymanski, Richard 5:17:06 (28,664)
Szynaka, Stefan 5:43:22 (31,708)
Tabaaro, Michael 5:44:27 (31,798)
Tabata, Yujin 4:47:33 (22,891)
Tabatabai-Madani, Seyed M 3:40:11 (6,038)
Tack, Ian R 2:57:50 (945)
Tadebois, Stellio 4:27:06 (17,775)
Tadesse, Kassa 2:15:09 (14)
Taevernier, Manu 4:20:47 (16,017)
Tafere, Mourad 4:18:19 (15,301)
Taffender, Ross 4:48:13 (23,056)
Taffs, Andrew J 6:11:23 (33,589)
Taggart, Simon T 4:31:01 (18,840)
Tagliarini, Rino 5:17:39 (28,738)
Tahan, Bijan M 6:23:12 (34,028)
Taiapa, Piripi H 4:25:10 (17,172)
Tait, Simon P 4:25:37 (17,321)
Taitz, Jonny 4:18:27 (15,350)
Takahashi, Koja 5:52:53 (32,490)
Takanishi, Masataka 5:12:04 (27,834)
Takano, Hideo 4:28:43 (18,225)
Takano, Satoshi 3:52:23 (8,574)
Takle, Andrew K 4:25:31 (17,290)
Talaron, Philippe 3:37:40 (5,599)
Talavera-Rivera, Jesus 3:25:11 (3,618)
Talbot, Jean-Luc 3:23:16 (3,345)
Talbot, Joshua J 5:00:52 (25,953)
Talbot, Mark B 4:22:17 (16,416)
Talbot, Nicholas M 4:03:03 (11,398)
Talbot, Richard J 3:31:28 (4,675)
Talbot, Robin H 3:58:57 (10,417)
Talevski, Robert 5:26:15 (29,897)
Talewar, Ghanaya S 6:27:29 (34,179)
Tallaron, Richard 3:47:16 (7,405)
Tallott, Giles 5:01:49 (26,109)
Tam, Patrick 3:49:00 (7,821)
Tame, Nick 4:53:10 (24,213)
Tame, Richard D 6:16:46 (33,810)
Tampin, Anthony J 3:53:37 (8,888)
Tams, Thomas 4:34:30 (19,711)
Tan, Joon Y 4:13:37 (14,046)
Tancer, Jaroslav 3:34:45 (5,151)
Tancock, Stephen J 3:05:22 (1,505)
Tandy, Ian J 5:24:43 (29,710)
Tang, Julian 5:53:27 (32,531)
Tang, Sammer H 5:57:40 (32,817)
Tanker, Peter N 3:36:08 (5,360)
Tann, Simon C 4:14:11 (14,207)
Tanna, Dev 4:50:24 (23,596)
Tanna, Rajin K 5:54:00 (32,564)
Tanneau, Joel 4:21:59 (16,326)
Tanner, Daniel 3:53:18 (8,801)
Tanner, Ian D 3:31:31 (4,682)
Tanner, Jean-Paul 4:50:26 (23,608)
Tanner, Jonathan B 4:50:24 (23,596)
Tanner, Vaughan 4:34:54 (19,825)
Tanser, Simon P 3:55:03 (9,245)
Tansey, Robert 3:05:33 (1,523)
Tantalo, Vittorio M 4:19:37 (15,699)

Tanti, Robert A	4:23:42 (16,776)	
Tanujaya, Johny	5:12:56 (27,988)	
Tanzer, William J	5:07:32 (27,150)	
Tao, Tony C	4:17:38 (15,118)	
Taplin, Derek R	6:06:23 (33,352)	
Taplin, Steve P	3:18:48 (2,861)	
Tappin, Nick D	4:05:57 (12,085)	
Tapster, Martin A	5:45:36 (31,903)	
Taranco, Daniel	4:17:43 (15,145)	
Taranik, Dan	5:33:26 (30,714)	
Tarbyat, Mahmoud	4:53:11 (24,217)	
Tareilus, Erwin	3:23:57 (3,441)	
Targett, David G	4:40:36 (21,285)	
Tarleton, James W	4:05:15 (11,929)	
Tarling, Stephen B	3:52:51 (8,695)	
Tarpey, Chris M	3:06:06 (1,559)	
Tarpey, Matthew	4:53:25 (24,281)	
Tarr, John F	6:03:30 (33,190)	
Tarrant, James P	4:00:45 (10,899)	
Tarrant, Nick G	3:56:40 (9,714)	
Tarrant, Richard J	5:30:37 (30,426)	
Tarry, Mark H	4:18:05 (15,231)	
Tarver, Andrew D	5:05:09 (26,713)	
Tassafout, Kamal	2:51:22 (554)	
Tassell, Andrew D	4:52:27 (24,041)	
Tassell, Stephen	5:58:13 (32,858)	
Tassinari, Giancarlo	3:59:04 (10,456)	
Tatam, John C	3:06:52 (1,624)	
Tate, Benjamin L	4:57:37 (25,251)	
Tate, Chris N	3:16:06 (2,590)	
Tate, Paul	4:13:54 (14,112)	
Tate, Steve J	3:38:09 (5,674)	
Tatoud, Philippe	3:38:44 (5,759)	
Tattam, David J	5:37:53 (31,180)	
Tattersall, Alan	5:21:16 (29,271)	
Tattersall, Ryan D	3:38:59 (5,812)	
Tatum, Steven J	4:44:44 (22,255)	
Taun, Alastair G	5:27:16 (30,010)	
Tauschinski, Alexander N	3:38:26 (5,714)	
Taverna, Thierry J	2:49:13 (475)	
Taverner, Philip J	4:56:53 (25,110)	
Taverner, Tony J	5:21:56 (29,345)	
Tawse, Alister W	4:20:47 (16,017)	
Taylo, Gary J	3:27:38 (4,042)	
Taylor, Adam C	4:17:01 (14,962)	
Taylor, Adam M	4:19:48 (15,754)	
Taylor, Alan G	4:34:09 (19,608)	
Taylor, Alan L	4:26:17 (17,527)	
Taylor, Andrew	5:16:40 (28,571)	
Taylor, Andrew D	3:47:00 (7,350)	
Taylor, Andrew P	3:30:43 (4,561)	
Taylor, Barry J	6:02:48 (33,126)	
Taylor, Ben N	4:34:06 (19,591)	
Taylor, Benjamin J	4:28:36 (18,195)	
Taylor, Bernard F	5:36:08 (31,007)	
Taylor, Bolwale O	6:00:33 (33,003)	
Taylor, Brian	3:33:29 (4,957)	
Taylor, Brian	4:42:09 (21,664)	
Taylor, Brian J	3:41:39 (6,313)	
Taylor, Bryon A	5:28:56 (30,240)	
Taylor, Charles G	3:13:44 (2,330)	
Taylor, Chris	4:08:26 (12,681)	
Taylor, Christian S	5:40:20 (31,447)	
Taylor, Christopher	4:21:53 (16,304)	
Taylor, Christopher J	3:42:58 (6,537)	
Taylor, Christopher M	4:23:49 (16,808)	
Taylor, Colin	4:50:14 (23,545)	
Taylor, Colin D	3:28:29 (4,194)	
Taylor, Craig	5:18:13 (28,820)	
Taylor, Dan G	4:26:10 (17,498)	
Taylor, David A	5:10:28 (27,565)	
Taylor, David G	6:06:39 (33,365)	
Taylor, David J	4:08:38 (12,722)	
Taylor, David W	2:18:47 (23)	
Taylor, Dean	4:54:46 (24,614)	
Taylor, Dean R	4:01:36 (11,066)	
Taylor, Derrick R	4:56:55 (25,117)	
Taylor, Drew	2:53:57 (681)	
Taylor, Duncan S	3:56:53 (9,781)	
Taylor, Eddie	5:41:32 (31,556)	
Taylor, Edward W	5:05:23 (26,771)	
Taylor, Eric	3:05:11 (1,483)	
Taylor, Ewan D	3:54:43 (9,158)	
Taylor, Glen	4:15:22 (14,540)	
Taylor, Graham C	2:58:47 (1,014)	
Taylor, Graham J	4:25:59 (17,429)	
Taylor, Greg N	4:42:07 (21,657)	
Taylor, Howard	3:53:20 (8,813)	
Taylor, Iain M	5:02:57 (26,329)	
Taylor, Ian	3:15:07 (2,487)	
Taylor, Ian	4:02:42 (11,315)	
Taylor, Ian C	5:00:35 (25,893)	
Taylor, Ian D	3:18:47 (2,858)	
Taylor, Ian R	4:28:26 (18,146)	
Taylor, Ian R	4:38:46 (20,821)	
Taylor, James	4:49:25 (23,342)	
Taylor, James	5:05:31 (26,798)	
Taylor, James R	5:10:52 (27,628)	
Taylor, James S	5:03:04 (26,352)	
Taylor, Jeffrey T	4:53:27 (24,290)	
Taylor, Jeremy D	4:56:34 (25,029)	
Taylor, Jeremy J	5:14:48 (28,313)	
Taylor, Jesse D	3:54:26 (9,086)	
Taylor, John	4:10:10 (13,133)	
Taylor, John C	3:03:48 (1,389)	
Taylor, John D	4:22:36 (16,503)	
Taylor, John I	4:51:53 (23,905)	
Taylor, John L	5:22:45 (29,458)	
Taylor, John L	5:46:20 (31,966)	
Taylor, Jonathan S	5:02:23 (26,216)	
Taylor, Keith	4:15:01 (14,457)	
Taylor, Keith R	3:59:32 (10,582)	
Taylor, Kenneth B	4:43:14 (21,919)	
Taylor, Kevin	3:58:58 (10,423)	
Taylor, Kevin A	4:33:58 (19,560)	
Taylor, Kevin J	3:36:56 (5,487)	
Taylor, Lance	3:33:10 (4,908)	
Taylor, Laurence S	6:02:49 (33,128)	
Taylor, Lee	4:43:38 (22,019)	
Taylor, Lewis R	6:35:48 (34,405)	
Taylor, Marcus J	4:50:31 (23,630)	
Taylor, Mark	3:09:34 (1,865)	
Taylor, Mark	4:08:28 (12,687)	
Taylor, Martin J	3:54:43 (9,158)	
Taylor, Martin J	4:37:11 (20,408)	
Taylor, Martin R	5:20:57 (29,231)	
Taylor, Matthew J	3:11:38 (2,093)	
Taylor, Michael J	3:40:27 (6,080)	
Taylor, Michael M	3:49:33 (7,944)	
Taylor, Neil	3:17:14 (2,706)	
Taylor, Neil C	3:57:07 (9,864)	
Taylor, Nicholas C	3:55:42 (9,429)	
Taylor, Nicholas D	3:57:28 (9,969)	
Taylor, Nicholas E	5:20:39 (29,202)	
Taylor, Niel	5:57:59 (32,833)	
Taylor, Nigel	5:02:44 (26,281)	
Taylor, Nigel J	3:35:18 (5,224)	
Taylor, Nigel R	3:46:21 (7,211)	
Taylor, Nikki	4:33:00 (19,316)	
Taylor, Owain J	5:21:44 (29,318)	
Taylor, Paul	4:59:11 (25,600)	
Taylor, Paul J	3:14:05 (2,364)	
Taylor, Paul M	6:05:10 (33,282)	
Taylor, Paul R	3:46:53 (7,326)	
Taylor, Paul R	4:32:33 (19,219)	
Taylor, Paul S	4:59:32 (25,670)	
Taylor, Pete R	4:42:15 (21,689)	
Taylor, Peter F	4:33:40 (19,477)	
Taylor, Peter J	4:09:16 (12,900)	
Taylor, Peter M	5:02:54 (26,320)	
Taylor, Peter S	3:56:35 (9,687)	
Taylor, Philip	6:24:03 (34,067)	
Taylor, Philip J	4:29:01 (18,318)	
Taylor, Philip M	3:56:51 (9,769)	
Taylor, Philip R	4:04:19 (11,705)	
Taylor, Phillip G	2:47:18 (378)	
Taylor, Phillip R	7:01:37 (34,888)	
Taylor, Richard	4:46:27 (22,657)	
Taylor, Richard T	5:40:31 (31,469)	
Taylor, Robert F	4:44:09 (22,129)	
Taylor, Robert M	3:50:10 (8,077)	
Taylor, Robert S	5:16:09 (28,498)	
Taylor, Roger N	5:56:11 (32,717)	
Taylor, Ross S	4:19:20 (15,619)	
Taylor, Scott J	4:07:41 (12,493)	
Taylor, Shaun P	4:16:38 (14,871)	
Taylor, Simeon	4:43:22 (21,949)	
Taylor, Simon D	3:33:47 (5,006)	
Taylor, Simon M	4:27:39 (17,937)	
Taylor, Simon R	5:28:13 (30,147)	
Taylor, Stephen J	3:37:06 (5,515)	
Taylor, Steve	4:09:11 (12,882)	
Taylor, Steven J	4:37:32 (20,502)	
Taylor, Stewart P	3:49:49 (8,000)	
Taylor, Stuart	4:48:12 (23,054)	
Taylor, Stuart A	5:16:43 (28,582)	
Taylor, Stuart E	4:05:00 (11,862)	
Taylor, Timothy J	6:46:22 (34,637)	
Taylor, Timothy M	4:38:39 (20,786)	
Taylor, William J	6:31:18 (34,287)	
Taylor-Gill, Robert	4:47:20 (22,840)	
Taylor-Schofield, Nigel C	4:57:56 (25,307)	
Taylorson, Simon L	3:51:05 (8,278)	
Taylor-Wilkin, Nigel D	4:19:43 (15,727)	
Teague, Stephen J	3:35:27 (5,249)	
Teatino, Raphael E	5:10:30 (27,572)	
Tebbutt, Chris M	4:58:10 (25,364)	
Tebbutt, Stuart J	3:44:50 (6,919)	
Tee, Paul K	3:19:41 (2,964)	
Telelis, Konstantinos	4:28:14 (18,095)	
Telfer, George	4:49:38 (23,408)	
Telford, Andrew D	3:27:00 (3,929)	
Telling, Barry J	4:05:05 (11,889)	
Temple, James D	3:36:59 (5,499)	
Temple, James M	3:43:02 (6,556)	
Temple, Neil K	4:01:13 (10,985)	
Temple, Roger J	4:28:46 (18,237)	
Templeman, Paul	4:42:08 (21,661)	
Templeman, Wayne A	4:40:47 (21,332)	
Tengawarima, Nyasha	4:01:41 (11,086)	
Tennant, Christopher D	5:42:22 (31,618)	
Tennant, Craig T	4:28:23 (18,137)	
Tennant, David M	5:02:53 (26,316)	
Tennant, Edward	4:42:34 (21,761)	
Tennekoon, Milinda	4:33:54 (19,546)	
Tennent, Daniel	4:14:47 (14,372)	
Tergat, Paul	2:11:38 (8)	
Terkelsen, Karl R	4:02:31 (11,276)	
Terrail, Jacques	3:29:26 (4,344)	
Terrier, Eric	3:20:36 (3,058)	
Terry, Christopher W	4:20:25 (15,918)	
Terry, Hugh J	4:33:13 (19,363)	
Terry, Martin	3:03:36 (1,373)	
Terry, Michael B	6:12:03 (33,619)	
Terry, Michael D	4:51:30 (23,829)	
Terry, Michael E	3:58:24 (10,261)	
Terry, Paul D	4:54:48 (24,622)	
Terry, Richard E	4:54:08 (24,456)	
Terry, Simon	5:08:28 (27,281)	
Tesi, Neil J	3:47:17 (7,411)	
Tester, Michel C	3:37:20 (5,545)	
Tetamo, Romano	5:07:49 (27,192)	
Tether, Colin P	4:14:25 (14,280)	
Tetlow, Drew B	4:15:50 (14,673)	
Tew, Gavin S	4:00:02 (10,736)	
Tewater, Sam	4:18:48 (15,464)	
Thackeray, Brian	5:27:13 (30,003)	
Thackeray, Charlie W	4:25:57 (17,413)	
Thackeray, David	4:42:00 (21,627)	
Thackeray, Stephen	3:35:04 (5,194)	
Tham, Quy D	4:34:45 (19,777)	
Thango, Thulani	3:41:28 (6,271)	
Thatcher, Garath S	4:47:32 (22,889)	
Thatcher, Nick	3:54:58 (9,232)	
Thaw, George	5:54:42 (32,613)	
Thawaites, Mark W	3:09:23 (1,851)	
Theakston, Edward D	3:50:20 (8,112)	
Thelwell, Jason A	5:10:56 (27,642)	
Thelwell, Luke J	3:52:02 (8,490)	
Theocharous, Harris	5:30:56 (30,461)	
Theodoulou, Orthodoxos	5:11:12 (27,687)	
Theophilou, George	7:04:19 (34,915)	
Theron, Nicholas C	3:23:47 (3,416)	
Thery, Stephane	3:24:09 (3,464)	
Theuerkauf, Daniel	4:19:17 (15,604)	
Thickett, Keith	3:20:07 (3,012)	
Thimaya, Kongandra A	4:27:28 (17,875)	
Thing, James E	5:57:32 (32,806)	
Thirasilpa, Therothai	4:26:29 (17,593)	

Thirsk, Michael 5:01:55 (26,129)
Thoams, Derek W 5:40:06 (31,427)
Thoemel, Andreas 4:50:40 (23,669)
Thom, Michael W 4:00:30 (10,832)
Thomas, Alan 4:29:03 (18,326)
Thomas, Alan 5:16:22 (28,529)
Thomas, Alex K 5:25:53 (29,850)
Thomas, Alistair L 4:24:40 (17,032)
Thomas, Allun E 4:13:09 (13,922)
Thomas, Andrew D 5:10:53 (27,634)
Thomas, Andrew J 5:20:03 (29,107)
Thomas, Andrew L 5:36:53 (31,091)
Thomas, Austen J 2:58:57 (1,028)
Thomas, Barry 5:16:23 (28,530)
Thomas, Barry 5:29:35 (30,318)
Thomas, Bobby A 6:21:49 (33,981)
Thomas, Brian V 5:26:35 (29,931)
Thomas, Christopher 3:40:13 (6,040)
Thomas, Christopher 5:46:09 (31,946)
Thomas, Christopher D 5:14:15 (28,217)
Thomas, Darren M 3:15:26 (2,520)
Thomas, David 3:08:13 (1,735)
Thomas, David A 5:00:11 (25,813)
Thomas, David G 4:22:08 (16,380)
Thomas, David H 4:05:51 (12,057)
Thomas, David I 3:44:32 (6,845)
Thomas, David J 3:47:19 (7,419)
Thomas, David M 5:39:14 (31,342)
Thomas, David R 3:57:46 (10,058)
Thomas, Dean R 4:45:22 (22,406)
Thomas, Duncan B 4:01:40 (11,082)
Thomas, Francis G 4:50:17 (23,556)
Thomas, Frank W 3:29:54 (4,438)
Thomas, Gareth 2:49:48 (494)
Thomas, Gareth R 2:36:32 (127)
Thomas, Gary 3:07:36 (1,687)
Thomas, Gary 4:26:13 (17,511)
Thomas, Gavin 3:39:48 (5,963)
Thomas, George E 3:30:11 (4,475)
Thomas, Glyn D 4:51:09 (23,761)
Thomas, Glynn L 2:57:06 (891)
Thomas, Graham B 4:06:04 (12,114)
Thomas, Gwynfor J 5:14:40 (28,296)
Thomas, Hadrian 3:50:35 (8,166)
Thomas, Haydn 5:00:18 (25,845)
Thomas, Huw 4:49:33 (23,371)
Thomas, Huw G 3:26:53 (3,908)
Thomas, Ian M 5:58:29 (32,877)
Thomas, James R 6:13:33 (33,684)
Thomas, John 3:48:31 (7,715)
Thomas, John M 3:16:03 (2,580)
Thomas, John P 3:14:16 (2,388)
Thomas, Keeran J 5:51:47 (32,395)
Thomas, Kermann F 3:40:42 (6,117)
Thomas, Kevin O 4:33:30 (19,433)
Thomas, Leighton N 3:33:35 (4,970)
Thomas, Lennard 3:14:03 (2,362)
Thomas, Mark 4:55:45 (24,831)
Thomas, Mark J 5:27:17 (30,014)
Thomas, Mark S 3:35:50 (5,314)
Thomas, Matthew A 4:50:42 (23,675)
Thomas, Matthew B 4:02:30 (11,272)
Thomas, Michael I 5:51:51 (32,401)
Thomas, Miles H 3:28:51 (4,253)
Thomas, Neil 5:10:43 (27,604)
Thomas, Neil A 5:00:38 (25,906)
Thomas, Neil D 4:56:41 (25,064)
Thomas, Neil E 4:19:23 (15,632)
Thomas, Nicholas 3:46:24 (7,222)
Thomas, Nick D 2:58:25 (984)
Thomas, Nigel J 4:17:10 (15,004)
Thomas, Patrick 4:49:14 (23,288)
Thomas, Paul 3:39:22 (5,886)
Thomas, Peter 3:05:56 (1,548)
Thomas, Peter 3:21:40 (3,148)
Thomas, Peter E 4:06:14 (12,149)
Thomas, Raymond W 5:51:44 (32,392)
Thomas, Rhodri G 5:16:29 (28,547)
Thomas, Richard 3:58:22 (10,250)
Thomas, Richard 4:42:33 (21,751)
Thomas, Richard D 3:08:40 (1,775)
Thomas, Richard H 5:15:51 (28,462)
Thomas, Robert W 4:33:19 (19,390)
Thomas, Robin 5:30:52 (30,448)
Thomas, Roderick M 4:33:40 (19,477)
Thomas, Rodney M 6:11:29 (33,593)
Thomas, Russell 3:14:25 (2,406)
Thomas, Russell E 4:25:16 (17,206)
Thomas, Ryan M 4:55:34 (24,783)
Thomas, Sam 3:50:01 (8,042)
Thomas, Shaun D 4:54:12 (24,475)
Thomas, Simon J 5:18:39 (28,897)
Thomas, Simon P 5:11:00 (27,653)
Thomas, Steffan 3:45:57 (7,124)
Thomas, Stephen G 5:05:41 (26,821)
Thomas, Stephen J 3:57:13 (9,898)
Thomas, Stephen J 4:59:03 (25,574)
Thomas, Tom J 3:46:28 (7,236)
Thomas MBE, Michael J 5:06:21 (26,931)
Thomason, Alan E 5:18:11 (28,815)
Thomason, Francis L 3:56:41 (9,722)
Thomason, Richard 4:27:34 (17,912)
Thomason, Richard J 4:58:44 (25,493)
Thomelin, Pascal 3:48:09 (7,627)
Thompson, Adrian P 5:31:14 (30,489)
Thompson, Andrew 3:36:11 (5,369)
Thompson, Andrew 3:48:05 (7,614)
Thompson, Andrew 3:52:54 (8,700)
Thompson, Andrew J 3:46:14 (7,188)
Thompson, Anthony R 5:08:19 (27,262)
Thompson, Aron J 4:51:09 (23,761)
Thompson, Ben 4:52:35 (24,070)
Thompson, Ben 4:55:15 (24,728)
Thompson, Benjamin J 3:45:13 (6,993)
Thompson, Carl A 3:13:03 (2,251)
Thompson, Chris J 3:04:58 (1,465)
Thompson, Christopher M 3:23:09 (3,324)
Thompson, Colin D 3:29:04 (4,286)
Thompson, Colin W 3:47:35 (7,469)
Thompson, Craig R 4:50:08 (23,523)
Thompson, Darren J 4:16:24 (14,820)
Thompson, David 3:47:41 (7,496)
Thompson, David 4:07:32 (12,466)
Thompson, David A 4:00:09 (10,756)
Thompson, David M 3:13:33 (2,308)
Thompson, David S 4:19:47 (15,748)
Thompson, Derek 4:33:01 (19,317)
Thompson, Dominic 4:40:13 (21,191)
Thompson, Gavin J 3:36:19 (5,397)
Thompson, George 2:54:25 (705)
Thompson, George 4:38:30 (20,757)
Thompson, Gordon W 3:38:34 (5,735)
Thompson, Graeme M 3:51:39 (8,400)
Thompson, Guy 4:43:45 (22,049)
Thompson, James 3:10:06 (1,933)
Thompson, James A 4:49:03 (23,250)
Thompson, James E 4:59:53 (25,752)
Thompson, James J 3:03:28 (1,361)
Thompson, Jeremy G 4:36:37 (20,258)
Thompson, Jeremy W 4:23:47 (16,796)
Thompson, John 4:08:17 (12,632)
Thompson, John 4:48:14 (23,060)
Thompson, John 5:17:02 (28,652)
Thompson, John S 3:29:22 (4,333)
Thompson, Jonathan 5:35:22 (30,943)
Thompson, Jonathan A 4:09:16 (12,900)
Thompson, Julian W 4:12:40 (13,794)
Thompson, Justin D 3:56:04 (9,524)
Thompson, Keith R 4:55:09 (24,713)
Thompson, Kevin 5:36:17 (31,026)
Thompson, Kevin A 4:01:18 (11,001)
Thompson, Laurence 3:31:36 (4,694)
Thompson, Lawrence 4:34:06 (19,591)
Thompson, Luke D 4:22:24 (16,445)
Thompson, Mark J 4:00:34 (10,857)
Thompson, Mark R 3:47:43 (7,509)
Thompson, Matthew 4:36:26 (20,209)
Thompson, Melvyn R 4:40:55 (21,366)
Thompson, Michael 4:30:06 (18,621)
Thompson, Michael 5:18:35 (28,888)
Thompson, Michael J 3:44:10 (6,779)
Thompson, Neil 3:58:39 (10,323)
Thompson, Neil W 4:58:42 (25,483)
Thompson, Neville K 3:16:19 (2,620)
Thompson, Nicholas C 4:46:02 (22,557)
Thompson, Paul 6:08:45 (33,476)
Thompson, Paul G 2:30:45 (75)
Thompson, Paul J 3:53:42 (8,909)
Thompson, Paul R 4:33:57 (19,557)
Thompson, Paul R 4:36:42 (20,279)
Thompson, Peter 4:39:33 (21,027)
Thompson, Peter A 5:27:40 (30,063)
Thompson, Phillip M 3:50:58 (8,254)
Thompson, Ralph P 4:22:37 (16,514)
Thompson, Rex 7:35:59 (35,160)
Thompson, Robert A 5:24:59 (29,743)
Thompson, Robert G 4:04:38 (11,779)
Thompson, Ron K 5:16:29 (28,547)
Thompson, Ryan 4:37:17 (20,440)
Thompson, Sean M 3:32:58 (4,885)
Thompson, Simon 4:36:26 (20,209)
Thompson, Steven J 5:16:08 (28,494)
Thompson, Tony 3:08:34 (1,766)
Thompson, Trevor D 4:40:09 (21,171)
Thompson, Trevor G 4:34:32 (19,722)
Thomsen, Thomas 4:08:34 (12,705)
Thomson, Andrew 4:31:28 (18,962)
Thomson, Gordon 4:03:19 (11,465)
Thomson, Ivan 4:10:40 (13,257)
Thomson, Jeff P 4:52:41 (24,101)
Thomson, John W 4:13:02 (13,888)
Thomson, Matthew A 5:22:24 (29,404)
Thomson, Michael R 4:16:35 (14,854)
Thomson, Paul A 3:14:57 (2,476)
Thomson, Paul D 3:51:38 (8,398)
Thomson, Robert 4:03:38 (11,530)
Thomson, Robert H 5:17:46 (28,754)
Thomson, Simon J 5:25:45 (29,833)
Thomson, Stephen 3:02:50 (1,321)
Thorarinsson, Halldor 3:59:02 (10,443)
Thorley, Andy M 3:37:22 (5,551)
Thorley, Noel D 3:48:13 (7,636)
Thorn, Mike A 3:33:26 (4,951)
Thorn, Nigel E 5:40:39 (31,480)
Thorn, Richard I 3:15:12 (2,496)
Thorn, Richard M 4:48:16 (23,070)
Thorn, Stephen 4:13:36 (14,043)
Thornby, David G 3:39:42 (5,951)
Thorne, Ben D 4:15:21 (14,537)
Thorne, Colin 4:48:47 (23,189)
Thorne, Matthew J 5:39:14 (31,342)
Thorne, Steve J 4:38:32 (20,761)
Thorne, Thomas D 3:35:16 (5,217)
Thorne-Jones, Stuart 5:06:51 (27,029)
Thorner, Roddy B 4:24:45 (17,059)
Thornton, Dean A 3:01:26 (1,211)
Thornton, Dominic J 3:42:02 (6,385)
Thornton, James P 4:03:08 (11,416)
Thornton, James S 5:12:15 (27,863)
Thornton, Jason P 4:37:10 (20,405)
Thornton, John L 4:51:25 (23,816)
Thornton, Keith J 3:26:44 (3,891)
Thornton, Mark 4:07:52 (12,547)
Thornton, Mark S 3:22:35 (3,251)
Thornton, Paul 4:28:46 (18,237)
Thornton, Sean 5:41:23 (31,543)
Thornton, Stanley 4:51:57 (23,919)
Thornton, Will J 4:42:17 (21,696)
Thornton-Clarke, Jeremy 3:50:19 (8,109)
Thorogood, Charles C 5:31:29 (30,515)
Thorogood, Keith S 3:43:47 (6,703)
Thorp, Mark S 4:29:52 (18,555)
Thorpe, Dean 5:00:21 (25,856)
Thorpe, John E 5:39:13 (31,336)
Thorpe, John H 3:16:33 (2,638)
Thorpe, John M 2:56:26 (837)
Thorpe, Richard 3:44:05 (6,756)
Thorsteinsson, Jakob 2:57:44 (935)
Thouless, Gavin 3:46:12 (7,180)
Thrale, Daniel P 4:31:43 (19,024)
Thrall, Chris 3:56:30 (9,663)
Threadgold, Robin J 3:10:14 (1,951)
Threlfall, Mark S 5:12:04 (27,834)
Thrilling, David L 4:25:03 (17,137)
Thripp, Michael F 5:23:31 (29,546)
Throssell, David B 4:06:53 (12,311)
Thrower, David F 2:57:24 (914)
Thrower, Tomas M 3:45:14 (6,995)
Thubron, Neil A 2:59:10 (1,052)

Thuillier, Robin P 4:26:39 (17,648)
Thumath, Steven G 6:28:12 (34,202)
Thurbin, Julian R 4:15:46 (14,651)
Thurgood, Adrian M 3:41:21 (6,248)
Thurgood, Geoffrey A 6:32:08 (34,307)
Thurgood, Hugh A 3:52:45 (8,676)
Thurgood, Mark S 3:26:54 (3,911)
Thurley, Adam 4:38:17 (20,695)
Thurlow, Michael J 5:36:33 (31,062)
Thursby, Chris J 4:22:13 (16,399)
Thurstance, Anthony 4:58:44 (25,493)
Thursting, Paul D 4:45:37 (22,463)
Thurston, Ian 4:04:54 (11,839)
Tibaldi, Justin 3:23:51 (3,430)
Tibbals, Adam 4:00:28 (10,822)
Tibbles, Mark W 3:45:21 (7,017)
Tichelkamp, Josef 3:55:10 (9,268)
Ticker, Simon 4:47:09 (22,806)
Tickner, Scott D 4:57:06 (25,154)
Tidd, Damien 3:46:14 (7,188)
Tidder, Anthony R 4:15:43 (14,642)
Tideswell, David J 3:54:08 (9,005)
Tidiman, Steve 3:10:18 (1,958)
Tidman, Darryl A 4:12:41 (13,798)
Tidman, Simon 3:49:53 (8,014)
Tiernan, Patrick J 3:09:37 (1,875)
Tierney, Neil 3:48:49 (7,792)
Tierney, Trevor D 3:55:09 (9,263)
Tietz, Karl 3:10:16 (1,954)
Tiffin, Ian S 4:51:47 (23,888)
Tighe, Anthony 4:36:25 (20,203)
Tilbury, Neil A 3:51:23 (8,348)
Tildsley, David G 3:11:57 (2,136)
Tiley, Dave J 3:51:30 (8,369)
Tilford, Brent C 4:06:52 (12,303)
Tillbrooke, Tony 4:09:30 (12,963)
Tiller, David M 3:54:35 (9,119)
Tillery, Paul 4:13:53 (14,107)
Tillery, Richard 4:13:53 (14,107)
Tillett, Colin R 6:35:59 (34,408)
Tilley, Andrew 4:08:39 (12,728)
Tilley, David 3:00:16 (1,145)
Tilley, Ian R 4:23:47 (16,796)
Tilley, Jason 3:09:19 (1,844)
Tillott, Neil 3:55:52 (9,480)
Tilson, Scott A 3:32:26 (4,808)
Timanti, Claudio 4:18:31 (15,364)
Timbers, Ben 4:14:28 (14,289)
Timbers, David A 3:34:50 (5,162)
Timby, Paul 4:56:27 (25,001)
Timmermans, John R 3:42:09 (6,411)
Timewell, Andy 3:18:14 (2,807)
Timkow, Kieran 4:51:27 (23,824)
Timm, Ortwin 4:51:34 (23,846)
Timmen, Martin 2:55:26 (763)
Timmins, Adrian J 2:38:51 (172)
Timmins, Kieran J 4:02:47 (11,339)
Timmins, Steven 4:08:20 (12,655)
Timmis, Simon J 6:54:50 (34,796)
Timms, Nigel A 5:05:25 (26,781)
Timms, Trevor 4:18:12 (15,266)
Timpano, Roberto 3:15:13 (2,497)
Tindall, David 4:51:40 (23,863)
Tindall, Duncan B 4:17:22 (15,055)
Ting, Vincent 3:09:56 (1,912)
Tingling, Rudi E 5:50:05 (32,270)
Tinguely, Jean-Luc 3:33:19 (4,931)
Tinham, Andrew L 4:37:41 (20,547)
Tinker, Antony A 3:58:09 (10,178)
Tinson, Adam N 4:37:55 (20,600)
Tiplady, David R 4:57:17 (25,189)
Tipler, Philip 3:15:56 (2,560)
Tipler, Richard 5:31:52 (30,548)
Tippet, Simon J 4:50:22 (23,585)
Tippett, Paul 4:50:53 (23,708)
Tippett, Richard J 5:16:53 (28,620)
Tippett, Robert A 4:24:19 (16,932)
Tipping, John A 4:43:03 (21,881)
Tipping, Laurence A 4:36:46 (20,294)
Tipple, Gaven 4:20:35 (15,958)
Tirraoro, Marco 4:36:24 (20,195)
Titchener, Frank 5:16:45 (28,589)
Titchener, John B 4:18:15 (15,280)
Tither, Steven W 6:26:18 (34,138)
Tivadar, Daniel 4:54:17 (24,496)
Tjoenij, Robert E 4:32:16 (19,152)
Toach, Terence H 5:38:31 (31,253)
Tobback, Karel 4:52:42 (24,106)
Tobin, Andrew C 3:52:40 (8,651)
Tobisawa, Ikkei 5:30:58 (30,465)
Tocknell, Paul D 4:15:18 (14,527)
Tod, James M 4:39:40 (21,060)
Todd, Andy 3:50:33 (8,158)
Todd, David B 3:11:00 (2,032)
Todd, James E 4:38:04 (20,638)
Todd, Michael 6:03:51 (33,214)
Todd, Paul 2:38:57 (174)
Todd, Phil G 4:33:45 (19,506)
Todd, Richard A 4:59:42 (25,711)
Tofield, Philip A 4:47:03 (22,783)
Toft, Dave H 3:53:33 (8,871)
Tolan, Keith 3:48:42 (7,763)
Tolfrey, Neil 3:01:27 (1,213)
Tolhurst, Raymond 4:25:21 (17,227)
Toll, Alexander J 3:13:56 (2,352)
Tollner, Matin E 4:15:11 (14,498)
Tolson, Piers R 5:05:22 (26,768)
Toma, Manabu 2:37:50 (152)
Tomasini, Gianluca 3:38:23 (5,709)
Tombs, Ian A 4:51:48 (23,892)
Tombs, Jonathan M 3:28:26 (4,186)
Tominey, Andrew G 6:50:22 (34,733)
Tomkins, Alan 5:14:06 (28,189)
Tomkins, Paul J 3:41:53 (6,351)
Tomkinson, Nicholas P 4:53:09 (24,210)
Tomlin, Glenn L 5:05:18 (26,749)
Tomlinson, Dean L 4:28:49 (18,254)
Tomlinson, Fred 7:00:37 (34,880)
Tomlinson, Mark W 3:29:48 (4,417)
Tomos, Cris W 5:07:50 (27,196)
Tompson, Alan N 5:04:17 (26,568)
Toms, David A 4:16:49 (14,918)
Toms, John A 4:46:22 (22,639)
Toms, Neil 4:22:12 (16,397)
Toms, Paul J 4:15:32 (14,589)
Toms, Roy A 5:20:09 (29,122)
Toms, Simon P 4:28:25 (18,144)
Tomsett, Peter L 4:05:06 (11,897)
Tong, Simon F 3:35:05 (5,196)
Tonioni, Paolo 3:33:33 (4,962)
Tonkin, Craig 3:44:58 (6,954)
Tonkin, Michael J 5:36:25 (31,040)
Tooke, Brian C 7:29:41 (35,124)
Toole, Anthony M 4:49:32 (23,365)
Tooley, Mark A 3:59:50 (10,676)
Toomer, Alan L 4:27:07 (17,780)
Toon, Ian 4:14:59 (14,437)
Toon, Michael 5:12:42 (27,949)
Toop, James P 3:20:01 (2,998)
Tootal, Thomas D 4:48:27 (23,114)
Tootell, Andrew R 3:29:15 (4,321)
Toothill, Richard J 4:34:44 (19,774)
Topal, Sueleyman 4:11:00 (13,350)
Topham, John J 4:43:38 (22,019)
Topham, Roy 4:33:19 (19,390)
Toplis, Paul T 5:33:33 (30,732)
Topper, Stephen 3:56:00 (9,513)
Topper, Tim 3:07:43 (1,693)
Topping, Bill 4:06:11 (12,137)
Topping, Colin A 4:49:32 (23,365)
Topping, Matthew S 4:47:25 (22,861)
Topping, Stephen F 3:34:59 (5,181)
Torfason, Omar 3:58:28 (10,278)
Tornbom, Dan T 3:50:02 (8,047)
Torp, Morten 4:44:22 (22,186)
Torr, Peter M 3:26:15 (3,801)
Torralba, Manuel 4:26:01 (17,441)
Torre, Peter 5:13:12 (28,023)
Toseland, Christopher W 6:21:45 (33,976)
Toseland, David 3:55:42 (9,429)
Tosswell, Jerry 4:29:07 (18,345)
Tostevin, Craig W 5:00:34 (25,890)
Tourdes, Alain 3:17:45 (2,761)
Toury, Didier 4:06:46 (12,277)
Tovell, Angus D 4:49:55 (23,477)
Tovey, Gareth D 4:11:58 (13,614)
Towell, Robert W 4:20:05 (15,826)
Towers, Darren 5:25:06 (29,760)
Towler, Hans 3:59:07 (10,473)
Towler, Tim J 3:59:01 (10,439)
Towne, Peter G 4:59:09 (25,593)
Townend, John F 4:01:06 (10,962)
Townhill, Steven H 4:37:14 (20,423)
Townley, Wayne 5:08:04 (27,229)
Towns, Robin 4:22:55 (16,585)
Towns, Simon M 3:15:59 (2,570)
Townsend, Andrew 4:23:25 (16,715)
Townsend, Craig B 4:35:28 (19,968)
Townsend, Dominic R 5:47:23 (32,049)
Townsend, Martin B 3:37:25 (5,559)
Townsend, Nicholas C 4:02:08 (11,190)
Townsend, Philip 2:54:07 (694)
Townsend, Tim J 3:22:00 (3,186)
Townsend, Zach 4:26:22 (17,555)
Townsley, Steve J 3:05:23 (1,507)
Townson, Ken 3:14:40 (2,440)
Townson, Matthew J 4:06:15 (12,154)
Towse, Paul 3:45:37 (7,068)
Toy, Jonathon F 4:33:23 (19,403)
Toye, Ken C 4:14:54 (14,412)
Toyer, Michael A 4:37:39 (20,529)
Tozer, Ross W 3:05:21 (1,502)
Tozer, Shaun A 3:00:14 (1,143)
Trabanino, Herbert 3:53:32 (8,866)
Tracey, Colin 4:32:27 (19,196)
Tracey, Francis J 3:45:56 (7,122)
Tracey, Mathew C 3:38:04 (5,661)
Traill, Gordon D 3:57:57 (10,127)
Train, Paul 4:46:28 (22,661)
Tran, Francis 4:55:13 (24,722)
Tran, Quan L 3:01:48 (1,247)
Trant, Andrew W 4:36:46 (20,294)
Tranter, Adrian J 2:48:50 (460)
Trappett, Dean M 3:57:59 (10,138)
Trapps, Christopher P 3:38:40 (5,749)
Trauboth, Frank 4:52:33 (24,065)
Travers, Guy 3:47:29 (7,454)
Travers, Matthew W 4:18:11 (15,261)
Travers, Tim 3:50:26 (8,133)
Trawinski, Dieter 3:56:35 (9,687)
Traynor, Mark W 2:55:33 (775)
Traynor, Patrick 5:27:38 (30,059)
Traynor, Peter A 3:48:27 (7,692)
Treagust, Daniel J 4:02:08 (11,190)
Treasure, Benjamin M 4:04:38 (11,779)
Treby, Malcolm J 3:18:44 (2,854)
Tredray, Geoffrey 5:11:27 (27,731)
Tree, Chris J 4:33:51 (19,533)
Tregaskes, Andy J 3:12:18 (2,175)
Tregaskiss, Stephen D 3:34:33 (5,128)
Tregoning, James 4:55:04 (24,693)
Treilhaud, Olivier 3:15:47 (2,547)
Tremelling, Paul 4:14:32 (14,300)
Tremlett, Anthony 5:48:55 (32,175)
Trenbath, Ernest G 5:10:01 (27,513)
Trent, Richard J 6:13:47 (33,691)
Trentham, Ian A 4:52:18 (24,014)
Tresler, Martin R 4:15:21 (14,537)
Trevail, Charles R 3:52:38 (8,641)
Trevarthen, Richard W 4:11:40 (13,525)
Trevethan, Liam M 4:33:58 (19,560)
Trevett, Gordon A 4:11:37 (13,508)
Trevett, John 3:45:08 (6,979)
Trevisan, Giuliano 3:27:11 (3,958)
Trew, Michael S 3:15:31 (2,526)
Trew, Oliver J 4:58:03 (25,338)
Trice, Robert K 4:16:43 (14,893)
Trick, Mark J 4:29:42 (18,520)
Trickett, Joel D 5:21:37 (29,302)
Trickett, Philip J 4:09:29 (12,955)
Trickey, Christopher P 4:54:52 (24,636)
Trickey, Lawrence A 3:16:02 (2,579)
Trigger, Mark E 3:49:48 (7,998)
Triggs, Chris 4:27:03 (17,759)
Triggs, Malcolm D 3:49:29 (7,929)
Trigwell, Stuart J 3:26:09 (3,788)
Trimble, Chris 3:51:54 (8,461)
Trimble, Gareth 3:57:04 (9,843)
Trimby, Paul J 4:48:36 (23,147)

Trimnell, Terance L	4:18:40 (15,420)
Trinder, Richard	3:53:45 (8,922)
Trinelli, Roberto	4:12:35 (13,769)
Triplow, George R	4:36:03 (20,093)
Tripp, Michael D	5:02:17 (26,200)
Trippel, Roland	3:12:44 (2,218)
Trodd, Ron	4:22:30 (16,472)
Trodden, John E	4:39:43 (21,070)
Tromans, Benjamin A	4:17:24 (15,068)
Troon, Nicholas J	5:39:03 (31,314)
Troop, Nicholas	3:13:45 (2,333)
Trory, John A	3:32:13 (4,777)
Trotman, Michael J	4:32:21 (19,176)
Trotter, Brian P	3:48:22 (7,677)
Trotter, Ian H	4:55:21 (24,747)
Trotter, Paul	5:10:20 (27,546)
Troup, Andy D	4:18:09 (15,249)
Troup, Michael G	3:22:06 (3,199)
Trout, Gordon	4:03:17 (11,455)
Trowbridge, Nicholas E	3:52:24 (8,578)
Trowbridge, Tony T	3:55:27 (9,353)
Trowell, Paul M	4:20:10 (15,846)
Trower, Nicholas J	4:55:54 (24,874)
Trowsdale, John	4:52:12 (23,985)
Troy, Christopher	5:42:35 (31,636)
Truan, Steven A	3:57:04 (9,843)
Trudgen, Russell C	4:32:58 (19,307)
Trudgill, Alan C	5:33:45 (30,754)
Trudgill, Graham J	4:00:15 (10,778)
True, David W	4:01:48 (11,112)
Truelove, Michael J	4:34:47 (19,786)
Trueman, Kevin T	4:05:30 (11,985)
Trueman, Peter	4:53:48 (24,383)
Truepenny, David J	2:48:31 (439)
Truman, Chris P	5:12:35 (27,923)
Truman, Jason M	3:57:45 (10,051)
Trumper, Paul M	3:54:48 (9,184)
Trundle, Gary	3:44:48 (6,904)
Trunty, Scott	4:47:16 (22,831)
Truran, Martin G	3:27:42 (4,061)
Trussell, Marc	3:56:21 (9,620)
Trussler, Mark J	3:30:55 (4,594)
Truswell, Simon G	5:39:04 (31,316)
Try, Christopher E	2:52:50 (628)
Tryvers, Roel	3:40:18 (6,050)
Tsang, Philip M	4:10:23 (13,194)
Tsavliris, George A	5:49:39 (32,239)
Tse, Andrew W	3:59:36 (10,599)
Tsui, Hudson H	5:19:19 (28,993)
Tu, Hien	4:22:37 (16,514)
Tucker, Andrew J	4:39:42 (21,067)
Tucker, Andy J	3:03:49 (1,390)
Tucker, Barry R	3:28:05 (4,120)
Tucker, Benjamin A	4:42:03 (21,634)
Tucker, Brian	5:38:23 (31,235)
Tucker, Colin	5:15:20 (28,390)
Tucker, Gareth A	4:42:29 (21,739)
Tucker, Graham A	3:43:19 (6,622)
Tucker, Graham J	3:13:55 (2,347)
Tucker, Guy	4:17:19 (15,042)
Tucker, Jeremy A	3:03:26 (1,358)
Tucker, Mark R	3:34:52 (5,166)
Tucker, Paul D	3:52:22 (8,569)
Tucker, Paul W	5:55:36 (32,689)
Tucker, Philip	5:08:47 (27,317)
Tucker, Simon C	3:35:34 (5,272)
Tucker, William F	3:56:45 (9,736)
Tucker Feltham, Jason	5:04:42 (26,631)
Tuckey, Andrew P	2:51:36 (570)
Tudball, Chris	4:37:03 (20,370)
Tudor, Stephen J	3:19:51 (2,981)
Tueter, Trygue K	3:24:15 (3,478)
Tuff, Vincent R	5:32:57 (30,666)
Tuffnell, Dennis	3:57:49 (10,080)
Tufton, John	6:09:47 (33,527)
Tufts, Mark J	4:53:11 (24,217)
Tugman, John	5:09:48 (27,485)
Tull, David	3:29:58 (4,381)
Tullett, Adam	3:33:48 (5,008)
Tullett, Peter	3:15:36 (2,531)
Tullo, Peter C	4:19:16 (15,596)
Tulloch, Freddie	4:04:45 (11,803)
Tulloch, Jim M	5:09:41 (27,469)

Tulloch, Robert M	4:49:37 (23,402)
Tully, Adam	5:24:06 (29,629)
Tully, John	4:40:49 (21,340)
Tumulty, Owen G	4:04:07 (11,665)
Tunn, Martin P	5:31:23 (30,505)
Tunnicliffe, John M	4:18:32 (15,368)
Tuppen, Darren J	3:58:12 (10,193)
Turberfield, Craig D	3:41:21 (6,248)
Turberville-Smith, Rupert J	4:17:39 (15,125)
Turek, Jeremy	4:05:24 (11,967)
Turk, David R	4:00:21 (10,794)
Turley, James C	3:49:05 (7,843)
Turley, Jonathan C	4:04:34 (11,761)
Turnball, Bill	4:32:46 (19,264)
Turnbull, Christopher D	4:38:34 (20,767)
Turnbull, David R	3:40:16 (6,044)
Turnbull, James S	4:36:08 (20,113)
Turnbull, Keith	4:56:35 (25,035)
Turnbull, Mark I	3:57:05 (9,850)
Turnbull, Matthew N	4:11:11 (13,402)
Turnbull, Robert P	4:38:09 (20,660)
Turnbull, Si	4:21:10 (16,102)
Turner, Andrew	4:53:30 (24,300)
Turner, Andrew K	3:08:35 (1,768)
Turner, Andrew P	3:32:41 (4,842)
Turner, Christopher D	4:12:15 (13,685)
Turner, Christopher G	4:24:01 (16,857)
Turner, Christopher J	4:27:25 (17,862)
Turner, Duncan A	4:15:40 (14,624)
Turner, Duncan J	6:57:52 (34,840)
Turner, Geoff P	3:14:23 (2,404)
Turner, Gerald J	4:10:39 (13,254)
Turner, Glenn M	3:41:50 (6,343)
Turner, Graeme M	3:38:57 (5,807)
Turner, Graham	4:51:45 (23,881)
Turner, Graham N	4:47:34 (22,902)
Turner, Grant W	5:25:45 (29,833)
Turner, Hugh	5:52:09 (32,422)
Turner, Ian A	4:06:08 (12,130)
Turner, James	4:24:23 (16,949)
Turner, James P	5:04:29 (26,595)
Turner, John A	3:56:33 (9,675)
Turner, Jonathan R	4:58:08 (25,355)
Turner, Keith	4:04:24 (11,721)
Turner, Mark J	5:45:58 (31,931)
Turner, Mark S	3:04:19 (1,415)
Turner, Martin J	5:14:27 (28,256)
Turner, Martin R	5:07:54 (27,201)
Turner, Matthew A	4:36:34 (20,238)
Turner, Matthew C	2:58:58 (1,031)
Turner, Michael A	6:24:41 (34,081)
Turner, Michael J	4:52:50 (24,134)
Turner, Michael S	3:36:29 (5,425)
Turner, Mike	4:42:36 (21,769)
Turner, Paul	4:08:14 (12,622)
Turner, Paul A	6:31:50 (34,300)
Turner, Paul R	5:11:29 (27,735)
Turner, Peter J	2:53:08 (642)
Turner, Richard D	4:17:18 (15,036)
Turner, Robert	3:48:28 (7,699)
Turner, Simon W	3:52:29 (8,599)
Turner, Stephen	3:45:16 (7,000)
Turner, Stephen	4:17:05 (14,977)
Turner, Vince N	4:22:39 (16,523)
Turner, Will R	4:50:39 (23,662)
Turnill, Richard J	3:38:00 (5,648)
Turpie, Michael	5:34:53 (30,894)
Turpin, Robert J	4:26:17 (17,527)
Turrell, Jeff W	4:07:06 (12,372)
Turrell, Peter F	2:47:32 (389)
Turrini, Roberto	5:09:12 (27,387)
Turton, David	3:44:09 (6,774)
Turton, Les J	3:10:04 (1,928)
Turvey, Stephen K	5:02:40 (26,268)
Tushingham, John P	4:21:13 (16,113)
Tuson, William K	4:01:44 (11,097)
Tutt, Kevin B	4:01:26 (11,032)
Tuttle, Peter A	2:50:33 (518)
Twaddle, Stuart H	4:05:49 (12,053)
Tweddle, Richard J	2:44:27 (307)
Tweed, Andrew P	3:58:22 (10,250)
Tweed, Daniel C	4:18:34 (15,382)
Tweed, John L	4:30:06 (18,621)

Tweeddale, Eoin K	4:51:45 (23,881)
Tweedie, Peter J	4:20:26 (15,922)
Tweedy, Chris J	4:30:06 (18,621)
Tween, Ian S	4:50:38 (23,658)
Twell, Andy	3:30:27 (4,515)
Twells, Liam K	5:49:19 (32,214)
Twemlow, Christopher M	4:48:19 (23,077)
Twigg, Andrew P	5:04:25 (26,589)
Twigge, Mark	4:26:43 (17,667)
Twiggs, Matthew A	4:35:21 (19,931)
Twinn, John	6:01:14 (33,037)
Twiston-Davies, Ben	4:29:10 (18,359)
Twizell, David W	4:24:56 (17,104)
Twombley, Andrew	4:44:38 (22,233)
Twomey, Eamonn B	3:07:35 (1,684)
Twomey, Humphrey	2:56:28 (840)
Twose, Paul	3:58:06 (10,169)
Tyalor, Graham	4:34:13 (19,634)
Tye, Geoffrey C	5:06:52 (27,036)
Tyerman, Graham	3:51:58 (8,476)
Tyler, Anthony J	5:36:39 (31,072)
Tyler, Daniel	3:37:46 (5,612)
Tyler, David P	4:39:01 (20,885)
Tyler, Dean M	3:39:06 (5,834)
Tyler, Jeffrey S	5:01:46 (26,101)
Tyler, John	3:02:12 (1,278)
Tyler, Jonathan	4:05:20 (11,955)
Tyler, Keith	4:50:09 (23,528)
Tyler, Michael E	3:50:46 (8,200)
Tyler, Nigel P	4:59:08 (25,591)
Tyler, Simon	3:05:03 (1,470)
Tyler, Stephen	5:06:30 (26,964)
Tyley, Gwynpor P	3:32:34 (4,830)
Tyrrell, Bryan K	5:42:48 (31,662)
Tyrrell, Chris	4:58:35 (25,463)
Tyrrell, Christopher	4:54:13 (24,479)
Tyrrell, Mark R	4:58:37 (25,472)
Tyrrell, Nigel P	4:14:15 (14,229)
Tyrrell, Stephen J	4:38:54 (20,849)
Tyrrell, Steven M	4:58:08 (25,355)
Tyson, Craig J	4:36:33 (20,237)
Tyson, Iain R	4:59:31 (25,668)
Tyszkiewicz, John Z	4:48:54 (23,212)
Ubsdell, Simon	2:56:15 (826)
Uebelguenne, Ruediger	4:26:27 (17,585)
Uff, Frederick	3:56:15 (9,585)
Uff, Stephen M	4:50:30 (23,626)
Uglow, John D	3:56:23 (9,634)
Ugwumadu, Austin H	4:01:27 (11,038)
Ulakanathan, Suthan	5:47:24 (32,051)
Ullah, Anis J	4:29:52 (18,555)
Ulloa, Karl	3:29:51 (4,428)
Ulrich, Erich	5:41:02 (31,517)
Ulrich, Kai-Uwe	3:23:11 (3,329)
Umpleby, Christian T	5:12:48 (27,969)
Umpleby, Martin F	3:50:57 (8,248)
Underhill, Jim S	4:07:43 (12,503)
Underhill, Richard	4:12:49 (13,887)
Underwood, Andrew	3:30:30 (4,526)
Underwood, David	5:55:33 (32,684)
Underwood, Scott	3:45:24 (7,030)
Underwood, Victor E	4:39:46 (21,084)
Unerman, Martin H	3:55:28 (9,358)
Ung, Hy C	4:29:18 (18,406)
Ungi, Thomas	5:22:36 (29,440)
Ungi, Tom E	5:22:36 (29,440)
Unitt, Dennis J	5:33:13 (30,691)
Unrau, Juergen	4:56:24 (24,990)
Unwin, Will	3:15:56 (2,560)
Upcott, Nigel	4:38:57 (20,860)
Uppal, Amaritpal S	4:20:26 (15,922)
Uprichard, Mark	6:24:56 (34,096)
Upson, Kevin	5:48:54 (32,172)
Upstone, Alan J	4:51:05 (23,749)
Upton, Andrew P	4:29:15 (18,379)
Upton, James B	4:21:40 (16,247)
Upton, Kevin P	4:01:09 (10,971)
Upton, Laurence A	5:10:58 (27,648)
Upton, Mark	4:48:22 (23,095)
Upton, Martin J	4:51:19 (23,800)
Ural, Jon	4:53:50 (24,389)
Urbahn, Peter	2:52:45 (624)

Ure, Bruce C....4:52:42 (24,106)
Uren, Martyn....4:47:15 (22,828)
Urmston, Michael....4:12:24 (13,726)
Urron, Geoffrey....4:03:03 (11,398)
Urry, Martyn J....4:00:46 (10,902)
Urwin, Alan....3:47:16 (7,405)
Urwin, Corey J....3:18:43 (2,852)
Urwin, Jeremy T....4:09:08 (12,870)
Urwin, Robert J....3:14:14 (2,385)
Urwin, Roger C....4:42:05 (21,645)
Usai, Gianluca....3:19:45 (2,972)
Useli, Bruno....3:49:30 (7,933)
Usher, John W....4:34:13 (19,634)
Usher, Keith J....6:34:41 (34,373)
Uthamakunan, Lavan....4:23:28 (16,725)
Utterson, Colin....3:17:50 (2,774)
Utting, Roy C....3:56:25 (9,637)
Uttley, Jonathan R....4:26:32 (17,612)
Uwins, John W....6:07:06 (33,394)
Vacalopoulos, Alex P....3:27:34 (4,031)
Vael, Marc....4:52:43 (24,108)
Vahl, Joachim....4:09:43 (13,016)
Vahrenhorst, Wolfgang....3:58:02 (10,152)
Vaiders, Peter....4:47:28 (22,880)
Valbonesi, Michael G....4:27:24 (17,857)
Vale, Christopher A....5:18:44 (28,910)
Vale, David J....5:20:03 (29,107)
Valek, Paul I....3:09:36 (1,872)
Valentine, Jonathan D....3:56:19 (9,609)
Valentine-Penney, Daniel J....4:05:01 (11,864)
Valeriani, Bruno....3:30:44 (4,565)
Valge, Ivar....4:39:22 (20,980)
Valia, Permjot S....7:40:55 (35,177)
Vallance, Jason A....4:24:04 (16,870)
Vallance, Louis....3:45:51 (7,106)
Valle, Juan W....3:59:28 (10,560)
Valleau, Christopher....4:42:21 (21,705)
Vallis, John H....3:29:37 (4,376)
Vallis, Stuart M....6:59:42 (34,863)
Valls, Jean-Claude....4:22:04 (16,360)
Valner, Olavi....3:15:42 (2,541)
Valouin, Kenneth F....3:46:56 (7,336)
Valsborg, Jacob Stenmann....3:18:37 (2,837)
Vamben, Eric S....2:36:52 (134)
Van Alderwegen, Damian E....4:30:43 (18,772)
Van Alderwegen, Francis S....4:21:55 (16,311)
Van Basten Batenburg, Robert A....4:08:00 (12,571)
Van Beek, Gerrit C....4:25:57 (17,413)
Van Bommel, Jos E....4:44:05 (22,113)
Van Den Berg, Brian A....3:14:18 (2,392)
Van Den Bon, Erik....4:41:31 (21,529)
Van Den Bosch, Paul....4:40:10 (21,175)
Van Den Broek, Paul....4:14:14 (14,220)
Van Der Horst, Rupert C....4:08:19 (12,645)
Van Der Linden, Robert J....4:18:10 (15,253)
Van Der Merwe, Eric W....3:37:04 (5,507)
Van Der Merwe, Willem B....4:09:57 (13,082)
Van Der Ploeg, Danny....3:57:52 (10,102)
Van Der Pol, Jaap....3:58:40 (10,338)
Van Der Westhuizen, Johan....4:23:52 (16,818)
Van Drunen, Wout....3:53:07 (8,748)
Van Hal, Erik J....3:40:32 (6,089)
Van Hilst, Rudolf....3:30:33 (4,538)
Van Hooland, Bart....4:59:57 (25,766)
Van Hoorn, Alje C....4:50:51 (23,703)
Van Isterdael, Daniel....3:44:29 (6,833)
Van Keulen, Martyn....4:11:53 (13,581)
Van Klaveren, Mark J....4:43:56 (22,081)
Van Kleef, Johannes J....4:27:26 (17,864)
Van Kuyk, Daniel A....4:38:57 (20,860)
Van Lokven, Ian H....2:39:45 (198)
Van Niekerk, Derek....3:36:07 (5,358)
Van Niekerk, Pieter B....4:29:28 (18,453)
Van Nuffelen, Nicholas L....5:33:30 (30,725)
Van Spall, Damian....4:48:06 (23,031)
Van Veen, Janec L....3:53:04 (8,733)
Van Warden, Ian....3:06:25 (1,585)
Van Wonderen, Jan J....3:12:47 (2,223)
Van Zyl, Anton....2:26:23 (52)
Vandeleur-Boorer, Simon J....5:30:56 (30,461)
Vanderlinden, René M....5:27:44 (30,068)
Vandermark, Richard J....3:26:23 (3,824)
Vaney, David C....4:46:22 (22,639)
Vanhegan, Tristan D....3:20:59 (3,086)
Vanhove, Frederic....4:15:40 (14,624)
Vanhove, Frederic J....5:21:10 (29,261)
Vankempen, Daniel L....4:18:08 (15,242)
Vanluchene, Henri....3:49:24 (7,914)
Van-Orden, Simon B....3:07:08 (1,643)
Vanson, Ed H....4:39:13 (20,937)
Vanstone, Adrian....3:44:57 (6,949)
Vanstone, Martin....4:20:14 (15,866)
Vanstone, Martin I....5:17:27 (28,705)
Vanstone, Neil A....5:18:34 (28,877)
Van-Thal, Robert J....3:53:10 (8,762)
Vantsiotis, Anasthase....3:06:24 (1,581)
Varady-Szabo, Bence....4:49:33 (23,371)
Varah, Andrew....4:18:58 (15,502)
Varden, Mark G....2:52:34 (614)
Vareyon, Philippe....3:43:16 (6,610)
Varlet, Bruno....3:10:24 (1,967)
Varley, Neil....4:03:54 (11,606)
Varnals, Aaron....4:14:35 (14,315)
Varndell, David G....4:23:47 (16,796)
Varney, Kenneth M....4:42:25 (21,722)
Varnish, James M....4:25:37 (17,321)
Vasallo, Juan I....6:01:33 (33,057)
Vaschalde, Michel....4:25:19 (17,221)
Vasey, Brian G....4:20:28 (15,933)
Vasiliou, Steven....3:23:12 (3,331)
Vassiliou, Vasso....4:09:36 (12,983)
Vaughan, Bryan....2:44:49 (314)
Vaughan, Bryan J....3:35:28 (5,255)
Vaughan, Christian P....4:21:28 (16,195)
Vaughan, Christian S....5:05:25 (26,781)
Vaughan, David A....3:50:37 (8,173)
Vaughan, Duncan....3:54:21 (9,062)
Vaughan, Jason P....3:40:02 (6,002)
Vaughan, Neil S....3:46:35 (7,258)
Vaughan, Neville A....3:25:24 (3,656)
Vaughan, Paul....5:03:04 (26,352)
Vaughan, Rhodri....3:50:39 (8,180)
Vaughan, Richard....5:09:04 (27,362)
Vaughan, Stephen S....4:31:15 (18,898)
Vaughan, Steven J....4:41:14 (21,454)
Vaughan, Todd M....4:05:15 (11,929)
Vawda, Farouk....4:06:27 (12,201)
Vazquez-Rosa, Juan H....5:09:37 (27,458)
Vdberg, Jack S....7:38:20 (35,168)
Vea, Staale....3:42:51 (6,518)
Veal, Gareth....4:30:29 (18,722)
Veall, Philip....4:10:49 (13,292)
Veasey, Andrew S....4:18:14 (15,273)
Veasey, Dominick J....3:25:59 (3,755)
Veder, Thomas J....5:36:28 (31,048)
Vedrine, David....2:25:25 (49)
Veeren, Jaysen....4:48:01 (23,014)
Vegro, Symon....4:21:05 (16,089)
Veiga, Jaime P....3:55:08 (9,258)
Veitch, Alister W....4:43:36 (22,007)
Veitch, Andrew....3:37:32 (5,584)
Veitch, Nicholas A....4:11:48 (13,564)
Veitch, Richard I....4:53:38 (24,338)
Veitch, Sam G....4:48:53 (23,205)
Vella, Clive A....4:18:13 (15,269)
Vellenoweth, Andrew S....5:22:21 (29,395)
Venables, Edward B....4:48:00 (23,011)
Venzor, Hugo A....4:24:12 (16,901)
Verboon, Wouter....4:15:10 (14,493)
Verdult, Peter H....3:34:51 (5,164)
Verghese, Rahul S....4:29:40 (18,510)
Verguet, Jean Luc....3:21:52 (3,170)
Verhagen, Jacob....4:43:40 (22,026)
Verity, Lee R....4:25:24 (17,246)
Vermeulen, Jonathan L....4:15:19 (14,532)
Vernal, Derrick....6:07:02 (33,391)
Vernhes, Laurent....3:10:50 (2,013)
Vernon, Darren....2:50:59 (541)
Vernon, Mike J....4:33:08 (19,347)
Vernon, Peter G....4:44:24 (22,193)
Vernon, Shaun....4:19:39 (15,709)
Vernoux, Olivier....3:56:16 (9,589)
Verpoest, Frederik M....3:55:43 (9,435)
Verrall, Thomas W....5:34:26 (30,840)
Verrie, Jonathan....4:09:19 (12,915)
Verulento, Salvatore....3:12:55 (2,240)
Verwanger, Roland....3:42:57 (6,535)
Vestey, George....3:36:07 (5,358)
Vesty, Colin R....4:44:11 (22,138)
Vesty, Robin L....4:50:08 (23,523)
Vetter, Rolf....3:31:17 (4,649)
Vettoretti, Tiziano....3:44:36 (6,860)
Vey, Stephen C....3:55:48 (9,461)
Veysey, Wayne....4:45:24 (22,414)
Vialls, Terry....5:32:46 (30,649)
Viana, Joe....4:36:12 (20,127)
Viatte, René....4:15:12 (14,502)
Vicary, Tim....5:24:32 (29,687)
Vicedo, Bruno....3:38:46 (5,772)
Vicentini, Andrea....4:40:48 (21,338)
Vick, Gary C....6:28:07 (34,198)
Vickers, David....4:34:50 (19,800)
Vickers, David A....5:41:20 (31,539)
Vickers, Donald F....4:58:27 (25,429)
Vickers, Douglas P....4:08:35 (12,711)
Vickers, Jeremy....4:40:41 (21,303)
Vickery, Andrew B....4:13:46 (14,083)
Vieiro, Juan C....4:32:12 (19,134)
Vieli, Andreas....3:18:39 (2,843)
Vienne, Bertrand....3:29:56 (4,444)
Vieyra, Igor....3:22:30 (3,242)
Vigar, Simon....4:35:39 (20,005)
Vigara, Eloy....2:57:19 (908)
Vigneron, Gerard....5:51:22 (32,359)
Vikshaaland, Geir....3:33:42 (4,990)
Vikshaaland, Georg....3:43:51 (6,713)
Vikstrem, Magnus....4:01:24 (11,024)
Villalard, Michael C....5:09:06 (27,370)
Villalon, Antonio....4:24:22 (16,944)
Villars, Philip....5:05:16 (26,741)
Villaume, Cyrille....2:55:49 (794)
Villiers, David....6:38:37 (34,476)
Vinall, Chris J....4:19:44 (15,733)
Vince, Ian F....6:05:30 (33,298)
Vincent, Andrew J....4:48:13 (23,056)
Vincent, David....7:31:39 (35,139)
Vincent, Edward M....3:27:58 (4,098)
Vincent, Mark D....4:42:34 (21,761)
Vincent, Nicholas....4:42:21 (21,705)
Vincent, Nick A....4:28:00 (18,032)
Vincent, Paul J....5:17:02 (28,652)
Vincent, Ron....5:03:06 (26,362)
Vincent, Russell J....3:58:04 (10,161)
Vincent, Wayne A....3:00:36 (1,163)
Vine, Desmond G....4:26:02 (17,447)
Vine, Peter J....3:54:42 (9,154)
Viney, Michael A....5:14:16 (28,221)
Viney, Steve....3:59:37 (10,608)
Vinson, John W....5:37:03 (31,104)
Vint, Peter J....5:07:11 (27,096)
Virdee, Gary....6:52:43 (34,765)
Visram, Neil....5:38:58 (31,306)
Visser, Daniel....6:09:28 (33,517)
Vissers, Dirk J....3:17:02 (2,680)
Vitale, Vincenzo....3:46:03 (7,147)
Vituli, Thomas....5:18:47 (28,917)
Vivian, Charles C....3:54:45 (9,171)
Vivian, Hugh C....4:13:54 (14,112)
Vivian, Mark C....5:51:28 (32,369)
Vivian, Matt....3:41:53 (6,351)
Voegel, Thomas....4:36:02 (20,091)
Vogado, Jonathan....4:05:04 (11,882)
Vogan, Ian....4:25:45 (17,365)
Voisey, Ian S....4:14:42 (14,346)
Voisey, Keith....5:04:20 (26,573)
Voituron, Christian....4:18:03 (15,220)
Volans, Ian J....3:35:48 (5,309)
Vollmer, Dieter....4:19:36 (15,692)
Voltzenlogel, Thierry....3:53:42 (8,909)
Von Der Stueck, Ingo....3:37:45 (5,609)
Von Doetinchem, Joachim A....3:17:40 (2,752)
Von Doussa, Carl W....3:53:41 (8,904)
Von Holten, Paul....5:09:31 (27,440)
Vonderlinden, Marius J....5:27:43 (30,067)
Vonlanthen, Marc R....4:57:33 (25,239)
Vorster, Rowan N....4:07:45 (12,516)
Vose, Arymond W....3:18:42 (2,849)
Vosloo, Andries H....6:07:17 (33,403)
Vosper, Mark R....4:27:37 (17,926)

Vout, Tony 2:52:43 (621)
Vouziotis, Nicholas 4:47:06 (22,796)
Vowles, James H 3:40:21 (6,064)
Vowles, Nick G 3:31:36 (4,694)
Voyce, Daniel J 3:42:17 (6,431)
Voyse, Dale R 6:12:15 (33,629)
Vymeris, Alex 3:55:26 (9,347)
Vyvyan, James H 5:19:09 (28,963)
Waby, Paul 2:47:50 (404)
Waddell, Douglas R 4:18:23 (15,319)
Waddup, Darren J 5:52:54 (32,491)
Waddup, Peter 5:53:05 (32,506)
Wade, Calvin R 4:45:44 (22,483)
Wade, Ian J 4:20:54 (16,051)
Wade, Mark A 4:01:36 (11,066)
Wade, Mark D 4:05:16 (11,936)
Wade, Neil S 4:04:55 (11,843)
Wade, Nick D 4:07:46 (12,523)
Wade, Stephan 3:48:51 (7,800)
Wade, William M 4:30:27 (18,712)
Waden, Robin C 6:57:11 (34,832)
Wadhwa, Tushar 4:58:51 (25,524)
Wadhwana, Hitesh 7:16:30 (35,043)
Wadie, Iain 4:08:26 (12,681)
Wadkin, Mark L 4:44:25 (22,199)
Wadley, Mark J 3:33:55 (5,030)
Wadsworth, Adrian M 5:52:02 (32,416)
Wadsworth, John 5:28:59 (30,243)
Wadsworth, Paul 4:53:58 (24,415)
Wadsworth, Richard 4:14:49 (14,385)
Waers, Paul D 4:17:23 (15,063)
Wagner, Marco 2:43:19 (276)
Wagstrom, Michael 3:29:49 (4,423)
Wahlberg, Anders 4:31:32 (18,978)
Wain, Paul C 4:37:54 (20,596)
Waine, Mark 2:49:54 (495)
Waine, Michael T 2:39:17 (181)
Wainewright, David M 5:54:31 (32,603)
Wainwright, Robert 4:59:38 (25,697)
Wainwright, Samuel T 5:06:08 (26,899)
Wainwright, Shane E 4:31:34 (18,989)
Wainwright, Stephen A 4:14:36 (14,318)
Wait, Andrew J 3:09:07 (1,823)
Waite, Ashly 4:48:06 (23,031)
Waite, Christopher J 4:48:37 (23,154)
Waite, Jeremy C 3:42:08 (6,408)
Waite, Rob H 4:41:14 (21,454)
Waite, Trevor J 5:31:04 (30,474)
Waites, Steve 5:20:27 (29,171)
Wake, Adrian P 3:55:29 (9,364)
Wake, Alan 4:26:08 (17,487)
Wake, Charles 5:25:27 (29,795)
Wake, Simon C 3:44:42 (6,880)
Wakefield, Andy M 3:15:16 (2,501)
Wakefield, David R 4:22:33 (16,486)
Wakefield, Iain S 3:55:13 (9,280)
Wakefield, Robin M 4:43:30 (21,980)
Wakefield, Sally 5:25:44 (29,829)
Wakefled, Simon D 3:39:28 (5,904)
Wakeford, Andrew E 4:49:25 (23,342)
Wakeford, Martin P 3:40:19 (6,052)
Wakeham, Alexander W 4:33:06 (19,343)
Wakelin, Grant 3:42:15 (6,425)
Wakeling, John F 5:17:28 (28,709)
Wakeling, Michael 4:21:59 (16,326)
Walaszczyk, Wojciech 2:58:27 (985)
Walburn, Michael J 5:23:14 (29,510)
Walburn, Stephen R 4:33:36 (19,465)
Walby, Chris 3:48:10 (7,629)
Walden, James D 3:43:53 (6,717)
Waldie, Brian 3:20:04 (3,009)
Waldie, Christopher S 3:47:17 (7,411)
Waldram, Stephen 3:21:55 (3,174)
Waldron, Anthony 4:05:22 (11,961)
Waldron, Simon G 4:14:57 (14,425)
Waldron, William B 4:59:17 (25,623)
Walduck, Anthony G 5:02:03 (26,155)
Walduck, Jason A 3:33:19 (4,931)
Walford, Keith S 4:13:32 (14,024)
Walford, Michael J 4:09:24 (12,933)
Walker, Adam 4:39:04 (20,896)
Walker, Allan P 4:36:41 (20,274)
Walker, Andrew M 4:31:50 (19,049)
Walker, Andrew N 5:07:04 (27,072)
Walker, Andy J 5:53:14 (32,518)
Walker, Ben 5:10:00 (27,512)
Walker, Bill 4:10:55 (13,323)
Walker, Bruce K 3:44:32 (6,845)
Walker, Chris 3:05:32 (1,522)
Walker, Christopher 4:19:54 (15,775)
Walker, Christopher P 3:38:34 (5,735)
Walker, Ciaran F 5:16:11 (28,503)
Walker, Colin K 3:37:50 (5,623)
Walker, Craig 4:23:15 (16,669)
Walker, Daniel J 5:44:05 (31,768)
Walker, David 3:26:46 (3,896)
Walker, David 4:26:34 (17,623)
Walker, David F 6:20:05 (33,920)
Walker, Derek A 2:59:02 (1,039)
Walker, Dominic 4:24:06 (16,876)
Walker, Doug 4:24:32 (17,001)
Walker, Gary A 2:58:21 (977)
Walker, Gary J 4:25:14 (17,196)
Walker, Geoffrey A 4:19:53 (15,770)
Walker, Graham J 4:30:16 (18,672)
Walker, Ian 4:28:41 (18,212)
Walker, James C 4:50:57 (23,719)
Walker, James D 6:20:05 (33,920)
Walker, Jason 3:53:13 (8,774)
Walker, Jonathan A 3:22:45 (3,267)
Walker, Joseph A 3:26:23 (3,824)
Walker, Keith E 5:13:41 (28,113)
Walker, Kieran W 3:31:26 (4,668)
Walker, Lewis L 4:02:21 (11,234)
Walker, Mark 7:08:39 (34,964)
Walker, Mark D 2:59:42 (1,103)
Walker, Martin J 3:26:33 (3,857)
Walker, Michael A 4:31:02 (18,843)
Walker, Neal 3:02:40 (1,311)
Walker, Neil 3:30:39 (4,552)
Walker, Patrick W 5:49:58 (32,259)
Walker, Phil 2:45:53 (344)
Walker, Robert 3:48:29 (7,702)
Walker, Robert J 2:59:48 (1,112)
Walker, Roy C 4:03:05 (11,406)
Walker, Samuel H 3:38:13 (5,682)
Walker, Samuel S 4:10:41 (13,261)
Walker, Shane M 3:58:00 (10,142)
Walker, Simon 5:01:10 (26,002)
Walker, Stephen A 3:48:20 (7,664)
Walker, Steven W 3:01:36 (1,232)
Walker, Stuart 3:25:06 (3,606)
Walker, Stuart D 3:15:40 (2,537)
Walker, Vincent J 5:23:34 (29,553)
Walker Buckton, Tristan J 4:10:16 (13,160)
Walkerdine, Martin 3:55:21 (9,321)
Walker-Okeover, Ralph 4:20:32 (15,943)
Wall, Alex J 5:44:33 (31,809)
Wall, James H 4:17:31 (15,094)
Wall, Stephen 4:31:40 (19,011)
Wall, Tony 5:16:48 (28,601)
Wall Persson, Lars I 3:54:08 (9,005)
Wallace, Bryan 3:53:42 (8,909)
Wallace, David D 3:41:12 (6,215)
Wallace, David E 4:57:19 (25,196)
Wallace, Iain J 3:37:02 (5,503)
Wallace, Jim 2:59:06 (1,046)
Wallace, Malcolm B 5:36:44 (31,081)
Wallace, Michael 5:39:00 (31,310)
Wallace, Stephen C 3:52:05 (8,500)
Wallace, Steve 4:14:58 (14,430)
Wallace, Steven M 3:24:17 (3,480)
Wallace, Tom W 5:14:01 (28,175)
Walland, John 5:48:58 (32,180)
Waller, Anthony 2:56:34 (848)
Waller, David 5:19:23 (29,007)
Waller, Douglas W 3:39:17 (5,864)
Waller, Gareth 5:58:49 (32,894)
Waller, James 4:12:07 (13,642)
Waller, James A 3:50:50 (8,219)
Waller, John 4:45:49 (22,504)
Waller, Richard J 5:31:54 (30,550)
Wallin, Ingvar R 5:44:08 (31,774)
Wallington, Darren J 4:13:25 (13,993)
Wallis, Dale E 3:49:04 (7,840)
Wallis, Derrick G 3:47:51 (7,539)
Wallis, Gordon W 4:49:04 (23,259)
Wallis, John 3:07:25 (1,667)
Wallis, John J 5:44:39 (31,814)
Wallis, Joseph G 4:57:04 (25,146)
Wallis, Oliver J 5:22:56 (29,477)
Wallis, Ronald 7:04:26 (34,917)
Wallman, Peter J 4:48:03 (23,022)
Wallman, Scott 3:55:17 (9,307)
Walls, Angus W 5:41:45 (31,571)
Walls, David I 4:18:35 (15,388)
Wallwork, Graham R 4:19:35 (15,686)
Wallwork, Robert A 5:13:53 (28,149)
Wallwork, Tim P 4:25:58 (17,423)
Walmsley, Paul 4:38:57 (20,860)
Waln, Jason G 4:08:48 (12,769)
Walpole, Maurice 5:30:05 (30,369)
Walsh, Alan 4:14:49 (14,385)
Walsh, Alex 3:26:38 (3,876)
Walsh, Colm P 4:37:41 (20,547)
Walsh, Damien J 4:04:05 (11,657)
Walsh, David 3:59:03 (10,451)
Walsh, Enda M 3:42:21 (6,441)
Walsh, Harry 4:22:53 (16,576)
Walsh, James C 3:16:18 (2,618)
Walsh, John 4:25:59 (17,429)
Walsh, Mark 3:11:22 (2,068)
Walsh, Michael D 3:29:02 (4,277)
Walsh, Michael I 3:40:50 (6,148)
Walsh, Michael J 4:33:14 (19,366)
Walsh, Neil B 4:48:59 (23,231)
Walsh, Nicholas J 3:10:49 (2,012)
Walsh, Nick 3:58:29 (10,288)
Walsh, Peter J 5:32:13 (30,579)
Walsh, Phillip I 3:36:31 (5,430)
Walsh, Steve R 3:18:10 (2,797)
Walsh, Timothy S 4:14:41 (14,343)
Walshe, Damian 5:39:13 (31,336)
Walter, David 4:59:47 (25,736)
Walter, Felchlin 4:15:20 (14,534)
Walter, Matthew H 5:06:00 (26,875)
Walter, Michael D 3:27:20 (3,983)
Walter, Peter K 5:33:02 (30,672)
Walters, Dennis A 5:15:32 (28,422)
Walters, Gregory J 3:17:53 (2,780)
Walters, Gyp M 3:08:52 (1,797)
Walters, Humphrey J 5:00:26 (25,868)
Walters, Kenneth 3:58:47 (10,382)
Walters, Matthew J 4:37:40 (20,539)
Walters, Meirion 4:30:02 (18,600)
Walters, Paul 3:37:29 (5,578)
Walters, Paul A 4:30:57 (18,826)
Walters, Spencer 3:57:44 (10,045)
Walther, Eberhard 4:28:06 (18,057)
Walthew, Mark 3:44:28 (6,827)
Waltho, David 4:21:17 (16,140)
Walton, Andrew M 3:55:44 (9,443)
Walton, Colin S 4:20:39 (15,978)
Walton, Dave J 3:54:24 (9,077)
Walton, David 4:14:03 (14,164)
Walton, David S 5:17:50 (28,763)
Walton, Ian D 4:31:41 (19,016)
Walton, James M 5:08:14 (27,253)
Walton, Jim P 4:15:32 (14,589)
Walton, John R 5:08:42 (27,311)
Walton, Paul G 4:36:30 (20,228)
Walton, Paul J 5:15:41 (28,441)
Wand, Alex J 4:31:57 (19,073)
Wanford, Matthew 2:52:20 (603)
Wanner, Ralf 3:54:49 (9,187)
Wanyoike, Henry 2:32:51 (91)
Wapples, Darren L 4:04:23 (11,718)
Warburton, Andrew J 4:14:24 (14,273)
Warburton, Hamish A 3:21:08 (3,097)
Warburton, James P 3:55:25 (9,342)
Warburton, Thomas A 4:50:54 (23,711)
Warbuton, John 4:28:50 (18,258)
Ward, Adrian J 4:26:03 (17,455)
Ward, Alan 3:52:34 (8,622)
Ward, Alvin M 3:24:41 (3,538)
Ward, Anthony 4:47:53 (22,985)
Ward, Anthony J 4:13:03 (13,894)
Ward, Anthony J 4:38:01 (20,627)
Ward, Anthony J 4:39:56 (21,122)

Ward, Anthony J	5:01:23	(26,039)
Ward, Carl	3:43:27	(6,645)
Ward, Charles	3:40:56	(6,169)
Ward, Charles P	5:20:08	(29,120)
Ward, Chris	4:03:28	(11,490)
Ward, Christopher J	4:51:18	(23,793)
Ward, Christopher M	3:59:47	(10,661)
Ward, Christopher R	7:26:19	(35,111)
Ward, Daniel R	4:18:25	(15,334)
Ward, Darren	3:55:51	(9,477)
Ward, Grahame L	4:06:46	(12,277)
Ward, Ian J	3:07:08	(1,643)
Ward, James S	2:52:14	(602)
Ward, Jason	5:01:19	(26,031)
Ward, Jeremy A	5:13:28	(28,076)
Ward, Jeremy B	3:26:19	(3,814)
Ward, John M	3:27:40	(4,054)
Ward, Jolyon	5:12:55	(27,985)
Ward, Jonathan T	4:13:14	(13,948)
Ward, Julian T	4:24:23	(16,949)
Ward, Karl C	3:09:32	(1,861)
Ward, Kevin P	4:48:58	(23,227)
Ward, Martin B	4:33:52	(19,538)
Ward, Melvin R	3:51:13	(8,305)
Ward, Michael S	4:35:25	(19,955)
Ward, Mick	3:27:10	(3,951)
Ward, Nicholas K	4:27:02	(17,755)
Ward, Paul	4:36:01	(20,087)
Ward, Paul A	3:54:07	(8,999)
Ward, Paul H	4:04:10	(11,674)
Ward, Pete A	5:02:00	(26,143)
Ward, Peter	4:17:37	(15,115)
Ward, Peter J	5:19:37	(29,051)
Ward, Richard B	3:42:59	(6,545)
Ward, Rob	7:11:35	(34,998)
Ward, Roland	3:50:32	(8,153)
Ward, Roland G	4:33:54	(19,546)
Ward, Simon G	4:03:32	(11,510)
Ward, Simon J	4:20:22	(15,903)
Ward, Simon L	3:34:21	(5,101)
Ward, Stephen D	4:27:57	(18,022)
Ward Brown, Jonathan M	4:40:07	(21,157)
Wardell, Chris	3:36:14	(5,378)
Wardell, Dave A	4:12:26	(13,734)
Wardell, Jamie	4:02:02	(11,167)
Wardell, Stephen J	3:33:21	(4,938)
Warden, Alan J	3:36:52	(5,473)
Warden, Malcolm G	6:43:54	(34,597)
Wardlaw, Robert G	3:32:54	(4,873)
Wardlaw, Steven	4:17:06	(14,982)
Wardle, David	4:22:10	(16,389)
Wardle, Mark	4:18:07	(15,239)
Wardley, Thomas E	3:21:23	(3,121)
Wardley, Tim O	4:03:54	(11,606)
Wardman, Andrew E	4:54:02	(24,436)
Ware, Mathew D	3:44:13	(6,788)
Wariebi, Adule M	5:16:01	(28,482)
Waring, Brett I	3:34:06	(5,061)
Waring, Matthew P	5:51:20	(32,356)
Waring, Nicholas	4:34:19	(19,668)
Warman, Robert I	3:51:48	(8,441)
Warn, Francis T	5:35:17	(30,931)
Warn, Timothy J	3:28:03	(4,113)
Warne, Barnaby	4:01:29	(11,047)
Warne, David J	4:24:57	(17,107)
Warne, James	3:46:44	(7,290)
Warner, Alan	3:25:19	(3,647)
Warner, Brian R	4:20:59	(16,071)
Warner, David R	4:47:45	(22,953)
Warner, Edmond W	3:19:03	(2,885)
Warner, Edward	3:50:13	(8,089)
Warner, Gary	3:49:14	(7,872)
Warner, George D	6:35:37	(34,401)
Warner, Graham K	4:18:05	(15,231)
Warner, Keith	4:25:53	(17,396)
Warner, Kim	3:37:13	(5,525)
Warner, Martin H	3:27:32	(4,028)
Warner, Michael	4:35:59	(20,081)
Warner, Michael	6:21:27	(33,960)
Warner, Michael B	3:24:00	(3,446)
Warner, Michael K	4:15:00	(14,448)
Warner, Paul C	3:20:21	(3,031)
Warner, Philip	5:12:45	(27,959)

Warner, Robert E	4:06:20	(12,177)
Warner, Simon	4:26:30	(17,600)
Warner, Simon E	5:58:49	(32,894)
Warner, Tony D	3:16:46	(2,660)
Warnes, Andrew	5:19:56	(29,087)
Warnett, Steven	4:33:40	(19,477)
Warnock, John	4:51:18	(23,793)
Warr, John E	6:02:52	(33,134)
Warr, Timothy S	4:53:57	(24,411)
Warren, David P	4:38:26	(20,736)
Warren, Garry	4:38:48	(20,830)
Warren, Gordon	5:18:30	(28,865)
Warren, Jamie D	3:37:47	(5,615)
Warren, John D	5:15:48	(28,457)
Warren, John E	4:48:31	(23,125)
Warren, John M	5:03:00	(26,341)
Warren, Neil P	3:44:10	(6,779)
Warren, Paul	4:12:20	(13,707)
Warren, Paul D	4:56:43	(25,073)
Warren, Richard K	4:18:08	(15,242)
Warren, Wayne	4:43:21	(21,946)
Warrender, Jonathan J	4:25:51	(17,387)
Warrick, Michael J	3:12:50	(2,232)
Warrilow, Walt	5:40:06	(31,427)
Warriner, Roddy A	4:12:14	(13,679)
Warrington, David A	2:42:20	(249)
Warwick, Gary A	4:26:55	(17,724)
Warwick, Paul N	5:44:16	(31,785)
Warwick, Steven J	5:06:48	(27,017)
Wash, Darren C	4:50:39	(23,662)
Washbourne, Darren R	5:23:28	(29,538)
Washington, Darren	2:51:59	(589)
Wassermann, Karl	3:07:27	(1,672)
Wastnage, Benjamin M	3:26:18	(3,810)
Watanabe, Daiki	5:34:13	(30,809)
Watanabe, Haruyuki	4:23:53	(16,822)
Watanabe, Noriaki	5:54:04	(32,572)
Waterfall, Sam	3:46:57	(7,338)
Waterhouse, Paul	3:32:54	(4,873)
Waterman, Christopher S	6:12:58	(33,661)
Waterman, David J	3:13:35	(2,314)
Waterman, David W	4:10:30	(13,227)
Waterman, James R	3:15:19	(2,506)
Waterman, Kevin D	3:07:43	(1,693)
Waterman, Ryan R	2:57:28	(920)
Waters, Colin A	5:03:25	(26,420)
Waters, David M	4:10:05	(13,109)
Waters, Geoff	4:29:51	(18,551)
Waters, John H	4:21:34	(16,221)
Waters, Mark L	5:35:09	(30,925)
Waterston, Laughlan L	3:53:42	(8,909)
Waterston, Paul	3:06:44	(1,611)
Watford, Adam J	4:53:25	(24,281)
Watkin, Alexander J	5:04:14	(26,558)
Watkins, Alastair J	3:48:20	(7,664)
Watkins, Andy J	5:40:34	(31,475)
Watkins, Anthony C	5:54:48	(32,622)
Watkins, Brian	7:27:59	(35,117)
Watkins, Paul	4:49:32	(23,365)
Watkins, Philip	4:21:44	(16,266)
Watkins, Philip R	4:28:03	(18,043)
Watkins, Rhys	3:40:07	(6,019)
Watkins, Robert	5:35:24	(30,947)
Watkins, Thomas A	3:59:52	(10,688)
Watkins, Tom	4:26:58	(17,745)
Watkinson, Peter G	3:18:13	(2,806)
Watkiss, Jonathan D	4:02:07	(11,186)
Watmough, Stephen J	3:51:57	(8,473)
Watson, Andrew J	3:38:40	(5,749)
Watson, Andrew L	3:16:33	(2,638)
Watson, Bob	5:12:06	(27,845)
Watson, Bruce M	3:46:41	(7,279)
Watson, Daniel A	4:24:02	(16,863)
Watson, David	3:17:06	(2,689)
Watson, David T	4:44:29	(22,210)
Watson, David W	4:50:13	(23,539)
Watson, Don A	4:36:38	(20,263)
Watson, Gary J	4:17:58	(15,194)
Watson, Ian A	4:25:31	(17,290)
Watson, Ian P	4:51:38	(23,859)
Watson, James	4:33:13	(19,363)
Watson, Jerry R	2:44:22	(305)
Watson, John	5:45:10	(31,865)

Watson, John F	5:21:30	(29,294)
Watson, Jonathan R	3:23:20	(3,355)
Watson, Mark	4:27:21	(17,838)
Watson, Mark A	5:08:02	(27,224)
Watson, Michael J	3:49:44	(7,985)
Watson, Nicholas R	3:25:46	(3,714)
Watson, Paul	3:02:29	(1,297)
Watson, Paul	4:29:08	(18,350)
Watson, Peter	4:39:33	(21,027)
Watson, Peter A	3:26:34	(3,859)
Watson, Peter D	3:05:59	(1,550)
Watson, Peter L	4:25:34	(17,307)
Watson, Phil G	3:37:53	(5,631)
Watson, Stephen	2:59:17	(1,067)
Watson, Stephen T	5:43:35	(31,727)
Watson, Steve	4:19:03	(15,527)
Watson, Stuart	2:56:47	(872)
Watson, Thomas	6:43:42	(34,587)
Watson, William	3:21:41	(3,151)
Watson, William	3:41:38	(6,310)
Watson, William D	4:10:04	(13,106)
Watt, Ashley L	4:16:10	(14,759)
Watt, Barry	4:06:56	(12,324)
Watt, Brian G	4:06:15	(12,154)
Watt, Brian J	4:08:40	(12,733)
Watt, Christopher	4:39:51	(21,100)
Watt, David	4:53:55	(24,398)
Watt, Guy	4:49:58	(23,488)
Watt, Kieran	5:35:56	(30,985)
Watters, Ian M	4:22:51	(16,568)
Wattley, Travis	5:15:42	(28,443)
Watton, Matthew J	5:14:34	(28,273)
Watts, Allen E	5:52:11	(32,423)
Watts, Andrew J	3:12:34	(2,200)
Watts, Barry F	4:05:54	(12,073)
Watts, Charlie T	5:14:42	(28,303)
Watts, David	4:26:50	(17,694)
Watts, David	4:39:03	(20,894)
Watts, Graham A	5:19:02	(28,948)
Watts, Graham J	5:50:30	(32,300)
Watts, Jonathan	4:15:03	(14,464)
Watts, Lee J	4:07:30	(12,460)
Watts, Matthew L	3:40:32	(6,089)
Watts, Michael B	4:36:28	(20,220)
Watts, Michael B	5:02:09	(26,174)
Watts, Paul J	3:54:50	(9,193)
Watts, Peter	3:52:54	(8,700)
Watts, Richard M	3:46:49	(7,308)
Watts, Stephen J	4:45:52	(22,513)
Waudby, Trevor W	4:22:11	(16,392)
Waude, Ian S	3:18:04	(2,792)
Waugh, Ryan D	4:42:33	(21,751)
Waugh, Stuart R	3:20:20	(3,029)
Waumsley, Peter	2:48:26	(430)
Wavell, Adam M	3:35:51	(5,315)
Way, Peter M	4:49:03	(23,250)
Waye, Antony D	5:09:39	(27,463)
Waylen, Craig J	4:04:34	(11,761)
Waymark, Chris P	5:53:49	(32,552)
Waymark, Karl G	4:26:17	(17,527)
Wayne, David H	4:25:50	(17,383)
Weait, James	6:48:42	(34,687)
Weal, Jonathan	5:23:32	(29,547)
Weall, Paul	3:12:50	(2,232)
Wearing, Michael J	6:05:11	(33,284)
Weatherall, Mark	4:32:48	(19,270)
Weatherby, Johnny R	6:10:14	(33,541)
Weatherill, Alex L	3:27:23	(3,988)
Weatherley, Alex W	4:14:22	(14,263)
Weaver, Andrew	3:53:04	(8,733)
Weaver, Anthony M	3:27:25	(4,000)
Weaver, Danny	4:00:51	(10,913)
Weaver, David P	4:19:52	(15,767)
Weaver, Luke N	4:32:02	(19,098)
Weaver, Robert M	3:46:55	(7,333)
Weaver, William J	4:39:21	(20,977)
Weavers, Terry P	3:15:02	(2,481)
Weaving, Peter P	4:51:11	(23,769)
Weavis, Darren	3:27:45	(4,067)
Webb, Adrian J	3:15:24	(2,513)
Webb, Alan	4:05:49	(12,053)
Webb, Alan	4:29:00	(18,306)
Webb, Alex	3:02:06	(1,268)

Webb, Andrew J	3:06:53 (1,626)	Wehling, Ansgar	5:18:06 (28,798)	West, Kenneth J	4:05:30 (11,985)
Webb, Flemmich	4:27:43 (17,955)	Wehner, Oliver	4:18:05 (15,231)	West, Kevin M	2:43:42 (285)
Webb, Graham	4:05:52 (12,063)	Wehrle, Stephen R	3:57:34 (10,003)	West, Nicholas S	4:05:25 (11,971)
Webb, Harvey J	3:25:30 (3,672)	Wehrle, Uwe	4:09:17 (12,903)	West, Rob	4:47:02 (22,777)
Webb, Ian	4:24:48 (17,071)	Weider, Frank	4:46:24 (22,648)	West, Rob G	4:24:39 (17,026)
Webb, Ian J	6:37:13 (34,438)	Weider, Karl-Ludwig	4:46:23 (22,645)	West, Robert N	4:20:49 (16,026)
Webb, Jack	4:27:44 (17,963)	Weighell, Robert D	3:42:10 (6,413)	West, Rory J	4:52:07 (23,970)
Webb, Jason	4:50:22 (23,585)	Weightman, Edward C	4:45:37 (22,463)	West, Stephen	3:38:15 (5,689)
Webb, John	4:27:36 (17,921)	Weijts, Nico E	3:49:40 (7,972)	West, Stephen A	3:44:59 (6,955)
Webb, John	4:39:55 (21,117)	Weilkiens, Tim	3:58:50 (10,397)	West, Steve	4:56:26 (24,996)
Webb, Justin	3:17:35 (2,746)	Weinkove, Robert	3:51:03 (8,265)	West, Stuart A	5:03:46 (26,476)
Webb, Justin S	5:45:10 (31,865)	Weinstein, David M	5:57:05 (32,782)	West, Timothy O	3:47:59 (7,573)
Webb, Laurence P	5:40:20 (31,447)	Weinstein, Morris A	4:40:22 (21,225)	West, Toby J	5:04:24 (26,583)
Webb, Lewis	3:37:29 (5,578)	Weir, Andrew P	2:24:21 (42)	West, Tom	3:56:04 (9,524)
Webb, Mark T	5:07:26 (27,135)	Weir, David	5:53:23 (32,526)	Westcott, David J	4:58:05 (25,347)
Webb, Martin D	4:15:18 (14,527)	Weir, David C	3:48:47 (7,780)	Western, Ivan M	4:56:28 (25,006)
Webb, Mathew P	4:30:03 (18,608)	Weir, Martin	4:01:21 (11,012)	Western, Phillip F	3:10:02 (1,924)
Webb, Matthew S	5:19:13 (28,976)	Weir, Paul	3:58:38 (10,318)	West-Evans, Errol L	3:54:09 (9,013)
Webb, Michael J	4:47:33 (22,891)	Weir, Peter T	4:21:22 (16,164)	Westgaard, Halvor	4:52:47 (24,123)
Webb, Neil F	5:24:43 (29,710)	Weiss, Christophe J	2:42:08 (246)	Westgarth, Christopher	4:20:52 (16,039)
Webb, Nicholas H	4:31:32 (18,978)	Welbury, James H	3:32:08 (4,764)	Westgate, Andrew M	4:26:34 (17,623)
Webb, Nick J	4:04:53 (11,834)	Welby-Everard, Guy J	3:31:55 (4,733)	Westgate, Nicholas R	3:54:20 (9,053)
Webb, Nigel	3:59:37 (10,608)	Welch, Alan J	2:57:22 (911)	Westgate, Stuart M	4:22:35 (16,497)
Webb, Paul I	6:36:59 (34,432)	Welch, Joseph S	3:22:02 (3,191)	Westhead, Andrew	3:49:26 (7,917)
Webb, Paul J	5:18:42 (28,906)	Welch, Keith W	4:01:32 (11,055)	Westhead, Nick C	4:24:29 (16,984)
Webb, Peter	5:10:34 (27,582)	Welch, Neil M	3:59:30 (10,571)	Westlake, Allan G	5:42:43 (31,653)
Webb, Peter J	5:33:58 (30,777)	Welch, Paul M	3:39:55 (5,982)	Westlake, Graham E	4:03:13 (11,435)
Webb, Philip	5:05:39 (26,813)	Welch, Richard H	5:45:41 (31,911)	Westlake-Bryant, Tim S	6:25:05 (34,099)
Webb, Richard	4:56:29 (25,014)	Weldin, Phillipe C	4:41:06 (21,422)	Weston, Andy F	4:51:48 (23,892)
Webb, Richard J	4:49:44 (23,435)	Welford, Justin J	4:59:30 (25,663)	Weston, Edward	4:19:10 (15,567)
Webb, Robert G	4:13:49 (14,093)	Weller, Allan	4:06:25 (12,193)	Weston, Jeff K	3:32:39 (4,836)
Webb, Robert J	3:50:51 (8,224)	Weller, Paul L	3:34:33 (5,128)	Weston, Mark	5:31:08 (30,481)
Webb, Sean M	3:03:53 (1,393)	Wellfair, Peter	6:18:36 (33,878)	Weston, Paul M	4:52:32 (24,061)
Webb, Simon R	3:31:11 (4,625)	Wellington, Stephen J	4:28:39 (18,203)	Weston, Simon M	4:05:30 (11,985)
Webb, Trevor	4:22:06 (16,367)	Wells, Alan M	4:15:57 (14,698)	Weston, Trevor	3:59:16 (10,513)
Webber, Adam D	3:47:55 (7,553)	Wells, Andrew J	3:25:38 (3,692)	Westropp, Patrick J	3:50:43 (8,192)
Webber, Adam R	4:28:45 (18,234)	Wells, Brian R	5:13:55 (28,153)	Westwood, Jamie I	4:49:04 (23,259)
Webber, Anthony	5:23:24 (29,529)	Wells, Colin	6:03:54 (33,217)	Westwood, Nick M	3:56:09 (9,552)
Webber, Anthony D	3:42:20 (6,438)	Wells, Colin N	5:22:02 (29,352)	Weton, Mark J	4:22:20 (16,429)
Webber, Christopher E	5:03:54 (26,503)	Wells, Daniel P	5:12:05 (27,839)	Wetterwald, Pascal	3:52:04 (4,758)
Webber, Gary P	3:48:21 (7,672)	Wells, David J	4:48:32 (23,130)	Wetton, David E	3:48:04 (7,606)
Webber, Ian C	4:03:45 (11,559)	Wells, David P	3:26:20 (3,816)	Wetton, Michael L	4:43:20 (21,943)
Webber, James M	4:40:44 (21,315)	Wells, Garry W	5:03:04 (26,352)	Weyell, Peter W	4:49:21 (23,326)
Webber, Mark D	4:05:41 (12,023)	Wells, Keith W	3:25:17 (3,641)	Whale, Richard C	4:38:13 (20,674)
Webber, Matthew J	3:55:47 (9,457)	Wells, Laurence	3:55:51 (9,477)	Whalen, Paul M	4:40:17 (21,203)
Webb-Peploe, Alex M	4:00:33 (10,852)	Wells, Michael	6:37:32 (34,442)	Whaley, Henry	4:55:23 (24,754)
Weber, Alain E	2:35:41 (119)	Wells, Peter J	5:17:53 (28,768)	Whalley, Adrian H	3:26:54 (3,911)
Weber, Gerhard	3:31:15 (4,643)	Wells, Philip I	4:58:00 (25,329)	Whalley, Robin M	3:51:24 (8,353)
Weber, Ruedi H	3:59:25 (10,548)	Wells, Steven W	4:43:52 (22,064)	Whann, Andrew J	4:24:29 (16,984)
Webster, Alan	3:00:52 (1,183)	Wells, Stuart	4:21:14 (16,124)	Wharton, Kevin	5:11:17 (27,701)
Webster, Alan	3:44:51 (6,928)	Wells, Tony	4:53:43 (24,358)	Wharton, Nick J	3:52:13 (8,532)
Webster, Andrew N	3:51:22 (8,346)	Wells, William G	4:07:04 (12,360)	Whatley, Philip J	3:23:08 (3,321)
Webster, Christopher R	6:22:37 (34,012)	Wells-Cole, James	3:54:47 (9,179)	Whatmore, Gary A	4:06:56 (12,324)
Webster, David	3:48:35 (7,736)	Welsh, Barry G	3:39:18 (5,868)	Wheale, Jack L	4:47:36 (22,907)
Webster, David G	4:02:04 (11,175)	Welsh, Berny M	4:05:15 (11,929)	Wheat, Richard J	4:59:40 (25,705)
Webster, Gilbert	4:51:53 (23,905)	Welsh, Christopher J	4:58:31 (25,448)	Wheatcroft, Mark A	3:48:31 (7,715)
Webster, Graeme J	5:07:43 (27,179)	Welsh, Mike	5:17:52 (28,767)	Wheatcroft, Russell S	5:23:46 (29,581)
Webster, Jim R	3:27:11 (3,958)	Welsh, Stephen J	5:42:57 (31,676)	Wheatley, Andrew	3:43:00 (6,549)
Webster, Jon R	3:25:06 (3,606)	Welshman, Andy C	2:45:58 (347)	Wheatley, Ian M	4:29:00 (18,306)
Webster, Jonathan P	3:45:49 (7,098)	Welton, Peter M	4:16:14 (14,775)	Wheatley, John J	3:53:23 (8,826)
Webster, Mark	4:12:12 (13,664)	Wemms, Matthew G	4:56:19 (24,967)	Wheatley, Stephen A	4:22:37 (16,514)
Webster, Nick	3:52:22 (8,569)	Wennek, Benjamin	4:42:29 (21,739)	Wheeldon, Scott A	3:48:29 (7,702)
Webster, Paul J	3:08:02 (1,718)	Wenning, Thomas	3:54:49 (9,187)	Wheeler, Ben D	4:26:24 (17,570)
Webster, Philip	4:39:59 (21,136)	Went, Marc R	4:25:38 (17,330)	Wheeler, Brian	3:44:23 (6,815)
Webster, Richard W	3:33:46 (5,003)	Wentworth, Alfred	4:48:31 (23,125)	Wheeler, Christopher J	3:22:13 (3,217)
Webster, Russell K	4:15:33 (14,593)	Wenz, Marc A	3:27:41 (4,057)	Wheeler, David L	4:31:29 (18,965)
Webster, Terry M	4:06:53 (12,311)	Wernberg, Stephen P	4:40:08 (21,164)	Wheeler, Ewan J	4:05:31 (11,991)
Wedderburn, Peter H	4:06:43 (12,270)	Werner, Thomas	4:31:09 (18,866)	Wheeler, Geoffrey S	4:26:07 (17,482)
Wedge, Iain D	2:53:00 (637)	Wesbroom, Adam	4:33:17 (19,377)	Wheeler, Harry	5:36:56 (31,096)
Wedgwood, Michael A	4:06:55 (12,323)	Wescombe, Christopher P	3:07:21 (1,656)	Wheeler, Jason C	5:03:00 (26,341)
Wedlake, Ryan S	5:13:26 (28,067)	Wesley, Neil R	4:26:09 (17,492)	Wheeler, Jeremy J	5:01:34 (26,076)
Weedon, Philip J	3:53:18 (8,801)	Wessels, Andrew M	4:20:42 (15,991)	Wheeler, John G	4:13:36 (14,043)
Weekes, Derek	4:22:59 (16,595)	West, Anthony	4:33:30 (19,433)	Wheeler, John W	5:25:32 (29,809)
Weeks, Christopher	5:23:56 (29,609)	West, Arnold	5:20:23 (29,158)	Wheeler, Michael J	3:56:26 (9,645)
Weeks, Joseph P	3:13:47 (2,337)	West, Christopher J	3:39:28 (5,904)	Wheeler, Miles S	3:27:59 (4,102)
Weeks, Michael R	2:40:33 (212)	West, Clive	4:05:42 (12,026)	Wheeler, Peter	4:18:08 (15,242)
Weeks, Neil	6:04:20 (33,234)	West, Colin	2:47:50 (404)	Wheeler, Richard A	4:03:31 (11,504)
Weeks, Simon J	4:57:03 (25,143)	West, Dean T	4:38:36 (20,777)	Wheeler, Simon P	5:05:40 (26,817)
Weetch, Royston J	4:38:32 (20,761)	West, Fintan J	5:02:17 (26,200)	Wheeler, Stephen A	4:25:05 (17,146)
Weetman, Stephen G	3:13:49 (2,341)	West, Graham J	3:49:14 (7,872)	Wheeler, Sydney J	3:57:44 (10,045)
Wegerhoff, Sean	3:30:04 (4,463)	West, Ian	5:09:42 (27,470)	Whelan, Andrew M	4:36:42 (20,279)
Weggen, Bjorn	3:56:59 (9,809)	West, James P	5:25:36 (29,817)	Whelan, Andrew M	4:43:58 (22,090)
Weggen, Eckhard	3:56:59 (9,809)	West, John S	3:17:06 (2,689)	Whelan, Dominic M	3:43:25 (6,642)

Whelan, Ryan P	4:53:07 (24,201)	
Whelehan, Oliver	3:49:02 (7,831)	
Wheller, Stephen	5:56:36 (32,742)	
Whetherly, Alan	5:34:08 (30,796)	
Whetlor, James K	4:42:39 (21,786)	
Wheway, Mark	3:59:58 (10,717)	
Whewell, Sean	4:42:05 (21,645)	
Whiddett, Oliver A	3:52:11 (8,523)	
Whiffen, Brian J	4:31:15 (18,898)	
Whiffin, Christopher M	4:37:57 (20,606)	
Whiffin, James L	4:25:10 (17,172)	
Whilan, Garry	4:56:10 (24,932)	
Whillans, David B	4:59:33 (25,674)	
Whimpenny, Dave J	4:03:45 (11,559)	
Whincup, Stephen P	4:20:37 (15,968)	
Whipp, Mark W	4:22:15 (16,407)	
Whippy, John A	4:23:23 (16,710)	
Whitaker, Christopher D	3:27:31 (4,025)	
Whitaker, Grant M	3:56:42 (9,726)	
Whitaker, Keith H	3:42:13 (6,420)	
White, Ade	3:27:37 (4,039)	
White, Adrian	3:15:15 (2,499)	
White, Alec	3:45:10 (6,984)	
White, Andrew	4:13:05 (13,906)	
White, Andrew	5:31:52 (30,548)	
White, Andrew J	3:35:32 (5,267)	
White, Andrew R	3:49:35 (7,948)	
White, Andrew T	4:34:35 (19,736)	
White, Anthony	4:29:17 (18,396)	
White, Anthony R	5:25:55 (29,858)	
White, Bijan V	3:54:11 (9,022)	
White, Brian A	4:10:57 (13,333)	
White, Brian J	3:59:22 (10,538)	
White, Colin W	5:52:21 (32,443)	
White, Craig A	4:05:07 (11,903)	
White, Dan D	2:58:41 (1,003)	
White, David	3:53:06 (8,743)	
White, David G	4:54:10 (24,463)	
White, David J	4:28:55 (18,279)	
White, David R	3:47:34 (7,468)	
White, Dean G	4:16:27 (14,828)	
White, Dean T	7:04:36 (34,920)	
White, Derek G	4:40:23 (21,228)	
White, Douglas M	6:14:23 (33,714)	
White, Duncan I	3:39:13 (5,854)	
White, Gary	4:10:54 (13,317)	
White, Geoff W	6:08:21 (33,460)	
White, Grahame K	4:20:41 (15,986)	
White, Ian	6:07:40 (33,423)	
White, Ian A	4:21:32 (16,213)	
White, Ian P	4:11:37 (13,508)	
White, Ian R	5:03:46 (26,476)	
White, James P	4:06:52 (12,303)	
White, John A	3:37:59 (5,644)	
White, John L	5:41:48 (31,578)	
White, Keith	5:28:56 (30,240)	
White, Kenneth R	4:56:38 (25,050)	
White, Kevin P	5:02:36 (26,250)	
White, Kristian H	5:23:14 (29,510)	
White, Louis	5:07:00 (27,057)	
White, Malcolm D	6:08:21 (33,460)	
White, Malcolm J	4:17:45 (15,149)	
White, Malcolm N	4:39:32 (21,022)	
White, Mark	3:57:04 (9,843)	
White, Mark	4:35:21 (19,931)	
White, Martin D	3:28:59 (4,269)	
White, Michael	3:06:27 (1,592)	
White, Michael D	3:54:52 (9,202)	
White, Michael P	3:02:10 (1,275)	
White, Neil M	4:55:40 (24,804)	
White, Nick R	4:36:09 (20,117)	
White, Paul	3:36:18 (5,392)	
White, Paul	3:41:18 (6,236)	
White, Paul	5:05:03 (26,693)	
White, Paul	5:55:44 (32,696)	
White, Paul A	5:44:10 (31,777)	
White, Peter	4:08:40 (12,733)	
White, Philip C	3:54:25 (9,081)	
White, Phillip D	4:47:36 (22,907)	
White, Richard	4:29:48 (18,545)	
White, Robert A	4:24:18 (16,924)	
White, Robert P	4:41:13 (21,451)	
White, Robin J	3:57:16 (9,909)	
White, Scott	3:32:33 (4,826)	
White, Scott D	5:48:17 (32,123)	
White, Simon	4:24:24 (16,956)	
White, Simon J	4:18:38 (15,408)	
White, Stephen	3:03:05 (1,335)	
White, Stephen B	4:29:15 (18,379)	
White, Stephen R	3:09:24 (1,852)	
White, Steven R	5:04:03 (26,522)	
Whitear, Roy E	5:34:17 (30,817)	
Whitefield, Rupert H	4:02:07 (11,186)	
Whitefoot, Ian R	4:28:08 (18,067)	
Whitehall, Robert P	2:51:19 (551)	
Whitehead, Gary	3:55:33 (9,385)	
Whitehead, Joshua C	2:48:53 (461)	
Whitehead, Kevin A	5:46:29 (31,976)	
Whitehead, Peter G	5:47:37 (32,069)	
Whitehead, Reno A	4:21:40 (16,247)	
Whitehouse, Andrew G	3:38:31 (5,729)	
Whitehouse, Ian R	3:14:58 (2,477)	
Whitehouse, John	5:34:01 (30,783)	
Whitehouse, Terry	4:54:21 (24,515)	
Whitelam, Gary	4:37:16 (20,433)	
Whitelaw, Andrew	4:03:19 (11,465)	
Whitelaw, Patrick J	4:05:36 (12,006)	
Whiteley, Iain N	3:53:19 (8,809)	
Whiteley, John	5:34:46 (30,882)	
Whiteley, Mike	3:33:00 (4,889)	
Whiteley, Nigel P	4:30:12 (18,655)	
Whitelock, Neil P	3:43:23 (6,633)	
Whiteman, Greg P	4:22:51 (16,568)	
Whiter, George A	4:35:20 (19,919)	
Whitfield, Karl J	5:20:25 (29,165)	
Whitfield, Matthew	3:02:04 (1,266)	
Whiting, David C	5:05:50 (26,848)	
Whiting, Dominic J	3:36:09 (5,365)	
Whiting, Mark E	3:38:03 (5,656)	
Whiting, Richard	5:24:31 (29,686)	
Whitley, John S	5:13:56 (28,156)	
Whitlock, Anthony R	4:04:48 (11,817)	
Whitlock, Russell A	3:30:26 (4,511)	
Whitlock, Tony R	3:17:17 (2,714)	
Whitmarsh, Jim F	3:25:07 (3,609)	
Whitmore, Clive C	4:01:21 (11,012)	
Whitmore, Ivon E	3:02:05 (1,267)	
Whitmore, Jamie R	4:14:10 (14,201)	
Whitmore, Kris	3:48:40 (7,756)	
Whitmore, Timothy G	5:37:59 (31,196)	
Whitnall, Simon R	4:18:58 (15,502)	
Whitney, Thomas O	4:19:31 (15,668)	
Whittaker, Anthony J	5:39:20 (31,358)	
Whittaker, James D	4:26:21 (17,548)	
Whittaker, Keith	4:20:38 (15,975)	
Whittaker, Mark	3:31:24 (4,663)	
Whittaker, Michael	4:32:40 (19,244)	
Whittam, Michael	5:17:23 (28,695)	
Whittem, Alex J	3:17:26 (2,726)	
Whittenbury, Robert J	4:42:00 (21,627)	
Whittingham, Conrad A	5:19:47 (29,075)	
Whittingham, Paul	3:27:36 (4,036)	
Whittington, Chayne K	4:28:00 (18,032)	
Whittington, David H	6:03:05 (33,149)	
Whittington, Richard H	3:58:43 (10,354)	
Whittington, Russell	3:00:57 (1,189)	
Whittington, Stuart M	3:41:43 (6,319)	
Whittle, Dominic P	4:07:52 (12,547)	
Whittle, John A	4:44:17 (22,167)	
Whittle, Jonathon B	4:04:04 (11,654)	
Whittle, Nigel J	5:41:53 (31,592)	
Whittle, Nigel R	3:17:42 (2,754)	
Whittle, Rohan E	4:59:48 (25,742)	
Whittle, Stephen J	4:14:03 (14,164)	
Whitton, Mark J	6:05:52 (33,320)	
Whitty, Gerard W	3:59:49 (10,667)	
Whitty, Graeme C	3:38:30 (5,726)	
Whitwell, Jamie A	3:31:49 (4,722)	
Whitworth, Bill J	3:56:45 (9,736)	
Whitworth, Dane C	3:56:06 (9,538)	
Whitworth, David	3:45:31 (7,050)	
Whitworth, Nicholas C	5:22:52 (29,467)	
Whysall, Michael G	3:48:24 (7,685)	
Whyte, Alistair J	4:02:05 (11,181)	
Whyte, Greg P	3:24:45 (3,548)	
Whyte, Jonathan D	3:39:00 (5,817)	
Wibbeke, Ludger B	4:17:33 (15,102)	
Wibberley, Donald J	5:20:31 (29,182)	
Wichmann, Hermann	4:48:21 (23,088)	
Wickenden, James M	6:30:43 (34,267)	
Wicker, Jorg J	3:26:08 (3,783)	
Wicker, Richard I	5:27:53 (30,086)	
Wickham, Stephen A	3:16:07 (2,593)	
Wickramasinghe, Eranda P	3:46:26 (7,228)	
Wicks, Daniel B	5:42:40 (31,649)	
Wicks, Jonathan R	3:28:47 (4,240)	
Wicks, Matthew S	5:11:42 (27,769)	
Wicks, Nathan	3:58:28 (10,278)	
Widdows, Bob	5:25:57 (29,864)	
Widdowson, John C	3:57:00 (9,815)	
Widdowson, Steven J	4:04:11 (11,678)	
Wideqvist, Lars Erik	5:18:10 (28,812)	
Widlez, David	2:43:45 (288)	
Wieland, Martin	3:04:51 (1,457)	
Wienecke, Juergen	5:18:16 (28,831)	
Wiesner, Norbert	3:58:41 (10,341)	
Wiffin, Damian M	3:25:53 (3,739)	
Wigdawl, Nicholas	3:57:22 (9,939)	
Wigfall, Tristan B	3:58:28 (10,278)	
Wiggall, Steve M	3:56:18 (9,605)	
Wiggans, Andy K	3:23:10 (3,326)	
Wiggin, Alexander J	4:22:07 (16,375)	
Wiggins, Andrew	3:10:51 (2,014)	
Wiggins, Darren	5:20:16 (29,136)	
Wiggins, David	3:54:41 (9,149)	
Wigginton, Richard	4:34:16 (19,654)	
Wigley, Andrew J	4:41:08 (21,428)	
Wigley, Timothy J	2:49:08 (473)	
Wigmore, Graham J	3:40:47 (6,136)	
Wigmore, Nick I	2:44:15 (303)	
Wignell, Marcus J	3:14:40 (2,440)	
Wigston, Andrew J	3:53:21 (8,820)	
Wigzell, Edward W	4:18:20 (15,307)	
Wijte, Kees	3:43:17 (6,613)	
Wikeley, Alan F	3:55:43 (9,435)	
Wilbourn, Chris	4:41:23 (21,489)	
Wilbraham, Paul	3:22:39 (3,257)	
Wilby, Garin J	3:32:18 (4,787)	
Wilcke, Heiko H	3:06:24 (1,581)	
Wilcock, Iain C	5:48:32 (32,137)	
Wilcock, Martin	2:55:58 (806)	
Wilcox, Michael	3:13:31 (2,304)	
Wilcox, Robert P	4:20:03 (15,813)	
Wilcox, Stephan	4:58:26 (25,425)	
Wild, Charles F	4:24:14 (16,912)	
Wild, David	4:24:14 (16,912)	
Wild, James D	4:14:24 (14,273)	
Wild, Oscar	3:58:00 (10,142)	
Wild, Reginald R	3:16:24 (2,627)	
Wild, Sam	5:00:32 (25,881)	
Wilde, Chris D	4:40:00 (21,142)	
Wilde, Philip G	3:24:50 (3,556)	
Wilde, Stephen	4:06:02 (12,102)	
Wilden, Stuart J	5:28:05 (30,115)	
Wilder, Paul	5:25:29 (29,803)	
Wilder, Peter	3:53:24 (8,831)	
Wilding, Andrew S	5:31:04 (30,474)	
Wilding, Keith	4:30:06 (18,621)	
Wildman, Alistair J	4:05:17 (11,944)	
Wildman, Fraser	3:06:30 (1,595)	
Wildman, Paul A	3:57:02 (9,828)	
Wiles, Andrew J	3:59:47 (10,661)	
Wiles, Christopher A	4:34:18 (19,665)	
Wiles, Gerald R	4:30:56 (18,823)	
Wilfin, Andrew	5:26:55 (29,964)	
Wilhelm, Blasius	3:47:46 (7,517)	
Wiliams, David M	3:59:39 (10,615)	
Wiliams, Gareth-Rhys	3:16:24 (2,627)	
Wiliamson, Anthony M	5:29:25 (30,293)	
Wiliamson, Darren A	3:45:51 (7,106)	
Wiliamson, Ian P	3:06:26 (1,590)	
Wilikinson, Jonathan M	6:25:09 (34,101)	
Wililams, Jeremy D	4:29:26 (18,442)	
Wilkes, Adrian N	4:26:17 (17,527)	
Wilkes, Anthony N	3:12:08 (2,156)	
Wilkes, Bernard T	3:37:56 (5,636)	
Wilkes, Julian S	4:36:31 (20,231)	
Wilkes, Neil H	4:08:27 (12,684)	
Wilkes, Oliver J	4:05:12 (11,921)	

Wilkie, Colin	4:54:42	(24,594)
Wilkie, Ronald J	5:05:10	(26,718)
Wilkins, Denis P	5:27:00	(29,977)
Wilkins, Derek	4:30:56	(18,823)
Wilkins, Ian	3:44:35	(6,857)
Wilkins, Jeremy	4:02:36	(11,294)
Wilkins, Keith R	4:15:24	(14,551)
Wilkins, Michael	4:56:45	(25,083)
Wilkins, Ryan	6:18:20	(33,863)
Wilkins, Simon	4:27:58	(18,025)
Wilkinson, Anthony	4:51:10	(23,766)
Wilkinson, Barry H	4:38:01	(20,627)
Wilkinson, Darren	2:52:01	(591)
Wilkinson, David R	3:35:25	(5,243)
Wilkinson, Duncan L	4:20:14	(15,866)
Wilkinson, Graham	4:29:15	(18,379)
Wilkinson, Graham A	2:58:31	(993)
Wilkinson, Ian B	4:38:47	(20,825)
Wilkinson, Ian J	3:36:13	(5,374)
Wilkinson, Ian M	3:51:17	(8,324)
Wilkinson, James A	4:19:32	(15,674)
Wilkinson, John A	3:50:24	(8,122)
Wilkinson, John A	4:40:59	(21,385)
Wilkinson, Kevin	4:17:24	(15,068)
Wilkinson, Mark A	4:58:51	(25,524)
Wilkinson, Martin	4:34:30	(19,711)
Wilkinson, Martin J	3:13:09	(2,263)
Wilkinson, Matt P	4:26:20	(17,545)
Wilkinson, Michael	5:45:02	(31,850)
Wilkinson, Murray J	3:18:54	(2,873)
Wilkinson, Neil	2:22:12	(33)
Wilkinson, Neil	3:47:10	(7,384)
Wilkinson, Nick L	5:04:21	(26,575)
Wilkinson, Nigel J	3:51:48	(8,441)
Wilkinson, Philip C	4:24:24	(16,956)
Wilkinson, Richard	4:02:03	(11,170)
Wilkinson, Robert M	5:34:23	(30,828)
Wilkinson, Sean M	4:04:54	(11,839)
Wilkinson, Stephen A	3:33:10	(4,908)
Wilkinson, Steven M	3:43:14	(6,595)
Wilkinson, Stuart	4:46:21	(22,635)
Wilkinson, Tim C	4:50:37	(23,655)
Wilkinson, Tim R	4:16:22	(14,814)
Wilkinson, Trevor	3:55:12	(9,276)
Wilkinson, Wayne I	4:53:03	(24,190)
Will, Andrew J	4:06:27	(12,201)
Willats, Philip	5:36:49	(31,088)
Willcocks, Ben W	4:03:30	(11,498)
Willdridge, William D	3:55:20	(9,315)
Willems, Winifried	3:17:16	(2,711)
Willerkens, Gunter	3:14:41	(2,443)
Willett, Lee A	4:35:56	(20,070)
Willett, Richard C	5:49:58	(32,259)
Willett, Sam M	5:24:39	(29,701)
Willett, Stephen M	4:58:58	(25,552)
Willett, Timothy	3:53:05	(8,739)
Willetts, Colin G	3:49:32	(7,940)
Willey, Martin J	3:36:03	(5,346)
Williams, Adrian P	3:41:04	(6,196)
Williams, Aled P	7:30:33	(35,131)
Williams, Alex	4:08:38	(12,722)
Williams, Allan	3:35:03	(5,191)
Williams, Alun	3:21:46	(3,159)
Williams, Andrew P	3:28:03	(4,113)
Williams, Andrew P	6:29:48	(34,249)
Williams, Andrew R	4:55:19	(24,738)
Williams, Angus J	4:21:19	(16,147)
Williams, Anton F	3:40:19	(6,052)
Williams, Antony J	3:57:24	(9,949)
Williams, Arthur C	5:45:21	(31,887)
Williams, Arwyn	3:58:00	(10,142)
Williams, Barrie A	4:15:16	(14,520)
Williams, Benjamin R	3:09:16	(1,838)
Williams, Bradley R	4:23:38	(16,761)
Williams, Brian G	5:02:03	(26,155)
Williams, Chad M	4:52:06	(23,966)
Williams, Chris A	3:11:41	(2,102)
Williams, Chris D	3:44:25	(6,823)
Williams, Christopher	5:05:32	(26,801)
Williams, Christopher	7:40:31	(35,175)
Williams, Christopher M	3:24:14	(3,476)
Williams, Christopher M	4:11:18	(13,428)
Williams, Christopher P	5:17:29	(28,713)
Williams, Clive T	5:10:42	(27,603)
Williams, Colin	3:43:37	(6,672)
Williams, Colin	3:46:52	(7,318)
Williams, Dafydd F	3:31:03	(4,613)
Williams, Dai	5:01:31	(26,069)
Williams, Daniel	3:53:19	(8,809)
Williams, Danny G	4:26:07	(17,482)
Williams, Darren P	2:42:05	(243)
Williams, Darren P	6:46:23	(34,641)
Williams, David C	3:58:41	(10,341)
Williams, David E	4:58:37	(25,472)
Williams, David G	4:39:10	(20,916)
Williams, David J	4:34:04	(19,583)
Williams, David T	3:57:17	(9,915)
Williams, Dennis R	4:54:50	(24,628)
Williams, Dennis S	3:16:04	(2,584)
Williams, Derek J	3:56:11	(9,571)
Williams, Derek J	3:59:44	(10,641)
Williams, Dominic M	5:21:21	(29,283)
Williams, Donald A	5:00:40	(25,915)
Williams, Dylan	3:51:31	(8,373)
Williams, Edward	4:42:22	(21,714)
Williams, Edward Ian	3:57:56	(10,123)
Williams, Frank A	6:20:05	(33,920)
Williams, Gareth	4:26:05	(17,469)
Williams, Gareth	4:36:50	(20,314)
Williams, Gareth	6:26:38	(34,146)
Williams, Gareth H	3:08:27	(1,753)
Williams, Gareth I	3:59:32	(10,582)
Williams, Gareth J	2:33:51	(101)
Williams, Gary	4:53:06	(24,199)
Williams, Gary	5:06:45	(27,008)
Williams, Geraint	3:27:01	(3,931)
Williams, Glen A	6:35:29	(34,395)
Williams, Graham J	2:47:46	(398)
Williams, Graham P	4:59:53	(25,752)
Williams, Grant C	4:57:59	(25,324)
Williams, Gwyn R	3:55:01	(9,241)
Williams, Harry	3:27:17	(3,973)
Williams, Haydn J	3:16:52	(2,665)
Williams, Iain	4:13:00	(13,878)
Williams, Ian	4:34:30	(19,711)
Williams, Ian	6:32:51	(34,325)
Williams, Iwan M	3:25:00	(3,583)
Williams, Iwan W	3:35:18	(5,224)
Williams, Jack	3:13:46	(2,335)
Williams, James H	4:01:08	(10,968)
Williams, James T	5:18:01	(28,788)
Williams, Jason M	2:43:05	(268)
Williams, Jason M	4:15:38	(14,617)
Williams, Jeremy M	4:40:58	(21,381)
Williams, Jim J	3:19:10	(2,896)
Williams, Jim R	4:12:07	(13,642)
Williams, John D	3:37:13	(5,525)
Williams, John W	5:14:51	(28,320)
Williams, Jonathan	4:17:11	(15,007)
Williams, Jonathan D	3:32:53	(4,868)
Williams, Jonathan D	4:19:56	(15,782)
Williams, Jonathan D	5:08:23	(27,268)
Williams, Jonathan M	3:57:41	(10,035)
Williams, Ken M	4:12:17	(13,692)
Williams, Kevin	4:42:26	(21,725)
Williams, Malcolm B	4:58:47	(25,506)
Williams, Mark	3:25:58	(3,748)
Williams, Mark	4:04:14	(11,691)
Williams, Mark K	3:05:12	(1,486)
Williams, Mark N	4:13:10	(13,928)
Williams, Mark P	4:06:50	(12,297)
Williams, Martin F	4:33:22	(19,400)
Williams, Martin J	3:14:19	(2,394)
Williams, Martin P	4:22:54	(16,579)
Williams, Matt O	4:04:18	(11,701)
Williams, Matthew D	3:28:50	(4,249)
Williams, Matthew D	5:14:01	(28,175)
Williams, Meirion	4:35:48	(20,042)
Williams, Meirion T	5:38:24	(31,237)
Williams, Michael	3:42:50	(6,514)
Williams, Michael	4:41:09	(21,432)
Williams, Neal R	4:08:17	(12,632)
Williams, Neil R	5:44:07	(31,771)
Williams, Nelson D	4:27:41	(17,947)
Williams, Nicholas R	3:22:47	(3,271)
Williams, Nick	5:24:33	(29,693)
Williams, Nigel	4:06:43	(12,270)
Williams, Owain L	4:24:36	(17,016)
Williams, Paul	5:01:37	(26,083)
Williams, Paul C	4:29:00	(18,306)
Williams, Paul D	4:58:09	(25,359)
Williams, Paul J	5:14:50	(28,317)
Williams, Paul M	3:55:16	(9,298)
Williams, Paul R	5:00:52	(25,953)
Williams, Paul R	5:15:26	(28,410)
Williams, Peter	3:32:27	(4,811)
Williams, Phil A	4:32:06	(19,109)
Williams, Philip M	6:50:55	(34,735)
Williams, Phillip T	3:19:07	(2,893)
Williams, Prys	4:21:14	(16,124)
Williams, Ray A	4:36:19	(20,168)
Williams, Ray G	3:13:45	(2,333)
Williams, Raymond	4:36:56	(20,339)
Williams, Red	3:48:23	(7,681)
Williams, Rhydian V	4:40:04	(21,151)
Williams, Rhys A	4:50:51	(23,703)
Williams, Richard K	4:59:00	(25,559)
Williams, Richard L	4:23:44	(16,788)
Williams, Richard P	4:20:21	(15,898)
Williams, Richard W	3:19:30	(2,937)
Williams, Robert E	4:42:41	(21,795)
Williams, Robin J	4:09:45	(13,029)
Williams, Shane F	4:25:52	(17,392)
Williams, Simon C	3:46:54	(7,330)
Williams, Stan	3:14:59	(2,480)
Williams, Stephen J	4:30:39	(18,760)
Williams, Stephen L	2:53:53	(679)
Williams, Steven	4:35:25	(19,955)
Williams, Steven Y	2:56:49	(874)
Williams, Stuart	4:35:36	(19,998)
Williams, Stuart J	4:45:52	(22,513)
Williams, Stuart M	2:55:16	(751)
Williams, Tim P	4:08:26	(12,681)
Williams, Timothy	4:58:27	(25,429)
Williams, Trevor	5:19:58	(29,091)
Williams-Gunn, Andrew	4:09:11	(12,882)
Williamson, Adrian E	3:39:02	(5,823)
Williamson, Alisdair G	4:03:59	(11,626)
Williamson, Andrew J	4:10:30	(13,227)
Williamson, Bruce G	3:00:42	(1,173)
Williamson, Colin	6:48:22	(34,682)
Williamson, David	5:11:26	(27,729)
Williamson, David F	4:00:27	(10,818)
Williamson, David M	3:27:10	(3,951)
Williamson, Gary J	4:20:01	(15,807)
Williamson, Ian D	4:28:43	(18,225)
Williamson, James A	3:52:37	(8,636)
Williamson, Keith	5:24:41	(29,708)
Williamson, Lee B	5:05:10	(26,718)
Williamson, Mark	3:23:24	(3,362)
Williamson, Neil R	4:35:30	(19,975)
Williamson, Neil R	5:23:39	(29,564)
Williamson, Nick	3:29:43	(4,397)
Williamson, Oliver R	4:59:10	(25,598)
Williamson, Paul	4:40:59	(21,385)
Williamson, Philip	4:05:47	(12,047)
Williamson, Tom R	3:50:03	(8,051)
Willingham, Edward	3:48:48	(7,788)
Willis, Bernard W	4:19:09	(15,562)
Willis, Crispin	3:40:22	(6,072)
Willis, David K	3:50:18	(8,104)
Willis, Gary S	3:50:57	(8,248)
Willis, James A	5:25:48	(29,842)
Willis, John A	4:11:56	(13,602)
Willis, Mark D	2:58:55	(1,025)
Willis, Matthew	4:34:41	(19,762)
Willis, Matthew J	2:53:32	(661)
Willis, Paul	4:31:09	(18,866)
Willis, Robert C	4:25:28	(17,273)
Willis, Roger T	5:26:11	(29,893)
Willis, Stephen	4:15:14	(14,511)
Willis, Tony N	5:34:24	(30,833)
Willis, Trevor	4:31:11	(18,879)
Willis Fleming, Sebastian J	3:50:42	(8,189)
Willmitt, William J	3:17:21	(2,718)
Willmott, Andrew G	4:06:30	(12,213)
Willmott, Ian	5:36:07	(31,005)
Willmott, Jon S	3:59:56	(10,705)
Willmott, Martin G	4:00:34	(10,857)

Willoughby, Stefan J	4:21:20 (16,155)	
Wills, Colin	5:34:08 (30,796)	
Wills, James	4:31:10 (18,876)	
Wills, Martin I	4:17:24 (15,068)	
Wills, Tim	4:07:27 (12,448)	
Willson, Anthony J	3:55:40 (9,416)	
Willson, Danny	4:24:54 (17,094)	
Willson, Darren J	4:42:39 (21,786)	
Willson, Nicholas M	3:42:06 (6,401)	
Willson, Spencer E	5:10:12 (27,528)	
Wills-Wilson, Graham S	4:58:23 (25,412)	
Wilmot, Andrew H	3:16:11 (2,602)	
Wilmshurst, Andrew P	2:55:16 (751)	
Wilsher, Tim A	4:34:13 (19,634)	
Wilsmore, Paul H	3:21:57 (3,180)	
Wilson, Alan	4:03:48 (11,576)	
Wilson, Alan	5:21:00 (29,236)	
Wilson, Alastair S	3:57:31 (9,988)	
Wilson, Alexander G	3:31:44 (4,708)	
Wilson, Andrew	5:05:16 (26,741)	
Wilson, Andrew G	3:31:35 (4,690)	
Wilson, Andrew P	3:58:52 (10,402)	
Wilson, Andrew R	4:34:36 (5,135)	
Wilson, Andy	3:26:29 (3,844)	
Wilson, Campbell	3:55:06 (9,256)	
Wilson, Christopher G	3:41:52 (6,348)	
Wilson, Christopher L	2:44:52 (315)	
Wilson, Craig	5:08:31 (27,287)	
Wilson, Craig W	4:40:49 (21,340)	
Wilson, Curtis	6:10:41 (33,560)	
Wilson, Damian R	3:32:05 (4,759)	
Wilson, David	4:31:16 (18,904)	
Wilson, David J	4:39:24 (20,989)	
Wilson, David W	4:56:33 (25,026)	
Wilson, Desmond A	5:52:23 (32,446)	
Wilson, Donough	6:09:25 (33,512)	
Wilson, Douglas J	6:38:55 (34,484)	
Wilson, Ewan R	3:47:29 (7,454)	
Wilson, Gary	4:29:58 (18,577)	
Wilson, Gary J	4:03:11 (11,427)	
Wilson, Gavin D	5:05:06 (26,700)	
Wilson, Geoffrey	3:08:30 (1,757)	
Wilson, Guy M	3:47:23 (7,434)	
Wilson, Iain A	3:07:37 (1,689)	
Wilson, Ian H	4:59:09 (25,593)	
Wilson, James M	3:40:42 (6,117)	
Wilson, Jamie R	5:13:50 (28,138)	
Wilson, John	4:32:53 (19,285)	
Wilson, John	4:52:34 (24,067)	
Wilson, John	5:29:22 (30,289)	
Wilson, John A	4:38:20 (20,704)	
Wilson, John B	4:26:10 (17,498)	
Wilson, Kenneth	3:48:16 (7,648)	
Wilson, Kevin A	5:49:15 (32,207)	
Wilson, Kevin P	3:54:00 (8,977)	
Wilson, Lee A	3:24:05 (3,456)	
Wilson, Lloyd J	4:11:22 (13,444)	
Wilson, Luke A	4:59:43 (25,717)	
Wilson, Marc	3:36:31 (5,430)	
Wilson, Mark A	4:39:59 (21,136)	
Wilson, Mark J	3:37:26 (5,564)	
Wilson, Mark T	4:08:49 (12,773)	
Wilson, Martin	3:29:00 (4,273)	
Wilson, Matthew G	5:26:41 (29,943)	
Wilson, Matthew L	5:10:26 (27,560)	
Wilson, Matthew R	4:52:01 (23,939)	
Wilson, Michael G	3:49:16 (7,883)	
Wilson, Mike P	4:07:18 (12,421)	
Wilson, Nick	3:06:39 (1,606)	
Wilson, Patrick	3:23:22 (3,359)	
Wilson, Patrick N	4:49:47 (23,444)	
Wilson, Paul J	3:26:31 (3,853)	
Wilson, Paul K	5:24:15 (29,653)	
Wilson, Paul S	6:31:12 (34,285)	
Wilson, Philip J	4:05:10 (11,916)	
Wilson, Rhydderch	3:54:01 (8,979)	
Wilson, Richard	4:49:41 (23,424)	
Wilson, Richard A	6:08:54 (33,482)	
Wilson, Richard V	4:30:30 (18,731)	
Wilson, Robert	2:48:45 (452)	
Wilson, Robert J	4:02:09 (11,195)	
Wilson, Robin F	4:43:16 (21,926)	
Wilson, Robin H	4:44:38 (22,233)	
Wilson, Rupert J	4:38:59 (20,871)	
Wilson, Samuel D	3:40:26 (6,077)	
Wilson, Shane	3:40:07 (6,019)	
Wilson, Stephen W	3:41:56 (6,366)	
Wilson, Steven R	5:28:26 (30,180)	
Wilson, Stuart	3:23:20 (3,355)	
Wilson, Thomas	4:12:54 (13,857)	
Wilson, Tom	3:35:54 (5,323)	
Wilson-Roberts, Michael J	3:45:24 (7,030)	
Wilton, Julian C	3:57:10 (9,880)	
Wilton, Philip J	4:00:03 (10,741)	
Wiltshire, John R	3:46:27 (7,232)	
Wiltshire, Lee M	4:02:54 (11,367)	
Wiltshire, Nicholas P	3:34:33 (5,128)	
Winch, Kevin E	4:21:37 (16,234)	
Winch, Kevin J	6:17:34 (33,842)	
Winder, Bill R	6:13:48 (33,694)	
Winder, David R	3:04:52 (1,459)	
Winder, Mark E	4:25:50 (17,383)	
Windle, Lee T	4:10:24 (13,204)	
Window, Anthony C	4:18:28 (15,354)	
Windridge, David F	4:17:22 (15,055)	
Windsor, John	4:33:44 (19,499)	
Windsor, John J	4:52:56 (24,156)	
Winehouse, Michael B	6:51:16 (34,743)	
Winfield, David J	3:57:09 (9,875)	
Winfield, Richard J	4:39:14 (20,942)	
Winfield, Steven P	3:26:13 (3,797)	
Wing, Gareth M	4:21:27 (16,190)	
Wing, Matthew D	4:01:11 (10,977)	
Wing, Stephen	6:08:29 (33,464)	
Winkler, Ruediger	4:50:40 (23,669)	
Winn, Matthew P	4:41:38 (21,552)	
Winning, David J	3:04:30 (1,426)	
Winning, Glen	3:25:14 (3,631)	
Winsbury, Mark W	3:52:19 (8,560)	
Winskell, Tim	4:18:47 (15,460)	
Winslet, Daniel J	4:24:11 (16,898)	
Winslet, Nick E	4:08:05 (12,587)	
Winslow, Michael P	4:06:42 (12,266)	
Winson, Dan	3:55:35 (9,401)	
Winsor, Peter K	3:56:37 (9,696)	
Winstanley, David N	4:39:23 (20,985)	
Winstone, Neil D	4:34:15 (19,649)	
Wint, Andrew	3:49:35 (7,948)	
Winter, Alan T	4:27:49 (17,987)	
Winter, Geoffrey P	4:26:50 (17,694)	
Winter, John R	4:01:59 (11,150)	
Winter, Mark J	4:41:43 (21,569)	
Winter, Martin	3:56:52 (9,775)	
Winter, Michael	3:44:36 (6,860)	
Winter, Richard J	4:17:33 (15,102)	
Winter, Robert J	3:51:03 (8,265)	
Winter, Thomas B	3:44:15 (6,792)	
Winter, Timothy	3:26:00 (3,757)	
Winter, Udo	3:45:20 (7,012)	
Winterbone, Ian M	4:59:53 (25,752)	
Winterbottom, Toby F	3:41:20 (6,247)	
Winterburn, Mark A	5:04:53 (26,666)	
Winterflood, David	4:22:41 (16,532)	
Winteringham, Paul M	4:12:55 (13,862)	
Winters, George M	4:44:08 (22,126)	
Winters, John T	3:45:07 (6,974)	
Winters, Stephen	5:23:34 (29,553)	
Wintershoven, Patrick E	6:03:24 (33,183)	
Wintle, Dave A	2:55:45 (791)	
Wintle, George	4:29:03 (18,326)	
Winton, Scott	2:17:01 (18)	
Wintour, Marcus	4:08:29 (12,690)	
Winwood, Craig	4:52:44 (24,111)	
Winzer, William G	4:24:20 (16,938)	
Wiquel, Dante	3:47:19 (7,419)	
Wire, Paul A	4:47:27 (22,875)	
Wirges, Thierry M	3:48:41 (7,757)	
Wirth, Wolfgang	4:41:05 (21,412)	
Wise, Nicholas D	3:53:17 (8,792)	
Wise, Roger S	5:10:16 (27,534)	
Wise, Seth D	4:47:37 (22,915)	
Wise, Stephen D	4:37:19 (20,451)	
Wisham, Wes	4:24:55 (17,096)	
Wishart, David R	4:13:42 (14,068)	
Wishart, James	5:41:53 (31,592)	
Wiskin, Mark S	4:45:38 (22,467)	
Witcomb, Alan R	3:55:45 (9,450)	
Withers, Andrew R	4:14:54 (14,412)	
Withers, David G	5:02:09 (26,174)	
Withers, Dominic P	4:22:31 (16,476)	
Withers, Donald W	6:16:58 (33,824)	
Withers, Gareth R	4:14:42 (14,346)	
Withers, Giselle F	4:39:09 (20,911)	
Withers, Paul J	3:39:28 (5,904)	
Witherstone, Matthew P	4:26:11 (17,503)	
Withinshaw, Warwick G	4:40:37 (21,289)	
Withouck, Serge	5:37:34 (31,150)	
Wittenberg, Derek B	5:38:03 (31,200)	
Wittering, Mark A	2:54:31 (715)	
Wittet, Pascal	3:25:37 (3,689)	
Witts, Graham P	4:37:56 (20,603)	
Witts, Nicholas K	4:27:37 (17,926)	
Wix, John J	4:16:04 (14,730)	
Wizard, Danny N	3:10:57 (2,026)	
Wojcik, Pieter J	3:56:26 (9,645)	
Wold, Richard L	3:24:57 (3,578)	
Woledge, William E	3:25:51 (3,730)	
Wolfe, Patrick	3:01:32 (1,223)	
Wolfendale, Stewart	3:41:31 (6,276)	
Wolff, David A	4:09:11 (12,882)	
Wolfgarten, Wilgried	5:42:47 (31,660)	
Wolger, James A	5:40:21 (31,452)	
Wollaston, Sam	4:17:05 (14,977)	
Wollington, Jason E	5:33:25 (30,708)	
Wolman, Merrick	5:00:46 (25,929)	
Wolovitz, Lionel	3:26:23 (3,824)	
Wolton, Peter H	4:44:29 (22,210)	
Wong, Chi H	4:47:54 (22,990)	
Wong, Kwan	5:36:50 (31,089)	
Wong, Michael	4:32:53 (19,285)	
Wontumi, Joseph A	5:23:27 (29,534)	
Wood, Adam J	3:51:12 (8,303)	
Wood, Alistair H	4:57:00 (25,128)	
Wood, Alistair M	4:08:32 (12,697)	
Wood, Andrew	3:20:17 (3,023)	
Wood, Andrew P	3:57:39 (10,027)	
Wood, Angus	4:34:44 (19,774)	
Wood, Benjamin D	3:34:44 (5,150)	
Wood, Brian E	3:55:28 (9,358)	
Wood, Christopher J	4:04:11 (11,678)	
Wood, Christopher M	3:38:16 (5,693)	
Wood, Colin	3:54:10 (9,019)	
Wood, Daniel N	4:03:46 (11,567)	
Wood, Dave	3:32:27 (4,811)	
Wood, David	5:36:24 (31,039)	
Wood, David A	5:13:26 (28,067)	
Wood, David J	4:39:30 (21,013)	
Wood, David M	4:17:49 (15,163)	
Wood, David S	4:52:13 (23,995)	
Wood, David T	4:21:32 (16,213)	
Wood, Derek J	3:41:03 (6,192)	
Wood, Douglas G	3:07:48 (1,699)	
Wood, Fred J	4:59:06 (25,586)	
Wood, Gareth D	3:08:09 (1,729)	
Wood, Gary R	3:28:47 (4,240)	
Wood, Gavin B	4:10:42 (13,267)	
Wood, Geoff P	4:14:38 (14,325)	
Wood, Graham R	4:07:12 (12,393)	
Wood, Ian D	3:24:22 (3,502)	
Wood, Ian S	5:14:40 (28,296)	
Wood, James J	4:38:45 (20,814)	
Wood, James M	5:01:23 (26,039)	
Wood, Jeremy C	5:40:02 (31,419)	
Wood, Jeremy R	3:56:09 (9,552)	
Wood, John M	4:09:07 (12,865)	
Wood, John R	3:34:34 (5,133)	
Wood, Marc A	5:27:20 (30,017)	
Wood, Mark S	5:59:12 (32,926)	
Wood, Mark T	3:10:47 (2,006)	
Wood, Michael	4:30:37 (18,750)	
Wood, Michael	4:43:07 (21,891)	
Wood, Michael A	4:21:12 (16,111)	
Wood, Nathan M	4:31:36 (18,997)	
Wood, Neil C	3:53:49 (8,938)	
Wood, Neil D	4:16:23 (14,817)	
Wood, Nick K	4:37:58 (20,610)	
Wood, Nigel G	5:02:04 (26,160)	
Wood, Nik	4:22:18 (16,421)	
Wood, Paul	4:20:47 (16,017)	

Wood, Paul W	5:09:14	(27,395)
Wood, Peter R	4:57:02	(25,138)
Wood, Peter T	5:06:27	(26,953)
Wood, Philip R	5:40:07	(31,431)
Wood, Richard C	3:08:49	(1,792)
Wood, Robert	6:50:00	(34,708)
Wood, Roy	4:49:04	(23,259)
Wood, Sam	4:59:35	(25,682)
Wood, Stephen J	5:48:09	(32,108)
Wood, Stephen L	4:40:17	(21,203)
Wood, Steve W	3:22:47	(3,271)
Wood, Steven C	5:43:23	(31,709)
Wood, Stirling M	6:28:09	(34,199)
Wood, Thomas J	3:12:19	(2,178)
Wood, Will	3:45:06	(6,972)
Woodall, Eric M	4:16:36	(14,862)
Woodberry, Dean T	5:40:59	(31,510)
Woodberry-Watts, Peter	5:29:58	(30,358)
Woodbridge, James P	4:28:53	(18,270)
Woodburn, James	4:19:28	(15,654)
Woodburn, Peter J	2:46:53	(368)
Woodcock, Brian	4:47:01	(22,774)
Woodcock, Jim	4:26:37	(17,636)
Woodcock, Kevin	3:39:40	(5,945)
Woodcock, Martin	4:10:23	(13,194)
Woodcock, Stephen	4:03:30	(11,498)
Woodford, Michael A	5:00:32	(25,881)
Woodgate, Paul J	5:13:10	(28,017)
Woodhead, John-Lee	4:45:04	(22,342)
Woodhead, Peter P	3:36:17	(5,387)
Woodhead, Stephen R	4:53:00	(24,174)
Woodhouse, Brian	4:13:17	(13,964)
Woodhouse, Christopher N	3:44:57	(6,949)
Woodhouse, Mark	4:08:44	(12,749)
Woodhouse, Richard J	3:56:37	(9,696)
Wooding, Peter D	4:06:17	(12,163)
Wooding, Stephen	3:57:51	(10,094)
Woodison, Graham J	4:00:40	(10,879)
Woodland, Mark	5:32:18	(30,590)
Woodley, David W	4:05:03	(11,878)
Woodley, David W	4:39:10	(20,916)
Woodley, James R	4:12:43	(13,809)
Woodley, Julian	5:45:39	(31,905)
Woodman, Anthony J	7:00:14	(34,872)
Woodman, Grant C	4:41:30	(21,523)
Woodman, John M	3:58:21	(10,243)
Woodman, Mark J	2:37:36	(147)
Woodman, William C	4:18:31	(15,364)
Woodman, William J	3:45:25	(7,037)
Woodroof, Alan R	4:30:59	(18,831)
Woodrow, Jonathan L	4:18:14	(15,273)
Woodruff, Andrew A	6:04:22	(33,235)
Woodruff, Jeffrey H	4:58:52	(25,527)
Woods, Alan G	5:13:51	(28,141)
Woods, Alec T	2:38:02	(160)
Woods, Andrew	3:59:05	(10,462)
Woods, Barry G	5:53:15	(32,520)
Woods, Carl A	3:29:07	(4,300)
Woods, Christopher	6:44:12	(34,602)
Woods, David	4:35:39	(20,005)
Woods, David J	5:26:31	(29,925)
Woods, Don W	3:39:51	(5,975)
Woods, Eric	5:32:15	(30,585)
Woods, Garry	3:29:38	(4,381)
Woods, Graham	7:38:34	(35,170)
Woods, Graham D	4:50:32	(23,636)
Woods, James D	4:30:23	(18,698)
Woods, Jason R	5:18:49	(28,922)
Woods, John D	5:34:23	(30,828)
Woods, John D	6:04:17	(33,231)
Woods, Mark R	5:23:47	(29,585)
Woods, Mark W	4:55:57	(24,888)
Woods, Michael	6:25:06	(34,100)
Woods, Paul W	4:55:57	(24,888)
Woods, Roger	4:25:48	(17,377)
Woods, Roger K	4:13:03	(13,894)
Woods, Simon	4:27:33	(17,906)
Woods, Thomas J	4:22:03	(16,356)
Woodthorpe, Andrew	6:08:15	(33,456)
Woodvine, David E	3:52:17	(8,551)
Woodward, Alex J	5:28:05	(30,115)
Woodward, Chad I	4:58:49	(25,515)
Woodward, Chris M	3:38:54	(5,793)

Woodward, Christopher	4:30:02	(18,600)
Woodward, Ian	4:21:02	(16,083)
Woodward, Keiron	7:02:56	(34,903)
Woodward, Kevin W	4:26:12	(17,508)
Woodward, Mark	6:16:06	(33,786)
Woodward, Michael	4:48:19	(23,077)
Woodward, Paul G	4:37:24	(20,472)
Woodward, Richard J	5:38:13	(31,224)
Woodward, Robert	3:50:28	(8,142)
Woodward, Robert A	4:29:24	(18,436)
Woodward, Stephen R	5:16:54	(28,624)
Woodward, Steve J	5:34:22	(30,824)
Woodward, Tristan D	4:54:44	(24,603)
Woodworth, James P	4:10:43	(13,271)
Wookey, David	5:21:14	(29,265)
Woolcott, Stuart E	6:01:19	(33,040)
Wooldridge, Peter R	4:51:41	(23,869)
Woolerton, Philip J	4:37:40	(20,539)
Woolf, Ian J	4:42:50	(21,830)
Woolgrove, David R	5:30:39	(30,427)
Woolhouse, John	6:06:43	(33,372)
Woolhouse, Michael G	3:55:00	(9,238)
Woolhouse, Neal	4:36:30	(20,228)
Woollard, Justin D	4:38:51	(20,840)
Wooller, John J	5:38:54	(31,296)
Woolley, Gilbert	4:24:26	(16,970)
Woolley, Martin	2:57:21	(909)
Woollon, Andy	3:35:27	(5,249)
Woolman, James	4:08:19	(12,645)
Woolmer, Alastair J	4:23:03	(16,612)
Woolmer, Timothy L	3:56:48	(9,753)
Wooloff, Geoffrey P	4:45:07	(22,357)
Woolrych, Simon J	3:52:07	(8,508)
Woon, Jayson M	3:55:51	(9,477)
Woonton, Stephen A	3:17:37	(2,749)
Woosey, Mark A	4:13:54	(14,112)
Wootten, Keith R	4:34:21	(19,676)
Wootton, Graham R	3:39:41	(5,949)
Wootton, Terence E	4:25:57	(17,413)
Worby, Martin	3:51:20	(8,336)
Wormald, John M	3:58:07	(10,171)
Worrall, Anthony G	4:06:59	(12,340)
Worrow, Jeff	3:42:27	(6,464)
Worsdell, Will	3:48:33	(7,727)
Worsfold, Davy T	4:49:39	(23,411)
Worsfold, Philip	4:14:44	(14,358)
Worsfold, Richard A	3:43:00	(6,549)
Worsley, Martin S	4:26:55	(17,724)
Worth, Byron K	4:09:05	(12,853)
Worth, Elliot	4:33:36	(19,465)
Worth, Philip G	3:54:41	(9,149)
Worthington, Brendan J	4:08:15	(12,628)
Worthington, Nicholas	5:26:14	(29,896)
Worthington, Paul	4:45:35	(22,453)
Worthington, Stephen	4:34:53	(19,819)
Worthington, Stuart W	3:59:31	(10,576)
Worthy, David S	5:03:19	(26,407)
Worthy, Ian	4:27:18	(17,825)
Wortley, Steve	5:49:39	(32,239)
Wotton, Mark A	4:38:56	(20,857)
Woznica, Maciej T	4:04:55	(11,843)
Wragg, Anthony A	4:33:38	(19,470)
Wragg, David A	4:58:43	(25,489)
Wragg, Robin G	6:43:48	(34,592)
Wrangle, Les J	3:01:35	(1,231)
Wray, Paul S	5:30:11	(30,381)
Wreglesworth, Edward	4:44:12	(22,142)
Wren, Colin J	3:43:35	(6,665)
Wren, Mark	3:44:54	(6,937)
Wren, Stewart K	5:16:17	(28,515)
Wrench, Benjamin M	4:49:54	(23,473)
Wrenn, Stuart A	4:05:53	(12,068)
Wride, Chris J	3:38:13	(5,682)
Wride, Robert	6:50:00	(34,718)
Wright, Adam G	3:54:58	(9,232)
Wright, Alan M	3:37:18	(5,536)
Wright, Alexander E	4:46:41	(22,704)
Wright, Andrew L	3:17:06	(2,689)
Wright, Andrew N	4:23:14	(16,661)
Wright, Andrew P	2:33:29	(98)
Wright, Andy	4:26:09	(17,492)
Wright, Anthony A	5:05:31	(26,798)
Wright, Anthony J	4:21:41	(16,252)

Wright, Benjamin N	4:22:19	(16,425)
Wright, Brian D	3:39:10	(5,843)
Wright, Christopher	5:00:29	(25,878)
Wright, Christopher J	3:56:48	(9,753)
Wright, Christopher P	3:55:28	(9,358)
Wright, Christopher P	5:35:59	(30,990)
Wright, Colin	4:08:18	(12,636)
Wright, Daniel J	4:38:03	(20,632)
Wright, David	4:10:28	(13,218)
Wright, David G	2:55:47	(792)
Wright, David J	4:00:50	(10,910)
Wright, David J	4:12:45	(13,817)
Wright, David J	4:19:44	(15,733)
Wright, David M	4:47:33	(22,891)
Wright, Felix J	4:20:22	(15,903)
Wright, Graham	5:37:24	(31,127)
Wright, John C	5:18:56	(28,934)
Wright, John S	5:28:06	(30,124)
Wright, John T	4:43:50	(22,061)
Wright, Jonathan C	5:58:44	(32,891)
Wright, Jonathan J	4:33:40	(19,477)
Wright, Joshua M	4:15:38	(14,617)
Wright, Justin J	4:16:38	(14,871)
Wright, Keith A	3:37:28	(5,575)
Wright, Kevin T	4:34:13	(19,634)
Wright, Lee W	4:39:09	(20,911)
Wright, Leon D	4:05:09	(11,914)
Wright, Mark D	4:12:19	(13,699)
Wright, Mark J	3:55:33	(9,385)
Wright, Martin	4:45:04	(22,342)
Wright, Matthew	4:58:03	(25,338)
Wright, Michael L	4:37:43	(20,559)
Wright, Neil D	3:45:44	(7,082)
Wright, Neil J	4:38:14	(20,678)
Wright, Nicholas J	5:55:12	(32,658)
Wright, Nick E	4:58:12	(25,375)
Wright, Noel N	3:58:12	(10,193)
Wright, Oliver	3:33:48	(5,008)
Wright, Oliver C	3:28:52	(4,256)
Wright, Paul P	4:07:48	(12,533)
Wright, Peter T	3:51:35	(8,386)
Wright, Philip	3:41:12	(6,215)
Wright, Phillip J	5:18:01	(28,788)
Wright, Robert	4:07:55	(12,557)
Wright, Robert K	4:40:12	(21,188)
Wright, Robin C	5:28:42	(30,207)
Wright, Russell I	5:19:27	(29,022)
Wright, Simon	4:10:15	(13,153)
Wright, Stephen	4:32:17	(19,158)
Wright, Stephen	7:10:25	(34,982)
Wright, Stephen G	4:23:43	(16,781)
Wright, Steve T	4:01:46	(11,104)
Wright, Steven F	4:56:40	(25,061)
Wright, Stewart J	6:02:23	(33,102)
Wright, Thomas	4:49:45	(23,438)
Wright, Timothy J	5:55:27	(32,675)
Wright, Wilton	3:52:56	(8,705)
Wrightson, John J	6:06:51	(33,383)
Wrigley, Henry	3:46:14	(7,188)
Wrigley, Joseph S	3:35:55	(5,324)
Wrigley, Mark	5:53:27	(32,531)
Wrigley, Matthew C	4:46:08	(22,585)
Wrind, Hans M	6:37:01	(34,433)
Wroth, James J	5:09:32	(27,442)
Wuensche, Gerd	3:48:44	(7,770)
Wuermli, Sam	3:06:35	(1,602)
Wyatt, Andrew D	5:40:17	(31,445)
Wyatt, Cliff L	3:49:18	(7,893)
Wyatt, Colin A	6:19:09	(33,894)
Wyatt, David R	4:55:23	(24,754)
Wyatt, Esmond J	4:05:58	(12,087)
Wyatt, George	5:11:48	(27,788)
Wyatt, Jon	3:49:59	(8,033)
Wyatt, Neil S	4:55:51	(24,862)
Wyatt, Norman	6:34:18	(34,362)
Wyatt, Philip	3:27:31	(4,025)
Wyatt, Philip	5:04:47	(26,647)
Wyatt, Robert P	4:51:45	(23,881)
Wyatt, Steve P	5:18:16	(28,831)
Wykes, Charlie F	5:23:33	(29,550)
Wylde, Andrew N	6:40:08	(34,510)
Wylder, Sebastian	4:59:11	(25,600)
Wylie, Colin A	5:02:20	(26,207)

Wylie, Mark J	3:59:29 (10,567)
Wylie, Matthew R	3:22:02 (3,191)
Wylie, Rick P	5:57:51 (32,827)
Wylie, Robert S	5:50:29 (32,297)
Wyllie, Alan E	4:45:36 (22,458)
Wymark, Andrew C	4:30:41 (18,765)
Wynarczyk, Raymond	5:27:30 (30,046)
Wynn, Eddie	4:07:04 (12,360)
Wynn, Richard D	4:13:03 (13,894)
Wynne, John H	5:11:16 (27,700)
Wynne-Hughes, Gareth R	4:19:47 (15,748)
Wynne-Jones, Owen	4:52:37 (24,080)
Wyre, Adam J	4:05:02 (11,871)
Wysocki, Edward J	4:04:45 (11,803)
Wyss, André	3:30:33 (4,538)
Wyss, Laurent	3:57:39 (10,027)
Yabandzhiru, Tsuyatko	5:54:34 (32,608)
Yadave, Rush L	4:03:53 (11,602)
Yamamoto, Katsuyuki	7:18:33 (35,066)
Yamamoto, Ryuji	3:44:57 (6,949)
Yamamura, Jun	5:26:03 (29,877)
Yanagawa, Masaoki	4:31:57 (19,073)
Yapp, Andrew W	5:38:19 (31,231)
Yard, David J	4:49:25 (23,342)
Yarde, Eddie	5:01:16 (26,019)
Yardley, Duane R	3:49:14 (7,872)
Yardley, Steve J	3:41:26 (6,266)
Yarnall, Mark E	5:51:52 (32,406)
Yarranton, David	4:09:30 (12,963)
Yarrow, Andrew J	3:27:39 (4,047)
Yarrow, Hugh W	3:51:18 (8,328)
Yarrow, Thomas J	3:38:59 (5,812)
Yates, Alan	3:28:44 (4,229)
Yates, Anthony J	4:02:40 (11,307)
Yates, Anthony J	4:34:06 (19,591)
Yates, David J	4:45:17 (22,390)
Yates, Jon	3:41:03 (6,192)
Yates, Michael B	4:14:12 (14,213)
Yates, Neil A	4:16:35 (14,854)
Yates, Philip	4:07:00 (12,343)
Yates, Richard B	4:01:24 (11,024)
Yates, Sean P	5:23:16 (29,514)
Yates, Simon R	3:53:12 (8,770)
Yates, Steven	4:31:54 (19,060)
Yau, Kinwo K	4:20:04 (15,817)
Yaxley, Edward W	3:26:16 (3,803)
Yazaki, Etsuro	3:06:57 (1,631)
Yeadon, Alexander J	4:22:39 (16,523)
Yeadon, Andrew	6:07:34 (33,420)
Yeates, Daniel R	4:42:36 (21,769)
Yeates, Harry S	3:55:59 (9,263)
Yeates, Keith	4:29:15 (18,379)
Yebra, José	4:18:03 (15,220)
Yee, David M	4:27:42 (17,951)
Yelding, Steven R	5:17:16 (28,684)
Yendall, Keith A	3:24:17 (3,480)
Yendell, Tim P	4:31:10 (18,876)
Yeoman, Chris H	4:39:53 (21,106)
Yeoman, Derek I	4:36:56 (20,339)
Yeoman, Justin	4:19:24 (15,636)
Yeoman, Mark	3:03:25 (1,356)
Yeomans, Michael R	4:19:57 (15,788)
Yeung, Chi-Wai	4:29:25 (18,439)
Yexley, John	4:31:07 (18,858)
Yianni, Nick	3:51:49 (8,445)
Yip, Tim	3:32:01 (4,751)
Yobera, Cyprian G	3:50:11 (8,081)
Yocum, Richard	5:28:05 (30,115)
York, Andrew P	4:14:15 (14,229)
York, David	5:38:09 (31,213)
Yoshida, Keigo	2:45:20 (331)
Youlden, James A	3:03:29 (1,363)
Young, Adam	3:57:22 (9,939)
Young, Alastair J	3:17:46 (2,762)
Young, Allan J	5:29:55 (30,352)
Young, Andrew G	4:14:47 (14,372)
Young, Barry	4:06:15 (12,154)
Young, Barry D	6:40:53 (34,521)
Young, Chris D	3:12:11 (2,163)
Young, Christopher A	4:10:39 (13,254)
Young, Christopher J	5:12:52 (27,980)
Young, Christopher R	3:41:37 (6,302)
Young, Clinton J	3:52:31 (8,609)

Young, Derek H	5:52:57 (32,493)
Young, Edward C	4:42:32 (21,747)
Young, George	5:23:08 (29,497)
Young, George E	4:46:43 (22,714)
Young, George E	6:40:18 (34,513)
Young, Harry S	4:26:23 (17,561)
Young, Ian	4:10:06 (13,115)
Young, James G	4:52:50 (24,134)
Young, John F	5:46:57 (32,012)
Young, Kevin	4:42:53 (21,847)
Young, Leon	3:53:18 (8,801)
Young, Malcolm W	4:23:48 (16,804)
Young, Mark D	3:23:18 (3,351)
Young, Martin	4:26:26 (17,580)
Young, Michael	4:13:32 (14,024)
Young, Michael M	3:57:12 (9,891)
Young, Murray V	7:23:15 (35,089)
Young, Neil J	5:44:55 (31,840)
Young, Paul W	4:11:48 (13,564)
Young, Peter F	4:13:35 (14,037)
Young, Peter W	4:45:15 (22,381)
Young, Philip	4:17:52 (15,174)
Young, Robert J	6:02:58 (33,141)
Young, Roy	4:12:13 (13,670)
Young, Simon K	3:42:19 (6,435)
Young, Stephen	5:24:09 (29,638)
Young, Stephen A	4:25:26 (17,262)
Young, Stuart B	4:28:28 (18,156)
Young, Stuart J	3:49:41 (7,976)
Young, Stuart J	5:11:54 (27,805)
Younge, Steven M	4:43:29 (21,974)
Youngs, George R	4:37:24 (20,472)
Youster, Tony E	5:20:47 (29,213)
Yoxall, Bill	3:27:38 (4,042)
Yoxall, Stuart	4:26:58 (17,745)
Yu, Kenny K	4:56:44 (25,078)
Yuill, Chick L	5:12:38 (27,934)
Yuill, Edward	4:11:55 (13,597)
Yuille, Robert	4:28:22 (18,129)
Yvard, Claude	4:11:55 (13,597)
Yvart, Alain	4:14:14 (14,220)
Yxne, Per E	3:41:50 (6,343)
Zabel, Joern	4:05:04 (11,882)
Zaheer, Imran	4:53:57 (24,411)
Zahler, Horst	3:36:25 (5,412)
Zamora, Daniel	3:52:16 (8,547)
Zanetti, John P	3:31:13 (4,634)
Zangrandi, Michele	4:42:04 (21,640)
Zaninelli, Gianfranco	3:42:14 (6,422)
Zanol, Giorgio	3:38:39 (5,745)
Zarri, John R	4:46:58 (22,765)
Zatyko, Donald R	4:25:34 (17,307)
Zebracki, Jaroslaw	3:43:42 (6,684)
Zech, Johann	3:53:25 (8,835)
Zeegers, Paul	5:12:02 (27,826)
Zeff, Daniel R	5:02:23 (26,216)
Zeglany, Jean-Marc	4:40:17 (21,203)
Zeitlin, Jonathan H	4:40:52 (21,352)
Zeller, Andrew Z	3:47:48 (7,525)
Zenato, Claudio	2:56:02 (808)
Zentner, Marcus O	3:35:21 (5,232)
Zhang, Zheng	5:33:31 (30,729)
Zidon, Kabiru	3:59:04 (10,456)
Zielinski, Konrad	5:37:50 (31,173)
Ziff, Alex L	3:39:28 (5,904)
Zillwood, Jason L	4:52:51 (24,140)
Zimmermann, Jean-Claude	3:27:44 (4,064)
Zimmermann, Jurgen P	3:38:52 (5,789)
Zimmt, Martin G	4:02:58 (11,383)
Ziolkowski-Evans, Paul R	5:29:53 (30,347)
Znetyniak, Mykolaj D	4:44:45 (22,262)
Zoll, Timothy E	6:26:54 (34,156)
Zollo, Andrew C	4:42:04 (21,640)
Zolty, Xavier	4:30:49 (18,799)
Zornoza, Agustin	3:26:22 (3,822)
Zottoli, Alessandro	3:26:34 (3,859)
Zoumides, John	4:17:58 (15,194)
Zuberi, Khawar R	3:15:43 (2,542)
Zucca, Nazario	4:04:46 (11,807)
Zuccardi-Merli, Gianluigi	2:55:31 (771)
Zuckerman, Jake M	4:06:56 (12,324)
Zurawlin, Paul A	3:28:55 (4,263)
Zwaenpoel, Karel	4:36:20 (20,172)

FEMALE RUNNERS

Aaron, Oghene	4:52:28 (24,045)
Abadzis, Natalie J	5:02:02 (26,152)
Abbott, Megan A	6:00:24 (32,997)
Abbotts, Marianna B	4:42:43 (21,804)
Abhyankar, Tay N	4:49:49 (23,454)
Abiad, Helen E	4:37:18 (20,445)
Abraham, Kirsten	4:20:41 (15,986)
Abraham, Maria E	3:59:58 (10,711)
Abrahams, Hilary	4:26:50 (17,694)
Abram, Elizabeth A	6:04:37 (33,250)
Abrams, Yvonne S	4:37:00 (20,357)
Ace, Clare J	4:59:35 (25,682)
Ackermann, Antoinette	5:24:15 (29,653)
Acott, Susan	4:44:24 (22,193)
Acton, Jane C	3:38:43 (5,757)
Adamou, Caroline	6:06:01 (33,330)
Adam-Reynolds, Sue L	5:13:15 (28,033)
Adams, Amanda J	4:56:20 (24,971)
Adams, Angela	4:59:29 (25,659)
Adams, Ann E	5:14:41 (28,301)
Adams, April	4:24:40 (17,032)
Adams, Eve L	5:33:25 (30,708)
Adams, Hazel R	4:27:15 (17,817)
Adams, Jane E	6:06:13 (33,342)
Adams, Jennifer L	5:29:03 (30,252)
Adams, Julie P	4:16:46 (14,907)
Adams, Linda	4:42:00 (21,627)
Adams, Polly H	3:28:05 (4,120)
Adams, Rebecca J	3:49:14 (7,872)
Adams, Samantha J	4:59:54 (25,759)
Adams, Victoria J	4:20:40 (15,981)
Adamson, Kathryn A	5:03:13 (26,387)
Adamson, Katie J	4:31:26 (18,951)
Adde, Annie C	5:50:58 (32,331)
Adderson, Emily C	5:09:21 (27,413)
Addison, Bernadette M	5:04:34 (26,608)
Addison, Christine E	4:26:56 (17,732)
Addison, Deborah I	4:06:22 (12,184)
Addison, Susan A	5:26:16 (29,898)
Adefajo, Bunmi R	4:45:22 (22,406)
Adeleye, Chantel O	5:19:35 (29,048)
Adeshara, Priti	6:26:50 (34,154)
Adey, Kate	4:18:36 (15,394)
Adkins, Louise Y	5:01:19 (26,031)
Adlam, Nicola	4:14:11 (14,207)
Adlard, Jane A	5:29:51 (30,345)
Adlum, Jane	4:28:07 (18,064)
Adriaanse, Julinda V	4:42:13 (21,683)
Aerchmann, Gaby	4:35:06 (19,873)
Afford, Suzanne N	5:20:20 (29,146)
Aftab, Fazilat-Jan	4:17:44 (15,147)
Aggett, Sian E	4:22:55 (16,585)
Agnew, Angela A	6:59:11 (34,855)
Agombar, Emma L	4:28:49 (18,254)
Agoro, Tayo	4:53:56 (24,402)
Agosti, Emanuela	4:07:00 (12,343)
Agostini, Fiorella	6:01:42 (33,065)
Aguilar-Stone, Shan E	3:47:47 (7,521)
Ahl, Lucie A	3:38:55 (5,798)
Ahlers, Dorotmee	4:55:30 (24,771)
Ahmed, Jusna	6:22:29 (34,007)
Aiken, Sian L	4:59:58 (25,771)
Ainge, Katie S	4:11:02 (13,361)
Ainslie, Samantha J	4:31:58 (19,078)
Ainsworth, Pat H	5:16:54 (28,624)
Aithfull, Donna M	7:21:24 (35,082)
Aitken, Claire L	5:16:52 (28,617)
Aitken, Dianne S	3:24:36 (3,527)
Aitken, Leila L	5:01:05 (25,994)
Aitken, Maryanne V	5:00:09 (25,803)
Aitken, Nicola A	3:10:25 (1,969)
Akehurst, Claire L	6:04:38 (33,251)
Akeroyd, Suzanne	3:20:51 (3,078)
Akhurst, Jennifer	4:33:01 (19,317)
Akin, Elo E	4:53:56 (24,402)
Al Lamee, Rasha K	4:48:14 (23,060)
Al-Bedri, Elaine	4:28:03 (18,043)
Alcorn, Janet A	6:14:23 (33,714)
Alder, Alice L	4:03:05 (11,406)
Alderson, Mark	6:15:26 (33,751)
Alderwick, Sally	5:06:27 (26,953)
Aldridge, Wendy J	4:12:36 (13,774)

Alexander, Helen A....4:10:05 (13,109)
Alexander, Jane....5:37:30 (31,142)
Alexander, Rachael H....4:55:02 (24,683)
Alexander, Sujatha J....4:55:07 (24,707)
Alexandrou, Tracey A....3:18:10 (2,797)
Allan, Dotty....4:35:40 (20,010)
Allan, Karen....5:20:27 (29,171)
Allan, Sarah J....5:00:55 (25,964)
Allaston, Alison J....3:54:03 (8,986)
Allcock, AS....5:23:23 (29,526)
Allcorn, Suzette....4:43:27 (21,964)
Allen, Angela M....6:26:02 (34,125)
Allen, Ashley H....6:12:29 (33,641)
Allen, Carla....3:56:26 (9,645)
Allen, Catherine J....6:01:57 (33,074)
Allen, Daphne I....5:25:03 (29,752)
Allen, Donna E....5:27:58 (30,097)
Allen, Donna M....4:33:44 (19,499)
Allen, Elisabeth J....4:25:37 (17,321)
Allen, Gill....7:09:10 (34,969)
Allen, Heather....3:48:48 (7,788)
Allen, Jennifer M....4:49:40 (23,422)
Allen, Joanna L....3:54:10 (9,019)
Allen, John F....6:03:05 (33,149)
Allen, Katie M....4:54:10 (24,463)
Allen, Lindsay H....4:16:01 (14,722)
Allen, Louisa E....5:09:24 (27,422)
Allen, Lucy D....4:55:00 (24,674)
Allen, Lynne....4:40:10 (21,175)
Allen, Mandy E....5:04:07 (26,541)
Allen, Marianne E....4:07:34 (12,467)
Allen, Sarah H....4:23:06 (16,631)
Allen, Sarah J....4:27:03 (17,759)
Allen, Susan M....4:37:44 (20,561)
Allibone, Tracey E....3:55:16 (9,298)
Allieri, Rossana....3:54:14 (9,029)
Allison, Julie....3:55:32 (9,376)
Allison, Kathleen M....5:24:47 (29,718)
Allison, Rachel M....6:15:28 (33,753)
Allison, Valerie....3:54:03 (8,986)
Allnutt, Louise....4:44:18 (22,169)
Almey, Helen L....5:16:48 (28,601)
Alton, Nina J....4:14:29 (14,290)
Alton, Tessa M....4:30:29 (18,722)
Alves, Virginia....4:40:32 (21,267)
Alves De Sousa, Sarah J....4:12:13 (13,670)
Alwis, Rosemary V....5:58:39 (32,887)
Amamoo, Rachel S....4:13:56 (14,125)
Amar, Marion....4:33:17 (19,377)
Ambler, Rebecca A....3:55:45 (9,450)
Ambler, Tracey A....6:12:45 (33,653)
Ambrosio, Lara....4:09:43 (13,016)
Amend, Samanatha....3:16:01 (2,577)
Amery, Jennifer E....5:17:28 (28,709)
Ames, Sara....5:34:56 (30,897)
Amos, Gina H....4:09:42 (13,012)
Amos, Vanessa J....6:08:36 (33,469)
Ampairee, Elizabeth E....4:30:25 (18,707)
Amrose, Wendy A....5:42:00 (31,597)
Anandakumaraswamy, Arani....7:02:46 (34,902)
Andersen, Kristin....3:59:20 (10,527)
Anderson, Carol A....5:30:22 (30,400)
Anderson, Carolyn L....6:57:14 (34,835)
Anderson, Cindy E....5:25:44 (29,829)
Anderson, Fiona J....4:37:12 (20,412)
Anderson, Hayley J....5:28:39 (30,204)
Anderson, Helen M....3:07:14 (1,650)
Anderson, Leanne M....6:46:31 (34,643)
Anderson, Louise....3:47:48 (7,525)
Anderson, Rachel....5:25:16 (29,775)
Anderson, Sally A....3:03:51 (1,392)
Anderson, Shanelle S....4:21:47 (16,280)
Anderson-Edward, Sarah E....3:53:48 (8,934)
Anderton, Fiona....3:43:36 (6,670)
Andrew, Sharon....4:36:55 (20,335)
Andrew, Susan L....3:14:11 (2,378)
Andrews, Amanda J....4:28:12 (18,085)
Andrews, Annalisa....4:39:28 (21,001)
Andrews, Carly H....3:53:09 (8,756)
Andrews, Claire....5:10:13 (27,530)
Andrews, Elizabeth....4:26:28 (17,590)
Andrews, Emma J....4:06:53 (12,311)
Andrews, Marie....5:26:13 (29,894)
Andrews, Maureen....6:42:22 (34,550)
Andrews, Penelope M....5:10:46 (27,610)
Andrews, Sarah....4:24:59 (17,117)
Andrews-King, Angela T....4:31:46 (19,038)
Angel, Melanie R....4:02:42 (11,315)
Angell, Lesley....4:26:24 (17,570)
Anghaee, Sholeh....4:42:33 (21,751)
Angus, Emily R....5:12:33 (27,919)
Annals, Jacqueline L....4:19:49 (15,756)
Annan, Amy E....3:17:37 (2,749)
Annetts, Elizabeth A....5:52:21 (32,443)
Annison, Heather K....6:45:12 (34,622)
Anscomb, Catherine M....4:45:26 (22,423)
Anscombe, Ann E....4:41:15 (21,460)
Ansell, Judith A....4:01:24 (11,024)
Anstee, Jessica....4:24:59 (17,117)
Anstey, Judith M....4:50:21 (23,579)
Antell, Helen O....4:49:07 (23,269)
Antonakas, Isabelle....4:24:37 (17,022)
Antoniou, Angela....6:44:31 (34,609)
Anwyll, Catarina C....4:39:01 (20,885)
Appleby, Helen J....5:23:01 (29,490)
Appleby, Melanie....4:32:30 (19,212)
Appleton, Andrea L....4:54:16 (24,492)
Appleton, Deborah J....2:42:24 (250)
Appleton, Linda....4:52:46 (24,119)
Appleton, Louise K....4:20:56 (16,061)
Appleyard, Sarah E....5:42:31 (31,628)
Apps, Tracey S....3:12:20 (2,179)
Apted, Kate L....3:49:40 (7,972)
Aquilina, Helen Y....6:18:23 (33,866)
Aranda, Nubia J....4:37:57 (20,606)
Aranki, Dima A....6:03:12 (33,160)
Arbery, Bethany C....4:04:54 (11,839)
Arcari, Lisa M....4:36:19 (20,168)
Archer, Emma J....2:51:36 (570)
Archer, Harriet L....3:35:57 (5,331)
Archer, Kate O....5:01:52 (26,118)
Archer, Melanie J....4:32:43 (19,250)
Archer, Nicole....3:11:38 (2,093)
Archer, Rosie....5:32:23 (30,603)
Archibold, Joyce....4:16:27 (14,828)
Arden, Victoria G....4:31:53 (19,059)
Argent, Patricia A....4:45:21 (22,401)
Ariff, Nicoli M....4:26:04 (17,462)
Arkinstall, Melissa....3:15:18 (2,504)
Armer, Sharon L....4:20:09 (15,840)
Armitage, Elise....5:02:38 (26,256)
Armitt, Margaret A....5:18:15 (28,828)
Armstrong, Elizabeth J....4:21:31 (16,211)
Armstrong, Helen J....5:33:30 (30,725)
Armstrong, Jessica....4:32:36 (19,228)
Armstrong, Karen R....6:21:36 (33,969)
Armstrong, Lucinda....4:52:18 (24,014)
Armstrong, Maja R....6:14:56 (33,731)
Armstrong, Miranda Y....6:03:19 (33,170)
Armstrong, Rosemary F....4:09:47 (13,035)
Armstrong, Susan E....4:35:39 (20,005)
Armstrong, Valerie A....5:05:28 (26,789)
Arnadottir, Bjorg....3:33:18 (4,928)
Arnold, Andrea A....4:21:13 (16,113)
Arnold, Jeanette C....6:33:11 (34,335)
Arnold, Louise E....6:27:05 (34,165)
Arrowsmith, Nicola J....5:48:18 (32,126)
Arsmtrong, Caroline W....4:39:23 (20,985)
Arthey, Carys L....4:58:05 (25,347)
Arthur, Zoe M....4:50:27 (23,612)
Asgeirsdottir, Svava Oddny....3:49:18 (7,893)
Asghar, Donna....3:52:53 (8,697)
Ashby, Karen L....3:41:07 (6,204)
Ashcroft, Cynthia....4:28:01 (18,034)
Ashdown, Cheryl D....4:13:48 (14,089)
Ashdown, Polly J....5:07:02 (27,061)
Ashdown, Sophie R....5:07:02 (27,061)
Asher, Carolyn J....5:24:58 (29,741)
Ashford-Smith, Paulette D....5:19:48 (29,076)
Ashley, Jo C....5:16:17 (28,515)
Ashley, Nicola K....4:12:04 (13,636)
Ashman, Claire E....5:00:09 (25,803)
Ashmore, Joanna C....3:39:28 (5,904)
Ashraf, Yasmin A....4:25:30 (17,286)
Ashton, Shirley L....3:48:22 (7,677)
Ashton, Susan....3:30:53 (4,588)
Ashworth, Tanya J....3:47:06 (7,372)
Askew, Hilary L....6:45:50 (34,626)
Askew, Zena L....6:09:50 (33,529)
Askwith, Celia....6:15:25 (33,750)
Aspinall, Suzanne J....5:48:43 (32,153)
Aston, Jennifer....3:57:07 (9,864)
Astor of Hever, Elizabeth....4:23:10 (16,647)
Asyhar, Anita....5:23:20 (29,519)
Atherfold, Karen....5:51:23 (32,362)
Atherton, Carolyn L....5:21:03 (29,244)
Atherton, Sereca L....3:26:52 (3,904)
Atiken, Gail I....4:25:14 (17,196)
Atkins, Heather K....4:37:55 (20,600)
Atkins, Jill E....4:57:24 (25,208)
Atkins, Michelle....5:01:56 (26,132)
Atkins, Rebecca J....4:55:00 (24,674)
Atkinson, Alison J....4:19:08 (15,558)
Atkinson, Darryl J....5:17:53 (28,768)
Atkinson, Elizabeth M....6:10:13 (33,539)
Atkinson, Fay....4:40:07 (21,157)
Atkinson, Fiona K....4:32:02 (19,098)
Atkinson, Jan M....5:39:58 (31,411)
Atkinson, Jan S....5:44:29 (31,801)
Atkinson, Janine M....4:41:03 (21,407)
Atkinson, Jessica J....4:23:45 (16,791)
Atkinson, Joanne....4:40:30 (21,259)
Atkinson, Sara L....4:36:15 (20,147)
Atkinson, Sarah....5:03:16 (26,397)
Attoe, Alyson J....6:03:09 (33,151)
Attrill, Patricia A....5:55:05 (32,645)
Attrill, Sarah L....4:52:47 (24,123)
Attrill, Victoria J....5:40:20 (31,447)
Attwell, Rachel....5:01:21 (26,035)
Au, Fiona S....4:29:30 (18,467)
Au, Lai Sze....4:59:02 (25,569)
Aubry, Véronique....4:36:04 (20,102)
Audenshaw, Ruth C....4:03:11 (11,427)
Auger, Shirley A....6:50:16 (34,729)
Augustinson, Lena....6:12:05 (33,621)
Aukofer, Renate....4:33:14 (19,366)
Auld, Susan....3:25:13 (3,627)
Aulsford, Elizabeth A....4:31:29 (18,965)
Aussenberg, Glenda J....7:59:06 (35,227)
Austen, Fiona....3:59:08 (10,479)
Austen-Brown, Sian E....3:51:36 (8,388)
Auster, Helen J....4:36:47 (20,298)
Austin, Elizabeth J....6:58:41 (34,847)
Austin, Jude A....3:33:49 (5,014)
Austin, Katie L....5:39:59 (31,415)
Austin, Lisa J....4:27:27 (17,869)
Austin, Sarah H....4:54:29 (24,550)
Austin, Teresa....6:31:45 (34,296)
Austin, Tina M....6:23:23 (34,035)
Austin, Una L....5:15:21 (28,394)
Avery, Sharon E....6:13:47 (33,691)
Avery Cornwall, June....4:14:02 (14,158)
Avey, Suzanne C....4:44:30 (22,214)
Axton, Louise M....6:02:45 (33,124)
Ayling, Joanne V....6:29:06 (34,222)
Ayodeji, Kim A....4:43:37 (22,015)
Ayrton, Michelle....7:07:21 (34,953)
Ayrton, Patricia M....5:14:18 (28,231)
Azzaro, Francesca....3:30:32 (4,533)
Azzolini, Arianna....3:46:41 (7,279)
Babb, Kim M....4:41:10 (21,439)
Babington, Amanda....4:58:15 (25,384)
Bache, Heather E....4:26:43 (17,667)
Bachert, Ina-Maria M....5:44:46 (31,825)
Bachmann, Lucy E....5:16:09 (28,498)
Backman, Gunilla I....3:55:33 (9,385)
Backstrand, Lena....5:03:47 (26,481)
Backus, Helen C....5:27:17 (30,014)
Bacon, Jessica C....4:25:28 (17,273)
Bacque, Patricia I....4:26:52 (17,706)
Badagliacco, Patrizia....3:21:44 (3,157)
Baerselman, Tessa A....4:21:24 (16,171)
Baettig, Petra....4:02:44 (11,329)
Baggio, Beverley....4:03:52 (11,598)
Baggott, Anne-Marie....5:43:44 (31,740)
Bagnall, Bridget C....4:46:04 (22,566)
Bagnall, Denise....5:40:30 (31,467)
Bagnall, Michelle A....6:11:41 (33,598)
Bahnam, Valerie....7:32:39 (35,149)

Bailey, Angela 5:29:00 (30,245)
Bailey, Anna 5:05:59 (26,868)
Bailey, Arabel E 4:07:39 (12,492)
Bailey, Caroline L 4:32:12 (19,134)
Bailey, Estina E 5:51:50 (32,400)
Bailey, Geraldine A 5:09:24 (27,422)
Bailey, Jayne L 4:58:44 (25,493)
Bailey, Joan V 5:18:01 (28,788)
Bailey, Leanne 4:35:46 (20,036)
Bailey, Lisa J 5:02:19 (26,206)
Bailey, Rowan I 6:31:42 (34,295)
Bailey, Sheila M 3:41:19 (6,238)
Bailey, Stephanie 4:13:28 (14,011)
Baillie, Susan E 5:05:24 (26,778)
Bainbridge, Alison L 5:44:03 (31,763)
Bainbridge, Jill 3:55:58 (9,508)
Bainbridge, Wendy E 5:04:34 (26,608)
Baines, Charlotte H 4:05:00 (11,862)
Baines, Jane 6:16:54 (33,820)
Baird, Karen 4:28:40 (18,206)
Baisley, Kathy J 5:07:16 (27,111)
Bajaj, Yogita 4:05:29 (11,983)
Bajaria, Sejal 4:49:47 (23,444)
Baker, Angela M 4:18:37 (15,399)
Baker, Anna R 5:45:45 (31,917)
Baker, Claire L 4:01:28 (11,041)
Baker, Deana E 4:14:45 (14,363)
Baker, Diane 5:18:28 (28,854)
Baker, Elizabeth C 4:24:23 (16,949)
Baker, Helen E 4:44:59 (22,321)
Baker, Joanne L 4:52:57 (24,158)
Baker, Kathryn C 4:52:48 (24,128)
Baker, Katrina M 5:31:26 (30,513)
Baker, Kirstin J 3:38:14 (5,684)
Baker, Louisa J 6:23:49 (34,052)
Baker, Louise 3:55:11 (9,273)
Baker, Louise G 4:38:06 (20,648)
Baker, Pauline A 5:19:49 (29,078)
Baker, Rachel 5:27:21 (30,021)
Baker, Sally H 3:02:07 (1,270)
Baker, Vivien L 4:52:52 (24,143)
Bakker, Claire F 4:37:58 (20,610)
Balance, Anna C 3:54:16 (9,038)
Balani, Jayshree 5:30:46 (30,439)
Balding, Anna 6:16:13 (33,795)
Baldock, Emily 4:13:48 (14,089)
Baldwin, Elizabeth A 4:22:32 (16,482)
Baldwin, Laura 5:18:38 (28,895)
Baldwin, Nicola J 6:19:13 (33,896)
Baldwin, Sophie J 5:02:50 (26,301)
Bales, Rowena J 3:15:22 (2,510)
Balfour, Jacky L 3:42:23 (6,448)
Balfour-Lynn, Leslie S 4:29:42 (18,520)
Ball, Amelia 4:12:21 (13,713)
Ball, Ann 4:22:49 (16,562)
Ball, Catherine J 4:38:55 (20,853)
Ball, Elizabeth L 6:25:49 (34,119)
Ball, Joanna E 3:14:45 (2,453)
Ball, Juliet 4:42:52 (21,838)
Ball, Lorraine M 5:04:40 (26,623)
Ball, Sarah L 5:14:51 (28,320)
Ball, Valarie G 4:08:29 (12,690)
Ballantyne, Jane 4:59:01 (25,565)
Ballard, Angela M 4:52:49 (24,131)
Ballard, Kathryn J 6:00:53 (33,023)
Ballard, Sue A 5:27:09 (29,992)
Ballinger, Nicola J 4:00:58 (10,941)
Bamber, Adela J 4:35:21 (19,931)
Bamford, Joanna L 4:42:57 (21,860)
Bamforth, Tracy J 4:13:50 (14,101)
Bamlett, Ara K 4:31:09 (18,866)
Banaghan, Glenda J 3:08:55 (1,802)
Bancroft, Karen A 5:42:53 (31,670)
Bancroft, Trish 3:46:48 (7,306)
Bandyopadhyay, Bidisha 6:02:49 (33,128)
Bane, Deony A 4:46:36 (22,688)
Bangsgaard, Eva 4:33:46 (19,513)
Banks, Angela L 3:38:23 (5,709)
Banks, Christine M 4:23:40 (16,766)
Banks, Claire J 4:09:50 (13,049)
Banks, Faye M 3:04:38 (1,439)
Banks, Samantha A 4:50:58 (23,726)
Bannink, Roniek 4:38:03 (20,632)
Bannister, Mandy 4:29:05 (18,334)
Bannister, Olive A 5:37:52 (31,178)
Bansal, Balwinder 5:24:06 (29,629)
Banszky, Elaine C 4:20:34 (15,954)
Baptiste, Alison 4:51:06 (23,751)
Barber, Fidelma J 7:00:34 (34,878)
Barber, Lyndsey H 5:01:28 (26,058)
Barboni, Lucie J 4:05:31 (11,991)
Barbour, Louise T 5:12:43 (27,953)
Barde, Christine 4:27:02 (17,755)
Bareham, Jennifer S 5:19:22 (29,002)
Bareille-St-Gaudens, Anne 4:06:47 (12,283)
Barford, Lorna J 4:56:16 (24,955)
Bargetto, Vanya 5:28:17 (30,164)
Bargh, Janet 4:50:13 (23,539)
Barker, Ann L 3:23:42 (3,402)
Barker, Jessie 3:42:19 (6,435)
Barker, Joanne M 5:19:30 (29,032)
Barker, Katie A 5:26:17 (29,901)
Barker, Pauline 5:53:38 (32,540)
Barker, Penny 3:38:02 (5,653)
Barker, Penny M 4:05:06 (11,897)
Barker, Ros J 3:16:31 (2,636)
Barker, Rosamund A 3:35:53 (5,320)
Barkman, Sally L 4:37:48 (20,580)
Barley, Julie A 3:07:25 (1,667)
Barlow, Alana M 4:35:30 (19,975)
Barlow, Amanda J 4:25:10 (17,172)
Barlow, Hazel G 5:30:21 (30,399)
Barlow, Jo 4:32:01 (19,093)
Barlow, Julie A 5:26:16 (29,898)
Barlow, Sally 4:01:42 (11,091)
Barltrop, Julia F 3:11:03 (2,038)
Barmby, Lois R 4:36:55 (20,335)
Barnard, Emma 6:55:18 (34,805)
Barnard, Heidi 4:38:57 (20,860)
Barnard, Shirley 5:52:57 (32,493)
Barnard, Susan E 4:54:33 (24,566)
Barnes, Debra A 6:14:14 (33,708)
Barnes, Eileen 5:10:28 (27,565)
Barnes, Emma 5:02:00 (26,143)
Barnes, Emma J 5:16:42 (28,578)
Barnes, Geraldine R 4:25:36 (17,315)
Barnes, Jane 4:20:16 (15,879)
Barnes, Jane J 6:04:24 (33,237)
Barnes, Jayne 3:49:47 (7,996)
Barnes, Nicola E 6:03:02 (33,145)
Barnes, Sue E 3:32:00 (4,748)
Barnes, Victoria 5:49:49 (32,246)
Barnes, Wendy A 3:35:26 (5,245)
Barnett, Claire E 4:06:11 (12,137)
Barnett, Hannah E 4:32:52 (19,279)
Barnett, Marion H 7:54:14 (35,222)
Barnett, Rebecca E 4:00:41 (10,883)
Barnett, Sarah L 5:38:57 (31,303)
Barnett, Tracy D 4:49:29 (23,355)
Barnfather, Nicola A 4:29:35 (18,491)
Barningham, Rebecca 3:51:51 (8,454)
Baron, Lorrain A 3:38:57 (5,807)
Barr, Evelyn 4:35:02 (19,860)
Barras, Sylvie E 5:03:45 (26,470)
Barratt, Anne 4:57:08 (25,161)
Barratt Smith, Angela S 3:48:27 (7,692)
Barre, Mylene 5:45:57 (31,928)
Barrell, Erica M 5:49:08 (32,192)
Barrett, Fiona C 4:42:52 (21,838)
Barrett, Linda J 4:06:23 (12,186)
Barrett, Lisa 4:37:10 (20,405)
Barrett, Lyndsay M 4:58:54 (25,536)
Barrett, Tracy 7:03:07 (34,906)
Barrett-Small, Elizabeth 5:38:12 (31,221)
Barrington Prowse, Melissa K 4:10:00 (13,092)
Barron, Amanda N 4:06:03 (12,107)
Barron, Hayley 3:51:07 (8,288)
Barron, Leigh E 4:36:44 (20,289)
Barron, Leonie K 4:15:35 (14,603)
Barrow, Michelle 5:20:01 (29,098)
Barrow-Green, June E 3:28:20 (4,164)
Barry, Amrie 5:52:11 (32,423)
Barry, Kay M 5:14:36 (28,279)
Barry, Maire N 5:12:46 (27,963)
Barsham, Hester R 5:51:44 (32,392)
Barter, Laura M 4:21:24 (16,171)
Barthel, Nelia 4:52:03 (23,948)
Bartholomew, Anna L 4:45:11 (22,369)
Bartholomew, Jayne C 8:03:01 (35,235)
Bartlett, Caroline M 4:52:48 (24,128)
Bartlett, Jackie A 4:14:22 (14,263)
Bartlett-Haynes, Kelly 5:05:44 (26,831)
Bartley, Maureen A 5:30:26 (30,408)
Barton, Frances C 5:53:07 (32,512)
Barton, Keely J 5:58:11 (32,855)
Barton, Tamsyn S 4:49:16 (23,296)
Bartram, Helen 4:25:06 (17,152)
Barty, Susan C 4:17:35 (15,110)
Barwell, Lorraine 4:35:11 (19,884)
Basic, Selma 5:28:37 (30,200)
Baskin, Tracy 6:05:28 (33,293)
Basquette, Rebekah 6:13:15 (33,670)
Bass, Irenie R 4:48:06 (23,031)
Bass, Josephine A 6:05:50 (33,317)
Bass, Nina J 4:59:11 (25,600)
Bassett, Alison F 4:39:30 (21,013)
Bassett, Sam J 5:07:30 (27,147)
Basu, Bulbul 5:30:44 (30,436)
Batchelor, Emma R 5:17:54 (28,771)
Batchelor, Julie W 4:12:36 (13,774)
Batchelor, Mary 3:47:06 (7,372)
Bateman, Hannah M 3:22:24 (3,233)
Bates, Catherine E 4:45:30 (22,432)
Bates, Claire L 3:42:56 (6,531)
Bates, Jane 4:36:17 (20,156)
Bates, Patricia M 5:44:41 (31,820)
Bates, Tracy A 5:19:39 (29,054)
Bates, Wendy J 4:49:35 (23,381)
Bath, Ann 3:51:09 (8,294)
Batson, Hannah R 6:09:40 (33,522)
Batt, Sarah L 4:16:35 (14,854)
Batt-Rawden, Linda A 6:05:36 (33,300)
Battson, Alexandra 5:12:13 (27,857)
Batty, Jane 3:16:48 (2,664)
Batty, Mia A 4:56:26 (24,996)
Bauckham, Nicky J 5:16:55 (28,629)
Baverstock, Antonia J 4:42:15 (21,689)
Baws, Rachel 5:05:24 (26,778)
Baxandall, Helen M 5:42:53 (31,670)
Baxter, Rebecca M 5:04:36 (26,612)
Baxter, Wendy S 4:44:26 (22,201)
Bayer, Leila R 4:42:51 (21,833)
Bayley, Jean 5:36:00 (30,992)
Baylis, Isobel 5:10:43 (27,604)
Baylis, Sarah 5:09:23 (27,417)
Baylis, Susan A 4:07:45 (12,516)
Bayliss, Deborah M 5:17:33 (28,726)
Bcbride, Catherine M 3:42:32 (6,472)
Beacham, Margaret E 5:39:21 (31,360)
Beal, Andrea M 5:12:01 (27,825)
Beale, Katie S 4:52:08 (23,972)
Bean, Christine M 5:27:49 (30,077)
Beardmore, Ange E 3:32:13 (4,777)
Beardmore, Donna M 3:18:10 (2,797)
Beardon, Sarah J 4:48:04 (23,024)
Beardshaw, Victoria L 5:24:37 (29,698)
Beardsmore, Julie E 5:29:50 (30,341)
Beardsmore, Nicola 4:36:54 (20,331)
Beare, Beth J 4:18:54 (15,483)
Bearman-Hayes, Sherrie-Ann 4:27:07 (17,780)
Beasley, Claire 6:05:35 (33,299)
Beasley, Debbie M 4:39:43 (21,070)
Beaton, Catherine E 6:22:26 (34,006)
Beattie, Michelle C 6:27:04 (34,162)
Beattie, Rachel C 5:06:33 (26,976)
Beaudoin, Jocelyne R 4:27:29 (17,884)
Beaumont, Eleanor L 4:01:45 (11,101)
Beavis, Birgitta S 4:35:49 (20,047)
Beazley, Sarah 5:54:43 (32,614)
Bebb, Kate E 3:43:44 (6,690)
Beckwith, Clare 4:45:00 (22,325)
Beckwith, Joanna L 4:25:18 (17,217)
Beckwith, Louise A 4:42:10 (21,670)
Beddard, Lorraine J 6:34:08 (34,359)
Beddoes, Yvonne J 4:13:32 (14,024)
Beddows, Marie P 4:27:04 (17,765)
Bedford, Suzanne J 3:56:22 (9,623)
Bedford, Vivienne E 5:41:29 (31,551)
Beecher, Sarah Lee 3:52:12 (8,526)

Beeching, Nichola A 6:03:11 (33,155)
Beecroft, Hayley C 6:08:39 (33,472)
Beecroft, Janet 4:19:04 (15,537)
Beecroft, Tarnya L 5:41:46 (31,575)
Beedham, Emily J 3:59:59 (10,724)
Beedham, Sue W 5:51:44 (32,392)
Beeke, Vikki C 5:00:11 (25,813)
Beeley, Jane 4:41:45 (21,578)
Beeson, Semirah 3:40:38 (6,108)
Begley, Carol J 6:40:54 (34,523)
Begley, Elizabeth A 5:39:23 (31,365)
Begum, Fatima 5:15:12 (28,369)
Beilby, Jayne C 4:21:47 (16,280)
Beith, Clare 5:37:43 (31,159)
Bekkers, Sarah 3:51:40 (8,405)
Belbin, Zoe N 5:33:26 (30,714)
Belcher, Joanne 3:41:37 (6,302)
Bell, Emily H 4:48:57 (23,224)
Bell, Fiona C 4:12:36 (13,774)
Bell, Helen L 5:04:18 (26,570)
Bell, Janet A 5:09:44 (27,475)
Bell, Jean A 5:44:08 (31,774)
Bell, Julia 6:03:45 (33,204)
Bell, Julia E 5:17:44 (28,745)
Bell, Julie D 4:31:11 (18,879)
Bell, Karen 4:37:29 (20,494)
Bell, Kate M 3:38:31 (5,729)
Bell, Katie 4:25:31 (17,290)
Bell, Lesli N 3:39:33 (5,923)
Bell, Lily E 6:37:20 (34,439)
Bell, Mary 5:41:01 (31,515)
Bell, Rachael S 3:50:56 (8,245)
Bell, Renée A 5:17:44 (28,745)
Bell, Serina K 3:36:14 (5,378)
Bell, Sheree S 4:38:49 (20,833)
Bell, Shona E 4:12:37 (13,781)
Bell, Susan 5:03:03 (26,350)
Bellamy, Ellen V 5:34:59 (30,902)
Belli, Sonia 3:59:52 (10,688)
Bellis, Julia 4:24:51 (17,085)
Bendeaux, Jill K 5:11:38 (27,760)
Bender, Melissa J 4:30:05 (18,615)
Benfield, Dianne M 5:27:56 (30,094)
Benger, Helen S 4:17:07 (14,991)
Benjamin, Floella 5:00:16 (25,838)
Benjamin, Kathleen E 6:16:47 (33,812)
Bennett, Christine 5:07:02 (27,061)
Bennett, Emma 6:29:36 (34,244)
Bennett, Georgina C 5:15:39 (28,440)
Bennett, Gillian C 5:19:19 (28,993)
Bennett, Helen 5:28:03 (30,109)
Bennett, Jane E 5:05:15 (26,738)
Bennett, Jennifer A 4:44:51 (22,285)
Bennett, Juliet D 4:31:16 (18,904)
Bennett, Linda 6:03:27 (33,184)
Bennett, Mandy J 5:57:27 (32,802)
Bennett, Michelle J 4:18:37 (15,399)
Bennett, Natalie 5:25:07 (29,763)
Bennett, Paula G 4:26:16 (17,521)
Bennett, Susan 4:09:53 (13,063)
Bennett-Hornsey, Lindsay 3:56:40 (9,714)
Benson, Catherine A 5:50:21 (32,290)
Bensouda, Nadia 3:59:56 (10,705)
Benstead, Amanda M 3:35:36 (5,279)
Benstead, Anne F 4:53:29 (24,297)
Benstead, Jane T 4:40:50 (21,346)
Bent, Angela M 3:42:02 (6,385)
Bentley, Theresa M 6:20:14 (33,928)
Benzinra, Ruth E 5:35:36 (30,959)
Beresford, Deborah A 4:17:06 (14,982)
Beresford, Lesley A 5:16:17 (28,515)
Berg, Jane C 4:57:20 (25,199)
Berger, Bertha 4:31:06 (18,853)
Bergevin, Anne 4:00:51 (10,913)
Berho, Gabriela L 3:45:43 (7,080)
Bernard, Lisa A 6:49:43 (34,703)
Bernhard, Bettina 4:41:58 (21,617)
Berrill, Anna 5:05:56 (26,858)
Berriman, Pamela P 4:11:06 (13,381)
Berrisford, Sandra 6:11:03 (33,575)
Berry, Caroline G 5:35:24 (30,947)
Berry, Catherine E 4:42:37 (21,776)
Berry, Cheryle J 6:34:27 (34,364)
Berry, Rosie 4:36:35 (20,243)
Berry, Ruth E 5:55:41 (32,693)
Berry, Samantha L 3:38:33 (5,732)
Berry, Vicky 4:38:59 (20,871)
Berwick, Helen D 5:37:23 (31,125)
Besley, Sally H 3:49:09 (7,854)
Besley, Siobhan 4:59:28 (25,655)
Besson, Lesley 4:20:55 (16,055)
Best, Emma E 5:16:42 (28,578)
Beteta, Patricia 3:47:48 (7,525)
Bethell, Dawn A 6:08:52 (33,481)
Bethune, Deirdre 3:53:41 (8,904)
Bettinson, Tracy 5:58:52 (32,902)
Betts, Helen 4:56:45 (25,083)
Beusch, Doris 3:46:35 (7,258)
Bevan, Helen J 5:06:53 (27,039)
Bevan, Joanne K 5:45:15 (31,875)
Beverley, Ruth R 4:51:59 (23,932)
Beverly, Cecilia B 4:48:40 (23,162)
Bevers, Emily C 5:03:57 (26,509)
Bevitt, Debbie M 6:37:41 (34,446)
Beyer, Jacqui G 5:49:18 (32,211)
Beynon, Juli 5:14:37 (28,283)
Bhatia, Gitty 5:00:12 (25,820)
Bhatt, Bhavna K 6:16:02 (33,780)
Biagioni, Lea 4:30:45 (18,784)
Biagioni, Paula A 4:45:58 (22,544)
Bibby, Caroline L 4:16:44 (14,898)
Bickell, Susan J 5:51:29 (32,372)
Bickerstaffe, Kate 4:04:41 (11,790)
Bicknell, Elizabeth 3:22:26 (3,236)
Biddiscombe, Sarah-Jane 4:34:06 (19,591)
Bidnell, Alison J 4:59:25 (25,647)
Bidston, Janet E 4:14:21 (14,257)
Bidston, Joanna H 3:39:49 (5,967)
Bielby, Jayne E 4:20:35 (15,958)
Biersani, Germana 5:35:43 (30,970)
Biggar, Alison J 3:48:44 (7,770)
Biggins, Sally E 4:29:00 (18,306)
Biggs-Hayes, Rachel L 4:45:35 (22,453)
Bigley, Venetia H 4:04:21 (11,712)
Bignell, Helena J 7:46:41 (35,199)
Bilcock, Heather M 4:19:40 (15,714)
Biles, Sonya 4:30:38 (18,755)
Bilgore, Sarah E 4:31:55 (19,064)
Billingham, Kim 4:36:11 (20,125)
Billson, Jackie L 6:50:04 (34,722)
Bilton, Jacqueline A 5:29:26 (30,297)
Binks, Susan E 4:16:30 (14,836)
Binks, Yvonne A 4:33:57 (19,557)
Binnendijk, Judy A 4:29:59 (18,583)
Binnington, Yvonne J 4:39:44 (21,077)
Binns, Sam 6:11:49 (33,605)
Birch, Annie M 4:00:34 (10,857)
Birch, Carole 5:05:02 (26,690)
Birch, Claire L 4:43:54 (22,070)
Birch, Francesca F 5:59:30 (32,949)
Birch, Hayley L 3:57:33 (9,999)
Birch, Jan 5:59:30 (32,949)
Bircham, Emma 6:34:48 (34,377)
Bird, Alice E 5:27:26 (30,034)
Bird, Christina 3:34:24 (5,110)
Bird, Emma L 5:09:40 (27,467)
Bird, Marion M 5:39:22 (31,363)
Bird, Nicola E 2:54:10 (696)
Bird, Norma 3:55:33 (9,385)
Bird, Rachel J 4:03:01 (11,393)
Bird, Sara N 5:49:55 (32,255)
Birkett, Joanne M 4:15:09 (14,491)
Birmingham, Sarah L 5:41:48 (31,578)
Birnie, Helen S 4:20:38 (15,975)
Birt, Louise H 4:20:34 (15,954)
Birtwistle, Esther G 5:14:36 (28,279)
Bishop, Cath J 4:06:49 (12,288)
Bishop, Clare D 4:40:09 (21,171)
Bishop, Louise S 4:28:20 (18,117)
Bishop, Lucy J 4:24:12 (16,901)
Bishop, Maria 5:54:02 (32,569)
Bishop, Nicola H 4:39:22 (20,980)
Bishop, Pauline B 3:57:54 (10,110)
Bishop, Rachel E 5:11:48 (27,788)
Bishop, Sam 5:04:05 (26,527)
Bishop, Stephanie R 3:19:59 (2,994)
Bishopp, Sara 3:01:09 (1,199)
Bisiker, Jane 4:10:54 (13,317)
Bissett, Debra J 5:01:25 (26,045)
Bissett, Pauline E 4:38:43 (20,803)
Bithray, Linda J 5:00:48 (25,935)
Black, Catriona F 4:12:47 (13,832)
Black, Helen 4:42:55 (21,855)
Black, Krisztina 6:14:49 (33,728)
Black, Maggie 4:58:27 (25,429)
Black, Nancy R 5:05:54 (26,853)
Black, Rachelle J 6:24:39 (34,079)
Black, Susan 3:29:49 (4,423)
Blackbourn, Ann E 5:33:46 (30,756)
Blacker, Renate C 4:33:07 (19,346)
Blackford, Lindsey J 4:44:09 (22,129)
Blackley, Heather W 5:37:30 (31,142)
Blacklock, Julie 5:08:08 (27,243)
Blackman, Melanie J 3:27:26 (4,005)
Blackmore, Ruth C 4:39:32 (21,022)
Blackmore, Sue C 5:11:30 (27,738)
Blackmore, Teila J 4:59:46 (25,730)
Blagden, Emma 5:13:14 (28,029)
Blair, Amanda J 5:33:31 (30,729)
Blair, Cindy R 5:24:49 (29,721)
Blair, Liz 4:10:50 (13,298)
Blake, Ann-Marie T 3:58:42 (10,347)
Blake, Emma J 5:29:52 (30,346)
Blake, Emma L 5:03:56 (26,507)
Blake, Sarah L 3:27:39 (4,047)
Blake, Susan E 4:30:29 (18,722)
Blakeham, Lesley A 4:25:42 (17,345)
Blakeley, Marie E 6:12:41 (33,651)
Blakey, Jean M 6:06:04 (33,332)
Blakey, Karen 5:55:06 (32,646)
Blakey, Kate L 3:54:13 (9,025)
Blanchard, Tracie J 5:51:09 (32,349)
Bland, Debbie L 3:57:23 (9,945)
Bland, Monique F 4:25:33 (17,302)
Bland, Sarah C 4:38:29 (20,756)
Bland, Thelma D 7:13:40 (35,023)
Blandford, Nicola J 3:37:43 (5,605)
Blandford, Sarah L 7:06:27 (34,943)
Blatchford, Isla K 7:42:25 (35,184)
Blatchly, Julia C 4:50:27 (23,612)
Blattler, Norma L 5:44:40 (31,816)
Blaylcok, Maggie A 5:51:57 (32,410)
Bleasdale, Kathleen V 6:32:13 (34,308)
Blenkinsop, Mandy S 3:45:45 (7,086)
Blewett, Lindsey 4:04:25 (11,724)
Blizard, Sarah K 4:47:24 (22,856)
Block, Doreen 3:46:20 (7,209)
Blofield, Janice M 5:24:26 (29,674)
Blomefield, Georgina G 5:26:10 (29,890)
Bloom, Deborah J 4:26:52 (17,706)
Bloom, Joanne L 5:26:04 (29,879)
Bloomfield, Christine A 4:53:42 (24,353)
Bloor, Debra 5:19:53 (29,084)
Blore Mitchell, Carolyn A 3:48:14 (7,641)
Blott, Emily A 5:25:00 (29,746)
Blott, Natasha L 5:04:21 (26,575)
Blow, Annabel L 5:08:06 (27,236)
Blowes, Kay L 7:08:37 (34,963)
Bloxham, Julie M 5:31:48 (30,545)
Blundell, Faye 5:22:23 (29,400)
Blunden, Kate E 7:00:29 (34,876)
Blunden, Maxine V 4:38:57 (20,860)
Blunt, Susan R 4:21:43 (16,259)
Blyth, Helen E 4:09:41 (13,007)
Blyth, Pamela 4:27:23 (17,853)
Boal, Lynn 4:24:18 (16,924)
Boanas, Susannah B 4:35:41 (20,016)
Boardley, Elizabeth 3:18:22 (2,818)
Boase, Monica G 4:38:22 (20,718)
Bodel, Alexa L 4:37:18 (20,445)
Bodenburg, Brigitte 3:58:11 (10,184)
Bodham-Thornhill, Katy F 3:22:30 (3,242)
Boelee, Scotia 5:21:55 (29,339)
Boffey, Anna K 5:27:52 (30,084)
Bogue, Mary T 4:36:35 (20,243)
Bohmer-Laubis, Jacqueline 4:26:42 (17,658)
Bolderston, Lucy E 5:35:05 (30,913)
Bolger, Mary P 5:00:37 (25,903)
Bolton, Jackie 5:32:45 (30,643)

Boman, Sophie 5:03:17 (26,400)
Bon, Caroline A 3:27:27 (4,008)
Bonas, Sophie 4:23:40 (16,766)
Bond, Patricia A 4:28:43 (18,225)
Bond, Sarah J 3:19:37 (2,957)
Bone, Jennie B 5:38:12 (31,221)
Bone, Norma R 4:29:24 (18,436)
Bongard, Denny 5:37:19 (31,118)
Bonnard, Olga 4:46:59 (22,770)
Bonnett, Suzanne 6:21:33 (33,966)
Bonney, Victoria L 4:11:13 (13,409)
Bonnick, Clare J 3:47:14 (7,398)
Bonning, Sandra E 4:53:52 (24,393)
Bonvini, Lena B 4:05:01 (11,864)
Booker, Donna M 5:04:41 (26,627)
Bookes, Melanie J 4:07:09 (12,382)
Boon, Corinne S 4:57:57 (25,314)
Boon, Karen 4:20:38 (15,975)
Boot, Sarah C 4:44:22 (22,186)
Booth, Helen M 4:24:55 (17,096)
Booth, Jamie 5:00:52 (25,953)
Booth, Sandra 4:34:50 (19,800)
Booth, Sarah 3:47:19 (7,419)
Booth, Tracey A 4:00:52 (10,922)
Booth, Victoria 3:36:53 (5,477)
Booth, Victoria J 6:16:28 (33,800)
Boothroyd, Claire M 4:58:26 (25,425)
Borbon, Elizabeth A 4:59:00 (25,559)
Bordenave, Michelle C 4:45:10 (22,368)
Boreham, Alison M 7:23:48 (35,094)
Borg, Christina M 3:49:22 (7,906)
Borthwick, Tracey 5:21:41 (29,309)
Bosac, Creana 4:35:40 (20,010)
Bosch, Sarah J 4:20:08 (15,838)
Bose, Angie K 4:19:02 (15,523)
Boshoff, Jeannine P 4:56:12 (24,940)
Bosley, Elizabeth 5:11:53 (27,802)
Boss, Sally R 4:24:41 (17,039)
Bostick, Dianna M 5:12:32 (27,915)
Bostock, Barbara Z 5:39:06 (31,322)
Bostock, Clare J 4:50:23 (23,592)
Bostock, Lucy C 5:17:32 (28,723)
Boston, Angela M 4:42:15 (21,689)
Boswell, Carol J 6:08:37 (33,471)
Boswell, Stephanie A 4:07:04 (12,360)
Boswell, Susan A 5:25:27 (29,795)
Botha, Jacinda M 4:48:36 (23,147)
Bott, Elisabeth J 3:48:17 (7,652)
Bott, Jenny H 4:56:32 (25,022)
Botting, Clair F 6:31:30 (34,290)
Botton, Anita M 4:00:32 (10,843)
Boucaud, Renée M 5:40:57 (31,501)
Bouchet, Evelyne 3:43:14 (6,595)
Boulger, Matilda 6:11:52 (33,606)
Bourke, Susan E 6:38:53 (34,483)
Bourne, Amanda 5:13:16 (28,036)
Bourne, Helen L 5:27:21 (30,021)
Bourne, Sarah 6:21:30 (33,961)
Bourne, Sarah L 4:34:53 (19,819)
Bourne, Suzanne 5:48:21 (32,129)
Bovio, Nina C 4:37:36 (20,523)
Bowcock, Joanne C 4:59:26 (25,651)
Bowden, Emma D 3:56:09 (9,552)
Bowden, Wendy R 4:34:51 (19,804)
Bowen, Colleen 4:52:20 (24,021)
Bowen, Jill A 6:13:51 (33,697)
Bowen, Mandy J 5:07:16 (27,111)
Bowen, Michelle A 3:46:43 (7,287)
Bowen, Rosemarie A 5:52:52 (32,489)
Bowen, Tracey 7:07:13 (34,951)
Bower, Kathryn N 5:47:54 (32,092)
Bower, Lisa R 6:37:46 (34,450)
Bower, Sarah 5:37:29 (31,141)
Bowers, Sandra 3:26:38 (3,876)
Bowery, Joanna C 5:37:32 (31,147)
Bowgen, Kelly Anne 4:49:17 (23,300)
Bowker, Carol M 3:13:43 (2,328)
Bowker, Margot C 4:03:47 (11,569)
Bowler, Heather L 4:33:59 (19,566)
Bowler, Karen E 4:57:04 (25,146)
Bowler, Lucie A 5:00:37 (25,903)
Bowler, Wendy K 4:36:12 (20,127)
Bowles, Ann 3:50:32 (8,153)
Bowles, Jacqueline F 4:12:46 (13,825)
Bowles, Katy L 5:47:49 (32,083)
Bowles, Sarah L 3:57:46 (10,058)
Bowman, Janice S 3:37:22 (5,551)
Bowman, Sharon A 5:06:36 (26,982)
Bown, Amanda 4:25:26 (17,262)
Bown, Rachel H 3:15:04 (2,483)
Bown, Sarah J 6:20:46 (33,944)
Bowsher, Judi 3:37:01 (5,500)
Bowtell, Lindsey M 3:30:58 (4,599)
Box, Rebecca 4:35:01 (19,855)
Boxall, Rachel C 6:21:11 (33,955)
Boxall, Sophie K 4:40:31 (21,263)
Boyd, Julie A 4:03:55 (11,608)
Boyden, Sally E 5:04:54 (26,672)
Boydon, Sandra J 3:35:00 (5,182)
Boylan, Frances B 4:24:32 (17,001)
Boylan, Jan V 3:42:10 (6,413)
Boyle, Irene E 5:56:57 (32,766)
Boyle, Marianne A 4:19:37 (15,699)
Boyle, Nicola A 3:29:38 (4,381)
Boyle, Shandi R 6:49:54 (34,707)
Boyle, Suzanne M 4:45:32 (22,439)
Boylett, Janet P 4:59:45 (25,725)
Boyne, Joyce M 4:23:32 (16,735)
Boys, Katie M 4:48:59 (23,231)
Brache, Jackie 5:55:09 (32,649)
Brack, Lucy 3:39:47 (5,960)
Brackenbury, Anita J 5:01:27 (26,054)
Brackley, Daphne A 7:38:50 (35,171)
Bradbrook, Emma A 5:55:40 (32,691)
Bradburn, Carol L 5:18:53 (28,930)
Bradbury, Taryn K 4:02:54 (11,367)
Braddock, Clare A 3:57:56 (10,123)
Bradeley, Alison 4:27:31 (17,894)
Bradford, Ruth C 3:55:41 (9,423)
Bradin, Victoria L 5:40:58 (31,505)
Bradle, Suzanne 5:34:36 (30,861)
Bradley, Carolyn M 4:38:44 (20,809)
Bradley, Christine A 4:43:12 (21,915)
Bradley, Eileen B 4:56:27 (25,001)
Bradley, Hannah V 5:11:55 (27,807)
Bradley, Jacqueline L 3:58:25 (10,266)
Bradley, Jayne F 4:26:53 (17,714)
Bradley, Jean 4:49:43 (23,429)
Bradshaw, Margaret A 5:56:52 (32,765)
Brady, Denise 5:16:34 (28,558)
Brady, Katherine L 4:49:45 (23,438)
Brady, Kieran 4:20:33 (15,948)
Brady, Pamela J 4:21:45 (16,271)
Bragg, Gillian 4:27:16 (17,818)
Braglewicz, Sarah 4:27:53 (18,007)
Braham, Alice R 2:45:06 (322)
Braham, Dawn L 5:18:34 (28,877)
Braid, Diane 3:31:35 (4,690)
Braid, Wendy 6:40:56 (34,524)
Brailsford, Victoria A 3:22:35 (3,251)
Brain, Heather 4:32:28 (19,204)
Brain, Helen C 6:24:31 (34,075)
Brana, Luisa P 3:42:54 (6,526)
Branch, Jo M 5:51:34 (32,379)
Branchett, Emma E 4:16:32 (14,842)
Brandhorst, Fiona J 5:35:01 (30,908)
Brandon, Susan 3:54:36 (9,124)
Brannick, Lesley Y 5:15:08 (28,356)
Branscombe, Faye A 4:55:23 (24,754)
Branson, Holly K 4:54:55 (24,641)
Bratell, Karin 3:48:04 (7,606)
Bray, Julie 5:40:30 (31,467)
Bray, Lesley C 4:52:55 (24,153)
Bray, Lisa 4:13:22 (13,982)
Bray, Sarah 3:56:57 (9,798)
Braybrook, Lauren H 6:54:36 (34,789)
Brayne, Julie A 4:10:20 (13,179)
Brayshaw, Karen 7:51:19 (35,209)
Brayshay, Margaret A 6:12:21 (33,631)
Breach, Martin J 4:33:04 (19,330)
Breaden, Donna A 5:37:21 (31,123)
Breagan, Heidi 5:02:42 (26,274)
Breakspeare, Hayley J 3:53:10 (8,762)
Breakwell, Sophie L 4:58:01 (25,333)
Breed, Wendy 3:50:06 (8,062)
Breeden, Susan C 4:31:36 (18,997)
Breeze, Victoria 6:23:40 (34,045)
Brekko, Tara 4:59:09 (25,593)
Brenna, Grethe 3:53:16 (8,786)
Brennan, Denise S 5:25:59 (29,867)
Brennan, Elizabeth G 3:58:53 (10,406)
Brennan, Jackie M 4:41:12 (21,446)
Brennan, Maureen 5:45:05 (31,854)
Brennan, Rebecca J 4:01:43 (11,095)
Brennan, Sharon 4:12:07 (13,642)
Brenner, Jane 3:11:46 (2,114)
Brentnall, Claire L 3:20:18 (3,026)
Brenton, Ellen J 7:11:16 (34,994)
Brenton, Sarah J 4:15:23 (14,547)
Brett, Mary 5:07:44 (27,180)
Brett, Sandra Y 3:09:12 (1,832)
Brett, Tina 5:11:30 (27,738)
Breuil, Laetitia 4:41:30 (21,523)
Breuling, Sabine C 4:19:45 (15,740)
Brewer, Karen D 4:54:14 (24,486)
Brewer, Sally 4:46:28 (22,661)
Brewis, Linda M 3:38:59 (5,812)
Brewster, Joanne C 5:40:50 (31,488)
Brian, Anna J 5:01:02 (25,983)
Brickland, Patricia 4:04:13 (11,687)
Brickley, Jacqueline 4:33:48 (19,518)
Bridge, Rita M 5:57:00 (32,772)
Bridger, Rachel J 5:13:58 (28,164)
Bridges, Pam M 5:58:02 (32,836)
Bridges, Rita S 6:02:34 (33,111)
Bridier, Genevieve 4:22:20 (16,429)
Brien, Maureen A 5:03:54 (26,503)
Brierley, Anne J 4:42:46 (21,817)
Briggs, Ana M 4:54:13 (24,479)
Briggs, Dawn 5:25:10 (29,768)
Briggs, Gail E 4:45:56 (22,539)
Briggs, Julie L 2:52:45 (624)
Briggs, Kathryn 4:31:32 (18,978)
Briggs, Katy V 5:10:54 (27,638)
Briggs, Kelly A 4:26:38 (17,643)
Briggs, Sandra C 5:20:30 (29,180)
Briggs, Sue 5:17:57 (28,773)
Brighouse, Diana 5:09:59 (27,509)
Bright, Anna M 5:00:11 (25,813)
Bright, Hetty K 4:24:01 (16,857)
Bright, Jane 3:45:24 (7,030)
Bright, Joanne E 4:06:37 (12,247)
Bright, Joanne E 4:25:14 (17,196)
Bright, Laura E 5:26:30 (29,922)
Bright, Margaret E 5:24:50 (29,726)
Brighton, Catherine M 3:20:01 (2,998)
Brimblecombe, Janette 6:40:59 (34,525)
Brindley, Anne 3:26:55 (3,914)
Brine, Lisa J 4:32:54 (19,289)
Bring, Manjit K 5:52:54 (32,491)
Bringloe, Juliette V 4:36:48 (20,306)
Brink, Elbie 6:29:57 (34,255)
Brinklow, Patricia M 6:04:44 (33,255)
Brinklow, Sarah L 5:10:48 (27,617)
Briscoe, Andrea 5:12:25 (27,890)
Bristow, Mary 4:56:24 (24,990)
Bristow Tyler, Linda 5:34:12 (30,805)
Brito, Kelly L 5:14:05 (28,182)
Brittney, Amanda L 4:18:23 (15,319)
Britton, Toni 3:42:12 (6,419)
Britz, Kirsten 3:59:20 (10,527)
Broadbent, Christine 3:58:49 (10,393)
Broadbent, Karen J 4:00:27 (10,818)
Broadby, Sonia P 7:43:21 (35,187)
Broadhurst, Claire 5:36:33 (31,062)
Broadley, Victoria J 4:41:21 (21,479)
Broadway, Tracey 4:47:24 (22,856)
Brock, Helen 3:32:54 (4,873)
Brock, Joanna L 4:49:36 (23,388)
Brocklesby, Edwina P 3:45:53 (7,114)
Broda, Krysia B 4:14:15 (14,229)
Broekhof, Kathleen 4:50:22 (23,585)
Brogan, Jennifer 5:41:16 (31,535)
Brokenshaw, Shirley J 3:37:23 (5,554)
Bromley, Elaine K 4:35:07 (19,878)
Bromley, Michaela G 3:34:11 (5,073)
Bromley, Patricia A 4:37:59 (20,616)
Brondoni, Federica 4:07:46 (12,523)
Brontesi, Giuliana 4:51:00 (23,734)

Brook, Lina M 3:54:43 (9,158)
Brook, Vivienne 5:37:49 (31,169)
Brooke, Flora 6:29:10 (34,226)
Brooke, Jennifer M 5:36:07 (31,005)
Brooke, Stacy A 5:02:53 (26,316)
Brooker, Annette 4:46:45 (22,719)
Brooker, Helen J 6:43:33 (34,583)
Brookes, Jennifer L 4:58:05 (25,347)
Brookes, Judith M 4:54:59 (24,668)
Brookes, Louise J 5:17:42 (28,742)
Brookes, Susan A 5:53:18 (32,524)
Brookhouse, Jane 4:40:17 (21,203)
Brooks, Georgiana E 4:14:46 (14,369)
Brooks, Jocelyne E 5:19:32 (29,038)
Brooks, Keelie 3:47:15 (7,403)
Brooks, Linda R 4:55:48 (24,841)
Brooks, Lucy J 2:57:36 (925)
Brooks, Melanie L 5:01:01 (25,978)
Brooks, Michelle D 6:05:07 (33,274)
Brooks, Sarah E 5:16:27 (28,540)
Brooks, Theresa 4:46:47 (22,727)
Brook-Walters, Natasha 6:08:27 (33,462)
Broome, Theresa D 6:42:01 (34,546)
Brough, Rachel 3:45:07 (6,974)
Broughall, Ceri E 4:54:41 (24,589)
Broughton, Andrea C 4:17:28 (15,088)
Broughton, Susan 7:25:06 (35,099)
Brower, Derek L 3:51:39 (8,400)
Brown, Aileen S 3:01:24 (1,209)
Brown, Alison 4:49:48 (23,449)
Brown, Alison R 3:50:07 (8,064)
Brown, Angela S 4:26:03 (17,455)
Brown, Anne M 5:15:15 (28,378)
Brown, Avril 4:48:57 (23,224)
Brown, Claire M 4:36:13 (20,135)
Brown, Debbie 5:38:25 (31,238)
Brown, Elizabeth L 6:16:41 (33,807)
Brown, Emma B 5:37:44 (31,161)
Brown, Fiona J 4:43:22 (21,949)
Brown, Francesca C 5:36:28 (31,048)
Brown, Gemma 5:15:21 (28,394)
Brown, Grace 4:24:40 (17,032)
Brown, Hayley S 5:17:29 (28,713)
Brown, Helen E 4:04:30 (11,746)
Brown, Ishbel K 5:01:06 (25,996)
Brown, Jane M 4:57:14 (25,181)
Brown, Janine E 3:11:25 (2,073)
Brown, Jessica C 5:34:48 (30,884)
Brown, Joanna H 4:44:21 (22,183)
Brown, Joanne L 4:14:54 (14,412)
Brown, Joanne L 4:25:04 (17,142)
Brown, Johanna E 4:30:28 (18,717)
Brown, Jude E 4:29:37 (18,499)
Brown, Judy 3:32:46 (4,853)
Brown, Julia T 6:48:08 (34,678)
Brown, Julie M 3:25:26 (3,659)
Brown, Karen 4:27:05 (17,771)
Brown, Karen 6:08:10 (33,453)
Brown, Karen A 4:06:46 (12,277)
Brown, Lindsey J 4:18:46 (15,452)
Brown, Louise P 5:02:57 (26,329)
Brown, Lucinda S 5:48:03 (32,097)
Brown, Lynne M 5:26:04 (29,879)
Brown, Mandy 4:25:16 (17,206)
Brown, Margaret 5:27:28 (30,039)
Brown, Margaret M 6:59:04 (34,853)
Brown, Marilyn F 4:41:04 (21,410)
Brown, Meilissa J 4:09:53 (13,063)
Brown, Merlyn 4:54:46 (24,614)
Brown, Moniea C 5:45:16 (31,876)
Brown, Nicola C 4:57:54 (25,302)
Brown, Nicola E 4:27:35 (17,915)
Brown, Patricia 4:47:22 (22,847)
Brown, Pauline 4:17:49 (15,163)
Brown, Rachel M 4:46:10 (22,599)
Brown, Rebecca E 3:57:35 (10,007)
Brown, Sally 5:39:25 (31,367)
Brown, Sally A 4:35:00 (19,853)
Brown, Samantha A 4:32:39 (19,238)
Brown, Sarah F 4:09:52 (13,059)
Brown, Sian C 4:08:24 (12,667)
Brown, Stefany A 6:25:58 (34,123)
Brown, Sue E 4:07:08 (12,379)
Brown, Sue J 5:07:10 (27,091)
Brown, Susan A 4:56:57 (25,122)
Brown, Susan F 4:02:22 (11,240)
Brown, Suzanne 4:55:50 (24,856)
Brown, Suzanne L 4:01:38 (11,075)
Brown, Valerie E 5:56:59 (32,769)
Brown, Wendy 6:46:45 (34,650)
Brown, Zoe 5:40:03 (31,421)
Browne, Helen 7:17:16 (35,057)
Browne, Kara 4:45:38 (22,467)
Browne, Sue M 4:10:49 (13,292)
Brownhill, Anne 4:21:21 (16,159)
Browning, Barbara 3:22:15 (3,223)
Browning, Clare E 4:40:24 (21,231)
Browning, Maryann 3:58:16 (10,210)
Browning, Monica I 5:13:46 (28,126)
Brownlee, Victoria A 4:25:42 (17,345)
Bruce, Libby E 6:18:38 (33,879)
Bruce, Lisa J 5:20:56 (29,229)
Bruce, Louise 4:41:38 (21,552)
Bruce, Sarah J 3:06:54 (1,627)
Bruce, Valerie M 4:27:28 (17,875)
Brueneheier, Sabine 4:35:55 (20,066)
Bruengger, Marcel 5:07:23 (27,126)
Bruff, Karen J 3:55:36 (9,403)
Bruggemann, Wibke 4:15:29 (14,573)
Brulet, Delphine 5:39:26 (31,368)
Brumfitt, Collette N 5:48:56 (32,178)
Brunning, Priscilla D 4:12:04 (13,636)
Bruno, Veronica F 4:50:39 (23,662)
Bruton, Charnelle D 5:04:47 (26,647)
Bruzek, Katja 3:49:29 (7,929)
Bryan, Delyth W 3:48:46 (7,777)
Bryan, Joanne M 4:53:17 (24,243)
Bryan, Louise A 5:25:27 (29,795)
Bryant, Caroline M 5:06:06 (26,890)
Bryant, Clare E 4:53:02 (24,183)
Bryant, Frances M 4:40:41 (21,303)
Bryant, Joanna E 4:42:05 (21,645)
Bryant, Susan A 6:43:23 (34,579)
Bryant-Jefferies, Lauren M 4:12:01 (13,628)
Bryson, Heidi 4:10:09 (13,127)
Buchan, June 3:55:19 (9,313)
Buchanan, Dianne E 4:31:38 (19,004)
Buchanan, Katie J 5:05:12 (26,725)
Buck, Jane F 3:45:34 (7,059)
Buck, Victoria C 3:49:35 (7,948)
Buckey, Emma L 6:35:36 (34,400)
Buckhorn, Lydia J 4:39:47 (21,089)
Buckingham, Fiona 3:53:31 (8,861)
Buckingham, Janet P 5:28:19 (30,170)
Buckland, Carol 3:50:28 (8,142)
Buckle, Tracey J 4:40:24 (21,231)
Buckley, Deborah A 5:25:56 (29,859)
Buckley, Janette M 4:28:22 (18,129)
Buckley, Katherine J 4:55:52 (24,868)
Buckley, Laura J 4:02:11 (11,201)
Buckley, Tracey 4:17:59 (15,201)
Buckley, Victoria 4:05:47 (12,047)
Buckwell, Zena K 4:26:14 (17,515)
Buda, Elena 5:01:46 (26,101)
Budd, Naomi S 4:36:39 (20,270)
Budd, Vivien K 5:37:21 (31,123)
Budge, Louise 5:12:22 (27,874)
Buffini, Lauren 3:51:05 (8,278)
Bufton, Teresea 4:26:22 (17,555)
Bugden, Charlotte S 5:16:31 (28,550)
Bugg, Alison 3:53:27 (8,848)
Buist, Michelle 5:47:29 (32,061)
Buitendag, Emma L 4:58:35 (25,463)
Buleux, Marie-Rose 4:46:45 (22,719)
Buley, Rona A 4:18:20 (15,307)
Bulgin, Victoria M 5:32:24 (30,605)
Bulkeley, Bayly J 3:26:53 (3,908)
Bull, Jacqueline L 5:17:14 (28,681)
Bull, Jill S 4:17:35 (15,110)
Bull, Mary T 4:03:29 (11,493)
Bull, Mike G 5:37:27 (31,136)
Bullen, Cristin K 5:15:17 (28,386)
Bullen, Kirsty J 5:27:29 (30,041)
Bullen, Nicola A 5:27:29 (30,041)
Bullimore, Jane 5:34:44 (30,880)
Bullman, Natalie L 6:01:30 (33,055)
Bullock, Elaine 4:24:13 (16,908)
Bullock, Janet M 5:52:26 (32,456)
Bullock, Jenny M 5:12:48 (27,969)
Bulman, Agnes 5:37:49 (31,169)
Bulmer, Louise 6:37:43 (34,448)
Bulpin, Susannah 3:22:53 (3,281)
Bumpus, Kathryn J 3:29:46 (4,414)
Bunch, Iona S 4:17:58 (15,194)
Bundy, Mary D 4:44:51 (22,285)
Bundy, Sabrina A 7:12:11 (35,005)
Bunker, Joanne 6:00:25 (33,001)
Bunn, Susan A 4:54:03 (24,439)
Bunten, Susan 3:24:37 (3,529)
Bunting, Jennie C 3:57:46 (10,058)
Bunting, Paula J 6:00:23 (32,996)
Buonsenso, Julia 3:45:08 (6,979)
Buratti, Elizabeth 5:06:38 (26,990)
Burbank, Louise B 5:09:09 (27,380)
Burbridge, Gillian F 4:55:40 (24,804)
Burchell, Sarah E 4:54:04 (24,443)
Burchell, Victoria L 5:57:16 (32,793)
Burchett, Judith S 4:11:42 (13,538)
Burchfield, Jo-Anne 4:28:31 (18,173)
Burden, Susan J 5:56:15 (32,722)
Burdess, Christine 5:33:12 (30,689)
Bureau, Sylvie 6:30:55 (34,273)
Burger, Estelle 5:29:58 (30,358)
Burger, Gemma S 4:51:46 (23,884)
Burger, Helen R 5:18:58 (28,940)
Burger, Lindy 5:13:18 (28,043)
Burgess, Ann 5:16:48 (28,601)
Burgess, Emily R 4:42:51 (21,833)
Burgess, Emma V 5:00:00 (25,776)
Burgess, Harriet K 4:19:36 (15,692)
Burgess, Helen L 4:00:44 (10,893)
Burgess, Joanne 4:58:23 (25,412)
Burgess, Kathryn M 3:50:21 (8,116)
Burgess, Nikki C 4:55:38 (24,799)
Burgess, Polly E 4:27:43 (17,955)
Burgess, Suzanne 5:18:45 (28,911)
Burgess, Tracy A 4:24:35 (17,010)
Burgin, Sandra 5:54:55 (32,634)
Burgoyne, Celia H 5:42:35 (31,636)
Burgoyne, Dionne 4:58:32 (25,452)
Burholt, Sarah J 3:56:37 (9,696)
Burke, Birgit 4:28:12 (18,085)
Burke, Catherine E 4:11:13 (13,409)
Burke, Eileen 4:30:48 (18,793)
Burke, Janet 5:14:26 (28,252)
Burke, Jill E 3:24:44 (3,544)
Burke, Lisa 3:36:15 (5,382)
Burke, Lisa 4:08:06 (12,590)
Burke, Lorraine 5:02:35 (26,245)
Burke, Martyna C 5:05:01 (26,687)
Burke, Sarah 4:39:26 (20,996)
Burkitt, Judi F 4:30:00 (18,584)
Burkitt, Sarah L 4:23:05 (16,625)
Burles-Nash, Karen D 4:29:12 (18,365)
Burley, Caroline L 4:57:32 (25,234)
Burley, Pamela D 5:42:45 (31,657)
Burman, Kathryn L 5:30:23 (30,402)
Burnard, Julie A 5:35:19 (30,935)
Burnell, Linda R 5:25:18 (29,781)
Burnett, Lucy M 3:42:04 (6,391)
Burnette, Linda 6:13:31 (33,681)
Burns, Caroline 4:53:48 (24,383)
Burns, Donna L 5:18:28 (28,854)
Burns, Moya 4:18:22 (15,315)
Burns, Nikki 4:43:59 (22,094)
Burns, Rebecca S 4:57:37 (25,251)
Burns, Tamsin T 5:05:45 (26,833)
Burrage, Amy C 3:41:36 (6,298)
Burridge, Helen J 4:14:51 (14,396)
Burrough, Sallie L 3:44:33 (6,848)
Burrow, Kirsty A 5:12:04 (27,834)
Burrows, Karen B 4:34:12 (19,624)
Burrows, Katy J 4:33:44 (19,499)
Bursnall, Deirdre M 6:04:26 (33,240)
Burstow, Diana K 4:04:01 (11,640)
Burt, Hannah L 6:31:46 (34,297)
Burt, Helen 4:42:24 (21,720)
Burton, Alexandra L 4:27:40 (17,942)
Burton, Christine J 4:22:22 (16,438)

Chaplin, Beverley A 3:52:03 (8,493)
Chapman, Ben M 4:27:11 (17,798)
Chapman, Caroline 4:36:12 (20,127)
Chapman, Ceri 3:58:01 (10,148)
Chapman, Cynthia M 4:18:32 (15,368)
Chapman, Gill 3:43:01 (6,553)
Chapman, Jacqueline L 4:09:05 (12,853)
Chapman, Julia M 4:35:01 (19,855)
Chapman, Katharine M 5:16:34 (28,558)
Chapman, Kathryn L 5:12:22 (27,874)
Chapman, Leila R 5:18:06 (28,798)
Chapman, Lesley 3:26:12 (3,794)
Chapman, Sally A 3:44:09 (6,774)
Chapman, Sarah 4:29:00 (18,306)
Chapman, Sarah E 5:16:05 (28,489)
Chapman, Sonia 4:54:25 (24,528)
Chappell, Julie L 4:15:50 (14,673)
Chardon, Mariette 4:14:04 (14,173)
Charge, Kellie J 5:55:31 (32,682)
Charkin, Susan 4:33:48 (19,518)
Charlannes, Agnes 6:02:00 (33,084)
Charlemagne, Angela 4:27:47 (17,980)
Charlery, Paulette A 3:21:31 (3,132)
Charles, Joanne 4:29:51 (18,551)
Charles, Joanne 6:09:19 (33,505)
Charles, Lorne K 4:42:17 (21,696)
Charles, Marvelyn 5:06:21 (26,931)
Charles, Sandra 3:52:27 (8,593)
Charlesworth, Claire 6:02:37 (33,114)
Charlesworth, Marian J 6:41:14 (34,531)
Charlton, Sarah 4:54:07 (24,454)
Charlton, Victoria 5:07:07 (27,079)
Charman, Mary L 5:48:54 (32,172)
Charnaud, Katherine F 4:59:24 (25,641)
Charter, Helen M 4:29:21 (18,416)
Charter, Lisa 6:47:32 (34,669)
Chase, Alison J 4:33:32 (19,444)
Chase, Hilary J 4:16:58 (14,948)
Chater, Frances L 6:02:51 (33,133)
Chatfield, Patricia M 4:55:16 (24,731)
Chauhan, Jyoti 5:21:00 (29,236)
Chauvin, Lauren 4:20:05 (15,826)
Chavda, Meena 6:51:09 (34,741)
Cheal, Suzanne L 3:53:14 (8,778)
Checketts, Wendy C 5:12:14 (27,858)
Chee, Wan Yee 5:14:37 (28,283)
Cheema, Kally K 6:40:14 (34,511)
Cheema, Rebecca 4:30:36 (18,747)
Cheetham, Denise E 4:28:52 (18,268)
Chen, Yi-Jing 5:09:19 (27,407)
Chepchumba, Joyce 2:27:01 (57)
Chepkemei, Susan 2:24:00 (38)
Chesney, Daniella P 3:22:10 (3,213)
Chestnutt, Sarah 3:41:36 (6,298)
Cheung, Jaimie W 4:09:17 (12,903)
Cheung, Lynn S 5:14:17 (28,225)
Cheung, Michelle O 5:30:24 (30,406)
Cheung, Sallie A 5:19:21 (28,998)
Cheung, Winnie 5:18:59 (28,943)
Cheverton, Dinah S 2:59:10 (1,052)
Chew, Shelby 3:41:37 (6,302)
Chia, Katharine J 5:30:17 (30,395)
Chidley, Charlotte A 4:44:29 (22,210)
Chidley, Isobel C 4:13:44 (14,076)
Chiffi, Anna Chiara 4:59:48 (25,742)
Chilcott, Melanie J 3:56:38 (9,707)
Child, Anne E 4:16:10 (14,759)
Chin, Cheryl 4:03:14 (11,440)
Chini, Antonella 3:20:47 (3,074)
Chinn, Rebecca 5:06:20 (26,926)
Chippendale, Helen 4:50:29 (23,623)
Chipperfield, Christine E 5:26:04 (29,879)
Chiswell, Stephanie A 4:48:21 (23,088)
Chiusoli, Marialetizia 4:55:24 (24,758)
Chivers, Ann E 5:13:59 (28,168)
Chivers, Karen L 5:31:39 (30,527)
Chiverton, Frances 5:05:59 (26,868)
Choglay, Shahina 4:58:04 (25,343)
Choy, Marcia F 5:35:07 (30,920)
Chrismas, Nicola E 4:56:30 (25,018)
Christ, Sarah J 3:31:59 (4,744)
Christensen, Jennifer W 4:22:33 (16,486)
Christensen, Mette P 4:34:22 (19,684)
Christian, Deborah A 4:55:19 (24,738)
Christie, Erica M 3:12:04 (2,148)
Christie, Nathalie 4:20:26 (15,922)
Church, Jo E 3:41:53 (6,351)
Church, Mary 4:56:52 (25,107)
Churchill, Margaret 6:12:12 (33,625)
Churchley, Caroline E 4:08:23 (12,664)
Churton, Kellie-Marie 7:11:45 (35,001)
Cicek, Sebnem 4:46:38 (22,696)
Clague, Jenny 2:41:21 (227)
Claisse, Caroline 5:16:07 (28,492)
Clampett, Linda S 4:13:41 (14,064)
Clanfield, Heather 5:01:39 (26,087)
Clare, Susanne 3:55:09 (9,263)
Clare, Sylvia R 4:27:35 (17,915)
Clark, Abbie 3:40:42 (6,117)
Clark, Angela 4:14:29 (14,290)
Clark, Barbara S 4:36:16 (20,149)
Clark, Caroline A 4:25:21 (17,227)
Clark, Catherine A 4:11:00 (13,350)
Clark, Emma L 4:03:24 (11,481)
Clark, Fiona L 4:43:44 (22,043)
Clark, Georgina J 5:54:33 (32,606)
Clark, Louise V 6:02:27 (33,104)
Clark, Marianne J 4:02:55 (11,374)
Clark, Nicola M 4:19:36 (15,692)
Clark, Sandra B 5:58:05 (32,844)
Clark, Sarah J 5:13:26 (28,067)
Clark, Susannah J 4:15:12 (14,502)
Clark, Zoe A 4:57:10 (25,169)
Clarke, Alison R 5:11:30 (27,738)
Clarke, Amanda 3:15:26 (2,520)
Clarke, Andrea L 4:11:05 (13,375)
Clarke, Annette J 3:24:56 (3,576)
Clarke, Carina M 5:32:02 (30,561)
Clarke, Carol J 4:11:08 (13,388)
Clarke, Caroline 5:10:46 (27,610)
Clarke, Debbie E 3:42:08 (6,408)
Clarke, Elizabeth F 5:16:34 (28,558)
Clarke, Elizabeth M 4:56:22 (24,981)
Clarke, Erika L 3:45:47 (7,091)
Clarke, Geraldine 4:39:54 (21,112)
Clarke, Helen 4:57:37 (25,251)
Clarke, Irene M 6:49:43 (34,703)
Clarke, Jessica 7:23:28 (35,091)
Clarke, Kate E 5:08:41 (27,308)
Clarke, Leander G 4:46:45 (22,719)
Clarke, Lesley 4:40:23 (21,228)
Clarke, Lindsay D 5:06:01 (26,876)
Clarke, Lorna 4:59:35 (25,682)
Clarke, Natacha D 4:34:39 (19,748)
Clarke, Nicola J 5:06:49 (27,020)
Clarke, Rita J 5:48:45 (32,156)
Clarke, Sally P 3:54:02 (8,983)
Clarke, Susan C 5:04:01 (26,519)
Clarke, Vanessa K 4:49:27 (23,350)
Clarke, Victoria A 4:34:22 (19,684)
Clarke, Victoria M 3:01:29 (1,218)
Clarke Noble, Désirée A 3:39:33 (5,923)
Clarkson, Hilary 4:43:30 (21,980)
Clarkson, Julia S 4:37:16 (20,433)
Clarkson, Linda P 3:04:12 (1,408)
Clarkson, Suzanne C 4:37:07 (20,391)
Clarvis, Julie A 3:47:23 (7,434)
Clatworthy, Patricia 4:31:56 (19,069)
Clawley, Charlotte 4:17:39 (15,125)
Claxton, Michelle A 6:05:53 (33,323)
Clay, Sil 5:03:25 (26,420)
Claydon, Helen J 5:24:30 (29,684)
Clayson, Lee 4:00:31 (10,841)
Clayton, Jaki 4:27:34 (17,912)
Clayton, Jennifer L 4:10:42 (13,267)
Clayton, Joanna L 4:25:51 (17,387)
Clayton, Lucy 4:52:50 (24,134)
Clayton, Sally M 5:26:01 (29,869)
Clayton, Samantha 4:33:04 (19,330)
Clayton, Siobhan M 3:58:25 (10,266)
Clayton, Valerie 6:47:41 (34,670)
Clea, Rebecca 5:58:11 (32,855)
Cleary, Lisa 4:00:33 (10,852)
Cleathero, Claire 3:30:19 (4,490)
Cleland-Smith, Sarah J 5:00:39 (25,909)
Clelland, Eleanor J 5:13:39 (28,110)
Clelland, Shirley A 5:06:48 (27,017)
Clemens, Linda A 4:10:12 (13,140)
Clements, Clair A 4:13:59 (14,141)
Clements, Mary E 4:09:12 (12,890)
Clements, Tina 6:18:07 (33,858)
Cleminson, Abigail S 4:38:00 (20,622)
Clerx, Hilde M 5:11:53 (27,802)
Cleverley, Helen K 5:03:51 (26,494)
Clews, Jan 4:34:55 (19,831)
Cliff, Anna 4:28:33 (18,181)
Clifford, Lizzie 3:14:42 (2,445)
Clifford, Rosemary L 5:29:18 (30,273)
Clift, Deborah R 3:41:10 (6,212)
Clifton, Amanda J 4:31:15 (18,898)
Clifton, Claire J 4:44:24 (22,193)
Clinch, Georgina 3:51:46 (8,429)
Clinton, Clare J 5:54:51 (32,628)
Clinton, Jane 4:31:12 (18,884)
Clinton, Karen M 5:22:34 (29,435)
Clist, Trudy C 4:16:58 (14,948)
Cloke, Yvonne M 4:27:11 (17,798)
Clough, Lucy M 3:46:41 (7,279)
Clover, Harriett C 4:40:34 (21,278)
Clowes, Janice 3:52:21 (8,566)
Clowes, Sophie 3:56:22 (9,623)
Clubb, Barbara 4:40:27 (21,243)
Clutton, Sharon 5:09:51 (27,490)
Coates, Jo C 4:41:44 (21,573)
Coates, Louise H 4:34:21 (19,676)
Coates, Michelle J 5:26:23 (29,908)
Coates, Paula 5:04:24 (26,583)
Coates, Rebecca C 5:44:10 (31,777)
Coatterwell, Nadia V 3:50:37 (8,173)
Cobby, Janet A 3:26:08 (3,783)
Cochrane, Anna C 6:10:21 (33,548)
Cockaday, Esther 5:28:49 (30,222)
Cocker, Abi L 5:56:02 (32,709)
Cocker, Jennifer S 4:06:45 (12,274)
Cockerill, Shannon L 3:31:12 (4,631)
Cockings, Ingrid J 4:48:33 (23,134)
Code, Joanne F 4:30:55 (18,821)
Coe, Fiona 4:43:36 (22,007)
Coe, Janet A 5:53:04 (32,504)
Coe, Kim G 5:10:50 (27,622)
Coe, Suzanne V 4:20:46 (16,010)
Coe, Victoria S 6:10:49 (33,568)
Coffey, Jill M 6:12:58 (33,661)
Coffey, Rachel T 6:02:59 (33,143)
Coffey, Rebecca J 6:12:59 (33,663)
Coffin, Maureen A 6:23:28 (34,036)
Cogan, Teresa T 5:31:30 (30,518)
Coggrave, Sarah H 5:01:42 (26,092)
Cohen, Rachel L 4:57:33 (25,239)
Cohen, Sharon 5:48:35 (32,140)
Colasurdo, Lydia G 4:25:54 (17,401)
Colbert, Susannah M 4:18:52 (15,479)
Colbourne, Nicola A 4:24:41 (17,039)
Colbridge, Ruth 5:39:05 (31,318)
Colburn, Melanie 4:17:32 (15,097)
Colclough, Helen L 4:27:40 (17,942)
Colclough, Louise 4:50:10 (23,531)
Cole, Ann 4:51:53 (23,905)
Cole, Julie 4:43:31 (21,988)
Cole, Mary 4:11:28 (13,477)
Cole, Michelle J 4:47:25 (22,861)
Cole, Patricia A 5:29:31 (30,310)
Cole, Rebecca 4:50:21 (23,579)
Cole, Sally T 4:08:49 (12,773)
Cole, Sally-Ann 4:39:47 (21,089)
Cole, Sarah E 5:24:59 (29,743)
Cole, Sherree G 5:04:52 (26,663)
Cole, Suzanne 4:48:55 (23,216)
Coleman, Lisa-Kay 3:40:52 (6,161)
Coleman, Patricia J 4:26:47 (17,687)
Colenutt, Margaret 6:10:40 (33,559)
Coles, Alice 4:55:06 (24,700)
Coles, Natalle J 3:44:59 (6,955)
Coles, Sharron J 5:07:21 (27,122)
Colgan, Lucy J 4:51:53 (23,905)
Collard-Odle, Tamara L 5:13:27 (28,071)
Collen, Gillian A 4:05:44 (12,036)
Collette, Jane M 6:15:09 (33,741)
Colley, Beth J 4:12:32 (13,752)

Colley, Gail	4:06:15 (12,154)
Collier, Amy L	5:19:55 (29,086)
Collier, Ann	5:22:57 (29,480)
Collier, Maggie L	6:12:34 (33,644)
Collier, Naomi L	4:00:41 (10,883)
Collin, Isabelle	3:48:41 (7,757)
Colling, Caron	5:06:50 (27,026)
Collingwood, Jane E	4:48:14 (23,060)
Collins, Alisa S	5:51:03 (32,341)
Collins, Becci S	5:21:00 (29,236)
Collins, Claire M	5:48:04 (32,099)
Collins, Emma	4:13:38 (14,053)
Collins, Gemma J	5:30:22 (30,400)
Collins, Helen	4:32:44 (19,256)
Collins, Joanne D	6:18:31 (33,872)
Collins, Margaret	4:20:25 (15,918)
Collins, Mary P	7:17:06 (35,055)
Collins, Tina	5:57:34 (32,808)
Collins, Virginia	4:14:05 (14,181)
Collinson, Audrey	5:58:21 (32,865)
Collinson, Libby H	4:39:11 (20,923)
Collinson, Lisa A	4:52:50 (24,134)
Collinson, Nicola J	4:40:59 (21,385)
Collison, Emma L	5:01:45 (26,099)
Collison, Sarah J	5:46:19 (31,965)
Colman, Jill M	3:48:20 (7,664)
Colquhoun, Lucy A	3:03:03 (1,332)
Colquhoun, Shirley J	3:24:55 (3,570)
Colson, Laura J	5:14:49 (28,314)
Colville, Rachel A	5:18:39 (28,897)
Colvin, Laura J	4:38:22 (20,718)
Colwell, Cathy	5:36:46 (31,085)
Combellack, Ruth D	4:31:45 (19,032)
Comber, Caroline	4:42:33 (21,751)
Comerford, Anna	3:42:06 (6,401)
Comerford, Helen	4:11:28 (13,477)
Comiskey, Carmel	3:18:38 (2,838)
Comolli, Christine	6:28:22 (34,208)
Conafray, Linda M	4:52:56 (24,156)
Coney, Deborah C	3:28:27 (4,188)
Coney, Diane J	3:30:56 (4,595)
Conlin, Clara M	4:55:18 (24,735)
Conlon, Joanna L	6:15:38 (33,767)
Connan, Fiona F	4:50:12 (23,534)
Connell, Keeley W	3:59:50 (10,676)
Connell, Susan P	5:01:15 (26,016)
Connelly, Jacqueline A	4:52:36 (24,074)
Connolly, Carolyne J	6:03:56 (33,219)
Connolly, Mary	3:58:21 (10,243)
Connolly, Mary	4:17:47 (15,154)
Connolly, Susan E	4:52:16 (24,006)
Connor, Dannielle	5:18:31 (28,866)
Connor, Dianne	5:20:19 (29,144)
Connor, Eleri J	4:48:22 (23,095)
Connor, Elisabeth C	5:12:49 (27,975)
Connor, Emma	7:20:07 (35,074)
Connor, Sheelagh M	5:16:20 (28,525)
Conrad-Pickles, Emily L	5:34:28 (30,845)
Conroy, Charlotte R	5:58:52 (32,902)
Constable, Rebecca J	4:05:18 (11,948)
Constantinou, Andyyoni	8:32:00 (35,246)
Constantinou, Marina	5:40:45 (31,484)
Conte, Immacolata	5:28:52 (30,229)
Conti, Jennifer E	4:23:49 (16,808)
Conway, Caroline J	6:06:27 (33,356)
Conway, Catherine H	3:53:34 (8,875)
Conway, Jackie	5:55:11 (32,654)
Cooil, Jan M	4:10:24 (13,204)
Cook, Alicia L	4:50:01 (23,500)
Cook, Alison D	5:00:13 (25,823)
Cook, Alissa B	4:17:08 (14,997)
Cook, Allison	4:24:11 (16,898)
Cook, Anne E	4:38:50 (20,836)
Cook, Debbie C	5:10:14 (27,531)
Cook, Elaine S	5:33:34 (30,734)
Cook, Gemma A	4:43:41 (22,028)
Cook, Jane M	3:55:29 (9,364)
Cook, Jennie	8:00:42 (35,232)
Cook, Joy	5:55:33 (32,684)
Cook, Justine S	5:12:43 (27,953)
Cook, Karen C	5:03:36 (26,446)
Cook, Lindsey J	4:25:05 (17,146)
Cook, Paula W	4:42:51 (21,833)

Cook, Phillippa J	3:47:22 (7,430)
Cook, Rachel	3:13:05 (2,255)
Cook, Samantha J	3:46:04 (7,153)
Cook, Samantha M	4:52:36 (24,074)
Cook, Sara J	4:24:24 (16,956)
Cook, Sarah E	4:36:27 (20,216)
Cook, Sharon J	5:43:59 (31,760)
Cook, Shirley K	5:13:56 (28,156)
Cook, Stephanie J	4:23:36 (16,754)
Cook, Stephanie M	3:16:00 (2,576)
Cook, Vanessa	4:30:06 (18,621)
Cooke, Florence E	3:30:03 (4,460)
Cooke, Jackie	5:42:56 (31,674)
Cooke, Lynette	4:41:49 (21,592)
Cooke, Tamara	5:57:33 (32,807)
Cooke-Simmons, Julia K	4:00:48 (10,905)
Cookson, Fiona	5:00:53 (25,958)
Cookson, Maria V	5:05:57 (26,862)
Coombe, Emma V	4:12:54 (13,857)
Coombe, Kathryn B	4:32:55 (19,295)
Coombs, Gemma L	6:43:37 (34,585)
Coop, Andrea V	5:29:35 (30,318)
Cooper, Alison C	6:30:54 (34,270)
Cooper, Caroline S	4:54:17 (24,496)
Cooper, Claire	5:38:04 (31,203)
Cooper, Heidi	5:04:41 (26,627)
Cooper, Heidi E	4:44:44 (22,255)
Cooper, Helen J	4:56:53 (25,110)
Cooper, Helene A	5:38:03 (31,200)
Cooper, Holly J	3:30:59 (4,601)
Cooper, Jill A	4:49:20 (23,320)
Cooper, Judith	4:51:33 (23,842)
Cooper, Julie A	7:12:48 (35,013)
Cooper, Kerri J	4:47:22 (22,847)
Cooper, Lindsey J	4:25:35 (17,310)
Cooper, Louise	6:03:02 (33,145)
Cooper, Louise J	2:56:30 (843)
Cooper, Patience A	4:38:33 (20,764)
Cooper, Rebecca J	4:25:06 (17,152)
Cooper, Susan	5:54:53 (32,631)
Cooper, Susan J	5:52:14 (32,431)
Cooper, Tracey E	5:11:22 (27,719)
Cooper, Tracey J	4:39:14 (20,942)
Cope, Amy L	4:05:41 (12,023)
Cope, Linda A	6:05:56 (33,329)
Cope, Samantha	4:20:10 (15,846)
Copeland, Lisa A	5:38:36 (31,265)
Copeman, Emma J	4:17:07 (14,991)
Coppens, An	6:07:32 (33,419)
Coppin, Anne W	5:56:45 (32,758)
Coppin, Emily J	4:30:36 (18,747)
Corbett, Tara J	3:59:47 (10,661)
Cordingley, Janet	3:36:46 (5,462)
Cork, Alison B	3:59:36 (10,599)
Cork, Clare R	5:09:16 (27,398)
Corkill, Verity S	5:52:23 (32,446)
Cormack, Sarah J	4:03:06 (11,411)
Corne, Hannah J	5:03:47 (26,481)
Cornell, Teresa	6:44:36 (34,611)
Cornes, Mary	6:25:27 (34,109)
Cornish, Charlotte R	5:34:01 (30,783)
Cornish, Leanne N	4:16:39 (14,876)
Cornwell, Lisa R	5:04:05 (26,527)
Cornwell, Michelle	4:17:06 (14,982)
Coronel, Monica V	5:38:34 (31,262)
Corpe, Angela L	6:57:08 (34,831)
Corrall, Karen A	5:15:11 (28,365)
Corsini, Susan J	3:27:20 (3,983)
Cosby, Beckie	4:44:23 (22,188)
Coslitt, Debbie	3:01:07 (1,198)
Costelloe, Jennifer C	4:08:11 (12,607)
Costiff, Christine	3:23:15 (3,343)
Cotin, Carole	4:04:47 (11,811)
Cotta, Sofia N	7:29:19 (35,121)
Cotterill, Caroline A	4:18:33 (15,373)
Cotterill, Fiona H	3:48:20 (7,664)
Cotton, Jody E	5:03:22 (26,414)
Couchman, Hannah A	4:51:04 (23,748)
Coughlan, Amanda	4:47:39 (22,927)
Coughlan, Norah E	6:26:00 (34,124)
Coughlin, Nicole M	3:35:57 (5,331)
Couling, Sally M	6:10:06 (33,536)
Coulson, Aileen F	4:57:25 (25,215)

Coulson, Diane	4:48:44 (23,175)
Coulter, Jenny	5:17:00 (28,645)
Coulthard, Helen T	4:37:34 (20,515)
Coultrip, Corrina J	5:45:44 (31,914)
Coultrup, Kathleen F	4:09:55 (13,074)
Coupland, Irene M	5:04:44 (26,636)
Coupland, Tracey	4:23:14 (16,661)
Courcier, Lorraine M	3:58:21 (10,243)
Cousen, Sharon L	3:51:52 (8,459)
Cousins, Suzanne M	5:00:03 (25,782)
Couzens, Clare L	6:12:06 (33,622)
Cova, Claire	4:59:01 (25,565)
Covarrubias, Alejandra	4:33:15 (19,370)
Cowan, Margaret M	6:03:10 (33,152)
Cowburn, Lucille M	4:58:03 (25,338)
Cowell, Julia	5:27:53 (30,086)
Cowen, Samantha J	3:59:52 (10,688)
Cowie, Felicity	5:14:36 (28,279)
Cowley, Laura J	2:53:47 (670)
Cowley, Rachel	4:25:27 (17,265)
Cowling, Gert T	3:54:47 (9,179)
Cowling, Margaret C	4:41:07 (21,424)
Cowling, Mary M	4:17:21 (15,050)
Cowling, Michelle	5:22:21 (29,395)
Cownden, Maggie A	7:25:35 (35,103)
Cox, Amanda L	4:28:58 (18,297)
Cox, Donna E	6:06:40 (33,366)
Cox, Dorothy	4:50:33 (23,642)
Cox, Hannah E	4:58:58 (25,552)
Cox, Jacqueline A	4:32:16 (19,152)
Cox, Jane	4:36:03 (20,093)
Cox, Jean	4:14:45 (14,363)
Cox, Joanne B	5:03:18 (26,404)
Cox, Julie C	6:09:03 (33,490)
Cox, Julie D	3:58:17 (10,220)
Cox, Lucy H	4:27:22 (17,845)
Cox, Mathilda M	5:10:30 (27,572)
Cox, Rachel E	4:05:18 (11,948)
Cox, Sally A	4:42:34 (21,761)
Cox, Samantha C	5:11:34 (27,752)
Cox, Sarah J	6:11:04 (33,577)
Cox, Sue M	5:48:17 (32,123)
Cox-Hoare, Olivia	5:10:30 (27,572)
Coxon, Alexandra E	5:07:52 (27,199)
Coxon, Leah S	4:59:46 (25,730)
Coxon, Linda	4:57:56 (25,307)
Coxon, Melanie J	5:09:42 (27,470)
Coyle, Elizabeth L	4:54:04 (24,443)
Coyle, Sara L	6:17:25 (33,837)
Crabb, Mary J	4:15:18 (14,527)
Cracknell, Beverley A	4:38:00 (20,622)
Cracknell, Joanne P	5:55:13 (32,660)
Craddock, Emma L	6:02:32 (33,107)
Cragg, Elizabeth J	4:48:20 (23,083)
Cragg, Louise	5:01:16 (26,019)
Craig, Maura B	3:59:12 (10,496)
Craig, Nicola A	3:52:21 (8,566)
Craig, Theresa K	4:51:33 (23,842)
Cramer, Suzy	5:57:26 (32,801)
Cramond, Catriona M	4:11:27 (13,474)
Cramp, Helen K	3:43:53 (6,717)
Crampton, Davina M	6:28:19 (34,207)
Crampton, Rachael A	3:35:10 (5,205)
Cramsie, Lara R	5:41:31 (31,553)
Crane, Karen	5:09:28 (27,432)
Cranmer, Angela M	4:08:57 (12,813)
Cranwell, Tricia S	4:15:39 (14,621)
Crask, Pauline L	6:51:53 (34,752)
Crate, Debbie C	4:26:40 (17,653)
Cravda, Jenny M	7:15:33 (35,037)
Crawford, Helen E	5:12:34 (27,921)
Crawford, Terry	4:41:02 (21,402)
Crawford, Zoe E	5:25:56 (29,859)
Crawley, Anita D	3:42:35 (6,477)
Crawley, Carol A	4:58:58 (25,552)
Crawley, Emma	3:57:12 (9,891)
Crawley, Victoria R	4:10:00 (13,092)
Cray, Janet M	4:36:35 (20,243)
Crayford, Jo C	4:19:03 (15,527)
Craze, Andrea L	4:44:20 (22,181)
Creasey, Cindy	5:20:54 (29,224)
Creasey, Tanya J	6:20:20 (33,931)
Creed, Natalie	4:42:39 (21,786)

Davis, Mary 4:38:28 (20,749)
Davis, Pauline M 6:15:47 (33,775)
Davis, Samantha M 3:56:16 (9,589)
Davis, Sarah L 6:46:53 (34,654)
Davison, Bridget J 4:31:05 (18,850)
Davison, Jane S 5:02:43 (26,278)
Davison, Julie C 4:10:18 (13,169)
Davison, Juliette T 5:14:55 (28,328)
Davy, Helen M 5:56:43 (32,749)
Davy, Peta Jane 5:13:51 (28,141)
Davy, Rosemary J 5:17:01 (28,648)
Davys, Heidi J 4:20:23 (15,909)
Dawe, Allison F 5:46:59 (32,018)
Dawes, Beverley A 4:38:06 (20,648)
Dawes, Janice E 3:47:36 (7,474)
Dawkins, Justine C 4:26:23 (17,561)
Dawkins, Margaret E 5:22:43 (29,456)
Dawoodi, Jane E 4:33:10 (19,355)
Dawrant, Emma J 4:54:10 (24,463)
Dawrant, Nancy J 3:45:48 (7,095)
Dawson, Deborah J 5:04:55 (26,676)
Dawson, Gail 2:58:43 (1,006)
Dawson, Gemma C 5:36:02 (30,998)
Dawson, Jahan 5:32:12 (30,576)
Dawson, Kay 6:26:20 (34,139)
Dawson, Metta 4:38:15 (20,683)
Dawson, Natalie S 4:15:28 (14,566)
Dawson, Nicole C 5:55:02 (32,643)
Day, Alison 4:28:02 (18,036)
Day, Emma 5:02:41 (26,270)
Day, Emma K 5:52:20 (32,442)
Day, Gill M 4:56:39 (25,056)
Day, Jill E 4:42:30 (21,742)
Day, Karen 4:18:36 (15,394)
Day, Lesley C 3:17:42 (2,754)
Day, Patrice R 4:33:43 (19,492)
Daynes, Catriona A 5:57:22 (32,797)
De Borr, Claudia M 3:48:30 (7,709)
De Carteret, Annette L 4:58:10 (25,364)
De Crespigny, Camilla 5:03:37 (26,448)
De Laage De Meux, Caroline 3:55:30 (9,368)
De Martino, Concetta 5:14:53 (28,324)
De Matos, Melanie M 4:02:51 (11,352)
De Meester, Michou 4:22:43 (16,540)
De Nadai, Raquel 5:36:34 (31,065)
De Paor, Aideen C 3:54:28 (9,093)
De Zoete, Fiona C 5:16:33 (28,556)
De Zoete, Susannah C 4:02:19 (11,225)
Deacon, Tracy L 5:21:09 (29,255)
Deakin, Anne M 4:55:58 (24,892)
Deakin, Sarah J 5:11:01 (27,658)
Deakins, Bethan J 4:58:34 (25,462)
Deal, Carole 6:48:19 (34,681)
Dean, Catherine 4:07:38 (12,486)
Dean, Charlotte 5:44:51 (31,836)
Dean, Dixie H 4:52:55 (24,153)
Dean, Helen 4:26:27 (17,585)
Dean, Julia M 5:28:39 (30,204)
Dean, Lucinda 4:36:21 (20,177)
Dean, Sarah J 4:45:28 (22,425)
Dean, Sharon J 3:59:49 (10,667)
Dean, Suzanne C 5:08:53 (27,337)
Dean, Zoe 3:50:53 (8,235)
Deane, Althea J 5:22:28 (29,415)
Dear, Sue W 4:45:17 (22,390)
Deasy, Margaret A 2:53:23 (654)
Deaves, Angela E 7:04:41 (34,921)
Deboumois, Andrée J 5:51:26 (32,366)
Decker, Eleanor 4:21:38 (16,238)
Deegan, Donna H 4:46:15 (22,611)
Deeks, Sara L 5:44:16 (31,785)
Deery, Sheila 9:08:10 (35,253)
Defis, Catrin L 5:08:57 (27,346)
De-Kisshazy, Michelle E 4:38:36 (20,777)
Dekkers, Carine M 5:04:12 (26,556)
Del Monte, Gloria J 5:30:55 (30,457)
Delaney, Jennifer J 5:17:07 (28,666)
Dell, Sally J 3:40:26 (6,077)
Delmar-Morgan, Kate S 4:58:35 (25,463)
Dempsey, Nicola 6:18:35 (33,877)
Denham-Cookes, Tessa L 5:00:06 (25,795)
Denham-Jones, Laura 4:27:29 (17,884)
Denley, Katrine 4:25:15 (17,203)
Denley, Loretto C 3:29:48 (4,417)
Denney, Cathy E 4:18:07 (15,239)
Dennis, Corrina E 5:22:46 (29,461)
Dennis, Gemma N 4:19:07 (15,553)
Dennison, Andrea M 2:56:07 (814)
Dennison, Deborah A 3:23:35 (3,387)
Dennison, Ruth E 5:16:38 (28,566)
Denniss, Stella S 4:24:36 (17,016)
Derrick, Claire L 5:22:57 (29,480)
Derrick, Sarah J 3:19:41 (2,964)
Desiderio, Philippa S 5:38:10 (31,217)
Desmond, Patricia 4:48:20 (23,083)
Desoutter, Briony S 5:22:30 (29,419)
Dessibourg, Jocelyne 4:32:34 (19,223)
Deutsch, Caroline 4:59:01 (25,565)
Deutzmann, Martina 5:21:07 (29,252)
Devenish-Meares, Sue E 5:20:42 (29,206)
Devereux, Jacqueline M 5:12:38 (27,934)
Devine, Kathryn J 5:01:36 (26,081)
Devine, Mairead 5:42:53 (31,670)
Devine, Nicola 5:17:19 (28,690)
Devlin, Bernadette 5:59:16 (32,931)
Devlin, Shirley 5:02:59 (26,338)
Devlin, Tina 4:06:33 (12,225)
Devonport, Kirsty L 3:46:45 (7,297)
Devoy, Anita E 4:33:53 (19,543)
Dewar, Emma 5:10:29 (27,569)
Dewinter, Margaret 5:01:06 (25,996)
Dews, Emma M 3:21:55 (3,174)
Dey, Elizabeth M 5:06:27 (26,953)
Dhariwal, Slinder 5:00:02 (25,779)
Dhupelia, Suniti R 3:29:38 (4,381)
Di Benedetto, Angela 3:54:51 (9,198)
Di Liello, Flaminia 3:37:27 (5,570)
Di Vita, Luisa 3:10:58 (2,029)
Diamente, Rosanna A 5:23:33 (29,550)
Diamond, Charlotte A 4:43:30 (21,980)
Diatta, Teba S 5:42:38 (31,642)
Dibb, Beth A 4:12:02 (13,630)
Dibb-Fuller, Verity E 3:49:50 (8,002)
Dibble, Deborah L 3:38:30 (5,724)
Dick, Eleanor M 3:55:17 (9,307)
Dick, Helen M 7:36:49 (35,164)
Dick, Patricia A 3:33:34 (4,966)
Dickie, Patricia 4:34:42 (19,771)
Dickinson, Lesley A 4:44:48 (22,275)
Dickinson, Lucy V 4:30:53 (18,815)
Dickinson, Sally 4:45:56 (22,539)
Dideron, Aline 5:43:25 (31,711)
Dietrich, Karyn L 4:28:10 (18,078)
Diffey, Joanne C 3:19:20 (2,913)
Difiore, Judy A 5:30:14 (30,390)
Digby, Pippa A 4:53:26 (24,288)
Diggins, Gemma M 5:07:25 (27,133)
Dimyan, Rebecca L 4:58:02 (25,335)
Dingle, Joanna E 5:13:20 (28,049)
Dinsdale, Helen 4:11:48 (13,564)
Dinsdale, Sarah L 3:57:55 (10,116)
Diprose, Caroline L 4:23:58 (16,840)
Diprose, Marion M 5:22:57 (29,480)
Di-Rienzo, Katia 5:19:26 (29,015)
Disbury, Rebecca 4:04:31 (11,749)
Disney, Glennys 3:15:32 (2,529)
Dita, Constantina 2:22:50 (36)
Ditchfield, Charlotte L 4:49:47 (23,444)
Dives, Helen 4:53:18 (24,251)
Dix, Annette 4:56:20 (24,971)
Dixon, Angela J 4:39:22 (20,980)
Dixon, Claire 4:37:15 (20,431)
Dixon, Clare H 6:12:38 (33,647)
Dixon, Hayley 4:25:11 (17,182)
Dixon, Jayne 5:09:06 (27,370)
Dixon, Karen 4:48:44 (23,175)
Dixon, Samantha J 4:57:46 (25,275)
Dlamini, Duduzile Revival 4:37:14 (20,423)
Dobie, Glenda L 3:46:35 (7,258)
Dobson, Janette 4:47:43 (22,948)
Dobson, Jeanette 4:51:09 (23,761)
Dobson, Katie A 4:09:35 (12,978)
Dobson, Meryl D 4:34:27 (19,703)
Dobson, Rachael M 4:09:19 (12,915)
Dobson, Theo M 5:40:05 (31,425)
Docherty, Caroline B 5:28:16 (30,160)
Docherty, Catherine C 4:28:16 (18,105)
Docherty, Daiana 5:02:16 (26,194)
Dodd, Rosanne G 4:05:02 (11,871)
Doddington, Denise A 3:26:25 (3,831)
Dodds, Vanessa J 4:02:33 (11,287)
Dodgson, Jocelyn F 5:12:56 (27,988)
Dods, Melissa S 3:58:11 (10,184)
Dodsworth, Catherine M 4:43:41 (22,028)
Doffman, Sarah R 6:02:06 (33,089)
Doherty, Carolyne F 3:42:25 (6,457)
Doherty, Hayley M 4:02:01 (11,161)
Doherty, Marian 6:37:51 (34,454)
Doherty, Maxine L 6:02:42 (33,121)
Dolamore, Tanya 4:43:24 (21,955)
Dolan, Anita M 4:13:14 (13,948)
Dolan, Jane M 5:04:03 (26,522)
Dolan, Lucy H 7:10:26 (34,983)
Dolan, Susan A 5:59:58 (32,979)
Dolphin, Alison 5:58:04 (32,840)
Domaille, Suzanna L 6:29:11 (34,229)
Doman, Tracey A 3:46:46 (7,302)
Dominey, Maureen 5:55:53 (32,702)
Domingo, Laurel P 7:14:30 (35,029)
Don, Nicola J 3:24:40 (3,536)
Donaghey, Gloria A 4:04:53 (11,834)
Donagrandi, Gaudenzia 3:36:14 (5,378)
Donahoe, Mary 4:24:04 (16,870)
Donald, Soizic M 4:08:42 (12,740)
Donald, Tanya E 4:53:36 (24,329)
Donaldson, Deborah 3:58:47 (10,382)
Donbavand, Nicky 5:03:49 (26,489)
Donkin, Anne 3:59:21 (10,533)
Donlan, Colleen 4:34:23 (19,689)
Donne, Danielle 5:15:24 (28,406)
Donnini, Linda J 5:14:00 (28,171)
Donoghue, Emma 5:07:29 (27,143)
Donohue, Sarah 5:09:49 (27,487)
Donovan, Laura J 4:16:47 (14,911)
Dooley, Ruth 4:07:50 (12,537)
Dooley, Sharon D 5:14:00 (28,171)
Dooley, Sonia 6:02:21 (33,100)
Dopson, Sarah L 4:59:02 (25,569)
Dorans, Claire L 5:04:21 (26,575)
Dore, Anita M 4:47:42 (22,945)
Dore, Emma J 5:10:31 (27,576)
Dormer, Harriet L 4:55:36 (24,789)
Dorrance, Priscilla 5:36:41 (31,077)
Dorrell, Patricia A 4:03:37 (11,528)
Dorrity, Miriam 4:25:47 (17,373)
Dos Santos, Celeste M 6:59:00 (34,852)
Dossett, Hannah L 4:52:57 (24,158)
Dougan, Kerry 4:35:24 (19,951)
Dougherty, Erin C 4:34:58 (19,847)
Douglas, Angela 4:25:57 (17,413)
Douglas, Emily P 3:27:23 (3,988)
Douglas, Sue 4:17:15 (15,021)
Douglas, Teresa 3:31:18 (4,651)
Doulton, Lindsay M 4:34:54 (19,825)
Dove, Tina L 5:34:57 (30,899)
Dover, Katherine L 4:29:00 (18,306)
Dover, Liz 3:54:50 (9,193)
Doveton, Michelle 4:08:13 (12,619)
Dow, Alexandra M 4:32:15 (19,149)
Dowbiggin, Nicola J 4:32:11 (19,131)
Dowdy, Paula L 4:15:29 (14,573)
Dowling, Louise 4:43:36 (22,007)
Down, Bernadette M 5:09:05 (27,365)
Down, Caroline L 5:08:57 (27,346)
Down, Sue K 5:21:49 (29,329)
Downes, Fiona 4:36:46 (20,294)
Downey, Fiona M 5:34:35 (30,858)
Downing, Caroline 7:18:23 (35,065)
Downing, Claire 5:01:26 (26,047)
Downing, Rebecca H 4:11:47 (13,559)
Downinton, Sally A 4:58:11 (25,367)
Downs, Ursula M 4:23:49 (16,808)
Dowse, Julie K 6:06:17 (33,347)
Dowsett, Pauline 4:45:31 (22,434)
Doyle, Claire L 4:25:14 (17,196)
Doyle, Emma T 4:49:18 (23,306)
Doyle, Glynis L 4:04:52 (11,829)
Doyle, Katrina H 4:56:47 (25,090)
Doyle, Niki 5:34:34 (30,854)

Doyle, Sylvia J 4:00:44 (10,893)
Drabble, Alison 6:02:49 (33,128)
Drake, Dawn A 4:29:31 (18,470)
Drake, Joanne L 5:42:22 (31,618)
Drake, Lesley A....4:19:10 (15,567)
Drake, Louisa J 4:12:53 (13,848)
Drake, Michala 4:44:56 (22,307)
Drake, Michelle....4:19:58 (15,792)
Drake, Natalie A....5:25:11 (29,769)
Drake, Wendy....5:11:38 (27,760)
Drakeley, Helena M 6:01:08 (33,032)
Draper, Eleanor....4:14:14 (14,220)
Drawbridge, Heidi L 4:01:38 (11,075)
Dreves-Van Rijswijk, Hanneke....5:53:38 (32,540)
Drew, Katherine R....3:31:05 (4,617)
Drewett, Cereta C....4:26:44 (17,672)
Dreze, Helene 4:29:23 (18,428)
Drinkwater, Rebecca L....4:49:36 (23,388)
Drinkwater, Renata 7:46:09 (35,196)
Driscoll, Emma J 4:26:17 (17,527)
Driver, Jane....4:48:21 (23,088)
Driver, Louise J....4:28:14 (18,095)
Drohan, Janice G 4:53:45 (24,366)
Drumm, Catherine C....5:23:33 (29,550)
Drummond, Paula M....5:50:14 (32,282)
Drummond, Sarah E....3:56:31 (9,670)
Drury, Catherine J....4:21:46 (16,276)
Drury, Rebecca....4:45:03 (22,338)
D'Souza, Anne S....6:50:04 (34,722)
Du Plessis, Julie 6:13:25 (33,673)
Du Plessis, Sonja....5:22:40 (29,452)
Du Toit, Aletta....5:38:39 (31,273)
Du Toit, Celeste....4:41:26 (21,506)
Duce, Lisa A....5:07:27 (27,138)
Duckling, Louise A....5:19:37 (29,051)
Duckworth, Sarah E....4:04:12 (11,684)
Ducret, Melanie M 5:28:04 (30,111)
Dudfield, Helen 4:12:50 (13,840)
Dudgeon, Sarah P 3:22:08 (3,204)
Dudley, Emer B 3:26:44 (3,891)
Dudley, Norma P 5:51:23 (32,362)
Duerden, Mandy 4:42:42 (21,800)
Duff, Hannah L....5:52:35 (32,470)
Duffield, Denise T....5:29:47 (30,337)
Duffy, Dalila A 4:36:59 (20,350)
Duffy, Fiona M....3:30:27 (4,515)
Duffy, Jo 4:59:48 (25,742)
Duffy, Patricia L....3:52:34 (8,622)
Duffy, Sarah F 4:20:13 (15,857)
Dufour, Fabienne....4:00:32 (10,843)
Dugdale, Elspeth L 4:40:38 (21,295)
Duggan, Andrea....4:50:01 (23,500)
Duggan, Elizabeth J 4:38:22 (20,718)
Duggan, Helen....4:22:26 (16,453)
Duggan, Martine....5:00:35 (25,893)
Duggins, Nicola J....5:25:28 (29,801)
Duggleby, Helen J 4:09:25 (12,936)
Duke, Julie C 4:08:21 (12,659)
Duke-Brown, Theresa J....4:10:44 (13,274)
Dumas, Sylvie....3:20:00 (2,996)
Dumbrell, Jeanette K....3:25:23 (3,654)
Dunbar, Elisa S 4:46:24 (22,648)
Dunbar, Sarah L....4:47:41 (22,941)
Duncan, Gillian....5:28:09 (30,134)
Duncan, June A....3:39:03 (5,830)
Duncombe, Rebecca....3:57:50 (10,089)
Dungate, Stephanie M....4:39:54 (21,112)
Dunham, Judith 5:11:07 (27,670)
Dunkerley, Deborah J 3:53:17 (8,792)
Dunkley, Joanna....4:20:04 (15,817)
Dunlop, Kirstie....3:55:53 (9,484)
Dunn, Fiona L....3:22:01 (3,189)
Dunn, Helen R....4:58:11 (25,367)
Dunn, Julia 5:27:11 (29,995)
Dunn, Karen R....5:19:06 (28,954)
Dunn, Tracey....6:16:08 (33,790)
Dunne, Kathleen....9:08:10 (35,253)
Dunning, Joan C 5:17:12 (28,674)
Dunstan, Charlotte M 4:17:39 (15,125)
Dunstan, Kate....5:27:25 (30,032)
Dunt, Claire A 4:46:32 (22,675)
Dunton, Joanne L 3:46:03 (7,147)
Dupain, Hannah J....3:26:41 (3,883)
Durand, Sophie....3:50:59 (8,256)
Durber, Sandra....5:11:27 (27,731)
Durbin, Julia....4:59:36 (25,691)
Durkin, Carmel F 5:09:51 (27,490)
Durn, Carol 5:15:37 (28,435)
Durnford, Sally C 4:48:57 (23,224)
Duroe, Fiona 3:43:19 (6,622)
Durrani, Monise....4:44:44 (22,255)
Durrant, Emma J....5:13:03 (28,007)
Dutch, Charlotte L....3:47:57 (7,560)
Dutton, Kerry 5:32:21 (30,595)
Dwyer, Laura E 4:55:01 (24,679)
Dwyer, Lucy J 3:57:28 (9,969)
Dwyer, Roslyn M 5:52:22 (32,445)
Dyakova, Olga....4:56:20 (24,971)
Dyble, Jayne....4:58:19 (25,395)
Dyde, Andrea....6:06:42 (33,370)
Dyer, Rachel F 5:48:28 (32,134)
Dyer, Sarah L 4:11:25 (13,458)
Dyett, Audrey A....4:01:37 (11,072)
Dyke, Sarah-Jane F 3:55:49 (9,467)
Dykes, Madeline C 4:09:31 (12,967)
Dykes, Rita....4:26:54 (17,718)
Dykins, Brenda A 6:08:42 (33,475)
Dylla, Barbara....4:56:51 (25,101)
Dymore-Brown, Linda S 4:18:44 (15,441)
Dyson, Clare 5:22:56 (29,477)
Dyson, Joanna L....4:32:58 (19,307)
Dyson, Natasha F....5:45:07 (31,856)
Dyter, Sarah 4:31:47 (19,042)
Dzialdow, Resi....4:15:15 (14,515)
Eagleson, Jill A 3:41:59 (6,372)
Ealand, Michelle 5:26:56 (29,968)
Eardley, Joanna E....4:26:00 (17,435)
Earlam, Joanna K....4:59:24 (25,641)
Earley, Fionnuala....4:54:40 (24,586)
Early, Lindsay A....5:50:30 (32,300)
Earthy, Kimberly....4:49:36 (23,388)
Earthy, Marianne....5:07:08 (27,081)
East, Charlotte E 4:01:04 (10,958)
East, Louise J 4:56:06 (24,918)
Easterbrook, Joanna C....4:33:50 (19,529)
Easterbrook, Liz 5:26:58 (29,975)
Easterbrook, Victoria E....4:45:45 (22,486)
Eastham, Dawn....4:32:52 (19,279)
Eastman, Jo....5:16:31 (28,550)
Eaton, Jane 3:50:26 (8,133)
Eccles, Kirstie A....6:21:30 (33,961)
Eccles, Tamsin J....6:59:23 (34,859)
Echlin, Helen 5:39:50 (31,400)
Eckett, Louise C 4:54:26 (24,534)
Eckles, Brenda J 4:48:27 (23,114)
Eddicott, Helen A 5:30:45 (30,438)
Eddleston, Susan P....5:54:09 (32,580)
Ede, Samantha 4:31:55 (19,064)
Eden, Julia R....5:17:47 (28,757)
Edgell, Nicole M....5:43:30 (31,717)
Edgerton, Sandra A 5:11:30 (27,738)
Edgson, Clare 5:42:52 (31,669)
Edmans, Gail B....4:55:42 (24,818)
Edmans, Jill K....6:08:49 (33,477)
Edmead, Tamara A....3:53:17 (8,792)
Edmiston, Portia C....4:37:41 (20,547)
Edmonds, Jill B....4:14:15 (14,229)
Edmonds, Lizzie....3:22:24 (3,233)
Edmondson, Jennifer 4:59:29 (25,659)
Edmondson, Penne L....5:38:32 (31,258)
Edmondson, Tanya E....4:43:08 (21,895)
Edmunds, Kim J 3:44:39 (6,868)
Edmunds, Pam J....5:24:01 (29,621)
Edmunds, Sarah F....3:20:18 (3,026)
Edson, Joanna H 3:42:50 (6,514)
Edwards, Alice V....3:38:09 (5,674)
Edwards, Brenda 5:04:09 (26,546)
Edwards, Christine E....7:31:56 (35,143)
Edwards, Claire J 4:05:45 (12,040)
Edwards, Debora G 5:36:29 (31,053)
Edwards, Elizabeth....6:35:25 (34,390)
Edwards, Emma L 5:08:17 (27,257)
Edwards, Fizzy G....5:19:30 (29,032)
Edwards, Gill 5:06:17 (26,917)
Edwards, Helen S 4:42:05 (21,645)
Edwards, Jane C 5:15:05 (28,346)
Edwards, Joanne K....3:52:56 (8,705)
Edwards, Julia E....4:18:44 (15,441)
Edwards, Katherine E 5:19:42 (29,060)
Edwards, Kelly....4:59:12 (25,607)
Edwards, Nadine M....5:44:06 (31,769)
Edwards, Natalie E 3:45:11 (6,988)
Edwards, Nicola L 4:10:34 (13,237)
Edwards, Nuala M 6:55:27 (34,807)
Edwards, Rebecca J 5:59:38 (32,954)
Edwards, Sharron....7:00:12 (34,870)
Edwards, Tracy B 4:55:40 (24,804)
Edwards, Verity J....4:22:54 (16,579)
Edwards, Yvonne 4:09:10 (12,878)
Edwardson, Jane A....3:46:51 (7,316)
Eeles, Karen J 5:52:13 (32,429)
Eerdekens, Maria 5:37:54 (31,184)
Egan, Mary E....3:51:11 (8,297)
Egan, Olivia M....5:02:35 (26,245)
Egmore, Jenni 4:37:58 (20,610)
Ehrat, Elizabeth....3:29:37 (4,376)
Ehrhardt, Adrienne S 3:56:07 (9,543)
Eiby, Donna 4:00:18 (10,787)
Eite, Rachael C....5:18:20 (28,841)
Elbro, Kate....4:36:55 (20,335)
Elder, Noeleen M....5:23:55 (29,607)
Eldridge, Anne E....6:36:49 (34,430)
Eldridge, Sally-Anne 5:16:30 (28,549)
Elengorn, Sarah J 4:30:24 (18,702)
Elgood, Zoe C....5:22:04 (29,362)
El-Hage, Marsha L....4:52:51 (24,140)
Elia, Roberta....3:17:57 (2,783)
Eling, Mikela 5:49:13 (32,201)
Ellacott, Suzy J 4:33:58 (19,560)
Ellender, Michelle A 6:19:23 (33,899)
Elliott, Caroline F....3:56:17 (9,599)
Elliott, Jenny L 3:45:27 (7,042)
Elliott, Joanne L 4:13:03 (13,894)
Elliott, Katrina J....6:32:16 (34,311)
Elliott, Linda 3:54:01 (8,979)
Elliott, Nicola E 4:47:34 (22,902)
Elliott, Nicola J....7:00:40 (34,882)
Elliott, Pauline M 5:13:35 (28,099)
Elliott, Penelope A....4:23:13 (16,655)
Elliott, Siobhan M....4:45:16 (22,384)
Elliott, Vanessa 4:51:59 (23,932)
Elliott, Zoe....4:27:32 (17,900)
Ellis, Carly....4:50:29 (23,623)
Ellis, Deborah F....5:54:20 (32,591)
Ellis, Janet A 5:03:21 (26,410)
Ellis, Janine E 3:54:44 (9,167)
Ellis, Jean 4:25:44 (17,359)
Ellis, Katie....5:32:54 (30,659)
Ellis, Melissa S 6:01:49 (33,071)
Ellis, Pauline D....4:24:56 (17,104)
Ellis, Sarah E....5:52:58 (32,496)
Ellis, Suzanne E....4:00:36 (10,867)
Ellis-Bell, Lucy R....6:40:22 (34,515)
Ellison, Annette....3:53:09 (8,756)
Ellison, Marnie J....4:44:24 (22,193)
Ellson, Jodie L 6:31:37 (34,293)
Ellson, Robyn 4:26:53 (17,714)
Elphinstone, May K....5:37:12 (31,116)
Else, Claire A....5:01:49 (26,109)
Elson, Rebecca L....4:52:11 (23,981)
Elsworth, Louise A 5:01:56 (26,132)
Elton, Jane....4:37:32 (20,502)
Elugbadebo, Adeola....4:47:26 (22,868)
Elvery, Donna M....5:22:13 (29,377)
Emerson, Katie....5:14:49 (28,314)
Emerton, Caroline M....4:14:08 (14,189)
Emery, Carol A 3:31:48 (4,718)
Emery, Kelly D....5:05:20 (26,756)
Emery, Tara S....4:31:20 (18,927)
Emilio, Shirley P....5:04:54 (26,672)
Emler, Charlotte....5:50:30 (32,300)
Emmerson, Janet A 4:46:41 (22,704)
Emmerson, Vicki....5:41:22 (31,542)
Emmett, Catriona R....5:42:39 (31,646)
Emond, Kathleen M....3:34:39 (5,142)
Endacott, Natasha K 5:37:01 (31,101)
Endicott, Patricia J 6:10:46 (33,567)
Endres, Christine E....5:22:33 (29,431)
Engdahl, Elin....3:02:32 (1,299)

England, Alma....5:12:57 (27,991)
England, Maureen....4:58:49 (25,515)
Englefield, Claire J....4:28:08 (18,067)
English, Amanda M....4:16:14 (14,775)
English, Teresa J....3:25:38 (3,692)
Engstrom, Cecilia....4:51:33 (23,842)
Ennis, Lynsey H....6:38:13 (34,460)
Ennis, Marie F....3:55:23 (9,332)
Ennis, Nicola R....4:56:11 (24,939)
Ennis, Philippa A....5:40:57 (31,501)
Entwisle, Elisabeth N....4:31:59 (19,083)
Epstein, Suzanne....5:11:12 (27,687)
Erasmus, Christie J....3:33:44 (4,995)
Eriksson, Lena....5:07:58 (27,211)
Eriksson, Nell....4:57:01 (25,135)
Errington, Justine D....4:39:05 (20,900)
Erritt, Sarah J....4:38:53 (20,848)
Ervin, Philippa....4:40:54 (21,361)
Escott, Mary A....5:11:39 (27,764)
Esdon, Jennifer....4:41:11 (21,443)
Espin, Melanie J....5:21:47 (29,324)
Esquilant, Karen....5:58:49 (32,894)
Essex, Claire E....5:33:29 (30,723)
Etchells, Barbara J....7:30:04 (35,126)
Etheridge, Beverley J....5:35:39 (30,962)
Etheridge, Nicola J....5:04:42 (26,631)
Eugster, Antoinette M....5:32:52 (30,658)
Evans, Alice H....2:57:24 (914)
Evans, Angela J....3:46:28 (7,236)
Evans, Angela M....5:51:43 (32,390)
Evans, Anigail L....6:41:09 (34,528)
Evans, Anne M....4:13:25 (13,993)
Evans, Carol A....3:00:56 (1,188)
Evans, Caroline....5:08:40 (27,305)
Evans, Catherine A....4:57:14 (25,181)
Evans, Christina J....3:09:35 (1,870)
Evans, Christina T....5:21:53 (29,337)
Evans, Denise A....4:21:16 (16,135)
Evans, Diane E....3:35:00 (5,182)
Evans, Elizabeth M....7:51:34 (35,212)
Evans, Helen C....5:02:01 (26,147)
Evans, Helen E....3:06:55 (1,629)
Evans, Jacqueline L....4:25:50 (17,383)
Evans, Jane C....5:21:32 (29,296)
Evans, Janet C....4:33:45 (19,506)
Evans, Julia A....4:51:35 (23,852)
Evans, Kathryn....5:45:38 (31,904)
Evans, Katrina J....4:02:49 (11,345)
Evans, Lisa....4:19:06 (15,547)
Evans, Lisa J....4:53:23 (24,270)
Evans, Lorraine T....4:42:45 (21,811)
Evans, Maggie E....4:49:18 (23,306)
Evans, Marie....4:24:07 (16,881)
Evans, Maureen H....4:47:56 (22,993)
Evans, Nicola C....5:02:02 (26,152)
Evans, Nicola H....4:50:57 (23,719)
Evans, Rebecca L....4:16:02 (14,724)
Evans, Rebecca W....6:13:27 (33,676)
Evans, Ria G....4:55:06 (24,700)
Evans, Rita....4:26:24 (17,570)
Evans, Samantha J....6:19:08 (33,892)
Evans, Sarah A....5:23:40 (29,569)
Evans, Sheelagh M....4:00:39 (10,877)
Evans, Stella....6:34:07 (34,357)
Evans, Susan....4:57:49 (25,282)
Evans, Tina....4:53:55 (24,398)
Evans, Tracey L....5:46:08 (31,944)
Evans, Vanessa E....5:14:10 (28,204)
Evans, Vicky J....6:34:42 (34,375)
Evans, Victoria L....5:02:03 (26,155)
Everding, Brigitte....4:38:39 (20,786)
Everett, Claire L....3:23:46 (3,411)
Everson, Sally....5:21:34 (29,297)
Everton, Kate E....5:59:44 (32,962)
Every, Ali P....5:36:42 (31,078)
Eves, Maggie M....6:01:12 (33,035)
Eveson, Samantha J....5:06:55 (27,045)
Evitt, Lydia J....5:43:42 (31,736)
Ewan, Christine....4:52:05 (23,961)
Ewen, Joanne C....3:52:50 (8,688)
Ewing, Jenny L....5:17:08 (28,669)
Eyes, Alexandra L....4:14:55 (14,417)
Eze, Gju....3:57:01 (9,820)
Ezekiel, Elizabeth....6:33:46 (34,349)
Ezuma, Chinyere U....5:45:12 (31,869)
Fabb, Rachel S....4:37:28 (20,489)
Faben, Jennifer....3:36:25 (5,412)
Fackerell, Karon L....3:51:24 (8,353)
Fagan, Laurraine D....5:34:12 (30,805)
Fagbohun, Ola....6:10:53 (33,570)
Fagg, Catherine M....3:57:47 (10,070)
Faherty, Louise J....3:16:03 (2,580)
Fairall, Karen....3:50:33 (8,158)
Fairbairn, Jeanine....4:31:40 (19,011)
Fairbairn, Lucy E....6:32:14 (34,310)
Fairbrother, Lisa M....6:43:53 (34,595)
Fairclough, Hayley G....6:27:17 (34,175)
Fairhead, Alison J....4:03:01 (11,393)
Fairweather, Sharon....4:18:58 (15,502)
Fairweather, Sonia....5:14:31 (28,263)
Fakande, Leanne....5:45:47 (31,919)
Fall, Sara....4:16:20 (14,805)
Fall, Suzanne L....4:46:29 (22,666)
Fallon, Bethan....3:19:33 (2,950)
Fallon, Patricia A....4:45:08 (22,363)
Fanning, Jane L....4:10:23 (13,194)
Fanning, Susan P....4:11:42 (13,538)
Farebrother, Helen M....5:53:02 (32,499)
Farey, Joan M....5:31:36 (30,522)
Fargher, Wenona S....5:13:56 (28,156)
Farman, Michelle C....3:18:32 (2,835)
Farmer, Jenny....4:23:32 (16,735)
Farmer, Juliet V....4:51:25 (23,816)
Farmer, Valerie M....5:06:37 (26,986)
Farmery, Joanne....4:13:53 (14,107)
Farmiloe, Kate P....4:58:50 (25,521)
Farnell, Shelley....5:23:10 (29,500)
Farnworth, Jayne E....4:19:08 (15,558)
Faron, Isabelle....4:09:33 (12,974)
Farquharson, Helen M....5:53:55 (32,559)
Farr, Elaine M....4:35:21 (19,931)
Farr, Michelle L....4:28:57 (18,292)
Farrall, Ali....3:35:01 (5,186)
Farrant, Catriona M....5:31:47 (30,542)
Farrell, Caroline....5:50:03 (32,268)
Farrell, Denise....5:12:26 (27,895)
Farrell, Jeanette....4:43:36 (22,007)
Farrell, Mo M....4:06:52 (12,303)
Farren, Amy....4:38:08 (20,656)
Farrer, Allison M....4:54:57 (24,658)
Farrow, Kay....4:45:28 (22,425)
Farrow, Patricia....4:01:33 (11,058)
Faulkner, Kelly A....4:45:00 (22,325)
Faulkner, Shannon I....4:56:15 (24,950)
Faure Walker, Julia....3:51:55 (8,466)
Faust, Nicola E....3:53:16 (8,786)
Fava, Cristina....3:19:42 (2,968)
Favell, Roz J....4:03:09 (11,421)
Fawbert, Lucy H....4:04:32 (11,756)
Fawcett, Sandra M....7:31:00 (35,134)
Fawcett, Sarah G....3:36:08 (5,360)
Fawcett, Sarah J....5:17:07 (28,666)
Fawcett, Trudy J....3:19:23 (2,921)
Fawcus, Sarah J....3:44:22 (6,811)
Fawkner-Corbett, Emma....4:04:42 (11,796)
Fearn, Margaret A....5:07:13 (27,106)
Fearne, Leila M....5:06:35 (26,980)
Feay, Sarah E....4:21:13 (16,113)
Feeley, Anne B....5:20:04 (29,111)
Feeney, Erin J....4:52:27 (24,041)
Feld, Joanne....5:49:10 (32,195)
Feldman, Sara J....5:46:09 (31,946)
Felgate, Helen E....4:43:41 (22,028)
Fell, Carol S....5:39:29 (31,375)
Fell, Karen....5:52:27 (32,459)
Fellowes, Tracey....5:14:41 (28,301)
Fellows, Joanne E....4:51:30 (23,829)
Felton, Ruth E....4:58:17 (25,390)
Felton, Sarah E....4:33:28 (19,421)
Feltwell, Anne L....4:51:11 (23,769)
Fenech, Donna....7:15:28 (35,035)
Fenn, Aimée L....4:32:57 (19,304)
Fenn, Catherine A....4:22:52 (16,574)
Fenn, Georgina A....4:56:30 (25,018)
Fenn, Maggie L....3:33:57 (5,036)
Fennah, Alison C....6:08:07 (33,450)
Fennell, Fiona M....4:22:33 (16,486)
Fennell, Shelley J....6:42:44 (34,562)
Fenwick, Rebecca H....5:08:05 (27,234)
Feraday, Caroline....4:40:45 (21,320)
Ferguson, Alice V....4:47:45 (22,953)
Ferguson, Barbara J....6:35:35 (34,398)
Ferguson, Caroline A....5:04:38 (26,618)
Ferguson, Christine....3:37:19 (5,539)
Ferguson, Elizabeth....3:33:43 (4,993)
Ferguson, Helen E....4:14:51 (14,396)
Ferguson, Lucy C....4:55:03 (24,687)
Ferguson, Shirley A....6:52:53 (34,770)
Fergusson, Christine A....4:00:46 (10,902)
Fernandes, Rachel E....5:24:06 (29,629)
Fernandes, Sofia....3:55:41 (9,423)
Fernee, Linda....5:24:26 (29,674)
Ferrari, Mariangela....5:34:45 (30,881)
Ferrari, Sandra....4:52:08 (23,972)
Ferraro, Sarah P....6:00:44 (33,013)
Ferris, Tanya L....5:28:05 (30,115)
Ferry, Emma....4:00:24 (10,804)
Ffoulkes-Morris, Helen....5:19:53 (29,084)
Ficken, Sarah E....5:36:25 (31,040)
Fiddament-Harris, Heather M....4:07:14 (12,399)
Fiddes, Gemma B....2:53:44 (667)
Field, Claire....6:12:36 (33,645)
Field, Claire M....4:48:29 (23,121)
Field, Jacqueline A....4:17:02 (14,967)
Field, Sally....5:05:44 (26,831)
Fielder, Jodie A....3:24:30 (3,516)
Fieldhouse, Jenny A....4:40:13 (21,191)
Filardi, Margarita....4:33:29 (19,425)
Filby, Catherine A....5:32:28 (30,612)
Fildes, Jennifer E....4:16:06 (14,738)
Filer, Daniela G....4:10:41 (13,261)
Filer, Sara-Marie....4:36:47 (20,298)
Filkins, Terri....4:26:16 (17,521)
Filsell, Susan S....4:48:54 (23,212)
Finch, Emma L....4:32:04 (19,104)
Finch, Janet R....5:03:45 (26,470)
Finch, Joanne E....5:27:59 (30,101)
Finch, Louise C....4:33:14 (19,366)
Finch, Lynn....5:26:23 (29,908)
Fincham, Donna L....6:07:58 (33,441)
Fincham, Sally J....4:28:09 (18,075)
Findel-Hawkins, Lisa J....5:46:02 (31,938)
Findlay, Celia A....3:26:35 (3,866)
Findlay, Debbie J....4:54:45 (24,610)
Findley, Judith A....3:54:40 (9,144)
Finegan, Elizabeth M....4:34:48 (19,789)
Finlay, Anita J....5:45:22 (31,888)
Finlayson, Karen A....5:57:03 (32,778)
Finlow, Pat C....7:19:57 (35,073)
Finn, Gabrielle L....5:03:44 (26,468)
Finn, Helen....5:10:24 (27,555)
Finnemore, Helen R....3:55:09 (9,263)
Fiori, Lucilla....3:08:49 (1,792)
Firman, Sarah-Jane....4:22:54 (16,579)
Firth, Emma J....4:58:57 (25,544)
Fish, Helen V....5:06:08 (26,899)
Fish, Sharon P....6:52:45 (34,766)
Fisher, Carla M....3:39:22 (5,886)
Fisher, Denise C....6:25:19 (34,102)
Fisher, Emma J....4:32:12 (19,134)
Fisher, Jane L....4:25:01 (17,130)
Fisher, Joanna....4:40:32 (21,267)
Fisher, Kay....4:41:21 (21,479)
Fisher, Lisa J....5:36:13 (31,014)
Fisher, Lyn-Si L....4:32:15 (19,149)
Fisher, Sarah-Jane M....6:35:18 (34,387)
Fisher, Victoria L....5:21:39 (29,306)
Fishlock, Hannah F....4:18:06 (15,236)
Fishwick, Leanne J....5:06:43 (27,004)
Fisichella, Annamaria....5:44:03 (31,763)
Fisk, Kirsty J....4:06:28 (12,204)
Fitch, Barbara Y....4:41:40 (21,558)
Fitzgerald, Claire....5:27:16 (30,010)
Fitzgerald, Jennifer H....4:08:02 (12,579)
Fitzgerald, Lesley....5:02:38 (26,256)
Fitzgerald, Ruth J....4:10:06 (13,115)
Fitzpatrick, Wendy L....3:54:25 (9,081)
Flaherty, Sian....3:45:35 (7,063)
Flatley, Anna....5:34:37 (30,863)

Fleckney, Abigail C 7:26:02 (35,108)	Foster, Beverley K 5:13:55 (28,153)	Froggatt, Julie A 4:22:33 (16,486)
Fleet-Milne, Sian E 6:42:04 (34,547)	Foster, Clare L 6:08:50 (33,478)	Froglia-Simmonds, Sonia M 6:49:06 (34,693)
Fleming, Dyan 4:28:32 (18,176)	Foster, Helen C 4:35:44 (20,026)	Frohn, Eva-Maria 5:12:07 (27,949)
Fleming, Georgina 4:50:19 (23,572)	Foster, Jennie 4:12:37 (13,781)	Frost, Claire 4:59:12 (25,607)
Fleming, Jean L 4:27:47 (17,980)	Foster, Joanna E 5:47:25 (32,052)	Frost, Emma 4:37:24 (20,472)
Fleming, Morna R 4:55:32 (24,777)	Foster, Joanne L 5:28:09 (30,134)	Frost, Ingrid C 3:26:40 (3,881)
Fleming, Nicola A 3:31:38 (4,699)	Foster, Lyn M 4:39:43 (21,070)	Frost, Kate A 4:09:59 (13,086)
Fletcher, Beverley 6:50:15 (34,728)	Foster, Rosalind C 3:29:32 (4,361)	Frost, Kerri E 5:12:47 (27,966)
Fletcher, Grace 7:33:35 (35,151)	Foster, Sara J 5:49:08 (32,192)	Frost, Sarah J 3:35:13 (5,212)
Fletcher, Jo H 4:23:23 (16,710)	Foster, Sharon 3:57:01 (9,820)	Froud, Victoria E 4:55:47 (24,837)
Fletcher, Julie A 7:33:35 (35,151)	Foulkes, Casey 4:41:10 (21,439)	Frrelk, Meghan M 3:45:58 (7,127)
Fletcher, Julie E 5:02:08 (26,172)	Found, Alaine C 4:38:14 (20,678)	Fry, Gillian E 5:49:55 (32,255)
Fletcher, Kathryn E 3:39:41 (5,949)	Fowler, Claire 3:27:27 (4,008)	Fry, Jennifer 4:35:50 (20,050)
Fletcher, Kathryn L 4:21:20 (16,155)	Fowler, Jessica 6:37:42 (34,447)	Fry, Karen L 3:31:35 (4,690)
Fletcher, Monica J 6:10:33 (33,556)	Fowler, Kay 3:36:17 (5,387)	Frye, Ruth M 7:22:59 (35,087)
Fletcher, Sarah 4:12:32 (13,752)	Fowler, Lindsey 4:17:33 (15,102)	Fryer, Jane E 4:56:05 (24,912)
Fletcher, Sheila R 6:05:29 (33,294)	Fowler, Rebecca L 5:49:50 (32,249)	Fryer, Natalie L 3:29:47 (4,416)
Fletcher, Susan J 7:33:35 (35,151)	Fowler, Sarah J 4:34:15 (19,649)	Fuchs, Michaela 4:00:33 (10,852)
Fletcher, Tracey 4:45:36 (22,458)	Fowler, Tina 4:20:13 (15,857)	Fudge, Amber 4:36:47 (20,298)
Fletcher, Victoria 4:27:36 (17,921)	Fowles, Nicola J 4:05:58 (12,087)	Fudge, Claire J 5:47:29 (32,061)
Fletcher, Zoe H 4:21:57 (16,317)	Fox, Anne 5:37:20 (31,121)	Fuentes, Teresa 4:24:05 (16,875)
Flexman, Anne-Marie C 5:12:58 (27,994)	Fox, Clair 4:08:01 (12,574)	Fuentes, Victoria H 4:49:14 (23,288)
Flisher, Sheena 5:29:50 (30,341)	Fox, Emma E 4:31:51 (19,052)	Fuerst, Julaine C 4:44:00 (22,099)
Floate, Mary A 4:54:41 (24,589)	Fox, Kay S 5:18:13 (28,820)	Fujita, Kaori 4:18:16 (15,283)
Flood, Jane L 5:46:36 (31,989)	Fox, Lisa J 3:20:17 (3,023)	Fulcher, Samantha M 4:04:06 (11,661)
Flook, Juoith A 5:04:48 (26,651)	Fox, Lorraine E 4:49:19 (23,315)	Fulford, Liz A 4:48:36 (23,147)
Flores, Vickie 3:49:45 (7,990)	Fox, Sally L 5:19:11 (28,970)	Fulk, Julie A 5:31:58 (30,557)
Flores-Laird, Dorina 5:50:30 (32,300)	Foxe Lowe, Angela L 5:15:09 (28,360)	Fullarton, Ailsa 5:39:37 (31,383)
Florio, Viviana 5:00:39 (25,909)	Foxton, Victoria 5:33:43 (30,747)	Fuller, Ann E 4:16:24 (14,820)
Flury, Patricia M 5:43:44 (31,740)	Foyster, Mandy L 3:31:36 (4,694)	Fuller, Emma L 5:31:29 (30,515)
Flux, Jane 4:58:11 (25,367)	Frame, Gill 5:00:53 (25,958)	Fuller, Michelle E 5:15:32 (28,422)
Flynn, Anne 4:07:29 (12,455)	Frampton, Lynn 4:22:40 (16,530)	Fuller, Sue J 4:19:19 (15,616)
Flynn, Karen L 4:21:02 (16,083)	France, Jacqueline R 3:12:42 (2,216)	Fulton, Laura K 3:43:03 (6,561)
Flynn, Mary 5:32:15 (30,585)	Francis, Andrea K 3:51:20 (8,336)	Funnell, Bridget M 4:11:58 (13,614)
Foale, Claire S 4:54:44 (24,603)	Francis, Julia D 5:48:12 (32,111)	Furbank, Valerie A 5:09:13 (27,392)
Foden, Tracy L 4:37:17 (20,440)	Francis, Michelle A 5:45:07 (31,856)	Furey, Caroline 4:32:27 (19,196)
Fogarty, Helen M 4:13:19 (13,968)	Francis, Paula J 6:52:23 (34,760)	Furhark, Lucy K 4:22:35 (16,497)
Fogden, Emma L 4:16:25 (14,825)	Francis, Susannah 3:30:20 (4,494)	Furnari, Megan E 4:28:44 (18,233)
Fogden, Polly A 4:16:25 (14,825)	Frank, Flora 6:15:28 (33,753)	Furse, Jennifer A 5:57:04 (32,781)
Foley, Cathy J 4:54:26 (24,534)	Frankish, Kim T 6:09:26 (33,514)	Fursman, Emma 4:10:22 (13,186)
Foley-French, Jessica 6:10:20 (33,547)	Frankland, Caroline S 6:26:14 (34,136)	Fursman, Joy 5:44:41 (31,820)
Folkerman, Britt 3:47:40 (7,494)	Frankland, Gail S 4:51:55 (23,915)	Furukawa, Keiko 6:03:14 (33,163)
Folkes, Liz S 4:36:50 (20,314)	Franklin, Jenny A 4:00:12 (10,766)	Furukawa, Sanae 7:23:56 (35,095)
Folland, Rachel K 4:22:31 (16,476)	Franklin, Roberta M 4:16:35 (14,854)	Fusco, Pamela F 4:34:07 (19,601)
Follows, Stella E 5:32:56 (30,663)	Franklin-Bruce, Patricia C 5:55:42 (32,694)	Futcher, Nicola K 6:27:40 (34,185)
Foote, Alice 4:26:36 (17,631)	Franks, David N 5:22:41 (29,453)	Futcher, Sarah 5:28:23 (30,177)
Foote, Judy 6:16:07 (33,788)	Franks, Georgina A 4:39:52 (21,101)	Fyfe, Rachel M 4:58:19 (25,395)
Footer, Katherine 3:50:08 (8,070)	Frappell, Lisa 5:51:00 (32,334)	Gabbott, Wendy 4:21:15 (16,129)
Foran, Gillian 5:06:22 (26,936)	Frary, Vanessa 6:54:47 (34,794)	Gaches, Annette J 4:40:36 (21,285)
Foran, Wendy E 3:57:45 (10,051)	Fraser, Alex K 4:02:51 (11,352)	Gadd, Eleanor M 5:08:08 (27,243)
Forbes, Lesley J 5:06:29 (26,959)	Fraser, Alyssa D 4:30:01 (18,591)	Gadd, Maxine J 5:11:13 (27,690)
Forbes, Leyonee M 4:44:19 (22,177)	Fraser, Annette J 3:47:49 (7,531)	Gadgill, Anjana R 3:54:06 (8,996)
Forbes, Liz J 4:27:48 (17,986)	Fraser, Lorna M 4:47:09 (22,806)	Gadhia, Nital 7:06:09 (34,940)
Ford, Carol A 5:25:47 (29,841)	Fraser, Samantha 4:09:59 (13,086)	Gadsby, Claire 4:52:32 (24,061)
Ford, Catherine J 3:58:10 (10,181)	Fraser, Susan B 4:31:20 (18,927)	Gaffney, Siobhan 6:54:49 (34,849)
Ford, Denise M 4:15:40 (14,624)	Fraser, Virginia 5:22:25 (29,407)	Gaillard De Laubenqu, Teresa J 3:51:58 (8,476)
Ford, Elaine L 4:09:05 (12,853)	Fraser-Moodie, Christine A 4:45:00 (22,325)	Gailrnella, Robin M 5:17:17 (28,685)
Ford, Kim M 5:19:28 (29,024)	Frassova, Lynda 4:44:46 (22,270)	Gaimster, Louisa J 4:40:58 (21,381)
Ford, Maggie 6:59:57 (34,866)	Frazier, Melanie J 6:05:36 (33,300)	Gale, Annie 4:35:32 (19,984)
Ford, Rebecca L 2:57:57 (951)	Freegard, Emilia 5:08:02 (27,224)	Gale, Jennifer 4:26:05 (17,469)
Ford, Sharon 3:16:04 (2,584)	Freeman, Anna 6:36:48 (34,429)	Galin, Catherine L 3:34:20 (5,098)
Forde, Hilary P 4:15:36 (14,607)	Freeman, Claire L 3:21:39 (3,144)	Gallacher, Jacki 4:40:54 (21,361)
Fordham, Angie C 5:10:41 (27,602)	Freeman, Elizabeth L 7:05:29 (34,930)	Gallagher, Jaime M 4:18:15 (15,280)
Foreman, Ally M 4:54:38 (24,581)	Freeman, Kerry M 5:17:12 (28,674)	Gallagher, Toni 6:06:30 (33,357)
Foreman, Julie 3:21:55 (3,174)	Freeman, Shirley 5:13:16 (28,036)	Galleway, Julia 5:39:06 (31,322)
Foreman, Sally E 3:19:14 (2,903)	French, Andrea 3:28:22 (4,169)	Gallivan, Angela K 6:10:17 (33,546)
Forman, Christine C 4:40:47 (21,332)	French, Jane C 4:13:15 (13,952)	Galloway, Denise 4:45:47 (22,491)
Forno, Joanne 4:32:43 (19,250)	French, Louise M 4:36:16 (20,149)	Gallup, Maria 5:03:23 (26,417)
Forrest, Ginny 6:05:53 (33,323)	French, Margaret A 4:36:36 (20,253)	Galpin, Karen M 4:14:15 (14,229)
Forrest, Melanie B 4:50:07 (23,518)	French, Michelle 5:54:43 (32,614)	Galvau, Carrie L 3:43:34 (6,661)
Forrest, Sarah 3:58:51 (10,401)	French, Stephanie J 3:43:39 (6,679)	Gambell, Hannah L 5:25:33 (29,811)
Forrester, Martine E 4:52:54 (24,149)	Frend, Claire E 4:47:39 (22,927)	Game, Fiona 4:31:31 (18,974)
Forsdyke, Verity 5:05:14 (26,734)	Frenken, Hildy 3:59:43 (10,635)	Gammon, Sarah L 4:26:37 (17,638)
Forster, Denise 4:49:13 (23,286)	Frerichs, Louise J 3:58:57 (10,417)	Gannon, Margaret E 7:08:54 (34,965)
Forster, Karen E 4:37:04 (20,372)	Friars, Claire 7:05:13 (34,928)	Gappy, Tina L 3:28:11 (4,141)
Forster, Kim 3:57:05 (9,850)	Fridiksdottir, Hafrun 4:02:21 (11,234)	Gappy, Tracy J 3:34:13 (5,082)
Forsyth, Eleanor C 5:49:51 (32,251)	Friel, Dympna V 3:49:26 (7,917)	Garad, Clare B 6:41:41 (34,538)
Forsyth, Karen L 4:49:24 (23,334)	Friel, Jackie 4:52:01 (23,939)	Garassini, Maria 5:14:21 (28,239)
Fortes Mayer, Gail E 3:18:38 (2,838)	Friend, Anita 4:48:47 (23,189)	Garcia, Glenn R 3:52:47 (8,682)
Fortescue, Clare E 5:11:30 (27,738)	Friend, Sue E 6:42:33 (34,556)	Garcia, Patricia 5:41:04 (31,520)
Fortune, Carole 3:26:47 (3,897)	Frilli, Jo 4:24:55 (17,096)	Garcia-Moya, Ghislaine 5:47:53 (32,088)
Forward, Claire P 4:10:17 (13,164)	Friskney, Ruth 4:54:23 (24,523)	Garciarguelles, Susana 4:52:06 (23,966)
Foskin, Patricia J 6:06:04 (33,332)	Frith, June 4:39:16 (20,957)	Gardener, Julie 6:46:16 (34,630)

Gardener, Sue E.......3:47:07 (7,377)
Gardiner, Elizabeth J.......4:54:49 (24,626)
Gardiner, Shelley D.......4:12:48 (13,833)
Gardner, Claire J.......5:02:21 (26,210)
Gardner, Gillian M.......4:30:49 (18,799)
Gardner, Julie R.......5:50:44 (32,322)
Gardner, Nicola E.......4:13:02 (13,888)
Gardner, Sally A.......4:37:00 (20,357)
Gardner, Sally E.......5:42:33 (31,634)
Gardner, Tina.......4:50:11 (23,533)
Gardner, Victoria C.......4:21:24 (16,171)
Gardner-Hall, Sarah J.......3:57:01 (9,820)
Garner-Jones, Annetta F.......3:51:10 (8,296)
Garnett, Emma A.......3:57:45 (10,051)
Garnett, Kathleen.......4:38:47 (20,825)
Garrad, Dianne R.......5:29:21 (30,285)
Garrard, Sharon D.......4:34:56 (19,836)
Garratt, Wendy A.......6:29:11 (34,229)
Garratty, Kelly.......5:19:28 (29,024)
Garrod, Lorna E.......3:52:13 (8,532)
Garry, Glenda.......4:05:08 (11,907)
Garside, Margaret C.......7:06:33 (34,945)
Gartell, Isabel S.......4:29:32 (18,476)
Gartland, Jane E.......4:24:07 (16,881)
Garton, Kate.......4:03:57 (11,617)
Gartshore, Elizabeth S.......4:50:38 (23,658)
Garzon, Maria J.......7:08:14 (34,959)
Gascoigne-Owens, Johanna S.......3:36:53 (5,477)
Gascoyne, Julie C.......5:54:02 (32,569)
Gash, Michelle.......5:32:54 (30,659)
Gaskell, Joanna M.......7:22:15 (35,085)
Gaskell, Sophie.......4:49:17 (23,300)
Gaskill, Claire L.......4:12:16 (13,688)
Gasque, Jeanette.......4:34:46 (19,781)
Gater, Carolyn.......4:29:23 (18,428)
Gates, Kathie P.......5:18:15 (28,828)
Gates, Rachel V.......4:27:13 (17,806)
Gatt, Donna M.......4:20:06 (15,832)
Gauci, Benny.......4:08:08 (12,598)
Gault, Elaine A.......3:41:09 (6,209)
Gault, Nicola J.......6:55:22 (34,806)
Gauvin, Sarah J.......3:58:44 (10,363)
Gavin, Una.......4:30:28 (18,717)
Gaw, Kirsty G.......3:33:26 (4,951)
Gawith, Marianne C.......4:11:01 (13,354)
Gaynor, Carole A.......5:12:45 (27,959)
Gaywood, Patricia M.......7:29:03 (35,119)
Gaze, Samantha.......6:00:33 (33,003)
Gaze-Fitzgibbon, Fiona.......5:01:14 (26,013)
Gazzani, Lena J.......4:15:04 (14,470)
Gazzard, Sarah J.......4:31:18 (18,918)
Gear, Julie M.......4:11:38 (13,518)
Gearing, Lesley.......4:59:57 (25,766)
Geary, Christine.......7:41:18 (35,179)
Geary, Michelle L.......5:03:31 (26,435)
Geddes, Carol A.......3:38:14 (5,684)
Geddes, Julie A.......5:21:57 (29,346)
Geddes, Sarah.......3:25:36 (3,686)
Gedney, Amanda.......5:13:32 (28,089)
Gee, Belinda.......5:28:28 (30,184)
Gee, Charlotte R.......3:56:07 (9,543)
Gee, Tracey M.......3:38:33 (5,732)
Geffen, Lisa.......3:46:44 (7,290)
Gellatly, Caroline M.......3:55:39 (9,411)
Gellett, Anne E.......4:11:13 (13,409)
Gellweiler, Michelle Y.......4:01:09 (10,971)
Gelsthorpe, Kirsty.......3:56:27 (9,652)
Genoud, Catherine.......4:21:13 (16,113)
Gent, Joanne C.......3:34:26 (5,116)
Gent, Sarah E.......3:51:47 (8,433)
Gentilcore, Elizabeth.......4:04:47 (11,811)
Gentile, Michelle S.......4:55:38 (24,799)
Gentile, Sandra.......4:28:53 (18,270)
George, Elinor E.......7:17:02 (35,049)
George, Emma L.......5:41:39 (31,568)
George, Rebecca A.......3:59:11 (10,493)
George, Teddy.......5:53:05 (32,506)
George, Vicky.......4:57:53 (25,296)
George, Zoe T.......5:52:17 (32,438)
Georghiou, Jane.......3:19:29 (2,934)
Georgiou, Anne L.......5:36:54 (31,092)
Gerada, Clare.......4:20:18 (15,889)
Geraghty, Faith R.......3:54:03 (8,986)
Gergelyne Mohacsy, Edit E.......4:10:56 (13,329)
Gerrard, Corinne.......4:17:16 (15,029)
Gerrard, Nicci.......3:58:50 (10,397)
Gettins, Lucy A.......3:53:20 (8,813)
Ghedini, Nadia.......4:42:00 (21,627)
Gheorge-Pickford, Laura.......4:43:10 (21,905)
Ghiroli, Susan.......5:41:53 (31,592)
Gibb, Wendy E.......4:14:24 (14,273)
Gibbins, Deborah K.......3:36:20 (5,399)
Gibbons, Amelia.......6:18:05 (33,856)
Gibbons, Helen.......4:10:58 (13,339)
Gibbons, Susan.......5:59:11 (32,925)
Gibbs, Dawn L.......3:08:42 (1,780)
Gibbs, Jean.......6:19:59 (33,915)
Gibbs, Karen L.......4:51:02 (23,741)
Gibbs, Kerry-Louise.......5:02:04 (26,160)
Gibbs, Marcia J.......5:11:22 (27,719)
Gibbs, Samantha L.......5:27:26 (30,034)
Gibbs, Susan.......6:33:37 (34,343)
Giblin, Julie.......4:18:04 (15,226)
Gibson, Alison C.......5:13:04 (28,011)
Gibson, Alison F.......4:50:27 (23,612)
Gibson, Catherine.......4:09:00 (12,826)
Gibson, Claire.......3:27:30 (4,020)
Gibson, Claire.......4:18:58 (15,502)
Gibson, Iris.......6:37:04 (34,434)
Gibson, Janet.......5:05:14 (26,734)
Gibson, Leanne.......4:50:41 (23,672)
Gibson, Lisa A.......5:10:20 (27,546)
Gibson, Margaret.......4:43:10 (21,905)
Gibson, Shirley R.......3:57:34 (10,003)
Gibson, Tracey A.......4:13:00 (13,878)
Gibson-Robinson, Angela.......4:14:53 (14,406)
Gidus, Tara J.......3:29:48 (4,417)
Giesler, Dawn S.......4:23:37 (16,756)
Gikunoo, Georgina A.......5:51:51 (32,401)
Gilbert, Carly A.......4:50:15 (23,548)
Gilbert, Lisha F.......5:23:50 (29,590)
Gilbert, Melinda C.......4:44:08 (22,126)
Gilbert, Sally A.......3:25:17 (3,641)
Gilbert, Tina M.......4:37:13 (20,416)
Gilbert, Tracey A.......5:32:14 (30,581)
Gilbertson, Katharine.......4:40:14 (21,196)
Gilby, Anne C.......3:27:01 (3,931)
Gilchrist, Anna.......5:04:22 (26,578)
Gilchrist, Helen L.......4:29:29 (18,457)
Gilchrist, Karen M.......4:48:53 (23,205)
Gildea, Sarah.......4:43:56 (22,081)
Gildener, Corey.......5:37:56 (31,189)
Giles, Jeannette L.......6:03:18 (33,168)
Giles, Joanna K.......4:36:00 (20,084)
Giles, Natalie J.......4:47:45 (22,953)
Giles, Nicola.......6:47:03 (34,658)
Gilhooley, Karen.......4:48:07 (23,037)
Gill, Amanda J.......4:49:54 (23,473)
Gill, Angela.......5:24:32 (29,687)
Gill, Diane M.......4:04:27 (11,734)
Gill, Gillian.......4:50:25 (23,603)
Gill, Nicky.......5:26:57 (29,973)
Gill, Tessa L.......5:03:29 (26,431)
Gill, Tracey E.......5:12:37 (27,929)
Gillam, Danielle.......3:53:39 (8,896)
Gillam, Lucy K.......3:42:15 (6,425)
Gillam, Sally E.......3:55:41 (9,423)
Gillespie, Jean.......4:10:49 (13,292)
Gillett, Lyn M.......5:22:56 (29,477)
Gilliard, Louise S.......4:30:04 (18,611)
Gillies, Susan.......4:27:54 (18,015)
Gillies, Tessa.......5:57:49 (32,824)
Gillings, Caroline.......5:24:23 (29,670)
Gillman, Katherine A.......3:46:04 (7,153)
Gillons, Carolyn J.......5:44:16 (31,785)
Gilmore, Joanna J.......4:40:08 (21,164)
Gilmour, Marie.......4:03:17 (11,455)
Gilpin, Jasmine E.......5:49:34 (32,229)
Gingell, Marian.......6:16:03 (33,781)
Gipson, Tamasine A.......4:23:49 (16,808)
Girard, Michele.......4:46:42 (22,709)
Gisby, Sharon L.......5:10:14 (27,531)
Gladman, Kirsty.......5:05:08 (26,710)
Gladstone, Jennifer C.......5:43:18 (31,702)
Gladstone, Julia L.......4:11:02 (13,361)
Glaister, Karen.......4:18:47 (15,460)
Glaister, Letitia P.......5:32:36 (30,625)
Glasby, Karen.......4:30:59 (18,831)
Glasgow, Emma J.......4:03:50 (11,590)
Glasgow, Katherine S.......4:09:41 (13,007)
Glass, Catherine M.......4:47:13 (22,823)
Gleadall, Vickie M.......4:51:41 (23,869)
Gleave, Maddie L.......3:56:00 (9,513)
Gleeson, Cheryl A.......6:14:38 (33,722)
Gleig, Katie.......5:11:43 (27,775)
Glencross, Julia L.......5:23:35 (29,559)
Glenister, Clare.......5:00:44 (25,923)
Glenn, Hester.......6:47:18 (34,661)
Glennane, Claire.......3:53:01 (8,720)
Glennie, Hannah D.......4:28:23 (18,137)
Glidewell, Gail F.......4:32:17 (19,158)
Glossop, Laetitia S.......5:08:33 (27,292)
Glover, Alyson J.......4:23:45 (16,791)
Glover, Rachel S.......4:08:51 (12,787)
Glyn, Margot.......4:12:37 (13,781)
Godage, Himali Y.......5:29:05 (30,258)
Goddard, Chloe.......4:22:39 (16,523)
Goddard, Thelma M.......4:57:32 (25,234)
Godden, Janet.......4:25:00 (17,125)
Godfrey, Annette.......4:21:27 (16,190)
Godfrey, Lesley C.......4:19:28 (15,654)
Godfrey, Rebecca A.......4:55:54 (24,874)
Godin, Susan M.......6:44:28 (34,607)
Goding, Dawn.......4:27:46 (17,973)
Godleman, Caroline.......5:02:33 (26,237)
Godney, Patricia A.......6:23:54 (34,056)
Godwin, Caroline.......7:20:08 (35,075)
Godwin, Juliet E.......4:15:29 (14,573)
Goerigk, Silvia.......4:12:46 (13,825)
Gold, Alexandra R.......4:30:32 (18,735)
Golden-Hann, Andrea C.......7:09:47 (34,973)
Goldie, Cheryl.......5:24:39 (29,701)
Golding, Deborah D.......5:14:31 (28,263)
Golding, Marina M.......6:08:55 (33,484)
Golding, Melanie J.......3:59:30 (10,571)
Golding, Nicola J.......4:20:45 (16,007)
Golding, Sarah J.......3:31:42 (4,706)
Goldring, Kirstin.......4:38:04 (20,638)
Goldring, Shayla.......4:47:28 (22,880)
Golds, Barbara.......5:58:43 (32,890)
Goldsmith, Claire L.......4:44:47 (22,272)
Goldsmith, Gail L.......4:04:49 (11,821)
Goldsmith, Jacqueline E.......3:42:35 (6,477)
Goldson, Sarah C.......4:25:21 (17,227)
Goldstein, Nathalie C.......4:24:13 (16,908)
Gomez, Brooke.......3:34:48 (5,160)
Gomm, Nicola J.......3:03:07 (1,339)
Goncalves, Anna.......5:04:46 (26,642)
Gonzalez Sanchez, Susana.......3:11:41 (2,102)
Gonzalez-Carranza, Zinnia H.......4:44:18 (22,169)
Goodall, Davina M.......5:39:19 (31,352)
Goodall, Jeanette A.......5:13:36 (28,101)
Goodband, Rachel M.......4:31:18 (18,918)
Goodchild, Alice M.......4:15:32 (14,589)
Goodchild, Heidi.......4:22:43 (16,540)
Goodchild, Tracy.......5:44:55 (31,840)
Gooden, Lesley B.......6:07:45 (33,425)
Goodes, Gillian C.......6:02:38 (33,116)
Goodman, Juliet D.......7:02:26 (34,899)
Goodwin, Denise E.......5:14:15 (28,217)
Goodwin, Emma.......5:42:39 (31,646)
Goodwin, Gemma J.......3:42:40 (6,495)
Goodwin, Jennnifer.......5:42:39 (31,646)
Goodwin, Karen J.......6:03:29 (33,189)
Goodwin, Lynda J.......4:52:04 (23,954)
Goodwin, Nina.......5:56:49 (32,762)
Goodwin, Pamela R.......7:42:00 (35,183)
Goodwin, Samantha C.......5:50:26 (32,294)
Goodwin, Sarah.......7:43:38 (35,188)
Goodwin, Vicky L.......5:07:46 (27,185)
Goodworth, Jean P.......4:48:25 (23,107)
Goorun, Rogie.......5:04:10 (26,548)
Gopal, Amar.......4:09:12 (12,890)
Gordon, Deborah.......4:28:02 (18,036)
Gordon, Elizabeth J.......4:42:09 (21,664)
Gordon, Laura A.......5:58:03 (32,839)
Gordon, Lyndsey J.......4:40:37 (21,289)
Gordon, Natasha M.......3:48:34 (7,730)
Gordzielik, Barbara M.......4:29:56 (18,573)

Gore, Kathleen A 6:06:07 (33,337)
Gore, Kathryn M 5:35:20 (30,938)
Gorham, Diana M 3:53:27 (8,848)
Gorman, Barbara 5:21:38 (29,305)
Gorman, Carlene M....5:51:59 (32,412)
Gorman, Jane 5:09:37 (27,458)
Gorman, Teresa P....6:51:04 (34,738)
Gorner, Joanne....6:47:01 (34,657)
Gorrie, Caroline L....5:00:04 (25,787)
Gorringe, Natalie 4:18:01 (15,212)
Gorry, Sally 4:55:04 (24,693)
Goscomb, Glenda I 4:28:51 (18,262)
Gosling, Laura C 3:49:00 (7,821)
Gosling, Tracy A 6:06:13 (33,342)
Gossage, Linda P 5:31:10 (30,482)
Gottschalk, Gisela....4:33:17 (19,377)
Goucher, Gillian M 6:07:50 (33,435)
Goudie, Angela M 6:29:46 (34,247)
Gough, Bridget I 5:11:21 (27,716)
Gough, Teresa 4:59:20 (25,633)
Gould, Elizabeth 4:39:12 (20,932)
Gould, Victoria J....5:05:56 (26,858)
Goulding, Michelle L....4:54:10 (24,463)
Gouldthorpe, Anne....5:55:20 (32,669)
Gouno, Mary N 4:08:52 (12,792)
Gourlay, Susan J 5:02:47 (26,292)
Gower, Denise 6:19:59 (33,915)
Gower, Gill P....5:44:29 (31,801)
Goyaud, France 3:52:10 (8,520)
Grace, Caroline M....4:25:02 (17,133)
Grace, Clare....6:17:14 (33,832)
Grace, Natasha 4:20:40 (15,981)
Grady, Jenny 4:36:03 (20,093)
Graham, Barbara E 4:15:07 (14,478)
Graham, Clare P....4:45:31 (22,434)
Graham, Janice A 3:44:45 (6,889)
Graham, Joanne E....4:45:41 (22,478)
Graham, Suriyati R....6:00:52 (33,019)
Graley, Joanne T....4:48:17 (23,073)
Grandison, Diane....4:59:58 (25,771)
Grandt, Anne 4:53:24 (24,275)
Grange, Nathalie....5:16:08 (28,494)
Grant, Alaison J 5:11:04 (27,665)
Grant, Anne Marie....4:40:21 (21,221)
Grant, Fiona R....5:10:52 (27,628)
Grant, Judith K....4:20:15 (15,875)
Grant, Julie M....4:37:28 (20,489)
Grant, Karen....4:08:32 (12,697)
Grant, Lesley C....4:55:13 (24,722)
Grant, Nicola J....5:03:04 (26,352)
Grant, Patricia A....5:54:01 (32,567)
Grant, Pauline S 5:58:06 (32,848)
Grant, Rebecca F....3:59:09 (10,485)
Grant-Ives, Bonnie 3:53:59 (8,972)
Grant-Riach, Heather A....4:09:14 (12,897)
Grassick, Katie L....5:06:26 (26,950)
Gravelin G, Ruth A....4:27:13 (17,806)
Graver, Emma....4:59:18 (25,628)
Gravestock, Rebecca J 4:37:46 (20,571)
Gravina-Coles, Maria M 5:05:06 (26,700)
Gravis, Karen H 6:29:31 (34,240)
Gray, Audrey B 4:22:47 (16,553)
Gray, Elaine....5:07:50 (27,196)
Gray, Elizabeth G....5:47:51 (32,086)
Gray, Helen L 4:02:48 (11,342)
Gray, Helen L 5:33:44 (30,751)
Gray, Jackie....5:50:43 (32,317)
Gray, Julie L....6:16:31 (33,801)
Gray, Karen J....4:28:58 (18,297)
Gray, Linoa A....5:02:54 (26,320)
Gray, Louise C 4:20:03 (15,813)
Gray, Lynne 4:54:33 (24,566)
Gray, Margaret R 4:50:55 (23,715)
Gray, Marian B....4:23:25 (16,715)
Gray, Natalie....4:12:00 (13,625)
Gray, Pauline E....4:34:52 (19,811)
Gray, Susan E....5:36:19 (31,031)
Gray, Valerie A....4:56:02 (24,907)
Graydon, Catherine 5:48:49 (32,163)
Greany, Kate E....4:23:59 (16,844)
Greatorex-Day, Suzanne L....4:31:01 (18,840)
Greaves, Amanda P 5:23:40 (29,569)
Greaves, Christine 6:30:46 (34,269)
Greaves, Tracey....4:28:08 (18,067)
Green, Ana-Maria....4:15:17 (14,524)
Green, Angela M....4:52:45 (24,114)
Green, Annie M 6:17:02 (33,825)
Green, Blandine....5:18:33 (28,875)
Green, Carle J....3:26:09 (3,788)
Green, Carole....4:19:06 (15,547)
Green, Catherine M....5:16:55 (28,629)
Green, Clare 4:14:15 (14,229)
Green, Clemency A....5:06:42 (27,003)
Green, Debra....6:18:46 (33,882)
Green, Diana M....6:34:04 (34,356)
Green, Elizabeth J 3:49:12 (7,863)
Green, Fiona....4:10:47 (13,281)
Green, Fiona....4:26:13 (17,511)
Green, Hannah 4:03:47 (11,569)
Green, Janet P 6:35:37 (34,401)
Green, Jenny M 4:16:13 (14,771)
Green, Jo-Anne....4:20:52 (16,039)
Green, Joanne D 5:06:32 (26,972)
Green, Julia E 4:55:48 (24,841)
Green, Julie C....5:08:27 (27,277)
Green, Karen 5:24:43 (29,710)
Green, Kathy 5:35:20 (30,938)
Green, Kirsty A 4:09:38 (12,991)
Green, Patricia K....5:12:50 (27,977)
Green, Rachael E 4:29:15 (18,379)
Green, Rachel E 4:24:26 (16,970)
Green, Sandra C....5:31:38 (30,524)
Green, Shannon....5:19:34 (29,044)
Green, Susan N 4:11:29 (13,482)
Green, Susannah C 4:43:35 (22,003)
Green, Suzanne....5:53:05 (32,506)
Green, Tracey A....4:20:13 (15,857)
Greenall, Vicki A 3:09:00 (1,812)
Greene, Gail 5:39:29 (31,375)
Greene, Rosemary A 5:58:27 (32,871)
Greenfield, Jane E....4:31:13 (18,888)
Greenfield, Kathryn P....5:04:01 (26,519)
Greenhill, Sophie P....4:00:32 (10,843)
Greenney, Anne B....4:18:37 (15,399)
Greenstreet, Elizabeth 5:33:43 (30,747)
Greenwell, Sally....6:43:54 (34,597)
Greenwood, Carol A 4:26:44 (17,672)
Greenwood, Jane E 4:53:11 (24,217)
Greenwood, Joanne R....4:34:12 (19,624)
Greenwood, Kathryn R 4:49:10 (23,277)
Greenwood, Nicola 5:44:16 (31,785)
Greer, Sara A 4:05:37 (12,008)
Greer, Sharon....5:18:59 (28,943)
Gregory, Adele 4:10:38 (13,248)
Gregory, Allison K....4:33:02 (19,320)
Gregory, Catherine L 5:36:52 (31,090)
Gregory, Elisabeth....5:01:44 (26,096)
Gregory, Kate L 4:45:06 (22,354)
Gregory, Ria C 4:14:33 (14,304)
Gregory, Tori 4:37:01 (20,360)
Gregson, Kerry A....5:19:30 (29,032)
Gregurec, Julia 5:02:04 (26,160)
Grehan, Monica 5:19:24 (29,009)
Grenville, Andrew R....3:40:00 (5,996)
Grewer, Laura....5:17:58 (28,776)
Grey, Karen E 4:57:25 (25,215)
Grice, Clare A....3:02:50 (1,321)
Grice, Helen G 3:59:53 (10,694)
Grice, Henrietta 3:54:37 (9,126)
Grice-Jackson, Nicole E 4:02:28 (11,262)
Grieve, Kathryn 4:31:50 (19,049)
Grieveson, Jane 4:45:25 (22,419)
Griffin, Carmel....3:49:00 (7,821)
Griffin, Jennie 4:02:20 (11,226)
Griffin, Lorne....5:04:20 (26,573)
Griffin, Sarah J 4:05:04 (11,882)
Griffith, Mari D 4:12:33 (13,760)
Griffith, Marion P 5:15:15 (28,378)
Griffith, Natalie....4:16:45 (14,902)
Griffith, Rachel S....4:28:06 (18,057)
Griffith-Jones, Pamela....4:08:35 (12,711)
Griffiths, Andrea M....5:35:52 (30,982)
Griffiths, Angela M....3:46:46 (7,302)
Griffiths, Carol A....5:34:37 (30,863)
Griffiths, Charlotte F....4:03:23 (11,476)
Griffiths, Diane M 6:11:06 (33,579)
Griffiths, Emma J 4:43:16 (21,926)
Griffiths, Hannah J....5:00:55 (25,964)
Griffiths, Jenny L....6:39:47 (34,504)
Griffiths, Karen J 5:49:28 (32,225)
Griffiths, Katie A 3:33:59 (5,045)
Griffiths, Lisa....4:00:16 (10,782)
Griffiths, Lynn 4:56:10 (24,932)
Griffiths, Madeline....3:40:08 (6,023)
Griffiths, Nicola....4:20:32 (15,943)
Griffiths, Rhiannon M 4:23:52 (16,818)
Griffiths, Rosie A....5:17:23 (28,695)
Griffiths, Sally C 4:04:14 (11,691)
Griffiths, Samantha J....6:20:39 (33,937)
Griffiths, Sharon 4:14:32 (14,300)
Grififths, Emma C 5:06:24 (26,946)
Grigg, Amanda E....4:21:20 (16,155)
Gril, Daniele 4:27:25 (17,862)
Grimaldi, Monica S 5:14:33 (28,268)
Grimes, Ciara....4:22:29 (16,467)
Grimshaw, Sarah M 4:34:16 (19,654)
Grindle, Corinna F....4:22:01 (16,343)
Grindu, Christiane 4:08:49 (12,773)
Grobler, Gina E 4:35:13 (19,887)
Groechenig, Monika 3:33:16 (4,923)
Groeger, Stephanie 5:38:18 (31,229)
Grogan, Michelle 5:08:25 (27,272)
Grogono, Joanna C....4:07:27 (12,448)
Groocock, Rosalyn T....5:04:49 (26,653)
Groombridge, Karen J 4:45:25 (22,419)
Grosboetzl, Ingrid....3:32:59 (4,886)
Gross, Judy C 6:03:19 (33,170)
Grosse, Emma K....4:56:34 (25,029)
Grossman, Deborah 6:40:53 (34,521)
Grout, Carol E 4:27:03 (17,759)
Grout, Jane A....4:11:58 (13,614)
Grover, Clare 6:50:18 (34,730)
Grover, Victoria L....4:56:16 (24,955)
Groves, Brigitte....4:50:57 (23,719)
Groves, Marie 6:02:57 (33,140)
Grower, Emma S....6:51:27 (34,746)
Gruffydd, Mari W 4:32:16 (19,152)
Grundy, Karen....5:12:05 (27,839)
Grundy, Madeleine 3:46:19 (7,207)
Grzelak, Bozena 4:27:59 (18,029)
Guard, Maureen....4:44:43 (22,253)
Gudgeon, Thea K....4:09:38 (12,991)
Gudger, Maryann F 4:46:34 (22,684)
Gueli, Paola 4:10:40 (13,257)
Guest, Claire L 5:20:51 (29,220)
Guest, Helen....4:20:42 (15,991)
Guild, Wendy B 5:02:14 (26,188)
Guillemain, Isabelle....6:04:35 (33,249)
Guillen, Constanza....4:04:29 (11,741)
Guinan, Dympna C 5:13:16 (28,036)
Gulteking, Necla 5:28:36 (30,195)
Gundle, Jo L....4:12:50 (13,840)
Gundry, Susan E....5:50:43 (32,317)
Gunn, Geraldine C 4:45:13 (22,374)
Gunn, Sally....5:22:02 (29,352)
Gunton, Sarah J....3:55:18 (9,310)
Gurkan, Suna 6:03:13 (33,161)
Gurr, Jessica S....5:20:19 (29,144)
Gurr, Tracey S....4:34:13 (19,634)
Gurtner, Pina....6:09:37 (33,521)
Guthrie, Alison M 5:07:08 (27,081)
Guthrie, Trudy E 5:22:49 (29,463)
Guttridge, Julia....6:04:53 (33,261)
Guy, Carol A 5:40:58 (31,505)
Guy, Samantha 3:23:11 (3,329)
Gwaderi, Razia....6:39:32 (34,495)
Gwinner, Stephanie A....5:27:22 (30,027)
Haar, Amber....4:32:39 (19,238)
Haase, Anita 4:10:10 (13,133)
Habgood, Sarah L....3:26:55 (3,914)
Hacker, Amanda....5:15:59 (28,476)
Hacker, Lisa C 3:29:46 (4,414)
Hackett, Corrinne M....7:27:17 (35,114)
Hackman, Sally-Anne....6:32:36 (34,321)
Haddican, Michele J 4:14:32 (14,300)
Hadfield, Elizabeth S 4:17:50 (15,168)
Hadley, Elizabeth A....4:47:57 (22,994)
Hadley, Emily M 4:01:56 (11,136)
Hadlow, Julia 5:16:53 (28,620)

Haesaert, Lies L....4:03:16 (11,449)
Haesendonck, Christiane....5:15:26 (28,410)
Hagan, Anne....4:09:16 (12,900)
Haggar, Rachel M....3:48:14 (7,641)
Haggar, Tracy K....4:30:50 (18,805)
Haggart, Nora....4:03:24 (11,481)
Haggett, Eimily F....4:43:17 (21,930)
Hahn, Cindy....5:19:13 (28,976)
Hahnel, Charlotte I....4:36:22 (20,188)
Haider, Zara J....4:30:32 (18,735)
Haight, Emma T....3:58:21 (10,243)
Hailey, Dee....3:57:37 (10,020)
Haines, Lesley L....3:20:41 (3,060)
Haines, Rachel G....5:22:37 (29,444)
Haines, Sarah L....3:17:15 (2,709)
Haines, Victoria J....3:53:58 (8,968)
Hainey, Louise J....4:56:08 (24,925)
Haining, Hayley....2:35:23 (116)
Halberda, Ruth M....4:23:06 (16,631)
Halden, Sophie K....4:16:15 (14,781)
Hale, Nicola J....3:40:18 (6,050)
Hales, Elizabeth S....3:09:21 (1,848)
Halfacree, Sheri L....4:56:20 (24,971)
Halfhead, Harriet L....4:07:04 (12,360)
Halford, Myrtle L....6:41:46 (34,541)
Hall, Amanda E....4:52:59 (24,170)
Hall, Beverley....5:26:09 (29,888)
Hall, Christine....5:21:16 (29,271)
Hall, Deborah A....3:56:59 (9,809)
Hall, Elizabeth A....5:17:12 (28,674)
Hall, Elizabeth J....4:59:03 (25,574)
Hall, Ginnie R....4:53:35 (24,323)
Hall, Jill....4:49:43 (23,429)
Hall, Julia A....5:09:07 (27,375)
Hall, Kate....3:45:29 (7,047)
Hall, Kate....4:49:18 (23,306)
Hall, Linda....5:28:51 (30,223)
Hall, Linda H....4:15:56 (14,696)
Hall, Lorna....7:25:29 (35,102)
Hall, Lynn....4:16:25 (14,825)
Hall, Melissa V....3:48:34 (7,730)
Hall, Mich J....4:43:30 (21,980)
Hall, Natasha M....4:40:12 (21,188)
Hall, Niki J....4:26:14 (17,515)
Hall, Polly C....4:15:49 (14,669)
Hall, Rachel A....5:44:47 (31,828)
Hall, Rebecca A....5:09:08 (27,377)
Hall, Rebecca J....4:32:06 (19,109)
Hall, Sarah....5:18:54 (28,932)
Hall, Sarah A....3:42:26 (6,460)
Hall, Sharon N....5:49:18 (32,211)
Hall, Sheila K....4:59:30 (25,663)
Hall, Susan F....5:14:27 (28,256)
Hall, Victoria A....5:52:06 (32,421)
Hallam, Tracey J....3:48:37 (7,745)
Hallecker, Andrea....3:46:46 (7,302)
Hallett, Carol....4:33:32 (19,444)
Hallett, Irene E....5:00:24 (25,863)
Halley, Susi M....4:24:26 (16,970)
Halliday, Susan....4:52:14 (24,001)
Halls, Emma L....5:28:34 (30,192)
Halme, Riikka E....3:28:42 (4,224)
Halsall, Helen M....3:57:25 (9,958)
Halsall, Lisa M....6:06:38 (33,364)
Hamada, Sachie....3:46:21 (7,211)
Hambleton, Karen....4:23:56 (16,834)
Hamblin, Sharron L....5:58:04 (32,840)
Hamblin, Susan....4:16:59 (14,951)
Hambly, Megan J....4:07:56 (12,561)
Hamel, Lynn....3:32:56 (4,880)
Hamer, Marie B....5:33:37 (30,738)
Hamilton, Annabel P....5:59:10 (32,923)
Hamilton, Christine....4:02:20 (11,226)
Hamilton, Deborah N....3:17:31 (2,736)
Hamilton, Eleanor M....5:12:17 (27,868)
Hamilton, Fiona....5:48:22 (32,131)
Hamilton, Julie....7:30:50 (35,132)
Hamilton-Fox, Fiona L....4:32:48 (19,270)
Hamlett, Alison E....4:20:37 (15,968)
Hamlin, Mollie J....5:13:47 (28,130)
Hammatt, Julie....5:54:18 (32,588)
Hammersland, Mette....4:16:23 (14,817)
Hammersley, Janine....5:04:54 (26,672)
Hammick, Jennie....5:47:26 (32,054)
Hammond, Carol L....4:20:46 (16,010)
Hammond, Louise....5:05:01 (26,687)
Hammond, Samantha L....3:26:22 (3,822)
Hammond, Tina L....4:20:33 (15,948)
Hamp, Jane A....4:03:35 (11,521)
Hampson, Tracey....6:39:57 (34,508)
Hampson, Victoria....3:46:58 (7,343)
Hampton, Jane M....5:07:41 (27,172)
Hampton, Lara M....4:01:47 (11,109)
Hamson, Julie C....4:16:20 (14,805)
Hancock, Karen E....3:07:46 (1,698)
Hancock, Matthew T....4:06:45 (12,274)
Hancock, Sarah....4:12:35 (13,769)
Handoll, Bethany V....3:41:22 (6,251)
Handson, Alison M....7:21:13 (35,081)
Hanks, Julie....4:27:14 (17,813)
Hanks, Tracey....5:50:14 (32,282)
Hanley, Patricia A....3:51:11 (8,297)
Hanley, Patricia J....4:20:31 (15,939)
Hann, Lavinia A....7:24:08 (35,097)
Hanna, Kristy M....3:35:52 (5,317)
Hannington, Tisha....5:49:59 (32,263)
Hannis, Natalie....4:04:56 (11,847)
Hanrahan, Niamh S....3:54:35 (9,119)
Hanratty, Krista A....4:14:18 (14,245)
Hansen, Aasta....3:53:25 (8,835)
Hansen, Inger H....4:22:38 (16,518)
Hansford, Lorraine K....4:10:37 (13,242)
Hanson, Kelly-Leanne....7:05:29 (34,930)
Hanson-Church, Claire L....6:09:10 (33,499)
Hansrani, Aarti....4:35:21 (19,931)
Hanwell, Janet....4:39:08 (20,907)
Harber, Teresa....4:32:39 (19,238)
Hardacre, Jane F....4:09:12 (12,890)
Hardern, Joanna E....5:51:06 (32,346)
Hardick, Sally C....5:20:31 (29,182)
Hardie, Petra....4:09:42 (13,012)
Harding, Belinda....4:20:43 (15,995)
Harding, Claire J....4:00:02 (10,736)
Harding, Elaine J....5:26:43 (29,949)
Harding, Elizabeth A....4:50:31 (23,630)
Harding, Giselle L....5:31:33 (30,521)
Harding, Helen L....5:16:08 (28,494)
Harding, Nancy J....4:26:23 (17,561)
Harding, Suvanne....5:27:37 (30,056)
Hardisty, Anne....5:15:05 (28,346)
Hardman, Joy....4:02:01 (11,161)
Hardman, Laura E....4:59:21 (25,635)
Hardwick, Clare....6:23:15 (34,031)
Hardwick, Helen....3:57:55 (10,116)
Hardwick, Karen J....6:44:20 (34,606)
Hardwick, Lucy J....3:57:15 (9,905)
Hardy, Frances A....7:15:27 (35,033)
Hardy, Karen M....5:07:17 (27,113)
Hardy, Kirsty D....5:44:55 (31,840)
Hardy, Lorna E....4:07:27 (12,448)
Hardy, Louise J....4:58:11 (25,367)
Hardy, Monique R....7:15:27 (35,033)
Hare Duke, Hilary....3:42:37 (6,486)
Hares, Lucy J....4:53:25 (24,281)
Hargie, Patricia G....5:19:44 (29,067)
Hargrave, Annie P....5:00:50 (25,942)
Hargrave, Sarah A....4:14:30 (14,297)
Hargraves, Victoria L....7:12:31 (35,011)
Hargreaves, Alison....4:12:46 (13,825)
Harikka, Regina....4:27:43 (17,955)
Harkin, Christina M....7:17:03 (35,050)
Harkins, Sally....4:34:07 (19,601)
Harling, Leanne....4:02:26 (11,255)
Harlow, Beverley....4:46:23 (22,645)
Harlow, Marian J....6:02:30 (33,106)
Harlow, Rebecca L....6:27:38 (34,183)
Harman, Sarah....4:07:23 (12,432)
Harmer, Rosie J....4:52:40 (24,096)
Harper, Alison C....5:06:36 (26,982)
Harper, Amy C....4:39:46 (21,084)
Harper, Karen....6:15:17 (33,748)
Harper, Louise A....4:04:25 (11,724)
Harrap, Linda R....8:52:31 (35,249)
Harries, Jacqui A....4:36:51 (20,319)
Harries, Victoria....6:53:05 (34,772)
Harrill, Dawn A....4:25:30 (17,286)
Harrington, Emma J....3:59:50 (10,676)
Harrington, Teresa B....4:08:56 (12,809)
Harris, Caroline H....5:50:31 (32,306)
Harris, Carolyn....4:17:00 (14,955)
Harris, Dianne L....4:54:55 (24,641)
Harris, Gillian R....5:11:44 (27,779)
Harris, Janet E....4:21:22 (16,164)
Harris, Jill....5:24:19 (29,660)
Harris, Joan K....4:26:43 (17,667)
Harris, Katie S....4:05:26 (11,978)
Harris, Laura....5:47:40 (32,073)
Harris, Lynne B....3:44:55 (6,940)
Harris, Melanie....4:26:56 (17,732)
Harris, Michael....5:31:44 (30,534)
Harris, Michele L....4:56:05 (24,912)
Harris, Millicent M....7:32:02 (35,144)
Harris, Nicola C....3:24:41 (3,538)
Harris, Nikki J....4:53:37 (24,333)
Harris, Sandra....5:27:40 (30,063)
Harris, Sarah A....5:06:56 (27,049)
Harris, Wendy A....4:30:19 (18,683)
Harrison, Amanda....6:23:45 (34,048)
Harrison, Angela T....4:37:04 (20,372)
Harrison, Anne-Marie....4:29:04 (18,330)
Harrison, Dawn E....5:17:13 (28,680)
Harrison, Donnie....7:53:08 (35,220)
Harrison, Gill M....3:22:57 (3,291)
Harrison, Hayley J....3:57:16 (9,909)
Harrison, Heather D....4:22:25 (16,449)
Harrison, Jane....4:51:20 (23,804)
Harrison, Karen....3:49:57 (8,026)
Harrison, Lesley C....4:05:07 (11,903)
Harrison, Lesley K....5:15:23 (28,401)
Harrison, Marie A....5:36:14 (31,018)
Harrison, Natalie S....6:12:39 (33,648)
Harrison, Paula J....6:10:09 (33,537)
Harrison, Stephanie....6:05:06 (33,272)
Harrison, Sue....2:39:54 (203)
Harrison, Susanna J....3:00:24 (1,151)
Harrison, Tina....5:15:01 (28,343)
Harrison, Tracy J....3:47:32 (7,465)
Harrold, Ruth....4:11:37 (13,508)
Harrop, Edwina....4:00:44 (10,893)
Harrow, Adele I....5:07:13 (27,106)
Harrow, Elspeth J....4:48:22 (23,095)
Hart, Becky J....3:31:24 (4,663)
Hart, Harriet....3:11:42 (2,105)
Hart, Hazel A....4:40:31 (21,263)
Hart, Jayne....3:53:07 (8,748)
Hart, Jennifer....3:58:04 (10,161)
Hart, Susan D....6:01:40 (33,063)
Hart, Victoria....4:03:32 (11,510)
Hart-Dale, Victoria H....5:27:30 (30,046)
Harte, Carina....6:14:28 (33,718)
Harte, Rachel....5:01:04 (25,988)
Hartland, Jennifer C....5:27:04 (29,982)
Hartley, Julia E....4:08:27 (12,684)
Hartley, Mary E....5:13:48 (28,137)
Hartley, Maureen....3:52:09 (8,517)
Hartley, Rebecca C....4:40:14 (21,196)
Hartley, Ruth....6:07:54 (33,438)
Hartmann, Karin....4:07:23 (12,432)
Hartney, Liz E....2:52:30 (609)
Hartridge, Ami L....5:04:37 (26,616)
Harvey, Carol....4:55:48 (24,841)
Harvey, Clare....4:52:39 (24,091)
Harvey, Colette....4:33:29 (19,425)
Harvey, Deborah A....5:37:47 (31,166)
Harvey, Julie....4:34:56 (19,836)
Harvey, Karen A....3:43:19 (6,622)
Harvey, Margo A....4:15:42 (14,636)
Harvey, Michelle S....3:43:53 (6,717)
Harvey, Ruth E....4:17:58 (15,194)
Harvey, Samantha L....4:59:35 (25,682)
Harvey, Sarah E....5:18:14 (28,824)
Harvey, Tina L....4:17:34 (15,106)
Harvey Franklin, Fiona D....4:48:27 (23,114)
Harvey-Smith, Laura J....4:23:03 (16,612)
Harward, Jennifer....4:25:46 (17,371)
Harwood, Abigail E....5:50:27 (32,295)
Harwood, Deborah J....4:48:29 (23,121)
Harwood, Debra L....4:06:53 (12,311)
Harwood, Jane M....4:36:41 (20,274)

Harwood, Lesley..............5:32:26 (30,609)
Harwood, Michaela L..........5:12:02 (27,826)
Harwood, Vanessa.............5:19:31 (29,035)
Hasebe, Miho.................5:37:55 (31,186)
Haselhurst, Sally L..........3:35:41 (5,293)
Haskell, Sarah L.............4:58:40 (25,479)
Haslam, Katherine A..........5:11:35 (27,754)
Haslam, Susan M..............4:17:49 (15,163)
Hasler, Penny M..............6:20:06 (33,925)
Hasler, Victoria L...........3:49:42 (7,978)
Haslett, Karen P.............5:29:59 (30,361)
Hassan, Yasemin L............5:33:58 (30,777)
Hassell, Amanda C............4:23:40 (16,766)
Hassell, Lucy................2:39:20 (182)
Hastilow, Victoria J.........5:15:44 (28,447)
Hastings, Linda..............4:14:09 (14,194)
Hatch, Alison................4:23:31 (16,732)
Hatcher, Jillian A...........5:13:09 (28,015)
Hatherley, Claire............4:44:11 (22,138)
Hathway, Seren...............5:03:48 (26,484)
Hatley, Tracey J.............6:07:59 (33,442)
Hatt, Clare L................4:03:08 (11,416)
Hattee, Caroline.............3:53:23 (8,826)
Hatto, Clare.................4:38:49 (20,833)
Hatton, Carol A..............4:10:59 (13,345)
Hatton, Karen L..............4:33:23 (19,403)
Hatton, Sally A..............4:01:00 (10,949)
Haugh, Jacqueline R..........5:09:35 (27,451)
Haughey, Michelle............5:05:47 (26,841)
Haughey, Moira A.............5:10:34 (27,582)
Haukeland, Gunhild...........5:20:39 (29,202)
Havard, Elizabeth............5:17:46 (28,754)
Haveron, Emma L..............4:25:08 (17,163)
Haviland, Fiona-Mary.........4:47:39 (22,927)
Havill, Andrea K.............4:31:35 (18,995)
Hawken, Valerie..............5:27:11 (29,995)
Hawker, Deborah J............5:01:40 (26,089)
Hawker, Elizabeth J..........3:02:54 (1,325)
Hawker, Sue D................5:01:34 (26,076)
Hawkes, Emma Z...............3:28:17 (4,155)
Hawkes, Melanie A............4:28:04 (18,047)
Hawkes, Ruth A...............5:09:38 (27,461)
Hawkes, Sian.................7:52:16 (35,215)
Hawkes, Tyrene...............7:20:13 (35,076)
Hawkes, Vicky S..............6:07:50 (33,435)
Hawking, Catherine...........5:13:30 (28,085)
Hawkins, Claire L............5:37:24 (31,127)
Hawkins, Jane................3:22:00 (3,186)
Hawkins, Joanna..............5:01:57 (26,136)
Hawkins, Louise..............5:45:11 (31,867)
Hawkins, Melanie.............4:23:32 (16,735)
Hawkins, Michala.............4:28:12 (18,085)
Hawkins, Patricia M..........4:40:26 (21,241)
Hawkins, Sharon J............3:00:43 (1,176)
Hawkins, Shirley.............5:54:04 (32,572)
Hawkins, Suzanne L...........4:01:25 (11,028)
Hawksworth, Sarah L..........6:16:07 (33,788)
Hawry Lyshyn, Kelly..........4:17:08 (14,997)
Hawthorne, Lauretta..........5:24:19 (29,660)
Hay, Anita M.................5:01:23 (26,039)
Hay, Anne E..................3:34:11 (5,073)
Hay, Debz A..................4:01:48 (11,112)
Hay, Julia M.................5:02:45 (26,284)
Hay, Stephanie L.............4:39:34 (21,032)
Hay, Sue.....................5:22:37 (29,444)
Haycock, Sonia M.............5:47:50 (32,085)
Haydon Rothwell, Lucy........6:14:47 (33,726)
Hayes, Carol A...............4:14:02 (14,158)
Hayes, Catherine B...........5:52:51 (32,485)
Hayes, Eranga................5:16:00 (28,479)
Hayes, Joanne................4:56:41 (25,064)
Hayes, Michelle P............7:05:10 (34,927)
Hayes, Pip A.................3:43:48 (6,706)
Hayes, Tracey................6:07:09 (33,397)
Hayhurst, Kathryn D..........4:20:26 (15,922)
Haykiran, Emel...............5:09:12 (27,387)
Haynes, Elizabeth C..........4:56:45 (25,083)
Haynes, Fiona A..............4:00:53 (10,927)
Haynes, Nicola-Jane..........5:31:36 (30,522)
Haynes, Sherie A.............7:09:42 (34,972)
Hays, Lynne..................4:42:56 (21,858)
Hayton, Diane E..............3:49:36 (7,956)
Hayward, Adele E.............4:52:59 (24,170)

Hayward, Jane E..............5:51:31 (32,374)
Hayward, Leanne M............4:36:54 (20,331)
Hayward, Nicky J.............4:37:54 (20,596)
Hayward, Samantha L..........4:11:37 (13,508)
Hayward, Toni S..............6:52:24 (34,762)
Haywood, Mia.................4:40:59 (21,385)
Hazard, Caroline J...........7:23:02 (35,088)
Hazelton, Arlene C...........4:04:52 (11,829)
Hazlitt, Karen...............2:55:44 (788)
Hazzard, Susan...............3:57:21 (9,933)
Head, Jean L.................6:07:46 (33,426)
Head, Samantha J.............6:36:35 (34,422)
Headon, Gail.................5:46:11 (31,954)
Heald, Claire L..............4:28:58 (18,297)
Heale, Caroline..............5:37:37 (31,152)
Heales, Naomi S..............5:18:21 (28,843)
Hean, Sarah C................4:38:47 (20,825)
Heap, Emma L.................4:47:44 (22,949)
Heap, Helen V................4:09:47 (13,035)
Heard, Geraldine A...........5:14:14 (28,214)
Heard, Lissa.................5:16:57 (28,637)
Hearn, Kathy.................5:36:55 (31,095)
Heasman, Lindsay.............3:25:26 (3,659)
Heath, Lorraine..............4:49:20 (23,320)
Heaton, Mathilde M...........2:56:46 (868)
Heaviside, Karen M...........3:11:39 (2,098)
Hebberd, Lisa A..............3:50:30 (8,150)
Hecher, Margareth............3:25:02 (3,589)
Heckel, Sally Ann............5:22:23 (29,400)
Heckman, Joyce...............5:12:02 (27,826)
Hedberg, May.................4:11:44 (13,548)
Heddon, Nicola A.............4:25:24 (17,246)
Heddon, Patricia A...........4:25:24 (17,246)
Hedges, Angela M.............3:59:31 (10,608)
Hedges, Anita E..............4:07:29 (12,455)
Hedges, Rebecca M............4:37:29 (20,494)
Hedges, Trudy................4:23:58 (16,840)
Heer, Bhupinder K............4:47:23 (22,851)
Heesom, Venetia..............5:50:17 (32,285)
Heighton, Bridie A...........4:38:46 (20,821)
Heighway, Jenny..............4:57:42 (25,263)
Hein-Hartmann, Rana..........4:58:55 (25,539)
Heldt, Caroline J............7:31:00 (35,134)
Hellier, Lindsay C...........4:18:54 (15,483)
Helliwell, Brenda L..........4:42:21 (21,705)
Hellmann, Sally..............5:14:11 (28,208)
Hellyar, Elizabeth A.........5:14:50 (28,317)
Helm, Laura A................4:32:16 (19,152)
Helme, Naomi.................3:45:08 (6,979)
Hemmaway, Claire J...........4:19:04 (15,537)
Hemsworth, Marion V..........3:57:39 (10,027)
Henbest, Louise M............4:53:12 (24,228)
Henbest, Melanie J...........5:21:55 (29,339)
Henderson, Katherine I.......4:31:42 (19,022)
Henderson, Louise E..........4:27:37 (17,926)
Henderson, Yvonne............6:10:33 (33,556)
Hendrickx, Veerle............3:50:35 (8,166)
Hendry, Margaret M...........4:21:36 (16,229)
Hendry, Sharon...............6:37:43 (34,448)
Hendy, Laura E...............5:46:24 (31,973)
Hennessy, Jean L.............4:17:04 (14,973)
Henning, Lucy................6:02:18 (33,097)
Henry, Ava A.................4:51:42 (23,876)
Henry, Belinda C.............4:19:59 (15,797)
Henry, Fredricka T...........4:29:43 (18,525)
Henry, Jane E................4:18:30 (15,361)
Henry, Shannon L.............4:55:06 (24,700)
Hensman, Ann B...............4:13:45 (14,077)
Hensman, Marianne Y..........4:03:17 (11,455)
Henton, Richard D............4:54:31 (24,558)
Henwood, Denise..............6:38:26 (34,467)
Heraty, Victoria L...........5:13:33 (28,091)
Herbert, Alison..............4:30:16 (18,672)
Herbert, Maria M.............5:03:36 (26,446)
Herbert, Marian E............6:06:41 (33,367)
Herbert, Penelope A..........4:10:22 (13,186)
Herbert, Rita................4:54:49 (24,626)
Herbert, Yvonne..............3:41:59 (6,372)
Herd, Sally E................4:14:14 (14,220)
Hermitage, Julia.............5:17:45 (28,750)
Herold, Anne.................3:25:44 (3,708)
Heron, Georgina..............3:53:31 (8,861)
Heron, Jennifer M............3:45:33 (7,057)

Herring, Jemma B.............4:54:41 (24,589)
Herring, Victoria S..........4:18:40 (15,420)
Herrington, Jane.............5:23:39 (29,564)
Herrmann, Ok-Sook............5:46:05 (31,940)
Herron, Elana A..............5:52:25 (32,454)
Heryet, Nicole...............3:43:20 (6,626)
Heseltine, Ingrid............5:18:33 (28,875)
Hessey, Karen C..............5:39:33 (31,379)
Hester, Amanda S.............3:21:44 (3,157)
Hetherington, Alexandra M....3:38:04 (5,661)
Hetherington, Tracey.........4:42:25 (21,722)
Hettle, Elizabeth C..........5:13:00 (27,998)
Heuveline, Georgette.........4:00:01 (10,732)
Hewer, Susan E...............4:56:45 (25,083)
Hewett, Joanna L.............5:18:10 (28,812)
Hewings, Sue Y...............3:23:48 (3,419)
Hewins, Katherine E..........7:17:44 (35,059)
Hewis, Sharon L..............3:31:46 (4,712)
Hewitt, Anita C..............6:10:16 (33,545)
Hewitt, Caroline J...........2:59:47 (1,110)
Hewitt, Catherine E..........3:14:27 (2,408)
Hewitt, Katy L...............4:47:36 (22,907)
Hewitt, Kirsty A.............5:58:05 (32,844)
Hewitt, Sarah................4:20:56 (16,061)
Hewlett, Vicki...............5:05:55 (26,855)
Heydecker, Deirdre...........3:59:58 (10,717)
Heyden, Margit...............4:19:13 (15,582)
Heygate, Fiona M.............5:09:23 (27,417)
Heywood, Kathryn.............5:00:51 (25,946)
Hickey, Ingrid...............6:47:49 (34,673)
Hickey, Julie E..............4:23:47 (16,796)
Hickling, Tania K............4:16:35 (14,854)
Hickman, Breeda M............3:41:04 (6,196)
Hickman, Charlotte...........5:39:15 (31,345)
Hicks, Alison L..............5:10:52 (27,628)
Hicks, Beverley..............5:53:24 (32,528)
Hicks, Beverley A............5:09:05 (27,365)
Hicks, Elizabeth.............5:50:36 (32,310)
Hicks, Georgette.............6:31:00 (34,274)
Hicks, Helen L...............3:57:31 (9,988)
Hicks, Karen J...............4:34:48 (19,789)
Hicks, Tracey................4:14:26 (14,283)
Hickson, Iram................4:29:22 (18,420)
Hickton, Valda D.............5:23:40 (29,569)
Hider, Geraldine L...........6:59:58 (34,867)
Higenbottam, Adele D.........3:57:23 (9,945)
Higgins, Alison V............4:40:08 (21,164)
Higgins, Anita P.............5:27:48 (30,075)
Higgins, Tanya D.............5:30:55 (30,457)
Higgins Zidar, Maggy.........3:48:04 (7,606)
Higgison, Sue................4:24:30 (16,994)
Higgott, Victoria L..........4:29:12 (18,365)
Higgs, Jody..................7:26:19 (35,111)
Higgs, Susan.................4:23:18 (16,690)
High, Charles................4:53:38 (24,338)
High, Sian L.................5:23:54 (29,602)
Highgate, Cath J.............4:21:13 (16,113)
Higson, Deborah J............3:37:51 (5,627)
Higton, Georgie..............5:19:05 (28,951)
Hilbery, Hannah..............5:10:35 (27,588)
Hiles, Jo R..................5:06:44 (27,017)
Hiley, Kimberley S...........6:27:47 (34,188)
Hill, Amanda J...............5:48:29 (32,135)
Hill, Andrea J...............3:03:31 (1,365)
Hill, Barbara................4:33:49 (19,523)
Hill, Carole J...............4:11:55 (13,597)
Hill, Catherine A............4:55:32 (24,777)
Hill, Charlotte..............4:19:35 (15,686)
Hill, Charlotte A............4:19:23 (15,632)
Hill, Cheryl W...............3:31:11 (4,625)
Hill, Diane C................5:11:01 (27,658)
Hill, Elizabeth..............5:20:55 (29,227)
Hill, Frances................5:43:41 (31,735)
Hill, Jacqueline A...........5:12:57 (27,991)
Hill, Janet E................3:41:02 (6,186)
Hill, Janet M................4:09:06 (12,860)
Hill, Jennifer N.............3:39:44 (5,956)
Hill, Julie J................3:33:15 (4,919)
Hill, Katherine H............4:17:55 (15,181)
Hill, Lorraine...............5:10:28 (27,545)
Hill, Lucy E.................4:28:55 (18,279)
Hill, Melanie J..............4:58:12 (25,375)
Hill, Melanie L..............4:21:34 (16,221)

Hill, Nicola H 3:12:10 (2,160)
Hill, Rebecca L 3:47:58 (7,568)
Hill, Samantha J 4:22:00 (16,335)
Hill, Sherry A 7:31:48 (35,141)
Hill, Tamasin 6:14:59 (33,733)
Hill, Tina 5:15:11 (28,365)
Hill, Tory M 5:02:13 (26,186)
Hill, Tracey J 4:28:19 (18,115)
Hillary, Elaine M 4:13:09 (13,922)
Hillier, Justine L 3:47:38 (7,482)
Hillier, Sally A 4:43:28 (21,969)
Hillier, Tamara R 4:46:04 (22,566)
Hillier, Zoe 4:38:52 (20,844)
Hillman, Donna S 3:23:02 (3,304)
Hills, Jennifer B 4:40:27 (21,243)
Hills, Leigh Ann 5:25:34 (29,813)
Hills, Linda 4:36:05 (20,104)
Hills, Nicole L 5:10:57 (27,645)
Hill-Trevor, Caroline A 4:42:49 (21,823)
Hill-Venning, Sue 4:48:14 (23,060)
Hilmarsdottir, Sigurlaug 3:58:27 (10,272)
Hilton, Deborah L 3:52:32 (8,612)
Hilton, Felicity V 4:40:08 (21,164)
Hilton, Rosemary 5:46:34 (31,985)
Hinchliffe, Emma 5:25:29 (29,803)
Hind, Jacky F 4:56:28 (25,006)
Hindlaugh, Shirley 5:15:15 (28,378)
Hindle, Karen L 4:37:23 (20,469)
Hinds, Amanda J 4:13:26 (13,998)
Hine, Laura 3:49:04 (7,840)
Hine, Lucy A 4:05:14 (11,926)
Hines, Karon A 5:42:21 (31,616)
Hini, Emmanuelle 4:46:52 (22,745)
Hinne, Stephanie J 4:02:50 (11,348)
Hinshelwood, Linda 4:35:16 (19,900)
Hinton, Catherine M 5:28:36 (30,195)
Hipkins, Cherie J 3:50:24 (8,122)
Hipwell, Carol D 5:02:07 (26,170)
Hirani, Jesal J 6:34:21 (34,363)
Hird, Elizabeth 4:27:08 (17,785)
Hird, Linda 4:07:42 (12,495)
Hird, Lucinda 5:47:05 (32,026)
Hird, Polly A 5:19:22 (29,002)
Hird, Tamara C 3:25:21 (3,651)
Hirniak, Sharon E 5:40:33 (31,473)
Hirons, Sarah R 4:16:00 (14,715)
Hirotsuna, Shoko 6:51:51 (34,750)
Hirst, Claire L 3:56:30 (9,663)
Hiscock, Trish M 4:24:09 (16,890)
Hitchmough, Charlotte L 4:20:19 (15,892)
Hithersay, Wendy 5:48:35 (32,140)
Hoare, Jessica A 6:07:18 (33,405)
Hoare, Katherine O 5:32:57 (30,666)
Hobbins, Catherine P 4:12:41 (13,798)
Hobbs, Angie L 5:05:04 (26,695)
Hobbs, Marie F 5:27:25 (30,032)
Hobday, Jackie 3:56:44 (9,734)
Hobden, Julie A 5:55:44 (32,696)
Hockin, Lorrayne 3:54:58 (9,232)
Hodder, Beth 4:07:16 (12,409)
Hodge, Philippa A 4:21:52 (16,302)
Hodge, Sally 4:00:11 (10,762)
Hodges, Deborah A 5:02:57 (26,329)
Hodges, Sonia 5:38:38 (31,271)
Hodgkins, Charlotte M 5:56:40 (32,747)
Hodgkins, Kathryn A 5:57:37 (32,812)
Hodgkinson, Mandy 4:20:46 (16,010)
Hodgson, Adrienne 4:37:38 (20,527)
Hodgson, Diane 5:29:25 (30,293)
Hodgson, Susan 4:25:23 (17,241)
Hodnett, Jenny 4:06:07 (12,126)
Hodson, Charles P 6:28:12 (34,202)
Hodson, Emma R 4:17:55 (15,181)
Hodson, Lucy C 4:36:00 (20,084)
Hodson, Nichola J 5:22:55 (29,473)
Hodson, Sarah C 4:52:45 (24,114)
Hoekstra, Venny 6:30:44 (34,268)
Hoey, Claire 4:24:27 (16,977)
Hoffman, Jane 3:27:06 (3,943)
Hogan, Anne E 5:00:26 (25,868)
Hogan, Jennie 5:07:45 (27,181)
Hogan, Sally R 4:33:25 (19,409)
Hogan, Simone C 7:07:08 (34,950)

Marathon medics

The original medical officer of the London Marathon, Dr Dan Tunstall Pedoe, ran in 1981 in a little over three hours. His medical team (in those days just four doctors plus St John Ambulance back-up) gathered in a draughty marquee in Green Park, set up as a field hospital on the mud and grass, with bales of hay in place of beds. Today there are 1,500 St John Ambulance volunteers including 20 medics on bikes. They dole out 100lbs of petroleum jelly, 200 bottles of baby oil and 200 plasters, and there are paramedics armed with defibrillators all along the course. 40,000 foil blankets will keep you warm at the finish.

Hogben, Carolyn A 4:16:40 (14,881)
Hohweiller, Nathalie 4:03:17 (11,455)
Hoile, Rita 4:00:16 (10,782)
Holbeck, Stephanie A 4:35:35 (19,992)
Holburn, Lucy C 7:25:12 (35,101)
Holdcroft, Clare L 3:48:50 (7,796)
Holden, Angela M 6:51:52 (34,751)
Holden, Heather J 3:50:13 (8,089)
Holden, Janet C 4:57:58 (25,319)
Holden, Lindsay A 5:10:57 (27,645)
Holden, Sandra M 5:42:36 (31,638)
Holden, Sarah 4:25:19 (17,221)
Holderness, Lucetta 4:19:52 (15,767)
Holding, Dawn 4:17:24 (15,068)
Holdsworth, Teddy 4:52:37 (24,080)
Hole, Sarah 4:35:04 (19,865)
Holgate, Ruth E 7:13:17 (35,019)
Holland, Aileen L 4:33:02 (19,320)
Holland, Fiona J 4:28:05 (18,049)
Holland, Liz J 6:24:46 (34,085)
Holland Lee, Amanda J 4:26:24 (17,570)
Hollands, Tracy J 5:18:04 (28,794)
Holley, Clare M 5:24:10 (29,640)
Holliday, Susan M 3:46:57 (7,338)
Hollinger, Ruth E 3:51:00 (8,257)
Hollingsworth, Juliet L 5:13:01 (28,000)
Hollington, Ali M 3:10:52 (2,017)
Hollins, Annick 4:30:27 (18,712)
Hollis, Lauren J 4:51:19 (23,800)
Holloway, Rachel A 5:42:09 (31,601)
Holloway-Vine, Diane L 4:38:46 (20,821)
Hollstein, Edeltraud Rita 4:40:57 (21,375)
Hollway, Jennifer A 5:44:07 (31,771)
Holly, Kim 5:03:52 (26,498)
Hollyhomes, Sandra K 6:14:24 (33,717)
Holmberg, Matilda 3:52:24 (8,578)
Holme, Olga M 5:25:28 (29,801)
Holmes, Alison M 4:13:23 (13,987)
Holmes, Anna C 5:00:13 (25,823)
Holmes, Anna L 4:58:00 (25,329)
Holmes, Carol E 5:23:56 (29,609)
Holmes, Catherine J 4:59:30 (25,663)
Holmes, Catherine J 5:10:45 (27,608)
Holmes, Deborah L 3:55:24 (9,337)
Holmes, Jane 6:24:46 (34,085)
Holmes, Janet M 5:13:44 (28,119)
Holmes, Julie 5:46:58 (32,014)
Holmes, Julie F 5:39:59 (31,415)
Holmes, Lesley 4:10:53 (13,310)
Holmes, Rachel J 5:24:52 (29,731)
Holmes, Ragin Z 5:14:25 (28,251)
Holmes, Samantha L 4:27:27 (17,869)
Holmes, Sandra D 3:11:44 (2,111)
Holmes, Sarah L 5:42:37 (31,639)
Holmes-Walker, Karen E 3:57:49 (10,080)

Holness, Deborah J 4:06:14 (12,149)
Holroyd, Jilly C 4:24:42 (17,043)
Holt, Carol J 7:41:40 (35,182)
Holt, Carolyn S 3:51:16 (8,321)
Holt, Kerry L 3:23:48 (3,419)
Holt, Marian L 5:50:18 (32,286)
Holt, Veronica A 4:59:03 (25,574)
Holt-Taylor, Charlette 5:03:35 (26,440)
Homan, Catherine M 5:44:44 (31,823)
Homan, Paula 4:11:56 (13,602)
Homersham, Nicola 5:12:30 (27,910)
Homersley, Claire J 4:20:24 (15,912)
Homewood, Karen E 4:57:49 (25,282)
Homewood, Kim L 4:49:16 (23,296)
Hone, Nyree L 4:41:54 (21,605)
Honekamp, Ivonne 4:58:32 (25,452)
Honess, Jo 4:41:44 (21,573)
Honey, Kathryn M 5:00:48 (25,935)
Honeyman, Diana E 5:28:12 (30,145)
Honnor, Lara 5:51:18 (32,354)
Hood, Flora 4:14:37 (14,323)
Hood, Jo-Anne M 6:19:42 (33,907)
Hood, Marion M 4:13:08 (13,916)
Hoodless, Charlotte G 6:18:20 (33,863)
Hooper, Helen A 5:43:46 (31,745)
Hooper, Juliette 4:49:37 (23,402)
Hooper, Louise A 3:52:16 (8,547)
Hooper-Smith, Rachel S 5:47:53 (32,088)
Hooson, Rhonda 7:43:08 (35,185)
Hopegood, Karen J 5:27:21 (30,021)
Hopes, Cheryl E 4:48:36 (23,147)
Hopgood, Deanna 7:10:19 (34,981)
Hopkins, Adrienne C 4:16:16 (14,786)
Hopkins, Clare M 4:44:59 (22,321)
Hopkins, Jodie P 5:04:41 (26,627)
Hopkins, Lisa 6:20:02 (33,918)
Hopkins, Susan V 5:06:36 (26,982)
Hopkinson, Lara L 5:56:09 (32,715)
Hopkinson, Louise 3:59:42 (10,630)
Hopkisson, Debbie 4:47:39 (22,927)
Hoppe, Gisela 3:27:23 (3,988)
Hopton, Lucy 4:51:19 (23,800)
Hopwood, Audrey J 6:29:11 (34,229)
Hopwood, Nicole M 4:52:20 (24,021)
Horne, Helen M 6:11:23 (33,589)
Horne, Joanna K 4:19:09 (15,562)
Horner, Elizabeth S 6:20:44 (33,943)
Horner, Jane L 5:20:32 (29,187)
Horner, Katy 4:41:49 (21,592)
Horrell, Tara 4:07:43 (12,503)
Horrobin, Susan A 5:43:47 (31,746)
Horsfall, Carole E 5:56:08 (32,714)
Horsley, Laura I 5:20:31 (29,182)
Horsman, Kathleen 3:47:14 (7,398)
Horton, Lisa M 5:26:55 (29,964)
Horton, Sally L 4:13:21 (13,978)
Horwood, Jo 5:36:23 (31,037)
Horwood, Melissa L 5:48:40 (32,149)
Hosey, Abbie E 6:04:25 (33,239)
Hosking, Amanda C 3:29:14 (4,317)
Hoskins, Alexandra K 6:17:47 (33,844)
Hotchin, Sally R 4:53:43 (24,358)
Houde, Leah D 5:48:36 (32,142)
Hough, Cara L 6:02:18 (33,097)
Hough, Charlotte A 5:35:05 (30,913)
Hough, Grace M 4:17:31 (15,094)
Hough, Jennifer 6:25:42 (34,117)
Hough, Sonia 4:22:30 (16,472)
Houghton, Lisa A 6:56:23 (34,819)
Houghton, Rebecca L 3:45:40 (7,073)
Houghton, Sharon D 4:40:35 (21,280)
Hoult, Amie J 5:19:44 (29,067)
Hoult, Anabel 4:25:28 (17,273)
Housden, Sharon 4:13:37 (14,046)
House, Rachel L 4:58:11 (25,367)
Housego, Grace H 5:34:41 (30,872)
Houston, Lucy 4:59:37 (25,692)
Hovden, Aase 3:29:31 (4,358)
Howad, Anne 5:42:30 (31,627)
Howard, Ann J 4:25:42 (17,345)
Howard, Beatrice A 3:55:27 (9,353)
Howard, Caroline L 3:16:44 (2,651)
Howard, Elisabeth A 4:36:26 (20,209)

Howard, Geraldine A	4:04:31 (11,749)
Howard, Julia	4:52:12 (23,985)
Howard, Kristen L	4:43:18 (21,935)
Howard, Louise M	4:55:16 (24,731)
Howard, Lucille J	4:31:25 (18,947)
Howard, Maggie	4:07:31 (12,463)
Howard, Mo	5:24:07 (29,633)
Howard, Nicky J	5:06:50 (27,026)
Howard, Samantha T	5:28:11 (30,139)
Howarth, Brenda C	4:27:49 (17,987)
Howatson, Graham	4:07:17 (12,413)
Howe, Angela D	2:56:14 (825)
Howe, Caroline A	5:51:42 (32,388)
Howe, Kate	4:51:15 (23,783)
Howe, Lynda C	5:27:14 (30,004)
Howe, Rachael E	5:51:37 (32,382)
Howell, Katrina E	5:28:17 (30,164)
Howell, Kim	4:17:54 (15,179)
Howell, Nicola S	4:22:43 (16,540)
Howells, Gwyneth E	5:24:48 (29,719)
Howells, Shirley	6:12:24 (33,635)
Howes, Pauline C	5:17:49 (28,762)
Howlett, Louise	5:14:04 (28,180)
Howse, Denise J	3:30:32 (4,533)
Howse, Jenny H	4:50:32 (23,636)
Howting, Sharyn	5:29:35 (30,318)
Hoye, Catherine L	5:32:46 (30,649)
Hoyle, Helen E	3:33:42 (4,990)
Hubbard, Rohanna J	5:34:09 (30,801)
Hubbard, Sandra L	6:45:05 (34,618)
Hubbick, Joanne S	4:55:57 (24,888)
Hubert, Ciaragh A	3:25:05 (3,602)
Huckfield, Tracey A	5:24:49 (29,721)
Huckle, Susan A	5:02:18 (26,202)
Hudson, Caroline V	5:11:11 (27,684)
Hudson, Kym	6:04:09 (33,227)
Hudson, Leila A	3:33:55 (5,030)
Hudson, Theresa	5:21:16 (29,271)
Huffer, Michaela A	5:34:03 (30,788)
Hufton, Elizabeth	5:15:15 (28,378)
Huggett, Bridget M	5:21:21 (29,283)
Huggett, Sylvia A	3:46:34 (7,254)
Hughes, Ali L	4:12:23 (13,721)
Hughes, Ann G	4:29:17 (18,396)
Hughes, Annie E	4:55:55 (24,883)
Hughes, Calre L	3:50:47 (8,204)
Hughes, Catherine L	7:24:46 (35,098)
Hughes, Charlotte E	5:00:14 (25,828)
Hughes, Debbie K	3:40:02 (6,002)
Hughes, Eimear	5:51:15 (32,352)
Hughes, Emma J	4:12:13 (13,670)
Hughes, Harriet C	3:51:32 (8,379)
Hughes, Helen	5:13:20 (28,049)
Hughes, Irene J	5:29:20 (30,279)
Hughes, James R	4:17:18 (15,036)
Hughes, Jane	6:15:53 (33,776)
Hughes, Jane M	5:31:29 (30,515)
Hughes, Janice M	4:15:37 (14,615)
Hughes, Jean M	5:45:04 (31,853)
Hughes, Judith R	4:18:25 (15,334)
Hughes, Kathleen	4:32:01 (19,093)
Hughes, Kathleen M	5:18:31 (28,866)
Hughes, Lisa M	4:11:57 (13,608)
Hughes, Louise E	4:16:38 (14,871)
Hughes, Nicola	5:14:32 (28,266)
Hughes, Nicola L	5:33:11 (30,686)
Hughes, Nicola R	5:01:05 (25,994)
Hughes, Philippa K	5:32:32 (30,618)
Hughes, Rebecca C	4:31:18 (18,918)
Hughes, Rebekah	4:18:45 (15,444)
Hughes, Rhian J	6:39:26 (34,491)
Hughes, Sue	6:46:21 (34,635)
Hughes, Suzanne L	4:59:45 (25,725)
Hughes, Tanya R	4:37:30 (20,498)
Hughes, Tina L	5:23:17 (29,516)
Hull, Natalie J	4:50:26 (23,608)
Hulme, Rebecca A	5:11:48 (27,788)
Hulme, Susanne	6:51:58 (34,755)
Hume, Alison C	4:30:22 (18,693)
Hume, Beverley A	5:48:32 (32,137)
Hume, Emmy	4:09:59 (13,086)
Hume, Ruth E	4:25:44 (17,359)
Hume, Sarah	5:36:00 (30,992)

Hume, Shirley	3:57:16 (9,909)
Hummel, Leslie H	5:16:57 (28,637)
Humpherston, Claire E	4:44:23 (22,188)
Humphrey, Michele	3:16:15 (2,611)
Humphreys, Claire E	5:34:21 (30,823)
Humphreys, Donna	5:04:53 (26,666)
Humphreys, Gillian	4:11:22 (13,444)
Humphreys, Julia E	5:38:45 (31,285)
Humphreys, Katrina J	5:00:21 (25,856)
Humphreys, Lorraine	6:01:18 (33,039)
Humphries, Heidrun	4:58:56 (25,541)
Humphries, Katherine J	6:21:31 (33,964)
Humphris, Susan M	5:39:58 (31,411)
Humphryson, Nicola J	5:43:20 (31,706)
Hunn, Aletheia K	4:22:27 (16,461)
Hunt, Julie L	6:56:18 (34,818)
Hunt, Lynda C	4:34:39 (19,748)
Hunt, Sarah L	4:42:53 (21,847)
Hunt, Sonia L	4:51:31 (23,836)
Hunt, Susan M	5:18:42 (28,906)
Hunt, Susannah	5:56:39 (32,745)
Hunt, Tamara G	4:31:05 (18,850)
Hunt, Terase	5:55:13 (32,660)
Hunter, Annette T	4:33:01 (19,317)
Hunter, Beth A	6:00:21 (32,995)
Hunter, Dawn	5:39:05 (31,318)
Hunter, Julia C	5:04:31 (26,602)
Hunter, Lorna K	5:37:37 (31,152)
Hunter, Marianne J	6:39:26 (34,491)
Hunter, Robyn B	5:21:48 (29,327)
Hunter, Sarah L	5:27:28 (30,039)
Hunter, Wendy	4:01:14 (10,991)
Huntingford, Gail A	5:47:47 (32,079)
Huntington, Christine A	4:37:27 (20,482)
Huntley, Susan J	4:54:43 (24,598)
Hurley, Marion J	6:49:03 (34,691)
Hurnell, Gill V	5:01:10 (26,002)
Hurrell, Kirsten	5:52:00 (32,413)
Hurwitz, Rebecca S	4:25:11 (17,182)
Hussain, Shaista	4:36:18 (20,164)
Hussein, Chaygin	5:59:18 (32,934)
Hussein, Suzanne	6:29:52 (34,251)
Hussey, Sue C	4:54:30 (24,551)
Hüsseyin, Çiğdem E	6:09:04 (33,492)
Hutchings, Ella C	6:42:45 (34,565)
Hutchings, Joanna C	4:34:57 (19,842)
Hutchings, Kate	4:23:47 (16,796)
Hutchings, Marie A	3:43:28 (6,647)
Hutchins, Johanna	4:57:12 (25,173)
Hutchinson, Deborah J	3:58:55 (10,412)
Hutchinson, Gillian	6:27:12 (34,172)
Hutchinson, Kate E	5:41:07 (31,522)
Hutchinson, Kathleen L	3:29:44 (4,401)
Hutchinson, Katie	4:39:46 (21,084)
Hutchinson, Keri L	5:01:27 (26,054)
Hutchinson, Sally	5:05:14 (26,734)
Hutchinson, Sian E	4:46:39 (22,698)
Hutchison, Claire A	3:53:17 (8,792)
Hutchison, Josephine	4:17:40 (15,130)
Hutt, Frances A	5:43:53 (31,751)
Hutton, Rosalind C	3:54:09 (9,013)
Hutton, Ruth	3:13:10 (2,265)
Huxley, Linda	3:27:29 (4,017)
Huxley, Tracey	5:11:55 (27,807)
Hvass, Louise J	5:50:12 (32,279)
Hyatt, Jenny C	4:20:10 (15,846)
Hyde, Georgina L	4:32:55 (19,295)
Hyde, Janette A	5:53:54 (32,558)
Hyde, Jodie	4:23:54 (16,827)
Hydon, Alison M	5:27:55 (30,092)
Hyland, Emma J	4:16:18 (14,793)
Hynd, Jennie L	3:34:09 (5,069)
Hyne, Jo	4:35:14 (19,895)
Hynes, Julia F	3:45:21 (7,017)
Hynes, Laurence	4:15:10 (14,493)
Iacovitti, Nina	4:18:53 (15,481)
Iannelli, Sarah L	3:19:30 (2,937)
Ieriti, Maddy	6:43:09 (34,573)
Igwe, Calista O	4:40:29 (21,257)
Ikeda, Hiromi	4:18:46 (15,452)
Ilaria, Ramazzotti	4:35:34 (19,988)
Iles, Patricia A	5:33:47 (30,757)
Illiar, Sharon D	4:21:49 (16,287)

Illingworth, Alexandra C	4:38:55 (20,853)
Illingworth, Barbara J	4:37:21 (20,457)
Illingworth, Karen A	5:48:07 (32,104)
Illingworth, Lindsay H	5:48:07 (32,104)
Illman, Susan C	3:36:36 (5,445)
Ilott, Karen E	5:06:59 (27,053)
Ilsley, Gillian	4:46:27 (22,657)
Impey, Cindy J	6:27:56 (34,194)
Impleton, Lisa J	5:25:16 (29,775)
Indresano, Assunta	4:26:23 (17,561)
Ineson, Emma L	5:38:29 (31,249)
Ingham, Caroline L	4:29:35 (18,491)
Ingham, Gareth M	3:53:32 (8,866)
Ingham, Louise A	5:05:16 (26,741)
Ingham, Yvonne A	6:34:41 (34,373)
Ingle, Kristy M	4:53:28 (24,294)
Inglis, Katherine L	4:19:16 (15,596)
Inglis, Wendy R	5:39:15 (31,345)
Ingwersen, Sarah J	3:32:25 (4,807)
Inman, Caroline W	7:29:29 (35,122)
Inman, Jane E	6:44:36 (34,611)
Inman, Sarah A	4:56:27 (25,001)
Innes, Fiona	5:22:37 (29,444)
Innes, Sarah L	3:55:21 (9,321)
Innes, Tracey	5:15:20 (28,390)
Ioannou, Angela H	4:56:59 (25,126)
Ioannou, Elizabeth Y	7:24:06 (35,096)
Iona, Heather	6:01:52 (33,073)
Ions, Alex R	3:55:16 (9,298)
Iorio, Lisa A	3:19:03 (2,885)
Ireland, Fiona M	6:22:29 (34,007)
Ireland, Lorna L	4:53:14 (24,231)
Ireland, Shahla M	6:07:49 (33,433)
Iremonger, Victoria K	4:53:43 (24,358)
Ireson, Alexandra C	4:25:09 (17,169)
Irimia, Gabriela	4:35:20 (19,919)
Irimia, Monica	4:35:21 (19,931)
Irlam, Lisa J	3:48:23 (7,681)
Irons, Tracey	5:48:05 (32,101)
Irvin, Laura C	4:27:24 (17,857)
Irvine, Elizabeth J	4:32:57 (19,304)
Irvine, Kelly	6:46:03 (34,628)
Irvine, Louise A	5:37:50 (31,173)
Irving, Jane	5:13:44 (28,119)
Irwin, Michaela B	4:38:25 (20,732)
Isaacs, Roisin	7:00:23 (34,874)
Isaacs, Sacha	3:39:17 (5,864)
Isgren, Cajsa	4:10:48 (13,289)
Isherwood, Amanda P	5:39:17 (31,348)
Isherwood, Catherine E	5:10:18 (27,541)
Issatt, Belinda J	4:37:44 (20,561)
Italinna, Heli I	3:53:19 (8,809)
Iversen, Ase	7:16:54 (35,047)
Ivey, Gretchen J	6:01:04 (33,029)
Jack, Elisabeth G	4:50:45 (23,683)
Jack, Kirsten N	4:54:53 (24,637)
Jack, Samantha W	5:08:01 (27,222)
Jack, Tanya L	3:22:50 (3,277)
Jackman, Emma	5:14:59 (28,338)
Jackson, Anne	3:40:08 (6,023)
Jackson, Avis-Joy	4:28:07 (18,064)
Jackson, Caroline F	6:13:48 (33,694)
Jackson, Cheryl	6:24:14 (34,071)
Jackson, Devi	4:12:03 (13,635)
Jackson, Glen	4:08:47 (12,764)
Jackson, Hannah L	4:47:10 (22,813)
Jackson, Jacqueline	4:55:20 (24,745)
Jackson, Karen E	4:31:11 (18,879)
Jackson, Laura A	4:03:14 (11,440)
Jackson, Lorraine	4:16:36 (14,862)
Jackson, Ruth J	4:38:38 (20,784)
Jackson, Samantha L	5:26:29 (29,920)
Jackson, Sarah L	3:06:25 (1,585)
Jackson, Shayne L	3:57:16 (9,909)
Jackson, Valerie	6:06:24 (33,354)
Jackson, Victoria F	3:27:25 (4,000)
Jackson Phillips, Victoria	6:27:11 (34,169)
Jackson-Spillman, Janie D	4:52:28 (24,045)
Jacobs, Caroline S	4:08:01 (12,574)
Jacobs, Jennifer E	4:27:09 (17,789)
Jacobs, Linda H	4:59:47 (25,736)
Jacques, Hayley L	5:04:40 (26,623)
Jacques, Sophie A	5:09:23 (27,417)

Jaeger, Katharina 4:04:45 (11,803)
Jafari, Shima 4:04:43 (11,798)
Jaffe, Jane S. 5:23:34 (29,553)
Jagger, Anne C. 4:02:09 (11,195)
Jakeman, Karen N 6:31:01 (34,276)
Jakeman, Marion J 6:31:01 (34,276)
Jakobsson, Claire E 4:33:15 (19,370)
Jalali, Helen P. 6:08:30 (33,465)
James, Alison C. 5:18:09 (28,808)
James, Anne Marie 7:15:47 (35,042)
James, Caroline A. 4:58:00 (25,329)
James, Claire S. 5:09:06 (27,370)
James, Clarissa L. 5:48:00 (32,096)
James, Hayley M 5:20:25 (29,165)
James, Heulwen J 4:36:25 (20,203)
James, Jo L. 5:02:56 (26,327)
James, Karen S. 5:11:00 (27,653)
James, Kerry L 3:58:11 (10,184)
James, Laura J. 5:18:02 (28,791)
James, Lucie F 4:16:45 (14,902)
James, Melanie D 6:13:29 (33,678)
James, Nicola M. 5:01:00 (25,975)
James, Rebecca C 6:13:29 (33,678)
James, Sharon L 5:24:49 (29,721)
James, Sian 5:58:27 (32,871)
James, Susan J. 4:32:18 (19,162)
James, Terri 4:14:59 (14,437)
Jameson, Susan 4:51:55 (23,915)
James-Owens, Rachel E 6:11:59 (33,614)
James-Thomas, Rosalyn Z 5:38:19 (31,231)
Jans, Chris E 4:33:43 (19,492)
Jansen, Patty E. 3:56:46 (9,740)
Januszewski, Evonne 5:15:12 (28,369)
Jappy, Lorraine 5:59:33 (32,951)
Jaques, Nicole L 4:04:35 (11,764)
Jarrard, Kelli D 5:16:21 (28,527)
Jarrett, Louise A 4:20:44 (16,001)
Jarrold, Nichola J 4:40:07 (21,157)
Jarrold, Tracy 4:59:05 (25,582)
Jarvis, Amy E. 5:44:50 (31,835)
Jarvis, Melanie L. 5:06:20 (26,926)
Jarvis, Myra 5:50:18 (32,286)
Jas, Karin J 4:18:20 (15,307)
Jeal, Caroline M 4:45:17 (22,390)
Jeant, Emmanuelle 3:46:17 (7,199)
Jeffers, Joumana 4:57:02 (25,138)
Jefferson, Sarah E. 3:38:23 (5,709)
Jefferson, Tara 4:37:53 (20,594)
Jeffery, Louise 5:13:41 (28,113)
Jeffrey, June R. 4:50:39 (23,662)
Jeffrey, Kerry J. 4:29:12 (18,365)
Jeffrey, Laura R. 4:46:06 (22,578)
Jeffs, Chris K. 3:59:38 (10,612)
Jelley, Diana M. 5:20:12 (29,132)
Jelonek, Martina 4:48:11 (23,048)
Jenkin, Tina M 5:21:15 (29,269)
Jenkins, Alison 5:00:42 (25,919)
Jenkins, Cara 5:32:58 (30,670)
Jenkins, Greta 3:37:29 (5,578)
Jenkins, Helen 3:57:22 (9,939)
Jenkins, Jennifer M 5:34:48 (30,884)
Jenkins, Karen F 4:42:42 (21,800)
Jenkins, Karen T. 4:03:29 (11,493)
Jenkins, Katherine S. 4:34:50 (19,800)
Jenkins, Lulu 4:53:12 (24,228)
Jenkins, Michelle 3:39:01 (5,821)
Jenkins, Sandra M 4:26:23 (17,561)
Jenkins, Sarah J 5:35:43 (30,970)
Jenkins, Susan J 5:22:02 (29,352)
Jenkins, Tracy I. 3:51:11 (8,297)
Jenks, Rebecca 3:39:58 (5,991)
Jenner, Jackie H 4:13:08 (13,916)
Jennings, Amanda S. 5:16:03 (28,485)
Jennings, Christina M 5:15:35 (28,432)
Jennings, Christine T 4:27:16 (17,818)
Jennings, Heather J. 5:10:55 (27,641)
Jennings, Kim M. 4:39:35 (21,037)
Jennings, Laura V. 5:11:37 (27,759)
Jennings, Linda A. 5:17:36 (28,733)
Jennings, Mary E 4:29:05 (18,334)
Jennings, Samantha 4:53:56 (24,402)
Jennings, Susan A. 5:42:41 (31,651)
Jens, Christina 4:14:19 (14,248)
Jensen, Anne H 5:12:07 (27,849)
Jensen, Sasha 5:47:25 (32,052)
Jenson, Elizabeth M 4:24:04 (16,870)
Jerams, Lesley 4:26:14 (17,515)
Jerram, Sarah A 5:59:16 (32,931)
Jerrom, Janice M 4:29:34 (18,486)
Jessop, Anita J 6:56:09 (34,814)
Jewell, Natalie A 4:46:46 (22,725)
Jewett, Melanie K 3:42:15 (6,425)
Jewson, Ann P. 6:14:50 (33,729)
Jhooti, Permi 5:16:54 (28,624)
Jimenez, Elvira 4:25:28 (17,273)
Jinks, Maureen A. 4:25:24 (17,246)
Job, Christy A. 3:56:55 (9,787)
Job, Genevieve 4:27:49 (17,987)
Jobling, Julie M 5:25:23 (29,787)
Jobson, Hazel 3:54:14 (9,029)
Jobson, Jan M 4:29:01 (18,318)
Johannes, Mairon 4:15:29 (14,573)
Johans, Anna M 5:54:58 (32,639)
John, Caroline V 3:38:07 (5,669)
John, Debbie N 5:27:51 (30,082)
John, Helen 3:51:49 (8,445)
John, Sarah 5:16:46 (28,594)
John, Victoria 4:05:01 (11,864)
Johns, Clare H 5:03:08 (26,369)
Johns, Emma V 5:05:11 (26,722)
Johns, Gemma C 6:17:28 (33,839)
Johns, Julie A. 4:21:05 (16,089)
Johns, Lisa M 4:45:48 (22,498)
Johnson, Angela 5:53:05 (32,506)
Johnson, Barbara A. 4:19:42 (15,721)
Johnson, Benita 2:26:32 (54)
Johnson, Blessing A 5:45:47 (31,919)
Johnson, Deborah A 4:00:14 (10,774)
Johnson, Debra A. 3:56:33 (9,675)
Johnson, Fiona H 6:25:24 (34,106)
Johnson, Gemma L 4:42:52 (21,838)
Johnson, Hayley 6:54:41 (34,792)
Johnson, Hayley J 4:19:54 (15,775)
Johnson, Heather 7:12:58 (35,015)
Johnson, Helen T. 5:10:53 (27,634)
Johnson, Joanna S 4:59:14 (25,614)
Johnson, Julianne K. 5:20:31 (29,182)
Johnson, Julie A 5:07:55 (27,205)
Johnson, Katie A 4:51:51 (23,900)
Johnson, Kirsty A. 7:33:47 (35,154)
Johnson, Linda J 6:03:04 (33,148)
Johnson, Lisa M. 3:35:56 (5,327)
Johnson, Lucinda C 4:37:36 (20,523)
Johnson, Michelle 5:44:11 (31,780)
Johnson, Nancy J 4:21:15 (16,129)
Johnson, Nicola J 5:32:08 (30,568)
Johnson, Norah L 4:53:59 (24,424)
Johnson, Rachael 3:59:49 (10,667)
Johnson, Riona M 5:55:27 (32,675)
Johnson, Sharron M. 4:55:06 (24,700)
Johnson, Sophie A 5:58:30 (32,880)
Johnson, Susan A 5:54:46 (32,620)
Johnson, Vikki L. 6:31:47 (34,298)
Johnson, Wendy J 4:36:19 (20,168)
Johnston, Alison J. 4:37:16 (20,433)
Johnston, Carron 4:18:55 (15,489)
Johnston, Catherine E 4:43:21 (21,946)
Johnston, Clare E 4:07:16 (12,409)
Johnston, Le-Anne 4:30:16 (18,672)
Johnston, Sarah L 4:26:16 (17,521)
Johnston, Stephanie D. 4:03:59 (11,626)
Johnston, Suzanne S 4:43:08 (21,895)
Johnstone, Helen J. 4:51:11 (23,769)
Johnstone, Laura H 4:53:17 (24,243)
Johnstone, Melanie 4:02:37 (11,296)
Johson, Molly 5:13:02 (28,003)
Joint, Holly 4:26:20 (17,545)
Jolly, Helen M. 4:11:17 (13,424)
Jolly, Stephen G. 4:22:31 (16,476)
Jonas, Ulrike 4:26:29 (17,593)
Jones, Alison J. 5:43:09 (31,693)
Jones, Alison M. 6:02:58 (33,141)
Jones, Alison W 3:40:24 (6,074)
Jones, Angela 4:19:11 (15,575)
Jones, Angela 5:33:56 (30,772)
Jones, Angela S. 4:52:37 (24,080)
Jones, Anne H 5:40:23 (31,458)
Jones, Anne-Marie 4:44:45 (22,262)
Jones, Barbara A. 4:32:48 (19,270)
Jones, Barbara A. 6:49:21 (34,697)
Jones, Belinda A 4:12:49 (13,837)
Jones, Bridget 5:36:16 (31,022)
Jones, Carlyn M 5:45:09 (31,862)
Jones, Carol A. 3:32:59 (4,886)
Jones, Carole B 5:07:48 (27,189)
Jones, Carolyn Ann 6:38:49 (34,482)
Jones, Carolynn S 4:53:35 (24,323)
Jones, Cath M 4:52:17 (24,010)
Jones, Catherine M 6:08:40 (33,473)
Jones, Ceri A. 5:26:02 (29,875)
Jones, Christina 5:10:31 (27,576)
Jones, Christine J. 4:19:05 (15,544)
Jones, Claire L 3:56:27 (9,652)
Jones, Claire L 5:01:56 (26,132)
Jones, Clare M 5:27:27 (30,037)
Jones, Dawn N 4:26:18 (17,538)
Jones, Debbie 3:44:07 (6,763)
Jones, Debbie 3:51:59 (8,483)
Jones, Deborah L 6:42:49 (34,571)
Jones, Dianne P 5:59:14 (32,927)
Jones, Elizabeth A 4:42:52 (21,838)
Jones, Ella L. 6:42:46 (34,567)
Jones, Gwynedd 4:59:44 (25,719)
Jones, Gwyneth A 4:04:20 (11,710)
Jones, Hannah 4:45:22 (22,406)
Jones, Helen 5:13:22 (28,053)
Jones, Helen 6:47:07 (34,660)
Jones, Helen E. 6:51:36 (34,747)
Jones, Helen G 5:18:34 (28,877)
Jones, Jan 4:57:52 (25,293)
Jones, Janine M 6:24:58 (34,097)
Jones, Jayne 4:54:25 (24,528)
Jones, Jayne E 4:39:11 (20,923)
Jones, Jean A. 6:05:37 (33,303)
Jones, Jessica M 5:18:12 (28,818)
Jones, Jill C 4:58:11 (25,367)
Jones, Jo 3:54:42 (9,154)
Jones, Joanne 4:16:22 (14,814)
Jones, Julia 4:21:38 (16,238)
Jones, Karen A. 5:46:47 (31,998)
Jones, Karin L. 5:17:57 (28,773)
Jones, Kate V 5:53:28 (32,533)
Jones, Katharine G 2:56:52 (878)
Jones, Kim N. 5:09:19 (27,407)
Jones, Laura A 4:56:23 (24,986)
Jones, Leanne 4:31:59 (19,083)
Jones, Linda 4:50:26 (23,608)
Jones, Lindsey J 4:59:35 (25,682)
Jones, Lucy J 4:49:09 (23,273)
Jones, Lucy M 5:02:12 (26,183)
Jones, Lucy-Ann R. 4:10:52 (13,307)
Jones, Margaret C. 7:22:11 (35,084)
Jones, Marie C 5:13:46 (28,126)
Jones, May 6:02:48 (33,126)
Jones, Melanie A 3:38:47 (5,774)
Jones, Menna 4:23:18 (16,690)
Jones, Menna L 5:16:55 (28,629)
Jones, Michelle N 4:01:41 (11,086)
Jones, Natalie 5:13:23 (28,055)
Jones, Natasha C 5:49:16 (32,208)
Jones, Nia W 3:48:28 (7,699)
Jones, Nia W 5:42:32 (31,630)
Jones, Nicola J 4:26:10 (17,498)
Jones, Nikki M 4:13:00 (13,878)
Jones, Nina L 4:11:02 (13,361)
Jones, Patricia 3:55:15 (9,292)
Jones, Paula M 5:58:27 (32,871)
Jones, Penny A. 3:48:47 (7,780)
Jones, Rachael A. 4:05:15 (11,929)
Jones, Rachel L. 4:40:50 (21,346)
Jones, Rebecca F 5:00:34 (25,890)
Jones, Rhian E 4:18:56 (15,494)
Jones, Samantha J 5:51:28 (32,369)
Jones, Sandra J 4:39:26 (20,996)
Jones, Sarah 5:31:20 (30,495)
Jones, Sarah 6:09:03 (33,490)
Jones, Sarah L. 4:46:05 (22,571)
Jones, Sarah L. 5:50:44 (32,322)
Jones, Sharon 3:54:08 (9,005)

Jones, Sharon 4:20:55 (16,055)
Jones, Sian M 4:37:40 (20,539)
Jones, Sian S 5:45:28 (31,893)
Jones, Sophie L 5:11:22 (27,719)
Jones, Sue 4:06:29 (12,209)
Jones, Tessa E 3:45:01 (6,958)
Jones, Tina 4:07:17 (12,413)
Jones, Victoria H 3:50:40 (8,182)
Jones, Wendy 3:08:23 (1,748)
Jones, Wendy A 5:23:23 (29,526)
Jones, Yvonne J 4:25:08 (17,163)
Jones, Yvonne T 5:00:08 (25,800)
Jones, Zoe H 3:28:15 (4,150)
Jones Cooper, Dawn P 4:07:15 (12,403)
Jones-Ulmer, Donna L 5:20:58 (29,232)
Jonsson, Agneta 3:13:29 (2,300)
Jordan, Aileen J 5:06:22 (26,936)
Jordan, Diane Louise 7:09:04 (34,966)
Jordan, Elizabeth A 4:08:43 (12,743)
Jordan, Fiona A 5:38:36 (31,265)
Jordan, Joy E 6:22:58 (34,019)
Jordan, Mary R 3:59:52 (10,688)
Jordan, Nikki M 4:29:23 (18,428)
Jordan, Sarah B 4:43:59 (22,094)
Jordan, Suzanne M 4:35:04 (19,865)
Jordan, Vicky E 3:43:26 (6,643)
Joshua, Katie E 4:52:43 (24,108)
Joslin, Evelyn M 3:51:48 (8,441)
Joslin, Lucy E 4:50:33 (23,642)
Joubin, Vanessa 5:11:55 (27,807)
Joyce, Carol B 5:10:44 (27,607)
Joyce, Ceara E 3:57:08 (9,870)
Joyce, Lisa A 5:36:28 (31,048)
Joyce, Maria C 4:25:33 (17,302)
Joyce, Susan 5:45:12 (31,869)
Joyce, Tamsin 4:28:05 (18,049)
Joye, Daisy C 4:01:14 (10,991)
Judson, Jill Y 4:28:21 (18,122)
Juett, Vickie 5:16:45 (28,589)
Juignet, Annie 4:04:27 (11,734)
Jukes, Victoria A 5:16:48 (28,601)
Juneau, Dawn 4:49:37 (23,402)
Jung, Carole 4:18:23 (15,319)
Jungnickel, Katrina E 4:14:48 (14,379)
Juniper, Michelle J 5:12:27 (27,901)
Junnila, Anna P 3:19:29 (2,934)
Justice, Jane S 5:42:46 (31,659)
Kaiser, Mirjam L 4:09:54 (13,071)
Kaiser-Davies, Joanne 4:23:37 (16,756)
Kamarainen-Cani, Paula M 5:50:53 (32,330)
Kane, Aine T 3:39:28 (5,904)
Kane, Carina J 3:54:59 (9,236)
Kane, Carol D 6:38:58 (34,485)
Kane, Deseree 5:53:12 (32,515)
Kaneen, Tina 7:32:25 (35,147)
Kanki Knight, Mayu 3:49:52 (8,011)
Kanthamani, Cherra 4:52:45 (24,114)
Karalius, Kate 5:38:40 (31,274)
Karooz, Julia M 4:57:50 (25,286)
Kaur, Hardeep 6:12:54 (33,657)
Kaur, Kal 6:51:16 (34,743)
Kavanagh, Anne M 4:17:06 (14,982)
Kavanagh, Jan S 4:23:16 (16,675)
Kawahara, Rieko 5:20:21 (29,151)
Kay, Caroline L 5:41:52 (31,587)
Kay, Pauline B 5:01:16 (26,019)
Kay, Sarah E 4:17:59 (15,201)
Kaye, Judith A 4:53:11 (24,217)
Kaye, Laura F 5:14:24 (28,245)
Kayley, Sarah L 5:26:55 (29,964)
Keam, Eleanor L 4:37:52 (20,591)
Keane, Susie 5:09:47 (27,482)
Kear, Catherine M 3:53:02 (8,727)
Kear, Tara V 6:03:44 (33,202)
Kear, Teri I 6:03:43 (33,199)
Kearney, Lesley 3:52:39 (8,646)
Kearney, Linda M 3:52:12 (8,526)
Kearns, Angela C 4:21:17 (16,140)
Kearon, Carmel 6:30:08 (34,260)
Kearsey, Helen S 5:59:25 (32,940)
Kearsley, Christine 5:04:12 (26,556)
Keartland, Susan L 4:14:15 (14,229)
Keating, Elizabeth 5:02:09 (26,174)
Keaton, Helen M 3:52:38 (8,641)
Keavney, Jacqueline S 3:29:26 (4,344)
Keay, Michelle M 3:25:59 (3,755)
Keddie, Gill 2:44:17 (304)
Keeber, Andrea J 6:12:37 (33,646)
Keel, Vicki A 6:33:18 (34,337)
Keeling, Clare E 3:53:55 (8,958)
Keenan, Jeanette 3:57:45 (10,051)
Keenan, Mandy 5:26:41 (29,943)
Keenan, Sarah J 5:51:26 (32,366)
Keet Marsh, Lorayne M 3:44:16 (6,794)
Keevill, Heather K 4:30:07 (18,630)
Kehoe, Megan 5:05:51 (26,851)
Keith, Tracy A 4:59:46 (25,730)
Kellaway, Kate S 4:54:32 (24,559)
Keller, Helge 4:41:23 (21,489)
Keller-Hoffmann, Ute 4:41:23 (21,489)
Kellert, Gisela 4:36:03 (20,093)
Kellett, Elin M 5:32:38 (30,632)
Kellie, Samantha C 4:33:38 (19,470)
Kelly, Debra J 4:49:54 (23,473)
Kelly, Diane 3:32:57 (4,882)
Kelly, Jane A 6:21:26 (33,959)
Kelly, Jemma M 5:54:07 (32,578)
Kelly, Lorraine 6:35:22 (34,389)
Kelly, Margaret M 4:16:57 (14,944)
Kelly, Maureen H 6:06:54 (33,384)
Kelly, Maureen P 4:04:00 (11,633)
Kelly, Susan C 5:14:17 (28,225)
Kelly, Trish 4:04:25 (11,724)
Kelly-White, Rhonda A 3:46:11 (7,176)
Kelsey, Elaine M 4:56:39 (25,056)
Kelso-Cross, Katherine 5:45:39 (31,905)
Kember, De-Ann 5:28:20 (30,173)
Kemp, Alice C 4:29:35 (18,491)
Kemp, Frances L 5:28:10 (30,137)
Kemp, Louisa J 4:30:18 (18,681)
Kemp, Nicola A 4:29:02 (18,320)
Kemp, Patricia 4:28:42 (18,219)
Kemp, Shannene M 3:42:18 (6,433)
Kemp, Tracy 4:17:59 (15,201)
Kench, Giselle M 6:16:45 (33,809)
Kenden, Fran 3:41:34 (6,290)
Kenneally, Karen 6:29:48 (34,249)
Kennedy, Alison 5:45:17 (31,878)
Kennedy, Anna 5:30:53 (30,451)
Kennedy, Audrey M 5:07:59 (27,215)
Kennedy, Helen P 3:51:02 (8,261)
Kennedy, Holly 4:27:30 (17,891)
Kennedy, Jane A 4:03:35 (11,521)
Kennedy, Katy 6:05:21 (33,291)
Kennedy, Linda 3:45:50 (7,101)
Kennedy, Lindsey D 5:16:39 (28,569)
Kennedy, Nicole T 4:35:19 (19,911)
Kennedy, Ruth A 4:31:44 (19,029)
Kennedy, Susan C 5:05:58 (26,864)
Kennerley, Polly 4:07:21 (12,429)
Kennerson, Emma M 4:40:16 (21,200)
Kennett, Deborah S 5:16:43 (28,582)
Kennett, Elizabeth J 3:28:39 (4,218)
Kenney, Hayley 4:06:34 (12,232)
Kenney, Megan R 3:59:35 (10,594)
Kenniford, Audrey B 7:11:13 (34,992)
Kenning, Julia A 4:01:36 (11,066)
Kenny, Ann C 5:14:43 (28,306)
Kenny, Elizabeth M 4:08:14 (12,622)
Kent, Fiona L 4:24:43 (17,047)
Kent, Lisa 5:01:53 (26,124)
Kent, Suzanne J 4:51:58 (23,925)
Kenworthy, Ruth A 4:21:13 (16,113)
Kenwright, Dawn L 3:16:15 (2,611)
Ker, Grace Mu Yun 5:12:35 (27,923)
Kerner, Caroll 3:38:51 (5,784)
Kerney, Sara 6:29:29 (34,239)
Kerr, Amanda J 3:18:25 (2,822)
Kerr, Sara J 7:09:30 (34,971)
Kerrison, Lois E 4:18:32 (15,368)
Kerry, Rebecca L 5:33:53 (30,763)
Kershaw, Helen E 5:50:43 (32,317)
Kesler, Andrea P 6:47:23 (34,664)
Kessel, Anne E 3:50:38 (8,178)
Kesson, Kathleen M 5:45:12 (31,869)
Ketchell, Emiley 4:52:04 (23,954)
Ketley, Fern E 3:48:03 (7,598)
Keylock, Louisa K 4:34:55 (19,831)
Keys, Deborah A 4:06:48 (12,286)
Keys, Emma 3:43:02 (6,556)
Keyte, Helen 4:33:17 (19,377)
Khadim, Shazia 7:06:09 (34,940)
Khaira, Akwal K 5:52:24 (32,451)
Khan, Carla L 6:45:51 (34,627)
Khan, Sara 5:00:27 (25,873)
Khan, Zena 5:07:19 (27,117)
Kharood, Kanwaljit K 4:54:59 (24,668)
Khedair, Jane Z 6:09:23 (33,508)
Khoo, Audrey L 3:56:34 (9,681)
Khoshnevis, Heather 3:19:19 (2,912)
Khouri, Carla L 4:13:40 (14,060)
Kibby, Gemma D 5:24:20 (29,666)
Kicks, Annabel 3:53:10 (8,762)
Kidd, Chico 5:29:08 (30,262)
Kidgell, Nicola L 4:26:10 (17,498)
Kidner, Karen J 4:15:07 (14,478)
Kidson, Beverley A 4:45:33 (22,445)
Kieran, Gwen M 3:10:18 (1,958)
Kiersey, Claire P 4:49:03 (23,250)
Kiggundu, Marianne 4:28:51 (18,262)
Kihlstrom, Lucy C 3:32:49 (4,859)
Kilgallen, Jayne S 4:55:51 (24,862)
Killean, Elizabeth J 4:58:57 (25,544)
Killough, Leana J 4:15:57 (14,698)
Kimberley, Simone 4:04:51 (11,825)
Kimmich-Laux, Dorothee 4:35:06 (19,873)
Kinch, Brenda E 4:26:01 (17,441)
Kinch, Henry W 3:40:42 (6,117)
King, Angela C 5:04:36 (26,612)
King, Anne M 5:23:30 (29,543)
King, Auriol 7:18:56 (35,069)
King, Caroline J 4:33:04 (19,330)
King, Christine A 3:29:39 (4,386)
King, Claire A 4:02:18 (11,222)
King, Emily S 4:50:00 (23,495)
King, Evelyn 5:08:54 (27,341)
King, Jackie S 5:19:41 (29,058)
King, Joanne 4:00:00 (10,728)
King, Katherine E 7:27:04 (35,113)
King, Lucy 4:18:51 (15,476)
King, Lyndsay A 4:58:40 (25,479)
King, Mandy L 4:44:39 (22,236)
King, Natalie A 6:00:39 (33,008)
King, Natalie B 4:50:05 (23,508)
King, Nichola 5:58:29 (32,877)
King, Patricia 4:25:14 (17,196)
King, Rachel 5:44:46 (31,825)
King, Rachel A 4:59:55 (25,761)
King, Rebecca E 6:09:34 (33,519)
King, Rosanna M 5:18:32 (28,869)
King, Sally 4:40:25 (21,238)
King, Tracey E 5:43:33 (31,724)
King, Virginia 4:27:38 (17,934)
King, Zoe R 4:19:06 (15,547)
Kingdon, Alexandra 4:52:41 (24,101)
Kingdon, Danielle 4:50:19 (23,572)
Kingdon, Fiona J 3:51:20 (8,336)
Kingdon, Jennie G 3:01:29 (1,218)
Kingdon, Rebecca L 3:43:17 (6,613)
Kingdon, Rita A 4:46:05 (22,571)
Kingsbeer, Glenda C 5:39:11 (31,332)
Kingsford, Juliet A 4:15:28 (14,566)
Kingston, Alison L 3:34:11 (5,073)
Kingston, Alison M 4:26:31 (17,608)
Kingston, Amy-Rose 4:28:56 (18,286)
Kingston, Carol 4:30:55 (18,821)
Kinloch, Heather A 4:43:46 (22,053)
Kinnaird, Helen E 5:09:36 (27,456)
Kinnes Nee Oldland, Katie L 6:04:27 (33,243)
Kinney, Gillian 5:21:03 (29,244)
Kinniburgh, Veronica J 7:11:43 (34,999)
Kinsella, Karen 6:43:52 (34,594)
Kinsley, Amanda L 4:45:03 (22,338)
Kipping, Sarah J 4:20:01 (15,807)
Kipping, Virginia L 6:12:18 (33,630)
Kirby, Denise E 5:00:36 (25,898)
Kirby, Julie 4:41:58 (21,617)
Kirby, Maureen 4:23:42 (16,776)
Kirby, Rebecca J 4:12:15 (13,685)

Kirby, Sara J 3:39:58 (5,991)
Kirk, Cheryl L 5:46:31 (31,981)
Kirk, Christine 4:11:32 (13,489)
Kirk, Emma J 5:07:37 (27,164)
Kirk, Lesley S 3:23:28 (3,370)
Kirk, Sally 3:57:48 (10,076)
Kirkby, Rachel 4:34:43 (19,772)
Kirkham, Myshola 3:26:57 (3,921)
Kirkland, Rita A 6:43:33 (34,583)
Kirkpatrick, Beth 4:27:26 (17,864)
Kirkpatrick, Dorothy M 3:49:35 (7,948)
Kirkpatrick, Hannah L 4:59:05 (25,582)
Kirkwood, Karla 4:53:25 (24,281)
Kirsop, Hayley 5:19:05 (28,951)
Kirwan, Cliona C 4:27:34 (17,912)
Kirwan, Julie A 4:42:57 (21,860)
Kirwin, Donna M 5:38:11 (31,218)
Kisbee, Louise V 5:46:41 (31,993)
Kitchen, Christine 5:57:24 (32,799)
Kitchener, Clare A 5:16:43 (28,582)
Kitchener, Janet 4:42:40 (21,793)
Kitchener, Tracey S 5:27:12 (29,999)
Kitching, Anna E 3:35:35 (5,276)
Kitt Gerraghty, Deborah A 5:27:51 (30,082)
Klaeijsen, Ester 5:24:08 (29,635)
Kleefisch, Angelika 4:12:58 (13,874)
Klevansky, Gillian 4:50:49 (23,697)
Klugman, Libby 3:37:35 (5,589)
Knapman, Beverley J 4:08:50 (12,782)
Knass, Jenny E 3:29:24 (4,338)
Knee, Wendy E 4:05:54 (12,073)
Knight, Amanda J 4:58:20 (25,400)
Knight, Catherine E 4:21:24 (16,171)
Knight, Eileen T 4:55:01 (24,679)
Knight, Kate 6:10:55 (33,571)
Knight, Kay A 4:44:21 (22,183)
Knight, Laura M 4:16:09 (14,755)
Knight, Samantha 7:11:47 (35,002)
Knight, Tracey M 5:49:01 (32,184)
Knighton, Jemma J 5:56:35 (32,738)
Knights, Diane S 3:50:54 (8,237)
Knights, Joanna C 4:45:04 (22,342)
Knights, Zoe M 4:18:59 (15,507)
Knock, Katy J 4:49:55 (23,477)
Knock, Louise 4:05:56 (12,080)
Knock, Susan 5:35:02 (30,910)
Knopp, Rosalind J 3:30:26 (4,511)
Knorpp, Nadine K 4:51:46 (23,884)
Knotwell, Zena A 5:15:41 (28,441)
Knowles, Alyson 4:32:35 (19,225)
Knowles, Dawn 5:46:09 (31,946)
Knowles, Debra 7:04:26 (34,917)
Knowles, Juliet S 3:12:33 (2,198)
Knox, Christine 5:28:11 (30,139)
Knuth, Helen K 4:44:40 (22,240)
Koerbel, Amy L 4:18:24 (15,327)
Koewler, Jannine S 4:02:39 (11,303)
Koiter, Caroline S 4:30:52 (18,813)
Koiter, Patricia E 6:09:13 (33,502)
Kokolay, Cheryl 6:34:39 (34,369)
Koltuniak, Gillian E 4:53:45 (24,366)
Kontos, Sandra M 4:45:21 (22,401)
Koontz, Denny L 5:37:51 (31,175)
Koppang, Deborah A 5:01:27 (26,054)
Korpancova, Jaroslara F 3:08:16 (1,739)
Korro, Helen 4:07:14 (12,399)
Kosela, Iris 4:40:10 (21,175)
Kozak, Rhiannon 5:17:22 (28,692)
Kraeuchi, Denise Y 4:46:58 (22,765)
Kraftaite, Vitalija 4:28:15 (18,101)
Krause, Eva 4:54:00 (24,428)
Krawec, Natalka Z 4:34:21 (19,676)
Kraxberger, Christine 4:35:25 (19,955)
Kriedemann, Bronwyn 5:29:43 (30,332)
Krill, Allison P 3:47:01 (7,354)
Kronis, Jennifer 5:16:20 (28,525)
Kruger, Iris 4:42:49 (21,823)
Kruger, Jeanette H 4:58:26 (25,425)
Kubiak, Zoe M 5:11:00 (27,653)
Kuhl, Debbie J 5:12:19 (27,871)
Kuijpers, Ann 4:18:23 (15,319)
Kularia, Kirndeep K 5:28:42 (30,207)
Kulikova, Tamara 5:57:50 (32,826)
Kumar, Ranjani 5:20:05 (29,115)
Kuntze, Heidi M 5:07:23 (27,126)
Kuritko, Christina P 4:36:54 (20,331)
Kuwamori, Kayoko 4:27:35 (17,915)
Kyle, Kirsty L 7:23:27 (35,090)
Laband, Caroline M 4:14:03 (14,164)
Labiner, Nancy 3:21:32 (3,135)
Lack, Victoria E 4:48:02 (23,017)
Lackey, Jean 4:43:04 (21,884)
Laffan, Donna M 7:51:54 (35,214)
Laffey, Siobhan C 5:49:37 (32,235)
Lagden, Natasha F 4:11:45 (13,552)
Lagedotter, Helena 7:16:54 (35,047)
Lagreve, Servane 4:06:29 (12,209)
Laing, Emma L 4:56:19 (24,967)
Laing, Janet 3:07:11 (1,648)
Laird, Amy D 4:25:44 (17,359)
Laird, Elizabeth 5:05:42 (26,827)
Laird, Nuala 4:31:21 (18,934)
Lake, Donna 5:35:05 (30,913)
Lake, Samantha 4:52:30 (24,055)
Laker, Joanne 4:21:15 (16,129)
Lalaguna, Claire 4:51:54 (23,913)
Lam, Ivy S 7:11:06 (34,989)
Lam, Sai Yee 4:23:47 (16,796)
Lam, Wendy S 5:04:25 (26,589)
Lam Nieto, Susanna 5:55:00 (32,641)
Lamalle, Sophie 4:26:46 (17,683)
Lambert, Denise 4:24:25 (16,965)
Lambert, Heather J 3:18:12 (2,804)
Lambert, Jennie 4:42:22 (21,714)
Lambert, Marion C 6:18:14 (33,861)
Lambert, Wendy 6:52:52 (34,769)
Lambrechts, Coralie 4:18:17 (15,290)
Lampard, Mary L 5:32:10 (30,572)
Lanaway, Claire M 4:00:55 (10,932)
Lancaster, Christine A 4:31:07 (18,858)
Lancaster, Katy 5:43:57 (31,756)
Lance, Karen P 5:30:15 (30,391)
Landeg, Nichula L 4:58:26 (25,425)
Lane, Dawn M 4:34:03 (19,579)
Lane, Helen 5:02:53 (26,316)
Lane, Irene 5:06:23 (26,942)
Lane, Karen J 4:28:26 (18,146)
Lane, Lynne J 6:21:43 (33,974)
Lane, Sallyann 5:41:11 (31,527)
Lane, Samantha L 4:44:39 (22,236)
Lang, Fiona C 3:25:04 (3,599)
Lang, Melanie J 4:44:10 (22,135)
Lang, Natalie J 5:19:14 (28,982)
Langford, Amber L 6:26:54 (34,156)
Langham, Charlotte R 4:04:41 (11,790)
Langham, Joanne C 4:10:16 (13,160)
Langham, Victoria R 3:47:45 (7,514)
Langley, Beth F 4:53:13 (24,230)
Langley, Carole 5:01:26 (26,047)
Langley, Jill R 4:22:11 (16,392)
Lanigan, Sue E 4:02:42 (11,315)
Lankester, Anna 3:40:50 (6,148)
Lankester, Anne M 6:54:37 (34,790)
Lanzersdorfer, Elisabeth 3:50:47 (8,204)
Lapham, Natalie 5:12:26 (27,895)
Lapthorn, Anna K 4:33:16 (19,375)
Larard, Victoria 5:02:48 (26,294)
Large, Karen 4:18:25 (15,334)
Lark, Emma 5:44:12 (31,782)
Larmer, Sara-Jane 4:27:22 (17,845)
Larobe, Françoise 4:38:22 (20,718)
Larsen, Rikke 3:18:53 (2,871)
Laschewski, Antje-Ellen 4:36:36 (20,253)
Laskey, Donna M 4:53:07 (24,201)
Lasseter, Amanda J 4:17:02 (14,967)
Latham, Lyn-Marie 4:20:41 (15,986)
Latham, Nicki 3:56:11 (9,571)
Lathbury, Louise A 5:57:25 (32,800)
Latoni, Lisa 4:47:11 (22,818)
Latter, Elizabeth H 4:45:48 (22,498)
Latto, Sheila C 5:41:00 (31,511)
Laud, Carolyn J 3:57:02 (9,828)
Laud, Katherine A 4:52:53 (24,146)
Lauder, Sarah 5:16:41 (28,573)
Laurence, Clare L 5:55:50 (32,700)
Laurence, Denzil J 5:39:13 (31,336)
Laurence, Jayne 3:29:54 (4,438)
Laurens, Kristin R 4:51:14 (23,782)
Lauryn, Shirley S 5:43:02 (31,679)
Lavelle, Carol J 4:55:19 (24,738)
Laver, Beverley A 4:38:46 (20,821)
Laver, Denise A 5:39:58 (31,411)
Lavers, Ann I 4:09:11 (12,882)
Lavies, Elizabeth J 4:33:04 (19,330)
Lavin, Bridget P 5:19:12 (28,974)
Law, Barbara D 4:00:12 (10,766)
Law, June A 4:56:43 (25,073)
Law, Sharon 4:30:07 (18,630)
Lawler, Emma R 6:03:46 (33,208)
Lawlor, Teresa 5:27:34 (30,052)
Lawrence, Amelia M 5:40:00 (31,417)
Lawrence, Deborah J 4:23:50 (16,815)
Lawrence, Janet A 5:32:17 (30,589)
Lawrence, Janet R 4:12:29 (13,742)
Lawrence, Julie 6:09:22 (33,507)
Lawrence, Julie 7:00:34 (34,878)
Lawrence, Katharine M 4:39:49 (21,094)
Lawrence, Kirsten A 5:47:35 (32,066)
Lawrence, Louise M 4:34:40 (19,753)
Lawrence, Miriam 4:59:52 (25,750)
Lawrence, Rebecca 6:43:17 (34,576)
Lawrence, Rosemary J 4:12:35 (13,769)
Lawrence, Sally E 4:25:17 (17,211)
Lawrence, Sarah J 4:28:04 (18,047)
Lawrence, Stephanie L 5:32:54 (30,659)
Lawrence, Suzanne J 4:25:46 (17,371)
Lawrey, Katherine J 5:17:47 (28,757)
Laws, Louise 4:01:39 (11,078)
Laws, Sally 7:01:40 (34,889)
Lawson, Louise 5:17:31 (28,719)
Lawson, Mandy 4:26:29 (17,593)
Lawson, Nicole 5:17:31 (28,719)
Lawson, Sarah 4:05:46 (12,041)
Lawson, Yvonne J 5:32:15 (30,585)
Lawton, Clare 5:35:51 (30,980)
Lawton, Jayne R 3:58:11 (10,184)
Lawton, Teresita 5:19:09 (28,963)
Lay, Natalie 5:16:16 (28,513)
Lay, Pamela I 4:44:40 (22,240)
Lazard, Penny J 4:35:39 (20,005)
Lazarova, Lepa 4:32:53 (19,285)
Lazarova, Stepana 4:47:31 (22,887)
Le Brocq, Sarah B 5:10:58 (27,648)
Le Chemianat, Anne 5:03:15 (26,392)
Le Claire, Nanette M 7:41:19 (35,180)
Le Good, Judith A 4:04:53 (11,834)
Le Good, Nicola J 2:54:30 (713)
Le Gresley, Lisa A 4:22:42 (16,538)
Le Grouyer, Josette 4:24:29 (16,984)
Le Guillou, Estelle A 4:16:37 (14,866)
Le Ruez, Susan J 3:18:51 (2,866)
Le Vay, Lulu D 5:29:04 (30,253)
Lea, Donna M 4:55:48 (24,841)
Leach, Anne E 4:44:07 (22,122)
Leach, Catherine M 4:51:38 (23,859)
Leach, Helen 5:18:45 (28,911)
Leach, Jude E 6:09:48 (33,528)
Leadbetter, Christine R 5:20:20 (29,146)
Leah, Katherine A 5:40:36 (31,478)
Leahy, Veronica E 4:52:47 (24,123)
Lear, Alison J 5:54:19 (32,589)
Learoyd, Jo 4:48:34 (23,135)
Leask, Annette B 4:27:09 (17,789)
Leather, Victoria 4:45:38 (22,467)
Leatherdale, Anna J 3:51:03 (8,265)
Leatherland, Catharine E 5:00:47 (25,932)
Leathers, Gillian S 3:22:10 (3,213)
Leathers, Samantha J 4:42:59 (21,871)
Leaviss, Isobel J 4:25:29 (17,280)
Leavitt, Sue 6:51:53 (34,752)
Leavy, Claire 6:23:11 (34,027)
Leavy, Paula M 5:02:54 (26,320)
Leckie, Norma G 4:06:41 (12,260)
Leder, Helen M 5:09:56 (27,501)
Le-Du, Christine 4:55:48 (24,841)
Lee, Abigail 5:26:25 (29,914)
Lee, Ava M 4:56:37 (25,045)
Lee, Felicity E 4:32:52 (19,279)
Lee, Hairee 5:11:10 (27,681)

Lee, Helen	4:06:58 (12,333)	
Lee, Insoon	4:29:28 (18,453)	
Lee, Joohee	5:05:06 (26,700)	
Lee, Lesley E	5:28:03 (30,109)	
Lee, Paula	5:01:22 (26,036)	
Lee, Sarah J	4:24:53 (17,090)	
Lee, Shelley M	5:25:00 (29,746)	
Lee, Susan L	5:14:38 (28,291)	
Lees, Caroline A	5:22:37 (29,444)	
Lees, Polly E	5:16:07 (28,492)	
Lefebvre, Catherine	5:21:37 (29,302)	
Lefton, Janet	4:56:02 (24,907)	
Lefton, Michelle K	4:42:33 (21,751)	
Legassick, Margaret C	4:43:21 (21,946)	
Leggett, Jenny J	6:04:08 (33,226)	
Legrave, Shelagh J	4:35:20 (19,919)	
Lehmann, Judith	5:07:23 (27,126)	
Leigh, Anne R	6:56:52 (34,829)	
Leigh, Emma M	4:45:55 (22,534)	
Leigh, Karen M	5:30:01 (30,363)	
Leigh, Rebecca	4:54:55 (24,641)	
Leighton, Adele	5:12:55 (27,985)	
Leighton, Michelle J	3:47:50 (7,533)	
Leiper, Jacqueline	4:44:15 (22,155)	
Lelegard, Rahnia	4:23:26 (16,718)	
Leleu, Roselyn	3:52:12 (8,526)	
Lemesle, Catherine	3:49:50 (8,002)	
Lemon, Ann	4:29:44 (18,530)	
Lenaghan, Moira	4:04:14 (11,691)	
Lennon, Myanna N	3:09:52 (1,905)	
Lennon, Susan H	3:58:39 (10,323)	
Leonard, Angela J	3:33:23 (4,944)	
Leonard, Bernie	5:55:28 (32,678)	
Leppard, Heather S	5:43:23 (31,709)	
Leppard, Julie D	4:32:02 (19,098)	
Lerner, Danielle	5:03:40 (26,456)	
Lesire, Patricia	4:06:53 (12,311)	
Lesley, Georgina	5:21:18 (29,277)	
Leslie, Jane A	4:31:57 (19,073)	
Leslie, Nicole	4:42:39 (21,786)	
Leslie, Samantha L	5:33:57 (30,776)	
Lester, Helen	4:09:23 (12,930)	
Lester, Helen E	3:46:33 (7,251)	
Letcher, Alison	4:03:04 (11,402)	
Letts, Tania	5:39:45 (31,391)	
Leuschke, Fiona M	4:15:19 (14,532)	
Levermore, Claire	4:18:39 (15,414)	
Levett, Denize C	6:00:33 (33,003)	
Levitz, Jane W	4:26:41 (17,656)	
Levy, Justine A	4:43:57 (22,089)	
Levy, Winsome	5:25:57 (29,864)	
Lewiecki, Marie	6:14:19 (33,711)	
Lewis, Abigail	4:54:46 (24,614)	
Lewis, Amanda M	4:58:48 (25,510)	
Lewis, Anna M	3:49:14 (7,872)	
Lewis, Bethan	4:59:07 (25,588)	
Lewis, Beti-Jane	4:11:41 (13,534)	
Lewis, Carol A	6:08:30 (33,465)	
Lewis, Celia M	6:03:28 (33,187)	
Lewis, Charlotte J	5:47:14 (32,037)	
Lewis, Christine M	6:35:08 (34,380)	
Lewis, Claire	4:44:50 (22,281)	
Lewis, Claire E	5:05:56 (26,858)	
Lewis, Heather R	3:57:52 (10,102)	
Lewis, Helen C	4:47:41 (22,941)	
Lewis, Helen V	5:04:51 (26,658)	
Lewis, Jackie A	4:10:54 (13,317)	
Lewis, Jennifer E	5:00:02 (25,779)	
Lewis, Jenny A	5:11:47 (27,784)	
Lewis, Julie	3:30:44 (4,565)	
Lewis, Kathy	3:55:48 (9,461)	
Lewis, Katy A	4:40:27 (21,243)	
Lewis, Kim	6:07:22 (33,412)	
Lewis, Linda J	6:39:35 (34,497)	
Lewis, Lynne	4:24:33 (17,007)	
Lewis, Pamela	6:04:55 (33,266)	
Lewis, Sally	4:45:01 (22,333)	
Lewis, Sandra E	4:56:12 (24,940)	
Lewis, Siobhan	5:22:03 (29,361)	
Lewis, Tanya M	5:07:53 (27,200)	
Lewis, Tracey A	3:27:45 (4,067)	
Lewis, Valerie J	6:45:04 (34,616)	
Lewis, Wendy A	6:24:13 (34,070)	
Lewis-Jones, Angharad C	4:48:15 (23,065)	
Lewis-Jones, Tracy E	4:46:11 (22,600)	
Lewtas, Susanne A	3:59:00 (10,430)	
Ley, Jacqueline	5:12:07 (27,849)	
Leyland, Linda A	3:42:36 (6,481)	
Leysner, Carmelita	4:39:41 (21,065)	
Li, Karen	6:15:29 (33,757)	
Lichtenstein, Jane M	4:59:51 (25,747)	
Lidbury, Suze	3:42:42 (6,498)	
Liddle, Helen J	4:55:46 (24,835)	
Lidste, Victoria	5:06:15 (26,911)	
Liepins, Victoria C	5:13:15 (28,033)	
Light, Erica	5:14:34 (28,273)	
Lightfoot, Emma	4:44:01 (22,105)	
Lightfoot, Isabel	4:43:07 (21,891)	
Lighton, Sarah K	4:56:53 (25,110)	
Li-Kwai-Cheung, Anne-Marie	3:36:49 (5,469)	
Lilley, Amy L	5:19:40 (29,056)	
Lilley, Claire M	4:45:12 (22,371)	
Lilly, Ashley R	3:34:57 (5,177)	
Lim, Audrey	3:58:11 (10,184)	
Lincoln-Burbidge, Monique	4:57:31 (25,230)	
Linden, Linda	4:13:40 (14,060)	
Lindley, Denise	4:39:52 (21,101)	
Lindley, Emma	4:44:06 (22,117)	
Lindley, Karen P	5:22:20 (29,388)	
Lindsay, Alison C	3:36:48 (5,468)	
Lindsay, Denise P	5:20:21 (29,151)	
Lindsay, Jackie A	3:22:39 (3,257)	
Lindsey, Karen A	4:07:37 (12,483)	
Lindsey, Valerie A	4:31:15 (18,898)	
Lineker, Michelle D	3:52:33 (8,615)	
Linford, Nicola	7:14:06 (35,026)	
Ling, Melanie	3:23:00 (3,294)	
Linguey, Nicole	4:39:35 (21,037)	
Linker, Kathryn A	4:18:39 (15,414)	
Linklater, Emily T	4:25:13 (17,189)	
Linnell, Suzanne M	5:01:10 (26,002)	
Lintern, Lyn J	4:18:12 (15,266)	
Linton, Anne	6:15:32 (33,759)	
Linton, Christine M	5:20:02 (29,102)	
Linton, Shirley M	4:58:24 (25,416)	
Linvik, Jenny	4:40:13 (21,191)	
Lipede, Kehinde F	4:14:23 (14,267)	
Lipman, Miriam	5:15:23 (28,401)	
Lisney, Lisa M	5:14:06 (28,189)	
Lister, Katherine E	5:05:21 (26,764)	
Listopad, Alina V	4:27:21 (17,838)	
Litchfield, Teresa M	5:35:48 (30,975)	
Lithun, Lise	3:57:29 (9,973)	
Litterick, Emma C	3:25:18 (3,646)	
Little, Amy	5:11:13 (27,690)	
Little, Gina M	4:31:27 (18,957)	
Little, Louise M	3:24:37 (3,529)	
Little, Rachael J	4:23:30 (16,728)	
Little, Shirley C	5:16:12 (28,504)	
Little, Susan E	4:23:43 (16,781)	
Littlefair, Gillian M	4:13:42 (14,068)	
Littler, Jan	3:24:24 (3,506)	
Livemore, Clare	5:48:52 (32,170)	
Liverani, Beatrice	3:33:53 (5,026)	
Livingstone, Helen	5:00:39 (25,909)	
Livingstone, Helen J	3:18:15 (2,809)	
Lloyd, Amy E	4:45:38 (22,467)	
Lloyd, Anne M	5:10:08 (27,521)	
Lloyd, Catrin L	5:11:14 (27,695)	
Lloyd, Deborah	6:36:36 (34,423)	
Lloyd, Diane E	7:09:56 (34,975)	
Lloyd, Karen J	5:53:16 (32,523)	
Lloyd, Natalie	3:57:19 (9,925)	
Lloyd, Philippa R	5:44:41 (31,820)	
Lloyd, Susan J	4:40:23 (21,228)	
Lloyd, Susanna A	4:05:40 (12,019)	
Lloyd-Bane, Joanna	4:29:47 (18,540)	
Lloyd-Williams, Emma	6:27:45 (34,187)	
Loach, Kate E	3:39:07 (5,836)	
Loader, Carole A	4:06:19 (12,171)	
Loble, Deborah M	4:07:48 (12,533)	
Lobley, Susan E	6:51:03 (34,737)	
Locci, Loredana	4:08:08 (12,598)	
Lock, Catherine M	3:44:31 (6,839)	
Lock, Claire	5:11:27 (27,731)	
Lock, Claire	6:26:30 (34,142)	
Lock, Deborah A	6:46:46 (34,651)	
Lock, Vanessa	4:23:05 (16,625)	
Locke, Ann V	6:07:47 (33,429)	
Locker, Christa J	4:57:04 (25,146)	
Lockerbie, Hayley A	5:06:16 (26,913)	
Lockett, Monica	5:21:20 (29,279)	
Lockwood, Linda A	4:02:11 (11,201)	
Lodewyke, Joanna	4:34:09 (19,608)	
Lodge, Judy A	4:31:39 (19,007)	
Loesch, Martina	4:23:40 (16,766)	
Loftus, Joan A	4:33:28 (19,421)	
Logan, Caroline A	5:52:15 (32,433)	
Logan, Marion S	4:08:20 (12,655)	
Logan, Sarah H	3:56:47 (9,749)	
Logue, Nicola	4:21:56 (16,312)	
Loizou, Helen	5:28:28 (30,184)	
Lomas, Hayley	4:00:53 (10,927)	
Lomax, Jayne D	4:05:22 (11,961)	
Lombard, Jeanine	4:27:21 (17,838)	
Lombard, Lize	4:25:51 (17,387)	
Lombardo, Jamie L	4:49:36 (23,388)	
London, Carolyn G	5:10:52 (27,628)	
Londt, Diane	6:05:29 (33,294)	
Long, Anne J	4:49:57 (23,483)	
Long, Caroline L	4:26:07 (17,482)	
Long, Danielle L	6:26:16 (34,137)	
Long, Janet N	4:32:28 (19,204)	
Long, Natasha K	3:50:32 (8,153)	
Long, Rachel H	4:56:57 (25,122)	
Long, Rita M	3:58:15 (10,206)	
Long, Stephanie A	5:15:07 (28,354)	
Long, Tracy A	6:22:10 (33,969)	
Long, Victoria	5:43:55 (31,754)	
Longfield, Nicola A	3:27:39 (4,047)	
Longhurst, Donna M	5:57:42 (32,820)	
Longley, Philippa	4:25:58 (17,423)	
Longley, Zira K	4:13:02 (13,888)	
Longmire, Susan	4:46:17 (22,621)	
Longstaff, Nina E	5:11:50 (27,792)	
Loosemore, Georgina C	3:57:30 (9,979)	
Loosemore, Melissa	6:02:41 (33,118)	
Loosemore, Rachel C	3:57:30 (9,979)	
Loosley, Karen M	4:26:03 (17,455)	
Lopez, Gillian P	4:33:10 (19,355)	
Lord, Alexandra C	4:29:02 (18,320)	
Lord, Catherine E	4:57:53 (25,296)	
Lord, Nicola J	3:57:45 (10,038)	
Lorente Ferrer, Carmen R	6:42:46 (34,567)	
Lorne, Catherine	4:26:20 (17,545)	
Loroupe, Tegla	2:34:42 (109)	
Losser, Elisabeth E	3:46:52 (7,318)	
Lotzke, Hanna M	4:38:37 (20,781)	
Loubser, Melanie A	4:15:22 (14,540)	
Loughrey, Elizabeth E	5:30:51 (30,445)	
Louka, Anne T	4:09:57 (13,082)	
Louth, Clare L	4:41:49 (21,592)	
Lovatt, Deborah	4:31:39 (19,007)	
Lovell, Pamela E	4:35:56 (20,070)	
Lovell, Sally J	3:23:18 (3,351)	
Lovelock, Suzie	5:38:27 (31,245)	
Lovering, Maria M	4:52:14 (24,001)	
Lovett, Emma	5:06:25 (26,948)	
Low, Alexandra D	4:45:32 (22,439)	
Low, Barbara E	7:02:28 (34,900)	
Low, Jeanette	5:46:56 (32,010)	
Lowe, Freda J	4:54:25 (24,528)	
Lowe, Jennifer S	5:06:20 (26,926)	
Lowe, Penny A	4:51:11 (23,769)	
Lowe, Vicki A	3:57:58 (10,135)	
Lowndes, Clare L	4:35:13 (19,887)	
Lowndes, Valerie	6:12:44 (33,652)	
Loy, Francesca	6:05:02 (33,270)	
Loyd, Jane	6:29:34 (34,243)	
Lubbock, Lucy E	4:15:39 (14,621)	
Lubikowski, Sarah A	6:03:11 (33,155)	
Lucas, Elaine M	5:04:07 (26,541)	
Lucas, Pauline A	3:52:13 (8,532)	
Lucas, Susan	3:55:51 (9,373)	
Luck, Annie M	4:36:36 (20,253)	
Luck, Louise A	4:45:07 (22,357)	
Ludford, Rebecca	5:46:34 (31,985)	
Luelsdorf, Constanze	3:25:49 (3,721)	
Lui, Yeun San	4:48:45 (23,182)	

Luker, Philippa C 5:57:00 (32,772)
Lummis, Elaine J 6:02:16 (33,094)
Lumsden, Anne R 4:53:25 (24,281)
Lumsden, Donna M 4:22:25 (16,449)
Lumsden, Jacqui 3:44:48 (6,904)
Lumsden, Sian M 4:40:57 (21,375)
Lundy, Claire 5:35:01 (30,908)
Lunn, Gemma E 4:24:29 (16,984)
Lunn, Lynn 4:30:01 (18,591)
Lunn, Susan 6:08:10 (33,453)
Lusthaus, Lauren 4:26:48 (17,690)
Lusty, Elizabeth R 3:53:59 (8,972)
Lutte, Julia F 3:53:23 (8,826)
Luxton, Jane N 3:40:37 (6,106)
Luxton, Pauline 5:46:13 (31,957)
Lyders, Cath 5:05:29 (26,793)
Lydon, Carole 4:43:44 (22,043)
Lyle, Rosemary P 5:46:14 (31,959)
Lymer, Claire E 4:53:27 (24,290)
Lynch, Allison D 6:51:58 (34,755)
Lynch, Joanna 6:16:55 (33,821)
Lynch, Julie M 5:15:23 (28,401)
Lynch, Susan E 4:03:48 (11,576)
Lyne, Lisette E 5:16:35 (28,561)
Lyne, Sarah 6:03:35 (33,193)
Lynn, Julie A 4:54:35 (24,576)
Lynn, Michaela M 4:09:47 (13,035)
Lyon, Anita K 4:36:08 (20,113)
Lyon, Helen L 4:12:25 (13,730)
Lyons, Claire L 4:43:53 (22,067)
Lyons, Dee M 4:21:54 (16,306)
Lyons, Helen C 4:28:42 (18,219)
Lyons, Julia F 4:43:05 (21,886)
Lyons, Kay 5:30:47 (30,441)
Lyons, Margaret A 4:27:26 (17,864)
Lyons, Patricia J 6:04:09 (33,227)
Lyttle, Elaine F 4:15:28 (14,566)
Mabs, Caroline S 6:21:30 (33,961)
Maby, Julie 7:40:59 (35,178)
Macaulay, Nicola A 4:39:50 (21,096)
Macbeth, Deanne V 4:30:14 (18,662)
MacConochie, Heloise A 4:22:47 (16,553)
MacCorquodale, Sophie 4:30:43 (18,772)
MacCurtain, Elizabeth M 3:54:32 (9,105)
Macdonald, Alexandra M 4:03:50 (11,590)
Macdonald, Claire A 6:17:58 (33,851)
Macdonald, Gillian 6:44:19 (34,603)
Macdonald, Helen P 4:57:59 (25,324)
Macdonald, Julie A 4:30:00 (18,584)
Macdonald, Kirsten 4:01:18 (11,001)
Macdonald, Margaret A 4:35:33 (19,986)
Macdonald, Rhiannon 4:18:10 (15,253)
Macdonald, Sally A 3:17:06 (2,689)
Macdonald, Soroya 4:34:41 (19,762)
Macedo, Lisa S 4:43:18 (21,935)
MacGregor, Fiona J 4:52:36 (24,074)
MacGregor, Shona M 4:52:29 (24,052)
MacGregor, Sue M 3:34:08 (5,066)
Machell, Ingrid J 3:24:15 (3,478)
Machell, Yvonne L 4:47:02 (22,777)
Machen, Suzanne C 4:27:42 (17,951)
Machin, Amanda 4:29:05 (18,334)
Machin, Victoria L 4:10:00 (13,092)
Macht, Judith C 3:28:24 (4,181)
MacInnes, Louise 4:49:46 (23,440)
Macintosh, Lucy J 5:24:45 (29,715)
Mack, Katie 5:43:07 (31,688)
Mack, Rosemary 4:34:13 (19,634)
Mackay, Lorna 5:09:26 (27,427)
Mackay, Lucy S 3:55:58 (9,508)
Mackay, Margaret M 4:34:48 (19,789)
Mackenzie, Hannah J 5:28:28 (30,184)
Mackenzie, Helen 5:50:29 (32,297)
Mackenzie, Kaeti A 3:07:25 (1,667)
Mackenzie, Liz G 4:29:42 (18,520)
MacKew, Kay 3:59:35 (10,594)
Mackie, Angela C 4:25:13 (17,189)
Mackie, Charlotte J 4:25:27 (17,265)
Mackie, Melanie J 4:36:34 (20,238)
Mackin, Mary 3:35:27 (5,249)
Mackinnon, Emma E 5:04:05 (26,527)
Mackintosh, Nicole L 4:36:46 (20,294)
Mackintosh, Rachel C 6:05:51 (33,319)
Mackley, Veronica M 4:06:32 (12,221)
Macklin, Sinead A 3:52:05 (8,500)
Mackrell, Jane A 8:05:59 (35,237)
MacLagan, Carolyn J 4:13:28 (14,011)
MacLaran, Philippa F 4:14:43 (14,352)
Maclean, Jennifer M 3:00:41 (1,172)
Maclean, Lara E 3:42:41 (6,497)
Maclean, Mairi T 4:49:20 (23,320)
MacLeary, Rebekah 4:36:59 (20,350)
MacLellan, Gail G 5:57:14 (32,791)
MacLellan-Smith, Rebecca L 5:03:51 (26,494)
MacMaster, Jennifer H 3:17:49 (2,770)
MacNab, Sheila M 4:02:35 (11,291)
MacPhee, Margaret L 4:37:07 (20,391)
Macpherson, Sarah J 4:29:08 (18,350)
Madden, Angela M 5:36:08 (31,007)
Madders, Rachel C 4:04:16 (11,698)
Maddison, Charlotte K 5:04:54 (26,672)
Maddocks, Hazel 6:40:19 (34,514)
Maddocks, Jennifer H 3:52:22 (8,569)
Maddocks, Joanne L 5:23:24 (29,529)
Maddows, Faye 4:31:20 (18,927)
Madgwick, Sarah L 4:52:31 (24,058)
Madsen, Janice M 4:10:05 (13,109)
Madsen, Sharon L 4:46:57 (22,761)
Mafham, Marion M 3:54:49 (9,187)
Maggs, Lisa 3:59:44 (10,641)
Magnusson, Anna S 5:02:49 (26,297)
Magnusson, Margaret I 5:02:49 (26,297)
Maguire, Fiona E 3:28:59 (4,269)
Maguire, Frederica L 7:11:12 (34,991)
Maguire, Jill C 4:13:40 (14,060)
Maguire, Joanna D 3:56:35 (9,687)
Maguire, Sandra 5:35:48 (30,975)
Maguire, Sarah 3:28:45 (4,234)
Mahli, Gee K 4:52:43 (24,108)
Mahmoud, Sonia E 4:01:45 (11,101)
Mahon, Mandy J 5:20:04 (29,111)
Mahoney, Deborah K 6:39:56 (34,507)
Mahony, Kathryn A 5:06:51 (27,029)
Maidment, Marilyn F 3:30:26 (4,511)
Main, Janice K 7:44:11 (35,190)
Main, Zoe A 4:16:14 (14,775)
Maines, Hazel J 4:43:11 (21,911)
Maisey, Margaret 5:33:22 (30,702)
Maison, Margaret C 4:08:44 (12,749)
Makin, Cheryl L 5:25:07 (29,763)
Makin, Penny L 3:45:41 (7,074)
Makino, Yukiyo 5:38:44 (31,283)
Makowska, Jolanta 3:40:29 (6,083)
Malam, Andrea 6:41:59 (34,545)
Malby, Rebecca L 4:13:16 (13,955)
Malcolm, Juidth M 4:27:28 (17,875)
Malecki, Kathryn A 5:01:48 (26,107)
Malin, Frances C 3:31:25 (4,666)
Malkinson, Caroline S 3:37:07 (5,518)
Mallery, Lynne 5:34:33 (30,850)
Mallin, Louise A 5:00:54 (25,962)
Mallon, Susan M 5:37:23 (31,125)
Mallory, Janet E 4:04:24 (11,721)
Malloth, Patricia 3:29:15 (4,321)
Malone, Rachel 5:37:52 (31,178)
Malric, Nelly F 4:22:59 (16,595)
Maltby, Emma S 4:10:17 (13,164)
Malyon, Julie 4:40:06 (21,154)
Mancell, Sara K 3:47:28 (7,449)
Manchego-Crisp, Adriana 5:47:17 (32,042)
Mancuso, Lucia C 4:07:22 (12,430)
Mandorlo, Jo 5:48:15 (32,117)
Mandozzi, Anna L 5:34:18 (30,818)
Manera, Claudia 3:51:55 (8,466)
Manfield, Mary 6:00:24 (32,997)
Manfield, Nicci D 4:35:24 (19,951)
Mangan, Christine 6:05:54 (33,326)
Mangelshot, Kimberley M 4:24:40 (17,032)
Manhoo-Robinson, Amanda M 5:32:45 (30,643)
Manifield, Catherine 6:06:48 (33,378)
Mankowitz, Olivia P 6:07:05 (33,392)
Manley, Angela J 4:09:53 (13,063)
Manley, Francine J 4:58:21 (25,402)
Manley, Hazel 4:58:54 (25,536)
Manly, Rita V 3:36:56 (5,487)
Mann, Andrea D 3:39:27 (5,899)
Mann, Hilary 5:12:50 (27,977)
Mann, Louise H 5:07:29 (27,143)
Mann, Polly R 4:14:54 (14,412)
Mann, Ruth T 4:56:09 (24,929)
Mann, Sarah A 4:54:20 (24,512)
Mann, Sophie 5:21:47 (29,324)
Manners, Janet 4:53:39 (24,344)
Manners, Mary 7:25:54 (35,105)
Manning, Charlotte L 4:35:00 (19,853)
Manning, Jane M 3:43:45 (6,693)
Manning, Karen S 3:58:01 (10,148)
Mannion, Laura 4:22:36 (16,503)
Mannis, Teresa 6:01:06 (33,030)
Manock, Vicky L 3:28:30 (4,198)
Mansfield, Helen C 3:26:35 (3,866)
Mansfield, Mahiran 4:54:58 (24,663)
Mansfield, Sally-Anne 5:27:20 (30,017)
Manze, Marilyn 4:44:52 (22,291)
Mapperson, Jackie S 5:26:38 (29,940)
Mapstone, Belinda 4:20:16 (15,879)
Mapstone, Sue E 5:04:29 (26,595)
Marais, Marlene 4:00:57 (10,938)
Marcer, Jane 4:15:48 (14,660)
Marchant, Claudine 5:14:15 (28,217)
Marchant, Judy C 3:59:35 (10,594)
Marchant, Zina D 3:17:38 (2,751)
Marchi, Miriam 7:23:38 (35,093)
Marder, Swee L 4:10:55 (13,323)
Margetson, Kasanna M 4:53:56 (24,402)
Marinetti, Febea 5:06:32 (26,972)
Marino, Sandra 4:54:01 (24,433)
Markey, Shelagh A 5:44:35 (31,811)
Markham, Lorna 4:25:06 (17,152)
Markram, Bianca 5:32:29 (30,613)
Marks, Jodie 5:25:40 (29,822)
Marks, Laura J 4:36:42 (20,279)
Markwell, Emma I 5:48:48 (32,162)
Marley, Amanda J 4:20:01 (15,807)
Marne, Pauline M 4:50:18 (23,564)
Marola, Tracy A 5:06:06 (26,890)
Marot, Véronique 3:29:39 (4,386)
Marrin, Kelly 5:24:17 (29,659)
Marrinan, Colette M 5:49:49 (32,246)
Marriot-Dodington, Sandra 4:13:27 (14,003)
Marriott, Catherine T 4:50:04 (23,505)
Marrow, Ursula M 6:07:59 (33,442)
Marsden, Ann E 5:02:08 (26,172)
Marsden, Debbie A 3:29:10 (4,306)
Marsden, Joanne E 4:31:32 (18,978)
Marsh, Candice 5:57:12 (32,788)
Marsh, Jane E 5:02:38 (26,256)
Marsh, Lisa C 7:45:08 (35,193)
Marsh, Pauline E 6:13:32 (33,682)
Marsh, Sara E 4:01:40 (11,082)
Marsh, Tracey L 4:03:11 (11,427)
Marshall, Angela S 5:44:40 (31,816)
Marshall, Elizabeth 4:15:22 (14,540)
Marshall, Emma C 4:03:47 (11,569)
Marshall, Georgina M 4:48:47 (23,189)
Marshall, Helen C 4:16:08 (14,751)
Marshall, Lisa R 4:26:32 (17,612)
Marshall, Sara M 5:50:36 (32,310)
Marshall, Sheila M 4:22:05 (16,362)
Marshall, Susan D 4:47:24 (22,856)
Marston, Caroline R 4:52:02 (23,944)
Marston, Lucy E 4:54:59 (24,668)
Marteau, Debbie S 4:55:54 (24,874)
Martensson, Elin 4:30:17 (18,678)
Marti, Maria 4:58:47 (25,506)
Martin, Alison L 5:09:09 (27,380)
Martin, Amanda J 3:14:29 (2,411)
Martin, Ann 5:17:51 (28,765)
Martin, Ashlea C 7:18:00 (35,062)
Martin, Carol A 3:39:39 (5,941)
Martin, Christianne M 4:16:17 (14,792)
Martin, Claire 4:33:04 (19,330)
Martin, Clare L 5:31:04 (30,474)
Martin, Debbie 4:23:08 (16,640)
Martin, Eleanor A 5:58:45 (32,892)
Martin, Elizabeth A 4:12:29 (13,742)
Martin, Elizabeth P 4:46:21 (22,635)
Martin, Emma C 7:11:09 (34,990)
Martin, Florence 4:59:37 (25,692)

Martin, Grace 5:35:42 (30,967)
Martin, Hayley 4:47:46 (22,960)
Martin, Heidi R 4:39:14 (20,942)
Martin, Helen 5:40:57 (31,501)
Martin, Helen J 5:05:34 (26,803)
Martin, Iona H 3:42:04 (6,391)
Martin, Jennifer R 4:48:43 (23,170)
Martin, Judith A 4:38:13 (20,674)
Martin, Kathryn E 5:33:13 (30,691)
Martin, Katie 4:47:23 (22,851)
Martin, Lucy R 6:55:09 (34,803)
Martin, Martha 7:02:13 (34,893)
Martin, Moira K 4:28:23 (18,137)
Martin, Natalie A 3:51:46 (8,429)
Martin, Nicola L 3:51:32 (8,379)
Martin, Nikki K 4:31:25 (18,947)
Martin, Rachel C 4:47:13 (22,823)
Martin, Rachel E 4:18:59 (15,507)
Martin, Rebecca L 4:46:03 (22,562)
Martin, Rosemary E 5:15:28 (28,415)
Martin, Sarah J 5:22:12 (29,375)
Martin, Sarah V 4:49:39 (23,411)
Martin, Sharon 5:49:22 (32,217)
Martin, Susan E 5:09:19 (27,407)
Martin, Teresa M 5:10:16 (27,534)
Martin, Véronique 3:27:36 (4,036)
Martin, Zoe K 3:18:04 (2,792)
Martindale, Kate 4:03:29 (11,493)
Martyn Smith, Patricia I 4:28:22 (18,129)
Maruyama, Chieko 5:06:40 (26,995)
Marvel, Alison J 3:57:47 (10,070)
Mascart, Deborah 4:42:59 (21,871)
Maskell, Susan 5:40:29 (31,465)
Maslen, Doninique 6:24:35 (34,077)
Mason, Ann B 5:09:38 (27,461)
Mason, Dawn 4:17:06 (14,982)
Mason, Debbie 2:36:59 (138)
Mason, Elizabeth M 4:18:40 (15,420)
Mason, Fiona M 4:33:43 (19,492)
Mason, Hayley 4:58:03 (25,338)
Mason, Jill M 5:20:02 (29,102)
Massard, Nathalie 3:48:41 (7,757)
Massari, Eliszbetta 3:56:34 (9,681)
Massey, Kara J 4:02:20 (11,226)
Massey, Kathryn L 3:54:08 (9,005)
Massey, Michelle M 5:07:00 (27,057)
Massey, Nikki J 5:51:49 (32,397)
Massie, Rosie M 5:20:27 (29,171)
Massimo, Michelle 4:41:23 (21,489)
Masterman, Julie 3:49:48 (7,998)
Masters, Claire L 5:26:51 (29,956)
Masters, Jane A 4:51:57 (23,919)
Masters, Nicole E 4:52:00 (23,936)
Masuda, Mitsuko 5:26:51 (29,956)
Mathen, Lucy C 3:41:48 (6,337)
Mathers, Jo-Anne 3:54:32 (9,105)
Mathers, Julie B 4:15:34 (14,599)
Mathers, Linda 3:38:01 (5,650)
Mathias, Lucy N 4:27:18 (17,825)
Mathie, Louise 5:16:57 (28,637)
Mathieson, Kirstie J 4:44:47 (22,272)
Matier, Ruth E 5:23:39 (29,564)
Maton, Jane 3:53:04 (8,733)
Matsuoka, Hideko 4:25:18 (17,217)
Mattarozzi, Donatella 4:29:17 (18,396)
Matthews, Denise 4:12:00 (13,625)
Matthews, Jennifer J 4:57:05 (25,151)
Matthews, Mary C 5:45:40 (31,910)
Matthews, Polly M 5:58:12 (32,857)
Matthews, Sarah 6:11:19 (33,585)
Mattick, Suzanne 3:51:18 (8,328)
Mattingley, Angela M 6:12:47 (33,655)
Maude, Karen M 3:54:32 (9,105)
Maule, Denise C 6:14:29 (33,719)
Maund, Louisa J 3:37:21 (5,548)
Maunder, Deborah M 4:26:59 (17,749)
Maunder, Sharon 5:23:15 (29,513)
Mausser, Sarah 5:41:52 (31,587)
Mawhinney, Ashley 5:17:32 (28,723)
Maxim, Jennie K 4:13:03 (13,894)
May, Elizabeth 5:02:14 (26,188)
May, Holly G 2:48:47 (455)
May, Jacqueline J 4:39:54 (21,112)
May, Marion K 4:47:01 (22,774)
Maycraft, Deborah 5:11:18 (27,706)
Mayes, Denise L 5:25:30 (29,806)
Mayhew, Kathryn 5:29:35 (30,318)
Mayle, Nicola M 4:19:51 (15,764)
Maynard, Helen P 7:07:55 (34,955)
Mayo, Caroline J 4:58:42 (25,483)
Mayor, Marie P 3:55:36 (9,403)
Mburu, Philomena W 4:04:10 (11,674)
McAlister Dunn, Maia 4:08:07 (12,597)
McAndrew, Nell 3:10:51 (2,014)
McAnulty, Jacqueline C 5:58:15 (32,859)
McArthur, Lucie J 4:16:50 (14,922)
McArthur, Lucy K 4:29:00 (18,306)
McAuliffe, Katherine M 4:56:13 (24,944)
McBride, Joanne T 4:26:57 (17,737)
McBride, Lisa A 4:47:25 (22,861)
McCabe, Julia A 6:10:30 (33,554)
McCabe, Lesley 5:53:04 (32,504)
McCabe, Pauline M 6:28:09 (34,199)
McCafferty, Marian D 5:22:25 (29,407)
McCaffrey, Anne 4:50:45 (23,683)
McCaffrey, Jenny L 5:53:13 (32,517)
McCaffrey, Linda A 6:47:44 (34,671)
McCagney, Katharine L 5:14:57 (28,332)
McCahill, Gabrielle M 4:41:56 (21,610)
McCall, Carol A 5:21:57 (29,346)
McCall, Marion S 3:26:12 (3,794)
McCann, Hilary 6:11:35 (33,596)
McCann, Mary 4:41:15 (21,460)
McCarrick, Caoilfhionn 4:20:13 (15,857)
McCarthy, Cara H 5:29:44 (30,333)
McCarthy, Cheryl A 6:39:37 (34,498)
McCarthy, Christine 3:08:41 (1,776)
McCarthy, Emma E 5:32:14 (30,581)
McCarthy, Sarah 3:55:44 (9,443)
McClelland, Suzanne J 6:02:55 (33,138)
McCloskey, Eimear 8:03:24 (35,236)
McCloy, Kairenjit K 5:04:45 (26,638)
McCluney, Fiona 5:20:51 (29,220)
McClure, Anne 4:04:40 (11,786)
McConochie, Jennifer L 5:31:45 (30,537)
McCormack, Stephanie M 5:30:03 (30,368)
McCormick, Susanne F 4:56:44 (25,078)
McCorry, Kitty P 4:32:07 (19,117)
McCourt, Maureen F 4:57:43 (25,270)
McCourt, Sophie J 5:24:15 (29,653)
McCracken, Catriona 3:40:10 (6,031)
McCreery, Claire E 3:17:31 (2,736)
McCrindle, Fiona A 5:18:18 (28,837)
McCrone, Alison D 6:11:58 (33,612)
McCrudden, Nicky C 4:47:08 (22,802)
McCudden-Hughes, Caroline G 4:13:35 (14,037)
McCulloch, Elaine 5:52:59 (32,497)
McCurdie, Susan M 4:45:47 (22,491)
McCusker, Victoria H 5:48:17 (32,123)
McDade, Donna M 4:59:51 (25,747)
McDaid, Dawn 4:07:35 (12,472)
McDaid, Susan J 4:48:45 (23,182)
McDermott, Claire 4:24:15 (16,915)
McDermott, Karen E 4:37:35 (20,520)
McDermott, Katie M 5:17:48 (28,760)
McDermott, Laura J 4:57:53 (25,296)
McDermott, Linda 3:12:51 (2,236)
McDermott, Lisa J 5:52:18 (32,440)
McDermott, Pamela J 5:14:53 (28,324)
McDiarmid, Jacoline C 4:49:19 (23,315)
McDonagh, Kay E 4:54:58 (24,663)
McDonald, Anne 5:43:19 (31,705)
McDonald, Candice R 3:11:42 (2,105)
McDonald, Fiona L 4:49:51 (23,461)
McDonald, Helen 4:05:02 (11,871)
McDonald, Isabel M 3:55:58 (9,508)
McDonald, Jacqui I 4:19:27 (15,649)
McDonald, Jean E 5:03:45 (26,470)
McDonald, Joanna C 3:49:14 (7,872)
McDonald, Joanne M 5:16:19 (28,523)
McDonald, Julia L 4:42:45 (21,811)
McDonald, Julie 3:35:05 (5,196)
McDonald, Karen 4:41:05 (21,412)
McDonald, Kelly A 5:07:20 (27,119)
McDonald, Kristal 3:49:35 (7,948)
McDonald, Shira S 4:22:09 (16,385)
McDonald, Susan E 4:27:27 (17,869)
McDonald, Tracy L 4:30:42 (18,769)
McDonnell, Joanne L 6:47:25 (34,666)
McDonnell, Natale 4:30:07 (18,630)
McDonough, Annie 3:30:21 (4,498)
McDougal, Jo 4:34:40 (19,753)
McDougall, Mae Lynne 4:42:49 (21,823)
McDougall, Samantha K 4:12:46 (13,825)
McElligott, Elma 4:57:50 (25,286)
McElroy, Eimear C 4:06:02 (12,102)
McEniery, Carmel M 3:49:14 (7,872)
McEntegart, Clair E 3:16:29 (2,632)
McEntegart, Margaret B 4:37:07 (20,391)
McEwan, Roseanne C 4:04:15 (11,696)
McFadyen, Clare J 3:57:02 (9,828)
McFall, Josie 6:44:31 (34,609)
McGaffney, Jane D 7:11:51 (35,003)
McGarraghy, Christina 4:24:35 (17,010)
McGarrick, Tracey 5:43:45 (31,742)
McGarry, Pauline A 5:00:53 (25,958)
McGarry, Yvonne C 3:20:21 (3,031)
McGeary, Kathryn S 5:25:38 (29,818)
McGee, Carmel 4:07:54 (12,553)
McGee, Leona 6:15:02 (33,736)
McGee, Tamala L 4:24:07 (16,881)
McGeough, Lucy E 5:18:46 (28,915)
McGhee, Claire M 5:15:00 (28,340)
McGill, Kirsty M 4:52:30 (24,055)
McGilloway, Paula A 3:59:06 (10,469)
McGimpsey, Rita J 3:52:26 (8,591)
McGinley, Alison E 4:34:09 (19,608)
McGinley, Valerie 6:06:49 (33,379)
McGinly, Helen 4:50:06 (23,514)
McGinnis, Holly D 6:14:03 (33,705)
McGlashan, Laura 5:24:50 (29,726)
McGlenatendolf, Lesline 4:39:35 (21,037)
McGonagle, Hilary M 6:52:22 (34,759)
McGovern, Kate F 5:02:27 (26,228)
McGovern, Leigh A 6:29:16 (34,234)
McGowan, Alice E 5:29:00 (30,245)
McGowan, Eileen 5:46:29 (31,976)
McGowan, Emma E 5:46:15 (31,961)
McGowan, Joanne 4:44:07 (22,122)
McGowan, Lindsay J 4:16:47 (14,911)
McGowan, Marianne 5:21:01 (29,242)
McGrady, Andrea 6:03:02 (33,145)
McGrath, Allison J 5:09:28 (27,432)
McGrath, Fiona M 4:21:00 (16,075)
McGrath, Jane H 5:54:02 (32,569)
McGregor, Amanda J 5:22:14 (29,379)
McGrillen, Louise M 3:49:39 (7,965)
McGuckin, Jacqui 4:33:02 (19,320)
McGuffin, Madeleine J 4:34:11 (19,617)
McGuigan, Michelle 4:16:59 (14,951)
McGuigan, Myra 6:40:34 (34,518)
McGuire, Mary C 5:52:16 (32,437)
McHugh, Sharon B 4:18:14 (15,273)
McIlwraith, Linda 4:10:36 (13,240)
McInnes, Fiona A 4:49:24 (23,334)
McIntosh, Joyce 6:27:03 (34,160)
McIntosh, Kerry L 5:43:57 (31,756)
McIntosh, Toni 2:53:39 (665)
McIvor, Shelley A 4:11:16 (13,419)
McKain, Shirley G 5:18:13 (28,820)
McKay, Caroline E 4:44:16 (22,160)
McKay, Eleanor 4:06:10 (12,134)
McKay, Fiona 5:34:18 (30,818)
McKay, Sheridan E 5:14:16 (28,221)
McKee, Emma J 6:09:50 (33,529)
McKee, Julia G 5:09:23 (27,417)
McKee, Mona 4:19:53 (15,770)
McKelvey, Judith A 4:45:07 (22,357)
McKenna, Christine M 5:07:36 (27,159)
McKenna, Julie 5:48:16 (32,120)
McKenzie, Kathryn 4:27:03 (17,759)
McKeon, Carol Y 3:53:25 (8,835)
McKie, Elizabeth A 3:01:05 (1,197)
McKinney, Anita 4:46:49 (22,738)
McKinnon, Susan W 4:08:46 (12,758)
McKune, Zoe F 4:09:44 (13,022)
McLachlan, Margaret E 3:37:04 (5,507)
McLaren, Gillian C 5:33:24 (30,706)
McLaren, Phyllis 6:59:08 (34,854)

McLaughlin, Alison C	4:41:39 (21,555)	
McLaughlin, Ann E	3:39:00 (5,817)	
McLaughlin, Elaine	4:39:19 (20,967)	
McLaughlin, Hannah	4:49:04 (23,259)	
McLaughlin, Sharon D	3:53:48 (8,934)	
McLaughlin, Siobhan	6:04:51 (33,259)	
McLean, Julian	5:16:27 (28,540)	
McLean, Kate	5:56:19 (32,726)	
McLean, Laison	4:36:25 (20,203)	
McLean, Laura S	5:00:51 (25,946)	
McLellan, Anne M	7:20:17 (35,078)	
McLeod, Mary F	4:55:54 (24,874)	
McLeod-Hatch, Hermione	6:16:08 (33,790)	
McLindon, Laura H	3:46:32 (7,247)	
McLoughlin, Rebecca M	3:42:04 (6,391)	
McMahon, Kathleen J	4:53:33 (24,313)	
McManus, Margaret J	5:46:54 (32,006)	
McManus, Sally A	4:10:36 (13,240)	
McMillan, Lesley D	5:32:10 (30,572)	
McMorrow, Philomena	4:34:33 (19,727)	
McNair, Helen-Marie	5:12:20 (27,872)	
McNally, Pamela	7:04:12 (34,913)	
McNally, Sally	4:43:44 (22,043)	
McNeill, Victoria E	4:25:43 (17,351)	
McNeilly, Yvonne J	5:33:11 (30,686)	
McNeish, Helen	4:09:50 (13,049)	
McNicol, Louise	6:43:47 (34,590)	
McNulty, Philippa J	4:52:10 (23,979)	
McNulty, Sharon M	4:43:35 (22,003)	
McNulty, Sonia T	4:56:41 (25,064)	
McPake, Ruth A	4:22:00 (16,335)	
McParland, Tracy	4:11:33 (13,494)	
McPaul, Carol A	4:19:43 (15,727)	
McPhail, Marian	4:17:13 (15,015)	
McPherson, Lucy	5:58:55 (32,905)	
McPherson, Samantha J	4:13:06 (13,910)	
McQuire, Zoe M	6:28:41 (34,209)	
McRae, Jenna L	4:01:57 (11,138)	
McRae, Katy A	4:53:56 (24,402)	
McRae, Sheryl E	4:47:40 (22,936)	
McRoberts, Briony	4:44:42 (22,249)	
McSharry, Janet	5:38:41 (31,277)	
McSpadden, Lisa D	3:44:34 (6,854)	
McTaggart, Vicky L	3:44:33 (6,848)	
McTeman, Jan	3:43:43 (6,686)	
McVay, Mary E	4:36:35 (20,243)	
McWilliams, Anne	6:10:41 (33,560)	
McWilliams, Carmel R	4:41:11 (21,443)	
McWilliams, Catherine	5:44:48 (31,829)	
McWilliams, Francesca	4:12:19 (13,699)	
McWilliams, Lisa	5:52:37 (32,472)	
McWilliams, Marian Lucia	4:38:33 (20,764)	
McWilliams, Marthena M	4:28:31 (18,173)	
McWilliams, Olivia A	6:58:59 (34,850)	
McWilliams-Gray, Antoinette	5:52:39 (32,473)	
Meacham, Hilary C	4:57:29 (25,226)	
Meacock, Joanna	4:00:24 (10,804)	
Mead, Colette S	4:41:27 (21,511)	
Mead, Linda N	5:40:03 (31,421)	
Meade, Jacqueline A	6:20:50 (33,946)	
Meadows, Katie	4:59:28 (25,655)	
Meakes, Caroline L	4:22:06 (16,367)	
Meakins, Teresa	7:14:48 (35,030)	
Mears, Kathryn S	6:18:49 (33,884)	
Measey, Debra J	7:12:07 (35,004)	
Medlycott, Abbey R	4:49:24 (23,334)	
Medwell, Jane A	4:48:41 (23,165)	
Mee, Kathryn A	5:05:45 (26,833)	
Meechan, Elizabeth	4:39:41 (21,065)	
Meeke, Joanna E	4:29:05 (18,334)	
Meer, Sophie	3:34:33 (5,128)	
Mein, Joanne E	5:50:59 (32,332)	
Meissner, Uta	3:45:28 (7,045)	
Melbourne, Rowena E	3:49:39 (7,965)	
Meldrum, Catherine A	4:34:26 (19,699)	
Melham, Gillian H	7:16:49 (35,045)	
Melkevik, Bodil	4:08:48 (12,769)	
Meller, Eira	4:11:58 (13,614)	
Meller, Helen C	4:35:06 (19,873)	
Mellor, Hayley A	4:39:39 (21,057)	
Mellors, Ruth M	4:31:15 (18,898)	
Mellows, Carol F	4:04:05 (11,657)	
Melluish, Susan C	4:35:16 (19,900)	

Melotte, Julie	4:18:41 (15,427)	
Melvin, Alexandra M	4:47:49 (22,967)	
Melvin, Alison M	3:58:46 (10,375)	
Mendenhall, Marybeth	4:49:55 (23,477)	
Mendez, Dalia D	6:09:05 (33,494)	
Menditta, Karen M	4:19:59 (15,797)	
Meng, Leona J	4:48:01 (23,014)	
Mensah, Abigail C	4:01:13 (10,985)	
Meran, Katharina	4:57:07 (25,157)	
Mercado, Rosa D	5:54:08 (32,579)	
Mercado, Yolanda	2:47:47 (401)	
Mercer, Elizabeth J	7:12:18 (35,006)	
Mercer, Laura J	4:39:33 (21,027)	
Mercer, Simone	5:00:05 (25,792)	
Merchant, Laura J	4:43:29 (21,974)	
Mercy, Jane E	4:39:42 (21,067)	
Meredith, Jean	4:56:10 (24,932)	
Merley, Jean A	3:38:52 (5,789)	
Merrick, Catherine V	4:55:35 (24,786)	
Merritt, Mandy J	4:24:17 (16,920)	
Merritt, Phillippa S	4:28:57 (18,292)	
Merritt, Rebecca E	6:56:38 (34,825)	
Merry, Lorna	4:03:18 (11,462)	
Merryfield, Liz M	5:32:07 (30,565)	
Messenger, Claire R	5:23:26 (29,531)	
Messenger, Julie I	4:00:55 (10,932)	
Meston, Niki	3:42:24 (6,450)	
Mestre, Paula	4:46:57 (22,761)	
Metcalf, Tracey	3:56:32 (9,671)	
Metcalf, Valerie M	3:06:46 (1,615)	
Metherell, Phillipa S	4:11:42 (13,538)	
Mettam, Sophie L	4:11:56 (13,602)	
Meyer, Alexandra P	4:43:56 (22,081)	
Meyer, Lindi E	3:56:10 (9,562)	
Meyer, Monika	3:51:27 (8,365)	
Michaelson, Lucie A	4:42:53 (21,847)	
Michalos, Julie	4:57:53 (25,296)	
Michelmore, Clare R	5:01:26 (26,047)	
Michels, Gerda	3:57:19 (9,925)	
Michelsen, Karen M	5:07:39 (27,167)	
Micklethwaite, Claire L	4:31:17 (18,913)	
Micklewright, Helen L	5:14:24 (28,245)	
Micklewright, Rosie C	5:14:23 (28,242)	
Mico, Stephanie	5:02:39 (26,263)	
Middle, Georgina S	4:27:39 (17,937)	
Middlehurst, Sue E	4:32:39 (19,238)	
Middleton, Caroline A	4:10:25 (13,211)	
Middleton, Linda A	5:20:35 (29,194)	
Middleton, Linda M	3:55:35 (9,401)	
Middleton, Luanne M	4:39:35 (21,037)	
Middleton, Marion R	3:56:18 (9,605)	
Middleton, Micky C	4:40:45 (21,320)	
Middlewick, Leah E	4:30:16 (18,672)	
Midmore, Caroline	5:20:34 (29,193)	
Miethke, Angela A	4:45:42 (22,480)	
Mifsud, Vivien M	4:25:37 (17,321)	
Mikhael, Joanna	4:54:30 (24,551)	
Milbourn, Helen F	4:41:20 (21,474)	
Miles, Anne Marie	5:09:18 (27,403)	
Miles, Genelle	5:44:04 (31,767)	
Miles, Helen	3:50:55 (8,239)	
Miles, Helen V	5:37:53 (31,180)	
Miles, Leanne	4:57:49 (25,282)	
Miles, Michelle A	4:41:18 (21,472)	
Miles, Rebecca L	4:44:55 (22,301)	
Miles, Sally A	4:01:00 (10,949)	
Miles, Susan	6:37:35 (34,444)	
Miles, Wendy A	5:21:04 (29,247)	
Milesi, Mariagrazia	6:51:07 (34,739)	
Milewski, Julie M	4:53:46 (24,374)	
Millar, Gillian M	3:27:05 (3,940)	
Millard, Alison J	4:26:22 (17,555)	
Millard, Fiona J	4:44:25 (22,199)	
Millard, Jacqueline	6:39:38 (34,501)	
Millard, Lynette	5:06:41 (26,998)	
Millard, Natasha J	5:50:09 (32,273)	
Millen, Lynda J	5:08:13 (27,248)	
Miller, Ann C	6:36:18 (34,416)	
Miller, Anna	4:17:11 (15,007)	
Miller, Carol	3:29:12 (4,315)	
Miller, Caroline M	5:03:46 (26,476)	
Miller, Claire L	4:30:44 (18,778)	
Miller, Irene J	4:26:07 (17,482)	

Miller, Lesley	3:27:41 (4,057)	
Miller, Mary D	5:49:33 (32,227)	
Miller, Natasha C	4:50:44 (23,680)	
Miller, Sharon	7:34:06 (35,155)	
Miller, Stephanie J	3:33:02 (4,892)	
Miller, Suzanne J	4:45:34 (22,448)	
Millgate, Heather	5:51:06 (32,346)	
Millichip, Jane A	4:39:36 (21,047)	
Millman, Sarah E	4:51:26 (23,821)	
Millray, Christine	7:06:38 (34,946)	
Mills, Anna R	4:48:43 (23,170)	
Mills, Clare	4:54:05 (24,447)	
Mills, Diana H	3:30:40 (4,556)	
Mills, Frances	6:34:46 (34,376)	
Mills, Francesca L	5:14:57 (28,332)	
Mills, Hayley T	7:02:24 (34,898)	
Mills, Jane E	4:26:01 (17,441)	
Mills, Joanne M	4:49:30 (23,359)	
Mills, Julia A	3:58:19 (10,232)	
Mills, Karen	5:32:48 (30,652)	
Mills, Kathryn A	5:09:27 (27,431)	
Mills, Laura E	5:00:55 (25,964)	
Mills, Lesley	4:06:00 (12,094)	
Mills, Susan C	5:47:39 (32,070)	
Mills, Tamogene A	5:42:00 (31,597)	
Mills, Vicky L	4:25:22 (17,235)	
Mills, Victoria C	6:46:36 (34,646)	
Mills-Jones, Delphina	4:44:41 (22,245)	
Milmo, Jax C	5:11:32 (27,745)	
Milne, Sandra J	3:31:15 (4,643)	
Milne, Sarah E	3:48:58 (7,815)	
Milner, Ronnie A	6:01:45 (33,069)	
Milnes, Dianne	5:03:18 (26,404)	
Milson, Sophie L	4:43:29 (21,974)	
Milton, Alison J	3:50:01 (8,042)	
Minhas, Gursharan K	4:45:19 (22,397)	
Minkner, Elisabeth	4:20:28 (15,933)	
Minns, June	6:56:43 (34,828)	
Minty, Michelle E	4:01:57 (11,138)	
Miskin, Emma L	6:22:33 (34,011)	
Mison, Kathryn	5:34:59 (30,902)	
Missen, Verity	3:47:25 (7,440)	
Mitchard, Sheila A	5:18:52 (28,927)	
Mitchell, Alison	6:39:59 (34,509)	
Mitchell, Alison L	5:07:36 (27,159)	
Mitchell, Caroline I	5:10:11 (27,525)	
Mitchell, Christine H	4:47:51 (22,979)	
Mitchell, Claire P	4:47:57 (22,994)	
Mitchell, Clare	3:46:04 (7,153)	
Mitchell, Elaine K	4:00:14 (10,774)	
Mitchell, Gemma S	4:03:44 (11,554)	
Mitchell, Heather H	3:48:35 (7,736)	
Mitchell, Jackie A	3:58:32 (10,296)	
Mitchell, Jane L	5:53:45 (32,550)	
Mitchell, Katie V	3:44:50 (6,919)	
Mitchell, Kay	5:37:04 (31,108)	
Mitchell, Michelle	5:27:10 (29,994)	
Mitchell, Ruth I	5:31:44 (30,534)	
Mitchell, Theresa	5:02:13 (26,186)	
Mitchell, Tracy	3:25:17 (3,641)	
Mitchell, Wendy M	4:31:14 (18,894)	
Miyamoto, Chieko	5:43:11 (31,695)	
Mizen, Angela J	4:18:38 (15,408)	
Mobbs, Vanessa M	5:09:12 (27,387)	
Moberg, Marianne	3:54:29 (9,096)	
Mocharrafie, Kim S	4:35:40 (20,010)	
Mockridge, Amanda G	4:58:24 (25,416)	
Mockridge, Nicki J	3:52:17 (8,551)	
Moe, Charlotte	4:14:35 (14,315)	
Mofatt, Virginia	6:15:12 (33,745)	
Moffat, Georgia E	5:34:25 (30,837)	
Moffat, Helen	4:08:42 (12,740)	
Moffat, Julie	6:06:17 (33,347)	
Moffat, Venessa	4:41:58 (21,617)	
Moffatt, Geeti A	6:26:07 (34,131)	
Moffatt, Kate S	4:33:33 (19,453)	
Mogridge, Tavy T	7:09:05 (34,967)	
Moir, Mhairi L	4:10:33 (13,232)	
Moir, Natasha C	5:12:06 (27,845)	
Moir, Natasha J	4:39:02 (20,890)	
Mok, May U	4:25:44 (17,359)	
Mole, Lisa M	5:35:26 (30,949)	
Mole, Patricia	4:50:13 (23,539)	

Mollard, Eileen M 5:56:30 (32,732)
Mollard, Rosalyn C 6:57:11 (34,832)
Molloy, Jane M 6:13:05 (33,666)
Molloy, Sarah Louise 6:13:05 (33,666)
Moloney, Donna M 3:35:09 (5,203)
Moloney, Jennifer M 3:59:31 (10,576)
Moloney, Susan M 5:17:45 (28,750)
Monaghan, Carrie A 4:32:58 (19,307)
Monahan, Nina L 4:57:45 (25,272)
Money, Vanessa E 3:44:15 (6,792)
Monkhouse, Claire 5:07:06 (27,076)
Monkhouse, Elaine P 4:03:41 (11,542)
Monks, Nicola E 4:55:59 (24,898)
Montague, Ruth 4:14:52 (14,403)
Monteiro, Michelle S 4:48:32 (23,130)
Monzani, Louisa C 4:02:43 (11,323)
Moodie, Clemmie F 4:06:57 (12,329)
Moody, Dawn K 4:02:54 (11,367)
Moody, Louise C 4:12:56 (13,865)
Moody, Margaret M 3:53:06 (8,743)
Moody, Pat R 4:54:22 (24,518)
Moon, Tracy Jane 4:05:05 (11,889)
Moon, Yvette E 4:55:19 (24,738)
Mooney, Catherine M 3:50:24 (8,122)
Moore, Emma L 4:35:13 (19,887)
Moore, Faye L 5:48:16 (32,120)
Moore, Harriet D 4:39:49 (21,094)
Moore, Joanne L 5:00:15 (25,831)
Moore, Karen 4:48:20 (23,083)
Moore, Karen 5:36:33 (31,062)
Moore, Kerry L 5:13:44 (28,119)
Moore, Laura J 5:31:21 (30,501)
Moore, Lesley S 4:22:44 (16,544)
Moore, Rachael M 3:14:05 (2,364)
Moore, Sally 4:08:49 (12,773)
Moore, Sarah C 5:45:12 (31,869)
Moore Fitzgerald, Lindsey 4:19:14 (15,589)
Moores, Helen L 4:24:00 (16,851)
Moores, Sarah E 3:40:45 (6,127)
Moorhouse, Dawn L 4:58:25 (25,422)
Moors, Annick M 4:41:51 (21,599)
Morales, Emma J 4:40:22 (21,225)
Morbey, Annabel S 4:37:05 (20,377)
Mordecai, Susan J 5:20:36 (29,197)
Morden, Amy 4:36:47 (20,298)
More-Molyneux, Sarah 6:32:21 (34,315)
Moreno, Josephine 6:39:13 (34,488)
Moreton, Penny 4:15:59 (14,710)
Morfill, Rochelle L 6:43:43 (34,588)
Morgan, Alison E 3:14:53 (2,470)
Morgan, Amanda J 4:49:14 (23,288)
Morgan, Angela B 6:22:25 (34,005)
Morgan, Anne R 5:36:28 (31,048)
Morgan, Ann-Marie 5:31:01 (30,472)
Morgan, Calire E 4:30:00 (18,584)
Morgan, Carole A 3:55:08 (9,258)
Morgan, Deborah A 4:26:00 (17,435)
Morgan, Edwina 5:56:44 (32,752)
Morgan, Frances A 5:18:34 (28,877)
Morgan, Joanne R 3:23:52 (3,434)
Morgan, Karen E 5:22:57 (29,480)
Morgan, Katherine L 3:54:25 (9,081)
Morgan, Katy E 5:45:39 (31,905)
Morgan, Kirsty 5:11:41 (27,766)
Morgan, Kylie 5:22:31 (29,423)
Morgan, Lon 3:51:44 (8,418)
Morgan, Mary B 5:28:48 (30,219)
Morgan, Melinda N 5:15:56 (28,472)
Morgan, Michelle P 5:25:23 (29,787)
Morgan, Nicola 4:15:14 (14,511)
Morgan, Polly C 4:21:44 (16,266)
Morgan, Rachel L 4:37:24 (20,472)
Morgan, Rowena E 3:57:10 (9,880)
Morgan, Rowena F 5:06:29 (26,959)
Morgan, Shan 3:02:26 (1,292)
Morgan, Sinead M 6:32:43 (34,323)
Morgan, Susan M 4:59:34 (25,675)
Moriarty, Sally A 4:47:09 (22,806)
Morley, Deborah C 5:40:12 (31,437)
Morley, Emma J 3:57:57 (10,127)
Morley, Jacqueline K 5:39:50 (31,400)
Morley, Katherine L 5:15:05 (28,346)
Morrell, Kate E 3:44:06 (6,761)
Morris, Alison A 3:58:46 (10,375)
Morris, Amanda J 4:49:21 (23,326)
Morris, Carole E 4:36:48 (20,306)
Morris, Ceinwen 5:05:38 (26,811)
Morris, Claire M 4:20:04 (15,817)
Morris, Colette M 5:50:34 (32,308)
Morris, Elin G 3:44:42 (6,880)
Morris, Julie A 5:04:05 (26,527)
Morris, June 4:39:24 (20,989)
Morris, Kathryn A 4:07:09 (12,382)
Morris, Kay 4:20:03 (15,813)
Morris, Louise T 7:54:06 (35,221)
Morris, Lynne P 4:39:11 (20,923)
Morris, Margaret A 4:37:49 (20,585)
Morris, Michelle J 6:03:35 (33,193)
Morris, Phillippa L 3:29:43 (4,397)
Morris, Sarah L 4:02:04 (11,175)
Morris, Sarah L 4:48:07 (23,037)
Morris, Sharon 2:40:18 (207)
Morris, Shona E 5:56:59 (32,769)
Morris, Susan G 4:50:00 (23,495)
Morris, Suzanne R 6:19:09 (33,894)
Morrish, Becky K 4:54:28 (24,548)
Morrison, Katie L 6:01:00 (33,027)
Morrison, Lindsay 4:41:43 (21,569)
Morrison, Moira L 5:29:01 (30,249)
Morrison, Rebecca K 4:49:55 (23,477)
Morrissey, Keely A 4:42:43 (21,804)
Morrow, Karen 4:21:25 (16,179)
Morrow, Karen L 4:42:07 (21,657)
Morrow, Rebecca J 4:54:27 (24,543)
Morshed, Sima 5:27:57 (30,095)
Mortimer, Amanda 4:33:31 (19,440)
Mortimer, Hilary 4:46:33 (22,679)
Mortimer, Pamela A 4:33:51 (19,533)
Mortimer, Sheila J 4:17:42 (15,140)
Mortlock, Zoe L 6:20:13 (33,927)
Morton, Collette A 5:26:37 (29,939)
Morton, Jacqueline A 3:50:45 (8,198)
Morton, Kathleen S 7:05:34 (34,933)
Morton, Lisa C 5:08:41 (27,308)
Morton, Marie K 4:04:51 (11,825)
Morton, Meryl E 5:18:18 (28,837)
Morton, Michele 7:12:51 (35,014)
Morton, Sarah A 6:12:00 (33,616)
Mosberger, Alexandra E 5:37:33 (31,148)
Moseley, Julie E 4:41:31 (21,529)
Mosley, Helen G 5:58:49 (32,894)
Mosley, Jane H 5:58:50 (32,900)
Mosley, Lynne D 5:58:50 (32,900)
Mosley, Sarah L 4:48:25 (23,107)
Moss, Ann 4:49:48 (23,449)
Moss, Jenny A 3:34:27 (5,121)
Moss, Kim E 3:58:58 (10,423)
Moss, Lisa J 6:38:03 (34,456)
Moss, Sophie A 5:15:32 (28,422)
Moss, Tracy A 5:53:23 (32,526)
Mossman, Bernadette 4:09:50 (13,049)
Motiwalla, Laila 5:43:32 (31,722)
Motley, Hilary A 4:57:24 (25,208)
Mould, Frances J 5:42:42 (31,652)
Mould, Jennifer A 4:59:41 (25,708)
Moulden, Adeline 4:36:45 (20,293)
Moulden, Helen 4:33:29 (19,425)
Moulder, Liz 5:16:12 (28,504)
Moullin, Alison 6:20:04 (33,919)
Mount, Katherine E 4:15:47 (14,656)
Mower, Julie M 5:23:28 (29,538)
Moyle, Avril J 4:33:58 (19,560)
Moynihan, Clare L 3:42:04 (6,391)
Moyse, Tracy O 4:51:58 (23,925)
Mpangile, Nancy L 7:41:35 (35,181)
Mrorison, Heather J 4:18:59 (15,507)
Mugford, Charlotte A 5:24:12 (29,644)
Mugford, Nicola 4:15:23 (14,547)
Mugridge, Danielle L 4:24:33 (17,007)
Muir, Brenda S 5:00:02 (25,779)
Muir, Emma L 4:25:57 (17,413)
Muir, Joanne L 4:26:42 (17,658)
Mulhaire, Nicola E 4:46:08 (22,585)
Mulhern, Lisa M 4:43:16 (21,926)
Mulholland, Vanessa J 3:12:47 (2,223)
Mulkerrins, Nuala M 5:39:10 (31,328)
Mullinger, Louise 4:13:08 (13,916)
Mullins, Gail D 5:27:49 (30,077)
Mullins, Heather L 4:43:53 (22,067)
Mullins-English, Linda 6:35:26 (34,392)
Mulvaney, Susan 4:20:10 (15,846)
Mulvey, Margaret B 3:00:06 (1,134)
Mulvihill, Catherine E 5:33:37 (30,738)
Mumby, Karen 4:06:11 (12,137)
Muminova, Ozoda 4:17:42 (15,140)
Muncey, Clare T 4:36:25 (20,203)
Muncey, Lynn 3:54:37 (9,126)
Mundy, Sangita 5:36:11 (31,012)
Munnery Cumper, Sharon M 5:32:08 (30,568)
Munro, Ann M 5:11:00 (27,653)
Munro, Annette C 6:55:02 (34,800)
Munro, Fiona D 5:15:26 (28,410)
Munro, Julie 5:23:13 (29,505)
Munro, Teresa E 6:40:17 (34,512)
Munroe, Debbie M 4:47:12 (22,821)
Munson, Kate L 5:43:00 (31,678)
Munton, Debbie S 3:58:40 (10,338)
Munzenhuter, Marie Jeanne 4:43:55 (22,077)
Muratori, Ana M 4:34:12 (19,624)
Murawska, Anna M 4:52:39 (24,091)
Murchie, Shonagh 4:55:29 (24,769)
Murdoch, Sharon 4:11:08 (13,388)
Murdock, Elish C 5:41:10 (31,525)
Murfin, Antonia E 5:46:55 (32,009)
Murphy, Angela 5:11:56 (27,813)
Murphy, Angela M 5:16:12 (28,504)
Murphy, Brenda M 4:13:10 (13,928)
Murphy, Caroline 5:03:47 (26,481)
Murphy, Caroline S 5:18:48 (28,920)
Murphy, Christine 2:55:53 (801)
Murphy, Elaine N 5:58:20 (32,864)
Murphy, Fiona C 3:58:12 (10,193)
Murphy, Hannah E 5:22:38 (29,449)
Murphy, Martina P 4:48:52 (23,202)
Murphy, Mary H 4:55:18 (24,735)
Murphy, Nicola 4:35:14 (19,895)
Murphy, Nicola R 4:49:01 (23,241)
Murphy, Patricia 4:39:06 (20,901)
Murphy, Patricia M 6:49:53 (34,706)
Murphy, Penny E 4:56:24 (24,990)
Murphy, Samantha 3:22:03 (3,194)
Murphy, Stacey 4:11:26 (13,467)
Murphy, Sue C 6:20:41 (33,939)
Murray, Anne 5:11:02 (27,661)
Murray, Annette 3:43:02 (6,556)
Murray, Charlotte L 4:37:27 (20,482)
Murray, Deb 4:18:46 (15,452)
Murray, Deborah J 3:57:42 (10,038)
Murray, Fiona H 4:37:50 (20,586)
Murray, Helen L 5:10:56 (27,642)
Murray, Jenny D 2:49:01 (469)
Murray, Morag 4:54:20 (24,512)
Murray, Petra 5:40:33 (31,473)
Murray, Sandra 5:49:11 (32,199)
Murray, Sharon 4:34:53 (19,819)
Murray, Sian F 3:53:35 (8,879)
Murrell, Sarah 7:03:29 (34,909)
Murtagh, Nuala C 4:37:39 (20,529)
Musgrave, Samantha A 5:08:13 (27,248)
Mustoe, Gemma M 6:59:13 (34,856)
Mutoowi, Kanini N 6:39:28 (34,494)
Muxagata, Roberta 6:06:54 (33,384)
Myer, Catherine 5:09:44 (27,475)
Myers, Amanda J 4:26:00 (17,435)
Myers, Ariana L 4:44:58 (22,316)
Myers, Malindi E 2:55:30 (767)
Myhill, Jane L 4:34:46 (19,781)
Mykura, Gillian M 3:09:00 (1,812)
Mynes, Amanda S 6:01:43 (33,068)
Myott, Kate M 5:08:48 (27,319)
Nadin, Sue 4:16:14 (14,775)
Nagel, Michelle 4:21:48 (16,284)
Nagell-Dahl, Halldis 4:10:47 (13,281)
Naidoo, Dulchardt 4:39:55 (21,117)
Naing, Claire L 4:05:31 (11,991)
Nairn, Fionn 3:11:11 (2,049)
Nairn, Susan M 5:48:16 (32,120)
Nana, Bhanomati 5:53:59 (32,562)
Nandra, Kirat K 4:31:20 (18,927)

Nangati, Zivai 5:22:55 (29,473)
Napper, Patricia 6:14:59 (33,733)
Narbey, Angela 5:55:12 (32,658)
Nardese, Marzia 4:45:40 (22,474)
Nardy, Sylviane 4:36:59 (20,350)
Narin, Emma D 4:31:07 (18,858)
Nash, Helen C 4:46:42 (22,709)
Nash, Jill P 6:04:53 (33,261)
Nash, Mary 7:08:22 (34,961)
Nash, Sharon L 4:59:11 (25,600)
Nasmyth-Miller, Sarah J 5:03:18 (26,404)
Nathan, Terrance R 5:49:58 (32,259)
Nathe, Natascha 5:49:22 (32,217)
Nathuran, Kathleen S 6:24:41 (34,081)
Nation, Lynn M 5:51:22 (32,359)
Natrajan, Rachael C 3:41:54 (6,360)
Natsas, Costa 4:00:59 (10,945)
Naughton, Denise 5:09:33 (27,447)
Naylor, Christine M 2:55:54 (803)
Naylor, Mary J 4:32:54 (19,289)
Naylor-Maury, Jane H 4:15:57 (14,698)
Neal, Jennifer S 3:59:03 (10,451)
Neal, Joanna 5:15:06 (28,351)
Neal, Kelli J 4:33:02 (19,320)
Neale, Kerry M 7:26:17 (35,110)
Neale, Mandy 4:22:38 (16,518)
Neale, Tamsin R 3:24:00 (3,446)
Neall, Alison C 4:26:36 (17,631)
Nechi, Kim 4:53:18 (24,251)
Nee, Xinxin 5:25:04 (29,754)
Needham, Christine M 5:42:44 (31,654)
Neely, Diana H 4:52:16 (24,006)
Neenan, Jacqueline 4:26:37 (17,636)
Neesom, Dawn 4:14:53 (14,406)
Neil, Rebecca 5:09:43 (27,473)
Neilson, Christine M 3:56:30 (9,663)
Neilson, Julie M 4:02:21 (11,234)
Nelson, Amanda L 5:37:28 (31,138)
Nelson, Gwen M 5:27:11 (29,995)
Nelson, Kate 3:22:10 (3,213)
Nelson, Kim F 3:32:59 (4,886)
Nelson, Lesley A 4:22:54 (16,579)
Nelson, Patsy 4:24:36 (17,016)
Nelson, Paula A 4:54:27 (24,543)
Nelson, Sarah L 4:24:26 (16,970)
Nelson, Vicki 5:23:49 (29,587)
Neocleous, Anna 4:03:12 (11,432)
Neocleous, Julia E 4:56:23 (24,986)
Nesdale, Kellie I 4:09:03 (12,838)
Nethercleft, Hollie A 4:28:56 (18,286)
Netherwood, Lyndsey D 4:58:33 (25,455)
Neufeld, Ulrike 5:09:40 (27,467)
Nevill, Ibby 3:24:30 (3,516)
Neville, Elizabeth 3:29:23 (4,336)
Nevin, Michelle J 6:38:13 (34,460)
New, Alexandra 4:49:18 (23,306)
New, Wendi M 5:28:11 (30,139)
Newbold, Sharon M 5:44:54 (31,839)
Newbury, Tracie L 4:30:47 (18,789)
Newell, Angela E 3:44:49 (6,915)
Newell, Angella 4:24:16 (16,918)
Newell, Jennifer F 4:41:26 (21,506)
Newell, Louise 3:46:23 (7,219)
Newing, Lisa 3:08:04 (1,721)
Newington-Bridges, Lucinda M 4:25:55 (17,404)
Newland, Rita 5:15:45 (28,451)
Newman, Annabel M 4:35:20 (19,919)
Newman, Brenda 6:21:06 (33,953)
Newman, Elizabeth H 4:10:11 (13,139)
Newman, Jane 4:23:12 (16,654)
Newman, Mary 5:10:49 (27,620)
Newman, Morwenna E 4:58:19 (25,395)
Newman, Tracey 4:35:20 (19,919)
Newman, Vivien A 6:01:51 (33,072)
Newman, Wendy M 5:54:49 (32,624)
Newport, Belinda J 4:39:28 (21,001)
Newrick, Victoira J 5:24:01 (29,621)
Newsholme, Pauline 6:00:50 (33,017)
Newsome, Julia D 5:11:01 (27,658)
Newstead, Johanne 3:24:10 (3,468)
Newton, Hilary A 3:58:05 (10,164)
Newton, Lois H 5:26:01 (29,869)
Newton, Maria T 5:03:35 (26,440)
Newton, Samantha 4:44:45 (22,262)
Newton, Sarah E 3:14:58 (2,477)
Newton, Vicky 4:53:31 (24,307)
Ng, Chin Chin 5:34:13 (30,809)
Ng, Yeelan 4:49:08 (23,271)
Nias, Helen J 10:06:32 (35,257)
Nicel, Jo K 4:33:55 (19,551)
Nichol, Janette E 4:47:46 (22,960)
Nicholas, Dominique L 4:28:56 (18,286)
Nicholas, Jennifer L 5:40:10 (31,436)
Nicholls, Claire E 6:23:13 (34,030)
Nicholls, Clare L 4:32:40 (19,244)
Nicholls, Elaine 4:48:53 (23,205)
Nicholls, Emily R 6:02:37 (33,114)
Nicholls, Janice J 5:40:12 (31,437)
Nicholls, Kate 5:59:01 (32,913)
Nicholls, Sally J 4:59:42 (25,711)
Nicholls, Sarah J 5:07:27 (27,138)
Nicholls, Yvonne L 3:42:34 (6,475)
Nichols, Karen J 5:09:10 (27,383)
Nichols, Lyn S 4:08:01 (12,574)
Nicholson, Clare J 2:58:20 (976)
Nicholson, Clare M 3:41:48 (6,337)
Nicholson, Emma L 4:24:02 (16,863)
Nicholson, Margaret A 5:59:49 (32,971)
Nicklen, Christina A 4:54:22 (24,518)
Nicol, Deborah J 4:46:49 (22,738)
Nicol, Linnea T 4:27:26 (17,864)
Nicolaou, Maria 5:10:17 (27,539)
Nicoletti, Lale 4:12:12 (13,664)
Nicoll, Lucy J 3:51:15 (8,316)
Nicoll, Rona 4:09:24 (12,933)
Nicolson, Rebecca J 4:25:13 (17,189)
Nieuwenhuysen, Sarah M 4:08:25 (12,675)
Niewczasinski, Jane M 4:14:00 (14,148)
Nightingale, Beverley A 4:46:19 (22,626)
Nightingale, Helen 4:31:20 (18,927)
Nightingale, Lisa M 5:17:33 (28,726)
Nilsson, Ann-Marie 4:02:54 (11,367)
Nimmo, Sarah L 4:47:23 (22,851)
Niziol, Michelle B 5:23:51 (29,593)
N'jie, Susan 4:53:01 (24,177)
Noble, Ailsa 6:11:57 (33,611)
Noble, Cate M 4:06:06 (12,121)
Noble, Eileen R 5:23:52 (29,599)
Noble, Heather L 4:32:18 (19,162)
Noble, Helen L 6:25:33 (34,114)
Noble, Pam 6:10:32 (33,555)
Noble, Sarah L 4:01:32 (11,055)
Noble, Sue P 3:57:46 (10,058)
Nobles, Margaret 4:28:26 (18,146)
Nock, Jeanette D 6:09:02 (33,489)
Nocker, Rosemarie 4:08:24 (12,667)
Noda, Marcia L 5:11:15 (27,698)
Noel, Maureen 3:29:36 (4,370)
Noke, Linda J 4:30:50 (18,805)
Nolan, Martine A 7:46:18 (35,198)
Nolan, Tina M 4:24:17 (16,920)
Nomoto, Kimie 6:12:51 (33,656)
Nones, Marina M 5:30:05 (30,369)
Noody, Carol J 6:15:40 (33,769)
Noot, Rhian 5:21:11 (29,262)
Norbury, Audrey 4:29:24 (18,436)
Nordin, Breege J 3:13:53 (2,343)
Norman, Alison L 4:52:12 (23,985)
Norman, Frances G 4:42:44 (21,809)
Norman, Laura E 4:26:03 (17,455)
Norman, Lucy A 4:07:30 (12,460)
Norman, Nikki 4:52:13 (23,995)
Norman, Patricia 4:18:57 (15,499)
Norman, Philippa 4:06:34 (12,232)
Norman, Sarah 5:12:55 (27,985)
Norquay, Megan J 3:28:33 (4,206)
Norrgard, Berit 4:23:32 (16,735)
Norris, Carole A 5:08:36 (27,298)
Norris, Christine B 4:39:31 (21,019)
Norris, Ellen 5:52:00 (32,413)
Norris, Fiona G 6:07:23 (33,414)
Norris, Samantha M 6:54:11 (34,785)
Norris, Sammy-Jo Y 4:34:47 (19,786)
North, Heather J 3:38:07 (5,669)
North, Stephanie 4:52:03 (23,948)
Northcott, Jennifer C 3:53:05 (8,739)
Norton, Ginny C 4:15:29 (14,573)
Norton, Karena C 3:43:55 (6,725)
Norton, Sharon Y 4:29:27 (18,448)
Norton, Yvette 5:19:01 (28,947)
Norton-Lay, Michaela F 4:15:28 (14,566)
Nowell, Jacqueline R 4:34:49 (19,797)
Nowell, Zoe 4:10:13 (13,146)
Ntekim, Maniza 4:54:23 (24,523)
Nudds, Fay L 5:05:17 (26,746)
Nuninger, Claudie 5:34:14 (30,811)
Nunn, Amy A 4:16:06 (14,738)
Nunn, Gill A 3:56:06 (9,538)
Nurcombe, Karen A 3:57:36 (10,015)
Nuttall, Philippa J 4:16:11 (14,762)
Nuttall, Susan M 5:38:42 (31,278)
Nutter, Glenys 5:38:25 (31,238)
Nutting, Annette 3:22:38 (3,256)
Nutting, Judy A 3:36:08 (5,360)
Nyman, Larissa 4:47:59 (23,004)
Oakes, Anne 4:16:40 (14,881)
Oakes, Fiona L 2:49:56 (497)
Oakes, Kathleen M 5:45:20 (31,883)
Oakes, Zoe L 5:01:17 (26,025)
Oakley, Joan 4:24:08 (16,886)
Oakley, Kirstie 5:13:32 (28,089)
Oaten, Lisa J 4:56:14 (24,946)
Oatham, Eleanor E 4:02:48 (11,342)
Obagi, Janine M 4:16:04 (14,730)
Obertell, Joanne E 4:22:13 (16,399)
O'Borne, Kathryn S 4:32:13 (19,141)
O'Boyle, Barbara J 4:49:55 (23,477)
O'Boyle, Olivia 6:41:09 (34,528)
O'Brien, Anne 4:18:35 (15,388)
O'Brien, Catherine J 4:10:22 (13,186)
O'Brien, Christine B 3:49:43 (7,981)
O'Brien, Dymphna M 4:44:45 (22,262)
O'Brien, Jennifer E 3:33:38 (4,979)
O'Brien, Kerry L 5:04:51 (26,658)
O'Brien, Nina 5:10:12 (27,528)
O'Callaghan, Joanne E 6:30:54 (34,270)
O'Carroll, Catherine A 3:30:39 (4,552)
Ochiltree, Elaine E 4:11:19 (13,434)
O'Connor, Elizabeth 4:03:14 (11,440)
O'Connor, Merryn 5:57:19 (32,796)
O'Connor, Miriam 4:21:34 (16,221)
O'Connor, Sinead M 4:31:38 (19,004)
Odell, Emma Kate 4:28:58 (18,297)
Odell, Sarah R 3:58:01 (10,148)
Odimayo, Benedicta 5:59:26 (32,942)
Odling, Barbara A 6:22:29 (34,007)
O'Doherty, Sinead 5:44:37 (31,812)
O'Donnell, Anne M 3:49:17 (7,887)
O'Donnell, Grainne 3:22:47 (3,271)
O'Donnell, Jo R 3:47:17 (7,411)
O'Donnell Spicer, Kay 5:25:02 (29,751)
O'Donoghue, Jenny A 6:34:03 (34,355)
O'Donovan, Bernie S 3:22:53 (3,281)
Odozi, Helen N 5:33:10 (30,685)
O'Dwyer, Rebecca K 3:59:32 (10,582)
O'Dwyer, Valerie J 5:28:46 (30,215)
Ody, Victoria H 5:56:40 (32,747)
Oeen, Gerda M 4:20:11 (15,852)
Offredi, Doreen 6:32:45 (34,324)
Ogden, Isabelle C 4:46:22 (22,639)
Oglesby, Gillian L 5:52:57 (32,493)
Ogorzalek, Maya 4:37:54 (20,596)
O'Grady, Mairead M 4:42:03 (21,634)
O'Grady, Paula 4:53:46 (24,374)
O'Grady, Sally J 4:03:55 (11,608)
Oguntokun, Abi 4:47:40 (22,936)
O'Hagan, Martina 4:36:21 (20,177)
O'Hagan, Rosie 4:36:54 (20,331)
O'Hanlon, Denise S 4:03:48 (11,576)
O'Hanlon, Rosie H 6:30:26 (34,263)
O'Hara, Jenny S 4:50:50 (23,699)
O'Hara, Karen M 4:06:58 (12,333)
O'Hara, Katy M 4:17:27 (15,084)
O'Hara, Maureen 3:44:31 (6,839)
Ohlsson, Carola 5:18:57 (28,937)
Ohlsson, Marita 5:18:57 (28,937)
Okayo, Margaret 2:25:22 (48)
O'Keefe, Collette L 4:18:21 (15,312)
O'Keefe, Patricia A 3:30:40 (4,556)

O'Keeffe, Natalie	5:11:15 (27,698)
Okwu, Antonia S	3:41:48 (6,337)
Old, Alexandra J	4:27:31 (17,894)
Old, Wendy D	7:45:59 (35,195)
Oldershaw, Tina J	3:24:19 (3,493)
Oldfield, Julie C	6:20:51 (33,947)
Oldfield, Kerry L	6:01:39 (33,060)
Oldfield, Leonora R	4:23:04 (16,619)
Oldman, Nicola M	4:02:53 (11,359)
Olds, Justine	4:28:22 (18,129)
Oliphant, Kim A	4:46:33 (22,679)
Oliver, Barbara	4:23:45 (16,791)
Oliver, Cara	3:35:27 (5,249)
Oliver, Joan E	3:46:41 (7,279)
Oliver, Joanne C	4:11:06 (13,381)
Oliver, Joanne P	4:56:38 (25,050)
Oliver, Karen T	5:23:57 (29,614)
Oliver, Sarah	6:01:29 (33,054)
Oliver, Tracy J	5:12:27 (27,901)
Olizeg, Anna-Maria	4:52:39 (24,091)
Ollerenshaw, Cherry M	5:12:14 (27,858)
Olliffe, Stephanie J	3:24:12 (3,472)
O'Loughlin, Christine S	6:01:57 (33,074)
O'Malley, Helen	4:20:00 (15,802)
O'Malley, Sarah M	4:07:13 (12,395)
O'Malley, Susan A	4:48:07 (23,037)
O'Neal, Joanna R	4:37:58 (20,610)
O'Neale, Dawn L	6:50:01 (34,709)
O'Neill, Ann	6:05:14 (33,285)
O'Neill, Catherine E	5:13:10 (28,017)
O'Neill, Catherine M	4:54:18 (24,505)
O'Neill, Cliona M	5:05:20 (26,756)
O'Neill, Deirdre M	3:32:33 (4,826)
O'Neill, Emma	4:38:26 (20,736)
O'Neill, Heike K	5:08:35 (27,296)
O'Neill, Judy E	6:36:22 (34,418)
O'Neill, Leigh H	4:35:43 (20,024)
O'Neill, Loraine J	5:21:43 (29,315)
O'Neill, Lynne M	4:35:44 (20,026)
O'Neill, Margaret C	4:40:55 (21,366)
O'Neill, Monica	5:36:35 (31,066)
O'Neill, Rachel	3:40:16 (6,044)
O'Neill, Rebecca	4:40:41 (21,303)
Ongert, Joanne M	5:55:01 (32,642)
Onley, Gillian L	4:53:54 (24,395)
Onslow, Sue	6:32:59 (34,329)
Openshaw, Jasmin	5:02:09 (26,174)
Oppmann, Simone	4:19:34 (15,684)
Orange, Liz E	5:04:05 (26,527)
Orban, Mary Bridget	4:07:01 (12,350)
Orchard, Nicola	4:58:00 (25,329)
O'Regan, Catherine P	4:10:49 (13,292)
O'Regan, Pippa J	4:38:54 (20,849)
O'Reilly, Claire K	4:18:37 (15,399)
O'Reilly, Melissa C	4:10:10 (13,133)
O'Reilly, Pauline C	4:57:09 (25,164)
O'Reilly, Yvonne G	4:29:26 (18,442)
Orenz, Anabell C	5:05:06 (26,700)
O'Riordan, Deirdre Ann	5:43:07 (31,688)
O'Riordan, Marion T	4:47:37 (22,915)
Orme, Rachel L	4:08:57 (12,813)
O'Rourke, Helen	4:38:31 (20,760)
O'Rourke, Louise M	4:53:37 (24,333)
Orrin, Zoe D	6:07:46 (33,426)
Orth, Barbara	3:23:51 (3,430)
Orton, Christine N	4:40:34 (21,278)
Orton, Paula L	4:31:39 (19,007)
Osborn, Laura	6:03:45 (33,204)
Osborn, Theresa M	6:03:45 (33,204)
Osborne, Carolyn S	4:15:24 (14,551)
Osborne, Claire J	3:55:16 (9,298)
Osborne, Gillian R	5:16:43 (28,582)
Osborne, Jane	6:03:19 (33,170)
Osborne, Jennifer C	4:18:30 (15,361)
Osborne, Katherine A	6:15:10 (33,744)
Osborne, Liz	6:39:18 (34,489)
Osborne, Nicole	5:40:21 (31,452)
Osei-Gyamfi, Vera	5:29:42 (30,331)
Osepian, Florence	6:32:16 (34,311)
O'Shea, Beverley J	5:05:25 (26,781)
O'Shea, Keely	5:05:23 (26,771)
O'Shea, Lindsay	4:56:07 (24,920)
Osman, Christina J	6:09:10 (33,499)

Osman, Christine	6:37:23 (34,440)
Ostler, Gillian H	4:58:08 (25,355)
Ostrow, Jamie B	4:28:18 (18,111)
O'Sullivan, Julie M	4:48:31 (23,125)
O'Sullivan, Lois	4:56:05 (24,912)
O'Sullivan, Maureen N	5:10:16 (27,534)
O'Sullivan, Sonia	2:29:01 (63)
O'Sullivan, Suzanne E	4:34:37 (19,740)
Otley, Deborah	3:54:32 (9,105)
O'Toole, Orna O	4:31:12 (18,884)
Ottaway, Julia Y	5:47:08 (32,030)
Ottewill, Brenda	5:32:15 (30,585)
Ovens, Dawn	6:29:25 (34,237)
Ovens, Jan	3:47:45 (7,514)
Ovens, Ruth C	4:36:07 (20,112)
Overbye, Gunvor	6:34:07 (34,357)
Overton, Terri	4:54:24 (24,525)
Ovry, Linda S	6:23:37 (34,043)
Owen, Alison J	4:46:50 (22,741)
Owen, Amanda T	5:02:36 (26,250)
Owen, Beverley P	5:15:09 (28,360)
Owen, Caroline J	5:58:37 (32,886)
Owen, Josephine	4:29:58 (18,577)
Owen, Kate	6:00:52 (33,019)
Owen, Katherine	4:38:25 (20,732)
Owen, Kira	4:48:19 (23,077)
Owen, Mary	3:32:20 (4,793)
Owen, Nicola S	5:16:32 (28,554)
Owen, Rachel E	5:05:15 (26,738)
Owen, Rachel L	5:50:07 (32,272)
Owen, Wendy P	7:13:29 (35,020)
Owens, Lorraine A	6:13:40 (33,686)
Oxley, Abigail R	5:51:48 (32,396)
Oxley, Samantha	5:27:41 (30,065)
Ozier, Patricia N	4:37:34 (20,515)
Ozkan, Gwen	7:39:08 (35,172)
Paavola, Paivi S	4:07:04 (12,360)
Packard, Janet F	6:19:43 (33,908)
Packham, Amanda J	6:34:50 (34,378)
Packman, Alison N	4:35:13 (19,887)
Packwood, Angela D	4:55:05 (24,697)
Padden, Shirley S	4:50:16 (23,551)
Paddington, Gemma	5:14:55 (28,328)
Padwick, Maria T	5:20:51 (29,220)
Page, Alison K	5:04:08 (26,544)
Page, Clare V	3:25:52 (3,734)
Page, Deborah	6:56:16 (34,816)
Page, Janet	6:36:18 (34,416)
Page, Janice	4:50:36 (23,649)
Page, Maria J	4:29:46 (18,537)
Page, Sarah	6:22:14 (34,000)
Paige, Helen	4:32:00 (19,087)
Pain, Ruth	4:05:42 (12,026)
Paine, Doreen M	4:36:17 (20,156)
Painter, Sarah L	3:48:03 (7,598)
Pakenham-Walsh, Rebecca C	4:09:35 (12,978)
Palfreeman, Julie	4:59:47 (25,736)
Pali, Tina M	4:32:08 (19,122)
Pall, Rema	6:34:40 (34,372)
Pallen, Clare E	4:53:27 (24,290)
Pallett, Joanne	3:34:04 (5,055)
Palmer, Amanda	5:31:04 (30,474)
Palmer, Beverley A	7:53:06 (35,219)
Palmer, Carol L	4:26:06 (17,475)
Palmer, Carolyn M	6:15:34 (33,763)
Palmer, Claire L	5:25:05 (29,757)
Palmer, Deborah	5:56:03 (32,710)
Palmer, Elaine A	4:32:37 (19,231)
Palmer, Ella L	4:16:41 (14,888)
Palmer, Jennie M	6:23:49 (34,052)
Palmer, Julia	3:14:19 (2,394)
Palmer, Lesley	5:45:06 (31,855)
Palmer, Lucy E	4:35:52 (20,058)
Palmer, Michelle L	4:50:01 (23,500)
Palmer, Pamela	4:42:53 (21,847)
Palmer, Virginia	4:28:59 (18,304)
Palser, Rebecca	5:33:07 (30,679)
Pamment, Lesley N	6:27:30 (34,180)
Pamplin, Diane R	3:42:05 (6,399)
Pandit, Shereen	5:18:22 (28,846)
Panella, Consuelo	5:19:26 (29,015)
Panes, Annabel R	4:36:39 (20,270)
Panetta, Thérèse A	3:50:46 (8,200)

Pang, Polly	5:29:28 (30,303)
Pang, Yinsan	5:32:11 (30,574)
Pannett, Claire E	4:53:33 (24,313)
Papaioannou, Joanna	6:15:42 (33,770)
Pape, Yvonne C	4:24:35 (17,010)
Papiez, Louise M	5:15:55 (28,471)
Papworth, Louise A	5:53:18 (32,524)
Pardo, Andrea H	5:38:51 (31,293)
Pardoe, Celia A	3:56:57 (9,798)
Parfitt, Pauline	3:43:07 (6,576)
Parfitt, Sarah	3:50:50 (8,219)
Parine, Anna J	4:16:50 (14,992)
Park, Cat A	4:50:49 (23,697)
Park, Karen	3:58:37 (10,314)
Park, Sharon M	5:38:40 (31,274)
Parke, Joanne M	4:57:58 (25,319)
Parke, Kay P	5:18:57 (28,937)
Parker, Elizabeth H	4:29:22 (18,420)
Parker, Emma J	4:43:33 (21,996)
Parker, Joanne K	4:23:54 (16,827)
Parker, Joanne M	3:38:45 (5,765)
Parker, Julia A	3:36:03 (5,346)
Parker, Kirsten B	5:30:41 (30,434)
Parker, Maureen	4:26:35 (17,629)
Parker, Mel S	4:23:59 (16,844)
Parker, Patricia	3:31:58 (4,742)
Parker, Simone L	4:28:26 (18,146)
Parker, Susy A	3:42:44 (6,504)
Parker-Seale, Debra J	4:53:22 (24,265)
Parkes, Jennifer A	3:53:35 (8,879)
Parkhouse, Juliet C	5:36:54 (31,092)
Parkin, Angela	4:19:08 (15,558)
Parkin, Jacqueline	5:54:43 (32,614)
Parkin, Sarah	6:09:23 (33,508)
Parkinson, Helen A	2:58:00 (957)
Parkinson, Helen A	5:11:42 (27,769)
Parkinson, Nicola H	4:44:26 (22,201)
Parkinson, Sandra E	4:37:16 (20,433)
Parnaby, Amanda C	4:50:21 (23,579)
Parnell, Kerry A	6:38:03 (34,456)
Parnell, Lindsey J	4:29:16 (18,390)
Parr, Susan J	5:15:57 (28,474)
Parr, Wendy	4:57:57 (25,314)
Parratt, Lesley H	7:02:45 (34,901)
Parris, Claire E	4:59:38 (25,697)
Parrott, Gena H	5:44:08 (31,774)
Parrott, Katherine A	5:45:18 (31,879)
Parry, Catehrine	3:52:14 (8,537)
Parry, Emma C	3:08:08 (1,727)
Parry, Isabel	4:53:30 (24,300)
Parry, Jacqui	5:50:45 (32,326)
Parry, Jennifer S	5:39:17 (31,348)
Parry, Louise H	4:21:33 (16,217)
Parry, Victoria L	5:04:18 (26,570)
Parsonage, Jane W	6:11:01 (33,573)
Parsons, Alex C	4:52:11 (23,981)
Parsons, Connie	5:50:10 (32,276)
Parsons, Elaine M	6:26:52 (34,155)
Parsons, Helen S	3:20:43 (3,068)
Parsons, Jemma J	7:00:41 (34,883)
Parsons, Judith	5:39:19 (31,352)
Parsons, Maxine	6:17:54 (33,848)
Parsons, Monique M	5:08:19 (27,262)
Parsons, Natalie E	5:48:45 (32,156)
Parsons, Pauline V	6:08:10 (33,453)
Parsons, Sandra I	4:04:31 (11,749)
Partridge, Harriet M	4:45:39 (22,472)
Partridge, Isobel S	3:03:45 (1,386)
Partridge, Sue	2:37:50 (152)
Pascoe, Angela	5:05:06 (26,700)
Pascoe, Claire A	6:01:57 (33,074)
Pascoe, Lindsey M	5:03:23 (26,417)
Passin, Licia J	4:32:33 (19,219)
Pastore, Kimberley J	4:22:48 (16,558)
Patching, Katrina J	4:27:05 (17,771)
Patel, Anita T	4:18:38 (15,408)
Patel, Bina J	6:37:40 (34,445)
Patel, Chhaya	4:58:53 (25,530)
Patel, Daksha	4:30:38 (18,755)
Patel, Emma N	2:59:45 (1,107)
Patel, Harshna	5:15:37 (28,435)
Patel, Laxmi	5:07:35 (27,156)
Patel, Sonal	4:32:15 (19,149)

Patel, Sonal....6:20:28 (33,936)
Patel, Sweta....4:39:19 (20,967)
Patel, Trupti J....6:21:43 (33,974)
Paterson, Anne-Marie....6:13:55 (33,703)
Paterson, Charlotte....5:13:18 (28,043)
Paterson, Gail M....4:53:33 (24,313)
Paterson, Helen C....4:12:40 (13,794)
Paterson, Karen....4:48:34 (23,135)
Paterson, Sarah....4:43:08 (21,895)
Paterson, Tracy C....4:55:24 (24,758)
Patmore, Ewa....4:13:19 (13,968)
Patmore, Lynne M....4:13:38 (14,053)
Paton, Vicky J....6:34:14 (34,360)
Patrick, Julie....4:16:24 (14,820)
Patrick, Karen J....4:57:31 (25,230)
Patrick, Katharine L....4:06:18 (12,166)
Patrick, Sarah L....4:28:53 (18,270)
Patterson, Anita....5:02:04 (26,160)
Patterson, Christine....4:35:49 (20,047)
Patterson, Jane....4:00:33 (10,852)
Pattinson, Frances E....6:22:46 (34,016)
Patton, Rachel B....4:26:55 (17,724)
Patykova, Hana....6:09:24 (33,510)
Paul, Carol....4:27:39 (17,937)
Pauzers, Clare E....3:11:56 (2,133)
Paver, Amanda....4:35:18 (19,908)
Pavlovic, Biserka....3:59:50 (10,676)
Pavlovic, Elizabeth....4:59:29 (25,659)
Pawson, Helen L....4:09:37 (12,987)
Pay, Claire L....4:22:22 (16,438)
Payne, Amanda L....6:03:19 (33,170)
Payne, Claire....4:35:03 (19,863)
Payne, Daphne....5:01:37 (26,083)
Payne, Gillian M....4:36:01 (20,087)
Payne, Helen A....3:47:28 (7,449)
Payne, Helen L....5:28:07 (30,126)
Payne, Joanna M....5:02:25 (26,223)
Payne, Juliet....5:15:50 (28,459)
Payne, Louisa....5:31:25 (30,510)
Payne, Nicola C....3:57:44 (10,045)
Payne, Rebecca A....4:24:56 (17,104)
Payne, Sara C....3:55:57 (9,501)
Payne, Susan....4:04:53 (11,834)
Payton, Susan C....4:03:50 (11,590)
Peace, Nicola E....5:22:23 (29,400)
Peach, Rachel L....5:14:40 (28,296)
Peacock, Claire....2:58:07 (964)
Peacock, Hannah C....4:17:58 (15,194)
Peacock, Hazel C....4:42:06 (21,653)
Peacock, Michelle....3:42:52 (6,521)
Peacock, Rachel....4:02:27 (11,261)
Peakman, Pip M....3:59:03 (10,451)
Peapell, Elizabeth F....5:30:40 (30,431)
Pearce, Clare L....5:36:35 (31,066)
Pearce, Janie....3:26:16 (3,803)
Pearce, Shannon M....3:46:59 (7,346)
Pearson, Anne....6:43:09 (34,573)
Pearson, Carol S....7:09:29 (34,970)
Pearson, Celine A....5:20:35 (29,194)
Pearson, Debra....4:40:46 (21,327)
Pearson, Jehanne....6:06:15 (33,345)
Pearson, Margaret A....5:56:44 (32,752)
Pearson, Melanie L....6:06:12 (33,340)
Pearson, Rebecca M....5:05:24 (26,778)
Pearson, Ruth E....5:51:29 (32,372)
Peasgood, Teresa J....3:44:47 (6,901)
Pech, Sylvie....4:21:05 (16,089)
Peck, Jaclyn E....5:06:45 (27,008)
Peck, Rita....3:58:25 (10,266)
Peck, Sarah J....4:33:44 (19,499)
Pedashenko, Tanya....4:53:11 (24,217)
Peden, Caroline....4:19:27 (15,649)
Pedersen-Wallin, Eva K....5:50:36 (32,310)
Pedro, Nusi J....4:28:25 (18,144)
Peek, Katy L....4:36:51 (20,319)
Peeters, Rita....4:26:57 (17,737)
Peever, Patricia S....4:58:44 (25,493)
Pegna, Alice....4:36:37 (20,258)
Peilow, Anne C....4:35:35 (19,992)
Pell, Susan F....4:57:32 (25,234)
Pell, Valerie M....4:25:54 (17,401)
Pellett, Carrie A....4:20:04 (15,817)
Pelta, Michelle D....5:04:08 (26,544)
Pelzer, Melanie....4:26:23 (17,561)
Pena, Ana M....4:39:31 (21,019)
Pender, Claire S....4:04:57 (11,849)
Pendlebury, Joanne....6:21:33 (33,966)
Pendleton, Debbie C....5:34:12 (30,805)
Pengelly, Carmela T....4:07:42 (12,495)
Penjon, Patrice....3:50:07 (8,064)
Penn, Emma....5:04:36 (26,612)
Pennell, Christine....3:37:14 (5,528)
Pennell, Victoria....5:18:09 (28,808)
Penneycard, Laura....5:19:19 (28,993)
Pennington, Sue....3:59:21 (10,533)
Penny, Gail E....6:33:13 (34,336)
Penrose, Anna M....4:43:30 (21,980)
Penrose, Janet M....4:31:40 (19,011)
Pentland, Debbie....4:57:30 (25,228)
Pentney, Fiona E....4:45:47 (22,491)
Pentol-Levy, Jacqueline J....6:03:54 (33,217)
Penton, Emma....6:06:30 (33,357)
Peppard, Jane....5:51:01 (32,338)
Pepper, Debbie A....3:47:42 (7,506)
Percy, Alexandra....4:35:40 (20,010)
Percy, Sharon L....3:21:31 (3,132)
Perdesi, Snita....4:51:07 (23,754)
Perdrisat, Odette....5:39:46 (31,393)
Perera, Helen A....4:06:31 (12,218)
Perera, Sukie R....7:11:02 (34,988)
Peres, Lara....4:25:01 (17,130)
Perez, Nadine A....4:57:23 (25,203)
Perkin, Helen M....4:33:51 (19,533)
Perkins, Kerry A....6:46:18 (34,632)
Perkins, Lucinda M....4:17:34 (15,106)
Perkins, Sheryl....4:35:21 (19,931)
Perron, Jenny C....5:33:22 (30,702)
Perry, Caroline L....5:04:48 (26,651)
Perry, Catherine A....3:49:57 (8,026)
Perry, Charlotte E....5:29:04 (30,253)
Perry, Christine M....4:30:31 (18,734)
Perry, Jayne....3:56:35 (9,687)
Perry, Karen L....6:13:54 (33,701)
Perry, Mandy J....4:01:44 (11,097)
Perry, Yvonne M....4:59:24 (25,641)
Persen, Madelein....4:50:07 (23,518)
Perz, Christine....4:24:11 (16,898)
Pessoa-Lopes, Isabel....5:48:03 (32,097)
Petchey, Louise E....5:41:39 (31,568)
Peters, Caroline T....5:41:59 (31,596)
Peters, Deirdre A....5:36:29 (31,053)
Peters, Michele T....5:38:49 (31,290)
Peters, Nicola J....4:19:35 (15,686)
Peters, Paula....4:09:37 (12,987)
Peters, Sarah P....4:14:51 (14,396)
Petri, Claudia....3:12:05 (2,152)
Petrie, Jenny....6:16:51 (33,816)
Petrova, Lyudmila....2:26:29 (53)
Pett, Alexandra M....5:45:35 (31,900)
Pett, Christine....6:53:50 (34,782)
Pettican, Kate....3:52:35 (8,625)
Pettinger, Arlene L....5:39:56 (31,407)
Pettit, Helena T....4:27:53 (18,007)
Petts, Jill....5:34:26 (30,840)
Petts, Sarah....5:17:06 (28,664)
Petzer, Alison C....3:53:17 (8,792)
Peverell, Tracey....4:40:27 (21,243)
Pfister, Arlette....4:04:21 (11,712)
Phaka, Kate M....3:58:24 (10,261)
Phelan, Dee C....4:37:11 (20,408)
Phelps, Melanie R....6:24:26 (34,074)
Philip, Katy J....4:03:20 (11,469)
Phillips, Alison J....4:00:28 (10,822)
Phillips, Beth E....5:36:26 (31,043)
Phillips, Catherine A....6:01:20 (33,041)
Phillips, Cheryl T....5:48:15 (32,117)
Phillips, Clare E....5:00:58 (25,970)
Phillips, Cynthia M....4:31:27 (18,957)
Phillips, Frances C....5:27:39 (30,061)
Phillips, Helen E....4:49:51 (23,461)
Phillips, Helen M....4:40:42 (21,310)
Phillips, Jacqui A....3:41:35 (6,294)
Phillips, Jacqui L....4:45:31 (22,434)
Phillips, Joanne C....5:09:56 (27,501)
Phillips, Joanne L....5:18:58 (28,940)
Phillips, Linda M....3:26:37 (3,872)
Phillips, Lisa....5:00:15 (25,831)
Phillips, Lisa A....5:28:54 (30,235)
Phillips, Michelle....4:50:00 (23,495)
Phillips, Morag....5:39:19 (31,352)
Phillips, Sarah L....7:33:02 (35,150)
Phillips, Sharon....4:20:33 (15,948)
Phillips, Tracy J....5:33:04 (30,675)
Philp, Nicola J....4:25:38 (17,330)
Philpot, Kelly....6:23:21 (34,033)
Phipps, Deborah J....4:06:08 (12,130)
Phipps, Elaine M....3:02:11 (1,277)
Phythian, Julie A....4:31:00 (18,837)
Piatkus, Leah D....5:00:24 (25,863)
Pickard, Deborah E....4:17:59 (15,201)
Pickard, Francesca A....4:57:36 (25,249)
Pickard, Kelly A....5:41:32 (31,556)
Pickering, Danielle....4:55:30 (24,771)
Pickering, Jane....3:50:24 (8,122)
Pickett, Helen....3:59:51 (10,682)
Pickles, Grace....5:18:25 (28,852)
Pickup, Andrea L....3:12:55 (2,240)
Pickup, Karen T....5:04:40 (26,623)
Picton, Pauline....4:37:48 (20,580)
Piddock, Helen C....6:05:39 (33,304)
Pidgeley, Michelle....4:42:53 (21,847)

Piechoczek, Dawn V....4:10:57 (13,333)

I was delighted and amazed to finish my first (and only) London Marathon, especially since I had been injured since February and unable to complete my training. A combination of painkillers, will-power and the support of friends, family and others along the route got me through. I was lucky enough to run about half of it with fellow runner Colin, and cross the finish line with Swee Lian. My motivation was the memory of my stepfather, George, who lost his battle with myeloma the previous year, and I had some generous sponsorship money at stake. I recall feeling pain, exhaustion, elation and relief at the end; a bit like giving birth but with a few more spectators!

Piehl, Hans-Dieter....4:01:34 (11,062)
Piercy, Angela C....4:27:02 (17,755)
Pike, Alison J....4:07:36 (12,479)
Pike, Jennifer J....4:34:46 (19,781)
Pike, Linda P....5:28:44 (30,211)
Pike, Lisa J....5:38:47 (31,288)
Pike, Zoe M....2:58:42 (1,005)
Pilc, Alexandra C....4:07:22 (12,430)
Pilch, Alexa....4:46:16 (22,615)

Quarini, Michelle 5:09:58 (27,508)
Quayle, Jenny C 6:06:08 (33,338)
Quellennel, Christel 4:28:15 (18,101)
Quibell, Lucinda 4:19:57 (15,788)
Quickenden, Michelle 5:06:01 (26,876)
Quigg, Deirdre 4:05:10 (11,916)
Quinn, Brigid 4:26:48 (17,690)
Quinn, Cora L 5:04:07 (26,541)
Quinn, Jamie 4:10:09 (13,127)
Quinn, Jamie E 3:50:26 (8,133)
Quinn, Joanne 4:28:05 (18,049)
Quinn, Marcia A 5:18:06 (28,798)
Quinnell, Lian M 4:19:27 (15,649)
Quinou, Christelle 5:02:04 (26,160)
Quirk, Trudi J 5:40:23 (31,458)
Quittner, Joanne 4:34:06 (19,591)
Raaijmakers, Monique M 3:29:45 (4,408)
Raby, Beth A 5:21:40 (29,307)

Radcliffe, Paula 2:17:42 (19)

Radford, Joy 3:28:05 (4,120)
Radford, Susan A 3:50:46 (8,200)
Rae, Jane E 4:28:41 (18,212)
Rafice, Bibi S 6:52:00 (34,757)
Rafii, Ella 4:26:02 (17,447)
Ragan, Karen 4:51:25 (23,816)
Rahman, Sarah 4:20:06 (15,832)
Raidy, Davina J 3:45:03 (6,963)
Raimondo, Amanda S 3:40:54 (6,166)
Raincock, Loraine E 4:44:58 (22,316)
Raine, Kate H 4:52:37 (24,080)
Raines, Margaret P 4:55:53 (24,871)
Rainford-Miller, Susan J 4:55:02 (24,683)
Rainger, Lesley 3:22:14 (3,219)
Raistrick, Carole 4:45:19 (22,397)
Rajasingham, Shirani 4:31:08 (18,862)
Rakusen, Deborah 6:07:06 (33,394)
Ralph, Barbara 3:20:29 (3,044)
Ralph, Helen F 4:19:28 (15,654)
Ralph, Julia M 5:30:09 (30,378)
Ralph, Karen 4:22:11 (16,392)
Ralston, Rhona 4:57:24 (25,208)
Ramisch, Monika 5:23:45 (29,576)
Ramos, Christina 4:41:26 (21,506)
Ramsay, Cayetana E 4:39:58 (21,129)
Ramsay, Fiona 6:00:53 (33,023)
Ramsay, Paula J 4:32:12 (19,134)
Ramsay, Rachel E 4:28:47 (18,241)
Ramsbotham, Leasa G 4:44:04 (22,108)
Ramsdale, Sue 4:04:00 (11,633)
Ramsden, Conor M 4:49:07 (23,269)
Ramsden, Jane 4:20:16 (15,879)
Ramsey, Helen J 5:17:47 (28,757)
Ramsey, Paula 3:48:25 (7,686)
Ramshaw, Sara L 4:33:18 (19,385)
Rance, Bryony L 3:50:09 (8,073)
Randal, Nicole E 4:33:21 (19,396)
Randall, Lee-Ann 5:04:17 (26,568)
Randall Johnson, Polly R 3:38:30 (5,724)
Randle, Vicky J 4:38:37 (20,781)
Ranft-Gerber, Wendy 4:55:01 (24,679)
Rankin, Alexandra C 4:11:39 (13,523)
Rankin, Kate 6:02:54 (33,136)
Ranoe-Hall, Dora C 4:53:05 (24,196)
Ransom, Lucy J 6:48:42 (34,687)
Ransome, Jane A 5:58:28 (32,875)
Ranson, Andrea S 4:26:03 (17,455)
Ranson, Pauline F 4:26:52 (17,706)
Raste, Yogini 4:00:28 (10,822)
Ratcliff, Nikki S 4:30:01 (18,591)
Ratcliffe, Jacqui L 4:48:29 (23,121)
Ratcliffe, Shelley 6:24:21 (34,072)
Ratcliffe, Victoria L 4:55:59 (24,898)
Ratsey, Nicola C 4:18:34 (15,382)
Rau, Angela 4:46:40 (22,701)
Rautiainen, Riina 4:39:25 (20,995)
Raveh, Terry 4:01:47 (11,109)
Raven, Vanessa J 5:54:52 (32,629)
Raw, Melody J 5:27:20 (30,017)
Rawles, Melanie D 5:21:49 (29,329)
Rawlings, Rebecca A 4:34:25 (19,695)
Rawlinson, Julia D 5:21:16 (29,271)
Rawlinson, Liz 4:47:25 (22,861)
Ray, Alison M 4:45:15 (22,381)
Ray, Mary 5:03:22 (26,414)
Ray, Rowena 4:12:54 (13,857)
Ray, Susannah H 4:25:33 (17,302)
Rayman, Alison G 6:11:29 (33,593)
Raynel, Natasha E 3:31:50 (4,724)
Rayner, Janice 6:01:46 (33,070)
Rayner, Julie A 4:09:15 (12,899)
Rayner, Marion R 3:11:55 (2,130)
Re, Stephanie 4:39:52 (21,101)
Rea, Pamela K 5:49:36 (32,234)
Read, Alison S 6:41:48 (34,542)
Read, Anna 3:30:51 (4,585)
Read, Clare L 3:09:44 (1,887)
Read, Genevieve C 6:41:49 (34,544)
Read, Jacqueline A 4:25:31 (17,290)
Read, June H 5:53:11 (32,514)
Read, Kathrine 4:39:18 (20,965)
Read, Teresa 4:47:06 (22,796)
Reader, Kim A 4:36:49 (20,311)
Reading, Celia J 5:11:29 (27,735)
Readman, Tamzin C 4:17:26 (15,081)
Ready, Deborah J 3:37:37 (5,590)
Reaper, Beckie 5:13:57 (28,161)
Reason, Glena R 3:55:52 (9,480)
Reay, Vivienne H 4:43:53 (22,067)
Reay Jones, Caroline 4:40:05 (21,153)
Rebbeck, Zoe 4:43:02 (21,878)
Recardo, Jacqueline R 6:00:47 (33,014)
Record, Jenny R 5:17:28 (28,709)
Record, Wendy H 4:31:29 (18,965)
Redden, Emma 5:22:33 (29,431)
Redden, Janet A 5:22:32 (29,427)
Redding, Rebecca J 4:23:27 (16,723)
Redford, Nicola A 5:43:03 (31,681)
Redhead, Abigail J 4:28:34 (18,187)
Redman, Lorna 5:06:20 (26,926)
Redman, Marie-Thérèse 4:46:21 (22,635)
Redman, Ruth 4:36:25 (20,203)
Redmond, Hazel 6:29:10 (34,226)
Redpath, Janet M 4:17:41 (15,134)
Reed, Catherine A 3:41:34 (6,290)
Reed, Claire 4:55:22 (24,751)
Reed, Katharine R 5:36:02 (30,998)
Reed, Moira J 4:56:41 (25,064)
Reed, Pamela 3:25:02 (3,589)
Reed, Sarah R 3:54:26 (9,086)
Rees, Bridget A 5:41:15 (31,532)
Rees, Catherine M 7:06:44 (34,947)
Rees, Delyth A 4:39:12 (20,932)
Rees, Elizabeth J 4:10:02 (13,098)
Rees, Jennifer 5:14:08 (28,198)
Rees, Kate 3:58:56 (10,414)
Rees, Penelope A 4:07:01 (12,350)
Rees, Samantha J 4:11:37 (13,508)
Reeve, Kate 6:46:47 (34,652)
Reeve, Lucy V 4:40:24 (21,231)
Reeve, Nicola C 4:56:22 (24,981)
Reeve, Sallyann 4:57:19 (25,196)
Reeve, Sarah F 4:17:38 (15,118)
Reeves, Dawn E 5:20:25 (29,165)
Reeves, Sara 5:34:19 (30,821)
Regan, Janet 5:05:17 (26,746)
Regan, Lara J 3:47:28 (7,449)
Reid, Amanda J 3:38:54 (5,793)
Reid, Carol A 3:31:04 (4,614)
Reid, Carole 5:27:12 (29,999)
Reid, Caroline E 5:07:37 (27,164)
Reid, Catriona M 4:43:55 (22,077)
Reid, Christine M 3:33:01 (4,890)
Reid, Claire L 4:18:17 (15,290)
Reid, Fiona 4:08:18 (12,636)
Reid, Jacqueline E 4:32:52 (19,279)
Reid, Morven A 3:12:36 (2,203)
Reid, Nickola 6:24:32 (34,076)
Reid, Pamela 5:03:57 (26,509)
Reid, Patricia 6:57:27 (34,837)
Reid, Rosemary M 4:49:15 (23,293)
Reid, Samantha 4:10:19 (13,176)
Reid, Sarah A 3:32:26 (4,808)
Reid, Sharon V 5:39:19 (31,352)
Reid, Tina 4:28:08 (18,067)
Reilly, Amanda J 4:59:34 (25,675)
Reilly, Cynthia A 5:28:51 (30,223)
Reinaldsdottir, Hafdis 3:49:30 (7,933)
Reinhardt, Margot 5:09:45 (27,477)
Reisman, Molly L 6:20:05 (33,920)
Remington, Joanne 3:32:20 (4,793)
Remond, Mauricette 4:18:40 (15,420)
Renard, Melanie 5:28:11 (30,139)
Renmant, Beverley 3:30:34 (4,541)
Rennie, Emma L 5:23:51 (29,593)
Rennie, Nina M 4:41:10 (21,439)
Rennings, Britta 3:54:49 (9,187)
Rennison, Charlotte J 5:25:56 (29,859)
Rennoldson, Sarah J 4:48:44 (23,175)
Renolds, Ksynia 5:52:45 (32,477)
Renoux, Chantal 4:08:17 (12,632)
Renson, Jill 4:30:19 (18,683)
Renwick, Dawne 3:30:03 (4,460)
Repton, Kirsty R 4:41:05 (21,412)
Rest, Elinor R 3:27:50 (4,082)
Retief, Chris-Marie 5:17:59 (28,779)
Revill, Helen P 4:39:56 (21,122)
Revill, Susan 4:14:20 (14,251)
Revolvo, Josefi 3:43:13 (6,593)
Rew, Katie A 5:14:01 (28,175)
Reynard, Stephanie M 4:54:56 (24,648)
Reynolds, Abigail M 4:27:23 (17,853)
Reynolds, Andrea 4:52:12 (23,985)
Reynolds, Barbara 6:42:44 (34,562)
Reynolds, Jacqui S 5:14:31 (28,263)
Reynolds, Joanne 4:24:57 (17,107)
Reynolds, Julie M 3:54:37 (9,126)
Reynolds, Kate L 4:48:39 (23,160)
Reynolds, Kelly P 4:48:56 (23,219)
Reynolds, Lee 3:54:16 (9,038)
Reynolds, Louise 4:29:53 (18,561)
Reynolds, Louise M 4:41:59 (21,623)
Rhoades-Smith, Lisa 4:54:57 (24,658)
Rhodes, Deborah A 3:28:02 (4,109)
Rhodes, Dusty 4:15:16 (14,520)
Rhodes, Frances J 4:49:10 (23,277)
Rhodes, Louise A 5:09:53 (27,493)
Rhodes, Nicola 5:24:01 (29,621)
Rhodes, Sarah L 5:01:28 (26,058)
Rhymes, Natasha A 3:33:39 (4,983)
Riccio, Virginia 4:38:04 (20,638)
Rice, Carly M 6:21:46 (33,978)
Rice, Lesley J 4:20:50 (16,030)
Rice, Lisa J 5:17:46 (28,754)

Rice, Lynsey J....5:54:40 (32,610)
Richard, Lil G....4:51:08 (23,759)
Richards, Alison J....5:22:15 (29,381)
Richards, Angela....5:41:36 (31,565)
Richards, Emma V....3:31:42 (4,706)
Richards, Faye L....4:50:18 (23,564)
Richards, Fenella C....4:31:24 (18,945)
Richards, Francesca E....4:37:03 (20,370)
Richards, Julia A....6:10:02 (33,535)
Richards, Kathryn L....3:47:41 (7,496)
Richards, Lucy G....3:52:27 (8,593)
Richards, Rachael R....5:13:54 (28,150)
Richards, Rachel....6:09:34 (33,519)
Richards, Ragnhild E....4:24:59 (17,117)
Richards, Ruth G....3:56:09 (9,552)
Richards, Wendy A....5:39:26 (31,368)
Richardson, Alice....3:54:39 (9,139)
Richardson, Amanda C....3:29:59 (4,451)
Richardson, Clare P....4:37:42 (20,554)
Richardson, Dawn P....3:03:33 (1,369)
Richardson, Julie A....4:15:54 (14,683)
Richardson, Myrl D....5:11:17 (27,701)
Richardson, Sally J....4:51:40 (23,863)
Richardson, Sarah J....4:47:27 (22,875)
Richardson, Sue L....4:52:25 (24,034)
Richardson, Susan C....6:05:19 (33,289)
Richardson, Susan P....4:42:49 (21,823)
Richert, Nathalie....4:03:17 (11,455)
Riches, Annalie....4:32:11 (19,131)
Riches, Omei....3:57:08 (9,870)
Richings, Deborah C....6:15:07 (33,739)
Richmond, Joanne L....4:46:09 (22,593)
Richmond, Katherine A....3:50:35 (8,166)
Richmond, Lillian M....4:29:52 (18,555)
Richmond, Raewyn G....5:09:56 (27,501)
Richmond, Sheryl A....3:34:56 (5,172)
Rickard, Donna....4:25:59 (17,429)
Rickard, Lisa D....5:55:30 (32,680)
Rickerby, Christina....5:06:05 (26,887)
Rickett, Jacqueline....5:35:47 (30,974)
Rickett, Jane K....3:56:22 (9,623)
Rickhuss, Joanne....5:53:38 (32,540)
Rickwood, Susan....8:52:31 (35,249)
Ridehalgh, Sarah E....3:37:28 (5,575)
Rideout, Natalie J....5:49:00 (32,182)
Ridgill, Emma F....4:25:38 (17,330)
Ridgley, Julie R....3:27:30 (4,020)
Ridgway, Frances....3:48:44 (7,770)
Ridgway, Joanna E....4:54:56 (24,648)
Riding, Jayne H....4:44:04 (22,108)
Riding, Liona....5:15:37 (28,435)
Riedmueller, Ute G....4:39:00 (20,879)
Rievel, Barbel....4:03:45 (11,559)
Rigby, Louise....4:17:10 (15,004)
Rigby-Hall, Siobhan....5:30:51 (30,445)
Rigg, Janine B....4:57:35 (25,247)
Rigg, Louise W....3:06:13 (1,569)
Riggs, Carole A....4:37:08 (20,399)
Rijsenbrij-Bredewoud, Hendrikje..4:17:25 (15,078)
Rikkerink, Zoe....4:15:46 (14,651)
Riley, Betty J....4:33:37 (19,468)
Riley, Caroline T....4:19:55 (15,779)
Riley-Jordan, Christine....4:15:43 (14,642)
Rimington, Jacqueline L....4:37:40 (20,539)
Rimmer, Dawn I....5:04:09 (26,546)
Ringham, Liz J....3:29:44 (4,401)
Ringheim, Marta....4:06:48 (12,286)
Ringwood, Ofelia....5:43:17 (31,701)
Risby, Kay E....4:04:07 (11,665)
Risely, Rachel....4:53:23 (24,270)
Risely, Rebecca R....4:53:23 (24,270)
Risely, Sarah....4:53:23 (24,270)
Ritchie, Deborah K....4:30:11 (18,652)
Ritchie, Kate E....5:45:20 (31,883)
Ritchie, Nicola D....3:34:33 (5,128)
Ritter, Joanne....6:02:32 (33,107)
Rivera, Veronica....3:45:30 (7,049)
Rivero, Michele....5:30:54 (30,454)
Rix, Miranda M....5:03:17 (26,400)
Roach, Denise V....4:53:05 (24,196)
Roach, Harriet L....4:57:39 (25,256)
Robb, Emily....4:42:57 (21,860)
Robbins, Jen C....4:12:07 (13,642)
Robbins, Joanna L....4:21:22 (16,164)
Robbins, Sarah R....4:42:33 (21,751)
Robert, Vanessa L....4:12:02 (13,630)
Roberts, Alexandra C....4:27:41 (17,947)
Roberts, Anne....5:49:03 (32,188)
Roberts, Annette....4:00:25 (10,808)
Roberts, Carole M....3:54:17 (9,043)
Roberts, Christine....5:48:09 (32,108)
Roberts, Claire P....5:45:48 (31,921)
Roberts, Clare L....5:26:01 (29,869)
Roberts, Collette....5:07:33 (27,152)
Roberts, Deborah A....4:56:13 (24,944)
Roberts, Elizabeth M....5:08:13 (27,248)
Roberts, Emma G....3:59:26 (10,552)
Roberts, Helen....4:22:58 (16,592)
Roberts, Helen C....4:37:47 (20,575)
Roberts, Jane A....4:29:00 (18,306)
Roberts, Jessica M....4:31:55 (19,064)
Roberts, Joan....6:21:16 (33,957)
Roberts, Karen R....5:58:27 (32,871)
Roberts, Kathryn....3:29:29 (4,351)
Roberts, Natalie E....3:45:45 (7,086)
Roberts, Penny M....4:28:41 (18,212)
Roberts, Ruth E....4:22:01 (16,343)
Roberts, Sharon M....4:49:24 (23,334)
Roberts, Sophie....4:13:52 (14,105)
Roberts, Trudy J....6:24:50 (34,089)
Roberts, Wanda K....3:57:10 (9,880)
Robertshaw, Diane....4:34:19 (19,668)
Roberts-Jones, Norah....7:05:28 (34,929)
Robertson, Bridget....4:06:05 (12,117)
Robertson, Dilys M....3:30:46 (4,576)
Robertson, Eileen T....4:30:35 (18,745)
Robertson, Elaine E....6:45:07 (34,619)
Robertson, Jennifer D....3:01:26 (1,211)
Robertson, Joanna C....5:37:31 (31,146)
Robertson, Katia....4:35:22 (19,940)
Robertson, Laura J....4:33:49 (19,523)
Robertson, Louise A....3:24:42 (3,540)
Robertson, Nicola....5:34:40 (30,870)
Robertson, Nicola C....3:52:17 (8,551)
Robertson, Sarah L....4:07:38 (12,486)
Robilliard, Mhairi T....5:46:23 (31,971)
Robinson, Alice E....5:24:45 (29,715)
Robinson, Ann Marie....6:16:01 (33,779)
Robinson, Anne R....5:46:52 (32,004)
Robinson, Cordelia A....3:45:07 (6,974)
Robinson, Daniele S....5:09:26 (27,427)
Robinson, Deborah J....5:59:38 (32,954)
Robinson, Deborah M....3:36:24 (5,405)
Robinson, Emily H....4:14:25 (14,280)
Robinson, Emma L....4:32:35 (19,225)
Robinson, Helen E....4:54:43 (24,598)
Robinson, Helen K....4:58:42 (25,483)
Robinson, Hilary C....4:59:39 (25,701)
Robinson, Jane....4:49:43 (23,429)
Robinson, Jane....7:00:12 (34,870)
Robinson, Jane P....4:02:31 (11,276)
Robinson, Joanna C....2:56:32 (845)
Robinson, Joanne....5:19:06 (28,954)
Robinson, Joanne M....6:05:48 (33,313)
Robinson, Joy....4:28:11 (18,084)
Robinson, Julie A....4:13:17 (13,964)
Robinson, Karen A....3:39:50 (5,971)
Robinson, Laura....4:24:09 (16,890)
Robinson, Louise E....4:49:33 (23,371)
Robinson, Lucy A....4:53:16 (24,239)
Robinson, Mary C....6:36:01 (34,411)
Robinson, Melanie J....4:33:19 (19,390)
Robinson, Melanie L....4:35:21 (19,931)
Robinson, Michele....4:06:07 (12,126)
Robinson, Nicola J....5:02:54 (26,320)
Robinson, Paula R....3:56:26 (9,645)
Robinson, Pauline L....4:53:35 (24,323)
Robinson, Sabine C....4:08:25 (12,675)
Robinson, Sara J....4:10:21 (13,182)
Robinson, Sarah A....4:09:39 (12,999)
Robinson, Sharron....4:54:05 (24,447)
Robinson, Wendy J....3:41:53 (6,351)
Robson, Amy F....4:35:03 (19,863)
Robson, Becky E....4:25:56 (17,409)
Robson, Clare L....7:00:46 (34,884)
Robson, Dany L....3:27:58 (4,098)
Robson, Deborah A....4:41:59 (21,623)
Robson, Jane....3:39:53 (5,979)
Robson, Laura J....4:34:45 (19,777)
Robson, Louise E....4:13:15 (13,952)
Robson, Lucy B....3:58:15 (10,206)
Robson, Suzi H....4:14:29 (14,290)
Roche, Julie L....4:10:40 (13,257)
Roche, Lucy G....3:42:15 (6,425)
Rockett, Gillian....5:19:13 (28,976)
Rockett, Lisa M....5:19:13 (28,976)
Rockliffe, Jacqueline M....3:31:59 (4,744)
Rodger, Amy H....4:27:43 (17,955)
Rodger, Diane....5:16:55 (28,629)
Rodger, Louise....5:48:55 (32,175)
Rodgers, Carolann....4:08:46 (12,758)
Rodgers, Caroline....4:58:30 (25,443)
Rodgers, Jennifer A....5:19:22 (29,002)
Rodgers, Mandy J....5:11:51 (27,795)
Rodricks, Sally....5:37:48 (31,168)
Roebuck, Denise....4:57:05 (25,151)
Rogan, Kerry J....5:33:56 (30,772)
Rogers, Claire V....4:14:44 (14,358)
Rogers, Diane E....3:57:54 (10,110)
Rogers, Jennifer....5:12:48 (27,969)
Rogers, Kerry A....5:47:14 (32,037)
Rogers, Rachel A....5:29:50 (30,341)
Rogers, Sarah J....4:09:26 (12,939)
Roine, Karen....3:58:39 (10,323)
Rojahn, Victoria....5:16:36 (28,564)
Rolfe, Marion F....6:15:44 (33,771)
Rolfe, Samantha....5:45:18 (31,879)
Rollason, Rachel A....4:26:30 (17,600)
Rollings, Ann B....3:58:43 (10,354)
Rollings, Fiona....4:57:49 (25,282)
Rollo, Theresa M....6:27:36 (34,182)
Roloff, Astrid....3:47:52 (7,541)
Rolph, Helen L....4:23:34 (16,746)
Romaine, Kimberly....3:40:00 (5,996)
Romans, Chloe E....3:43:16 (6,610)
Romecin, Lindsay H....3:48:38 (7,749)
Rooke, Samantha J....5:35:29 (30,953)
Rookes, Julie....5:19:46 (29,073)
Rookyard, Zoe A....5:25:50 (29,845)
Rooney, Ann F....4:21:42 (16,258)
Rooney, Kelly M....5:27:04 (29,982)
Roper, Amaryllis K....3:51:03 (8,265)
Roper, Louise J....4:25:12 (17,188)
Rosales, Ruth A....5:56:39 (32,745)
Roscoe, Susan L....5:31:11 (30,487)
Rose, Amy V....6:14:18 (33,709)
Rose, Carol A....4:58:35 (25,463)
Rose, Cath....7:09:59 (34,977)
Rose, Joanne....4:24:18 (16,924)
Rose, Julie....4:46:29 (22,666)
Rose, Karen....4:32:51 (19,276)
Rose, Katherine J....6:04:26 (33,240)
Rose, Lisa V....4:48:35 (23,143)
Rose, Melinda C....6:29:31 (34,240)
Rose, Rebecca R....4:56:15 (24,950)
Rose, Samantha L....7:10:59 (34,986)
Rose, Sharon E....5:28:35 (30,194)
Rose, Teresa....4:40:44 (21,315)
Rose, Vanessa D....5:56:16 (32,723)
Rose, Yasmine....3:51:42 (8,412)
Rosemann, Gabriele....5:22:31 (29,423)
Rosenbaum, Michele E....3:28:27 (4,188)
Rosenberg, Olivia....5:47:14 (32,037)
Rose-Quirie, Alison J....3:41:27 (6,268)
Ross, Billee....4:54:13 (24,479)
Ross, Catherine M....5:50:02 (32,267)
Ross, Clare A....6:05:06 (33,272)
Ross, Fiona F....4:36:31 (20,231)
Ross, Ian S....3:56:53 (9,781)
Ross, Jennifer A....5:54:56 (32,636)
Ross, Jillian....4:02:58 (11,383)
Ross, Mary E....5:09:09 (27,380)
Ross, Susan F....4:39:53 (21,106)
Ross Russell, Fiona M....3:15:17 (2,502)
Rossberg, Hildegard....5:07:34 (27,154)
Rossi, Laura A....4:43:20 (21,943)
Rossini, Alena....4:28:02 (18,036)
Rossiter, Carolyn A....5:02:18 (26,202)
Ross-Strong, Fiona C....4:46:41 (22,704)

Rostant, Johanna 7:10:38 (34,984)
Roughley, Megan E 5:52:41 (32,475)
Roughton, Louise J 5:16:19 (28,523)
Round, Helen J 4:19:39 (15,709)
Rouse, Hayley A 5:05:55 (26,855)
Rouse, Janice J 4:54:33 (24,566)
Rouse, Judy H 3:30:39 (4,552)
Routledge, Deborah J 4:55:48 (24,841)
Rowan Robinson, Katie 4:51:20 (23,804)
Rowe, Carole A 4:04:21 (11,712)
Rowe, Cynthia E 5:39:13 (31,336)
Rowe, Elizabeth A 4:37:02 (20,364)
Rowe, Jenifer J 6:23:01 (34,022)
Rowe, Jessica 5:24:08 (29,635)
Rowell, Wendy E 4:43:14 (21,919)
Rowelle, Joanna 5:37:38 (31,154)
Rowett, Ann 4:27:22 (17,845)
Rowland, Carly 6:24:01 (34,066)
Rowland, Georgia-Lee 4:54:51 (24,630)
Rowland, Louise S 6:13:51 (33,697)
Rowland, Patricia J 5:34:55 (30,896)
Rowlands, Angela 4:22:31 (16,476)
Rowley, Amanda J 6:25:23 (34,105)
Rowling, Karen L 5:11:47 (27,784)
Rowlinson, Helen 4:54:32 (24,559)
Rowlinson, Kathryn S 4:56:35 (25,035)
Rown, Wendy J 4:50:53 (23,708)
Rowson, Meriel C 3:59:08 (10,479)
Rowswell, Kathryn M 4:41:35 (21,544)
Royer, Simone 4:50:43 (23,678)
Rubidge, Tina M 4:41:27 (21,511)
Rucinski, Reni 6:00:55 (33,026)
Rudaz, Katie D 3:29:53 (4,435)
Rudd, Belinda J 4:22:54 (16,579)
Ruddy, Elaine C 4:59:42 (25,711)
Rudland, Deborah 6:33:53 (34,350)
Rudzki, Maria 5:30:08 (30,375)
Ruff, Susan E 4:44:28 (22,206)
Ruffle, Diane J 4:31:26 (18,951)
Ruhl, Georgina A 4:33:49 (19,523)
Rundle, Joanna 5:25:46 (29,837)
Rundle, Suzanne 4:25:06 (17,152)
Runnacles, Julia R 4:53:02 (24,183)
Rusca, Mirna G 5:18:35 (28,888)
Ruscoe, Janet E 4:38:40 (20,792)
Rushbrook, Louise E 5:15:44 (28,447)
Rushby, Sonia M 3:51:07 (8,288)
Rushton, Amanda C 4:43:04 (21,884)
Rushton, Victoria E 4:46:08 (22,585)
Rushworth, Ellie J 5:32:32 (30,618)
Rusinski, Eorgie 5:32:43 (30,639)
Rusling, Barbara 3:36:04 (5,350)
Rusling, Lucy J 6:55:01 (34,799)
Russ, Beverley A 6:13:41 (33,687)
Russel Ponte, Raqwel L 5:05:11 (26,722)
Russell, Christine A 4:22:36 (16,503)
Russell, Debbie L 3:00:22 (1,147)
Russell, Delma R 5:44:40 (31,816)
Russell, Dorothea 4:54:41 (24,589)
Russell, Gillian V 4:21:45 (16,271)
Russell, Hannah R 4:02:41 (11,309)
Russell, Judith E 4:14:21 (14,257)
Russell, Lesley D 3:45:00 (6,957)
Russell, Linda J 4:00:30 (10,832)
Russell, Louise E 5:31:47 (30,542)
Russell, Lucy E 5:12:29 (27,907)
Russell, Sarah J 3:37:17 (5,534)
Russell, Sophie 3:57:03 (9,837)
Russell Flint, Tamsin L 4:23:37 (16,756)
Russell-Fisk, Elizabeth 4:36:06 (20,108)
Russo, Deborah E 3:35:44 (5,303)
Russo, Elizabeth A 5:15:44 (28,447)
Russo, Vanessa M 4:53:25 (24,281)
Russon, Hannah L 5:16:48 (28,601)
Rutherford, Catherine 4:37:36 (20,523)
Rutherford, Nicola J 4:56:07 (24,920)
Ryan, Anne M 4:44:37 (22,231)
Ryan, Anne T 5:28:17 (30,164)
Ryan, Bernie H 4:03:11 (11,427)
Ryan, Dianne 6:28:11 (34,201)
Ryan, Jennifer A 4:36:22 (20,188)
Ryan, Jennifer H 4:49:50 (23,458)
Ryan, Karen L 4:44:19 (22,177)
Ryan, Kerry P 4:04:41 (11,790)
Ryan, Lea 6:09:21 (33,506)
Ryan, Lia 4:03:30 (11,498)
Ryan, Lisa 7:02:07 (34,892)
Ryan, Mairead 4:48:00 (23,011)
Ryan, Mary N 3:14:45 (2,453)
Ryan, Olive M 5:36:00 (30,992)
Rycroft-Malone, Joanne 4:33:32 (19,444)
Ryden, Catherine M 5:13:12 (28,023)
Ryder, Jennie C 3:33:58 (5,041)
Ryder, Lorna J 5:20:11 (29,129)
Sabin, Elizabeth J 4:05:35 (12,003)
Sabrosa, Vina 4:19:21 (15,624)
Sackville, Emma 5:13:10 (28,017)
Sadler, Rosemarie E 4:23:39 (16,764)
Sage, Helen M 6:05:44 (33,309)
Sainsbury, Eve T 5:20:55 (29,227)
Saint, Debbie M 3:49:26 (7,917)
Sainty, Mandy J 6:34:01 (34,354)
Salem, Lara 5:01:27 (26,054)
Salih, Samira 4:42:03 (21,634)
Salley, Joanne S 4:00:11 (10,762)
Salmon, Claire L 4:07:03 (12,356)
Salmon, Helen J 4:55:50 (24,856)
Salmond, Alison J 4:31:34 (18,989)
Salt, Adela M 2:53:59 (686)
Salter, Amanda J 4:49:20 (23,320)
Salter-Kipp, Ulrike 5:23:05 (29,494)
Sambrook, Louise 4:11:44 (13,548)
Sammons, Catherine F 4:53:31 (24,307)
Sammons, Rita E 4:21:07 (16,094)
Sampson, Helen M 4:20:41 (15,986)
Sampson, Leonie 6:29:27 (34,238)
Sampson, Lisa M 4:40:30 (21,259)
Sams, Katie J 4:24:52 (17,087)
Sams, Maddy 4:01:54 (11,128)
Sams, Patricia A 5:29:28 (30,303)
Samson, Maria 4:48:18 (23,075)
Samsudin, Cathy J 4:36:27 (20,216)
Samuels, Diana R 4:24:09 (16,890)
Samuels, Sidonie G 7:59:55 (35,228)
Sanchez De Muniain, Sol A 5:28:23 (30,177)
Sanday, Julia T 4:33:14 (19,366)
Sanders, Charlotte J 6:06:41 (33,367)
Sanderson, Catherine 4:43:16 (21,926)
Sanderson, Jayne 4:22:18 (16,421)
Sanderson, Julie L 5:01:31 (26,069)
Sanderson, Laura J 4:00:59 (10,945)
Sanderson, Polly 5:18:17 (28,833)
Sandhu, Ros M 4:22:02 (16,350)
Sands, Hilary M 4:02:31 (11,276)
Sang, Melanie A 4:13:25 (13,993)
Sanger, Wendy 4:33:51 (19,533)
Sanghera, Rajinder 5:38:31 (31,253)
Sangster, Fiona J 4:59:18 (25,628)
Sangster, Gillian 4:02:40 (11,307)
Sangster, Susan A 5:54:53 (32,631)
Sansom, Brenda 6:34:15 (34,361)
Sansome, Karen J 4:31:16 (18,904)
Sanson, Sylvie 4:22:26 (16,453)
Santar, Heather 4:53:41 (24,350)
Sanz, Catherin 3:47:14 (7,398)
Sapier, Tracy D 4:15:03 (14,464)
Sargant, Clare L 6:33:38 (34,344)
Sargeant, Pauline 3:46:33 (7,251)
Sargent, Janet C 5:05:00 (26,686)
Sarker, Gopa 3:56:51 (9,769)
Sarkin, Carrene 5:41:17 (31,537)
Sarkin, Janine 5:56:38 (32,744)
Sarti, Daniela E 4:50:58 (23,726)
Sarton, Emma L 5:33:26 (30,714)
Sarup, Louise S 4:38:14 (20,678)
Sato, Noriko 4:32:22 (19,179)
Sattaur-Olivi, Tanya M 6:15:37 (33,766)
Saulsbury, Nicki K 6:44:19 (34,603)
Saunders, Ann R 4:17:00 (14,955)
Saunders, Helen 5:14:42 (28,303)
Saunders, Helen E 4:33:04 (19,330)
Saunders, Jenna H 6:20:41 (33,939)
Saunders, Lynne A 4:08:58 (12,817)
Saunders, Ruth K 4:31:16 (18,904)
Saunders, Sarah E 5:44:29 (31,801)
Saunderson, Gillian M 4:31:09 (18,866)
Savage, Debbie L 4:08:02 (12,579)
Savage, Michelle L 4:16:51 (14,927)
Savill, Anna K 3:26:05 (3,779)
Savill, Melanie R 4:34:29 (19,706)
Sawdon, Julie P 5:24:55 (29,734)
Sawka, Helen A 6:34:36 (34,366)
Sawyer, Carolyn B 5:10:50 (27,622)
Sawyer, Catriona B 5:06:45 (27,008)
Sawyer, Julie 4:45:13 (22,374)
Sayers, Kimberley 6:46:18 (34,632)
Sayers, Rachel 4:55:40 (24,804)
Sayles, Louisa M 5:58:39 (32,887)
Scahill, Helen L 4:26:07 (17,482)
Scantlebury, Hannah 4:32:30 (19,212)
Scantlebury, Katherine 4:25:24 (17,246)
Scaramangas, Lisa 4:34:53 (19,819)
Scarfe, Jacqueline K 3:51:01 (8,259)
Scarrott, Yvonne C 3:18:26 (2,826)
Scarso, Véronique 4:36:38 (20,263)
Scarth, Anna M 4:20:15 (15,875)
Scarth, Gillian M 3:57:54 (10,110)
Scarth, Julia M 4:53:11 (24,217)
Sceats, Maureen A 6:16:38 (33,805)
Schaefer, Maren 4:12:06 (13,640)
Schirmer, Jacquelyn L 4:33:31 (19,440)
Schmid, Erika R 3:40:58 (6,173)
Schneiderman, Frances J 5:34:52 (30,891)
Schofield, Adele 4:11:57 (13,608)
Schofield, Amanda R 3:25:02 (3,589)
Schofield, Tracey J 3:56:35 (9,687)
Scholes, Helen E 4:42:06 (21,653)
Scholes, Rachel I 6:06:04 (33,332)
Scholey, Julie A 3:19:32 (2,946)
Schoovaerts, Liesbeth 4:45:16 (22,384)
Schreiber, Suzanne 4:51:34 (23,846)
Schroeder, Helga 3:56:43 (9,732)
Schuberth, Joanna 5:01:39 (26,087)
Schueler, Jennifer M 4:27:20 (17,833)
Schult, Barbara 4:51:02 (23,741)
Schumacher, Linda S 6:21:48 (33,980)
Schumann, Anne L 4:30:00 (18,584)
Schurmann, Deborah S 4:36:13 (20,135)
Schwarz, Gerlinde 4:04:21 (11,712)
Scot, Susan R 5:57:56 (32,829)
Scotland, Beverley 4:40:18 (21,209)
Scott, Alison 4:27:52 (18,005)
Scott, Amanda J 4:33:08 (19,347)
Scott, Bobbie A 4:26:33 (17,616)
Scott, Caroline 5:21:51 (29,334)
Scott, Claire A 5:49:22 (32,217)
Scott, Elaine L 4:44:45 (22,262)
Scott, Elisabeth M 4:26:26 (17,580)
Scott, Emily C 3:54:29 (9,096)
Scott, Jenny 4:22:40 (16,530)
Scott, Julia S 4:26:08 (17,487)
Scott, Karen L 6:56:26 (34,820)
Scott, Katie Jane 4:28:08 (18,067)
Scott, Louise A 4:04:57 (11,849)
Scott, Mary A 6:14:23 (33,714)
Scott, Michele 4:08:32 (12,697)
Scott, Rosemarie D 5:46:29 (31,976)
Scott, Wendy A 3:15:14 (2,498)
Scotter, Kate 4:04:33 (11,757)
Scowcroft, Cora M 4:34:34 (19,732)
Scrase, Linda E 4:08:19 (12,645)
Scully, Patricia J 4:39:35 (21,037)
Scully, Teresa N 3:02:07 (1,270)
Scurrell, Heather A 5:03:09 (26,376)
Seal, Janet L 6:46:43 (34,649)
Sealy, Wendy L 3:57:53 (10,107)
Searle, Amy 4:43:32 (21,990)
Searle, Christine J 3:57:52 (10,102)
Searle, Claire L 4:47:04 (22,784)
Searle, Emma 4:02:46 (11,335)
Sears, Michelle 7:23:33 (35,092)
Seaton, Michlle C 6:23:07 (34,025)
Sebba, Henrietta A 4:47:31 (22,887)
Seboka, Mulu 2:30:54 (77)
Sedgman, Katherine J 4:21:01 (16,078)
Sedgwick, Thérèse M 3:55:21 (9,321)
Seed, Andrea J 6:04:26 (33,240)
Seel, Georgina K 3:58:31 (10,293)
Seers, Sally C 5:16:06 (28,491)

Sees, Carly.....................................4:33:22 (19,400)
Seguss, Emma F............................3:38:26 (5,714)
Selby, Ann....................................4:13:54 (14,112)
Selby, Jennifer.............................5:15:24 (28,406)
Selby, Linda.................................4:11:07 (13,384)
Sellar, Julie M..............................3:53:15 (8,783)
Selley, Barbara K.........................5:48:06 (32,102)
Selman, Diane..............................6:01:25 (33,046)
Selman, Natasha R.......................6:16:20 (33,797)
Semmens, Tina S..........................5:54:05 (32,577)
Semonin, Hannah L......................5:05:59 (26,868)
Sendlhofer, Britta D......................4:39:12 (20,932)
Senior, Jane E...............................4:13:49 (14,093)
Sephton, Pamela J.........................4:22:00 (16,335)
Servatius, Julie A..........................4:47:49 (22,967)
Sethill, Lynsey.............................4:26:11 (17,503)
Seton, Fiona M.............................5:13:23 (28,055)
Severn, Zahra...............................5:27:00 (29,977)
Seville, Lucy E.............................6:54:09 (34,784)
Seward, Lavinia E..........................4:55:59 (24,898)
Sewart, Katie................................4:03:33 (11,514)
Sewell, Carina L...........................3:41:06 (6,203)
Sewell, Kathy M............................5:34:00 (30,782)
Sexton, Amy.................................3:41:38 (6,310)
Sexton, Julie A..............................4:36:35 (20,243)
Seymour, Charmaine A..................5:50:31 (32,306)
Seymour, Christine.......................4:54:03 (24,439)
Seymour, Ellen D..........................4:56:39 (25,056)
Seymour, Zoe...............................4:25:44 (17,359)
Shah, Nishma...............................4:55:54 (24,874)
Shakeshaft, Jilly A.........................5:39:05 (31,318)
Shakespeare, Jackie......................3:57:21 (9,933)
Shales, Jo.....................................4:22:00 (16,335)
Shallcross, Lynne J........................5:51:43 (32,390)
Shanahan, Erica F.........................5:23:10 (29,500)
Shanks, Jackie..............................3:02:43 (1,317)
Shanley, Lynne.............................3:56:12 (9,575)
Shannon, Audrey..........................3:35:28 (5,255)
Shannon-Jones, Sue.....................5:47:11 (32,032)
Shapter, Philippa E.......................4:50:17 (23,556)
Shapter, Sophie............................4:50:17 (23,556)
Share, Simone S............................5:04:05 (26,527)
Sharkie, Margaret.........................6:21:47 (33,979)
Sharland, Sharon L........................3:41:37 (6,302)
Sharma, Kusum L..........................5:12:21 (27,873)
Sharma, Rehana............................5:10:23 (27,551)
Sharman, Fiona A..........................4:49:41 (23,424)
Sharp, Christina M.........................7:49:25 (35,205)
Sharp, Michelle E..........................4:37:33 (20,509)
Sharp, Samantha M........................4:26:56 (17,732)
Sharp, Tracy M.............................4:31:09 (18,866)
Sharpe, Anthea L..........................3:33:54 (5,029)
Sharpe, Gillian H..........................4:11:39 (13,523)
Sharpe, Linda...............................5:01:57 (26,136)
Sharron, Hazel A...........................4:31:41 (19,016)
Shattock, Frances E.......................4:18:03 (15,220)
Shaughnessy, Lisa.........................5:41:24 (31,544)
Shaukat, Shabana.........................6:53:14 (34,774)
Shaw, Anne Maree V......................4:46:26 (22,655)
Shaw, Bridget L............................4:36:50 (20,314)
Shaw, Carol A...............................6:17:33 (33,840)
Shaw, Caroline M..........................4:03:43 (11,548)
Shaw, Diane.................................5:25:11 (29,769)
Shaw, Emma.................................4:13:48 (14,089)
Shaw, Esther................................4:33:42 (19,488)
Shaw, Janet M..............................4:58:49 (25,515)
Shaw, Lisa J.................................3:19:30 (2,937)
Shaw, Susan.................................4:41:12 (21,446)
Shea, Margaret.............................5:00:55 (25,964)
Shearing, Deborah E......................4:53:08 (24,205)
Shearn, Jessica J...........................5:30:53 (30,451)
Shears, Lucy J...............................4:59:55 (25,761)
Shea-Simonds, Claire....................3:27:05 (3,940)
Shedden, Felicity P........................4:04:21 (11,712)
Sheedy, Alison J............................5:24:14 (29,650)
Sheehan, Melanie Y.......................5:34:25 (30,837)
Sheldrake, Claire L........................4:48:45 (23,182)
Sheldrake, Debbie A......................4:45:32 (22,439)
Shellard, Katie E............................4:29:16 (18,390)
Shelley, Claire J.............................3:43:46 (6,698)
Shelley, Lauren K...........................2:41:42 (233)
Shellito, Diane P............................5:32:56 (30,663)
Shelton, Jill D...............................4:44:47 (22,272)

Shemmans, Kelly R.......................6:27:50 (34,191)
Shephard, Elizabeth A...................5:47:01 (32,020)
Shepherd, Janet M........................4:29:10 (18,359)
Shepherd, Janette L.......................3:11:13 (2,055)
Shepherd, Jennifer M.....................4:12:41 (13,798)
Shepherd, Julia M..........................4:18:31 (15,364)
Shepherd, Rhiannon......................4:43:59 (22,094)
Shepherd, Samantha J...................3:57:09 (9,875)
Shepherd, Samantha J...................4:17:03 (14,971)
Shepherd, Sarah J..........................4:40:20 (21,218)
Sheppard, Hayley L........................6:32:13 (34,308)
Sherard, Elaine M..........................5:55:55 (32,704)
Sheridan, Alison J..........................4:34:28 (19,704)
Sheridan, Alyson L.........................6:06:08 (33,338)
Sheridan, Tanya J...........................4:12:35 (13,769)
Sherwood, Emma C........................4:33:50 (19,529)
Sherwood, Heather J......................4:53:39 (24,344)
Shevchenko, Anna E.......................5:52:28 (32,460)
Shewbridge, Laura E......................4:41:14 (21,454)
Shewry, Jane L..............................3:59:44 (10,641)
Shields, Clare S.............................4:37:05 (20,377)
Shields, Diane C............................3:37:23 (5,554)
Shields, Hayley L...........................5:00:51 (25,946)
Shiels, Kathy................................4:58:22 (25,406)
Shier, Katherine L.........................5:16:54 (28,624)
Shillington, Anthea.......................4:12:19 (13,699)
Shipton, Alison M..........................5:10:39 (27,597)
Shirley, Anita R............................6:06:50 (33,381)
Shirley, Laura...............................4:40:44 (21,315)
Shoebridge, Polly A.......................4:15:04 (14,470)
Shore, Charlotte E.........................5:17:59 (28,779)
Shore, Elaine P.............................4:08:53 (12,797)
Short, Andrea J.............................5:39:58 (31,411)
Short, Claire E..............................5:11:40 (27,765)
Short, Emily.................................5:23:51 (29,593)
Short, Fiona.................................5:22:41 (29,453)
Shorter, Tracey C..........................5:09:21 (27,413)
Shortland, Sally............................6:31:22 (34,288)
Shortt, Jemma E............................4:48:34 (23,135)
Shpherd, Janie..............................5:19:19 (28,993)
Shrimpton, Sally-Anne R................7:09:05 (34,967)
Shrubb, Jane L..............................4:15:27 (14,563)
Shuttleworth, Christie....................4:11:12 (13,406)
Siao, Diane P................................4:30:03 (18,608)
Sibley, Jane.................................5:31:40 (30,529)
Sick, Claudia................................4:41:21 (21,479)
Siddall, Jacqueline........................5:38:12 (31,221)
Siddall, Nicola E............................4:46:32 (22,675)
Siebrits, Sarah S............................4:47:36 (22,907)
Sieloff, Cheryl..............................6:06:42 (33,370)
Signy, Helen................................4:38:35 (20,774)
Sihra, Virinder K...........................5:19:21 (28,998)
Silbermann, Kate E........................4:40:03 (21,150)
Silcock, Ann.................................4:23:30 (16,728)
Sill, Michaela...............................4:10:15 (13,153)
Sillitoe, Joanne L..........................4:00:15 (10,778)
Sills, Ruth M................................3:24:51 (3,562)
Silva, Joanna M............................5:26:36 (29,935)
Silvani, Anja.................................4:27:38 (17,934)
Silver, Jill F..................................6:46:21 (34,635)
Silverman, Ruth H.........................4:38:09 (20,660)
Silverthorn, Gillian.......................5:03:48 (26,484)
Silverwood, Emma........................4:42:33 (21,751)
Simmonds, Brigid M.......................4:20:14 (15,866)
Simmonds, Jennifer M....................4:36:41 (20,274)
Simmonds, Lorraine K....................5:56:43 (32,749)
Simmons, Ann E............................4:38:26 (20,736)
Simmons, Charlotte M....................4:53:35 (24,323)
Simmons, Emma L.........................3:51:03 (8,265)
Simmons, Melanie J.......................4:11:28 (13,477)
Simmons, Noelle E........................5:01:13 (26,010)
Simmons, Tracy A..........................4:21:51 (16,297)
Simms, Abigail..............................6:43:18 (34,578)
Simms, Annabel E..........................4:05:50 (12,055)
Simonetti, Marta...........................4:50:31 (23,630)
Simons, Anna K.............................5:09:15 (27,397)
Simons, Jenny..............................4:10:53 (13,310)
Simons, Louise C...........................6:05:07 (33,274)
Simpkins, Emma J.........................4:04:52 (11,829)
Simpson, Belinda A........................5:11:19 (27,708)
Simpson, Bryony R........................4:53:30 (24,300)
Simpson, Cecilia...........................4:51:50 (23,896)
Simpson, Elizabeth R.....................4:28:36 (18,195)

Simpson, Joanna E.........................3:25:30 (3,672)
Simpson, Kate L............................5:02:32 (26,234)
Simpson, Kathryn R.......................4:44:00 (22,099)
Simpson, Katie L...........................6:34:37 (34,367)
Simpson, Liz.................................4:05:17 (11,944)
Simpson, Louise I..........................3:53:21 (8,820)
Simpson, Rhia M...........................6:07:19 (33,409)
Simpson, Shona R.........................4:38:25 (20,732)
Simpson, Sonia.............................4:38:21 (20,709)
Sims, Ann C..................................5:09:18 (27,403)
Sims, Gillian.................................4:59:46 (25,730)
Sims-Stirling, Karen L.....................4:09:12 (12,890)
Sinclair, Barbara J..........................4:41:09 (21,432)
Sinclair, Judith A...........................4:31:32 (18,978)
Sinclair, Margaret B.......................5:27:42 (30,066)
Sinfield, Jenny..............................4:46:43 (22,714)
Sinfield, Judith A...........................4:08:54 (12,802)
Singer, Jo L...................................3:19:48 (2,978)
Singer, Lucia N..............................3:42:20 (6,438)
Singh, Kavita................................8:09:41 (35,240)
Singleton, Michelle.......................2:59:01 (1,036)
Singleton, Veronica C.....................3:35:36 (5,279)
Sinnamon, Margaret E....................5:18:29 (28,860)
Sinnott, June...............................4:54:19 (24,508)
Sira, Mandi..................................5:46:10 (31,952)
Siret, Nikki L................................5:34:54 (30,895)
Sirois, Shirley A............................4:47:49 (22,967)
Sittampalam, Mara J.......................4:39:22 (20,980)
Sjoo, Solweig...............................4:40:47 (21,332)
Skerritt, Tania..............................4:52:09 (23,977)
Skidmore, Flora............................3:15:54 (2,557)
Skilbeck, Mandy J..........................5:58:28 (32,875)
Skinner, Catherine J.......................3:29:11 (4,311)
Skinner, Elisabeth A.......................5:18:06 (28,798)
Skinner, Helen M...........................4:10:38 (13,248)
Skinner, Jane S..............................5:07:29 (27,143)
Skinner, Jo Anne M........................4:48:55 (23,216)
Skipper, Victoria T.........................4:16:01 (14,722)
Skipsey, Claire L............................4:33:02 (19,320)
Skitt, Angela M.............................6:24:53 (34,093)
Skitt, Jean A.................................5:36:01 (30,996)
Skitt, Sarah J................................4:17:53 (15,177)
Skittrall, Lucy I.............................6:00:39 (33,008)
Slack, Debbie A.............................3:44:55 (6,940)
Slade, Tracey C.............................3:24:21 (3,498)
Slamon, Lynne..............................4:07:35 (12,472)
Slater, Carolyn.............................4:44:26 (22,201)
Slater, Kerry L..............................4:13:58 (14,135)
Slater, Lesley L.............................3:51:31 (8,373)
Slattery, Helen A...........................4:52:25 (24,034)
Slaymaker, Dorte..........................4:02:10 (11,199)
Sledge, Charlotte E........................3:31:31 (4,682)
Sleeman, Sarah.............................5:28:51 (30,223)
Sleep, Laura J...............................6:23:50 (34,055)
Slevin, Sally.................................6:00:52 (33,019)
Slinn, Patricia M............................4:29:56 (18,573)
Sloan, Anna M..............................3:26:25 (3,831)
Sloan, Joanna E............................5:13:38 (28,106)
Slocock, Katherine........................4:59:02 (25,569)
Slocombe, Carly J..........................4:26:02 (17,447)
Sloper, Julie S...............................5:33:28 (30,719)
Small, Lisa J.................................5:03:17 (26,400)
Smallacombe, Geraldine M.............3:57:46 (10,058)
Smallman, Joanna E.......................4:54:38 (24,581)
Smallwood, Lucie E........................5:22:20 (29,388)
Smart, Jinty..................................4:06:35 (12,238)
Smart, Linda A..............................5:28:14 (30,155)
Smart, Michelle L...........................4:23:13 (16,655)
Smart, Samantha M........................5:42:11 (31,602)
Smeaton, Zoe C.............................4:11:42 (13,538)
Smedley, Josie A...........................5:28:05 (30,115)
Smethurst, Helen E........................3:10:09 (1,942)
Smiddy, Mary E.............................4:32:19 (19,170)
Smith, Adelaide.............................7:10:04 (34,979)
Smith, Adrienne M.........................6:11:53 (33,607)
Smith, Alison J..............................3:30:00 (4,454)
Smith, Amanda J............................5:58:33 (32,883)
Smith, Amy A................................4:18:33 (15,373)
Smith, Amy L................................3:37:50 (5,623)
Smith, Angela...............................5:02:25 (26,223)
Smith, Angela M............................4:05:37 (12,008)
Smith, Angela P.............................5:16:14 (28,511)
Smith, Angharad L.........................4:08:39 (12,728)

Smith, Anna M 4:14:34 (14,311)
Smith, Anna M 4:18:33 (15,373)
Smith, Anne 4:04:06 (11,661)
Smith, Barbara 4:58:49 (25,515)
Smith, Beverley A 4:39:11 (20,923)
Smith, Beverley M 4:06:54 (12,320)
Smith, Brenda 5:45:07 (31,856)
Smith, Bryony J 5:02:45 (26,284)
Smith, Carly S 4:06:12 (12,143)
Smith, Caroline 4:56:16 (24,955)
Smith, Catherine A 3:52:24 (8,578)
Smith, Celia 6:16:36 (33,804)
Smith, Charlene V 5:15:44 (28,447)
Smith, Charlotte E 4:31:29 (18,965)
Smith, Charlotte E 6:00:24 (32,997)
Smith, Clare L 4:57:56 (25,307)
Smith, Claudia M 5:44:58 (31,849)
Smith, Corin B 4:53:11 (24,217)
Smith, Debbie 4:08:24 (12,667)
Smith, Donna 5:02:35 (26,245)
Smith, Donna K 6:26:26 (34,140)
Smith, Donna M 4:48:19 (23,077)
Smith, Elaine G 4:14:33 (14,304)
Smith, Elizabeth A 4:06:06 (12,121)
Smith, Emma L 5:29:26 (30,297)
Smith, Emma-Louise F 4:47:04 (22,784)
Smith, Esra 4:59:07 (25,588)
Smith, Gemma M 6:38:14 (34,462)
Smith, Gillian E 5:00:52 (25,953)
Smith, Ginette 4:27:04 (17,765)
Smith, Glenys 4:34:21 (19,676)
Smith, Hayley E 4:26:44 (17,672)
Smith, Helen 4:41:45 (21,578)
Smith, Helen 6:54:41 (34,792)
Smith, Helene 6:05:40 (33,306)
Smith, Ian J 3:56:04 (9,524)
Smith, Jan 4:42:52 (21,838)
Smith, Jane C 5:32:44 (30,641)
Smith, Jane E 5:24:07 (29,633)
Smith, Jane R 3:52:39 (8,646)
Smith, Jemma L 5:02:57 (26,329)
Smith, Jessica A 5:56:33 (32,735)
Smith, Joanna 5:18:45 (28,911)
Smith, Joanne L 5:20:04 (29,111)
Smith, Josephine M 7:16:49 (35,045)
Smith, Julia K 5:34:36 (30,861)
Smith, Julia M 5:37:43 (31,159)
Smith, Justine 6:05:47 (33,312)
Smith, Karen 4:41:49 (21,592)
Smith, Karen C 4:31:33 (18,986)
Smith, Karen M 4:55:47 (24,837)
Smith, Kellymarie 5:35:19 (30,935)
Smith, Kerry 3:27:49 (4,079)
Smith, Kim C 5:10:52 (27,628)
Smith, Laura C 5:06:38 (26,990)
Smith, Lisa J 6:34:37 (34,367)
Smith, Maddy K 3:33:36 (4,974)
Smith, Mandy 5:08:36 (27,298)
Smith, Maria J 4:18:10 (15,253)
Smith, Melanie C 3:54:13 (9,025)
Smith, Melanie L 4:49:00 (23,235)
Smith, Mena B 4:17:57 (15,189)
Smith, Michelle L 4:53:35 (24,323)
Smith, Nicola J 4:09:47 (13,035)
Smith, Norma F 3:57:55 (10,116)
Smith, Pamela A 4:42:12 (21,676)
Smith, Pamela J 5:13:41 (28,113)
Smith, Patricia A 5:20:09 (29,122)
Smith, Paula J 4:53:14 (24,231)
Smith, Penny F 4:42:52 (21,838)
Smith, Philippa J 4:33:34 (19,455)
Smith, Rachel A 4:07:42 (12,495)
Smith, Rachel L 4:35:34 (19,988)
Smith, Rebecca J 4:33:35 (19,459)
Smith, Rebecca L 3:11:28 (2,076)
Smith, Richard L 4:18:35 (15,388)
Smith, Ruth M 5:26:33 (29,928)
Smith, Sally 6:28:53 (34,213)
Smith, Sara K 5:35:42 (30,967)
Smith, Sarah T 6:41:35 (34,534)
Smith, Sharon 3:54:53 (9,212)
Smith, Sharon H 3:08:24 (1,750)
Smith, Sian 6:27:49 (34,190)
Smith, Stephanie 3:54:14 (9,029)
Smith, Stephanie V 4:23:48 (16,804)
Smith, Suzanne 5:23:41 (29,574)
Smith, Tina 4:58:01 (25,333)
Smith, Tina M 4:45:53 (22,516)
Smith, Tracey 5:13:20 (28,049)
Smith, Verity 3:49:26 (7,917)
Smith, Veronica E 6:13:42 (33,689)
Smith, Wendy 5:43:38 (31,731)
Smith, Wendy A 4:34:39 (19,748)
Smith, Wendy E 6:19:05 (33,890)
Smith-Calvert, Elizabeth H 4:24:04 (16,870)
Smithson, Sonia A 5:15:12 (28,369)
Smyth, Anne E 3:55:49 (9,467)
Smyth, Cara A 5:19:42 (29,060)
Smyth, Yvonne M 4:07:58 (12,568)
Smythe, Anne 4:19:42 (15,721)
Snee, Julia A 5:02:49 (26,297)
Sneezum, Beverley 5:08:47 (27,317)
Snell, Allyson E 4:33:27 (19,417)
Snell, Beverly A 3:53:21 (8,820)
Snell, Claerwen R 4:54:46 (24,614)
Snell, Nicola L 4:10:17 (13,164)
Snellgrove, Emily R 6:35:01 (34,379)
Snellgrove, Kirste L 5:04:15 (26,561)
Snelling, Jean E 5:16:42 (28,578)
Snook, Beverley A 4:16:05 (14,734)
Snook, Davina 5:09:17 (27,400)
Snook, Rachel J 4:19:31 (15,668)
Snook, Sian J 5:07:03 (27,068)
Snook, Suzanne E 3:44:09 (6,774)
Snook, Tanya L 4:04:00 (11,633)
Snookes, Kathryn M 6:21:02 (33,952)
Snow, Alice F 3:50:37 (8,173)
Snowden, Bernadette M 6:01:28 (33,052)
Snowden, Dianne F 5:58:36 (32,885)
Snyman, Lisa 4:59:24 (25,641)
Soames, Camilla M 3:58:07 (10,171)
Soane, Lorie E 3:59:46 (10,654)
Sobenes, Suzanne B 4:34:53 (19,819)
Sohweitzer, Louise V 5:24:21 (29,668)
Sollim, Jessica 4:48:02 (23,017)
Solomon Williams, Rachel 4:07:10 (12,387)
Somers, Laura 4:11:47 (13,559)
Somers, Rhian E 3:26:59 (3,927)
Sommerton, Helen A 5:14:05 (28,182)
Sommerville, Lorna E 4:05:24 (11,967)
Soong, Nicola M 4:58:24 (25,416)
Sorensen, Lotte H 3:37:19 (5,539)
Sotheby, Angela 4:23:02 (16,607)
Sott, Andrea H 3:53:30 (8,855)
Soudine, Lynda 6:48:54 (34,689)
Souness, Liz 3:33:21 (4,938)
Sourlis, Dorothy A 4:14:09 (14,194)
Souster, Rachael 4:18:20 (15,307)
South, Erika P 5:07:09 (27,086)
South, Jayne E 4:49:27 (23,350)
Southall, Carolyn M 4:13:10 (13,928)
Southall, Mary 5:04:00 (26,516)
Southall, Sarah 5:04:00 (26,516)
Southen, Leanne J 4:12:39 (13,790)
Southgate, Kirsty L 4:23:34 (16,746)
Southworth, Anna E 4:31:19 (18,923)
Sowden, Miranda C 3:57:50 (10,089)
Sowry, Deborah A 4:38:28 (20,749)
Sowter, Elizabeth M 3:15:24 (2,513)
Sowter, Kathryn J 4:21:01 (16,078)
Spacey, Joanna R 3:57:25 (9,958)
Spain, Eileen I 5:13:56 (28,156)
Spalluto, Mirella C 5:09:32 (27,442)
Sparham, Michele D 6:01:25 (33,046)
Sparks, Laura J 4:44:49 (22,276)
Speake, Celia 3:41:46 (6,327)
Speechley, Bernadette 4:08:11 (12,607)
Speirs, Lynne 5:09:51 (27,490)
Speller, Christine 5:30:52 (30,448)
Speller, Vicki L 4:14:17 (14,241)
Spence, Isabella J 5:29:39 (30,325)
Spence, Pamela H 6:11:14 (33,584)
Spencer, Anna-Louise 4:55:43 (24,822)
Spencer, Caroline D 4:50:43 (23,678)
Spencer, Karen 5:53:31 (32,536)
Spencer, Sally A 3:33:03 (4,893)
Spencer, Sarah A 4:56:29 (25,014)
Spencer, Vicki 3:35:37 (5,285)
Spencer, Victoria J 4:09:27 (12,943)

Spens, Deborah S 4:33:19 (19,390)

My stepsister suggested we run London Marathon 2005 in memory of my father who died of myeloma the previous year. It seemed the perfect way to pay tribute to him, and to my mother who died of breast cancer in 1983. My strongest memory of the day is the camaraderie with fellow runners and the support you get from the crowd. When I hit 'the wall' at 20 miles it was a fellow runner who got me to the finish. My T-shirt was printed with the words 'For Mum and Dad, both lost to cancer', and this fellow runner came up and said: 'They would be very proud and they will be even more proud if you keep on running'. How could I *not* knock down that wall and press on to the end? The finish was very emotional, but the relief was overwhelming. I probably won't ever do the London Marathon again due to injuries but the memory of it will live with me forever.

Sperry, Lorraine Y 5:42:28 (31,624)
Sperry, Natalie D 4:47:58 (22,997)
Spick, Claire 4:00:58 (10,941)
Spiegel, Rosemarie 4:52:35 (24,070)
Spikes, Sarah E 3:54:03 (8,986)
Spillett, Nicola C 5:10:39 (27,597)
Spink, Jennifer G 4:45:14 (22,379)
Spong, Carole 3:32:33 (4,826)
Spong, Sue 3:10:16 (1,954)
Spooner, Amie L 4:07:50 (12,537)
Spooner, Cynthia J 6:01:09 (33,034)
Spooner, Jeannie M 5:21:51 (29,334)
Spooner, Jill 5:34:07 (30,791)
Spooner, Rosanna 4:28:16 (18,105)
Spouse, Kelly J 4:28:32 (18,176)
Spragg, Jane 4:14:03 (14,164)
Springall, Claire 4:22:30 (16,472)
Springall, Nicola 5:24:12 (29,644)
Springthorpe, Andrea 4:04:19 (11,705)
Spurdle, Yvonne M 5:16:31 (28,550)
Spurr, Sarah J 5:18:10 (28,812)
St Croix, Christina 5:24:51 (29,729)
St John-Ives, Githa T 4:54:39 (24,583)
Stableforth, Abigail C 4:38:16 (20,689)
Stacey, Elizabeth A 4:36:34 (20,238)
Stacey, Judith C 3:23:52 (3,434)
Stacey, Verity 3:05:17 (1,492)
Stach-Kevitz, Adele 3:35:23 (5,237)
Stack, Finola 5:04:50 (26,655)
Stackpool-Moore, Lucy R 4:37:14 (20,423)
Staff, Ruth S 3:38:08 (5,673)
Staines, Sharen 6:05:08 (33,278)
Stallard, Jennifer S 5:35:23 (30,945)
Stammers, Louisa C 5:35:32 (30,958)
Stamp, Jill 5:05:04 (26,695)
Stamp, Tracey C 3:38:15 (5,689)
Stampi, Elisabetta 3:24:50 (3,556)
Stanage, Bobbie 5:13:55 (28,153)
Standing, Angie C 4:51:40 (23,863)
Staniforth, Jane A 4:55:06 (24,700)
Staniforth, Kerry A 5:18:43 (28,908)
Staniforth, Louise M 6:31:50 (34,300)
Stanislaus, Charlotte V 4:55:59 (24,898)
Stanley, Andrea N 3:54:37 (9,126)
Stanley, Glenda M 4:11:52 (13,574)
Stanley-Hewitt, Mylene 4:52:34 (24,067)
Stannett, Kate F 4:25:24 (17,246)
Stansbie, Melissa J 4:47:26 (22,868)
Stansfield, Sarah M 5:39:22 (31,363)
Stanton, Catherine 5:20:07 (29,119)
Stanton, Mary 4:51:31 (23,836)
Stanton, Sandra 4:17:24 (15,068)
Stanton, Sharon D 6:23:57 (34,060)
Stanton, Tracy A 6:11:59 (33,614)
Stanyon, Jan A 5:52:26 (32,456)
Staples, Catherine R 4:53:08 (24,205)

Tagle, Lucero....4:12:53 (13,848)
Taiapa, Linda M....7:31:20 (35,137)
Tait, Gayle M....3:55:54 (9,488)
Tait, Nicola G....5:01:17 (26,025)
Taiwo, Ayo....4:34:16 (19,654)
Talbot, Katie J....5:02:48 (26,294)
Talbot, Nora....5:10:23 (27,551)
Talbot Rosner, Victoria H....3:49:55 (8,021)
Tallon, Sophie I....6:15:36 (33,765)
Tam, Emily W....4:03:50 (11,590)
Tame, Kate V....4:53:11 (24,217)
Tammen, Constance C....3:31:54 (4,732)
Tan, Janine Y....6:08:51 (33,479)
Tan, Poh....5:55:13 (32,660)
Tanner, Jane C....5:31:58 (30,557)
Tansey, Sara....3:48:32 (7,724)
Tansley, Rachel....5:36:44 (31,081)
Tapley, Julie....3:46:00 (7,133)
Tapper, Caroline R....5:30:29 (30,414)
Tapper, Liz J....3:29:25 (4,341)
Tapping, Katherine J....5:12:06 (27,845)
Tarpey, Maureen L....6:56:10 (34,815)
Tarrach, Zoe C....4:14:58 (14,430)
Tatchley, Maria....3:52:17 (8,551)
Tate, Roma E....5:19:05 (28,951)
Tate, Soriah....4:57:38 (25,254)
Tatoud, Laurence....4:14:59 (14,437)
Taun, Margaret R....6:16:03 (33,781)
Tavener, Diane....4:30:08 (18,636)
Tavernier, Brigitte....4:38:51 (20,840)
Tawiah, Jennifer C....5:31:12 (30,488)
Taylor, Alice M....5:19:12 (28,974)
Taylor, Andie J....4:01:58 (11,145)
Taylor, Ann....5:31:21 (30,501)
Taylor, Anne V....4:33:24 (19,407)
Taylor, Bridgeen M....5:21:17 (29,276)
Taylor, Claire H....4:50:44 (23,680)
Taylor, Corinna....5:01:08 (26,000)
Taylor, Emily-Jane....6:04:10 (33,229)
Taylor, Emma E....4:47:57 (22,994)
Taylor, Eve....5:23:22 (29,524)
Taylor, Gail....3:57:26 (9,961)
Taylor, Gwen....5:24:57 (29,739)
Taylor, Heather V....4:51:34 (23,846)
Taylor, Helen L....6:18:57 (33,888)
Taylor, Helen M....4:18:12 (15,266)
Taylor, Jacqueline F....6:09:11 (33,501)
Taylor, Janet....5:39:37 (31,383)
Taylor, Janine....5:43:45 (31,742)
Taylor, Jennie L....5:28:33 (30,191)
Taylor, Joan I....5:44:26 (31,796)
Taylor, Johanna....3:52:20 (8,563)
Taylor, Juliet M....5:14:57 (28,332)
Taylor, Karen....5:38:26 (31,243)
Taylor, Karen M....4:57:27 (25,219)
Taylor, Karen S....6:37:11 (34,436)
Taylor, Kate A....4:12:45 (13,817)
Taylor, Katherine L....5:19:25 (29,013)
Taylor, Kristine J....4:02:58 (11,383)
Taylor, Laura....5:58:18 (32,861)
Taylor, Leila....4:09:26 (12,939)
Taylor, Lisa M....6:27:11 (34,169)
Taylor, Lorna....5:29:20 (30,279)
Taylor, Lynda....4:34:32 (19,722)
Taylor, Lynn....4:45:38 (22,467)
Taylor, Marianne C....5:59:24 (32,939)
Taylor, Melanie A....4:54:00 (24,428)
Taylor, Michelle M....4:25:31 (17,290)
Taylor, Nicola A....6:24:37 (34,078)
Taylor, Pippa J....5:04:15 (26,561)
Taylor, Rachel J....5:19:52 (29,083)
Taylor, Rachel L....4:10:30 (13,227)
Taylor, Rebbeca....5:59:25 (32,940)
Taylor, Rebecca L....4:50:59 (23,728)
Taylor, Reisha M....5:49:20 (32,215)
Taylor, Ruth....6:46:22 (34,637)
Taylor, Sandra M....6:16:04 (33,784)
Taylor, Sara E....4:31:20 (18,927)
Taylor, Sarah E....4:05:44 (12,036)
Taylor, Sarah M....5:27:15 (30,008)
Taylor, Shona J....3:53:47 (8,930)
Taylor, Sophie....3:56:32 (9,671)
Taylor, Susan A....6:02:49 (33,128)
Taylor, Susan P....5:23:45 (29,576)
Taylor, Susie....5:02:58 (26,335)
Taylor, Tania E....3:42:21 (6,441)
Taylor, Tracy E....4:19:16 (15,596)
Taylor, Valerie E....5:37:58 (31,193)
Taylor Palmer, Jo....4:22:02 (16,350)
Taylor-Gill, Carol A....5:02:39 (26,263)
Taylor-Reid, Jane P....5:08:49 (27,324)
Teasdale, Susan....4:45:54 (22,524)
Teasel, Michelle T....3:26:20 (3,816)
Tebbutt, Carla G....3:48:18 (7,657)
Tee, Sarah L....4:26:53 (17,714)
Teeney, Clare....4:20:06 (15,832)
Teerlinck, Beatrijs K....4:48:22 (23,095)
Teixeira Gomes, Susana....4:14:23 (14,267)
Temple, Kenza....5:32:31 (30,616)
Temple, Lesley....5:07:39 (27,167)
Templeman, Clare E....5:29:11 (30,263)
Templeton, Jan S....5:55:11 (32,654)
Temprell, Michael....3:42:13 (6,420)
Ten Broeke, Vanessa J....6:31:07 (34,279)
Tennant, Jodie L....5:11:33 (27,749)
Tennant, Lisa M....6:36:47 (34,428)
Terenziani, Scristina....4:55:59 (24,898)
Terjesen, Siri A....3:05:30 (1,518)
Terriere, Annie....4:28:12 (18,085)
Terry, Carolyn A....4:52:14 (24,001)
Terry, Emma L....4:34:58 (19,847)
Terry, Kathryn A....7:17:38 (35,058)
Testo, Susan L....4:08:39 (12,728)
Tetlow, Pamela J....4:41:58 (21,617)
Teufel, Michelle....5:43:06 (31,686)
Tew, Donna M....3:31:27 (4,671)
Thacker, Helen....5:37:55 (31,186)
Thacker, Sarah L....4:40:57 (21,375)
Thain, Shona....5:06:53 (27,039)
Thakkar, Meera K....6:21:38 (33,971)
Thatcher, Sarah M....6:06:54 (33,384)
Thatcher, Victoria E....5:08:43 (27,313)
Thayan, Sumi....6:00:52 (33,019)
Thayer, Rosie E....6:07:46 (33,426)
Thaysen, Birgit....3:24:17 (3,480)
Thearle, Sue....6:59:38 (34,862)
Theed, Penny J....3:39:02 (5,823)
Theler, Irene....3:37:47 (5,615)
Theocharous, Amrit K....5:26:38 (29,940)
Thetford, Sally....5:50:10 (32,276)
Thevenet-Smith, Ramona E....3:27:51 (4,085)
Thistlethwaite, Anne M....5:07:57 (27,210)
Thistleton, Heather J....4:19:21 (15,624)
Thoemel, Sabine....4:50:41 (23,672)
Thom, Laura E....4:59:28 (25,655)
Thomas, Alexandra C....5:35:39 (30,962)
Thomas, Amy....4:23:00 (16,600)
Thomas, Barbara....4:41:20 (21,474)
Thomas, Beryl A....5:08:24 (27,269)
Thomas, Bianca M....3:23:38 (3,392)
Thomas, Caroline....5:32:11 (30,574)
Thomas, Catherine D....4:09:39 (12,999)
Thomas, Claire P....3:25:08 (3,612)
Thomas, Dawn A....4:13:21 (13,978)
Thomas, Debbie M....3:10:57 (2,026)
Thomas, Francesan....4:39:12 (20,932)
Thomas, Hayley....6:55:39 (34,808)
Thomas, Hilary N....6:15:21 (33,749)
Thomas, Jane B....4:37:50 (20,586)
Thomas, Jeanette....3:42:02 (6,385)
Thomas, Jennifer....3:52:24 (8,578)
Thomas, Judith A....4:28:36 (18,195)
Thomas, Karen....4:09:53 (13,063)
Thomas, Kerry L....4:19:18 (15,611)
Thomas, Lorenza M....4:46:15 (22,611)
Thomas, Lynn M....6:30:26 (34,263)
Thomas, Marion J....5:05:05 (26,698)
Thomas, Marion W....5:58:56 (32,908)
Thomas, Nicky J....4:10:40 (13,257)
Thomas, Olga....4:26:08 (17,487)
Thomas, Rebecca....6:14:32 (33,721)
Thomas, Rhianwen E....4:04:53 (11,834)
Thomas, Sharon....4:52:59 (24,170)
Thomas, Sian....4:24:12 (16,901)
Thomas, Sophie C....5:14:13 (28,213)
Thomas, Susan H....5:30:39 (30,427)
Thomas, Trudy....3:56:28 (9,656)
Thomas, Victoria K....5:51:51 (32,401)
Thompson, Angela A....4:15:48 (14,660)
Thompson, Carol L....5:25:54 (29,854)
Thompson, Emily J....4:16:35 (14,854)
Thompson, Gillian....5:12:43 (27,953)
Thompson, Gillian....5:18:40 (28,900)
Thompson, Helen L....4:13:32 (14,024)
Thompson, Helen L....4:20:27 (15,929)
Thompson, Jane E....3:48:00 (7,581)
Thompson, Julie A....4:21:56 (16,312)
Thompson, Karina....4:57:27 (25,219)
Thompson, Kate....4:34:08 (19,604)
Thompson, Kirsty....5:16:46 (28,594)
Thompson, Lesley A....4:43:59 (22,094)
Thompson, Linda....6:07:42 (33,424)
Thompson, Linda C....3:59:44 (10,641)
Thompson, Linda C....4:54:17 (24,496)
Thompson, Lisa J....4:26:27 (17,585)
Thompson, Lorraine....5:16:48 (28,601)
Thompson, Louise V....5:03:44 (26,468)
Thompson, Margaret....4:49:28 (23,353)
Thompson, Michelle P....4:37:39 (20,529)
Thompson, Rebecca L....6:23:59 (34,064)
Thompson, Stephanie J....5:08:45 (27,314)
Thomson, Jacqui M....3:05:40 (1,527)
Thomson, Jane S....4:14:10 (14,201)
Thomson, Joanne....6:31:39 (34,294)
Thomson, Kim....7:03:28 (34,908)
Thomson, Margaret F....6:10:42 (33,563)
Thomson, Maria....6:02:35 (33,112)
Thomson, Melanie L....8:54:53 (35,251)
Thomson, Sally N....3:52:34 (8,622)
Thorn, Cherie M....4:54:21 (24,515)
Thorn, Pauline M....4:50:13 (23,539)
Thornburgh, Zoe K....2:54:56 (738)
Thorne, Catherine....5:03:06 (26,362)
Thorne, Christine....3:56:08 (9,551)
Thorne, Elizabeth M....5:25:53 (29,850)
Thorne, Sarah K....5:40:12 (31,437)
Thornley, Nicki....4:43:19 (21,940)
Thorns, Colette M....4:44:58 (22,316)
Thornton, Christine....5:05:31 (26,798)
Thornton, Clair F....5:14:33 (28,268)
Thornton, Julie L....4:38:28 (20,749)
Thornton, Karen....5:52:51 (32,485)
Thornton, Lesley J....5:23:00 (29,489)
Thorpe, Alexandra J....5:19:25 (29,013)
Thorpe, Katie L....4:37:21 (20,457)
Thorpe, Sarah J....6:56:02 (34,813)
Thorpe, Shirley A....4:26:57 (17,737)
Thran, Amy L....4:34:13 (19,634)
Thurman, Alison....3:46:30 (7,243)
Thythian, Jamie....4:45:45 (22,486)
Tibbatts, Joanne....3:54:20 (9,053)
Tibble, Yvonne....3:14:29 (2,411)
Tibbott, Catherine R....4:34:06 (19,591)
Tibbs, Denise....3:25:30 (3,672)
Tickle, Linda A....4:42:05 (21,645)
Tideswell, Fiona J....3:34:12 (5,078)
Tidmarsh, Mary E....5:55:27 (32,675)
Tierney, Jill....5:05:46 (26,837)
Tift, Lindsay C....5:41:32 (31,556)
Tighe, Camilla R....5:26:42 (29,946)
Tighman, Teresa M....7:01:08 (34,887)
Tigneres, Isabelle....4:54:46 (24,614)
Tilby, Gaynor L....5:11:06 (27,669)
Tiley, Tina L....5:04:37 (26,616)
Tillett, Caroline....5:55:26 (32,673)
Tilley, Alexa....4:30:23 (18,698)
Tilley, Cathy F....3:57:05 (9,850)
Tilley, Julia C....4:59:47 (25,736)
Tillman, Fi E....5:19:23 (29,007)
Tillson, Lisa....5:12:48 (27,969)
Tilt, Carole A....4:56:35 (25,035)
Timmerman, Leentje C....4:17:12 (15,011)
Timms, Sophie A....3:55:52 (9,480)
Timothy, Catherine M....4:40:54 (21,361)
Timothy, Julie....6:03:11 (33,155)
Tims, Caroline A....5:47:27 (32,058)
Tims, Emily M....4:38:02 (20,631)
Tin, Lwin L....4:33:03 (19,327)
Tincknell, Karen....5:01:17 (26,025)

Tindill, Nicole L....4:24:55 (17,096)
Tinham, Ann J....5:57:42 (32,820)
Tinsley, Judith C....3:38:19 (5,702)
Tipper, Lucy F....4:52:03 (23,948)
Tipping, Michelle J....5:58:00 (32,834)
Tippins, Emma L....4:54:59 (24,668)
Tiptaft, Emma R....3:36:26 (5,415)
Tipton, Claire L....4:15:57 (14,698)
Tisdale, Catherine T....6:27:55 (34,193)
Titley, Jody....4:51:46 (23,884)
Titus, Heather L....5:34:52 (30,891)
Tivers, Jacqueline....5:38:05 (31,204)
Toach, Glenda....5:38:31 (31,253)
Tobin, Sue....5:17:00 (28,645)
Toby, Julia K....3:45:27 (7,042)
Tock, Sarah E....5:01:29 (26,061)
Todd, Kate....3:50:27 (8,138)
Todd, Lesley M....5:28:54 (30,235)
Todd, Lindsey C....5:33:07 (30,679)
Todd, Rebecca J....4:43:05 (21,886)
Todd, Vilma....6:39:25 (34,490)
Todd, Yvonne L....5:22:10 (29,372)
Todd-Lloyd, Samantha C....4:30:12 (18,655)
Todman, Christine M....5:52:24 (32,451)
Toft, Jacqueline A....5:16:55 (28,629)
Tolch, Leanne....4:50:59 (23,728)
Tollafield, Heather J....6:53:47 (34,781)
Tolman, Catherine E....5:07:04 (27,072)
Tolmie, Linda....4:59:10 (25,598)
Tomaine, Susan....3:58:23 (10,255)
Tomas, Lisa....4:31:46 (19,038)
Tombling, Karen....4:19:10 (15,567)
Tomkins, Beverly A....4:56:21 (24,977)
Tomkins, Paula A....3:42:46 (6,507)
Tomkins, Susannah C....4:29:37 (18,499)
Toner, Milla....5:33:35 (30,735)
Tongue, Catherine....5:47:21 (32,045)
Tonkin, Jane E....5:16:10 (28,502)
Tonks, Denise A....6:19:23 (33,899)
Tonna-Barthet, Daphne....6:27:53 (34,192)
Toofail, Rachel M....5:38:36 (31,265)
Tooher-Rodd, Rachael....5:47:03 (32,022)
Tooley, Rachel E....6:24:21 (34,072)
Toomer, Susan F....6:18:50 (33,886)
Toomey, Ann M....5:45:57 (31,928)
Toothill, Charlotte L....4:34:44 (19,774)
Toovey, Gail E....4:47:34 (22,902)
Tori, Tiziana....5:35:59 (30,990)
Torkington, Megan L....4:55:00 (24,674)
Toseland, Susan E....6:23:49 (34,052)
Tossani, Federica....5:29:40 (30,326)
Tournade, Sylvie....4:04:55 (11,843)
Towers, Julie A....3:56:04 (9,524)
Towers, Morag A....5:11:04 (27,665)
Towl, Clare V....4:54:20 (24,512)
Townend, Helen A....3:35:37 (5,285)
Towner, Hannah J....3:58:52 (10,402)
Townes, Suzanne M....4:07:44 (12,510)
Townley, Sharon....3:57:30 (9,979)
Towns, Jacqueline P....5:51:24 (32,365)
Towns, Jill M....4:57:17 (25,189)
Towns, Sharon....4:22:55 (16,585)
Townsend, Alice M....5:23:13 (29,505)
Townsend, Amanda J....7:51:20 (35,210)
Townsend, Caroline A....5:17:03 (28,656)
Townsend, Catherine A....6:35:52 (34,406)
Townsend, Emma C....5:23:13 (29,505)
Townsend, Janet....8:01:33 (35,234)
Townsend, Sarah C....5:23:12 (29,504)
Townsend, Tracy....4:05:01 (11,864)
Toye, Katy....5:18:00 (28,784)
Toye, Olivia....3:51:07 (8,288)
Tracey, Anita F....4:53:08 (24,205)
Tracey, June....4:31:17 (18,913)
Tracey, Lisa M....3:32:54 (4,873)
Tracey-Aguera, Mary-Anne A....4:30:00 (18,584)
Trafford, Katie F....3:48:44 (7,770)
Trafford, Rebecca J....6:03:20 (33,178)
Travell, Gemma....4:06:01 (12,096)
Travers, Gail M....6:21:31 (33,964)
Travers, Kirsty J....5:36:43 (31,079)
Traweek, Toya L....5:28:26 (30,180)
Trayhurn, Venetia H....5:37:49 (31,169)
Traynor, Mary P....3:56:46 (9,740)
Treacher, Alison H....5:55:37 (32,690)
Treadwell, Julie....4:23:17 (16,683)
Treadwell, Lorraine F....3:48:15 (7,645)
Tree, Brigid V....7:49:42 (35,206)
Tregidgo, Angela E....5:44:19 (31,790)
Tremlett, Rima M....4:22:38 (16,518)
Trendell, Susan....5:29:04 (30,253)
Trett, Ann D....5:19:43 (29,064)
Trevor, Kelly A....6:19:27 (33,903)
Trevorrow, Philippa A....3:42:18 (6,433)
Trew, Juliet A....4:00:04 (10,745)
Treweek, Gillian E....5:36:18 (31,029)
Triegaardt, Jeanette E....4:03:55 (11,608)
Tristram, Claire L....6:27:38 (34,183)
Trkulja, Clare A....5:35:26 (30,949)
Trollen, Carole....3:51:21 (8,343)
Troop, Alison....5:35:50 (30,979)
Trosh, Caroline....3:30:13 (4,480)
Trueman, Gwendoline A....4:52:49 (24,131)
Truesdale, Alexandra S....5:56:21 (32,729)
Truett, Dinah M....5:06:45 (27,008)
Trump, Keziah E....4:49:51 (23,461)
Trump, Stacey L....4:36:29 (20,223)
Trumpess, Nicola M....4:54:06 (24,453)
Trygger, Maria C....5:09:12 (27,387)
Tubbs, Sarah D....5:22:12 (29,375)
Tucker, Christine....5:14:50 (28,317)
Tucker, Diane....5:13:34 (28,098)
Tucker, Lucy....5:26:44 (29,950)
Tucker, Sarah J....3:01:57 (1,255)
Tucker, Tina L....3:55:32 (9,376)
Tuff, Estella....5:32:56 (30,663)
Tuffin, Rachel P....4:20:59 (16,071)
Tufft, Lindsay H....4:35:16 (19,900)
Tufnell, Chloe J....5:57:27 (32,802)
Tuineau, Mel....6:12:23 (33,633)
Tuke, Catherine A....5:05:38 (26,811)
Tull, Jane E....5:13:05 (28,012)
Tullis, Caroline....4:42:47 (21,819)
Tulloch, Sue....4:04:44 (11,801)
Tully, Lisa M....5:27:36 (30,054)
Tumber, Clara E....4:44:12 (22,142)
Tummons, Sharon L....4:54:33 (24,566)
Tuner, Joanne G....4:33:53 (19,543)
Tuplin, Catriona J....3:49:18 (7,893)
Turkington, Helen R....4:32:45 (19,258)
Turnbull, Tracey E....6:02:32 (33,107)
Turner, Adele....5:22:08 (29,370)
Turner, Anne E....4:40:28 (21,251)
Turner, Catherine L....5:31:56 (30,553)
Turner, Christine E....5:40:25 (31,462)
Turner, Claire E....5:12:16 (27,865)
Turner, Gemma....5:55:51 (32,701)
Turner, Hollie J....5:42:16 (31,606)
Turner, Jane L....5:21:55 (29,339)
Turner, Jennifer A....3:36:09 (5,365)
Turner, Jennifer C....3:19:38 (2,959)
Turner, Jo....5:00:05 (25,792)
Turner, Julie....5:12:00 (27,822)
Turner, Kenneth J....5:42:17 (31,609)
Turner, Lisa J....4:25:03 (17,137)
Turner, Lorraine....5:25:45 (29,833)
Turner, Louise....6:00:40 (33,010)
Turner, Mary....5:02:39 (26,263)
Turner, Melanie J....5:44:03 (31,763)
Turner, Sarah E....4:06:54 (12,320)
Turner, Sarah J....4:50:26 (23,608)
Turner, Teresa M....5:29:47 (30,337)
Turner, Tina....4:53:17 (24,243)
Turner-Stockham, Helen E....5:45:43 (31,913)
Turtle, Rachel....4:21:29 (16,200)
Tutcher, Hilary B....4:14:53 (14,406)
Tutin, Angela M....4:46:47 (22,727)
Tutton, Ruth L....6:10:29 (33,551)
Tweed, Jo L....3:05:43 (1,531)
Twilley, Victoria A....4:50:07 (23,518)
Twinn, Jason G....4:30:08 (18,636)
Twitchin, Claire V....5:55:24 (32,672)
Twitchin, Lucy R....4:12:22 (13,716)
Twomey, Emma V....5:06:43 (27,004)
Twyman, Lucy M....5:03:39 (26,453)
Tydd, Hilary A....6:06:23 (33,352)
Tye, Lisa....6:25:19 (34,102)
Tyler, Alison L....4:28:19 (18,115)
Tyler, Amy L....4:35:13 (19,887)
Tyler, Claire E....4:35:13 (19,887)
Tyler, Gillian C....5:19:34 (29,044)
Tyler, Jacky A....3:44:22 (6,811)
Tyler, Rosemary A....4:58:11 (25,367)
Tyrrell, Jill P....4:29:14 (18,375)
Tyrrell, Rosina R....4:54:13 (24,479)
Tyson, Deborah M....5:13:27 (28,071)
Tyson, Linda A....5:06:34 (26,979)
Ubierna, Maria L....3:05:40 (1,527)
Ugolini, Virginia....4:17:15 (15,021)
Ukiah, Nicola J....4:17:59 (15,201)
Ulliott, Cathy F....3:24:50 (3,556)
Umebuani, Yvonne A....6:17:26 (33,838)
Underwood, Holly....4:47:48 (22,965)
Underwood, Kerry L....5:27:58 (30,097)
Unite, Lesley A....4:53:06 (24,199)
Unitt, Angela....6:06:58 (33,387)
Unthank, Nina....3:47:38 (7,482)
Upton, Sybil J....3:48:30 (7,709)
Urban, Wendy H....3:23:00 (3,294)
Uren, Lisa U....3:34:31 (5,126)
Urmson, Janine K....5:53:38 (32,540)
Urquhart, Dawn J....3:41:02 (6,186)
Urquhart, Jennifer M....3:24:44 (3,544)
Urry, Jeanette....4:53:17 (24,243)
Urwin, Sinead....3:56:10 (9,562)
Urwin-Mann, Sarah L....3:13:20 (2,276)
Usher, Christine....4:36:03 (20,093)
Usher, Tanya I....3:40:36 (6,101)
Uzice, Doreen....5:28:34 (30,192)
Vakilpour, Janet....3:33:14 (4,915)
Valapinee, Anick M....3:18:54 (2,873)
Valente, Elisio M....5:53:02 (32,499)
Valiente, Gracia....3:05:21 (1,502)
Vallance, Lita D....5:20:24 (29,161)
Vallario, Anthony G....4:27:17 (17,822)
Valleau, Anne-Marie....4:42:21 (21,705)
Vallely, Karen J....4:44:51 (22,285)
Vallier, Louise A....3:43:29 (6,651)
Van Bergen, Lizette I....4:07:42 (12,495)
Van De Bourry, Carly....5:56:34 (32,736)
Van De Linden, Marietta L....2:58:41 (1,003)
Van Deelen, Jennifer M....3:15:20 (2,508)
Van Der Merwe, Maria P....4:23:32 (16,735)
Van Hoof, Esther....3:20:42 (3,062)
Van Hoof, Linda M....5:07:25 (27,133)
Van Hoof, Ria....4:00:02 (10,736)
Van Kerckudorde, Kristel....4:32:21 (19,176)
Van Rees, Stephanie I....4:35:37 (20,002)
Van Soeren, Julie R....4:58:13 (25,379)
Van Zantem, Jet Velohuijzen....5:15:34 (28,430)
Vanbetsbrugge, Anne-Lore....4:43:54 (22,070)
Vance, Fiona M....5:18:50 (28,926)
Vanhatalo, Anni T....3:40:34 (6,097)
Vanhatalo, Emmi M....3:40:33 (6,094)
Vann, Rachel....4:39:09 (20,911)
Van't Hoff, Angela J....6:14:43 (33,725)
Varga, Andrea....4:49:36 (23,388)
Varga, Cindy....3:57:01 (9,820)
Vargas, Patricia A....3:57:18 (9,920)
Varley, Nicola J....4:30:05 (18,615)
Varndell-Dawes, Paula....4:12:12 (13,664)
Varnish, Helen C....4:25:37 (17,321)
Varsani, Dilan V....5:50:11 (32,278)
Vasant, Mellissa....5:38:59 (31,308)
Vastola, Joyce A....4:10:12 (13,140)
Vaughan, Carole D....4:19:01 (15,519)
Veal, Sarah M....5:27:12 (29,999)
Vecchi Martini, Elda....4:13:47 (14,087)
Veenstra, Margriet....5:49:35 (32,230)
Vekariya, Premila P....5:04:00 (26,516)
Vellenoweth, Katie....5:04:27 (26,592)
Vellino, Joanne E....4:56:32 (25,022)
Veness, Leonie....4:14:38 (14,325)
Venn, Anna M....6:01:32 (33,056)
Venn, Rebecca L....5:13:58 (28,164)
Venn, Sally H....5:46:54 (32,006)
Verbic, Darja....5:43:26 (31,713)
Verde Nieto, Diana....4:07:05 (12,368)
Verga, Gillian....4:07:31 (12,463)

Watson, Laura 5:20:35 (29,194)
Watson, Lorna A.............4:14:52 (14,403)
Watson, Louise C.............2:47:00 (374)
Watson, Rebecca 4:39:47 (21,089)
Watson, Sarah L.............6:03:41 (33,197)
Watson, Su-Lin 5:12:35 (27,923)
Watson, Tanya C.............5:52:51 (32,485)
Watson, Victoria J.............5:45:58 (31,931)
Watson-Jones, Lucy C.............4:40:35 (21,280)
Watt, Caroline E.............3:55:44 (9,443)
Watt, Janet E.............4:27:20 (17,833)
Watt, Jayne 4:03:32 (11,510)
Watt, Nicola A.............5:56:18 (32,725)
Watton, Fiona L.............5:12:29 (27,907)
Watts, Amelia.............3:35:58 (5,337)
Watts, Dawn T.............5:37:36 (31,151)
Watts, Jane 4:40:21 (21,221)
Watts, Julia A 6:37:47 (34,451)
Watts, Justin M.............4:37:51 (20,590)
Watts, Kathleen M.............5:23:39 (29,564)
Watts, Kaye R.............5:13:19 (28,046)
Watts, Sally J.............4:58:22 (25,406)
Watts, Victoria J.............3:41:44 (6,322)
Way, Nicola J.............3:31:28 (4,675)
Weames, Joanne N.............4:54:21 (24,515)
Weatherill, Melissa J.............4:50:12 (23,534)
Webb, Carol A 4:10:38 (13,248)
Webb, Caroline L.............5:23:16 (29,514)
Webb, Dixie 7:21:45 (35,083)
Webb, Elizabeth 5:01:47 (26,103)
Webb, Gemma M 4:45:06 (22,354)
Webb, Helen M 5:27:45 (30,071)
Webb, Kerry A 7:12:18 (35,006)
Webb, Kim L.............4:27:44 (17,963)
Webb, Liza M.............4:26:55 (17,724)
Webb, Rosemarie A 6:02:50 (33,132)
Webb, Sophie 4:13:53 (14,107)
Webb, Vicki.............6:07:11 (33,400)
Webber, Kate 4:54:58 (24,663)
Webber, Sabina 4:41:31 (21,529)
Webber, Sarah 4:34:20 (19,671)
Webb-Greenwood, Sandra.............4:20:56 (16,061)
Weber, Claudia 3:54:49 (9,187)
Webster, Emma L 5:06:29 (26,959)
Webster, Kathie C.............4:18:22 (15,315)
Webster, Katy M.............2:50:46 (529)
Webster, Kirsty 4:41:37 (21,549)
Webster, Lucy S 5:46:21 (31,968)
Webster, Maggie 6:17:08 (33,829)
Webster, Michelle L.............4:35:20 (19,919)
Webster, Ruth C.............6:38:03 (34,456)
Webster, Sarah A 4:49:55 (23,477)
Wedgbury, Melanie J.............5:28:11 (30,139)
Wedlake, Deborah A 4:37:18 (20,445)
Weedon, Linda O.............5:20:06 (29,117)
Weekes, Bridgit 3:58:20 (10,237)
Weekes, Lisa J.............5:38:35 (31,264)
Weekes, Sarah.............7:44:28 (35,191)
Weeks, Kara L.............4:44:34 (22,222)
Weeks, Rosa 5:09:12 (27,387)
Weggen, Gisela 4:44:06 (22,117)
Wehling, Christina.............5:18:06 (28,798)
Wehrle, Vera.............3:24:18 (3,486)
Weightman, Tracey J.............4:19:10 (15,567)
Weil, Leonora G.............5:10:58 (27,648)
Weinands, Marion.............4:03:38 (11,530)
Weinstock, Michelle C 4:04:18 (11,701)
Weir, Jane M 4:57:16 (25,188)
Weiss, Karen 3:17:26 (2,726)
Weiss, Sabine 3:41:04 (6,196)
Welch, Jo.............6:17:14 (33,832)
Welch, Louise 3:43:14 (6,595)
Weldon, Georgina M.............5:20:48 (29,217)
Weldon, Liz-Ann 4:49:30 (23,359)
Welfare, Claudia.............4:11:35 (13,500)
Welland, Samantha J.............5:08:55 (27,342)
Weller, Amy L 4:14:07 (14,184)
Weller, Katharine C.............4:48:45 (23,182)
Weller, Ruth E 4:52:59 (24,170)
Weller, Susan J.............5:15:47 (28,455)
Wellfair, Nicola C 4:45:12 (22,371)
Wells, Belinda 5:18:41 (28,903)
Wells, Dianne B 5:25:01 (29,748)

Wells, Heather O.............4:00:59 (10,945)
Wells, Irene E 5:13:23 (28,055)
Wells, Jane K.............4:52:35 (24,070)
Wells, Lorraine 4:41:15 (21,460)
Wells, Lynn 5:44:33 (31,809)
Wells, Sharon N.............4:37:01 (20,360)
Wells, Tracey L.............5:36:21 (31,034)
Wells, Victoria C.............4:34:20 (19,671)
Wellum, Ruth 5:11:10 (27,681)
Welscher, Waltraud 5:41:01 (31,515)
Welsford, Louise J 5:13:39 (28,110)
Welsh, Catriona P.............3:28:44 (4,229)
Welsh, Clare.............4:36:35 (20,243)
Welsh, Louise M 4:20:04 (15,817)
Welsh, Susan A 3:41:27 (6,268)
Wemyss, Sarah B.............4:39:16 (20,957)
Wenman, Debbie C.............3:21:50 (3,168)
Wensaver, Brigitte.............4:46:13 (22,606)
Went, Angela 3:47:39 (7,492)
Wesling, Kresse A 3:55:44 (9,443)
Wesson, Anna C.............5:04:56 (26,677)
West, Amanda L.............4:42:05 (21,645)
West, Claire L.............5:50:05 (32,270)
West, Diane B 5:56:12 (32,719)
West, Donna 4:09:38 (12,991)
West, Maria 4:47:02 (22,777)
West, Melissa.............4:39:18 (20,965)
West, Nicola 4:20:36 (15,962)
West, Nikki J 4:40:15 (21,199)
West, Stephanie N 5:28:31 (30,188)
West, Susan.............6:21:11 (33,955)
West, Tracey J.............3:13:21 (2,281)
West, Victoria L.............5:59:02 (32,915)
Westbrook, Susan M.............6:23:29 (34,037)
Westerman, Jo 6:48:24 (34,683)
Weston, Alison E 4:50:25 (23,603)
Weston, Helen L.............3:36:41 (5,451)
Weston, Judith 4:45:07 (22,357)
Weston, Phylis A 5:07:45 (27,181)
Weston, Rebecca M 4:34:40 (19,753)
Weston, Sally.............4:54:02 (24,436)
Westover, Natasha J 5:18:28 (28,854)
Westwood, Greta P 3:42:06 (6,401)
Wetherall, Sally.............5:38:01 (31,197)
Wetherall, Suzanne E.............3:13:34 (2,310)
Wetherell, Julie E 6:57:12 (34,834)
Wetherill, Lara J.............4:16:02 (14,724)
Wetton, Katie M 4:20:18 (15,889)
Wharam, Hilary M 4:57:36 (25,249)
Wharnsby, Anita 4:34:38 (19,743)
Wharton, Emma L 3:40:51 (6,157)
Wheatley, Andrée A 3:57:02 (9,828)
Wheatley, Sarah M.............4:31:47 (19,042)
Wheeldon, Victoria L.............6:57:23 (34,836)
Wheeler, Adelle C 5:02:01 (26,147)
Wheeler, Clare J 3:55:03 (9,245)
Wheeler, Emma E 6:01:58 (33,078)
Wheeler, Helen E 3:58:43 (10,354)
Wheeler, Kim 4:16:06 (14,738)
Wheelhouse, Anne M 5:17:03 (28,656)
Whelan, Alison 5:25:24 (29,792)
Whetlor, Julia F.............4:13:17 (13,964)
Whidburn, Amy G.............5:06:51 (27,029)
Whiffin, Joanne 4:25:10 (17,172)
Whiley, Lesley 2:57:09 (893)
White, Ailsa R 4:30:15 (18,667)
White, Alison J.............4:13:11 (13,938)
White, Amanda J 4:34:56 (19,836)
White, Angela V 6:11:04 (33,577)
White, Caroline S 3:42:36 (6,481)
White, Elaine 5:29:47 (30,337)
White, Francesca A.............6:08:57 (33,486)
White, Gillian 3:52:03 (8,493)
White, Heidi L.............4:44:18 (22,169)
White, Jane L.............3:33:48 (5,008)
White, Jeanette 4:32:28 (19,204)
White, Jessica 3:40:42 (6,117)
White, Joan 4:36:22 (20,188)
White, Jodie-Anne 5:57:10 (32,784)
White, Kate 5:06:41 (26,998)
White, Kathryn S.............5:03:53 (26,500)
White, Katie H.............5:55:11 (32,654)
White, Laura L 5:20:48 (29,217)

White, Loretta A.............5:08:33 (27,292)
White, Lynsey M.............5:45:52 (31,927)
White, Michelle 4:36:21 (20,177)
White, Natalie L 4:56:01 (24,906)
White, Pamela L.............3:52:24 (8,578)
White, Rachel 4:47:59 (23,004)
White, Rebecca.............4:31:26 (18,951)
White, Sally A 3:58:16 (10,210)
White, Sandra 3:49:23 (7,908)
White, Sarah L.............4:48:43 (23,170)
White, Skye 3:58:46 (10,375)
White, Susan E 3:50:44 (8,194)
White, Suzanne 4:07:51 (12,543)
White, Teresa M 6:27:03 (34,160)
White, Theresa M.............4:33:29 (19,425)
White, Victoria 4:20:00 (15,802)
Whitehead, Bethan A.............5:15:16 (28,383)
Whitehead, Jackie 5:12:05 (27,839)
Whitehead, Liz 4:52:46 (24,119)
Whitehead, Sarah.............3:10:34 (1,985)
Whitehead, Sharon A.............4:30:29 (18,722)
Whitehouse, Anna C.............4:46:52 (22,745)
Whitehouse, Elizabeth 4:02:32 (11,283)
Whitehouse, Laura 4:01:26 (11,032)
Whitehouse, Mary 6:32:28 (34,317)
Whitehurst, Louise M 4:05:13 (11,924)
Whitelam, Hannah R 4:47:05 (22,790)
Whiteman, Eloise J.............5:34:37 (30,863)
Whiteman, Emily J 5:04:06 (26,538)
Whiteman, Gaynor 3:45:09 (6,983)
Whiteson, Denisa 4:22:36 (16,503)
Whitestone, Joanne D 5:04:50 (26,655)
Whitfield, Diane M.............4:36:20 (20,172)
Whitfield, Julia F 5:17:37 (28,735)
Whitley, Jane.............3:57:50 (5,623)
Whitling, Holly E.............5:32:09 (30,571)
Whitlock, Pat 4:49:02 (23,246)
Whitmore, Cara L 4:18:13 (15,269)
Whitmore, Hazel 5:32:21 (30,595)
Whitnall, Lynn K.............5:01:49 (26,109)
Whitney, Diana 4:20:31 (15,950)
Whitney, Kate J 3:39:37 (5,933)
Whitney, Vicky J.............4:44:18 (22,169)
Whittaker, Allison M 5:46:21 (31,968)
Whittaker, Joanne L 4:21:38 (16,238)
Whittaker, Rachel L 3:56:46 (9,740)
Whitten, Selina I 3:40:51 (6,157)
Whittington, Doreen A.............5:27:20 (30,017)
Whittington, Eve A.............5:59:45 (32,963)
Whittle, Carol E.............4:33:18 (19,385)
Whittle, Caroline J 4:28:42 (18,219)
Whittle, Debbie D 5:00:25 (25,866)
Whittle, Ersuline A.............4:33:40 (19,477)
Whittle, Tracy L.............5:32:25 (30,607)
Whittley, Janette 3:51:20 (8,336)
Whitton, Linda J.............5:15:45 (28,451)
Whyand, Sarah J.............3:58:24 (10,261)
Whyman, Kath 4:54:25 (24,528)
Whyte, Susan G 5:31:47 (30,542)
Whytefield, Collette 5:44:22 (31,792)
Wicht, Sandra J.............4:29:04 (18,330)
Wickens, Gillian A.............4:49:50 (23,458)
Wicks, Kay A 3:26:08 (3,783)
Widd, Sarah E.............6:18:25 (33,867)
Widdicombe, Helen 5:01:13 (26,010)
Widdicombe, Sarah J 5:01:13 (26,010)
Widdop, Paula J.............5:23:47 (29,585)
Widdowson, Diane 4:25:15 (17,203)
Widman, Gabriella 6:27:25 (34,177)
Widnell, Gina A.............6:13:42 (33,689)
Wigg, Alison H 4:47:49 (22,967)
Wiggett, Nina 3:35:16 (5,217)
Wiggins, Emma J 4:44:13 (22,147)
Wiggins, Ruth M.............4:08:38 (12,722)
Wiggins, Tamara J 3:44:35 (6,857)
Wightman, Annabel 4:58:17 (25,390)
Wightman, Helen.............4:23:43 (16,781)
Wilcock, Helen 3:13:39 (2,322)
Wild, Clare E 5:18:17 (28,833)
Wild, Elizabeth K.............4:17:39 (15,125)
Wild, Gillian 5:24:13 (29,647)
Wild, Lisa J.............4:17:05 (14,977)
Wild, Narisa 3:18:14 (2,807)

Wild, Susan M	6:29:19 (34,236)
Wilde, Rebecca D	4:38:16 (20,689)
Wildig, Kathryn A	5:18:48 (28,920)
Wildt, Olivia	6:10:00 (33,532)
Wiles, Elizabeth A	6:46:56 (34,655)
Wiles, Gillian	7:36:16 (35,161)
Wiley, Susan	5:46:33 (31,983)
Wilkes, Susan R	5:59:21 (32,936)
Wilkie, Gillian M	4:40:46 (21,327)
Wilkie, Gosia L	4:28:20 (18,117)
Wilkie, Rose	3:29:54 (4,438)
Wilkins, Anna	4:38:34 (20,767)
Wilkins, Denise S	5:07:12 (27,103)
Wilkins, Julie	5:50:28 (32,296)
Wilkins, Mary	4:44:49 (22,276)
Wilkins, Sarah L	5:56:10 (32,716)
Wilkinson, Carolyn S	3:30:34 (4,541)
Wilkinson, Emma K	3:51:44 (8,418)
Wilkinson, Holly	3:35:43 (5,299)
Wilkinson, Joy L	3:45:50 (7,101)
Wilkinson, Kate S	4:08:11 (12,607)
Wilkinson, Kirsty	4:43:36 (22,007)
Wilkinson, Laura	3:54:59 (9,236)
Wilkinson, Lisa	3:40:34 (6,097)
Wilkinson, Lisa	4:46:50 (22,741)
Wilkinson, Louise J	7:10:12 (34,980)
Wilkinson, Matthew J	5:44:38 (31,813)
Wilkinson, Sally J	4:02:00 (11,155)
Wilkinson, Susie M	5:59:42 (32,960)
Wilkinson, Victoria C	4:11:31 (13,486)
Willan, Amanda	4:46:12 (22,604)
Willbourne, Sian E	4:36:05 (20,104)
Willcox, Rebecca E	4:29:09 (18,354)
Willett, Pauline A	6:06:30 (33,357)
Williams, Alison M	6:03:51 (33,214)
Williams, Alison S	5:22:16 (29,383)
Williams, Amanda J	5:11:33 (27,749)
Williams, Amy D	4:45:04 (22,342)
Williams, Anita E	4:03:40 (11,538)
Williams, Ann C	5:28:52 (30,229)
Williams, Anne	6:02:41 (33,118)
Williams, Barbara E	6:05:08 (33,278)
Williams, Bernadine S	5:03:28 (26,428)
Williams, Beth L	6:00:35 (33,006)
Williams, Bridget	5:17:21 (28,691)
Williams, Carol	5:23:27 (29,534)
Williams, Catherine	3:56:16 (9,589)
Williams, Catherine L	4:45:35 (22,453)
Williams, Cathy J	4:46:15 (22,611)
Williams, Cherry A	5:08:41 (27,308)
Williams, Claire L	6:56:01 (34,812)
Williams, Dawn E	4:56:28 (25,006)
Williams, Deborah A	5:17:26 (28,701)
Williams, Elizabeth B	5:00:27 (25,873)
Williams, Elizabeth L	4:45:55 (22,534)
Williams, Elizabeth M	4:47:59 (23,004)
Williams, Ellie F	4:42:52 (21,838)
Williams, Emily	5:30:23 (30,402)
Williams, Emma L	3:41:00 (6,180)
Williams, Emma L	4:18:38 (15,408)
Williams, Frances A	5:08:30 (27,286)
Williams, Frances E	3:53:31 (8,861)
Williams, Gabriella	4:35:25 (19,955)
Williams, Gwen M	4:40:58 (21,381)
Williams, Gwenndolyn A	6:09:27 (33,516)
Williams, Helen	4:34:41 (19,762)
Williams, Helen L	5:13:17 (28,040)
Williams, James P	4:12:21 (13,713)
Williams, Jeany P	6:06:22 (33,350)
Williams, Jennefer	4:42:10 (21,670)
Williams, Jennifer D	5:19:39 (29,054)
Williams, Joanne	4:26:29 (17,593)
Williams, Julia C	5:28:08 (30,130)
Williams, June F	7:30:51 (35,133)
Williams, Karen B	5:28:16 (30,160)
Williams, Karen E	4:16:19 (14,799)
Williams, Kirsten A	5:23:50 (29,590)
Williams, Leah V	4:25:18 (17,217)
Williams, Lucy F	4:25:24 (17,246)
Williams, Madeleine M	4:37:57 (20,606)
Williams, Nest M	4:49:47 (23,444)
Williams, Nicola R	5:28:22 (30,175)
Williams, Nina E	4:38:43 (20,803)

Williams, Sarah L	5:03:09 (26,376)
Williams, Sharon	3:56:19 (9,609)
Williams, Shirley A	4:57:20 (25,199)
Williams, Teresa K	3:17:57 (2,783)
Williams, Tracey A	4:45:53 (22,516)
Williams, Tracey L	5:52:46 (32,479)
Williamson, Ann-Marie	6:24:45 (34,083)
Williamson, Elin	4:20:24 (15,912)
Williamson, Jessica M	5:26:41 (29,943)
Williamson, Julia	5:23:39 (29,564)
Williamson, Lucy A	6:01:58 (33,078)
Williamson, Rachel K	4:58:43 (25,489)
Williamson, Sue	3:27:24 (3,996)
Williams-Royal, Deborah	5:23:27 (29,534)
Williams-Thomas, Polly E	4:37:05 (20,377)
Willis, Anne-Marie	6:26:55 (34,158)
Willis, Julia S	4:56:24 (24,990)
Willis, Sarah	4:43:00 (21,876)
Willocks-Watts, Michelle S	5:21:14 (29,265)
Willox, Carola A	4:50:48 (23,694)
Wills, Dawn C	6:18:06 (33,857)
Wills, Romilly	3:37:43 (5,605)
Willson, Penelope K	3:05:23 (1,507)
Willson, Sarah J	5:15:09 (28,360)
Wilmot, Leah M	5:24:13 (29,647)
Wilshaw, Susan	4:49:37 (23,402)
Wilsher, Andrea	4:34:13 (19,634)
Wilsher, Rachael M	3:42:10 (6,413)
Wilson, Alison M	5:10:37 (27,595)
Wilson, Anne	3:43:19 (6,622)
Wilson, Antoinette S	4:31:03 (18,847)
Wilson, Carli S	5:22:21 (29,395)
Wilson, Cheryl A	4:47:16 (22,831)
Wilson, Denise P	7:11:13 (34,992)
Wilson, Elaine D	5:09:45 (27,477)
Wilson, Gillian	4:41:47 (21,585)
Wilson, Heather E	4:53:32 (24,310)
Wilson, Helen K	4:28:42 (18,219)
Wilson, Jan K	5:49:13 (32,201)
Wilson, Jane	5:06:37 (26,986)
Wilson, Janice M	4:12:39 (13,790)
Wilson, Jessica J	3:46:42 (7,284)
Wilson, Joanna L	3:33:24 (4,947)
Wilson, Joanne C	3:17:29 (2,733)
Wilson, Karen	5:49:13 (32,201)
Wilson, Karen J	3:38:44 (5,759)
Wilson, Karen J	3:49:31 (7,938)
Wilson, Kathleen	6:05:09 (33,281)
Wilson, Kirsty L	5:13:52 (28,144)
Wilson, Laura C	5:03:15 (26,392)
Wilson, Lauren H	5:12:23 (27,882)
Wilson, Louise V	4:54:11 (24,471)
Wilson, Lucinda S	3:32:30 (4,821)
Wilson, Michelle	5:41:00 (31,511)
Wilson, Nicola	4:34:54 (19,825)
Wilson, Nicola A	3:37:40 (5,599)
Wilson, Nicola A	4:47:36 (22,907)
Wilson, Nicola M	5:52:05 (32,418)
Wilson, Penelope B	4:34:23 (19,689)
Wilson, Phylly	4:53:43 (24,358)
Wilson, Rachel M	3:44:34 (6,854)
Wilson, Rebecca	4:05:39 (12,016)
Wilson, Revecca	3:58:16 (10,210)
Wilson, Roisin E	4:59:18 (25,628)
Wilson, Rosalyn D	6:30:13 (34,261)
Wilson, Sarah N	5:09:49 (27,487)
Wilson, Simone C	3:23:09 (3,324)
Wilson, Solange M	6:08:19 (33,458)
Wilson, Susan C	4:35:14 (19,895)
Wilson, Thea R	4:29:22 (18,420)
Wilson, Tracey C	6:35:29 (34,395)
Wilson, Zelda	6:13:25 (33,673)
Wimbleton, Tanya J	5:01:51 (26,117)
Winch, Carol-Anne	4:48:56 (23,219)
Winder, Laura F	4:36:21 (20,177)
Winders, Catherine F	4:26:52 (17,706)
Windle, Kim E	4:14:13 (14,217)
Windsor Smith, Rachel	7:11:20 (34,995)
Wing, Julia A	4:44:49 (22,276)
Wingate, Catherine	6:04:29 (33,246)
Winkworth, Shirley M	6:59:43 (34,864)
Winn, Heidi N	3:28:01 (4,107)
Winnall, Catharine E	5:12:11 (27,854)

Winnard, Diane E	3:57:46 (10,058)
Winslow, Nicola H	3:59:10 (10,488)
Winter, Fleur L	4:30:03 (18,608)
Winter, Flora R	5:28:29 (30,187)
Winter, Lin	4:46:54 (22,753)
Winter, Lindsey	4:26:50 (17,694)
Winter, Sarah J	5:55:18 (32,666)
Winter-Barker, Sally	4:32:29 (19,207)
Winters, Melissa H	3:13:17 (2,273)
Wintle, Sally A	3:59:04 (10,456)
Wintle, Sarah	3:52:36 (8,629)
Wintour, Alexsis	6:20:43 (33,941)
Winyard, Christina	5:30:44 (30,436)
Wisdom, Carole J	4:29:05 (18,334)
Wisdom, Linda A	5:38:13 (31,224)
Wise, Hannah L	4:54:58 (24,663)
Wise, Julie E	5:44:57 (31,845)
Wise, Paula M	5:14:24 (28,245)
Wiseman, Anna C	4:18:10 (15,253)
Wiseman, Julie L	6:58:46 (34,848)
Wiseman, Sally A	6:16:46 (33,810)
Wisson, Joanne Y	5:04:03 (26,522)
Wisson, Shirley A	4:59:20 (25,633)
Witham, Helen M	3:53:01 (8,720)
Withers, Patricia A	5:20:47 (29,213)
Withey, Sarah J	5:20:40 (29,204)
Witjens-Spoelstra, Laura J	5:11:07 (27,670)
Witton, Christine H	4:43:43 (22,039)
Witty, Margo J	5:36:08 (31,007)
Wohanka, Oonagh	3:37:14 (5,528)
Wold, Ellen S	4:25:22 (17,235)
Wolf, Ruth	3:48:54 (7,802)
Wolfe, Helen	4:49:16 (23,296)
Wolfendale, Rebecca R	5:03:45 (26,470)
Wollen, Jenna R	4:34:40 (19,753)
Wolstenholme, Helen S	4:16:46 (14,907)
Wolstenhoome, Susan A	4:22:05 (16,362)
Womack, Sharon A	4:27:53 (18,007)
Wong, Joanna	4:49:53 (23,469)
Wong, Patsy	4:26:59 (17,749)
Wong, Suzie	3:17:14 (2,706)
Woo, Rita	5:58:08 (32,851)
Wood, Barbara J	4:12:13 (13,670)
Wood, Caroline J	5:32:45 (30,643)
Wood, Dorothy J	4:37:50 (20,586)
Wood, Fiona A	4:57:17 (25,189)
Wood, Georgia E	3:24:06 (3,460)
Wood, Ger	4:42:26 (21,725)
Wood, Hannah C	6:20:09 (33,926)
Wood, Janet	5:37:47 (31,166)
Wood, Janice	4:32:13 (19,141)
Wood, Jennifer	5:54:16 (32,587)
Wood, Jo	4:36:29 (20,223)
Wood, Joanne	4:04:59 (11,856)
Wood, Lene	6:47:51 (34,675)
Wood, Lindsay	5:19:28 (29,024)
Wood, Lucy	6:04:07 (33,225)
Wood, Marie A	6:13:51 (33,697)
Wood, Marie D	5:12:26 (27,895)
Wood, Pauline E	5:20:16 (29,136)
Wood, Penny	4:29:48 (18,545)
Wood, Rebecca	5:36:44 (31,081)
Wood, Ruth	4:11:00 (13,350)
Wood, Sarah H	6:05:36 (33,300)
Wood, Sophie M	2:54:57 (739)
Wood, Suzanne L	5:14:37 (28,283)
Wood, Vivien J	5:18:34 (28,877)
Wood Page, Elen C	5:37:07 (31,111)
Woodall, Kate M	4:58:48 (25,510)
Woodbridge, Barbara	5:51:06 (32,346)
Woodbridge, Sandy	5:59:51 (32,976)
Wood-Brignall, Sandra G	6:33:33 (34,342)
Woodcock, Caroline J	5:14:00 (28,171)
Woodcock, Sarah A	4:49:33 (23,371)
Wooden, Caroline J	4:05:31 (11,991)
Woodhams, Emma L	3:49:02 (7,831)
Woodhead, Jane	4:32:27 (19,196)
Woodhead, June A	5:14:38 (28,291)
Woodhouse, Amanda M	7:15:32 (35,036)
Woodhouse, Emma L	6:38:18 (34,464)
Woodhouse, Julia B	7:15:33 (35,037)
Woodhouse, Margaret	3:56:10 (9,562)
Woodhouse, Susan L	5:45:29 (31,894)

Woodley, Sandra A 6:24:46 (34,085)
Woodman, Rebecca E 3:21:39 (3,144)
Woodrow, Joyce M 6:35:25 (34,390)
Woodruff, Lora A 6:04:22 (33,235)
Woods, Abigail L 3:56:28 (9,656)
Woods, Anne P 4:21:21 (16,159)
Woods, Janet E 5:40:54 (31,496)
Woods, Marion C 5:10:36 (27,592)
Woods, Samantha J 6:31:50 (34,300)
Woods, Susan C 5:36:39 (31,072)
Woodward, Alison 3:33:40 (4,985)
Woodward, Amanda C 4:26:58 (17,745)
Woodward, Anja J 6:52:16 (34,758)
Woodward, Lesley 3:48:11 (7,631)
Woodyatt, Lucie E 3:36:17 (5,387)
Woolgar, Nicola J 5:39:10 (31,328)
Woolhouse, Cheryl M 5:51:51 (32,401)
Wooller, Diane E 3:51:56 (8,470)
Woolley, Jennifer L 5:58:04 (32,840)
Woolliscroft, Rachel L 4:22:26 (16,453)
Woolmer, Susie A 3:50:50 (8,219)
Woonton-Pink, Patricia M 5:16:23 (28,530)
Wooster, Joanne C 5:01:35 (26,079)
Wooster, Yvonne M 3:28:20 (4,164)
Wootton, Kelly A 3:44:49 (6,915)
Wordsworth, Sarah 5:59:38 (32,954)
Workman, Hayley 4:44:05 (22,113)
Workman, Joanna M 4:58:56 (25,541)
Workman, Lilsa 5:13:30 (28,085)
Workman, Sarita 6:25:41 (34,116)
Worsfold, Shirley A 3:23:01 (3,300)
Worsley, Elizabeth C 4:25:57 (17,413)
Worth, Iris L 8:13:27 (35,241)
Worth, Maria J 4:00:25 (10,808)
Wotherspoon, Jane 3:55:56 (9,498)
Wozniak, Catherine A 4:54:30 (24,551)
Wraight, Claire L 4:57:42 (25,263)
Wright, Alexandra 3:58:47 (10,382)
Wright, Alison S 7:09:57 (34,976)
Wright, Catherine 4:47:38 (22,922)
Wright, Chloe N 5:31:10 (30,482)
Wright, Claire R 4:15:58 (14,707)
Wright, Diane 3:52:10 (8,520)
Wright, Esther 4:24:10 (16,894)
Wright, Fiona E 4:47:51 (22,979)
Wright, Hilary S 5:07:55 (27,205)
Wright, Hollie E 4:27:17 (17,822)
Wright, Jennifer L 5:45:20 (31,883)
Wright, Jessica C 6:05:07 (33,274)
Wright, Joanne F 5:28:09 (30,134)
Wright, Joanne L 4:19:47 (15,748)
Wright, Karena C 4:29:40 (18,510)
Wright, Kate 3:50:14 (8,095)
Wright, Laura J 3:26:17 (3,808)
Wright, Lynn 5:02:01 (26,147)
Wright, Mandy 3:39:02 (5,823)
Wright, Maureen A 4:08:47 (12,764)
Wright, Melanie M 4:32:55 (19,295)
Wright, Rachel L 4:21:25 (16,179)
Wright, Sian L 4:52:12 (23,985)
Wright, Tracy 6:24:46 (34,085)
Wright, Vicki 5:00:56 (25,968)
Wright, Vivienne M 7:25:56 (35,106)
Wright, Winsome 5:28:22 (30,175)
Wrightman, Lana 4:13:00 (13,878)
Wrigley, Pamela J 3:52:41 (8,657)
Wrothington, Ruth M 3:53:50 (8,942)
Wyatt, Janet 6:55:39 (34,808)
Wyatt, Lynne 6:06:12 (33,340)
Wyatt, Margaret A 5:29:23 (30,292)
Wyatt, Paula 4:39:28 (21,001)
Wyatt, Rebecca J 5:25:33 (29,811)
Wylie, Jayne L 4:51:54 (23,913)
Wyndham, Anna J 4:30:12 (18,655)
Wynes, Fiona E 6:11:28 (33,592)
Wynne, Inez H 4:51:01 (23,736)
Wynne, Theresa A 3:35:51 (5,315)
Wythe, Rosalind M 5:24:28 (29,679)
Yamaguchi, Sandy 5:36:02 (30,998)
Yamamoto, Junko 6:07:15 (33,402)
Yamauchi, Mara 2:31:52 (85)
Yan, Zhiyan 5:47:23 (32,049)
Yardy, Jane M 4:12:40 (13,794)

Yardy, Sharon............................6:59:14 (34,857)
Yarroll, Louise M 4:22:41 (16,532)
Yasso, Laura 4:08:25 (12,675)
Yate, June 6:42:24 (34,552)
Yates, Gill A 4:28:53 (18,270)
Yates, Marilyn 5:25:18 (29,781)
Yea, Nicola A 5:12:45 (27,959)
Yeap, Victoria E 6:54:11 (34,785)
Yeats, Denise 4:02:43 (11,323)
Yelling, Liz 2:37:42 (150)
Yendley, Susan E 3:52:14 (8,537)
Yeo, Catherine S 5:42:22 (31,618)
Yeoman, Vivienne Y 4:56:22 (24,981)
Yeomans, Debra A 4:26:29 (17,593)
Yeomans, Melanie D 5:13:54 (28,150)
Yerbury, Katrina J 3:59:45 (10,649)
Yetton, Ami M 4:20:29 (15,936)
Yiasoumi, Fanny 5:28:36 (30,195)
Yingjie, Sun 2:42:05 (243)
Yong, Gladys F 3:49:54 (8,017)
York, Marie L 3:39:25 (5,896)
Yorke, Laura 5:43:29 (31,715)
Youel, Karen Y 5:06:52 (27,036)
Youle, Katharine J 6:58:38 (34,844)
Young, Alejandra Aida 4:14:49 (14,385)
Young, Andrea S 6:14:05 (33,706)
Young, Anna J 3:58:58 (10,423)
Young, Carole A 5:23:56 (29,609)
Young, Christine A 3:59:49 (10,667)
Young, Deborah M 5:44:48 (31,829)
Young, Dianne 5:44:24 (31,794)
Young, Elizabeth H 5:44:55 (31,840)
Young, Helen L 5:12:17 (27,868)
Young, Kate L 5:14:05 (28,182)
Young, Katharine E 4:54:24 (24,525)
Young, Katie A 5:39:31 (31,378)
Young, Lesley A 6:19:08 (33,892)
Young, Linda 4:34:01 (19,569)
Young, Michelle A 4:04:01 (11,640)
Young, Nina P 6:14:52 (33,730)
Young, Polly E 3:54:38 (9,135)
Young, Ruth H 5:31:10 (30,482)
Young, Sally J 5:07:23 (27,126)
Young, Sophie A 4:40:42 (21,310)
Young, Susan J 4:46:56 (22,757)
Young, Vanessa 5:31:10 (30,482)
Younger, Janet A 4:20:15 (15,875)
Younghusband, Linda V 4:45:58 (22,544)
Yuill, Chris 3:32:23 (4,803)
Yuill, Kathryn H 6:07:06 (33,394)
Yuill, Margaret A 5:35:48 (30,975)
Yvard, Patricia 4:11:56 (13,602)
Zajac, Jacqueline 3:47:56 (7,557)
Zakiewicz, Samantha G 4:35:25 (19,955)
Zaman, Sherry 6:17:56 (33,849)
Zardo, Judith 5:28:07 (30,126)

Zdanowicz, Lisa M 5:02:07 (26,170)
Zeeman, Laetitia 4:11:12 (13,406)
Zellick, Adam D 3:58:31 (10,293)
Zenzer, Helen 4:19:33 (15,680)
Zeytin, Simone 3:55:26 (9,347)
Ziemann, Jutta 5:05:13 (26,729)
Ziepe, Sarah 6:35:26 (34,392)
Zillig, Peter D 4:07:24 (12,438)
Zingale, Silvia 4:21:30 (16,207)
Zuckerman, Rachel 3:19:59 (2,994)
Zulberg, Jodi 3:37:09 (5,519)
Zulver, Allyn 4:23:30 (16,728)
Zurawliw, Susan R 3:57:46 (10,058)
Zwinggi, Barbara 3:56:04 (9,524)

WHEELCHAIR ENTRANTS

Adams, Jeff 1:35:54 (2)
Alldis, Brian 1:50:35 (13)
Allen, Geof 2:22:16 (28)
Brennan, Deborah 2:18:42 (26)
Brogan, Chris 3:36:16 (39)
Cassell, Ric 3:27:53 (37)
Cheek, Andrew 1:57:01 (19)
Derwin, Steve 3:18:50 (36)
Downing, Peter 3:02:42 (35)
Ferchl, Gottfried 1:49:44 (11)
Forde, Jerry 3:28:17 (38)
Fuss, Alain 1:36:04 (7)
Gill, Jason 1:56:18 (16)
Grey-Thompson, Tanni 2:02:39 (22)
Hanley, Chris 2:25:38 (30)
Herriot, Kenny 1:41:58 (8)
Holding, David 1:50:26 (12)
Koysap, Supachai 1:49:41 (10)
Lemeunier, Denis 1:36:04 (6)
Lewis, Michelle 2:32:32 (32)
Marten, Michael 3:41:42 (40)
Mendoza, Saul 1:35:51 (1)
O'Connor, Gerald 2:18:55 (27)
Patel, Tushar 1:36:03 (4)
Piercy, Sarah 2:48:24 (34)
Porcellato, Francesca 1:56:59 (18)
Powell, Richie 1:54:14 (15)
Qadir, Shaho 1:59:00 (21)
Richards, Jason 1:54:13 (14)
Richardson, Lee 2:15:58 (24)
Riggs, Stuart 2:23:52 (29)
Smith, Robert 2:35:30 (33)
Tana, Rawat 1:46:10 (9)
Teurnier, Eric 1:36:03 (5)
Turner, James 2:26:49 (31)
Wallengren, Gunilla 2:16:03 (25)
Weir, David 1:36:03 (3)
Williamson, Steve 1:56:33 (17)
Woods, Shelly 1:57:03 (20)
Worrell, Wesley 2:10:50 (23)

The 2006 London Marathon

In steady rain, the 2006 London Marathon was hit by the non-appearance of Paula Radcliffe – who had pulled out of this race injured. But once again it produced a new women's champion, Deena Kastor, who joined the elite club of women to have broken the 2:20 barrier.

Kastor, 33 years of age from the United States and a creative writing student, ran 2:19:36, the fourth fastest female time ever, winning £59,000 in prize money and bonuses. She appeared to damage a wrist in the slippery conditions when she stumbled into one of the food tables while trying to grab a drink. But it didn't put her off her stride and Kastor finished well ahead of Russia's Lyudmila Petrova who ran 2:21:29 and Kenyan Susan Chepkemei who clocked 2:21:46.

'The drizzle worked in the runners' favour and it didn't dampen the day for the crowds either,' said race director Dave Bedford. 'And all six of the first women finishers ran faster than they had before.'

Britain's best performance came from Mara Yamauchi and, although the Oxford-born runner was unable to deliver a home victory, her personal best of 2:25:13 put her second on the UK all-time list.

The men's race was a far closer finish and once again it boasted one of the strongest fields ever. The crowds over the final mile were treated to a sprint finish worthy of a track race as the Kenyan team-mates Felix Limo and Martin Lel, the defending champion, ran side by side and stride for stride. Limo finally shook off Lel in the last 200 meters as they rounded the bend by Buckingham Palace to win in 2:06:39 with Lel just 2 seconds behind. South Africa's Hendrick Ramaala finished third in 2:06:55.

But perhaps the bigger story was Haile Gebrselassie who again failed to make the impression on the London Marathon that many experts predicted he would. There were hopes that he might deliver a world record but the Ethiopian, the double Olympic 10,000m champion, who has set world records over the half marathon and 25km, faded to ninth after running with the pack for most of the race.

The British men seemed unable to handle the pace of the leading pack but Peter Riley (12th), Huw Lobb (15th) and Tomas Abyu (16th) achieved the qualifying mark of 2:16 for the 2006 European Championships in Gothenburg.

Britain's David Weir won the London wheelchair marathon for a second time, defying the wet conditions and a troublesome cold to break the course record in 1:29:48, so becoming the first racer to dip under 1:30 on the challenging London course. He finished some 8 minutes ahead of two-time winner Saul Mendoza.

Former winners Ernst Van Dyk and Denis Lemeunier crashed at a roundabout after three miles and by the 15-mile mark Weir was some 5 minutes clear of the field.

Meanwhile, Italian Francesca Porcellato claimed her fourth straight women's title despite suffering a puncture around five miles from the finish. Porcellato clocked 1:59:57 ahead of British teenager Shelly Woods with a time of 2:04:37. Fellow Britons Deborah Brennan and Sarah Piercy (who had won the 2005 race as a teenager) were third and fourth.

As well as celebrities such as chef Gordon Ramsay and Olympian Sir Steve Redgrave, the runners included three inmates from Standford Hill prison in Kent. Lloyd Scott, who completed the 2002 race in a diving suit, this time wore a suit

of armour and dragged an 8ft dragon to mark St George's Day.

A bride and groom, Katie Austin and Gordon Fryer from Romsey, Hampshire, dressed in an ivory bridal gown and morning suit, were married on Tower Bridge – halfway round the marathon route. They asked friends and family to make donations to charity rather than buying wedding presents.

The late Jade Goody, a former Big Brother contestant, admitted to having run only 30 minutes on a treadmill before the event and having prepared with a diet of curries and Chinese meals. The inevitable happened and she collapsed and failed to make it to the finish.

Paramedics spent 50 minutes frantically trying to regulate her breathing before rushing her to hospital for emergency treatment. Jade jogged just eight miles of the 26.2 mile course then spent four hours walking another ten before calling it a day at 18 miles.

Explanation of placing system

Each London Marathon year in this register is divided up into four categories: first, a summary of the **Elite Athletes**, containing names (last, first) and times (hours : minutes : seconds) of the top 50 male runners, top 50 female runners, top 3 male and top 2 female wheelchair entrants; then **Male Runners**, **Female Runners** and **Wheelchair Entrants**. These last three sections display the individual names and times of *every* entrant, including elite athletes, alphabetically and with their overall finishing position in that year's Marathon displayed in brackets alongside.

Some entrants have chosen to enhance past London Marathon entries with photos and recollections online at www.aubreybooks.com. Please visit the website to find out more about appearing in future editions.

ELITE ATHLETES

Top 50 male runners

Limo, Felix	2:06:39
Lel, Martin	2:06:41
Ramaala, Hendrick	2:06:55
Khannouchi, Khalid	2:07:04
Baldini, Stefano	2:07:22
Rop, Rogers	2:07:34
Chatt, Hicham	2:07:59
Gharib, Jaouad	2:08:45
Gebrselassie, Haile	2:09:05
Rutto, Evans	2:09:35
El Mouaziz, Abdelkader	2:10:24
Riley, Peter	2:14:31
Aburaya, Shigeru	2:14:49
Ziani, Kamel	2:14:50
Lobb, Huw	2:15:38
Abyu, Tomas	2:15:50
Cortes, Javier	2:15:51
Idland, Trond	2:16:09
Sandstad, Henrik	2:16:48
Sly, Phil	2:16:53
Rasmussen, Karl Johan	2:17:20
Leighton, Nigel	2:18:25
Gardiner, Richard	2:18:41
Green, Michael	2:19:14
Jones, Andi	2:19:16
Ogata, Tsuyoshi	2:19:17
McFarlane, John	2:19:24
Jensen, Dennis	2:19:37
Marriott, Adrian	2:20:30
Fisher, Ian	2:20:38
Kero, Jaakko	2:20:43
Osterlund, Kristoffer	2:21:08
Bangani, Pumlani	2:22:27
Buud, Jonas	2:22:28
Kieser, Fred	2:23:03
Norman, Dave	2:23:26

Simons, Dan	2:23:29
Grodseth, Henrik	2:24:59
Birchall, Chris	2:25:10
Normington, Matthew	2:25:18
Wardle, David	2:25:39
Martyn, Nicholas A.	2:26:08
Plant, Ray	2:26:13
Barnett, Ed	2:26:14
Harkness, Ian R.	2:26:41
Hunt, Andrew D.	2:26:49
Harris, Rod	2:27:26
Barrett, Simon J.	2:27:40
Simpson, Eddie	2:27:46
Boral, Jacek	2:28:02

Top 50 female runners

Kastor, Deena	2:19:36
Petrova, Lyudmila	2:21:29
Chepkemei, Susan	2:21:46
Adere, Berhane	2:21:52
Bogomolova, Galina	2:21:58
Yamauchi, Mara	2:25:13
Dita, Constantina	2:27:51
Kosgei, Salina	2:28:40
Okayo, Margaret	2:29:16
Hayakawa, Eri	2:31:41
Clague, Jenny	2:36:10
Larsen, Stine	2:37:31
Braham, Alice	2:40:38
May, Holly	2:44:59
Laithwaite, Gill	2:45:24
Salt, Adela M	2:47:41
Thornburgh, Imogen L	2:48:43
Dagne, Birhan	2:49:48
Schmidt, Elke	2:50:04
McKinnon, Maxine J	2:50:27
Yff, Barbara	2:50:36

Oakes, Fiona L	2:51:38
Colquhoun, Lucy A	2:51:48
Davies, Fiona	2:51:50
Leservoisier, Michelle	2:52:54
Perry, Victoria A	2:53:11
Myers, Malindi E	2:53:25
Archer, Nicole	2:53:52
Neal, Nikki H.	2:54:19
Ellis, Melanie J	2:54:23
Wilson, Heidi J	2:54:26
Cowley, Laura J	2:54:27
Briggs, Julie L	2:54:33
Archer, Emma J	2:54:34
Alexander, Roz	2:54:41
Hyde Peters, Zara	2:54:49
Peacock, Claire E	2:54:59
Dennison, Andrea M	2:55:13
Crowle, Revis M	2:55:45
Wilson, Beverley J	2:55:45
Gordon, Claire	2:55:58
Critchell, Dawn A	2:56:02
Care, Angharad	2:56:03
Preen, Jane L	2:56:06
Guilfoyle, Tracy	2:56:21
Green, Kim	2:56:42
Scully, Teresa N	2:56:42
Decker, Helen J	2:56:52
Cann, Claire M	2:56:56
Morrall, Zelah M	2:56:58

Top 3 male and top 2 female wheelchair entrants

Weir, David	1:29:48
Mendoza, Saul	1:37:52
Fuss, Alain	1:39:37
Porcellato, Francesca	1:59:57
Woods, Shelly	2:04:37

MALE RUNNERS

Aaland, Per Einar 3:17:12 (2,908)
Aaronovitch, David 4:24:12 (17,714)
Aartse-Tuyn, Guy 3:55:05 (10,240)
Aasmot, Rune 4:54:40 (24,808)
Abaroa, José Manuel 5:13:47 (27,743)
Abb, Jochen 4:32:33 (19,910)
Abbey, Nick J 3:58:06 (11,185)
Abbey, Simon R 4:34:55 (20,466)
Abbott, Brian J 3:58:38 (11,375)
Abbott, Gyles 3:27:23 (4,311)
Abbott, Ian C 3:44:16 (7,511)
Abbott, Ioulios G 3:55:49 (10,482)
Abbott, Laurence 4:23:56 (17,633)
Abbott, Paul 3:49:47 (8,816)
Abbs, Theodore H 4:00:51 (12,005)
Abecassis, Remi 3:23:57 (3,782)
Abel, Lawrence J 2:58:18 (1,045)
Abel, Peter W 4:47:04 (23,226)
Ab-Elwyn, Rhys 2:49:01 (498)
Abernethy, Andrew G 3:47:36 (8,270)
Abid, Rahil 4:06:50 (13,308)
Ablett, Howard R 5:33:13 (29,831)
Ablett, Justin P 3:30:28 (4,886)
Ablonczy, David 5:48:33 (30,971)
Abraham, Brian P 5:35:44 (30,030)
Abraham, Francisco 3:59:17 (11,599)
Abraham, Philip I 3:32:37 (5,268)
Abraham, Richard J 4:00:02 (11,828)
Abraham, William 4:14:47 (15,284)
Abraham, William J 5:32:27 (29,765)
Abrahams, Ian 8:06:27 (33,182)
Abrahams, Michael S 3:52:17 (9,435)
Abrahim, Harold S 3:39:56 (6,614)
Abram, Andy P 3:06:58 (1,755)
Abrami, Mauro 3:57:42 (11,072)
Abrams, Gary P 3:55:33 (10,387)
Absolon, James A 3:41:18 (6,872)
Abson, Michael J 4:54:01 (24,679)
Absoud, Michael A 5:32:04 (29,743)
Abuhagiar, Sofian K 3:37:27 (6,121)
Aburaya, Shigeru 2:14:49 (13)
Abyu, Tomas 2:15:50 (16)
Acar, Bektas 5:15:05 (27,910)
Acheson, Marc 4:30:45 (19,485)
Achte, Jean-Luc M 4:07:00 (13,346)
Ackers, Jeremy W 4:45:35 (22,920)
Ackroyd, Andrew 3:31:01 (4,987)
Ackroyd, Patrick M 4:42:23 (22,198)
Acs, Laszlo 2:55:09 (797)
Acton, Keith J 4:34:32 (20,371)
Acton, Raymond K 5:28:49 (29,413)
Acton, Robert P 3:14:53 (2,650)
Adam, Arnaud 3:53:59 (9,917)
Adam, François-Xavier 3:54:00 (9,923)
Adami, Mauro 3:19:55 (3,250)
Adams, Andrew P 5:06:23 (26,768)
Adams, Antony J 5:47:30 (30,918)
Adams, Chris P 3:57:38 (11,056)
Adams, Christopher J 3:02:33 (1,411)
Adams, Colin J 4:00:12 (11,864)
Adams, Henry 3:44:12 (7,491)
Adams, Ian 3:59:18 (11,604)
Adams, Jason R 4:28:45 (18,962)
Adams, Jeff 4:58:27 (25,596)
Adams, John H 4:09:03 (13,872)
Adams, John R 3:05:57 (1,660)
Adams, Jon P 5:11:17 (27,425)
Adams, Keith J 3:41:11 (6,849)
Adams, Keith W 5:19:06 (28,385)
Adams, Kevin L 4:32:43 (19,939)
Adams, Leslie 4:46:31 (23,124)
Adams, Liam 3:19:03 (3,138)
Adams, Mark D 4:07:35 (13,501)
Adams, Nick L 4:26:57 (18,495)
Adams, Paul A 5:08:41 (27,103)
Adams, Paul R 3:15:09 (2,678)
Adams, Richard 4:37:14 (21,039)
Adams, Richard D 3:24:29 (3,861)
Adams, Robert F 5:24:07 (28,958)
Adams, Wayne B 4:38:09 (21,273)
Adams, William M 3:49:41 (8,793)
Adamson, Daniel S 4:43:55 (22,554)
Adamson, David M 6:37:03 (32,565)
Adamson, David W 3:21:37 (3,486)
Adamson, Francis B 5:21:15 (28,638)
Adamson, Ken W 3:35:02 (5,669)
Adamson, Paul D 4:30:57 (19,521)
Adby, Geoff C 3:51:19 (9,178)
Adcock, Chris J 4:12:38 (14,734)
Adcock, Nicholas S 4:25:22 (18,079)
Addis, Peter J 4:53:46 (24,633)
Addison, Stephen 5:23:18 (28,870)
Addy, Paul G 3:55:56 (10,519)
Ade, Bradley F 4:08:04 (13,632)
Adegoke, Yinka 4:55:43 (25,040)
Adekoya, Anthony 4:09:57 (14,091)
Adeleye, Dayo 4:06:40 (13,265)
Adelsberg, Steven G 3:50:18 (8,933)
Ader, John M 7:04:22 (32,933)
Adesina, Adeyemi A 6:19:59 (32,228)
Adey, Matt 3:12:52 (2,384)
Adkin, Ian 2:57:45 (1,006)
Adkins, Christopher D 3:30:54 (4,963)
Adkins, David D 3:39:54 (6,606)
Adkins, Peter J 3:39:51 (6,597)
Adlam, Hugh 3:36:57 (6,029)
Adlam, Michael J 3:54:46 (10,128)
Adley, Nicholas P 5:26:07 (29,139)
Adlington, Paul J 4:21:34 (16,989)
Adnitt, Robert I 3:29:03 (4,634)
Adrat, Marc 3:24:42 (3,896)
Affleck, Michael V 3:37:14 (6,079)
Affleck, Robert J 3:38:53 (6,408)
Afforselles, Ben J 3:06:22 (1,699)
Afonso Neto, Luis M 4:40:26 (21,756)
Afshar, Dan 3:10:44 (2,134)
Afzal, Sultan M 7:38:53 (33,139)
Agar, Alexander R 3:43:29 (7,350)
Agar, Thomas P 4:15:35 (15,491)
Agbeze, Kalu 4:12:31 (14,710)
Agbo, Celestine O 4:19:51 (16,568)
Agbohlah, Senyo K 6:11:43 (31,978)
Agenbag, Pieter C 4:32:41 (19,931)
Ager, Kieran G 5:13:26 (27,711)
Ager, Simon 4:06:04 (13,154)
Ageros, Benjamin 3:03:35 (1,485)
Ageros, James 4:52:21 (24,320)
Aggleton, Lawrence J 4:41:40 (22,030)
Agnew, Sam A 2:55:28 (814)
Agui, Taro 3:49:43 (8,802)
Aguilar, Juan P 4:24:59 (17,953)
Aguilar, Octavio 4:40:16 (21,726)
Ahearne, Matthew J 3:44:23 (7,536)
Ahern, Brian J 4:46:50 (23,182)
Ahmed, Ishamael 4:34:52 (20,449)
Ahmed, Jahangir 4:24:17 (17,742)
Ahmed, Naeem 4:59:46 (25,844)
Ahmed, Sadeque 4:30:43 (19,477)
Ahuja, Anand S 5:10:29 (27,332)
Ahuja, Puneet 4:36:41 (20,885)
Ahuja, Raju N 5:14:59 (27,904)
Ahuja, Vijay Y 2:50:04 (551)
Aiken, Iain J 5:49:08 (31,008)
Aiken, Todd T 4:25:59 (18,253)
Aikman, Jonathan S 4:35:32 (20,607)
Aimable, Michael H 7:19:58 (33,041)
Aina, Antonio 5:21:57 (28,712)
Aina, Benjamin A 6:11:02 (31,957)
Aindow, Colin J 3:53:39 (9,806)
Ainley, Richard D 5:49:52 (31,062)
Ainscow, Edward K 2:50:35 (569)
Ainsley, David B 5:08:58 (27,144)
Ainslie, Cameron 5:05:03 (26,589)
Ainslie, Paul 3:12:30 (2,342)
Ainsworth, Christopher B 6:12:09 (31,993)
Ainsworth, Paul A 3:48:23 (8,470)
Ainsworth, Peter J 3:26:13 (4,105)
Ainsworth-Smith, Richard 4:47:24 (23,294)
Aird, Alastair G 4:19:24 (16,448)
Aird, Haydn J 3:45:42 (7,851)
Airey, Giles C 4:45:53 (22,985)
Airey, John 4:26:22 (18,352)
Airlie, Brian S 4:14:23 (15,179)
Aitchison, Ronald 3:39:41 (6,570)
Aitken, Andrew R 3:46:15 (7,955)
Aitken, Jamie M 4:21:38 (17,006)
Aitken, Mark W 4:39:03 (21,454)
Aitken, Murray J 3:43:44 (7,402)
Aitken, Neil E 2:59:21 (1,182)
Aitken, Nigel J 3:40:06 (6,641)
Aitkins, Donald P 3:42:07 (7,046)
Akenhead, David 6:01:39 (31,633)
Akeroyd, Philip F 3:57:12 (10,920)
Akhtar, Rahim 5:01:07 (26,063)
Alam, Aftab 4:32:44 (19,944)
Alam, Matt 6:45:18 (32,696)
Al-Azzawi, Ali 5:15:38 (27,965)
Alberola-Catalan, Antonio 3:42:34 (7,126)
Albertyn, Gregory R 4:56:05 (25,117)
Albon, Steven 4:01:28 (12,140)
Albutt, John W 5:31:35 (29,713)
Alcock, David 2:44:20 (324)
Alcock, John 3:50:21 (8,943)
Alden, Mark D 4:13:09 (14,888)
Aldersley, Mark A 3:24:46 (3,908)
Alderson, Ian D 4:23:48 (17,589)
Alderson, Paul V 3:36:04 (5,845)
Alderton, Colin N 4:34:56 (20,471)
Aldewereld, Patrick 4:24:36 (17,842)
Aldis, David 3:24:51 (3,919)
Aldred, David J 4:03:02 (12,489)
Aldred, Jason L 4:49:04 (23,666)
Aldred, Peter 4:09:10 (13,895)
Aldred, Simon J 4:04:33 (12,825)
Aldridge, Angus C 4:55:24 (24,983)
Aldridge, Ian D 4:45:00 (22,786)
Aldridge, James 3:58:12 (11,233)
Aldridge, Lewis 3:55:13 (10,290)
Aldridge, Michael 5:17:09 (28,146)
Aleman, Justin D 5:18:40 (28,331)
Alexander, David W 4:40:44 (21,837)
Alexander, James R 4:55:51 (25,066)
Alexander, James W 3:34:54 (5,642)
Alexander, Mark J 2:47:27 (436)
Alexander, Michael 3:56:58 (10,838)
Alexander, Michael D 5:49:09 (31,012)
Alexander, Mike P 4:06:35 (13,250)
Alexander, Ryan R 3:51:05 (9,118)
Alexander, Scott 5:03:03 (26,322)
Alexandrou, Antony 6:53:26 (32,801)
Alfert, Roland 3:11:40 (2,233)
Alford, Andrew W 4:26:30 (18,384)
Alford, Neil B 4:18:07 (16,144)
Algacs, Paul D 5:21:39 (28,680)
Ali, Arif R 4:46:31 (23,124)
Ali, Imtiaz 6:43:13 (32,658)
Ali, Irfan A 5:31:12 (29,678)
Ali, Mao M 5:56:04 (31,355)
Ali, Mohammed K 3:11:01 (2,158)
Ali, Yassar 4:44:44 (22,716)
Alibert, Marc 3:17:55 (2,987)
Aliberti, Giuseppe 2:50:56 (586)
Allan, Alistair G 3:09:43 (2,038)
Allan, Brad L 4:32:38 (19,923)
Allan, Crawford 3:41:09 (6,841)
Allan, David 5:05:52 (26,690)
Allan, David G 4:09:27 (13,981)
Allan, Ian 3:41:44 (6,972)
Allan, Richard W 4:47:43 (23,364)
Allan, Rod 3:22:19 (3,573)
Allan, Simon R 3:03:02 (1,444)
Allan, Stephen 3:31:00 (4,984)
Allan, William 2:55:42 (828)
Allan-Stubbs, Andrew J 5:22:38 (28,791)
Allan-Stubbs, Richard D 4:10:10 (14,142)
Allard, John G 3:12:19 (2,326)
Allard, Charles J Jnr 3:00:04 (1,238)
Allardice, Stephen J 4:43:37 (22,471)
Allaway, Jeffrey A 4:24:17 (17,742)
Allchurch, Graham P 4:01:51 (12,225)
Allcock, Alan C 5:15:51 (27,982)
Alldis, Michael A 3:12:31 (2,345)
Allebon, Toby D 4:27:33 (18,638)
Allen, Andrew E 4:26:06 (18,286)
Allen, Andrew J 4:08:23 (13,712)
Allen, Andrew N 4:04:40 (12,847)
Allen, Andrew P 3:23:16 (3,682)
Allen, Andy 5:06:09 (26,733)

Allen, Antony 6:32:54 (32,497)
Allen, Brian M 4:14:39 (15,242)
Allen, Charles 4:21:04 (16,883)
Allen, Christopher 3:59:26 (11,651)
Allen, Christopher P 3:58:44 (11,417)
Allen, Christos T 4:22:10 (17,162)
Allen, Crispin R 2:58:01 (1,023)
Allen, David J 4:38:02 (21,231)
Allen, David P 4:30:37 (19,457)
Allen, David R 4:13:52 (15,034)
Allen, David R 5:06:15 (26,748)
Allen, Gavin R 2:58:55 (1,131)
Allen, George F 4:01:56 (12,244)
Allen, Graham A 3:25:14 (3,968)
Allen, Hugh N 3:21:37 (3,486)
Allen, James 4:51:33 (24,155)
Allen, Jeremy 6:05:15 (31,768)
Allen, Jez 4:26:44 (18,443)
Allen, Jim K 3:53:01 (9,630)
Allen, John 6:19:27 (32,217)
Allen, John L 6:00:59 (31,605)
Allen, Jonathan P 3:56:32 (10,694)
Allen, Kai 5:59:43 (31,542)
Allen, Keith W 4:51:55 (24,236)
Allen, Kevin J 4:56:06 (25,119)
Allen, Kevin M 4:11:19 (14,420)
Allen, Luke 5:59:44 (31,543)
Allen, Mark 5:22:15 (28,747)
Allen, Mark C 4:26:56 (18,489)
Allen, Mark D 4:12:59 (14,831)
Allen, Neil 4:04:58 (12,912)
Allen, Neil V 4:59:38 (25,818)
Allen, Nicholas 3:59:52 (11,780)
Allen, Nigel D 4:47:03 (23,222)
Allen, Paul 3:33:58 (5,474)
Allen, Paul D 3:49:38 (8,780)
Allen, Peter 4:31:28 (19,656)
Allen, Philip 3:41:54 (7,008)
Allen, Ralph 4:20:52 (16,827)
Allen, Richard J 4:37:27 (21,097)
Allen, Richard T 4:34:13 (20,294)
Allen, Roland 4:44:18 (22,638)
Allen, Scott 6:32:41 (32,495)
Allen, Terence C 5:20:00 (28,492)
Allen, Tim 3:56:40 (10,746)
Allen, Tim D 4:09:28 (13,988)
Allen, Tim J 5:09:42 (27,226)
Allibone, Michael 3:59:45 (11,747)
Allier, Frederic 4:55:05 (24,914)
Allingham, Daniel M 5:40:39 (30,403)
Allingham, Richard 4:50:10 (23,871)
Allington, Brian 5:29:06 (29,434)
Allison, David 4:48:31 (23,543)
Allison, Mark 4:07:27 (13,457)
Allison, Stuart 4:25:11 (18,023)
Alliston, Andrew J 4:33:35 (20,159)
Allsop, Tim D 3:52:16 (9,431)
Allsopp, Brian 5:11:31 (27,461)
Allsopp, Criag 3:02:56 (1,437)
Allsopp, James R 4:27:30 (18,621)
Allsup, Jeremy 5:00:07 (25,908)
Allum, John S 6:14:34 (32,071)
Allum, Martin J 4:14:43 (15,263)
Allum, Philip W 4:54:53 (24,868)
Almond, Stuart T 4:36:03 (20,736)
Alon, Shlomo 4:41:23 (21,966)
Alonso, Dave 4:22:33 (17,252)
Alonso, Ernesto 3:15:40 (2,737)
Aloof, Brian H 6:25:15 (32,359)
Alouani, Sami 3:48:26 (8,483)
Alpendre, Luis M 3:51:38 (9,252)
Alsaidi, Hashim T 5:23:05 (28,843)
Al-Salim, Atheer 4:32:43 (19,939)
Alsey, Simon J 4:01:44 (12,197)
Alsop, Mark F 3:58:38 (11,375)
Alston, Richard 3:31:18 (5,036)
Altham-Lewis, Paul 3:56:40 (10,746)
Altknecht, Holger 3:38:16 (6,285)
Alty, Robert L 5:13:16 (27,688)
Aluarez Meijide, José Luis 3:53:02 (9,638)
Alun Jones, Tom 5:06:49 (26,840)
Alvarenz, Angelo 3:40:51 (6,770)
Alvarez, Damian 3:52:26 (9,481)
Alvarez, Pedro 3:55:10 (10,264)
Alvarez, Salvador 3:54:28 (10,042)
Alzard, Alain 3:52:33 (9,506)
Alzard, Gerard 4:46:01 (23,008)
Amadi, Paul 4:20:09 (16,644)
Amarjit, Singh Gill 5:39:57 (30,359)
Amata, Kico 5:00:45 (26,000)
Amatt, Robert 3:34:30 (5,566)
Amatzidis, Jason J 5:08:58 (27,144)
Ambler, Ian C 4:55:19 (24,963)
Ambler, Richard C 4:19:39 (16,516)
Ambridge, Paul R 5:34:58 (29,964)
Ambrose, Mark S 3:35:04 (5,684)
Ambrose, Ronnie 4:12:40 (14,742)
Ambrose, Simon 4:45:13 (22,840)
Ambrosio, Carlos 4:40:31 (21,791)
Amer, Stephen 5:20:44 (28,584)
Amestoy, Christophe 3:05:52 (1,654)
Amestoy, Frederic 3:17:14 (2,915)
Amin, Saj 5:19:32 (28,441)
Amistani, Gabriel 4:16:05 (15,620)
Amla, Ismail 3:53:08 (9,672)
Amory, Stuart 5:31:34 (29,711)
Amos, James B 3:33:53 (5,460)
Amos, Mark D 3:02:46 (1,422)
Amos, Philip J 4:02:12 (12,305)
Amson, Derek 4:55:40 (25,032)
Amtmann, Werner 3:30:41 (4,929)
Amy, Thomas 3:54:39 (10,091)
Anand, Ankur 5:02:16 (26,215)
Ancona, Luca 3:49:40 (8,790)
Andersen, Anders Leon 4:15:38 (15,503)
Andersen, Benny 4:07:16 (13,415)
Andersen, Bo 3:38:00 (6,222)
Andersen, Reidar 3:23:01 (3,659)
Anderson, Alexander 5:44:06 (30,649)
Anderson, Andy D 4:36:58 (20,973)
Anderson, Anthony D 4:45:01 (22,791)
Anderson, Brian P 3:09:18 (1,983)
Anderson, Cameron J 4:10:51 (14,294)
Anderson, Christopher E 4:45:14 (22,845)
Anderson, Crawford G 3:51:21 (9,190)
Anderson, Daniel J 2:35:46 (125)
Anderson, David 4:35:35 (20,618)
Anderson, David K 3:56:05 (10,563)
Anderson, Dean S 5:41:12 (30,432)
Anderson, Derrick J 3:17:06 (2,899)
Anderson, Des J 4:12:09 (14,612)
Anderson, Ian 4:23:44 (17,571)
Anderson, Ian S 2:38:10 (169)
Anderson, James A 4:22:38 (17,283)
Anderson, James S 5:46:12 (30,802)
Anderson, Jamie T 4:27:07 (18,533)
Anderson, John M 4:27:39 (18,671)
Anderson, Kean J 2:53:47 (711)
Anderson, Kevin J 4:20:28 (16,727)
Anderson, Mark R 3:12:15 (2,317)
Anderson, Michael R 3:08:06 (1,871)
Anderson, Neil R 3:49:24 (8,718)
Anderson, Olle 4:09:04 (13,874)
Anderson, Stephen L 4:20:43 (16,793)
Anderson, Stuart J 5:59:52 (31,553)
Anderson, Terence W 3:48:14 (8,439)
Anderson, Tim R 3:51:53 (9,329)
Anderson, Tony 4:27:09 (18,542)
Anderson, Trevor M 4:55:56 (25,085)
Anderton, James P 3:32:25 (5,236)
Anderton-Brown, Robin J 3:28:16 (4,456)
Andrade, Pedro 5:13:34 (27,727)
Andreadis, Alexander 4:04:28 (12,810)
Andreotti, Jean-Louis 4:04:13 (12,760)
Andrew, Chris 4:35:20 (20,563)
Andrew, Darren M 3:45:53 (7,884)
Andrew, Kevin J 3:55:04 (10,233)
Andrew, Peter J 5:41:34 (30,460)
Andrew, Sam M 2:57:55 (1,015)
Andrews, Christopher D 5:27:37 (29,284)
Andrews, Christopher M 5:06:29 (26,785)
Andrews, David J 3:27:47 (4,375)
Andrews, David J 3:43:55 (7,443)
Andrews, Henry T 3:14:32 (2,600)
Andrews, Ian A 4:00:53 (12,012)
Andrews, Jeffrey B 5:11:55 (27,515)
Andrews, Julian R 4:10:06 (14,121)
Andrews, Kyle 3:26:08 (4,091)
Andrews, Mark P 5:31:59 (29,736)
Andrews, Mark V 3:14:24 (2,583)
Andrews, Neil K 4:00:52 (12,009)
Andrews, Richard M 3:52:04 (9,375)
Andrews, Ricky 4:54:33 (24,792)
Andrews, Robert J 3:20:18 (3,312)
Andrews, Steven J 4:10:46 (14,266)
Andrews, Terry 3:54:17 (9,997)
Angell, Dean P 2:58:20 (1,050)
Angiulli, Raffaele 4:34:23 (20,335)
Angol, Michael 5:14:00 (27,760)
Angove, Barry 4:19:49 (16,557)
Angus, Steve 2:51:30 (612)
Anjomshoaa, Ali 3:46:43 (8,066)
Anjum, Zabair 5:34:53 (29,958)
Ankers, Stephen A 3:45:20 (7,765)
Anley, Brian J 5:28:10 (29,349)
Annable, Jon 4:59:35 (25,807)
Annand, Nathan 4:53:50 (24,642)
Anne, Joel 3:52:34 (9,510)
Annecke, Andreas 3:14:36 (2,615)
Annells, Peter M 4:54:31 (24,781)
Annetts, Martyn 3:24:39 (3,889)
Annetts, Sean 4:23:07 (17,391)
Ansari, Asif S 5:21:02 (28,611)
Ansell, Andrew P 4:26:01 (18,263)
Ansell, David V 4:46:39 (23,147)
Ansell, Jack E 4:21:58 (17,108)
Ansell, Leonard A 5:48:50 (30,993)
Ansell, Martin J 4:09:17 (13,928)
Anstee, Nick J 4:50:00 (23,843)
Anstiss, Steven D 3:25:00 (3,931)
Antanelis, Ricardas 4:41:43 (22,039)
Antcliff, Andrew J 3:05:58 (1,663)
Antcliffe, Mark J 3:01:09 (1,314)
Antelme, Mark C 3:51:16 (9,165)
Anthony, Simon J 4:34:10 (20,286)
Antignac, Jean-Luc 4:30:34 (19,442)
Antolik, Bryan 3:43:22 (7,326)
Antomarchi, Olivier 3:55:39 (10,416)
Antonacci, Ignazio 2:53:31 (699)
Antonelos, Evaggelos 3:25:20 (3,980)
Antoniou, Alexandros 4:59:39 (25,823)
Antonoff, Nicolas 4:34:37 (20,391)
Antrobus, Daniel P 4:02:58 (12,470)
Antrobus, Philip R 4:29:48 (19,250)
Antscherl, Robert J 3:54:08 (9,953)
Appell, Nicholas P 4:53:49 (24,639)
Apperley, Ian J 3:01:11 (1,318)
Apperley, John 3:36:24 (5,914)
Applebee, John 5:25:02 (29,041)
Appleby, Bryan J 4:23:29 (17,496)
Appleby, David 3:14:35 (2,611)
Appleby, David 3:33:59 (5,479)
Appleby, John P 5:35:29 (30,011)
Appleby, Paul A 3:37:54 (6,208)
Appleby, Rodney J 3:26:58 (4,237)
Appleby, Tony 4:14:00 (15,067)
Applegate, Matthew R 4:12:17 (14,645)
Appleton, Andrew M 4:38:59 (21,436)
Appleyard, David K 3:45:12 (7,730)
Appleyard, Nyall L 4:37:37 (21,142)
Apps, Dan 4:13:21 (14,931)
Apps, Paul R 3:47:20 (8,200)
Apps, Phillip 5:00:54 (26,028)
Aprahamian, Miran W 3:42:43 (7,159)
Aptel, Steven 5:33:01 (29,818)
Aram, Jim W 5:08:02 (27,011)
Arbour, Adrian J 3:05:14 (1,597)
Arch, Cliff J 5:26:06 (29,136)
Archbold, Stuart 4:55:08 (24,926)
Archer, Anthony M 4:27:07 (18,533)
Archer, Anthony W 3:06:18 (1,695)
Archer, Brian P 4:49:45 (23,801)
Archer, Jeff 3:49:08 (8,653)
Archer, Mark J 3:00:32 (1,275)
Archer, Micah 4:03:46 (12,665)
Archer, Nathan P 3:56:03 (10,552)
Archer, Paul A 4:11:22 (14,432)
Archer, Paul D 5:53:06 (31,221)
Archer-Thomson, John H 4:42:33 (22,230)

Ardron, Simon A	3:55:43 (10,444)	
Arens, Michael	3:59:30 (11,672)	
Arentoft, Preben	5:06:33 (26,793)	
Arezoi, Fateh M	8:30:09 (33,207)	
Argent, Alan W	4:53:04 (24,468)	
Arguelles, Antonio	3:24:48 (3,912)	
Argyrou, Nicholas A	5:34:23 (29,920)	
Arias, Antonio	4:19:15 (16,408)	
Aries, James A	3:35:02 (5,669)	
Arkell, Chris	4:34:39 (20,397)	
Armist, Ronnie	3:52:40 (9,544)	
Armit, Neil	4:33:35 (20,159)	
Armitage, George B	3:42:39 (7,145)	
Armitage, John W	3:44:21 (7,533)	
Armitage, Philip	4:27:32 (18,633)	
Armitage, Richard	4:00:48 (11,993)	
Armitage, Richard G	4:26:18 (18,335)	
Armour, William	4:13:37 (14,979)	
Armstrong, Alexander	3:47:35 (8,266)	
Armstrong, Allister J	3:59:20 (11,617)	
Armstrong, Brendan J	3:13:29 (2,466)	
Armstrong, Craig D	5:00:57 (26,034)	
Armstrong, Graeme R	3:47:59 (8,378)	
Armstrong, Jack W	4:21:17 (16,934)	
Armstrong, Mark	3:38:51 (6,396)	
Armstrong, Mark A	2:44:08 (316)	
Armstrong, Mark F	5:16:43 (28,095)	
Armstrong, Matthew F	5:29:40 (29,502)	
Armstrong, Michael M	3:29:10 (4,649)	
Armstrong, Nigel J	2:44:32 (330)	
Armstrong, Peter H	3:07:58 (1,856)	
Armstrong, Robert B	5:49:50 (31,059)	
Armstrong, Robert G	4:13:39 (14,994)	
Armstrong, Shaun	3:51:20 (9,185)	
Armstrong, Stephen	3:19:45 (3,222)	
Armstrong, Thomas T	5:51:20 (31,146)	
Armstrong, Tom R	4:04:40 (12,847)	
Arndt, Detlef	3:55:40 (10,427)	
Arnett, Ellis O	4:11:17 (14,413)	
Arnett, Leslie F	4:11:17 (14,413)	
Arnold, Andy	4:11:06 (14,359)	
Arnold, Chris	4:25:51 (18,210)	
Arnold, Colin J	2:51:31 (613)	
Arnold, Daryl L	3:08:19 (1,887)	
Arnold, Dave	3:16:55 (2,868)	
Arnold, Gresham T	3:59:26 (11,651)	
Arnold, Jack S	3:20:12 (3,299)	
Arnold, Martin J	5:22:15 (28,747)	
Arnold, Matthew B	3:39:08 (6,462)	
Arnold, Philippe	6:15:32 (32,102)	
Arnold, Richard E	3:54:11 (9,972)	
Arnold, Simon P	3:54:51 (10,160)	
Arnold, Stephen M	3:57:48 (11,115)	
Arnold, Stuart M	4:17:20 (15,940)	
Arnott, Alan M	3:48:02 (8,392)	
Arnott, Richard J	5:08:52 (27,129)	
Arnoux, Alain	4:01:43 (12,192)	
Aronowitz, Daniel	3:40:37 (6,731)	
Arribas Perez, Javier	3:45:10 (7,723)	
Arrowsmith, James R	3:43:42 (7,389)	
Arrowsmith, Mark	2:57:56 (1,017)	
Arthey, Chris	3:09:23 (1,998)	
Arthur, John	3:28:56 (4,609)	
Arthur, Nigel A	3:38:43 (6,367)	
Arthur, Richard	3:57:59 (11,153)	
Arthur, Steve	4:21:20 (16,941)	
Ash, Daniel K	3:55:24 (10,345)	
Ash, Dominic S	3:45:55 (7,889)	
Ash, Justinian	3:58:46 (11,431)	
Ash, Peter D	3:34:47 (5,626)	
Ash, Roger G	4:28:14 (18,820)	
Ashburn, Justin P	4:16:24 (15,691)	
Ashby, Charles E	3:15:25 (2,710)	
Ashby, Jonathan	4:59:20 (25,750)	
Ashby, Mark	2:57:56 (1,017)	
Ashby, Stephen D	4:38:06 (21,261)	
Ashcroft, Anthony G	4:38:58 (21,434)	
Ashcroft, Paul S	4:01:35 (12,168)	
Ashfield, Jody R	5:01:14 (26,078)	
Ashfield, Thomas A	4:05:23 (12,994)	
Ashford, Brian C	5:18:28 (28,304)	
Ashford, Lee G	4:47:48 (23,382)	
Ashford, Martin K	4:25:32 (18,123)	
Ashley, Jonathan P	3:56:19 (10,630)	
Ashley, Philip J	4:15:40 (15,512)	
Ashley, Stephen R	4:21:56 (17,095)	
Ashley, Steven A	4:29:17 (19,115)	
Ashman, Rod J	4:34:16 (20,302)	
Ashmead, Shaun	5:11:49 (27,496)	
Ashmore, Mark	3:55:11 (10,275)	
Ashpool, Gavin D	3:33:24 (5,388)	
Ashraf, Muhammad	4:24:55 (17,930)	
Ashraf, Shahbaz	4:15:20 (15,425)	
Ashton, Jim E	3:50:09 (8,902)	
Ashton, Mark S	3:57:30 (11,014)	
Ashton, Martin	5:25:02 (29,041)	
Ashton, Robert G	5:18:04 (28,248)	
Ashton, Simon	3:47:12 (8,168)	
Ashton, Timothy C	4:00:35 (11,946)	
Ashurst, Stephen	3:44:09 (7,480)	
Ashwood, Brian	4:36:11 (20,774)	
Ashworth, Andrew	4:03:50 (12,681)	
Ashworth, John H	4:31:23 (19,638)	
Ashworth, Jonathan D	3:06:07 (1,678)	
Ashworth, Mike I	3:35:39 (5,775)	
Ashworth, Trevor	4:21:41 (17,018)	
Asiedu, Eric K	4:17:34 (16,003)	
Askew, David	4:05:34 (13,040)	
Askew, Gerald A	4:44:10 (22,598)	
Askew, Jason M	4:50:02 (23,848)	
Askew, Mark D	4:00:07 (11,851)	
Askew, Nick J	3:05:49 (1,646)	
Askey, Gareth E	4:42:18 (22,176)	
Askey, Paul K	5:37:56 (30,198)	
Askin, Daron G	3:54:24 (10,028)	
Aspden, Kester D	4:22:03 (17,130)	
Aspden, Stephen	3:58:05 (11,178)	
Aspinall, Nathan E	2:44:41 (338)	
Aspinall, Steven	5:44:37 (30,687)	
Aspland, Jason R	3:39:13 (6,484)	
Astier, Christophe	4:44:55 (22,763)	
Astle, Thomas W	2:59:37 (1,212)	
Astley, David	3:24:12 (3,821)	
Aston, Andrew	2:51:17 (605)	
Aston, Andrew J	4:50:55 (24,028)	
Aston, Christopher	3:29:05 (4,638)	
Aston, Darren R	5:45:13 (30,732)	
Aston, David J	4:33:00 (20,008)	
Aston, Edgar	3:29:20 (4,684)	
Aston, Jeffrey R	3:47:50 (8,336)	
Aston, John	3:06:02 (1,670)	
Aston, Jon R	4:35:08 (20,516)	
Aston, Michael J	3:53:22 (9,736)	
Astridge, Andrew W	6:13:04 (32,021)	
Atefi, Paul	3:45:16 (7,745)	
Athawes, Jon	4:00:30 (11,934)	
Atherfold, Paul	4:21:41 (17,018)	
Atherton, Dennis	4:40:32 (21,797)	
Atherton, John L	4:25:43 (18,163)	
Atherton, Jonathon	7:03:23 (32,913)	
Atherton, Lawrence J	4:56:45 (25,249)	
Athwal, Ranjeet	4:14:52 (15,303)	
Atkin, Antony C	3:42:56 (7,217)	
Atkin, Rob J	2:34:28 (107)	
Atkins, Craig G	5:59:58 (31,560)	
Atkins, Edward A	3:56:04 (10,558)	
Atkins, Gary	3:33:36 (5,421)	
Atkins, James P	3:21:15 (3,431)	
Atkins, John P	3:33:00 (5,322)	
Atkins, Michael J	4:05:00 (12,918)	
Atkins, Paul K	2:58:47 (1,112)	
Atkins, Robert W	4:32:42 (19,934)	
Atkins, Samuel	4:13:48 (15,023)	
Atkins, Sean	3:47:49 (8,332)	
Atkins, Ted R	4:32:59 (20,000)	
Atkins, Tim J	3:38:40 (6,360)	
Atkinson, Andrew S	3:51:19 (9,178)	
Atkinson, Bernard T	6:25:20 (32,353)	
Atkinson, Chris J	3:19:53 (3,246)	
Atkinson, Colin C	3:06:26 (1,706)	
Atkinson, David A	4:05:49 (13,103)	
Atkinson, David S	3:12:35 (2,351)	
Atkinson, Ian A	3:02:08 (1,387)	
Atkinson, Ian J	3:54:25 (10,030)	
Atkinson, Ian J	4:03:43 (12,654)	
Atkinson, James S	4:49:05 (23,669)	
Atkinson, Lewis P	5:26:40 (29,182)	
Atkinson, Paul J	4:18:17 (16,178)	
Atkinson, Tony J	3:28:05 (4,420)	
Attar-Zadeh, Darush	4:44:13 (22,615)	
Attfield, Jeremy M	4:40:11 (21,708)	
Attfield, Richard	4:08:44 (13,792)	
Atton, Karl R	3:18:39 (3,088)	
Attrell, Ben S	4:10:19 (14,176)	
Attri, Krishan Kant	5:49:18 (31,024)	
Attwood, Anthony N	5:22:35 (28,786)	
Atwell, Christopher	3:11:53 (2,256)	
Atwill, David	4:24:21 (17,764)	
Audas, Algie J	3:21:20 (3,445)	
Audenshaw, Tony	2:58:49 (1,117)	
Audis, David W	3:29:21 (4,689)	
Auf der Heiden, Friedrich	4:56:00 (25,105)	
Auger, Martin J	3:38:24 (6,303)	
Augeri, John Paul	3:56:15 (10,610)	
Aukett, John P	4:18:15 (16,169)	
Auld, Chris W	3:29:17 (4,671)	
Auld, Gary	5:23:59 (28,935)	
Aulinger, Albert	4:23:20 (17,452)	
Ault, Stephen W	3:55:56 (10,519)	
Austen, Simon J	5:12:02 (27,527)	
Austen-Reed, Phillip M	4:40:47 (21,848)	
Austin, Alan	4:05:27 (13,011)	
Austin, Christopher W	3:19:46 (3,225)	
Austin, Clive	3:37:53 (6,206)	
Austin, Craig S	3:55:55 (10,514)	
Austin, Derek G	4:06:51 (13,311)	
Austin, Frederick J	8:27:42 (33,203)	
Austin, Huw R	3:42:02 (7,030)	
Austin, Michael B	4:55:57 (25,091)	
Austin, Paul A	4:58:21 (25,578)	
Austin, Robert W	7:37:36 (33,132)	
Austin, Shaun	5:04:24 (26,513)	
Austin, Simon J	3:49:57 (8,857)	
Austin, William R	3:44:46 (7,631)	
Avantario, Giuseppe	4:44:46 (22,724)	
Avanzato, Roberto	2:56:12 (869)	
Avara, Oner	3:45:07 (7,712)	
Avery, Joe A	3:04:59 (1,573)	
Avery, Leo J	3:24:29 (3,861)	
Avery, Matthew	5:08:27 (27,070)	
Aves, Clayton A	3:11:22 (2,203)	
Avey, Lee K	4:16:54 (15,833)	
Avey, Terry J	4:14:01 (15,074)	
Avigad, Daniel	2:58:41 (1,094)	
Aviles, Elias Z	3:27:55 (4,397)	
Avison, Matthew F	4:04:49 (12,880)	
Aviss, Tim H	4:52:25 (24,334)	
Avital, Yoni	4:27:27 (18,600)	
Avramovich, Ruben	4:16:34 (15,743)	
Awad, Samer	4:50:57 (24,037)	
Axam, Gary L	3:29:12 (4,654)	
Axon, Terry	3:41:51 (6,999)	
Axten, Godfrey	4:33:18 (20,085)	
Ayam-Lau, Genaro	4:59:46 (25,844)	
Ayers, Robert	3:18:00 (2,996)	
Ayers, Tim S	5:14:57 (27,899)	
Ayinbode, Augustine	4:02:08 (12,295)	
Ayles, Duncan M	4:10:38 (14,240)	
Aylett, Jason R	3:50:09 (8,902)	
Ayling, John	5:31:15 (29,687)	
Ayling, Samuel J	3:30:58 (4,976)	
Aylott, Michael C	3:22:36 (3,613)	
Aylott, Wayne T	4:06:49 (13,303)	
Aynge, Alan W	4:54:06 (24,695)	
Aynsley, Graham D	4:50:55 (24,028)	
Ayo, Leon P	4:05:22 (12,991)	
Ayres, Alan	3:04:05 (1,519)	
Ayres, Andrew E	4:55:50 (25,061)	
Ayres, Arthur J	4:01:28 (12,140)	
Ayres, Paul A	3:18:51 (3,114)	
Ayres, Roger M	4:13:07 (14,878)	
Azad, Iqbal S	3:58:01 (11,156)	
Azevedo, Miiguel J	4:43:46 (22,510)	
Aziz, Damian	4:18:34 (16,248)	
Baarlid, Christian	3:59:48 (11,762)	
Babajide, Michael O	5:38:23 (30,240)	
Babb, Ian	4:21:31 (16,977)	
Babbage, Jason A	5:00:00 (25,884)	
Babington, Duncan	4:03:51 (12,683)	

Babynec, Wayne A 4:11:47 (14,516)
Bacchi-Andreoli, James 5:27:27 (29,265)
Baci, Arber 2:40:49 (227)
Bacon, Christopher F 4:13:10 (14,893)
Bacon, Guy T 3:59:09 (11,560)
Bacon, James M 3:14:34 (2,608)
Bacon, Jonathan P 3:58:51 (11,464)
Bacon, Matthew J 3:57:12 (10,920)
Bacon, Matthew J 4:24:31 (17,806)
Bacon, Nick A 4:07:04 (13,360)
Bacon, Walter R 4:24:01 (17,661)
Badcock, Fraser O 5:47:44 (30,931)
Baddeley, Steve P 3:53:07 (9,665)
Badder, Stephen 4:35:59 (20,718)
Bader, Brett S 6:21:16 (32,263)
Bader, Ronald 3:50:25 (8,959)
Badger, Jonathan 3:36:52 (6,012)
Badger, Lew 3:36:05 (5,851)
Badham, Neil A 3:30:39 (4,924)
Badillo, José 3:57:18 (10,949)
Baechler, Stefan 4:02:52 (12,449)
Baehrens, Christian 3:28:50 (4,585)
Baessler-Vogel, Cerret 4:15:48 (15,544)
Baggaley, Clive R 3:20:42 (3,363)
Baggaley, Paul 4:26:35 (18,403)
Baggaley, Philip J 3:36:04 (5,845)
Baggaley, Stephen 4:13:48 (15,023)
Baggott, Barry J 6:52:07 (32,783)
Bagley, John R 5:28:02 (29,326)
Bagnall, Gary B 2:57:03 (947)
Bagshaw, Andrew 3:57:53 (11,130)
Bagshaw, John A 4:36:14 (20,791)
Bagshaw, Ross A 4:26:51 (18,475)
Baguley, Paul A 3:24:22 (3,844)
Bahadursingh, Prithiviraj 5:21:56 (28,709)
Bahra, Davinder S 6:10:20 (31,935)
Baigent, Derek 2:56:06 (857)
Bailes, Jonathan P 5:08:37 (27,094)
Bailes, Peter L 5:51:44 (31,168)
Bailey, Andreas N 6:11:37 (31,972)
Bailey, Andy M 5:01:23 (26,095)
Bailey, Andy N 3:53:05 (9,660)
Bailey, Bernard J 5:12:35 (27,599)
Bailey, Brian P 3:32:08 (5,184)
Bailey, Chris 5:09:05 (27,158)
Bailey, Cliff P 2:55:44 (830)
Bailey, Daniel R 5:24:50 (29,020)
Bailey, David B 4:40:08 (21,697)
Bailey, David F 6:18:30 (32,184)
Bailey, Dennis J 5:38:53 (30,272)
Bailey, Frank 4:35:07 (20,513)
Bailey, Geoff S 3:47:12 (8,168)
Bailey, Harry B 6:18:27 (32,181)
Bailey, Ian 3:07:47 (1,837)
Bailey, Ian M 4:35:19 (20,559)
Bailey, Jess R 5:12:54 (27,632)
Bailey, Joseph 4:31:23 (19,638)
Bailey, Justin J 3:53:27 (9,755)
Bailey, Kevin 4:12:10 (14,616)
Bailey, Kevin D 6:38:49 (32,596)
Bailey, Mark J 4:35:55 (20,692)
Bailey, Michael J 5:03:23 (26,373)
Bailey, Michael J 5:09:20 (27,187)
Bailey, Mrcus P 4:29:29 (19,174)
Bailey, Nicholas M 4:08:35 (13,766)
Bailey, Nigel A 4:05:59 (13,137)
Bailey, Richard J 4:29:19 (19,122)
Bailey, Robert O 4:40:19 (21,737)
Bailey, Thomas B 4:12:11 (14,620)
Bailey, Thomas W 5:45:03 (30,721)
Bailey Wood, Colin M 2:51:08 (600)
Bailie, Derrick 3:25:22 (3,991)
Baillie, Andrew N 3:57:34 (11,033)
Baillie, Kenneth 5:47:03 (30,864)
Baillie, Michael J 2:44:06 (315)
Baillie, Stephen 3:49:14 (8,674)
Bain, Alan T 4:27:58 (18,739)
Bain, Andrew G 4:11:58 (14,566)
Bainbridge, Andrew 4:05:25 (13,003)
Bainbridge, Daniel J 4:30:09 (19,335)
Baines, Jonathan N 4:16:14 (15,652)
Baines, Mark A 5:10:33 (27,342)
Baines, Michael 3:37:41 (6,163)
Baines, Paul J 3:52:37 (9,526)
Bainger, Graham E 3:58:32 (11,350)
Baird, Danny 4:27:41 (18,677)
Baisden, Kevin J 5:05:12 (26,611)
Baixauli, José B 5:24:11 (28,964)
Bajaj, Robert 3:59:12 (11,577)
Bakacs, Gyorgy 3:58:38 (11,375)
Baker, Andrew H 3:38:22 (6,297)
Baker, Bjorn P 3:39:37 (6,557)
Baker, Christopher 3:57:06 (10,883)
Baker, Christopher C 3:20:09 (3,289)
Baker, Clive A 3:00:50 (1,291)
Baker, David J 4:51:49 (24,214)
Baker, David J 6:00:29 (31,582)
Baker, Duncan 3:18:19 (3,034)
Baker, Eamon J 4:04:39 (12,845)
Baker, Gary 5:06:38 (26,807)
Baker, Gary A 4:21:58 (17,108)
Baker, Graham 3:11:22 (2,203)
Baker, Gregory P 3:45:01 (7,693)
Baker, Ian D 3:57:34 (11,033)
Baker, Ian R 4:38:03 (21,239)
Baker, Jason G 3:47:37 (8,276)
Baker, Julian D 2:37:00 (145)
Baker, Justin P 4:13:49 (15,025)
Baker, Justin R 3:20:31 (3,340)
Baker, Kim P 3:34:34 (5,585)
Baker, Leslie 5:29:47 (29,518)
Baker, Luke 4:05:46 (13,090)
Baker, Mark 3:05:26 (1,620)
Baker, Mark N 4:55:53 (25,074)
Baker, Martin 4:27:09 (18,542)
Baker, Martyn J 3:53:47 (9,853)
Baker, Michael P 5:11:41 (27,479)
Baker, Neal 4:53:17 (24,520)
Baker, Neil S 4:56:15 (25,150)
Baker, Newar 4:19:30 (16,478)
Baker, Nicholas 3:42:02 (7,030)
Baker, Nick M 2:40:44 (225)
Baker, Nigel G 5:27:19 (29,254)
Baker, Patrick 4:05:34 (13,040)
Baker, Paul A 5:04:15 (26,480)
Baker, Philip 4:28:41 (18,940)
Baker, Richard H 4:47:37 (23,347)
Baker, Richard W 4:24:26 (17,785)
Baker, Robin 4:42:47 (22,278)
Baker, Simon R 4:39:16 (21,505)
Baker, Stuart 3:49:37 (8,775)
Baker, Tony 4:20:35 (16,754)
Baker, Trevor D 5:36:30 (30,094)
Baker-Smith, Hugh 4:18:16 (16,174)
Balcombe, Darren 4:01:52 (12,228)
Baldeo, André D 4:29:52 (19,261)
Baldini, Stefano 2:07:22 (5)
Baldock, Neil S 4:40:26 (21,756)
Baldwin, Adrian N 4:59:52 (25,862)
Baldwin, David 6:32:33 (32,490)
Baldwin, David S 2:59:11 (1,161)
Baldwin, Elwyn 3:02:07 (1,385)
Baldwin, Gareth R 4:36:50 (20,945)
Baldwin, James A 2:44:27 (329)
Baldwin, Kelvin J 4:32:43 (19,939)
Baldwin, Paul 6:38:00 (32,579)
Baldwin, Sam 3:58:26 (11,319)
Baldwin, Simon 2:59:06 (1,150)
Baldwin, Steven M 3:41:03 (6,815)
Bale, Mons 3:08:01 (1,861)
Bale, Simon M 3:25:00 (3,931)
Bales, Kieron J 4:17:32 (15,992)
Bali, Utsav 4:23:14 (17,427)
Balich, Mark 5:13:13 (27,679)
Ball, Anthony R 4:42:46 (22,274)
Ball, Christopher W 5:57:09 (31,410)
Ball, David M 3:46:58 (8,112)
Ball, Dean A 3:48:49 (8,583)
Ball, Douglas 5:24:01 (28,940)
Ball, James W 4:25:03 (17,976)
Ball, Jason K 3:27:28 (4,326)
Ball, Mark J 4:56:15 (25,150)
Ball, Martin D 2:48:51 (486)
Ball, Matthew D 4:09:10 (13,895)
Ball, Michael C 4:33:41 (20,185)
Ball, Michael D 3:39:46 (6,582)
Ball, Stephen J 3:11:10 (2,171)
Ball, Tim J 5:56:00 (31,353)
Ballantyne, Barrie J 4:41:28 (21,986)
Ballantyne, David F 3:14:48 (2,642)
Ballard, Alex M 4:07:13 (13,406)
Ballard, Jim P 4:45:18 (22,856)
Ballard, Neil 3:27:38 (4,357)
Baller, Steve 3:53:57 (9,908)
Ballet, Michel 3:06:12 (1,687)
Balliana, Angelo 3:52:08 (9,390)
Ballisai, Antonello 5:00:35 (25,981)
Balls, Edmund W 5:14:39 (27,869)
Ballsdon, Edward 4:07:48 (13,555)
Balman, Mark G 3:34:48 (5,627)
Balmer, Martin H 4:37:38 (21,144)
Baltazar, Nicolas 3:09:31 (2,015)
Bamber, Dean R 5:23:14 (28,861)
Bamford, Alex T 5:01:33 (26,112)
Bamford, David 2:52:22 (648)
Bamford, David R 5:00:41 (25,994)
Bamford, Reg L 4:29:46 (19,246)
Bampfylde, Richard W 4:53:32 (24,575)
Bampton, Christopher 3:18:04 (3,007)
Bampton, James 5:22:34 (28,778)
Bamsey, Philip L 3:34:59 (5,659)
Banach, Alberto 4:07:57 (13,602)
Banbury, David P 4:24:37 (17,845)
Banbury, John M 4:10:43 (14,251)
Bance, Elliott J 4:16:25 (15,695)
Bancroft, Ian R 3:44:20 (7,530)
Bancroft, Simon R 6:47:06 (32,724)
Bandry, Michael D 3:58:59 (11,500)
Banfield, Alistair 3:52:20 (9,445)
Banfield, Martin H 3:29:09 (4,644)
Banfield, Simon 3:05:03 (1,579)
Banford, David J 4:31:06 (19,555)
Bangani, Pumlani 2:22:27 (38)
Banham, Mark R 4:29:19 (19,122)
Banks, Ian M 5:11:46 (27,490)
Banks, Kenneth 4:20:26 (16,717)
Banks, Richard D 3:32:21 (5,228)
Banks, Simon J 4:25:33 (18,126)
Banks, Thomas M 3:59:48 (11,762)
Banks, Timothy D 3:43:31 (7,354)
Banks, Tom 4:12:22 (14,677)
Banner, Charles E 3:20:15 (3,305)
Bannister, Brendan J 4:45:47 (22,965)
Bannister, Mark H 4:30:25 (19,407)
Bannister, Peter J 4:29:10 (19,076)
Bannister, Philip A 5:07:26 (26,923)
Bannister, Stuart 4:10:00 (14,098)
Bansback, Mike J 4:42:01 (22,116)
Bansept, Dan 3:34:43 (5,616)
Bant, Philip 3:58:24 (11,306)
Bantin, Laurie 3:14:55 (2,655)
Banton, Jonathan D 4:05:40 (13,070)
Banwait, Sukhjit 5:36:53 (30,124)
Bara, James 3:24:32 (3,870)
Barachetti, Antonio 3:35:32 (5,755)
Barber, Eugene P 4:18:43 (16,286)
Barber, Ian B 3:14:26 (2,588)
Barber, Kyle G 3:09:40 (2,034)
Barber, Neill 4:21:48 (17,062)
Barber, Nic 3:21:28 (3,464)
Barber, Paul E 4:36:41 (20,885)
Barber, Ric O 3:25:05 (3,939)
Barbet, Andy J 7:18:48 (33,034)
Barbieri, Filippo 3:21:03 (3,405)
Barbone, Alan 4:55:00 (24,895)
Barclay, Craig 4:07:04 (13,360)
Barclay, James 5:20:18 (28,537)
Barclay, Luke J 4:08:53 (13,830)
Barclay, Robert S 4:46:30 (23,120)
Barden, John G 4:15:25 (15,454)
Barden, Roy 3:36:02 (5,842)
Bardll, George 4:15:44 (15,529)
Bardsley, David W 3:45:39 (7,833)
Bardwell, Julian E 3:29:17 (4,671)
Bareham, Patrick W 3:23:57 (3,782)
Barf, David C 5:03:47 (26,428)
Barfety, Christian 3:54:31 (10,057)
Bargh, Donald M 3:48:16 (8,442)
Bargier, Jacques R 4:10:58 (14,322)

Barham, Jeffrey P 4:25:58 (18,249)
Barham, Malcolm R 4:14:58 (15,325)
Barham, Richard 3:58:40 (11,388)
Barham, Stephen L 3:56:27 (10,672)
Barke, Christopher P 4:45:18 (22,856)
Barker, Alistair P 5:11:31 (27,461)
Barker, Antony T 4:29:16 (19,107)
Barker, Craig 3:47:34 (8,259)
Barker, Dean 4:14:20 (15,169)
Barker, Jonathan E 4:13:42 (15,005)
Barker, Joseph A 4:05:39 (13,067)
Barker, Lee A 3:38:52 (6,402)
Barker, Michael M 4:38:40 (21,365)
Barker, Michael W 3:32:53 (5,305)
Barker, Nicholas D 4:07:09 (13,390)
Barker, Peter D 4:10:25 (14,196)
Barker, Ralph 3:04:14 (1,529)
Barker, Ryan 2:58:19 (1,047)
Barker-Wyatt, Edward J 4:50:10 (23,871)
Barkes, Christopher P 5:21:13 (28,632)
Barkes, Tom R 4:09:24 (13,963)
Barkhouse, Jeremy J 4:39:23 (21,542)
Bark-Jones, Michael D 3:52:03 (9,372)
Barley, Alan C 5:36:17 (30,080)
Barley, Clive 4:53:21 (24,538)
Barley, Gary P 4:06:12 (13,177)
Barley, Paul 3:27:50 (4,387)
Barling, Timothy C 3:54:28 (10,042)
Barlow, Chris 4:03:08 (12,516)
Barlow, Daniel W 3:54:47 (10,138)
Barlow, Gary M 4:26:25 (18,365)
Barlow, Matthew E 3:50:36 (9,003)
Barlow, Matthew V 3:47:42 (8,298)
Barlow, Michael R 3:31:33 (5,073)
Barlow, Paul A 2:55:24 (811)
Barlow, Paul M 3:18:11 (3,018)
Barlow, Richard G 3:57:05 (10,870)
Barlow, Simon E 4:11:10 (14,380)
Barlow, Stephen T 3:06:26 (1,706)
Barltrop, Verne 3:54:18 (10,004)
Barnaby, Harold M 5:30:57 (29,644)
Barnard, Antony E 6:10:46 (31,950)
Barnard, Carl A 4:49:30 (23,754)
Barnard, Daniel R 4:13:02 (14,856)
Barnard, Graeme R 5:53:17 (31,231)
Barnard, Guy G 3:19:18 (3,172)
Barnard, Jem J 4:03:28 (12,598)
Barnard, Michael 3:35:43 (5,789)
Barnard, Simon J 4:35:02 (20,498)
Barnes, Adam R 5:19:32 (28,441)
Barnes, Adam R 5:46:18 (30,810)
Barnes, Alan C 3:15:39 (2,733)
Barnes, Andrew 4:16:46 (15,793)
Barnes, Andrew R 4:34:01 (20,249)
Barnes, Christopher J 4:08:46 (13,805)
Barnes, Daniel C 4:30:49 (19,497)
Barnes, Daniel L 5:18:16 (28,279)
Barnes, David G 3:01:41 (1,349)
Barnes, David J 3:33:34 (5,410)
Barnes, Frederick 5:11:10 (27,407)
Barnes, Gary R 4:53:22 (24,539)
Barnes, James A 3:58:06 (11,185)
Barnes, Keith J 4:49:52 (23,815)
Barnes, Mark 4:45:03 (22,804)
Barnes, Nick A 3:54:10 (9,968)
Barnes, Nigel 3:51:31 (9,222)
Barnes, Terence A 4:16:28 (15,714)
Barnes, Trevor 3:40:24 (6,692)
Barnes-Smith, Martin J 3:12:45 (2,369)
Barnett, Andrew G 4:36:12 (20,779)
Barnett, Ed 2:26:14 (50)
Barnett, Matthew A 5:51:56 (31,181)
Barnett, Matthew D 5:08:24 (27,064)
Barnett, Robert S 3:34:18 (5,533)
Barnett, Stefan M 3:47:28 (8,234)
Barney, Dean C 4:14:45 (15,272)
Barney, Luke 4:03:09 (12,520)
Barnfield, Mark J 4:25:12 (18,027)
Barnstaple, Craig J 5:46:28 (30,822)
Barnstaple, Glen 4:33:41 (20,185)
Baron, Andy 3:54:34 (10,069)
Baron, Carl J 3:39:38 (6,564)
Barr, Andrew P 4:52:04 (24,260)

Barr, David 3:48:31 (8,504)
Barr, James D 3:46:08 (7,929)
Barr, James E 3:41:26 (6,900)
Barr, Robert D 4:03:11 (12,524)
Barr, Roger W 2:49:49 (535)
Barr, Travers R 3:23:33 (3,717)
Barra, Patric 3:11:10 (2,171)
Barraclough, Clive A 3:27:11 (4,271)
Barralet-Leak, Tim 3:54:38 (10,086)
Barrand, William J 3:31:10 (5,020)
Barrass, Barnaby J 3:06:55 (1,748)
Barrass, Simon 3:32:22 (5,231)
Barrass, Tim J 4:18:31 (16,238)
Barratt, Adam M 4:46:03 (23,016)
Barratt, Lee 3:21:53 (3,520)
Barratt, Matthew L 4:22:57 (17,356)
Barratt, Raymond C 4:25:57 (18,244)
Barratt, Richard J 4:05:10 (12,950)
Barratt, Thomas O 5:21:03 (28,615)
Barratt, Trevor J 5:07:50 (26,978)
Barrell, Stuart 4:28:19 (18,847)
Barren, Mark I 4:08:10 (13,656)
Barrett, Gerry 4:04:26 (12,801)
Barrett, Gordon D 3:05:10 (1,590)
Barrett, Joseph 3:57:13 (10,928)
Barrett, Lance 5:35:21 (29,999)
Barrett, Michael A 5:34:14 (29,906)
Barrett, Michael P 5:18:54 (28,358)
Barrett, Nigel 3:41:39 (6,954)
Barrett, Paul A 4:31:55 (19,776)
Barrett, Paul A 4:33:12 (20,062)
Barrett, Phil J 3:51:31 (9,222)
Barrett, Simon J 2:27:40 (54)
Barrett, Stephen J 3:16:34 (2,823)
Barribal, Scott L 4:30:19 (19,380)
Barrie, Allan G 4:00:01 (11,820)
Barrie, William E 3:49:38 (8,780)
Barron, Jeremy D 4:23:23 (17,468)
Barron, Peter 3:26:57 (4,234)
Barron, Robert M 4:50:52 (24,021)
Barron, Steven R 3:59:40 (11,715)
Barron, Stuart D 3:03:35 (1,485)
Barros, Paulo M 3:26:18 (4,114)
Barros, Ricardo C 3:35:05 (5,690)
Barrott, Michael J 3:50:53 (9,072)
Barrow, Dean 4:53:04 (24,468)
Barrow, Duncan A 4:38:04 (21,245)
Barrow, Keith 5:22:08 (28,730)
Barrow, Michael 3:47:35 (8,266)
Barrowman, Michael S 3:49:54 (8,846)
Barrows, Anthony J 4:18:30 (16,231)
Barrow-Williams, Timothy D 4:27:16 (18,572)
Barrs, Gary E 4:49:17 (23,714)
Barry, Daniel J 4:08:29 (13,738)
Barry, John 3:52:24 (9,473)
Barry, Julian A 2:59:37 (1,212)
Barry, Patrick A 3:47:32 (8,246)
Barry, Paul D 3:16:44 (2,845)
Barry, Sean J 3:39:16 (6,493)
Barry, Simon 3:30:30 (4,895)
Barsby, Paul S 4:14:45 (15,272)
Barstow, Michael P 3:56:35 (10,717)
Barteczko, Igor 3:28:09 (4,433)
Barter, Peter W 5:21:10 (28,625)
Bartlett, Anthony 4:20:17 (16,678)
Bartlett, Edwin H 4:37:45 (21,167)
Bartlett, Robin L 4:54:49 (24,855)
Bartley, Maddhew 4:41:00 (21,895)
Barton, Alan J 4:32:41 (19,931)
Barton, Bruce D 2:53:17 (687)
Barton, David G 3:06:53 (1,745)
Barton, David R 4:29:17 (19,115)
Barton, Desmond P 4:20:12 (16,662)
Barton, Glynn E 4:28:33 (18,910)
Barton, Michael 3:59:30 (11,672)
Barton, Neil P 3:53:59 (9,917)
Barton, Patrick J 4:04:35 (12,829)
Barton, William 4:21:39 (17,012)
Bartram, David C 5:08:19 (27,052)
Bartrip, Lee 4:15:04 (15,355)
Baruah, Dean 3:30:36 (4,914)
Barwell, Matthew R 4:36:47 (20,933)
Barwise, Russell P 5:05:12 (26,611)

Bashford, Kevin P 3:54:39 (10,091)
Basletta, Fausto 3:35:04 (5,684)
Bass, Andrew P 2:53:00 (678)
Bass, David 3:48:18 (8,450)
Bassan, Gwynn 3:28:10 (4,436)
Basset, Bruno C 2:53:36 (704)
Basset, Thomas M 4:22:11 (17,171)
Bassett, Neville 5:30:10 (29,558)
Bassett, Nicholas D 4:00:51 (12,005)
Bassett, Peter J 4:25:43 (18,163)
Bassi, Corrado 3:30:05 (4,843)
Bassi, Jaspreet S 5:28:38 (29,389)
Bassi, Marco 3:28:23 (4,489)
Bassi, Stefano 4:20:29 (16,733)
Bassu, Gianfranco 3:13:19 (2,436)
Bastable, Jonathan M 4:49:22 (23,729)
Bastin, Colin 5:38:15 (30,226)
Bastyan, Terrence J 4:48:13 (23,474)
Basu, Subhashis 3:20:53 (3,390)
Bataille, Frederic 4:26:26 (18,368)
Batchelor, Alan 4:51:07 (24,063)
Batchelor, Gary M 4:22:52 (17,336)
Batchelor, Robert J 5:06:49 (26,840)
Batchelor, Steven R 6:06:23 (31,797)
Bate, Darryl P 5:04:04 (26,463)
Bate, David L 3:14:08 (2,546)
Bate, Lawrence M 3:33:44 (5,440)
Bate, Storm 3:29:53 (4,802)
Bateman, Adam 4:44:59 (22,778)
Bateman, Alan S 4:05:02 (12,923)
Bateman, Andrew B 5:03:35 (26,400)
Bateman, Daniel J 3:36:29 (5,928)
Bateman, Danny A 5:20:13 (28,521)
Bateman, Delano I 3:28:51 (4,590)
Bateman, Jeremy D 2:53:35 (702)
Bateman, Jonathan S 2:58:38 (1,083)
Bateman, Mervin C 5:51:46 (31,171)
Bater, Bernie 3:02:20 (1,394)
Bates, Edward A 4:06:49 (13,303)
Bates, Ian 4:53:11 (24,504)
Bates, John D 3:35:02 (5,669)
Bates, Kenneth J 4:15:43 (15,524)
Bates, Matthew A 4:31:39 (19,711)
Bates, Richard 3:36:11 (5,872)
Bates, Simon M 4:29:02 (19,034)
Bates, Steven P 6:06:47 (31,816)
Bates, Tony 4:27:59 (18,745)
Bateson, Nick J 3:00:07 (1,240)
Batey, Keith B 3:54:48 (10,145)
Bath, Steven P 5:37:29 (30,163)
Bathgate, Robert J 3:43:36 (7,370)
Batista, Mark A 4:20:03 (16,613)
Batley, Lloyd E 4:41:23 (21,966)
Batrick, Lee 4:24:15 (17,732)
Batson, Nicholas 5:24:45 (29,012)
Batten, Kenneth M 4:50:55 (24,028)
Battersby, William C 4:54:10 (24,720)
Battrick, Colin 4:57:39 (25,424)
Battrick, Neil A 6:07:39 (31,846)
Batty, Mark K 3:39:03 (6,445)
Batty, Peter 4:33:34 (20,157)
Baty, Andrew 3:51:15 (9,160)
Baucutt, Graham M 5:14:01 (27,767)
Baudois, Jacques 3:23:24 (3,697)
Baudois, Jean M 3:21:49 (3,515)
Baudouin, Michel 4:23:49 (17,598)
Baughan, Christopher A 4:28:46 (18,965)
Bauhs, Henrik 3:53:51 (9,882)
Baujon, Alain 3:31:37 (5,089)
Baukham, Jonathan E 4:59:39 (25,823)
Baumfield, Nicholas J 4:31:23 (19,638)
Baumfield, Tim G 4:21:35 (16,993)
Bawa, Ahmed 4:27:35 (18,650)
Bax, William R 4:59:27 (25,773)
Baxendale, Samuel G 3:49:42 (8,799)
Baxendale, Toby O 3:18:32 (3,073)
Baxter, Andrew D 6:05:05 (31,763)
Baxter, David 3:59:11 (11,570)
Baxter, Eric 3:29:12 (4,654)
Baxter, Ewart J 4:28:34 (18,917)
Baxter, Glenn A 4:52:17 (24,303)
Baxter, Gordon S 3:18:07 (3,012)
Baxter, Ian R 4:13:33 (14,965)

Baxter, James N 4:47:23 (23,287)
Baxter, Lindsay J 3:49:46 (8,813)
Baxter, Noel C 3:59:42 (11,728)
Baxter, Rick D 4:26:22 (18,352)
Bayer, Boris M 4:16:33 (15,737)
Bayer, Malcolm E 2:50:49 (579)
Bayes, Graham P 4:24:18 (17,750)
Bayes, Peter 4:47:38 (23,349)
Bayford, Thomas F 3:29:42 (4,759)
Bayley, Ian 5:31:06 (29,672)
Bayley, Ian P 3:51:16 (9,165)
Bayley, Mark A 3:44:49 (7,645)
Bayley-Dainton, Stuart J 3:34:35 (5,591)
Baylis, Edward J 4:48:27 (23,527)
Bayliss, Chris B 4:56:49 (25,259)
Bayliss, Emma J 5:20:26 (28,556)
Bayliss, Geoffrey 3:51:14 (9,156)
Bayly, Robin M 5:15:11 (27,924)
Baynes, Charles B 3:17:12 (2,908)
Baynes, Chris P 3:23:02 (3,661)
Baynes, Neil 3:49:42 (8,799)
Bayon, Tony 4:04:52 (12,888)
Bazley, Peter G 3:31:57 (5,152)
Beach, Paul A 4:33:14 (20,067)
Beacham, Rob 4:14:04 (15,092)
Beacock, John P 3:47:02 (8,127)
Beadell, Ray W 4:30:07 (19,328)
Beadle, Matthew J 4:18:27 (16,218)
Beagley, Mark A 3:19:25 (3,182)
Beale, Darren 3:57:08 (10,893)
Beale, Fraser B 5:20:22 (28,550)
Beales, Chris H 3:56:30 (10,685)
Beales, Robert D 4:50:43 (23,988)
Beany, Captain 5:38:26 (30,245)
Beard, Adrian R 3:56:43 (10,758)
Beard, Michael C 3:04:37 (1,557)
Beard, Nigel M 3:56:49 (10,790)
Beard, Russell J 3:13:05 (2,411)
Beard, Simon 4:23:34 (17,523)
Beardmore, Martin J 3:52:10 (9,402)
Beardmore, Paul 3:55:51 (10,490)
Beardsall, Richard G 4:41:54 (22,085)
Beardsworth, Dominic P 4:09:00 (13,859)
Beardsworth, Jamie 3:56:38 (10,734)
Bearn, Mark J 4:55:00 (24,895)
Bearwish, Neil S 3:09:19 (1,986)
Beasley, Emma V 4:34:08 (20,278)
Beasley, Mark G 3:46:04 (7,918)
Beathe, Carl J 3:08:01 (1,861)
Beaton, Michael F 2:56:56 (935)
Beattie, Brian W 3:28:57 (4,612)
Beattie, Ian J 3:12:06 (2,288)
Beattie, James H 4:38:57 (21,430)
Beattie, Michael J 2:55:45 (832)
Beattie, Philip G 4:48:37 (23,571)
Beattie, Tim 4:18:15 (16,169)
Beatty, John D 4:09:21 (13,946)
Beaty-Pownall, Paul J 4:20:03 (16,613)
Beaumont, Alex 4:12:51 (14,796)
Beaumont, Charles H 4:18:52 (16,318)
Beaumont, Kim D 4:55:02 (24,904)
Beaumont, Richard G 3:51:20 (9,185)
Beaumont, Steven 5:06:04 (26,723)
Beauvisage, Bruno 3:39:16 (6,493)
Beavan, David E 4:07:58 (13,606)
Beaven, Roger 3:33:21 (5,378)
Beaver, Thomas E 3:26:34 (4,168)
Beavis, John A 4:07:53 (13,579)
Beck, Paul R 3:27:26 (4,320)
Beck, Robert J 5:34:48 (29,954)
Beck, Russell 4:00:46 (11,985)
Beck, Stephen A 5:10:22 (27,313)
Beckerman, Chris 4:17:13 (15,910)
Beckett, Darren M 2:54:02 (727)
Beckett, Peter G 3:37:03 (6,047)
Beckett, William G 6:18:30 (32,184)
Beckingham, Ian J 3:05:10 (1,590)
Beckingham, Neil D 3:22:21 (3,577)
Beckley, David W 3:54:04 (9,936)
Beddard, Carl F 5:21:57 (28,712)
Bedder, Stephen R 3:33:16 (5,364)
Beddoe, Stewart R 4:28:47 (18,969)
Beddoe, Toby C 4:59:47 (25,847)
Bedford, Geoffrey 4:30:23 (19,398)
Bedford, Graham J 3:53:28 (9,760)
Bedford, Greg P 3:55:44 (10,453)
Bedford, Paul 4:16:48 (15,798)
Bedford, Terence L 4:32:15 (19,845)
Bedington, Terence J 3:35:19 (5,723)
Bedlow, Richard 3:54:24 (10,028)
Bednall, Michael 4:38:33 (21,349)
Bedwell, Ian C 3:58:39 (11,382)
Bedwell, Peter R 3:57:44 (11,087)
Beeby, Ian R 3:46:46 (8,074)
Beech, David A 4:17:34 (16,003)
Beech, David C 4:00:27 (11,927)
Beech, Geoff 3:35:32 (5,755)
Beech, Jeremy W 3:56:49 (10,790)
Beech, Stephen J 3:22:29 (3,591)
Beecham, George E 6:03:43 (31,715)
Beechey, Andrew 3:29:28 (4,708)
Beechey, Benjamin J 4:44:44 (22,716)
Beecroft, David 3:04:28 (1,541)
Beeks, Darren C 4:37:19 (21,061)
Beeks, Ramon A 5:04:15 (26,480)
Beer, Edward 5:02:43 (26,275)
Beer, Michael R 4:57:39 (25,424)
Beer, Simon A 4:43:06 (22,346)
Beesley, Graham J 3:25:12 (3,960)
Beesley, Ian S 3:46:02 (7,907)
Beeston, Tim R 3:59:37 (11,698)
Begg, Graham J 4:48:31 (23,543)
Beguier, Jean-Mary 3:53:02 (9,638)
Behrens, Gordon G 4:34:48 (20,436)
Behrman, Ryan 5:10:21 (27,309)
Beillon, Jean-Michel 3:53:08 (9,672)
Beken, Matt C 3:39:05 (6,451)
Beketov, Andrei 3:20:15 (3,305)
Beland, Paul 4:23:25 (17,474)
Belassie, Simon D 3:53:45 (9,844)
Belbeck, Daniel A 3:55:19 (10,320)
Belbin, Rich H 4:04:16 (12,770)
Belbin, Simon J 4:52:19 (24,312)
Belcher, Ian C 5:54:39 (31,297)
Belcher, Mark A 3:17:42 (2,966)
Belcher, Paul F 3:07:16 (1,779)
Belcher, Victor 4:45:00 (22,786)
Belchior, Pedro 3:07:16 (1,779)
Belda-Cano, José M 3:51:45 (9,287)
Beldon, Richard G 4:17:13 (15,910)
Belfield, David C 4:54:20 (24,754)
Belgrove, Carl R 4:19:37 (16,505)
Bell, Anthony C 4:08:49 (13,818)
Bell, Bernard 4:53:11 (24,504)
Bell, Colin 7:44:10 (33,153)
Bell, David A 5:32:39 (29,781)
Bell, David J 3:08:49 (1,937)
Bell, David J 3:27:51 (4,391)
Bell, David M 2:58:25 (1,060)
Bell, Duncan 2:43:03 (289)
Bell, Duncan E 5:00:56 (26,031)
Bell, Frederick M 3:37:43 (6,171)
Bell, Geoffrey D 4:55:05 (24,914)
Bell, Graeme E 3:25:50 (4,052)
Bell, Graham A 3:41:34 (6,933)
Bell, James 4:08:34 (13,761)
Bell, James J 4:29:27 (19,160)
Bell, Jason 5:12:59 (27,649)
Bell, Jimmy 2:47:47 (448)
Bell, John 2:51:58 (633)
Bell, John D 3:03:27 (1,477)
Bell, Lindsay M 3:40:02 (6,633)
Bell, Martin A 3:52:02 (9,369)
Bell, Matthew J 2:30:45 (73)
Bell, Nick 3:32:31 (5,256)
Bell, Nick G 3:32:06 (5,180)
Bell, Peter A 3:57:21 (10,966)
Bell, Peter W 3:53:15 (9,706)
Bell, Richard C 4:50:10 (23,871)
Bell, Simon J 2:40:33 (218)
Bell, Steven J 4:38:31 (21,344)
Bell, Steven M 5:06:33 (26,793)
Bell, Wayne P 2:52:37 (656)
Bellamy, Andrew 4:09:54 (14,084)
Bellamy, Darren W 4:26:09 (18,296)
Bellamy, Edward J 3:12:27 (2,339)
Bellamy, Guy S 5:49:08 (31,008)
Bellandi, Oscar 3:40:59 (6,799)
Bellass, Andy 4:28:56 (19,006)
Belleguelle, Russell J 5:14:16 (27,807)
Beller, André 3:37:37 (6,155)
Belletty, Steven C 4:28:32 (18,904)
Belleville, Paul C 2:53:26 (696)
Bellingham, Neil J 4:56:19 (25,168)
Bellis, Deryn S 3:00:12 (1,247)
Bello, Aurelio M 3:51:40 (9,260)
Belperche, Philippe 4:11:55 (14,555)
Belsham, Paul M 4:22:53 (17,339)
Belson, Steven J 4:45:33 (22,913)
Belton, Andrew W 3:35:32 (5,755)
Belton, Christopher C 3:26:22 (4,130)
Belton, Richard W 4:53:13 (24,512)
Ben Halim, Amr M 4:54:08 (24,704)
Bena, Stefano 4:48:01 (23,430)
Benali, Francis V 3:31:09 (5,017)
Benamara, Samir 3:56:57 (10,828)
Benassi, Stefano 4:43:07 (22,355)
Benbow, Joe 4:08:21 (13,704)
Benbow, Steve S 4:10:49 (14,282)
Bence, Christopher G 4:30:35 (19,446)
Bencer, Roland H 3:34:18 (5,533)
Bendel, Daryl 4:03:59 (12,710)
Bender, Etienne A 3:58:58 (11,497)
Bendle, Jeremy P 4:03:59 (12,710)
Benedick, Darren M 4:07:20 (13,429)
Benford, Michael J 2:51:14 (603)
Benham, Kevin D 3:30:16 (4,862)
Beninga, Holger 5:40:50 (30,418)
Benjamin, Michael A 3:57:06 (10,883)
Benjaminsen, Tor A 4:33:02 (20,013)
Benke, Graham N 5:29:48 (29,523)
Benn, Guy H 3:38:43 (6,367)
Benn, Karl E 4:58:30 (25,607)
Benn, Mark R 4:42:18 (22,176)
Benn, Matthew J 4:42:17 (22,172)
Benn, William 5:34:53 (29,958)
Bennellick, Darren A 4:02:48 (12,438)
Bennett, Andrew 4:13:07 (14,878)
Bennett, Andrew D 3:59:11 (11,570)
Bennett, Bernard T 4:14:46 (15,279)
Bennett, Brendan J 4:35:08 (20,516)
Bennett, Brian S 4:19:58 (16,594)
Bennett, Daniel J 4:34:27 (20,350)
Bennett, Darren M 4:41:13 (21,927)
Bennett, David A 4:02:54 (12,458)
Bennett, David M 4:20:08 (16,636)
Bennett, David P 4:45:40 (22,935)
Bennett, Duncan P 3:25:45 (4,034)
Bennett, George B 7:22:34 (33,053)
Bennett, Gregory R 4:17:33 (15,999)
Bennett, James E 4:26:32 (18,391)
Bennett, John J 4:05:21 (12,988)
Bennett, Jon A 3:50:05 (8,880)
Bennett, Julian F 4:58:03 (25,513)
Bennett, Kevin M 2:58:46 (1,106)
Bennett, Marc 3:28:43 (4,560)
Bennett, Mark 4:44:10 (22,598)
Bennett, Martin J 4:07:02 (13,351)
Bennett, Neil 3:30:58 (4,976)
Bennett, Nigel J 4:32:23 (19,884)
Bennett, Paul 3:18:06 (3,011)
Bennett, Raymond 4:02:49 (12,441)
Bennett, Richard A 4:53:17 (24,520)
Bennett, Richard M 3:38:51 (6,396)
Bennett, Roger 3:07:12 (1,778)
Bennett, Roger 5:30:33 (29,598)
Bennett, Scott 3:53:06 (9,662)
Bennett, Sean W 3:40:37 (6,731)
Bennett, Simon J 3:38:05 (6,247)
Bennett, Simon P 4:36:34 (20,861)
Bennett, Steven A 3:09:19 (1,986)
Bennett, Tom J 3:20:03 (3,273)
Bennington, Roy J 3:54:45 (10,124)
Bennion, Chris 3:46:39 (8,048)
Benny, Peter M 4:12:29 (14,699)
Benoit, Nicolas 3:58:44 (11,417)
Bensen, Nicolas E 4:08:44 (13,792)
Bensetti, Abdelkader 5:00:19 (25,946)
Benson, Ian C 3:06:57 (1,751)

Benson, Ian E....3:45:04 (7,704)
Benson, James....2:39:31 (201)
Benson, Justin J....3:34:38 (5,597)
Benson, Mark M....3:47:12 (8,168)
Benson, Neil....3:48:14 (8,439)
Benson, Richard M....4:10:39 (14,242)
Benson, Stpehen G....3:48:08 (8,414)
Benstead, Robin....3:52:05 (9,381)
Bent, Graham A....3:49:19 (8,697)
Bentley, David R....3:24:22 (3,844)
Bentley, Derek....4:49:25 (23,739)
Bentley, Gary C....4:02:50 (12,445)
Bentley, Jon....4:12:47 (14,769)
Bentley, Mark....3:18:20 (3,039)
Bentley, Pauls D....6:21:55 (32,282)
Bentley, Stephen....4:42:34 (22,234)
Benton, Brian E....4:21:08 (16,902)
Benton, Derek R....4:22:22 (17,215)
Benton, Kevin L....3:39:16 (6,493)
Benton, Mark A....4:44:06 (22,583)
Benton, Richard H....3:38:55 (6,418)
Benton, Wesley....3:48:04 (8,398)
Benwell, Nigel R....4:48:03 (23,438)
Berard, Philippe F....3:44:30 (7,567)
Berends, Dieter....4:34:00 (20,245)
Beresford, David C....4:21:30 (16,975)
Beresford, Martin P....4:35:36 (20,624)
Beretta, Corrado....3:56:10 (10,587)
Berezowski, Robert J....5:04:58 (26,578)
Berger, Jamie....4:54:09 (24,712)
Bergin, Mark R....4:00:43 (11,979)
Bergozza, Marco....4:24:50 (17,898)
Berg-Sorensen, Leif....6:06:38 (31,809)
Berkman, Steven....4:12:42 (14,749)
Berks, Peter R....4:34:43 (20,416)
Berlan, Philippe....4:01:14 (12,105)
Bermingham, Andrew....3:28:04 (4,416)
Bernabe-Palacios, Bernabe....3:47:36 (8,270)
Bernaers, Juul....3:42:38 (7,138)
Bernal, Nicholas....4:23:49 (17,598)
Bernard, François C....4:19:34 (16,497)
Bernard, Olivier N....4:56:45 (25,249)
Bernard, Patrice D....4:21:40 (17,015)
Bernard, Ralph M....5:01:13 (26,074)
Bernard, Simon A....3:40:37 (6,731)
Bernardo, Alessandro....3:26:59 (4,241)
Bernascone, Ralph....3:34:49 (5,628)
Bernhardt, Mark J....3:18:34 (3,077)
Bernolet, Luc G....4:17:52 (16,076)
Berquez, Leon....4:17:17 (15,923)
Berry, Anthony J....4:54:00 (24,677)
Berry, David J....4:14:41 (15,255)
Berry, Gavin R....3:19:05 (3,140)
Berry, Graham D....4:04:20 (12,782)
Berry, Grant....4:35:57 (20,709)
Berry, Ian J....3:59:37 (11,698)
Berry, Luke J....4:33:58 (20,244)
Berry, Mark....2:59:01 (1,143)
Berry, Martin G....4:55:44 (25,043)
Berry, Mike J....4:54:57 (24,880)
Berry, Mike P....3:11:13 (2,182)
Berry, Paul R....2:58:58 (1,138)
Berry, Ray....4:43:04 (22,339)
Berry, Stephen F....5:10:47 (27,363)
Berryman, Tony S....4:19:25 (16,455)
Bertagne, Michael G....4:00:27 (11,927)
Bertherin, Claude....4:41:56 (22,095)
Bertocchi, Roberto....3:32:30 (5,252)
Bertoli, Angelo....4:53:44 (24,626)
Bertolone, Enzo....5:17:40 (28,213)
Bertoni, Alberto....2:56:13 (871)
Bertram, Ivan A....3:28:15 (4,452)
Bertram, Roger C....5:28:35 (29,380)
Bertrand, Robin G....5:00:22 (25,954)
Bertucat, Laurent....3:28:17 (4,464)
Bertuccelli, Paolo....3:47:24 (8,213)
Berueso, Manuel....4:06:51 (13,311)
Besnard, Bernie....6:34:19 (32,521)
Bessho, Tatsuya....3:44:14 (7,501)
Bessi, Alessandro....3:58:00 (11,154)
Besson, Pascal....4:35:20 (20,563)
Best, David C....4:29:38 (19,213)
Best, James F....3:44:25 (7,543)
Best, Mark....3:38:15 (6,280)
Best, Philip N....3:14:24 (2,583)
Best, Simon A....5:35:27 (30,008)
Best, Steven G....4:56:22 (25,179)
Bethell, Daniel R....4:12:04 (14,586)
Bethell, Jeremy J....3:31:07 (5,010)
Bethune, Richard A....3:18:51 (3,114)
Betoni, Fabrizio....3:21:40 (3,495)
Betson, Richard P....4:17:17 (15,923)
Betsworth, Glyn L....4:48:33 (23,552)
Bettany, Darrell P....4:55:32 (25,003)
Betteridge, Neil R....4:10:07 (14,127)
Bettersby, John A....3:08:05 (1,869)
Bettington, Gordon J....4:55:52 (25,070)
Bettinson, Paul R....3:55:16 (10,305)
Bettison, Colin....5:03:09 (26,335)
Betts, Gary C....3:57:30 (11,014)
Betts, Mark P....2:54:21 (749)
Betts, Timothy R....3:30:38 (4,921)
Beuchling, Michael....4:28:28 (18,889)
Beulich, Uwe....4:06:16 (13,185)
Bevan, Chris M....4:20:18 (16,684)
Bevan, David....7:16:58 (33,020)
Bevan, Gavin....4:59:12 (25,736)
Bevan, James....4:30:24 (19,400)
Bevan, Neil....2:52:54 (671)
Bevan, Philip C....4:26:39 (18,421)
Bevan, Steve....3:42:00 (7,024)
Bevan, Tim J....4:32:46 (19,952)
Beveridge, Ian R....5:09:01 (27,148)
Beveridge, Robert J....4:15:17 (15,408)
Beverly, Michael....4:11:45 (14,508)
Bevil, Robert G....5:03:52 (26,441)
Bevis, Andrew....4:18:35 (16,252)
Bewsey, Benjamin E....4:46:17 (23,073)
Bewtra, Vineet....4:09:52 (14,072)
Beynon, Robert....5:36:13 (30,073)
Bezance, Max....2:50:47 (578)
Bezoari, Carlo J....5:11:21 (27,434)
Bezoodis, Mark S....4:39:27 (21,554)
Bhagat, Lee....3:39:23 (6,514)
Bhalla, Ajay....4:01:54 (12,236)
Bhalla, Surjit S....5:10:08 (27,279)
Bhambra, Gurpal S....4:40:06 (21,691)
Bhargava, Vijay....4:08:11 (13,663)
Bhirth, Gurvinder S....6:14:29 (32,068)
Bhoja, Narshi....4:46:39 (23,147)
Bhreathnach, Adrian J....5:56:50 (31,395)
Bhugon, Daniel M....3:16:54 (2,864)
Bhullar, Pavenpal S....4:32:14 (19,839)
Biagioni, Carl....3:34:42 (5,611)
Bianchetto Songia, Alberto....4:54:32 (24,785)
Bianco, Federico....4:38:04 (21,245)
Bibby, James A....3:10:10 (2,084)
Bichard, Joe L....4:12:14 (14,634)
Bickerstaffe, Rob N....4:55:02 (24,904)
Bickerstaffe, Simon M....4:06:27 (13,219)
Bickhan, Zakir....5:56:28 (31,378)
Bickles, Gary A....5:12:53 (27,629)
Bickley, Jonathan R....4:01:38 (12,179)
Bicknell, Jonathan....4:02:34 (12,391)
Bicknell, Richard A....4:01:24 (12,133)
Bicknell, Richard J....3:54:33 (10,066)
Biddis, Mark G....3:51:09 (9,135)
Biddiscombe, Rupert S....4:29:26 (19,153)
Bidgood, Gavin J....6:40:13 (32,614)
Bidgood, Martyn J....3:57:55 (11,139)
Bidmead, Christopher I....4:54:42 (24,816)
Bidston, Mark J....4:02:02 (12,274)
Biederman, Carlos....3:09:34 (2,020)
Bielby, Richard S....3:39:43 (6,574)
Bier, Nicholas A....4:46:18 (23,075)
Bierton, Kelvin J....3:52:32 (9,501)
Biesold, Frank....3:33:13 (5,357)
Biffin, Mark S....6:24:13 (32,334)
Biggart, Douglas....4:38:50 (21,400)
Biggs, Gerard M....5:42:41 (30,547)
Biggs, Simon J....4:15:24 (15,449)
Biggs, Stuart J....5:57:19 (31,425)
Biggs-Hayes, Thomas W....4:51:56 (24,239)
Bigham, Colin....3:25:46 (4,040)
Bigley, Matthew R....2:46:30 (404)
Bigmore, Jonathan P....3:12:58 (2,393)
Bigmore, Paul T....4:17:01 (15,867)
Bignell, Philip J....3:32:03 (5,169)
Bilato, Roberto....3:45:08 (7,715)
Bilcock, Graham W....3:53:40 (9,810)
Biles, Dominic P....3:53:04 (9,655)
Bilke, David C....4:33:20 (20,092)
Billin, Peter A....4:08:21 (13,704)
Billingham, David P....3:13:28 (2,462)
Billington, Andrew....4:47:12 (23,260)
Billington, Gary....3:38:44 (6,374)
Billows, Jon....6:14:09 (32,057)
Bills, Chris G....4:17:09 (15,894)
Bills, Robert....4:31:01 (19,537)
Billy, Andrew T....5:40:11 (30,380)
Biltcliffe, Steven J....4:17:47 (16,056)
Bilton, Carl R....4:50:21 (23,917)
Bilton, Jason C....4:21:58 (17,108)
Binch, Trevor A....6:50:43 (32,770)
Binder, Peter J....5:24:49 (29,018)
Bindra, Amrit P....5:20:08 (28,510)
Binfield, Geoffrey C....4:30:06 (19,324)
Bingham, Graham W....4:53:55 (24,663)
Bingham, Hugh....2:55:11 (798)
Bingham, Kenneth....4:27:39 (18,671)
Bingham, Kevin R....4:47:23 (23,287)
Bingham, Stephen M....3:30:14 (4,858)
Bingham, Stuart J....3:36:00 (5,836)
Binner, Daniel J....3:37:54 (6,208)
Binns, Daniel J....4:52:27 (24,343)
Binstead, Simon J....5:04:19 (26,491)
Bionaz, Franck....3:31:34 (5,082)
Birch, Andy J....4:37:10 (21,017)
Birch, Christopher B....3:19:11 (3,156)
Birch, Eric....4:58:31 (25,614)
Birch, Kevin D....4:21:42 (17,023)
Birch, Sean W....3:30:19 (4,867)
Birch, Stephen....4:59:47 (25,847)
Birchall, Chris....2:25:10 (44)
Birchmore, Trevor M....5:44:27 (30,678)
Bircumshaw, Nigel A....4:17:56 (16,088)
Bird, Andrew D....4:36:47 (20,933)
Bird, Andrew P....3:08:42 (1,926)
Bird, Christopher....3:55:33 (10,387)
Bird, Christopher I....4:57:20 (25,371)
Bird, Colin C....5:11:32 (27,464)
Bird, David J....3:12:27 (2,339)
Bird, James A....6:48:53 (32,742)
Bird, James M....5:52:09 (31,187)
Bird, Jamie E....3:23:24 (3,697)
Bird, John....4:39:18 (21,514)
Bird, Jonathan C....4:11:35 (14,475)
Bird, Melvyn....4:09:32 (14,000)
Bird, Vincent J....5:36:16 (30,077)
Birk, Yves....4:21:51 (17,076)
Birkby, David P....4:10:09 (14,135)
Birkens, John B....3:29:01 (4,624)
Birkett, Harokd H....5:10:43 (27,354)
Birks, Kevin....4:40:30 (21,777)
Birley, Carl S....5:02:46 (26,284)
Birley, Patrick....4:16:40 (15,773)
Birmingham, Bill....3:08:27 (1,904)
Birnie, Andrew E....2:52:08 (643)
Birt, Ashley S....3:22:43 (3,626)
Biscoe, Simon J....5:04:51 (26,561)
Biscomb, Geoffrey C....3:21:27 (3,460)
Bish-Jones, Trevor C....4:46:11 (23,047)
Bishop, Andrew L....3:28:44 (4,561)
Bishop, Andy....3:23:24 (3,697)
Bishop, Antony D....3:04:30 (1,548)
Bishop, Calvin....3:28:35 (4,528)
Bishop, Daniel T....2:44:33 (332)
Bishop, Darren B....3:12:10 (2,302)
Bishop, David....4:41:59 (22,110)
Bishop, David A....3:48:02 (8,392)
Bishop, David S....4:59:25 (25,764)
Bishop, Graham A....4:45:30 (22,904)
Bishop, John F....5:33:50 (29,876)
Bishop, Karl M....5:03:35 (26,400)
Bishop, Mark D....4:36:19 (20,809)
Bishop, Michael J....6:11:21 (31,965)
Bishop, Oli....4:09:53 (14,076)
Bishop, Paul M....4:29:04 (19,041)
Bishop, Simon....4:41:43 (22,039)

Bishop, Stephen	3:40:04 (6,636)	
Bishop, Stephen D	4:21:56 (17,095)	
Bishop, Steven D	2:48:06 (455)	
Bisiker, Stephen R	4:24:26 (17,785)	
Bisla, Navtes	4:37:27 (21,097)	
Bisley, William T	4:45:22 (22,877)	
Biss, Neil	4:12:22 (14,677)	
Bissett, Richard	4:25:02 (17,972)	
Bissett, Tim J	4:13:18 (14,917)	
Bissig, Stephan	3:57:34 (11,033)	
Bissoli, Franco	2:55:06 (794)	
Bissoli, Gianni	2:49:36 (522)	
Bitmead, Martin	3:59:40 (11,715)	
Bivens, John H	6:17:44 (32,166)	
Bixter, Mark	3:45:14 (7,737)	
Bizby, David C	4:39:20 (21,528)	
Bjelanovic, Predrag	3:57:39 (11,060)	
Bjerrum, Mads	3:26:58 (4,237)	
Bjornermark, Thomas	3:41:32 (6,926)	
Bjornsson, Ingolfur	4:18:18 (16,183)	
Blaafjelldal, Vidar	3:54:50 (10,156)	
Blaber, Edward T	4:46:14 (23,056)	
Black, Alistair	2:58:42 (1,097)	
Black, Alistair M	4:16:50 (15,811)	
Black, Richard	4:42:49 (22,288)	
Black, Richard A	4:22:35 (17,260)	
Black, Samuel H	5:22:48 (28,811)	
Black, Steven E	4:33:20 (20,092)	
Black, Stuart R	3:40:58 (6,798)	
Blackaller, Russell	3:48:15 (8,441)	
Blackburn, Andrew P	4:32:04 (19,808)	
Blackburn, Andrew R	3:45:46 (7,863)	
Blackburn, Daniel T	4:15:44 (15,529)	
Blackburn, David	4:16:03 (15,609)	
Blackburn, Graham M	3:00:59 (1,302)	
Blackburn, Guy V	4:23:29 (17,496)	
Blackburn, Ian	4:17:48 (16,060)	
Blackburn, Jonathan	5:34:37 (29,945)	
Blackburn, Jonathan C	4:55:59 (25,103)	
Blackburn, Joseph C	4:11:31 (14,462)	
Blackburn, Paul	3:52:36 (9,520)	
Blackburn, Simon J	3:54:58 (10,194)	
Blackford, Robert G	4:56:11 (25,135)	
Blackham, Robin J	4:24:18 (17,750)	
Blackie, David	4:49:40 (23,786)	
Blackman, David A	3:12:13 (2,311)	
Blackman, Gary N	4:15:41 (15,514)	
Blackman, Jamie	3:53:24 (9,738)	
Blackman, Keith W	4:44:10 (22,598)	
Blackman, Leslie K	4:49:21 (23,724)	
Blackman, Roger A	4:38:14 (21,287)	
Blackmore, Anthony M	4:41:46 (22,052)	
Blackmore, Daniel C	3:48:38 (8,535)	
Blackmore, Darren T	3:37:00 (6,042)	
Blackmore, Mark	5:04:06 (26,466)	
Blackmore, Matthew	3:54:52 (10,165)	
Blackmore, Stephen D	3:04:05 (1,519)	
Blackshaw, Steve M	3:59:12 (11,577)	
Blackwel, Phillip N	3:11:51 (2,252)	
Blackwell, Martin E	3:55:29 (10,369)	
Blackwell, Nicholas A	3:11:50 (2,249)	
Blades, Kenneth	4:05:24 (13,000)	
Blades, Nicholas A	3:10:40 (2,128)	
Bladon, Andrew	4:44:15 (22,625)	
Blain, Christopher J	4:21:38 (17,006)	
Blaine, John S	3:09:56 (2,056)	
Blair, Alan J	3:12:16 (2,319)	
Blake, James D	3:18:23 (3,045)	
Blake, James M	4:48:52 (23,623)	
Blake, Kevin M	4:11:28 (14,452)	
Blake, Marcus T	3:18:33 (3,076)	
Blake, Neil A	3:49:07 (8,650)	
Blake, Nicholas M	3:15:37 (2,727)	
Blake, Peter G	4:54:47 (24,840)	
Blake, Simon	3:52:20 (9,445)	
Blakeley, Mark A	5:05:13 (26,616)	
Blakey, Brian	5:07:36 (26,947)	
Blakey, David M	4:10:53 (14,301)	
Blakie, Gary	3:20:45 (3,371)	
Blamey, Jonathan M	3:23:28 (3,706)	
Bland, Adam	4:29:08 (19,065)	
Bland, David J	4:07:45 (13,545)	
Bland, Steven M	4:13:39 (14,994)	

Blaney, Neil A	4:00:13 (11,869)	
Blank, Jonathan J	4:30:22 (19,393)	
Blank, Tony J	5:37:42 (30,180)	
Blankendaal, Jeroen A	3:56:38 (10,734)	
Blanshard, Neil D	3:31:44 (5,109)	
Blantz, Andrew	4:30:52 (19,509)	
Blanvillain, Dominique	4:08:18 (13,689)	
Blaser, Patrick P	3:09:57 (2,058)	
Blasques Da Rosa Lea, JM	4:19:37 (16,505)	
Blaxter, James D	4:30:13 (19,357)	
Blazquez, José L	3:44:56 (7,677)	
Bleach, Paul A	2:39:03 (189)	
Bleaken, Daniel G	4:07:29 (13,470)	
Bleakley, Alasdair P	4:56:21 (25,175)	
Blenkhorn, John W	4:26:45 (18,452)	
Blevins, Alistair S	5:03:58 (26,453)	
Blevins, Stewart	4:50:53 (24,023)	
Blewett, Stephen G	3:12:40 (2,358)	
Bligh, William A	6:24:56 (32,352)	
Bliss, David	5:24:55 (29,031)	
Bliss, Robert G	5:00:54 (26,028)	
Blissett, Luther L	5:09:47 (27,240)	
Bliszko, Ferenc	5:07:49 (26,976)	
Blizzard, Gareth D	2:56:23 (882)	
Bloemsma, Jeroen	4:34:57 (20,473)	
Blofeld, Stuart R	3:57:47 (11,110)	
Blois, Richard	6:56:19 (32,845)	
Blok, André	3:23:42 (3,742)	
Blokland, Koos	5:48:16 (30,961)	
Blondel, Thomas L	3:47:48 (8,326)	
Bloom, Andrew	4:30:31 (19,432)	
Bloom, Marc	4:25:15 (18,042)	
Bloomer, Peter	4:45:50 (22,977)	
Bloomfield, Barry F	3:20:18 (3,312)	
Bloomfield, Colin	3:50:54 (9,077)	
Bloomfield, David J	4:11:45 (14,508)	
Bloomfield, Mark A	4:01:10 (12,092)	
Bloor, Charles D	3:42:28 (7,106)	
Bloss, Richard J	3:08:09 (1,873)	
Blot, David	3:54:04 (9,936)	
Blount, Christopher	5:27:22 (29,258)	
Blower, David E	4:07:08 (13,385)	
Blower, John L	5:37:42 (30,180)	
Blower, Lee	4:02:18 (12,331)	
Blowes, Benjamin D	3:06:30 (1,709)	
Blowin, Gregory	4:33:30 (20,135)	
Blowing, Michael	4:25:52 (18,215)	
Bloxam, Andrew	3:34:33 (5,581)	
Bloxham, Clive	5:21:21 (28,652)	
Bloxham, Roy W	4:06:38 (13,256)	
Bluck, Gavin W	3:48:29 (8,495)	
Bluhm, Peter	4:32:21 (19,873)	
Blunn, Andrew	3:14:18 (2,567)	
Blunt, Peter E	4:48:34 (23,556)	
Blunt, Richard L	3:52:22 (9,458)	
Bluteau, Jean-Claude	4:35:56 (20,698)	
Blyth, Graham R	4:39:17 (21,509)	
Blyth, John R	3:46:41 (8,057)	
Blyth, Paul J	4:34:34 (20,382)	
Blyth, Ric M	4:40:48 (21,855)	
Blythe, Dominic	3:45:43 (7,854)	
Blythe, Kenneth C	4:15:04 (15,355)	
Blythe, Roy A	3:26:00 (4,074)	
Blythen, Timothy R	3:19:07 (3,145)	
Boal, Calvin	5:46:24 (30,818)	
Board, Chris	4:50:41 (23,979)	
Board, Jonathan M	4:39:38 (21,584)	
Boardley, Ian	3:03:03 (1,447)	
Boardley, John T	4:46:53 (23,192)	
Boardley, Neal J	3:13:36 (2,476)	
Boardman, Keith	2:56:17 (875)	
Boardman, Wayne J	4:27:50 (18,703)	
Boas, Jason M	3:55:36 (10,405)	
Bober, Richard J	3:48:23 (8,470)	
Bocchetti, Katio	5:14:01 (27,767)	
Bocock, Ian T	5:50:19 (31,096)	
Bocock, Stephen P	4:42:11 (22,153)	
Boddy, Christopher S	6:50:27 (32,766)	
Boddy, Michael J	3:31:52 (5,138)	
Boddy, Paul J	5:08:16 (27,045)	
Boden, Lazloe	2:52:01 (638)	
Boden, Marc I	3:59:17 (11,599)	
Boden, Mark A	4:42:39 (22,249)	

Boden, Sam L	3:11:28 (2,211)	
Bodenham, David	4:22:21 (17,209)	
Body, Robert D	5:54:37 (31,294)	
Bofill, Laurent	4:32:11 (19,827)	
Bogaert, Jan R	3:26:35 (4,173)	
Bogg, Charles H	3:31:49 (5,125)	
Boggild, Esben K	4:48:34 (23,556)	
Boggis, Mark A	3:49:22 (8,707)	
Bogle, Thomas P	3:07:32 (1,807)	
Bogue, Christopher	5:21:29 (28,663)	
Bogush, Jeremy H	3:59:59 (11,808)	
Bohm, Peter	4:25:40 (18,153)	
Bohm, Urs	2:48:34 (476)	
Boillereau, Frederick	3:34:55 (5,646)	
Boivin, Philippe	3:26:10 (4,096)	
Bolam, Kevin F	4:21:16 (16,932)	
Bold, Paul G	4:32:09 (19,820)	
Bold, Stewart R	6:58:03 (32,864)	
Bolden, David K	3:30:04 (4,838)	
Bole, Frederic	2:48:39 (481)	
Bolewski, Bernd	4:48:31 (23,543)	
Bollington, Simon S	4:16:07 (15,627)	
Bolton, Andrew J	4:55:38 (25,023)	
Bolton, Ashley J	3:59:12 (11,577)	
Bolton, David J	4:55:22 (24,976)	
Bolton, David R	5:52:16 (31,192)	
Bolton, Delme J	3:51:48 (9,303)	
Bolton, Jeffrey R	4:43:06 (22,346)	
Bolton, Marc	5:37:38 (30,176)	
Bolton, Ross E	4:20:08 (16,636)	
Bolton, Simon	4:10:06 (14,121)	
Bolton, Steve	2:55:32 (819)	
Bolton, Wayne L	4:13:34 (14,968)	
Bolus, Richard W	5:00:39 (25,990)	
Bolvig, Thomas	4:23:47 (17,582)	
Bolwell, Guy R	4:27:18 (18,578)	
Bombardi, Luca	4:38:05 (21,251)	
Bonacini, Ermanno	4:54:47 (24,840)	
Bonass, Carl	4:05:41 (13,074)	
Bond, Daniel M	4:49:13 (23,694)	
Bond, Leon P	3:16:44 (2,845)	
Bond, Mark G	5:33:32 (29,849)	
Bond, Martin A	4:45:01 (22,791)	
Bond, Robin G	4:06:57 (13,337)	
Bond, Stewart	3:32:05 (5,178)	
Bondioli, Luca	4:06:25 (13,215)	
Bone, Kenneth C	5:01:57 (26,171)	
Bone, Morgan	3:27:34 (4,344)	
Bone, Paul	5:23:11 (28,853)	
Bonelli, Anthony S	4:38:40 (21,365)	
Boney, Christian	3:28:49 (4,578)	
Boniface, Andrew	4:41:27 (21,982)	
Bonito, José A	3:42:00 (7,024)	
Bonner, Dannie J	4:07:21 (13,433)	
Bonner, Mark	5:11:13 (27,415)	
Bonnet, Jean-Claude C	5:02:44 (26,278)	
Bonnick, Ian N	3:49:10 (8,661)	
Bont, Jacobus G	4:01:07 (12,077)	
Bontoft, Alan	2:57:09 (956)	
Booker, John D	3:57:12 (10,920)	
Booker, Paul T	4:19:18 (16,422)	
Bookham, Colin D	3:53:07 (9,665)	
Bookham, Kevin J	3:22:51 (3,641)	
Boom, Gary	4:05:32 (13,034)	
Boon, Matthew J	3:17:04 (2,885)	
Boon, Richard	3:36:34 (5,947)	
Boon, Robert	2:57:35 (992)	
Boorman, Bill	7:08:17 (32,964)	
Boorman, Jon C	5:05:00 (26,581)	
Boorman, Nickolas	4:09:07 (13,881)	
Boosey, Robert G	4:11:10 (14,380)	
Booth, Andrew J	4:20:08 (16,636)	
Booth, Bernard J	5:49:31 (31,046)	
Booth, George	3:12:39 (2,356)	
Booth, Julian	3:54:11 (9,972)	
Booth, Levi J	3:00:20 (1,256)	
Booth, Mark	3:26:13 (4,105)	
Booth, Nigel	6:05:34 (31,779)	
Booth, Paul D	4:08:56 (13,846)	
Booth, Roger	3:03:25 (1,474)	
Booth, Simon M	4:16:54 (15,833)	
Booth, Steve H	5:47:06 (30,870)	
Booth, Terence	4:56:30 (25,204)	

Booth, Allan 3:54:11 (9,972)
Boother, Mark 4:37:29 (21,108)
Boquillet, Laurent 3:15:48 (2,753)
Boral, Jacek 2:28:02 (57)
Bordes, Patrick 4:47:11 (23,255)
Bordilion, Marco 3:23:48 (3,755)
Boreel, Jacob 4:02:15 (12,319)
Boreham, Martin J 3:51:37 (9,247)
Borejszo, Sean 5:29:57 (29,540)
Borges, Yann 3:12:04 (2,285)
Borghi, Cristiano 3:53:31 (9,771)
Borgini, Mario 5:47:17 (30,892)
Borgman, Paul S 3:43:36 (7,370)
Borgund, Ole Jan 4:31:22 (19,630)
Bork, Ralf-Rainer 4:45:04 (22,807)
Borland, John A 4:41:49 (22,060)
Borley, Harry W 4:17:18 (15,929)
Borondy, Steve 3:40:55 (6,786)
Borrelli, Piero 4:24:40 (17,864)
Borrowdale, David 3:06:10 (1,682)
Borsley, Stephen J 3:33:13 (5,357)
Bortoft, Arron 3:17:25 (2,934)
Borton, Simon A 3:05:46 (1,639)
Borup, Kell 4:43:43 (22,499)
Bos, Yvo B 4:35:01 (20,496)
Bosch, Ulf 3:10:36 (2,124)
Boschetti, Paolo 3:40:50 (6,765)
Bose, Jamie 5:08:01 (27,007)
Bosence, Mark 4:55:52 (25,070)
Bosse, Thomas 3:41:31 (6,922)
Bosson, Paul J 2:50:57 (588)
Bostock, Colin R 4:00:36 (11,948)
Bostock, Malcolm S 2:51:31 (613)
Boston, Barry T 5:01:29 (26,106)
Boston, David T 4:21:43 (17,026)
Boston, Nasser 4:06:57 (13,337)
Bostrom, Sven Erik 5:13:19 (27,692)
Boswell, Lindsay S 4:18:25 (16,212)
Boswell, Matthew J 4:29:48 (19,250)
Boswell, Robert J 4:50:03 (23,850)
Boswell, Scott 4:05:32 (13,034)
Botalla, Gilles 3:23:00 (3,656)
Botelho, Pedro 3:37:06 (6,058)
Botfield, Andrew R 4:42:45 (22,269)
Botfield, Glyn J 4:07:49 (13,564)
Botha, Theunis L 3:29:17 (4,671)
Botha, William J 4:59:37 (25,815)
Botham, Stephen A 3:40:04 (6,636)
Bott, Jonathan R 3:05:50 (1,648)
Bottomley, Christopher I 3:43:57 (7,449)
Bottwood, Guy W 4:01:40 (12,186)
Botwright, Robert 4:15:06 (15,366)
Boucault, Darren S 4:09:41 (14,026)
Boucher, Ian T 4:03:46 (12,665)
Boucher, Michael B 2:29:35 (69)
Boucher, Stuart C 5:02:29 (26,246)
Boudreault, Jean Michel 3:15:04 (2,667)
Boudry, Fenwick 5:26:33 (29,177)
Boudry, Stephen F 4:00:00 (11,810)
Boughton, Ellis J 3:59:24 (11,638)
Bouhy, Alain 5:09:32 (27,210)
Boukhelif, Akim 4:35:05 (20,508)
Boulding, Simon J 5:07:12 (26,892)
Boulton, David 4:55:56 (25,085)
Boulton, Jude D 3:25:07 (3,949)
Boulton, Samuel J 3:55:47 (10,472)
Bourdillat, Loic 3:39:05 (6,451)
Bourdillon, Luke E 4:50:16 (23,898)
Bourdonnais, Alain 4:00:58 (12,040)
Bourgaize, Andrew 3:41:06 (6,827)
Bourguignon, Eril 3:35:52 (5,810)
Bourke, Dominic 4:55:04 (24,908)
Bourke, Stephen J 4:02:30 (12,374)
Bourla, Marcel A 2:30:57 (75)
Bourn, David J 4:37:15 (21,045)
Bourne, Michael J 3:54:59 (10,196)
Bourne, Richard L 3:50:44 (9,037)
Bourne, Simon C 4:09:21 (13,946)
Bournes, Michael J 4:55:54 (25,077)
Bousfield, Mark 5:30:03 (29,549)
Bousfield, Tim G 5:17:17 (28,164)
Boutell, Richard J 3:28:11 (4,438)
Bouziani, Rachid 4:12:03 (14,585)
Bove, Nicola 3:07:55 (1,847)
Bovey, Cedric 3:29:48 (4,782)
Bovill, Peter J 3:25:57 (4,066)
Bovone, Arnaldo 3:58:58 (11,497)
Bowd, Ryan 4:37:06 (21,002)
Bowden, Bill 4:28:17 (18,833)
Bowden, Daniel 3:16:34 (2,823)
Bowden, Paul 4:11:44 (14,503)
Bowden, Richard 5:31:04 (29,664)
Bowden, William J 4:28:49 (18,976)
Bowdery, Scott J 4:31:35 (19,692)
Bowell, John D 5:11:21 (27,434)
Bowell, Mark A 5:24:43 (29,008)
Bowen, Alister S 4:44:45 (22,721)
Bowen, Andy 3:19:50 (3,238)
Bowen, Anthony J 4:08:10 (13,656)
Bowen, Anthony J 4:47:58 (23,422)
Bowen, David I 3:38:44 (6,374)
Bowen, David R 4:59:37 (25,815)
Bowen, Geraint R 4:23:35 (17,527)
Bowen, James 2:57:25 (975)
Bowen, Keith J 3:40:26 (6,698)
Bowen, Meurig 4:53:17 (24,520)
Bowen, Nigel T 4:06:34 (13,243)
Bowen, Robert M 4:29:56 (19,276)
Bowen, Simon J 3:47:12 (8,168)
Bowen, William 4:14:37 (15,237)
Bower, Edward T 4:22:12 (17,174)
Bower, Julian C 3:33:51 (5,456)
Bower, Michael L 3:44:15 (7,507)
Bower, Richard E 4:12:51 (14,796)
Bower, Scott D 3:57:50 (11,121)
Bowern, Jonathan M 5:03:57 (26,451)
Bowers, Adam J 5:28:08 (29,342)
Bowers, Jared P 4:22:46 (17,315)
Bowers, Nigel L 4:39:50 (21,636)
Bowes, Andrew J 4:32:13 (19,836)
Bowes, David 4:09:11 (13,903)
Bowes, David H 6:25:47 (32,372)
Bowhay, Paul C 5:24:03 (28,949)
Bowie, Bill B 4:03:21 (12,565)
Bowker, Richard 4:57:20 (25,371)
Bowker, Robert J 4:00:39 (11,965)
Bowkett, Andrew 4:26:31 (18,389)
Bowler, Dean J 4:58:34 (25,625)
Bowler, Paul L 4:08:55 (13,842)
Bowles, Alastair E 4:23:26 (17,478)
Bowles, Darren D 5:54:43 (31,300)
Bowles, James W 3:55:33 (10,387)
Bowles, Jason F 4:46:28 (23,113)
Bowles, Neil 5:07:33 (26,939)
Bowles, Stephen J 4:15:17 (15,408)
Bowles, Steven J 4:09:14 (13,919)
Bowling, Roy P 3:11:04 (2,165)
Bowling, Shane 3:23:13 (3,676)
Bowman, Benjamin W 2:39:30 (199)
Bowman, Geoff M 3:25:50 (4,052)
Bowman, John 4:59:48 (25,852)
Bowman, Mark O 3:54:17 (9,997)
Bowman, Nicholas 4:30:57 (19,521)
Bowman, Paul M 4:18:25 (16,212)
Bownes, Kevin G 3:26:34 (4,168)
Bowry, William J 3:52:56 (9,604)
Bowser, Phillip R 4:44:57 (22,770)
Bowyer, Glenn A 3:43:49 (7,427)
Bowyer, Ian 4:04:20 (12,782)
Bowyer, Ian 5:13:09 (27,671)
Bowyer, Malcolm J 2:57:11 (959)
Bowyer, Stephen W 5:13:00 (27,653)
Box, Adam J 3:49:01 (8,630)
Box, James A 3:23:37 (3,728)
Box, Mark A 4:02:44 (12,420)
Boxall, John E 4:31:45 (19,733)
Boxall, Peter J 5:16:21 (28,051)
Boxall-Hunt, Stuart A 4:42:38 (22,242)
Boxer, Nicholas 4:07:35 (13,501)
Boxford, Stephen H 4:38:47 (21,387)
Boy, Graeme I 3:51:26 (9,204)
Boyall, Timothy J 3:19:28 (3,191)
Boyce, Christopher J 5:22:12 (28,743)
Boyce, Jesse A 4:12:37 (14,729)
Boyce, Richard E 3:06:14 (1,690)
Boyd, Gareth J 4:49:58 (23,838)
Boyd, Keith 4:24:53 (17,917)
Boyd, Kenneth A 3:47:00 (8,119)
Boyd, Timothy 4:19:09 (16,379)
Boyes, Andrew 3:19:02 (3,136)
Boyes, James W 4:17:00 (15,860)
Boyett, Dakius P 4:47:34 (23,339)
Boyle, Kieron J 3:53:47 (9,853)
Boyle, Mark C 4:13:52 (15,034)
Boyle, Robert J 4:53:50 (24,642)
Boynton, Christopher H 5:12:05 (27,537)
Boyter, Gavin 3:11:43 (2,238)
Brabin, James H 3:48:09 (8,422)
Brabyn, Matthew P 3:50:02 (8,871)
Bracegirdle, Paul A 3:52:29 (9,488)
Bracey, Nick 3:55:43 (10,444)
Bracey, Paul R 4:22:09 (17,157)
Brachet, Loic 4:50:11 (23,876)
Brackstone, Lawrence C 4:07:49 (13,564)
Bracqbien, Denis B 4:03:02 (12,489)
Bradburn, Robert K 3:51:59 (9,361)
Bradbury, Alan K 3:23:30 (3,713)
Bradbury, Kelvin E 3:40:23 (6,687)
Bradbury, Mark 4:35:36 (20,624)
Bradbury, Stephen A 3:55:55 (10,514)
Bradbury, Tom 4:17:06 (15,886)
Bradford, Karl M 4:02:52 (12,449)
Bradford, Luke R 4:23:42 (17,560)
Bradford, Matt S 3:26:23 (4,134)
Bradford, Roy 5:19:27 (28,428)
Bradford, Simon D 4:11:35 (14,475)
Bradley, Barrington J 4:03:36 (12,624)
Bradley, David M 3:44:26 (7,547)
Bradley, Harvey 3:52:51 (9,578)
Bradley, Ian 4:00:26 (11,921)
Bradley, Ian B 4:57:53 (25,475)
Bradley, Jack 4:36:30 (20,844)
Bradley, Jeremy 3:50:00 (8,868)
Bradley, Leslie J 4:32:10 (19,825)
Bradley, Mark 3:48:00 (8,382)
Bradley, Matthew J 4:57:54 (25,479)
Bradley, Michael J 4:13:52 (15,034)
Bradley, Michael J 5:02:31 (26,251)
Bradley, Paul 4:38:56 (21,426)
Bradley, Philip A 3:19:57 (3,259)
Bradley, Phillip 4:48:15 (23,483)
Bradley, Robert J 4:55:38 (25,023)
Bradley, Russell J 4:58:23 (25,584)
Bradley, William P 3:33:58 (5,474)
Bradley MBE, Raymond 5:44:01 (30,642)
Bradnock, Tim J 5:47:04 (30,867)
Bradshaw, Adam 3:58:47 (11,440)
Bradshaw, Eric G 4:14:50 (15,292)
Bradshaw, Karl R 5:46:38 (30,835)
Bradshaw, Mark 3:47:48 (8,326)
Bradshaw, Thomas W 4:15:52 (15,569)
Bradwell, Andrew D 4:39:25 (21,548)
Brady, Gerald 5:41:46 (30,481)
Brady, John C 3:30:41 (4,929)
Brady, Joseph M 2:57:18 (967)
Brady, Luke W 4:41:45 (22,048)
Brady, Martin A 4:19:58 (16,594)
Brady, Owen D 4:27:26 (18,606)
Brady, Paul A 5:39:17 (30,301)
Bragg, Jeremy P 2:47:21 (429)
Bragg, Simon A 4:26:27 (18,371)
Braid, David P 4:31:00 (19,533)
Braidwood, Billy G 3:14:18 (2,567)
Braidwood, Ian 4:53:52 (24,652)
Brain, Robert E 4:23:42 (17,560)
Braithwaite, Andrew J 3:53:41 (9,816)
Braithwaite, Jonathan P 6:17:41 (32,163)
Braithwaite, Lee A 4:42:21 (22,190)
Braithwaite, Stephen A 4:54:52 (24,866)
Braizat, Pascal 3:33:23 (5,386)
Brake, Martin J 5:04:18 (26,489)
Bramall, Hugh 4:01:45 (12,199)
Brame, Paul F 4:13:01 (14,850)
Bramhald, Simon H 3:36:55 (6,024)
Bramhall, Christopher P 5:03:52 (26,441)
Bramham, Lee 4:44:29 (22,678)
Bramley, George E 3:10:57 (2,152)
Bramley, Jonathan 4:06:44 (13,285)
Bramley, Mark R 3:40:59 (6,799)

Bramley, Tony D 4:37:06 (21,002)
Bramwell, Joel 4:48:05 (23,446)
Bramwell, Jonathon D 5:03:56 (26,448)
Bran, Thomas M 4:18:09 (16,151)
Branch, Jon S 4:16:26 (15,704)
Branch, Staurt 4:26:07 (18,291)
Branco, Miguel R 2:49:10 (507)
Brand, Ian G 4:06:27 (13,219)
Brand, Neil G 4:56:01 (25,106)
Brand, Philip 4:08:14 (13,674)
Brand, Roger J 3:32:08 (5,184)
Brandish, Stephen E 4:13:49 (15,025)
Brandon, Dirk 2:50:50 (581)
Brandon, Simon J 5:08:33 (27,084)
Brandt, David A 4:13:47 (15,018)
Brandt, Francisco J 4:40:36 (21,810)
Brannican, Niall S 5:19:24 (28,425)
Brannigan, Damien T 3:10:04 (2,070)
Brannon, Guy 4:31:19 (19,618)
Bransby, Guy A 5:19:11 (28,403)
Branson, Martin C 4:32:15 (19,845)
Branson, Robert J 4:36:46 (20,924)
Brant, John R 4:19:08 (16,374)
Brant, Raymond P 4:21:01 (16,873)
Brant, William 3:27:42 (4,365)
Branthwaite, Ian C 3:48:34 (8,517)
Brasher, Martin L 3:38:24 (6,303)
Brask, Anders 3:48:53 (8,603)
Brassington, Jonathan C 3:47:03 (8,133)
Bratchell, Roger T 4:14:27 (15,197)
Brattoli, Raffaele 3:35:29 (5,747)
Bratton, Mark Q 3:55:23 (10,339)
Bratton, Timothy J 3:57:07 (10,888)
Braunton, David W 4:48:43 (23,587)
Brawn, Jason 4:07:58 (13,606)
Bray, Alan 3:41:19 (6,876)
Bray, Chris J 4:31:46 (19,738)
Bray, Edward P 4:27:56 (18,733)
Bray, James E 4:05:11 (12,951)
Bray, Simon G 4:56:20 (25,172)
Braybrook, Colin A 2:46:22 (401)
Braybrook, Mark W 2:56:06 (857)
Brayn, Warren P 5:06:00 (26,710)
Brayshaw, Chris D 3:33:57 (5,473)
Brazier, Jeff 4:27:08 (18,538)
Brazil, John 5:18:09 (28,262)
Breach, Hamish 4:23:21 (17,454)
Breadmore, Nigel D 3:43:33 (7,361)
Brearley, Andrew S 3:03:03 (1,447)
Brecht, Philip T 3:53:30 (9,766)
Breda, Errol 5:14:38 (27,860)
Breen, Christopher C 4:00:00 (11,810)
Breen, Francis G 3:56:45 (10,766)
Breen, Paul A 3:46:18 (7,970)
Breese, Trevor N 3:58:24 (11,306)
Breeze, Christopher J 4:24:08 (17,697)
Bregeau, Dominique 4:17:11 (15,905)
Brehaut, Matthew 4:06:14 (13,181)
Brehmer, Henrik 3:24:14 (3,831)
Breidenbach, Hubert E 4:55:23 (24,980)
Bremner, Walter J 3:47:19 (8,196)
Brenchley, Michael L 4:28:03 (18,762)
Brend, Colin A 5:08:57 (27,143)
Brennan, Chris 4:48:53 (23,625)
Brennan, David 4:52:52 (24,431)
Brennan, David K 7:03:23 (32,913)
Brennan, Eamon C 4:51:49 (24,214)
Brennan, Joe C 4:25:56 (18,238)
Brennan, Kevin 3:29:12 (4,654)
Brennan, Neill 3:28:11 (4,438)
Brennan, Niall P 4:39:36 (21,577)
Brennan, Patrick P 4:52:31 (24,358)
Brennan, Paul M 5:47:16 (30,886)
Brennan, Stephen A 4:08:08 (13,648)
Brennan, Timothy R 3:50:19 (8,937)
Brentnall, Dean M 5:07:00 (26,861)
Brequeville, David 4:20:09 (16,644)
Breslin, Dave 6:51:14 (32,777)
Breslin, Declan 3:44:10 (7,486)
Breslin, Edward D 3:58:16 (11,253)
Breslin, John 3:47:03 (8,133)
Bressington, Darrell C 3:41:30 (6,914)
Breton, Edward H 3:57:03 (10,861)
Brett, Christopher J 5:35:01 (29,967)
Brett, Colin M 3:40:04 (6,636)
Brett, Gary R 4:06:38 (13,256)
Brett, Mark I 4:53:04 (24,468)
Brett, Rory M 4:36:53 (20,960)
Brett, Stephen 2:58:46 (1,106)
Brettell, John M 4:51:52 (24,225)
Breuker, Casper J 4:08:04 (13,632)
Brew, Patrick 3:15:31 (2,722)
Brewer, John 3:48:09 (8,422)
Brewer, John S 4:50:04 (23,855)
Brewer, Joseph T 3:29:08 (4,643)
Brewer, Lyndon D 3:51:38 (9,252)
Brewer, Michael D 3:44:24 (7,538)
Brewster, Graham 4:31:32 (19,678)
Breydin, Patrick J 4:46:48 (23,171)
Brian, Paul 5:07:31 (26,932)
Briant, Laurent M 4:51:50 (24,218)
Briche, Eric 3:29:42 (4,759)
Bridge, Adrian 3:59:43 (11,738)
Bridge, Adrian R 3:44:52 (7,658)
Bridge, Matthew J 3:10:08 (2,076)
Bridge, Peter E 5:26:59 (29,224)
Bridger, Andrew J 3:31:42 (5,101)
Bridger, Mark 5:13:57 (27,757)
Bridges, Alex J 5:42:01 (30,497)
Bridges, Anthony M 2:42:24 (260)
Bridges, Donald J 3:44:09 (7,480)
Bridges, Simon E 4:58:47 (25,658)
Bridgewater, Keith 4:21:45 (17,045)
Bridle, Lee J 4:46:21 (23,091)
Brien, James 3:31:04 (4,998)
Brier, Anthony J 4:53:23 (24,544)
Brierley, Andrew S 2:57:25 (975)
Briers, Craig A 3:45:37 (7,826)
Briffitt, Charlie W 3:58:38 (11,375)
Briggs, Gary 4:00:12 (11,864)
Briggs, Iain A 4:46:37 (23,144)
Briggs, Jonathan D 5:48:09 (30,953)
Briggs, Jonathan M 3:59:26 (11,651)
Briggs, Karl D 4:11:09 (14,377)
Briggs, Michael C 3:35:38 (5,774)
Briggs, Paul G 3:49:03 (8,637)
Briggs, Peter I 3:41:34 (6,933)
Briggs, Robert 5:21:13 (28,632)
Briggs, Timothy P 3:32:46 (5,287)
Bright, Andrew A 4:25:03 (17,976)
Bright, Mark 4:03:06 (12,504)
Bright, Mark A 4:16:16 (15,660)
Bright, Simon 4:36:43 (20,901)
Brignall, David M 3:28:32 (4,522)
Brigstock, Jamie R 4:08:47 (13,809)
Briley, Colin 3:54:13 (9,983)
Brill, Nicholas 4:35:11 (20,527)
Brindle, Stephen 4:52:33 (24,365)
Brining, Steven N 4:02:05 (12,280)
Brinkley, David P 3:51:52 (9,324)
Brinklow, David A 5:35:13 (29,988)
Briozzo, Mirko G 4:36:45 (20,919)
Brisco, Douglas A 2:52:43 (662)
Brister, David J 5:31:42 (29,719)
Bristow, Benjamin J 3:39:02 (6,438)
Bristow, Mark J 4:03:24 (12,579)
Brito, Matt J 4:07:22 (13,439)
Brito Pereira, Jorge M 4:39:45 (21,612)
Britt, Andi J 3:24:44 (3,901)
Brittain, Stefan E 3:36:31 (5,936)
Britten, Daniel 3:46:23 (7,979)
Britten, Kevin 3:34:27 (5,558)
Britten, Tony R 3:18:19 (3,034)
Brittle, John P 5:06:33 (26,793)
Brizzell, Sam 4:29:51 (19,259)
Broad, Guy S 4:02:33 (12,387)
Broadbent, Edward G 3:39:11 (6,471)
Broadbent, James P 3:57:16 (10,937)
Broadbent, Steven S 3:28:54 (4,606)
Broadhead, Robert W 5:55:54 (31,349)
Broadhurst, Jack F 3:45:16 (7,745)
Broadley, Alan G 3:55:36 (10,405)
Broadway, Matthew E 4:26:29 (18,381)
Brochetti, Luigi 3:56:08 (10,577)
Brochman, Luciano 3:21:34 (3,481)
Brock, Barry O 3:14:09 (2,549)
Brock, Graham S 4:19:26 (16,460)
Brock, Matthew R 3:40:53 (6,776)
Brockelhurst-Burton, Patrick M 6:19:12 (32,210)
Brockhurst, Daniel L 3:48:58 (8,623)
Brocklebank, Michael 4:41:54 (22,085)
Brockway, Darren J 4:07:15 (13,412)
Brodrick, Ian S 3:16:47 (2,850)
Brodziak, Andrew 2:57:13 (963)
Broere, John 3:14:51 (2,646)
Brogan, Ed 3:55:43 (10,444)
Brogan, Philip S 4:57:44 (25,441)
Brogden, Richard A 3:44:36 (7,596)
Bromage, Charles N 3:42:40 (7,150)
Bromhead, Andrew F 3:49:19 (8,697)
Bromley, Nigel G 3:48:54 (8,609)
Bromley, Stephen W 4:40:53 (21,869)
Bronder, Timothy J 2:48:37 (478)
Brook, Anthony T 4:05:20 (12,985)
Brook, Geoffrey A 6:16:23 (32,131)
Brook, Graham J 2:41:26 (236)
Brook, Jeremy D 5:25:51 (29,116)
Brook, Nigel G 3:31:52 (5,138)
Brook, Roland S 3:52:35 (9,515)
Brooke, Anthony D 3:07:51 (1,843)
Brooke, Craig D 3:38:13 (6,270)
Brooke, David A 6:36:36 (32,553)
Brooke, David J 3:44:57 (7,681)
Brooke, Jason C 5:30:35 (29,604)
Brooke, John J 4:13:15 (14,910)
Brooker, James A 5:30:28 (29,586)
Brooker, Philip 4:02:48 (12,438)
Brookes, John L 5:14:28 (27,837)
Brookes, Nicholas C 3:41:03 (6,815)
Brookes, Nigel A 3:19:37 (3,202)
Brookes, Roger D 5:08:04 (27,018)
Brookling, Ryan J 3:07:57 (1,852)
Brooks, Adrian 4:07:48 (13,555)
Brooks, Aidam T 4:03:49 (12,677)
Brooks, Alex D 2:48:07 (456)
Brooks, Andrew D 5:39:27 (30,317)
Brooks, Andrew P 4:13:36 (14,975)
Brooks, Dave A 5:26:59 (29,224)
Brooks, Derek F 5:14:53 (27,892)
Brooks, Edward G 4:57:38 (25,423)
Brooks, Graham L 5:29:05 (29,431)
Brooks, Ian P 3:54:51 (10,160)
Brooks, Jonathan C 4:00:18 (11,887)
Brooks, Joseph G 3:50:26 (8,966)
Brooks, Kevin 3:20:51 (3,385)
Brooks, Michael 3:09:10 (1,972)
Brooks, Mike 3:51:56 (9,346)
Brooks, Nigel 4:05:47 (13,096)
Brooks, Paul K 3:46:27 (8,000)
Brooks, Paul S 3:58:58 (11,497)
Brooks, Richard A 3:51:40 (9,260)
Brooks, Richard A 4:31:50 (19,755)
Brooks, Richard D 4:12:01 (14,577)
Brooks, Steven 4:28:58 (19,018)
Brooks, Timothy J 4:19:24 (16,448)
Brooks, Wayne 3:25:36 (4,021)
Brookshaw, Ben I 3:26:00 (4,074)
Broom, Oliver 4:30:41 (19,473)
Broom, Richard A 5:23:24 (28,883)
Broomhead, Peter D 3:46:38 (8,043)
Brosnan, Michael J 5:36:42 (30,112)
Brost, Henry A 5:34:16 (29,911)
Brotherton, Colin R 4:00:41 (11,973)
Brotherton, Michael G 3:34:00 (5,484)
Brough, Dickon M 3:02:53 (1,429)
Brough, Jon R 3:07:00 (1,759)
Broughton, Alan 2:42:18 (256)
Broughton, James E 3:38:26 (6,313)
Broughton, Mike 4:45:23 (22,885)
Broughton, Peter J 3:46:22 (7,976)
Broughton, Richard A 5:12:26 (27,583)
Brouner, James 3:20:20 (3,316)
Brouson, Beniot P 5:37:15 (30,149)
Browett, Mark 4:03:08 (12,516)
Brown, Aaron Rhys 5:32:07 (29,748)
Brown, Adrian P 4:41:09 (21,923)
Brown, Ainsley P 4:51:44 (24,192)
Brown, Alan J 4:43:51 (22,534)
Brown, Alastair I 4:36:40 (20,879)

Brown, Alastair M........................4:06:00 (13,140)
Brown, Alex G............................4:21:38 (17,006)
Brown, Alex W............................3:50:08 (8,895)
Brown, Alexander J.......................4:08:02 (13,621)
Brown, Andrew............................5:30:31 (29,594)
Brown, Andrew C..........................4:33:54 (20,225)
Brown, Andrew C..........................4:58:05 (25,525)
Brown, Andrew J..........................4:37:01 (20,985)
Brown, Andy J............................3:13:44 (2,493)
Brown, Angus A...........................3:27:36 (4,353)
Brown, Anthony R.........................3:56:56 (10,822)
Brown, Anthony S.........................5:54:04 (31,264)
Brown, Antony N..........................4:08:06 (13,641)
Brown, Barney C..........................3:55:20 (10,325)
Brown, Barry.............................3:58:16 (11,253)
Brown, Benjamin..........................3:34:03 (5,491)
Brown, Cabot.............................3:41:47 (6,983)
Brown, Chris.............................4:57:34 (25,411)
Brown, Chris V...........................3:07:22 (1,790)
Brown, Colin S...........................5:00:07 (25,908)
Brown, Craig.............................3:47:49 (8,332)
Brown, Daniel............................3:10:13 (2,087)
Brown, Daniel A..........................4:56:48 (25,256)
Brown, David A...........................4:05:27 (13,011)
Brown, David A...........................4:36:14 (20,791)
Brown, David C...........................7:09:53 (32,975)
Brown, David J...........................3:12:58 (2,393)
Brown, David J...........................4:34:24 (20,341)
Brown, David M...........................4:30:15 (19,367)
Brown, David P...........................4:42:40 (22,254)
Brown, David W...........................3:45:15 (7,742)
Brown, Dennis N..........................3:59:04 (11,534)
Brown, Derek.............................6:08:08 (31,863)
Brown, Derek.............................6:59:16 (32,871)
Brown, Dominic...........................4:28:20 (18,854)
Brown, Dominic A.........................3:45:20 (7,765)
Brown, Doug S............................2:59:59 (1,233)
Brown, Duncan M..........................4:30:12 (19,350)
Brown, Gareth............................4:12:59 (14,831)
Brown, Gavin P...........................4:21:35 (16,993)
Brown, Geoff S...........................4:28:21 (18,858)
Brown, Gordon............................3:35:54 (5,818)
Brown, Graeme J..........................3:36:15 (5,884)
Brown, Graham D..........................4:10:15 (14,161)
Brown, Grahame S.........................4:40:12 (21,713)
Brown, Henry J...........................3:37:24 (6,114)
Brown, Howard R..........................5:47:59 (30,943)
Brown, Ian...............................4:26:39 (18,421)
Brown, James.............................3:49:30 (8,747)
Brown, James H...........................3:06:54 (1,747)
Brown, James R...........................4:19:52 (16,571)
Brown, Jason M...........................3:52:47 (9,564)
Brown, Jason P...........................4:58:55 (25,692)
Brown, John..............................5:49:06 (31,005)
Brown, John A............................5:32:35 (29,777)
Brown, John W............................4:42:30 (22,217)
Brown, Jonathan P........................4:16:12 (15,644)
Brown, Justin L..........................4:30:30 (19,428)
Brown, Kale W............................4:00:15 (11,879)
Brown, Keith.............................3:33:26 (5,394)
Brown, Keith A...........................3:18:30 (3,065)
Brown, Kevin G...........................3:22:36 (3,613)
Brown, Leslie W..........................5:36:29 (30,093)
Brown, Lindsay...........................4:15:19 (15,421)
Brown, Malcolm C.........................4:52:10 (24,285)
Brown, Mark F............................4:21:38 (17,006)
Brown, Mark J............................4:44:05 (22,582)
Brown, Mark P............................4:22:14 (17,185)
Brown, Martin I..........................4:30:03 (19,309)
Brown, Martin J..........................3:49:37 (8,775)
Brown, Michael J.........................2:58:57 (1,135)
Brown, Mike T............................3:27:49 (4,385)
Brown, Neil C............................3:43:54 (7,439)
Brown, Nicholas..........................3:11:58 (2,271)
Brown, Nicholas..........................4:39:06 (21,465)
Brown, Nicholas J........................5:04:34 (26,533)
Brown, Nicholas L........................3:15:27 (2,714)
Brown, Nicholas R........................3:54:40 (10,099)
Brown, Nick P............................3:50:58 (9,091)
Brown, Noramn C..........................3:41:03 (6,815)
Brown, Owen..............................3:44:31 (7,570)
Brown, Patrick...........................4:24:33 (17,824)
Brown, Paul M............................3:43:08 (7,269)
Brown, Paul W............................4:01:31 (12,148)
Brown, Peter.............................4:37:21 (21,072)
Brown, Peter G...........................4:41:46 (22,052)
Brown, Peter N...........................4:50:23 (23,920)
Brown, Philip J..........................4:45:12 (22,834)
Brown, Philip W..........................5:35:02 (29,969)
Brown, Piers A...........................4:00:20 (11,896)
Brown, Ray...............................3:28:16 (4,456)
Brown, Raymond P.........................3:49:36 (8,769)
Brown, Richard...........................4:35:45 (20,661)
Brown, Richard E.........................4:25:56 (18,238)
Brown, Richard J.........................4:48:51 (23,620)
Brown, Robert............................4:27:43 (18,680)
Brown, Robert A..........................4:06:01 (13,143)
Brown, Robert J..........................3:39:56 (6,614)
Brown, Robert N..........................4:41:37 (22,017)
Brown, Rodger............................5:09:10 (27,169)
Brown, Roger J...........................5:27:22 (29,258)
Brown, Roger S...........................2:57:40 (1,000)
Brown, Rowan M...........................4:33:55 (20,229)
Brown, Russell M.........................4:04:15 (12,766)
Brown, Simon.............................4:50:24 (23,926)
Brown, Simon H...........................5:09:13 (27,175)
Brown, Simon T...........................4:54:08 (24,704)
Brown, Stephen...........................4:40:58 (21,884)
Brown, Stephen J.........................3:38:33 (6,343)
Brown, Stephen P.........................3:47:55 (8,360)
Brown, Steve.............................4:33:21 (20,099)
Brown, Stewart S.........................5:29:42 (29,507)
Brown, Stewart W.........................5:19:45 (28,464)
Brown, Stuart C..........................3:20:27 (3,332)
Brown, Stuart P..........................3:39:43 (6,574)
Brown, Stuart S..........................4:09:49 (14,065)
Brown, Stuart W..........................6:05:48 (31,789)
Brown, Thomas R..........................5:00:29 (25,968)
Brown, Tony..............................4:07:37 (13,512)
Brown, Tristan R.........................4:40:22 (21,744)
Brown, Wiliam............................7:05:01 (32,940)
Brown, William R.........................4:05:16 (12,974)
Browne, Alasdair E.......................3:20:27 (3,332)
Browne, Justin C.........................4:23:54 (17,623)
Browne, Nathan J.........................4:30:21 (19,388)
Browne, Peter............................4:20:00 (16,602)
Browne, Robert G.........................4:59:31 (25,792)
Browne, Shaun............................4:43:40 (22,481)
Browne, Simon M..........................4:22:38 (17,283)
Browne, Simon R..........................3:49:15 (8,682)
Browne, Timothy J........................4:19:10 (16,382)
Browning, David C........................3:59:19 (11,611)
Browning, David E........................4:08:37 (13,773)
Browning, Gareth D.......................4:06:27 (13,219)
Browning, Paul...........................3:14:34 (2,608)
Browning, Peter N........................3:50:39 (9,016)
Brownlee, Tom S..........................4:13:37 (14,979)
Brownlie, James M........................6:50:51 (32,773)
Brownlie, Peter R........................3:59:55 (11,790)
Brownsdon, Michael E.....................5:13:23 (27,701)
Brownsword, Nigel P......................4:31:12 (19,581)
Bruce, David.............................3:45:39 (7,833)
Bruce, Gary..............................3:27:33 (4,342)
Bruce, John A............................3:52:03 (9,372)
Bruce, Jonathan P........................4:33:50 (20,209)
Bruce, Paul A............................5:00:59 (26,039)
Bruce, Richard J.........................3:46:13 (7,947)
Bruce, Robert L..........................4:10:43 (14,251)
Bruce, Thomas O..........................3:38:54 (6,412)
Bruce-Ball, James E......................4:19:14 (16,398)
Brudenell, Ryan J........................5:07:54 (26,991)
Bruford, Henry J.........................4:01:03 (12,058)
Brule, Herve.............................3:55:54 (10,507)
Brumby, Ged..............................4:16:37 (15,761)
Brun, Alexis R...........................3:06:51 (1,740)
Brundle, Alan G..........................6:16:55 (32,139)
Brunel, Gregory..........................3:41:20 (6,882)
Brunelli, Nicola.........................3:44:35 (7,591)
Brunelli Bonetti, Alberto................4:11:51 (14,534)
Brunn, Ole...............................4:58:49 (25,667)
Brunner, René............................3:40:55 (6,786)
Brunning, James J........................3:09:35 (2,023)
Bruno, Umberto...........................3:56:25 (10,660)
Brunskill, Michael.......................4:19:26 (16,460)
Brunton, William R.......................4:42:19 (22,180)
Brunyee, John S..........................3:43:18 (7,308)
Bruschi, Benedetto.......................5:06:00 (26,710)
Brusut, Stephane J.......................4:19:33 (16,491)
Bryan, Anthony P.........................5:36:16 (30,077)
Bryan, Mike A............................5:17:08 (28,142)
Bryan, Paul D............................5:29:43 (29,511)
Bryan, Peter.............................4:49:11 (23,686)
Bryan, Rory..............................3:38:02 (6,234)
Bryan, Tim...............................5:48:44 (30,983)
Bryan, Timothy A.........................4:30:00 (19,297)
Bryan-Brown, Nicholas....................4:02:51 (12,448)
Bryant, Andrew...........................4:37:38 (21,144)
Bryant, Andrew D.........................3:23:26 (3,702)
Bryant, John.............................4:56:44 (25,247)
Bryant, John.............................5:40:16 (30,382)
Bryant, Keith A..........................3:41:22 (6,891)
Bryant, Michael R........................4:37:03 (20,989)
Bryant, Simon J..........................3:02:15 (1,388)
Bryant, Tony W...........................3:51:39 (9,255)
Bryer, Steven M..........................3:26:08 (4,091)
Brynie, Jens H...........................3:49:02 (8,634)
Bryon, Paul..............................5:20:38 (28,579)
Bubb, Nick J.............................3:45:30 (7,805)
Bucerius, Matthias.......................3:36:25 (5,919)
Buchan, Kevin A..........................4:56:33 (25,216)
Buchan, Peter J..........................4:00:57 (12,030)
Buchan, Stuart...........................2:38:19 (174)
Buchanan, Ian R..........................6:17:42 (32,165)
Buchanan, Peter S........................2:59:36 (1,210)
Buchterkirche, Klaus.....................3:42:09 (7,055)
Buckeldee, Martin S......................4:16:29 (15,724)
Buckett, Thomas..........................4:03:06 (12,504)
Buckingham, Graham L.....................3:13:05 (2,411)
Buckingham, Peter J......................3:18:34 (3,077)
Buckingham, Philip C.....................4:34:06 (20,274)
Buckland, Michael P......................4:44:34 (22,686)
Buckle, Graham M.........................4:34:48 (20,436)
Buckle, Stephen G........................4:03:51 (12,683)
Buckley, Adrian P........................5:04:53 (26,567)
Buckley, Damian..........................5:12:39 (27,606)
Buckley, Frank...........................6:54:26 (32,814)
Buckley, George..........................3:46:15 (7,955)
Buckley, Graeme..........................3:59:34 (11,689)
Buckley, Howard A........................4:18:03 (16,119)
Buckley, Jason R.........................5:06:35 (26,802)
Buckley, Lee.............................4:07:12 (13,403)
Buckley, Michael.........................7:05:54 (32,947)
Buckley, Paul A..........................2:52:01 (638)
Buckley, Paul R..........................4:07:12 (13,403)
Buckley, Robert A........................3:45:56 (7,893)
Buckley, Robert P........................4:13:17 (14,914)
Bucknall, Clive..........................3:47:01 (8,123)
Buckton, Tim.............................3:49:27 (8,731)
Budd, Kevin P............................4:39:02 (21,447)
Budd, Stephen A..........................5:22:29 (28,770)
Budge, Kurt R............................3:43:35 (7,366)
Budgen, Ian P............................6:00:07 (31,570)
Budgen, Paul G...........................4:27:38 (18,666)
Budnick, Pablo...........................3:54:10 (9,968)
Budroni, Paolino Massimo.................3:04:31 (1,551)
Buecker, Karsten.........................3:19:03 (3,138)
Buffham, Andrew D........................4:16:34 (15,743)
Bugby, Tony..............................5:18:38 (28,326)
Bugeja, Philip A.........................4:28:25 (18,874)
Bugg, Richard J..........................3:31:32 (5,070)
Buggy, Stephen J.........................4:01:19 (12,118)
Buglass, Thomas..........................6:50:10 (32,764)
Bugler, Andrew T.........................4:17:17 (15,923)
Buhr, Keith..............................3:13:43 (2,487)
Buick, Jim...............................3:22:35 (3,608)
Buis, James C............................2:43:28 (300)
Buisson, Rory G..........................3:28:49 (4,578)
Bulessi, Andrea..........................3:46:48 (8,081)
Bull, Andrew R...........................6:04:13 (31,732)
Bull, Derek..............................5:09:41 (27,225)
Bull, Geoffrey S.........................4:16:05 (15,620)
Bull, Ian P..............................4:32:36 (19,916)
Bull, John M.............................4:42:25 (22,203)
Bull, John R.............................6:56:09 (32,841)
Bull, Martin J...........................6:00:54 (31,601)
Bull, Martyn G...........................7:19:09 (33,039)
Bull, Peter B............................3:44:50 (7,650)
Bull, Peter M............................4:22:13 (17,179)
Bull, Ross...............................8:17:19 (33,192)

Buwalda, Steve J 3:36:20 (5,900)
Buxton, Thomas X 3:35:30 (5,749)
Byansi, Malachi 2:38:18 (173)
Byard, James A 4:20:25 (16,713)
Byass, Andrew 3:46:11 (7,939)
Byatt, James E 4:46:28 (23,113)
Byatt, Mark 4:15:03 (15,351)
Bycroft, Jeremy N 4:06:54 (13,328)
Bye, Alan F 3:23:44 (3,750)
Bye, Jonathan E 4:28:29 (18,894)
Bye, Jonathan T 4:27:26 (18,606)
Bye, Rod J 4:03:07 (12,509)
Byers, Anthony S 4:47:59 (23,426)
Byers, Ian K 5:35:10 (29,982)
Bygrave, Simon R 3:10:17 (2,095)
Bygrave, Stephen J 3:24:46 (3,908)
Byham, Anthony L 5:20:45 (28,586)
Byham, Paul W 5:40:19 (30,386)
Byott, Sam W 3:31:20 (5,044)
Byram, Wayne P 5:10:30 (27,336)
Byrne, Anthony W 4:37:10 (21,017)
Byrne, David A 2:43:01 (287)
Byrne, Duncan J 4:03:46 (12,665)
Byrne, first name unknown 4:36:41 (20,885)
Byrne, Gerard J 3:44:06 (7,472)
Byrne, Keith M 4:44:37 (22,693)
Byrne, Kevin C 3:25:39 (4,025)
Byrne, Neil S 4:03:13 (12,532)
Byrne, Paul A 4:24:09 (17,702)
Byrne, Paul E 4:36:08 (20,763)
Byrom, Christopher E 4:24:33 (17,824)
Byrom, Matthew W 3:17:57 (2,991)
Byron, Christopher J 5:10:25 (27,323)
Byron, Michael J 3:15:16 (2,691)
Byron, Paul K 4:49:53 (23,817)
Bywater, Michael J 4:44:12 (22,610)
Caalsen, Darryl 4:18:09 (16,151)
Cable, David A 4:38:06 (21,261)
Cable, Stephen J 3:05:03 (1,579)
Cable, Tim N 3:48:17 (8,447)
Cabot, Tristan J 5:42:22 (30,522)
Cabrera, Mariano 2:56:42 (916)
Caddy, David J 2:46:59 (415)
Caddy, Derek 3:34:40 (5,604)
Cade, Alan 3:34:57 (5,653)
Cadena, Pierre A 3:50:08 (8,895)
Cader, Dominic S 5:02:34 (26,258)
Cadiou, Loic H 3:16:20 (2,806)
Cadman, David 5:25:42 (29,102)
Cadman, Michael T 3:35:36 (5,769)
Caesar, Benjamin C 3:59:55 (11,790)
Caesar, Edward W 4:29:10 (19,076)
Caffetti, Angiolino 4:58:30 (25,607)
Cahill, Graham 4:23:22 (17,464)
Cahill, Phillip J 4:58:39 (25,636)
Cahill, Stephen C 3:50:48 (9,055)
Cain, Paul S 4:47:10 (23,247)
Cain, Rory 3:26:29 (4,149)
Caine, Robert S 3:31:04 (4,998)
Cainer, Geoff 3:51:20 (9,185)
Cairns, John G 4:20:57 (16,853)
Cairns, John S 4:14:11 (15,137)
Cairns, Roger W 4:57:04 (25,328)
Cakebread, George H 8:32:58 (33,209)
Calabrese, Vito 3:45:41 (7,844)
Calascione, Ben F 3:36:50 (6,001)
Calcagnini, Aldo 4:13:23 (14,940)
Calcutt, Colin N 4:32:06 (19,814)
Calcutt, Howard J 3:51:41 (9,269)
Caldas, Giovane 3:18:38 (3,087)
Calder, Ian W 4:06:01 (13,143)
Calder, Sean M 4:50:13 (23,885)
Calderon, Carlos 3:58:45 (11,422)
Caldicott, Peter J 2:49:21 (514)
Caldon, Kevin T 4:15:44 (15,529)
Callaghan, Adrian 3:07:03 (1,763)
Callaghan, Dominic J 5:12:05 (27,537)
Callaghan, Michael 5:25:36 (29,090)
Callaghan, Nicholas J 4:27:12 (18,555)
Callaghan, Philip D 4:54:37 (24,803)
Callaghan, Stephen R 5:35:50 (30,041)
Callaghan, Timothy A 3:05:59 (1,665)
Callaghan Wetton, James A 3:57:23 (10,974)
Callagher, Damien J 3:27:00 (4,246)
Callaway, Richard 4:24:10 (17,707)
Callcott, Andrew J 3:59:26 (11,651)
Calleja-Martin, Miguel A 3:36:49 (5,997)
Caller, Mark J 4:43:28 (22,425)
Calles, Ignacio 3:18:31 (3,069)
Callister, Ian D 4:21:05 (16,886)
Callister, Paul 4:34:31 (20,365)
Callow, Ian 4:10:15 (14,161)
Callow, James R 4:56:40 (25,236)
Callow, James S 3:35:23 (5,732)
Callow, Leo J 4:00:01 (11,820)
Callow, Martin 6:40:47 (32,622)
Calmonson, Byron 3:52:11 (9,408)
Calow, Mark V 4:56:19 (25,168)
Calthrop, Benjamin C 3:45:41 (7,844)
Calvert, Jonathon 3:35:09 (5,701)
Calvert, Mark A 3:29:33 (4,731)
Calvert, Paul W 3:30:43 (4,935)
Calvert, Rodney P 3:58:26 (11,319)
Calvo-Jimenez, Abel 4:57:13 (25,354)
Camara, Cirilo J 4:42:59 (22,325)
Camara, Mauricio 3:17:09 (2,903)
Cambell, Ewan J 4:41:37 (22,017)
Camber, Benn R 3:58:48 (11,447)
Cambiano, Dario 3:34:46 (5,624)
Cambiano, Giorgio 3:50:50 (9,062)
Cambridge, Matthew 4:18:57 (16,344)
Cambridge, Rickie S 4:17:25 (15,960)
Cameron, Alex C 3:17:49 (2,979)
Cameron, Alisdair J 4:41:05 (21,913)
Cameron, Graham J 7:11:27 (32,992)
Cameron, Iain S 5:01:48 (26,147)
Cameron, Neil 4:03:49 (12,677)
Cameron, Niall G 4:14:09 (15,122)
Cameron, Paul A 3:25:31 (4,005)
Cameron, Richard J 5:28:29 (29,374)
Camfield, Bryan 3:01:32 (1,340)
Camilleri, Nathan M 4:26:30 (18,384)
Camp Overy, Mark 4:12:32 (14,716)
Campagne, Ragnar 3:11:06 (2,166)
Campbell, Andrew 4:57:48 (25,455)
Campbell, Andy 4:37:20 (21,066)
Campbell, Christopher J 3:21:48 (3,509)
Campbell, Clarke I 4:15:00 (15,338)
Campbell, Craig 3:28:13 (4,445)
Campbell, Darren W 4:31:46 (19,738)
Campbell, David 4:19:54 (16,578)
Campbell, Geoff 2:55:21 (806)
Campbell, Graeme J 3:23:10 (3,672)
Campbell, Grant S 4:05:50 (13,106)
Campbell, Kenny 3:17:59 (2,994)
Campbell, Mark 5:29:43 (29,511)
Campbell, Mark A 2:35:28 (121)
Campbell, Matt I 3:59:26 (11,651)
Campbell, Maurice J 5:35:01 (29,967)
Campbell, Nicholas A 6:44:08 (32,674)
Campbell, Pete J 4:57:48 (25,455)
Campbell, Peter A 4:06:43 (13,278)
Campbell, Robert K 3:19:45 (3,222)
Campbell, Russell C 4:35:43 (20,655)
Campbell, Simon A 3:50:03 (8,874)
Campbell, Stuart 5:03:03 (26,322)
Campbell, Timothy A 4:35:05 (20,508)
Campion, Daniel J 3:27:36 (4,353)
Campion, James P 3:54:07 (9,949)
Campion, Mark A 2:55:50 (839)
Campion, Stephen W 3:10:03 (2,069)
Campion, Timothy C 3:51:30 (9,215)
Campodonico, Federico 4:23:31 (17,509)
Camponi, Peter 5:53:41 (31,247)
Cancelliere, Jean-Michel 4:18:13 (16,162)
Candy, Matthew S 4:19:07 (16,368)
Cane, John E 5:11:04 (27,394)
Cane, Mark R 3:37:46 (6,180)
Cane, Peter S 3:58:10 (11,218)
Cangiano, Marino 5:03:11 (26,343)
Canham, Michael 5:30:18 (29,576)
Canipel, Timothy P 4:54:47 (24,840)
Cannavina, Michael 5:35:19 (29,998)
Canning, David J 3:56:05 (10,563)
Cannon, Colin R 4:48:49 (23,613)
Cannon, David D 5:28:36 (29,385)
Cannon, John 3:09:28 (2,010)
Cannon, Les 3:43:58 (7,452)
Cannon, Russell G 3:07:26 (1,797)
Cant, Chris W 4:03:55 (12,695)
Cantarini, Sandro 4:34:09 (20,280)
Cantle, Vincent W 5:01:13 (26,074)
Cantlon, Adam M 4:11:12 (14,388)
Cantrill, Roderick G 3:27:17 (4,287)
Canty, Michael N 4:34:55 (20,466)
Capel, Alan S 3:53:03 (9,647)
Capel, Daren P 3:34:14 (5,518)
Capeling, Michael 5:01:54 (26,164)
Capener, John R 3:53:21 (9,731)
Capetti, Giacomo 2:46:32 (405)
Capjon, Ben A 3:52:14 (9,422)
Caplen, Stephen 3:44:52 (7,658)
Capocci, Marco 4:10:52 (14,299)
Capon, Ian H 4:36:40 (20,879)
Capone, Nicholas 6:33:37 (32,507)
Caponera, Roberto 4:01:43 (12,192)
Caporale, Eduardo 4:52:41 (24,399)
Caposano, Guiseppe 3:09:48 (2,044)
Capp, Alastair C 3:42:30 (7,114)
Cappelletti, Mario 3:46:42 (8,060)
Cappucci, Luigi 3:51:07 (9,125)
Capra, Giovanni A 4:10:59 (14,325)
Capstick, Chris C 4:25:21 (18,075)
Capuano, Vincenzo 3:20:11 (3,295)
Caputo, Donato 3:38:35 (6,346)
Caramatti, Niccolo L 4:17:26 (15,965)
Carberry, Colm 4:16:48 (15,798)
Carcassola, Arturo 3:35:31 (5,753)
Card, Simon J 4:21:54 (17,088)
Cardew, James M 4:03:46 (12,665)
Cardiff, Patrick J 5:56:48 (31,394)
Cardona, Christopher A 4:09:26 (13,976)
Cardoso, Joachim 3:20:23 (3,324)
Cardoso, Roland 2:50:31 (566)
Carey, Allan R 4:02:36 (12,400)
Carey, Andrew J 5:31:22 (29,696)
Carey, Chris 4:58:05 (25,525)
Carey, Stephen R 4:18:46 (16,298)
Cargan, Peter J 3:59:46 (11,753)
Cargill, Jamie T 4:11:11 (14,383)
Carimchael, Ian J 4:25:41 (18,159)
Carini, Giulio 4:32:52 (19,970)
Carleschi, Renzo 4:29:35 (19,194)
Carlisle, Wayne 4:21:27 (16,968)
Carlsson, Dick 3:31:19 (5,038)
Carlyon, Oliver C 4:12:48 (14,773)
Carlyon, Simon 3:23:33 (3,717)
Carmichael, Jeremy R 3:26:23 (4,134)
Carmichael, Luke 3:12:31 (2,345)
Carmichael, Robert C 3:55:42 (10,441)
Carmichael Hussain, Tareen 5:34:21 (29,918)
Carmody, Kieran A 3:38:04 (6,242)
Carnelley, David H 4:32:07 (19,818)
Carnet, Michel 4:53:39 (24,607)
Carney, Gary A 3:41:32 (6,926)
Carney, Michael 4:17:50 (16,067)
Carniato, Massimo 2:55:35 (822)
Carnie, Andrew 4:11:16 (14,406)
Carno, Diogo O 3:45:41 (7,844)
Caroe, Chris 3:59:42 (11,728)
Carol, Riel 3:33:59 (5,479)
Carolan, Thomas J 4:00:48 (11,993)
Caron, Erik 3:45:47 (7,866)
Carpenter, Andrew 4:27:34 (18,644)
Carpenter, Colin B 5:06:19 (26,757)
Carpenter, Julian 3:36:59 (6,037)
Carpenter, Mark P 5:06:58 (26,854)
Carpenter, Nick S 3:59:49 (11,770)
Carpenter, Paul 4:12:50 (14,786)
Carpenter, Paul M 4:32:29 (19,900)
Carpenter, Peter G 3:27:18 (4,293)
Carpenter, Trevor A 4:18:26 (16,216)
Carr, Adrian N 3:55:00 (10,204)
Carr, David 4:22:40 (17,291)
Carr, David G 4:28:08 (18,785)
Carr, Graham E 4:00:35 (11,946)
Carr, Jason M 5:35:36 (30,022)
Carr, Malcolm A 3:30:55 (4,968)
Carr, Michael J 3:55:28 (10,361)

Carr, Mike....4:35:42 (20,650)
Carr, Phillip R....3:19:55 (3,250)
Carr, Robert....3:27:58 (4,403)
Carr, Robert B....5:02:12 (26,201)
Carr, Steven D....4:46:14 (23,056)
Carre, Giles....3:50:28 (8,972)
Carre, Scott....5:35:26 (30,006)
Carrea, Michael....4:28:58 (19,018)
Carrera, Pablo....2:46:52 (412)
Carreras, Pascal....4:40:11 (21,708)
Carrigan, Paul....4:29:45 (19,238)
Carrillo, Freddy G....5:08:19 (27,052)
Carrillo, Oscar M....3:25:34 (4,014)
Carrington, Darren R....4:44:46 (22,724)
Carrivick, Gareth A....4:40:09 (21,703)
Carroll, Charlie....5:32:07 (29,748)
Carroll, John....3:31:05 (5,002)
Carroll, Kevin....3:34:43 (5,616)
Carroll, Paul....4:18:05 (16,137)
Carroll, Paul C....4:00:59 (12,045)
Carroll, Paul N....3:54:26 (10,033)
Carroll, Paul S....4:07:18 (13,420)
Carroll, Scott L....3:29:45 (4,771)
Carroll, Sean J....4:07:39 (13,519)
Carroll, Steven....4:03:58 (12,708)
Carroll, Stuart P....3:54:26 (10,033)
Carruthers, Andy P....4:24:27 (17,789)
Carruthers, David V....3:46:02 (7,907)
Carsberg, Simon P....4:14:06 (15,104)
Carson, Brian....4:34:41 (20,406)
Carson, Ian....2:57:41 (1,001)
Carson, Jon G....3:51:14 (9,156)
Carswell, Ian B....4:46:48 (23,171)
Carter, Adam....4:22:36 (17,271)
Carter, Adam....5:21:33 (28,671)
Carter, Andrew J....5:23:51 (28,921)
Carter, Darren R....5:25:19 (29,070)
Carter, Dave....4:10:04 (14,115)
Carter, Dave S....5:14:42 (27,872)
Carter, Dominic J....4:36:42 (20,896)
Carter, Graham M....4:04:56 (12,903)
Carter, Harry J....3:28:53 (4,601)
Carter, John....4:27:46 (18,686)
Carter, John D....3:31:19 (5,038)
Carter, Jonathan....3:44:31 (7,570)
Carter, Jonathan A....4:22:37 (17,277)
Carter, Lee D....5:14:31 (27,845)
Carter, Leigh C....4:22:39 (17,287)
Carter, Nicolas D....3:53:12 (9,689)
Carter, Norman J....3:55:44 (10,453)
Carter, Randolph H....4:25:06 (17,990)
Carter, Roger J....4:35:22 (20,573)
Carter, Stephen....6:02:15 (31,653)
Carter, Stephen G....3:51:54 (9,334)
Carter, Stephen G....4:35:23 (20,577)
Carter, Stuart....5:10:15 (27,298)
Carthew, Michael J....4:39:20 (21,528)
Carthy, Daniel M....4:38:41 (21,368)
Carton, Kenneth....3:57:35 (11,036)
Carton, Philip....4:25:53 (18,224)
Cartwright, Adrian....3:43:22 (7,326)
Cartwright, Clay....4:25:02 (17,972)
Cartwright, Darren....4:43:46 (22,510)
Cartwright, Gordon....4:08:54 (13,838)
Cartwright, Matthew L....3:36:24 (5,914)
Cartwright, Paul....4:29:49 (19,252)
Cartwright, Stephen M....4:34:39 (20,397)
Carty, Damien....5:19:08 (28,393)
Caruana, Paul....4:05:40 (13,070)
Carvalho, Jorge....4:26:37 (18,413)
Carvalho, Pedro L....3:47:51 (8,344)
Carvelle, Jean Pierre....4:50:12 (23,881)
Carver, Christopher....3:20:33 (3,341)
Carver, Paul....5:19:22 (28,417)
Cascella, Vincenzo....2:45:27 (356)
Casci, Mark J....5:51:55 (31,176)
Case, Andrew W....3:23:39 (3,735)
Caseman, Richard....5:03:22 (26,371)
Casey, Daniel J....4:58:03 (25,513)
Casey, Michael P....3:13:33 (2,472)
Casey, Terence M....3:44:39 (7,603)
Cash, Simon R....3:53:50 (9,873)
Cason, Christopher J....3:37:05 (6,053)

Casotto, Mauro....4:22:18 (17,199)
Casquinho, Pedro M....4:19:37 (16,505)
Cassels, Paul C....3:16:08 (2,793)
Cassidy, Bernard....3:32:14 (5,211)
Cassidy, Brian....3:48:30 (8,501)
Cassidy, James T....5:27:52 (29,316)
Cassidy, Stuart J....3:45:27 (7,798)
Cassini, Dario....3:28:15 (4,452)
Castagnaro, Silvio....4:54:36 (24,800)
Castagnola, Barry....4:00:48 (11,993)
Castanheira, Nuno....4:40:22 (21,744)
Castellano, Luis....4:08:42 (13,789)
Castellini, Lorenzo....5:24:44 (29,010)
Castet, Didier....3:48:06 (8,403)
Castillo, Raul....3:41:26 (6,900)
Castillo, Thierry....3:47:36 (8,270)
Castle, Brianj J....3:57:43 (11,082)
Castle, John A....3:01:06 (1,309)
Castle, Toby....3:20:37 (3,350)
Castledine, Nicholas J....2:59:33 (1,198)
Castro-Carollo, José....4:53:36 (24,599)
Caswell-Jones, Kevin....4:45:30 (22,904)
Catanach, David J....4:58:52 (25,679)
Catchpole, Andrew J....5:18:09 (28,262)
Catchpole, Charles F....3:59:03 (11,526)
Catchpole, Christopher R....3:17:05 (2,891)
Catchpole, Philip....3:49:40 (8,790)
Catchpole, Tony....4:32:35 (19,912)
Catchpole, William A....4:32:55 (19,982)
Catehrine, Christian N....3:48:41 (8,551)
Cater, Gary R....6:53:10 (32,798)
Cates, Michael J....3:25:21 (3,987)
Cathcart, George....4:38:50 (21,400)
Cation, James N....4:19:13 (16,393)
Catmull, Julian....2:58:52 (1,125)
Catmull, Trevor P....5:11:09 (27,403)
Caton, Eliot....3:54:26 (10,033)
Caton, Tony....4:39:09 (21,481)
Catt, Mark R....5:07:30 (26,930)
Catt, Stephen A....3:56:49 (10,790)
Cattell, James P....4:41:14 (21,930)
Catterall, David M....4:36:44 (20,910)
Cattley, Steve....3:33:25 (5,391)
Catto, John W....3:15:09 (2,678)
Caudwell, John B....4:59:47 (25,847)
Caulder, Graham A....3:38:51 (6,396)
Caulfield, Michael A....4:48:57 (23,640)
Caulton, Anthony....2:51:40 (621)
Caunce, Peter....3:46:42 (8,060)
Cavailere, Francesco....3:29:28 (4,708)
Cavanagh, Andy....3:12:04 (2,285)
Cavanagh, Kenneth J....4:42:23 (22,198)
Cavanagh, Mark T....4:44:20 (22,645)
Cavanagh, Sean A....4:09:53 (14,076)
Cavanna, Pietro....3:59:18 (11,604)
Cave, Andy M....3:42:04 (7,040)
Cave, Colin....3:44:15 (7,507)
Caves, Trevor J....4:31:01 (19,537)
Cavill, Anthony....3:55:12 (10,282)
Cawley, John W....3:41:58 (7,018)
Cawood, Kevin R....4:26:19 (18,342)
Cawthray, Chris....5:08:06 (27,024)
Cayton, Neil H....2:37:56 (167)
Cazenave, Philippe....3:47:41 (8,290)
Cazenove, George D....3:59:08 (11,555)
Cebula, Jaco A....4:01:32 (12,153)
Cederstrom, Bengt....5:04:15 (26,480)
Celoria, Marco....3:04:21 (1,533)
Cena, Bernard....4:16:18 (15,668)
Cenci, Maurizio....3:15:44 (2,745)
Cerisex, Jean-Claude....3:44:38 (7,600)
Cerri, Stefano....4:24:54 (17,925)
Cerrutti Biondino, Piero....3:39:30 (6,541)
Cesarani, David....5:27:48 (29,303)
Ceseracciu, Tomaso Luigi....3:08:48 (1,935)
Chadaway, Paul R....4:54:43 (24,820)
Chadderton, Martin G....5:49:12 (31,017)
Chadwick, Nicholas C....3:58:40 (11,388)
Chadwick, Peter J....4:47:44 (23,368)
Chadwick, Peter J....5:00:57 (26,034)
Chaffer, Dale R....4:08:13 (13,669)
Chaffin, John R....5:35:00 (29,966)
Chahal, Maninder S....5:04:05 (26,465)

Chaimowitz, Anthony M....3:12:26 (2,337)
Chainey, Ross A....3:19:46 (3,225)
Chalasani, Venkat S....4:55:48 (25,054)
Chalk, Ian....4:32:00 (19,791)
Chalk, Lee C....3:55:13 (10,290)
Chalk, Simon B....4:50:07 (23,862)
Chalkley, John W....4:12:31 (14,710)
Challis, Simon....3:41:57 (7,012)
Challoner, Robert....3:37:46 (6,180)
Chalmers, Alexander J....5:11:30 (27,459)
Chalmers, David....3:55:28 (10,361)
Chalmers, Robert A....5:07:12 (26,892)
Chalus, Jean Pierre M....4:46:31 (23,124)
Chalvet, Jean Claude....5:20:21 (28,548)
Chamberlain, Brian....4:22:25 (17,229)
Chamberlain, Gary....3:54:49 (10,154)
Chamberlain, James W....4:34:19 (20,310)
Chamberlain, Mark J....2:52:22 (648)
Chamberlain, Martin....3:39:41 (6,570)
Chamberlain, Roger B....5:15:12 (27,926)
Chambers, Alistair....2:46:59 (415)
Chambers, Craig....3:32:42 (5,279)
Chambers, John P....3:12:01 (2,278)
Chambers, Joseph....4:22:06 (17,146)
Chambers, Michael F....4:58:53 (25,684)
Chambers, Neil A....3:26:10 (4,096)
Chambers, Nick....4:52:58 (24,448)
Chambers, Philip....3:54:56 (10,187)
Chambers, Richard E....4:53:13 (24,512)
Chambers, Steve....5:23:35 (28,893)
Champ, Ian A....4:37:52 (21,189)
Champion, Stuart D....4:58:05 (25,525)
Chana, Jaswant S....4:02:50 (12,445)
Chance, Rickey A....3:27:35 (4,348)
Chandler, Anthony J....4:27:16 (18,572)
Chandler, Gary W....2:37:45 (160)
Chandler, James A....4:24:01 (17,661)
Chandler, Karl....3:21:55 (3,524)
Chandler, Michael J....4:31:31 (19,668)
Chandler, Paul....4:20:04 (16,622)
Chandler, Ross A....3:33:08 (5,339)
Chandley, Paul J....4:12:35 (14,725)
Chandramohan, Vyramuthu....7:17:45 (33,028)
Channon, Mark G....3:56:19 (10,630)
Channon, Michael K....4:20:26 (16,717)
Chant, Adam P....3:08:14 (1,877)
Chanter, Iain W....5:11:29 (27,455)
Chanter, Trevor....4:41:10 (21,924)
Chantrey, David F....6:41:49 (32,635)
Chapel, Jerome....3:32:03 (5,169)
Chapellier, Alexis....3:09:46 (2,042)
Chaplin, David I....2:58:31 (1,068)
Chaplin, Ian D....3:00:13 (1,251)
Chaplin, Michael G....3:20:25 (3,330)
Chapman, Adam P....3:06:21 (1,698)
Chapman, Andrew J....3:51:47 (9,300)
Chapman, Anthony C....4:23:39 (17,546)
Chapman, Brian....4:19:25 (16,455)
Chapman, Brian A....3:54:19 (10,009)
Chapman, Chris P....4:28:16 (18,831)
Chapman, Christopher R....4:05:26 (13,005)
Chapman, Christopher S....4:18:52 (16,318)
Chapman, Craig G....3:12:58 (2,393)
Chapman, David J....3:43:09 (7,274)
Chapman, Garry R....5:35:23 (30,001)
Chapman, Gary I....2:49:56 (545)
Chapman, Gary T....4:58:16 (25,563)
Chapman, Graeme....4:19:20 (16,430)
Chapman, Howard R....4:34:19 (20,310)
Chapman, Ian G....4:56:22 (25,179)
Chapman, James....3:50:08 (8,895)
Chapman, Jim S....3:49:47 (8,816)
Chapman, Jody C....3:36:34 (5,947)
Chapman, John....2:59:26 (1,189)
Chapman, John....4:10:01 (14,103)
Chapman, Leslie R....7:16:39 (33,018)
Chapman, Nigel J....5:19:30 (28,435)
Chapman, Paul....4:36:23 (20,820)
Chapman, Paul A....4:02:53 (12,455)
Chapman, Peter....3:03:02 (1,444)
Chapman, Peter....4:31:30 (19,665)
Chapman, Peter J....5:12:33 (27,594)
Chapman, Philip....4:29:26 (19,153)

Chapman, Reg M 3:09:25 (2,003)
Chapman, Richard 3:51:10 (9,140)
Chapman, Rod D 4:05:36 (13,053)
Chapman, Roy 5:01:34 (26,113)
Chapman, Shane 4:26:19 (18,342)
Chapman, Simon 4:13:06 (14,874)
Chapman, Stephen R 3:05:49 (1,646)
Chapman, Tim 3:01:52 (1,362)
Chapman, Tim W 4:06:39 (13,259)
Chappell, Aaron 3:39:26 (6,529)
Chappell, Daniel M 2:39:41 (204)
Chappell, Darren J 4:40:44 (21,837)
Chappell, Ian 3:58:32 (11,350)
Chappell, Michael J 3:18:59 (3,131)
Chapple, Andy T 2:56:52 (926)
Chapple, Tony 3:47:13 (8,180)
Charalambous, Marios 4:20:36 (16,759)
Chard, Daniel T 3:57:45 (11,093)
Chard, Ken R 3:07:22 (1,790)
Chard, Mark W 5:53:05 (31,218)
Chard, Michael R 3:50:56 (9,083)
Chard, Stephen 4:38:50 (21,400)
Chardet, Dolf 4:09:28 (13,988)
Charles, Chris J 4:20:45 (16,795)
Charles, Jeremy D 4:40:07 (21,695)
Charles, Michael 4:21:03 (16,880)
Charles, Michael M 4:01:18 (12,115)
Charles, Paul J 3:24:35 (3,878)
Charles, Phillip A 4:36:17 (20,802)
Charles-Jones, Peter M 4:55:19 (24,963)
Charleston, Brandon M 4:57:07 (25,338)
Charlesworth, Adam 2:59:58 (1,232)
Charlesworth, Michael D 3:52:28 (9,485)
Charlton, Alan 3:59:31 (11,677)
Charlton, Christopher J 3:53:08 (9,672)
Charlton, Martin J 3:58:08 (11,203)
Charlton, Mike 3:44:31 (7,570)
Charlton, Ray 4:43:58 (22,566)
Charlton, Simon 3:55:42 (10,441)
Charlwood, Richard S 4:33:17 (20,080)
Charman, Dan 3:07:55 (1,847)
Charman, Philip G 4:25:24 (18,090)
Charnley, Patrick M 3:34:20 (5,543)
Charpentier, Frederic 3:15:21 (2,702)
Charsley, Darren J 3:57:31 (11,020)
Chart, Mike C 4:42:21 (22,190)
Chart, Robert J 3:48:07 (8,411)
Charters, Paul W 3:51:33 (9,234)
Chase, Edward J 3:55:31 (10,382)
Chatainier, Jean-Marc 3:27:24 (4,314)
Chataway, Matthew C 4:20:38 (16,769)
Chatburn, Dean P 3:41:22 (6,891)
Chater, John D 4:46:23 (23,098)
Chatt, Hicham 2:07:59 (7)
Chatten, Simon 3:40:55 (6,786)
Chaudry, Imran A 6:02:54 (31,675)
Chaufournais, Franck 4:02:09 (12,296)
Chaufournais, Michel 3:09:12 (1,976)
Chauhan, Preetesh 5:01:46 (26,143)
Chaussard, François X 2:41:10 (229)
Chawke, Tony 4:21:45 (17,045)
Cheal, Jonathan I 3:57:44 (11,087)
Cheape, Henry B 4:28:51 (18,983)
Checchia, Frank 2:57:38 (996)
Cheesebrough, Timothy L 3:48:00 (8,382)
Cheeseman, Bruce A 4:57:13 (25,354)
Cheeseman, Christopher R 3:26:00 (4,074)
Cheeseman, Daniel V 6:10:56 (31,953)
Cheesman, Charles R 4:43:19 (22,392)
Cheetham, Mark S 3:48:03 (8,396)
Cheetham, Simon 4:11:48 (14,524)
Cheetham, Stephen G 3:28:52 (4,595)
Cheffins, Patrick M 3:58:57 (11,490)
Chell, Philip 5:00:09 (25,915)
Chelton, Lee 4:23:47 (17,582)
Chen, Andrew R 4:33:14 (20,067)
Chen, Shih Pin 4:08:20 (13,701)
Chenery, Matthew O 5:04:26 (26,515)
Cheney, Leslie 4:02:52 (12,449)
Cheng, Andrew 5:14:02 (27,770)
Chereau, Jacques L 3:48:38 (8,535)
Cherniavsky, Lexi 3:19:56 (3,255)
Cherrett, Richard M 3:50:37 (9,009)
Cherry, Robert J 3:25:07 (3,949)
Cherry, Steven 3:49:43 (8,802)
Cherukur, Venkateswaralu J 7:25:57 (33,075)
Cheshire, Anthony P 4:34:54 (20,463)
Cheshire, Darren E 4:14:59 (15,332)
Cheshire, Geoffrey M 2:55:52 (841)
Chesman, Alan J 5:09:44 (27,233)
Chesney, Paul D 4:46:15 (23,062)
Chesser, Alistair M 3:17:31 (2,945)
Chester, Martin G 3:03:14 (1,460)
Chester, Richard 4:29:29 (19,174)
Chesterfield, Nick J 4:20:03 (16,613)
Chestney, Jon 2:59:32 (1,194)
Chetcuti, Gino 3:14:07 (2,543)
Cheung, Andrew 3:31:51 (5,134)
Cheung, Vincent W 5:12:07 (27,542)
Cheung, Walter 4:05:28 (13,018)
Chevannes, Errol 5:25:04 (29,046)
Chevassut, Timothy J 4:41:45 (22,048)
Cheyne, Timothy 5:15:29 (27,950)
Chick, Alexander W 3:43:10 (7,281)
Chick, Hayden J 3:39:07 (6,458)
Chick, Jonathan B 4:00:38 (11,958)
Chicktay, Ishmail 5:39:10 (30,297)
Chidambi, Athreya 3:41:49 (6,994)
Chidley, Daivd A 4:25:09 (18,008)
Chigioni, Mauro 3:26:50 (4,210)
Chilcott, Darren 4:19:01 (16,356)
Child, Jeff J 5:01:00 (26,042)
Childers, Andrew D 4:48:57 (23,640)
Childs, Daniel W 5:15:37 (27,964)
Childs, Nicholas J 5:11:09 (27,403)
Childs, Paul A 2:54:15 (742)
Childs, Peter J 4:11:13 (14,391)
Chiles, Adrian 3:59:42 (11,728)
Chiles, Lawrence 3:24:51 (3,919)
Chiles, Matthew 3:09:26 (2,006)
Chiles, Thomas 6:07:42 (31,848)
Chilvers, Daniel J 4:38:03 (21,239)
Chilvers, Steve R 4:11:03 (14,346)
Chinn, Rodney D 3:28:49 (4,578)
Chiplin, Gerald 4:26:05 (18,281)
Chipperfield, Mark 4:12:16 (14,643)
Chippington, Max 3:46:24 (7,989)
Chisholm, Barry J 3:09:02 (1,961)
Chittenden, Paul 4:09:51 (14,069)
Chivers, Andy 3:42:42 (7,157)
Chivers, Richard 3:38:50 (6,393)
Chomette, Philippe 3:17:59 (2,994)
Chong, Zhe Wei 4:38:27 (21,325)
Chorley, Marcus J 4:03:32 (12,611)
Chorlton, Gordon C 4:05:01 (12,920)
Choudhry, Muhammad N 4:45:43 (22,947)
Choudhry, Muneeb 4:36:57 (20,970)
Choudhry, Shahzeb A 4:10:18 (14,170)
Choules, David 3:11:12 (2,177)
Chow, Gary C 3:45:02 (7,697)
Chow, Richard J 5:10:24 (27,319)
Chowdhry, Tarik 4:10:00 (14,098)
Chowdhury, Mikail M 4:26:02 (18,271)
Chowles, Dennis E 5:28:22 (29,365)
Chownsmith, Laurence 3:36:11 (5,872)
Chrisostome, Thierry 2:55:13 (800)
Christensen, Thomas B 3:54:03 (9,930)
Christian, Marc 3:56:39 (10,739)
Christian, Paul R 3:36:50 (6,001)
Christian, Robin P 3:25:27 (3,999)
Christie, Campbell S 3:26:52 (4,217)
Christie, David 3:23:48 (3,755)
Christie, Emlyn D 2:57:07 (953)
Christie, Gary 3:28:45 (4,566)
Christie, George E 5:47:22 (30,908)
Christie, Graham J 4:48:29 (23,538)
Christie, Michael 4:11:07 (14,364)
Christie, Paul 4:28:44 (18,956)
Christie, Sandy 3:11:49 (2,247)
Christie, Steve R 4:14:20 (15,169)
Christison, Clive R 3:44:14 (7,501)
Christmas, Lee 2:50:54 (584)
Christopher, John M 3:11:53 (2,256)
Christopher, Jonathan 3:52:37 (9,526)
Christopher, Michael J 4:43:58 (22,566)
Chritchlow, Philip 2:39:32 (202)
Chu, Brian 3:22:40 (3,620)
Chu, Vy X 4:54:16 (24,738)
Chubb, Jonathan 4:12:16 (14,643)
Chubb, William J 6:07:46 (31,852)
Chudasama, Vijay H 5:28:20 (29,360)
Chung, Kinming 5:30:42 (29,618)
Church, Colin W 4:01:34 (12,165)
Church, Matthew J 5:52:39 (31,204)
Church, Ron A 3:43:55 (7,443)
Church, Steven W 4:28:51 (18,983)
Church, Stewart A 6:01:31 (31,628)
Church, Warren 4:36:13 (20,786)
Churcher, Stephen 5:23:51 (28,921)
Churchill, Duncan R 4:14:24 (15,180)
Churchill, George M 3:51:07 (9,125)
Churchill, Mark J 4:21:56 (17,095)
Churchill, Nigel 3:42:20 (7,084)
Churchill, Steve 4:46:21 (23,091)
Churton, Mark A 3:41:18 (6,872)
Chuter, Timothy A 3:19:05 (3,140)
Ciaccia, Filippo Pio 3:38:22 (6,297)
Cimino, Gennaro 3:36:21 (5,904)
Cimino, Vincenzo 3:18:02 (3,002)
Cimminiello, Giovanni 3:21:37 (3,486)
Cinnamon, Paul T 5:27:50 (29,312)
Cino, Claudio 4:42:31 (22,226)
Cinque, Giulio A 3:11:27 (2,210)
Cinquetti, Lucio 3:42:54 (7,206)
Ciofani, Claudio 3:29:52 (4,800)
Cioffi, Attilio 3:51:04 (9,116)
Ciravegna, Ernesto 2:57:50 (1,011)
Cistac, Christian 4:56:18 (25,164)
Civetta, Christophe 3:21:55 (3,524)
Clack, Paul R 4:39:16 (21,505)
Clague, Mark W 3:01:23 (1,330)
Clamp, Andrew C 3:40:25 (6,695)
Clamp, Paul J 4:08:29 (13,738)
Clampin, Geoffrey A 5:14:54 (27,895)
Clancy, Brian 4:28:02 (18,757)
Clapham, Jeremy A 3:51:08 (9,131)
Clapham, Peter B 4:53:05 (24,473)
Clapp, David A 4:34:21 (20,328)
Clapp, Michael J 5:12:06 (27,539)
Clapson, Martin R 4:17:04 (15,877)
Clapton, Roland A 4:04:02 (12,723)
Clare, Andrew D 6:36:43 (32,555)
Clare, Daniel M 4:55:55 (25,080)
Clare, Jonathan R 4:36:23 (20,820)
Clare, Martin 6:23:39 (32,322)
Clarehugh, Mark 2:34:27 (106)
Claridge, Simon J 2:57:17 (966)
Clark, Adrian 4:07:05 (13,370)
Clark, Adrian P 4:31:40 (19,717)
Clark, Alex 4:07:04 (13,360)
Clark, Allan 4:03:36 (12,624)
Clark, Allan G 3:48:46 (8,570)
Clark, Andrew J 4:24:08 (17,697)
Clark, Andrew R 3:22:06 (3,544)
Clark, Benjamin 4:08:40 (13,781)
Clark, Billy 3:17:47 (2,975)
Clark, Colin 4:29:31 (19,184)
Clark, Daniel E 5:05:09 (26,606)
Clark, Darren 3:01:58 (1,373)
Clark, Darrin 4:24:07 (17,691)
Clark, David 5:30:28 (29,586)
Clark, David C 3:41:11 (6,849)
Clark, David R 4:56:58 (25,302)
Clark, Derek W 4:25:36 (18,136)
Clark, Gareth C 4:27:19 (18,584)
Clark, Geoffrey M 6:53:28 (32,803)
Clark, Gorodn D 3:49:44 (8,808)
Clark, Graham A 4:22:45 (17,310)
Clark, Graham S 3:15:01 (2,661)
Clark, Gregg 7:10:12 (32,981)
Clark, Ian 3:43:34 (7,362)
Clark, John 4:30:48 (19,495)
Clark, Jonathan D 5:25:58 (29,125)
Clark, Jonathan J 4:50:57 (24,037)
Clark, Jonathan S 4:44:07 (22,589)
Clark, Kevin 4:03:39 (12,640)
Clark, Mark 3:26:43 (4,193)
Clark, Mark A 3:07:32 (1,807)
Clark, Martin J 4:06:18 (13,194)

Clark, Martin T	4:42:25 (22,203)	Clarke, Robert J	3:58:18 (11,266)	Clifford, Peter P	3:25:48 (4,049)
Clark, Matthew	4:51:26 (24,132)	Clarke, Simon J	4:37:22 (21,083)	Clifford, Richard C	3:18:42 (3,094)
Clark, Matthew	5:52:08 (31,186)	Clarke, Sion	5:13:15 (27,686)	Clifford, Stephen J	3:05:12 (1,593)
Clark, Michael A	4:18:59 (16,351)	Clarke, Stephen T	4:16:27 (15,711)	Clifford, Stephen W	3:50:14 (8,920)
Clark, Michael J	3:40:30 (6,713)	Clarke, Steven	4:31:26 (19,649)	Clifford, Steve W	3:30:17 (4,864)
Clark, Neil J	3:56:17 (10,624)	Clarke, Toby J	3:51:29 (9,214)	Clifford, Tom A	4:47:23 (23,287)
Clark, Neil R	3:37:21 (6,105)	Clarke, Tony J	5:44:37 (30,687)	Clift, Daniel J	5:17:20 (28,172)
Clark, Neil R	4:21:00 (16,867)	Clarkson, Alan	3:12:53 (2,385)	Clift, Paul	4:00:06 (11,843)
Clark, Nicholas J	4:59:51 (25,858)	Clarkson, Craig W	3:27:42 (4,365)	Cline, Michael P	4:40:15 (21,724)
Clark, Nigel V	5:15:09 (27,916)	Clarkson, Rick J	3:42:59 (7,227)	Clinnick, Stephen C	4:14:24 (15,180)
Clark, Oliver	4:55:51 (25,066)	Clatworthy, Graham P	4:49:53 (23,817)	Clinton, Brian G	4:50:03 (23,850)
Clark, Oliver G	3:13:58 (2,524)	Claus, Jean Paul	3:02:30 (1,406)	Clinton, Peter	3:54:05 (9,940)
Clark, Paul	6:12:36 (32,009)	Clausen, Simon P	4:19:26 (16,460)	Clipson, Paul	4:55:41 (25,035)
Clark, Paul W	3:41:07 (6,831)	Claverie, Arnaud H	2:39:02 (188)	Clish, Andrew	3:53:20 (9,726)
Clark, Peter G	5:18:39 (28,330)	Clavijo, Jorge	4:30:26 (19,412)	Clissold, Cole	3:20:24 (3,326)
Clark, Richard H	3:13:32 (2,470)	Clawson, Mark	3:46:17 (7,963)	Cloherty, John M	4:38:44 (21,380)
Clark, Richard L	4:25:48 (18,194)	Clay, Christopher	3:32:08 (5,184)	Cloke, Andy	3:52:20 (9,445)
Clark, Robert G	3:36:29 (5,928)	Clay, Jamie C	3:54:02 (9,928)	Cloonan, Peter G	3:54:37 (10,083)
Clark, Robert V	3:51:46 (9,294)	Clay, Nigel R	4:45:41 (22,942)	Clossais, Jerome	3:10:02 (2,066)
Clark, Roger J	4:46:24 (23,103)	Clay, Paul	4:25:25 (18,095)	Clothier, Alex H	3:50:26 (8,966)
Clark, Rupert J	3:52:31 (9,497)	Clay, Paul M	4:34:23 (20,335)	Clough, Trevor	2:54:34 (766)
Clark, Russell G	5:04:29 (26,523)	Clay, Richard M	4:53:38 (24,604)	Clow, Simon	6:11:52 (31,983)
Clark, Sam R	4:30:09 (19,335)	Clayden, Andrew	4:31:11 (19,575)	Clowes, Andrew J	5:26:22 (29,159)
Clark, Samuel T	4:19:14 (16,398)	Clayden, Steve R	4:50:55 (24,028)	Clubb, Stuart A	4:30:26 (19,412)
Clark, Simon C	3:36:48 (5,993)	Claydon, Nicky A	4:15:58 (15,592)	Clues, Mark A	3:35:16 (5,717)
Clark, Simon M	3:48:22 (8,466)	Clayforth-Carr, Edward	4:36:47 (20,933)	Cluley, David	5:00:52 (26,023)
Clark, Stephen	4:39:53 (21,651)	Clayton, Andrew R	3:46:23 (7,979)	Clune, Raymond	5:29:12 (29,443)
Clark, Stephen A	3:27:22 (4,306)	Clayton, Francis M	3:36:54 (6,020)	Clure, Jason K	6:17:16 (32,151)
Clark, Steve	4:42:12 (22,156)	Clayton, Ian	2:40:01 (211)	Clusker, Dean	3:58:01 (11,156)
Clark, Steven V	3:38:51 (6,396)	Clayton, Peter J	4:38:34 (21,354)	Clutterbuck, Christopher J	4:21:45 (17,045)
Clark, Stu T	4:44:00 (22,572)	Clayton, Peter P	2:54:24 (755)	Clyde, David J	3:45:00 (7,689)
Clark, Stuart I	4:41:25 (21,973)	Clayton, Rob T	3:43:14 (7,295)	Clyne, Mike	3:55:38 (10,415)
Clark, Stuart W	4:20:52 (16,827)	Clayton, Thomas E	3:38:49 (6,386)	Clynes, Declan P	3:11:03 (2,161)
Clark, Timothy	4:09:27 (13,981)	Clayton, Tristan T	5:14:30 (27,841)	Coales, David	2:45:28 (358)
Clarke, Aaron P	4:31:27 (19,651)	Cleal, Simon J	4:52:55 (24,441)	Coals, Adam J	4:46:05 (23,022)
Clarke, Alan P	3:44:52 (7,658)	Cleall, Leonard	4:41:42 (22,036)	Coan, Paul	3:56:25 (10,660)
Clarke, Alan R	3:56:12 (10,593)	Cleaver, James P	3:29:23 (4,693)	Coates, Alan P	4:47:33 (23,334)
Clarke, Andrew	3:55:44 (10,453)	Cleaver, Jim	4:34:54 (20,463)	Coates, Brian W	3:06:51 (1,740)
Clarke, Andrew	3:56:57 (10,828)	Clegg, Gavin J	4:18:42 (16,281)	Coates, Kenneth H	5:11:28 (27,452)
Clarke, Andrew	4:39:22 (21,537)	Clegg, Keith R	5:25:50 (29,114)	Coates, Michael J	3:36:35 (5,952)
Clarke, Andrew J	5:52:31 (31,198)	Clegg, Steven B	4:38:56 (21,426)	Coates, Nigel J	2:50:44 (575)
Clarke, Andrew T	4:18:30 (16,231)	Cleland, Mark D	4:36:10 (20,771)	Coates, Richard C	3:42:21 (7,088)
Clarke, Ben	3:54:11 (9,972)	Clelland, Craig M	2:59:02 (1,145)	Cobb, Godfrey	5:58:21 (31,478)
Clarke, Ben E	4:54:32 (24,785)	Clemens, John B	3:10:49 (2,139)	Cobb, Graham E	4:47:30 (23,319)
Clarke, Brian M	4:24:14 (17,725)	Clemens, Nigel	3:36:35 (5,952)	Cobbold, Andy P	3:55:41 (10,431)
Clarke, Chris A	4:36:32 (20,853)	Clement, Paul	3:50:43 (9,033)	Cobbold, Ryan J	4:44:07 (22,589)
Clarke, Dave E	4:05:40 (13,070)	Clement, Tim N	3:58:54 (11,476)	Cobill, Sebastian C	2:59:32 (1,194)
Clarke, David	3:55:44 (10,453)	Clemente, Vitantonio	4:08:42 (13,789)	Cocarane, Philip	4:59:02 (25,713)
Clarke, David	4:38:03 (21,239)	Clements, David	4:49:05 (23,669)	Cocco, Massimo	3:17:35 (2,950)
Clarke, David J	4:00:46 (11,985)	Clements, Gavin G	3:53:50 (9,873)	Cochran, Jason I	4:20:32 (16,742)
Clarke, David J	4:16:50 (15,811)	Clements, Graham	3:55:37 (10,409)	Cochrane, Robert W	3:19:15 (3,167)
Clarke, Douglas S	3:03:41 (1,492)	Clements, Ian J	4:34:15 (20,300)	Cochrane, Timothy	4:03:45 (12,661)
Clarke, Edward M	3:20:49 (3,377)	Clements, John M	3:52:57 (9,610)	Cockayne, James P	4:18:20 (16,193)
Clarke, Gary	4:12:09 (14,612)	Clements, Jon A	4:15:20 (15,425)	Cockbill, Brett	4:36:24 (20,827)
Clarke, George	4:33:18 (20,085)	Clements, Miall C	3:53:26 (9,749)	Cockbill, Martin D	5:04:22 (26,499)
Clarke, Gervase	3:56:22 (10,643)	Clements, Nick B	3:54:30 (10,051)	Cockburn, Jason G	3:51:54 (9,334)
Clarke, Ian	4:32:13 (19,836)	Clements, Paul D	4:31:54 (19,772)	Cocker, Paul	3:45:20 (7,765)
Clarke, James	4:27:33 (18,638)	Clements, Peter	3:34:40 (5,604)	Cockerell, Richard	4:31:45 (19,733)
Clarke, James A	2:53:48 (713)	Clements, Robert	4:21:35 (16,993)	Cockerill, Peter	5:18:52 (28,351)
Clarke, James A	3:56:15 (10,610)	Clements, Tim P	4:24:13 (17,717)	Cockroft, Guy H	5:47:15 (30,883)
Clarke, James B	2:54:21 (749)	Cleminson, Jeff	3:43:44 (7,402)	Cockshott, David L	3:49:24 (8,718)
Clarke, James M	3:59:35 (11,694)	Clemson, Jonathan B	3:06:37 (1,718)	Coculet, Gilles	4:25:50 (18,202)
Clarke, John E	5:07:37 (26,950)	Clenaghan, Stuart	4:24:15 (17,732)	Codd, Paul M	3:21:41 (3,498)
Clarke, John G	3:49:18 (8,691)	Clench, James A	3:29:47 (4,779)	Coen, Daniel J	3:49:17 (8,688)
Clarke, John P	2:30:31 (72)	Clerc, Andy S	4:00:55 (12,019)	Coenen, Dirk	4:44:27 (22,666)
Clarke, Jonathan J	3:48:54 (8,609)	Clere, David	2:59:19 (1,178)	Coey, Stephen	3:56:06 (10,568)
Clarke, Joseph C	6:27:56 (32,421)	Cleveland, Paul F	4:03:29 (12,601)	Coggan, Ben	5:23:14 (28,861)
Clarke, Liston	5:20:45 (28,586)	Cleveland, Richard R	4:10:41 (14,245)	Coggan, Thomas M	5:23:26 (28,884)
Clarke, Matthew B	4:39:35 (21,571)	Cleves, Andrew J	2:49:53 (542)	Coggin, Richard	4:15:03 (15,351)
Clarke, Michael E	4:01:03 (12,058)	Clewlow, Melvin T	3:12:36 (2,353)	Coggins, Ric	4:55:00 (24,895)
Clarke, Michael F	3:48:39 (8,541)	Clews, Stuart P	3:58:16 (11,253)	Coghill, Ian A	4:01:54 (12,236)
Clarke, Michael G	4:11:50 (14,528)	Clews, William J	4:49:37 (23,778)	Cohen, Colin S	4:50:18 (23,905)
Clarke, Michael P	4:28:53 (18,991)	Cliff, Paul	4:59:56 (25,875)	Cohen, Daniel N	4:59:45 (25,840)
Clarke, Neil J	4:10:49 (14,282)	Cliff, Simon R	4:17:49 (16,065)	Cohen, David B	4:37:19 (21,061)
Clarke, Nicholas J	3:54:34 (10,069)	Cliff, Thomas R	3:26:50 (4,210)	Cohen, Howard	3:16:46 (2,849)
Clarke, Owen	4:46:19 (23,080)	Cliffe, Neil S	3:29:26 (4,704)	Cohen, Joseph B	4:21:23 (16,955)
Clarke, Patrick J	4:04:52 (12,888)	Cliffe, Richard M	4:45:49 (22,971)	Cohen, Mauricio	2:48:47 (484)
Clarke, Paul M	4:57:29 (25,395)	Cliffe, Shane	3:55:01 (10,209)	Cohen, Michael S	4:33:14 (20,067)
Clarke, Peter	5:09:22 (27,190)	Cliffe, Simon D	4:13:49 (15,025)	Cohen, Roger C	5:27:13 (29,246)
Clarke, Philip	4:04:21 (12,787)	Clifford, Alexander	3:51:13 (9,151)	Cohen, Samuel	4:06:02 (13,147)
Clarke, Philip L	3:19:13 (3,159)	Clifford, John	4:56:58 (25,302)	Cohen-Price, Daniel L	6:46:18 (32,716)
Clarke, Phillip T	3:39:08 (6,462)	Clifford, John A	4:18:35 (16,252)	Cohring, John P	5:33:02 (29,819)
Clarke, Robert A	4:29:41 (19,222)	Clifford, Michael K	3:23:42 (3,742)	Cojeen, Victoria M	3:53:30 (9,766)

Coker, Jeremy 5:07:31 (26,932)
Coker, Jonathan E 3:24:12 (3,821)
Coker, Matthew R 6:09:33 (31,915)
Colbet, Denzil 3:19:22 (3,179)
Colbourne, Steve J 3:02:30 (1,406)
Colby, Christopher D 4:24:53 (17,917)
Colby, Philip G 5:58:05 (31,460)
Colclough, Nicholas M 4:11:56 (14,559)
Coldridge, Jonathan C 4:47:46 (23,377)
Cole, Adam K 3:52:02 (9,369)
Cole, Alan E 4:05:06 (12,939)
Cole, Andrew 3:41:04 (6,820)
Cole, Brian J 2:29:11 (65)
Cole, Edward J 5:49:57 (31,068)
Cole, Jamie A 4:26:38 (18,417)
Cole, Jonathan 4:04:41 (12,853)
Cole, Jonathan E 4:16:10 (15,639)
Cole, Josh 4:51:17 (24,089)
Cole, Kevin D 2:49:57 (547)
Cole, Mark D 3:30:03 (4,836)
Cole, Martin B 5:02:06 (26,187)
Cole, Melvyn 3:43:41 (7,386)
Cole, Michael K 5:27:03 (29,230)
Cole, Neil C 5:44:19 (30,666)
Cole, Paul 4:47:49 (23,386)
Cole, Paul T 4:16:52 (15,817)
Cole, Ray 2:47:23 (430)
Cole, Reg 5:05:41 (26,665)
Cole, Robert J 3:22:40 (3,620)
Cole, Scott A 3:47:13 (8,180)
Cole, Stephen F 4:14:45 (15,272)
Cole, Stephen H 4:00:24 (11,919)
Cole, Stephen M 3:52:47 (9,564)
Colebrook, Chris J 3:53:35 (9,787)
Coleby, James W 5:14:26 (27,834)
Colegate, Andrew 2:45:15 (351)
Colegrave, John B 3:44:54 (7,669)
Coleman, Andrew P 3:06:11 (1,685)
Coleman, Ben E 4:59:35 (25,807)
Coleman, Darran P 3:15:04 (2,667)
Coleman, Fergus C 3:09:41 (2,036)
Coleman, James C 4:33:57 (20,238)
Coleman, John 4:25:51 (18,210)
Coleman, John P 6:17:26 (32,155)
Coleman, Mike 2:35:13 (117)
Coleman, Paul J 3:51:58 (9,356)
Coleman, Rory J 5:36:59 (30,134)
Coleman, Stanley W 5:32:30 (29,771)
Coleman, Terry P 5:27:27 (29,265)
Coleman, William A 5:51:08 (31,132)
Coles, Andrew 4:46:13 (23,051)
Coles, Christopher L 4:19:50 (16,562)
Coles, Daryl J 3:43:46 (7,411)
Coles, David L 4:23:44 (17,571)
Coles, Ian B 3:31:42 (5,101)
Coles, Mark 3:33:34 (5,410)
Coles, Peter D 4:58:05 (25,525)
Coles, Robert J 4:53:32 (24,575)
Coles, Samuel 4:12:25 (14,684)
Coles, Scott 3:29:19 (4,679)
Coles, Terence G 3:29:17 (4,671)
Coles, Vernon E 5:31:12 (29,678)
Coley, David 4:25:41 (18,159)
Coley, Giles A 3:42:45 (7,176)
Colfer, James J 3:21:33 (3,477)
Colgin, Everard 4:01:08 (12,082)
Colitti, Antonio 4:44:44 (22,716)
Coll, Robin P 2:40:02 (212)
Collard, Alister K 4:06:18 (13,194)
Collard, Robert J 3:55:27 (10,358)
Collazos, Alex 3:56:57 (10,828)
Collenette, John P 4:05:03 (12,928)
Coller, Jonny C 3:44:53 (7,665)
Coll-Escolano, Gines 3:44:34 (7,585)
Collett, Les 3:59:00 (11,511)
Collett, Richard M 4:32:57 (19,992)
Collett, Timothy E 5:26:57 (29,218)
Colley, Darren 4:52:47 (24,420)
Colley, John W 4:30:25 (19,407)
Collie, James I 3:55:41 (10,431)
Collie, Philip F 4:23:34 (17,523)
Collier, Christopher J 5:33:28 (29,846)
Collier, Darren W 3:35:20 (5,726)
Collier, David S 2:52:47 (664)
Collier, Hadrian R 4:09:42 (14,029)
Collier, John S 5:16:53 (28,115)
Collier, Paul D 3:50:13 (8,915)
Collier, Tony R 4:20:28 (16,727)
Collinge, Andrew 2:44:37 (336)
Collinge, Stephen A 3:18:21 (3,042)
Collingridge, Graham L 3:47:49 (8,332)
Collingwood, Paul S 3:02:24 (1,399)
Collins, Andrew T 3:47:34 (8,259)
Collins, Andy 2:53:50 (715)
Collins, Duncan 4:50:40 (23,976)
Collins, Gary D 3:25:17 (3,972)
Collins, Grahame F 3:16:39 (2,834)
Collins, Grant R 4:24:44 (17,880)
Collins, James C 3:20:01 (3,270)
Collins, James M 4:06:22 (13,204)
Collins, John 3:53:41 (9,816)
Collins, Jonathan G 3:00:58 (1,299)
Collins, Lance K 4:24:25 (17,777)
Collins, Lee 4:32:25 (19,891)
Collins, Mark S 5:18:27 (28,302)
Collins, Martin A 3:27:22 (4,306)
Collins, Matthew C 3:26:28 (4,142)
Collins, Maurice S 2:55:40 (826)
Collins, Michael 3:15:06 (2,671)
Collins, Michael 3:59:49 (11,770)
Collins, Michael 5:07:56 (26,996)
Collins, Michael J 4:39:45 (21,612)
Collins, Michael P 4:55:17 (24,957)
Collins, Michael T 3:39:26 (6,529)
Collins, Nigel A 3:19:18 (3,172)
Collins, Paul 3:47:54 (8,354)
Collins, Paul J 2:57:09 (956)
Collins, Paul J 3:55:27 (10,358)
Collins, Peter M 4:01:05 (12,067)
Collins, Peter R 3:47:54 (8,354)
Collins, Russell 2:54:33 (761)
Collins, Sean 4:28:24 (18,871)
Collins, Simon L 3:08:58 (1,952)
Collins, Stephen 2:52:00 (634)
Collins, Steve 3:42:51 (7,193)
Collinson, Anthony 3:15:53 (2,767)
Collis, Andrew S 4:56:57 (25,295)
Collis, James G 3:36:57 (6,029)
Collison, Brian G 4:51:03 (24,049)
Collyer, Nick M 5:14:55 (27,898)
Colman, Norman 5:26:50 (29,204)
Colman, Paul M 3:18:23 (3,045)
Colton, John J 3:53:41 (9,816)
Colwell, Andy J 4:41:07 (21,918)
Colwell, Stephen J 4:52:29 (24,349)
Combat, Jean-Paul 3:37:52 (6,202)
Combat, Raphael 2:35:47 (126)
Combes, Stephen N 4:13:18 (14,917)
Combrinck, Paul J 5:11:13 (27,415)
Comerford, Samuel 3:21:30 (3,471)
Comerford, Sean 4:58:25 (25,589)
Comette, Allan J 4:43:27 (22,421)
Comins, Jonathan P 6:26:59 (32,402)
Commander, Richard A 3:34:34 (5,585)
Comper, Paul 3:51:58 (9,356)
Compte, Philip 3:26:56 (4,229)
Compton, Claude J 4:13:50 (15,030)
Compton, David J 4:11:48 (14,524)
Compton, Oliver S 3:25:04 (3,936)
Compton, Peter A 5:30:16 (29,569)
Comyn, James A 5:12:55 (27,637)
Condello, Christian 5:04:11 (26,474)
Condon, Richard 3:09:15 (1,980)
Coney, Richard I 3:26:36 (4,177)
Congdon, Andrew J 3:47:38 (8,279)
Congreve, Raymond A 4:22:47 (17,318)
Conley, Neil M 3:48:46 (8,570)
Conlin, Paul J 3:13:06 (2,414)
Conlon, Gary A 4:22:28 (17,237)
Conlon, Kevan M 4:49:27 (23,746)
Conn, Greg M 4:32:43 (19,939)
Conn, Peter W 3:21:40 (3,495)
Connaughton, Peter K 4:55:54 (25,077)
Connearn, Dale 3:05:11 (1,592)
Conneely, Paul J 3:58:05 (11,178)
Conneely, Stephen J 4:51:19 (24,097)
Connell, Anthony 4:33:33 (20,149)
Connell, Benjamin J 2:56:27 (888)
Connell, James T 5:06:33 (26,793)
Connell, Michael 6:55:37 (32,835)
Connell, Stephen J 4:28:17 (18,833)
Connell, Steven 3:05:41 (1,633)
Connell-Wynne, Nicholas W 3:52:09 (9,398)
Connelly, Mark D 4:51:05 (24,057)
Connery, Neil E 4:05:47 (13,096)
Connett, David J 4:59:00 (25,708)
Connick, Lee J 5:29:32 (29,489)
Connolly, Daniel 3:59:34 (11,689)
Connolly, Ger M 4:51:42 (24,188)
Connolly, James 4:41:00 (21,895)
Connolly, James P 3:41:51 (6,999)
Connolly, Michael R 5:33:21 (29,836)
Connolly, Patrick W 4:03:33 (12,614)
Connolly, Paul E 4:32:15 (19,845)
Connolly, Peter A 3:22:08 (3,550)
Connolly, Tommy 5:45:40 (30,760)
Connoly, Charles D 3:43:46 (7,411)
Connor, David P 2:35:01 (115)
Connor, Paul W 4:14:09 (15,122)
Connor, Ray O 3:46:39 (8,048)
Connor, Sean 3:48:45 (8,569)
Connors, Michael 6:11:37 (31,972)
Connor-Scahill, Wayne P 4:48:54 (23,628)
Conole, Bevan A 5:03:11 (26,343)
Conoley, Michael 4:48:09 (23,459)
Conquest, Doug 4:52:34 (24,371)
Conrad-Pickles, Harry C 3:51:01 (9,102)
Conridge, Philip 3:31:33 (5,073)
Conroy, Bill 4:13:37 (14,979)
Conroy, Chris 4:20:14 (16,673)
Conroy, Paul L 5:05:33 (26,647)
Conroy, Stephen W 3:28:56 (4,609)
Considine, John 4:08:04 (13,632)
Constable, Christopher J 4:02:05 (12,280)
Contessi, Leandro 2:53:55 (722)
Contractor, Bhadresh R 4:39:23 (21,542)
Contreras-Ramis, José M 3:42:59 (7,227)
Conway, Ian P 4:22:13 (17,179)
Conway, John 3:52:32 (9,501)
Conway, Mark I 4:22:05 (17,141)
Conway, Matt J 4:05:33 (13,038)
Conway, Paul I 5:02:00 (26,177)
Conway, Paul M 3:26:44 (4,197)
Conway, Robert M 4:26:06 (18,286)
Conway, Stuart 3:29:24 (4,696)
Conyers-Silverthorn, Rex M 4:40:06 (21,691)
Cooil, Richard B 3:40:14 (6,663)
Cook, Adrian R 5:08:44 (27,110)
Cook, Alan 3:05:48 (1,642)
Cook, Andrew J 3:45:36 (7,821)
Cook, Barry T 3:42:24 (7,098)
Cook, Daniel J 3:17:23 (2,929)
Cook, David J 3:56:50 (10,799)
Cook, David S 3:43:08 (7,269)
Cook, Duncan R 4:55:11 (24,936)
Cook, Jacob 3:55:55 (10,514)
Cook, John 2:56:30 (896)
Cook, John 3:45:34 (7,814)
Cook, Keith N 5:45:13 (30,732)
Cook, Michael G 4:04:00 (12,714)
Cook, Nicholas A 4:17:31 (15,987)
Cook, Nicholas I 4:29:56 (19,276)
Cook, Philip M 5:08:47 (27,114)
Cook, Robert J 4:58:42 (25,644)
Cook, Roy 4:37:59 (21,216)
Cook, Simon C 3:58:07 (11,195)
Cook, Stuart P 3:43:05 (7,261)
Cook, Terence 4:37:27 (21,097)
Cook, Tony 4:18:32 (16,243)
Cook, William R 4:29:07 (19,062)
Cooke, Andrew J 4:52:12 (24,289)
Cooke, Anthony J 4:56:02 (25,107)
Cooke, Gary 4:27:32 (18,633)
Cooke, Guy E 4:53:26 (24,553)
Cooke, Jason L 2:41:16 (232)
Cooke, Jonathan D 4:25:29 (18,114)
Cooke, Jonathan P 3:31:07 (5,010)
Cooke, Joseph G 3:54:52 (10,165)
Cooke, Julian C 4:14:51 (15,298)

Name	Time	Name	Time	Name	Time
Cooke, Kevin J	4:22:16 (17,191)	Copeland, Kevin M	4:35:27 (20,594)	Cosco, Antonio	5:23:54 (28,928)
Cooke, Paul	5:55:38 (31,339)	Copeland, Matthew S	4:51:19 (24,097)	Cosgrave, James	2:58:35 (1,072)
Cooke, Peter J	4:51:24 (24,121)	Copeland, Maurice H	6:10:41 (31,948)	Cosham, Derek	6:11:20 (31,964)
Cooke, Stephen	4:34:17 (20,303)	Copeland, Terry	4:40:43 (21,831)	Cossar, Dave	5:11:21 (27,434)
Cooke, Tim	3:28:40 (4,543)	Copeman, Colin T	4:39:15 (21,502)	Cossette, Darren A	4:41:37 (22,017)
Cooksey, Andrew P	3:48:01 (8,387)	Copestick, Robin	2:30:58 (76)	Cosson, Stuart	4:42:16 (22,167)
Coolbear, David	5:07:35 (26,944)	Copland, Christopher N	4:25:56 (18,238)	Cossu, Maurizio	4:04:36 (12,831)
Coomber, Jamie R	3:48:55 (8,614)	Coppard, Kenneth P	4:00:14 (11,874)	Costa, Luigi	4:15:54 (15,578)
Coombes, Chad L	5:43:37 (30,613)	Coppin, Paul	5:31:29 (29,704)	Costa-D'Sa, Richard A	3:42:14 (7,072)
Coombes, Jo	5:06:31 (26,790)	Copsey, Richard J	4:11:25 (14,445)	Costard, Martin D	5:05:17 (26,620)
Coombs, Christopher K	3:28:22 (4,486)	Copus, Christopher D	3:18:39 (3,088)	Costas, Paraskeva B	3:23:57 (3,782)
Coombs, David T	4:03:32 (12,611)	Copus, Martin R	3:32:39 (5,272)	Costas, Paul	3:13:03 (2,406)
Coombs, Michael W	4:29:30 (19,179)	Corbet Burcher, James A	3:34:34 (5,585)	Costello, Anthony G	4:06:36 (13,251)
Coombs, Nicholas M	5:12:55 (27,637)	Corbett, Gavin F	4:30:34 (19,442)	Costello, Michael P	4:40:23 (21,747)
Cooner, Jagdeep	5:24:38 (28,998)	Corbett, Richard C	3:53:33 (9,778)	Costello, Peter J	5:29:42 (29,507)
Cooney, Andrew S	2:43:58 (311)	Corbett, Richard J	5:07:05 (26,874)	Costello, Samuel J	2:48:17 (462)
Cooney, John J	4:33:32 (20,142)	Corbetta, Angelo	3:41:00 (6,805)	Costello, Stephen W	3:38:19 (6,292)
Cooney, Kevin	3:45:48 (7,873)	Corbetta, Massimo	3:17:17 (2,920)	Costin, Paul	3:51:18 (9,173)
Cooney, Stephen	3:26:35 (4,173)	Corbishley, John	4:35:04 (20,504)	Cote, André-Denis	4:41:28 (21,986)
Cooney, Stephen	4:42:47 (22,278)	Corby, Anthony	3:31:27 (5,062)	Cote, Sean A	4:49:34 (23,769)
Cooper, Adrian D	3:03:53 (1,507)	Corby, Colin D	4:56:25 (25,191)	Cottee, Ian S	3:59:29 (11,668)
Cooper, Allan	3:59:31 (11,677)	Corby, Michael J	4:29:27 (19,160)	Cottell, Martin W	5:04:22 (26,499)
Cooper, Andrew J	5:18:25 (28,300)	Corby, Nick	4:54:56 (24,875)	Cottenham, Ian P	4:28:37 (18,924)
Cooper, Andrew K	2:46:21 (399)	Corcoran, Chris	3:16:49 (2,854)	Cotter, Ian J	2:59:41 (1,218)
Cooper, Anthony J	4:20:17 (16,678)	Corcoran, John M	5:06:16 (26,750)	Cotter, Michael S	4:22:58 (17,358)
Cooper, Arthur J	5:01:52 (26,154)	Corcoran, Kevin M	4:07:02 (13,351)	Cotter, Stephen	4:11:36 (14,479)
Cooper, Ben J	3:28:05 (4,420)	Corcoran, Peter	4:26:19 (18,342)	Cotterill, Mark A	3:14:04 (2,539)
Cooper, Brendan R	4:43:28 (22,425)	Cordeel, Filip	4:52:31 (24,358)	Cotterill, Phillip	3:29:32 (4,725)
Cooper, Christopher J	3:59:48 (11,762)	Corden, James M	2:56:27 (888)	Cottingham, Matthew S	4:52:36 (24,380)
Cooper, Christopher J	4:44:12 (22,610)	Corder, Christopher C	4:47:52 (23,400)	Cottingham, Tim	4:53:43 (24,622)
Cooper, Christopher R	5:35:07 (29,978)	Corder, Michael P	3:22:13 (3,558)	Cottington, Graham A	4:15:29 (15,474)
Cooper, Clive A	3:55:46 (10,468)	Cordery, Lee F	5:00:21 (25,952)	Cottle, James H	3:33:53 (5,460)
Cooper, Conrad P	3:58:48 (11,447)	Cordiner, Andrew J	5:06:03 (26,722)	Cotton, Anthony E	3:34:38 (5,597)
Cooper, Darren	5:41:47 (30,484)	Cording, Steve	3:42:51 (7,193)	Cotton, Chris	4:02:54 (12,458)
Cooper, Darren J	3:57:06 (10,883)	Cordingley, Simon N	3:58:16 (11,253)	Cotton, David M	4:41:58 (22,101)
Cooper, David	4:09:47 (14,054)	Cordner, Stuart	3:10:58 (2,153)	Cotton, Ian J	4:07:44 (13,543)
Cooper, David A	2:54:06 (734)	Core, Kevin A	4:34:45 (20,424)	Cotton, John D	3:53:58 (9,912)
Cooper, David A	4:23:29 (17,496)	Core, Peter J	4:43:06 (22,346)	Cotton, Mark J	4:21:06 (16,892)
Cooper, Dick	4:49:35 (23,774)	Corfield, Paul D	4:06:44 (13,285)	Cottrell, David F	4:52:34 (24,371)
Cooper, Gary L	4:26:22 (18,352)	Corker, David	3:57:19 (10,953)	Cottrell, Michael J	4:50:55 (24,028)
Cooper, Geoffrey R	4:03:06 (12,504)	Corkett, Tony	4:14:45 (15,272)	Cottrell, Neil	4:38:08 (21,268)
Cooper, George S	3:42:53 (7,202)	Corless, David	3:46:16 (7,960)	Couch, Barry J	4:28:01 (18,753)
Cooper, Glenn	3:04:07 (1,523)	Corley, Daniel	4:47:30 (23,319)	Couch, Duncan	4:31:44 (19,729)
Cooper, Glenn A	3:50:30 (8,984)	Corley, John	4:55:11 (24,936)	Couchman, Neil B	4:16:35 (15,747)
Cooper, Ian P	4:17:13 (15,910)	Corley, Steve M	3:35:19 (5,723)	Coudert, Gerard	3:04:48 (1,566)
Cooper, Ian R	3:39:44 (6,579)	Cormaud, Doyato	5:00:49 (26,015)	Coughlan, Anthony M	4:14:28 (15,202)
Cooper, Ian T	4:29:35 (19,194)	Corn, Jonathan G	3:59:18 (11,604)	Coulaud, Jean-Christophe	5:08:24 (27,064)
Cooper, James A	4:20:51 (16,820)	Cornacchia, Biagio	4:44:59 (22,778)	Couling, Neil J	3:48:16 (8,442)
Cooper, James H	3:33:47 (5,447)	Cornacchia, Nicola	4:25:19 (18,065)	Coull, Graham	4:07:04 (13,360)
Cooper, John	4:42:48 (22,285)	Cornelius, Neil R	4:15:39 (15,508)	Coulson, Bryan	4:25:33 (18,126)
Cooper, John A	4:56:59 (25,307)	Cornell, Andrew R	5:41:20 (30,442)	Coulson, Stephen M	4:06:53 (13,321)
Cooper, John M	3:36:33 (5,943)	Cornell, Mark K	3:26:26 (4,140)	Coulter, Barry A	2:55:24 (811)
Cooper, John M	3:55:45 (10,460)	Cornell, Matt	5:42:10 (30,516)	Coulter, David A	4:45:43 (22,947)
Cooper, Mark A	4:05:23 (12,994)	Corneloues, Roy	5:05:23 (26,635)	Councell, Mathew	4:09:05 (13,878)
Cooper, Mark C	5:02:59 (26,314)	Corney, John E	4:40:56 (21,877)	Coupe, Benjamin J	5:24:03 (28,949)
Cooper, Martin	3:31:51 (5,134)	Cornford, Adrian W	3:02:02 (1,378)	Coupe, David A	3:44:34 (7,585)
Cooper, Martin S	4:08:19 (13,695)	Cornish, Alan G	3:48:44 (8,565)	Coupe, Matthew R	3:18:20 (3,039)
Cooper, Matthew J	3:39:25 (6,523)	Cornish, Nathan J	4:27:34 (18,644)	Court, Alan R	3:18:24 (3,049)
Cooper, Michael	3:14:01 (2,534)	Cornish, Simon	3:46:14 (7,953)	Court, Jonathan P	3:24:36 (3,879)
Cooper, Michael P	5:16:09 (28,021)	Cornwall, Dale M	4:02:31 (12,376)	Court, Philip A	4:09:18 (13,934)
Cooper, Neil V	3:14:55 (2,655)	Cornwall, Kieran	4:06:40 (13,265)	Courtade, Joel	4:29:45 (19,238)
Cooper, Nick J	3:35:40 (5,777)	Cornwell, Clive	4:35:27 (20,594)	Courtenay Clack, Thomas M	5:39:31 (30,326)
Cooper, Paul A	4:18:02 (16,114)	Corona, Pietro	5:32:19 (29,762)	Courtney, Anthony G	6:07:19 (31,831)
Cooper, Paul D	4:36:34 (20,861)	Correa, Alexis	5:26:45 (29,193)	Courtney, John	5:14:00 (27,760)
Cooper, Paul E	4:43:38 (22,474)	Correia, Marcelo	3:56:36 (10,726)	Courtney, Kevin S	2:51:45 (625)
Cooper, Philip J	2:54:07 (736)	Correia Dos Santos, Julio A	2:47:13 (423)	Courtney, Roy	5:56:59 (31,405)
Cooper, Philip R	4:31:17 (19,606)	Corrie, Darren	5:07:32 (26,934)	Courtney, Trevor A	4:41:59 (22,110)
Cooper, Rafi	4:32:21 (19,873)	Corrie Hill, James A	3:31:47 (5,115)	Cousens, Charles L	5:01:10 (26,065)
Cooper, Richard J	3:58:49 (11,452)	Corrigan, Andrew	4:05:11 (12,951)	Cousins, Andy G	5:20:10 (28,516)
Cooper, Robert J	4:01:32 (12,153)	Corrigan, Gerald S	4:04:15 (12,766)	Cousins, James	4:11:41 (14,494)
Cooper, Roddy D	3:48:41 (8,551)	Corrigan, Kevin J	5:11:24 (27,442)	Cousins, Patrick C	3:30:48 (4,944)
Cooper, Ronald C	5:35:08 (29,980)	Corringham, Barry	4:03:40 (12,644)	Cousins, Roger N	4:24:53 (17,917)
Cooper, Shaun A	5:14:42 (27,872)	Corry, James M	3:53:29 (9,762)	Coutinho, Joao	4:19:33 (16,491)
Cooper, Simon J	3:38:20 (6,293)	Corry, Timothy D	3:22:30 (3,594)	Coutts, Gordon A	4:34:13 (20,294)
Cooper, Stephen J	4:09:50 (14,067)	Corsini, Russell	2:55:53 (843)	Coverdale, John E	3:28:08 (4,431)
Cooper, Steve	6:41:02 (32,627)	Corteletti, Claudio	4:23:31 (17,509)	Coves-Arquez, José	3:18:22 (3,044)
Cooper, Wilfred N Jnr	3:19:58 (3,262)	Cortes, Eric	4:24:42 (17,869)	Covington, Richard M	4:12:45 (14,761)
Coote, Jon M	2:54:46 (780)	Cortes, Javier	2:15:51 (17)	Cowan, Alan J	4:24:36 (17,842)
Coote, Shaun L	3:36:27 (5,925)	Cortese, Guiseppe	4:40:47 (21,848)	Cowan, Andrew D	4:36:46 (20,924)
Coote, Wayne J	3:55:28 (10,361)	Corti, Dominic F	4:27:50 (18,703)	Cowan, Christopher	4:35:35 (20,618)
Cope, Peter	4:31:40 (19,717)	Cortinhas-Carvalhido, Santiago	3:55:02 (10,217)	Cowan, Mark	5:43:53 (30,632)
Cope, Trevor A	4:07:54 (13,581)	Cortinovis, Paolo	4:28:00 (18,749)	Cowan, Nick	3:42:50 (7,191)
Copeland, Gary E	4:03:28 (12,598)	Corton, James R	4:34:23 (20,335)	Cowdrill, Andrew G	4:35:12 (20,531)

Cowdrill, Gary T	4:35:12 (20,531)	
Cowell, Courtney J	4:46:26 (23,108)	
Cowell, Jon M	3:01:38 (1,346)	
Cowell, Martin F	4:03:21 (12,565)	
Cowell, TJ	4:12:24 (14,681)	
Cowen, Andrew J	4:14:50 (15,292)	
Cowhig, Philip J	3:57:10 (10,911)	
Cowie, Duncan	3:31:10 (5,020)	
Cowley, David	3:22:08 (3,550)	
Cowley, John	4:09:53 (14,076)	
Cowley, Keith	3:01:54 (1,367)	
Cowley, Morgan J	3:22:02 (3,539)	
Cowley, Nicholas	4:27:11 (18,551)	
Cowley, Simon	3:53:56 (9,902)	
Cowling, Jeff	3:06:25 (1,705)	
Cowling, Jonathan P	5:25:33 (29,087)	
Cowling, Stephen K	3:46:17 (7,963)	
Cowling, Tim	5:55:35 (31,333)	
Cowman, Christopher R	3:21:57 (3,529)	
Cowpe, Matthew D	4:01:33 (12,158)	
Cox, Alan	3:17:20 (2,923)	
Cox, Alan	3:28:40 (4,543)	
Cox, Alex P	4:04:27 (12,804)	
Cox, Alistair N	4:12:21 (14,670)	
Cox, Andrew C	2:56:41 (915)	
Cox, Andrew L	5:05:28 (26,641)	
Cox, Barry S	3:32:08 (5,184)	
Cox, Brian A	5:44:12 (30,662)	
Cox, Brian L	4:43:20 (22,395)	
Cox, Daniel R	3:31:36 (5,087)	
Cox, Daniel R	5:02:06 (26,187)	
Cox, Darren J	5:38:26 (30,245)	
Cox, David A	4:14:42 (15,260)	
Cox, David C	3:53:07 (9,665)	
Cox, David R	3:50:05 (8,880)	
Cox, Gareth B	6:08:18 (31,870)	
Cox, Ian	4:02:23 (12,347)	
Cox, Ian D	3:44:22 (7,534)	
Cox, Ian G	3:59:17 (11,599)	
Cox, James A	3:51:31 (9,222)	
Cox, Jason	3:40:14 (6,663)	
Cox, Jonathan R	3:26:10 (4,096)	
Cox, Justin A	2:58:17 (1,043)	
Cox, Mark A	3:38:51 (6,396)	
Cox, Michael	3:29:43 (4,765)	
Cox, Mick	4:25:45 (18,176)	
Cox, Paul	2:40:43 (224)	
Cox, Peter M	4:10:28 (14,206)	
Cox, Richard	5:23:37 (28,896)	
Cox, Steve R	3:03:54 (1,508)	
Cox, Steven W	4:53:49 (24,639)	
Cox, Stewart J	2:49:42 (528)	
Cox, Toby	4:57:41 (25,431)	
Cox, Troy T	5:48:09 (30,953)	
Coxall, Steven	3:43:10 (7,281)	
Coxley, Philip R	5:59:45 (31,544)	
Coxon, Peter J	3:47:31 (8,242)	
Coyle, Alasdair J	3:35:57 (5,828)	
Coyle, Terry P	2:48:14 (461)	
Coyle, William J	3:07:28 (1,800)	
Coyne, Colin P	3:20:33 (3,341)	
Crabb, Graham L	7:47:54 (33,167)	
Crabot, Jean-François	4:45:04 (22,807)	
Crabtree, Jason W	3:28:35 (4,528)	
Crabtree, Julian S	5:19:21 (28,413)	
Crabtree, Mark A	2:58:26 (1,061)	
Crack, Alastair J	5:30:54 (29,636)	
Cracker, Michael	5:19:31 (28,438)	
Cracknell, James E	3:00:10 (1,242)	
Cradden, Brendan P	3:29:28 (4,708)	
Craddock, Kevin J	4:48:27 (23,527)	
Craft, Nicolas E	3:14:33 (2,603)	
Crafter, Daniel J	4:53:52 (24,652)	
Cragg, Adrian P	4:12:38 (14,734)	
Cragg, Melvyn J	2:56:43 (919)	
Cragg, Stephen	4:19:07 (16,368)	
Cragg, Stephen J	4:37:40 (21,152)	
Craggs, Darren M	4:07:16 (13,415)	
Cragie, Robert C	4:24:02 (17,666)	
Crahart, Lee J	4:15:39 (15,508)	
Craig, Brett	4:32:30 (19,903)	
Craig, Christopher	3:22:58 (3,653)	
Craig, Darren	5:03:03 (26,322)	

Craig, Duncan E	4:30:35 (19,446)	
Craig, Gerard	2:51:04 (596)	
Craig, Kenneth R	4:20:32 (16,742)	
Craig, Michael	2:51:35 (617)	
Craig, Philip A	4:07:33 (13,486)	
Craig, Scott	3:28:29 (4,506)	
Craig, Steve	4:23:02 (17,369)	
Cramer, Nicholas R	3:13:52 (2,509)	
Cramer, Stuart J	3:37:05 (6,053)	
Cramm, Falk	4:42:25 (22,203)	
Cramp, Howard J	5:05:17 (26,620)	
Cramp, John W	4:00:30 (11,934)	
Crampsey, James	2:48:53 (491)	
Crampton, Paul S	5:13:19 (27,692)	
Crandon, David	4:40:41 (21,825)	
Crane, Al	4:28:46 (18,965)	
Crane, Andrew J	4:44:19 (22,639)	
Crane, Barry M	3:53:13 (9,697)	
Crane, Basil F	5:09:34 (27,216)	
Crane, Christopher M	4:09:11 (13,903)	
Crane, Gregory L	5:07:41 (26,962)	
Crane, Neil	5:17:32 (28,198)	
Crane, Peter J	3:38:17 (6,289)	
Crane, Russell P	4:51:49 (24,214)	
Crane, Sean A	4:25:46 (18,184)	
Crane, Steven T	5:17:24 (28,183)	
Crane, William T	3:34:16 (5,523)	
Cranfield, Glen	5:12:24 (27,575)	
Crannage, Jonathan	3:12:13 (2,311)	
Cranstoun, Simon D	4:43:06 (22,346)	
Cranwell, Mark A	3:20:54 (3,392)	
Crashaw, Justin R	4:24:02 (17,666)	
Crassier, Lionel	3:25:48 (4,049)	
Crassweller, Kenneth G	3:22:18 (3,572)	
Craven, Paul A	4:36:43 (20,901)	
Craven, Paul V	4:15:20 (15,425)	
Crawford, Alan J	3:39:31 (6,543)	
Crawford, Anthony	5:37:23 (30,155)	
Crawford, Bryan R	2:57:28 (983)	
Crawford, David	4:26:05 (18,281)	
Crawford, David A	3:53:02 (9,638)	
Crawford, George	4:21:05 (16,886)	
Crawford, James D	4:32:32 (19,908)	
Crawford, Miles H	5:19:45 (28,464)	
Crawford, Philip	4:52:24 (24,333)	
Crawford, Richard H	3:14:20 (2,573)	
Crawford, Richard P	3:01:57 (1,371)	
Crawford, Robert K	4:13:30 (14,955)	
Crawford, Victor S	4:17:00 (15,860)	
Crawley, Bryan R	4:56:25 (25,191)	
Crawley, William	4:04:03 (12,726)	
Crawte, Antony M	3:52:57 (9,610)	
Crayston, David	3:09:21 (1,993)	
Creane, John E	2:37:39 (158)	
Crease, Gregory B	4:11:14 (14,396)	
Crease, Tony	3:43:31 (7,354)	
Creasey, Timothy J	3:42:28 (7,106)	
Creasy, Ian A	4:50:35 (23,956)	
Creber, Jim E	3:51:57 (9,351)	
Creber, Theodore S	4:20:41 (16,783)	
Creech, Stuart D	3:05:02 (1,578)	
Creed, Gareth	3:13:04 (2,410)	
Creedon, Adam	3:35:27 (5,742)	
Creese, Jeremy D	4:01:49 (12,219)	
Cregan, Jack N	5:49:18 (31,024)	
Creigh, David	3:50:32 (8,997)	
Creighton, Luke T	3:14:18 (2,567)	
Creighton, Paul L	5:18:06 (28,252)	
Creighton, Peter	4:05:26 (13,005)	
Crenol, Kevin N	2:35:25 (118)	
Crespo, José Manuel	3:59:56 (11,795)	
Cresswell, Jeremy P	6:16:04 (32,120)	
Cretton, Scott P	4:12:21 (14,670)	
Crews, Jon	3:17:48 (2,978)	
Cribb, Stephen T	4:35:34 (20,615)	
Cribier, Guillaume J	2:38:49 (184)	
Crick, Mark F	4:59:04 (25,718)	
Crick, Steve	4:23:14 (17,427)	
Cridland, Dean R	4:41:16 (21,943)	
Cridland, Peter R	3:49:10 (8,661)	
Crighton, Thomas G	4:17:47 (16,056)	
Crippa, Corrado	4:11:06 (14,359)	
Cripps, Graham K	5:07:24 (26,918)	

Cripps, Jason K	4:17:41 (16,031)	
Crisp, Kev P	4:27:34 (18,644)	
Crisp, Martin T	5:08:52 (27,129)	
Crisp, Matthew D	3:38:15 (6,280)	
Crisp, Trevor D	3:11:03 (2,161)	
Crispin, Jason D	3:57:01 (10,847)	
Crispin, Nick J	4:01:07 (12,077)	
Crispin, Stuart J	3:46:41 (8,057)	
Critchley, David J	4:34:03 (20,267)	
Critchley, Gavin	3:42:02 (7,030)	
Critchley, Neil J	3:24:39 (3,889)	
Critchlow, Nigel	3:14:19 (2,572)	
Crocker, Edward	6:31:09 (32,477)	
Crocker, John A	4:30:49 (19,497)	
Crocker, Paul D	4:15:35 (15,491)	
Crocker, Paul D	4:29:17 (19,115)	
Crocket, Graham P	3:47:20 (8,200)	
Crockford, John G	2:53:45 (710)	
Croft, James	6:13:13 (32,028)	
Croft, James O	3:10:51 (2,143)	
Croft, James S	5:11:32 (27,464)	
Croft, Jared	3:12:10 (2,302)	
Croft, Paul A	3:30:54 (4,963)	
Crofts, Joe N	4:56:32 (25,213)	
Croker, Philip	4:55:25 (24,985)	
Croker, Robert J	4:18:24 (16,209)	
Croll, Darren L	5:16:18 (28,045)	
Cromar, Ion W	3:37:04 (6,048)	
Cromhout, Ian	6:02:09 (31,649)	
Crompton, Neil W	2:36:27 (135)	
Crompton, Robert	4:26:29 (18,381)	
Cronin, Michael J	4:31:08 (19,566)	
Cronk, David W	3:25:19 (3,978)	
Crook, Andrew	3:25:45 (4,034)	
Crook, Philip J	5:20:33 (28,567)	
Crook, Richard R	3:23:46 (3,752)	
Crook, Warren S	3:04:29 (1,544)	
Crookall, Jonathan M	3:45:41 (7,844)	
Crookes, Edward M	3:28:57 (4,612)	
Crookes, Paul M	4:19:10 (16,382)	
Crooks, Cedric	3:19:44 (3,220)	
Crosbie, Ben W	3:32:30 (5,252)	
Crosbie, Raymond W	5:02:30 (26,249)	
Crosland, Tom D	4:58:35 (25,627)	
Crosnier Leconte, Thibault R	3:32:36 (5,265)	
Cross, Adam	4:04:51 (12,885)	
Cross, Darren R	4:39:47 (21,624)	
Cross, Ian N	4:12:44 (14,756)	
Cross, Jeremy A	3:28:37 (4,533)	
Cross, Jeremy S	3:14:38 (2,619)	
Cross, Matt R	3:31:02 (4,990)	
Cross, Matthew J	4:58:27 (25,596)	
Cross, Paul S	4:01:56 (12,244)	
Cross, Peter	4:38:51 (21,404)	
Cross, Peter H	5:13:31 (27,724)	
Cross, Peter R	3:33:41 (5,435)	
Cross, Philip J	3:04:23 (1,527)	
Cross, Stephen A	3:15:40 (2,737)	
Cross, Terry	4:02:43 (12,415)	
Cross, Will	3:13:17 (2,430)	
Crosse, Lee W	5:12:27 (27,585)	
Crossland, Brian C	4:06:08 (13,167)	
Crossland, Timothy J	2:30:26 (71)	
Crossley, Gareth M	3:01:51 (1,359)	
Crotty, Simon M	4:17:30 (15,981)	
Crouch, Christopher C	6:11:47 (31,980)	
Crouch, Graham	3:54:17 (9,997)	
Crouch, Michael	4:44:39 (22,695)	
Crouch, Nicholas	5:36:56 (30,128)	
Crouch, Robert J	4:15:05 (15,363)	
Crouch, Simon	4:47:46 (23,377)	
Crouch, Stephen P	4:44:19 (22,639)	
Croucher, Graham J	4:23:02 (17,369)	
Croucher, Ken	4:25:03 (17,976)	
Crowcombe, David N	5:01:51 (26,152)	
Crowder, John R	4:07:24 (13,451)	
Crowe, Adrian V	4:41:54 (22,085)	
Crowe, James A	6:15:25 (32,097)	
Crowe, Liam A	4:35:53 (20,686)	
Crowe, Simon P	4:15:37 (15,498)	
Crowhurst, Paul A	5:30:24 (29,580)	
Crowle, Christopher	4:20:36 (16,759)	
Crowle, Mark	3:46:17 (7,963)	

Crowley, Ben 4:51:26 (24,132)
Crowley, David M 3:29:29 (4,713)
Crowley, Gregory S 2:59:12 (1,164)
Crowley, Julian F 3:41:47 (6,983)
Crowley, Richard J 7:10:05 (32,979)
Crowley, Stuart A 5:15:15 (27,932)
Crowley, Vincent P 3:29:16 (4,667)
Crowson, Kevin W 4:07:10 (13,396)
Crowson, Michael 4:20:36 (16,759)
Crowson, Paul J 3:46:29 (8,008)
Crowther, Julian G 2:51:25 (610)
Croydon, Stuart A 3:39:22 (6,512)
Crozier, Adam 4:14:01 (15,074)
Crozier, Peter 3:07:57 (1,852)
Crozier, Rob 3:13:18 (2,433)
Crudgington, James W 3:47:36 (8,270)
Crudgington, Tom G 3:59:38 (11,702)
Cruickshank, David A 3:53:12 (9,689)
Cruickshank, George A 4:28:38 (18,929)
Cruickshank, Sandy 3:34:06 (5,498)
Crumley, Euan J 3:51:31 (9,222)
Crummack, Matthew 4:44:32 (22,683)
Crummett, Steve P 3:57:07 (10,888)
Crump, Oliver C 3:59:57 (11,801)
Crutchley, Philip R 4:29:38 (19,213)
Cruz, Arman 4:50:34 (23,953)
Cruz Rosa, Hector M 3:27:05 (4,258)
Cryer, Patrick W 4:40:11 (21,708)
Cryer, Simon 5:05:37 (26,655)
Cubbon, Andrew K 4:07:39 (13,519)
Cuddeford, Paul M 4:27:06 (18,527)
Cudlipp, Jonathan 4:32:13 (19,836)
Cudmore, Ian M 3:55:41 (10,431)
Cuesta, Rafael 2:56:01 (848)
Cuff, Paul E 2:47:13 (423)
Cuffie, Floyd J 3:47:02 (8,127)
Cull, Simon M 5:24:19 (28,973)
Cullen, Andrew J 5:58:22 (31,482)
Cullen, Denis G 7:09:03 (32,971)
Cullen, Martin J 4:13:20 (14,924)
Cullender, Marc 4:42:41 (22,259)
Cullern, Doug 4:40:27 (21,761)
Culley, Simon J 3:41:36 (6,945)
Cullimore, Scot 4:08:17 (13,686)
Cullinane, John 3:28:44 (4,561)
Cullinane, Martin J 5:44:30 (30,680)
Culling, Adam 4:22:37 (17,277)
Cullingworth, Ian 3:20:11 (3,295)
Cullom, Jonathan M 2:56:52 (926)
Cullum, Ian 4:27:19 (18,584)
Culpan, Charlie J 3:58:42 (11,401)
Culpan, Philip S 2:45:11 (349)
Cultrera, Marcello 4:57:09 (25,346)
Culverwell, Steven 4:47:55 (23,414)
Culwin, Fintan 4:07:29 (13,470)
Cumber, Geoffrey 3:00:25 (1,264)
Cumbers, Leonard 5:11:49 (27,496)
Cumberworth, Paul L 3:53:44 (9,833)
Cumer, Gerard 3:11:33 (2,218)
Cumiskey, Alexander H 3:50:43 (9,033)
Cumiskey, Michael J 3:52:08 (9,390)
Cumming, Andrew F 4:41:33 (22,001)
Cumming, Rob G 4:24:06 (17,683)
Cummings, Chris E 5:18:12 (28,269)
Cummings, Ian J 4:23:55 (17,630)
Cummings, Mark D 3:14:00 (2,530)
Cummings, Simon J 3:27:03 (4,253)
Cummins, James B 4:41:25 (21,973)
Cummins, Mark C 3:40:08 (6,645)
Cumper, Stephen M 3:30:51 (4,952)
Cumpsty, Samuel F 5:47:30 (30,918)
Cundy, Kevin J 3:54:38 (10,086)
Cunliffe, Bill J 3:17:39 (2,958)
Cunningham, David 4:17:22 (15,947)
Cunningham, Gavin J 3:58:10 (11,218)
Cunningham, Jason 4:48:45 (23,596)
Cunningham, John A 4:03:57 (12,704)
Cunningham, Martin A 3:50:58 (9,091)
Cunningham, Michael 2:53:36 (704)
Cunningham, Michael J 4:24:32 (17,809)
Cunningham, Nicholas A 4:16:26 (15,704)
Cunningham, Paul 5:05:45 (26,671)
Cunningham, Peter T 6:56:28 (32,847)
Cunningham, Philip P 2:50:55 (585)
Cunningham, Ryan G 4:40:24 (21,751)
Cunningham, Shane A 3:52:01 (9,365)
Cunningham, Steve 2:46:41 (407)
Cunningham, Stuart J 3:27:58 (4,403)
Cunningham, Thomas S 4:08:14 (13,674)
Cunningham, Tony 3:08:43 (1,927)
Cunningham, William G 4:20:51 (16,820)
Cunnington, David A 4:10:29 (14,212)
Curlew, Simon 4:47:32 (23,329)
Curphey, Paul T 3:03:01 (1,443)
Currams, Neil 3:42:09 (7,055)
Curran, Gavin 3:33:34 (5,410)
Curran, Len 4:44:42 (22,711)
Curran, Michael F 5:08:28 (27,071)
Curran, Patrick L 2:34:18 (103)
Curran, Phil 5:18:59 (28,370)
Curran, Shaun M 4:23:40 (17,552)
Curran, William R 3:08:00 (1,858)
Currell, Barry 2:51:03 (594)
Currell, Mark W 4:42:40 (22,254)
Currie, Douglas Q 3:45:53 (7,884)
Currington, Robert J 5:29:27 (29,480)
Curtin, Matthew J 3:53:15 (9,706)
Curtis, Alec 4:16:35 (15,747)
Curtis, Darren 5:16:29 (28,068)
Curtis, David M 7:12:21 (32,998)
Curtis, Gavin 4:17:48 (16,060)
Curtis, Ivan 4:16:59 (15,854)
Curtis, Mark R 4:55:58 (25,097)
Curtis, Matthew J 4:25:07 (17,996)
Curtis, Michael H 5:27:05 (29,235)
Curtis, Nathan J 3:59:25 (11,641)
Curtis, Paul F 2:48:23 (464)
Curtis, Robert O 4:13:53 (15,039)
Curtis, Stephen 3:37:26 (6,119)
Curtis-Evans, Philip A 4:52:18 (24,307)
Curzon, David B 3:43:46 (7,411)
Curzon, Frank 4:30:49 (19,497)
Cusack, Jake 3:43:53 (7,437)
Cusack, Seamus 4:42:03 (22,123)
Cusick, Peter 3:09:26 (2,006)
Cusimano, Paul 2:58:38 (1,083)
Cussell, Richard M 4:12:40 (14,742)
Cuthbert, Allan R 3:58:07 (11,195)
Cuthbert, Andrew J 5:03:40 (26,413)
Cuthbert, James R 3:56:03 (10,552)
Cuthbert, John P 4:28:21 (18,858)
Cuthbert, Morgan C 3:15:22 (2,704)
Cuthbert, Philip D 3:25:50 (4,052)
Cuthbert, Richard H 5:23:17 (28,865)
Cuthbert, Simon 3:44:34 (7,585)
Cuthbertson, Alistair M 4:02:24 (12,351)
Cuthbertson, James 6:19:24 (32,216)
Cutts, Nigel P 4:09:00 (13,859)
Cutts, Philip M 4:06:07 (13,163)
Czerniewski, Peter M 4:05:34 (13,040)
D'Heygere, François 4:00:50 (12,002)
Da Cruz, Manuel S 3:46:44 (8,069)
Da Gama, Paul S 5:22:25 (28,768)
Da Silva, Edmundo N 4:19:46 (16,544)
Da Silva, Panta 3:51:45 (9,287)
Da Silva Velhas, Ismael J 4:13:41 (15,000)
Dabas, Hubert M 4:11:56 (14,559)
Dabbs, Jonathan M 2:37:50 (163)
Dable, Neil A 3:47:25 (8,219)
Daborn, David R 3:54:42 (10,114)
Dacey, Patrick W 3:49:10 (8,661)
Dachtler, Christopher 3:39:55 (6,610)
Dack, Paul J 3:38:13 (6,270)
Dackmo, Pontus 3:43:18 (7,308)
Dacosta, John W 4:08:52 (13,825)
Dadd, James E 4:01:17 (12,114)
Dadd, Matthew S 3:32:23 (5,232)
Dadd, Tony 4:36:42 (20,896)
Dadomo, Robert 3:31:11 (5,026)
Dady, Simon 5:16:17 (28,039)
Daga, Renato 3:24:28 (3,857)
Dagger, Matthew R 4:41:42 (22,036)
Dagger, Robert 6:02:59 (31,680)
Dagnino, Angelo 3:34:29 (5,560)
Dahlborg, Gunnar 3:00:51 (1,292)
Dahle Meidell, Oeystein T 4:35:51 (20,683)
Dahlstrom, Bjorn A 4:00:53 (12,012)
Daily, Robert M 5:10:17 (27,303)
Daily, Simon 3:51:09 (9,135)
Dainton, Andrew 4:21:44 (17,036)
Daish, Lee J 4:13:43 (15,007)
Daish, Stephen R 3:27:00 (4,246)
Daldorph, Thomas C 4:21:37 (17,003)
Daldry, Simon J 4:14:50 (15,292)
Dale, Adrian B 3:23:19 (3,686)
Dale, Glenn J 4:30:40 (19,467)
Dale, Graham 4:43:19 (22,392)
Dale, Kevin M 3:47:23 (8,208)
Dale, Paul R 3:37:31 (6,136)
Dale, Shaun M 3:42:31 (7,115)
Dale, Stephen G 3:53:47 (9,853)
Dale, Steven R 6:36:18 (32,548)
Dales, Ben S 4:37:15 (21,045)
Dales, Lee A 4:37:15 (21,045)
Daley, Andrew 5:04:56 (26,573)
Dalitz, Martin 3:13:35 (2,474)
Dalla Via, Luca 4:00:37 (11,953)
Dallas, Barry 4:51:19 (24,097)
Dallas, Bruce R 4:51:18 (24,092)
Dallas, Ian A 4:21:59 (17,112)
Dallaway, Neil P 3:08:30 (1,909)
Dalli, Marc J 4:59:32 (25,794)
Dalloz, Vincent M 3:11:59 (2,274)
Dalrymple Smith, James 3:24:08 (3,812)
Dalston, Michael N 4:04:57 (12,907)
Dalton, Paul W 4:54:47 (24,840)
Dalton, Robert 3:43:40 (7,383)
D'Alton, Simon V 3:15:29 (2,719)
Daly, Francis J 3:55:34 (10,390)
Daly, Hugh D 3:33:34 (5,410)
Daly, Jamie J 4:56:37 (25,223)
Daly, John 4:11:46 (14,513)
Daly, Neil R 4:31:19 (19,618)
Daly, Rob C 5:05:57 (26,700)
Dalziel, Henry J 4:47:16 (23,272)
Damas, Raul A 3:50:29 (8,977)
D'Ambrosio, Gino 3:58:44 (11,417)
Damle, Sameer D 4:29:37 (19,206)
Damour, Gerard 3:05:05 (1,585)
Danby, Tom J 3:00:22 (1,258)
Dance, Ian A 4:31:47 (19,743)
Dance, Kevin A 4:25:28 (18,110)
Danciger, Simon L 2:55:19 (804)
Dandrea, Renzo 3:43:15 (7,300)
Daneo, Giorgio 4:49:21 (23,724)
Danes, Chris M 4:24:14 (17,725)
Dangerfield, Matt J 4:19:49 (16,557)
Dangoor, Daniel E 2:54:23 (752)
Daniel, Jean-Pierre 3:29:29 (4,713)
Daniel, Richard W 4:11:49 (14,527)
Daniel, Rodney J 4:43:57 (22,563)
Daniells, Andy 4:04:51 (12,885)
Daniels, Andrew 5:26:07 (29,139)
Daniels, Gary M 3:44:16 (7,511)
Daniels, Jonathan L 4:32:04 (19,808)
Daniels, Michael J 4:44:54 (22,756)
Daniels, Mike 5:04:41 (26,541)
Daniels, Nicholas J 2:58:58 (1,138)
Daniels, Paul 4:13:26 (14,949)
Daniels, Paul K 3:20:51 (3,385)
Danis, Serge 3:29:48 (4,782)
Danks, Simon J 3:20:37 (3,350)
Dann, Neil R 3:19:56 (3,255)
Dannatt, Richard D 4:35:38 (20,637)
Dansey, Mathew T 5:29:41 (29,503)
Danson, Robert P 4:18:20 (16,193)
Darby, Iain M 2:51:31 (613)
Darby, Matthew J 4:00:20 (11,896)
Darby, Paul A 4:31:34 (19,686)
Darby, Richard A 4:25:21 (18,075)
Darbyshire, Phillip B 2:34:21 (105)
Darch, Gary C 5:19:22 (28,417)
Darcy, Toby M 3:53:55 (9,897)
Darcy-Evans, Patrick J 3:21:01 (3,401)
Dare, Martin L 3:48:40 (8,545)
Dargan, Frank 4:11:19 (14,420)
Dargue, Karl J 5:46:44 (30,842)
Dari, Marco 3:44:02 (7,462)
Darke, Christopher J 3:40:45 (6,752)

Darkins, Peter S............4:31:47 (19,743)
Darling, Richard J 2:49:01 (498)
Darlow, John R 5:12:57 (27,642)
Darnell, Neil M............4:33:13 (20,066)
Darnell, Peter 4:18:02 (16,114)
Darrie, James 5:07:49 (26,976)
Dart, Ian 3:02:52 (1,427)
Dartington, Daniel J............5:20:38 (28,579)
Dartington, Jake J............3:44:46 (7,631)
Darvill, Neil J............4:49:21 (23,724)
Das, Anupam 3:17:58 (2,993)
Dasey, Mark G............3:56:15 (10,610)
Da-Silva, Pierre 3:15:12 (2,683)
Dass, Narinder B 4:33:00 (20,008)
Datar, Rajan 4:53:33 (24,581)
Dates, Alex V 4:44:35 (22,688)
Dathan, David P 4:26:34 (18,397)
Dattani, Dilip 3:12:44 (2,367)
Daub-Klose, Stefan 3:11:16 (2,193)
Daubney, Alisdair J............4:45:34 (22,916)
Daucheez, Julien F 3:49:12 (8,668)
Daugherty, Brian 3:47:24 (8,213)
Daugherty, Duane W............3:09:44 (2,039)
Dauncey, James A 4:29:36 (19,199)
Dauncey, Stephen B............4:31:21 (19,625)
Davall, Ian 4:14:04 (15,092)
Dave, Vikash 4:30:01 (19,299)
Davenport, Danny J............5:39:07 (30,293)
Davenport, Kenny G 4:26:00 (18,258)
Davenport, Stuart............4:09:17 (13,928)
Davey, Anthony J............4:41:30 (21,994)
Davey, Graham P 4:47:28 (23,311)
Davey, Ian 4:18:14 (16,165)
Davey, James O 3:43:38 (7,375)
Davey, John S 4:17:14 (15,914)
Davey, Martin C 3:45:39 (7,833)
Davey, Paul J 3:27:31 (4,336)
Davey, Paul K 4:59:40 (25,826)
Davey, Russ M 4:48:43 (23,587)
Davey, Terry 5:13:53 (27,748)
David, John............4:27:00 (18,504)
David, Mark J 3:34:43 (5,616)
David, Zoltan D 3:57:46 (11,100)
Davidge, Nicholas P 5:47:33 (30,921)
Davidson, Brian R 4:59:03 (25,715)
Davidson, Graeme W 4:07:27 (13,457)
Davidson, Ian C............3:51:21 (9,190)
Davidson, Jamie O 3:34:19 (5,538)
Davidson, Len 3:41:29 (6,909)
Davidson, Michael............3:59:25 (11,641)
Davidson, Ross............3:08:06 (1,871)
Davidson, Steven A............6:20:12 (32,237)
Davie, John C............3:22:49 (3,638)
Davie, Michael C 4:16:25 (15,695)
Davie, Robert............5:56:50 (31,395)
Davies, Adam 5:15:19 (27,938)
Davies, Adrian H 4:28:31 (18,901)
Davies, Alan 5:23:21 (28,878)
Davies, Alexander G............3:02:30 (1,406)
Davies, Allan R 3:39:37 (6,557)
Davies, Alun J............4:57:44 (25,441)
Davies, Andrew C 4:59:56 (25,875)
Davies, Angus S 3:36:10 (5,868)
Davies, Carl J 4:01:47 (12,209)
Davies, Carl T 3:33:27 (5,398)
Davies, Charles M 4:51:09 (24,069)
Davies, Chris J............3:57:05 (10,870)
Davies, Chris N............3:53:02 (9,638)
Davies, Christopher A............4:20:38 (16,769)
Davies, Christopher G............3:07:29 (1,803)
Davies, Clive J 4:43:22 (22,404)
Davies, Colin M 3:35:14 (5,712)
Davies, Craig 3:38:03 (6,239)
Davies, David 4:23:23 (17,468)
Davies, David M 3:30:50 (4,947)
Davies, Dilwyn E 4:25:05 (17,989)
Davies, Eric B............3:41:42 (6,967)
Davies, Gareth E............3:37:08 (6,062)
Davies, Gareth J 4:12:55 (14,816)
Davies, Gareth R............3:58:21 (11,288)
Davies, Gareth R............4:50:56 (24,035)
Davies, Gareth W............7:02:56 (32,906)
Davies, Gavin R............2:42:07 (253)

Davies, Guy M............4:37:32 (21,117)
Davies, Haydn............5:24:03 (28,949)
Davies, Huw............3:43:02 (7,242)
Davies, Hywel J 4:15:45 (15,535)
Davies, Ian 3:28:16 (4,456)
Davies, Ivor J............4:45:40 (22,935)
Davies, James 4:14:08 (15,117)
Davies, James 4:20:20 (16,695)
Davies, Jamie P 4:32:40 (19,925)
Davies, Jason 6:52:13 (32,786)
Davies, Jeffrey P 2:53:44 (709)
Davies, John 3:20:27 (3,332)
Davies, John A 3:53:32 (9,774)
Davies, John D 4:17:19 (15,933)
Davies, John G 3:58:39 (11,382)
Davies, John H 3:54:47 (10,138)
Davies, John I 4:57:13 (25,354)
Davies, John N 4:31:49 (19,750)
Davies, John P............4:36:34 (20,861)
Davies, John R 4:22:05 (17,141)
Davies, Jonathan 3:13:43 (2,487)
Davies, Jonathan C 3:23:48 (3,755)
Davies, Jonathan P 3:49:22 (8,707)
Davies, Keith J 2:48:59 (497)
Dauncey, Kerry............3:04:44 (1,563)
Davies, Kevin 5:26:57 (29,218)
Davies, Kevin J 3:23:50 (3,767)
Davies, Kevin M 4:08:01 (13,616)
Davies, Lawrence F............4:11:29 (14,456)
Davies, Lee 3:33:27 (5,398)
Davies, Lee T 3:50:09 (8,902)
Davies, Leighton 4:16:58 (15,851)
Davies, Mark R............4:23:57 (17,641)
Davies, Martin L 3:38:00 (6,222)
Davies, Matt J............5:37:25 (30,158)
Davies, Max............5:08:58 (27,144)
Davies, Michael H 3:30:08 (4,851)
Davies, Michael J............5:28:50 (29,415)
Davies, Mike 3:03:11 (1,455)
Davies, Neil S 4:13:16 (14,911)
Davies, Nicholas 5:37:05 (30,142)
Davies, Nick J............3:26:33 (4,164)
Davies, Paul 5:32:04 (29,743)
Davies, Peter G 3:38:48 (6,383)
Davies, Peter G 4:32:15 (19,845)
Davies, Peter M 5:51:55 (31,176)
Davies, Phil R............3:45:27 (7,798)
Davies, Philip L 3:46:16 (7,960)
Davies, Rhys 3:49:18 (8,691)
Davies, Richard J 5:20:04 (28,501)
Davies, Richard L 3:27:17 (4,287)
Davies, Richard V 3:47:41 (8,290)
Davies, Rob I 4:08:18 (13,689)
Davies, Robert 4:20:51 (16,820)
Davies, Robert R............3:56:57 (10,828)
Davies, Ross 4:25:51 (18,210)
Davies, Simon G 2:47:05 (419)
Davies, Simon L 4:49:13 (23,694)
Davies, Stephen 3:55:55 (10,514)
Davies, Stephen J............3:40:27 (6,703)
Davies, Stephen K 4:26:10 (18,302)
Davies, Steve P 4:14:31 (15,209)
Davies, Stuart M 5:03:16 (26,354)
Davies, Thomas 4:27:22 (18,595)
Davies, Thomas G 6:49:07 (32,747)
Davies, Thomas V............5:44:47 (30,700)
Davies, Timothy P 4:32:46 (19,952)
Davies, Tony............5:28:24 (29,368)
Davies, Vivian H 5:39:36 (30,332)
Davies, Warren S 5:48:33 (30,971)
Davies, Will 4:00:06 (11,843)
Davies, William M 3:46:16 (7,960)
Davies Knapp, Jack............4:06:28 (13,224)
Davies MBE, Christopher 4:14:52 (15,303)
Davies-Holmes, Robin W 3:59:28 (11,662)
Davis, Adrian J............5:17:36 (28,209)
Davis, Andrew R 3:06:06 (1,676)
Davis, Andy W............4:10:18 (14,170)
Davis, Anthony 4:13:14 (14,906)
Davis, Anthony D 3:07:43 (1,826)
Davis, Anthony J............4:41:15 (21,934)
Davis, Anthony L............3:20:37 (3,350)
Davis, Anthony P............3:38:55 (6,418)

Davis, Benjamin J 3:26:55 (4,225)
Davis, Brian 3:13:58 (2,524)
Davis, Christopher A............4:26:48 (18,464)
Davis, Christopher S 3:52:52 (9,585)
Davis, Colin R 4:13:52 (15,034)
Davis, Darryl K............3:37:27 (6,121)
Davis, David M 4:33:11 (20,055)
Davis, Glen 3:46:03 (7,916)
Davis, Haydn P 3:48:57 (8,620)
Davis, Hugh A............4:09:23 (13,954)
Davis, James R 4:53:41 (24,613)
Davis, Jim 4:20:31 (16,738)
Davis, John W 4:30:39 (19,462)
Davis, Jonathan S 3:15:27 (2,714)
Davis, Justin 4:55:31 (25,001)
Davis, Marc 3:24:12 (3,821)
Davis, Mark 2:45:51 (368)
Davis, Mark R 3:16:31 (2,821)
Davis, Martin B 3:31:37 (5,089)
Davis, Martin J 2:53:16 (686)
Davis, Martin J 5:49:10 (31,014)
Davis, Nicholas G 2:54:20 (747)
Davis, Nigel C 3:52:13 (9,419)
Davis, Noel D 4:26:56 (18,489)
Davis, Paul 3:57:30 (11,014)
Davis, Paul A 5:27:34 (29,281)
Davis, Paul J 3:13:23 (2,450)
Davis, Paul J 3:58:09 (11,209)
Davis, Paul M 4:10:35 (14,232)
Davis, Paul R 6:08:30 (31,876)
Davis, Richard J 3:46:09 (7,935)
Davis, Richard J 5:19:10 (28,397)
Davis, Richard M 3:04:29 (1,544)
Davis, Richard M 3:14:40 (2,625)
Davis, Roger M 4:40:51 (21,865)
Davis, Simon J 4:16:36 (15,756)
Davison, Christopher 4:58:47 (25,658)
Davison, Ian M 3:52:13 (9,419)
Davison, Jeremy A 3:47:46 (8,313)
Davison, Lee R............4:45:28 (22,901)
Davison, Peter 4:24:44 (17,880)
Davison, Scott H 3:53:04 (9,655)
Davison, Sean W 4:24:49 (17,895)
Davison, William G............4:31:13 (19,586)
Davy, John R 5:38:16 (30,231)
Davy, Martin S 4:36:25 (20,828)
Dawber, Nigel 3:19:25 (3,182)
Dawe, Grahame T 4:56:52 (25,276)
Dawes, Matthew 4:23:43 (17,565)
Dawes, Matthew G 3:23:39 (3,735)
Dawkins, Jason............4:03:15 (12,863)
Dawodu, James F 3:58:46 (11,431)
Daws, Peter M 3:22:07 (3,548)
Dawson, Alex 4:02:17 (12,328)
Dawson, Allen J 4:48:31 (23,543)
Dawson, Andrew L 4:07:33 (13,486)
Dawson, Bernard J 4:08:45 (13,800)
Dawson, Gary............4:48:30 (23,540)
Dawson, James C 5:19:09 (28,395)
Dawson, James P............7:15:31 (33,009)
Dawson, Jamie C 4:34:58 (20,480)
Dawson, Jason L 3:08:41 (1,925)
Dawson, John C 5:38:10 (30,215)
Dawson, Jonathan 2:49:51 (539)
Dawson, Lee 4:57:22 (25,380)
Dawson, Mark A 5:10:41 (27,352)
Dawson, Mark S 5:18:33 (28,314)
Dawson, Matthew 3:54:30 (10,051)
Dawson, Neil A 4:20:33 (16,749)
Dawson, Neil J 4:19:59 (16,598)
Dawson, Philip J 3:48:26 (8,483)
Dawson, Stuart P 4:44:59 (22,778)
Dawwas, Haitham 5:33:55 (29,881)
Day, Adrian P............4:37:28 (21,102)
Day, Alec S 3:48:16 (8,442)
Day, Arron J 4:15:16 (15,403)
Day, Duncan C 4:51:20 (24,101)
Day, Ian 2:54:08 (737)
Day, John 3:42:55 (7,212)
Day, John 5:06:27 (26,783)
Day, Jonathan G 3:22:00 (3,533)
Day, Kevin J............4:42:48 (22,285)

Day, Michael D	4:09:26 (13,976)	
Day, Nicholas J	4:15:46 (15,537)	
Day, Paul E	4:49:50 (23,810)	
Day, Philip B	4:20:48 (16,810)	
Day, Richard N	4:01:36 (12,174)	
Day, Russell J	3:59:37 (11,698)	
Day, Thomas F	4:07:09 (13,390)	
Days, Anthony G	4:42:53 (22,301)	
Days, Jonathan A	4:24:38 (17,851)	
De Angelo, Christian	5:18:37 (28,323)	
De Bie, Frank	4:06:24 (13,212)	
De Boer, Peter	3:16:42 (2,841)	
De Boise, Matthew J	4:12:25 (14,684)	
De Bomdt, Jan	3:52:05 (9,381)	
De Boos, Paul M	4:21:43 (17,026)	
De Buhr, Ingo	4:01:10 (12,092)	
De Burca, Ronan M	5:15:44 (27,970)	
De Causmaecker, Frans	2:56:32 (898)	
De Clercq, Peter	4:15:10 (15,383)	
De Coverly, Edd	4:21:29 (16,973)	
De Croos, Douglas J	5:14:47 (27,880)	
De Filippo, Armand F	3:27:55 (4,397)	
De Knop, Jean	3:58:50 (11,460)	
De Kok, Ramon	3:27:14 (4,276)	
De La Fuente, Gearado	3:43:31 (7,354)	
De Longhi, Michele	4:57:06 (25,334)	
De Luca, Paolo A	3:13:31 (2,467)	
De Masi, Luca	4:56:40 (25,236)	
De Montfort, Guy	4:49:53 (23,817)	
De Munnik, Grant	3:15:29 (2,719)	
De Parterroyo, Roberto	3:30:02 (4,830)	
De Ryche, Koenraad	3:35:04 (5,684)	
De Schrynmakers, Frederic	3:41:32 (6,926)	
De Smet, Christof	4:44:27 (22,666)	
De Sousa, Joe A	3:36:15 (5,884)	
De Spaeth, Carsten	4:09:12 (13,909)	
De Villiers, David J	4:08:01 (13,616)	
De Vooght Johnson, Ryan L	6:39:55 (32,609)	
De Vrind, Johanus H	3:50:01 (8,869)	
De Vrind, Johaus M	5:55:27 (31,323)	
De Wit, Nico	4:06:22 (13,204)	
De Zordo, Massimo	3:29:41 (4,756)	
Deacon, Simon	5:59:58 (31,560)	
Deadman, Sean A	3:58:27 (11,327)	
Deakin, Nicholas J	4:14:22 (15,175)	
Deakin, Paul L	3:44:40 (7,612)	
Dean, Garry J	3:26:19 (4,119)	
Dean, Gary J	2:56:27 (888)	
Dean, James R	3:55:19 (10,320)	
Dean, Ken	4:31:07 (19,557)	
Dean, Malcolm B	6:52:20 (32,788)	
Dean, Martin J	4:41:36 (22,014)	
Dean, Michael R	3:55:08 (10,255)	
Dean, Philip A	3:48:39 (8,541)	
Dean, Stephen M	4:54:23 (24,765)	
Dean, Stuart	4:58:22 (25,583)	
Deane, Michael J	4:36:14 (20,791)	
Deans, Frank	5:16:33 (28,075)	
Dearden, Alan R	3:27:22 (4,306)	
Dearden, Jonny M	3:38:25 (6,309)	
Dearing, Anthony J	4:14:36 (15,233)	
Dearing, Joanathan A	3:33:58 (5,474)	
Dearing, Niki	4:44:00 (22,572)	
Dearmer, Christopher W	4:37:04 (20,993)	
Dearsley, Arthur M	3:20:23 (3,324)	
Deas, Jonathan B	5:03:50 (26,431)	
Deason, Dave	4:12:58 (14,828)	
Deaville, Andrew J	5:18:14 (28,277)	
Debarros, Jason M	3:53:06 (9,662)	
Debernard, François	6:48:53 (32,742)	
Debnam, David J	3:32:42 (5,279)	
Deboos, Mark A	3:18:17 (3,029)	
Dee, Michael	5:06:17 (26,754)	
Dee, Philip T	4:54:43 (24,820)	
Deeprose, Simon C	4:29:16 (19,107)	
Deffenbaugh, John L	3:54:28 (10,042)	
Deftereos, Phillip	4:20:19 (16,688)	
Degaigne, Nicolas	3:23:48 (3,755)	
Degez, Philippe	3:35:09 (5,701)	
Degia, Ilyas	4:51:35 (24,164)	
Deibert, Edward A	5:37:30 (30,166)	
Deighan, Hugh A	3:43:02 (7,242)	
Deith, Matthew	4:54:09 (24,712)	

Deja, Philip A	4:29:27 (19,160)	
Dekker, Jean Pierre	4:53:22 (24,539)	
Dekkers, Ivo	3:45:51 (7,878)	
Dela-Haye, Terry	3:48:29 (8,495)	
Delaney, Anthony	4:49:55 (23,831)	
Delany, John F	4:36:13 (20,786)	
Delattre, Frederic	5:24:47 (29,015)	
Delaudi, Giancarlo	5:51:45 (31,170)	
Delay, Harjit	3:53:55 (9,897)	
Delderfield, Kris	3:22:54 (3,648)	
Delduca, Matthew V	3:40:47 (6,760)	
Delea, Marc S	3:07:50 (1,842)	
Delevic, Zdravko Zack	5:00:45 (26,000)	
Delew, Russell	3:42:10 (7,061)	
Delile, Bruno	3:16:23 (2,808)	
Delingpole, Charles K	3:55:39 (10,416)	
Delisle, Stephane	4:01:35 (12,168)	
Dell, Andrew G	3:02:34 (1,414)	
Dell, Graeme J	3:56:08 (10,577)	
Dell, Jack W	4:11:48 (14,524)	
Dellamano, Rocky	4:42:31 (22,226)	
Dellar, Peter R	2:59:01 (1,143)	
Delmartino, Dirk	4:33:09 (20,047)	
Delport, Carl E	5:02:34 (26,258)	
Del-Vecchio, Jerome	3:30:36 (4,914)	
Del-Vecchio, Patrick	3:10:10 (2,084)	
Demeyere, Jan	5:23:01 (28,830)	
Dempsey, Nick	5:25:37 (29,093)	
Demuynck, Paul G	3:54:47 (10,138)	
Denbow, Nicholas P	3:52:33 (9,506)	
Denbow, Richard J	4:48:34 (23,556)	
Dench, Gary	3:01:08 (1,313)	
Denenis, Alex	5:26:52 (29,210)	
Denham, Jay	4:08:18 (13,689)	
Denham, John P	3:45:39 (7,833)	
Denham, Roddy J	5:04:27 (26,517)	
Denley, Chris	4:30:42 (19,476)	
Denman, Paul D	4:51:38 (24,177)	
Denman, Stephen	7:57:52 (33,174)	
Denmead, Matthew J	2:48:37 (478)	
Dennell, Keith	5:03:50 (26,431)	
Dennes, Robert J	4:06:47 (13,298)	
Dennie, James	4:34:50 (20,444)	
Dennis, Andrew R	5:03:09 (26,335)	
Dennis, Geoffrey A	5:16:55 (28,118)	
Dennis, Ian E	5:27:18 (29,250)	
Dennis, John L	3:33:35 (5,418)	
Dennis, Matthew R	5:01:19 (26,086)	
Dennis, Paul J	3:15:03 (2,664)	
Dennis, Shane	5:00:02 (25,888)	
Dennison, James E	4:29:13 (19,088)	
Dennison, Mark E	3:55:10 (10,264)	
Dennison, Matthew	3:52:52 (9,585)	
Dennison, Michael R	4:09:12 (13,909)	
Denny, Matthew J	3:42:03 (7,036)	
Denny, Paul	4:38:12 (21,282)	
Denny, Paul G	4:06:41 (13,271)	
Denny, Paul T	4:31:52 (19,766)	
Denny, Richard W	4:14:16 (15,155)	
Densley, Sam A	5:35:53 (30,045)	
Dent, David R	3:30:02 (4,830)	
Dent, James P	4:51:48 (24,210)	
Dent, Stefan I	3:44:26 (7,547)	
Denton, David G	3:57:32 (11,022)	
Denton, Jeremy P	4:29:37 (19,206)	
Derbyshire, Ian J	4:21:50 (17,074)	
Derbyshire, Phil J	3:59:05 (11,538)	
Derham, Keith A	5:25:58 (29,125)	
Dering, David	3:59:31 (11,677)	
Dermody, Justin P	4:17:04 (15,877)	
Derow, Paul	4:37:21 (21,072)	
Derrett, Joe E	3:46:52 (8,097)	
Derrick, Ian M	3:46:22 (7,976)	
Derriman, Duncan	5:00:53 (26,026)	
Derville, Bruno	3:52:12 (9,410)	
Derzypilskyj, John	4:06:26 (13,218)	
Desborough, Simon J	4:18:37 (16,259)	
Desborough, Valerie C	4:17:55 (16,083)	
Deschamps, Pascal	3:36:34 (5,947)	
D'Escrivan, Julio C	3:52:35 (9,515)	
Desmond, James	3:27:40 (4,360)	
Desnoyers, Olivier	3:29:25 (4,698)	

Desousa, Alex	5:26:16 (29,152)	
Despres, Jason J	4:17:26 (15,965)	
Despretz, Christophe	4:19:14 (16,398)	
Dessau, Ben D	4:39:07 (21,469)	
Dettman, Joerg M	3:20:40 (3,359)	
Deutsch, Robert V	4:38:58 (21,434)	
Deutschen, Aloysius	3:50:56 (9,083)	
Dev, Vivek	6:03:59 (31,728)	
Devaney, Gearoid	3:35:25 (5,736)	
Devaney, Neil M	2:57:43 (1,004)	
Dever, Noel T	4:17:20 (15,940)	
Devereaux, John	5:01:13 (26,074)	
Devereux, James	4:09:44 (14,039)	
Deviercy, Stephane	3:12:02 (2,280)	
Deville, Simon	5:18:22 (28,290)	
Deville, Steven	4:53:08 (24,489)	
Devine, Andrew T	3:05:03 (1,579)	
Devine, Brian P	3:54:22 (10,021)	
Devine, Gary R	3:23:41 (3,739)	
Devine, Kieran	7:08:05 (32,963)	
Devine, Peter J	5:40:00 (30,365)	
Devine, William	5:05:44 (26,669)	
Devins, Marc	3:26:44 (4,197)	
Devitt, Russell E	3:13:06 (2,414)	
Devlin, Brendan J	3:38:01 (6,230)	
Devlin, Jerry F	4:23:52 (17,613)	
Devlin, Paul D	4:21:20 (16,941)	
Devney, Carl L	3:54:15 (9,993)	
Devonish, Neil	6:17:11 (32,147)	
Devoto, Shaun A	4:01:46 (12,205)	
Dewar, Gordon	4:20:50 (16,817)	
Dewar, Michael	3:52:20 (9,445)	
Dewey, Brian	4:16:59 (15,854)	
Dewick, Mark C	4:42:18 (22,176)	
Dewing, David S	4:35:09 (20,521)	
Dews, Trevor W	8:13:05 (33,187)	
Dewulf, Mark L	3:50:56 (9,083)	
Dexter, Colin G	5:26:04 (29,133)	
Dexter, Gareth	4:35:56 (20,698)	
Dhaussy, Pierre	2:56:27 (888)	
Dhesi, Kuljit S	5:47:20 (30,901)	
Dhillon, Mandeep S	4:04:00 (12,714)	
Dhirubhai, Prakash	5:59:38 (31,541)	
Di Cara, Nino	4:45:10 (22,825)	
Di Ck, Graham R	4:57:20 (25,371)	
Di Giacomo, Thierry	3:08:02 (1,863)	
Di Giovanni, Carlo	4:32:45 (19,945)	
Di Mario, Bruno	4:46:07 (23,031)	
Di Molfetta, Pasquale	3:30:18 (4,865)	
Di Properzio, Roberto	3:21:33 (3,477)	
Di Stefano, Corrado	4:21:28 (16,971)	
Diacon, Jean-François	4:20:24 (16,711)	
Diagana, Stephane	2:59:15 (1,170)	
Diamond, Ian C	3:57:05 (10,870)	
Diamond, Stephen P	3:30:59 (4,981)	
Diaz, Francisco	2:37:38 (157)	
Diaz-Canales, José L	3:39:39 (6,565)	
Dibben, Martin	4:33:22 (20,103)	
Dibden, Terence J	4:26:44 (18,443)	
Diciollo, Francesco	3:24:37 (3,883)	
Dick, Alistair	2:58:48 (1,116)	
Dick, Michael J	3:31:33 (5,073)	
Dick, Simon C	3:46:49 (8,088)	
Dickens, David S	4:39:32 (21,562)	
Dickens, Paul A	3:28:25 (4,499)	
Dickenson, Robert	2:52:32 (652)	
Dicker, Clive A	4:09:00 (13,859)	
Dickerson, Thomas	4:58:54 (25,687)	
Dickins, Philip C	4:24:05 (17,680)	
Dickinson, Christopher T	5:06:00 (26,710)	
Dickinson, David J	4:23:41 (17,555)	
Dickinson, David T	2:45:12 (350)	
Dickinson, Dharam R	4:55:20 (24,969)	
Dickinson, Kelvin B	2:58:46 (1,106)	
Dickinson, Ralph	3:57:16 (10,937)	
Dickinson, Richard	3:44:19 (7,525)	
Dickinson, Robert A	3:20:10 (3,291)	
Dickinson, Ross A	3:55:32 (10,385)	
Dickinson, Simon G	4:42:07 (22,138)	
Dickson, Adam R	4:52:22 (24,325)	
Dickson, Alan R	3:16:50 (2,859)	
Dickson, Darren	3:37:43 (6,171)	
Dickson, David R	4:14:15 (15,150)	

Dickson, Ken 4:37:28 (21,102)
Dickson, Paul D 4:17:34 (16,003)
Dickson, Paul J 4:12:25 (14,684)
Dickson, Richard G 4:49:37 (23,778)
Dickson, Stephen A 3:24:41 (3,893)
Diddams, Greg 2:53:51 (716)
Didelot, Bruno 4:10:30 (14,214)
Diella, Ruggiero 3:24:30 (3,864)
Dieppe, Edward 3:53:51 (9,882)
Dierickx, Steven 3:53:20 (9,726)
Diethe, Tom R 3:41:41 (6,961)
Diffey, Andrew J 3:05:58 (1,663)
Diffey, John G 3:26:41 (4,189)
Difranco, Mike D 3:45:50 (7,877)
Digby, Benjamin T 5:24:07 (28,958)
Digman, Ian R 3:55:29 (10,369)
Dignan, Robert 6:23:57 (32,327)
Digweed, John N 5:21:55 (28,704)
Dillon, Andrew 4:32:59 (20,000)
Dillon, John E 4:20:52 (16,827)
Dillon, Kevin J 5:41:28 (30,454)
Dillon, Richard A 4:08:50 (13,821)
Dilnot, Noel 5:31:14 (29,684)
Dilworth, Mark T 4:06:59 (13,345)
Dilworth, Robby A 3:52:48 (9,569)
Dimarco, Kevin M 4:14:49 (15,288)
Dimbleby, Peter J 2:46:01 (385)
Dimelow, Geoffrey 3:48:01 (8,387)
Dimmock, Graeme D 6:22:20 (32,298)
Dimond, Martyn 5:27:05 (29,235)
Dineen, William A 4:52:16 (24,296)
Dines, Ross P 4:04:12 (12,756)
Dingle, Neil M 4:05:37 (13,055)
Dingley, Graham J 3:21:27 (3,460)
Diniz, Joao Paulo F 3:49:53 (8,843)
Dinneen, Miles T 4:05:21 (12,988)
Dinning, Max W 4:34:02 (20,260)
Dinning, Robert P 5:20:52 (28,597)
Dionisio, Tiago B 4:21:47 (17,058)
Dirienzo, Marco 4:00:06 (11,843)
Disley, Ben 4:57:56 (25,484)
Disley, Hugh 5:27:27 (29,265)
Ditcham, Robert 3:34:31 (5,571)
Dite, Christopher J 5:30:45 (29,622)
Divani, Gordhan V 5:27:09 (29,240)
Divittorio, Francesco 3:55:27 (10,358)
Diwell, Nicholas S 4:37:04 (20,993)
Dix, Nigel 3:56:35 (10,717)
Dix, Philip J 3:39:32 (6,547)
Dixon, Andy M 4:03:49 (12,677)
Dixon, Billy 3:52:40 (9,544)
Dixon, Clem N 3:03:46 (1,498)
Dixon, Dave 3:55:12 (10,282)
Dixon, David 3:10:02 (2,066)
Dixon, David A 3:54:15 (9,993)
Dixon, Garry J 2:34:53 (113)
Dixon, Gary 3:50:08 (8,895)
Dixon, Gary 4:24:08 (17,697)
Dixon, Geoff P 4:39:13 (21,496)
Dixon, Ian H 3:25:47 (4,042)
Dixon, John J 3:44:16 (7,511)
Dixon, Neil 5:27:18 (29,250)
Dixon, Sean H 3:10:05 (2,072)
Dixon, Simon S 4:11:36 (14,479)
Dixon, Thomas B 3:49:55 (8,848)
Dixon-Box, Russell B 3:55:05 (10,240)
Doake, James 3:57:10 (10,911)
Dobbs, Colin M 3:51:34 (9,238)
Dobbs, Patrick A 3:12:08 (2,292)
Dobbs, Peter G 4:34:19 (20,310)
Dobedoe, Richard S 3:10:54 (2,148)
Dobie, Angus J 2:57:32 (986)
Dobie, Ronald 4:25:06 (17,990)
Dobkin, Russell M 5:06:06 (26,726)
Doble, Clive A 4:02:34 (12,391)
Doble, Lee R 3:58:13 (11,238)
Doble, Robin 3:13:25 (2,453)
Dobres, Michael S 3:47:46 (8,313)
Dobson, Andrew M 3:39:53 (6,602)
Dobson, David A 3:48:25 (8,477)
Dobson, Jonathan E 2:47:03 (418)
Dobson, Jonathan J 4:13:36 (14,975)
Dobson, Mark J 5:03:31 (26,392)
Dobson, Spencer B 3:40:37 (6,731)
Dobuisson, Afzal 4:41:47 (22,056)
Docherty, Christopher D 4:13:21 (14,931)
Docherty, Richard 2:56:09 (863)
Dockar, Andrew D 3:13:11 (2,424)
Dockerill, Steven C 4:01:34 (12,165)
Dodanis, Christos 3:10:53 (2,146)
Dodd, Andrew K 4:22:10 (17,162)
Dodd, Clive C 3:59:18 (11,604)
Dodd, Jason 4:00:59 (12,045)
Dodd, Michael R 3:53:56 (9,902)
Dodd, Neal C 4:05:37 (13,055)
Dodd, Roy A 5:49:24 (31,036)
Dodd, Stephen J 3:56:17 (10,624)
Doddq, Howard 4:11:29 (14,456)
Dodds, Jeffrey 4:29:12 (19,085)
Dodds, Matthew L 4:48:07 (23,453)
Dodds, Rupert 3:30:58 (4,976)
Doddy, John A 4:14:06 (15,104)
Dodhia, Shilan R 4:44:55 (22,763)
Dodridge, Ashley 4:00:10 (11,859)
Dodsley, Keith M 3:42:50 (7,191)
Dodson, Edward C 3:58:49 (11,452)
Dodson, Matthew S 3:23:38 (3,732)
Doelling, Robert 4:26:49 (18,468)
Doelling, Volker 4:31:07 (19,557)
Doelwijt, Albert 3:50:44 (9,037)
Doerr, Dean S 5:24:39 (29,000)
Doggett, Christopher J 5:58:46 (31,496)
Doherty, Andrew 5:34:23 (29,920)
Doherty, Chris 5:29:18 (29,456)
Doherty, Christopher 4:12:42 (14,749)
Doherty, Clifford A 6:03:38 (31,710)
Doherty, Daniel 4:12:38 (14,734)
Doherty, Danny M 4:20:23 (16,706)
Doherty, Hugh M 4:48:26 (23,520)
Doherty, Jackie J 2:58:36 (1,075)
Doherty, John C 4:19:13 (16,393)
Doherty, Kevin 4:03:51 (12,683)
Doherty, Kieran M 3:15:24 (2,707)
Doherty, Mark 6:04:36 (31,748)
Doherty, Stephen 3:23:00 (3,656)
Doherty, Timothy B 4:18:55 (16,331)
Doig, Gavin A 4:14:24 (15,180)
Dolan, Aidan C 4:34:53 (20,459)
Dolan, Brent L 4:54:32 (24,785)
Dolan, Gary 4:15:23 (15,442)
Dolan, Robert M 3:12:38 (2,355)
Dolan, Vincent J 4:30:26 (19,412)
Dolding, Philip J 4:37:15 (21,045)
Dolle, Wilhelm 3:32:03 (5,169)
Dolman, Antony R 4:14:41 (15,255)
Dolphin, Christopher C 4:16:12 (15,644)
Domaille, Mark 3:32:48 (5,291)
Domaingue, Jean-Claude P 3:50:30 (8,984)
Dome, Andrew J 4:06:57 (13,337)
Dommett, Paul M 3:51:18 (9,173)
Dommett, Robert A 6:15:11 (32,089)
Donaghy, James H 6:00:27 (31,580)
Donald, Andrew J 3:15:08 (2,674)
Donald, Christopher 5:30:35 (29,604)
Donald, Paul 3:50:29 (8,977)
Donald, Robert D 4:05:32 (13,034)
Donaldson, Alan 4:21:15 (16,927)
Donaldson, Craig E 4:14:28 (15,202)
Donaldson, Drew 3:02:23 (1,397)
Donaldson, Gordon W 4:21:21 (16,947)
Donaldson, Kenneth B 3:58:16 (11,253)
Donaldson, Matthew S 4:10:51 (14,294)
Donaldson, Robert S 4:34:06 (20,274)
Donaldson, Thomas A 4:08:55 (13,842)
Donaldson, Walter J 3:56:35 (10,717)
Donegan, Barry J 4:35:56 (20,698)
Donegan, Paul W 4:57:47 (25,454)
Donetti, Stephane 4:39:30 (21,560)
Donker, Margitta 4:37:32 (21,117)
Donnan, Graeme E 3:19:47 (3,230)
Donneky, John S 2:48:57 (495)
Donnelly, Adrian J 5:11:10 (27,407)
Donnelly, Andrew G 3:57:09 (10,902)
Donnelly, Colm 3:35:14 (5,712)
Donnelly, Stephen P 3:36:50 (6,001)
Donoghue, Chris 2:56:49 (922)
Donohoe, Orlf 5:08:18 (27,050)
Donohue, Ronan M 4:11:33 (14,471)
Donohue, Stephen 4:54:25 (24,773)
Donovan, Clive 3:15:13 (2,687)
Donovan, James D 4:05:12 (12,958)
Donovan, Steven P 5:37:51 (30,193)
Donovan, Wayne P 4:21:44 (17,036)
Doogan, Sean B 4:54:06 (24,695)
Doolan, James E 4:17:35 (16,011)
Doolan, John A 4:26:01 (18,263)
Dooley, John P 4:00:34 (11,945)
Dooley, Jonathan 5:08:25 (27,068)
Dooley, Joseph 4:22:22 (17,215)
Dooley, Michael P 4:58:40 (25,638)
Dooley, Victor J 4:08:29 (13,738)
Dooling, Colin M 3:55:20 (10,325)
Dooling, Graham C 3:18:28 (3,059)
Doppagne, Paul M 3:22:26 (3,589)
Doran, Andrew T 3:39:15 (6,489)
Doran, Matt J 4:19:39 (16,516)
Doran, Patrick 6:11:34 (31,969)
Doran, Paul J 3:51:30 (9,215)
Dorey, Ralph C 4:20:36 (16,759)
Dorgan, J 6:06:11 (31,793)
Dorian, Douglas 4:43:40 (22,481)
Dorian, Matthew J 4:56:21 (25,175)
Dorling, George R 4:43:53 (22,543)
Dorman, Edgar K 3:56:48 (10,785)
Dormer, Benjamin 3:48:51 (8,591)
Dorrell, Trevor D 4:01:32 (12,153)
Dorriam, Matthew J 5:16:51 (28,110)
Dorrian, John 4:42:43 (22,264)
Dorrington, Mark 4:34:24 (20,341)
Dorrington, Rodney A 5:45:59 (30,782)
Dorward, Neil L 2:57:02 (944)
Dosanjh, Jatinder 5:44:03 (30,645)
Dosansh, Gurpreet S 4:39:56 (21,662)
Doster, Stephen 4:14:25 (15,185)
Douek, Edward 4:34:35 (20,383)
Dougal, Andrew 3:58:23 (11,298)
Dougherty, David J 4:15:56 (15,583)
Doughty, Chris J 3:48:34 (8,517)
Douglas, Charles R 4:30:41 (19,473)
Douglas, David 4:14:41 (15,255)
Douglas, Gavin H 3:25:23 (3,994)
Douglas, George J 4:19:51 (16,568)
Douglas, James A 3:04:29 (1,544)
Douglas, Kenneth J 3:39:46 (6,582)
Douglas, Kent N 6:10:20 (31,935)
Douglas, Leo E 4:36:47 (20,933)
Douglas, Michael P 3:09:36 (2,026)
Douglas, Neil 2:44:51 (341)
Douglas, Neil A 2:50:59 (591)
Douglas, Nial 3:26:33 (4,164)
Douglas, Richard A 3:47:54 (8,354)
Douglas, Stuart D 3:37:01 (6,043)
Douglas, Stuart J 3:46:36 (8,034)
Douglass, Paul M 3:28:48 (4,573)
Dourdin, David 3:22:49 (3,638)
Doust, Peter R 4:55:27 (24,993)
Douthwaite, Neil 4:10:28 (14,206)
Dove, Christopher W 3:56:32 (10,694)
Dove, Jeffrey R 4:31:28 (19,656)
Dove, Nick S 3:23:48 (3,755)
Dove, Paul 4:48:44 (23,594)
Dover, Gary W 3:13:07 (2,416)
Dover, Terry 5:05:22 (26,634)
Dovey, Darren W 5:55:37 (31,338)
Dovey, Tim J 4:00:00 (11,810)
Dow, Andrew C 4:30:27 (19,416)
Dow, Peter J 4:26:44 (18,443)
Dow, Simon J 5:20:35 (28,575)
Dowdall, Kevin R 4:17:24 (15,954)
Dowdall, Martin J 3:34:25 (5,551)
Dowdall, Stuart M 5:12:16 (27,560)
Dowdle, Ian J 5:32:48 (29,798)
Dowers, Alan L 4:24:32 (17,809)
Dowle, Matthew J 4:14:15 (15,150)
Dowler, John J 4:53:28 (24,556)
Dowling, Jonathan M 3:20:07 (3,282)
Dowling, Shaun 4:01:36 (12,174)
Down, Christopher G 5:00:57 (26,034)
Down, James 4:53:53 (24,655)

Down, James C	4:10:49 (14,282)	
Down, Lawrence	4:42:18 (22,176)	
Down, Malcolm R	3:04:13 (1,528)	
Downard, David J	5:56:03 (31,354)	
Downer, Allen L	3:12:23 (2,333)	
Downer, Gregory O	3:26:23 (4,134)	
Downes, Kevin R	3:26:10 (4,096)	
Downes, Philip J	4:19:50 (16,562)	
Downes, Robert A	4:08:58 (13,853)	
Downes, Thomas	3:59:06 (11,543)	
Downey, Desmond D	3:55:45 (10,460)	
Downey, Kevin	5:07:34 (26,941)	
Downham, Antony S	4:14:19 (15,165)	
Downham, David I	4:44:10 (22,598)	
Downham, John J	3:06:44 (1,732)	
Downie, Colin M	4:57:34 (25,411)	
Downie, James A	3:44:39 (7,603)	
Downing, Oliver J	3:18:26 (3,053)	
Downing, Terence R	3:57:36 (11,045)	
Downs, Alistair J	4:49:35 (23,774)	
Downs, David J	3:08:22 (1,892)	
Downs, Peter E	4:24:34 (17,830)	
Dowse, Peter M	4:43:43 (22,499)	
Dowse, Ray	4:06:31 (13,238)	
Dowsett, Frederick J	3:36:33 (5,943)	
Dowsett, Kevin R	4:12:07 (14,603)	
Dowsett, Mike J	3:40:13 (6,659)	
Dowsett, Peter C	3:16:00 (2,780)	
Dowson, John	3:33:40 (5,433)	
Doxford, Stuart R	3:34:42 (5,611)	
Doye, Julian	4:28:51 (18,983)	
Doye, Ryan	4:16:28 (15,714)	
Doyle, Alan R	4:05:02 (12,923)	
Doyle, Alastair K	2:58:34 (1,069)	
Doyle, Andrew	3:46:53 (8,098)	
Doyle, Andrew	5:08:23 (27,063)	
Doyle, Andrew J	4:41:58 (22,101)	
Doyle, Bradley	4:51:50 (24,218)	
Doyle, Edward	3:21:20 (3,445)	
Doyle, Gavin J	4:27:29 (18,618)	
Doyle, Geoffrey E	3:12:12 (2,306)	
Doyle, James L	4:11:38 (14,487)	
Doyle, John M	3:22:42 (3,623)	
Doyle, Kevin	3:21:13 (3,427)	
Doyle, Kirk	4:54:11 (24,724)	
Doyle, Mark J	3:09:33 (2,018)	
Doyle, Michael D	2:50:16 (558)	
Doyle, Raphael	6:05:05 (31,763)	
Doyle, Thomas A	3:37:09 (6,067)	
Drabwell, Alan L	5:58:07 (31,465)	
Drackford, Mark R	3:37:52 (6,202)	
Drain, Brendon I	3:52:40 (9,544)	
Drake, Brendan J	3:28:31 (4,514)	
Drake, Brian	7:07:14 (32,953)	
Drake, Justin A	3:56:10 (10,587)	
Drake, Oliver	5:01:19 (26,086)	
Drake, Richard M	4:25:11 (18,023)	
Drake, Steve R	3:54:57 (10,190)	
Draper, Christopher D	4:56:03 (25,109)	
Draper, David	3:58:55 (11,483)	
Draper, Dennis W	4:56:14 (25,146)	
Draper, Lee M	3:47:43 (8,301)	
Draysey, John R	4:42:24 (22,202)	
Dreadon, Kent B	3:31:19 (5,038)	
Dreher, Simon M	3:51:41 (9,269)	
Drew, Ian	3:07:06 (1,768)	
Drew, Kieron	3:51:46 (9,294)	
Drewe, Gareth S	4:52:09 (24,279)	
Drewett, Adrian M	5:50:02 (31,076)	
Drewett, Jamie R	3:57:20 (10,961)	
Drewry, Thomas L	4:30:41 (19,473)	
Drinkell, Andrew L	4:34:31 (20,365)	
Driscoll, Richard W	4:28:32 (18,904)	
Driver, Andrew P	3:35:08 (5,697)	
Driver, Gary	3:52:28 (9,485)	
Driver, Marlon	4:06:50 (13,308)	
Driver, Richard P	4:41:22 (21,965)	
Drozario, Warren F	5:28:59 (29,427)	
Drummond, Colin	3:45:24 (7,783)	
Drummond, John R	5:03:30 (26,389)	
Drummond, Samuel	3:50:51 (9,066)	
Drummond, Steven	4:08:10 (13,656)	
Drury, Ian P	5:36:57 (30,129)	

Drury, James S	3:54:05 (9,940)	
Dry, Peter F	3:32:00 (5,158)	
Dryland, Keith	4:09:50 (14,067)	
Drysoale, Euan G	3:44:59 (7,684)	
Du Plessis, Jacques	4:09:23 (13,954)	
Du Preez, Jason	4:06:43 (13,278)	
Dubock, Warren R	4:36:40 (20,879)	
Dubois, Christian	2:39:48 (208)	
Dubouloz, Hubert J	2:59:42 (1,220)	
Ducharme, Richard I	3:15:38 (2,729)	
Duck, Alexander M	3:19:14 (3,164)	
Duckenfield, Adam C	4:59:21 (25,754)	
Duckett, Alex J	4:15:54 (15,578)	
Duckgeischel, Hubertus	4:24:32 (17,809)	
Duckworth, Anthony J	5:38:14 (30,224)	
Duckworth, Kevin	2:43:57 (310)	
Duckworth, Matthew P	4:07:36 (13,506)	
Duclos, Eric	4:33:07 (20,036)	
Ducrocq, Patrick	3:27:48 (4,379)	
Dudbridge, Frank	2:40:06 (213)	
Duddell, Michael A	4:57:36 (25,417)	
Dude, Viesturs	2:43:06 (290)	
Duder, James H	3:58:54 (11,476)	
Dudgeon, Benjamin P	3:44:18 (7,521)	
Dudley, Dennis C	3:46:48 (8,081)	
Dudley, Paul J	3:58:16 (11,253)	
Duehmke, Rudolf M	4:48:32 (23,551)	
Duetthorn, Wolfram	3:42:52 (7,196)	
Duff, Craig R	4:07:31 (13,479)	
Duff, Forbes	4:50:24 (23,926)	
Duff, Nigel R	3:54:39 (10,091)	
Duff, Robert	6:18:45 (32,192)	
Duff Gordon, William	3:36:14 (5,882)	
Duffait, Jean-Luc	3:25:34 (4,014)	
Duffey, John P	3:59:41 (11,723)	
Duffield, Andrew	4:56:16 (25,155)	
Duffin, Adrian J	4:48:34 (23,556)	
Duffours, Paul	4:54:38 (24,804)	
Duffus, Stewart W	3:48:47 (8,572)	
Duffy, Andrew D	2:55:54 (845)	
Duffy, Arthur J	4:02:47 (12,436)	
Duffy, Brendan M	6:23:23 (32,312)	
Duffy, Brian W	2:59:13 (1,166)	
Duffy, Christopher J	4:58:39 (25,636)	
Duffy, David M	5:00:42 (25,995)	
Duffy, Gavin	3:49:32 (8,753)	
Duffy, John F	4:16:43 (15,783)	
Duffy, Jonathan R	4:49:06 (23,677)	
Duffy, Kevin	3:48:20 (8,460)	
Duffy, Liam J	3:13:48 (2,505)	
Duffy, Michael J	3:17:00 (2,877)	
Duffy, Michael V	4:42:51 (22,294)	
Duffy, Steven J	4:04:05 (12,736)	
Dufour, Yves	4:17:44 (16,038)	
Dugerdil, Raymond H	3:56:13 (10,599)	
Duggan, Brian T	4:12:11 (14,620)	
Duggan, Mike A	3:21:29 (3,468)	
Duggan, Patrick J	3:53:30 (9,766)	
Duhamel, David A	4:31:22 (19,630)	
Duhutrel, Patrick	4:21:33 (16,985)	
Duhutrel, Vincent	4:35:33 (20,612)	
Duke, Chris A	2:59:34 (1,206)	
Duke, Nicholas C	4:01:28 (12,140)	
Dukelow, Steven J	3:42:36 (7,134)	
Dukes, Nicholas J	2:49:39 (524)	
Dulai, Gurjit S	3:55:54 (10,507)	
Dullaghan, Sean R	3:46:08 (7,929)	
Dullehan, Michael F	4:05:53 (13,115)	
Dumartin, Jerome	4:45:36 (22,926)	
Dumican, Paul	4:21:51 (17,076)	
Dumpleton, Chris	3:59:38 (11,702)	
Dunbar, Christopher J	5:00:22 (25,954)	
Duncan, Adrian	3:54:08 (9,953)	
Duncan, Alan	2:58:50 (1,120)	
Duncan, Alasdair W	3:20:54 (3,392)	
Duncan, Barry A	4:03:25 (12,582)	
Duncan, George B	4:53:06 (24,479)	
Duncan, Gordon I	5:47:18 (30,898)	
Duncan, James A	4:04:31 (12,821)	
Duncan, Paul	3:50:40 (9,021)	
Duncan, Tony J	3:35:02 (5,669)	
Duncan, William A	4:20:18 (16,684)	
Dunce, Andrew H	4:18:50 (16,308)	

Duncton, Ross	4:53:03 (24,467)	
Dunford, Michael B	3:48:57 (8,620)	
Dunford, Nicholas R	3:55:01 (10,209)	
Dunford, Timothy J	5:18:53 (28,354)	
Dungey, Kevin M	5:09:55 (27,256)	
Dunham, Alan D	4:19:04 (16,360)	
Dunham, Mark P	3:28:33 (4,525)	
Dunk, Steve	4:22:08 (17,155)	
Dunkerley, Andrew J	4:17:50 (16,067)	
Dunkerley, Paul	2:59:07 (1,151)	
Dunkley, Kerry	3:42:08 (7,050)	
Dunkley, Stephen H	3:46:46 (8,074)	
Dunlea, Brian	4:17:32 (15,992)	
Dunleavy, Martin	3:23:56 (3,780)	
Dunlop, Adam	4:23:15 (17,433)	
Dunlop, Andrew W	3:54:54 (10,182)	
Dunlop, Ian S	3:34:54 (5,642)	
Dunn, Barrie	3:11:10 (2,171)	
Dunn, Chris	4:31:19 (19,618)	
Dunn, George	2:54:23 (752)	
Dunn, George	3:11:13 (2,182)	
Dunn, Matthew	5:16:10 (28,025)	
Dunn, Matthew P	3:36:15 (5,884)	
Dunn, Norman F	4:15:07 (15,372)	
Dunn, Sam D	4:58:21 (25,578)	
Dunn, Simon J	4:14:33 (15,216)	
Dunn, Thomas J	3:50:55 (9,080)	
Dunne, Damien	5:36:49 (30,118)	
Dunne, Frank	3:42:59 (7,227)	
Dunne, Mark P	3:40:19 (6,678)	
Dunne, Stephen	3:44:05 (7,470)	
Dunnenberger, Rolf	3:42:21 (7,088)	
Dunnett, Keith	5:13:23 (27,701)	
Dunnett, Robert J	4:42:47 (22,278)	
Dunning, Michael J	4:47:17 (23,274)	
Dunn-Parrant, Glenn D	2:58:15 (1,037)	
Dunscombe, Guy C	3:48:06 (8,403)	
Dunscombe, Mark	3:02:45 (1,421)	
Dunsdon, Chris	3:47:54 (8,354)	
Dunsmuir-Watts, Andrew	3:33:01 (5,326)	
Dunstall, Ian R	4:24:53 (17,917)	
Dunster, Robert A	4:45:48 (22,968)	
Dunwoody, Guy	3:36:05 (5,851)	
Duong, Ceyn	4:42:38 (22,242)	
Duplaa, Ivan	3:22:34 (3,604)	
Dupouy, Cyril	4:18:58 (16,348)	
Dupuis, Thierry	5:01:02 (26,048)	
Duquesnois, Laurent	3:04:51 (1,569)	
Durand, David	3:05:15 (1,601)	
Durant, Paul A	5:06:46 (26,830)	
Durao, Joao P	3:21:25 (3,456)	
Durban, Christian S	4:22:00 (17,118)	
Durdy, Steven	3:04:55 (1,571)	
Duret, Yannick	6:23:23 (32,312)	
Durkan, Gregory	4:19:15 (16,408)	
Durkan, Kevin J	4:19:14 (16,398)	
Duron, Gerald	4:57:42 (25,433)	
Durrani, Amer J	4:43:03 (22,335)	
Durrant, Ian P	2:42:20 (257)	
Durrant, Marc	4:23:35 (17,527)	
Durrant, Mark	4:17:30 (15,981)	
Dursley, Paul W	3:34:08 (5,503)	
Durst, Michael B	4:12:50 (14,786)	
Durston, Alan O	4:03:12 (12,530)	
Durston, Richard W	3:47:34 (8,259)	
Durteste, Patrick F	3:51:32 (9,229)	
Dussart, Luc	3:13:51 (2,507)	
Dussek, Jeremy N	4:36:09 (20,768)	
Dussuyer, Christian	3:11:10 (2,171)	
Dussuyer, Serge	3:31:16 (5,034)	
Dutch, David J	4:36:41 (20,885)	
Dutch, James	4:35:24 (20,579)	
Dutnall, Kevin J	5:08:56 (27,140)	
Duton, Patrick	2:47:13 (423)	
Dutt, Devesh	5:39:41 (30,336)	
Duttfield, Tim	3:44:27 (7,553)	
Dutton, David	3:33:46 (5,445)	
Dutton, Gavin M	4:43:45 (22,506)	
Dutton, Paul A	4:05:05 (12,936)	
Dutton, Richard J	4:19:23 (16,442)	
Dvergsnes, Erik	3:59:08 (11,555)	
Dvey, Keiron	4:23:54 (17,623)	
Dwyer, Andrew	3:17:09 (2,903)	

Dwyer, Carl 4:18:09 (16,151)
Dwyer, Gary F 3:38:43 (6,367)
Dwyer, Stephen J 4:35:11 (20,527)
Dyas, Ben 4:34:29 (20,360)
Dyas, James 4:34:28 (20,356)
Dyble, Steven J 5:15:10 (27,921)
Dyckes, John J 3:29:48 (4,782)
Dyde, Jon A 3:40:29 (6,709)
Dyde, Martin C 3:42:20 (7,084)
Dyde, Robert A 2:57:11 (959)
Dyer, Gary R 4:30:28 (19,419)
Dyer, Glen L 4:44:06 (22,583)
Dyer, Jonathan P 4:58:56 (25,697)
Dyer, Matthew D 3:27:16 (4,284)
Dyer, Matthew R 4:10:34 (14,226)
Dyer, Rod 4:45:27 (22,898)
Dyer, William J 4:43:11 (22,366)
Dyirakumunda, Benjamin 3:50:13 (8,915)
Dyke, Chris G 5:17:48 (28,221)
Dyke, Matthew K 6:04:36 (31,748)
Dyke, Steven A 5:21:49 (28,692)
Dykes, Chris J 3:17:11 (2,906)
Dykes, Terry E 3:53:35 (9,787)
Dymond, Jonathan D 4:47:42 (23,360)
Dyson, Andy I 3:41:43 (6,970)
Dyson, Howard 5:22:06 (28,725)
Dyson, Paul 5:18:55 (28,361)
Dyson, Philip A 4:35:25 (20,583)
Dyson, Stephen 4:05:32 (13,034)
Dziewulski, Peter 5:41:53 (30,492)
Dziubak, Stefan J 4:50:56 (24,035)
Eade, Benjamin D 4:15:50 (15,559)
Eade, Robert J 5:41:19 (30,441)
Eaden, Mark G 4:35:42 (20,650)
Eades, James W 3:08:22 (1,892)
Eades, Kevin M 3:11:33 (2,218)
Eadon, Roger A 4:21:44 (17,036)
Eagar, Christopher M 3:30:52 (4,955)
Eales, Paul S 4:30:15 (19,367)
Eames, Andrew E 4:18:35 (16,252)
Eames Illingworth, Jason P 4:32:21 (19,873)
Eardley, Craig 4:33:37 (20,170)
Earl, Andrew D 3:50:42 (9,031)
Earl, David W 4:29:38 (19,213)
Earl, Derek W 3:51:13 (9,151)
Earl, John W 3:13:37 (2,479)
Earl, Jonathan A 5:11:57 (27,521)
Earl, Martin J 4:07:26 (13,453)
Earl, Sam 6:07:50 (31,856)
Earl, Stephen J 3:26:45 (4,202)
Earlam, Nicholas P 4:10:48 (14,277)
Earle, Stephen 3:26:18 (4,114)
Earlie, Hughie 4:22:18 (17,199)
Earp, Spencer J 3:51:50 (9,313)
Earthy, Paul S 3:52:38 (9,534)
Easlea, Paul J 4:10:49 (14,282)
Easom, Michael D 4:06:36 (13,251)
East, David A 5:38:01 (30,203)
East, Graeme 4:40:08 (21,697)
East, Lloyd J 3:42:34 (7,126)
East, Michael D 4:20:20 (16,695)
East, Trevor S 3:07:22 (1,790)
Eastaugh, Chris D 2:54:29 (759)
Easter, Christopher 4:25:51 (18,210)
Easterbrook, Joseph D 4:19:22 (16,439)
Easterbrook, Richard J 4:55:01 (24,899)
Eastham, Fred 4:56:59 (25,307)
Eastham, John M 4:36:00 (20,722)
Easton, Mark A 4:48:31 (23,543)
Easton, Terry A 5:00:47 (26,006)
Eastwood, Hywell D 5:42:02 (30,502)
Eastwood, Mark I 5:16:09 (28,021)
Eastwood, Paul M 3:13:20 (2,438)
Eastwood, Robert J 3:52:19 (9,441)
Eaton, Andrew R 4:02:13 (12,308)
Eaton, Anthony 3:43:06 (7,264)
Eaton, Daniel A 4:38:02 (21,231)
Eaton, Ken C 5:24:20 (28,978)
Eaton, Michael 4:24:42 (17,869)
Eaton, Nick 3:52:37 (9,526)
Eaton, Philip A 3:21:35 (3,483)
Eaton, Raymond 5:51:29 (31,155)
Eaton, Stephen D 5:46:10 (30,799)
Ebbage, Alan C 4:10:14 (14,156)
Ebbesen, Eskild 3:28:58 (4,615)
Ebdon, Matthew S 4:18:03 (16,119)
Ebrahim, Brian 5:24:48 (29,016)
Eccles, Michael 4:47:46 (23,377)
Eccles, Peter T 4:38:48 (21,391)
Eccleston, John S 3:09:35 (2,023)
Eddis, Tim 3:27:28 (4,326)
Eddleston, Michael J 3:35:12 (5,706)
Ede, Alistair 3:49:59 (8,863)
Edelsbrunner, Dieter 4:10:49 (14,282)
Edelsbrunner, Michael 4:10:49 (14,282)
Eden, Geoffrey 4:20:34 (16,750)
Eden, Paul 4:23:02 (17,369)
Eden, Timothy M 4:28:18 (18,842)
Edensor, Ray J 4:45:05 (22,810)
Edery, Steven R 3:49:28 (8,734)
Edgar, Iwan 3:11:00 (2,157)
Edge, Howard 3:42:35 (7,132)
Edge, Jonathan D 5:04:06 (26,466)
Edge, Michael 3:44:26 (7,547)
Edge, Shane D 3:18:24 (3,049)
Edgecliffe-Johnson, Robin R 4:27:22 (18,595)
Edgell, Jonathan L 3:20:07 (3,282)
Edgell, Rhys 4:43:10 (22,362)
Edgington, Adrian M 3:38:43 (6,367)
Edginton, Mark P 4:24:46 (17,884)
Ediker, Simon C 4:33:33 (20,149)
Edington, Paul F 5:27:50 (29,312)
Edis, Anthony J 5:18:37 (28,323)
Edlin, David A 4:36:28 (20,836)
Edlin, Guy A 4:28:04 (18,767)
Edmands, Simon F 5:30:31 (29,594)
Edmond, Michael J 3:52:25 (9,477)
Edmonds, Christopher J 3:59:16 (11,591)
Edmonds, Neil 5:49:26 (31,038)
Edmonds, Richard G 4:41:18 (21,952)
Edmondson, James 4:23:58 (17,644)
Edmondson, Peter M 3:59:41 (11,723)
Edmondson-Jones, Andrew M 3:06:34 (1,716)
Edmundson, Joe 3:53:48 (9,861)
Edmundson, Russell 4:24:28 (17,792)
Edwards, Andrew L 4:40:29 (21,771)
Edwards, Andrew P 4:29:35 (19,194)
Edwards, Barry 4:07:06 (13,374)
Edwards, Barry L 4:22:15 (17,188)
Edwards, Ben J 5:12:26 (27,583)
Edwards, Chris H 3:55:25 (10,349)
Edwards, Chris I 4:43:45 (22,506)
Edwards, Christopher D 4:43:41 (22,490)
Edwards, Colin 4:45:25 (22,895)
Edwards, Darren 3:49:50 (8,828)
Edwards, David 3:27:09 (4,267)
Edwards, David A 4:02:24 (12,351)
Edwards, David J 4:43:03 (22,335)
Edwards, Eirwyn 3:58:48 (11,447)
Edwards, Garry O 3:46:35 (8,030)
Edwards, Gary 6:11:36 (31,971)
Edwards, Gary S 4:37:50 (21,186)
Edwards, George W 6:03:04 (31,686)
Edwards, Glyn P 3:39:39 (6,565)
Edwards, Jamie 5:49:51 (31,060)
Edwards, Jason 4:07:56 (13,593)
Edwards, Jonathan M 3:53:50 (9,873)
Edwards, Keith 3:48:31 (8,504)
Edwards, Kevin D 3:00:59 (1,302)
Edwards, Kevin J 3:43:14 (7,295)
Edwards, Kristian P 4:54:53 (24,868)
Edwards, Lee S 3:58:13 (11,238)
Edwards, Malcolm J 3:57:15 (10,934)
Edwards, Marc 5:00:33 (25,976)
Edwards, Mark 3:10:15 (2,089)
Edwards, Mark 4:05:02 (12,923)
Edwards, Mark 4:59:48 (25,852)
Edwards, Martin 4:20:31 (16,738)
Edwards, Matthew R 3:27:22 (4,306)
Edwards, Neil 3:07:16 (1,779)
Edwards, Norman 3:56:19 (10,630)
Edwards, Oliver R 4:03:25 (12,582)
Edwards, Paul 5:17:12 (28,151)
Edwards, Paul T 4:29:22 (19,138)
Edwards, Philip M 3:56:32 (10,694)
Edwards, Rhys 4:15:53 (15,576)
Edwards, Richard C 4:15:21 (15,432)
Edwards, Richard H 4:03:14 (12,535)
Edwards, Ross A 6:09:59 (31,926)
Edwards, Simon 3:47:27 (8,225)
Edwards, Stephen D 3:54:46 (10,128)
Edwards, Stephen F 4:26:09 (18,296)
Edwards, Stephen P 6:22:32 (32,300)
Edwards, Stephen R 3:39:00 (6,434)
Edwards, Steve 3:03:30 (1,480)
Edwards, Trevor A 5:16:19 (28,047)
Edwards, William J 5:56:43 (31,391)
Eels, Stuart W 4:17:02 (15,870)
Eely, Justin M 4:46:40 (23,153)
Effenberger, Timo 4:52:45 (24,409)
Efthimiou, Panikos 4:12:50 (14,786)
Egan, Christopher J 4:41:33 (22,001)
Egan, David 5:14:38 (27,860)
Egan, Dominic J 4:03:40 (12,644)
Egan, Paul A 4:55:53 (25,074)
Egan, Peter G 3:32:13 (5,206)
Egbor, Michael A 5:00:19 (25,946)
Egelie, Eduard C 3:08:33 (1,914)
Eggers, Mattias 3:50:48 (9,055)
Eggerschwiler, Viktor E 4:06:16 (13,185)
Eggett, Jonathan M 3:37:33 (6,140)
Eggington, Simon 4:31:27 (19,651)
Eggink, Robert 3:55:51 (10,490)
Egglestone, Mark A 5:31:02 (29,659)
Eggleton, Bernard J 3:44:59 (7,684)
Egleton, Steve J 3:47:32 (8,246)
Egli, Lauren 2:48:27 (468)
Egre, Alain N 6:07:38 (31,845)
Ehren, Gary R 4:20:54 (16,838)
Eikemo, Martin 3:48:23 (8,470)
Eikermann, Christian 4:23:49 (17,598)
Eikill, Gunnar 3:44:43 (7,621)
Eirmbter, Wolfgang K 3:48:07 (8,411)
Ekanayake, Anil I 4:48:19 (23,496)
El Atribi, Omar I 4:27:36 (18,655)
El Hout, Adam 5:24:19 (28,973)
El Khoury, Jihad 4:26:49 (18,468)
El Mouaziz, Abdelkader 2:10:24 (11)
El Sharkawy, Mohamed A 4:47:02 (23,220)
Elarkam, Rachid 4:52:35 (24,377)
Elbert, Philippe M 5:18:36 (28,321)
Elborough, Justin D 3:58:56 (11,487)
Elbourne, Lawrence 4:09:48 (14,061)
Elby, Stephen H 4:53:41 (24,613)
Elder, Daniel 3:28:38 (4,537)
Elder, Jeffrey 4:11:45 (14,508)
Elia, Charlie 5:58:11 (31,468)
Elia, Nicholas 5:58:11 (31,468)
Elias, Georgios 5:24:19 (28,973)
Elkan, Stephen J 3:59:10 (11,563)
Elkerton, William J 3:33:17 (5,365)
Elkins, David 5:56:05 (31,358)
Elkins, John B 4:34:19 (20,310)
Elleman, Anthony P 5:15:28 (27,948)
Ellens, Nigel A 3:22:54 (3,648)
Ellery, John 3:12:55 (2,388)
Ellicott, Kevin 5:41:44 (30,476)
Elliker-Reebe, Andrew 4:39:07 (21,469)
Elling, Mark 4:49:11 (23,686)
Elling, Paul L 4:28:12 (18,812)
Ellingford, David P 5:03:38 (26,409)
Ellingham, Mark A 3:39:23 (6,514)
Ellingham, Simon R 4:04:53 (12,893)
Ellinor, Nigel P 5:22:56 (28,818)
Elliot, Joe J 3:59:25 (11,641)
Elliot, Natalie L 4:28:14 (18,820)
Elliott, Andrew J 3:43:13 (7,292)
Elliott, Andrew P 3:28:26 (4,500)
Elliott, Charles R 4:51:09 (24,069)
Elliott, Corin C 5:02:32 (26,254)
Elliott, Daivd W 4:25:22 (18,079)
Elliott, Daryl 4:21:50 (17,074)
Elliott, David 3:28:41 (4,549)
Elliott, Derrick J 4:29:41 (19,222)
Elliott, Gary 3:37:08 (6,062)
Elliott, Howard C 3:01:46 (1,354)
Elliott, Iain G 5:23:18 (28,870)
Elliott, James G 5:27:39 (29,287)
Elliott, Jarrad R 3:39:47 (6,587)

Elliott, John 3:16:00 (2,780)
Elliott, Kevin M 4:18:17 (16,178)
Elliott, Michael H........4:58:29 (25,602)
Elliott, Neill A........3:34:03 (5,491)
Elliott, Paul S........3:18:07 (3,012)
Elliott, Peter 5:02:52 (26,299)
Elliott, Richard J........3:31:21 (5,046)
Elliott, Scott........4:27:54 (18,722)
Elliott, Stephen J 4:06:30 (13,233)
Elliott, Stephen K........4:54:08 (24,704)
Elliott, Stuart E........3:10:06 (2,073)
Ellis, Adam R 4:43:35 (22,462)
Ellis, Andrew J 3:28:34 (4,526)
Ellis, Andy........5:41:05 (30,428)
Ellis, Elisabeth I........5:06:23 (26,768)
Ellis, Garry........4:51:41 (24,183)
Ellis, Ian N 4:27:14 (18,564)
Ellis, Jeremy P........3:55:39 (10,416)
Ellis, John R........5:19:07 (28,390)
Ellis, John W........3:40:08 (6,645)
Ellis, John W........4:32:54 (19,979)
Ellis, Kevin 4:35:18 (20,553)
Ellis, Mark........3:59:37 (11,698)
Ellis, Matthew 4:55:15 (24,949)
Ellis, Michael A........5:20:48 (28,593)
Ellis, Michael B........3:43:30 (7,351)
Ellis, Myles P 5:36:50 (30,121)
Ellis, Ralph........4:45:22 (22,877)
Ellis, Ralph........4:55:14 (24,945)
Ellis, Robert H........4:50:22 (23,919)
Ellis, Samuel J 4:15:24 (15,449)
Ellis, Simon C 3:32:30 (5,252)
Ellis, Stephen........5:31:00 (29,650)
Ellis, Steve 3:40:50 (6,765)
Ellis, Steven P 3:52:57 (9,610)
Ellis, Tim........2:44:26 (328)
Ellison, David T........3:01:07 (1,310)
Ellison, Mark W........3:17:05 (2,891)
Ellis-Paul, Henry E 4:15:37 (15,498)
Elliston, Barry A 5:01:45 (26,138)
Elliston, Barry A 5:03:46 (26,422)
Ellithorn, Mark R........3:00:12 (1,247)
Ellsbury, Stuart J........3:57:45 (11,093)
Ellse, Simon R 4:48:24 (23,515)
Ellsmore, Lee D........6:45:26 (32,701)
Ellson, Matthew J 3:23:46 (3,752)
Elmer, Gregory G 5:16:15 (28,035)
Elsas, Herbert A Jnr 3:47:53 (8,351)
Elsby, Dominic A........2:38:16 (171)
Elsden, Kevin F........4:12:04 (14,586)
El-Sheikh, Ahmed 4:40:30 (21,777)
Elson, Michael P........4:48:10 (23,464)
Elston, Frank G 3:48:17 (8,447)
Elsworth, Lester J 4:14:08 (15,117)
Elsworth, Stephen I........3:47:15 (8,184)
Elton, Colin 4:53:29 (24,562)
Elton, Colin R........4:41:19 (21,956)
Elton, Mark A........3:32:50 (5,300)
Elton, Matthew R 3:45:45 (7,858)
Elverd, Stephen C 3:42:21 (7,088)
Elvin, Anders........4:12:55 (14,816)
Elvin, Andrew B........4:48:53 (23,625)
Elwell, Richard J........4:26:02 (18,271)
Elwood, Mark A........4:26:09 (18,296)
Embleton, David T........3:59:25 (11,641)
Emerre, Robert 4:14:04 (15,092)
Emerson, Bruce M 3:30:28 (4,886)
Emerson, Steven J 4:58:14 (25,555)
Emery, David M........5:21:39 (28,680)
Emery, Michael........2:48:28 (471)
Emery, Peter K........3:08:48 (1,935)
Emery, Robert M 5:33:32 (29,849)
Emge, Stephen M........4:27:33 (18,638)
Emm, Stephen D........4:50:41 (23,979)
Emmerich, Armin 3:45:16 (7,745)
Emmerich, Neil C 3:53:44 (9,833)
Emmerson, Anthony H........4:11:11 (14,383)
Emmerson, Bob 4:33:41 (20,185)
Emmerson, Don J........6:13:11 (32,026)
Emmerson, Jeffrey 4:44:25 (22,662)
Emmerson, John Paul........4:59:27 (25,773)
Emmerson, Neil C........3:51:52 (9,324)
Emmett, Simon E........4:53:34 (24,588)
Emorfopoulos, George 8:10:50 (33,185)
Emprin, Alain........4:21:19 (16,938)
Emprin, Jean-Michel........5:30:53 (29,634)
Emsden, John A 4:20:03 (16,613)
Endemano, Mark 3:17:05 (2,891)
Enders, David J........4:01:57 (12,249)
Engel, Richard L 4:57:43 (25,436)
Engelund, Elo I 4:26:16 (18,328)
England, Lee 4:12:59 (14,831)
England, Nicholas P........3:14:35 (2,611)
England, Russell M 4:16:25 (15,695)
English, Bryan K........3:45:04 (7,704)
English, Jamieson J 3:42:14 (7,072)
English, Kevin........5:15:46 (27,975)
English, Mark J........2:50:36 (570)
English, Mike........4:33:18 (20,085)
English, Rob J........3:48:50 (8,585)
English, Robert J 3:28:12 (4,441)
English, Stephen D 4:25:03 (17,976)
Enmalm, Timo P........4:02:45 (12,424)
Ennion, Matthew J 3:19:47 (3,230)
Ennis, Martin J 3:18:44 (3,097)
Ennis, Stephen 3:58:45 (11,422)
Enoch, Anthony B........4:45:35 (22,920)
Enticknap, Nicholas C 4:15:03 (15,351)
Entwistle, Iain P........4:55:19 (24,963)
Entwistle, Peter R........2:47:24 (433)
Eppleston, James J........3:53:13 (9,697)
Epps, Ian........4:35:26 (20,588)
Epps, Terry A........3:08:59 (1,957)
Epsom, Joseph........4:05:39 (13,067)
Erbar, Torsten........5:04:23 (26,508)
Erdal, Helge M........4:03:54 (12,690)
Erdmann, Christoph........2:58:46 (1,106)
Ergas, Alfredo........3:41:31 (6,922)
Erikson, Tore........3:24:18 (3,839)
Eriksson, Duncan........5:31:02 (29,659)
Erincx, David J........3:59:40 (11,715)
Erni, Patrick........4:24:56 (17,938)
Ernst, Frank K........4:32:29 (19,900)
Erotocritou, Harry 6:44:21 (32,681)
Errington, John........3:33:38 (5,427)
Errington, Mark F........3:32:10 (5,193)
Erskine, Kevin A........2:57:54 (1,013)
Erve, Martin........3:59:57 (11,801)
Escott, Philip B........6:03:00 (31,681)
Eshelby, Mark S 3:44:56 (7,677)
Eskandarzadeh, Mansour G 4:55:10 (24,928)
Espejo, José........3:31:33 (5,073)
Espinasa, Jorge 4:03:43 (12,654)
Espinasa, Jorge 4:21:06 (16,892)
Espitalier, Vincent........3:22:19 (3,573)
Espley, Thomas P 5:18:38 (28,326)
Esplin, Stephen F 3:15:48 (2,753)
Esposito, Vincenzo........4:14:19 (15,165)
Essex, Francis-John 4:22:13 (17,179)
Essex, Gavin C 3:26:06 (4,088)
Essigman, Martin 3:55:57 (10,527)
Essilfie-Quaye, Edmund K........3:53:48 (9,861)
Esslemont, Paul N........4:29:34 (19,190)
Essoufi, Driss 5:04:46 (26,553)
Essunger, Lennart S 5:09:12 (27,172)
Estall, Jim H........4:10:57 (14,315)
Esterhuizen, Philip........5:40:03 (30,367)
Estevez-Lopez, Luis 2:52:10 (645)
Estill, Michael R 3:55:11 (10,275)
Estrada, Diego........3:58:49 (11,452)
Estua Belaunzaran, Armando........3:28:30 (4,512)
Etchells, Robert P........3:11:26 (2,208)
Ethelston, Gary........4:06:39 (13,259)
Etheridge, Brian R 4:24:47 (17,891)
Etheridge, Martin........4:51:45 (24,198)
Etherington, Simon D 4:42:26 (22,208)
Ettlinger, Anthony C........5:16:52 (28,113)
Ettlinger, Roy A 4:26:58 (18,497)
Evans, Aled 4:19:52 (16,571)
Evans, Alun T 3:21:18 (3,440)
Evans, Andrew........4:25:12 (18,027)
Evans, Andrew D 4:31:15 (19,599)
Evans, Anthony........4:21:32 (16,981)
Evans, Barrie J 4:18:03 (16,119)
Evans, Ben 5:32:30 (29,771)
Evans, Ben T........4:57:28 (25,392)
Evans, Ceri........5:27:33 (29,279)
Evans, Clive E 3:44:31 (7,570)
Evans, Daniel........2:46:13 (390)
Evans, Daniel M........5:10:23 (27,316)
Evans, Daniel S........3:13:20 (2,438)
Evans, Dave G........3:27:48 (4,379)
Evans, David E........4:44:22 (22,651)
Evans, David J........4:29:14 (19,093)
Evans, David K........4:46:23 (23,098)
Evans, David M........4:45:46 (22,961)
Evans, David W........4:15:44 (15,529)
Evans, Declan 5:43:23 (30,601)
Evans, Edwin........3:37:42 (6,166)
Evans, Elfyn 5:23:36 (28,895)
Evans, Emlyn E........4:37:07 (21,007)
Evans, Gareth P 5:35:16 (29,995)
Evans, Gary........5:47:52 (30,939)
Evans, Gavin M........2:52:35 (655)
Evans, Geraint W........4:26:52 (18,479)
Evans, Glyn R........3:08:44 (1,929)
Evans, Graham A........3:45:20 (7,765)
Evans, Greg J 4:25:08 (18,004)
Evans, Gwyn W 3:54:47 (10,138)
Evans, Iain J 4:00:07 (11,851)
Evans, Ian A........5:23:38 (28,899)
Evans, Ian E 3:11:38 (2,227)
Evans, James B........4:00:01 (11,820)
Evans, Jamie D........4:25:17 (18,051)
Evans, John L........4:03:29 (12,601)
Evans, Jonathan D........4:43:46 (22,510)
Evans, Jonathan P 6:55:27 (32,830)
Evans, Julian D 4:49:21 (23,724)
Evans, Justyn D 4:45:26 (22,896)
Evans, Mark A........4:46:49 (23,177)
Evans, Mark T........2:44:59 (343)
Evans, Martin........3:48:34 (8,517)
Evans, Martin G........3:27:50 (4,387)
Evans, Mattehw G........3:37:34 (6,145)
Evans, Matthew G........3:25:04 (3,936)
Evans, Michael B 4:35:13 (20,540)
Evans, Michael C........4:58:31 (25,614)
Evans, Michael J 5:10:47 (27,363)
Evans, Mike........4:24:34 (17,830)
Evans, Neil R 5:07:55 (26,995)
Evans, Nicholas R........3:47:01 (8,123)
Evans, Paul........5:38:14 (30,224)
Evans, Paul D........4:28:58 (19,018)
Evans, Paul J 5:12:09 (27,544)
Evans, Paul M 4:50:15 (23,893)
Evans, Peter J 3:43:44 (7,402)
Evans, Peter M........4:33:16 (20,077)
Evans, Peter R........5:57:29 (31,434)
Evans, Philip J........3:13:41 (2,484)
Evans, Phillip J........3:32:54 (5,307)
Evans, Richard........4:40:01 (21,679)
Evans, Richard C 4:21:03 (16,880)
Evans, Richard C 6:55:28 (32,831)
Evans, Richard D 4:01:10 (12,092)
Evans, Richard P 4:17:44 (16,038)
Evans, Robert J 4:07:56 (13,593)
Evans, Robert Z 3:45:24 (7,783)
Evans, Shane........4:23:52 (17,613)
Evans, Simon L........3:34:54 (5,642)
Evans, Simon T........4:43:24 (22,411)
Evans, Stephen 6:11:37 (31,972)
Evans, Stephen P........5:31:22 (29,696)
Evans, Steve J 6:19:03 (32,204)
Evans, Stuart C 4:01:03 (12,058)
Evans, Thomas D........4:01:48 (12,214)
Evans, Thomas R........4:09:01 (13,865)
Evans, Thomas R........4:31:07 (19,557)
Evans, Timothy E 3:56:08 (10,577)
Evans, Timothy H........4:35:47 (20,670)
Evans, Vaughan 3:35:21 (5,727)
Evans, William D 3:31:26 (5,057)
Eveleigh, Samuel J........4:10:46 (14,266)
Evenden, Derek R 4:32:16 (19,853)
Everard, Roger P 3:10:45 (2,136)
Everest, Adam R 4:18:25 (16,212)
Everest, Terry J 3:15:24 (2,707)
Everett, Barry........4:25:06 (17,990)
Everett, Mike J 4:30:57 (19,521)
Everitt, Nick A 4:33:07 (20,036)

Everitt, Shaun A 4:16:45 (15,789)
Evers, Ben P 3:45:20 (7,765)
Eversdijk, Jacobys 4:28:59 (19,024)
Everson, Eugene 4:10:21 (14,183)
Everson, Matthew 4:14:34 (15,226)
Eves, Terence 3:43:09 (7,274)
Ewart, Michael D 3:40:45 (6,752)
Ewer, Andrew K 4:20:58 (16,857)
Ewing, Andy J 4:03:08 (12,516)
Ewing, Paul N 4:22:37 (17,277)
Ewing, Tom 5:30:28 (29,586)
Exham, Henry A 3:57:40 (11,065)
Exley, Jonathan N 3:30:30 (4,895)
Exley, Martin J 2:47:24 (433)
Exley, Steven J 4:31:53 (19,769)
Exworth, Matthew R 3:24:09 (3,815)
Eykyn, Alastair O 3:55:18 (10,314)
Eyles, George P 3:32:19 (5,226)
Eynon, Wayne 4:46:43 (23,163)
Eyre, Douglas 4:25:26 (18,103)
Eyre, Joseph J 3:52:55 (9,597)
Eyre, Richard J 3:27:28 (4,326)
Ezard, Paul 3:06:41 (1,726)
Fabbro, Maurizio 3:35:30 (5,749)
Fabra-Andreu, Aurelio 4:04:44 (12,862)
Facey, Tony 3:43:00 (7,231)
Fack, Erik F 6:06:35 (31,807)
Facon, Jean O 4:28:10 (18,799)
Faes, Nikolaas F 4:14:36 (15,233)
Fafalios, Stavros A 5:00:04 (25,899)
Fagnou, François 3:50:05 (8,880)
Fahey, Timmy 3:36:22 (5,908)
Fahrer, Gauthier 4:15:05 (15,363)
Faigan, Mitchell P 4:36:52 (20,955)
Faik, Can C 5:53:55 (31,260)
Faint, Jeremy 4:13:40 (14,997)
Faint, Richard J 6:51:13 (32,776)
Fairbrother, George B 4:46:33 (23,133)
Fairbrother, Leon M 3:52:22 (9,458)
Fairburn, David L 3:59:05 (11,538)
Fairclough, Stuart J 2:55:31 (817)
Fairclough, William J 3:22:23 (3,582)
Fairfield, Thomas M 4:07:41 (13,528)
Fairhall, Benjamin S 3:05:14 (1,597)
Fairhurst, Victor 4:36:05 (20,746)
Fairlie, Kenneth W 3:46:02 (7,907)
Fairlie, Nicholas C 4:36:00 (20,722)
Fairs, Rob E 3:57:26 (10,989)
Fakande, Olugbenga 5:28:54 (29,419)
Fakhry, Husam 5:46:06 (30,793)
Falck-Therkelsen, Erik G 4:02:15 (12,319)
Falcon, Michael 3:44:42 (7,618)
Falconer, Gordon 3:22:08 (3,550)
Falconi, Massimo 3:09:57 (2,058)
Falk, Seb 3:17:07 (2,900)
Falkner, Jonathan N 3:14:45 (2,635)
Falla, Matthew P 5:00:02 (25,888)
Fallaize, Mike 3:58:52 (11,470)
Fallon, Mark 6:38:51 (32,597)
Fallon, Michael C 5:23:43 (28,911)
Fallon, Michael J 4:54:48 (24,848)
Fangueiro, Joaquim G 2:47:12 (422)
Fanin, Gary S 4:37:28 (21,102)
Fanning, Carl P 5:21:20 (28,649)
Fanning, Kieran E 3:45:56 (7,893)
Fanning, Richard D 3:27:47 (4,375)
Fanshawe, Robert L 4:36:10 (20,771)
Fara, Gerardo 3:40:28 (6,706)
Faraday, Joseph M 3:47:43 (8,301)
Farag, Sharif M 4:34:21 (20,328)
Farah, Rami 4:02:04 (12,277)
Farano, Giuseppe 3:51:28 (9,212)
Farcas, David 3:13:18 (2,433)
Fargnoli, Paolo D 3:45:38 (7,830)
Faria, Benedict E 3:29:04 (4,636)
Farina, Richard A 4:03:37 (12,629)
Farley, Adam M 4:43:41 (22,490)
Farley, Tim J 3:55:58 (10,531)
Farlow, Andy C 3:17:29 (2,942)
Farmer, Anthony R 3:49:41 (8,793)
Farmer, Clive 3:51:40 (9,260)
Farmer, David P 4:31:37 (19,701)
Farmer, Ian 4:04:17 (12,774)
Farmer, Mark E 5:11:57 (27,521)
Farmer, Michael J 5:39:54 (30,352)
Farmer, Nigel K 3:43:10 (7,281)
Farmer, Paul S 4:07:41 (13,528)
Farnell, Lee E 3:35:40 (5,777)
Farnell, Mark A 2:51:29 (611)
Farnes, Jack 3:27:47 (4,375)
Farnese, Darren B 4:12:50 (14,786)
Farnham, Lyndon J 5:14:02 (27,770)
Farnhill, John H 5:05:18 (26,624)
Farnsworth, Graham 3:10:01 (2,064)
Farnworth, Ian D 3:46:39 (8,048)
Farook, Ansar 3:58:06 (11,185)
Farquhar, Gordon J 4:48:43 (23,587)
Farquhar, Graeme E 5:42:33 (30,539)
Farquhar, Richard D 4:52:04 (24,260)
Farquharson, Andrew J 2:35:38 (124)
Farquharson, John 2:54:53 (784)
Farquharson, Rob 4:36:33 (20,857)
Farrant, Nick M 5:10:38 (27,346)
Farrar, Barry B 4:23:59 (17,648)
Farrar, Brian 4:23:59 (17,648)
Farrar, Richard W 4:11:51 (14,534)
Farrell, Edward 4:27:15 (18,567)
Farrell, John 3:53:09 (9,676)
Farrell, Keith P 4:46:16 (23,069)
Farrell, Michael G 5:33:33 (29,853)
Farrelly, Paul H 5:54:35 (31,291)
Farrer, Mark A 3:57:54 (11,134)
Farrier, Robert D 4:34:59 (20,483)
Farrimond, Jonathan M 7:48:27 (33,169)
Farrington, Eddie P 4:25:35 (18,135)
Farrow, Brian S 3:47:18 (8,191)
Farrow, Jeffrey P 6:53:27 (32,802)
Farrow, Matthew S 4:44:07 (22,589)
Farrow, Nigel A 3:56:25 (10,660)
Farrow, Peter 4:03:18 (12,552)
Farrow-Smith, Mark 3:58:26 (11,319)
Farthing, David J 3:57:30 (11,014)
Farthing, Rhodri T 5:24:40 (29,002)
Fass, David 4:23:48 (17,589)
Fassnidge, Matt J 4:24:42 (17,869)
Fatemian, Kaveh R 4:57:40 (25,428)
Fatoba, Oluwajimi R 4:24:51 (17,903)
Faubel, Alan D 6:13:38 (32,038)
Faul, Ian D 6:13:24 (32,032)
Faulkner, Andrew J 5:06:08 (26,729)
Faulkner, James W 3:29:37 (4,746)
Faulkner, Kevin J 6:07:57 (31,858)
Faulkner, Kevin M 3:20:39 (3,357)
Faulkner, Simon P 3:10:35 (2,122)
Faulks, Dan A 3:41:40 (6,958)
Faust, Hans 4:36:10 (20,771)
Faver, Steven G 4:23:21 (17,454)
Fawcett, Nicholas E 4:13:59 (15,063)
Fawcett, Peter W 3:38:26 (6,313)
Fawcett, Phillip J 3:18:48 (3,106)
Fawcett, Rupert G 3:26:47 (4,205)
Fawthrop, Richard K 4:00:10 (11,859)
Fay, Andrew S 2:52:55 (673)
Fay, Ciarian G 3:54:43 (10,120)
Fay, Michael J 4:39:17 (21,509)
Fazio, Pietro 4:08:59 (13,856)
Feakes, Kieren L 3:24:27 (3,853)
Fear, Alan J 4:21:25 (16,960)
Fear, David 4:54:20 (24,754)
Fear, Paul D 4:28:43 (18,951)
Fearn, David 4:04:58 (12,912)
Fearnley, Ian 6:49:45 (32,757)
Fearon, Alexander L 4:01:31 (12,148)
Fearon, Graeme C 4:08:15 (13,677)
Feasey, Robert D 4:11:08 (14,370)
Feather, Michael J 4:39:36 (21,577)
Featherstone, Mark A 3:55:59 (10,537)
Feddal, Michel 3:32:18 (5,222)
Federico, Ronti 3:22:08 (3,550)
Feeney, John P 5:14:08 (27,790)
Feeney, John R 4:32:45 (19,945)
Fegan, Daniel P 3:28:01 (4,411)
Feger, Andreas 5:31:33 (29,707)
Feilder, James 4:20:59 (16,861)
Feld, David 3:24:08 (3,812)
Feldman, Paul S 5:55:20 (31,317)
Feldt, Waldemar 5:54:30 (31,284)
Fell, David H 3:58:59 (11,500)
Fell, Graeme L 5:03:23 (26,373)
Fell, Joe 4:21:55 (17,091)
Fell, Russell 4:05:33 (13,038)
Fell, Stuart P 4:47:38 (23,349)
Fellman, David H 4:11:14 (14,396)
Fellows, David J 4:36:50 (20,945)
Fellows, Edward 4:33:51 (20,216)
Fellows, Mark 4:36:40 (20,879)
Fellows, Paul A 4:46:36 (23,143)
Fellows, Stephen E 5:03:58 (26,453)
Fells, Daniel 4:47:03 (23,222)
Felter, Christian T 4:47:41 (23,357)
Feltham, Barry 5:05:58 (26,704)
Felton, Christopher G 3:39:36 (6,554)
Felton, David J 3:07:10 (1,774)
Felton, Tim 3:49:18 (8,691)
Feltwell, Ian 4:09:55 (14,088)
Femia, Andrés 3:50:23 (8,951)
Fendley, Peter A 3:19:10 (3,152)
Fenelon, Michael 4:06:02 (13,147)
Fenn, Russell K 4:31:07 (19,557)
Fennell, Jim R 4:07:27 (13,457)
Fenney, Eric 3:49:20 (8,703)
Fenney, Paul E 4:14:16 (15,155)
Fenney, Steven 2:45:40 (361)
Fenn-Healey, Cheryl Anne 5:13:06 (27,666)
Fenny, Richard 4:13:24 (14,943)
Fent, Martin J 4:13:57 (15,051)
Fenton, Andrew P 4:32:40 (19,925)
Fenton, Ian 3:13:38 (2,483)
Fenton, Jeffrey A 3:50:02 (8,871)
Fenwick, James H 4:59:34 (25,804)
Ferebee, David S 4:35:12 (20,531)
Fereday, David H 4:07:08 (13,385)
Fereday, Graham N 4:14:45 (15,272)
Ferguson, Alex 4:40:58 (21,884)
Ferguson, Anthony J 6:21:21 (32,268)
Ferguson, Cameron 3:15:05 (2,670)
Ferguson, David A 4:20:56 (16,850)
Ferguson, Dean J 4:16:32 (15,736)
Ferguson, Gary 3:02:16 (1,389)
Ferguson, Ian 3:44:31 (7,570)
Ferguson, James G 4:12:15 (14,640)
Ferguson, Mark 3:15:24 (2,707)
Ferguson, Mark W 3:23:42 (3,742)
Ferguson, Richard B 5:24:29 (28,988)
Ferguson, William J 3:35:27 (5,742)
Fergusson, Andrew 4:24:53 (17,917)
Fergusson, Colin M 4:57:07 (25,338)
Fergusson, Euan R 2:58:03 (1,027)
Fergusson, Frederick W 3:45:11 (7,725)
Fermi, Giuseppe 3:46:15 (7,955)
Fernandes, A 4:16:39 (15,769)
Fernandes, Ezequiel A 3:12:58 (2,393)
Fernandes, Ian B 4:43:04 (22,339)
Fernandes, Luis F 4:40:49 (21,858)
Fernando, Michael D 4:22:03 (17,130)
Fernhombreg, Burkhard 3:28:01 (4,411)
Fernie, Ken J 4:06:33 (13,242)
Ferns, Ged V 4:49:30 (23,754)
Feron, Nicolas R 4:02:25 (12,355)
Ferran, Oriol 3:12:13 (2,311)
Ferrar, Ian 5:36:19 (30,083)
Ferrara, Guiseppe 3:11:12 (2,177)
Ferrari, Michael 3:39:03 (6,445)
Ferrario, Luca 3:46:18 (7,970)
Ferraris, Paolo 4:41:10 (21,924)
Ferraro, Julian D 2:45:06 (346)
Ferres, Peter 3:34:46 (5,624)
Ferrett, Kenneth 3:57:26 (10,989)
Ferri, Claudio 4:09:12 (13,909)
Ferriday, Ernest J 4:40:43 (21,831)
Ferrier, Richard N 5:09:45 (27,238)
Ferris, Glenn 4:00:53 (12,012)
Ferris, Kevin J 5:05:35 (26,650)
Ferris, Peter A 3:55:12 (10,282)
Ferris, Peter J 3:30:39 (4,924)
Festersen, Tage 3:32:17 (5,220)
Few, Gregory M 5:13:53 (27,748)
Fewell, Darren A 4:13:04 (14,862)
Fey, Keith R 3:51:07 (9,125)

Feydeau, Gilles M	3:21:04 (3,408)
Ffoulkes, Nick	3:47:19 (8,196)
Fiddis, Richard W	3:47:40 (8,285)
Fidge, John M	4:03:19 (12,556)
Fidler, Liam B	3:20:03 (3,273)
Fidler, Michael P	4:39:06 (21,465)
Field, Andrew E	3:18:32 (3,073)
Field, Andrew M	4:43:15 (22,376)
Field, David	4:39:43 (21,605)
Field, David G	3:49:01 (8,630)
Field, Geoffrey	3:52:54 (9,595)
Field, Lee D	5:15:53 (27,987)
Field, Matthew J	5:07:07 (26,883)
Field, Nigel J	4:16:34 (15,743)
Field, Robert O	5:38:34 (30,257)
Field, Steve	3:07:08 (1,771)
Field, Timothy N	2:39:33 (203)
Fielden, Peter G	4:37:58 (21,213)
Fielder, Dave	3:59:48 (11,762)
Fielder, Simon	3:43:12 (7,289)
Fielder, Stuart P	5:51:43 (31,166)
Fieldhouse, Richard M	4:23:27 (17,486)
Fielding, Andy M	4:23:11 (17,410)
Fielding, Michael	4:23:11 (17,410)
Fielding, Paul A	5:14:20 (27,817)
Fierro, Mark	5:01:20 (26,091)
Fifield, Ben J	4:53:50 (24,642)
Figge, Jason K	3:57:18 (10,949)
Figoni, Giovanni	4:51:21 (24,105)
Figueiredo, Carlos M	5:00:21 (25,952)
File, Richard F	3:54:44 (10,123)
Fileccia, Marco	3:28:08 (4,431)
Filer, Paul E	4:57:49 (25,459)
Filippini, Daniel	4:16:52 (15,817)
Filkin, Neil C	4:49:30 (23,754)
Fillbrook, Neil R	4:28:18 (18,842)
Filloux, Alain	3:10:32 (2,119)
Filmer, Greg P	4:11:34 (14,473)
Filtness, Paul M	3:48:13 (8,434)
Finbow, Mark F	4:35:17 (20,548)
Finch, David E	3:49:35 (8,765)
Finch, Edward	5:24:20 (28,978)
Finch, Ernie J	4:08:31 (13,748)
Finch, Glen M	4:30:47 (19,491)
Finch, Graham J	3:55:02 (10,217)
Finch, Jason	3:26:56 (4,229)
Finch, Jason T	5:28:29 (29,374)
Finch, John F	4:34:18 (20,307)
Finch, Paul B	3:14:47 (2,637)
Finch, Peter L	3:11:40 (2,233)
Fincham, Daron A	3:56:23 (10,650)
Findel-Hawkins, David P	3:14:53 (2,650)
Finden-Crofts, Toby A	3:59:49 (11,770)
Findlay, Alan J	2:56:22 (880)
Findlay, Gordon	3:02:50 (1,425)
Fine, Martin H	3:50:56 (9,083)
Finegan, Tim	4:24:26 (17,785)
Finerty, Bernard F	3:53:15 (9,706)
Finill, Chris T	2:48:25 (465)
Finlay, Michael J	3:47:27 (8,225)
Finlayson, Robert D	4:33:23 (20,106)
Finlayson, Stephen G	5:53:34 (31,244)
Finlayson, Wayne	6:16:33 (32,134)
Finn, Allan G	5:07:54 (26,991)
Finn, Andrew M	2:39:06 (191)
Finn, Julian A	5:26:26 (29,168)
Finn, Matthias	2:44:20 (324)
Finn, Stephen P	4:33:21 (20,099)
Finnemore, Bernard G	4:33:51 (20,216)
Finnerty, Andrew T	3:29:21 (4,689)
Finney, Mark	4:01:43 (12,192)
Finney, Mark R	3:19:58 (3,262)
Finnie, Kenneth J	3:53:25 (9,741)
Fiorentino, Tonino	3:54:31 (10,057)
Firmin, Michael P	2:53:59 (726)
Firouzi, Mazeyar	3:06:35 (1,717)
Firth, Colin	4:20:57 (16,853)
Firth, Daniel J	4:15:47 (15,540)
Firth, Edward	4:10:03 (14,111)
Firth, James D	5:18:06 (28,252)
Firth, Justin P	4:00:08 (11,855)
Firth, Matthew S	4:04:31 (12,821)
Fischer, Soren	3:34:50 (5,631)
Fischlein, Steffen	4:20:32 (16,742)
Fish, Bradley D	5:01:39 (26,128)
Fish, Brian W	3:59:21 (11,621)
Fish, Rhys J	3:45:12 (7,730)
Fish, Richard M	3:56:41 (10,750)
Fishel, Mathew	4:53:50 (24,642)
Fishel, Simon B	3:47:12 (8,168)
Fisher, Alistair R	3:54:49 (10,154)
Fisher, Angela	6:03:18 (31,695)
Fisher, Anthony P	7:03:58 (32,928)
Fisher, Barry	4:15:00 (15,338)
Fisher, Derek G	5:14:09 (27,791)
Fisher, Gary J	4:46:15 (23,062)
Fisher, Gary M	4:48:12 (23,471)
Fisher, Geoff	3:18:44 (3,097)
Fisher, Graham V	5:05:35 (26,650)
Fisher, Ian	2:20:38 (31)
Fisher, Ian	2:34:06 (100)
Fisher, Ian	3:55:02 (10,217)
Fisher, Ian M	3:22:22 (3,581)
Fisher, John D	4:13:23 (14,940)
Fisher, John E	6:13:21 (32,030)
Fisher, John T	4:44:22 (22,651)
Fisher, Martin J	3:21:50 (3,517)
Fisher, Martin L	3:31:20 (5,044)
Fisher, Michael L	4:18:56 (16,337)
Fisher, Michael W	4:07:31 (13,479)
Fisher, Neil M	3:42:54 (7,206)
Fisher, Nicholas C	3:26:08 (4,091)
Fisher, Paul A	5:57:48 (31,446)
Fisher, Roderick M	4:33:11 (20,055)
Fisher, Scott E	4:40:45 (21,841)
Fisher, Simon	3:20:39 (3,357)
Fisher, Simon R	4:21:49 (17,067)
Fisher, Stephen	3:58:43 (11,405)
Fisher, William E	4:20:05 (16,626)
Fishpool, Sean D	3:22:16 (3,566)
Fishwick, Nicholas G	4:13:58 (15,054)
Fishwick, Peter J	7:16:29 (33,017)
Fishwick, Rob	6:44:04 (32,673)
Fiske, Neal	5:17:27 (28,191)
Fitch, Ian R	4:34:42 (20,411)
Fitch, Jamie F	4:08:36 (13,769)
Fitt, James	4:44:33 (22,685)
Fitter, Carl	3:40:16 (6,671)
Fitzduff, David	3:53:19 (9,722)
Fitzgerald, Alistair J	3:37:22 (6,109)
Fitzgerald, Brian	4:33:14 (20,067)
Fitzgerald, James	4:59:14 (25,738)
Fitzgerald, Richard	4:09:21 (13,946)
Fitzgerald, William	3:49:48 (8,822)
Fitzgerald-O'Connor, Henry	4:01:26 (12,137)
Fitzgibbon, Francis	4:20:00 (16,602)
Fitzgibbon, Robin	3:08:44 (1,929)
Fitzjohn, Colin	3:01:37 (1,345)
Fitzpatrick, Eamonn M	3:55:26 (10,354)
Fitzpatrick, John K	3:19:54 (3,248)
Fitzpatrick, Peter	3:07:03 (1,763)
Fitzpatrick, Shane J	4:33:33 (20,149)
Fitzsimon, David A	4:08:40 (13,781)
Fjelostad, Lars Helge	3:35:52 (5,810)
Flack, David T	4:10:25 (14,196)
Flack, Simon A	5:16:00 (27,999)
Fladung, Matt	3:53:44 (9,833)
Flaherty, John	4:54:57 (24,880)
Flaherty, Patrick J	4:21:33 (16,985)
Flaherty, Peter	5:27:13 (29,246)
Flamant, François	3:18:34 (3,077)
Flanagan, Andrew C	4:29:10 (19,076)
Flanagan, Brian J	3:33:13 (5,357)
Flanagan, David C	4:12:10 (14,616)
Flanagan, Paul A	4:51:45 (24,198)
Flanagan, Tadhg J	4:07:34 (13,496)
Flanders, Geoff G	5:18:23 (28,294)
Flannery, John	3:30:33 (4,904)
Flannery, John J	3:40:44 (6,749)
Flannery, Raymond	3:52:17 (9,435)
Flannigan, Peter	4:56:39 (25,229)
Flatter, Ben	5:01:34 (26,113)
Flatter, Michael	5:01:34 (26,113)
Flavell, Christopher J	2:45:57 (378)
Flavell, Paul	2:57:10 (958)
Flaxman, John	4:57:05 (25,332)
Fleckney, Paul T	5:23:58 (28,934)
Fleeman, Nicholas J	5:19:46 (28,467)
Fleet, Keith	4:13:21 (14,931)
Fleetwood, Ashley I	4:21:34 (16,989)
Fleischman, Victor	5:28:53 (29,416)
Fleming, Albert P	3:46:04 (7,918)
Fleming, Ian J	6:11:49 (31,981)
Fleming, Ian M	4:36:46 (20,924)
Fleming, Lee	4:37:55 (21,202)
Fleming, Martin	4:17:17 (15,923)
Fleming, Paul A	3:05:50 (1,648)
Fleming, Richard D	4:28:27 (18,882)
Fleming, Simon L	4:29:20 (19,130)
Fletcher, Alister T	4:26:49 (18,468)
Fletcher, Chris J	3:00:46 (1,285)
Fletcher, Christopher P	4:39:55 (21,658)
Fletcher, Eddie G	4:14:07 (15,108)
Fletcher, Gordon	3:22:49 (3,638)
Fletcher, Ion M	3:16:02 (2,783)
Fletcher, Jason	3:57:04 (10,865)
Fletcher, John H	4:09:34 (14,007)
Fletcher, Patrick J	4:08:22 (13,708)
Fletcher, Paul D	3:37:39 (6,159)
Fletcher, Richard M	4:57:46 (25,448)
Fletcher, Robert W	4:18:19 (16,190)
Fletcher, Simon	4:11:44 (14,503)
Fletcher, Simon	5:15:50 (27,977)
Fletcher, Simon A	4:57:19 (25,369)
Fletcher, Stephen J	4:56:39 (25,229)
Fleuret, Alain	4:02:25 (12,355)
Flewitt, Peter M	2:38:26 (176)
Flint, James M	4:36:58 (20,973)
Flint, Tony J	4:56:31 (25,210)
Flintham, Frazer	4:20:00 (16,602)
Flintoff, James S	3:59:21 (11,621)
Flitton, John	6:14:21 (32,064)
Floch, Ludovic	3:58:03 (11,168)
Flockhart, Kevin R	4:55:57 (25,091)
Flood, Kevin M	4:30:22 (19,393)
Flor, German E	4:06:46 (13,297)
Flores-Dominguez, Antonio	2:43:26 (298)
Florida-James, Michael D	3:00:36 (1,280)
Florio, Lorenzo	3:56:23 (10,650)
Flower, Kevin M	3:49:25 (8,725)
Flower, Martin R	5:56:37 (31,388)
Flower, Marty R	2:45:53 (371)
Flower, Michael J	4:10:57 (14,315)
Flowers, Mark A	3:28:24 (4,495)
Flowers, Michael J	3:30:48 (4,944)
Flowers, Simon R	3:47:35 (8,266)
Floyd, Maynard	5:08:54 (27,135)
Floyd, Neville	4:12:14 (14,634)
Floyd, Robert J	3:48:01 (8,387)
Floyd, Russell	5:59:59 (31,564)
Flude, Robert	6:14:01 (32,049)
Flynn, Alexander C	4:25:44 (18,169)
Flynn, Anthony M	5:04:11 (26,474)
Flynn, Ben E	3:35:49 (5,801)
Flynn, Carl	4:26:41 (18,426)
Flynn, John	4:45:35 (22,920)
Flynn, John K	3:07:44 (1,830)
Flynn, John P	4:39:39 (21,588)
Flynn, Kellan	3:58:10 (11,218)
Flynn, Patrick	4:38:41 (21,368)
Flynn, Patrick K	5:10:15 (27,298)
Flynn, Paul	5:02:29 (26,246)
Flynn, Simon J	3:47:33 (8,249)
Flynn, Stephen E	4:35:35 (20,618)
Foddering, Ian J	4:24:54 (17,925)
Foddy, Matthew D	3:09:48 (2,044)
Foden, John E	3:41:46 (6,978)
Fodor, Juergen F	2:58:24 (1,057)
Foehner, Dan	3:11:37 (2,223)
Foertsch, Thomas G	3:35:34 (5,763)
Fogarty, Chris	3:46:54 (8,101)
Fogden, Gary	4:58:51 (25,675)
Fogden, Terry R	5:11:03 (27,390)
Fogg, Brian	4:23:04 (17,378)
Fogg, Steve T	4:16:55 (15,839)
Fogg, Trevor	5:11:03 (27,390)
Fogwill, Alex S	3:47:30 (8,239)
Foireau, Guy	4:10:07 (14,127)
Folan, Chris	2:53:42 (708)

Foley, James E	4:51:55 (24,236)
Foley, James J	4:17:15 (15,918)
Foley, John	3:20:55 (3,394)
Folkard, Melvyn	3:39:46 (6,582)
Folland, Mike	3:39:45 (6,581)
Folland, Richard	6:01:21 (31,620)
Folliot, Eric	4:36:59 (20,976)
Follis, Tim M	4:58:42 (25,644)
Fonsela, Armando S	3:45:14 (7,737)
Fontana, Francisco J	3:21:37 (3,486)
Fontanille, Philippe	3:14:05 (2,540)
Fonteneau, Dominique	4:30:24 (19,400)
Fontimpe, Marc	3:15:21 (2,702)
Foord, Daniel J	3:58:46 (11,431)
Foord, Timothy J	4:57:01 (25,315)
Foot, Paul M	3:13:43 (2,487)
Foot, Peter G	5:49:28 (31,043)
Foote, Johnathan P	4:06:25 (13,215)
Foran, Andrew	4:05:27 (13,011)
Forbes, Justin D	4:28:00 (18,749)
Forbes, Mike	3:57:15 (10,934)
Forcer, Iain	4:42:17 (22,172)
Ford, Christopher J	3:55:08 (10,255)
Ford, David	4:05:08 (12,946)
Ford, David I	4:00:22 (11,906)
Ford, David J	6:03:48 (31,718)
Ford, Graham	4:09:48 (14,061)
Ford, Graham K	3:36:38 (5,962)
Ford, James A	5:05:45 (26,671)
Ford, James D	4:01:34 (12,165)
Ford, Joseph T	6:08:51 (31,891)
Ford, Martin C	3:11:46 (2,244)
Ford, Matthew R	3:19:40 (3,206)
Ford, Michael	4:12:29 (14,699)
Ford, Neil A	3:51:20 (9,185)
Ford, Nicholas J	4:45:51 (22,978)
Ford, Paul J	3:51:32 (9,229)
Ford, Robert	4:18:09 (16,151)
Ford, Timothy	4:16:42 (15,779)
Forde, Michael	4:07:33 (13,486)
Forder, Martin J	2:40:29 (215)
Forder, Matthew A	4:15:16 (15,403)
Fordham, Colin M	4:20:03 (16,613)
Fordham, Paul	3:55:22 (10,337)
Fordyce, Alex	4:17:12 (15,909)
Foreman, Antony E	4:11:05 (14,354)
Foreman, Timothy F	3:24:49 (3,915)
Forkin, Harry	4:39:21 (21,533)
Forman, Timothy M	4:19:34 (16,497)
Formuli, Naeem	4:49:12 (23,690)
Foronda, Alberto R	3:11:44 (2,241)
Forrest, Andrew	5:15:09 (27,916)
Forrest, Darryl T	4:52:56 (24,443)
Forrest, Gordon W	4:42:13 (22,162)
Forrest, Ian	4:24:13 (17,717)
Forrest, Stephen A	4:14:02 (15,080)
Forrester, Alexander	4:10:54 (14,305)
Forrester, Andrew P	4:33:29 (20,131)
Forrester, Ian W	3:46:34 (8,026)
Forrester, Paul	4:30:35 (19,446)
Forrester, Peter J	4:03:07 (12,509)
Forster, Adrian J	4:59:27 (25,773)
Forster, Frank	4:08:42 (13,789)
Forster, Nicholas A	3:44:47 (7,638)
Forte, Phil	3:32:29 (5,246)
Forte, Sandro	4:44:57 (22,770)
Fortea, Agustin	4:02:07 (12,289)
Forth, Michael A	4:02:53 (12,455)
Fortune, David J	4:02:14 (12,312)
Forty, Peter J	3:23:28 (3,670)
Forward, David J	4:04:27 (12,804)
Foskett, Matthew O	3:51:55 (9,341)
Foss, David	4:50:16 (23,898)
Foss, Jan	4:33:04 (20,019)
Foss, Robert J	3:54:14 (9,988)
Foster, Andrew	3:51:45 (9,287)
Foster, David	4:26:09 (18,296)
Foster, David I	4:52:00 (24,253)
Foster, David J	3:52:12 (9,410)
Foster, Graham J	3:37:55 (6,213)
Foster, James J	4:14:43 (15,263)
Foster, Jeremy N	3:17:37 (2,953)
Foster, John	7:29:43 (33,092)

Foster, Leonard J	3:35:49 (5,801)
Foster, Paul R	6:22:42 (32,302)
Foster, Paul W	3:53:55 (9,897)
Foster, Quentin S	5:48:40 (30,980)
Foster, Robert N	3:19:27 (3,188)
Foster, Robert S	4:55:23 (24,980)
Foster, Steven	4:47:28 (23,311)
Foster, Steven	5:20:52 (28,597)
Fotherby, Kenneth J	2:56:26 (885)
Fotheringham, Neil H	3:56:49 (10,790)
Foucaud, Michel	4:03:07 (12,509)
Foudy, Peter J	4:32:35 (19,912)
Foulds, John	3:21:25 (3,456)
Foulds, Steven A	4:41:51 (22,069)
Foulkes, Llifon A	3:36:22 (5,908)
Found, Stuart D	4:32:18 (19,859)
Fountain, Colin A	3:37:30 (6,133)
Fourquet, Jean-Pierre	5:00:38 (25,989)
Fourriques, Thierry	5:57:20 (31,428)
Fowler, Alan R	3:14:09 (2,549)
Fowler, Cedric	5:33:06 (29,823)
Fowler, Darran	3:27:07 (4,263)
Fowler, David R	4:07:50 (13,568)
Fowler, Ian G	4:59:26 (25,767)
Fowler, Jonathan D	3:57:56 (11,144)
Fowler, Kevin	3:04:07 (1,523)
Fowler, Martin G	3:05:16 (1,603)
Fowler, Matthew	3:08:02 (1,863)
Fowler, Nicholas P	3:30:54 (4,963)
Fowler, Nigel C	3:26:39 (4,184)
Fowler, Paul R	4:32:05 (19,812)
Fowler, Richard A	3:06:08 (1,680)
Fowler, Stephen P	3:43:37 (7,373)
Fowlie, Stuart	4:04:46 (12,872)
Fox, Brian T	3:05:16 (1,603)
Fox, Darren M	4:53:24 (24,549)
Fox, David T	4:24:52 (17,906)
Fox, John	4:58:46 (25,656)
Fox, Martin	3:00:59 (1,302)
Fox, Martin	3:35:47 (5,796)
Fox, Martin R	4:05:35 (13,047)
Fox, Michael V	3:45:21 (7,771)
Fox, Neil B	4:08:25 (13,722)
Fox, Paul E	4:26:36 (18,408)
Fox, Robert A	3:54:42 (10,114)
Fox, Stuart	2:45:18 (352)
Fox, Trevor J	4:38:17 (21,299)
Fox, William S	3:32:58 (5,319)
Foxall, Peter L	3:13:21 (2,443)
Foxcroft, Andrew J	5:02:20 (26,230)
Foxley, Nick C	3:55:31 (10,382)
Foxton, Graham E	4:17:07 (15,891)
Foxton, Justin R	3:36:53 (6,016)
Foxwell, James R	3:49:02 (8,634)
Foy, Jamie M	3:58:45 (11,422)
Foy, Leslie M	4:57:43 (25,436)
Frackiewicz, Neil A	3:44:52 (7,658)
Fradley, William T	4:03:15 (12,538)
Frain, David	4:10:31 (14,217)
Frampton, Glyn L	4:47:52 (23,329)
Franca, José V	4:31:46 (19,738)
France, Ashley S	4:35:48 (20,673)
France, Peter J	3:52:45 (9,557)
Franceschini, Pietro D	3:43:03 (7,251)
Francis, Anthony J	4:18:04 (16,128)
Francis, Brian P	4:20:05 (16,626)
Francis, Christopher T	4:02:18 (12,331)
Francis, Daniel	3:30:45 (4,936)
Francis, Ian	4:33:09 (20,047)
Francis, James D	4:35:24 (20,579)
Francis, Michael A	3:53:47 (9,853)
Francis, Michael J	3:59:06 (11,543)
Francis, Richard	4:52:09 (24,279)
Francis, Richard C	3:41:35 (6,941)
Francis, Richard J	3:18:14 (3,022)
Francis, Richard W	3:45:01 (7,693)
Francis, Robert J	4:30:11 (19,345)
Francis, Stephen W	3:53:02 (9,638)
Francis, Steve	3:43:51 (7,431)
Francksen, John D	4:34:53 (20,459)
François, Alan J	3:24:07 (3,808)
Frankland, David A	4:11:13 (14,391)
Frankland, Michael D	3:56:32 (10,694)

Franklin, David P	4:26:48 (18,464)
Franklin, Glenn	4:08:09 (13,652)
Franklin, John K	3:00:33 (1,278)
Franklin, Joseph D	4:23:53 (17,618)
Franklin, Mark R	3:38:43 (6,367)
Franklin, Neil P	4:49:00 (23,649)
Franklin, Neil W	3:28:21 (4,480)
Franklin, Nicholas	5:28:35 (29,380)
Franklin, Robert C	3:36:24 (5,914)
Franklin, Sam	4:28:09 (18,792)
Franklin, Shane V	3:46:08 (7,929)
Franklin, Simon A	3:26:22 (4,130)
Franks, Alasdair B	3:53:41 (9,816)
Franks, Andrew P	5:12:08 (27,543)
Franks, Keith	3:40:25 (6,695)
Franks, Mark W	4:00:28 (11,930)
Fransson, Bo I	5:14:37 (27,857)
Frantz, Patrick	5:45:52 (30,768)
Franz, Jonathon W	4:24:31 (17,806)
Franzon, Gunnar	4:37:07 (21,007)
Fraser, Andrew J	4:23:49 (17,598)
Fraser, David	4:43:30 (22,435)
Fraser, Edward	4:23:58 (17,644)
Fraser, Graeme A	4:21:45 (17,045)
Fraser, Matthew J	4:35:18 (20,553)
Fraser, Neil M	5:16:38 (28,087)
Fraser, Simon N	2:57:15 (965)
Fraser, Simon W	5:38:05 (30,211)
Fraser-Looen, Oliver J	3:55:04 (10,233)
Fray, Martin D	2:56:22 (880)
Frazer, Ben	5:59:11 (31,515)
Frazer, Michael	3:45:16 (7,745)
Fred, Dadzie	4:40:05 (21,690)
Fredericks, Simon K	4:39:43 (21,605)
Free, Alexander J	3:41:21 (6,887)
Freedman, Ben M	4:24:11 (17,709)
Freedman, Clive	4:53:53 (24,655)
Freedman, Paul	5:50:15 (31,092)
Freel, Christopher J	3:25:35 (4,017)
Freeland, Dominic S	4:28:17 (18,833)
Freeland, Lee	3:32:55 (5,311)
Freeland, Tony R	6:51:19 (32,778)
Freeman, Anthony W	4:33:56 (20,231)
Freeman, Darren	3:53:15 (9,706)
Freeman, David J	3:25:10 (3,955)
Freeman, Gary	4:38:12 (21,282)
Freeman, Ian J	3:58:24 (11,306)
Freeman, Jonathan M	4:09:58 (14,093)
Freeman, Kevin C	3:47:47 (8,318)
Freeman, Kirk G	5:06:19 (26,757)
Freeman, Matthew A	3:54:45 (10,124)
Freeman, Matthew D	4:49:16 (23,707)
Freeman, Murray J	3:51:27 (9,209)
Freeman, Neil D	4:41:11 (21,926)
Freeman, Paul	2:50:46 (577)
Freeman, Paul R	3:15:31 (2,722)
Freeman, Paul W	3:18:52 (3,119)
Freeman, Randall	3:31:38 (5,094)
Freeman, Robin A	4:42:19 (22,180)
Freeman, Samuel E	3:44:49 (7,645)
Freeman, Scott L	4:24:20 (17,759)
Freeman, Simon K	4:58:19 (25,572)
Freeman, Walter L	4:55:33 (25,007)
Freestone, Andy	3:56:37 (10,730)
Frei, Nikolaus	3:25:05 (3,939)
Freire, Antonio J	4:38:30 (21,340)
Freire, Flavio M	5:05:25 (26,638)
French, Christopher	4:38:27 (21,325)
French, David J	3:33:41 (5,435)
French, Freddie A	4:40:30 (21,777)
French, Graham J	3:50:43 (9,033)
French, Graham T	3:07:18 (1,785)
French, Julian C	4:18:16 (16,174)
French, Kevin	3:23:38 (3,732)
French, Kevin R	5:22:11 (28,739)
French, Nick	3:29:19 (4,679)
French, Paul I	4:32:21 (19,873)
French, Richard J	5:11:28 (27,452)
French, Sean	4:03:49 (12,677)
Frenzer, Jurgen	4:03:29 (12,601)
Fresson, Edward J	4:38:53 (21,413)
Fretwell, Des	4:42:52 (22,297)
Freudenfeld, Tony	4:30:27 (19,416)

Gass, Alexander F....3:44:00 (7,456)
Gaston, Paul....4:08:32 (13,750)
Gaston, Reginald L....4:10:45 (14,259)
Gaston Grubb, Kevin A....3:56:15 (10,610)
Gates, Andrew S....3:38:31 (6,329)
Gates, Gary A....3:44:19 (7,525)
Gates, Tommy....4:54:50 (24,856)
Gatherer, William A....3:29:56 (4,813)
Gatt, Garry M....4:20:46 (16,803)
Gatt, Robert....4:20:02 (16,607)
Gattrell, William T....4:24:24 (17,774)
Gauch, Chantal....4:01:31 (12,148)
Gaudu, Remi....4:52:44 (24,405)
Gauge, Michael J....6:18:55 (32,198)
Gaughan, Andrew I....4:29:53 (19,264)
Gaulder, Nicholas R....3:16:09 (2,795)
Gaunt, Martin S....2:44:17 (322)
Gaunt, Mike....4:56:28 (25,201)
Gausden, Neil B....4:24:35 (17,837)
Gauthier, James D....3:14:03 (2,538)
Gautier, Mark A....6:09:07 (31,898)
Gautier, Patrice....4:12:29 (14,699)
Gavaghan, James C....5:20:16 (28,530)
Gavin, Michael....3:39:49 (6,592)
Gay, Anthony B....3:18:07 (3,012)
Gay, Christopher D....3:49:51 (8,831)
Gay, Paul E....4:17:31 (15,987)
Gay, Richard....3:19:45 (3,222)
Gaydon, Adam....3:55:43 (10,444)
Gayle, Terry....3:28:48 (4,573)
Gayler, Duncan R....4:27:52 (18,714)
Gayler, Ryan....3:47:14 (8,182)
Gaynor, Nigel....5:05:19 (26,628)
Gaytten, James....4:22:12 (17,174)
Gaze, Peter J....4:12:48 (14,773)
Gazzari, Giuseppe....2:45:52 (370)
Gebbie, Andrew M....5:27:43 (29,296)

Gebrselassie, Haile....2:09:05 (9)

Geddes, Ian....4:31:42 (19,721)
Geddes, Paul B....3:56:05 (10,563)
Geddes, Readford....4:47:53 (23,403)
Gedin, Mats R....2:37:49 (161)
Gee, Alexander P....3:56:24 (10,656)
Gee, Andrew D....4:10:06 (14,121)
Gee, Christopher....4:12:29 (14,699)
Gee, David....4:19:38 (16,509)
Gee, David....4:57:54 (25,479)
Gee, Raymond....3:55:24 (10,345)
Geekie, Stuart....4:00:07 (11,851)
Geekie, Thomas....4:10:08 (14,133)
Geelhoed, Dirk....3:56:31 (10,691)
Geert, Dhaens....3:33:21 (5,378)
Geert, Verdoodt....3:40:59 (6,799)
Geerts, Francis....3:12:25 (2,335)
Geh, Eddie....4:46:35 (23,139)
Gelb, Sivan....4:33:42 (20,188)
Geldard, Wayne....3:49:08 (8,653)
Gelister, Benjamin....3:15:14 (2,690)
Gell, Colin....2:38:17 (172)
Gellatly, Nairn J....3:50:53 (9,072)
Gelok, Jeroen W....4:06:23 (13,207)
Gendrot, Bruno....3:52:49 (9,572)
Generalis, Sotos C....5:14:59 (27,904)
Genever, Mark A....4:52:28 (24,347)
Gennery, Michael J....4:21:57 (17,102)
Gennery, Paul....5:46:52 (30,853)
Genovese, Erico....4:37:13 (21,037)
Gent, Barrie....5:55:32 (31,327)
Gent, Douglas....3:31:41 (5,099)
Gent, John A....4:57:07 (25,338)
Gent, Michael....5:13:24 (27,705)
Gentili, Alessandro....4:50:47 (24,001)
Gentili, Massimo Paolo....3:30:42 (4,933)
Gentle, Chris R....3:21:21 (3,449)
Gentle, John F....4:19:24 (16,448)
Gentzel, Ingo....4:31:22 (19,630)
Geoghegan, Michael F....6:01:01 (31,606)
George, Craig A....3:46:34 (8,026)
George, David J....3:56:37 (10,730)
George, Derek....2:57:12 (961)
George, Ferdinand K....6:58:59 (32,868)
George, Frederic M....4:59:23 (25,758)
George, Iain P....4:56:57 (25,295)
George, Ian R....3:05:39 (1,629)
George, Jason B....3:13:58 (2,524)
George, Lenny....3:11:07 (2,167)
George, Mark....3:22:31 (3,598)
George, Martin J....3:11:51 (2,252)
George, Maurice....3:15:46 (2,748)
George, Michael J....5:09:52 (27,249)
George, Michael P....3:01:14 (1,320)
George, Neil D....4:09:42 (14,029)
George, Philip....4:22:18 (17,199)
George, Phillip M....2:52:00 (634)
George, Stephen W....5:38:10 (30,215)
Georges, Matthieu....3:50:59 (9,095)
Georgiades, Tony J....4:57:53 (25,475)
Gepp, John A....5:29:14 (29,449)
Geraghty, Michael G....3:39:37 (6,557)
Gerbaud, Alain....3:52:17 (9,435)
German, Noel J....3:22:21 (3,577)
Germany, Colin....4:20:11 (16,656)
Gernes, Christopher M....3:44:53 (7,665)
Gerom, Rainer....3:43:35 (7,366)
Gerrard, Chris M....3:34:09 (5,505)
Gerrard, Mark A....4:24:41 (17,868)
Gerrard, Matthew P....4:05:42 (13,078)
Gerrard, Simon C....3:43:01 (7,236)
Gerrard, Timothy W....3:21:49 (3,515)
Gerritsen, Rolf....4:39:04 (21,458)
Gershon, Mike J....4:54:08 (24,704)
Gertel, Eloi L....5:04:23 (26,508)
Gessat, Manfred....4:41:15 (21,934)
Gesset, Claude....3:18:01 (2,998)
Getliffe, Martin....4:55:04 (24,908)
Geurts, Benoit A....3:56:26 (10,668)
Gharib, Jaouad....2:08:45 (8)
Ghelani, Deven....3:52:56 (9,604)
Ghezzi, Giampiero....3:59:06 (11,543)
Ghosh, Neill....4:42:43 (22,264)
Giannerini, Paolo....5:17:20 (28,172)
Gibb, Martin C....4:32:20 (19,869)
Gibben, John G....6:12:18 (31,998)
Gibbens, David J....6:42:56 (32,655)
Gibbens, Philip M....3:44:59 (7,684)
Gibbes, Edward A....3:55:06 (10,246)
Gibbins, Richard....4:31:01 (19,537)
Gibbon, John....4:17:23 (15,951)
Gibbons, Andrew....4:45:49 (22,971)
Gibbons, Christopher P....3:35:13 (5,709)
Gibbons, Eamonn....4:02:28 (12,368)
Gibbons, John T....4:10:19 (14,176)
Gibbons, Paul J....4:33:29 (20,131)
Gibbs, Ben L....3:46:55 (8,105)
Gibbs, Darren E....4:24:50 (17,898)
Gibbs, David J....4:29:36 (19,199)
Gibbs, David W....3:48:43 (8,561)
Gibbs, Edward B....3:11:52 (2,254)
Gibbs, Hugh T....3:47:48 (8,326)
Gibbs, Mark A....4:57:53 (25,475)
Gibbs, Mark B....4:25:04 (17,982)
Gibbs, Mark T....3:54:30 (10,051)
Gibbs, Martin R....4:24:56 (17,938)
Gibbs, Simon....3:49:34 (8,761)
Gibier, Julien....2:56:12 (869)
Giblin, John F....5:24:54 (29,028)
Gibson, Andrew....4:01:44 (12,197)
Gibson, Carl J....5:06:13 (26,740)
Gibson, Carl P....3:55:50 (10,485)
Gibson, Craig J....4:50:46 (23,995)
Gibson, Dale M....5:58:24 (31,483)
Gibson, David S....3:15:28 (2,717)
Gibson, Dean....3:09:39 (2,031)
Gibson, Fergus H....4:16:33 (15,737)
Gibson, Jay D....4:28:46 (18,965)
Gibson, John D....3:56:42 (10,757)
Gibson, Mark J....4:17:16 (15,921)
Gibson, Oliver....3:44:32 (7,578)
Gibson, Paul K....4:25:52 (18,215)
Gibson, Paul R....5:00:03 (25,894)
Gibson, Richard H....3:58:47 (11,440)
Gibson, Robert....3:55:51 (10,490)
Gibson, Roger B....4:37:14 (21,039)
Gibson, Ryan S....4:29:36 (19,199)
Gibson, Stephen....4:04:38 (12,837)
Gibson, Stephen J....3:58:03 (11,168)
Gidade P Moura, Luis M....4:26:15 (18,323)
Giddins, Stephen J....5:10:43 (27,354)
Giek, Johannes....3:32:31 (5,256)
Gigg, Julian A....3:21:09 (3,415)
Giggs, Ian C....3:35:22 (5,729)
Gilad, Roey....3:46:45 (8,071)
Gilbert, Anthony J....5:44:51 (30,707)
Gilbert, Ashley J....3:58:33 (11,357)
Gilbert, David....3:37:07 (6,059)
Gilbert, David L....3:50:29 (8,977)
Gilbert, James....5:09:03 (27,154)
Gilbert, Jonathan P....3:58:44 (11,417)
Gilbert, Mark J....3:55:00 (10,204)
Gilbert, Max M....4:18:16 (16,174)
Gilbert, Nicholas J....3:38:13 (6,270)
Gilbert, Paul J....4:17:18 (15,929)
Gilbert, Peter D....4:09:10 (13,895)
Gilbert, Ralph R....3:20:22 (3,320)
Gilbert, Robert J....4:04:56 (12,903)
Gilbert, Simon M....3:24:11 (3,820)
Gilbey, Ian J....4:56:40 (25,236)
Gilbourne, James A....5:44:21 (30,670)
Gilby, Barry....3:57:05 (10,870)
Gilchrist, Robert D....5:57:09 (31,410)
Gilchrist, Tyrone....5:08:41 (27,103)
Gildea, Richard J....5:45:55 (30,772)
Gilding, Neil M....5:36:18 (30,081)
Giles, Alan....5:01:56 (26,168)
Giles, Christopher A....3:46:19 (7,972)
Giles, David W....3:33:21 (5,378)
Giles, Kirk A....3:15:25 (2,710)
Giles, Martin R....2:53:52 (718)
Giles, Matt J....2:33:06 (90)
Giles, Nikki....4:01:09 (12,089)
Giles, Peter....3:16:34 (2,823)
Giles, Thomas E....4:51:11 (24,074)
Gilio, Lee R....3:16:36 (2,828)
Gill, Andrew D....4:24:49 (17,895)
Gill, Brian J....5:20:18 (28,537)
Gill, David K....4:32:16 (19,853)
Gill, David P....4:38:05 (21,251)
Gill, James S....3:16:43 (2,844)
Gill, Michael B....4:13:09 (14,888)
Gill, Parmjit S....4:18:18 (16,183)
Gill, Ray....4:33:31 (20,138)
Gill, Raymond I....5:29:20 (29,460)
Gill, Richard....4:05:15 (12,971)
Gill, Robert N....3:01:56 (1,368)
Gill, Simon....4:10:57 (14,315)
Gill, Simon M....6:00:43 (31,590)
Gill, Tallan M....4:13:11 (14,897)

Gillard, David J	4:01:33	(12,158)
Gilleen, John	4:49:46	(23,803)
Gilles, Daniel M	5:08:19	(27,052)
Gillespie, Andrew J	3:33:50	(5,454)
Gillespie, Andrew J	4:27:14	(18,564)
Gillespie, Charles	3:52:23	(9,466)
Gillespie, Frank G	3:57:09	(10,902)
Gillespie, Gordon M	3:21:56	(3,526)
Gillespie, Joe R	3:37:59	(6,220)
Gillespie, Peter R	2:53:33	(700)
Gillett, Daniel J	2:53:14	(685)
Gillett, Edward S	3:27:14	(4,276)
Gillett, Peter	3:31:56	(5,148)
Gillett, Philip L	3:49:38	(8,780)
Gillies, Julian R	4:37:33	(21,125)
Gillies, Robert	3:18:05	(3,009)
Gillies, Stuart G	4:41:35	(22,008)
Gilligan, Jon	4:27:33	(18,638)
Gilliland, Mark F	4:57:45	(25,445)
Gilling, Jonathan C	2:42:02	(249)
Gilliver, Matthew G	4:57:53	(25,475)
Gillman, Chris	5:19:06	(28,385)
Gillon, Charles A	3:22:13	(3,558)
Gillon, Jasneet	4:42:17	(22,172)
Gillon, Nav	4:27:57	(18,737)
Gillooly, Timothy J	4:40:14	(21,720)
Gillott, Seb D	3:56:45	(10,766)
Gillott, Stuart J	4:31:34	(19,686)
Gillson, Stephen P	3:27:15	(4,280)
Gilman, Andrew C	4:17:19	(15,933)
Gilmore, Cormac J	4:52:39	(24,393)
Gilmore, Stephen	5:08:03	(27,014)
Gilmore, Steve	3:57:37	(11,051)
Gilmour, Duncan N	3:51:58	(9,356)
Gilpin, John R	3:59:22	(11,630)
Gilroy, Caspar	4:45:20	(22,870)
Gilroy, Francis J	3:09:35	(2,023)
Gimeno, José Ignacio	3:25:28	(4,001)
Ginevro, Oliviero	3:54:18	(10,004)
Ginn, Andrew P	4:19:34	(16,497)
Ginn, Richard C	3:20:28	(3,336)
Ginnaw, Gary R	4:39:18	(21,514)
Giovannini, Luca	2:58:40	(1,090)
Girard, Thierry	3:51:54	(9,334)
Girardi, Pietro	5:09:04	(27,155)
Gireau, Daniel	5:16:22	(28,054)
Girlanda, Raffaele	3:15:35	(2,726)
Girling, Russell W	3:41:55	(7,011)
Girling, Simon N	3:40:57	(6,793)
Girondier, Jacques	3:25:55	(4,061)
Giroux, Ward W	4:32:10	(19,825)
Gisby, Matthew T	3:51:15	(9,160)
Gisby, Robin W	4:06:56	(13,333)
Gisby, Simon J	3:41:47	(6,983)
Gittins, Paul	3:04:32	(1,552)
Giuseppetti, Fernando	5:52:38	(31,203)
Given, Paul A	2:46:00	(382)
Gjini, James	3:31:23	(5,050)
Gjorloff, Lars	5:23:34	(28,892)
Gladkow, Alexei S	4:07:54	(13,581)
Gladstone, David R	3:44:35	(7,591)
Gladwin, Harry J	4:42:35	(22,235)
Gladwin, Philip P	4:46:18	(23,075)
Glancy, Stephen	3:46:02	(7,907)
Glass, Andy J	3:27:30	(4,334)
Glass, David	4:04:58	(12,912)
Glass, Geoff	4:21:56	(17,095)
Glass, Ian P	3:36:27	(5,925)
Glass, James	4:47:29	(23,317)
Glassock, Stephen M	5:18:59	(28,370)
Glasson, Richard	3:48:53	(8,603)
Glaysher, Stefan N	2:52:37	(656)
Glazebrook, Roger L	5:39:39	(30,334)
Gleadall, Stephen	3:31:38	(5,094)
Gledhill, Andrew M	4:33:42	(20,188)
Gledhill, Liam F	3:55:07	(10,250)
Gledhill, Marc S	6:10:11	(31,930)
Gleed, Ian P	4:34:03	(20,267)
Gleed, Kevin P	4:14:51	(15,298)
Gleeson, Alan	4:36:03	(20,736)
Gleeson, Declan V	5:37:32	(30,171)
Gleeson, Michael J	4:12:24	(14,681)
Gleicher, Adam J	4:34:38	(20,395)
Glen, Andrew	3:05:20	(1,612)
Glen, John T	5:27:42	(29,293)
Glendinning, Marcus J	5:22:19	(28,757)
Glenister, Graham	3:57:41	(11,067)
Glenn, Anthony J	5:40:17	(30,383)
Glennon, Guy W	3:18:02	(3,002)
Glenny, Alexander C	4:53:07	(24,485)
Glew, David V	5:38:34	(30,257)
Glew, Ramsay M	3:26:40	(4,187)
Glinka, Arkadiusz	4:30:02	(19,305)
Glock, Hans F	3:22:45	(3,628)
Glossop, Peter	4:34:28	(20,356)
Gloster, James	3:59:10	(11,563)
Gloudemans, Kyle M	5:23:08	(28,847)
Glover, Adrian D	4:45:19	(22,867)
Glover, Brian R	4:32:56	(19,987)
Glover, Graeme	3:54:03	(9,930)
Glover, Ian	3:02:05	(1,383)
Glover, Lee A	4:28:38	(18,929)
Glover, Mark J	3:55:39	(10,416)
Glover, Mark T	4:20:17	(16,678)
Glover, Martin J	3:20:27	(3,332)
Glover, Nicholas	5:36:23	(30,088)
Glyn, Caspar	4:28:29	(18,894)
Glynn, Matthew E	3:12:08	(2,292)
Glynn, Paul M	5:16:35	(28,082)
Glynn, Stephen C	3:28:49	(4,578)
Goakes, Andy	4:00:12	(11,864)
Goalen, Iain M	3:48:48	(8,578)
Goasdoue, Yves	3:51:00	(9,100)
Goblet D Alviella, Charles N	4:10:07	(14,127)
Godbee, Peter J	3:56:32	(10,694)
Godber, Matthew J	3:45:40	(7,841)
Goddard, Alan J	4:54:13	(24,732)
Goddard, Craig J	3:58:20	(11,280)
Goddard, Mark S	3:01:33	(1,342)
Goddard, Paul E	3:31:24	(5,055)
Goddard, Robert D	4:28:17	(18,833)
Goddard, Tom M	4:13:44	(15,010)
Goddard, William R	5:22:14	(28,745)
Godden, Ian D	3:13:27	(2,459)
Godden, James P	3:06:03	(1,673)
Godden, Keith R	3:43:04	(7,255)
Godfrey, Bruce C	4:40:43	(21,831)
Godfrey, Martin D	4:34:32	(20,371)
Godfrey, Peter	4:11:29	(14,456)
Godley, John	3:27:24	(4,314)
Godley, Mark A	3:01:44	(1,352)
Godowin, Neil	4:54:07	(24,700)
Goerlich, Oliver	4:08:34	(13,761)
Goessweiner, Herwig C	3:40:36	(6,728)
Goetschi, Bernard	3:38:29	(6,324)
Goff, Tim R	4:53:54	(24,660)
Goford, Giles J	3:58:07	(11,195)
Goglio, Piero	4:56:59	(25,307)
Gohring, Heinz	3:47:57	(8,374)
Going, David	4:01:16	(12,109)
Gold, Damian	3:12:12	(2,306)
Gold, Daniel	3:33:42	(5,438)
Gold, David A	4:03:54	(12,690)
Gold, Paul A	3:56:14	(10,603)
Goldberg, James E	4:54:11	(24,724)
Golden, Brian C	2:44:20	(324)
Golden, Peter	3:55:48	(10,479)
Goldie, Chris	4:07:07	(13,377)
Goldie, Mark A	3:14:33	(2,603)
Goldie-Scot, Duncan J	3:45:51	(7,878)
Goldin, Adam J	4:35:37	(20,632)
Golding, Andrew	4:20:22	(16,700)
Golding, Clive J	3:36:18	(5,895)
Golding, John F	3:23:10	(3,672)
Golding, Stuart	4:34:50	(20,444)
Golds, Nigel J	6:56:28	(32,847)
Goldsbrough, James	4:05:03	(12,928)
Goldsmid, Robert R	3:56:03	(10,552)
Goldsmith, Crispin	4:13:07	(14,878)
Goldsmith, Stuart G	4:16:35	(15,747)
Goldsmith, Tim	4:15:07	(15,372)
Goldstone, Simon L	4:32:58	(19,997)
Goldsworthy-Trapp, Maurice A	4:23:43	(17,565)
Goldthorp, Alan	4:14:11	(15,137)
Goldwater, Jonathan A	3:46:58	(8,112)
Golebiewski, Edward	3:29:17	(4,671)
Goligher, Scott	4:12:56	(14,820)
Golisz, Kamil	4:44:25	(22,662)
Golledge, Nicholas J	3:57:29	(11,008)
Gollogly, Brendan R	4:29:25	(19,150)
Gomersall, Richard	4:15:02	(15,349)
Gomez, Juan A	2:42:53	(282)
Gomez, Matt L	4:56:20	(25,172)
Gomez-Heredia, Fernando	3:06:07	(1,678)
Gompertz, Simon M	3:54:59	(10,196)
Goncalves, Albino	4:17:57	(16,095)
Gonde, Chris	3:41:24	(6,895)
Goniszewski, Jan	5:57:11	(31,415)
Gonzalez, Carlos	4:29:41	(19,222)
Gonzalez, Miguel A	3:34:11	(5,511)
Gonzalez, Pablo	3:47:37	(8,276)
Gonzalez, Paul J	4:24:27	(17,789)
Gonzalez, Richard D	5:04:31	(26,528)
Gonzalez, Silvio	3:21:19	(3,442)
Gooch, Clive A	4:17:04	(15,877)
Gooch, Warwick	3:40:54	(6,783)
Good, Christopher R	3:31:42	(5,101)
Goodair, Alec N	5:10:15	(27,298)
Goodall, Colin R	4:56:06	(25,119)
Goodall, Malcolm	3:16:03	(2,784)
Goodall, Malcolm A	5:40:24	(30,389)
Goodall, Terence V	5:00:36	(25,985)
Goodall, Thomas	4:43:52	(22,537)
Goodbun, Mark	4:14:25	(15,185)
Goodchild, Mark A	3:36:01	(5,837)
Goodchild, Nicholas J	3:42:18	(7,079)
Goodchild, Philip M	3:19:46	(3,225)
Goodchild, Robert C	4:47:49	(23,386)
Goode, Philip	3:08:20	(1,889)
Goode, Tom	5:31:48	(29,725)
Gooder, Stephen A	4:40:38	(21,816)
Gooderick, Robert L	5:36:22	(30,086)
Gooderson, Ross J	4:52:18	(24,307)
Goodeve, Andrew	4:34:48	(20,436)
Goodfellow, Peter B	3:05:46	(1,639)
Goodfellow, Stephen C	4:24:40	(17,864)
Goodfield, Paul M	3:55:52	(10,496)
Gooding, Michael J	3:07:32	(1,807)
Goodliff, David M	6:22:08	(32,294)
Goodman, Ashley J	4:04:38	(12,837)
Goodman, Robbie P	4:29:01	(19,031)
Goodman, Simon J	4:12:58	(14,828)
Goodman, Simon R	4:02:01	(12,269)
Goodridge, Dominic	4:17:03	(15,873)
Goodridge, Ian D	5:08:38	(27,097)
Goodridge, Paul J	3:49:41	(8,793)
Goodrum, Paul J	3:11:10	(2,171)
Goodson, Andrew M	3:55:58	(10,531)
Goodson, Edward	4:36:46	(20,924)
Goodwin, Alan J	5:46:15	(30,806)
Goodwin, Andrew T	4:54:11	(24,724)
Goodwin, Ashley	5:34:54	(29,960)
Goodwin, Bernard J	3:13:12	(2,426)
Goodwin, Daniel J	6:22:44	(32,303)
Goodwin, David A	4:27:49	(18,697)
Goodwin, Geoff B	4:21:05	(16,886)
Goodwin, Julian	3:20:24	(3,326)
Goodwin, Justin S	4:28:11	(18,802)
Goodwin, Keith D	3:49:32	(8,753)
Goodwin, Leon	3:13:03	(2,406)
Goodwin, Mark H	3:38:50	(6,393)
Goodwin, Mike	4:53:57	(24,669)
Goodwin, Peter S	5:26:14	(29,144)
Goodwin, Ryan T	3:40:14	(6,663)
Goodwin, Stephen H	3:02:42	(1,418)
Goodwin, Sydney C	5:16:16	(28,037)
Goodworth, David J	3:32:54	(5,307)
Goody, Chris A	4:58:01	(25,508)
Goody, Mark J	5:34:37	(29,945)
Goody, Stephen	4:04:07	(12,744)
Googe, Michael	4:53:33	(24,581)
Goombes, Timothy G	4:27:14	(18,564)
Gopal, Daniel	4:35:04	(20,504)
Gordon, Adrian T	4:10:14	(14,156)
Gordon, Aidan J	4:53:35	(24,592)
Gordon, Charlie E	4:57:18	(25,368)
Gordon, Dominic A	4:25:18	(18,054)
Gordon, Jeffrey	4:08:34	(13,761)
Gordon, Keith	4:09:25	(13,969)

Gordon, Keith D 4:47:04 (23,226)
Gordon, Paul A 4:30:39 (19,462)
Gordon, Rob M 4:43:17 (22,387)
Gordon-Brown, Paul D 3:47:50 (8,336)
Gordonshute, David..........4:02:35 (12,395)
Gore, Jonathan G..........2:53:18 (688)
Gorin, Pascal 3:20:37 (3,350)
Gorman, Anthony J..........4:54:33 (24,792)
Gorman, David..........4:15:00 (15,338)
Gorman, Denis..........3:03:04 (1,450)
Gorman, Douglas R 3:55:30 (10,374)
Gorman, Justin S..........4:26:15 (18,323)
Gorman, Kieran P..........4:32:03 (19,801)
Gorman, Martin 3:48:13 (8,434)
Gorman, Nigel..........3:39:12 (6,475)
Gorman, Patrick M 3:22:16 (3,566)
Gorman, Thomas..........5:05:37 (26,655)
Gormley, Eugene M..........4:09:27 (13,981)
Gornowicz, Tomasz..........4:21:10 (16,908)
Gorozpe, Arturo..........4:07:30 (13,475)
Gorringe, Benjamin M..........4:38:52 (21,406)
Gorringe, Darren A..........4:50:45 (23,992)
Gorst, Richard T..........2:47:37 (442)
Gorton, Michael J..........4:04:36 (12,831)
Gosbee, Norman..........3:55:39 (10,416)
Gosden, Mark S..........5:43:19 (30,594)
Gosling, Christopher P..........4:47:26 (23,304)
Gosling, Gary R..........3:37:34 (6,145)
Gosling, William S..........3:58:32 (11,350)
Gosnell, Andy..........3:20:50 (3,382)
Gosney, Max L..........3:12:00 (2,276)
Goss, James S..........3:37:27 (6,121)
Goss, Paul D..........3:50:39 (9,016)
Goss, Reginald W..........4:48:55 (23,632)
Goss, Stuart D..........3:55:35 (10,399)
Gossage, Alan C..........6:13:52 (32,045)
Gothard, Maxwell..........6:08:44 (31,884)
Gottfredsson, Magnus..........3:04:28 (1,541)
Gottlieb, Craig H..........5:50:36 (31,115)
Goudin, Franck..........3:24:04 (3,803)
Gough, Carl A..........3:46:38 (8,043)
Gough, James..........5:03:09 (26,335)
Gough, Kenneth..........4:02:17 (12,328)
Gough, Mike..........4:02:17 (12,328)
Gough, Paul..........3:40:35 (6,726)
Gough, Robert J..........5:21:56 (28,709)
Goughlan, Kevin G..........4:25:53 (18,224)
Gould, Bill G..........5:33:37 (29,860)
Gould, Bruce K..........8:35:50 (33,210)
Gould, Henry H..........4:19:48 (16,552)
Gould, Jeremy J..........4:35:18 (20,553)
Gould, Leo A..........4:03:56 (12,702)
Gould, Norman S..........8:35:51 (33,211)
Goulding, Steven R..........4:14:10 (15,133)
Gourlay, David J..........3:36:55 (6,024)
Goverdhan, Srini..........6:16:15 (32,126)
Govier, Antony D..........4:58:29 (25,602)
Govier, Jamie M..........3:05:48 (1,642)
Gow, Chris W..........4:07:11 (13,401)
Gowans, Sonny D..........3:39:26 (6,529)
Gowar, Michael P..........3:52:35 (9,515)
Gower, Matt R..........3:13:00 (2,397)
Gower, Simon P..........3:43:42 (7,389)
Gower, Steve..........4:46:48 (23,171)
Gowers, Richard W..........3:32:09 (5,190)
Gowers, Stephen J..........4:01:24 (12,133)
Gowland, James..........4:42:53 (22,301)
Goy, Adam J..........4:46:14 (23,056)
Grace, Anthony S..........2:51:52 (630)
Grace, Colin..........3:31:50 (5,128)
Grace, Philip J..........3:41:53 (7,004)
Grace, Raymond W..........4:18:48 (16,304)
Grace, William..........4:33:10 (20,051)
Gracey, John D..........4:12:06 (14,595)
Gracia, Adrian..........5:19:23 (28,421)
Grady, David C..........4:42:58 (22,322)
Grady, Mark S..........4:08:13 (13,669)
Graf, Olivier..........3:38:55 (6,418)
Graf, Wilhelm..........3:57:39 (11,060)
Graham, Alan B..........5:06:53 (26,844)
Graham, Alexander S..........4:39:14 (21,498)
Graham, Bill..........2:50:50 (581)
Graham, Carroll..........3:42:22 (7,093)
Graham, Ewan H..........3:48:20 (8,460)
Graham, Hugh..........3:32:44 (5,284)
Graham, Ian C..........3:45:57 (7,898)
Graham, Michael P..........5:36:31 (30,098)
Graham, Neil..........3:56:50 (10,799)
Graham, Ray K..........4:06:40 (13,265)
Graham, Rod D..........4:39:16 (21,505)
Graham, Steven E..........4:45:21 (22,874)
Graham, Stuart..........4:03:59 (12,710)
Graham, Tim J..........3:23:59 (3,790)
Graham, Warren V..........4:24:43 (17,875)
Graham-Smith, James A..........3:41:14 (6,858)
Grahan, Kieron L..........4:39:58 (21,668)
Grainger, James B..........4:29:15 (19,102)
Grainger, Richard J..........5:08:00 (27,005)
Grainger, Steve..........2:53:27 (697)
Graley, Christopher D..........4:10:28 (14,206)
Granby, Mark L..........3:40:57 (6,793)
Grandison, James W..........5:58:10 (31,467)
Grandison, Rowen D..........3:16:59 (2,875)
Grange, Ian V..........4:00:36 (11,948)
Granger, Andrew D..........5:06:39 (26,809)
Granier, Olivier D..........5:28:35 (29,380)
Grant, Daniel J..........3:51:45 (9,287)
Grant, David B..........5:42:28 (30,532)
Grant, Eugene J..........2:51:07 (599)
Grant, Frank..........4:52:07 (24,275)
Grant, James J..........4:15:49 (15,552)
Grant, Ken P..........4:59:26 (25,767)
Grant, Lee..........4:31:33 (19,681)
Grant, Mick J..........3:39:27 (6,535)
Grant, Peter..........4:22:06 (17,146)
Grant, Robert A..........5:04:22 (26,499)
Grant, Stephen P..........3:52:52 (9,585)
Grant, Stewart G..........4:33:20 (20,092)
Grasset, Christopher J..........4:53:40 (24,610)
Grassetto, Alessandro..........4:15:30 (15,476)
Gratton, Mark K..........4:38:01 (21,227)
Graveney, Timothy J..........4:37:32 (21,117)
Graves, Daniel M..........5:18:55 (28,361)
Graves, Derek R..........3:38:46 (6,380)
Graves, Ian C..........4:29:28 (19,167)
Graves, Markus..........6:19:06 (32,206)
Graves, Paul M..........3:05:27 (1,621)
Gravestock, Mark..........3:49:37 (8,775)
Gravis, Craig B..........4:23:46 (17,578)
Gray, Adam D..........3:57:41 (11,067)
Gray, Andrew C..........6:52:07 (32,783)
Gray, Andrew R..........3:58:59 (11,500)
Gray, Anthony D..........3:18:30 (3,065)
Gray, Brendan P..........4:51:57 (24,242)
Gray, Chris J..........4:14:09 (15,122)
Gray, Christopher D..........3:30:01 (4,829)
Gray, Craig P..........3:10:31 (2,117)
Gray, David R..........4:37:42 (21,160)
Gray, James C..........4:28:53 (18,991)
Gray, Jamie..........4:45:01 (22,791)
Gray, John A..........4:01:38 (12,179)
Gray, Joseph B..........4:16:17 (15,664)
Gray, Lee..........5:24:24 (28,983)
Gray, Malcolm J..........6:30:13 (32,454)
Gray, Matthew..........3:31:33 (5,073)
Gray, Matthew A..........4:50:27 (23,935)
Gray, Neil..........3:23:54 (3,775)
Gray, Patrick J..........4:40:31 (21,791)
Gray, Peter..........4:40:21 (21,741)
Gray, Richard..........4:57:26 (25,386)
Gray, Richard S..........3:32:00 (5,158)
Gray, Robert..........5:11:13 (27,415)
Gray, Ronald A..........7:26:25 (33,078)
Gray, Sam M..........3:37:15 (6,082)
Gray, Simon O..........4:40:30 (21,777)
Gray, Steve C..........5:24:00 (28,936)
Gray, Stuart..........6:55:33 (32,833)
Gray, Stuart D..........4:47:28 (23,311)
Gray, Terence A..........3:40:45 (6,752)
Gray, Trevor..........6:02:46 (31,670)
Graybrook, Richard H..........3:54:52 (10,165)
Graziosi, Max..........5:07:06 (26,878)
Grazzini, Romeo..........3:14:22 (2,579)
Greaves, Andrew..........5:34:35 (29,940)
Greaves, Andrew J..........4:29:27 (19,160)
Greaves, Jonathan M..........4:55:10 (24,928)
Greaves, Mark F..........3:12:13 (2,311)
Greaves, Martyn J..........3:57:41 (11,067)
Greaves, Paul..........3:48:31 (8,504)
Greaves, Paul M..........3:00:10 (1,242)
Greaves, Philip A..........4:20:51 (16,820)
Greaves, Robert C..........4:16:14 (15,652)
Greaves, Stuart..........4:37:24 (21,086)
Grecu, Tudor..........4:31:41 (19,719)
Green, Aidan C..........3:45:08 (7,715)
Green, Alan D..........3:13:56 (2,517)
Green, Andy J..........4:08:40 (13,781)
Green, Ben J..........4:39:52 (21,645)
Green, Benjamin R..........3:57:46 (11,100)
Green, Carle J..........2:48:12 (459)
Green, Charles R..........3:12:13 (2,311)
Green, Charles R..........4:33:52 (20,221)
Green, Christopher N..........5:41:50 (30,488)
Green, Christopher S..........3:28:03 (4,413)
Green, Clive A..........4:17:01 (15,867)
Green, Colin..........6:14:19 (32,061)
Green, Daniel..........5:31:01 (29,654)
Green, Dave..........3:50:45 (9,045)
Green, David..........3:03:57 (1,510)
Green, David C..........4:54:09 (24,712)
Green, David D..........5:48:43 (30,981)
Green, Gary..........3:55:56 (10,519)
Green, Gary A..........4:50:46 (23,995)
Green, Geoffrey H..........5:47:05 (30,868)
Green, James..........4:26:45 (18,452)
Green, James B..........3:02:25 (1,401)
Green, James O..........4:03:37 (12,629)
Green, Jerry..........4:03:47 (12,673)
Green, John J..........4:05:18 (12,978)
Green, John K..........2:53:03 (681)
Green, Jonathan D..........4:38:17 (21,299)
Green, Jonathan P..........4:51:05 (24,057)
Green, Lucas..........3:40:44 (6,749)
Green, Malcolm..........4:10:47 (14,270)
Green, Marcus C..........4:47:34 (23,339)
Green, Mark A..........4:21:51 (17,076)
Green, Michael..........2:19:14 (24)
Green, Michael D..........5:23:19 (28,873)
Green, Michal G..........3:13:08 (2,418)
Green, Mick..........2:59:22 (1,184)
Green, Mike D..........3:21:40 (3,495)
Green, Nick D..........3:49:54 (8,846)
Green, Nick E..........3:52:52 (9,585)
Green, Nigel J..........3:53:48 (9,861)
Green, Paul D..........3:13:57 (2,521)
Green, Paul L..........4:40:48 (21,855)
Green, Peter..........2:59:53 (1,230)
Green, Robert J..........4:08:29 (13,738)
Green, Sam..........3:06:00 (1,667)
Green, Sean S..........4:51:21 (24,105)
Green, Shane A..........3:54:37 (10,083)
Green, Shaun F..........4:37:10 (21,017)
Green, Simon J..........4:35:17 (20,548)
Green, Stephen..........4:45:13 (22,840)
Green, Thomas C..........3:00:31 (1,273)
Greenall, Daniel..........4:51:55 (24,236)
Greenall, John C..........3:29:38 (4,749)
Greenaway, Alex B..........3:53:43 (9,827)
Greene, Gavin R..........3:22:45 (3,628)
Greene, Harvey..........6:12:16 (31,995)
Greene, Jonathan..........3:57:24 (10,979)
Greene, Martin E..........5:26:03 (29,131)
Greene, Terence..........3:53:36 (9,793)
Greener, John S..........3:54:08 (9,953)
Greenfield, Andrew D..........4:37:25 (21,090)
Greenfield, David A..........4:15:26 (15,460)
Greenfield, Philip..........3:46:08 (7,929)
Greenfield, Sam J..........4:48:14 (23,477)
Greenhalf, Richard W..........4:00:32 (11,943)
Greenhalgh, Andrew F..........4:23:30 (17,505)
Greenhalgh, Clifford..........4:42:54 (22,309)
Greenham, David H..........4:09:46 (14,048)
Greenhow, James H..........4:54:45 (24,828)
Greening, Martin R..........6:49:14 (32,751)
Greenland, Richard D..........4:34:27 (20,350)
Greenshields, Martin J..........3:45:37 (7,826)
Greenslade, Adam..........4:30:19 (19,380)
Greenslade, Oliver..........3:59:55 (11,790)
Greenslade, Tim N..........5:28:40 (29,397)

Greenup, Julian I 4:05:01 (12,920)
Greenwood, Andrew J 3:39:31 (6,543)
Greenwood, David J 4:50:28 (23,939)
Greenwood, Jonathan 3:58:34 (11,362)
Greenwood, Keith J 4:09:48 (14,061)
Greenwood, Mark A 2:45:45 (363)
Greenwood, Paul 4:10:02 (14,107)
Greenwood, Paul 4:41:04 (21,910)
Greenwood, Paul A 3:25:22 (3,991)
Greenwood, Peter 4:43:25 (22,414)
Greenwood, Roger V 5:54:33 (31,289)
Greeson, Warren A 3:24:38 (3,886)
Greevy, John 4:13:32 (14,962)
Gregg, William S 3:38:14 (6,278)
Gregor, Daniel M 4:05:13 (12,963)
Gregor, Zdenek J 3:54:34 (10,069)
Gregory, Bruce T 4:24:32 (17,809)
Gregory, Darren A 5:49:07 (31,007)
Gregory, David A 2:48:51 (486)
Gregory, David K 3:49:28 (8,734)
Gregory, George N 4:18:29 (16,228)
Gregory, Graham N 3:42:57 (7,221)
Gregory, Guy 4:23:45 (17,574)
Gregory, Mark J 3:02:28 (1,403)
Gregory, Michael J 3:54:08 (9,953)
Gregory, Michael P 3:32:57 (5,315)
Gregory, Nicholas A 3:11:53 (2,256)
Gregory, Paul 5:02:54 (26,304)
Gregory, Paul F 2:42:23 (258)
Gregory, Peter A 3:57:08 (10,893)
Gregory, Stephen R 4:17:10 (15,898)
Gregory, Stewart J 2:32:36 (87)
Gregory, Trevor P 3:53:29 (9,762)
Grehan, Mark 3:23:59 (3,790)
Greig, Donald B 4:20:27 (16,723)
Greig, Jonathan M 3:05:59 (1,665)
Greig, William N 4:12:59 (14,831)
Greiss, Rafik 3:26:20 (4,124)
Grenier, Stephen M 4:36:05 (20,746)
Gresswell, David J 3:17:45 (2,972)
Gresty, Paul J 3:17:03 (2,882)
Grew, Adama D 3:38:31 (6,329)
Grewar, Donald C 3:55:02 (10,217)
Grey, William M 3:07:43 (1,826)
Greyling, Robert R 4:27:45 (18,684)
Gribbin, Graham 5:34:45 (29,950)
Grice, Andrew 4:10:51 (14,294)
Gridley, David P 3:58:59 (11,500)
Gridley, Marc 3:47:02 (8,127)
Gridley, Stephen A 4:45:37 (22,930)
Grierson, James 3:39:18 (6,500)
Grieve, Craig W 3:37:21 (6,105)
Grieve, Graham D 3:13:26 (2,457)
Griffen, Richard D 4:35:46 (20,666)
Griffies, Miles J 4:25:28 (18,110)
Griffin, Andrew G 4:17:02 (15,870)
Griffin, Charles 3:44:29 (7,563)
Griffin, Danny 5:39:23 (30,309)
Griffin, Dick 4:25:20 (18,067)
Griffin, Garry E 4:37:07 (21,007)
Griffin, John 2:52:00 (634)
Griffin, Julian L 3:51:45 (9,287)
Griffin, Kenneth M 4:14:58 (15,325)
Griffin, Liam 3:40:41 (6,742)
Griffin, Paul W 5:55:36 (31,336)
Griffin, Richard F 4:29:02 (19,034)
Griffin, Roger F 3:33:10 (5,347)
Griffin, Simon B 3:51:30 (9,215)
Griffin, Steven M 4:42:29 (22,212)
Griffin, Thomas 5:22:37 (28,789)
Griffin, Tom R 3:20:05 (3,277)
Griffith, Jackson E 3:57:05 (10,870)
Griffith, John O 3:29:13 (4,658)
Griffiths, Alan 4:42:21 (22,190)
Griffiths, Alan P 3:42:29 (7,111)
Griffiths, Andrew 5:33:44 (29,872)
Griffiths, Antony D 4:01:58 (12,255)
Griffiths, Bryn L 7:03:59 (32,929)
Griffiths, David J 4:00:21 (11,902)
Griffiths, David R 4:13:37 (14,979)
Griffiths, Gareth 4:35:17 (20,548)
Griffiths, Gregory G 3:09:44 (2,039)
Griffiths, Hugh A 4:29:28 (19,167)
Griffiths, Huw A 4:20:17 (16,678)
Griffiths, Huw D 3:32:13 (5,206)
Griffiths, John B 5:57:46 (31,442)
Griffiths, John R 5:30:33 (29,598)
Griffiths, Keith I 4:24:01 (17,661)
Griffiths, Kevin J 6:26:41 (32,395)
Griffiths, Leigh A 4:18:43 (16,286)
Griffiths, Mark A 3:53:21 (9,731)
Griffiths, Mark D 3:47:14 (8,182)
Griffiths, Michael 5:22:53 (28,815)
Griffiths, Mike J 3:33:55 (5,468)
Griffiths, Neville 3:14:49 (2,644)
Griffiths, Paul D 2:44:25 (327)
Griffiths, Paul W 3:10:31 (2,117)
Griffiths, Peter 3:14:30 (2,596)
Griffiths, Robert E 4:21:47 (17,058)
Griffiths, Timothy E 4:28:19 (18,847)
Griffiths, Tom L 4:35:57 (20,709)
Grigg, Duncan J 4:19:38 (16,509)
Grigg, Iain F 4:49:24 (23,734)
Griggs, Michael 5:06:21 (26,761)
Griggs, Thomas C 3:56:12 (10,593)
Grigny, Olivier 3:00:23 (1,262)
Grigoleit, Peter M 3:19:42 (3,213)
Grill, David R 5:02:52 (26,299)
Grillo, James W 4:38:05 (21,251)
Grimault, Fabrice 3:26:34 (4,168)
Grimes, Anthony J 3:38:36 (6,349)
Grimes, Kevin J 4:13:19 (14,920)
Grimes, Norman S 4:50:50 (24,010)
Grimes, Sean M 3:57:55 (11,139)
Grimmer, Rudolf K 4:29:56 (19,276)
Grimmette, John A 4:29:14 (19,093)
Grimmond, Adrian 3:22:35 (3,608)
Grimmond, David M 4:12:23 (14,679)
Grimsey, James A 4:46:03 (23,016)
Grimshaw, Dave 4:39:11 (21,486)
Grimshaw, Grahame D 4:03:23 (12,574)
Grimwood, Graham A 4:13:35 (14,973)
Grimwood, Mark A 3:59:04 (11,534)
Grindu, Louis 4:04:41 (12,853)
Grinshaw, Kevin W 4:23:48 (17,589)
Grinsted, James M 4:10:41 (14,245)
Grinter, Carl E 3:21:31 (3,472)
Grist, Anthony P 4:59:18 (25,743)
Grist, Kevin R 3:15:06 (2,671)
Grist, Stuart M 4:39:42 (21,599)
Gristwood, Andrew T 3:22:37 (3,616)
Groce, Ken W 5:46:21 (30,814)
Grocott, Anthony 5:16:12 (28,031)
Grocott, David G 5:17:46 (28,216)
Grocutt, Anthony E 3:55:50 (10,485)
Grodseth, Henrik 2:24:59 (43)
Groen, Maarten C 4:37:15 (21,045)
Groesz, Hans-Juergen 3:46:00 (7,902)
Grogan, Stephen B 3:21:29 (3,468)
Grondal, Hallgrimur H 3:55:02 (10,217)
Groom, Christopher F 4:55:50 (25,061)
Groom, Gary 3:28:39 (4,541)
Groom, Jon 4:21:07 (16,897)
Groom, Stephen 3:22:13 (3,558)
Groom, Steven 3:12:48 (2,376)
Groombridge, Christopher J 3:53:34 (9,782)
Groombridge, Michael J 4:55:24 (24,983)
Groombridge, Stephen P 2:59:12 (1,164)
Groppe, Markus 6:04:26 (31,742)
Groskamp, Pieter 3:17:02 (2,880)
Groso, Vincent 3:52:43 (9,551)
Grosse, Joshua 3:36:01 (5,837)
Grosskopf, Harry 3:26:18 (4,114)
Grosso, Giulio G 3:55:15 (10,298)
Grosvenor, Michael W 4:52:58 (24,448)
Grosvenor, Phillip A 5:01:38 (26,124)
Grotto, Antonio 3:22:14 (3,563)
Grout, Ian D 4:51:26 (24,132)
Grout, Steve R 3:33:34 (5,410)
Grove, Andrew 3:29:45 (4,771)
Grove, Christopher J 4:03:20 (12,559)
Grove, Darren 3:35:00 (5,661)
Grove, Nigel E 2:55:04 (792)
Grove, Shaun D 3:57:09 (10,902)
Grove, Terry 4:25:18 (18,054)
Grove, Thomas H 4:01:09 (12,089)
Grover, David 3:18:43 (3,096)
Grover, John M 3:27:35 (4,348)
Groves, Anthony 4:03:27 (12,592)
Groves, Glen 2:28:58 (62)
Groves, Ian J 3:24:28 (3,857)
Groves, Peter J 4:07:08 (13,385)
Groves, Richard J 4:29:20 (19,130)
Groves, William R 4:59:35 (25,807)
Grubb, Andrew D 3:11:14 (2,188)
Grubb, Martyn P 3:00:51 (1,292)
Grubb, Timothy J 4:17:37 (16,022)
Grundy, Alex J 3:21:37 (3,486)
Grundy, Andrew S 3:49:29 (8,743)
Grunmill, Wayne E 5:01:16 (26,084)
Grunwald, Thomas S 4:35:20 (20,563)
Guaschi, Darren 4:38:53 (21,413)
Gubbins, Matthew J 4:11:30 (14,459)
Guccione, Edward J 4:09:09 (13,892)
Gudgeon, Shane A 3:05:23 (1,617)
Gudka, Piyush 3:35:02 (5,669)
Gudmundsson, Einar R 4:09:27 (13,981)
Guedes, Paulo J 3:12:35 (2,351)
Gueit, Jean-Claude 4:15:38 (15,503)
Guenaricheau, Sam-James 4:39:28 (21,555)
Guendouz, Omar 4:57:51 (25,463)
Guerin, Jean Marc 2:58:06 (1,032)
Guest, Ian S 4:59:29 (25,784)
Guest, Simon L 3:39:12 (6,475)
Gueutal, Pierre 3:35:06 (5,693)
Gugelmann, Christoph 4:37:51 (21,188)
Guglielmi, Thomas A 5:27:08 (29,238)
Guidotti, Antonio Umberto 4:13:04 (14,862)
Guihen, Patrick 5:07:38 (26,954)
Guilloux, Loic 3:38:29 (6,324)
Guinan, Paul E 2:39:46 (206)
Guiney, William F 3:17:35 (2,950)
Guire, Russell 4:25:47 (18,189)
Guiseley, Andrew 2:59:08 (1,152)
Guitard, Ludoviv 4:01:41 (12,187)
Guitton, Dominique 3:52:30 (9,496)
Guitton, Serge 4:33:32 (20,142)
Guiver, Richard J 3:06:31 (1,711)
Gulc, Peter 3:42:12 (7,065)
Guldner, Bernd 3:41:36 (6,945)
Gulliver, Andrew 6:40:13 (32,614)
Gulliver, John P 4:31:00 (19,533)
Gulsin, Gaurav 3:28:42 (4,556)
Gumbleton, Michael J 3:42:13 (7,069)
Gumbley, Edward W 3:17:04 (2,885)
Gummer, Matthew 3:40:27 (6,703)
Gundry, Martin 3:38:42 (6,365)
Gunn, Graham 4:22:53 (17,339)
Gunn, Mark L 4:22:54 (17,345)
Gunn, Peter R 3:22:17 (3,571)
Gunn, Stephen R 4:19:16 (16,413)
Gunnarsson, Claes 4:26:23 (18,357)
Gunnarsson, Dan 4:38:33 (21,349)
Gunnell, Julian M 3:41:06 (6,827)
Gunson, Martin D 5:53:27 (31,239)
Gunston, Andrew C 4:06:01 (13,143)
Gunton, Gary J 3:36:36 (5,958)
Gupta, Neeraj K 3:36:38 (5,962)
Gupta, Sanjay 4:52:38 (24,388)
Gurbutt, James 4:11:16 (14,406)
Gurd, Richard 2:47:19 (428)
Gurden, Matthew J 4:14:08 (15,117)
Gurnell, Adrian P 3:28:21 (4,480)
Gurnett, Tim 3:47:04 (8,140)
Gurney, Darren 3:07:07 (1,769)
Gurney, Hugh R 4:39:25 (21,548)
Gurney, Nigel J 4:20:24 (16,711)
Gurr, Stuart 2:54:19 (744)
Gurria, Angel 4:02:09 (12,296)
Gurrieri, Jonathan 4:36:36 (20,868)
Gurung, Devendra 3:53:54 (9,893)
Gush, Michael H 4:11:03 (14,346)
Gustavsson, Bernth T 3:53:28 (9,760)
Gustavsson, Thomas N 3:43:21 (7,320)
Gut, Hugo 3:06:50 (1,738)
Guthrie, Duncan 3:31:14 (5,030)
Guthrie, Matthew J 3:47:26 (8,223)
Guthrie, Neville 4:33:10 (20,051)
Guthrie, Peter 5:27:12 (29,245)

Gutternplan, Don D	4:24:10 (17,707)	
Guy, Christopher D	5:33:11 (29,830)	
Guy, David J	4:21:48 (17,062)	
Guy, John A	4:40:26 (21,756)	
Guy, Keith	4:54:03 (24,684)	
Guy, Stephen J	3:25:14 (3,968)	
Guy, Victor	7:15:57 (33,012)	
Guyatt, Robert J	4:48:17 (23,489)	
Guyon, Pierre	3:48:57 (8,620)	
Guyver, Chris J	4:48:24 (23,515)	
Gwatkin, Clive E	3:38:23 (6,301)	
Gwilliam, David J	3:50:45 (9,045)	
Gwilliam, Paul A	3:36:10 (5,868)	
Gwynne, James R	4:24:34 (17,830)	
Gwyther, Andrew G	3:28:24 (4,495)	
Gwyther, David P	4:40:37 (21,814)	
Gyles, Mike A	3:55:51 (10,490)	
Gyselinck, Dirk	4:09:34 (14,007)	
Haas, Otto K	2:46:09 (387)	
Haase, Mark P	4:24:31 (17,806)	
Haasner, Adrian	4:31:34 (19,686)	
Habberley, Scott W	3:57:16 (10,937)	
Habbestad, Olav	3:18:48 (3,106)	
Haberbauer, Christoph	3:52:39 (9,538)	
Habib, Rami	4:29:46 (19,246)	
Hack, Raymond	3:28:16 (4,456)	
Hacker, Paul	4:42:48 (22,285)	
Hacker, Peter J	4:02:29 (12,371)	
Hackett, Hugh	4:25:30 (18,118)	
Hackett, Wayne I	4:58:26 (25,594)	
Hacking, Guy C	3:32:00 (5,158)	
Hackwell, John A	4:28:22 (18,863)	
Hacquard, Eric	4:23:54 (17,623)	
Haddock, Lee P	5:18:38 (28,326)	
Haddock, Paul A	3:57:55 (11,139)	
Haden, Michael J	4:43:22 (22,404)	
Haden, Tony F	2:55:30 (815)	
Hadfield, Graham	6:45:17 (32,695)	
Hadfield, Tom D	2:39:30 (199)	
Hadjigeorgiou, George	4:53:42 (24,620)	
Hadley, Dan	3:45:17 (7,751)	
Hadley, Darren J	5:36:12 (30,071)	
Hadley, Peter E	3:22:36 (3,613)	
Hadlow, Edward	3:29:19 (4,679)	
Hadwin, Stuart	3:57:17 (10,944)	
Hafsaas, Helge	2:31:29 (78)	
Hagan, Daniel S	3:56:28 (10,676)	
Hagan, Keith H	3:46:48 (8,081)	
Hageman, Mark R	3:59:40 (11,715)	
Hagen, Divind Ravn	4:44:16 (22,629)	
Haggas, Neil	2:47:55 (450)	
Haggerty, Derek	4:47:01 (23,218)	
Haggett, Raymond	4:48:14 (23,477)	
Hagon, Daniel J	4:58:03 (25,513)	
Hahlbohn, Jens	3:54:31 (10,057)	
Hahnel, Mario	2:59:15 (1,170)	
Haigh, Jason S	3:16:47 (2,850)	
Haigh, Martin J	4:30:06 (19,324)	
Haigh, Michael D	3:57:38 (11,056)	
Haigh, Philip A	3:22:02 (3,539)	
Haigh, Robert J	4:49:57 (23,835)	
Hails, Philip J	2:44:46 (339)	
Haiman, Tamas	4:28:44 (18,956)	
Haines, Andrew J	4:12:49 (14,779)	
Haines, Dan W	4:34:52 (20,449)	
Haines, David J	5:30:33 (29,598)	
Haines, Ian	3:33:10 (5,347)	
Haines, Stephen	3:33:37 (5,424)	
Haines, Tim	3:47:56 (8,363)	
Haining, Andrew	4:25:58 (18,249)	
Haining, William	3:17:53 (2,983)	
Hainsworth, Paul J	3:09:59 (2,062)	
Hair, Ryan N	5:28:20 (29,360)	
Haire, Kenneth V	4:04:05 (12,736)	
Haith, Peter	3:49:46 (8,813)	
Hajime, Gen	4:48:31 (23,543)	
Hajji, Tim	4:39:22 (21,537)	
Hakansson, Michael	4:15:01 (15,342)	
Hal, Keith R	6:27:43 (32,418)	
Haldane, Andrew G	4:40:28 (21,763)	
Haldane, Graham C	4:25:50 (18,202)	
Hale, Darren C	3:45:04 (7,704)	
Hale, Ian	4:45:01 (22,791)	
Hale, John R	4:49:18 (23,717)	
Hales, Andrew M	4:54:44 (24,823)	
Hales, Colin S	4:14:12 (15,142)	
Hales, Jonathan P	4:30:27 (19,416)	
Hales, Kenneth H	4:47:45 (23,374)	
Hales, Matthew J	3:01:25 (1,333)	
Hales, Nigel J	5:17:11 (28,149)	
Haley, Alan K	4:37:54 (21,196)	
Haley, Lee	6:12:25 (32,002)	
Halford, Stewart M	4:01:02 (12,055)	
Halifax, Martin C	4:32:23 (19,884)	
Halkin, Cosh	5:21:27 (28,660)	
Hall, Adam D	3:56:02 (10,549)	
Hall, Alex	3:11:30 (2,215)	
Hall, Andrew	3:19:50 (3,238)	
Hall, Arnold	6:30:55 (32,474)	
Hall, Bengt	3:55:02 (10,217)	
Hall, Chris J	4:12:58 (14,828)	
Hall, Christopher	3:35:52 (5,810)	
Hall, Christopher J	3:33:02 (5,328)	
Hall, Christopher J	3:56:00 (10,543)	
Hall, Christopher R	4:28:27 (18,882)	
Hall, David A	3:12:50 (2,381)	
Hall, David J	2:42:42 (271)	
Hall, David J	3:37:57 (6,217)	
Hall, David J	4:45:01 (22,791)	
Hall, Dominic J	3:55:08 (10,255)	
Hall, Doug J	4:53:35 (24,592)	
Hall, Edward J	5:00:00 (25,884)	
Hall, Elvis	4:11:08 (14,370)	
Hall, Gareth D	4:28:42 (18,944)	
Hall, Geoffrey A	4:12:53 (14,806)	
Hall, James A	7:03:23 (32,913)	
Hall, James M	4:56:50 (25,264)	
Hall, Jason	7:05:59 (32,948)	
Hall, John	3:25:06 (3,942)	
Hall, John A	4:16:49 (15,804)	
Hall, Jonathan M	4:22:09 (17,157)	
Hall, Jonathan N	3:26:39 (4,184)	
Hall, Ken	4:19:48 (16,552)	
Hall, Kieron P	4:43:33 (22,452)	
Hall, Leigh N	3:55:21 (10,332)	
Hall, Leslie	5:17:01 (28,131)	
Hall, Martin K	2:41:31 (237)	
Hall, Matthew	3:34:53 (5,639)	
Hall, Micahel	3:06:57 (1,751)	
Hall, Michael C	3:51:26 (9,204)	
Hall, Michael D	3:50:27 (8,971)	
Hall, Michael R	5:00:10 (25,918)	
Hall, Peter	3:32:16 (5,218)	
Hall, Peter J	4:24:56 (17,938)	
Hall, Peter L	4:09:30 (13,996)	
Hall, Peter V	4:57:02 (25,319)	
Hall, Richard	4:29:23 (19,143)	
Hall, Richard A	3:39:44 (6,579)	
Hall, Richard J	5:54:06 (31,267)	
Hall, Rob	2:40:38 (221)	
Hall, Robert	4:18:11 (16,157)	
Hall, Robert E	5:32:40 (29,784)	
Hall, Sam T	4:16:55 (15,839)	
Hall, Simon	3:35:59 (5,832)	
Hall, Thomas H	3:24:07 (3,808)	
Hall, Tom I	2:59:17 (1,174)	
Halladay, Andrew P	3:54:48 (10,145)	
Hallam, Colin	3:48:12 (8,432)	
Hallam, David L	3:51:51 (9,318)	
Hallas, Steve J	2:36:34 (137)	
Hallden, Dave	3:10:22 (2,102)	
Hallett, Paul	5:03:55 (26,447)	
Hallett, Richard B	4:28:55 (18,998)	
Halliday, Andrew D	5:00:24 (25,960)	
Halliday, Neil	4:03:22 (12,570)	
Halliday, Peter	5:42:50 (30,562)	
Hallifax, Benjamin G	3:36:59 (6,037)	
Halligan, James K	3:14:34 (2,608)	
Halliwell, Gareth J	4:50:11 (23,876)	
Halliwell, Grant L	3:52:26 (9,481)	
Halliwell, John K	3:13:46 (2,498)	
Halliwell, Martin P	3:52:04 (9,375)	
Hall-Matthews, Berners	4:31:38 (19,705)	
Hallows, Jon A	4:06:18 (13,194)	
Halls, Mark A	3:03:20 (1,466)	
Halluska, Richard J	3:37:47 (6,188)	
Hallworth, Bill	4:15:34 (15,489)	
Halmshaw, Damian A	5:16:08 (28,018)	
Halpin, Alexander J	4:32:14 (19,839)	
Halsey, Glenn	5:19:21 (28,413)	
Halsey, Grant A	4:18:35 (16,252)	
Halsey, Mark I	4:43:12 (22,367)	
Halsey, Michael W	5:07:48 (26,973)	
Halsey, Stephen J	2:58:30 (1,065)	
Halstead, Peter J	3:44:13 (7,495)	
Halvatzis, Nicos A	3:16:41 (2,838)	
Halvey, Martin	2:45:56 (376)	
Ham, David W	3:53:14 (9,703)	
Hama, Tariq M	4:07:48 (13,555)	
Hamadi, Rabah	4:03:43 (12,654)	
Hamblen, Jonathan M	3:34:29 (5,560)	
Hamblin, Paul M	3:57:05 (10,870)	
Hamblin, Steven H	4:05:30 (13,022)	
Hambling, James D	4:36:46 (20,924)	
Hambling, Philip	5:04:33 (26,532)	
Hambly, Rory M	3:23:41 (3,739)	
Hamblyn, Mark A	4:04:36 (12,831)	
Hamdorff, David	3:32:25 (5,236)	
Hamer-Hodges, Gareth W	4:06:51 (13,311)	
Hamerston, Gerald J	4:18:16 (16,174)	
Hames, Michael D	3:47:40 (8,285)	
Hamill, Andrew R	3:28:29 (4,506)	
Hamilton, Alistair	3:40:53 (6,776)	
Hamilton, Anthony P	4:03:05 (12,500)	
Hamilton, Damon J	4:27:25 (18,604)	
Hamilton, David	4:56:56 (25,290)	
Hamilton, Derek J	3:55:25 (10,349)	
Hamilton, Edward	3:09:09 (1,969)	
Hamilton, Graham M	3:02:59 (1,441)	
Hamilton, Ian	4:16:20 (15,678)	
Hamilton, James	4:50:38 (23,971)	
Hamilton, James R	3:35:33 (5,759)	
Hamilton, Kevin	5:59:05 (31,506)	
Hamilton, Liam T	3:44:31 (7,570)	
Hamilton, Peter R	5:19:27 (28,428)	
Hamilton, Philip W	3:59:28 (11,662)	
Hamilton, Robert J	3:38:13 (6,270)	
Hamilton, Robin M	3:48:48 (8,578)	
Hamilton, Rod T	3:27:33 (4,342)	
Hamilton, Scott	3:57:52 (11,128)	
Hamilton, Sebastian	3:47:48 (8,326)	
Hamilton, Simon	3:33:40 (5,433)	
Hamilton, Stuart	4:32:52 (19,970)	
Hamilton-Fletcher, Adam	5:59:58 (31,560)	
Hamlbeton, Stephen W	4:34:08 (20,278)	
Hamling, Mark	3:16:26 (2,813)	
Hamlyn, Peter J	5:11:20 (27,431)	
Hammacott, Paul	4:17:41 (16,031)	
Hamment, Michael G	4:52:44 (24,405)	
Hammersley, Chris A	3:54:03 (9,930)	
Hammersley, Nigel P	3:52:36 (9,520)	
Hammond, Glyn L	3:55:00 (10,204)	
Hammond, Ian	4:04:02 (12,723)	
Hammond, John S	3:30:00 (4,827)	
Hammond, Jonathan S	4:51:30 (24,144)	
Hammond, Mark E	4:40:30 (21,777)	
Hammond, Richard B	3:17:25 (2,934)	
Hammond, Stephen M	4:00:48 (11,993)	
Hammonds, George E	5:12:54 (27,632)	
Hamon, James L	3:40:02 (6,633)	
Hamon, Patrick	3:45:05 (7,709)	
Hampe, Eberhard	4:56:32 (25,213)	
Hampshire, Graeme R	4:04:00 (12,714)	
Hampshire, Neil C	3:39:12 (6,475)	
Hampson, Andy M	4:08:25 (13,722)	
Hampson, Jonathan W	3:36:31 (5,936)	
Hampson, Michael R	4:05:18 (12,978)	
Hampton, Anthony N	3:50:33 (8,998)	
Hampton, Christopher D	3:28:21 (4,480)	
Hampton, Edward T	4:21:49 (17,067)	
Hampton, James E	3:28:20 (4,477)	
Hampton, Ray	3:17:20 (2,923)	
Hamsher, Mark W	4:44:07 (22,589)	
Hamslton, Andrew M	4:11:05 (14,354)	
Hamson, Peter J	4:09:25 (13,969)	
Hamzic, Edin	4:45:49 (22,971)	
Hanan, Tim J	4:01:14 (12,105)	
Hance, Freddie A	6:14:33 (32,070)	
Hancock, Anthony	3:26:32 (4,162)	

Hancock, Jonathan P.....3:22:25 (3,585)
Hancock, Keith G.....4:54:47 (24,840)
Hancock, Mark A.....4:39:12 (21,490)
Hancock, Nicholas D.....4:03:26 (12,589)
Hancock, Rhys G.....4:23:26 (17,478)
Hancock, Tim M.....3:47:19 (8,196)
Hancox, Grenville R.....4:19:59 (16,598)
Hancox, Robert G.....3:25:29 (4,002)
Hand, Michael.....3:21:48 (3,509)
Hand, Simon.....3:35:28 (5,745)
Handley, Fraser.....5:22:16 (28,749)
Handley, Graham.....4:08:49 (13,818)
Handley, James J.....3:45:00 (7,689)
Handley, Matt.....4:52:36 (24,380)
Handley, Matthew D.....5:28:02 (29,326)
Handley, Stephen.....3:37:17 (6,088)
Handley, Thomas M.....4:08:03 (13,628)
Handscombe, Paul.....4:51:35 (24,164)
Handslip, Nicholas F.....3:01:51 (1,359)
Handy, David.....4:34:49 (20,441)
Handy, Lionel P.....3:08:36 (1,918)
Handy, Paul.....3:50:31 (8,989)
Hanlay, Christopher J.....3:55:37 (10,409)
Hanley, Brian S.....2:36:15 (132)
Hanlon, Paul G.....4:23:46 (17,578)
Hann, Kevin P.....4:17:01 (15,867)
Hanna, Josh J.....3:39:52 (6,599)
Hanna, Mark.....3:43:28 (7,344)
Hannah, Colin D.....4:11:59 (14,569)
Hannah, David W.....4:13:03 (14,858)
Hannah, Tom.....3:24:49 (3,915)
Hannam, Scott A.....5:19:41 (28,457)
Hannan, Mark R.....4:35:40 (20,645)
Hannibal, Alan R.....3:01:36 (1,343)
Hannington, Ben.....4:49:53 (23,817)
Hannington, Janmes.....4:29:45 (19,238)
Hannington, Warren.....3:22:21 (3,577)
Hannon, Jason P.....4:11:54 (14,549)
Hannon, Martin J.....4:02:43 (12,415)
Hanratty, Daniel R.....3:34:06 (5,498)
Hansard, Mark.....4:37:47 (21,173)
Hanscomb, John W.....4:29:14 (19,093)
Hansel, John M.....4:39:03 (21,454)
Hansell, Jack W.....5:09:11 (27,170)
Hansen, Karsten R.....3:08:58 (1,952)
Hansen, Michael R.....4:12:06 (14,595)
Hansen, Paul.....3:09:56 (2,056)
Hansen, Paul S.....3:42:55 (7,212)
Hansen, Rune.....3:52:20 (9,445)
Hanson, David P.....4:34:29 (20,360)
Hanson, David P.....7:09:53 (32,975)
Hanson, Gareth M.....3:38:24 (6,303)
Hanson, James D.....4:03:03 (12,492)
Hanson, Paul.....3:59:24 (11,638)
Hanson, Paul.....4:24:19 (17,754)
Hanson, Simon T.....3:35:41 (5,783)
Hanson, Thomas.....3:22:42 (3,623)
Hanson, Thomas L.....7:37:18 (33,124)
Hanson Akins, Alexander H.....4:43:16 (22,383)
Hans-Rudolph, Weibel.....4:08:56 (13,846)
Hansson, Sten.....4:56:56 (25,290)
Hanton, Glenn M.....5:14:20 (27,817)
Haq, Jai.....4:44:40 (22,700)
Haragan, Scott.....4:01:39 (12,184)
Haraldsson, Haraldur.....3:08:14 (1,877)
Haraldsson, Jon K.....3:31:25 (5,056)
Harbon, Richard I.....3:04:30 (1,548)
Harbottle, Keith.....4:21:43 (17,026)
Hardacre, Timothy A.....3:28:40 (4,543)
Hardaker, Christopher D.....3:33:55 (5,468)
Hardaker, Steve.....3:01:44 (1,352)
Hardie, Shaun.....4:04:40 (12,847)
Hardiman, Dominic.....3:40:10 (6,652)
Hardiman, Lance S.....5:22:48 (28,811)
Harding, Alan S.....4:14:01 (15,074)
Harding, Clive G.....5:55:21 (31,319)
Harding, Harvey J.....4:32:20 (19,869)
Harding, James D.....3:29:30 (4,718)
Harding, Jason P.....3:16:19 (2,804)
Harding, John.....5:08:49 (27,120)
Harding, John A.....4:38:14 (21,287)
Harding, Jonathan.....4:36:09 (20,768)
Harding, Kevin.....5:39:30 (30,324)
Harding, Lee B.....2:52:43 (662)
Harding, Peter M.....3:53:42 (9,824)
Harding, Philip.....4:38:14 (21,287)
Harding, Robert M.....3:25:33 (4,011)
Hardman, Benjamin C.....3:55:42 (10,441)
Hardman, James C.....4:44:41 (22,707)
Hardman, Keith.....4:07:22 (13,439)
Hardman, Nigel P.....4:23:37 (17,535)
Hardman, Paul.....4:03:37 (12,629)
Hardman, Richard J.....5:31:20 (29,694)
Hardstaff, Ian N.....3:16:06 (2,788)
Hardwell, Keith J.....3:36:17 (5,891)
Hardwick, Alex J.....4:17:06 (15,886)
Hardwick, John R.....4:30:44 (19,480)
Hardwicke, Edward.....3:46:34 (8,026)
Hardwicke, Humphrey.....4:26:48 (18,464)
Hardy, Danny P.....3:43:38 (7,375)
Hardy, Geoffrey P.....4:03:42 (12,652)
Hardy, Glen G.....4:08:32 (13,750)
Hardy, John C.....4:23:03 (17,374)
Hardy, Jon A.....4:12:02 (14,580)
Hardy, Russell.....3:12:36 (2,353)
Hardy, Sean.....4:05:19 (12,982)
Hardy, Thomas A.....3:28:52 (4,595)
Hardy, Ty F.....4:02:44 (12,420)
Hardyman, Christopher J.....4:48:23 (23,510)
Hare, David N.....3:52:56 (9,604)
Hare, Phillip P.....5:43:42 (30,621)
Hare, Stephen C.....5:31:11 (29,677)
Harfield, Patrick D.....6:23:14 (32,309)
Harfield, Stephen P.....6:23:14 (32,309)
Harfst, Richard.....4:08:53 (13,830)
Hargrave, David.....3:31:50 (5,128)
Hargrave, Gordon.....5:44:05 (30,648)
Hargreaves, David.....3:39:54 (6,606)
Hargreaves, Gary D.....4:59:57 (25,879)
Hargreaves, Michael S.....4:48:39 (23,576)
Hargreaves, Richard N.....3:56:04 (10,558)
Haria, Rahul.....4:56:48 (25,256)
Harji, Sameer.....3:55:19 (10,320)
Harker, Andrew J.....3:13:28 (2,462)
Harkin, Tony.....5:55:45 (31,346)
Harkness, Ian R.....2:26:41 (51)
Harkness, Sean M.....4:08:01 (13,616)
Harkus, Gavin M.....2:49:20 (513)
Harland, Andrew N.....4:03:30 (12,606)
Harland, David.....4:56:03 (25,109)
Harland, Matthew J.....3:46:13 (7,947)
Harley, Allan F.....4:23:04 (17,378)
Harley, Colin P.....3:12:27 (2,339)
Harley, Darren J.....3:24:41 (3,893)
Harley, Jan.....3:37:19 (6,097)
Harley, Robert A.....3:17:13 (2,911)
Harman, Alan.....3:39:26 (6,529)
Harman, David J.....3:39:03 (6,445)
Harman, Mark.....4:26:57 (18,495)
Harmel, Steven T.....6:52:45 (32,793)
Harnett, Dennis.....3:21:15 (3,431)
Harney, Brian.....3:17:10 (2,905)
Harper, Christopher J.....4:06:23 (13,207)
Harper, Clive A.....4:26:51 (18,475)
Harper, George H.....4:05:14 (12,967)
Harper, Graham.....4:26:06 (18,286)
Harper, James H.....5:04:07 (26,468)
Harper, Jeffrey F.....2:46:27 (402)
Harper, Justin M.....3:53:12 (9,689)
Harper, Kenneth J.....4:22:48 (17,322)
Harper, Kevin F.....4:39:24 (21,545)
Harper, Michael E.....4:15:46 (15,537)
Harper, Nicholas J.....6:17:45 (32,167)
Harper, Paul W.....2:32:29 (86)
Harper, Simon P.....4:00:47 (11,989)
Harper, Simon R.....4:14:01 (15,074)
Harper, Stuart J.....4:31:30 (19,665)
Harre, Ian J.....4:59:01 (25,710)
Harrhy, David A.....3:47:40 (8,285)
Harries, Richard.....4:47:23 (23,287)
Harrild, Mark W.....4:17:39 (16,026)
Harrington, Alexander.....4:14:16 (15,155)
Harrington, Richard P.....4:46:34 (23,137)
Harrington, Robert D.....4:52:33 (24,365)
Harris, Adrian.....4:16:52 (15,817)
Harris, Andrew D.....3:32:10 (5,193)
Harris, Andrew J.....5:33:56 (29,885)
Harris, Andrew N.....3:21:57 (3,529)
Harris, Barnaby R.....4:16:31 (15,732)
Harris, Chris J.....3:47:44 (8,306)
Harris, Chris P.....4:28:27 (18,882)
Harris, Colin R.....5:27:31 (29,277)
Harris, Daniel M.....4:12:33 (14,720)
Harris, Danny P.....3:57:45 (11,093)
Harris, David.....4:30:24 (19,400)
Harris, David I.....4:48:21 (23,500)
Harris, Dominic.....3:25:25 (3,995)
Harris, Edward J.....5:43:59 (30,637)
Harris, Giles.....2:59:28 (1,193)
Harris, Graham D.....6:13:27 (32,035)
Harris, Graham M.....4:26:38 (18,417)
Harris, James A.....4:39:34 (21,567)
Harris, Jason.....2:59:36 (1,210)
Harris, Jason.....5:47:47 (30,934)
Harris, John D.....3:17:46 (2,973)
Harris, John T.....4:15:04 (15,355)
Harris, Jonathan G.....5:02:06 (26,187)
Harris, Keith G.....4:58:07 (25,533)
Harris, Mark.....2:50:19 (561)
Harris, Mark E.....4:41:04 (21,910)
Harris, Mark P.....5:21:58 (28,715)
Harris, Martin G.....4:35:55 (20,692)
Harris, Matthew C.....3:18:17 (3,029)
Harris, Michael.....5:14:57 (27,899)
Harris, Nick E.....4:11:04 (14,353)
Harris, Nigel.....5:02:23 (26,236)
Harris, Nigel R.....3:44:43 (7,621)
Harris, Paul D.....3:30:05 (4,843)
Harris, Paul J.....6:00:56 (31,602)
Harris, Peter M.....4:11:51 (14,534)
Harris, Phillip I.....3:59:31 (11,677)
Harris, Raymond A.....3:41:27 (6,904)
Harris, Reg.....4:49:34 (23,769)
Harris, Richard W.....4:37:17 (21,054)
Harris, Robert E.....4:23:04 (17,378)
Harris, Robert I.....5:31:33 (29,707)
Harris, Robin.....4:02:15 (12,319)
Harris, Rod.....2:27:26 (53)
Harris, Ronald M.....4:59:47 (25,847)
Harris, Simon.....4:58:16 (25,563)
Harris, Steven.....5:34:29 (29,932)
Harris, Steven C.....4:33:19 (20,088)
Harris, Stuart.....4:22:30 (17,242)
Harris, Terry D.....3:42:18 (7,079)
Harris, Timothy E.....4:14:04 (15,092)
Harris, Timothy J.....4:11:03 (14,346)
Harris, William R.....3:59:04 (11,534)
Harrison, Adrian J.....6:01:39 (31,633)
Harrison, Alex J.....4:11:21 (14,429)
Harrison, Andrew J.....3:18:05 (3,009)
Harrison, Andrew M.....4:11:52 (14,542)
Harrison, Bob M.....3:05:23 (1,617)
Harrison, Brian.....3:57:35 (11,036)
Harrison, Charles D.....2:50:22 (563)
Harrison, Daniel N.....4:23:49 (17,598)
Harrison, David J.....4:59:50 (25,857)
Harrison, David S.....3:56:25 (10,660)
Harrison, Dennis H.....5:58:37 (31,491)
Harrison, Derek J.....3:08:20 (1,889)
Harrison, Derek V.....4:31:31 (19,668)
Harrison, Gary P.....4:07:27 (13,457)
Harrison, Jack.....4:08:17 (13,686)
Harrison, James B.....3:21:16 (3,434)
Harrison, John.....4:25:20 (18,067)
Harrison, John F.....4:45:09 (22,820)
Harrison, John T.....4:01:29 (12,146)
Harrison, Jonathan S.....5:28:27 (29,372)
Harrison, Kevin P.....7:37:19 (33,126)
Harrison, Malcolm J.....3:58:41 (11,396)
Harrison, Mark A.....5:46:53 (30,855)
Harrison, Mark J.....4:22:35 (17,260)
Harrison, Matthew J.....4:52:31 (24,358)
Harrison, Mike J.....3:28:21 (4,480)
Harrison, Paul E.....4:54:30 (24,780)
Harrison, Paul J.....3:39:43 (6,574)
Harrison, Peter J.....4:36:32 (20,853)
Harrison, Simon G.....4:25:09 (18,008)
Harrison, Simon J.....3:50:40 (9,021)
Harrison, Stephen.....3:47:56 (8,363)

Harrison, Stewart H 3:32:06 (5,180)
Harrison, Stuart 3:45:23 (7,781)
Harrison, Thomas J 3:52:24 (9,473)
Harrison, Thomas J 4:53:33 (24,581)
Harrison, Tim J 4:19:20 (16,430)
Harrison, Tom 4:11:41 (14,494)
Harrison, Tony 3:35:57 (5,828)
Harrison Church, John N 3:23:23 (3,694)
Harris-Smith, Richard J 4:01:07 (12,077)
Harrod, Matthew 4:18:14 (16,165)
Harron, Philip G 3:57:15 (10,934)
Harry, Richard D 2:57:32 (986)
Harryman, Ian L 3:50:26 (8,966)
Harshaw, Robert J 4:29:49 (19,252)
Harston, Dale 4:00:38 (11,958)
Hart, Al 2:33:01 (88)
Hart, Andrew D 2:45:06 (346)
Hart, Anthony M 4:39:54 (21,656)
Hart, Ashley J 6:14:22 (32,065)
Hart, Brett R 4:33:12 (20,062)
Hart, Colin A 3:31:37 (5,089)
Hart, Daniel A 3:22:29 (3,591)
Hart, Edward 4:55:59 (25,103)
Hart, Graham W 3:15:47 (2,751)
Hart, Gregory P 3:34:09 (5,505)
Hart, Ian D 5:10:21 (27,309)
Hart, Jason C 4:34:35 (20,383)
Hart, Mark A 3:37:12 (6,075)
Hart, Michael A 4:13:04 (14,862)
Hart, Peter J 3:17:57 (2,991)
Hart, Roy 3:08:55 (1,948)
Hart, Russell L 3:12:17 (2,320)
Hart, Steven 3:45:26 (7,789)
Hart, Stuart P 4:23:12 (17,414)
Hart, Timothy P 4:25:00 (17,964)
Harte, James 3:53:34 (9,782)
Harte, Michael J 5:24:23 (28,982)
Harten, Kieran 3:51:02 (9,110)
Hartie, Matthew 4:17:59 (16,106)
Hartill, Andrew J 3:51:40 (9,260)
Hartill, James E 3:31:06 (5,005)
Hartley, Adrian J 3:58:01 (11,156)
Hartley, Allan 4:03:41 (12,646)
Hartley, Andrew N 3:07:43 (1,826)
Hartley, James R 7:03:25 (32,922)
Hartley, James V 3:47:07 (8,149)
Hartley, Julian A 3:51:35 (9,242)
Hartley, Nigel 3:46:09 (7,935)
Hartley, Patrick G 3:50:55 (9,080)
Hartley, Richard A 3:48:18 (8,450)
Hartley, Simon G 4:25:27 (18,105)
Hartley, Steve 3:55:28 (10,361)
Hartley, Thomas W 4:04:33 (12,825)
Hartman, Steven 5:02:12 (26,201)
Hartnett, Matthew J 3:58:21 (11,288)
Hartnett, Peter J 4:44:07 (22,589)
Hartwell, David K 2:49:53 (542)
Hartwell, Toby J 4:06:07 (13,163)
Harvey, Adam J 4:35:56 (20,698)
Harvey, Adrian J 5:31:05 (29,669)
Harvey, Alex 3:29:39 (4,753)
Harvey, Andrew N 4:19:23 (16,442)
Harvey, Dan 4:17:31 (15,987)
Harvey, Geoffrey 3:37:26 (6,119)
Harvey, Geoffrey M 5:17:02 (28,133)
Harvey, John 3:26:19 (4,119)
Harvey, Jonathan M 5:48:13 (30,958)
Harvey, Matthew M 4:52:20 (24,317)
Harvey, Michael S 4:55:58 (25,097)
Harvey, Nick 6:20:52 (32,250)
Harvey, Paul 3:45:55 (7,889)
Harvey, Paul 5:51:10 (31,135)
Harvey, Paul M 3:54:57 (10,190)
Harvey, Philip J 4:12:52 (14,803)
Harvey, Richard 3:30:29 (4,889)
Harvey, Robert L 3:25:32 (4,008)
Harvey, Stephen L 4:39:22 (21,537)
Harvey, Stephen R 3:49:23 (8,715)
Harvey, Warren D 5:04:57 (26,576)
Harvey, William P 3:51:54 (9,334)
Harvie, Gavin D 2:52:56 (674)
Harwood, Adam P 3:33:07 (5,335)
Harwood, Andrew S 4:40:18 (21,732)
Harwood, David J 4:41:30 (21,994)
Harwood, Greg D 3:43:01 (7,236)
Harwood, Paul 2:49:48 (533)
Harwood, Paul 4:55:32 (25,003)
Haseldine, Daren P 3:56:47 (10,778)
Hashem, Loui 3:14:22 (2,579)
Hashim, Simon J 4:35:54 (20,690)
Haskin, Garth F 5:31:46 (29,724)
Haslam, David A 5:02:20 (26,230)
Hasler, Tom 3:28:36 (4,532)
Haslett, Francis P 6:21:43 (32,275)
Haslinger, Hubert 5:08:21 (27,058)
Hassall, Richard J 4:29:20 (19,130)
Hassan, Andrew P 3:30:32 (4,902)
Hassan, Syed I 4:00:13 (11,869)
Hassan, Tarek M 4:23:10 (17,406)
Hassan, Yasemin L 4:41:14 (21,930)
Hassard, Darren J 3:37:28 (6,127)
Haste, David P 6:38:18 (32,586)
Hastie, Martin P 4:44:55 (22,763)
Hastings, Kenneth D 3:57:30 (11,014)
Hastings, Roger D 4:57:32 (25,403)
Hastings, Terence A 5:02:15 (26,210)
Haszko, Michael S 4:17:34 (16,003)
Hatch, Clive R 4:39:14 (21,498)
Hatch, David M 5:01:56 (26,168)
Hatcher, Kevin C 4:08:22 (13,708)
Hatcliff, Stuart G 4:02:06 (12,285)
Hateley, John J 5:08:38 (27,097)
Hathaway, Edward T 4:41:58 (22,101)
Hattersley, David L 4:09:24 (13,963)
Hattersley, Mark A 4:27:02 (18,511)
Hatton, Michael 2:42:05 (251)
Hatton, Stephen J 3:24:12 (3,821)
Hatvany, Alan P 3:09:10 (1,972)
Hauffels, Paul 4:03:18 (12,552)
Haughey, Duncan J 3:02:57 (1,439)
Haughey, Edward G 3:44:59 (7,684)
Haughney, Paul 5:03:44 (26,420)
Haurant, Olivier B 3:39:21 (6,510)
Hauschild, Armin 3:38:38 (6,356)
Hausken, Oddvar 3:06:16 (1,692)
Hausladen, Rudolf 4:54:09 (24,712)
Havenhand, David C 3:03:07 (1,453)
Havill, Neil S 3:44:22 (7,534)
Havis, Gareth J 3:31:04 (4,998)
Havrylov, Volodymyr 4:07:43 (13,540)
Haw, Matt R 4:55:02 (24,904)
Haward, Robert 3:56:14 (10,603)
Hawcroft, Matthew K 2:50:20 (562)
Hawcutt, Michael J 4:13:41 (15,000)
Hawes, Bill R 2:59:33 (1,198)
Hawes, Dougie 4:07:08 (13,385)
Hawes, Patrick J 4:09:08 (13,885)
Hawes, Peter 4:25:08 (18,004)
Hawke, Gregory J 4:51:22 (24,112)
Hawke, Kevin 4:41:28 (21,986)
Hawken, Alexander J 5:10:56 (27,378)
Hawker, Ian 5:07:35 (26,944)
Hawker, Jason R 4:25:22 (18,079)
Hawker, Kevin R 2:49:09 (506)
Hawker, Marc H 3:41:33 (6,932)
Hawkes, Jeff 6:04:12 (31,731)
Hawkes, Matthew R 4:53:05 (24,473)
Hawkes, Neil D 3:47:47 (8,318)
Hawkes, Sean C 8:56:44 (33,215)
Hawkings, John 4:05:48 (13,100)
Hawkins, Andrew R 2:58:21 (1,051)
Hawkins, Andrew S 2:45:54 (373)
Hawkins, Craig S 4:55:05 (24,914)
Hawkins, Daniel 4:50:08 (23,865)
Hawkins, David J 3:53:01 (9,630)
Hawkins, David J 3:58:20 (11,280)
Hawkins, Graeme 3:10:34 (2,120)
Hawkins, Les 4:31:12 (19,581)
Hawkins, Martin S 3:14:21 (2,575)
Hawkins, Michael J 5:18:06 (28,252)
Hawkins, Peter 3:53:50 (9,873)
Hawkins, Richard J 5:32:57 (29,813)
Hawkins, Robbie A 3:58:20 (11,280)
Hawkins, Roger L 4:32:25 (19,891)
Hawkins, Steve C 4:11:38 (14,487)
Hawkins, Steve J 4:07:23 (13,447)
Hawkins, Steven D 4:25:54 (18,233)
Hawkshaw, Paul 4:00:10 (11,859)
Hawkshaw-Burn, Charles 3:57:25 (10,984)
Hawksley, Gary J 3:58:03 (11,168)
Hawksworth, Keith J 4:08:32 (13,750)
Hawley, Craig S 4:02:38 (12,408)
Hawley, Philip J 3:56:25 (10,660)
Hawliczek, Edward J 3:40:41 (6,742)
Hawliczek, Simon E 3:44:14 (7,501)
Haws, Barry J 4:05:46 (13,090)
Hawser, Paul J 3:42:53 (7,202)
Hawthorn, Jamie 3:28:56 (4,609)
Hay, Andrew 3:24:30 (3,864)
Hay, Christian 3:41:09 (6,841)
Hay, Graeme J 6:10:17 (31,932)
Hay, James M 4:13:01 (14,850)
Hay, Mick 4:16:49 (15,804)
Hay, Paul N 3:19:25 (3,182)
Hay, Peter S 2:57:43 (1,004)
Hay, Stuart 3:07:56 (1,849)
Hay, Stuart 4:49:14 (23,699)
Hayburn, Ian 2:54:16 (743)
Haycock, Edward G 4:30:22 (19,393)
Haycock, Patrick M 6:28:25 (32,429)
Haycocks, Steven C 4:41:35 (22,008)
Hayden, Barry 4:26:44 (18,443)
Hayden, Darrin P 4:26:51 (18,475)
Haydon, Andrew C 3:14:15 (2,559)
Haydon, David J 5:16:24 (28,057)
Haydon, Patrick C 5:03:16 (26,354)
Hayes, Andrew B 3:49:57 (8,857)
Hayes, Charles F 4:03:15 (12,538)
Hayes, Chris 4:23:22 (17,464)
Hayes, Christopher C 3:46:23 (7,979)
Hayes, Colin 4:47:12 (23,260)
Hayes, David 4:37:18 (21,060)
Hayes, Johnathan 3:53:27 (9,755)
Hayes, Julian 3:41:38 (6,950)
Hayes, Ken 4:29:37 (19,206)
Hayes, Kieron T 6:09:16 (31,904)
Hayes, Kim J 6:06:39 (31,810)
Hayes, Lee R 6:22:02 (32,290)
Hayes, Martin J 4:40:04 (21,688)
Hayes, Michael A 3:25:21 (3,987)
Hayes, Patrick J 2:59:02 (1,145)
Hayes, Peter J 4:13:41 (15,000)
Hayes, Richard 3:11:25 (2,206)
Hayes, Richard S 3:07:18 (1,785)
Hayes, Roger B 2:57:12 (961)
Hayes, Stephen A 4:21:13 (16,920)
Hayes, Stephen A 5:06:35 (26,802)
Hayfield, Matthew G 3:21:58 (3,531)
Hayhow, Christopher 3:53:38 (9,802)
Hayler, Robert 4:20:59 (16,861)
Haylock, Ian D 3:59:04 (11,534)
Hayman, Christopher D 4:12:53 (14,806)
Hayman, Joseph 4:55:57 (25,091)
Haynes, David 4:17:03 (15,873)
Haynes, Jeffrey J 3:05:48 (1,642)
Haynes, Mark 4:12:34 (14,723)
Haynes, Russell J 4:14:33 (15,216)
Haynes, Stewart 3:17:33 (2,947)
Hayns, Stephen J 4:26:19 (18,342)
Hays, Anthony D 3:51:58 (9,356)
Hayter, Ian M 4:35:39 (20,639)
Hayton, Bernard J 3:21:43 (3,502)
Hayton, David M 3:08:17 (1,882)
Hayward, Alexander D 3:51:17 (9,168)
Hayward, Philip G 4:45:06 (22,815)
Hayward, Steven 4:55:25 (24,985)
Haywood, Andy 4:17:31 (15,987)
Haywood, Dexter 3:05:28 (1,622)
Haywood, Nick R 3:11:09 (2,170)
Haywood, Rusell G 5:04:23 (26,508)
Hazard, John R 3:46:42 (8,060)
Hazelden, David J 4:20:31 (16,738)
Hazelden, Peter 3:57:29 (11,008)
Hazell, Damon P 5:47:59 (30,943)
Hazell, Justin L 3:51:23 (9,196)
Hazell, Martin J 4:00:00 (11,810)
Hazell, Peter L 3:55:16 (10,305)
Hazell, Tony 2:48:30 (473)
Hazell, Trevor 3:48:12 (8,432)

Hazlehurst, Daniel J....5:56:06 (31,359)
Head, Adrian P....4:04:14 (12,764)
Head, Andrew D....4:21:59 (17,112)
Head, Anthony R....5:16:02 (28,002)
Head, Jonathan M....3:54:03 (9,930)
Head, Keith J....4:16:05 (15,620)
Head, Paul J....4:39:50 (21,636)
Head, Peter J....5:22:19 (28,757)
Head, Robert W....6:40:35 (32,617)
Head, Tony....4:36:07 (20,759)
Headley, Stephen R....3:51:53 (9,329)
Headly, Nicholas I....4:37:26 (21,094)
Headon, David L....3:07:17 (1,783)
Heafey, Christopher....3:56:11 (10,591)
Heal, Gareth A....3:55:03 (10,227)
Heal, Matthew W....3:27:27 (4,321)
Heal, Steven J....4:43:18 (22,391)
Healey, Ben A....3:16:17 (2,801)
Healey, Christopher....4:36:18 (20,803)
Healey, William T....4:32:56 (19,987)
Healy, Lee J....3:25:20 (3,980)
Healy, Luke....3:52:34 (9,510)
Healy, Michael....3:27:09 (4,267)
Healy, Paul R....3:53:44 (9,833)
Healy, William J....4:41:18 (21,952)
Heaney, Sean A....4:12:02 (14,580)
Heap, Clive R....4:16:36 (15,756)
Heap, Jonathan....4:25:34 (18,132)
Heap, Nigel R....3:52:40 (9,544)
Heard, Andrew J....4:58:31 (25,614)
Heard, David C....4:58:14 (25,555)
Heard, Mark....2:41:54 (244)
Heard, Michael J....5:09:14 (27,178)
Heard, Peter A....4:01:08 (12,082)
Hearn, Edward J....4:21:14 (16,924)
Hearn, Martin J....4:41:53 (22,081)
Hearnden, Philip J....4:11:47 (14,516)
Hearne, Matthew....3:48:09 (8,422)
Hearson, James L....4:14:58 (15,325)
Heartford, Damian D....4:44:46 (22,724)
Heaselgrave, Albert W....5:33:38 (29,862)
Heasman, Dan....3:28:46 (4,569)
Heath, Barry R....4:21:09 (16,904)
Heath, David....6:28:11 (32,425)
Heath, Dominic P....5:29:18 (29,456)
Heath, Frederick C....3:53:31 (9,771)
Heath, Howard J....3:42:36 (7,134)
Heath, Jack M....3:03:49 (1,501)
Heath, James L....2:45:00 (345)
Heath, James R....3:40:25 (6,695)
Heath, Lee....5:28:46 (29,408)
Heath, Rob D....3:51:30 (9,215)
Heathcote, Michael....3:15:38 (2,729)
Heathcote, Rupert D....4:17:25 (15,960)
Heather, Richard G....4:48:50 (23,616)
Heathfield, Adrian....4:22:17 (17,194)
Heathorn, Anthony K....4:55:10 (24,928)
Heaton, Chris C....4:05:21 (12,988)
Heaton, Ian M....4:05:51 (13,109)
Heaven, James A....4:35:15 (20,544)
Heaver, John P....3:44:51 (7,655)
Heaviside, Ben....5:49:36 (31,048)
Hebditch, George....4:16:24 (15,691)
Heck, Matthew J....3:29:49 (4,790)
Heckford, Richard J....3:55:37 (10,409)
Heckford, William J....4:18:45 (16,291)
Hedgecock, Jonathan....4:16:53 (15,827)
Hedger, Graham....2:49:50 (537)
Hedges, Robert D....3:36:29 (5,928)
Hedgethorne, Peter J....4:12:53 (14,806)
Hedley, Martin....4:37:28 (21,102)
Heeley, David G....3:30:55 (4,968)
Heeley, Paul....2:55:27 (813)
Heeley, Richard....3:56:20 (10,635)
Heeney, Roy A....3:23:30 (3,713)
Hefferman, Terry....6:36:00 (32,543)
Heffernan, Darren M....4:52:23 (24,330)
Heffernan, James....4:30:19 (19,380)
Hegan, Colin M....4:51:34 (24,156)
Hegarty, Dennis J....3:49:15 (8,682)
Hegarty, Hugh....3:22:25 (3,585)
Hegarty, Simon D....4:18:27 (16,218)
Hegen, Erwin....3:51:51 (9,318)
Heggenberger, Ulf....3:47:10 (8,158)
Hegley, Marc....5:35:51 (30,042)
Hehir, Christopher....4:13:45 (15,012)
Hehir, Gerry....3:32:49 (5,296)
Heighton, Ben....4:24:09 (17,702)
Heine, Michael....3:27:03 (4,253)
Heinskou, Torben....3:56:21 (10,638)
Heiron, Andrew G....4:08:31 (13,748)
Heke, Aiden T....5:28:54 (29,419)
Helbich, Martin....4:07:34 (13,496)
Helleken, Frank....4:17:33 (15,999)
Hellen, David J....4:04:11 (12,755)
Heller, Slawomir....4:14:06 (15,104)
Hellier, Andrew J....3:53:44 (9,833)
Hellings, Jan E....5:03:27 (26,386)
Hellmers, Christopher L....3:07:36 (1,813)
Helmantel, Herman M....3:10:08 (2,076)
Helmn, Luke....3:56:56 (10,822)
Helmy, Amir E....4:28:11 (18,802)
Helps, David....4:11:11 (14,383)
Hemingway, Maurice....4:00:23 (11,910)
Hemmila, Jari....2:58:55 (1,131)
Hemming Tayler, Paul D....4:12:50 (14,786)
Hemmings, Simon T....4:12:37 (14,729)
Hemmings, Stephen....3:48:43 (8,561)
Hemmington, James....4:38:23 (21,314)
Hemms, Martin R....3:34:38 (5,597)
Hempstead, Charles N....3:44:16 (7,511)
Hemsley, Paul....3:59:56 (11,795)
Hemson, Robert A....5:44:22 (30,672)
Hemy, Vaughan....2:57:22 (972)
Henderson, Andrew T....7:03:24 (32,920)
Henderson, Anthony W....5:31:01 (29,654)
Henderson, Bernard J....5:08:40 (27,101)
Henderson, Craig S....4:13:16 (14,911)
Henderson, Daivd J....4:52:53 (24,433)
Henderson, David B....4:30:58 (19,526)
Henderson, David G....3:32:56 (5,312)
Henderson, Desmond G....4:43:38 (22,474)
Henderson, Duncan L....5:14:43 (27,875)
Henderson, Ian....3:59:51 (11,776)
Henderson, James R....4:16:23 (15,688)
Henderson, Jason A....3:50:49 (9,058)
Henderson, John J....4:30:44 (19,480)
Henderson, Mark....5:39:07 (30,293)
Henderson, Mark J....4:01:42 (12,190)
Henderson, Neil C....5:15:16 (27,934)
Henderson, Neil D....4:08:32 (13,750)
Henderson, Paul....4:02:10 (12,299)
Henderson, Robert C....3:27:00 (4,246)
Henderson, Rory E....3:57:51 (11,124)
Henderson, Steve....4:47:11 (23,255)
Henderson, Stuart J....3:51:37 (9,247)
Henderson, Thomas A....4:10:03 (14,111)
Hendley, Darren P....3:58:47 (11,440)
Hendon, Stuart C....5:14:16 (27,807)
Hendra, Kevin P....5:22:11 (28,739)
Hendry, Ian P....4:40:29 (21,771)
Hendry, John S....3:19:13 (3,159)
Hendry, Philip H....4:00:14 (11,874)
Hendry, Richard M....3:54:00 (9,923)
Hendry, Simon F....3:55:08 (10,255)
Hendrysson, Lars H....4:54:02 (24,681)
Hendy, Adrian....5:51:02 (31,130)
Hendy, Peter M....3:51:36 (9,243)
Heney, Kenneth J....3:02:50 (1,425)
Hengartner, Urs....2:52:01 (638)
Henley, Wayne D....3:09:18 (1,983)
Henly, Steve P....3:58:02 (11,163)
Hennequin, Eric....3:07:29 (1,803)
Hennessey, Iain....5:47:18 (30,898)
Hennessy, James A....4:10:38 (14,240)
Hennis, Richard B....3:43:03 (7,251)
Henriques, Steven A....3:50:31 (8,989)
Henry, Andrew J....4:45:59 (23,001)
Henry, Barry....6:43:21 (32,659)
Henry, Kieran....3:56:11 (10,591)
Henry, Nigel J....3:39:10 (6,467)
Hense, Antonius M....3:57:27 (10,996)
Hensen, Titus....3:19:50 (3,238)
Henshall, Richard A....4:07:09 (13,390)
Henshaw, Christopher....4:15:27 (15,466)
Henshaw, Paul A....5:21:48 (28,691)
Henshaw, Richard D....5:25:59 (29,128)
Henton, Ian....4:23:54 (17,623)
Henwood, Stuart....4:23:48 (17,589)
Henwood Fox, Gary....4:51:23 (24,117)
Heppell, Andrew B....4:54:25 (24,773)
Hepple, Jason N....4:43:15 (22,376)
Hepsoe, Thor M....4:11:25 (14,445)
Hepworth, Ian D....3:55:15 (10,298)
Herb, Ray D....5:09:12 (27,172)
Herb, Stephen J....5:32:32 (29,773)
Herbert, Alexander P....6:23:39 (32,322)
Herbert, Andrew R....3:48:26 (8,483)
Herbert, Brian E....3:56:14 (10,603)
Herbert, James....5:10:12 (27,289)
Herbert, Matthew C....3:06:37 (1,718)
Herbert, Raymond L....7:09:54 (32,978)
Herbert, Richard D....3:44:54 (7,669)
Herbert, Robert....5:21:21 (28,652)
Herbert, Simon....4:15:55 (15,581)
Herbert, Stephen J....4:23:38 (17,542)
Herbert, Thomas A....2:55:52 (841)
Herd, Darren G....4:20:29 (16,733)
Herd, Jonathan J....4:45:40 (22,935)
Herdman, Dominic W....5:05:19 (26,628)
Herdman, Seamus J....5:50:24 (31,102)
Herity, John....3:52:12 (9,410)
Herlihy, Dion J....4:10:27 (14,204)
Herlin, Thierry....3:35:33 (5,759)
Herman, Christopher R....7:27:49 (33,084)
Herman, Marc S....4:25:15 (18,042)
Hermann, Wilfried....4:06:42 (13,275)
Hermer, Duncan J....3:41:04 (6,820)
Hernandez, Miguel....3:21:24 (3,455)
Hernandez Aramburo, Carlos A....4:51:44 (24,192)
Heron, Clinton....4:20:35 (16,754)
Heron, James....3:04:41 (1,560)
Herrero, Gustavo....4:30:07 (19,328)
Herrero, José I....3:15:18 (2,695)
Herrick, Timothy P....2:47:13 (423)
Herring, Jonathan I....2:58:35 (1,072)
Herrington, Richard C....3:00:28 (1,269)
Herriott, Bryan P....4:26:13 (18,316)
Herry, Yves....2:41:53 (243)
Herst, Peter....4:19:11 (16,390)
Hervy, Christophe....3:33:44 (5,440)
Herz, David....4:21:49 (17,067)
Heseltine, Michael D....5:04:11 (26,474)
Hesketh, Benjamin H....4:30:54 (19,511)
Heslop, Garry....4:29:14 (19,093)
Heslop, Ian....3:31:15 (5,032)
Heslop, Paul D....4:27:54 (18,722)
Heslop, Timothy C....4:04:15 (12,766)
Hesten, Paul....5:54:35 (31,291)
Hester, Douglas P....4:52:27 (24,343)
Hester, Richard C....4:28:42 (18,944)
Heuman, Adam J....4:10:34 (14,226)
Hevey, Darren J....4:36:04 (20,742)
Heward, Neil I....5:53:05 (31,218)
Hewer, Tom....4:48:54 (23,628)
Hewerdine, Joshua G....3:16:49 (2,854)
Hewett, Alan....3:47:10 (8,158)
Hewett, Arron....6:14:45 (32,080)
Hewett, James P....4:08:36 (13,769)
Hewitson, Robert A....3:22:53 (3,644)
Hewitt, Damien F....5:02:49 (26,291)
Hewitt, David E....5:41:34 (30,460)
Hewitt, David J....4:16:52 (15,817)
Hewitt, Kevan J....3:50:31 (8,989)
Hewitt, Leslie D....4:08:03 (13,628)
Hewitt, Liam T....4:32:53 (19,974)
Hewitt, Michael....3:18:50 (3,111)
Hewitt, Nick....3:33:06 (5,333)
Hewitt, Simon....3:14:17 (2,565)
Hewson, Anthony J....3:28:04 (4,416)
Hex, Dominic C....4:02:52 (12,449)
Heyden, Andrew P....2:37:29 (151)
Heyes, Richard C....3:40:14 (6,663)
Heyl, Peter....3:32:28 (5,245)
Heys, Simon R....3:08:30 (1,909)
Heyworth, Reginald P....5:20:53 (28,601)
Hiatt, David A....3:39:25 (6,523)
Hibberd, David J....3:21:59 (3,532)
Hibberd, Duncan S....4:56:42 (25,243)

Hibberd, Raymond T.....5:53:49 (31,255)
Hibberd, Roy G.....4:08:22 (13,708)
Hibbert, Alex P.....3:25:29 (4,002)
Hibbert, Chris A.....4:29:28 (19,167)
Hibbert, Christopher.....3:34:16 (5,523)
Hibbert, Grant D.....3:19:07 (3,145)
Hibbert, Mathew.....3:51:44 (9,284)
Hibbert, Michael G.....3:26:04 (4,083)
Hibbert, Paul T.....5:18:59 (28,370)
Hibbert, Warren T.....4:14:54 (15,311)
Hibbin, Peter.....3:54:28 (10,042)
Hick, Brian K.....5:31:48 (29,725)
Hick, Jameson F.....5:04:16 (26,485)
Hickling, Jeffery P.....4:45:21 (22,874)
Hickling, Robert L.....4:03:39 (12,640)
Hickman, Andrew D.....4:27:46 (18,686)
Hickman, Edward C.....3:24:56 (3,924)
Hickman, Ian J.....3:24:32 (3,870)
Hickman, Michael J.....3:51:45 (9,287)
Hickman, Stephen P.....3:49:08 (8,653)
Hickmott, Andy.....4:46:28 (23,113)
Hicks, Alan.....3:59:40 (11,715)
Hicks, Barry M.....4:48:43 (23,587)
Hicks, Brian.....4:59:45 (25,840)
Hicks, Dylan J.....5:18:16 (28,279)
Hicks, Paul.....3:36:08 (5,860)
Hicks, Robert I.....3:08:19 (1,887)
Hicks, Robin.....3:29:01 (4,624)
Hicks, Simon J.....5:16:42 (28,093)
Hicks, Stephen A.....4:59:36 (25,811)
Hickson, Amy H.....5:26:15 (29,147)
Hickson, Ken W.....3:28:53 (4,601)
Hiddleston, David M.....3:22:01 (3,537)
Hide, George.....2:34:07 (101)
Hides, Nicholas B.....2:42:27 (262)
Higgins, Adrian J.....3:47:12 (8,168)
Higgins, Bernard.....3:33:26 (5,394)
Higgins, Daniel J.....2:43:16 (296)
Higgins, Daniel P.....3:57:48 (11,115)
Higgins, Kevin.....3:51:03 (9,113)
Higgins, Neil D.....3:29:20 (4,684)
Higgins, Philip B.....4:38:32 (21,347)
Higginson, Jamie P.....3:38:10 (6,260)
Higginson, Martin J.....3:43:46 (7,411)
Higglesden, Matthew W.....3:17:24 (2,931)
Higgs, Andrew D.....6:00:52 (31,600)
Higgs, David W.....3:39:28 (6,538)
Higgs, Mark A.....3:15:39 (2,733)
Higgs, Mark W.....2:53:55 (722)
Higgs, Matthew.....4:01:06 (12,072)
Higgs, Paul D.....4:50:18 (23,905)
Higgs, Phil.....4:40:00 (21,674)
Higgs, Philip A.....3:25:20 (3,980)
Higgs, Richard M.....3:34:11 (5,511)
Higgs, Simon J.....4:07:51 (13,570)
Higgs, Stephen J.....4:02:46 (12,430)
High, Matthew P.....4:54:58 (24,887)
Higham, Robert A.....3:32:33 (5,260)
Highfield, Colin R.....3:03:20 (1,466)
Highfield, Mark.....3:49:52 (8,837)
Hight, Christopher H.....4:38:15 (21,292)
Higlett, Kevin.....5:07:36 (26,947)
Higson, James F.....4:03:36 (12,624)
Hijkoop, Frans.....3:34:13 (5,515)
Hikosaka, Yasuyuki.....4:22:16 (17,191)
Hilal, Haithem.....4:16:08 (15,629)
Hild, Harry.....4:15:42 (15,521)
Hild, Jens.....4:35:39 (20,639)
Hild, Rudi.....4:21:46 (17,052)
Hildebrandt, Charles R.....3:46:26 (7,998)
Hilder, Adam.....3:22:23 (3,582)
Hilder, Mark.....3:53:48 (9,861)
Hill, Andrew J.....5:09:14 (27,178)
Hill, Austin.....4:06:29 (13,228)
Hill, Christopher D.....3:49:51 (8,831)
Hill, Christopher D.....5:11:48 (27,492)
Hill, David A.....4:14:56 (15,317)
Hill, Dominic.....4:20:53 (16,833)
Hill, Edward C.....3:33:38 (5,427)
Hill, Gavin.....3:54:40 (10,099)
Hill, Glen.....2:49:40 (525)
Hill, Iain D.....3:53:59 (9,917)
Hill, James N.....5:19:52 (28,479)
Hill, James R.....5:09:20 (27,187)
Hill, Jonathan.....4:06:29 (13,228)
Hill, Joseph.....4:44:53 (22,752)
Hill, Justin B.....3:02:04 (1,381)
Hill, Kenneth.....3:12:14 (2,316)
Hill, Mark A.....3:01:59 (1,374)
Hill, Martin J.....3:37:17 (6,088)
Hill, Michael.....3:26:03 (4,082)
Hill, Michael A.....3:29:29 (4,713)
Hill, Michael G.....4:39:04 (21,458)
Hill, Michael J.....4:43:27 (22,421)
Hill, Nicholas M.....4:43:49 (22,523)
Hill, Nicholas P.....3:31:52 (5,138)
Hill, Nick E.....4:48:31 (23,543)
Hill, Paul D.....3:52:35 (9,515)
Hill, Richard E.....4:46:46 (23,166)
Hill, Richard W.....5:40:50 (30,418)
Hill, Robert E.....4:12:18 (14,652)
Hill, Roger L.....3:40:19 (6,678)
Hill, Simon A.....4:54:27 (24,777)
Hill, Simon C.....3:07:28 (1,800)
Hill, Stephen C.....4:02:23 (12,347)
Hill, Steven.....4:05:55 (13,125)
Hill, Terence.....4:56:35 (25,220)
Hill, Terry.....4:45:47 (22,965)
Hill, Tim.....3:28:19 (4,475)
Hill, Tim J.....3:18:24 (3,049)
Hill, Tommy J.....4:15:23 (15,442)
Hill, Walter J.....2:58:37 (1,081)
Hillard, Timothy C.....3:57:46 (11,100)
Hillery, Carl J.....3:55:09 (10,263)
Hilliar, Zel D.....4:55:36 (25,017)
Hillier, Mick.....5:29:20 (29,460)
Hillier, Stephen M.....4:43:55 (22,554)
Hilllier, Adam I.....4:38:25 (21,316)
Hillman, Mark R.....5:42:54 (30,566)
Hillman, Mark W.....4:16:43 (15,783)
Hills, Adam S.....3:46:29 (8,008)
Hills, David J.....4:18:30 (16,231)
Hills, Mils P.....4:00:18 (11,887)
Hills, Nigel G.....5:00:18 (25,944)
Hills, Stuart.....4:19:29 (16,474)
Hills, Vernon J.....4:10:34 (14,226)
Hillsley, Glen A.....3:57:02 (10,852)
Hilton, Alan G.....4:29:36 (19,199)
Hilton, John.....4:10:47 (14,270)
Hilton, Jon Paul C.....3:07:39 (1,820)
Hilton, Paul.....4:10:48 (14,277)
Hilton, Stephen.....2:51:06 (598)
Himade, Frank.....3:39:07 (6,458)
Hinchcliffe, Scott M.....4:24:19 (17,754)
Hinchliffe, Paul G.....5:08:36 (27,090)
Hinchliffe, Robert J.....4:09:38 (14,019)
Hinchliffe, Steven W.....5:08:36 (27,090)
Hind, Andy.....4:15:17 (15,408)
Hind, Gareth R.....3:42:07 (7,046)
Hinder, Gavin A.....4:50:10 (23,871)
Hindhaugh, Andrew M.....6:17:45 (32,167)
Hindle, Norman.....4:14:59 (15,332)
Hindle, Oliver G.....3:12:22 (2,330)
Hindley, Mark C.....3:10:09 (2,081)
Hindmarch, Nicholas J.....3:53:56 (9,902)
Hinds, Carlos R.....4:58:38 (25,632)
Hinds, Jeremy.....5:07:51 (26,981)
Hinds, William.....4:33:06 (20,030)
Hine, Adrian J.....4:07:00 (13,346)
Hine, Mark A.....4:00:13 (11,869)
Hingley, Chris G.....4:58:49 (25,667)
Hingley, Gregory N.....3:52:29 (9,488)
Hinman, Peter M.....5:23:17 (28,865)
Hinojosa, José Antonio.....3:48:06 (8,403)
Hinsley, Jeff.....3:54:18 (10,004)
Hinson, Michael C.....4:29:59 (19,288)
Hinson, Robert.....4:30:21 (19,388)
Hinson, Robert J.....4:29:59 (19,288)
Hinton, Alexander C.....3:43:39 (7,380)
Hinton, Andrew R.....3:47:27 (8,225)
Hinton, Joshua J.....5:13:11 (27,673)
Hinton, Lee S.....3:57:28 (11,003)
Hinton, Matthew H.....3:45:23 (7,781)
Hinton, Stephen N.....5:37:29 (30,163)
Hinz, Olav.....3:20:24 (3,326)
Hiorns, Stephen R.....3:12:43 (2,363)
Hipkin, John W.....3:57:50 (11,121)
Hipshon, John W.....4:46:15 (23,062)
Hipshon, Mark J.....3:43:41 (7,386)
Hirani, Zain.....4:12:11 (14,620)
Hirst, Andrew D.....4:30:21 (19,388)
Hirst, John.....5:39:48 (30,346)
Hirst, Russell J.....5:37:14 (30,148)
Hiscock, Andy.....4:33:57 (20,238)
Hiscock, Jonathan N.....2:44:33 (332)
Hiscox, John.....3:29:41 (4,756)
Histon, David A.....3:37:43 (6,171)
Histon, John M.....4:40:47 (21,848)
Hita-Hita, Luis.....3:29:50 (4,795)
Hitch, Chris A.....4:33:46 (20,199)
Hitchmough, Andrew.....3:39:21 (6,510)
Hithersay, Simon M.....3:55:20 (10,325)
Hittinger Roux, Giles.....4:50:08 (23,865)
Hixson, Stuart D.....4:24:35 (17,837)
Hjorth, Tommy.....4:21:00 (16,867)
Hlobo, Rampeoane.....4:48:27 (23,527)
Ho, Alex.....3:00:15 (1,252)
Ho, Andrew.....4:41:07 (21,918)
Ho, Stephen.....6:10:45 (31,949)
Hoad, Ian A.....3:19:52 (3,244)
Hoang, David.....3:58:12 (11,233)
Hoar, Alan F.....5:42:16 (30,518)
Hoare, Alex J.....4:39:03 (21,454)
Hoare, Chris J.....3:10:41 (2,130)
Hoare, Chris P.....5:10:14 (27,295)
Hoare, Daniel J.....3:57:41 (11,067)
Hoare, Ian P.....2:53:24 (692)
Hoare, Sam P.....4:22:02 (17,126)
Hoban, Maurice.....4:49:30 (23,754)
Hobbs, Andrew.....5:49:03 (31,002)
Hobbs, Chris G.....3:20:00 (3,268)
Hobbs, Craig A.....5:33:08 (29,826)
Hobbs, David.....3:54:46 (10,128)
Hobbs, Desmond A.....3:48:29 (8,495)
Hobbs, Gary P.....5:04:39 (26,539)
Hobbs, Greg M.....4:51:20 (24,101)
Hobbs, Jonathan M.....2:42:32 (266)
Hobbs, Kurt P.....4:56:39 (25,229)
Hobbs, Mark.....3:52:07 (9,387)
Hobbs, Michael J.....3:00:52 (1,294)
Hobbs, Paul J.....5:16:44 (28,097)
Hobbs, Philip.....4:02:36 (12,400)
Hobbs, Ryan C.....4:57:51 (25,463)
Hobbs, Sebastian.....4:30:59 (19,528)
Hobbs, Simon A.....4:46:14 (23,056)
Hobbs, Stephen.....6:50:04 (32,762)
Hobbs, Stephen M.....3:29:47 (4,779)
Hobday, Michael E.....3:20:11 (3,295)
Hobden, Brendan C.....3:45:11 (7,725)
Hobin, Mark J.....3:10:11 (2,086)
Hobson, Kevin M.....5:56:50 (31,395)
Hobson, Kirk M.....3:28:37 (4,533)
Hobson, Robert D.....3:57:33 (11,028)
Hobson, Simon A.....4:34:17 (20,303)
Hocart, Nicholas.....4:11:51 (14,534)
Hockey, Ian O.....5:13:32 (27,726)
Hocking, Michael J.....5:29:26 (29,475)
Hocking, Steve J.....4:56:59 (25,307)
Hoddinott, Andy.....3:46:05 (7,922)
Hodge, Steve.....4:20:34 (16,750)
Hodges, Allan.....4:51:31 (24,151)
Hodges, Christopher S.....3:29:35 (4,739)
Hodges, Darren P.....3:49:29 (8,743)
Hodges, Jon.....4:20:09 (16,644)
Hodges, Michael J.....4:33:32 (20,142)
Hodges, Nick B.....2:43:14 (293)
Hodges, Simon C.....3:36:18 (5,895)
Hodgetts, Matthew J.....4:12:17 (14,645)
Hodgkins, Andrew S.....5:39:44 (30,340)
Hodgkiss, Callen.....3:07:37 (1,816)
Hodgon, Tim D.....5:12:00 (27,525)
Hodgson, James T.....4:07:53 (13,579)
Hodgson, Jeremy.....6:19:05 (32,205)
Hodgson, Kevin I.....4:50:39 (23,973)
Hodgson, Martin C.....3:35:44 (5,792)
Hodgson, Matthew.....3:30:46 (4,940)
Hodgson, Matthew.....4:24:11 (17,709)
Hodgson, Matthew W.....3:31:05 (5,002)
Hodgson, Steven N.....5:02:05 (26,185)

Hodgson, Stuart A........................3:44:49 (7,645)
Hodgson, Toby H........................4:07:37 (13,512)
Hodgson, Tony........................3:09:39 (2,031)
Hodossy, Peter........................3:13:27 (2,459)
Hodson, Adrian........................4:03:06 (12,504)
Hodson, Alan D........................6:14:20 (32,062)
Hodson, David........................3:19:27 (3,188)
Hodson, James A........................4:18:49 (16,305)
Hodson, Oliver C........................3:50:06 (8,885)
Hodson, Stephen........................4:39:35 (21,571)
Hoeke, Jan-Michael........................3:21:48 (3,509)
Hoeke, Joachim E........................3:26:31 (4,158)
Hoenle, Martin........................4:21:26 (16,965)
Hoermann, Peter........................3:48:44 (8,565)
Hoertnagl, Thomas I........................5:06:33 (26,793)
Hoey, Michael A........................2:44:14 (320)
Hoey, William F........................4:18:00 (16,108)
Hoez, Jean-Luc C........................4:30:20 (19,384)
Hoff, Kevin M........................3:54:22 (10,021)
Hofferberth, Volkmar........................3:41:57 (7,012)
Hoffman, Chris P........................4:38:06 (21,261)
Hoffman, Lance D........................3:56:48 (10,785)
Hoffman, Paul D........................5:01:27 (26,101)
Hoffman, Wlater........................3:10:15 (2,089)
Hoffmann, Claus A........................3:39:02 (6,438)
Hofmann, Ralf........................3:41:45 (6,974)
Hofstetter, Peter M........................3:25:47 (4,042)
Hogan, Garry R........................3:40:38 (6,737)
Hogan, Graham S........................2:56:56 (935)
Hogan, James........................3:24:32 (3,870)
Hogan, John........................4:36:46 (20,924)
Hogan, John M........................4:57:42 (25,433)
Hogan, Michael........................3:17:04 (2,885)
Hogan, Michael P........................5:17:03 (28,135)
Hogarth, Malcolm........................4:29:19 (19,122)
Hogberg, Christer........................3:42:08 (7,050)
Hogenbirk, Nicolaas........................3:58:21 (11,288)
Hogenelst, Sicco........................4:03:15 (12,538)
Hogg, Andrew A........................3:59:27 (11,659)
Hogg, Andrew J........................4:26:58 (18,497)
Hogg, Douglas C........................4:07:11 (13,401)
Hogg, John........................4:51:03 (24,049)
Hogg, Michael J........................5:03:12 (26,349)
Hogg, Peter W........................3:44:45 (7,629)
Hogg, Roland........................4:23:48 (17,589)
Hoggan, Brent C........................3:38:00 (6,222)
Hogger, Harry B........................3:18:14 (3,022)
Hoglund, Greger........................5:34:33 (29,936)
Hoile, Kevin P........................4:29:41 (19,222)
Holah, Daniel J........................3:42:28 (7,106)
Holbourne, Alex E........................5:15:35 (27,960)
Holbrook, Edward........................4:11:19 (14,420)
Holbrook, Steve........................4:28:47 (18,969)
Holburn, Angus........................5:26:53 (29,213)
Holcombe, Andrew P........................4:46:02 (23,012)
Holcroft, Clyde M........................4:42:06 (22,134)
Holdaway, Kevin W........................4:26:34 (18,397)
Holden, Adrian........................4:43:55 (22,554)
Holden, David........................3:55:56 (10,519)
Holden, Frank........................4:37:11 (21,025)
Holden, Ian N........................4:14:32 (15,213)
Holden, John........................4:37:30 (21,111)
Holden, Martin........................4:56:26 (25,198)
Holden, Peter........................5:21:29 (28,663)
Holden, Raymond J........................3:08:25 (1,899)
Holden, Stephen........................3:29:32 (4,725)
Holden, Warren J........................4:20:58 (16,857)
Holden, Wayne........................3:36:45 (5,982)
Holden-Brown, Nicholas S........................3:43:04 (7,255)
Holder, John A........................5:40:59 (30,425)
Holder, Julian T........................4:24:14 (17,725)
Holder, Timothy J........................4:10:03 (14,111)
Holder, Wayne C........................5:26:14 (29,144)
Holderness, Kevin........................4:20:28 (16,727)
Holdich, Stephen W........................4:57:04 (25,328)
Holding, Brett........................3:56:03 (10,552)
Holding, Phil R........................4:49:13 (23,694)
Holding Parsons, David T........................5:57:55 (31,452)
Holditch, Karl........................4:08:44 (13,792)
Holdswortth, Sam........................4:04:59 (12,915)
Hole, James C........................3:53:04 (9,655)
Hole, Mark R........................4:23:32 (17,513)
Holehouse, Benjamin W........................4:56:23 (25,185)
Holgate, Paul........................4:14:17 (15,161)
Holiday, David M........................4:21:13 (16,920)
Holladay, Andrew C........................3:32:36 (5,265)
Holladay, Norman C........................4:49:34 (23,769)
Holland, Adam J........................2:51:56 (632)
Holland, Alistair R........................3:01:30 (1,337)
Holland, Christopher S........................6:24:34 (32,346)
Holland, Dale A........................5:25:45 (29,109)
Holland, John D........................3:11:15 (2,191)
Holland, Matthew T........................4:15:07 (15,372)
Holland, Stephen J........................4:07:21 (13,433)
Holland, Vincent........................4:28:22 (18,863)
Holland, William........................4:04:19 (12,780)
Hollands, Mark T........................2:39:52 (209)
Holleron, Dominic P........................4:38:31 (21,344)
Holley, Amanda........................4:33:20 (20,092)
Holley, David J........................5:10:19 (27,307)
Hollick, Kevin........................5:00:42 (25,995)
Holliday, Vincent J........................5:18:01 (28,239)
Hollier, Steve........................2:48:51 (486)
Holling, Anthony........................3:37:44 (6,176)
Hollingsworth, Noel........................3:15:13 (2,687)
Hollingsworth, Richard........................4:01:54 (12,236)
Hollington, Allan........................5:02:35 (26,260)
Hollington, Ben........................4:49:17 (23,714)
Hollinshead, Christopher D........................2:46:49 (411)
Hollis, Barry........................4:17:48 (16,060)
Hollis, Gavin R........................4:05:50 (13,106)
Hollis, Stephen P........................3:59:21 (11,621)
Hollisey, Lee........................5:36:52 (30,123)
Hollister, Ray P........................4:27:32 (18,633)
Hollobone, Philip T........................4:41:20 (21,960)
Hollow, Martin........................6:25:29 (32,364)
Holloway, Adrian........................3:46:33 (8,021)
Holloway, Damien S........................4:27:27 (18,609)
Holloway, Daniel........................4:16:44 (15,788)
Holloway, Darren P........................4:29:24 (19,146)
Holloway, Melvyn J........................3:25:33 (4,011)
Holloway, Nick........................4:09:31 (13,997)
Holloway, Richard B........................3:47:28 (8,234)
Holloway, Stephen........................4:55:55 (25,080)
Holloway, Steven J........................3:33:02 (5,328)
Hollowell, Graham J........................3:17:04 (2,885)
Hollowell, James........................3:34:53 (5,639)
Holly, Paul M........................4:39:45 (21,612)
Hollyhead, Simon J........................4:19:10 (16,382)
Hollywood, Bernie P........................5:37:45 (30,189)
Holman, Dave P........................4:14:51 (15,298)
Holman, James C........................3:50:37 (9,009)
Holman, Steve........................3:51:10 (9,140)
Holman, Tom O........................3:48:27 (8,489)
Holmes, Aaron R........................3:51:23 (9,196)
Holmes, Dennis........................3:28:58 (4,615)
Holmes, Derrick W........................4:18:28 (16,223)
Holmes, Frank C........................3:28:34 (4,526)
Holmes, Fraser........................4:12:02 (14,580)
Holmes, Gary........................3:54:20 (10,011)
Holmes, Gavin W........................6:26:38 (32,391)
Holmes, John H........................3:08:15 (1,880)
Holmes, John W........................5:30:10 (29,558)
Holmes, Karl........................6:07:12 (31,828)
Holmes, Leigh D........................4:17:19 (15,933)
Holmes, Matt N........................3:31:13 (5,028)
Holmes, Nicholas........................3:29:58 (4,818)
Holmes, Nicholas M........................3:06:23 (1,701)
Holmes, Nicholas R........................3:39:24 (6,518)
Holmes, Nick J........................3:26:21 (4,128)
Holmes, Patrick M........................3:22:03 (3,542)
Holmes, Paul A........................4:05:31 (13,027)
Holmes, Peter H........................3:49:07 (8,650)
Holmes, Peter I........................3:07:16 (1,779)
Holmes, Richard........................4:40:41 (21,825)
Holmes, Richard........................5:29:39 (29,497)
Holmes, Richard A........................3:18:02 (3,002)
Holmes, Rob J........................4:00:29 (11,932)
Holmes, Robert W........................4:26:42 (18,430)
Holmes, Stephen........................2:58:19 (1,047)
Holmes, Steve M........................4:42:07 (22,138)
Holmes, Stuart M........................6:12:35 (32,008)
Holpin, Stuart R........................5:57:13 (31,416)
Holroyd-Smith, Alex J........................3:46:19 (7,972)
Holsetin, Flemming........................4:34:59 (20,483)
Holst, Hans........................3:19:35 (3,200)
Holt, Alan W........................3:50:06 (8,885)
Holt, Alexander R........................6:07:31 (31,841)
Holt, Brian P........................4:36:31 (20,849)
Holt, Craig........................5:35:27 (30,008)
Holt, David J........................4:02:32 (12,382)
Holt, John F........................3:54:07 (9,949)
Holt, Jonathan D........................4:20:00 (16,602)
Holt, Julian D........................4:26:10 (18,302)
Holt, Mark L........................4:23:04 (17,378)
Holt, Peter A........................3:54:47 (10,138)
Holt, Philip C........................3:44:39 (7,603)
Holt, Sean P........................3:30:57 (4,973)
Holt, Tim C........................4:50:51 (24,016)
Holte, Soren........................3:49:39 (8,786)
Holthe, Helge........................2:35:48 (127)
Holton, Peter A........................2:58:57 (1,135)
Holton, Peter R........................4:21:32 (16,981)
Holwell, Steven........................3:28:35 (4,528)
Holzapfel, Helmut H........................4:00:04 (11,836)
Home, Steven........................2:43:40 (304)
Homer, James N........................4:32:11 (19,827)
Homer, Mark R........................2:59:11 (1,161)
Homes, Simon P........................5:37:20 (30,153)
Homewood, Max........................4:48:39 (23,576)
Hone, Angus........................4:15:23 (15,442)
Hone, Mark S........................3:56:43 (10,758)
Honey, Matthew J........................4:25:37 (18,140)
Honeyball, John K........................5:25:44 (29,107)
Honeycombe, Peter D........................4:09:26 (13,976)
Honeyman, Ross........................6:07:05 (31,824)
Hong, Dengli........................4:15:35 (15,491)
Honnor, Ian C........................3:14:32 (2,600)
Honour, Darren........................3:50:46 (9,050)
Hood, Anthony J........................4:41:27 (21,982)
Hood, Graeme........................4:25:06 (17,990)
Hood, Graeme J........................3:32:31 (5,256)
Hood, Mark O........................3:50:39 (9,016)
Hooft, Patrick........................3:40:33 (6,721)
Hook, Edward J........................4:51:25 (24,129)
Hook, John C........................3:11:17 (2,194)
Hook, Philip F........................3:45:19 (7,760)
Hook, Robert........................4:37:00 (20,979)
Hooke, Andrew P........................4:51:56 (24,239)
Hooke, Bob G........................4:57:40 (25,428)
Hooke, Danny R........................4:09:42 (14,029)
Hoolahan, Roy........................4:24:05 (17,680)
Hooper, Chris J........................4:23:27 (17,486)
Hooper, Daniel........................4:05:44 (13,082)
Hooper, Graham P........................4:48:57 (23,640)
Hooper, Mark R........................4:29:15 (19,102)
Hooper, Nicholas N........................4:26:18 (18,335)
Hooper, Patrick D........................5:01:45 (26,138)
Hooper, Paul A........................3:47:09 (8,156)
Hooper, Rodney........................3:57:37 (11,051)
Hooper, Ronald L........................4:54:08 (24,704)
Hooper, Samuel H........................4:25:00 (17,964)
Hooper, Steven C........................3:01:23 (1,330)
Hooson, Shaun........................3:11:37 (2,223)
Hopcraft, Geoffrey M........................4:51:49 (24,214)
Hopcraft, Robert J........................4:03:26 (12,589)
Hope, Alan C........................4:05:27 (13,011)
Hope, Alex........................2:38:28 (178)
Hope, Andrew S........................4:22:21 (17,209)
Hope, David E........................5:18:32 (28,313)
Hope, Gary J........................2:38:49 (184)
Hope, Lee C........................6:26:23 (32,387)
Hope, Neil P........................4:05:34 (13,040)
Hope, Richard J........................3:48:42 (8,558)
Hope, Stuart........................3:21:12 (3,423)
Hopegood, James........................4:43:22 (22,404)
Hopgood, Martin A........................3:54:10 (9,968)
Hopkins, Andrew J........................4:00:19 (11,892)
Hopkins, Carl D........................5:20:04 (28,501)
Hopkins, Darren........................5:03:43 (26,418)
Hopkins, Elwyn M........................3:50:17 (8,931)
Hopkins, Graham J........................5:07:51 (26,981)
Hopkins, Greg........................3:57:56 (11,144)
Hopkins, Lee M........................4:53:32 (24,575)
Hopkins, Mark........................4:14:56 (15,317)
Hopkins, Martin J........................4:07:48 (13,555)
Hopkins, Paul A........................4:57:52 (25,470)
Hopkins, Peter C........................4:31:42 (19,721)
Hopkins, Robert........................3:02:41 (1,416)

Hopkins, Stephen D	3:35:51 (5,808)	
Hopkins, Stephen M	3:35:37 (5,773)	
Hopkins, Stuart	2:55:00 (790)	
Hopkinson, Tom	3:45:11 (7,725)	
Hopp, Brian K	6:34:47 (32,524)	
Hopper, Nicholas J	3:58:36 (11,370)	
Hopps, Peter W	3:11:45 (2,243)	
Hopton, Christopher P	4:49:34 (23,769)	
Hopton, Tim P	4:51:05 (24,057)	
Hopwood, Tony R	3:08:58 (1,952)	
Horan, David J	3:42:39 (7,145)	
Horan, Iwan W	3:26:07 (4,089)	
Horan, Paul J	4:18:41 (16,278)	
Horan, Scott	4:44:36 (22,690)	
Horbert, Peter	4:27:19 (18,584)	
Horn, Jeff	3:53:48 (9,861)	
Horncastle, Kevin C	4:03:53 (12,687)	
Horne, Archie	4:49:31 (23,760)	
Horne, Chad M	3:21:56 (3,526)	
Horne, Graham R	4:53:06 (24,479)	
Horne, Nicholas N	3:38:53 (6,408)	
Horne, Shaine P	5:03:35 (26,400)	
Horne, Simon P	3:34:25 (5,551)	
Horner, Alan	5:51:17 (31,140)	
Hornigold, Simon J	4:47:25 (23,296)	
Horniman, John	6:42:38 (32,650)	
Hornsey, Lee C	3:40:03 (6,635)	
Hornsey, Mark R	3:45:08 (7,715)	
Hornshaw, Aleck E	4:37:52 (21,189)	
Hornung, Marc	3:57:32 (11,022)	
Hornung, Michael B	4:43:56 (22,558)	
Horowitz, Gabriel	4:32:17 (19,857)	
Horowitz, Jack	3:57:47 (11,110)	
Horrell, Robert	3:53:25 (9,741)	
Horrocks, Nicholas P	3:28:16 (4,456)	
Horschig, Kai	2:58:45 (1,103)	
Horseman, Jeffrey C	3:01:31 (1,339)	
Horsfall, John L	6:32:33 (32,490)	
Horsfield, Craig L	3:52:37 (9,526)	
Horsley, Graham M	2:58:01 (1,023)	
Horsman, Joseph	3:39:25 (6,523)	
Horstead, Graeme K	3:46:30 (8,010)	
Horton, Andrew R	3:55:15 (10,298)	
Horton, Clive	3:17:54 (2,985)	
Horton, Clive	3:33:24 (5,388)	
Horton, David L	4:44:19 (22,639)	
Horton, Leslie	3:07:52 (1,844)	
Horton, Michael E	3:45:03 (7,701)	
Horton, Patrick A	4:02:35 (12,395)	
Horton, Peter H	3:14:10 (2,551)	
Horton, Rob	4:23:32 (17,513)	
Horton, Rob	4:29:19 (19,122)	
Horton, Robert M	5:26:41 (29,187)	
Horton, Stephen J	5:46:47 (30,847)	
Horwood, Mike J	3:29:59 (4,822)	
Horwood, Thomas H	4:09:10 (13,895)	
Hosegood, Barry	4:35:41 (20,647)	
Hosegood, Martin	3:25:55 (4,061)	
Hosey, Richard P	3:37:20 (6,098)	
Hoske, Oliver	3:35:54 (5,818)	
Hosken, Simon W	4:01:49 (12,219)	
Hoskin, Jeremy D	4:03:27 (12,592)	
Hoskin, Niall P	4:11:07 (14,364)	
Hoskins, Dean M	4:53:05 (24,473)	
Hoskins, Steve	3:59:23 (11,634)	
Hoskyn, John	4:57:59 (25,500)	
Hosler, Darren J	4:05:11 (12,951)	
Hosny, Sherif A	5:29:21 (29,463)	
Hossack, John	4:12:32 (14,716)	
Hossain, Syed	4:28:21 (18,858)	
Hossick, Ian M	4:20:32 (16,742)	
Hothum, Ralf	3:15:17 (2,694)	
Houchell, Oliver A	3:59:42 (11,728)	
Houden, Jon	3:27:48 (4,379)	
Hough, Alan	3:34:32 (5,575)	
Hough, Dermot P	4:01:08 (12,082)	
Hough, Michael P	5:15:11 (27,924)	
Hough, Philip S	4:29:31 (19,184)	
Hougham, Gary C	4:33:21 (20,099)	
Houghton, Alex B	4:01:47 (12,209)	
Houghton, David J	5:49:22 (31,034)	
Houghton, Greg	3:40:52 (6,774)	
Houghton, Michael J	4:25:19 (18,065)	

Houghton, Patrick J	3:29:15 (4,663)	
Houghton, Philip D	4:02:14 (12,312)	
Houghton, Robert	3:37:11 (6,072)	
Houghton, Robin J	2:37:21 (149)	
Houlden, Grant P	4:40:30 (21,777)	
Houldsworth, Richard J	4:53:24 (24,549)	
Houlihan, Patrick J	5:35:57 (30,051)	
Houlot, Geoffrey M	3:36:35 (5,952)	
Houlot, Vincent N	3:39:19 (6,503)	
Hoult, Spencer	5:19:46 (28,467)	
Houlton, Nicholas J	2:40:35 (219)	
Hounsell, John M	4:25:15 (18,042)	
House, David	3:51:41 (9,269)	
House, Ed R	3:53:11 (9,686)	
Houseago, Daniel O	3:49:13 (8,671)	
Household, Richard E	4:44:07 (22,589)	
Housley, Alex M	3:46:35 (8,030)	
Houtby, John F	4:02:05 (12,280)	
How, Chris	3:50:31 (8,989)	
How, Nicholas R	3:51:15 (9,160)	
Howard, Alan M	3:53:59 (9,917)	
Howard, Andrew	4:46:32 (23,129)	
Howard, Andrew J	5:29:44 (29,516)	
Howard, Andrew P	4:18:40 (16,270)	
Howard, David R	3:18:15 (3,024)	
Howard, David R	4:20:18 (16,684)	
Howard, Edward J	4:49:45 (23,801)	
Howard, Ian T	3:47:52 (8,347)	
Howard, James A	4:02:52 (12,449)	
Howard, Julian	4:28:29 (18,894)	
Howard, Kelvin D	4:20:08 (16,636)	
Howard, Kevin S	6:38:41 (32,592)	
Howard, Kevin W	5:07:33 (26,939)	
Howard, Leigh M	3:38:13 (6,270)	
Howard, Martin J	3:27:57 (4,402)	
Howard, Michael P	4:01:23 (12,129)	
Howard, Paul J	3:47:59 (8,378)	
Howard, Philip E	3:17:05 (2,891)	
Howard, Richard P	4:22:19 (17,206)	
Howard, Robin J	3:49:41 (8,793)	
Howard, Roger J	4:02:26 (12,361)	
Howard, Stephen	3:36:02 (5,842)	
Howard, Timothy J	4:06:44 (13,285)	
Howarth, Adam	4:34:55 (20,466)	
Howarth, Christopher	3:15:30 (2,721)	
Howarth, John	5:26:18 (29,153)	
Howarth, Mark	4:38:26 (21,320)	
Howarth, Raymond	4:28:13 (18,817)	
Howarth, Raymond P	3:04:04 (1,518)	
Howarth, Steve	4:42:07 (22,138)	
Howat, Paul	4:28:08 (18,785)	
Howden, Andrew K	4:02:06 (12,285)	
Howden, Matthew A	4:54:46 (24,833)	
Howden-Windell, Nicholas J	5:46:07 (30,794)	
Howe, James E	4:56:14 (25,146)	
Howe, Nicholas J	5:07:48 (26,973)	
Howe, Paul	3:34:18 (5,533)	
Howe, Steven C	4:23:39 (17,546)	
Howe, Steven J	4:00:59 (12,045)	
Howe, Stewart L	4:51:34 (24,156)	
Howell, Christopher E	6:54:49 (32,824)	
Howell, Malcolm J	4:22:23 (17,221)	
Howell, Scott J	2:59:10 (1,157)	
Howell, Sebastian E	3:16:11 (2,797)	
Howell, Stuart	3:07:56 (1,849)	
Howell, Vaughan B	5:46:26 (30,819)	
Howells, Adrian C	5:24:27 (28,986)	
Howells, Alistair	3:14:13 (2,555)	
Howells, Andrew C	3:57:36 (11,045)	
Howells, David S	3:53:24 (9,738)	
Howells, Denis M	4:07:36 (13,506)	
Howells, John M	5:48:45 (30,985)	
Howells, Malcolm	3:21:22 (3,452)	
Howells, Matt	4:14:42 (15,260)	
Howells, Robert B	4:37:17 (21,054)	
Howells, Robert D	3:18:16 (3,025)	
Howes, Colin T	3:28:47 (4,570)	
Howes, David R	3:37:21 (6,105)	
Howes, David W	3:35:08 (5,697)	
Howes, William J	3:56:32 (10,694)	
Howett, Ian R	3:31:55 (5,146)	
Howett, Tim D	3:51:36 (9,243)	
Howgego, Peter G	3:20:42 (3,363)	

Howie, Charles	4:10:28 (14,206)	
Howie, Dan J	3:44:25 (7,543)	
Howitt, Alistair J	4:16:28 (15,714)	
Howlett, Aaron W	4:57:02 (25,319)	
Howlett, Kevin C	3:22:33 (3,603)	
Howlett, Steve	4:41:03 (21,906)	
Howley, Martyn D	4:25:22 (18,079)	
Howorth, Keith	4:15:25 (15,454)	
Howsham, John P	3:38:02 (6,234)	
Howson, Philip D	3:38:05 (6,247)	
Howson, Stephen J	4:05:26 (13,005)	
Hoy, Nicholas M	3:57:21 (10,966)	
Hoyland, Bradley J	4:24:46 (17,884)	
Hoyland, Jim A	4:07:13 (13,406)	
Hoyldsworth, Graham M	6:04:54 (31,759)	
Hoyle, Ian R	5:02:36 (26,262)	
Hoyle, Mark J	4:50:15 (23,893)	
Hoyle, Nick M	4:55:30 (24,997)	
Hoyle, Raymond J	7:30:10 (33,095)	
Huard, Patrick	3:37:46 (6,180)	
Hubbard, John R	4:03:01 (12,481)	
Hubbard, Scott	4:05:37 (13,055)	
Hubbard, Simon W	5:28:27 (29,372)	
Hubbard, Steve J	4:04:22 (12,790)	
Hubble, David W	4:00:52 (12,009)	
Huber, Peter	4:25:52 (18,215)	
Hubert, Steven S	3:56:35 (10,717)	
Huby, Paul	3:44:57 (7,681)	
Huck, Dave	2:58:46 (1,106)	
Huck, Ernest F	3:33:21 (5,378)	
Huckle, Alan P	3:12:34 (2,349)	
Huckle, Ryan J	3:32:58 (5,319)	
Hucknell, David N	4:07:39 (13,519)	
Hudd, Tony A	4:23:27 (17,486)	
Huddart, Andrew J	4:10:35 (14,232)	
Huddart, Matthew J	3:24:22 (3,844)	
Hudjec, Thomas	4:57:24 (25,382)	
Hudson, Andrew D	5:26:06 (29,136)	
Hudson, Ben R	4:59:05 (25,720)	
Hudson, Damian R	4:15:32 (15,484)	
Hudson, Jason	4:43:53 (22,543)	
Hudson, John W	5:24:15 (28,968)	
Hudson, Kenneth	3:38:32 (6,334)	
Hudson, Mat J	4:10:06 (14,121)	
Hudson, Michael J	4:22:17 (17,194)	
Hudson, Paul W	4:37:16 (21,050)	
Hudson, Philip	4:14:33 (15,216)	
Hudson, Richard H	4:21:17 (16,934)	
Hudspith, John E	3:50:41 (9,027)	
Hueber, Didier	3:32:03 (5,169)	
Huebner, Reiner	5:10:18 (27,305)	
Huenermann, Georg	4:30:30 (19,428)	
Hufton, Tim N	3:52:58 (9,617)	
Huggins, Andrew M	5:39:07 (30,293)	
Huggins, Jason F	5:28:02 (29,326)	
Huggins, Malcolm I	3:37:46 (6,180)	
Huggins, Mervyn	5:12:54 (27,748)	
Hughes, Adam R	3:00:10 (1,242)	
Hughes, Ben A	4:54:05 (24,689)	
Hughes, Ceri	4:01:58 (12,255)	
Hughes, Chris	4:20:39 (16,774)	
Hughes, Daniel J	4:10:33 (14,220)	
Hughes, Darren A	3:45:25 (7,787)	
Hughes, Darren G	6:57:09 (32,856)	
Hughes, David A	4:35:43 (20,655)	
Hughes, David R	3:04:28 (1,541)	
Hughes, David R	4:16:28 (15,714)	
Hughes, Frank D	3:20:06 (3,278)	
Hughes, Gareth J	5:16:59 (28,122)	
Hughes, Gareth J	5:45:53 (30,770)	
Hughes, Gary	3:20:46 (3,372)	
Hughes, Gary	4:02:14 (12,312)	
Hughes, Geriant	2:52:28 (651)	
Hughes, Glenn J	4:36:29 (20,842)	
Hughes, Graeme	3:46:05 (7,922)	
Hughes, Graeth	4:35:28 (20,598)	
Hughes, Hywel L	4:36:12 (20,779)	
Hughes, James	5:14:00 (27,760)	
Hughes, Jimmy P	5:58:33 (31,489)	
Hughes, John H	3:57:55 (11,139)	
Hughes, Ken	3:51:10 (9,140)	
Hughes, Leonard M	3:32:33 (5,260)	
Hughes, Leslie	3:39:02 (6,438)	

Hughes, Marc.......4:18:45 (16,291)
Hughes, Marc A.......4:11:21 (14,429)
Hughes, Mark C.......3:27:35 (4,348)
Hughes, Mark D.......3:52:45 (9,557)
Hughes, Mark J.......3:41:42 (6,967)
Hughes, Martin A.......4:45:45 (22,958)
Hughes, Peter H.......4:12:59 (14,831)
Hughes, Peter M.......4:23:15 (17,433)
Hughes, Richard A.......4:37:56 (21,204)
Hughes, Ritchie N.......3:46:26 (7,998)
Hughes, Robert G.......3:41:48 (6,988)
Hughes, Sean P.......5:05:05 (26,596)
Hughes, Simon.......3:56:57 (10,828)
Hughes, Simon G.......4:18:57 (16,344)
Hughes, Stephen R.......3:50:51 (9,066)
Hughes, Stephen R.......4:04:48 (12,879)
Hughes, Terence.......3:01:03 (1,306)
Hughes, Terry.......4:11:14 (14,396)
Hughes, William.......7:29:41 (33,091)
Hughes, William.......7:29:45 (33,093)
Hughes, William D.......4:08:12 (13,666)
Hughes MBE, Evan.......4:05:31 (13,027)
Hugill, Gary W.......3:13:47 (2,501)
Hugo, Jeremy K.......4:46:21 (23,091)
Huke, Michael C.......3:29:19 (4,679)
Hukin, Danny.......3:05:57 (1,660)

Hulcoop, Stephen V.......4:35:45 (20,661)

I always had an ambition to run the London Marathon and finally got accepted in 1989, aged 44. Since then I have run all bar one, with a range of times from 3hrs 37mins in 1995, to 5hrs 33mins in 2010. I have always had the ability to stand on my head and about 2000 decided to incorporate this into my race to prove that running the Marathon is 'as easy as standing on your head'. I did this at various landmarks on the course such as Cutty Sark, Tower Bridge, Canary Wharf and at the finish line in The Mall. About 5 years ago I decided to incorporate another activity in to my antics by taking a skipping rope and skipping as well as standing on my head at the landmark positions. I look upon these activities as an extra way to entertain the crowds, who provide such great support, as well as hopefully giving extra publicity for the charity I am running for.

Hull, Adrian F.......3:53:39 (9,806)
Hull, Andrew M.......5:17:02 (28,133)
Hull, Derek R.......4:07:09 (13,390)
Hull, Keith.......3:27:06 (4,259)
Hull, Rich J.......3:12:22 (2,330)
Hull, Richard P.......3:51:34 (9,238)
Hull, Richard T.......5:25:30 (29,086)
Hull, Richard W.......3:55:15 (10,298)
Hull, Stephen.......4:19:10 (16,382)
Hulm, Simon J.......4:27:04 (18,517)
Hulme, David.......7:09:53 (32,975)
Hulme, Ged.......4:35:48 (20,673)
Hulme, Jack H.......3:30:36 (4,914)
Hulme, Lee H.......5:08:00 (27,005)
Hulme, Thomas A.......4:28:19 (18,847)
Hulse, Christopher T.......3:54:40 (10,099)
Hulse, Michael W.......6:05:16 (31,769)
Hume, Adam R.......3:41:05 (6,826)
Hume, Christopher J.......3:55:26 (10,354)
Hume, Guy V.......3:13:52 (2,509)
Hume, James S.......3:48:40 (8,545)
Hume, Jamie R.......4:00:45 (11,983)
Hume, Richard T.......3:56:22 (10,643)
Humes, Alan.......3:41:50 (6,996)
Hummel, Martin H.......4:36:43 (20,901)
Humphrey, Adam D.......3:51:56 (9,346)
Humphrey, David J.......6:00:22 (31,578)
Humphrey, Matthew D.......3:34:06 (5,498)
Humphrey, Richard A.......3:18:13 (3,021)
Humphrey, Thomas.......4:51:40 (24,179)
Humphreys, Alun W.......3:33:49 (5,451)
Humphreys, Ian S.......3:05:19 (1,608)
Humphreys, Paul T.......4:09:22 (13,950)
Humphries, Barrie J.......4:49:26 (23,740)
Humphries, David J.......3:43:27 (7,342)
Humphries, Graham.......6:30:34 (32,465)
Humphries, Michael.......4:18:56 (16,337)
Humphries, Michael J.......3:53:36 (9,793)
Humphries, Murray.......3:45:43 (7,854)
Humphries, Stephen A.......4:29:44 (19,235)
Humphry, Richard.......3:58:30 (11,340)
Hunphries, Kevin F.......4:46:21 (23,091)
Hunt, Andrew D.......2:26:49 (52)
Hunt, Andrew J.......3:25:56 (4,065)
Hunt, Anthony.......3:54:42 (10,114)
Hunt, Christopher E.......3:47:03 (8,133)
Hunt, David V.......2:54:19 (744)
Hunt, Gary.......4:16:02 (15,604)
Hunt, Ian H.......4:52:52 (24,431)
Hunt, James C.......4:11:03 (14,346)
Hunt, Jeffrey P.......4:46:47 (23,169)
Hunt, Jon R.......3:27:20 (4,301)
Hunt, Matt E.......3:35:55 (5,823)
Hunt, Nick A.......4:53:02 (24,463)
Hunt, Paul D.......3:57:54 (11,134)
Hunt, Peter.......2:50:58 (590)
Hunt, Peter.......3:48:09 (8,422)
Hunt, Peter J.......5:00:05 (25,902)
Hunt, Richard.......4:27:05 (18,524)
Hunt, Richard A.......4:20:54 (16,838)
Hunt, Richard J.......4:47:50 (23,394)
Hunt, Richard J.......4:50:23 (23,920)
Hunt, Rob.......3:49:04 (8,643)
Hunt, Robert P.......3:28:49 (4,578)
Hunt, Shane P.......3:11:26 (2,208)
Hunt, Simon A.......3:20:28 (3,336)
Hunt, Simon M.......2:53:58 (724)
Hunt, Steve B.......3:54:59 (10,196)
Hunt, Steve P.......2:56:47 (921)
Hunter, Aitken.......4:15:23 (15,442)
Hunter, Gareth R.......3:44:39 (7,603)
Hunter, Graham.......5:18:52 (28,351)
Hunter, James.......5:02:07 (26,194)
Hunter, Mark J.......4:29:53 (19,264)
Hunter, Martyn.......4:55:12 (24,941)
Hunter, Miles K.......3:55:51 (10,490)
Hunter, Robert.......3:45:26 (7,789)
Hunter, Ross M.......5:02:05 (26,185)
Hunter, Roy.......4:53:29 (24,562)
Hunter, Steven P.......3:56:32 (10,694)
Hunter Smart, Edward.......3:51:18 (9,173)
Huntley, George E.......4:47:56 (23,417)
Huntley, Neil J.......4:11:15 (14,402)
Hurcom, Melvin G.......3:42:28 (7,106)
Hurd, Andrew J.......3:51:09 (9,135)
Hurd, Philip G.......3:44:42 (7,618)
Hurdle, Gary J.......4:12:06 (14,595)
Hurdley, Paul.......4:31:22 (19,630)
Hurford, Mike J.......3:05:22 (1,616)
Hurley, Ben.......3:49:35 (8,765)
Hurley, Joe G.......3:09:48 (2,044)
Hurley, Mark.......3:57:49 (11,119)
Hurley, Steven D.......3:08:03 (1,865)
Hurn, Anthony.......3:17:13 (2,911)
Hurn, Paul A.......4:05:46 (13,090)
Hurrell, Mark J.......3:11:02 (2,159)
Hurren, Mark A.......4:22:25 (17,229)
Hurry, Richard J.......4:40:50 (21,863)
Hurst, Alan.......4:53:06 (24,479)
Hurst, Alastair.......5:38:11 (30,218)
Hurst, Geoff.......4:37:21 (21,072)
Hurst, Peter.......4:40:02 (21,682)
Hurst, Steven J.......3:38:49 (6,386)
Hursthouse, Carl D.......4:20:09 (16,644)
Hurtado, Joe L.......3:21:18 (3,440)
Husher, Robert J.......4:30:01 (19,299)
Hussain, Khuzema.......4:23:39 (17,546)
Hussain, Sajid.......5:39:04 (30,289)
Hussain, Shahzada H.......4:30:31 (19,432)
Hussain, Tariq.......3:46:23 (7,979)
Hussell, Vincent P.......3:46:30 (8,010)
Hussey, Dominick.......4:13:22 (14,937)
Hussey, Paul.......3:58:10 (11,218)
Hutcheson, Adam J.......4:16:40 (15,773)
Hutcheson, Christopher.......4:04:43 (12,861)
Hutcheson, Luke.......3:48:04 (8,398)
Hutcheson, Mark M.......5:42:17 (30,520)
Hutchings, Andy J.......3:33:45 (5,442)
Hutchings, Gerard.......3:45:48 (7,873)
Hutchings, Lian R.......3:52:08 (9,390)
Hutchings, Richard G.......4:37:45 (21,167)
Hutchings, Terrence R.......8:09:36 (33,184)
Hutchings, Wayne R.......4:05:16 (12,974)
Hutchins, Gareth.......3:31:08 (5,015)
Hutchinson, Alan K.......3:07:11 (1,776)
Hutchinson, Brett G.......3:04:08 (1,525)
Hutchinson, Craig.......3:09:11 (1,974)
Hutchinson, David E.......4:09:20 (13,940)
Hutchinson, David R.......4:52:28 (24,347)
Hutchinson, Doulgas J.......3:08:27 (1,904)
Hutchinson, John.......3:47:41 (8,290)
Hutchinson, Malcolm D.......4:11:59 (14,569)
Hutchinson, Nicholas M.......5:42:54 (30,566)
Hutchinson, Paul W.......4:38:19 (21,305)
Hutchinson, Peter.......4:21:33 (16,985)
Hutchinson, Peter R.......3:58:49 (11,452)
Hutchison, Robert B.......4:05:44 (13,082)
Hutchison, Ross P.......3:31:26 (5,057)
Hutko, Gregory L.......3:54:28 (10,042)
Hutson, Peter R.......3:37:07 (6,059)
Hutson, Raymond C.......4:28:07 (18,780)
Hutt, Mark C.......4:17:19 (15,933)
Hutton, Glenn J.......6:32:27 (32,488)
Hutton, Gregory S.......5:34:19 (29,915)
Hutton, Keith D.......4:49:32 (23,764)
Hutton, Kenneth M.......3:12:40 (2,358)
Hutton, Mark.......3:38:42 (6,365)
Hutton, Martin.......6:41:32 (32,630)
Huxley, André.......3:58:05 (11,178)
Huxley, Philip J.......3:56:21 (10,638)
Huysman, Thierry L.......3:26:31 (4,158)
Hyams, David.......4:46:20 (23,086)
Hyams, John R.......4:58:56 (25,697)
Hyams, Paul R.......3:26:41 (4,189)
Hyatt, Gary F.......3:26:54 (4,223)
Hyde, Gordon E.......5:58:20 (31,477)
Hyde, John N.......3:47:34 (8,259)
Hyde, Nick P.......4:01:07 (12,077)
Hyde, Paul J.......4:52:25 (24,334)
Hyde, Richard T.......3:47:57 (8,374)
Hyde, Stephen.......5:26:19 (29,155)
Hyder, Malcolm C.......3:10:17 (2,095)
Hyder, Richard F.......3:55:29 (10,369)
Hydes, Nigel S.......4:10:37 (14,236)
Hyland, Anthony.......3:06:42 (1,728)
Hyland, Edward T.......3:57:24 (10,979)
Hyland, Timothy C.......4:03:26 (12,589)
Hylands, Christopher.......4:26:44 (18,443)
Hymans, Michael H.......3:52:51 (9,578)
Hymas, Dan G.......5:04:16 (26,485)
Hymas, Max J.......4:20:20 (16,695)
Hynd, Andrew.......3:48:56 (8,618)
Hynes, Richard J.......4:44:01 (22,576)
Hynes, Simon A.......4:03:30 (12,606)
Iacono, David.......3:40:16 (6,671)

I'Anson, Anthony	4:14:18	(15,163)
Ibanez, Gilles	3:45:17	(7,751)
Ibberson, Alan	4:01:33	(12,158)
Ibberson, Hugh B	6:21:30	(32,272)
Ibbotson-Ducker, Andrew	3:47:04	(8,140)
Icely, Nick	4:39:51	(21,640)
Idland, Trond	2:16:09	(18)
Ieda, Giuseppe	4:25:47	(18,189)
Ifcher, Daniel M	2:59:10	(1,157)
Ikediashi, George	5:48:58	(30,998)
Iles, Martin D	4:17:13	(15,910)
Ilic, Nicholas	4:22:51	(17,333)
Illinesi, Anthony M	3:38:27	(6,316)
Illing, Paul	2:58:19	(1,047)
Illingworth, Colin J	4:47:26	(23,304)
Illingworth, David C	3:27:29	(4,330)
Illsley, Robert J	5:35:42	(30,025)
Ilott, Martin C	3:36:11	(5,872)
Ilott, Paul J	2:43:31	(301)
Imanaka, Ichiju	3:46:32	(8,019)
Imbriaco, Guglielmo	5:00:53	(26,026)
Imbriaco, Maurizio	3:34:52	(5,636)
Imperiale, Christian	4:04:28	(12,810)
Imrie, William R	4:21:22	(16,953)
Inamoto, Kenichi	5:04:44	(26,548)
Inamoto, Kenichi	5:06:43	(26,820)
Incardona, Bruno	3:13:18	(2,433)
Ince, Ian J	3:14:46	(2,636)
Ince, Mark G	3:14:42	(2,628)
Ince, Paul J	3:38:54	(6,412)
Inchley, Richard A	3:48:26	(8,483)
Inchley, Thomas J	2:56:34	(900)
Ingason, Haukur	3:58:49	(11,452)
Ingason, Snorri	3:55:34	(10,390)
Ingham, John J	4:01:33	(12,158)
Ingham, Lee	4:40:12	(21,713)
Ingle, Steven J	3:13:02	(2,403)
Ingledew, Neil	3:20:46	(3,372)
Ingles, Colin	5:05:45	(26,671)
Ingles, John L	5:03:07	(26,330)
Inglis, Alexander A	3:32:35	(5,264)
Ingoe, Phill E	3:05:14	(1,597)
Ingold, Andrew J	4:00:28	(11,930)
Ingram, Anthony	5:15:18	(27,936)
Ingram, Charles W	4:52:38	(24,388)
Ingram, Jonathan V	4:31:52	(19,766)
Ingram, Kevin A	4:30:16	(19,371)
Ingram, Lee P	3:48:31	(8,504)
Ingram, Michael J	3:59:03	(11,526)
Ingram, Steven J	4:09:12	(13,909)
Ingram, Stewart W	4:32:45	(19,945)
Inisan, Gildas	3:32:42	(5,279)
Inman, Lawrence A	4:14:34	(15,226)
Innes, Danny N	3:55:19	(10,320)
Innes, Hamish A	3:29:43	(4,765)
Innes, Jason S	4:57:16	(25,364)
Innes, Richard G	3:55:15	(10,298)
Innes Ker, Edward A	4:21:43	(17,026)
Innocenti, Mark J	3:15:51	(2,761)
Inns, Howard G	4:15:20	(15,425)
Inwood, Anthony R	3:54:39	(10,091)
Inwood, Martin J	5:27:30	(29,274)
Ioannou, Yianny	3:57:13	(10,928)
Ion, William J	3:50:36	(9,003)
Ions, Philip J	3:35:35	(5,765)
Iqbal, Lateef	5:59:59	(31,564)
Iqbal, Omar	3:26:28	(4,142)
Ireland, John E	4:07:16	(13,415)
Ireland, Philip S	3:53:17	(9,718)
Irens, Angus	4:04:29	(12,815)
Irish, John C	3:11:17	(2,194)
Irlam, James C	3:19:21	(3,177)
Irons, Alan G	5:16:50	(28,107)
Irons, Graham	3:21:28	(3,464)
Irons, Graham	4:42:07	(22,138)
Irons, Matthew F	4:23:48	(17,589)
Irvine, Angus D	4:32:57	(19,992)
Irvine, Geoffrey P	4:21:00	(16,867)
Irvine, Sam G	3:44:39	(7,603)
Irving, Colin A	5:03:21	(26,364)
Irving, Roger W	3:00:58	(1,299)
Irwin, Dale	4:27:04	(18,517)
Irwin, David T	4:26:45	(18,452)
Isaac, Gareth D	3:44:30	(7,567)
Isaac, Nicholas D	3:13:55	(2,513)
Isaacs, Mark W	4:12:09	(14,612)
Isbill, Robert W	5:19:01	(28,377)
Iseke, Hans	3:35:36	(5,769)
Isely, Robert E	4:07:09	(13,390)
Isenman, Andrew C	3:58:05	(11,178)
Isenmann, Albert	4:14:33	(15,216)
Isherwood, Paul R	2:49:11	(508)
Isherwood, Steven	7:03:23	(32,913)
Islam, Rejaul	5:11:55	(27,515)
Ismail Mohamed, Mohammed	4:27:01	(18,509)
Isman, Renaud H	4:17:17	(15,923)
Ison, Daniel	3:37:34	(6,145)
Issa, Mohsin	3:17:02	(2,880)
Issa, Salim	5:22:44	(28,804)
Issaacs, Jason	3:32:30	(5,252)
Issatt, Howard T	3:28:58	(4,615)
Issatt, Martin	4:00:43	(11,979)
Isted, Stephen G	4:55:48	(25,054)
Ito, Masahiko	3:58:54	(11,476)
Ittershagen-Strauss, Lukas	4:20:08	(16,636)
Iuliano, Domenico	4:29:54	(19,267)
Ivarsson, Goran	6:33:26	(32,504)
Ivens, Derek M	3:10:49	(2,139)
Iversen, Jon Geir	3:13:19	(2,436)
Ives, Andrew E	3:17:29	(2,942)
Ives, Anthony W	3:59:02	(11,523)
Ives, Kevin R	4:57:51	(25,463)
Ives, Stephen J	4:39:56	(21,662)
Ives, Stuart J	3:05:13	(1,596)
Ives, Wayne	3:51:52	(9,324)
Ivory, Damien R	4:49:40	(23,786)
Ivory, Kenneth J	3:04:01	(1,512)
Iwlson, James	3:30:34	(4,907)
Izza, Michael D	4:58:12	(25,549)
Jabbar, Ayaz	7:44:38	(33,156)
Jachens, Victor	3:47:06	(8,145)
Jack, Fergus R	3:50:15	(8,924)
Jack, Nicholas R	4:58:47	(25,658)
Jackett, Mark	3:21:53	(3,520)
Jackson, Andrew	2:38:15	(170)
Jackson, Andrew J	4:29:06	(19,057)
Jackson, Andy W	5:32:06	(29,747)
Jackson, Anthony C	3:22:13	(3,558)
Jackson, Bob	3:14:41	(2,627)
Jackson, Brett A	3:13:56	(2,517)
Jackson, Chris M	4:56:38	(25,226)
Jackson, Christopher A	4:05:03	(12,928)
Jackson, Christopher K	5:06:25	(26,774)
Jackson, Clive J	5:18:13	(28,273)
Jackson, Daniel L	4:14:14	(15,148)
Jackson, Daniel R	6:29:55	(32,446)
Jackson, Darren A	4:26:04	(18,279)
Jackson, David G	4:02:57	(12,467)
Jackson, David P	5:32:59	(29,815)
Jackson, George D	2:59:46	(1,225)
Jackson, Guy	3:41:39	(6,954)
Jackson, Guy	3:55:52	(10,496)
Jackson, Ian	3:51:01	(9,102)
Jackson, Ian	5:21:07	(28,618)
Jackson, Ian	5:36:05	(30,059)
Jackson, Ian G	3:44:18	(7,521)
Jackson, James	6:05:17	(31,771)
Jackson, Joel A	4:24:03	(17,672)
Jackson, Kenneth P	4:47:31	(23,324)
Jackson, Lee A	4:53:33	(24,581)
Jackson, Leslie	4:09:14	(13,919)
Jackson, Luke	2:58:54	(1,129)
Jackson, Mark R	4:04:03	(12,726)
Jackson, Mark R	4:17:58	(16,100)
Jackson, Martin A	4:34:07	(20,276)
Jackson, Martyn R	4:18:51	(16,310)
Jackson, Matthew	3:32:11	(5,198)
Jackson, Mick E	4:28:57	(19,012)
Jackson, Neil	2:55:20	(805)
Jackson, Neil W	5:28:45	(29,406)
Jackson, Nigel A	4:25:04	(17,982)
Jackson, Nigel W	2:52:38	(658)
Jackson, Paul S	3:34:36	(5,593)
Jackson, Paul T	4:02:24	(12,351)
Jackson, Peter E	6:41:48	(32,634)
Jackson, Peter M	4:17:51	(16,072)
Jackson, Peter N	4:33:39	(20,177)
Jackson, Philip C	4:10:19	(14,176)
Jackson, Phillip A	4:27:18	(18,578)
Jackson, Robert C	4:11:06	(14,359)
Jackson, Robert J	4:02:22	(12,345)
Jackson, Robert L	5:14:47	(27,880)
Jackson, Simon C	4:35:31	(20,605)
Jackson, Simon W	3:39:46	(6,582)
Jackson, Stephen C	3:36:31	(5,936)
Jackson, Stephen N	4:10:09	(14,135)
Jacob, Kevin M	3:34:03	(5,491)
Jacob, Owen	4:22:23	(17,221)
Jacobi, Michael A	4:09:58	(14,093)
Jacobi, Sean T	5:56:23	(31,374)
Jacobs, Alan G	4:50:12	(23,881)
Jacobs, Christopher J	5:11:47	(27,491)
Jacobs, Colin R	3:55:36	(10,405)
Jacobs, Darrell M	3:59:02	(11,523)
Jacobs, Darren W	4:58:24	(25,585)
Jacobs, Doug	5:22:43	(28,801)
Jacobs, Jeff	4:01:21	(12,122)
Jacobs, Kenneth J	5:34:25	(29,925)
Jacobs, Nick E	3:17:42	(2,966)
Jacobs, Nicolas P	4:51:32	(24,153)
Jacobs, Philip J	3:41:02	(6,809)
Jacobs, Robert E	4:08:51	(13,824)
Jacobs, Samuel	5:46:59	(30,859)
Jacobsen, Alexander N	5:07:08	(26,884)
Jacobson, Gary T	4:10:45	(14,259)
Jacobson, Paul	4:42:22	(22,197)
Jacques, Marc	2:58:36	(1,075)
Jacquot, Daniel M	5:17:22	(28,180)
Jacqz, Maxime	5:03:11	(26,343)
Jaeckel, Harald	4:12:27	(14,693)
Jaeggi, Heinrich	3:48:35	(8,526)
Jaffe, Peter S	3:27:22	(4,306)
Jaffrey, Farooq	5:05:14	(26,617)
Jagdev, Hartej S	5:09:59	(27,263)
Jagger, Mark A	4:02:04	(12,277)
Jagpal, Raman	5:45:09	(30,727)
Jaime, Ricardo	3:15:20	(2,699)
Jain, Ajay K	4:27:36	(18,655)
Jaines, Simon W	4:49:43	(23,795)
Jaka, Petrit	5:21:08	(28,620)
Jakes, Colin	4:45:00	(22,786)
Jakubowski, Juergen	5:40:17	(30,383)
Jalabert, Laurent	2:57:39	(998)
Jalloh, Aberaham A	2:49:57	(547)
James, Adam T	5:12:54	(27,632)
James, Adrian C	6:12:41	(32,010)
James, Andrew D	3:38:23	(6,301)
James, Andrew M	4:49:05	(23,669)
James, Anthony	5:13:36	(27,729)
James, Ashley	3:53:03	(9,647)
James, Bradley G	2:59:33	(1,198)
James, Charles J	4:04:26	(12,801)
James, Daniel	7:18:30	(33,031)
James, David	3:43:31	(7,354)
James, Dean R	4:24:17	(17,742)
James, Derek J	3:42:47	(7,182)
James, Hylton H	3:26:22	(4,130)
James, Ian F	2:43:01	(287)
James, John M	4:28:45	(18,962)
James, Mark D	3:33:47	(5,447)
James, Mark F	4:39:23	(21,542)
James, Mark R	4:13:58	(15,054)
James, Matt	3:24:33	(3,874)
James, Mike	4:13:36	(14,975)
James, Pete	3:54:17	(9,997)
James, Philip L	4:36:33	(20,857)
James, Rob D	3:31:48	(5,123)
James, Robert S	2:40:36	(220)
James, Robert W	3:53:49	(9,870)
James, Simon	4:28:27	(18,882)
James, Stafford A	3:58:20	(11,280)
James, Steve A	4:03:01	(12,481)
James, Susan C	4:49:05	(23,669)
James, Thomas A	3:28:41	(4,549)
James, Thomas W	3:18:32	(3,073)
James, Timothy C	4:49:13	(23,694)
James, Vernon L	4:03:01	(12,481)
James, William G	3:57:08	(10,893)
James Bowen, Roderick M	4:45:33	(22,913)

Jameson, Andrew D	4:07:10	(13,396)
Jameson, Andrew D	4:40:32	(21,797)
Jameson, Paul	4:57:32	(25,403)
Jamieson, Christopher J	3:52:39	(9,538)
Jamieson, Conor	3:53:00	(9,626)
Jamieson, Robin L	4:16:05	(15,620)
Jan Rooyen, Malcolm J	4:03:16	(12,546)
Janaway, Oliver M	4:45:52	(22,983)
Janbon, Frederic	3:23:17	(3,684)
Jandu, Dhanwant	6:02:07	(31,643)
Jandu, Randeep	6:02:07	(31,643)
Jandu, Sandeep	6:02:08	(31,645)
Jandu, Sukhbindar	4:39:34	(21,567)
Janes, Jeremy N	3:09:11	(1,974)
Janes, Michael R	4:46:02	(23,012)
Janes, Peter A	3:45:18	(7,758)
Jania, Thilo	4:06:21	(13,202)
Jankowski, Jamie L	3:54:59	(10,196)
Janna, Roger	4:19:57	(16,589)
Janoskey, James W	4:01:06	(12,072)
Janot, Lionel	4:31:11	(19,575)
Jans, Ruud	3:59:15	(11,585)
Jansen, Bart I	4:12:21	(14,670)
Jansen, Tom	4:48:46	(23,602)
Janssen, Raf	4:12:21	(14,670)
Janssens, Jean Philippe	3:00:48	(1,289)
Japes, Richard B	4:25:21	(18,075)
Jaques, Mark J	4:05:38	(13,061)
Jaques, Richard C	4:19:26	(16,460)
Jaques, Robert	5:02:49	(26,291)
Jardine, Gary E	4:34:58	(20,480)
Jardine, Graham A	3:51:00	(9,100)
Jardine, Howard W	3:10:51	(2,143)
Jared, Matthew J	4:47:30	(23,319)
Jarlett-Green, Andrew	6:01:55	(31,638)
Jarman, Mark A	4:28:56	(19,006)
Jarrett, Jermaine L	3:59:09	(11,560)
Jarrett, Mark	6:43:23	(32,662)
Jarrett, Nicholas D	3:59:10	(11,563)
Jarrey, Michael C	4:40:12	(21,713)
Jarrold, Darren M	3:21:16	(3,434)
Jarvis, Barry J	4:18:00	(16,108)
Jarvis, James P	4:23:46	(17,578)
Jarvis, Richard P	4:08:47	(13,809)
Jarvis, Simon A	4:11:54	(14,549)
Jarvis, Steve	4:38:02	(21,231)
Jarvis, William M	4:26:02	(18,271)
Jarvis, William R	4:27:20	(18,590)
Jarvisalo, Juha	4:13:50	(15,030)
Jasinevicius, Mindaugas	4:59:10	(25,733)
Jasnoch, Paul	3:14:58	(2,657)
Jason, Robert J	3:31:32	(5,070)
Jaspers, Volker	3:36:08	(5,860)
Jassi, Jagdish R	6:18:57	(32,199)
Javquin, Daniel R	3:49:05	(8,645)
Jay, Eric	4:57:32	(25,403)
Jay, Lee W	4:13:49	(15,025)
Jay, Nick	3:45:14	(7,737)
Jayes, Neil J	4:14:22	(15,175)
Jbara, Nasreddine	4:48:04	(23,442)
Jeacock, Paul A	4:31:14	(19,593)
Jealouse, Arthur R	3:55:54	(10,507)
Jean, Loic	2:54:20	(747)
Jean-Jacques, Patrick J	3:59:02	(11,523)
Jeanne, Lee	3:47:12	(8,168)
Jeatt, Stephen	4:44:14	(22,622)
Jeavons, Stephen M	4:26:53	(18,483)
Jefcoate, Simon N	3:32:57	(5,315)
Jeffcoate, Thomas A	3:24:13	(3,826)
Jefferies, Christopher	3:02:30	(1,406)
Jefferies, Nick	3:44:20	(7,530)
Jefferies, Stacey	3:09:00	(1,959)
Jefferis, Chris J	4:33:25	(20,113)
Jeffery, Adam P	3:38:41	(6,362)
Jeffery, Adrian G	4:13:45	(15,012)
Jeffery, Christopher S	3:36:56	(6,027)
Jeffery, Craig N	2:39:45	(205)
Jeffery, David L	2:56:13	(871)
Jeffery, Jason T	5:32:02	(29,741)
Jeffery, Michael D	4:11:09	(14,377)
Jeffery, Mike S	7:15:41	(33,010)
Jeffery, Robert I	3:33:14	(5,361)
Jeffery, Stephen P	3:01:22	(1,329)
Jefford, Andy	4:33:51	(20,216)
Jeffrey, Allister	4:20:11	(16,656)
Jeffrey, Andrew M	4:12:19	(14,659)
Jeffrey, Jonathon	4:13:19	(14,920)
Jeffrey, Tom	3:48:34	(8,517)
Jeffreys, Adrian C	5:45:56	(30,775)
Jeffreys, Aled R	2:58:35	(1,072)
Jeffries, William	3:32:34	(5,262)
Jeffs, Ptere R	3:44:48	(7,643)
Jeffs, Richard G	4:02:14	(12,312)
Jelden, Wendy J	5:10:58	(27,380)
Jelley, David	2:56:52	(926)
Jelley, Jonathan A	4:35:26	(20,588)
Jelley, Matthew A	4:35:27	(20,594)
Jelley, Peter J	4:24:07	(17,691)
Jelley, Roger	4:56:42	(25,243)
Jellis, David	3:54:17	(9,997)
Jenkin, Daniel J	3:13:10	(2,421)
Jenkin, Huw D	2:42:14	(255)
Jenkin, Phil	5:28:02	(29,326)
Jenkins, Andrew	3:51:57	(9,351)
Jenkins, Andrew	5:36:07	(30,061)
Jenkins, Barnaby G	3:52:58	(9,617)
Jenkins, Brian	3:53:44	(9,833)
Jenkins, Christopher J	3:38:25	(6,309)
Jenkins, Christopher J	4:13:07	(14,878)
Jenkins, David Emyr	5:08:50	(27,122)
Jenkins, David P	4:52:32	(24,363)
Jenkins, David S	3:58:31	(11,344)
Jenkins, Gerraint H	4:22:04	(17,137)
Jenkins, Huw A	4:06:20	(13,201)
Jenkins, Huw W	2:55:04	(792)
Jenkins, Jonathan M	3:56:59	(10,842)
Jenkins, Mark P	4:24:14	(17,725)
Jenkins, Martyn	4:29:56	(19,276)
Jenkins, Paul A	3:16:39	(2,834)
Jenkins, Peter	5:07:00	(26,861)
Jenkins, Peter J	4:03:55	(12,695)
Jenkins, Philip J	4:18:05	(16,137)
Jenkins, Robert	4:48:56	(23,636)
Jenkins, Robert	5:07:13	(26,895)
Jenkins, Robert A	4:13:27	(14,951)
Jenkins MBE, Ian C	6:32:27	(32,488)
Jenkinson, Damian F	4:34:32	(20,371)
Jenkinson, David M	5:22:09	(28,733)
Jenkinson, Jonathan G	3:33:24	(5,388)
Jenkinson, Peter J	4:18:14	(16,165)
Jenks, Andrew M	5:00:09	(25,915)
Jenn, Michael	5:02:43	(26,275)
Jenner, Adam	4:38:00	(21,223)
Jenner, Marc E	4:31:35	(19,692)
Jennings, Barrie C	3:52:12	(9,410)
Jennings, Cliff	3:56:46	(10,769)
Jennings, Jason	5:18:24	(28,297)
Jennings, Keenan	3:05:01	(1,576)
Jennings, Kenneth E	4:48:33	(23,552)
Jennings, Mark	2:39:06	(191)
Jennings, Mike	3:52:26	(9,481)
Jennings, Neil R	3:22:34	(3,604)
Jennings, Paul	3:16:07	(2,792)
Jennings, Paul D	4:04:27	(12,804)
Jennings, Shaun A	4:38:11	(21,280)
Jennings, Stephen C	4:51:20	(24,101)
Jennison, Richard	5:15:57	(27,995)
Jennkins, Stuart P	3:46:46	(8,074)
Jensen, Cameron	4:20:21	(16,699)
Jensen, David A	3:43:30	(7,351)
Jensen, Dennis	2:19:37	(29)
Jensen, Erik L	3:34:51	(5,633)
Jensen, Henrik H	3:52:38	(9,534)
Jensen, Lars B	3:10:35	(2,122)
Jeong, Dong Chang	5:17:09	(28,146)
Jephson, Bill	4:29:09	(19,070)
Jepps, Neil J	5:00:35	(25,981)
Jepson, Paul	4:22:18	(17,199)
Jepson, Stuart I	4:36:18	(20,803)
Jerman, Richard G	4:07:02	(13,351)
Jerome, Mark E	5:01:34	(26,113)
Jerome-Ball, Graham S	3:54:48	(10,145)
Jerrom, Barry	6:46:25	(32,718)
Jessop, Allan B	4:45:51	(22,978)
Jessop, Christopher H	3:57:22	(10,969)
Jessup, Peter	5:25:10	(29,055)
Jethwa, Paras	3:16:55	(2,868)
Jethwa, Tejal K	4:18:04	(16,128)
Jewell, Adam	4:39:12	(21,490)
Jewell, Mark G	4:23:48	(17,589)
Jewell, Martin R	3:29:31	(4,723)
Jewkes, Richard S	3:06:59	(1,758)
Jezowski, Slawomir	3:08:05	(1,869)
Jhaveri, Noormahomed O	5:15:29	(27,950)
Jicquel, Gerard	3:52:48	(9,569)
Jinivizian, Alex B	3:52:45	(9,557)
Jinks, Nicholas P	5:12:53	(27,629)
Joad, Dave W	4:38:05	(21,251)
Joannou, Philip A	5:05:06	(26,599)
Jobling, Justin P	5:52:29	(31,196)
Jobson, Martin	5:32:51	(29,804)
Jocelyn, Steven M	3:56:12	(10,593)
Jochym, Bogdan	4:24:30	(17,802)
Joel, Geoff	4:30:40	(19,467)
Johan J, Van Dijk	3:57:42	(11,072)
Johansson, Kent	3:48:19	(8,457)
Johansson, Lars Ake	3:52:48	(9,569)
John, Andrew M	4:21:17	(16,934)
John, Chris	7:54:24	(33,172)
John, Gareth	4:20:41	(16,783)
John, Gareth N	3:45:17	(7,751)
John, Gilbert G	4:50:33	(23,949)
John, Harry S	3:25:22	(3,991)
John, Lewis D	5:14:57	(27,899)
John, Nicholas	6:36:40	(32,554)
John, Steven W	4:32:40	(19,925)
Johnes, Christopher I	4:07:36	(13,506)
Johnes, Simon H	3:26:38	(4,182)
Johns, Christopher J	3:36:15	(5,884)
Johns, Gavin P	4:15:28	(15,469)
Johns, Mark	4:27:34	(18,644)
Johnson, Adrian L	4:37:26	(21,094)
Johnson, Andrew	3:37:50	(6,198)
Johnson, Andrew R	4:33:28	(20,126)
Johnson, Arthur N	4:34:19	(20,310)
Johnson, Ben	3:48:02	(8,392)
Johnson, Brian J	4:05:18	(12,978)
Johnson, Carl W	6:35:31	(32,536)
Johnson, Christopher	4:38:02	(21,231)
Johnson, Christopher M	4:15:38	(15,503)
Johnson, Colin	5:15:42	(27,968)
Johnson, Craig K	4:47:56	(23,417)
Johnson, Daniel L	3:39:48	(6,589)
Johnson, Daniel W	5:04:14	(26,479)
Johnson, David	3:23:01	(3,659)
Johnson, Dominic J	5:15:07	(27,912)
Johnson, Gary	3:37:33	(6,140)
Johnson, George D	3:50:12	(8,911)
Johnson, Gerald C	4:15:14	(15,398)
Johnson, Graham L	6:35:55	(32,542)
Johnson, Henry T	4:15:36	(15,496)
Johnson, Howard A	5:04:16	(26,485)
Johnson, Ian	6:36:18	(32,548)
Johnson, Ian A	4:45:58	(22,998)
Johnson, James E	5:18:59	(28,370)
Johnson, James G	6:59:56	(32,881)
Johnson, Joe C	4:12:02	(14,580)
Johnson, John S	3:56:07	(10,573)
Johnson, Jonathan	3:39:54	(6,606)
Johnson, Lee	3:05:39	(1,629)
Johnson, Malcolm	3:48:35	(8,526)
Johnson, Maxwell	4:41:57	(22,098)
Johnson, Michael I	5:03:38	(26,409)
Johnson, Mike	3:55:30	(10,374)
Johnson, Nathaniel L	3:59:40	(11,715)
Johnson, Neale	4:19:20	(16,430)
Johnson, Neil	3:42:12	(7,065)
Johnson, Neil A	5:23:13	(28,859)
Johnson, Nick	3:31:45	(5,112)
Johnson, Paul	4:20:57	(16,853)
Johnson, Paul A	4:00:46	(11,985)
Johnson, Paul S	7:18:01	(33,029)
Johnson, Paul W	3:14:52	(2,647)
Johnson, Ray D	3:49:50	(8,828)
Johnson, Raymond	4:55:20	(24,969)
Johnson, Richard	5:00:01	(25,886)
Johnson, Richard J	4:07:40	(13,525)
Johnson, Richard M	3:47:41	(8,290)
Johnson, Robert G	4:26:44	(18,443)

Johnson, Robert P.................7:28:03 (33,087)
Johnson, Robert S.................4:01:22 (12,125)
Johnson, Simon K.................3:49:28 (8,734)
Johnson, Stephen P.................5:06:09 (26,733)
Johnson, Steven.................5:36:07 (30,061)
Johnson, Tony.................2:56:36 (903)
Johnson, Walter D.................5:18:51 (28,350)
Johnson, William E.................4:28:16 (18,831)
Johnston, Adrian.................4:52:20 (24,317)
Johnston, Andrew I.................3:43:48 (7,422)
Johnston, Andrew P.................3:50:12 (8,911)
Johnston, Angus.................4:07:36 (13,506)
Johnston, Barry.................4:52:49 (24,426)
Johnston, David A.................4:06:54 (13,328)
Johnston, David N.................4:01:04 (12,063)
Johnston, Gordon M.................5:10:22 (27,313)
Johnston, Harry G.................3:51:27 (9,209)
Johnston, James.................4:36:53 (20,960)
Johnston, Kevin D.................3:26:39 (4,184)
Johnston, Kim H.................3:52:32 (9,501)
Johnston, Lee J.................6:22:17 (32,297)
Johnston, Mark N.................3:26:55 (4,225)
Johnston, Mark W.................3:56:38 (10,734)
Johnston, Richard A.................4:06:56 (13,333)
Johnston, Robert D.................3:42:20 (7,084)
Johnston, Sandy M.................3:04:03 (1,515)
Johnston, Scott.................4:24:13 (17,717)
Johnstone, Neil.................3:27:36 (4,353)
Johnstone, Paul S.................4:16:25 (15,695)
Johnstone, Robert M.................3:54:18 (10,004)
Johntop Flat, Gareth H.................5:56:13 (31,368)
Johri, Kapil K.................4:12:14 (14,634)
Jokhan, Martin.................6:23:37 (32,320)
Jollie, David M.................3:59:48 (11,762)
Jolliffe, Darron J.................4:33:11 (20,055)
Jolliffe, David T.................4:12:57 (14,824)
Jolliffe, Robert J.................3:30:47 (4,942)
Jolly, Stephen G.................4:19:07 (16,368)
Jolly, Victoria A.................5:22:18 (28,753)
Joly, Pascal C.................3:52:51 (9,578)
Jomehri, Ali B.................5:28:43 (29,402)
Jonas, Andy C.................4:05:12 (12,958)
Jonas, Warren L.................4:28:02 (18,757)
Jonathan, Hugh O.................3:46:44 (8,069)
Jones, Adam.................3:18:45 (3,100)
Jones, Adrian.................4:27:02 (18,511)
Jones, Adrian.................4:48:02 (23,434)
Jones, Adrian D.................3:38:02 (6,234)
Jones, Alan.................3:50:53 (9,072)
Jones, Alan.................5:47:26 (30,913)
Jones, Aled R.................3:41:07 (6,831)
Jones, Alexander A.................5:00:24 (25,960)
Jones, Alexander W.................5:30:09 (29,556)
Jones, Alistair T.................3:53:52 (9,887)
Jones, Allan.................5:15:12 (27,926)
Jones, Allen D.................2:41:38 (238)
Jones, Alun.................4:46:48 (23,171)
Jones, Andi.................2:19:16 (25)
Jones, Andrew D.................3:48:08 (8,414)
Jones, Andrew F.................4:15:39 (15,508)
Jones, Andrew F.................4:54:44 (24,823)
Jones, Andrew L.................3:48:35 (8,526)
Jones, Andrew M.................5:38:21 (30,237)
Jones, Andrew N.................5:12:38 (27,605)
Jones, Anthony A.................4:59:36 (25,811)
Jones, Arwel W.................3:11:03 (2,161)
Jones, Ben.................4:45:02 (22,798)
Jones, Bernad.................3:53:55 (9,897)
Jones, Bradford.................4:41:50 (22,062)
Jones, Brian.................5:02:57 (26,310)
Jones, Brian P.................3:57:54 (11,134)
Jones, Bruce A.................3:44:31 (7,570)
Jones, Chris.................5:06:38 (26,807)
Jones, Chris H.................3:47:12 (8,168)
Jones, Chris P.................3:42:20 (7,084)
Jones, Christopher L.................5:08:13 (27,037)
Jones, Christopher M.................5:15:55 (27,993)
Jones, Craig P.................4:56:16 (25,155)
Jones, Cyril.................4:11:36 (14,479)
Jones, Daniel.................4:27:47 (18,693)
Jones, Daniel.................5:22:59 (28,824)
Jones, Daniel T.................3:31:09 (5,017)
Jones, Danny.................4:06:52 (13,316)

Jones, Darren L.................6:18:54 (32,196)
Jones, Darren R.................3:17:03 (2,882)
Jones, Darron S.................2:46:55 (413)
Jones, Dave.................4:08:14 (13,674)
Jones, David.................3:52:59 (9,623)
Jones, David.................4:18:55 (16,331)
Jones, David.................5:49:26 (31,038)
Jones, David A.................4:45:18 (22,856)
Jones, David H.................3:19:55 (3,250)
Jones, David K.................3:54:35 (10,074)
Jones, David M.................4:28:58 (19,018)
Jones, David R.................2:50:53 (583)
Jones, David R.................2:56:21 (878)
Jones, David R.................4:23:32 (17,513)
Jones, David T.................3:50:37 (9,009)
Jones, David T.................5:22:57 (28,819)
Jones, Dennis R.................4:55:06 (24,920)
Jones, Dominic N.................3:59:19 (11,611)
Jones, Donald L.................3:31:32 (5,070)
Jones, Duncan J.................3:29:48 (4,782)
Jones, Francis D.................5:32:56 (29,811)
Jones, Gareth.................4:08:02 (13,621)
Jones, Gareth D.................5:55:38 (31,339)
Jones, Gareth H.................4:04:55 (12,899)
Jones, Gareth J.................3:58:46 (11,431)
Jones, Gareth K.................4:15:06 (15,366)
Jones, Gareth L.................4:41:07 (21,918)
Jones, Garry D.................3:51:50 (9,313)
Jones, George W.................3:35:53 (5,814)
Jones, Geraint R.................4:17:14 (15,914)
Jones, Glyn.................3:39:27 (6,535)
Jones, Glyn.................3:58:07 (11,195)
Jones, Graeme S.................3:38:49 (6,386)
Jones, Graham A.................5:38:31 (30,253)
Jones, Graham E.................4:03:10 (12,522)
Jones, Graham P.................4:48:58 (23,644)
Jones, Grahame.................3:48:44 (8,565)
Jones, Grant F.................3:49:14 (8,674)
Jones, Hadyn H.................3:00:19 (1,255)
Jones, Howard N.................3:03:19 (1,464)
Jones, Huw.................4:16:42 (15,779)
Jones, Huw.................5:35:39 (30,024)
Jones, Huw G.................3:44:28 (7,558)
Jones, Ian.................3:56:28 (10,676)
Jones, Ian D.................4:51:25 (24,129)
Jones, Ian O.................5:20:13 (28,521)
Jones, John.................4:00:26 (11,921)
Jones, John E.................6:49:07 (32,747)
Jones, John O.................4:12:45 (14,761)
Jones, Justin G.................4:58:33 (25,623)
Jones, Keith G.................3:47:43 (8,301)
Jones, Keith R.................6:12:10 (31,994)
Jones, Kenning I.................4:29:59 (19,288)
Jones, Kev.................4:22:15 (17,188)
Jones, Kevin.................4:21:35 (16,993)
Jones, Kevin T.................4:05:06 (12,939)
Jones, Laurence W.................6:41:55 (32,639)
Jones, Leslie A.................5:21:21 (28,652)
Jones, Llewelyn.................3:17:47 (2,975)
Jones, Malcolm J.................6:19:21 (32,215)
Jones, Marc D.................4:29:11 (19,079)
Jones, Meirion.................5:46:28 (30,822)
Jones, Merrick A.................4:22:56 (17,350)
Jones, Michael D.................2:58:54 (1,129)
Jones, Michael E.................4:35:09 (20,521)
Jones, Michael W.................3:45:22 (7,777)
Jones, Milton P.................4:30:40 (19,467)
Jones, Neil.................4:52:14 (24,292)
Jones, Neil A.................3:45:12 (7,730)
Jones, Neil B.................4:29:28 (19,167)
Jones, Neil G.................4:24:17 (17,742)
Jones, Neil R.................3:52:32 (9,501)
Jones, Nicholas M.................5:30:45 (29,622)
Jones, Nick A.................4:59:53 (25,866)
Jones, Nigel.................4:35:00 (20,491)
Jones, Nigel D.................3:09:23 (1,998)
Jones, Nigel F.................3:00:34 (1,279)
Jones, Norman V.................7:32:23 (33,103)
Jones, Oliver.................2:52:50 (665)
Jones, Oliver S.................4:04:38 (12,837)
Jones, Owen L.................4:31:39 (19,711)
Jones, Paul.................3:46:06 (7,926)
Jones, Paul.................4:30:29 (19,424)

Jones, Paul.................4:30:56 (19,515)
Jones, Paul.................4:57:43 (25,436)
Jones, Paul.................5:07:18 (26,906)
Jones, Paul L.................4:31:31 (19,668)
Jones, Paul M.................4:10:48 (14,277)
Jones, Paul T.................5:08:44 (27,110)
Jones, Peter.................4:10:56 (14,312)
Jones, Peter.................4:17:36 (16,018)
Jones, Peter C.................4:07:02 (13,351)
Jones, Peter G.................3:13:28 (2,462)
Jones, Peter L.................3:36:58 (6,035)
Jones, Petre T.................5:26:48 (29,201)
Jones, Philip A.................4:50:15 (23,893)
Jones, Philip L.................5:19:51 (28,475)
Jones, Philip O.................3:58:40 (11,388)
Jones, Ralph W.................4:18:27 (16,218)
Jones, Raymond G.................6:26:31 (32,390)
Jones, Rhodri D.................4:36:52 (20,955)
Jones, Rhodri L.................4:07:56 (13,593)
Jones, Richard A.................4:48:18 (23,493)
Jones, Richard H.................5:12:27 (27,585)
Jones, Richard M.................3:41:14 (6,858)
Jones, Richard R.................3:14:47 (2,637)
Jones, Robert P.................3:30:24 (4,878)
Jones, Robin C.................3:41:52 (7,002)
Jones, Russell.................3:29:30 (4,718)
Jones, Sam.................3:19:56 (3,255)
Jones, Simon.................2:33:04 (89)
Jones, Simon.................3:35:11 (5,705)
Jones, Simon G.................3:21:50 (3,517)
Jones, Stephen.................2:59:19 (1,178)
Jones, Stephen.................3:59:05 (11,538)
Jones, Stephen A.................3:55:41 (10,431)
Jones, Stephen N.................5:16:29 (28,068)
Jones, Steve.................4:38:20 (21,308)
Jones, Steve N.................3:01:52 (1,362)
Jones, Thomas.................4:07:12 (13,403)
Jones, Thomas H.................3:21:06 (3,411)
Jones, Tim.................3:00:32 (1,275)
Jones, Tom W.................3:13:02 (2,403)
Jones, Tony J.................5:21:29 (28,663)
Jones, Vernon.................4:29:41 (19,222)
Jones, Vincent A.................3:10:29 (2,110)
Jones, Walter.................5:28:41 (29,401)
Jones, William J.................4:42:59 (22,325)
Jonker, Jan J.................4:03:15 (12,538)
Jonsson, Jon G.................3:38:13 (6,270)
Jonsson, Lars.................3:27:40 (4,360)
Jonsson, Magnus T.................3:23:28 (3,706)
Jooste, Conrad G.................3:50:17 (8,931)
Jordan, Andrew P.................4:08:01 (13,616)
Jordan, Andy.................3:55:31 (10,382)
Jordan, Ed.................4:06:41 (13,271)
Jordan, Frenny W.................4:41:13 (21,927)
Jordan, Kevin M.................4:32:12 (19,833)
Jordan, Mark A.................3:56:44 (10,763)
Jordan, Matthew P.................3:45:40 (7,841)
Jordan, Paul.................3:56:46 (10,769)
Jordan, Philip J.................4:23:00 (17,366)
Jordan, Richard W.................2:42:39 (269)
Jordan, Shaun G.................3:52:28 (9,485)
Jordan, Simon K.................3:58:13 (11,238)
Jorna, Thomas A.................3:59:01 (11,517)
Jorritsma, Sjoerd.................3:38:58 (6,428)
Joseph, Paul B.................5:05:40 (26,663)
Josephs, Gideon.................6:17:41 (32,163)
Josephs, Merrick.................3:58:24 (11,306)
Josephson, Erik W.................5:12:58 (27,645)
Joshi, Anil.................3:52:59 (9,623)
Joshi, Raj.................6:01:31 (31,628)
Joslin, Christopher A.................4:45:18 (22,856)
Joslin, Shaun.................4:13:25 (14,948)
Josseron, Herve.................3:38:49 (6,386)
Jotcham, Daniel J.................3:40:42 (6,746)
Joules, Keith.................2:48:13 (460)
Jourbert, Frederick.................5:53:45 (31,251)
Jourdain, Pierre.................3:04:11 (1,526)
Jourdan-Brown, Mark A.................4:39:29 (21,556)
Jowatte, Christophe.................3:23:33 (3,717)
Jowett, Chris J.................3:58:20 (11,280)
Jowett, Iain A.................5:34:24 (29,923)
Jowett, Kenneth W.................5:34:30 (29,933)
Joy, Mark.................4:48:28 (23,532)

Joyce, Alan D	4:08:57 (13,852)
Joyce, Alistair W	4:00:53 (12,012)
Joyce, Ciaran S	3:30:02 (4,830)
Joyce, Daniel J	4:27:10 (18,548)
Joyce, Jim	4:23:29 (17,496)
Joyce, John E	5:15:09 (27,916)
Joyce, Paul W	3:28:55 (4,608)
Joyce, Ryan J	3:44:55 (7,674)
Joyce, Stephen	3:49:15 (8,682)
Joyner, Jim B	3:51:13 (9,151)
Jubb, Michael	3:59:38 (11,702)
Judd, Guy A	4:13:14 (14,906)
Judge, Bruce G	2:38:31 (180)
Judge, Ciaran C	5:10:35 (27,344)
Judge, Gregory W	4:25:13 (18,033)
Judge, Michael R	4:25:58 (18,249)
Judge, Sean P	3:36:42 (5,976)
Jukes, Daman	3:31:06 (5,005)
Jukes, Jeremy D	4:13:30 (14,955)
Juliusson, Gunnlaugur A	3:30:18 (4,865)
Julyan, Martin	4:43:54 (22,549)
Jumani, Ish A	4:06:08 (13,167)
Jummon, Arnold	4:22:01 (17,121)
Juniper, Gavin S	5:25:43 (29,104)
Jurgens, Mark J	3:11:54 (2,262)
Jusgen, Roger A	3:53:52 (9,887)
Justice, James J	4:46:15 (23,062)
Jutson, Kevin T	4:16:18 (15,668)
Juul, Niels	3:33:59 (5,479)
Juzaszek, Dawid J	3:44:34 (7,585)
Kabaria, Nilesh	4:32:03 (19,801)
Kadiwar, Kantilal	7:00:52 (32,889)
Kaempfer, Alexander	4:08:09 (13,652)
Kaempfer, Matthias	5:55:53 (31,348)
Kaess, Hermann	3:33:34 (5,410)
Kaestele, Thomas	3:52:42 (9,549)
Kahlon, Amarjit	4:08:08 (13,648)
Kahnau, Raoul W	3:45:17 (7,751)
Kainth, Ranjiet	3:08:26 (1,902)
Kaligotla, Sudhir	5:18:13 (28,273)
Kalinski, Stephan	4:20:39 (16,774)
Kallgarden, Per	2:43:07 (292)
Kalymnios, Hari	3:43:35 (7,366)
Kamal, Faisal	5:27:05 (29,235)
Kamalanathan, Selladurai	5:07:43 (26,964)
Kamara, Lamin	4:28:53 (18,991)
Kambara, Koji	5:55:33 (31,331)
Kamji, Mohamed	5:30:48 (29,629)
Kan, Simon C	3:59:15 (11,585)
Kanarski, Jaroslaw	5:16:41 (28,091)
Kandola, Harpinder S	4:09:36 (14,016)
Kane, Gary	3:30:40 (4,926)
Kane, Iain G	3:58:18 (11,266)
Kane, Jonathan J	3:24:38 (3,886)
Kane, Nicholas M	3:11:53 (2,256)
Kanikanian, Armen	5:45:34 (30,755)
Kanyua, John G	4:55:10 (24,928)
Kapadia, Hatim	4:23:19 (17,448)
Kaplan, David	4:36:25 (20,828)
Kapoor, Neil	3:02:48 (1,424)
Kara, Zaahid G	3:51:31 (9,222)
Karim, Aziz E	4:14:15 (15,150)
Karim, Majid	4:14:15 (15,150)
Karim, Muqu	3:38:10 (6,260)
Karim, Rauf	5:40:42 (30,406)
Karklins, Gunars	5:47:35 (30,924)
Karlcut, Harpal	4:22:56 (17,350)
Karlsen, Morten	4:02:52 (12,449)
Karlsson, Mats	3:43:14 (7,295)
Karlsson, Ola A	3:32:31 (5,256)
Karnfalt, Goran	3:13:00 (2,397)
Karran, Andrew	4:52:02 (24,256)
Karski, Alexander J	3:36:49 (5,997)
Kasprzak, Mark	3:35:02 (5,669)
Kass, Mark L	2:56:02 (850)
Kat, Gregory	3:01:47 (1,355)
Katchi, Stephen D	3:40:53 (6,776)
Kato, Hiromichi	4:45:56 (22,994)
Katow, Gennady	4:22:58 (17,358)
Katz, Jason J	5:37:30 (30,166)
Kauffman, Jean Marc	3:59:55 (11,790)
Kaufman, Daniel E	4:34:43 (20,416)
Kaulgud, Dinesh S	7:11:49 (32,995)

Kavanagh, Anthony E	4:12:32 (14,716)
Kavanagh, Declan B	5:23:48 (28,919)
Kavanagh, Kevin S	4:19:32 (16,489)
Kavanagh, Peter	3:59:03 (11,526)
Kavanagh, Steven	4:48:26 (23,520)
Kavanagh, Terence W	5:17:59 (28,237)
Kavanagh, Terry F	4:12:07 (14,603)
Kay, Chris	4:35:36 (20,624)
Kay, David E	5:11:25 (27,444)
Kay, Julian	5:01:02 (26,048)
Kay, Matthew S	2:55:11 (798)
Kay, Paul	3:19:35 (3,200)
Kay, Peter A	5:11:56 (27,519)
Kay, Peter M	3:15:56 (2,772)
Kay, Robert	2:59:39 (1,217)
Kaye, Ben A	5:12:15 (27,555)
Kaye, Ian	5:31:04 (29,664)
Kaye, Martin	4:23:40 (17,552)
Kayum, Donald A	3:00:28 (1,269)
Kealy, Alan	5:01:38 (26,124)
Kean, Adam	3:57:03 (10,861)
Kean, Jonathan	3:21:19 (3,442)
Keane, Denis	4:38:04 (21,245)
Keane, John P	4:09:53 (14,076)
Keane, Padraig	3:55:37 (10,409)
Keane, Patrick C	3:34:25 (5,551)
Keane, Peter T	3:35:02 (5,669)
Keane, Simon J	3:28:53 (4,601)
Keaney, Kilian J	4:44:16 (22,629)
Kearney, Brian P	7:25:01 (33,069)
Kearney, Edward	3:40:39 (6,741)
Kearns, Alex J	4:04:50 (12,882)
Kearns, James P	3:53:03 (9,647)
Kearns, Joe	3:44:47 (7,638)
Kearns, Liam J	3:54:03 (9,930)
Kearns, Simon J	3:15:57 (2,776)
Kearsey, Ray C	3:43:34 (7,362)
Kearsey, Timothy J	5:23:57 (28,933)
Kearsley, Mark P	5:04:51 (26,561)
Keast, Richard L	3:43:20 (7,315)
Keat, Daniel E	4:18:57 (16,344)
Keates, Garry C	3:46:42 (8,060)
Keating, John B	4:00:06 (11,843)
Keating, Mark A	4:01:18 (12,115)
Keating, Patrick N	5:01:17 (26,085)
Keating, Rory B	3:20:41 (3,360)
Keating, Timothy	3:50:15 (8,924)
Keay, Kevin W	4:43:01 (22,331)
Kebbell, Richard	4:41:17 (21,948)
Kee, Howard W	3:10:53 (2,146)
Keeble, Ian R	2:44:10 (317)
Keeble, Jamie M	3:39:57 (6,620)
Keech, Edward J	5:55:44 (31,344)
Keech, Leonard R	4:38:42 (21,371)
Keech, Paul A	3:25:20 (3,980)
Keech, Tony	3:36:41 (5,972)
Keegan, Andy J	3:50:44 (9,037)
Keegan, James M	6:03:54 (31,723)
Keegan, Nicholas J	4:45:35 (22,920)
Keegan, Paul M	4:44:46 (22,724)
Keegan, Robert	3:44:43 (7,621)
Keehner, Robert E	6:00:20 (31,576)
Keelan, Edward P	4:05:24 (13,000)
Keeler, Andrew	3:18:12 (3,019)
Keeley, David A	4:48:56 (23,636)
Keeling, Colin L	4:16:56 (15,843)
Keeling, Dean C	4:55:57 (25,091)
Keely, Paddy	4:26:01 (18,263)
Keen, Bob	3:50:46 (9,050)
Keen, Howard S	4:20:28 (16,727)
Keen, Jason W	4:17:25 (15,960)
Keen, Leslie M	5:25:05 (29,050)
Keen, Michael G	3:54:14 (9,988)
Keenan, Brian	4:07:40 (13,525)
Keenan, David M	3:07:30 (1,806)
Keenan, Frank E	3:57:42 (11,072)
Keenan, Graeme A	4:38:55 (21,423)
Keenan, Ian	4:00:51 (12,005)
Keenan, Mark J	5:00:31 (25,970)
Keene, Benjamin G	3:16:30 (2,819)
Keene, Graham L	3:52:50 (9,576)
Keenleyside, Piers B	4:12:13 (14,629)
Keep, Robert P	3:54:51 (10,160)

Keep, Trevor	3:15:55 (2,769)
Keeping, James P	3:51:48 (9,303)
Keighley, Charles J	3:58:50 (11,460)
Keiller, Robert	5:35:13 (29,988)
Keilloh, Richard J	4:29:16 (19,107)
Keilty, Sean C	4:31:04 (19,544)
Keily, John F	4:51:22 (24,112)
Keith, Ian N	3:49:14 (8,674)
Keizer, Rekky	4:18:46 (16,298)
Kelf, Paul D	4:36:26 (20,832)
Kellermayr, Sebastian	3:02:28 (1,403)
Kellett, Gary K	3:03:05 (1,452)
Kellie, Thomas J	4:41:44 (22,046)
Kelly, Adam J	5:10:15 (27,298)
Kelly, Andrew J	5:01:34 (26,113)
Kelly, Christopher J	3:34:16 (5,523)
Kelly, Christopher J	3:44:28 (7,558)
Kelly, Christopher J	4:43:27 (22,421)
Kelly, Christopher P	4:56:18 (25,164)
Kelly, Christopher T	3:07:48 (1,840)
Kelly, Daniel I	3:58:39 (11,382)
Kelly, Daniel P	4:14:02 (15,080)
Kelly, David C	5:21:50 (28,694)
Kelly, Dominic J	3:07:35 (1,811)
Kelly, Graham E	3:44:47 (7,638)
Kelly, Hugh	3:29:50 (4,795)
Kelly, John M	3:56:41 (10,750)
Kelly, John S	6:08:49 (31,889)
Kelly, Kevin P	2:54:33 (761)
Kelly, Liam P	4:08:32 (13,750)
Kelly, Martin C	4:25:27 (18,105)
Kelly, Michael G	5:58:27 (31,484)
Kelly, Michael J	3:58:51 (11,464)
Kelly, Michael T	4:15:20 (15,425)
Kelly, Patrick	3:23:33 (3,717)
Kelly, Paul	4:41:23 (21,966)
Kelly, Peter J	4:20:30 (16,736)
Kelly, Richard	3:55:32 (10,385)
Kelly, Richard	4:39:34 (21,567)
Kelly, Richard J	3:19:31 (3,194)
Kelly, Sean	3:14:32 (2,600)
Kelly, Sebastian	3:08:37 (1,920)
Kelly, Stefan A	4:25:26 (18,103)
Kelly, Stephen P	5:25:15 (29,065)
Kelly, Thomas P	3:55:53 (10,505)
Kelly, Tim C	3:09:37 (2,027)
Kelman, Bob M	6:11:01 (31,955)
Kelsey, David W	4:20:20 (16,695)
Kelsey, Peter R	5:30:00 (29,546)
Kelso, Robert P	4:00:20 (11,896)
Kemish, Kingsley P	4:02:31 (12,376)
Kemp, Albert L	3:32:10 (5,193)
Kemp, Andrew S	4:51:04 (24,053)
Kemp, Barry R	3:32:43 (5,283)
Kemp, Benjamin J	2:42:50 (280)
Kemp, Edward C	4:09:23 (13,954)
Kemp, Ian	5:28:08 (29,342)
Kemp, James	3:58:34 (11,362)
Kemp, Jon C	3:43:23 (7,329)
Kemp, Jon M	2:57:04 (948)
Kemp, Jonathan	4:59:40 (25,826)
Kemp, Martyn	4:10:07 (14,127)
Kemp, Peter J	4:19:50 (16,562)
Kemp, Peter P	5:43:14 (30,588)
Kemp, Philip A	3:30:21 (4,874)
Kemp, Sam J	3:48:07 (8,411)
Kemp, Stephen D	3:11:49 (2,247)
Kemp, Stephen J	3:57:39 (11,060)
Kemp, Stephen P	3:53:15 (9,706)
Kemp, Stewart J	3:19:48 (3,233)
Kempgens, Arndt W	4:15:37 (15,498)
Kemple, Terry J	4:14:42 (15,260)
Kempster, David	4:38:26 (21,320)
Kemsley, Peter R	5:56:10 (31,361)
Kenan, Garry	3:47:03 (8,133)
Kenchington, Christopher J	2:58:37 (1,081)
Kenchington, Guy D	4:46:30 (23,120)
Kendall, Graham P	2:58:42 (1,097)
Kendall, Jason R	3:41:09 (6,841)
Kendall, Kevin	4:14:21 (15,173)
Kendall, Richard I	3:11:39 (2,229)
Kendall, Rowland W	4:07:03 (13,356)
Kendall, William S	3:45:26 (7,789)

Kirby, Robin W 4:47:08 (23,240)
Kirby, Simon K 4:36:41 (20,885)
Kirby, Steven E 2:58:29 (1,064)
Kirby, Trevor A 5:27:44 (29,297)
Kirchin, Stephen M 3:01:42 (1,351)
Kirchner, Richard P 4:47:57 (23,421)
Kirk, Elliott 3:27:07 (4,263)
Kirk, John M 3:43:07 (7,265)
Kirk, Michael J 5:21:29 (28,663)
Kirk, Nicholas J 4:47:18 (23,276)
Kirk, Nick 4:14:34 (15,226)
Kirk, Paul C 3:59:39 (11,711)
Kirk, Roger A 3:50:20 (8,940)
Kirkby, James A 3:44:40 (7,612)
Kirkby, Lee 4:03:19 (12,556)
Kirkby, Leonard 3:47:34 (8,259)
Kirkham, Adie 4:30:20 (19,384)
Kirkham, Daniel R 4:56:39 (25,229)
Kirkham, Richard A 4:19:21 (16,433)
Kirkland, Christopher E 3:51:45 (9,287)
Kirkland, Jim P 4:32:42 (19,934)
Kirkpatrick, Ben 4:34:02 (20,260)
Kirk-Wilson, Ed 3:28:52 (4,595)
Kirkwood, Graham A 3:56:46 (10,769)
Kirton, Akira 3:56:43 (10,758)
Kirton, Ken J 5:10:38 (27,346)
Kirwin, Philip A 2:34:49 (112)
Kis, Janos 3:48:52 (8,598)
Kitahara, Hirotaka 3:58:33 (11,357)
Kitchen, Ben 4:08:26 (13,728)
Kitchen, David M 5:13:27 (27,712)
Kitchen, Gerald T 5:31:10 (29,676)
Kitchen, Jim 5:02:07 (26,194)
Kitchen, Jon 4:45:39 (22,934)
Kitchen, Neil D 4:04:45 (12,868)
Kitching, Darren 4:22:55 (17,347)
Kitching, Ian D 2:42:59 (284)
Kitching, Wayne 5:05:11 (26,608)
Kitchman, Stephen M 3:46:39 (8,048)
Kiteley, Mark 5:29:27 (29,480)
Kitson, John N 4:35:10 (20,525)
Kitson, Paul J 4:05:23 (12,994)
Kitson, Tom P 4:53:33 (24,581)
Kittler, Robert L 5:16:17 (28,039)
Kivlehan, David P 4:03:33 (12,614)
Klein, Christoph M 4:05:38 (13,061)
Klein, Peter 3:58:19 (11,275)
Klein, Peter W 3:44:14 (7,501)
Kleinman, Martin P 5:26:48 (29,201)
Klinger, Peter 4:11:50 (14,528)
Kluger, Jason L 4:18:43 (16,286)
Kluger, Robert J 5:20:17 (28,533)
Kluth, Andrew 4:37:45 (21,167)
Knapman, Simon H 4:48:57 (23,640)
Knapp, John M 3:37:46 (6,180)
Knapp, Raymond B 5:37:06 (30,144)
Knapp, Robert J 4:15:25 (15,454)
Knebel, Richard P 5:29:26 (29,475)
Knee, David J 4:03:41 (12,646)
Kneeshaw, Paul 4:34:35 (20,383)
Knibb, John W 2:47:01 (417)
Knibbs, Alec V 5:47:48 (30,938)
Knickenberg, Anthony P 4:10:21 (14,183)
Knight, Alastair 3:43:40 (7,383)
Knight, Andrew D 3:54:59 (10,196)
Knight, Anthony D 3:55:14 (10,293)
Knight, Benjamin C 3:34:01 (5,486)
Knight, Bruce 3:54:18 (10,004)
Knight, Craig S 4:50:45 (23,992)
Knight, Daniel J 4:24:05 (17,680)
Knight, Dave A 4:23:45 (17,574)
Knight, David L 3:51:30 (9,215)
Knight, David T 4:15:12 (15,387)
Knight, Gareth C 3:19:19 (3,174)
Knight, Graham D 3:47:33 (8,249)
Knight, Jason 3:16:17 (2,801)
Knight, John R 3:28:40 (4,543)
Knight, Malcolm J 3:31:19 (5,038)
Knight, Mark 4:10:42 (14,248)
Knight, Mark C 3:58:23 (11,298)
Knight, Mark J 4:20:13 (16,666)
Knight, Michael J 4:03:45 (12,661)
Knight, Peter C 4:28:38 (18,929)
Knight, Richard J 5:36:59 (30,134)
Knight, Richard P 6:54:26 (32,814)
Knight, Robert 4:58:48 (25,662)
Knight, Robert L 4:06:05 (13,157)
Knight, Steven P 4:11:26 (14,448)
Knight, William J 3:30:59 (4,981)
Knightley, James W 3:44:55 (7,674)
Knighton, Simon J 3:25:17 (3,972)
Knights, Andrew J 3:47:46 (8,313)
Knights, Bruce J 5:26:15 (29,147)
Knights, Charles E 3:57:49 (11,119)
Knights, Christopher F 4:27:07 (18,533)
Knights, Howard J 3:46:01 (7,905)
Knights, Jim 4:53:34 (24,588)
Knockaert, Koen 3:44:03 (7,463)
Knolles, David S 3:21:56 (3,526)
Knott, Geoff P 4:25:12 (18,027)
Knott, John W 4:44:22 (22,651)
Knott, Kevin A 4:41:35 (22,008)
Knott, Peter 4:40:41 (21,825)
Knott, Peter J 4:08:53 (13,830)
Knott, Shane 4:46:59 (23,210)
Knott, Stephen G 5:16:16 (28,037)
Knott, Trevor L 3:45:26 (7,789)
Knoupe, Adam W 4:25:18 (18,054)
Knowles, Andrew 3:31:10 (5,020)
Knowles, John 3:22:42 (3,623)
Knowles, Michael A 3:24:08 (3,812)
Knowles, Neil J 4:35:16 (20,546)
Knowles, Peter K 4:25:32 (18,123)
Knowles, Stephen 4:08:34 (13,761)
Knox, Douglas J 3:58:40 (11,388)
Knox, George W 2:57:05 (951)
Knudsen, Knud Erik 3:52:15 (9,429)
Knutson, Randy 4:48:35 (23,563)
Kobayashi, Akira 4:57:46 (25,448)
Kobayashi-Hillary, Mark R 4:05:03 (12,928)
Kocen, Andrew S 3:36:24 (5,914)
Koch, Michael 3:29:37 (4,746)
Kocsis, Arpad 4:24:39 (17,858)
Koerner, Felix 4:38:49 (21,396)
Koike, Hirotsugu 6:02:17 (31,655)
Kojima, Andrew T 3:45:05 (7,709)
Kojima, Giichi 7:22:54 (33,055)
Kok, Arnout T 4:48:21 (23,500)
Kokel, Julien 4:09:38 (14,019)
Kolbe, Stefan 2:50:42 (572)
Kolodziej, Jerzy 8:29:28 (33,204)
Komenda, Peter 3:08:45 (1,932)
Kominek, Pavel 4:06:55 (13,330)
Konarowski, Martin 5:19:21 (28,413)
Kondo, Kuninori 4:29:45 (19,238)
Konlechner, Konrad J 4:11:47 (14,516)
Konrad, Ingo 4:25:50 (18,202)
Konstantinidis, Marios 4:18:03 (16,119)
Koohyar, Ali 3:52:22 (9,458)
Kopiecki, Stefan J 5:51:24 (31,150)
Kordts, Michael 3:20:14 (3,303)
Kormornick, Lawrence M 4:13:09 (14,888)
Kornas, Antony S 4:15:01 (15,342)
Kornicki, Edmund B 3:42:43 (7,159)
Korobejko, Stephen M 3:32:04 (5,175)
Korthigon, Ravindrov 3:31:34 (5,082)
Kostanjevec, John C 6:17:25 (32,154)
Koszegi, Istvan 4:15:41 (15,514)
Kotecha, Priten 3:43:52 (7,432)
Kottek, Michael H 3:38:18 (6,291)
Kotze, Deon C 4:03:21 (12,565)
Kotze, Jean-Pierre 4:39:56 (21,662)
Kotze, Martin A 3:48:28 (8,493)
Koudoua, Abbey 4:26:29 (18,381)
Koulakis, David 4:53:10 (24,500)
Koulioumba, Nicolaos I 7:33:36 (33,107)
Koutsounouris, Antonios 5:22:20 (28,761)
Kovacs, James 2:33:59 (98)
Kowolik, David J 4:29:11 (19,079)
Krafft, Philip J 4:22:10 (17,162)
Krajcar, Zelko 3:31:26 (5,057)
Kramp, Clemens 3:57:31 (11,020)
Kratz, James P 4:46:49 (23,177)
Kratz, Philip R 5:42:59 (30,577)
Krause, Christian 4:24:25 (17,777)
Krauspe, Lothar 4:20:16 (16,676)
Krauth, Michael H 4:38:00 (21,223)
Kremer, John 3:23:28 (3,706)
Kreth, Reinhard 3:34:15 (5,520)
Krien, Alexander D 3:43:48 (7,422)
Krohn, Christian 3:41:49 (6,994)
Krol, Dariusz 2:57:04 (948)
Krosnar, Thomas 4:11:11 (14,383)
Krug, Klaus P 4:03:22 (12,570)
Krumins, John 4:04:05 (12,736)
Kruppa, Peter R 3:49:59 (8,863)
Krzak, Robert 2:45:30 (359)
Ksiaszkiewicz, Jacek 3:03:50 (1,502)
Kuamme, Gustan 6:16:08 (32,122)
Kudla, Leon D 4:45:14 (22,845)
Kuehne, Martin 2:53:29 (698)
Kuehne, Raphael 3:17:12 (2,908)
Kuehnl, Andreas 5:39:27 (30,317)
Kula-Przezwanski, Wlodzimierz G 3:47:29 (8,237)
Kumar, Pardeep 4:37:32 (21,117)
Kumar, Raman 5:05:08 (26,605)
Kumar, Verender 5:36:49 (30,118)
Kumar, Vishal 4:29:14 (19,093)
Kunugi, Seiichi 5:07:46 (26,972)
Kunz, Albert 3:54:21 (10,018)
Kunz, Stefan 3:14:26 (2,588)
Kupfer, Uwe 3:45:22 (7,777)
Kusnick, Peter 3:43:43 (7,396)
Kutner, David B 4:30:39 (19,462)
Kutzner, Micahel 3:38:00 (6,222)
Kuzinski, Matthias 4:04:33 (12,825)
Kvamme, Ole Magnar 4:09:04 (13,874)
Kvassheim, Einar 3:41:11 (6,849)
Kvassheim, Torbjorn 3:31:13 (5,028)
Kwan, Jonathan 4:02:00 (12,267)
Kwarteng, Eric 3:44:33 (7,582)
Kyallo, Joshua 4:25:47 (18,189)
Kyd, Laurence D 4:14:17 (15,161)
Kyereme, Kojo A 2:28:35 (60)
Kyjak-Lane, Stephen Z 5:24:35 (28,993)
Kyne, David M 3:14:00 (2,530)
Kynoch, Graham R 3:13:58 (2,524)
Kyritsis, Neoclis 4:28:01 (18,753)
Kyte, Tony S 4:41:45 (22,048)
La Bray, Andrew D 3:56:20 (10,635)
Laban, James T 4:15:17 (15,408)
Labas, Sean M 5:58:01 (31,456)
Labianca, Luca 3:54:17 (9,997)
Laboyrie, Thijs 4:07:22 (13,439)
Labuschagne, Petrus I 4:32:03 (19,801)
Labuschagne, Timothy 3:58:05 (11,178)
Lacey, Charlie E 4:55:35 (25,015)
Lacey, Paul W 4:15:29 (15,474)
Lacey, Sean P 4:58:10 (25,540)
Lacey, Will R 3:24:09 (3,815)
Lach, Guenter 4:00:36 (11,948)
Lackey, Peter J 3:46:27 (8,000)
Lacour, Christiane 4:00:27 (11,927)
Lad, Darren 5:00:51 (26,020)
Lad, Mahesh 5:51:01 (31,129)
Ladd, Andrew R 4:22:27 (17,235)
Ladd, Joe 3:24:04 (3,803)
Ladd, Mayank 4:53:34 (24,588)
Lafave, Wendell M 4:14:41 (15,255)
Laffar, James V 4:06:58 (13,341)
Lafford, John A 5:28:58 (29,424)
Lagaht, Jean-Louis 5:46:09 (30,797)
Lagan, Paul J 7:21:36 (33,050)
Lagarde, Bruno 3:42:31 (7,115)
Lagnado, Max 3:12:25 (2,335)
Lague, David 3:25:39 (4,025)
Laguillo, George 3:21:27 (3,460)
Lahert, Paul A 4:24:42 (17,869)
Laidler, Stephen T 2:58:43 (1,100)
Laier, Robert P 4:05:37 (13,055)
Laine, Franck 3:23:19 (3,686)
Laing, David J 2:36:47 (142)
Laing, Nicholas P 3:36:57 (6,029)
Laing, Philip 5:45:53 (30,770)
Laird, Allister 3:44:19 (7,525)
Lais, Alexander 4:03:17 (12,549)
Laiz, Maximiliano 3:29:57 (4,815)
Lake, Oliver J 4:08:47 (13,809)
Lake, Philip N 5:18:29 (28,310)

Lake, Robert J 4:07:33 (13,486)
Lake, Wally S 3:24:32 (3,870)
Lakey, Daniel J 3:55:44 (10,453)
Lakhani, Muzzamil 4:36:41 (20,885)
Lall, Michael J 3:31:50 (5,128)
Lalla, Karol 4:28:37 (18,924)
Lallier, Jacques 3:52:53 (9,593)
Lalnne, Patrick 3:58:06 (11,185)
Lam, Chi-Wai 5:42:28 (30,532)
Lamacraft, Mervyn 5:07:03 (26,867)
Lamb, Adrian R 4:16:39 (15,769)
Lamb, Andrew M 3:32:12 (5,203)
Lamb, Giles R 4:21:36 (16,999)
Lamb, Ian S 3:02:41 (1,416)
Lamb, Jason 4:15:52 (15,569)
Lamb, Ken D 3:29:25 (4,698)
Lamb, Kevin 4:37:14 (21,039)
Lamb, Phillip 4:37:50 (21,186)
Lamb, Spencer C 5:14:49 (27,884)
Lamb, William I 5:14:21 (27,821)
Lambard, David G 3:35:03 (5,679)
Lambden, Keith S 3:48:51 (8,591)
Lambden, Murray M 3:22:20 (3,575)
Lambden, Richard D 4:29:30 (19,179)
Lambert, Andrew D 3:37:08 (6,062)
Lambert, Daniel P 3:51:13 (9,151)
Lambert, Guy R 2:57:48 (1,009)
Lambert, Ian L 3:07:37 (1,816)
Lambert, Jon P 4:28:43 (18,951)
Lambert, Marcus 4:02:29 (12,371)
Lambert, Nigel K 4:39:47 (21,624)
Lambert, Richard P 4:43:00 (22,329)
Lambert, Roland 3:28:52 (4,595)
Lambert, Stephen A 4:16:25 (15,695)
Lambert, Timothy D 5:09:51 (27,245)
Lambie, George 3:47:31 (8,242)
Lambillion-Jameson, Peter W 3:21:06 (3,411)
Lambkin, Gary P 3:29:36 (4,743)
Lambley, Charles J 3:39:12 (6,475)
Lambrou, Tony 4:54:20 (24,754)
Lamkin, David S 4:12:17 (14,645)
Lamkin, Simon 4:14:03 (15,086)
Lammali, Aziouz 3:08:43 (1,927)
Lammas, Edward 3:30:26 (4,882)
Lammy, Simon P 4:23:56 (17,633)
Lamond, Michael B 4:20:27 (16,723)
Lampe, Wolfgang 4:12:43 (14,754)
Lamper, Mark A 4:32:09 (19,820)
Lamza, Ernie W 3:07:01 (1,760)
Lan, Kevin 3:55:46 (10,468)
Lancashire, Tony C 3:37:42 (6,166)
Lancaster, Gary J 4:32:18 (19,859)
Lancaster, Philip A 4:32:46 (19,952)
Lancaster, Simon J 5:24:48 (29,016)
Lance, Timothy G 4:17:22 (15,947)
Lanceley, Jon N 6:00:06 (31,569)
Lancetti, Luciano 3:22:52 (3,642)
Lander, Christopher M 4:05:29 (13,021)
Lander, David L 4:51:13 (24,078)
Lander, Mark N 4:51:13 (24,078)
Landquist, Bengt 3:58:24 (11,306)
Lane, Alistair J 5:18:24 (28,297)
Lane, Andrew G 3:28:31 (4,514)
Lane, Barnard R 5:14:11 (27,796)
Lane, Brian 3:29:15 (4,663)
Lane, Gary L 3:57:29 (11,008)
Lane, Graham R 4:20:47 (16,806)
Lane, Kevin R 4:27:31 (18,628)
Lane, Lewis S 4:22:41 (17,294)
Lane, Luke 4:16:28 (15,714)
Lane, Malcolm R 3:36:44 (5,981)
Lane, Matthew J 4:02:14 (12,312)
Lane, Michael J 2:42:06 (252)
Lane, Nathaniel R 2:31:40 (81)
Lane, Norman J 4:30:35 (19,446)
Lane, Paul R 3:05:39 (1,629)
Lane, Philip J 4:55:01 (24,899)
Lane, Richard N 4:23:47 (17,582)
Lane, Ronald F 3:36:49 (5,997)
Lang, Andrew M 4:07:26 (13,453)
Lang, Angus I 4:54:08 (24,704)
Lang, Chris 4:48:13 (23,474)
Lang, John N 4:31:22 (19,630)
Lang, Steven M 4:24:43 (17,875)
Lang, Johann 3:28:00 (4,408)
Langan, Stephen 3:18:41 (3,091)
Langdon, Ben 3:46:30 (8,010)
Langdon, Jeremy 3:45:02 (7,697)
Langdon, Mark J 4:26:43 (18,439)
Langdon, Martin J 3:55:26 (10,354)
Lange, Dietmar 4:01:57 (12,249)
Lange, Eric W 5:45:52 (30,768)
Lange, Patrice 3:14:15 (2,559)
Lange, Wilhelm 4:28:02 (18,757)
Langen, Alex F 4:24:57 (17,946)
Langford, Dan J 4:05:58 (13,135)
Langford, David 5:19:09 (28,395)
Langford, Martyn 4:01:10 (12,092)
Langham, Peter A 4:37:17 (21,054)
Langham, Phillip N 4:26:35 (18,403)
Langholz, Peter 5:25:14 (29,064)
Langley, Alex 4:41:25 (21,973)
Langley, Andrew T 5:17:08 (28,142)
Langley, Colin 2:58:38 (1,083)
Langley, Daniel R 4:00:19 (11,892)
Langley, Michael C 4:40:38 (21,816)
Langley, Paul 7:03:24 (32,920)
Langley, Robert F 3:00:32 (1,275)
Langley, Robert J 4:18:11 (16,157)
Langley, Simon J 5:17:08 (28,142)
Langlois, André R 5:16:05 (28,012)
Langridge, Jamie 2:52:25 (650)
Langridge-Brown, Gary M 3:48:18 (8,450)
Langrish, David R 5:21:52 (28,698)
Langton, John S 3:21:07 (3,413)
Langton, Philip D 4:19:43 (16,534)
Lanham, James P 4:10:36 (14,235)
Lankester, Mark R 3:32:13 (5,206)
Lannigan, James J 7:47:05 (33,166)
Lanoe, Kjell 3:51:51 (9,318)
Lansbury, Mark P 4:27:06 (18,527)
Lansdell, Jeff S 3:19:42 (3,213)
Lanyon, Richard W 3:33:21 (5,378)
Lanza, Giuseppe 3:51:49 (9,307)
Laoudi, Merzouk 3:35:07 (5,696)
Lapierre, Oliver 3:36:34 (5,947)
Lapins, Terry D 3:29:49 (4,790)
Lappin, Noel G 5:48:13 (30,958)
Lapsley, Robert I 4:17:23 (15,951)
Lapworth, David M 3:49:47 (8,816)
Laranjeira, Vitor M 4:57:32 (25,403)
Lard, Frederic 2:53:41 (707)
Large, Paul 3:52:22 (9,458)
Large, Phillip H 3:03:44 (1,496)
Large, Steven G 2:59:10 (1,157)
Larham, Kevin A 3:26:37 (4,179)
Larke, Barry 3:37:40 (6,161)
Larkin, David A 4:17:10 (15,898)
Larkin, Kevin M 4:26:33 (18,396)
Larking, Richard P 5:14:14 (27,803)
Larmet, Michel 4:19:45 (16,539)
Larmignat, Daniel 4:28:49 (18,976)
Larocca, José M 3:53:12 (9,689)
Larsen, Bernt M 4:58:38 (25,632)
Larsson, Rasmus 4:07:42 (13,536)
Larsson, Ruben 4:15:48 (15,544)
Lartey, Lawrence 4:41:37 (22,017)
Larvin, Tim D 4:33:25 (20,113)
Lasaosa, Bruno 3:47:41 (8,290)
Lasham, Nick B 4:57:22 (25,380)
Lashmar, Ben 3:01:57 (1,371)
Lashmar, Tony 2:40:45 (226)
Lasio, Enrico 4:31:38 (19,705)
Lassalle, Daniel 4:21:21 (16,947)
Lasserre, Fabrice 2:59:43 (1,222)
Lasslett, Matthew J 4:44:27 (22,666)
Last, Peter 4:10:31 (14,217)
Laszczok, Henryk J 3:40:57 (6,793)
Latham, Andrew K 3:52:19 (9,441)
Latham, Andrew S 5:14:21 (27,821)
Latham, Stan F 4:25:16 (18,050)
Latham, Steven G 3:35:02 (5,669)
Latham, Tony 5:00:14 (25,934)
Lathwell, Simon G 3:14:07 (2,543)
Latif, Ali 4:55:01 (24,899)
Latif, Iqbal 4:43:05 (22,343)
Latif, Ismael 5:15:45 (27,971)
Latter, Darren J 3:35:08 (5,697)
Latter, Michael J 5:38:33 (30,256)
Latter, Peter E 5:43:43 (30,623)
Lau, Chak Sing Wallace 5:11:22 (27,441)
Lau, Hing L 3:17:20 (2,923)
Laubscher, Dirk 3:33:59 (5,479)
Lauchlan, Robert A 4:25:23 (18,087)
Laud, Brian D 4:19:07 (16,368)
Laud, Nathan J 4:14:04 (15,092)
Laudato, Adriano 3:45:47 (7,866)
Lauder, Ryan N 4:14:05 (15,098)
Laughton, Anthony 3:57:01 (10,847)
Laughton, Douglas E 4:15:53 (15,576)
Laurence, Garry S 4:01:05 (12,067)
Laurie, Dominic W 5:50:02 (31,076)
Laurie, Steven 2:57:41 (1,001)
Laurier, Phillip B 4:18:40 (16,270)
Lauritsen, Kurt 4:51:46 (24,202)
Lavan, Michael J 3:38:03 (6,239)
Lavan, Nick 3:57:01 (10,847)
Lavatelli, Giuseppe 4:19:22 (16,439)
Lavelle, John R 3:23:32 (3,716)
Laver, Toby 2:46:13 (390)
Lavers, Roderick J 3:04:44 (1,563)
Laverty, Hugh 3:30:57 (4,973)
Laverty, Sean 3:13:35 (2,474)
Lavery, Joe 6:19:11 (32,209)
Lavery, Michael 5:23:17 (28,865)
Lavin, Norman J 6:23:58 (32,328)
Law, Alistair D 3:21:21 (3,449)
Law, Andrew P 4:49:26 (23,740)
Law, Christopher K 5:36:58 (30,132)
Law, Christopher N 3:10:04 (2,070)
Law, Dominic D 3:43:02 (7,242)
Law, James K 5:29:11 (29,441)
Law, Matthew 5:33:55 (29,881)
Law, Peter M 4:27:37 (18,662)
Law, Peter W 4:08:45 (13,800)
Law, Richard D 5:15:45 (27,971)
Law, Simon N 3:05:19 (1,608)
Lawes, Chris P 3:34:17 (5,529)
Lawes, Graeme 4:12:17 (14,645)
Lawford, Nicholas M 4:45:40 (22,935)
Lawler, Alex 4:27:06 (18,527)
Lawley, Steven G 4:00:06 (11,843)
Lawlor, Paul A 3:12:17 (2,320)
Lawlor, Robert W 4:56:04 (25,114)
Lawrance, Richard S 3:18:59 (3,131)
Lawrence, Aaron A 4:49:34 (23,769)
Lawrence, Andrew D 4:13:43 (15,007)
Lawrence, David J 3:09:18 (1,983)
Lawrence, Donald L 5:57:53 (31,451)
Lawrence, Gavin J 3:26:01 (4,079)
Lawrence, Ivor A 3:55:30 (10,374)
Lawrence, Martin 4:08:46 (13,805)
Lawrence, Michael P 5:10:43 (27,354)
Lawrence, Neil J 4:54:14 (24,736)
Lawrence, Nick 3:34:17 (5,529)
Lawrence, Philip M 4:58:52 (25,679)
Lawrence, Richard N 3:55:58 (10,531)
Lawrence, Robert W 3:19:51 (3,242)
Lawrence, Sean 5:01:06 (26,061)
Lawrence, Simon 5:10:47 (27,363)
Lawrence, Tim 3:19:23 (3,180)
Lawrence, Tim N 3:57:16 (10,937)
Lawrenson, Paul 5:22:44 (28,804)
Lawrey, David K 4:43:21 (22,398)
Lawrie, Charles 3:28:18 (4,468)
Lawrie, Daniel C 3:28:18 (4,468)
Lawrie, David 3:49:38 (8,780)
Lawrie, Dennis M 5:21:34 (28,672)
Lawrie, Jonathan W 4:34:15 (20,300)
Laws, Damon 6:06:13 (31,794)
Laws, Richard 4:47:45 (23,374)
Lawson, Alan 2:57:13 (963)
Lawson, David K 3:58:01 (11,156)
Lawson, Don M 4:22:45 (17,310)
Lawson, Guy 4:27:46 (18,686)
Lawson, James D 3:49:43 (8,802)
Lawson, Scott 3:21:42 (3,500)
Lawson, Steve A 4:08:41 (13,786)
Lawson, Thomas G 4:43:36 (22,467)

Lawther, Dennis	4:53:35 (24,592)	Lee, Brian M.	5:07:37 (26,950)	Leivers, Garry	5:27:30 (29,274)
Lawton, Bruce W	3:18:54 (3,123)	Lee, Brian R.	5:22:19 (28,757)	Lel, Martin	2:06:41 (2)
Lawton, Bryan W	3:16:12 (2,799)	Lee, Charles	3:31:07 (5,010)	Lemanski, James M	3:52:47 (9,564)
Lawton, Michael L	4:39:51 (21,640)	Lee, Charles T	4:27:19 (18,584)	Le-Mene, Jacques	4:13:10 (14,893)
Lawton, Peter J	3:34:17 (5,529)	Lee, Chris	2:59:03 (1,148)	Lemin, Michael J	3:31:05 (5,002)
Lay, John L	4:04:30 (12,816)	Lee, Clyde E	3:52:35 (9,515)	Lemon, Daniel R	3:29:46 (4,778)
Lay, Peter A	3:04:30 (1,548)	Lee, Daniel	3:46:48 (8,081)	Lemon, Darren M	5:02:41 (26,273)
Laycock, Graeme J	3:59:24 (11,638)	Lee, Daren M	3:44:33 (7,582)	Lemon, James C	3:58:23 (11,298)
Laycock, Jon S	3:43:35 (7,366)	Lee, Gareth J	3:53:36 (9,793)	Lemon, Mark L	5:09:21 (27,189)
Layton, Adrian	5:06:25 (26,774)	Lee, Gary S	4:15:32 (15,484)	Lempereur, Jean Luc	3:43:12 (7,289)
Layton, David B	3:57:19 (10,953)	Lee, James N	4:14:07 (15,108)	Lempke, Edward A	4:04:21 (12,787)
Layton, Erik J	3:25:35 (4,017)	Lee, James Y	4:14:09 (15,122)	Lengthorn, Philip	4:29:42 (19,228)
Layton, Stephen A	5:12:15 (27,555)	Lee, John	3:39:07 (6,458)	Lengyel, Andrea	4:14:36 (15,233)
Laywood, Mark	6:34:31 (32,523)	Lee, Jon	4:46:37 (23,144)	Lenihan, Kevin G	3:00:46 (1,285)
Lazos, Antonios	4:34:28 (20,356)	Lee, Jonathan M	3:50:45 (9,045)	Lennard, David A	4:55:43 (25,040)
Le Bihan, Neil E	4:12:06 (14,595)	Lee, Jong Hun	4:36:32 (20,853)	Lennon, Christopher M	4:39:47 (21,624)
Le Blevennec, Gilles H	3:06:37 (1,718)	Lee, Joo Sin	3:46:42 (8,060)	Lennox, Barry	4:01:18 (12,115)
Le Cornu, Marcus D	3:44:24 (7,538)	Lee, Marcus P	5:24:20 (28,978)	Lennox, Gordon J	2:54:03 (730)
Le Delmat, Xavier	3:27:23 (4,311)	Lee, Martin A	4:52:43 (24,402)	Lenthall, Martyn B	5:29:50 (29,527)
Le Fanu, Tom M	4:18:26 (16,216)	Lee, Martyn A	4:22:30 (17,242)	Lenton, Steven R	5:31:14 (29,684)
Le Good, Daniel S	3:39:03 (6,445)	Lee, Moon Hee	3:27:40 (4,360)	Lenza, Ugo	3:42:54 (7,206)
Le Good, Graham P	3:10:39 (2,127)	Lee, Nick	3:41:27 (6,904)	Leon, Mauricio	5:07:24 (26,918)
Le Gouill, Bernard E	4:17:31 (15,987)	Lee, Nigel	3:15:53 (2,767)	Leonard, John F	5:23:21 (28,878)
Le Gouill, Michel H	4:07:22 (13,439)	Lee, Patrick S	5:29:04 (29,430)	Leonard, Matthew M	3:33:35 (5,418)
Le Gresley, Edward Marc	3:20:14 (3,303)	Lee, Paul	5:07:35 (26,944)	Leonard, Paul G	3:31:52 (5,138)
Le Hen, Laurent	4:19:55 (16,581)	Lee, Perry S	3:44:39 (7,603)	Leonard, Richard	5:28:06 (29,334)
Le Jeune, Martin E	4:45:16 (22,852)	Lee, Peter G	2:54:04 (731)	Leonard, Stuart	3:09:37 (2,027)
Le Jollec, Jean-Luc	3:47:08 (8,151)	Lee, Philip A	4:20:41 (16,783)	Leonard, Thomas A	5:40:47 (30,412)
Le Marie, Andy J	5:14:42 (27,872)	Lee, Richard	5:51:34 (31,160)	Leonidas, Diogo	4:22:39 (17,287)
Le Mercier, Eric	3:25:42 (4,028)	Lee, Richard C	4:44:40 (22,700)	Lequitte, Didier	3:21:47 (3,507)
Le Roux, Fanus	6:00:42 (31,588)	Lee, Richard G	3:03:40 (1,490)	Leroy, Gilles	3:42:42 (7,157)
Lea, Jason	3:49:51 (8,831)	Lee, Richard J	4:37:16 (21,050)	Lescott, Rupert A	3:38:39 (6,358)
Lea, Nigel	5:36:49 (30,118)	Lee, Richard J	4:47:31 (23,324)	Leservoisier, Patrick	2:43:26 (298)
Lea, Robert K	4:33:25 (20,113)	Lee, Robert S	4:24:48 (17,892)	Lesley, Richard J	4:20:32 (16,742)
Leach, Chris M	6:26:45 (32,396)	Lee, Robert W	4:17:58 (16,100)	Leslie, Ben	4:47:09 (23,243)
Leach, Chris S	3:58:14 (11,245)	Lee, Robin A	4:03:01 (12,481)	Leslie, Graham W	3:45:27 (7,798)
Leach, David A	4:42:33 (22,230)	Lee, Roger D	4:47:48 (23,382)	Leslie, Marc P	4:54:40 (24,808)
Leach, David A	5:16:30 (28,073)	Lee, Royston A	2:52:08 (643)	Leslie, Mark	3:53:40 (9,810)
Leach, Matthew C	3:45:51 (7,878)	Lee, Ryan	4:27:05 (18,524)	Leslie, Max A	3:47:24 (8,213)
Leach, Norman	5:31:40 (29,717)	Lee, Suet Y	5:42:55 (30,571)	Leslie, Neil	5:07:51 (26,981)
Leach, Oliver J	3:25:42 (4,028)	Lee, Tim J	3:49:45 (8,811)	Leslie, Robert J	4:31:21 (19,625)
Leach, Robert	3:11:54 (2,262)	Lee, Yoon Soo	4:15:20 (15,425)	Lessiter, Brian C	3:40:23 (6,687)
Leach, Stuart M	4:03:23 (12,574)	Lee, Young G	3:50:54 (9,077)	Lester, Mark A	3:48:06 (8,403)
Lead, Tony	4:43:16 (22,383)	Leech, Lewis W	4:31:55 (19,776)	Lester, Paul D	2:55:21 (806)
Leadbetter, Keith J	5:11:07 (27,399)	Leek, Peter J	2:39:46 (206)	Lester-Owen, Peter	4:17:56 (16,088)
Leadbetter, Martin	4:40:45 (21,841)	Leek, Steven	3:53:07 (9,665)	L'Estrange, Paul J	4:41:32 (22,000)
Leader, Stephen	5:58:32 (31,488)	Leen, David S	3:52:31 (9,497)	Letford, John	3:25:15 (3,970)
Leader, Stewart D	6:11:19 (31,963)	Lees, Alex	3:47:52 (8,347)	Lethaby, Raymond J	4:18:08 (16,146)
Leaf, Simon L	4:30:28 (19,419)	Lees, Allan D	3:46:37 (8,040)	Letham, Matthew E	3:44:40 (7,612)
Leahy, Malcolm E	6:07:20 (31,832)	Lees, Fraser J	4:03:41 (12,646)	Leung, Victor A	4:10:03 (14,111)
Leahy, Richard P	3:11:53 (2,256)	Leeson, John P	5:25:15 (29,065)	Levasier, James A	4:16:53 (15,827)
Leak, Andrew S	5:53:06 (31,221)	Leeson, Tom D	5:25:15 (29,065)	Leveille, Robert A	4:35:40 (20,645)
Leak, Christopher S	4:20:59 (16,861)	Leete, Matthew A	4:12:45 (14,761)	Lever, Paul A	4:06:43 (13,278)
Leak, Steven	5:20:32 (28,565)	Lefebvre, Serge	2:56:06 (857)	Leverett, Craig A	4:06:53 (13,321)
Leal, Pedro	3:37:25 (6,116)	Lefranc, Alain	3:53:25 (9,741)	Leverett, Ivan	3:39:14 (6,486)
Leal-Acuna, Agustin	3:28:51 (4,590)	Le-Gallou, Philippe	3:04:03 (1,515)	Leverett, Peter	4:55:52 (25,070)
Leaning, Wayne	3:48:29 (8,495)	Legendre, Stephane	2:46:09 (387)	Levermore, Paul	5:12:59 (27,649)
Leaper, Tim R	4:45:55 (22,992)	Legg, Daniel H	3:36:41 (5,972)	Leverton, Jack	3:03:17 (1,462)
Learmouth, Terry D	3:27:19 (4,297)	Legg, Jonathan	3:43:09 (7,274)	Leveson, Joseph	4:41:24 (21,971)
Learner, Huw	5:44:57 (30,712)	Legg, Trevor	5:27:00 (29,227)	Levett, Peter D	4:32:22 (19,879)
Leary, Julian P	4:47:54 (23,407)	Leggatt, Nigel A	5:20:21 (28,548)	Levick, John W	3:09:23 (1,998)
Leary, Paul A	3:45:32 (7,811)	Legge, Jonathan M	5:33:02 (29,819)	Levick, Paul E	3:00:24 (1,263)
Leary-Joyce, John S	4:53:12 (24,510)	Legge, Timothy T	2:53:13 (684)	Levin, Joseph	4:20:51 (16,820)
Leat, Martin	3:41:28 (6,906)	Leggett, Malcolm V	3:38:07 (6,253)	Levine, Luke H	5:16:50 (28,107)
Lebaudy, Guy	3:41:43 (6,970)	Legras, Jean-Pierre	3:35:28 (5,745)	Levine, Pascal	4:18:12 (16,159)
Leblanc, Joel R	3:50:15 (8,924)	Le-Hir, Patrice	3:42:31 (7,115)	Levine, Saul	4:23:07 (17,391)
Leblond, Herve	4:09:00 (13,859)	Leigh, Adrian P	3:54:21 (10,018)	Levitt, Brian F	4:51:41 (24,183)
Lebret, Jean	4:16:48 (15,798)	Leigh, Christopher W	3:56:02 (10,549)	Levitt, Julian E	4:10:47 (14,270)
Lebris, Patrick	4:20:11 (16,656)	Leigh, David P	3:52:16 (9,431)	Levitt, Martyn J	4:12:29 (14,699)
Leccardi, Alexander	4:41:08 (21,922)	Leigh, David R	5:08:37 (27,094)	Levitz, Michael D	4:37:12 (21,032)
Lech, David G	4:05:15 (12,971)	Leigh, Jon	3:29:59 (4,822)	Levy, Arron R	5:29:21 (29,463)
Lechtermann, Ulrich	3:50:22 (8,945)	Leigh, Michel E	5:03:52 (26,441)	Levy, Elliot	4:59:30 (25,786)
Leck, Michael	3:25:27 (3,999)	Leigh, Timothy I	3:58:57 (11,490)	Levy, Gus M	2:55:21 (806)
Leclerc, Stephane	3:40:00 (6,626)	Leighfield, Stephen P	3:09:33 (2,018)	Levy, Guy G	4:01:08 (12,082)
Leclerc-Chalvet, Matthieu	4:00:13 (11,869)	Leighton, Gareth J	3:13:43 (2,487)	Levy, Stuart B	6:13:25 (32,034)
Ledder, Paul R	3:40:15 (6,669)	Leighton, James O	4:13:43 (15,007)	Levy-Rueff, Bruno	3:32:41 (5,277)
Ledgard, Simon O	3:39:55 (6,610)	Leighton, Nigel	2:18:25 (22)	Levy-Rueff, Guy	3:21:32 (3,475)
Ledra, Harvey	3:46:54 (8,101)	Leighton, Paul	6:05:45 (31,787)	Lewars, Richard C	7:21:03 (33,048)
Ledsam, Charles E	4:40:28 (21,763)	Leiper, John E	3:56:13 (10,599)	Lewer, Aidan P	3:29:38 (4,749)
Ledwidge, Alan	4:02:12 (12,305)	Leiter, Wolfgang	3:34:59 (5,659)	Lewin, Barnaby	5:47:22 (30,908)
Lee, Andrew G	5:03:24 (26,377)	Leith, Wynne A	3:55:05 (10,240)	Lewin, Michael	4:05:53 (13,115)
Lee, Andrew J	3:03:03 (1,447)	Leiva-Ramirez, Fabio	4:33:50 (20,209)	Lewin, Stephen J	3:40:00 (6,626)
Lee, Ben	4:20:46 (16,803)	Leive, Adam	2:42:57 (283)	Lewington-Bracey, Barry J	4:37:00 (20,979)

Lewis, Adrian 4:07:18 (13,420)
Lewis, Adrian J 4:13:03 (14,858)
Lewis, Alex 4:48:02 (23,434)
Lewis, Andrew 4:09:27 (13,981)
Lewis, Andrew C 4:45:14 (22,845)
Lewis, Andrew R 4:17:00 (15,860)
Lewis, Benjamin 4:29:42 (19,228)
Lewis, Benjamin P 5:44:32 (30,682)
Lewis, Colin 3:20:21 (3,317)
Lewis, Daniel 2:43:54 (307)
Lewis, Darren J 2:56:54 (931)
Lewis, David A 5:09:25 (27,194)
Lewis, David G 4:25:59 (18,253)
Lewis, David J 3:51:18 (9,173)
Lewis, Dennis J 4:25:30 (18,118)
Lewis, Dylan R 4:01:58 (12,255)
Lewis, Elliot A 3:40:26 (6,698)
Lewis, Gerald S 6:36:50 (32,559)
Lewis, Glenn J 3:24:28 (3,857)
Lewis, Graham L 4:09:25 (13,969)
Lewis, Graham R 3:11:39 (2,229)
Lewis, Gwilym H 4:14:07 (15,108)
Lewis, Iain B 4:38:29 (21,335)
Lewis, Ian A 5:24:26 (28,984)
Lewis, Ian F 4:38:06 (21,261)
Lewis, James S 5:04:46 (26,553)
Lewis, Jamie 3:23:02 (3,661)
Lewis, John D 3:25:53 (4,058)
Lewis, John M 4:32:37 (19,920)
Lewis, Mark L 3:29:12 (4,654)
Lewis, Marten G 4:17:22 (15,947)
Lewis, Martin 3:51:34 (9,238)
Lewis, Martin J 6:46:12 (32,711)
Lewis, Martin W 5:14:43 (27,875)
Lewis, Matthew G 3:58:43 (11,405)
Lewis, Michael W 4:59:26 (25,767)
Lewis, Neil J 4:17:21 (15,944)
Lewis, Paul G 4:40:01 (21,679)
Lewis, Paul J 4:11:00 (14,329)
Lewis, Peter J 5:38:57 (30,277)
Lewis, Rhys T 4:33:11 (20,055)
Lewis, Richard J 3:53:26 (9,749)
Lewis, Rob 6:12:30 (32,004)
Lewis, Seth 3:17:05 (2,891)
Lewis, Simon 2:56:37 (907)
Lewis, Simon 4:53:09 (24,491)
Lewis, Simon J 4:23:21 (17,454)
Lewis, Simon M 3:48:51 (8,591)
Lewis, Stephen 6:52:18 (32,787)
Lewis, Stephen B 3:32:00 (5,158)
Lewis, Steven J 3:32:11 (5,198)
Lewis, Steven J 4:40:32 (21,797)
Lewis, Tevor A 3:02:58 (1,440)
Lewis, Thomas R 3:29:33 (4,731)
Lewis, Tim 2:42:52 (281)
Lewis, Tony W 5:21:10 (28,625)
Lewis, Vaughan S 3:57:19 (10,953)
Lewis-Aburn, Matthew J 3:36:18 (5,895)
Lewisman, Hagan 3:34:33 (5,581)
Leworthy, David 4:27:40 (18,676)
Lewton, Sean A 3:58:45 (11,422)
Lewy, Steven J 4:06:12 (13,177)
Lewys-Lloyd, Gareth 4:18:56 (16,337)
Ley, Kevin 4:30:26 (19,412)
Ley, Stephen J 5:45:22 (30,746)
Leyenda, Manuel 3:30:50 (4,947)
Lharidon, Jean-Luc 3:42:13 (7,069)
Li, Sammy 3:36:42 (5,976)
Li, Wing H 6:46:10 (32,710)
Liamo, Arne 3:11:29 (2,214)
Lichtenstern, Albert 3:07:18 (1,785)
Lichtenthaeler, Stefan 3:09:25 (2,003)
Lickman, Paul R 4:47:07 (23,238)
Liddell, Richard I 3:55:07 (10,250)
Liddle, Alexander B 3:36:20 (5,900)
Liddle, Kevin 6:41:50 (32,636)
Liddle, Scott R 5:00:35 (25,981)
Liddon, Gerard R 4:34:32 (20,371)
Lidgate-Taylor, Steven P 2:56:09 (863)
Liebers, Jonathan 3:50:07 (8,890)
Liffen, Neil J 3:47:33 (8,249)
Liger, Alain J 4:59:23 (25,758)
Light, Darren A 5:42:43 (30,552)
Light, Mark P 5:05:59 (26,708)
Light, Richard D 3:53:37 (9,800)
Lighterness, David 5:12:30 (27,588)
Lightfoot, Andrew 4:03:28 (12,598)
Lightfoot, Ian 5:23:33 (28,889)
Lightfoot, Ian A 3:38:36 (6,349)
Lightfoot, Philip A 3:54:41 (10,109)
Lightman, Shaun 5:37:15 (30,149)
Lightning, David W 4:10:34 (14,226)
Lightwood, Paul 5:32:59 (29,815)
Ligot, Xavier 4:16:52 (15,817)
Lill, Gary 3:32:40 (5,273)
Lilley, David 4:20:03 (16,613)
Lilley, Jeffrey D 4:23:56 (17,633)
Lilley, Philip J 4:09:28 (13,988)
Lillo De La Cruz, Marco 3:37:17 (6,088)
Lilly, Robert J 5:04:22 (26,499)
Lim, Eng B 4:31:29 (19,661)
Lim, Guan 4:12:52 (14,803)
Lim, Mike P 4:46:30 (23,120)
Lima Da Silva, Luis A 4:31:35 (19,692)
Limb, David 3:08:44 (1,929)
Limm, Anthony B 4:02:11 (12,302)

Limo, Felix 2:06:39 (1)

Felix Limo (born 22 August 1980) is a Kenyan long-distance and marathon runner. He held the 15km road running word record of 41:29 minutes, run in November 2001 in the Netherlands (Deriba Merga of Ethiopia matched his time in 2009). He won the Portuguese half marathon in 2002 and ran his first marathon in 2003 at Amsterdam. There he finished second in 2:06.42, just 3 seconds behind William Kipsang who set a course record. Limo won the 2005 Chicago Marathon, as well as Berlin and Rotterdam in 2004. When winning at Rotterdam he set a personal best of 2:06:14. Limo won the 2006 London Marathon in a time of 2:06:39, the third fastest marathon that year. He beat the defending champion Martin Lel by one second in a 100-metre sprint finish.

Lin, Zuojun 4:26:23 (18,357)
Linares, Charles A 4:34:01 (20,249)
Linathan, Craig 5:59:19 (31,529)
Linathan, Julian 3:19:40 (3,206)
Lind, Kenneth R 3:55:10 (10,264)
Linder, Franz 3:46:46 (8,074)
Lindesay, Matthew W 5:28:07 (29,339)
Lindesay, William D 4:22:40 (17,291)
Lindfield, Anthony 4:09:24 (13,963)
Lindley, James N 3:35:00 (5,661)
Lindley, Tom 5:25:52 (29,119)
Lindner, Andrew J 3:26:33 (4,164)
Lindner, Matthias 4:41:06 (21,916)
Lindsay, Arran M 4:29:45 (19,238)
Lindsay, Brendan T 4:30:13 (19,357)
Lindsay, David N 5:08:03 (27,014)
Lindsay, Donald 3:37:59 (6,220)
Lindsay, Iain 3:24:50 (3,918)
Lindsay, Iain S 3:35:24 (5,735)
Lindsay, Nick B 5:12:10 (27,545)
Lindstrom, Richard E 5:09:52 (27,249)
Line, Sam 5:48:11 (30,955)
Linehan, Kevin P 3:07:09 (1,773)
Lines, Derek C 2:38:50 (186)
Lines, John R 4:47:54 (23,407)
Lines, Paul A 3:57:19 (10,953)
Lingard, Richard 4:34:30 (20,362)
Lingard, Tom E 4:43:40 (22,481)
Linger, Steven P 4:45:44 (22,952)
Link, Simon J 2:43:00 (285)
Linney, John G 3:54:53 (10,173)
Linstead, Michael D 5:19:07 (28,390)
Lintern, Anthony E 3:28:09 (4,433)
Linton, John 4:41:55 (22,093)
Lintott, Daniel A 4:09:23 (13,954)
Lion, Rupert J 4:13:58 (15,054)
Lipczynski, Nicholas J 4:58:58 (25,704)
Lipka, Lawrence A 5:24:11 (28,964)
Lipscomb, David W 4:48:22 (23,506)
Lipscomb, Scott 3:58:10 (11,218)
Lipscombe, Paul D 4:43:31 (22,443)
Lipscombe, Sam 4:17:33 (15,999)
Lipton, Tim P 5:23:12 (28,858)
Liptrott, Mark 4:48:19 (23,496)
Lis, David G 4:13:08 (14,883)
Lischewski, Johann 5:09:36 (27,218)
Lisle, Richard A 3:23:13 (3,676)
Lisney, Peter J 5:53:53 (31,258)
Lister, Andrew R 4:09:17 (13,928)
Lister, Daniel 3:28:14 (4,448)
Lister, Darron 4:25:18 (18,054)
Lister, James S 4:06:18 (13,194)
Lister, Joseph W 5:34:26 (29,928)
Lister, Michael J 4:24:06 (17,683)
Lister, Nicholas P 3:19:49 (3,234)
Litchfield, David A 3:53:10 (9,679)
Little, Chris J 3:21:39 (3,492)
Little, David W 4:47:22 (23,285)
Little, Martin R 3:44:33 (7,582)
Little, Neil C 3:41:29 (6,909)
Little, Nicholas W 6:43:28 (32,665)
Little, Oliver R 4:31:31 (19,668)
Little, Peter R 5:59:36 (31,539)
Little, Richard M 5:59:36 (31,539)
Little, Ronald J 4:27:38 (18,666)
Little, Thomas J 4:07:46 (13,547)
Littlechild, Justin P 2:53:00 (678)
Littlejohn, Robert E 4:29:58 (19,285)
Littleproud, James 3:56:27 (10,672)
Littler, Frank H 3:45:15 (7,742)
Littler, Stephen T 2:28:25 (59)
Littleton, David 5:18:50 (28,348)
Littlewood, Mike H 4:25:07 (17,996)
Littlewood, Philip M 4:36:28 (20,836)
Littlewood, Richard S 3:10:08 (2,076)
Littlewood, Stephen J 3:24:56 (3,924)
Litvin, Norman P 2:57:25 (975)
Liu, David 4:08:50 (13,821)
Liu, Lewis 4:47:41 (23,357)
Liuzzi, Stephen M 4:26:37 (18,413)
Livermore, Benjamin J 3:18:19 (3,034)
Livermore, Colin B 6:00:08 (31,571)
Livesey, John A 5:48:25 (30,965)
Livesey, Mark 5:17:05 (28,139)
Livingston, Ian J 4:09:24 (13,963)
Livingston, Roy H 4:50:10 (23,871)
Livingstone, David 2:59:08 (1,152)
Llewelly-Jones, Charles B 4:21:05 (16,886)
Llewellyn, Richard D 5:40:15 (30,381)
Lloyd, Christopher 4:23:18 (17,443)
Lloyd, Colin J 6:19:10 (32,207)
Lloyd, David R 3:31:33 (5,073)
Lloyd, Gavin G 3:45:39 (7,833)

Lloyd, Jonathan D........................4:25:13 (18,033)
Lloyd, Jonathan S........................4:53:01 (24,459)
Lloyd, Kevin S...........................4:31:21 (19,625)
Lloyd, Martin P..........................3:26:11 (4,101)
Lloyd, Matthew J.........................4:25:14 (18,038)
Lloyd, Matthew L.........................5:30:38 (29,608)
Lloyd, Paul A............................3:28:21 (4,480)
Lloyd, Philip M..........................4:14:57 (15,319)
Lloyd, Richard R.........................4:25:22 (18,079)
Lloyd, Richard W.........................4:44:54 (22,756)
Lloyd, Robin.............................3:29:35 (4,739)
Lloyd, Stuart G..........................5:42:03 (30,506)
Lloyd, Thomas M..........................3:47:27 (8,225)
Lloyd, Tom D.............................3:38:05 (6,247)
Lloyd, Tom H.............................3:15:57 (2,776)
Lloyd, Tony A............................5:29:41 (29,503)
Lloyd-Brennan, Andrew S..................6:15:50 (32,110)
Lloyd-Davies, Gareth W...................3:50:09 (8,902)
Lloyd-Gane, Jonathan.....................4:09:07 (13,881)
Lndblow, Stefan..........................3:24:02 (3,799)
Lo, Luke C...............................6:02:56 (31,678)
Lo Scalzo, Dario.........................3:21:50 (3,517)
Loake, Stephen D.........................4:55:36 (25,017)
Loan, Nick W.............................4:25:22 (18,079)
Lobb, Huw................................2:15:38 (15)
Lober, Howard A..........................3:40:18 (6,676)
Lobley, David P..........................3:52:20 (9,445)
Lock, Alan...............................3:28:18 (4,468)
Lock, Benjamin...........................4:57:57 (25,487)
Lock, Christopher P......................4:10:41 (14,245)
Lock, Darren.............................4:06:55 (13,330)
Lock, David S............................4:49:23 (23,730)
Lock, David S............................5:42:07 (30,509)
Lock, Ian D..............................5:53:03 (31,216)
Lock, Ian J..............................3:37:13 (6,076)
Lock, Ian K..............................4:21:25 (16,960)
Lock, Michael............................4:54:51 (24,864)
Lock Necrews, Christian..................4:26:12 (18,313)
Locke, Eric V............................4:46:49 (23,177)
Locke, Ernie.............................4:19:33 (16,491)
Locke, Laurent...........................6:34:05 (32,517)
Locke, Mark S............................3:54:52 (10,165)
Locker, Rick.............................5:16:59 (28,122)
Lockett, Andrew P........................3:08:03 (1,865)
Lockett, Patrick.........................2:59:16 (1,172)
Lockett, Phillip J.......................5:47:17 (30,892)
Lockey, Alistair J.......................2:46:16 (394)
Lockey, Matthew J........................4:02:20 (12,337)
Lockie, Steve J..........................5:02:36 (26,262)
Lockley, Darren S........................4:07:04 (13,360)
Lockwood, Paul R.........................4:02:55 (12,462)
Lockyear, Kevin R........................3:23:39 (3,735)
Lockyer, Derek...........................2:56:17 (875)
Lockyer, Michael W.......................4:36:04 (20,742)
Lodge, Andrew V..........................4:44:48 (22,734)
Loeber, Peter J..........................3:42:57 (7,221)
Loeng, Kaare.............................4:08:40 (13,781)
Loenning, Eivino.........................4:45:40 (22,935)
Loertscher, Mathias A....................3:46:02 (7,907)
Loewe, Andreas...........................3:01:20 (1,327)
Lofthouse, Daniel P......................4:55:35 (25,015)
Loftus, Jacob N..........................6:14:03 (32,050)
Loftus, Kevin J..........................3:03:28 (1,478)
Logan, Alan S............................4:46:51 (23,185)
Logan, Gregory D.........................4:36:13 (20,786)
Logan, Michael B.........................4:28:06 (18,773)
Logan, Paul..............................5:23:32 (28,888)
Logan, Robert P..........................4:41:50 (22,062)
Loi, Mervin..............................4:20:40 (16,781)
Lomas, Darren............................4:20:45 (16,795)
Lomas-Brown, Richard E...................3:03:43 (1,494)
Lomax, Chris.............................3:03:29 (1,479)
Lomax, Simon.............................5:20:13 (28,521)
Lombardi, Giulio.........................4:19:49 (16,557)
Lombardi, Sergio.........................4:53:05 (24,473)
Lombroso, Eytan J........................5:19:06 (28,385)
Londesborough, Jim.......................3:13:12 (2,426)
London, David A..........................5:41:15 (30,435)
Lonergan, Stephen........................3:24:17 (3,836)
Long, Adrian P...........................4:01:19 (12,118)
Long, Alan M.............................4:24:13 (17,717)
Long, Brandon L..........................4:29:02 (19,034)
Long, Bryan G............................4:26:32 (18,391)

Long, Daniel P...........................5:04:49 (26,558)
Long, Darrell P..........................3:35:47 (5,796)
Long, Darren S...........................3:41:48 (6,988)
Long, David J............................3:50:25 (8,959)
Long, Jeremy C...........................3:48:37 (8,531)
Long, Marc K.............................4:51:59 (24,249)
Long, Oliver J...........................4:46:59 (23,210)
Long, Shaun D............................3:51:33 (9,234)
Longbottom, Andrew J.....................4:22:41 (17,294)
Longhi, Carlo M..........................3:55:47 (10,472)
Longhurst, Martin J......................3:12:03 (2,283)
Longhurst, Paul R........................4:07:10 (13,396)
Longhurst, Philip J......................4:05:56 (13,129)

Longland, Ian M..........................4:15:24 (15,449)

London 2006 was my very first marathon and was such an overwhelming emotional experience. Tower Bridge brought me to tears when I saw my family and from then on I just lapped up the amazing atmosphere. You realise how important London is with the masses of people there for a reason, either the loss of a friend, loved one or to raise money. Seeing the finish line tipped my emotions over the top and I blabbered down The Mall, looking at everything, not wanting to forget. I had done it. I had done the world's biggest marathon – London. I just thank my wife Helen, and daughters Caitlin and Brianna, for their love and support through my highs and lows before, during and after.

Longlands, Richard M.....................3:51:05 (9,118)
Longley, Gavin D.........................3:19:57 (3,259)
Longley, Robert C........................4:44:13 (22,615)
Longman, James A.........................3:30:26 (4,882)
Longman, Michael P.......................4:46:05 (23,022)
Longson, Gavin...........................4:52:21 (24,320)
Longstaff, Chris.........................3:34:16 (5,523)
Longstaff, Mark L........................4:09:01 (13,865)
Longstaff, Martin W......................4:23:57 (17,641)
Longstaff, Tony..........................4:34:44 (20,421)
Longthorn, Alan..........................4:53:05 (24,473)
Longthorpe, Andrew J.....................3:40:07 (6,643)
Longthorpe, Simon........................2:45:40 (361)
Longwill, Andrew.........................5:28:24 (29,368)
Longworth, Ben T.........................4:21:43 (17,026)
Lonrigg, Seb S...........................4:09:08 (13,885)
Lonsdale, Andrew M.......................4:27:28 (18,614)

Lonsdale, Richard I......................4:27:16 (18,572)
Lonsdale, Tony...........................4:13:01 (14,850)
Lonsdale, William G......................3:30:52 (4,955)
Looby, Adrian L..........................4:33:26 (20,121)
Looby, Stephen...........................5:07:25 (26,921)
Looms, Iain R............................3:34:24 (5,547)
Lopes, Octavio C.........................3:41:14 (6,858)
Lopes, Roger.............................3:17:21 (2,928)
Lopes Jesus, Paulo S.....................2:36:32 (136)
Lopez Diaz, Basilio M....................4:01:55 (12,242)
Lopez-Granados, Amador...................3:31:33 (5,073)
Lord, Adam P.............................6:04:48 (31,754)
Lord, Ben................................5:18:40 (28,331)
Lord, David..............................3:02:02 (1,378)
Lord, John F.............................5:06:29 (26,785)
Lord, Ken L..............................4:17:58 (16,100)
Lord, Mike A.............................4:57:10 (25,349)
Lord, Robert R...........................3:33:49 (5,451)
Lord, Steven T...........................2:58:04 (1,028)
Lore, Nicola.............................3:29:40 (4,754)
Lorentsen, Ragnar........................3:52:31 (9,497)
Lorenz, Jorg.............................4:06:05 (13,157)
Lorgat, Ziyaad...........................5:03:50 (26,431)
Lornco, Serafin..........................4:46:01 (23,008)
Lorriman, Steve..........................4:12:59 (14,831)
Lossen, Ulaus W..........................3:23:09 (3,671)
Loth, Wilhelm............................4:20:06 (16,629)
Lotherington, Stuart A...................3:59:38 (11,702)
Lott, Andrew.............................3:33:17 (5,365)
Loubert, Sebastien.......................3:48:18 (8,450)
Louchart, Marc...........................3:15:16 (2,691)
Louden, Adrian R.........................4:23:50 (17,605)
Louden, Paul T...........................4:13:01 (14,850)
Loughnane, Martin C......................2:58:15 (1,037)
Loughran, Raymond........................4:52:43 (24,402)
Louisnard, Thierry M.....................3:18:56 (3,126)
Loureiro, Antonio........................3:46:23 (7,979)
Loury, John H............................4:03:09 (12,520)
Louth, Shaun M...........................5:00:17 (25,941)
Louw, Bertus J...........................3:49:19 (8,697)
Louw, Jason..............................4:08:39 (13,780)
Lovatt, Gary P...........................4:37:10 (21,017)
Lovatt, Steven M.........................3:24:37 (3,883)
Love, Brian J............................5:58:53 (31,499)
Love, David S............................3:57:32 (11,022)
Love, Jay D..............................4:01:49 (12,219)
Loveday, Terry...........................4:16:47 (15,795)
Lovegrove, Dominic.......................4:59:13 (25,737)
Lovegrove, Melvyn R......................5:35:44 (30,030)
Lovegrove, Paul D........................3:56:29 (10,681)
Lovegrove, Paul D........................4:16:25 (15,695)
Lovekin, Jeremy..........................3:39:11 (6,471)
Lovelace, Craig B........................3:51:12 (9,147)
Lovelady, John...........................4:59:24 (25,761)
Loveless, Martin G.......................3:18:47 (3,104)
Lovell, James............................3:53:41 (9,816)
Lovell, John C...........................4:12:48 (14,773)
Lovell, Peter............................3:45:36 (7,821)
Lovelock, Ian............................5:31:19 (29,693)
Lovelock, Richard C......................3:31:58 (5,156)
Lovelock, Steven D.......................3:24:26 (3,850)
Loveridge, Ian...........................5:13:03 (27,663)
Loveridge, Paul J........................3:13:45 (2,495)
Loveridge, Trevor J......................5:30:17 (29,573)
Lovett, Nick.............................4:33:42 (20,188)
Loveys, Neil P...........................3:26:18 (4,114)
Lovick, Andrew J.........................4:17:56 (16,088)
Lovidge, Leslie J........................3:49:47 (8,816)
Low, Daniel C............................4:14:33 (15,216)
Low, Li Chun.............................3:31:40 (5,098)
Low, Nicholas............................5:20:14 (28,524)
Low, Nick M..............................4:42:21 (22,190)
Low, Philip J............................4:27:12 (18,555)
Low, Roger L.............................3:44:07 (7,475)
Low, Steven D............................3:23:54 (3,775)
Lowbridge, David.........................3:12:02 (2,280)
Lowde, Kim R.............................3:58:08 (11,203)
Lowden, Paul C...........................5:07:19 (26,907)
Lowden, Richard C........................2:57:26 (979)
Lowe, Andrew J...........................4:58:55 (25,692)
Lowe, Andrew W...........................3:48:00 (8,382)
Lowe, Gary M.............................4:03:46 (12,665)
Lowe, Ian................................3:32:44 (5,284)

Lowe, James A	4:18:30 (16,231)	
Lowe, Jeremy J	4:23:50 (17,605)	
Lowe, John O	5:09:38 (27,222)	
Lowe, Jonathon E	3:06:55 (1,748)	
Lowe, Joseph	5:23:44 (28,914)	
Lowe, Karl R	4:29:39 (19,216)	
Lowe, Martin D	5:35:03 (29,970)	
Lowe, Michael P	4:02:18 (12,331)	
Lowe, Paul	4:27:49 (18,697)	
Lowe, Paul A	3:42:11 (7,063)	
Lowe, Paul T	4:37:56 (21,204)	
Lowe, Peter N	4:19:30 (16,478)	
Lowe, Richard C	3:43:50 (7,429)	
Lowe, Richards S	4:24:43 (17,875)	
Lowe, Sean B	5:33:40 (29,869)	
Lowe, Simon J	3:14:20 (2,573)	
Lowen, Christopher	4:06:08 (13,167)	
Lower, Rob W	3:16:27 (2,817)	
Lowery, Daniel L	5:05:48 (26,676)	
Lowndes, Nigel A	4:53:30 (24,569)	
Lowrie, Andrew D	4:17:57 (16,095)	
Lowrie, Martyn	3:36:52 (6,012)	
Lowry, Alexander M	3:37:33 (6,140)	
Lowry, Hugo A	4:18:54 (16,325)	
Lowson, Richard J	2:47:11 (421)	
Lowther, Mark J	5:20:33 (28,567)	
Lowther, Richard C	5:13:12 (27,676)	
Loxley, Steven J	5:16:22 (28,054)	
Loy, Martin	3:02:04 (1,381)	
Loydale, John E	4:29:22 (19,138)	
Lttler, Michael I	4:06:29 (13,228)	
Lubbock, David R	4:12:10 (14,616)	
Lucarotti, John R	4:13:32 (14,962)	
Lucas, Andrew	3:38:13 (6,270)	
Lucas, Andrew	3:57:28 (11,003)	
Lucas, Bernard S	3:33:07 (5,335)	
Lucas, Derek R	4:23:41 (17,555)	
Lucas, Graham C	5:34:08 (29,897)	
Lucas, John A	4:58:34 (25,625)	
Lucas, Jonathan R	3:29:04 (4,636)	
Lucas, Kevin J	3:10:30 (2,113)	
Lucas, Mike G	4:52:43 (24,402)	
Lucas, Rick	4:04:53 (12,893)	
Lucas, Stephen C	4:21:02 (16,875)	
Lucey, Gareth A	4:28:45 (18,962)	
Luck, Andrew P	4:25:34 (18,132)	
Luck, Jamie D	3:23:26 (3,702)	
Luckett, David M	3:54:16 (9,996)	
Luckey, Scott J	4:59:16 (25,742)	
Lucy, Paul	4:41:40 (22,030)	
Luddon, Simon J	6:03:34 (31,707)	
Ludlam, Graham A	4:31:18 (19,613)	
Ludlow, Trevor	4:24:50 (17,898)	
Ludwig, Frank-Markus	4:02:05 (12,280)	
Luebke, Peter	3:47:56 (8,363)	
Luecke, Peter	4:22:06 (17,146)	
Luehrig, Tobias	4:39:18 (21,514)	
Luengo-Fernandez, Ramon	3:54:53 (10,173)	
Luepkes, Joerg	4:24:25 (17,777)	
Luesley, Christopher J	3:59:07 (11,553)	
Luff, Bradley I	5:26:56 (29,217)	
Luis, Joao M	4:35:29 (20,601)	
Lukasik, Matthew A	6:37:37 (32,571)	
Luke, Theo R	3:56:51 (10,804)	
Lukins, Colin I	3:19:13 (3,159)	
Lulham, Andy J	3:57:28 (11,003)	
Lumb, Stuart A	5:53:45 (31,251)	
Lumber, Nigel	3:11:12 (2,177)	
Lumley, Roger A	5:49:59 (31,091)	
Lumsden, William	4:37:42 (21,160)	
Lumsdon, Michael	4:30:01 (19,299)	
Lund, Simon	3:02:18 (1,391)	
Lund, Tim J	4:02:45 (12,424)	
Lundemose, Anker	4:25:37 (18,140)	
Lundgren, Eric	3:54:30 (10,051)	
Lundie, Blair A	5:41:44 (30,476)	
Lundon, Sean	4:39:24 (21,545)	
Lundy, Mark	4:05:12 (12,958)	
Lunn, Andrew P	3:23:29 (3,710)	
Lunn, Gary J	3:10:06 (2,073)	
Lunn, Timothy J	4:15:57 (15,587)	
Lunt, David W	5:05:02 (26,585)	
Lunt, Michael J	4:42:53 (22,301)	
Luong, Vu T	4:44:17 (22,636)	
Lupton, Paul A	3:51:40 (9,260)	
Luscombe, Adrian R	4:50:27 (23,935)	
Luscombe, Neil D	5:07:59 (27,004)	
Lush, Robert G	4:04:01 (12,721)	
Luther, Siegmar Paul	3:36:07 (5,858)	
Lutje Wagelaar, Benno	3:08:11 (1,874)	
Lutman, Damien	4:30:51 (19,504)	
Lutz, Herbert	4:45:41 (22,942)	
Luxford, Andrew W	5:03:36 (26,406)	
Luxford, Kevin J	5:03:35 (26,400)	
Luxton, Nicholas P	4:49:21 (23,724)	
Lyall, Graham	3:02:28 (1,403)	
Lydon, Stuart R	5:07:17 (26,904)	
Lye, Robert	3:56:13 (10,599)	
Lyle, Robert M	4:38:28 (21,329)	
Lyle, Tobias S	4:28:41 (18,940)	
Lynam, Robert G	3:10:36 (2,124)	
Lynch, Andrew J	4:16:03 (15,609)	
Lynch, Barry J	4:37:33 (21,125)	
Lynch, Benjamin J	4:55:27 (24,993)	
Lynch, Damian M	4:17:36 (16,018)	
Lynch, Elliott	3:53:36 (9,793)	
Lynch, Jim E	5:36:26 (30,090)	
Lynch, John	5:49:18 (31,024)	
Lynch, Matthew P	4:19:14 (16,398)	
Lynch, Peter A	5:29:06 (29,434)	
Lynch, Philip J	5:17:45 (28,215)	
Lynch, Richard B	4:52:19 (24,312)	
Lynch, Robert G	5:44:57 (30,712)	
Lynch, Robert M	5:28:07 (29,339)	
Lynch, Steven R	3:48:39 (8,541)	
Lynderup, Ejvind	4:00:46 (11,985)	
Lyne, Andrew G	2:52:50 (665)	
Lynn, Jeff	3:14:23 (2,581)	
Lynn, Michael	7:30:14 (33,096)	
Lynn, Philip M	3:54:13 (9,983)	
Lynn, Stuart W	3:12:31 (2,345)	
Lynock, Mark	3:37:54 (6,208)	
Lyon, Mark	4:34:30 (20,362)	
Lyon, Roger	5:49:10 (31,014)	
Lyons, Dale R	4:45:05 (22,810)	
Lyons, David S	4:29:09 (19,070)	
Lyons, Denys	3:37:42 (6,166)	
Lyons, Edward A	4:21:48 (17,062)	
Lyons, Gary	4:13:54 (15,042)	
Lyons, Henry T	4:22:55 (17,347)	
Lyons, Michael J	3:27:14 (4,276)	
Lyons, Michael W	3:09:59 (2,062)	
Lyons, Stuart	5:46:12 (30,802)	
Lyons Lowe, Damian	4:57:33 (25,410)	
Lysak, Anthony E	3:38:56 (6,423)	
Lyse, Remy	4:56:11 (25,135)	
Lythgoe, Nicholas G	4:23:16 (17,437)	
Lythgoe, Richard	4:07:42 (13,536)	
Maake Ka-McUbe, Sello	4:36:23 (20,820)	
Maali, Jamal	2:54:48 (781)	
Mabbott, Iain	4:25:18 (18,054)	
Mabbs, Alan J	7:42:24 (33,149)	
Mabey, Peter F	3:18:00 (2,996)	
Mabille, Ludovic	2:58:36 (1,075)	
Mabin, Pdro A	4:08:47 (13,809)	
Macarthur, John L	5:00:26 (25,965)	
Macartney, Michael G	4:49:33 (23,766)	
MacAskill, John R	4:54:45 (24,828)	
Macaulay, Bruce M	3:52:25 (9,477)	
Macbeth, Kenneth D	2:57:32 (986)	
Maccarrone, Franck	4:23:03 (17,374)	
MacCormick, Ian	5:47:17 (30,892)	
Macdiarmid, Robert B	4:25:52 (18,215)	
Macdonald, Alex	7:03:25 (32,922)	
Macdonald, Charles P	4:30:11 (19,345)	
Macdonald, Colin	4:14:51 (15,298)	
Macdonald, David M	2:56:59 (941)	
Macdonald, Greg	2:51:18 (606)	
Macdonald, James M	3:50:13 (8,915)	
Macdonald, John	4:36:49 (20,941)	
Macdonald, John D	5:12:17 (27,563)	
Macdonald, Keith W	4:04:35 (12,829)	
Macdonald, Scott R	4:19:29 (16,474)	
Macdonald, Shane A	5:13:49 (27,746)	
Macdonald, Steve C	3:56:18 (10,628)	
Macdonald, Stuart K	3:57:47 (11,110)	
Macdonald, Thomas	3:13:57 (2,521)	
Macdonald Brown, James G	4:22:58 (17,358)	
Macdonald-Williams, Emile	5:30:38 (29,608)	
MacDougall, Gary A	4:43:31 (22,443)	
MacDougall, Ian D	2:34:39 (108)	
MacDowall, Simon J	4:32:30 (19,903)	
Macey, Mark R	4:49:58 (23,838)	
Macey, Stuart	4:37:32 (21,117)	
Macey, Terence J	3:54:50 (10,156)	
MacFadyen, Alasdair L	5:16:27 (28,065)	
Macfarlan, Andrew	4:18:38 (16,262)	
Macfarlane, Alexander J	4:45:36 (22,926)	
MacGregor, Calum D	3:45:37 (7,826)	
MacGregor, David J	5:38:59 (30,280)	
MacGregor, John C	3:21:48 (3,509)	
MacGregor, Philip R	3:31:52 (5,158)	
Machado, Mario C	3:24:44 (3,901)	
Machin, Jason R	4:10:21 (14,183)	
Machray, Simon M	3:28:42 (4,556)	
Maciejewski, Christopher A	3:46:38 (8,043)	
Maciejkowicz, Rudolf	3:12:51 (2,383)	
MacInnes, Donald P	4:52:26 (24,339)	
MacInnes, John C	3:28:58 (4,615)	
Macintyre, Daniel G	4:45:32 (22,910)	
Macintyre, Ivan G	6:30:01 (32,449)	
MacIver, Nick G	4:32:45 (19,945)	
MacIver, Robert M	3:18:50 (3,111)	
Mack, Chris C	3:55:01 (10,209)	
Mack, Darren R	2:48:10 (458)	
Mack, Nick J	4:48:49 (23,613)	
MacKaskill, Andy K	2:35:27 (120)	
Mackay, Alexander J	3:57:18 (10,949)	
Mackay, Andrew	4:18:45 (16,291)	
Mackay, Andrew J	3:38:27 (6,316)	
Mackay, Frazer D	3:41:48 (6,988)	
Mackay, Gordon	4:12:59 (14,831)	
Mackay, Iain	4:55:45 (25,047)	
Mackay, James	4:54:41 (24,814)	
Mackay, Paul M	6:04:15 (31,733)	
Mackeith, Pieter R	3:21:10 (3,417)	
MacKenney, Stephen M	4:11:53 (14,547)	
Mackenzie, Adam Z	4:02:45 (12,424)	
Mackenzie, David W	4:58:15 (25,560)	
Mackenzie, Michael A	4:00:21 (11,902)	
Mackenzie, Rob J	3:23:52 (3,770)	
Mackenzie, Scott	3:37:36 (6,154)	
Mackenzie, Steve J	3:12:11 (2,305)	
Mackertich, David S	3:13:17 (2,430)	
Mackey, Brian R	3:20:09 (3,289)	
Mackey, Paul	3:49:28 (8,734)	
Mackie, Brian	2:52:15 (646)	
Mackie, Neil E	4:29:21 (19,136)	
Mackie, Simon	3:45:47 (7,866)	
Mackinnon, Angus E	4:58:42 (25,644)	
Mackinnon, Stephen	4:19:18 (16,422)	
Mackley, John S	3:49:28 (8,734)	
Macklin, Martin D	5:27:53 (29,317)	
Macklin, Matt J	3:55:10 (10,264)	
MacKonochie, Robin H	4:58:59 (25,706)	
Mackrill, Colin	3:55:07 (10,250)	
MacLachlan, Alastair J	2:54:04 (731)	
MacLagan, Ross A	4:18:51 (16,310)	
Maclean, Alastair R	3:27:35 (4,348)	
Maclean, Fraser W	3:43:47 (7,419)	
Maclean, Graham F	3:33:51 (5,456)	
Macleod, Assynt M	3:18:45 (3,100)	
Macleod, Douglas G	4:28:46 (18,965)	
Macleod, Murdo	3:47:56 (8,363)	
Macleod Carey, Timothy C	5:12:16 (27,560)	
Macleod-Miller, Leslie	3:34:24 (5,547)	
MacLure, Steven A	3:38:28 (6,321)	
MacManus, Paul A	3:09:39 (2,031)	
Macmillan, John R	4:14:40 (15,249)	
Macmillan, Mark	4:56:50 (25,264)	
MacNamara, Neil	7:05:51 (32,946)	
MacNaughton, Iain S	5:22:20 (28,751)	
MacNeil, Ernest A	3:20:56 (3,396)	
MacNicol, Neil	2:50:01 (549)	
Macpherson, Angus	3:14:12 (2,554)	
Macpherson, Hamish I	4:08:11 (13,663)	
MacQueen, Ian M	4:06:36 (13,251)	
Macrae, Duncan J	2:33:11 (92)	

MacTavish, Ian	5:51:55	(31,176)
Madarbux, Rahim	4:09:29	(13,992)
Maddams, Russell	2:31:50	(83)
Madden, Eamonn	8:58:11	(33,216)
Madden, Ian S	4:23:29	(17,496)
Madden, Paul C	4:00:01	(11,820)
Madder, Michael J	3:37:38	(6,158)
Maddern, Chris R	4:11:03	(14,346)
Madders, Thomas M	4:19:15	(16,408)
Madders, Thomas P	3:46:48	(8,081)
Maddock, Alistair D	4:04:40	(12,847)
Maddock, Andrew R	3:59:27	(11,659)
Maddock, Chris	3:40:41	(6,742)
Maddock, William A	3:57:56	(11,144)
Maddocks, Jordan	3:07:22	(1,790)
Maddox, Colin	4:16:22	(15,684)
Madeira, Pedro	3:34:01	(5,486)
Madeley, Sean A	4:44:23	(22,656)
Madgwick, Ian A	4:35:19	(20,559)
Madiba, James J	3:18:26	(3,053)
Madine, Jarlath	4:36:08	(20,763)
Madisclaire, Thierry	3:40:56	(6,791)
Madrigal, Alejandro	5:09:01	(27,148)
Madsen, Harald	5:18:57	(28,367)
Maerz, Frank W	3:23:57	(3,782)
Magan, Edward	3:40:10	(6,652)
Magee, Don F	3:48:20	(8,460)
Magee, Niall	3:59:38	(11,702)
Magee, Richard P	5:25:52	(29,119)
Maggee, Robett D	5:16:29	(28,068)
Maggs, Nigel	3:35:58	(5,830)
Maggs, Philip R	3:31:06	(5,005)
Magill, John A	3:36:54	(6,020)
Maginness, Patrick	5:30:37	(29,607)
Magnall, Stephen	5:52:11	(31,188)
Magnos, Gary C	4:53:35	(24,592)
Magueur, Philippe	4:00:57	(12,030)
Maguire, Bob	3:23:30	(3,713)
Maguire, Kevin J	5:05:50	(26,685)
Maguire, Marcus J	3:55:18	(10,314)
Maguire, Stephen	4:28:33	(18,910)
Maguire, Terence J	6:12:33	(32,005)
Maguire, Trevor A	2:58:36	(1,075)
Mahajan, Rajat	4:44:32	(22,683)
Maher, Alastair J	3:28:23	(4,489)
Maher, David D	3:45:04	(7,704)
Maher, David E	3:45:59	(7,901)
Maher, Derek P	4:19:44	(16,537)
Maher, Keith P	4:38:27	(21,325)
Maher, Patrick	3:29:29	(4,713)
Maheswaran, Shanmuga S	5:18:20	(28,286)
Mahil, Shaninder	4:55:16	(24,955)
Mahmood, Kamran A	3:55:03	(10,227)
Mahmood, Khalid	4:11:15	(14,402)
Mahmood, Talat	4:57:05	(25,332)
Mahon, Michael	3:51:44	(9,284)
Mahoney, Jonathan	4:18:51	(16,310)
Mahoney, Matthew	3:14:54	(2,653)
Mahony, David A	3:35:53	(5,814)
Mahood, John M	3:45:29	(7,802)
Mahoukou, Felix	4:17:58	(16,100)
Mahsoudi, Bruno E	3:20:08	(3,284)
Mahuma, Kenneth B	4:01:41	(12,187)
Maiden, Arthur J	3:58:11	(11,225)
Maiden, Chris H	4:59:38	(25,818)
Maiden, Richard P	4:54:17	(24,742)
Maidment, Jeffrey C	5:14:36	(27,854)
Maidment, Paul	4:51:18	(24,092)
Maigret, Philippe P	4:54:46	(24,833)
Maile, John	5:28:47	(29,410)
Maillard De La Moran, Hubert	4:01:01	(12,054)
Maillot, Renaud	3:44:50	(7,650)
Mailly, Jean-Pierre J	3:04:21	(1,533)
Main, Vincent G	3:26:19	(4,119)
Mainwaring, Michael R	3:36:04	(5,845)
Mainwaring, Robert E	5:18:07	(28,257)
Mainwaring, Russell A	3:27:44	(4,368)
Mair, Colin	3:55:14	(10,293)
Mair, Ian W	3:32:18	(5,222)
Mair, Robert	6:01:59	(31,639)
Mairot, Jocelyn	3:38:30	(6,327)
Mairs, Stuart	5:01:11	(26,069)
Maitland, Charles M	3:23:53	(3,771)

Performance measures

Fred Lebow, founder of the New York Marathon that inspired the London race, was obsessive about his own performance. At various points he trained himself to exist on practically no sleep, dropped regular meals, and in one particularly bizarre experiment, deliberately went without sex for a year to see what effect it would have on his running.

Majer, Peter E	3:32:59	(5,321)
Major, David	3:43:24	(7,333)
Major, Paul L	2:39:24	(198)
Major, William G	3:26:17	(4,113)
Maker, Michael J	3:54:14	(9,988)
Makings, Philip C	3:26:57	(4,234)
Makuwa, Bill	3:31:31	(5,068)
Mal, Firouz	3:28:15	(4,452)
Malan, Christian G	3:46:01	(7,905)
Malcolm, Thomas E	3:36:25	(5,919)
Male, Chris	4:22:24	(17,226)
Male, David	5:49:28	(31,043)
Male, David R	4:41:31	(21,997)
Male, Tony K	5:14:15	(27,806)
Maleedy, Christian A	4:21:14	(16,924)
Males, Anthony R	3:07:39	(1,820)
Males, Nik B	5:11:59	(27,523)
Malik, Abdul	6:17:01	(32,143)
Malik, Alan	4:00:40	(11,969)
Malin, Brian C	3:35:16	(5,717)
Mall, Jasbir	6:24:33	(32,345)
Mall, Sadik	4:41:29	(21,989)
Mallard, Lee J	3:57:45	(11,093)
Mallen, James P	3:26:33	(4,164)
Mallen, John S	4:11:45	(14,508)
Mallet, Clude	4:46:44	(23,164)
Mallet, Sonny	4:24:39	(17,858)
Mallett, Keith A	4:26:45	(18,452)
Malley, Adam J	4:50:23	(23,920)
Malley, Michael A	3:47:33	(8,249)
Mallin, Christopher G	3:57:05	(10,870)
Mallinson, James R	3:42:16	(7,076)
Mallison, Conrad J	3:47:31	(8,242)
Mallon, Cornelius B	3:29:26	(4,704)
Mallon, Padraig N	5:50:27	(31,110)
Malloy, Colin J	4:54:57	(24,880)
Malmqvist, Tony	3:47:19	(8,196)
Malone, Paul M	4:32:22	(19,879)
Maltby, Daniel E	4:24:24	(17,774)
Maltby, John N	3:49:18	(8,691)
Maltby, Robert J	4:02:25	(12,355)
Malton, John R	4:13:20	(14,924)
Malzer, Alex P	3:25:38	(4,023)
Mammon, Adam D	4:03:37	(12,629)
Man, Anthony	4:54:22	(24,761)
Man, Christopher C	4:43:14	(22,372)
Man, Jonathan	4:21:00	(16,867)
Man, Si-Chong	4:43:12	(22,367)
Mandelbaum, Matt C	5:46:21	(30,814)
Mander, David	4:34:57	(20,473)
Mander, Geoffrey F	4:52:53	(24,433)
Mandrell, Matthew	3:37:21	(6,105)
Manfrini, Leonardo	3:00:06	(1,239)
Mangat, Jasdip S	2:57:04	(948)
Mangelshot, Larry P	2:57:27	(981)
Mangion, Ted	3:41:31	(6,922)
Mangos, Nicholas A	3:02:24	(1,399)
Manir, Mohammed	2:36:34	(137)
Mann, Alan S	3:50:16	(8,929)
Mann, Alex J	3:12:08	(2,292)
Mann, Anthony J	5:34:14	(29,906)
Mann, Chris B	4:43:33	(22,452)
Mann, Christopher	3:51:41	(9,269)

Mann, Craig	3:14:38	(2,619)
Mann, Dave K	4:03:30	(12,606)
Mann, David G	4:25:10	(18,016)
Mann, Dean	3:17:27	(2,939)
Mann, Jason	4:13:13	(14,901)
Mann, Jason P	3:41:53	(7,004)
Mann, Jeremy D	3:52:17	(9,435)
Mann, Julian	2:36:34	(137)
Mann, Malcolm J	4:26:13	(18,316)
Mann, Malvinder S	3:44:16	(7,511)
Mann, Nicholas J	3:33:14	(5,361)
Mann, Paul A	3:07:56	(1,849)
Mann, Perry	4:39:46	(21,622)
Mann, Pete C	2:45:46	(364)
Mann, Phil	3:07:42	(1,825)
Mann, Rajpal S	4:09:33	(14,004)
Mann, Rodger P	4:31:03	(19,542)
Mann, Stuart	4:23:26	(17,478)
Mann, Tony W	4:19:23	(16,442)
Mannering, Ryan E	4:10:04	(14,115)
Mannheim, Ben	3:53:54	(9,893)
Manning, David P	7:33:13	(33,106)
Manning, Jason I	3:53:19	(9,722)
Manning, Julian H	2:56:09	(863)
Manning, Karl A	4:18:23	(16,204)
Manning, Paul	4:07:19	(13,427)
Manning, Paul J	3:53:27	(9,755)
Manning, Stephen	3:52:01	(9,365)
Manning, Terence G	3:46:51	(8,095)
Mannion, Dermot	3:22:16	(3,566)
Mannion, John R	4:41:15	(21,934)
Mannoni, Carlo	3:41:01	(6,807)
Manoharan, Arun P	5:11:33	(27,467)
Mansbridge, Stephen J	4:42:47	(22,278)
Mansell, Anthony M	3:46:59	(8,116)
Mansell, Phillip M	4:58:25	(25,589)
Mansfield, David S	3:36:21	(5,904)
Mansfield, Derek L	4:26:35	(18,403)
Mansfield, Jonathan D	3:59:44	(11,741)
Mansfield, Simon O	3:49:14	(8,674)
Mansfield, Terrence A	3:33:19	(5,370)
Mansi, Andrew J	3:07:28	(1,800)
Mansilla, Francisco J	5:08:47	(27,114)
Mansilla, Mario H	4:56:51	(25,270)
Manson, David C	3:59:34	(11,689)
Mansouri, Bruno	3:59:25	(11,641)
Mantle, Jason L	4:37:10	(21,017)
Manton, Christopher J	4:46:04	(23,019)
Manuel, David	3:41:09	(6,841)
Manuel, Dominic J	4:12:42	(14,749)
Manwaring, Mark T	4:45:43	(22,947)
Manze, David P	5:08:12	(27,035)
Mapp, Daniel P	3:28:31	(4,514)
Maqsood, Zayarat	4:33:48	(20,206)
Marais, Chris J	4:52:33	(24,365)
Marcato, Germano	5:19:12	(28,406)
March, Geoffrey W	3:48:33	(8,512)
March, Jason J	5:22:40	(28,796)
March, Richard P	3:44:05	(7,470)
March, Steve P	2:57:05	(951)
Marchant, Gary J	7:52:51	(33,171)
Marchant, Ian P	5:02:26	(26,242)
Marchant, Matthew F	4:54:32	(24,785)
Marchant, Michael C	3:32:46	(5,287)
Marciniak, Cezary	3:27:46	(4,373)
Marcinowicz, Adam L	3:16:25	(2,811)
Marck, Bertrand	3:55:18	(10,314)
Marcos, Miguel	4:26:11	(18,310)
Marcuz, Philippe	3:01:09	(1,314)
Mardisalu, Mart	4:13:00	(11,093)
Marengo Lopez, Raul A	7:32:14	(33,101)
Marfell-Jones, Elwyn J	3:44:52	(7,658)
Margerie, Robert	3:11:28	(2,211)
Margetts, Owen E	5:59:20	(31,531)
Margolis, Geoffrey A	4:46:32	(23,129)
Marianelli, Federico	6:57:22	(32,858)
Marie, Cyprien C	4:28:25	(18,874)
Marie De Lisle, Igor	4:04:19	(12,780)
Mariette, Louis	4:14:09	(15,122)
Mariis, Roland	3:57:45	(11,093)
Marinari, Stefano	3:26:59	(4,241)
Mariner, Timothy C	3:15:38	(2,729)
Marini, Marco	5:03:09	(26,335)

McFadyen, John ... 3:27:52 (4,394)
McFall, Patrick N ... 3:14:31 (2,598)
McFarlane, Barry J ... 3:48:08 (8,414)
McFarlane, James ... 4:33:12 (20,062)
McFarlane, John ... 2:19:24 (27)
McFarlane, Michael ... 4:43:14 (22,372)
McFarlane, Ronald ... 5:29:17 (29,455)
McGee, David M ... 4:23:13 (17,421)
McGeough, Peter F ... 3:18:03 (3,005)
McGhee, Alexander F ... 5:10:34 (27,343)
McGhie, Christopher ... 3:58:22 (11,293)
McGill, Colin A ... 2:42:02 (249)
McGilligan, Hugh P ... 2:44:54 (342)
McGilloway, Paul J ... 4:00:55 (12,019)
McGinley, Ciaran ... 5:00:13 (25,929)
McGinn, Michael E ... 4:06:37 (13,254)
McGinn, Nicholas J ... 4:11:16 (14,406)
McGinnes, Maurice F ... 3:36:11 (5,872)
McGinty, Martyn J ... 3:40:54 (6,783)
McGivern, Kieran M ... 5:14:50 (27,885)
McGivern, Peter L ... 6:02:18 (31,656)
McGlennon, David L ... 3:39:56 (6,614)
McGlynn, Peter J ... 4:24:26 (17,785)
McGonagle, John ... 3:45:35 (7,819)
McGonagle, Joseph M ... 4:01:43 (12,192)
McGonnell, John ... 3:42:07 (7,046)
McGough, Paul G ... 3:39:17 (6,499)
McGowan, Brian P ... 4:05:48 (13,100)
McGowan, Kevin ... 3:49:43 (8,802)
McGowan, Peter ... 4:00:39 (11,965)
McGowen, Paul S ... 4:02:56 (12,464)
McGown, Joe F ... 5:22:30 (28,773)
McGrath, Alex J ... 5:17:01 (28,131)
McGrath, Brendan A ... 4:57:57 (25,487)
McGrath, David ... 3:19:46 (3,225)
McGrath, Declan ... 3:56:46 (10,769)
McGrath, Gerard F ... 4:09:16 (13,926)
McGrath, Graham ... 4:43:16 (22,383)
McGrath, Matthew ... 4:21:59 (17,112)
McGrath, Michael C ... 4:43:57 (22,563)
McGrath, Neil J ... 5:30:31 (29,594)
McGrath, Oliver J ... 3:31:02 (4,990)
McGraw, Gary T ... 3:48:26 (8,483)
McGread, Michael P ... 3:11:57 (2,268)
McGreal, Kevin ... 3:58:19 (11,275)
McGregor, Calum A ... 3:54:41 (10,109)
McGregor, Campbell S ... 3:56:22 (10,643)
McGregor, Gordon R ... 2:55:08 (795)
McGregor, Keith D ... 5:27:28 (29,269)
McGregor, Ranald ... 3:45:01 (7,693)
McGregor-Cheers, Philip A ... 6:55:53 (32,837)
McGregor-Macdonald, Francis ... 3:49:48 (8,822)
McGroarty, Patrick J ... 3:54:12 (9,980)
McGroarty, Paul ... 4:24:06 (17,683)
McGroggan, Sean ... 4:58:41 (25,641)
McGrory, Paul ... 5:32:55 (29,809)
McGuigan, Michael V ... 3:28:18 (4,468)
McGuigan, Paul J ... 3:03:59 (1,511)
McGuinness, Daniel H ... 4:00:15 (11,879)
McGuire, Arthur ... 4:28:26 (18,879)
McGuire, Benjamin S ... 5:59:08 (31,509)
McGuire, Craig T ... 4:20:15 (16,675)
McGuire, Dominic M ... 3:25:09 (3,953)
McGuire, James T ... 4:52:46 (24,414)
McGuirk, David J ... 7:26:50 (33,081)
McHale, Austin P ... 4:36:23 (20,820)
McHardy, Simon J ... 4:14:48 (15,286)
McHenry, Desi ... 2:59:33 (1,198)
McHugh, Noel P ... 3:47:57 (8,374)
McHugh, Sean ... 3:51:57 (9,351)
McIlroy, Glenn ... 4:17:42 (16,033)
McIlvenna, Luke ... 4:05:46 (13,090)
McIlwee, Ian ... 2:45:59 (381)
McInally, Jason ... 3:54:27 (10,038)
McInally, Stephen A ... 3:31:54 (5,144)
McInerney, Michael A ... 3:22:25 (3,585)
McInerney, Paul A ... 3:12:07 (2,291)
McInnes, Colin G ... 3:35:05 (5,690)
McInnes, James A ... 4:20:31 (16,738)
McInnes, John A ... 3:41:39 (6,954)
McIntosh, Christopher G ... 3:57:02 (10,852)
McIntosh, Craig I ... 4:19:10 (16,382)
McIntosh, Doug A ... 4:24:52 (17,906)
McIntosh, James A ... 3:59:32 (11,682)
McIntosh, Malcolm ... 4:01:10 (12,092)
McIntosh, Mark S ... 3:11:43 (2,238)
McIntyre, Alan ... 4:54:50 (24,856)
McIntyre, Andrew J ... 3:57:06 (10,883)
McIntyre, Neil A ... 3:57:05 (10,870)
McIvor, Aaron ... 3:07:26 (1,797)
McKay, Daniel I ... 4:27:48 (18,696)
McKay, Ian A ... 4:47:10 (23,247)
McKay, John C ... 3:56:35 (10,717)
McKay, Paul W ... 3:22:46 (3,631)
McKay, Robert ... 3:28:19 (4,475)
McKeating, Neil P ... 3:53:15 (9,706)
McKechnie, Ian ... 5:36:46 (30,114)
McKechnie, James D ... 4:54:48 (24,848)
McKee, Ray ... 3:56:15 (10,610)
McKee, Robert P ... 4:50:35 (23,956)
McKeen, Kenneth ... 4:07:30 (13,475)
McKeeney, Paul ... 4:52:53 (24,433)
McKell, Laurence E ... 4:10:44 (14,256)
McKellar, James R ... 4:24:52 (17,906)
McKellow, Stephen N ... 5:47:35 (30,924)
McKelvey, Grant A ... 3:14:33 (2,603)
McKelvey, Stephen J ... 4:25:23 (18,087)
McKendrick, Alastair W ... 4:58:24 (25,585)
McKendry, Glenn ... 2:55:38 (823)
McKenna, Aidan M ... 5:55:05 (31,306)
McKenna, Gary P ... 2:58:47 (1,112)
McKenna, Malcolm J ... 4:55:00 (24,895)
McKenna, Richard C ... 4:57:28 (25,392)
McKenzie, Andrew H ... 5:02:45 (26,282)
McKenzie, Gavin ... 4:30:28 (19,419)
McKeown, Damian ... 4:18:47 (16,303)
McKeown, Des M ... 3:33:17 (5,365)
McKerrow, Alastair I ... 3:53:21 (9,731)
McKetty, Marlon C ... 4:39:54 (21,656)
McKevitt, Simon ... 2:29:04 (64)
McKibbin, Keri H ... 3:50:57 (9,090)
McKidd, Laurence R ... 3:49:15 (8,682)
McKimm, David ... 4:57:57 (25,487)
McKinlay, Jamie R ... 4:31:07 (19,557)
McKirdy, Gordon J ... 3:49:09 (8,658)
McKnight, Steven ... 3:58:34 (11,362)
McKown-Lunt, Iain G ... 7:06:47 (32,952)
McLachlan, Michael I ... 3:39:27 (6,535)
McLain, Christopher M ... 5:01:20 (26,091)
McLaren, Bruce J ... 3:24:14 (3,831)
McLaren, Guy N ... 3:17:20 (2,923)
McLaren, James C ... 3:38:49 (6,386)
McLaren, John J ... 3:51:19 (9,178)
McLaren, Lawrence ... 5:21:52 (28,698)
McLaren, Neil M ... 3:49:28 (8,734)
McLaren, Paul ... 3:56:06 (10,568)
McLaughlin, Aiden J ... 5:58:01 (31,456)
McLaughlin, Brian J ... 3:41:03 (6,815)
McLaughlin, Daniel M ... 4:03:07 (12,509)
McLaughlin, David E ... 5:35:58 (30,053)
McLaughlin, Declan ... 3:39:37 (6,557)
McLaughlin, Liam ... 4:56:57 (25,295)
McLaughlin, Philip ... 5:48:32 (30,970)
McLaughlin, Philip R ... 4:41:04 (21,910)
McLay, Stephen H ... 4:22:43 (17,303)
McLean, Darryl ... 4:35:57 (20,709)
McLean, Henry ... 3:58:49 (11,452)
McLean, Vincent T ... 5:44:37 (30,687)
McLean-Reid, David J ... 4:39:48 (21,630)
McLeish, Andrew J ... 5:51:28 (31,153)
McLelland, David ... 2:45:55 (375)
McLelland, Steve ... 3:40:14 (6,663)
McLeod, Andrew J ... 2:38:30 (179)
McLeod, Kirk ... 4:09:47 (14,054)
McLernon, Paul ... 4:23:48 (17,589)
McLintock, Ian J ... 4:39:52 (21,645)
McLornan, Donal P ... 3:34:03 (5,491)
McLoughlin, Robert J ... 3:45:34 (7,814)
McLoughlin, Stephen ... 3:59:19 (11,611)
McLurcan, Iain J ... 4:05:08 (12,946)
McMahon, Bernard J ... 3:45:14 (7,737)
McMahon, James H ... 4:10:00 (14,098)
McMahon, James T ... 4:49:15 (23,702)
McMahon, Jamie ... 3:36:08 (5,860)
McMahon, John P ... 3:37:46 (6,180)
McMahon, Paul ... 3:46:13 (7,947)
McMahon, Raymond F ... 3:55:20 (10,325)
McMahon, Simon A ... 3:42:43 (7,159)
McMahon, Stephen B ... 3:54:03 (9,930)
McManamon, Martin ... 4:47:09 (23,243)

McManmon, Pascal J ... 4:34:31 (20,365)

As I and fellow runners from my Ware Joggers Running Club gathered on Blackheath the anticipation rose. Although it was my 5th London Marathon the nervous excitement was the same. Despite a bit of rain, which cooled the runners, spirits of the many thousands of supporters was not dampened. Seeing my friends and family twice on the Isle of Dogs really spurred me on. Although I had a few minor problems with cramp at about 23 miles I reached the finish with a time of 4hrs 34mins raising £1,551 for Marie Curie Cancer Care, feeling tired, elated and proud that I had completed this marathon in memory of my dear sister Bernie who had recently died of cancer.

McManus, Kevin A ... 3:09:21 (1,993)
McManus, Peter J ... 4:30:03 (19,309)
McManus, Simon ... 4:11:03 (14,346)
McMeekin, Aaron T ... 3:42:55 (7,212)
McMeekin, James W ... 4:10:12 (14,149)
McMeekin, Lee W ... 2:36:13 (131)
McMenamin, Paul A ... 4:12:10 (14,616)
McMillan, Alastair ... 5:22:59 (28,824)
McMillan, Craig L ... 4:22:43 (17,303)
McMillan, Duncan R ... 3:50:56 (9,083)
McMillan, Kevin G ... 3:19:56 (3,255)
McMillan, Nelson ... 3:59:38 (11,702)
McMillan, Russell B ... 6:04:17 (31,734)
McMillen, Richard L ... 4:09:41 (14,026)
McMonagle, Noel ... 3:46:24 (7,989)
McMullen, John E ... 4:26:32 (18,391)
McMullen, Rory J ... 3:58:43 (11,405)
McMyler, Sean A ... 2:46:15 (393)
McNab, David ... 3:17:46 (2,973)
McNair, Martin A ... 4:27:31 (18,628)
McNally, Brian L ... 5:31:29 (29,704)
McNally, David J ... 4:33:40 (20,183)
McNally, John R ... 3:15:50 (2,759)
McNamara, David M ... 3:20:43 (3,366)
McNamara, James P ... 5:43:11 (30,587)
McNamara, Stephen C ... 3:11:31 (2,217)
McNaught, Chilton J ... 5:07:23 (26,915)
McNaught, Roger S ... 4:17:21 (15,944)
McNaull, Allisdhair I ... 3:38:02 (6,234)
McNeil, Martin R ... 5:46:29 (30,824)
McNeil, Neil J ... 3:49:39 (8,786)
McNeila, Joseph ... 4:27:04 (18,517)
McNeill, Andrew S ... 2:34:58 (114)
McNeill, Andrew V ... 4:11:58 (14,566)
McNeill, Rory ... 3:48:31 (8,504)
McNelis, Robin N ... 2:56:37 (907)
McNelliey, John J ... 6:26:23 (32,387)
McNestrie, Nigel R ... 5:05:02 (26,585)
McNicholas, Joe N ... 5:12:12 (27,551)
McNicholas, Paul ... 3:53:07 (9,665)
McNulty, Alun A ... 3:25:01 (3,934)
McNulty, Myles F ... 4:20:56 (16,850)

McParland, Francis 4:01:14 (12,105)
McPartlan, Paul 3:49:03 (8,637)
McPaul, Robert 4:14:20 (15,169)
McPeake, Francis B 3:49:21 (8,705)
McPhail, Colin D 3:23:42 (3,742)
McPhail, Stephen A 5:04:21 (26,498)
McPherson, George A 2:58:46 (1,106)
McPherson, Steven R 4:51:51 (24,222)
McPherson, William A 5:44:51 (30,707)
McPhillips, Kevin R 3:28:31 (4,514)
McQuade, Bryan M 4:29:27 (19,160)
McQueen, Robert J 3:31:07 (5,010)
McQuellen, Gordon J 5:28:48 (29,411)
McRae-Adams, Ian D 5:11:45 (27,488)
McRae-Spencer, Duncan M 5:54:12 (31,272)
McShane, Desmond C 2:59:09 (1,154)
McShane, Francis 4:42:15 (22,165)
McSharry, Alexander J 3:44:45 (7,629)
McSweeney, Brian G 4:23:18 (17,443)
McTigue, Joseph 3:59:22 (11,630)
McVey, Geoffrey P 3:51:40 (9,260)
McVickers, Declan J 4:50:41 (23,979)
McWhirter, Alan J 4:49:02 (23,658)
McWilliam, Stuart J 4:10:18 (14,170)
Mead, Adrian 3:09:58 (2,061)
Mead, Derek G 4:50:38 (23,971)
Mead, Mark 4:43:47 (22,514)
Mead, Steve J 2:52:57 (676)
Meaden, John G 4:31:07 (19,557)
Meader, Paul 5:20:23 (28,552)
Meadowcroft, Ian C 2:58:45 (1,103)
Meadows, Craig 4:46:23 (23,098)
Meadows, John D 4:45:53 (22,985)
Meadows, John W 4:59:30 (25,786)
Meager, John B 3:46:28 (8,004)

Meagor, Lucas B 3:54:05 (9,940)

My best ever London time of my six entries. 2007 and 2009 went a bit wrong! It was a damper start but a good day. My brother had to withdraw so we ran together in 2007. I seemed to enjoy the cooler air as I had a good first half – with encouragement from the crowds I seemed to be flying! I finally finished London in sub 4 hours – the one and only time. I went on to run Belfast Marathon 8 days later in 3:44 and Cardiff in the October in 3:31 – my best of 19 Marathons at time of going to print. I ran for four charities – MRDF, NCH, RICE and CLIC Sargent – and raised over £3,000 between them. Had blonde and purple hair, and started my website to mark it all www.lucaskeepsrunning.co.uk

Meakes, Timothy G 4:17:24 (15,954)
Meakin, Ian R 4:21:10 (16,908)
Meakins, Chris 5:54:23 (31,278)
Mealing, Jonathan W 3:33:55 (5,468)
Mears, Mark W 4:11:20 (14,426)
Measday, Byron O 4:08:41 (13,786)
Medalin-Moret, Michel 3:48:38 (8,535)
Medcalf, Peter 4:46:08 (23,033)
Medcraft, David 3:58:20 (11,280)
Medcraft, Jonathan P 3:21:39 (3,492)
Medeiros, Marcelo P 3:30:09 (4,852)
Medler, Neil F 4:31:41 (19,719)
Medlock, Scott 4:19:08 (16,374)
Medrano, Antonio 3:15:42 (2,741)
Medway, Jim S 3:42:02 (7,030)
Mee, Chris D 5:45:58 (30,777)
Mee, Darren 4:41:43 (22,039)
Meech, Laurence 4:14:16 (15,155)
Meehan, David J 3:33:48 (5,449)
Meehan, John P 3:41:34 (6,933)
Meehan, Tony 4:36:06 (20,752)
Meek, Andrew J 4:33:51 (20,216)
Meek, Jon M 3:11:13 (2,182)
Meeking, Christopher G 4:31:04 (19,544)
Meekings, Philip J 5:29:41 (29,503)
Mees, Alex 4:32:50 (19,963)
Meggitt, Ashley J 4:29:14 (19,093)
Mehat, Raminder 3:47:42 (8,298)
Mehew, Bruce 4:24:34 (17,830)
Mehlhorn, Siegfried 4:27:30 (18,621)
Mehmed, Deniz 3:20:46 (3,372)
Mehmet, Erol R 5:07:29 (26,927)
Mehta, Ajay 5:08:13 (27,037)
Mehta, Mayur 5:13:41 (27,734)
Mehta, Paresh 4:33:23 (20,106)
Meier, Robert P 3:56:00 (10,543)
Meier, Stefan M 5:20:17 (28,533)
Mein, William 5:17:00 (28,126)
Meldoli, Massimo 3:22:06 (3,544)
Meldrum, David 5:29:21 (29,463)
Meldrum, Peter 4:23:56 (17,633)
Melhuish, Paul 4:41:02 (21,905)
Melhuish, Stuart J 5:01:59 (26,174)
Melia, Dean P 3:38:22 (6,297)
Melia, John F 4:42:50 (22,291)
Melis, Jochem 3:46:37 (8,040)
Mellem, Ola 2:57:18 (967)
Melling, Anthony 4:31:59 (19,786)
Melling, Nicholas J 3:29:09 (4,644)
Mellon, James 5:48:29 (30,966)
Mellon, Mark L 3:05:47 (1,641)
Mellor, Dennis 4:54:06 (24,695)
Mellor, Martyn 6:59:04 (32,869)
Mellor, Robert J 3:25:45 (4,034)
Melluish, Stephen A 3:37:13 (6,076)
Melly, William J 4:10:07 (14,127)
Melton, Steve P 6:23:49 (32,325)
Melville, Greg 6:21:57 (32,284)
Melville, Leigh 6:21:57 (32,284)
Melville Smith, John D 5:21:26 (28,659)
Membribe-Sola, Antonio 3:41:02 (6,809)
Memmott, Neil 3:48:26 (8,483)
Mendick, David 4:53:07 (24,485)
Mendum, David J 5:37:35 (30,173)
Menegassi, Jorge C 4:04:06 (12,739)
Meneses, Joaquim C 3:26:45 (4,202)
Mennell, Simon R 3:21:34 (3,481)
Menozzi, Guido 2:41:49 (240)
Mercer, Ian J 3:50:19 (8,937)
Mercer, Peter J 5:56:14 (31,369)
Mercer, Richard 3:53:57 (9,908)
Mercer, Roland C 5:24:00 (28,936)
Meredith, Christopher J 4:56:47 (25,254)
Meredith, David 4:07:01 (13,349)
Meredith, Roy 4:00:17 (11,884)
Meredith, Tim D 3:55:44 (10,453)
Meredith, Tobias A 5:10:11 (27,284)
Meredith-Hardy, Charlie A 4:38:44 (21,380)
Merley, Christian 3:51:32 (9,229)
Merlin, Ben H 3:12:23 (2,333)
Merlin, Pierre 3:46:28 (8,004)
Merrall, Grant L 3:35:54 (5,818)
Merrey, James 3:29:13 (4,658)
Merrick, Simon 5:36:58 (30,132)
Merritt, Nicholas A 3:58:07 (11,195)
Merritt-Holmes, Mike 4:29:04 (19,041)
Merriweather, Aaron 3:52:15 (9,429)
Merriweather, Brian 5:02:27 (26,244)
Merron, Bernard J 3:09:25 (2,003)
Merry, Russell A 5:04:24 (26,513)
Merry, William G 4:46:49 (23,177)
Meschini, Alessandro 3:18:37 (3,084)
Mesney, Peer M 4:04:04 (12,732)
Messenger, Mark 3:54:36 (10,080)
Messinger, William T 3:53:25 (9,741)
Meston, Thomas J 3:09:24 (2,002)
Meta, James B 4:24:25 (17,777)
Metcalf, Alan E 2:46:28 (403)
Metcalf, John D 3:59:34 (11,689)
Metcalf, Lester 4:42:12 (22,156)
Metcalf, Peter C 3:19:25 (3,182)
Metcalf, Steven N 3:52:19 (9,441)
Metcalfe, John H 4:36:28 (20,836)
Metcalfe, Len 4:38:05 (21,251)
Metcalfe, Tim C 3:02:01 (1,376)
Metral, Jean-Claude 3:14:28 (2,591)
Metzgen, Richard A 4:07:50 (13,568)
Meumann, Mark D 3:20:38 (3,354)
Mewse, Dale L 4:08:04 (13,632)
Meyer, Franck 5:05:07 (26,602)
Meyer, Lars O 3:58:02 (11,163)
Meyer, Nicholas S 4:22:43 (17,303)
Meyer, Paul D 2:59:52 (1,229)
Meyrick, Andrew P 4:39:25 (21,548)
Meyrick, Miles W 2:57:19 (969)
Mgaleka, Paul 3:31:42 (5,101)
Miah, Afsor 5:27:28 (29,269)
Miah, Atik 5:26:26 (29,168)
Micallef, Charles 3:32:14 (5,211)
Michael, Nick 4:22:13 (17,179)
Michael, Paul J 3:21:43 (3,502)
Michaelides, Christos I 5:26:15 (29,147)
Michaels, Simon J 5:14:29 (27,839)
Michales, Stephen A 4:36:06 (20,752)
Michel, Pascal 2:36:54 (143)
Michel, Roelandt 5:38:13 (30,220)
Michel, Roland P 4:04:16 (12,770)
Michell, Nick 3:58:16 (11,253)
Michler, Peter 3:40:32 (6,718)
Michol, Gary T 3:54:19 (10,009)
Micklem, Duncan 5:14:04 (27,776)
Micklethwaite, Todd 5:34:36 (29,943)
Middlemas, Bruce M 3:41:12 (6,854)
Middlemas, Ian 3:47:23 (8,208)
Middlemass, Andrew 4:18:51 (16,310)
Middleton, Andrew G 7:20:25 (33,044)
Middleton, Craig G 4:19:01 (16,356)
Middleton, Robin J 3:35:50 (5,807)
Middleton, Robin J 4:23:26 (17,478)
Middleton, Thomas E 3:54:11 (9,972)
Middleton, Thomas F 3:01:25 (1,333)
Middleton, William G 4:15:59 (15,596)
Middlewick, Andrew R 4:39:47 (21,624)
Midworth, Nick S 3:39:31 (6,543)
Miers, James A 3:32:17 (5,220)
Mifsud, Daniel J 3:58:31 (11,344)
Migne, Patrick 3:26:51 (4,214)
Mikellides, Andy 4:04:13 (12,760)
Mikkelsen, Vidar 3:32:15 (5,217)
Mikolajczewski, Pawel 4:08:24 (13,717)
Mikulski, Richard N 4:47:40 (23,353)
Milburn, Alastair G 4:29:47 (19,248)
Milburn, Mark W 5:44:06 (30,649)
Milcent, Stephen 3:42:39 (7,145)
Miles, Carl 3:51:17 (9,168)
Miles, Chris 3:28:41 (4,549)
Miles, Christopher T 4:31:24 (19,645)
Miles, David 4:10:15 (14,161)
Miles, David M 3:07:45 (1,833)
Miles, Dominic 3:53:12 (9,689)
Miles, Gary 3:33:18 (5,369)
Miles, James J 3:08:28 (1,908)
Miles, James W 4:12:51 (14,796)
Miles, Laurence 2:41:10 (229)
Miles, Nicholas J 3:41:18 (6,872)
Miles, Noel R 3:02:56 (1,437)
Miles, Paul W 2:58:51 (1,123)
Miles, Philip B 4:07:41 (13,528)
Miles, Stephen M 3:55:08 (10,255)
Milford, Simon J 4:15:26 (15,460)
Millar, Alexander J 6:21:27 (32,271)
Millar, Andrew P 3:36:43 (5,979)
Millar, Barry N 4:57:10 (25,349)
Millar, Gordon N 4:25:00 (17,964)
Millar, Ralph S 4:27:18 (18,578)
Millar, Robert D 4:56:06 (25,119)

Millard, Duncan R 3:35:26 (5,738)
Millard, Iain V 5:22:22 (28,764)
Millard, Simon 5:02:06 (26,187)
Miller, Adrian D 3:17:41 (2,962)
Miller, Alexander C 3:17:30 (2,944)
Miller, Andrew 6:03:23 (31,700)
Miller, Andrew R 5:43:44 (30,625)
Miller, Brent A 4:28:08 (18,785)
Miller, Calum A 3:38:06 (6,250)
Miller, Charles M 4:17:30 (15,981)
Miller, Christopher R 3:15:46 (2,748)
Miller, Craig J 3:44:35 (7,591)
Miller, Daniel J 3:17:27 (2,939)
Miller, David 3:29:47 (4,779)
Miller, David 4:58:19 (25,572)
Miller, David A 5:08:51 (27,125)
Miller, Elliott 4:42:20 (22,185)
Miller, Frank 3:44:50 (7,650)
Miller, Graeme 3:12:45 (2,369)
Miller, Graham F 3:49:58 (8,860)
Miller, Ian E 4:06:27 (13,219)
Miller, James 6:03:24 (31,702)
Miller, James G 4:43:30 (22,435)
Miller, John C 4:29:50 (19,256)
Miller, Keith D 4:25:55 (18,237)
Miller, Len V 4:09:36 (14,016)
Miller, Les D 5:36:36 (30,107)
Miller, Marc J 4:44:37 (22,693)
Miller, Mark P 4:49:41 (23,789)
Miller, Michael J 3:09:05 (1,964)
Miller, Paul B 4:53:22 (24,539)
Miller, Paul D 4:40:59 (21,891)
Miller, Peter 3:08:31 (1,912)
Miller, Philip J 5:08:35 (27,089)
Miller, Robert J 4:59:01 (25,710)
Miller, Steven 2:41:59 (247)
Miller, Steven J 5:17:24 (28,183)
Miller, Tom 3:52:13 (9,419)
Millership, Stephen J 4:31:14 (19,593)
Millhouse, Craig J 5:19:25 (28,427)
Millican, Graham J 3:12:26 (2,337)
Millican, Keith M 4:11:31 (14,462)
Millichamp, James J 5:29:05 (29,431)
Milligan, Derrick 4:21:46 (17,052)
Milligan, Gordon 3:50:53 (9,072)
Milligan, Graham 3:47:23 (8,208)
Milliner, Kenneth L 4:06:44 (13,285)
Millington, Matthew A 5:20:50 (28,595)
Millington, Scott 6:21:05 (32,257)
Millington, Simon A 3:23:55 (3,778)
Millns, Tom J 3:45:24 (7,783)
Millott, Niku A 3:03:02 (1,444)
Mills, Andrew 5:24:59 (29,039)
Mills, Andrew D 4:12:08 (14,608)
Mills, Blair I 4:22:56 (17,350)
Mills, Chris J 5:19:56 (28,483)
Mills, Dane 4:34:09 (20,280)
Mills, Edward J 4:11:59 (14,569)
Mills, Frank 4:25:07 (17,996)
Mills, Gregory D 3:47:52 (8,347)
Mills, John A 3:30:50 (4,947)
Mills, Jonathan J 3:28:14 (4,448)
Mills, Michael 4:45:34 (22,916)
Mills, Michael O 4:21:56 (17,095)
Mills, Paul K 8:15:10 (33,191)
Mills, Shaun 3:41:41 (6,961)
Mills, Stephen J 4:33:40 (20,183)
Mills, Tim 3:39:04 (6,449)
Mills, Tim S 4:21:07 (16,897)
Mills, Trevor D 4:13:26 (14,949)
Millsom, Tony 5:47:09 (30,875)
Millward, Paul 5:07:29 (26,927)
Millward, Wayne 4:38:53 (21,413)
Milmine, James D 5:01:32 (26,110)
Milmoe, Michael 3:19:41 (3,211)
Milne, Andrew K 3:29:45 (4,771)
Milne, Anthony F 5:18:12 (28,269)
Milne, Ian H 5:03:58 (26,453)
Milne, Ian J 4:10:44 (14,256)
Milne, Ian S 3:46:38 (8,043)
Milne, Jeremy 3:50:39 (9,016)
Milne, Jonathan 4:54:20 (24,754)
Milne, Ronald W 3:31:54 (5,144)
Milne, Stephen 3:44:46 (7,631)
Milne, Stuart 4:23:52 (17,613)
Milner, James S 3:57:21 (10,966)
Milner, Nigel F 3:35:01 (5,668)
Milner, Stephen C 4:33:35 (20,159)
Milns, Barry 3:47:00 (8,119)
Milson, Paul J 3:48:40 (8,545)
Milton, Andrew 3:37:48 (6,191)
Milton, David R 3:42:22 (7,093)
Milton, John S 4:44:42 (22,711)
Minchin, Andrew E 4:21:43 (17,026)
Minchin, Patrick M 2:59:26 (1,189)
Mingay, Simon 3:06:27 (1,708)
Minguez-Lassa, Angel E 5:05:37 (26,655)
Minhall, Martin P 4:11:54 (14,549)
Minhas, Pardip S 3:45:19 (7,760)
Minns, Daniel C 4:19:49 (16,557)
Minns, Richard H 5:06:25 (26,774)
Minns, Roger 4:18:05 (16,137)
Minoos, Simon 4:54:08 (24,704)
Mint, Anthony H 4:07:36 (13,506)
Mintram, Ian 3:59:56 (11,795)
Mintrim, David R 3:42:24 (7,098)
Miracca, Angelo 3:47:47 (8,318)
Miranda, Stan 4:23:09 (17,397)
Mir-Puche, Miguel A 4:10:33 (14,220)
Miskelly, Fergus P 4:37:03 (20,989)
Misra, Akshay 4:32:22 (19,879)
Misselbrook, Mike J 4:59:25 (25,764)
Misselbrook, Neil G 4:37:56 (21,204)
Missingham, Andrew 3:58:13 (11,238)
Mistry, Bipin 4:53:09 (24,491)
Mistry, Hitesh S 3:10:28 (2,109)
Mistry, Jayanti 4:13:02 (14,856)
Mistry, Shashikant M 6:53:16 (32,799)
Mistry, Shashikant V 5:17:50 (28,224)
Mistry, Surrendra 5:01:28 (26,104)
Mitchell, Alan 4:42:21 (22,190)
Mitchell, Barry W 4:43:26 (22,417)
Mitchell, Damian P 4:39:04 (21,458)
Mitchell, David 3:49:24 (8,718)
Mitchell, Eriq 5:45:55 (30,772)
Mitchell, George 2:52:00 (634)
Mitchell, Gideon F 4:26:49 (18,468)
Mitchell, Gordon D 4:39:52 (21,645)
Mitchell, Gregory 5:14:52 (27,889)
Mitchell, Ian P 5:53:11 (31,228)
Mitchell, James K 3:44:24 (7,538)
Mitchell, Justin A 2:58:38 (1,083)
Mitchell, Karl 3:51:48 (9,303)
Mitchell, Keith 5:45:55 (30,772)
Mitchell, Keith S 3:21:02 (3,403)
Mitchell, Kevin 4:06:39 (13,259)
Mitchell, Martin R 3:52:56 (9,604)
Mitchell, Mathew 4:33:39 (20,177)
Mitchell, Nick 4:32:18 (19,859)
Mitchell, Nigel M 3:14:02 (2,537)
Mitchell, Paul R 2:50:13 (556)
Mitchell, Raymond 3:06:00 (1,667)
Mitchell, Richard H 3:44:32 (7,578)
Mitchell, Robert G 4:44:04 (22,578)
Mitchell, Robert J 3:14:33 (2,603)
Mitchell, Sean 3:18:19 (3,034)
Mitchell, Simon L 4:18:28 (16,223)
Mitchell, Stuart A 3:27:56 (4,401)
Mitchell, Stuart R 6:17:31 (32,158)
Mitchell, Wayne G 3:31:57 (5,152)
Mitchener, Paul J 3:37:51 (6,199)
Mitford, Timothy B 4:43:48 (22,521)
Mitsch, Ralf 3:46:23 (7,979)
Mitsumizo, Ken 3:05:31 (1,624)
Mitton, Matt P 4:37:11 (21,025)
Mivaro, Marco 3:47:08 (8,151)
Mizzi, Robert 4:55:17 (24,957)
Mkhize, Fortune M 4:48:40 (23,579)
Mo, Heine 3:40:24 (6,692)
Moat, Darren E 3:24:03 (3,800)
Moate, Simon R 3:50:28 (8,972)
Moate, Toby J 3:49:53 (8,843)
Moberly, James P 4:24:04 (17,675)
Mocetti, Ivano 3:25:52 (4,057)
Mocharrafie, Bassam M 4:49:15 (23,702)
Mockett, Thomas 4:51:05 (24,057)
Modaher, Jasvir S 5:35:21 (29,999)
Modderman, Siert A 3:44:09 (7,480)
Modi, Mitul 6:06:43 (31,814)
Moffat, Christopher A 4:04:45 (12,868)
Moffat, Stephen H 2:59:19 (1,178)
Moffett, David J 3:26:28 (4,142)
Moger, Christian F 5:12:22 (27,573)
Mogford, Andrew M 4:26:43 (18,439)
Mogford, David J 4:53:55 (24,663)
Mogg, Anthony R 4:44:57 (22,770)
Moggridge, Jonathan D 4:32:00 (19,791)
Mogridge, Chris 4:37:39 (21,149)
Mohamed, Jamal D 2:45:32 (360)
Mohamed, Salin 3:42:34 (7,126)
Mohr, Jason 4:13:03 (14,858)
Mohr, Nikolaus 4:56:13 (25,142)
Mohun, Timothy J 3:17:38 (2,956)
Moir, Michael C 4:12:50 (14,786)
Moir, Richard J 3:30:37 (4,918)
Moisson, Edward P 3:51:44 (9,284)
Mole, Denis H 4:09:40 (14,024)
Mole, James 4:53:41 (24,613)
Mole, Stephen J 3:10:49 (2,139)
Molefi, Amal L 3:31:37 (5,089)
Moles, Chris 4:20:54 (16,838)
Moles, David W 4:51:04 (24,053)
Molesworth, Jason 4:42:20 (22,185)
Molina Silva, José J 4:06:49 (13,303)
Molins, Greg P 5:41:42 (30,472)
Moll, Simon T 4:33:05 (20,025)
Moller, Robert 4:27:26 (18,606)
Mollet, Frederic J 3:06:47 (1,735)
Mollison, Rowan A 5:17:37 (28,210)
Molloy, Wayne 3:57:24 (10,979)
Moloney, Darren 3:16:06 (2,788)
Moloney, Michael D 5:00:47 (26,006)
Molony, Neil 3:59:01 (11,517)
Moltrasio, Renzo 4:16:58 (15,851)
Molyneux, Graham J 2:58:47 (1,112)
Molyneux, Sidney A 4:27:13 (18,560)
Mometti, Maurizio 4:02:12 (12,305)
Monaghan, Martin J 4:30:04 (19,315)
Monaghan, Paul E 3:54:46 (10,128)
Monaghan, Robin N 4:31:29 (19,661)
Monaghan, Stephen C 3:41:41 (6,961)
Moncrief, Edward R 3:51:43 (9,278)
Moncur, Iain M 5:27:34 (29,281)
Monczakowski, Marek 3:12:21 (2,329)
Mondello, Pasqualino 4:10:14 (14,156)
Money, Antony H 4:16:13 (15,650)
Monferrer, Manuel 4:12:05 (14,591)
Mong Thiong, Gilles 3:09:03 (1,963)
Monk, Howard 4:17:56 (16,088)
Monk, Mike J 4:19:56 (16,584)
Monk, Sam 4:14:44 (15,267)
Monk, Will S 5:09:58 (27,262)
Monkhouse, Christopher F 4:07:27 (13,457)
Monks, Gavin S 2:49:42 (528)
Monks, Raoull J 2:49:42 (528)
Monnickendam, Giles C 2:49:40 (525)
Montacute, Nigel J 5:21:55 (28,704)
Montague, Peter A 6:04:33 (31,747)
Montana, Carl 3:55:24 (10,345)
Montanari, Gino 4:09:12 (13,909)
Monteiro, Paulo A 5:20:23 (28,552)
Montero, José M 3:37:08 (6,062)
Montgomerie, James 5:43:50 (30,631)
Montgomery, Andy 4:04:09 (12,751)
Montgomery, Matthew L 3:38:27 (6,316)
Montgomery, Richard W 4:10:01 (14,103)
Montgomery, Will B 3:53:36 (9,793)
Monti, Sandro 4:44:53 (22,752)
Monticelli, Franco 5:11:03 (27,390)
Moodley, Allan 3:45:26 (7,789)
Moody, Andrew 4:28:42 (18,944)
Moody, Antony 5:16:20 (28,049)
Moody, Colin A 3:05:04 (1,583)
Moody, David A 5:34:46 (29,953)
Moody, Douglas G 3:42:41 (7,156)
Moody, James 4:32:06 (19,814)
Moody, Paul E 5:34:19 (29,915)
Moody, Robert H 4:44:21 (22,647)
Moody, Stephen J 4:47:12 (23,260)

Moolman, William W 4:13:46 (15,016)
Moon, Chris 5:16:17 (28,039)
Moon, James A 4:39:20 (21,528)
Moon, James K 3:07:44 (1,830)
Moon, Paul 4:10:09 (14,135)
Moon, Stephen A 4:43:39 (22,476)
Mooney, Andy P 3:58:11 (11,225)
Mooney, Dave E 5:46:30 (30,826)
Mooney, Gordon B 3:55:25 (10,349)
Mooney, Richard J 3:48:11 (8,431)
Mooney, Sacha J 4:38:04 (21,245)
Mooney, Trevor J 5:18:13 (28,273)
Moorby, Andrew 5:58:05 (31,460)
Moore, Andrew 3:45:53 (7,884)
Moore, Andrew C 3:50:49 (9,058)
Moore, Andrew J 4:58:18 (25,570)
Moore, Andrew M 3:10:09 (2,081)
Moore, Andrew P 3:41:34 (6,933)
Moore, Andrew P 5:13:23 (27,701)
Moore, Andy D 3:56:32 (10,694)
Moore, Christopher 3:28:06 (4,425)
Moore, Christopher R 3:30:34 (4,907)
Moore, Colin D 4:14:57 (15,319)
Moore, Darren E 3:51:39 (9,255)
Moore, Daryl L 4:41:51 (22,069)
Moore, David G 2:49:18 (512)
Moore, Gary W 4:33:07 (20,036)
Moore, Graham S 3:09:15 (1,980)
Moore, Ian 3:37:27 (6,121)
Moore, Ian 4:34:57 (20,473)
Moore, James A 3:22:08 (3,550)
Moore, Jimmy C 4:27:34 (18,644)
Moore, Jonathan 3:55:30 (10,374)
Moore, Joseph I 4:46:05 (23,022)
Moore, Julian M 3:53:57 (9,908)
Moore, Karl D 2:52:42 (661)
Moore, Kevin 5:38:15 (30,226)
Moore, Martin J 4:10:00 (14,098)
Moore, Martin L 5:06:21 (26,761)
Moore, Melwyn J 4:26:56 (18,489)
Moore, Michael F 2:56:54 (931)
Moore, Michael J 3:33:20 (5,373)
Moore, Michael J 4:44:25 (22,662)
Moore, Murray 3:34:36 (5,593)
Moore, Nicholas 4:44:58 (22,775)
Moore, Nigel J 5:25:00 (29,040)
Moore, Nigel T 3:26:30 (4,155)
Moore, Oliver P 3:43:14 (7,295)
Moore, Paul 3:55:16 (10,305)
Moore, Richard J 2:55:44 (830)
Moore, Richard J 3:10:17 (2,095)
Moore, Roger P 4:17:35 (16,011)
Moore, Roger W 4:51:16 (24,086)
Moore, Sebastian H 5:25:19 (29,070)
Moore, Simon P 3:46:03 (7,916)
Moore, Stephen R 3:05:15 (1,601)
Moore, Thomas P 4:36:01 (20,725)
Moore, Trevor A 3:05:14 (1,597)
Moores, Guy C 5:53:40 (31,246)
Moores, Mattehew P 4:31:13 (19,586)
Moorley, Calvin R 5:29:58 (29,543)
Mora, Giuseppe 4:14:57 (15,319)
Mora, Jorge 4:08:10 (13,656)
Morales Gonzales, David J 4:36:18 (20,803)
Moran, Andrew 3:02:47 (1,423)
Moran, Christopher J 4:32:35 (19,912)
Moran, David 3:15:01 (2,661)
Moran, David F 4:10:51 (14,294)
Moran, James C 5:34:34 (29,939)
Moran, John B 3:28:12 (4,441)
Moran, John P 4:38:53 (21,413)
Moran, Lee 5:07:25 (26,921)
Moran, Lee D 3:29:18 (4,677)
Moran, Michael M 3:57:12 (10,920)
Moran, Michael S 5:34:35 (29,940)
Moran, Nicholas 4:43:47 (22,514)
Moran, Paschal P 3:41:42 (6,967)
Moran, Stuart S 4:29:04 (19,041)
Morcombe, Lloyd S 7:07:48 (32,959)
Mordain, Richard 4:23:21 (17,454)
Mordelet, Erwan 4:24:38 (17,851)
Mordue, Christopher P 3:52:58 (9,617)
More, Nicholas J 4:35:47 (20,670)
Moreau, Marc 4:50:13 (23,885)
Morel, Franck 3:33:34 (5,410)
Morel, Ivan 4:24:11 (17,709)
Morel, Philip B 4:02:07 (12,289)
Moreland, David E 3:52:23 (9,466)
More-Molyneux, Michael G 5:39:45 (30,342)
Morenas, Ransley P 4:09:43 (14,035)
Moreno-Rodriguez, Luis 3:06:19 (1,697)
Moret, Teynis 3:42:43 (7,159)
Moreton, Darren J 3:49:49 (8,825)
Moreton, Neil A 3:46:05 (7,922)
Moreve, Guy L 3:26:31 (4,158)
Morfey, Michael J 5:29:54 (29,535)
Morgan, Andrew P 3:26:41 (4,189)
Morgan, Andrew P 5:19:02 (28,381)
Morgan, Christopher 4:19:06 (16,366)
Morgan, Darren M 3:29:09 (4,644)
Morgan, David J 3:48:38 (8,535)
Morgan, David K 3:37:15 (6,082)
Morgan, David R 3:52:08 (9,390)
Morgan, Emyr W 3:18:56 (3,126)
Morgan, Gregory A 3:50:25 (8,959)
Morgan, Ian 5:16:08 (28,018)
Morgan, Iver W 4:18:51 (16,310)
Morgan, John G 5:45:59 (30,782)
Morgan, Jonathan P 3:45:36 (7,821)
Morgan, Kenneth L 4:24:00 (17,656)
Morgan, Kristian M 3:31:10 (5,020)
Morgan, Marlon J 6:18:27 (32,181)
Morgan, Neil 3:21:15 (3,431)
Morgan, Neil 4:24:22 (17,770)
Morgan, Nicholas G 4:12:38 (14,734)
Morgan, Oliver W 3:39:40 (6,567)
Morgan, Owen 4:45:03 (22,804)
Morgan, Paul 3:37:20 (6,098)
Morgan, Paul 4:15:01 (15,342)
Morgan, Philip 3:42:32 (7,121)
Morgan, Richard J 3:50:07 (8,890)
Morgan, Robert A 5:03:56 (26,448)
Morgan, Robert D 4:44:21 (22,647)
Morgan, Robert W 3:31:23 (5,050)
Morgan, Robin M 5:18:01 (28,239)
Morgan, Ronald G 3:51:23 (9,196)
Morgan, Russell B 3:34:02 (5,490)
Morgan, Russell J 4:40:30 (21,777)
Morgan, Simon A 4:54:32 (24,785)
Morgan, Simon C 3:55:28 (10,361)
Morgan, Steve 4:21:29 (16,973)
Morgan, Thomas 4:39:53 (21,651)
Morgan, Thomas J 5:33:33 (29,853)
Morgan, Timothy P 3:45:08 (7,715)
Morgenstern, Christoph 5:17:07 (28,141)
Moriarty, Michael J 4:49:57 (23,835)
Morin, Michel 3:58:45 (11,422)
Morison, Ian J 3:57:27 (10,996)
Morita, Yasumichi 5:57:35 (31,436)
Moritz, David A 3:38:45 (6,376)
Morley, Colin J 4:12:32 (14,716)
Morley, Eric H 6:48:59 (32,746)
Morley, Ian 4:17:46 (16,052)
Morley, James E 3:34:16 (5,523)
Morley, Lee S 5:19:27 (28,428)
Morley, Nick 5:49:26 (31,038)
Morley, Philip A 3:06:58 (1,755)
Morley, Philip E 4:01:36 (12,174)
Morley, Raymond 4:38:16 (21,295)
Morley, Stewart J 4:10:04 (14,115)
Morlock, Guy H 3:37:56 (6,215)
Moro, Paolo 3:52:16 (9,431)
Moroney, Alan J 4:07:20 (13,429)
Morpuss, Guy 3:53:49 (9,870)
Morrall, Alexander 3:12:09 (2,299)
Morrans, Neil 3:19:15 (3,167)
Morreale, Paz 5:33:15 (29,832)
Morrell, David J 4:17:24 (15,954)
Morrelle, Mark 6:36:16 (32,547)
Morrice, Andrew 4:43:42 (22,495)
Morrin, Damian J 4:03:45 (12,661)
Morris, Aidan J 3:47:41 (8,290)
Morris, Aled J 4:03:53 (12,687)
Morris, Andrew J 3:57:29 (11,008)
Morris, Chris J 2:56:38 (909)
Morris, Colin R 4:23:20 (17,452)
Morris, David J 4:50:02 (23,848)
Morris, David J 5:42:59 (30,577)
Morris, David P 3:50:06 (8,885)
Morris, David P 3:53:44 (9,833)
Morris, Garth 3:13:00 (2,397)
Morris, Glyn E 3:14:08 (2,546)
Morris, Gregory E 4:32:14 (19,839)
Morris, James 4:07:27 (13,457)
Morris, James 4:12:31 (14,710)
Morris, John S 4:42:55 (22,310)
Morris, Jonathan C 3:40:36 (6,728)
Morris, Mark 2:58:41 (1,094)
Morris, Mark G 4:41:43 (22,039)
Morris, Paul D 3:35:46 (5,794)
Morris, Paul M 3:03:24 (1,472)
Morris, Paul S 5:10:11 (27,284)
Morris, Paul W 3:11:14 (2,188)
Morris, Peter T 4:42:53 (22,301)
Morris, Philip 3:33:39 (5,430)
Morris, Philip J 3:41:29 (6,909)
Morris, Philip J 4:44:48 (22,734)
Morris, Richard D 4:09:31 (13,997)
Morris, Robert P 3:59:35 (11,694)
Morris, Robert P 4:47:36 (23,342)
Morris, Robin 4:02:22 (12,345)
Morris, Ross B 4:28:25 (18,874)
Morris, Ryan M 3:41:48 (6,988)
Morris, Sheridan J 3:13:45 (2,495)
Morris, Simon P 5:10:12 (27,289)
Morris, Steven 4:05:35 (13,047)
Morris, Stuart 5:50:48 (31,121)
Morris, Thomas A 3:12:19 (2,326)
Morris, Tomos P 4:26:01 (18,263)
Morris, Trevor 3:06:52 (1,744)
Morrish, Simon H 4:19:09 (16,379)
Morrison, Andrew 4:22:59 (17,363)
Morrison, Benjamin L 4:17:28 (15,972)
Morrison, Christopher F 2:49:12 (509)
Morrison, Clive 5:21:35 (28,673)
Morrison, David M 3:47:27 (8,225)
Morrison, Fraser C 6:01:44 (31,635)
Morrison, Ian 3:34:45 (5,621)
Morrison, James M 4:16:54 (15,833)
Morrison, John E 3:35:56 (5,825)
Morrison, Michael 3:34:34 (5,585)
Morrison, Paul S 5:50:20 (31,097)
Morrison, Shaun B 5:02:51 (26,295)
Morrison, Sid 3:40:29 (6,709)
Morrison, Steven 3:39:01 (6,436)
Morrison, Thomas 4:58:45 (25,654)
Morrow, David G 3:38:32 (6,334)
Morrow, Nicholas E 3:05:12 (1,593)
Morrs, John D 3:07:04 (1,765)
Morse, Jeremy 5:34:16 (29,911)
Morshead, Ross J 4:37:12 (21,032)
Mort, Allan D 4:46:42 (23,160)
Mort, Stephen 3:49:37 (8,775)
Mortazavi, Omid 4:53:44 (24,626)
Morter, Lee 4:51:34 (24,156)
Mortimer, Andrew P 4:30:56 (19,515)
Mortimer, Crispin J 3:44:10 (7,486)
Mortimer, Gerard A 3:59:23 (11,634)
Mortimer, Ian A 4:34:40 (20,402)
Mortimer, John G 4:19:36 (16,504)
Mortimer, Simon T 2:47:57 (452)
Mortimer, Stephen B 4:06:44 (13,285)
Mortimore, Andrew J 5:38:36 (30,260)
Mortley, Michael P 4:22:06 (17,146)
Morton, Adam T 3:40:09 (6,649)
Morton, Alan C 6:25:30 (32,365)
Morton, Brian G 4:57:40 (25,428)
Morton, Chris J 4:27:58 (18,739)
Morton, Christopher J 4:47:58 (23,422)
Morton, Gary E 3:14:33 (2,603)
Morton, Glenn M 3:42:27 (7,102)
Morton, Ian 4:19:06 (16,366)
Morton, Jonathan M 3:36:38 (5,962)
Morton, Paul 3:56:53 (10,812)
Morton, Paul 4:55:48 (25,054)
Morton, Steven J 2:49:12 (509)
Morton, Stuart C 4:13:18 (14,917)
Morton-Holmes, Gavin J 5:55:35 (31,333)
Morwood, David W 2:37:36 (156)

Morwood, Ian	4:42:33 (22,230)	
Mosawy, Zaid	3:46:50 (8,093)	
Mosca, Alberto	4:11:21 (14,429)	
Mosca, Lorenzo	3:50:25 (8,959)	
Moscrop, David	3:57:57 (11,150)	
Moscrop, Mark A	4:44:45 (22,721)	
Mosedale, Warren	4:46:21 (23,091)	
Moseley, James C	3:58:23 (11,298)	
Moses, John J	5:12:24 (27,575)	
Mosley, Martin R	3:11:55 (2,265)	
Moss, Andrew J	5:00:02 (25,888)	
Moss, Anthony J	5:02:18 (26,224)	
Moss, David	4:01:33 (12,158)	
Moss, David R	3:31:27 (5,062)	
Moss, Gary T	3:28:13 (4,445)	
Moss, Gavin P	3:27:18 (4,293)	
Moss, Graham R	5:18:55 (28,361)	
Moss, Grant R	3:48:08 (8,414)	
Moss, Jonathan D	5:47:47 (30,934)	
Moss, Jonathan R	4:24:21 (17,764)	
Moss, Mark V	3:48:06 (8,403)	
Moss, Moddy J	3:47:33 (8,249)	
Moss, Robert M	4:05:52 (13,111)	
Moss, Stephen D	3:43:42 (7,389)	
Moss, Trevor A	5:13:30 (27,721)	
Mostue, Sverre	3:59:00 (11,511)	
Mosuro, Folarin	7:02:20 (32,898)	
Mothersole, Richard G	5:45:07 (30,726)	
Motherway, Thomas J	3:27:07 (4,263)	
Motson, Nicholas E	4:27:49 (18,697)	
Mott, Alexander J	4:31:25 (19,648)	
Mott, Iain G	4:09:12 (13,909)	
Mott, Neil	4:57:30 (25,397)	
Mottram, Andrew	3:41:08 (6,835)	
Mottram, Jason	4:43:10 (22,362)	
Mottram, Matthew	3:58:32 (11,350)	
Motylak, Michael	4:41:55 (22,093)	
Mould, Brent L	5:46:03 (30,789)	
Mould, John R	4:22:06 (17,146)	
Moulden, Paul A	4:26:09 (18,296)	
Moulden, Simon R	4:21:30 (16,975)	
Moulding, Declan L	5:43:21 (30,596)	
Moules, Paul W	5:02:22 (26,234)	
Moules, Robert	4:13:24 (14,943)	
Moulins, Christian	4:19:40 (16,522)	
Moulson, Stuart C	5:06:45 (26,829)	
Moulton, Robert	3:01:30 (1,337)	
Moultrie, Paul H	4:36:15 (20,799)	
Mouncey, David J	3:28:23 (4,489)	
Mounsey-Heysham, Toby	4:18:09 (16,151)	
Mountain, Joe	3:30:05 (4,843)	
Mounter, Garry	5:21:49 (28,692)	
Mountford, Andrew	4:00:58 (12,040)	
Mountford, Michael A	3:47:29 (8,237)	
Mountford, Paul J	2:32:11 (84)	
Mountford, Peter R	5:23:02 (28,832)	
Mountney, Andrew R	3:47:23 (8,208)	
Mourgues, André	3:14:23 (2,581)	
Moursy, Kamal M	4:46:57 (23,198)	
Moussa, Hany	5:43:00 (30,579)	
Moutrey, John	6:10:05 (31,927)	
Mowat, Raymond J	3:57:10 (10,911)	
Mowbray, Paul	4:07:30 (13,475)	
Mowle, Chris B	2:56:35 (901)	
Mowle, Lee C	3:09:41 (2,036)	
Moxey, Chris	4:15:52 (15,569)	
Moxon, Richard	4:29:54 (19,267)	
Moy, Andrew O	4:10:54 (14,305)	
Moye, Andrew D	3:48:05 (8,401)	
Moyes, Peter D	4:19:17 (16,418)	
Moyes, Stuart J	3:47:33 (8,249)	
Moyle, Chris	3:34:49 (5,628)	
Moyns, Daniel	3:45:45 (7,858)	
Moyse, Gary P	4:03:11 (12,524)	
Muboro, Edward	3:12:43 (2,363)	
Muccioli, Walter	4:42:28 (22,211)	
Mudd, Christopher J	5:47:28 (30,916)	
Muddeman, John A	2:38:51 (187)	
Mudge, Ian D	3:14:52 (2,647)	
Mueller, Holger	4:29:14 (19,093)	
Mueller, Peter H	5:05:11 (26,608)	
Mueller, Werner	3:58:06 (11,185)	
Muff, Darren M	4:44:22 (22,651)	
Muhlmann, Michael H	3:16:50 (2,859)	
Muir, Graham M	3:37:48 (6,191)	
Muir, Malcolm J	2:35:26 (119)	
Muir, Roger C	5:10:02 (27,273)	
Muirhead, Gordon E	4:28:38 (18,929)	
Muirhead, Linus	4:31:51 (19,760)	
Mukadam, Hussain	5:26:24 (29,165)	
Mulcahy, Garry J	3:59:01 (11,517)	
Mulder, Jacco A	4:17:35 (16,011)	
Mulhall, Patrick B	4:53:19 (24,529)	
Mulhern, Gary	3:43:11 (7,285)	
Mulholland, Keith R	3:36:53 (6,016)	
Mullally, Aidan J	4:08:03 (13,628)	
Mullan, Paul	3:46:25 (7,993)	
Mullaney, Christopher	4:18:25 (16,212)	
Mullaney, James P	4:41:29 (21,989)	
Mullany, Chris P	3:50:47 (9,053)	
Mullany, Paul B	4:40:08 (21,697)	
Mullarkey, Peter J	3:26:45 (4,202)	
Muller, Marcus B	2:52:01 (638)	
Muller, Marius A	5:30:26 (29,583)	
Muller, Michael	4:42:02 (22,121)	
Muller-Weyermuller, Raoul	3:05:36 (1,627)	
Mullery, Peter J	3:16:49 (2,854)	
Mulley, Jim	3:58:52 (11,470)	
Mullick, Biman	6:42:38 (32,650)	
Mulligan, Michael	3:57:42 (11,072)	
Mullin, Michael A	4:25:10 (18,016)	
Mullins, Paul A	3:35:35 (5,765)	
Mullins, Sean	3:58:18 (11,266)	
Mullins, Sean	4:16:33 (15,737)	
Mullis, Justin	4:58:51 (25,675)	
Mullis, Thomas	3:32:49 (5,296)	
Mulliss, Rowan J	4:15:14 (15,398)	
Mulraney, Peter	5:51:20 (31,146)	
Mulvaney, David J	4:09:41 (14,026)	
Mulvenna, Stephen	3:19:14 (3,164)	
Mumford, Bill L	4:05:26 (13,005)	
Mumford, Paul R	2:58:45 (1,103)	
Munasinghe, Indumina C	4:29:34 (19,190)	
Munday, David A	5:14:38 (27,860)	
Munday, James	4:37:21 (21,072)	
Munday, Lee	5:40:03 (30,367)	
Munden, Barry R	5:06:49 (26,840)	
Munden, David	4:35:56 (20,698)	
Munn, Patrick J	3:54:13 (9,983)	
Munro, Anthony	5:42:34 (30,540)	
Munro, Hugh	5:15:50 (27,977)	
Munro, John T	7:05:45 (32,943)	
Munro, Jonathan C	4:02:37 (12,405)	
Munro, Kenneth	5:23:50 (28,920)	
Munro, Matt E	3:26:53 (4,219)	
Munro, Phillip	3:06:13 (1,688)	
Munroe, Andy J	3:36:17 (5,891)	
Munroe, Patrick	4:37:14 (21,039)	
Muorah, Mordi E	4:53:29 (24,562)	
Murayama, Takumi	3:54:09 (9,962)	
Murdey, Ian D	3:05:55 (1,656)	
Murdey, Lawrie P	5:36:25 (30,089)	
Murdoch, Andrew M	3:59:51 (11,776)	
Murdoch, Graeme A	3:08:59 (1,957)	
Murdoch, Michael	3:13:44 (2,493)	
Murdoch, Paul B	4:32:45 (19,945)	
Murdoch, Steven J	2:45:19 (353)	
Murfin, Andrew J	3:18:26 (3,053)	
Murfin, Steven A	5:02:00 (26,177)	
Murgatroyd, Lee J	3:57:14 (10,932)	
Murisier, Jean-François	3:36:47 (5,990)	
Murley, Shaun P	6:47:41 (32,733)	
Murphy, Alan	4:16:35 (15,747)	
Murphy, Alan J	6:09:21 (31,908)	
Murphy, Allan J	4:39:47 (21,624)	
Murphy, Andrew J	3:29:25 (4,698)	
Murphy, Andrew P	3:30:29 (4,889)	
Murphy, Andy	4:40:30 (21,777)	
Murphy, Brendan	4:36:20 (20,812)	
Murphy, Brendan M	4:45:14 (22,845)	
Murphy, Brian P	4:38:10 (21,276)	
Murphy, David J	3:50:08 (8,895)	
Murphy, Edward T	6:30:16 (32,456)	
Murphy, Gerard	5:58:56 (31,501)	
Murphy, Gerry	3:52:02 (9,369)	
Murphy, Glenn P	3:49:10 (8,661)	
Murphy, Jack	3:58:15 (11,249)	
Murphy, Jeff	3:52:57 (9,610)	
Murphy, John	4:07:57 (13,602)	
Murphy, John C	4:22:33 (17,252)	
Murphy, John E	3:18:29 (3,063)	
Murphy, John P	3:19:13 (3,159)	
Murphy, Kevin	2:58:59 (1,142)	
Murphy, Lee J	4:18:28 (16,223)	
Murphy, Mark P	4:41:17 (21,948)	
Murphy, Mark P	6:08:39 (31,880)	
Murphy, Martin P	5:11:43 (27,480)	
Murphy, Michael	5:02:53 (26,302)	
Murphy, Mike D	4:16:30 (15,727)	
Murphy, Nicholas	4:34:44 (20,421)	
Murphy, Paul G	3:36:59 (6,037)	
Murphy, Peter J	3:17:41 (2,962)	
Murphy, Peter J	4:11:23 (14,434)	
Murphy, Scott	4:08:06 (13,641)	
Murphy, Shaun	4:37:23 (21,084)	
Murphy, Tom	4:07:55 (13,587)	
Murphy, William J	2:56:36 (903)	
Murr, Angus J	5:34:51 (29,956)	
Murray, Andrew	4:40:51 (21,865)	
Murray, Andy	3:28:35 (4,528)	
Murray, Benjamin	5:50:12 (31,087)	
Murray, Brian J	5:22:18 (28,753)	
Murray, Daniel	4:47:51 (23,396)	
Murray, Daniel C	4:38:25 (21,316)	
Murray, David J	3:51:07 (9,125)	
Murray, David J	4:07:23 (13,447)	
Murray, David J	4:29:04 (19,041)	
Murray, Iain	3:06:10 (1,682)	
Murray, James B	4:39:26 (21,552)	
Murray, James J	4:20:59 (16,861)	
Murray, John	5:48:47 (30,989)	
Murray, Lee S	4:32:11 (19,827)	
Murray, Martin	4:38:57 (21,430)	
Murray, Neil A	3:53:48 (9,861)	
Murray, Paul A	4:22:04 (17,137)	
Murray, Robert J	4:34:41 (20,406)	
Murray, Scott	5:02:59 (26,314)	
Murray, Stephen J	5:05:04 (26,591)	
Murray, Stephen M	4:24:13 (17,717)	
Murray, William	4:44:39 (22,695)	
Murrell, Philip E	5:05:29 (26,644)	
Murrin, Kevin	4:26:45 (18,452)	
Mursell, Dean J	3:09:31 (2,015)	
Mursell, John W	3:28:54 (4,606)	
Murtagh, Simon J	3:48:40 (8,545)	
Murthwaite, Robert	5:00:24 (25,960)	
Musgrave, Paul K	5:09:43 (27,229)	
Musgrove, David J	4:18:18 (16,183)	
Musk, Paul J	4:01:36 (12,174)	
Musker, Jonathan G	3:58:20 (11,280)	
Muskett, Andy W	5:50:42 (31,118)	
Mussi, Aldo	4:39:24 (8,718)	
Musson, Michael S	4:45:13 (22,840)	
Musumeci, Sebastiano	3:53:24 (9,738)	
Musyoki, Patrick M	2:39:10 (193)	
Mutch, Graeme P	3:14:21 (2,575)	
Mutsaers, Adrian R	3:29:01 (4,624)	
Mutschler, Jock	4:10:56 (14,312)	
Muttett, David C	4:36:31 (20,849)	
Mutyaba, Robert	4:51:22 (24,112)	
Mvubu, Mispah D	4:06:11 (13,174)	
Mycock, Gareth J	3:37:49 (6,194)	
Myers, Allen A	4:25:44 (18,169)	
Myers, Aron	3:28:37 (4,533)	
Myers, Iain D	3:46:32 (8,019)	
Myers, Jonathan B	4:35:25 (20,583)	
Myers, Nick A	4:19:40 (16,522)	
Myerscough, Andrew M	5:38:01 (30,203)	
Myles, Glenn O	5:30:53 (29,634)	
Mynard, David J	2:58:01 (1,023)	
Mynard, Paul S	4:54:46 (24,833)	
Myres, Peter J	4:54:19 (24,749)	
Mytton, Neil M	2:38:41 (181)	
Naber, Grant E	4:46:08 (23,033)	
Nadali, Michele	3:08:40 (1,924)	
Nadalutti, Mauro	5:17:18 (28,167)	
Nagata, Masato	4:03:42 (12,652)	
Nagel, Arthur L	4:53:05 (24,473)	
Nagel, David C	4:58:30 (25,607)	

Nagel, Reto 4:01:49 (12,219)
Nagle, Tim 4:49:53 (23,817)
Naidoo, Kamlan 4:45:21 (22,874)
Naidoo, Kebsi R 5:19:45 (28,464)
Naik, Rav 5:24:41 (29,006)
Nair, Vinay 4:15:18 (15,415)
Nairn, Darren 4:18:13 (16,162)
Najurally, Nashir A 3:19:40 (3,206)
Nale, Claudio 3:02:27 (1,402)
Nanavati, Mayur 4:51:53 (24,228)
Nancarrow, James 4:09:09 (13,892)
Nandha, Bhavesh P 4:30:33 (19,439)
Nangs, Nicholas N 4:34:00 (20,245)
Napier, Rick M 3:42:34 (7,126)
Napolitano, Sergio 4:06:57 (13,337)
Napper, Chris J 3:39:46 (6,582)
Napper, James B 3:26:26 (4,140)
Nappi, Thomas M 6:03:06 (31,687)
Nar, Satbinder S 5:30:57 (29,644)
Narain, Gregory 3:27:17 (4,287)
Nareike, Uwe 3:48:33 (8,512)
Narinesingh, Gareth 4:02:14 (12,312)
Narracott, Simon G 5:03:30 (26,389)
Nascimento, Pablo J 4:17:20 (15,940)
Naseem, Muhammad S 4:33:05 (20,025)
Nash, Andrew 4:24:14 (17,725)
Nash, Colin P 4:14:37 (15,237)
Nash, David A 4:42:57 (22,316)
Nash, Mark S 5:28:43 (29,402)
Nash, Neil J 5:20:47 (28,591)
Nash, Paul S 3:16:03 (2,784)
Nash, Steven 4:50:04 (23,855)
Nasir, Behram 5:29:06 (29,434)
Natali, Paul E 3:43:04 (7,255)
Natali, Pierfranco 4:17:10 (15,898)
Nathan, Paul 3:24:48 (3,912)
Nathwani, Neeraj 4:34:19 (20,310)
Nation, Paul 4:11:52 (14,542)
Nation, Robert J 3:30:38 (4,921)
Naughton, John 4:37:04 (20,993)
Nauth-Misir, Rohan R 5:39:28 (30,320)
Navesey, Ged 3:48:33 (8,512)
Navin-Jones, Michael G 5:46:00 (30,787)
Naylor, Dave G 3:14:25 (2,587)
Naylor, Donald E 2:30:55 (74)
Naylor-Smith, Nigel 4:40:03 (21,684)
Ndekwe, Jonn 5:02:06 (26,187)
Neads, Kevin M 3:12:46 (2,373)
Neal, Jonathan 4:55:55 (25,080)
Neal, Steven J 3:41:02 (6,809)
Neal, Thomas D 4:45:16 (22,852)
Neal, Trevor J 5:31:16 (29,689)
Neale, David A 3:41:02 (6,809)
Neale, Michael G 5:12:04 (27,532)
Neale, Richard G 5:54:32 (31,285)
Neale, Robert A 3:34:13 (5,515)
Neale, Robert J 4:08:45 (13,800)
Neale, Simon M 3:44:26 (7,547)
Neale, Warren C 3:43:52 (7,432)
Nearney, Pat W 5:31:55 (29,733)
Neary, Benjamin F 4:24:55 (17,930)
Neate, Philip 5:14:04 (27,776)
Neaves, Antony B 4:18:52 (16,318)
Nederstigt, Antonius J 4:06:23 (13,207)
Needham, David M 4:15:36 (15,496)
Needham, Patrick 4:41:37 (22,017)
Needham, Peter J 4:16:30 (15,727)
Neethling, Edward C 3:37:56 (6,215)
Neil, Kevan R 4:20:32 (16,742)
Neil, Martin L 4:45:18 (22,856)
Neill, Adrian S 6:46:50 (32,721)
Neill, Francis J 3:25:25 (3,995)
Neillis, John N 3:59:20 (11,617)
Neilly, Mark 3:41:59 (7,022)
Neilson, Graham A 3:56:30 (10,685)
Neilson, Paul J 4:34:13 (20,294)
Neligan, Tim S 3:48:19 (8,457)
Nellins, Christopher T 3:09:46 (2,042)
Nellis, Joseph G 4:23:30 (17,505)
Nelson, Andrew B 4:01:09 (12,089)
Nelson, Anthony 4:36:06 (20,752)
Nelson, Carl 4:40:46 (21,844)
Nelson, Craig W 4:35:35 (20,618)
Nelson, Gary E 5:03:11 (26,343)
Nelson, John E 4:32:28 (19,898)
Nelson, Kenneth B 4:28:44 (18,956)
Nelson, Kevin P 4:08:23 (13,712)
Nelson, Michael J 4:38:08 (21,268)
Nelson, Peter C 4:11:51 (14,534)
Nelson, Richard D 3:15:11 (2,681)
Nelson, Stephen J 4:45:31 (22,908)
Nemcek, Jozef 2:34:19 (104)
Nemodruk, Oleg 3:52:36 (9,520)
Neocleous, Petros 4:58:00 (25,505)
Neocleous, Richard R 4:38:47 (21,387)
Neophytou, Christopher 3:25:26 (3,997)
Neophytou, Neiphitos 5:06:01 (26,716)
Nery, Simon J 3:41:46 (6,978)
Nesbit, Chris N 4:40:11 (21,708)
Nesbitt, Jonathan 4:08:54 (13,838)
Nesom, Chris 3:38:58 (6,428)
Nester, Michael J 2:42:34 (268)
Nethercleft, Andrew J 4:41:50 (22,062)
Nethercott, Steve J 3:41:41 (6,961)
Netherthorpe, James F 4:34:09 (20,280)
Neto, José 4:07:59 (13,612)
Nettleton, Philip D 4:00:37 (11,953)
Neumann, David J 3:51:58 (9,356)
Neumann, Lee 3:33:14 (5,361)
Neumann, Stephen R 3:56:06 (10,568)
Nevelos, Paul 4:53:47 (24,635)
Neveux, Alban 3:24:27 (3,853)
Neviani, Andrea 5:22:37 (28,789)
Nevill, David 4:48:04 (23,442)
Nevill, Peter C 3:30:16 (4,862)
Neville, Laurence P 4:31:28 (19,656)
Neville, Michael D 4:42:16 (22,167)
Neville, Paul R 4:31:54 (19,772)
Neville, Simon G 3:08:22 (1,892)
Nevola, Venturino R 2:44:04 (314)
New, Simon D 3:50:50 (9,062)
Newall, Oliver J 3:51:43 (9,278)
Newbert, Richard J 3:45:58 (7,899)
Newbold, Kevin J 4:02:48 (12,438)
Newbury, Andrew W 3:53:50 (9,873)
Newbury, Paul 5:05:18 (26,624)
Newby, Robert T 3:54:14 (9,988)
Newcombe, Oliver C 4:23:52 (17,613)
Newell, John P 4:29:04 (19,041)
Newell, Mark S 4:17:09 (15,894)
Newell, Russell T 4:24:52 (17,906)
Newell, Terry 6:01:04 (31,608)
Newey, Chris 3:53:37 (9,800)
Newham, Michael A 4:58:57 (25,701)
Newins, Mathew D 3:49:28 (8,734)
Newitt, Frank S 4:55:45 (25,047)
Newland, Alan J 3:50:38 (9,013)
Newland, David J 3:38:09 (6,256)
Newley, David 4:10:15 (14,161)
Newman, Adrian 4:08:56 (13,846)
Newman, Alan P 4:42:27 (22,210)
Newman, Bryan J 3:48:01 (8,387)
Newman, Clive W 3:41:51 (6,999)
Newman, David A 4:43:33 (22,452)
Newman, David J 4:31:51 (19,760)
Newman, Edward 4:38:29 (21,335)
Newman, Gavin J 3:48:53 (8,603)
Newman, Graeme R 3:29:48 (4,782)
Newman, Graham 4:22:35 (17,260)
Newman, Graham D 3:49:06 (8,648)
Newman, Irwin G 5:39:29 (30,323)
Newman, John M 5:32:14 (29,757)
Newman, Mark R 6:09:04 (31,897)
Newman, Martin C 3:37:17 (6,088)
Newman, Neil K 4:36:07 (20,759)
Newman, Neville J 4:15:52 (15,569)
Newman, Paul S 5:20:06 (28,503)
Newman, Paul S 5:58:21 (31,478)
Newman, Peter J 5:34:22 (29,919)
Newman, Philip 3:58:18 (11,266)
Newman, Philip 4:05:54 (13,118)
Newman, Ralph J 3:32:11 (5,198)
Newman, Sean 4:13:31 (14,960)
Newman, Stuart E 5:18:30 (28,311)
Newnes, Robert J 4:43:52 (22,537)
Newnham, Robin P 3:18:24 (3,049)
Newnham Reeve, Mark A 3:44:11 (7,488)
Newsham, David A 5:51:46 (31,171)
Newsome, Paul 3:46:39 (8,048)
Newson, Timothy 3:55:30 (10,374)
Newton, David P 4:06:31 (13,238)
Newton, Gavin J 3:20:43 (3,366)
Newton, Harry J 3:54:35 (10,074)
Newton, James 4:07:14 (13,410)
Newton, James A 4:27:38 (18,666)
Newton, James E 3:38:22 (6,297)
Newton, Keith 4:00:25 (11,920)
Newton, Malcolm A 5:27:42 (29,293)
Newton, Mark S 3:42:11 (7,063)
Newton, Nicholas M 3:10:58 (2,153)
Newton, Oliver 4:18:08 (16,146)
Newton, Paul 4:06:05 (13,157)
Newton, Richard C 4:23:04 (17,378)
Newton, Rodger 5:52:58 (31,213)
Newton, Ronald A 4:14:27 (15,197)
Newton, Simon 2:42:44 (275)
Newton, Simon J 3:14:07 (2,543)
Newton, Tim 4:24:46 (17,884)
Newton-Lee, Andy 3:50:31 (8,989)
Neylon, Kevin P 3:56:23 (10,650)
Ng, Anthony 3:59:16 (11,591)
Ng, Joe C 4:42:07 (22,138)
Ng, Nigel R 4:21:49 (17,067)
Ng, Paul W 4:18:40 (16,270)
Ng, Stephen 5:39:04 (30,289)
Ng Oma, Stephen M 4:33:15 (20,074)
Nice, Gary R 6:00:16 (31,574)
Nicell, Patrick J 2:59:35 (1,209)
Nichol, John P 4:13:05 (14,872)
Nicholas, Adam K 3:48:47 (8,572)
Nicholas, Barry J 5:07:38 (26,954)
Nicholas, Dean T 3:00:11 (1,246)
Nicholas, Kevin 4:47:56 (23,417)
Nicholas, Michael 6:06:24 (31,798)
Nicholas, Philip J 4:19:14 (16,398)
Nicholason, Brian 3:56:27 (10,672)
Nicholls, Andrew S 3:06:51 (1,740)
Nicholls, Gavin 5:57:50 (31,449)
Nicholls, Grant M 4:55:55 (25,080)
Nicholls, Ian K 4:29:23 (19,143)
Nicholls, Keith A 4:43:37 (22,471)
Nicholls, Mark A 3:56:34 (10,714)
Nicholls, Michael J 3:35:04 (5,684)
Nicholls, Michael R 4:26:47 (18,461)
Nicholls, Peter 5:18:28 (28,304)
Nicholls, Phil T 4:15:44 (15,529)
Nicholls, Steve J 3:41:26 (6,900)
Nichols, Gary 4:35:58 (20,715)
Nichols, Gavin E 3:16:27 (2,817)
Nichols, Lee 5:08:15 (27,042)
Nichols, Michael 2:56:24 (884)
Nichols, Paul A 4:12:36 (14,726)
Nichols, Scott 6:27:50 (32,420)
Nicholson, Alan 5:16:49 (28,105)
Nicholson, Andrew 4:22:03 (17,130)
Nicholson, Andrew R 4:27:09 (18,542)
Nicholson, Angus 4:49:16 (23,707)
Nicholson, Ben 4:07:27 (13,457)
Nicholson, James 4:49:01 (23,654)
Nicholson, Jeremy M 4:11:37 (14,484)
Nicholson, Luke A 4:43:28 (22,425)
Nicholson, Phil H 3:26:21 (4,128)
Nicholson, Simon J 4:49:18 (23,717)
Nickau, Hanno C 2:58:58 (1,138)
Nicklas, Carl D 3:14:16 (2,563)
Nicklin, Paul J 3:55:52 (10,496)
Nicol, Colin 4:43:10 (22,362)
Nicol, Gary 3:42:27 (7,102)
Nicol, Graeme D 4:24:37 (17,845)
Nicol, Peter 3:59:49 (11,770)
Nicol, Scott A 3:32:06 (5,180)
Nicolaou, Gabriel A 4:22:49 (17,326)
Nicoli, Luke G 3:43:20 (7,315)
Nicoll, Angus 3:15:00 (2,660)
Nicoll, Chris 2:51:19 (607)
Nicosia, Vincenzo 4:14:05 (15,098)
Nida, James D 4:07:55 (13,587)
Niederberger, Othmar 3:21:27 (3,460)
Niederer, Marc 3:37:05 (6,053)

Niederkofler, Herbert............3:28:58 (4,615)
Niedringhaus, George W..........4:34:02 (20,260)
Nielsen, Finn 3:11:44 (2,241)
Nielsen, James C.................3:19:10 (3,152)
Nielsen, Kai.....................4:34:59 (20,483)
Nielsen, Patrick W...............4:28:08 (18,785)
Nielsen, Soren...................4:33:56 (20,231)
Nienaber, Thomas.................3:52:08 (9,390)
Niesen, Frank H..................3:27:29 (4,330)
Nieto, Angel.....................4:22:11 (17,171)
Nightingale, Keith P.............4:45:26 (22,896)
Nightingale, Kevin P 3:39:16 (6,493)
Nightingale, Mark J..............3:17:01 (2,878)
Nightingale, Peter J.............4:46:06 (23,027)
Nightingale, Thomas W............3:26:24 (4,138)
Nijhawan, Anil...................5:54:13 (31,273)
Nijjar, Avtar S..................4:34:39 (20,397)
Nike, John L.....................6:11:14 (31,962)
Nilsen, Tor......................3:25:58 (4,069)
Nilsson, Bo Egon.................3:18:34 (3,077)
Nimmo, Howard G..................5:00:01 (25,886)
Ninivaggi, Arcangelo 2:50:57 (588)
Nisbet, David B..................4:49:03 (23,663)
Nisbet, Jack.....................3:14:06 (2,542)
Nittel, Hans-Joachim.............3:53:26 (9,749)
Nixon, Arum......................3:59:05 (11,538)
Nixon, David 4:43:40 (22,481)
Nixon, Jon J.....................3:28:27 (4,503)
Niziol, Marian...................3:27:50 (4,387)
Nizzo, Andrea....................3:58:59 (11,500)
Nkenko, Marius...................3:48:06 (8,403)
Noad, Ian D......................3:03:15 (1,461)
Noad, Peter J....................3:41:16 (6,866)
Noakes, Gary.....................3:49:30 (8,747)
Noakes, Matthew S................3:44:13 (7,495)
Noakes, Michael A 3:56:14 (10,603)
Nobbs, Martin R..................3:29:20 (4,684)
Nobes, Lee A.....................3:53:15 (9,706)
Nobili, Enrico...................3:47:18 (8,191)
Noble, Angus.....................4:34:57 (20,473)
Noble, Christopher J.............4:05:57 (13,132)
Noble, Ian.......................3:32:18 (5,222)
Noble, Jeff......................3:08:32 (1,913)
Noble, Kim.......................5:19:12 (28,406)
Noble Clarke, Matthew............3:01:19 (1,326)
Noblett, Thomas G 7:28:03 (33,087)
Nock, Graham S...................3:10:42 (2,133)
Noel, Vernon L...................5:50:45 (31,120)
Noga, Jeff A.....................4:45:30 (22,904)
Nolan, Brian.....................3:01:53 (1,366)
Nolan, David.....................3:03:30 (1,480)
Nolan, Frank.....................3:41:47 (6,983)
Nolan, James M...................4:40:50 (21,863)
Nolan, Kevin.....................4:31:49 (19,750)
Nolan, Phelim J..................3:59:21 (11,621)
Nolan, Timothy M.................3:43:52 (7,432)
Nonino, Alberto..................2:57:56 (1,017)
Noon, Jonathan A 4:52:21 (24,320)
Noonan, Patrick B................3:07:52 (1,844)
Noone, Christopher W 4:07:18 (13,420)
Noone, Richard...................3:11:17 (2,194)
Noorbaccus, Mike.................5:11:54 (27,514)
Noormahomed, Hassif A............3:24:05 (3,805)
Nopck, Gerhard...................4:57:57 (25,487)
Norbury, Antony 3:54:35 (10,074)
Norbury, Gareth C 4:46:42 (23,160)
Nordam, Odd N....................4:08:47 (13,809)
Nordboee, Jarl Inge 3:56:19 (10,630)
Nordstroem, Knut.................3:27:10 (4,269)
Norfield, Benjamin E.............3:55:20 (10,325)
Norfolk, Ben H...................3:15:10 (2,680)
Norgaard, Jan O..................5:05:49 (26,680)
Norman, Ben E 3:22:28 (3,590)
Norman, Daniel G.................3:35:40 (5,777)
Norman, Dave.....................2:23:26 (41)
Normanton, Ian...................3:55:43 (10,444)
Normington, Matthew..............2:25:18 (46)
Norridge, Christopher............3:50:26 (8,966)
Norris, Andrew...................4:44:07 (22,589)
Norris, Chris....................4:49:00 (23,649)
Norris, Gary.....................4:37:33 (21,125)
Norris, Graham L.................4:16:35 (15,747)
Norris, Jonathan A 5:57:25 (31,430)

Norris, Kieron J.................4:04:26 (12,801)
Norris, Leigh J..................5:21:15 (28,638)
Norris, Liam 4:43:52 (22,537)
Norris, Martin J.................4:28:43 (18,951)
Norris, Matthew J................4:02:15 (12,319)
Norris, Matthew P 4:13:01 (14,850)
Norris, Paul M...................3:23:21 (3,691)
Norris, Peter J..................2:55:23 (810)
Norris, Philip L.................3:07:40 (1,822)
Norris, Richard A................3:00:00 (1,234)
Norris, Simon R..................4:12:31 (14,710)
Norris, Steve....................5:06:32 (26,792)
Norris-Grey, Robert..............3:36:05 (5,851)
Norsworthy, Mark D...............4:19:45 (16,539)
Norsworthy, Michael P............4:24:19 (17,754)
North, Andrew P..................3:53:16 (9,713)
North, Ernest F..................4:34:22 (20,331)
North, Glenn R...................2:46:00 (382)
North, Ian K.....................3:50:23 (8,951)
North, Jonathan T................4:32:00 (19,791)
North, Mark......................5:53:44 (31,249)
North, Shaun R...................2:42:43 (272)
Northcott, Stewart...............4:23:16 (17,437)
Northern, Paul...................3:19:15 (3,167)
Northey, Kevin...................3:53:06 (9,662)
Norton, Colin J..................3:47:47 (8,318)
Norton, David R..................4:50:36 (23,960)
Norton, Graham R.................4:29:19 (19,122)
Norton, Jonathon P 4:31:55 (19,776)
Norton, Matthew P................3:58:17 (11,262)
Norton, Michael A 4:31:45 (19,733)
Norwood, Barry T 4:03:57 (12,704)
Noschese, Giuseppe 4:52:25 (24,334)
Nott, Daniel D...................3:43:46 (7,411)
Nott, David M....................5:22:54 (28,816)
Nott, Mark W.....................5:19:29 (28,433)
Nott, Russell P..................3:28:14 (4,448)
Nottage, Miles...................5:07:37 (26,950)
Nottidge, Richard R..............3:47:54 (8,354)
Nouillan, William 4:39:29 (21,556)
Nout, Martinus J.................4:36:23 (20,820)
Nouze, Richard...................4:44:11 (22,606)
Novell, Simon L..................3:26:04 (4,083)
Novick, Steven...................3:20:08 (3,284)
Nowak, Detlev Paul...............5:37:37 (30,175)
Nowak, Matthias..................3:31:29 (5,065)
Nowakowski, David L..............4:40:28 (21,763)
Nowicki, Matthew P...............4:58:53 (25,684)
Ntende, Robert 5:41:48 (30,487)
Ntuli, Dumisani..................4:36:35 (20,865)
Nubert, Edgar....................3:29:32 (4,725)
Nudd, Peter M....................3:44:13 (7,495)
Nugent, Brian M..................5:47:11 (30,877)
Nugent, David S..................3:31:02 (4,990)
Nugent, James P..................4:17:39 (16,026)
Nugent, John G...................4:50:29 (23,943)
Nugent, Robert L.................3:32:10 (5,193)
Nugus, John P 2:46:45 (409)
Nunn, David P....................4:08:56 (13,846)
Nunn, James L....................4:26:23 (18,357)
Nunn, Peter E....................5:28:35 (29,380)
Nunn, Peter J....................5:50:08 (31,084)
Nunn, Peter M....................4:54:21 (24,760)
Nurrish, David L.................4:08:53 (13,830)
Nussbaumer, Jean-Marc............3:27:54 (4,396)
Nussey, Mark.....................3:31:47 (5,115)
Nute, Dominic L..................4:42:13 (22,162)
Nutt, Matthew D..................3:29:56 (4,813)
Nutt, Matthew R..................2:53:38 (706)
Nutt, William....................3:27:29 (4,330)
Nuttall, Ian.....................4:45:58 (22,998)
Nuttall, Roger...................4:21:55 (17,091)
Nutter, Eric.....................4:06:13 (13,180)
Nuzzo, Giovanni..................5:08:55 (27,137)
Nwani, Okorie....................4:15:00 (15,338)
Nyamundanda, George 8:14:17 (33,188)
Nye, Derek.......................4:59:38 (25,818)
Nye, John........................5:14:44 (27,878)
Nys, Jean-François...............3:40:19 (6,678)
Nyss, David L....................4:22:46 (17,315)
Oades, Andy G 4:31:12 (19,581)
Oakes, Harold W..................5:14:01 (27,767)
Oakes, Simon C...................4:44:57 (22,770)

Oakes, Tom W.....................3:44:34 (7,585)
Oakes, Tony J....................4:48:20 (23,498)
Oakley, Andrew...................3:41:18 (6,872)
Oakley, Stuart J.................4:31:45 (19,733)
Oakshett, Charles H..............3:39:08 (6,462)
Oakton, Neil R...................4:38:17 (21,299)
Oakwell, Paul D..................3:55:29 (10,369)
Oaten, Colin M...................4:22:56 (17,350)
Oates, Neil......................5:00:16 (25,937)
Oatham, Paul W...................5:26:40 (29,182)
Oatham, Philip W.................3:06:02 (1,670)
Oatts, Martin J..................4:55:53 (25,074)
O'Beirne, Gerry B................3:17:11 (2,906)
Obembe, Robert...................6:50:58 (32,774)
Oberg, Paul G....................3:28:29 (4,506)
O'Boyle, Brendan D...............2:53:52 (718)
O'Boyle, Richard A 3:03:26 (1,475)
Obree, Mike......................4:37:04 (20,993)
O'Brien, Adrian..................4:02:41 (12,413)
O'Brien, Adrian..................5:30:54 (29,636)
O'Brien, Anthony S...............3:20:57 (3,399)
O'Brien, Chris R.................3:58:14 (11,245)
O'Brien, David J.................4:20:52 (16,827)
O'Brien, Dominic.................5:28:16 (29,352)
O'Brien, Kieran A................3:00:10 (1,242)
O'Brien, Martin I 4:36:52 (20,955)
O'Brien, Martin J................4:42:19 (22,180)
O'Brien, Michael A...............5:05:04 (26,591)
O'Brien, Nigel D.................4:25:07 (17,996)
O'Brien, Peter...................5:21:59 (28,718)
O'Brien, Robin E 4:38:19 (21,305)
O'Byrne, Andrew..................4:36:03 (20,736)
O'Callaghan, Pat.................4:16:57 (15,847)
O'Callaghan, Paul................4:48:45 (23,596)
Occelli, Christophe 3:24:06 (3,806)
O'Ceallaigh, Eoghan 3:42:47 (7,182)
Ockenman, Dirk...................4:12:59 (14,831)
Ockwell, Miles G 4:16:36 (15,756)
O'Connell, Andrew M 4:04:40 (12,847)
O'Connell, Brendan M.............3:48:29 (8,495)
O'Connell, Damian................4:28:33 (18,910)
O'Connell, Darren J 4:54:48 (24,848)
O'Connell, David M...............4:01:45 (12,199)
O'Connell, Gerry N 4:43:51 (22,534)
O'Connell, Timothy F 5:28:46 (29,408)
O'Connor, Alan...................3:16:42 (2,841)
O'Connor, Anthony 2:54:57 (787)
O'Connor, Daniel F...............3:41:30 (6,914)
O'Connor, Huw....................4:18:04 (16,128)
O'Connor, Jason..................2:54:55 (785)
O'Connor, Kevin..................3:14:30 (2,596)
O'Connor, Kieron J...............4:28:48 (18,973)
O'Connor, Liam...................5:21:54 (28,702)
O'Connor, Michael A..............3:21:33 (3,477)
O'Connor, Niall J................3:20:41 (3,360)
O'Connor, Raymond................7:42:12 (33,148)
O'Connor, Rory...................3:56:46 (10,769)
O'Connor, Shane..................3:33:12 (5,353)
O'Connor, Shane..................3:46:00 (7,902)
O'Connor, Terence A 4:47:30 (23,319)
O'Connor, William J 4:47:49 (23,386)
O'Cuilleanain, Cian 4:38:26 (21,320)
Oddy, Huw M......................4:29:25 (19,150)
Odell, Andrew H..................5:15:30 (27,953)
Odell, Graham A..................4:04:14 (12,764)
O'Dell, John P...................4:10:57 (14,315)
Odgers, Ian......................3:57:46 (11,100)
O'Donnell, Brian F 4:45:05 (22,810)
O'Donnell, Chris.................3:53:12 (9,689)
O'Donnell, Jonathan 3:29:44 (4,768)
O'Donnell, Liam..................5:50:32 (31,112)
O'Donnell, Owen..................3:38:06 (6,250)
O'Donnell, Tom E.................3:34:05 (5,496)
O'Donoghue, Brett................4:07:58 (13,606)
O'Donoghue, John P...............3:48:52 (8,598)
O'Donoghue, Mark.................3:17:38 (2,956)
O'Donoghue, Scott D 4:38:52 (21,406)
O'Donoghue, Thomas...............3:11:35 (2,221)
O'Donovan, Brian.................5:05:36 (26,653)
O'Donovan, Colin.................5:08:16 (27,045)
O'Driscoll, Barry 3:23:48 (3,755)
O'Dwyer, John T..................3:42:44 (7,167)
O'Dwyer, Luke C..................4:23:39 (17,546)

O'Dwyer, Paul A 5:42:54 (30,566)
Oehlert, Andreas K 3:51:26 (9,204)
Offler, Gordon I 3:52:12 (9,410)
O'Flynn, Thomas 5:00:46 (26,004)
Ogata, Tsuyoshi 2:19:17 (26)
Ogbonna, Joseph C 4:28:06 (18,773)
Ogborn, Steve D 2:37:35 (155)
Ogden, Daniel C 4:04:28 (12,810)
Ogden, Paul J 3:27:44 (4,368)
Ogden, Peter 4:41:59 (22,110)
Ogden, Robert 4:02:49 (12,441)
Ogilvie, Ian P 7:10:15 (32,982)
O'Gorman, Barry A 4:00:22 (11,906)
O'Gorman, Edward P 3:37:20 (6,098)
O'Gorman, Mark C 4:16:50 (15,811)
O'Gorman, Timothy J 4:08:45 (13,800)
O'Grady, Geoff V 3:39:53 (6,602)
O'Grady, Henry T 4:38:27 (21,325)
O'Grady, Martin J 4:52:15 (24,294)
O'Griallais, Mairtin S 3:15:51 (2,761)
Ogundare, Rotimi 4:38:43 (21,378)
Ogunnaike, Michael A 4:25:17 (18,051)
Ogunyemi, Jackson 5:41:17 (30,436)
O'Hagan, Bernard 3:58:43 (11,405)
O'Hanlon, John E 3:51:33 (9,234)
O'Hanlon, Mark 4:15:58 (15,592)
O'Hanlon, Nicholas 6:36:50 (32,559)
O'Hara, Kieran 4:19:25 (16,455)
O'Hara, Simon D 4:39:04 (21,458)
O'Hare, Brendan J 4:28:06 (18,773)
O'Hare, Liam 3:02:18 (1,391)
O'Hare, Niall M 4:46:58 (23,200)
O'Herne, Bernard 3:50:15 (8,924)
Ohlek, Derk 3:21:10 (3,417)
Ojeda, Idelfonso 5:39:35 (30,330)
O'Kane, Brian J 2:52:51 (667)
O'Kane, Sean G 4:46:09 (23,038)
Okano, Kiichiro 4:01:11 (12,099)
O'Keefe, Steven J 4:30:56 (19,515)
O'Keeffe, David A 6:18:03 (32,174)
O'Keeffe, Terence G 3:55:39 (10,416)
Okhrimenko, Ihor 3:35:35 (5,765)
Oku, Yoshimitsu 4:37:21 (21,072)
Olarte, David J 5:48:56 (30,996)
Olavarria, Eduardo 3:23:14 (3,680)
Oldaker, David J 4:56:03 (25,109)
Oldcroft, Charlie 5:45:23 (30,748)
Older, Robert H 4:26:50 (18,473)
Older, Tim 3:21:23 (3,454)
Oldershaw, Jonathan G 5:00:03 (25,894)
Oldfield, Alex 3:13:10 (2,421)
Oldfield, Richard 5:32:44 (29,789)
Oldham, Simon G 3:29:09 (4,644)
Oldridge, Daniel J 4:11:00 (14,329)
Oldroyd, Stuart J 4:37:59 (21,216)
Olds, Joe 3:46:48 (8,081)
O'Leary, Chris J 4:41:15 (21,934)
O'Leary, Grant 3:47:10 (8,158)
O'Leary, John 5:34:13 (29,903)
O'Leary, Kevin R 4:29:32 (19,187)
O'Leary, Steven J 5:24:50 (29,020)
Olejak, Ivo 2:54:36 (772)
Oliphant, Mark J 3:39:18 (6,500)
Olivan, José I 3:47:28 (8,234)
Olive, Richard T 3:07:37 (1,816)
Oliveira, Carlos A 5:18:10 (28,266)
Oliveira, Paul 4:30:45 (19,485)
Oliveira, Silvi 5:18:09 (28,262)
Oliver, Danny D 3:12:41 (2,360)
Oliver, John C 4:08:44 (13,792)
Oliver, Jonathan P 4:30:13 (19,357)
Oliver, Michael F 3:18:20 (3,039)
Oliver, Owen W 3:34:55 (5,646)
Oliver, Phillip J 4:37:14 (21,039)
Oliver, Richard H 4:09:20 (13,940)
Oliver, Richard T 3:47:47 (8,318)
Oliver, Simon L 5:25:23 (29,076)
Oliver, Stephen 5:20:14 (28,524)
Oliver, Steven 3:56:26 (10,668)
Oliver-Bellasis, Richard C 4:30:01 (19,299)
Olivo, Alberto 4:46:33 (23,133)
Ollerton, David B 4:07:16 (13,415)
Ollett, Kevin J 4:39:39 (21,588)
Ollington, Jonathan 4:16:45 (15,789)
Olner, Steven J 3:58:47 (11,440)
Olney, Richard J 4:57:35 (25,416)
O'Loughlin, Shaun P 3:52:54 (9,595)
O'Loughlin, Trevor 5:15:10 (27,921)
Olsen, Daginn 4:22:49 (17,326)
Olsen, Erik 4:14:30 (15,206)
Olsen, Lars P 3:08:34 (1,915)
Olsson, Folke 3:58:06 (11,185)
O'Mahoney, Gerard F 4:02:31 (12,376)
O'Mahony, John A 3:43:41 (7,386)
O'Mahony, Lee S 3:55:40 (10,427)
O'Malley, John R 4:25:50 (18,202)
Omar, Said T 3:40:48 (6,762)
Omar, Taufik 5:02:16 (26,215)
O'Mara, Craig A 4:15:06 (15,366)
O'Mara, Robert C 4:20:04 (16,622)
O'Meara, Philip 3:10:51 (2,143)
O'Neill, Aidan 4:58:09 (25,539)
O'Neill, Donal J 5:02:18 (26,224)
O'Neill, Eamonn 2:49:34 (521)
O'Neill, Edward F 3:21:25 (3,456)
O'Neill, James 3:19:41 (3,211)
O'Neill, John A 4:47:52 (23,400)
O'Neill, Patrick 4:14:57 (15,319)
O'Neill, Robert J 3:09:30 (2,011)
O'Neill, Stephen 3:24:51 (3,919)
Ong, Soon Seng 3:18:10 (3,015)
O'Nions, Darren 4:47:54 (23,407)
Onody, Ryan M 3:28:17 (4,464)
Oo, Tun 4:56:09 (25,130)
Oosterneuk, Jeroen 3:57:37 (11,051)
Opdahl, Geir 4:08:52 (13,825)
Oppenheimer, David W 3:51:19 (9,178)
Oppong-Adarkwa, Chrisotpher ...4:49:15 (23,702)
Oram, Andrew 4:31:07 (19,557)
Oram, Andrew N 4:08:02 (13,621)
Orange, Darren G 4:36:21 (20,816)
Orange, Jon 2:36:43 (141)
Orchard, Mark 5:27:57 (29,322)
Orde, Hugh S 3:56:01 (10,547)
O'Regan, Deri P 5:01:51 (26,152)
O'Regan, John A 4:21:07 (16,897)
O'Regan, Leon 3:14:18 (2,567)
O'Reilly, Damien R 4:30:11 (19,345)
O'Reilly, James A 5:41:34 (30,460)
O'Reilly, John 6:04:50 (31,757)
O'Reilly, Michael J 4:30:51 (19,504)
O'Reilly, Patrick G 3:49:08 (8,653)
O'Reilly, Paul J 5:23:00 (28,829)
Organ, Adrian C 3:48:32 (8,510)
Orgill, Robert C 3:49:21 (8,705)
Orkamfat, Patrick N 5:02:15 (26,210)
Orlov, Valery 5:26:36 (29,179)
Orme, Jonathan N 3:54:48 (10,145)
Ormerod, Mark I 4:15:11 (15,384)
Ormond, John M 4:51:03 (24,049)
Ormond, Paul A 3:37:41 (6,163)
Ormsby, Roy 3:26:04 (4,083)
O'Rourke, Declan M 4:01:10 (12,092)
O'Rourke, Patrick 3:52:01 (9,365)
O'Rourke, Philip J 4:16:23 (15,688)
Orr, Billy 2:56:50 (923)
Orr, Craig A 4:38:16 (21,295)
Orr, James 6:39:14 (32,599)
Orsenigo, Corrado 4:30:15 (19,367)
Orton, John R 3:25:32 (4,008)
Orton, Steven D 6:39:31 (32,604)
Oryan, David H 4:15:13 (15,392)
Osborn, Colin H 4:03:23 (12,574)
Osborn, Jonathan R 4:41:20 (21,960)
Osborn, Kevan C 4:22:01 (17,121)
Osborn, Matthew N 4:13:08 (14,883)
Osborne, Ian 3:18:40 (3,090)
Osborne, Kenneth 4:13:35 (14,973)
Osborne, Steve 4:24:44 (17,880)
Osborne, Tristan 4:09:52 (14,072)
Osburn, Barry A 3:34:42 (5,611)
O'Seaghoha, Diarmuid 2:33:55 (96)
Osgathorpe, Andy F 5:04:36 (26,535)
Osguthorpe, Aaron 3:59:23 (11,634)
O'Shaughnessy, Justin 3:36:04 (5,845)
O'Shaughnessy, Michael S 5:06:26 (26,781)
O'Shea, David R 4:01:02 (12,055)
O'Shea, Denis 3:53:33 (9,778)
O'Shea, Jonathan M 5:11:48 (27,492)
O'Shea, Ronan 4:58:49 (25,667)
Osiepa, Dominique 5:15:57 (27,995)
Osinowo, Remi 3:51:10 (9,140)
Oskarsson, Knutur 3:55:34 (10,390)
Osman, Adib 3:52:42 (9,549)
Osman, Paul M 4:34:10 (20,286)
Osma-Torres, Antonio 3:06:40 (1,723)
Ossitt, Simon D 4:07:54 (13,581)
Osterlund, Kristoffer 2:21:08 (33)
Ostermann, Frederic 4:44:36 (22,690)
Osterwalder, Ilja 3:42:34 (7,126)
Ostinelli, John M 4:21:43 (17,026)
O'Sullivan, Barry 4:07:29 (13,470)
O'Sullivan, Christopher M 4:22:32 (17,251)
O'Sullivan, Donal G 4:08:15 (13,677)
O'Sullivan, James 4:17:35 (16,011)
O'Sullivan, John V 4:25:52 (18,215)
O'Sullivan, Michael G 4:28:43 (18,951)
O'Sullivan, Michael P 3:15:57 (2,776)
O'Sullivan, Nick 4:29:07 (19,062)
O'Sullivan, Sonny T 4:40:59 (21,891)
O'Sullivan, Thomas P 5:51:17 (31,140)
Osvath, Istvan M 4:09:13 (13,916)
Oswald, Robin J 3:46:25 (7,993)
Oswin, Christopher J 3:51:48 (9,303)
Otkay, Emir 4:37:19 (21,061)
O'Toole, Jamie 3:49:35 (8,765)
O'Toole, Kevin 5:30:20 (29,578)
O'Toole, Martin K 5:34:45 (29,950)
O'Toole, Patrick 4:37:28 (21,102)
O'Toole, Peter J 3:49:51 (8,831)
Otten, Remco 3:50:24 (8,955)
Otter, Simon T 3:51:52 (9,324)
Otto, Kevin 3:29:49 (4,790)
Ough, Anthony J 3:29:44 (4,768)
Oulton, Rupert F 4:45:44 (22,952)
Oury, Loren H 4:53:32 (24,575)
Outram, Daniel 4:41:29 (21,989)
Outten, Jonathan C 4:19:15 (16,408)
Outten, Simon B 3:51:37 (9,247)
Overall, Mark 4:24:55 (17,930)
Overgaard, Henning 3:36:50 (6,001)
Overstall, Gerald D 5:50:56 (31,128)
Overvoorde, Peter A 4:39:53 (21,651)
Owen, Chris D 4:54:24 (24,770)
Owen, Christopher A 5:31:53 (29,731)
Owen, Christopher S 4:56:30 (25,204)
Owen, David J 4:42:19 (22,180)
Owen, David R 3:49:26 (8,730)
Owen, Derek 4:24:38 (17,851)
Owen, Gareth W 4:31:15 (19,599)
Owen, Gary J 3:43:04 (7,255)
Owen, Gwilym N 5:04:19 (26,491)
Owen, H 4:15:49 (15,552)
Owen, Hugh T 2:38:43 (182)
Owen, James E 5:02:20 (26,230)
Owen, John S 3:55:10 (10,264)
Owen, Kevin 2:57:49 (1,010)
Owen, Martin J 3:28:50 (4,585)
Owen, Mike D 4:39:19 (21,521)
Owen, Patrick 3:50:51 (9,066)
Owen, Robert 4:01:35 (12,168)
Owen, Robert F 3:56:36 (10,726)
Owen, Simon J 3:26:44 (4,197)
Owen, Stephen 3:50:30 (8,984)
Owen, Stephen R 3:39:30 (6,541)
Owen, Steven R 3:31:51 (5,134)
Owen, Tim H 5:14:52 (27,889)
Owens, Andrew J 3:51:02 (9,110)
Owens, David A 3:44:11 (7,488)
Owens, Kevin N 5:50:24 (31,102)
Owens, Matthew 4:49:40 (23,786)
Owens, Robert C 4:43:29 (22,431)
Owers, Andrew J 4:45:06 (22,815)
Owers, Ian H 5:36:41 (30,110)
Owers, Stuart T 4:24:24 (17,774)
Owusuansa, Stefane 3:16:54 (2,864)
Oxborrow, Trevor 4:06:43 (13,278)
Oxenham, Simon T 4:10:12 (14,149)
Oxley, Chris 4:05:06 (12,939)

Oxley, Philip	3:48:47 (8,572)	
Oxley, Scott A	4:13:04 (14,862)	
Oxley, Simon C	4:15:12 (15,387)	
Oyarzun, Roland	4:24:29 (17,797)	
Oyeyinka, Samuel D	3:35:00 (5,661)	
Oyston, Nigel	6:15:15 (32,094)	
Oza, Amit M	5:25:29 (29,084)	
Ozcoz, Lionel	3:40:23 (6,687)	
Ozenbrook, Damian	4:24:57 (17,946)	
Paardekooper, Wim	3:41:32 (6,926)	
Pace, Edward	4:09:43 (14,035)	
Pack, Andy	4:30:29 (19,424)	
Packer, Jonathan	4:34:02 (20,260)	
Packer, Leigh J	2:53:33 (700)	
Packer, Malcolm P	2:48:50 (485)	
Packer, Robert G	5:33:32 (29,849)	
Paddon, Guy	3:42:39 (7,145)	
Paddon, Neil B	3:17:51 (2,980)	
Padhiar, Raj	5:13:21 (27,699)	
Padley, Roger P	3:18:28 (3,059)	
Paez, Mario	3:36:56 (6,027)	
Page, Andrew J	3:41:16 (6,866)	
Page, Bob	5:49:09 (31,012)	
Page, David	4:47:47 (23,381)	
Page, David R	3:48:13 (8,434)	
Page, Emmanuel	3:10:56 (2,150)	
Page, Gary B	4:01:16 (12,109)	
Page, James	3:46:45 (8,071)	
Page, Keith D	5:24:11 (28,964)	
Page, Kevin F	3:34:38 (5,597)	
Page, Martin C	5:30:05 (29,554)	
Page, Matthew	4:19:52 (16,571)	
Page, Matthew P	3:13:36 (2,476)	
Page, Neal S	2:59:33 (1,198)	
Page, Nicholas	4:31:17 (19,606)	
Page, Nick V	2:46:09 (387)	
Page, Robin	3:32:04 (5,175)	
Page, Shane M	4:01:04 (12,063)	
Paget, Ben J	4:45:24 (22,890)	
Paget, Martin J	4:45:24 (22,890)	
Paget, Timothy J	4:08:46 (13,805)	
Pagett, Stephen C	5:27:03 (29,230)	
Pago, Joao	4:40:20 (21,739)	
Paice, Jonathan B	5:28:25 (29,370)	
Paige, Richard P	3:38:11 (6,264)	
Pain, Dominique	4:35:58 (20,715)	
Painigra, Jacques	3:25:26 (3,997)	
Paint, Christopher D	5:06:13 (26,740)	
Painter, Benjamin E	3:54:20 (10,011)	
Painter, Mark D	4:53:44 (24,626)	
Painter, Paul W	4:03:12 (12,530)	
Pairman, John	3:33:27 (5,398)	
Pairman, Steven	3:06:57 (1,751)	
Paiva, Carlos	4:50:35 (23,956)	
Paiva, Joao Manuel C	4:12:12 (14,625)	
Pajak, Stan	3:48:34 (8,517)	
Pake, Fraser J	4:17:05 (15,883)	
Pake, Rees P	4:32:14 (19,839)	
Palasciano, Francesco	4:22:58 (17,358)	
Palasciano, Giuseppe	3:33:07 (5,335)	
Palasciano, Luca	3:34:29 (5,560)	
Palazzimi, Giovambattista	2:47:17 (427)	
Paley, Stuart J	3:46:31 (8,017)	
Palfreeman, Mark A	4:51:34 (24,156)	
Palfreman, Michael J	5:11:34 (27,469)	
Palfrey, Daryl B	3:14:05 (2,540)	
Palgi, Boaz	4:22:23 (17,221)	
Palikiras, Andreas	3:46:13 (7,947)	
Pallant, Richard G	4:53:37 (24,602)	
Pallas, Jonathan	4:50:24 (23,926)	
Pallister, Stephen P	3:25:08 (3,951)	
Palma, Arturo	4:21:09 (16,904)	
Palmer, Alex	5:29:24 (29,469)	
Palmer, Allan	4:30:31 (19,432)	
Palmer, Andrew	3:27:07 (4,263)	
Palmer, Charles T	4:53:58 (24,670)	
Palmer, Christopher J	5:21:50 (28,694)	
Palmer, David C	3:41:28 (6,906)	
Palmer, David T	3:24:52 (3,922)	
Palmer, Garry S	3:07:41 (1,823)	
Palmer, Geoff	4:05:06 (12,939)	
Palmer, Graeme K	5:18:19 (28,284)	
Palmer, Ian J	4:22:17 (17,194)	

Palmer, Ian L	4:02:11 (12,302)	
Palmer, Kenneth L	3:00:40 (1,281)	
Palmer, Leon D	5:44:37 (30,687)	
Palmer, Mark J	5:14:03 (27,772)	
Palmer, Richard J	3:26:30 (4,155)	
Palmer, Roy N	2:47:40 (443)	
Palmer, Simon C	4:12:26 (14,689)	
Palmer, Steven E	3:57:25 (10,984)	
Palmer, Steven F	4:00:55 (12,019)	
Palmer, Stuart C	4:44:54 (22,756)	
Palmer, Stuart G	4:39:17 (21,509)	
Palomares-Rico, José E	3:11:43 (2,238)	
Palser, Graham	3:56:59 (10,842)	
Pamboris, Nicholas	3:34:20 (5,543)	
Pamplin, John	4:25:10 (18,016)	
Pandit, Digish	4:31:33 (19,681)	
Pando, Fabio	3:28:52 (4,595)	
Pandya, Sunil D	5:06:31 (26,790)	
Pang, Philip	4:34:57 (20,473)	
Pangbourne, Roger W	3:59:39 (11,711)	
Panoscha, Gunar	4:34:05 (20,273)	
Panoscha, Matthias	4:11:22 (14,432)	
Pansera, Fabio	4:22:07 (17,152)	
Panter, John A	4:07:15 (13,412)	
Paolo, Casadei	4:26:41 (18,426)	
Papageorgiou, Andros	4:07:05 (13,370)	
Pape, James W	4:54:07 (24,700)	
Papen, Edward F	4:47:53 (23,403)	
Papenfus, François P	4:39:59 (21,670)	
Papps, Damien A	4:29:55 (19,273)	
Papworth, Michael J	6:02:11 (31,651)	
Papworth, Stephen T	4:07:19 (13,427)	
Paramor, Joshua K	4:48:50 (23,616)	
Paramore, Ian	3:43:00 (7,231)	
Paraskeva, Mario	4:03:24 (12,579)	
Parasram, Anthony R	4:23:08 (17,393)	
Parby, Birger T	4:00:05 (11,839)	
Pardey, David A	3:51:20 (9,185)	
Pardy, Darren	4:44:53 (22,752)	
Parekh, David H	4:43:01 (22,331)	
Parello, Salvatore	3:12:06 (2,288)	
Parfitt, Alex R	3:26:58 (4,237)	
Parfitt, Dean J	4:31:28 (19,656)	
Parfitt, James A	4:03:03 (12,492)	
Parfitt, Martin J	4:03:30 (12,606)	
Parikh, Michael W	4:11:52 (14,542)	
Paris, Michael J	3:55:37 (10,409)	
Parish, Andrew	4:45:20 (22,870)	
Parish, David J	3:29:42 (4,759)	
Parish, Duncan G	3:38:06 (6,250)	
Parish, Timoghy F	3:44:25 (7,543)	
Park, Cameron	5:16:26 (28,062)	
Park, Edward	3:54:35 (10,074)	
Park, Grahame	4:36:20 (20,812)	
Park, Gregor J	3:27:17 (4,287)	
Park, Iain M	3:52:14 (9,422)	
Park, John A	2:56:10 (867)	
Park, Simon	4:35:34 (20,615)	
Parke, Kevin D	3:32:51 (5,302)	
Parker, Adam J	5:24:30 (28,990)	
Parker, Allan J	3:46:53 (8,098)	
Parker, Andrew C	4:43:36 (22,467)	
Parker, Andrew C	4:48:01 (23,430)	
Parker, Andrew P	4:12:23 (14,679)	
Parker, Charles E	4:29:05 (19,053)	
Parker, Colin B	3:54:10 (9,968)	
Parker, Colin W	3:56:50 (10,799)	
Parker, Damen L	4:13:22 (14,937)	
Parker, Dave C	4:30:20 (19,384)	
Parker, David J	3:24:42 (3,896)	
Parker, Dominic J	4:43:06 (22,346)	
Parker, Gary P	4:03:54 (12,690)	
Parker, Ian	3:16:49 (2,854)	
Parker, James T	3:54:36 (10,080)	
Parker, John B	5:31:20 (29,694)	

Parker, John J	4:21:09 (16,904)	
Parker, Jonathan C	5:19:23 (28,421)	
Parker, Kent A	3:32:40 (5,273)	
Parker, Lee	5:59:15 (31,523)	
Parker, Malcolm G	4:15:24 (15,449)	
Parker, Mike	4:11:32 (14,470)	
Parker, Nick J	5:24:31 (28,991)	
Parker, Oliver J	5:28:08 (29,342)	
Parker, Paul T	4:47:12 (23,260)	
Parker, Richard N	4:43:40 (22,481)	
Parker, Robert B	4:24:02 (17,666)	
Parker, Russell J	3:39:18 (6,500)	
Parker, Shane A	5:39:17 (30,301)	
Parker, Simon J	5:39:18 (30,304)	
Parker, Simon P	3:52:12 (9,410)	
Parker, Stephen	3:13:25 (2,453)	
Parker, Stuart C	3:44:09 (7,480)	
Parker, Terence R	4:33:19 (20,088)	
Parker, Terence T	5:10:30 (27,336)	
Parkes, Brandon L	3:42:44 (7,167)	
Parkes, David A	3:27:27 (4,321)	
Parkes, Jeffrey R	4:08:44 (13,792)	
Parkes, Matthew W	4:56:57 (25,295)	
Parkes, Tony G	5:43:14 (30,588)	
Parkin, David L	3:54:51 (10,160)	
Parkin, Ian	4:19:04 (16,360)	
Parkin, Nicholas	4:49:53 (23,817)	
Parkin, Oliver F	4:06:43 (13,278)	
Parkin, Philip E	3:48:41 (8,551)	
Parkin, Shaun M	2:57:23 (973)	
Parkington, David A	2:40:18 (214)	
Parkins, Derek W	3:11:08 (2,169)	
Parkinson, Andrew	4:04:55 (12,899)	
Parkinson, Andrew	5:00:16 (25,937)	
Parkinson, Jon J	2:53:19 (689)	
Parkinson, Mike L	4:44:16 (22,629)	
Parkinson, Paul D	3:12:39 (2,356)	
Parkinson, Roy	3:38:15 (6,280)	
Parkinson, Terry	3:23:34 (3,723)	
Park-Ross, Sean M	3:47:22 (8,206)	
Parks, Raymund B	4:45:23 (22,885)	
Parks, Robbie M	3:20:00 (3,268)	
Parks, Sidney	5:30:29 (29,590)	
Parle, James M	3:34:57 (5,653)	
Parmar, Rakesh K	5:22:58 (28,822)	
Parmenter, Robert A	4:34:12 (20,292)	
Parmiter, Thomas M	4:28:42 (18,944)	
Parncutt, Andrew J	4:28:56 (19,006)	
Parnell, Peter J	4:21:23 (16,955)	
Parnell, Steve A	6:12:59 (32,018)	
Parr, John R	3:17:43 (2,969)	
Parr, Jonathan M	4:22:36 (17,271)	
Parr, Matthew J	3:17:08 (2,902)	
Parr, Richard P	4:05:14 (12,967)	
Parr, Tim	3:53:44 (9,833)	
Parra-Arredondo, Pedro	2:53:25 (694)	
Parrett, Craig	4:12:20 (14,664)	
Parri, Gianmarco	3:01:49 (1,358)	
Parris, Andrew W	4:30:23 (19,398)	
Parrish, James	4:35:26 (20,588)	
Parrott, John	6:27:49 (32,419)	
Parrott, Lee B	5:00:29 (25,968)	
Parry, Andrew I	6:43:32 (32,667)	
Parry, Christopher A	4:47:25 (23,296)	
Parry, Colin R	5:17:34 (28,202)	
Parry, David	5:28:59 (29,427)	
Parry, David J	3:14:36 (2,615)	
Parry, Jonathan R	3:45:34 (7,814)	
Parry, Malcolm	3:52:24 (9,473)	
Parry, Peter	3:34:41 (5,610)	
Parry, Ross W	4:55:15 (24,949)	
Parry, Stephen	4:31:39 (19,711)	
Parry, Stephen B	4:04:50 (12,882)	
Parry, Tony	3:06:04 (1,674)	
Parry, William	4:26:07 (18,291)	
Parry Jones, Ashley H	4:20:36 (16,759)	
Parsison, Keith R	4:29:11 (19,079)	
Parsley, Elvis I	2:51:37 (618)	
Parson, Gordon I	4:51:30 (24,144)	
Parsons, Andrew D	4:42:45 (22,269)	
Parsons, Charles H	5:08:18 (27,050)	
Parsons, Iain A	6:21:17 (32,264)	
Parsons, John	4:01:38 (12,179)	

LONDON MARATHON

Parsons, Mark A	3:50:24 (8,955)	
Parsons, Matthew R	4:42:45 (22,269)	
Parsons, Michael E	4:39:45 (21,612)	
Parsons, Phillip I	5:29:12 (29,443)	
Parsons, Phillip R	4:28:57 (19,012)	
Parsons, Ronald H	5:31:44 (29,720)	
Parsons, Steve B	5:05:59 (26,708)	
Parsons, Steve M	6:47:04 (32,723)	
Parsons, Tim D	4:03:00 (12,477)	
Parsons, William	5:13:27 (27,712)	
Partaix, Didier	4:03:34 (12,617)	
Parton, Ian A	4:13:00 (14,842)	
Parton, Terence	3:25:12 (3,960)	
Partridge, Darren J	4:26:13 (18,316)	
Partridge, David A	4:18:21 (16,199)	
Partridge, Dominic G	3:53:45 (9,844)	
Partridge, Keith G	2:57:54 (1,013)	
Partridge, Roland W	5:47:05 (30,868)	
Partridge, Simon D	3:20:49 (3,377)	
Partridge, Simon P	4:26:00 (18,258)	
Pasanisi, Gianluca	4:04:37 (12,834)	
Pascoe, Barry	3:50:41 (9,027)	
Pascoe, Shaun	4:23:33 (17,520)	
Pascoe, Simon P	3:42:48 (7,185)	
Pashby, David	5:00:19 (25,946)	
Paskins, Paul N	3:23:15 (3,681)	
Pasqualini, Alain	3:06:23 (1,701)	
Pass, Terry M	3:39:12 (6,475)	
Passaro, Enzo	6:45:29 (32,702)	
Pasternakiewicz, Mark	3:28:29 (4,506)	
Pasztor, John L	4:58:08 (25,537)	
Patchett, Gareth R	3:20:21 (3,317)	
Patchett, Robert N	4:36:42 (20,896)	
Patel, Ajay	4:24:53 (17,917)	
Patel, Atulkumar S	4:19:22 (16,439)	
Patel, Balwant K	5:32:01 (29,739)	
Patel, Bejal K	6:52:05 (32,782)	
Patel, Bhavesh	5:53:41 (31,247)	
Patel, Bipin	5:40:04 (30,371)	
Patel, Brijesh	4:18:35 (16,252)	
Patel, Dee	3:00:40 (1,281)	
Patel, Gokul	3:06:11 (1,685)	
Patel, Haroon	4:31:53 (19,769)	
Patel, Hasu	4:14:59 (15,332)	
Patel, Kelpen	3:51:09 (9,135)	
Patel, Kiran D	5:12:39 (27,606)	
Patel, Mahendra K	3:59:29 (11,668)	
Patel, Mahesh M	5:18:23 (28,294)	
Patel, Naran M	5:11:05 (27,396)	
Patel, Nilesh	4:44:20 (22,645)	
Patel, Prakash	4:21:42 (17,023)	
Patel, Pratap	5:47:47 (30,934)	
Patel, Puneet R	5:34:27 (29,930)	
Patel, Rahul	4:08:15 (13,677)	
Patel, Rakesh	4:48:48 (23,609)	
Patel, Ramesh	6:53:30 (32,804)	
Patel, Sacha	4:16:22 (15,684)	
Patel, Sanjay	5:59:56 (31,556)	
Patel, Sanjiv	3:29:10 (4,649)	
Patel, Satish K	4:25:20 (18,067)	
Patel, Shameer S	5:56:44 (31,392)	
Patel, Shivlal H	4:17:54 (16,080)	
Patel, Siraj	3:27:40 (4,360)	
Patel, Sirish J	5:20:48 (28,593)	
Patel, Sunil	5:50:49 (31,122)	
Patel, Tapan	4:39:32 (21,562)	
Patel, Vimal	3:38:07 (6,253)	
Pateman, Andrew G	4:10:01 (14,103)	
Paterlini, Marco	3:44:35 (7,591)	
Paterson, Edward	4:33:50 (20,209)	
Paterson, Keith	3:16:55 (2,868)	
Paterson, Paul D	3:57:53 (11,130)	
Paterson, Stephen	7:02:08 (32,896)	
Paterson, Stephen JJ	2:55:50 (839)	
Pates, Jeremy N	3:56:56 (10,822)	
Patey, Daniel F	7:00:10 (32,884)	
Pather, Rubin	4:14:49 (15,288)	
Patience, James	4:13:20 (14,924)	
Patmore, Scott	5:44:19 (30,666)	
Paton, Colin G	2:36:37 (140)	
Paton, Douglas A	3:26:08 (4,091)	
Paton, Ian D	3:34:32 (5,575)	
Paton, Jason A	5:59:33 (31,536)	
Paton, Richard S	4:13:10 (14,893)	
Paton, Samantha A	4:31:49 (19,750)	
Patrick, Noel M	4:50:07 (23,862)	
Patruno, Christophe D	3:56:20 (10,635)	
Pattas, Nicholas G	4:43:53 (22,543)	
Patten, Francis D	4:15:13 (15,392)	
Patten, Kevin A	4:13:42 (15,005)	
Patterson, Andy	3:14:18 (2,567)	
Patterson, Dean K	4:05:31 (13,027)	
Patterson, John	3:31:08 (5,015)	
Patterson, Mark	4:30:24 (19,400)	
Patterson, Mark T	4:58:25 (25,589)	
Patterson, Patrick	3:39:00 (6,434)	
Patterson, Richard E	4:31:03 (19,542)	
Pattinson, Thomas	4:54:48 (24,848)	
Pattison, Graham	4:16:12 (15,644)	
Pattison, Keith S	3:23:59 (3,790)	
Pattison, Lee	2:50:11 (555)	
Pattison, Nigel A	4:13:23 (14,940)	
Pattison, Paul G	6:00:36 (31,586)	
Pattni, Sharad B	5:50:26 (31,108)	
Patton, Dominic E	4:55:29 (24,995)	
Patzlsperger, Josef G	4:23:30 (17,505)	
Paul, Cruise	4:05:54 (13,118)	
Paul, Daniel	3:59:15 (11,585)	
Paul, Douglas W	4:52:23 (24,330)	
Paul, Eric A	2:49:37 (523)	
Paul, Matthew	4:50:07 (23,862)	
Paul, Ray J	4:22:45 (17,310)	
Paul, Robert J	5:40:54 (30,421)	
Pauley, George D	3:06:53 (1,745)	
Pauline, Alistair D	4:15:39 (15,508)	
Paull, Gren T	6:48:15 (32,739)	
Paull, Stephen F	3:50:14 (8,920)	
Paulson, Darryll A	3:49:05 (8,645)	
Paulson, Michael R	5:12:03 (27,530)	
Pauw, Theo	4:41:01 (21,900)	
Pavan, Marco	3:17:13 (2,911)	
Paveling, Chris J	5:12:11 (27,547)	
Pavey, Andrew D	5:36:35 (30,106)	
Pavitt, Peter	4:20:59 (16,861)	
Pavitt, Stuart	5:12:53 (27,629)	
Pawson, Mark D	6:22:22 (32,299)	
Pawson, Nicholas J	3:57:11 (10,917)	
Paxton, Kevin J	3:37:34 (6,145)	
Paydon, Marc B	4:38:25 (21,316)	
Payen, Frank	4:07:21 (13,433)	
Payne, Alan K	4:25:27 (18,105)	
Payne, Alastair W	2:51:23 (608)	
Payne, Anthony	3:14:43 (2,631)	
Payne, Barry M	7:06:22 (32,949)	
Payne, Bradley S	3:57:32 (11,022)	
Payne, Colin A	4:29:08 (19,065)	
Payne, Colin J	4:21:47 (17,058)	
Payne, Darren	4:32:45 (19,945)	
Payne, David N	5:42:01 (30,497)	
Payne, Garry P	2:34:14 (102)	
Payne, Gary F	4:49:58 (23,838)	
Payne, George W	3:30:26 (4,882)	
Payne, Ian K	4:29:26 (19,153)	
Payne, Kevin K	4:50:36 (23,960)	
Payne, Kevin N	4:09:22 (13,950)	
Payne, Marcus L	3:39:12 (6,475)	
Payne, Nick T	7:03:14 (32,908)	
Payne, Paul	4:02:18 (12,331)	
Payne, Philip	4:03:39 (12,640)	
Payne, Philip L	5:05:39 (26,661)	
Payne, Robert	3:29:32 (4,725)	
Payne, Russ	3:09:30 (2,011)	
Payne, Stephen G	4:51:26 (24,132)	
Payne, Stephen K	3:56:44 (10,763)	
Payne, Steve	2:37:02 (146)	
Payne, Stuart B	3:56:25 (10,660)	
Payne, Tim	4:31:09 (19,571)	
Payne, Trevor C	4:27:29 (18,618)	
Payton, John R	6:05:22 (31,774)	
Peace, Christopher M	3:54:09 (9,962)	
Peace, Kevin M	4:26:31 (18,389)	
Peace, Michael S	3:15:56 (2,772)	
Peace, Tim D	5:08:15 (27,042)	
Peach, Chris	5:42:25 (30,526)	
Peach, James A	3:53:01 (9,630)	
Peach, Nick	3:26:12 (4,103)	
Peacher, Mark S	5:04:56 (26,573)	
Peacher, Ricky C	3:37:34 (6,145)	
Peachey, Michael	3:18:23 (3,045)	
Peacock, David	4:27:57 (18,737)	
Peacock, David M	3:50:02 (8,871)	
Peacock, James K	3:37:23 (6,111)	
Peacock, Jody	5:22:55 (28,817)	
Peacock, Mark	4:42:57 (22,316)	
Peacock, Oliver M	5:23:07 (28,845)	
Peak, Daniel	4:06:43 (13,278)	
Peake, Graham D	4:58:07 (25,533)	
Peake, Leigh F	4:36:48 (20,937)	
Peake, Tim	4:37:31 (21,113)	
Peaple, Derek J	3:02:07 (1,385)	
Pearce, Andrew P	3:29:17 (4,671)	
Pearce, Andrew R	3:51:46 (9,294)	
Pearce, Andy M	4:18:52 (16,318)	
Pearce, Brendan G	4:21:49 (17,067)	
Pearce, Christopher J	4:47:05 (23,231)	
Pearce, David	2:56:10 (867)	
Pearce, David K	4:35:59 (20,718)	
Pearce, Duncan	8:14:34 (33,190)	
Pearce, Glyn	6:02:33 (31,660)	
Pearce, Harry	4:06:06 (13,161)	
Pearce, Ian P	3:48:18 (8,450)	
Pearce, John D	4:16:41 (15,777)	
Pearce, Mark A	6:15:31 (32,101)	
Pearce, Nicholas R	3:58:11 (11,225)	
Pearce, Raymond	2:44:32 (330)	
Pearce, Richard	4:00:49 (12,001)	
Pearce, Robert E	4:00:13 (11,869)	
Pearce, Stefan C	5:32:52 (29,805)	
Pearce, Stephen A	4:45:57 (22,995)	
Pearce, Steve J	4:19:52 (16,571)	
Pearcey, David F	4:17:19 (15,933)	
Pearch, Benjamin J	4:24:52 (17,906)	
Pearman, Lee C	5:33:57 (29,887)	
Pears, Adam J	3:54:46 (10,128)	
Pears, Bryan M	3:41:08 (6,835)	
Pearsall, Steven J	3:49:14 (8,674)	
Pearse, Wiliam J	3:27:32 (4,339)	
Pearson, Andrew	4:16:26 (15,704)	
Pearson, Andrew D	4:30:38 (19,458)	
Pearson, Anthony	3:51:30 (9,215)	
Pearson, Anthony M	4:13:20 (14,924)	
Pearson, Carey J	4:03:25 (12,582)	
Pearson, Charlie L	3:23:00 (3,656)	
Pearson, Christopher J	3:11:12 (2,177)	
Pearson, Gavin J	3:19:49 (3,234)	
Pearson, Geoff	5:12:14 (27,554)	
Pearson, Huh A	3:38:57 (6,425)	
Pearson, John H	3:51:47 (9,300)	
Pearson, Peter	4:32:25 (19,891)	
Pearson, Peter J	4:13:14 (14,906)	
Pearson, Philip J	4:10:50 (14,291)	
Pearson, Richard M	3:30:20 (4,872)	
Pearson, Simon	4:11:10 (14,380)	
Pearson, Stephen	5:18:55 (28,361)	
Pearson, Toby S	2:51:38 (619)	
Peart, Gary R	4:23:32 (17,513)	
Pease, Ian R	5:03:50 (26,431)	
Pease, Kevin J	3:46:56 (8,106)	
Pease, Steven A	3:33:29 (5,403)	
Pease, Steven A	4:18:07 (16,144)	
Peasgood, Andrew D	4:56:07 (25,124)	
Peate, Michael D	5:32:36 (29,778)	
Peats, Michael D	4:01:42 (12,190)	
Peck, Boris W	4:28:33 (18,910)	
Pecoraro, Antonio	2:54:12 (739)	
Peddie, Ronald D	4:06:05 (13,157)	
Peddie, Steven	2:55:47 (835)	
Pedersen, Erling	4:55:56 (25,085)	
Pedlar, Charlie	2:56:39 (911)	
Pedrazzini, Marco	3:42:36 (7,134)	
Peebles, Keith A	4:26:58 (18,497)	
Peel, Ben	5:00:33 (25,976)	
Peel, Christopher J	3:39:49 (6,592)	
Peel, David J	4:45:02 (22,798)	
Peel, Jonathan	3:42:27 (7,102)	
Peel, Jonathan	4:36:58 (20,973)	
Peel, Mike	5:25:11 (29,057)	
Peel, Phil D	3:45:19 (7,760)	
Peel, Stephen	6:36:49 (32,557)	

Peers, Alan...........3:45:15 (7,742)	Percival, Martin R...........4:51:51 (24,222)	Petrides, John G...........6:18:01 (32,171)
Peers, Mark A...........4:00:23 (11,910)	Percival Smith, Paul E...........3:21:17 (3,437)	Petrie, Christopher...........4:08:06 (13,641)
Peers, Richard...........3:36:59 (6,037)	Percy, Matthew...........3:36:17 (5,891)	Petrou, Peter...........4:47:33 (23,334)
Peers, Stephen N...........4:00:00 (11,810)	Perdaan, Nicolaas H...........3:47:06 (8,145)	Petrovic, Alexander...........5:27:56 (29,319)
Peers, Wayne V...........4:24:54 (17,925)	Pereira, Joaquim J...........3:54:46 (10,128)	Petrovic, Darko...........4:27:15 (18,567)
Peersen, Reidar...........4:01:56 (12,244)	Pereira, Vitor...........2:48:27 (468)	Petrovic, Milan...........4:28:14 (18,820)
Peers-Jones, Richard L...........4:32:03 (19,801)	Perera-Sweetman, Martin J...........4:26:42 (18,430)	Petruso, Tony...........3:34:32 (5,575)
Peet, David J...........3:32:34 (5,262)	Peretto, Franck J...........3:58:39 (11,382)	Pettigrew, James W...........3:54:09 (9,962)
Peet, Steven...........4:19:08 (16,374)	Perez, Angel A...........4:29:29 (19,174)	Pettit, Daniel S...........3:24:00 (3,793)
Peevor, Robert F...........4:07:33 (13,486)	Perez, Daniel...........3:55:02 (10,217)	Pettitt, Dean A...........5:21:53 (28,701)
Pegg, Jonathan C...........3:47:48 (8,326)	Perez, John...........3:39:37 (6,557)	Pettitt, Martin J...........4:12:36 (14,726)
Pegg, Kenneth R...........5:58:41 (31,493)	Perez, Juan-Antonio...........4:17:50 (16,067)	Pettitt, Nigel M...........4:01:26 (12,137)
Pegni, Sandro...........3:49:43 (8,802)	Perez, Rafael...........3:24:26 (3,850)	Pettitt, Robin A...........4:16:48 (15,798)
Peichl, Gerald...........3:25:20 (3,980)	Perez Bermejo, Luis...........4:49:02 (23,658)	Petty, Chris P...........5:04:01 (26,459)
Peirce, David...........3:25:11 (3,958)	Perez De Herrasti, Andrés...........4:58:04 (25,520)	Petty, Gareth...........4:07:04 (13,360)
Peirce, Nicholas...........4:17:40 (16,029)	Perez Rodriguez, Marcos...........4:01:55 (12,242)	Petty, Phil D...........4:39:07 (21,469)
Pelella, Angelo...........3:03:22 (1,471)	Perez-Aguilar, Francisco J...........4:15:57 (15,587)	Petty, Richard J...........2:46:56 (414)
Pelizzaro, Mario...........3:59:21 (11,621)	Peri, Francesco...........4:50:01 (23,845)	Petz, Roberto...........4:10:02 (14,107)
Pell, Bengt E...........4:40:39 (21,820)	Perkins, David...........4:05:06 (12,939)	Pewter, Andrew...........5:04:41 (26,541)
Pelliccia, Giancarlo...........3:19:15 (3,167)	Perkins, Dominic G...........4:31:44 (19,729)	Pewtner, Joseph P...........3:57:05 (10,870)
Pellicciari, Michele...........3:38:34 (6,344)	Perkins, Jon...........4:38:52 (21,406)	Pez, Jacques...........4:25:00 (17,964)
Pellicciotti, Paolo...........4:03:41 (12,646)	Perkins, Mark...........3:53:27 (9,755)	Pezzolla, Leonardo...........4:18:33 (16,246)
Pellikaan, Hugo...........4:31:17 (19,606)	Perkins, Matt...........4:38:14 (21,287)	Pfaff, Marcus...........3:31:38 (5,094)
Pelling, Charlie...........4:39:51 (21,640)	Perkins, Matthew J...........3:44:20 (7,530)	Pfarl, Eric...........4:42:13 (22,162)
Pellottiero, Patrick M...........3:38:11 (6,264)	Perkins, Nicholas...........4:16:54 (15,833)	Phair, Liam G...........4:03:53 (12,687)
Pellow, Matthew J...........3:16:42 (2,841)	Perkins, Tom G...........3:29:30 (4,718)	Pheasant, Colin R...........4:48:17 (23,489)
Pelly, Stephen G...........4:41:01 (21,900)	Perlmutter, Antony...........4:33:31 (20,138)	Phelan, Chris...........2:42:27 (262)
Pemberton, Alan R...........3:14:24 (2,583)	Perrault, Michel...........4:19:56 (16,584)	Phelan, James F...........3:21:13 (3,427)
Pemberton, Gareth J...........3:05:21 (1,613)	Perret, Olivier G...........2:59:24 (1,188)	Phelps, Lee M...........3:49:11 (8,666)
Pembroke, Michael J...........3:25:08 (3,951)	Perrett, Stephen...........5:17:21 (28,177)	Phelvin, Robert S...........4:23:18 (17,443)
Pena, Pedro L...........3:48:23 (8,470)	Perrill, Joseph J...........5:02:54 (26,304)	Philbin, Jason V...........2:59:26 (1,189)
Pendleton, Lee J...........4:11:34 (14,473)	Perrin, Andrew...........4:31:18 (19,613)	Philips, Richard N...........3:59:54 (11,786)
Pendleton, Nick S...........5:33:38 (29,862)	Perrin, David B...........3:43:19 (7,312)	Philipsen, Henning...........4:34:59 (20,483)
Pendleton-Hughes, Simon M...........3:59:35 (11,694)	Perrin, Jonathan A...........3:58:11 (11,225)	Phillips, Alan C...........6:14:38 (32,076)
Penfold, Christian R...........4:43:52 (22,537)	Perrin, Marc E...........3:48:52 (8,598)	Phillips, Alec W...........5:18:12 (28,269)
Penfold, Jonathan M...........3:57:11 (10,917)	Perrin, Stephen R...........2:58:39 (1,089)	Phillips, Anthony C...........4:22:22 (17,215)
Penfold, Keith J...........5:07:43 (26,964)	Perring, David W...........4:24:43 (17,875)	Phillips, Anthony M...........3:48:36 (8,530)
Penfold, Mungo...........3:59:40 (11,715)	Perrott, Nicholas E...........3:37:33 (6,140)	Phillips, Benedict L...........4:16:52 (15,817)
Pengelly, Andrew J...........3:24:10 (3,818)	Perry, Andrew...........3:46:21 (7,974)	Phillips, Chris...........4:27:00 (18,504)
Penicaud, Jean-Claude...........3:40:13 (6,659)	Perry, Ashley A...........4:22:59 (17,363)	Phillips, Daniel...........4:49:44 (23,797)
Penk, Christopher C...........4:10:30 (14,214)	Perry, Ben...........3:59:42 (11,728)	Phillips, David J...........3:21:44 (3,505)
Penka, Wolfgang...........4:05:14 (12,967)	Perry, Christopher...........3:40:32 (6,718)	Phillips, David M...........4:15:43 (15,524)
Penman, Adam W...........3:58:16 (11,253)	Perry, Darren...........3:07:02 (1,762)	Phillips, David S...........3:55:23 (10,339)
Penman, Jeffrey T...........5:01:02 (26,048)	Perry, Edward J...........3:18:42 (3,094)	Phillips, Duncan C...........4:05:47 (13,096)
Pennacchia, Francesco...........3:14:39 (2,623)	Perry, Giles C...........4:52:16 (24,296)	Phillips, Gareth T...........3:32:14 (5,211)
Pennal, Robin J...........3:42:29 (7,111)	Perry, Hamish B...........3:53:00 (9,626)	Phillips, Gavin M...........4:31:21 (19,625)
Pennell, David...........5:45:59 (30,782)	Perry, Ian G...........4:01:23 (12,129)	Phillips, Ian J...........4:35:16 (20,546)
Pennells, Geoffrey R...........3:57:00 (10,846)	Perry, John F...........4:08:30 (13,745)	Phillips, James...........5:26:22 (29,159)
Penner, Alexander C...........4:55:34 (25,010)	Perry, Luke B...........4:52:16 (24,296)	Phillips, James A...........4:34:39 (20,397)
Penner, Dan A...........4:46:28 (23,113)	Perry, Marcus C...........4:24:25 (17,777)	Phillips, Jason...........5:05:07 (26,602)
Penney, Andrew D...........2:50:42 (572)	Perry, Mark T...........3:46:35 (8,030)	Phillips, John...........4:35:22 (20,573)
Penney, Nicholas R...........4:34:44 (20,421)	Perry, Nicholas...........4:23:59 (17,648)	Phillips, Mervyn...........3:37:54 (6,208)
Penney, Simon...........3:14:38 (2,619)	Perry, Paul J...........2:47:07 (420)	Phillips, Michael...........4:43:14 (22,372)
Pennick, Gordon C...........5:44:26 (30,677)	Perry, Ross M...........3:48:32 (8,510)	Phillips, Nicholas A...........4:13:13 (14,901)
Pennicott, James...........3:15:03 (2,664)	Perry, Seth...........3:47:57 (8,374)	Phillips, Paul...........3:55:47 (10,472)
Pennington, Jason...........3:47:45 (8,311)	Perry, Simon...........5:18:56 (28,365)	Phillips, Paul G...........4:12:15 (14,640)
Pennington, John...........4:20:23 (16,706)	Perry, Simon W...........3:43:44 (7,402)	Phillips, Rhodri P...........3:29:30 (4,718)
Pennington, Jon M...........6:00:46 (31,592)	Perry, Steve...........5:06:48 (26,836)	Phillips, Richard M...........3:45:12 (7,730)
Pennington, Liam J...........3:18:23 (3,045)	Perry, Thomas E...........4:31:14 (19,593)	Phillips, Rob...........2:47:41 (444)
Pennington, Oliver J...........3:09:26 (2,006)	Perry, Wayne I...........3:56:55 (10,817)	Phillips, Robert A...........4:12:21 (14,670)
Penny, Brian...........2:49:51 (539)	Perry Lewis, Matt...........5:07:19 (26,907)	Phillips, Robert W...........4:55:13 (24,942)
Penny, Craig...........4:45:44 (22,952)	Peruzzo, Alberto...........5:00:13 (25,929)	Phillips, Shaun P...........2:58:24 (1,057)
Penny, Kristian...........4:33:53 (20,224)	Pescod, Daniel...........3:06:39 (1,722)	Phillips, Simon...........4:48:23 (23,510)
Pennycook, Robert...........4:55:04 (24,908)	Peskett, Stuart J...........4:56:14 (25,146)	Phillips, Stephen P...........4:25:23 (18,087)
Penrice, Frank...........6:15:04 (32,087)	Pesquero, Gary D...........2:59:17 (1,174)	Phillips, Steven J...........5:07:19 (26,907)
Penrose, Ian R...........3:56:33 (10,708)	Pestell, Adrian F...........3:15:41 (2,739)	Phillips, Steven P...........6:17:24 (32,152)
Penrose, Noel R...........4:22:44 (17,307)	Petagna, Marco...........3:26:34 (4,168)	Phillips, Timothy C...........5:03:26 (26,382)
Penter, David R...........3:33:59 (5,479)	Peters, Charles M...........4:57:25 (25,383)	Phillips, Trevor...........4:48:09 (23,459)
Penter, Graham...........3:41:40 (6,958)	Peters, David S...........3:08:24 (1,897)	Phillipson, Jason J...........5:01:13 (26,061)
Pentke, Siegfried...........3:57:43 (11,082)	Peters, Gary R...........3:30:41 (4,929)	Phillipson, Laurie C...........4:33:45 (20,196)
Pentland, Bob...........2:59:14 (1,169)	Peters, Kenneth...........4:15:09 (15,380)	Phillis, Timothy J...........3:34:40 (5,604)
Pentland, Paul D...........4:21:46 (17,052)	Peters, Michael...........2:54:50 (783)	Phillpotts, Garfield S...........4:57:21 (25,375)
Penton, David C...........5:48:45 (30,985)	Peters, Nicholas J...........3:28:04 (4,416)	Philp, Brian...........3:37:10 (6,069)
Penton, Philip...........5:48:44 (30,983)	Peters, Paul L...........4:37:36 (21,137)	Philp, Bruce...........5:04:57 (26,567)
Pentony, Liam...........4:13:37 (14,979)	Peters, Philip C...........4:08:53 (13,830)	Philpot, Saul T...........4:25:25 (18,095)
Pepes, Peter S...........3:39:19 (6,503)	Peterson, Calum H...........3:39:02 (6,438)	Philpott, Alan G...........4:22:48 (17,322)
Peploe, Seth...........5:59:12 (31,520)	Peterson, Garth D...........2:54:26 (756)	Philpott, Garry C...........5:03:49 (26,430)
Pepper, Jonathan...........3:49:58 (8,860)	Peterson, Mark J...........4:17:53 (16,079)	Philpott, Mark A...........3:36:32 (5,940)
Pepper, Matthew J...........5:21:15 (28,638)	Petit, Christophe...........3:20:41 (3,360)	Philpott, Timothy R...........3:48:41 (8,551)
Peppiatt, Malcolm W...........5:00:31 (25,970)	Petit, Didier...........3:06:23 (1,701)	Philpotts, Robert...........3:11:55 (2,265)
Peppiatt, Samuel S...........4:38:48 (21,391)	Petite, Alain...........3:39:10 (6,467)	Phipps, David J...........3:50:13 (8,915)
Perchard, Mike...........3:34:57 (5,653)	Petreni, Enzo G...........5:39:31 (30,326)	Phipps, Kevin M...........3:35:22 (5,729)
Percival, Mark N...........4:21:45 (17,045)	Petri, Stephen J...........4:17:39 (16,026)	Phipps, Patrick...........3:51:53 (9,329)

Phipps-Jones, Arnold	4:18:40 (16,270)	
Phoenix, Andrew	4:23:19 (17,448)	
Phoenix, Mike B	4:54:52 (24,866)	
Piana, Gianluca	3:38:16 (6,285)	
Pibworth, Keith A	4:44:06 (22,583)	
Pichler, Peter	3:41:45 (6,974)	
Pick, Daniel M	4:22:03 (17,130)	
Pick, Robert M	3:27:27 (4,321)	
Pick, Stephen E	3:57:08 (10,893)	
Pickard, Graham J	4:17:49 (16,065)	
Pickard, John F	3:23:53 (3,771)	
Pickard, Mark J	3:56:22 (10,643)	
Pickard, Toby M	3:36:36 (5,958)	
Picken, Nigel M	5:20:00 (28,492)	
Pickerill, Mark	3:32:52 (5,304)	
Pickering, Daniel N	3:22:53 (3,644)	
Pickering, David C	3:03:55 (1,509)	
Pickering, David T	4:11:35 (14,475)	
Pickering, Derrick J	5:33:43 (29,870)	
Pickering, Jon	3:38:00 (6,222)	
Pickering, Richard	3:06:42 (1,728)	
Pickering, Steven	3:16:52 (2,861)	
Pickert, Alan M	4:48:22 (23,506)	
Pickett, Donald G	3:53:29 (9,762)	
Pickett, Gary J	6:09:27 (31,911)	
Pickett, Ian	3:36:54 (6,020)	
Pickett, Kenneth G	5:15:06 (27,911)	
Pickett, Nigel	4:48:14 (23,477)	
Pickhaver, Tony	4:37:20 (21,066)	
Pickup, Stephen	3:45:40 (7,841)	
Pickup, Stephen J	3:30:30 (4,895)	
Picola, José L	5:04:00 (26,457)	
Picot, Michael J	4:03:29 (12,601)	
Pidgeon, Steve T	5:17:35 (28,204)	
Piepoli, Gennaro	3:50:04 (8,878)	
Pierce, Christian W	3:11:13 (2,182)	
Pierce, Dominic J	3:05:44 (1,636)	
Pierce, Stewart W	4:02:59 (12,474)	
Piersall, Anthony C	5:02:50 (26,293)	
Pierson, Richrad M	3:52:39 (9,538)	
Pieterse, Jacobus N	4:36:53 (20,960)	
Pietrosanti, Massimiliano	2:52:16 (647)	
Pighills, Stephen G	4:34:55 (20,466)	
Pigram, Matthew D	4:48:50 (23,616)	
Piguet, Vincent	3:29:13 (4,658)	
Pike, Daniel J	3:54:39 (10,091)	
Pike, Daniel R	3:16:53 (2,862)	
Pike, Darren J	3:45:33 (7,812)	
Pike, David	3:43:34 (7,362)	
Pike, David J	3:17:34 (2,949)	
Pike, Derek J	4:29:58 (19,285)	
Pike, Graham J	4:40:17 (21,729)	
Pike, Graham J	4:47:10 (23,247)	
Pike, Iain R	4:17:06 (15,886)	
Pike, John	4:16:52 (15,817)	
Pike, Michael S	4:20:13 (16,666)	
Pike, Richard G	5:42:00 (30,496)	
Pilarczyk, Ralf F	3:58:59 (11,500)	
Pilbeam, David J	3:22:14 (3,563)	
Pilbeam, David M	4:27:00 (18,504)	
Pilcher, Sean M	4:54:03 (24,684)	
Pilgrim, Ben	4:57:46 (25,448)	
Piliszczuk, Thomas	3:50:44 (9,037)	
Pilkington, Adrian	3:23:49 (3,764)	
Pilkington, Brydon J	4:29:24 (19,146)	
Pilkington, Michael	4:27:59 (18,745)	
Pilkington, Rory I	4:02:46 (12,430)	
Pill, Stephen	3:16:39 (2,834)	
Pilling, David M	4:10:18 (14,170)	
Pilling, Gregory	3:42:21 (7,088)	
Pilorge, Bertrand	2:54:35 (770)	
Pils, Jon	4:01:16 (12,109)	
Pim, Brian	3:18:59 (3,131)	
Pimentel, José W	4:05:37 (13,055)	
Pimlott, David	4:14:44 (15,267)	
Pimm, Stephen	4:32:53 (19,974)	
Pinardi, Alessandro	3:43:21 (7,320)	
Pinches, Joss P	3:06:48 (1,737)	
Pinder, Mark	3:49:12 (8,668)	
Pinder, Nick G	4:14:45 (15,272)	
Pinder, Roger J	3:55:15 (10,298)	
Pinder, William T	6:15:38 (32,105)	
Pindoria, Hitesh R	4:37:31 (21,113)	

Pinfold, David R	4:52:23 (24,330)	
Pinfold, Mark A	5:30:56 (29,640)	
Ping, Darren J	3:41:08 (6,835)	
Pinha, Pedro	3:10:09 (2,081)	
Pini, Stefano	5:34:06 (29,896)	
Pink, Michael S	5:44:25 (30,676)	
Pinkerton, Charles J	3:20:03 (3,273)	
Pinkney, Tedd	4:24:15 (17,732)	
Pinnell, Kevin A	4:53:17 (24,520)	
Pinner, James R	3:51:05 (9,118)	
Pinner, Stephen A	5:51:31 (31,156)	
Pinnick, David	3:56:12 (10,593)	
Pinnick, Richard D	4:27:56 (18,733)	
Pino, Andrew	4:11:20 (14,426)	
Pinsent, Matthew C	4:08:03 (13,628)	
Pinto, Carlos Miguel C	4:09:08 (13,885)	
Piper, David J	4:37:02 (20,987)	
Piper, Neil	3:55:01 (10,209)	
Pipes, Ian R	3:48:51 (8,591)	
Piron, Richard	4:36:39 (20,876)	
Pisani, Dino L	4:29:59 (19,288)	
Pitchell, Ian	3:24:36 (3,879)	
Pitcher, Julian N	4:14:19 (15,165)	
Piterzak, John	4:12:26 (14,689)	
Pitt, Alan	2:59:23 (1,186)	
Pitt, Chris J	3:54:06 (9,946)	
Pittard, Jonathan D	4:25:51 (18,210)	
Pittaway, Mark	2:44:12 (318)	
Pitters, Harry J	4:45:43 (22,947)	
Pittman, Andrew A	4:52:46 (24,414)	
Pittman, Andrew R	2:54:38 (775)	
Pittman, Michael J	4:13:09 (14,888)	
Pittman, Simon J	5:54:23 (31,278)	
Pitts, Damien T	3:17:16 (2,918)	
Pitts, Simon M	3:45:02 (7,697)	
Pitz, Friedrich	3:58:09 (11,209)	
Pivi, Danilo	4:42:29 (22,212)	
Piwecki, Paul S	4:50:11 (23,876)	
Pizzey, Kevin J	4:58:43 (25,650)	
Place, David	4:24:06 (17,683)	
Placet, David C	4:21:55 (17,091)	
Plaka, Ozer	4:12:00 (14,573)	
Plan, Jean-Luc H	4:19:47 (16,547)	
Planch, Dominique	4:04:24 (12,796)	
Planche, Richard Y	3:31:31 (5,068)	
Planchon, Mathieu	4:16:38 (15,766)	
Planner, Donald	6:55:33 (32,833)	
Plant, Ben	4:13:03 (14,858)	
Plant, Gareth A	3:15:42 (2,741)	
Plant, John L	5:36:48 (30,116)	
Plant, Lee A	4:02:07 (12,289)	
Plant, Ray	2:26:13 (49)	
Plant, Stuart M	5:40:30 (30,392)	
Platt, Gary A	3:03:39 (1,488)	
Platt, Martin C	2:57:24 (974)	
Platt, Nigel H	4:26:19 (18,342)	
Platts, Charles A	3:46:28 (8,004)	
Platts, Glen	4:25:24 (18,090)	
Platts, Rob	3:08:20 (1,889)	
Platts, Stephen D	3:54:48 (10,145)	
Platts, Tom N	3:22:39 (3,619)	
Player, Ben L	3:58:43 (11,405)	
Player, William G	3:16:33 (2,822)	
Playford, Ian	5:06:47 (26,833)	
Playle, David J	5:46:03 (30,789)	
Pleasance, Stephen	3:51:01 (9,102)	
Pleass, David I	3:58:15 (11,249)	
Plenderleith, Scott M	3:51:41 (9,269)	
Plews, Anrew	3:49:34 (8,761)	
Plimmer, Peter S	3:25:35 (4,017)	
Plowman, Robin	4:24:17 (17,742)	
Plows, Trevor	3:41:57 (7,012)	
Pluck, Neil W	4:38:33 (21,349)	
Pluckrose, Allan	3:55:26 (10,354)	
Pluckrose, Michael D	2:43:44 (305)	
Plum, Hans J	3:24:36 (3,879)	
Plumer, Keith	3:06:32 (1,713)	
Plumley, Royston K	4:07:37 (13,512)	
Plummer, Bradley C	3:13:56 (2,517)	
Plummer, James W	3:56:03 (10,552)	
Plummer, Julian	5:56:42 (31,389)	
Plummer, Martin C	5:47:38 (30,927)	
Plump, Brent	3:22:58 (3,653)	

Plumridge, Neil J	3:10:30 (2,113)	
Plumstead, Mark K	3:23:48 (3,755)	
Plumstead, Pat	3:01:14 (1,320)	
Plunkett, Douglas T	4:03:21 (12,565)	
Plunkett, Steve K	4:03:29 (12,601)	
Pluviaud, Herve	4:43:17 (22,387)	
Pockett, Simon C	5:26:51 (29,209)	
Pocklington, David	3:46:00 (7,902)	
Pockney, Timothy E	4:28:07 (18,780)	
Pocock, Frank A	4:32:15 (19,845)	
Pocock, John W	3:28:07 (4,427)	
Pocock, Toby	4:27:59 (18,745)	
Podda, Aldo	4:49:12 (23,690)	
Podevin, Jean Claud	3:45:55 (7,889)	
Pointel, Yves	3:39:34 (6,551)	
Pointer, Daniel M	4:18:27 (16,218)	
Pokroy, Craig A	3:55:22 (10,337)	
Polhill, Dean M	4:24:21 (17,764)	
Pollack, Mark	4:20:11 (16,656)	
Pollard, Ian F	2:56:09 (863)	
Pollard, Joseph A	3:36:13 (5,880)	
Pollard, Michael J	3:47:21 (8,202)	
Pollard, Simon J	3:55:25 (10,349)	
Pollard, Tim J	3:39:24 (6,518)	
Pollen, Samuel	3:35:00 (5,661)	
Pollett, Derek J	3:51:01 (9,102)	
Pollexfen, Andy	4:21:57 (17,102)	
Polley, Keith A	4:34:09 (20,280)	
Polley, Richard	3:40:53 (6,776)	
Pollock, Allister D	4:37:42 (21,160)	
Pollock, Andrew J	4:27:49 (18,697)	
Pollock, David W	4:41:16 (21,943)	
Pollock, Jeremy R	2:44:47 (340)	
Pollock, Nicholas S	2:53:35 (702)	
Pollock, Robert A	3:16:54 (2,864)	
Pollock, Wayne B	3:56:40 (10,746)	
Pomford, Colin	4:22:36 (17,271)	
Pomfret, Graham L	3:24:41 (3,893)	
Pomroy, Timothy J	4:00:57 (12,030)	
Poncelet, Yves	4:24:20 (17,759)	
Pond, Andrew J	4:10:21 (14,183)	
Pond, Chris R	3:56:47 (10,778)	
Pond, Christopher M	3:38:28 (6,321)	
Pond, Jeffery I	3:30:06 (4,847)	
Ponder, Carl B	5:30:40 (29,613)	
Ponsford, David E	3:24:18 (3,839)	
Ponsford, Richard	3:24:28 (3,857)	
Ponter, Ian R	6:08:14 (31,868)	
Ponting, David K	3:17:44 (2,971)	
Pontoglio, Claudio	3:36:40 (5,970)	
Ponty, Christian	4:51:11 (24,074)	
Pool, Jim W	4:09:01 (13,865)	
Pool, Robert C	4:43:49 (22,523)	
Poole, Andrew M	4:25:13 (18,033)	
Poole, James A	4:09:28 (13,988)	
Poole, Matthew	3:58:08 (11,203)	
Poole, Phil	4:23:47 (17,582)	
Poole, Philip N	4:36:57 (20,970)	
Pooley, Martin	4:09:42 (14,029)	
Poolman, Ian	3:38:24 (6,303)	
Poon, Cornelius N	5:23:41 (28,906)	
Pope, Charles A	3:36:01 (5,837)	
Pope, Christopher L	4:24:32 (17,809)	
Pope, Ed	4:35:39 (20,639)	
Pope, James W	5:11:04 (27,394)	
Pope, Robert P	4:49:35 (23,774)	
Pope, Roger	5:29:08 (29,438)	
Pope, Thomas J	3:03:31 (1,483)	
Pope, Christopher J Snr	4:24:32 (17,809)	
Popple, Martin A	4:56:25 (25,191)	
Port, Gary W	4:13:58 (15,054)	
Porteous, Andrew C	4:04:30 (12,816)	
Porteous, David J	5:20:45 (28,586)	
Porteous, Henry J	3:20:06 (3,278)	
Porter, Adam J	4:41:15 (21,934)	
Porter, Alan	4:29:15 (19,102)	
Porter, Christopher J	4:57:30 (25,397)	
Porter, Danny	4:17:06 (15,886)	
Porter, David N	3:50:12 (8,911)	
Porter, David R	5:05:26 (26,639)	
Porter, Garry S	5:47:34 (30,922)	
Porter, Lee D	5:06:00 (26,710)	
Porter, Martin R	4:00:59 (12,045)	

Porter, Patrick W ... 3:52:33 (9,506)
Porter, Robert J ... 4:50:42 (23,985)
Porter, Roger A ... 3:32:53 (5,305)
Porter, Stuart ... 4:00:41 (11,973)
Porter, Ted H ... 4:58:16 (25,563)
Porter, Tom ... 4:19:33 (16,491)
Portnell, Nicholas J ... 4:28:04 (18,767)
Portsmouth, Stephen G ... 5:52:46 (31,207)
Portus, James O ... 3:58:43 (11,405)
Posgate, Robert W ... 4:02:55 (12,462)
Potash, Steven ... 5:07:08 (26,884)
Potier, Bernard ... 3:40:36 (6,728)
Potkin, Leigh ... 4:47:44 (23,368)
Potter, Adam D ... 4:38:45 (21,382)
Potter, Alan W ... 3:58:13 (11,238)
Potter, Colin ... 4:29:31 (19,184)
Potter, David M ... 3:01:36 (1,343)
Potter, Gary ... 5:04:04 (26,463)
Potter, Iain V ... 4:50:44 (23,991)
Potter, James M ... 3:13:03 (2,406)
Potter, John H ... 6:07:05 (31,824)
Potter, Keith ... 3:44:36 (7,596)
Potter, Marc J ... 4:51:48 (24,210)
Potter, Mark J ... 3:06:44 (1,732)
Potter, Matt ... 4:41:26 (21,978)
Potter, Matthew C ... 4:06:27 (13,219)
Potter, Stephen ... 3:45:26 (7,789)
Potter, Stephen E ... 4:36:45 (20,919)
Potts, Colin I ... 2:39:11 (195)
Potts, Daniel J ... 3:57:43 (11,082)
Potts, Duncan M ... 3:58:46 (11,431)
Potts, Jonathan E ... 4:15:55 (15,581)
Potts, Kevin J ... 4:49:26 (23,740)
Potts, Richard A ... 4:11:09 (14,377)
Potts, William A ... 3:57:07 (10,888)
Poulsom, Giles ... 3:54:45 (10,124)
Poulter, Kim ... 4:12:00 (14,573)
Poulter, Michael J ... 3:57:22 (10,969)
Poulton, David J ... 5:20:16 (28,530)
Poulton, Kristopher M ... 5:45:25 (30,750)
Poulton, Thomas E ... 4:28:44 (18,956)
Poulton, Timothy ... 4:02:54 (12,458)
Pouncett, Ian M ... 3:29:16 (4,667)
Pouncey, David A ... 3:21:14 (3,429)
Pound, Daniel R ... 4:27:56 (18,733)
Pounder, Michael J ... 3:33:11 (5,351)
Pout, James C ... 3:28:15 (4,452)
Povey, Kenneth G ... 4:34:22 (20,331)
Povey, Kevin R ... 4:18:35 (16,252)
Povinelli, Raymond A ... 3:50:56 (9,083)
Pow, Jack P ... 4:20:12 (16,662)
Powell, Adrian D ... 3:16:09 (2,795)
Powell, Alun ... 4:27:36 (18,655)
Powell, Andrew ... 4:12:17 (14,645)
Powell, Christopher J ... 3:58:51 (11,464)
Powell, David D ... 3:53:44 (9,833)
Powell, Dean W ... 5:27:49 (29,308)
Powell, Gary ... 6:27:01 (32,404)
Powell, Ian J ... 3:29:29 (4,713)
Powell, Ian S ... 3:47:50 (8,336)
Powell, James L ... 5:44:49 (30,704)
Powell, Jason D ... 3:23:13 (3,676)
Powell, John ... 4:46:58 (23,200)
Powell, John C ... 4:43:56 (22,558)
Powell, John D ... 5:05:10 (26,607)
Powell, John E ... 4:37:59 (21,216)
Powell, Jonathon ... 3:43:46 (7,411)
Powell, Keith T ... 4:22:41 (17,294)
Powell, Mark D ... 3:55:54 (10,507)
Powell, Martin A ... 5:55:20 (31,317)
Powell, Martin P ... 4:20:38 (16,769)
Powell, Michael L ... 4:55:44 (25,043)
Powell, Nick J ... 4:47:55 (23,414)
Powell, Richard ... 3:27:59 (4,406)
Powell, Thomas W ... 3:41:54 (7,008)
Powell, Tony ... 5:32:04 (29,743)
Power, Gary ... 4:11:27 (14,450)
Power, Rolf G ... 3:37:18 (6,095)
Powers, Sean ... 5:24:00 (28,936)
Powles, Frederick R ... 4:42:42 (22,260)
Powney, John M ... 4:21:44 (17,036)
Poxon, Roy ... 5:42:40 (30,546)
Pozzoli, Giovanni ... 4:12:50 (14,786)

Prada, Graziano A ... 3:49:55 (8,848)
Pradhan, Sanjay K ... 5:12:50 (27,624)
Prag, Ben D ... 3:19:10 (3,152)
Prangle, Christopher P ... 4:32:16 (19,853)
Prasad, Manish ... 5:45:16 (30,736)
Pratt, Adam C ... 5:10:13 (27,291)
Pratt, Alan J ... 3:54:48 (10,145)
Pratt, David J ... 3:49:27 (8,731)
Pravato, Claudio ... 4:14:20 (15,169)
Prazsky, Tom F ... 4:38:28 (21,329)
Preece, David J ... 3:28:11 (4,438)
Preece, Howard J ... 4:27:33 (18,638)
Preece, Jon A ... 4:54:46 (24,833)
Preen, Gregory L ... 4:46:19 (23,080)
Prendergast, Andrew ... 4:34:47 (20,433)
Prendergast, Matthew C ... 3:25:06 (3,942)
Prentice, Stuart N ... 3:28:27 (4,503)
Prenzel, Siegfried ... 3:59:11 (11,570)
Prescott, Edward J ... 4:04:23 (12,793)
Prescott, Richard W ... 4:20:22 (16,700)
Prescott, Stephen H ... 4:50:20 (23,914)
Prescott, Tom E ... 3:18:27 (3,058)
Presdee, Julian M ... 4:11:38 (14,487)
Preshous, Andrew D ... 3:50:59 (9,095)
Press, Andrew J ... 4:35:22 (20,573)
Pressley, Ashley M ... 4:41:16 (21,943)
Pressley, Mark J ... 2:49:46 (531)
Prest, Gordon J ... 3:59:06 (11,543)
Presti, Giovanni ... 5:29:48 (29,523)
Prestidge, Alistair T ... 4:40:55 (21,875)
Prestidge, Caspar ... 3:03:20 (1,466)
Preston, Andy P ... 3:58:41 (11,396)
Preston, Jeremy ... 5:05:52 (26,690)
Preston, Kevin ... 4:00:26 (11,921)
Preston, Leigh P ... 4:32:48 (19,959)
Preston, Mark S ... 3:42:40 (7,150)
Preston, Ross W ... 3:20:49 (3,377)
Preston, Stephen ... 3:22:06 (3,544)
Preston, Stuart D ... 3:49:18 (8,691)
Prestridge, Jeffrey J ... 3:55:50 (10,485)
Pretorius, Walter ... 4:21:00 (16,867)
Pretsell, Barry C ... 3:58:37 (11,372)
Prettyman, Richard J ... 4:12:29 (14,699)
Prewett, Christian D ... 4:13:27 (14,951)
Price, Alan J ... 3:55:08 (10,255)
Price, Andrew D ... 3:59:20 (11,617)
Price, Anthony R ... 5:01:50 (26,151)
Price, Christopher D ... 4:48:05 (23,446)
Price, Curt ... 4:20:48 (16,810)
Price, Daniel A ... 5:00:40 (25,991)
Price, Dave J ... 2:56:27 (888)
Price, David C ... 3:14:42 (2,628)
Price, David C ... 4:04:07 (12,744)
Price, Gareth A ... 3:36:25 (5,919)
Price, Howard P ... 4:00:55 (12,019)
Price, Ian ... 3:15:39 (2,733)
Price, Ian R ... 3:07:38 (1,819)
Price, James ... 3:12:09 (2,299)
Price, James ... 4:48:35 (23,563)
Price, Jim R ... 5:09:55 (27,256)
Price, Jonathan ... 4:11:20 (14,426)
Price, Keith S ... 3:57:20 (10,961)
Price, Kevin J ... 3:57:16 (10,937)
Price, Marcus P ... 3:21:12 (3,423)
Price, Martin G ... 2:43:34 (302)
Price, Matt ... 3:57:42 (11,072)
Price, Neil J ... 3:48:25 (8,477)
Price, Neil R ... 3:58:59 (11,500)
Price, Nicholas ... 6:15:49 (32,109)
Price, Nigel T ... 3:55:05 (10,240)
Price, Paul T ... 3:14:59 (2,658)
Price, Richard A ... 4:51:25 (24,129)
Price, Richard T ... 2:50:45 (576)
Price, Sean C ... 4:01:28 (12,140)
Price, Simon R ... 3:24:13 (3,826)
Price, Stephen ... 4:07:51 (13,570)
Price, Stephen ... 5:15:53 (27,987)
Price, Stephen J ... 2:59:34 (1,206)
Price, Tim C ... 4:11:47 (14,516)
Price, Tim R ... 2:48:33 (475)
Price, Trevor I ... 3:25:13 (3,966)
Prichard, Euan D ... 4:15:02 (15,349)
Prichard, Michael J ... 4:11:23 (14,434)

Prickett, Clive A ... 4:23:42 (17,560)
Priday, James A ... 5:17:48 (28,221)
Pride, Chris J ... 4:25:44 (18,169)
Pride, Tristan ... 4:55:49 (25,059)
Priekulis, Bernie ... 3:15:20 (2,699)
Priest, Andrew J ... 3:57:09 (10,902)
Priestley, Richard D ... 5:23:09 (28,850)
Priestley, Spencer D ... 3:42:46 (7,178)
Priestman, Murray B ... 3:56:35 (10,717)
Prietzel, Christopher H ... 3:47:33 (8,249)
Prime, David D ... 4:14:33 (15,216)
Prime, Glenn ... 5:40:36 (30,398)
Prime, Royston ... 5:22:40 (28,796)
Primrose, Noel ... 4:08:36 (13,769)
Prin, Frank A ... 3:16:25 (2,811)
Prince, Daniel J ... 5:01:43 (26,136)
Prince, Ian A ... 5:44:11 (30,658)
Prince, Kevin J ... 4:52:30 (24,355)
Pring, Richard A ... 4:37:12 (21,032)
Pringle, Grix ... 6:10:30 (31,944)
Pringle, Kevin ... 3:35:53 (5,814)
Pringle, Mark A ... 3:37:30 (6,133)
Pringle, Nigel P ... 4:57:31 (25,401)
Pringle, Robert A ... 4:41:41 (22,035)
Prior, Charlie H ... 3:58:33 (11,357)
Prior, Philip W ... 4:48:25 (23,517)
Pritchard, David A ... 5:39:35 (30,330)
Pritchard, David F ... 4:22:38 (17,283)
Pritchard, David G ... 4:14:59 (15,332)
Pritchard, William ... 3:32:18 (5,222)
Privitera, Frankie L ... 5:16:11 (28,026)
Probert, Jeremy H ... 6:21:04 (32,266)
Probert, Mark E ... 3:06:06 (1,676)
Procter, Russell ... 3:31:19 (5,038)
Proctor, Benjamin M ... 3:57:46 (11,100)
Proctor, Richard ... 4:20:19 (16,688)
Proctor, Richard J ... 3:23:38 (3,732)
Proctor, Simon J ... 3:31:27 (5,062)
Prodger, Gary M ... 5:21:58 (28,715)
Prod'homme, Patrice ... 3:26:20 (4,124)
Proffitt, Edward N ... 4:26:05 (18,281)
Proietti, Roberto F ... 3:41:58 (7,018)
Pronger, Andrew R ... 4:42:17 (22,172)
Prono, Guido ... 4:23:09 (17,397)
Prosser, James P ... 5:35:23 (30,001)
Prosser, Paul A ... 5:35:23 (30,001)
Prothero, Robert A ... 2:58:38 (1,083)
Proudley, Gavin J ... 2:54:31 (760)
Proudlove, Mike ... 2:33:51 (95)
Proven, Mike J ... 3:07:25 (1,795)
Prowting, Michael H ... 4:15:59 (15,596)
Pruce, Daniel R ... 5:04:29 (26,523)
Prudence, Perry A ... 4:55:25 (24,985)
Prudham, Joseph P ... 3:32:50 (5,300)
Pryce, Andrew J ... 4:11:35 (14,475)
Pryke, Andrew M ... 3:37:30 (6,133)
Pryke, Keith R ... 4:13:40 (14,997)
Pryor, Benjamin J ... 3:46:13 (7,947)
Pryor, Mark A ... 3:12:48 (2,376)
Pryor, Steven ... 3:56:56 (10,822)
Pryor, Tom ... 4:29:22 (19,138)
Puddefoot, Ian M ... 4:19:18 (16,422)
Puddick, Julian U ... 3:20:12 (3,299)
Pudsey, David J ... 3:20:22 (3,320)
Pugh, Ben M ... 4:54:18 (24,747)
Pugh, Eddie ... 4:25:10 (18,016)
Pugh, John D ... 4:14:03 (15,086)
Pugh, Neale ... 3:54:04 (9,936)
Pugh, Patrick F ... 3:12:18 (2,323)
Pugh, Robert M ... 7:03:23 (32,913)
Pugh, Roderick M ... 3:07:11 (1,776)
Pugliese, Leroy ... 6:53:01 (32,795)
Pugsley, Gareth J ... 4:48:11 (23,466)
Pugsley, Simon C ... 3:50:59 (9,095)
Puig, Santiago ... 3:59:07 (11,553)
Pulfer, Anthony ... 4:38:00 (21,223)
Pulford, Tom G ... 7:45:04 (33,158)
Pullen, John M ... 3:38:15 (6,280)
Pullen, Leslie C ... 5:27:51 (29,315)
Pullen, Matthew T ... 3:37:57 (6,217)
Pullen, Miles ... 4:33:35 (20,159)
Pullen, Toby H ... 3:50:29 (8,977)
Pullinger, Lars E ... 3:49:28 (8,734)

Pullman, Mark G 5:14:30 (27,841)
Pulman, Jon J 5:51:35 (31,161)
Puntan, Piers 3:27:27 (4,321)
Purcell, Ian S 3:58:04 (11,174)
Purcell, Jim 7:44:56 (33,157)
Purdie, Alexander 4:09:07 (13,881)
Purdom, Lee D 4:08:54 (13,838)
Purdy, Justin 3:49:52 (8,837)
Purdy, Richard 5:14:18 (27,811)
Purewal, Paul 4:14:33 (15,216)
Purkiss, Mark C 4:03:07 (12,509)
Purkiss, Michael T 5:26:28 (29,171)
Purkiss-McEndoo, Shaun 2:50:43 (574)
Purnell, Andrew G 4:22:44 (17,307)
Purnell, Colin 4:08:32 (13,750)
Purnell, James M 4:37:47 (21,173)
Purser, Kevin A 4:17:48 (16,060)
Pursey, Len 4:18:08 (16,146)
Purvey, Alan 4:47:00 (23,215)
Purvis, Darren M 2:37:55 (166)
Puszet, Ian J 5:02:40 (26,270)
Putland, Richard 4:05:02 (12,923)
Puttick, Timothy 4:57:21 (25,375)
Puzin, Joel 3:54:36 (10,080)
Puzio, Jan D 3:49:19 (8,697)
Pye, Clifford M 4:31:43 (19,725)
Pye, David L 4:10:54 (14,305)
Pye, Roy F 4:01:22 (12,125)
Pye, Shaw D 3:04:33 (1,555)
Pyke, Thomas R 4:39:45 (21,612)
Pyne, David J 4:20:10 (16,652)
Pyne, Steven R 3:57:45 (11,093)
Pyper, Darryl J 3:48:40 (8,545)
Quaeck, Mathew J 4:41:43 (22,039)
Quaile, Ian J 4:34:11 (20,288)
Quantrill, Philip 2:55:33 (821)
Quarendon, James 4:32:46 (19,952)
Quarry, Jamie 3:29:48 (4,782)
Quartly, Leonard S 3:55:28 (10,361)
Quattromini, Gianriccardo 4:37:37 (21,142)
Quayle, Scott J 3:53:02 (9,638)
Quelch, Christopher J 4:37:00 (20,979)
Quelch, Paul 5:54:34 (31,290)
Quennell, Richard G 2:56:36 (903)
Quest, Paul A 4:39:49 (21,632)
Quick, Jonathan A 4:31:22 (19,630)
Quickenden, Timothy P 2:57:42 (1,003)
Quigley, James E 4:23:41 (17,555)
Quigley, John M 4:52:30 (24,355)
Quigley, Philip A 4:53:32 (24,575)
Quill, Tony 4:25:50 (18,202)
Quillet, Jean-Pierre 4:15:45 (15,535)
Quin, Paul 5:01:53 (26,158)
Quinby, Richard 3:44:50 (7,650)
Quinlan, Edward A 6:23:09 (32,306)
Quinlan, Warren 3:42:31 (7,115)
Quinn, Anthony 5:00:59 (26,039)
Quinn, Antony 3:46:07 (7,928)
Quinn, Benedict J 3:46:11 (7,939)
Quinn, Daniel J 3:10:08 (2,076)
Quinn, David A 3:22:53 (3,644)
Quinn, Eamon G 3:54:20 (10,011)
Quinn, Eamonn 6:07:31 (31,841)
Quinn, Greg 3:12:44 (2,367)
Quinn, Gregory 3:41:16 (6,866)
Quinn, James B 5:34:28 (29,931)
Quinn, John E 4:21:02 (16,875)
Quinn, Malcolm K 4:32:17 (19,857)
Quinn, Mark J 3:51:41 (9,269)
Quinn, Michael A 3:24:29 (3,861)
Quinn, Michael J 4:52:48 (24,422)
Quinn, Sean P 4:38:56 (21,426)
Quinn, Simon P 4:08:40 (13,781)
Quinn, Tomas 3:34:55 (5,646)
Quinsee, Paul A 3:51:33 (9,234)
Quintrell, Troy 4:57:49 (25,459)
Quirighetti, Paul 3:56:22 (10,643)
Quslch, Daniel A 3:57:54 (11,134)
Raanes, Deyvind 6:23:49 (32,325)
Rabazzi, Giancarlo 4:32:24 (19,889)
Rabbetts, Mark A 2:51:31 (613)
Rabensteiner, Gerhard 3:24:45 (3,905)
Rabett, Justin R 3:25:05 (3,939)

Rabey, Derrick A 3:14:47 (2,637)
Rabiet, Frederic 3:08:18 (1,884)
Rabin, Nicholas P 3:47:06 (8,145)
Rabinowitz, Gideon P 4:27:51 (18,708)
Rabjohns, Peter 3:12:34 (2,349)
Raboldt, Marco 4:22:22 (17,215)
Race, Andrew M 4:43:21 (22,398)
Race, Barnaby 3:45:41 (7,844)
Race, Stuart 5:27:03 (29,230)
Rackham, Nigel D 2:45:47 (365)
Rackstraw, Stephen 4:45:17 (22,855)
Racle, Denis 3:30:53 (4,960)
Racy, Emmanuel 4:43:29 (22,431)
Radbourne, Mathew 4:58:55 (25,692)
Radcliffe, Jamie W 4:21:41 (17,018)
Radcliffe, Richard 3:13:20 (2,438)
Radford, Brian 4:59:15 (25,740)
Radford, Colin 4:08:58 (13,853)
Radford, James 3:43:15 (7,300)
Radford, Nicholas L 3:52:23 (9,466)
Radford, Sean R 3:30:02 (4,830)
Radigan, John 3:54:20 (10,011)
Radley, Adam D 5:35:31 (30,016)
Radley, Wayne 4:50:25 (23,930)
Radusch, Joerg 5:35:57 (30,051)
Rae, Alex 7:36:51 (33,122)
Rae, Ewan G 5:19:48 (28,471)
Rae, Steven 3:56:04 (10,558)
Raffagnini, Simone 2:32:28 (85)
Raft, Anders 3:59:00 (11,511)
Ragatzu, Pierpaolo 3:27:28 (4,326)
Ragg, David 4:28:06 (18,773)

Raghwani, Vimal K 5:05:19 (26,628)

My first ever marathon and what a day. Plagued with injuries and lack of long runs, started on the start line with pain and nerves. As soon as the race kicked off, it all seemed to disappear, and I realised that I was doing this for people less fortunate than me. Knowing this and the amazing London crowds helped over the 26.2-mile course, and I finished with great satisfaction. The wet weather did not help with blisters, but sure did keep us nice and cool throughout the course. Will never forget that moment of hitting the wall at 19 miles, kept ploughing on. Thanks you all for supporting me, and thank you Sense for giving me the chance to make a difference. Vimal Kalyan Raghwani

---

Ragless, Ben 4:24:02 (17,666)
Rahman, Bobby 4:33:11 (20,055)
Rahman, Emdad 5:43:15 (30,590)
Rai, Eddie 6:08:44 (31,884)
Rai, James P 4:48:28 (23,532)

Rai, Sean M 5:46:44 (30,842)
Raia, Bruno 3:55:08 (10,255)
Raikes, Fred 3:28:26 (4,500)
Raimondo, René P 2:55:38 (823)
Rainbird, Stephen J 4:53:11 (24,504)
Rainbow, Matthew S 3:53:20 (9,726)
Rainer, Thomas W 3:43:18 (7,308)
Rainey, Chris 4:30:44 (19,480)
Rainey, Ira L 4:06:39 (13,259)
Rainey, Timothy 3:59:52 (11,780)
Rains, John G 4:27:17 (18,576)
Rains, Kevin J 4:08:09 (13,652)
Rait, Richard J 3:18:28 (3,059)
Raitzl, Tranz 3:44:00 (7,456)
Rajani, Jayprakash 5:49:58 (31,070)
Ralfe, Philip 4:06:06 (13,161)
Ralley, Paul D 4:13:06 (14,874)
Ralph, Lew 5:21:10 (28,625)
Ralph, Michael 4:31:36 (19,698)
Ralton, Paul J 2:52:56 (674)
Ramaala, Hendrick 2:06:55 (3)
Ramage, Stephen J 3:58:04 (11,174)
Ramakrishna, Suresha 5:35:54 (30,046)
Ramalhal, Rui M 3:30:31 (4,899)
Raman, Manoj 4:25:09 (18,008)
Ramanaharan, Venugopal 4:23:26 (17,478)
Ramchandani, Parkash 4:55:55 (25,080)
Ramella Pajrin, Fausto 3:56:22 (10,643)
Ramesh, Siva 5:22:11 (28,739)
Ramirez, Santiago 3:31:41 (5,099)
Ramond, Patrick 3:49:47 (8,816)
Rampersad, Prashan M 4:39:03 (21,454)
Ramsay, Adam D 4:15:17 (15,408)
Ramsay, Daniel 4:06:16 (13,185)
Ramsay, Gordon 3:46:10 (7,937)
Ramsay, Graeme 5:30:56 (29,640)
Ramsay, Grant M 2:37:34 (154)
Ramsay, Jonathan R 3:11:12 (2,177)
Ramsay, Malcolm C 4:15:06 (15,366)
Ramsdale, Mark 3:04:26 (1,540)
Ramsden, Anthony J 4:28:23 (18,867)
Ramsden, Stephen C 3:58:45 (11,422)
Ramsell, Chris D 3:08:25 (1,899)
Ramsell, Ian R 4:38:11 (21,280)
Ramsey, John S 5:41:46 (30,481)
Ramsey, John W 3:08:25 (1,899)
Ramsey, Martin S 4:46:51 (23,185)
Ramsey-Smith, David 3:57:27 (10,996)
Ramuscello, Patrick 3:56:41 (10,750)
Rand, Edward C 4:52:06 (24,268)
Randall, Dave W 4:06:53 (13,321)
Randall, Jeremy R 3:13:52 (2,509)
Randall, Stephen E 4:52:26 (24,339)
Randell, Paul N 3:47:21 (8,202)
Randerson, Philip E 5:06:08 (26,729)
Randle, Sean M 5:00:46 (26,004)
Randles, Malcolm P 4:09:51 (14,069)
Rands, John 5:00:37 (25,987)
Range, Fred 4:58:49 (25,667)
Ranger, Terry E 3:41:19 (6,876)
Ranieri, Cesare G 3:31:46 (5,113)
Rankin, David J 4:40:29 (21,771)
Rankin, Matthew 3:20:55 (3,394)
Rankin, Michael C 4:23:10 (17,406)
Ranns, Ian 5:17:13 (28,155)
Ransom, Jeremy C 3:10:22 (2,102)
Ranson, Ashleigh V 3:45:16 (7,745)
Rantell, David A 2:45:06 (346)
Raper, John C 3:30:52 (4,955)
Raper, Jonathan M 5:32:57 (29,813)
Raper, Ray J 3:20:06 (3,278)
Raphael, Michael 5:34:11 (29,899)
Rapley, Nicholas 4:14:03 (15,086)
Rasmussen, Graeme P 2:43:06 (290)
Rasmussen, Jesper 3:12:53 (2,385)
Rasmussen, Karl Johan 2:17:20 (21)
Rasmussen, Tore 3:24:18 (3,839)
Rason, Steven A 3:44:38 (7,600)
Rassim, Ertan 5:39:26 (30,314)
Ratchford, Daniel J 4:20:39 (16,774)
Ratchford, David L 3:33:49 (5,451)
Ratcliffe, Andrew P 4:45:11 (22,830)
Ratcliffe, John D 3:42:40 (7,150)

Ratcliffe, Jonathan D	5:16:43 (28,095)	
Ratcliffe, Julian	3:54:39 (10,091)	
Ratcliffe, Mark A	5:20:14 (28,524)	
Ratcliffe, Steven	3:28:20 (4,477)	
Rathe, Austin E.	3:54:05 (9,940)	
Rattigan, John G.	5:12:41 (27,613)	
Raueiser, Georg H	4:27:54 (18,722)	
Rault, Matthew A.	4:03:39 (12,640)	
Rauschnabel, Markus	3:34:23 (5,546)	
Raven, Alec J.	4:22:39 (17,287)	
Raveney, Samuel J	3:24:27 (3,853)	
Rawden, Douglas M	4:46:30 (23,120)	
Rawlings, Christopher	6:00:48 (31,593)	
Rawlings, Jonathan G.	3:20:48 (3,376)	
Rawlinson, Lee	4:33:08 (20,043)	
Rawlinson, Robert J.	4:48:18 (23,493)	
Rawson, David	3:29:25 (4,698)	
Rawson, Paul J	3:43:20 (7,315)	
Rawson, Simon J.	4:12:05 (14,591)	
Ray, Duncan	4:17:45 (16,046)	
Ray, Geoffrey J	3:53:03 (9,647)	
Ray, Ripon	4:08:38 (13,778)	
Rayers, Matthew R.	4:18:45 (16,291)	
Rayfield, Benjamin L	4:37:26 (21,094)	
Rayfield, Brian S.	5:11:49 (27,496)	
Rayfield, David W	2:58:47 (1,112)	
Rayment, Matthew D.	3:49:09 (8,658)	
Raymond, Bruce E	4:07:58 (13,606)	
Raymond, Byron J	3:11:40 (2,233)	
Raymond, Mark	4:53:47 (24,635)	
Raymond, Rupert G	4:40:58 (21,884)	
Raynaud, Christopher A	3:28:45 (4,566)	
Rayner, Andrew	4:31:50 (19,755)	
Rayner, Anthony J	5:00:45 (26,000)	
Rayner, Ben J	4:14:16 (15,155)	
Rayner, Danny	4:34:48 (20,436)	
Rayner, David A	2:50:34 (568)	
Rayner, Gary R.	2:57:36 (994)	
Rayner, Mark A	5:27:26 (29,263)	
Rayner, Sean	5:33:24 (29,840)	
Rayner, Steve H	4:20:35 (16,754)	
Rayner, Trevor D	2:56:59 (941)	
Raynes, David	4:14:50 (15,292)	
Raynes, Richard	8:20:51 (33,198)	
Raynor, John	4:30:19 (19,380)	
Raynsford, Jody	4:54:32 (24,785)	
Rayson, Christopher J	4:36:12 (20,779)	
Raza, Abdul R	4:01:33 (12,158)	
Raza, Mark I.	4:29:19 (19,122)	
Rea, Christopher J.	4:29:27 (19,160)	
Rea, Martin	3:24:13 (3,826)	
Rea, Nicholas	4:03:05 (12,500)	
Rea, Peter S	4:42:52 (22,297)	
Read, Alan W	3:58:54 (11,476)	
Read, Anthony J	4:04:40 (12,847)	
Read, Chris M.	3:54:00 (9,923)	
Read, David W	3:50:09 (8,902)	
Read, Kevin R	6:31:21 (32,479)	
Read, Mark	4:46:54 (23,195)	
Read, Martin G	4:08:28 (13,735)	
Read, Martin R	4:16:02 (15,604)	
Read, Nicholas W	4:15:43 (15,524)	
Read, Paul	2:57:34 (991)	
Read, Paul J	3:39:25 (6,523)	
Read, Peter B	3:15:51 (2,761)	
Read, Sean A	4:18:51 (16,310)	
Read, Steven A	4:16:25 (15,695)	
Reader, John	4:42:01 (22,116)	
Reader, Paul T	4:39:21 (21,533)	
Reader, Simon W	3:28:10 (4,436)	
Reading, David	4:01:46 (12,205)	
Readings, Gavin	5:29:56 (29,538)	
Readman, Ben G	3:26:04 (4,083)	
Ready, Christopher	4:18:56 (16,337)	
Real Cabo, Paul	4:44:40 (22,700)	
Reami, Roberto	3:35:42 (5,786)	
Rean, Peter J	3:29:23 (4,693)	
Reaney, Patrick M.	3:32:29 (5,246)	
Reardon, Matthew C	5:08:20 (27,056)	
Reavey, Matthew R	4:53:23 (24,544)	
Reavley, John	3:56:46 (10,769)	
Reay-Jones, Simon H.	4:29:03 (19,040)	
Rebelo, Dominic L	4:11:36 (14,479)	
Recchia, Christopher J	4:08:27 (13,732)	
Reddard, Roger	4:17:03 (15,873)	
Redden, Phil	2:56:14 (873)	
Reddicliffe, Alexander	4:05:54 (13,118)	
Redding, Chris	4:06:01 (13,143)	
Reddy, Luke A	2:42:43 (272)	
Redfern, Neal	3:43:19 (7,312)	
Redfern, Simon	4:38:37 (21,360)	
Redgrave, Steve	5:29:06 (29,434)	
Redhead, Richard M	4:23:52 (17,613)	
Reding, Tom	4:31:12 (19,581)	
Redknapp, Mark J	4:54:34 (24,798)	
Redman, Andrew M	4:20:55 (16,842)	
Redman, Andy	3:17:41 (2,962)	
Redman, Christopher M	5:15:13 (27,928)	
Redman, Neil A	4:29:20 (19,130)	
Redman, Paul	2:58:26 (1,061)	
Redmond, Alasdair I	4:06:24 (13,212)	
Redsell, John D	4:54:48 (24,848)	
Redwood, Derek	5:09:11 (27,170)	
Redwood, Leslie W	3:19:42 (3,213)	
Reece, Oliver	5:10:10 (27,282)	
Reed, Andrew E.	6:18:44 (32,191)	
Reed, Andrew G	5:22:08 (28,730)	
Reed, David R	2:37:40 (159)	
Reed, Declan A	3:09:13 (1,978)	
Reed, James S	4:52:48 (24,422)	
Reed, Malcolm	4:40:22 (21,744)	
Reed, Peter A.	4:29:04 (19,041)	
Reed, Phil W	4:44:23 (22,656)	
Reed, Richard M	4:00:58 (12,040)	
Reed, Rob J	4:54:10 (24,720)	
Reed, Simon M.	5:24:54 (29,028)	
Reede, Willem	4:41:50 (22,062)	
Reeder, Roy W	2:33:55 (96)	
Rees, Alun K	5:04:48 (26,557)	
Rees, Anthony	4:54:04 (24,687)	
Rees, Christopher O	4:40:17 (21,729)	
Rees, Christopher R	4:17:58 (16,100)	
Rees, Colin D	5:45:16 (30,736)	
Rees, Colin J	3:21:32 (3,475)	
Rees, Daniel A	3:26:50 (4,210)	
Rees, David B	5:12:41 (27,613)	
Rees, David P	3:44:52 (7,658)	
Rees, John J	3:45:37 (7,826)	
Rees, Richard	4:58:16 (25,563)	
Rees, Robert H	4:00:50 (12,002)	
Rees, Stephen J	3:50:22 (8,945)	
Reeve, Alistair	3:50:34 (9,000)	
Reeve, David M.	4:50:04 (23,855)	
Reeve, Martin	4:15:37 (15,498)	
Reeve, Stephen M	4:18:56 (16,337)	
Reeves, Andrew B	2:44:35 (335)	
Reeves, Gavin J	4:14:10 (15,133)	
Reeves, James A	3:13:32 (2,470)	
Reeves, Mark J	4:14:16 (15,155)	
Reeves, Robb J	3:24:37 (3,883)	
Reeves, Steve	3:20:50 (3,382)	
Reeves, Steven E	4:05:39 (13,067)	
Reeves, Stuart N	2:48:21 (463)	
Reeves, William G	6:11:30 (31,967)	
Regan, Andy P	4:04:07 (12,744)	
Regan, James W	3:33:20 (5,373)	
Regan, Sean	3:34:43 (5,616)	
Regan, Tom J	4:30:28 (19,419)	
Regulski, Brett R	4:24:49 (17,895)	
Rehn, Lars	3:26:28 (4,142)	
Reibeiro, Fernando	3:30:04 (4,838)	
Reich, Kenneth E	3:43:45 (7,408)	
Reid, Adam J.	4:07:34 (13,496)	
Reid, Adam P	3:46:11 (7,939)	
Reid, Brian D	4:28:14 (18,820)	
Reid, Clive S	4:10:47 (14,270)	
Reid, Daniel J	3:34:19 (5,538)	
Reid, Gareth M	5:12:42 (27,615)	
Reid, Gavin	2:55:56 (846)	
Reid, Gavin	3:06:24 (1,704)	
Reid, Gavin J	4:21:02 (16,875)	
Reid, Ian D	2:49:56 (545)	
Reid, James R	5:37:27 (30,159)	
Reid, Martin A	4:23:12 (17,414)	
Reid, Nicholas I	2:51:40 (621)	
Reid, Paul	4:26:56 (18,489)	
Reid, Paul	4:43:06 (22,346)	
Reid, Paul	6:48:56 (32,745)	
Reid, Peter K	2:56:23 (882)	
Reid, Tim J	4:25:12 (18,027)	
Reil, Hermann G	4:42:52 (22,297)	
Reilly, Angus D	4:23:09 (17,397)	
Reilly, Darren	4:56:47 (25,254)	
Reilly, Harry J	3:35:14 (5,712)	
Reilly, Matt	5:08:12 (27,035)	
Reilly, Peter A	3:43:42 (7,389)	
Reilly, Peter J	5:28:38 (29,389)	
Reilly, Stephen J	3:39:35 (6,553)	
Reilly, Stuart C	3:52:51 (9,578)	
Reilly, William	5:17:50 (28,224)	
Reinhardt, Andreas	4:22:41 (17,294)	
Reis, Dieter	4:52:03 (24,257)	
Reiss, Manfred	3:58:06 (11,185)	
Reithmuller, Drew	4:08:05 (13,639)	
Relton, Richard D	4:55:49 (25,059)	
Remfry, Gideon J	3:54:30 (10,051)	
Remnant, Trevor M	5:34:14 (29,906)	
Renals, Paul	4:58:19 (25,572)	
Renard, Olivier	4:50:28 (23,939)	
Rendall, David K	4:37:54 (21,196)	
Rendall, Julian I	2:33:08 (91)	
Rendall, Mark W	4:41:58 (22,101)	
Rendu, Matthew	5:09:01 (27,148)	
René, Fiorese	3:57:29 (11,008)	
Rennie, Gavin A	3:19:06 (3,144)	
Rennie, Gregor	5:27:39 (29,287)	
Rennie, Les	4:17:44 (16,038)	
Rennison, Mark	3:19:13 (3,159)	
Renshaw, Ben	4:38:05 (21,251)	
Renwick, Simon M	4:49:05 (23,669)	
Renz, Karlheinz	3:34:50 (5,631)	
Resnick, Brian L	5:03:04 (26,326)	
Reston, Rhydian H	3:34:52 (5,636)	
Retalic, Paul P	4:42:53 (22,301)	
Retallick, Timothy	4:50:26 (23,932)	
Revel, Ghislain	4:24:39 (17,858)	
Revell, David J	4:48:34 (23,556)	
Revell, Peter A	4:56:27 (25,199)	
Revill, Keith	5:13:38 (27,731)	
Revill, Paul R	4:17:29 (15,978)	
Revill, Steven J	5:19:58 (28,487)	
Revolvo, Tomas	2:54:14 (741)	
Rew, Nick	3:43:01 (7,236)	
Reyneke, Arnoldus M	5:02:30 (26,249)	
Reynolds, Andrew K	3:49:32 (8,753)	
Reynolds, Andy J	4:51:54 (24,229)	
Reynolds, Damian P	4:56:16 (25,155)	
Reynolds, David A	3:53:50 (9,873)	
Reynolds, Derek A	5:35:12 (29,985)	
Reynolds, Graham	3:40:13 (6,659)	
Reynolds, Guy J	4:51:37 (24,171)	
Reynolds, James F	4:46:39 (23,147)	
Reynolds, Jason	4:20:49 (16,814)	
Reynolds, John A	5:00:07 (25,908)	
Reynolds, Jon	5:02:38 (26,266)	
Reynolds, Mark	4:41:59 (22,110)	
Reynolds, Mark A	3:46:08 (7,929)	
Reynolds, Mark P	3:42:38 (7,138)	
Reynolds, Martin L	3:28:51 (4,590)	
Reynolds, Matthew J	3:54:23 (10,023)	
Reynolds, Nick J	3:56:30 (10,685)	
Reynolds, Paul	4:45:43 (22,947)	
Reynolds, Paul A	5:07:43 (26,964)	
Reynolds, Paul C	4:28:17 (18,833)	
Reynolds, Paul J	3:57:14 (10,932)	
Reynolds, Peter	4:09:49 (14,065)	
Reynolds, Peter W	4:26:22 (18,352)	
Reynolds, Stephen J	4:30:58 (19,526)	
Reynolds, Thomas A	3:27:00 (4,246)	
Reynolds, Tim	4:37:00 (20,979)	
Rham, Steve	4:41:53 (22,081)	
Rhead, Robert J	3:53:43 (9,827)	
Rhimes, Godfrey H	2:47:27 (436)	
Rhind, Thomas J	3:48:08 (8,414)	
Rhoades, Andy B	3:19:49 (3,234)	
Rhodes, Christopher J	5:14:38 (27,860)	
Rhodes, Gary W	5:08:36 (27,090)	
Rhodes, Graeme P	4:16:11 (15,643)	
Rhodes, Graham A	4:42:00 (22,115)	

Roberts, Nicholas	4:19:40 (16,522)	
Roberts, Nicholas A	4:11:24 (14,442)	
Roberts, Nigel D	4:52:49 (24,426)	
Roberts, Nigel S	3:46:51 (8,095)	
Roberts, Paul A	3:57:01 (10,847)	
Roberts, Paul G	5:16:41 (28,091)	
Roberts, Paul M	4:09:33 (14,004)	
Roberts, Peter	4:42:45 (22,269)	
Roberts, Peter D	4:47:27 (23,308)	
Roberts, Peter W	4:46:10 (23,043)	
Roberts, Philip	4:53:09 (24,491)	
Roberts, Richard H	3:01:15 (1,322)	
Roberts, Robin B	3:28:03 (4,413)	
Roberts, Simon C	4:22:36 (17,271)	
Roberts, Simon D	4:29:15 (19,102)	
Roberts, Simon J	3:02:23 (1,397)	
Roberts, Simon M	4:26:16 (18,328)	
Roberts, Simon N	3:35:15 (5,715)	
Roberts, Stephen	4:59:48 (25,852)	
Roberts, Stephen J	3:37:09 (6,067)	
Roberts, Stephen W	3:20:10 (3,291)	
Roberts, Steve J	3:31:58 (5,156)	
Roberts, Thomas J	5:22:06 (28,725)	
Roberts, Tony	4:04:49 (12,880)	
Roberts, Tony N	5:27:28 (29,269)	
Roberts, Trevor J	3:52:01 (9,365)	
Roberts, Vincent C	4:07:27 (13,457)	
Roberts, Wyn	4:52:49 (24,426)	
Robertshaw, Tom	2:57:57 (1,021)	
Robertson, Alex A	4:11:51 (14,534)	
Robertson, Alexander S	4:04:20 (12,782)	
Robertson, Andrew H	6:26:53 (32,400)	
Robertson, Frank C	4:49:27 (23,746)	
Robertson, Graham F	4:29:18 (19,119)	
Robertson, Iain T	4:45:41 (22,942)	
Robertson, Ian D	5:05:42 (26,666)	
Robertson, James	3:21:11 (3,420)	
Robertson, Keith J	3:42:59 (7,227)	
Robertson, Neil	5:27:22 (29,258)	
Robertson, Paul	3:02:20 (1,394)	
Robertson, Paul T	4:58:40 (25,638)	
Robertson, Peter C	4:10:30 (14,214)	
Robertson, Peter J	5:12:20 (27,566)	
Robertson, Philip	5:11:09 (27,403)	
Robertson, Stewart D	3:14:31 (2,598)	
Robertson, William A	3:55:39 (10,416)	
Robineau, Philipe	4:25:40 (18,153)	
Robins, David J	5:03:52 (26,441)	
Robins, Michael J	3:19:40 (3,206)	
Robinson, Aaron	3:49:51 (8,831)	
Robinson, Adam G	4:41:05 (21,913)	
Robinson, Alex	3:49:46 (8,813)	
Robinson, Antony J	4:47:15 (23,271)	
Robinson, Dale	3:49:51 (8,831)	
Robinson, Damian C	5:01:57 (26,171)	
Robinson, Daniel	4:11:23 (14,434)	
Robinson, Dave	4:49:33 (23,766)	
Robinson, David A	2:56:53 (930)	
Robinson, David A	5:28:14 (29,351)	
Robinson, David J	4:17:06 (15,886)	
Robinson, David K	3:12:08 (2,292)	
Robinson, Gerard	3:38:11 (6,264)	
Robinson, Glen J	4:28:32 (18,904)	
Robinson, Glenn A	3:05:21 (1,613)	
Robinson, Howard J	4:32:57 (19,992)	
Robinson, James B	4:22:30 (17,242)	
Robinson, James D	4:31:16 (19,602)	
Robinson, John G	3:36:29 (5,928)	
Robinson, John L	4:40:25 (21,753)	
Robinson, Jonathan D	4:55:31 (25,001)	
Robinson, Jonathan H	2:56:38 (909)	
Robinson, Jonathan M	4:29:16 (19,107)	
Robinson, Kenneth	4:15:18 (15,415)	
Robinson, Mark	4:16:34 (15,743)	
Robinson, Martin	3:56:07 (10,573)	
Robinson, Martyn P	4:24:21 (17,764)	
Robinson, Matthew J	5:01:56 (26,168)	
Robinson, Neil M	3:53:50 (9,873)	
Robinson, Patrick A	5:35:42 (30,025)	
Robinson, Peter	3:51:28 (9,212)	
Robinson, Peter P	4:28:50 (18,979)	
Robinson, Reece R	3:19:05 (3,140)	
Robinson, Robert	4:20:54 (16,838)	
Robinson, Simon C	3:53:47 (9,853)	
Robinson, Steven	3:49:44 (8,808)	
Robinson, Thomas H	4:07:51 (13,570)	
Robinson, Tom D	5:29:35 (29,493)	
Robinson, Tommy M	5:14:14 (27,803)	
Robinson, Tristan O	4:46:20 (23,086)	
Robinson, Victor P	3:29:16 (4,667)	
Robles, Emanuel	3:08:26 (1,902)	
Robotham, David W	3:59:10 (11,563)	
Robshaw, Craig L	2:52:40 (659)	
Robson, Alan	3:15:28 (2,717)	
Robson, Andrew J	5:47:17 (30,892)	
Robson, Angus	4:12:12 (14,625)	
Robson, Darrell M	7:42:00 (33,147)	
Robson, Darren P	5:55:34 (31,332)	
Robson, Fred T	4:46:54 (23,195)	
Robson, John M	4:09:04 (13,874)	
Robson, Jon D	4:59:14 (25,738)	
Robson, Mark	4:15:21 (15,432)	
Robson, Mark N	4:44:46 (22,724)	
Robson, Nicholas P	4:59:15 (25,740)	
Robson, Philip J	2:44:00 (312)	
Robson, Rob J	4:05:41 (13,074)	
Robson, Simon P	4:29:23 (19,143)	
Robson, Timothy M	4:40:00 (21,674)	
Roby, John A	5:45:09 (30,727)	
Roca, Vincent	3:51:39 (9,255)	
Rocco, Guillermo F	3:30:07 (4,849)	
Roche, Anthony J	5:08:49 (27,120)	
Roche, Francis A	4:31:51 (19,760)	
Roche, Michael J	4:08:00 (13,615)	
Roche, Paul G	3:51:12 (9,147)	
Roche, Richard A	3:51:19 (9,178)	
Roche, Shaun P	5:05:56 (26,699)	
Rocher, Herve	5:01:59 (26,174)	
Rochford, Danny J	5:21:38 (28,677)	
Rochford, James A	4:24:20 (17,759)	
Rochussen, Gavin M	3:59:30 (11,672)	
Rocke, Alan	3:39:53 (6,602)	
Rockcliffe, Albert E	3:41:08 (6,835)	
Rockman, James M	5:18:20 (28,286)	
Rodacan, David T	5:05:50 (26,685)	
Roddis, Alan J	3:54:41 (10,109)	
Roderick, Kevin	4:01:35 (12,168)	
Rodford, Graham	4:54:02 (24,681)	
Rodgers, Stuart A	4:54:57 (24,880)	
Rodia, Antonio C	3:54:09 (9,962)	
Rodmell, Darren A	3:28:24 (4,495)	
Rodot, Christia	5:34:15 (29,909)	
Rodrigues, Antonio G	4:40:30 (21,777)	
Rodrigues, Bernardo G	4:28:28 (18,889)	
Rodrigues, Mervyn A	3:10:41 (2,130)	
Rodrigues, Stephen G	3:52:06 (9,385)	
Rodriguez, Daniel	5:28:58 (29,424)	
Rodriguez, Francisco	3:58:06 (11,185)	
Rodriguez Diez, Ramon	3:16:26 (2,813)	
Roe, David G	5:14:09 (27,791)	
Roe, Richard R	4:13:31 (14,960)	
Roebuck, Tony	3:27:58 (4,403)	
Roehm, Walter C	3:43:26 (7,338)	
Roff, James A	4:10:37 (14,236)	
Roffey, William J	4:16:09 (15,634)	
Rogan, Francis A	5:27:56 (29,319)	
Rogers, Bradley S	4:30:11 (19,345)	
Rogers, Brendan F	5:27:44 (29,297)	
Rogers, Brian C	5:57:56 (31,453)	
Rogers, Brian J	3:28:44 (4,561)	
Rogers, Christopher J	3:46:33 (8,021)	
Rogers, Colin K	4:52:51 (24,430)	
Rogers, George E	5:11:21 (27,434)	
Rogers, Geraint	3:53:17 (9,718)	
Rogers, Ian P	4:43:03 (22,335)	
Rogers, Jeremy	2:41:17 (233)	
Rogers, Kevin R	3:35:26 (5,738)	
Rogers, Lee	5:22:32 (28,774)	
Rogers, Lloyd M	5:22:58 (28,822)	
Rogers, Nigel M	3:30:21 (4,874)	
Rogers, Paul	4:24:58 (17,951)	
Rogers, Paul	5:22:32 (28,774)	
Rogers, Pete D	4:24:34 (17,830)	
Rogers, Peter J	3:33:21 (5,378)	
Rogers, Philip A	3:26:48 (4,208)	
Rogers, Philip J	4:16:47 (15,795)	
Rogers, Philip T	4:32:55 (19,982)	
Rogers, Simon P	7:10:37 (32,986)	
Rogers, Steve	4:13:00 (14,842)	
Rogers, Timothy M	6:25:08 (32,354)	
Rogerson, Adam R	4:30:15 (19,367)	
Rogerson, Andrew	3:42:37 (7,137)	
Rogerson, Paul	3:51:24 (9,200)	
Rohleder, Michael D	3:35:22 (5,729)	
Rohrlach, Greg	4:49:01 (23,654)	
Roi, Mike	4:52:18 (24,307)	
Rojas, Javier	3:41:15 (6,863)	
Rokenson, Gary J	4:49:39 (23,782)	
Roleston, John P	3:56:44 (10,763)	
Rolfe, Alan T	4:21:26 (16,965)	
Rolfe, James	3:24:43 (3,900)	
Rolfe, Les	3:25:38 (4,023)	
Rolfe, Michael	5:49:11 (31,016)	
Rolfe, Michael A	3:24:33 (3,874)	
Rolig, Torsten	3:54:38 (10,086)	
Roling, David P	4:25:29 (18,114)	
Rollaston, Lee J	3:47:02 (8,127)	
Rollings, Adam M	5:04:23 (26,508)	
Rollings, Matt J	4:12:56 (14,820)	
Rollinson, Jason	4:56:33 (25,216)	
Rolls, Terence F	4:47:36 (23,342)	
Romagny, Jean-Christophe	2:57:35 (992)	
Romamini, Giovanni	3:13:22 (2,447)	
Romani, Sergio R	4:43:35 (22,462)	
Romero, Antonio	2:57:33 (990)	
Romprey, David A	5:49:00 (31,000)	
Ronayne, Ian M	2:58:08 (1,034)	
Ronchi, Bernard P	4:00:48 (11,993)	
Ronnan, Andrew	4:52:39 (24,393)	
Rono, Edwin K	5:16:05 (28,012)	
Rook, John	3:58:12 (11,233)	
Rook, Spencer J	2:56:36 (903)	
Rooney, Christopher P	4:13:17 (14,914)	
Rooney, Michael J	3:52:09 (9,398)	
Rooney, Peter	4:26:55 (18,487)	
Rooney, Philip	6:04:20 (31,735)	
Rooney, Ryan A	4:30:44 (19,480)	
Rooney, Tom	4:19:28 (16,469)	
Root, Richard J	4:07:39 (13,519)	
Rop, Rogers	2:07:34 (6)	
Rope, Kevin P	4:51:59 (24,249)	
Roper, Chris B	3:47:33 (8,249)	
Roper, Ian R	3:57:04 (10,865)	
Roper, Luke J	3:40:30 (6,713)	
Roper, Martin J	4:38:42 (21,371)	
Rosa, Domenico	3:36:13 (5,880)	
Rosak, Anthony R	2:47:32 (440)	
Rosario, José F	4:17:45 (16,046)	
Rosbrook, Simon J	3:55:02 (10,217)	
Rose, Andrew	3:26:43 (4,193)	
Rose, Andrew M	3:27:46 (4,373)	
Rose, Andrew M	4:35:24 (20,579)	
Rose, Anthony G	3:35:47 (5,796)	
Rose, Benjamin J	4:39:35 (21,571)	
Rose, Charlie T	4:22:56 (17,350)	
Rose, David	4:01:37 (12,178)	
Rose, David A	3:38:09 (6,256)	
Rose, Gary	3:42:52 (7,196)	
Rose, Gary D	5:04:00 (26,457)	
Rose, Harvey D	2:43:56 (308)	
Rose, Ian	5:22:10 (28,735)	
Rose, Martin D	3:44:00 (7,456)	
Rose, Michael E	4:09:35 (14,011)	
Rose, Nicholas J	3:43:08 (7,269)	
Rose, Paul	2:47:56 (451)	
Rose, Simon P	3:58:24 (11,306)	
Rose, Stuart K	4:11:08 (14,370)	
Rosedale, Benjamin J	3:12:12 (2,306)	
Rosell, Martin J	3:36:51 (6,008)	
Rosellini, Aldo	4:14:40 (15,249)	
Rosen, Simon N	4:06:43 (13,278)	
Rosendale, Craig	7:09:39 (32,974)	
Rosendale, Philip J	7:06:44 (32,951)	
Rosenfeld, David J	4:15:51 (15,564)	
Rosher, Paul M	3:45:22 (7,777)	
Rosie, John	4:18:17 (16,178)	
Rosie, William	4:13:59 (15,063)	
Ross, Cameron R	3:15:47 (2,751)	
Ross, Charles W	4:09:20 (13,940)	

Ross, Christopher J 3:25:12 (3,960)
Ross, David M 3:20:18 (3,312)
Ross, Duncan J 4:54:56 (24,875)
Ross, Garry S 4:15:12 (15,387)
Ross, Iain D 5:21:09 (28,623)
Ross, Ian D 3:17:43 (2,969)
Ross, Jamie A 4:46:53 (23,192)
Ross, Jonathan W 5:25:13 (29,062)
Ross, Keiron C 3:11:52 (2,254)
Ross, Kenneth J 5:14:00 (27,760)
Ross, Nick M 4:42:30 (22,217)
Ross, Oliver 4:11:52 (14,542)
Ross, Simon 3:31:47 (5,115)
Ross, Simon J 3:15:49 (2,755)
Rosser, David A 3:37:05 (6,053)
Rosser, David R 4:40:48 (21,855)
Rossi, Alessandro 3:51:41 (9,269)
Rossi, Giusepee 7:07:23 (32,956)
Rossi, Paolo 4:43:37 (22,471)
Rossi, Stefano 3:29:37 (4,746)
Rossiter, Philippe R 4:55:50 (25,061)
Ross-Jones, John 5:15:10 (27,921)
Rossmann, Bernd 3:52:49 (9,572)
Ross-McNairn, Jonathon E 3:48:33 (8,512)
Rossouw, François J 4:27:20 (18,590)
Rostant, Joseph A 5:47:34 (30,922)
Rostern, Paul 3:11:28 (2,211)
Rotat, Michel 5:37:38 (30,176)
Roth, Alexander 3:13:36 (2,476)
Rothera, David J 4:38:46 (21,385)
Rothermundt, Cyrill M 4:04:23 (12,793)
Rothwell, Alan 3:52:12 (9,410)
Rothwell, Colin 3:10:54 (2,148)
Rothwell, Duncan A 4:37:59 (21,216)
Rothwell, Simon J 3:20:24 (3,326)
Rottenberg, Jacques 5:24:05 (28,953)
Rottenbert, Philippe 5:17:15 (28,158)
Rouault, Louis 3:52:26 (9,481)
Roudeau, Bernard 3:24:14 (3,831)
Rouet, Philippe 3:46:28 (8,004)
Rouffa, Urbain A 3:56:30 (10,685)
Rough, Christopher J 3:53:14 (9,703)
Roulleau, Christian 3:52:49 (9,572)
Roulleau, Guy 4:49:53 (23,817)
Roulston, Barrie W 4:03:38 (12,637)
Rounce, Neil J 4:32:20 (19,869)
Rounce, Phil 4:42:53 (22,301)
Round, John D 5:30:16 (29,569)
Round, Stephen J 3:25:47 (4,042)
Rourke, Simon M 3:20:43 (3,366)
Rourke, Thomas E 4:20:09 (16,644)
Rouse, Aaron F 5:18:58 (28,368)
Rouse, David 4:44:55 (22,763)
Rouse, James 4:01:35 (12,168)
Rousham, David B 5:39:10 (30,297)
Roussel, Felix 3:03:47 (1,500)
Rousselle, Bernard 5:15:57 (27,995)
Routledge, John F 3:05:01 (1,576)
Routley, Luke J 3:37:16 (6,086)
Rouzic, Michel 3:57:18 (10,949)
Rowan, John S 3:57:19 (10,953)
Rowberry, William M 4:31:47 (19,743)
Rowden, David J 3:05:31 (1,624)
Rowe, Adam 4:20:22 (16,700)
Rowe, Alex R 2:46:16 (394)
Rowe, Christopher 3:40:45 (6,752)
Rowe, Daniel R 3:55:12 (10,282)
Rowe, Mark 4:55:20 (24,969)
Rowe, Michael C 4:31:48 (19,748)
Rowe, Paul R 4:27:20 (18,590)
Rowe, Philip 4:05:55 (13,125)
Rowell, Barry M 4:03:21 (12,565)
Rowell, Jason L 4:01:35 (12,168)
Rowell, Maxwell T 3:39:26 (6,529)
Rowell, Richard 3:58:43 (11,405)
Roweth, Stephen M 3:55:59 (10,537)
Rowland, Andrew R 2:48:07 (456)
Rowland, Colin M 5:08:05 (27,021)
Rowland, David R 4:36:21 (20,816)
Rowland, Ian 2:56:28 (894)
Rowland, Jonathan 4:28:19 (18,847)
Rowland, Lawrence E 4:39:12 (21,490)
Rowland, Michael J 5:35:29 (30,011)
Rowland, Robert A 2:58:49 (1,117)
Rowlands, Anthony F 3:44:34 (7,585)
Rowlands, Iain S 4:07:13 (13,406)
Rowlands, John E 4:16:41 (15,777)
Rowlands, Marc N 3:50:53 (9,072)
Rowlands, Nicholas K 4:58:25 (25,589)
Rowlands, Peter 4:21:21 (16,947)
Rowley, Andrew J 3:58:29 (11,333)
Rowley, Chris R 4:06:52 (13,316)
Rowley, Grant P 3:41:34 (6,933)
Rowley, John 3:30:37 (4,918)
Rowntree, Timothy N 4:07:33 (13,486)
Rowton-Lee, Nick D 4:57:03 (25,324)
Roy, Andrew R 3:52:09 (9,398)
Roy, Steve M 4:46:11 (23,047)
Royce, Andrew D 3:32:26 (5,240)
Royle, Dean A 4:57:57 (25,487)
Rozemeijer, Kees 4:03:01 (12,481)
Ruane, Woody 4:35:46 (20,666)
Rubel, Simon 4:14:09 (15,122)
Ruben, Alan S 2:42:01 (248)
Rubio, Juan 3:28:41 (4,549)
Rudall, David C 2:59:42 (1,220)
Rudd, Darran J 3:06:41 (1,726)
Rudd, Michael 5:32:05 (29,746)
Ruddick, Mike J 4:33:56 (20,231)
Ruddle, Paul D 3:03:11 (1,455)
Ruddock, Ian E 4:08:26 (13,728)
Ruddy, Patrick R 3:47:52 (8,347)
Ruddy, Simon 4:56:25 (25,191)
Rudge, Michael J 5:24:40 (29,002)
Rudge, Nicholas P 4:14:50 (15,292)
Rudge, Nick S 3:45:00 (7,689)
Rudisuli, Pius A 2:55:53 (843)
Rudkin, Karl 4:27:27 (18,609)
Rudnik, Maciej 3:13:33 (2,472)
Rudnik, Peter 3:57:42 (11,072)
Rudoni, Jeffrey J 3:43:56 (7,447)
Rudrum, Martyn Q 5:38:42 (30,266)
Rueda, Antonio 2:59:41 (1,218)
Rueda, Emmanuel 4:55:15 (24,949)
Ruelens, Blair S 3:59:17 (11,599)
Ruellan, Gregory I 4:12:27 (14,693)
Ruff, Elliot M 4:18:19 (16,190)
Ruff, Keith P 4:18:19 (16,190)
Ruff, Stephen C 6:40:09 (32,613)
Ruffell, Graham A 4:00:02 (11,828)
Ruffle, Steve 4:10:48 (14,277)
Ruffley, Stephen E 3:58:09 (11,209)
Rugg, Vincent C 4:22:53 (17,339)
Rugg-Easey, Paul J 4:58:58 (25,704)
Rughani, Indulal K 5:22:17 (28,751)
Rugman, Stanley J 5:06:43 (26,820)
Ruhland, Karl 3:32:48 (5,291)
Ruia, Alok 4:33:10 (20,051)
Ruia, Sunil 4:59:54 (25,870)
Ruiz, Bruno 3:42:48 (7,185)
Ruiz, Miguel 4:39:19 (21,521)
Ruiz, Salvador 4:40:04 (21,688)
Ruiz-Nieto, José M 3:17:01 (2,878)
Rumble, David J 4:52:41 (24,399)
Rumbles, Chris R 3:55:56 (10,519)
Rumsey, Steve 5:05:12 (26,611)
Rumson, Alexander G 3:11:50 (2,249)
Runacres, Mark J 3:29:02 (4,631)
Runacus, Alan 4:21:31 (16,977)
Runciman, Lee 3:56:54 (10,814)
Rundle, Christopher R 4:01:58 (12,255)
Runnacles, Stephen J 5:59:18 (31,526)
Rusbridge, Keith R 5:43:42 (30,621)
Rush, Kristopher A 3:36:45 (5,982)
Rush, Martin 4:33:00 (20,008)
Rush, Nick W 4:19:00 (16,354)
Rush, Tom 4:33:00 (20,008)
Rushbrooke, James W 3:37:53 (6,206)
Rushby, Ian J 4:02:20 (12,337)
Rushby, Philip J 3:56:55 (10,817)
Rushden, Max P 4:40:34 (21,804)
Rushmer, Gary 2:58:04 (1,028)
Rushmere, Philip J 4:34:33 (20,379)
Rushworth, Peter N 4:04:22 (12,790)
Russ, Brian N 3:57:22 (10,969)
Russ, Nicholas 4:30:34 (19,442)
Russell, Arthur J 3:52:10 (9,402)
Russell, Colin D 4:40:55 (21,875)
Russell, Damian J 4:12:20 (14,664)
Russell, Derek J 3:09:54 (2,055)
Russell, George 3:16:37 (2,830)
Russell, Ian J 4:48:55 (23,632)
Russell, James A 4:34:32 (20,371)
Russell, James E 4:51:26 (24,132)
Russell, John R 3:05:55 (1,656)
Russell, Jonathan C 4:07:20 (13,429)
Russell, Joseph G 4:24:03 (17,672)
Russell, Mark 5:00:11 (25,924)
Russell, Michael G 3:15:26 (2,713)
Russell, Michael J 3:38:30 (6,327)
Russell, Mike 4:37:41 (21,156)
Russell, Nigel D 3:01:05 (1,308)
Russell, Oliver M 5:45:58 (30,777)
Russell, Paul T 5:08:52 (27,129)
Russell, Phillip 3:26:11 (4,101)
Russell, Raymond J 3:55:04 (10,233)
Russell, Shaun G 4:04:20 (12,782)
Russell, Shaune D 3:14:43 (2,631)
Russell, Steve M 4:03:34 (12,617)
Russell, Steven C 4:26:01 (18,263)
Russell, Toby P 3:40:50 (6,765)
Russell, William E 4:24:13 (17,717)
Russell-Jones, James D 4:28:44 (18,956)
Russell-Smith, Robert D 4:07:47 (13,552)
Russo, Jean Marc T 3:18:01 (2,998)
Rust, Daniel 8:01:09 (33,177)
Rust, Matthew J 4:50:03 (23,850)
Rusterholz, Bruno 4:03:34 (12,617)
Ruth, Michael 4:15:16 (15,403)
Rutherford, Ian 3:47:27 (8,225)
Rutherford, Kevin 3:42:02 (7,030)
Rutherford, Neil 3:04:59 (1,573)
Rutherford, Paul A 3:14:13 (2,555)
Rutherford, Philip 4:20:08 (16,636)
Rutherford, Tristan R 4:18:42 (16,281)
Rutjes, Grame W 3:50:28 (8,972)
Rutkowski, Paul H 3:40:44 (6,749)
Rutland, Craig N 3:50:36 (9,003)
Rutledge, Alan C 3:06:44 (1,732)
Rutt, Carl J 3:55:23 (10,339)
Rutt, David J 5:13:48 (27,745)
Rutter, Alexander M 5:39:39 (30,334)
Rutter, Mark P 4:47:54 (23,407)
Rutter, Neil B 6:06:10 (31,792)
Rutter, Neil E 4:17:46 (16,052)
Rutto, Evans 2:09:35 (10)
Ryall, Samuel 2:50:01 (549)
Ryan, Andrew P 4:44:06 (22,583)
Ryan, Chris 3:42:23 (7,097)
Ryan, Garrett E 4:48:42 (23,583)
Ryan, Jon 4:44:27 (22,666)
Ryan, Julian M 4:35:12 (20,531)
Ryan, Lee 3:42:13 (7,069)
Ryan, Liam P 3:24:01 (3,796)
Ryan, Martin 5:32:44 (29,789)
Ryan, Matthew C 4:33:50 (20,209)
Ryan, Matthew J 3:38:28 (6,321)
Ryan, Michael 4:16:03 (15,609)
Ryan, Michael C 4:35:25 (20,583)
Ryan, Michael C 4:37:33 (21,125)
Ryan, Michael J 4:20:03 (16,613)
Ryan, Paul F 4:36:43 (20,901)
Ryan, Richrd J 4:32:37 (19,920)
Ryan, Sean 3:40:26 (6,698)
Ryan, Trevor J 5:45:06 (30,724)
Ryder, Clive S 3:16:54 (2,864)
Ryder, David A 3:23:54 (3,775)
Ryder, Jonathan M 4:21:52 (17,081)
Ryder, Tom A 5:53:27 (31,239)
Ryding, James K 5:13:47 (27,743)
Rydout, Damian E 4:01:53 (12,230)
Rye, Andrew E 3:11:21 (2,202)
Rye, Joseph M 2:43:56 (308)
Rye, Kim B 5:07:05 (26,874)
Ryles, David J 4:46:32 (23,129)
Ryznar, Joshua E 4:51:48 (24,210)
Sabberton, Ben A 3:57:02 (10,852)
Sabino, José F 3:28:41 (4,549)
Sachet, Philippe 3:23:37 (3,728)

Sachs, Victor M....4:00:26 (11,921)
Sacks, Brian Z....3:38:32 (6,334)
Saddington, William K....3:57:29 (11,008)
Sadler, Benjamin J....3:25:34 (4,014)
Sadler, David....5:20:56 (28,602)
Sadler, Dexter R....4:29:30 (19,179)
Sadler, Joel P....4:54:00 (24,677)
Sadler, Jon D....4:27:09 (18,542)
Sadler, Keith C....5:07:19 (26,907)
Sadler, Mark....3:25:12 (3,960)
Sagar, Nicholas J....4:43:49 (22,523)
Saggers, Martin S....3:37:40 (6,161)
Saggers, Stuart C....3:20:15 (3,305)
Saggs, Mark....4:31:30 (19,665)
Saha, Soumen S....5:36:04 (30,058)
Sahodree, Mike....4:47:35 (23,341)
Saigal, Kabir K....5:28:08 (29,342)
Saini, Ravinder....3:59:28 (11,662)
Saini, Sukhwinder....3:28:05 (4,420)
Saint, Alastair J....4:46:39 (23,147)
Saintpierre, Olivier....4:15:21 (15,432)
Sainty, Martin....4:10:39 (14,242)
Saito, Toshihiko....4:20:37 (16,766)
Saiz, Gabriel J....2:47:58 (454)
Saker, Andrew M....3:43:30 (7,351)
Salam, Abdul....3:58:22 (11,293)
Salathiel, Mark R....5:13:54 (27,753)
Saldutti, Robert L....4:43:35 (22,462)
Sale, Antonio....4:10:57 (14,315)
Saleem, Maz....4:35:28 (20,598)
Salemi, Francesco....4:54:13 (24,732)
Salimbene, Giorgio....3:58:18 (11,266)
Salinger, Mark F....4:18:28 (16,223)
Salisbury, James R....5:00:47 (26,006)
Salisbury, Paul M....4:24:46 (17,884)
Salisbury, Stuart B....5:00:47 (26,006)
Salkus, Peter A....4:36:46 (20,924)
Sallent, André....4:35:48 (20,673)
Sallnow, Andrew J....3:31:43 (5,106)
Salmon, Jonathan....3:47:10 (8,158)
Salmond, George....2:59:13 (1,166)
Salomons, Nico....3:39:36 (6,554)
Salt, Jeff B....4:23:37 (17,535)
Salt, Peter W....5:24:52 (29,023)
Salt, Phillip M....4:23:21 (17,454)
Salter, Alan C....3:41:45 (6,974)
Salter, Chris J....3:22:48 (3,635)
Salter, Edward B....3:31:50 (5,128)
Salter, John Paul S....3:40:32 (6,718)
Salter, Neil G....3:23:29 (3,710)
Saltmer, Nick P....4:58:03 (25,513)
Saltrick, Christopher J....3:47:43 (8,301)
Salzburg, Karsten....3:28:12 (4,441)
Sambhi, Sarwjit....3:59:27 (11,659)
Sambridge, Ron....5:23:20 (28,875)
Sammon, Paul....4:37:20 (21,066)
Sampath, Niels M....4:36:48 (20,937)
Sampietro, Giorgio....3:56:24 (10,656)
Sample, Timothy M....5:01:48 (26,147)
Sampson, James....3:13:37 (2,479)
Sampson, Ralph O....3:19:57 (3,259)
Sampson, Roger W....5:27:47 (29,302)
Sampson, Stephen P....4:44:10 (22,598)
Sams, Ronald A....5:27:35 (29,283)
Samson, James R....3:37:08 (6,062)
Samson, Paul A....5:06:13 (26,740)
Samsudin, Azi....5:35:33 (30,018)
Samuel, Edward R....3:40:00 (6,626)
Samuel, James W....4:10:29 (14,212)
Samuel, Timothy J....3:43:39 (7,380)
Samuels, Adam E....4:23:58 (17,644)
Samuels, David L....5:23:56 (28,932)
Samuels, Simon E....4:09:54 (14,084)
Samways, Paul....4:53:01 (24,459)
Sanahuja, José L....5:38:43 (30,268)
Sanchez, André....4:15:27 (15,466)
Sanchez-Vidal, Roberto....4:04:45 (12,868)
Sandall, Michael....4:52:04 (24,260)
Sandeluss, Asher T....4:34:35 (20,383)
Sandercock, Mark....4:37:36 (21,137)
Sandercombe, Robert S....3:45:58 (7,899)
Sanders, Andrew L....5:03:50 (26,431)
Sanders, Dale P....4:33:42 (20,188)
Sanders, Gary A....4:40:37 (21,814)
Sanders, Paul R....3:54:39 (10,091)
Sanders, Shane C....3:52:14 (9,422)
Sanders, Simon A....4:12:02 (14,580)
Sanderson, Andrew R....4:06:07 (13,163)
Sanderson, Brian J....3:24:03 (3,800)
Sanderson, David J....5:15:08 (27,915)
Sanderson, Gordon N....4:25:33 (18,126)
Sanderson, Nicholas M....3:41:48 (6,988)
Sanderson, William F....3:45:43 (7,854)
Sandford, Alan J....3:59:17 (11,599)
Sandford, Jeremy W....4:35:57 (20,709)
Sandford-Hart, John....6:50:31 (32,767)
Sandham, Richard W....4:49:11 (23,686)
Sandhu, Dilbag S....4:58:04 (25,520)
Sandhu, Ranjeet S....4:10:28 (14,206)
Sandhu, Satwant S....5:39:01 (30,282)
Sandilands, William....3:56:31 (10,691)
Sandland, Daniel P....4:15:04 (15,355)
Sandri, Giuseppe....4:54:01 (24,679)
Sands, Jonathon P....6:20:22 (32,240)
Sandstad, Henrik....2:16:48 (19)
Sandy, Daniel....5:22:34 (28,778)
Sandys, Rowland G....4:09:51 (14,069)
Sanger, Philip B....2:36:25 (134)
Sangha, Charanjit....4:23:08 (17,393)
Sangha, Jas....4:23:09 (17,397)
Sanghera, Davindera S....6:46:50 (32,721)
Sanham, Robert A....3:42:40 (7,150)
Sanmartin Losada, Roberto....3:39:22 (6,512)
Sano, Naoshige....5:24:05 (28,953)
Sansom, Chris J....3:34:49 (5,628)
Sansom, Derek J....4:10:23 (14,192)
Santambrogio, Luca....3:31:07 (5,010)
Santi, Massimo....4:14:18 (15,163)
Santi Laurini, Gabriele....3:46:17 (7,963)
Santinato, Fabio....3:57:26 (10,989)
Santos, Antonio R....4:00:58 (12,040)
Santos, José E....4:12:49 (14,779)
Saouli, Mood....4:34:00 (20,245)
Saperia, Matthew S....4:07:46 (13,547)
Sappor, Henry....4:11:00 (14,329)
Sapwell, Andrew K....3:31:44 (5,109)
Saracino, Vincenzo....3:33:21 (5,378)
Saraiva, Arthur S....4:28:26 (18,879)
Sardone, Angelo....3:30:49 (4,946)
Sareen, Ellis W....4:30:36 (19,454)
Saretta, Giorgio....4:58:31 (25,614)
Sargeant, Jonathan D....3:10:18 (2,099)
Sargent, Lee....5:16:50 (28,107)
Sargent, Peter....4:40:36 (21,810)
Sargisson, Christopher H....4:58:29 (25,602)
Sarkar, Mustafa G....4:53:01 (24,459)
Sarno, Raffaele....3:15:23 (2,705)
Sarson, Peter....4:28:34 (18,917)
Sartain, John R....4:25:29 (18,114)
Sarthou, Philippe A....3:33:10 (5,347)
Sartorello, Ivan....4:57:07 (25,338)
Sarveswaran, Paul C....3:59:30 (11,672)
Saucedo Vargas, Roberto....4:25:18 (18,054)
Saude, Sergio S....4:25:24 (18,090)
Saudners, Matthew....4:23:30 (17,505)
Sauer, Ulrich....3:40:59 (6,799)
Saunder, Ben....2:55:18 (802)
Saunders, David A....4:25:01 (17,969)
Saunders, Gary....3:32:46 (5,287)
Saunders, Gavin....4:09:35 (14,011)
Saunders, Ian N....4:12:20 (14,664)
Saunders, Jamie....4:56:51 (25,270)
Saunders, Kier P....3:51:08 (9,131)
Saunders, Malcolm J....4:25:49 (18,199)
Saunders, Marc P....5:20:17 (28,533)
Saunders, Mark....6:34:53 (32,527)
Saunders, Richard....3:15:56 (2,772)
Saunders, Robert....5:23:19 (28,873)
Saunders, Rowan G....3:16:45 (2,847)
Saunders, Timothy G....4:12:39 (14,740)
Saunderson, Eric M....4:42:25 (22,203)
Saunderson, Mark....3:19:11 (3,156)
Savage, Andrew R....4:22:10 (17,162)
Savage, Bryn J....4:38:09 (21,273)
Savage, James....2:52:06 (642)
Savage, James....3:28:48 (4,573)
Savage, James E....4:24:28 (17,792)
Savage, James G....4:34:36 (20,390)
Savage, James R....4:36:09 (20,768)
Savage, Jeff M....4:43:34 (22,458)
Savage, Michael....4:01:57 (12,249)
Savage, Philip B....4:31:31 (19,668)
Savage, Richard A....3:53:30 (9,766)
Savage, Robin J....3:55:57 (10,527)
Savignac, Gerard....3:45:17 (7,751)
Savimaki, Ilkka M....4:12:49 (14,779)
Savin, Guy P....5:08:33 (27,084)
Savjani, Kalpesh....5:01:20 (26,091)
Savoia, Luigi....5:30:15 (29,566)
Saw, Martin S....3:36:01 (5,837)
Sawbridge, Mark T....4:16:35 (15,747)
Sawdon, Paul....4:52:45 (24,409)
Sawer, Martin....3:15:31 (2,722)
Sawers, Iain A....3:57:05 (10,870)
Sawers, Kevin J....7:10:20 (32,984)
Sawford, Steven....3:58:29 (11,333)
Sawko, Peter W....3:57:09 (10,902)
Sawyer, Andrew J....4:16:16 (15,660)
Sawyer, Duncan M....4:05:04 (12,933)
Saxby, Jeff A....3:58:53 (11,473)
Saxton, Jeremy....5:14:25 (27,832)
Sayburn, Robert P....4:19:37 (16,505)
Sayburn, Ronan J....4:11:02 (14,339)
Sayer, Gabriel L....3:22:05 (3,543)
Sayer, Mark K....3:26:19 (4,119)
Sayer, Timothy M....5:18:54 (28,358)
Sayers, Greg....4:33:06 (20,030)
Sayers, Matthew T....3:42:52 (7,196)
Sayers, Steve....3:17:41 (2,962)
Saywell, Stephen H....5:23:20 (28,875)
Scaglione, Antonio....6:00:21 (31,577)
Scaife, Nick F....4:53:29 (24,562)
Scales, Kevin S....4:17:45 (16,046)
Scalia, Antonio....4:57:36 (25,417)
Scamans, Oliver M....4:28:18 (18,842)
Scammell, Steve J....4:18:42 (16,281)
Scanlan, Chris R....5:34:16 (29,911)
Scanlon, John....3:56:16 (10,618)
Scanlon, Sean T....4:19:57 (16,589)
Scapolo, Fabio....3:35:41 (5,783)
Scapolo, Gianpaolo....4:46:03 (23,016)
Scarbrough, Matthew J....5:17:53 (28,232)
Scarlett, Dominic....5:30:30 (29,593)
Schabram, Stuart A....3:50:37 (9,009)
Schafer, Wolfgang....3:32:02 (5,168)
Schaller, Hermann....3:33:23 (5,386)
Schapira, Paul S....3:49:23 (8,715)
Scheidegger, Karl....3:35:05 (5,690)
Scheinkonig, Joseph....4:13:00 (14,842)
Scheuermann, Ralph....3:51:50 (9,313)
Schewitz, Kelvan....4:07:26 (13,453)
Schieler, Klas....3:30:34 (4,907)
Schiffer, Hans-Wilhelm....4:03:18 (12,552)
Schiffer, Karl....3:35:42 (5,786)
Schilling, Thomas....4:11:23 (14,434)
Schimmel, Martin....4:36:15 (20,799)
Schindler, Jo....3:14:21 (2,575)
Schirmeisen, Tim G....4:57:58 (25,498)
Schlender, Marten....3:21:05 (3,409)
Schmidt, Enrico....3:42:03 (7,036)
Schmidt-Soltau, Nils S....5:25:24 (29,078)
Schmidt-Soltau, Peer....4:01:59 (12,264)
Schmitz, Dirk....3:58:25 (11,317)
Schmitz, Marcus....3:56:55 (10,817)
Schneider, Michael....3:41:21 (6,887)
Schneider, Michael F....3:34:01 (5,486)
Schoenbuehler, Werner....4:15:16 (15,403)
Schoenmann, Hermann....4:37:06 (21,002)
Schofield, Alan....3:52:58 (9,617)
Schofield, Dominic....4:57:43 (25,436)
Schofield, Mark P....4:14:22 (15,175)
Schofield, Paul N....4:18:20 (16,193)
Schofield, Peter....3:54:56 (10,187)
Scholefield, Philip O....4:29:13 (19,088)
Schooling, Robert J....3:19:10 (3,152)
Schoppe, Rainer....4:11:05 (14,354)
Schormann, Mark....3:41:14 (6,858)
Schrantz, Olivier....5:25:34 (29,088)
Schrenk, Georg....4:00:14 (11,874)

Name	Time	(Position)
Schroll, Guenther	4:34:31	(20,365)
Schubert, Dave J	3:02:55	(1,435)
Schuener, Pierre	4:42:03	(22,123)
Schull, Ottmar	4:02:05	(12,280)
Schultes, Olaf	3:36:06	(5,855)
Schulz, Christian	3:52:33	(9,506)
Schulz, Roman J	3:49:24	(8,718)
Schulze, Karl J	4:02:26	(12,361)
Schumann, Jason	3:31:43	(5,106)
Schumann, Matthew A	3:58:35	(11,368)
Schumann, Paul	2:53:03	(681)
Schuster, Ralf	4:37:19	(21,061)
Schutte, Andrew C	3:54:47	(10,138)
Schwartz, Steven J	4:00:48	(11,993)
Schwarz, Stefan	3:11:59	(2,274)
Schweinberger, Bernhard	4:22:59	(17,363)
Schwendenmann, Claude	3:59:54	(11,786)
Schwinger, Gerd	4:00:23	(11,910)
Sciancalepore, Alberto	3:29:34	(4,736)
Sciardo, Antonio	3:15:23	(2,705)
Sciusco, Francesco	3:30:02	(4,830)
Scobie, Stephen B	4:03:57	(12,704)
Scoffham, Alastair W	4:01:21	(12,122)
Scoffings, Peter J	3:52:55	(9,597)
Scofield, Michael J	4:28:15	(18,829)
Scollin, Nigel R	3:59:03	(11,526)
Scorthorne, Richard J	4:44:49	(22,736)
Scott, Alistair	3:57:05	(10,870)
Scott, Andrew	3:38:04	(6,242)
Scott, Andrew D	3:44:27	(7,553)
Scott, Brough	4:18:44	(16,290)
Scott, Chris	4:34:25	(20,347)
Scott, Chris R	3:54:46	(10,128)
Scott, Craig	4:50:57	(24,037)
Scott, Daniel	4:03:20	(12,559)
Scott, Danny A	3:00:12	(1,247)
Scott, David A	4:34:54	(20,463)
Scott, David C	4:36:11	(20,774)
Scott, Derek G	4:37:34	(21,131)
Scott, Douglas F	3:32:48	(5,291)
Scott, Gareth	4:32:03	(19,801)
Scott, George	3:20:33	(3,341)
Scott, Iain H	4:24:29	(17,797)
Scott, Ian T	4:00:47	(11,989)
Scott, Ian V	5:05:48	(26,676)
Scott, James A	2:59:37	(1,212)
Scott, Jason	5:12:20	(27,566)
Scott, Jon M	5:03:48	(26,429)
Scott, Jordan	4:41:53	(22,081)
Scott, Kevin	3:51:09	(9,135)
Scott, Kieran A	4:18:02	(16,114)
Scott, Matthew J	9:23:14	(33,218)
Scott, Michael A	3:47:38	(8,279)
Scott, Michael J	6:50:07	(32,763)
Scott, Neil	4:26:42	(18,430)
Scott, Nicholas G	2:59:10	(1,157)
Scott, Paul	3:56:04	(10,558)
Scott, Petr	3:37:37	(6,155)
Scott, Philip I	3:32:42	(5,279)
Scott, Robert A	4:44:27	(22,666)
Scott, Robert J	3:48:21	(8,465)
Scott, Robin H	3:05:41	(1,633)
Scott, Russell A	4:12:57	(14,824)
Scott, Simon A	3:57:51	(11,124)
Scott, Steve A	4:09:25	(13,969)
Scott, Stewart D	4:36:14	(20,791)
Scott, Stuart D	5:09:32	(27,210)
Scott, Terence	3:57:10	(10,911)
Scott, Thomas C	4:00:30	(11,934)
Scott, Timothy J	5:12:33	(27,594)
Scott, Tom	3:51:01	(9,102)
Scott, William A	4:07:41	(13,528)
Scott-Bell, Gareth S	5:05:53	(26,693)
Scott-Buccleuch, James	3:26:29	(4,149)
Scott-Douglas, Christopher	4:04:27	(12,804)
Scott-Ellis, Tim	3:59:45	(11,747)
Scott-Priestley, Simon C	5:19:23	(28,421)
Scott-Richardson, Paul M	4:25:17	(18,051)
Scoular, Oliver W	3:13:17	(2,430)
Scourfield, John D	3:58:15	(11,249)
Scowcroft, Andrew K	3:09:37	(2,027)
Scranage, David	4:19:27	(16,466)
Scrase, Philip W	4:39:41	(21,596)
Scriven, Christopher B	3:32:10	(5,193)
Scrivener, Aaron	4:59:41	(25,831)
Scrivener, Chris	2:59:18	(1,176)
Scrivener, Russell J	4:52:54	(24,437)
Scruton, Neil	3:06:05	(1,675)
Scullion, David W	4:29:53	(19,264)
Scully, Stephen J	4:51:24	(24,121)
Scutchings, Glen D	5:06:53	(26,844)
Scutt, Oliver G	3:28:48	(4,573)
Scyner, Mark A	3:50:03	(8,874)
Seaberg, Alan	3:57:58	(11,152)
Seabourne, Ben	4:04:54	(12,897)
Seach, Michael	5:14:27	(27,835)
Seager, Daniel D	4:27:39	(18,671)
Seager, Neil J	4:45:53	(22,985)
Seakens, Clive M	5:27:33	(29,279)
Seal, Donald S	4:20:52	(16,827)
Seal, Julian D	4:22:44	(17,307)
Sealey, Robert M	6:53:37	(32,805)
Seaman, Kelvin P	5:02:12	(26,201)
Seaman, Paul H	4:47:11	(23,255)
Seamark, Jamie R	2:54:55	(785)
Sear, Richard A	4:06:34	(13,243)
Searle, Adrian E	4:14:07	(15,108)
Searle, Daivd A	3:45:42	(7,851)
Searle, Martin D	3:39:14	(6,486)
Searle, Stephen P	4:23:37	(17,535)
Searle, Wayne R	4:16:21	(15,681)
Sears, John	4:09:32	(14,000)
Sears, Tony S	4:52:41	(24,399)
Seaton, Mark I	5:24:43	(29,008)
Seaton, Steven A	4:46:51	(23,185)
Seatter, Marc C	3:38:11	(6,264)
Seaward, Nigel P	4:49:52	(23,815)
Sebba, Adam L	3:55:52	(10,496)
Sebille, Pierre	2:55:32	(819)
Seddon, Dwaine P	5:05:04	(26,591)
Seddon, Jeff	3:08:55	(1,948)
Seddon, Ronald J	5:46:16	(30,808)
Sedge, Martyn J	2:57:08	(955)
Sedgwick, Glenn C	4:45:44	(22,952)
Sedgwick, Stephan	4:34:19	(20,310)
Sedgwick, Stephen J	3:56:32	(10,694)
Seehafer, Holger	3:07:41	(1,823)
Seelandt, Frank	3:27:21	(4,303)
Seeley, Graham J	4:08:28	(13,735)
Sefton, Paul S	3:21:45	(3,506)
Segal, Eliezer S	4:28:36	(18,922)
Segall, Philip G	3:47:34	(8,259)
Segen, Joseph C	5:33:34	(29,857)
Segreto, Filippo	3:40:38	(6,737)
Sehnke, Peter	3:26:32	(4,162)
Seidel, Darren S	4:44:57	(22,770)
Seifert, Christiau	3:31:36	(5,087)
Sekeram, Mohan S	4:42:20	(22,185)
Sekiguchi, Mashahi	3:50:04	(8,878)
Sekito, Ryoji	3:53:16	(9,713)
Sel, Trond D	5:29:48	(29,523)
Selby, Adam L	4:35:19	(20,559)
Selby, Martin	4:45:59	(23,001)
Selby, Paul	4:45:59	(23,001)
Selby, Robin C	3:54:56	(10,187)
Seldon, Keith	4:28:20	(18,854)
Selfe, Christopher P	4:18:23	(16,204)
Sell, Alexander D	3:35:39	(5,775)
Sell, David J	4:41:56	(22,095)
Sellars, John G	4:01:06	(12,072)
Selley, Andrew M	5:07:15	(26,898)
Sels, Carl	4:05:56	(13,129)
Selvan, Jonathan	3:43:26	(7,338)
Selves, Stephen J	4:25:57	(18,244)
Selwood, David J	3:45:12	(7,730)
Semmence, Philip J	4:08:59	(13,856)
Semmo, Nasser	3:03:42	(1,493)
Sena, Richard A	3:25:53	(4,058)
Senaldi, Giorgio	4:10:34	(14,226)
Senard, Christophe	3:24:16	(3,835)
Sencier, David	3:47:33	(8,249)
Senelier, Didier	3:57:09	(10,902)
Senior, Richard P	5:59:06	(31,508)
Senior, Stephen P	3:19:37	(3,202)
Senior, Timothy J	3:40:31	(6,715)
Sensier, James J	3:39:19	(6,503)
Sequeira, Edgar	3:24:38	(3,886)
Sercombe, Andrew G	3:50:18	(8,933)
Sercombe, Stephen J	3:47:07	(8,149)
Sergeant, Jonathan C	4:04:22	(12,790)
Sergeant, Robert W	4:25:29	(18,114)
Sermon, Gavin	4:12:29	(14,699)
Serra, Jorge	2:59:21	(1,182)
Seth, Steve	4:30:14	(19,364)
Sette, Antonio	3:11:46	(2,244)
Setterfield, Aaron D	4:38:08	(21,268)
Severeide, Hans Petter	4:10:49	(14,282)
Severeide Hopsoal, Leif Einar	5:29:32	(29,489)
Severn, David	5:10:31	(27,341)
Seviour, Justin	4:15:28	(15,469)
Sewell, Andrew P	3:01:56	(1,368)
Sewell, Ben	4:12:08	(14,608)
Sewell, Colin P	3:26:14	(4,108)
Sewell, David J	4:16:40	(15,773)
Sexton, Carl S	4:46:06	(23,027)
Sexton, Christopher P	3:28:42	(4,556)
Sexton, David H	3:07:57	(1,852)
Sexton, Robert P	4:29:26	(19,153)
Sextone, John E	6:00:03	(31,568)
Seymour, David A	2:58:55	(1,131)
Seymour, David J	4:24:23	(17,772)
Seymour, Jack A	3:36:51	(6,008)
Seymour, John F	5:14:34	(27,851)
Seymour, Julian J	3:51:17	(9,168)
Seymour, Mark	4:26:51	(18,475)
Seymour, Oliver	3:52:12	(9,410)
Seymour, Thomas J	4:16:55	(15,839)
Seymour, Tim D	4:18:05	(16,137)
Seys, Paul	4:00:37	(11,953)
Sgalbiero, Orazio	4:16:26	(15,704)
Shacklady, Bryan R	3:47:05	(8,142)
Shackleton, Richard P	3:24:31	(3,869)
Shafier, Lawrence E	3:10:15	(2,089)
Shah, Dharmesh	4:36:36	(20,868)
Shah, Kaushik	4:12:15	(14,640)
Shah, Minesh	4:23:12	(17,414)
Shah, Minesh	4:27:51	(18,708)
Shah, Nishan	3:54:20	(10,011)
Shah, Panash	6:20:11	(32,236)
Shah, Priyen	4:15:48	(15,544)
Shah, Romal	3:26:29	(4,149)
Shaikly, Darin	3:33:00	(5,322)
Shale, John	4:37:21	(21,072)
Shallis, Paul C	5:29:59	(29,545)
Shanahan, Andy D	3:41:15	(6,863)
Shanahan, Edward J	4:21:20	(16,941)
Shanahan, Gregory K	5:13:08	(27,669)
Shanahan, Leon P	5:44:01	(30,642)
Shand, Alan J	4:12:30	(14,707)
Shand, Iain C	4:13:04	(14,862)
Shand, Michael	5:28:21	(29,364)
Shandley, Adrian P	4:07:27	(13,457)
Shanks, Andrew J	4:17:34	(16,003)
Shanks, Dan	3:41:19	(6,876)
Shanks, Mark	6:27:31	(32,411)
Shannon, Andrew	4:05:44	(13,082)
Shapland, Mark	4:21:52	(17,081)
Shapland, Martin J	2:48:56	(494)
Shardlow, Richard J	5:43:25	(30,606)
Sharghy, Shahram	4:48:36	(23,569)
Sharif, Basharat A	4:35:50	(20,680)
Sharkett, Spencer	4:39:42	(21,599)
Sharkey, Gary H	3:29:22	(4,692)
Sharkey, Jonathan D	2:49:01	(498)
Sharland, Paul R	4:19:48	(16,552)
Sharland, Richard J	3:11:20	(2,201)
Sharma, Kishore K	3:47:27	(8,225)
Sharma, Sanjai	2:57:58	(1,022)
Sharma, Sanjeeve	4:08:23	(13,712)
Sharma, Sunil	3:42:38	(7,138)
Sharma, Sunil D	4:25:59	(18,253)
Sharman, Ben	4:03:24	(12,579)
Sharman, Mark A	4:53:23	(24,544)
Sharp, Benjamin J	5:23:43	(28,911)
Sharp, Christopher	5:02:37	(26,265)
Sharp, Jeremy F	3:21:26	(3,459)
Sharp, Nick	3:39:08	(6,462)
Sharp, Richard	4:25:46	(18,184)
Sharp, Steve M	4:16:18	(15,668)

Sharp, Stuart G....4:19:13 (16,393)
Sharp, Warren J....4:59:30 (25,786)
Sharp, William....5:21:10 (28,625)
Sharpe, Anthony C....4:28:04 (18,767)
Sharpe, Christopher A....4:22:35 (17,260)
Sharpe, Damien R....4:51:27 (24,140)
Sharpe, David W....5:14:38 (27,860)
Sharpe, Fraser T....3:42:35 (7,132)
Sharpe, Ian D....4:47:03 (23,222)
Sharpe, Ian D....6:18:21 (32,178)
Sharpe, Martyn G....4:24:23 (17,772)
Sharpe, Michael A....3:54:09 (9,962)
Sharpe, Richard P....4:23:06 (17,387)
Sharples, Stephen....4:36:31 (20,849)
Sharpley, David R....5:51:33 (31,159)
Sharpley, Robert D....4:19:40 (16,522)
Shattock, Edward F....3:42:03 (7,036)
Shaw, Adam J....4:30:12 (19,350)
Shaw, Alec E....3:23:18 (3,685)
Shaw, Andrew D....5:31:52 (29,730)
Shaw, Anthony T....4:25:02 (17,972)
Shaw, Colin E....4:31:16 (19,602)
Shaw, David I....3:54:45 (10,124)
Shaw, David J....5:01:40 (26,131)
Shaw, Gary L....4:58:10 (25,540)
Shaw, Geoff....3:41:08 (6,835)
Shaw, Gerry A....3:03:52 (1,505)
Shaw, Ian....5:59:22 (31,532)
Shaw, Jeremy D....4:23:56 (17,633)
Shaw, Jonathan P....4:03:25 (12,582)
Shaw, Julian Q....3:25:06 (3,942)
Shaw, Matthew....4:02:01 (12,269)
Shaw, Michael L....5:19:30 (28,435)
Shaw, Paul A....3:49:12 (8,668)
Shaw, Paul F....4:09:43 (14,035)
Shaw, Peter E....3:13:03 (2,406)
Shaw, Robert....3:38:04 (6,242)
Shaw, Robert....5:17:51 (28,226)
Shaw, Robert D....4:33:19 (20,088)
Shaw, Steven....3:30:13 (4,857)
Shaw, Stuart A....2:48:26 (467)
Shaw, Thomas A....4:18:46 (16,298)
Shaw, Timothy M....5:57:37 (31,438)
Shaw, Tom....5:04:28 (26,521)
Shaya, Darrin M....3:45:12 (7,730)
Shayler, Daniel J....3:58:09 (11,209)
Shcade, Christian....2:49:29 (520)
Sheahan, David J....3:43:53 (7,437)
Sheard, Brian A....3:26:00 (4,074)
Sheard, Bryan A....3:44:31 (7,570)
Sheard, Steven P....2:53:01 (680)
Shearer, Andrew J....3:34:30 (5,566)
Shearer, Andrew J....4:36:14 (20,791)
Shearer, Jason....4:36:30 (20,844)
Shearing, Philip R....4:58:01 (25,508)
Shearn, Nick....2:53:52 (718)
Sheather, Cameron C....4:00:07 (11,851)
Sheedy, Mike P....5:47:23 (30,910)
Sheehan, Brian D....4:15:28 (15,469)
Sheehan, Jonathan A....4:05:46 (13,090)
Sheehan, Martin G....2:49:26 (518)
Sheehan, Nicholas P....4:37:25 (21,090)
Sheehan, Nigel P....3:56:08 (10,577)
Sheehan, Paul....3:17:52 (2,982)
Sheehy, Robert P....4:43:25 (22,414)
Sheen, Graham....4:05:01 (12,920)
Sheikh, Affy....4:24:12 (17,714)
Shek, Duncan....5:15:59 (27,998)
Sheldon, Anthon J....3:02:53 (1,429)
Sheldon, J Chris P....3:23:23 (3,694)
Sheldon, Matthew....4:06:32 (13,241)
Sheldon, Mike D....3:23:05 (3,666)
Sheliker, John....4:32:26 (19,896)
Shellard, Russell G....3:29:53 (4,802)
Shelley, James C....4:17:43 (16,034)
Shelley, Peter M....4:10:34 (14,226)
Shelock, Paul W....6:47:47 (32,735)
Shelton, John C....4:15:05 (15,363)
Shelton, Richard C....3:53:17 (9,718)
Shemar, Raji L....3:54:28 (10,042)
Shepard, Simon R....4:41:54 (22,085)
Shephard, Craig A....4:36:12 (20,779)
Shephard, Mark S....4:00:40 (11,969)
Shepheard, Nicholas S....2:59:02 (1,145)
Shepherd, Adam....4:07:06 (13,374)
Shepherd, Andrew....4:24:02 (17,666)
Shepherd, Andrew....4:50:17 (23,901)
Shepherd, Ben....3:58:08 (11,203)
Shepherd, Craig P....4:51:58 (24,246)
Shepherd, David P....4:55:57 (25,091)
Shepherd, Philip H....4:25:03 (17,976)
Sheppard, Jay W....4:53:09 (24,491)
Sheppard, Jonathan N....7:45:29 (33,161)
Sheppard, Michael T....4:31:00 (19,533)
Sheppard, Peter J....4:20:55 (16,842)
Sheppard, Simon....4:00:16 (11,883)
Sherbourne, Howard....7:27:59 (33,086)
Shercliff, Simon....4:05:27 (13,011)
Sheridan, Andrew....4:26:36 (18,408)
Sheridan, Christopher T....4:01:25 (12,135)
Sheridan, Michael J....4:21:05 (16,886)
Sheridan, Paul J....3:06:57 (1,751)
Sheriff, Antony....4:37:34 (21,131)
Sheriff, John....3:47:56 (8,363)
Sherlock, Brian J....3:54:46 (10,128)
Sherratt, Mark A....5:19:40 (28,452)
Sherratt, Matthew A....4:13:08 (14,883)
Sherriffs, Duncan C....4:51:08 (24,066)
Sherrin, Neil K....3:37:37 (6,155)
Sherry, Padraig H....3:25:21 (3,987)
Sherry, Thomas....3:35:21 (5,727)
Shersby, Paul A....4:34:21 (20,328)
Sherston, Nicholas C....4:53:28 (24,556)
Shetty, Sanjeev....5:48:07 (30,952)
Shevlin, Colm....3:56:30 (10,685)
Shew, Peter....3:56:21 (10,638)
Sheward, Adam....4:53:23 (24,544)
Shewbridge, Paul L....4:20:16 (16,676)
Shiang, Steve....3:36:29 (5,928)
Shickell, John....3:41:30 (6,914)
Shiel, Stephen W....3:56:36 (10,726)
Shield, Jerry M....3:04:06 (1,522)
Shields, Allan B....4:47:05 (23,231)
Shields, Dominic J....4:01:00 (12,052)
Shields, Mark T....5:09:27 (27,199)
Shields, Martin....4:28:05 (18,771)
Shields, Matthew J....5:44:16 (30,664)
Shields, Michael....7:01:05 (32,890)
Shields, Travis A....2:47:57 (452)
Shiels, Eddie J....4:14:11 (15,137)
Shillabeer, Edmund H....4:54:03 (24,684)
Shilton, Carl J....4:53:02 (24,463)
Shimell, Luke J....4:03:07 (12,509)
Shimizu, first name unknown....6:07:17 (31,830)
Shimmin, Robert J....3:47:49 (8,332)
Shiner, James P....4:13:37 (14,979)
Shiner, Richard E....3:54:55 (10,184)
Shingfield, Jonathan A....5:24:02 (28,943)
Shipley, James....3:33:12 (5,353)
Shipman, James M....3:31:10 (5,020)
Shipman, John....6:09:44 (31,917)
Shipman, Oliver A....3:56:28 (10,676)
Shipway, Nickolas P....3:47:55 (8,360)
Shipway, Richard M....2:47:42 (446)
Shirlaw, Robert P....5:15:50 (27,977)
Shirley, John L....3:51:57 (9,351)
Shirreff, Simon....4:08:19 (13,695)
Shirt, Paul A....4:29:40 (19,219)
Shohid, Abdul....5:13:18 (27,691)
Shone, Grahame P....3:42:38 (7,138)
Shooter, Neil R....4:24:04 (17,675)
Shore, Benjamin J....3:40:33 (6,721)
Shore, Martin A....5:30:51 (29,631)
Shore, Paul....4:25:31 (18,122)
Shore, Richard E....3:27:31 (4,336)
Shorrock, Adrian B....3:09:30 (2,011)
Shorrocks, David....3:44:56 (7,677)
Short, Andrew J....4:38:33 (21,349)
Short, Arthur....3:09:38 (2,030)
Short, David....4:07:21 (13,433)
Short, Garry J....3:13:14 (2,428)
Short, Kevin....3:14:17 (2,565)
Short, Kevin A....4:03:38 (12,637)
Short, Steven....4:27:45 (18,684)
Shotbolt, Adrian W....3:39:48 (6,589)
Shotton, Richard A....4:28:53 (18,991)
Shout, Andrew M....4:38:05 (21,251)
Shrestha, Autar....3:25:31 (4,005)
Shrimpton, Benjamin J....3:07:05 (1,767)
Shrubsole, Paul D....5:08:30 (27,078)
Shuck, Stephen P....3:03:18 (1,463)
Shucksmith, David....4:10:33 (14,220)
Shurlock, Timothy W....3:52:46 (9,563)
Shute, David M....4:35:26 (20,588)
Shute, Jack....4:33:39 (20,177)
Shute, Kevin E....4:01:19 (12,118)
Shute, Rupert N....2:49:02 (502)
Shutt, Allan D....6:42:50 (32,654)
Shuttleworth, Gregory D....2:42:46 (277)
Shuttleworth, Hugo W....5:19:19 (28,412)
Sibbald, Andrew....4:09:23 (13,954)
Sibie, Kees....4:23:13 (17,421)
Sibley, Graham R....6:14:06 (32,051)
Sibson, Keith R....4:24:09 (17,702)
Sibson, Phil....3:43:05 (7,261)
Sibson, Terry....5:22:44 (28,804)
Sidaway, David J....3:55:52 (10,496)
Siddiqui, Muhammed S....5:39:41 (30,336)
Siddons, Barrie J....4:01:16 (12,109)
Sidell, Brian M....4:18:05 (16,137)
Sidhu, Duljinder S....4:26:18 (18,335)
Sidhu, Jatinder....4:09:02 (13,870)
Sidik, Osman G....4:35:18 (20,553)
Siemons, Wilhelm....4:22:12 (17,174)
Siendones, Rafael....3:49:01 (8,630)
Sig, Robert F....4:02:11 (12,302)
Sigand, Daniel M....4:57:10 (25,349)
Sigrist, Hugh....4:41:43 (22,039)
Sigston, Derek....4:51:08 (24,066)
Sigsworth, Lewis A....3:42:00 (7,024)
Sigurbjornsson, Sigurjon....2:49:06 (504)
Sigurdsson, Bjarni O....3:25:49 (4,051)
Sigurdsson, Engilbert....3:15:04 (2,667)
Sikatzis, Bakis....3:19:50 (3,238)
Siklos, Jonathan A....3:53:02 (9,638)
Silasi, Octavian S....6:29:50 (32,445)
Silberwasser, Luis....4:36:02 (20,731)
Sillence, Paul....4:12:42 (14,749)
Sillett, Graham M....4:28:17 (18,833)
Silva, Alvaro L....3:37:15 (6,082)
Silva, Graham V....6:15:14 (32,092)
Silva, Joseph A....6:01:14 (31,614)
Silvani, Christian P....3:18:44 (3,097)
Silver, Nicholas A....3:25:33 (4,011)
Silverman, Barry....5:51:59 (31,184)
Silverstone, Terence P....4:48:09 (23,459)
Silverton, Ross L....3:33:29 (5,403)
Silvestre, Pascal....2:42:40 (270)
Silvey, Adrian....3:50:44 (9,037)
Simal-Hernandez, Fernando....3:37:20 (6,098)
Simcock, Ian C....3:43:24 (7,333)
Simkins, Ian R....4:29:20 (19,130)
Simkins, John P....4:58:07 (25,533)
Simkins, Paul F....4:02:44 (12,420)
Simkins, Paul J....3:49:55 (8,848)
Simkiss, Gary J....4:26:18 (18,335)
Simmonds, James....4:06:14 (13,181)
Simmonds, Martin....3:46:42 (8,060)
Simmonds, Paul A....4:47:32 (23,329)
Simmonds, Roger....3:35:15 (5,715)
Simmons, Cyril H....7:16:25 (33,016)
Simmons, Edward....3:27:19 (4,297)
Simmons, Gary C....4:38:30 (21,340)
Simmons, Steve....3:44:49 (7,645)
Simms, Andrew D....3:44:04 (7,465)
Simms, Chris J....3:55:08 (10,255)
Simms, Mike G....4:19:31 (16,482)
Simoes, Carlos A....5:10:39 (27,349)
Simon, Anthony J....3:45:56 (7,893)
Simon, Paul F....5:22:36 (28,787)
Simon, Steven A....4:12:05 (14,591)
Simon, Van Der Marel....5:42:43 (30,552)
Simons, Dan....2:23:29 (42)
Simons, Michael J....4:10:58 (14,322)
Simpson, Alistair....5:47:16 (30,886)
Simpson, Andrew D....2:50:22 (563)
Simpson, Andrew P....4:03:11 (12,524)
Simpson, Barry S....3:29:49 (4,790)
Simpson, Brigg....4:28:27 (18,882)

Simpson, Colin L	3:15:41	(2,739)
Simpson, David R	4:28:17	(18,833)
Simpson, David T	3:42:49	(7,188)
Simpson, Dominic	4:00:39	(11,965)
Simpson, Eddie	2:27:46	(55)
Simpson, Edward	3:52:06	(9,385)
Simpson, Garry J	3:52:22	(9,458)
Simpson, Gerry M	4:02:39	(12,412)
Simpson, Graham W	3:15:25	(2,710)
Simpson, John N	4:40:54	(21,873)
Simpson, Louis M	5:26:41	(29,187)
Simpson, Matt S	4:00:30	(11,934)
Simpson, Matthew E	5:14:34	(27,851)
Simpson, Paul H	3:43:57	(7,449)
Simpson, Peter J	3:23:43	(3,746)
Simpson, Richard	3:40:53	(6,776)
Simpson, Richard H	4:29:45	(19,238)
Simpson, Richard J	4:28:12	(18,812)
Simpson, Robert J	4:06:51	(13,311)
Simpson, Robert M	5:13:56	(27,755)
Simpson, Robert R	3:08:36	(1,918)
Sims, David P	4:16:47	(15,795)
Sims, Lee	3:37:24	(6,114)
Sims, Mark A	4:10:33	(14,220)
Sinclair, Doug	3:49:58	(8,860)
Sinclair, Graeme	4:22:23	(17,221)
Sinclair, James M	5:23:02	(28,832)
Sinclair, Malcolm	3:01:56	(1,368)
Sinclair, Nicholas	3:41:07	(6,831)
Sinclair, Oliver J	2:56:39	(911)
Sinclair, Richard I	4:00:23	(11,910)
Sinclair, Robert C	3:56:08	(10,577)
Sinclair, Steven R	5:03:14	(26,351)
Sinclair, Terence F	3:13:24	(2,451)
Sinclair, Thomas F	5:49:08	(31,008)
Sinclair, Thomas G	4:12:20	(14,664)
Singal, Ash K	4:44:06	(22,583)
Singer, Laurence A	5:32:32	(29,773)
Singh, Charanjeet	5:01:19	(26,086)
Singh, David	3:55:49	(10,482)
Singh, George G	4:04:01	(12,721)
Singh, Harbhag	4:27:54	(18,722)
Singh, Hardev	4:46:58	(23,200)
Singh, Harjinder	5:50:13	(31,088)
Singh, Harjit	5:22:34	(28,778)
Singh, Harmander	7:27:41	(33,083)
Singh, Hartej B	5:12:58	(27,645)
Singh, Jagjit	4:52:29	(24,349)
Singh, Karan M	6:28:46	(32,433)
Singh, Keelan K	4:36:52	(20,955)
Singh, Lall	4:58:57	(25,701)
Singh, Makhan	4:27:13	(18,560)
Singh, Manjit	3:32:51	(5,302)
Singh, Manjit	4:14:00	(15,067)
Singh, Parminder	4:50:52	(24,021)
Singh, Parmjit	6:10:19	(31,934)
Singh, Sukhjinder	5:19:41	(28,457)
Singh Shokar, Sukhdip	6:22:08	(32,294)
Singh-Digpal, Surinder	5:20:01	(28,495)
Singlehurst, Thomas A	4:54:13	(24,732)
Singleton, Colin	4:16:42	(15,779)
Singleton, Karl W	5:09:59	(27,263)
Singleton, Mark D	3:28:50	(4,585)
Sinha, Ian	5:18:04	(28,248)
Sinha, Ramesh C	4:20:25	(16,713)
Sinnott, Colin E	3:46:14	(7,953)
Sinnott, David	4:03:03	(12,492)
Sinnott, Guy	3:58:01	(11,156)
Sinnott, Matt A	3:11:53	(2,256)
Sinnott, Philip J	4:40:08	(21,697)
Sinton, James	4:22:37	(17,277)
Sinton, Kevin N	3:39:11	(6,471)
Sippitt, Ian J	4:22:54	(17,345)
Sirdefield, Stephen	3:29:15	(4,663)
Sire, Alain	3:09:08	(1,967)
Sire, Patrick	5:16:34	(28,079)
Sirett, Nicholas J	5:55:32	(31,327)
Sirra, Kamalakar	4:19:18	(16,422)
Sirs, Nicholas	2:44:19	(323)
Sissons, Richard J	3:46:36	(8,034)
Sisto, Egidio	5:38:22	(30,239)
Siva, José L	3:41:17	(6,869)
Sjogreen, Steen	3:59:18	(11,604)
Skaife, Mark A	2:59:34	(1,206)
Skeeles, Damian R	3:59:13	(11,582)
Skelding, Matthew W	3:37:52	(6,202)
Skelly, Brian E	4:51:37	(24,171)
Skelton, John	3:17:20	(2,923)
Skelton, Kevan A	3:56:57	(10,828)
Skelton, Patrick A	5:02:18	(26,224)
Skelton, Raymond D	3:16:37	(2,830)
Skerratt, Clark I	3:00:25	(1,264)
Skett, Mark A	4:13:34	(14,968)
Skidmore, Dean J	4:41:52	(22,074)
Skidmore, Jonathan	3:18:35	(3,082)
Skidmore, Nicholas A	5:01:48	(26,147)
Skidmore, Paul	3:58:09	(11,209)
Skidmore, Paul	4:25:33	(18,126)
Skingley, Ian D	3:12:42	(2,361)
Skinitis, Constantinos J	5:00:03	(25,894)
Skinkis, Michael	4:15:54	(15,578)
Skinner, Chris	4:23:17	(17,440)
Skinner, Christian J	4:28:33	(18,910)
Skinner, Christopher J	4:57:13	(25,354)
Skinner, David K	4:44:28	(22,675)
Skinner, Graham	4:41:51	(22,069)
Skinner, John M	4:25:20	(18,067)
Skinner, Mark S	4:09:27	(13,981)
Skinner, Matthew J	3:59:40	(11,715)
Skinner, Neil A	5:29:56	(29,538)
Skipp, Paul A	4:00:38	(11,958)
Skipper, Michael B	4:25:56	(18,238)
Skivington, Brian D	4:00:19	(11,892)
Skjoldan, Michael	2:49:49	(535)
Skjoldborg, Mikael	4:55:05	(24,914)
Skorubskas, Andriy	2:37:49	(161)
Skov, Henrik	2:46:42	(408)
Skrine, Alexander M	3:35:04	(5,684)
Skryseth, Bjoern	4:18:32	(16,243)
Sladden, Mark	4:11:55	(14,555)
Slade, Francis L	6:00:02	(31,566)
Slade, Glen	3:31:56	(5,148)
Slade, Nigel R	5:35:23	(30,001)
Slagel, Craig A	2:58:30	(1,065)
Slaiding, Ian R	4:22:31	(17,247)
Slape, James C	3:41:32	(6,926)
Slate, Brian R	4:51:21	(24,105)
Slater, Alfred C	5:17:00	(28,126)
Slater, Andrew E	3:33:13	(5,357)
Slater, Carl W	4:11:52	(14,542)
Slater, Daniel P	3:22:34	(3,604)
Slater, Michael R	4:10:10	(14,142)
Slater, Paul N	3:27:24	(4,314)
Slater, Paul W	3:43:10	(7,281)
Slater, Peter E	4:59:58	(25,883)
Slater, Philip H	4:07:28	(13,467)
Slatford, Andrew W	4:24:52	(17,906)
Slaughter, Ashley	4:19:55	(16,581)
Slaughter, Daniel	4:30:49	(19,497)
Slavicky, Stuart J	3:34:40	(5,604)
Slee, Ian S	4:11:47	(14,516)
Sleeman, Dominic P	3:58:32	(11,350)
Slimane, Karim D	3:45:11	(7,725)
Slinn, Gregory J	4:37:11	(21,025)
Sliwerski, Trevor Z	5:20:20	(28,544)
Sloan, Harry	3:11:36	(2,222)
Sloan, Ronald W	4:48:00	(23,428)
Sloane, Sidney	4:52:33	(24,365)
Sloman, Gary	4:03:19	(12,556)
Sloman, Hywel	3:58:36	(11,370)
Sloss, Ian J	4:01:22	(12,125)
Slot, Peter	3:55:47	(10,472)
Slowik, Pawel	4:34:14	(20,298)
Sluman, Jon D	4:15:41	(15,514)
Slutter, Ben	4:26:45	(18,452)
Sly, Andrew	2:57:55	(1,015)
Sly, Phil	2:16:53	(20)
Slyman, Mark	4:08:18	(13,689)
Smailes, Paul	3:59:22	(11,630)
Smale, Chris	3:45:17	(7,751)
Small, Alexander D	4:50:01	(23,845)
Small, Matthew P	4:08:56	(13,846)
Small, Roderick S	5:07:23	(26,915)
Smalley, Michael A	4:37:24	(21,086)
Smalley, Robert	4:28:52	(18,989)
Smalls, Allen	2:35:37	(123)
Smallwood, Timothy J	3:54:59	(10,196)
Smart, Albert M	6:15:00	(32,085)
Smart, Craig F	4:27:53	(18,717)
Smart, Darren I	3:16:15	(2,800)
Smart, Ian L	4:07:56	(13,593)
Smart, James H	3:41:24	(6,895)
Smart, Matthew N	4:29:20	(19,130)
Smart, Philip J	3:42:48	(7,185)
Smart, Richard	4:08:09	(13,652)
Smart, Richard E	4:36:02	(20,731)
Smeed, Michael J	4:37:44	(21,165)
Smiles, Peter A	4:59:36	(25,811)
Smillie, Paul	4:25:52	(18,215)
Smink, Luc J	3:50:07	(8,890)
Smit, Abraham M	4:16:33	(15,737)
Smit, Daniel J	4:16:48	(15,798)
Smith, Aaron P	4:35:32	(20,607)
Smith, Adam K	4:27:58	(18,739)
Smith, Adrian G	4:50:23	(23,920)
Smith, Adrian S	4:10:49	(14,282)
Smith, Alan	3:39:23	(6,514)
Smith, Alan	3:50:15	(8,924)
Smith, Alan K	2:28:02	(57)
Smith, Alexander T	3:55:35	(10,399)
Smith, Alistair F	2:58:34	(1,069)
Smith, Andrew B	3:52:14	(9,422)
Smith, Andrew C	3:33:20	(5,373)
Smith, Andrew D	3:58:47	(11,440)
Smith, Andrew D	4:22:23	(17,221)
Smith, Andrew J	2:48:37	(478)
Smith, Andrew J	3:19:58	(3,262)
Smith, Andrew J	4:01:51	(12,225)
Smith, Andrew J	5:41:14	(30,434)
Smith, Andrew J	6:07:41	(31,847)
Smith, Andrew L	3:25:12	(3,960)
Smith, Andrew P	5:02:53	(26,302)
Smith, Andrew T	5:27:30	(29,274)
Smith, Andy M	4:15:18	(15,415)
Smith, Andy M	4:40:57	(21,882)
Smith, Barry	5:34:31	(29,934)
Smith, Barry C	3:56:34	(10,714)
Smith, Barry S	3:36:38	(5,962)
Smith, Ben	3:48:34	(8,517)
Smith, Ben W	3:57:03	(10,861)
Smith, Bill	3:01:18	(1,324)
Smith, Brian	4:55:30	(24,997)
Smith, Brian R	3:58:49	(11,452)
Smith, Carl P	3:34:33	(5,581)
Smith, Chris E	3:58:55	(11,483)
Smith, Chris J	4:05:13	(12,963)
Smith, Chris J	4:30:45	(19,485)
Smith, Chris M	3:47:48	(8,326)
Smith, Chris R	5:36:50	(30,121)
Smith, Christopher A	3:57:46	(11,100)
Smith, Christopher M	3:43:56	(7,447)
Smith, Christopher M	4:49:08	(23,681)
Smith, Christopher P	3:48:55	(8,614)
Smith, Cliff	3:30:04	(4,838)
Smith, Clifford D	5:19:13	(28,409)
Smith, Colin R	4:08:12	(13,666)
Smith, Daniel	3:54:05	(9,940)
Smith, Daniel A	5:03:17	(26,359)
Smith, Darren	4:09:43	(14,035)
Smith, Darren J	4:52:32	(24,363)
Smith, Darren K	3:58:40	(11,388)
Smith, Darren M	4:30:02	(19,305)
Smith, Darren P	5:15:54	(27,992)
Smith, David	5:04:10	(26,471)
Smith, David B	3:54:52	(10,165)
Smith, David C	4:59:34	(25,804)
Smith, David E	3:26:22	(4,130)
Smith, David E	3:41:50	(6,996)
Smith, David G	3:36:28	(5,927)
Smith, David G	5:06:21	(26,761)
Smith, David K	4:59:20	(25,750)

LONDON MARATHON

Smith, David K 6:14:16 (32,060)
Smith, David M............2:48:25 (465)
Smith, David M............3:29:19 (4,679)
Smith, David P............4:26:15 (18,323)
Smith, David S............5:14:00 (27,760)
Smith, David W............4:29:18 (19,119)
Smith, Dean............3:58:10 (11,218)
Smith, Dean M............5:36:36 (30,107)
Smith, Derek 2:57:39 (998)
Smith, Derek R............4:49:04 (23,666)
Smith, Derek W............6:24:31 (32,343)
Smith, Dominic T............4:21:26 (16,965)
Smith, Edwin J............3:33:35 (5,418)
Smith, Garry A............4:13:24 (14,943)
Smith, Garvan............4:59:47 (25,847)
Smith, Gary............4:12:37 (14,729)
Smith, Gary............4:52:05 (24,263)
Smith, Gary B............3:50:45 (9,045)
Smith, Gary D............4:27:24 (18,602)
Smith, Gary J............3:45:08 (7,715)
Smith, Gary J............4:14:55 (15,315)
Smith, Geoffrey B............3:40:41 (6,742)
Smith, George L............8:25:41 (33,201)
Smith, George M............5:47:15 (30,883)
Smith, Gerry C............2:45:49 (367)
Smith, Giles E............4:53:19 (24,529)
Smith, Graeme J............3:41:21 (6,887)
Smith, Graham............3:50:23 (8,951)
Smith, Graham............4:57:52 (25,470)
Smith, Graham D............4:16:43 (15,783)
Smith, Graham T............3:47:05 (8,142)
Smith, Grant D............4:33:16 (20,077)
Smith, Gregory G............3:58:13 (11,238)
Smith, Guy D............5:26:39 (29,181)
Smith, Guy O............3:50:18 (8,933)
Smith, Harry J............4:01:10 (12,092)
Smith, Hillas R............3:59:01 (11,517)
Smith, Howard M............3:54:41 (10,109)
Smith, Iain A............3:39:34 (6,551)
Smith, Ian G............3:33:06 (5,333)
Smith, Ian J............3:57:32 (11,022)
Smith, Ian M............3:36:35 (5,952)
Smith, Ian S............4:08:56 (13,846)
Smith, Ian S............5:14:24 (27,826)
Smith, Ian T............3:49:03 (8,637)
Smith, James A............3:59:38 (11,702)
Smith, James D............3:29:54 (4,806)
Smith, James D............5:12:11 (27,547)
Smith, Jamie............4:23:43 (17,565)
Smith, Jeremy............5:00:23 (25,958)
Smith, Jeremy B............4:28:41 (18,940)
Smith, Jeremy P............3:34:27 (5,558)
Smith, John............3:39:56 (6,614)
Smith, John............4:25:20 (18,067)
Smith, John J............2:59:18 (1,176)
Smith, John K............3:04:20 (1,532)
Smith, John M............3:53:10 (9,679)
Smith, John R............4:08:02 (13,621)
Smith, Jonathan............4:58:30 (25,607)
Smith, Jonathan D............3:33:54 (5,464)
Smith, Jonathan D............4:13:55 (15,045)
Smith, Jonathan J............4:02:59 (12,474)
Smith, Jonathan M............5:06:47 (26,833)
Smith, Keith A............4:12:49 (14,779)
Smith, Kenny D............5:42:24 (30,525)
Smith, Kevin P............3:34:54 (5,642)
Smith, Kevin P............3:52:39 (9,538)
Smith, Kevin R............3:38:41 (6,362)
Smith, Kevin W............2:49:54 (544)
Smith, Lee E............4:53:17 (24,520)
Smith, Les............4:33:33 (20,149)
Smith, Malcolm............4:13:33 (14,965)
Smith, Malcolm C............4:43:47 (22,514)
Smith, Mark............4:21:38 (17,006)
Smith, Mark A............3:15:49 (2,755)
Smith, Mark A............4:03:35 (12,621)
Smith, Mark A............4:10:18 (14,170)
Smith, Mark A............4:53:18 (24,527)
Smith, Mark A............5:36:32 (30,102)
Smith, Mark N............4:34:07 (20,276)
Smith, Mark R............4:36:40 (20,879)
Smith, Martin A............3:53:38 (9,802)
Smith, Martin J............2:58:26 (1,061)

Smith, Martin S............3:29:50 (4,795)
Smith, Martyn A............5:01:14 (26,078)
Smith, Matthew............5:16:17 (28,039)
Smith, Matthew D............4:29:24 (19,146)
Smith, Matthew E............4:25:43 (18,163)
Smith, Matthew J............3:47:24 (8,213)
Smith, Matthew J............4:05:20 (12,985)
Smith, Matthew W............5:43:40 (30,618)
Smith, Matthew S............5:07:54 (26,991)
Smith, Michael............4:38:57 (21,430)
Smith, Michael A............3:46:24 (7,989)
Smith, Michael J............2:54:38 (775)
Smith, Michael J............3:49:52 (8,837)
Smith, Michael P............3:55:16 (10,305)
Smith, Mick A............4:34:27 (20,350)
Smith, Mike............3:30:22 (4,877)
Smith, Mike R............3:58:55 (11,483)
Smith, Neil A............4:43:19 (22,392)
Smith, Neil C............3:57:48 (11,115)
Smith, Neil F............3:10:16 (2,093)
Smith, Neil M............5:29:43 (29,511)
Smith, Niall F............4:16:21 (15,681)
Smith, Nicholas............4:19:39 (16,516)
Smith, Nicholas A............5:17:12 (28,151)
Smith, Nicholas L............4:07:58 (13,606)
Smith, Nigel A............3:39:29 (6,540)
Smith, Oliver B............3:50:10 (8,908)
Smith, Paul............3:53:36 (9,793)
Smith, Paul............4:21:41 (17,018)
Smith, Paul............4:23:29 (17,496)
Smith, Paul............4:56:12 (25,139)
Smith, Paul A............4:32:14 (19,839)
Smith, Paul A............4:54:54 (24,871)
Smith, Paul D............4:26:05 (18,281)
Smith, Paul J............4:06:11 (13,174)
Smith, Paul J............4:06:56 (13,333)
Smith, Paul M............4:16:49 (15,804)
Smith, Paul R............3:56:27 (10,672)
Smith, Paul S............5:09:59 (27,263)
Smith, Paul W............4:26:32 (18,391)
Smith, Peter............4:27:00 (18,504)
Smith, Peter C............4:01:58 (12,255)
Smith, Peter D............5:57:26 (31,431)
Smith, Peter G............6:44:11 (32,676)
Smith, Philip............4:39:52 (21,645)
Smith, Philip E............3:53:16 (9,713)
Smith, Philip J............3:50:21 (8,943)
Smith, Phillip G............4:41:19 (21,956)
Smith, Rhodri L............3:48:08 (8,414)
Smith, Richard............4:06:02 (13,147)
Smith, Richard............4:14:33 (15,216)
Smith, Richard A............4:16:51 (15,815)
Smith, Richard M............3:32:16 (5,218)
Smith, Robert............4:02:01 (12,269)
Smith, Robert D............4:21:36 (16,999)
Smith, Robert J............3:37:52 (6,202)
Smith, Robert M............2:53:51 (716)
Smith, Robert M............4:20:02 (16,607)
Smith, Robert M............4:26:01 (18,263)
Smith, Robert M............5:08:47 (27,114)
Smith, Robert W............4:37:06 (21,002)
Smith, Robin O............4:24:27 (17,789)
Smith, Rod............4:26:20 (18,348)
Smith, Roger............3:40:38 (6,737)
Smith, Ronald............4:20:10 (16,652)
Smith, Rory O............3:52:44 (9,554)
Smith, Roy............4:07:23 (13,447)
Smith, Roy D............4:58:48 (25,662)
Smith, Russell D............5:34:45 (29,950)
Smith, Russell H............3:28:22 (4,486)
Smith, Sean............2:54:22 (751)
Smith, Shaun R............4:16:29 (15,724)
Smith, Simon............4:04:38 (12,837)
Smith, Simon A............2:55:21 (806)
Smith, Simon C............4:18:40 (16,270)
Smith, Simon M............3:35:09 (5,701)
Smith, Simon M............3:43:43 (7,396)
Smith, Simon P............4:23:22 (17,464)
Smith, Stephen............4:55:41 (25,035)
Smith, Stephen J............4:15:26 (15,460)
Smith, Stephen M............6:18:32 (32,187)
Smith, Stephen P............6:47:51 (32,737)
Smith, Stephen R............5:53:08 (31,226)

Smith, Steve J............4:01:13 (12,103)
Smith, Steve M............4:42:04 (22,128)
Smith, Steve R............3:07:47 (1,837)
Smith, Steven............3:04:32 (1,552)
Smith, Steven D............6:13:05 (32,022)
Smith, Steven J............4:13:10 (14,893)
Smith, Stuart C............4:45:15 (22,850)
Smith, Stuart D............2:56:07 (862)
Smith, Stuart H............3:50:28 (8,972)
Smith, Terrance............3:58:31 (11,344)
Smith, Thomas O............6:04:39 (31,750)
Smith, Thomas W............4:39:19 (21,521)
Smith, Timothy D............4:42:57 (22,316)
Smith, Tom R............4:58:27 (25,596)
Smith, Tony R............4:09:45 (14,044)
Smith, Trevor............3:55:12 (10,282)
Smith, Trevor A............4:34:09 (20,240)
Smith, Trevor J............4:12:33 (14,720)
Smith, Vincent F............4:25:20 (18,067)
Smith, Wayne J............4:14:43 (15,263)
Smith, Wayne M............4:21:53 (17,084)
Smith, William E............4:06:44 (13,285)
Smith, William G............5:16:17 (28,039)
Smith Filho, Fernando F 4:11:16 (14,406)
Smitham, David R 4:11:50 (14,528)
Smitheman, Alan............4:02:26 (12,361)
Smithers, Charles E............4:40:49 (21,858)
Smithers, David P............4:34:43 (20,416)
Smithers, Keith B............4:38:49 (21,396)
Smith-Halvorsen, Paul J............4:42:03 (22,123)
Smithies, Chad............4:50:33 (23,949)
Smith-Morgan, Richard 4:26:08 (18,293)
Smithson, Neil J............4:27:43 (18,680)
Smolik, Greg............4:39:45 (21,612)
Smtih, Wayne............4:02:43 (12,415)
Smy, David J............3:46:39 (8,048)
Smyth, Andrew D............5:53:16 (31,229)
Smyth, Andrew J............3:40:49 (6,764)
Smyth, David A............3:39:28 (6,538)
Smyth, Derek A............3:36:29 (5,928)
Smyth, James............4:12:12 (14,625)
Smyth, John H............2:45:51 (368)
Smyth, Kevin J............3:54:32 (10,061)
Smyth, Nick J............3:23:43 (3,746)
Smyth, Patrick E............4:59:20 (25,750)
Smyth, Trevor I............5:46:00 (30,787)
Smythe, Benjamin D............5:07:56 (26,996)
Smythe, Stephen J............2:43:53 (306)
Smythe, Steve............2:55:30 (815)
Smythe, Todd B............3:51:41 (9,269)
Snaith, Darren G............4:47:38 (23,349)
Snaith, David M............3:32:05 (5,178)
Snape, Geoffrey K............4:18:04 (16,128)
Snape, Joe............3:52:53 (9,593)
Snape, Jonathan P............4:24:16 (17,735)
Snape, Mark............5:06:22 (26,767)
Snead, Martin P............4:07:18 (13,420)
Sneddon, John M............3:46:49 (8,088)
Sneezum, Patrick L............4:55:38 (25,023)
Snelgrove, William............3:10:23 (2,105)
Snell, Peter A............8:18:58 (33,195)
Snelling, David E............7:03:23 (32,913)
Snelling, Liam M............4:06:42 (13,275)
Snelson, Gavin R............5:30:54 (29,816)
Snelson, Michael R............3:59:29 (11,668)
Snelson, Stuart J............3:52:21 (9,456)
Sneyd, Paul B............4:36:06 (20,752)
Snook, Daniel G............3:17:42 (2,966)
Snook, Gareth............3:52:29 (9,488)
Snook, Matt............4:26:35 (18,403)
Snow, David R............4:25:10 (18,016)
Snow, Mark C............4:48:43 (23,587)
Snowball, Peter............3:58:29 (11,333)
Snowden, Kevin............4:06:48 (13,302)
Snowdon, Peter J............3:22:14 (3,563)
Snoxell, Mark J............5:29:20 (29,460)
Snyder, Adam E............4:45:00 (22,786)
Soane, Ian P............4:07:32 (13,484)
Soar, Andrew M............4:05:12 (12,958)
Soares Dos Santos, José M............4:50:35 (23,956)
Socquet-Clerc, Julien E............3:27:21 (4,303)
Sodeinde, Opeoluwa............4:27:36 (18,655)
Soden, Christopher............3:32:14 (5,211)

Soden, Matt	5:20:29 (28,559)
Soderberg, Philip D	3:45:28 (7,801)
Soereide, Thor B	4:27:02 (18,511)
Soerensen, Steen	3:03:46 (1,498)
Softly, Georges	3:29:50 (4,795)
Sohanpal, Amandeep	4:26:45 (18,452)
Soldano, James W	2:43:18 (297)
Soliman, Mohamed T	5:09:36 (27,218)
Solley, Theo	3:51:10 (9,140)
Solly, John C	2:45:54 (373)
Solomon, Selwyn	4:20:19 (16,688)
Soltysik, Andrew	3:07:48 (1,840)
Somaita, Pranav	4:30:56 (19,515)
Somerfield, Christopher D	4:08:25 (13,722)
Somers, Vince	4:30:51 (19,504)
Somerset, Quentin	3:57:12 (10,920)
Somerville, Gerald F	7:24:56 (33,068)
Someya, Takehiko	4:53:38 (24,604)
Sommerlad, Brian C	3:39:40 (6,567)
Somner, John	5:47:06 (30,870)
Sondh, Javaher S	5:32:53 (29,807)
Songhurst, Andrew K	5:34:33 (29,936)
Sonoda, Toyoyki	3:59:44 (11,741)
Sony, Paul T	5:44:22 (30,672)
Sood, Amit	5:16:45 (28,099)
Soper, Thomas	3:23:34 (3,723)
Soraf, David	4:57:01 (25,315)
Sorby, Oliver E	4:05:54 (13,118)
Sorg, Michael	3:50:59 (9,095)
Sorley, Neil P	4:44:16 (22,629)
Sorrentino, Ferdinando	3:28:42 (4,556)
Sorrie, Paul D	2:38:25 (175)
Sorrill, Denis S	5:00:50 (26,016)
Sortwell, Andrew J	3:34:40 (5,604)
Sortwell, Robert M	3:34:40 (5,604)
Sosick, Alex J	3:59:25 (11,641)
Sotheran, Gavin J	4:29:25 (19,150)
Sothinathan, Roshan	5:50:49 (31,122)
Souchon, Pascal	4:05:00 (12,918)
Soulier, Gerard	3:26:55 (4,225)
Sousa, Luis	3:30:25 (4,880)
Souter, James	5:17:21 (28,177)
South, Clayton J	3:12:15 (2,317)
South, Clifford R	4:06:44 (13,285)
South, David I	4:49:54 (23,826)
Southall, Ben I	3:47:39 (8,282)
Southall, David O	4:25:33 (18,126)
Southall, Paul C	4:00:06 (11,843)
Southam, Christopher	2:33:59 (98)
Southart, Stephen A	4:40:43 (21,831)
Southcott, Mark K	5:32:39 (29,781)
Southern, Anthony C	3:57:26 (10,989)
Southern, Mark J	5:02:58 (26,311)
Southey, David H	5:07:40 (26,961)
Southgate, Christopher A	3:56:39 (10,739)
Southgate, Mathew J	4:52:29 (24,349)
Southwell-Sander, Tim	3:42:57 (7,221)
Southworth, Timothy J	4:41:16 (21,943)
Spacey, Graham B	5:27:21 (29,255)
Spalding, Nicholas J	5:59:18 (31,526)
Spall, Michael J	3:34:30 (5,566)
Spalton, Phil N	3:55:21 (10,332)
Spanswick, Kurt T	4:11:18 (14,418)
Sparber, Ernst	3:25:29 (4,002)
Spare, Tracey P	4:07:03 (13,356)
Sparey, Christian	3:58:40 (11,388)
Sparey, Simon A	5:04:51 (26,561)
Sparks, Daniel P	5:02:59 (26,314)
Sparks, Steven	3:29:05 (4,638)
Sparling, Gari	4:09:25 (13,969)
Sparrey, Graham M	3:06:32 (1,713)
Sparrow, Alen J	3:59:01 (11,517)
Sparrow, Chris E	4:02:28 (12,368)
Sparrow, Chris R	5:56:34 (31,385)
Sparrow, Ian S	4:00:57 (12,030)
Sparrow, Matthew S	3:17:47 (2,975)
Sparrow, Roger L	3:52:25 (9,477)
Sparsis, Andrew	6:21:15 (32,262)
Spawton, Robert J	4:37:53 (21,194)
Speake, Brian A	3:26:50 (4,210)
Speake, Malcolm D	3:59:11 (11,570)
Speakman, Gary T	4:17:17 (15,923)
Speakman, Paul D	4:48:17 (23,489)

Spear, Derek	4:12:47 (14,769)
Spear, John	4:05:35 (13,047)
Spear, Richard G	5:20:28 (28,558)
Specht, Simon W	4:32:51 (19,967)
Speck, Adam B	3:12:09 (2,299)
Spedding, Robert I	5:07:08 (26,884)
Speed, Christopher A	4:20:22 (16,700)
Speed, Morley W	3:46:11 (7,939)
Speelman, Anthony A	4:14:03 (15,086)
Speller, Richard	3:24:44 (3,901)
Spelman, Nigel D	4:11:19 (14,420)
Spelman, Peter J	3:27:19 (4,297)
Spence, Craig	5:10:26 (27,326)
Spence, Daniel J	4:10:10 (14,142)
Spence, James O	4:58:54 (25,687)
Spence, Leon D	4:42:42 (22,260)
Spence, Martin T	3:42:01 (7,028)
Spence, Steven R	4:23:27 (17,486)
Spence, Will D	3:56:21 (10,638)
Spencer, Andrew M	2:56:06 (857)
Spencer, Andrew M	3:41:20 (6,882)
Spencer, Andrew N	3:49:30 (8,747)
Spencer, Colin D	3:09:51 (2,053)
Spencer, Ian	3:21:12 (3,423)
Spencer, Ian H	3:13:55 (2,513)
Spencer, Ian J	4:06:11 (13,174)
Spencer, Jamie L	4:31:20 (19,622)
Spencer, Jeremy H	3:10:16 (2,093)
Spencer, Julian T	2:57:30 (985)
Spencer, Kevin P	4:23:51 (17,609)
Spencer, Matthew J	5:38:15 (30,226)
Spencer, Nigel R	5:01:31 (26,109)
Spencer, Paul A	4:50:36 (23,960)
Spencer, Robert P	3:59:56 (11,795)
Spencer, Stephen N	5:14:21 (27,821)
Spencer-Adams, Stephan A	6:55:06 (32,828)
Spencer-Brunt, Simon	5:42:27 (30,529)
Spencer-Perkins, Michael D	5:01:52 (26,154)
Spendlove, Terence D	3:50:41 (9,027)
Spensley, Daniel J	3:24:10 (3,818)
Sperling, Kevin A	5:43:35 (30,612)
Sperling, Thomas	3:27:06 (4,259)
Spicer, Andrew O	4:25:25 (18,095)
Spicer, Graham F	4:05:31 (13,027)
Spicer, James	6:30:21 (32,459)
Spiers, Roger	3:48:47 (8,572)
Spiller, Mark J	4:31:35 (19,692)
Spiller, Stephen D	5:45:39 (30,759)
Spinelli, Riccardo	3:30:58 (4,976)
Spinks, Mark P	4:09:32 (14,000)
Spinks, Oliver P	5:12:54 (27,632)
Spinks, Roger E	4:29:04 (19,041)
Spires, David	6:16:18 (32,129)
Spittle, Andrew M	3:44:47 (7,638)
Spolander, Brandon G	3:30:19 (4,867)
Spong, Albert W	5:17:23 (28,181)
Spooner, Maurice	4:10:32 (14,219)
Spooner, Richard	4:25:18 (18,054)
Spotswood, Robert	3:36:21 (5,904)
Spouse, Iain	3:04:21 (1,533)
Spragg, Christian M	4:16:05 (15,620)
Spraggett, Simon J	4:36:00 (20,722)
Spraggs, Frank	4:25:10 (18,016)
Spratt, Anthony	3:22:37 (3,616)
Spratt, Graham K	5:24:19 (28,973)
Spreadbury, Kevin I	3:32:40 (5,273)
Spriggs, Andrew J	3:46:53 (8,098)
Spriggs, Benjamin W	4:19:18 (16,422)
Spriggs, Will	3:54:46 (10,128)
Spring, William J	4:37:09 (21,013)
Springer, Andrew J	4:32:06 (19,814)
Springer, Marcellus A	3:12:30 (2,342)
Springett, Adrian	4:13:41 (15,000)
Sprules, Anthony J	3:03:00 (1,442)
Spurdle, Derek	4:24:11 (17,709)
Spurgeon, Nigel F	3:05:17 (1,606)
Spurling, Peter	4:11:31 (14,462)
Spurr, Robert	4:13:50 (15,030)
Squier, Jonathan J	4:12:44 (14,756)
Squillante, Maurizio	3:42:01 (7,028)
Squire, Anthony	2:56:40 (913)
Squire, Leon E	5:14:18 (27,811)
Squire, Mark L	4:03:43 (12,654)

Squire, Winston	5:43:37 (30,613)
Squires, Gary R	4:36:11 (20,774)
Squires, Graham	4:03:58 (12,708)
Srikandakumar, Anton	5:16:29 (28,068)
St Clair, Richard	2:54:04 (731)
St Croix, Dennis C	4:13:30 (14,955)
St John, Anthony	4:25:54 (18,233)
Staas, Oliver	3:22:30 (3,594)
Stacey, Gary J	5:32:45 (29,794)
Stacey, Graham L	4:39:19 (21,521)
Stacey, Jonathan A	4:39:20 (21,528)
Stacey, Paul A	3:10:45 (2,136)
Stacey, Robin D	6:15:13 (32,091)
Stacey, Steve J	4:01:53 (12,230)
Stack, Nick	4:55:21 (24,972)
Stackhouse, Daniel W	4:30:06 (19,324)
Staddon, Andrew	5:56:32 (31,383)
Staddon, Graeme J	3:19:32 (3,195)
Stadtel, Bjoern	3:08:35 (1,917)
Staedele, Norbert	4:40:32 (21,797)
Stafford, John	5:22:11 (28,739)
Stafford, Matthew C	3:53:05 (9,660)
Stafford, Matthew R	3:46:05 (7,922)
Stafford, Peter R	3:53:03 (9,647)
Stafford, Thomas	4:43:10 (22,362)
Stagg, Andrew	5:12:32 (27,592)
Stagg, Anthony J	3:32:46 (5,287)
Stagg, Christopher J	4:45:10 (22,825)
Staggs, Robert J	5:42:27 (30,529)
Stainer, Peter	2:39:10 (193)
Staines, Michael J	5:56:21 (31,371)
Staines, Michael R	3:59:39 (11,711)
Stainsby, Chris	5:59:11 (31,515)
Stainsby, Philip M	3:56:12 (10,593)
Stait, Haydn W	4:17:24 (15,954)
Stait, Timothy	3:38:45 (6,376)
Staite, Richard J	2:47:34 (441)
Stalker, Howard J	4:36:51 (20,952)
Stallard, Philip	3:43:40 (7,383)
Stamp, Richard M	3:28:16 (4,456)
Stamper, Nicholas J	3:18:48 (3,106)
Stanbrook, Richard J	4:02:16 (12,327)
Stancliffe, George	5:14:29 (27,839)
Stancliffe, Harry J	4:55:07 (24,922)
Stancliffe, Tom J	4:20:01 (16,606)
Stancombe, Mark R	5:00:51 (26,020)
Standing, Deano J	4:25:57 (18,244)
Standring, Robert D	5:04:36 (26,535)
Standring, Richard A	4:20:36 (16,759)
Stanfield, Michael J	5:10:29 (27,332)
Stanford, Ian R	4:03:03 (12,492)
Stanger, Christopher J	3:22:21 (3,577)
Stanger, Michael J	3:36:59 (6,037)
Stanhope, Boyd E	4:11:44 (14,503)
Stanhope, Ian C	3:50:31 (8,989)
Staniard, Bill J	3:38:37 (6,353)
Staniland, Anthony	3:37:18 (6,095)
Staniland, David	3:35:36 (5,769)
Stanley, David M	3:44:12 (7,491)
Stanley, Guy	6:36:20 (32,550)
Stanley, Shaun	3:43:09 (7,274)
Stanley-Evans, Charles B	3:48:58 (8,623)
Stannard, Alan	3:36:10 (5,868)
Stannard, Eric E	3:44:32 (7,578)
Stannard, Ian	4:31:55 (19,776)
Stannard, Paul L	3:26:12 (4,103)
Stannett, Charlie	4:43:35 (22,462)
Stano, Vincenzo	4:35:21 (20,568)
Stansfield, Andrew	6:08:57 (31,893)
Stansfield, Graham	3:49:29 (8,743)
Stansfield, Spencer J	5:04:44 (26,548)
Stanton, Neil	4:49:43 (23,795)
Stanton, Nigel J	3:58:18 (11,266)
Stanton, Peter	3:27:25 (4,319)
Stanway, Anthony J	6:47:33 (32,731)
Stanyon, Andrew D	4:21:44 (17,036)
Staplehurst, David	6:22:06 (32,292)
Staples, Andrew V	4:36:05 (20,746)
Staples, Francis A	3:58:54 (11,476)
Stapleton, Alan J	3:41:54 (7,008)
Stapleton, Phillip R	3:37:02 (6,045)
Stapley, Benjamin G	3:22:57 (3,652)
Stapley, Phillip D	5:17:20 (28,172)

Starbrook, Samuel J 4:53:02 (24,463)
Starbuck, Robert 4:53:52 (24,652)
Stark, David N 2:59:33 (1,198)
Stark, Richard 4:04:41 (12,853)
Stark, Stephen 2:58:44 (1,101)
Stark, Warren 4:16:56 (15,843)
Starkey, Jason P 5:55:55 (31,350)
Starkey, Tom P 4:41:50 (22,062)
Starrs, Paul R 3:23:33 (3,717)
Stas, Jo 4:05:56 (13,129)
Stasch, Horst 4:52:45 (24,409)
Stasiuk, Stefan 3:43:11 (7,285)
Statham, Jason K 3:08:58 (1,952)
Statham, Malcolm J 3:27:45 (4,372)
Staton, Derek L 4:30:10 (19,340)
Statter, Graham J 3:19:42 (3,213)
Staunton, Dominic M 3:14:53 (2,650)
Staunton, Michael 4:13:37 (14,979)
Staunton, Richard J 4:00:04 (11,836)
Staurland, Gunnar 3:51:52 (9,324)
Staveley, Andy J 2:59:33 (1,198)
Stead, Andrew R 4:26:02 (18,271)
Stead, Colin 3:42:49 (7,188)
Stead, Jeffery 5:39:55 (30,354)
Stead, John 3:32:00 (5,158)
Stead, Jonathan P 2:52:51 (667)
Steadman, John F 4:27:50 (18,703)
Steadman, Jon G 4:08:24 (13,717)
Steadman, Mark R 4:09:42 (14,029)
Steady, Clive J 4:41:50 (22,062)
Stearn, Nick A 3:29:27 (4,707)
Stears, Terry R 4:22:55 (17,347)
Stedman, Alun J 4:06:39 (13,259)
Steedman, David P 3:36:50 (6,001)
Steel, Guy S 3:39:24 (6,518)
Steel, Ian S 4:27:38 (18,666)
Steel, John R 4:28:55 (18,998)
Steel, Jonathan E 3:56:41 (10,750)
Steel, Mark I 3:51:04 (9,116)
Steele, Ian 5:47:32 (30,920)
Steele, James K 6:27:42 (32,416)
Steele, Ray K 4:39:38 (21,584)
Steele, Roy 3:07:01 (1,760)
Steele, Shaun 4:38:40 (21,365)
Steele, William R 4:51:57 (24,242)
Steeles, Simon P 3:15:08 (2,674)
Steen, Peter R 4:23:28 (17,493)
Steer, Christopher R 5:12:16 (27,560)
Steer, John 3:38:32 (6,334)
Stefan, Martin D 4:01:05 (12,067)
Steffan, Enzo 4:20:52 (16,827)
Stegner, Zygmunt J 2:58:41 (1,094)
Steiger, Malcolm J 3:26:53 (4,219)
Steimel, Juergen 3:12:12 (2,306)
Steinig, Georg 3:51:22 (9,193)
Steinpress, Laurence D 4:53:23 (24,544)
Stell, Anthony J 4:51:09 (24,069)
Stene, Lasse 4:56:17 (25,159)
Stenhouse, Jamieson M 4:10:57 (14,315)
Stenhouse, Lawrie J 3:58:33 (11,357)
Stenner, Roger A 4:30:13 (19,357)
Stenning, Savin B 4:40:14 (21,720)
Stenson, Michael 5:23:05 (28,843)
Steortz, James E 5:12:31 (27,591)
Stephan, Wolfhard 4:10:26 (14,200)
Stephen, Jason M 5:32:48 (29,798)
Stephens, Andrew 5:09:52 (27,249)
Stephens, Christopher J 6:04:23 (31,737)
Stephens, Daniel M 4:48:03 (23,438)
Stephens, David C 4:02:56 (12,464)
Stephens, Garry A 4:36:41 (20,885)
Stephens, Goerge H 3:00:28 (1,269)
Stephens, Graham C 2:47:24 (433)
Stephens, Marc R 4:19:11 (16,390)
Stephens, Mark J 3:21:09 (3,415)
Stephens, Neale G 2:58:40 (1,090)
Stephens, Nicholas 2:57:21 (971)
Stephens, Paul 4:20:35 (16,754)
Stephenson, Andrew 3:03:33 (1,484)
Stephenson, Andrew J 4:42:38 (22,242)
Stephenson, Anthony M 3:50:13 (8,915)
Stephenson, Brian 5:18:58 (28,368)
Stephenson, Charlie D 3:55:46 (10,468)
Stephenson, Damian P 4:24:40 (17,864)
Stephenson, James 4:13:21 (14,931)
Stephenson, Jeffrey B 3:35:59 (5,832)
Steptoe, Colin F 2:37:53 (165)
Steptoe, Paul J 3:19:12 (3,158)
Sterland, David M 3:23:29 (3,710)
Stern, Andrew J 5:41:24 (30,450)
Sterry, John 5:37:48 (30,190)
Steven, Dhaens 4:13:00 (14,842)
Steven, Paul 4:53:39 (24,607)
Stevens, Anthony 4:45:51 (22,978)
Stevens, Bob G 6:54:32 (32,821)
Stevens, Darren 3:45:31 (7,808)
Stevens, David R 4:11:28 (14,452)
Stevens, Gary 7:37:28 (33,127)
Stevens, Graham J 3:18:51 (3,114)
Stevens, Grant A 4:40:28 (21,763)
Stevens, Greg P 2:40:32 (217)
Stevens, Mark G 4:59:41 (25,831)
Stevens, Mark P 7:42:28 (33,150)
Stevens, Matthew 4:10:50 (14,291)
Stevens, Matthew T 4:04:44 (12,862)
Stevens, Michael A 4:55:04 (24,908)
Stevens, Neil 4:57:31 (25,401)
Stevens, Paul 4:42:19 (22,180)
Stevens, Peter J 4:08:23 (13,712)
Stevens, Phil G 5:41:42 (30,472)
Stevens, Phillip J 3:49:23 (8,715)
Stevens, Robert 3:18:01 (2,998)
Stevens, Robert C 3:36:23 (5,912)
Stevens, Terry 5:52:50 (31,208)
Stevens, Thomas L 4:41:46 (22,052)
Stevens, Wayne 4:49:50 (23,810)
Stevenson, Andrew G 3:37:55 (6,213)
Stevenson, Clive 3:39:59 (6,624)
Stevenson, Colin W 3:58:54 (11,476)
Stevenson, David M 3:28:59 (4,620)
Stevenson, Huw 5:01:53 (26,158)
Stevenson, James E 4:23:47 (17,582)
Stevenson, Justin J 4:56:59 (25,307)
Stevenson, Martin L 4:46:58 (23,200)
Stevenson, Michael J 3:42:40 (7,150)
Stevenson, Robert 4:46:49 (23,177)
Stewart, Brian P 3:42:04 (7,040)
Stewart, Bryan J 3:17:39 (2,958)
Stewart, Daniel T 4:53:43 (24,622)
Stewart, Darren I 4:47:00 (23,215)
Stewart, David A 4:47:48 (23,382)
Stewart, Duncan J 3:21:16 (3,434)
Stewart, Evan J 4:37:09 (21,013)
Stewart, Iain 3:58:07 (11,195)
Stewart, Ian 4:22:02 (17,126)
Stewart, James I 4:15:21 (15,432)
Stewart, Jon R 4:34:11 (20,288)
Stewart, Joseph A 5:55:27 (31,323)
Stewart, Kenneth G 4:05:22 (12,991)
Stewart, Lee E 4:11:40 (14,493)
Stewart, Mark A 4:00:22 (11,906)
Stewart, Mark J 4:10:59 (14,325)
Stewart, Michael D 4:17:08 (15,893)
Stewart, Nathan J 3:49:14 (8,674)
Stewart, Neville 5:49:46 (31,054)
Stewart, Robert 3:36:07 (5,858)
Stewart, Robert 5:00:48 (26,013)
Stewart, Robert A 3:19:14 (3,164)
Stewart, Ryan J 3:33:03 (5,330)
Steyn, André 4:19:18 (16,422)
Steyn, Joe S 4:23:06 (17,387)
Stiasny, Jonathan D 4:35:45 (20,661)
Stick, Carl R 3:53:19 (9,722)
Stickley, John F 6:26:11 (32,384)
Stiff, Ben S 5:42:07 (30,509)
Stiff, Gafyn S 4:26:44 (18,443)
Stiff, Michael 3:26:37 (4,179)
Stileman, Mark R 2:48:44 (483)
Stiles, Andrew D 3:11:58 (2,271)
Still, Ben 3:13:42 (2,485)
Still, Martin D 4:19:15 (16,408)
Still, Robert 6:12:49 (32,014)
Still, Stuart J 3:33:09 (5,342)
Stillwell, David 4:08:52 (13,825)
Stimpson, Andrew J 6:03:08 (31,691)
Stinchcombe, Nigel S 3:24:00 (3,793)
Stinson, William R 3:58:13 (11,238)
Stirk, Harry R 4:19:42 (16,531)
Stirland, Richard J 4:28:04 (18,767)
Stirling, Mark 4:39:46 (21,622)
Stoakley, Robin E 4:14:03 (15,086)
Stoate, Howard G 4:04:20 (12,782)
Stock, Andrew N 3:25:32 (4,008)
Stock, Daniel J 3:55:34 (10,390)
Stock, Richard D 4:35:59 (20,718)
Stock, Tim 2:56:50 (923)
Stock, Timothy 5:32:03 (29,742)
Stock, Vincent J 3:49:59 (8,863)
Stockdale, Mark R 4:33:27 (20,123)
Stocker, Daniel A 3:53:43 (9,827)
Stocker, Jim 3:51:55 (9,341)
Stocker, John L 4:16:59 (15,854)
Stocking, Marc 3:54:59 (10,196)
Stocking, Peter R 4:10:06 (14,121)
Stockley, Hal 2:56:54 (931)
Stockley, Mike 5:11:02 (27,388)
Stockley, Robert J 5:45:34 (30,755)
Stocks, Adrian P 4:12:01 (14,577)
Stocks, Christopher W 3:30:54 (4,963)
Stockwell, Jonathan P 3:40:42 (6,746)
Stockwell, Peter R 4:24:28 (17,792)
Stoddard, Mark 3:01:38 (1,346)
Stoddart, Christopher K 3:53:26 (9,749)
Stoerel, Thomas 3:42:52 (7,196)
Stokes, Clifford R 4:07:52 (13,574)
Stokes, Daniel L 4:51:24 (24,121)
Stokes, David K 4:14:27 (15,197)
Stokes, Graham B 3:55:41 (10,431)
Stokes, Jamie E 4:07:32 (13,484)
Stokes, Kevin 2:45:53 (371)
Stokes, Michael 4:20:39 (16,774)
Stokes, Paul A 4:11:01 (14,336)
Stokes, Rob A 5:14:14 (27,803)
Stone, Andy 3:03:09 (1,454)
Stone, Barry C 3:21:11 (3,420)
Stone, Christian A 4:52:38 (24,388)
Stone, Christopher J 4:07:13 (13,406)
Stone, David M 2:37:21 (149)
Stone, Derek C 2:55:40 (826)
Stone, Gab 4:40:38 (21,816)
Stone, Ian 4:50:33 (23,949)
Stone, John 4:15:38 (15,503)
Stone, Jonathan D 5:13:31 (27,724)
Stone, Jonathan P 4:01:05 (12,067)
Stone, Mark D 3:41:45 (6,974)
Stone, Martin 3:39:20 (6,507)
Stone, Michael D 4:29:49 (19,252)
Stone, Nicholas 3:46:30 (8,010)
Stone, Nigel J 4:02:10 (12,299)
Stone, Peter 4:53:44 (24,626)
Stone, Peter K 6:12:08 (31,990)
Stone, Richard J 4:59:24 (25,761)
Stone, Steven D 4:13:47 (15,018)
Stone, Terry 4:38:53 (21,413)
Stoneley, Norman W 4:33:03 (20,016)
Stoneley, Paul A 3:25:06 (3,942)
Stoneman, Christopher J 4:19:38 (16,509)
Stoney, Martin J 4:43:15 (22,376)
Stonham, Albert A 5:42:34 (30,540)
Stopford, Jeremy L 5:39:33 (30,329)
Stopher, Jed 4:51:57 (24,242)
Storck, Christian 2:56:26 (885)
Storer, David A 3:52:08 (9,390)
Storer, Graham N 3:41:15 (6,863)
Storey, John A 5:16:59 (28,122)
Storey, Peter 4:32:18 (19,859)
Storie, Chris J 4:07:18 (13,420)
Storkaas, Geir 3:36:47 (5,990)
Storrie, Giles D 5:13:00 (27,653)
Storrie, Martin J 3:35:27 (5,742)
Story, Terry D 3:48:20 (8,460)
Story, Thomas E 3:45:55 (7,889)
Stothard, Peter 4:30:38 (19,458)
Stott, Richard L 5:46:08 (30,795)
Stovell, Paul A 5:06:30 (26,789)
Stow, Martin P 3:16:24 (2,809)
Stowe, Andrew W 2:42:30 (265)
Strachan, Darren 3:29:16 (4,667)
Strachan, David 4:05:19 (12,982)

Syrett, Jason K 3:39:47 (6,587)
Szczepaniak, Daniel 5:06:00 (26,710)
Szelwach, Artur 4:12:46 (14,765)
Szponar, John P 4:01:53 (12,230)
Szulc, Terracne C 5:34:23 (29,920)
Szuplak, Henryk C 4:20:45 (16,795)
Szwinto, Henry 2:46:19 (398)
Szymokowiak, Christophe 3:48:04 (8,398)
Szynaka, Stefan 4:38:19 (21,305)
Taaffe, Peter H 4:19:04 (16,360)
Tabellion, Guy 4:10:14 (14,156)
Tabor, Paul A 3:55:58 (10,531)
Tadie, Alexis J 3:06:51 (1,740)
Taffinder, Robert F 5:42:43 (30,552)
Taft, Michael 3:56:14 (10,603)
Taggart, Simon T 4:37:10 (21,017)
Tagney, Gregory P 3:47:32 (8,246)
Tai, William K 4:37:52 (21,189)
Tailor, Umesh 5:39:01 (30,282)
Tait, Christopher I 4:00:29 (11,932)
Tait, Colin A 4:52:48 (24,422)
Tait, David J 5:26:50 (29,204)
Tait, John S 3:33:51 (5,456)
Tait, Philippe D 4:19:29 (16,474)
Taitt, Jonathan P 5:15:09 (27,916)
Takahashi, Sadad 4:50:30 (23,945)
Takaku, Hirofumi 3:56:41 (10,750)
Takano, Satoshi 3:44:01 (7,460)
Talbot, Andrew 3:53:53 (9,890)
Talbot, Bruno 4:20:19 (16,688)
Talbot, Colin A 3:24:14 (3,831)
Talbot, Edward C 4:24:17 (17,742)
Talbot, Gavin 4:53:28 (24,556)
Talbot, Michael A 4:15:30 (15,476)
Talbot, Simon A 4:43:04 (22,339)
Talbot-Jones, Ian 3:57:28 (11,003)
Talbott, Mark T 5:20:45 (28,586)
Talibart, Peter 4:49:56 (23,832)
Tallents, Godfrey 5:58:27 (31,484)
Tam, Patrick 3:47:08 (8,151)
Tamblyn, David S 7:11:12 (32,990)
Tambour, Torbjoru 3:27:20 (4,301)
Tamburini, Daniele 4:23:29 (17,496)
Tame, David J 3:09:02 (1,961)
Tame, Nick 4:34:18 (20,307)
Tan, Adrian S 3:48:09 (8,422)
Tan, Joon Y 4:17:33 (15,999)
Tanaka, Hitotaka 4:34:01 (20,249)
Tancock, Stephen 3:06:55 (1,748)
Tandy, Andrew D 4:03:15 (12,538)
Tandy, Simon 5:52:43 (31,206)
Tang, Hong 5:38:32 (30,255)
Taniguchi, Kazuma 4:31:22 (19,630)
Tanini, Matteo 5:57:19 (31,425)
Tanner, Adrian G 2:44:34 (334)
Tanner, Colin R 4:10:10 (14,142)
Tanner, Ian D 3:18:16 (3,025)
Tanner, Jean-Paul 4:40:47 (21,848)
Tanner, John R 4:06:16 (13,185)
Tanner, Jonathan E 3:24:22 (3,844)
Tanner, Keith E 4:05:28 (13,018)
Tansey, Robert J 2:46:18 (397)
Tansley, Kim 5:01:41 (26,132)
Tansley, Timothy C 3:19:28 (3,191)
Tapley, Colin R 3:48:31 (8,504)
Taplin, Christopher I 4:00:20 (11,896)
Taplin, Derek R 4:58:24 (25,585)
Taplin, Simon J 3:18:41 (3,091)
Tapster, Martin A 5:20:20 (28,544)
Taranik, Dan L 6:42:34 (32,647)
Tardy, Enrico 4:21:24 (16,959)
Tarrant, Dominic N 4:50:58 (24,042)
Tarrant, James R 3:17:04 (2,885)
Tarratt, Christopher S 3:40:45 (6,752)
Tarravello, Gilles 4:19:48 (16,552)
Tarrier, Peter I 2:59:32 (1,194)
Tasker, Austin 5:12:03 (27,530)
Tasquiier, Nick 4:07:06 (13,374)
Tassell, Andrew D 6:21:17 (32,264)
Tassetti, Roberto 3:14:42 (2,628)
Tate, Alexander J 2:58:21 (1,051)
Tate, Andrew P 3:49:13 (8,671)
Tate, Kevin 3:42:46 (7,178)

Tate, Mark 4:07:57 (13,602)
Tate, Neville A 3:58:04 (11,174)
Tatham, Alasdair G 2:39:57 (210)
Tatsumi, Ikuo 4:36:19 (20,809)
Tattersall, Alan 4:48:39 (23,576)
Tatum, Nicholas B 4:06:18 (13,194)
Tavinor, Steven M 4:27:15 (18,567)
Tawn, Paul R 3:56:17 (10,624)
Tayeb, Rawand 2:39:15 (196)
Tayler, Martin J 4:08:21 (13,704)
Taylor, Adam D 6:03:24 (31,702)
Taylor, Alan C 4:44:24 (22,660)
Taylor, Alston 4:57:14 (25,359)
Taylor, Andrew 4:37:02 (20,987)
Taylor, Andrew M 4:22:01 (17,121)
Taylor, Andrew P 4:07:48 (13,555)
Taylor, Andrew P 4:24:48 (17,892)
Taylor, Ashley D 3:56:16 (10,618)
Taylor, Ben M 4:08:26 (13,728)
Taylor, Ben N 4:12:06 (14,595)
Taylor, Benjamin M 3:56:19 (10,630)
Taylor, Brant 3:11:13 (2,182)
Taylor, Brian G 3:57:44 (11,087)
Taylor, Brian R 4:24:16 (17,735)
Taylor, Campbell 3:54:04 (9,936)
Taylor, Charles P 3:36:12 (5,878)
Taylor, Chris 4:36:13 (20,786)
Taylor, Christopher B 4:56:50 (25,264)
Taylor, Colin 2:48:55 (492)
Taylor, Colin 3:28:26 (4,500)
Taylor, Colin 4:36:45 (20,919)
Taylor, Dan 5:54:07 (31,269)
Taylor, Darren L 4:23:43 (17,565)
Taylor, David 5:46:14 (30,805)
Taylor, David E 3:18:18 (3,032)
Taylor, David I 4:29:04 (19,041)
Taylor, David J 5:23:11 (28,853)
Taylor, David L 4:20:06 (16,629)
Taylor, Drew 2:50:13 (556)
Taylor, Duncan A 4:53:20 (24,535)
Taylor, Edward 4:37:49 (21,181)
Taylor, Edward J 4:36:57 (20,970)
Taylor, Eric 5:11:35 (27,473)
Taylor, Gary 4:01:23 (12,129)
Taylor, Gary 4:20:13 (16,666)
Taylor, Gary S 4:13:56 (15,049)
Taylor, George K 2:49:46 (531)
Taylor, Glenn 4:01:38 (12,179)
Taylor, Graeme K 7:04:22 (32,933)
Taylor, Graham 3:57:04 (10,865)
Taylor, Graham 4:05:11 (12,951)
Taylor, Graham P 3:55:47 (10,472)
Taylor, Guy A 3:37:17 (6,088)
Taylor, Iain M 5:13:41 (27,734)
Taylor, Ian 3:56:35 (10,717)
Taylor, Ian D 3:58:02 (11,163)
Taylor, Ian R 3:57:20 (10,961)
Taylor, James T 3:28:18 (4,468)
Taylor, Jeremy F 5:52:28 (31,195)
Taylor, Jeremy N 3:44:04 (7,465)
Taylor, Jeremy P 3:55:59 (10,416)
Taylor, Jim A 5:43:59 (30,637)
Taylor, John 4:14:43 (15,263)
Taylor, John 4:37:08 (21,012)
Taylor, John C 3:21:39 (3,492)
Taylor, John C 3:38:24 (6,303)
Taylor, John M 5:19:23 (28,421)
Taylor, Jonathan C 3:57:26 (10,989)
Taylor, Joost 4:04:37 (12,834)
Taylor, Jordan M 3:54:51 (10,160)
Taylor, Keith 4:08:27 (13,732)
Taylor, Keith D 4:17:32 (15,992)
Taylor, Keith R 4:21:04 (16,883)
Taylor, Kevin A 4:12:44 (14,756)
Taylor, Leslie R 3:59:45 (11,747)
Taylor, Malcolm D 5:37:58 (30,200)
Taylor, Marcus J 4:41:29 (21,989)
Taylor, Mark B 3:14:54 (2,653)
Taylor, Mark C 4:14:19 (15,165)
Taylor, Mark E 4:37:39 (21,149)
Taylor, Mark J 4:29:18 (19,119)
Taylor, Matthew 3:54:26 (10,033)
Taylor, Melvyn R 3:24:57 (3,927)

Taylor, Michael J 3:34:42 (5,611)
Taylor, Nathan S 4:49:24 (23,734)
Taylor, Neil A 3:40:26 (6,698)
Taylor, Neil B 4:29:09 (19,070)
Taylor, Nicholas 5:29:18 (29,456)
Taylor, Nicholas J 3:21:22 (3,452)
Taylor, Nigel G 4:25:25 (18,095)
Taylor, Nigel J 3:16:30 (2,819)
Taylor, Nigel R 3:38:32 (6,334)
Taylor, Owain 4:11:02 (14,339)
Taylor, Patrick A 4:04:37 (12,834)
Taylor, Paul R 4:33:46 (20,199)
Taylor, Pete R 4:13:11 (14,897)
Taylor, Peter 5:39:58 (30,360)
Taylor, Peter G 4:06:22 (13,204)
Taylor, Phil D 4:02:27 (12,366)
Taylor, Philip 2:49:01 (498)
Taylor, Philip 4:30:34 (19,442)
Taylor, Philip C 3:20:35 (3,346)
Taylor, Philip J 4:16:53 (15,827)
Taylor, Phillip G 2:45:57 (378)
Taylor, Richard 3:58:43 (11,405)
Taylor, Rob 5:51:02 (31,130)
Taylor, Robert G 6:03:01 (31,682)
Taylor, Ryan P 3:28:07 (4,427)
Taylor, Simon B 3:08:54 (1,947)
Taylor, Stewart P 3:54:46 (10,128)
Taylor, Stuart 4:39:12 (21,490)
Taylor, Thomas W 4:06:19 (13,200)
Taylor, Vincent G 4:49:10 (23,683)
Taylor, Wilfrid R 3:06:22 (1,699)
Taylorson, Adrian S 4:31:43 (19,725)
Taylorson, Simon L 3:38:57 (6,425)
Taylor-Stoddard, Nicolas J 4:35:25 (20,583)
Taylor-Wilkin, Nigel D 4:42:08 (22,146)
Teager, Richard J 4:51:29 (24,142)
Teague, Nick R 5:35:37 (30,023)
Teague, Steven R 5:40:40 (30,404)
Teall, Michael J 3:38:21 (6,295)
Tebbit, Paul D 3:42:05 (7,043)
Tebbutt, Gary D 4:32:55 (19,982)
Tedder, Roger C 4:39:33 (21,564)
Tedoldi, Alessandro 4:34:02 (20,260)
Tedstone, Gavin M 3:50:31 (8,989)
Tee, Andrew 4:59:41 (25,831)
Teer, Ryan C 3:35:03 (5,679)
Tegala, Praag 5:25:57 (29,124)
Teitz, Karl 2:58:36 (1,075)
Teixeira, Jorge V 3:30:53 (4,960)
Teixeira-Duarte, Antonio 4:46:09 (23,038)
Teixeira-Duarte, Antonio C 3:52:05 (9,381)
Teixeira-Duarte, Miguel C 4:44:40 (22,700)
Teixeira-Duarte, Pedro M 4:40:30 (21,777)
Teixgira-Duarte, Manuel M 5:03:08 (26,332)
Teji, Shalinder 3:29:45 (4,771)
Telfer, George M 4:35:30 (20,603)
Telfer, Scott R 3:36:21 (5,904)
Telford, Christopher H 3:45:51 (7,878)
Telgenkamp, Maurits 4:48:03 (23,438)
Temple, Adam 4:07:07 (13,377)
Templeman, Paul 4:25:28 (18,110)
Templeton, Philip S 4:35:23 (20,577)
Tennant, Alastair P 4:24:38 (17,851)
Tennant, John 3:07:36 (1,813)
Tennent, Thomas D 4:40:28 (21,763)
Terrill, Chris F 4:02:56 (12,464)
Terry, Andrew 4:59:19 (25,746)
Terry, Andrew L 5:06:57 (26,853)
Terry, Colin D 4:11:50 (14,528)
Terry, Craig A 6:49:30 (32,754)
Terry, George A 4:28:40 (18,936)
Terry, Martin 2:59:11 (1,161)
Tervit, Leighton A 4:01:07 (12,077)
Tesfai, Awot 4:34:39 (20,397)
Tesolin, Tiziano 4:31:11 (19,575)
Tesoro, Giovanni 4:21:51 (17,076)
Testa, Mario 3:56:51 (10,804)
Tester, Andrew F 4:08:58 (13,853)
Tester, Victor E 4:45:48 (22,968)
Tevenan, John 4:42:32 (22,229)
Thackeray, Richard P 3:09:09 (1,969)
Thackray, David J 4:39:39 (21,588)
Thakrar, Bharat 5:30:57 (29,644)

Thapa, Ben V	4:33:33 (20,149)	Thomas, Robert M	3:41:03 (6,815)	Thoms, Michael A	3:34:31 (5,571)
Thaw, George T	5:48:17 (30,962)	Thomas, Robert L	5:23:47 (28,916)	Thomson, Alex J	3:26:02 (4,081)
Thayre, Mark	5:09:53 (27,253)	Thomas, Ron J	5:16:07 (28,017)	Thomson, Bob	4:56:24 (25,189)
Theakstone, Ian L	3:43:46 (7,411)	Thomas, Roy D	3:37:20 (6,098)	Thomson, Brendan K	3:52:45 (9,557)
Thein, Alan	3:41:09 (6,841)	Thomas, Rupert T	3:53:59 (9,917)	Thomson, Martin	4:59:24 (25,761)
Theobald, Jonathan G	3:15:08 (2,674)	Thomas, Russ J	4:58:02 (25,511)	Thomson, Robert	4:06:03 (13,152)
Theobold, Nigel G	3:52:22 (9,458)	Thomas, Russell	5:25:59 (29,128)	Thomson, Robert H	5:08:01 (27,007)
Theophanous, Gabriel	5:55:08 (31,310)	Thomas, Shaun	4:17:09 (15,894)	Thomson, Stephen	3:03:51 (1,503)
Thewlis, Andrew R	4:47:25 (23,296)	Thomas, Simon A	4:12:39 (14,740)	Thomson, Steven R	4:59:52 (25,862)
Thibault, Jacques	3:31:30 (5,066)	Thomas, Simon H	4:51:34 (24,156)	Thorarinsson, Sigurdur	2:56:57 (939)
Thillaye Du Boullay, Chrstian	3:34:15 (5,520)	Thomas, Simon R	3:03:21 (1,469)	Thordarson, Birgir	3:21:53 (3,520)
Thing, James E	3:34:51 (5,633)	Thomas, Stephen	2:40:41 (223)	Thoren, Bjorn	4:24:32 (17,809)
Thiongo, Simon K	4:51:22 (24,112)	Thomas, Stephen G	4:45:47 (22,965)	Thorington, Peter J	4:30:10 (19,340)
Tholen, Michael W	4:20:26 (16,717)	Thomas, Stephen J	3:20:08 (3,284)	Thorley, Matthew S	3:47:56 (8,363)
Tholome, Luc H	3:05:37 (1,628)	Thomas, Stuart W	3:59:35 (11,694)	Thorn, Jonathan D	4:02:07 (12,289)
Thomas, Adrian	3:12:42 (2,361)	Thomas, Wayne	5:37:18 (30,152)	Thorn, Keith R	4:00:56 (12,027)
Thomas, Alan	4:44:44 (22,716)	Thomas, Will D	4:38:55 (21,423)	Thorn, Mike A	3:45:26 (7,789)
Thomas, Alan D	5:57:04 (31,409)	Thomason, Francis L	3:40:53 (6,776)	Thorn, Richard I	3:03:19 (1,464)
Thomas, Alex	4:08:04 (13,632)	Thomason, Richard P	3:21:21 (3,449)	Thorn, Tony M	5:22:39 (28,795)
Thomas, Allan	3:36:24 (5,914)	Thomassin, Mathias	2:47:23 (430)	Thorne, Colin	4:54:11 (24,724)
Thomas, Alun	5:19:37 (28,449)	Thompson, Alan B	4:45:28 (22,901)	Thorne, Gerrard J	3:58:00 (11,154)
Thomas, Andrew K	3:32:44 (5,284)	Thompson, Allan J	4:11:01 (14,336)	Thorne, Harold C	3:36:10 (5,868)
Thomas, Austen J	3:02:43 (1,419)	Thompson, Andrew	3:16:56 (2,871)	Thorne, John W	4:22:50 (17,331)
Thomas, Barry H	4:09:56 (14,089)	Thompson, Andrew D	2:47:44 (447)	Thorne, Robert E	4:17:27 (15,969)
Thomas, Ben	6:10:27 (31,943)	Thompson, Andrew J	3:08:53 (1,945)	Thorneloe, Guy R	3:18:31 (3,069)
Thomas, Callum A	3:47:44 (8,306)	Thompson, Andrew P	2:48:34 (476)	Thorner, Roddy B	4:13:32 (14,962)
Thomas, Carl	4:57:54 (25,479)	Thompson, Ashley	3:52:38 (9,534)	Thorneton-Field, Matthew	5:48:49 (30,991)
Thomas, Christopher P	3:49:33 (8,759)	Thompson, Barry J	3:26:59 (4,241)	Thornett, Greg J	3:54:48 (10,145)
Thomas, Clive	2:59:37 (1,212)	Thompson, Ben G	4:19:19 (16,429)	Thornhill, Ernest J	3:43:32 (7,358)
Thomas, Colin R	3:54:34 (10,069)	Thompson, Ben J	3:32:29 (5,246)	Thornhill, Roger	4:48:20 (23,498)
Thomas, Darren M	5:21:41 (28,682)	Thompson, Colin D	5:58:21 (31,478)	Thornton, Gary M	4:17:51 (16,072)
Thomas, David	4:07:56 (13,593)	Thompson, Colin W	3:39:37 (6,557)	Thornton, James S	5:11:21 (27,434)
Thomas, David I	3:49:55 (8,848)	Thompson, David A	5:06:13 (26,740)	Thornton, Jonathan D	4:53:10 (24,500)
Thomas, David R	4:23:26 (17,478)	Thompson, David P	3:17:54 (2,985)	Thornton, Keith J	3:01:38 (1,346)
Thomas, Dean A	3:09:19 (1,986)	Thompson, David W	4:23:25 (17,474)	Thornton, Kevin J	3:43:45 (7,408)
Thomas, Eric J	3:07:34 (1,810)	Thompson, Delme R	4:34:48 (20,436)	Thornton, Paul A	4:24:19 (17,754)
Thomas, Gareth	3:04:41 (1,560)	Thompson, Denis M	3:41:38 (6,950)	Thornton, Stanley	6:08:56 (31,892)
Thomas, Gareth L	5:17:59 (28,237)	Thompson, Derek C	4:59:33 (25,799)	Thornton, Thomas F	5:44:40 (30,697)
Thomas, Gareth R	2:31:22 (77)	Thompson, Dominic J	5:14:16 (27,807)	Thorogood, Spencer	5:39:26 (30,314)
Thomas, Gavin	3:23:40 (3,738)	Thompson, Gary H	3:10:38 (2,126)	Thorpe, Gary R	2:43:37 (303)
Thomas, George A	4:07:23 (13,447)	Thompson, George	2:44:16 (321)	Thorpe, Ian M	5:45:59 (30,782)
Thomas, George A	4:50:40 (23,976)	Thompson, Ian	3:27:13 (4,274)	Thorpe, Nick J	4:21:06 (16,892)
Thomas, Glyn A	4:34:20 (20,321)	Thompson, Ian P	3:34:57 (5,653)	Thorpe, Paul J	3:29:55 (4,809)
Thomas, Glynn L	2:50:07 (554)	Thompson, James L	4:20:29 (16,733)	Thorsteinsson, Vilhelm M	3:15:18 (2,695)
Thomas, Graham N	4:56:56 (25,290)	Thompson, James W	4:43:09 (22,360)	Thorstensson, Eirikur	3:55:34 (10,390)
Thomas, Grant	3:54:06 (9,946)	Thompson, Jane S	6:52:41 (32,791)	Thranberend, Klaus	4:29:16 (19,107)
Thomas, Gwyn	4:16:35 (15,747)	Thompson, Jeremy P	5:42:44 (30,556)	Threadgould, Michael D	5:20:06 (28,503)
Thomas, Hadrian	3:35:56 (5,825)	Thompson, John	5:17:14 (28,157)	Throssell, Stephen	3:09:12 (1,976)
Thomas, Henry J	3:21:11 (3,420)	Thompson, John D	4:16:28 (15,714)	Thrower, Nigel R	3:59:56 (11,795)
Thomas, Huw	4:57:57 (25,487)	Thompson, John S	3:19:07 (3,145)	Thubron, Neil A	3:00:15 (1,252)
Thomas, Ian	4:02:57 (12,467)	Thompson, Jonathan	5:22:34 (28,778)	Thuning, Hannes	3:59:31 (11,677)
Thomas, Ian P	3:21:33 (3,477)	Thompson, Jonathan P	3:41:48 (6,988)	Thurgood, Colin H	5:46:40 (30,836)
Thomas, Ian W	4:02:19 (12,336)	Thompson, Julian W	4:16:12 (15,644)	Thurgood, Colin M	5:46:40 (30,836)
Thomas, Jeffrey C	3:54:23 (10,023)	Thompson, Keith N	3:13:51 (2,507)	Thurgood, Hugh A	3:38:45 (6,376)
Thomas, John	3:42:18 (7,079)	Thompson, Lawrence	4:26:09 (18,296)	Thurman, Ian J	6:20:21 (32,239)
Thomas, John D	7:12:45 (33,000)	Thompson, Marcus R	5:20:57 (28,605)	Thursfield, Steven A	4:37:57 (21,211)
Thomas, John P	3:36:08 (5,860)	Thompson, Mark D	5:31:00 (29,650)	Thurston, Leslie J	3:39:07 (6,458)
Thomas, Justin	3:10:13 (2,087)	Thompson, Mark E	3:37:42 (6,166)	Thurtle, David G	5:50:30 (31,111)
Thomas, Kevin	3:23:57 (3,782)	Thompson, Mark L	3:30:38 (4,921)	Thwaites, David M	3:41:53 (7,004)
Thomas, Kevin P	3:29:36 (4,743)	Thompson, Mark R	4:32:02 (19,798)	Thwaites, Gary M	3:42:04 (7,040)
Thomas, Leighton N	3:43:49 (7,427)	Thompson, Martyn J	5:10:53 (27,374)	Thwaites, Laurie M	3:11:11 (2,176)
Thomas, Lennard	3:24:01 (3,796)	Thompson, Matthew	3:55:30 (10,374)	Tibbalds, Benedict M	3:48:54 (8,609)
Thomas, Lucien	3:25:55 (4,061)	Thompson, Michael P	4:02:18 (12,331)	Tibbles, Mark W	3:28:40 (4,543)
Thomas, Malcolm C	5:12:25 (27,581)	Thompson, Mike	3:49:19 (8,697)	Tibero, Magnus	3:46:56 (8,106)
Thomas, Mark D	3:47:12 (8,168)	Thompson, Mike	3:58:32 (11,350)	Tickle, David C	3:40:34 (6,724)
Thomas, Martin L	5:51:28 (31,153)	Thompson, Neil C	3:23:07 (3,668)	Tidbury, Colin E	5:12:37 (27,602)
Thomas, Michael	4:44:11 (22,606)	Thompson, Nigel P	2:41:43 (239)	Tidd, Damien	3:39:12 (6,475)
Thomas, Miles H	3:18:55 (3,124)	Thompson, Paul	2:29:56 (70)	Tidd, Matthew L	6:41:13 (32,628)
Thomas, Neil R	4:24:32 (17,809)	Thompson, Paul C	3:23:16 (3,682)	Tidder, Anthony R	4:53:47 (24,635)
Thomas, Nicholas J	3:43:44 (7,402)	Thompson, Paul D	3:51:02 (9,110)	Tidey, Keith	4:49:41 (23,789)
Thomas, Nicholas P	4:59:51 (25,858)	Thompson, Paul J	3:58:56 (11,487)	Tidey, William M	3:54:40 (10,099)
Thomas, Nick E	3:15:45 (2,747)	Thompson, Paul R	4:39:59 (21,670)	Tidiman, Steve	2:56:20 (877)
Thomas, Paul	4:06:30 (13,233)	Thompson, Peter A	5:03:13 (26,350)	Tidswell, Daniel J	4:34:24 (20,341)
Thomas, Paul A	4:26:35 (18,403)	Thompson, Philip	3:49:55 (8,848)	Tiedeman, Simon A	4:29:42 (19,228)
Thomas, Paul B	4:44:30 (22,680)	Thompson, Robert	4:13:38 (14,991)	Tiernan, John	4:41:00 (21,895)
Thomas, Paul J	4:58:15 (25,560)	Thompson, Robert E	3:26:47 (4,205)	Tiernan, Patrick J	3:02:54 (1,431)
Thomas, Paul S	3:52:52 (9,585)	Thompson, Robert L	3:10:02 (2,066)	Tiernan, Paul	4:57:32 (25,403)
Thomas, Peter	3:01:48 (1,356)	Thompson, Roger	5:47:28 (30,916)	Tierney, David A	3:40:29 (6,709)
Thomas, Peter C	5:18:43 (28,339)	Thompson, Russell L	5:45:49 (30,766)	Tierney, John K	4:34:52 (20,449)
Thomas, Peter R	6:01:08 (31,611)	Thompson, Sean M	3:33:00 (5,322)	Tighe, Anthony R	4:26:26 (18,368)
Thomas, Philip J	3:34:17 (5,529)	Thompson, Simon	4:56:08 (25,128)	Tighe, Christopher J	4:38:54 (21,420)
Thomas, Richard	3:41:09 (6,841)	Thompson, Tony	2:59:09 (1,154)	Tighe, Jonathan A	4:38:53 (21,413)
Thomas, Richard	4:03:20 (12,559)	Thoms, Holger	4:19:34 (16,497)	Tighe, Matthew	4:38:52 (21,406)

Tigue, Daniel S....3:44:59 (7,684)
Tilbury, Neil....3:51:26 (9,204)
Tildsley, David G....5:53:46 (31,253)
Tilke, Warren....3:55:25 (10,349)
Tillbrooke, Tony....4:22:58 (17,358)
Tiller, Mark A....3:41:24 (6,895)
Tillery, Andrew J....2:59:44 (1,223)
Tillett, Ian M....3:51:43 (9,278)
Tillett, Matthew R....3:51:24 (9,200)
Tilley, Ian R....4:42:35 (22,235)
Tilley, Robert E....5:18:27 (28,302)
Tilling, Stuart J....3:17:51 (2,980)
Tillotson, Marcus J....2:58:50 (1,120)
Tillott, Neil D....3:11:17 (2,194)
Tillyard, Robert F....4:51:54 (24,229)
Tillyer, David W....5:18:28 (28,304)
Tilson, Scott A....3:24:13 (3,826)
Timlin, Bryan....3:19:52 (3,244)
Timlin, Jonathan E....4:37:11 (21,025)
Timmermann, Kai....3:20:16 (3,309)
Timmins, Adrian....2:43:00 (285)
Timmins, Colin W....3:26:54 (4,223)
Timmins, James....4:45:54 (22,989)
Timmins, Michael....3:30:33 (4,904)
Timmins, Steven....4:14:34 (15,226)
Timmis, Jonathan P....3:43:20 (7,315)
Timms, Lee A....4:00:59 (12,045)
Timms, Richard V....4:16:16 (15,660)
Timothy, Andrew M....4:31:11 (19,575)
Timothy, Kevin M....4:34:45 (20,424)
Tinarelli, Edigio....3:55:59 (10,537)
Tindall, Alexander P....5:12:47 (27,622)
Tindall, Dave....4:43:06 (22,346)
Tingley, Thomas A....4:22:07 (17,152)
Tinline, David P....4:34:03 (20,267)
Tinline, Robert J....3:50:34 (9,000)
Tinney, Graham....5:16:54 (28,116)
Tinnyunt, Roebrt....6:33:18 (32,501)
Tinsey, Jason....4:20:47 (16,806)
Tinsley, Grahame M....3:55:16 (10,305)
Tinston, Joseph F....3:23:48 (3,755)
Tiozzo, Angelo....5:57:19 (31,425)
Tippen, Ian F....5:19:48 (28,471)
Tippet, Simon J....4:37:17 (21,054)
Tipping, Niall M....5:38:50 (30,271)
Tippu, Naveed....5:57:18 (31,422)
Tisi, Simon J....4:58:38 (25,632)
Tissa, Remi N....3:58:46 (11,431)
Titchener, John B....4:01:03 (12,058)
Tite, Julian C....3:58:19 (11,275)
Titlestad, Kjell....2:58:40 (1,090)
Titley, Adam J....4:14:30 (15,206)
Titt, John K....3:18:26 (3,053)
Tittley, Stephen A....5:00:08 (25,913)
Tivella, Leonardo....3:41:00 (6,805)
Tizzard, Raymond P....5:31:57 (29,734)
Toal, Declan D....5:19:10 (28,397)
Tobin, Dominick....5:10:14 (27,295)
Tobutt, Nicholas A....3:48:10 (8,430)
Tod, Jonathan....3:19:00 (3,135)
Tod, Simon J....3:56:08 (10,577)
Todd, Alastair....4:15:28 (15,469)
Todd, David B....3:29:02 (4,631)
Todd, David C....4:14:25 (15,185)
Todd, James K....5:05:06 (26,599)
Todd, Kevin J....5:12:50 (27,624)
Todd, Olly J....3:27:06 (4,259)
Todd, Richard P....4:02:33 (12,387)
Todd, Ross....3:44:12 (7,491)
Todeschini, Flavio....4:39:25 (21,548)
Toft, Dave H....3:31:30 (5,066)
Tointon, Mark J....4:18:55 (16,331)
Tojeiro, Rob....2:49:16 (511)
Toledano, Simon....3:40:18 (6,676)
Tolfrey, Neil....2:50:05 (553)
Toll, Alexander J....3:00:57 (1,297)
Tollan, Gerard....5:19:57 (28,486)
Tomblin, Matthew J....4:08:33 (13,759)
Tombling, Anthony....5:19:01 (28,377)
Tombs, Jonathan M....3:23:36 (3,726)
Tomco, Jan....3:41:58 (7,018)
Tomita, Hiroshi....3:56:26 (10,668)
Tomkins, James A....4:39:49 (21,632)
Tomkins, Paul J....3:46:38 (8,043)
Tomlins, Mike J....5:29:28 (29,485)
Tomlinson, Ben....5:57:10 (31,414)
Tomlinson, Charles M....4:28:48 (18,973)
Tomlinson, Clive....5:52:16 (31,192)
Tomlinson, Dean L....4:50:50 (24,010)
Tomlinson, Francis G....4:56:55 (25,287)
Tomlinson, Frderick G....7:32:46 (33,104)
Tomlinson, Gavin....2:34:48 (111)
Tomlinson, Howard C....5:02:35 (26,260)
Tomlinson, James C....5:33:28 (29,846)
Tomlinson, Mark W....2:51:43 (624)
Tomlinson, Ryan....3:14:08 (2,546)
Tomlinson, Scott J....4:34:11 (20,288)
Tommasini, Claudio....3:31:15 (5,032)
Tompsett, Gary....4:21:58 (17,108)
Toms, David A....4:03:14 (12,535)
Toms, Malcolm....5:47:11 (30,877)
Tomson, Allan....4:48:52 (23,623)
Tomuseni, Dominic....5:02:17 (26,222)
Tondo, Renato....5:31:12 (29,678)
Tonge, Andrew J....3:25:51 (4,055)
Tonkin, Mike J....5:32:28 (29,767)
Tonkin, Simon E....4:11:02 (14,339)
Tonks, Nigel J....3:22:00 (3,533)
Tonndorf, Joerg M....3:23:10 (3,672)
Tononi, Aldo....3:28:30 (4,512)
Tookey, Andrew....4:38:02 (21,231)
Toolis, Patrick F....3:23:49 (3,764)
Toomey, Sean....3:58:12 (11,233)
Toon, Andrew R....4:56:58 (25,302)
Toon, Royston L....3:56:09 (10,585)
Tootal, Thomas D....4:43:50 (22,533)
Tootell, Alex J....5:14:45 (27,879)
Top, Gerrit....3:52:57 (9,610)
Tope, Clare....4:40:47 (21,848)
Topham, Daren R....5:22:34 (28,778)
Topham, Matthew P....3:19:05 (3,140)
Topham, Nigel R....4:20:34 (16,750)
Topper, Steve....3:50:58 (9,091)
Topping, Benjamin J....3:24:01 (3,796)
Topping, Stephen J....4:33:35 (20,159)
Topping, Troy....3:44:26 (7,547)
Torbet, Alex....4:53:58 (24,670)
Torelli, Marco....3:46:22 (7,976)
Tornari, Tommy....5:36:41 (30,110)
Torode, John D....5:28:43 (29,402)
Torrance, Andrew....4:04:52 (12,888)
Torrens, Jamie....4:10:42 (14,248)
Torti, Enzo....4:50:37 (23,966)
Toscano, Joseph....4:45:55 (22,992)
Tou, Daniel P....4:32:12 (19,833)
Toubiana, Stephane....4:24:51 (17,903)
Touhey, Christopher K....4:35:00 (20,491)
Toulemonde, Pierre H....5:02:44 (26,278)
Toulson, Simon J....5:09:38 (27,222)
Toumazis, Tom....4:31:00 (19,533)
Toumazo, Dimitri....6:33:53 (32,513)
Tourret, Eric....4:50:54 (24,025)
Tout, John....5:25:21 (29,074)
Towell, Robert W....3:58:09 (11,209)
Towell, Shaun A....4:24:30 (17,802)
Towers, Stephen....4:14:24 (15,180)
Towers, William B....3:57:12 (10,920)
Townley, Mike D....3:05:51 (1,652)
Townsend, Andy R....4:03:08 (12,516)
Townsend, David S....4:54:57 (24,880)
Townsend, John B....6:41:50 (32,636)
Townsend, Martin B....3:15:03 (2,664)
Townsend, Michael....5:05:48 (26,676)
Townsend, Richard L....4:19:32 (16,489)
Townsend, Stuart....3:38:51 (6,396)
Townsend, Tim J....3:29:31 (4,723)
Townsend, Victor J....5:33:22 (29,837)
Townshend, David....3:52:14 (9,422)
Townsley, Scott P....4:16:08 (15,629)
Townsley, Steve J....2:59:37 (1,212)
Toy, Jonathon F....4:13:07 (14,878)
Toye, Anthony....3:15:12 (2,683)
Toye, Ken C....4:18:31 (16,238)
Toyne, Adam C....3:20:17 (3,310)
Tozer, Peter....4:23:55 (17,630)
Tozer, Ross W....3:14:40 (2,625)
Tozer, Shaun A....2:51:42 (623)
Tracey, Andrew D....3:07:46 (1,834)
Tracey, Ciaran....4:59:25 (25,764)
Tracey, Graham R....3:08:51 (1,940)
Tracey, Simon J....4:24:06 (17,683)
Trafford, Stephen J....4:57:03 (25,324)
Train, Terence S....4:16:14 (15,652)
Tranah, Troy A....4:19:57 (16,589)
Trant, Mike....3:41:20 (6,882)
Tranter, Alex J....4:23:31 (17,509)
Trape, Florent J....4:20:25 (16,713)
Trapp, Neil T....4:05:31 (13,027)
Trasler, Andrew M....4:27:54 (18,722)
Travers, Andrew R....4:56:40 (25,236)
Travers, Duncan J....4:22:47 (17,318)
Travers, Paul J....3:56:38 (10,734)
Traversa, Nicola Vito....3:48:47 (8,572)
Travert, Stephane....5:10:19 (27,307)
Traynor, Mark W....2:56:35 (901)
Traynor, Patrick....5:51:09 (31,134)
Traynor, Simon J....3:43:13 (7,292)
Treacher, Adam P....4:09:25 (13,969)
Treadgold, Paul J....4:56:49 (25,259)
Trebilcock, Norman A....4:41:34 (22,004)
Trede, Volker....3:34:24 (5,547)
Tredget, Richard D....4:51:22 (24,112)
Tregaskiss, Stephen D....3:34:32 (5,575)
Tregubov, Victor....3:02:01 (1,376)
Tregurtha, Warren....4:48:56 (23,636)
Treleaven, James G....5:03:50 (26,431)
Tremain, Cameron L....4:08:24 (13,717)
Tremeaud, Louezig....3:29:36 (4,743)
Tremolada, Lorenzo....3:51:40 (9,260)
Trenchard, Wiliam J....3:24:45 (3,905)
Trend, Stephen A....4:06:52 (13,316)
Trenerry, Jacob....4:32:09 (19,820)
Trennery, David S....4:22:13 (17,179)
Trenoowicz, Christopher J....4:11:36 (14,479)
Trent, Dean....5:43:22 (30,598)
Tresca, Arnaud M....3:25:20 (3,980)
Trettin, Reinhard....3:16:26 (2,813)
Trevail, Benjamin W....3:51:31 (9,222)
Trevail, Tim J....4:25:36 (18,136)
Trevelyan, Adrian....3:22:35 (3,608)
Trevelyan, Colin G....4:40:40 (21,823)
Trevelyan, Oliver....4:07:31 (13,479)
Trevenna, Adam C....4:00:17 (11,884)
Trevenna, Steven G....4:06:52 (13,316)
Treves, Alex K....4:11:00 (14,329)
Trevisani, Marco....3:45:47 (7,866)
Trevorrow, James....5:34:56 (29,962)
Trevorrow, Kaylene E....5:31:04 (29,664)
Trew, Michael J....3:03:39 (1,488)
Trewhitt, Gary M....3:47:37 (8,276)
Triballeau, Michel....4:04:30 (12,816)
Trice, Robert K....4:04:06 (12,739)
Trice, Stephen J....3:48:51 (8,591)
Trichot, Guy A....2:59:22 (1,184)
Trickett, Paul R....4:15:23 (15,442)
Trickett, Philip J....3:50:28 (8,972)
Trickey, Christopher P....6:26:53 (32,400)
Trigg, Christopher....4:54:09 (24,712)
Trigger, Mark E....3:51:17 (9,168)
Trigger, Matthew W....4:22:50 (17,331)
Trigger, Roger M....4:11:27 (14,450)
Triggs, Tim R....5:12:42 (27,615)
Trigwell, Peter G....5:41:38 (30,469)
Trim, Christopher E....3:33:52 (5,459)
Trimmer, Benjamin J....5:08:32 (27,083)
Tringham, Nicholas J....4:39:41 (21,596)
Triquet, Yves....4:36:42 (20,896)
Triscott, Simon D....4:00:30 (11,934)
Trodd, Ron....5:07:04 (26,869)
Troidl, Reinhard....3:36:32 (5,940)
Troke, Christopher B....4:51:50 (24,218)
Trommel, Bastiaan....3:42:28 (7,106)
Troon, Nicholas J....4:22:35 (17,260)
Troop, Nicholas J....4:02:32 (12,382)
Trory, John A....3:33:54 (5,464)
Troth, Anthony....4:31:18 (19,613)
Trott, Alan....5:09:59 (27,263)
Trotter, Douglas I....4:31:14 (19,593)
Trotter, Ian H....4:44:53 (22,752)

Troup, Michael G	3:16:37 (2,830)	
Trowbridge, Tony T	3:40:14 (6,663)	
Trower, Patrick A	5:40:10 (30,378)	
Trowsdale, John	4:47:13 (23,266)	
Trowsdale, Paul J	3:27:19 (4,297)	
Trudgen, Russell C	4:14:26 (15,190)	
Truman, Matthew A	3:37:32 (6,137)	
Truran, Martin G	3:24:34 (3,876)	
Truscott, Robert K	6:07:30 (31,838)	
Trussler, Mark J	3:33:38 (5,427)	
Truter, René	4:04:24 (12,796)	
Try, Christopher E	3:07:59 (1,857)	
Tsang, Philip M	3:54:23 (10,023)	
Tsavalos, John S	3:58:06 (11,185)	
Tschurr, Enrico	3:35:04 (5,684)	
Tsiokanos, Evangelos	5:23:27 (28,885)	
Tsoi, Andy C	3:24:09 (3,815)	
Tsopotsa, Vimbai	4:28:42 (18,944)	
Tsutsumi, Hatsuji	3:36:35 (5,952)	
Ttouli, Peter	7:17:30 (33,024)	
Tubbs, Trevor D	3:55:03 (10,227)	
Tuck, Paul	3:37:34 (6,145)	
Tuck, Russell	4:24:21 (17,764)	
Tuck, Stephen G	4:10:23 (14,192)	
Tucker, Allan J	3:45:48 (7,873)	
Tucker, Andy J	3:03:26 (1,475)	
Tucker, David K	3:16:05 (2,787)	
Tucker, Gareth J	4:31:42 (19,721)	
Tucker, Graham J	3:09:50 (2,049)	
Tucker, Guy	3:34:55 (5,646)	
Tucker, Harry T	3:36:20 (5,900)	
Tucker, Jeffrey	4:07:02 (13,351)	
Tucker, Mark W	5:33:44 (29,872)	
Tucker, Russell	4:26:38 (18,417)	
Tucker, Stephen P	4:12:18 (14,652)	
Tuckett, Mark A	2:49:06 (504)	
Tuckey, Andrew P	2:37:52 (164)	
Tudge, Scott	3:23:43 (3,746)	
Tudor, Steve	3:10:06 (2,073)	
Tufts, Mark J	4:31:26 (19,649)	
Tugwell, Peter M	5:47:37 (30,926)	
Tullett, Andrew J	3:53:01 (9,630)	
Tulloch, Kevin J	2:56:27 (888)	
Tune, Christopher J	4:30:30 (19,428)	
Tune, Darran J	4:34:53 (20,459)	
Tunn, Martin P	4:54:46 (24,833)	
Tunstall, Paul	4:00:05 (11,839)	
Tuplin, Lee J	3:32:04 (5,175)	
Turek, Jeremy	4:24:39 (17,858)	
Turello, Naldo	4:32:47 (19,958)	
Turl, Gary	4:09:12 (13,909)	
Turley, Jonathan C	4:16:26 (15,704)	
Turley, Richard P	3:41:46 (6,978)	
Turnbull, Alexander B	3:28:23 (4,489)	
Turnbull, David R	2:52:33 (654)	
Turnbull, Douglas	5:10:45 (27,350)	
Turnbull, James H	3:45:26 (7,789)	
Turnbull, James T	3:24:27 (3,853)	
Turnbull, Martin	4:03:20 (12,559)	
Turnbull, Simon R	4:07:41 (13,528)	
Turner, Andrew C	4:42:06 (22,134)	
Turner, Andrew J	2:53:47 (711)	
Turner, Andy J	3:42:44 (7,167)	
Turner, Brian W	5:20:22 (28,550)	
Turner, Carl J	4:46:13 (23,051)	
Turner, Christopher J	4:48:40 (23,579)	
Turner, Colin	3:53:43 (9,827)	
Turner, Colin E	5:21:37 (28,674)	
Turner, Danny C	4:15:09 (15,380)	
Turner, Emmett A	5:42:36 (30,543)	
Turner, Glyn R	4:38:38 (21,363)	
Turner, Grahame E	3:30:12 (4,854)	
Turner, Ian A	3:57:47 (11,110)	
Turner, James	5:46:48 (30,848)	
Turner, Jeremy	4:38:56 (21,426)	
Turner, Jonathan C	3:43:48 (7,422)	
Turner, Joshua M	4:49:23 (23,730)	
Turner, Julian P	4:29:34 (19,190)	
Turner, Kevin	4:45:18 (22,856)	
Turner, Kevin L	4:08:05 (13,639)	
Turner, Kevin N	5:47:18 (30,898)	
Turner, Lee M	4:04:16 (12,770)	
Turner, Mark A	4:11:39 (14,491)	

Turner, Mark A	5:58:31 (31,487)	
Turner, Mark J	4:28:56 (19,006)	
Turner, Martin	4:18:39 (16,266)	
Turner, Martyn J	5:08:43 (27,107)	
Turner, Michael S	3:12:56 (2,390)	
Turner, Neil	3:10:41 (2,130)	
Turner, Nicholas	4:16:43 (15,783)	
Turner, Nick M	3:32:24 (5,234)	
Turner, Nigel P	3:46:13 (7,947)	
Turner, Paul	4:54:46 (24,833)	
Turner, Paul M	5:22:48 (28,811)	
Turner, Paul R	4:48:21 (23,500)	
Turner, Peter A	3:41:01 (6,807)	
Turner, Peter J	2:55:48 (837)	
Turner, Raymond J	4:40:34 (21,804)	
Turner, Richard M	3:48:09 (8,422)	
Turner, Richard M	4:26:06 (18,286)	
Turner, Robert L	4:38:49 (21,396)	
Turner, Sean	3:46:54 (8,101)	
Turner, Simon W	3:49:14 (8,674)	
Turner, Stephen J	3:38:54 (6,412)	
Turner, Steven J	4:36:51 (20,952)	
Turner, Terence W	3:58:18 (11,266)	
Turner, Tristan N	5:21:02 (28,611)	
Turner, Andrew K	3:09:09 (1,969)	
Turner Smith, David	6:02:37 (31,664)	
Turney, Michael P	3:12:18 (2,323)	
Turney, Wade	4:20:10 (16,652)	
Turnock, Jason R	4:12:53 (14,806)	
Turp, Roy W	5:19:01 (28,377)	
Turpie, Gordon H	3:04:29 (1,544)	
Turpin, Charles E	5:42:37 (30,544)	
Turrell, Jeff W	3:54:59 (10,196)	
Turrell, Shane M	5:19:44 (28,462)	
Turrell-Croft, Thomas C	4:08:16 (13,683)	
Turton, Andrew J	4:36:01 (20,725)	
Turton, Les J	3:10:27 (2,108)	
Turvey, Andrew P	3:44:24 (7,538)	
Turzynski, Maciej	4:28:31 (18,901)	
Tushingham, John P	3:59:47 (11,755)	
Tustain, Adam R	4:52:45 (24,409)	
Tustin, Bayley J	3:34:45 (5,621)	
Tveter, Trygve K	3:09:48 (2,044)	
Tvilde, Tore	3:06:50 (1,738)	
Tweddle, Andrew	4:17:47 (16,056)	
Tweddle, John C	3:12:57 (2,391)	
Tweddle, Richard J	2:46:46 (410)	
Tweed, Andy M	3:30:31 (4,899)	
Tweedle, Allan	5:57:48 (31,446)	
Tweedle, Tom	4:35:39 (20,639)	
Twidale, Richard J	4:24:38 (17,851)	
Twigg, Graham J	4:46:58 (23,200)	
Twigger, Andrew N	5:09:33 (27,214)	
Twitchen, Roger W	4:50:47 (24,001)	
Tye, Colin I	4:34:58 (20,480)	
Tye, Dominic M	7:04:30 (32,937)	
Tyers, Gregory C	4:01:57 (12,249)	
Tyldesley, Mark J	3:38:49 (6,386)	
Tyler, Anthony H	3:14:01 (2,534)	
Tyler, Anthony R	4:21:15 (16,927)	
Tyler, Graham A	4:03:16 (12,546)	
Tyler, Graham J	4:55:11 (24,936)	
Tyler, Joe J	4:14:37 (15,237)	
Tyler, John	3:02:06 (1,384)	
Tyler, Keith	4:25:41 (18,159)	
Tyler, Richar C	3:42:19 (7,082)	
Tyler, Simon J	4:06:28 (13,224)	
Tyler, Stephen	4:49:57 (23,835)	
Tyman, Robert M	3:26:29 (4,149)	
Tynan, John	4:16:51 (15,815)	
Tynan, Martin C	4:36:02 (20,731)	
Tyrrell, Andrew J	3:34:22 (5,545)	
Tyrrell, Bryan K	4:18:38 (16,262)	
Tyrrell, Chris	4:53:40 (24,610)	
Tyrrell, Liam J	4:26:18 (18,335)	
Tyrrell, Mark	4:56:22 (25,179)	
Tyrrell, Nigel P	3:29:52 (4,800)	
Tyrrell, Oliver	4:42:49 (22,288)	
Tyrrell, Patrick B	3:29:48 (4,782)	
Tyrrell, Philip G	6:54:05 (32,808)	
Tyson, Graham	4:02:32 (12,382)	
Tyson, Simon J	3:53:51 (9,882)	
Tyszkiewicz, John Z	3:57:09 (10,902)	

Tyzack, David J	4:56:49 (25,259)	
Tyzack, William	4:12:18 (14,652)	
Uberschar, Tony	3:24:17 (3,836)	
Ubsdell, Simon	3:02:44 (1,420)	
Uddin, Mohib	4:51:26 (24,132)	
Uden, Simon	9:00:55 (33,217)	
Udraufski, Glyn	5:01:21 (26,094)	
Uff, Andrew J	5:54:32 (31,285)	
Uff, Frederick	4:08:37 (13,773)	
Uffendell, James S	4:11:01 (14,396)	
Uglow, Bruce C	4:49:54 (23,826)	
Ugwumadu, Austin H	4:07:10 (13,396)	
Ujihashi, Motoshige	5:05:28 (26,641)	
Ukrasin, Igor	4:19:54 (16,578)	
Ulargui, Mauricio	4:11:51 (14,534)	
Uljasz, Patrice	4:14:32 (15,213)	
Ulliott, Tom	2:51:55 (631)	
Ulrich, Kai-Uwe	3:27:21 (4,303)	
Ulvoeen, Jon Arne	5:51:42 (31,165)	
Umpleby, Philip	6:27:19 (32,410)	
Umweni, Ighodaro	5:46:48 (30,848)	
Underhill, Giles	4:35:02 (20,498)	
Underhill, Paul	4:27:35 (18,650)	
Undrell, Jonathan M	5:00:03 (25,894)	
Unerman, David B	5:26:10 (29,142)	
Unger, Christoph	4:11:28 (14,452)	
Ungi, Tom	4:53:58 (24,670)	
Unia, Nasir	4:43:55 (22,554)	
Unibaso, Antonio	3:38:53 (6,408)	
Unitt, Andrew V	3:09:22 (1,996)	
Unsal, Deniz	4:46:27 (23,112)	
Unsted, Paul S	3:46:11 (7,939)	
Unsworth, Mark	3:43:14 (7,295)	
Unwin, Richard J	3:08:30 (1,909)	
Unwin, Will	2:54:02 (727)	
Uphill, Kevin J	3:55:02 (10,217)	
Upsdell, Dafydd B	4:35:06 (20,512)	
Upson, Mark	3:53:13 (9,697)	
Upton, Christopher R	4:53:12 (24,510)	
Upton, James A	4:43:32 (22,447)	
Upton, Martin J	4:14:48 (15,286)	
Upton, Nick C	3:38:31 (6,329)	
Upton, Stewart	4:45:18 (22,856)	
Upward, Mark	6:09:08 (31,899)	
Upward, Michael R	4:14:51 (15,298)	
Ural, Jon	4:23:56 (17,633)	
Urban, Alexander R	3:13:56 (2,517)	
Urch, Tyrone	5:26:28 (29,171)	
Ure, Bruce C	4:18:56 (16,337)	
Ure, Stuart C	4:35:56 (20,698)	
Uribe, Philip G	3:45:03 (7,701)	
Urie, Andrew G	5:04:51 (26,561)	
Ursfalt, Hasse	5:19:11 (28,403)	
Urwin, Alan	3:30:29 (4,889)	
Usher, John W	4:01:47 (12,209)	
Usher, Keith J	3:31:19 (5,038)	
Utterson, Colin	3:16:35 (2,826)	
Uttim, Paul	5:09:06 (27,161)	
Utley, Jonathan	3:02:33 (1,411)	
Utz, Pascal	3:34:38 (5,597)	
Uzzell, Kevin	3:10:15 (2,089)	
Vabre, Guy	4:40:31 (21,791)	
Vacalopoulos, Robert P	2:48:52 (490)	
Vaccaro, Giuseppe	4:46:37 (23,144)	
Vadgama, Nilesh B	4:35:50 (20,680)	
Vaghela, Kishor	6:39:58 (32,611)	
Vaghjiani, Vijay	4:56:03 (25,109)	
Vailes, Christopher R	5:11:05 (27,396)	
Vale, Christopher A	4:21:06 (16,892)	
Vale, David J	5:18:24 (28,297)	
Valena, Mark	4:14:31 (15,209)	
Valente, Simon C	4:24:59 (17,953)	
Valentine, David A	4:22:27 (17,235)	
Valentine, Keith R	4:50:51 (24,016)	
Valentini, Mick	2:58:21 (1,051)	
Valjy, Mohammed	6:22:14 (32,296)	
Valla, Nico S	3:43:42 (7,389)	
Vallance, Andrew	3:05:12 (1,593)	
Vallance, Roger W	3:02:16 (1,389)	
Vallario, Anthony G	4:44:27 (22,666)	
Valle, Svein	3:49:56 (8,853)	
Vallejo, Manuel	3:26:53 (4,219)	
Valler, Alfred	4:09:18 (13,934)	

Vallett, Lee J 4:05:54 (13,118)
Vallis, John H 3:09:20 (1,989)
Vally, Bashir A 4:16:17 (15,664)
Vamben, Eric S 2:37:57 (168)
Van Acker, Luc A 2:59:32 (1,194)
Van Aller, Bert 4:33:29 (20,131)
Van Beek, Andrew J 3:10:34 (2,120)
Van Blerk, Daryl A 4:11:00 (14,329)
Van De Plassche, Rob 4:12:33 (14,720)
Van Den Akker, Henk Jan 3:58:11 (11,225)
Van Den Vlekkert, Hendrik A 5:04:02 (26,462)
Van Der Sijde, Daan 4:18:55 (16,331)
Van Der Heyden, Kurt G 3:53:26 (9,749)
Van Der Hoff, Jack 4:35:12 (20,531)
Van Der Horst, Gerard 3:56:43 (10,758)
Van Der Horst, Tim 4:39:18 (21,514)
Van Der Linden, Gary O 3:39:16 (6,493)
Van Der Logt, Paul C 3:40:29 (6,709)
Van Der Meer, Jurian 4:36:43 (20,901)
Van Der Meijden, Gijs J 3:51:39 (9,255)
Van Der Merne, Willem B 3:44:54 (7,669)
Van Der Merwe, André J 3:05:19 (1,608)
Van Der Stoep, Bert 3:58:46 (11,431)
Van Der Stoep, Clemens 4:05:18 (12,978)
Van Der Stoep, Floris 3:44:29 (7,563)
Van Der Zee, Pieter 3:07:10 (1,774)
Van Deursen, Ulf 4:29:14 (19,093)
Van Dyk, William 3:38:54 (6,412)
Van Eck, Teuns H 3:31:14 (5,030)
Van Eerden, Henk 4:33:27 (20,123)
Van Egeraat, Frans 4:54:40 (24,808)
Van Eihan, Dean 4:29:36 (19,199)
Van Franck, Mark 4:23:47 (17,582)
Van Gennip, Josephys 3:37:07 (6,059)
Van Hal, Erik 3:42:09 (7,055)
Van Hecke, Georges 3:14:35 (2,611)
Van Heerden, Deon 4:46:41 (23,156)
Van Heiningen, Andrew 3:59:42 (11,728)
Van Holsteijn, Hein 3:37:27 (6,121)
Van Hulder, Michel 4:11:44 (14,503)
Van Huysteen, Detleff 6:02:37 (31,664)
Van Hyfte, Dirk 2:53:58 (724)
Van Kats, Petrus Z 4:05:44 (13,082)
Van Kerkwijk, Gerard 5:34:58 (29,964)
Van Klaveren, Mark J 5:16:20 (28,049)
Van Knippenberg, Nico 3:26:13 (4,105)
Van Nieuwkoop, Jacco 4:24:20 (17,759)
Van Oostaijen, Clemens 6:03:54 (31,723)
Van Pletsen, Schalk Merwe 3:55:03 (10,227)
Van Reenen, Rijk 4:06:00 (13,140)
Van Rij, Jaap 4:11:55 (14,555)
Van Schalkwyk, Rian 4:51:40 (24,179)
Van Tuijl, Hendrik 5:14:05 (27,781)
Van Welie, Theo W 2:56:04 (854)
Van Wijk, Mieke P 4:14:00 (15,067)
Van Wyk, Anore 4:16:29 (15,724)
Vann, David J 4:30:47 (19,491)
Vanneck, Mark A 4:38:30 (21,340)
Vanneste, Xavier J 3:13:16 (2,429)
Vanniasingham, Daniel J 5:35:55 (30,049)
Vanotti, Alfredo E 4:04:00 (12,714)
Vanpeperstraete, Eric 4:04:08 (12,749)
Vanwalscappel, Philippe 3:54:00 (9,923)
Vanwanseele, Remi L 4:05:52 (13,111)
Vara, Sanjay 3:41:50 (6,996)
Varden, Mark G 3:01:09 (1,314)
Vardy, Scott M 4:14:55 (15,315)
Varey, Thaddaeus E 4:58:56 (25,697)
Varga, Laszlo 3:02:18 (1,391)
Vargas, Guillermo 3:55:05 (10,240)
Vargin, Pier Paolo 4:42:23 (22,198)
Varley, Andrew J 4:58:38 (25,632)
Varley, Ben D 3:15:46 (2,748)
Varley, James R 4:15:19 (15,421)
Varney, Adrian J 4:39:10 (21,483)
Varney, David E 4:55:51 (25,066)
Varney, Richard C 6:19:27 (32,217)
Varnham, Keith 4:48:22 (23,506)
Varty, Christopher P 4:25:28 (18,110)
Vasconcellos, José C 2:58:22 (1,056)
Vasilescu, Laurent A 3:27:49 (4,385)
Vass, Simon O 2:58:49 (1,117)
Vassiliou, Vasso 4:36:04 (20,742)

Vaudin, John 5:28:34 (29,378)
Vaughan, Andrew J 4:39:42 (21,599)
Vaughan, Bryan J 3:48:25 (8,477)
Vaughan, Floyd 4:11:28 (14,452)
Vaughan, Gareth L 4:23:26 (17,478)
Vaughan, Mark 3:58:37 (11,372)
Vaughan, Michael A 7:07:27 (32,957)
Vaughan, Neville A 3:26:44 (4,197)
Vaughan, Rhodri 3:28:53 (4,601)
Vaughan, Robert J 6:08:12 (31,865)
Vaughan, Tim W 4:19:05 (16,363)
Vazquez, Javier J 4:36:43 (20,901)
Veasey, Andrew S 3:56:48 (10,785)
Veasey, David P 3:20:35 (3,346)
Vecchio, Leonardo 3:56:15 (10,610)
Velho, Helder 5:06:42 (26,815)
Vellensworth, Matthew 5:21:00 (28,609)
Velluet, Peter 3:47:17 (8,187)
Venables, David C 2:55:47 (835)
Venamore, Lee 5:23:22 (28,881)
Venison, Tim P 4:08:32 (13,750)
Venn, Chris J 3:54:29 (10,049)
Ventom, Mark F 3:35:02 (5,669)
Ventress, Mark A 4:24:39 (17,858)
Vera, Luis 4:55:40 (25,032)
Vera Bacallado, Juan M 4:50:18 (23,905)
Verborgt, Oliver 4:17:55 (16,083)
Vercoe, Rik J 5:50:43 (31,119)
Verdebello, Paolo 5:20:41 (28,581)
Verdejo, Juan P 3:26:28 (4,142)
Vere, Derek 4:54:56 (24,875)
Vergez, Juan A 4:07:35 (13,501)
Vergnet, Roger 4:26:14 (18,320)
Verhaere, Anthony 3:45:17 (7,751)
Verhulst, Georges 3:52:57 (9,610)
Verity, Lee R 4:00:44 (11,982)
Verlaan, Brian P 4:02:49 (12,441)
Verling, Benjamin F 3:18:10 (3,015)
Verma, Gagan 4:22:05 (17,141)
Verma, Manish 4:59:42 (25,836)
Verma, Rahul 6:13:51 (32,044)
Vermeulen, Stefaan 3:47:50 (8,336)
Vermont, Matthew D 4:28:28 (18,889)
Vern, Wayne 3:56:32 (10,694)
Vernal, Derrick 5:56:34 (31,385)
Vernon, Anthony M 8:04:24 (33,180)
Vernon, Chris M 4:51:41 (24,183)
Vernon, Christopher R 3:52:29 (9,488)
Vernon, Darren 2:56:26 (885)
Verrecchia, Steven A 3:50:52 (9,070)
Verrier, Jonathan P 4:35:37 (20,632)
Versolato, Michele 5:13:59 (27,758)
Vesey, David 5:58:38 (31,492)
Vesey, Derek 3:45:19 (7,760)
Vessey, David S 2:57:29 (984)
Vest, Torben 3:33:54 (5,464)
Vettasseri, Reji 3:54:53 (10,173)
Vey, Stephen C 3:44:47 (7,638)
Veysey, Craig L 5:03:00 (26,318)
Veysey, Wayne 4:07:01 (13,349)
Vial, Eric 3:41:35 (6,941)
Vial, Simon T 3:42:05 (7,043)
Vialls, Terry 5:11:10 (27,407)
Vianello, Federico 4:30:57 (19,521)
Vicente Do Souto, Carlos 3:25:59 (4,072)
Vichion, Mark P 4:31:24 (19,645)
Vickers, Bernard 3:00:07 (1,240)
Vickers, David 3:57:09 (10,902)
Vickers, David A 5:27:29 (29,273)
Vickers, Douglas P 4:10:51 (14,294)
Vickers, James 6:37:45 (32,574)
Vickers, Jason B 6:19:15 (32,211)
Vickers, Jay G 4:05:48 (13,100)
Vickers, Robin P 3:37:17 (6,088)
Vickery, Richard 4:08:25 (13,722)

LONDON MARATHON

Vickery, Richard J 4:11:23 (14,434)
Victor, David 4:33:43 (20,193)
Vidal, Frederic 4:38:51 (21,404)
Vidiella, Fernando 4:02:33 (12,387)
Vidion, Neil R 3:57:22 (10,969)
Vidoe, Thomas 2:59:26 (1,189)
Vieira, Erik R 3:42:38 (7,138)
Vieira, Michael A 5:13:22 (27,700)
Vigano, Federico 3:55:21 (10,332)
Viguri, Victor 5:28:17 (29,354)
Vikhammermo, Bjoern 4:22:34 (17,257)
Vikshaaland, Georg 3:41:17 (6,869)
Vilanoba, Philippe I 3:23:25 (3,701)
Vilar, José L 4:30:07 (19,328)
Vilar, Roberto 4:30:07 (19,328)
Vile, Alistair J 3:53:34 (9,782)
Vilela, Filpe 4:45:31 (22,908)
Viljoen, Philip C 6:00:42 (31,588)
Villa, Emilio C 3:37:45 (6,178)
Villa, Manuel 2:56:05 (855)
Villalard, Michael C 5:03:46 (26,422)
Villari, Nino 5:47:12 (30,880)
Villodres, Ricardo 4:08:02 (13,621)
Vincent, David J 4:00:55 (12,019)
Vincent, Edward M 3:41:59 (7,022)
Vincent, John A 5:35:43 (30,028)
Vincent, Mark D 5:02:23 (26,236)
Vincent, Paul E 5:28:18 (29,355)
Vincent, Ron 4:50:46 (23,995)
Vincenz, Claudia 4:31:53 (19,769)
Viney, Steve 4:15:23 (15,442)
Vinken, Adrian C 3:53:03 (9,647)
Vinten, Stephen 3:02:03 (1,380)
Vinter, Philip 4:56:35 (25,220)
Viray, Arlan 4:55:08 (24,926)
Vireswer, Selvavinayagam 5:18:16 (28,279)
Virgin, David A 4:25:15 (18,042)
Virgo, Damian F 4:21:43 (17,026)
Virgo, Jonathan D 4:48:28 (23,532)
Virgone, Giovanni 3:28:31 (4,514)
Visintin, Stefano 3:00:26 (1,268)
Vitulli, Tom 4:42:21 (22,190)
Viva, Giuseppe A 4:37:21 (21,072)
Vivash, Paul R 3:51:37 (9,247)
Viveash, Ian 5:14:00 (27,760)
Vlasblom, Xander 3:32:19 (5,226)
Vobe, Rees N 3:57:05 (10,870)
Voet, Pascal 3:16:11 (2,797)
Vogan, Ian 4:33:04 (20,019)
Vogel, William G 3:33:33 (5,408)
Voigt, Andreas 3:12:06 (2,288)
Volans, Ian J 3:39:14 (6,486)
Voller, Mark J 3:14:15 (2,559)
Voller, Philip 3:01:03 (1,306)
Volpi, Mario A 3:46:41 (8,057)
Volz, Hansjoerg 4:36:55 (20,963)
Volz, Karl A 4:17:55 (16,083)
Von Bechtolsheim, Matthias 3:16:48 (2,853)
Von Habsburg Lothringen, MP 3:20:52 (3,387)
Voora, Deepak 4:36:05 (20,746)
Voralia, Len G 4:49:15 (23,702)
Voskuhl, Justin B 4:52:33 (24,365)
Vosper, Matthew P 4:30:21 (19,388)
Voss, Ben 4:20:38 (16,769)
Voss, Dave R 3:51:03 (9,113)
Voss, Neil M 4:51:13 (24,078)
Vowles, Jonathan S 4:56:23 (25,185)
Voysey, Andrew J 3:45:52 (7,882)
Vrind, Gijs 4:29:33 (19,188)
Vrind, Hans N 4:23:14 (17,427)
Vyvyan-Robinson, Mark W 3:29:11 (4,651)
Waby, Paul 2:38:26 (176)
Wachter, Marc S 3:51:31 (9,222)
Wackenhut, Rainer 4:23:25 (17,474)
Waddell, Douglas R 3:22:44 (3,627)
Waddell, James 4:42:30 (22,217)
Waddington, Mark 3:49:32 (8,753)
Wade, Ian J 4:12:53 (14,806)
Wade, James A 3:46:56 (8,106)
Wade, Stuart A 4:48:47 (23,606)
Wadeson, Ivan 3:30:20 (4,872)
Wadey, Christopher C 4:12:11 (14,620)
Wadey, Graham P 4:19:03 (16,359)

Wadey, Ian D.	3:26:18 (4,114)	
Wadham, Tim	3:18:47 (3,104)	
Wadhams, Mark A	4:25:39 (18,145)	
Wadley, Mark	3:45:07 (7,712)	
Wadsworth, Adrian M	2:59:45 (1,224)	
Wadsworth, Alan D	6:43:55 (32,670)	
Wadsworth, John	2:57:32 (986)	
Wadsworth, Martin G	5:28:48 (29,411)	
Waelti, Philippe	3:55:19 (10,320)	
Wager, Ashley	4:00:23 (11,910)	
Wager, Robert P	5:12:30 (27,588)	
Wagland, Gareth W	3:02:32 (1,410)	
Wagner, Juersen	2:48:51 (486)	
Wagner, Paul	4:14:44 (15,267)	
Wagner, Robert	5:15:09 (27,916)	
Wagstaff, James C	3:35:49 (5,801)	
Wagstaff, Michael	4:54:28 (24,778)	
Wagstaff, Simon	4:55:56 (25,085)	
Wagstaff, Thomas R	3:57:42 (11,072)	
Waheed, Khan	3:43:38 (7,375)	
Wahl, Max	3:03:11 (1,455)	
Wahlgren, Lennart	4:07:00 (13,346)	
Waiman, Alexander H	6:12:59 (32,018)	
Waiman, Joseph	4:45:32 (22,910)	
Wain, John	3:47:15 (8,184)	
Wainewright, David M	5:19:58 (28,487)	
Wainhouse, Paul S	5:11:56 (27,519)	
Wainwright, Jonathan M	3:04:48 (1,566)	
Wainwright, Robert T	3:36:45 (5,982)	
Waistell, Lisa M	5:41:32 (30,458)	
Waite, Ashley W	4:55:39 (25,028)	
Waite, Gary	3:55:57 (10,527)	
Waite, Stephen D	4:58:12 (25,549)	
Waiting, Robert A	4:36:11 (20,774)	
Wake, Alan	4:48:35 (23,563)	
Wakefield, Ben	4:45:45 (22,958)	
Wakefield, George D	4:01:47 (12,209)	
Wakefield, Iain S	3:44:08 (7,478)	
Wakefield, Terry	4:34:42 (20,411)	
Wakeford, Edward D	3:46:50 (8,093)	
Wakeford, Thomas B	3:36:50 (6,001)	
Wakeham, David R	3:59:06 (11,543)	
Wakeham, Simon R	3:56:22 (10,643)	
Wakelen, Kevin H	4:05:30 (13,022)	
Wakelin, Kevin J	5:52:15 (31,191)	
Wakelin, Simon	5:36:16 (30,077)	
Wakely, Chris T	4:02:33 (12,387)	
Wakenshaw, Trevor	3:51:32 (9,229)	
Wakerley, Nick	4:29:39 (19,216)	
Walden, Darren	3:42:51 (7,193)	
Walden, Kris	4:17:29 (15,978)	
Walden, Mark	3:28:44 (4,561)	
Walden, Steve	4:35:17 (20,548)	
Walder, Nigel D	3:43:02 (7,242)	
Walder, Steven J	3:44:08 (7,478)	
Waldergrave, Scott	3:55:30 (10,374)	
Waldron, Bernard	4:47:43 (23,364)	
Walduck, Charles A	6:45:20 (32,698)	
Waler, David B	3:36:18 (5,895)	
Walford, Lawrence	4:33:54 (20,225)	
Walford, Neil J	3:00:46 (1,285)	
Walker, Adam	4:24:42 (17,869)	
Walker, Adam N	4:31:16 (19,602)	
Walker, Alan	5:31:30 (29,706)	
Walker, Andrew M	3:20:11 (3,295)	
Walker, Barry	5:44:37 (30,687)	
Walker, Bruce K	3:44:44 (7,627)	
Walker, Chris	3:53:44 (9,833)	
Walker, Christopher P	3:27:48 (4,379)	
Walker, Colin	3:46:46 (8,074)	
Walker, Daniel	3:45:39 (7,833)	
Walker, David F	4:04:09 (12,751)	
Walker, David J	4:17:43 (16,034)	
Walker, Derek A	4:21:56 (17,095)	
Walker, Derek M	3:13:25 (2,453)	
Walker, Derry J	3:27:39 (4,359)	
Walker, Gareth C	5:10:21 (27,309)	
Walker, Garry A	4:37:19 (21,061)	
Walker, Gary	4:06:53 (13,321)	
Walker, Gary A	2:55:42 (828)	
Walker, Ian	4:16:03 (15,609)	
Walker, James	4:46:59 (23,210)	
Walker, Jason	3:49:32 (8,753)	
Walker, John C	4:34:52 (20,449)	
Walker, Joseph A	3:28:31 (4,514)	
Walker, Ken B	2:58:58 (1,138)	
Walker, Mark D	2:58:16 (1,040)	
Walker, Mark G	3:15:39 (2,733)	
Walker, Martin	3:18:51 (3,114)	
Walker, Martin J	4:56:48 (25,256)	
Walker, Martin P	3:31:47 (5,115)	
Walker, Matthew J	4:41:57 (22,098)	
Walker, Michael J	4:18:46 (16,298)	
Walker, Mike	3:02:33 (1,411)	
Walker, Neil	4:50:05 (23,860)	
Walker, Oliver	4:30:18 (19,378)	
Walker, Paul	5:37:42 (30,180)	
Walker, Paul A	4:20:51 (16,820)	
Walker, Peter R	4:38:28 (21,329)	
Walker, Philip	6:37:15 (32,568)	
Walker, Richard M	3:20:08 (3,284)	
Walker, Robert F	5:18:19 (28,284)	
Walker, Robert J	4:23:47 (17,582)	
Walker, Simon A	4:10:43 (14,251)	
Walker, Stephen J	4:45:36 (22,926)	
Walker, Steven J	4:57:26 (25,386)	
Walker, Steven W	3:05:56 (1,659)	
Walker, Stewart	3:47:47 (8,318)	
Walker, Stuart D	3:09:20 (1,989)	
Walker, Stuart D	4:11:33 (14,471)	
Walker, Tim	4:37:21 (21,072)	
Walker, Vincent J	4:53:20 (24,535)	
Walker, Warren R	3:54:33 (10,066)	
Walker-Arnott, William D	4:16:19 (15,674)	
Walkind, David R	5:46:42 (30,839)	
Walklett, Philip D	4:32:02 (19,798)	
Walkley, Darrell T	4:17:18 (15,929)	
Wall, Alexander P	3:27:23 (4,311)	
Wall, Alexander P	5:04:01 (26,459)	
Wall, Anthony	5:29:03 (29,429)	
Wall, David V	5:20:06 (28,503)	
Wall, Edwin J	5:11:29 (27,455)	
Wall, Lee R	4:48:55 (23,632)	
Wall, Stephen M	4:51:54 (24,229)	
Wallace, David E	5:23:41 (28,906)	
Wallace, Garry J	4:32:00 (19,791)	
Wallace, Ian M	3:48:09 (8,422)	
Wallace, James S	4:17:58 (16,100)	
Wallace, Jamie	4:29:28 (19,167)	
Wallace, Jason P	4:43:28 (22,425)	
Wallace, John F	4:21:37 (17,003)	
Wallace, Mark	2:51:15 (604)	
Wallace, Mark	3:44:17 (7,519)	
Wallace, Mark P	4:16:08 (15,629)	
Wallace, Sam	3:59:44 (11,741)	
Walland, John R	5:20:26 (28,556)	
Wallen, Mikael	3:42:38 (7,138)	
Waller, Bob W	3:33:28 (5,402)	
Waller, Graham J	4:30:22 (19,393)	
Waller, John	4:36:01 (20,725)	
Walley, Jeremy J	4:14:54 (15,311)	
Walliker, Alexander C	3:55:10 (10,264)	
Wallington, Anthony J	6:46:23 (32,717)	
Wallington, Lee	3:36:34 (5,947)	
Wallis, Andrew M	4:19:10 (16,382)	
Wallis, David	3:51:50 (9,313)	
Wallis, David T	4:40:31 (21,791)	
Wallis, James	3:17:13 (2,911)	
Wallis, Patrick B	3:44:42 (7,618)	
Wallis, Paul S	4:10:11 (14,147)	
Wallis, Peter J	3:33:25 (5,391)	
Wallis, Scott D	3:55:12 (10,282)	
Wallman, Scott L	3:49:48 (8,822)	
Wallnutt, John	3:56:46 (10,769)	
Wallwork, David M	3:41:46 (6,978)	
Wallwork, Mark A	3:52:07 (9,387)	
Walmsley, Alastair	3:10:56 (2,150)	
Walmsley, Chris	2:49:52 (541)	
Walmsley, Dave M	2:54:34 (766)	
Walmsley, Paul G	4:04:41 (12,853)	
Walne, John N	3:40:51 (6,770)	
Walne, Simon	5:09:43 (27,229)	
Walpole, Geoffrey C	4:37:11 (21,025)	
Walsby, Ricky D	5:08:16 (27,045)	
Walsh, Alan P	4:00:59 (12,045)	
Walsh, Andrew D	3:29:48 (4,782)	
Walsh, Andrew R	3:34:56 (5,651)	
Walsh, Carl	5:03:10 (26,339)	
Walsh, Charles T	3:35:56 (5,825)	
Walsh, Colin P	4:37:56 (21,204)	
Walsh, David A	2:52:51 (667)	
Walsh, Guy A	5:00:11 (25,924)	
Walsh, Ian L	3:05:19 (1,608)	
Walsh, Kevin M	3:51:12 (9,147)	
Walsh, Michael J	4:04:42 (12,858)	
Walsh, Neil B	5:32:13 (29,754)	
Walsh, Nicholas J	2:58:36 (1,075)	
Walsh, Nigel	3:50:40 (9,021)	
Walsh, Nigel J	3:34:00 (5,484)	
Walsh, Patrick J	5:36:48 (30,116)	
Walsh, Raymond F	3:15:38 (2,729)	
Walsh, Steve R	3:23:21 (3,691)	
Walsh Woolcott, Matt J	5:31:15 (29,687)	
Walsham, John	5:20:29 (28,559)	
Walshe, Donal	5:11:21 (27,434)	
Walshe, Kevin	5:18:46 (28,343)	
Walshe, William	3:42:34 (7,126)	
Waltenspul, Christoph	3:57:46 (11,100)	
Walter, Dominik	3:38:00 (6,222)	
Walter, Robert I	4:09:52 (14,072)	
Walter, Stefan	4:39:00 (21,441)	
Walters, Adrian N	4:03:43 (12,654)	
Walters, Alan A	5:02:16 (26,215)	
Walters, Bryn L	4:33:54 (20,225)	
Walters, Clint L	4:26:16 (18,328)	
Walters, Edmund J	5:23:02 (28,832)	
Walters, Edwyn J	4:00:56 (12,027)	
Walters, Humphrey J	4:42:53 (22,301)	
Walters, John	4:50:34 (23,953)	
Walters, Karl	4:11:31 (14,462)	
Walters, Lee	4:36:08 (20,763)	
Walters, Matthew J	3:35:31 (5,753)	
Walters, Morgan	2:46:14 (392)	
Walters, Paul	3:34:33 (5,581)	
Walters, Stephen	5:41:22 (30,447)	
Waltho, Jonathan G	5:18:42 (28,335)	
Walton, Anthony R	4:35:48 (20,673)	
Walton, David J	3:28:13 (4,445)	
Walton, James M	5:10:49 (27,369)	
Walton, John	4:21:12 (16,915)	
Walton, Michael E	5:17:48 (28,221)	
Walton, Michael M	4:35:04 (20,504)	
Walton, Paul D	3:30:50 (4,895)	
Walton, Richard	4:08:13 (13,669)	
Walton, Richard J	4:28:40 (18,936)	
Walton, Simon M	3:56:47 (10,778)	
Walton, Stuart	3:44:57 (7,681)	
Walvius, Joop	3:35:36 (5,769)	
Wan, Kenny Y	3:41:22 (6,891)	
Wan, Peter S	4:35:45 (20,661)	
Wands, Andrew C	4:04:03 (12,726)	
Wands, Chris	4:15:59 (15,596)	
Wands, Stephen L	4:20:13 (16,666)	
Wanford, Matthew	3:05:41 (1,633)	
Wanlin, Gregory	4:17:56 (16,088)	
Wanning, Helmut	6:05:03 (31,762)	
Want, Daniel T	3:30:55 (4,968)	
Wappat, Bryan	4:36:28 (20,836)	
Warburton, David	4:42:08 (22,146)	
Warburton, James P	4:09:44 (14,039)	
Warburton, Richard C	5:21:17 (28,644)	
Warby, Adam H	4:11:30 (14,459)	
Ward, Adam	4:32:56 (19,987)	
Ward, Andrew J	5:21:46 (28,686)	
Ward, Charles W	3:45:41 (7,844)	
Ward, Christopher E	4:09:23 (13,954)	
Ward, Christopher J	4:32:31 (19,905)	
Ward, Colin	3:39:49 (6,592)	
Ward, David	3:35:26 (5,738)	
Ward, David J	3:08:51 (1,940)	
Ward, David J	4:06:34 (13,243)	
Ward, David R	4:38:59 (21,436)	
Ward, Grahame L	4:14:39 (15,242)	
Ward, Ian J	3:08:04 (1,868)	
Ward, Ian R	4:15:48 (15,544)	
Ward, James S	2:47:28 (438)	
Ward, Jamie	4:25:09 (18,008)	
Ward, John C	3:26:52 (4,217)	
Ward, John P	3:29:54 (4,806)	

Ward, Jonathan 3:57:08 (10,893)
Ward, Julian T 4:22:37 (17,277)
Ward, Keith 4:22:18 (17,199)
Ward, Kevan M 5:27:44 (29,297)
Ward, Laurence J 4:31:50 (19,755)
Ward, Matthew C 4:08:44 (13,792)
Ward, Michael A 3:42:08 (7,050)
Ward, Peter J 4:45:02 (22,798)
Ward, Richard H 5:20:52 (28,597)
Ward, Robert J 3:36:08 (5,860)
Ward, Robert M 5:05:58 (26,704)
Ward, Simon 5:55:36 (31,336)
Ward, Simon J 3:31:42 (5,101)
Ward, Spencer 3:47:55 (8,360)
Ward, Stuart E 4:22:05 (17,141)
Ward, Stuart J 5:06:47 (26,833)
Ward, Vernon 4:45:10 (22,825)
Warden, Jonathan P 5:10:13 (27,291)
Warden, Paul 3:52:52 (9,585)
Wardlaw, Robert G 3:26:29 (4,149)
Wardle, Anthony J 4:33:06 (20,030)
Wardle, David 2:25:39 (47)
Wardle, Kim 4:09:53 (14,076)
Wardley, Dean 5:40:03 (30,367)
Wardley-Kershaw, Keith 5:19:08 (28,393)
Wardman, Ben P 3:58:59 (11,500)
Wardman, Tom A 3:58:59 (11,500)
Wardrope, Drew 4:12:43 (14,754)
Ware, David J 4:07:52 (13,574)
Ware, Graham H 4:43:26 (22,417)
Ware, Simon J 3:25:02 (3,935)
Wareing, Joseph B 5:21:12 (28,631)
Wareman, Stuart R 4:36:19 (20,809)
Warhurst, Anthony R 3:56:30 (10,685)
Waring, Keith J 3:35:41 (5,783)
Waring, Paul R 3:24:30 (3,864)
Warlow, Gynfor J 5:14:24 (27,826)
Warminger, Paul 4:22:14 (17,185)
Warn, Derek W 3:53:10 (9,679)
Warn, Francis T 5:22:29 (28,770)
Warne, Barry A 3:10:59 (2,155)
Warne, Mark 4:31:14 (19,593)
Warne, Richard P 4:45:16 (22,852)
Warner, Andrew R 3:51:53 (9,329)
Warner, Carl J 4:47:27 (23,308)
Warner, Daniel J 4:19:21 (16,433)
Warner, David J 4:16:55 (15,839)
Warner, Gavin L 4:46:06 (23,027)
Warner, James R 4:41:27 (21,982)
Warner, Joe 3:53:21 (9,731)
Warner, Kim 3:25:55 (4,061)
Warner, Luc A 3:34:11 (5,511)
Warner, Mark A 3:49:39 (8,786)
Warner, Michael K 4:05:31 (13,027)
Warner, Philip 4:39:17 (21,509)
Warner, Steve R 3:36:09 (5,867)
Warner, Stuart J 2:48:31 (474)
Warner, Tim 3:24:13 (3,826)
Warner, Tony D 3:08:39 (1,922)
Warner, Wayne 4:57:15 (25,362)
Warnes, Kristian D 3:59:28 (11,662)
Warnes, Peter E 4:03:59 (12,710)
Warr, John E 5:54:36 (31,293)
Warrand, Jerome 3:12:00 (2,276)
Warren, Edward R 6:57:24 (32,859)
Warren, Geoff E 3:43:36 (7,370)
Warren, John D 4:38:15 (21,292)
Warren, John M 4:24:53 (17,917)
Warren, Michael E 3:35:08 (5,697)
Warren, Oliver J 4:13:57 (15,051)
Warren, Paul J 4:16:04 (15,617)
Warren, Paul N 4:05:06 (12,939)
Warren, Peter J 4:08:24 (13,717)
Warren, Peter J 5:16:59 (28,122)
Warren, Peter L 4:35:18 (20,553)
Warren, Philip N 4:39:45 (21,612)
Warren, Shaun 4:24:35 (17,837)
Warren, Simon 3:56:15 (10,610)
Warren, Toby 5:10:14 (27,295)
Warrender, Wililam J 4:15:56 (15,583)
Warrick, Michael J 3:15:33 (2,725)
Warrilow, Paul 4:36:21 (20,816)
Warrington, Greig C 5:51:49 (31,174)
Warters, Eamonn P 5:00:20 (25,950)
Warwick, Derrick 5:26:52 (29,210)
Warwick, Gary D 5:02:02 (26,182)
Warwick, Oliver W 4:41:59 (22,110)
Warwicker, Paul 6:07:49 (31,855)
Warwick-Munday, Paul R 4:56:27 (25,199)
Washington, Darren 2:47:52 (449)
Washington, Gary 3:42:12 (7,065)
Wasmayr, Dietrich 3:25:18 (3,977)
Wassel, Jonathan D 3:52:18 (9,440)
Wasson, Christopher W 3:46:35 (8,030)
Watanabe, Kazuki 3:18:28 (3,059)
Waterfield, Jonathan L 3:31:23 (5,050)
Waterhouse, Andrew S 4:43:32 (22,447)
Wateridge, Justin L 5:11:20 (27,431)
Waterman, David K 3:41:53 (7,004)
Waterman, Dov 4:48:51 (23,620)
Waterman, Steven M 3:45:52 (7,882)
Waterman-Smith, Thomas E 4:13:04 (14,862)
Waters, Anthony T 5:41:25 (30,452)
Waters, Cedric D 5:39:23 (30,309)
Waters, Chris C 5:09:14 (27,178)
Waters, David M 4:04:06 (12,739)
Waters, Gareth A 4:48:21 (23,500)
Waters, Geoff 4:53:10 (24,500)
Waters, George C 3:29:25 (4,698)
Waters, James 3:13:09 (2,420)
Waters, Matthew F 4:37:24 (21,086)
Waters, Matthew J 4:26:54 (18,486)
Waters, Richard C 3:23:49 (3,764)
Waters, Timothy J 5:00:51 (26,020)
Waters, Trevor D 4:49:24 (23,734)
Waterton, Nik T 4:13:45 (15,012)
Wates, Tom J 5:06:21 (26,761)
Watford, Neil J 4:11:43 (14,500)
Watherson, Jamie H 4:54:40 (24,808)
Watkin, Chris P 4:38:07 (21,266)
Watkins, Andrew J 4:16:25 (15,695)
Watkins, Charles 4:20:37 (16,766)
Watkins, Darren J 4:11:15 (14,402)
Watkins, Dennis C 4:37:58 (21,213)
Watkins, Gavin T 2:56:40 (913)
Watkins, Huw 4:11:14 (14,396)
Watkins, Ian 4:19:57 (16,589)
Watkins, Jonathan M 4:19:00 (16,354)
Watkins, Martin 5:02:22 (26,234)
Watkins, Nicholas 4:00:37 (11,953)
Watkins, Simon D 4:01:58 (12,255)
Watkins, Simon P 4:35:09 (20,521)
Watkins, Steve 2:58:18 (1,045)
Watkinson, Graham 4:58:48 (25,662)
Watkinson, Kenneth 4:15:06 (15,366)
Watkinson, Michael 3:43:25 (7,337)
Watkinson, Peter G 3:14:29 (2,594)
Watkinson, Richard A 2:54:44 (779)
Watmough, Stephen J 3:12:47 (2,374)
Watson, Aerwyn R 5:09:26 (27,197)
Watson, Alex F 4:18:31 (16,238)
Watson, Andrew N 4:57:34 (25,411)
Watson, Anthony 4:56:53 (25,278)
Watson, Ashley J 3:48:43 (8,561)
Watson, Bob S 4:52:05 (24,263)
Watson, Christopher 3:25:20 (3,980)
Watson, Craig J 4:56:08 (25,128)
Watson, David 3:19:17 (3,171)
Watson, David J 3:07:29 (1,803)
Watson, Denise M 4:41:52 (22,074)
Watson, Derek S 3:35:35 (5,765)
Watson, Gary C 4:38:17 (21,299)
Watson, Jerry R 3:06:30 (1,709)
Watson, Ken 3:18:41 (3,091)
Watson, Kevin 3:49:29 (8,743)
Watson, Kevin B 5:08:06 (27,024)
Watson, Laurence F 3:58:48 (11,447)
Watson, Lester W 3:59:51 (11,776)
Watson, Mark 4:17:00 (15,860)
Watson, Martin 4:15:25 (15,454)
Watson, Matthew R 4:30:24 (19,400)
Watson, Paul A 5:43:37 (30,613)
Watson, Peter D 2:58:50 (1,120)
Watson, Peter J 4:25:45 (18,176)
Watson, Phillip 3:07:46 (1,834)
Watson, Richard W 3:03:13 (1,458)
Watson, Robert S 4:33:07 (20,036)
Watson, Russell A 5:16:46 (28,100)
Watson, Stephen L 5:23:54 (28,928)
Watson, Steven P 3:47:21 (8,202)
Watson, Tom D 3:21:35 (3,483)
Watson, Tom P 2:58:16 (1,040)
Watson, Troy H 3:38:21 (6,295)
Watson-Steward, Duncan H 3:53:32 (9,774)
Watt, Andrew 4:20:53 (16,833)
Watt, Brian J 4:15:41 (15,514)
Watt, Christopher A 4:45:40 (22,935)
Watt, Michael 3:42:45 (7,176)
Watt, Michael 5:04:26 (26,515)
Watters, Simon G 5:01:05 (26,059)
Watton, Andrew 4:15:32 (15,484)
Watts, Andrew 4:44:10 (22,598)
Watts, Andrew J 3:08:34 (1,915)
Watts, Andrew N 4:57:01 (25,315)
Watts, Barry F 4:07:03 (13,356)
Watts, Gary 3:59:41 (11,723)
Watts, Glenn W 4:45:22 (22,877)
Watts, Jeffrey F 5:28:02 (29,326)
Watts, Lee 3:54:43 (10,120)
Watts, Matthew 4:36:44 (20,910)
Watts, Matthew L 3:36:32 (5,940)
Watts, Matthew P 4:57:51 (25,463)
Watts, Michael 4:29:58 (19,285)
Watts, Michael B 4:55:51 (25,066)
Watts, Michael J 5:00:47 (26,006)
Watts, Paul D 3:50:01 (8,869)
Watts, Peter A 3:56:25 (10,660)
Watts, Robert 2:33:33 (94)
Watts, Robert E 4:40:11 (21,708)
Waudby, Trevor W 4:34:59 (20,483)
Waumsley, Peter 2:35:58 (128)
Way, Lawrence C 3:57:08 (10,893)
Way, Steven J 3:07:08 (1,771)
Waye, Osy 6:18:59 (32,200)
Wayland, James A 3:43:08 (7,269)
Waylett, Daniel J 4:39:40 (21,592)
Wayman, David G 4:28:33 (18,910)
Wayne, Matt 4:08:34 (13,761)
Wayne, Robert 3:25:04 (3,936)
Weals, David A 4:15:58 (15,592)
Weals, Richard J 4:19:10 (16,382)
Weatherill, William P 3:47:02 (8,127)
Weatherley, Adam R 4:41:18 (21,952)
Weatherley, Ian 5:51:22 (31,149)
Weaver, Brian 5:31:00 (29,650)
Weaver, John M 3:35:16 (5,717)
Weaver, Michael 3:49:38 (8,780)
Weaver, Simon C 3:23:24 (3,697)
Weavers, Terry P 3:06:16 (1,692)
Weaving, Peter G 3:01:07 (1,310)
Weavis, Darren 3:19:44 (3,220)
Webb, Alan 3:53:32 (9,774)
Webb, Alan D 4:15:46 (15,537)
Webb, Andrew P 5:03:11 (26,343)
Webb, Antony L 3:23:48 (3,755)
Webb, Barry 5:48:56 (30,996)
Webb, Brian 5:09:09 (27,167)
Webb, Denys W 3:26:30 (4,155)
Webb, Garry 4:51:06 (24,061)
Webb, Harvey J 3:46:02 (7,907)
Webb, Ian A 5:35:43 (30,028)
Webb, Ian J 5:37:57 (30,199)
Webb, Jack 4:25:48 (18,194)
Webb, James 3:44:16 (7,511)
Webb, James J 3:32:54 (5,307)
Webb, Jamie 4:06:03 (13,152)
Webb, Lewis 3:29:59 (4,822)
Webb, Martin D 4:51:37 (24,171)
Webb, Matthew J 3:48:37 (8,531)
Webb, Nicholas 5:06:13 (26,740)
Webb, Nick 4:27:31 (18,628)
Webb, Nigel 3:51:18 (9,173)
Webb, Patrick J 6:12:41 (32,010)
Webb, Richard 5:07:15 (26,898)
Webb, Robert J 3:55:20 (10,325)
Webber, Daniel J 3:11:39 (2,229)
Webber, Don 4:12:18 (14,652)
Webber, Ian C 3:52:50 (9,576)
Webber, Matthew F 3:19:40 (3,206)

Webber, Matthew J 4:12:14 (14,634)
Webber, Michael 4:58:01 (25,508)
Webber, Robert G 5:15:07 (27,912)
Webbon, John M 5:02:12 (26,201)
Weber, Reto 3:30:46 (4,940)
Weber, Richard G 4:39:11 (21,486)
Weber, Urs S 3:15:58 (2,779)
Webster, Alan 4:43:36 (22,467)
Webster, Andrew J 5:12:18 (27,565)
Webster, Christopher R 6:16:05 (32,121)
Webster, David 3:27:55 (4,397)
Webster, Gilbert 4:52:55 (24,441)
Webster, James M 4:24:59 (17,953)
Webster, Jon 3:30:06 (4,847)
Webster, Jonathan P 3:28:23 (4,489)
Webster, Karl M 4:59:54 (25,870)
Webster, Mark A 4:51:17 (24,089)
Webster, Matthew G 3:42:53 (7,202)
Webster, Michael G 3:38:31 (6,329)
Webster, Paul A 4:19:50 (16,562)
Webster, Paul J 3:04:43 (1,562)
Webster, Richard W 3:08:52 (1,942)
Webster, Sam 5:27:40 (29,289)
Webster, Simon 3:56:49 (10,790)
Webster, Terry N 3:21:47 (3,507)
Webster, Tim S 3:54:08 (9,953)
Webster-Smith, Richard S 3:44:12 (7,491)
Wedick, David J 4:40:52 (21,867)
Wedley, John R 4:42:46 (22,274)
Weed, Christopher T 4:09:52 (14,072)
Weekes, John L 3:53:34 (9,782)
Weeks, Ian 4:14:39 (15,242)
Weeks, Richard 5:28:37 (29,387)
Weeks, Timothy J 3:34:09 (5,505)
Weernink, Eric 3:10:23 (2,105)
Weetman, Jason 3:07:04 (1,765)
Weetman, Stephen 2:35:29 (122)
Wehner, Oliver 4:14:45 (15,272)
Wehrhahn, Thorsten 3:32:29 (5,246)
Wehrle, Stephen R 4:31:33 (19,681)
Weichhart, Anthony W 3:23:37 (3,728)
Weickhardt, David L 3:57:37 (11,051)
Weidle, Hans Dieter 3:32:03 (5,169)
Weidling, Nicholas E 4:53:50 (24,642)
Weighell, Robert D 3:38:52 (6,402)
Weighill, Robert P 3:57:17 (10,944)
Weikert-Picker, Christian D 2:56:15 (874)
Weil, Dany 4:18:58 (16,348)
Weir, Barry 3:18:10 (3,015)
Weir, Colin 5:13:25 (27,708)
Weir, Paul 3:57:36 (11,045)
Weir, Russell G 4:53:35 (24,592)
Weir, Stephen 4:08:37 (13,773)
Welby, Mark B 4:40:18 (21,732)
Welch, Alan 3:27:17 (4,287)
Welch, Andy C 5:19:58 (28,487)
Welch, David 4:00:47 (11,989)
Welch, David J 4:13:04 (14,862)
Welch, Graham J 4:36:44 (20,910)
Welch, James R 3:31:43 (5,106)
Welch, Michael J 3:59:48 (11,762)
Welch, Miles 3:58:51 (11,464)
Welch, Richard K 3:51:49 (9,307)
Welch, Sam P 3:57:35 (11,036)
Welch, Simon A 4:50:00 (23,843)
Welch, Simon D 5:14:50 (27,885)
Welch, Timothy 2:58:21 (1,051)
Welch, Tom 4:27:12 (18,555)
Welchman, Alan E 3:57:23 (10,974)
Weldon, Brent J 3:59:21 (11,621)
Welham, Robert A 4:09:14 (13,919)
Weller, Ian W 5:49:19 (31,028)
Weller, Sam W 4:20:23 (16,706)
Wellfair, Peter J 5:57:09 (31,410)
Welling, Keith 3:58:15 (11,249)
Wells, Adrian 3:13:55 (2,513)
Wells, Brian R 5:38:27 (30,247)
Wells, Christopher H 5:09:01 (27,148)
Wells, Colin J 4:55:19 (24,963)
Wells, David J 4:49:39 (23,782)
Wells, David P 5:02:38 (26,266)
Wells, Mark E 4:14:00 (15,067)
Wells, Martin 4:56:46 (25,251)
Wells, Paul D 3:06:43 (1,731)
Wells, Paul R 3:39:23 (6,514)
Wells, Roland A 3:44:36 (7,596)
Wells, Tony S 4:08:08 (13,648)
Wells, William D 4:13:30 (14,955)
Welsh, James 5:07:52 (26,985)
Welton, Mark J 4:12:52 (14,803)
Wemhoener, Frank 3:57:04 (10,865)
Wenger, Jean Luc 4:10:19 (14,176)
Wengraf-Townsend, James A 4:12:48 (14,773)
Wenlock, Tony 3:56:47 (10,778)
Wennevold, Peter 3:29:13 (4,658)
Went, Trevor 3:38:36 (6,349)
Wentworth, Alfred 4:29:28 (19,167)
Wentzell, David J 5:00:52 (26,023)
Weppler, Ezequiel 4:10:09 (14,135)
Werder, Gary J 3:58:43 (11,405)
Wernicke, Eckhard 3:52:37 (9,526)
Werry-Easterbrook, James N 5:31:00 (29,650)
Wespi, Marcel 3:53:30 (9,766)
Wessels, Herman 3:27:15 (4,280)
Wessinghage, Thomas 3:07:07 (1,769)
West, Brent H 4:21:46 (17,052)
West, Brian J 4:54:17 (24,742)
West, Christopher 4:45:00 (22,786)
West, Clive B 4:06:08 (13,167)
West, Colin 2:50:16 (558)
West, Dean T 4:18:23 (16,204)
West, Ian M 4:38:59 (21,436)
West, James D 3:55:59 (10,537)
West, James M 5:11:18 (27,427)
West, Kevin M 2:42:28 (264)
West, Michael 3:42:31 (7,115)
West, Paul J 4:18:32 (16,243)
West, Paul R 3:49:03 (8,637)
West, Rob 4:15:47 (15,540)
West, Stephen 3:21:43 (3,502)
West, Stephen A 3:28:31 (4,514)
West, Steve 4:37:09 (21,013)
West, William 4:07:31 (13,479)
Westacott, Martin 3:30:41 (4,929)
Westaway, Julian C 3:36:41 (5,972)
Westbrook, Dean M 4:22:38 (17,283)
Westbrook, Ernest W 3:55:21 (10,332)
Westbrook, James 4:38:08 (21,268)
Westcott, David J 4:46:33 (23,133)
Westcough, Steven 3:58:11 (11,225)
Westerman, Lee 4:12:37 (14,729)
West-Evans, Errol L 4:06:28 (13,224)
Westgate, Andrew M 4:52:18 (24,307)
Westhead, Andrew 5:57:39 (31,440)
Westhead, Roger W 4:03:55 (12,695)
Westhead, Sam J 2:42:46 (277)
Westlake, Andrew 4:15:15 (15,402)
Westley, Ian C 4:03:05 (12,500)
Westmore, Peter J 4:53:51 (24,647)
Weston, Barnaby E 4:38:03 (21,239)
Weston, Christopher M 5:23:01 (28,830)
Weston, Jason 3:24:42 (3,896)
Weston, Jeff K 3:58:24 (11,306)
Weston, Mark R 3:27:18 (4,293)
Weston, Neil 4:10:43 (14,251)
Weston, Oliver R 4:31:33 (19,681)
Weston, Wayne G 4:45:34 (22,916)
Westray, Oliver 3:49:53 (8,843)
Westropp, James 3:25:47 (4,042)
Westwood, David A 3:56:52 (10,809)
Westwood, Jason D 2:58:55 (1,131)
Westwood, Michael J 3:44:35 (7,591)
Westwood, Paul J 3:29:44 (4,768)
Wetherhill, Tim J 4:43:47 (22,514)
Wethers, Nigel 3:25:54 (4,060)
Wettner, David P 4:35:55 (20,692)
Wettone, Pete J 4:55:50 (25,061)
Wetzel, Eberhard 4:01:04 (12,063)
Whale, Chris A 4:50:41 (23,979)
Whale, Colin 4:17:56 (16,088)
Whalley, Adrian H 3:09:06 (1,965)
Whalley, Jason P 4:55:58 (25,097)
Whalley, Steve 3:27:30 (4,334)
Whapshott, Darren W 4:52:16 (24,296)
Wharton, Adam J 3:17:05 (2,891)
Wharton, Anthony J 4:02:45 (12,424)
Wharton, George J 4:40:25 (21,753)
Wharton, Nick J 3:36:57 (6,029)
Whatford, Howard M 4:08:48 (13,815)
Whatley, Gavin J 4:15:49 (15,552)
Whatmore, Darren 5:21:04 (28,616)
Whatson, Simon M 3:39:54 (6,606)
Wheatley, Adrian J 4:02:58 (12,470)
Wheatley, Craig S 4:24:20 (17,759)
Wheatley, Iain E 4:02:25 (12,355)
Wheatley, Nick C 4:06:23 (13,207)
Wheaton, Antony R 4:32:09 (19,820)
Wheddon, Charles A 3:43:02 (7,242)
Wheeldon, Scott A 3:38:04 (6,242)
Wheeldon-Wright, John T 4:21:10 (16,908)
Wheeler, Andrew W 3:50:40 (9,021)
Wheeler, Benjamin J 5:44:04 (30,646)
Wheeler, Christopher E 6:54:56 (32,827)
Wheeler, Daniel W 3:16:04 (2,786)
Wheeler, David L 4:35:14 (20,542)
Wheeler, Dean 4:03:34 (12,617)
Wheeler, Duncan S 4:52:10 (24,285)
Wheeler, Ian C 3:38:48 (6,383)
Wheeler, Michael J 7:37:36 (33,132)
Wheeler, Ralph E 3:38:15 (6,280)
Wheeler, Richard 4:35:56 (20,698)
Wheeler, Richard A 3:57:25 (10,984)
Wheeler, Sydney J 3:57:24 (10,979)
Whelan, Dominic 3:41:04 (6,820)
Whelan, Liam 5:48:34 (30,974)
Whelband, Marcus J 3:08:03 (1,865)
Wheldon, Jim 3:08:17 (1,882)
Whenlock, Benjamin M 3:54:32 (10,061)
Whettlock, Phillip J 4:21:41 (17,018)
Whetton, Lawrence C 6:33:59 (32,516)
Whewell, Sean 3:31:21 (5,046)
Whewell, Thomas S 3:41:13 (6,856)
Whibley, Jack 2:59:20 (1,181)
Whiffen, David P 4:45:27 (22,898)
Whiles, Stephen J 4:29:41 (19,222)
Whillier, Roy T 4:22:33 (17,252)
Whippa, Graham 5:46:48 (30,848)
Whishaw, Bernard W 3:58:26 (11,319)
Whitaker, Christopher D 3:28:16 (4,456)
Whitaker, David S 4:00:57 (12,030)
Whitaker, Iain R 3:23:21 (3,691)
Whitaker, Paul 4:04:06 (12,739)
Whitbread, Scott J 5:15:19 (27,938)
Whitby, Ben J 5:41:04 (30,427)
Whitby, Simon M 4:37:59 (21,216)
Whitby-Samways, Greg 4:18:04 (16,128)
White, Adrian 3:14:36 (2,615)
White, Adrian J 4:15:56 (15,583)
White, Andrew S 3:59:21 (11,621)
White, Anthony E 4:30:39 (19,462)
White, Anthony F 3:39:12 (6,475)
White, Chris F 4:50:57 (24,037)
White, Christopher F 4:16:49 (15,804)
White, Colin S 5:16:04 (28,007)
White, Daniel J 5:30:39 (29,611)
White, Danny 5:11:15 (27,421)
White, Darren W 3:32:21 (5,228)
White, David C 4:02:31 (12,376)
White, Douglas M 5:53:17 (31,231)
White, Edward J 3:13:46 (2,498)
White, Geoffrey B 3:04:49 (1,568)
White, George 5:17:51 (28,226)
White, Glynn 4:21:32 (16,981)
White, Grahame K 4:09:45 (14,044)
White, Gregory R 4:14:52 (15,303)
White, Ian 3:52:55 (9,597)
White, Ian A 4:10:15 (14,161)
White, Ian G 4:31:31 (19,668)
White, James M 4:41:05 (21,913)
White, James N 4:55:15 (24,949)
White, Jamie 5:09:42 (27,226)
White, Jamie L 4:53:00 (24,455)
White, John A 3:59:03 (11,526)
White, John L 4:47:31 (23,324)
White, Julian F 3:55:14 (10,293)
White, Kevin J 5:53:06 (31,221)
White, Kevin M 4:58:43 (25,650)
White, Kevin P 4:06:31 (13,238)
White, Laurence A 5:10:16 (27,302)

White, Luke....4:40:09 (21,703)
White, Malcolm D....5:37:28 (30,162)
White, Mark....3:45:49 (7,876)
White, Mark....3:49:41 (8,793)
White, Mark....4:21:20 (16,941)
White, Martin....4:18:34 (16,248)
White, Martin D....3:56:54 (10,814)
White, Martyn P....4:53:56 (24,666)
White, Michael....5:31:01 (29,654)
White, Michael E....4:14:07 (15,108)
White, Michael P....2:54:59 (788)
White, Neil....4:16:42 (15,779)
White, Oliver L....4:32:56 (19,987)
White, Paul....5:44:23 (30,674)
White, Paul M....4:22:21 (17,209)
White, Peter J....3:57:28 (11,003)
White, Peter J....4:30:16 (19,371)
White, Philip D....4:40:19 (21,737)
White, Richard C....4:00:58 (12,040)
White, Richard D....3:16:08 (2,793)
White, Robert P....4:51:04 (24,053)
White, Robert P....5:08:05 (27,021)
White, Roger A....6:06:41 (31,812)
White, Roland....3:17:56 (2,988)
White, Samuel....4:35:39 (20,639)
White, Simon C....4:45:12 (22,834)
White, Simon J....4:04:18 (12,776)
White, Steve R....3:39:19 (6,503)
White, Stuart J....4:28:32 (18,904)
White, Terence A....4:09:05 (13,878)
White, Tony S....3:28:52 (4,595)
Whiteaker, James H....6:01:11 (31,612)
Whitear, Roy E....5:34:40 (29,948)
Whitehead, Alan G....5:16:05 (28,012)
Whitehead, Anthony....4:48:41 (23,582)
Whitehead, Carl....3:12:08 (2,292)
Whitehead, Glen....5:21:30 (28,668)
Whitehead, John....4:44:13 (22,615)
Whitehead, Joshua C....2:39:05 (190)
Whitehead, Justin R....4:39:14 (21,498)
Whitehead, Michael L....3:47:50 (8,336)
Whitehead, Stephen....2:46:17 (396)
Whitehorn, Robert J....4:06:04 (13,154)
Whitehouse, David B....3:07:36 (1,813)
Whitehouse, Ian R....2:51:03 (594)
Whitehouse, Michael L....3:37:54 (6,208)
Whitehouse, Simon....5:24:51 (29,022)
Whitelaw, Robert J....4:23:57 (17,641)
Whitelegg, Richard....2:44:01 (313)
Whiteley, David R....4:48:27 (23,527)
Whiteley, Jonathan....4:29:37 (19,206)
Whiteley, Richard K....5:06:59 (26,858)
Whiteley, Stephen P....3:17:16 (2,918)
Whitelock, Danny R....5:32:44 (29,789)
Whitelock, Neil P....3:34:13 (5,515)
Whiteman, Aaron D....3:37:29 (6,131)
Whiteside, Chris....5:45:47 (30,765)
Whitfield, Adam....4:01:15 (12,108)
Whitfield, Gary J....3:44:16 (7,511)
Whitfield, Graeme....4:18:13 (16,162)
Whitfield, Jean-Pierre....3:37:20 (6,098)
Whitfield, Matthew....3:13:20 (2,438)
Whitford, Richard D....3:58:32 (11,350)
Whithouse, Mark T....5:13:53 (27,748)
Whithouse, Richard F....5:13:53 (27,748)
Whiting, Andrew P....3:53:39 (9,806)
Whiting, Richard....5:07:36 (26,947)
Whiting, Stephen J....2:56:32 (898)
Whitley, Michael P....3:45:38 (7,830)
Whitley, Nathaniel T....3:18:51 (3,114)
Whitmarsh, Jim F....3:25:40 (4,027)
Whitmore, Ivon E....3:09:50 (2,049)
Whitmore, James R....3:52:55 (9,597)
Whitmore, John....4:03:27 (12,592)
Whitmore, Paul T....4:33:57 (20,238)
Whitrod, Simon....4:49:19 (23,720)
Whittaker, Michael....4:38:07 (21,266)
Whittaker, Philip A....3:38:53 (6,408)
Whittall, Richard P....4:37:36 (21,137)
Whittall, Robert J....3:54:32 (10,061)
Whittem, Alex J....2:50:16 (558)
Whittingham, Andrew J....3:26:35 (4,173)
Whittingham, Kevin....4:35:28 (20,598)
Whittingham, Kevin....4:40:49 (21,858)
Whittington, Harvey....4:19:18 (16,422)
Whittington, Joshua B....3:35:12 (5,706)
Whittington, Richard H....3:55:43 (10,444)
Whittington, Russell....2:52:32 (652)
Whittington, Tom K....3:33:10 (5,347)
Whittle, Arthur H....3:53:58 (9,912)
Whittle, Domonic P....4:08:06 (13,641)
Whittle, Rob J....4:48:14 (23,477)
Whittley, Shane....3:43:02 (7,242)
Whitton, Mark....4:27:53 (18,717)
Whitty, Graeme C....3:19:58 (3,262)
Whitty, Iain A....3:55:13 (10,290)
Whitworth, Bill J....4:00:02 (11,828)
Whitworth, David....3:52:51 (9,578)
Whitworth, Nicholas C....5:16:40 (28,090)
Whyatt, Paul D....5:27:46 (29,301)
Whybrow, Sammy M....4:40:07 (21,695)
Whyman, Len M....5:20:31 (28,563)
Whyte, Alistair J....4:12:09 (14,612)
Whyte, Bruce W....4:39:07 (21,469)
Whyte, Kieran E....4:36:30 (20,844)
Whyte, Michael E....3:06:18 (1,695)
Whyte, Shamus C....4:52:34 (24,371)
Whyton, Christopher M....5:20:19 (28,541)
Wiblin, David J....5:09:22 (27,190)
Wichman, Carl C....3:43:23 (7,329)
Wickenden, Lee C....4:50:34 (23,953)
Wickens, Samuel P....4:30:51 (19,504)
Wickham, Martin J....4:40:15 (21,724)
Wickham, Rowan D....4:56:55 (25,287)
Wickramasinghe, Eranda P....3:43:50 (7,429)
Wicks, Timothy L....4:42:35 (22,235)
Wickstead, Edward L....3:02:54 (1,431)
Widdowson, Paul E....4:10:22 (14,189)
Widelski, Gregg P....3:58:14 (11,245)
Wider, Marcel....3:41:21 (6,887)
Wieckowski, Andrzej T....4:18:55 (16,331)
Wield, Christopher....4:35:31 (20,605)
Wientjens, Peter....3:59:25 (11,641)
Wiggans, Andy K....3:48:13 (8,434)
Wiggins, Coiln....4:35:03 (20,501)
Wiggins, Ian D....4:14:39 (15,242)
Wiggins, Michael....3:35:00 (5,661)
Wiggins, Michael K....3:43:52 (7,432)
Wiggins, Robert C....2:56:51 (925)
Wigginton, Luke A....4:35:48 (20,673)
Wight, Jeremy P....3:40:42 (6,746)
Wignall, Edward J....4:58:35 (25,627)
Wignall, Richard E....5:10:24 (27,319)
Wignall, Ross....4:30:14 (19,364)
Wigren, Hakan....5:12:24 (27,575)
Wilbourn, Chris....4:35:36 (20,624)
Wilby, Guy D....5:02:59 (26,314)
Wilcock, Brian....5:18:09 (28,262)
Wilcock, Martin....2:58:02 (1,026)
Wilcockson, Ian E....4:02:38 (12,408)
Wilcockson, Simon P....3:57:16 (10,937)
Wilcox, Dale R....3:58:09 (11,209)
Wilcox, Stephan....4:00:56 (12,027)
Wilcox, Timothy J....4:18:49 (16,305)
Wilcox-Smith, Myles....4:43:41 (22,490)
Wilczkiewilcz, Henryk W....6:56:36 (32,851)
Wild, Adrian T....3:33:37 (5,424)
Wild, Richard S....3:31:47 (5,115)
Wildbore, James M....4:51:35 (24,164)
Wilde, Gareth J....4:13:44 (15,010)
Wilde, Mark J....4:34:42 (20,411)
Wilder, Chris R....3:47:11 (8,163)
Wildey, Andrew R....3:26:35 (4,173)
Wildey, Lee D....3:23:36 (3,726)
Wilding, Paul....4:20:36 (16,759)
Wilding, Stephen....4:04:18 (12,776)
Wildisen, Greg J....3:32:38 (5,270)
Wildsmith, Sam....4:18:18 (16,183)
Wileman, Paul....4:27:03 (18,515)
Wiles, Andrew J....4:20:23 (16,706)
Wiley, Kevin J....4:25:12 (18,027)
Wiley, Peter C....4:58:50 (25,671)
Wiliams, Gerwyn I....3:46:56 (8,106)
Wilkerson, Paul J....3:16:53 (2,862)
Wilkes, Andrew....4:28:07 (18,780)
Wilkes, Anthony N....3:16:35 (2,826)
Wilkes, Bernard T....3:48:40 (8,545)
Wilkes, Peter E....4:19:27 (16,466)
Wilkie, James P....4:47:01 (23,218)
Wilkie, Stuart H....3:21:31 (3,472)
Wilkins, Derek....3:57:38 (11,056)
Wilkins, Duncan K....4:14:49 (15,288)
Wilkins, Jeremy C....3:50:10 (8,908)
Wilkins, John....3:52:56 (9,604)
Wilkins, Scott J....3:59:03 (11,526)
Wilkins, Thomas C....3:50:47 (9,053)
Wilkinson, Andy E....3:00:55 (1,295)
Wilkinson, Ben L....3:24:19 (3,842)
Wilkinson, David J....4:12:56 (14,820)
Wilkinson, Geoffrey....4:54:33 (24,792)
Wilkinson, Graham A....2:44:37 (336)
Wilkinson, Henry A....4:50:04 (23,855)
Wilkinson, James E....4:43:00 (22,329)
Wilkinson, Jason....4:00:18 (11,887)
Wilkinson, Mark D....2:58:07 (1,033)
Wilkinson, Martin J....3:07:43 (1,826)
Wilkinson, Matthew L....5:01:53 (26,158)
Wilkinson, Michael....6:27:08 (32,406)
Wilkinson, Michael J....5:46:13 (30,804)
Wilkinson, Nicholas R....5:13:14 (27,681)
Wilkinson, Nick L....4:50:49 (24,007)
Wilkinson, Paul T....5:00:42 (25,995)
Wilkinson, Peter J....3:39:13 (6,484)
Wilkinson, Richard J....3:56:58 (10,838)
Wilkinson, Robert....4:29:33 (19,188)
Wilkinson, Ronald J....5:00:13 (25,929)
Wilkinson, Steven M....3:28:23 (4,489)
Wilkinson, Stuart....4:43:36 (22,467)
Wilkinson, Tony....3:39:06 (6,454)
Wilkinson, Trevor....3:17:26 (2,936)
Willbourne, Paul S....5:20:08 (28,510)
Willems, Geert....3:47:38 (8,279)
Willett, Lee A....4:40:34 (21,804)
Willey, Duncan J....3:46:12 (7,945)
Willfratt, Kevin M....4:19:59 (16,598)
Williams, Alastair P....3:09:53 (2,054)
Williams, Aled R....5:39:58 (30,360)
Williams, Alex....3:45:39 (7,833)
Williams, Alexander C....4:35:01 (20,496)
Williams, Alun....4:41:51 (22,069)
Williams, Andrew G....4:33:51 (20,216)
Williams, Andrew J....4:24:38 (17,851)
Williams, Andrew J....4:53:40 (24,610)
Williams, Andrew P....3:31:04 (4,998)
Williams, Andrew R....4:10:40 (14,244)
Williams, Andy J....4:12:07 (14,603)
Williams, Anthony....4:15:01 (15,342)
Williams, Anthony D....5:06:08 (26,729)
Williams, Anthony E....4:18:43 (16,286)
Williams, Antony J....4:41:15 (21,934)
Williams, Arwel....4:30:02 (19,305)
Williams, Ashley....3:18:03 (3,005)
Williams, Brian....3:18:58 (3,129)
Williams, Bryn....5:02:31 (26,251)
Williams, Charles K....6:03:50 (31,720)
Williams, Clark....4:00:09 (11,858)
Williams, Colin....3:53:55 (9,897)
Williams, Colin C....3:52:34 (9,510)
Williams, Craig W....4:24:02 (17,666)
Williams, Dafydd....4:57:06 (25,334)
Williams, Damian....3:07:25 (1,795)
Williams, Daniel H....3:33:36 (5,421)
Williams, Daniel J....4:29:13 (19,088)
Williams, Daniel M....3:18:34 (3,077)
Williams, David....3:54:11 (9,972)
Williams, David G....4:51:26 (24,132)
Williams, David M....3:47:40 (8,285)
Williams, David O....3:12:47 (2,374)
Williams, David R....4:10:01 (14,103)
Williams, Dean....5:12:56 (27,640)
Williams, Dennis S....3:27:55 (4,397)
Williams, Edward A....6:50:48 (32,772)
Williams, Edward G....4:16:04 (15,617)
Williams, Edward I....4:22:08 (17,155)
Williams, Emlyn G....3:20:29 (3,338)
Williams, Gareth....3:47:11 (8,163)
Williams, Gareth I....3:38:03 (6,239)
Williams, Gareth J....2:33:21 (93)
Williams, Gareth P....3:08:14 (1,877)

Williams, Gareth P	4:13:13 (14,901)	
Williams, Gary	3:04:23 (1,537)	
Williams, Gavin	4:35:37 (20,632)	
Williams, Geoffrey D	3:19:54 (3,248)	
Williams, Glenn	4:21:56 (17,095)	
Williams, Glenn	5:43:22 (30,598)	
Williams, Graham	4:20:50 (16,817)	
Williams, Graham J	4:45:09 (22,820)	
Williams, Guy	4:44:52 (22,748)	
Williams, Guy M	4:21:59 (17,112)	
Williams, Gwion O	3:45:09 (7,721)	
Williams, Harry G	4:26:14 (18,320)	
Williams, Huw C	4:37:32 (21,117)	
Williams, Ian D	5:14:50 (27,885)	
Williams, Ian P	4:43:33 (22,452)	
Williams, Iolo	3:41:08 (6,835)	
Williams, Jack	3:31:56 (5,148)	
Williams, James	5:10:28 (27,330)	
Williams, James	6:08:45 (31,886)	
Williams, James T	5:15:01 (27,906)	
Williams, Jamie A	4:00:55 (12,019)	
Williams, Jeremy J	3:30:24 (4,878)	
Williams, John	3:26:51 (4,214)	
Williams, John D	3:48:22 (8,466)	
Williams, John S	3:31:00 (4,984)	
Williams, Jonathan D	3:19:43 (3,217)	
Williams, Julian I	3:56:32 (10,694)	
Williams, K J	4:22:26 (17,234)	
Williams, Keith	3:28:29 (4,506)	
Williams, Kevin	4:18:00 (16,108)	
Williams, Kevin	5:04:56 (26,573)	
Williams, Kevin S	4:19:31 (16,482)	
Williams, Lee	4:34:19 (20,310)	
Williams, Leighton R	3:46:23 (7,979)	
Williams, Leslie	4:23:08 (17,393)	
Williams, Lewis W	6:16:27 (32,132)	
Williams, Lindsay R	3:22:37 (3,616)	
Williams, Mark	3:53:45 (9,844)	
Williams, Mark L	3:29:57 (4,815)	
Williams, Martin P	3:32:25 (5,236)	
Williams, Martin R	4:50:03 (23,850)	
Williams, Matthew I	3:54:48 (10,145)	
Williams, Michael	3:52:08 (9,390)	
Williams, Michael H	4:59:40 (25,826)	
Williams, Michael J	4:22:03 (17,130)	
Williams, Michael S	3:18:49 (3,110)	
Williams, Mike	4:04:55 (12,899)	
Williams, Neil F	3:49:17 (8,688)	
Williams, Nigel	3:48:01 (8,387)	
Williams, Nigel P	3:53:25 (9,741)	
Williams, Nigel S	4:35:24 (20,579)	
Williams, Oliver	3:29:15 (4,663)	
Williams, Owain	4:26:41 (18,426)	
Williams, Owain L	4:04:38 (12,837)	
Williams, Owen M	4:17:19 (15,933)	
Williams, Paul	4:12:07 (14,603)	
Williams, Paul	4:28:59 (19,024)	
Williams, Paul C	3:39:02 (6,438)	
Williams, Paul D	4:46:23 (23,098)	
Williams, Paul D	4:50:37 (23,966)	
Williams, Paul E	4:14:38 (15,240)	
Williams, Paul L	4:54:08 (24,704)	
Williams, Paul M	5:01:00 (26,042)	
Williams, Peter	5:39:53 (30,350)	
Williams, Peter E	3:30:51 (4,952)	
Williams, Peter H	3:29:09 (4,644)	
Williams, Peter R	5:36:11 (30,069)	
Williams, Philip J	4:41:25 (21,973)	
Williams, Phillip T	3:38:55 (6,418)	
Williams, Ray W	4:14:53 (15,309)	
Williams, Red	3:45:35 (7,819)	
Williams, Rhys G	4:55:22 (24,976)	
Williams, Rhys L	3:35:18 (5,721)	
Williams, Richard B	3:55:02 (10,217)	
Williams, Richard C	3:52:14 (9,422)	
Williams, Richard O	4:16:28 (15,714)	
Williams, Richard W	3:15:20 (2,699)	
Williams, Rik S	5:18:43 (28,339)	
Williams, Robert C	3:51:11 (9,145)	
Williams, Robert G	5:52:35 (31,201)	
Williams, Sean	5:07:00 (26,861)	
Williams, Simon B	4:57:07 (25,338)	
Williams, Simon G	4:34:46 (20,430)	

Williams, Simon P	3:43:03 (7,251)	
Williams, Stan	3:14:59 (2,658)	
Williams, Stephen	5:24:09 (28,961)	
Williams, Stephen A	4:06:34 (13,243)	
Williams, Stephen E	5:42:43 (30,552)	
Williams, Stephen I	4:29:57 (19,282)	
Williams, Stephen J	3:58:59 (11,500)	
Williams, Stephen J	4:29:15 (19,102)	
Williams, Stephen M	2:56:31 (897)	
Williams, Thomas A	2:58:52 (1,125)	
Williams, Timothy J	4:22:46 (17,315)	
Williams, Tony R	4:33:32 (20,142)	
Williams, Trevor	4:57:25 (25,383)	
Williams, Warren J	4:35:12 (20,531)	
Williams-Gunn, Andrew	3:52:52 (9,585)	
Williamson, Adam	4:07:29 (13,470)	
Williamson, Alexander K	4:20:22 (16,700)	
Williamson, Alexander T	4:00:05 (11,839)	
Williamson, Anthony M	5:02:07 (26,194)	
Williamson, Bruce G	2:56:05 (855)	
Williamson, Colin	6:34:29 (32,522)	
Williamson, Dave B	4:13:06 (14,874)	
Williamson, David A	4:22:51 (17,333)	
Williamson, Guy B	4:17:51 (16,072)	
Williamson, John B	3:50:31 (8,989)	
Williamson, Mark	4:20:09 (16,644)	
Williamson, Mark	4:44:54 (22,756)	
Williamson, Matthew C	2:41:57 (245)	
Williamson, Michael	4:26:20 (18,348)	
Williamson, Neil R	4:03:52 (12,686)	
Williamson, Robin D	3:53:19 (9,722)	
Williamson, Ron G	4:16:05 (15,620)	
Williamson, Ross	3:46:49 (8,088)	
Williamson, Rupert J	3:33:09 (5,342)	
Williamson, Steven W	4:17:00 (15,860)	
Williamson, Toby	5:43:24 (30,605)	
Willicott, Mark	3:38:32 (6,334)	
Willingham, James J	3:35:40 (5,777)	
Willington, Simon H	3:57:42 (11,072)	
Willis, Andrew J	4:21:45 (17,045)	
Willis, Andrew J	5:20:12 (28,519)	
Willis, David	5:40:06 (30,372)	
Willis, David J	4:20:55 (16,842)	
Willis, David J	4:35:35 (20,618)	
Willis, Ian J	3:30:45 (4,936)	
Willis, Matthew J	2:45:47 (365)	
Willis, Paul	4:40:53 (21,869)	
Willis, Peter A	4:16:12 (15,644)	
Willis, Regan	3:21:19 (3,442)	
Willis, Robert C	4:11:56 (14,559)	
Willis, Robert H	3:26:07 (4,089)	
Willis, Rupert	5:43:29 (30,609)	
Willis, Sean G	3:58:17 (11,262)	
Willis, Simon L	4:16:19 (15,674)	
Willis, Stephen P	4:47:06 (23,235)	
Willis, Steve J	3:52:09 (9,398)	
Willis, Tim J	4:31:36 (19,698)	
Willis-Fleming, Sebastian J	3:48:48 (8,578)	
Willmitt, William J	3:16:06 (2,788)	
Willmott, Martin G	3:51:56 (9,346)	
Willmott, Stephen L	4:36:34 (20,861)	
Willock, Lee	4:24:33 (17,824)	
Willott, Guy	5:20:03 (28,500)	
Willoughby, Ian	4:48:31 (23,543)	
Willoughby, Stephen J	3:55:49 (10,482)	
Willox, Shaun	4:08:53 (13,830)	
Wills, Dennis A	3:53:04 (9,655)	
Wills, Kevin J	3:44:06 (7,472)	
Willsher, Neil D	3:24:48 (3,912)	
Willson, Anthony J	3:23:26 (3,702)	
Willson, David R	4:31:23 (19,638)	
Wilman, David R	4:54:32 (24,785)	
Wilmot, Andrew	3:22:30 (3,594)	
Wilmot, Andrew H	3:27:24 (4,314)	
Wilmott, Peter	3:04:40 (1,559)	
Wilmshurst, Andrew P	2:55:48 (837)	
Wilsmore, Paul H	4:51:54 (24,229)	
Wilson, Alan	3:58:04 (11,174)	
Wilson, Alex H	4:00:18 (11,887)	
Wilson, Andrew P	3:50:41 (9,027)	
Wilson, Andrew R	4:46:08 (23,033)	
Wilson, Barry	2:54:36 (772)	
Wilson, Ben A	4:08:19 (13,695)	

Wilson, Benjamin J	3:44:29 (7,563)	
Wilson, Campbell	4:06:17 (13,192)	
Wilson, Charles R	4:40:06 (21,691)	
Wilson, Charlie S	5:25:11 (29,057)	
Wilson, Chris	2:43:15 (295)	
Wilson, Colin J	4:49:48 (23,806)	
Wilson, Daren M	5:01:39 (26,128)	
Wilson, David H	3:12:49 (2,380)	
Wilson, David P	4:46:31 (23,124)	
Wilson, David P	5:11:26 (27,446)	
Wilson, David R	3:43:02 (7,242)	
Wilson, Donough	6:25:52 (32,375)	
Wilson, Eugene	4:59:57 (25,879)	
Wilson, Frank	4:45:23 (22,885)	
Wilson, Gareth E	2:41:20 (234)	
Wilson, Gary	2:45:58 (380)	
Wilson, Gary E	5:39:22 (30,308)	
Wilson, Gary J	3:13:21 (2,443)	
Wilson, Geoff M	4:36:25 (20,828)	
Wilson, Geoffrey	3:05:21 (1,613)	
Wilson, Glenn T	4:44:58 (22,775)	
Wilson, Graham	5:21:25 (28,658)	
Wilson, Iain	4:25:01 (17,969)	
Wilson, Ian C	4:26:42 (18,430)	
Wilson, James G	4:39:41 (21,596)	
Wilson, James I	3:30:45 (4,936)	
Wilson, James M	3:24:47 (3,911)	
Wilson, Jamie R	5:25:38 (29,094)	
Wilson, Jeffrey R	3:52:20 (9,445)	
Wilson, John A	4:16:40 (15,773)	
Wilson, John C	3:18:50 (3,111)	
Wilson, John R	3:55:52 (10,496)	
Wilson, Keith R	3:48:25 (8,477)	
Wilson, Kenneth J	3:43:21 (7,320)	
Wilson, Lee R	3:33:41 (5,435)	
Wilson, Luke A	3:59:01 (11,517)	
Wilson, Mark	3:49:52 (8,837)	
Wilson, Mark	3:59:08 (11,555)	
Wilson, Mark	5:06:56 (26,852)	
Wilson, Mark A	3:18:55 (3,124)	
Wilson, Mark G	4:36:03 (20,736)	
Wilson, Mark G	4:39:49 (21,632)	
Wilson, Mark R	4:41:52 (22,074)	
Wilson, Michael G	3:31:50 (5,128)	
Wilson, Michael R	3:30:28 (4,886)	
Wilson, Neil M	4:13:08 (14,883)	
Wilson, Nicholas M	3:14:26 (2,588)	
Wilson, Nick	3:09:23 (1,998)	
Wilson, Patrick N	5:12:11 (27,547)	
Wilson, Paul	2:36:23 (133)	
Wilson, Paul	4:08:49 (13,818)	
Wilson, Paul M	4:40:09 (21,703)	
Wilson, Peter	3:13:37 (2,479)	
Wilson, Richard A	6:35:35 (32,538)	
Wilson, Robert	3:20:13 (3,302)	
Wilson, Robert	4:18:49 (16,305)	
Wilson, Robert F	4:02:14 (12,312)	
Wilson, Robin H	4:55:34 (25,010)	
Wilson, Scott A	4:55:17 (24,957)	
Wilson, Sean M	3:28:17 (4,464)	
Wilson, Shane	3:12:48 (2,376)	
Wilson, Stephen D	4:46:11 (23,047)	
Wilson, Stephen P	4:24:01 (17,661)	
Wilson, Stuart J	4:20:56 (16,850)	
Wilson, Tony D	4:28:58 (19,018)	
Wilson, Trevor R	3:20:12 (3,299)	
Wilson, William T	7:26:15 (33,076)	
Wilson Stephens, Simon J	4:29:16 (19,107)	
Wilson-Phesse, Paul	4:05:04 (12,933)	
Wilton, Graham G	2:48:58 (496)	
Wilton, John F	4:43:52 (22,537)	
Wiltshire, Ian	4:40:39 (21,820)	
Wiltshire, Lee M	3:50:09 (8,902)	
Wiltshire, Martin J	6:17:31 (32,158)	
Wimble, Lance A	4:23:37 (17,535)	
Wimblett, Peter	5:04:15 (26,480)	
Windebank, Richard J	4:14:34 (15,226)	
Winder, David J	3:09:08 (1,967)	
Winder, Robert W	6:56:33 (32,849)	
Windle, Daron K	4:01:45 (12,199)	
Windle, Jason M	3:49:00 (8,628)	
Windle, Paul J	4:12:06 (14,595)	
Windorfer, Gerhard	4:28:19 (18,847)	

Windover, Jonathan M	5:03:23	(26,373)
Windybank, David J	4:27:51	(18,708)
Winfield, David	3:59:53	(11,784)
Winfield, Philip	4:36:18	(20,803)
Winfield, Stephen J	3:40:47	(6,760)
Winfield, Steven P	3:19:30	(3,193)
Wing, John S	3:55:07	(10,250)
Wing, Stephen	5:48:38	(30,979)
Wingate, Matthew D	3:31:57	(5,152)
Wingate, Tom M	5:29:38	(29,495)
Wingham, Mark	3:22:16	(3,566)
Wingrove, Andrew R	3:58:24	(11,306)
Wingrove, Tommy P	4:30:05	(19,320)
Winkelmann, Juergen	3:41:35	(6,941)
Winkelmann, Robert	3:51:54	(9,334)
Winkler, Gregor	2:53:21	(690)
Winkworth, Guy H	4:28:39	(18,935)
Winn, Julian K	4:00:53	(12,012)
Winsborough, Mike S	3:27:48	(4,379)
Winship, Julian A	4:03:01	(12,481)
Winslet, Daniel J	4:11:05	(14,354)
Winslow, Michael P	3:54:39	(10,091)
Winslow, Tony	4:02:27	(12,366)
Winston, Geoffrey N	3:45:24	(7,783)
Winstone, Andrew C	4:32:42	(19,934)
Winstone, Martin	4:21:48	(17,062)
Winter, Colin G	3:58:17	(11,262)
Winter, Dean W	4:25:54	(18,233)
Winter, Geoff	4:15:51	(15,564)
Winter, Kevin J	6:03:03	(31,683)
Winter, Paul G	4:20:28	(16,727)
Winter, Paul L	5:01:54	(26,164)
Winter, Paul M	5:22:19	(28,757)
Winterbottom, Nicholas P	4:52:54	(24,437)
Winterflood, David	4:03:23	(12,574)
Winterflood, Simon P	4:39:56	(21,662)
Winterhagen, Wolf Rainer	5:43:07	(30,582)
Winters, Daniel	4:39:11	(21,486)
Winters, John T	3:50:30	(8,984)
Winthrod, Paul	5:45:03	(30,721)
Winton, Piers N	5:02:09	(26,197)
Wipp, Jonathan P	5:05:23	(26,635)
Wirsing, Vwe	3:07:19	(1,789)
Wisbey, Matthew J	4:47:30	(23,319)
Wisdom, Martin J	3:40:16	(6,671)
Wise, Andrew S	4:11:30	(14,459)
Wise, Jason	4:20:57	(16,853)
Wise, Robert A	3:39:01	(6,436)
Wise, Roger S	4:25:45	(18,176)
Wiseman, Michael A	3:36:52	(6,012)
Witcomb, Mark	3:32:06	(5,180)
Witcombe, Paul C	3:00:42	(1,283)
Witherall, Robert P	3:12:48	(2,376)
Witherington, Kieran D	4:29:11	(19,079)
Withers, Bill	3:24:42	(3,896)
Withers, David G	4:47:28	(23,311)
Withers, Richard J	3:29:01	(4,624)
Withington, Terry	4:50:40	(23,976)
Witt, Jonathan J	3:54:31	(10,057)
Witte, Andrew C	3:48:02	(8,392)
Witts, Andrew	3:43:24	(7,333)
Witts, Nicholas K	4:04:44	(12,862)
Wizard, Danny N	3:01:41	(1,349)
Wodu, Chinna O	5:12:29	(27,587)
Wojcik, Pieter J	3:43:58	(7,452)
Wolf, Joachim	2:37:33	(153)
Wolf, Klas Uwe	5:07:14	(26,897)
Wolfe, Dave B	4:15:47	(15,540)
Wolfe, Lee	4:21:33	(16,985)
Wolfe, Patrick J	2:56:56	(935)
Wolfendale, Stewart	4:06:10	(13,173)
Wolfensohn, Simon V	4:10:20	(14,181)
Wolfgramme, Mark H	5:56:06	(31,359)
Wolland, Brian	4:19:33	(16,491)
Wolman, Merrick	4:53:25	(24,551)
Wolovitz, Lionel	3:16:17	(2,801)
Wolsey, Peter	3:45:43	(7,854)
Wolstencroft, John A	4:07:48	(13,555)
Wolstenholme, Patrick J	4:23:36	(17,530)
Wolton, Timothy M	4:21:43	(17,026)
Womack, Simon T	3:36:58	(6,035)
Wong, Baldwin	3:47:51	(8,344)
Wong, Chi T	4:52:10	(24,285)
Wong, Hing	4:24:46	(17,884)
Wong, Justin	4:19:16	(16,413)
Wong, Lawrence	4:34:47	(20,433)
Wong, Marie	4:32:54	(19,979)
Wooby, Neil R	3:06:58	(1,755)
Wood, Alan	5:55:26	(31,322)
Wood, Alistair A	5:11:43	(27,480)
Wood, Alun	2:41:49	(240)
Wood, Andrew P	5:45:58	(30,777)
Wood, Andrew T	4:52:44	(24,405)
Wood, Angus D	4:09:27	(13,981)
Wood, Brian E	3:56:41	(10,750)
Wood, Chris	3:44:56	(7,677)
Wood, Chris	4:20:05	(16,626)
Wood, Christopher J	4:05:03	(12,928)
Wood, Darrell J	4:43:57	(22,563)
Wood, David	4:34:20	(20,321)
Wood, David A	4:21:36	(16,999)
Wood, David A	5:00:16	(25,937)
Wood, David M	3:57:53	(11,130)
Wood, Gareth D	2:54:06	(734)
Wood, Haydn C	3:58:38	(11,375)
Wood, Ian G	5:17:18	(28,167)
Wood, Ian S	4:58:48	(25,662)
Wood, Jeremy	4:18:41	(16,278)
Wood, John	3:17:24	(2,931)
Wood, John B	4:16:14	(15,652)
Wood, John R	3:47:12	(8,168)
Wood, Jonathan P	4:08:28	(13,735)
Wood, Keith A	3:29:55	(4,809)
Wood, Kenneth J	6:18:29	(32,183)
Wood, Kevin B	3:49:59	(8,863)
Wood, Kevin T	3:57:57	(11,150)
Wood, Lewis G	5:30:47	(29,626)
Wood, Marc A	4:59:45	(25,840)
Wood, Mark T	3:00:01	(1,235)
Wood, Martin I	3:03:30	(1,480)
Wood, Martin J	3:03:04	(1,450)
Wood, Martyn	4:52:01	(24,254)
Wood, Matthew P	5:26:48	(29,201)
Wood, Matthew R	4:39:22	(21,537)
Wood, Max D	3:54:35	(10,074)
Wood, Michael	3:36:49	(5,997)
Wood, Michael	4:02:37	(12,405)
Wood, Michael J	3:30:45	(4,936)
Wood, Michael L	3:52:57	(9,610)
Wood, Nigel	4:18:36	(16,258)
Wood, Nigel	4:39:13	(21,496)
Wood, Nigel O	3:45:45	(7,858)
Wood, Nigel T	4:20:55	(16,842)
Wood, Paul	3:59:08	(11,555)
Wood, Paul J	2:54:10	(738)
Wood, Peter	3:55:36	(10,405)
Wood, Peter J	4:16:49	(15,804)
Wood, Philip A	4:44:17	(22,636)
Wood, Philip M	3:37:04	(6,048)
Wood, Reece H	3:31:44	(5,109)
Wood, Richard	4:28:50	(18,979)
Wood, Richard C	3:09:22	(1,996)
Wood, Robert M	3:57:02	(10,852)
Wood, Robert T	4:40:56	(21,877)
Wood, Steve W	3:32:27	(5,243)
Wood, Stuart J	4:15:09	(15,380)
Wood, Timothy S	3:19:53	(3,246)
Wood, Will	3:43:44	(7,402)
Woodard, Gary J	4:17:15	(15,918)
Woodcock, Clive A	3:33:01	(5,326)
Woodcock, Martin J	4:23:32	(17,513)
Woodcock, Paul V	4:39:07	(21,469)
Woodcock, Stephen	4:04:54	(12,897)
Wooderson, Andrew D	4:07:08	(13,385)
Woodfield, Ben M	6:03:43	(31,715)
Woodfine, Gary P	5:00:44	(25,999)
Woodfine, Owen	4:33:43	(20,193)
Woodford, Matt	4:44:08	(22,596)
Woodgate, Marc A	3:53:01	(9,630)
Woodhall, Darren M	3:25:06	(3,942)
Woodham, James M	4:23:09	(17,397)
Woodhams, Elliot W	4:02:01	(12,269)
Woodhead, Andrew C	4:30:04	(19,315)
Woodhead, Richard J	3:35:18	(5,721)
Woodhouse, Ben	3:52:10	(9,402)
Woodhouse, Paul D	4:36:06	(20,752)
Woodhouse-Roe, Douglas K	4:02:01	(12,269)
Wooding, John	3:29:49	(4,790)
Wooding, Stephen R	4:16:00	(15,599)
Woodley, James R	3:50:03	(8,874)
Woodman, Mark J	2:37:04	(147)
Woodman, Philip C	3:36:23	(5,912)
Woodroof, Neil D	4:07:22	(13,439)
Woodrow, Austin K	3:57:17	(10,944)
Woodrow, George F	4:29:54	(19,267)
Woodrow, James M	4:29:54	(19,267)
Woodruff, Raymond	3:23:46	(3,752)
Woods, Andrew J	3:34:25	(5,551)
Woods, Andrew J	4:28:18	(18,842)
Woods, Chris M	3:26:19	(4,119)
Woods, Colin P	4:23:18	(17,443)
Woods, George H	3:59:34	(11,689)
Woods, Jason R	4:16:37	(15,761)
Woods, Kevin	3:39:11	(6,471)
Woods, Lee M	3:33:11	(5,351)
Woods, Leo	4:25:58	(18,249)
Woods, Michael	6:13:09	(32,024)
Woods, Nathanael D	3:50:25	(8,959)
Woods, Paul	5:06:40	(26,811)
Woods, Pete T	3:49:44	(8,808)
Woods, Philip R	3:51:19	(9,178)
Woodward, Chad I	5:20:45	(28,586)
Woodward, David T	4:29:40	(19,219)
Woodward, George W	4:11:41	(14,494)
Woodward, James D	3:30:29	(4,889)
Woodward, Jamie	5:11:14	(27,418)
Woodward, Jeremy M	3:34:44	(5,620)
Woodward, Keiron	5:21:32	(28,669)
Woodward, Kevin K	3:25:43	(4,031)
Woodward, Matthew S	4:00:03	(11,834)
Woodward, Michael	4:52:50	(24,429)
Woodward, Philip P	4:29:59	(19,288)
Woodward, Robert	3:28:09	(4,433)
Woodward, Robert A	4:47:12	(23,260)
Woolcock, Anthony	4:09:23	(13,954)
Woolcock, Charlie	4:34:45	(20,424)
Woolcock, Martin K	3:53:21	(9,731)
Woolerton, Mark I	6:27:10	(32,407)
Woolerton, Philip J	4:37:41	(21,156)
Wooley, Alan N	4:14:27	(15,197)
Woolf, Neal J	4:26:47	(18,461)
Woolf, Oliver	3:50:06	(8,885)
Woolf, Paul	3:27:01	(4,251)
Woolford, Mark C	4:55:13	(24,942)
Woolgar, Nick R	4:50:17	(23,901)
Woolgar, Terry	3:37:47	(6,188)
Woolhouse, Michael G	3:24:30	(3,864)
Wooller, Tristan J	3:30:03	(4,836)
Woolley, David	4:43:04	(22,339)
Woolley, David J	4:54:18	(24,747)
Woolley, Ian G	4:29:35	(19,194)
Woolley, Jonathan J	3:48:55	(8,614)
Woolley, Laurence M	4:23:58	(17,644)
Woolley, Simon M	3:27:35	(4,348)
Woollon, Andy	3:47:10	(8,158)
Woolston, Thomas H	5:05:35	(26,650)
Woolven, Adrian D	3:36:39	(5,967)
Woolward, Darryl	3:46:40	(8,055)
Woonton, Stephen A	3:29:20	(4,684)
Wootten, Ronald	4:14:26	(15,190)
Wootton, Richard O	3:58:55	(11,483)
Wootton, Robert O	4:22:53	(17,339)
Wootton, Rod	4:29:52	(19,261)
Wootton, Terence E	4:28:29	(18,894)
Worcester, David R	6:20:00	(32,229)
Workman, Anthony C	3:42:56	(7,217)
Workman, Richard	3:38:16	(6,285)
Worley, Ben A	4:25:09	(18,008)
Worrall, Chris L	4:05:31	(13,027)
Worrall, Richard G	4:06:47	(13,298)
Worrall, Richard L	3:29:28	(4,708)
Worsdell, Philip	4:16:31	(15,732)
Worsfold, Paul	3:27:40	(4,360)
Worsfold, Philip	3:36:37	(5,961)
Worsley, Martin S	3:48:42	(8,558)
Worsley, Martyn C	4:59:38	(25,818)
Worsnip, Ian A	3:59:14	(11,583)
Worsnip, James C	4:11:51	(14,534)
Worster, Peter J	4:14:06	(15,104)

Wort, Peter M 4:13:41 (15,000)
Worth, Laurence M 5:16:26 (28,062)
Worth, Ryan J 3:13:11 (2,424)
Worthington, John A 2:36:59 (144)
Worthington, Paul 4:56:12 (25,139)
Worthington, Sam T 3:19:55 (3,250)
Wostenholm, Maurice T 4:35:08 (20,516)
Wotherspoon, Michael J 4:26:42 (18,430)
Wotton, Kevin M 3:09:06 (1,965)
Wrage, George D 5:50:06 (31,081)
Wragg, Anthony A 4:52:07 (24,275)
Wragg, David A 4:14:46 (15,279)
Wraight, Oliver R 3:35:59 (5,832)
Wray, Alan J 3:08:27 (1,904)
Wray, Michael A 3:43:08 (7,269)
Wren, Edwin F 4:36:50 (20,945)
Wren, James A 4:36:37 (20,872)
Wren, Martin C 4:21:17 (16,934)
Wrench, James R 3:02:55 (1,435)
Wrenn, Chris B 3:56:28 (10,676)
Wrenn, Nicholas J 3:27:34 (4,344)
Wrenn, Simon A 5:05:49 (26,680)
Wrenn, Stuart A 3:43:01 (7,236)
Wretham, Russell J 5:33:43 (29,870)
Wride, Chris J 3:45:26 (7,789)
Wride, Robert 7:03:22 (32,910)
Wright, Alan 4:16:22 (15,684)
Wright, Alan 4:21:16 (16,932)
Wright, Andrew J 4:15:13 (15,392)
Wright, Andrew J 5:18:13 (28,273)
Wright, Andrew L 3:10:59 (2,155)
Wright, Andrew S 3:51:57 (9,351)
Wright, Anthony J 4:51:35 (24,164)
Wright, Chris 5:07:51 (26,981)
Wright, Christopher I 5:50:01 (31,075)
Wright, Christopher S 5:02:36 (26,262)
Wright, David 4:16:09 (15,634)
Wright, David A 4:43:21 (22,398)
Wright, David J 3:03:52 (1,505)
Wright, David J 3:14:00 (2,530)
Wright, David J 5:29:48 (29,523)
Wright, David K 3:56:47 (10,778)
Wright, David K 5:37:23 (30,155)
Wright, David P 3:53:56 (9,902)
Wright, David W 5:51:17 (31,140)
Wright, Derek 3:25:31 (4,005)
Wright, Duncan A 4:25:07 (17,996)
Wright, Duncan P 4:46:09 (23,038)
Wright, Elliot F 3:26:56 (4,229)
Wright, Felipe 3:04:02 (1,514)
Wright, Gary S 3:37:42 (6,166)
Wright, Ian S 5:01:30 (26,107)
Wright, James D 3:37:43 (6,171)
Wright, Jason A 4:12:49 (14,779)
Wright, John C 4:54:26 (24,776)
Wright, John J 4:51:24 (24,121)
Wright, John K 3:46:39 (8,048)
Wright, John T 4:20:11 (16,656)
Wright, Lee A 3:36:48 (5,993)
Wright, Mark 4:53:06 (24,479)
Wright, Mark D 3:51:07 (9,125)
Wright, Matthew 3:51:55 (9,341)
Wright, Matthew J 3:56:49 (10,790)
Wright, Michael R 3:37:32 (6,137)
Wright, Neil D 3:35:03 (5,679)
Wright, Nicholas 4:44:59 (22,778)
Wright, Nicholas K 3:46:36 (8,034)
Wright, Nick J 3:29:38 (4,749)
Wright, Nik S 3:05:48 (1,642)
Wright, Oliver C 3:21:00 (3,400)
Wright, Oliver G 2:56:44 (920)
Wright, Oliver T 5:08:41 (27,103)
Wright, Paul 4:53:01 (24,459)
Wright, Paul J 4:25:48 (18,194)
Wright, Peter A 3:19:49 (3,234)
Wright, Peter R 3:53:40 (9,810)
Wright, Philip A 5:05:49 (26,680)
Wright, Spencer 4:29:55 (19,273)
Wright, Stephen J 3:59:42 (11,728)
Wright, Stephen T 3:51:14 (9,156)
Wright, Steven P 3:58:18 (11,266)
Wright, Stuart 3:46:02 (7,907)
Wright, Stuart E 4:40:29 (21,771)
Wright, Williams 3:58:29 (11,333)
Wrighton, Christopher J 2:36:11 (130)
Wrightson, James A 3:17:37 (2,953)
Wriglesworth, John 3:14:28 (2,591)
Wriglesworth, John L 4:38:02 (21,231)
Wrigley, David 4:30:04 (19,315)
Wrigley, Joseph S 3:14:50 (2,645)
Wrigley, Peter J 3:46:43 (8,066)
Writer, Keith D 4:32:45 (19,945)
Wrobel, Joao A 4:20:41 (16,783)
Wroblewski, Steve J 3:16:24 (2,809)
Wroe, Andrew D 4:34:17 (20,303)
Wroot, Andrew J 3:50:25 (8,959)
Wrout, Andrew P 3:19:59 (3,267)
Wuerz, Thomas H 3:21:28 (3,464)
Wyatt, Darren S 3:28:00 (4,408)
Wyatt, David R 4:09:47 (14,054)
Wyatt, Richard W 5:20:14 (28,524)
Wye, Mark A 4:44:19 (22,639)
Wyer, Martin J 4:07:04 (13,360)
Wyeth, Stephen 6:03:58 (31,727)
Wyke, James A 5:45:20 (30,741)
Wyld, Mark R 4:02:09 (12,296)
Wylie, Robert S 5:05:15 (26,618)
Wylie, Stephen J 5:03:16 (26,354)
Wyllie, Peter B 4:35:08 (20,516)
Wyllie, Robert 4:27:04 (18,517)
Wyman, Todd 4:18:52 (16,318)
Wyn-Jones, Neil 4:48:33 (23,552)
Wynn, Anthony J 4:28:28 (18,889)
Wynne, Gronwy 5:46:09 (30,797)
Wynn-Jones, William B 3:24:17 (3,836)
Wysome, Anthony 3:29:58 (4,818)
Wyson, Richard J 3:36:47 (5,990)
Xenophontos, Chris 3:57:02 (10,852)
Yabsley, Edward J 4:27:55 (18,729)
Yabu, Kenji 5:16:14 (28,034)
Yadave, Rush L 3:55:48 (10,479)
Yamashita, Shigeru 4:25:02 (17,972)
Yamazaki, Takeshi 3:00:25 (1,264)
Yan, Henry 4:31:39 (19,711)
Yannick, Delaunay 4:21:22 (16,953)
Yapp, Peter D 4:56:43 (25,245)
Yard, Phil 4:19:13 (16,393)
Yardley, Robert H 4:45:02 (22,798)
Yarnell, Jonathan N 5:30:33 (29,598)
Yarrow, Hugh W 4:14:26 (15,190)
Yarrow, Nick S 5:47:58 (30,942)
Yarrow, Tom J 3:29:33 (4,731)
Yasumatsu, Kazuhiko 4:13:27 (14,951)
Yates, Anthony J 3:57:19 (10,953)
Yates, David A 5:40:20 (30,388)
Yates, Eric W 5:26:24 (29,165)
Yates, Ian J 4:16:03 (15,609)
Yates, Michael 5:11:34 (27,469)
Yates, Nicholas M 4:45:57 (22,995)
Yates, Peter E 4:22:53 (17,339)
Yates, Robert 3:20:18 (3,312)
Yates, Robert J 5:07:05 (26,874)
Yazaki, Etsuro 3:08:24 (1,897)
Yeadon, Alex J 4:14:03 (15,086)
Yearsley, Fred A 3:36:01 (5,837)
Yeates, Daniel R 4:31:37 (19,701)
Yellop, Antony 4:35:43 (20,655)
Yeoman, Dean P 3:13:02 (2,403)
Yeoman, Justin 3:57:27 (10,996)
Yeoman, Lloyd A 4:59:53 (25,866)
Yetman, Martyn E 3:56:06 (10,568)
Yip, Timothy 3:26:15 (4,109)
Yiu, Joseph M 4:26:48 (18,464)
Yoon, I Cheol 3:55:21 (10,332)
Yore, Gavin 5:35:35 (30,020)
York, Anthony G 3:58:38 (11,375)
York, Clive D 5:39:58 (30,360)
York, Richard J 4:50:21 (23,917)
York, Richard K 3:59:54 (11,786)
Yorke, Richard 5:05:12 (26,611)
Yoshida, Genechi 3:13:47 (2,501)
Yoshida, Tamotsu 4:15:31 (15,481)
Yoshida, Toshiharu 4:39:18 (21,514)
You, Jeong Hah 5:35:15 (29,993)
Youdan, Ben J 3:56:45 (10,766)
Youds, Daniel O 4:04:57 (12,907)
Youens, Kenneth 4:10:12 (14,149)
Youens, Robert 3:38:36 (6,349)
Youl, Christopher S 3:56:33 (10,708)
Youlden, James A 2:55:18 (802)
Young, Adam 3:38:25 (6,309)
Young, Adam G 4:31:31 (19,668)
Young, Andrew H 3:30:07 (4,849)
Young, Andrew J 3:07:47 (1,837)
Young, Andrew W 4:57:44 (25,441)
Young, Brian J 5:10:48 (27,367)
Young, Chris D 3:23:53 (3,771)
Young, Christopher J 3:35:53 (5,814)
Young, David J 3:48:42 (8,558)
Young, Graham 5:15:56 (27,994)
Young, Grant R 4:49:30 (23,754)
Young, Harvey T 4:50:27 (23,935)
Young, Ian 4:55:56 (25,085)
Young, Jim 3:43:07 (7,265)
Young, Joe 3:29:41 (4,756)
Young, John B 3:34:32 (5,575)
Young, Kevin A 5:09:22 (27,190)
Young, Mark D 3:14:38 (2,619)
Young, Mark T 3:37:35 (6,152)
Young, Michael M 3:41:30 (6,914)
Young, Philip 4:08:45 (13,800)
Young, Robin D 4:11:14 (14,396)
Young, Roland J 4:40:29 (21,771)
Young, Shaun 5:05:55 (26,698)
Young, Simon D 4:09:16 (13,926)
Young, Thomas D 3:15:52 (2,765)
Young, Tom J 4:21:12 (16,915)
Young, Trevor J 3:42:03 (7,036)
Younger, Peter J 4:35:03 (20,501)
Youngman, Adrian R 4:02:45 (12,424)
Youngman, James D 4:11:56 (14,559)
Youngs, Stephen J 4:18:30 (16,231)
Youngson, Derek K 3:28:38 (4,537)
Yoxall, Ned O 4:06:28 (13,224)
Ysern, Ricardo 4:24:59 (17,953)
Ytreland, Kristian G 4:33:56 (20,231)
Yuen, Alfred H 3:44:30 (7,567)
Yukler, Yusyf 3:32:08 (5,184)
Yuksel, Hakan 3:48:50 (8,585)
Yull, Alan R 4:16:00 (15,599)
Yuste, Hector 4:09:08 (13,885)
Zachariasse, Andries 4:00:12 (11,864)
Zacho, Torben M 4:31:09 (19,571)
Zanetto, Jean 2:51:05 (597)
Zanol, Giorgio 3:36:11 (5,872)
Zansi, Antonio 4:51:41 (24,183)
Zaremba, Mark 5:49:26 (31,038)
Zbyszewski, Dinusha I 5:47:08 (30,873)
Zealey, Nicholas C 3:58:49 (11,452)
Zehnder, Brian 3:52:44 (9,554)
Zeindler, Roland 3:48:48 (8,578)
Zellick, Adam D 3:45:30 (7,805)
Zenone, Gennaro 6:36:01 (32,544)
Zerban, Aziz 3:40:46 (6,759)
Zeroski, Dan 4:06:50 (13,308)
Zettl, Guenter 5:20:56 (28,602)
Zhuk, Mark 5:05:20 (26,632)
Ziani, Kamel 2:14:50 (14)
Zielinski, Jeremy V 2:58:24 (1,057)
Zingarelli, Sergio 4:24:55 (17,930)
Zinni, Vincenzo 3:55:43 (10,444)
Zipperle, Volker 3:13:37 (2,479)
Zirngast, Philip J 4:03:56 (12,702)
Zivan Sussholz, Philippe 3:31:22 (5,049)
Zoller, Gary J 3:20:15 (3,305)
Zollo, Andy C 4:20:08 (16,636)
Zouras, Arthur 4:06:16 (13,185)
Zubairu, Abdul 4:54:47 (24,840)
Zucconi, Anthony 4:33:28 (20,126)
Zucker, Jamie 3:52:36 (9,520)
Zuendorf, Franz P 3:56:06 (10,568)
Zumiani, Giuseppe 3:30:51 (4,952)
Zunde, Nigel D 3:45:21 (7,771)

FEMALE RUNNERS

Aarthun, Marit 3:03:51 (1,503)
Abb, Hannelore 5:32:55 (29,809)
Abbott, Charmian J 4:33:57 (20,238)
Abbott, Eileen B 5:08:47 (27,114)

Abbott, Joanna 4:22:42 (17,300)
Abbott, Kathryn E 4:17:44 (16,038)
Abbott, Pamela L 4:52:37 (24,384)
Abbott, Tracey E 4:52:58 (24,448)
Abbs, Wendy 5:03:07 (26,330)
Abdul Rahim, Suha 6:56:42 (32,852)
Abel, Katherine A 3:57:44 (11,087)
Abel, Lanie 4:26:44 (18,443)
Abela, Cheryl 4:35:32 (20,607)
Abell, Kathryn A 4:20:55 (16,842)
Abercrombie, Mary 3:56:39 (10,739)
Abercromby, Amanda 4:53:13 (24,512)
Abiola, Waliyah O 6:35:16 (32,530)
Ablethorpe, Clare L 4:03:00 (12,477)
Abraham, Claire M 5:29:23 (29,466)
Abraham, Corinne S 3:43:15 (7,300)
Abraham, Faye 4:28:29 (18,894)
Abram, Amanda J 5:46:23 (30,817)
Abramson, Caron 4:28:19 (18,847)
Abramson, Katie L 4:28:20 (18,854)
Achten, Renilda 4:15:42 (15,521)
Ackooij Van, Louise J 5:06:07 (26,727)
Ackroyd, Jacqueline A 3:37:10 (6,069)
Ackroyd, Susan 5:04:22 (26,499)
Acton, Jane C 3:37:10 (6,069)
Acton, Laura M 5:20:34 (28,573)
Adam, Charlotte 6:06:26 (31,801)
Adams, Alexandra C 3:49:02 (8,634)
Adams, Alison J 5:17:19 (28,170)
Adams, Dawn 5:45:17 (30,740)
Adams, Deborah 6:09:08 (31,899)
Adams, Elizabeth 4:25:49 (18,199)
Adams, Gillian C 3:43:54 (7,439)
Adams, Hazel R 4:07:04 (13,360)
Adams, Julianne 5:24:55 (29,031)
Adams, Julie A 5:12:59 (27,649)
Adams, Julie A 7:27:53 (33,085)
Adams, Kerri J 5:26:52 (29,210)
Adams, Paula L 2:57:37 (995)
Adams, Polly H 3:16:00 (2,780)
Adams, Susan P 5:02:47 (26,285)
Adams, Tara D 3:44:55 (7,674)
Adams, Teresa B 4:46:40 (23,153)
Adams, Victoria J 4:57:52 (25,470)
Adamson, Alison M 4:43:21 (22,398)
Adcock, Rosemary A 4:52:46 (24,414)
Addelsee, Helen M 4:42:04 (22,128)
Adderley-Speke, Sadie J 5:16:58 (28,121)
Adere, Berhane 2:21:52 (36)
Adesemoxe, Wole 4:33:46 (20,199)
Adiseshiah, Maria 5:50:51 (31,124)
Adlard, Jane A 5:18:28 (28,304)
Aerne Rusterholz, Susanne 3:53:47 (9,853)
Agnew, Angela A 6:30:41 (32,468)
Agnew, Rebecca E 4:04:27 (12,804)
Ahearn, Ginette 6:03:57 (31,726)
Ahl, Lucie A 3:22:09 (3,555)
Ahmed, Nadia 5:47:21 (30,904)
Ahmed, Shehneela J 6:08:00 (31,859)
Aiken, Ceri J 5:00:37 (25,987)
Ainscough, Kirsty A 3:54:05 (9,940)
Ainslie, Tina L 5:21:52 (28,698)
Ainsworth, Laura J 4:41:15 (21,934)
Ainsworth, Pat 5:12:30 (27,588)
Aird, Nerys W 4:16:10 (15,639)
Aird, Sue 5:54:37 (31,294)
Airlie, Shona M 5:01:15 (26,083)
Aitchison, Pauline A 3:31:50 (5,128)
Aithwaite, Beverley S 4:27:04 (18,517)
Aitken, Leila L 4:25:49 (18,199)
Aiyela, Remi 5:03:33 (26,398)
Akeroyd, Lisa 3:56:29 (10,681)
Albutt, Denise 5:31:35 (29,713)
Alcock, Emma L 3:59:50 (11,774)
Alder, Marie L 5:03:11 (26,343)
Aldersley, Helen C 4:14:46 (15,279)
Alderton, Ann 5:06:51 (26,843)
Aldgate, Hannah J 5:02:48 (26,288)
Aleknavicius, Carol 4:34:59 (20,483)
Alepuz, Marta 4:33:08 (20,043)
Alexander, Jacqueline 5:25:28 (29,081)
Alexander, Jane 5:54:43 (31,300)
Alexander, Roz 2:54:41 (777)
Alexander, Samantha 4:57:36 (25,417)
Alford, Holly A 4:36:11 (20,774)
Alford, Rebecca J 3:43:00 (7,231)
Alger, Diane L 4:47:50 (23,394)
Al-Hashimi, Tamara 4:58:42 (25,644)
Ali, Simeen 6:15:25 (32,097)
Allan, Elizabeth A 3:58:37 (11,372)
Allan, Emily P 4:35:37 (20,632)
Allan, Faye 5:14:03 (27,772)
Allan, Heather A 4:40:28 (21,763)
Allan, Jean M 6:06:24 (31,798)
Allan, Katie 4:01:59 (12,264)
Allan, Nicola 6:38:58 (32,598)
Allan, Tania 6:17:29 (32,156)
Allan, Wendy J 4:53:43 (24,622)
Allcock, Elizabeth M 5:15:51 (27,982)
Allen, Catherine J 3:56:58 (10,838)
Allen, Coral P 3:48:55 (8,614)
Allen, Diane L 5:47:45 (30,932)
Allen, Heather 3:44:28 (7,558)
Allen, Jennifer G 5:16:04 (28,007)
Allen, Joanne R 5:22:45 (28,808)
Allen, Joy 4:02:46 (12,430)
Allen, Julie A 4:58:35 (25,627)
Allen, Lisa P 3:44:27 (7,553)
Allen, Lucy M 3:40:28 (6,706)
Allen, Rachael C 6:29:30 (32,441)
Allen, Sarah 6:49:18 (32,752)
Allen, Tricia M 4:47:25 (23,296)
Allen, Valerie J 5:30:18 (29,576)
Allender, Pat 7:05:04 (32,941)
Allgood, Angela 4:19:08 (16,374)
Allgood, Michelle L 5:37:06 (30,144)
Allingham, Ann 4:40:24 (21,751)
Allingham, Lucy J 5:26:22 (29,159)
Allinson, Caroline F 4:48:45 (23,596)
Allison, Carolina L 5:50:41 (31,116)
Allison, Karen L 4:26:46 (18,459)
Allison, Sophie J 4:24:56 (17,938)
Allsopp, Lucy V 5:45:50 (30,767)
Allum, Julie 4:33:14 (20,067)
Almond, Tracy J 4:07:43 (13,540)
Alon, Sheila 4:49:46 (23,803)
Alson, Kirsty H 5:01:04 (26,056)
Alves De Sousa, Sarah J 4:03:11 (12,524)
Amakasu, Ririko 5:06:43 (26,820)
Amarquaye, Ruth A 6:09:02 (31,895)
Ambrose, Jane 5:50:23 (31,099)
Ambrose, Shaheda 5:43:49 (30,627)
Amend, Samantha 3:01:52 (1,362)
Amer, Claire L 3:58:14 (11,245)
Amesbury, Rosie 5:09:50 (27,244)
Ameur, Angela 5:25:12 (29,059)
Amondi, Olukemi J 5:43:23 (30,601)
Amson-Orth, Karyn 4:54:47 (24,840)
Amy, Chris 4:33:56 (20,231)
Anait, Rehana 6:25:19 (32,361)
Anderson, Alexandra E 4:05:12 (12,958)
Anderson, Ashley C 4:19:14 (16,398)
Anderson, Bridget C 5:31:17 (29,690)
Anderson, Britta 3:42:32 (7,121)
Anderson, Caroline R 3:58:21 (11,288)
Anderson, Clare 5:23:40 (28,901)
Anderson, Deborah L 6:14:32 (32,069)
Anderson, Elaine 4:41:19 (21,956)
Anderson, Hazel A 3:52:43 (9,551)
Anderson, Irit R 4:48:03 (23,438)
Anderson, Jennifer L 4:56:29 (25,202)
Anderson, Jessica M 5:44:07 (30,653)
Anderson, Judith A 5:19:15 (28,410)
Anderson, Katy M 3:50:46 (9,050)
Anderson, Kim P 4:51:11 (24,074)
Anderson, Layla E 4:50:39 (23,973)
Anderson, Martha M 3:49:47 (8,816)
Anderson, Michelle L 5:22:21 (28,763)
Anderson, Samara D 3:48:18 (8,450)
Anderson, Sara M 4:58:20 (25,577)
Andersson, Eva C 5:29:47 (29,518)
Andersson Drugge, Inemarie 6:44:21 (32,681)
Anderton, Sophie 5:49:48 (31,056)
Andew, Vera 5:10:29 (27,332)
Andreassen, Nichola M 5:22:18 (28,753)
Andrew, Beth L 3:16:59 (2,875)
Andrew, Kim 5:42:02 (30,502)
Andrew, Pamela M 5:41:34 (30,460)
Andrews, Cathy M 5:30:03 (29,549)
Andrews, Deborah L 5:12:51 (27,627)
Andrews, Emma C 7:23:07 (33,056)
Andrews, Katie H 4:00:36 (11,948)
Andrews, Kim M 5:08:56 (27,140)
Andrews, Linda 4:32:11 (19,827)
Andrews, Mandy T 4:20:06 (16,629)
Andrews, Margaret H 4:17:18 (15,929)
Andrews, Sarah 4:14:02 (15,080)
Angel, Melanie R 3:57:35 (11,036)
Angeli, Angela 5:46:43 (30,840)
Angell, Sarah J 5:08:10 (27,028)
Anghaee, Sholeh 4:23:28 (17,493)
Aninat, Caroline 3:45:46 (7,863)
Ankarett, Helen 4:40:12 (21,713)
Anley, Kerry A 3:24:30 (3,864)
Annetts, Elizabeth A 4:22:35 (17,260)
Annis, Sarah J 5:01:04 (26,056)
Annyaegbunam, Ify 5:20:19 (28,541)
Ansell, Eloise 5:36:22 (30,086)
Ansfield, Rebecca A 3:30:04 (4,838)
Antanelis, Sue-Ellen 4:01:57 (12,249)
Antomarchi, Fabienne 4:20:45 (16,795)
Applebee, Christina H 4:58:04 (25,520)
Applebee, Margot 3:58:43 (11,405)
Appleby, Lesley 5:40:45 (30,408)
Aragao, Sandra 3:55:45 (10,460)
Arav, Deborah L 5:34:26 (29,928)
Arbery, Bethany C 4:02:35 (12,395)
Arch, Helen R 5:24:55 (29,031)
Arch, Jodie E 5:24:55 (29,031)
Archbold, Catherine C 5:30:39 (29,611)
Archer, Caroline M 4:42:30 (22,217)
Archer, Emma J 2:54:34 (766)
Archer, Katherine E 5:06:44 (26,824)
Archer, Nicole 2:53:52 (718)
Archer, Rachel M 5:47:17 (30,892)
Archer, Sarah L 4:46:58 (23,200)
Archer, Skye J 4:02:29 (12,371)
Archer, Susan K 5:05:00 (26,581)
Archibald, Fiona E 5:02:51 (26,295)
Argent, Patricia A 4:26:05 (18,281)
Aries, Felicity J 5:49:16 (31,023)
Aris, Gillian M 4:52:06 (24,268)
Arkle, Rachel M 4:18:03 (16,119)
Armitage, Caroline L 5:45:43 (30,761)
Armitage, Geraldine 5:13:12 (27,676)
Armstrong, Dawn M 5:05:18 (26,624)
Armstrong, Donna L 3:40:54 (6,783)
Armstrong, Jessica 4:46:05 (23,022)
Armstrong, Julie B 5:31:33 (29,707)
Armstrong, Rachel D 3:46:25 (7,993)
Armstrong, Sarah 3:36:48 (5,993)
Arnfield, Alison M 4:12:55 (14,816)
Arnold, Hannah R 3:36:45 (5,982)
Arnold, Lousie E 4:55:14 (24,945)
Arnold, Marie E 4:55:43 (25,040)
Arnold, Trisha S 4:43:12 (22,367)
Arnold-Masters, Katrina L 5:46:04 (30,792)
Arola, Satu 3:59:19 (11,611)
Arora, Shelley 4:38:01 (21,227)
Arpino, Tanya F 6:42:31 (32,646)
Arrowood, Catherine A 3:43:39 (7,380)
Arrowsmith, Katherine A 4:13:39 (14,994)
Arundale, Lisa J 3:27:03 (4,253)
Aryeetey, Camille 4:07:38 (13,516)
Asakawa, Miyuki 4:39:02 (21,447)
Ascott, Claire 5:40:48 (30,414)
Ash, Hayley E 5:01:45 (26,138)
Ash, Lydia R 5:47:16 (30,886)
Ash, Rebecca 3:51:25 (9,203)
Ashby, Karen L 3:47:40 (8,285)
Ashby, Susan J 5:44:00 (30,640)
Ashcroft, Cynthia 4:15:38 (15,503)
Ashcroft, Laura 4:44:54 (22,756)
Ashdown, Diane M 5:49:33 (31,047)
Ashdown, Jane M 5:13:27 (27,712)
Ashdown, Rebecca L 3:53:36 (9,793)
Ashdown, Sophie R 5:13:28 (27,717)
Ashe, Deborah 3:55:39 (10,416)
Ashe, Rachel J 4:19:24 (16,448)

Ashenden, Tracey 5:06:40 (26,811)
Ashley, Debbi J 6:48:55 (32,744)
Ashley, Jean B 4:34:01 (20,249)
Ashley, Lisa J 3:58:47 (11,440)
Ashley, Sarah L 6:08:29 (31,875)
Ashpole, Linda 4:59:09 (25,730)
Ashton, Adele P 6:23:30 (32,317)
Ashton, Anne E 4:04:24 (12,796)
Ashton, Jane F 4:25:04 (17,982)
Ashton, Jennifer 4:57:56 (25,484)
Ashton, Julie 4:26:24 (18,361)
Ashton, Shirley L 3:42:06 (7,045)
Ashton, Tracey 4:21:32 (16,981)
Ashurst, Catherine M 4:10:26 (14,200)
Ashwell, Gemma K 3:56:32 (10,694)
Askam, Virginia L 4:16:00 (15,599)
Askew, Sharon G 3:39:15 (6,489)
Aspden, Samantha J 7:09:36 (32,973)
Aspland, Helen C 5:13:27 (27,712)
Aston, Christine M 4:43:17 (22,387)
Aston, Felicity D 5:34:02 (29,893)
Atchison, Edda I 4:20:12 (16,662)
Atkin, Louanne 5:35:13 (29,988)
Atkins, Carolyn E 3:56:52 (10,809)
Atkins, Mandy J 5:37:52 (30,195)
Atkins, Michelle L 4:59:30 (25,786)
Atkins, Nichola A 3:42:12 (7,065)
Atkins, Sharon E 4:14:52 (15,303)
Atkins, Sheryl 5:40:19 (30,386)
Atkins, Wendy J 4:35:56 (20,698)
Atkinson, Alison J 3:55:15 (10,298)
Atkinson, Cathy 3:38:32 (6,334)
Atkinson, Elaine 5:13:40 (27,733)
Atkinson, Jan 5:20:01 (28,495)
Atkinson, Nina V 3:53:45 (9,844)
Atkinson, Rebecca 4:03:23 (12,574)
Atkinson, Sue E 6:17:09 (32,146)
Atladottir, Hildur 4:39:07 (21,469)
Atrride, Hannah M 4:04:32 (12,824)
Attrill, Patricia A 5:00:13 (25,929)
Attwell, Christine E 4:01:16 (12,109)
Attwood, Catherine M 5:31:59 (29,736)
Attwood, Helen M 4:40:14 (21,720)
Audis, Patricia M 5:20:02 (28,497)
Auguste, Jacqueline 5:01:53 (26,158)
Augustus, Diane R 4:11:37 (14,484)
Aussenberg, Glenda J 7:36:37 (33,120)
Austin, Allison 4:37:00 (20,979)
Austin, Carol L 3:39:06 (6,454)
Austin, Jude A 3:25:19 (3,978)
Austin, Katie L 7:37:38 (33,134)
Austin, Rebecca 4:32:01 (19,797)
Austin, Rebecca L 5:07:32 (26,934)
Austin-Brydon, Tracy E 6:13:41 (32,039)
Authers, Sandra D 4:00:54 (12,017)
Auton, Rachael C 3:51:49 (9,307)
Avery, Amanda J 3:18:29 (3,063)
Avery, June 3:42:40 (7,150)
Avery, Natalie 5:14:32 (27,849)
Aves, Susan M 4:11:59 (14,569)
Aveyard, Katherine 5:42:07 (30,509)
Aviet, Anne-Marie 4:31:17 (19,606)
Avramovich, Patricia 4:09:54 (14,084)
Axelsson, Brittzi 5:53:05 (31,218)
Axelsson, Susanne 4:35:48 (20,673)
Axford, Minna V 4:14:04 (15,092)
Ayas, Nour 6:03:42 (31,712)
Ayas, Rima 6:20:04 (32,234)
Aydelott, Dee Ann 5:34:10 (29,898)
Ayers, Emily 4:52:30 (24,355)
Ayers, Jane E 7:20:18 (33,043)
Ayers, Samantha J 3:23:41 (3,739)
Ayling, Tia Ia J 5:27:49 (29,308)
Aylmer, Sarah J 3:51:51 (9,318)
Ayre, Ally J 3:51:14 (9,156)
Ayres, Mandy 4:39:00 (21,441)
Ayriss, Fay 5:32:43 (29,788)
Ayscough, Ursula J 3:22:52 (3,642)
Babb, Kathryn G 4:39:36 (21,577)
Babb, Kim M 4:55:19 (24,963)
Bach, Rowena Y 5:49:53 (31,066)
Bache, Suzanne 4:56:50 (25,264)
Bach-Petersen, Kirsten 5:08:10 (27,028)
Backshell, Kerry M 3:28:16 (4,456)
Bacon, Deborah M 4:42:01 (22,116)
Bacon, Gemma E 5:13:20 (27,695)
Badel, Maria 3:55:23 (10,339)
Badger, Joanne V 4:27:06 (18,527)
Badman, Dawn 4:12:01 (14,577)
Badock, Lesley J 4:50:50 (24,010)
Badowska, Constance D 6:32:34 (32,493)
Baechler Preu, Beate B 4:39:49 (21,632)
Baggaley, Elizabeth J 4:30:25 (19,407)
Baggs, Julia C 4:32:56 (19,987)
Bagnall, Pauline 5:55:57 (31,351)
Bailes, Joanne D 5:51:44 (31,168)
Bailey, Cassell M 4:13:56 (15,049)
Bailey, Christine 7:35:16 (33,118)
Bailey, Fiona K 3:04:57 (1,572)
Bailey, Jenny M 5:38:53 (30,272)
Bailey, Karen A 6:54:55 (32,826)
Bailey, Kay M 4:15:26 (15,460)
Bailey, Laura N 4:57:36 (25,417)
Bailey, Liz F 5:03:26 (26,382)
Bailey, Marie-Clare 4:46:08 (23,033)
Bailey, Roni 5:15:35 (27,960)
Bailey, Rowan I 8:00:26 (33,176)
Bailey, Sarah L 3:12:17 (2,320)
Bailey, Sharon M 4:45:08 (22,818)
Bailey, Sheila M 3:37:41 (6,163)
Bailey, Tina L 3:18:59 (3,131)
Bailey, Tracey L 3:53:49 (9,870)
Bailey, Victoria L 4:24:12 (17,714)
Baillie, Ann C 5:23:21 (28,878)
Bain, Karen A 3:45:09 (7,721)
Bain, Natasha J 4:05:47 (13,096)
Baines, Charlotte 3:21:20 (3,445)
Baines, Valerie G 6:25:10 (32,357)
Bains, Surjit 4:54:10 (24,720)
Bainton, Alice E 5:42:22 (30,522)
Baird, Angela A 5:08:19 (27,052)
Baird, Julie M 4:18:37 (16,259)
Baird, Katherine S 4:30:47 (19,491)
Baird, Sarah 3:50:24 (8,955)
Bajohra, Kristina 5:13:35 (27,728)
Baker, Alexis Z 4:51:51 (24,222)
Baker, Angelina A 4:50:13 (23,885)
Baker, Anna R 5:10:58 (27,380)
Baker, Bridget D 3:18:37 (3,084)
Baker, Cassandra J 6:30:59 (32,475)
Baker, Ceri L 4:43:49 (22,523)
Baker, Clare 5:11:50 (27,501)
Baker, Deana E 3:56:46 (10,769)
Baker, Denise 4:21:27 (16,968)
Baker, Dianne M 4:27:52 (18,714)
Baker, Jan 4:06:37 (13,254)
Baker, Julia K 5:40:40 (30,404)
Baker, Julie P 6:38:34 (32,590)
Baker, Louise C 4:57:43 (25,436)
Baker, Lucy E 3:59:52 (11,780)
Baker, Sally J 3:57:36 (11,045)
Baker, Samantha 4:04:28 (12,810)
Baker, Sarah V 4:27:09 (18,542)
Baker, Sheryl V 4:09:10 (13,895)
Baker, Sue C 5:01:01 (26,045)
Baker, Teresa A 5:48:49 (30,991)
Bakker, Claire F 4:27:30 (18,621)
Bakoulis, Gordon 3:01:27 (1,336)
Balani, Jay 5:03:36 (26,406)
Balazs, Jane T 5:42:27 (30,529)
Balch, Wendy 5:02:20 (26,230)
Balchin, Kate 3:17:56 (2,988)
Balcombe, Rebecca K 5:43:10 (30,586)
Balduck, Nadine D 3:19:08 (3,149)
Baldvinsdottir, Eyrun 4:20:27 (16,723)
Baldwin, Jan 5:08:22 (27,061)
Baldwin, Joanna F 5:03:20 (26,362)
Bales, Rowena J 3:17:33 (2,947)
Ball, Becky J 5:07:48 (26,973)
Ball, Corinna 5:59:56 (31,556)
Ball, Gillian L 5:49:23 (31,035)
Ball, Joanna E 3:13:59 (2,528)
Ball, Kay 4:00:23 (11,910)
Ball, Laura 4:42:43 (22,264)
Ball, Linda J 6:36:50 (32,559)
Ball, Lorraine M 5:28:43 (29,402)
Ball, Stephanie 3:48:53 (8,603)
Ball, Tina 5:00:31 (25,970)
Ballard, Jane S 5:19:31 (28,438)
Ballard, Kate L 4:05:52 (13,111)
Ballard, Storm 4:39:52 (21,645)
Ballarini, Tracy L 6:23:09 (32,306)
Ballinger, Anne B 4:19:45 (16,539)
Ballisat, Emily M 4:52:53 (24,433)
Balmer, Sarah L 5:16:03 (28,005)
Balmforth, Claire 5:35:27 (30,008)
Bamber, Sara 3:44:17 (7,519)
Bamford, Janet M 5:23:39 (28,900)
Bamforth, Tracy J 3:56:55 (10,817)
Banerjee, Tamara P 4:59:52 (25,862)
Banerjee, Tyara P 5:14:27 (27,835)
Banfield, Hazel J 3:47:11 (8,163)
Bangham, Kirsty 4:26:28 (18,376)
Banks, Charlie 6:19:10 (32,207)
Banks, Chris M 4:49:20 (23,722)
Banks, Claire J 4:03:20 (12,559)
Banks, Donna M 5:09:02 (27,152)
Banks, Faye M 2:57:38 (996)
Banks, Jane W 3:57:27 (10,996)
Banks, Joanna 5:32:07 (29,748)
Banks, Lucy 5:49:21 (31,032)
Banks, Victoria C 5:11:50 (27,501)
Bannister, Pamela J 5:33:39 (29,866)
Bannister, Victoria C 6:15:50 (32,110)
Banville, Elaine M 3:49:22 (8,707)
Banwait, Harjinder 6:33:26 (32,504)
Baran, Liz J 4:07:52 (13,574)
Barber, Elizabeth M 3:48:30 (8,501)
Barber, Jeanette E 4:04:27 (12,804)
Barber, Jenny L 4:12:13 (14,629)
Barber, Lyn K 5:14:10 (27,794)
Barber, Ruth 3:51:50 (9,313)
Barber, Ruth M 6:14:37 (32,074)
Barber, Sue 4:15:57 (15,587)
Barber, Tonya Q 4:07:56 (13,593)
Barbone, Catriona E 4:29:26 (19,153)
Barcella, Roberta 4:17:22 (15,947)
Barcella, Sara 4:13:00 (14,842)
Barclay, Jessica E 5:11:44 (27,482)
Barden, Sandra L 5:25:04 (29,046)
Bardsley, Lisa C 6:09:37 (31,916)
Bardswell, Isabella L 4:54:06 (24,695)
Bareham, Jennifer S 5:02:15 (26,210)
Barfield, Abigail C 3:58:39 (11,382)
Bargary, Teresa P 5:11:27 (27,449)
Bargetto, Vanya 5:41:22 (30,447)
Barke, Jill 6:01:15 (31,616)
Barker, Anne S 5:54:04 (31,264)
Barker, Joan C 4:59:07 (25,726)
Barker, Joanne M 4:49:02 (23,658)
Barker, Katie A 4:20:25 (16,713)
Barker, Nicola J 5:13:04 (27,664)
Barker, Nicole D 4:23:04 (17,378)
Barker, Rosamund A 3:11:25 (2,206)
Barker, Sian M 4:54:59 (24,891)
Barkman, Sally L 4:59:19 (25,746)
Barley, Julie A 3:14:15 (2,559)
Barlow, Jo 5:10:11 (27,284)
Barlow, Sally 3:44:39 (7,603)
Barltrop, Julia F 3:05:03 (1,579)
Barnard, Heidi A 4:27:04 (18,517)
Barnard, Monica J 5:39:53 (30,350)
Barnard, Nicola 4:25:04 (17,982)
Barnard Hankey, Alexandra M 3:46:06 (7,926)
Barnes, Amy J 5:44:47 (30,700)
Barnes, Christine M 3:53:01 (9,630)
Barnes, Elaine A 6:17:40 (32,162)
Barnes, Lesley A 4:35:43 (20,655)
Barnes, Lorna J 5:59:12 (31,520)
Barnes, Lynne C 5:31:57 (29,734)
Barnes, Osphia M 4:59:33 (25,799)
Barnes, Sue C 6:19:49 (32,224)
Barnes, Victoria L 5:43:58 (30,634)
Barnett, Jenny 5:15:51 (27,982)
Barnett, Kate E 5:09:27 (27,199)
Barnett, Lisa 4:24:03 (17,672)
Barnett, Marion H 7:37:30 (33,130)
Barnett, Sarah L 5:55:47 (31,347)
Baron, Sarah J 4:43:42 (22,495)

Baron, Tabitha C....5:47:20 (30,901)
Barraclough, Helen L....3:50:22 (8,945)
Barrass, Sandra....5:04:55 (26,571)
Barratt, Catherine....5:14:06 (27,785)
Barratt-Smith, Angela....3:38:45 (6,376)
Barrett, Amy....4:54:05 (24,689)
Barrett, Anne S....5:25:41 (29,099)
Barrett, Caroline....4:26:52 (18,479)
Barrett, Gillian M....3:56:24 (10,656)
Barrett, Heather....4:38:16 (21,295)
Barrett, Jan....4:38:06 (21,261)
Barrett, Jeannette C....6:27:01 (32,404)
Barrett, Louise C....4:32:46 (19,952)
Barrett, Nicola J....6:08:03 (31,860)
Barrett, Rebecca V....4:23:44 (17,571)
Barrett, Ruth....5:17:30 (28,195)
Barrett, Sam....4:30:10 (19,340)
Barrett, Shelley....4:10:58 (14,322)
Barribal, Judith E....5:35:45 (30,035)
Barrier, Bridget A....4:43:07 (22,355)
Barrington, Heather....4:48:25 (23,517)
Barron, Alison L....5:44:48 (30,702)
Barron, Emma....5:44:32 (30,682)
Barron, Julie....6:12:50 (32,016)
Barron, Julie A....6:00:49 (31,595)
Barrow, Cara L....4:23:15 (17,433)
Barrow, Kathryn R....4:55:33 (25,007)
Barrow, Michelle....5:22:08 (28,730)
Barrow-Green, June E....3:29:53 (4,802)
Barrows, Eleanor....6:35:30 (32,535)
Barter, Lucy A....5:11:30 (27,459)
Barter, Naomi J....5:26:31 (29,175)
Bartimote, Joan A....4:49:17 (23,714)
Bartlam, Sian E....5:51:18 (31,144)
Bartlett, Denise A....5:59:04 (31,505)
Bartlett, Julia E....4:43:31 (22,443)
Barton, Georgia C....5:50:34 (31,114)
Barton, Kate R....6:38:11 (32,582)
Barton, Lin A....4:09:00 (13,859)
Barton, Nina E....4:14:26 (15,190)
Barton, Sophie....5:38:29 (30,251)
Barton Atkinson, Kate....5:53:04 (31,217)
Bartram, Anna M....5:36:31 (30,098)
Bartrip, Laura J....5:33:56 (29,885)
Bartrum, Susan....5:09:59 (27,263)
Barwell, Harriet M....5:02:10 (26,198)
Barzellotti, Camilla....4:17:37 (16,022)
Basford, Lisa....4:30:14 (19,364)
Basham, Caroline C....4:00:57 (12,030)
Baskerville, Kathryn....5:38:35 (30,259)
Bassi, Tanya....4:07:52 (13,574)
Bassil, Anna K....3:38:52 (6,402)
Bassinder, Clare....4:31:18 (19,613)
Bastian, Melissa J....4:51:37 (24,171)
Bastyan, Catherine....4:48:14 (23,477)
Bateman, Avrel....4:17:44 (16,038)
Bateman, Hannah M....3:22:06 (3,544)
Bateman, Penelope L....5:54:09 (31,270)
Bates, Claire L....3:30:32 (4,902)
Bates, Sarah L....4:37:52 (21,189)
Bates, Wendy J....4:26:37 (18,413)
Bath, Doreen A....4:16:46 (15,793)
Bathard, Wendy M....4:36:41 (20,885)
Batheja, Maya....3:48:22 (8,466)
Batram, Nicola....3:59:11 (11,570)
Batt, Louise E....5:43:09 (30,584)
Batts, Caroline S....6:02:10 (31,650)
Battson, Elaine C....4:12:44 (14,756)
Batty, Jane C....5:35:07 (29,978)
Baty, Catherine A....4:57:32 (25,403)
Baty, Louise E....4:54:05 (24,689)
Bauer, Wendy M....5:27:15 (29,248)
Bauldry, Georgina L....4:50:37 (23,966)
Baumanis, Michelle L....4:10:24 (14,194)
Baumgartner, Stephanie....4:28:29 (18,894)
Baverstock, Julia L....3:43:21 (7,320)
Bawden, Sarah-Leigh E....4:06:24 (13,212)
Baxandall, Helen M....5:22:38 (28,791)
Baxendale, Amanda L....4:01:12 (12,102)
Baxter, Carys....5:56:29 (31,380)
Baxter, Kate....4:46:09 (23,038)
Baxter, Wendy S....4:36:12 (20,779)
Bayford, Georgie L....6:44:20 (32,680)
Bayley, Lisa N....3:39:41 (6,570)
Bayne, Carolyn J....6:21:03 (32,254)
Baynton-Glen, Claire V....6:11:52 (31,983)
Baynton-Glen, Sarah L....6:11:39 (31,976)
Bazeley, Judith M....4:48:15 (23,483)
Bazley, Ali J....4:34:42 (20,411)
Beacham, Marion S....6:21:03 (32,254)
Beadle, Suzanne....4:45:20 (22,870)
Beagrie, Lynn....5:18:46 (28,343)
Beale, Kathryn J....6:07:30 (31,838)
Beale, Nicola J....4:52:44 (24,405)
Beall, Liza....4:52:34 (24,371)
Bean, Ruth....4:08:25 (13,722)
Beard, Candice L....7:20:32 (33,045)
Beard, Josephine A....6:18:23 (32,180)
Beard, Kelly A....4:42:50 (22,291)
Beardall, Victoria C....4:20:34 (16,750)
Beare, Paula L....6:33:03 (32,498)
Beasley, Claire....5:49:52 (31,062)
Beastall, Sally J....4:52:29 (24,349)
Beaton, Ann F....6:33:46 (32,512)
Beaton, Pauline....5:00:34 (25,979)
Beattie, Heather....4:19:56 (16,584)
Beattie, Monique....3:57:04 (10,865)
Beauchamp, Clare F....4:37:31 (21,113)
Beauchamp, Tina-Camilla....5:46:59 (30,859)
Beaumont, Diane....6:13:13 (32,028)
Beaumont, Laura C....4:04:03 (12,726)
Beavan, Faye....5:41:28 (30,454)
Beavis, Marianne J....5:01:25 (26,099)
Beazer, Elizabeth J....4:01:47 (12,209)
Bebbington, Keren....5:09:28 (27,201)
Beck, Alison....4:56:54 (25,281)
Beck, Claire E....5:17:28 (28,192)
Becker, Diana....6:02:57 (31,679)
Becker, Gabriele....4:30:12 (19,350)
Beckett, Kim....4:33:22 (20,103)
Beckett, Sarah L....5:03:34 (26,399)
Beckham, Catherine J....4:55:58 (25,097)
Beckingsale, Louise M....3:13:31 (2,467)
Beckman, Jennifer....5:20:12 (28,519)
Beddard, Emily J....4:31:18 (19,613)
Beddows, Karen....4:16:33 (15,737)
Bedeau, Rebecca J....3:58:41 (11,396)
Bedford, Judith A....4:14:12 (15,142)
Bedwell, Maggie J....4:11:39 (14,491)
Bee, Paul....4:39:42 (21,599)
Bee, Peta....4:15:26 (15,460)
Beech, Jane L....3:45:01 (7,693)
Beech, Janet M....5:55:07 (31,309)
Beecham, Helen C....4:12:40 (14,742)
Beecham, Rachel M....3:38:47 (6,382)
Beecroft, Jennifer A....4:39:04 (21,458)
Beedham, Ruth H....4:27:10 (18,548)
Beedles, Jillian....5:12:39 (27,606)
Beer, Beverley....6:12:49 (32,014)
Beer, Louise M....4:36:07 (20,759)
Beese, Anna E....6:06:26 (31,801)
Beesley, Marlene....5:02:02 (26,182)
Beeson, Michelle A....4:47:29 (23,317)
Beeson, Semirah....3:20:10 (3,291)
Beffa, Heidi....3:03:21 (1,469)
Begbie, Hannah M....4:32:36 (19,916)
Begg, Liz A....4:15:25 (15,454)
Begum, Shajue....4:13:47 (15,018)
Beilby, Sharon D....6:20:58 (32,252)
Belcham, Kay E....5:08:22 (27,061)
Belcher, Joanne....3:21:31 (3,472)
Belfi, Elizabeth G....4:45:04 (22,807)
Bell, Corrie A....5:13:29 (27,718)
Bell, Fiona A....5:03:30 (26,389)
Bell, Jayne A....4:32:54 (19,979)
Bell, Joanna....5:44:57 (30,712)
Bell, Julie D....5:01:02 (26,048)
Bell, Kathleen P....6:39:35 (32,605)
Bell, Kerrie M....5:32:39 (29,781)
Bell, Laura F....4:46:52 (23,189)
Bell, Lesli....3:24:45 (3,905)
Bell, Nia J....4:57:19 (25,369)
Bell, Rachel A....4:06:29 (13,228)
Bell, Rebecca E....4:19:23 (16,442)
Bell, Shirley H....4:41:18 (21,952)
Bell, Sophie L....4:20:18 (16,684)
Bell, Tina....6:23:32 (32,318)
Bell, Zoe....3:30:40 (4,926)
Bellamy, Karen....5:06:34 (26,799)
Bellarby, Helen C....6:19:18 (32,212)
Bellerby, Alexandra J....4:21:52 (17,081)
Bellerby-Brown, Helen R....3:12:20 (2,328)
Bello, Rashidat K....4:37:49 (21,181)
Belton, Moerida....5:25:28 (29,081)
Belyavin, Julia R....3:22:31 (3,598)
Benad-Smith, Sharon P....4:23:29 (17,496)
Bendall, Nicola....4:00:42 (11,976)
Bendall, Sarah....6:24:24 (32,338)
Bender, Jennifer S....4:12:40 (14,742)
Benet, Carol D....4:40:06 (21,691)
Benfield, Sarah J....6:05:29 (31,776)
Benham, Sally M....5:19:51 (28,475)
Benham-Clarke, Anne....4:59:06 (25,723)
Benjamin, Floella....4:46:10 (23,043)
Benktander, Caroline....5:03:35 (26,400)
Bennett, Andrea M....4:22:18 (17,199)
Bennett, Anne Marie....5:09:33 (27,214)
Bennett, Celina K....4:19:29 (16,474)
Bennett, Elizabeth C....3:26:59 (4,241)
Bennett, Fiona J....6:06:33 (31,804)
Bennett, Georgina E....3:43:24 (7,333)
Bennett, Gillian C....4:59:26 (25,767)
Bennett, Jennifer....5:21:58 (28,715)
Bennett, Kathleen E....5:41:24 (30,450)
Bennett, Kelly N....5:07:04 (26,869)
Bennett, Lisa J....3:33:00 (5,322)
Bennett, Maxine M....7:22:34 (33,053)
Bennett, Natalie D....6:21:26 (32,270)
Bennett, Patricia A....4:40:58 (21,884)
Bennett, Rebecca J....6:56:22 (32,846)
Bennett, Sarah....3:43:11 (7,285)
Bennett, Susan E....5:59:31 (31,535)
Bennett, Yolanda....5:47:26 (30,913)
Bennett, Yvonne....4:00:32 (11,943)
Bensen, Geri D....4:08:44 (13,792)
Benson, Elizabeth J....4:32:19 (19,866)
Benson, Gaynor A....3:49:25 (8,725)
Benson, Lucy V....4:27:36 (18,655)
Benson, Wendy L....5:01:37 (26,121)
Bensusan, Iona....6:27:15 (32,408)
Bent, Alison E....3:33:17 (5,365)
Bent, Jaclyn....3:58:26 (11,319)
Bentham, Karen....4:06:47 (13,298)
Benton, Julie A....4:57:21 (25,375)
Benzinra, Ruth E....5:44:38 (30,694)
Beresford, Lesley C....3:23:19 (3,686)
Beresford, Nicola M....3:42:46 (7,178)
Bergin, Sara A....5:44:43 (30,698)
Berke, Shree....5:00:34 (25,979)
Berkovitch, Michelle A....4:17:11 (15,905)
Berlevy, Samantha....6:09:54 (31,922)
Bernardini, Cecilia....4:34:01 (20,249)
Berney, Rachel....3:45:34 (7,814)
Berry, Carol A....4:55:44 (25,043)
Berry, Cheryle J....6:16:03 (32,119)
Berry, Heidi J....6:56:33 (32,849)
Berry, Jaqueline E....5:03:51 (26,439)
Berry, Michiko C....3:55:17 (10,311)
Berry, Moya....5:58:02 (31,458)
Berry, Sarah A....4:30:12 (19,350)
Berryman, Catherine....3:52:22 (9,458)
Berryman, Rebecca E....4:21:46 (17,052)
Bertaiola, Patrizia....4:22:35 (17,260)
Berthould, Tamara K....4:34:41 (20,406)
Bertin, Gabrielle L....5:18:22 (28,290)
Bertram, Jo....4:26:10 (18,302)
Bertram, Wendy D....4:39:59 (21,670)
Besley, Siobham....5:18:22 (28,290)
Besson, Lesley F....4:24:52 (17,906)
Best, Rachel M....3:21:02 (3,403)
Best, Suzanne E....4:52:01 (24,254)
Best, Zoe A....4:48:09 (23,459)
Bester, Elisca M....5:01:52 (26,154)
Beswick, Kate....4:37:25 (21,090)
Bethune, Deirdre....4:10:09 (14,135)
Bettridge, Allyson L....4:50:16 (23,898)
Betts, Fiona H....3:25:10 (3,955)
Betts, Sally-Ann L....4:33:28 (20,126)
Betts, Victoria....3:35:00 (5,661)

Bevan, Caryl M 5:05:26 (26,639)
Bevan, Julie 5:18:53 (28,354)
Beverley, Felicity J 5:53:54 (31,259)
Beverly, Alice 3:28:06 (4,425)
Bewson, Anna 4:16:39 (15,769)
Bexson, Emma J 4:02:44 (12,420)
Bhagrath, Serena J 4:49:42 (23,791)
Bhana, Sara 4:37:10 (21,017)
Bhandari, Seema 4:57:26 (25,386)
Bhudia, Jessica 6:25:09 (32,355)
Biagioni, Liz P 5:26:00 (29,130)
Biancalana, Sharon A 4:40:33 (21,802)
Biba, Angie 6:24:15 (32,336)
Bibby, Elizabeth A 7:49:46 (33,170)
Bickerdike, Suzanne A 3:53:17 (9,718)
Bickerstaffe, Kate 4:06:30 (13,233)
Bicknell, Elizabeth 3:29:01 (4,624)
Biddell, Jane 6:08:12 (31,865)
Bidgood, Susan E 3:38:46 (6,380)
Bidnell, Alison J 4:57:00 (25,314)
Bidston, Joanna H 3:46:36 (8,034)
Biedley, Helen J 5:27:40 (29,289)
Bieniek, Sherrie 4:03:38 (12,637)
Bierton, Vanessa C 4:34:20 (20,321)
Bilcock, Heather M 4:28:19 (18,847)
Billson, Jackie L 5:51:31 (31,156)
Bilton, Jacqueline A 4:23:36 (17,530)
Binfield, Susan C 4:34:24 (20,341)
Bingham, Jan 4:10:53 (14,301)
Bingham, Lisa V 7:25:01 (33,069)
Bingham, Sandy J 6:02:55 (31,677)
Binks, Susan E 3:45:21 (7,771)
Binks, Yvonne A 4:26:58 (18,497)
Binnell, Bridgid M 4:00:38 (11,958)
Binns, Janet 3:18:26 (3,053)
Binns, Laura 4:13:58 (15,054)
Binstead, Julia G 3:52:58 (9,617)
Birch, Annie M 4:10:45 (14,259)
Birch, Bridget 3:55:17 (10,311)
Birch, Hayley J 6:14:42 (32,078)
Birch, Jan 4:47:08 (23,240)
Birch, Lisa 5:23:42 (28,909)
Birch, Natasha L 4:35:17 (20,548)
Birch, Penny C 5:04:55 (26,571)
Bird, Alice E 4:50:26 (23,932)
Bird, Jacqui M 4:25:45 (18,176)
Bird, Norma 3:58:24 (11,306)
Bird, Rona 5:11:44 (27,482)
Birgisdottir, Lilja 3:55:01 (10,209)
Birks, Hilary E 4:15:35 (15,491)
Birley, Susanne J 4:46:58 (23,200)
Bishop, Cathryn J 4:21:57 (17,102)
Bishop, Claire 5:49:20 (31,031)
Bishop, Elizabeth A 5:38:09 (30,214)
Bishop, Fiona J 3:36:39 (5,967)
Bishop, Gemma M 5:10:37 (27,345)
Bishop, Hayley S 4:12:50 (14,786)
Bishop, Maria 5:09:38 (27,222)
Bishop, Sophie A 3:56:48 (10,785)
Bissell, Janice 7:19:00 (33,036)
Biswell, Rebecca L 4:02:23 (12,347)
Bjorkevoll, Kjersti Eitrheim 3:56:55 (10,817)
Bjornstrom, Gullan 4:04:56 (12,903)
Blaber, Amanda Y 5:25:53 (29,121)
Blaber, Elizabeth L 4:46:10 (23,043)
Black, Bryony R 4:12:46 (14,765)
Black, Debbie J 5:04:41 (26,541)
Black, Jeanette M 4:13:57 (15,051)
Black, Linda M 4:29:55 (19,273)
Black, Rachel P 6:20:46 (32,246)
Black, Susannah A 4:06:08 (13,167)
Black, Zoe M 6:44:59 (32,690)
Blackburn, Amanda C 5:02:01 (26,181)
Blackburn, Helen E 3:58:54 (11,476)
Blackburn, Madeleine C 4:45:10 (22,825)
Blackburn, Tracey J 6:10:24 (31,939)
Blacker, Claire L 4:32:00 (19,791)
Blackford, Hilary A 5:45:20 (30,741)
Blacklock, Julie 6:19:35 (32,220)
Blackmore, Dianne H 4:37:54 (21,196)
Blackmore, Emma J 5:12:40 (27,611)
Blackmore, Ruth C 4:44:46 (22,724)
Blagbrough, Eleanor 4:12:54 (14,815)
Blain, Lindsey A 4:11:46 (14,513)
Blair, Liz 3:49:01 (8,630)
Blake, Claire 3:43:45 (7,408)
Blake, Joanna 5:18:08 (28,260)
Blake, Judy M 5:08:11 (27,032)
Blake, Sarah L 3:18:37 (3,084)
Blake, Stephanie A 3:50:44 (9,037)
Blakeman, Lesley A 4:33:37 (20,170)
Blakemore, Lucy C 5:16:09 (28,021)
Blanchard, Danielle M 4:24:46 (17,884)
Bland, Anne L 5:39:21 (30,307)
Bland, Debbie L 3:59:19 (11,611)
Blanvillain, Claudia 4:58:06 (25,529)
Blaukopf, Clare L 4:39:05 (21,463)
Bleach, Jeanette A 5:57:17 (31,419)
Bleksley, Katie R 3:52:17 (9,435)
Blencowe, Carla M 4:47:21 (23,283)
Blencowe, Jenna L 4:47:21 (23,283)
Blenkinsop, Catherine 5:36:32 (30,102)
Blenkinsop, Mandy S 3:43:46 (7,411)
Blenkinsop, Samantha 4:18:40 (16,270)
Blessett, Marianne N 5:16:51 (28,110)
Blewden, Tina S 4:43:41 (22,490)
Blewitt, Rachel M 5:47:21 (30,904)
Bligh, Ellen L 4:05:30 (13,022)
Blissett, Annie C 4:36:23 (20,820)
Blissett, Nastasya 5:45:02 (30,720)
Blofield, Carol F 3:55:58 (10,531)
Blomqvist, Katarina 3:50:45 (9,045)
Blood, Alison J 4:31:50 (19,755)
Bloomer, Joanne E 5:34:35 (29,940)
Bloomer, Sharon K 5:44:09 (30,655)
Bloomfield, Christine A 4:33:02 (20,013)
Bloomfield, Emma C 3:45:14 (7,737)
Blott, Natasha L 4:48:30 (23,540)
Blower, Susan 4:56:57 (25,295)
Bloxham, Laura M 5:20:47 (28,591)
Blum, Christine 4:13:37 (14,979)
Blundell, Jane 4:52:21 (24,320)
Blunt, Michelle S 4:56:30 (25,204)
Blyth, Pamela 4:19:57 (16,589)
Blythe, Amy J 3:45:33 (7,812)
Boal, Lynn 4:19:52 (16,571)
Boal, Wendy A 3:48:17 (8,447)
Bocock, Jennifer R 4:42:11 (22,153)
Boden, Patricia A 3:51:16 (9,165)
Boggis, Emma L 3:40:55 (6,786)
Bogie, Alison 3:09:30 (2,011)
Bogomolova, Galina 2:21:58 (37)
Bolcina, Valeria S 5:31:17 (29,690)
Bolden, Michelle L 4:23:38 (17,542)
Bolla, Jaskamal K 3:53:40 (9,810)
Bolton, Carol L 4:35:36 (20,624)
Bolton, Helen J 4:16:43 (15,783)
Bolton, Joanna 5:01:28 (26,104)
Bolton, Marie-Claire 5:28:57 (29,423)
Bolton, Rowena A 4:54:11 (24,724)
Bolton, Victoria J 4:21:51 (17,076)
Boltong, Anna G 4:13:58 (15,054)
Bolwell, Vicky C 3:58:40 (11,388)
Bombroffe, Gwen J 4:03:01 (12,481)
Bomphray, Sandi 3:58:10 (11,218)
Bond, Amanda C 5:20:34 (28,573)
Bond, Caroline J 4:56:21 (25,175)
Bond, Catheirne L 4:14:07 (15,108)
Bond, Gemma J 6:30:20 (32,458)
Bond, Katherine A 4:03:37 (12,629)
Bond, Lynn O 4:45:54 (22,989)
Bond, Nicola 5:14:12 (27,799)
Bonete, Lucy-Anne 5:05:40 (26,663)
Bonner, Joanna 3:23:12 (3,675)
Bonnick, Clare J 3:33:36 (5,421)
Bonnick, Nicola B 6:03:48 (31,718)
Bont Schilder, Catharina E 3:32:48 (5,291)
Boomer, Nicola J 4:16:27 (15,711)
Boon, Georgina R 6:20:03 (32,233)
Boon, Patricia 4:35:08 (20,516)
Boora, Harvi 5:02:50 (26,293)
Boote, Philippa H 3:49:56 (8,853)
Booth, Charlotte J 4:32:59 (20,000)
Booth, Elizabeth J 4:07:55 (13,587)
Booth, Jamie 5:18:15 (28,278)
Booth, Melanie J 3:56:49 (10,790)
Booth, Shirley 3:40:27 (6,703)
Booth, Tineke 5:28:08 (29,342)
Booth, Victoria 3:35:03 (5,679)
Bore, Caroline 5:42:46 (30,558)
Borg, Amanda T 5:21:19 (28,647)
Borg, Coltte E 4:19:39 (16,516)
Borkett, Denise 5:44:00 (30,640)
Borland, Katie S 4:07:30 (13,475)
Borrett, Dawn 4:58:21 (25,578)
Borten, Janet H 6:50:37 (32,769)
Borthwick, Sally A 9:43:49 (33,220)
Boscarino, Simonetta 4:10:20 (14,181)
Bosch, Sarah J 3:58:23 (11,298)
Bossema, Gineke 4:28:12 (18,812)
Bostock, Barbara Z 4:46:06 (23,027)
Boston, Alexandra K 3:44:38 (7,600)
Boston, Colleen G 5:01:30 (26,107)
Bosworth, Mary T 4:47:51 (23,396)
Bott, Elisabeth J 3:48:06 (8,403)
Botten, Tina C 3:25:45 (4,034)
Bottero, Cecile 4:07:36 (13,506)
Bouhy, Brigitte 5:09:32 (27,210)
Boulger, Anne E 4:06:41 (13,271)
Boulger, Matilda 6:11:01 (31,955)
Bound, Elizabeth A 3:44:26 (7,547)
Bourke, Imogen E 4:40:58 (21,884)
Bourne, Amber K 6:38:03 (32,580)
Bourne, Anna J 5:12:36 (27,601)
Bourne, Naomi A 3:47:39 (8,282)
Bourne, Wendy 5:48:29 (30,966)
Bousfield, Clare J 4:41:20 (21,960)
Bousfield, Susan K 5:39:56 (30,358)
Boustead, Jill 4:14:22 (15,175)
Bouston, Sarah J 4:04:52 (12,888)
Bouvet, Emma F 5:16:44 (28,097)
Bovey, Claire L 4:49:30 (23,754)
Bowden, Annie 3:36:29 (5,928)
Bowden, Elizabeth A 4:01:21 (12,122)
Bowden, Jenny 4:40:44 (21,837)
Bowdler, Sian E 4:28:27 (18,882)
Bowen, Caroline A 4:29:50 (19,256)
Bowen, Elizabeth S 4:09:58 (14,093)
Bowen, Michelle A 3:33:53 (5,460)
Bowen, Natasha 4:22:04 (17,137)
Bower, Donna 5:42:09 (30,514)
Bower, Penny J 4:07:21 (13,433)
Bowers, Sandra 3:17:14 (2,915)
Bowler, Heather L 4:41:49 (22,060)
Bowles, Jacqueline F 3:48:50 (8,585)
Bowles, Nicola L 5:33:39 (29,866)
Bowley, Carmen L 4:26:16 (18,328)
Bowman, Gemma E 4:46:15 (23,062)
Bown, Rachel H 3:15:01 (2,661)
Bowry, Stacey J 5:44:04 (30,646)
Bowsher, Judi S 3:37:28 (6,127)
Bowsher, Nicola C 5:02:16 (26,215)
Bowyer, Ruth C 5:13:00 (27,653)
Bowyer-Jones, Pauline J 4:36:44 (20,910)
Boxall, Sarah V 5:14:24 (27,826)
Boyd, Carol A 3:46:49 (8,088)
Boyd, Clare E 4:41:37 (22,017)
Boyd, Jennie S 4:18:29 (16,228)
Boyd, Judith 3:44:13 (7,495)
Boyd, Rosemary S 6:38:23 (32,587)
Boyd, Sophie A 5:57:58 (31,454)
Boyd, Stephanie J 3:00:22 (1,258)
Boyd, Valerie 5:31:23 (29,699)
Boyett, Nicola 5:22:10 (28,735)
Boyle, Brenda M 4:32:21 (19,873)
Boyle, Carole A 4:23:39 (17,546)
Boyle, Louise M 3:40:00 (6,626)
Boyle, Melissa A 4:47:23 (23,287)
Boyle, Vicki J 3:10:40 (2,128)
Boynton, Carol E 4:03:10 (12,522)
Bracewell, Anna M 6:10:52 (31,951)
Bradbourn, Maria D 5:17:06 (28,140)
Bradburn, Nina L 3:51:59 (9,361)
Bradbury, Georgina A 4:49:56 (23,832)
Bradbury, Helen M 5:03:32 (26,393)
Braden, Pat A 5:33:00 (29,817)
Bradford, Nikki 3:49:08 (8,653)
Bradford, Sarah L 6:38:47 (32,595)
Bradford, Valerie T 3:54:55 (10,184)

Bradley, Alexa 5:09:19 (27,185)
Bradley, Catherine J 4:35:42 (20,650)
Bradley, Collette 4:54:45 (24,828)
Bradley, Debbie 4:08:30 (13,745)
Bradley, Jayne F 5:50:24 (31,102)
Bradley, Jayne M 4:33:54 (20,225)
Bradley, Karen 3:11:39 (2,229)
Bradley, Rachael L 5:00:04 (25,899)
Bradshaw, Louise C 4:14:52 (15,303)
Bradshaw, Suzanne M 4:39:45 (21,612)
Brady, Carrie T 2:58:17 (1,043)
Brady, Emma 4:33:07 (20,036)
Brady, Katherine L 4:20:14 (16,673)
Brady, Sandra C 4:45:49 (22,971)
Brady, Tina A 4:52:08 (24,277)
Bragg, Clare 4:49:24 (23,734)
Bragg, Gillian 4:43:29 (22,431)
Bragg, Susie D 5:36:32 (30,102)
Braham, Alice 2:40:38 (221)
Braham, Neasa A 5:33:08 (29,826)
Brailsford, Victoria A 3:27:03 (4,253)
Brain, Suzanne 4:01:56 (12,244)
Braithwaite, Jo M 4:28:56 (19,006)
Braithwaite, Karen J 4:39:40 (21,592)
Brana, Luisa P 3:48:50 (8,585)
Brand, Cassandra L 4:27:56 (18,733)
Brandie, Pamela M 4:03:48 (12,675)
Brannigan, Charlotte E 4:24:42 (17,869)
Branscombe, Karen L 5:32:13 (29,754)
Brant, Nicola J 4:52:06 (24,268)
Brardmore, Donna 3:35:25 (5,736)
Braude, Leora J 4:46:19 (23,080)
Braun, Babette 5:06:26 (26,781)
Braunold, Aviva S 6:56:09 (32,841)
Braunton, Lisa J 4:10:46 (14,266)
Braverman, Susana 5:28:49 (29,413)
Bray, Alana 5:28:00 (29,324)
Bray, Laura L 3:58:57 (11,490)
Brayne, Julie A 4:12:51 (14,796)
Brazier, Tanya D 5:30:14 (29,564)
Breaker, Linda F 5:17:52 (28,230)
Breakwell, Wendy J 4:18:05 (16,137)
Brearley, Carly J 5:48:13 (30,958)
Brearley, Janet 6:15:14 (32,092)
Breed, Wendy 3:29:24 (4,696)
Breen, Michelle 6:18:02 (32,172)
Breeze, Mary F 4:35:12 (20,531)
Bregan, Heidi B 5:03:50 (26,431)
Brekenfeld, Katrin 4:24:13 (17,717)
Bremner, Jane S 3:20:08 (3,284)
Bremner, Nicole S 4:00:43 (11,979)
Brench, Alison M 4:44:16 (22,629)
Brennan, Louise E 4:58:26 (25,594)
Brennan, Sharon 3:37:39 (6,159)
Brentnall, Clare A 5:06:59 (26,858)
Brentnall, Lucy E 4:48:05 (23,446)
Brereton, Tammy 5:07:53 (26,990)
Breuil, Laetitia 4:07:04 (13,360)
Brew, Charlotte 4:01:49 (12,219)
Brewer, Linda M 4:27:50 (18,703)
Brewster, Clare V 5:04:37 (26,538)
Brewster, Elaine 5:19:56 (28,483)
Brewster, Vanessa M 4:30:07 (19,328)
Brickell, Sarah L 4:33:06 (20,030)
Brickley, Katherine E 4:10:59 (14,325)
Bridel, Anna K 5:22:52 (28,814)
Bridge, Paula A 6:52:10 (32,785)
Bridge, Rachael E 5:42:54 (30,566)
Bridges, Allison 4:32:31 (19,905)
Bridges, Val P 4:33:24 (20,111)
Brierley, Anne 5:46:51 (30,851)
Briggs, Camilla 3:15:44 (2,745)
Briggs, Caroline J 4:23:17 (17,440)
Briggs, Julie L 2:54:33 (761)
Briggs, Kathryn J 4:13:04 (14,862)
Briggs, Minna C 4:42:38 (22,242)
Briggs, Nicola S 4:31:50 (19,755)
Bright, Jane 3:50:12 (8,911)
Bright, Margaret E 5:39:27 (30,317)
Bright, Sharon J 4:33:33 (20,149)
Brightman, Pat A 6:28:47 (32,435)
Brightmore, Emma 5:44:02 (30,644)
Brighton, Susan L 3:42:43 (7,159)
Brimble, Su 4:56:53 (25,278)
Brimley, Jennifer L 4:39:39 (21,588)
Brindley, Anne 3:15:27 (2,714)
Brindley, Joanne 3:57:43 (11,082)
Bringlow, Véronique 3:04:39 (1,558)
Briscoe, Jackie 5:49:15 (31,020)
Bristow, Lucy M 4:26:24 (18,361)
Bristow, Mary 5:19:28 (28,431)
Bristow Tyler, Linda 5:07:03 (26,867)
Britland, Toni 5:37:53 (30,196)
Britton, Jenny 4:09:25 (13,969)
Britton, Louise 5:38:25 (30,243)
Broad, Lucinda 4:49:44 (23,797)
Broad, Sarah L 4:27:27 (18,609)
Broadbent, Clare E 4:16:27 (15,711)
Broadley, Michelle D 4:48:54 (23,628)
Broadway, Louise H 3:53:45 (9,844)
Brock, Helen 3:25:17 (3,972)
Brockbank, Susanna 5:16:03 (28,005)
Brockhurst, Elise 5:17:21 (28,177)
Brockies, Jane C 3:42:14 (7,072)
Brocklebank, Victoria E 4:37:41 (21,156)
Brocklesby, Edwina P 3:56:12 (10,593)
Brockman, Miranda H 5:00:31 (25,970)
Brockway, Angela K 4:37:14 (21,039)
Broda, Krysia B 4:11:25 (14,445)
Broderick, Laura 3:51:36 (9,243)
Brodie, Jacquie D 6:45:44 (32,707)
Broekhof, Mary K 4:03:54 (12,690)
Bromley, Lauren E 3:41:02 (6,809)
Bromley, Lysa A 6:42:36 (32,648)
Bromley, Sally A 5:11:18 (27,427)
Brons, Glenda L 4:22:09 (17,157)
Bronsdon, Pandie 4:38:29 (21,335)
Brook, Christine E 3:52:43 (9,551)
Brook, Diana L 4:28:11 (18,802)
Brook, Katharine 4:44:30 (22,680)
Brook, Laura J 3:55:10 (10,264)
Brook, Sally C 4:32:12 (19,833)
Brookbanks, Adele L 3:41:29 (6,909)
Brooke, Anna L 4:09:46 (14,048)
Brooke, Bronwen T 4:56:59 (25,307)
Brooke, Jennifer M 5:28:03 (29,332)
Brooke, Kathryn 5:25:29 (29,084)
Brooker, Carol 4:11:19 (14,420)
Brooker, Lisa J 4:46:04 (23,019)
Brookes, Sophie L 5:09:52 (27,249)
Brooks, Claire H 4:16:18 (15,668)
Brooks, Claire J 5:39:01 (30,282)
Brooks, Debbie 4:47:25 (23,296)
Brooks, Helen 4:39:19 (21,521)
Brooks, Mary 5:20:20 (28,544)
Brooks, Melanie L 5:14:10 (27,794)
Brooks, Sara 4:53:17 (24,520)
Brooks, Sarah 3:53:39 (9,806)
Brooks, Susan 5:42:02 (30,502)
Broom, Debbie A 5:37:35 (30,173)
Broom, Louise 4:35:22 (20,573)
Broome, Catherine J 4:00:14 (11,874)
Broomfield, Diane M 5:20:57 (28,605)
Broomfield, Susannah E 3:56:07 (10,573)
Brorsson, Asa M 4:25:57 (18,244)
Broughton, Jennifer A 4:06:40 (13,265)
Broughton, Maryann S 4:29:28 (19,167)
Broughton, Steven 6:33:54 (32,514)
Broughton-Head, Nicola C 4:56:25 (25,191)
Brown, Abigail G 4:46:04 (23,019)
Brown, Alison R 3:38:37 (6,353)
Brown, Angela 6:59:16 (32,871)
Brown, Angela P 4:34:46 (20,430)
Brown, Angela S 4:14:09 (15,122)
Brown, Avril 4:31:29 (19,661)
Brown, Cate 4:22:09 (17,157)
Brown, Cayetana 5:07:16 (26,903)
Brown, Claire 5:15:31 (27,955)
Brown, Elizabeth A 5:15:36 (27,963)
Brown, Elizabeth A 5:58:05 (31,460)
Brown, Elma 4:36:26 (20,832)
Brown, Eloisa D 4:07:54 (13,581)
Brown, Fiona C 4:57:45 (25,445)
Brown, Freya A 4:09:06 (13,880)
Brown, Gudrun E 4:41:44 (22,046)
Brown, Hannah E 4:23:03 (17,374)
Brown, Heather 4:17:25 (15,960)
Brown, Heather 4:31:20 (19,622)
Brown, Helen 4:24:55 (17,930)
Brown, Helen E 3:53:00 (9,626)
Brown, Janet H 3:35:12 (5,706)
Brown, Jennifer 6:21:44 (32,276)
Brown, Jill C 4:44:46 (22,724)
Brown, Josie 5:06:29 (26,785)
Brown, Judy 3:29:01 (4,624)
Brown, Julie A 4:24:55 (17,930)
Brown, Julie C 5:41:37 (30,467)
Brown, Karen 4:49:26 (23,740)
Brown, Karen L 4:47:43 (23,364)
Brown, Katie L 4:32:04 (19,808)
Brown, Kristy E 4:41:35 (22,008)
Brown, Lisa M 4:31:21 (19,625)
Brown, Lorraine 6:06:53 (31,819)
Brown, Lynn 6:26:18 (32,386)
Brown, Mandy 3:40:55 (6,786)
Brown, Margaret M 6:30:41 (32,468)
Brown, Maxine 4:14:46 (15,279)
Brown, Michelle L 4:31:13 (19,586)
Brown, Monica 5:48:02 (30,946)
Brown, Nicky 5:24:18 (28,971)
Brown, Pauline 4:38:36 (21,359)
Brown, Petrena E 4:45:37 (22,930)
Brown, Rachel M 4:41:00 (21,895)
Brown, Rachel R 4:16:31 (15,732)
Brown, Samantha E 4:20:28 (16,727)
Brown, Sara J 4:40:53 (21,869)
Brown, Sarah A 4:16:00 (15,599)
Brown, Stephanie 7:15:14 (33,008)
Brown, Sue 3:45:02 (7,697)
Brown, Valerie 4:34:41 (20,406)
Brown, Veronica P 5:17:20 (28,172)
Browne, Debbie J 5:07:45 (26,970)
Browne, Gabrielle 3:41:10 (6,847)
Brownhill, Alison 3:03:24 (1,472)
Bruce, Elise J 4:58:31 (25,614)
Bruce, Joan 4:25:44 (18,169)
Bruce, Kathryn R 4:40:31 (21,791)
Bruce, Rebecca 4:55:21 (24,972)
Bruce, Sarah J 3:06:08 (1,680)
Bruce, Sarah J 4:08:36 (13,769)
Brugha, Lia P 4:26:12 (18,313)
Brule, Maryse 3:54:53 (10,173)
Brumble, Rebecca 4:59:40 (25,826)
Brumby, Leonie J 3:58:30 (11,340)
Brummellq, Zoe A 4:15:34 (15,489)
Brumwell, Sue E 3:41:11 (6,849)
Bruneau, Rosalyn A 4:13:09 (14,888)
Brunskill, Iain R 5:11:34 (27,469)
Brunton, Suzanna 3:38:31 (6,329)
Brusels, Linzi M 4:25:10 (18,016)
Bruun, Helen E 4:58:50 (25,671)
Bruun, Susanne 3:53:58 (9,912)
Bryan, Delyth W 3:53:43 (9,827)
Bryan, Jeanette 4:55:37 (25,020)
Bryan, Leoni 4:24:56 (17,938)
Bryan, Terrie 5:29:42 (29,507)
Bryans, Fiona 3:53:47 (9,853)
Bryant, Helen 5:03:06 (26,329)
Bryant, Lynn D 4:56:57 (25,295)
Brydon, Marina E 5:30:29 (29,590)
Bryson, Felicity V 4:29:37 (19,206)
Buccolini, Mariella 4:50:47 (24,001)
Buchanan, Aileen M 4:44:12 (22,610)
Buchanan, Ingrid J 4:48:35 (23,563)
Buck, Janet L 6:08:03 (31,860)
Buck, Rachel 4:12:19 (14,659)
Buck, Victoria C 3:37:14 (6,079)
Buckingham, Fiona 3:54:07 (9,949)
Buckingham, Laura C 5:35:13 (29,988)
Buckland, Carol 3:46:23 (7,979)
Buckle, Emma J 5:11:51 (27,507)
Buckle, Kirsten 4:26:47 (18,461)
Buckle, Michelle 3:05:23 (1,617)
Buckle, Polly 4:14:09 (15,122)
Buckley, Alison J 3:43:01 (7,236)
Buckley, Diane 4:32:50 (19,963)
Buckley, Julie 5:15:34 (27,958)
Buckley, Kelly E 4:14:05 (15,098)
Buckley, Natasha K 3:37:05 (6,053)

Buckley, Susan L 7:02:43 (32,902)
Buckley, Tracie 5:05:42 (26,666)
Buckley, Victoria 3:49:10 (8,661)
Buckwell, Zena K 4:21:42 (17,023)
Budd, Sarah 5:29:14 (29,449)
Budden, Rosemary C 4:59:03 (25,715)
Buddle, Clare R 3:58:47 (11,440)
Bula, Deborah A 4:25:44 (18,169)
Bulkeley, Lucy J 4:41:56 (22,095)
Bull, Nicola L 6:26:06 (32,377)
Bullingham, Ella J 5:25:02 (29,041)
Bullivant, Sharon 5:41:39 (30,470)
Bullman, Claire 4:27:51 (18,708)
Bullock, Janet M 5:23:03 (28,837)
Bullock, Jennifer M 5:08:02 (27,011)
Bullock, Katie A 4:41:40 (22,030)
Bullough, Martina C 4:33:39 (20,177)
Bulman, Susan 5:52:53 (31,210)
Bulmer, Samantha C 3:57:33 (11,028)
Bultitude, Melanie M 7:07:22 (32,955)
Bunch, Iona S 4:28:01 (18,753)
Bunn, Annette I 5:25:13 (29,062)
Bunston, Clare A 4:02:31 (12,376)
Bunten, Susan 3:40:37 (6,731)
Bunting, Tina H 6:06:01 (31,791)
Bunyan, Frances S 4:32:53 (19,974)
Burch, Samanatha 4:57:57 (25,487)
Burdall, Lucy K 4:27:05 (18,524)
Burdekin, Samantha L 6:38:46 (32,593)
Burdekova, Marketa 4:00:02 (11,828)
Burden, Alexandra M 4:18:27 (16,218)
Burden, Angela M 4:36:03 (20,736)
Burden, Jeanette M 4:25:53 (18,224)
Burden, Karen E 5:28:39 (29,395)
Burdess, Christine 5:20:23 (28,552)
Burgdorf, Katherine S 4:57:57 (25,487)
Burge, Claire P 4:10:21 (14,183)
Burger, Estelle 5:14:13 (27,800)
Burgess, Catherine 4:06:53 (13,321)
Burgess, Linda C 6:56:53 (32,854)
Burgess, Tracy A 4:22:10 (17,162)
Burke, Birgit 4:15:49 (15,552)
Burke, Deborah E 5:14:24 (27,826)
Burke, Jacqui 4:26:56 (18,489)
Burke, Jill E 3:07:17 (1,783)
Burke, Victoria L 4:40:03 (21,684)
Burkett, Mary 5:41:12 (30,432)
Burlace, Erica L 4:40:26 (21,756)
Burles, Julie A 5:27:25 (29,262)
Burley, Emma L 6:10:21 (31,937)
Burnand, Elizabeth M 4:59:19 (25,746)
Burnand, Lesley C 5:09:04 (27,155)
Burnard, Philippa 4:56:50 (25,264)
Burnell, Gillian 4:04:17 (12,774)
Burnell, Linda R 4:56:34 (25,218)
Burnett, Angela R 5:09:51 (27,245)
Burnett, Anita J 4:17:59 (16,106)
Burnett, Kristi J 4:19:33 (16,491)
Burnett, Zoe M 4:29:52 (19,261)
Burnham, Frances L 4:07:39 (13,519)
Burnicle, Jacqueline L 5:38:25 (30,243)
Burns, Carla C 4:45:09 (22,820)
Burns, Charlotte M 5:33:58 (29,888)
Burns, Donna L 5:14:24 (27,826)
Burns, Eilis J 4:56:40 (25,236)
Burns, Ilze 4:54:42 (24,816)
Burns, Marion 4:17:35 (16,011)
Burns, Yvonne B 4:20:19 (16,688)
Burrard-Lucas, Megan 4:35:48 (20,673)
Burrell, Kate A 4:45:18 (22,856)
Burrows, Alison J 5:21:37 (28,674)
Burrows, Catherine A 4:27:08 (18,538)
Burrows, Clare L 5:22:00 (28,719)
Burrows, Harriet 6:56:06 (32,839)
Burt, Helen 4:30:59 (19,528)
Burthem, Joanne 4:49:51 (23,813)
Burton, Amy L 5:20:23 (28,552)
Burton, Dionne 6:16:18 (32,129)
Burton, Janet 6:05:45 (31,787)
Burton, Jennifer N 3:35:49 (5,801)
Burton, Lynette J 3:57:52 (11,128)
Burton, Michelle M 5:10:52 (27,372)
Burton, Nicky A 4:28:55 (18,998)
Burton, Ruth E 4:53:36 (24,599)
Burton, Sarah J 5:08:53 (27,132)
Burton, Sharon 3:30:12 (4,854)
Burwood, Kelly 3:50:38 (9,013)
Burwood-Taylor, Olivia M 4:24:00 (17,656)
Busby, Amanda M 7:03:52 (32,925)
Bush, Heather M 3:43:15 (7,300)
Bush, Josephine R 4:22:52 (17,336)
Bushell, Claire R 5:42:53 (30,564)
Bushell, Nicky G 3:22:01 (3,537)
Bushnell, Julie A 4:42:46 (22,274)
Bushnell, Margaret C 4:53:58 (24,670)
Butcher, Catherine L 3:41:36 (6,945)
Butcher, Emily J 4:53:11 (24,504)
Butcher, Lisa E 4:22:21 (17,209)
Butcher, Lucy C 5:03:35 (26,400)
Butland, Olly C 3:43:15 (7,300)
Butler, Clare E 6:07:42 (31,848)
Butler, Gillian 5:09:18 (27,183)
Butler, Jane 5:17:13 (28,155)
Butler, Kate L 4:16:07 (15,627)
Butler, Laura 4:54:41 (24,814)
Butler, Michelle B 4:09:20 (13,940)
Butler, Rowena T 3:56:59 (10,842)
Butler, Sandra J 4:53:06 (24,479)
Butler, Sarah 3:29:58 (4,818)
Butler, Vanessa L 3:27:31 (4,336)
Butterfield, Caroline A 6:57:42 (32,863)
Butterfield, Katharine L 3:32:57 (5,315)
Butterill, Carol 4:11:57 (14,563)
Butters, Jo L 5:24:01 (28,940)
Butterworth, Jill E 4:31:08 (19,566)
Butterworth, Julie 7:16:58 (33,020)
Butterworth, Suzanne E 4:59:52 (25,862)
Button, Justine C 4:39:36 (21,577)
Button, Zoe C 4:04:38 (12,837)
Buxton, Sarah E 5:49:51 (31,060)
Byard, Jill 5:12:12 (27,551)
Byas, Rachael E 3:50:07 (8,890)
Bye, Louise A 4:24:52 (17,906)
Byford, Kirsty L 5:41:27 (30,453)
Byrne, Jassodra 5:24:13 (28,967)
Byrne, Susan J 4:53:29 (24,562)
Byrom, Lynda G 6:05:44 (31,786)
Byron, Glynnis 3:48:38 (8,535)
Byvelds, Reta A 5:30:59 (29,648)
Caalsen, Amelia 4:18:09 (16,151)
Cable, Vicky J 5:18:01 (28,239)
Cade, Lindsey A 5:34:00 (29,890)
Cadman, Rachael L 4:47:25 (23,296)
Cadwallader, Sarah 3:22:31 (3,598)
Caeiro, Susana 4:00:02 (11,828)
Caesar, Felicity J 4:58:30 (25,607)
Cafferkey, Annette 4:06:15 (13,184)
Caffyn, Sarah J 6:54:31 (32,819)
Cahill, Paulina 6:07:22 (31,833)
Cahill, Pauline J 4:26:00 (18,258)
Cahillane, Lucy C 4:46:29 (23,118)
Cahusac, Nicola C 3:13:07 (2,416)
Cain, Ingrid M 4:20:39 (16,774)
Cain, Susan P 3:57:17 (10,944)
Caine, Samantha E 4:39:37 (21,581)
Caira, Trudy 5:47:38 (30,927)
Cairney, Anna E 4:54:38 (24,804)
Cairns, Jacqueline 6:14:10 (32,058)
Cakebread, Sarah L 4:39:30 (21,560)
Caket, Deborah J 4:42:53 (22,301)
Caldecott, Jessica 6:45:29 (32,702)
Caldeira, Allison M 4:42:58 (22,322)
Calder, Sarah L 3:49:52 (8,837)
Calderon, Sofia 3:51:32 (9,229)
Caldwell, Amy C 3:41:38 (6,950)
Caldwell, Andrea T 4:37:49 (21,181)
Caldwell, Gillian M 4:54:33 (24,792)
Caleffi, Tania 3:38:54 (6,412)

LONDON MARATHON

Caligari, Carole J 4:19:01 (16,356)
Callaghan, Michelle 4:25:11 (18,023)
Calmeyer, Laura J 6:12:19 (32,000)
Calnan, Ann R 3:28:38 (4,537)
Calne, Stephanie D 4:45:27 (22,898)
Calver, Katy A 4:00:50 (12,002)
Calvert, Jennifer E 5:21:51 (28,697)
Calvey, Danette E 4:26:08 (18,293)
Calvo-Jimenez, Amanda J 4:57:14 (25,359)
Camberon, Annabele L 4:08:20 (13,701)
Cameron, Jo-Anna 4:25:06 (17,990)
Cameron, Lee D 4:27:50 (18,703)
Cameron, Mary M 4:30:13 (19,357)
Cameron, Victoria L 5:01:14 (26,078)
Cameron-Jung, Susan M 5:05:47 (26,675)
Cameron-Mowat, Mary A 5:07:00 (26,861)
Camfield, Carol P 5:09:18 (27,183)
Camilleri, Karen 5:15:25 (27,945)
Camm, Joanne 4:56:10 (25,133)
Campana, Alessandra 4:53:29 (24,562)
Campbell, Amanda J 5:36:39 (30,109)
Campbell, Annie L 4:24:11 (17,709)
Campbell, Brigette C 4:59:21 (25,754)
Campbell, Gail F 3:59:47 (11,755)
Campbell, Georgina J 3:28:18 (4,468)
Campbell, Gill 5:29:43 (29,511)
Campbell, Helen K 5:07:52 (26,985)
Campbell, Maureen 6:05:39 (31,782)
Campbell, Nancy M 5:41:58 (30,494)
Campbell, Nina R 3:46:17 (7,963)
Campbell, Phyllis 5:14:43 (27,875)
Campbell, Rosie E 4:44:41 (22,707)
Campbell, Shona A 5:11:29 (27,455)
Campion, Heather 7:10:07 (32,980)
Campion, Jane 3:14:28 (2,591)
Campion, Stephanie J 3:33:09 (5,342)
Camplin, Jennifer A 7:00:14 (32,885)
Canavan, Lucia 6:35:29 (32,534)
Canham, Tracey L 4:32:23 (19,884)
Cann, Claire M 2:56:56 (935)
Cann, Lee-Anne M 3:01:23 (1,330)
Cann, Sarah E 3:59:21 (11,621)
Cannell, Susan H 6:04:03 (31,729)
Cannon, Jessica L 4:14:33 (15,216)
Cant, Denise C 4:35:26 (20,588)
Cantlay, Kaye L 3:15:49 (2,755)
Cantrill, Lisa 3:53:48 (9,861)
Capener, Rebecca A 3:43:03 (7,251)
Carberry, Suzanne 4:33:57 (20,238)
Cardale, Kate J 3:54:42 (10,114)
Cardell, Sarah F 4:08:54 (13,838)
Cardno-Strachan, Gillian 3:38:58 (6,428)
Care, Angharad 2:56:03 (853)
Carew, Funmi 3:58:06 (11,185)
Carey, Jane 4:33:17 (20,080)
Carey, Laura 3:55:01 (10,209)
Carey, Linda M 4:17:52 (16,076)
Carleton, Lynne 5:02:29 (26,246)
Carlin, Annette K 3:18:12 (3,019)
Carlin, Julie E 4:25:12 (18,027)
Carlsson, Sara 3:32:49 (5,296)
Carlyle, Heather 4:36:29 (20,842)
Carman, Stacey J 4:08:08 (13,648)
Carmentran, Agnes 4:24:01 (17,661)
Carmichael, Linda J 4:59:28 (25,780)
Carney, Jean D 6:00:12 (31,572)
Carney, Ruth 4:53:28 (24,556)
Carr, Alex J 3:57:24 (10,979)
Carr, Karen 5:17:33 (28,199)
Carr, Simone E 5:22:46 (28,809)
Carrington, Elizabeth 5:07:06 (26,878)
Carrington Birch, Catherine E 3:57:22 (10,969)
Carritt, Joanna 3:06:38 (1,721)
Carroll, Anita P 4:45:58 (22,998)
Carroll, Cecilia A 4:57:59 (25,500)
Carroll, Joanne C 4:13:20 (14,924)
Carroll, Kirsty J 4:22:42 (17,300)
Carroll, Lucy 4:03:55 (12,695)
Carroll, Pamela 4:53:42 (24,620)
Carson, Edwina S 4:39:38 (21,584)
Carswell, Brynna 3:59:06 (11,543)
Carswell, Emma L 5:20:08 (28,510)
Carter, Alex M 4:43:23 (22,408)

Carter, Alexandra....4:33:27 (20,123)
Carter, Carol A....3:56:57 (10,828)
Carter, Elizabeth J....4:30:32 (19,436)
Carter, Fiona L....4:25:04 (17,982)
Carter, Janet....3:57:40 (11,065)
Carter, Lucy J....4:28:00 (18,749)
Carter, Nicola M....4:03:20 (12,559)
Carter, Nicola M....4:53:36 (24,599)
Carter, Noreen....6:35:31 (32,536)
Carter, Patricia R....5:26:57 (29,218)
Carter, Rachael H....6:04:57 (31,760)
Carter, Rachel L....4:12:42 (14,749)
Carter, Ruth H....3:50:26 (8,966)
Carter, Theresa A....4:15:17 (15,408)
Cartmill, Alana M....4:55:22 (24,976)
Cartner, Jackie....4:39:15 (21,502)
Cartwright, Carole....5:11:09 (27,403)
Cartwright, Kady....4:27:03 (18,515)
Cartwright, Sadie M....5:15:33 (27,957)
Cartwright, Shirley J....5:28:37 (29,387)
Cartwright, Susan M....5:39:28 (30,320)
Carullo, Stephanie....4:42:40 (22,254)
Carver, Jackie A....5:08:11 (27,032)
Cary, Catherine J....4:17:45 (16,046)
Casanova, Imelda L....6:00:27 (31,580)
Case, Suzanne J....4:42:16 (22,167)
Caseley, Julie A....4:27:00 (18,504)
Casey, Nicola J....4:37:55 (21,202)
Cashmore, Ann L....4:07:45 (13,545)
Cass, Dawn M....4:39:44 (21,610)
Cass, Jennifer M....5:41:21 (30,444)
Cassamally, Laura....4:56:46 (25,251)
Casserly, Julia M....5:08:55 (27,137)
Cassey, Vanessa J....3:45:11 (7,725)
Cassidy, Lydia A....5:03:10 (26,339)
Cassidy, Vanessa S....4:16:54 (15,833)
Castelen, Shirley....4:23:27 (17,486)
Castell, Sarah A....5:00:31 (25,970)
Castelluccio, Lesleyann....4:52:18 (24,307)
Castle, Carolyn A....5:18:03 (28,245)
Castle, Rosemary A....4:45:02 (22,798)
Castles, Lesley A....4:56:54 (25,281)
Caswell, Helen L....3:28:22 (4,486)
Caswell, Louisa M....5:00:09 (25,915)
Cater, Lisa J....5:19:00 (28,375)
Caterino, Anna-Maria....5:14:05 (27,781)
Catlin, Louise....5:39:17 (30,301)
Catlow, Sarah L....5:56:10 (31,361)
Caton, Claire J....4:00:30 (11,934)
Catt, Vicky E....5:50:23 (31,099)
Cattell, Sarah J....3:57:30 (11,014)
Catterall, Tracey D....4:56:55 (25,287)
Caudwell, Vanessa L....4:31:59 (19,786)
Caulfield, Vanda....3:18:17 (3,029)
Caunt, Charlotte A....3:48:56 (8,618)
Causer, Linda S....5:27:26 (29,263)
Cavanagh, Carmel M....5:02:58 (26,311)
Cavanagh, Kwendy S....4:42:57 (22,316)
Cave, Elizabeth A....4:05:08 (12,946)
Cavelle, Ruth....5:11:52 (27,510)
Caven, Alexandra J....3:15:19 (2,698)
Cawley, Jacqueline....6:15:24 (32,096)
Cawston, Sarah A....4:00:08 (11,855)
Celestino, Fatima M....4:25:45 (18,176)
Cesarani, Carla....4:10:14 (14,156)
Chadfield, Sarah....4:51:23 (24,117)
Chadwick, Joanne....4:38:05 (21,251)
Chadwick, Lindsey P....6:22:03 (32,291)
Chadwick, Rebecca J....4:21:35 (16,993)
Chadwick, Sandrine....4:49:29 (23,752)
Chaffer, Oonagh C....4:08:13 (13,669)
Chaffey, Heather C....4:38:26 (21,320)
Chalkley, Sharon....3:56:50 (10,799)
Challenger, Glenys B....4:37:49 (21,181)
Challis, Debbie A....5:46:46 (30,846)
Challis, Patricia A....4:20:09 (16,644)
Chalmers, Gillian F....4:25:50 (18,202)
Chalmers, Louise J....5:24:42 (29,007)
Chalmers, Tracy T....5:17:35 (28,204)
Chalton, Sophie....3:46:46 (8,074)
Chamayou, Sadrine....5:00:42 (25,995)
Chamberlain, Diane L....4:50:11 (23,876)
Chamberlain, Elizabeth J....4:10:16 (14,167)
Chamberlain, Laura M....3:59:51 (11,776)
Chambers, Joanne S....4:02:03 (12,276)
Chambers, Kelly L....4:45:05 (22,810)
Chambers, Sophie A....4:35:02 (20,498)
Champion, Emma J....4:38:29 (21,335)
Champion, Liz J....6:02:54 (31,675)
Chan, Harriet....4:19:51 (16,568)
Chan, Ling K....3:46:25 (7,993)
Chan, Martha K....4:22:17 (17,194)
Chan, Suiling....4:54:48 (24,848)
Chan, Woon....4:55:48 (25,054)
Chana, Raj....6:23:37 (32,320)
Chance, Katherine E....3:57:23 (10,974)
Chancellor, Caron L....4:54:58 (24,887)
Chandaman, Edwina C....4:04:06 (12,739)
Chandler, Selina....5:08:14 (27,040)
Chandler, Trudi....6:31:14 (32,478)
Chandolia, Alka....6:57:00 (32,855)
Channer, Debbie....4:33:42 (20,188)
Chaplin, Nicola J....5:15:34 (27,958)
Chapman, Alison C....4:52:12 (24,289)
Chapman, Brigid T....4:19:23 (16,442)
Chapman, Corinne W....4:38:33 (21,349)
Chapman, Cynthia M....4:03:36 (12,624)
Chapman, Emily S....5:23:17 (28,865)
Chapman, Gill....3:41:35 (6,941)
Chapman, Kate....5:16:33 (28,075)
Chapman, Kelly A....4:51:30 (24,144)
Chapman, Lesley....3:27:10 (4,269)
Chapman, Lorraine A....5:05:57 (26,700)
Chapman, Louise....4:39:20 (21,528)
Chapman, Sarah L....4:18:34 (16,248)
Chappell, Annelie K....4:07:34 (13,496)
Chappell, Jane....3:20:02 (3,272)
Charapentier, Dominique M....3:21:05 (3,409)
Chard, Lucy C....4:00:12 (11,864)
Charles, Joanne....4:35:41 (20,647)
Charles, Kate P....4:56:54 (25,281)
Charles, Lisa J....5:02:16 (26,215)
Charles, Lorne K....4:23:08 (17,393)
Charles, Marvelyn....4:41:54 (22,085)
Charleton, Andrea Z....6:09:50 (31,919)
Charlton, Avril C....5:29:15 (29,453)
Charlton, Dee-Ann....4:50:09 (23,869)
Charlton, Mary P....4:35:26 (20,588)
Charlton, Rachel J....4:55:22 (24,976)
Charman, Mary L....5:07:26 (26,923)
Charmley, Susan E....6:18:45 (32,192)
Charnley, Victoria M....4:56:16 (25,155)
Charrington, Susie J....4:14:07 (15,108)
Charter, Gloria....4:42:47 (22,278)
Chaston, Lisa A....5:38:31 (30,253)
Chatterton, Sarah E....3:58:18 (11,266)
Chaudhri, Sarah E....4:22:12 (17,174)
Chaudoin, Leah C....5:36:14 (30,075)
Chaundy, Alison J....4:49:02 (23,658)
Cheesman, Jessica....7:38:18 (33,135)
Chepkemei, Susan....2:21:46 (35)
Chera, Olwen M....6:47:43 (32,734)
Cheriton, Deborah....6:54:15 (32,811)
Cheshire, Lynette M....4:40:58 (21,884)
Chesley, Anne-Marie....5:17:31 (28,196)
Chessum, Deborah S....4:35:32 (20,607)
Chester, Richard W....4:24:28 (17,792)
Chesterman, Carron L....5:13:08 (27,669)
Chestnutt, Sarah A....3:31:21 (5,046)
Chesworth, Caroline A....4:06:58 (13,341)
Cheung, Philippa K....4:35:15 (20,544)
Cheung, Winnie....5:08:55 (27,137)
Chevassut, Ann C....4:41:45 (22,048)
Chick, Amanda K....4:37:40 (21,152)
Chigwedere, Terry Z....4:46:13 (23,051)
Child, Anne E....4:46:32 (23,129)
Child, Hayley V....5:48:02 (30,946)
Child, Mary Anne....7:25:05 (33,072)
Childs, Stacy A....5:33:08 (29,826)
Chilvers, Ruth M....5:15:50 (27,977)
Chilvers, Sarah F....4:01:48 (12,214)
Chin, Rhian E....4:40:08 (21,697)
Ching, Jaqueline M....5:05:57 (26,700)
Chisholm, Gina....4:39:06 (21,465)
Chittenden, Thea....6:08:19 (31,871)
Chivers, Janine....5:23:52 (28,924)
Chivers, Susan A....4:44:04 (22,578)
Chodosh, Abi E....4:51:16 (24,086)
Choi, Jocelyn J....4:58:54 (25,687)
Chomka, Krysia....4:17:44 (16,038)
Chopra, Perveen....4:57:39 (25,424)
Choy, Tina....4:43:44 (22,502)
Chriostofides, Ana....6:30:13 (32,454)
Christie, Erica M....3:12:45 (2,369)
Christie, Nathalie....3:39:12 (6,475)
Christopher, Claire L....4:13:14 (14,906)
Christophers, Fiona L....5:15:52 (27,986)
Christophorou, Penelope J....3:38:50 (6,393)
Christy, Morisha K....4:58:33 (25,623)
Chubb, Fiona R....4:36:40 (20,879)
Chung, May....6:23:22 (32,311)
Church, Christine M....3:53:13 (9,697)
Church, Jo....5:18:59 (28,370)
Church, Susan A....6:01:31 (31,628)
Churches, Louise M....5:38:16 (30,231)
Churchill, Alison L....4:25:22 (18,079)
Churchill, Lesley J....4:50:49 (24,007)
Chuter, Tracey M....4:25:08 (18,004)
Ciavarini Azzi, Valerie H....4:36:33 (20,857)
Ciccarelli, Gabriella....4:14:59 (15,332)
Ciccioriccio, Maria Carla....5:09:29 (27,203)
Ciccotosto, Sabine....4:18:03 (16,119)
Cinnamon, Amy E....5:27:50 (29,312)
Cistac, Yolande....3:22:02 (3,539)
Clack, Jacqueline....4:31:02 (19,541)
Clague, Alexi....4:37:20 (21,066)
Clague, Jenny....2:36:10 (129)
Clamp, Joanne E....3:31:00 (4,984)
Clampett, Linda S....4:09:44 (14,039)
Clancy, Alison....4:20:10 (16,652)
Clare, Stephanie....4:34:45 (20,424)
Claridge, Tina J....4:38:05 (21,251)
Clark, Alison I....4:48:28 (23,532)
Clark, Angela....5:42:01 (30,497)
Clark, Anna....4:42:33 (22,230)
Clark, Bev....4:07:41 (13,528)
Clark, Billie....4:07:05 (13,370)
Clark, Caroline P....6:04:25 (31,739)
Clark, Catherine J....5:11:38 (27,475)
Clark, Charlie....4:44:00 (22,572)
Clark, Corinne M....3:49:34 (8,761)
Clark, Dawn....3:42:10 (7,061)
Clark, Glenda....4:20:53 (16,833)
Clark, Janet M....4:26:16 (18,328)
Clark, Jennie E....5:22:38 (28,791)
Clark, Kathleen....4:42:25 (22,203)
Clark, Lisa Jane....5:58:12 (31,471)
Clark, Lynsey S....5:44:19 (30,666)
Clark, Meg B....5:06:00 (26,710)
Clark, Rebecca....5:00:02 (25,888)
Clark, Sarah....4:42:12 (22,156)
Clark, Sarah J....4:20:45 (16,795)
Clark, Shona....6:10:26 (31,942)
Clark, Victoria J....5:14:35 (27,853)
Clark, Zoe A....4:12:06 (14,595)
Clarke, Alison M....4:18:00 (16,108)
Clarke, Anna E....3:53:10 (9,679)
Clarke, Annette J....3:23:27 (3,705)
Clarke, Caroline E....6:27:56 (32,421)
Clarke, Christina G....4:24:09 (17,702)
Clarke, Janice C....4:28:14 (18,820)
Clarke, Jessica....6:37:37 (32,571)
Clarke, Katherine E....4:06:44 (13,285)
Clarke, Katie M....4:28:02 (18,757)
Clarke, Kay M....5:52:31 (31,198)
Clarke, Laura S....4:13:58 (15,054)
Clarke, Melanie....4:46:41 (23,156)
Clarke, Patricia M....5:38:13 (30,220)
Clarke, Rebecca J....4:43:30 (22,435)
Clarke, Rebecca J....4:48:28 (23,532)
Clarke, Renée M....7:24:18 (33,065)
Clarke, Sharon M....4:39:45 (21,612)
Clarke, Sherrese A....6:20:17 (32,238)
Clarke, Terri J....4:13:20 (14,924)
Clarke, Victoria M....2:57:19 (969)
Clarke, Vivienne M....5:42:07 (30,509)
Clarke Noble, Desiree A....3:23:58 (3,788)
Clarkson, Hilary....5:15:45 (27,971)
Clarkson, Kim....5:48:11 (30,955)

Clarkson, Linda P 3:04:12 (1,527)
Clarkson, Lorna K 5:30:29 (29,590)
Claudy, Marion 3:28:51 (4,590)
Claughton, Alexandra M 5:06:12 (26,738)
Claxton, Frances J 5:44:35 (30,685)
Clay, Sharon J 3:14:14 (2,557)
Clayton, Collette 4:05:27 (13,011)
Clayton, Jane E 3:58:38 (11,375)
Clayton, Lindsay J 5:16:24 (28,057)
Clayton, Sharon E 4:33:04 (20,019)
Cleere, Genevieve R 5:08:25 (27,068)
Clegg, Karly D 6:00:51 (31,598)
Clelland, Sarah E 3:45:21 (7,771)
Clement, Toya S 5:49:59 (31,071)
Clement, Vivienne P 3:27:15 (4,280)
Clements, Clair A 3:57:42 (11,072)
Clements, Deborah M 3:39:24 (6,518)
Clements, Mary E 4:05:58 (13,135)
Clews, Jan 4:47:04 (23,226)
Clews, Joanne 3:46:33 (8,021)
Cliff, Alison J 4:23:19 (17,448)
Clifford, Lizzie J 3:03:13 (1,458)
Climo, Joan K 7:33:52 (33,109)
Clinch, Georgina 3:46:31 (8,017)
Clingham, Gillian 4:57:49 (25,459)
Clink, Jenny 4:07:26 (13,453)
Clinton, Jacqueline W 4:49:10 (23,683)
Close, Claire L 4:18:17 (16,178)
Close, Sarah L 4:59:37 (25,815)
Close, Sian E 5:57:09 (31,410)
Close-Smith, Kelli A 5:49:04 (31,004)
Clossais, Martine 3:40:50 (6,765)
Clouting, Heather E 5:07:06 (26,878)
Clughen, Susan M 4:07:54 (13,581)
Cluitt, Sonia 4:26:12 (18,313)
Clutton, Hayley L 4:47:04 (23,226)
Clutton, Sharon E 4:38:42 (21,371)
Cluver, Cathryn A 4:36:15 (20,799)
Coastsmith, Louise S 5:54:49 (31,303)
Coates, Lousie H 5:06:54 (26,848)
Coates, Mikki K 4:05:36 (13,053)
Coates, Tracy A 4:33:09 (20,047)
Coats, Alison J 5:59:47 (31,547)
Coats, Caroline J 5:47:21 (30,904)
Cobaine, Faith A 4:23:26 (17,478)
Cobb, Jenny A 5:59:45 (31,544)
Cobbold, Marie D 4:49:27 (23,746)
Cobbold, Rebecca J 4:15:42 (15,521)
Cobby, Janet A 3:30:31 (4,899)
Coca, Florentina 3:45:54 (7,887)
Cochrane, Alice A 4:01:45 (12,199)
Cochrane, Tamzin J 5:43:33 (30,610)
Cockayne, Yael 4:25:56 (18,238)
Cocker, Laura E 4:28:14 (18,820)
Cockerell, Diana J 4:41:17 (21,948)
Cockerton, Christine E 5:20:56 (28,602)
Cockill, Hazel V 5:56:53 (31,400)
Cockill, Melanie 5:56:53 (31,400)
Cockle, Caroline E 4:45:08 (22,818)
Cocks, Elaine 5:54:41 (31,299)
Codelia, Adriene B 6:34:12 (32,519)
Coffey, Rebecca L 4:38:01 (21,227)
Coffman, Lynn M 4:36:43 (20,901)
Cogan, Lindesay A 5:28:25 (29,370)
Cohen, Ellana 3:56:51 (10,804)
Cojeen, Simon J 4:37:06 (21,002)
Cokell, Sian E 4:34:45 (20,424)
Cole, Deborah J 6:13:12 (32,027)
Cole, Helen G 5:07:37 (26,950)
Cole, Joanne S 4:09:31 (13,997)
Cole, Rachel A 4:51:36 (24,168)
Cole, Salena L 5:40:07 (30,373)
Cole, Sarah L 5:07:28 (26,926)
Cole, Sofie 4:36:41 (20,885)
Cole, Tracy J 4:53:53 (24,655)
Colebrook, Amanda 4:11:19 (14,420)
Coleby, Gillian F 7:07:55 (32,962)
Coleman, Abigail M 6:09:22 (31,909)
Coleman, Heidi L 3:01:32 (1,340)
Coleman, Kaye M 5:40:57 (30,423)
Coleman, Rhene 4:45:37 (22,930)
Coleman, Tamar R 4:21:15 (16,927)
Coles, Amanda J 5:39:55 (30,354)
Coles, Melissa 4:44:23 (22,656)
Colfer, Rochelle S 4:43:16 (22,383)
Collerton, Carol-Ann 4:18:21 (16,199)
Colley, Jeanette L 4:52:10 (24,285)
Colley, Lucy D 5:33:31 (29,848)
Colley, Rachael S 4:22:10 (17,162)
Collinge, Susan 4:36:31 (20,849)
Collingwood, Anya 5:03:32 (26,393)
Collins, Agneta B 6:08:40 (31,882)
Collins, Joanna C 5:20:08 (28,510)
Collins, Kate 4:59:30 (25,786)
Collins, Kate E 3:57:44 (11,087)
Collins, Kathryn D 4:09:29 (13,992)
Collins, Lindsey S 5:24:02 (28,943)
Collins, Louise J 5:24:52 (29,023)
Collins, Luisa Z 4:44:51 (22,745)
Collins, Nicola K 4:43:49 (22,523)
Collins, Nicola L 4:34:13 (20,294)
Collins, Nicola L 7:17:43 (33,027)
Collins, Patricia E 4:48:18 (23,493)
Collins, Rebecca 4:18:42 (16,281)
Collins, Sandra 4:11:13 (14,391)
Collins, Victoria 5:21:05 (28,617)
Collis, Rebecca C 4:54:22 (24,761)
Colllier, Sonia K 3:53:38 (9,802)
Colman, Julie A 4:59:06 (25,723)
Colquhoun, Lucy A 2:51:48 (627)
Coltart, Clementine L 5:46:45 (30,845)
Coltro, Ana L 4:28:06 (18,773)
Colwell, Cathy 4:28:12 (18,812)
Comiskey, Carmel A 3:15:12 (2,683)
Comyns, Claire 4:12:00 (14,573)
Condon, Deborah L 4:21:10 (16,908)
Coney, Deborah C 3:36:45 (5,982)
Coney, Diane J 3:30:15 (4,860)
Confait, Rachel 4:26:01 (18,263)
Conhye, Devina E 5:19:46 (28,467)
Conklin, Linda 4:17:45 (16,046)
Conley, Julie 6:14:08 (32,054)
Connaughton, Emma L 4:20:48 (16,810)
Conneally, Sarah-Jane 4:32:18 (19,859)
Connell, Keeley W 3:48:23 (8,470)
Connell, Kristina P 7:34:09 (33,115)
Connell, Natalie A 5:48:02 (30,946)
Connell, Sandra I 3:58:45 (11,422)
Connell, Tracy 3:14:35 (2,611)
Connelly, Helen R 3:42:47 (7,182)
Connelly, Samantha J 7:03:57 (32,927)
Connolly, Breege V 3:01:07 (1,310)
Connolly, Claire 3:56:07 (10,573)
Connolly, Mary P 6:08:45 (31,886)
Connolly, Sian M 4:22:36 (17,271)
Conroy, Julie C 4:36:38 (20,875)
Constable, Gillian E 4:07:35 (13,501)
Constable, Rebecca J 3:42:16 (7,076)
Constantinou, Marina 6:04:51 (31,758)
Conte, Franca 4:46:14 (23,056)
Convery, Susan C 4:28:47 (18,969)
Conway, Catherine H 3:50:40 (9,021)
Conway, Eloise C 5:23:40 (28,901)
Conway, Helen M 6:13:59 (32,047)
Coogan, Rebecca E 3:56:39 (10,739)
Cooil, Jan M 3:59:30 (11,672)
Cook, Alissa B 4:11:11 (14,383)
Cook, Ann E 3:28:07 (4,427)
Cook, Elaine J 4:24:46 (17,884)
Cook, Elaine S 5:08:48 (27,118)
Cook, Erica J 4:47:06 (23,235)
Cook, Jackie A 4:56:04 (25,114)
Cook, Katherine E 4:58:18 (25,570)
Cook, Lindsay J 4:29:19 (19,122)
Cook, Loretta 4:59:53 (25,866)
Cook, Natasha H 5:10:30 (27,336)
Cook, Paula W 4:28:40 (18,936)
Cook, Rachel J 3:10:50 (2,142)
Cook, Rachel Y 4:28:11 (18,802)
Cook, Sharon A 4:40:23 (21,747)
Cook, Shirley K 5:11:48 (27,492)
Cook, Susan A 5:07:01 (26,865)
Cook, Vanessa 4:27:39 (18,671)
Cook, Wendy J 4:51:13 (24,078)
Cooke, Anna K 4:48:16 (23,487)
Cooke, Lucy 5:22:41 (28,798)
Cooke, Susie L 4:44:46 (22,724)
Cooke, Suzi J 3:59:28 (11,662)
Cooke, Tina R 5:46:11 (30,800)
Cooke, Zoe 5:13:11 (27,673)
Cooke-Simmons, Julia K 4:03:47 (12,673)
Cooley, Martina 5:01:38 (26,124)
Coombs, Sarah L 6:03:54 (31,723)
Cooney, Ann L 6:47:48 (32,736)
Cooney, Victoria C 4:07:07 (13,377)
Cooper, Alison 3:19:47 (3,230)
Cooper, Anna 5:13:50 (27,747)
Cooper, Anne 4:25:53 (18,224)
Cooper, Anne M 5:37:24 (30,157)
Cooper, Carol J 3:28:40 (4,543)
Cooper, Catriona J 4:53:28 (24,556)
Cooper, Elaine D 3:57:35 (11,036)
Cooper, Eleanor J 5:56:29 (31,380)
Cooper, Helen 4:18:23 (16,204)
Cooper, Jacqueline 3:39:36 (6,554)
Cooper, Jean F 4:30:35 (19,446)
Cooper, Judith 4:21:39 (17,012)
Cooper, Julia R 4:48:29 (23,538)
Cooper, Justine C 5:04:46 (26,553)
Cooper, Lindsey J 3:56:02 (10,549)
Cooper, Louise J 3:00:55 (1,295)
Cooper, Patience A 3:53:20 (9,726)
Cooper, Penelope J 4:40:36 (21,810)
Cooper, Rosie C 4:22:02 (17,126)
Cooper, Sonia O 5:32:28 (29,767)
Cooper, Susannah C 4:26:04 (18,279)
Cooper, Tracey J 4:06:04 (13,154)
Cooper, Valerie J 5:03:46 (26,422)
Cope, Beth M 5:04:50 (26,560)
Cope, Sally 4:58:11 (25,544)
Copeland, Julia A 5:03:57 (26,451)
Copeland, Karen L 5:16:09 (28,021)
Copp, Rhona 3:38:00 (6,222)
Copp, Sharon P 4:24:04 (17,675)
Copus, Suzanne M 4:14:10 (15,133)
Corbett, Alison J 4:11:08 (14,370)
Corbett, Anne M 4:57:11 (25,352)
Corbett, Nathalie J 5:08:30 (27,078)
Corbetta, Simonetta 3:30:50 (4,947)
Corbin, Sally 3:37:46 (6,180)
Corby, Clare E 4:45:40 (22,935)
Corcoran, Catherine E 4:46:26 (23,108)
Cord, Susan M 3:45:08 (7,715)
Cordery, Emma L 4:42:57 (22,316)
Cordingley, Janet P 3:42:55 (7,212)
Cordrey, Tina 7:08:21 (32,965)
Cordwell, June 3:58:53 (11,473)
Corkovic, Tanja 3:44:28 (7,558)
Cormack, Christine J 5:04:15 (26,480)
Cornell, Janet 4:51:58 (24,246)
Cornell, Stephanie L 5:11:44 (27,482)
Cornforth, Maggie F 4:34:46 (20,430)
Cornwell, Helen E 3:34:09 (5,505)
Corrall, Karen A 6:30:47 (32,473)
Corrigan, Amy R 4:59:48 (25,852)
Corrigan, Philomena 4:33:47 (20,203)
Corsini, Anna 4:41:37 (22,017)
Corsini, Susan J 3:25:17 (3,972)
Cosby, Beckie A 4:15:48 (15,544)
Coster, Debbie A 3:41:20 (6,882)
Costiff, Christine 3:11:19 (2,199)
Cottaris, Tracy M 4:16:52 (15,817)
Cottell, Robyn A 6:03:12 (31,692)
Cottell, Sarah L 3:40:34 (6,724)
Cotter, Joanne L 4:53:49 (24,639)
Cotter, Louise E 5:03:38 (26,409)
Cotter, Sarah 4:04:12 (12,756)
Cotterill, Fiona 3:37:34 (6,145)
Cotton, Nicola E 4:14:33 (15,216)
Cotton, Rebecca L 6:19:38 (32,222)
Cottrell, Maureen J 5:09:17 (27,181)
Cottrell, Sally 3:32:12 (5,203)
Couch, Elizabeth J 4:43:20 (22,395)
Couch, Lisa A 5:41:47 (30,484)
Coulbert, Julie A 3:58:31 (11,344)
Coulthard, Sally E 4:48:59 (23,648)
Coulthard, Tamsin V 5:06:05 (26,724)
Courage, Jennifer M 5:39:44 (30,340)
Court, Jilly P 5:26:40 (29,182)

Court, Ruth C....4:24:35 (17,837)
Courtauld, Sarah L....5:13:30 (27,721)
Courtman, Karin A....6:28:12 (32,426)
Courtney, Lucy V....4:43:21 (22,398)
Courtney-Smith, Lesley....6:39:14 (32,599)
Cousins, Lisa....4:59:32 (25,794)
Cousins, Wendy A....6:35:41 (32,539)
Covey, Jenny M....3:59:47 (11,755)
Cowan, Eleanor F....4:06:49 (13,303)
Cowan, Emma S....3:36:16 (5,888)
Cowan, Michelle....4:46:09 (23,038)
Cowdall, Alison....4:43:34 (22,458)
Cowdry, Rosalyne A....4:46:14 (23,056)
Cowell, Lucy N....5:04:27 (26,517)
Cowell, Ruth....3:48:35 (8,526)
Cowie, Laura....4:06:42 (13,275)
Cowley, Annie C....4:27:12 (18,555)
Cowley, Hillary....4:24:32 (17,809)
Cowley, Laura J....2:54:27 (758)
Cowling, Bronwen R....7:41:59 (33,146)
Cowling, Gert T....4:03:17 (12,549)
Cox, Alexandra L....4:23:34 (17,523)
Cox, Ann....5:17:52 (28,230)
Cox, Anna M....4:53:20 (24,535)
Cox, Charlotte....4:58:51 (25,675)
Cox, Donna....6:09:13 (31,902)
Cox, Emma A....5:31:33 (29,707)
Cox, Emma K....5:07:38 (26,954)
Cox, Fran H....5:05:29 (26,644)
Cox, Georgina F....4:41:40 (22,030)
Cox, Jacqueline M....5:13:09 (27,671)
Cox, Janice A....7:00:51 (32,888)
Cox, Michelle J....5:38:27 (30,247)
Cox, Sarah....5:35:09 (29,981)
Cox, Sharon E....4:57:34 (25,411)
Cox, Sonia C....3:53:50 (9,873)
Cox, Susannah C....5:43:58 (30,634)
Coxall, Sian M....5:23:02 (28,832)
Coxeter Smith, Helen J....4:25:52 (18,215)
Coxhead, Dawn....4:00:31 (11,941)
Coxon, Linda J....4:33:50 (20,209)
Coyle, Colette E....5:10:23 (27,316)
Coyle, Janice....4:00:03 (11,834)
Coyne, Glenis V....4:55:21 (24,972)
Coyne, Jenny....5:32:45 (29,794)
Coyne, Mary B....4:38:25 (21,316)
Crabb, Mary J....4:12:06 (14,595)
Crabtree, Linda C....3:31:35 (5,084)
Cracknell, Joanne P....5:25:27 (29,079)
Craddock, Elizabeth A....5:06:44 (26,824)
Craig, Charlotte J....4:01:58 (12,255)
Craig, Evelyn J....5:26:50 (29,204)
Craig, Liz L....4:47:32 (23,329)
Craig, Mary....3:47:42 (8,298)
Craig, Sue....5:45:16 (30,736)
Craig-Humphreys, Joanne....5:19:52 (28,479)
Craigie, Eve N....5:58:21 (31,478)
Cramer, Suzanne....5:46:37 (30,833)
Crampton, Rachael A....3:34:31 (5,571)
Crane, Alison K....3:20:52 (3,387)
Crane, Denise....4:25:47 (18,189)
Crane, Roberta....4:33:46 (20,199)
Crane, Victoria L....3:36:26 (5,923)
Cranmer, Rosamund H....4:49:51 (23,813)
Crassier-Mokdad, Cecile....3:51:55 (9,341)
Craven, Laura E....6:29:23 (32,438)
Craven, Ruth O....4:30:36 (19,454)
Crawford, Beverly J....5:45:58 (30,777)
Crawford, Glynis....4:23:53 (17,618)
Crawford, Helen E....4:49:29 (23,752)
Crawford, Katherine J....4:29:36 (19,199)
Crawford, Lisa C....4:33:04 (20,019)
Crawford, Lynsey J....4:37:47 (21,173)
Crawford, Rebecca J....3:38:32 (6,334)
Crawford, Sarah R....4:29:37 (19,206)
Crawley, Amy G....4:00:06 (11,843)
Crawley, Anita D....3:33:29 (5,403)
Crawley, Victoria R....4:05:46 (13,090)
Crawshaw, Katherine....4:31:27 (19,651)
Cray, Clare I....4:57:15 (25,362)
Crayford, Joanne C....4:45:18 (22,856)
Crealy, Louise....3:55:48 (10,479)
Cream, Tania J....3:31:47 (5,115)
Crean, Amy....4:35:32 (20,607)
Creasey, Lin L....6:08:49 (31,889)
Creasy, Carol....5:56:26 (31,377)
Creed, Jo C....5:00:03 (25,894)
Creed, Julie J....5:13:24 (27,705)
Creely, Siobhan H....5:16:00 (27,999)
Creighton, Denise M....6:01:26 (31,623)
Cremen, Sandra....4:21:44 (17,036)
Cremin, Hannah V....6:07:04 (31,821)
Cremmer, Jennifer A....4:28:55 (18,998)
Crerar, Joanna D....5:47:56 (30,941)
Crews, Sharon....4:07:48 (13,555)
Crick, Judy A....4:46:31 (23,124)
Cripps, Ruth A....5:09:09 (27,167)
Crisp, Jodie....3:56:32 (10,694)
Critchell, Dawn A....2:56:02 (850)
Critchley, Barbara A....3:43:32 (7,358)
Critchley, Marlene J....4:34:03 (20,267)
Crocker, Habe....3:44:11 (7,488)
Crocker, Jennifer H....5:57:47 (31,444)
Crocker, Jessica J....4:52:35 (24,377)
Crockett, Kim J....5:32:54 (29,808)
Crockett, Phillipa M....4:09:10 (13,895)
Crofton, Sue A....6:45:35 (32,705)
Croker, Laura J....3:55:53 (10,505)
Croker, Sarah J....5:01:19 (26,086)
Cronin-Jones, Susan....4:07:18 (13,420)
Crook, Amanda E....4:14:02 (15,080)
Crook, Amy L....7:16:20 (33,014)
Crook, Nicola....4:38:24 (21,315)
Crook, Sally A....4:18:03 (16,119)
Crook, Tanya....3:54:08 (9,953)
Crookes, Vanessa-Jane....3:28:05 (4,420)
Crooks, Alison....5:19:04 (28,383)
Crooks, Lynn S....3:58:28 (11,329)
Crook-Wiliams, Lusette M....5:20:10 (28,516)
Crosland, Rachel S....3:57:26 (10,989)
Cross, Anna C....4:45:44 (22,952)
Cross, Charmaine G....3:54:38 (10,086)
Cross, Christine E....5:29:13 (29,445)
Cross, Dee C....5:05:54 (26,695)
Cross, Denise....3:40:10 (6,652)
Cross, Jillian L....4:35:56 (20,698)
Cross, Kate....3:55:34 (10,390)
Cross, Marion....5:54:21 (31,275)
Cross, Mary B....5:05:17 (26,620)
Crossland, Natalie C....3:48:34 (8,517)
Crotty, Iryna E....4:59:09 (25,730)
Crouch, Amy L....5:07:05 (26,874)
Croucher, Helen....4:18:37 (16,259)
Crow, Karen....4:47:08 (23,240)
Crowe, Chantal M....3:28:24 (4,495)
Crowe, Katie A....3:45:34 (7,814)
Crowe, Lynda A....6:21:58 (32,287)
Crowe, Rebecca L....6:21:58 (32,287)
Crowe, Sue M....4:16:45 (15,789)
Crowe, Suzy....3:29:35 (4,739)
Crowhurst, Paula L....4:27:37 (18,662)
Crowl, Charlotte A....5:19:35 (28,448)
Crowle, Revis M....2:55:45 (832)
Crowley, Sharon....4:01:48 (12,214)
Crowson, Jackie A....5:43:23 (30,601)
Crowther, Ann....5:54:24 (31,280)
Crowther, Lucy A....4:51:24 (24,121)
Crowther, Lucy E....5:29:26 (29,475)
Crowther, Rachel P....4:19:28 (16,469)
Crowther, Sarah J....4:17:30 (15,981)
Croxford, Liza J....5:11:06 (27,398)
Crozier, Lisa M....4:34:03 (20,267)
Cruickshank, Emma....4:47:13 (23,266)
Crummay, Fiona M....4:32:03 (19,801)
Cruz, Katie A....4:27:18 (18,578)
Cubberley, Rachael R....3:37:49 (6,194)
Cuckney, Kate J....4:37:01 (20,985)
Cuelton, Sian L....4:54:51 (24,864)
Culham, Larraine A....4:30:33 (19,439)
Culkin, Sandra A....4:58:31 (25,614)
Cullen, Jennifer R....4:31:31 (19,668)
Cullen, Violet R....5:24:06 (28,956)
Culliford, Nicola A....5:18:53 (28,354)
Cullum, Gail P....3:47:54 (8,354)
Cullum, Sue M....3:57:01 (10,847)
Culshaw, Janice E....3:42:55 (7,212)
Cumber, Claire L....4:48:44 (23,594)
Cumming, Henrietta....4:43:25 (22,414)
Cummings, Emma L....4:23:09 (17,397)
Cummins, Brooke N....4:41:25 (21,973)
Cummins, Fiona S....3:39:10 (6,467)
Cummins, Karen T....4:25:11 (18,023)
Cunliffe, Jane....5:06:25 (26,774)
Cunliffe, Jessica J....3:28:04 (4,416)
Cunningham, Alichea A....7:09:24 (32,972)
Cunningham, Fay L....4:07:33 (13,486)
Cunningham, Lindsay....5:09:45 (27,238)
Curlew, Jennifer C....5:10:01 (27,271)
Curling, Clare A....4:32:11 (19,827)
Curno, Melanie J....4:10:17 (14,169)
Curnock, Emma J....4:25:18 (18,054)
Curnow, Denise C....5:46:30 (30,826)
Curran, Sarah T....4:07:03 (13,356)
Currell, Justine A....4:35:11 (20,527)
Currie, Misha....5:36:26 (30,090)
Currimjee, Nadine....4:28:24 (18,871)
Currington, Debra J....4:44:59 (22,778)
Curry, Helen L....4:52:16 (24,296)
Curry, Joanna....3:57:12 (10,920)
Curry, Peter J....3:53:00 (9,626)
Curry, Susan M....3:17:24 (2,931)
Curtin, Eimear C....3:39:32 (6,547)
Curtin, Helen M....3:23:33 (3,717)
Curtis, Janet....5:30:01 (29,547)
Curtis, Sarah L....4:22:56 (17,350)
Cuthbertson, Sarah J....5:21:16 (28,642)
Cutler, Deborah E....4:35:52 (20,685)
Cutner, Christine J....4:01:54 (12,236)
Cutting, Donna M....5:28:40 (29,397)
Cwiklinski, Laura J....6:59:52 (32,879)
Czerniewska, Pam R....4:20:30 (16,736)
D Alton, Emma K....3:19:32 (3,195)
Da Silva, Katherine M....4:49:53 (23,817)
Da Silva, Sophie....3:54:52 (10,165)
Dable, Pauline M....4:19:17 (16,418)
Dack, Anne E....5:36:20 (30,084)
Dadds, Rachel E....4:54:07 (24,700)
Dagestad, Inger J....4:52:22 (24,325)
Dagger, Bethany....4:58:44 (25,653)
Daglish, Tracy M....4:51:24 (24,121)
Dagne, Birhan....2:49:48 (533)
Dahle, Astrid....3:52:39 (9,538)
Dakin, Sue M....6:47:54 (32,738)
Dal Pozzo, Sarah....5:37:27 (30,159)
Dale, Joy....4:10:10 (14,142)
Dale, Kate....4:53:19 (24,529)
Dale, Natalie....5:32:45 (29,794)
Dale, Nicola I....4:16:23 (15,688)
Dale, Sue I....3:41:06 (6,827)
Dale, Zoe L....5:12:21 (27,568)
Daley, Loretta E....3:50:10 (8,908)
Daley, Rachel A....5:51:20 (31,146)
Daley, Susan....7:24:41 (33,066)
Daley, Susan H....4:04:42 (12,858)
Dalgarno, Charlotte E....6:01:12 (31,613)
Dalglish, Emma-Rose J....5:12:04 (27,532)
Dalladay, Carmen J....4:30:21 (19,388)
Dallimore, Caroline E....4:09:10 (13,895)
Dalrymple, Susan....4:29:02 (19,034)
Dalton, Lettie P....5:38:16 (30,231)
Daly, Gwen....4:07:09 (13,390)
Dalzell, Julie....4:11:31 (14,462)
Dalziel, Margaret R....6:51:11 (32,775)
Damen, Janet M....3:46:43 (8,066)
Dammone, Karen L....4:58:43 (25,650)
Damore, Maureen....4:12:24 (14,681)
Daniel, Claire....3:57:02 (10,852)
Daniel, Lynn C....4:38:22 (21,310)
Daniel, Ramona....5:55:11 (31,314)
Daniels, Catrin....3:56:03 (10,552)
Daniels, Irena....4:46:48 (23,171)
Daniels, Michelle....6:32:14 (32,486)
Dansey, Susanne E....5:32:08 (29,751)
Danvers, Natalie S....4:30:31 (19,432)
Darbey, Andrea C....3:46:40 (8,055)
Darby, Catherine M....3:13:21 (2,443)
Darby, Sarah L....6:56:14 (32,843)
Dargan, Tracey....4:33:23 (20,106)
Dargie, Kate E....4:12:50 (14,786)

Dargiel, Aleksandra......5:10:44 (27,358)
Darke, Tracy A......3:19:20 (3,175)
Darkin, Beverley......4:16:57 (15,847)
Darley, Claire L......5:59:27 (31,533)
Darmody, Penelope E......4:09:19 (13,937)
Darsley, Anne L......3:35:54 (5,818)
Darvill, Nicola J......5:34:24 (29,923)
Das Simpson, Sonali N......6:06:35 (31,807)
Dav Ies, Emma J......5:16:52 (28,113)
Davanzo, Alison......4:19:07 (16,368)
Davenport, Angela M......5:26:54 (29,215)
Davenport, Diane T......5:43:49 (30,627)
Davenport, Janet L......5:36:08 (30,067)
Davey, Antoinette M......6:20:40 (32,244)
Davey, Madeleine L......4:28:50 (18,979)
Davey, Tina D......6:54:27 (32,816)
David, Anna......3:23:06 (3,667)
Davidoff, Vanessa......4:12:55 (14,816)
Davidson, Amanda......4:20:02 (16,607)
Davidson, Ann......4:18:24 (16,209)
Davidson, Anne......4:18:54 (16,325)
Davidson, Christiana C......4:16:50 (15,811)
Davidson, Deborah J......4:53:43 (24,622)
Davidson, Karen......4:37:40 (21,152)
Davidson, Nicki J......3:47:06 (8,145)
Davidson, Sharon G......4:30:03 (19,309)
Davidson, Susanna C......4:58:11 (25,544)
Davidson, Valerie M......4:54:45 (24,828)
Davidson, Violet......4:07:55 (13,587)
Davies, Adele M......6:08:30 (31,876)
Davies, Adele R......4:16:28 (15,714)
Davies, Amy F......5:37:41 (30,179)
Davies, Anneli......6:12:41 (32,010)
Davies, Belinda......3:08:18 (1,884)
Davies, Carol-Ann......3:22:45 (3,628)
Davies, Caroline M......4:41:26 (21,978)
Davies, Caryl M......5:32:37 (29,779)
Davies, Ceri-Anne......3:22:35 (3,608)
Davies, Cynthia......6:17:15 (32,149)
Davies, Esther M......5:03:17 (26,359)
Davies, Fiona......2:51:50 (629)
Davies, Harriet E......4:09:29 (13,992)
Davies, Helen E......4:43:53 (22,543)
Davies, Helen E......4:45:01 (22,791)
Davies, Jackie S......6:21:45 (32,277)
Davies, Jacqueline......4:55:39 (25,028)
Davies, Jacqueline A......4:56:17 (25,159)
Davies, Jane A......3:55:00 (10,204)
Davies, Jane K......6:28:45 (32,432)
Davies, Jean M......4:30:17 (19,374)
Davies, Joanne L......4:15:19 (15,421)
Davies, Josephine......4:19:39 (16,516)
Davies, Joy L......4:27:53 (18,717)
Davies, Julie C......5:10:22 (27,313)
Davies, Karen......6:05:39 (31,782)
Davies, Karen E......3:53:10 (9,679)
Davies, Kate R......5:51:48 (31,173)
Davies, Kathryn E......5:34:20 (29,917)
Davies, Kim......4:51:34 (24,156)
Davies, Lisa......4:29:05 (19,053)
Davies, Lisa J......5:22:25 (28,768)
Davies, Rachel M......3:41:26 (6,900)
Davies, Rebecca H......5:56:11 (31,367)
Davies, Samantha J......6:49:57 (32,760)
Davies, Susan W......4:53:58 (24,670)
Davies, Wendy......5:16:04 (28,007)
Davies, Wendy A......3:18:48 (3,106)
Davies, Yvonne M......3:34:10 (5,509)
Davies, Zoe......5:24:53 (29,025)
Davis, Abigail A......5:39:04 (30,289)
Davis, Elizabeth J......5:21:19 (28,647)
Davis, Emma L......4:05:27 (13,011)
Davis, Emma L......4:51:54 (24,229)
Davis, Esther......4:11:45 (14,508)
Davis, Janet......4:10:04 (14,115)
Davis, Joanne C......5:18:07 (28,257)
Davis, Katie......4:42:20 (22,185)
Davis, Katie......4:44:15 (22,625)
Davis, Mary J......4:34:20 (20,321)
Davis, Natalie E......4:59:42 (25,836)
Davis, Pauline M......5:03:21 (26,364)
Davis, Rachel F......5:07:13 (26,895)
Davis, Sarah J......3:14:47 (2,637)
Davis, Tracey J......5:00:23 (25,958)
Davison, Michele A......6:43:30 (32,666)
Davy, Peta Jane......4:36:25 (20,828)
Daw, Sharon L......3:05:39 (1,629)
Dawe, Barbara A......4:56:53 (25,278)
Dawe, Esther E......4:54:40 (24,808)
Dawes, Lisa......4:05:15 (12,971)
Dawkins, Justine C......4:55:03 (24,907)
Dawkins, Kerry J......4:25:57 (18,244)
Dawkins, Pauline D......5:06:25 (26,774)
Dawkins, Yvonne J......6:26:06 (32,377)
Dawson, Amy L......4:26:18 (18,335)
Dawson, Chrissie......5:42:39 (30,545)
Dawson, Christine R......3:24:59 (3,930)
Dawson, Gail......2:59:09 (1,154)
Dawson, Joanna M......4:31:43 (19,725)
Dawson, Kelly A......4:53:44 (24,626)
Dawson, Lisa J......6:42:02 (32,641)
Dawson, Sally H......5:24:18 (28,971)
Dawson, Sara L......5:18:41 (28,333)
Dawson, Sophie J......3:31:02 (4,990)
Dawson, Zoe A......3:25:58 (4,069)
Day, Elaine A......7:56:15 (33,173)
Day, Helen V......4:30:44 (19,480)
Day, Joanne......6:31:02 (32,476)
Day, Joanne L......4:26:30 (18,384)
Day, Jodie L......5:19:02 (28,381)
Day, Julia M......4:46:50 (23,182)
Day, Karen M......4:28:11 (18,802)
Day, Michelle A......5:47:43 (30,930)
Day, Tina A......5:28:56 (29,422)
Dayde, Sylvie......4:16:13 (15,650)
De Asha, Anne L......4:20:42 (16,789)
De Boer, Shelley D......5:35:29 (30,011)
De Boer Van Dam, Claudia M......3:52:22 (9,458)
De Boltz, Deborah M......6:42:27 (32,645)
De Boos, Claire F......4:17:56 (16,088)
De Bruin, Margrete I......5:14:11 (27,796)
De Bues, Jennifer M......5:34:33 (29,936)
De Cothi, Elizabeth......3:41:57 (7,012)
De Gouveia, Ana......4:36:30 (20,844)
De Heveningham, Emma A......4:51:10 (24,072)
De Hol, Micheline......4:22:15 (17,188)
De La Mothe, Emma J......5:30:25 (29,582)
De Moraes, Camilla A......5:22:16 (28,749)
De Salis, Karen L......6:26:06 (32,377)
De Souza, Yoko......6:18:02 (32,172)
De Zoete, Fiona C......5:04:49 (26,558)
Deacon, Angela M......4:10:25 (14,196)
Deacon, Catherine S......5:41:52 (30,491)
Deakin, Karen J......4:29:13 (19,088)
Dean, Cathy N......5:34:49 (29,955)
Dean, Dixie H......4:38:13 (21,284)
Deans, Carla J......4:55:30 (24,997)
Deans, Michelle A......5:00:27 (25,967)
Dear, Jane H......3:45:03 (7,701)
Dear, Sarah L......6:36:49 (32,557)
Dearlove, Annabel C......4:37:52 (21,189)
Deas, Margaret......4:19:53 (16,577)
Deasy, Joanne......4:39:01 (21,444)
Debleu, Claire......4:52:54 (24,437)
Decker, Helen J......2:56:52 (926)
Dedman, Shelley......4:49:16 (23,707)
Deegan, Julie......3:09:50 (2,049)
Deery, Anny C......4:00:20 (11,896)
Defries, Julie T......4:23:10 (17,406)
Dejager, Nicole......4:52:56 (24,443)
Delahunt, Miriam......5:01:36 (26,120)
Deller, Suzanne......5:26:14 (29,144)
Dell-Price, Carol......4:15:11 (15,384)
Demery, Julia C......4:21:48 (17,062)
Dempsey, Helen C......5:21:38 (28,677)
Dempsey, Katherine M......4:31:49 (19,750)
Dempsey, Kira......5:46:03 (30,789)
Den Ouden, Tarynne J......5:35:54 (30,046)
Denby, Lucinda......4:23:14 (17,427)
Dench, Rachel E......4:15:48 (15,544)
Denham, Jo N......4:01:54 (12,236)
Denker, Ann Lynn......5:38:19 (30,235)
Denman, Emma J......3:56:37 (10,730)
Denmead, Dianne......4:25:40 (18,153)
Denne, Linda J......5:29:31 (29,487)
Dennis, Catherine T......4:25:41 (18,159)
Dennis, Cheryl A......5:20:30 (28,561)
Dennis, Maxine S......5:27:18 (29,250)
Dennison, Andrea M......2:55:13 (800)
Dennison, Audra L......3:08:15 (1,880)
Denny, Lorna......6:21:46 (32,278)
Denslow, Alison......4:31:33 (19,681)
Denton, Susan......3:53:38 (9,802)
Denyer, Alice L......4:34:02 (20,260)
Der Weduwen, Simone......4:37:39 (21,149)
Derbyshire, Elvira T......3:29:26 (4,704)
Dervish, Sheree......6:29:35 (32,443)
Deschamps, Christine......3:34:18 (5,533)
Desmond, Lara G......4:33:05 (20,025)
Dessuet, Isabelle......4:55:48 (25,054)
Deters, Kerstin......4:20:06 (16,629)
Devecchis, Kerrie M......5:14:32 (27,849)
Devereux, Alana C......3:53:46 (9,850)
Devereux, Kate A......5:24:37 (28,994)
Deville, Kim N......5:26:45 (29,193)
Devine, Andrea J......3:32:24 (5,234)
Devlin, Bernadette M......5:18:42 (28,335)
Devonish, Angela M......6:17:11 (32,147)
Dew, Fay......5:50:16 (31,094)
Dewar, Joanne P......4:14:50 (15,292)
Dewhirst, Nicola C......4:56:18 (25,164)
Dewhurst, Ingrid......4:31:07 (19,557)
Dewhurst, Sheila B......5:46:52 (30,853)
Dews, Emma M......3:06:31 (1,711)
Dey, Jane L......5:36:20 (30,084)
Dharmapriya, Melum......5:02:00 (26,177)
Dhupelia, Suni R......3:08:50 (1,939)
Di Franco, Sheena J......5:19:54 (28,482)
Di Tullio, Anne......3:29:34 (4,736)
Diaz, Rhessa......5:48:30 (30,969)
Dick, Katrina......4:29:06 (19,057)
Dick, Patricia A......3:27:13 (4,274)
Dickens, Joanna P......5:11:51 (27,507)
Dicker, Faye S......4:27:30 (18,621)
Dickerson, Anne M......3:52:10 (9,402)
Dickinson, Lesley A......4:39:12 (21,490)
Dickinson, Maxine......4:34:09 (20,280)
Dickinson, Sally......4:51:24 (24,121)
Dickinson, Tamsin K......4:19:35 (16,503)
Dickson, Leonora......5:46:16 (30,808)
Didovich, Diane M......4:35:30 (20,603)
Dieulefit, Nadine......4:06:40 (13,265)
Diffey, Joanne C......3:22:20 (3,575)
Dillon, Trina A......4:55:40 (25,032)
Dimmock, Kate......5:03:41 (26,415)
Dinnage, Tracy J......4:14:30 (15,206)
Dior, Suzy......5:08:50 (27,122)
Disbury, Rebecca......4:38:05 (21,251)
Disney, Glennys......3:15:18 (2,695)
Dita, Constantina......2:27:51 (56)
Ditchfield, Penny......3:36:45 (5,982)
Dix, Annette......3:59:56 (11,795)
Dix-Baker, Joanne E......3:59:21 (11,621)
Dixon, Chantelle E......4:34:40 (20,402)
Dixon, Karen......4:31:35 (19,692)
Dixon, Patricia M......4:07:27 (13,457)
Dixon, Tina K......5:34:13 (29,903)
Doake, Rebecca K......4:06:18 (13,194)
Dobbin, Caroline J......3:52:52 (9,585)
Dobbin, Gillian M......3:55:41 (10,431)
Dobie, Glenda L......3:36:51 (6,008)
Dobriskey, Sarah......7:13:41 (33,003)
Dobson, Caroline C......5:08:28 (27,071)
Dobson, Lesley A......3:39:37 (6,557)
Docherty, Helen R......4:48:34 (23,556)
Docherty, Kathleen......4:36:52 (20,955)
Dock, Katie......4:46:24 (23,103)
Dodd, Tara L......5:00:32 (25,975)
Dodd, Tracy......4:47:55 (23,414)
Doddington, Denise A......3:30:53 (4,960)
Dodds, Emma J......6:33:42 (32,511)
Dodgson, Stacey L......4:21:05 (16,886)
Doe, Emma L......6:18:30 (32,184)
Doel Van Den, Jorien L......3:52:14 (9,422)
Doheny, Laura M......4:18:54 (16,325)
Doherty, Bernadette T......6:12:34 (32,006)
Doherty, Clare......5:39:43 (30,339)
Doherty, Madeleine S......4:08:19 (13,695)
Dolan, Anne......4:42:40 (22,254)

Dolan, Carla 5:05:49 (26,680)
Dolan, Christine 6:46:09 (32,709)
Dolding, Lorraine J 4:33:39 (20,177)
Doleman, Samantha 4:25:18 (18,054)
Dollery, Sara L 4:53:41 (24,613)
Donald, Charmaine R 4:26:24 (18,361)
Donald, Julie 4:33:11 (20,055)
Donald, Kate L 3:44:53 (7,665)
Donald, Pauline A 3:49:22 (8,707)
Donaldson, Mandy S 4:10:53 (14,301)
Donaldson, Rosemary J 3:47:17 (8,187)
Donato, Alice N 3:43:02 (7,242)
Donin, Brunella 4:15:31 (15,481)
Donkersley, Kirsty J 4:43:48 (22,521)
Donnachie, Fiona J 5:11:28 (27,452)
Donnell, Laura A 6:15:03 (32,086)
Donnelly, Elaine M 4:22:25 (17,229)
Donnelly, Katherine S 4:14:25 (15,185)
Donnelly, Seaneen C 4:37:44 (21,165)
Donovan, Clare E 4:23:02 (17,369)
Donovan, Julie D 4:42:39 (22,249)
Donovan, Julie P 3:57:07 (10,888)
Donovan, Mary-Ellen I 4:30:11 (19,345)
Doodson, Sandra J 4:17:02 (15,870)
Dooley, Lauren C 4:52:58 (24,448)
Doores, Katie J 4:09:33 (14,004)
Dopson, Sarah L 3:52:49 (9,572)
Doria, Louise M 4:54:58 (24,887)
Dorman, Rosalind A 4:51:07 (24,063)
Dormer, Katherine J 3:54:53 (10,173)
Dorrance, Priscilla 5:45:12 (30,731)
Dorrell, Patricia A 4:08:16 (13,683)
Dorrington, Sandra M 6:25:43 (32,370)
Dorta, Cristina 5:55:32 (31,327)
Dossin, Teresinha S 5:29:35 (29,493)
Dotzek, Jane 4:18:17 (16,178)
Doubleday, Heather M 4:39:55 (21,658)
Dougall, Anne K 3:59:38 (11,702)
Doughty, Lucy C 4:43:59 (22,570)
Doughty, Victoria A 4:08:25 (13,722)
Douglas, Amanda J 4:39:55 (21,658)
Douglas, Cheryl 6:18:59 (32,200)
Douglas, Helen L 4:51:23 (24,117)
Douglas, Michelle C 4:51:13 (24,078)
Douglas, Trudy L 5:30:40 (29,613)
Douglass, Carolyn L 4:00:06 (11,843)
Doutaz Pingeon, Martine 4:07:41 (13,528)
Douthwaite, Donna M 4:10:28 (14,206)
Douthwaite, Hatty A 4:45:41 (22,942)
Dove, Amy J 3:54:41 (10,109)
Dover, Liz 3:43:52 (7,432)
Dowall, Karen A 5:15:40 (27,967)
Dowling, Gabrielle M 6:27:17 (32,409)
Down, Bernadette M 4:39:01 (21,444)
Downes, Ellen J 5:38:19 (30,235)
Downey, Fiona M 4:56:06 (25,119)
Downham, Diana 5:57:38 (31,439)
Downing, Rebecca 5:14:38 (27,860)
Downs, Gabrielle A 3:37:15 (6,082)
Downton, Julie A 6:11:23 (31,966)
Downton, Rachel H 4:54:06 (24,695)
Dowse, Gaye 5:29:27 (29,480)
Dowse, Julie K 5:48:29 (30,966)
Dowsett, Pauline 4:28:17 (18,833)
Dowty, Cynthia I 4:25:15 (18,042)
Doyle, Judith C 6:25:30 (32,365)
Doyle, Lisa R 5:19:56 (28,483)
Doyle, Nancy 6:00:56 (31,602)
Drake, Amanda K 4:47:18 (23,276)
Drake, Cheryl D 4:54:50 (24,856)
Drake, Michala 4:23:17 (17,440)
Drake, Sophie J 5:18:36 (28,321)
Drangsholt, Elin 3:20:06 (3,278)
Draper, Eleanor N 4:22:14 (17,185)
Draper, Kathryn L 4:43:23 (22,408)
Draper, Sara F 4:50:54 (24,025)
Draper, Stephanie C 5:16:11 (28,026)
Drew, Hayley A 6:32:33 (32,490)
Drewe, Kathleen A 4:52:09 (24,279)
Drewett, Aidan 4:48:23 (23,510)
Drinnan, Cindy 4:40:42 (21,829)
Driscoll, Glenis K 3:34:15 (5,520)
Driscoll, Helen T 4:39:47 (21,624)
Driscoll, Jean M 5:01:47 (26,145)
Driscoll, Sarah H 4:31:05 (19,548)
Driver, Carole D 4:23:45 (17,574)
Driver, Tracy 3:55:52 (10,496)
Droogan, Jacqueline M 4:58:30 (25,607)
Druitt, Catherine L 4:19:21 (16,433)
Drummond, Paula M 5:10:08 (27,279)
Drummond, Terrie A 5:12:21 (27,568)
Druvaskalns, Lina E 5:27:32 (29,278)
Dryden, Jennifer A 4:20:50 (16,817)
Dryhurst, Eleanor 4:35:58 (20,715)
Dryhurst, Sarah E 4:35:57 (20,709)
Drysdale, Jennifer C 6:53:54 (32,806)
D'Souza, Lynn J 4:53:26 (24,553)
Du Plessis, Louise 4:09:24 (13,963)
Dubeau, Sandra J 5:58:53 (31,499)
Dubery, Lindsay M 6:05:08 (31,766)
Dubois, Ann M 3:50:33 (8,998)
Dubouloz, Martine M 3:48:06 (8,403)
Duce, Lisa A 4:54:48 (24,848)
Ducker, Jackie A 3:59:16 (11,591)
Duff, Alicia 6:15:34 (32,103)
Duff, Leesa 3:39:15 (6,489)
Duffell, Linda J 3:38:55 (6,418)
Duffin, Janet K 4:55:30 (24,997)
Duffy, Catherine T 7:10:51 (32,988)
Duffy, Rita 4:00:45 (11,983)
Dufour, Mireille 4:18:59 (16,351)
Duggan, Andrea 4:49:16 (23,707)
Duggan, Elizabeth J 4:08:37 (13,773)
Duggan, Lorraine 5:04:43 (26,547)
Duigley, Kirsty L 6:27:41 (32,415)
Duijkers, Lieveke 4:59:43 (25,839)
Duke, Joanne D 4:52:45 (24,409)
Duling, Brittany 5:00:14 (25,934)
Dulley, Katherine T 3:42:17 (7,078)
Dumpleton, Julie N 4:47:00 (23,215)
Dunbar, Amanda K 4:18:08 (16,146)
Dunbar, Katrina M 5:59:09 (31,512)
Duncan, Catriona 3:51:49 (9,307)
Duncan, June A 3:41:25 (6,898)
Duncan, Katharine 5:07:44 (26,967)
Duncan, Lucy D 4:36:36 (20,868)
Duncan, Lucy J 4:44:11 (22,606)
Duncan, Tara J 4:37:29 (21,108)
Dungate, Stephanie M 4:41:13 (21,927)
Dunglinson, Helen 3:54:08 (9,953)
Dunham, Helen J 4:31:05 (19,548)
Dunley, Caroline J 5:03:10 (26,339)
Dunlop, Susan F 5:50:00 (31,074)
Dunn, Anna 6:52:22 (32,789)
Dunn, Caroline A 4:02:36 (12,400)
Dunn, Julie 4:49:05 (23,669)
Dunn, Julie E 4:21:21 (16,947)
Dunn, Lesley M 4:02:43 (12,415)
Dunn, Prunella 4:27:29 (18,618)
Dunphy, Sinead 5:14:36 (27,854)
Dunster, Carol A 5:06:54 (26,848)
Dupain, Hannah J 3:14:24 (2,583)
Duplessis, Sonja 5:04:19 (26,491)
Dupont, Beatrice 4:40:03 (21,684)
Durber, Vanessa A 5:23:04 (28,840)
Durn, Carol 4:42:04 (22,128)
Duro, Joanne L 5:37:50 (30,192)
Durow, Sandra 4:43:09 (22,360)
Durrant, Alison J 5:40:00 (30,365)
Durrant, Ann T 4:35:34 (20,615)
Dury, Beverley K 4:34:52 (20,449)
Duthie, Fiona E 5:04:19 (26,491)
Duthie, Mary J 5:47:25 (30,912)
Dutton, Clare E 5:22:34 (28,778)
Dutton, Kerry 5:27:48 (29,303)
Dwyer, Brenda J 5:31:25 (29,701)
Dyball, Laura 4:09:44 (14,039)
Dyde, Andrea F 5:44:21 (30,670)
Dyde, Rosalind H 4:54:42 (24,816)
Dye, Rachel H 4:14:05 (15,098)
Dyer, Caroline H 4:44:52 (22,748)
Dyer, Louise 4:49:06 (23,677)
Dyke, Rebecca K 7:18:30 (33,031)
Dykes, Victoria J 3:53:35 (9,787)
Dyson-Brown, Joanna 4:47:25 (23,296)
Eade, Barbara L 5:06:24 (26,772)
Eade, Elisa 4:49:02 (23,658)
Eade, Tara 5:41:18 (30,440)
Eagle, Lynda 3:57:51 (11,124)
Eaglesham, Claire A 8:42:55 (33,213)
Eardley, Jane R 3:27:38 (4,357)
Earl-Johnson, Rae A 7:14:43 (33,004)
Earnshaw, Dawn 4:59:10 (25,733)
Easdale, Sandra 5:03:20 (26,362)
East, Charlotte 3:31:37 (5,089)
East, Janet 5:38:02 (30,206)
East, Jennifer A 5:38:02 (30,206)
Eastaugh, Tina T 4:23:33 (17,520)
Eastham, Jane E 3:57:16 (10,937)
Easthill, Joanna W 4:30:04 (19,315)
Eastlake, Jenna C 4:25:08 (18,004)
Eastman, Alison C 3:20:10 (3,291)
Easton, Nicola J 5:24:09 (28,961)
Eaton, Emma J 3:51:51 (9,318)
Ebdon, Alison 4:00:21 (11,902)
Eckelmann, Baerbel 5:35:44 (30,030)
Eckersley, Lucy A 4:26:18 (18,335)
Eddington, Marianne 5:46:56 (30,858)
Eddleston, Susan P 5:32:40 (29,784)
Edenbrow, Amber C 4:05:30 (13,022)
Edet, Sara E 5:33:50 (29,876)
Edge, Diane E 4:09:04 (13,874)
Edgerton, Antonia C 4:13:04 (14,862)
Edgson, Zoe L 4:04:07 (12,744)
Edis, Sally-Anne E 5:02:39 (26,269)
Edmead, Tammy A 3:43:15 (7,300)
Edmondson, Rowena M 3:43:21 (7,320)
Edmunds, Kim Joy 3:30:19 (4,867)
Edmunds, Sarah 3:11:13 (2,182)
Edward, Philippa J 4:54:59 (24,891)
Edwards, Alexandra A 5:31:05 (29,669)
Edwards, Alwyn 5:35:06 (29,976)
Edwards, Amanda F 5:12:58 (27,645)
Edwards, Christine E 7:28:46 (33,090)
Edwards, Claire 4:31:37 (19,701)
Edwards, Clare D 4:30:28 (19,419)
Edwards, Clare R 5:10:00 (27,269)
Edwards, Fiona V 5:48:53 (30,994)
Edwards, Fizzy G 5:44:29 (30,679)
Edwards, Frances K 3:18:58 (3,129)
Edwards, Hannah M 3:43:22 (7,326)
Edwards, Jane A 4:37:05 (21,000)
Edwards, Joanna L 4:37:03 (20,989)
Edwards, Juliet J 4:02:36 (12,400)
Edwards, Karen L 4:36:12 (20,779)
Edwards, Kelly J 5:03:54 (26,446)
Edwards, Linda K 4:11:57 (14,563)
Edwards, Lisa 5:09:48 (27,241)
Edwards, Lucy J 3:21:53 (3,520)
Edwards, Maria J 4:51:54 (24,229)
Edwards, Maria M 4:59:27 (25,773)
Edwards, Natalie E 3:44:28 (7,558)
Edwards, Nicola L 6:30:41 (32,468)
Edwards, Nicola R 3:17:56 (2,988)
Edwards, Patricia 4:18:21 (16,199)
Edwards, Penny J 3:11:07 (2,167)
Edwards, Sally 4:58:42 (25,644)
Edwards, Sharon L 5:17:12 (28,151)
Edwards, Traci 3:53:26 (9,749)
Edwards, Wendy M 3:25:21 (3,987)
Egerton, Ingrid J 6:10:36 (31,947)
Egerton, Joanne M 5:58:29 (31,486)
Eggerstsdottir, Johanna K 4:04:04 (12,732)
Eggett, Heather 5:21:55 (28,704)
Eggleton, Jacqueline A 5:56:57 (31,404)
Egli, Nicole 3:25:13 (3,966)
Ehrenberg, Margaret 3:30:19 (4,867)
Eilerts De Haan, Carin 4:14:09 (15,122)
Eilertsen, Jennifer J 4:04:04 (12,732)
Einarsdottir, Anna 3:25:58 (4,069)
Eitrheim, Elisabeth 4:10:49 (14,282)
Ekanger, Morag 4:03:00 (12,477)
Eke, Tina H 4:16:36 (15,756)
Elachkar, Hala 4:39:29 (21,556)
Elder, Charlotte J 4:34:25 (20,347)
Eldred, Linda J 5:28:23 (29,366)
Eldridge, Samantha L 4:26:42 (18,430)
Elgar, Catherine J 4:22:45 (17,310)
El-Hage, Marsha L 4:21:25 (16,960)

Elkins, Sue 4:23:21 (17,454)
Ellerton, Joanne M 3:13:26 (2,457)
Ellery, Lucy E 3:50:18 (8,933)
Elleson, Elizabeth R 5:01:03 (26,054)
Ellingham, Caroline M 7:25:10 (33,073)
Elliot, Imogen G 6:14:47 (32,082)
Elliott, Anne 7:39:10 (33,140)
Elliott, Dawn 5:06:28 (26,784)
Elliott, Faith V 5:05:01 (26,583)
Elliott, Gemma V 4:39:29 (21,556)
Elliott, Jeanette M 5:03:03 (26,322)
Elliott, Katherine R 4:48:45 (23,596)
Elliott, Susie 4:35:20 (20,563)
Elliott, Vanessa 4:33:20 (20,092)
Elliott-Guest, Christine L 4:28:49 (18,976)
Ellis, Dee-Anne 4:35:20 (20,563)
Ellis, Denise E 4:12:29 (14,699)
Ellis, Jane E 4:41:58 (22,101)
Ellis, Laura J 4:54:31 (24,781)
Ellis, Lucy A 4:41:39 (22,028)
Ellis, Mary 5:13:23 (27,701)
Ellis, Melanie J 2:54:23 (752)
Ellis, Michelle A 4:48:35 (23,563)
Ellis, Pandora J 4:43:49 (22,523)
Ellis, Sally 4:34:50 (20,444)
Ellis, Suzanne 5:31:04 (29,664)
Ellis, Teresa L 4:42:07 (22,138)
Ellison, Jane 4:17:04 (15,877)
Ellison, Jane E 5:11:26 (27,446)
Ellison, Sherine 5:29:14 (29,449)
Ellman, Lucia 5:04:18 (26,489)
Elmes, Flavia C 4:13:54 (15,042)
Eloquin, Sophie C 4:19:43 (16,534)
Elphick, Katie J 4:45:22 (22,877)
Else, Claire A 4:24:59 (17,953)
Elsley, Sharon E 5:26:47 (29,199)
Elsmore, Di C 4:11:15 (14,402)
Elston, Frances M 4:52:31 (24,358)
Elswood, Sacha 5:49:03 (31,002)
Elverd, Narlap 5:56:22 (31,373)
Elwin, Jean E 4:24:14 (17,725)
Emerson, Katie M 4:58:14 (25,555)
Emery, Sophie C 5:33:32 (29,849)
Emmerson, Lara R 4:38:08 (21,268)
Emmott, Rebecca J 4:59:05 (25,720)
Emsley, Victoria L 3:46:21 (7,974)
Enderby, Valerie A 5:46:11 (30,800)
Endicott, Linda 4:02:20 (12,337)
Endres, Vanessa 4:55:32 (25,003)
Engen, Beathe 4:38:59 (21,436)
England, Debra J 5:16:18 (28,045)
England, Helen 4:46:51 (23,185)
Engler, Anna 4:11:16 (14,406)
Enhard, Susanne 3:32:29 (5,246)
Ennis, Marie F 4:16:17 (15,664)
Ennor, Zoe 5:59:10 (31,513)
Enright, Esther 5:12:17 (27,563)
Ensil, Mairon J 5:57:17 (31,419)
Ensor, Joanna 4:43:06 (22,346)
Eriksson, Nel 5:31:02 (29,659)
Eriksson, Sarah L 3:59:22 (11,630)
Erlach, Andrea 3:27:44 (4,368)
Erskine, Lorraine A 5:23:33 (28,889)
Erskine, Rosemary G 4:10:09 (14,135)
Ersking, Linda 5:39:55 (30,354)
Ertel, Whitney L 4:42:12 (22,156)
Eson, Sharon A 4:08:01 (13,616)
Espey, Jennifer M 4:02:21 (12,342)
Esser, Amy F 3:57:46 (11,100)
Esterhuysen, Danielle 3:55:46 (10,468)
Etchells, Sarah J 5:07:39 (26,957)
Etheridge, Helen D 4:24:33 (17,824)
Etheridge, Nicola J 4:42:02 (22,121)
Etherington, Catherine L 4:40:08 (21,697)
Euart-James, Elizabeth 6:37:59 (32,578)
Evanglista, Elizabeth C 4:26:28 (18,376)
Evans, Alison R 4:20:37 (16,766)
Evans, Angela 3:09:49 (2,048)
Evans, Anne-Marie 3:46:23 (7,979)
Evans, Bernadette M 4:25:25 (18,095)
Evans, Beth L 6:48:42 (32,740)
Evans, Catherine L 4:06:29 (13,228)
Evans, Claire L 4:15:01 (15,342)
Evans, Debbie 5:01:43 (26,136)
Evans, Denise 3:47:36 (8,270)
Evans, Emily J 5:34:25 (29,925)
Evans, Felicity C 4:28:03 (18,762)
Evans, Glenys 6:17:06 (32,144)
Evans, Hannah E 5:57:28 (31,432)
Evans, Hannah M 5:18:04 (28,248)
Evans, Helen E 3:05:16 (1,603)
Evans, Isabel 4:24:43 (17,875)
Evans, Jane D 5:06:14 (26,746)
Evans, Jessica S 3:57:27 (10,996)
Evans, Joan M 6:32:48 (32,496)
Evans, Jocelyn L 4:14:26 (15,190)
Evans, Karen 4:29:09 (19,070)
Evans, Kim E 5:42:18 (30,521)
Evans, Lucy M 4:23:28 (17,493)
Evans, Maggie E 5:22:07 (28,728)
Evans, Marian 4:50:12 (23,881)
Evans, Myfanwy A 4:33:08 (20,043)
Evans, Natalie A 4:30:40 (19,467)
Evans, Natasha R 4:15:56 (15,583)
Evans, Nicola J 4:34:01 (20,249)
Evans, Rachel 4:26:34 (18,397)
Evans, Rowena F 3:28:37 (4,533)
Evans, Sandra D 4:46:20 (23,086)
Evans, Sara 6:17:29 (32,156)
Evans, Sian E 3:51:15 (9,160)
Evans, Steph 7:18:22 (33,030)
Evans, Susan 5:15:20 (27,940)
Evans, Terri 4:33:33 (20,149)
Evans, Victoria J 4:29:57 (19,282)
Evelyn, Sabina S 6:56:42 (32,852)
Everett, Julie 4:17:04 (15,877)
Evert, Belinda J 4:00:40 (11,969)
Evtushenko, Lana 4:50:36 (23,960)
Ewaterman, Kerry 6:26:24 (32,389)
Eyles, Rebecca 5:23:47 (28,916)
Eyre, Annabelle C 5:35:33 (30,018)
Eyre, Helen M 4:16:30 (15,727)
Eyres, Michelle M 4:48:37 (23,571)
Ezekiel, Nina 5:08:11 (27,032)
Ezugwu, Ginika L 5:56:32 (31,383)
Fabrini, Francesca 3:44:43 (7,621)
Fackerell, Karon L 3:44:16 (7,511)
Fagan, Laurraine D 5:09:30 (27,205)
Faherty, Louise J 3:15:12 (2,683)
Fahy, Aodhnait S 4:27:36 (18,655)
Fahy, Clodagh B 4:16:16 (15,660)
Fairbrother, Davina 4:09:47 (14,054)
Fairbrother, Jodie M 4:24:52 (17,906)
Fairclough, Gail J 4:30:32 (19,436)
Fairclough, Janet 4:56:54 (25,281)
Fairlamb, Patricia A 4:33:25 (20,113)
Fairs, Jeanne M 4:37:54 (21,196)
Fairweather, Sharon 3:59:58 (11,806)
Falconer, Kay I 6:24:50 (32,351)
Falconi, Ricardo 3:29:43 (4,765)
Falkner, Emma C 5:07:56 (26,996)
Falkner, Jane E 4:18:01 (16,113)
Fall, Suzanne L 4:53:11 (24,504)
Falsey, Maura B 3:55:59 (10,537)
Fanning, Jane L 3:40:10 (6,652)
Fantom, Amy 6:37:56 (32,577)
Farbridge, Nicola L 4:31:38 (19,705)
Farebrother, Alice J 5:25:27 (29,079)
Farley, Carol J 4:23:12 (17,414)
Farley, Dannielle L 6:08:27 (31,873)
Farley, Janice D 5:55:09 (31,313)
Farley, Mary 7:34:11 (33,116)
Farley, Sarah 5:30:03 (29,549)
Farman, Michelle M 3:18:36 (3,083)
Farmer, Alice 4:45:30 (22,904)
Farmer, Elizabeth A 4:16:45 (15,789)
Farmer, Jenny 3:45:29 (7,802)
Farnall, Rebecca 4:30:06 (19,324)
Farnell, Tanya C 6:13:24 (32,032)
Farney, Sarah L 3:54:32 (10,061)
Farquhar, Alexandra E 4:15:41 (15,514)
Farquhar, Karen A 4:54:44 (24,823)
Farr, Natasha 3:55:04 (10,233)
Farrall, Ali 3:38:35 (6,346)
Farrant, Catriona M 5:53:26 (31,237)
Farrell, Frances M 5:15:29 (27,950)
Farrell, Julia D 5:33:33 (29,853)
Farrell, Megan L 4:07:07 (13,377)
Farrell, Sandra A 4:32:52 (19,970)
Farren, Joanna M 6:19:29 (32,219)
Farrer, Lucy E 4:22:24 (17,226)
Farrow, Jane L 3:51:51 (9,318)
Farrow, Lin 4:36:44 (20,910)
Farrow, Sharon B 4:23:12 (17,414)
Farrugia, Claire 4:44:36 (22,690)
Faulkner, Angela-Louise 5:22:43 (28,801)
Faulkner, Jodie M 4:15:12 (15,387)
Favero, Susi A 4:42:37 (22,241)
Favre, Aline 5:18:28 (28,304)
Fawcett, Trudy J 3:14:10 (2,551)
Fawcett-Eustace, Zoe A 5:18:38 (28,326)
Fay, Helen J 3:59:45 (11,747)
Fay, Sandra A 4:30:55 (19,512)
Fearnside, Maureen 5:11:44 (27,482)
Featherstone, Kate V 3:59:26 (11,651)
Featherstone, Suzanne 8:19:11 (33,196)
Fee, Monica M 3:27:32 (4,339)
Feeney, Jaimie L 3:55:50 (10,485)
Feeney, Kelly M 7:03:32 (32,924)
Feeney, Lynnette 5:51:35 (31,161)
Felkl, Peter 4:56:31 (25,210)
Fell, Carol S 5:24:03 (28,949)
Fellingham, Emma L 4:28:47 (18,969)
Felstead, Michelle A 5:13:14 (27,681)
Feltham, Rebecca T 4:06:21 (13,202)
Feneley, Jane 3:35:13 (5,709)
Fenelon, Patsy E 3:51:12 (9,147)
Fenn, Catherine A 3:52:34 (9,510)
Fenn, Fiona H 4:15:13 (15,392)
Fenner, Nicola C 5:02:23 (26,236)
Fenner, Sarah E 4:33:03 (20,016)
Fenton, Nicki C 4:22:35 (17,260)
Ferguson, Elaine L 4:12:36 (14,726)
Ferguson, Heather J 4:12:37 (14,729)
Ferguson, Lorna 4:22:01 (17,121)
Ferguson, Naomi L 3:41:37 (6,948)
Ferguson, Tracey B 5:27:48 (29,303)
Fergusson, Leanne 3:53:47 (9,853)
Fergusson-Kelly, Helen 5:17:47 (28,219)
Fernhomberg, Angelika 5:02:38 (26,266)
Ferrand, Helen M 5:14:31 (27,845)
Ferrari, Anita C 6:30:11 (32,451)
Ferrari, Claire E 4:25:39 (18,145)
Ferrier, Joanna 4:33:32 (20,142)
Ferrin-Erdozarn, Maite 4:39:19 (21,521)
Ferriroli, Sarah 4:49:32 (23,764)
Ferris, Alisa M 4:33:36 (20,166)
Ferris, Anne E 5:30:46 (29,625)
Fever, Sheryl J 4:31:08 (19,566)
Fewins, Alison 6:45:08 (32,693)
Fickling, Emma J 5:40:48 (30,414)
Field, Anna L 3:30:35 (4,911)
Field, Sue M 5:11:18 (27,427)
Field, Vanessa E 5:42:42 (30,549)
Filby, Melissa P 6:03:52 (31,722)
Filewood, Fiona 4:07:40 (13,525)
Fillekes, Fieke 4:41:27 (21,982)
Filloux, Catherine 4:45:57 (22,995)
Filsell, Vikki C 3:28:14 (4,448)
Finch, Amanda J 4:26:59 (18,503)
Finch, Charlotte E 6:15:11 (32,089)
Finch, Samantha J 3:56:29 (10,681)
Findlater, Jean 4:33:25 (20,113)
Findlay, Celia A 3:35:33 (5,759)
Findlay, Joanne 4:15:14 (15,398)
Findlay, Susan A 3:42:08 (7,050)
Findlay, Vanessa Z 5:12:45 (27,621)
Finkel, Joanne 5:08:42 (27,106)
Finlay, Heather A 5:13:02 (27,659)
Finlay, Helga J 4:45:15 (22,850)
Finlayson, Mary L 7:17:38 (33,026)
Finley, Joan 5:35:23 (30,001)
Finn, Anna K 4:21:49 (17,067)
Finnamore, Rebecca J 4:30:12 (19,350)
Finnegan, Anna E 4:17:27 (15,969)
Finney, Louise K 5:05:04 (26,591)
Finnie, Emma V 4:57:59 (25,500)
Fionda, Helen 5:26:06 (29,136)
Firman, Sarah-Jane 4:18:33 (16,246)

Firth, Diane 5:07:32 (26,934)
Firth, Emma J 4:56:17 (25,159)
Firth, Louise A.................4:42:49 (22,288)
Firth, Mellissa 3:59:39 (11,711)
Fischer, Carmen 4:22:22 (17,215)
Fischer, Helga..................4:40:03 (21,684)
Fish, Kathryn J 4:51:45 (24,198)
Fisher, Abigail C...............5:35:32 (30,017)
Fisher, Catrina J...............4:22:22 (17,215)
Fisher, Hope 3:49:36 (8,769)
Fisher, Jane B....................4:13:53 (15,039)
Fisher, Lynsey A................5:13:13 (27,679)
Fisher, Natasha M..............4:47:05 (23,231)
Fisher, Rispa J...................5:06:11 (26,737)
Fisher, Samantha S............4:27:46 (18,686)
Fisher, Sarah E..................4:29:26 (19,153)
Fisher, Susan J..................5:35:46 (30,038)
Fisher, Victoria J...............4:09:18 (13,934)
Fitchett, Eve.....................5:12:21 (27,568)
Fitt, Suzy 3:06:13 (1,688)
Fitzgerald, Emma L............5:14:31 (27,845)
Fitzgerald, Jillian M...........4:37:54 (21,196)
Fitzgerald, Kristina M.........5:06:42 (26,815)
Fitzgerald, Nicola C 5:25:08 (29,053)
Fitzpartrick, Rachel M 4:41:37 (22,017)
Fitzpatric, Wendy L 3:30:54 (4,963)
Fitzpatrick, Sue 5:08:29 (27,077)
Fitzsimmons, Anna P 4:55:45 (25,047)
Fitzsimon, Bethan 5:26:57 (29,218)
Fitzwater, Helen 4:55:16 (24,955)
Fitzwater, Trudy A.............5:03:18 (26,361)
Flanders, Olga 5:18:23 (28,294)
Fleckney, Rebecca G 5:23:54 (28,928)
Flello, Lianne 5:29:58 (29,543)
Fleming, Bridget T.............4:37:47 (21,173)
Fleming, Helen 3:26:00 (4,074)
Fleming, Morna R..............4:02:15 (12,319)
Flemons, Kirstie J 4:10:53 (14,301)
Fletcher, Alison C..............5:48:59 (30,999)
Fletcher, Angela F..............5:24:40 (29,002)
Fletcher, Dani E.................4:50:23 (23,920)
Fletcher, Dawn J................4:14:07 (15,108)
Fletcher, Grace M..............6:35:14 (32,529)
Fletcher, Johanna 3:05:55 (1,656)
Fletcher, Julie A.................6:35:13 (32,528)
Fletcher, Kathryn E 3:25:44 (4,033)
Fletcher, Leanne 5:47:11 (30,877)
Fletcher, Lisa A.................4:11:12 (14,388)
Fletcher, Lisa M................5:42:16 (30,518)
Fletcher, Michelle 6:31:38 (32,481)
Fletcher, Patricia A............4:25:46 (18,184)
Fletcher, Rose 4:57:46 (25,448)
Fletcher, Sarah 3:55:34 (10,390)
Fletcher, Stephanie 4:12:51 (14,796)
Fletcher, Susan J...............5:29:30 (29,486)
Fletcher, Susan M..............4:06:23 (13,207)
Fletcher, Tracey 5:14:22 (27,825)
Fletcher, Vivienne A...........6:58:55 (32,866)
Flett, Nadine L 4:36:06 (20,752)
Flew, Elizbeth J 5:45:20 (30,741)
Fligg, Jayne A....................5:12:02 (27,527)
Flint, Michelle E.................4:01:00 (12,052)
Flint, Sharon....................5:58:57 (31,502)
Flitcroft, Shelley 5:34:13 (29,903)
Flitton, Rowan 4:07:42 (13,536)
Flower, Virginia L...............5:01:11 (26,069)
Flude, Amanda J.................4:50:19 (23,911)
Flury, Joanna C..................3:34:24 (5,547)
Flynn, Karen L...................5:39:59 (30,363)
Flynn Burnett, Kathleen M........5:25:04 (29,046)
Flynn-Samuels, Mary B.................5:02:19 (26,227)
Focke, Britta 3:46:08 (7,929)
Fogarty, Clare A.................5:59:47 (31,547)
Fogarty, Gail M.................4:17:40 (16,029)
Fogarty, Valerie 4:45:45 (22,958)
Foley, Cathy J....................4:27:32 (18,633)
Foley, Doreen 5:50:24 (31,102)
Foley, Finola B...................5:35:35 (30,020)
Foley, Sarah 5:32:23 (29,763)
Folkard, Heidi C.................3:53:01 (9,630)
Folks, Sarah K....................3:36:22 (5,908)
Follan, Anne 3:51:39 (9,255)
Follis, Sarah E....................4:58:42 (25,644)

The Wall

Hitting 'The Wall' is something every marathoner dreads. It is that moment somewhere around the 19-mile mark when both physical and mental energy seems to desert you. It seems easy for the champions. Former world-marathon record holder Steve Jones once said of the marathon: 'I just run as hard as I can for 20 miles and then I race.' That sounds like good advice if you are a world-beater, but most mere mortals try other tricks. They try to dodge The Wall by carrying extra carbohydrate in the form of sports drinks and gels. Other strategies include running 'negative splits' (running the first half of the race slower that the second) and writing your name on the front of your shirt so the crowd will yell it out. The most notorious point for hitting The Wall on the London course is at Heron Quays, just after the 18-mile mark – you have been warned.

Fong, Anne E......................5:00:10 (25,918)
Fontanarosa, Gina...............4:54:05 (24,689)
Fontanille, Catherine.........3:59:50 (11,774)
Fooks, Kathy 3:42:46 (7,178)
Foong, Wendy....................6:08:13 (31,867)
Foord, Doreen M 5:10:17 (27,303)
Foote, Tamsin J.................5:38:15 (30,226)
Foots, Alison F..................4:58:06 (25,529)
Forbes, Karen 4:41:23 (21,966)
Forbes, Lesley J.................4:55:21 (24,972)
Forbes, Leyonee M.............4:27:25 (18,604)
Forbes, Linda A.................5:26:59 (29,224)
Ford, Amy B......................4:39:22 (21,537)
Ford, Antonia G 4:45:41 (22,942)
Ford, Carol A....................4:43:05 (22,343)
Ford, Denise M..................3:46:46 (8,074)
Ford, Gail B......................3:48:18 (8,450)
Ford, Jodie L.....................4:42:29 (22,212)
Ford, Julia R 5:06:07 (26,727)
Ford, Lida 4:22:10 (17,162)
Ford, Rosalind 6:30:29 (32,462)
Ford, Sue A.......................4:51:48 (24,210)
Forde, Claire F 5:09:30 (27,205)
Forde, Moji 3:53:44 (9,833)
Fordham, Jacqueline M 4:20:03 (16,613)
Fordham, Janet 4:30:36 (19,454)
Fordham, Linda J................7:33:54 (33,110)
Foreman, Alison 5:00:59 (26,039)
Foreman, Clare V...............4:34:37 (20,391)
Formby, Emma L................4:37:38 (21,144)
Forshaw, Sarah J 4:42:29 (22,212)
Forster, Karen E 4:56:11 (25,135)
Forster, Romy 6:00:56 (31,602)
Forster, Tracy A.................5:06:37 (26,805)
Forsyth, Imogen S 4:34:22 (20,331)
Forsyth, Taryn M 4:07:04 (13,360)
Forsythe, Emily M 4:32:59 (20,000)
Fortes Mayer, Gail E...........3:22:30 (3,594)
Fortune, Carole M.............3:15:55 (2,769)
Forward, Rosemary P.........5:54:03 (31,262)
Foster, Alexandra 4:46:02 (23,012)
Foster, Debra J..................4:44:59 (22,778)
Foster, Jane 4:17:50 (16,067)
Foster, Kate L....................3:55:11 (10,275)
Foster, Laura A 4:02:21 (12,342)
Foster, Louise M................4:16:04 (15,617)
Foster, Lucy......................6:46:13 (32,712)

Foster, Sharon 4:31:38 (19,705)
Foster, Sonja A..................4:15:41 (15,514)
Foster, Sue 4:36:43 (20,901)
Fournat, Stephanie 4:58:31 (25,614)
Fourriques, Michele..........5:57:20 (31,428)
Fowler, Ann 5:33:06 (29,823)
Fowler, Claire....................3:13:00 (2,397)
Fowler, Karen J 4:29:06 (19,057)
Fowler, Kay 3:15:43 (2,743)
Fowler, Louise H 3:38:26 (6,313)
Fowler, Michelle L..............4:50:36 (23,960)
Fowler, Natalie S................6:27:42 (32,416)
Fowler, Sara A...................5:32:01 (29,739)
Fowles, Nicola J.................4:11:02 (14,339)
Fox, Gillian 4:58:17 (25,569)
Fox, Jannine M..................4:18:45 (16,291)
Fox, Joan M......................4:35:43 (20,655)
Fox, Penelope J.................4:33:35 (20,159)
Fox, Stephanie 4:52:39 (24,393)
Fox, Sue 4:57:09 (25,346)
Fox, Suzi M.......................4:11:05 (14,354)
Foxe Lowe, Angela L 4:34:02 (20,260)
Foy, Amy..........................5:37:12 (30,146)
Foy, Elisabeth P 5:51:40 (31,164)
Foyster, Mandy L...............3:40:01 (6,632)
Fradgley, Emma R..............4:58:57 (25,701)
Frampton, Anne E 4:53:16 (24,517)
Frampton, Beverley A.........6:19:20 (32,214)
Frampton, Gemma J 4:41:15 (21,934)
Frampton, Julie 6:36:27 (32,551)
Frampton, Kimberley J 4:19:31 (16,482)
Frampton, Lenni A 4:57:28 (25,392)
Frampton, Susie E..............4:26:15 (18,323)
Francioso, Monica.............5:26:45 (29,193)
Francis, Andrea K...............3:40:07 (6,643)
Francis, Charlotte R 3:40:22 (6,684)
Francis, Ellen 4:39:07 (21,469)
Francis, Janine M...............3:14:44 (2,633)
Francis, Jemima K..............4:18:04 (16,128)
Francis, Kristin R................4:21:35 (16,993)
Francis, Lucy L...................5:07:39 (26,957)
Francis, Nicola 4:32:59 (20,000)
Francis, Sarah K 3:48:49 (8,583)
Francis Williams, Carly.............4:33:09 (20,047)
Frank, Flora 5:55:58 (31,352)
Frankis, Karen 4:15:57 (15,587)
Frankish, Sally C.................4:11:24 (14,442)
Franklin, Frances 4:23:04 (17,378)
Franklin, Joanne C..............4:23:51 (17,609)
Franklin, Niamh 4:23:04 (17,378)
Franklin, Rebecca E 4:07:48 (13,555)
Franklin, Sarah E................3:38:01 (6,230)
Franks, Mary-Liz A 5:48:19 (30,963)
Franon, Anita 4:23:21 (17,454)
Fransson, Karin M..............5:14:37 (27,857)
Franzon, Stina 4:40:56 (21,877)
Fraser, Anna C...................4:30:40 (19,467)
Fraser, Elinor J..................5:30:26 (29,583)
Fraser, Lorraine J...............5:39:38 (30,333)
Fraser, Susan B 4:20:06 (16,629)
Fraser Moodie, Christine A 4:48:46 (23,602)
Fraytet, Jane D..................7:04:29 (32,936)
Frazier, Melanie J...............5:23:33 (28,889)
Fredenham, Nancy A..........6:47:40 (32,732)
Freegard, Emilia 5:10:21 (27,309)
Freegard, Julie...................5:34:52 (29,957)
Freeland, Dawn A...............6:55:28 (32,831)
Freelove, Lynn M 5:37:31 (30,168)
Freeman, Beth...................4:32:14 (19,839)
Freeman, Caroline A...........4:54:45 (24,828)
Freeman, Claire A...............3:40:08 (6,645)
Freeman, Debra J...............6:21:38 (32,274)
Freeman, Louissa A............4:32:42 (19,934)
Freeman, Sarah J................4:57:04 (25,328)
Freer, Kathryn J 4:36:55 (20,963)
French, Gaynor T...............4:27:16 (18,572)
French, Margaret A............4:05:11 (12,951)
French, Victoria 5:30:16 (29,569)
Frerichs, Carley V...............4:26:03 (18,277)
Freshwater, Dawn S 4:36:50 (20,945)
Fricker, Lorna....................5:03:41 (26,415)
Fricker, Sarah J 4:13:37 (14,979)
Friedman, Jodie L 4:53:07 (24,485)

Friedrick, Lynn D....4:09:47 (14,054)
Friel, Kathleen M....7:34:08 (33,114)
Fripp, Charlotte M....4:10:35 (14,232)
Frisby, Tracy F....4:57:36 (25,417)
Froome, Victoria A....4:35:12 (20,531)
Frost, Angela J....5:11:11 (27,412)
Frost, Laura E....4:30:09 (19,335)
Frost, Lisa A....5:41:17 (30,436)
Frost, Sarah J....3:36:55 (6,024)
Frost, Sarah R....4:51:58 (24,246)
Frost, Theresa E....3:30:25 (4,880)
Froud, Helen K....4:46:52 (23,189)
Frulloni, Clare L....3:49:25 (8,725)
Fry, Samantha L....4:09:14 (13,919)
Fry, Sue....3:22:24 (3,584)
Fryer, Natalie L....3:34:35 (5,591)
Fryer, Rebecca M....4:53:41 (24,613)
Fryett, Angie D....5:26:45 (29,193)
Fuce, Maria L....5:30:45 (29,622)
Fuhr, Simone....3:55:35 (10,399)
Fulcher, Gillian....5:08:21 (27,058)
Fulford, Liz....4:23:24 (17,472)
Fulluck, Abi....4:38:54 (21,420)
Fullwood, Lesley J....4:44:27 (22,666)
Fullylove, Rosamund J....5:40:08 (30,375)
Fulton, Laura K....3:31:23 (5,050)
Funk, Johanna L....4:58:36 (25,631)
Funnell, Bridget M....4:51:57 (24,242)
Fuqua Jones, Linda L....5:57:59 (31,455)
Furbank, Valerie A....5:20:42 (28,582)
Furlong, Elizabeth....4:05:30 (13,022)
Furnival, Clare....4:21:54 (17,088)
Furreboee, Randi....4:52:22 (24,325)
Fyfe, Frippy G....4:41:33 (22,001)
Fyfe, Paula I....5:45:57 (30,776)
Gabe, Lucy S....5:31:01 (29,654)
Gaches, Anna C....4:31:19 (19,618)
Gaches, Annette J....4:36:41 (20,885)
Gadd, Deborah J....5:06:34 (26,799)
Gadd, Eleanor M....6:05:11 (31,767)
Gadgil, Anjana R....3:39:06 (6,454)
Gadkowski, Lynne B....4:32:38 (19,923)
Gaechter, Joyce H....5:38:36 (30,260)
Gaffney, Naomi S....5:17:15 (28,158)
Gagan, Sarah....4:41:26 (21,978)
Gahagan, Marie....4:42:30 (22,217)
Gaham, Zoe....4:54:39 (24,806)
Gahan, Anna E....4:26:17 (18,334)
Gaillard De Laubenqu, Teresa J....3:13:55 (2,513)
Gaines, Sue J....4:47:49 (23,386)
Gales, Eleanor L....4:27:18 (18,578)
Gall, Joanne L....5:15:18 (27,936)
Gall, Lorna P....4:11:57 (14,563)
Gallagher, Elizabeth A....5:31:18 (29,692)
Gallagher, Joan....6:33:55 (32,515)
Gallagher, Kirsty A....3:56:26 (10,668)
Gallagher, Lorraine S....5:12:01 (27,526)
Gallagher, Meabh C....4:11:13 (14,391)
Gallagher, Tess M....4:54:55 (24,873)
Gallego, Paula....6:23:24 (32,314)
Gallia, Daniela....4:50:37 (23,966)
Gallichan, Sharon....4:14:59 (15,332)
Galligan, Katherine M....4:55:26 (24,992)
Galligan, Sarah E....4:34:32 (20,371)
Gallo Carrabba, Larissa....4:17:37 (16,022)
Gallop, Carolyn B....4:46:19 (23,080)
Gallup Black, Adria....3:52:19 (9,441)
Galpin, Karen M....3:50:34 (9,000)
Gamble, Natasha....5:47:13 (30,881)
Gambrill, Barbara....4:31:38 (19,705)
Gander, Emma....4:29:29 (19,174)
Gannon, Sophie H....4:43:32 (22,447)
Gant, Clare A....5:05:58 (26,704)
Gappy, Tina L....3:35:23 (5,732)
Garb, Karen D....6:26:59 (32,402)
Garbarz, Zoe H....4:58:41 (25,641)
Garbutt, Cassandra B....3:58:23 (11,298)
Garcia Hernandez, Alejandra....4:30:48 (19,495)
Garciarguelles, Susana....4:32:22 (19,879)
Gard, Jemma....7:18:49 (33,035)
Garden, Laura....6:29:16 (32,436)
Garden, Philippa L....5:08:03 (27,014)
Gardener, Tracy....4:59:34 (25,804)
Gardiner, Charlotte L....4:21:15 (16,927)
Gardiner, Elizabeth S....6:40:55 (32,624)
Gardiner, Gillian....4:52:37 (24,384)
Gardiner, Janeen M....5:19:21 (28,413)
Gardiner, Julia....3:43:12 (7,289)
Gardiner, Mychaela A....7:17:24 (33,022)
Gardiner, Susan M....4:12:53 (14,806)
Gardiner, Victoria M....3:34:30 (5,566)
Gardner, Dawn A....7:23:43 (33,060)
Gardner, Donna M....6:00:02 (31,566)
Gardner, Harriette S....4:59:06 (25,723)
Gardner, Julie....5:07:19 (26,907)
Gardner, Julie R....5:24:06 (28,956)
Gardner, Rosie J....4:40:01 (21,679)
Gardner, Sally H....6:00:29 (31,582)
Gardner, Sandra....5:10:24 (27,319)
Gardner, Tina F....3:39:57 (6,620)
Gardner-Hall, Sarah J....3:45:38 (7,830)
Gare, Louise A....4:09:32 (14,000)
Garland, Jackie M....4:46:01 (23,008)
Garner, Amanda J....5:18:07 (28,257)
Garner, Julie A....4:27:28 (18,614)
Garner, Sue....4:15:16 (15,403)
Garnett, Kathleen....4:57:44 (25,441)
Garnham, Carey R....4:28:11 (18,802)
Garnham, Martina....5:29:27 (29,480)
Garnham, Samantha L....4:48:48 (23,609)
Garrard, Minnie D....4:32:59 (20,000)
Garratt, Amy J....5:08:01 (27,007)
Garrett, Dena....5:25:04 (29,046)
Garrod, Lorna E....3:44:14 (7,501)
Garrod, Zoe....4:48:45 (23,596)
Garside, Claire L....4:46:26 (23,108)
Garside, Heather M....5:30:10 (29,558)
Garvey, Marianne....4:45:23 (22,885)
Garwood, Emma L....4:50:20 (23,914)
Gascoigne, Emma J....4:38:37 (21,360)
Gascoigne-Owens, Johanna S....3:16:39 (2,834)
Gascoyne, Julie C....5:38:38 (30,263)
Gaskell, Sophie....4:02:42 (12,414)
Gaskill, Claire L....3:24:49 (3,915)
Gaskin, Bridget D....4:39:43 (21,605)
Gates, Fulcia....6:21:50 (32,280)
Gates, Nicol....5:30:34 (29,603)
Gatland, Deborah A....3:59:52 (11,780)
Gauci, Benny....4:13:21 (14,931)
Gaule, Zoe A....4:44:49 (22,736)
Gaulton, Amy V....3:47:56 (8,363)
Gaunt, Abigail C....4:41:14 (21,930)
Gaunt, Catherine A....3:52:07 (9,387)
Gauvin, Sarah J....3:39:43 (6,574)
Gavin, Eleanor Z....5:13:44 (27,740)
Gavin, Rachael....6:04:48 (31,754)
Gawler, Louise A....4:59:45 (25,840)
Gawne-Cain, Mary L....4:48:21 (23,500)
Gawthorpe, Lesley....4:52:33 (24,365)
Gay, Claudine....3:56:36 (10,726)
Gay, Francesca....3:43:38 (7,375)
Gay, Gerald....5:42:13 (30,517)
Gay, Heather T....4:38:16 (21,295)
Gay, Nicola J....4:51:14 (24,084)
Gay, Suzanne C....5:54:32 (31,285)
Gaylor, Barbara A....4:52:21 (24,320)
Gaylor, Victoria J....4:16:59 (15,854)
Gaymer, Anna L....4:54:23 (24,765)
Gaymer, Katie L....4:54:23 (24,765)
Gaymer, Rebecca C....4:54:23 (24,765)
Gaynor, Carole A....5:24:16 (28,970)
Gaynor, Zoe C....5:30:58 (29,647)
Gazzard, Debbie A....4:47:22 (23,285)
Gazzard, Mary J....6:45:00 (32,691)
Geall, Caroline....4:37:16 (21,050)
Geary, Victoria J....6:44:50 (32,689)
Gebbett, Emily S....4:45:05 (22,810)
Geddes, Julie A....6:03:32 (31,706)
Gee, Elaine....4:31:37 (19,701)
Gee, Sarah R....3:08:52 (1,942)
Geerts, Laila....4:33:21 (20,099)
Gelder, Emily....3:31:55 (5,146)
Gelson, Emily S....3:26:59 (4,241)
Genovese, Lia....5:48:54 (30,995)
Gent, Claire L....5:05:48 (26,676)
Gent, Joanne C....3:37:04 (6,048)
Gent, Karen L....4:04:18 (12,776)
Gentilcore, Elizabeth....3:58:50 (11,460)
Gentle, Linda J....3:45:47 (7,866)
Gentzel, Margrit....4:31:22 (19,630)
Geoghegan, Lynn M....4:03:03 (12,492)
George, Claire L....3:59:44 (11,741)
George, Irene E....6:02:44 (31,667)
George, Johanna L....4:32:05 (19,812)
George-Plunkett, Abey S....4:06:55 (13,330)
Georghiou, Jane....3:24:46 (3,908)
Geran, Janine....5:57:28 (31,432)
Gerdom, Diana....3:48:41 (8,551)
Germain, Heather....7:15:13 (33,007)
German, Gemma T....5:25:56 (29,123)
German, Sarah L....6:28:37 (32,431)
Gerrard, Dani L....5:25:50 (29,114)
Gerrard, Julie....3:58:34 (11,362)
Gerrard, Maria E....4:49:42 (23,791)
Gerson, Greer....4:55:04 (24,908)
Gessey, Joanne....5:09:26 (27,197)
Ghaleb, Ursula L....4:45:46 (22,961)
Ghose, Victoria J....5:00:47 (26,006)
Ghosh, Rosalind N....4:46:47 (23,169)
Gibb, Donna A....5:02:25 (26,241)
Gibbard, Emma....8:14:28 (33,189)
Gibbes, Barbara....3:55:59 (10,537)
Gibbin, Hannah V....3:39:55 (6,610)
Gibbin, Vanessa M....4:19:31 (16,482)
Gibbins, Deborah K....3:32:01 (5,166)
Gibbon, Juliet R....5:29:26 (29,475)
Gibbons, Carleen J....4:36:35 (20,865)
Gibbons, Lynda....4:25:07 (17,996)
Gibbs, Anita M....4:28:28 (18,889)
Gibbs, Christine G....3:58:23 (11,298)
Gibbs, Dawn L....2:58:04 (1,028)
Gibbs, Kim E....5:26:13 (29,143)
Gibbs, Philippa L....4:04:47 (12,876)
Gibbs, Samantha J....3:57:05 (10,870)
Gibbs, Samantha L....4:50:26 (23,932)
Gibson, Cathee A....5:06:25 (26,774)
Gibson, Julie....3:47:25 (8,219)
Gibson, Lesley A....5:58:51 (31,498)
Gibson, Nicole S....4:25:52 (18,215)
Gibson, Shirley R....3:47:18 (8,191)
Gibson, Tracy....4:53:31 (24,571)
Gibson-Robinson, Angela....4:06:45 (13,294)
Gibson-Sexton, Anne L....5:21:08 (28,620)
Gifford, Virginia R....3:54:17 (9,997)
Gignoux, Camilla....5:12:50 (27,624)
Gilbert, Anne E....5:24:10 (28,963)
Gilbert, Helen K....3:55:47 (10,472)
Gilbert, Lisa....5:45:31 (30,754)
Gilbert, Sally A....3:21:10 (3,417)
Gilbert, Tina M....4:31:23 (19,638)
Gilby, Pete R....3:56:39 (10,739)
Gilby, Sue N....3:47:09 (8,156)
Gilchrist, Kerry A....5:29:24 (29,469)
Gilchrist, Lucy....4:18:15 (16,169)
Gilderdale Scott, Heather....4:36:51 (20,952)
Gilding, Sally J....5:20:14 (28,524)
Giles, Catherine....4:26:53 (18,483)
Giles, Catherine H....4:19:42 (16,531)
Giles, Emma....6:16:10 (32,124)
Giles, Heather L....6:59:55 (32,880)
Gilkes, Susan J....4:42:20 (22,185)
Gill, Anne M....5:22:10 (28,735)
Gill, Debbie....5:42:01 (30,497)
Gill, Diane C....5:04:27 (26,517)
Gill, Emma....5:42:45 (30,557)
Gill, Gillian....4:41:24 (21,971)
Gill, Joan E....4:42:15 (22,165)
Gill, Lindsey A....4:43:45 (22,506)
Gill, Lise M....7:46:55 (33,164)
Gill, Ruth....5:29:53 (29,532)
Gill, Susan M....5:04:27 (26,517)
Gillan, Katy L....4:40:46 (21,844)
Gillard, Margaret C....3:59:19 (11,611)
Gillbe, Clare L....4:44:43 (22,714)
Gillespie, Carol....5:10:46 (27,362)
Gillespie, Catehrine R....4:36:05 (20,746)
Gillies, Barbara....4:59:05 (25,720)
Gillies, Gillian F....5:45:14 (30,734)
Gilligan, Carmel F....6:06:13 (31,794)

Gillingham, Katie L......6:03:18 (31,695)
Gilliver, Sarah E......5:12:24 (27,575)
Gillman, Faye D......5:11:17 (27,425)
Gilmartin, Clare......3:50:30 (8,984)
Gilmor, Carole......3:16:58 (2,874)
Gilmore, Alexandra H......4:49:58 (23,838)
Gilpin, Jasmine E......5:52:58 (31,213)
Gilson, Susan F......4:48:40 (23,579)
Ging, Sarah P......4:23:36 (17,530)
Gingell, Hanna......4:51:37 (24,171)
Ginns, Madeleine A......3:35:51 (5,808)
Giordanengo, Rebecca L......4:15:33 (15,487)
Giorgi, Joy E......3:54:50 (10,156)
Gipp, Diana M......3:26:42 (4,192)
Gipson, Ongeleigh......4:48:07 (23,453)
Girling, Hannah K......3:58:09 (11,209)
Girling, Tanya L......5:00:07 (25,908)
Girvan, Cara L......2:59:13 (1,166)
Giusta, Laura......3:43:26 (7,338)
Gjikokaj, Kaori H......5:02:54 (26,304)
Glanvile, Francesca V......5:44:30 (30,680)
Glanville, Danielle C......3:42:44 (7,167)
Glass, Jane F......5:01:53 (26,158)
Glass, Joanne E......4:21:57 (17,102)
Glassey, Joanne......4:30:05 (19,320)
Gledhill, Sara J......6:03:19 (31,698)
Glen, Janet P......5:07:50 (26,978)
Glendonl, Sharon......3:37:04 (6,048)
Glenn, Svanaug......4:30:25 (19,407)
Glennane, Claire M......3:39:52 (6,599)
Glennerster, Corrina A......4:56:15 (25,150)
Gloor, Barbara......5:55:44 (31,344)
Gloor, Susanne......4:25:18 (18,054)
Glover, Louise......6:15:50 (32,110)
Glover, Michelle......5:17:29 (28,193)
Glowka, Maja......3:31:48 (5,123)
Glynn, Diane......4:07:35 (13,501)
Glynn, Lorna M......4:19:44 (16,537)
Goalby, Kate J......5:37:15 (30,149)
Gobey, Tracey......4:45:22 (22,877)
Goble, Tracy S......4:15:13 (15,392)
Goddard, Sarah C......5:14:36 (27,854)
Godefroy, Isabelle......4:58:30 (25,607)
Godfrey, Annette S......4:40:42 (21,829)
Godfrey, Jacqueline A......5:05:19 (26,628)
Godfrey, Louise J......4:03:11 (12,524)
Godridge, Nicky N......4:34:32 (20,371)
Godwin, Nancy......5:38:13 (30,220)
Godwin, Salome A......3:59:05 (11,538)
Godwin, Sarah L......3:54:53 (10,173)
Gold, Lauren A......6:48:43 (32,741)
Gold, Liane M......3:18:01 (2,998)
Gold, Stephanie......5:56:30 (31,382)
Golding, Katherine M......4:33:38 (20,173)
Goldsack, Elizabeth A......5:09:12 (27,172)
Goldsmith, Alexandra J......4:44:47 (22,732)
Goldstone, Lisa R......6:24:40 (32,349)
Goldstone, Patricia J......4:28:55 (18,998)
Goldthorp, Wendy H......4:48:46 (23,602)
Golenberg, Emily R......3:49:25 (8,725)
Golland, Rebecca L......6:37:24 (32,569)
Golland, Sally C......5:53:06 (31,221)
Gomes, Elizabeth......4:27:55 (18,729)
Goncalves, Anna......4:47:19 (23,280)
Gonzalez, Susana......3:46:36 (8,034)
Gonzalez, Susana......4:16:19 (15,674)
Gooch, Rebecca J......4:39:11 (21,486)
Good, Lorraine......5:31:45 (29,722)
Goodall, Jayne......4:49:28 (23,750)
Goodall, Joanne M......4:31:15 (19,599)
Goodall, Suzanne R......4:41:03 (21,906)
Goodband, Rachel M......4:18:04 (16,128)
Goode, Charlotte......4:16:30 (15,727)
Goode, Lisa C......4:06:08 (13,167)
Goode, Sarah J......4:13:04 (14,862)
Goodearl, Kerry L......7:00:07 (32,883)
Goodenough, Victoria E......4:27:13 (18,560)
Gooderham, Christine......5:49:18 (31,024)
Goodey, Jane E......3:56:51 (10,804)
Goodey, Nicola L......4:52:03 (24,257)
Goodman, Hannah C......3:58:57 (11,490)
Goodman, Janet......5:11:10 (27,407)
Goodman, Madeline......4:31:11 (19,575)
Goodman, Tracy......7:32:18 (33,102)
Goodrick, Gail......4:23:59 (17,648)
Goodridge, Ruth D......4:07:46 (13,547)
Goodwin, Denise M......5:25:35 (29,089)
Goodwin, Ruth J......4:47:14 (23,268)
Goodwyn, Camilla......4:47:07 (23,238)
Goody, Samantha......4:16:28 (15,714)
Goodyer, Megan C......4:27:07 (18,533)
Goorney, Hilary R......6:18:54 (32,196)
Goorney, Joanna M......3:38:34 (6,344)
Goorun, Rogie......4:46:41 (23,156)
Gopalan, Geeta......6:26:12 (32,385)
Gorasia, Asmita......5:26:43 (29,191)
Gordon, Claire......2:55:58 (847)
Gordon, Jacqueline I......5:02:14 (26,209)
Gordon, Karen......4:09:46 (14,048)
Gordon, Kirsty......4:37:45 (21,167)
Gore, Sophie J......4:28:08 (18,785)
Gorga, Toni......5:28:38 (29,389)
Gorgeon, Laurence......4:52:06 (24,268)
Gorham, Diana M......3:23:55 (3,778)
Gorio, Federica......5:15:24 (27,944)
Gormley, Alison R......3:41:39 (6,954)
Gormley, Caroline......4:35:41 (20,647)
Gormley, Teresa M......4:53:58 (24,670)
Gorrie, Annabel J......4:04:00 (12,714)
Gosling, Laura J......4:57:52 (25,470)
Gosney, Jenny L......4:29:54 (19,267)
Goss, Breda M......4:23:16 (17,437)
Gough, Bridget I......4:51:43 (24,190)
Gough, Helen J......5:16:49 (28,105)
Gough, Martine W......6:06:26 (31,801)
Gough, Sharon......5:33:18 (29,833)
Gough, Teresa......5:06:21 (26,761)
Goujet, Helene......3:32:12 (5,203)
Gould, Sue......4:50:46 (23,995)
Gouldthorpe, Anne......5:23:28 (28,886)
Gow, Jennifer A......5:19:07 (28,390)
Gowar, Sarah L......6:34:18 (32,520)
Goward, Lynn M......3:47:34 (8,259)
Gowen, Julia M......4:13:00 (14,842)
Gower-Quiroga, Catherine J......4:04:16 (12,770)
Gowlett, Michelle A......4:19:23 (16,442)
Graat, Mirian......3:40:06 (6,641)
Grace, Amanda J......4:36:46 (20,924)
Grace, Jade......5:37:02 (30,136)
Grace, Janet E......3:31:02 (4,990)
Grady, Helen C......4:55:58 (25,097)
Graham, Danielle......4:35:46 (20,666)
Graham, Elizabeth S......3:57:20 (10,961)
Graham, Jenny M......4:43:23 (22,408)
Graham, Jody......6:45:38 (32,706)
Graham, Julie E......4:22:19 (17,206)
Graham, Kerry......5:40:24 (30,389)
Graham Wood, Camilla S......4:09:01 (13,865)
Grahamslaw, Margaret......6:14:37 (32,074)
Grainger, Michele D......3:42:27 (7,102)
Grandison, Diane......5:56:04 (31,355)
Grandy, Sarah A......4:33:17 (20,080)
Granger, Dawn E......5:36:28 (30,092)
Grant, Alison......4:45:44 (22,952)
Grant, Elizabeth A......4:11:03 (14,346)
Grant, Fiona......4:56:30 (25,204)
Grant, Kathryn A......5:17:23 (28,181)
Grant, Liza M......6:17:31 (32,158)
Grant, Michelle J......5:28:06 (29,334)
Grant, Pamela C......3:42:49 (7,188)
Grant, Paulette L......4:03:14 (12,535)
Grant, Sophie J......4:24:09 (17,702)
Grant, Vicki M......4:00:01 (11,820)
Grant, Victoria......4:31:56 (19,782)
Grantz, Alexandra......4:38:52 (21,406)
Grasset, Laurel......5:50:52 (31,125)
Grave, Linda M......3:32:00 (5,158)
Graves, Kirsten......5:48:33 (30,971)
Graves, Sarah J......3:44:09 (7,480)
Graves, Sharon D......5:54:45 (31,302)
Grawehr, Cezanne M......5:40:07 (30,373)
Gray, Adele......3:22:41 (3,622)
Gray, Alison......4:35:39 (20,639)
Gray, Anna S......5:05:49 (26,680)
Gray, Caroline......4:49:00 (23,649)
Gray, Caroline A......4:40:43 (21,831)
Gray, Hannah E......6:02:33 (31,660)
Gray, Jacqui M......5:05:44 (26,669)
Gray, Jean......6:32:03 (32,484)
Gray, Juanita......4:38:43 (21,378)
Gray, Kat M......6:45:22 (32,699)
Gray, Katherine E......4:29:54 (19,267)
Gray, Lisa A......5:49:52 (31,062)
Gray, Lucinda......5:02:47 (26,285)
Gray, Lydia N......4:53:44 (24,626)
Gray, Marian B......5:03:43 (26,418)
Gray, Nicola J......5:58:19 (31,475)
Gray, Rosaire P......3:44:53 (7,665)
Gray, Sam L......6:15:35 (32,104)
Gray, Wendy J......5:09:48 (27,241)
Grayson, Penny A......3:50:29 (8,977)
Grazioli, Gaia......3:38:10 (6,260)
Greasley, Lucinda C......4:12:25 (14,684)
Greaves, Elaine......4:57:21 (25,375)
Greaves, Kate......3:52:23 (9,466)
Greaves, Susan M......4:43:26 (22,417)
Green, Aleksandra C......4:44:50 (22,741)
Green, Alison......3:54:58 (10,194)
Green, Ana-Maria......4:05:49 (13,103)
Green, Caroline J......6:16:08 (32,122)
Green, Claire......4:18:54 (16,325)
Green, Diana M......6:13:29 (32,037)
Green, Elizabeth J......3:55:11 (10,275)
Green, Emily J......5:17:47 (28,219)
Green, Emma L......5:07:57 (27,000)
Green, Gail......4:44:50 (22,741)
Green, Helena L......4:41:26 (21,978)
Green, Janet E......3:53:58 (9,912)
Green, Jenny K......4:33:17 (20,080)
Green, Jill L......5:20:02 (28,497)
Green, Jo......3:48:19 (8,457)
Green, Joanne L......3:49:24 (8,718)
Green, Judith M......4:18:56 (16,337)
Green, Katina K......4:11:55 (14,555)
Green, Kim......2:56:42 (916)
Green, Lisa J......5:16:36 (28,085)
Green, Molly......5:06:29 (26,785)
Green, Nicola......3:35:55 (5,823)
Green, Rachel V......5:32:18 (29,761)
Green, Sarah J......4:16:03 (15,609)
Green, Terrie M......5:21:27 (28,660)
Green, Theodosia......3:59:44 (11,741)
Green, Tiffany J......4:20:45 (16,795)
Green, Valerie D......4:18:08 (16,146)
Greenacre, Louisa......3:45:30 (7,805)
Greenaway, Natalie P......4:10:47 (14,270)
Greenburg, Elizabeth A......4:17:55 (16,083)
Greene, Jenny K......4:16:25 (15,695)
Greenfield, Jacqueline D......5:21:28 (28,662)
Greenfield, Jane E......6:49:18 (32,752)
Greenfield, Lisa C......3:04:47 (1,565)
Greenhalf, Zoe E......4:02:35 (12,395)
Greenhalgh, Ruth H......5:58:11 (31,468)
Greenland, Philippa M......4:18:04 (16,128)
Greenslade, Deborah......4:48:38 (23,574)
Greenwood, Celia......3:59:47 (11,755)
Greenwood, Clare......4:25:48 (18,194)
Greenwood, Eleanor......3:44:41 (7,616)
Greenwood, Jane E......4:40:23 (21,747)
Gregg, Catherine......4:26:26 (18,368)
Gregory, Cindy......6:06:42 (31,813)
Gregory, Elizabeth D......4:22:48 (17,322)
Gregory, Helen J......4:42:52 (22,297)
Gregory, Ria C......3:59:32 (11,682)
Gregory, Sarah L......3:41:37 (6,948)
Greis, Christina A......3:26:15 (4,109)
Grennan, Sharon......4:55:04 (24,908)
Gresty, Sarah L......4:59:55 (25,874)
Grewal, Harjit......4:47:42 (23,360)
Grey, Mei-Ling......6:03:03 (31,683)
Grierson, Corinna......4:25:45 (18,176)
Grierson-Jackson, Sarah J......3:44:27 (7,553)
Griffies, Helen L......5:07:44 (26,967)
Griffin, Angela C......6:11:30 (31,967)
Griffin, Barbara F......3:46:57 (8,111)
Griffin, Chanese C......3:26:49 (4,209)
Griffin, Linda A......3:28:03 (4,413)
Griffin, Lorne......4:32:15 (19,845)
Griffin, Susan L......5:17:44 (28,214)

Griffith, Becky L....3:24:26 (3,850)
Griffith, Rachel S....4:16:21 (15,681)
Griffiths, Andrea M....5:10:18 (27,305)
Griffiths, Becky A....3:30:58 (4,976)
Griffiths, Donna M....5:14:06 (27,785)
Griffiths, Heather R....3:49:27 (8,731)
Griffiths, Helen J....4:33:31 (20,138)
Griffiths, Jane E....5:00:19 (25,946)
Griffiths, Lorraine....4:40:17 (21,729)
Griffiths, Madelaine....3:19:02 (3,136)
Griffiths, Natalie....6:54:41 (32,822)
Griffiths, Nicola A....5:26:15 (29,147)
Griffiths, Sarah J....7:02:04 (32,895)
Griffiths, Sian....4:57:42 (25,433)
Griffiths, Terri A....4:29:01 (19,031)
Grigor, Sarah-Louise....4:36:39 (20,876)
Grimble, Katherine....4:07:55 (13,587)
Grindley, Suzannah M....3:53:41 (9,816)
Grindu, Christiane....4:17:24 (15,954)
Grist, Samantha....3:55:39 (10,416)
Grocott, Colette....4:09:22 (13,950)
Gromett, Samantha....3:38:39 (6,358)
Grooby, Janis A....5:46:34 (30,830)
Groppe, Dilupa....6:04:27 (31,744)
Grose, Catherine A....5:21:18 (28,646)
Gross, Natalie S....4:41:54 (22,085)
Grossman, Claire J....5:41:05 (30,428)
Grosvenor, Catherine A....5:08:53 (27,132)
Grosvenor, Susan A....5:40:34 (30,396)
Grotzki, Anja....4:29:02 (19,034)
Groucott, Leesa....4:01:31 (12,148)
Grout, Jackie....4:03:17 (12,549)
Grove, Gay....4:52:06 (24,268)
Grove, Jennet M....5:08:01 (27,007)
Grove, Julie A....5:54:04 (31,264)
Grover, Maria L....5:24:37 (28,994)
Grover, Sonia J....5:24:37 (28,994)
Groves, Brigitte....4:28:13 (18,817)
Groves, Lianne C....5:17:35 (28,204)
Groves, Susan M....6:32:13 (32,485)
Gruijters, Tracey....4:46:57 (23,198)
Grum, Catherine I....4:51:38 (24,177)
Grylls, Samantha....4:27:09 (18,542)
Gualco, Francesca....3:19:58 (3,262)
Gualtieri, Wendy J....3:20:04 (3,276)
Gudbjornsdottir, Lilja....4:31:51 (19,760)
Gudmundsdottir, Birna....4:30:05 (19,320)
Gueit, Françoise....5:00:36 (25,985)
Guest, Helen....4:00:04 (11,836)
Guest, Lisa C....5:07:57 (27,000)
Guest, Sarah....3:09:50 (2,049)
Guild, Rhona M....5:15:28 (27,948)
Guilfoyle, Tracy....2:56:21 (878)
Guillaume, Claudia....3:30:56 (4,972)
Guise, Monica....5:02:32 (26,254)
Guiz, Esther....4:48:11 (23,466)
Gulland, Monica R....5:36:30 (30,094)
Gullick, Helen L....3:55:24 (10,345)
Gundle, Jo L....3:57:08 (10,893)
Gunn, Claire R....5:36:07 (30,061)
Gunn, Elaine J....5:07:29 (26,927)
Gunn, Geraldine C....4:09:13 (13,916)
Gunn, Nichola L....5:38:15 (30,226)
Gunning, Carolyn R....5:23:11 (28,853)
Gunning, John L....5:23:11 (28,853)
Gunnlaugsdottir, Anna....4:39:40 (21,592)
Gunnlaugsdottir, Vilborg....5:11:55 (27,515)
Gunter, Sarah....4:39:05 (21,463)
Gurmin, Victoria J....4:28:14 (18,820)
Gurr, Tracey S....4:50:43 (23,988)
Gurry, Gaye....4:13:59 (15,063)
Guthrie, Michelle....4:02:32 (12,382)
Guttridge, Nancy J....4:27:58 (18,739)
Guy, Sylvia J....4:37:12 (21,032)
Guyton, Teresa M....5:42:56 (30,572)
Guzman Reyes, Deborah....3:18:53 (3,121)
Gwaderi, Razia....6:54:42 (32,823)
Haagsman V Straalen, Wilma....4:42:10 (22,151)
Haan, Alison J....4:37:34 (21,131)
Hacker, Lisa C....3:42:44 (7,167)
Hackett, Karen....5:20:14 (28,524)
Hacon, Gweneth....4:35:09 (20,521)
Hadcroft, Shiona M....4:19:28 (16,469)
Haddon, Imogen F....5:05:11 (26,608)
Haddon, Natalie A....3:52:20 (9,445)
Haden, Deborah E....4:22:53 (17,339)
Hadley, Gina L....3:51:42 (9,277)
Hadley, Sarah L....4:44:01 (22,576)
Hagan, Anne....3:37:02 (6,045)
Hagemann, Britta....4:24:25 (17,777)
Hagg, Kirsty J....4:46:46 (23,166)
Haggerty, Nuala....4:41:54 (22,085)
Hailey, Dee....4:08:15 (13,677)
Haine, Susan....5:19:32 (28,441)
Haines, Caroline....5:40:55 (30,422)
Haines, Lesley L....3:05:30 (1,623)
Haines, Lorna J....4:14:02 (15,080)
Haines, Marie Claire....4:32:06 (19,814)
Haines, Nicola L....5:36:42 (30,112)
Haines, Philippa A....5:10:25 (27,323)
Hainsworth, Kim....4:09:11 (13,903)
Hairsine, Janet E....3:17:23 (2,929)
Hake, Ursula....3:47:25 (8,219)
Halai, Bhupa V....4:56:31 (25,210)
Halder, Caroline....4:59:51 (25,858)
Hale, Caroline J....3:22:46 (3,631)
Hale, Catriona J....7:23:43 (33,060)
Hale, Claire....3:36:41 (5,972)
Hale, Tamzin C....6:16:54 (32,137)
Hales, Alison....5:00:10 (25,918)
Hales, Elizabeth S....3:29:59 (4,822)
Hales, Henrietta E....4:12:47 (14,769)
Hales, Katrina J....6:24:25 (32,340)
Halfhead, Harriet L....3:45:21 (7,771)
Halkett, Siobhan....4:56:38 (25,226)
Hall, Carol....3:55:10 (10,264)
Hall, Daphne S....3:46:37 (8,040)
Hall, Deborah A....3:42:08 (7,050)
Hall, Elizabeth M....5:10:54 (27,376)
Hall, Gillian M....4:27:38 (18,666)
Hall, Jayne A....4:03:30 (12,606)
Hall, Julie M....5:16:35 (28,082)
Hall, Kate....4:37:38 (21,144)
Hall, Kate S....4:30:35 (19,446)
Hall, Linda....4:18:38 (16,262)
Hall, Linda....5:09:31 (27,207)
Hall, Moira....4:42:01 (22,116)
Hall, Pauline N....3:55:04 (10,233)
Hall, Sally A....4:34:37 (20,391)
Hall, Sarah E....4:04:56 (12,903)
Hall, Suzanne....4:37:34 (21,131)
Hallam, Jane S....3:54:25 (10,030)
Hallas, Shareen....4:19:16 (16,413)
Hallett, Carol M....4:50:59 (24,044)
Halls, Charlotte W....4:55:34 (25,010)
Halsall, Karen A....5:08:33 (27,084)
Halse, Katy R....5:56:50 (31,395)
Hambling, Margaret A....6:07:37 (31,844)
Hamblyn, Sam....3:45:54 (7,887)
Hameed, Alia S....4:58:52 (25,679)
Hamilton, Erni....3:15:51 (2,761)
Hamilton, Lindsay....4:06:12 (13,177)
Hamilton, Patricia....6:21:09 (32,259)
Hamilton, Susan....5:07:32 (26,934)
Hamilton Duff, Lisa M....4:26:28 (18,376)
Hamilton-Fox, Fiona L....3:58:31 (11,344)
Hamlett, Alison....4:49:54 (23,826)
Hamm, Sarah L....4:38:22 (21,310)
Hammersley, Colleen A....4:41:03 (21,906)
Hammersley, Margaret....4:39:08 (21,478)
Hammerton, Louise S....3:58:42 (11,401)
Hammond, Elizabeth....6:02:08 (31,645)
Hammond, Michelle....6:12:04 (31,988)
Hammond, Sanantha L....3:26:51 (4,214)
Hammond, Sarah....4:50:45 (23,992)
Hammond, Stacey T....5:57:46 (31,442)
Hammond, Susan I....5:01:10 (26,065)
Hampshire, Susan J....5:11:51 (27,507)
Hampson, Amanda J....4:27:55 (18,729)
Hampson, Heather H....4:59:54 (25,870)
Hampson, Victoria....3:42:31 (7,115)
Hampton, Giselle M....5:38:59 (30,280)
Hamshere, Jane....5:07:45 (26,970)
Hamson, Clare L....3:39:25 (6,523)
Hancock, Dawn L....5:06:09 (26,733)
Hancock, Elizabeth....4:00:55 (12,019)
Handoll, Bethany V....3:33:08 (5,339)
Handslip, Susanna F....3:36:04 (5,845)
Hanks, Joanna R....5:33:55 (29,881)
Hanlen, Karen L....3:13:47 (2,501)
Hanley, Debbie L....5:42:51 (30,563)
Hanlon, Françoise....3:35:32 (5,755)
Hannaford, Elizabeth....4:12:26 (14,689)
Hanney, Nina....5:32:34 (29,776)
Hannington, Patricia....5:43:47 (30,626)
Hanrahan, Cara A....6:08:27 (31,873)
Hansen, Aasta....3:45:36 (7,821)
Hansen, Eline V....5:01:05 (26,059)
Hansen, Mette....3:56:16 (10,618)
Hansen, Teresa A....5:59:08 (31,509)
Hansford, Laura E....4:53:51 (24,647)
Hansford, Tracy J....4:32:43 (19,939)
Hanson, Karen N....7:37:18 (33,124)
Hanson, Sally M....4:26:42 (18,430)
Happs, Gillian S....4:47:36 (23,342)
Harber, Sandra A....5:12:33 (27,594)
Harber, Teresa....4:08:21 (13,704)
Harbon, Joanne....3:45:19 (7,760)
Hardcastle, Kim T....4:47:10 (23,247)
Hardick, Natalie T....4:31:47 (19,743)
Hardiman, Lisa V....4:24:48 (17,892)
Harding, Caroline....4:36:44 (20,910)
Harding, Deirdre A....5:06:44 (26,824)
Harding, Hazel....4:24:16 (17,735)
Harding, Jane S....3:47:56 (8,363)
Harding, Jodie M....5:46:33 (30,829)
Harding, Laura A....5:18:01 (28,239)
Harding, Laura E....3:20:34 (3,345)
Harding, Lesley J....4:08:15 (13,677)
Harding, Louise....3:41:34 (6,933)
Harding, Louise M....5:58:06 (31,463)
Hardman, Jackie S....4:36:48 (20,937)
Hardman, Pamela M....4:47:28 (23,311)
Hards, Tracie J....5:29:26 (29,475)
Hardwick, Valma J....7:34:23 (33,117)
Hardy, Claire L....4:58:07 (25,533)
Hardy, Karen M....4:57:46 (25,448)
Hardy, Lynne C....5:16:24 (28,057)
Hardy, Maria L....3:57:03 (10,861)
Hardy, Rachel M....4:01:03 (12,058)
Hardy, Sarah M....3:46:49 (8,088)
Hardy, Susan....5:01:23 (26,095)
Hardy, Victoria L....4:23:13 (17,421)
Hare Duke, Hilary....3:30:00 (4,827)
Hares, Caroline....5:59:19 (31,529)
Hargie, Patricia G....4:55:54 (25,077)
Hargrave, Emma L....3:27:02 (4,252)
Hargreaves, Alison....3:54:11 (9,972)
Hargreaves, Jean H....6:29:57 (32,447)
Harland, Claire A....5:17:55 (28,233)
Harmer, Jenny A....4:59:19 (25,746)
Harmer, Rachel E....5:31:41 (29,718)
Harney, Sorsha....4:29:12 (19,085)
Harp, Kristina E....3:22:46 (3,631)
Harper, Carole A....4:35:36 (20,624)
Harper, Caroline H....4:53:26 (24,553)
Harper, Kate....5:19:51 (28,475)
Harpham, Angela Y....4:23:40 (17,552)
Harrhy, Jeny L....6:14:14 (32,059)
Harries, Katherine J....5:50:26 (31,108)
Harrington, Emma....4:48:34 (23,556)
Harrington, Karen....3:54:06 (9,946)
Harrington, Naoimh S....5:14:47 (27,880)
Harris, Abi....3:52:25 (9,477)
Harris, Anne M....4:01:53 (12,230)
Harris, Charlotte E....4:48:36 (23,569)
Harris, Charlotte M....3:32:56 (5,312)
Harris, Danielle M....4:57:07 (25,338)
Harris, Dawn....4:01:53 (12,230)
Harris, Georgina K....6:20:49 (32,247)
Harris, Gillian R....4:49:19 (23,720)
Harris, Heather....3:56:25 (10,660)
Harris, Jane E....3:40:38 (6,737)
Harris, Jane L....4:44:59 (22,778)
Harris, Jo....5:18:01 (28,239)
Harris, Joanna L....3:52:23 (9,466)
Harris, Karen J....4:22:33 (17,252)
Harris, Katie M....3:51:49 (9,307)
Harris, Kerry A....3:54:40 (10,099)

Harris, Lauren I 6:43:58 (32,671)
Harris, Michelle 4:27:41 (18,677)
Harris, Nicola C 3:25:57 (4,066)
Harris, Nikki J 5:02:41 (26,273)
Harris, Rebecca 3:48:34 (8,517)
Harris, Rebecca E 4:44:39 (22,695)
Harris, Samantha J 3:38:58 (6,428)
Harris, Sarah L 4:30:24 (19,400)
Harris, Sophie H 4:44:24 (22,660)
Harris, Victoria E 4:54:20 (24,754)
Harris, Victoria J 4:31:54 (19,772)
Harrisberg, Sue 3:30:33 (4,904)
Harrison, Abigail S 4:26:27 (18,371)
Harrison, Amanda J 5:56:59 (31,405)
Harrison, Claire 5:39:30 (30,324)
Harrison, Elizabeth E 4:19:26 (16,460)
Harrison, Gill M 3:30:55 (4,968)
Harrison, Jane B 5:28:19 (29,357)
Harrison, Karen 3:35:03 (5,679)
Harrison, Rochelle C 5:46:53 (30,855)
Harrison, Roger 4:38:22 (21,310)
Harrison, Shirley 5:26:23 (29,164)
Harrison, Stephanie 5:33:06 (29,823)
Harrison, Susanna J 3:05:04 (1,583)
Harrison, Tracy J 4:24:34 (17,830)
Harrop, Bernadete L 3:28:41 (4,549)
Harrop, Michele 4:23:54 (17,623)
Harrowby, Jenny 5:22:29 (28,770)
Harry, Anna N 4:35:19 (20,559)
Harsent, Jill E 4:29:45 (19,238)
Harston, Naomi M 4:32:36 (19,916)
Hart, Caroline J 4:17:55 (16,083)
Hart, Emma C 3:43:09 (7,274)
Hart, Jackie 4:54:50 (24,856)
Hart, Jayne C 4:59:28 (25,780)
Hart, Kathryn 3:58:29 (11,333)
Hart, Lisa M 4:49:18 (23,717)
Hart, Sarah D 4:11:07 (14,364)
Hart, Victoria 5:50:14 (31,090)
Hart, Yvonne R 4:14:12 (15,142)
Harte, Catherine A 4:51:13 (24,078)
Harter- Miles, Theresa 6:26:47 (32,397)
Hartin, Deborah S 5:15:50 (27,977)
Harting, Marlis 4:13:40 (14,997)
Hartley, Jeanette 5:48:11 (30,955)
Hartley, Jillian K 4:19:14 (16,398)
Hartley, Lindsey A 4:39:02 (21,447)
Hartley, Maureen 4:13:34 (14,968)
Hartley, Wendy L 4:04:04 (12,732)
Hartmann, Anke C 4:28:25 (18,874)
Hartney, Astra 4:01:43 (12,192)
Hartnoll, Samantha J 5:50:09 (31,085)
Hartogs, Jessica A 5:46:19 (30,813)
Hartshorne, Pauline M 4:32:49 (19,961)
Hartwell, Angela 5:12:24 (27,575)
Hartwell, Victoria 5:16:54 (28,116)
Hartwright, Caryl E 4:10:19 (14,176)
Harty, Majella 3:39:20 (6,507)
Harvey, Angie J 3:53:07 (9,665)
Harvey, Deborah A 5:33:55 (29,881)
Harvey, Hazel J 5:06:09 (26,733)
Harvey, Jayne 5:58:15 (31,472)
Harvey, Julie 4:33:00 (20,008)
Harvey, Rosalind 6:04:31 (31,746)
Harvey, Ruth E 4:20:26 (16,717)
Harwood-Mann, Bethany J 4:18:58 (16,348)
Hasegawa, Naomi 4:45:12 (22,834)
Hasell, Bridget L 4:16:57 (15,847)
Hashimoto, Naoko 6:31:52 (32,483)
Haslam, Joanne 3:31:26 (5,057)
Hass, Inga J 5:08:37 (27,094)
Hassell, Marion 3:56:23 (10,650)
Hassett, Lynn 4:53:13 (24,512)
Hassett, Sinead 3:57:39 (11,060)
Hastie, Emma K 5:24:27 (28,986)
Hastings, Samantha J 4:09:09 (13,892)
Hatch, Louise E 5:20:19 (28,541)
Hatcher, Lynn M 7:38:26 (33,136)
Hatcher, Ollie. A 4:58:00 (25,505)
Hatfield, Sue 4:54:23 (24,765)
Hathaway, Daphne L 4:54:54 (24,871)
Hatherley, Marilyn J 4:02:38 (12,408)
Hatto, Clare E 4:29:01 (19,031)
Hatton, Ingrid R 3:43:00 (7,231)
Hatton, Jenny A 4:31:16 (19,602)
Hatts, Daphne J 5:30:40 (29,613)
Haughey, Michelle 5:16:17 (28,039)
Haussermann, Eveline 5:16:13 (28,033)
Haward, SA 4:23:23 (17,468)
Hawcutt, Karen V 5:07:56 (26,996)
Hawes, Emma L 5:15:02 (27,908)
Hawk, Sarah 4:39:07 (21,469)
Hawken, Amy K 4:43:15 (22,376)
Hawken, Valerie E 5:02:32 (26,254)
Hawker, Lesley C 5:41:17 (30,436)
Hawker, Penny J 5:41:17 (30,436)
Hawker, Rosemary K 3:34:19 (5,538)
Hawkes, Emma Z 3:30:57 (4,973)
Hawkes, Tyrene R 8:52:47 (33,214)
Hawkings, Kelly N 5:06:16 (26,750)
Hawkins, Debbie L 4:38:45 (21,382)
Hawkins, Emma L 4:47:26 (23,304)
Hawkins, Jacqui 4:44:26 (22,665)
Hawkins, Juliet 4:09:59 (14,097)
Hawkins, Laura 3:32:09 (5,190)
Hawkins, Melissa 4:09:23 (13,954)
Hawkins, Sharon J 2:58:15 (1,037)
Hawkins, Sharon T 4:15:57 (15,587)
Hawkrigg, Bridget R 4:47:54 (23,407)
Hawkrigg, Elizabeth A 4:47:54 (23,407)
Haworth, Emma L 3:48:24 (8,475)
Hay, Anne E 3:37:35 (6,152)
Hay, Beryl 4:47:23 (23,287)
Hayakawa, Eri 2:31:41 (82)
Hayden-Pepper, Michelle C 4:49:31 (23,760)
Haydu, Andrea 4:24:07 (17,691)
Hayes, Beverley S 4:02:53 (12,455)
Hayes, Carol A 4:21:08 (16,902)
Hayes, Joanne 5:05:50 (26,685)
Hayes, Rosemary J 5:56:10 (31,361)
Hayhow, Prunella V 3:22:07 (3,548)
Hayles, Linda M 4:00:00 (11,810)
Haylett, Ainslie J 3:54:00 (9,923)
Haynes, Jane 3:58:22 (11,293)
Haynes, Julie A 4:47:40 (23,353)
Haynes, Pamela M 5:14:20 (27,817)
Haynes, Susan J 5:11:26 (27,446)
Haynes, Vivien J 4:07:57 (13,602)
Hayter, Ann W 4:14:38 (15,240)
Hayward, Carla 4:48:55 (23,632)
Hayward, Leanne M 5:01:02 (26,048)
Hayward, Samantha L 4:11:31 (14,462)
Haywood, Michelle 6:03:42 (31,712)
Haywood, Sally M 5:04:22 (26,499)
Hazel, Gillian R 3:53:50 (9,873)
Hazel, Victoria J 4:01:08 (12,082)
Hazeldon, Layla J 5:02:44 (26,278)
Hazell, Katharine E 4:29:56 (19,276)
Hazzard, Susan 3:42:52 (7,196)
Hazzledine, Helen 4:48:42 (23,583)
Head, Emma M 5:02:15 (26,210)
Headley, Fiona J 3:51:53 (9,329)
Heal, Lorraine J 4:20:59 (16,861)
Heald, Marie L 4:15:01 (15,342)
Heaney, Kelli 4:53:29 (24,562)
Hearn, Alison C 4:49:06 (23,677)
Hearn, Amy L 3:43:58 (7,452)
Hearn, John M 4:32:16 (19,853)
Heath, Heather 5:07:15 (26,898)
Heath, Kirsty 5:52:58 (31,213)
Heath, Natalie C 4:09:38 (14,019)
Heath, Rebecca J 4:02:13 (12,308)
Heath, Sarah D 3:33:20 (5,373)
Heath, Sheryl L 3:31:47 (5,115)
Heathcote, Emma 6:43:51 (32,669)
Heathfield, Deanna 4:22:17 (17,194)
Heathwood, Jane 3:53:13 (9,697)
Heaton, Mathilde M 3:12:08 (2,292)
Heaviside, Karen M 3:03:40 (1,490)
Hebberd, Lisa A 4:00:01 (11,820)
Hebblethwaite, Claire 3:49:00 (8,628)
Hebden, Kathryn L 4:55:32 (25,003)
Hedberg, Haj 4:12:00 (14,573)
Hedden, Ruth 4:41:40 (22,030)
Hedditch, Anita E 4:28:22 (18,863)
Heddon, Karen A 5:01:53 (26,158)
Hedges, Julie A 3:46:15 (7,955)
Hedgley, Denise M 5:00:06 (25,904)
Hedley, Krista 5:15:23 (27,942)
Hedley, Lesley J 6:20:36 (32,242)
Hedley Lewis, Penny 4:08:50 (13,821)
Heeneman, Alicia 3:45:22 (7,777)
Heffer, Katharine L 4:27:27 (18,609)
Hefferon, Becky M 4:57:07 (25,338)
Heggarty, Helen G 6:02:46 (31,670)
Heine, Christl 4:03:37 (12,629)
Hellblom, Ann 4:34:40 (20,402)
Heller, Charlie 5:37:29 (30,163)
Hellman, Lou F 6:05:32 (31,778)
Helm, Natalie J 4:21:44 (17,036)
Hemingway, Pamela C 5:12:55 (27,637)
Hemingway Arnold, Kirsten 5:31:03 (29,662)
Hemming, Amanda J 6:24:10 (32,333)
Hempsall, Theresa K 3:27:47 (4,375)
Hemsley, Iveta 4:07:59 (13,612)
Hemsworth, Marion V 3:51:43 (9,278)
Hemy, Pauline 3:49:39 (8,786)
Henderson, Allison 4:30:00 (19,297)
Henderson, Claudia C 5:23:43 (28,911)
Henderson, Elizabeth K 5:35:03 (29,970)
Henderson, Jamie J 5:58:15 (31,472)
Henderson, Jane A 4:36:50 (20,945)
Henderson, Jane C 4:24:59 (17,953)
Henderson, Jemma R 4:40:46 (21,844)
Henderson, Jenny J 3:57:20 (10,961)
Henderson, Karen 4:05:59 (13,137)
Henderson, Lynn A 3:25:47 (4,042)
Henderson, Nicola 4:39:35 (21,571)
Henderson, Noreen B 4:05:35 (13,047)
Henderson, Rayna 6:18:38 (32,188)
Henderson, Ruth I 5:04:40 (26,540)
Henderson, Sarah E 4:31:01 (19,537)
Henderson, Sarah L 5:44:59 (30,718)
Hendry, Allison J 5:13:25 (27,708)
Hendry, Sharon 5:58:07 (31,465)
Heneage, Charlotte E 5:16:02 (28,002)
Heneghan, Kate M 4:27:51 (18,708)
Henley, Ann E 4:55:05 (24,914)
Henley, Ashley M 4:58:48 (25,662)
Henley, Kate E 4:48:37 (23,571)
Hennessy, Annabel I 5:45:21 (30,745)
Hennessy, Kay B 6:12:03 (31,987)
Henning, Lucy 5:18:50 (28,348)
Henriksen, Shila 5:29:23 (29,466)
Henry, Caren M 6:00:41 (31,587)
Henry, Emma 5:33:44 (29,872)
Henry, Jean M 3:27:16 (4,284)
Henry, Kirsty A 4:28:37 (18,924)
Henry, Victoria A 6:41:44 (32,632)
Henry-Brown, Rebecca L 4:27:12 (18,555)
Henshaw, Sheila M 5:37:31 (30,168)
Hentley, Fiona E 4:19:42 (16,531)
Henwood-Fox, Keryn 5:38:46 (30,269)
Heppolette, Nicola 6:15:55 (32,115)
Hepworth, Jennifer 4:30:01 (19,299)
Heracleous, Kate A 3:48:53 (8,603)
Herbert, Asha T 4:46:01 (23,008)
Herbert, Julie J 6:47:15 (32,727)
Herbert, Rita 5:19:15 (28,410)
Herbert, Sarah 3:29:28 (4,708)
Hermitage, Julia 4:39:02 (21,447)
Heron, Joan E 4:15:30 (15,476)
Heron, Judith A 5:02:11 (26,200)
Heron, Martina 5:46:18 (30,810)
Heron, Sharon E 5:19:53 (28,481)
Herring, Louise S 4:01:50 (12,224)
Herring, Susan M 4:25:15 (18,042)
Herring, Victoria S 3:49:36 (8,769)
Herringshaw, Emily M 4:59:33 (25,799)
Herrington, Kathy 4:42:56 (22,314)
Hershman, Abigail H 4:36:01 (20,725)
Heryet, Nicole 3:43:05 (7,261)
Heslegrave, Amanda J 4:26:41 (18,426)
Heslip, Andrea L 4:16:09 (15,634)
Heslop, Sally E 3:49:30 (8,747)
Hester, Lesley A 7:35:22 (33,119)
Hetherington, Alexandra M 3:53:45 (9,844)
Hevingham, Rebecca C 4:09:58 (14,093)
Hewer, Susan E 4:52:56 (24,443)

Hewett, Carolyn L	3:54:40 (10,099)	
Hewett, Sandy R	6:28:27 (32,430)	
Hewings, Sue Y	3:23:34 (3,723)	
Hewitson, Jolyn	5:57:45 (31,441)	
Hewitt, Amanda Jane	4:51:02 (24,047)	
Hewitt, Caroline J	3:06:10 (1,682)	
Hewitt, Catherine E	3:09:34 (2,020)	
Hewson, Sarah J	4:48:08 (23,457)	
Hexter, Francesca J	5:54:26 (31,281)	
Heydecker, Deirdre A	3:35:49 (5,801)	
Heyer, Sim	5:18:48 (28,347)	
Heyes, Carla L	6:02:50 (31,673)	
Heywood, Elizabeth K	4:45:35 (22,920)	
Heywood, Kathryn	4:47:10 (23,247)	
Heywood, Rebecca L	6:05:17 (31,771)	
Hibbert, Leanne	3:11:42 (2,237)	
Hibbs, Angela E	3:10:01 (2,064)	
Hickey, Joanne C	5:10:02 (27,273)	
Hickie, Emma L	4:24:25 (17,777)	
Hickman, Helen E	4:45:54 (22,989)	
Hickman, Sarah	6:03:51 (31,721)	
Hicks, Alison	5:00:06 (25,904)	
Hicks, Beverley A	5:20:02 (28,497)	
Hicks, Elizabeth	5:19:01 (28,377)	
Hicks, Emma J	4:33:07 (20,036)	
Hicks, Wendy A	4:14:57 (15,319)	
Hickson, Sandra J	4:59:32 (25,794)	
Hier, Diane R	3:26:57 (4,234)	
Higginbottom, Wendy E	3:28:21 (4,480)	
Higgins, Angela	3:41:04 (6,820)	
Higgins, Bernadette	5:17:17 (28,164)	
Higgins, Merrin E	4:42:10 (22,151)	
Higgins, Sandra G	4:31:29 (19,661)	
Higgs, Deborah G	5:37:31 (30,168)	
Higgs, Elaine S	3:46:48 (8,081)	
Higgs, Lynda A	5:30:40 (29,613)	
Highgate, Cath J	4:14:44 (15,267)	
Higley, Katherine M	4:26:20 (18,348)	
Higne, Annie	3:42:57 (7,221)	
Higson, Emily	4:56:02 (25,107)	
Hild, Christine	5:13:59 (27,758)	
Hild, Petra	5:16:26 (28,062)	
Hildingsson, Karin B	3:45:36 (7,821)	
Hilditch, Jane E	4:57:41 (25,431)	
Hiley, Kayleigh M	6:16:55 (32,139)	
Hiley, Kimberley J	6:16:58 (32,141)	
Hill, Alison	4:45:22 (22,877)	
Hill, Andrea J	3:14:47 (2,637)	
Hill, Briony J	4:01:28 (12,140)	
Hill, Caroline L	4:00:51 (12,005)	
Hill, Catherine A	4:50:58 (24,042)	
Hill, Catherine E	4:50:51 (24,016)	
Hill, Cheryl W	3:36:43 (5,979)	
Hill, Debbie	4:39:43 (21,605)	
Hill, Debbie M	5:14:40 (27,871)	
Hill, Jane	4:54:58 (24,887)	
Hill, Jane F	4:49:14 (23,699)	
Hill, Janet M	3:54:54 (10,182)	
Hill, Jenny A	4:44:22 (22,651)	
Hill, Jessica L	5:08:59 (27,147)	
Hill, Julianne	4:40:44 (21,837)	
Hill, Karen E	3:41:12 (6,854)	
Hill, Melanie S	5:46:44 (30,842)	
Hill, Michelle H	4:11:07 (14,364)	
Hill, Paula K	3:31:11 (5,026)	
Hill, Rachel E	5:24:32 (28,992)	
Hill, Samantha J	4:31:32 (19,678)	
Hill, Sarah L	3:49:57 (8,857)	
Hill, Simona	5:37:05 (30,142)	
Hiller, Eileen M	4:07:21 (13,433)	
Hilliam, Pam A	5:21:54 (28,702)	
Hilliard, Marie T	6:37:14 (32,567)	
Hillier, Kirsty L	3:53:03 (9,647)	
Hillman, Donna M	5:51:50 (31,175)	
Hillman, Kate	4:58:29 (25,602)	
Hills, Linda K	4:33:04 (20,019)	
Hills, Lynne	4:57:57 (25,487)	
Hills, Samantha L	4:17:34 (16,003)	
Hills, Tonya	5:35:06 (29,976)	
Hilman, Paula	5:04:22 (26,499)	
Hilton, Helen L	4:24:52 (17,906)	
Hilton, Lyndsay J	4:34:37 (20,391)	
Hilton, Rachel	4:37:27 (21,097)	
Hinc, Nina R	5:05:02 (26,585)	
Hindlaugh, Wendy L	3:41:19 (6,876)	
Hindley, Laura A	4:43:42 (22,495)	
Hinds-Sotomey, Lorna M	4:23:09 (17,397)	
Hine, Sophie	3:43:48 (7,422)	
Hiner, Tansy L	3:40:00 (6,626)	
Hinshelwood, Linda	4:25:59 (18,253)	
Hinton, Clare L	3:54:53 (10,173)	
Hinxman, Kathryn E	4:07:15 (13,412)	
Hiorns, Caroline E	3:51:49 (9,307)	
Hird, Polly A	5:02:15 (26,210)	
Hirotsuna, Shoko	6:25:23 (32,362)	
Hirsch, Annie	3:55:45 (10,460)	
Hirst, Nicola A	3:58:56 (11,487)	
Hirst, Rebecca L	4:46:10 (23,043)	
Hirst, Susan E	4:40:33 (21,802)	
Hisa, Keiko	5:30:17 (29,573)	
Hische, Debra	5:01:01 (26,045)	
Hiscox, Sarah M	3:38:20 (6,293)	
Hishin, Gina	5:10:55 (27,377)	
Hitchcock, Nicky J	3:47:05 (8,142)	
Hitman, Avril F	6:11:57 (31,986)	
Ho, Bridget L	7:02:55 (32,905)	
Ho, Olivia I	3:45:25 (7,787)	
Hoad, Elizabeth K	7:10:48 (32,987)	
Hoad-Reddick, Anna K	4:21:53 (17,084)	
Hoarau, Rachel L	6:46:06 (32,708)	
Hoare, Carol A	4:39:53 (21,651)	
Hoare, Emma	3:43:23 (7,329)	
Hobbs, Deborah A	5:23:16 (28,864)	
Hobbs, Jane M	3:48:29 (8,495)	
Hobbs, Joanne S	7:10:28 (32,985)	
Hobbs, Kathryn F	5:16:36 (28,085)	
Hobbs, Shirley	5:49:38 (31,052)	
Hobin, Carolyne	4:30:03 (19,309)	
Hobson, Emma M	4:21:59 (17,112)	
Hobson, Louise F	3:41:10 (6,847)	
Hobson, Sarah M	4:44:40 (22,700)	
Hochfeld, Kim	3:37:33 (6,140)	
Hockey, Hannah J	4:21:55 (17,091)	
Hodge, Alexandra J	5:41:45 (30,480)	
Hodge, Nicky J	5:26:44 (29,192)	
Hodgkinson, Jane E	3:53:20 (9,726)	
Hodgkinson, Tara	4:34:52 (20,449)	
Hodgson, Kathryn W	3:48:52 (8,598)	
Hodkins, Amanda	5:13:12 (27,676)	
Hodkinson, Joanna G	4:44:14 (22,622)	
Hodson, Caroline S	6:14:20 (32,062)	
Hoertnagl, Katharina	4:05:57 (13,132)	
Hoey, Jacqueline A	3:52:20 (9,445)	
Hofmeyr, Debbie	4:32:22 (19,879)	
Hogarth-Smith, Katy	5:26:22 (29,159)	
Hogben, Christine	5:10:40 (27,351)	
Hogg, Pauline L	4:24:29 (17,797)	
Hogg, Sophie A	5:43:33 (30,610)	
Holappa, Karen G	5:37:03 (30,138)	
Holbrook, Felicity C	5:00:08 (25,913)	
Holbrough, Jayne M	4:09:53 (14,076)	
Holden, Fiona A	5:39:28 (30,320)	
Holden, Genevieve R	4:26:25 (18,365)	
Holden, Katy J	4:19:50 (16,562)	
Holden, Sarah	3:54:29 (10,049)	
Holden, Sarah J	4:59:27 (25,773)	
Holden, Tracey	4:17:19 (15,933)	
Holder, Belinda J	5:50:17 (31,095)	
Holder, Jeanette	4:23:35 (17,527)	
Holdsworth, Joanna V	4:28:03 (18,762)	
Hole, Maureen A	4:42:57 (22,316)	
Hole, Sarah	4:10:25 (14,196)	
Holford, Kay	5:15:32 (27,956)	
Holland, Elizabeth J	6:24:35 (32,347)	
Holland, Kim E	4:27:11 (18,551)	
Holland, Sally A	6:27:40 (32,414)	
Holland, Sarah C	6:40:46 (32,621)	
Holland, Victoria M	5:14:07 (27,788)	
Holland Lee, Amanda J	4:22:30 (17,242)	
Hollands, Emma L	4:41:19 (21,956)	
Holleran, Christine	3:56:57 (10,828)	
Holliday, Alison V	4:54:44 (24,823)	
Holliday, Karen L	4:50:29 (23,943)	
Holliday, Susan M	3:52:40 (9,544)	
Hollington, Alison M	3:15:16 (2,691)	
Hollins, Annick	4:42:38 (22,242)	
Hollinshead, Monique G	3:12:10 (2,302)	
Holloway, Allison M	4:20:03 (16,613)	
Holloway, Beverley	4:41:34 (22,004)	
Holloway, Tracy M	5:35:48 (30,040)	
Holman, Melanie	4:15:22 (15,437)	
Holmes, Caroline T	3:58:26 (11,319)	
Holmes, Catherine J	4:47:19 (23,280)	
Holmes, Gillian M	4:51:46 (24,202)	
Holmes, Heather O	5:45:16 (30,736)	
Holmes, Jan	4:18:21 (16,199)	
Holmes, Jessica L	4:02:25 (12,355)	
Holmes, Julie J	6:43:22 (32,661)	
Holmes, Kelly S	4:08:26 (13,728)	
Holmes, Lorna M	4:40:41 (21,825)	
Holmes, Rachel	4:55:39 (25,028)	
Holmes, Samantha L	4:23:14 (17,427)	
Holroyd, Julie	4:27:54 (18,722)	
Holst, Sonza I	4:02:21 (12,342)	
Holt, Genevieve C	4:50:51 (24,016)	
Holt, Jessica A	5:02:32 (26,254)	
Holt, Kerry L	3:32:11 (5,198)	
Holt, Linda M	5:17:00 (28,126)	
Holt, Tina	5:23:03 (28,837)	
Homer, Allison M	4:54:09 (24,712)	
Homer, Britta	3:38:49 (6,386)	
Honey, Johanna N	4:57:39 (25,424)	
Honour, Helen E	4:55:42 (25,037)	
Hood, Jo-Anne M	5:23:41 (28,906)	
Hooley, Sarah	5:06:46 (26,830)	
Hooper, Elin C	4:57:30 (25,397)	
Hooper, Patricia A	5:31:13 (29,681)	
Hooper, Tina J	5:20:42 (28,582)	
Hope, Helen J	3:54:15 (9,993)	
Hopkins, Alexandra	5:19:10 (28,397)	
Hopkins, Joanne	4:16:02 (15,604)	
Hopkins, Julia M	5:21:02 (28,611)	
Hopkinson, Anne E	4:38:49 (21,396)	
Hopkinson, Nicola	3:26:31 (4,158)	
Hopp, Terry A	6:34:48 (32,525)	
Hoppe, Gisela	3:22:59 (3,655)	
Hopper, Wendy	6:18:42 (32,190)	
Hopwell, Sally A	5:10:02 (27,273)	
Hopwood, Rosalind J	4:31:05 (19,548)	
Horan, Jennifer S	3:59:18 (11,604)	
Horne, Amanda	6:45:00 (32,691)	
Horne, Jemma A	4:48:13 (23,474)	
Horne, Joanne C	5:42:07 (30,509)	
Horne, Margaret A	5:45:22 (30,746)	
Horner, Angela	5:41:34 (30,460)	
Horner, Jacqueline M	5:51:16 (31,138)	
Horner, Nicola	5:24:15 (28,968)	
Hornsby, Julian E	5:59:05 (31,506)	
Horrabin, Elizabeth A	4:00:23 (11,910)	
Horrell, Rebecca J	5:16:35 (28,082)	
Horrell, Sophie A	5:14:57 (27,899)	
Horrell, Tara	3:53:25 (9,741)	
Horsfall, Sam L	3:53:40 (9,810)	
Horsley, Laura I	4:49:04 (23,666)	
Horsman, Kathleen	3:47:51 (8,344)	
Horta Osorio, Ana C	4:24:36 (17,842)	
Horton, Elizabeth A	4:40:25 (21,753)	
Horton, Lisa M	5:38:58 (30,279)	
Horton, Lucy A	4:50:30 (23,945)	
Horwood, Katy A	4:19:41 (16,527)	
Hoskin, Julie	6:12:48 (32,013)	
Hoskinson, Mollie C	5:48:46 (30,988)	
Hossack, Susan L	4:08:29 (13,738)	
Hotston, Jane L	4:14:09 (15,122)	
Houchen, Margaret P	6:15:16 (32,095)	
Houden, Aase S	3:27:48 (4,379)	
Hough, Lindsay J	5:38:24 (30,242)	
Hought, Louise	6:54:05 (32,808)	
Houghton, Tracy A	5:15:22 (27,941)	
Houghton, Tracy A	5:37:43 (30,184)	
Houlder, Alice	4:33:28 (20,126)	
Houlder, Sophie E	4:28:03 (18,762)	
Hounza, Chantal	5:23:45 (28,915)	
House, Annabel S	5:10:24 (27,319)	
House, Jayne	6:21:33 (32,273)	
Housley, Helena J	4:55:10 (24,928)	
Housley, Julie	4:58:35 (25,627)	
Houston, Catherine M	4:40:34 (21,804)	
Howard, Alexandra S	5:04:32 (26,529)	

Howard, Christine E....4:26:44 (18,443)
Howard, Corty....3:58:43 (11,405)
Howard, Ginny....5:09:59 (27,263)
Howard, Jo....6:09:31 (31,912)
Howard, Joanne C....4:47:51 (23,396)
Howard, Judy G....5:13:06 (27,666)
Howard, Kristen L....4:40:21 (21,741)
Howard, Lynn....4:43:30 (22,435)
Howard, Suzanne K....6:39:55 (32,609)
Howarth, Brenda C....4:16:05 (15,620)
Howarth, Marie....4:58:08 (25,537)
Howe, Jane....4:24:07 (17,691)
Howe, Patricia A....6:19:18 (32,212)
Howell, Jude....4:21:02 (16,875)
Howell, Katrina E....5:41:22 (30,447)
Howells, Anwen....3:55:18 (10,314)
Howells, Debbie J....5:01:25 (26,099)
Howells, Deirdre B....4:25:36 (18,136)
Howells, Hannah R....5:38:39 (30,264)
Howells, Nicholas J....4:22:45 (17,310)
Howells, Rachael J....4:12:45 (14,761)
Howick, Tiffeny....4:40:30 (21,777)
Howlett, Annelise M....5:06:55 (26,850)
Howlett, Midge E....4:11:37 (14,484)
Howroyd, Anne-Marie R....3:57:46 (11,100)
Howse, Denise J....3:33:46 (5,445)
Howting, Sharyn....5:32:40 (29,784)
Hoy, Donna M....4:40:47 (21,848)
Hoyland, Joanne M....3:30:35 (4,911)
Hoyland, Sharon D....5:17:58 (28,236)
Hoyle, Helen E....3:32:09 (5,190)
Hoyle, Helen P....4:19:25 (16,455)
Hoyle, Sarah G....5:40:45 (30,408)
Huber-Berger, Rosmarie....5:15:17 (27,935)
Hubert, Nicola....4:25:45 (18,176)
Hudson, Jane A....6:26:49 (32,399)
Hudson, Karen E....4:43:08 (22,357)
Hudson, Kym....4:34:35 (20,383)
Hudson, Leila A....3:38:58 (6,428)
Hudson, Louise M....4:51:30 (24,144)
Hudson, Lucy C....4:23:51 (17,609)
Hudson, Sarah J....5:15:38 (27,965)
Hudson-Cooper, Claire....4:37:03 (20,989)
Hufford, Sarah L....3:53:13 (9,697)
Hufton, Elizabeth J....3:35:29 (5,747)
Huggett, Bridget M....5:39:15 (30,299)
Huggins, Michelle....5:37:04 (30,140)
Hughes, Alison....4:12:38 (14,734)
Hughes, Anna C....3:58:25 (11,317)
Hughes, Carly M....4:23:12 (17,414)
Hughes, Caroline....4:56:39 (25,229)
Hughes, Christina....4:55:37 (25,020)
Hughes, Debbie K....3:23:53 (3,771)
Hughes, Donna....5:13:17 (27,689)
Hughes, Eimear R....4:16:20 (15,678)
Hughes, Eleanor J....6:44:11 (32,676)
Hughes, Helen....6:00:51 (31,598)
Hughes, Jean....4:54:24 (24,770)
Hughes, Karren....5:27:48 (29,303)
Hughes, Kelly....5:13:17 (27,689)
Hughes, Margret....7:17:35 (33,025)
Hughes, Nana H....4:32:02 (19,798)
Hughes, Natasha L....4:42:46 (22,274)
Hughes, Pauline....6:03:23 (31,700)
Hughes, Rachel C....5:18:34 (28,316)
Hughes, Rebekah....3:52:51 (9,578)
Hughes, Shirley M....4:21:12 (16,915)
Hukins, Caroline A....3:41:30 (6,914)
Hull, Christine M....4:38:46 (21,385)
Hull, Tracey E....6:11:45 (31,979)
Hull, Yvonne M....6:46:40 (32,720)
Hullett, Andrea G....5:06:23 (26,768)
Hulley, Susie M....3:58:28 (11,329)
Hulme, Lea V....4:12:53 (14,806)
Hulme, Lindsay F....4:35:18 (20,553)
Humberstone, Josephine C....3:32:29 (5,246)
Humbles, Patricia D....5:49:14 (31,019)
Hume, Shirley....3:35:30 (5,749)
Humpherston, Claire E....4:37:21 (21,072)
Humphrey, Kate....4:08:53 (13,830)
Humphreys, Alison....4:22:40 (17,291)
Humphreys, Rachel H....6:02:08 (31,645)
Humphreys, Sally L....5:20:33 (28,567)
Humphries, Julie E....4:02:07 (12,289)
Humphries, Suzanne T....4:52:54 (24,437)
Humphris, Debra A....5:43:49 (30,627)
Hung, Kitty S....4:52:59 (24,453)
Hungerford, Melinda F....4:56:49 (25,259)
Hunt, Caoimhe B....3:13:08 (2,418)
Hunt, Helen D....5:31:26 (29,702)
Hunt, Julie A....5:03:01 (26,319)
Hunt, Wendy....4:19:10 (16,382)
Hunter, Caroline A....5:18:52 (28,351)
Hunter, Gillian....5:01:14 (26,078)
Hunter, Joanna K....4:26:15 (18,323)
Hunter, Judy E....4:29:04 (19,041)
Hunter, Julia C....4:40:21 (21,741)
Hunter, Mary....3:44:39 (7,603)
Hunter, Sarah G....5:39:09 (30,296)
Hunter, Sarah R....3:58:31 (11,344)
Hunter, Wendy....3:47:08 (8,151)
Hunter Smart, Georgina J....3:51:17 (9,168)
Huntrods, Alison J....5:40:47 (30,412)
Hurcombe, Fiona M....5:21:46 (28,686)
Hurd, Joanna H....4:39:06 (21,465)
Hurford, Kate J....4:41:21 (21,963)
Hurran, Elizabeth J....6:10:17 (31,932)
Hurrell, Anne....4:53:31 (24,571)
Hurst, Caroline J....4:58:00 (25,505)
Hurst, Rachel J....3:37:49 (6,194)
Hussey, Sara....5:12:35 (27,599)
Hüsseyin, Çiğdem E....6:05:29 (31,776)
Huston, Jacqui N....5:21:47 (28,689)
Hustwit, Julie A....3:47:21 (8,202)
Hutchings, Debbie J....6:35:25 (32,533)
Hutchins, Patricia....5:23:40 (28,901)
Hutchinson, Elizabeth A....4:28:11 (18,802)
Hutchinson, Nicola M....3:29:45 (4,771)
Hutchinson, Sally....5:07:50 (26,978)
Hutchinson, Sophie M....5:36:07 (30,061)
Hutchison, Atlanta....6:07:04 (31,821)
Hutchison, Claire T....4:29:14 (19,093)
Huthwaite, Leigh A....7:08:42 (32,967)
Hutner, Hazel C....3:56:50 (10,799)
Hutt, Darice E....6:37:08 (32,566)
Hutton, Hannah E....6:54:49 (32,824)
Hutton, Nicola C....4:43:54 (22,549)
Hutton, Ruth....3:06:02 (1,670)
Huws, Meinir....4:17:52 (16,076)
Huxster, Victoria F....5:05:06 (26,599)
Huxtable, Emily M....4:51:21 (24,105)
Huynh, Nga....3:59:59 (11,808)
Huzzey, Sarah J....5:24:07 (28,958)
Hyde, Julie A....4:35:00 (20,491)
Hyde, Laura....5:29:45 (29,517)
Hyde, Lindsay J....4:00:57 (12,030)
Hyde, Mandy J....5:35:44 (30,030)
Hyde, Natasha L....5:04:44 (26,548)
Hyde Peters, Zara....2:54:49 (782)
Hymers, Katherine M....3:50:50 (9,062)
Hynd, Jennie L....3:13:05 (2,411)
Hynd, Julie....3:51:08 (9,131)
Iannelli, Sarah L....3:06:17 (1,694)
Ianson, Rachel A....6:42:48 (32,653)
Ibbitson, Julia....5:43:07 (30,582)
Ibrahim, Layla....5:07:06 (26,878)
Ibrahim, Samira....5:19:40 (28,452)
Igoe, Josephine R....3:29:11 (4,651)
Ikeda, Tomoko....3:49:20 (8,703)
Iles, Denise E....5:29:47 (29,518)
Illingworth, Alexandra C....4:45:11 (22,830)
Illman, Susan C....3:09:44 (2,039)
Imkamp, Maroula W....3:47:45 (8,311)
Inbeay-Ampiah, Dinah....5:29:43 (29,511)
Inch, Christine A....3:44:32 (7,578)
Ingham, Jill....5:09:22 (27,190)
Ingman, Rebecca L....4:58:21 (25,578)
Ingwersen, Sarah J....3:28:29 (4,506)
Inkster, Becky....4:51:42 (24,188)
Inman, Katie E....5:35:59 (30,055)
Innes, Louise A....5:48:37 (30,977)
Inness, Vicky L....3:29:42 (4,759)
Instance, Nicola J....5:22:18 (28,753)
Ioannou, Monica....4:52:29 (24,349)
Iona, Nicola....6:39:19 (32,601)
Irani, Hana....5:25:12 (29,059)
Ireland, Caroline D....4:12:57 (14,824)
Ireland, Esme....3:53:53 (9,890)
Ireland, Janis....4:41:52 (22,074)
Irory, Sarah V....3:56:57 (10,828)
Irvine, Margaret A....4:29:04 (19,041)
Irving, Joanne....5:03:22 (26,371)
Irving, Joanne M....5:06:44 (26,824)
Irwin, Maya....4:23:43 (17,565)
Irwin, Michaela B....4:21:12 (16,915)
Irwin, Ronaele....5:12:43 (27,617)
Isaac, Helen L....4:06:51 (13,311)
Isaac, Judith A....6:05:28 (31,775)
Isbill, Joanna F....4:51:50 (24,218)
Ison, Margaret....6:39:24 (32,602)
Ison, Rebecca....5:30:13 (29,563)
Issott, Tracey....4:52:06 (24,268)
Isturis, Bernadette....4:46:16 (23,069)
Ivarsson, Maria....6:18:14 (32,177)
Ivinson, Sarah....6:15:41 (32,106)
Izquierdo, Ella....6:03:37 (31,708)
Jack, Carolyn L....5:44:38 (30,694)
Jack, Elizabeth....4:34:11 (20,288)
Jack, Tanya L....3:22:31 (3,598)
Jacks, Annette F....5:04:44 (26,548)
Jackson, Adele L....5:21:32 (28,669)
Jackson, Carol A....6:33:37 (32,507)
Jackson, Cheryl....4:56:25 (25,191)
Jackson, Debby....5:21:45 (28,684)
Jackson, Emma J....4:18:18 (16,183)
Jackson, Emma J....5:08:51 (27,125)
Jackson, Glen P....3:45:47 (7,866)
Jackson, Jen A....5:15:14 (27,930)
Jackson, Kirsten....3:10:30 (2,113)
Jackson, Lisa....6:44:15 (32,678)
Jackson, Lucy....5:09:56 (27,258)
Jackson, Mary A....5:09:57 (27,260)
Jackson, Nicky J....5:07:09 (26,887)
Jackson, Penny J....5:26:57 (29,218)
Jackson, Ruth E....4:17:21 (15,944)
Jackson, Sarah A....4:28:18 (18,842)
Jackson, Susan K....4:59:28 (25,780)
Jackson, Tracy....5:47:16 (30,886)
Jackson, Vivienne A....4:48:47 (23,606)
Jacobs, Kate....3:22:56 (3,651)
Jacobs, Nicole A....4:53:41 (24,613)
Jacobs, Tracey....3:58:27 (11,327)
Jacobsen, Natasha B....4:02:38 (12,408)
Jacobson, Beverley L....3:58:46 (11,431)
Jacquemart, Angela J....4:11:08 (14,370)
Jacques, Claire L....4:15:24 (15,449)
Jaffe, Jane S....4:56:56 (25,290)
Jagan, Karen....4:43:26 (22,417)
Jagger, Jennifers E....3:02:36 (1,415)
Jagger, Joanne....4:11:18 (14,418)
Jahn, Sigrid C....4:16:57 (15,847)
Jalabert, Sylvie....4:50:51 (24,016)
James, Cherry A....5:20:16 (28,530)
James, Emma L....5:36:54 (30,127)
James, Helen....5:51:08 (31,132)
James, Jennifer....4:35:29 (20,601)
James, Jo....5:19:40 (28,452)
James, Kate J....6:01:15 (31,616)
James, Lisa....4:11:43 (14,500)
James, Nicola M....4:48:38 (23,574)
James, Sally-Anne....5:32:15 (29,758)
James, Zoe M....4:09:35 (14,011)
James Roger, Kimberley....5:23:52 (28,924)
Jameson-O'Neill, Tara A....4:52:38 (24,388)
Jamieson, Hilary....4:11:47 (14,516)
Jandrell, Rhiannon B....4:53:33 (24,581)
Jane, Zoe....6:45:25 (32,700)
Jang, Hemabha....4:47:14 (23,268)
Janseen, Heike....4:43:02 (22,334)
Janssen, Naomi S....4:09:20 (13,940)
Januszewski, Evonne....4:51:44 (24,192)
Janvrin, Genevieve....4:47:17 (23,274)
Jaques, Carly S....4:57:16 (25,364)
Jaques, Hayley J....4:57:16 (25,364)
Jaques, Hilary A....3:43:28 (7,344)
Jaques, Nicole L....4:04:09 (12,751)
Jaques, Tracey A....5:41:41 (30,471)
Jardon, Iris....4:57:37 (25,422)
Jarrold, Claire....5:42:22 (30,522)

Jarrold, Tracy	5:05:18 (26,624)
Jarvis, Angela M	5:46:51 (30,851)
Jarvis, Beverley A	4:56:07 (25,124)
Jarvis, Jackie L	3:33:37 (5,424)
Javaudin, Celine	4:49:54 (23,826)
Jay, Hannah F	5:26:24 (29,165)
Jay, Karen R	5:11:59 (27,523)
Jayant, Tracy J	4:05:22 (12,991)
Jeacock, Jackie S	4:48:05 (23,446)
Jeavons, Megan E	5:23:11 (28,853)
Jebson, Elspeth A	3:37:28 (6,127)
Jeffcoat, Rosalind	5:11:55 (27,515)
Jefferies, Helen P	5:47:16 (30,886)
Jefferies, Rebecca	3:50:43 (9,033)
Jefferis, Jenny M	4:33:25 (20,113)
Jeffers, Joumana	5:15:53 (27,987)
Jeffers, Lisa A	5:15:53 (27,987)
Jeffery, Louise	5:14:04 (27,776)
Jeffery, Natalie D	5:12:39 (27,606)
Jefferys, Emma K	5:03:25 (26,379)
Jeffrey, Annie	5:54:09 (31,270)
Jeffs, Chris K	3:56:23 (10,650)
Jelley, Diana M	4:16:18 (15,668)
Jelley, Susan M	3:20:01 (3,270)
Jellis, Rebecca M	5:17:11 (28,149)
Jelsig, Anne Marie	3:22:12 (3,557)
Jemmett-Allen, Michelle	4:35:00 (20,491)
Jenkin, Linda	6:30:36 (32,466)
Jenkins, Abi C	5:07:17 (26,904)
Jenkins, Beverley	5:31:35 (29,713)
Jenkins, Elise A	4:40:35 (21,809)
Jenkins, Greta S	3:39:32 (6,547)
Jenkins, Helen	4:57:29 (25,395)
Jenkins, Mary E	6:24:27 (32,341)
Jenkins, Michelle	3:42:58 (7,226)
Jenkins, Ruth E	4:41:58 (22,101)
Jenkins, Sylvia	4:14:15 (15,150)
Jenkins, Tracy A	5:41:05 (30,428)
Jenkins, Tracy I	3:38:43 (6,367)
Jenkinson, Gary	3:41:04 (6,820)
Jenkinson, Karen M	4:09:15 (13,923)
Jenkinson, Karen S	5:22:09 (28,733)
Jenks, Jennifer C	3:47:44 (8,306)
Jenner, Belinda J	5:20:06 (28,503)
Jenner, Ruth K	4:25:09 (18,008)
Jennings, Catherine L	6:26:06 (32,377)
Jennings, Jennifer	6:24:03 (32,330)
Jennings, Kim M	4:36:18 (20,803)
Jennings, Linda A	5:00:24 (25,960)
Jennings, Mary E	4:25:04 (17,982)
Jennings, Teresa B	5:02:00 (26,177)
Jennings, Val A	3:23:07 (3,668)
Jensen, Merete B	4:24:38 (17,851)
Jensen, Victoria A	4:24:06 (17,683)
Jepson, Ivy A	4:03:57 (12,704)
Jermain, Jennifer L	4:35:36 (20,624)
Jermyn, Claire K	4:15:58 (15,592)
Jerner, Marie A	5:46:35 (30,832)
Jerrett, Suzanna L	3:58:26 (11,319)
Jersild, Helle	3:19:20 (3,175)
Jeschke, Louisa	3:53:04 (9,655)
Jess, Samantha J	4:38:35 (21,357)
Jessen, Gianna	8:20:51 (33,198)
Jessen, Phillippa M	4:29:30 (19,179)
Jesson-Heslin, Maree	3:21:17 (3,437)
Jessop, Christina D	6:06:14 (31,796)
Jessop, Gina	4:15:40 (15,512)
Jessop, Jacqueline	4:54:56 (24,875)
Jevons, Amy L	4:34:50 (20,444)
Jewett, Melanie K	3:33:19 (5,370)
Jimenez-Royo, Pilar	5:07:04 (26,869)
Jin, Kazuko	4:26:28 (18,376)
Jinkerson, Mandy	4:50:23 (23,920)
Jobson, Amber J	5:21:38 (28,657)
Jobson, Hannah	5:40:45 (30,408)
Johal, Hardeep K	8:29:32 (33,206)
Johal, Jaymini	4:05:59 (13,137)
Johal, Parveen	4:28:13 (18,817)
Johansson, Linda C	4:37:21 (21,072)
John, Caroline V	3:42:44 (7,167)
John, Glynis A	5:19:00 (28,375)
John, Nicki J	4:50:59 (24,044)
John, Sophie	4:13:58 (15,054)
Johns, Emma	4:45:22 (22,877)
Johns, Julie A	4:21:21 (16,947)
Johnson, Amanda J	4:28:51 (18,983)
Johnson, Amanda J	4:58:12 (25,549)
Johnson, Amy E	4:29:44 (19,235)
Johnson, Anna	5:04:08 (26,470)
Johnson, Charlotte J	5:51:31 (31,156)
Johnson, Cher L	6:09:57 (31,924)
Johnson, Christine A	3:57:12 (10,920)
Johnson, Debbie	5:03:38 (26,409)
Johnson, Debbie	5:44:11 (30,658)
Johnson, Elizabeth S	4:20:13 (16,666)
Johnson, Fiona	3:21:14 (3,429)
Johnson, Fiona M	4:27:28 (18,614)
Johnson, Fiona S	4:30:39 (19,462)
Johnson, Hayley J	3:43:57 (7,449)
Johnson, Jean A	4:08:18 (13,689)
Johnson, Julie A	4:10:00 (14,098)
Johnson, Kathleen	4:30:35 (19,446)
Johnson, Kirsty C	4:48:05 (23,446)
Johnson, Linda E	3:25:06 (3,942)
Johnson, Lisa M	3:26:28 (4,142)
Johnson, Louise M	5:14:09 (27,791)
Johnson, Lucinda C	4:05:45 (13,087)
Johnson, Maggie A	4:25:18 (18,054)
Johnson, Michelle G	6:01:37 (31,632)
Johnson, Michelle L	7:00:05 (32,882)
Johnson, Rachel C	5:12:32 (27,592)
Johnson, Riona	5:36:53 (30,124)
Johnson, Sandra	3:53:11 (9,686)
Johnson, Sarah J	5:17:46 (28,216)
Johnson, Shanti M	3:58:11 (11,225)
Johnson, Simone L	3:58:23 (11,298)
Johnson, Sophie A	4:55:52 (25,070)
Johnson, Veera	5:42:32 (30,538)
Johnson, Vicky	5:53:31 (31,241)
Johnson Cox, Kirsty E	4:00:48 (11,993)
Johnston, Alison J	4:34:31 (20,365)
Johnston, Carron	4:11:16 (14,406)
Johnston, Emma V	6:42:09 (32,643)
Johnston, Hazel	5:08:31 (27,081)
Johnston, Lisa M	3:50:36 (9,003)
Johnston, Lynn M	5:04:16 (26,485)
Johnston, Patricia	5:11:53 (27,513)
Johnston, Sarah E	4:44:28 (22,675)
Johnston, Yvette	4:11:08 (14,370)
Johnstone, Anne L	5:16:21 (28,051)
Johnstone, Janice	4:13:47 (15,018)
Johnstone, Ruth	3:21:42 (3,500)
Johnstone, Sarah E	5:25:07 (29,052)
Johnstone, Sophie	4:55:38 (25,023)
Johnstone, Victoria	4:58:40 (25,638)
Joint, Elizabeth H	5:25:45 (29,109)
Jolly, Elizabeth J	4:35:25 (20,583)
Jones, Alice A	5:17:31 (28,196)
Jones, Amanda C	4:32:37 (19,920)
Jones, Amanda E	4:07:31 (13,479)
Jones, Andrea I	5:08:33 (27,084)
Jones, Andrea J	4:34:19 (20,310)
Jones, Angela	3:12:02 (2,280)
Jones, Ann	4:43:43 (22,499)
Jones, Anna	4:23:18 (17,443)
Jones, Anna M	4:25:47 (18,189)
Jones, Carol	4:00:39 (11,965)
Jones, Carol L	5:10:10 (27,282)
Jones, Carole	3:41:32 (6,926)
Jones, Cathy L	5:40:45 (30,408)
Jones, Ceri L	5:03:53 (26,445)
Jones, Ceri L	6:12:25 (32,002)
Jones, Claire E	5:15:14 (27,930)
Jones, Daphne L	4:18:40 (16,270)
Jones, Deirdre R	3:46:30 (8,010)
Jones, Dianne P	4:46:08 (23,033)
Jones, Ellen M	4:54:09 (24,712)
Jones, Emma C	3:56:35 (10,717)
Jones, Ffion C	5:42:54 (30,566)
Jones, Fiona L	4:05:34 (13,040)
Jones, Gwyneth A	4:07:37 (13,512)
Jones, Hannah J	4:19:21 (16,433)
Jones, Hazel	3:15:37 (2,727)
Jones, Helen	4:44:21 (22,647)
Jones, Helen C	3:59:03 (11,526)
Jones, Jane E	7:33:54 (33,110)
Jones, Jayne	4:37:38 (21,144)
Jones, Jenna L	6:02:49 (31,672)
Jones, Jennifer E	5:05:03 (26,589)
Jones, Jenny E	5:01:32 (26,110)
Jones, Judith B	3:53:53 (9,890)
Jones, Julia L	4:40:16 (21,726)
Jones, Juliette	5:19:34 (28,446)
Jones, Justine	3:49:33 (8,759)
Jones, Karen J	5:20:33 (28,567)
Jones, Karen L	5:16:46 (28,100)
Jones, Kate E	3:58:12 (11,233)
Jones, Kerry J	4:58:03 (25,513)
Jones, Kim A	4:28:58 (19,018)
Jones, Kim D	5:15:07 (27,912)
Jones, Kirsty D	4:24:07 (17,691)
Jones, Laura A	4:54:15 (24,737)
Jones, Lauren	4:19:05 (16,363)
Jones, Leontine	4:04:30 (12,816)
Jones, Liz A	4:51:46 (24,202)
Jones, Louise F	5:48:35 (30,976)
Jones, Lowri	4:04:30 (12,816)
Jones, Lyndsey	5:28:00 (29,324)
Jones, Marie E	4:02:20 (12,337)
Jones, Mary	5:25:40 (29,097)
Jones, Meryl	6:20:30 (32,241)
Jones, Moira	5:18:05 (28,251)
Jones, Natalie L	4:43:49 (22,523)
Jones, Nia	4:50:06 (23,861)
Jones, Nicola L	4:51:30 (24,144)
Jones, Pauline	4:22:06 (17,146)
Jones, Rachael A	3:55:51 (10,490)
Jones, Rachel B	4:28:56 (19,006)
Jones, Rebecca F	4:34:01 (20,249)
Jones, Rebecca M	3:36:11 (5,872)
Jones, Rhian E	3:59:06 (11,543)
Jones, Rhian E	5:00:16 (25,937)
Jones, Rosalind A	4:23:38 (17,542)
Jones, Sarah A	3:32:54 (5,307)
Jones, Sarah J	4:33:10 (20,051)
Jones, Sharon	4:02:50 (12,445)
Jones, Sian	6:01:59 (31,639)
Jones, Tracey	4:04:13 (12,760)
Jones, Tracy J	3:35:23 (5,732)
Jones, Tricia	4:40:57 (21,882)
Jones, Vanessa D	4:35:51 (20,683)
Jones, Vera E	5:44:14 (30,663)
Jones, Vicky	4:37:04 (20,993)
Jones, Victoria M	4:29:59 (19,288)
Jones, Yvonne I	3:40:16 (6,671)
Jones, Yvonne J	4:16:08 (15,629)
Jones-Crofts, Helen L	4:02:15 (12,319)
Jonsdottir, Valgerdur E	3:36:51 (6,008)
Jonsson, Kristina	4:18:53 (16,323)
Jordaan, Antalene N	4:50:46 (23,995)
Jordan, Anna F	4:16:58 (15,851)
Jordan, Deborah M	4:43:56 (22,558)
Jordan, Julie L	3:50:20 (8,940)
Jordan Spence, Julie	6:11:38 (31,975)
Jordansen, Karin I	3:26:40 (4,187)
Joseph, Stephanie T	5:39:59 (30,363)
Joshua, Katie E	5:03:02 (26,321)
Jourbert, Glenys	5:14:13 (27,800)
Jousselin, Helen E	4:56:51 (25,270)
Jowett, Tracey A	5:19:47 (28,470)
Joy, Amelia J	4:50:15 (23,893)
Joy, Caroline	5:04:41 (26,541)
Joyce, Annette	4:46:58 (23,200)
Joyce, Linda	5:10:11 (27,284)
Joyce, Sinead M	4:29:36 (19,199)
Juby, Sarah J	5:12:21 (27,568)
Juchau, Nathalie G	4:04:53 (12,893)
Jucker, Pia	3:19:51 (3,242)
Judd, Hayley	4:41:38 (22,026)
Jude, Abi	5:24:29 (28,988)
Jude, Angela S	7:39:39 (33,142)
Judson, Jill Y	4:33:16 (20,077)
Jukes, Victoria A	5:06:58 (26,854)
Jules, Frederique	3:15:49 (2,755)
Julian, Nicola J	5:41:36 (30,465)
Jung, Joann H	5:35:15 (29,993)
Juniper, Heather E	5:16:55 (28,118)
Jupp, Rebecca	4:43:49 (22,523)
Jupp, Tracy S	5:03:56 (26,448)

Jury, Martina M	4:17:57 (16,095)
Justice, Victoria J	5:00:33 (25,976)
Kabza, Clare V	3:12:30 (2,342)
Kadejo, Remi	5:00:45 (26,000)
Kafadar, Helon	5:31:51 (29,729)
Kallmeyer, Janice	4:28:27 (18,882)
Kalve, Christin	5:10:43 (27,354)
Kaminski, Audrey C	5:45:27 (30,753)
Kamvissidis, Sarah	4:35:53 (20,686)
Kane, Kerry	5:21:56 (28,709)
Kane, Sasha S.	4:50:17 (23,901)
Kane, Sidell	4:58:06 (25,529)
Kane, Theresa M	6:20:01 (32,230)
Karen, Pickering	5:28:02 (29,326)
Karin Vango, Jeannette	4:42:44 (22,267)
Karp, Anna	4:12:31 (14,710)
Karvonen, Liisa E	4:04:59 (12,915)
Kasa, Annamaria	5:50:02 (31,076)

Kastor, Deena 2:19:36 (28)

Deena Kastor (born 14 February 1973 in Waltham, Massachusetts) holds American records in the marathon, half-marathon, and numerous road distances. Kastor's most noted accomplishment is winning marathon bronze at the 2004 Olympics in Athens. She became the first American marathoner to win an Olympic medal for twenty years in the brutally hot conditions. Two years later in 2006, she set the American women's marathon record of 2:19:36 at the London Marathon. She won silver medals in the World Cross Country Championships in 2002 and 2003. In August 2008, Kastor pulled out of the women's marathon at the Beijing Olympics with a foot injury. At about the 5km mark, she dropped to one knee and was forced to withdraw from the race with a broken foot. Kastor lives with her husband Andrew Kastor in Mammoth Lakes, California, where she is coached by Terrence Mahon. She trains 140 miles a week.

Kastor was forced to take a tiring two-day journey to London via Paris to run in the 2010 London Marathon following airline chaos cause by the Icelandic volcanic ash cloud. Understandably, she had a rare off-day, struggling to finish 18th in 2:36:20. It was the slowest time for any marathon she had completed in her career since taking up the event in 2001.

Katz, Joanna	4:12:08 (14,608)
Kavanagh, Barbara T	4:30:46 (19,488)
Kavanagh, Jan	4:25:44 (18,169)
Kavanagh, Joanne	4:04:00 (12,714)
Kavanagh, Kerry A	5:29:55 (29,536)
Kay, Diana M	4:44:04 (22,578)
Kay, Rebecca J	4:47:31 (23,324)
Kay, Susan	4:20:41 (16,783)
Keane, Bronagh P	4:19:30 (16,478)
Kearney, Alexandra R	4:42:58 (22,322)
Kearney, Linda M	4:18:29 (16,228)
Kearney, Lyndsay M	3:53:48 (9,861)
Kearney, Rachel	5:11:50 (27,501)
Kearns, Zannah C	5:18:56 (28,365)
Kearsey, Rachel	4:54:17 (24,742)
Keating, Lucy K	4:43:03 (22,335)
Keats, Susan	3:59:47 (11,755)
Keck, Michaela	4:46:16 (23,069)
Keddilty, Sarah L	5:38:10 (30,215)
Keeble, Dawn M	5:43:49 (30,627)
Keeble, Mandy J	4:50:03 (23,850)
Keefe, Neilma J	5:29:27 (29,480)
Keegan, Helen E	4:03:25 (12,582)
Keehner, Claire E	6:00:19 (31,575)
Keelan, Annika E	4:47:10 (23,247)
Keen, Diana J	4:39:34 (21,567)
Keenan, Helen B	5:34:38 (29,947)
Keenan, Mandy	4:50:18 (23,905)
Keene, Alison T	4:51:47 (24,207)
Keep, Jocelyn E	4:16:53 (15,827)
Kefford-Watson, Angela F	3:16:26 (2,813)
Keighley, Lesley A	4:34:23 (20,335)
Keilty, Veronica A	4:56:14 (25,146)
Keitch, Jane M	5:18:11 (28,268)
Kelly, Caroline	6:33:21 (32,503)
Kelly, Carolyn	4:27:24 (18,602)
Kelly, Geraldine P	4:43:44 (22,502)
Kelly, Jennifer	4:52:17 (24,303)
Kelly, Justine P	3:57:45 (11,093)
Kelly, Maureen T	5:20:44 (28,584)
Kelly, Nicky	3:27:43 (4,367)
Kelly, Rebecca L	5:21:08 (28,620)
Kelly, Rosalind	5:05:01 (26,583)
Kelly, Tara J	5:04:29 (26,523)
Kelly, Theresa M	4:59:57 (25,879)
Kelly, Tracy	3:40:20 (6,681)
Kelsey, Gita M	4:28:09 (18,792)
Kelso, Melany	5:01:24 (26,098)
Kemma, Horst	4:38:03 (21,239)
Kemp, Anne R	3:46:27 (8,000)
Kemp, Carolyn P	3:48:44 (8,565)
Kemp, Cecilia	4:19:50 (16,562)
Kemp, Helene L	6:17:07 (32,145)
Kemp, Hilary D	3:47:18 (8,191)
Kemp, Jessica L	3:56:24 (10,656)
Kemsley, Olivia J	5:56:10 (31,361)
Kendall, Sarah	4:33:25 (20,113)
Kenden, Fran	3:48:34 (8,517)
Kenley, Natalie N	5:35:04 (29,973)
Kennard, Terri	7:13:26 (33,001)
Kenneally, Andrea	5:00:07 (25,908)
Kenneally, Tanya	3:45:46 (7,863)
Kennedy, Audrey M	5:03:21 (26,364)
Kennedy, Caroline A	4:54:24 (24,770)
Kennedy, Evelyn	4:23:02 (17,369)
Kennedy, Iryana	4:00:01 (11,820)
Kennedy, Lesley	5:28:38 (29,389)
Kennedy, Linda	3:42:54 (7,206)
Kennedy, Monnelia	5:29:55 (29,536)
Kennedy, Nari	4:23:50 (17,605)
Kennedy, Susan E	4:21:13 (16,920)
Kennell, Donna S	5:09:48 (27,241)
Kennelly, Michelle R	5:53:19 (31,233)
Kenney, Bianca	6:59:10 (32,870)
Kennon, Katie V	4:05:54 (13,118)
Kenny, Nicola J	6:07:42 (31,848)
Kenrick, Kate M	4:12:53 (14,806)
Kent, Christine	5:48:43 (30,981)
Kent, Jenny A	4:27:21 (18,594)
Kent, Katherine M	7:30:25 (33,097)
Kent, Lorraine M	4:00:20 (11,896)
Kent, Rosie	3:41:04 (6,820)
Kent, Ruth	4:06:16 (13,185)

Kent, Ruth M	4:32:36 (19,916)
Kent, Sarah M	4:42:55 (22,310)
Kenward, Cassie J	5:14:04 (27,776)
Kenward, Judy A	5:36:57 (30,129)
Kenwright, Dawn L	3:15:50 (2,759)
Keogh, Samantha R	5:13:01 (27,657)
Keough, Lisa A	5:19:06 (28,385)
Keppel, Luci E	5:19:32 (28,441)
Kernaghan, Hilary A	3:22:29 (3,591)
Kerner, Caroll	3:40:45 (6,752)
Kerr, Angela	3:53:59 (9,917)
Kerr, Cath	4:51:02 (24,047)
Kerr, Emma J	4:56:21 (25,175)
Kerr, Gina	5:17:51 (28,226)
Kerr, Lucy J	4:45:36 (22,926)
Kerr, Raewyne J	4:01:39 (12,184)
Kerry, Patricia	3:51:19 (9,178)
Kershen, Amanda-Jane	4:33:56 (20,231)
Kerslake, Julia M	6:14:36 (32,073)
Ketchen, Susan	4:42:39 (22,249)
Kettle, Anthea J	4:15:07 (15,372)
Kettle, Charlotte S	5:18:54 (28,358)
Kettle, Helen E	4:52:05 (24,263)
Key, Cherry	4:47:05 (23,231)
Keys, Christine E	6:26:07 (32,382)
Keys, Emma Jane	4:49:48 (23,806)
Keyte, Julie D	5:03:46 (26,422)
Keyworth, Helen L	3:57:07 (10,888)
Keyworth, Nicky J	4:54:59 (24,891)
Khaghani, Clare S	5:07:01 (26,865)
Khaleque, Shahara	4:25:40 (18,153)
Khan, Ayesha	6:03:42 (31,712)
Khan, Eleanor J	4:04:55 (12,899)
Khan, Faheen	5:16:34 (28,079)
Khan, Lucy C	3:42:32 (7,121)
Khan, Norren	6:44:18 (32,679)
Khan, Ubeda N	5:52:11 (31,188)
Khan, Zena	5:49:37 (31,049)
Khimji, Rekha R	6:23:32 (32,318)
Khoo, Eileen A	5:43:41 (30,619)
Khoshnevis, Heather	3:40:08 (6,645)
Kidd, Chico	5:37:58 (30,200)
Kidd, Gillian	3:48:54 (8,609)
Kidd, Lindsey	4:23:32 (17,513)
Kidman, Tracey D	5:33:23 (29,839)
Kier, Rebecca M	5:35:11 (29,984)
Kilcast, Sharon	6:21:54 (32,281)
Kilch, Aryn A	4:16:39 (15,769)
Kilgallon, Geraldine	4:12:11 (14,620)
Kilgour, Alexandra H	3:52:16 (9,431)
Killen Quinan, Fiona M	4:49:00 (23,649)
Killick, Julia	4:29:43 (19,234)
Kilmartin, Sarah L	3:55:11 (10,275)
Kilmnartin, Claire E	4:49:27 (23,746)
Kilner, Annabel E	4:55:38 (25,023)
Kim, Christina	5:36:09 (30,068)
Kim, Clara H	4:21:40 (17,015)
Kimberley, Michelle	3:58:22 (11,293)
Kimbley, Liz	3:53:09 (9,676)
Kinber, Lorraine A	7:23:45 (33,062)
Kinch, Brenda E	4:09:38 (14,019)
King, Annette S	5:22:13 (28,744)
King, Chris A	3:19:55 (3,250)
King, Claire L	3:49:37 (8,775)
King, Fiona	5:49:19 (31,028)
King, Hannah C	7:26:37 (33,080)
King, Helen E	5:15:53 (27,828)
King, Janette	5:16:00 (27,999)
King, Janey G	4:48:12 (23,471)
King, Karen	5:07:52 (26,985)
King, Liz C	7:02:42 (32,900)
King, Nadine M	5:25:41 (29,099)
King, Natalie M	5:08:39 (27,100)
King, Nichola I	5:29:47 (29,518)
King, Penny A	4:26:00 (18,258)
King, Philippa C	4:58:12 (25,549)
King, Rebecca L	5:44:07 (30,653)
King, Rowena J	4:07:48 (13,555)
King, Sharon	3:38:52 (6,402)
King, Shirley C	5:47:39 (30,929)
Kingdon, Fiona J	3:33:45 (5,442)
Kingdon, Paula	4:11:44 (14,503)
Kingdon, Samantha L	5:19:38 (28,450)

Lee, Nicola J 3:39:55 (6,610)
Lee, Ruth 3:53:34 (9,782)
Lee, Sarah J 4:26:28 (18,376)
Lee, Sharon D 6:28:13 (32,428)
Lee, Sonia K 4:35:53 (20,686)
Lee, Susan L 5:07:09 (26,887)
Leech, Jane E 3:34:07 (5,502)
Leech, Sheila V 5:10:47 (27,363)
Leefe, Joy F 4:39:42 (21,599)
Lees, Jennifer I 4:08:55 (13,842)
Leeson, Yvonne 3:35:54 (5,818)
Leete, Jenny M 4:28:10 (18,799)
Legallais, Sylvie 3:12:53 (2,385)
Legg, Charlotte H 4:34:28 (20,356)
Legg, Tessa L 4:38:48 (21,391)
Leggett, Anne 3:39:51 (6,597)
Leggett, Janet D 3:52:34 (9,510)
Leggett, Karen P 4:57:01 (25,315)
Leggott, Louise 4:28:17 (18,833)
Legoff, Sonia 4:35:50 (20,680)
Lehmann, Lumen 6:38:31 (32,589)
Lehmer, Christine 4:40:49 (21,858)
Leibbrandt, Dedj D 5:04:51 (26,561)
Leigh, Katie L 4:59:10 (25,733)
Leigh-Pemberton, Lucy R 5:01:27 (26,101)
Leighton, Michelle J 3:37:11 (6,072)
Leitch, Claire S 3:58:26 (11,319)
Leitch, Jessica R 3:11:19 (2,199)
Lejeune, Rose 4:33:14 (20,067)
Leleu, Roselyn 4:22:47 (17,318)
Lemon, Jennifer V 4:52:46 (24,414)
Lemon, Katy J 5:55:29 (31,326)
Lemon, Tessa A 4:25:25 (18,095)
Lenaghan, Donna 3:38:25 (6,309)
Lench, Angela J 4:55:15 (24,949)
Lennon, Emma K 5:03:21 (26,364)
Lennon, Myanna N 3:07:57 (1,852)
Lennon, Susan H 3:38:04 (6,242)
Lentell, Nicki J 5:40:33 (30,393)
Leonard, Bernadette 5:30:21 (29,579)
Leonard, Catherine 3:43:17 (7,306)
Leonard, Gillian D 4:15:22 (15,437)
Leonard, Karen 4:27:46 (18,686)
Leonard, Kirsten A 4:27:08 (18,538)
Leonard, Philippa M 4:50:33 (23,949)
Leonard, Sally E 4:59:38 (25,818)
Leonard, Vanessa K 4:42:08 (22,146)
Leonard-Morgan, Samantha 5:14:39 (27,869)
Lerner, Daniella 4:51:17 (24,089)
Leservoisier, Michelle 2:52:54 (671)
Leslie, Thérèse 4:33:26 (20,121)
Lester, Helen E 3:33:12 (5,353)
Lester, Melanie 4:47:16 (23,272)
Lester, Rebecca L 5:44:10 (30,657)
Letchford, Sally M 5:14:30 (27,841)
Leupold-Langauer, Ingrid C 4:09:22 (13,950)
Levene, Karen A 3:41:11 (6,849)
Leveque, Jean Loup 4:08:16 (13,683)
Leveque, Julie 3:54:57 (10,190)
Leverett, Ann E 4:24:39 (17,858)
Levey, Mary 6:52:34 (32,790)
Levinson, Jacqueline E 5:37:44 (30,185)
Levinson, Susanne 5:30:56 (29,640)
Levitt, Fiona E 3:50:22 (8,945)
Levitt, Julie M 5:33:34 (29,857)
Levoir, Judi L 4:01:25 (12,135)
Levy, Jacqueline V 4:59:07 (25,726)
Levy, Karen I 3:27:06 (4,259)
Levy, Nadine E 6:13:09 (32,024)
Lewington-Bracey, Charlie M 4:36:59 (20,976)
Lewis, Alexandra M 4:06:38 (13,256)
Lewis, Amanda J 5:21:16 (28,642)
Lewis, Amanda S 4:19:31 (16,482)
Lewis, Anne J 4:57:26 (25,386)
Lewis, Carole J 8:27:16 (33,202)
Lewis, Caroline A 4:02:37 (12,405)
Lewis, Caroline A 4:56:57 (25,295)
Lewis, Catrin 6:56:15 (32,844)
Lewis, Eileen 4:08:55 (13,842)
Lewis, Gilly S 5:22:01 (28,720)
Lewis, Heather R 4:33:02 (20,013)
Lewis, Jenny D 5:27:48 (29,303)
Lewis, Jodie A 4:53:09 (24,491)
Lewis, Julie 3:37:51 (6,199)
Lewis, Julie M 6:36:51 (32,562)
Lewis, Karen L 4:38:47 (21,387)
Lewis, Kate E 5:23:02 (28,832)
Lewis, Kathy 3:55:01 (10,209)
Lewis, Lindsay J 3:56:21 (10,638)
Lewis, Lisa J 3:47:00 (8,119)
Lewis, Lucie J 8:38:51 (33,212)
Lewis, Mererid 6:16:17 (32,128)
Lewis, Natalie 5:04:20 (26,496)
Lewis, Rebecca G 4:00:18 (11,887)
Lewis, Ruth F 4:15:50 (15,559)
Lewis, Sarah J 5:39:03 (30,288)
Lewis, Sarah N 3:46:23 (7,979)
Lewis, Sophie C 4:17:09 (15,894)
Lewis, Susie 4:37:57 (21,211)
Leyne, Breda M 4:14:49 (15,288)
Li, May-Fay J 4:54:50 (24,856)
Liberty, Darrelyn J 5:22:59 (28,824)
Lichtenstein, Jane M 4:52:09 (24,279)
Lid, Turid 5:00:50 (26,016)
Liddell, Lindsey C 4:09:29 (13,992)
Liddle, Hilary 6:41:51 (32,638)
Liddle, Pauline 6:25:40 (32,368)
Liesenfelt, Barbara A 4:28:21 (18,858)
Liggins, Tracy A 6:01:30 (31,627)
Lightfoot, Michele B 5:25:39 (29,095)
Liley, Clare E 4:05:35 (13,047)
Lilley, Jennifer M 4:37:36 (21,137)
Lilley, Rozalind K 3:37:22 (6,109)
Lilley, Sophie J 3:59:23 (11,634)
Lillyman, Helen L 5:46:43 (30,840)
Lillywhite, Rebecca K 4:31:47 (19,743)
Lim, A Kim 3:57:10 (10,911)
Limer, Joanne 5:29:50 (29,527)
Limmer, Caitlin R 5:18:53 (28,354)
Linaker, Karen P 4:44:27 (22,666)
Lind, Sharleen 4:35:07 (20,513)
Lindenberg, Sue 4:30:13 (19,357)
Lindley, Toinette E 4:39:50 (21,636)
Lindner, Jana 4:41:07 (21,918)
Lindsay, Heather A 5:09:02 (27,152)
Lindsey, Claire E 4:56:20 (25,172)
Lines, Deborah F 5:12:15 (27,555)
Lines, Susan J 4:36:22 (20,819)
Ling, Ann E 6:18:50 (32,194)
Ling, Kathy M 6:44:29 (32,684)
Ling, Melanie 3:22:32 (3,602)
Ling, Melanie J 4:58:03 (25,513)
Lingiah, Shereena M 4:34:22 (20,331)
Linsey, Clare 4:24:37 (17,845)
Linton, Sara J 4:36:20 (20,812)
Linwood, Joanna K 4:43:54 (22,549)
Linzell, Laraine A 5:56:42 (31,389)
Lion, Charlotte 4:08:17 (13,686)
Lion, Sharon R 6:47:08 (32,725)
Lipede, Kehinde F 4:03:46 (12,665)
Lis, Emily 3:21:03 (3,405)
Lishman, Tracy L 3:58:57 (11,490)
Lisney, Lisa M 5:19:40 (28,452)
Lister, Evelyne 4:24:16 (17,735)
Lister, Jane A 4:48:46 (23,602)
Lister, Jessica A 4:30:16 (19,371)
Lister, Jill F 4:53:09 (24,491)
Lister, Katherine M 5:39:46 (30,343)
Littell, Sarah A 4:54:53 (24,868)
Litterick, Emma C 3:37:46 (6,180)
Little, Gina M 4:27:22 (18,595)
Little, Maxine 4:03:41 (12,646)
Little, Norma E 5:29:19 (29,459)
Little, Rachael 4:34:52 (20,449)
Little, Sarah J 7:05:46 (32,944)
Little, Susan A 3:31:35 (5,084)
Little, Susan E 4:38:04 (21,245)
Little, Zoe C 4:32:21 (19,873)
Littlefair, Gillian M 4:07:51 (13,570)
Liu, Michelle 3:43:11 (7,285)
Livemore, Clare 5:06:05 (26,724)
Livermore, Sarah S 5:58:42 (31,495)
Livingston, Joanne I 4:52:06 (24,268)
Livingston, Kirsty J 4:36:05 (20,746)
Livingstone, Karen A 6:21:25 (32,269)
Lizzimore, Lisa J 4:33:50 (20,209)
Llewellyn, Catherine 5:20:52 (28,597)
Llewellyn, David E 5:38:02 (30,206)
Llewellyn, Janice 4:36:23 (20,820)
Lloyd, Amelia J 3:50:59 (9,095)
Lloyd, Amy 4:33:20 (20,092)
Lloyd, Camilla F 4:35:21 (20,568)
Lloyd, Catherine 4:51:10 (24,072)
Lloyd, Helen A 3:57:33 (11,028)
Lloyd, Jackalene J 4:42:07 (22,138)
Lloyd, Jennifer A 4:37:09 (21,013)
Lloyd, Karen J 4:32:51 (19,967)
Lloyd, Laura V 4:35:21 (20,568)
Lloyd, Margaret H 5:37:20 (30,153)
Lloyd, Nancy W 5:18:28 (28,304)
Lloyd, Philippa R 6:10:31 (31,945)
Lloyd, Sarah L 4:47:03 (23,222)
Lloyd, Susan M 4:24:57 (17,946)
Lloyd Richards, Veronica M 5:07:44 (26,967)
Loach, Kate E 3:39:24 (6,518)
Loader, Jackie A 4:23:59 (17,648)
Loake, Catherine J 3:20:49 (3,377)
Local, Michelle 5:01:41 (26,132)
Loch, Julie 6:00:49 (31,595)
Lock, Claire 5:32:12 (29,753)
Lock, Katy 5:08:04 (27,018)
Lock, Maria E 3:56:32 (10,694)
Lock, Suzanne V 4:12:05 (14,591)
Lockett, Joanne H 6:05:01 (31,761)
Lockhart, Jean M 5:21:09 (28,623)
Lockie, Joanne L 3:45:56 (7,893)
Lockton, Julie E 5:17:29 (28,193)
Lockwood, Claire L 4:47:49 (23,386)
Lockwood, Linda A 4:00:42 (11,976)
Lodder, Anje 4:37:32 (21,117)
Lodge, Judy A 4:29:47 (19,248)
Lodge, Kimberley J 6:20:43 (32,245)
Lodge, Tara 4:34:59 (20,483)
Lodwig, Clare E 3:53:51 (9,882)
Logan, Caroline A 5:22:07 (28,728)
Logan, Cathryn 5:00:10 (25,918)
Logue, Aoife C 6:05:42 (31,785)
Logue, Donna M 4:28:05 (18,771)
Logue, Nicola 4:05:42 (13,078)
Loillier, Christine 4:08:32 (13,750)
Lomas, Hayley 3:44:46 (7,631)
Lombardo, Elise 4:50:04 (23,855)
Long, Ann 5:36:57 (30,129)
Long, Deborah L 4:05:41 (13,074)
Long, Felicia F 5:08:51 (27,125)
Long, Helen P 5:18:21 (28,289)
Long, Janet N 4:33:05 (20,025)
Long, Marlies O 4:51:52 (24,225)
Long, Mary E 5:37:49 (30,191)
Long, Samantha J 5:56:54 (31,403)
Long, Sandra J 4:07:10 (13,396)
Longden, Lorraine L 3:54:30 (10,051)
Longhurst, Jane R 4:54:12 (24,730)
Longhurst, Karen E 5:59:34 (31,537)
Longley, Zira K 4:53:46 (24,633)
Lonsdale, Hannelore 4:27:39 (18,671)
Lonsdale, Rachel E 5:23:17 (28,865)
Loomes, Lynda A 6:58:55 (32,866)
Loos, Rebecca 4:47:18 (23,276)
Loosemore, Kathryn M 4:33:31 (20,138)
Lopez-Turner, Ana 5:04:01 (26,459)
Loprete, Fabiola 4:51:19 (24,097)
Lord, Julia 3:59:25 (11,641)
Lord, Katherine L 4:26:27 (18,371)
Lord, Nicola J 4:02:06 (12,285)
Lorrimer-Roberts, Claire 4:32:29 (19,900)
Losito, Jo Ann 6:26:47 (32,397)
Lothe, Grete H 4:48:27 (23,527)
Loughrey, Elizabeth E 5:27:37 (29,284)
Loughrey-Jennings, Sarah C 4:15:11 (15,384)
Loury, Sebastien 4:15:47 (15,540)
Lousada, Alison R 4:10:47 (14,270)
Lovatt, Ellen L 4:45:14 (22,845)
Love, Gail E 3:58:30 (11,340)
Loveday, Melanie A 5:46:26 (30,819)
Loveless, Sarah 5:02:51 (26,295)
Lovell, Sally J 3:31:03 (4,996)
Lovelock, Karen 5:49:59 (31,071)
Lovensheimer, Kelly 3:09:57 (2,058)

Marsh, Chloe	5:09:04 (27,155)	
Marsh, Clare L	4:50:54 (24,025)	
Marsh, Lucy J	5:19:42 (28,460)	
Marsh, Nicola C	4:32:40 (19,925)	
Marsh, Sara E	4:25:25 (18,095)	
Marsh, Tamzin E	4:22:29 (17,240)	
Marshall, Catriona F	4:12:59 (14,831)	
Marshall, Cindy C	3:51:46 (9,294)	
Marshall, Heather	3:47:16 (8,186)	
Marshall, Heather	3:55:12 (10,282)	
Marshall, Helen M	8:02:49 (33,179)	
Marshall, Liz	4:46:53 (23,192)	
Marshall, Michala M	5:59:57 (31,559)	
Marshall, Sheila M	4:05:23 (12,994)	
Marshall, Susan	4:17:46 (16,052)	
Marshall, Susan E	3:28:53 (4,601)	
Marshall, Teresa A	4:46:45 (23,165)	
Marshall, Tracy A	4:44:34 (22,686)	
Martell, Barbara	5:24:40 (29,002)	
Martin, Amanda J	3:22:13 (3,558)	
Martin, Anna G	4:16:02 (15,604)	
Martin, Anne C	4:36:35 (20,865)	
Martin, Beverley J	5:06:24 (26,772)	
Martin, Brenda	3:41:06 (6,827)	
Martin, Brinder	4:22:09 (17,157)	
Martin, Carol A	3:28:57 (4,612)	
Martin, Caroline R	3:47:18 (8,191)	
Martin, Cathleen A	4:30:18 (19,378)	
Martin, Cheryl T	5:29:05 (29,431)	
Martin, Clare E	3:00:22 (1,258)	
Martin, Dawn R	3:47:50 (8,336)	
Martin, Debbie	3:50:51 (9,066)	
Martin, Esme M	4:27:22 (18,595)	
Martin, Jill E	5:08:28 (27,071)	
Martin, Joanne	4:11:53 (14,547)	
Martin, Nicola	4:58:54 (25,687)	
Martin, Rebecca	5:12:23 (27,574)	
Martin, Sam J	4:54:57 (24,880)	
Martin, Sarah E	5:52:37 (31,202)	
Martin, Sarah L	5:38:21 (30,237)	
Martin, Sharon	4:46:46 (23,166)	
Martin, Shirley	5:26:32 (29,176)	
Martinez, Catherine	4:15:48 (15,544)	
Martinez, Susan C	4:41:21 (21,963)	
Martino, Orsolina I	3:58:07 (11,195)	
Maruyama, Chieko	5:04:10 (26,471)	
Marval, Anitia L	4:25:20 (18,067)	
Marvel, Alison J	3:40:50 (6,765)	
Marzaioli, Sarah L	3:53:48 (9,861)	
Masding, Deborah J	4:46:59 (23,210)	
Mash, Jane E	7:31:53 (33,100)	
Maskell, Amanda J	4:43:29 (22,431)	
Mason, Camilla	4:04:12 (12,756)	
Mason, Claire E	5:37:39 (30,178)	
Mason, Dawn	4:24:50 (17,898)	
Mason, Gayle A	4:31:38 (19,705)	
Mason, Hayley	4:52:22 (24,325)	
Mason, Helen R	5:00:25 (25,964)	
Mason, Janet S	4:29:59 (19,288)	
Mason, Kate E	4:16:36 (15,756)	
Mason, Sarah A	5:08:50 (27,122)	
Mason, Wendy A	3:58:03 (11,168)	
Massarella, Francesca	5:48:37 (30,977)	
Massetti, Caterina	5:14:54 (27,895)	
Massetti, Noemi	4:27:11 (18,551)	
Massey, Diane B	4:19:46 (16,544)	
Massey, Kara J	3:40:21 (6,682)	
Massingham, Andrea M	5:12:04 (27,532)	
Masson, Kim C	3:12:03 (2,283)	
Masuda, Junko	5:27:38 (29,286)	
Mate, Suzanne J	4:34:35 (20,383)	
Matharu, Charanjeet K	4:26:23 (18,357)	
Mather, Christine	4:07:22 (13,439)	
Mathers, Julie B	4:21:14 (16,924)	
Mathers, Linda	3:35:52 (5,810)	
Mathers, Sarah L	4:38:14 (21,287)	
Matheson, Patricia E	3:18:30 (3,065)	
Mathews, Eleanor	3:45:42 (7,851)	
Mathews, Laura	5:14:13 (27,800)	
Mathias, Simone	3:24:58 (3,928)	
Mathieson, Emma L	4:47:36 (23,342)	
Mathieu, Penelope D	4:40:26 (21,756)	
Mathis, Sylvie	3:47:56 (8,363)	
Matsuzaki, Masako	5:50:03 (31,079)	
Matta, Sara L	4:19:54 (16,578)	
Mattar, Carole E	5:28:34 (29,378)	
Mattes, Antoinette	4:03:48 (12,675)	
Matthews, Clare	4:14:11 (15,137)	
Matthews, Clare L	4:47:23 (23,287)	
Matthews, Denise	3:59:06 (11,543)	
Matthews, Di J	5:52:06 (31,185)	
Matthews, Hayley E	6:10:54 (31,952)	
Matthews, Jean M	7:03:56 (32,926)	
Matthews, Jo L	6:03:13 (31,693)	
Matthews, Judith A	4:50:55 (24,028)	
Matthews, Kelly M	5:28:11 (29,350)	
Matthews, Lorraine	5:25:53 (29,121)	
Matthews, Zoe E	4:56:24 (25,189)	
Mattingley, Angela M	5:37:44 (30,185)	
Mattson, Jennifer M	5:09:43 (27,229)	
Maudsley, Barbara M	5:32:48 (29,798)	
Maund, Louisa J	3:39:58 (6,623)	
Maunder, Tamsin	4:28:52 (18,989)	
Maxted, Margaret A	4:16:17 (15,664)	
Maxwell, Sinead M	5:43:37 (30,613)	
May, Andrea E	4:47:45 (23,374)	
May, Ellie-Louise	3:53:57 (9,908)	
May, Holly	2:44:59 (343)	
May, Lucy R	4:57:52 (25,470)	
May, Marion K	4:34:51 (20,448)	
Maycock, Fiona J	3:32:08 (5,184)	
Mayers, Karen L	7:23:40 (33,059)	
Mayes, Katherine L	5:02:13 (26,208)	
Mayhew, Danielle	5:14:04 (27,776)	
Mayhew, Linda A	5:08:08 (27,026)	
Maynard, Linda H	6:07:48 (31,854)	
Maynard, Samantha L	4:56:22 (25,179)	
Maynard, Zara V	4:55:25 (24,985)	
Maynes, Helena	3:52:47 (9,564)	
Mayo, Clare L	5:58:57 (31,502)	
Mayo, Janet	5:55:08 (31,310)	
Mayo, Jenni M	5:00:35 (25,981)	
Mayor, Marie P	4:59:39 (25,823)	
Mays, Carly A	4:55:07 (24,922)	
Maziere, Angela M	3:43:28 (7,344)	
Mazza, Roseleen P	4:37:56 (21,204)	
Mazzuca, Marzia	4:26:36 (18,408)	
McAdam, Julia F	5:11:08 (27,400)	
McAlindon, Elisa J	4:40:54 (21,873)	
McAllister, Allison M	4:05:42 (13,078)	
McAllister, Orlaith	5:49:48 (31,056)	
McAlpine, Cheryl	4:03:03 (12,492)	
McAndrew, Bernadette A	5:25:51 (29,116)	
McArdle, Deirdre M	4:45:09 (22,820)	
McArthur, Lucy-Jane	3:54:08 (9,953)	
McAulay, Frances M	5:06:43 (26,820)	
McAuslane, Amy	4:48:02 (23,434)	
McBeth, Colene	3:37:23 (6,111)	
McBride, Susan L	4:47:04 (23,226)	
McCabe, Anni	5:29:39 (29,497)	
McCabe, Julia A	6:23:24 (32,314)	
McCabe, Laura	4:58:14 (25,555)	
McCabe, Veronica M	4:47:54 (23,407)	
McCall, Julie L	4:33:30 (20,135)	
McCall, Marion S	3:28:49 (4,578)	
McCallum, Caroline R	5:12:04 (27,532)	
McCallum, Lucy	5:07:52 (26,985)	
McCalvey, Clare	4:20:51 (16,820)	
McCann, Mary	4:21:53 (17,084)	
McCardle, Rebecca	4:31:13 (19,586)	
McCart, Nicola	6:42:37 (32,649)	
McCarthy, Abby	5:12:34 (27,598)	
McCarthy, Anna E	6:19:52 (32,225)	
McCarthy, Bernadette	4:46:35 (23,139)	
McCarthy, Beth A	5:34:57 (29,963)	
McCarthy, Christine	3:03:38 (1,487)	
McCarthy, Deirdre O	5:16:23 (28,056)	
McCarthy, Hilary A	4:00:00 (11,810)	
McCarthy, Martin	4:43:27 (22,421)	
McCarthy, Patricia	5:00:12 (25,927)	
McCartney, Gillian L	4:25:54 (18,233)	
McCleary, Samantha J	5:41:43 (30,475)	
McCleave, Veronica M	6:25:25 (32,363)	
McClure, Kathryn E	6:55:53 (32,837)	
McCluskey, Hazel M	3:32:40 (5,273)	
McCluskey, Sarah E	4:48:51 (23,620)	
McCluskie, Caroline E	3:50:05 (8,880)	
McCole, Selina I	3:39:15 (6,489)	
McCombe, Collette	4:55:34 (25,010)	
McCombie, Sarah L	5:07:26 (26,923)	
McConley, Susan K	4:23:12 (17,414)	
McConnell, Gemma L	5:24:05 (28,953)	
McConnell, Julie	3:34:37 (5,596)	
McConnell, Ruth A	6:05:16 (31,769)	
McCoy, Joanne K	3:01:52 (1,362)	
McCrakle, Karen	4:07:47 (13,552)	
McCreery, Claire E	3:22:48 (3,635)	
McCrow, Clare L	4:48:30 (23,540)	
McCullagh, Carole I	3:51:47 (9,300)	
McCulloch, Ellyn S	4:33:43 (20,193)	
McCutcheon, Jacqui A	5:22:17 (28,751)	
McDavid, Jennifer	4:22:13 (17,179)	
McDermott, Ailish M	3:49:14 (8,674)	
McDermott, Caroline J	4:56:39 (25,229)	
McDermott, Claire	4:01:45 (12,199)	
McDermott, Teresa	5:53:58 (31,261)	
McDevitt, Kathleen	5:26:50 (29,204)	
McDonagh, Lorraine M	3:40:16 (6,671)	
McDonald, Joanne M	5:45:15 (30,735)	
McDonald, Julie	3:25:42 (4,028)	
McDonald, Karen	4:41:01 (21,900)	
McDonald, Katherine G	4:23:15 (17,433)	
McDonald, Morven I	3:41:30 (6,914)	
McDonald, Phoebe	4:22:28 (17,237)	
McDonald, Roslyn	6:21:19 (32,266)	
McDonnell, Louise	7:03:14 (32,908)	
McDonough, Annie	3:19:24 (3,181)	
McDougall, Andrea	4:25:27 (18,105)	
McEneaney, Susan	3:59:48 (11,762)	
McEwan, Paula J	5:50:41 (31,116)	
McFall, Josie	6:28:09 (32,424)	
McFarlane, Gillian	4:01:08 (12,082)	
McGarraghy, Christina	4:33:28 (20,126)	
McGauley, Samantha L	5:05:17 (26,620)	
McGee, Edel	5:29:47 (29,518)	
McGeehan, Rhona A	4:32:18 (19,859)	
McGettigan, Donna M	4:12:13 (14,629)	
McGhie, Caroline	5:23:04 (28,840)	
McGill, Charlotte A	5:09:44 (27,233)	
McGilloway, Pavia	4:00:54 (12,017)	
McGimpsey, Rita J	3:57:02 (10,852)	
McGinty, Hannah L	4:13:37 (14,979)	
McGivern, Deborah P	4:15:22 (15,437)	
McGlade, Pamela	4:17:35 (16,011)	
McGloin, Eileen A	5:16:19 (28,047)	
McGlynn, Kathleen M	4:19:34 (16,497)	
McGoldrick, Kathleen	4:23:34 (17,523)	
McGovern, Ann	4:19:41 (16,527)	
McGowan, Eileen	5:16:06 (28,015)	
McGowan, Emma E	4:58:02 (25,511)	
McGowan, Emma J	6:11:10 (31,961)	
McGowan, Marianne	5:47:03 (30,864)	
McGrath, Kathryn J	5:08:43 (27,107)	
McGrath, Laura	4:27:06 (18,527)	
McGrath, Maria J	4:46:56 (23,197)	
McGrath, Patricia B	6:25:51 (32,373)	
McGreevy, Adele M	3:52:58 (9,617)	
McGreevy, Sally	4:30:03 (19,309)	
McGrory, Jennifer L	5:35:30 (30,014)	
McGuane, Caroline M	5:40:38 (30,401)	
McGuigan, Julie A	5:09:44 (27,233)	
McGuiness, Joan T	4:21:19 (16,938)	
McGuinness, Sharon A	4:04:08 (12,749)	
McGuire, Mary	6:30:00 (32,448)	
McHale, Victoria J	4:17:28 (15,972)	
McIndoe, Caroline D	3:27:00 (4,246)	
McInnes, Carol B	5:30:24 (29,580)	
McInnes, Suzanne	4:34:35 (20,383)	
McIntosh, Kerry L	5:06:42 (26,815)	
McIntyre, Karen E	4:18:39 (16,266)	
McIntyre, Kathryn A	5:51:55 (31,176)	
McKay, Anna L	4:39:38 (21,584)	
McKay, Deborah S	3:59:41 (11,723)	
McKay, Kathie T	4:12:07 (14,603)	
McKay, Nola E	4:09:54 (14,084)	
McKeating, Sarah H	3:21:29 (3,468)	
McKee, Gillian C	7:45:15 (33,160)	
McKelvey, Judith L	5:31:01 (29,654)	
McKenary, Joanne	4:47:48 (23,382)	

McKenna, Edel P	4:15:08 (15,378)
McKenzie, Kathryn	4:37:36 (21,137)
McKenzie, Laura A	6:43:21 (32,659)
McKenzie, Sarah	4:05:11 (12,951)
McKeon, Glynis A	4:37:05 (21,000)
McKeon, Joanne	5:32:32 (29,773)
McKeown, Jacqueline	4:42:47 (22,278)
McKeown, Sarah	4:44:12 (22,610)
McKerral, Lesley P	4:25:07 (17,996)
McKey, Katharine L	5:20:37 (28,578)
McKiernan, Bernadette M	5:13:43 (27,739)
McKinnon, Maxine J	2:50:27 (565)
McLachlan, Kim S	4:49:39 (23,782)
McLaren, Heather	3:47:00 (8,119)
McLaren, Phyllis	6:30:41 (32,468)
McLaren, Sue R	4:33:37 (20,170)
McLaughlan, Claire A	5:56:24 (31,375)
McLaughlan, Gil L	5:13:53 (27,748)
McLaughlin, Claire	4:07:22 (13,439)
McLaughlin, Dei	4:22:03 (17,130)
McLaughlin, Frances	3:23:23 (3,694)
McLaughlin, Joanne	4:30:46 (19,488)
McLean, Alison L	4:10:26 (14,200)
McLean, Helen E	4:16:33 (15,737)
McLean, Jillian	4:27:46 (18,686)
McLean, Julie	3:53:31 (9,771)
McLean, Louisa	4:27:30 (18,621)
McLean, Lucie	6:00:15 (31,573)
McLean, Tracy	5:45:44 (30,763)
McLellan, Natasha	5:24:44 (29,010)
McLeod, Alexandra J	4:09:40 (14,024)
McLeod, Anna C	5:07:34 (26,941)
McLindon, Laura	4:00:38 (11,958)
McLoughlin, Mary T	3:36:50 (6,001)
McLoughlin, Sarah L	7:25:15 (33,074)
McLucas, Janice	6:09:53 (31,921)
McMahon, Laura R	5:53:08 (31,226)
McManus, Maggie J	4:54:22 (24,761)
McManus, Tereza	4:58:04 (25,520)
McMichael, Laine	4:34:03 (20,267)
McMillan, Lesley D	5:41:09 (30,431)
McMillan, Marion C	4:11:47 (14,516)
McMinn, Anita J	5:18:06 (28,252)
McNair, Vikki M	4:29:34 (19,190)
McNally, Pamela	7:08:51 (32,969)
McNally, Sally	4:48:35 (23,563)
McNamara, Adelle A	4:03:06 (12,504)
McNaught-Davis, Beth A	4:58:11 (25,544)
McNeill, Lucy A	5:45:34 (30,755)
McNeish, Helen	4:15:25 (15,454)
McNelis, Jan	5:11:44 (27,482)
McNickle, Judith	4:18:24 (16,209)
McParland, Christine T	4:55:25 (24,985)
McParland, Tracy	3:50:58 (9,091)
McPartlan, Ruth A	4:29:08 (19,065)
McPherson, Trish	4:42:08 (22,146)
McQuaid, Linda	5:06:21 (26,761)
McQuaker, Janet M	3:29:33 (4,731)
McQueen, Toni C	4:11:02 (14,339)
McRae, Linda A	4:46:18 (23,075)
McRobert, Nicola J	4:24:40 (17,864)
McRory, Helen M	4:27:23 (18,600)
McShane, Leanne E	5:49:37 (31,049)
McSloy Poli, Caroline M	5:37:44 (30,185)
McStravick, Frances	3:31:33 (5,073)
McVeigh, Rebecca E	4:52:19 (24,312)
McWeeney, Mary C	4:15:17 (15,408)
McWilliams, Anne P	6:24:18 (32,337)
McWilliams, Carmel R	4:35:59 (20,718)
McWilliams, Jane M	2:57:02 (944)
McWilliams, Marian L	4:14:10 (15,133)
McWilliams, Marthena M	4:29:30 (19,179)
Mead, Jill L	4:59:26 (25,767)
Mead, Natalie I	3:36:06 (5,855)
Meader, Sacha	5:23:37 (28,896)
Meadows, Joni A	4:56:46 (25,251)
Meadows, Patricia	4:31:36 (19,698)
Meads, Roberta R	5:19:10 (28,397)
Meadway, Jennie L	4:07:33 (13,486)
Meah, Shira	5:13:41 (27,734)
Meakes, Caroline L	4:37:49 (21,181)
Meakin, Lisa	6:18:51 (32,195)
Meakin, Penny A	5:59:12 (31,520)

Measures, Josephine	3:58:52 (11,470)
Mecking, Bettina	4:12:17 (14,645)
Meech, Michele E	5:08:09 (27,027)
Meeds, Sandra W	5:12:24 (27,575)
Meek, Jacqueline	6:10:22 (31,938)
Meek, Rachael J	4:12:40 (14,742)
Meekins, Joanne L	4:16:20 (15,678)
Meenan, Colette P	4:52:22 (24,325)
Mehmet, Ava	4:49:23 (23,730)
Mehrabian, Julie N	4:43:32 (22,447)
Meier-Spitz, Claudia A	5:56:10 (31,361)
Meiklejohn, Janice G	5:19:34 (28,446)
Mein, Michaela	5:14:47 (27,880)
Melandri, Katherine B	6:17:57 (32,170)
Melling, Alexia	4:36:03 (20,736)
Mellor, Anne E	4:40:18 (21,732)
Mellor, Catherine J	4:46:00 (23,005)
Mellor, Sarah L	4:33:48 (20,206)
Melly, Faye C	5:03:51 (26,439)
Melville, Susan M	6:21:57 (32,284)
Mendham, Katie E	5:13:56 (27,755)
Mennella, Janira	4:27:44 (18,682)
Mensah, Cassie	4:39:53 (21,651)
Menschel, Sabina C	3:52:55 (9,597)
Menzies, Issy	3:04:18 (1,531)
Mercer, Ruth J	4:19:05 (16,363)
Mercer, Susan E	5:38:00 (30,202)
Mercer-Leach, Lisa A	4:40:59 (21,891)
Mercier, Adele F	5:08:28 (27,071)
Meredith, Jean	4:59:18 (25,743)
Merritt, Claire L	5:26:09 (29,141)
Merryweather, Marilyn	5:03:16 (26,354)
Mesher, Helen M	5:53:44 (31,249)
Messenger, Claire E	3:33:48 (5,449)
Messenger, Clare H	6:04:41 (31,752)
Messervy-Evans, Anna K	5:03:21 (26,364)
Meston, Niki	3:35:47 (5,796)
Metcalfe, Margaret R	3:52:10 (9,402)
Metcalfe, Sally-Ann	5:41:32 (30,458)
Metcalfe, Sarah J	4:48:25 (23,517)
Metha, Colleen B	4:54:05 (24,689)
Meyer, Corrina J	5:24:02 (28,943)
Meyer, Elizabeth J	5:04:36 (26,535)
Meyer, Jane	4:27:55 (18,729)
Meyers, Della	6:36:59 (32,563)
Meyrick, Sarah C	4:33:08 (20,043)
Michaels, Victoria L	5:14:30 (27,841)
Michel, Cristina	5:04:54 (26,569)
Michel, Gillian P	4:03:37 (12,629)
Michelitsch, Verena B	6:58:36 (32,865)
Michell, Rebecca J	4:33:38 (20,173)
Michon, Sylvie	3:48:25 (8,477)
Middlebrook, Sophia C	4:22:18 (17,199)
Middleton, Anna L	3:42:54 (7,206)
Middleton, Katrine	5:42:25 (30,526)
Middleton, Laura	3:43:19 (7,312)
Middleton, Marion R	3:55:40 (10,427)
Middleton-Hockin, Caroline J	5:13:45 (27,741)
Midgley, Chantal	5:47:21 (30,904)
Midgley, Nicola	3:40:48 (6,762)
Midren, Kerry L	5:01:34 (26,113)
Mifsud, Vivien M	4:28:36 (18,922)
Mignon, Natasja	4:14:44 (15,267)
Mileham, Claire E	4:27:06 (18,527)
Miles, Belinda J	3:57:44 (11,087)
Miles, Emma J	3:52:12 (9,410)
Miles, Helen	5:06:15 (26,748)
Miles, Joanne M	4:12:51 (14,796)
Miles, Nicola W	5:13:20 (27,695)
Miles, Nikki	6:22:32 (32,300)
Miles, Wendy J	7:38:47 (33,137)
Milinkovic, Amy	5:01:10 (26,065)
Mill, Sophie M	4:56:03 (25,109)
Millar, Berenice J	5:36:32 (30,102)
Millar, Gillian M	3:48:00 (8,382)
Millar, Hilary A	3:18:21 (3,042)
Millar, Julie	4:46:29 (23,118)
Millard, Fiona J	4:23:53 (17,618)
Miller, Amber	6:25:16 (32,360)
Miller, Carol	3:35:16 (5,717)
Miller, Christine	5:17:26 (28,188)
Miller, Elizabeth C	5:24:26 (28,984)
Miller, Gillian	4:10:52 (14,299)

Miller, Hannah J	4:29:09 (19,070)
Miller, Helene P	4:40:27 (21,761)
Miller, Irene J	3:43:04 (7,255)
Miller, Katy L	5:26:55 (29,216)
Miller, Khadijah	4:43:24 (22,411)
Miller, Lucy	3:41:20 (6,882)
Miller, Rebecca C	5:47:03 (30,864)
Miller, Samantha L	4:14:54 (15,311)
Miller, Susan A	5:46:34 (30,830)
Miller, Suzanne M	5:00:22 (25,954)
Miller, Wendy J	6:09:52 (31,920)
Millican, Amanda J	4:22:25 (17,229)
Millican, Joanna L	3:46:58 (8,112)
Millichap, Eunice L	4:38:42 (21,371)
Millichap, Suzanne	5:05:43 (26,668)
Milligan, Felicity A	5:09:19 (27,185)
Milligan, Sue	5:30:11 (29,561)
Mills, Charlotte L	5:19:04 (28,383)
Mills, Elaine D	5:23:09 (28,850)
Mills, Frances W	4:21:36 (16,999)
Mills, Francesca L	5:07:39 (26,957)
Mills, Gemma K	5:59:49 (31,551)
Mills, Jacqueline	4:16:59 (15,854)
Mills, Joanne	5:30:06 (29,555)
Mills, Joanne	6:27:57 (32,423)
Mills, Lesley	3:59:33 (11,686)
Mills, Nichola	5:39:54 (30,352)
Mills, Paula J	4:17:07 (15,891)
Mills, Sharon L	6:00:50 (31,597)
Mills, Tracy D	6:59:45 (32,878)
Millson, Carrie H	3:06:32 (1,713)
Millward, Andrea E	5:35:03 (29,970)
Millward, Katie	5:19:31 (28,438)
Millward, Liz J	5:32:48 (29,798)
Milne, Caroline	4:41:51 (22,069)
Milne, Fiona	5:37:27 (30,159)
Milne, Kiriana M	5:27:44 (29,297)
Milne, Lindsey	4:10:44 (14,256)
Milne, Penelope	4:19:27 (16,466)
Milne, Ray W	4:55:56 (25,085)
Milne, Sandra J	3:58:07 (11,195)
Milne, Sarah	3:51:13 (9,151)
Milne, Sarah L	3:23:02 (3,661)
Milner, Jo M	7:37:29 (33,128)
Milnes, Chris M	5:30:33 (29,598)
Milone, Sheri	5:57:17 (31,419)
Milsom, Amanda J	4:40:43 (21,831)
Milsom, Mary E	5:12:37 (27,602)
Milson, Sophie L	5:00:06 (25,904)
Milton, Amanda E	3:55:03 (10,227)
Milton, Lucie C	5:58:19 (31,475)
Minshull, Amanda	7:02:51 (32,904)
Minter, Juliette L	3:09:20 (1,989)
Minty, Elaine M	4:01:33 (12,158)
Minty, Victoria	4:28:53 (18,991)
Mitchell, Alison A	6:21:56 (32,283)
Mitchell, Alison L	5:25:51 (29,116)
Mitchell, Avril C	4:36:02 (20,731)
Mitchell, Catherine P	4:29:29 (19,174)
Mitchell, Elaine	5:56:20 (31,370)
Mitchell, Emma W	5:07:34 (26,941)
Mitchell, Gaynor	7:00:14 (32,885)
Mitchell, Heather M	4:20:55 (16,842)
Mitchell, Helen C	3:47:56 (8,363)
Mitchell, Jackie A	4:02:31 (12,376)
Mitchell, Kerry J	4:15:08 (15,378)
Mitchell, Kim	7:07:49 (32,961)
Mitchell, Kirsty L	4:51:23 (24,117)
Mitchell, Moira	6:49:56 (32,759)
Mitchell, Quona	5:02:54 (26,304)
Mitchell, Susan P	4:23:33 (17,520)
Mitchell, Theresa A	5:01:49 (26,150)
Mitchell, Trudy	6:53:01 (32,795)
Mitchell, Vanessa J	3:51:05 (9,118)
Mitchell, Victoria J	4:43:28 (22,425)
Mitchell, Wendy A	6:04:28 (31,745)
Mitchell, Zona T	4:35:53 (20,686)
Mitchell-Heggs, Caroline A	4:14:09 (15,122)
Mitchinson, Jo L	5:11:16 (27,423)
Mithcell, Denise A	5:06:12 (26,738)
Mitra, Anna	4:53:55 (24,663)
Mitton, Liz N	4:42:07 (22,138)
Mizen, Lucy-Anne	4:11:08 (14,370)

Moan, Susanna 3:36:48 (5,993)
Moffatt, Fiona H 3:40:28 (6,706)
Mogan, Sandra A 4:30:49 (19,497)
Moger, Arabella 4:55:58 (25,097)
Mohammed, Tara E 4:56:25 (25,191)
Mohomed, Fathima 4:52:12 (24,289)
Mollin, Aoife 4:18:45 (16,291)
Mollitt, Lillian 4:17:43 (16,034)
Mollitt, Sarah E 4:17:44 (16,038)
Molnar Broander, Eua 4:43:49 (22,523)
Moloney, Ann M 4:36:50 (20,945)
Moloney, Jenny 3:16:38 (2,833)
Molyneux, Mandy S 3:46:17 (7,963)
Moncaster, Rachel S 4:11:43 (14,500)
Money, Vanessa E 3:29:23 (4,693)
Monk, Clare 4:24:32 (17,809)
Monks, Nicola E 4:59:20 (25,750)
Monks, Nikki 6:19:38 (32,222)
Monod, Lesley A 4:51:30 (24,144)
Montacute, Hannah L 4:50:09 (23,869)
Montagu, Minnie 4:45:51 (22,978)
Montague, Tracy E 5:28:55 (29,421)
Monteith, Michaela G 4:23:27 (17,486)
Monti, Kim E 4:54:44 (24,823)
Montrone, Nunzia 4:40:00 (21,674)
Moody, Christine M 4:33:36 (20,166)
Moody, Dianne 4:36:56 (20,967)
Moody, Pat 4:49:10 (23,683)
Mooney, Lisa M 5:06:23 (26,768)
Moore, Alice M 5:09:28 (27,201)
Moore, Alison J 3:53:41 (9,816)
Moore, Charlotte L 3:53:11 (9,686)
Moore, Emily C 4:18:45 (16,291)
Moore, Fiona C 3:24:07 (3,808)
Moore, Helen L 5:20:18 (28,537)
Moore, Jenny E 4:21:57 (17,102)
Moore, Karen 7:06:39 (32,950)
Moore, Karen I 5:10:07 (27,278)
Moore, Katherine 5:09:43 (27,229)
Moore, Katherine M 5:43:41 (30,619)
Moore, Kerry L 5:35:47 (30,039)
Moore, Kirsty H 4:27:07 (18,533)
Moore, Lucinda 4:23:59 (17,648)
Moore, Mandy 4:41:29 (21,989)
Moore, Meredith G 4:26:03 (18,277)
Moore, Nelly C 3:39:48 (6,589)
Moore, Pamela E 4:12:51 (14,796)
Moore, Patricia E 4:30:09 (19,335)
Moore, Sarah 5:03:16 (26,354)
Moore, Sarah E 5:36:30 (30,094)
Moore, Sophie 4:05:14 (12,967)
Moore, Susan E 4:40:09 (21,703)
Moore, Tessa K 4:47:40 (23,353)
Moores, Helen L 3:40:51 (6,770)
Moores, Sarah E 3:19:07 (3,145)
Moorhouse, Penelope A 4:49:36 (23,777)
Moran, Michelle 3:52:05 (9,381)
Moraru, Emilia M 5:30:03 (29,549)
Moreau, Linda 3:26:29 (4,149)
More-Molyneux, Sarah 5:52:55 (31,211)
Moreton, Helen C 7:21:01 (33,047)
Moreton, Penny 4:08:44 (13,792)
Morey, Danielle E 4:55:15 (24,949)
Morgan, Amanda-Jane 4:06:41 (13,271)
Morgan, Ann L 5:15:45 (27,971)
Morgan, Bethan R 5:45:06 (30,724)
Morgan, Carole A 3:38:41 (6,362)
Morgan, Christine 5:58:15 (31,472)
Morgan, Christine E 4:22:39 (17,287)
Morgan, Claire S 4:22:52 (17,336)
Morgan, Colette 4:01:58 (12,255)
Morgan, Ellen 5:11:29 (27,455)
Morgan, Joanna R 4:33:12 (20,062)
Morgan, Kathryn L 6:13:03 (32,020)
Morgan, Katie A 4:53:18 (24,527)
Morgan, Lon 4:08:35 (13,766)
Morgan, Margaret A 4:13:30 (14,955)
Morgan, Philippa J 5:06:44 (26,824)
Morgan, Tracey A 4:44:21 (22,647)
Morgan, Zoe A 4:58:21 (25,578)
Morgans, Paulette 4:00:30 (11,934)
Morjaria, Neema 4:43:31 (22,443)
Morley, Amy O 5:47:26 (30,913)
Morley, Christine 6:14:58 (32,084)
Morley, Elizabeth A 4:18:04 (16,128)
Morley, Sarah 3:59:16 (11,591)
Morley, Sarah K 5:30:31 (29,594)
Morley, Suzanne 7:39:10 (33,140)
Morrall, Zelah M 2:56:58 (940)
Morris, Abigail 3:44:04 (7,465)
Morris, Alexandra G 5:07:15 (26,898)
Morris, Amanda J 4:23:23 (17,468)
Morris, Angela S 5:29:13 (29,445)
Morris, Ann M 4:52:47 (24,420)
Morris, Beth 4:08:06 (13,641)
Morris, Cindy A 4:54:50 (24,856)
Morris, Claire L 4:03:05 (12,500)
Morris, Colleen A 4:28:11 (18,802)
Morris, Diane K 5:27:18 (29,250)
Morris, Helen E 6:47:20 (32,729)
Morris, Helen M 7:33:49 (33,108)
Morris, Hilary F 5:06:46 (26,830)
Morris, Jennifer C 3:58:57 (11,490)
Morris, Kate A 5:43:00 (30,579)
Morris, Katy H 4:39:07 (21,469)
Morris, Kay 3:49:22 (8,707)
Morris, Kirsty A 6:19:56 (32,227)
Morris, Margaret A 4:03:11 (12,524)
Morris, Mary 5:52:18 (31,194)
Morris, Nicola 4:53:35 (24,592)
Morris, Penelope L 4:30:10 (19,340)
Morris, Phillippa L 3:17:40 (2,961)
Morris, Rachel 4:47:09 (23,243)
Morris, Sara J 6:06:33 (31,804)
Morris, Sarah L 4:20:55 (16,842)
Morris, Susan 4:21:34 (16,989)
Morris, Yvonne 5:37:53 (30,196)
Morris, Yvonne J 4:13:55 (15,045)
Morrison, Angelica 6:45:19 (32,697)
Morrison, Christa E 4:25:14 (18,038)
Morrison, Erica 6:34:11 (32,518)
Morrison, Gillian A 6:01:44 (31,635)
Morrison, Kimberley E 4:24:50 (17,898)
Morrissey, Helen S 5:40:17 (30,383)
Morrissey, Ian 4:06:58 (13,341)
Morrissey, Laura S 5:18:42 (28,335)
Morrow, Laura 4:13:22 (14,937)
Morse, Joanna E 4:43:40 (22,481)
Morse, Kaitlin 3:58:42 (11,401)
Mort, Helen R 3:35:46 (5,794)
Mortier, Andrea 5:27:49 (29,308)
Mortimer, Clare L 4:27:59 (18,745)
Mortimer, Heather M 4:50:53 (24,023)
Mortimore, Julia A 4:15:21 (15,432)
Mortlock, Zoe L 5:38:55 (30,275)
Morton, Clare N 4:49:24 (23,734)
Morton, Collette A 5:13:05 (27,665)
Morton, Helen 4:29:40 (19,219)
Morton, Jacqueline A 3:39:16 (6,493)
Morton, Joanna S 4:00:57 (12,030)
Morton, Lisa 5:03:24 (26,377)
Morton, Meryl G 5:28:39 (29,395)
Morton, Paula F 5:03:25 (26,379)
Morton-Holmes, Ivana R 7:36:44 (33,121)
Morwood, Lorraine 4:38:59 (21,436)
Moseley, Donna L 4:45:51 (22,978)
Moseley, Julie E 4:13:16 (14,911)
Moseley, Victoria 4:22:11 (17,171)
Moseley Payne, Carleene S 7:23:57 (33,064)
Mosley, Jane H 5:22:14 (28,745)
Moss, Briony 4:22:20 (17,208)
Moss, Jayne 5:59:27 (31,533)
Moss, Sarah F 3:53:58 (9,912)
Moss, Susan J 4:32:00 (19,791)
Mott, Claire 4:53:22 (24,539)
Mott, Jacqueline A 4:56:13 (25,142)
Mottershead, Ema L 4:01:57 (12,249)
Mottley, Bev A 4:50:19 (23,911)

LONDON MARATHON

Mouat, Deborah E 4:23:49 (17,598)
Mould, Jennifer A 5:18:22 (28,290)
Mould, Jo E 4:53:51 (24,647)
Moulder, Katherine J 5:19:33 (28,445)
Mounsey, Philippa H 3:49:24 (8,718)
Mountain, Alison J 4:59:53 (25,866)
Mountain, Mary C 4:51:36 (24,168)
Mountford, Valerie A 6:11:53 (31,985)
Mouton, Nathalie 5:13:29 (27,718)
Moye, Jennifer E 4:40:32 (21,797)
Moyes, Hazel L 4:14:34 (15,226)
Moynihan, Claire 6:41:18 (32,629)
Moynihan, Maria 5:41:37 (30,467)
Moyse, Tracy O 4:38:34 (21,354)
Mozzanica, Louise F 4:44:40 (22,700)
Mpangile, Nancy L 8:20:08 (33,197)
Muchenje, Juliet 4:21:49 (17,067)
Mudd, Rebecca J 3:54:42 (10,114)
Mudge, Jacki 7:11:36 (32,993)
Mudhar, Sukhdeep 5:20:09 (28,515)
Muid, Stephanie 4:53:22 (24,539)
Muir, Clare E 4:48:07 (23,453)
Muir, Denise 4:44:51 (22,745)
Muir, Karen M 4:09:20 (13,940)
Muir, Kirsty F 5:47:17 (30,892)
Muir, Luz D 4:26:10 (18,302)
Muirhead, Sarah J 3:37:11 (6,072)
Mulcaster, Sally A 5:16:28 (28,066)
Mulder, Christina M 4:58:06 (25,529)
Mulhaire, Nicola E 4:18:55 (16,331)
Mulhall, Helen J 3:36:31 (5,936)
Mulhall, Sarah L 3:52:37 (9,526)
Mulholland, Karen 4:36:55 (20,963)
Mulkerrin, Christine A 6:37:01 (32,564)
Mullan, Emily K 4:54:16 (24,738)
Mulley, Janet 5:35:12 (29,985)
Mulligan, Sarah E 4:40:45 (21,841)
Mullin, Annabel J 4:28:08 (18,785)
Mulliner, Penny 5:05:38 (26,659)
Mullins, Andrea C 4:57:45 (25,445)
Mullins, Gillian M 5:21:13 (28,632)
Mulraine-Simkin, Rebecca J 5:01:12 (26,071)
Mulvey, Margaret B 5:38:11 (30,218)
Mumford, Joanne L 3:39:10 (6,467)
Muncey, Clare T 4:31:05 (19,548)
Munday, Paula J 5:21:13 (28,632)
Munday, Sophie F 5:36:07 (30,061)
Mundinger, Amber E 5:29:53 (29,532)
Mundy, Claire 5:40:49 (30,417)
Munn, Patricia 5:58:02 (31,458)
Munnings, Sarah J 4:40:30 (21,777)
Munns, Hannah L 4:50:47 (24,001)
Munro, Erica C 4:58:12 (25,549)
Munro, Patricia A 3:32:57 (5,315)
Munroe, Jo L 5:01:12 (26,071)
Munson, Gillian F 5:01:57 (26,171)
Munton, Deborah S 3:44:07 (7,475)
Munton, Karen A 4:33:05 (20,025)
Murch, Harriet J 4:35:42 (20,650)
Murchie, Shonagh 4:44:49 (22,736)
Murdoch, Elizabeth J 4:50:27 (23,935)
Murgatroyd, Ami K 6:18:10 (32,175)
Murphy, Carol A 4:51:21 (24,105)
Murphy, Caroline M 3:55:30 (10,374)
Murphy, Chris M 5:47:20 (30,901)
Murphy, Danielle L 3:46:17 (7,963)
Murphy, Emma C 4:40:40 (21,823)
Murphy, Gillian 7:20:55 (33,046)
Murphy, Jacqueline A 4:16:02 (15,604)
Murphy, Joanne E 4:20:48 (16,810)
Murphy, Karen E 3:05:50 (1,648)
Murphy, Kate 4:51:36 (24,168)
Murphy, Maurya 3:23:13 (3,676)
Murphy, Michelle 5:57:49 (31,448)
Murphy, Nicola 4:46:39 (23,147)
Murphy, Nicola T 4:47:10 (23,247)
Murphy, Olive M 4:21:06 (16,892)
Murphy, Patricia 4:14:12 (15,142)
Murphy, Rebecca F 4:10:12 (14,149)
Murphy, Ruth E 4:14:00 (15,067)
Murphy, Sharon A 3:09:00 (1,959)
Murphy, Susan E 6:04:26 (31,742)
Murphy, Teresa 3:27:04 (4,257)

Murphy, Tracey M	3:55:47 (10,472)	
Murphy, Una J	4:14:27 (15,197)	
Murphy, Vicky C	5:03:01 (26,319)	
Murphy, Virginie	3:49:22 (8,707)	
Murray, Andrea C	3:42:00 (7,024)	
Murray, Annette	3:29:03 (4,634)	
Murray, Carol M	5:22:02 (28,722)	
Murray, Catriona A.	5:02:16 (26,215)	
Murray, Catriona H	3:21:03 (3,405)	
Murray, Fiona	3:58:44 (11,417)	
Murray, Jacqueline	4:41:36 (22,014)	
Murray, Morag	4:55:50 (25,061)	
Murray, Rebecca	3:57:42 (11,072)	
Murray, Susan L	4:50:48 (24,005)	
Murray, Tracy	4:37:45 (21,167)	
Murray-Smith, Sonia	4:20:58 (16,857)	
Murton, Karen J	6:10:58 (31,954)	
Mussett, Jackie A	5:20:58 (28,608)	
Musson, Sally M	3:01:10 (1,317)	
Mutersbaugh, Julie Anne	4:24:17 (17,742)	
Mutschler, Linda J	4:10:56 (14,312)	
Mutter, Charlene A	4:12:28 (14,696)	
Myers, Catherine B	4:04:18 (12,776)	
Myers, Felicity M	5:52:30 (31,197)	
Myers, Kate	5:08:21 (27,058)	
Myers, Malindi E	2:53:25 (694)	
Myford, Sarah J	5:38:04 (30,210)	
Myles, Jenna	6:49:13 (32,750)	
Myres, Emma	4:54:19 (24,749)	
Nabarro, Laura E	4:14:08 (15,117)	
Nabben, Jennifer P	5:30:51 (29,631)	
Naden, Clare	3:23:58 (3,788)	
Naess, Bjoerg	5:25:10 (29,055)	
Nagell Dahl, Halldis	4:12:34 (14,723)	
Nagra, Rashpal K	5:34:32 (29,935)	
Naicker, Kosiladeui	5:25:23 (29,076)	
Naicker, Kubeshini	3:52:04 (9,375)	
Nairn, Fionn	3:11:14 (2,188)	
Naish, Rachel M	4:17:20 (15,940)	
Nalikka, Angela N	4:54:07 (24,700)	
Nally, Theresa	5:01:54 (26,164)	
Nandra, Kirat K	4:33:19 (20,088)	
Nanhoo-Robinson, Amanda M	6:02:08 (31,645)	
Nappi, Laura T	6:07:51 (31,857)	
Narang, Satwant K.	5:23:20 (28,875)	
Nash, Chavonne	5:44:19 (30,666)	
Nash, Doireann	3:49:36 (8,769)	
Nash, Lesley P	4:51:21 (24,105)	
Nash, Lisa	3:43:55 (7,443)	
Nash, Sharlene J	5:08:51 (27,125)	
Nash, Vicky K	6:25:09 (32,355)	
Nasmyth-Miller, Sarah J	4:49:05 (23,669)	
Nason, Melanie J	4:52:26 (24,339)	
Nasser, Sara	5:03:32 (26,393)	
Natrajan, Rachael C	3:44:46 (7,631)	
Naughton, Rebecca	5:22:01 (28,720)	
Naylor, Sarah F	4:53:51 (24,647)	
Neachell, Emma A	5:22:46 (28,809)	
Neal, Elise	4:19:48 (16,552)	
Neal, Jennifer S	3:55:01 (10,209)	
Neal, Nikki H	2:54:19 (744)	
Neal, Susan E	6:17:48 (32,169)	
Neale, Jaime A	7:13:26 (33,001)	
Neale, Mandy	4:31:59 (19,786)	
Neary, Helen P	3:54:27 (10,038)	
Needham, Lindsay J	4:05:57 (13,132)	
Neely, Diana H	4:26:42 (18,430)	
Neivens, Barbara E	5:29:25 (29,473)	
Nelson, Bibiana C	5:56:21 (31,371)	
Nelson, Francesca	3:37:16 (6,086)	
Nelson, Kate	3:08:55 (1,948)	
Nelson, Lesley K	6:30:38 (32,467)	
Nelson, Marion C	4:11:26 (14,448)	
Neocleous, Anna	4:00:01 (11,820)	
Neocleous, Julia E	4:38:48 (21,391)	
Nerva, Anne R	5:08:03 (27,014)	
Nesbitt, Sarah R	5:35:30 (30,014)	
Ness, Janet	6:43:10 (32,656)	
Nestor, Frances M	4:56:34 (25,218)	
Neto, Sarita	4:19:45 (16,539)	
Neubauer, Deborah A	6:20:55 (32,251)	
Neubecker, Leslie	4:04:59 (12,915)	
Neufville, Gillian	4:19:59 (16,598)	
Neuhaus, Kathy J	5:08:34 (27,088)	
Neumann, Ulrike	4:39:33 (21,564)	
Neurisse, Bernadette	4:43:30 (22,435)	
Nevill, Ibby	3:21:48 (3,509)	
Neville, Fiona A	4:39:26 (21,552)	
Neville, Julie	4:29:16 (19,107)	
New, Kim E	4:25:30 (18,118)	
Newbery, Tara J	4:25:50 (18,202)	
Newbury, Christine	4:31:48 (19,748)	
Newby-Stubbs, Rebecca L	4:17:03 (15,873)	
Newcombe, Barbara	5:23:18 (28,870)	
Newell, Claire F	4:25:53 (18,224)	
Newell, Sharon	3:53:33 (9,778)	
Newham, Judith A	3:36:04 (5,845)	
Newham, Kate J	4:14:53 (15,309)	
Newing, Lisa M	3:02:00 (1,375)	
Newington, Samantha J	4:19:17 (16,418)	
Newman, Annette C	4:53:02 (24,463)	
Newman, Carol A	5:49:21 (31,032)	
Newman, Claire M	6:39:24 (32,602)	
Newman, Jenny	4:42:12 (22,156)	
Newman, Kim L	4:33:47 (20,203)	
Newman, Lisa J	4:56:38 (25,226)	
Newman, Margaret R	4:34:20 (20,321)	
Newman, Miranda R	7:10:15 (32,982)	
Newman, Pauline A	6:25:40 (32,368)	
Newman, Samantha H	4:24:32 (17,809)	
Newman, Tracey	4:24:35 (17,837)	
Newns, Elizabeth	4:57:34 (25,411)	
Newstead, Johanne	3:43:20 (7,315)	
Newton, Florence	3:09:21 (1,993)	
Newton, Linette	4:28:22 (18,863)	
Newton, Lynda J	5:58:47 (31,497)	
Newton, Merab	4:33:56 (20,231)	
Newton, Phyllis A	5:00:06 (25,904)	
Newton, Sally C	4:13:55 (15,045)	
Newton-Dunn, Tracey	7:08:21 (32,965)	
Nichol, Donna M	5:00:40 (25,991)	
Nichol, Jan	6:03:07 (31,689)	
Nicholas, Hannah M	3:59:09 (11,560)	
Nicholl, Kay W	5:32:26 (29,764)	
Nicholls, Alison J	6:50:18 (32,765)	
Nicholls, Gaynor M	5:29:53 (29,532)	
Nicholls, Kathryn	6:07:44 (31,851)	
Nicholls, Melanie D	4:05:34 (13,040)	
Nicholson, Emma D	5:44:38 (30,694)	
Nicholson, Rebecca E	4:48:28 (23,532)	
Nicholson, Sue	3:57:09 (10,902)	
Nicklen, Margaret E	5:25:49 (29,113)	
Nicklin, Debbie E	5:11:14 (27,418)	
Nicklin, Jacqueline K	4:45:24 (22,890)	
Nicol, Anne	5:50:52 (31,125)	
Nicol, Eileen N	3:49:36 (8,769)	
Nicol, Jackie A	3:34:29 (5,560)	
Nicol, Linnea T	4:24:37 (17,845)	
Nicolino, Catherine	4:07:56 (13,593)	
Nicolof, Maria	4:41:14 (21,930)	
Nicolson, Krissie B	4:41:35 (22,008)	
Nightingale, Mary	3:50:44 (9,037)	
Nightingale, Sharon J	5:14:19 (27,816)	
Nigro, Leanne N	4:32:50 (19,963)	
Nijhar, Jag K	5:21:50 (28,694)	
Nilsson, Ann-Marie	3:55:06 (10,246)	
Nin, Elisabetta	4:48:26 (23,520)	
Nineberg, Roz	5:21:55 (28,704)	
Nippress, Michelle H	5:16:08 (28,018)	
Nissim, Rachel	5:11:50 (27,501)	
Niven, Audrey	6:49:37 (32,756)	
Niven, Nicola J	7:02:42 (32,900)	
Niven, Sandy C	7:02:43 (32,902)	
Nixon, Gail L	4:44:39 (22,695)	
Nixon, Lisa J	6:54:27 (32,816)	
Noad, Joy	3:25:47 (4,042)	
Noble, Eileen R	5:14:54 (27,895)	
Noble, Joanne	5:22:36 (28,787)	
Noble, Karen L	3:54:34 (10,069)	
Noble, Monica	4:58:52 (25,679)	
Nobles, Margaret	4:40:31 (21,791)	
Nock, Jeanette D	5:17:15 (28,158)	
Noel, Maureen	3:29:42 (4,759)	
Nolan, Christina N	4:24:07 (17,691)	
Nones, Marina M	5:27:55 (29,318)	
Nonoo, Rebecca H	4:49:56 (23,832)	
Noonoo, Barbara E	5:04:42 (26,545)	
Norbury, Audrey	4:53:33 (24,581)	
Nordberg, Micaela M	5:38:57 (30,277)	
Nordin, Breege J	3:25:06 (3,942)	
Norfolk, Kate A	5:32:28 (29,767)	
Norgrove, Kate J	4:24:56 (17,938)	
Norman, Carmen A	4:57:51 (25,463)	
Norman, Michelle	4:45:49 (22,971)	
Norman-Thorpe, Lesley	5:01:10 (26,065)	
Normington, Michelle	4:26:39 (18,421)	
Norquay, Megan J	3:24:40 (3,892)	
Norrington, Alison R	4:43:33 (22,452)	
Norris, Caroline E	5:26:19 (29,155)	
Norris, Katherine	4:22:34 (17,257)	
Norris, Louise J	4:34:01 (20,249)	
Norris, Rachael E	5:57:36 (31,437)	
Norris, Sally V	5:21:15 (28,638)	
Norris, Samantha A	5:28:45 (29,406)	
North, Heather J	3:34:52 (5,636)	
North, Philipa	4:41:52 (22,074)	
Northey, Teresa J	4:26:32 (18,391)	
Northwood, Tina	5:25:44 (29,107)	
Norton, Julie A	4:18:31 (16,238)	
Norton, Karena C	3:55:45 (10,460)	
Norton, Sarah J	4:36:27 (20,835)	
Norton, Sophie	5:00:10 (25,918)	
Nothard, Gillian R	4:53:41 (24,613)	
Nott, Jo	3:24:23 (3,848)	
Nottage, Angela D	5:37:13 (30,147)	
Nourse, Katy L	5:30:38 (29,608)	
Nouze, Vanessa	4:28:54 (18,996)	
Noyce, Stephanie J	3:32:11 (5,198)	
Nucci, Julie A	4:45:46 (22,961)	
Nuckhir, Charlotte E	7:01:08 (32,891)	
Nudds, Fay	4:32:59 (20,000)	
Nunes, Pedro	3:45:39 (7,833)	
Nunn, Caroline L	3:59:47 (11,755)	
Nurse, Linda J	4:27:46 (18,686)	
Nutter, Glenys	5:21:11 (28,629)	
Nutting, Julie A	4:52:14 (24,292)	
Nyoni, Charity	5:12:59 (27,649)	
Oakes, Anne	4:19:26 (16,460)	
Oakes, Fiona L	2:51:38 (619)	
Oakes, Sarah A	5:35:55 (30,049)	
Oakley, Carole L	5:29:51 (29,530)	
Oakley, Frances D	4:26:25 (18,365)	
Oakley, Wnifred J	6:56:08 (32,840)	
Oates, Jenna L	5:50:09 (31,085)	
Oathout, Monica F	4:23:06 (17,387)	
Obertelli, Kelly M	3:54:57 (10,190)	
Obomeli, Obianagha D	4:53:39 (24,607)	
O'Brien, Angela M	3:58:53 (11,473)	
O'Brien, Eve M	3:17:03 (2,882)	
O'Brien, Haley J	5:33:33 (29,853)	
O'Brien, Jennifer K	5:11:33 (27,467)	
O'Brien, Meghan G	5:09:07 (27,163)	
O'Callaghan, Clarissa J	5:00:50 (26,016)	
O'Callaghan, Jennifer	4:07:07 (13,377)	
O'Callaghan, Kate E	5:26:40 (29,182)	
O'Callaghan, Susan	5:45:34 (30,755)	
O'Connor, Ainslie B	4:10:57 (14,315)	
O'Connor, Caroline	5:22:59 (28,824)	
O'Connor, Elaine M	4:15:04 (15,355)	
O'Connor, Helen L	3:56:51 (10,816)	
O'Connor, Keeley C	4:52:26 (24,339)	
O'Connor, Maria	6:25:51 (32,373)	
O'Connor, Merryn L	5:27:27 (29,265)	
O'Connor, Ruth F	5:39:24 (30,311)	
O'Connor, Susan E	5:02:03 (26,184)	
O'Connor, Tanya L	3:06:47 (1,735)	
Odayar, Mano	4:36:28 (20,836)	
Odell, Sarah R	3:53:27 (9,755)	
Odell, Siggy	4:28:54 (18,994)	
O'Donnell, Anne M	3:43:43 (7,396)	
O'Donnell, Grainne M	2:57:27 (981)	
O'Donnell, Kelly	4:35:05 (20,508)	
O'Donnell, Patricia K	5:29:38 (29,495)	
O'Donnell, Sarah	4:06:30 (13,233)	
O'Donoghue, Sarah J	3:51:26 (9,204)	
O'Donovan, Annette E	4:28:51 (18,983)	
O'Donovan, Elizabeth J	4:19:30 (16,478)	
O'Donovan, Emma J	5:22:57 (28,819)	
O'Donovan, Karen	4:55:36 (25,017)	

Oelkuch, Heidrun....4:19:47 (16,547)
Offley, Sue....5:59:56 (31,556)
Offredi, Doreen....6:31:32 (32,480)
Ogden, Sarah C....4:18:00 (16,108)
Ogilvy, Kirstin A....4:38:52 (21,406)
Ogita, Yumi....3:41:34 (6,933)
O'Grady, Martina....5:57:15 (31,418)
Ogundari, Tinu....6:40:58 (32,626)
O'Hagan, Collette M....4:57:57 (25,487)
O'Hagan, Katherine....3:59:42 (11,728)
O'Halloran, Jacqueline E....9:28:17 (33,219)
O'Halloran, Madeline J....6:23:09 (32,306)
O'Hanlon, Denise S....4:23:48 (17,589)
O'Hara, Sue B....5:42:48 (30,561)
O'Hare, Elizabeth A....4:36:32 (20,853)
Oja, Clair M....3:42:44 (7,167)
Okadera, Hiromi....4:30:52 (19,509)
Okayo, Margaret....2:29:16 (67)
O'Keeffe, Clare E....4:47:28 (23,311)
O'Keeffe, Patricia A....5:19:38 (28,450)
Okogba, Jane E....7:43:04 (33,151)
Okwu, Antonia S....3:29:40 (4,754)
Olafsdottir, Unnur M....4:15:06 (15,366)
Olafsdottir, Valegerdur....4:17:10 (15,898)
Oldfield, Donna....5:43:22 (30,598)
Oldfield, Lisa J....4:54:43 (24,820)
Oldham, Katie E....5:55:24 (31,320)
Oldham, Michelle....3:25:35 (4,017)
Oldham, Nicola S....3:30:47 (4,942)
Oldknow, Jenny L....6:13:27 (32,035)
Olds, Denise....4:43:49 (22,523)
O'Leary, Emma J....6:15:48 (32,108)
Olfert, Michaelia G....3:54:28 (10,042)
Oliver, Barbara....4:21:25 (16,960)
Oliver, Cara....3:19:25 (3,182)
Oliver, Deborah K....3:40:52 (6,774)
Oliver, Emma L....4:29:21 (19,136)
Oliver, Hannah....4:11:42 (14,498)
Oliver, Hayley....5:54:22 (31,277)
Oliver, Kate E....4:30:51 (19,504)
Oliver, Lynn M....4:28:35 (18,920)
Oliver, Lynne M....4:55:25 (24,985)
Oliver-Welsh, Lucy G....3:33:58 (5,474)
Olivi, Carla....5:40:58 (30,424)
Olivier, Melissa....4:13:34 (14,968)
Ollerton, Lucinda J....4:13:45 (15,012)
Olliffe, Stephanie J....3:31:51 (5,134)
O'Loughlin, Jane....4:45:18 (22,856)
Olsson, Britt Viol....4:47:46 (23,377)
Olsson, Taina....4:03:55 (12,695)
Olusanya, Ronke....4:27:04 (18,517)
O'Mahoney, Sharon E....7:04:09 (32,930)
O'Mara, Nicola J....5:43:20 (30,595)
O'Neill, Catherine E....4:48:10 (23,464)
O'Neill, Doreen....4:25:27 (18,105)
O'Neill, Elizabeth E....5:10:05 (27,277)
O'Neill, Johanna M....4:12:49 (14,779)
O'Neill, Lisa M....4:32:53 (19,974)
O'Neill, Patricia A....3:49:30 (8,747)
Onions, Gillian A....5:34:55 (29,961)
Oosthuizen, Riette....3:36:05 (5,851)
Open, Ann M....6:29:20 (32,437)
Oppmann, Simone....4:17:57 (16,095)
Orban, Mary B....4:14:57 (15,319)
Orchard, Joanne C....4:43:59 (22,570)
Orchard, Nicola....4:42:38 (22,242)
Ord, Louise M....5:42:03 (30,506)
O'Regan, Catherine P....4:09:11 (13,903)
O'Reilly, Claire K....3:52:03 (9,372)
O'Reilly, Gayle L....4:49:14 (23,699)
O'Reilly, Pauline....3:48:38 (8,535)
O'Reilly, Pauline CC....5:26:20 (29,158)
O'Riordan, Aisling....4:18:38 (16,262)
O'Riordan, Fiona....5:24:38 (28,998)
Orme, Anita S....4:07:42 (13,536)
O'Rourke, Joanna E....4:59:02 (25,713)
Orphant, Carla L....4:33:39 (20,177)
Orr, Jennifer A....4:30:30 (19,428)
Orr, Sally....3:38:27 (6,316)
Orridge, Sharon....4:45:19 (22,867)
Orrone, Lindsey E....4:41:53 (22,081)
Oruche, Grace....8:29:29 (33,205)
Oruche, Phina....5:49:06 (31,005)
Orum, Nicola J....3:59:26 (11,651)
Osborn, Gemma V....4:38:37 (21,360)
Osborne, Fiona M....4:33:20 (20,092)
Osborne, Katherine A....4:55:18 (24,962)
Osborne, Kathleen A....4:29:27 (19,160)
Osborne, Margaret....6:46:13 (32,712)
Osborne, Penny R....7:14:55 (33,005)
O'Shea, Lindsay....4:26:02 (18,271)
O'Shea, Mary P....3:26:20 (4,124)
Osler, Karen D....5:06:55 (26,850)
Osowska, Francesca....3:23:19 (3,686)
Ostermeier, Simone....4:03:46 (12,665)
Ostrehan, Bridget L....3:29:21 (4,689)
O'Sullivan, Britt....5:03:40 (26,413)
O'Sullivan, Deborah S....4:54:22 (24,761)
O'Sullivan, Joanne K....4:52:36 (24,380)
O'Sullivan, Julie M....4:48:00 (23,428)
O'Sullivan, Maureen N....5:32:28 (29,767)
O'Sullivan, Michele....4:22:33 (17,252)
O'Sullivan, Tina....5:32:27 (29,765)
Oswald, Jennefer E....4:52:08 (24,277)
Otonari, Masako....4:44:41 (22,707)
O'Toole, Anne M....7:34:06 (33,113)
O'Toole, Karen P....4:26:50 (18,473)
Ott, Elmarie....4:33:57 (20,238)
Ottaway, Samantha E....5:10:48 (27,367)
Otter, Sally H....5:38:23 (30,240)
Otterstedt, Elisabet....4:46:40 (23,153)
Otto, Juliet L....4:32:15 (19,845)
Ouassa, Rebecca D....4:47:06 (23,235)
Oughton, Emma C....3:35:30 (5,749)
Outhwaite, Wendy H....4:32:40 (19,925)
Overall, Sarah....6:11:50 (31,982)
Overy, Nicolette M....3:41:46 (6,978)
Oviatt, Val....5:17:26 (28,188)
Ovington, Anna....2:57:26 (979)
Ovstedal, Jenny L....4:24:54 (17,925)
Owen, Alexandra M....7:44:13 (33,154)
Owen, Alison F....5:09:08 (27,165)
Owen, Anna L....5:11:15 (27,421)
Owen, Bernadette A....4:14:24 (15,180)
Owen, Catherine R....3:46:15 (7,955)
Owen, Ceridwen....4:41:46 (22,052)
Owen, Emma....4:19:43 (16,534)
Owen, Emma L....4:54:50 (24,856)
Owen, Gabrielle A....5:14:52 (27,889)
Owen, Helen S....4:52:09 (24,279)
Owen, Josephine....4:30:50 (19,503)
Owen, Julie....5:16:11 (28,026)
Owen, Katherine A....6:57:30 (32,860)
Owen, Kira....5:01:06 (26,061)
Owen, Linda P....6:36:15 (32,545)
Owen, Lucy M....4:24:59 (17,953)
Owen, Mary B....3:11:48 (2,246)
Owen, Melanie A....6:04:24 (31,738)
Owen, Rosalind M....5:32:44 (29,789)
Owens, Amanda J....5:21:37 (28,674)
Owens, Caroline....4:37:11 (21,025)
Owens, Juliet M....4:34:33 (20,379)
Owens, Karen M....5:32:44 (29,789)
Owers, Catharine A....4:38:26 (21,320)
Owers, Helen T....5:44:11 (30,658)
Owles, Amanda L....5:30:09 (29,556)
Oxberry, Sarah R....4:51:32 (24,153)
Oxborrow, Melissa....4:26:46 (18,459)
Oxlade, Louisa M....6:12:34 (32,006)
Oxley, Rosemary J....5:04:19 (26,491)
Oxley, Samantha....4:32:52 (19,970)
Oyre, Tamara....3:41:30 (6,914)
Paananen, Johanna M....3:34:11 (5,511)
Pacey, Deborah J....4:58:46 (25,656)
Pacey, Sabrina A....4:26:34 (18,397)
Pack, Caroline M....4:29:09 (19,070)
Padfield, Clare L....4:39:16 (21,505)
Padgham, Melanie A....3:59:33 (11,686)
Padley, Gemma S....5:33:38 (29,862)
Page, Clare V....3:19:21 (3,177)
Page, Janice....4:37:00 (20,979)
Page, Katherine....5:18:46 (28,343)
Page, Katie....4:25:32 (18,123)
Page, Laura E....4:17:35 (16,011)
Paget, Jane....7:29:45 (33,093)
Paige, Alison D....6:47:12 (32,726)
Pain, Deborah K....4:57:57 (25,487)
Paine, Doreen M....4:48:58 (23,644)
Paine, Samantha J....4:37:54 (21,196)
Painter, Claire E....4:54:36 (24,800)
Painter, Elizabeth....4:37:20 (21,066)
Painter, Mary H....4:00:23 (11,910)
Pak, Minsun....5:59:02 (31,504)
Palacios Martinez, Rachael....3:55:14 (10,293)
Palframan, Laura....4:32:46 (19,952)
Palfreman, Suzy....4:33:22 (20,103)
Palin, Angharad M....3:29:25 (4,698)
Paling, Judith E....4:37:58 (21,213)
Palladino, Camilla A....4:35:35 (20,618)
Pallen, Clare E....5:19:42 (28,460)
Pallett, Joanne....3:38:52 (6,402)
Pallett, Suzy C....3:55:10 (10,264)
Pallister, Valerie H....4:08:06 (13,641)
Palmer, Ann E....7:46:39 (33,163)
Palmer, Barbara A....5:32:41 (29,787)
Palmer, Heloise V....4:51:04 (24,053)
Palmer, Joanne E....4:48:23 (23,510)
Palmer, Julia....3:05:08 (1,588)
Palmer, Karen M....3:48:48 (8,578)
Palmer, Kathryn J....4:01:48 (12,214)
Palmer, Kerenza M....4:56:30 (25,204)
Palmer, Michelle....5:10:29 (27,332)
Palmer, Rachel A....4:00:52 (12,009)
Palmer, Tara M....4:39:21 (21,533)
Palombo, Sonja C....4:48:26 (23,520)
Palomino, Patricia....5:48:48 (30,990)
Pamplin, Diane R....3:36:16 (5,888)
Panayiotou, Vicky J....4:13:46 (15,016)
Pankhurst, Emily C....5:11:35 (27,473)
Pannett, Claire E....4:45:13 (22,840)
Panoscha, Heidrun....4:47:19 (23,280)
Panting, Caroline J....4:39:42 (21,599)
Papagni, Lorraine M....4:30:09 (19,335)
Pape, Emma....4:47:11 (23,255)
Parchment, Marion....3:43:38 (7,375)
Pardoe, Jane....4:17:36 (16,018)
Parfitt, Dena B....3:00:22 (1,258)
Parfitt, Pauline....3:39:05 (6,451)
Paris, Clare L....5:01:45 (26,138)
Parish, Emma....5:07:19 (26,907)
Parish, Joanna C....4:21:44 (17,036)
Parish, Karina W....5:32:13 (29,754)
Parish, Tanya E....4:11:58 (14,566)
Parisotto, Elisabetta....5:17:20 (28,172)
Park, Amanda L....6:30:32 (32,464)
Park, Diane....6:04:10 (31,730)
Park, Elizabeth R....4:54:25 (24,773)
Park, Lynne A....3:41:41 (6,961)
Parker, Audrey A....5:04:32 (26,529)
Parker, Catherine E....3:57:13 (10,928)
Parker, Elizabeth R....4:33:33 (20,149)
Parker, Emma....4:14:00 (15,067)
Parker, Glenda A....5:19:58 (28,487)
Parker, Helen M....4:28:12 (18,812)
Parker, Julia A....3:34:42 (5,611)
Parker, Justine D....5:58:06 (31,463)
Parker, Karen E....5:11:12 (27,413)
Parker, Karen L....5:10:59 (27,384)
Parker, Kathrine....4:03:22 (12,570)
Parker, Pamela A....4:22:43 (17,303)
Parker, Patricia A....3:26:25 (4,139)
Parker, Sally J....4:31:09 (19,571)
Parker, Samantha L....4:52:39 (24,393)
Parker, Sarah A....3:53:35 (9,787)
Parker, Sarah J....3:56:16 (10,618)
Parker, Sarah M....4:58:12 (25,549)
Parker, Shelia....5:31:04 (29,664)
Parker, Stacy L....7:05:50 (32,945)
Parker, Tarnya....4:51:14 (24,084)
Parkes, Samantha....5:23:35 (28,893)
Parkin, Kate S....4:44:56 (22,768)
Parkinson, Helen A....3:00:18 (1,254)
Parkinson, Margaret E....6:20:01 (32,230)
Parkinson, Maria L....5:53:19 (31,233)
Parkinson, Sally....5:21:22 (28,655)
Parkinson, Sylvie....4:44:16 (22,629)
Parnacott, Sarah M....4:56:11 (25,135)
Parnell, Lindsey J....4:31:51 (19,760)
Parrott, Frances M....6:00:45 (31,591)

Parry, Anne M.	4:21:02 (16,875)	
Parry, Claire	4:56:44 (25,247)	
Parry, Emma C.	3:01:48 (1,356)	
Parry, Isabel	5:22:33 (28,777)	
Parry, Jemma	4:59:23 (25,758)	
Parry, Nicola J.	5:54:38 (31,296)	
Parry, Robbi L.	4:37:13 (21,037)	
Parry, Wendy	3:53:33 (9,778)	
Parson, Emma C.	4:08:04 (13,632)	
Parson, Erica J.	5:03:10 (26,339)	
Parson, Philippa J.	3:57:35 (11,036)	
Parsons, Caroline C.	5:06:58 (26,854)	
Parsons, Connie	5:53:06 (31,221)	
Parsons, Heather E	4:05:55 (13,125)	
Parsons, Helen S	3:09:40 (2,034)	
Parsons, Jackie A	3:58:09 (11,209)	
Parsons, Jane	4:51:46 (24,202)	
Parsons, Karen J	4:48:16 (23,487)	
Parsons, Karen J	5:07:32 (26,934)	
Parsons, Nicola A	5:14:11 (27,796)	
Parsons, Sarah J	4:33:29 (20,131)	
Parsons, Sarah M	5:26:42 (29,189)	
Partridge, Amanda-Jane	4:37:56 (21,204)	
Partridge, Bonnie	5:37:04 (30,140)	
Pasolini, Isa	5:03:41 (26,415)	
Pasquier, Marion	2:57:56 (1,017)	
Patching, Katrina J	3:49:32 (8,753)	
Patel, Amisha	5:41:00 (30,426)	
Patel, Chantal	4:59:29 (25,784)	
Patel, Dimple	3:54:43 (10,120)	
Patel, Heena	5:14:53 (27,892)	
Patel, Priya	6:21:02 (32,253)	
Patel, Pushpa	4:47:25 (23,296)	
Patel, Samanthi	4:22:48 (17,322)	
Pateman, Rachell A	4:26:10 (18,302)	
Paterson, Allyson	4:31:24 (19,645)	
Paterson, Annabel J	4:51:41 (24,183)	
Paterson, Georgina M	3:44:48 (7,643)	
Paterson, Susan	4:32:31 (19,905)	
Patience, Nikki J	3:54:52 (10,165)	
Paton, Hilda C	4:15:07 (15,372)	
Paton, Jessie	5:16:15 (28,035)	
Paton, Karen R	3:42:43 (7,159)	
Patrick, Claire H	5:06:01 (26,716)	
Patten, Rachel S	5:10:58 (27,380)	
Patterson, Jacqueline R	4:23:37 (17,535)	
Patterson, Karen	4:40:29 (21,771)	
Pattison, Deborah	4:12:47 (14,769)	
Pattison, Vanessa	4:19:16 (16,413)	
Patwari, Jagriti	4:26:53 (18,483)	
Paul, Carol	4:05:50 (13,106)	
Paul, Michelle	3:58:51 (11,464)	
Paulin, Susan M	3:59:25 (11,641)	
Pauw, Elise	5:02:44 (26,278)	
Pauzers, Clare	3:05:32 (1,626)	
Paver, Amanda	4:25:39 (18,145)	
Pavlof, Nadia N.	5:17:25 (28,187)	
Paxinou Paraskevi, Viviane	5:57:18 (31,422)	
Payne, Claire	3:55:05 (10,240)	
Payne, Daphne	5:14:53 (27,892)	
Payne, Elizabeth	5:04:34 (26,533)	
Payne, Francesca	5:09:25 (27,194)	
Payne, Gilian	4:39:35 (21,571)	
Payne, Karen M	4:47:31 (23,324)	
Payne, Kathryn S	7:08:42 (32,967)	
Payne, Richard M	3:57:46 (11,100)	
Payne, Susan	4:04:39 (12,845)	
Paynter, Nicky K	5:28:36 (29,385)	
Payton, Heather	4:23:10 (17,406)	
Peace, Angela	4:17:54 (16,080)	
Peace, Mandy J	3:32:13 (5,206)	
Peace, Michaela	4:44:59 (22,778)	
Peacefull, Catherine	6:09:55 (31,923)	
Peachey, Pamela	5:28:53 (29,416)	
Peacock, Claire E	2:54:59 (788)	
Peacock, Madeline	4:35:07 (20,513)	
Peacock, Suzy D.	4:36:01 (20,725)	
Peacock, Theresa	6:07:04 (31,821)	
Peake, Emily L.	4:36:48 (20,937)	
Peake, Jennifer	5:07:12 (26,892)	
Pearce, Chay L.	4:03:44 (12,659)	
Pearce, Cressida J	4:24:59 (17,953)	
Pearce, Helen M.	3:35:13 (5,709)	
Pearce, Janet A	4:46:24 (23,103)	
Pearce, Katie A	3:47:24 (8,213)	
Pearl, Lindsay J	6:47:15 (32,727)	
Pearson, Carolyn A	3:50:49 (9,058)	
Pearson, Carolyn J	4:15:28 (15,469)	
Pearson, Christina C	5:29:57 (29,540)	
Pearson, Claire B.	5:07:11 (26,890)	
Pearson, Elizabeth A	4:59:41 (25,831)	
Pearson, Helen J	2:57:02 (944)	
Pearson, Jennifer A	4:34:19 (20,310)	
Pearson, Rebecca M	4:03:00 (12,477)	
Pearson, Samantha	6:04:39 (31,750)	
Pearson, Zoe M	5:27:21 (29,255)	
Pease, Zoe	5:29:57 (29,540)	
Peasgood, Teresa J	3:48:39 (8,541)	
Peck, Gillian	4:35:03 (20,501)	
Peck, Juliette A	4:46:22 (23,096)	
Peck, Rita	3:56:56 (10,822)	
Peckett, Clare	4:46:12 (23,050)	
Pedersen, Jessie	4:47:02 (23,220)	
Pedersen, Linda	4:18:15 (16,169)	
Peers, Christine A	5:01:52 (26,154)	
Peeters, Anja	4:46:18 (23,075)	
Pegg, Gemma L	5:26:46 (29,198)	
Pegrum, Carly L	4:27:47 (18,693)	
Peirce, Claire	5:20:07 (28,508)	
Pell, Valerie M	4:25:15 (18,042)	
Pemberton, Katherine E	4:29:08 (19,065)	
Pemberton, Stephanie J	5:31:45 (29,722)	
Pembridge, Holly J	5:26:42 (29,189)	
Pembroke, Debbie J	4:18:12 (16,159)	
Pendaries, Claire Y	4:34:55 (20,466)	
Pendered, Jane	3:44:07 (7,475)	
Pendleton, Deborah C	5:09:29 (27,203)	
Pendleton-Hughes, Paula A	4:42:55 (22,310)	
Penfold, Celine L	5:00:52 (26,023)	
Penfold, Susan	5:02:23 (26,236)	
Penman, Victoria S	4:05:20 (12,985)	
Pennell, Christine	3:47:31 (8,242)	
Pennells, Nicki C	5:19:30 (28,435)	
Penner, Lorie E	4:01:06 (12,072)	
Penney, Carol A	4:44:13 (22,615)	
Pennycook, Sarah	4:27:42 (18,679)	
Penrose, Fran	3:37:58 (6,219)	
Penrose, Katherine M	4:10:45 (14,259)	
Penrose, Robina C	5:12:48 (27,623)	
Pentland, Debbie G	5:29:39 (29,497)	
Pentland, Emma L	4:44:16 (22,629)	
Penton, Emma	5:17:24 (28,183)	
Penty, Becky H	3:40:00 (6,626)	
Pepper, Debbie	3:49:52 (8,837)	
Percival, Violando H	4:00:57 (12,030)	
Perez-Ruiz, Ascension	4:27:36 (18,655)	
Perkins, Gaynor F	5:14:16 (27,807)	
Perkins, Kathryn A	4:42:35 (22,235)	
Perkins, Lisa A	4:57:02 (25,319)	
Perkins, Suzanne J	4:31:13 (19,586)	
Peronnet, Josiane	3:42:57 (7,221)	
Perriman, Jarqui	4:05:41 (13,074)	
Perrin, Louise M	3:33:43 (5,439)	
Perron, Jenny C	5:09:31 (27,207)	
Perry, Claire L	5:53:52 (31,257)	
Perry, Elizabeth J	6:38:11 (32,582)	
Perry, Fiona M	4:41:43 (22,039)	
Perry, Natasha S	3:24:53 (3,923)	
Perry, Ruth	4:15:31 (15,481)	
Perry, Victoria A	2:53:11 (683)	
Persaud, Marcia C	5:09:05 (27,158)	
Persson, Karin M	3:39:04 (6,449)	
Perugini, Nicola F	5:04:59 (26,579)	
Peters, Andrea C	6:57:16 (32,857)	
Peters, Joanna R	4:25:13 (18,033)	
Peters, Louise R	3:29:58 (4,818)	
Peters, Sharon L	3:56:23 (10,650)	
Peterson, Shelley L	4:30:25 (19,407)	
Petit-Zeman, Sophie	4:12:31 (14,710)	
Petrelli, Valentina	3:45:41 (7,844)	
Petrova, Lyudmila	2:21:29 (34)	
Petulla, Kerry L	3:14:14 (2,557)	
Pezzolla, Michela	4:14:25 (15,185)	
Pharoah, Fiona M	4:33:32 (20,142)	
Pheazey, Charlotte M	4:02:32 (12,382)	
Phelps, Jane	5:11:48 (27,492)	
Philip, Charlotte	4:36:56 (20,967)	
Philip, Kirsty R	3:39:33 (6,550)	
Philip, Laura M	4:25:44 (18,169)	
Philips, Elizabeth J	5:43:37 (30,613)	
Phillip Celine, Jacinta M	6:03:37 (31,708)	
Phillips, Aimée	6:14:08 (32,054)	
Phillips, Anna M	4:15:43 (15,524)	
Phillips, Anna M	5:11:08 (27,400)	
Phillips, Carole	3:29:05 (4,638)	
Phillips, Clare	3:10:29 (2,110)	
Phillips, Hazel	6:13:52 (32,045)	
Phillips, Helen L	5:02:43 (26,275)	
Phillips, Jacqueline	4:21:23 (16,955)	
Phillips, Jemma S	5:12:33 (27,594)	
Phillips, Joanne L	5:11:12 (27,413)	
Phillips, Kathryn M	3:48:16 (8,442)	
Phillips, Lisa A	5:26:03 (29,131)	
Phillips, Meg J	3:56:39 (10,739)	
Phillips, Pamela J	5:11:39 (27,476)	
Phillips, Rhian M	5:23:54 (28,928)	
Phillips, Sasha	4:50:46 (23,995)	
Phillips, Sonia E	3:34:31 (5,571)	
Phillips, Susan J	6:17:24 (32,152)	
Phillipson, Sarah	5:25:02 (29,041)	
Philp, Linda K	3:31:03 (4,996)	
Philp, Louise	4:56:15 (25,150)	
Philp, Nicky	5:02:26 (26,242)	
Philpot, Leonie Y	4:21:07 (16,897)	
Philps, Christine H	5:53:50 (31,256)	
Phin, Catriona M	3:34:58 (5,658)	
Phippen, Polli A	4:22:57 (17,356)	
Phipps, Katie E	4:08:47 (13,809)	
Phipps, Sarah A	5:21:22 (28,655)	
Piccolo, Alessandra	5:41:50 (30,488)	
Pichler, Silke C	2:59:50 (1,228)	
Pichon, Hannah	4:43:35 (22,462)	
Pick, Katherine	6:16:10 (32,124)	
Pickard, Francesca M	6:54:29 (32,818)	
Pickering, Nicola J	4:17:28 (15,972)	
Pickering, Tracy	5:05:05 (26,596)	
Pickert, Linda C	4:48:22 (23,506)	
Pickett, Jill	4:37:12 (21,032)	
Pickles, Andrea J	4:17:51 (16,072)	
Pienaar, Louise A	4:30:46 (19,488)	
Pierce, Pearl	3:58:05 (11,178)	
Piggott, Penny J	4:27:19 (18,584)	
Piipponen, Eero O	4:53:06 (24,479)	
Pike, Karen S	4:55:47 (25,052)	
Pike, Lisa J	5:30:02 (29,548)	
Pike, Zoe M	3:02:20 (1,394)	
Pilbeam, René E	4:45:18 (22,856)	
Pilbrow, Nik	3:51:59 (9,361)	
Pilcher, Sarah L	4:55:01 (24,899)	
Pilkington, Laura F	5:36:07 (30,061)	
Pilling, Angela M	5:23:03 (28,837)	
Pinder, Katherine V	5:25:28 (29,081)	
Pinder, Susan	3:20:26 (3,331)	
Pini, Daniela	5:01:04 (26,056)	
Pini, Divina A	6:30:12 (32,453)	
Pinner, Audrey L	5:36:13 (30,073)	
Pinney, Nicola	3:30:19 (4,867)	
Pinnock, Helen L	4:11:17 (14,413)	
Pinter, Maki	4:44:13 (22,615)	
Piper, Carolyn J	4:10:04 (14,115)	
Piper, Fiona E	3:45:05 (7,709)	
Pirie, Karen B	4:33:45 (20,196)	
Pirie, Laura J	4:50:37 (23,966)	
Pithie, Jane L	4:17:38 (16,025)	
Pitt, Emma	3:55:43 (10,444)	
Pitt, Emma	4:40:30 (21,777)	
Pitt, Maresa E	3:10:19 (2,100)	
Pitt, Nicola S	4:19:24 (16,448)	
Pitt, Samantha J	5:52:32 (31,200)	
Pittard, Debbie A	5:46:41 (30,838)	
Pitts, Lisa M	5:27:42 (29,293)	
Pitts, Ruth F	5:53:46 (31,253)	
Plant, Nciola J	4:10:43 (14,123)	
Playford, Marie B	3:41:38 (6,950)	
Plowright, Linda C	4:31:05 (19,548)	
Plumb, Leza J	5:26:19 (29,155)	
Plume, Jennifer L	5:25:41 (29,099)	
Plummer, Lucy C	5:59:10 (31,513)	
Plummer, Victoria A	3:29:57 (4,815)	

Pode, Miranda 5:22:44 (28,804)
Poingdestre, Elizabeth A 4:04:38 (12,837)
Pointon, Amy K 4:17:34 (16,003)
Poler, Kirsten C 3:57:37 (11,051)
Pollard, Gemma C 4:35:56 (20,698)
Pollard, Linda 4:22:24 (17,226)
Polosse, Jacqueline 5:09:31 (27,207)
Pomeroy, Louise 5:08:05 (27,021)
Ponchia, Lorenza 4:04:03 (12,726)
Pond, Gill J 4:39:43 (21,605)
Ponting, Kim M 4:49:53 (23,817)
Poole, Abigail E 4:00:59 (12,045)
Poole, Claire J 5:31:39 (29,716)
Poole, Jane 3:33:08 (5,339)
Poole, Janet A 4:16:14 (15,652)
Poole, Liz 4:01:32 (12,153)
Poole, Olivia 4:15:41 (15,514)
Pooley, Ellen 3:17:04 (2,885)
Pooley, Susan J 5:10:13 (27,291)
Poore, Kate A 5:25:43 (29,104)
Pope, Clare 6:28:46 (32,433)
Pope, Margaret G 4:21:23 (16,955)
Pope, Suzanne E 4:41:35 (22,008)
Popham, Lorraine H 4:37:59 (21,216)
Popple, Jasmin M 6:41:56 (32,640)
Popplewell, Jo S 5:22:32 (28,774)
Popplewell, Katie J 5:22:34 (28,778)
Porter, Annabel J 4:48:47 (23,606)
Porter, Charlotte E 3:26:05 (4,087)
Porter, Gertrud F 3:56:43 (10,758)
Porter, Helen J 5:01:12 (26,071)
Porter, Jane A 5:03:37 (26,408)
Porter, Laura A 5:17:55 (28,233)
Porter, Linda J 4:37:17 (21,054)
Porter, Lynette A 3:11:18 (2,198)
Porter, Susan 5:08:48 (27,118)
Porter, Zoe G 3:19:32 (3,195)
Portlock, Elizabeth A 5:33:53 (29,880)
Portsmouth, Helen 4:23:13 (17,421)
Postlethwaite, Becky 4:37:29 (21,108)
Pote, Catherine 5:39:01 (30,282)
Potgieter, Andrea 3:35:34 (5,763)
Potlin, Gwen F 4:09:35 (14,011)
Pottage, Sandie 3:45:29 (7,802)
Potter, Dawn T 4:46:48 (23,171)
Potter, Dianne E 5:31:06 (29,672)
Potter, Jean J 4:36:06 (20,752)
Potter, Patricia 4:53:54 (24,660)
Potter, Sarah L 6:20:36 (32,242)
Potterton, Kirsty A 4:29:00 (19,028)
Potts, Joanne 5:16:56 (28,120)
Potts, Samantha J 4:05:19 (12,982)
Poulter, Deborah A 5:08:14 (27,040)
Poulter, Jacqueline 4:54:35 (24,799)
Poultney, Candice R 5:31:03 (29,662)
Poulton, Esther R 5:19:10 (28,397)
Pounds, Carolyn C 4:59:51 (25,858)
Pountney, Pippa K 4:51:31 (24,151)
Povey, Sonia 3:43:42 (7,389)
Powell, Alison J 4:22:51 (17,333)
Powell, Lisa D 4:49:01 (23,654)
Powell, Mariann 3:38:48 (6,383)
Powell, Nicola A 4:04:46 (12,872)
Powell, Pauline A 4:50:57 (24,037)
Powell, Rosemary J 5:08:20 (27,056)
Power, Clare 6:01:05 (31,609)
Power, Diana M 5:54:32 (31,285)
Power, Julie 5:01:42 (26,135)
Power, Rebecca C 4:34:38 (20,395)
Power, Wenda M 4:42:21 (22,190)
Powers, Sabrina 5:24:00 (28,936)
Powles, Jacqueline 5:20:07 (28,508)
Powls, Nicola L 5:30:51 (29,631)
Powrie, Catherine 3:31:46 (5,113)
Powrie, Honor E 4:37:28 (21,102)
Powrie, Kathryn E 4:28:41 (18,940)
Powsey, Emma L 6:08:22 (31,872)
Poyner, Jane 4:05:49 (13,103)
Poynton, Linda M 5:18:43 (28,339)
Prajapati, Urmila B 4:02:35 (12,395)
Prance, Carole 3:50:03 (8,874)
Prange, Helen A 5:17:46 (28,216)
Pratt, Joanna K 4:00:55 (12,019)

Pratt, Keeley M 5:14:28 (27,837)
Pratt, Margaret C 4:20:43 (16,793)
Preece, Mary 6:05:37 (31,781)
Preece, Ruth J 5:56:50 (31,395)
Preen, Jane L 2:56:06 (857)
Prentice, Linda 4:43:40 (22,481)
Preston, Chloe R 4:59:30 (25,786)
Preston, Emma M 5:23:37 (28,896)
Preston, Joanne 4:13:52 (15,034)
Preston, Lila M 5:03:05 (26,327)
Preston, Nicola M 4:20:17 (16,678)
Preston, Samantha 5:07:30 (26,930)
Preston, Susan M 4:09:34 (14,007)
Prestwich, Janet 6:01:01 (31,606)
Price, Claire L 5:06:16 (26,750)
Price, Evette L 4:09:35 (14,011)
Price, Hannah K 5:12:39 (27,606)
Price, Joanne E 3:49:19 (8,697)
Price, Julie 4:01:11 (12,099)
Price, Julie J 5:09:53 (27,253)
Price, Katie J 4:40:34 (21,804)
Price, Kirsty E 4:02:25 (12,355)
Price, Lorraine 4:30:29 (19,424)
Price, Louise R 4:49:48 (23,806)
Price, Rebecca C 6:01:28 (31,624)
Price, Rhiannon M 4:57:16 (25,364)
Price, Ruth 5:45:09 (30,727)
Price, Shelley M 4:43:13 (22,370)
Prichard, Pamela I 3:43:28 (7,344)
Prideaux, Lesley A 3:58:39 (11,382)
Pridmore, Nicola 4:44:13 (22,615)
Pridmore, Teresa 4:03:35 (12,621)
Priestley, Carole I 4:36:04 (20,742)
Prince, Debbie J 4:14:01 (15,074)
Prince, Louise 3:59:10 (11,563)
Pring, Caroline D 5:27:24 (29,261)
Pring, Fiona E 4:38:42 (21,371)
Prinsley, Emma L 5:28:06 (29,334)
Prior, Clare 4:17:43 (16,034)
Pritchett, Jennifer A 4:23:46 (17,578)
Proctor, Janet S 5:13:37 (27,730)
Proctor, Joanna C 5:36:18 (30,081)
Proctor, Madeleine H 4:00:00 (11,810)
Proddow, Louise 3:29:11 (4,651)
Prosser, Kathryn 4:21:25 (16,960)
Prosser, Laura 5:42:58 (30,576)
Protasomi, Laura E 4:11:00 (14,329)
Prowse, Elaine 7:01:54 (32,894)
Prowse, Wendy 3:48:25 (8,477)
Prust, Marie-Claire A 4:43:30 (22,435)
Pruzina, Stephanie 3:42:09 (7,055)
Pryke, Gail 3:14:21 (2,575)
Pryor, Shona A 3:57:19 (10,953)
Psatha, Maria 3:43:23 (7,329)
Pugh, Daphne W 5:11:32 (27,464)
Pugh, Gillian E 3:32:36 (5,265)
Pugh, Jane M 3:59:32 (11,682)
Pugh, Rachel C 4:57:27 (25,390)
Pugh, Tracy M 4:37:53 (21,194)
Pullan, Belinda J 3:25:47 (4,042)
Purkiss, Sheila T 5:26:29 (29,174)
Purnell, Kim 5:08:45 (27,112)
Purser, Stephanie 4:46:23 (23,098)
Purton, Charlotte E 4:34:57 (20,473)
Putland, Helen 4:35:45 (20,661)
Putt, Louise J 4:54:56 (24,875)
Puttick, Megan 4:57:21 (25,375)
Puzzarini, Andrea 5:35:58 (30,053)
Pye, Judith 4:55:19 (24,963)
Pye, Tessa 6:46:13 (32,712)
Pyman, Melanie R 5:43:21 (30,596)
Pyne, Janet L 5:24:55 (29,031)
Quail, Lisa R 6:03:45 (31,717)
Quaile, Jackie 5:18:10 (28,266)
Quarmby, Shirley M 3:58:08 (11,203)

LONDON MARATHON

Quartermaine, Paulette D 5:56:59 (31,405)
Quatresols, Alison 5:05:57 (26,700)
Quawson, Nana N 3:58:41 (11,396)
Queally, Gemma L 3:52:51 (9,578)
Quelch, Nicola A 4:22:21 (17,209)
Quigley, Marian 4:22:35 (17,260)
Quigley, Sharon P 4:27:19 (18,584)
Quinlan, Barbara P 5:24:58 (29,038)
Quinlivan, Claire M 4:56:10 (25,133)
Quinn, Jamie E 3:32:38 (5,270)
Quinn, Karen M 5:59:48 (31,550)
Quinn, Laura-Ann 6:01:25 (31,621)
Raaijmakers, Monique M 3:30:42 (4,933)
Rabe, Martina 3:47:27 (8,225)
Raborn, Janelle 5:30:59 (29,648)
Rabuka, Marica E 7:16:44 (33,019)
Race, Julia E 3:33:56 (5,472)
Rackett, Peta N 4:49:28 (23,750)
Radford, Joy C 3:35:47 (5,796)
Raeburn, Elizabeth A 5:34:02 (29,893)
Raeside, Karen J 4:47:44 (23,368)
Rafferty, Diane M 6:59:22 (32,874)
Rago, Judit 5:41:44 (30,476)
Rahimi, Galavish 6:59:23 (32,875)
Rahman, Huma 3:29:54 (4,806)
Rainey, Sarah C 6:54:31 (32,819)
Rainger, Lesley 3:24:34 (3,876)
Rainwood, Katherine 6:10:12 (31,931)
Ralph, Andrea F 5:07:22 (26,914)
Ralph, Caroline J 4:39:37 (21,581)
Ramadan, Manal 5:47:14 (30,882)
Ramsay, Amanda G 3:41:30 (6,914)
Ramsay, Jacqueline 4:55:10 (24,928)
Ramsay, Tana 4:16:35 (15,747)
Ramsbotham, Leasa G 4:16:03 (15,609)
Ramsden, Pippa 4:18:20 (16,193)
Ramsell, Victoria J 4:01:54 (12,236)
Ramsey, Paula 3:48:58 (8,623)
Ramsey Smith, Sarah 3:57:26 (10,989)
Ranby, Emma J 4:01:45 (12,199)
Rand, Louise F 4:35:33 (20,612)
Rand, Sarah 4:05:05 (12,936)
Randall, Ceri L 4:43:08 (22,357)
Randall, Rebecca A 5:51:17 (31,140)
Randalls, Brian 5:01:02 (26,048)
Randerson, Caroline M 5:59:47 (31,547)
Randle, Anna 5:00:47 (26,006)
Randolph, Rachel L 5:06:34 (26,799)
Rangeard, Fabienne C 4:15:07 (15,372)
Rankin, Alison L 4:23:11 (17,410)
Rankin, Cate 5:54:55 (31,305)
Rannard, Anne C 5:51:24 (31,150)
Ransome, Gail A 6:59:26 (32,876)
Ranson, Pauline F 4:07:41 (13,528)
Rapp, Avgelika 4:02:49 (12,441)
Rapson, Kathy T 5:50:25 (31,106)
Rapson, Nicola M 5:50:25 (31,106)
Rashid, Husna 6:44:33 (32,685)
Rasmussen, Hanne K 4:34:56 (20,471)
Ratcliffe, Martine A 4:45:03 (22,804)
Rathbone, Melissa 4:13:20 (14,924)
Rathie, Sophia M 5:23:53 (28,927)
Ratnavira, Clare B 4:43:32 (22,447)
Rattu, Lisa M 3:43:01 (7,236)
Raub-Segall, Elke 5:18:06 (28,252)
Raundell, Victoria A 7:26:34 (33,079)
Rausch, Manuela 4:40:49 (21,858)
Rawlings, Donna M 4:31:07 (19,557)
Rawlings, Zoe J 3:23:57 (3,782)
Rawlinson, Annie 4:47:43 (23,364)
Rawlinson, Emma 4:19:34 (16,497)
Rawsthorne, Kim F 4:13:38 (14,991)
Ray, Alison M 4:29:22 (19,138)
Rayat, Amrit 6:13:50 (32,042)
Raynel, Natasha E 3:56:08 (10,577)
Rayner, Andrea J 4:56:32 (25,213)
Rayner, Denise M 7:21:31 (33,049)
Rayner, Diana E 6:38:06 (32,581)
Rayner, Lisa 4:46:13 (23,051)
Rayner, Marion R 3:13:50 (2,506)
Raynes, Julie A 5:17:04 (28,137)
Rea, Maureen 4:09:38 (14,019)
Read, Gemma 4:54:19 (24,749)

Read, Henrietta M	4:16:10 (15,639)
Read, Jackie S	4:14:40 (15,249)
Read, Jennifer M	4:02:45 (12,424)
Read, Natalie C	5:43:09 (30,584)
Read, Susan D	5:10:56 (27,378)
Reader, Sarah J	4:28:57 (19,012)
Reader, Susan J	4:50:13 (23,885)
Reading, Barbara	4:14:58 (15,325)
Reading, Gabriella	5:10:26 (27,326)
Readman, Penny J	4:58:19 (25,572)
Readman, Tamzin C	4:10:22 (14,189)
Ready, Deborah J	3:56:15 (10,610)
Reale, Diane	4:59:08 (25,729)
Reaney, Bridget	4:04:13 (12,760)
Reanney, Victoria E	4:22:12 (17,174)
Reaper, Beckie L	4:58:31 (25,614)
Reavill, Jacqueline	4:59:01 (25,710)
Redding, Rebecca	4:25:01 (17,969)
Reddish, Kerrie S	5:07:15 (26,898)
Reddy, Kay	4:18:14 (16,165)
Redgrave, Ann	7:10:55 (32,989)
Redgrave-Evans, Leizabeth J	7:19:35 (33,040)
Redington, Anna C	4:20:13 (16,666)
Redmond, Anne S	5:21:20 (28,649)
Redmond, Caroline	3:59:00 (11,511)
Redmond, Deborah J	4:15:27 (15,466)
Redmond, Sarah L	7:25:01 (33,069)
Redpath, Corin R	4:34:47 (20,433)
Redstone, Jenni E	3:57:51 (11,124)
Reed, Charlotte O	5:05:39 (26,661)
Reed, Georgette L	5:07:41 (26,962)
Reed, Gina A	5:18:20 (28,286)
Reed, Sue	4:45:37 (22,930)
Reeder, Heather J	5:33:10 (29,829)
Reeder, Louise E	5:24:45 (29,012)
Reedy, Jane A	4:56:06 (25,119)
Rees, Joanna H	4:57:07 (25,338)
Rees, Ruth	4:58:03 (25,513)
Rees, Sara C	4:58:25 (25,589)
Reeve, Emma	3:52:23 (9,466)
Reeve, Helen L	5:06:48 (26,836)
Reeve, Lucy V	4:28:09 (18,792)
Reeve, Penny J	4:26:08 (18,293)
Reeve, Rachel	4:49:33 (23,766)
Reeve, Rebecca L	4:42:30 (22,217)
Reeves, Annabelle N	5:44:57 (30,712)
Reeves, Jules A	3:50:56 (9,083)
Reeves, Justine	4:41:47 (22,056)
Regan, Sarah J	5:09:06 (27,161)
Regan, Suzanne E	4:30:57 (19,521)
Reid, Carol A	3:26:36 (4,177)
Reid, Jacqueline E	4:39:44 (21,610)
Reid, Katy H	4:24:59 (17,953)
Reid, Lesley A	7:02:56 (32,906)
Reid, Margaret	3:48:03 (8,396)
Reid, Sandy	4:23:51 (17,609)
Reid, Sarah A	3:12:22 (2,330)
Reid, Shelley L	4:24:55 (17,930)
Reid, Sheridan P	4:16:49 (15,804)
Reilly, Kerry-Jo	4:56:19 (25,168)
Reilly, Michael W	3:28:50 (4,585)
Reilly, Victoria D	6:16:00 (32,117)
Relf, Jennifer C	4:34:19 (20,310)
Remington, Jo	3:33:19 (5,370)
Renfrey, Gemma L	4:15:50 (15,559)
Renmant, Beverley J	3:28:47 (4,570)
Rennie, Kaytherine L	3:50:22 (8,945)
Rennie, Nina M	4:38:03 (21,239)
Renshaw, Amelia L	4:59:22 (25,757)
Resker, Diane	4:23:42 (17,560)
Reyneke, Letitia N	5:02:31 (26,251)
Reynolds, Abigail M	4:09:37 (14,018)
Reynolds, Alison J	4:20:19 (16,688)
Reynolds, Ellen	5:22:59 (28,824)
Reynolds, Fiona M	4:43:17 (22,387)
Reynolds, Gillian P	5:09:56 (27,258)
Reynolds, Julie	3:44:18 (7,521)
Reynolds, Lesley E	4:28:55 (18,998)
Reynolds, Lisa C	6:06:33 (31,804)
Reynolds, Rachel	3:54:23 (10,023)
Reynolds, Sally A	4:32:50 (19,963)
Reynolds, Sian V	4:59:36 (25,811)
Reynolds, Stephanie A	5:09:57 (27,260)

Rhoderick-Jones, Annabel C	5:06:19 (26,757)
Rhodes, Catherine	4:59:27 (25,773)
Rhodes, Dusty	4:08:20 (13,701)
Rhodes, Elizabeth	5:46:37 (30,833)
Rhodes, Jessica J	4:31:31 (19,668)
Rhodes, Lucy J	5:21:46 (28,686)
Rhodes, Mary	5:07:11 (26,890)
Rhys, Jennifer C	3:21:35 (3,483)
Rice, Sheila A	5:36:46 (30,114)
Richards, Alison	4:25:59 (18,253)
Richards, Anne	4:46:24 (23,103)
Richards, Benyna M	6:38:36 (32,591)
Richards, Dawn	5:22:42 (28,799)
Richards, Emily E	5:03:05 (26,327)
Richards, Faye L	4:10:45 (14,259)
Richards, Jan N	4:08:32 (13,750)
Richards, Jennifer A	6:44:22 (32,683)
Richards, Jennifer M	5:47:06 (30,870)
Richards, Katie	5:02:16 (26,215)
Richards, Linda G	6:06:49 (31,817)
Richards, Lise E	4:08:19 (13,695)
Richards, Pauline A	5:38:30 (30,252)
Richards, Romana D	4:34:30 (20,362)
Richards, Ruth G	3:37:20 (6,098)
Richardson, Amanda R	6:07:02 (31,820)
Richardson, Bridget S	4:16:15 (15,658)
Richardson, Jill C	3:53:25 (9,741)
Richardson, Julie	3:50:16 (8,929)
Richardson, Julie	4:57:14 (25,359)
Richardson, Leanda	4:39:02 (21,447)
Richardson, Lesley C	3:30:26 (4,882)
Richardson, Samantha	4:21:54 (17,088)
Richardson, Stella C	5:17:18 (28,167)
Richardson, Val	4:34:27 (20,350)
Riches, Annalie	4:34:31 (20,365)
Rickaby, Emma J	4:42:45 (22,269)
Rickard, Donna	4:28:42 (18,944)
Rickerby, Christina	4:59:32 (25,794)
Rickett, Leanne	4:58:28 (25,600)
Ricketts, Clare J	4:38:42 (21,371)
Ridd, Emma	5:38:02 (30,206)
Ridd, Karen L	5:42:28 (30,532)
Riddell, Grainne	3:37:51 (6,199)
Ridehalgh, Sarah E	3:24:03 (3,800)
Ridgley, Julie R	3:32:00 (5,158)
Ridgway, Frances	3:42:56 (7,217)
Ridgway, Hayley	4:35:05 (20,508)
Ridgway, Sandy	3:54:11 (9,972)
Riding, Liona	4:08:18 (13,689)
Ridings, Samantha J	4:40:00 (21,674)
Ridley, Angela C	4:33:23 (20,106)
Ridon, Marie Anne	4:36:01 (20,725)
Rigby, Brenda E	5:33:18 (29,833)
Rigby, Rachael L	4:45:11 (22,830)
Rigby, Wendy	4:31:13 (19,586)
Rigg, Katie S	4:05:44 (13,082)
Rigg, Susan P	4:18:39 (16,266)
Riley, Belinda J	4:21:34 (16,989)
Riley, Carol A	4:38:22 (21,310)
Riley, Diana L	5:15:15 (27,932)
Riley, Donna R	4:00:15 (11,879)
Riley, Françoise	4:26:30 (18,384)
Riley, Louise	3:51:46 (9,294)
Rimmington, Carole L	4:33:35 (20,159)
Ring, Claire	4:57:25 (25,383)
Ring, Tina	4:58:16 (25,563)
Ringwood, Ofelia	5:12:40 (27,611)
Risbridger, Petra A	4:07:07 (13,377)
Risk, Elizabeth	4:21:04 (16,883)
Ritch, Charlene A	5:28:06 (29,334)
Ritchie, Christine M	4:57:48 (25,455)
Ritchie, Nicola D	4:13:27 (14,951)
Ritchie, Shanna L	5:49:43 (31,053)
Rivera Luna, Deyawira E	3:22:25 (3,585)
Riveron, Lisette C	5:26:05 (29,134)
Rivers, Charmaine	4:03:22 (12,570)
Rivers, Valerie	4:29:05 (19,053)
Rix, Mandy J	5:32:17 (29,759)
Rizal, Radiah	6:47:30 (32,730)
Rizmal, Ivana	5:00:15 (25,936)
Robb, Kathryn	5:08:36 (27,090)
Robb, Tracy A	3:55:56 (10,519)
Robert, Marie-Claude	4:16:37 (15,761)

Roberts, Alison	4:05:02 (12,923)
Roberts, Alison M	3:49:16 (8,686)
Roberts, Amy H	6:10:06 (31,928)
Roberts, Bee	3:57:06 (10,883)
Roberts, Beverley A	6:37:43 (32,573)
Roberts, Carly	4:55:05 (24,914)
Roberts, Carole M	4:46:20 (23,086)
Roberts, Denise L	7:45:14 (33,159)
Roberts, Emma G	3:43:54 (7,439)
Roberts, Faye	4:14:58 (15,325)
Roberts, Fiona C	5:01:39 (26,128)
Roberts, Fleur E	3:49:59 (8,863)
Roberts, Gillian A	5:25:17 (29,068)
Roberts, Glenda	4:01:41 (12,187)
Roberts, Hannah E	4:05:25 (13,003)
Roberts, Joan	6:40:43 (32,620)
Roberts, Josephine E	4:36:30 (20,844)
Roberts, Karen	4:56:37 (25,223)
Roberts, Katherine S	3:24:07 (3,808)
Roberts, Kylie B	4:50:08 (23,865)
Roberts, Lisa J	4:05:11 (12,951)
Roberts, Mari A	6:02:53 (31,674)
Roberts, Michelle	4:58:54 (25,687)
Roberts, Nicola J	4:29:26 (19,153)
Roberts, Nyssa	3:40:59 (6,799)
Roberts, Ruth E	4:26:37 (18,413)
Roberts, Sharon C	5:43:57 (30,633)
Roberts, Sharon M	4:40:14 (21,720)
Roberts, Steffani S	4:31:31 (19,668)
Roberts, Suzanne	8:18:03 (33,194)
Roberts, Trudy J	5:36:31 (30,098)
Robertson, Caroline P	4:58:19 (25,572)
Robertson, Dilys M	3:19:34 (3,199)
Robertson, Katherine E	5:07:20 (26,913)
Robertson, Katia	4:18:46 (16,298)
Robertson, Louise	6:02:30 (31,658)
Robin, Marg	4:30:43 (19,477)
Robins, Mia	5:02:12 (26,201)
Robinson, Anna	4:38:28 (21,329)
Robinson, Anne	4:53:45 (24,632)
Robinson, Carina N	3:46:24 (7,989)
Robinson, Carol	5:35:18 (29,996)
Robinson, Catriona M	4:28:02 (18,757)
Robinson, Charlotte	4:25:13 (18,033)
Robinson, Deborah H	4:18:41 (16,278)
Robinson, Deborah M	3:30:40 (4,926)
Robinson, Eleanor	3:36:53 (6,016)
Robinson, Emily H	3:55:11 (10,275)
Robinson, Jackie	4:51:07 (24,063)
Robinson, Julia A	4:17:45 (16,046)
Robinson, Julie A	3:55:52 (10,496)
Robinson, June A	3:33:39 (5,430)
Robinson, Karen A	3:25:57 (4,066)
Robinson, Kerry Lyn	5:59:08 (31,509)
Robinson, Leisa F	4:25:06 (17,990)
Robinson, Lisa M	7:26:17 (33,077)
Robinson, Lucy A	4:11:23 (14,434)
Robinson, Lucy J	3:57:08 (10,893)
Robinson, Michelle H	4:23:43 (17,565)
Robinson, Sarah L	4:43:56 (22,558)
Robinson, Sophie E	4:17:23 (15,951)
Robinson, Wendy J	3:30:15 (4,860)
Robjohns, Karen S	4:25:53 (18,224)
Robson, Amanda J	5:11:25 (27,444)
Robson, Anne M	3:41:13 (6,856)
Robson, Dawn E	3:40:51 (6,770)
Robson, Erin D	5:38:55 (30,275)
Robson, Jane M	4:58:15 (25,560)
Robson, Lorraine D	5:44:57 (30,712)
Robson, Nadine E	5:55:35 (31,333)
Robson, Rebecca M	4:22:49 (17,326)
Robson, Rosalyn	6:43:26 (32,664)
Robson, Sarah	4:48:07 (23,453)
Roby-Welford, Anna C	4:39:02 (21,447)
Roche, Alison D	4:54:11 (24,724)
Roche, Catherine A	4:16:38 (15,766)
Roche-Kelly, Lelia A	4:09:57 (14,091)
Rocher, Laure	5:01:47 (26,145)
Rocholl, Zoe	5:14:20 (27,817)
Rock, Lois M	5:30:15 (29,566)
Rockliffe, Jacqueline M	3:20:43 (3,366)
Rockman, Diana L	5:27:10 (29,242)
Rodger, Camilla L	4:50:24 (23,926)

Rodgers, Faye A....4:27:35 (18,650)
Rodgers, Louise K....4:50:17 (23,901)
Rodrigues, Odete M....3:46:34 (8,026)
Roe, Avril R....4:47:42 (23,360)
Roffey, Alison J....4:47:14 (23,268)
Rogan, Emma B....3:36:39 (5,967)
Rogers, Anne....4:55:23 (24,980)
Rogers, Corinna A....5:00:02 (25,888)
Rogers, Emma....4:29:59 (19,288)
Rogers, Kate....4:39:33 (21,564)
Rogers, Kerry A....6:07:46 (31,852)
Rogers, Laura R....3:59:46 (11,753)
Rogers, Lisa C....5:35:54 (30,046)
Rogers, Lisa M....5:07:39 (26,957)
Rogers, Rebecca E....4:24:19 (17,754)
Rogers, Rosemary....4:36:49 (20,941)
Rogers, Sarah J....3:49:41 (8,793)
Rolfe, Marion F....6:20:01 (32,230)
Rolfe, Sally H....4:54:40 (24,808)
Rolfe, Virignia A....4:26:52 (18,479)
Rollason, Sarah E....4:46:24 (23,103)
Rollason, Stephen G....4:22:42 (17,300)
Rollings, Ann B....3:42:33 (7,124)
Rollinson, Lorraine....3:28:27 (4,503)
Rollo, Theresa M....6:01:17 (31,618)
Rolph, Claire L....5:10:45 (27,359)
Rolt, Georgina A....3:30:50 (4,947)
Romaine, Kimberly K....4:16:59 (15,854)
Romecin, Lindsay H....3:35:49 (5,801)
Ronan, Lindsay C....4:39:51 (21,640)
Ronan, Nadine....5:10:23 (27,316)
Roohi, Bejan....4:28:10 (18,799)
Rooke, Samantha J....5:54:06 (31,267)
Rooke, Vicki....5:11:27 (27,449)
Rooker, Jemma C....3:55:54 (10,507)
Rooker, Jessica....4:52:05 (24,263)
Rooney, Alison J....4:16:52 (15,817)
Rooney, Clare J....4:13:17 (14,914)
Roose, Kathleen A....4:41:47 (22,056)
Roper, Helen....4:50:14 (23,889)
Roper, Jessica C....4:11:06 (14,359)
Roper, Niki J....6:57:31 (32,861)
Rose, Caroline....5:28:19 (29,357)
Rose, Catherine J....5:50:07 (31,082)
Rose, Eileen M....4:48:17 (23,489)
Rose, Emma L....3:47:03 (8,133)
Rose, Heidi....5:22:24 (28,766)
Rose, J....6:10:24 (31,939)
Rose, Janice A....6:20:09 (32,235)
Rose, Julie M....4:43:30 (22,435)
Rose, Kirsty J....5:27:03 (29,230)
Rose, Sylvie J....5:05:15 (26,618)
Rose, Vicki A....6:44:40 (32,688)
Rose, Yasmine....3:57:17 (10,944)
Rosekilly, Julie A....4:46:42 (23,160)
Rosen, Deborah Z....4:11:17 (14,413)
Rosewarne, Amanda C....4:50:20 (23,914)
Ross, Fiona F....4:15:13 (15,392)
Ross, Jacqueline M....4:57:04 (25,328)
Ross, Jacqueline M....5:09:35 (27,217)
Ross, Kirsty E....3:59:32 (11,682)
Ross, Nicola J....4:08:27 (13,732)
Ross, Rosanna S....3:57:25 (10,984)
Ross, Susan....5:14:00 (27,760)
Rossall, Cassi S....5:44:06 (30,649)
Rossall, Sue....5:44:06 (30,649)
Rossi, Abigail J....4:02:34 (12,391)
Rossiter, Helene L....5:15:43 (27,969)
Ross-Russell, Rachel S....3:08:49 (1,937)
Rostampour, Janey....4:39:12 (21,490)
Rostron, Lucy H....5:13:29 (27,718)
Roth, Katharine M....4:25:43 (18,163)
Rother, Marion....4:12:13 (14,629)
Rothwell, Tania....4:46:00 (23,005)
Roughton, Louise J....4:06:02 (13,147)
Roulstone, Suzanne....4:53:31 (24,571)
Round, Kathleen....4:08:41 (13,786)
Rourke, Sarah L....5:08:24 (27,064)
Rouse, Linda....4:44:55 (22,763)
Roussel, Kay A....7:41:44 (33,144)
Rout, Marie....4:27:01 (18,509)
Routledge, Joanne....4:05:24 (13,000)
Rovida, Vincenza....3:50:25 (8,959)

Rowberry, Amy V....4:31:46 (19,738)
Rowe, Shirley A....4:59:27 (25,773)
Rowell, Vicky L....4:43:52 (22,537)
Rowett, Ann....4:24:33 (17,824)
Rowland, Carole....5:42:41 (30,547)
Rowland, Jane E....5:17:08 (28,142)
Rowland, Keirina A....4:19:31 (16,482)
Rowley, Jennifer A....5:03:21 (26,364)
Rowling, Karen L....4:52:39 (24,393)
Roy, Isabelle R....4:49:16 (23,707)
Roy, Lucy S....5:11:40 (27,477)
Royan, Deborah....6:16:52 (32,136)
Ruby, Kerry J....6:11:42 (31,977)
Rudge, Sarah J....3:44:00 (7,456)
Rudkin, Nicola....4:19:12 (16,392)
Rudrum, Stefanie A....5:38:42 (30,266)
Rueda, Fanny....4:55:11 (24,936)
Rueda, Marianne....4:55:11 (24,936)
Rugani, Anna A....4:24:59 (17,953)
Rugg Easey, Elizabeth A....4:55:39 (25,028)
Ruhl, Georgina A....4:00:47 (11,989)
Rumbelow, Antonia F....4:18:50 (16,308)
Rumbelow, Joanna L....4:15:50 (15,559)
Rumbold, Naomi....5:35:44 (30,030)
Rupillo, Maria....4:34:01 (20,249)
Rush, Sharon L....5:06:02 (26,720)
Rush, Suzanne C....4:28:26 (18,879)
Rushbrook, Julia E....4:13:55 (15,045)
Rushbury, Michelle E....4:33:55 (20,229)
Rushby, Sonia M....4:03:18 (12,552)
Rushford, Anita P....5:27:49 (29,308)
Rushforth, Kay....3:39:49 (6,592)
Rushmer, Louise K....4:11:54 (14,549)
Rushton, Laurie E....5:50:22 (31,098)
Rushton, Lucy J....4:02:23 (12,347)
Rushton, Lynne....5:17:34 (28,202)
Rushton, Michelle....3:42:38 (7,138)
Rushton, Nicki J....4:01:48 (12,214)
Rushworth, Belinda M....4:04:21 (12,787)
Rusinowski, Karen L....5:36:14 (30,075)
Rusk, Jennifer E....4:41:31 (21,997)
Russell, Cathryn S....5:08:30 (27,078)
Russell, Lenore A....4:02:54 (12,458)
Russell, Lesley D....3:40:53 (6,776)
Russell, Lisa T....4:15:52 (15,569)
Russell, Mark....4:27:44 (18,682)
Russell, Sarah J....5:05:07 (26,602)
Russell, Sophie C....3:52:04 (9,375)
Russell-Grant, Helen....5:13:11 (27,673)
Russett, Julia....5:15:27 (27,947)
Rust, Susanna E....3:59:16 (11,591)
Rutherford, Julia....3:50:14 (8,920)
Rutherford, Lynne M....6:12:08 (31,990)
Rutherford, Nicola N....4:08:29 (13,738)
Rutter, Helen K....4:11:54 (14,549)
Rutter, Karen J....8:32:25 (33,208)
Ryan, Catherine P....5:42:28 (30,532)
Ryan, Debbie....5:42:42 (30,549)
Ryan, Deirdre E....4:20:40 (16,781)
Ryan, Dorothea E....4:23:04 (17,378)
Ryan, Kim....4:25:34 (18,132)
Ryan, Lisa M....7:37:29 (33,128)
Ryan, Louise....4:33:34 (20,157)
Ryan, Nichola M....5:18:17 (28,283)
Ryan, Olive M....5:48:45 (30,985)
Ryder, Helen S....3:39:31 (6,543)
Ryder, Sherie J....4:59:56 (25,875)
Ryecart, Mariella....3:23:37 (3,728)
Rylatt, Suzie M....4:20:26 (16,717)
Rymer, Jane....5:38:01 (30,203)
Ryness, Dena....5:54:52 (31,304)
Sabanta, Jasmin....4:00:48 (11,993)
Sadler, Angela S....3:06:00 (1,667)
Safaty, Elaine C....4:42:29 (22,212)
Sage, Isabel J....5:25:21 (29,074)
Sage, Mary J....6:59:44 (32,877)
Sagoo, Randeep....6:39:36 (32,606)
Saigal, Priyanka....4:43:20 (22,395)
Sail, Annette R....5:09:17 (27,181)
Sainsbury, Anita....3:41:57 (7,012)
Saint, Debbie M....3:54:40 (10,099)
Sakotic, Claire K....7:30:46 (33,099)
Salazar, Gisele G....4:43:53 (22,543)

Sale, Nicola....4:32:57 (19,992)
Sales, Anne....4:23:31 (17,509)
Sales, Lisa J....4:45:01 (22,791)
Salisbury, Helen R....4:53:31 (24,571)
Salisbury, Patricia....5:24:02 (28,943)
Sallis, Caroline J....4:02:13 (12,308)
Salmeron-Diaz, Luisa S....5:08:15 (27,042)
Salmon, Elaine....3:54:35 (10,074)
Salmon, Zoe....5:31:27 (29,703)
Salt, Adela M....2:47:41 (444)
Salter, Jen A....3:26:44 (4,197)
Salvadori, Bea....3:01:21 (1,328)
Salvoni, Samantha....4:46:19 (23,080)
Sammes, Rachel....3:48:59 (8,627)
Sammons, Rita E....4:21:59 (17,112)
Sampson, Kathryn A....6:12:24 (32,001)
Sampson, Marilyn D....5:13:01 (27,657)
Sams, Maddy....5:02:48 (26,288)
Samson Huston, Bernadette R....3:53:35 (9,787)
Samuel, Katharine L....5:44:48 (30,702)
Samuelson-Dean, Katie M....3:27:50 (4,387)
Sanchez, Clare L....4:12:30 (14,707)
Sandberg, Lucy....4:50:19 (23,911)
Sandbrook, Catherine J....4:16:19 (15,674)
Sandell, Elizabeth....5:46:08 (30,795)
Sanders, Caroline....4:36:49 (20,941)
Sanders, Chloe A....4:56:04 (25,114)
Sanders, Janet H....4:25:53 (18,224)
Sanderson, Alyson J....4:28:43 (18,951)
Sanderson, Jordan L....4:48:43 (23,587)
Sanderson, Krista....4:45:32 (22,910)
Sanderson, Saskia C....4:24:34 (17,830)
Sanderson, Sylvia E....6:24:44 (32,350)
Sanderson, Tracey B....4:12:27 (14,693)
Sandford, Gillian....6:07:24 (31,834)
Sandford, Natalie....5:55:14 (31,316)
Sandhu, Joanne....5:39:01 (30,282)
Sandilands, Julie....4:02:59 (12,474)
Sang, Melanie A....3:57:38 (11,056)
Sankey, Julie C....4:32:25 (19,891)
Santi, Karen....5:30:12 (29,562)
Santos, Ceres L....4:11:17 (14,413)
Santos, Deolinda F....4:40:30 (21,777)
Sapstead, Nicole Z....4:45:02 (22,798)
Sarah, Donohue....4:55:33 (25,007)
Sardar, Jane....6:07:35 (31,843)
Sargeant, Pauline....4:08:02 (13,621)
Sargent, Joanna....3:49:13 (8,671)
Sarker, Gopa....4:49:05 (23,669)
Sarker Bell, Sunanda....4:07:25 (13,452)
Sarre, Lucy C....6:12:51 (32,017)
Sarup, Louise S....3:59:41 (11,723)
Sarvari, Diana C....3:25:46 (4,040)
Sarvey, Rachel E....4:12:56 (14,820)
Sato, Kanami....7:19:59 (33,042)
Sato, Yasuko....4:53:19 (24,529)
Sattentau, Jane....4:25:33 (18,126)
Saunders, Alison J....3:54:07 (9,949)
Saunders, Elizabeth J....4:05:35 (13,047)
Saunders, Helen C....4:39:56 (21,662)
Saunders, Kathryn R....4:08:11 (13,663)
Saunders, Linda K....7:07:17 (32,954)
Saunders, Michele A....5:16:02 (28,002)
Saunt, Tonia E....4:18:34 (16,248)
Savage, Charlotte E....4:53:53 (24,655)
Savage, Claire L....5:50:55 (31,127)
Savage, Clare L....5:47:45 (30,932)
Savage, Katie V....5:24:49 (29,018)
Savage, Nicola J....6:00:48 (31,593)
Savarino, Sarah L....6:08:39 (31,880)
Savill, Anna K....3:16:21 (2,807)
Saville, Emma L....4:52:38 (24,388)
Savoy-Havck, Barbara....4:35:13 (20,540)
Sawdon, Julie....4:54:31 (24,781)
Sawkins, Deborah A....5:11:45 (27,488)
Sawyer, Carolyn B....5:16:06 (28,015)
Sayer, Nicholette....4:49:03 (23,663)
Sayers, Janet F....4:50:12 (23,881)
Sayliss, Lesley....4:53:16 (24,517)
Scaife, Ann M....4:53:28 (24,556)
Scales, Emma E....6:37:35 (32,570)
Scales, Wendy....5:20:20 (28,544)
Scammell, Claire L....4:32:09 (19,820)

Scanlan, Marzena M	4:57:56	(25,484)
Scannell, Mary T	4:12:20	(14,664)
Scarfe, Jacqueline K	3:56:33	(10,708)
Scarlett, Kathi	5:41:47	(30,484)
Scarr, Nikki K	4:53:56	(24,666)
Scattergood, Anna E	5:21:29	(28,663)
Schadschneider, Sabine	4:25:30	(18,118)
Schaefer, Maren	4:15:18	(15,415)
Schafer, Catherine A	4:20:58	(16,857)
Schever, Ina	3:27:44	(4,368)
Schiffer, Maria	5:38:06	(30,212)
Schiffo, Cinzia	4:59:57	(25,879)
Schimpf, Cheryl M	4:07:20	(13,429)
Schimpf, Jennifer A	4:54:59	(24,891)
Schmaltz, Virginie	3:25:10	(3,955)
Schmid, Erika R	3:27:34	(4,344)
Schmidt, Elke	2:50:04	(551)
Schmidt, Marianne	4:35:54	(20,690)
Schmidt, Tonja	6:01:14	(31,614)
Schmiegelow, Antonia J	5:02:10	(26,198)
Schmitt, Diane R	5:18:34	(28,316)
Schmitt, Kathryn M	5:42:42	(30,549)
Schneider, Susanne M	5:27:02	(29,229)
Schoeman, Ulrike	5:38:07	(30,213)
Schoeman, Vera	3:47:59	(8,378)
Schoenfeldt, Dagmar	3:51:54	(9,334)
Schofield, Amanda R	3:21:17	(3,437)
Schofield, Andrea J	6:39:36	(32,606)
Schofield, Jane	4:56:49	(25,259)
Scholey, Lindsay J	3:28:59	(4,620)
Schools, Barbara G	4:51:16	(24,086)
Schouwenaar, Heleen	3:37:32	(6,137)
Schraut, Corinna M	3:32:03	(5,169)
Schugel, Theresa L	4:27:49	(18,697)
Schuller, Ildiko	5:36:30	(30,094)
Schulz, Adele K	4:10:48	(14,277)
Schulz, Ursula G	3:28:51	(4,590)
Schuster, Monika	3:55:54	(10,507)
Schutz, Megan A	4:02:26	(12,361)
Schwazz, Mazion	3:52:36	(9,520)
Schwede, Dagni	4:50:49	(24,007)
Schwinger, Inge	4:52:20	(24,317)
Scoles, Cara L	4:09:45	(14,044)
Scotland, Brenda	6:09:24	(31,910)
Scott, Aileen	3:26:55	(4,225)
Scott, Alex L	4:52:27	(24,343)
Scott, Alison V	5:51:57	(31,183)
Scott, Angela G	4:41:58	(22,101)
Scott, Barbara A	4:39:59	(21,670)
Scott, Caroline M	3:45:56	(7,893)
Scott, Danielle K	4:16:28	(15,714)
Scott, Elinor J	3:47:24	(8,213)
Scott, Eve A	6:15:55	(32,115)
Scott, Helen	4:07:44	(13,543)
Scott, Jo L	4:50:42	(23,985)
Scott, Julia S	3:57:33	(11,028)
Scott, Kate J	4:38:28	(21,329)
Scott, Kim	4:00:10	(11,859)
Scott, Kirsty	4:46:35	(23,139)
Scott, Lucy	3:29:45	(4,771)
Scott, Lucy J	5:23:30	(28,887)
Scott, Michele	4:21:12	(16,915)
Scott, Rosemarie D	4:21:09	(16,904)
Scott, Sophie	4:00:38	(11,958)
Scott, Teresa	4:43:39	(22,476)
Scott, Wendy E	3:51:43	(9,278)
Scott Knight, Gemma	4:51:27	(24,140)
Scott-Hayward, Cassandra L	6:21:47	(32,279)
Scrivener, Perrine	5:18:01	(28,239)
Scrivens, Hannah	4:16:38	(15,766)
Scroggs, Deborah	4:01:11	(12,099)
Scully, Teresa N	2:56:42	(916)
Scully, Veronica F	5:37:02	(30,136)
Seabrook, Patricia H	5:35:18	(29,996)
Seal, Carly J	4:58:41	(25,641)
Sealey, Helen	4:34:52	(20,449)
Search, Elizabeth A	4:20:49	(16,814)
Searle, Amber J	3:52:37	(9,526)
Searle, Jane C	3:56:49	(10,790)
Searle, Wendy	4:11:38	(14,487)
Seas, Jane	5:32:38	(29,780)
Seath, Patricia M	5:45:26	(30,752)
Secher, Rachel K	4:30:49	(19,497)

Secker, Nicola J	4:38:41	(21,368)
Sedman, Alison	3:08:46	(1,933)
Sedman, Charlotte A	4:31:27	(19,651)
See, Peta N	4:22:34	(17,257)
Seear, Olwen M	5:18:08	(28,260)
Seed, Alexandra A	6:55:16	(32,829)
Seeff, Nicole S	4:55:01	(24,899)
Seel, Katy A	4:40:52	(21,867)
Seers, Camilla A	4:52:17	(24,303)
Seetharam, Sunanda	6:40:31	(32,616)
Seeviour, Rebecca J	6:17:34	(32,161)
Sefton, Emma A	4:10:45	(14,259)
Sejersen, Gitte	4:25:20	(18,067)
Sekhon, Suni	6:02:14	(31,652)
Selby, Linda	3:59:08	(11,555)
Selby, Pamela J	4:46:07	(23,031)
Seletsky, Joy P	4:48:54	(23,628)
Self, Charlotte L	3:57:19	(10,953)
Self, Deb C	3:53:10	(9,679)
Selfe, Linda A	7:07:48	(32,959)
Sella, Joelle J	5:34:01	(29,892)
Sellers, Maria H	4:25:24	(18,090)
Sendall, Catherine M	6:49:32	(32,755)
Senior, Gill V	3:41:07	(6,831)
Seredynsky, Karen	4:28:59	(19,024)
Servadei, Karen	6:06:46	(31,815)
Sessions, Clare A	4:07:59	(13,612)
Setter, Katy I	3:58:24	(11,306)
Settle, Clare R	3:27:32	(4,339)
Sewell, Emma J	4:00:40	(11,969)
Sewell, Helen	4:51:26	(24,132)
Sexton, Baeni	4:49:16	(23,707)
Seymour, Christine	5:02:47	(26,285)
Seymour, Samantha L	5:16:04	(28,007)
Shackleton, Dawn	4:27:15	(18,567)
Shacklock, Jackie S	6:46:13	(32,712)
Shadbolt, Veronica M	3:42:14	(7,072)
Shah, Nishma	3:47:44	(8,306)
Shah, Pragna	6:03:15	(31,694)
Shah, Prisha	4:55:13	(24,942)
Shales, Jo	4:02:47	(12,436)
Shales, Louise A	4:09:03	(13,872)
Shambrook, Alex M	5:17:37	(28,210)
Shams, Fari	2:59:56	(1,231)
Shannon, Angela D	5:00:40	(25,991)
Sharkey, Mali	5:45:10	(30,730)
Sharkey, Vanessa C	4:56:51	(25,270)
Sharman, Charlotte A	3:54:50	(10,156)
Sharman, Suzanne C	3:22:34	(3,604)
Sharp, Claire L	8:05:44	(33,181)
Sharp, Helen C	4:07:28	(13,467)
Sharp, Renata	5:03:32	(26,393)
Sharp, Sandy L	5:16:34	(28,079)
Sharp, Victoria M	4:35:21	(20,568)
Sharp, Zoe A	4:44:15	(22,625)
Sharpe, Amy J	4:12:49	(14,779)
Sharpe, Laura	4:56:09	(25,130)
Shave, Sarah J	4:05:42	(13,078)
Shaw, Deborah A	3:33:55	(5,468)
Shaw, Felicity J	4:44:50	(22,741)
Shaw, Hester E	5:24:19	(28,973)
Shaw, Joanna R	5:08:24	(27,064)
Shaw, Judy	7:12:26	(32,999)
Shaw, Lisa	3:50:06	(8,885)
Shaw, Megan J	5:49:55	(31,067)
Shaw, Natasha J	4:38:02	(21,231)
Shaw, Rachael N	3:57:39	(11,060)
Shaw, Sarah	3:48:51	(8,591)
Shaw, Susan P	4:35:55	(20,692)
Shayler, Carrie	5:17:35	(28,204)
Sheaf, Wendy L	4:49:37	(23,778)
Shearer, Jennifer W	4:07:05	(13,370)
Shearer, Joanna M	3:57:33	(11,028)
Shearon, Ellen	5:33:37	(29,860)
Shedden, Kathryn E	6:24:07	(32,332)
Sheehan, Belinda M	3:53:46	(9,850)
Sheehan, Deirdre B	3:54:53	(10,173)
Sheehan, Georgina A	4:37:25	(21,090)
Sheehan, Margot V	3:43:27	(7,342)
Sheehy, Mary Kay	4:52:17	(24,303)
Sheen, Pamela	4:56:56	(25,290)
Sheldrake, Sophie L	4:01:51	(12,225)
Shelley, Claire J	3:44:43	(7,621)

Shelley, Jo	4:15:22	(15,437)
Shelley, Victoria E	4:15:52	(15,569)
Shelton, Leigh	4:57:59	(25,500)
Shenton, Fiona C	3:15:11	(2,681)
Shepherd, Amanda	5:02:45	(26,282)
Shepherd, Christina	5:29:24	(29,469)
Shepherd, Sally A	5:24:45	(29,012)
Shepherd, Suzie E	4:59:04	(25,718)
Sheppard, Gail	5:36:12	(30,071)
Sheppard, Sandra E	4:45:20	(22,870)
Sheppard, Tracey	5:19:06	(28,385)
Sheriff, Victoria J	4:21:46	(17,052)
Sherratt, Lyndsay	6:05:18	(31,773)
Sherriff, Lucinda M	5:48:02	(30,946)
Shevlin, Claire H	5:51:55	(31,176)
Shewbridge, Laura E	4:19:38	(16,509)
Shewell, Sarah J	3:55:10	(10,264)
Shields, Julia D	4:17:16	(15,921)
Shiels, Tracey	6:51:19	(32,778)
Shimmin, Margaret G	5:03:59	(26,456)
Shinners, Kathryn	4:55:17	(24,957)
Shipley, Adele V	4:14:47	(15,284)
Shipp, Katherine	4:07:22	(13,439)
Shipp, Rachel E	4:24:33	(17,824)
Shipton, Karon A	3:10:44	(2,134)
Shirley, Jana	4:28:09	(18,792)
Shoemark, Amelia N	3:32:48	(5,291)
Shooter, Caroline R	5:49:24	(31,036)
Short, Colette	4:58:28	(25,600)
Short, Lisa C	5:37:44	(30,185)
Short, Sian M	5:24:02	(28,943)
Shorter, Carly L	6:07:24	(31,834)
Shorter, Tracey C	4:53:51	(24,647)
Shorthouse, Kirsty A	3:44:06	(7,472)
Shorthouse, Lucy I	5:25:42	(29,102)
Shotton, Bryanie S	4:28:09	(18,792)
Shreeve, Helen L	4:22:37	(17,277)
Shrimpton, Annette C	4:07:33	(13,486)
Shrimpton, Elizabeth	5:13:02	(27,659)
Shrimpton, Karen B	5:50:23	(31,099)
Shrimpton, Susan	4:57:12	(25,353)
Shubotham, Christine A	4:36:37	(20,872)
Shurville, Sheryl	4:45:22	(22,877)
Sibilla, Barbara	4:49:13	(23,694)
Sibley, Emma H	5:42:56	(30,572)
Sibson, Helen L	5:26:22	(29,159)
Siddle, Anita I	5:29:11	(29,441)
Sidford, Sali W	5:21:02	(28,611)
Sidhwa, Ruki V	3:52:08	(9,390)
Sidney, Catharina M	7:44:16	(33,105)
Siemons, Susanne	3:30:02	(4,830)
Sieracki, Helen J	4:28:32	(18,904)
Sihra, Virinder K	4:38:02	(21,231)
Sill, Michaela	3:58:05	(11,178)
Silva-Fletcher, Ayona	4:57:51	(25,463)
Silveira, Maria M	6:22:00	(32,289)
Silverman, Ruth H	3:33:26	(5,394)
Silverstone, Corinne P	4:48:08	(23,457)
Silverthorne, Karen	4:40:18	(21,732)
Silverwood, Emma	3:47:17	(8,187)
Silwal, Catherine E	5:20:00	(28,492)
Simcock, Christine R	4:11:02	(14,339)
Simek, Zoe C	4:09:15	(13,923)
Simeon, Helga L	5:05:36	(26,653)
Simkin, Elizabeth R	4:27:51	(18,708)
Simm, Melanie J	4:25:40	(18,153)
Simmonds, Jacqueline	5:32:52	(29,805)
Simmonite, Emma-Jayne	4:06:45	(13,294)
Simmons, Kate V	5:14:31	(27,845)
Simmons, Kathy	3:59:38	(11,702)
Simmons, Lucinda J	3:59:16	(11,591)
Simms, Donna L	4:38:10	(21,276)
Simms, Julia H	4:31:08	(19,566)
Simms, Lisa J	5:12:06	(27,539)
Simms, Maxine J	3:46:36	(8,034)
Simonds, Fran J	4:39:21	(21,533)
Simons, Eleanor	4:43:15	(22,376)
Simpkin, Julie	5:46:15	(30,806)
Simpkins, Rachel M	5:14:38	(27,860)
Simpson, Abigail P	3:58:59	(11,500)
Simpson, Janine	4:04:38	(12,837)
Simpson, Janis P	7:16:21	(33,015)
Simpson, Joanna C	4:14:40	(15,249)

Simpson, Julie A....3:42:44 (7,167)
Simpson, June....4:31:06 (19,555)
Simpson, June A....4:39:18 (21,514)
Simpson, Laura J....5:51:26 (31,152)
Simpson, Lisa V....5:41:53 (30,492)
Simpson, Shona R....4:16:14 (15,652)
Simpson-Eyre, Irene....4:12:14 (14,634)
Sims, Amanda C....6:02:36 (31,663)
Sims, Belinda G....3:58:03 (11,168)
Sims, Noeline D....5:28:38 (29,389)
Sims, Rosie G....3:43:47 (7,419)
Sinclaid, Ailson....5:31:13 (29,681)
Sinclair, Emma....6:04:49 (31,756)
Sinclair, Joanna L....4:30:59 (19,528)
Sinclair, Lesley....4:58:31 (25,614)
Sinclair, Zoe E....6:16:46 (32,135)
Sindole, Eileen P....4:16:09 (15,634)
Singer, Lucia N....3:29:53 (4,802)
Singh, Sandra D....4:55:07 (24,922)
Singleton, Michelle....3:10:24 (2,107)
Singleton, Veronica C....3:21:48 (3,509)
Sinnett, Ann E....3:20:38 (3,354)
Sinton, Tracey J....4:15:04 (15,355)
Sirett, Linda J....5:55:32 (31,327)
Sivakumaran, Sharmi....6:16:02 (32,118)
Sivier, Becky M....4:56:15 (25,150)
Sjollema, Jenny L....4:59:46 (25,844)
Sjoo, Solweig....4:55:37 (25,020)
Skarnes, Tove....5:16:21 (28,051)
Skeels, Katie L....6:30:17 (32,457)
Skelding-Millar, Liesl J....6:38:29 (32,588)
Skellett, Emily L....5:54:18 (31,274)
Skelton, Catherine B....5:25:06 (29,051)
Skelton, Kelly T....5:10:26 (27,326)
Skelton, Vicky G....3:08:13 (1,876)
Skidmore, Flora....3:05:07 (1,586)
Skidmore, Sarah H....4:47:56 (23,417)
Skilbeck, Samantha W....4:33:06 (20,030)
Skinner, Claire A....3:33:58 (5,474)
Skinner, Clare....5:33:27 (29,845)
Skinner, Corrina....4:21:31 (16,977)
Skinner, Jo Anne....4:29:06 (19,057)
Skinner, Wendy A....6:18:41 (32,189)
Skippen, Jayne I....6:33:36 (32,506)
Skipper, Victoria T....4:04:57 (12,907)
Skuce, Karen....4:20:08 (16,636)
Slack, Debbie A....3:37:29 (6,131)
Slade, Anna....4:38:42 (21,371)
Slade, Catherine J....5:05:58 (26,704)
Slade, Elisabeth....5:28:20 (29,360)
Slade, Elizabeth S....4:56:59 (25,307)
Slade, Emma C....4:08:10 (13,656)
Slaghekke, Nicole C....4:52:29 (24,349)
Slater, Cheryl A....4:41:16 (21,943)
Slater, Danielle L....4:27:53 (18,717)
Slater, Gillian A....5:15:23 (27,942)
Slater, Olga....5:00:50 (26,016)
Slaughter, Anna....4:29:42 (19,228)
Slawinski, Regine....4:31:57 (19,783)
Slay, Kimberley....5:00:02 (25,888)
Slaymaker, Kelly....4:49:39 (23,782)
Sleaford, Gillian E....4:58:55 (25,692)
Sleep, Laura J....5:32:50 (29,803)
Sloan, Jacqueline E....5:06:41 (26,813)
Sloan-Brinkley, Ashly....4:42:11 (22,153)
Sloly, Hope A....3:55:35 (10,399)
Sloman, Penny J....4:23:56 (17,633)
Smailes, Jules....4:21:37 (17,003)
Smale, Dee....3:01:51 (1,359)
Small, Elizabeth A....4:56:17 (25,159)
Small, Elizabeth A....5:09:51 (27,245)
Smallman, Emma L....3:55:39 (10,416)
Smallwood, Mary E....3:48:37 (8,531)
Smallwood, Nicola J....4:54:19 (24,749)
Smallwood, Sylvia....4:59:33 (25,799)
Smart, Charmin....5:53:26 (31,237)
Smart, Elizabeth V....4:30:56 (19,515)
Smart, Felicity J....5:33:59 (29,889)
Smart, Fiona J....5:14:25 (27,832)
Smedley, Dionne....5:39:46 (30,343)
Smillie, Carolyn....5:00:57 (26,034)
Smillie, Lesley H....4:30:47 (19,491)
Smillie, Susan....5:00:58 (26,038)
Smit, Rennette....5:16:42 (28,093)
Smith, Adrienne M....5:27:40 (29,289)
Smith, Alexandra G....4:04:03 (12,726)
Smith, Ali C....6:39:46 (32,608)
Smith, Alison B....5:03:27 (26,386)
Smith, Alison J....3:26:43 (4,193)
Smith, Amanda H....4:31:59 (19,786)
Smith, Amy L....3:34:08 (5,503)
Smith, Andrea....3:44:43 (7,621)
Smith, Andrea J....3:58:17 (11,262)
Smith, Angela J....4:18:31 (16,238)
Smith, Angela P....4:58:10 (25,540)
Smith, Angharad L....4:04:51 (12,885)
Smith, Ashley P....5:39:02 (30,287)
Smith, Brenda-Joyce J....5:28:18 (29,355)
Smith, Carol A....3:57:41 (11,067)
Smith, Carol A....4:50:50 (24,010)
Smith, Caroline A....4:24:16 (17,735)
Smith, Carolyn A....3:32:23 (5,232)
Smith, Catherine....3:53:03 (9,647)
Smith, Cathy M....4:19:21 (16,433)
Smith, Celia....6:08:17 (31,869)
Smith, Charlotte J....4:10:27 (14,204)
Smith, Charlotte L....5:04:51 (26,561)
Smith, Christine....4:29:06 (19,057)
Smith, Christine....4:30:35 (19,446)
Smith, Corin B....4:43:34 (22,458)
Smith, Davina L....4:08:38 (13,778)
Smith, Deborah E....6:13:06 (32,023)
Smith, Deborah J....4:33:07 (20,036)
Smith, Debra....3:30:52 (4,955)
Smith, Denise C....6:07:15 (31,829)
Smith, Elaine G....4:16:52 (15,817)
Smith, Emily F....4:03:46 (12,665)
Smith, Emma J....5:29:16 (29,454)
Smith, Fiona A....5:16:32 (28,074)
Smith, Fiona C....5:22:06 (28,725)
Smith, Germaine....5:12:15 (27,555)
Smith, Halcyon A....6:33:37 (32,507)
Smith, Hannah....3:51:01 (9,102)
Smith, Hazel....4:18:06 (16,143)
Smith, Hazel D....4:39:08 (21,478)
Smith, Helen....4:10:33 (14,220)
Smith, Helen....4:25:03 (17,976)
Smith, Helen....6:51:44 (32,780)
Smith, Helen X....5:25:02 (29,041)
Smith, Helena L....4:42:50 (22,291)
Smith, Hilary S....4:05:26 (13,005)
Smith, Irene....5:59:11 (31,515)
Smith, Ita....5:12:25 (27,581)
Smith, Jackie L....4:27:10 (18,548)
Smith, Jacqueline....4:22:07 (17,152)
Smith, Jane L....6:34:50 (32,526)
Smith, Jean....3:45:16 (7,745)
Smith, Jennie L....4:29:04 (19,041)
Smith, Jennifer....3:47:41 (8,290)
Smith, Jennifer....5:49:52 (31,062)
Smith, Joan L....5:59:49 (31,551)
Smith, Joanna....4:52:56 (24,443)
Smith, Joy A....6:01:18 (31,619)
Smith, Julien R....4:31:42 (19,721)
Smith, Kate....5:48:00 (30,945)
Smith, Kathleen M....3:55:04 (10,233)
Smith, Kim J....5:30:14 (29,564)
Smith, Laura....4:42:42 (22,260)
Smith, Laura A....4:18:21 (16,199)
Smith, Laura A....4:56:51 (25,270)
Smith, Laura J....6:30:23 (32,460)
Smith, Linda M....5:57:52 (31,450)
Smith, Linda M....7:22:00 (33,051)
Smith, Linda S....4:18:18 (16,183)
Smith, Louisa K....5:18:37 (28,323)
Smith, Louise....5:06:01 (26,716)
Smith, Margaret A....6:44:10 (32,675)
Smith, Maria J....3:59:33 (11,686)
Smith, Megan A....4:25:36 (18,136)
Smith, Mhairi K....5:14:18 (27,811)
Smith, Natalie A....5:30:17 (29,573)
Smith, Nicola J....4:03:27 (12,592)
Smith, Nikki J....5:06:16 (26,750)
Smith, Nuala P....4:53:09 (24,491)
Smith, Pamela A....4:27:32 (18,633)
Smith, Rebecca J....5:08:16 (27,045)
Smith, Roseline....5:04:59 (26,579)
Smith, Rowan L....4:01:53 (12,230)
Smith, Rowena H....5:41:20 (30,442)
Smith, Ruth E....4:31:08 (19,566)
Smith, Samantha J....3:28:05 (4,420)
Smith, Samantha L....5:56:24 (31,375)
Smith, Sarah A....5:47:47 (30,934)
Smith, Sarah J....7:01:51 (32,893)
Smith, Serena R....5:38:18 (30,234)
Smith, Shan A....5:17:00 (28,126)
Smith, Sharon H....3:04:54 (1,570)
Smith, Sharon K....6:15:50 (32,110)
Smith, Sheena....6:44:03 (32,672)
Smith, Sheila....6:02:16 (31,654)
Smith, Sian....6:16:58 (32,141)
Smith, Sophie C....5:59:52 (31,553)
Smith, Sue J....4:32:55 (19,982)
Smith, Susan....4:27:37 (18,662)
Smith, Suzanne L....4:05:05 (12,936)
Smith, Suzanne M....3:48:50 (8,585)
Smith, Tamsin A....4:41:31 (21,997)
Smith, Terri E....4:34:23 (20,335)
Smith, Una J....4:21:20 (16,941)
Smith, Vanessa H....4:54:50 (24,856)
Smith, Wendy M....4:18:18 (16,183)
Smith-Calvert, Elizabeth H....4:11:23 (14,434)
Smithson, Anne M....5:51:16 (31,138)
Smithson, Helen M....4:43:13 (22,370)
Smith-Topp, Lesley J....4:36:20 (20,812)
Smittle, Linda....5:00:17 (25,941)
Smyth, Cara A....5:20:11 (28,518)
Smyth, Catherine C....7:04:09 (32,930)
Smyth, Fiona A....4:28:25 (18,874)
Smyth, Helena A....7:22:20 (33,052)
Smyth, Michelle M....7:04:09 (32,930)
Smyth, Moira M....6:49:47 (32,758)
Smyth, Nicola....4:03:16 (12,546)
Smyth, Ruth J....4:14:21 (15,173)
Snaith, Krystina....4:28:23 (18,867)
Snape, Kathleen M....4:50:28 (23,939)
Sneddon, Emma....4:34:14 (20,298)
Sneddon, Stephanie....4:24:56 (17,938)
Sneezum, Beverley E....4:48:14 (23,477)
Snelgrove, Elizabeth A....4:36:18 (20,803)
Snell, Claire J....4:26:27 (18,371)
Snell, Victoria L....4:44:56 (22,768)
Snellgrove, Claire J....7:23:46 (33,063)
Snellgrove, Kirste L....4:59:48 (25,852)
Snelling, Laura L....4:02:26 (12,361)
Snook, Davina....5:06:17 (26,754)
Snook, Lisa J....6:20:49 (32,247)
Snook, Suzanne E....3:25:00 (3,931)
Snow, Tanya....6:03:03 (31,683)
Snowden, Carol A....4:56:29 (25,202)
Soane, Laurie J....4:24:30 (17,802)
Soar, Susan R....4:06:53 (13,321)
Sohm, Amelie....4:17:11 (15,905)
Solari, Chiara....5:33:51 (29,879)
Sole, Samantha....5:44:55 (30,710)
Sollom, Jessica....4:47:33 (23,334)
Solomon, Julie A....5:23:04 (28,840)
Solomon Williams, Rachel....3:56:04 (10,558)
Solomons, Helen C....5:06:59 (26,858)
Somerville, Andrea....6:24:27 (32,341)
Sommerton, Helen A....5:33:05 (29,822)
Son, Jane....4:20:38 (16,769)
Soper, Claire E....5:37:33 (30,172)
Soper, Katherine E....4:43:22 (22,404)
Sorensen, Lotte H....3:26:38 (4,182)
Sorensen, Meta M....4:24:59 (17,953)
Sorrell-Barry, Susan....4:56:51 (25,270)
Southall, Caroline....3:58:02 (11,163)
Southern, Deborah A....4:35:37 (20,632)
Southon, Lisa J....3:57:36 (11,045)
Sowden, Miranda C....3:51:03 (9,113)
Sowerby, Hetty T....4:21:20 (16,941)
Sowerby, Susan J....4:41:38 (22,026)
Spalding, Carole A....5:59:18 (31,526)
Spargo, Gail A....4:19:41 (16,527)
Sparham, Michele....5:50:32 (31,112)
Sparrow, Gillian L....4:08:23 (13,712)
Spaughton, Natalie C....5:56:44 (31,392)
Speake, Celia....3:39:56 (6,614)

Spearman, Isabel 5:21:13 (28,632)
Spearman, Natalia 4:28:09 (18,792)
Speed, Susan M 4:25:25 (18,095)
Spence, Gemma A 4:59:56 (25,875)
Spence, Jannett C 7:04:40 (32,939)
Spence, Jayne A 5:33:24 (29,840)
Spencer, Caroline D 4:47:24 (23,294)
Spencer, Claire L 4:37:33 (21,125)
Spencer, Debbie 6:14:42 (32,078)
Spencer, Jill M 4:48:11 (23,466)
Spencer, Sally A 3:25:17 (3,972)
Spencer, Shelley A 4:21:10 (16,908)
Spencer-Ward, Annabelle J 5:44:09 (30,655)
Spick, Claire 3:47:53 (8,351)
Spinks, Rozlyn S 5:27:10 (29,242)
Spittles, Sharon 7:08:51 (32,969)
Spivey, Carolyn 4:34:42 (20,411)
Spleiss, Janine 4:26:14 (18,320)
Spnecer-Bruce, Tamieka N 4:47:36 (23,342)
Spong, Carole 3:38:56 (6,423)
Spong, Sue 3:11:57 (2,268)
Spoor, Kathleen M 5:12:57 (27,642)
Spoor, Laura E 6:37:45 (32,574)
Spragg, Jane 3:59:25 (11,641)
Sprake, Juliet A 4:02:30 (12,374)
Spratt, Shirley 4:35:11 (20,527)
Spring, Nicola K 4:23:13 (17,421)
Springthorpe, Rebecca L 6:43:24 (32,663)
Sproson, Alison 5:29:09 (29,440)
Sproston, Rachel M 3:08:23 (1,896)
Sprules, Nicky D 3:45:21 (7,771)
Sprules, Tracey 5:49:15 (31,020)
Spry, Emily F 5:12:58 (27,645)
Spurr, Sarah J 5:03:26 (26,382)
Spurrier, Alexandra V 3:56:49 (10,790)
Spyvee, Zoe 4:42:44 (22,267)
Squelch, Dana K 4:38:04 (21,245)
Squicciarini, Annalisa 3:35:40 (5,777)
Squire, Helen 4:44:52 (22,748)
Staas, Kirsten 3:42:43 (7,159)
Stabile, Donna M 5:16:12 (28,031)
Stacey, Judith C 3:56:33 (10,708)
Stacey, Tracy 4:24:18 (17,750)
Staff, Claire J 5:23:22 (28,881)
Stafford, Fay 4:23:56 (17,633)
Staite, Jane C 3:31:35 (5,084)
Stallard, Angela 4:35:47 (20,670)
Stallard, Elizabeth F 4:16:24 (15,691)
Stallard, Rebecca C 5:49:26 (31,038)
Stammers, Faye L 3:36:36 (5,958)
Stamp, Katherine J 5:14:38 (27,860)
Stamp, Margaret A 4:40:23 (21,747)
Stamp, Tracey C 3:27:27 (4,321)
Stamper, Linda 3:45:47 (7,866)
Stancliffe, Jane M 5:20:17 (28,533)
Stancliffe, Josephine C 4:58:11 (25,544)
Stanfield, Janet 6:50:47 (32,771)
Stanfield, Nicola J 5:10:28 (27,330)
Stanislawski, Belinda A 4:44:31 (22,682)
Stanley, Catherine 5:17:33 (28,199)
Stanley, Joanna 5:14:58 (27,903)
Stanley, Lisa D 4:14:40 (15,249)
Stannett, Jennifer 3:48:53 (8,603)
Stansfield, Kerry G 4:40:39 (21,820)
Stanton, Deborah 6:09:14 (31,903)
Stanton, Sandra 4:21:43 (17,026)
Staples, Pamela M 4:29:56 (19,276)
Stapley, Louise Y 4:13:38 (14,991)
Star, Stacey M 4:08:13 (13,669)
Stark, Diana R 4:07:38 (13,516)
Starr, Victoria J 5:03:15 (26,352)
Staunton, Joanne E 3:50:54 (9,077)
Staunton, Rebecca L 4:06:34 (13,243)
Staveley, Eve M 5:32:56 (29,811)
Staynor, Christine A 7:45:48 (33,162)
Stearn, Michelle L 4:53:37 (24,602)
Steel, Hannah C 4:56:13 (25,142)
Steel, Julie N 5:41:50 (30,488)
Steele, Julia A 3:34:29 (5,560)
Steele, Julie V 6:14:52 (32,083)
Steele, Penny J 4:28:08 (18,785)
Steels, Sandra 4:07:18 (13,420)
Steer, Deborah A 2:57:51 (1,012)

Steers, Angela M 5:20:08 (28,510)
Steeves, Elizabeth B 5:11:52 (27,510)
Steggles, Andrea 5:13:20 (27,695)
Stehle, Daniela 4:00:19 (11,892)
Stein, Kate A 5:25:58 (29,125)
Steiner Gardner, Susan M 3:55:45 (10,460)
Stenhouse, Michelle J 4:29:42 (19,228)
Stenner, Sarah V 5:19:41 (28,457)
Stenner, Sue C 5:03:50 (26,431)
Stenning, Gemma E 4:52:59 (24,453)
Stenton, Moira L 6:27:34 (32,412)
Stephens, Anna L 4:55:46 (25,051)
Stephens, Jane 3:04:59 (1,573)
Stephens, Jayne S 4:39:14 (21,498)
Stephens, Jean 4:59:07 (25,726)
Stephens, Natalie J 4:23:21 (17,454)
Stephens, Patricia 5:25:12 (29,059)
Stephenson, Joanne 4:15:14 (15,398)
Stephenson, Kim 3:31:52 (5,138)
Steptoe, Charlotte 3:29:55 (4,809)
Steptoe, Helen 5:02:12 (26,201)
Stern, Helen L 4:44:40 (22,700)
Steven, Jill 5:08:38 (27,097)
Stevens, Anne L 4:08:30 (13,745)
Stevens, Charlie 6:09:58 (31,925)
Stevens, Claire E 4:26:30 (18,384)
Stevens, Emily V 5:13:14 (27,681)
Stevens, Gillian 3:21:08 (3,414)
Stevens, Janine E 3:34:39 (5,603)
Stevens, Joanna 6:32:37 (32,494)
Stevens, Kelli L 4:41:06 (21,916)
Stevens, Kerry J 5:11:03 (27,390)
Stevens, Marie J 4:10:06 (14,121)
Stevens, Miranda 5:08:16 (27,045)
Stevens, Wendy 5:42:47 (30,559)
Stevenson, Clarissa 4:41:17 (21,948)
Stevenson, Kate 4:42:36 (22,239)
Stevenson, Louise M 4:19:45 (16,539)
Stevenson, Nicola 4:13:37 (14,979)
Stevenson, Rachel J 4:16:08 (15,629)
Steward, Amanda L 5:10:51 (27,371)
Steward, Claire E 3:27:52 (4,394)
Steward, Michelle S 5:45:05 (30,723)
Stewart, Amy D 4:24:29 (17,797)
Stewart, Andrea 4:10:13 (14,153)
Stewart, Helen C 6:33:09 (32,499)
Stewart, Jennifer 3:36:38 (5,962)
Stewart, Jennifer A 4:15:04 (15,355)
Stewart, Jennifer J 5:00:56 (26,031)
Stewart, Julie 3:40:45 (6,752)
Stewart, Karen 5:14:51 (27,888)
Stewart, Karen M 5:25:47 (29,111)
Stewart, Patricia M 5:18:12 (28,269)
Stewart, Sophie 4:27:20 (18,590)
Stewart, Susan A 4:07:58 (13,606)
Stibbs, Helen J 4:07:56 (13,593)
Stickland, Davina C 5:35:45 (30,035)
Stickland, Marysia L 4:36:44 (20,910)
Stickland, Rebecca J 3:20:44 (3,370)
Stiff, Lindsey A 6:11:06 (31,960)
Stiff, Tracy L 5:14:18 (27,811)
Stileman, Elizabeth J 3:38:58 (6,428)
Still, Carol A 3:37:45 (6,178)
Stimpson, Christine J 4:45:46 (22,961)
Stimpson, Jennifer 6:03:07 (31,689)
Stimpson, Lucy R 6:36:15 (32,545)
Stimson, Donna L 4:01:32 (12,153)
Stirrup, Carole M 4:17:44 (16,038)
Stock, Katy L 5:23:08 (28,847)
Stockan, Jennifer A 5:35:13 (29,988)
Stockdale, Julie 5:29:08 (29,438)
Stockham, Elizabeth A 4:32:27 (19,897)
Stockley, Gemma L 4:24:21 (17,764)
Stockley, Nicola 4:19:14 (16,398)
Stockton, Elizabeth S 4:12:46 (14,765)
Stockton, Paula. J 3:25:45 (4,034)
Stoddard, Amy S 3:48:27 (8,489)
Stoddart, Rachel 6:21:19 (32,266)
Stoft, Suzanne 4:37:33 (21,125)
Stokes, Elizabeth R 5:17:03 (28,135)
Stokes, Marie A 4:13:51 (15,033)
Stokes, Sharon J 5:53:33 (31,243)
Stone, Anna K 5:07:57 (27,000)

LONDON MARATHON

Stone, Gina 4:26:01 (18,263)
Stone, Janet E 4:27:33 (18,638)
Stone, Laura A 5:16:38 (28,087)
Stone, Leanne 4:53:04 (24,468)
Stone, Lisa M 4:00:41 (11,973)
Stone, Marie L 4:10:26 (14,200)
Stone, Sally A 3:54:12 (9,980)
Stone, Veronica M 4:23:32 (17,513)
Stone, Wendy A 6:12:08 (31,990)
Stonebanks, Frances J 5:33:22 (29,837)
Stoneman, Samantha J 4:19:39 (16,516)
Stones, Elizabeth M 5:03:44 (26,420)
Stones, Janine A 3:24:24 (3,849)
Stopforth, Karen N 4:58:24 (25,585)
Storck, Christiane 3:53:12 (9,689)
Storey, Katherine 3:55:11 (10,275)
Storey, Kelly A 4:23:19 (17,448)
Storey, Leigh-Anne 4:32:18 (19,859)
Storey, Pamela 6:11:02 (31,957)
Stott, Dhavala 3:13:01 (2,402)
Stott, Sandra 4:55:14 (24,945)
Stovell, Leonora M 5:18:35 (28,320)
Stracey, Victoria J 4:20:06 (16,629)
Strain, Caitriona C 4:53:30 (24,569)
Straker, Elizabeth J 4:03:54 (12,690)
Strang, Dianne 3:59:44 (11,741)
Strange, Sarah E 4:10:07 (14,127)
Stranks, Elizabeth A 4:57:06 (25,334)
Stray, Rachael E 4:36:56 (20,967)
Streater, Jill W 4:56:17 (25,159)
Street, Charlotte E 4:40:36 (21,810)
Street, Helen 4:03:50 (12,681)
Street, Louise A 5:47:02 (30,863)
Street, Stephanie A 4:50:59 (24,044)
Stretton, Moira K 3:25:45 (4,034)
Strevens, Anna Verity 6:02:32 (31,659)
Stringer, Christine 4:45:49 (22,971)
Stringer, Vikki A 2:58:44 (1,101)
Strode, Yvonne N 4:16:56 (15,843)
Strong, Anne 4:29:04 (19,041)
Strong, Heidi 5:25:18 (29,069)
Stroud, Clover 4:43:40 (22,481)
Stroud, Sue C 5:43:23 (30,601)
Strouts, Fiona 3:44:49 (7,645)
Strowger, Victoria L 4:14:07 (15,108)
Stuart, Elizabeth M 3:45:00 (7,689)
Stuart, Fiona 5:26:26 (29,168)
Stuart, Fiona C 5:35:59 (30,055)
Stuart, Jane E 4:01:31 (12,148)
Stubbs, Sally J 3:21:41 (3,498)
Stuckey, Elizabeth A 3:56:59 (10,842)
Stuckey, Sarah E 4:49:59 (23,842)
Sturgeon, Tina 5:55:13 (31,315)
Sturgess, Ann C 5:13:20 (27,695)
Sturt, Sarah L 4:56:41 (25,242)
Styler, Wendy J 4:56:54 (25,281)
Styles, Louise C 5:34:17 (29,914)
Styles, Philippa Z 5:43:59 (30,637)
Suckling, Alison J 4:27:58 (18,739)
Suddick, Julie 5:04:12 (26,477)
Suddrey, Sarah L 5:02:24 (26,240)
Sufflico, Mariagrazia 3:58:02 (11,163)
Sugarman, Rachel E 4:12:04 (14,586)
Sugden, Ingrid 5:12:11 (27,547)
Sugita, Chiyuki 5:16:33 (28,075)
Suleck, Claudia 4:15:01 (15,342)
Sullivan, Angela T 4:54:36 (24,800)
Sullivan, Anita 5:00:22 (25,954)
Sullivan, Barbara A 3:42:52 (7,196)
Sullivan, Carmel M 4:04:46 (12,872)
Sullivan, Caroline E 5:51:36 (31,163)
Sullivan, Deborah A 4:10:42 (14,248)
Sullivan, Janis K 4:56:54 (25,281)
Sullivan, Joanne V 3:38:09 (6,256)
Sullivan, Meaveen 4:28:59 (19,024)
Sullivan, Nicola 4:33:24 (20,111)

Sullivan, Nicole L 3:26:56 (4,229)
Sullivan, Victoria C 4:32:04 (19,808)
Sum, Susan 4:42:30 (22,217)
Sumal, Raman 5:43:03 (30,581)
Summer, Eileen D 3:46:27 (8,000)
Summerfield, Wendy A 3:42:29 (7,111)
Summerscale, Claire E 6:50:01 (32,761)
Summerson, Una 4:38:57 (21,430)
Sumption, Frederique R 6:35:24 (32,532)
Suominen, Heini E 5:12:43 (27,617)
Supple, Felicity J 4:41:52 (22,074)
Surman, Jessica A 3:57:54 (11,134)
Surman, Joanne L 5:33:39 (29,866)
Surrell, Lisa R 5:38:28 (30,250)
Surti, Jay 5:55:41 (31,342)
Suttle, Selina S 4:58:45 (25,654)
Suttleworth, Hayley J 5:46:29 (30,824)
Sutton, Amy 4:57:30 (25,397)
Sutton, Helen F 4:30:24 (19,400)
Sutton, Jane 4:47:33 (23,334)
Sutton-Smith, Elizabeth A 4:46:58 (23,200)
Suwalski, Karen 6:43:10 (32,656)
Suy, Anja 3:51:01 (9,102)
Swadling, Victoria M 4:44:41 (22,707)
Swain, Emma L 4:12:30 (14,707)
Swaine, Samantha J 5:07:57 (27,000)
Swainson, Joanna 5:11:18 (27,427)
Swallow, Eileen M 4:43:39 (22,476)
Swallow, Jodie 4:52:40 (24,398)
Swallow, Kate C 7:24:44 (33,067)
Swan, Eileen M 4:52:15 (24,294)
Swan, Emma P 4:28:15 (18,829)
Swan, Fiona M 5:12:15 (27,555)
Swan, Suzanne 3:24:58 (3,928)
Swann, Claire E 4:25:14 (18,038)
Swanson, Katherine M 3:26:43 (4,193)
Swanson, Lorraine J 6:30:46 (32,472)
Swart, Chantelle 4:19:31 (16,482)
Swart, Marizelle 3:51:07 (9,125)
Swaysland, Sarah L 3:34:45 (5,621)
Sweeting, Alison J 5:09:13 (27,175)
Sweetlove, Jennifer A 4:15:23 (15,442)
Sweetman, Kathryn 5:25:36 (29,090)
Swift, Amanda A 6:07:10 (31,826)
Swift, Claire M 4:18:54 (16,325)
Swift, Helen A 4:21:11 (16,914)
Swift, Jaine E 3:08:00 (1,858)
Swift, Julie 6:54:17 (32,812)
Swift, Julie T 4:27:30 (18,621)
Swinburn, Rachel L 4:41:34 (22,004)
Swinburne, Tracey J 4:20:53 (16,833)
Swindell, Mary C 4:44:14 (22,622)
Swingler, Val 3:16:57 (2,873)
Sword, Nicola M 3:47:23 (8,208)
Sworn, Carol A 4:09:15 (13,923)
Syed, Nelofer 3:46:04 (7,918)
Syers, Clare L 4:25:04 (17,982)
Sykes, Christine A 4:48:05 (23,446)
Sykes, Julie 4:42:03 (22,123)
Sylvester, Gemma A 4:23:21 (17,454)
Syme, Dawn I 4:22:05 (17,141)
Symmonds, Deborah 5:49:49 (31,058)
Symmons, Elaine 5:52:55 (31,211)
Symonds, Claire B 4:10:02 (14,107)
Symonds, Michelle 5:42:56 (30,572)
Symons, Kristina M 4:43:08 (22,357)
Szczotka, Ewa 4:49:08 (23,681)
Taberner, Ruth C 3:42:22 (7,093)
Tabor, Ros 3:14:16 (2,563)
Tabraham, Amy E 4:33:25 (20,113)
Tagg, Lynn 8:12:21 (33,186)
Tagg, Susan G 3:28:18 (4,468)
Taggart, Ailsa 4:37:10 (21,017)
Tagliavini, Paola 3:16:06 (2,788)
Tai, Samantha 4:42:05 (22,131)
Taillandier, Dominique 4:24:29 (17,797)
Talbot, Dana 6:10:24 (31,939)
Talbot, Julie 4:42:56 (22,314)
Talbot, Nicola 5:13:14 (27,681)
Talbot Rosner, Victoria H 3:36:40 (5,970)
Taliadoros, Helen 4:54:16 (24,738)
Talks, Clare 3:36:20 (5,900)
Tam, Judy 5:01:41 (26,132)
Tamblyn, Rosalind K 7:11:12 (32,990)
Tanaka, Chieko 3:37:25 (6,116)
Tanner, Anita 4:46:35 (23,139)
Tanner, Joanna 4:42:16 (22,167)
Tanner, Tracey 7:05:13 (32,942)
Tanner, Victoria A 5:46:18 (30,810)
Tanner, Wendy 4:16:49 (15,804)
Tansey, Alison 6:31:51 (32,482)
Tansey, Barbara 6:09:32 (31,913)
Tansey, Sharon D 5:04:22 (26,499)
Tapper, Caroline R 5:16:33 (28,075)
Tapper, Liz J 3:15:43 (2,743)
Tapster, Louise J 4:27:58 (18,739)
Taranowski, Helen L 3:18:31 (3,069)
Tarleton, Gillian M 5:42:47 (30,559)
Tarplee, Katy M 4:28:11 (18,802)
Tarr, Robyn B 3:45:18 (7,758)
Tarry, Beverley H 4:09:45 (14,044)
Tarry, Laura L 5:03:46 (26,422)
Tatsumi, Wako 5:40:33 (30,393)
Tattersall, Kathryn M 4:50:14 (23,889)
Tatton, Melissa J 4:31:10 (19,574)
Taverner, Zoe 4:56:22 (25,179)
Tawiah, Jennifer C 4:35:42 (20,650)
Tayhlor, Laura J 6:40:55 (32,624)
Taylor, Alana R 4:41:58 (22,101)
Taylor, Brenda C 5:39:51 (30,349)
Taylor, Charlotte L 5:26:47 (29,199)
Taylor, Charlotte R 6:44:39 (32,687)
Taylor, Claire E 4:40:53 (21,869)
Taylor, Claire V 4:56:05 (25,117)
Taylor, Deborah M 4:31:45 (19,733)
Taylor, Fiona J 3:43:47 (7,419)
Taylor, Gemma L 4:05:13 (12,963)
Taylor, Jacqueline F 6:30:25 (32,461)
Taylor, Joyce M 4:51:21 (24,105)
Taylor, Julia K 5:05:38 (26,659)
Taylor, Julie S 4:27:35 (18,650)
Taylor, Karen P 3:29:42 (4,759)
Taylor, Katherine A 6:36:34 (32,552)
Taylor, Katherine E 5:57:47 (31,444)
Taylor, Kathryn R 3:30:10 (4,853)
Taylor, Katy L 4:01:04 (12,063)
Taylor, Lee 4:23:41 (17,555)
Taylor, Leila 4:10:13 (14,153)
Taylor, Lisa 4:48:33 (23,552)
Taylor, Lorna 6:14:06 (32,051)
Taylor, Louise M 4:12:48 (14,773)
Taylor, Lynda A 4:48:01 (23,430)
Taylor, Melanie 5:04:10 (26,471)
Taylor, Pauline 5:41:46 (30,481)
Taylor, Rachel H 4:48:12 (23,471)
Taylor, Rachelle F 4:54:04 (24,687)
Taylor, Reisha M 5:44:36 (30,686)
Taylor, Sara 5:35:10 (29,982)
Taylor, Sarah A 4:03:35 (12,621)
Taylor, Sharon 4:32:53 (19,974)
Taylor, Sharon A 3:54:47 (10,138)
Taylor, Shirley A 5:35:12 (29,985)
Taylor, Stephanie A 5:11:21 (27,434)
Tayor, Louise M 4:58:10 (25,540)
Teague, Natalie H 4:16:26 (15,704)
Teasdale, Sarah 6:13:49 (32,041)
Teasdale, Sarah L 3:56:58 (10,838)
Teasdale, Sophie A 4:49:31 (23,760)
Tebbatt, Elizabeth M 5:43:17 (30,591)
Tebbutt, Zoe E 5:18:33 (28,314)
Teed, Dawn N 3:35:42 (5,786)
Teferi, Sarah E 4:50:30 (23,945)
Tegtmeier, Simonis 5:13:41 (27,734)
Telford, Angela 3:34:38 (5,597)
Temple, Sally J 4:25:48 (18,194)
Temple, Victoria J 5:17:09 (28,146)
Templeman, Clare E 4:26:39 (18,421)
Teper, Nikki 5:19:49 (28,473)
Terblanche, Tania 6:20:49 (32,247)
Terjesen, Siri 5:17:51 (28,226)
Terrier, Stephanie M 3:59:11 (11,570)
Terry, Carolyn A 5:33:26 (29,842)
Terry, Rachel 4:50:36 (23,960)
Tesser, Nadia 3:52:47 (9,564)
Tetlow, Christine 4:17:50 (16,067)
Tewkesbury, Rachael L 4:11:54 (14,549)
Thakar, Clare C 5:59:17 (31,524)
Thake, Sue J 3:56:16 (10,618)
Thatcher, Hannah 4:43:15 (22,376)
Thawley, Angela J 5:53:31 (31,241)
Thebault, Elisabelle 5:26:58 (29,223)
Theodosiou, Eirini 4:16:24 (15,691)
Thijm, Jacqueline A 4:35:57 (20,709)
Thircuir, Jeanne 4:36:33 (20,857)
Thistleton, Heather J 4:23:00 (17,366)
Tholen, Elaine 4:51:54 (24,229)
Thom, Laura E 4:14:31 (15,209)
Thomas, Ann 2:58:30 (1,065)
Thomas, Annette P 4:20:46 (16,803)
Thomas, Carol E 4:58:11 (25,544)
Thomas, Caroline 5:30:44 (29,620)
Thomas, Caroline F 4:27:08 (18,538)
Thomas, Carolyn 4:59:32 (25,794)
Thomas, Claire P 5:10:38 (27,346)
Thomas, Clara B 5:21:45 (28,684)
Thomas, Debbie M 3:10:22 (2,102)
Thomas, Emma L 5:59:45 (31,544)
Thomas, Fiona C 5:19:24 (28,425)
Thomas, Hope M 5:14:05 (27,781)
Thomas, Jayne 4:22:29 (17,240)
Thomas, Karen 3:55:41 (10,431)
Thomas, Kathryn 4:47:51 (23,396)
Thomas, Linda M 5:11:34 (27,469)
Thomas, Louise 5:18:42 (28,335)
Thomas, Michelle A 6:42:38 (32,650)
Thomas, Michelle A 7:04:23 (32,935)
Thomas, Rebecca M 4:55:42 (25,037)
Thomas, Samantha J 3:34:19 (5,538)
Thomas, Stephanie 5:01:07 (26,063)
Thomas, Susan 5:40:42 (30,406)
Thomas, Tracy A 5:10:52 (27,372)
Thomas-Branch, Lynda M 3:59:16 (11,591)
Thomason, Gale 8:23:03 (33,200)
Thomason, Jean 6:07:26 (31,836)
Thompson, Adele M 5:20:36 (28,577)
Thompson, Alexandra 5:06:58 (26,854)
Thompson, Andrea 5:40:09 (30,376)
Thompson, Angela M 3:59:58 (11,806)
Thompson, Claire A 5:01:37 (26,121)
Thompson, Clare 5:03:08 (26,332)
Thompson, Erica L 3:56:17 (10,624)
Thompson, Gillian 5:07:52 (26,985)
Thompson, Helen L 3:42:02 (7,030)
Thompson, Helen V 4:43:58 (22,566)
Thompson, Jacqueline 3:59:29 (11,668)
Thompson, Jane Z 3:43:02 (7,242)
Thompson, Jemma E 4:59:41 (25,831)
Thompson, Jenny M 4:38:10 (21,276)
Thompson, Josie C 3:51:40 (9,260)
Thompson, Karen E 4:37:24 (21,086)
Thompson, Katharine V 4:09:11 (13,903)
Thompson, Linda C 3:40:35 (6,726)
Thompson, Lisa J 5:13:02 (27,659)
Thompson, Lisa T 5:27:40 (29,289)
Thompson, Louise M 5:54:26 (31,281)
Thompson, Margaret 4:38:31 (21,344)
Thompson, Mary A 5:35:52 (30,043)
Thompson, Mary R 4:10:18 (14,170)
Thompson, Melody R 3:46:54 (8,101)
Thompson, Nicola E 3:21:12 (3,423)
Thompson, Pauline J 4:20:45 (16,795)
Thompson, Philippa 3:59:57 (11,801)
Thompson, Rachael E 3:55:40 (10,427)
Thompson, Rosie J 4:23:25 (17,474)
Thompson, Sharon A 4:19:24 (16,448)
Thompson, Susan A 4:40:46 (21,844)
Thompson, Tania S 5:28:30 (29,376)
Thomson, Abigail 5:06:39 (26,809)
Thomson, Arabel 4:09:47 (14,054)
Thomson, Elizabeth I 4:45:12 (22,834)
Thomson, Helen 6:30:31 (32,463)
Thomson, Jacqueline P 4:19:25 (16,455)
Thomson, Jill L 4:45:12 (22,834)
Thomson, Julia M 3:42:39 (7,145)
Thomson, Nicola J 4:47:09 (23,243)
Thomson, Sally N 3:31:10 (5,020)
Thorarinsdottir, Katrin 3:38:29 (6,324)
Thorington, Katie J 4:30:10 (19,340)
Thorley, Naomi 4:26:42 (18,430)

Thorn, Pauline 4:43:42 (22,495)
Thorn, Penny J 3:19:08 (3,149)
Thornburgh, Imogen L 2:48:43 (482)
Thorne, Christine 4:01:06 (12,072)
Thorne, Harriet A 4:23:21 (17,454)
Thorne, Joanne R 4:52:48 (24,422)
Thorne, Olivia M 4:04:57 (12,907)
Thorne, Paula L 4:36:13 (20,786)
Thornes, Sheila M 4:30:59 (19,528)
Thornton, Carmel M 3:57:25 (10,984)
Thornton, Jane M 4:44:49 (22,736)
Thornton, Laura 4:13:00 (14,842)
Thornton, Lesley J 5:26:45 (29,193)
Thornton, Sharon 3:30:37 (4,918)
Thorpe, Alexandra J 4:43:39 (22,476)
Thorpe, Angie M 3:35:26 (5,738)
Thorpe, Beverley 4:25:09 (18,008)
Thorpe, Sarah J 5:45:58 (30,777)
Threadgold, Susan K 5:48:02 (30,946)
Thresher, Dora 3:46:02 (7,907)
Thrower, Michelle 4:41:37 (22,017)
Thurgood, Julia C 4:38:34 (21,354)
Thursfield, Angela M 4:31:44 (19,729)
Tibbett-Amps, Angela 8:08:40 (33,183)
Tieghi, Chiara Angela 3:49:45 (8,811)
Tildesley, Catherine C 6:18:22 (32,179)
Tiller, Samantha K 4:41:01 (21,900)
Tillman, Fi E 4:27:54 (18,722)
Tillson, Lisa 4:47:44 (23,368)
Tilt, Carole A 4:42:03 (22,123)
Tilt, Pamela M 5:10:30 (27,336)
Timbrell, Jodie 4:09:34 (14,007)
Timlin, Theresa E 5:26:50 (29,204)
Timlin, Victoria R 4:57:46 (25,448)
Timmins, Elizabeth 5:48:03 (30,951)
Timmins, Nicola M 3:43:07 (7,265)
Timms, Louise 5:22:22 (28,764)
Timothy, Julie 5:26:38 (29,180)
Timothy, Karen A 4:15:48 (15,544)
Timson, Catherine J 4:53:04 (24,468)
Timson, Charlotte E 4:42:05 (22,131)
Timson, Nicola L 4:36:43 (20,901)
Tin, Lwin 4:19:47 (16,547)
Tingle, Rachael 4:04:47 (12,876)
Tinnyunt, Mary E 6:33:18 (32,501)
Tinsley, Judith C 3:32:56 (5,312)
Tinsley, Sarah E 6:38:15 (32,585)
Tipping, Julie A 5:06:37 (26,805)
Tipping, Nicki L 6:00:31 (31,584)
Tiptaft, Emma R 3:41:19 (6,876)
Tirotto, Josie 5:16:47 (28,103)
Titler, Kerry L 4:38:35 (21,357)
Titlestad, Ingrid 4:02:20 (12,337)
Tizard, Sue M 5:44:24 (30,675)
Todd, Helen J 4:28:11 (18,802)
Todd, Lindsey C 5:18:34 (28,316)
Todd, Lindsey C 5:18:34 (28,316)
Todd, Yvette E 4:43:30 (22,435)
Tole, Maria E 4:31:46 (19,738)
Toley, Nicola 4:23:53 (17,618)
Toll, Lorraine M 4:24:30 (17,802)
Tolson, Sharon 5:11:40 (27,477)
Tomas, Rachel H 4:36:08 (20,763)
Tomes, Jean 4:46:22 (23,096)
Tomic, Olga 4:58:51 (25,675)
Tomkins, Lucy A 4:48:11 (23,466)
Tomkins, Natalie K 7:16:12 (33,013)
Tomkins, Paula A 4:04:23 (12,793)
Tomlin, Tina 4:10:54 (14,305)
Tomlinson, Cheryl P 6:11:35 (31,970)
Tomlinson, Laura 5:35:05 (29,974)
Toms, Philippa M 3:59:10 (11,563)
Tomsett, Ruth 4:09:02 (13,870)
Tong, Caroline E 5:45:25 (30,750)
Tonge, Katherine E 5:55:41 (31,342)
Tongue, Jo 4:52:19 (24,312)
Tonner, Sharon 5:38:36 (30,260)
Toogood, Clare A 4:33:17 (20,080)
Toon, Kathy S 4:52:27 (24,343)
Topp, Vanessa J 4:30:38 (19,458)
Tori, Tiziana 5:39:32 (30,328)
Tormey, Orla M 3:31:06 (5,005)
Tornari, Katerina 5:26:15 (29,147)
Toro, Carla T 4:15:43 (15,524)
Toubiana, Sophie 4:24:51 (17,903)
Tout, Helen A 4:34:20 (20,321)
Tout, Linda K 4:30:55 (19,512)
Tovey, Elizabeth G 4:06:30 (13,233)
Towers, Emily R 3:46:11 (7,939)
Towers, Julie A 3:43:28 (7,344)
Townend, Claire E 5:34:12 (29,900)
Townend, Laura 5:34:12 (29,900)
Townend, Rebecca 4:41:00 (21,895)
Townley, Claire H 6:22:44 (32,303)
Townsend, Charlotte 6:18:59 (32,200)
Townsend, Charlotte T 4:12:14 (14,634)
Townsend, Diane 3:34:06 (5,498)
Townsend, Diane 6:03:25 (31,704)
Townsend, Jane E 4:52:19 (24,312)
Trace, Ella E 4:31:27 (19,651)
Tracey, June A 4:17:00 (15,860)
Traille, Eugene C 5:43:27 (30,608)
Traversone, Elizabeth 4:28:20 (18,854)
Traylen, Sophie M 4:01:52 (12,228)
Trayling, Denise 4:06:45 (13,294)
Trayner, Gail 4:35:33 (20,612)
Treacher, Natalie 4:22:31 (17,247)
Treadgold, Amanda J 4:57:54 (25,479)
Treadwell, Lorraine F 3:42:07 (7,046)
Tredant, Anna M 6:03:41 (31,711)
Trembath, Elianne M 3:42:09 (7,055)
Tres, Jessica 4:20:55 (16,842)
Trevaskis, Janet M 4:05:17 (12,977)
Trevis, Maria 5:19:11 (28,403)
Triegaardt, Jeanette E 3:45:07 (7,712)
Trigg, Amy M 4:06:07 (13,163)
Trigg, Michelle M 4:45:48 (22,968)
Trigwell, Carolyn J 5:41:31 (30,457)
Tripp, Kate M 4:54:10 (24,720)
Troni, Elizabeth 3:55:58 (10,531)
Tropeano, Mandy A 4:45:24 (22,890)
Troth, Joan 5:30:43 (29,619)
Trott, Claire L 4:29:13 (19,088)
Trotter, Kirsty V 4:46:19 (23,080)
Trueman, Michelle J 4:19:38 (16,509)
Trumper, Lynn E 4:58:56 (25,697)
Tryssesoone, Ann 5:39:41 (30,336)
Tseng, Joyce 6:37:55 (32,576)
Tucker, Carrie J 3:48:24 (8,475)
Tucker, Clare J 6:09:44 (31,917)
Tucker, Jayne E 4:51:34 (24,156)
Tucker, Lucy 5:40:09 (30,376)
Tucker, Sarah S 3:00:44 (1,284)
Tucker, Serena 5:09:44 (27,233)
Tucker, Tina L 3:58:28 (11,329)
Tuer, Nicky 4:13:33 (14,965)
Tuffney, Rachel Z 4:42:26 (22,208)
Tugman, Gill 4:03:04 (12,499)
Tullis, Caroline 4:15:12 (15,387)
Tully, Julia R 3:28:41 (4,549)
Tuohy, Lauren 4:39:50 (21,636)
Tuppen, Melissa 5:19:22 (28,417)
Tupping, Elaine 4:45:13 (22,840)
Turbinskys, Stephanie I 4:37:59 (21,216)
Turgoose, Susannah J 3:25:16 (3,971)
Turk, Elizabeth J 3:39:20 (6,507)
Turk, Ozgun 4:43:06 (22,346)
Turkington, Helen R 4:32:28 (19,898)
Turnbull, Clare L 4:00:31 (11,941)
Turnbull, Darielle D 4:23:11 (17,410)
Turnbull, Vida J 6:21:14 (32,261)
Turner, Anna M 3:40:23 (6,687)
Turner, Christine A 4:57:13 (25,354)
Turner, Elisabeth C 4:19:17 (16,418)
Turner, Elizabeth C 4:14:12 (15,142)
Turner, Fiona R 3:46:30 (8,010)
Turner, Hollie 5:41:29 (30,456)
Turner, Jacqueline 4:20:22 (16,700)
Turner, Jean K 3:44:54 (7,669)
Turner, Lisa C 3:43:09 (7,274)
Turner, Lorraine 4:49:15 (23,702)
Turner, Natalie E 5:31:07 (29,674)
Turner, Nicola 3:50:38 (9,013)
Turner, Nicola J 6:19:37 (32,221)
Turner, Rebecca 4:10:02 (14,107)
Turner, Sarah J 3:52:23 (9,466)
Turner, Sian E 5:49:46 (31,054)
Turner, Valerie 5:30:15 (29,566)
Turner, Victoria E 4:54:09 (24,712)
Turner, Victoria J 4:25:21 (18,075)
Turner, Yvonne A 4:12:44 (14,756)
Turrell, Tracy M 4:14:39 (15,242)
Turrent, Ana 3:44:44 (7,627)
Turton, Helen 3:31:47 (5,115)
Turvey, Helen R 4:49:48 (23,806)
Tutin, Angela M 4:10:50 (14,291)
Tweddell, Susan 4:47:26 (23,304)
Tweed, Jo L 3:12:12 (2,306)
Tweedie, Rachel A 3:56:13 (10,599)
Tweedle, Kathryn H 4:30:20 (19,384)
Tweedy, Sue A 5:55:28 (31,325)
Twelftree, Gillian E 4:15:52 (15,569)
Twelvetree, Yvonne 3:44:15 (7,507)
Tye, Caroline J 7:04:30 (32,937)
Tyler, Carly E 4:41:57 (22,098)
Tyler, Karen 3:54:38 (10,086)
Tyler, Kati F 4:09:10 (13,895)
Tyler, Linda 3:55:43 (10,444)
Tyler, Susan M 5:51:12 (31,136)
Tyrer, Tracey A 3:55:28 (10,361)
Tyrrell, Elaine 6:54:04 (32,807)
Tyrrell, Jill P 5:15:26 (27,946)
Tyrrell, Jodie E 5:14:03 (27,772)
Tyrrell, Josephine 3:58:11 (11,225)
Tyrrell, Nicola D 3:19:25 (3,182)
Tyrrell, Rosina A 5:29:41 (29,503)
Tytherleigh, Catherine L 5:23:51 (28,921)
Uccomte, Summer K 4:27:22 (18,595)
Uju, Ujh 4:03:37 (12,629)
Ulrich, Katrin 5:16:25 (28,060)
Underdown, Marion L 5:27:59 (29,323)
Underhill, Ann B 4:27:35 (18,650)
Underwood, Caroline L 4:57:32 (25,403)
Underwood, Claire C 4:01:46 (12,205)
Underwood, Hilary K 5:03:08 (26,332)
Unseld, Anne P 4:29:22 (19,138)
Unsted, Claire L 4:04:00 (12,714)
Upton, Alexandra 4:19:55 (16,581)
Upton, Ann E 4:48:43 (23,587)
Upton, Jemma 5:28:53 (29,416)
Upton, Joanna W 4:37:41 (21,156)
Upton, Stephanie E 3:40:31 (6,715)
Urand, Sarah M 6:42:16 (32,644)
Urch, Gillian E 5:26:28 (29,171)
Uren, Louisa J 6:13:50 (32,042)
Usher, Christine 4:31:17 (19,606)
Usher, Jane M 4:27:34 (18,644)
Usher, Sarah 4:15:18 (15,415)
Uthauakumar, Nilani 6:01:29 (31,625)
Vagle, Wenche H 7:18:34 (33,033)
Vahiboglu, Ayse 3:46:10 (7,937)
Vallier, Louise A 3:08:27 (1,904)
Vam Kerckvoodre, Christella 4:30:12 (19,350)
Van Deelen, Jennifer N 3:14:00 (2,530)
Van Den Bergh, Lucey M 4:03:45 (12,661)
Van Den Merwe, Christelle 3:44:54 (7,669)
Van Der Horst, Belinda J 4:36:44 (20,910)
Van Der Merwe, Caren L 4:48:45 (23,596)
Van Der Merwe, Ronel 4:22:16 (17,191)
Van Der Walt, Estee 4:04:57 (12,907)
Van Dijk, Ellen 3:49:36 (8,769)
Van Doorn, Cressida A 4:50:42 (23,985)
Van Dyk, Tharina S 4:19:38 (16,509)
Van Egeraat, Mariala 4:54:39 (24,806)
Van Huysteeen, Julia 4:56:13 (25,142)
Van Jaarsveld, Magdalena F 4:24:32 (17,809)
Van Kets, Karen M 4:30:05 (19,320)
Van Lint, Sallie E 4:22:36 (17,271)
Van Reenen, Michelle T 5:15:51 (27,982)
Van Rooyen, Elzare 4:49:38 (23,781)
Van Schalkwyk, Annelene 4:51:40 (24,179)
Van Tiel, Cara L 4:44:15 (22,625)
Vand Er Lelie, Helen 4:19:56 (16,584)
Vandersypen, Sarah J 4:04:15 (12,766)
Vandevelde, Martine 4:56:52 (25,276)
Vangaveti, Awani 6:25:44 (32,371)
Vanlint, Alisa 3:49:56 (8,853)
Vanstone, Nicky A 4:31:58 (19,785)
Vargas, Patricia A 3:47:02 (8,127)

Varley, Paula A 4:02:58 (12,470)
Vary, Carmel E 5:02:40 (26,270)
Vary, Josephine A 5:21:23 (28,657)
Vasey, Natalie 3:38:32 (6,334)
Vassallo, Valerie A 6:32:15 (32,487)
Vaughan, Susan M 7:07:28 (32,958)
Vautier, Jackie-Helene 7:15:55 (33,011)
Vaux, Nicola E 4:40:38 (21,816)
Veale, Jackie D 5:08:46 (27,113)
Vellino, Joanne E 5:34:02 (29,893)
Venamore, Zoe L 6:24:24 (32,338)
Verduyn, Christine M 3:55:06 (10,246)
Verga, Gillian 3:54:13 (9,983)
Verhoeven, Vreni 3:28:31 (4,514)
Vermeersch, Heidi N 4:13:13 (14,901)
Vernazza, Patricia 3:42:54 (7,206)
Verner, Susan M 5:04:54 (26,569)
Verrill, Freda 3:54:40 (10,099)
Versey, Amanda C 3:20:38 (3,354)
Vescovi, Giuliana 4:17:14 (15,914)
Vescovi, Luisa 4:31:57 (19,783)
Vestey, Flora G 4:53:00 (24,455)
Vestey, Rose A 3:58:42 (11,401)
Vettorsllo, Renée M 5:57:31 (31,435)
Vicary, Sue K 4:11:50 (14,528)
Vickers, Heather 7:19:00 (33,036)
Vickers, Louise 3:53:25 (9,741)
Vickers, Louise S 6:12:18 (31,998)
Victor, Christina R 4:05:34 (13,040)
Vigar, Patricia E 4:39:10 (21,483)
Vigneswaran, Trisha 3:56:54 (10,814)
Vinall, Lucie E 4:04:53 (12,893)
Vince, Pamela 4:15:19 (15,421)
Vincent, Julie 5:12:02 (27,527)
Vincent, Verity 4:02:57 (12,467)
Vine, Susan E 4:29:17 (19,115)
Vinicombe, Karen L 4:08:53 (13,830)
Vint, Georgia F 4:58:53 (25,684)
Vint, Helen 5:07:04 (26,869)
Virk, Amrit P 4:47:42 (23,360)
Virley, Nicola S 5:03:32 (26,393)
Visal, Marina L 5:01:46 (26,143)
Visser, Isla 5:30:28 (29,586)
Vitale-Cumper, Giulietta 3:12:43 (2,363)
Vivash, Claire M 6:05:36 (31,780)
Vivian, Christina 3:43:07 (7,265)
Vivian, Lynn 4:53:19 (24,529)
Vlassak, Ruth E 3:59:12 (11,577)
Volckaerts, Diane 4:05:40 (13,070)
Volpi, Annalisa 4:50:41 (23,979)
Von Arx, Valerie J 4:56:43 (25,245)
Von Buren, Jane C 6:00:23 (31,579)
Von Klemperer, Jane 4:37:46 (21,172)
Von Knobloch, Ursula 3:11:15 (2,191)
Vossler, Dana 4:26:58 (18,497)
Vowels, Helen J 4:43:53 (22,543)
Vowles, Leanne J 4:56:23 (25,185)
Vowles, Tracy 4:56:22 (25,179)
Voymann, Sally 4:25:00 (17,964)
Voysey, Alison R 4:28:55 (18,998)
Vucenovic, Dani 4:42:39 (22,249)
Vuille, Nathalie 4:20:45 (16,795)
Vyas, Sima 4:17:30 (15,981)
Wadforth, Catherine 3:48:30 (8,501)
Wadge, Nilufer 4:08:37 (13,773)
Wager, Carol A 5:30:40 (29,613)
Waggott, Penny A 4:09:26 (13,976)
Wagh, Claire U 3:36:18 (5,895)
Waghorn, Tamsin R 4:19:52 (16,571)
Wagland, Karen F 4:29:11 (19,079)
Wagner, Avital 5:11:50 (27,501)
Wagner, Esther Joy 4:56:07 (25,124)
Wagstaff, Nina E 3:13:45 (2,495)
Wahab, Aliya E 3:28:38 (4,537)
Wain, Rebecca 4:42:31 (22,226)
Waistell, Zoe 5:23:07 (28,845)
Wait, Debra E 3:07:53 (1,846)
Waite, Alison 4:10:11 (14,147)
Waite, Kathryn J 5:04:13 (26,478)
Waite, Sally A 5:30:56 (29,640)
Wake, Nina A 4:45:11 (22,830)
Wakefield, Caroline W 3:36:17 (5,891)
Wakefield, Elizabeth 5:48:34 (30,974)
Wakefield, Kelly J 7:37:11 (33,123)
Wakefield, Lorna J 4:07:14 (13,410)
Wakefield, Lucy J 4:16:31 (15,732)
Wakefield, Sally 4:28:57 (19,012)
Wakeham, Katie 4:58:27 (25,596)
Wakelin, Louise J 5:52:12 (31,190)
Wakeling, Anna 4:54:17 (24,742)
Wakeling, Helen C 4:54:17 (24,742)
Walder, Claire L 6:43:49 (32,668)
Walder, Kirsty G 4:53:58 (24,670)
Waldoch, Lorraine M 3:37:23 (6,111)
Waldock, Clare B 5:18:47 (28,346)
Waldron, Linda 5:11:49 (27,496)
Wale, Caroline A 6:22:07 (32,293)
Walecki, Michelle L 5:03:46 (26,422)
Wales, Paula E 5:32:47 (29,797)
Walker, Abigail V 3:28:49 (4,578)
Walker, Amanda J 4:34:52 (20,449)
Walker, Amanda J 6:04:43 (31,753)
Walker, Bronwyn A 4:27:52 (18,714)
Walker, Christina M 5:10:53 (27,374)
Walker, Ellen M 7:26:54 (33,082)
Walker, Gary 3:39:02 (6,438)
Walker, Hilary 4:33:15 (20,074)
Walker, Jayne B 4:32:40 (19,925)
Walker, Julia 5:51:12 (31,136)
Walker, Julia C 3:54:09 (9,962)
Walker, Katrina J 4:10:22 (14,189)
Walker, Lillian H 4:51:56 (24,239)
Walker, Linda-Jean 5:17:16 (28,161)
Walker, Lucy J 5:47:08 (30,873)
Walker, Lynn 4:32:55 (19,982)
Walker, Nicola M 4:48:42 (23,583)
Walker, Sarah M 7:46:55 (33,164)
Walker, Sue 4:20:13 (16,666)
Walker, Suzanne 5:44:37 (30,687)
Walker, Tracy 3:17:15 (2,917)
Walker, Wendy J 5:42:01 (30,497)
Walker Kirby, Elizabeth C 6:15:47 (32,107)
Walkerden, Laura M 4:57:02 (25,319)
Walklate, Anna R 3:57:56 (11,144)
Walklate, Rachel J 3:57:56 (11,144)
Wall, Judith M 3:56:14 (10,603)
Wall, Michala C 3:17:26 (2,936)
Wall, Pamela H 4:22:31 (17,247)
Wall, Rebecca J 3:43:09 (7,274)
Wallace, Anna W 3:23:51 (3,769)
Wallace, Caroline S 3:51:23 (9,196)
Wallace, Jennifer L 4:52:25 (24,334)
Wallace, Louisa 4:29:51 (19,259)
Wallace, Nicola K 4:25:46 (18,184)
Wallace, Rosemary 6:14:23 (32,066)
Wallace, Sarah 5:24:55 (29,031)
Waller, Charlotte A 4:06:58 (13,341)
Waller, Emma C 5:00:56 (26,031)
Wallis, Diana P 5:19:58 (28,487)
Wallis, Samantha J 3:42:44 (7,167)
Wallis, Vicky J 5:28:05 (29,333)
Wallis, Yvonne L 3:18:16 (3,025)
Walls, Fiona 6:09:17 (31,905)
Walls, Ursula C 4:27:37 (18,662)
Walpole, Jan 4:23:55 (17,630)
Walsh, Angela J 5:00:26 (25,965)
Walsh, Beverley A 4:23:36 (17,530)
Walsh, Christine M 6:26:39 (32,392)
Walsh, Clair F 4:56:23 (25,185)
Walsh, Edit 4:08:52 (13,825)
Walsh, Jillian R 3:50:08 (8,895)
Walsh, Mary B 3:48:16 (8,442)
Walsh, Mary S 8:17:28 (33,193)
Walsh, Olivia J 5:08:13 (27,037)
Walsh, Terri 4:41:01 (21,900)
Walshe, Juliet Mary 5:42:34 (30,540)
Walter, Janis 4:40:12 (21,713)
Walters, Candisse F 5:19:10 (28,397)

LONDON MARATHON

Walters, Deborah J 2:58:40 (1,090)
Walters, Gail R 3:18:53 (3,121)
Walters, Karen G 4:39:18 (21,514)
Walters, Linda J 5:25:36 (29,090)
Walton, Barbara H 4:48:04 (23,442)
Walton, Hayley A 4:51:06 (24,061)
Walton, Jan D 4:09:19 (13,937)
Walton, Robyn 4:34:57 (20,473)
Walton, Victoria R 5:42:53 (30,564)
Walton-Peile, Michala 5:23:52 (28,924)
Wan, Joycelyn Y 4:15:18 (15,415)
Wang, Mary E 5:33:36 (29,859)
Wanklyn, Ann 6:29:23 (32,438)
Wanning, Sabine B 6:05:06 (31,765)
Wansbrough-Jones, Anna M 3:56:28 (10,676)
Warburton, Claire L 4:23:37 (17,535)
Ward, Claire A 4:44:04 (22,578)
Ward, Cressida E 4:47:11 (23,255)
Ward, Denise M 4:34:00 (20,245)
Ward, Diana 5:46:21 (30,814)
Ward, Felicity J 3:31:56 (5,148)
Ward, Helen M 4:22:31 (17,247)
Ward, Katie 4:31:34 (19,686)
Ward, Lisa J 4:56:19 (25,168)
Ward, Maxine 3:38:14 (6,278)
Ward, Nichola 5:29:14 (29,449)
Ward, Penny J 5:36:31 (30,098)
Ward, Rachel A 3:40:59 (6,799)
Ward, Sharon A 5:20:30 (28,561)
Ward, Stella 4:28:55 (18,998)
Ward, Zoe M 4:42:40 (22,254)
Ward-Booth, Sara 4:44:19 (22,639)
Wardrop, Ann M 4:14:52 (15,303)
Wardropper, Barbara 7:34:04 (33,112)
Warman, Wendy J 4:36:55 (20,963)
Warne, Sharon L 4:11:50 (14,528)
Warner, Anne 4:38:13 (21,284)
Warner, Debbie E 5:27:04 (29,234)
Warnes, Diane M 6:27:34 (32,412)
Warnes, Simone 4:01:56 (12,244)
Warnett, Amanda L 4:54:12 (24,730)
Warnke, Emily R 4:30:56 (19,515)
Warren, Katie M 5:48:24 (30,964)
Warren, Lee W 5:16:38 (28,087)
Warren, Louise C 4:45:53 (22,985)
Warren, Lucy C 5:38:13 (30,220)
Warren, Susan 4:38:09 (21,273)
Warrener, Lucy A 4:37:42 (21,160)
Warrick, Stephanie M 4:26:49 (18,468)
Warrior, Julia 4:00:26 (11,921)
Warsap, Tonia J 4:47:10 (23,247)
Warwick, Cathy 5:30:26 (29,583)
Warwick, Karen 4:24:04 (17,675)
Wasmeier, Christina 3:43:13 (7,292)
Wasmuth, Cheryl K 6:25:52 (32,375)
Watchorn-Rice, Ruth F 3:32:37 (5,268)
Waterfield, Jan 6:01:05 (31,609)
Waterhouse, Abby 5:36:11 (30,069)
Waterhouse, Dawn M 7:41:10 (33,143)
Waters, Alison J 4:24:58 (17,951)
Waters, Anne-Marie 4:34:12 (20,292)
Waters, Claire 3:23:02 (3,661)
Waters, Ellen M 4:46:15 (23,062)
Waters, Hazel 3:54:33 (10,066)
Waters, Sandra M 4:37:17 (21,054)
Wates, Amanda J 3:59:26 (11,651)
Wathen, Diana C 5:13:42 (27,738)
Watkin, Joanne L 5:28:09 (29,348)
Watkin, Sarah K 5:14:05 (27,781)
Watkins, Charlotte 3:48:09 (8,422)
Watkins, Jeannie S 5:13:19 (27,692)
Watkins, Lara 5:03:15 (26,352)
Watkins, Rachel 4:07:43 (13,540)
Watkins, Sally A 3:44:19 (7,525)
Watkins, Sophie H 4:47:52 (23,400)
Watkinson, Kate 4:39:19 (21,521)
Watkinson, Lynne L 3:29:00 (4,623)
Watling, Andrea 3:52:55 (9,597)
Watling, Jo 4:46:50 (23,182)
Watson, Christie J 7:15:02 (33,006)
Watson, Emily M 4:14:05 (15,098)
Watson, Irene 5:40:37 (30,399)
Watson, Julie C 5:10:25 (27,323)

Watson, Karen L	3:19:33	(3,198)
Watson, Lyndal C	4:12:25	(14,684)
Watson, Ruth B.	5:39:16	(30,300)
Watson, Susan J	3:14:11	(2,553)
Watson, Susan M	6:14:00	(32,048)
Watson, Yvonne E	3:57:43	(11,082)
Watters, Claire J	5:03:26	(26,382)
Watters, Jude C	4:12:19	(14,659)
Watts, Alison J	6:03:06	(31,687)
Watts, Amelia	3:28:07	(4,427)
Watts, Anne-Marie	4:53:35	(24,592)
Watts, Caroline A	5:06:42	(26,815)
Watts, Charlotte H	4:33:47	(20,203)
Watts, Heather E	4:32:35	(19,912)
Watts, Jean L	5:40:29	(30,391)
Watts, Linda	4:48:42	(23,583)
Watts, Nicola A	4:13:37	(14,979)
Watts, Tracey L	5:40:48	(30,414)
Watts, Tracy J	5:16:04	(28,007)
Wauchope, Rachael D	5:04:23	(26,508)
Waugh, Catriona W	4:57:09	(25,346)
Waugh, Charlie M	5:06:33	(26,793)
Waugh, Karen	6:14:08	(32,054)
Way, Kathleen	5:52:42	(31,205)
Wayman, Chantal L	4:24:37	(17,845)
Waymark, Leanne	4:24:13	(17,717)
Weatherall, Gayle M	4:46:17	(23,073)
Weaver, Caren A	4:34:18	(20,307)
Weaver, Nicola	5:29:13	(29,445)
Weaver, Tina	6:44:34	(32,686)
Webb, Caroline R	3:58:29	(11,333)
Webb, Julia	4:53:09	(24,491)
Webb, Karla	5:06:14	(26,746)
Webb, Lorna P	5:46:59	(30,859)
Webb, Rebecca A	5:00:11	(25,924)
Webb, Sally	4:28:00	(18,749)
Webb, Samantha L	4:44:43	(22,714)
Webb, Sarah E	4:56:50	(25,264)
Webb-Carter, Rose E	4:29:00	(19,028)
Webber, Jackie	3:52:32	(9,501)
Webber, Nancy A	5:35:42	(30,025)
Webber, Nicola E	4:23:59	(17,648)
Webber, Tracey A	4:53:32	(24,575)
Webdale, Thelma L	5:31:22	(29,696)
Weber, Elise	4:26:19	(18,342)
Webster, Anne-Marie H	4:14:00	(15,067)
Webster, Emma	4:22:35	(17,260)
Webster, Emma L	3:58:28	(11,329)
Webster, Issy C	4:31:55	(19,776)
Webster, Jennifer A	6:55:39	(32,836)
Webster, Julia E	3:53:22	(9,736)
Webster, Nicola L	7:23:18	(33,058)
Webster, Sophie V	4:51:45	(24,198)
Webster, Susan	4:03:02	(12,489)
Webster, Yvonne L	3:43:17	(7,306)
Weddell, Paula L	4:55:25	(24,985)
Wedgwood, Andrés F	5:22:24	(28,766)
Weekes, Bridgit C	4:11:00	(14,329)
Weeks, Constantina B	4:56:18	(25,164)
Weeks, Rebecca J	5:21:11	(28,629)
Weetch, Amy J	4:19:08	(16,374)
Wehbe, Angeline	3:28:39	(4,541)
Weibel, Klara	3:55:50	(10,485)
Weichert, Heike	4:51:34	(24,156)
Weil, Kristelle R	5:46:32	(30,828)
Welch, Clare P	5:18:43	(28,339)
Welch, Emily L	5:39:05	(30,292)
Welch, Emma V	3:19:43	(3,217)
Welch, Louise A	3:36:26	(5,923)
Welch, Lucy C	3:19:43	(3,217)
Welch, Zoe P	5:06:25	(26,774)
Weldon, Georgina M	5:33:50	(29,876)
Welke, Luise	5:27:21	(29,255)
Weller, Jane E	5:49:19	(31,028)
Wells, Belinda	4:36:41	(20,885)
Wells, Louise C	5:17:35	(28,204)
Wells, Louise E	5:49:57	(31,068)
Wells, Sara L	4:02:34	(12,391)
Wells, Sara L	4:28:06	(18,773)
Wells, Sophie J	4:52:03	(24,257)
Wells, Victoria	4:34:24	(20,341)
Wells, Victoria F	4:09:26	(13,976)
Wels, Jane F	4:48:06	(23,452)
Welsh, Angeline M	3:56:39	(10,739)
Welsh, Bridget A	5:12:44	(27,619)
Welsh, Clare	4:48:11	(23,466)
Welsh, Jaime	5:54:21	(31,275)
Welsh, Louise M	3:54:13	(9,983)
Welsh, Sarah J	3:36:12	(5,878)
Wendel, Rebecca	6:06:24	(31,798)
Wenham, Judith A	5:28:35	(29,380)
Wensley, Helen R	3:40:04	(6,636)
Went, Angela	4:44:52	(22,748)
Wertli, Beatrice	3:09:15	(1,980)
Wespi, Beatrice	3:51:43	(9,278)
West, Carolyn E	4:44:29	(22,678)
West, Diane B	6:23:59	(32,329)
West, Jennifer	3:54:14	(9,988)
West, Louise S	4:25:24	(18,090)
West, Sara J	4:47:49	(23,386)
West, Tracey J	3:08:00	(1,858)
West, Zoe	3:27:15	(4,280)
Westaway, Helen J	3:56:33	(10,708)
Westgarth, Natalia L	6:01:25	(31,621)
Westgate, Jacqueline L	4:34:23	(20,335)
Westlake, Sonia A	4:40:00	(21,674)
Weston, Deborah M	4:49:12	(23,690)
Weston, Denise	3:56:00	(10,543)
Weston, Helen L	3:36:33	(5,943)
Weston, Susan	3:59:20	(11,617)
Westray, Katharine L	3:47:12	(8,168)
Whale, Sonia L	5:05:02	(26,585)
Whalley, Susie	3:55:35	(10,399)
Wharton, Emma L	3:29:55	(4,809)
Whayman, Taryna	4:45:09	(22,820)
Wheadon, Louise L	4:39:58	(21,668)
Wheatley, Andrée A	3:55:17	(10,311)
Wheatley, Josephine B	5:02:54	(26,304)
Wheeler, Fiona M	4:49:42	(23,791)
Wheeler, Jane E	3:49:49	(8,825)
Wheeler, Katherine E	4:17:28	(15,972)
Whelan, Francesca K	3:51:01	(9,102)
Whelan, Jeni	6:06:52	(31,818)
Whetlor, Julia F	3:38:27	(6,316)
Whiley, Lesley	3:04:01	(1,512)
Whinn, Julie	5:00:17	(25,941)
Whinney, Christine C	4:39:15	(21,502)
Whiston, Nicola C	5:12:06	(27,539)
Whitaker, Ffreuer H	5:21:55	(28,704)
Whitbourn, Ruth E	5:49:13	(31,018)
Whitby, Nicola H	3:47:44	(8,306)
Whitchurch, Annette J	4:43:47	(22,514)
White, Alice K	3:56:47	(10,778)
White, Alison J	3:58:01	(11,156)
White, Angela W	4:28:51	(18,983)
White, Anna L	4:35:10	(20,525)
White, Caroline S	3:48:37	(8,531)
White, Christine A	5:24:37	(28,994)
White, Elaine	4:39:40	(21,592)
White, Emma J	5:14:21	(27,821)
White, Helen L	5:11:16	(27,423)
White, Jane L	3:20:33	(3,341)
White, Jane M	6:24:35	(32,347)
White, Janis V	4:20:32	(16,742)
White, Julianne L	5:06:53	(26,844)
White, Karen	4:54:20	(24,754)
White, Kate J	4:43:58	(22,566)
White, Kelly S	4:20:06	(16,629)
White, Lesley A	4:46:18	(23,075)
White, Lindsay F	3:52:39	(9,538)
White, Lindsay J	4:31:17	(19,606)
White, Nicola S	3:44:09	(7,480)
White, Nicole N	5:47:16	(30,886)
White, Pamela L	3:24:44	(3,901)
White, Rebecca	4:36:14	(20,791)
White, Rebecca L	3:56:52	(10,809)
White, Sara E	5:31:05	(29,669)
White, Sarah C	3:47:43	(8,301)
White, Victoria M	4:26:39	(18,421)
Whitehad, Amanda J	4:20:53	(16,833)
Whitehead, Alice H	4:36:37	(20,872)
Whitehead, Claire A	4:28:31	(18,901)
Whitehead, Louise	5:11:02	(27,388)
Whitehead, Michelle	3:57:56	(11,144)
Whitehouse, Karen	5:10:59	(27,384)
Whitehouse, Mary	6:13:42	(32,040)
Whitehurst, Tracy	4:12:38	(14,734)
Whiteley, Christine	5:12:04	(27,532)
Whiteley, Jacqueline E	4:39:08	(21,478)
Whiteley, Sarah J	6:41:32	(32,630)
Whiteley, Sarah K	5:08:28	(27,071)
Whitelock, Anne M	3:59:15	(11,585)
Whitely, Meredith S	4:28:07	(18,780)
Whiteside, Lynda J	5:20:35	(28,575)
Whitfield, Lorraine	4:59:18	(25,743)
Whitham, Emma J	4:05:45	(13,087)
Whitington, Zoe C	5:31:13	(29,681)
Whitley, Jane	3:27:34	(4,344)
Whitman, Maureen P	5:20:32	(28,565)
Whitmore, Gill R	4:10:33	(14,220)
Whitnall, Lynn K	4:52:58	(24,448)
Whitney, Karla D	5:16:11	(28,026)
Whittaker, Claire E	5:44:18	(30,665)
Whittaker, Elizabeth A	4:15:49	(15,552)
Whittaker, Rosemary	4:26:58	(18,497)
Whittaker, Sarah	4:41:15	(21,934)
Whittall, Liz A	6:38:12	(32,584)
Whitten, Lisa	5:27:08	(29,238)
Whitters, Caralea	4:39:57	(21,667)
Whittington, Sally Ann	4:48:26	(23,520)
Whittle, Carol E	4:08:04	(13,632)
Whittle, Sally	4:14:39	(15,242)
Whitworth, Karen T	4:46:58	(23,200)
Whitworth, Natalie A	4:25:07	(17,996)
Wholgemuth, Alison A	5:54:03	(31,262)
Whorton, Helen	6:08:06	(31,862)
Why, Christina J	4:49:26	(23,740)
Whybrow, Jennifer A	4:12:18	(14,652)
Whyke, Josy	5:35:26	(30,006)
Whyne, Janice M	6:13:21	(32,030)
Whyte, Kerry A	5:28:38	(29,389)
Whythe, Caterhine M	5:57:18	(31,422)
Wickert, Katie A	3:33:34	(5,410)
Wickham, Rachel C	4:33:50	(20,209)
Wickham, Sue	5:22:04	(28,724)
Wicks, Amey L	5:20:06	(28,503)
Widdowson, Karen E	3:47:39	(8,282)
Wiezel, Melanie J	4:55:10	(24,928)
Wiggett, Jo	5:22:10	(28,735)
Wiggins, Catherine	5:19:28	(28,431)
Wigmore, Tina	4:45:59	(23,001)
Wijesingha, Savini	4:44:09	(22,597)
Wijesooriya, Naomi A	4:20:42	(16,789)
Wilbraham, Annabel C	5:20:50	(28,595)
Wilbrey, Susan E	6:01:53	(31,637)
Wilby, Sarah J	3:39:59	(6,624)
Wilcox, Jo S	4:22:21	(17,209)
Wild, Louise	3:16:41	(2,838)
Wilenius, Laura J	4:49:54	(23,826)
Wilford, Fiona L	4:03:15	(12,538)
Wilford, Laison L	4:34:24	(20,341)
Wilgoss, Linda J	6:14:34	(32,071)
Wilkes, Harriet C	5:31:08	(29,675)
Wilkie, Gosia L	4:06:17	(13,192)
Wilkins, Eleanor J	4:55:29	(24,995)
Wilkins, Frances M	3:37:01	(6,043)
Wilkins, Julie Y	3:57:47	(11,110)
Wilkins, Mary	4:14:01	(15,074)
Wilkinson, Beth	5:04:42	(26,545)
Wilkinson, Carole E	4:18:51	(16,310)
Wilkinson, Carolyn S	3:17:26	(2,936)
Wilkinson, Daney S	5:12:37	(27,602)
Wilkinson, Dawn	5:14:06	(27,785)
Wilkinson, Dorothy A	3:37:27	(6,121)
Wilkinson, Holly	3:06:40	(1,723)
Wilkinson, Lisa	3:38:57	(6,425)
Willans, Gemma L	5:13:30	(27,721)
Willbond, Andrea F	4:36:28	(20,836)
Willbourne, Sian E	4:59:26	(25,767)
Willcock, Louise E	4:57:02	(25,319)
Willcocks, Jayne	5:01:55	(26,167)
Willdigg, Jane H	4:04:12	(12,756)
Willett, Pauline A	5:35:05	(29,974)
Williams, Alex	4:38:48	(21,391)
Williams, Alexandra C	5:58:33	(31,489)
Williams, Alison S	5:56:34	(31,385)
Williams, Anita M	6:19:02	(32,203)
Williams, Bernice T	6:53:01	(32,795)
Williams, Caitlin J	4:32:20	(19,869)

Williams, Cara B 5:33:04 (29,821)
Williams, Carol 5:56:10 (31,361)
Williams, Caroline 4:18:53 (16,323)
Williams, Catherine 3:29:45 (4,771)
Williams, Catherine F 4:49:26 (23,740)
Williams, Catherine M 4:17:15 (15,918)
Williams, Clare 5:19:50 (28,474)
Williams, Dawn E 4:54:28 (24,778)
Williams, Deanna M 4:04:47 (12,876)
Williams, Elizabeth A 4:27:31 (18,628)
Williams, Fiona C 4:57:27 (25,390)
Williams, Fiona K 5:02:06 (26,187)
Williams, Gabriella 4:57:06 (25,334)
Williams, Gail A 3:23:19 (3,686)
Williams, Gail H 4:22:03 (17,130)
Williams, Jacqueline A 3:34:05 (5,496)
Williams, Jane M 4:39:17 (21,509)
Williams, Jane P 6:02:44 (31,667)
Williams, Janet 4:43:34 (22,458)
Williams, Julia J 4:42:08 (22,146)
Williams, Julie 4:50:08 (23,865)
Williams, Justine M 4:47:41 (23,357)
Williams, Karen L 4:07:07 (13,377)
Williams, Kate A 5:02:19 (26,227)
Williams, Kathleen 6:17:15 (32,149)
Williams, Kathryn H 3:41:02 (6,809)
Williams, Katie 4:35:55 (20,692)
Williams, Katie E 4:26:22 (18,352)
Williams, Katie O 6:26:39 (32,392)
Williams, Katie R 3:58:35 (11,368)
Williams, Kym 6:40:50 (32,623)
Williams, Lesley K 5:21:17 (28,644)
Williams, Louise 3:55:54 (10,507)
Williams, Madeleine M 4:29:35 (19,194)
Williams, Margaret C 3:47:25 (8,219)
Williams, Mary B 3:51:22 (9,193)
Williams, Mel C 4:10:21 (14,183)
Williams, Nerys 6:08:57 (31,893)
Williams, Rebecca C 4:38:30 (21,340)
Williams, Sarah 4:09:42 (14,029)
Williams, Sarah 5:53:25 (31,236)
Williams, Sarah J 5:23:14 (28,861)
Williams, Sharon A 4:55:10 (24,928)
Williams, Teresa 4:13:36 (14,975)
Williams, Teresa K 3:23:45 (3,751)
Williamson, Andrea 5:10:39 (27,349)
Williamson, Fiona 3:52:04 (9,375)
Williamson, Julia F 4:44:44 (22,716)
Williamson, Kate 3:40:11 (6,657)
Williamson, Kerry S 4:57:54 (25,479)
Williamson, Laura E 4:31:04 (19,544)
Williamson, Linda M 6:59:21 (32,873)
Williamson, Lisa A 5:49:37 (31,049)
Williamson, Michelle B 5:26:40 (29,182)
Williamson, Naomi L 4:29:05 (19,053)
Willings, Maria L 5:23:08 (28,847)
Willis, Abigail E 4:31:20 (19,622)
Willis, Amy L 5:27:01 (29,228)
Willis, Caroline A 4:42:59 (22,325)
Willis, Debra J 4:43:33 (22,452)
Willis, Elen 4:31:59 (19,786)
Willis, Elizabeth J 4:20:17 (16,678)
Willis, Elizabeth L 3:53:14 (9,703)
Willis, Kay 4:35:27 (20,594)
Willis, Pamela S 5:22:42 (28,799)
Willis, Rachel E 3:42:24 (7,098)
Willmington, Lesley A 4:12:08 (14,608)
Wills, Romilly 3:38:37 (6,353)
Wilmot, Kathryn L 4:19:49 (16,557)
Wilson, Alison M 5:11:01 (27,387)
Wilson, Beverley J 2:55:45 (832)
Wilson, Christine M 4:07:07 (13,377)
Wilson, Claire L 3:55:23 (10,339)
Wilson, Elaine E 5:06:08 (26,729)
Wilson, Elizabeth R 3:57:23 (10,974)
Wilson, Emily 4:53:09 (24,491)
Wilson, Emma 4:55:34 (25,010)
Wilson, Emma-Beth 5:47:23 (30,910)
Wilson, Fiona K 5:41:42 (30,472)
Wilson, Gillian 4:42:55 (22,310)
Wilson, Gillian A 3:46:59 (8,116)
Wilson, Heather E 4:22:49 (17,326)
Wilson, Heidi J 2:54:26 (756)
Wilson, J 4:28:14 (18,820)
Wilson, Jacqueline L 3:27:16 (4,284)
Wilson, Jane 4:47:58 (23,422)
Wilson, Janet 3:49:25 (8,725)
Wilson, Janice M 3:47:03 (8,133)
Wilson, Jennifer I 6:21:05 (32,257)
Wilson, Jo 4:44:58 (22,775)
Wilson, Jo C 4:20:39 (16,774)
Wilson, Joanne C 3:13:00 (2,397)
Wilson, Joanne E 3:34:56 (5,651)
Wilson, Julie A 4:27:31 (18,628)
Wilson, Karen 3:41:47 (6,983)
Wilson, Kathryn M 4:40:10 (21,707)
Wilson, Kim J 4:22:30 (17,242)
Wilson, Lisa J 3:59:55 (11,790)
Wilson, Lizzie A 4:39:09 (21,481)
Wilson, Lucy R 4:16:53 (15,827)
Wilson, Lynne 6:28:12 (32,426)
Wilson, Michelle A 3:43:43 (7,396)
Wilson, Nicola A 3:30:29 (4,889)
Wilson, Nicola C 6:02:03 (31,642)
Wilson, Patricia M 3:55:44 (10,453)
Wilson, Philippa L 4:05:07 (12,945)
Wilson, Phillipa R 4:06:49 (13,303)
Wilson, Rosemary E 3:30:05 (4,843)
Wilson, Ruth 3:52:11 (9,408)
Wilson, Sally M 5:29:50 (29,527)
Wilson, Samantha N 4:10:59 (14,325)
Wilson, Sarah J 4:21:13 (16,920)
Wilson, Sarah L 3:33:04 (5,332)
Wilson, Simone C 3:32:01 (5,166)
Wilson, Susan C 4:20:42 (16,789)
Wilson, Susan D 4:22:35 (17,260)
Wilson, Tina 4:44:19 (22,639)
Wilson, Traci J 4:39:52 (21,645)
Wilson, Ursula R 3:48:58 (8,623)
Wilson, Vanessa 6:09:08 (31,899)
Wilson-Phesse, Sarah 4:05:04 (12,933)
Wilton, Susan E 5:02:40 (26,270)
Wiltshire, Cheryl K 5:43:58 (30,634)
Wimms, Lizzie 6:04:20 (31,735)
Winder, Caroline L 5:05:04 (26,591)
Windle, Jane A 4:30:08 (19,334)
Windle, Kim E 4:22:49 (17,326)
Windley, Elizabeth J 6:24:06 (32,331)
Windram, Andrea 5:31:59 (29,736)
Wing, Julia A 4:51:08 (24,066)
Wingfield, Joan 3:20:21 (3,317)
Winkworth, Lucy C 4:38:54 (21,420)
Winn, Heidi N 3:31:26 (5,057)
Winn-Smith, Joanna E 4:31:17 (19,606)
Winstanley, Louise J 4:28:07 (18,780)
Wint, Georgina M 5:27:09 (29,240)
Winter, Anne-Marie 4:15:35 (15,491)
Winter, Kirsty M 6:46:30 (32,719)
Winter, Lindsey 4:15:51 (15,564)
Winter-Barker, Sally A 5:21:20 (28,649)
Winterhagen, Roswitha 4:19:09 (16,379)
Winters, Helen 4:10:24 (14,194)
Winters, Melissa H 3:04:23 (1,537)
Winterson, Victoria 3:29:33 (4,731)
Winthrop, Shona A 5:49:08 (31,008)
Winward, Sarah 4:01:05 (12,067)
Winwood, Marion J 5:01:03 (26,054)
Wiscombe, Rebecca A 3:47:30 (8,239)
Wise, Gay 5:52:51 (31,209)
Wise, Shirley A 4:33:48 (20,206)
Wiseman, Katie S 4:50:39 (23,973)
Wiseman, Nicole L 6:22:47 (32,305)
Wiseman, Tammy M 6:53:20 (32,800)
Wiser, Joanna L 4:34:32 (20,371)
Wisson, Shirley A 4:35:04 (20,504)
Witek, Samantha J 5:44:37 (30,687)
Witham, Nondyebo 5:41:44 (30,476)
Withycombe, Kim L 3:44:13 (7,495)
Witton, Christine 4:42:51 (22,294)
Witty, Emily V 3:36:08 (5,860)
Wohanka, Donagh 3:44:24 (7,538)
Wolff, Bernadette 4:10:54 (14,305)
Wolff, Olivia L 4:44:11 (22,606)
Wollaston, Esther 3:50:49 (9,058)
Wolstenholme, Susan A 4:05:55 (13,125)
Wood, Anna M 4:22:41 (17,294)
Wood, Anne 5:29:23 (29,466)
Wood, Elizabeth A 4:43:56 (22,558)
Wood, Elizabeth G 3:59:57 (11,801)
Wood, Elizabeth G 4:49:06 (23,677)
Wood, Ellen C 4:11:41 (14,494)
Wood, Emma S 3:52:56 (9,604)
Wood, Gaynor 5:42:05 (30,508)
Wood, Jennifer S 5:21:57 (28,712)
Wood, Joanne L 4:49:12 (23,690)
Wood, Kelly S 4:26:24 (18,361)
Wood, Kerrie J 3:04:22 (1,536)
Wood, Lesley 5:24:53 (29,025)
Wood, Linda 5:55:06 (31,308)
Wood, Linda J 5:08:56 (27,140)
Wood, Marie A 5:45:24 (30,749)
Wood, Marion E 3:19:39 (3,205)
Wood, Nicola 3:44:29 (7,563)
Wood, Rachel H 3:30:14 (4,858)
Wood, Rachel J 4:48:09 (23,459)
Wood, Rebecca J 3:50:48 (9,055)
Wood, Rebecca J 4:59:09 (25,730)
Wood, Rosalind M 4:34:27 (20,350)
Wood, Sharon J 5:15:30 (27,953)
Wood, Tamara C 5:24:22 (28,981)
Woodard, Ann K 4:58:47 (25,658)
Woodburn, Jennifer M 5:27:16 (29,249)
Woodcock, Anne 4:28:33 (18,910)
Woodcock, Sarah 4:53:17 (24,520)
Woodford, Carol A 5:00:54 (26,028)
Woodgate, Marie 5:12:57 (27,642)
Woodhouse, Ann E 5:29:24 (29,469)
Woodhouse, Melanie J 3:38:13 (6,270)
Woodhouse, Natalie L 6:40:36 (32,618)
Woodhouse, Rebecca K 4:08:48 (13,815)
Woodhouse, Susan L 5:28:20 (29,360)
Woodings, Katie J 4:05:26 (13,005)
Woodland, Calre L 4:08:33 (13,759)
Woodrow, Kerry P 6:14:46 (32,081)
Woodrow, Roberta K 5:28:23 (29,366)
Woods, Abigail L 3:23:56 (3,780)
Woods, Bernadette 4:05:13 (12,963)
Woods, Caroline M 4:37:35 (21,136)
Woods, Marion C 4:32:32 (19,908)
Woods, Sophie E 6:26:08 (32,383)
Woodward, Anne M 7:28:35 (33,089)
Woodward, Carol S 3:37:13 (6,076)
Woodward, Emma C 4:35:14 (20,542)
Wooff, Katherine 4:24:32 (17,809)
Wooldridge, Kate R 4:06:34 (13,243)
Woolford, Anna R 3:34:34 (5,585)
Woolgrove, Catherine J 5:39:26 (30,314)
Wooller, Diane E 3:52:29 (9,488)
Woolley, Anne-Marie E 4:42:01 (22,116)
Woolley, Laura C 5:14:18 (27,811)
Woolley, Lauren F 3:20:52 (3,387)
Woolley, Lesley A 5:09:08 (27,165)
Woolley, Theresa 3:26:23 (4,134)
Woolnough, Jennifer L 4:05:38 (13,061)
Woolnough, Samantha 4:47:49 (23,386)
Woon, Christine D 5:43:25 (30,606)
Wooster, Samantha J 4:48:58 (23,644)
Wooster, Yvonne M 3:28:48 (4,573)
Worboys-Hodgson, Joanne 4:23:03 (17,374)
Worden, Maxine C 3:27:11 (4,271)
Wordsworth, Sarah 5:30:16 (29,569)
Wormell, Joanna C 4:23:09 (17,397)
Worsley, Kim L 5:31:34 (29,711)
Worthington, Ann 4:48:53 (23,625)
Worthington, Carol L 5:44:50 (30,705)
Worwood, Emma V 5:13:27 (27,712)
Wotherspoon, Jane D 3:31:01 (4,987)
Wotherspoon, Wendy D 4:03:03 (12,492)
Wotton, Alison M 7:12:19 (32,997)
Wouda, Sharon L 3:52:45 (9,557)
Wragg, Jane M 5:03:25 (26,379)
Wratten, Katherine E 5:12:21 (27,568)
Wray, Harriet A 5:29:39 (29,497)
Wray, Shelley A 4:34:45 (20,424)
Wren, Aly K 3:58:45 (11,422)
Wren, Sally R 4:41:54 (22,085)
Wrenn, Sara 5:31:54 (29,732)
Wright, Anita D 7:00:15 (32,887)
Wright, Carolyn L 4:43:46 (22,510)

Wright, Denise.............6:09:03 (31,896)
Wright, Emilie L.............4:48:23 (23,510)
Wright, Erin B.............3:50:39 (9,016)
Wright, Gael E.............4:54:13 (24,732)
Wright, Helen E.............4:59:03 (25,715)
Wright, Jackie.............4:34:33 (20,379)
Wright, Jeannie.............5:06:48 (26,836)
Wright, Jo E.............4:26:10 (18,302)
Wright, Joan M.............4:09:11 (13,903)
Wright, Joanne L.............3:56:46 (10,769)
Wright, Julia L.............4:36:49 (20,941)
Wright, Julia T.............5:56:53 (31,400)
Wright, Kate.............3:22:53 (3,644)
Wright, Laura J.............3:36:45 (5,982)
Wright, Lucie.............5:50:07 (31,082)
Wright, Maureen A.............3:58:16 (11,253)
Wright, Sandy J.............5:28:30 (29,376)
Wright, Stephanie.............5:01:23 (26,095)
Wright, Tracey.............4:48:15 (23,483)
Wrigley, Helen.............6:06:40 (31,811)
Wuilloud, Mary.............4:16:26 (15,704)
Wyatt, Paula.............4:28:42 (18,944)
Wyer, Karen P.............3:30:34 (4,907)
Wyllie, Denise L.............4:45:12 (22,834)
Wyndham, Megan L.............4:21:21 (16,947)
Wyngard, Clare E.............3:31:01 (4,987)
Wynn, Alison T.............3:54:52 (10,165)
Wynn, Elizabeth J.............3:27:17 (4,287)
Wynn, Linda Z.............4:33:06 (20,030)
Wysocki, Jacqueline.............4:34:41 (20,406)
Yamashita, Satoko.............4:32:58 (19,997)

Yamauchi, Mara.............2:25:13 (45)

Yamazaki, Mieko.............5:18:03 (28,245)
Yard, Gemma V.............5:13:54 (27,753)

Yardley, Catherine A.............5:40:03 (30,367)
Yates, Alison M.............4:14:28 (15,202)
Yates, Clemency.............6:10:33 (31,946)
Yates, Louise M.............4:51:20 (24,101)
Yates, Michelle A.............5:11:08 (27,400)
Yates, Victoria E.............4:49:44 (23,797)
Yearley, Lesley C.............4:08:48 (13,815)
Yeeles, Marion.............5:36:06 (30,060)
Yeo, Anna R.............4:21:44 (17,036)
Yeomans, Joanna.............5:07:10 (26,889)
Yeomans, Victoria L.............4:28:50 (18,979)
Yevko, Nicola.............2:58:42 (1,097)
Yff, Barbara.............2:50:36 (570)
Yogaratnam, Helena.............4:38:55 (21,423)
York, Marie L.............3:44:18 (7,521)
Youel, Karen J.............4:50:50 (24,010)
Youell, Karen A.............5:29:32 (29,489)
Young, Angela B.............4:25:39 (18,145)
Young, Bobbie Joe.............3:50:29 (8,977)
Young, Catherine F.............3:29:34 (4,736)
Young, Elinor.............4:45:23 (22,885)
Young, Justine M.............4:49:00 (23,649)
Young, Katherine E.............4:04:24 (12,796)
Young, Lesley A.............5:39:48 (30,346)
Young, Libby J.............5:04:22 (26,499)
Young, Melanie.............3:36:42 (5,976)
Young, Nathalie L.............3:58:40 (11,388)
Young, Sarah D.............3:50:50 (9,062)
Young, Sarah E.............4:29:07 (19,062)
Younghusband, Tracey J.............5:09:32 (27,210)
Ytreland, Gerd Marit.............4:29:44 (19,235)
Yu, Donna K.............5:42:28 (30,532)
Yuill, Chris.............3:40:56 (6,791)
Yuill, Helen L.............4:13:06 (14,874)
Yuill, Kathryn H.............5:29:25 (29,473)
Yupanqui Bazan, Maria.............4:32:49 (19,961)
Zabihi, Helena M.............4:38:28 (21,329)
Zaccagni, Ilaria.............3:36:54 (6,020)
Zak, Minoda J.............5:25:09 (29,054)
Zammit, Lisa M.............4:42:30 (22,217)
Zammit, Sandra J.............6:36:44 (32,556)
Zanda, Federica.............4:52:09 (24,279)
Zanoline, Barbar M.............5:26:18 (29,153)
Zarpanely, Renée.............5:44:56 (30,711)
Zenobi-Bird, Luisa.............5:06:48 (26,836)
Zettl, Melitta.............5:20:57 (28,605)
Zie, Ann A.............4:10:47 (14,270)
Zielke, Laila.............4:17:00 (15,860)
Zielke, Maj-Britt.............4:31:35 (19,692)
Zieve, Sharon E.............5:11:50 (27,501)
Zonnevylle, Caroline.............5:02:52 (26,299)
Zuber, Julita B.............4:05:37 (13,055)
Zucker, Dalia.............6:01:29 (31,625)
Zulberg, Jodie.............3:05:07 (1,586)
Zwarthoed Schilder, Maria C.............3:32:49 (5,296)

WHEELCHAIR ENTRANTS

Adams, Jeff.............1:53:24 (6)
Alldis, Brian.............1:47:34 (5)
Brennan, Deborah.............2:21:02 (17)
Cassell, Ric.............3:10:54 (23)
Cheek, Andrew.............2:16:31 (15)
Derwin, Steve.............3:10:10 (22)
Downing, Peter.............3:04:10 (21)
Forde, Jerry.............3:39:45 (25)
Fuss, Alain.............1:39:37 (3)
Gill, Jason.............2:02:47 (10)
Holliday, Rob.............3:26:01 (24)
Hunt, Paul.............2:12:11 (14)
Marten, Michael.............4:09:28 (26)
Mendoza, Saul.............1:37:52 (2)
Patel, Tushar.............2:06:44 (13)
Piercy, Sarah.............2:39:10 (20)
Porcellato, Francesca.............1:59:57 (8)
Qadir, Shaho.............2:00:52 (9)
Richards, Jason.............1:53:29 (7)
Riggs, Stuart.............2:27:22 (18)
Smith, Robert.............2:33:02 (19)
Stone, Douglas.............2:17:20 (16)
Teurnier, Eric.............1:43:52 (4)
Weir, David.............1:29:48 (1)
Williamson, Steve.............2:03:23 (11)
Woods, Shelly.............2:04:37 (12)

In 2005 Paula Radcliffe was caught short and had to relieve herself late in the race. But she still won.

The same thing happened to Steve Jones when he ran 2:08:16 to win in 1985.

These days there are 900 portable loos along the course. So don't be discouraged by an unscheduled pit-stop. It shouldn't ruin your time.

InterContinental Hotels Group

2007

The 2007 London Marathon

Runners knew they were in for a hard time with the sun blazing strongly well before the start of the 2007 London Marathon. Temperatures seemed likely to rise to produce a race that would be the hottest in the event's history. The sweltering heat left hundreds needing medical treatment. Temperatures almost hit 21°C at midday, just about equalling the 1996 record in this race as runners reported 'nightmare' conditions. St John Ambulance treated over 5,000 people.

Celebrity chef Gordon Ramsay, who was running his eighth marathon, said the conditions were, 'Extraordinary. It was like running in a desert today. They were dropping like flies.'

An extra 30,000 bottles of water were rushed out along the route, but even so some feeding stations still ran dry. The organisers had issued many warnings to take care in the heat, yet there was no shortage of contestants in fancy dress – with costumes that must have felt like ovens, and a foolhardy scattering of outsize 'rhinos' defying the challenging conditions.

Suffering alongside the fun runners were two strong fields in the men's and women's races, though there were some surprise dropouts – the most notable being Haile Gebrselassie. The Ethiopian ground to a halt shortly before the 20-mile mark. The double Olympic 10,000m champion pulled out of the lead group clutching his stomach.

He said: 'I had a stitch here in my chest and could not continue. I'm not injured, I just could not breathe.' The marathon is no respecter of reputations, and even this genius of the track could be laid low by every beginner jogger's bugbear – the 'stitch'.

Kenya's Martin Lel won the men's race in what many regarded as an upset, not just for

Gebrselassie, but for the reigning world marathon record holder Paul Tergat. Lel had won the race in 2005.

Lel regained the men's title running 2:07:41 thanks to a tremendous turn of pace in the final 300 metres. The 28-year-old Kenyan won the sprint, narrowly beating Abderrahim Goumri. Lel, one of ten siblings from a very poor background, walked away with £40,000 in prize money which he planned to invest in grocery stores and an apartment block back home in Kenya.

Commonwealth Games bronze medallist Dan Robinson was the first Briton, finishing ninth as he came home in 2:14:14. Jon Brown, expected to lead the home challenge, was a non-starter, pulling out of the race early in the morning after a bout of sickness.

The Chinese athlete Zhou Chunxiu became the first Chinese winner of the women's race. A punishing burst just over three miles from the finish (her 24th mile was timed at a blistering 5 minutes 9 seconds) pulled her clear of the rest of the field to win in 2:20:38.

Chunxiu, who was 2006 Asian Games champion, blew away the challenges of Ethiopia's Gete Wami (2:21:45) and Constantina Tomescu-Dita of Romania (2:23:55). Britain's Mara Yamauchi ran a fine race in the heat, finishing in sixth place for the second successive year in 2:25:41, while Liz Yelling also reached the top 10 and qualified for the 2008 Olympics, finishing eighth in 2:30:44.

Britons David Weir and Shelly Woods won the wheelchair races. Weir, 27, won a sprint finish to defend his wheelchair title in a time of 1:30:49. Meanwhile, Shelly Woods, 20, took the women's race, finishing in 1:50:40, just outside her personal best time.

A 22-year-old runner, David Rogers, who collapsed after completing the London Marathon

died on the day after the 2007 Marathon. Rogers had completed the course in 3:56 but collapsed suffering from 'water intoxication'. Water intoxication (also known as hyper-hydration or water poisoning) is a disturbance in brain functions that results when the normal balance of electrolytes in the body is pushed beyond safe limits by over-consumption of water. Marathon runners are susceptible to water intoxication if they drink too much, and medics at marathon events are trained to suspect water intoxication immediately if runners collapse or show signs of confusion.

One wonderful British performance came from the 42-year-old former champion Liz McColgan, who won London way back in 1996. Running in memory of her father, Martin, who died in 2007, she lined up in the mass start. But even so this formidable former winner finished inside 2:51.

Explanation of placing system

Each London Marathon year in this register is divided up into four categories: first, a summary of the **Elite Athletes**, containing names (last, first) and times (hours : minutes : seconds) of the top 50 male runners, top 50 female runners, top 3 male and top 2 female wheelchair entrants; then **Male Runners**, **Female Runners** and **Wheelchair Entrants**. These last three sections display the individual names and times of *every* entrant, including elite athletes, alphabetically and with their overall finishing position in that year's Marathon displayed in brackets alongside.

Some entrants have chosen to enhance past London Marathon entries with photos and recollections online at **www.aubreybooks.com**. Please visit the website to find out more about appearing in future editions.

ELITE ATHLETES

Top 50 male runners

Lel, Martin	2:07:41
Goumri, Abderrahim	2:07:44
Limo, Felix	2:07:47
Gharib, Jaouad	2:07:54
Ramaala, Hendrick	2:07:56
Tergat, Paul	2:08:06
Hall, Ryan	2:08:24
Gomes, Marilson	2:08:37
Robinson, Dan	2:14:14
Jones, Andi	2:17:49
Cherono, Benson	2:18:55
Lunde, Orjan	2:20:21
Gardiner, Richie	2:20:26
Driscoll, Joe	2:20:49
McFarlane, John	2:22:18
Raven, Gareth	2:23:27
Renault, Neil	2:23:44
Miles, Mark	2:24:20
Bilton, Darran E	2:25:10
Carroll, Michael J	2:25:19
Hoiom, Runar	2:26:23
Tschopp, Marcel	2:26:56
McAlister, Joseph	2:27:10
Martyn, Nicholas A	2:27:11
Bangani, Pumlani	2:28:26
Mustafa, Daoud	2:28:29
Smith, Michael J	2:28:36
Macdonald, Stewart F	2:28:39
McGuinness, Nicky	2:29:03
Hasler, Paul G	2:29:11
Bizuneh, Fasil	2:29:30
Byansi, Malachi	2:29:40
Nurse, Ian A	2:29:51
Clarke, John P	2:29:57
Weir, Andrew P	2:30:22
Cockerell, William V	2:30:39

Galpin, Peter C	2:30:49
Fisher, Ian R	2:31:01
North, Steffan J	2:31:39
Thompson, Paul	2:31:47
Baker, Julian D	2:31:49
Nicolson, Christian	2:31:52
Frost, Jonathan	2:32:20
Coleman, Michael	2:32:45
Boucher, Michael B	2:32:51
Littler, Stephen T	2:33:07
Adams, Paul R	2:33:15
Hart, Al	2:33:30
Wilson, Graeme S	2:33:40
Van Zyl, Anton	2:33:43

Top 50 female runners

Chunxiu, Zhou	2:20:38
Wami, Gete	2:21:45
Tomescu-Dita, Constantina	2:23:55
Kosgei, Salina	2:24:13
Kiplagat, Lornah	2:24:46
Yamauchi, Mara	2:25:41
Johnson, Benita	2:29:47
Yelling, Liz	2:30:44
Abitova, Inga	2:34:25
Adere, Berhane	2:39:11
Donta, Helen	2:40:42
Mihaylova, Milka	2:44:35
Mercado Torres, Yolanda	2:44:58
Clay, Nicola K	2:46:25
Schmidt, Elke	2:47:09
Hawker, Liz	2:47:55
Kelsey, Jo R	2:47:59
Natoli, Karen	2:48:23
Laithwaite, Gill	2:48:32
Cowley, Laura J	2:48:46
Wilding, Catherine M	2:49:07

Howe, Angela D	2:49:57
Mackenzie, Kaeti A	2:50:28
Murphy, Gemma B	2:50:34
McColgan, Liz	2:50:38
Webster, Katy M	2:52:05
Powell, Pauline P	2:52:47
Burke, Melanie	2:52:52
Whitehead-Waterlow, Amy	2:53:34
Stuart, Helen M	2:53:38
McIntosh, Shona	2:54:04
Perry, Victoria A	2:54:29
Foundling-Hawker, Heather R	2:54:56
Heaton, Mathilde M	2:54:56
Steer, Deborah A	2:55:05
Lawrence, Helen	2:55:19
Holloway-Guilfoyle, Tracy	2:56:03
Menzies, Issy	2:56:04
Mansbridge, Kaye	2:56:27
Monahan, Sian E	2:56:28
Banks, Faye M	2:56:34
Decker, Helen J	2:56:36
Thomas, Ann	2:57:29
Wilson, Heidi J	2:57:43
Fleming, Zoe	2:57:59
Leitch, Jessica R	2:58:11
Wooley, Theresa	2:58:13
Baumann, Margaretha	2:58:36
Newing, Lisa M	2:58:36
Parfitt, Dena B	2:59:05

Top 3 male and top 2 female wheelchair entrants

Weir, David	1:30:49
Fearnley, Kurt	1:30:50
Mendoza, Saul	1:33:46
Woods, Shelly	1:50:40
Porcellato, Francesca	1:59:46

MALE RUNNERS

Aabat Oliba, Jordi 3:50:57 (7,127)
Aalbers, Jan 4:29:10 (15,900)
Aanensen, Arne 3:11:15 (1,651)
Aanensen, Kaare 2:58:08 (757)
Aanensen, Stein 3:00:57 (954)
Aarsland, Ole-Andreas 4:04:01 (9,969)
Aarstad Odgaard, Christian 2:44:37 (229)
Aatkar, Paresh 4:52:33 (21,626)
Abbas, Khawar S 5:08:39 (25,217)
Abbas, Mujtaba 5:43:29 (30,992)
Abbey, David 4:57:42 (22,956)
Abbey, Nick J 4:32:59 (16,780)
Abbott, Colin 6:50:05 (34,934)
Abbott, Gordon D 4:18:09 (13,108)
Abbott, Graham 4:25:22 (14,913)
Abbott, Jason J 6:03:08 (32,829)
Abbott, Julian C 3:50:13 (6,977)
Abbott, Justin J 4:47:01 (20,286)
Abbott, Martin J 4:11:47 (11,568)
Abbott, Patrick N 3:38:02 (4,837)
Abbott, Phil A 3:25:42 (3,088)
Abbott, Robin D 4:08:34 (10,882)
Abbott, Ryan J 3:16:36 (2,134)
Abbott, Steven C 7:00:10 (35,126)
Abbott, Stuart I 4:39:56 (18,520)
Abbou, Alex 4:04:41 (10,089)
Abbs, Richard R 4:52:10 (21,533)
Abel, Clive E 5:24:51 (28,250)
Abel, Lawrence J 3:32:47 (4,102)
Ab-Elwyn, Rhys 3:00:33 (934)
Abenaim, Norbert N 4:13:03 (11,847)
Abercrombie, Kelvin 4:43:49 (19,482)
Aberdeen, Bobby Z 4:51:00 (21,242)
Aberdour, George E 4:36:48 (17,740)
Abigail, Chris 5:30:14 (29,179)
Abolin, Patrice 3:02:08 (1,008)
Abou Chedid, Naji K 3:17:12 (2,197)
Abraham, Martin J 4:11:09 (11,413)
Abraham, Nigel H 4:12:17 (11,681)
Abraham, Richard J 4:15:10 (12,360)
Abrahams, Robert S 4:40:20 (18,615)
Abrahim, Harry 3:47:34 (6,438)
Abram, Barry 2:59:24 (854)
Abram, Shaun B 3:54:42 (7,945)
Abundis, Francisco 6:01:50 (32,743)
Accalai, Fabrizio 4:08:03 (10,778)
Acheampong, Kawabana 6:24:25 (34,095)
Acheson, James N 4:21:41 (13,999)
Acheson, Marc 5:32:40 (29,561)
Acheson, Timothy I 3:47:49 (6,499)
Achour, Francis 3:45:40 (6,130)
Acker, Leo 4:01:48 (9,568)
Ackers, Chris J 4:27:09 (15,366)
Acklam, Stefan P 4:43:57 (19,520)
Ackland, Adam J 4:45:43 (19,993)
Ackroyd, David R 5:21:51 (27,766)
Ackroyd, Jacob 3:40:41 (5,299)
Ackroyd, John S 3:57:12 (8,528)
Acon, Ruben 4:04:20 (10,030)
Acons, Stephen M 5:09:49 (25,434)
A'Court, Darren J 4:42:11 (19,089)
Acton, Robert P 3:25:30 (3,063)
Acuna, Roy F 4:26:23 (15,155)
Adam, Miles S 5:59:25 (32,545)
Adami, Alberto 2:44:45 (234)
Adams, Alastair H 3:28:53 (3,553)
Adams, Chris A 3:38:23 (4,901)
Adams, Clive 3:27:50 (3,388)
Adams, Dan K 3:59:29 (9,091)
Adams, Darren 6:10:06 (33,311)
Adams, David E 4:14:15 (12,152)
Adams, Douglas V 4:44:08 (19,571)
Adams, James W 5:27:13 (28,667)
Adams, Jason 4:45:49 (20,010)
Adams, Jason R 4:17:35 (12,975)
Adams, John H 4:29:35 (16,034)
Adams, Joseph 4:39:09 (18,320)
Adams, Kenny 4:14:25 (12,192)
Adams, Leslie 4:13:49 (12,048)
Adams, Paul R 2:33:15 (55)
Adams, Raymond J 5:39:20 (30,494)
Adams, Richard I 5:20:59 (27,604)
Adams, Robert 5:09:38 (25,400)
Adams, Roger 4:30:50 (16,320)
Adams, Ronnie E 2:40:54 (156)
Adams, Russ J 4:25:09 (14,859)
Adams, Russell 4:51:37 (21,402)
Adams, Stephen D 6:32:10 (34,415)
Adams, Stephen J 6:01:55 (32,747)
Adams, Steve 3:03:35 (1,082)
Adams, Terence P 4:24:56 (14,809)
Adams, Timothy P 4:07:13 (10,610)
Adams, Tom M 5:43:20 (30,976)
Adams, William F 3:48:14 (6,567)
Adamson, Kenneth J 4:33:20 (16,879)
Adamson, Mark D 4:33:02 (16,795)
Adamson, Matthew D 5:26:04 (28,470)
Adamson, Paul M 5:34:16 (29,806)
Adamson, Stuart 4:24:06 (14,598)
Adan, Iain A 5:04:54 (24,501)
Adcock, James R 4:03:33 (9,878)
Adcock, Norman A 5:11:57 (25,846)
Adcock, Toby H 4:50:36 (21,151)
Addis, Christopher C 4:52:49 (21,706)
Addis, Stefano M 4:01:43 (9,554)
Addrison, Martin K 5:10:16 (25,536)
Adeboyeku, David 4:54:44 (22,207)
Adekoya, Anthony 3:53:19 (7,648)
Adey, Matt 3:08:44 (1,447)
Adey, Tomas 4:23:33 (14,459)
Adisa, Timothy A 4:22:38 (14,241)
Adisi, John K 5:44:29 (31,092)
Adkin, Ian 2:57:16 (695)
Adkins, David D 3:40:10 (5,212)
Adlam, David P 5:11:55 (25,838)
Adlan-Merini, Mehdi 3:07:53 (1,379)
Adlard, Simon C 3:34:18 (4,316)
Adlem, Wayne S 3:47:45 (6,488)
Adler, Philip 4:28:44 (15,796)
Adnitt, Gary A 4:53:35 (21,909)
Adnitt, Robert I 3:22:18 (2,727)
Adolfo, Benedetto 3:50:00 (6,942)
Adolfsson, Lennart 3:26:24 (3,186)
Adolph, Richard V 4:36:49 (17,747)
Aeugle, Wolfgang B 3:56:50 (8,439)
Affleck, Robert J 5:48:00 (31,466)
Afford, Richard A 5:02:08 (23,956)
Afinowi, Rasheed A 3:45:54 (6,163)
Agarwal, Atul 5:59:16 (32,534)
Agates, Alan R 4:53:45 (21,951)
Agathangelou, Lex 5:08:43 (25,229)
Agbayai, Rafael 5:10:45 (25,617)
Ager, Iain N 4:49:08 (20,803)
Ager, Matthew D 3:42:11 (5,549)
Ager, Nick P 4:21:41 (13,999)
Ageros, Benjamin 3:19:27 (2,433)
Agg, Philip J 4:42:05 (19,060)
Aggett, Leslie J 4:57:19 (22,860)
Aghanian, Raffi 4:45:49 (20,010)
Agrawal, Sanjay 4:35:40 (17,446)
Agrusta, Domenico E 4:22:30 (14,205)
Aguirre, José I 2:46:44 (277)
Aguirre, Oscar I 5:50:18 (31,708)
Agul, Taro 2:46:15 (265)
Agulleiro-Diaz, Jesus P 3:22:29 (2,746)
Ahmad, Karim 4:15:39 (12,474)
Ahmad, Rafat 4:13:30 (11,963)
Ahmad, Sardar A 4:38:22 (18,117)
Ahmed, Amjad K 5:32:22 (29,504)
Ahmed, Jahangir 4:42:13 (19,101)
Ahmet, Sol 4:09:57 (11,156)
Ahouiyek, Said C 4:41:40 (18,958)
Ahsunollah, Paul 3:58:26 (8,816)
Aiken, Scott M 3:05:44 (1,220)
Aikin, Tim 5:47:06 (31,360)
Ailio, Antti A 4:57:07 (22,800)
Aimable, Michael H 6:42:36 (34,738)
Ainge, Philip D 4:39:59 (18,533)
Ainger, Mark S 4:29:44 (16,070)
Ainsley, Christopher J 3:28:09 (3,424)
Ainslie, Paul 3:19:39 (2,448)
Ainslie, Stuart 4:44:00 (19,538)
Ainsworth, John J 5:23:45 (28,063)
Ainsworth, Neil D 5:06:26 (24,778)
Ainsworth, Peter J 3:43:57 (5,856)
Aird, James A 3:39:17 (5,061)
Airey, Bob 6:27:35 (34,236)
Aitchinson, Liam 4:18:22 (13,165)
Aitchison, Alan C 4:28:41 (15,781)
Aitchison, John 5:00:03 (23,517)
Aitchison, Mark C 4:18:44 (13,273)
Aitchison, Robert J 3:42:28 (5,593)
Aitken, George 3:29:57 (3,709)
Aitken, Troy A 4:16:22 (12,665)
Aizman, Efrain 3:51:59 (7,363)
Ajibawo, Babatunde 4:16:02 (12,575)
Ajona, José A 3:35:32 (4,490)
Akast, William L 4:53:06 (21,779)
Akenhead, David 5:56:06 (32,246)
Akerman, Nick J 4:10:42 (11,313)
Akerman, Paul R 5:43:43 (31,016)
Akeroyd, Alan 6:20:59 (33,950)
Akeroyd, Charles 5:01:29 (23,827)
Akeroyd, Richard C 2:59:08 (835)
Akers, Jonathan 3:54:23 (7,880)
Akhras, Edward J 3:43:47 (5,826)
Akhtar, Rahim 5:20:51 (27,581)
Akiyama, Takeshi 3:34:19 (4,318)
Akkerhuys, Willem L 4:38:29 (18,146)
Akpojaro, Princeton E 4:04:17 (10,022)
Alberdi, Mikel 4:23:56 (14,549)
Alberg, Richard D 5:35:20 (29,956)
Albert, Michael J 6:27:34 (34,235)
Alberto, Zanotti 3:29:41 (3,671)
Albon, Christopher J 5:45:07 (31,169)
Albrighton, Matthew 4:37:49 (17,960)
Albrow, Jonathan M 4:16:12 (12,621)
Albury, Adrian T 4:31:52 (16,538)
Alcaraz, Ramon J 3:41:11 (5,396)
Alcober, Miguel 3:30:54 (3,827)
Alcock, Andrew G 5:16:58 (26,852)
Alcock, John 3:56:16 (8,290)
Alcock, Robert W 5:35:51 (30,031)
Alden, Gareth J 4:39:12 (18,335)
Alden, Kieran 5:12:23 (25,936)
Alder, Chris M 3:46:49 (6,307)
Alder, Edward M 4:15:31 (12,445)
Alder, Jason P 3:44:36 (5,959)
Alderman, Wulston C 5:27:11 (28,658)
Alderson, Paul M 3:51:33 (7,266)
Aldis, David 4:34:54 (17,248)
Aldis, Gary 4:17:40 (12,989)
Aldis, Roger 2:46:15 (265)
Aldous, Matthew J 4:06:50 (10,537)
Aldous, Rod B 6:33:04 (34,441)
Aldred, David J 4:46:48 (20,229)
Aldred, Mark D 3:00:53 (948)
Aldred, Mark K 4:42:44 (19,238)
Aldridge, Lewis W 4:17:29 (12,940)
Aldridge, Sam 5:29:03 (28,992)
Aldus, Barry 6:31:49 (34,395)
Aldus, Graham 6:31:49 (34,395)
Aleksic, Vladimir 3:29:09 (3,596)
Alessandrini, Christian 3:53:13 (7,626)
Alexander, Jeff R 4:22:27 (14,184)
Alexander, Lee 3:44:36 (5,959)
Alexander, Miles A 4:54:45 (22,212)
Alexander, Philip G 5:20:15 (27,467)
Alexander, Richard 4:35:42 (17,460)
Algar, Barry 5:34:01 (29,764)
Ali, Asif R 4:45:57 (20,050)
Ali, Erol 3:38:48 (4,973)
Ali, Imtiaz 3:46:47 (6,301)
Ali, Nazim 6:20:28 (33,919)
Aliis, Jeff 4:23:52 (14,536)
Allan, Andrew 4:16:56 (12,798)
Allan, Douglas R 3:31:40 (3,936)
Allan, Paul 6:31:49 (34,395)
Allanach, Greg R 5:37:13 (30,199)
Allanson, Martin G 5:17:35 (26,976)
Allard, Claude 4:17:20 (12,887)
Allard, Tim 4:49:16 (20,831)
Allard, Charles J Jnr 3:08:32 (1,433)
Allday, Paul J 6:08:27 (33,199)
Alldis, Michael A 3:32:53 (4,118)
Allen, Alexander J 6:01:44 (32,736)
Allen, Andrew S 5:23:35 (28,026)
Allen, Charles 4:03:06 (9,801)

Allen, Christopher M 4:38:30 (18,153)
Allen, Crispin R 3:17:22 (2,212)
Allen, David G 4:50:03 (21,007)
Allen, David H 5:29:30 (29,070)
Allen, David J 5:03:49 (24,294)
Allen, David T 6:06:16 (33,065)
Allen, Gareth J 5:55:47 (32,217)
Allen, Gavin P 4:22:31 (14,209)
Allen, Graeme J 3:45:34 (6,107)
Allen, Graham G 4:10:09 (11,194)
Allen, Hugh N 3:31:54 (3,972)
Allen, James N 3:09:32 (1,519)
Allen, John 6:54:58 (35,033)
Allen, Joseph J 3:30:01 (3,725)
Allen, Keith W 5:19:58 (27,420)
Allen, Kelvin I 4:06:38 (10,490)
Allen, Ken R 3:23:55 (2,896)
Allen, Kevin M 4:25:51 (15,025)
Allen, Luke 4:14:05 (12,120)
Allen, Martin C 3:41:26 (5,434)
Allen, Matthew D 4:39:40 (18,454)
Allen, Michael B 7:02:36 (35,170)
Allen, Michael J 5:03:35 (24,251)
Allen, Nicholas 4:47:10 (20,328)
Allen, Nick H 4:46:07 (20,086)
Allen, Nicolas D 4:36:40 (17,708)
Allen, Paul J 4:02:30 (9,699)
Allen, Philip J 4:28:17 (15,666)
Allen, Roger H 4:35:05 (17,291)
Allen, Stephen D 4:05:47 (10,304)
Allen, Steve 3:31:57 (3,985)
Allen, Stuart 3:52:59 (7,564)
Allen, Stuart K 5:02:31 (24,045)
Allen, Stuart R 4:39:17 (18,357)
Allen, Terence C 6:26:25 (34,191)
Allen, Tim 4:01:42 (9,551)
Allen, Tim C 4:13:19 (11,912)
Allen, Tim P 3:43:37 (5,801)
Allen, Tristan M 5:08:21 (25,162)
Allender, Karl A 4:36:19 (17,614)
Allerton, David M 5:02:14 (23,974)
Allford, Neil J 4:03:32 (9,874)
Allin, Howard A 4:14:53 (12,292)
Allingham, Richard 5:20:14 (27,466)
Allison, Andrew I 3:03:16 (1,064)
Allison, Clive J 2:57:11 (689)
Allison, Jason C 3:31:36 (3,927)
Allison, Jonathan M 6:20:24 (33,913)
Allison, Neil J 6:06:00 (33,050)
Allison, Richard J 3:25:36 (3,076)
Allison, Robert M 4:32:15 (16,620)
Allison, Tim 4:15:33 (12,450)
Alliston, Andrew J 4:31:26 (16,447)
Allitt, James D 4:31:33 (16,471)
Allitt, Paul F 4:45:38 (19,977)
Allmark, Terence V 4:23:21 (14,408)
Allpass, Samuel R 3:09:11 (1,485)
Allport, Trevor A 3:28:00 (3,407)
Allsop, Timothy K 3:03:00 (1,049)
Allsopp, Brian 5:28:06 (28,818)
Allsopp, Jonathan 4:23:09 (14,366)
Allton, Paul G 4:30:58 (16,347)
Allton, Roger A 4:58:10 (23,067)
Allum, Andrew M 3:54:56 (7,995)
Allum, John P 3:16:52 (2,165)
Allum, John W 6:37:29 (34,591)
Allum, Steve 5:28:13 (28,840)
Allward, Stuart J 6:03:37 (32,861)
Allwright, Sebastian K 5:16:41 (26,787)
Almeida, Alvaro 3:37:23 (4,730)
Almond, James W 3:49:40 (6,862)
Alquraishi, Assaf 5:31:19 (29,347)
Alred, Nigel M 4:22:44 (14,268)
Alsford, Benjamin J 4:07:21 (10,626)
Alsop, Doug A 3:26:51 (3,249)
Alston, Richard 3:28:12 (3,434)
Alston, Sean 4:42:45 (19,245)
Altenbach, Stefan 3:11:25 (1,664)
Altoft, Paul C 3:36:39 (4,634)
Alvarez, Humberto C 3:23:52 (2,888)
Amaral, Pedro G 3:16:36 (2,134)
Ambler, Ian J 4:24:25 (14,685)
Ambrose, Gary J 4:30:14 (16,202)

Ambrose, Keith J 5:46:55 (31,348)
Ambrosi, Luca 4:34:06 (17,050)
Ames, Ashley E 4:11:14 (11,433)
Ames, Ashley P 4:41:35 (18,944)
Ames, Mark L 4:03:30 (9,869)
Amin, Assad 3:39:23 (5,082)
Amin, Saj 5:45:42 (31,228)
Amin, Yashmit N 5:32:30 (29,525)
Amla, Ismail 4:51:13 (21,292)
Amoah, Richard 4:56:39 (22,679)
Amodei, Giuseppe 4:38:15 (18,068)
Amoore, James 5:02:29 (24,033)
Amooty, Brendan 3:55:59 (8,221)
Amor, Ross 4:27:26 (15,458)
Amore, Stefano 3:32:47 (4,102)
Amoretti, Federico 4:24:02 (14,580)
Amos, Kelvin J 3:16:08 (2,093)
Amos, Mark D 3:29:17 (3,614)
Amos, Martin C 4:37:11 (17,820)
Amos, Phil J 4:44:59 (19,833)
Amos, Simon 4:55:28 (22,386)
Amy, Thomas 3:42:22 (5,579)
Ancrum, Richard C 4:40:47 (18,728)
Anda, Prakash 6:01:41 (32,732)
Andersen, Jens Rambeck 3:36:48 (4,657)
Anderson, Alan T 4:53:23 (21,854)
Anderson, Alexander R 4:55:09 (22,305)
Anderson, Brian P 3:27:37 (3,364)
Anderson, Daniel J 2:46:33 (274)
Anderson, Dave R 4:27:48 (15,541)
Anderson, David K 3:57:02 (8,487)
Anderson, David R 5:14:22 (26,305)
Anderson, Dean M 5:46:08 (31,278)
Anderson, Derrick J 3:14:05 (1,902)
Anderson, Douglas E 3:41:40 (5,465)
Anderson, Ed 5:15:02 (26,464)
Anderson, Gavin 4:31:55 (16,549)
Anderson, Gavin S 3:57:58 (8,712)
Anderson, Graeme A 5:41:27 (30,762)
Anderson, Graham 3:30:32 (3,790)
Anderson, Graham M 3:06:28 (1,271)
Anderson, Ian S 2:47:25 (297)
Anderson, Jamie K 3:34:45 (4,368)
Anderson, Jamie R 2:56:52 (663)
Anderson, Jeffrey M 5:01:30 (23,829)
Anderson, John 4:05:37 (10,268)
Anderson, Kean J 3:10:46 (1,611)
Anderson, Kevin P 5:55:38 (32,204)
Anderson, Lee J 4:16:16 (12,639)
Anderson, Mark 5:14:17 (26,288)
Anderson, Mark R 3:12:14 (1,749)
Anderson, Neil F 4:57:44 (22,966)
Anderson, Neil R 3:49:46 (6,886)
Anderson, Nicholas 5:24:48 (28,238)
Anderson, Peter N 5:48:16 (31,502)
Anderson, Richard J 3:16:15 (2,099)
Anderson, Robbie E 4:06:14 (10,399)
Anderson, Simon P 3:18:15 (2,319)
Anderson, Stephen L 5:25:05 (28,286)
Anderson, Tony 5:06:54 (24,861)
Anderson, Victor 6:07:43 (33,146)
Anderson, Wayne J 5:23:07 (27,951)
Anderssen, Knut 4:34:29 (17,143)
Andersson, Christer L 4:29:30 (16,007)
Andersson, Goran 5:59:46 (32,563)
Andersson, Ulf 3:06:26 (1,268)
Anderton, James P 4:58:48 (23,206)
Anderton, Rupert J 4:32:16 (16,623)
Andrade, Luis M 5:49:57 (31,671)
Andre, Anthony L 6:39:06 (34,644)
Andreae-Jones, William P 4:51:59 (21,483)
Andreou, Andy 3:18:21 (2,330)
Andrew, Christopher P 4:43:21 (19,394)
Andrew, Darren M 3:54:04 (7,806)
Andrew, Kevin J 3:42:31 (5,599)

Andrew, Nick W 5:41:18 (30,740)
Andrew, Timothy M 4:33:31 (16,916)
Andrews, Benjamin C 3:35:26 (4,474)
Andrews, Christopher S 5:09:10 (25,306)
Andrews, David 4:35:15 (17,348)
Andrews, James P 4:17:57 (13,058)
Andrews, Jamie 4:19:34 (13,471)
Andrews, John 3:45:12 (6,052)
Andrews, John I 4:27:09 (15,366)
Andrews, John W 4:32:07 (16,584)
Andrews, Jon W 3:28:35 (3,502)
Andrews, Jonathan C 7:20:59 (35,396)
Andrews, Mark V 3:20:46 (2,584)
Andrews, Martin J 3:10:14 (1,582)
Andrews, Martin N 4:38:18 (18,093)
Andrews, Matthew R 4:35:22 (17,375)
Andrews, Michael A 5:05:24 (24,573)
Andrews, Michael J 5:29:09 (29,011)
Andrews, Oliver W 4:16:50 (12,770)
Andrews, Paul 6:24:36 (34,111)
Andrews, Paul J 3:40:17 (5,227)
Andrews, Philip 3:38:39 (4,949)
Andrews, Simon 4:48:19 (20,613)
Andrews, Stuart E 5:50:56 (31,766)
Andrews, Stuart G 4:08:26 (10,859)
Andrews, Thomas 4:44:46 (19,763)
Andrews, Thomas J 4:30:59 (16,349)
Andrietti, Sergio 4:50:07 (21,026)
Andrus, Mark 4:53:31 (21,892)
Angel, Anthony L 4:47:16 (20,347)
Angel, Jonathan A 5:07:17 (24,951)
Angel, Martin 4:03:03 (9,797)
Angel, Richard J 3:53:29 (7,683)
Angell, Phil 4:24:26 (14,691)
Angell, Robin B 5:19:07 (27,271)
Angelopoulos, Panos 3:40:14 (5,220)
Angelucci, Valerio 4:58:34 (23,163)
Angier, John B 3:48:26 (6,604)
Angilley, David 3:11:22 (1,660)
Anglem, Ryan A 4:21:36 (13,985)
Angove, Mark J 3:50:13 (6,977)
Angsund, Bjoern 4:16:14 (12,630)
Angus, Henry G 4:22:35 (14,224)
Anis, Hisham D 6:05:05 (32,970)
Anjomshoaa, Ali 3:45:55 (6,166)
Ankers, Stephen A 3:47:38 (6,460)
Annals, Marc J 5:09:31 (25,375)
Annarumma, Christian 3:47:03 (6,355)
Anne, Mickael 5:17:28 (26,951)
Anness, Richard 4:09:02 (10,956)
Annigoni, Franco 4:29:50 (16,101)
Ansah, Julian 4:55:53 (22,483)
Ansell, David V 4:54:55 (22,250)
Ansell, Gary J 3:54:14 (7,848)
Ansell, Martin J 4:19:34 (13,471)
Anstead, Matthew 3:53:58 (7,785)
Anstee, Nick J 4:18:01 (13,080)
Anstee, Nigel 5:14:53 (26,426)
Anthonio, Ernesto 4:21:36 (13,985)
Anthony, Ian J 3:11:57 (1,721)
Antolik, Bryan C 4:14:01 (12,101)
Antonelli, Roberto 5:11:14 (25,709)
Antonowicz, Daniel 4:24:50 (14,793)
Antony, Scott G 2:41:17 (160)
Antrobus, John 5:25:06 (28,289)
Anyangwe, Baron 5:09:41 (25,411)
Anzalichi, Said 5:09:25 (25,358)
Aparicio, Alejandro 2:59:54 (893)
Aparisi Insa, José Ignacio 4:41:07 (18,817)
Apperley, Hugh C 3:44:27 (5,933)
Appleby, Gary M 4:35:52 (17,502)
Appleby, Luke P 4:21:54 (14,066)
Appleby, Luke R 4:50:02 (21,003)
Appleby, Rod J 3:42:52 (5,661)
Appleby, Stephen J 5:17:12 (26,895)
Applegate, Jeffrey 4:14:21 (12,175)
Appleton, Ben 4:39:56 (18,520)
Appleton, Mark R 3:14:43 (1,962)
Appleton, Robert J 3:43:03 (5,698)
Appleton, Steven R 4:50:50 (21,200)
Applin, Kerry J 5:33:59 (29,756)
Apps, Dan 4:28:41 (15,781)
Apted, Brian G 5:23:54 (28,093)

LONDON MARATHON

Aquiliva, Christopher P 5:58:19 (32,445)
Arafa, Tariq M 5:14:18 (26,292)
Arago Martinez, Salvador D 3:57:50 (8,677)
Arawwawala, Dilshan 4:45:25 (19,927)
Arbour, Adrian J 3:30:05 (3,731)
Arcache, Alexander 3:19:12 (2,414)
Archell, Nicholas K 4:24:13 (14,634)
Archer, Andrew N 3:27:29 (3,353)
Archer, Michael 3:24:33 (2,964)
Archer, Nicholas J 5:33:28 (29,675)
Archer, Paul 4:50:21 (21,080)
Archibald, Andrew D 4:09:32 (11,080)
Archman, Philip A 4:58:26 (23,143)
Arckless, Neil J 4:28:54 (15,835)
Arendt, Mike 3:11:52 (1,711)
Aresvik, Lars 3:56:08 (8,259)
Arfield, David J 5:07:37 (25,023)
Argir, Thorbjorn 4:29:04 (15,875)
Argyle, Dennis C 3:40:02 (5,195)
Argyrou, Nicholas A 5:54:19 (32,082)
Arias, Pedro 4:25:22 (14,913)
Aries, Nick J 3:39:35 (5,121)
Arkill, Lloyd A 4:27:52 (15,556)
Arkinstall, Ivan P 4:11:25 (11,478)
Arleri, Carol 3:17:52 (2,268)
Arlett, Neil A 6:06:25 (33,078)
Armas, Segundo 3:18:44 (2,362)
Armella Sanchez, Sergio 4:00:57 (9,409)
Armist, Ronald 4:36:05 (17,553)
Armitage, Alex 3:33:02 (4,141)
Armitage, Michael R 4:33:46 (16,983)
Armitage, Neil 3:26:22 (3,182)
Armitage, Patrick A 4:22:48 (14,286)
Armitage, Richard G 4:34:25 (17,118)
Armitage, Steve L 4:13:01 (11,833)
Armstrong, Alasdair M 3:56:16 (8,290)
Armstrong, Alexander B 3:50:38 (7,062)
Armstrong, Allister J 4:22:45 (14,272)
Armstrong, Darren 5:11:43 (25,793)
Armstrong, John 4:11:27 (11,490)
Armstrong, John 4:18:13 (13,129)
Armstrong, Liam 5:21:45 (27,741)
Armstrong, Mark S 5:05:08 (24,532)
Armstrong, Martin J 5:35:07 (29,929)
Armstrong, Nigel J 2:53:19 (485)
Armstrong, Peter H 3:31:44 (3,944)
Armstrong, Robert J 3:12:24 (1,766)
Armstrong, Russell J 3:56:48 (8,431)
Armstrong, Simon P 4:48:38 (20,676)
Armstrong, Stephen 3:09:40 (1,530)
Armstrong, Thomas T 6:49:31 (34,920)
Arnell, Ian J 4:24:57 (14,814)
Arnell, Nicholas C 5:23:54 (28,093)
Arnold, Adrian T 4:24:44 (14,756)
Arnold, Andy 3:51:17 (7,200)
Arnold, Benjamin 3:50:02 (6,951)
Arnold, Christopher 4:01:34 (9,529)
Arnold, Darren J 5:43:05 (30,944)
Arnold, Daryl L 3:30:19 (3,767)
Arnold, James 5:09:38 (25,400)
Arnold, John A 6:02:35 (32,790)
Arnold, Mark 4:08:12 (10,811)
Arnold, Mark J 3:42:15 (5,561)
Arnold, Martin A 5:06:46 (24,837)
Arnold, Phillip J 5:30:11 (29,174)
Arnold, Richard E 6:37:08 (34,585)
Arnold, Roland A 4:13:57 (12,084)
Arnold, Tom J 6:02:17 (32,770)
Arnold, William M 4:16:21 (12,660)
Arnott, Gary 4:17:20 (12,887)
Arnott, Richard 5:38:55 (30,443)
Arnott, Stephen D 5:50:09 (31,685)
Arnott, Tom 4:12:14 (11,666)
Arpaia, Gabriel 3:45:15 (6,056)
Arrachart, Didier 5:17:32 (26,964)
Arrowsmith, Leslie 4:39:54 (18,508)
Arrowsmith, Mark A 3:21:38 (2,667)
Arrowsmith, Paul M 3:58:03 (8,735)
Arrowsmith, Timothy J 4:52:15 (21,556)
Arshad, Shahzad 6:14:20 (33,571)
Artes Garcia, Manuel 3:36:24 (4,602)
Arthur, Antony 4:12:09 (11,644)
Arthur, David 4:06:11 (10,390)
Arthur, Huw W 3:43:35 (5,797)
Arthur, John 4:18:20 (13,159)
Arthur, Steven P 4:24:40 (14,739)
Arthurton, Anthony W 4:25:15 (14,884)
Artis, Daniel J 4:59:31 (23,390)
Artus, Tim 2:47:51 (305)
Arufe, Mario 3:34:16 (4,309)
Arundel, Michael J 4:27:57 (15,571)
Arup, Jan 5:20:18 (27,477)
Arup, Martin 4:38:18 (18,093)
Asante, Christen J 5:23:02 (27,941)
Ash, Adrian R 4:54:50 (22,234)
Ash, David 6:04:35 (32,923)
Ash, Graeme C 4:33:18 (16,867)
Ash, Hayley E 5:26:23 (28,529)
Ash, Martin 5:48:31 (31,524)
Ash, Matthew J 5:11:52 (25,827)
Ash, Samuel 5:57:41 (32,382)
Ashby, Antony S 4:00:12 (9,250)
Ashby, Ben C 4:07:38 (10,686)
Ashby, Charles E 3:11:57 (1,721)
Ashby, Gerald 5:27:48 (28,761)
Ashby, James 3:27:47 (3,385)
Ashby, Jonathan 4:46:19 (20,130)
Ashby, Mark 3:00:01 (901)
Ashby, Mike J 3:29:57 (3,709)
Ashby, Thomas S 3:49:37 (6,854)
Ashcroft, Benjamin J 3:25:46 (3,097)
Ashcroft, Derek 3:19:59 (2,493)
Ashcroft, Neil H 2:56:30 (633)
Ashcroft, Paul S 4:17:55 (13,047)
Ashdown, Jeremy C 4:55:23 (22,361)
Ashdown, Piers R 4:37:31 (17,892)
Ashdown, Roger W 5:46:03 (31,266)
Ashe, Richard 2:49:47 (368)
Asher, Darren G 4:57:12 (22,821)
Asher, Stephen A 5:54:23 (32,095)
Ashford, Damien 5:17:20 (26,925)
Ashford, Justin M 4:53:43 (21,948)
Ashforth, Alan 3:18:30 (2,343)
Ashington, Michael S 4:43:18 (19,372)
Ashley, Ian 4:26:39 (15,223)
Ashley, Jonathan M 6:32:30 (34,424)
Ashley, Philip J 4:15:45 (12,495)
Ashley, Stephen R 4:46:30 (20,178)
Ashley, Tiernan A 5:13:45 (26,178)
Ashman, Alvin M 4:59:08 (23,295)
Ashman, Joe 3:39:41 (5,141)
Ashman, Rod J 5:03:59 (24,322)
Ashmead, Gareth 3:17:50 (2,265)
Ashment, Mathew 4:42:20 (19,129)
Ashmore, Lee J 6:11:06 (33,377)
Ashmore, Mark A 4:40:58 (18,777)
Ashmore, Terry C 4:18:32 (13,221)
Ashmore-Short, Benedick 3:44:35 (5,955)
Ashraf, Muhammad 4:03:57 (9,958)
Ashraf, Shahbaz 4:23:54 (14,544)
Ashrafi, Reza 3:37:26 (4,741)
Ashton, Alan 2:56:38 (648)
Ashton, Alan G 3:15:10 (2,010)
Ashton, John 3:42:06 (5,538)
Ashton, Kevin R 5:21:33 (27,701)
Ashton, Michael J 5:27:53 (28,776)
Ashton, Neil K 3:19:32 (2,437)
Ashton, Nigel P 4:19:46 (13,532)
Ashton, Stephen J 5:05:44 (24,642)
Ashwell, Simon M 4:39:13 (18,340)
Ashwood, Keith E 3:48:24 (6,595)
Ashworth, Chris 3:58:47 (8,906)
Ashworth, Edward 6:04:54 (32,950)
Ashworth, Mike 5:46:39 (31,324)
Ashworth, Tom W 4:23:44 (14,497)
Asiedu, Eric 4:27:33 (15,477)
Askew, David 4:39:30 (18,415)
Askew, Michael J 4:06:21 (10,423)
Askew, Philip M 4:21:41 (13,999)
Askey, Michael 4:39:00 (18,283)
Askildsen, Morthen 4:00:03 (9,216)
Aslam, Qasir 4:51:13 (21,292)
Aspell, Andrew D 5:31:21 (29,351)
Aspenstrom, Pontus 4:06:26 (10,450)
Aspin, Chris J 4:47:57 (20,520)
Aspin, James 3:03:10 (1,058)
Aspinall, Aaron J 3:34:30 (4,340)
Aspinall, Nathan E 2:53:12 (477)
Aspland, Jason R 3:38:36 (4,939)
Asplin, Robert A 5:01:53 (23,909)
Asser, Jeffrey D 3:11:22 (1,660)
Asser, Mihir 6:59:42 (35,121)
Ast, Gregoire 3:35:24 (4,470)
Astaire, Daniel P 4:21:27 (13,952)
Astbury, Daniel 4:14:41 (12,253)
Asten, Mark 4:43:06 (19,318)
Astephen, John 3:53:37 (7,709)
Astesiano, Marco 3:56:05 (8,244)
Astin, Russell J 6:11:00 (33,368)
Astle, Paul 4:32:15 (16,620)
Astle, Thomas W 3:13:29 (1,862)
Astley, Richard T 3:26:39 (3,216)
Astley, Robert 4:05:57 (10,342)
Aston, Andrew 2:59:09 (837)
Aston, Jeffrey R 4:25:01 (14,829)
Aston, John 3:29:14 (3,607)
Aston, Peter E 4:30:12 (16,196)
Aston, Peter G 4:30:28 (16,250)
Aston O'Donovan, Marc A 3:46:45 (6,291)
Astridge, Andrew W 7:04:56 (35,203)
Athanas, Jim 5:33:10 (29,629)
Atherton, John L 4:17:02 (12,822)
Atherton, Joseph J 4:45:53 (20,029)
Athreya, Kannan 4:02:41 (9,725)
Atkin, Paul C 5:10:05 (25,501)
Atkins, Andrew K 3:26:01 (3,131)
Atkins, Barry L 3:07:58 (1,385)
Atkins, Benjamin 2:39:18 (129)
Atkins, Danny 4:23:17 (14,397)
Atkins, David J 4:05:58 (10,348)
Atkins, Jimmy A 4:02:49 (9,757)
Atkins, Michael J 4:38:52 (18,246)
Atkins, Richard D 3:27:41 (3,370)
Atkins, Stephen L 4:31:22 (16,438)
Atkins, Steve W 4:07:45 (10,712)
Atkins, Steven L 5:27:14 (28,669)
Atkins, Ted R 4:42:10 (19,082)
Atkinson, Alexis L 3:44:52 (6,004)
Atkinson, Christopher J 3:25:06 (3,030)
Atkinson, David 3:19:48 (2,466)
Atkinson, David J 4:05:22 (10,212)
Atkinson, Gary J 3:19:54 (2,479)
Atkinson, Ian 3:44:31 (5,945)
Atkinson, Ian C 4:48:43 (20,700)
Atkinson, Ian J 4:41:25 (18,896)
Atkinson, John 2:56:01 (610)
Atkinson, John M 3:48:26 (6,604)
Atkinson, Lee J 4:51:15 (21,298)
Atkinson, Neil 5:29:08 (29,005)
Atkinson, Paul S 5:04:56 (24,506)
Atkinson, Peter A 4:42:23 (19,146)
Atkins-Smith, Andy 5:14:08 (26,253)
A'ts, Laszlo 4:00:49 (9,378)
Attanayake, Julian R 5:07:29 (24,995)
Attar-Zadeh, Darush 5:47:00 (31,355)
Attenborough, Mark 4:27:36 (15,491)
Atter, Darren L 3:21:06 (2,615)
Attewell, Gary 4:04:09 (9,994)
Attlee, Rupert J 4:54:07 (22,048)
Attram, Isaac M 5:54:05 (32,060)
Attridge, Joseph 3:46:59 (6,342)
Attwood, Howard M 4:39:23 (18,388)
Attwood, Mark J 4:43:40 (19,456)
Attwood, Tom 4:05:34 (10,256)
Atwa Mansour, Mohamed H 4:48:08 (20,560)
Atwal, Kulwant S 4:01:48 (9,568)
Atwal, Sarvjit S 4:01:47 (9,564)
Atwell, Christopher 3:29:14 (3,607)
Atwell, Harry J 5:35:49 (30,025)
Audas, Allen J 3:22:59 (2,794)
Auden, Edward G 3:11:58 (1,724)
Auden, Thomas W 3:11:58 (1,724)
Audenshaw, Tony 3:15:04 (2,003)
Audouin, Jacky 3:31:27 (3,898)
Aufenacker, Jan C 4:38:21 (18,113)
Auger, Eric 3:25:06 (3,030)
Aujla, Jagdeep S 5:48:03 (31,472)
Aukett, John 4:40:29 (18,654)
Auld, Alan A 3:09:29 (1,515)

Aumeeruddy, Altaff	5:39:42 (30,558)
Austen, William S	4:12:25 (11,705)
Austin, Andrew N	4:01:08 (9,444)
Austin, Christopher	3:47:41 (6,473)
Austin, Clive	3:50:57 (7,127)
Austin, Daniel	5:12:57 (26,033)
Austin, David A	4:26:53 (15,288)
Austin, David J	4:42:24 (19,152)
Austin, Dean	3:54:03 (7,803)
Austin, Malcolm D	5:08:32 (25,193)
Austin, Matthew E	4:43:41 (19,459)
Austin, Melvyn R	4:36:32 (17,677)
Austin, Michael B	4:40:33 (18,666)
Austin, Nicholas J	3:21:30 (2,650)
Austin, Richard	4:36:25 (17,644)
Austin, Russell J	4:35:45 (17,473)
Autenried, Roger	3:41:21 (5,418)
Autie, Sam J	5:27:33 (28,719)
Autin, Christian	4:25:39 (14,985)
Avanzi, Rolando	3:38:07 (4,857)
Avara, Oner	3:51:58 (7,359)
Avenell, Garry	3:03:51 (1,097)
Avery, Joe A	5:52:36 (31,927)
Avery, Mike A	4:55:21 (22,349)
Avery, Paul J	4:53:54 (21,991)
Avery, Thomas P	3:22:04 (2,711)
Aves, Clayton A	3:15:29 (2,028)
Aveyard, Carl	3:44:56 (6,017)
Avigad, Daniel	3:23:56 (2,898)
Avignon, Lionel T	3:42:37 (5,611)
Aviles, Elias Z	3:46:31 (6,249)
Avitabile, Alfredo	4:10:34 (11,283)
Awadzi, Albert A	6:38:44 (34,627)
Awcock, Colin S	4:32:40 (16,709)
Awofolaju, Tunde	4:50:47 (21,189)
Axellod, David	5:18:56 (27,239)
Axon, Terry	4:18:15 (13,135)
Axon, Tim E	3:53:33 (7,698)
Aylen, Joseph	4:04:13 (10,010)
Ayles, Duncan M	4:40:34 (18,673)
Ayling, Terry J	3:47:30 (6,424)
Aylmore, James R	3:16:36 (2,134)
Aylott, Michael C	3:29:39 (3,669)
Ayo, James D	4:18:24 (13,174)
Ayres, Alan	3:09:20 (1,503)
Ayres, Dean	6:09:17 (33,253)
Ayres, Paul A	3:23:52 (2,888)
Ayres, Richard J	4:27:57 (15,571)
Ayres, Tim F	3:28:46 (3,534)
Ayres, William H	4:18:56 (13,314)
Ayrton, David R	4:25:58 (15,049)
Ayscough, Matt C	3:48:58 (6,723)
Azad, Iqbal S	4:14:48 (12,271)
Azevedo, Luis	4:17:33 (12,961)
Aziz, Paul I	4:31:40 (16,500)
Aziz, Yasin M	4:36:25 (17,644)
Baardsen, Audun	2:44:57 (238)
Babaian, Nicholas	4:14:03 (12,112)
Babar, Rehan	5:48:35 (31,531)
Babb, Steve M	3:00:54 (952)
Babbage, Stuart D	4:21:42 (14,003)
Babe, Colin J	5:31:12 (29,335)
Baber, Guy F	4:05:02 (10,150)
Babington, Duncan	3:51:29 (7,250)
Babu, Dal	5:12:28 (25,948)
Bacchiavini, Alessandro	4:00:56 (9,405)
Bach, François	4:07:49 (10,730)
Bach, Paul F	4:52:03 (21,499)
Bachra, Surtar S	4:22:32 (14,213)
Bachu, Abdalla	4:11:53 (11,588)
Baci, Arber	2:47:23 (296)
Back, Adam R	4:44:24 (19,649)
Backhouse, John S	4:17:45 (13,010)
Backstrand, Tommy	7:03:21 (35,179)
Bacon, James W	4:14:59 (12,318)
Bacon, Lee	5:35:33 (29,984)
Bacon, Martin S	3:05:40 (1,213)
Bacon, Neil C	4:26:06 (15,074)
Bacon, Robert A	4:38:40 (18,188)
Bacon, Russell G	5:46:06 (31,272)
Badcock, David B	4:29:43 (16,064)
Badcock, Fraser O	4:51:58 (21,477)
Badenoch, Patrick R	4:36:51 (17,754)

Bader, Brett S	8:01:54 (35,641)
Bader, Ronald	4:22:43 (14,264)
Badgen, Steven	4:06:07 (10,376)
Badr, Ishmail	3:09:11 (1,485)
Badzek, Karl	4:38:52 (18,246)
Baerwald, Oliver	4:39:01 (18,288)
Baga, Satvinder	6:19:42 (33,878)
Bagan, Ryan M	4:34:50 (17,234)
Bagdady, Lee	5:19:27 (27,327)
Bage, Steven	3:52:58 (7,557)
Baggaley, Clive R	3:24:39 (2,977)
Bagge, Per	3:58:29 (8,838)
Baggs, Stewart A	4:20:47 (13,792)
Bagha, Sanjay	5:39:25 (30,510)
Baghino, Alessandro	5:04:27 (24,411)
Baghino, Stefano	2:50:23 (385)
Baglin, David	3:50:39 (7,066)
Bagnall, Gary B	3:03:48 (1,093)
Bagnoli, Nicola	3:24:37 (2,972)
Bagshaw, Stephen J	4:35:13 (17,338)
Baguley, Paul A	3:41:08 (5,387)
Baig, Nasir	5:20:27 (27,504)
Baik, Kwang Hyun	4:11:32 (11,508)
Baile, James N	4:43:21 (19,394)
Bailes, Lindsay	4:26:08 (15,081)
Bailey, Adam	4:58:22 (23,124)
Bailey, Alan	3:34:33 (4,348)
Bailey, Alyn H	5:18:52 (27,226)
Bailey, Benjamin J	3:52:47 (7,520)
Bailey, Cliff P	2:57:07 (683)
Bailey, David M	4:32:59 (16,780)
Bailey, George P	4:35:43 (17,463)
Bailey, Guy C	4:37:46 (17,951)
Bailey, Guy M	4:04:29 (10,054)
Bailey, Howard	4:18:42 (13,264)
Bailey, Ian M	4:52:28 (21,609)
Bailey, Jason D	3:59:49 (9,166)
Bailey, Mark J	4:44:29 (19,677)
Bailey, Martyn R	4:21:14 (13,901)
Bailey, Michael G	5:10:00 (25,477)
Bailey, Nicholas M	5:12:59 (26,046)
Bailey, Nick G	5:07:37 (25,023)
Bailey, Paul A	4:21:26 (13,947)
Bailey, Philip	5:28:53 (28,963)
Bailey, Richard C	4:14:25 (12,192)
Bailey, Richard J	4:21:29 (13,963)
Bailey, Richard P	4:29:11 (15,906)
Bailey, Robert	4:26:01 (15,061)
Bailey, Roydon C	5:04:31 (24,422)
Bailey, Russell J	5:10:49 (25,630)
Bailey, Steven R	5:15:16 (26,518)
Bailey, Stuart G	4:33:00 (16,785)
Bailey, Stuart M	4:38:36 (18,177)
Bailey, Terence	4:13:26 (11,944)
Bailey, Thomas W	5:08:21 (25,162)
Bailey, Tim	5:59:05 (32,516)
Bailey, Toby	3:56:49 (8,435)
Baillie, Doug A	4:24:18 (14,654)
Baillie, Robert P	4:31:01 (16,357)
Baily, Alexander M	4:09:42 (11,116)
Bain, Fraser D	4:50:19 (21,070)
Bain, John	4:04:30 (10,057)
Bainbridge, Daniel J	4:21:58 (14,080)
Bainbridge, Michael J	2:58:22 (777)
Bainbridge, Paul	5:18:22 (27,140)
Bainbridge, Steven R	4:08:01 (10,769)
Bainbridge, Thomas	3:52:01 (7,366)
Baines, Charles H	5:34:34 (29,859)
Baines, Michael	4:00:49 (9,378)
Baines, Robert	4:44:29 (19,677)
Bainger, Graham E	4:06:24 (10,439)
Bains, Shamsher S	4:51:51 (21,453)
Bains, Yijaypal S	6:20:30 (33,921)
Baird, Julian M	4:24:22 (14,669)
Bajaj, Robert	6:56:04 (35,053)
Baker, Andrew	6:05:57 (33,041)
Baker, Andy	5:46:54 (31,344)
Baker, Anthony	3:36:30 (4,609)
Baker, Brendan P	3:42:48 (5,648)
Baker, Carl	3:12:39 (1,792)
Baker, Charles J	4:51:47 (21,434)
Baker, Christopher	4:08:29 (10,868)
Baker, Christopher C	3:34:26 (4,334)

Baker, Christopher T	4:07:00 (10,575)
Baker, Cliff J	5:10:36 (25,594)
Baker, Daniel	4:26:19 (15,136)
Baker, Daniel	4:33:46 (16,983)
Baker, Daniel D	5:17:48 (27,011)
Baker, Darren	4:54:34 (22,158)
Baker, Duncan N	3:28:45 (3,531)
Baker, Eamon	3:58:00 (8,725)
Baker, Frank J	4:39:27 (18,404)
Baker, Gary J	4:25:25 (14,930)
Baker, Gary P	3:17:06 (2,190)
Baker, George A	5:47:07 (31,361)
Baker, Graham	3:12:31 (1,778)
Baker, Hugh	6:45:49 (34,822)
Baker, Ian D	4:07:53 (10,742)
Baker, James E	5:23:00 (27,939)
Baker, Jason	4:32:07 (16,584)
Baker, Jof M	6:28:46 (34,274)
Baker, John B	4:01:37 (9,538)
Baker, Jon M	4:46:19 (20,130)
Baker, Jonathan A	4:09:33 (11,085)
Baker, Julian D	2:31:49 (49)
Baker, Karl G	4:46:15 (20,115)
Baker, Kevin N	5:05:52 (24,666)
Baker, Lee W	6:17:23 (33,742)
Baker, Leon A	3:39:59 (5,185)
Baker, Mark D	5:06:41 (24,811)
Baker, Mark E	3:26:58 (3,272)
Baker, Mark H	4:09:32 (11,080)
Baker, Mark J	4:15:40 (12,478)
Baker, Mark S	3:21:28 (2,646)
Baker, Martin	4:15:13 (12,397)
Baker, Martin G	4:38:29 (18,146)
Baker, Matthew R	4:35:04 (17,288)
Baker, Michael A	3:48:13 (6,565)
Baker, Michael G	4:30:05 (16,170)
Baker, Neil	5:38:09 (30,325)
Baker, Nick	3:34:19 (4,318)
Baker, Nick M	2:39:21 (132)
Baker, Paul E	4:23:31 (14,451)
Baker, Philip J	4:42:09 (19,076)
Baker, Richard J	3:40:15 (5,225)
Baker, Roger E	3:31:01 (3,840)
Baker, Ross D	3:54:21 (7,877)
Baker, Simon	4:27:39 (15,501)
Baker, Simon B	5:15:59 (26,654)
Baker, Stephen B	5:43:48 (31,022)
Baker, Stuart	5:32:23 (29,507)
Baker, Trevor D	5:09:24 (25,353)
Baker, Wayne W	5:13:23 (26,096)
Bakker, Holger	4:30:01 (16,151)
Bakker, Peter	4:27:39 (15,501)
Balaam, Laurence R	5:32:31 (29,533)
Balaam, Simon R	4:25:30 (14,945)
Balakrishna, Rangappa	4:23:49 (14,518)
Balan, Mihai D	4:13:39 (12,007)
Balard, Patrice	2:44:26 (226)
Balcer, Matthew A	3:54:52 (7,978)
Balcombe, Sebastian	4:01:30 (9,515)
Balconi, Carlo	4:40:39 (18,687)
Balding, Terry S	4:50:31 (21,129)
Baldock, Andrew R	4:23:16 (14,393)
Baldock, Michael J	3:41:50 (5,491)
Baldry, Jon	3:46:34 (6,263)
Baldwin, Anthony M	5:39:58 (30,584)
Baldwin, David M	5:43:10 (30,957)
Baldwin, Elwyn	3:08:01 (1,392)
Baldwin, Nick P	6:00:53 (32,657)
Baldwin, Peter S	5:17:25 (26,943)
Bale, Mons	2:49:28 (358)
Bale, Simon M	3:01:20 (977)
Balfour, James J	5:56:57 (32,329)
Balfour, James M	4:20:32 (13,738)
Balfour, Robbie C	5:16:18 (26,722)
Ball, Adrian P	4:38:06 (18,040)
Ball, Andrew	3:14:05 (1,902)
Ball, Andrew J	4:04:33 (10,067)
Ball, Christopher	5:58:12 (32,433)
Ball, David S	3:25:59 (3,123)
Ball, Douglas	6:22:44 (34,035)
Ball, Gary M	4:38:06 (18,040)
Ball, Graham	3:01:28 (983)
Ball, James	4:34:44 (17,211)

Ball, Justin....4:45:49 (20,010)
Ball, Kevin J....4:23:56 (14,549)
Ball, Kristopher W....6:10:07 (33,313)
Ball, Martin D....2:49:10 (351)
Ball, Michael C....5:39:43 (30,560)
Ball, Nicholas T....3:28:55 (3,561)
Ball, Peter....4:47:14 (20,340)
Ball, Richard....5:23:28 (28,004)
Ball, Richard L....7:12:55 (35,320)
Ball, Stanley....6:12:31 (33,461)
Ball, Stephen....4:21:43 (14,009)
Ballam, Paul A....4:36:40 (17,708)
Ballantine, Guy H....4:13:33 (11,984)
Ballantyne, David F....3:21:11 (2,622)
Ballantyne, Stephen J....4:13:14 (11,889)
Ballard, Christian....4:55:55 (22,493)
Ballard, David J....3:33:54 (4,254)
Ballard, Richard T....5:44:26 (31,085)
Ballen, Lee R....3:58:53 (8,938)
Ballinger, Mike E....5:19:08 (27,276)
Ballsdon, Edward J....4:19:36 (13,486)
Baltzer, Daniel....6:08:32 (33,206)
Bamber, Richard W....5:31:48 (29,419)
Bamford, Alex T....4:02:19 (9,671)
Bamford, Robert W....3:55:08 (8,039)
Bamlett, Richard A....5:14:17 (26,288)
Bampton, Nick K....4:58:16 (23,093)
Bampton, Richard J....4:05:39 (10,277)
Bamsey, Philip L....3:29:37 (3,663)
Banani, Dinesh D....4:18:45 (13,276)
Bance, Elliott J....5:06:11 (24,734)
Bancroft, Andrew J....3:49:56 (6,923)
Bancroft, Greg H....4:31:49 (16,530)
Bandharangshi, Prateep....5:20:57 (27,598)
Banerji, Udai B....6:16:17 (33,702)
Banfi, Paolo....3:51:44 (7,303)
Banfield, Alistair....3:52:09 (7,400)
Banfield, Simon R....3:09:37 (1,524)
Bangani, Pumlani....2:28:26 (31)
Bangert, Neil A....4:09:00 (10,949)
Banham, Joseph....4:27:02 (15,331)
Banin, Daniel....4:44:45 (19,758)
Banks, Adrian....5:19:29 (27,334)
Banks, Davey R....4:14:56 (12,306)
Banks, David....4:35:01 (17,278)
Banks, Martin P....4:14:37 (12,235)
Banks, Scott A....4:16:38 (12,723)
Banks, Stephen....3:48:01 (6,529)
Banner, Charles E....3:24:02 (2,909)
Bannerman, Keith....4:31:28 (16,457)
Bannerman, Lee J....3:44:04 (5,875)
Bannister, Joseph R....4:49:45 (20,943)
Bannister, Mark H....5:21:20 (27,663)
Bannon, Damian J....5:23:46 (28,071)
Bannon, Mark....5:31:26 (29,371)
Bansal, Jitendra....5:22:20 (27,825)
Bansal, Ravi S....5:49:41 (31,647)
Bansal, Vikrant....3:09:04 (1,472)
Bant, Phil J....4:15:08 (12,351)
Bantin, Laurie A....3:13:18 (1,852)
Banwell, Christopher....5:26:39 (28,566)
Bara, Philippe....3:40:27 (5,253)
Barazzuol, Angelo....5:29:51 (29,114)
Barbed, Felipe....2:48:02 (310)
Barber, Allan J....4:26:11 (15,091)
Barber, Christopher W....4:43:34 (19,434)
Barber, Daniel....3:16:51 (2,164)
Barber, Doug L....5:15:42 (26,602)
Barber, Ian B....3:52:58 (7,557)
Barber, Ian J....2:59:47 (884)
Barber, Ian M....3:51:09 (7,171)
Barber, Jon....4:57:55 (23,012)
Barber, Leon....5:15:09 (26,490)
Barber, Nick....4:11:27 (11,490)
Barber, Paul J....5:25:50 (28,431)
Barber, Richard P....5:38:31 (30,384)
Barberye, Philippe....3:53:49 (7,746)
Barbet, Andy J....6:44:32 (34,790)
Barbieri, Giancarlo....3:38:50 (4,983)
Barbosa, Rodrigo C....3:03:20 (1,066)
Barbour, Dave....4:17:44 (13,006)
Barbour, Richard N....4:28:35 (15,754)
Barclay, David....4:29:48 (16,090)
Bardell, Daniel J....4:28:38 (15,768)
Barden, David S....4:14:37 (12,235)
Barden, Stefan....4:06:40 (10,494)
Barder, Owen....3:04:09 (1,109)
Bardon, Richard B....3:15:37 (2,040)
Bardou, Laurent....4:51:13 (21,292)
Bardsley, Adam....2:59:42 (878)
Bareham, Nicholas J....5:17:57 (27,041)
Baren, David J....4:16:24 (12,670)
Barfield, Mark J....4:11:36 (11,527)
Barfield, Richard T....4:04:16 (10,017)
Barfoot, Anthony I....3:59:05 (8,981)
Barge, Alistair D....4:36:43 (17,718)
Baricsa, Janos....3:17:07 (2,192)
Bark, Nick S....4:02:08 (9,626)
Bark, Peter G....4:46:26 (20,164)
Barker, Adam J....4:04:05 (9,983)
Barker, Benjamin D....4:06:04 (10,364)
Barker, Daniel K....6:24:04 (34,083)
Barker, David....3:07:28 (1,347)
Barker, Douglas M....4:54:47 (22,223)
Barker, Edward....3:26:40 (3,217)
Barker, Ernest....4:40:46 (18,722)
Barker, Fredrick....5:39:41 (30,555)
Barker, Gavin....4:48:36 (20,669)
Barker, John H....4:00:10 (9,242)
Barker, Jonathan A....4:09:09 (10,993)
Barker, Keith M....6:09:20 (33,258)
Barker, Lee A....3:57:11 (8,520)
Barker, Matt J....5:14:41 (26,379)
Barker, Michael W....3:26:55 (3,261)
Barker, Nicholas J....5:12:09 (25,888)
Barker, Paul....6:15:55 (33,678)
Barker, Stuart C....4:40:24 (18,632)
Barker, Tim M....4:07:26 (10,641)
Barkhuysen, Rodney P....3:36:09 (4,565)
Barkley, Peter J....3:53:24 (7,668)
Barksby, Keith....6:12:51 (33,482)
Barla, Luigi....4:25:49 (15,022)
Barley, Allan C....6:11:17 (33,391)
Barley, Clive....5:23:04 (27,945)
Barley, David P....4:25:46 (15,009)
Barley, Kevin....4:45:59 (20,059)
Barley, Paul J....4:49:39 (20,926)
Barley, Richard....3:59:02 (8,965)
Barlow, Chris....4:43:13 (19,343)
Barlow, Kevin W....3:11:11 (1,646)
Barlow, Neil....4:05:26 (10,228)
Barlow, Peter....3:10:45 (1,610)
Barlow, Stephen J....4:23:43 (14,493)
Barlow, Stephen T....3:23:27 (2,848)
Barnard, Adrian J....5:21:24 (27,680)
Barnard, Daniel G....5:24:45 (28,230)
Barnard, Daniel T....4:55:27 (22,377)
Barnard, Neil A....3:57:37 (8,629)
Barne, John D....3:28:48 (3,539)
Barnes, Adrian....3:54:35 (7,917)
Barnes, Alan P....2:42:48 (194)
Barnes, Andrew R....4:52:15 (21,556)
Barnes, Andy G....3:05:55 (1,229)
Barnes, Anthony J....5:30:27 (29,210)
Barnes, Chris J....4:33:56 (17,016)
Barnes, Daryl A....5:38:15 (30,342)
Barnes, David G....3:08:27 (1,428)
Barnes, David M....5:53:52 (32,041)
Barnes, Garry R....5:20:08 (27,444)
Barnes, Gary J....4:14:16 (12,157)
Barnes, James R....3:36:29 (4,608)
Barnes, Max....4:45:28 (19,938)
Barnes, Michael D....4:41:26 (18,901)
Barnes, Nick....4:55:26 (22,372)
Barnes, Nigel....4:18:21 (13,163)
Barnes, Paul A....3:05:20 (1,186)
Barnes, Rob W....4:59:57 (23,490)
Barnes, Robert B....4:38:18 (18,093)
Barnes, Simon A....4:45:48 (20,007)
Barnes, Simon P....2:56:44 (654)
Barnes-Smith, Martin J....3:16:45 (2,152)
Barnett, Christopher J....5:26:45 (28,585)
Barnett, David J....3:36:38 (4,632)
Barnett, Gary R....5:00:19 (23,581)
Barnett, James M....3:54:50 (7,970)
Barnett, Jonathan....5:21:08 (27,621)
Barnett, Michael W....6:05:32 (33,008)
Barnett, Nick....4:04:34 (10,071)
Barnett, Simon J....3:37:26 (4,741)
Barnett, Tony P....5:04:21 (24,390)
Barningham, Richard A....5:12:12 (25,897)
Barnsley, Paul P....4:17:33 (12,961)
Barnwell, Leigh C....5:35:33 (29,984)
Baro, Soulemane....4:08:02 (10,774)
Baron, Andrew D....4:19:09 (13,367)
Baron, Gerald J....4:00:03 (9,216)
Baron, John R....5:08:55 (25,266)
Barr, Dave A....3:54:18 (7,872)
Barr, David....3:54:13 (7,843)
Barr, David M....3:38:00 (4,830)
Barr, Jonathan D....5:13:38 (26,146)
Barr, Robert D....3:51:13 (7,191)
Barr, Tom....3:40:29 (5,261)
Barraclough, Clive A....3:44:50 (5,997)
Barraclough, Ian D....4:16:44 (12,748)
Barraclough, Richard M....3:51:45 (7,305)
Barrance, Tony R....5:26:20 (28,516)
Barrantes, Francisco V....3:31:31 (3,914)
Barrass, Daniel J....5:00:51 (23,696)
Barratt, Daniel D....5:43:41 (31,013)
Barratt, Ian R....5:24:10 (28,134)
Barratt, Lee....3:14:53 (1,978)
Barratt, Nick....4:47:49 (20,482)
Barratt, Nick....4:54:12 (22,079)
Barratt, Richard J....3:43:18 (5,739)
Barreiros, Custodio M....5:41:12 (30,728)
Barrell, Justin J....4:37:39 (17,922)
Barrena, Luis S....3:15:28 (2,027)
Barrenger, Leigh R....3:28:31 (3,490)
Barrett, Alan....3:49:42 (6,872)
Barrett, Antony....4:55:49 (22,461)
Barrett, Clayton N....2:52:13 (452)
Barrett, Craig A....4:13:26 (11,944)
Barrett, George G....4:53:41 (21,937)
Barrett, Gorodn D....3:10:35 (1,600)
Barrett, Ian....3:53:55 (7,769)
Barrett, James M....5:20:30 (27,517)
Barrett, James P....4:42:10 (19,082)
Barrett, John C....5:01:58 (23,929)
Barrett, Matt J....4:34:37 (17,181)
Barrett, Matthew....5:34:52 (29,896)
Barrett, Michael....4:35:11 (17,323)
Barrett, Michael P....5:57:09 (32,345)
Barrett, Mike....7:29:26 (35,485)
Barrett, Paul A....5:37:40 (30,257)
Barrett, Roger K....4:21:55 (14,069)
Barrett, Simon J....2:46:25 (270)
Barrett, Simon P....4:41:42 (18,966)
Barrett, Stephen J....3:35:08 (4,427)
Barretta, José A....3:07:45 (1,367)
Barrie, Martin J....4:22:45 (14,272)
Barritt, Robert J....4:08:25 (10,856)
Barron, Gavin M....6:13:22 (33,511)
Barron, George....3:18:19 (2,328)
Barron, James....3:58:14 (8,772)
Barron, Kevin J....5:16:47 (26,802)
Barron, Mark....4:38:33 (18,163)
Barron, Russell L....2:58:25 (782)
Barron, Shawn N....3:41:10 (5,390)
Barrow, Julian....3:39:06 (5,033)
Barrow, Paul J....4:04:19 (10,028)
Barrow, Peter M....4:34:21 (17,104)
Barrowman, Michael S....3:51:38 (7,283)
Barry, Andrew J....3:20:38 (2,570)
Barry, Brian A....3:48:25 (6,598)
Barry, Caswell J....4:27:44 (15,529)
Barry, Cornelius....3:56:08 (8,259)
Barry, John G....4:03:31 (9,873)
Barry, Joseph....4:57:10 (22,811)
Barry, Steven....3:44:25 (5,926)
Barsby, Paul S....5:13:50 (26,197)
Barsdell, David J....4:55:15 (22,331)
Bartell, Martin....5:05:03 (24,520)
Bartholomew, Adam T....5:09:47 (25,431)
Bartholomew, David....5:04:21 (24,390)
Bartholomew, Peter S....4:23:51 (14,530)
Bartholomew, Simon S....5:01:23 (23,811)
Bartholomew-Biggs, David A....4:39:06 (18,306)
Bartkowiak, Dariusz....3:11:51 (1,708)

Bartle, Phillip P	5:01:13	(23,776)
Bartle-Jones, Guy	3:57:15	(8,542)
Bartlett, Andy W	4:59:14	(23,319)
Bartlett, Ben	5:19:19	(27,313)
Bartlett, Chris N	4:34:09	(17,062)
Bartlett, David	5:04:53	(24,496)
Bartlett, Edwin H	5:36:02	(30,054)
Bartlett, James	3:51:44	(7,303)
Bartlett, Oliver P	4:14:02	(12,106)
Bartlett, Paul R	3:11:37	(1,686)
Bartlett, Peter G	5:27:07	(28,640)
Bartlett, Rodney W	5:27:58	(28,789)
Bartman, Nicholas	4:09:42	(11,116)
Barton, Charles L	4:59:37	(23,417)
Barton, Gareth C	4:14:42	(12,257)
Barton, Graham A	4:50:22	(21,087)
Barton, James P	4:24:23	(14,675)
Barton, Paul S	4:11:09	(11,413)
Barton, Stephen	3:48:50	(6,694)
Barton, Thomas E	4:20:03	(13,611)
Barton, Tom D	4:54:41	(22,194)
Barton-White, Nigel G	5:57:47	(32,390)
Bartram, Clive	5:21:43	(27,734)
Bartram, Ian J	3:49:46	(6,886)
Bartrip, Lee	4:37:58	(17,999)
Barwell, James M	3:41:00	(5,365)
Barwell, Matthew R	4:35:09	(17,315)
Barwick, Carl W	7:06:24	(35,227)
Barwick, Charles G	3:54:16	(7,861)
Barwise, Tony	4:27:01	(15,326)
Bas, Luc M	3:09:12	(1,490)
Basham, David P	4:12:17	(11,681)
Basham, Leslie J	4:25:51	(15,025)
Basher, Adel B	5:05:26	(24,584)
Basil, Philip	4:57:50	(22,995)
Basini, Justin S	4:49:33	(20,900)
Baskind, Adam	3:54:49	(7,965)
Bason, Peter J	4:09:24	(11,048)
Bass, Andrew P	2:51:14	(418)
Bass, David	3:58:48	(8,910)
Bass, Julian L	4:41:30	(18,920)
Bass, Neil J	4:40:06	(18,556)
Bass, Richard	2:59:35	(869)
Bassendowski, Piotr	2:57:58	(743)
Bassett, Christopher J	4:57:50	(22,995)
Bassett, Cliff S	5:27:42	(28,744)
Bassett, Malcolm P	5:21:50	(27,762)
Bassett, Nicholas D	4:12:08	(11,639)
Bassett, Vincent	3:50:41	(7,075)
Bassinder, John	3:59:35	(9,114)
Basso, Gianpaolo	5:12:02	(25,861)
Basso, Luca A	3:53:07	(7,594)
Basson, Coen	4:01:44	(9,555)
Baster, Tom	5:17:32	(26,964)
Bastick, Damian	3:51:24	(7,225)
Bastick, Mark P	5:11:43	(25,793)
Basu, Subhashis	3:18:57	(2,385)
Bataille, Jean François	5:22:49	(27,909)
Batcheler, William J	5:15:33	(26,577)
Batchelor, Alan	4:35:00	(17,270)
Batchelor, James S	3:14:58	(1,991)
Batchelor, Stuart	5:06:04	(24,707)
Bateman, Alastair	3:41:50	(5,491)
Bateman, Danny A	5:06:11	(24,734)
Bateman, Jeremy D	3:03:36	(1,083)
Bateman, Jonathan S	2:41:31	(168)
Bateman, Jonathan S	3:26:32	(3,199)
Bater, Bernie P	4:28:22	(15,689)
Bates, Alex V	5:50:43	(31,749)
Bates, Anthony S	4:15:15	(12,376)
Bates, David A	3:41:24	(5,428)
Bates, Ian	4:20:21	(13,697)
Bates, Jason J	5:43:26	(30,987)
Bates, Matthew J	5:08:48	(25,242)
Bates, Michael G	5:06:23	(24,764)
Bates, Nigel M	3:54:47	(7,958)
Bates, Oliver J	3:57:58	(8,712)
Bates, Philip M	5:36:56	(30,167)
Bates, Terry	3:44:40	(5,972)
Bates, Thomas W	3:49:00	(6,736)
Bateson, Daniel J	4:35:32	(17,410)
Bateson, Garry	3:36:44	(4,651)
Bateson, Graham A	3:38:09	(4,864)

Batey, Mark R	4:03:46	(9,919)
Batey, Paul T	6:09:12	(33,248)
Batho, Charles R	5:01:09	(23,761)
Bathurst, Andrew W	4:05:08	(10,169)
Batkin, Ian P	4:50:27	(21,109)
Batley, Lloyd E	4:56:38	(22,672)
Batra, Amul	5:00:56	(23,715)
Batrick, Lee	4:38:55	(18,258)
Batson, Adrian B	5:12:34	(25,961)
Batstone, Andrew J	6:56:35	(35,064)
Batt, Michael H	3:40:59	(5,361)
Battavoine, Robert	6:07:50	(33,157)
Batterbee, Ian	6:18:21	(33,793)
Batters, Nigel I	3:53:58	(7,785)
Battersby, Anthony K	2:59:11	(839)
Battersby, Ian W	4:20:50	(13,814)
Battersby, John A	3:14:15	(1,919)
Battersby, Nicholas J	4:14:18	(12,169)
Battershall, Tim J	3:16:29	(2,127)
Battershill, Stephen	5:24:50	(28,243)
Battrick, Thomas C	5:02:09	(23,961)
Batty, Alex J	5:12:14	(25,904)
Batty, Nigel P	5:21:52	(27,769)
Battye, John R	4:16:43	(12,741)
Battye, Michael J	4:08:14	(10,821)
Battye, Michael L	4:13:56	(12,079)
Baty, Adrian J	3:57:51	(8,680)
Baty, Andrew	3:55:53	(4,535)
Baudet, Ghislain J	5:04:09	(24,350)
Baudini, Claudio	3:57:35	(8,619)
Baugniet, William	3:50:11	(6,973)
Baumgartner, Siegfried	3:43:07	(5,711)
Baumgartner, Thomas W	5:39:43	(30,560)
Baumker, Werner M	4:41:30	(18,920)
Baun, John B	4:30:14	(16,202)
Bautista, Daniel	4:35:10	(17,316)
Bavington, Michael	3:57:49	(8,676)
Bavister, Richard M	3:47:37	(6,454)
Baxendale, Samuel G	4:01:27	(9,506)
Baxendell, Roy W	4:21:09	(13,889)
Baxter, Adam C	4:21:50	(14,044)
Baxter, Andrew W	5:15:42	(26,602)
Baxter, Carl	6:01:04	(32,682)
Baxter, Duncan R	4:49:10	(20,813)
Baxter, Eric	3:50:36	(7,054)
Baxter, Greg	2:49:51	(372)
Baxter, John T	6:44:34	(34,792)
Baxter, Kenneth	4:43:11	(19,337)
Baxter, Mike	5:00:38	(23,645)
Baxter, Paul M	5:09:20	(25,342)
Baxter, Ramy L	5:48:20	(31,512)
Baxter, Robert	4:39:19	(18,368)
Baxter, Tony J	4:47:42	(20,457)
Baybutt, Charles P	4:24:42	(14,747)
Bayer, Malcolm E	2:53:17	(482)
Bayes, Jonathan	4:34:14	(17,085)
Bayissa, Tegegn	4:06:17	(10,414)
Bayle, Daniel	3:58:53	(8,938)
Bayley, David A	3:55:05	(8,026)
Bayley, Ian P	4:01:33	(9,521)
Bayliss, Danny J	4:06:23	(10,435)
Bayliss, Garry	5:15:21	(26,531)
Bayliss, Gerald	4:37:22	(17,852)
Bayliss, Michael C	4:19:06	(13,355)
Bayliss, Steve	4:14:05	(12,120)
Bayliss, Steven J	4:25:19	(14,898)
Baynes, Chris P	3:13:43	(1,876)
Baynton, Tom E	5:20:46	(27,567)
Bayntun-Roberts, Neil J	3:26:57	(3,270)
Bazley, Aaron G	3:28:47	(3,537)
Bazzard, Andrew M	4:36:11	(17,576)
Bdesha, Bub S	5:13:24	(26,102)
Beacham, James A	5:17:38	(26,987)
Beadle, David	3:19:49	(2,469)
Beadle, Michael S	3:19:24	(2,429)
Beal, Neville H	4:54:54	(22,246)
Beale, Cameron C	4:09:02	(10,956)
Beale, Darren	4:26:10	(15,089)
Beale, Nicholas C	4:20:55	(13,833)
Beaman, Richard A	3:14:28	(1,938)
Beamish, Charles W	5:22:47	(27,906)
Beamish, David	5:48:33	(31,528)
Beamish, Simon H	5:08:22	(25,165)

Bean, Chris P	4:34:37	(17,181)
Bean, Graham M	4:59:42	(23,433)
Bean, James	3:59:42	(9,142)
Beaney, Jason W	5:52:50	(31,953)
Beany, Captain	6:46:05	(34,831)
Beard, Alen	6:00:49	(32,647)
Beard, Daniel A	4:44:20	(19,630)
Beard, Mark J	4:35:20	(17,368)
Beard, Michael	5:38:18	(30,360)
Beard, Michael C	3:09:53	(1,546)
Beard, Peter	4:47:45	(20,470)
Beard, Richard L	5:10:51	(25,633)
Beard, Robert A	5:10:51	(25,633)
Beard, Russell J	3:19:41	(2,452)
Beard, Thomas G	4:01:56	(9,592)
Beardshall, Martin J	4:45:54	(20,033)
Beardsmore, Keith J	3:09:17	(1,500)
Beare, Nicholas A	3:27:03	(3,290)
Bearman, Jamie R	4:35:35	(17,427)
Bearsley, Peter D	4:29:09	(15,898)
Bearwish, Neil S	3:25:53	(3,112)
Beasant, Campbell A	4:06:12	(10,396)
Beasley, Noel M	5:19:14	(27,297)
Beasley, Roderick J	4:43:51	(19,497)
Beastall, Fraser A	4:36:27	(17,653)
Beathe, Carl J	3:18:24	(2,334)
Beaton, Euan K	3:23:05	(2,804)
Beaton, Finlay K	5:54:52	(32,133)
Beattie, Alastair J	4:01:08	(9,444)
Beattie, David	5:30:38	(29,241)
Beattie, David I	3:16:28	(2,124)
Beattie, Sean P	5:21:23	(27,673)
Beatty, Nicholas C	5:40:16	(30,622)
Beatty, Steven	5:02:03	(23,943)
Beaty-Pownall, Paul J	4:41:18	(18,862)
Beaubois, Xavier	3:49:08	(6,756)
Beauchamp, Charlie F	5:06:57	(24,872)
Beauchamp, Keith M	3:39:47	(5,155)
Beaumont, Angus	3:58:50	(8,921)
Beaumont, Graham	4:53:25	(21,868)
Beaumont, Jon K	4:22:23	(14,170)
Beaumont, Mark J	3:46:23	(6,233)
Beaumont, Mark S	3:19:54	(2,479)
Beaumont, Richard	3:12:24	(1,766)
Beaumont, Richard M	3:56:35	(8,379)
Beaumont, Thomas M	4:45:27	(19,934)
Beaumont, Tony R	6:29:59	(34,325)
Beauverger, Mickael G	3:29:00	(3,577)
Beavan, Carl A	5:35:39	(30,007)
Beaver, Robert	5:12:09	(25,888)
Beazeley, Chris D	3:34:46	(4,371)
Bebbington, Graeme R	4:28:27	(15,715)
Bebbington, Mark C	3:28:05	(3,416)
Becart, Bernard	2:58:15	(766)
Becerril, Juan C	4:47:02	(20,295)
Beck, Anthony R	3:50:45	(7,097)
Beck, Eric	3:38:26	(4,908)
Beck, Gary R	4:20:01	(13,602)
Beck, James	5:26:48	(28,587)
Beck, John W	3:20:15	(2,523)
Beck, Richard P	3:42:59	(5,689)
Beckett, Carl A	5:51:54	(31,864)
Beckett, Graham	5:28:25	(28,891)
Beckford, Scott W	4:26:12	(15,102)
Beckrich, Xavier	3:31:26	(3,896)
Beckwith, Mervyn J	4:31:48	(16,527)
Bedder, Stephen R	3:41:00	(5,365)
Bedford, Geoff	7:02:58	(35,175)
Bedford, John H	3:38:15	(4,877)
Bedford, Paul	4:43:18	(19,372)
Bedson, Simon D	3:50:48	(7,095)
Bedwell, Neil	4:46:25	(20,157)
Bedwell, Peter R	4:16:04	(12,585)
Bedwell, Steven L	3:54:42	(7,945)
Bedworth, Jeffrey R	5:05:59	(24,691)
Bee, Alexander	4:10:19	(11,231)
Bee, Giles S	4:28:04	(15,614)
Beech, David A	4:39:06	(18,306)
Beechey, Neil	4:35:54	(17,515)
Beechey, Paul D	3:31:26	(3,896)
Beecroft, David	3:06:05	(1,238)
Beedie, Neil	3:31:43	(3,943)
Beedle, Stephen	3:34:13	(4,299)

Beeken, Julian 4:39:18 (18,364)
Beeks, Darren C 4:49:47 (20,951)
Beeks, Ramon A 5:15:07 (26,484)
Beeley, Will 3:55:50 (8,190)
Beer, Craig A 5:43:26 (30,987)
Beer, Peter G 2:57:45 (725)
Beesley, Paul J 5:09:32 (25,381)
Beeston, James E 3:51:23 (7,221)
Beeston, Richard 5:30:29 (29,218)
Beeston, Tim R 4:27:15 (15,407)
Beet, Andrew J 4:54:08 (22,054)
Beetham, Stephen 3:54:37 (7,925)
Beeton, Andrew J 3:49:36 (6,851)
Beever, Matthew P 4:48:40 (20,682)
Beevers, Dashal 4:20:06 (13,624)
Begert, Marc 2:56:27 (629)
Beggan, Shane J 3:30:20 (3,771)
Beggs, Geoff T 5:10:14 (25,530)
Beggs, Timothy A 5:12:04 (25,868)
Beggs, William K 4:19:08 (13,365)
Begi, Alberto 3:56:23 (8,330)
Behan, Kenneth J 3:24:55 (3,011)
Behl, Edward J 5:07:38 (25,025)
Beighton, Conrad A 3:43:24 (5,754)
Beinart, Eldon 4:40:52 (18,752)
Beirne, Christopher J 5:22:07 (27,797)
Bekemyer, Dennis L 4:30:07 (16,177)
Bekerman, Marek 4:12:41 (11,767)
Beketov, Andrei 3:37:05 (4,698)
Belcher, Matthew J 4:10:07 (11,186)
Belcher, Peter A 2:41:12 (158)
Belcher, Simon A 3:25:07 (3,033)
Belfield, David C 5:07:47 (25,054)
Belk, Alan R 4:28:53 (15,828)
Belk, Chris 4:41:22 (18,879)
Bell, Adriann M 5:13:33 (26,131)
Bell, Andrew 4:31:16 (16,416)
Bell, Austin 4:00:38 (9,342)
Bell, Bernard 4:57:02 (22,782)
Bell, Chris J 3:03:29 (1,078)
Bell, Christopher E 4:41:40 (18,958)
Bell, Colin A 4:48:27 (20,639)
Bell, Craig J 3:20:41 (2,575)
Bell, David J 3:38:00 (4,830)
Bell, David P 6:27:30 (34,231)
Bell, Duncan 6:05:01 (32,964)
Bell, Graham 2:58:37 (801)
Bell, John 3:17:55 (2,277)
Bell, Jonathan 3:56:40 (8,396)
Bell, Karl E 3:58:12 (8,760)
Bell, Mark D 5:35:40 (30,009)
Bell, Martin 3:58:51 (8,930)
Bell, Mathew D 4:45:08 (19,867)
Bell, Matthew D 4:12:15 (11,670)
Bell, Michael D 4:26:50 (15,275)
Bell, Michael D 4:39:52 (18,500)
Bell, Nick 5:55:38 (32,204)
Bell, Nick G 3:41:33 (5,448)
Bell, Oliver J 3:50:44 (7,084)
Bell, Phil J 6:45:15 (34,804)
Bell, Simon J 2:48:52 (340)
Bell, Simon J 3:46:47 (6,301)
Bell, Steven M 4:44:49 (19,784)
Bell, Timothy F 4:17:33 (12,961)
Bell, Wayne P 2:56:50 (662)
Bellacosa, Maurizio 4:37:42 (17,937)
Bellamy, Darren W 4:50:14 (21,055)
Bellamy, Fraser S 5:30:27 (29,210)
Bellamy, Guy 2:57:10 (687)
Bellamy, Simon 3:30:18 (3,763)
Bellani, Flavio 4:14:32 (12,211)
Belleguelle, Russell J 5:08:03 (25,105)
Belleville, Paul C 3:14:49 (1,971)
Bellicaud, Fabrice J 4:08:27 (10,862)
Bellingham, Neil J 4:43:40 (19,456)
Bellingham, Steve J 4:00:10 (9,242)
Bellis, Deryn S 3:06:14 (1,249)
Bellis, Ian T 4:08:35 (10,888)
Bellman, David 6:09:08 (33,244)
Bellman, Jason A 6:09:08 (33,244)
Bello, Aurelio M 4:33:09 (16,823)
Bellwood, Simon 3:07:03 (1,314)
Belmonte, José L 3:11:27 (1,667)
Belsom, Robin S 3:45:11 (6,047)
Belson, Robin T 6:01:45 (32,737)
Belton, Andrew W 4:36:20 (17,621)
Belton, Chris C 3:10:53 (1,620)
Belton, Richard W 5:41:09 (30,723)
Belton, Robert B 4:02:14 (9,659)
Beltran, Renato 3:43:13 (5,723)
Ben Ismail, Maaouia 3:10:35 (1,600)
Ben Tanfous, Souhail B 3:37:45 (4,783)
Benagla, Giuseppe 4:00:55 (9,402)
Benardout, Neil B 4:59:56 (23,484)
Benbow, Simon 5:40:29 (30,650)
Bence-Trower, Nicholas A 5:51:27 (31,822)
Bendal, Mark W 2:38:15 (112)
Bendall, Colin 7:29:20 (35,478)
Bendle, Stephen A 4:09:14 (11,014)
Benedik, Arpad 5:14:33 (26,350)
Beneke, Rainer 4:44:53 (19,803)
Benfield, Graham 4:47:10 (20,328)
Benfield, Martin 4:53:56 (22,000)
Benford, Tim S 4:15:49 (12,511)
Benham, Karl H 4:35:59 (17,532)
Benie, Noel 6:15:58 (33,681)
Beningfield, Paul R 5:32:50 (29,582)
Benitez, Antonio 3:51:14 (7,194)
Benn, Matthew J 5:35:12 (29,940)
Ben-Nathan, Marc I 4:44:47 (19,772)
Bennett, Adam 4:18:07 (13,103)
Bennett, Alex A 5:15:52 (26,634)
Bennett, Andrew J 4:06:42 (10,502)
Bennett, Andy S 3:53:44 (7,737)
Bennett, Daniel E 5:14:05 (26,243)
Bennett, David 4:37:35 (17,906)
Bennett, David A 4:12:09 (11,644)
Bennett, David E 5:32:22 (29,504)
Bennett, David G 4:20:15 (13,665)
Bennett, Elliot S 4:52:20 (21,581)
Bennett, Gary J 3:52:56 (7,551)
Bennett, John E 4:42:16 (19,117)
Bennett, Jonathon R 4:37:35 (17,906)
Bennett, Julian R 4:51:53 (21,463)
Bennett, Kevin M 2:58:25 (782)
Bennett, Lee 4:44:28 (19,670)
Bennett, Mark A 4:47:27 (20,394)
Bennett, Mark T 6:02:21 (32,774)
Bennett, Martin J 5:29:09 (29,011)
Bennett, Michael J 3:59:58 (9,201)
Bennett, Neil A 4:45:37 (19,970)
Bennett, Owen D 3:36:19 (4,589)
Bennett, Paul 3:16:28 (2,124)
Bennett, Raymond 4:13:24 (11,936)
Bennett, Richard J 3:35:42 (4,514)
Bennett, Richard K 4:52:36 (21,642)
Bennett, Russell J 3:43:03 (5,698)
Bennett, Stephen J 4:35:11 (17,323)
Bennett, Steven W 6:26:07 (34,176)
Bennett-King, Peter F 5:50:27 (31,722)
Bennetts, Colin 4:26:58 (15,314)
Bennetts, Philip 4:42:50 (19,264)
Bennis, Ahmed 3:06:12 (1,248)
Benoy, Gillon 4:27:13 (15,396)
Benskin, Ian D 3:08:10 (1,403)
Benson, Bruce 4:08:19 (10,835)
Benson, Daniel J 5:12:17 (25,917)
Benson, Daniel M 5:17:07 (26,882)
Benson, Ian C 3:09:57 (1,554)
Benson, James 2:44:16 (223)
Benson, Joel W 3:25:27 (3,059)
Benson, Jonathan W 5:18:28 (27,158)
Benson, Justin J 3:45:09 (6,041)
Benson, Mark M 4:19:45 (13,524)
Benson, Neil D 5:35:33 (29,984)
Benson, Preston P 3:54:56 (7,995)
Benson, Richard J 3:51:10 (7,177)
Benson, Rodney D 5:46:19 (31,294)
Bensouda, Nordine 3:46:35 (6,267)
Benstock, Brian 4:24:25 (14,685)
Bent, Alan 3:28:55 (3,561)
Bent, Nicholas 4:06:24 (10,439)
Bent, Richard A 5:32:47 (29,574)
Bentley, Alan H 3:41:57 (5,509)
Bentley, David R 4:15:36 (12,460)
Bentley, Ian R 5:20:00 (27,424)
Bentley, James M 4:41:08 (18,823)
Bentley, Justin D 3:35:30 (4,480)
Bentley, Mark 3:18:24 (2,334)
Bentley, Mark A 4:25:48 (15,018)
Bentley, Michael P 4:12:14 (11,666)
Bentley, Paul D 5:59:45 (32,562)
Bentley, Richard C 4:18:39 (13,252)
Bentley, Robin J 2:42:41 (191)
Bentley, Simon J 4:25:23 (14,918)
Bentley, Timothy W 3:11:11 (1,646)
Benton, Derek R 4:33:33 (16,928)
Benton, Kevin L 4:05:43 (10,293)
Benton, Mark 4:07:33 (10,662)
Benton, Mark P 4:22:45 (14,272)
Benton, Tom R 3:39:01 (5,021)
Benwell, Nigel R 4:34:33 (17,159)
Ben-Yehuda, Niv 5:00:56 (23,715)
Benyon, Pete 3:06:51 (1,303)
Beraki, Negabelay 4:21:26 (13,947)
Berastegui, Oscar 4:10:03 (11,176)
Berbeck, Charles 6:37:12 (34,587)
Beresford, John P 3:37:25 (4,739)
Beresford, Martin P 4:27:37 (15,493)
Beresford, Simon C 6:15:21 (33,637)
Berg, Jack S 8:01:49 (35,640)
Berg, Jens-Kristian 2:41:22 (163)
Berg, Olan 5:56:56 (32,327)
Berg, Per-Hans 6:06:21 (33,071)
Berg, Stewart 4:20:38 (13,764)
Berger, Hugo J 3:45:22 (6,077)
Berger, Jamie 5:08:00 (25,093)
Bergin, Chris 4:40:13 (18,581)
Bergin, Ian R 4:18:28 (13,201)
Berglund, Anders 3:28:25 (3,466)
Bergozza, Marco 4:44:20 (19,630)
Berhe, Elias 3:18:54 (2,381)
Berisford, Andrew J 3:59:33 (9,108)
Berkeley, Jason J 5:27:16 (28,672)
Berkman, Steven B 4:35:06 (17,298)
Berkovits, Matthew 5:30:40 (29,246)
Berks, Peter R 4:28:19 (15,679)
Berleen, Abdi-Karim 4:01:16 (9,474)
Berlie, Adrian J 3:34:54 (4,395)
Berlyn, Paul P 4:04:54 (10,129)
Bernard, Christophe 4:09:21 (11,041)
Bernard, Ralph M 5:38:00 (30,303)
Bernard-Brunel, Denis 3:16:02 (2,081)
Bernardi, Graziano 4:23:42 (14,490)
Bernhardt, Andreas 3:47:40 (6,468)
Bernhardt, Mark J 3:32:51 (4,115)
Bernini, Giancarlo U 4:30:25 (16,237)
Bernstein, Peter S 4:15:00 (12,325)
Bernstein, Richard P 3:13:23 (1,856)
Berrecloth, Neil 5:04:09 (24,350)
Berridge, James 4:28:01 (15,592)
Berriman, Paul G 5:19:30 (27,337)
Berrisford, Leigh C 3:54:56 (7,995)
Berrow, Andrew D 3:40:52 (5,337)
Berrow, Paul E 4:45:37 (19,970)
Berry, Adam 5:25:26 (28,351)
Berry, Christopher W 4:55:53 (22,483)
Berry, Craig 4:32:52 (16,758)
Berry, Daniel R 4:23:57 (14,555)
Berry, David J 4:19:00 (13,328)
Berry, Duncan G 4:11:45 (11,558)
Berry, Gavin R 4:05:08 (10,169)
Berry, Ian J 3:32:08 (4,017)
Berry, James E 4:33:10 (16,830)
Berry, James L 5:14:38 (26,369)
Berry, Jamie M 3:51:52 (7,330)
Berry, Jason 3:34:06 (4,280)
Berry, Mark S 4:20:05 (13,622)
Berry, Paul R 3:55:22 (8,099)
Berry, Robin S 4:41:32 (18,932)
Berry, Stephen F 6:03:27 (32,849)
Bertdcchi, Yvan 3:41:07 (5,384)
Bertoldi, Giorgio 5:20:45 (27,565)
Bertoncini, Vincent 3:27:52 (3,390)
Bertrand, Patrice O 3:44:37 (5,963)
Bertrano, Verona 4:22:17 (14,148)
Bertschin, Keith E 4:14:21 (12,175)
Beschizza, Mark S 4:59:30 (23,384)
Bescoby, Tim J 3:56:19 (8,307)

Besly, Adrian	5:14:14 (26,278)	Biggs, Matthew J	4:16:01 (12,570)	Bishop, Jonathan R	3:29:25 (3,637)
Besnard, Bernie	6:47:52 (34,885)	Bigley, Andrew T	5:53:26 (31,998)	Bishop, Michael J	6:46:37 (34,847)
Besnard, Jean-Pierre	4:44:11 (19,594)	Biglin, Andrew	4:30:47 (16,313)	Bishop, Mike A	4:31:15 (16,415)
Best, Andrew F	5:22:19 (27,822)	Bignell, Stephen W	5:21:36 (27,712)	Bishop, Roger D	4:51:52 (21,459)
Best, Anthony W	5:31:02 (29,302)	Bila, Antonio	4:02:14 (9,659)	Bishop, Simon	4:22:52 (14,303)
Best, David	6:33:55 (34,463)	Bilbrey, Clifford F	3:47:37 (6,454)	Bishop, Stuart T	5:07:55 (25,080)
Best, David C	4:34:04 (17,043)	Biles, Dominic P	3:44:40 (5,972)	Bishop, Timothy S	3:11:53 (1,713)
Best, David P	6:08:32 (33,206)	Biller, Andrew	3:35:23 (4,467)	Bishopp, Stephen R	5:16:38 (26,778)
Best, Peter A	3:50:40 (7,071)	Billing, Brian A	6:02:28 (32,784)	Bisiker, Martin	4:16:24 (12,670)
Best, Steven G	5:12:08 (25,879)	Billing, Shaun A	2:52:31 (459)	Bispo, Ronaldo A	4:55:31 (22,395)
Bestwick, Christopher D	5:42:48 (30,909)	Billinger, Jan C	4:55:14 (22,325)	Bisschop, Murray	4:35:07 (17,303)
Bestwick, Tim	4:39:54 (18,508)	Billingham, David P	3:16:06 (2,089)	Bissell, Peter	3:50:08 (6,967)
Bethell, Cyril H	6:42:24 (34,735)	Billington, Gary	3:48:05 (6,539)	Bisset, Ian A	4:21:58 (14,080)
Bethell, Jeremy J	4:19:55 (13,578)	Billington, John	4:37:23 (17,855)	Bissett, Andy P	4:53:57 (22,006)
Bethell, Peter H	5:38:13 (30,339)	Billington, Keith S	4:34:35 (17,169)	Bissoli, Gianni	2:54:48 (569)
Betjes, Sjaak	3:02:43 (1,038)	Billington, Kevin F	4:27:02 (15,331)	Bisson, Antoine S	4:20:50 (13,814)
Betley, Paul J	6:10:33 (33,339)	Billington, Michael	4:46:52 (20,243)	Biswas, Santonu K	3:37:02 (4,695)
Betson, Mark J	4:44:51 (19,791)	Billington, William	5:00:31 (23,617)	Bitton, John F	6:30:34 (34,343)
Bett, Tim	3:49:13 (6,779)	Billy, Andrew T	5:47:32 (31,411)	Bizjak, Craig A	4:09:06 (10,973)
Betti, Alessio	2:54:45 (565)	Biltcliffe, Steven J	4:28:41 (15,781)	Bizuneh, Fasil	2:29:30 (37)
Bettis, Carl	5:18:15 (27,113)	Bilton, Darran E	2:25:10 (24)	Bjornermark, Thomas	4:26:47 (15,260)
Bettis, Lee	4:35:02 (17,284)	Bilton, Jason C	3:49:13 (6,779)	Bjornsson, Magnus J	4:37:45 (17,948)
Betts, Delmont M	4:29:53 (16,118)	Bilton, Matt	3:41:58 (5,511)	Bjornsson, Mikael B	3:43:43 (5,816)
Betts, Jonathan	4:05:32 (10,245)	Binder, Jan K	5:32:16 (29,492)	Black, Alistair M	4:23:33 (14,459)
Betts, Mark P	2:50:37 (397)	Binding, Robert J	4:50:40 (21,159)	Black, Daniel C	4:16:01 (12,570)
Betts, Noel L	4:41:21 (18,875)	Binet, Sam	3:49:52 (6,911)	Black, Darren R	4:40:57 (18,775)
Bettsworth, Richard G	3:07:23 (1,343)	Bingham, Christian	5:13:57 (26,222)	Black, David A	4:48:30 (20,647)
Betty, Stphen J	4:46:48 (20,229)	Bingham, Hugh	2:58:02 (749)	Black, John A	5:03:42 (24,271)
Betz, Gregory H	4:42:28 (19,171)	Bingham, Iain S	4:16:02 (12,575)	Black, Paul	4:41:56 (19,026)
Beutter, Ralph M	4:41:27 (18,902)	Bingham, Paul D	3:28:09 (3,424)	Black, Richard J	4:08:34 (10,882)
Bevan, Darren	5:15:58 (26,652)	Bingham, Roger C	5:50:39 (31,744)	Black, Stuart R	4:55:42 (22,429)
Bevan, David H	4:55:08 (22,298)	Bingham, Stephen M	3:39:50 (5,164)	Blackburn, Graham M	3:10:56 (1,627)
Bevan, Gavin	4:56:13 (22,570)	Bingham, Stuart J	4:10:42 (11,313)	Blackburn, Ian	4:08:24 (10,848)
Bevan, Jonathan N	5:14:19 (26,294)	Bingley, Kenneth	4:53:05 (21,771)	Blackburn, Richard	4:57:10 (22,811)
Bevan, Kristian J	4:24:49 (14,785)	Binnendijk, Andrew R	4:11:02 (11,380)	Blackburn, Simon	3:59:13 (9,017)
Bevan, Neil	2:57:33 (713)	Binning, Paul	5:09:02 (25,283)	Blackburn, Stephen T	6:51:07 (34,960)
Bevan-Smith, Sean B	4:47:52 (20,494)	Binns, Daye B	5:34:15 (29,803)	Blackburn, Tim J	4:17:19 (12,880)
Beveridge, Findlay B	5:54:00 (32,054)	Binns, John J	4:19:26 (13,440)	Blackburne, Robert C	4:21:20 (13,918)
Beverley, Chad	5:07:33 (25,010)	Binns, Richard M	4:17:33 (12,961)	Blackford, Colin H	4:02:42 (9,729)
Beverley, Thor	4:51:27 (21,356)	Binyon, Trevor J	3:48:31 (6,625)	Blackham, Benjamin R	6:49:29 (34,919)
Bevington, Victor D	3:41:26 (5,434)	Birch, Christopher B	3:35:35 (4,497)	Blackham, Paul R	6:42:54 (34,747)
Bevis, Simon J	4:56:28 (22,628)	Birch, Graeme	4:50:57 (21,230)	Blackledge, Simon A	3:40:00 (5,189)
Bewick, Martin J	4:42:52 (19,273)	Birch, Nick	4:00:59 (9,417)	Blacklock, Kevin	5:01:50 (23,897)
Beyer, Paul K	3:39:37 (5,131)	Birch, Nigel P	4:57:30 (22,904)	Blackman, Leslie K	6:15:27 (33,644)
Beyneveldt, Willem H	3:29:21 (3,627)	Birch, Philip M	4:13:52 (12,056)	Blackman, Ricci D	4:59:57 (23,490)
Bezance, Tom	4:00:53 (9,393)	Birch, Richard J	3:54:40 (7,937)	Blackman, Roger A	4:39:21 (18,381)
Bhachoo, Arvinder	4:43:48 (19,478)	Birchall, Brian	4:44:06 (19,563)	Blackmore, Charles	3:38:57 (5,008)
Bhagalia, Jiten R	6:10:29 (33,334)	Birchall, Matthew J	3:44:41 (5,977)	Blackmore, Chris M	3:41:03 (5,372)
Bhakar, Surinder S	5:03:26 (24,224)	Birchley, Robert A	3:47:37 (6,454)	Blackmore, Matthew A	3:50:19 (7,003)
Bhakri, Harbans L	4:49:14 (20,828)	Birchnall, Sean P	4:14:23 (12,183)	Blackmore, Michael T	2:37:30 (104)
Bharadwa, Kam	7:41:23 (35,576)	Bird, Alan D	4:44:04 (19,556)	Blackmore, Philip W	5:03:34 (24,250)
Bhatia, Vikas	5:42:40 (30,890)	Bird, Gareth A	4:26:53 (15,288)	Blackstock, Alanzo	3:50:50 (7,102)
Bhogal, Jasdeep	5:38:25 (30,374)	Bird, Gareth R	7:02:27 (35,167)	Blackstone, Marc	3:36:55 (4,677)
Bhogal, Mick	4:43:11 (19,337)	Bird, Graham G	5:23:17 (27,974)	Blackwell, Kevin M	4:29:15 (15,926)
Bhuoia, Mehul N	5:21:11 (27,631)	Bird, James A	3:31:25 (3,892)	Blackwell, Oliver	4:46:39 (20,208)
Bhupal, Kulvinder S	4:36:53 (17,763)	Bird, James A	7:10:53 (35,287)	Blackwell, Paul A	4:17:34 (12,969)
Bianco, Filippo	3:41:26 (5,434)	Bird, Jamie E	3:32:54 (4,123)	Blackwell, Philip N	3:21:15 (2,628)
Bianconi, Paolo	4:52:26 (21,604)	Bird, Mark	4:42:20 (19,129)	Blackwell, Richard	5:15:31 (26,567)
Bibby, Andy M	6:24:33 (34,103)	Bird, Melvyn	4:22:30 (14,205)	Blackwell, Will S	3:49:57 (6,927)
Bibby, David M	7:17:16 (35,360)	Bird, Nicholas J	4:39:35 (18,433)	Blackwood, Graeme	4:49:50 (20,959)
Bibby, Jay D	3:38:08 (4,860)	Bird, Paul A	3:07:41 (1,359)	Bladen, Alan J	5:17:41 (26,998)
Bibby, Matthew W	3:51:09 (7,171)	Bird, Richard	3:47:35 (6,441)	Blades, Nicholas A	3:22:36 (2,755)
Bibonas, Leonidas	4:50:03 (21,007)	Birdsall, Shaun	5:51:20 (31,810)	Blades, Richard J	3:28:22 (3,459)
Bickers, Christopher J	6:47:37 (34,874)	Birdseye, Michael R	5:22:20 (27,825)	Bladley, Paul	5:16:29 (26,755)
Bickers, Michael A	3:44:46 (5,989)	Birkbeck, Stephen P	4:13:01 (11,833)	Blaine, John S	3:19:46 (2,462)
Bickerstaffe, Rob	5:08:22 (25,165)	Birkby, Nicholas F	3:40:49 (5,324)	Blair, Alan J	3:57:51 (8,680)
Bickerton, Ian	4:22:17 (14,148)	Birkett, Charles	5:24:16 (28,151)	Blair, Ian	5:23:06 (27,948)
Bickerton, Richard	4:00:31 (9,314)	Birkholm, Jon	5:47:25 (31,400)	Blair, Matthew J	5:23:13 (27,961)
Bicket, Jamie A	5:32:20 (29,501)	Birks, Ian D	4:07:54 (10,748)	Blair, Simon H	6:27:25 (34,228)
Bicknell, Ellis J	3:57:05 (8,497)	Birley, Carl S	5:48:01 (31,468)	Blair-Smith, Andrew C	4:06:26 (10,610)
Bicknell, Guy	4:10:41 (11,310)	Birmingham, Bill	3:50:59 (7,135)	Blaize, Andy	3:02:07 (1,007)
Bicknell, Jonathan	3:48:36 (6,645)	Birmingham, Joseph C	5:01:49 (23,894)	Blake, Daniel C	5:59:55 (32,568)
Biddell, Christopher D	5:05:58 (24,689)	Birnie, Andrew E	3:05:44 (1,220)	Blake, David J	5:55:22 (32,180)
Bidgood, Harry S	3:45:41 (6,132)	Birt, Ashley S	3:26:51 (3,249)	Blake, Dominic W	3:34:03 (4,274)
Bidwell, Alex S	4:08:41 (10,907)	Bisby, Paul R	3:40:13 (5,219)	Blake, John H	3:55:21 (8,093)
Bienkowski, Stephen	4:27:14 (15,400)	Bishop, Andrew J	3:27:55 (3,398)	Blake, Kevin C	3:57:26 (8,588)
Bienvenu, Steve M	4:16:05 (12,589)	Bishop, Ben	4:56:26 (22,622)	Blake, Mark R	4:56:08 (22,543)
Bieris, Stan	4:20:07 (13,629)	Bishop, Benjamin L	4:07:02 (10,580)	Blake, Neil A	4:00:33 (9,322)
Bierton, Kelvin J	3:37:21 (4,726)	Bishop, Christopher R	3:47:14 (6,384)	Blake, Stephen J	3:06:21 (1,257)
Bige, Pierre	4:02:45 (9,742)	Bishop, Daniel C	5:07:46 (25,052)	Blake, Steve J	4:55:50 (22,468)
Biggar, Andrew	3:40:42 (5,302)	Bishop, Daniel T	2:56:32 (637)	Blake, Tim E	4:46:06 (20,082)
Biggerstaff, Stuart J	3:22:30 (2,747)	Bishop, Danny	4:17:52 (13,034)	Blakeborough, Tony J	5:13:50 (26,197)
Biggs, Geoff D	4:28:33 (15,745)	Bishop, Edward T	6:17:16 (33,740)	Blakeley, Mark A	5:22:10 (27,804)

Blakeley, Paul 5:33:25 (29,667)
Blakeley, Stuart A 3:30:13 (3,750)
Blakelock, John F 5:36:40 (30,132)
Blakemore, Stephen S 3:40:53 (5,343)
Blanchard, Anthony J 3:24:51 (3,002)
Blanchard, Henry C 4:35:49 (17,491)
Blanco, Felipe 5:05:16 (24,552)
Bland, Kevin C 4:00:11 (9,247)
Blaney, Simon 4:58:33 (23,159)
Blaney, Stephen A 7:10:52 (35,284)
Blanks, Douglas T 5:31:59 (29,448)
Blannin, Andrew K 3:20:19 (2,531)
Blard, Yann P 4:21:44 (14,012)
Blaskey, Jay E 5:29:14 (29,031)
Blass, Frank 5:11:18 (25,719)
Blatch, Sebastian B 4:51:54 (21,466)
Blaxill, Ray 6:53:01 (34,993)
Blazquez, José L 4:48:23 (20,631)
Bleasdale, John M 4:41:19 (18,867)
Blease, James W 4:26:09 (15,084)
Blevins, Willard L 5:42:40 (30,890)
Blewitt, Tim A 5:34:22 (29,820)
Blin, Christopher J 4:43:49 (19,482)
Blizzard, Gareth 3:18:04 (2,291)
Block, Robert A 3:49:32 (6,839)
Blockley, Mark A 4:35:12 (17,333)
Blocksidge, Gareth M 4:58:44 (23,193)
Blodr, Kenneth 3:49:28 (6,821)
Bloemsma, Deroen 4:16:22 (12,665)
Bloese, Ian P 4:50:20 (21,075)
Blois, Richard H 7:37:38 (35,550)
Blom, Matt A 4:52:21 (21,583)
Blomfield, Chris J 5:47:55 (31,454)
Blomfield, David M 5:02:30 (24,040)
Blomley, Greg 4:06:11 (10,390)
Blondel, Benoit A 2:50:24 (386)
Blondel, Brice 3:30:38 (3,798)
Bloom, Ryan 4:51:17 (21,307)
Bloom, Tged D 4:47:16 (20,347)
Bloomfield, Clive W 7:24:02 (35,425)
Bloomfield, Colin 4:29:10 (15,900)
Bloomfield, Ian G 2:43:25 (206)
Bloomfield, John B 4:28:01 (15,592)
Bloomfield, Phil 5:40:53 (30,693)
Blossfeldt, Patrick 4:02:05 (9,617)
Blot, David 3:51:54 (7,337)
Blowers, Peter 4:03:19 (9,835)
Blowing, Michael F 4:37:10 (17,817)
Bloxam, Andrew 3:07:02 (1,311)
Bloxham, Robert J 3:49:33 (6,842)
Bloxham, Robert J 5:42:46 (30,903)
Blum, Richard G 5:41:08 (30,721)
Blundell, Issy 4:40:23 (18,628)
Blundell, Mark 5:43:10 (30,957)
Blundell, Neil 4:38:30 (18,153)
Blundell, Paul D 4:16:10 (12,612)
Blunden, Keith 4:51:37 (21,402)
Blyth, Kenny S 4:06:07 (10,376)
Blyth, Richard J 4:23:59 (14,566)
Blyth, William H 4:38:01 (18,015)
Blythe, Colin W 3:45:32 (6,097)
Blythe, Gary M 3:49:03 (6,743)
Blythe, Kenneth C 4:57:56 (23,014)
Blythe, Toby C 3:53:14 (7,631)
Blythe, Tony J 4:40:17 (18,597)
Boa, Peter M 4:10:02 (11,173)
Boan, Robert I 4:17:08 (12,837)
Board, Jonathan M 5:12:13 (25,901)
Board, Phillip J 4:34:23 (17,111)
Board, Roy 4:19:12 (13,375)
Boardley, Ian 3:02:19 (1,016)
Boardley, John T 5:09:51 (25,439)
Boardman, Allan N 5:24:23 (28,171)
Bobbert, Coenraad W 3:57:51 (8,680)
Bobineau, Claude 3:34:25 (4,330)
Bock, Alois M 4:54:49 (22,229)
Bodart, Claude G 5:05:20 (24,558)
Boddington, Roy 4:56:56 (22,759)
Boden, Matthew D 4:28:14 (15,653)
Boden, Robert 4:35:40 (17,446)
Bodfish, Stephen 6:11:36 (33,405)
Bodley-Scott, Peter G 3:59:07 (8,990)
Bodson, Patrick 5:01:37 (23,856)

Body, Paul A 3:15:30 (2,030)
Boehm, Volker 5:46:10 (31,280)
Boeke, André 5:05:06 (24,527)
Boeke, Thies 4:23:49 (14,518)
Boesch, Olaf 3:46:44 (6,289)
Boettcher, Jens-Carsten 4:04:53 (10,127)
Boettiger, Oliver 4:13:40 (12,012)
Bogle, Thomas P 3:28:38 (3,511)
Bogue, James Y 4:16:05 (12,589)
Bogush, Jeremy 4:13:56 (12,079)
Bohannon, Paul W 4:14:05 (12,120)
Bohnert, Matthew 3:45:52 (6,157)
Boileau, John A 5:41:31 (30,770)
Boitiere, Mickael 3:03:54 (1,100)
Bolam, John P 5:01:00 (23,725)
Bold, Matthew M 5:19:40 (27,369)
Boldero, Ian G 4:52:47 (21,689)
Bole, Robert D 3:28:39 (3,516)
Bollore, Thierry C 3:18:08 (2,302)
Bolman, Justin A 4:15:12 (12,368)
Bolton, Adam J 3:17:42 (2,253)
Bolton, David J 5:24:09 (28,132)
Bolton, Gavin 5:11:25 (25,744)
Bolton, Julian C 4:04:38 (10,080)
Bolton, Neil D 4:42:53 (19,278)
Bolton, Roger M 4:42:52 (19,273)
Bolton, Steve 3:00:10 (906)
Bolton, Stuart 4:30:20 (16,223)
Bolton, Wayne L 4:18:57 (13,319)
Bolzer, Pascal 4:28:26 (15,709)
Bon, Nicolas 3:07:28 (1,347)
Bonavita, Nunzio 3:26:41 (3,221)
Bond, Adrian D 4:57:19 (22,860)
Bond, Andrew 5:03:44 (24,276)
Bond, Barry J 5:13:00 (26,048)
Bond, Chris 4:41:13 (18,844)
Bond, Daniel M 4:22:07 (14,110)
Bond, Francis D 3:48:31 (6,625)
Bond, Maurice T 5:51:33 (31,833)
Bond, Michael J 5:03:51 (24,298)
Bond, Robert J 4:52:47 (21,689)
Bond, Simon P 3:00:58 (957)
Bond, Stewart A 3:28:42 (3,524)
Bond, Tristan 5:44:17 (31,078)
Bone, Andy G 3:18:34 (2,348)
Bone, Darren 5:20:56 (27,595)
Bone, Kenneth C 5:02:34 (24,055)
Bone, Mark 4:42:38 (19,214)
Bone, Martin 5:27:03 (28,628)
Bone, Michael A 4:47:54 (20,505)
Bonell, Simon J 3:55:10 (8,051)
Bonelli, Anthony S 3:46:23 (6,233)
Bonfrate, Vincenzo 3:56:17 (8,297)
Bonilla, Marco T 4:01:04 (9,429)
Bonnaz, Christophe 4:13:46 (12,035)
Bonner, Clive D 4:11:10 (11,417)
Bonner, Jonathan L 4:21:56 (14,073)
Bonner, Mark L 5:48:01 (31,468)
Bonner, Matthew 5:00:47 (23,683)
Bonnet, Olivier H 5:40:07 (30,609)
Bonnett, Curtis 3:34:47 (4,377)
Bonnett, Stephen 4:44:51 (19,791)
Bonney, Graham 6:23:23 (34,049)
Bonniec, Philippe 2:54:17 (532)
Bonora, Liam 5:03:28 (24,230)
Bonser, Derek A 5:50:26 (31,720)
Boocock, Paul A 4:22:23 (14,170)
Boocock, Scott A 4:44:03 (19,552)
Booker, Alex D 3:45:45 (6,139)
Booker, Steve R 3:11:57 (1,721)
Boon, Julian M 4:28:15 (15,657)
Boon, Neil 4:12:16 (11,677)
Boon, Robert 3:08:25 (1,423)
Boorer, Bryan H 4:38:41 (18,195)
Boorman, Bill 7:19:03 (35,381)
Boorman, Nickolas S 4:55:05 (22,285)
Boorsma, Mark D 5:32:01 (29,459)
Booter, Joel 5:39:53 (30,577)
Booth, Alan 6:23:52 (34,069)
Booth, Alistair J 4:33:15 (16,857)
Booth, Andrew J 5:02:02 (23,941)
Booth, Gareth M 3:19:34 (2,440)
Booth, John P 4:53:34 (21,904)

Booth, Jonathan 4:05:03 (10,153)
Booth, Mark A 4:45:03 (19,852)
Booth, Martin 4:25:23 (14,918)
Booth, Paul A 5:14:40 (26,377)
Booth, Roger 3:05:14 (1,178)
Booth, Stephen G 2:57:11 (689)
Booth, Terence 5:38:34 (30,390)
Booth, Vincent A 2:52:05 (444)
Boother, Mark 5:02:16 (23,982)
Boothman, John D 4:13:16 (11,899)
Boothman, Stuart R 4:33:37 (16,942)
Boothroyd, Alastair 5:00:02 (23,512)
Bootle, Andrew W 5:49:51 (31,667)
Booty, Graham 3:12:07 (1,742)
Boram, John 4:33:54 (17,007)
Bore, Alan D 5:41:50 (30,811)
Boreel, Jacob 4:20:20 (13,691)
Borel-Saladin, Jean-Pierre A 4:56:37 (22,665)
Borg, Alan 5:28:12 (28,838)
Borg, Henric 3:55:01 (8,011)
Borgars, Robert W 4:47:14 (20,340)
Borgerson, Graham 4:58:56 (23,238)
Borgund, Ole J 4:36:58 (17,779)
Boris-Moller, Jan 6:10:39 (33,345)
Borland, John A 5:14:14 (26,278)
Borley, David C 4:51:59 (21,483)
Borley, Harry W 4:23:50 (14,525)
Born, Chris 5:29:53 (29,118)
Bornand, Olivier P 3:23:49 (2,879)
Boross, Paul 4:55:02 (22,271)
Borowski, Mark N 4:08:50 (10,928)
Borri, Alessandro 3:52:40 (7,494)
Borri, Domenico 4:57:07 (22,800)
Borrowdale, David 4:41:22 (18,879)
Borthwick, Daniel C 4:14:50 (12,273)
Borucki, Kuba J 5:05:26 (24,584)
Bory, Jacques 4:19:19 (13,410)
Bos, Egbert P 4:14:23 (12,183)
Bos, Peter 4:24:44 (14,756)
Bosch, Ulf 3:10:17 (1,586)
Bosek, Robert 4:01:27 (9,506)
Bosence, Mark 4:52:36 (21,642)
Bosi, Valerio 4:14:49 (12,272)
Bosley, Philip M 4:42:09 (19,076)
Bosquet, Jean-Jacques G 3:50:27 (7,029)
Bosse, Thomas 3:54:56 (7,995)
Bostock, Colin R 4:14:26 (12,194)
Bostock, Lee A 3:56:42 (8,406)
Bostock, Malcolm S 3:16:02 (2,081)
Bostock, Will 4:50:26 (21,107)
Boston, David T 4:54:57 (22,257)
Boswell, Robert J 6:31:10 (34,367)
Boswell, Stuart N 3:27:41 (3,370)
Bosworth, Mark R 3:34:49 (4,381)
Botfield, Glyn J 4:10:20 (11,233)
Botha, Leo 4:27:49 (15,543)
Botha, Matt W 5:25:20 (28,327)
Botham, Christo 6:41:04 (34,691)
Botreau, Yves 3:06:46 (1,295)
Bott, Jonathan R 3:31:34 (3,919)
Botting, Brian J 4:55:10 (22,309)
Bottomley, Simon J 5:08:46 (25,237)
Bouaziz, Fessal 4:45:54 (20,033)
Bouchard, Jean-Paul 3:52:23 (7,448)
Bouchard, Martin 3:39:45 (5,152)
Boucher, Llewellyn P 3:50:43 (7,082)
Boucher, Michael B 2:32:51 (53)
Boucher, Paul M 5:11:07 (25,693)
Boucher, William J 3:39:29 (5,104)
Bouda, Christopher M 4:48:46 (20,711)
Boulby, Kenneth A 4:02:35 (9,705)
Boullard, Jerome 4:13:41 (12,014)
Boult, Jonathan 4:51:54 (21,466)
Boult, Stephen W 4:14:11 (12,134)
Boulter, Adam C 5:19:14 (27,297)
Boulter, David 4:07:04 (10,587)
Boulton, John R 4:05:47 (10,304)
Boulton, Stephen P 4:28:42 (15,789)
Boulton-Jones, Nicholas M 4:43:06 (19,318)
Bouma, Klaas K 5:32:44 (29,569)
Bouman, Christiaaan 4:31:50 (16,533)
Bourgain, Christian 3:14:38 (1,958)
Bouri, Chandra M 7:20:40 (35,393)

Bourke, Robert A 3:58:28 (8,832)
Bourletias, Gilles 4:34:15 (17,088)
Bourne, David R 3:48:23 (6,587)
Bourne, Paul R 5:39:24 (30,507)
Bourne, Stanley B 6:54:17 (35,024)
Bourne, Stuart J 4:47:20 (20,367)
Bourne, Wayne 4:22:49 (14,290)
Bousfield, Richard S 3:55:08 (8,039)
Bousquet, Philippe 5:20:38 (27,545)
Boussenot, Jean-Luce 5:12:06 (25,870)
Boutcher, Jonathan M 4:38:14 (18,064)
Boutellier, Eric 3:00:30 (931)
Bovenzi, Bruno 3:53:34 (7,702)
Bovill, David 3:56:10 (8,267)
Bovill, Peter 2:41:46 (174)
Bowden, Alexander C 3:44:11 (5,890)
Bowden, David A 4:13:14 (11,889)
Bowden, Nicholas P 4:10:22 (11,240)
Bowden, Paul 3:08:01 (1,392)
Bowden, Raymond F 4:25:02 (14,834)
Bowden, Rodney A 4:12:12 (11,655)
Bowden, Stephen 5:15:17 (26,520)
Bowden, Trevor W 4:03:37 (9,889)
Bowden-Brown, Andrew 5:16:07 (26,687)
Bowen, Andy 3:22:06 (2,714)
Bowen, Anthony J 5:18:01 (27,060)
Bowen, Anthony M 4:50:47 (21,189)
Bowen, Corin J 4:08:50 (10,928)
Bowen, James K 2:56:16 (624)
Bowen, Julian C 5:44:04 (31,049)
Bowen, Kirk 5:05:20 (24,558)
Bowen, Laurence J 4:41:40 (18,958)
Bowen, Leslie A 4:46:19 (20,130)
Bowen, Sean 3:03:47 (1,091)
Bower, Brian 3:23:40 (2,866)
Bower, Sean A 4:52:53 (21,721)
Bowerman, Paddy E 4:15:37 (12,468)
Bowers, Gerald I 5:59:40 (32,556)
Bowers, Stuart E 4:37:17 (17,838)
Bowes, Christopher D 3:35:59 (4,545)
Bowie, Randy C 5:31:05 (29,312)
Bowker, Lyndon T 4:44:42 (19,744)
Bowker, Paul H 5:31:20 (29,349)
Bowler, Jamie C 4:43:18 (19,372)
Bowler, Jason 4:13:02 (11,840)
Bowles, Andrew M 4:21:16 (13,905)
Bowles, David L 4:12:02 (11,619)
Bowles, Keith D 4:37:24 (17,862)
Bowles, Neil 4:05:11 (10,184)
Bowles, William 5:29:07 (28,998)
Bowlzer, Nicholas M 4:01:47 (9,564)
Bowman, Fred G 4:52:33 (21,626)
Bowman, Harry J 4:47:50 (20,489)
Bowman, Ian 4:16:58 (12,808)
Bowman, John 5:25:42 (28,406)
Bowman, Nick 5:38:03 (30,310)
Bowman, Nick K 4:41:20 (18,869)
Bowman, Nigel P 5:14:43 (26,389)
Bowman, Nicholas D 4:28:43 (15,792)
Bowman, Steve A 3:52:43 (7,506)
Bowmer, Shaun J 7:14:20 (35,335)
Bownes, George H 3:20:56 (2,603)
Bownes, Kevin G 3:57:09 (8,511)
Bowran, Stephen J 3:32:08 (4,017)
Bowyer, Barry W 6:04:41 (32,932)
Bowyer, Malcolm 3:01:11 (970)
Bowyer, Oliver 4:19:18 (13,405)
Box, Richard H 4:54:05 (22,037)
Boxall, Simon J 4:19:55 (13,578)
Boxford, Stephen H 5:04:24 (24,403)
Boxhall, Richard J 4:51:58 (21,477)
Boxley, Keith W 4:23:30 (14,444)
Boyall, Tim J 4:13:55 (12,073)
Boyce, Benjamin M 5:05:40 (24,628)
Boyce, Glen J 4:59:06 (23,287)
Boyce, John J 5:25:38 (28,391)
Boyce, Richard E 3:09:59 (1,557)
Boyd, Andrew 4:17:00 (12,814)
Boyd, Billy 4:55:01 (22,267)
Boyd, Gavin E 5:12:30 (25,951)
Boyd, Richard S 4:36:31 (17,671)
Boyd, Robert P 3:49:51 (6,908)
Boyd, Steven P 5:18:48 (27,214)
Boyden, Mark P 4:58:10 (23,067)
Boyden, Richard 4:43:43 (19,466)
Boyd-Vandeleur, Paul W 6:22:28 (34,021)
Boyes, Andrew 3:51:35 (7,274)
Boyes, Simon J 3:58:19 (8,790)
Boyle, Anthony 4:55:48 (22,455)
Boyle, Brendan J 4:56:51 (22,735)
Boyle, David A 4:05:40 (10,280)
Boyle, Jamie E 4:01:00 (9,420)
Boyman, Matthew J 4:36:00 (17,534)
Boyne, Benjamin T 4:04:43 (10,095)
Boyne, Robert 3:41:08 (5,387)
Boysen, Claus 3:49:21 (6,805)
Bozier, Chris M 4:02:18 (9,668)
Bozzoli, Andrea 4:17:33 (12,961)
Brabner, Nicholas S 5:45:59 (31,256)
Brace, Anthony G 4:25:11 (14,867)
Brace, Simon P 3:08:58 (1,466)
Bracegirdle, Ian 5:19:38 (27,365)
Bracey, James C 3:54:34 (7,914)
Bracey, Nick 4:23:27 (14,432)
Bracey, Richard W 6:00:08 (32,589)
Bracher, Phil S 4:09:48 (11,127)
Brack, Peter 5:44:14 (31,069)
Brackstone, Paul S 4:13:38 (12,004)
Bradbeer, Alex 3:38:47 (4,971)
Bradburn, Paul J 4:05:53 (10,327)
Bradbury, Alan K 3:20:19 (2,531)
Bradbury, David 4:46:59 (20,274)
Bradbury, Gary J 4:14:55 (12,302)
Bradbury, Paul A 4:17:28 (12,932)
Bradbury, Steven P 5:41:52 (30,816)
Bradbury, Thomas J 4:19:57 (13,589)
Braddon, Anthony A 4:52:22 (21,589)
Bradford, Luke 3:34:09 (4,286)
Bradford, Malcolm J 7:36:48 (35,541)
Bradford, Paul S 4:05:56 (10,338)
Bradford, Peter S 4:36:29 (17,659)
Bradford, Simon D 4:37:09 (17,814)
Bradley, Alan M 3:36:08 (4,562)
Bradley, Andrew R 5:23:31 (28,013)
Bradley, Barrington J 3:58:50 (8,921)
Bradley, Ben P 4:06:58 (10,566)
Bradley, Eamon 3:32:14 (4,036)
Bradley, Harvey 4:16:00 (12,562)
Bradley, Ian 4:40:02 (18,543)
Bradley, Mark 3:58:23 (8,805)
Bradley, Mark 4:44:34 (19,705)
Bradley, Mikk J 3:03:27 (1,073)
Bradley, Neil J 3:50:59 (7,135)
Bradley, Nigel T 4:26:39 (15,223)
Bradley, Paul 3:39:37 (5,131)
Bradley, Philip A 3:07:19 (1,336)
Bradley, Philip D 5:36:51 (30,156)
Bradley, Richard 4:24:15 (14,643)
Bradley, Russell D 4:13:53 (12,062)
Bradley, Scott 2:45:30 (250)
Bradley, William A 4:43:05 (19,315)
Bradshaw, Allan 3:56:14 (8,284)
Bradshaw, Brian S 5:24:18 (28,157)
Bradshaw, Chris A 3:35:55 (4,538)
Bradshaw, Colin R 5:23:54 (28,093)
Bradshaw, Eric G 4:20:18 (13,679)
Bradshaw, Gary J 3:35:32 (4,490)
Bradshaw, Jeff 4:18:27 (13,196)
Bradshaw, Jonathan 3:30:24 (3,778)
Bradshaw, Lee J 4:17:40 (12,989)
Bradshaw, Mark 4:28:32 (15,738)
Bradshaw, Nigel T 5:07:16 (24,947)
Bradshaw, Stephen 4:25:12 (14,875)
Bradshaw, Terence A 3:41:07 (5,384)
Bradshaw, Thomas 4:26:23 (15,155)
Bradshaw, Thomas J 3:53:54 (7,765)
Brady, Anthony 4:50:59 (21,240)
Brady, Des C 4:26:18 (15,130)
Brady, Gerald J 5:56:00 (32,240)
Brady, John C 3:57:21 (8,567)
Brady, Joseph M 3:23:47 (2,876)
Brady, Michael S 4:38:01 (18,015)
Brady, Peter E 4:46:57 (20,267)
Braham, Zak G 6:48:06 (34,890)
Braham-Everett, Daniel A 4:19:58 (13,594)
Brahams, Gareth E 4:24:31 (14,710)
Brahams, Nigel R 4:10:14 (11,212)
Brailsford, Adam J 4:04:15 (10,014)
Brain, John 5:38:23 (30,367)
Brain, Paul M 5:19:52 (27,402)
Braithwaite, Carl S 3:41:58 (5,511)
Braithwaite, Mark 5:14:50 (26,415)
Brakenbury, Matthew G 4:39:58 (18,531)
Brakes, William R 5:58:19 (32,445)
Brambles, Neil 3:32:15 (4,038)
Brameld, Dominic 6:55:25 (35,046)
Bramley, Damian J 4:56:56 (22,759)
Brammer, David J 4:01:38 (9,539)
Brammer, Michael 5:02:33 (24,051)
Brammer, Paul 5:38:16 (30,350)
Bramwell, James A 5:14:27 (26,321)
Branch, Christopher P 4:53:00 (21,756)
Branch, Jason A 4:15:34 (12,453)
Branch, Malcolm F 4:11:44 (11,554)
Brand, Kevin J 5:30:02 (29,147)
Brand, Philip 4:08:30 (10,871)
Brand, Thomas E 4:27:59 (15,582)
Brandon, Graham T 5:36:36 (30,125)
Brandon-Trye, Christopher P 3:34:15 (4,302)
Brandrick, Paul 3:15:55 (2,072)
Brandt, Dan G 4:40:47 (18,728)
Brandwood, Tim 4:41:11 (18,836)
Branford, Michael R 5:32:40 (29,561)
Brannigan, Malachy 4:22:55 (14,313)
Bransom, Kenneth A 4:52:42 (21,668)
Branson, Gary 7:31:18 (35,505)
Brant, Andrew 4:47:53 (20,502)
Brant, Raymond P 5:00:07 (23,526)
Brasted, Dominic 3:31:10 (3,858)
Bratchell, Roger 4:43:20 (19,390)
Bratton, Graham J 4:48:32 (20,656)
Bratttoli, Raffaele 3:51:25 (7,231)
Braun, Eric 4:41:16 (18,855)
Braunton, David W 5:16:32 (26,763)
Bravo, Antonio 6:31:22 (34,376)
Bravo, Ramiro 4:54:09 (22,062)
Brawn, Nick 3:08:02 (1,394)
Bray, Alan 3:59:36 (9,119)
Bray, Chris J 4:09:03 (10,966)
Bray, Matthew J 4:19:05 (13,350)
Bray, Michael A 5:10:29 (25,574)
Bray, Michael G 3:54:29 (7,899)
Bray, Robert J 5:21:36 (27,712)
Bray, Stuart 4:08:51 (10,933)
Bray, Vivian F 4:03:50 (9,935)
Braybrook, Colin A 3:15:41 (2,046)
Braybrook, James W 5:28:28 (28,896)
Brayne, Chris 4:53:59 (22,016)
Brayne, Martin S 4:15:46 (12,501)
Brayshaw, Jeremy D 4:12:21 (11,690)
Brazendale, David A 4:49:34 (20,908)
Brazier, Bill S 4:20:43 (13,778)
Brazier, Matthew R 4:23:30 (14,444)
Brazier, Russell 5:31:06 (29,317)
Brazier, Tony M 3:39:13 (5,048)
Brazil, John E 4:39:20 (18,379)
Brazil, Simon A 3:29:31 (3,650)
Brdoa, Roland T 5:26:58 (28,618)
Breadmore, Nigel D 3:51:43 (7,297)
Breaker, Ben 3:25:44 (3,094)
Breaker, Derek 5:05:28 (24,595)
Breaks, Adam B 2:40:20 (145)
Brearley, Michael 2:58:59 (821)
Brebnor, Lance J 4:29:27 (15,993)
Breeden, Martin R 4:44:28 (19,670)
Breen, Derek 2:53:26 (491)
Breen, James 3:23:05 (2,804)
Breens, Stuart J 7:08:11 (35,247)
Breese, Allan 3:46:01 (6,182)
Breese, Ian C 4:26:11 (15,091)
Breetzke, Gavin 4:25:08 (14,856)
Brehaut, Matthew 3:47:44 (6,486)
Brench, Gary 4:47:30 (20,407)
Brennan, Daniel J 4:11:51 (11,585)
Brennan, Daniel J 5:06:13 (24,744)
Brennan, Justin P 5:05:10 (24,538)
Brennan, Lorcan 3:26:58 (3,272)
Brennan, Michael E 4:31:59 (16,557)
Brennan, Miles R 4:21:00 (13,853)

Brennan, Noel	5:05:25 (24,577)
Brennan, Paul M	3:44:00 (5,867)
Brennan, Toby J	4:57:49 (22,991)
Brent, Roger M	3:59:21 (9,053)
Brereton, Andrew J	4:13:20 (11,917)
Brereton, Matthew R	4:56:05 (22,532)
Breslin, John J	4:18:18 (13,149)
Bretherton, Edward M	4:38:47 (18,226)
Bretherton, Neil	4:07:21 (10,626)
Brett, Barry J	4:29:13 (15,915)
Brett, Colin M	3:56:23 (8,330)
Brett, John R	6:30:45 (34,348)
Brett, Richard M	3:38:32 (4,926)
Brett, Stephen	3:24:03 (2,914)
Brettell, Angus G	4:38:16 (18,077)
Breuer, John P	3:39:15 (5,055)
Breuning, Sam M	3:28:21 (3,457)
Brew, Patrick	3:23:03 (2,801)
Brew, Robin	5:54:24 (32,097)
Brewer, Adam	4:20:50 (13,814)
Brewer, John	4:09:28 (11,066)
Brewer, John S	4:18:14 (13,132)
Brewin, Nicholas	5:19:44 (27,379)
Brewis, Henry S	5:22:53 (27,918)
Brewis, Matthew	3:22:48 (2,777)
Breydin, Patrick J	5:16:17 (26,719)
Brian, Geoffrey S	7:05:07 (35,205)
Bric, Garrett D	3:36:21 (4,594)
Briddon, Simon J	4:22:47 (14,281)
Bridge, Andrew K	4:52:44 (21,677)
Bridge, Grantley S	3:37:47 (4,786)
Bridge, James	4:25:59 (15,054)
Bridge, John D	3:39:59 (5,185)
Bridge, Karl R	4:28:42 (15,789)
Bridge, Peter E	5:47:26 (31,403)
Bridgeman, Gary	4:28:08 (15,629)
Bridgeman, Paul	4:11:24 (11,474)
Bridgens, John M	4:16:33 (12,704)
Bridger, Gary S	4:49:13 (20,824)
Bridger, John D	4:34:13 (17,079)
Bridges, Alex J	5:48:57 (31,578)
Bridges, Anthony M	2:50:34 (395)
Bridges, Barry F	4:23:26 (14,427)
Bridges, Douglas J	3:57:28 (8,594)
Bridges, Graham R	3:54:16 (7,861)
Bridges, Mark	5:27:39 (28,736)
Bridges, Oliver R	5:46:20 (31,295)
Bridges, Russell T	3:15:02 (2,001)
Bridgewater, Benjamin H	4:58:25 (23,136)
Bridgeworth, Paul	5:43:59 (31,039)
Bridgman, Peter J	4:18:25 (13,181)
Bridgman, Tim R	4:23:16 (14,393)
Brien, James	3:38:35 (4,937)
Briens, Eric	3:24:00 (2,904)
Briens, Jean-Marc G	2:58:26 (786)
Brierley, Andrew S	3:08:29 (1,430)
Brierley, Benjamin	5:52:30 (31,919)
Brierley, Peter J	5:06:11 (24,734)
Brierley, Simon P	4:20:03 (13,611)
Brigg, Nick J	4:52:31 (21,618)
Briggs, Adam D	3:36:53 (4,672)
Briggs, Andi M	5:52:40 (31,935)
Briggs, Andrew J	5:11:54 (25,834)
Briggs, Ben J	4:52:11 (21,537)
Briggs, Clifford J	5:30:07 (29,165)
Briggs, Gareth	2:35:36 (79)
Briggs, Martin P	4:48:01 (20,535)
Briggs, Mike A	5:09:59 (25,473)
Briggs, Nicholas N	3:59:41 (9,136)
Briggs, Timothy P	3:38:55 (5,000)
Bright, Andrew A	4:13:22 (11,926)
Bright, Dennis	5:50:20 (31,709)
Bright, Kevin J	3:47:14 (6,384)
Bright, Mark	4:55:17 (22,337)
Bright, Matthew	4:36:44 (17,723)
Bright, Nick	4:43:24 (19,400)
Bright, Simon	5:51:57 (31,870)
Brightling, David	3:42:07 (5,540)
Brightman, Scott	4:40:23 (18,628)
Brightwell, Simon L	3:17:26 (2,221)
Brighty, Keith G	5:01:17 (23,789)
Brigstock, Tim W	4:35:57 (17,524)
Bril, Ronan O	4:58:11 (23,070)

Briley, Colin J	4:45:49 (20,010)
Brill, Jonathon R	4:54:32 (22,150)
Brinck, David J	4:56:53 (22,743)
Brind, Kevin N	5:22:19 (27,822)
Brindle, Nian D	3:50:27 (7,029)
Brindle, Paul J	4:15:16 (12,383)
Brining, Steven N	4:01:48 (9,568)
Brink, Christian P	3:30:12 (3,749)
Brinkley, Peter	5:17:04 (26,871)
Brisco, Douglas A	2:49:10 (351)
Briscoe, Wesley W	3:50:25 (7,024)
Brisley, Michael J	3:52:16 (7,425)
Brister, Gregory	3:57:09 (8,511)
Bristow, Colin R	5:37:17 (30,212)
Bristow, James L	3:55:45 (8,175)
Bristow, Richard E	4:41:14 (18,848)
Bristow, Simon J	5:03:29 (24,235)
Brittain, Elliott	5:02:00 (23,934)
Brittain, Peter	7:29:26 (35,485)
Brittle, Peter G	3:56:20 (8,314)
Britton, Alan R	4:37:26 (17,874)
Britton, Brett J	5:39:34 (30,541)
Britton, Jeremy E	6:03:55 (32,881)
Britton, Jonathan	4:53:32 (21,894)
Britton, Matthew C	4:10:07 (11,186)
Britton, Richard W	6:44:15 (34,781)
Britton, Timothy J	4:33:41 (16,955)
Britton Hall, Stephen J	3:37:31 (4,754)
Britz, Andries	4:23:19 (14,402)
Briwwant-Jones, Gwyn	4:59:02 (23,264)
Broad, Dan J	5:45:36 (31,218)
Broad, Joel	5:15:38 (26,590)
Broad, Nigel P	3:43:09 (5,714)
Broadbent, David I	3:55:46 (8,178)
Broadbent, Peter	4:06:25 (10,445)
Broadbent, Steven S	3:48:16 (6,568)
Broadhead, Andrew	5:07:15 (24,942)
Broadhurst, Andrew W	5:09:10 (25,306)
Broadley, Duncan K	4:03:04 (9,798)
Broadribb, William	3:28:35 (3,502)
Brock, Christopher T	5:32:01 (29,459)
Brock, Claus	3:47:06 (6,364)
Brock, Michael H	4:24:48 (14,777)
Brockington, Martin J	5:24:51 (28,250)
Brocklehurst, Aaron	4:14:18 (12,169)
Brocklehurst, Robert	3:58:33 (8,849)
Brocklesby, Keith A	4:28:10 (15,640)
Brockley, Mark	6:01:00 (32,671)
Brodie, David A	4:22:52 (14,303)
Brodie, Gordon R	6:31:49 (34,395)
Brodie, Tom D	4:22:52 (14,303)
Brodziak, Andy	3:05:04 (1,167)
Brogden, Thomas G	3:34:17 (4,312)
Bromley, Adam J	3:40:27 (5,253)
Bromley, Danny J	5:08:23 (25,172)
Bromley, Ian D	4:05:19 (10,206)
Bromley, John W	6:36:53 (34,577)
Bromley, Nigel G	4:07:54 (10,748)
Brook, Anthony T	3:21:42 (2,675)
Brook, Ashley	3:00:03 (903)
Brook, Giles T	3:58:43 (8,887)
Brook, Graham J	2:47:59 (308)
Brook, Paul G	4:48:18 (20,605)
Brook, Quentin S	4:31:04 (16,368)
Brook, Roland S	4:06:10 (10,385)
Brooke, Andrew	3:50:01 (6,948)
Brooke, Angus J	3:32:47 (4,102)
Brooke, Anthony C	3:47:05 (6,361)
Brooke, Anthony D	3:01:18 (975)
Brooke, David A	6:22:40 (34,031)
Brooke, Orlando D	3:52:09 (7,400)
Brooker, Bruce	4:52:30 (21,612)
Brooker, Kevin	4:29:25 (15,980)
Brooker-Corcoran, Tom P	4:22:14 (14,137)
Brookes, Andrew W	4:34:06 (17,050)
Brookes, Anthony E	5:58:55 (32,498)
Brookes, Jamie	4:00:58 (9,411)
Brookes, John G	6:09:32 (33,275)
Brookes, Nigel A	3:20:56 (2,603)
Brookes, Paul	4:42:07 (19,071)
Brookes-Smith, Bryan J	6:24:33 (34,103)
Brooking, Gary A	4:47:47 (20,478)
Brooks, Adam J	3:39:19 (5,067)

Brooks, Adrian C	4:18:31 (13,217)
Brooks, Alexander D	3:55:24 (8,105)
Brooks, Andrew D	5:38:03 (30,310)
Brooks, Anthony N	4:11:01 (11,371)
Brooks, Ashley	5:37:56 (30,291)
Brooks, Charles V	6:36:30 (34,557)
Brooks, Danny L	4:28:31 (15,730)
Brooks, Duncan G	5:43:45 (31,019)
Brooks, Gary	4:23:40 (14,484)
Brooks, James D	6:05:36 (33,016)
Brooks, Michael	3:24:47 (2,994)
Brooks, Stephen R	6:11:07 (33,378)
Brooks, Thomas	4:09:17 (11,024)
Brooksbank, Jake A	6:21:53 (33,991)
Brookshaw, Ben I	3:57:51 (8,680)
Broom, Graham M	5:19:10 (27,283)
Broom, John	2:50:12 (379)
Broom, Michael D	5:49:01 (31,588)
Broom, Robert	6:22:15 (34,009)
Broom, Will	3:17:53 (2,272)
Broome, Christopher	5:15:15 (26,513)
Broomfield, James H	4:48:20 (20,620)
Broomfield, Ken W	5:05:11 (24,541)
Brophy, Michael J	4:11:20 (11,456)
Brosend, Marcel	5:05:27 (24,588)
Brosnan, Michael F	5:01:56 (23,920)
Brosnan, Paul	4:57:13 (22,827)
Brotherton, Chris A	3:10:19 (1,588)
Brotherton, Stuart	5:25:13 (28,308)
Brough, Dickon M	3:28:49 (3,541)
Brough, Terry W	3:51:34 (7,269)
Brougham, Charlie W	4:31:54 (16,542)
Brougham, Samuel M	6:48:24 (34,897)
Broughton, Anthony C	5:12:58 (26,039)
Broughton, Colin J	4:57:28 (22,900)
Broughton, Martin F	5:49:36 (31,638)
Brouwer, Henk	4:24:29 (14,701)
Browes, Graham	5:08:19 (25,158)
Browett, Mark	4:45:46 (20,001)
Brown, Adrian P	3:59:08 (8,992)
Brown, Alan	5:31:41 (29,402)
Brown, Alan R	4:09:25 (11,053)
Brown, Alan R	4:45:20 (19,914)
Brown, Alastair M	4:28:15 (15,657)
Brown, Alex	3:38:43 (4,960)
Brown, Alexander N	4:04:38 (10,080)
Brown, Alistair R	4:10:13 (11,209)
Brown, Andrew	3:53:13 (7,626)
Brown, Andrew J	4:14:52 (12,284)
Brown, Anthoney	5:23:38 (28,039)
Brown, Anthony S	6:08:07 (33,181)
Brown, Barnaby J	3:41:12 (5,398)
Brown, Bruce M	4:55:27 (22,377)
Brown, Charles M	6:40:11 (34,671)
Brown, Chris	4:15:26 (12,426)
Brown, Chris V	3:38:30 (4,922)
Brown, Christopher	3:56:26 (8,338)
Brown, Christopher	4:02:45 (9,742)
Brown, Christopher M	3:25:18 (3,044)
Brown, Christopher W	5:01:00 (23,725)
Brown, Craig	3:47:16 (6,389)
Brown, Danny	4:40:45 (18,714)
Brown, David A	4:36:18 (17,612)
Brown, David A	4:39:26 (18,400)
Brown, David B	5:42:41 (30,892)
Brown, David C	7:18:25 (35,376)
Brown, David D	5:14:57 (26,439)
Brown, David G	5:29:13 (29,027)
Brown, David J	4:19:26 (13,440)
Brown, David J	4:27:07 (15,357)
Brown, David K	4:57:58 (23,025)
Brown, Dean C	4:56:12 (22,564)
Brown, Delaney J	4:28:32 (15,738)
Brown, Derek	2:43:56 (212)
Brown, Derek A	5:33:08 (29,624)
Brown, Derek A	7:25:17 (35,433)
Brown, Duncan J	4:22:44 (14,268)
Brown, Duncan J	4:26:46 (15,255)
Brown, Gary	3:07:02 (1,311)
Brown, Gary	5:16:52 (26,829)
Brown, Gavin J	3:56:53 (8,452)
Brown, Geoffrey	3:57:10 (8,518)
Brown, Geoffrey	5:38:45 (30,423)

Brown, Gordon 4:10:12 (11,205)
Brown, Iain P 5:33:07 (29,622)
Brown, Iain R 4:19:13 (13,379)
Brown, Ian 4:07:53 (10,742)
Brown, Ian M 3:05:31 (1,203)
Brown, James A 4:40:25 (18,634)
Brown, James H 3:08:54 (1,458)
Brown, James M 3:20:30 (2,553)
Brown, John W 4:59:35 (23,407)
Brown, Jonathan J 2:54:34 (552)
Brown, Jonathan L 3:51:58 (7,359)
Brown, Joseph S 3:23:25 (2,842)
Brown, Julian D 5:25:29 (28,367)
Brown, Karl C 6:07:58 (33,167)
Brown, Kevin J 3:42:58 (5,682)
Brown, Kevin P 4:20:07 (13,629)
Brown, Kieran P 4:16:18 (12,650)
Brown, Lee E 4:06:09 (10,383)
Brown, Mark J 4:23:50 (14,525)
Brown, Martin S 3:42:23 (5,581)
Brown, Matt 5:42:34 (30,884)
Brown, Matthew 3:34:54 (4,395)
Brown, Michael J 3:35:14 (4,438)
Brown, Michael N 4:55:05 (22,285)
Brown, Neil E 5:15:48 (26,625)
Brown, Nicholas 3:05:36 (1,209)
Brown, Nicholas E 4:25:08 (14,856)
Brown, Nick 5:44:00 (31,042)
Brown, Nick C 4:15:04 (12,336)
Brown, Nick E 4:33:47 (16,987)
Brown, Paul A 4:30:32 (16,261)
Brown, Paul R 4:46:28 (20,170)
Brown, Peter 4:17:25 (12,914)
Brown, Peter 5:09:35 (25,395)
Brown, Peter T 4:02:28 (9,692)
Brown, Peter W 4:28:28 (15,720)
Brown, Phil A 3:40:33 (5,278)
Brown, Ray D 3:41:37 (5,458)
Brown, Raymond P 3:58:44 (8,893)
Brown, Richard E 4:54:08 (22,054)
Brown, Robert L 3:37:50 (4,794)
Brown, Robert S 4:13:29 (11,956)
Brown, Roger T 4:32:59 (16,780)
Brown, Sam E 4:45:39 (19,983)
Brown, Scott E 4:42:25 (19,156)
Brown, Shaun 3:17:55 (2,277)
Brown, Shaun J 4:41:21 (18,875)
Brown, Simon J 2:49:26 (357)
Brown, Stephen A 3:52:54 (7,544)
Brown, Stephen B 3:39:29 (5,104)
Brown, Steve 4:54:24 (22,123)
Brown, Steve M 4:23:46 (14,505)
Brown, Stuart 4:15:15 (12,376)
Brown, Terry 4:19:10 (13,370)
Brown, Tommie 6:05:56 (33,040)
Brown, Tony 4:44:27 (19,663)
Brown, Warren 5:06:08 (24,723)
Brown, Wayne 5:32:29 (29,520)
Brown, William B 4:08:35 (10,888)
Brown, William R 4:27:49 (15,543)
Browne, Alasdair E 3:49:43 (6,879)
Browne, Arthur J 4:48:24 (20,633)
Browne, James A 3:35:26 (4,474)
Browne, John J 4:09:11 (11,002)
Browne, Michael T 5:06:54 (24,861)
Browne, Patrick J 4:27:27 (15,460)
Browne, Richard M 2:56:06 (617)
Browne, Roger 5:09:14 (25,323)
Browne, Steve S 4:36:34 (17,686)
Brownie, Christopher A 4:17:07 (12,833)
Browning, Daniel J 5:33:50 (29,736)
Browning, David C 4:32:49 (16,744)
Browning, Kenneth M 6:03:03 (32,822)
Browning, Meil R 3:15:41 (2,046)
Browning, Peter E 6:32:45 (34,431)
Brownlee, Ricky J 4:51:49 (21,440)
Brownlee, Scott 4:54:07 (22,048)
Brownlee, Shane G 4:27:22 (15,436)
Brownlee, Steven S 6:02:31 (32,787)
Brownless, Stephen A 5:11:12 (25,703)
Brownlie, Francis 4:12:45 (11,775)
Brownsmith, Graham P 3:54:49 (7,965)
Broxton, Mark D 4:13:52 (12,056)
Brtadley, Tony 4:49:53 (20,970)
Bruce, Andrew 4:56:11 (22,559)
Bruce, Andrew K 3:43:37 (5,801)
Bruce, Chris J 3:53:33 (7,698)
Bruce, Clive J 4:33:02 (16,795)
Bruce, Craig 5:13:36 (26,141)
Bruce, Gerald R 5:13:32 (26,129)
Bruce, Henry 4:19:15 (13,395)
Bruce, John 5:32:30 (29,525)
Bruce, Jonathan P 4:39:18 (18,364)
Bruce, Martyn J 4:42:28 (19,171)
Bruce, Perry C 4:27:22 (15,436)
Bruce, Robert A 4:02:06 (9,622)
Bruce, Sam 3:57:33 (8,610)
Bruce, Sandy 4:58:01 (23,039)
Brudenell, Ryan J 3:39:39 (5,135)
Brudenell, Victor W 2:49:25 (356)
Brueck, Thomas 3:58:44 (8,893)
Bruenen, Andreas 4:03:39 (9,891)
Bruil, Jan 4:07:21 (10,626)
Bruneau, Dominic 4:11:57 (11,603)
Brunelli Bonetti, Alberto 4:08:27 (10,862)
Brunier, Remi 4:22:11 (14,121)
Brunning, Peter E 4:47:16 (20,347)
Brunsdon, Richard M 5:51:18 (31,808)
Brunskill, Simon N 4:41:00 (18,791)
Brunt, Frederick R 3:42:20 (5,577)
Brunt, Martyn J 3:15:35 (2,034)
Brunyee, John S 3:53:26 (7,673)
Bruty, James C 4:36:01 (17,540)
Bryan, Adam 4:13:13 (11,883)
Bryan, Philip E 2:51:07 (414)
Bryans, Chris 4:49:26 (20,867)
Bryant, Andrew D 3:16:43 (2,150)
Bryant, Ben L 5:28:31 (28,903)
Bryant, Chris 3:34:19 (4,318)
Bryant, Dan J 4:50:28 (21,114)
Bryant, David J 5:48:39 (31,539)
Bryant, Edmund B 3:44:54 (6,013)
Bryant, Geoffrey J 5:44:38 (31,116)
Bryant, George I 3:44:38 (5,964)
Bryant, John M 4:09:31 (11,078)
Bryant, John W 5:26:41 (28,574)
Bryant, Matthew A 3:30:48 (3,820)
Bryant, Michael B 5:25:53 (28,439)
Bryant, Michael R 4:52:22 (21,589)
Bryant, Paul D 4:09:04 (10,969)
Bryant, Peter R 5:01:07 (23,755)
Bryant, Robert E 4:26:32 (15,201)
Bryant, Simon L 4:19:49 (13,544)
Bryant, Wayne 3:54:54 (7,991)
Bryant, Will 5:26:41 (28,574)
Bryar, Carl 5:19:30 (27,337)
Bryce, Donal K 5:56:14 (32,259)
Bryce, Graeme E 3:28:38 (3,511)
Bryon, Paul A 5:25:01 (28,272)
Bryson, Rob P 3:09:38 (1,525)
Bryson, William G 4:52:36 (21,642)
Bubb, Philip G 5:07:45 (25,044)
Bubloz, David 5:30:27 (29,210)
Bucerius, Matthias 3:42:49 (5,650)
Buch, Dhaval 5:30:04 (29,155)
Buchan, Andrew 3:09:23 (1,509)
Buchan, Kevin A 5:23:42 (28,055)
Buchan, Steven 3:59:59 (9,205)
Buchan, Stuart 3:37:00 (4,686)
Buchan, Stuart 3:48:28 (6,612)
Buchanan, Iain C 5:02:41 (24,074)
Buchanan, Jonathan A 4:21:39 (13,995)
Buchanan, Mark K 3:35:31 (4,486)
Buchmann, Laurence J 5:15:54 (26,643)
Buchmeier, Christian 5:16:07 (26,687)
Buck, Chris G 5:11:00 (25,665)
Buck, Neil R 4:25:14 (14,882)
Buckingham, David K 3:29:58 (3,714)
Buckingham, Graham L 3:29:10 (3,600)
Buckingham, Matthew 4:43:42 (19,463)
Buckingham, Nicholas J 4:31:54 (16,542)
Buckingham, Peter J 3:11:39 (1,691)
Buckingham, Stephen G 5:12:54 (26,022)
Buckinx, Etienne 3:14:16 (1,921)
Buckland, Keith 5:25:35 (28,388)
Buckland, Paul 4:12:13 (11,662)
Buckle, David G 4:55:22 (22,353)
Buckle, Neil A 4:38:59 (18,280)
Buckle, Timothy J 3:55:18 (8,077)
Buckley, Brian W 3:27:20 (3,330)
Buckley, Darrel 4:21:55 (14,069)
Buckley, Lucky G 5:48:14 (31,494)
Buckley, Mark P 4:49:05 (20,789)
Buckley, Matthew W 5:30:52 (29,274)
Buckley, Neil 5:00:11 (23,547)
Buckley, Paul J 3:35:59 (4,545)
Buckley, Robert N 4:29:03 (15,867)
Buckley, Ronnie 5:02:08 (23,956)
Buckley, Simon J 5:35:52 (30,033)
Buckley, Steven W 3:49:32 (6,839)
Bucknall, David E 3:40:01 (5,192)
Bucknell, Daniel F 5:18:28 (27,158)
Buckpitt, Allan M 4:36:36 (17,692)
Budd, Christopher P 4:21:35 (13,980)
Budd, Peter C 5:19:10 (27,283)
Budd, Steven J 5:14:31 (26,341)
Budden, Colin D 5:50:56 (31,766)
Budden, David 5:04:23 (24,399)
Budge, Grant 4:50:51 (21,204)
Budge, Kurt R 4:29:04 (15,875)
Budroni, Paolino 3:05:56 (1,231)
Buecker, Karsten 3:11:35 (1,679)
Bueckers, Dominik 4:10:14 (11,212)
Buenger, Jens-Uwe 3:46:10 (6,204)
Bufton, Glyn J 5:50:10 (31,687)
Bugby, Tony R 5:25:52 (28,437)
Bugeja, Philip A 4:39:26 (18,400)
Bugg, Steven M 3:51:07 (7,161)
Buggy, Donal 4:36:47 (17,739)
Buglass, Mark A 3:56:38 (8,392)
Buglass, Thomas 7:05:28 (35,209)
Bugler, Patrick F 4:40:59 (18,780)
Bugler, Paul 3:47:05 (6,361)
Buick, Jim 3:00:49 (944)
Buijs, Marco 3:59:24 (9,068)
Buis, James C 2:42:45 (193)
Bulaitis, Peter A 3:54:10 (7,833)
Bulbaczynskyj, Stefan W 5:03:07 (24,153)
Buley, Mark J 4:49:22 (20,853)
Bulger, Steven J 3:49:20 (6,800)
Bull, John M 6:10:35 (33,343)
Bull, Keith 4:30:15 (16,210)
Bull, Martyn G 7:49:59 (35,617)
Bull, Richard E 3:34:57 (4,403)
Bull, Robert O 4:19:54 (13,574)
Bull, Ross D 7:45:59 (35,605)
Bull, Simon J 3:58:56 (8,947)
Bull, Stephen H 3:42:29 (5,597)
Bullen, Andrew G 5:48:11 (31,486)
Bullen, David A 4:29:05 (15,880)
Bullen, Simon J 5:47:41 (31,427)
Bullen, Timothy F 5:58:19 (32,445)
Buller, James R 3:52:48 (7,524)
Bullivant, Paul A 4:33:58 (17,027)
Bullock, Andrew J 3:23:36 (2,858)
Bullock, Paul D 3:11:34 (1,676)
Bullock, Stephen J 6:09:06 (33,242)
Bullock, Terry 3:16:33 (2,130)
Bumstead, Ivan V 3:57:45 (8,665)
Bunbury, Anthony G 5:02:02 (23,941)
Bunce, Gerald 3:47:06 (6,364)
Bunce, James 3:41:46 (5,480)
Bunce, Paddy A 4:57:21 (22,875)
Bunclark, Nick J 3:59:17 (9,037)
Bunday, Simon P 4:19:56 (13,582)
Bundey, Paul 3:51:15 (7,197)
Bungay, Alan M 5:20:34 (27,534)
Bunn, David A 3:00:37 (937)
Bunn, Philip J 3:17:20 (2,209)
Bunnage, Russ 4:25:35 (14,963)
Bunner, Colin 3:48:25 (6,598)
Bunnett, Graham R 3:37:01 (4,689)
Bunston, Michael J 3:15:45 (2,055)
Bunt, Jonathan 5:35:00 (29,915)
Bunting, Gary 4:53:35 (21,909)
Bunting, Simon J 4:57:17 (22,847)
Bunting, William C 5:59:43 (32,558)
Bunton, Neil 4:14:39 (12,247)
Bunyan, Roberts G 3:22:47 (2,774)

Buonfrate, Aleksandra B 5:39:35 (30,543)
Burbanks, Magnus P 3:56:25 (8,336)
Burbanks, Petri A 3:00:29 (930)
Burbidge, Craig M 4:17:59 (13,072)
Burbidge, Mark 4:19:53 (13,569)
Burbidge, Reginald 6:53:27 (35,004)
Burch, Jonathon D 4:02:48 (9,753)
Burchell, Neil 5:07:34 (25,015)
Burchett, Gary P 3:33:18 (4,179)
Burchett, Rainer H 4:04:12 (10,006)
Burden, Andrew 4:38:48 (18,234)
Burden, Andrew R 5:16:32 (26,763)
Burden, Mark J 3:34:17 (4,312)
Burden, Neil J 5:49:44 (31,649)
Burdett, Ian J 3:49:47 (6,894)
Burdon, Brian 5:13:59 (26,227)
Burette, Emmanuel L 4:40:46 (18,722)
Burfitt, Stephen J 5:06:53 (24,859)
Burford, Bruce W 4:32:31 (16,667)
Burford, Colin J 4:32:40 (16,709)
Burford, Peter D 3:35:25 (4,471)
Burge, Raymond L 4:37:19 (17,845)
Burger, Carl M 6:16:40 (33,721)
Burgess, Andrew R 4:32:37 (16,695)
Burgess, Euan 3:51:22 (7,213)
Burgess, James A 4:51:29 (21,368)
Burgess, Jason 3:45:52 (6,157)
Burgess, John 4:08:49 (10,924)
Burgess, John A 3:31:37 (3,931)
Burgess, John G 5:40:14 (30,617)
Burgess, Ken 6:01:07 (32,689)
Burgess, Mark I 4:58:19 (23,109)
Burgess, Michael P 3:59:24 (9,068)
Burgess, Neil A 4:44:01 (19,542)
Burgess, Paul J 5:06:14 (24,749)
Burgess, Richard M 3:51:18 (7,202)
Burgess, Simon D 3:25:03 (3,025)
Burgess, Stuart 6:00:48 (32,645)
Burgin, Christopher J 3:37:23 (4,730)
Burgoyne, Christopher S 3:18:33 (2,346)
Buri, Pitiphatr 4:36:05 (17,553)
Burke, Alastair 4:25:36 (14,970)
Burke, Darren M 5:44:12 (31,064)
Burke, Darren P 4:35:35 (17,427)
Burke, David A 3:11:31 (1,674)
Burke, Desmond 3:56:37 (8,385)
Burke, James 6:35:52 (34,532)
Burke, Jonjo 3:57:51 (8,680)
Burke, Kevin 3:09:34 (1,521)
Burke, Mark J 5:05:50 (24,659)
Burke, Martin J 4:39:13 (18,340)
Burke, Martin J 4:58:46 (23,198)
Burke, Michael J 3:59:31 (9,097)
Burke, Robert 3:31:27 (3,898)
Burke, Steve 6:23:59 (34,078)
Burke, Terence J 3:36:23 (4,599)
Burke, Thomas 4:46:54 (20,254)
Burke, Tom 5:30:22 (29,195)
Burkhill, John 6:10:47 (33,353)
Burkinshaw, Jon 3:50:48 (7,095)
Burland, David 3:48:48 (6,687)
Burman, James E 4:52:58 (21,748)
Burmeister, Daniel P 3:34:07 (4,281)
Burn, Anthony A 3:17:19 (2,205)
Burn, Christopher J 3:36:35 (4,625)
Burnell, Frank 6:01:46 (32,739)
Burnell, Henry 6:01:46 (32,739)
Burnett, Bryan 3:05:59 (1,232)
Burnett, Christopher 4:42:43 (19,233)
Burnett, David A 4:24:31 (14,710)
Burnett, John D 3:55:00 (8,009)
Burnett, Lawson 4:44:46 (19,763)
Burnett-Hall, Graham D 4:08:23 (10,846)
Burnham, Darrell R 5:02:20 (23,998)
Burns, Alastair 4:51:12 (21,286)
Burns, Daniel E 5:23:19 (27,980)
Burns, David 3:41:34 (5,451)
Burns, Michael L 3:38:49 (4,978)
Burns, Robert E 4:19:46 (13,532)
Burns, Robert J 3:37:08 (4,705)
Burns, Simon J 3:54:49 (7,965)
Burnside, Kenneth 4:35:24 (17,382)
Burr, Christopher P 4:00:36 (9,330)
Burrage, Adam 5:16:10 (26,692)
Burrard-Lucas, William B 4:18:24 (13,174)
Burrell, John F 5:05:05 (24,526)
Burrett, Mark P 4:37:36 (17,911)
Burrett, Mike 2:33:56 (60)
Burridge, Mike J 5:00:53 (23,708)
Burridge, Stephen 4:51:56 (21,473)
Burrows, Alan D 3:43:04 (5,701)
Burrows, Christopher E 5:25:05 (28,286)
Burslem, Paul 3:12:49 (1,810)
Burston, Geoffrey P 4:02:54 (9,767)
Burstow, Mark P 5:53:17 (31,984)
Burt, Alistair J 5:18:35 (27,178)
Burt, Gary M 5:00:23 (23,595)
Burtenshaw, Noel P 5:04:04 (24,337)
Burton, Alex J 3:22:37 (2,757)
Burton, Andrew J 3:41:46 (5,480)
Burton, Cliff 4:44:41 (19,740)
Burton, David 5:40:02 (30,595)
Burton, Hugh R 3:49:46 (6,886)
Burton, James W 3:33:24 (4,194)
Burton, Jeff P 3:09:38 (1,525)
Burton, John L 3:42:51 (5,657)
Burton, Michael F 3:53:04 (7,582)
Burton, Neal 4:56:40 (22,686)
Burton, Neil A 3:17:53 (2,272)
Burton, Paul 4:51:23 (21,339)
Burton, Robert J 2:44:19 (224)
Burton, Robin C 3:49:53 (6,914)
Burton, Russell E 3:12:12 (1,748)
Burton, Terence C 5:21:37 (27,715)
Burton-Page, Tom A 3:47:23 (6,405)
Burton-Thorne, Andrew B 3:41:22 (5,421)
Burvill, Chris R 4:40:48 (18,733)
Burwood, Christopher M 4:27:17 (15,416)
Busaidy, Nabil 5:25:21 (28,330)
Busby, Steven R 3:58:11 (8,755)
Bush, Adam J 4:20:34 (13,745)
Bush, Andrew P 4:30:50 (16,320)
Bush, Christopher J 4:51:12 (21,286)
Bush, James 4:30:59 (16,349)
Bush, Kevin R 3:43:35 (5,797)
Bush, Martin R 6:00:01 (32,576)
Bush, Nigel L 4:03:36 (9,886)
Bush, Paul W 3:49:12 (6,774)
Bush, Timothy J 4:15:57 (12,543)
Bushell, David 4:02:01 (9,605)
Bushell, Gary J 5:04:02 (24,332)
Bushell, Philip E 4:11:08 (11,407)
Bushell, Stephen L 5:35:04 (29,922)
Bushnell-Wye, Graham 4:53:17 (21,831)
Buskwood, Mark 3:26:01 (3,131)
Buso, Achille 3:22:26 (2,741)
Buss, Steven 7:01:01 (35,146)
Busse, Jakob 3:41:25 (5,433)
Buswell, Andy M 3:50:28 (7,039)
Butcher, Alec H 5:09:22 (25,344)
Butcher, Andy 4:36:30 (17,664)
Butcher, Antony 5:37:01 (30,172)
Butcher, Geoffrey C 3:51:22 (7,213)
Butcher, Ian 4:28:45 (15,799)
Butcher, Jeremy E 3:27:20 (3,330)
Butcher, John W 4:12:39 (11,751)
Butcher, Neil A 3:34:02 (4,273)
Butcher, Tom G 3:46:56 (6,332)
Butcher, Tom P 3:46:58 (6,338)
Butland, Jonty 4:30:19 (16,218)
Butler, Andrew D 6:15:07 (33,625)
Butler, Chayne C 7:00:06 (35,124)
Butler, David G 5:06:59 (24,876)
Butler, David J 5:21:22 (27,667)
Butler, David R 4:22:50 (14,295)
Butler, David R 4:35:33 (17,415)
Butler, Eoin W 3:53:17 (7,638)
Butler, George A 4:27:14 (15,400)
Butler, Grant J 2:56:29 (632)
Butler, Ian R 6:07:01 (33,108)
Butler, Jason P 4:18:32 (13,221)
Butler, Jeffrey 3:34:39 (4,358)
Butler, Kenneth J 5:01:27 (23,821)
Butler, Malcolm 4:31:07 (16,386)
Butler, Matthew 3:46:55 (6,327)
Butler, Matthew A 3:48:56 (6,712)
Butler, Matthew P 5:30:11 (29,174)
Butler, Michael F 4:06:05 (10,367)
Butler, Peter 3:57:09 (8,511)
Butler, Peter 5:30:11 (29,174)
Butler, Peter P 4:18:50 (13,291)
Butler, Robert A 3:30:07 (3,737)
Butler, Robert A 3:49:26 (6,818)
Butler, Scott J 5:42:42 (30,896)
Butler, Simon 5:11:16 (25,712)
Butler, Stanley C 6:12:16 (33,441)
Butler, Stephen M 4:02:42 (9,729)
Butler, Steven C 3:48:19 (6,578)
Butler, Tim D 4:13:25 (11,940)
Butler, Tom E 5:00:10 (23,541)
Butlin, Anthony G 4:39:38 (18,445)
Butlin, Nicholas A 4:33:09 (16,823)
Butt, Jawaad 5:06:27 (24,782)
Butt, Najam 6:26:05 (34,173)
Butt, Nicholas J 3:57:53 (8,693)
Buttenshaw, Barry 5:34:59 (29,911)
Butterfield, Karl M 5:37:44 (30,266)
Butterlin, Marc B 4:45:55 (20,040)
Butterworth, Graeme J 4:15:31 (12,445)
Butterworth, Graham 4:23:30 (14,444)
Butterworth, Simon M 4:25:10 (14,862)
Buttery, Chris 5:08:49 (25,244)
Buttery, Darren J 5:46:13 (31,285)
Buttle, Kevin J 5:03:39 (24,266)
Button, David 6:19:32 (33,864)
Button, Mark 5:25:24 (28,341)
Button, Phillip D 4:32:33 (16,675)
Buvira, Herbert J 3:19:54 (2,479)
Buxani, Dipak 5:35:07 (29,929)
Buxton, Mark S 4:41:32 (18,932)
Buxton, Paul D 3:21:59 (2,705)
Buxton, Rupert J 4:15:28 (12,435)
Buzzel, James R 5:31:53 (29,431)
Byansi, Malachi 2:29:40 (38)
Byard, Edward M 3:36:34 (4,621)
Byas, David 4:01:58 (9,597)
Byberg, Jan Lai 4:27:50 (15,552)
Bydlowski, Jayme M 5:18:17 (27,117)
Bye, Alan F 3:40:59 (5,361)
Bye, Edward D 5:04:43 (24,452)
Bye, Jonathan E 5:04:43 (24,452)
Bye, Jonathan T 4:14:42 (12,257)
Byerley, Andrew L 3:37:06 (4,700)
Byers, John H 5:09:06 (25,295)
Byers, Richard J 2:53:18 (483)
Byford, Richard D 4:29:39 (16,056)
Bygrave, Kelvin R 5:06:16 (24,754)
Byram, Wayne P 3:56:17 (8,297)
Byres, Kelvin J 3:45:02 (6,031)
Byrne, Adrian 5:36:37 (30,127)
Byrne, Brendan 4:42:12 (19,095)
Byrne, Dan 3:36:21 (4,594)
Byrne, David 4:34:25 (17,118)
Byrne, David A 2:46:30 (273)
Byrne, David M 5:06:50 (24,850)
Byrne, Edmund J 4:12:04 (11,624)
Byrne, Fiacre J 3:24:07 (2,922)
Byrne, Francis G 6:13:53 (33,541)
Byrne, Gerry J 3:32:41 (4,094)
Byrne, Kevin C 3:47:21 (6,397)
Byrne, Matthew 4:46:49 (20,232)
Byrne, Matthew J 5:00:16 (23,568)
Byrne, Neil S 4:23:02 (14,340)
Byrne, Robert A 4:32:01 (16,562)
Byrnes, Damian T 3:06:41 (1,286)
Byrom, Christopher E 5:03:32 (24,243)
Byrom, David 4:22:02 (14,095)
Byrom, Matthew W 3:18:12 (2,310)
Byron, Paul W 4:09:08 (10,986)
Byron, Shawn P 4:19:31 (13,463)
Bywater, Andrew W 4:14:01 (12,101)
Cabanes, José 3:56:28 (8,352)
Cable, Andrew J 4:05:17 (10,202)
Cable, Geoffrey 5:40:37 (30,665)
Cable, Paul A 4:06:10 (10,385)
Cable, Stephen J 3:40:56 (5,353)
Cabrera, Edwin V 5:53:11 (31,977)
Cabrol, Louis-Noel 4:24:56 (14,809)
Caddick, Mark 5:10:29 (25,574)

Caddock, Graham T 4:50:09 (21,034)
Caddy, David J 2:50:27 (390)
Caddy, Derek 3:38:38 (4,945)
Cadiou, Dougal A....4:54:18 (22,101)
Cadman, John Paul....4:07:25 (10,636)
Cadogan, John L....7:11:51 (35,303)
Cadogan, Paul D 3:58:38 (8,867)
Cadogan, Stephen....7:29:15 (35,472)
Caertledge, Ben....5:28:16 (28,855)
Caesar, Colin 5:00:51 (23,696)
Caffery, John P 4:34:35 (17,169)
Caffrey, Mark....5:31:03 (29,307)
Cahill, Gerard O 5:32:58 (29,601)
Cahill, Lee J....5:06:39 (24,809)
Cahill, Paul....4:25:39 (14,985)
Cahnbley, Martin L 4:26:26 (15,170)
Caiger, John F....4:54:14 (22,085)
Caillaud, Herve 5:19:07 (27,271)
Cain, Christopher E 3:26:58 (3,272)
Cain, Frank P....3:31:27 (3,898)
Cain, Jeremy T....4:28:32 (15,738)
Cain, Paul S 4:59:17 (23,335)
Cain, Steve E....3:40:30 (5,266)
Caine, Steven R 5:30:49 (29,267)
Cairns, Andy....4:28:05 (15,616)
Cairns, Daniel J 5:20:11 (27,453)
Cairns, John L 5:28:19 (28,871)
Cairns, John M 3:28:16 (3,442)
Cairns, John S....4:18:10 (13,112)
Cairns, Philip J 4:26:37 (15,214)
Cairns, Steve M....2:41:36 (169)
Cairns, William J....4:37:48 (17,955)
Cake, James 5:31:48 (29,419)
Calascione, Ben F....3:56:21 (8,319)
Calcraft, Robert M 3:50:58 (7,131)
Calcutt, Howard J....4:30:19 (16,218)
Calcutt, Roy V....3:39:12 (5,046)
Calderbank, Michael....5:58:56 (32,502)
Calderon, George J 5:29:25 (29,061)
Calderwood, Craig 3:16:21 (2,111)
Caldow, Peter J 3:43:27 (5,769)
Caldwell, Ian....5:32:57 (29,599)
Calford, David 4:43:33 (19,426)
Callachan, David 4:13:43 (12,022)
Callaghan, Harry....4:04:35 (10,074)
Callaghan, Peter J 3:59:26 (9,075)
Callaghan, William....5:03:29 (24,235)
Callanan, Mike M....5:58:24 (32,459)
Callcott, Andrew J 4:09:39 (11,103)
Calleja, Miguel A....3:41:44 (5,474)
Callister, Ian....4:39:24 (18,389)
Callow, James S....4:03:52 (9,939)
Callow, Leo J....4:28:55 (15,838)
Callow, Martin J....3:31:55 (3,976)
Callow, Samuel R....4:12:38 (11,748)
Calloway, Ian P 5:45:47 (31,236)
Calloway, Philip W....3:34:17 (4,312)
Calthrop, Benjamin C....3:53:12 (7,618)
Calton, Iain. W 3:39:18 (5,064)
Calver, Laurence 3:33:13 (4,168)
Calverley, James I 6:42:22 (34,732)
Calvert, John G....3:20:50 (2,589)
Calvert, Jonathan R....4:05:04 (10,156)
Calvert, Paul V....4:56:10 (22,555)
Cambounet, Jean-Jacques....3:41:22 (5,421)
Cambridge, Rickie S 4:37:17 (17,838)
Cambuli, Enrico....4:50:56 (21,227)
Camenzino, Peter....2:40:15 (144)
Cameron, Alan 3:45:33 (6,103)
Cameron, Alastair A....4:10:53 (11,345)
Cameron, Jeremy A....6:15:05 (33,621)
Cameron, Mark I....5:04:50 (24,476)
Cameron, Neil....4:13:54 (12,068)
Cameron, Neil D....4:52:33 (21,626)
Cameron, Neil D....5:07:49 (25,064)
Cameron, Paul A....3:28:03 (3,413)
Cameron, Ray J....4:45:17 (19,900)
Cameron, Stuart....3:52:38 (7,485)
Cameron-Wood, Robert A....3:25:52 (3,108)
Camez, Salomon 5:14:09 (26,257)
Camfield, Bryan 2:55:27 (591)
Camley, Mark....5:52:11 (31,891)
Campbell, Brian A....4:07:47 (10,721)
Campbell, Brian J....3:31:38 (3,933)
Campbell, Charlie....4:47:29 (20,401)
Campbell, Christopher W....3:57:36 (8,624)
Campbell, Daniel 5:21:12 (27,633)
Campbell, Daniel A....5:56:21 (32,271)
Campbell, Duncan J....3:48:21 (6,584)
Campbell, Eric M 4:42:11 (19,089)
Campbell, Geoff....2:51:09 (415)
Campbell, Graeme J....3:37:38 (4,768)
Campbell, Graeme T 4:30:14 (16,202)
Campbell, Harry....4:56:32 (22,640)
Campbell, James P 4:12:40 (11,761)
Campbell, Kenneth M 3:53:39 (7,717)
Campbell, Kenton C....5:43:36 (31,001)
Campbell, Leroy A....4:46:02 (20,067)
Campbell, Logan J 3:20:34 (2,565)
Campbell, Malcolm S....4:28:26 (15,709)
Campbell, Mark A....2:45:58 (261)
Campbell, Mark J 3:57:34 (8,615)
Campbell, Matthew I....4:43:13 (19,343)
Campbell, Neil 4:15:20 (12,404)
Campbell, Paul....6:12:30 (33,459)
Campbell, Peter I 4:54:11 (22,076)
Campbell, Robert W 5:14:34 (26,354)
Campbell, Scott P....4:15:51 (12,526)
Campbell, Scott R 5:28:06 (28,818)
Campbell, Stephen A....4:54:22 (22,114)
Campbell, Stuart D 4:08:38 (10,900)
Campbell, Thomas G....5:10:27 (25,566)
Campbell, Wilfred G....4:33:25 (16,895)
Campbell-Barr, Gordon 4:21:50 (14,044)
Campey, Paul....4:05:28 (10,236)
Campion, Mark A....2:54:12 (525)
Campion, Paul....6:06:52 (33,101)
Campion, Stephen 3:07:15 (1,330)
Campion, Timothy C 4:12:45 (11,775)
Campos, José F 3:18:54 (2,381)
Canacott, John A....4:15:57 (12,543)
Canavan, Martin J 2:54:42 (560)
Candi, Silvano 3:50:42 (7,078)
Candy, Mattehw S....4:28:33 (15,745)
Cane, Ben R....4:56:06 (22,535)
Cane, John E 5:20:07 (27,440)
Cane, Mark S....3:47:16 (6,389)
Cane, Peter S....4:01:50 (9,574)
Caney, Simon G....3:36:52 (4,669)
Canham, Colin....4:47:00 (20,280)
Canham, Matthew J....3:18:19 (2,328)
Canham, Ray D 4:29:21 (15,956)
Cann, Andrew G....4:36:17 (17,606)
Cann, Gary J 4:37:16 (17,834)
Cann, Graeme A....4:32:13 (16,613)
Cann, Jonathan 4:41:52 (19,013)
Cann, Paul....4:37:00 (17,786)
Cannell, David A 3:42:17 (5,566)
Canning, Johnny A....3:20:16 (2,527)
Canning, Stephen P....4:10:35 (11,286)
Cannon, John....5:21:47 (27,751)
Cannon, John L....3:31:50 (3,959)
Cannon, Stephen....4:22:44 (14,268)
Cant, Andrew M 4:38:44 (18,208)
Cant, Christopher P....5:10:15 (25,534)
Cant, Paul F....4:42:12 (19,095)
Cantwell, Matthew D....3:08:56 (1,464)
Capecci, Elio....4:22:58 (14,322)
Capelin-Jones, Kevin S....4:52:02 (21,492)
Capelli, Donaro....4:45:07 (19,863)
Capilla Alonso, Manuel 3:01:54 (999)
Caplan, Daniel M 4:33:04 (16,803)
Capon, Daniel J 4:08:19 (10,835)
Capon, Ian H....5:36:45 (30,138)
Capon, Malcolm K 5:23:44 (28,059)
Caponnetto, Antonio....5:52:43 (31,941)
Caporiccio, Dino....4:40:55 (18,768)
Capp, Michael D 6:26:44 (34,203)
Cappuccio, Peter....4:02:47 (9,747)
Capron, Pascal....3:36:40 (4,637)
Caps, Chris S....3:17:07 (2,192)
Caps, Stephen....5:40:19 (30,630)
Caramatti, Niccolo L....4:35:48 (17,487)
Carass, Neil L....5:16:57 (26,850)
Caravaggio, Valentino....2:58:55 (817)
Carden, Michael C....4:33:07 (16,816)
Cardenal, Ivan M....4:49:56 (20,980)
Carder, Richard A 4:39:44 (18,471)
Cardetta, Leonardo....3:58:01 (8,728)
Cardona, Kenneth J 4:09:50 (11,134)
Cardoso, Abel....3:53:06 (7,591)
Cardy, Tom J 4:13:02 (11,840)
Care, Thomas J....4:09:44 (11,120)
Carey, Adrian....5:55:45 (32,213)
Carey, Andrew J 5:31:42 (29,406)
Carey, Keith 5:19:25 (27,324)
Carey, Kevin A 5:09:49 (25,434)
Cargill, David S....6:17:46 (33,770)
Cargill, Rebecca M 5:57:59 (32,412)
Carissimi, Daniel 4:05:50 (10,314)
Carles, Claude 3:06:34 (1,276)
Carleton, Alister M....5:56:37 (32,300)
Carley, Ian P 3:09:35 (1,522)
Carley, Kevin J 5:42:50 (30,919)
Carley, Martin T 4:36:20 (17,621)
Carlier, Nick 3:55:45 (8,175)
Carlin, Paul J 3:41:10 (5,390)
Carlisle, Stephen 3:35:17 (4,445)
Carlon, Martin....3:54:16 (7,861)
Carlson, David....4:49:55 (20,976)
Carmichael, Jeremy R....3:45:40 (6,130)
Carmichael, Peter J 5:50:49 (31,759)
Carmichael, Tom A 5:30:23 (29,197)
Carmichael-Hussain, Tareen 5:38:08 (30,322)
Carminati, Adrien 4:31:41 (16,504)
Carmo, Fernando M 2:38:24 (116)
Carmody, Kieran A....3:37:14 (4,716)
Carnall, Philip B....6:11:11 (33,381)
Carnall, Simon J 4:06:46 (10,521)
Carne, Peter R....3:26:59 (3,278)
Carnegie, David C 5:21:33 (27,701)
Carnell, Robert C 5:09:22 (25,344)
Carney, Leon 4:27:46 (15,535)
Carney, Patrick M 5:48:39 (31,539)
Carnus, Charles....3:46:54 (6,321)
Carnwath, Alexander P....4:52:21 (21,583)
Carol, Riel....4:23:03 (14,346)
Carolan, Kevin....4:56:13 (22,570)
Carolan, Malcom V 6:17:29 (33,748)
Carolan, Patrick J 3:27:55 (3,398)
Carolan, Thomas J 4:41:05 (18,807)
Carosella, Federico 4:31:04 (16,368)
Carpenter, Geoffrey R....4:59:41 (23,427)
Carpenter, Jonathan A....2:43:54 (211)
Carpenter, Mark R 4:27:37 (15,493)
Carpenter, Trevor A 5:03:00 (24,121)
Carr, Adrian....3:33:21 (4,187)
Carr, Adrian N....3:41:34 (5,451)
Carr, Andrew T....6:55:23 (35,044)
Carr, Anthony....3:35:17 (4,445)
Carr, Anthony....5:37:58 (30,297)
Carr, Clive A 3:33:54 (4,254)
Carr, Derek C 5:57:13 (32,347)
Carr, Ian....4:15:20 (12,404)
Carr, Ian J 3:59:36 (9,119)
Carr, Joe....3:30:26 (3,781)
Carr, John 2:45:30 (250)
Carr, John V....4:19:03 (13,337)
Carr, Keith S 3:39:19 (5,067)
Carr, Leigh G....3:46:13 (6,207)
Carr, Malcolm A 3:43:04 (5,701)
Carr, Martin G 4:33:47 (16,987)
Carr, Matthew J....4:16:30 (12,698)
Carr, Michael J....4:14:38 (12,242)
Carr, Michelle P....6:25:42 (34,154)
Carr, Paul B 5:21:22 (27,667)
Carr, Paul J....4:45:09 (19,870)
Carr, Phillip R....3:26:02 (3,133)
Carr, Roderick 4:25:51 (15,025)
Carr, Ronan P 4:55:01 (22,267)
Carr, Scott R 4:41:15 (18,851)
Carr, Steven P 5:44:37 (31,111)
Carr, Stuart 4:46:20 (20,135)
Carrick, Paul J 5:53:34 (32,017)
Carrillo, Emilio A 3:05:22 (1,190)
Carrington, Keith....4:32:04 (16,574)
Carrington, Simon 4:00:15 (9,263)
Carrion, Alejandro....3:24:05 (2,918)
Carroll, Anthony 3:58:28 (8,832)

Carroll, Darragh S......6:29:34 (34,310)
Carroll, Derek A......4:02:24 (9,682)
Carroll, James......4:31:33 (16,471)
Carroll, John......3:27:40 (3,368)
Carroll, John G......4:09:42 (11,116)
Carroll, Kevin......3:12:01 (1,729)
Carroll, Mark......4:50:03 (21,007)
Carroll, Michael J......2:25:19 (25)
Carroll, Paul A......3:12:40 (1,795)
Carroll, Paul L......3:29:57 (3,709)
Carroll, Paul R......2:45:57 (260)
Carroll, Raymond L......5:27:41 (28,739)
Carroll, Shaun P......5:46:44 (31,329)
Carroll, Stuart P......3:19:40 (2,450)
Carsberg, Simon P......4:19:46 (13,532)
Carson, Clarke R......4:24:47 (14,773)
Carson, James D......4:13:08 (11,865)
Carson, John......5:57:40 (32,379)
Carson, Jon G......3:54:55 (7,992)
Carson, Michael D......5:01:12 (23,773)
Carson, Rory J......4:19:27 (13,446)
Carson, Steven J......5:14:12 (26,267)
Carson, Tom P......4:19:27 (13,446)
Cartailler, Mathias......2:57:00 (676)
Carter, Adam D......3:36:10 (4,566)
Carter, Adam L......4:43:20 (19,390)
Carter, Alun J......3:37:54 (4,806)
Carter, Andrew E......4:40:11 (18,578)
Carter, Andrew S......2:58:05 (754)
Carter, Andy......5:41:19 (30,744)
Carter, Chris......4:39:05 (18,303)
Carter, Christopher......4:43:56 (19,517)
Carter, Colin D......5:23:14 (27,966)
Carter, Daniel R......4:13:10 (11,871)
Carter, Darren D......4:24:39 (14,735)
Carter, Dave......2:38:30 (117)
Carter, Dave......4:55:45 (22,444)
Carter, David F......5:31:07 (29,320)
Carter, David J......5:12:09 (25,888)
Carter, Denis J......4:19:41 (13,504)
Carter, Eric J......4:09:37 (11,100)
Carter, Grant......3:46:42 (6,283)
Carter, Harry J......4:10:14 (11,212)
Carter, Jake......4:53:55 (21,997)
Carter, James R......5:01:52 (23,905)
Carter, Jamie......4:34:09 (17,062)
Carter, Joel G......3:56:36 (8,381)
Carter, John......3:40:30 (5,266)
Carter, John D......3:40:09 (5,209)
Carter, John H......5:38:28 (30,380)
Carter, Keith G......4:39:08 (18,314)
Carter, Kevin P......4:56:47 (22,710)
Carter, Luke D......4:27:05 (15,350)
Carter, Malcolm L......4:39:02 (18,293)
Carter, Mark R......3:26:49 (3,244)
Carter, Melvyn J......5:28:32 (28,907)
Carter, Michael J......4:30:01 (16,151)
Carter, Nigel G......4:23:16 (14,393)
Carter, Patrick J......4:30:16 (16,213)
Carter, Paul......5:50:49 (31,759)
Carter, Paul J......4:26:11 (15,091)
Carter, Paul T......4:29:33 (16,028)
Carter, Phillip. E......4:32:30 (16,662)
Carter, Richard A......5:21:43 (27,734)
Carter, Robert J......5:25:30 (28,372)
Carter, Ross......4:32:16 (16,623)
Carter, Rumon......3:14:11 (1,910)
Carter, Simon G......3:59:43 (9,144)
Carter, Steve J......3:22:13 (2,721)
Carter, Thomas P......4:17:00 (12,814)
Carter, Timothy......3:56:22 (8,324)
Carter, Trevor......5:54:14 (32,073)
Carter-Lee, Andrew R......4:01:25 (9,503)
Carton, Andy D......3:11:14 (1,649)
Carton, Keith S......4:02:03 (9,612)
Cartwright, Daniel T......4:28:24 (15,703)
Cartwright, David M......6:36:41 (34,567)
Cartwright, Joseph J......5:01:21 (23,803)
Cartwright, Richard L......5:07:02 (24,892)
Cartwright, Spencer F......5:00:36 (23,634)
Cartwright, Stephen M......5:06:06 (24,712)
Carty, Paul T......5:56:42 (32,308)
Caruana, John A......4:22:56 (14,317)

Carvalho, Augusto......4:49:26 (20,867)
Carvalho, Maritz T......3:42:04 (5,530)
Carvell, Rob D......3:19:11 (2,413)
Carver, Peter......4:35:05 (17,291)
Carver, Ricki A......4:37:36 (17,911)
Carvill, Stephen......5:33:25 (29,667)
Cary, Clive S......4:56:16 (22,580)
Cary, Thomas J......4:44:30 (19,681)
Case, Anthony V......6:19:12 (33,850)
Case, Christopher J......5:26:16 (28,503)
Case, Mick......4:11:39 (11,537)
Casella, Dean......3:25:29 (3,061)
Casement, William R......4:30:59 (16,349)
Casey, Anthony D......3:06:16 (1,251)
Casey, Brian......3:34:30 (4,340)
Casey, Daniel J......6:52:04 (34,977)
Casey, Darren J......6:00:51 (32,650)
Casey, David......5:16:47 (26,802)
Casey, Jody P......6:08:50 (33,228)
Casey, Mark F......5:00:46 (23,680)
Casey, Michael P......3:28:26 (3,468)
Casey, Warren N......5:13:09 (26,071)
Cash, Peter......4:42:02 (19,047)
Cashman, Andrew F......5:29:35 (29,082)
Cashman, Lee R......6:34:49 (34,488)
Cason, Christopher J......4:04:44 (10,100)
Cason, Nicholas......4:54:38 (22,179)
Caspari, Thomas......4:29:51 (16,110)
Cass, John E......4:05:41 (10,286)
Cass, John W......4:39:40 (18,454)
Cassidy, Dermot F......6:07:44 (33,152)
Cassidy, James W......4:01:50 (9,574)
Cassidy, Jonathan M......4:17:35 (12,975)
Cassie, Philip S......4:42:03 (19,054)
Castano Lara, John M......5:26:35 (28,555)
Castellani, Ercole......3:27:24 (3,341)
Castelletto, Federico......3:44:26 (5,928)
Castle, John A......2:52:34 (461)
Castle, Robert E......4:54:32 (22,150)
Castle, Toby......3:32:16 (4,040)
Castle, William J......5:32:29 (29,520)
Castleton, Mark......3:26:28 (3,194)
Castro, Carlos A......3:29:36 (3,660)
Castro Suarez, Gustavo......3:48:54 (6,703)
Caswell, Gary P......4:57:38 (22,939)
Cataldo, Luigi......4:17:26 (12,921)
Catchpole, Anthony......4:55:21 (22,349)
Catchpole, Daniel......3:35:30 (4,480)
Catchpole, Ian L......4:11:28 (11,495)
Catchpole, Phil......4:08:53 (10,940)
Catchpole, Steven J......4:44:23 (19,645)
Cater, George E......5:20:37 (27,544)
Cates, Liam......4:20:10 (13,645)
Catmull, Julian A......3:20:13 (2,521)
Caton, Eliot......3:51:10 (7,177)
Caton, Mark......3:50:55 (7,120)
Caton, Michael H......4:44:58 (19,828)
Cattanach, Alasdair B......4:42:06 (19,064)
Catterall, Adam......6:27:38 (34,238)
Catterall, Chris......4:05:35 (10,262)
Catterall, David C......4:48:59 (20,765)
Cattle, Larry A......3:50:07 (6,964)
Cattley, Steven J......3:54:55 (7,992)
Caudrelier, Tim......3:31:34 (3,919)
Caudwell, Neil P......4:39:19 (18,368)
Caul, Scott E......4:08:24 (10,848)
Caulder, Graham A......3:49:33 (6,842)
Caulfield, Michael......5:47:15 (31,375)
Caunce, Peter......4:05:13 (10,187)
Causey, Mark J......3:53:18 (7,641)
Causon, Roger A......5:08:00 (25,093)
Cavaciuti, Anthony......3:52:33 (7,473)
Cavaglieri, Daniel J......4:12:14 (11,666)
Cavallaro, Angelo......3:16:14 (2,097)
Cavallaro, James M......4:43:32 (19,421)
Cavanagh, Andy D......3:06:36 (1,279)
Cavanagh, David C......6:21:50 (33,989)
Cavanagh, Martyn......4:40:31 (18,660)
Cavanagh, Sean A......4:17:16 (12,866)
Cavasinni, Lino......3:19:10 (2,411)
Cave, Adrian J......4:06:18 (10,417)
Cave, Peter S......4:30:36 (16,280)
Cave, Richard J......3:53:41 (7,725)

Cave, Richard J......4:54:46 (22,216)
Cavener, Craig......5:23:36 (28,029)
Caveney, Craig D......3:51:11 (7,182)
Caves, Trevor J......4:17:04 (12,825)
Cavner, Kevin J......5:52:40 (31,935)
Cavozzi, Gerardo A......4:13:52 (12,056)
Cawley, Alexander W......4:49:45 (20,943)
Cawley, John W......3:56:35 (8,379)
Cawley, Mark......4:04:44 (10,100)
Cawley, Peter J......4:56:53 (22,743)
Cawston, Derek A......5:26:52 (28,602)
Cawthorne, Mark A......6:06:24 (33,076)
Cayley, Adam C......4:25:20 (14,904)
Cayley, Brett......4:36:30 (17,664)
Ceccarelli, Marco......4:43:45 (19,471)
Cecchi, Alessanard......4:41:59 (19,033)
Cedrone, Christopher A......3:57:11 (8,520)
Celotto, Alfonso......4:23:56 (14,549)
Cendrowicz, Leo......3:35:41 (4,511)
Centeno, Alex K......5:18:42 (27,199)
Centeno, Joau......3:58:00 (8,725)
Cepparalo, Robert......5:13:26 (26,110)
Cerda, Antoni......3:41:44 (5,474)
Cermolacce, Christophe......3:33:02 (4,141)
Cerveny, Frank S......3:38:33 (4,929)
Cessford, James......5:57:46 (32,389)
Chabod, Philippe......5:57:46 (32,389)
Chadaway, Andrew K......4:50:47 (21,189)
Chadwick, Andrew M......4:21:59 (14,085)
Chadwick, Chris G......3:44:42 (5,978)
Chadwick, Peter......4:41:44 (18,969)
Chadwick, Peter J......4:45:49 (20,010)
Chadwick, Peter J......5:12:34 (25,961)
Chadwick, Philip......5:04:30 (24,421)
Chadwick, Shaun A......4:30:03 (16,159)
Chafer, Anthony......5:08:53 (25,261)
Chaffe, Gary A......4:47:47 (20,478)
Chaffe, Richard W......3:54:25 (7,887)
Chaffin, John R......4:23:02 (14,340)
Chakraverty, Julian......4:38:37 (18,181)
Chakraverty, Ronjon......4:15:06 (12,342)
Chalk, Jason A......4:20:46 (13,790)
Chalk, Steven J......3:35:53 (4,535)
Chalke, Steve J......3:58:40 (8,877)
Chalkley, Phillip C......4:59:29 (23,379)
Challand, Robin H......5:19:55 (27,412)
Challinor, Edward W......5:02:40 (24,069)
Challis, Mark......5:12:08 (25,879)
Challis, Shaun M......3:53:37 (7,709)
Challoner, Robert......4:09:38 (11,101)
Chalmers, Alexander J......4:55:39 (22,418)
Chalmers, Daniel J......3:48:40 (6,659)
Chalmers, Mark D......4:00:36 (9,330)
Chalmers, Michael N......4:02:52 (9,763)
Chalmers, Philip J......5:51:26 (31,818)
Chaloner, Andrew......6:16:27 (33,716)
Chamberlain, Andrew R......3:13:11 (1,836)
Chamberlain, Brian......4:43:13 (19,343)
Chamberlain, Mark J......2:45:31 (253)
Chamberlain, Michael D......3:17:20 (2,209)
Chamberlain, Nicholas J......4:35:18 (17,359)
Chamberlain, Roger B......6:00:25 (32,614)
Chamberlain, Stephen F......4:38:35 (18,170)
Chamberlain, Stephen P......4:03:34 (9,880)
Chambers, Adrian P......5:30:00 (29,137)
Chambers, Alastair......2:48:10 (318)
Chambers, Brian D......4:51:53 (21,463)
Chambers, Craig......4:20:07 (13,629)
Chambers, Dean K......4:05:36 (10,265)
Chambers, Gordon L......4:06:04 (10,364)
Chambers, Keith......3:40:57 (5,356)
Chambers, Mark R......3:44:42 (5,978)
Chambers, Noel M......3:23:32 (2,853)
Chambers, Steve......5:39:11 (30,475)
Chamiga, Andrzej......3:34:46 (4,371)
Chaminadas, Francis M......3:51:47 (7,314)
Champetier, Bruno......5:37:59 (30,298)
Champion, Christophe......3:52:41 (7,497)
Champion, Steven......4:32:46 (16,729)
Champion, Stuart M......3:52:17 (7,429)
Chan, Aaron......4:38:01 (18,015)
Chan, Alan K......5:26:08 (28,479)

Chan, Chong 3:04:30 (1,131)
Chan, Ken C 6:24:37 (34,112)
Chan, Peter 5:05:52 (24,666)
Chan, Tim P 4:33:44 (16,976)
Chana, Jaswant S 4:38:32 (18,159)
Chanal, Gilles 3:04:46 (1,146)
Chanat, Jean-Luc 5:21:19 (27,660)
Chand, Kieran 6:15:30 (33,651)
Chande, Raj S 4:47:55 (20,509)
Chandler, Conrad M 4:56:07 (22,540)
Chandler, David G 5:31:43 (29,409)
Chandler, Gary W 2:40:46 (153)
Chandler, Michael J 4:05:57 (10,342)
Chandler, Michael. C 3:50:51 (7,107)
Chandler, Paul 4:47:56 (20,512)
Chandler, Paul H 3:47:52 (6,504)
Chandler, Peter J 3:42:33 (5,604)
Chandler, Simon D 3:30:18 (3,763)
Chandley, Paul J 4:23:03 (14,346)
Chanell, Philip 4:11:00 (11,369)
Chang, Joseph E 3:29:28 (3,643)
Chant, Ian R 3:09:29 (1,515)
Chapman, Anthony C 4:41:27 (18,902)
Chapman, Anthony J 4:07:04 (10,587)
Chapman, Benjamin E 4:29:57 (16,134)
Chapman, Christopher R 4:38:31 (18,157)
Chapman, Colin F 5:39:53 (30,577)
Chapman, Colin W 5:33:05 (29,617)
Chapman, Daniel J 4:37:09 (17,814)
Chapman, Daniel M 4:41:20 (18,869)
Chapman, David C 5:15:52 (26,634)
Chapman, Edward R 4:08:50 (10,928)
Chapman, Gary 5:15:26 (26,548)
Chapman, Gary I 3:28:42 (3,524)
Chapman, Grant J 5:27:39 (28,736)
Chapman, Ian 6:25:37 (34,153)
Chapman, Jason T 3:51:55 (7,342)
Chapman, Mark E 3:12:35 (1,788)
Chapman, Mark G 5:14:56 (26,435)
Chapman, Mark R 3:25:20 (3,047)
Chapman, Mark S 3:57:35 (8,619)
Chapman, Neil A 4:04:08 (9,991)
Chapman, Neville 4:01:26 (9,505)
Chapman, Nicholas 4:23:43 (14,493)
Chapman, Nigel A 5:26:15 (28,502)
Chapman, Nigel J 5:18:30 (27,164)
Chapman, Nik E 4:52:01 (21,489)
Chapman, Olly V 3:51:52 (7,330)
Chapman, Paul A 4:27:14 (15,400)
Chapman, Paul D 3:28:38 (3,511)
Chapman, Peter L 4:17:26 (12,921)
Chapman, Philip D 4:20:03 (13,611)
Chapman, Philip D 4:45:37 (19,970)
Chapman, Robert H 3:29:40 (3,670)
Chapman, Simon 4:37:48 (17,955)
Chapman, Stephen R 3:44:57 (6,021)
Chapman, Tim 4:12:29 (11,718)
Chapman, Toby 2:50:58 (406)
Chapman, Trevor S 4:34:53 (17,244)
Chappell, Darren R 3:47:25 (6,413)
Chappell, David 5:27:25 (28,699)
Chappell, Gareth 4:01:15 (9,470)
Chappell, Graham 5:23:27 (28,001)
Chapple, Andy T 3:07:50 (1,372)
Chapple, David A 6:04:07 (32,896)
Chapple, Owen 3:50:41 (7,075)
Charalambous, Apostolis 5:48:40 (31,547)
Charalambous, Kyriacos 4:09:16 (11,020)
Chard, Ken R 3:18:46 (2,364)
Chard, Mark W 4:39:52 (18,500)
Chardet, Dolf 4:17:39 (12,988)
Charhoillaux, Didier 4:58:12 (23,076)
Charles, Clive L 5:27:18 (28,677)
Charles, Gregory G 4:01:29 (9,512)
Charles, Henry W 4:22:23 (14,170)
Charles, Jonathan P 4:28:36 (15,761)
Charles, Paul J 3:27:22 (3,336)
Charles, Simon P 3:56:59 (8,476)
Charles, Stuart 4:52:21 (21,583)
Charles, Tom R 4:10:05 (11,180)
Charleston, Dan J 3:03:57 (1,102)
Charlesworth, Lee J 4:44:30 (19,681)
Charlesworth, Simon 4:00:58 (9,411)
Charlesworth, Stephen 6:17:33 (33,755)
Charlish, Peter G 5:25:05 (28,286)
Charlton, Kevin A 3:29:49 (3,691)
Charlton, Martin J 3:49:02 (6,740)
Charlton, Michael O 3:31:36 (3,927)
Charman, Dan 3:30:56 (3,833)
Charnley, Edward J 4:39:29 (18,414)
Charnley, William 4:41:13 (18,844)
Charnock, Graham H 4:36:17 (17,606)
Charrier, Nicolas 3:09:30 (1,517)
Charrington, Huw A 4:46:53 (20,247)
Charron, Philippe 3:38:19 (4,889)
Chart, Robert J 3:49:28 (6,821)
Charter, Nicholas V 4:48:22 (20,628)
Charters, Paul W 4:41:24 (18,889)
Chartlton, Michael D 4:19:05 (13,350)
Chartres, Jon 5:04:05 (24,340)
Chase, Daniel J 4:57:56 (23,014)
Chase, James W 4:57:56 (23,014)
Chase, Kelvin M 3:40:37 (5,287)
Chase, Mark 4:32:52 (16,758)
Chassot, Patrick 3:29:49 (3,691)
Chattaway, Robert 4:23:51 (14,530)
Chattell, Brian 5:41:48 (30,809)
Chatten, Simon 4:40:15 (18,589)
Chatten, Simon M 2:53:26 (491)
Chatterjee, Karl 4:04:47 (10,110)
Chatterton, Nicholas P 4:25:01 (14,829)
Chatterton, Richard S 4:39:52 (18,500)
Chaudhry, Zahid 5:41:36 (30,780)
Chauhan, Jiten 5:50:14 (31,697)
Chauvet, Christophe 3:34:53 (4,392)
Chavarria, Oldemar 3:40:59 (5,361)
Chavda, Gordhan 5:53:18 (31,986)
Chaytow, Ben K 3:57:36 (8,624)
Cheal, John M 3:56:07 (8,254)
Chebab, Abderrahim 4:45:43 (19,993)
Chebab, Nassira 4:52:47 (21,689)
Checchia, Frank 3:06:23 (1,261)
Checkley, Matthew 4:24:42 (14,747)
Cheek, Christopher A 3:34:01 (4,270)
Cheek, Nigel 4:31:41 (16,504)
Cheema, Barinderjit S 6:33:45 (34,456)
Cheesebrough, Timothy L 4:08:36 (10,893)
Cheeseman, Robert S 4:29:46 (16,080)
Cheesman, Bruce 4:46:23 (20,151)
Cheesman, Charles 5:30:32 (29,227)
Cheesmur, Stephen 4:18:09 (13,108)
Cheetham, Mark S 3:58:28 (8,832)
Chell, Darren P 3:47:06 (6,364)
Chell, Ian M 3:25:21 (3,051)
Chell, Philip 4:40:22 (18,624)
Chen, Eewei 4:40:57 (18,775)
Chen, Jack C 4:12:36 (11,737)
Chen, Lei 5:08:55 (25,266)
Chenery, Alexander M 5:30:22 (29,195)
Chenery, Tobe 5:22:31 (27,860)
Chenguiti, Salaheddine 4:32:21 (16,636)
Chenhall, Richard J 4:38:15 (18,068)
Cherono, Benson 2:18:55 (11)
Cherrill, Graham C 5:14:06 (26,247)
Cherruau, Armand-Phillippe 3:23:11 (2,820)
Cherry, Marcus 4:00:23 (9,287)
Cherry, Nick W 4:07:59 (10,764)
Cheseloine, Noel A 4:03:11 (9,813)
Chesney, Andrew N 4:48:51 (20,732)
Chesnutt, Jonathan 4:22:39 (14,246)
Chessell, Bruce 4:51:15 (21,298)
Chessell, Guy 3:57:41 (8,649)
Chester, Martin G 3:24:02 (2,909)
Chester, Neil J 3:24:20 (2,942)
Chesterton, Allen J 5:17:02 (26,863)
Chesterton, Neil D 4:19:42 (13,510)
Chesterton, Peter B 4:20:48 (13,799)
Chestney, Jon 4:53:34 (21,904)
Chetty, Devanand 3:39:18 (5,064)
Cheung, Desmond 7:41:10 (35,574)
Cheung, Jerome 6:12:56 (33,488)
Cheung, Kein Y 5:56:46 (32,316)
Cheung, Raymond 4:42:11 (19,089)
Cheung, Ronny L 5:22:28 (27,842)
Cheung, Simon 4:51:18 (21,315)
Chevalier, Lauren 2:57:24 (703)
Chevassu, Jean-Felix F 2:40:12 (143)
Chewter, Alan 4:31:16 (16,416)
Chewter, David J 4:26:52 (15,285)
Chichorek, Piotr R 4:04:13 (10,010)
Chiddention, Sean 4:06:55 (10,554)
Chidley, David A 4:22:01 (14,089)
Chidley, Kester 5:54:51 (32,130)
Chidlow, Matthew P 4:48:07 (20,555)
Chilcott, Darren W 4:33:11 (16,838)
Chilcott, Peter 5:19:11 (27,290)
Child, Mark 4:19:36 (13,486)
Childers, Andrew D 5:09:24 (25,353)
Childs, Jordan T 4:52:45 (21,681)
Childs, Paul A 2:57:03 (682)
Childs, Peter J 3:57:12 (8,528)
Childs, Samuel J 5:23:21 (27,984)
Chiles, Andrew D 4:01:49 (9,572)
Chiles, John 6:58:16 (35,095)
Chiles, Matthew 3:39:35 (5,121)
Chilton, Andrew C 4:12:25 (11,705)
Chilton, Christopher J 3:26:52 (3,251)
Chin, Raymond A 5:09:28 (25,366)
Chinhirun, Kriangsak 4:16:09 (12,609)
Chiorando, Enrico Z 4:30:03 (16,159)
Chippendale, Alan 7:29:17 (35,476)
Chislett, David W 3:07:51 (1,373)
Chittell, Chris 4:47:39 (20,441)
Chittem, David J 4:12:31 (11,726)
Chittick, William B 5:14:14 (26,278)
Chitty, Gavyn D 4:55:31 (22,395)
Chivers, Ashley 4:13:37 (11,999)
Chivers, Craig 4:13:37 (11,999)
Chivers, Mark 5:14:13 (26,270)
Chlebus, Marvin 3:32:47 (4,102)
Chmara, Edward Z 5:26:01 (28,458)
Cho, Leung K 4:55:42 (22,429)
Chojnacki, Mitchell D 6:08:36 (33,213)
Chong, Heong P 3:46:45 (6,291)
Chonstkowsky, Salomon 4:04:07 (9,989)
Chopra, Narinder K 4:46:08 (20,090)
Choquet, Didier M 2:52:15 (454)
Chorley, Martin 3:26:33 (3,201)
Choukeir, Mouhammed 5:04:53 (24,496)
Chouksey, Nikhil 3:55:22 (8,099)
Chow, Kun Fai 4:14:00 (12,096)
Chow, Richard J 5:49:22 (31,616)
Chowles, Dennis E 5:18:57 (27,242)
Chraibi, Salah E 4:47:25 (20,387)
Chrisafis, Alexis 3:44:47 (5,991)
Christensen, Bente A 3:46:20 (6,225)
Christensen, Simon P 4:53:06 (21,779)
Christiansen, Klaus 3:59:28 (9,087)
Christie, Campbell S 3:44:35 (5,955)
Christie, David 3:22:52 (2,785)
Christie, David 3:58:25 (8,812)
Christie, Emlyn D 2:52:36 (463)
Christie, Grant S 5:50:46 (31,753)
Christie, James 5:15:17 (26,520)
Christie, Michael 4:56:34 (22,647)
Christie, Neil A 3:46:17 (6,216)
Christie, Sandy 3:37:44 (4,780)
Christie, Terry S 3:02:19 (1,016)
Christiensen, Roman S 5:02:50 (24,093)
Christmas, Julian 4:52:18 (21,568)
Christofields, George 3:31:57 (3,985)
Christopher, Derek 3:53:20 (7,655)
Christopher, John M 3:09:04 (1,472)
Christopher, Leonard A 2:58:59 (821)
Christopher, Lynsey G 3:49:07 (6,754)
Christy, Ian 4:41:33 (18,939)
Christy, James R 5:31:09 (29,329)
Christy, John R 3:05:10 (1,172)
Chritchlow, Philip 2:35:38 (80)
Chrystal, John 3:48:58 (6,723)
Chu, Lai A 5:39:26 (30,514)
Chu, Vy X 4:32:50 (16,748)
Chudy, Bernard 5:04:40 (24,443)
Chughtai, Javed S 4:04:38 (10,080)
Chui, Wai H 4:35:45 (17,473)
Chumaceiro, Ronald 4:10:23 (11,244)
Chumber, Jas S 3:50:50 (7,102)
Chung, Alex 5:15:53 (26,638)
Chung, Kam K 3:09:07 (1,480)

Chung, Laurence C....5:08:17 (25,152)
Chung, Tony....4:33:31 (16,916)
Church, David B....4:57:59 (23,032)
Church, Jeremy S....4:14:10 (12,130)
Church, John W....4:00:32 (9,318)
Church, Paul....4:52:20 (21,581)
Church, Trevor E....4:42:57 (19,289)
Churchard, Christopher J....4:12:23 (11,697)
Churcher, Joe....5:00:19 (23,581)
Churchill, Adam D....3:08:39 (1,441)
Churchill, Andrew E....3:39:48 (5,157)
Churchill, Duncan R....3:29:59 (3,717)
Churchill, Jack A....4:56:04 (22,528)
Churchill, Neil R....4:49:55 (20,976)
Churchill, Nigel....4:03:30 (9,869)
Churchward, Ian....3:06:51 (1,303)
Churton, Mark A....4:05:38 (10,273)
Chuter, Charles S....3:47:45 (6,488)
Ciaccia, Filippo....3:35:08 (4,427)
Cillard, Jean-François....4:05:06 (10,164)
Cima, Edward....4:25:20 (14,904)
Cima, Keith H....4:12:04 (11,624)
Cimini, Nicola....4:09:24 (11,048)
Cinnamon, Paul T....3:40:11 (5,213)
Cinque, Giulio A....3:07:05 (1,320)
Cipes, Luc....3:59:11 (9,008)
Circus, James A....5:22:43 (27,892)
Cirelli, Andrea....3:17:24 (2,217)
Claber, Martyn G....3:22:51 (2,783)
Clachers, Liam L....4:31:26 (16,447)
Clack, Christopher T....5:58:50 (32,492)
Clack, Paul A....3:13:07 (1,828)
Claessen, Eggert....6:00:37 (32,632)
Clague, Mark W....3:11:36 (1,680)
Clague, William T....5:39:02 (30,454)
Claire, Kanwaljit S....4:42:49 (19,260)
Clampin, Anthony M....7:26:49 (35,443)
Clancy, Andrew....3:11:18 (1,653)
Clancy, Paul F....4:26:43 (15,242)
Clapp, Matthew N....2:46:48 (280)
Clapperton, Mike....6:49:07 (34,915)
Clapton, John M....4:49:29 (20,885)
Clapton, Roland A....4:10:17 (11,226)
Clare, Danny....4:48:17 (20,597)
Clare, Edward....4:49:27 (20,874)
Clare, Jonathan R....3:08:59 (1,468)
Clare, Tom....5:32:00 (29,451)
Clarehugh, Mark....2:40:51 (155)
Claridge, David....5:02:39 (24,066)
Claridge, Robert A....5:15:57 (26,650)
Clark, Adrian....4:38:47 (18,226)
Clark, Alan G....6:19:54 (33,885)
Clark, Andrew A....4:39:40 (18,454)
Clark, Andrew D....5:19:58 (27,420)
Clark, Andrew J....4:36:33 (17,681)
Clark, Andrew M....6:02:10 (32,758)
Clark, Antony S....4:35:05 (17,291)
Clark, Billy C....4:08:30 (10,871)
Clark, Brent J....5:26:20 (28,516)
Clark, Chris E....4:17:58 (13,064)
Clark, Christopher J....3:47:36 (6,447)
Clark, Craig....3:57:36 (8,624)
Clark, Daniel....3:57:30 (8,600)
Clark, Daniel J....4:46:40 (20,210)
Clark, Danny J....5:22:18 (27,820)
Clark, Darren G....5:58:44 (32,486)
Clark, David....5:54:55 (32,142)
Clark, Derek J....4:25:55 (15,037)
Clark, Graham R....5:51:16 (31,804)
Clark, Gren E....4:05:10 (10,179)
Clark, Hamish I....3:36:34 (4,621)
Clark, James R....4:56:34 (22,647)
Clark, James S....4:24:56 (14,809)
Clark, Jamie C....5:28:24 (28,888)
Clark, Jason....4:46:41 (20,212)
Clark, Joel S....4:23:27 (14,432)
Clark, John....4:11:57 (11,603)
Clark, John R....4:31:34 (16,475)
Clark, Jonathan L....5:32:34 (29,545)
Clark, Kevin P....4:41:27 (18,902)
Clark, Lauder P....4:16:26 (12,681)
Clark, Malcolm A....6:43:16 (34,757)
Clark, Mark A....3:32:47 (4,102)
Clark, Martin D....4:57:00 (22,772)
Clark, Martin J....4:00:54 (9,399)
Clark, Mel....4:54:39 (22,185)
Clark, Michael J....3:16:24 (2,118)
Clark, Michael J....4:50:13 (21,051)
Clark, Neil J....4:00:34 (9,326)
Clark, Neil R....4:00:19 (9,275)
Clark, Nicholas....4:55:59 (22,508)
Clark, Oliver G....3:44:20 (5,916)
Clark, Paul....5:56:29 (32,285)
Clark, Paul D....4:33:51 (17,002)
Clark, Paul J....4:32:51 (16,755)
Clark, Pete J....4:58:09 (23,063)
Clark, Richard....4:53:08 (21,788)
Clark, Richard H....3:33:05 (4,150)
Clark, Robert G....3:58:31 (8,842)
Clark, Robert M....4:01:59 (9,600)
Clark, Robin....4:23:26 (14,427)
Clark, Robin A....4:17:20 (12,887)
Clark, Robin H....4:53:57 (22,006)
Clark, Roger....4:35:27 (17,389)
Clark, Russell J....3:47:22 (6,401)
Clark, Simon....4:17:45 (13,010)
Clark, Simon A....4:28:01 (15,592)
Clark, Simon T....3:59:39 (9,129)
Clark, Steven V....3:55:05 (8,026)
Clark, William....4:51:02 (21,248)
Clark, William A....4:16:28 (12,692)
Clarke, Andrew J....5:10:31 (25,580)
Clarke, Andrew J....5:53:35 (32,020)
Clarke, Andrew M....4:32:28 (16,652)
Clarke, Andrew R....6:32:08 (34,414)
Clarke, Ben....4:17:50 (13,029)
Clarke, Benjamin J....4:18:17 (13,142)
Clarke, Brian T....5:17:23 (26,937)
Clarke, Christopher J....4:27:07 (15,357)
Clarke, Dave A....4:25:05 (14,842)
Clarke, Dave S....6:53:11 (34,997)
Clarke, David....5:01:42 (23,869)
Clarke, David A....5:28:44 (28,936)
Clarke, David G....6:14:45 (33,596)
Clarke, Douglas S....2:57:02 (680)
Clarke, Fintan J....3:55:09 (8,044)
Clarke, Gareth R....3:34:38 (4,356)
Clarke, Gary G....7:09:49 (35,269)
Clarke, Gavin....5:17:31 (26,960)
Clarke, Glenn....3:55:08 (8,039)
Clarke, Graham G....5:51:09 (31,789)
Clarke, Iain D....3:49:09 (6,758)
Clarke, Ian....4:51:16 (21,300)
Clarke, James A....3:21:39 (2,672)
Clarke, James D....3:45:20 (6,070)
Clarke, James J....3:55:44 (8,171)
Clarke, John B....5:23:46 (28,071)
Clarke, John E....4:50:45 (21,177)
Clarke, John F....6:18:52 (33,828)
Clarke, John P....2:29:57 (41)
Clarke, John P....4:59:43 (23,436)
Clarke, Jonathan P....5:33:32 (29,693)
Clarke, Kenny W....3:13:37 (1,866)
Clarke, Lorne D....5:57:20 (32,358)
Clarke, Martin H....3:15:05 (2,005)
Clarke, Michael B....4:44:30 (19,681)
Clarke, Michael E....3:31:16 (3,875)
Clarke, Michael F....3:58:01 (8,728)
Clarke, Neil J....4:18:30 (13,211)
Clarke, Neville P....4:32:03 (16,569)
Clarke, Nicholas J....3:11:18 (1,653)
Clarke, Nicholas J....5:17:21 (26,927)
Clarke, Owen D....4:38:48 (18,234)
Clarke, Patrick J....3:32:27 (4,059)
Clarke, Patrick J....4:59:04 (23,277)
Clarke, Paul D....3:43:57 (5,856)
Clarke, Paul J....4:19:13 (13,379)
Clarke, Peter....6:36:13 (34,546)
Clarke, Peter R....4:14:02 (12,106)
Clarke, Philip....4:50:42 (21,168)
Clarke, Richard....5:24:39 (28,207)
Clarke, Robert....5:17:23 (26,937)
Clarke, Robert E....5:17:37 (26,984)
Clarke, Roger S....3:42:05 (5,534)
Clarke, Russell....3:48:41 (6,663)
Clarke, Simon....3:55:08 (8,039)
Clarke, Simon....4:42:25 (19,156)
Clarke, Simon D....5:02:27 (24,026)
Clarke, Stephen J....4:54:11 (22,076)
Clarke, Stephen P....5:28:59 (28,979)
Clarke, Steven R....4:31:37 (16,490)
Clarke, Stuart....4:50:13 (21,051)
Clarke, Toby J....4:07:40 (10,695)
Clark-Savage, Gary....5:03:11 (24,170)
Clarkson, Dean....5:33:20 (29,653)
Clarkson, Graham....3:04:09 (1,109)
Clarkson, Graham J....5:44:42 (31,124)
Clarkson, Thomas P....3:22:24 (2,739)
Clatworthy, Graham P....5:15:32 (26,575)
Claude, Millet....4:49:55 (20,976)
Clausen, Jake....4:21:22 (13,926)
Claverie, Arnaud H....2:39:01 (126)
Clawson, Mark....4:02:19 (9,671)
Clay, Alexander L....4:42:20 (19,129)
Clay, Andrew M....5:32:30 (29,525)
Clay, Christopher....3:33:21 (4,187)
Clay, Nigel R....4:48:11 (20,573)
Clay, Paul....5:09:34 (25,391)
Clay, Trevor....5:14:04 (26,242)
Clayden, Robert A....4:52:04 (21,503)
Claydon, Jack R....4:19:44 (13,520)
Claydon, Paul....4:41:24 (18,889)
Clayton, Andrew P....4:19:51 (13,559)
Clayton, Andy S....6:15:48 (33,671)
Clayton, Carl S....4:51:16 (21,300)
Clayton, Chris S....5:06:49 (24,844)
Clayton, Christopher P....3:28:05 (3,416)
Clayton, Harry C....4:58:12 (23,076)
Clayton, Iain R....5:18:28 (27,158)
Clayton, Ian....2:57:46 (727)
Clayton, Jonathan C....4:27:41 (15,512)
Clayton, Lee M....6:53:50 (35,017)
Clayton, Peter J....4:17:29 (12,940)
Clayton, Peter P....2:58:45 (808)
Clayton, Richard J....5:48:07 (31,481)
Clayton, Richard S....4:20:36 (13,752)
Clayton, Robert....3:42:37 (5,611)
Clayton, Robert J....5:05:25 (24,577)
Clayton, Stephen F....3:51:30 (7,256)
Clayton, Steve....4:33:24 (16,892)
Clear, Nigel T....4:33:48 (16,991)
Cleary, Christopher F....3:10:51 (1,618)
Cleary, Richard....4:12:09 (11,644)
Cleasby, Neil M....3:49:18 (6,796)
Cleave, Richard J....4:20:48 (13,799)
Cleaves, Trevor A....7:11:35 (35,298)
Clegg, Alastair B....4:36:02 (17,544)
Clegg, Jeremy D....4:37:15 (17,831)
Clegg, Steven....5:24:49 (28,240)
Cleland, James R....3:23:12 (2,823)
Cleland, Jonathan B....4:23:59 (14,566)
Cleland, Mark D....5:00:01 (23,508)
Cleland, Ross J....3:48:48 (6,687)
Clemens, John B....3:31:51 (3,963)
Clemenson, David M....4:04:30 (10,057)
Clement, Alain....3:56:48 (8,431)
Clement, Matthew D....4:43:03 (19,306)
Clement, Morgan L....4:44:47 (19,772)
Clement, Nigel....3:26:48 (3,240)
Clements, Andrew C....2:42:06 (181)
Clements, Edward....5:19:49 (27,396)
Clements, John R....5:45:46 (31,235)
Clements, Philip E....4:53:08 (21,788)
Clements, Thomas K....4:43:59 (19,535)
Clements, Thomas R....4:25:09 (14,859)
Clements, Trevor W....3:25:30 (3,063)
Clenaghan, Stuart J....4:32:00 (16,560)
Clendon, Daniel G....2:37:46 (107)
Clephane, Gordon A....7:30:18 (35,496)
Cleugh, Tony P....5:47:18 (31,386)
Cleveland, Kevin....6:07:08 (33,114)
Cleveley, Mike J....5:01:34 (23,848)
Clevett, Neil D....6:08:52 (33,229)
Clewley, Thomas....3:56:29 (8,355)
Clewlow, Melvin T....3:15:00 (1,995)
Clews, Charlie....4:58:51 (23,218)
Cliff, Thomas R....3:38:32 (4,926)
Cliffe, Daniel J....5:55:29 (32,190)
Cliffe, Shane....4:06:01 (10,353)

Clifford, Edward A....3:45:10 (6,044)
Clifford, Robin P....2:57:07 (683)
Clifford, Steve W....4:05:50 (10,314)
Clifton, Dale B....6:00:56 (32,661)
Clinch, Mike....4:39:00 (18,283)
Clinch, Peter D....4:56:54 (22,749)
Clint, Jonathan E....4:36:25 (17,644)
Clinton, Peter....4:06:22 (10,429)
Clipper, Alexander S....3:42:47 (5,643)
Clive, Adrian....5:01:28 (23,823)
Cloarec, Cedric....4:47:51 (20,493)
Cloherty, Tommy M....6:09:00 (33,237)
Clohesy, Jamie....4:37:58 (17,999)
Cloke, Daniel....4:59:57 (23,490)
Close, Edward....3:40:14 (5,220)
Close, Steven T....3:45:04 (6,033)
Clough, Andrew B....4:13:19 (11,912)
Clough, Darren....4:02:59 (9,781)
Clough, Lee....3:44:23 (5,922)
Clough, Robin D....3:28:37 (3,507)
Clough, Trevor....3:00:57 (954)
Clowes, Dan....3:28:19 (3,452)
Clowes, Jamie....4:09:17 (11,024)
Clowes, John D....5:09:54 (25,451)
Clubley, Steve R....4:29:56 (16,128)
Clulow, Jolyon S....4:49:13 (20,824)
Clune, Raymond M....6:21:04 (33,958)
Clusker, Dean....3:45:21 (6,072)
Clutterbuck, Andrew M....4:12:47 (11,786)
Clutterbuck, Barnaby T....4:19:16 (13,402)
Clutterbuck, Christopher J....5:11:13 (25,706)
Clutterbuck, Jeremy....5:15:44 (26,612)
Clutterbuck, Nathan B....4:31:39 (16,497)
Clutterbuck, Stephen A....5:01:40 (23,864)
Clutton, Paul A....4:29:05 (15,880)
Cluzet, Bernard....4:19:56 (13,582)
Clyaton, Mark....4:05:55 (10,332)
Clyne, Dave J....4:59:43 (23,436)
Clyne, Mike....4:47:43 (20,459)
Clynes, Declan P....2:57:37 (716)
Coade, David....4:04:39 (10,087)
Coales, David J....2:54:38 (554)
Coates, Alan....6:30:46 (34,351)
Coates, Brian W....3:10:48 (1,616)
Coates, Craig J....3:57:39 (8,639)
Coates, George A....6:18:37 (33,812)
Coates, Jonathon L....3:31:38 (3,933)
Coates, Nigel J....3:08:19 (1,417)
Coates, Stephen T....3:09:06 (1,477)
Cobb, Ben....4:48:16 (20,595)
Cobb, Edward....6:10:38 (33,344)
Cobbett, Peter L....4:48:40 (20,682)
Cobbin, Terry....4:46:53 (20,247)
Cobill, Sebastian C....3:28:53 (3,553)
Cobley, Gareth J....5:16:33 (26,767)
Cobley, Kevin N....6:44:06 (34,778)
Cobley, Phillip....5:29:27 (29,065)
Cocco, Massimo....3:24:41 (2,984)
Cochran, Mark C....4:26:09 (15,084)
Cochrane, Alistair D....5:20:27 (27,504)
Cochrane, David....5:07:58 (25,088)
Cochrane, Jason I....4:18:34 (13,230)
Cochrane, Robert W....4:35:55 (17,519)
Cockbain, Mark....3:31:20 (3,881)
Cockburn, Andrew D....3:58:20 (8,793)
Cockburn, Nat B....4:11:30 (11,501)
Cockburn, Robert A....4:52:50 (21,711)
Cockell, James W....5:25:01 (28,272)
Cocker, David J....3:41:44 (5,474)
Cockerell, William V....2:30:39 (43)
Cockhill, Andy J....4:21:56 (14,073)
Cocking, Sam C....4:00:04 (9,221)
Cockings, Antony P....6:39:18 (34,651)
Cocklin, Matthew....5:33:41 (29,711)
Cockram, Kevin J....4:09:57 (11,156)
Cockram, Simon J....5:26:40 (28,571)
Cocksedge, Lynn A....4:11:07 (11,401)
Cocksedge, Mark J....3:44:51 (5,999)
Cockshott, David L....4:00:37 (9,337)
Codling, Ian R....5:18:11 (27,098)
Coe, Gavin J....6:24:40 (34,115)
Coelus, Lieven....4:55:19 (22,341)
Coffey, Damian N....3:03:20 (1,066)
Coffey, Matthew....3:13:02 (1,821)
Coghill, Craig....5:17:24 (26,941)
Coglan, Julian J....4:47:30 (20,407)
Cohen, Howard....3:15:07 (2,006)
Cohen, Paul....4:14:22 (12,180)
Cohen, Steffan K....2:58:31 (790)
Cohen, Stuart T....4:51:33 (21,383)
Cohen-Price, Daniel L....5:56:17 (32,264)
Coke, Ken J....5:16:52 (26,829)
Coker, Kenneth N....4:12:34 (11,731)
Colborne, Graham....5:57:04 (32,337)
Colborne, Jonathan....5:57:04 (32,337)
Colbourne, Melvin P....4:23:46 (14,505)
Colbourne, Richard S....3:50:39 (7,066)
Colbourne, Steve J....3:02:30 (1,029)
Colburn, James A....4:36:56 (17,774)
Colclough, Richard J....5:18:30 (27,164)
Colcombe, Paul A....6:12:06 (33,432)
Coldridge, Terry J....5:42:28 (30,876)
Coldron, Andrew....3:51:46 (7,311)
Cole, Alan M....4:50:58 (21,233)
Cole, Anthony W....3:43:52 (5,838)
Cole, Brian J....2:35:31 (75)
Cole, Brian T....4:54:49 (22,229)
Cole, Christopher J....6:19:46 (33,880)
Cole, Dan J....5:56:05 (32,245)
Cole, Ian A....4:53:58 (22,012)
Cole, James....4:31:14 (16,411)
Cole, Martin....4:20:36 (13,752)
Cole, Martin A....5:00:55 (23,712)
Cole, Martin R....5:25:11 (28,300)
Cole, Michael G....5:02:40 (24,069)
Cole, Paul S....4:38:13 (18,062)
Cole, Paul T....4:06:58 (10,566)
Cole, Rob E....3:52:23 (7,448)
Cole, Robert B....5:26:11 (28,487)
Cole, Robert J....5:31:29 (29,376)
Cole, Stephen H....5:27:09 (28,646)
Cole, Stephen M....3:19:07 (2,405)
Cole, Thomas S....4:34:05 (17,046)
Colegate, Andrew....3:12:31 (1,778)
Coleman, Andrew J....5:19:30 (27,337)
Coleman, Andy....2:59:23 (852)
Coleman, Dominic....5:12:01 (25,858)
Coleman, Glen....3:13:50 (1,887)
Coleman, Glenn R....5:29:25 (29,061)
Coleman, Graham....4:10:40 (11,307)
Coleman, Ian R....5:24:01 (28,109)
Coleman, Jamie C....4:15:16 (12,383)
Coleman, Jason E....5:14:33 (26,350)
Coleman, John P....4:15:50 (12,518)
Coleman, John P....6:53:27 (35,004)
Coleman, Mark....4:10:08 (11,190)
Coleman, Martin J....3:59:12 (9,011)
Coleman, Martin R....6:46:52 (34,853)
Coleman, Michael....2:32:45 (52)
Coleman, Paul J....5:51:25 (31,816)
Coleman, Paul N....4:18:40 (13,258)
Coleman, Phil....4:26:22 (15,149)
Coleman, Richard J....3:27:04 (3,293)
Coleman, Rory J....5:35:46 (30,018)
Coleman, Ross J....5:18:23 (27,144)
Coleman, Steve J....3:29:08 (3,593)
Coleman, Terry P....5:55:58 (32,237)
Coleman, Tom S....4:24:41 (14,745)
Coleman, William A....5:37:54 (30,287)
Coles, Clive A....4:06:34 (10,480)
Coles, Mark....4:03:49 (9,930)
Coles, Matthew T....6:17:54 (33,774)
Coles, Nathan M....4:37:40 (17,926)
Coles, Paul....3:40:18 (5,231)
Coles, Richard J....4:24:29 (14,701)
Coles, Russell K....4:37:53 (17,977)
Coles, Terence D....4:40:24 (18,632)
Coles, Terry G....4:42:48 (19,255)
Coles, Thomas A....6:02:02 (32,754)
Coleshill, James....3:54:04 (7,806)
Coleshill, Paul G....4:04:26 (10,045)
Coley, Mark D....4:59:11 (23,302)
Colfer, James J....4:07:36 (10,680)
Colgin, Everard....4:20:38 (13,764)
Colinet, Yves....3:51:03 (7,145)
Collard, David M....5:37:03 (30,177)
Collard, Dominic P....4:35:45 (17,473)
Collard, Mark P....6:15:19 (33,634)
Collard, Robert....6:20:15 (33,901)
Colle, Ronnie....4:51:14 (21,297)
Coller, Jonny C....3:49:56 (6,923)
Collerton, Liam....3:57:55 (8,702)
Collett, Graham J....3:35:42 (4,514)
Collett, Jamie....5:13:00 (26,048)
Collett, John D....5:04:15 (24,363)
Collier, Adrian L....4:13:40 (12,012)
Collier, Edward W....3:19:59 (2,493)
Collier, Ian D....3:21:11 (2,622)
Collier, Jeffrey E....4:34:26 (17,131)
Collier, John S....5:26:53 (28,607)
Collier, Peter F....4:41:55 (19,020)
Collier, Robert G....3:43:17 (5,734)
Collier, Steve....6:37:17 (34,588)
Collin, Edmund....4:26:47 (15,260)
Colling, Joseph C....4:17:27 (12,927)
Collingbourne, Robert J....4:48:33 (20,661)
Collinge, Andrew....2:56:59 (673)
Collings, Murray E....3:58:10 (8,750)
Collings, Stuart A....4:37:57 (17,993)
Collingwood, Edwin J....4:15:21 (12,406)
Collingwood, Paul S....3:05:21 (1,188)
Collins, Alex G....3:06:36 (1,279)
Collins, Bruce P....4:40:28 (18,644)
Collins, Clive D....5:37:50 (30,274)
Collins, Daniel J....3:43:06 (5,707)
Collins, David....3:42:37 (5,611)
Collins, David....9:04:43 (35,694)
Collins, Dennis A....4:25:55 (15,037)
Collins, Duncan....2:49:03 (346)
Collins, Glen J....4:32:14 (16,616)
Collins, Jonathan M....3:20:46 (2,584)
Collins, Lance K....4:44:45 (19,758)
Collins, Liam R....4:20:10 (13,645)
Collins, Mark....3:56:13 (8,279)
Collins, Mark....5:09:44 (25,422)
Collins, Martin A....3:09:12 (1,490)
Collins, Matthew J....2:42:01 (180)
Collins, Maurice S....2:57:00 (676)
Collins, Michael....3:24:37 (2,972)
Collins, Michael....4:31:32 (16,466)
Collins, Michael J....5:30:40 (29,246)
Collins, Michael P....5:12:56 (26,027)
Collins, Michael T....3:29:23 (3,633)
Collins, Peter....5:57:39 (32,378)
Collins, Peter R....4:00:16 (9,266)
Collins, Richard D....4:38:47 (18,226)
Collins, Robert A....3:54:29 (7,899)
Collins, Robert P....4:51:47 (21,434)
Collins, Ronnie....5:30:00 (29,137)
Collins, Shaun....4:50:44 (21,172)
Collins, Stephen D....6:26:41 (34,199)
Collins, Stephen M....3:49:49 (6,899)
Collins, Tom H....4:01:57 (9,594)
Collinson, Anthony....3:12:59 (1,819)
Collinson, Bobby....4:57:43 (22,963)
Collinson, Mark W....2:52:43 (467)
Collinson, Richard J....3:08:03 (1,395)
Collinwood, James....4:29:13 (15,915)
Collis, Guy W....3:22:56 (2,789)
Collis, Simon....4:27:09 (15,366)
Collishaw, Andrew....4:12:08 (11,639)
Collishe, Robert E....6:50:37 (34,948)
Collis-Smith, David F....4:29:34 (16,031)
Collyer, Chris S....4:43:14 (19,349)
Collymore, Lance V....4:59:41 (23,427)
Colman, Ivan N....4:15:41 (12,480)
Colman, Scott....4:54:10 (22,069)
Colquhoun, Robert W....4:13:35 (11,990)
Colquitt, Andrew....5:53:07 (31,971)
Coltart, Mark C....5:26:19 (28,512)
Coltart, William J....5:26:19 (28,512)
Colton, Ivan P....3:55:36 (8,138)
Colton, Matthew J....4:40:40 (18,694)
Colverson, Matthew M....5:04:15 (24,363)
Colyer, Sam....4:59:30 (23,384)
Coman, Brian D....6:05:44 (33,025)
Combis, Narcis....4:11:36 (11,527)
Combs, Richard W....4:09:00 (10,949)
Comer, Roy F....6:27:43 (34,243)

LONDON MARATHON

Comerford, Sean	5:17:53	(27,025)
Comette, Allan J	5:07:40	(25,030)
Comins, Allan H	5:19:52	(27,402)
Comish, David	3:18:50	(2,370)
Common, Robert	4:03:29	(9,866)
Compagnino, Alessandro	4:14:15	(12,152)
Compton, David	5:03:53	(24,305)
Compton, Derek K	5:44:41	(31,122)
Compton, Jeff	5:39:41	(30,555)
Compton, John P	3:34:25	(4,330)
Compton, Nicholas D	3:59:18	(9,043)
Comte, Dominique	3:45:09	(6,041)
Comyn, James A	5:20:54	(27,587)
Conaghan, Martin	3:26:09	(3,149)
Conchar, Stewart R	4:54:46	(22,216)
Condotti, Matthew	5:22:20	(27,825)
Conduit, Timothy C	3:20:44	(2,580)
Coney, Richard I	3:23:13	(2,825)
Congreve, David	5:54:36	(32,113)
Congreve, Steve C	3:58:29	(8,838)
Coningham, Jason M	4:54:34	(22,158)
Coningham, Matthew	2:54:43	(562)
Conlan, Stephen	4:08:04	(10,782)
Conley, David C	4:55:55	(22,493)
Conley, Neil M	4:15:58	(12,551)
Conlin, Paul J	3:13:05	(1,826)
Conlon, Henry	4:55:49	(22,461)
Conlon, John J	4:25:43	(14,998)
Conlon, Toby J	3:42:42	(5,627)
Connaughton, Simon I	5:37:52	(30,281)
Connell, Ashley	6:29:13	(34,294)
Connell, Robert M	4:31:08	(16,395)
Connell, Stephen J	4:49:33	(20,900)
Connell, Steven	3:15:50	(2,064)
Connelly, Mark	4:50:41	(21,164)
Conner, Luke A	4:12:30	(11,721)
Connery, Douglas G	3:42:25	(5,587)
Connery, Matthew B	5:06:25	(24,772)
Connery, Neil E	3:56:15	(8,286)
Connolly, Gary	3:52:42	(7,503)
Connolly, James P	3:48:41	(6,663)
Connolly, Michael P	3:15:55	(2,072)
Connolly, Paul	5:35:54	(30,038)
Connolly, Seamus	5:44:20	(31,080)
Connolly, Shane R	2:54:31	(547)
Connolly, Tommy	6:20:33	(33,924)
Connor, Andrew F	4:13:45	(12,030)
Connor, David P	2:36:50	(95)
Connor, Edward	5:08:46	(25,237)
Connor, Ian G	3:47:52	(6,504)
Connor, John R	4:26:13	(15,105)
Connor, Noel S	3:23:01	(2,798)
Connor, Peter	3:38:48	(4,973)
Connors, Des	5:45:31	(31,210)
Connor-Stead, Philip	4:17:24	(12,908)
Conoley, Michael	4:46:35	(20,196)
Conophy, Thomas M	5:14:32	(26,344)
Conoplia, Bernhard	3:24:40	(2,980)
Conoplia, Sasha S	3:24:40	(2,980)
Conquest, Doug	4:40:39	(18,687)
Conrad, David J	5:06:25	(24,772)
Conrad, Stephen M	5:03:19	(24,197)
Conran, Alex S	5:31:07	(29,320)
Conroy, Chris	3:51:45	(7,305)
Conroy, Christopher C	5:17:31	(26,960)
Conroy, Frank	5:24:37	(28,200)
Conroy, Grayson R	4:59:27	(23,363)
Conroy, Jude J	6:36:35	(34,561)
Conroy, Stephen C	4:22:19	(14,157)
Consantini, Marco	4:53:08	(21,788)
Constable, Adrian J	3:37:56	(4,814)
Constanti, Theodoros	6:22:37	(34,028)
Constantino, Carlos M	3:59:46	(9,158)
Convert, Pierre	3:23:26	(2,845)
Convery, John J	2:54:46	(566)
Conway, John N	5:29:50	(29,112)
Cooda, Andrew H	3:06:07	(1,240)
Coode, David J	6:35:13	(34,509)
Coode, Matthew J	4:07:35	(10,676)
Coode, Richard W	6:04:27	(32,915)
Cook, Adam J	4:11:49	(11,573)
Cook, Adam M	3:43:21	(5,746)
Cook, Alan	4:33:11	(16,838)

Cook, Alastair A	4:20:55	(13,833)
Cook, Alistair	4:51:02	(21,248)
Cook, David J	3:57:54	(8,698)
Cook, David J	5:55:44	(32,211)
Cook, David S	3:33:51	(4,243)
Cook, David V	4:59:07	(23,292)
Cook, Dean	4:44:02	(19,548)
Cook, Gary	3:12:53	(1,813)
Cook, Gary J	3:09:52	(1,544)
Cook, Glenn	4:48:41	(20,689)
Cook, Graham F	5:12:12	(25,897)
Cook, James E	4:48:43	(20,700)
Cook, Jamie M	4:00:21	(9,278)
Cook, Jason L	4:32:55	(16,768)
Cook, Jason M	5:04:54	(24,501)
Cook, Jonathan M	5:15:53	(26,638)
Cook, Lee A	3:32:29	(4,065)
Cook, Len J	4:48:02	(20,541)
Cook, Malcolm J	4:34:47	(17,218)
Cook, Mark D	5:39:47	(30,570)
Cook, Matt D	5:14:27	(26,321)
Cook, Neil J	3:13:41	(1,872)
Cook, Nigel W	3:21:23	(2,638)
Cook, Paul	5:18:12	(27,103)
Cook, Paul A	5:14:28	(26,328)
Cook, Roy P	5:55:46	(32,216)
Cook, Stephen	3:59:42	(9,142)
Cook, Stephen	4:32:31	(16,667)
Cook, Stephen	5:41:27	(30,762)
Cook, Stephen G	4:22:23	(14,170)
Cook, Steve	3:13:13	(1,843)
Cook, Terry	3:36:06	(4,557)
Cook, Timothy	6:05:58	(33,044)
Cook, Timothy P	5:05:13	(24,545)
Cooke, Alistair	5:16:42	(26,789)
Cooke, Craig G	5:16:42	(26,789)
Cooke, David J	4:45:59	(20,059)
Cooke, Gareth	4:30:50	(16,320)
Cooke, Graham S	5:29:47	(29,107)
Cooke, Ian	4:15:45	(12,495)
Cooke, Ian J	4:20:12	(13,655)
Cooke, James A	4:09:16	(11,020)
Cooke, Jason L	2:57:31	(711)
Cooke, Jeremy H	4:24:44	(14,756)
Cooke, Paul M	5:45:26	(31,195)
Cooke, Peter J	5:08:50	(25,247)
Cooke, Stephen	3:55:03	(8,019)
Cooke, Trevor B	4:46:07	(20,086)
Cooknell, David J	4:47:55	(20,509)
Cooksey, Neil A	3:53:24	(7,668)
Cooley, John M	4:53:04	(21,769)
Cooling, Philip M	4:11:21	(11,459)
Cooling, Richard J	5:52:41	(31,937)
Cools, Raf	3:29:06	(3,591)
Coombe, Nicholas S	4:45:00	(19,836)
Coomber, Jamie R	3:50:51	(7,107)
Coomber, Kevin A	5:28:06	(28,818)
Coombes, Jan P	6:06:19	(33,068)
Coombs, Del	5:51:42	(31,846)
Coombs, Philip J	5:28:52	(28,962)
Cooney, Andrew G	4:15:34	(12,453)
Cooper, Aaron C	3:43:57	(5,856)
Cooper, Ben R	4:22:05	(14,105)
Cooper, Benjamin	4:50:35	(21,145)
Cooper, Chris A	3:38:05	(4,850)
Cooper, Christian A	6:02:45	(32,802)
Cooper, Clive A	4:11:06	(11,397)
Cooper, Dana K	5:03:57	(24,317)
Cooper, Daniel W	5:38:37	(30,400)
Cooper, David A	3:53:19	(7,648)
Cooper, David G	5:36:45	(30,138)
Cooper, David J	3:20:57	(2,608)
Cooper, Edward	3:58:46	(8,903)
Cooper, Gary	5:06:37	(24,801)
Cooper, Gary D	4:01:01	(9,423)

Cooper, George S	4:47:46	(20,475)
Cooper, Glenn A	3:37:21	(4,726)
Cooper, Grahame F	4:57:10	(22,811)
Cooper, Ian	4:34:25	(17,118)
Cooper, Ian R	3:48:43	(6,672)
Cooper, Ian T	4:36:37	(17,696)
Cooper, Jamie	4:39:47	(18,483)
Cooper, Jon D	3:38:01	(4,833)
Cooper, Lee J	4:52:59	(21,749)
Cooper, Mark	7:10:48	(35,283)
Cooper, Mark J	4:51:27	(21,356)
Cooper, Mark T	3:39:03	(5,025)
Cooper, Matthew J	3:42:04	(5,530)
Cooper, Michael	3:19:54	(2,479)
Cooper, Michael	5:10:10	(25,522)
Cooper, Michael F	5:17:29	(26,956)
Cooper, Neil V	3:20:36	(2,569)
Cooper, Nicholas J	4:43:41	(19,459)
Cooper, Nick A	4:20:37	(13,758)
Cooper, Nick J	5:17:01	(26,861)
Cooper, Nigel D	4:03:35	(9,883)
Cooper, Paul A	4:42:32	(19,187)
Cooper, Robert	4:55:24	(22,366)
Cooper, Robert	5:21:45	(27,741)
Cooper, Robert C	6:04:27	(32,915)
Cooper, Robert H	4:29:58	(16,139)
Cooper, Robert J	4:39:12	(18,335)
Cooper, Roddy J	3:42:15	(5,561)
Cooper, Russell J	3:46:24	(6,237)
Cooper, Ryan S	4:32:22	(16,640)
Cooper, Shaun L	2:59:30	(865)
Cooper, Simon	5:54:25	(32,099)
Cooper, Simon J	4:27:22	(15,436)
Cooper, Stefan	4:33:06	(16,810)
Cooper, Stephen J	4:06:59	(10,572)
Cooper, Stephen J	4:33:42	(16,962)
Cooper, Stephen J	4:39:15	(18,351)
Cooper, Stephen P	4:45:16	(19,896)
Cooper, Tim E	3:38:50	(4,983)
Cooper-Tydeman, Simon	7:29:17	(35,476)
Coote, Jon M	2:56:34	(641)
Cooymans, Patrick	3:09:28	(1,513)
Copas, Nicholas	3:46:46	(6,296)
Cope, Benjamin T	3:25:00	(3,019)
Cope, Trevor A	4:41:36	(18,948)
Copeland, Scott A	5:10:20	(25,546)
Copeland, Terry R	4:25:07	(14,852)
Copeland, Tom J	5:10:30	(25,578)
Copeman, Mark D	4:36:13	(17,585)
Copeman, Tony	4:44:34	(19,705)
Copland, David J	4:45:52	(20,024)
Copleston, Edward M	6:31:12	(34,370)
Copley, Sebastian J	4:38:56	(18,265)
Coppard, Kenneth [	4:01:44	(9,555)
Coppelov, Michael I	3:38:13	(4,871)
Coppelov, Wally S	3:23:49	(2,879)
Coppin, Andrew	4:33:17	(16,863)
Coppin, John	3:45:01	(6,029)
Copping, Thomas R	3:41:47	(5,482)
Coppock, John D	5:35:39	(30,007)
Copps, Philip	4:39:40	(18,454)
Cops, Matthew	5:16:55	(26,845)
Copsey, Nick R	4:28:41	(15,781)
Copsey, Richard J	4:55:40	(22,421)
Copsey, Robert W	5:50:10	(31,687)
Copus, Christopher D	3:38:26	(4,908)
Cora Decunto, Adrian	4:37:03	(17,796)
Corbelli, Enrico	4:19:44	(13,520)
Corbett, Colin F	4:59:31	(23,390)
Corbett, David T	3:48:08	(6,550)
Corbett, Ed C	5:25:26	(28,351)
Corbett, Graham	4:04:47	(10,110)
Corbett, Michael T	4:13:19	(11,912)
Corbin, Matthew W	3:34:48	(4,379)
Corbishley, Graeme C	5:31:58	(29,444)
Corbould, Clive R	6:04:33	(32,920)
Corbould, Stephen P	5:18:05	(27,074)
Corby, Matthew T	3:24:02	(2,909)
Corcoran, Andrew P	4:22:20	(14,162)
Corcoran, John	4:36:49	(17,747)
Corden, James M	2:50:25	(388)
Corderoy, Richard J	4:32:33	(16,675)
Cordoliani, Nonce	3:24:04	(2,915)

Cordwell, Gary D....6:06:00 (33,050)
Cordwell, Julian C....4:25:53 (15,032)
Corfe, Julian A....3:30:22 (3,777)
Corfield, John W....5:19:03 (27,255)
Corfield, Mike H....3:33:08 (4,158)
Cork, John....4:20:16 (13,670)
Corker, Barry J....4:21:26 (13,947)
Corlett, Brian J....4:52:56 (21,735)
Corley, Steven M....3:43:45 (5,820)
Cormack, Hamish G....3:56:26 (8,338)
Cormery, Denis G....3:09:31 (1,518)
Cornall, Jon H....5:59:12 (32,529)
Cornell, Stephen W....3:24:41 (2,984)
Cornell, Timothy J....3:50:18 (6,998)
Cornew, Steven P....3:29:18 (3,618)
Corney, Andy J....4:49:52 (20,968)
Corney, Robert A....3:47:48 (6,496)
Cornford, Adrian W....3:14:18 (1,925)
Cornish, Clive....7:09:34 (35,267)
Cornish, David P....5:47:36 (31,414)
Cornish, Lee Dominic....4:36:30 (17,664)
Cornwall, John B....5:00:39 (23,648)
Cornwall-Legh, George....4:50:20 (21,075)
Cornwell, Clive....4:44:25 (19,654)
Cornwell, Nick R....3:55:38 (8,146)
Corr, James J....5:07:14 (24,938)
Corr, Liam J....4:15:07 (12,345)
Corre, Christophe....4:19:53 (13,569)
Corriette, Michael....5:07:01 (24,887)
Corrigan, Edward....5:26:05 (28,472)
Corrigan, John J....5:03:16 (24,185)
Corry Reid, Edward B....4:40:50 (18,740)
Corsini, Russell G....2:58:22 (777)
Cortes, Xavier....4:48:45 (20,708)
Cortese, Guiseppe....4:42:04 (19,059)
Corton, Mark....4:33:18 (16,867)
Cory, Timothy I....3:30:00 (3,719)
Cosco, Antonio....5:11:50 (25,820)
Cosgrove, David A....3:43:59 (5,865)
Cosgrove, Neil R....3:59:15 (9,027)
Cosham, Derek....6:46:39 (34,848)
Cosher, Jamie J....5:22:24 (27,833)
Cosnard, Patrick....4:31:01 (16,357)
Cossar, Dave....5:36:29 (30,111)
Cossins, Brian....5:05:25 (24,577)
Costa, Bob....4:02:19 (9,671)
Costain, Nigel M....3:35:33 (4,495)
Costall, Steve J....2:58:31 (790)
Costas, Paul....3:14:59 (1,994)
Costella, Marco F....4:29:13 (15,915)
Costello, Kevin....4:41:06 (18,811)
Costello, Michael J....3:28:18 (3,449)
Coster, Malcolm....4:39:35 (18,433)
Costerton, Andrew S....4:44:22 (19,639)
Cotta, Jason A....5:46:54 (31,344)
Cottam, Dale A....4:17:23 (12,904)
Cotteleer, Christiaan F....5:26:36 (28,557)
Cotter, Ian J....2:59:21 (850)
Cotter, Michael S....4:19:22 (13,424)
Cotterill, Mark A....3:27:13 (3,312)
Cotterill, Richard G....6:23:57 (34,075)
Cottier, Andrew C....2:57:30 (710)
Cottingham, David A....5:29:51 (29,114)
Cottington, Graham....3:54:33 (7,911)
Cottis, John D....3:06:37 (1,282)
Cottis, Roy A....4:14:29 (12,200)
Cotton, Anthony E....4:03:40 (9,896)
Cotton, Antony N....4:49:34 (20,908)
Cotton, Roger B....4:56:02 (22,522)
Cottrell, Brendan M....3:27:53 (3,394)
Cottrell, Michael J....5:08:33 (25,195)
Cottrell, Stephen R....3:51:52 (7,330)
Cottrell, Tim....5:00:09 (23,535)
Cottrell, Tom....6:48:11 (34,892)
Couch, Barry J....4:06:43 (10,507)
Couch, Gareth J....4:41:27 (18,902)
Couch, Ian....4:45:49 (20,010)
Couchman, Ian B....5:07:25 (24,980)
Coughlan, Kevin G....4:30:55 (16,339)
Coughlan, Peter....4:51:09 (21,278)
Coughlan, Simon D....4:30:04 (16,165)
Couling, Steven....4:34:05 (17,046)
Coulot, François....4:47:56 (20,512)
Coulson, Andrew J....4:13:11 (11,874)
Coulson, Paul....5:02:43 (24,079)
Coulson, Stephen M....4:15:51 (12,526)
Coulson, Wayne A....3:12:45 (1,802)
Coulter, Barry A....3:36:49 (4,659)
Coulthurst, Andrew J....3:15:07 (2,006)
Coupe, David A....4:08:49 (10,924)
Coupe, Stanley....5:34:16 (29,806)
Coupy, Partice....3:44:23 (5,922)
Courage, Toby B....2:53:14 (479)
Cournee, Michel....4:12:39 (11,751)
Courrmont, Alain....3:20:59 (2,610)
Court, Alan R....3:18:07 (2,298)
Court, Daniel J....4:53:56 (22,000)
Court, David L....4:44:55 (19,812)
Court, John W....4:55:52 (22,479)
Court, Robert I....3:32:54 (4,123)
Court, Simon....6:44:20 (34,785)
Courtauld, Thomas....4:35:08 (17,310)
Courtenay, Timothy W....4:12:26 (11,710)
Courtman-Stock, Paul S....4:15:21 (12,406)
Courtney, John....6:00:31 (32,626)
Courtney, Kevin S....3:16:22 (2,112)
Courtney, Max M....6:00:31 (32,626)
Courtney, Trevor A....5:15:59 (26,654)
Courville, Guillaume....3:11:34 (1,676)
Cousens, Charles L....4:56:26 (22,622)
Cousens, Simon J....5:43:38 (31,005)
Cousin, Xavier....5:00:45 (23,676)
Cousins, Andy....5:33:43 (29,715)
Cousins, Gavin....4:00:35 (9,327)
Cousins, Geoffrey R....4:48:47 (20,717)
Cousins, Nicholas J....3:15:50 (2,064)
Cousins, Roger N....4:55:16 (22,333)
Coutard, Jean-Yves....4:17:31 (12,951)
Coutard, Pascal....4:02:54 (9,767)
Coutnt, Patrick....3:08:00 (1,389)
Coutts, Phillip H....4:47:45 (20,470)
Coutts, Richard A....5:01:29 (23,827)
Couzens, Michael W....5:18:19 (27,128)
Covey, Sean A....3:31:44 (3,944)
Covey, Wayne....6:12:53 (33,486)
Covre, Fabio....3:30:54 (3,827)
Cowan, Andrew D....4:39:35 (18,433)
Cowan, Nicholas E....4:27:21 (15,433)
Coward, Alan....5:36:48 (30,148)
Cowdrey, Matthew R....4:43:31 (19,419)
Cowdrill, Andrew G....4:47:18 (20,359)
Cowell, Antony J....3:32:04 (4,003)
Cowell, Jon M....3:01:40 (991)
Cowen, Andy....5:19:09 (27,280)
Cowen, Daniel W....4:13:49 (12,048)
Cowie, Duncan....3:30:46 (3,815)
Cowie, Stuart R....5:03:00 (24,121)
Cowland, Dan....4:58:37 (23,171)
Cowley, Richard J....4:58:04 (23,050)
Cowley, Simon....3:49:21 (6,805)
Cowlin, Robert....6:53:48 (35,016)
Cowling, Paul A....4:22:33 (14,217)
Cowlishaw, Simon J....4:30:51 (16,324)
Cowls, Stephen J....4:58:41 (23,186)
Cowper, Jonathan....4:08:01 (10,769)
Cowpertwait, Colin J....5:10:51 (25,633)
Cox, Alan....3:15:47 (2,057)
Cox, Alan D....4:52:29 (21,611)
Cox, Allan....5:30:49 (29,267)
Cox, Allan J....3:41:05 (5,378)
Cox, Andrew D....4:24:44 (14,756)
Cox, Andrew M....3:36:34 (4,621)
Cox, Andrew P....5:05:53 (24,672)
Cox, Barry R....4:25:18 (14,894)
Cox, Brian A....5:25:23 (28,335)
Cox, Christopher S....4:32:37 (16,695)
Cox, Darren J....3:43:00 (5,692)
Cox, David A....4:49:07 (20,798)
Cox, David G....3:16:49 (2,161)
Cox, Duncan....3:22:39 (2,762)
Cox, Fergus D....4:22:58 (14,322)
Cox, Gareth B....6:30:32 (34,342)
Cox, Gary H....3:43:32 (5,787)
Cox, Geoff....4:38:08 (18,047)
Cox, Graham A....6:26:12 (34,182)
Cox, Graham R....4:03:39 (9,891)
Cox, Ian D....4:27:37 (15,493)
Cox, Ian G....4:24:03 (14,585)
Cox, Justin A....3:05:20 (1,186)
Cox, Mark A....3:21:37 (2,663)
Cox, Mark M....3:18:23 (2,333)
Cox, Marty J....6:03:58 (32,885)
Cox, Matthew....4:18:54 (13,306)
Cox, Matthew D....4:28:23 (15,695)
Cox, Matthew J....3:50:00 (6,942)
Cox, Michael....4:47:29 (20,401)
Cox, Nicholas R....3:32:12 (4,030)
Cox, Paul D....5:47:36 (31,414)
Cox, Peter A....4:15:21 (12,406)
Cox, Philip S....4:14:34 (12,222)
Cox, Richard....5:27:47 (28,759)
Cox, Richard A....5:01:14 (23,782)
Cox, Richard D....3:31:36 (3,927)
Cox, Sean....4:18:11 (13,121)
Cox, Steve R....2:51:19 (420)
Cox, Stewart J....2:54:42 (560)
Cox, Tim H....3:50:20 (7,008)
Cox, Vivion S....3:55:43 (8,169)
Coxall, Chris....4:19:03 (13,337)
Coxhead, Ian S....3:17:02 (2,183)
Coxhead, Mark A....4:40:28 (18,644)
Cox-Nicol, James....4:24:30 (14,704)
Coxon, Andrew....3:51:27 (7,243)
Coxon, Marcus J....5:09:33 (25,384)
Coy, Edward P....4:32:08 (16,591)
Coyle, David N....4:05:16 (10,197)
Coyle, James....4:24:39 (14,735)
Coyle, Michael J....5:14:27 (26,321)
Coyle, Nicholas S....4:56:40 (22,686)
Coyle, Terry P....2:51:36 (425)
Coyne, Craig....4:59:46 (23,448)
Coyne, David....4:29:11 (15,906)
Coyne, Martin T....4:17:38 (12,982)
Coyne, Martyn P....4:56:33 (22,643)
Cozens, David G....4:40:01 (18,539)
Crabb, Richard J....3:38:15 (4,877)
Crabb, Stephen....5:13:41 (26,161)
Crabbie, Colin J....3:41:48 (5,484)
Crabtree, David W....5:23:10 (27,956)
Crabtree, Ian P....3:28:59 (3,575)
Crabtree, Mark A....2:52:09 (449)
Cracknell, Adam D....5:28:31 (28,903)
Cracknell, Kenny J....5:01:38 (23,860)
Cracknell, Paul....6:22:12 (34,007)
Cracknell, Samuel C....5:28:31 (28,903)
Cradden, Brendan P....4:04:58 (10,139)
Craddock, Daniel A....5:03:37 (24,261)
Craddock, Richard....3:52:25 (7,455)
Cradock, Neil D....5:33:27 (29,672)
Cragg, Stuart J....2:48:03 (311)
Craggs, Douglas....4:43:08 (19,329)
Crahart, Lee J....4:33:19 (16,876)
Craig, Ben J....4:55:26 (22,372)
Craig, Brian C....4:16:22 (12,665)
Craig, Christopher....3:52:29 (7,464)
Craig, Darren P....4:45:53 (20,029)
Craig, Gerard....2:59:56 (897)
Craig, Jamie C....4:50:56 (21,227)
Craig, Robert C....4:24:10 (14,622)
Craig, Scott....5:05:17 (24,555)
Craigen, Gregory J....4:40:21 (18,618)
Craigie, David G....4:33:43 (16,970)
Craik, Nicholas J....5:00:50 (23,693)
Crake, Toby....5:13:23 (26,096)
Crameri, Michael....4:59:10 (23,299)
Crameri, Remo....3:28:23 (3,460)
Crammond, James....3:42:47 (5,643)
Cramp, Phil....4:52:12 (21,541)
Cramp, Richard....5:00:33 (23,624)
Crampete, Louis....4:42:48 (19,255)
Crampsey, James M....2:52:00 (439)
Crampton, Ian....2:36:24 (90)
Crampton, Leslie D....5:29:01 (28,988)
Crampton, Peter....4:25:11 (14,867)
Crandon, David....4:41:07 (18,817)
Crane, Duncan....3:51:39 (7,285)
Crane, Melvin I....5:03:23 (24,213)
Crane, Peter....6:07:24 (33,123)
Crane, Richard....5:19:46 (27,386)

Crane, Stephen 3:57:47 (8,671)
Crane, Stephen D..............4:08:29 (10,868)
Crane, William T..............3:25:17 (3,042)
Crangle, Robert..............3:31:07 (3,853)
Cranmer, Kevin 4:20:17 (13,674)
Cranwell, Mark A 2:55:31 (594)
Crate, Daniel P..............4:50:09 (21,034)
Craveiro, Joao..............4:15:15 (12,376)
Craven, Kevin D 4:15:29 (12,439)
Craven, Paul..............4:41:54 (19,017)
Craven, Philip J..............4:37:35 (17,906)
Crawford, Alan 5:27:48 (28,761)
Crawford, Alasdair O 5:17:57 (27,041)
Crawford, Christopher J 6:05:16 (32,981)
Crawford, Darran A 5:09:53 (25,449)
Crawford, David 4:29:21 (15,956)
Crawford, Jared K..............3:53:18 (7,641)
Crawford, Joff..............4:10:50 (11,335)
Crawford, Joseph M 4:40:45 (18,714)
Crawford, Stuart J..............4:54:40 (22,190)
Crawford, Trevor 4:53:11 (21,804)
Crawley, Matthew E 5:23:45 (28,063)
Crawley, Steven K 4:02:49 (9,757)
Crawshaw, Charles J 3:58:14 (8,772)
Crawshaw, John S 4:22:40 (14,248)
Crawshaw, Richard 5:48:32 (31,526)
Cray, Richard..............4:45:19 (19,908)
Crayford, Paul S 4:18:02 (13,083)
Crayson, Nicholas M 6:20:19 (33,907)
Craze, Andrew..............5:17:21 (26,927)
Crean, Adrian P..............3:53:12 (7,618)
Crease, Gregory B 5:56:20 (32,269)
Creaton, Donald I 4:57:02 (22,782)
Creaven, Dylan 4:28:05 (15,616)
Creber, Kevin 5:29:02 (28,990)
Creech, Jeremy 5:36:10 (30,064)
Creed, Gareth..............3:28:28 (3,477)
Creed, Hugh M 3:52:24 (7,451)
Creedon, John J 5:24:37 (28,200)
Creely, Sean 4:41:47 (18,989)
Crees, Stuart E..............2:40:38 (151)
Cregor, Paul D 4:10:13 (11,209)
Crehan, John..............5:28:21 (28,880)
Creighton, Luke T 3:19:05 (2,401)
Creixell, Lluis M 6:30:51 (34,359)
Cremen, Vincent P..............5:12:05 (25,869)
Cremonte, Giovanni 2:47:17 (291)
Cresswell, Brent A 3:28:53 (3,553)
Cresswell, Stephen C..............5:24:09 (28,132)
Cresswell, Wayne 4:24:22 (14,669)
Crestan, Gabriele 3:59:15 (9,027)
Crew, Danny E 4:35:42 (17,460)
Crewe, David O 3:48:32 (6,630)
Crewe, Fraser H..............4:55:22 (22,353)
Cribier, Guillaume J 2:38:14 (111)
Crich, Andrew D 5:18:00 (27,058)
Crichton, Simon 5:01:25 (23,815)
Cridland, Barry J 5:31:22 (29,355)
Crimmings, Andrew C 5:16:14 (26,706)
Crimmins, Perry 5:45:04 (31,162)
Cripps, Ben R 4:07:10 (10,601)
Crisp, Charles P..............5:19:03 (27,255)
Crisp, Clive 3:41:48 (5,484)
Crisp, David D 5:07:02 (24,892)
Crisp, John F..............3:09:25 (1,511)
Crisp, Martin T..............5:46:41 (31,327)
Crisp, Matthew D 3:29:32 (3,652)
Crisp, Nicholas 5:14:26 (26,318)
Crisp, Paul G 5:26:39 (28,566)
Crisp, Richard J 4:21:11 (13,896)
Crispin, Andrew 4:23:37 (14,470)
Crispin, Jason D 4:15:17 (12,391)
Crispin, Stuart J..............4:27:22 (15,436)
Crist, Giles R..............3:47:28 (6,420)
Critchley, Alan 3:49:54 (6,918)
Critchley, Gavin 4:01:21 (9,490)
Critchley, Neil J 3:42:12 (5,554)
Critchley, Paul M 4:23:04 (14,348)
Critchlow, Nigel..............3:27:58 (3,403)
Critoph, Jason 4:29:30 (16,007)
Croal, Jeremy 4:53:19 (21,842)
Croasdell, Neil A 3:52:41 (7,497)
Crocker, James P 5:07:49 (25,064)

Crocker, Matthew..............4:59:00 (23,253)
Crocker, Paul D 4:29:47 (16,087)
Crocker, Robert W 3:54:40 (7,937)
Crocket, Graham D 3:16:41 (2,147)
Crockett, Edward J 3:15:14 (2,015)
Crockett, Leon 5:08:02 (25,101)
Crockford, John G 3:38:31 (4,924)
Crockwell, David 4:09:53 (11,147)
Croft, Daniel R 4:33:07 (16,816)
Croft, Darren S 4:48:36 (20,669)
Croft, James C 4:06:33 (10,476)
Croft, James C 4:07:31 (10,655)
Croft, Jared 3:16:50 (2,163)
Croft, Stuart K 6:05:09 (32,975)
Crofts, Joe N 5:32:38 (29,557)
Crofts, Mark D 3:49:13 (6,779)
Croker, Matthew I 6:53:00 (34,992)
Croker, Shaun 5:59:25 (32,545)
Crole-Rees, Matthew J 4:24:10 (14,622)
Crombie, Hugh D 4:47:01 (20,286)
Crompton, Gary D 3:47:46 (6,492)
Crompton, John K 5:13:13 (26,083)
Crompton, Jonathan P 6:16:41 (33,722)
Crone, Gary S 3:13:13 (1,843)
Cronin, Paul 3:44:23 (5,922)
Cronk, John..............4:20:18 (13,679)
Crook, Andrew P..............4:29:58 (16,139)
Crook, Andrew T..............5:40:32 (30,657)
Crook, Gavin 5:15:04 (26,475)
Crook, Jason 4:35:22 (17,375)
Crook, Jonathan S..............2:44:51 (236)
Crook, Paul A 4:26:33 (15,205)
Crook, Philip A..............6:17:31 (33,752)
Crook, Richard C 4:35:42 (17,460)
Crook, Stuart R 3:57:15 (8,542)
Crook, Warren S..............3:25:05 (3,028)
Crosbie, Stuart F..............3:57:02 (8,487)
Crosbie, Tobias 5:19:51 (27,401)
Crosby, Damian E 5:03:36 (24,258)
Crosby, David J 4:22:17 (14,148)
Cross, Andrew 5:03:40 (24,269)
Cross, Andrew D..............4:21:29 (13,963)
Cross, Anthony W..............3:15:48 (2,061)
Cross, Ian R 4:51:33 (21,383)
Cross, James 3:40:25 (5,250)
Cross, James A 5:37:01 (30,172)
Cross, Jeremy S 3:33:20 (4,184)
Cross, John 4:39:15 (18,351)
Cross, Matthew C 6:15:53 (33,675)
Cross, Michael 3:53:38 (7,713)
Cross, Paul S 4:11:29 (11,496)
Cross, Peter H 6:00:28 (32,618)
Cross, Peter R 3:28:49 (3,541)
Cross, Philip J 3:08:35 (1,436)
Cross, Roger J 4:11:22 (11,466)
Crosse, Matthew P 3:10:53 (1,620)
Crossingham, Rowan A..............4:11:08 (11,407)
Crossley, James 4:24:22 (14,669)
Crossley, Mark 4:25:57 (15,043)
Crossley, Paul G 4:19:07 (13,359)
Crossley, Peter J 5:50:46 (31,753)
Crossman, Edward J 4:16:56 (12,798)
Crosswell, Christopher W 4:44:31 (19,692)
Crosthwaite, Giles 4:43:04 (19,310)
Crothers, Alastair C..............4:10:47 (11,324)
Crothers, Gordon A 4:24:23 (14,675)
Crouch, David J 4:55:59 (22,508)
Crouch, Marc R..............4:19:15 (13,395)
Crouch, Oliver T 4:21:30 (13,967)
Crouch, Robert J 4:46:51 (20,239)
Crouch, Stephen P..............5:21:13 (27,637)
Crouchman, Graham L 5:27:01 (28,623)
Crouzat, Didier 4:15:06 (12,342)
Crow, George..............4:53:24 (21,862)
Crow, Peter 3:48:44 (6,674)
Crowe, Graham 5:21:15 (27,644)
Crowe, Liam C..............3:50:22 (7,014)
Crowe, Wayne 4:17:38 (12,982)
Crowhurst, Jake 4:05:05 (10,160)
Crowley, David M 3:34:26 (4,334)
Crowley, Greg S 3:12:17 (1,756)
Crowley, Stuart A..............5:32:10 (29,477)
Crowley, Vincent P 3:40:44 (5,306)

Crown, Giles H 4:27:01 (15,326)
Crowson, Andrew J..............5:27:19 (28,682)
Croxford, Philip A..............4:57:05 (22,792)
Croydon, Stuart A 3:23:19 (2,834)
Crozier, Peter..............3:39:22 (5,079)
Cruard, Philippe 3:23:15 (2,829)
Crudgington, James W..............4:41:08 (18,823)
Cruickshank, Brian 2:56:06 (617)
Cruickshank, George A..............5:06:12 (24,741)
Cruickshank, Kevin 4:55:28 (22,386)
Cruickshank, Michael A..............6:20:09 (33,893)
Cruickshank, Neil P 4:40:34 (18,673)
Cruiks, Andrew..............4:47:09 (20,322)
Cruise, Jonathon 4:32:17 (16,625)
Cruise, Paul S 4:54:38 (22,179)
Crummack, Ian J 4:45:52 (20,024)
Crump, Stephen J 5:09:41 (25,411)
Crumpton, Anthony L 4:21:05 (13,868)
Crush, Stephen K 4:37:58 (17,999)
Crussell, Nicholas..............5:18:39 (27,189)
Crust, Richard C..............6:08:59 (33,236)
Crutcher, Alexander J 3:27:38 (3,365)
Crutchley, Philip R..............4:20:59 (13,850)
Cruttenden, Joe..............4:33:22 (16,884)
Cruyt, Rudy..............3:46:40 (6,277)
Cruz, Joel 5:23:33 (28,021)
Cryer, Simeon E 3:52:38 (7,485)
Crysell, Trevor 4:09:48 (11,127)
Crystal, Roger 4:21:20 (13,918)
Cubbin, John 5:58:19 (32,445)
Cubis, Brent A 3:43:01 (5,694)
Cucignatto, Mauro Luigi 4:14:16 (12,157)
Cucis, Jean-Claude 3:50:41 (7,075)
Cudby, Paul..............5:22:54 (27,921)
Cuddeford, Paul M 4:30:16 (16,213)
Cuddy, Brian..............4:27:03 (15,339)
Cudmore, Miles A 3:48:49 (6,692)
Cudworth, Christopher J 4:16:48 (12,762)
Cudworth, Ryan N 4:21:52 (14,055)
Cuell, Wesley P 4:58:58 (23,244)
Cuff, Pete 3:45:04 (6,033)
Cuffe, John G 6:00:01 (32,576)
Cuffley, David M 4:58:55 (23,230)
Cull, Matthew J..............3:57:12 (8,528)
Cullen, Christopher P..............4:04:10 (10,000)
Cullen, David T 5:24:02 (28,110)
Cullen, Edward A 5:38:52 (30,436)
Cullen, Martin J..............4:10:29 (11,261)
Cullen, Matthew B 3:42:47 (5,643)
Cullen, Stephen 4:41:59 (19,033)
Cullen, Steve..............4:38:52 (18,246)
Cullen, Tom R 4:03:12 (9,818)
Cullern, Doug A 4:42:15 (19,110)
Culleton, Philip 5:04:56 (24,506)
Culley, Spencer W 5:14:54 (26,428)
Culligan, Stephen E 3:10:06 (1,571)
Culling, Jonathan B 6:31:59 (34,406)
Culora, Mario S 4:01:14 (9,466)
Culpan, Charlie J..............4:47:04 (20,305)
Culshaw, Tim 4:44:27 (19,663)
Culver, Jeremy S 4:02:41 (9,725)
Culver, Peter J..............3:18:28 (2,340)
Culwin, Fintan 4:40:32 (18,662)
Cumber, Geoffrey..............2:53:51 (516)
Cumisky, Nicholas J..............4:36:01 (17,540)
Cumming, James R 4:06:21 (10,423)
Cummings, Alan 3:44:59 (6,025)
Cummings, Christopher R 4:39:56 (18,520)
Cummings, Graham P 5:35:53 (30,035)
Cummings, Neil M 5:58:06 (32,420)
Cummins, Liam J 4:14:52 (12,284)
Cummins, Nicholas J 4:44:00 (19,538)
Cummins, Thomas J 3:17:24 (2,217)
Cummins, Timothy D 4:22:09 (14,116)
Cundy, Andrew P..............4:55:56 (22,499)
Cunego, Piergiorgio..............4:20:27 (13,719)
Cunliffe, Graham A..............3:05:38 (1,211)
Cunliffe, Rory 3:13:41 (1,872)
Cunnane, Matt 3:33:38 (4,220)
Cunnane, Noel 5:59:11 (32,526)
Cunniffe, Dean 4:29:03 (15,867)
Cunningham, Craig D 4:18:56 (13,314)
Cunningham, Damien..............4:51:39 (21,409)

Cunningham, Iain W 4:42:44 (19,238)
Cunningham, Ian 5:02:01 (23,938)
Cunningham, Jim D 4:12:47 (11,786)
Cunningham, Kevin 5:11:38 (25,784)
Cunningham, Michael A 2:52:37 (465)
Cunningham, Michael R 3:33:35 (4,210)
Cunningham, Peter 3:12:17 (1,756)
Cunningham, Phil L 4:26:25 (15,164)
Cunningham, Philip P 3:04:00 (1,105)
Cunningham, Steve 3:13:12 (1,840)
Cunningham, Stuart J 2:52:36 (463)
Cunningham, Tony 3:04:21 (1,123)
Cunnison, Martin P 5:04:43 (24,452)
Cunnngham, Steve 5:23:19 (27,980)
Cupitt, Eddie 3:56:53 (8,452)
Curd, Robert S 6:04:50 (32,946)
Curle, Piers 3:01:43 (992)
Curless, Brent 3:52:46 (7,517)
Curley, Philip D 4:02:47 (9,747)
Curliss, Kevin 6:36:13 (34,546)
Curll, Arran N 4:13:08 (11,865)
Curme, Ian M 5:32:08 (29,474)
Curphey, Paul R 3:08:24 (1,422)
Curran, Gavin 3:27:34 (3,359)
Curran, Len 4:33:04 (16,803)
Curran, Liam K 5:33:20 (29,653)
Curran, Michael F 4:48:53 (20,740)
Curran, Tom 3:50:48 (7,095)
Curren, Gerard S 4:47:09 (20,322)
Currie, Stephen G 4:27:10 (15,375)
Curry, Andrew J 5:06:18 (24,757)
Curry, Robert 3:57:09 (8,511)
Curt, Gareth 4:28:51 (15,822)
Curtin, Giles P 5:11:13 (25,706)
Curtis, Alan M 4:21:49 (14,036)
Curtis, Andrew B 3:43:46 (5,822)
Curtis, Daniel 4:28:03 (15,608)
Curtis, David A 3:54:31 (7,908)
Curtis, Dean 3:05:17 (1,183)
Curtis, Gary L 6:24:51 (34,120)
Curtis, Graham R 5:34:10 (29,788)
Curtis, Ian S 5:35:51 (30,031)
Curtis, Kevin R 4:59:05 (23,284)
Curtis, Lee A 6:03:59 (32,887)
Curtis, Marc S 3:33:05 (4,150)
Curtis, Matthew J 4:09:29 (11,068)
Curtis, Paul 4:33:35 (16,930)
Curtis, Paul 4:36:23 (17,637)
Curtis, Paul F 3:18:35 (2,351)
Curtis, Sean 4:30:09 (16,188)
Curtis, Steven A 2:53:09 (476)
Curwood, Steven 4:39:39 (18,449)
Cusack, David M 3:35:17 (4,445)
Cusack, John K 4:29:55 (16,123)
Cusack, Seamus 5:03:09 (24,160)
Cushing, Nicholas E 6:06:43 (33,091)
Cushway, William 4:21:51 (14,049)
Cusick, Peter 3:11:36 (1,680)
Custance, Thomas A 4:19:58 (13,594)
Cuthbert, James A 4:09:18 (11,031)
Cuthbert, Paul J 4:09:17 (11,024)
Cuthbert, Simon 4:17:17 (12,871)
Cutler, Nick M 3:39:03 (5,025)
Cutler, Peitr M 4:45:28 (19,938)
Cutress, Paul A 4:47:46 (20,475)
Cutter, Georges 4:03:32 (9,874)
Cuttle, Ben 4:10:39 (11,300)
Cutts, Nigel P 4:17:58 (13,064)
Czaja, Alan J 3:33:55 (4,257)
Czaya, Christian 4:13:29 (11,956)
Da Costa, Shane 3:32:40 (4,093)
Da Silva, Deolor 5:15:35 (26,582)
Da Silva, Henrique 4:05:00 (10,143)
Dabbadie, François X 5:36:29 (30,111)
Daborn, David R 4:26:11 (15,091)
Dachtler, Christopher 3:51:28 (7,246)
Dada, Mohamed S 4:38:19 (18,101)
Dade, Richard C 4:41:27 (18,902)
Daemen, Joes A 4:07:42 (10,704)
Daga, Renato 3:35:09 (4,431)
Daga, Sandro 4:33:45 (16,978)
Dagger, Matthew R 4:20:27 (13,719)
Dagger, Robbie W 4:57:52 (23,002)
D'Ahbrosio, Gino 4:02:47 (9,747)
Dahdouh, Fadi 4:39:02 (18,293)
Dahl, Terje 3:04:34 (1,136)
Daish, Richard J 4:58:48 (23,206)
Daish, Sam G 3:36:50 (4,665)
Daivson, Darryl 3:58:47 (8,906)
Daji, Noman M 5:10:37 (25,599)
Dakin, Keith 4:00:48 (9,372)
Dakin-White, Giles K 5:14:12 (26,267)
Dal Vecchio, Enrico 4:41:08 (18,823)
Dalby, Paul A 4:00:33 (9,322)
Daldry, Simon J 4:53:56 (22,000)
Dale, Adrian 3:56:06 (8,247)
Dale, Graham T 5:02:09 (23,961)
Dale, Jim 3:58:52 (8,934)
Dale, John H 5:42:55 (30,924)
Dale, Matthew J 3:57:20 (8,561)
Dale, Paul R 3:41:59 (5,518)
Dale, Robert A 4:54:20 (22,106)
Dale, Stephen G 3:39:23 (5,082)
Dale, Thomas 5:07:59 (25,091)
Dales, Lee A 4:40:18 (18,603)
D'Alessio, Giovanni 3:59:14 (9,021)
Daley, Justin M 5:31:03 (29,307)
Daley, Neil R 4:55:36 (22,410)
Daley, Philip A 5:55:58 (32,237)
Daley, Susan 7:05:55 (35,217)
Daley, Trevor 5:56:22 (32,272)
D'All, Gordon C 4:43:48 (19,478)
Dallas, Ian A 5:20:41 (27,554)
Dalley, Alex D 3:40:46 (5,312)
Dalrymple, Charlie D 4:22:16 (14,142)
Dalrymple, David W 3:52:32 (7,472)
Dalsania, Ameet 4:40:36 (18,680)
Dalton, Anthony J 5:01:51 (23,902)
Dalton, James R 4:31:36 (16,484)
Dalton, Mark S 2:59:43 (879)
Dalton, Robert P 3:56:27 (8,346)
Dalton, William A 3:57:41 (8,649)
Daly, Bryan C 5:02:37 (24,060)
Daly, Gerard M 4:11:02 (11,380)
Daly, Hugh D 4:11:35 (11,518)
Daly, Jamie J 5:32:48 (29,578)
Daly, John 4:34:16 (17,091)
Daly, John A 4:44:20 (19,630)
Daly, Mark 7:29:29 (35,488)
Daly, Mark A 4:04:29 (10,054)
Daly, Matthew L 3:42:39 (5,618)
Daly, Michael J 4:27:13 (15,396)
Daly, Neil R 4:38:47 (18,226)
Daly, Nial 5:37:42 (30,262)
Daly, Paul 4:14:21 (12,175)
Daly, Stephen 3:49:16 (6,792)
Dam, Diego 2:36:13 (88)
Damelin, Errol 3:37:48 (4,788)
Damerell, Robert W 6:41:58 (34,716)
Danaher, James D 4:48:08 (20,560)
Dance, Ian A 4:10:06 (11,185)
Dance, Richard 4:00:14 (9,261)
Dancer, Andrew 3:44:20 (5,916)
Danckert, Russell J 4:29:10 (15,900)
Dancy, Darren D 5:12:07 (25,874)
Daneels, Thomas 3:53:16 (7,634)
Dangelo, Kirk A 4:07:39 (10,690)
Daniel, David 3:55:46 (8,178)
Daniel, David L 3:46:55 (6,327)
Daniel, David M 3:05:25 (1,195)
Daniel, Neil J 8:26:32 (35,675)
Daniel, Ron B 4:44:38 (19,726)
Daniells, Sam J 4:58:17 (23,098)
Daniels, Alan 4:55:55 (22,493)
Daniels, Henry 4:19:12 (13,375)
Daniels, Lee 3:35:04 (4,415)
Daniels, Michael 2:56:56 (669)
Daniels, Michael J 4:15:26 (12,426)
Daniels, Mike 5:23:32 (28,018)
Daniels, Paul 3:18:27 (2,338)
Daniels, Paul K 3:32:32 (4,076)
Dann, Christopher 5:32:29 (29,520)
Dann, Mitchell 3:55:15 (8,067)
Dann, Peter 5:12:40 (25,982)
Dann, Steve J 4:46:55 (20,257)
Dannatt, Simon J 4:01:06 (9,436)
Dannert, Carsten 5:15:45 (26,618)
Dansey, Mathew T 5:10:08 (25,513)
Danvers, Benjamin 3:12:23 (1,764)
Danziger, Neil A 4:56:26 (22,622)
Darbon, Clive C 6:15:29 (33,648)
Darby, John 4:26:59 (15,321)
Darby, Matthew J 3:56:56 (8,461)
Darby, Paul 4:50:46 (21,183)
Darby, Paul S 4:49:47 (20,951)
Darby, Richard A 5:03:09 (24,160)
Darby, Stephen J 3:29:22 (3,629)
Darbyshire, Colin 4:30:35 (16,276)
Darbyshire, Malcolm 3:24:20 (2,942)
Darceaux, Jean-Michel 4:12:26 (11,710)
Darch, Rhodri M 2:53:35 (499)
Darcy, Kevin J 2:49:08 (349)
D'Arcy, Luke J 3:34:50 (4,384)
D'Arcy-Evans, Stephen 4:32:08 (16,591)
Darcy-Evans, Patrick J 3:39:44 (5,148)
Dargue, Kevin R 4:16:22 (12,665)
Dark, Jason P 3:37:39 (4,770)
Darke, Adam 3:59:24 (9,068)
Darken, Stephen B 5:28:15 (28,849)
Darkins, Peter S 3:57:35 (8,619)
Darley, Richard G 4:22:17 (14,148)
Darling, Richard J 2:52:09 (449)
Darnell, Derek M 3:21:44 (2,677)
Dartington, Daniel J 5:02:36 (24,057)
Dartois, David 3:39:43 (5,146)
Dartois, Yves 4:31:22 (16,438)
Darton, Peter J 4:10:26 (11,253)
Darvill, Malcolm 5:46:07 (31,275)
Das, Bhakta G 5:47:54 (31,449)
Das, Sanjay 6:38:23 (34,619)
Das Gupta, Noresh 5:23:05 (27,947)
Datema, Bonne A 4:17:27 (12,927)
Dattani, Dilip 3:06:11 (1,245)
Daubignard, Xavier 5:33:46 (29,726)
Dauchy, Eric 4:02:43 (9,733)
Daugherty, Duane W 3:24:41 (2,984)
D'Auvergne, Luke A 6:52:59 (34,991)
Dav Ies, Jeffrey 3:52:46 (7,517)
Davaine, Stephane 4:56:35 (22,656)
Davainne, Philippe 3:57:06 (8,502)
Davda, Hemal 5:41:01 (30,710)
Dave, Bhavesh 5:09:58 (25,469)
Davenport, Carl N 4:28:10 (15,640)
Davenport, Dylan 3:20:56 (2,603)
Davenport, Mark J 4:33:49 (16,995)
Davenport, Roy 5:18:04 (27,071)
Davenport, Stephen J 3:48:39 (6,656)
Davey, Adrian R 3:11:05 (1,640)
Davey, Anthony 5:14:30 (26,334)
Davey, Craig 2:35:16 (73)
Davey, Jon B 4:07:24 (10,634)
Davey, Mark 4:19:15 (13,395)
Davey, Mark R 4:13:08 (11,865)
Davey, Martin 5:30:49 (29,267)
Davey, Matthew J 5:03:08 (24,156)
Davey, Philip C 4:56:02 (22,522)
Davey, Simon P 6:47:12 (34,866)
David, Adrian 4:57:25 (22,889)
David, Brent 4:23:06 (14,355)
Davids, Luke A 4:01:12 (9,459)
Davidson, Andy W 3:45:11 (6,047)
Davidson, Christopher L 4:50:08 (21,030)
Davidson, Eric R 4:35:05 (17,291)
Davidson, George F 3:28:08 (3,423)
Davidson, Gordon I 5:24:17 (28,155)
Davidson, Jamie O 3:56:30 (8,360)
Davidson, Kevin J 3:30:47 (3,817)
Davidson, Martin G 4:59:01 (23,259)
Davidson, Richard M 5:24:15 (28,148)
Davidson, Stuart 5:01:28 (23,823)
Davidson, William 7:15:20 (35,347)
Davie, Barry 4:56:38 (22,672)
Davie, Ian 4:23:11 (14,374)
Davie, Joe 4:40:05 (18,552)
Davies, Adrian H 5:23:39 (28,040)
Davies, Alan J 7:27:07 (35,450)
Davies, Alexander J 4:36:34 (17,686)
Davies, Alun 5:20:13 (27,459)
Davies, Alun L 4:46:29 (20,174)

Davies, Andrew....4:53:01 (21,758)
Davies, Andrew K....2:45:34 (254)
Davies, Andrew L....2:58:32 (793)
Davies, Andrew T....3:29:16 (3,611)
Davies, Byron J....5:23:25 (27,992)
Davies, Chris....4:12:28 (11,715)
Davies, Christopher G....5:06:11 (24,734)
Davies, Christopher J....4:42:52 (19,273)
Davies, Christopher M....3:53:30 (7,689)
Davies, Clive T....3:04:01 (1,106)
Davies, Colij....5:47:36 (31,414)
Davies, Darren M....6:50:13 (34,935)
Davies, David....3:16:05 (2,087)
Davies, David....4:36:40 (17,708)
Davies, David....5:04:14 (24,362)
Davies, David T....5:37:19 (30,218)
Davies, David W....3:38:10 (4,865)
Davies, Delfryn A....4:32:28 (16,652)
Davies, Gareth....4:07:25 (10,636)
Davies, Gareth I....5:53:43 (32,029)
Davies, Gareth M....2:54:30 (545)
Davies, Gareth M....4:48:40 (20,682)
Davies, Gareth R....3:43:52 (5,838)
Davies, Gary P....4:42:59 (19,291)
Davies, Geoffrey F....4:21:00 (13,853)
Davies, Grant....3:48:23 (6,587)
Davies, Gregg....5:47:27 (31,405)
Davies, Guy F....3:53:49 (7,746)
Davies, Hadleigh J....3:48:57 (6,717)
Davies, Haydn....5:48:17 (31,503)
Davies, Howard A....3:38:26 (4,908)
Davies, Hywel J....3:57:11 (8,520)
Davies, Ian....3:38:59 (5,012)
Davies, Ian M....3:21:57 (2,702)
Davies, Ian M....3:31:57 (3,985)
Davies, Ian P....4:23:57 (14,555)
Davies, James....3:37:13 (4,713)
Davies, James T....4:32:08 (16,591)
Davies, Jason....6:45:28 (34,809)
Davies, John A....3:35:23 (4,467)
Davies, John H....4:14:40 (12,249)
Davies, John W....5:06:01 (24,696)
Davies, John-Paul R....5:17:50 (27,013)
Davies, Jonathan....5:56:22 (32,272)
Davies, Jonathan C....3:38:40 (4,953)
Davies, Jonathan P....3:44:26 (5,928)
Davies, Keith J....3:03:20 (1,066)
Davies, Kevin M....4:54:06 (22,041)
Davies, Kevin P....4:58:57 (23,241)
Davies, Laurie D....3:56:08 (8,259)
Davies, Leighton B....5:24:04 (28,116)
Davies, Leighton E....3:47:02 (6,352)
Davies, Mark....4:39:53 (18,504)
Davies, Mark C....3:18:39 (2,356)
Davies, Mark M....3:42:33 (5,604)
Davies, Martin....4:56:57 (22,763)
Davies, Martin L....3:29:38 (3,665)
Davies, Martin R....5:21:09 (27,624)
Davies, Martin V....3:11:46 (1,699)
Davies, Michael F....4:56:24 (22,613)
Davies, Michael H....3:41:21 (5,418)
Davies, Neil S....3:52:52 (7,537)
Davies, Nicholas J....4:36:31 (17,671)
Davies, Nick J....3:46:46 (6,296)
Davies, Nick J....4:47:03 (20,299)
Davies, Nigel H....3:57:38 (8,634)
Davies, Patrick E....5:24:50 (28,243)
Davies, Paul....3:47:36 (6,447)
Davies, Paul A....2:51:11 (417)
Davies, Paul D....3:52:08 (7,398)
Davies, Paul S....5:11:05 (25,682)
Davies, Paul W....2:54:53 (573)
Davies, Pete H....3:47:34 (6,438)
Davies, Philip T....4:44:25 (19,654)
Davies, Raymond....4:25:38 (14,977)
Davies, Richard J....6:50:23 (34,942)
Davies, Richard L....6:21:07 (33,962)
Davies, Richard R....4:30:25 (16,237)
Davies, Robert....4:51:40 (21,412)
Davies, Robert....4:52:51 (21,715)
Davies, Robert....5:16:13 (26,705)
Davies, Robert P....4:18:53 (13,304)
Davies, Robert R....3:36:18 (4,588)
Davies, Samuel....4:29:01 (15,861)
Davies, Scott....4:32:46 (16,729)
Davies, Shane....3:36:59 (4,682)
Davies, Simon R....4:42:00 (19,038)
Davies, Stephen....3:26:07 (3,143)
Davies, Stephen C....2:47:39 (302)
Davies, Stephen J....3:21:31 (2,651)
Davies, Stephen J....3:32:05 (4,004)
Davies, Stephen L....5:53:43 (32,029)
Davies, Stephen P....4:40:07 (18,560)
Davies, Steve P....4:23:53 (14,540)
Davies, Steven B....4:29:55 (16,123)
Davies, Stuart M....5:12:17 (25,917)
Davies, Thomas G....3:31:05 (3,846)
Davies, Thomas R....3:12:18 (1,760)
Davies, Tim....5:16:25 (26,742)
Davies, Tim W....4:27:27 (15,460)
Davies, Truphena L....4:54:26 (22,132)
Davies-Knapp, Gethin....4:49:50 (20,959)
Davis, Alan....6:12:40 (33,469)
Davis, Andrew R....3:22:08 (2,717)
Davis, Ashley....3:15:51 (2,068)
Davis, Ben J....3:46:03 (6,186)
Davis, Benjamin E....4:57:11 (22,819)
Davis, Brent A....3:20:38 (2,570)
Davis, Brian K....4:43:07 (19,324)
Davis, Carl....3:51:05 (7,158)
Davis, Charles....3:09:57 (1,554)
Davis, Colin....4:35:36 (17,431)
Davis, Danny....4:28:20 (15,680)
Davis, Darryl K....3:19:46 (2,462)
Davis, Evan....4:17:12 (12,853)
Davis, Gareth....3:55:13 (8,061)
Davis, George....4:40:56 (18,772)
Davis, Glen....4:16:55 (12,792)
Davis, Jeremy P....4:44:22 (19,639)
Davis, John E....4:28:49 (15,814)
Davis, Kevin D....5:03:38 (24,263)
Davis, Kevin J....3:51:53 (7,335)
Davis, Lee A....6:27:42 (34,241)
Davis, Mark....2:48:37 (332)
Davis, Mark H....3:35:43 (4,517)
Davis, Martin B....3:36:37 (4,629)
Davis, Martin J....3:13:19 (1,853)
Davis, Matthew J....5:01:14 (23,782)
Davis, Matthew L....5:21:23 (27,673)
Davis, Michael B....4:22:36 (14,230)
Davis, Nicholas G....2:57:28 (707)
Davis, Pascal....4:33:20 (16,879)
Davis, Paul J....4:16:53 (12,778)
Davis, Paul M....3:42:27 (5,592)
Davis, Paul N....5:31:34 (29,384)
Davis, Peter....4:10:32 (11,274)
Davis, Phillip E....5:28:51 (28,957)
Davis, Richard M....3:09:05 (1,475)
Davis, Robert A....4:27:56 (15,567)
Davis, Robert R....3:55:15 (8,067)
Davis, Simon P....4:47:58 (20,525)
Davis, Simon W....4:11:44 (11,554)
Davis, Stephen K....4:26:14 (15,114)
Davis, Stuart G....6:48:48 (34,905)
Davis, Wayne....5:23:56 (28,097)
Davison, Gary R....5:32:32 (29,539)
Davison, James T....4:40:17 (18,597)
Davison, Lee R....4:46:07 (20,086)
Davison, Scott H....4:29:31 (16,013)
Davitt, Mark J....5:15:16 (26,518)
D'Avola, Giovanni P....3:57:56 (8,705)
Davy, James R....3:53:11 (7,610)
Davy, Olivier....4:52:46 (21,685)
Davy, Simon....4:32:14 (16,616)
Davy, Stephen P....4:05:44 (10,295)
Daw, Richard J....4:08:33 (10,879)
Dawber, Andrew J....5:13:39 (26,150)
Dawber, Nigel....3:48:46 (6,682)
Dawber, Steven....5:10:10 (25,522)
Dawe, James A....4:48:54 (20,745)
Dawe, Nicholas C....3:45:26 (6,088)
Dawes, Chris....3:30:20 (3,771)
Dawes, Ian P....4:48:26 (20,638)
Dawkins, Andrew D....4:18:36 (13,240)
Dawkins, Colin....3:59:34 (9,111)
Dawkins, Robert J....3:46:52 (6,314)
Dawney, Kevin R....5:16:53 (26,835)
Daws, Paul....4:16:06 (12,596)
Dawson, Alan R....2:58:02 (749)
Dawson, Bernard J....4:16:08 (12,604)
Dawson, Carl....6:11:55 (33,419)
Dawson, Elliott....4:17:31 (12,951)
Dawson, Gary J....4:37:24 (17,862)
Dawson, Gordon....5:13:28 (26,116)
Dawson, Hilton....5:17:10 (26,886)
Dawson, John....6:15:21 (33,637)
Dawson, Keith....3:03:48 (1,093)
Dawson, Kirk J....4:46:10 (20,095)
Dawson, Lee....5:00:29 (23,610)
Dawson, Liam J....4:33:02 (16,795)
Dawson, Matthew S....4:35:39 (17,440)
Dawson, Michael J....4:45:23 (19,922)
Dawson, Michael J....5:13:55 (26,213)
Dawson, Neil A....4:53:59 (22,016)
Dawson, Patrick J....3:52:18 (7,434)
Dawson, Peter J....5:15:00 (26,449)
Dawson, Phillip C....4:26:20 (15,142)
Dawson, Roy W....4:59:02 (23,264)
Dawson, Simon J....4:28:45 (15,799)
Dawson, Steve....3:23:07 (2,812)
Dawson, Thomas D....3:41:48 (5,484)
Dawson, Warren L....6:30:23 (34,336)
Dawson-Wink, John....3:28:37 (3,507)
Day, Andrew D....3:55:41 (8,161)
Day, Barnaby....3:39:44 (5,148)
Day, Brian D....6:05:47 (33,031)
Day, Christopher M....4:44:48 (19,780)
Day, David A....3:16:52 (2,165)
Day, Grant J....4:16:00 (12,562)
Day, Ian M....2:58:52 (815)
Day, John....5:00:41 (23,652)
Day, John W....5:05:30 (24,602)
Day, Jonathan G....3:16:10 (2,094)
Day, Julian E....4:23:40 (14,484)
Day, Kevin....6:36:12 (34,543)
Day, Matthew J....3:38:29 (4,917)
Day, Paul....3:41:12 (5,398)
Day, Russell J....5:25:29 (28,367)
Day, Simon C....3:40:18 (5,231)
Day, Steve....3:35:18 (4,449)
Day, Thomas F....4:00:39 (9,345)
Day, Thomas W....4:28:45 (15,799)
Dayman, Guy H....4:06:21 (10,423)
Daynes, Michael D....3:57:43 (8,657)
Days, Anthony G....5:20:42 (27,555)
Days, Jonathan A....5:00:51 (23,696)
Dayton, Andrew P....4:25:22 (14,913)
Daziano, Alberto....4:42:27 (19,164)
Dazo, Herbert F....5:30:41 (29,251)
De Almeida, Martin W....5:35:42 (30,011)
De Beer, Russell E....4:47:22 (20,374)
De Beer, Zach J....3:42:04 (5,530)
De Boer, Erik R....4:43:57 (19,520)
De Cicco, Massimo....4:56:25 (22,616)
De Francesco, Fabrizio....4:06:45 (10,513)
De Francisci, Francesco....4:33:45 (16,978)
De Gobbi, Marco....2:58:23 (780)
De Hita, José M....4:36:04 (17,549)
De Jager, Johan Y....5:35:06 (29,926)
De Jager, Petrus J....5:35:06 (29,926)
De La Barreda, Ruben....6:07:44 (33,152)
De La Haye, Terry....3:49:13 (6,779)
De Luzan, Philippe....3:03:01 (1,051)
De Marco, Chris....6:06:04 (33,054)
De Marco, Luciano....4:16:56 (12,798)
De Mulder, Jan L....3:09:11 (1,485)
De Palma, Rodney....5:13:05 (26,060)
De Pastors, Olivier....4:05:22 (10,212)
De Praeter, Jurgen....3:51:51 (7,327)
De Sanctis, Saverio....3:37:48 (4,788)
De Santis, Francesco....4:30:45 (16,307)
De Silva, Nigel A....4:06:21 (10,423)
De Silva, Suresh P....5:40:58 (30,702)
De Simone, Daniel....5:28:01 (28,801)
De Souza, Derek P....5:39:10 (30,472)
De Souza Brady, Shaun M....4:34:54 (17,248)
De Val, Thomas E....4:16:15 (12,634)
Deacon, Michael L....5:30:36 (29,235)
Deacon, Richard....6:55:20 (35,043)

Deacy, Anthony J 3:46:32 (6,254)
Deadman, Stephen J 3:18:12 (2,310)
Deakes, Karl A 5:36:10 (30,064)
Deakin, Mark A 5:34:14 (29,801)
Deakins, Christopher J 3:57:33 (8,610)
Deal, Sacha 4:22:28 (14,190)
Deaman, Peter E 3:19:42 (2,453)
Dean, Alastair M 5:20:17 (27,472)
Dean, Alexander D 5:04:38 (24,434)
Dean, Anthony 6:33:42 (34,455)
Dean, Benjamin F 3:49:10 (6,761)
Dean, Brian 4:43:50 (19,489)
Dean, Clive G 5:30:41 (29,251)
Dean, Gary 2:56:57 (670)
Dean, Josh 3:35:30 (4,480)
Dean, Ken 4:36:07 (17,563)
Dean, Kevin G 4:05:03 (10,153)
Dean, Mark R 3:17:15 (2,202)
Dean, Matthew F 6:02:47 (32,807)
Dean, Michael R 3:27:54 (3,396)
Dean, Scott 4:51:39 (21,409)
Deane, John P 3:57:54 (8,698)
Deaner, Peter C 4:00:40 (9,349)
Deans, Donald 4:41:59 (19,033)
Deans, Frank 5:03:19 (24,197)
Deanus, Del 6:02:11 (32,761)
Dear, Andrew J 5:07:12 (24,929)
Dear, James E 3:43:17 (5,734)
Dear, Michael W 7:36:04 (35,540)
Dear, Richard A 4:08:26 (10,859)
Dearden, Alan R 3:50:27 (7,029)
Dearing, Stephen C 4:57:33 (22,914)
Dearman, Jonathan A 4:29:19 (15,943)
Dearson, Michael E 6:57:02 (35,073)
Deas, Jon 4:44:32 (19,697)
Deason, Dave 3:55:28 (8,114)
Deason-Barrow, Julian 7:52:53 (35,630)
Debelder, Daniel L 3:48:42 (6,666)
Debenham, James R 3:42:47 (5,643)
Debenham, Shaun P 6:13:56 (33,545)
Debergh, Bruno 3:46:33 (6,257)
Deboute, Jerome 4:16:40 (12,729)
Debray, Philippe P 3:22:32 (2,750)
Debricon, Jean-Marc 4:21:08 (13,882)
Debrosse, Didier 4:30:51 (16,324)
Decair, Thomas W 7:26:22 (35,438)
Decol, Paolo 2:53:38 (502)
Decrouez, Gerard 7:14:24 (35,337)
Dede, Armand 3:46:59 (6,342)
Dedow, Eike 4:36:50 (17,752)
Dee, John A 3:53:53 (7,761)
Deeks, Andrew W 5:34:25 (29,833)
Deeley, Stuart 6:18:59 (33,836)
Deen, Alivin F 4:26:58 (15,314)
Deen, Naren 5:46:50 (31,339)
Deer, Colin S 4:51:06 (21,266)
Deery, Francis E 3:55:23 (8,102)
Deffontaine, Vincent 3:07:44 (1,366)
Deftereos, Phillip 5:02:53 (24,102)
Degia, Ilyas 5:09:34 (25,391)
Degroot, Thomas J 4:41:06 (18,811)
Dehoyos, Jesse L 3:38:38 (4,945)
Del Gaudio, Ennio 3:16:02 (2,081)
Del Papa, Pasqualino 3:10:03 (1,563)
Del Rosario, Gennuino 5:32:48 (29,578)
Delahoy, Trevor R 4:13:38 (12,004)
Delaine, Karl 4:50:58 (21,233)
Delaney, Christopher P 4:56:38 (22,672)
Delaney, James N 5:03:03 (24,139)
Delaney, Joe 4:50:14 (21,055)
Delaney, Lee D 5:01:21 (23,803)
Delaney, Owen S 4:44:53 (19,803)
De-Lapeyre, Bruno 3:56:40 (8,396)
Delderfield, Kris 4:58:12 (23,076)
Delderfield, Luke F 3:04:22 (1,125)
Delepoulle, Alexis 3:33:18 (4,179)
Deleurme, Stephane 2:34:05 (64)
Delew, Russell P 4:05:41 (10,286)
Delf, Mike J 4:29:49 (16,095)
Delgado Lorenzo, Ramon 4:50:50 (21,200)
Delille, Thierry O 3:48:33 (6,637)
Dell, Graeme J 4:43:19 (19,383)
Dell'Abate, Romolo 4:06:51 (10,540)
Dellbridge, Andrew 5:34:11 (29,791)
Dellen, David C 3:16:39 (2,138)
Delliston, Alan K 4:24:19 (14,658)
Delogne, Jean-Claude 3:14:44 (1,963)
Delph, Paul S 5:39:28 (30,521)
Delubac, Hugo 3:38:10 (4,865)
Demaerschalk, Patrick A 3:41:41 (5,466)
Demaid, Simon D 4:32:24 (16,644)
Demaine, Michael 4:31:07 (16,386)
Demarco, Edward V 3:08:53 (1,456)
Demarecaux, Pascal 3:20:11 (2,517)
Demay, Frederic 5:15:47 (26,621)
Demetrious, Philip S 4:00:45 (9,365)
Demong, Peter B 4:21:04 (13,864)
Dempsey, Peter D 5:02:51 (24,095)
Dempster, Andrew B 3:52:17 (7,429)
Den Hartog, Jan A 3:27:29 (3,353)
Denby-Hollis, Luke 3:58:48 (8,910)
Dench, Marc S 3:36:14 (4,577)
Dendy, Michael 3:58:22 (8,800)
Denfeld, Hans Jvergen 3:46:55 (6,327)
Denham, Brian R 3:53:12 (7,618)
Denham, Toby P 3:44:52 (6,004)
Denis, Romain S 3:18:33 (2,346)
Denis Romero, Roberto 5:45:49 (31,240)
Denison, Ross D 4:01:04 (9,429)
Deniz, Tim 6:34:30 (34,477)
Denke, Wernfried 3:52:15 (7,421)
Dennell, Keith 5:26:44 (28,581)
Dennett, Peter A 3:47:03 (6,355)
Dennington, Tom J 4:16:28 (12,692)
Dennis, Matthew R 5:37:53 (30,285)
Dennis, Neil R 4:57:08 (22,805)
Dennis, Paul J 3:21:45 (2,680)
Dennis, Philip G 4:08:46 (10,916)
Dennis, Steven P 6:00:02 (32,582)
Dennis, William J 5:30:17 (29,181)
Dennison, Daniel 5:27:55 (28,781)
Dennison, Michael R 4:33:52 (17,005)
Dennison, Nicholas J 4:58:49 (23,211)
Denny, Alan 5:00:47 (23,683)
Denny, Jason 4:24:51 (14,797)
Denny, Jonny A 5:12:48 (26,000)
Dent, James P 4:25:57 (15,043)
Dent, Paul S 4:49:23 (20,858)
Denton, Jon W 3:20:11 (2,517)
Denton, Pete 4:51:22 (21,334)
Denton, Roger S 3:04:36 (1,138)
Denwood, Thomas J 3:10:33 (1,598)
Denye, Andrew J 4:30:43 (16,295)
Denyer, Andrew 4:25:27 (14,934)
Denyer, John F 4:00:18 (9,273)
Denyer, Peter R 3:32:37 (4,086)
Deol, Harjit 4:10:59 (11,365)
Der Duijn Schouten, Niek Van P 3:28:20 (3,454)
Derby, Nigel M 3:41:58 (5,511)
Derbyshire, Ian 5:22:39 (27,882)
Derbyshire, Phil 4:59:31 (23,390)
Derbyshire, Stephen 6:15:36 (33,657)
Derbyshire, Todd 4:09:10 (10,997)
Derham, Jason P 5:09:37 (25,399)
Derome, Philippe 3:31:54 (3,972)
Derow, Paul E 4:43:03 (19,306)
Derrett, Joseph E 3:56:29 (8,355)
Derrington, Richard P 4:23:55 (14,547)
Derry, Mark 3:14:56 (1,985)
Dervis, Cengiz 3:43:52 (5,838)
Derwas, Philip C 4:13:54 (12,068)
Derwent, Gary G 5:17:32 (26,964)
Desborough, Steve 2:52:45 (468)
Desmond, Paul 4:17:12 (12,853)
Despic, John 3:46:46 (6,296)
Despretz, Christophe 4:14:59 (12,318)
Devadason, Dev S 4:02:54 (9,767)
Devaney, Gearoid E 3:50:15 (6,984)
Devanney, Tim M 3:12:39 (1,792)
De-Varine, Davier 3:50:56 (7,123)
Deveney, Callum M 5:00:30 (23,613)
Devenish, Brett D 5:48:26 (31,520)
Deverill, John E 5:00:55 (23,712)
Devey, Dennis 5:25:12 (28,302)
Devine, Ciaran C 5:48:42 (31,553)
Devine, Michael J 3:51:30 (7,256)
Devitt, Russell 4:35:51 (17,499)
Devlin, Brendan J 3:39:48 (5,157)
Devlin, Robert 5:03:07 (24,153)
Devonshire, Stephen 5:20:25 (27,497)
Devoy, Richard S 4:22:28 (14,190)
Dewfall, Nicholas J 5:00:54 (23,709)
Dewick, Mark C 5:35:12 (29,940)
Dewire, Richard A 4:10:32 (11,274)
Dewood, Richard N 4:38:29 (18,146)
Dewson, Neville R 5:21:20 (27,663)
Dexter, Adam P 4:24:21 (14,665)
Dexter, Colin G 5:54:44 (32,119)
Dexter, Dave 5:42:12 (30,847)
Dexter, Matthew J 4:04:22 (10,032)
Dexter, Phillip M 4:50:59 (21,240)
Dey, Andrew 4:42:13 (19,101)
Dharimal, Navraj S 4:53:42 (21,942)
Dhaussy, Pierre 2:57:13 (692)
Dhellin, Pascal 3:23:51 (2,886)
Dherbecourt, Gerard M 3:51:55 (7,342)
Dhesi, Manjinder S 5:19:43 (27,376)
Dhital, Anish 6:22:36 (34,026)
Dhooper, Nick J 5:06:06 (24,712)
Di Biase, Fausto 5:07:05 (24,905)
Di Ciacca, Paul 3:29:28 (3,643)
Di Clemente, Antonio 5:06:11 (24,734)
Di Corato, Massimo 5:08:09 (25,126)
Di Falco, Domenico 4:26:50 (15,275)
Di Leo, Daniele 3:42:58 (5,682)
Di Martino, Tommy 3:47:38 (6,460)
Di Mucci, Paul P 3:30:47 (3,817)
Di Nardo, Renzo 3:02:00 (1,003)
Di Nunzio, Giuseppe 4:09:26 (11,057)
Di Rubba, Domenico 4:38:32 (18,159)
Diaj, Mark 4:26:38 (15,218)
Diamond, Samuel P 3:28:15 (3,438)
Diaper, Jonathan P 3:56:23 (8,330)
Dias, José J 4:57:36 (22,932)
Diasparra, Didier 4:38:35 (18,170)
Diaz, José A 4:24:36 (14,727)
Diaz, Julio 4:02:26 (9,687)
Dibb Fuller, Jason 3:38:20 (4,892)
Dibley, Bob J 6:15:44 (33,665)
Dichi, Abraham 3:28:18 (3,449)
Dick, Alastair 4:52:53 (21,721)
Dick, Alistair 3:10:06 (1,571)
Dick, Jim 4:13:47 (12,040)
Dick, Michael J 3:30:32 (3,790)
Dick, Stewart J 4:36:17 (17,606)
Dickens, George 4:41:40 (18,958)
Dickens, Mark I 4:59:01 (23,259)
Dickens, Peter K 4:47:59 (20,531)
Dickenson, Darren M 7:42:28 (35,587)
Dicker, Clive A 4:37:27 (17,883)
Dickie, Ewan T 4:01:41 (9,549)
Dickinson, Christopher T 6:08:11 (33,185)
Dickinson, David M 6:26:35 (34,195)
Dickinson, David T 2:41:29 (166)
Dickinson, Kelvin B 2:59:12 (840)
Dickinson, Mark 2:47:36 (300)
Dickinson, Mark A 5:16:44 (26,794)
Dickinson, Martin D 3:35:00 (4,409)
Dickinson, Michael 4:57:41 (22,954)
Dickinson, Oliver P 4:20:22 (13,700)
Dickinson, Peter 4:59:46 (23,448)
Dickinson, Phillip G 3:47:28 (6,420)
Dickinson, Ralph W 3:28:58 (3,569)
Dickinson, Stephen 4:43:56 (19,517)
Dickinson, Stephen J 4:47:09 (20,322)
Dickman, Andrew 4:22:17 (14,148)
Dickson, Andrew 4:09:11 (11,002)
Dickson, David R 4:43:58 (19,527)
Dickson, Graham 3:45:30 (6,095)
Dickson, Ian C 4:46:51 (20,239)
Dickson, Ken J 6:51:13 (34,962)
Dickson, Kevin 4:14:16 (12,157)
Dickson, Paul D 3:59:35 (9,114)
Dickson, Stephen A 3:58:41 (8,880)
Dickson, Stuart J 5:45:14 (31,175)
Dides, Simon 5:02:53 (24,102)
Didsbury, Christopher J 4:00:41 (9,354)
Diegnan, Lee C 4:47:50 (20,489)
Diesel, Wayne J 3:28:15 (3,438)

Diesner, Stephen G	3:33:22	(4,191)
Digby, Stephen J	4:11:40	(11,542)
Digby-Baker, Hugh J	4:03:42	(9,902)
Diggens, Timothy M	5:03:12	(24,173)
Diggins, Oliver T	4:53:52	(21,980)
Digholm, Bjorn	3:54:49	(7,965)
Dighton, Terry	4:04:31	(10,059)
Dignan, Jay M	3:37:01	(4,689)
Diliberto, Fabio	3:42:59	(5,689)
Dilley, Nicholas A	4:58:20	(23,115)
Dillin, Jason P	3:58:26	(8,816)
Dillon, Andrew P	4:36:33	(17,681)
Dillow, Gavin	4:12:44	(11,774)
Dillow, Peter L	3:58:24	(8,809)
Dilloway, Luke E	4:00:23	(9,287)
Dilmi, Ludovic	2:45:30	(250)
Dilworth, Robby A	4:35:52	(17,502)
Dimbleby, Peter J	2:43:11	(202)
Dimelow, Geoffrey	4:02:06	(9,622)
Dimelow, Glenn	4:04:56	(10,133)
Dimeo, Alfredo	4:32:04	(16,574)
Dimmock, Chris P	4:14:04	(12,118)
Dimond, Stephen J	3:26:11	(3,155)
Dinger, Willem N	4:07:05	(10,592)
Dingle, Adam D	7:19:49	(35,384)
Dingle, Neil M	4:20:24	(13,707)
Dingley, Christopher S	4:43:18	(19,372)
Diniz, Clauder	3:53:36	(7,708)
Dinler, Kerim	5:41:44	(30,802)
Dionisio, Tiago B	4:16:56	(12,798)
Dipersio, David G	4:38:19	(18,101)
Disley, Christopher J	3:59:45	(9,152)
Ditcham, Robert	3:44:39	(5,967)
Dix, Stuart B	4:59:39	(23,423)
Dixon, Andrew	3:54:53	(7,982)
Dixon, Andrew	5:40:07	(30,609)
Dixon, Andrew J	4:25:37	(14,973)
Dixon, Andrew P	4:21:27	(13,952)
Dixon, Andy	4:32:10	(16,599)
Dixon, Ben	4:05:11	(10,184)
Dixon, Christopher	5:28:36	(28,918)
Dixon, Clem	3:02:20	(1,018)
Dixon, Colin J	5:30:23	(29,197)
Dixon, David	3:58:58	(8,954)
Dixon, David A	4:05:33	(10,250)
Dixon, David J	3:43:57	(5,856)
Dixon, David W	3:32:29	(4,065)
Dixon, Edward J	4:29:08	(15,895)
Dixon, Garry J	2:39:31	(136)
Dixon, Hugh R	4:39:12	(18,335)
Dixon, Ian H	4:27:09	(15,366)
Dixon, John	5:18:21	(27,135)
Dixon, John J	3:42:55	(5,672)
Dixon, Jonathan H	3:21:31	(2,651)
Dixon, Joshua P	5:08:45	(25,234)
Dixon, Kevin A	4:42:24	(19,152)
Dixon, Marhsall L	5:14:24	(26,312)
Dixon, Mark	5:14:37	(26,365)
Dixon, Nicholas J	4:17:14	(12,861)
Dixon, Nigel	3:49:05	(6,747)
Dixon, Paul A	4:08:41	(10,907)
Dixon, Paul D	3:43:03	(5,698)
Dixon, Robert A	5:39:57	(30,580)
Dixon, Robert J	5:07:48	(25,058)
Dixon, Sam	5:35:03	(29,920)
Dixon, Scott	4:25:15	(14,884)
Dixon, Steve	5:05:40	(24,628)
Djavanian, Hassan	5:00:18	(23,575)
Djellas, Ryad	3:51:23	(7,221)
Dlamini, Jacob S	4:59:53	(23,470)
Dlubala, Lech	5:30:00	(29,137)
Dmello, Kevin A	4:44:33	(19,703)
Dmitrzak, Michael	3:20:33	(2,562)
Doak, Ian D	4:43:17	(19,367)
Dobbin, Andrew D	3:58:16	(8,783)
Dobbin, David J	4:39:46	(18,476)
Dobbs, Patrick A	3:35:51	(4,528)
Dobbs, Simon C	2:56:32	(637)
Dobby, Adam	4:23:31	(14,451)
Dobby, Andrew M	2:59:03	(829)
Dobeson, Geoff J	4:36:13	(17,585)
Dobie, Ronald	4:26:40	(15,231)
Doblas-Reyes, Francisco J	4:51:43	(21,424)
Doble, Paul W	5:12:02	(25,861)
Dobson, Andrew	3:54:26	(7,889)
Dobson, Douglas	4:45:26	(19,930)
Dobson, Jonathan E	2:48:13	(322)
Dobson, Jonathan S	4:14:02	(12,106)
Dobson, Michael	3:46:24	(6,237)
Dobson, Neal R	4:38:15	(18,068)
Dobson, Neil J	4:07:47	(10,721)
Dobson, Nicholas J	4:23:12	(14,379)
Dobson, Robin	3:46:25	(6,240)
Dobson, Spencer B	3:53:33	(7,698)
Dobson, Stephen M	5:14:20	(26,300)
Docherty, Alasdair	5:05:21	(24,564)
Docherty, Kevin J	4:18:07	(13,103)
Docherty, Richard	3:09:02	(1,471)
Docherty, Stephen	4:41:33	(18,939)
Dockerill, David A	3:35:01	(4,411)
Dockerill, Steven C	3:37:55	(4,809)
Dodanis, Christos	3:36:59	(4,682)
Dodd, Andrew C	3:53:27	(7,677)
Dodd, David	4:42:47	(19,251)
Dodd, Geoff	5:07:54	(25,077)
Dodd, Paul F	3:03:02	(1,052)
Dodd, Richard S	4:52:55	(21,730)
Dodd, Rodney H	5:02:53	(24,102)
Dodds, David	4:36:53	(17,763)
Dodds, Jeffrey	4:44:34	(19,705)
Dodds, Nigel R	4:35:36	(17,431)
Doderer, Hartwig	4:12:54	(11,806)
Dodge, Richard M	5:18:50	(27,219)
Dodson, Andrew J	3:55:09	(8,044)
Dodson, Edward C	3:56:41	(8,399)
Doe, Don G	3:12:51	(1,812)
Doe, Keith E	5:04:53	(24,496)
Doherty, Barry	5:25:42	(28,406)
Doherty, Ben J	5:13:24	(26,102)
Doherty, Brendan D	5:45:57	(31,249)
Doherty, Christopher	7:12:59	(35,322)
Doherty, Daniel	4:54:00	(22,022)
Doherty, David	4:56:29	(22,631)
Doherty, Declan P	3:57:37	(8,629)
Doherty, Jackie J	3:26:55	(3,261)
Doherty, James	5:21:52	(27,769)
Doherty, Kieran M	3:47:28	(6,420)
Doherty, Liam	4:17:16	(12,866)
Doherty, Martin J	4:49:10	(20,813)
Doherty, Matthew J	4:39:33	(18,424)
Doherty, Patrick	6:15:42	(33,661)
Doherty, Patrick A	6:32:44	(34,429)
Doherty, Peter	3:56:57	(8,466)
Doherty, Stuart	4:20:14	(13,660)
Doherty, Tom A	3:41:10	(5,390)
Doherty Moore, Paddy	3:21:00	(2,611)
Doig, Henry R	4:23:21	(14,408)
Dokotum, Joseph S	6:55:24	(35,045)
Doktor, Bernd	4:39:57	(18,527)
Dolan, Christopher J	4:24:44	(14,756)
Dolan, Robert	3:38:05	(4,850)
Dolan, Robert	3:38:06	(4,856)
Dolan, Trevor	4:37:22	(17,852)
Dolman, Antony R	4:18:36	(13,240)
Dolman, Paul J	5:11:18	(25,719)
Dolphin, Christopher C	4:52:35	(21,635)
Dolphin, James H	3:06:44	(1,292)
Dolphin, Oliver V	4:15:15	(12,376)
Domaingue, Jean Claude P	4:18:17	(13,142)
Dome, Andrew J	3:50:12	(6,974)
Dommersnes, Sam	6:05:28	(32,999)
Dommett, Robert A	6:42:11	(34,726)
Don, Ian G	5:36:45	(30,138)
Donald, Alex	2:48:38	(334)
Donaldson, Drew	3:09:05	(1,475)
Donaldson, Kelvin W	4:38:46	(18,220)
Donaldson, Neil J	5:03:23	(24,213)
Donaldson, Thomas A	3:37:52	(4,802)
Donaldson, Tony	4:58:58	(23,244)
Donato, Lorenzo	3:40:18	(5,231)
Done, Andrew J	8:24:37	(35,674)
Done, Mike J	4:25:18	(14,894)
Donegan, Marc	5:31:35	(29,387)
Donelli, Mirco	4:32:57	(16,773)
Donetti, Stephane	4:24:11	(14,627)
Donkin, Andrew N	7:14:39	(35,342)
Donkin, Robert J	4:54:45	(22,212)
Donnellan, Leo	4:36:02	(17,544)
Donnelly, Arthur	3:18:12	(2,310)
Donnelly, Dean P	5:23:31	(28,013)
Donnelly, Gerard M	4:34:06	(17,050)
Donnelly, John	4:51:58	(21,477)
Donnelly, Philip S	4:15:57	(12,543)
Donnelly, Stephen	3:06:14	(1,249)
Donnelly, Steven M	5:08:38	(25,213)
Donoghue, Anthony	6:57:16	(35,078)
Donoghue, Christopher	3:13:11	(1,836)
Donoghue, Christopher	4:19:21	(13,420)
Donoghue, Gerard	6:17:32	(33,753)
Donoho, Gideon	3:26:05	(3,140)
Donohue, Carl A	3:38:59	(5,012)
Donovan, Clive	3:16:58	(2,176)
Dook, Hadrian	3:52:50	(7,534)
Doolan, James	4:02:11	(9,642)
Doolan, John A	5:01:59	(23,933)
Doolan, Kristian E	4:12:06	(11,630)
Dooley, Joseph	5:42:04	(30,834)
Dooley, Michael	5:28:48	(28,952)
Dooley, Michael S	2:59:37	(870)
Doran, Andrew T	3:46:34	(6,263)
Doran, Benjamin	3:32:03	(3,995)
Doran, Chris J	5:40:03	(30,598)
Doran, Colin C	4:07:46	(10,719)
Doran, David	3:24:32	(2,958)
Doran, Jeremy J	4:27:04	(15,345)
Doran, Nicholas S	3:09:06	(1,477)
Doran, Rian P	7:50:36	(35,624)
Dorenbos, Ron	4:24:06	(14,598)
Dorey, Arnaud	5:15:35	(26,582)
Dorey, Colin R	3:29:14	(3,607)
Dorkin, Jonathan	4:33:17	(16,863)
Dorling, David C	5:20:21	(27,485)
Dorman, Lawrence	3:54:14	(7,848)
Dorney, Mark J	5:53:36	(32,022)
Dorney, Robert A	4:25:04	(14,837)
Dorrell, Trevor D	4:09:21	(11,041)
Dorrington, Robert E	4:35:41	(17,456)
Dorward, Neil L	3:24:20	(2,942)
Dosanjh, Jatinder	5:27:49	(28,766)
Dossena, Paolo	3:51:04	(7,154)
Dotta, Gianmarco	3:30:31	(3,788)
Double, Graham H	6:08:27	(33,199)
Douch, Martin	5:16:04	(26,674)
Dougall, Robert	5:26:22	(28,524)
Dougan, Andy	5:45:33	(31,215)
Dougherty, Andrew D	5:52:02	(31,874)
Dougherty, Simon J	4:13:27	(11,947)
Doughty, Andrew J	4:05:32	(10,245)
Doughty, Mark I	5:47:48	(31,438)
Douglas, George J	4:44:39	(19,727)
Douglas, Greg	5:28:53	(28,963)
Douglas, Ian M	3:52:55	(7,549)
Douglas, Neil A	2:59:48	(886)
Douglas, Noel M	4:32:30	(16,662)
Douglas, Paul D	2:58:48	(813)
Douglas, Philip	3:39:11	(5,045)
Douglas, Richard A	4:28:20	(15,680)
Douglas, Stuart J	2:58:44	(807)
Douglas-Pennant, Ian C	5:00:43	(23,664)
Douglis, Matthew G	5:21:59	(27,778)
Doumenc, Benoit	5:01:13	(23,776)
Dousset, Pierre J	3:28:45	(3,531)
Dove, Christopher W	4:24:08	(14,610)
Dove, Paul J	4:59:28	(23,369)
Dover, Gary W	3:25:54	(3,115)
Dover, Victor B	5:15:58	(26,652)
Dow, Andrew J	3:26:22	(3,182)
Dow, Peter J	3:19:27	(2,433)
Dowald, Andrew J	4:03:32	(9,874)
Dowall, Kevin R	5:56:34	(32,296)
Dowdall, Jim	9:16:39	(35,697)
Dowdney, Harry A	3:52:53	(7,540)
Dowdney, Ruari B	3:52:53	(7,540)
Dowdy, Michael T	4:31:34	(16,475)
Dowdy, Nicholas H	4:57:34	(22,919)
Dowell, John W	5:57:53	(32,402)
Dowie, Paul	4:10:19	(11,231)
Dowle, Matthew P	3:03:32	(1,079)
Dowling, David	5:55:10	(32,163)

Dowling, Michael G	4:06:46 (10,521)
Down, Malcolm R	3:10:01 (1,562)
Downer, Allen L	3:06:43 (1,290)
Downer, Edward F	5:02:30 (24,040)
Downer, Greg O	3:57:10 (8,518)
Downer, Harvey P	5:08:20 (25,161)
Downes, Andrew R	5:17:57 (27,041)
Downes, Augustin A	3:31:19 (3,880)
Downes, Gareth	3:47:36 (6,447)
Downes, Mark	4:08:01 (10,769)
Downes, Ryk G	5:17:24 (26,941)
Downey, Desmond D	4:57:43 (22,963)
Downey, Gary A	4:20:30 (13,732)
Downey, James	6:26:00 (34,164)
Downey, Kevin	5:29:44 (29,100)
Downie, Kevin C	5:33:49 (29,734)
Downie, Matthew	5:37:54 (30,287)
Downing, Oliver J	3:25:42 (3,088)
Downs, David J	3:26:38 (3,212)
Downs, Mitchell L	5:17:10 (26,886)
Downs, Timothy C	4:09:16 (11,020)
Dowsett, Frederick J	4:06:48 (10,530)
Dowsett, Jeff	4:02:48 (9,753)
Dowsett, Peter C	3:42:20 (5,577)
Dowsett, William	4:42:18 (19,123)
Dowson, Andrew M	3:14:27 (1,936)
Dowson, Paul A	4:35:52 (17,502)
Dowton, Alan P	3:31:18 (3,877)
Doxat-Purser, Alistair R	4:55:04 (22,282)
Doyle, Alastair K	3:03:51 (1,097)
Doyle, Andrew	4:48:10 (20,566)
Doyle, Andrew J	5:18:07 (27,084)
Doyle, Dave R	3:47:24 (6,410)
Doyle, Frank A	5:27:04 (28,631)
Doyle, Frank P	3:56:31 (8,364)
Doyle, Gavin S	6:07:43 (33,146)
Doyle, Geoffrey E	3:07:17 (1,332)
Doyle, James H	4:04:11 (10,002)
Doyle, Jeremy S	3:49:59 (6,934)
Doyle, John	4:39:24 (18,389)
Doyle, John P	4:54:59 (22,261)
Doyle, Jonathan	4:51:00 (21,242)
Doyle, Kevin S	3:24:05 (2,918)
Doyle, Kirk	4:54:08 (22,054)
Doyle, Marek E	5:19:36 (27,360)
Doyle, Matthew L	3:53:43 (7,733)
Doyle, Michael D	3:27:44 (3,378)
Doyle, Nicholas A	6:10:59 (33,367)
Doyle, Patrick D	3:18:15 (2,319)
Doyle, Peter T	5:16:52 (26,829)
Doyle, Richard	4:20:37 (13,758)
Doyle, Robert F	4:29:38 (16,048)
Doyle, Sean J	4:19:43 (13,515)
Doyle, Simon J	3:37:50 (4,794)
Drabble, Dean	4:18:39 (13,252)
Dragazis, Demetri	6:40:45 (34,681)
Drake, Adam C	4:23:04 (14,348)
Drake, Martin	4:13:32 (11,980)
Drake, Nathan	4:51:03 (21,255)
Drake, Peter L	4:28:39 (15,773)
Drake, Richard J	3:26:14 (3,163)
Draper, Ben	3:31:28 (3,905)
Draper, Darren	5:30:26 (29,205)
Draper, Dennis W	4:36:19 (17,614)
Draper, Kevin J	4:10:11 (11,201)
Draper, Martin D	4:45:37 (19,970)
Draper, Martin J	5:29:23 (29,054)
Draper, Paul S	4:54:10 (22,069)
Draper, Thomas C	3:21:56 (2,700)
Dray, Philip A	5:43:28 (30,990)
Drayton, Mark A	3:43:10 (5,720)
Drew, Ian	3:35:22 (4,465)
Drew, Kieron	4:31:06 (16,381)
Drew, Philip	5:02:08 (23,956)
Drewell, Daniel	5:27:57 (28,786)
Drewett, Jamie R	4:04:54 (10,129)
Drexler, Martin W	4:10:18 (11,228)
Dreyfus, Alain	4:37:40 (17,926)
Drinkwater, James R	5:03:44 (24,276)
Drinkwater, Tom	4:11:01 (11,371)
Driscoll, Joe	2:20:49 (15)
Driscoll, Stephen M	5:03:05 (24,145)
Driscoll, Terence	4:06:02 (10,355)

Driver, Gary G	4:13:00 (11,827)
Driver, Jim	4:21:58 (14,080)
Driver, John	4:51:32 (21,376)
Driver, Matthew G	3:49:41 (6,868)
Driver, Philip J	4:00:49 (9,378)
Driver, Richard P	5:31:00 (29,294)
Driver, Roebrt C	5:02:22 (24,008)
Drozario, Lance	4:01:17 (9,477)
Drozario, Nathan	3:49:26 (6,818)
Druitt, Thomas A	4:58:55 (23,230)
Drummond, Alan P	5:00:13 (23,557)
Drummond, Alastair C	3:55:42 (8,164)
Drummond, Christopher J	4:50:21 (21,080)
Drummond, Connell	3:02:25 (1,021)
Drummond, James A	4:26:26 (15,170)
Drummond, Samuel	3:09:08 (1,481)
Drury, Adrian J	3:48:47 (6,685)
Drury, Ian C	4:16:07 (12,602)
Drury, Stephen J	4:14:14 (12,149)
Dryden, Colin M	5:12:52 (26,014)
Drysdale, James	4:54:52 (22,238)
Du, Dafydd	3:30:20 (3,771)
Du Plessis, Jacques	4:34:25 (17,118)
Du Plessis, Jean P	4:25:23 (14,918)
Duan, Alei	3:38:17 (4,885)
Duarte Nuno, Andrade	4:02:09 (9,630)
Dubery, Robert P	6:00:51 (32,650)
Ducarre, Nicolas	4:44:36 (19,718)
Duckels, Carl	3:57:07 (8,504)
Ducker, Michael P	4:24:24 (14,681)
Duckett, Simon J	3:55:32 (8,121)
Duckgeischel, Hubertus	4:22:11 (14,121)
Duckworth, Caleb J	5:37:47 (30,269)
Duckworth, Ian J	3:42:48 (5,648)
Duckworth, Kevin P	2:49:17 (354)
Ducros, Laurent	4:08:21 (10,842)
Ducy, Jean-Pierre	3:16:11 (2,095)
Duddell, Stephen T	2:50:28 (391)
Dudden, Tom	2:58:38 (803)
Duddy, Gerard M	2:58:15 (766)
Duddy, Paul	3:46:19 (6,222)
Dudley, Dennis C	3:41:30 (5,445)
Dudley, George B	5:12:14 (25,904)
Dudley, Michael P	4:00:39 (9,345)
Dudley, Peter	5:34:15 (29,803)
Dudley, Toby A	3:38:34 (4,934)
Dudman, Richard J	4:54:55 (22,250)
Dudney, Alan G	4:49:35 (20,912)
Dudok, John	3:57:59 (8,718)
Duesterhoeft, Stefan	4:17:55 (13,047)
Dufeu, Jacques	4:21:28 (13,957)
Duff, Craig	4:44:35 (19,712)
Duff, Fraser J	4:18:51 (13,296)
Duff, Jonathan P	4:10:16 (11,222)
Duffield, Andrew	5:22:40 (27,885)
Duffield, Paul R	7:29:22 (35,479)
Duffield, Richard J	3:53:56 (7,775)
Duffy, Adam	4:49:35 (20,912)
Duffy, Andrew	4:19:00 (13,328)
Duffy, Andrew D	3:12:15 (1,750)
Duffy, Clive	4:10:16 (11,222)
Duffy, Dean	4:29:43 (16,064)
Duffy, Laurence B	3:12:44 (1,800)
Duffy, Liam J	3:37:18 (4,722)
Duffy, Mark J	5:20:06 (27,439)
Duffy, Michael J	4:42:32 (19,187)
Duffy, Michael V	4:41:35 (18,944)
Duffy, Paul	4:24:40 (14,739)
Duffy, Paul D	4:19:10 (13,370)
Duffy, Roger A	4:52:09 (21,527)
Duffy, Scott G	5:38:18 (30,360)
Duffy, William R	4:41:47 (18,989)
Duffy-Penny, Keith	4:13:18 (11,909)
Dufour, Leon	5:38:11 (30,333)
Dugan, Peter	4:43:40 (19,456)
Dugard, Kirk	4:39:48 (18,488)
Dugdale, Andrew G	4:59:04 (23,277)
Duggal, Sunil K	4:50:19 (21,070)
Duggan, David J	4:37:24 (17,862)
Duggan, James D	4:19:41 (13,504)
Duggan, John M	5:14:26 (26,318)
Duggan, Mike A	3:38:18 (4,888)
Duggan, Nicholas D	4:50:09 (21,034)

Duke, Chris A	3:12:23 (1,764)
Duke, Steven D	3:33:56 (4,258)
Duke, Trevor N	7:32:11 (35,509)
Dukelow, Steven J	3:18:14 (2,315)
Duke-Low, Simon D	5:17:02 (26,863)
Dukes, Mark C	6:06:49 (33,097)
Dukes, Nicholas J	2:52:01 (440)
Dulai, Gurjit S	4:56:25 (22,616)
Dulay, Bali S	3:59:21 (9,053)
Dulieu, Billy R	5:15:23 (26,540)
Dumas, Denis M	4:59:33 (23,399)
Dumas, Pierre	3:52:41 (7,497)
Dumbrell, Stephen D	4:44:45 (19,758)
Dumoulin, Patrice	4:09:07 (10,979)
Dumper, Simon	3:57:50 (8,677)
Dumps, Joel C	5:19:17 (27,308)
Dun, Craig	4:02:27 (9,690)
Duncalf, Matt	3:27:03 (3,290)
Duncalf, Timothy G	4:10:29 (11,261)
Duncan, Gary	5:06:59 (24,876)
Duncan, Glen E	4:06:06 (10,370)
Duncan, Mark G	3:39:48 (5,157)
Duncan, Mark R	3:25:33 (3,072)
Duncan, Matthew J	3:17:33 (2,233)
Duncker, Tim M	5:27:18 (28,677)
Dunckley, Chris	4:17:45 (13,010)
Duncombe, Andrew	3:19:52 (2,475)
Duncombe, Ian P	5:10:35 (25,591)
Dunford, Michael B	4:21:51 (14,049)
Dungate, Christopher A	4:18:18 (13,149)
Dungate, Keith S	3:31:25 (3,892)
Dunk, Christopher	5:12:07 (25,874)
Dunk, Oliver M	3:56:19 (8,307)
Dunk, Steve	5:37:41 (30,258)
Dunlea, Brian	4:45:07 (19,863)
Dunleavy, Martin	3:23:56 (2,898)
Dunlop, Barney J	4:38:03 (18,024)
Dunlop, Ian S	3:32:14 (4,036)
Dunlop, Paul	6:15:32 (33,653)
Dunlop, Shaun A	3:24:25 (2,949)
Dunn, Andrew J	4:19:27 (13,446)
Dunn, Christopher	3:03:46 (1,090)
Dunn, George	3:37:33 (4,760)
Dunn, James W	4:50:57 (21,230)
Dunn, Joseph P	3:59:52 (9,173)
Dunn, Mark J	5:06:25 (24,772)
Dunn, Mark J	8:05:53 (35,651)
Dunn, Matt	3:58:39 (8,871)
Dunn, Matthew M	4:20:49 (13,807)
Dunn, Mike J	3:34:40 (4,361)
Dunn, Peter M	4:30:22 (16,229)
Dunn, Sam	4:31:43 (16,511)
Dunn, Simon J	4:13:24 (11,936)
Dunn, Stuart C	5:27:56 (28,784)
Dunn Parrant, Glenn D	3:08:09 (1,401)
Dunnage, Niel A	4:10:08 (11,190)
Dunne, Andrew J	4:13:36 (11,996)
Dunne, Brian M	5:10:59 (25,662)
Dunne, Cormac	4:33:39 (16,947)
Dunne, Gerry A	3:34:19 (4,318)
Dunne, Kenneth B	4:29:37 (16,042)
Dunne, Michael J	5:51:26 (31,818)
Dunne, Michael P	4:57:42 (22,956)
Dunne, Paul A	4:56:30 (22,633)
Dunnett, Keith	4:35:01 (17,278)
Dunning, Adrian J	4:57:23 (22,883)
Dunning, David	4:37:56 (17,989)
Dunphy, Matthew	4:42:08 (19,073)
Dunscombe, Mark	3:14:10 (1,908)
Dunsmuir-Watts, Andrew	3:22:01 (2,708)
Dunstan, Matthew W	4:31:07 (16,386)
Dunstan, Richard E	4:58:00 (23,036)
Dunstone, Nicholas A	4:14:24 (12,189)
Duo, Elmes	4:06:46 (10,521)
Dupe, Bruce R	5:01:11 (23,768)
Dupe, Dominique	4:41:18 (18,862)
Duplock, Michael L	5:35:36 (29,996)
Dupont, Eric	3:32:26 (4,058)
Duran Carredano, Ignacio	4:32:40 (16,709)
Durante, Gareth J	4:37:32 (17,897)
Durber, Marcus L	5:10:31 (25,580)
Durbin, John	5:05:03 (24,520)
Durbin, Matthew J	3:39:18 (5,064)

Durbin, Paul M..................4:51:02 (21,248)
Durham, Neil J...................4:51:40 (21,412)
Durick, Gary I...................3:59:10 (9,003)
Durkin, Barry P.................5:15:52 (26,634)
Durkin, Glenn...................5:08:41 (25,220)
Durkin, Richard A...............3:29:29 (3,646)
Durnall, Paul M.................3:25:13 (3,039)
Durrani, Amer J.................5:14:30 (26,334)
Durrant, James M...............3:59:23 (9,065)
Durrant, James R................3:51:55 (7,342)
Durrant, Mark R.................4:32:08 (16,591)
Durrant, Martin A...............4:38:32 (18,159)
Durrant, Matthew R.............4:16:10 (12,612)
Durrant, Richard...............4:06:47 (10,526)
Dursley, Paul W.................4:00:07 (9,230)
Dussaux, Eric...................4:07:33 (10,662)
Duston, Andrew J................4:14:58 (12,313)
Dutfield, Martyn G..............5:47:29 (31,407)
Dutfield, Peter C...............4:26:18 (15,130)
Dutfield, Robert J..............4:24:30 (14,704)
Duthie, Ian S...................5:14:20 (26,300)
Dutnall, Julian R...............5:14:17 (26,288)
Dutton, Alex J..................4:37:09 (17,814)
Dutton, Jack....................4:22:21 (14,164)
Dutton, John R..................5:26:52 (28,602)
Dutton, Paul J..................4:27:37 (15,493)
Dutton, Peter G.................5:01:03 (23,739)
Dutton, Richard E...............4:50:35 (21,145)
Dutton, Timothy N..............4:03:40 (9,896)
Duxfield, Robin................5:28:17 (28,858)
Dvergsnes, Erik................4:07:14 (10,611)
Dwyer, John B..................3:40:01 (5,192)
Dwyer, John W..................6:25:44 (34,159)
Dwyer, Kevin J.................5:46:03 (31,266)
Dyce, Craig S..................3:07:58 (1,385)
Dyckes, John J.................3:28:29 (3,483)
Dyde, Alasdair L...............4:51:26 (21,352)
Dye, Neeriem T.................5:51:48 (31,855)
Dye, Richard J.................3:30:55 (3,831)
Dyer, John B...................5:20:22 (27,488)
Dyer, Kevin....................4:58:38 (23,176)
Dyer, Robert...................4:13:11 (11,874)
Dyer, Simon A..................7:25:15 (35,432)
Dyke, Alan J...................5:34:57 (29,907)
Dymond, Garry..................3:40:29 (5,261)
Dymond, Huw C..................4:26:30 (15,195)
Dymond, Sam....................5:01:32 (23,835)
Dyson, Andrew I................3:59:22 (9,061)
Dyson, Graham..................4:19:25 (13,436)
Dyson, Neil R..................6:33:46 (34,457)
Dyson, Nicholas A..............3:14:32 (1,947)
Dyson, Phillip A...............4:25:36 (14,970)
Dyson, Stephen E...............6:00:56 (32,661)
Eacock, Les A..................4:45:36 (19,967)
Eager, Christian B.............4:33:09 (16,823)
Eagle, Paul G..................4:19:39 (13,494)
Eagles, Graham R...............4:17:44 (13,006)
Eagles, John M.................5:27:54 (28,780)
Eaglesham, Spencer F...........6:13:35 (33,529)
Eaglestone, Jason M............3:25:24 (3,055)
Eaglestone, William............4:27:07 (15,357)
Eales, Darryl..................5:07:30 (24,999)
Eames, John S..................5:06:42 (24,817)
Eames, Michael.................4:01:00 (9,420)
Eardley, Neil..................4:44:10 (19,587)
Earl, David....................5:12:50 (26,005)
Earl, David W..................5:00:41 (23,652)
Earl, Dennis...................3:38:08 (4,860)
Earl, Jonathan R...............4:17:42 (12,996)
Earle, Douglas.................5:37:14 (30,203)
Earle, Stuart C................3:33:17 (4,176)
Earley, James J................4:39:34 (18,427)
Earnshaw, Paul F...............4:19:42 (13,510)
Earnshaw, Philip A.............6:20:20 (33,909)
Earp, Kenneth E................5:23:56 (28,097)
Eason, Adam D..................3:48:59 (6,729)
Eason, Benjamin J..............3:41:45 (5,479)
Eason, Simon D.................5:09:04 (25,289)
Easson, James M................3:19:08 (2,408)
East, David A..................6:22:20 (34,014)
East, Gordon R.................3:47:13 (6,381)
East, Grant P..................3:43:10 (5,720)
East, Richard..................5:39:29 (30,523)

Eastabrook, Paul J.............4:51:28 (21,363)
Eastaff, John..................5:21:24 (27,680)
Easterbrook, Steven J..........3:53:23 (7,660)
Eastes, Steven J...............5:34:30 (29,851)
Eastham, Fred..................4:42:03 (19,054)
Eastham, John M................4:19:34 (13,471)
Eastham, Theo A................4:44:40 (19,734)
Eastman, John..................3:20:33 (2,562)
Easto, Simon P.................3:45:39 (6,125)
Easton, Andrew.................3:25:39 (3,083)
Easton, Edmund R...............3:53:04 (7,582)
Eastwood, Colin R..............6:02:11 (32,761)
Eastwood, Robert L.............4:27:05 (15,350)
Eastwood, Sean B...............5:00:52 (23,704)
Eat, Raymond P.................3:27:11 (3,308)
Eaton, Andrew C................5:11:17 (25,714)
Eaton, Gareth R................4:29:51 (16,110)
Eaton, John D..................6:00:50 (32,648)
Eaton, Kevin...................5:45:15 (31,177)
Eaton, Kevin P.................5:21:59 (27,778)
Eaton, Matthew.................4:24:26 (14,691)
Eaton, Michael T...............4:07:21 (10,626)
Eaton, Nick....................4:02:43 (9,733)
Eaton, Paul J..................5:16:48 (26,805)
Eaton, Peter R.................5:02:03 (23,943)
Eaton, Simon A.................3:43:39 (5,805)
Eaton, Stephen D...............6:20:39 (33,936)
Eaves, Sean A..................5:32:50 (29,582)
Eavis, Winston H...............4:51:11 (21,281)
Ebbage, Peter R................4:01:27 (9,506)
Ebbage, Richard J..............5:22:29 (27,844)
Ebner, Martin..................3:32:42 (4,096)
Eccles, Antony D...............5:31:25 (29,367)
Eccles, David N................4:09:32 (11,080)
Eccleston, John S..............3:12:28 (1,775)
Eckersley, Neil................5:41:51 (30,814)
Eckett, Simon M................5:09:52 (25,444)
Eckford, Matthew A.............4:22:49 (14,290)
Ecob, Richard..................4:44:40 (19,734)
Eddolls, Haldon................4:02:09 (9,630)
Eddy, Antony S.................4:47:16 (20,347)
Ede, Alistair..................4:20:21 (13,697)
Ede, David G...................5:22:27 (27,841)
Ede, Russ......................5:19:42 (27,373)
Ede, Stuart J..................4:21:43 (14,009)
Edecox, Robert J...............5:37:11 (30,195)
Edelmann, Anton S..............4:59:26 (23,359)
Edgar, Ian J...................4:52:25 (21,600)
Edgar, John....................5:46:25 (31,302)
Edgar, Ross R..................4:17:57 (13,058)
Edgar, Simon...................3:30:41 (3,805)
Edgcumbe, Neil.................7:03:34 (35,184)
Edge, Chris....................4:05:10 (10,179)
Edge, Daniel...................4:57:46 (22,973)
Edge, Michael..................4:16:53 (12,778)
Edge, Shane D..................3:38:16 (4,883)
Edgeworth, Brett I.............3:00:53 (948)
Edlin, David A.................5:05:07 (24,530)
Edlin, Mark S..................4:35:05 (17,291)
Edmeades, Allan J..............4:49:46 (20,947)
Edmond, Michael J..............4:11:18 (11,448)
Edmond, Paul C.................4:15:17 (12,391)
Edmonds, Benjamin..............3:37:01 (4,689)
Edmonds, Gary N................3:43:50 (5,835)
Edmonds, Joe...................4:19:39 (13,494)
Edmondson, Colin J.............6:02:52 (32,812)
Edmondson, Keith M.............4:51:37 (21,402)
Edmunds, Michael J.............4:20:01 (13,602)
Edmunds, Richard J.............4:06:48 (10,530)
Edney, Alan....................5:09:59 (25,473)
Edney, Lewis...................5:11:34 (25,773)
Edwards, Adrian................3:42:03 (5,529)
Edwards, Alan R................4:48:10 (20,566)
Edwards, Barry.................3:49:38 (6,858)
Edwards, Christopher D.........4:53:55 (21,997)
Edwards, Colin.................4:36:49 (17,747)
Edwards, Craig S...............4:21:46 (14,025)
Edwards, Darren C..............3:26:16 (3,169)
Edwards, Darren M..............3:08:41 (1,444)
Edwards, David A...............4:00:03 (9,216)
Edwards, David A...............4:14:21 (12,175)
Edwards, David C...............4:16:56 (12,798)
Edwards, David F...............3:08:54 (1,458)

Edwards, Duncan P..............5:36:24 (30,097)
Edwards, Gavin P...............5:16:12 (26,700)
Edwards, Geoffrey P............5:14:32 (26,344)
Edwards, Geraint V.............5:02:21 (24,001)
Edwards, Ian M.................4:26:58 (15,314)
Edwards, Ieuan R...............4:53:44 (21,950)
Edwards, Jason A...............5:27:33 (28,719)
Edwards, Jeremy S..............3:43:54 (5,850)
Edwards, Joe J.................4:10:08 (11,190)
Edwards, Jonathan I............4:00:28 (9,303)
Edwards, Julian................6:47:45 (34,880)
Edwards, Kevin D...............3:21:25 (2,641)
Edwards, Mark..................3:00:24 (924)
Edwards, Mark A................4:16:36 (12,716)
Edwards, Mark A................5:49:22 (31,616)
Edwards, Matthew R.............6:14:22 (33,572)
Edwards, Neil S................3:16:12 (2,096)
Edwards, Paul A................3:54:39 (7,934)
Edwards, Paul G................6:43:10 (34,755)
Edwards, Paul K................3:37:01 (4,689)
Edwards, Paul T................4:48:04 (20,547)
Edwards, Peter A...............4:44:37 (19,720)
Edwards, Peter R...............4:17:11 (12,871)
Edwards, Phillip J.............5:18:19 (27,128)
Edwards, Richard D.............5:10:09 (25,517)
Edwards, Richard G.............3:48:30 (6,619)
Edwards, Robert S..............3:19:43 (2,457)
Edwards, Robert T..............4:59:28 (23,369)
Edwards, Ross..................3:55:55 (8,212)
Edwards, Samuel I..............4:28:44 (15,796)
Edwards, Stephen P.............3:22:04 (2,711)
Edwards, Steve.................3:12:44 (1,800)
Edwards, Stuart J..............5:42:24 (30,867)
Edwards, Terry P...............4:49:05 (20,789)
Edwards, Thomas P..............3:42:42 (5,627)
Edwards, William...............3:21:48 (2,685)
Efthimiou, Panikos.............4:02:41 (9,725)
Egan, David J..................5:10:35 (25,591)
Egan, John P...................3:49:59 (6,934)
Egan, Paul.....................3:28:27 (3,471)
Egan, Peter G..................3:47:13 (6,381)
Egan, Thomas M.................4:17:34 (12,969)
Egedesoe, Klaus................4:40:44 (18,706)
Egelie, Edward C...............3:19:00 (2,392)
Egelie, Norbert C..............4:17:21 (12,895)
Egers, Marco...................4:47:39 (20,441)
Eggar, Christopher N...........4:25:48 (15,018)
Eggbeer, Peter K...............3:28:24 (3,462)
Eggett, Christopher J..........3:48:16 (6,568)
Eggleston, Peter...............3:26:48 (3,240)
Eggleton, Bernard J............3:47:11 (6,375)
Eguia, Felix...................3:52:44 (7,511)
Ehlert, Thomas.................4:05:10 (10,179)
Ehren, Gary R..................4:27:14 (15,400)
Eichelmann, Eckhard............5:07:45 (25,044)
Eichin, Uwe....................3:39:56 (5,179)
Eickelberg, Jan M..............4:23:04 (14,348)
Eide, Knut N...................4:12:01 (11,617)
Eidelman, Raymond..............4:31:50 (16,533)
Einarsson, Arni E..............4:02:13 (9,652)
Einarsson, Jens G..............4:07:02 (10,580)
Eisenhofer, Alexis.............3:27:58 (3,403)
Ek, Anders.....................4:32:03 (16,569)
El Kardoudi, Said..............4:13:11 (11,874)
El Mansouri, Nabil.............3:05:42 (1,217)
Elam, Tom......................4:33:10 (16,830)
El-Atribi, Omar I..............3:41:32 (5,447)
Eldred, Nigel..................4:39:44 (18,471)
Eldrett, Christian A...........4:50:05 (21,020)
Eldridge, Darren L.............4:47:03 (20,299)
Eldridge, Joshua P.............3:27:09 (3,302)
Eldridge, Thomas C.............3:33:40 (4,224)
Eley, David C..................4:54:40 (22,190)
Eley, Nick G...................4:20:40 (13,768)
Elfant, David J................5:44:22 (31,082)
Elgohary, Mostafa..............5:14:06 (26,247)
Elhag, Omar M..................5:01:04 (23,745)
El-Hamamsy, Ismail.............3:29:04 (3,583)
Elia, Charlie..................5:49:04 (31,593)
Elia, Nick.....................5:42:14 (30,856)
Elias, Elyn B..................5:18:36 (27,180)
Elias, Simon J.................4:44:49 (19,784)
Elkan, Stephen.................4:20:48 (13,799)

LONDON MARATHON, 2007: MALE RUNNERS 833

Elkerton, Andrew P......4:38:04 (18,028)
Elkhadraoui, Anouar......5:20:10 (27,449)
Elkhadraoui, Aziz......4:19:27 (13,446)
Elkhadraoui, Mohamed......5:53:50 (32,037)
Elkihel, Abderazzak......3:32:05 (4,004)
Elkington, Jason E......3:12:32 (1,782)
Elkins, John B......5:32:49 (29,581)
Ellard, Matthew J......4:40:50 (18,740)
Ellender, Mark J......7:48:03 (35,611)
Ellesser, Joerg......4:19:14 (13,387)
Ellett, Ryan......4:53:17 (21,831)
Ellice, Simon......3:50:16 (6,991)
Ellice, William A......4:26:47 (15,260)
Ellingham, Mark A......3:30:25 (3,779)
Ellingham, Simon R......4:23:42 (14,490)
Ellingsen, Michael J......3:44:53 (6,007)
Elliot, Kenton R......4:00:05 (9,224)
Elliot, Kevin......4:43:51 (19,497)
Elliot, Robin C......4:00:00 (9,208)
Elliott, Andy J......3:59:08 (8,992)
Elliott, Chris......4:25:49 (15,022)
Elliott, David......5:26:01 (28,458)
Elliott, James G......6:21:07 (33,962)
Elliott, Joe V......3:40:47 (5,318)
Elliott, Jonathan P......5:18:03 (27,068)
Elliott, Jonathan P......5:30:12 (29,177)
Elliott, Keith......4:00:37 (9,337)
Elliott, Mark C......3:22:41 (2,764)
Elliott, Matthew J......3:48:06 (6,543)
Elliott, Neill A......3:19:09 (2,409)
Elliott, Paul F......4:14:23 (12,183)
Elliott, Richard J......3:37:58 (4,826)
Elliott, Ross A......5:05:21 (24,564)
Elliott, Simon G......3:21:37 (2,663)
Elliott, Simon L......5:15:11 (26,495)
Elliott, Steven J......3:56:00 (8,226)
Elliott, Thomas......7:29:40 (35,493)
Ellis, Andrew J......3:30:47 (3,817)
Ellis, Benjamin......6:13:38 (33,531)
Ellis, Carl......3:02:51 (1,042)
Ellis, Dan......3:49:29 (6,827)
Ellis, Darren J......3:45:26 (6,088)
Ellis, Dave H......4:05:38 (10,273)
Ellis, David A......4:57:50 (22,995)
Ellis, Edward J......4:10:50 (11,335)
Ellis, Gareth S......3:13:56 (1,897)
Ellis, Garry E......5:12:39 (25,974)
Ellis, Grant......4:49:31 (20,892)
Ellis, Jack......5:03:53 (24,305)
Ellis, John......4:55:22 (22,353)
Ellis, Kevan P......3:30:14 (3,753)
Ellis, Mark R......5:29:56 (29,124)
Ellis, Michael......7:31:00 (35,502)
Ellis, Michael C......5:27:45 (28,754)
Ellis, Mike......3:58:47 (8,906)
Ellis, Ralph......4:44:29 (19,677)
Ellis, Ralph R......4:23:56 (14,549)
Ellis, Richard F......5:00:52 (23,704)
Ellis, Samuel J......4:49:13 (20,824)
Ellis, Simon J......7:01:39 (35,152)
Ellis, Simon K......4:25:23 (14,918)
Ellis, Stephen D......5:16:31 (26,759)
Ellis, Steve......4:05:47 (10,304)
Ellis, Tim......2:48:23 (325)
Ellis, Tony......3:48:52 (6,697)
Ellis, Vince......3:24:38 (2,976)
Ellis-Jones, Thomas D......4:28:25 (15,707)
Ellis-Keeler, Christopher J......5:09:32 (25,381)
Ellison, Andrew J......2:51:51 (435)
Ellison, Ray J......6:18:44 (33,821)
Ellison, Robert G......4:07:31 (10,655)
Ellison, Wayne A......5:16:53 (26,835)
Ellison, Zachary......5:33:37 (29,705)
Elliston, Robert W......4:24:10 (14,622)
Ellithorn, Mark R......3:18:46 (2,364)
Ellsbury, Stuart J......3:58:49 (8,913)
Ellson, Matthew J......3:40:18 (5,231)
Ellson, Michael......5:46:46 (31,330)
Ellsworth, Stuart A......4:50:35 (21,145)
Ellwood, Jamie J......5:56:42 (32,308)
Ellwood, John H......5:17:55 (27,036)
Ellwood, Tim J......3:48:27 (6,608)
Elmer, Christopher A......6:22:03 (33,998)

Elmes, George......4:13:15 (11,896)
Elmhirst, Tristram R......3:55:05 (8,026)
Elms, Michael R......4:15:22 (12,411)
Elms, Nicholas R......3:54:08 (7,823)
Elms, Robert J......5:11:06 (25,687)
Elsby, Dominic A......2:41:24 (164)
Elscey, Kevin M......7:20:17 (35,391)
Else, Richard A......4:11:20 (11,456)
Elsmere, Alan F......3:24:31 (2,957)
Elsmore, Nigel R......3:56:49 (8,435)
Elson, Nigel C......3:24:35 (2,968)
Elston, David C......5:36:59 (30,170)
Elton, Paul B......4:29:37 (16,042)
Elvin, Jonathan......4:27:11 (15,381)
Elwell, Kenneth J......6:16:24 (33,712)
Elwell, Thomas W......5:52:43 (31,941)
Elwick, Peter M......5:32:37 (29,551)
Elworthy, Christopher C......4:27:38 (15,498)
Emanuel, Geoffrey......4:47:07 (20,317)
Emanuel, Llyr......3:53:18 (7,641)
Embiricos, Nicholas S......4:24:37 (14,733)
Embling, Jonathan D......3:09:43 (1,533)
Emeny, Matthew......6:37:56 (34,603)
Emeny, Simon......3:32:03 (3,995)
Emerson, Alastair......4:54:16 (22,095)
Emerson, Bruce M......3:14:25 (1,935)
Emery, Brian G......6:12:47 (33,478)
Emery, Daniel S......3:22:45 (2,769)
Emery, David W......5:22:29 (27,844)
Emery, Graham......5:17:21 (26,927)
Emery, Michael P......3:52:04 (7,386)
Emery, Nathan T......3:55:45 (8,175)
Emery, Paul S......4:46:03 (20,070)
Emery, Peter K......3:17:35 (2,237)
Emery, Peter M......5:35:18 (29,953)
Emery, Robert P......4:36:44 (17,723)
Emes, Mark......3:44:05 (5,878)
Emm, Martin J......3:57:07 (8,504)
Emment, Phillip D......5:27:19 (28,682)
Emmerson, Anthony H......4:04:54 (10,129)
Emmerson, Bob......5:05:15 (24,549)
Emmerson, John Paul......5:15:51 (26,630)
Emmerson, Steven G......3:47:54 (6,512)
Emmett, Edward......4:29:15 (15,926)
Emmett, William J......3:53:04 (7,582)
Emos, Filipe......3:40:00 (5,189)
Emoto, Yoshikazu......5:08:50 (25,247)
Emperor, David J......3:31:48 (3,954)
Empson, Robert J......4:49:43 (20,936)
Emtage, James N......4:39:54 (18,508)
Enaloei, Mohammad......3:34:46 (4,371)
Engel, Jorgen......4:07:07 (10,595)
Engelbrecht, Jacus......3:58:14 (8,772)
Engelmann, Paul M......4:20:57 (13,840)
England, Daryn J......4:46:58 (20,269)
England, John R......5:27:17 (28,675)
England, Nicholas P......3:10:05 (1,569)
England, Russell......4:46:57 (20,267)
Englert, Thomas......3:40:50 (5,329)
English, Robert J......3:48:28 (6,612)
English, Tony......4:24:10 (14,622)
Ennion, Matthew J......2:59:02 (827)
Ennis, Kevin M......3:37:46 (4,784)
Enock, Eric B......4:53:56 (22,000)
Enright, Edward F......4:09:33 (11,085)
Enright, Ger......4:58:13 (23,080)
Enright, Paul J......3:40:20 (5,240)
Entwistle, James......4:19:44 (13,520)
Entwistle, Simon G......4:14:13 (12,141)
Enujioke, Emmanuel A......4:40:40 (18,694)
Enville, Paul......6:32:16 (34,419)
Eperon, Alastair D......3:36:30 (4,609)
Epps, Terry A......3:11:38 (1,690)
Epsom, Joseph H......4:52:34 (21,629)
Ericcson, Ivan E......4:33:12 (16,846)
Eriksen, Joergen S......4:50:22 (21,087)

Erikson, Tore......3:32:53 (4,118)
Ernalsteen, Philip......4:01:57 (9,594)
Ernst, Kurt......3:48:16 (6,568)
Errington, John......3:35:18 (4,449)
Erskine, Andrew K......3:39:05 (5,030)
Erskine, Grant S......3:20:40 (2,573)
Erskine, Kevin A......2:57:50 (733)
Erwin, Ben......4:11:45 (11,558)
Eslick, Leigh......5:18:05 (27,074)
Esmeraldo, Alexandre P......4:23:43 (14,493)
Esnault, Loic......3:38:31 (4,924)
Espiritusanto, José A......4:26:38 (15,218)
Essex, Francis-John......4:43:51 (19,497)
Essex, Richard......3:24:01 (2,905)
Esson, Stephen G......5:12:44 (25,990)
Essoufi, Driss......4:46:27 (20,166)
Esterhuizen, Philip......5:26:51 (28,599)
Esthofer, Gustav......3:26:26 (3,190)
Estrada, German J......3:58:37 (8,857)
Estrade, Daniel......4:25:04 (14,837)
Esward, Sam......3:44:31 (5,945)
Etchegoinberry, Rodolphe......3:27:55 (3,398)
Etchells, Kevin......3:33:16 (4,174)
Etchells, Robert P......3:28:10 (3,430)
Etheridge, Brian R......4:36:04 (17,549)
Etheridge, Desmond......5:11:12 (25,703)
Etheridge, Paul A......3:38:58 (5,009)
Etherington, Stephen P......4:42:24 (19,152)
Etherton, Tom......4:32:38 (16,701)
Evan-Hughes, Jonathan D......4:11:03 (11,383)
Evans, Aaron......6:29:02 (34,285)
Evans, Aled M......3:29:08 (3,593)
Evans, Alun......5:34:29 (29,845)
Evans, Andrew......4:07:35 (10,676)
Evans, Anthony J......5:16:59 (26,855)
Evans, Anthony R......3:51:18 (7,202)
Evans, Benjamin R......4:03:19 (9,835)
Evans, Bernard H......4:46:53 (20,247)
Evans, Chris......5:16:36 (26,771)
Evans, Christopher D......6:09:26 (33,264)
Evans, Christopher J......4:17:20 (12,887)
Evans, Christopher J......4:42:27 (19,164)
Evans, Christopher M......3:31:50 (3,959)
Evans, Clive E......3:51:56 (7,351)
Evans, Colin C......3:45:32 (6,097)
Evans, Daniel......2:58:17 (770)
Evans, Daniel......4:29:10 (15,900)
Evans, Daniel S......3:18:10 (2,306)
Evans, Daniel S......6:06:32 (33,080)
Evans, Daren J......4:18:30 (13,211)
Evans, David......3:39:32 (5,113)
Evans, David I......5:04:50 (24,476)
Evans, David M......5:15:44 (26,612)
Evans, Declan......6:19:36 (33,868)
Evans, Edwin......3:39:13 (5,048)
Evans, Frank C......3:40:30 (5,266)
Evans, Gareth C......3:32:32 (4,076)
Evans, Gareth J......4:12:37 (11,743)
Evans, Gary E......3:48:37 (6,648)
Evans, Gavin M......2:59:46 (883)
Evans, Geraint W......3:51:10 (7,177)
Evans, Gerald H......3:27:01 (3,286)
Evans, Gerald R......4:57:05 (22,792)
Evans, Glyn......3:35:40 (4,508)
Evans, Glyn R......3:13:09 (1,831)
Evans, Guy M......3:48:39 (6,656)
Evans, Gwyn W......3:42:17 (5,566)
Evans, Gwynn M......5:28:04 (28,812)
Evans, Harford......3:34:42 (4,365)
Evans, Harri L......4:21:08 (13,882)
Evans, Iain J......4:10:40 (11,307)
Evans, Ian......5:35:04 (29,922)
Evans, Ian E......3:51:13 (7,191)
Evans, Iolo......4:26:33 (15,205)
Evans, Jason T......4:13:42 (12,018)
Evans, Jeffrey......4:54:11 (22,076)
Evans, John A......4:38:46 (18,220)
Evans, John B......3:33:22 (4,191)
Evans, John C......3:33:56 (4,258)
Evans, John D......4:56:39 (22,679)
Evans, John E......3:45:59 (6,176)
Evans, John E......5:44:00 (31,042)
Evans, John L......3:51:07 (7,161)

Feltham, Ellis L 5:25:09 (28,297)
Felton, Daniel P 4:19:33 (13,469)
Felton, David J 3:12:36 (1,789)
Felton, Keith D 4:16:34 (12,708)
Fender, Richard J 5:42:44 (30,898)
Fender, Tom H 3:48:28 (6,612)
Fendley, Peter A 3:24:41 (2,984)
Fenick, William T 4:49:08 (20,803)
Fenn, David T 6:55:04 (35,036)
Fenn, Nigel R 3:53:52 (7,757)
Fennell, David A 3:51:20 (7,208)
Fennell, Martin L 3:37:50 (4,794)
Fennell, Sean P 3:58:27 (8,822)
Fenner, Damon R 3:02:25 (1,021)
Fenner, Martin R 4:58:04 (23,050)
Fennessy, Sean 6:04:34 (32,921)
Fenney, Steven 3:06:09 (1,242)
Fensome, Garry C 4:32:07 (16,584)
Fenson, Graham R 3:59:59 (9,205)
Fenston, Edward F 4:19:57 (13,589)
Fentham-Fletcher, Simon 5:05:49 (24,657)
Fenton, Richard J 5:02:42 (24,078)
Fenton, Tom 4:53:52 (21,980)
Fenwick, Dale K 5:12:35 (25,965)
Fenwick, Gary J 4:16:49 (12,765)
Fenwick, Paul K 5:07:50 (25,066)
Fereday, David H 4:06:32 (10,471)
Ferenczy, Peter D 3:09:14 (1,496)
Ferguson, Andrew M 3:46:40 (6,277)
Ferguson, Antony C 3:57:28 (8,594)
Ferguson, Carl A 3:30:15 (3,758)
Ferguson, David A 4:26:41 (15,238)
Ferguson, Ian C 5:15:42 (26,602)
Ferguson, John 5:29:59 (29,129)
Ferguson, John W 3:26:02 (3,133)
Ferguson, Kenneth A 5:06:30 (24,784)
Ferguson, Mark 4:12:21 (11,690)
Ferguson, Samuel 5:03:45 (24,282)
Ferguson, Sandy 4:52:57 (21,742)
Ferguson, William 3:58:11 (8,755)
Fermie, Peter G 5:14:28 (26,328)
Fermor, Nicholas R 5:46:55 (31,348)
Fernandes, Charles V 6:36:12 (34,543)
Fernandes, Joe 5:00:43 (23,664)
Fernandes, Luis F 4:39:09 (18,320)
Fernandez, Arturo 3:15:19 (2,021)
Fernandez, John 5:04:23 (24,399)
Fernandez, Manuel A 6:22:50 (34,037)
Fernandez, Matthew J 5:47:09 (31,364)
Fernandez, Wesley D 6:11:01 (33,371)
Fernie, Ken J 3:47:55 (6,514)
Ferrao, Julian D 2:42:53 (197)
Ferrar, Ian 5:41:01 (30,710)
Ferrara-Forbes, Patrick 4:58:49 (23,211)
Ferrarini, Graziano 3:59:19 (9,045)
Ferreira, Alcides 4:50:51 (21,204)
Ferreira, Dimas A 4:06:32 (10,471)
Ferrett, Christopher S 4:57:27 (22,896)
Ferriday, Ernest J 5:17:30 (26,958)
Ferrigno, Robson 3:32:51 (4,115)
Ferris, Graham A 4:05:01 (10,147)
Ferris, Ian J 3:50:21 (7,013)
Ferris, Martin R 4:59:51 (23,467)
Festa, Felice 3:58:46 (8,903)
Fetherston, Christopher E 5:32:50 (29,582)
Fetherston, Richard W 5:26:22 (28,524)
Feuvrier, Philippe 4:33:30 (16,911)
Few, Bradley 4:26:49 (15,270)
Fewell, Darren A 4:44:07 (19,568)
Fhima, Meyer 4:43:57 (19,520)
Ficheux, Damien 4:43:22 (19,397)
Ficuccilli, Fabrizio 5:08:49 (25,244)
Fiddes, Mark 4:43:01 (19,300)
Fiddes, Paul 5:02:18 (23,988)
Fiddis, Richard W 4:19:23 (13,427)
Fiddy, Jonathan O 5:24:05 (28,120)
Fidler, Michael I 4:44:51 (19,791)
Field, Andrew E 3:23:52 (2,888)
Field, Ashleigh K 3:13:25 (1,859)
Field, Brian J 5:35:07 (29,929)
Field, Christopher L 4:11:08 (11,407)
Field, David 4:58:36 (23,166)
Field, Donald A 3:41:05 (5,378)
Field, Ivan 3:10:33 (1,598)
Field, Lee-Paul 3:11:03 (1,637)
Field, Nicholas G 3:48:00 (6,526)
Field, Paul D 2:59:24 (854)
Field, Paul W 6:03:22 (32,842)
Field, Robert D 5:10:48 (25,628)
Field, Robert M 4:01:16 (9,474)
Field, Stephen P 3:27:47 (3,385)
Field, Terry C 4:27:12 (15,387)
Field, Tim 6:08:43 (33,220)
Fielden, Nicholas J 4:18:02 (13,083)
Fielder, James 4:33:13 (16,852)
Fielder, Raymond 4:32:36 (16,690)
Fieldgrass, Victor 6:53:37 (35,009)
Fielding, Ian L 4:49:31 (20,892)
Fielding, Michael 4:53:25 (21,868)
Fielding, Simon 3:08:58 (1,466)
Field-Johnson, Anthony R 4:54:56 (22,254)
Fifield, Stephen W 5:40:29 (30,650)
Figgins, David M 6:47:52 (34,885)
Figgitt, Richard W 3:59:28 (9,087)
Fildes, Richard P 3:50:05 (6,960)
Fillery, Craig M 4:27:04 (15,345)
Filmer, Graham 4:20:14 (13,660)
Filmer, Greg P 5:05:29 (24,600)
Filtness, Paul M 4:18:51 (13,296)
Finch, David M 3:16:40 (2,141)
Finch, Ernie J 4:03:52 (9,939)
Finch, Glen M 5:08:00 (25,093)
Finch, Paul B 3:19:03 (2,397)
Finch, Peter 4:08:03 (10,778)
Finch, Peter S 6:08:39 (33,215)
Finch, Robert A 5:02:30 (24,040)
Finch, Simon 4:27:59 (15,582)
Finch, Stephen P 4:04:49 (10,116)
Findlay, Gary S 5:56:15 (32,263)
Findlay, Samuel D 5:16:00 (26,662)
Findlay, Scott J 4:50:44 (21,172)
Findley, Iain J 6:14:57 (33,610)
Fine, Adam 4:59:56 (23,484)
Fine, Jon 4:24:12 (14,630)
Fine, Martin H 4:07:35 (10,676)
Fine, Yoni 6:15:07 (33,625)
Finegan, Timothy 4:13:41 (12,014)
Fineron, Alan G 4:11:21 (11,459)
Finerty, Bernard F 4:17:52 (13,034)
Finill, Chris T 2:49:04 (347)
Finill, Thomas 4:12:12 (11,655)
Finlay, David B 4:08:50 (10,928)
Finlay, Douglas K 4:25:58 (15,049)
Finlay, Jim 4:33:49 (16,995)
Finlay, Malcolm C 3:38:45 (4,967)
Finlay, Stewart 4:08:52 (10,937)
Finlay-Newton, Richard J 5:32:31 (29,533)
Finley, Aidan M 5:10:53 (25,641)
Finn, Allan G 4:45:35 (19,962)
Finn, Andrew M 2:38:44 (120)
Finn, Julian A 5:10:58 (25,660)
Finn, Peter J 4:04:26 (10,045)
Finn, Stephen 4:28:40 (15,780)
Finn, Stephen P 4:45:11 (19,884)
Finnegan, Samuel G 5:00:42 (23,661)
Finnegan, Stephen M 4:24:48 (14,777)
Finney, Paul J 5:03:01 (24,129)
Fiol, Stewart C 4:35:39 (17,440)
Fiorini, Francesco 4:28:22 (15,689)
Firdion, Denis 3:54:02 (7,799)
Firman, Martin I 5:23:23 (27,988)
Firouzi, Mazeyar 2:54:27 (542)
Firth, Alistair 3:28:58 (3,569)
Firth, Bryan 5:25:33 (28,379)
Firth, Malcolm R 4:25:38 (14,977)
Fischer, Martin 2:58:21 (775)
Fish, Ben R 3:14:37 (1,956)
Fish, Ian 5:20:27 (27,504)
Fish, Matthew S 5:16:40 (26,784)
Fish, Tom F 3:33:38 (4,220)
Fishbourne, James R 3:51:35 (7,274)
Fisher, Adam N 5:13:26 (26,110)
Fisher, Alistair R 4:48:47 (20,717)
Fisher, Brian A 4:11:26 (11,486)
Fisher, Damian R 3:55:48 (8,185)
Fisher, Derek G 6:09:42 (33,285)
Fisher, Dominic F 4:05:34 (10,256)
Fisher, Ian 4:01:28 (9,510)
Fisher, Ian M 3:28:05 (3,416)
Fisher, Ian R 2:31:01 (46)
Fisher, James A 4:29:14 (15,924)
Fisher, James W 4:29:13 (15,915)
Fisher, Jason R 4:14:43 (12,260)
Fisher, John D 4:45:48 (20,007)
Fisher, Julian C 3:54:36 (7,921)
Fisher, Lee J 5:52:32 (31,921)
Fisher, Martin J 3:20:51 (2,591)
Fisher, Michael 5:21:45 (27,741)
Fisher, Michael J 7:29:15 (35,472)
Fisher, Neil M 3:53:49 (7,746)
Fisher, Neil R 5:23:40 (28,044)
Fisher, Nicholas C 3:46:53 (6,318)
Fisher, Richard P 6:09:52 (33,297)
Fisher, Robert P 5:33:04 (29,612)
Fisher, Stephen 3:48:54 (6,703)
Fisher, Stephen R 4:51:07 (21,271)
Fisher, Tim B 4:01:08 (9,444)
Fisher, Tony R 5:57:59 (32,412)
Fisher-Pascall, Kenneth G 6:04:07 (32,896)
Fishlock, Dave J 4:24:01 (14,576)
Fishlock, David J 5:56:03 (32,242)
Fishwick, Guy 4:51:17 (21,307)
Fishwick, John 4:47:30 (20,407)
Fishwick, Sam J 4:36:35 (17,689)
Fisne, Gerard 3:29:41 (3,671)
Fitch, Adam T 3:28:57 (3,565)
Fitch, Andrew 3:46:19 (6,222)
Fitch, Gregory C 5:35:23 (29,965)
Fitch, Ian R 4:48:34 (20,663)
Fitch, Simon C 4:38:29 (18,146)
Fitt, Norman R 5:18:09 (27,091)
Fitz, Colin D 4:42:49 (19,260)
Fitzgerald, Colin M 6:27:32 (34,233)
Fitzgerald, James W 5:47:51 (31,444)
Fitzgerald, Lloyd C 4:55:03 (22,274)
Fitzgerald, Loman 5:42:42 (30,896)
Fitzgerald, Michael 4:42:02 (19,047)
Fitzgerald, Michael D 5:24:22 (28,168)
Fitzgerald, Richard 4:30:15 (16,210)
Fitzgerald-O'Connor, Henry L 4:37:31 (17,892)
Fitzgibbon, Francis 4:03:40 (9,896)
Fitzgibbon, John F 4:45:08 (19,867)
Fitzgibbon, Robin 3:26:56 (3,265)
Fitzherbert, Richard G 3:56:47 (8,428)
Fitzjohn, Graeme E 4:21:08 (13,882)
Fitzjohn, Malcolm G 5:31:22 (29,355)
Fitzmaurice, James P 4:24:14 (14,638)
Fitzpatrick, Anthony J 5:22:10 (27,804)
Fitzpatrick, John P 4:44:57 (19,820)
Fitzpatrick, N 5:38:55 (30,443)
Fitzpatrick, Richard D 4:45:00 (19,836)
Fitzsimmons, Paul 5:40:44 (30,675)
Flack, Alan A 4:19:41 (13,504)
Flaherty, Adrian I 4:27:12 (15,387)
Flaherty, Danny A 6:11:58 (33,424)
Flaherty, Michael A 3:33:08 (4,158)
Flaherty, Patrick S 5:38:59 (30,450)
Flaherty, Peter F 5:49:10 (31,601)
Flanagan, Brian J 3:36:30 (4,609)
Flanagan, Conor 4:27:02 (15,331)
Flanagan, David C 4:19:40 (13,499)
Flanagan, Tony 3:10:08 (1,574)
Flanigan, Barry J 5:03:02 (24,135)
Flannery, Hugh 3:50:22 (7,014)
Flannery, Mark 5:05:55 (24,682)
Flannery, Martin T 5:06:36 (24,798)
Flannery, Patrick 4:50:29 (21,116)
Flannery, Peter 5:54:25 (32,099)
Flannery, Raymond 5:27:27 (28,704)
Flannigan, Paul 3:33:51 (4,243)
Flatau, William D 4:33:10 (16,830)
Flatley, John 4:24:13 (14,634)
Flatt, Christopher J 3:34:04 (4,276)
Flavell, Paul 3:21:17 (2,633)
Flavin, Paul N 3:44:02 (5,871)
Flaxman, John W 5:11:29 (25,750)
Flecheau, Bruno 4:17:54 (13,043)
Fleeman, Nicholas 4:59:09 (23,297)
Fleetwood, Ashley I 4:17:24 (12,908)

Fleetwood, Daniel	4:18:14	(13,132)
Fleismaher, Arnaud	3:31:48	(3,954)
Fleming, Bradley J	4:09:29	(11,068)
Fleming, Chris	5:11:05	(25,682)
Fleming, Desmond H	5:19:44	(27,379)
Fleming, Ian	4:27:05	(15,350)
Fleming, Michael J	4:11:14	(11,433)
Fleming, Nicholas J	4:05:57	(10,342)
Fleming, Paul A	3:12:33	(1,785)
Fleming, Paul S	5:18:15	(27,113)
Fleming, Roy	5:23:56	(28,097)
Fleming, William A	4:16:26	(12,681)
Fleming-Gale, Jacob T	3:24:44	(2,991)
Fletcher, Andrew D	3:32:58	(4,134)
Fletcher, Andrew J	4:08:51	(10,933)
Fletcher, Anthony J	4:35:31	(17,407)
Fletcher, Cedric J	2:45:39	(255)
Fletcher, Chris	3:12:48	(1,808)
Fletcher, Christopher D	2:58:39	(805)
Fletcher, Eddie	3:39:00	(5,017)
Fletcher, Gordon	4:15:35	(12,456)
Fletcher, Graham W	5:40:18	(30,627)
Fletcher, John A	4:47:21	(20,370)
Fletcher, John S	3:25:54	(3,115)
Fletcher, Joseph E	4:42:02	(19,047)
Fletcher, Julian D	3:41:57	(5,509)
Fletcher, Paul D	3:54:13	(7,843)
Fletcher, Peter R	4:31:52	(16,538)
Fletcher, Robert W	4:51:28	(21,363)
Fletcher, Robin J	4:38:43	(18,205)
Fletcher, Simon M	4:15:24	(12,418)
Fletcher, Stephen J	5:32:38	(29,557)
Fletcher, Timothy	4:13:45	(12,030)
Flett, Matt B	4:28:56	(15,842)
Fleury, Thierry M	3:26:12	(3,157)
Flind, Jonathan	3:28:40	(3,518)
Flindall, Andrew M	3:59:32	(9,104)
Flint, Chris G	3:47:13	(6,381)
Flint, Daniel	3:21:31	(2,651)
Flint, Mark A	4:13:31	(11,969)
Flint, Steven	4:02:36	(9,708)
Flint, Stuart J	4:29:29	(15,998)
Flint, Thomas P	3:52:30	(7,468)
Flint, Wayne B	4:13:30	(11,963)
Flitton, Paul A	5:27:44	(28,751)
Flockhart, Kevin R	5:31:49	(29,423)
Florentin, Pierre	4:03:00	(9,785)
Flores, Christopher B	4:07:46	(10,719)
Florid James, Michael D	3:18:52	(2,374)
Florida-James, Peter J	3:12:40	(1,795)
Florisca, Octavian	4:24:53	(14,801)
Flower, Edward S	4:45:05	(19,857)
Flower, Kevin M	3:40:46	(5,312)
Flowerdew, Tom D	4:02:37	(9,716)
Flowers, Adam P	4:53:36	(21,913)
Flowers, Mark A	3:55:42	(8,164)
Floyd, Darren L	4:49:00	(20,769)
Floyd, Geoffrey	4:54:05	(22,037)
Floyd, Robert J	3:35:13	(4,437)
Flynn, Jamie	4:10:36	(11,287)
Flynn, Jan J	4:50:02	(21,003)
Flynn, John	5:38:22	(30,365)
Flynn, John K	3:40:40	(5,293)
Flynn, John P	4:18:19	(13,155)
Flynn, Matthew R	5:03:04	(24,140)
Flynn, Richard J	3:51:31	(7,259)
Flynn, Simon J	3:56:11	(8,270)
Flynn, Thomas F	5:35:06	(29,926)
Foard, Martyn R	3:43:19	(5,742)
Foat, John R	5:00:04	(23,520)
Foerster, Peter	3:22:44	(2,766)
Fogarty, William J	3:19:57	(2,489)
Fogg, Brian	4:28:00	(15,586)
Fojadelli, Tomaso	3:38:01	(4,833)
Folan, Mark Lawrence	5:01:34	(23,848)
Folan, Paul D	4:20:59	(13,850)
Foley, Darren	4:33:09	(16,823)
Foley, Elias C	3:54:29	(7,899)
Foley, Frank P	6:02:12	(32,766)
Foley, Giles T	4:30:11	(16,192)
Foley, Peter L	4:43:00	(19,297)
Foley, Terry	5:29:18	(29,039)
Folgado, Ricardo D	4:43:28	(19,409)

Folkesson, Erik A	3:26:32	(3,199)
Folley, Stuart J	3:55:16	(8,070)
Folliot, Eric	4:18:53	(13,304)
Follis, Timothy M	4:23:00	(14,334)
Follot, Martial	3:34:18	(4,316)
Folt, Patrick A	4:04:12	(10,006)
Fones, Richard D	3:37:33	(4,760)
Fontimpe, Marc	3:31:50	(3,959)
Fontimpe, Paul	3:31:15	(3,872)
Foo, Kim	3:00:12	(907)
Foo, Shane S	3:28:10	(3,430)
Foord, Michael R	6:34:52	(34,492)
Foord, Tony	4:24:11	(14,627)
Foot, Jon R	4:56:20	(22,598)
Foot, Nigel P	4:06:48	(10,530)
Foot, Peter G	6:02:07	(32,756)
Foran, Clark	4:46:21	(20,144)
Forbes, Christopher L	3:43:46	(5,822)
Forbes, Emile P	4:28:10	(15,640)
Forbes, Gary	6:09:58	(33,302)
Forbes, Matthew J	4:32:18	(16,627)
Ford, Adrian M	4:56:12	(22,564)
Ford, Andrew M	5:09:10	(25,306)
Ford, Ben G	4:00:52	(9,392)
Ford, Darran	3:28:28	(3,477)
Ford, David	6:16:45	(33,724)
Ford, David R	4:30:03	(16,159)
Ford, Don S	5:01:54	(23,913)
Ford, Howard J	3:44:03	(5,873)
Ford, John	3:50:57	(7,127)
Ford, John M	4:43:14	(19,349)
Ford, Jonathan R	4:55:12	(22,318)
Ford, Lee	6:08:26	(33,198)
Ford, Mark K	7:00:44	(35,142)
Ford, William C	4:29:03	(15,867)
Forde, James	4:20:58	(13,845)
Fordham, Craig J	3:56:34	(8,376)
Fordham, David I	4:14:40	(12,249)
Fordham, David M	4:20:59	(13,850)
Fordham, Steven E	6:20:12	(33,896)
Fordrey, Thomas D	4:11:25	(11,478)
Fordyce, Bruce	3:58:42	(8,882)
Forecast, Allen B	4:47:18	(20,359)
Foreman, Colin P	3:53:42	(7,728)
Foreman, Ian	3:32:27	(4,059)
Foreman, Keith D	4:45:32	(19,958)
Foreman, Kevin N	3:23:44	(2,870)
Foreman, Simeon A	4:03:17	(9,832)
Foreman, Timothy F	3:28:01	(3,409)
Foreman, William	3:34:35	(4,352)
Forester, Peter J	2:49:37	(363)
Forey, Simon	4:51:31	(21,371)
Forgan, Jamie	5:12:03	(25,865)
Forman, Ian T	3:48:37	(6,648)
Formhals, Don C	4:18:47	(13,281)
Forrest, Darryl T	5:49:45	(31,653)
Forrest, Ian	5:12:39	(25,974)
Forrest, Ian M	3:51:41	(7,290)
Forrest, Thomas	3:34:40	(4,361)
Forrester, Ian W	4:15:45	(12,495)
Forrester, Martin	4:53:05	(21,771)
Forrester, Paul	5:26:16	(28,503)
Forrester, Peter J	4:02:51	(9,760)
Forsdike, Adam J	5:16:32	(26,763)
Forsdike, Mark A	5:25:32	(28,376)
Forsdyke, David S	5:10:28	(25,571)
Forshaw, Darren	5:44:23	(31,083)
Forshew, Jeremy	3:45:28	(6,092)
Forster, Adrian J	5:17:08	(26,884)
Forster, Andrew T	3:26:50	(3,247)
Forster, Guy W	3:36:06	(4,557)
Forster, Stephen	4:14:31	(12,207)
Forte, Phil	3:23:28	(2,849)
Fortin, Jean-Christophe	3:34:09	(4,286)
Fortis, Dean	4:03:44	(9,911)
Fortuna, Wayne F	3:48:29	(6,618)
Foscolo, Richard T	5:17:22	(26,935)
Fosh, Michael J	3:26:27	(3,193)
Foskew, Ian P	3:07:00	(1,308)
Fossett, James J	3:26:42	(3,223)
Fossey, Chris	4:51:27	(21,356)
Foster, Darren R	5:33:29	(29,678)
Foster, David	4:40:07	(18,560)

Foster, David I	3:34:15	(4,302)
Foster, David M	4:30:55	(16,339)
Foster, David M	4:34:56	(17,253)
Foster, Gary	4:40:21	(18,618)
Foster, Gavin R	5:30:01	(29,144)
Foster, Graham I	3:46:04	(6,189)
Foster, Graham J	4:24:12	(14,630)
Foster, Jason C	4:50:30	(21,120)
Foster, Jason T	4:14:32	(12,211)
Foster, Jeremy N	3:48:32	(6,630)
Foster, Karl M	3:28:38	(3,511)
Foster, Kevin	4:06:44	(10,509)
Foster, Lee T	5:13:10	(26,075)
Foster, Mark D	5:31:03	(29,307)
Foster, Mark J	4:00:53	(9,393)
Foster, Neil S	4:29:57	(16,134)
Foster, Peter	4:16:02	(12,575)
Foster, Philip A	3:56:26	(8,338)
Foster, Robert	4:35:53	(17,508)
Foster, Robert S	4:34:40	(17,196)
Foster, Simon P	5:48:33	(31,528)
Foster, Steven M	5:23:30	(28,010)
Foster, Timothy R	5:15:41	(26,600)
Fotherby, Kenneth J	3:06:08	(1,241)
Fothergill, Luke F	4:40:51	(18,747)
Fothergill, Ross	4:35:13	(17,338)
Fotheringham, Blair A	4:22:41	(14,253)
Foual, Alain	4:12:12	(11,655)
Foucault, Pierre	3:59:08	(8,992)
Foucher, Christophe J	3:15:37	(2,040)
Foucher, François	4:05:13	(10,187)
Foulds, John	3:30:02	(3,727)
Foulkes, Ashley S	5:17:51	(27,018)
Foulkes, Llifon A	3:39:39	(5,135)
Foulston, Neil	4:41:38	(18,955)
Fountain, Andrew M	5:48:29	(31,522)
Fountain, Simon G	5:09:17	(25,330)
Fountain, Tony	4:23:43	(14,493)
Fourie, Stephanus	4:34:51	(17,236)
Fowler, Andrew M	3:25:18	(3,044)
Fowler, Cedric	6:47:58	(34,888)
Fowler, Charlie N	4:54:25	(22,128)
Fowler, Ian J	3:53:51	(7,753)
Fowler, Keith E	4:12:12	(11,655)
Fowler, Martin G	3:37:15	(4,719)
Fowler, Matthew	3:14:33	(1,949)
Fowler, Matthew D	2:59:40	(876)
Fowler, Matthew J	3:39:08	(5,039)
Fowler, Matthew W	3:36:06	(4,557)
Fowler, Paul W	4:34:43	(17,206)
Fowler, Richard I	3:49:53	(6,914)
Fowler, Steve	7:19:27	(35,382)
Fowler, Vincent C	3:23:00	(2,796)
Fowles, Peter	3:48:53	(6,700)
Fox, Barrie R	3:38:59	(5,012)
Fox, Brendan	4:47:00	(20,280)
Fox, Brian T	3:46:57	(6,335)
Fox, Christian T	3:48:59	(6,729)
Fox, Daniel J	4:52:14	(21,552)
Fox, David P	4:29:22	(15,964)
Fox, David T	3:28:41	(3,520)
Fox, Fred J	4:09:10	(10,997)
Fox, James A	5:25:15	(28,315)
Fox, Joseph T	5:04:27	(24,411)
Fox, Malcolm F	6:11:12	(33,382)
Fox, Martin	4:20:29	(13,729)
Fox, Martyn D	5:10:31	(25,580)
Fox, Nicholas J	4:20:08	(13,637)
Fox, Robin E	4:45:58	(20,054)
Fox, Sam	4:51:27	(21,356)
Fox, Simon A	4:56:57	(22,763)
Fox, Stephen L	6:09:50	(33,293)
Fox, Stuart	2:41:26	(165)
Fox, Thomas	4:18:18	(13,149)
Fox Joyce, Edward	4:32:43	(16,720)
Foxall, Martin P	4:02:44	(9,740)
Foxall, Rob J	4:22:05	(14,105)
Foxley, David	5:56:11	(32,254)
Foy, Garry J	5:15:42	(26,602)
Fraga, David	4:14:33	(12,219)
Frain, David	4:45:07	(19,863)
Frain, Peter J	4:19:03	(13,337)
Fraiz, Wayne	5:05:52	(24,666)

Frame, Kip A 4:58:25 (23,136)
Frampton, Christopher J 4:28:45 (15,799)
Frampton, Robert 3:48:48 (6,687)
France, Ashley 5:05:53 (24,672)
France, James R 5:58:08 (32,426)
France, Timothy J 4:56:48 (22,715)
Francescon, Marco 5:27:08 (28,644)
Francey, Andrew R 6:56:34 (35,063)
Francis, Alen 6:08:14 (33,189)
Francis, Brian P 4:29:37 (16,042)
Francis, Chad 4:06:24 (10,439)
Francis, Charles 5:10:37 (25,599)
Francis, Christopher T 4:13:49 (12,048)
Francis, Daniel 4:26:16 (15,123)
Francis, Daniel J 4:49:57 (20,984)
Francis, David 3:33:09 (4,161)
Francis, Dennis P 6:02:30 (32,785)
Francis, Grant 4:58:44 (23,193)
Francis, Ian D 4:26:48 (15,267)
Francis, Nick 4:22:35 (14,224)
Francis, Pete J 4:00:13 (9,259)
Francis, Richard C 3:52:46 (7,517)
Francis, Richard D 6:02:30 (32,785)
Francis, Robert J 5:18:12 (27,103)
Francis, Sean 5:27:09 (28,646)
Francis, Stephen W 4:55:26 (22,372)
Francisci, Marc-Paul 4:16:20 (12,654)
Frank, Glen D 5:15:06 (26,479)
Frank, Wayne G 4:36:00 (17,534)
Franke, Werner 4:38:32 (18,159)
Frankland, Anthony J 3:27:16 (3,320)
Frankland, Neil A 5:06:37 (24,801)
Frankland, Paul M 4:12:23 (11,697)
Franklin, Andy C 4:25:51 (15,025)
Franklin, Harry C 5:55:08 (32,158)
Franklin, John K 3:04:43 (1,144)
Franklin, John P 4:15:49 (12,511)
Franklin, Martin A 4:40:09 (18,566)
Franklin, Paul 3:58:26 (8,816)
Franklin, Robert M 4:20:56 (13,838)
Franklin, Shane V 3:45:52 (6,157)
Franklin, Simon A 3:25:58 (3,122)
Franklin, Stephen M 3:45:18 (6,068)
Franks, David A 4:45:01 (19,842)
Frankum, Martin J 4:57:00 (22,772)
Franz, Jonathan W 4:10:38 (11,296)
Fraser, Anthony 3:42:33 (5,604)
Fraser, Charles A 4:53:26 (21,876)
Fraser, David 5:13:34 (26,134)
Fraser, David D 3:49:14 (6,788)
Fraser, Derek 3:23:23 (2,839)
Fraser, Edward 3:55:34 (8,131)
Fraser, Graeme S 4:54:46 (22,216)
Fraser, Keith A 3:23:21 (2,838)
Fraser, Kevin J 5:08:22 (25,165)
Fraser, Matthew J 4:38:54 (18,254)
Fraser, Neil A 4:12:49 (11,793)
Fraser, Neil G 4:09:58 (11,159)
Fraser, Paul G 4:13:02 (11,840)
Fraser, Phillip J 5:30:40 (29,246)
Fraser, Stephen 4:28:00 (15,586)
Fraser, Stuart J 2:59:29 (861)
Fraser, Thomas P 4:50:11 (21,042)
Frater, Bruce 4:21:32 (13,973)
Frattaroli, David 4:09:09 (10,993)
Fray, Martin D 3:03:09 (1,057)
Fream, Stephen G 4:15:08 (12,351)
Frean, Michael E 3:56:31 (8,364)
Frecknall, James R 5:51:27 (31,822)
Frederick, James D 4:29:55 (16,123)
Frederiksen, Lars 3:22:26 (2,741)
Fredriksen, Rune 2:54:51 (571)
Free, Charles A 4:17:27 (12,927)
Free, Gary E 6:26:07 (34,176)
Free, John C 4:59:58 (23,497)
Freeder, David B 5:14:59 (26,447)
Freedman, Jonathan M 5:34:48 (29,886)
Freedman, Paul 5:45:40 (31,222)
Freeland, Lee 3:31:32 (3,915)
Freeman, Andrew R 4:57:10 (22,811)
Freeman, Angus J 5:28:13 (28,840)
Freeman, David A 5:03:18 (24,191)
Freeman, David J 2:50:47 (402)
Freeman, Dennis G 3:46:00 (6,178)
Freeman, Jason W 5:14:44 (26,393)
Freeman, Julian P 4:40:45 (18,714)
Freeman, Paul 2:58:59 (821)
Freeman, Paul R 4:16:54 (12,785)
Freeman, Paul W 3:56:18 (8,304)
Freeman, Roy H 4:50:14 (21,055)
Freeman, Scott 4:14:28 (12,199)
Freeman, Simon H 4:12:18 (11,685)
Freeman, Simon K 5:59:46 (32,563)
Freeman, Tony W 5:15:29 (26,560)
Freestone, Matt G 4:43:15 (19,355)
Freeze, David L 4:59:30 (23,384)
Freeze, John D 5:32:13 (29,485)
Freitas, Carlos A 4:10:12 (11,205)
Fremantle, Thomas 4:38:42 (18,201)
Fremlin, Harvey D 4:38:34 (18,168)
French, Anthony T 4:42:52 (19,273)
French, Freddie 5:18:08 (27,089)
French, Graham T 4:36:54 (17,768)
French, James 5:06:47 (24,840)
French, Kevin J 3:38:33 (4,929)
French, Mark 4:55:52 (22,479)
French, Nicholas J 5:12:58 (26,039)
French, Paul I 4:44:39 (19,727)
French, Peter 4:44:39 (19,727)
French, Philip R 6:52:40 (34,985)
French, Sean 4:40:23 (18,628)
French, Tim 3:48:47 (6,685)
Fretton, Robert H 5:03:28 (24,230)
Fretwell, Scott D 4:52:35 (21,635)
Frewer, Martyn A 5:05:52 (24,666)
Fribbens, Mark I 4:42:16 (19,117)
Fribbins, Michael G 5:22:58 (27,932)
Fricker, Lee T 4:01:38 (9,539)
Friden, Jan D 4:01:31 (9,516)
Fried, Andrew M 4:48:34 (20,663)
Friedlander, Jeremy I 4:25:33 (14,955)
Friel, Robert H 4:23:49 (14,518)
Friend, Andrew S 5:01:43 (23,871)
Friend, Brian S 3:21:01 (2,612)
Friend, Bryan J 3:48:49 (6,692)
Friend, Graham P 4:24:30 (14,704)
Friend-James, Mark 3:09:22 (1,506)
Friery, Andrew M 5:28:51 (28,957)
Fries, Axel 3:53:06 (7,591)
Fright, Tim R 4:24:42 (14,747)
Frisby, Brian J 3:55:02 (8,015)
Friscia, Marco 5:14:19 (26,294)
Frith, Andy J 3:52:25 (7,455)
Frith, Anthony J 4:53:58 (22,012)
Frith, John C 4:14:54 (12,297)
Fritzsch, Matthias 4:58:51 (23,218)
Fritzsch, Tobias 4:58:51 (23,218)
Froestad, Kaare 3:50:17 (6,995)
Froggatt, Nick J 3:56:42 (8,406)
Froment, Michel 3:21:16 (2,631)
Fromont, Christophe 4:41:37 (18,952)
Frosdick, Stephen 4:05:19 (10,206)
Frost, Alex J 2:59:40 (876)
Frost, Gary 5:28:25 (28,891)
Frost, Jonathan 2:32:20 (51)
Frost, Kevin 4:25:08 (14,856)
Frost, Mark H 3:12:01 (1,729)
Frost, Mark P 3:34:53 (4,392)
Frost, Martin A 3:53:38 (7,713)
Frost, Matthew G 4:49:59 (20,990)
Frost, Peter R 4:40:21 (18,618)
Frost, Stephen 4:44:10 (19,587)
Frost, Steve P 4:38:49 (18,239)
Froud, James D 5:18:46 (27,207)
Froude, Gregory P 4:32:54 (16,763)
Fry, Bernard S 4:20:41 (13,773)
Fry, John 4:03:50 (9,935)
Fry, John W 3:45:22 (6,077)
Fry, Kevin P 4:16:11 (12,620)
Fry, Les D 4:49:35 (20,912)
Fry, Malcolm M 4:32:28 (16,652)
Fry, Matthew 5:50:20 (31,709)
Fry, Nigel J 3:40:05 (5,203)
Frydman, Olivier 4:25:11 (14,867)
Fryer, Andy J 5:35:37 (30,000)
Fryer, Grant C 6:02:27 (32,783)
Fryer, Paul M 4:04:00 (9,967)
Fryer, Peter 4:19:48 (13,542)
Fryman, Neil 5:06:16 (24,754)
Frymann, David 4:10:34 (11,283)
Fuat, Koray 5:36:40 (30,132)
Fubel, Jorg 3:52:29 (7,464)
Fudge, Lloyd J 5:51:50 (31,858)
Fudulu, Livin 3:50:39 (7,066)
Fuerst, René 3:33:51 (4,243)
Fuggle, Tony J 5:00:01 (23,508)
Fujimura, Ikuo 4:47:30 (20,407)
Fulker, Duncan J 5:47:39 (31,422)
Fullalove, Paul A 3:47:26 (6,417)
Fullbrook, Richard 3:57:57 (8,708)
Fuller, Adrian H 2:51:47 (432)
Fuller, Chris 2:55:58 (609)
Fuller, Gregory J 3:46:03 (6,186)
Fuller, Justin 5:25:21 (28,330)
Fuller, Lee 5:14:27 (26,321)
Fuller, Mark 5:51:55 (31,866)
Fuller, Martin G 2:56:34 (641)
Fuller, Paul 4:32:58 (16,777)
Fuller, Richard N 3:09:15 (1,498)
Fuller, Stephen 5:35:33 (29,984)
Fuller, William F 5:10:22 (25,549)
Fullilove, Charly L 4:25:24 (14,927)
Fulton, Peter 4:37:32 (17,897)
Fulton, William J 4:14:58 (12,313)
Fumagalli, Carlo 4:12:15 (11,670)
Funayama, Kenji 3:56:12 (8,274)
Fung, William 6:06:59 (33,105)
Funnell, Keith A 4:47:49 (20,482)
Funnell, Roger A 4:26:41 (15,238)
Furley, Andy 3:37:13 (4,713)
Furlong, Michael J 4:16:16 (12,639)
Furlong, Rob A 5:15:36 (26,586)
Furmidge, Sean A 4:12:48 (11,789)
Furness, Christopher B 3:42:39 (5,618)
Furness, Simon D 5:06:56 (24,865)
Furness, Tom 4:55:41 (22,423)
Furniss, Andy 3:49:42 (6,872)
Furry, Kevin C 3:55:18 (8,077)
Fursey, Matthew J 5:02:26 (24,024)
Fursey, Robert G 3:41:31 (5,446)
Furzer, Paul M 4:30:20 (16,223)
Furzer, Shaun A 4:45:54 (20,033)
Fusaro, Roberto D 3:27:42 (3,373)
Fusillo, Donato 4:15:44 (12,491)
Futcher, Mark E 4:10:10 (11,196)
Futcher, Peter J 5:26:33 (28,548)
Fyall, Drummond D 5:06:31 (24,786)
Fyfe, Andrew T 5:22:35 (27,873)
Fyffe, Margaret M 6:37:55 (34,601)
Fynn, Adrian J 4:31:18 (16,423)
Gabriel, Brian J 4:45:38 (19,977)
Gabriel, Heinz 5:13:05 (26,060)
Gabriel, Julian C 4:19:26 (13,440)
Gabriel, Martin J 3:46:11 (6,205)
Gabriele, Palmino 3:22:23 (2,736)
Gaby, James 5:10:55 (25,648)
Gaches, Anton M 4:05:53 (10,327)
Gadd, Adam 5:03:00 (24,121)
Gadgil, Devendra V 6:00:56 (32,661)
Gaertner, Volkmar 4:03:02 (9,791)
Gaffney, David P 4:44:26 (19,660)
Gager, Andrew W 5:05:02 (24,518)
Gager, Terry C 4:04:47 (10,110)
Gahagan, Jonathan M 4:56:49 (22,719)
Gahagan, Patrick A 4:04:06 (9,985)
Gains, Keith S 4:46:10 (20,095)
Gajbutowicz, Andrzej 4:18:38 (13,250)
Gale, Andrew M 4:04:28 (10,052)
Gale, Matthew T 3:35:44 (4,518)
Gale, Peter D 4:04:38 (10,080)
Galeckyj, Andrew 5:05:37 (24,621)
Galissard, Alain 3:52:11 (7,406)
Gallacher, Edward 7:16:22 (35,356)
Gallacher, Gerard J 5:44:55 (31,142)
Gallacher, Russell S 3:58:13 (8,769)
Gallagher, Andrew J 3:33:27 (4,200)
Gallagher, Colin J 3:23:05 (2,804)
Gallagher, Daniel J 4:30:46 (16,308)
Gallagher, Harvey 4:32:18 (16,627)

Gallagher, Joseph P	4:42:21 (19,139)
Gallagher, Kevin J	4:16:37 (12,720)
Gallagher, Mark A	4:49:59 (20,990)
Gallagher, Michael	4:36:32 (17,677)
Gallagher, Michael A	2:58:36 (797)
Gallagher, Michael H	4:31:27 (16,451)
Gallagher, Patrick J	3:18:37 (2,354)
Gallagher, Samuel G	6:51:26 (34,967)
Gallanagh, Peter	2:58:49 (814)
Gallant, Lee A	6:15:34 (33,656)
Gallaway, Ben J	4:24:02 (14,580)
Gallaway-Meyer, Tony	6:22:00 (33,994)
Gallen, Brendan E	3:26:08 (3,146)
Gallen, Kieren M	6:14:48 (33,603)
Galleri, Enrico	3:43:38 (5,804)
Gallese, Nando	3:03:45 (1,089)
Galli, Erio	3:32:33 (4,079)
Galli, Giuliano	3:23:56 (2,898)
Gallien, Olivier P	4:25:12 (14,875)
Gallimore, Adam	4:03:08 (9,806)
Gallivan, John F	7:13:42 (35,330)
Gallo, Simon J	5:56:33 (32,294)
Galloway, Alan P	5:03:59 (24,322)
Gallucci, Enrico	4:37:31 (17,892)
Gallus, John S	5:44:59 (31,152)
Galpin, Peter C	2:30:49 (45)
Galvin, Michael	5:31:13 (29,337)
Gambino, Andrew	4:59:14 (23,319)
Gamble, Andrew S	4:21:28 (13,957)
Gamble, John A	3:42:59 (5,689)
Gamble, Keith M	5:59:21 (32,541)
Gamble, Steven W	3:52:02 (7,370)
Gamborg, Tom	4:39:50 (18,494)
Gambrill, James	6:02:37 (32,794)
Gambrill, Simon	6:02:37 (32,794)
Gambs, Christopher D	3:52:03 (7,378)
Gamby, Graham L	4:20:51 (13,817)
Game, Kevin J	3:21:54 (2,696)
Game, Matthew	3:54:08 (7,823)
Game, Paul J	3:15:18 (2,020)
Game, Robert W	3:30:42 (3,806)
Gami, Jay B	5:33:29 (29,678)
Gammage, Tom J	4:13:49 (12,048)
Gammell, Alastair D	5:14:34 (26,354)
Gammon, Adrian	5:28:36 (28,918)
Gammon, Malcolm D	3:25:10 (3,037)
Gammon, Vincent J	4:06:22 (10,429)
Gamsby, Spencer J	5:03:54 (24,310)
Gan, Heng	4:16:37 (12,720)
Gander, Ashley	4:54:42 (22,198)
Gander, Ian	5:21:05 (27,615)
Gandhi, Bharat	5:07:48 (25,058)
Gandhi, Shirish	3:49:12 (6,774)
Ganguly, Stephen R	4:53:24 (21,862)
Gannon, Paul M	4:45:45 (19,998)
Gannon, Richard J	2:48:52 (340)
Gannon, Stephen C	3:46:54 (6,321)
Garaasen, Gar	6:42:12 (34,728)
Garasa, Sergio	3:56:13 (8,279)
Garcha, Parvinder S	5:57:08 (32,344)
Garcia, Andy	5:15:22 (26,535)
Garcia, Antony M	4:55:55 (22,493)
Garcia, Fernando	3:53:33 (7,698)
Garcia, José A	4:56:09 (22,550)
Garcia, Juan	4:36:16 (17,602)
Garcia, Luis	4:48:36 (20,669)
Garcia, Luiz César	4:00:30 (9,311)
Garcia, Salvador	2:57:42 (720)
Gard, Merlin A	7:00:22 (35,133)
Gardener, Geoffrey T	5:05:09 (24,536)
Gardener, Philip W	4:16:49 (12,765)
Gardener, Richard	4:32:55 (16,768)
Gardener, Sean	5:47:44 (31,435)
Gardent, Thierry	2:54:29 (543)
Gardiner, Charles H	5:06:45 (24,831)
Gardiner, Glen W	6:00:52 (32,653)
Gardiner, John P	3:50:00 (6,942)
Gardiner, Jonathan L	7:43:29 (35,592)
Gardiner, Richie	2:20:26 (13)
Gardiner, Simon	3:57:42 (8,654)
Gardner, Andrew	4:08:18 (10,833)
Gardner, Barry	3:20:25 (2,547)
Gardner, Barry	3:47:56 (6,516)

Gardner, Craig	5:39:27 (30,518)
Gardner, David J	3:35:25 (4,471)
Gardner, John A	5:27:15 (28,671)
Gardner, Keith D	4:57:14 (22,828)
Gardner, Keith I	5:03:46 (24,284)
Gardner, Leighton J	3:08:50 (1,454)
Gardner, Mark S	3:27:52 (3,390)
Gardner, Matthew	3:58:40 (8,877)
Gardner, Neal T	5:09:26 (25,362)
Gardner, Nicholas J	3:30:07 (3,737)
Gardner, Philip M	3:59:31 (9,097)
Gardner, Stephen J	5:05:41 (24,631)
Gardner, Tony	3:36:52 (4,669)
Gardner, Trevor	5:03:28 (24,230)
Gardner, Wayne	4:07:19 (10,621)
Gardner, William R	4:40:28 (18,644)
Gargan, Nick	4:31:27 (16,451)
Gargaro, Steven	5:16:18 (26,722)
Gargiulo, Bruno	3:56:12 (8,274)
Garham, Thomas P	5:23:15 (27,970)
Garland, Christopher J	4:15:26 (12,426)
Garland, Jonathan A	5:23:08 (27,953)
Garland, Michael J	4:46:46 (20,224)
Garlick, Paul A	3:52:02 (7,370)
Garlick, Peter A	4:46:03 (20,070)
Garman, John P	3:59:51 (9,171)
Garner, Les	4:56:43 (22,700)
Garner, Michael	5:11:00 (25,665)
Garner, Paul D	5:02:21 (24,001)
Garner, Simon G	3:29:05 (3,590)
Garnett, Andrew	3:13:10 (1,834)
Garnett, Chris J	4:24:23 (14,675)
Garnham, Andrew K	5:53:30 (32,008)
Garnham, Gary G	4:10:33 (11,281)
Garrard, Simon D	4:41:46 (18,983)
Garratt, Brett S	3:32:06 (4,011)
Garratt, Christopher	4:09:22 (11,044)
Garratt, Colin J	5:08:10 (25,131)
Garratt, Mark	2:54:48 (569)
Garratt, Matthew	4:57:36 (22,932)
Garratt, Paul T	4:03:47 (9,924)
Garrett, Alan F	5:28:21 (28,880)
Garrett, Anthony P	5:01:43 (23,871)
Garrett, Darren	5:23:10 (27,956)
Garrett, Michael A	2:57:07 (683)
Garrett, Phil A	4:26:00 (15,058)
Garrett, Sean	5:52:11 (31,891)
Garrity, Martin J	5:24:44 (28,224)
Garrity, Nicholas S	4:44:28 (19,670)
Garrity, Roger P	4:36:13 (17,585)
Garrod, Adrian L	6:41:43 (34,709)
Garrod, Leslie	4:05:30 (10,240)
Garrod, Miles J	4:11:50 (11,578)
Garrood, Steve J	3:52:40 (7,494)
Garside, Roger	5:15:09 (26,490)
Garside, Simon D	3:20:44 (2,580)
Garside, Steve	5:00:10 (23,541)
Garty, Dominic R	5:11:18 (25,719)
Garvey, Daniel J	4:26:53 (15,288)
Garvey, Pete	5:05:15 (24,549)
Garvey, Stephen	3:08:49 (1,451)
Garwell, Tom J	4:55:29 (22,389)
Garwood, James R	3:46:59 (6,342)
Garwood, Jason P	4:50:41 (21,164)
Garwood-Watkins, Andrew P	5:01:05 (23,750)
Garza, Roberto	4:33:58 (17,027)
Garzelli, Gianpiero	5:31:56 (29,437)
Gascoine, Andrew M	4:37:16 (17,834)
Gascoyne, Chris	5:38:42 (30,417)
Gashe, Terry A	4:17:14 (12,861)
Gaskell, Ben	5:05:34 (24,616)
Gaskell, David J	4:44:26 (19,660)
Gaskell, Phil	4:59:05 (23,284)
Gaskin, Martin J	4:41:16 (18,855)
Gasparini, Alessandro	3:03:40 (1,086)
Gasparotto, Manlio	5:07:00 (24,883)
Gasteen, James A	5:28:49 (28,954)
Gaston, Paul	4:39:39 (18,449)
Gateley, Jonathan	3:59:23 (9,065)
Gates, Anthony	4:33:18 (16,867)
Gates, David W	5:11:05 (25,682)
Gates, Gary A	3:45:37 (6,120)
Gates, Michael	5:53:18 (31,986)

Gateshill, Daniel M	4:28:15 (15,657)
Gatherer, William A	4:11:01 (11,371)
Gatlin, Stephen	5:20:48 (27,573)
Gatti, Renato	3:11:28 (1,671)
Gatto, Marco	3:06:44 (1,292)
Gattoni, Robert J	5:00:46 (23,680)
Gauchi, Damen	3:42:57 (5,677)
Gauden-Ing, Stephen D	4:29:58 (16,139)
Gauiter, Yvon P	4:00:01 (9,211)
Gaukroger, Antony J	4:53:34 (21,904)
Gaukroger, Jonathan	4:23:14 (14,385)
Gaulder, Nicholas R	3:48:56 (6,712)
Gaume, Marcelo J	3:13:16 (1,849)
Gaunt, Martin	3:09:54 (1,548)
Gaunt, Oliver	5:42:13 (30,852)
Gauthier, James D	3:30:14 (3,753)
Gavaghan, James C	5:38:08 (30,322)
Gavagnin, Cinzio	4:03:28 (9,860)
Gavin, Anthony	6:24:35 (34,110)
Gavin, Malcolm F	5:54:14 (32,073)
Gavin, Michael J	4:00:51 (9,386)
Gawen, Bruce	3:38:53 (4,995)
Gawron, Michal B	5:57:31 (32,371)
Gay, Anthony B	3:28:14 (3,437)
Gay, Antony J	5:32:46 (29,571)
Gay, Christopher D	3:51:11 (7,182)
Gay, Daniel	4:34:53 (17,244)
Gay, Edward J	5:27:01 (28,623)
Gay, John R	4:46:35 (20,196)
Gay, Peter	5:12:08 (25,879)
Gay, Richard	3:29:35 (3,659)
Gay, Stephen	6:05:30 (33,004)
Gayer, David J	3:46:31 (6,249)
Gaylard, Jonathan	3:38:01 (4,833)
Gayner, Ronald G	4:17:11 (12,848)
Gaze, Nicholas C	4:31:02 (16,364)
Gbadamassi, Tounde	3:25:26 (3,056)
Geaney, John S	4:24:43 (14,753)
Gear, David J	4:45:26 (19,930)
Gear, Martin S	5:21:48 (27,756)
Gearing, Mark	5:03:48 (24,292)
Geary, Darin	5:28:15 (28,849)
Geary, David E	5:46:33 (31,313)
Geddes, Daniel P	4:22:36 (14,230)
Geddes, Fraser H	5:27:16 (28,672)
Geddes, Ian	4:10:00 (11,166)
Geddes, Nicholas M	5:25:26 (28,351)
Gedin, Mats R	2:47:37 (301)
Gee, Christopher W	4:28:02 (15,602)
Gee, Dylan	4:16:36 (12,716)
Gee, Fenton B	6:12:16 (33,441)
Gee, Harry	3:39:40 (5,138)
Gee, Michael B	4:11:29 (11,496)
Gee, Raymond	4:25:35 (14,963)
Geerts, Walter	5:46:02 (31,263)
Gehin, Stephane	3:45:41 (6,132)
Gehlen, Bernd	4:14:41 (12,253)
Geiger, Klaus	4:06:07 (10,376)
Geiger, Steffen C	3:58:27 (8,822)
Geldart, Richard J	4:46:01 (20,062)
Gelder, Philip	5:20:13 (27,459)
Gell, Colin	2:39:02 (127)
Geney, Jerome	3:45:27 (6,091)
Genge, Berard J	3:34:12 (4,293)
Gent, Russell A	6:09:20 (33,256)
Gentle, Chris R	3:30:48 (3,820)
Gentle, John F	5:52:06 (31,881)
Gentle, Paul E	3:10:00 (1,559)
Gentry, Mark E	5:17:53 (27,025)
Gentry, Ross D	5:26:07 (28,477)
George, Derek	4:17:12 (12,853)
George, Edward D	5:13:02 (26,054)
George, Kevin L	3:38:19 (4,889)
George, Michael E	4:29:06 (15,888)
George, Phillip M	2:48:54 (343)
George, Steve D	3:58:15 (8,780)
Georgiou, George A	5:28:45 (28,941)
Geraghty, Donal	4:03:42 (9,902)
Gerard, Thomas J	3:42:04 (5,530)
Gerber, Alain	3:46:46 (6,296)
Gerber, Frans J	5:20:56 (27,595)
Gerber, Hans-Ulrich	4:00:02 (9,214)
Gercke, Chris J	5:38:46 (30,425)

Gerhardsen, Karl H..................4:18:42 (13,264)
Gerlack, Matthew D 4:37:26 (17,874)
Germain, Paul S 4:24:17 (14,651)
German, Paul 5:53:12 (31,978)
Germinario, Giuseppe 2:56:33 (639)
Gerrard, Andrew D 5:19:24 (27,319)
Gerrard, James R..................4:55:02 (22,271)
Gershon, Mike J 6:08:04 (33,176)
Gerundini, Richard P 3:50:59 (7,135)
Gestin, Gerard R 4:43:32 (19,421)
Gething, Colin J 4:43:04 (19,310)
Gevers, Peter M 3:44:06 (5,881)
Gharib, Jaouad 2:07:54 (4)
Ghatge, Arun 5:46:32 (31,312)
Ghazi-Nouri, Seyed M..................5:15:34 (26,579)
Ghosh, Navin K 4:37:26 (17,874)
Giacopazzi, Peter..................4:52:10 (21,533)
Giancristofano, Dario J..................4:34:31 (17,154)
Giansante, Roberto 4:28:23 (15,695)
Giardelli, Adrian N 4:46:21 (20,144)
Gibb, Andy L 3:50:04 (6,957)
Gibb, Martin C 5:22:32 (27,862)
Gibbard, Adrian B..................3:38:34 (4,934)
Gibbins, Alexander N 2:42:23 (186)
Gibbins, Chris S..................2:54:51 (571)
Gibbins, Martin T..................5:48:18 (31,505)
Gibbins, Peter..................4:10:56 (11,358)
Gibbon, Adrian 3:49:32 (6,839)
Gibbon, David E..................4:58:18 (23,103)
Gibbons, Alastair R 3:07:52 (1,375)
Gibbons, Andrew P 4:30:22 (16,229)
Gibbons, Bob..................5:13:22 (26,094)
Gibbons, Christopher P..................5:24:19 (28,160)
Gibbons, David W 4:18:35 (13,234)
Gibbons, Michael P..................3:08:06 (1,397)
Gibbons, Nigel F 5:04:53 (24,496)
Gibbons, Robert..................5:11:43 (25,793)
Gibbons, Ronald 5:25:29 (28,367)
Gibbs, Andrew P..................5:18:37 (27,186)
Gibbs, Aran E 4:39:32 (18,421)
Gibbs, Benjamin L 3:27:09 (3,302)
Gibbs, David W 3:58:43 (8,887)
Gibbs, Gregory 4:58:35 (23,164)
Gibbs, James 4:28:17 (15,666)
Gibbs, James A..................5:32:47 (29,574)
Gibbs, Marcus..................3:39:56 (5,179)
Gibbs, Philip 4:13:14 (11,889)
Gibbs, Timothy..................5:26:10 (28,483)
Gibbs-Jones, Colin G..................5:20:29 (27,513)
Giblenn, Tom 4:07:48 (10,724)
Gibney, Michael..................4:19:51 (13,559)
Gibs, Bob J 5:46:00 (31,259)
Gibson, Alistair J..................5:00:16 (23,568)
Gibson, Bryan M 3:47:30 (6,424)
Gibson, David 3:29:19 (3,620)
Gibson, David P..................5:26:24 (28,531)
Gibson, David T 5:07:17 (24,951)
Gibson, Ian C 6:09:53 (33,299)
Gibson, Ian G 4:52:14 (21,552)
Gibson, James M 4:45:31 (19,954)
Gibson, Jeremy J..................4:39:54 (18,508)
Gibson, John D..................4:49:14 (20,828)
Gibson, Leslie W 4:32:47 (16,735)
Gibson, Neal M 3:33:31 (4,205)
Gibson, Neal M 3:43:09 (5,714)
Gibson, Oliver 5:25:26 (28,351)
Gibson, Paul H 4:12:36 (11,737)
Gibson, Paul P 6:37:54 (34,600)
Gibson, Paul R..................5:38:47 (30,426)
Gibson, Peter..................3:46:54 (6,321)
Gibson, Robert 3:55:35 (8,133)
Gibson, Robert E..................4:11:06 (11,397)
Gibson, Stuart W 5:19:05 (27,262)
Gibson, Thomas D 4:24:34 (14,721)
Gibson, Timothy M 3:19:06 (2,404)
Gibson, Tom R 3:44:36 (5,959)
Gibson, Tony P 4:25:12 (14,875)
Giddings, Stephen J..................5:34:48 (29,886)
Gidney, Graham M..................3:26:40 (3,217)
Gielgen, Raphael..................4:55:12 (22,318)
Giering, Dieter 3:41:48 (5,484)
Gieseler, Morsert..................6:11:34 (33,401)
Giesen, Raimond..................5:15:30 (26,563)

Don't sweat it

The weather is often a huge factor in the London Marathon. Runners find that throwaway clothes or even black bin-bags come in useful if the weather is cold, they can easily be discarded long after the start. But heat is the deadliest enemy. The most gruelling London Marathon ever was in 2007 when thousands suffered from heat exhaustion as temperatures reached 23.5°C. There was no rain and over seven hours of sunshine. St John Ambulance treated 5,032 people, 73 of whom were sent to hospital for further treatment. One died. Celebrity chef Gordon Ramsay said: 'It was like running in a desert ... They were dropping like flies.' The coldest Marathon was in 1994. The temperature at the start was 5.9°C. Chris Brasher blamed wind chill for yet another death.

Giffin, André 4:16:00 (12,562)
Gifford, Simon D..................3:53:19 (7,648)
Giggs, Ian..................3:33:04 (4,148)
Gilbert, Christopher 3:43:32 (5,787)
Gilbert, David G 5:43:04 (30,942)
Gilbert, Howard G 4:42:23 (19,146)
Gilbert, Ian J..................5:08:31 (25,191)
Gilbert, Joe 6:47:49 (34,882)
Gilbert, Jonathan P 4:27:34 (15,480)
Gilbert, Mark R 5:22:51 (27,915)
Gilbert, Matthew C..................5:16:42 (26,789)
Gilbert, Simon J..................3:52:58 (7,557)
Gilbert, Simon M 3:09:44 (1,535)
Gilbert, Terence M..................5:56:18 (32,266)
Gilbert, William R 4:32:37 (16,695)
Gilbey, Ian J..................4:51:41 (21,419)
Gilboy, Gary P 4:56:25 (22,616)
Gilbranch, Daniel..................5:45:18 (31,182)
Gilchrist, David S..................2:52:01 (440)
Gilchrist, Ewan R 6:17:37 (33,761)
Gilchrist, Tyrone 5:23:34 (28,024)
Gilding, Barry J..................5:35:17 (29,951)
Giles, Alan 4:15:26 (12,426)
Giles, Austin A..................5:24:13 (28,140)
Giles, Ian R 3:07:28 (1,347)
Giles, Matt J..................2:34:15 (68)
Giles, Nicholas S..................4:21:06 (13,874)
Giles, Nikki 3:56:29 (8,355)
Giles, Paul R..................4:07:38 (10,686)
Giles, Steven J..................4:55:06 (22,289)
Gilfillan, Dean A 3:58:17 (8,786)
Gilgallon, Chris 3:55:52 (8,200)
Gilhooly, Michael 4:22:26 (14,181)
Gill, Amarjit S..................6:33:12 (34,444)
Gill, Andrew D..................4:50:03 (21,007)
Gill, Andrew M 4:38:04 (18,028)
Gill, Anthony 4:10:23 (11,244)
Gill, David K 3:57:20 (8,561)
Gill, Ewean J..................3:38:26 (4,908)
Gill, Jeffrey I 5:13:24 (26,102)
Gill, Jonathan D 4:01:33 (9,521)
Gill, Mark H..................4:51:19 (21,321)
Gill, Michael 4:40:59 (18,780)
Gill, Nicholas C 5:38:01 (30,306)
Gill, Pau J..................5:45:54 (31,245)
Gill, Paul D 4:03:21 (9,840)
Gill, Paul. D 3:58:27 (8,822)
Gill, Ray 5:18:07 (27,084)

Gill, Richard J..................4:39:18 (18,364)
Gill, Thomas W 3:47:48 (6,496)
Gillard, Terence J..................4:26:29 (15,184)
Gillard-Moss, Peter K 3:47:43 (6,482)
Gillen, Mark J..................5:43:41 (31,013)
Gillespie, Frank G 4:18:17 (13,142)
Gillespie, Simon M..................4:24:02 (14,580)
Gillespie, Stuart T 5:02:41 (24,074)
Gillett, Daniel J..................3:24:56 (3,012)
Gillett, Stephen M..................4:03:45 (9,916)
Gillham, Garth K..................5:17:12 (26,895)
Gilliam, Robert J..................4:23:34 (14,463)
Gillian, David J..................4:10:12 (11,205)
Gilliard, Ken J..................4:39:53 (18,504)
Gillibrand, Christian S..................3:35:37 (4,501)
Gillick, Kieran P 2:59:50 (889)
Gillies, Mark R..................5:26:41 (28,574)
Gillies, Robert..................3:42:10 (5,547)
Gillies, Stuart 4:44:09 (19,579)
Gilligan, Richard A 5:10:07 (25,509)
Gillingham, Craig..................3:49:53 (6,914)
Gillis, Andrew J..................3:37:58 (4,826)
Gillis, John W 3:47:34 (6,438)
Gill-Martin, Rupert P 3:47:26 (6,417)
Gillon, Charles A..................3:30:45 (3,814)
Gillot, Jean-Charles 3:27:04 (3,293)
Gillott, Stuart J..................4:50:46 (21,183)
Gillson, Charles E..................4:20:30 (13,732)
Gillson, Scott 3:36:30 (4,609)
Gillson, Stephen P 3:24:17 (2,939)
Gilmore, Dominic P..................3:51:05 (7,158)
Gilmore, James H..................5:50:25 (31,718)
Gilmore, Mark..................4:47:44 (20,464)
Gilmour, Duncan N 2:55:53 (606)
Gilmour, Rory C 4:00:35 (9,327)
Gilmour, Stephen G 3:47:31 (6,432)
Gilpin, John R 4:26:13 (15,105)
Gilroy, Robson M 5:38:31 (30,384)
Gilsenan, William H..................5:00:26 (23,603)
Gimeno, Manuel 4:47:02 (20,295)
Gimre, Michael C..................4:01:08 (9,444)
Ginger, Oliver J 5:17:06 (26,877)
Ginks, Matthew..................4:04:35 (10,074)
Ginman, Anthony 5:58:06 (32,420)
Ginn, Alan P 3:38:42 (4,956)
Ginnaw, Colin 5:47:57 (31,462)
Ginnaw, Gary R 5:02:58 (24,116)
Ginzinger, Helmut 4:40:40 (18,694)
Giochini, Alessandro..................3:20:27 (2,549)
Gipp, Peter R..................4:15:23 (12,416)
Gipson, Adam..................5:28:04 (28,812)
Girardelli, Adrian O..................3:43:17 (5,734)
Girbal, Joel..................4:25:26 (14,931)
Gireau, Daniel 5:33:29 (29,678)
Girling, James C 4:27:40 (15,509)
Girling, Stephen M 4:17:40 (12,989)
Githui, Davidson M 5:26:50 (28,597)
Gittings, Paul 4:09:50 (11,134)
Gittins, James R 4:36:48 (17,740)
Gittins, Paul 3:11:49 (1,705)
Gittoes, Jonathan M 3:52:01 (7,366)
Giuffrida, Giuseppe 4:13:53 (12,062)
Giugno, Carlo 3:26:49 (3,244)
Glade, Stefan 4:12:30 (11,721)
Gladman, Alan 4:54:56 (22,254)
Gladwell, Ian D..................2:58:20 (774)
Glancy, Paul 4:29:46 (16,080)
Glandfield, Tom G 3:12:09 (1,745)
Glanville, Richard 4:25:05 (14,842)
Glass, Douglas J..................4:29:31 (16,013)
Glass, Frank 4:09:50 (11,134)
Glass, Stephen 4:29:46 (16,080)
Glassford, Richard..................5:38:11 (30,333)
Glassock, Chris P..................5:23:45 (28,063)
Glastonbury, Martin K 4:07:42 (10,704)
Glattes, Marc O 3:40:46 (5,312)
Glaysher, Stefan N..................2:55:00 (578)
Glazier, Darren 4:53:03 (21,762)
Gleave, Alistair R 4:56:58 (22,768)
Gleave, Harold 4:38:33 (18,163)
Gledhill, Peter M..................4:07:52 (10,741)
Gleed, Kevin P 4:30:27 (16,246)
Gleeson, Christopher L 6:23:50 (34,067)

Gleeson, Daniel M 6:22:52 (34,038)
Gleeson, Declan V 4:14:54 (12,297)
Gleeson, Michael J 3:24:51 (3,002)
Gleeson, Michael J 4:53:16 (21,828)
Gleeson, Nathan 5:00:12 (23,551)
Gleeson, Paul 6:22:48 (34,036)
Gleghorn, Gary W 4:47:12 (20,334)
Glen, Andrew 3:30:48 (3,820)
Glen, Colin 4:36:44 (17,723)
Glendennan, Paul 4:13:26 (11,944)
Glendinning, Thomas B 3:46:47 (6,301)
Glenister, Kevin A 3:50:23 (7,018)
Gless, Gerard 4:34:56 (17,253)
Glossy, David A 5:00:19 (23,581)
Glover, Adrian D 4:31:00 (16,354)
Glover, Dominic S 4:24:50 (14,793)
Glover, Francis 3:56:46 (8,423)
Glover, Hugo 4:19:36 (13,486)
Glover, Ian 2:59:56 (897)
Glover, Ian G 4:12:53 (11,803)
Glover, Nicholas W 6:37:46 (34,597)
Glover, Paul 4:45:56 (20,042)
Glover, Paul 6:12:15 (33,439)
Gloyens, Mark A 3:46:01 (6,182)
Glynn, Graham J 3:45:55 (6,166)
Glynn, Mark J 3:38:20 (4,892)
Glynn, Paul F 3:47:22 (6,401)
Goadsby, William 6:03:31 (32,852)
Goakes, Andrew 3:37:52 (4,802)
Goalen, Iain M 4:18:25 (13,181)
Godbee, Peter J 4:12:00 (11,613)
Godber, Paul J 5:28:08 (28,826)
Godbold, Brian 4:16:08 (12,604)
Godbold, Douglas L 3:59:31 (9,097)
Goddard, Alex B 4:12:15 (11,670)
Goddard, Barry 5:36:13 (30,075)
Goddard, Chris A 5:14:07 (26,251)
Goddard, Martyn J 5:26:38 (28,560)
Goddard, Neil D 4:42:41 (19,227)
Goddard, Paul S 5:11:47 (25,808)
Goddard, Paul S 5:48:49 (31,562)
Goddard, Peter 4:15:06 (12,342)
Goddard, Russell M 3:27:13 (3,312)
Goddard, Stephen C 4:27:04 (15,345)
Godde, Joel P 4:37:04 (17,801)
Godden, Ian D 3:21:51 (2,690)
Godden, Jim P 3:26:29 (3,196)
Godec, Thomas R 4:51:34 (21,387)
Goden, Peter J 4:29:27 (15,993)
Godet, Patrick 4:38:56 (18,265)
Godfrey, Alfred A 4:10:31 (11,273)
Godfrey, Christopher A 5:07:21 (24,967)
Godfrey, Christopher J 4:48:47 (20,717)
Godfrey, Jonathan M 6:30:58 (34,362)
Godfrey, Leigh R 5:11:49 (25,817)
Godfrey, Michael S 6:01:07 (32,689)
Godfrey, Peter 5:58:44 (32,486)
Godfrey, Thomas A 3:48:54 (6,703)
Godly, Anton J 4:51:22 (21,334)
Godman, Michael L 3:58:37 (8,857)
Godrich, Shane R 4:58:24 (23,134)
Godskesew, Thomas 3:32:35 (4,082)
Godwin, Adrian N 5:03:20 (24,202)
Godwin, Daniel 3:22:23 (2,736)
Godwin, Ross 3:56:02 (8,231)
Godwin, Simon J 5:42:26 (30,874)
Godzisz, Wojtek M 5:10:05 (25,501)
Goehring, Stefan 4:15:14 (12,374)
Goel, Amit 5:02:21 (24,001)
Goessweiner, Herwig C 3:37:50 (4,794)
Goetti, Thomas R 2:57:00 (676)
Goetzfried, Alfons 3:58:51 (8,930)
Goff, Graham D 5:31:23 (29,359)
Goff, Matthew P 4:11:01 (11,371)
Goffe, James R 3:55:07 (8,035)
Gohil, Sunil R 3:19:43 (2,457)
Gois, Manuel V 5:29:07 (28,998)
Gold, Lawrence F 4:10:03 (11,176)
Gold, Peter 4:07:47 (10,721)
Goldener, Emil 4:28:02 (15,602)
Golder, Sean M 5:08:42 (25,226)
Goldie, John 5:06:42 (24,817)
Goldie-Scot, Duncan J 4:12:07 (11,637)
Golding, Daniel 5:21:39 (27,726)
Golding, Daniel J 2:38:40 (119)
Golding, David A 4:09:06 (10,973)
Golding, Mark 5:31:31 (29,378)
Goldman, Michael 6:13:53 (33,541)
Goldsbrough, Kenneth 4:30:18 (16,216)
Goldsmid, Robert R 4:44:49 (19,784)
Goldsmith, Ian R 4:55:07 (22,296)
Goldsmith, Mark J 5:13:06 (26,063)
Goldsmith, Nicholas 4:37:25 (17,870)
Goldsmith, Nick J 4:00:36 (9,330)
Goldsmith, Oliver P 5:28:44 (28,936)
Goldsmith, Robert R 4:39:43 (18,466)
Goldsmith, Simon J 5:08:42 (25,226)
Goldsmith, Steven 3:56:23 (8,330)
Goldsmith, Stuart G 3:42:49 (5,650)
Goldspink, Graham J 4:20:12 (13,655)
Goldstein, Jayme R 5:00:45 (23,676)
Goldstein, Mark A 2:59:31 (866)
Goldsworthy, John 4:57:57 (23,022)
Goldup, Robert J 4:54:42 (22,198)
Golfieri, Antonio 4:08:25 (10,856)
Goligher, Scott W 3:20:34 (2,565)
Golisz, Kamil 4:52:43 (21,673)
Golledge, Clive G 3:46:04 (6,189)
Gollings, David J 3:54:05 (7,812)
Gollings, Michael S 3:38:15 (4,877)
Gollner, Heinz 3:57:56 (8,705)
Gombert, Alain 4:55:19 (22,341)
Gomes, Marilson 2:08:37 (8)
Gomez, Francisco J 3:31:20 (3,881)
Gomez, José L 5:14:52 (26,422)
Gomez, Luis F 2:56:46 (658)
Gomez Flores, Pedro Carlos 3:44:07 (5,883)
Gomez-Perales, Jorge E 4:06:18 (10,417)
Goncalves, Pedro M 4:53:49 (21,972)
Gonde, Chris 3:53:27 (7,677)
Goniszewski, Jan 6:03:03 (32,822)
Gonnella, Josh 4:36:26 (17,649)
Gonsalves, Armindo 3:09:41 (1,531)
Gonsalves, Raphael 6:01:43 (32,735)
Gonsalves, Victor 4:42:39 (19,215)
Gonzalez, Angel 4:06:35 (10,482)
Gonzalez, Carlos 2:54:16 (530)
Gonzalez, David 3:24:33 (2,964)
Gonzalez, Donald 3:27:14 (3,318)
Gonzalez, José 3:57:31 (8,602)
Gonzalez, José D 2:42:52 (196)
Gonzalez, Luis M 3:31:32 (3,915)
Gonzalez, Victor 4:01:28 (9,510)
Gonzalez Valenzuela, Miguel A 5:15:01 (26,456)
Gonzalez-Diaz, Francisco F 2:57:27 (706)
Good, Hervay 5:01:53 (23,909)
Good, Michael E 3:51:57 (7,356)
Goodall, Adam T 4:35:11 (17,323)
Goodall, James N 5:36:07 (30,062)
Goodall, Jonathan S 4:40:07 (18,560)
Goodall, Kevin J 5:47:01 (31,356)
Goodall, Martin J 5:27:43 (28,747)
Goodall, Terence V 5:15:10 (26,493)
Goodall, William K 5:12:50 (26,005)
Goodbun, Mark 4:14:02 (12,106)
Goodchild, James L 3:55:21 (8,093)
Goodchild, Julian P 5:04:26 (24,407)
Goodchild, Keith 5:04:31 (24,422)
Goodchild, Paul D 3:52:43 (7,506)
Gooddy, John F 4:07:11 (10,606)
Goode, Andrew 4:50:24 (21,097)
Goode, Jonny M 3:51:29 (7,250)
Goode, Nigel C 3:20:00 (2,497)
Goode, Paul J 4:04:27 (10,049)
Goode, Philip 2:59:53 (891)
Goode, Tom A 6:37:55 (34,601)
Gooden, Howard M 5:38:39 (30,409)
Gooder, Steve A 5:01:54 (23,913)
Goodeve, Andrew 4:47:52 (20,494)
Goodey, Matthew 4:51:18 (21,315)
Goodey, Vincent G 4:43:09 (19,330)
Goodhead, Christopher J 4:30:12 (16,196)
Goodhind, Colin 4:33:56 (17,016)
Gooding, Adrian 4:16:08 (12,604)
Gooding, Michael J 2:59:00 (824)
Gooding, Peter R 3:25:42 (3,088)
Goodlad, Chris S 4:14:10 (12,130)
Goodman, James 3:44:30 (5,942)
Goodman, James N 4:59:14 (23,319)
Goodman, Simon D 5:15:00 (26,449)
Goodman, Spencer E 5:02:43 (24,079)
Goodrick, Paul J 6:14:24 (33,576)
Goodright, Ray 4:43:15 (19,355)
Goodrum, Paul J 3:10:46 (1,611)
Goodrum, Richard 3:41:05 (5,378)
Goodsall, James A 3:42:40 (5,622)
Goodsir, Mark A 4:47:12 (20,334)
Goodson, Andrew M 6:54:43 (35,029)
Goodson, Mark 4:16:16 (12,639)
Goodway, Dean 5:25:22 (28,334)
Goodwin, Alan J 4:53:37 (21,919)
Goodwin, Andrew P 4:26:50 (15,275)
Goodwin, David 5:24:33 (28,188)
Goodwin, Frederick V 4:45:56 (20,042)
Goodwin, Ian V 3:42:19 (5,572)
Goodwin, Jack 4:55:31 (22,395)
Goodwin, John 4:53:54 (21,991)
Goodwin, Julian 3:21:46 (2,682)
Goodwin, Kevin 4:33:40 (16,952)
Goodwin, Michael J 5:47:38 (31,420)
Goodwin, Paul D 4:29:55 (16,123)
Goodwin, Ryan T 3:33:36 (4,213)
Goodwin, Scott W 4:07:30 (10,651)
Goodwin, Stephen H 3:23:59 (2,903)
Goodyear, David M 5:12:39 (25,974)
Goold, Andrew M 4:03:07 (9,804)
Goosen, Jacobus J 4:37:31 (17,892)
Gopalakrishnan, Luckshman H 4:57:24 (22,887)
Gopalan, Srinivasan 5:12:07 (25,874)
Gordine, Hayden V 4:19:32 (13,467)
Gordon, Adrian T 4:16:34 (12,708)
Gordon, Alan D 3:35:56 (4,540)
Gordon, Chris J 6:17:05 (33,735)
Gordon, Christopher R 5:32:10 (29,477)
Gordon, Daniel J 3:48:59 (6,729)
Gordon, David 4:32:33 (16,675)
Gordon, Garry H 4:23:01 (14,337)
Gordon, Jeffrey 5:23:51 (28,085)
Gordon, Jonathan N 3:08:07 (1,399)
Gordon, Keith 4:29:54 (16,121)
Gordon, Keith D 5:19:53 (27,405)
Gordon, Lee K 5:19:06 (27,267)
Gordon, Luke J 4:35:19 (17,363)
Gordon, Michael W 4:36:19 (17,614)
Gordon, Peter C 3:28:41 (3,520)
Gordon, Stephen J 3:07:51 (1,373)
Gordon, Stewart 5:12:27 (25,946)
Gordon-Wilkin, Gareth I 4:23:58 (14,562)
Gore, Andrew K 3:09:48 (1,539)
Gore, Anthony J 3:52:59 (7,564)
Gore, Bob 4:54:18 (22,101)
Gore, Jonathan P 5:58:24 (32,459)
Gore, Lawrence 4:15:14 (12,374)
Gore, Martin D 4:11:29 (11,496)
Gore, Martin P 3:07:43 (1,364)
Gore, Matthew H 5:01:16 (23,787)
Gorham, Matthew R 4:43:19 (19,383)
Gorioux, Franco-Xavi 3:59:12 (9,011)
Gorman, Martin A 4:27:10 (15,375)
Gormley, Bernard P 5:45:06 (31,167)
Gormley, G A 3:30:59 (3,838)
Gornall, Nicholas W 5:29:44 (29,100)
Gorst, Richard T 2:57:16 (695)
Gorthy, Bhanu P 7:24:28 (35,427)
Gosbee, Norman 4:21:15 (13,903)
Gosling, Christopher P 5:01:08 (23,759)
Gosling, Mark W 3:54:12 (7,839)
Gosling, Richard N 4:40:50 (18,740)
Gosney, Paul J 5:11:58 (25,848)
Goss, Andrew K 4:23:00 (14,334)
Goss, Clive M 4:54:29 (22,145)
Goss, David R 5:30:44 (29,259)
Goss, John D 4:43:26 (19,405)
Goss, Jonathan A 4:52:02 (21,492)
Goss, Paul D 3:50:51 (7,107)
Gossage, Michael J 4:59:03 (23,272)
Gossop, Stephen B 5:07:35 (25,017)
Gostelow, Neil D 4:51:28 (21,363)
Gostling, John P 3:59:48 (9,162)

Gothard, Derek I.	3:38:51 (4,988)	
Gothard, Maxwell S.	6:30:49 (34,356)	
Gotlieb, Rob	3:53:47 (7,743)	
Gottlieb, Craig H.	5:51:35 (31,836)	
Gottlieb, Kim A	5:36:01 (30,050)	
Gotz, Mohindra	5:37:14 (30,203)	
Goucher, Dave	5:07:17 (24,951)	
Goude, Christian	4:28:33 (15,745)	
Goudge, Adam E.	4:35:28 (17,397)	
Gough, Antony R	4:41:47 (18,989)	
Gough, Brian E	7:26:48 (35,442)	
Gough, Charles V	5:53:08 (31,973)	
Gough, David R.	3:19:42 (2,453)	
Gough, James	5:28:20 (28,877)	
Gough, Mike	4:33:10 (16,830)	
Gough, Neil M.	5:24:12 (28,137)	
Gough, Paul B	3:56:54 (8,457)	
Gould, Andrew J.	4:54:20 (22,106)	
Gould, Bruce K.	7:32:28 (35,511)	
Gould, Edmund A.	4:42:13 (19,101)	
Gould, Martin	3:26:30 (3,197)	
Gould, Norman S.	7:32:44 (35,512)	
Gould, Thomas	3:54:15 (7,855)	
Goulding, Geoffrey W.	5:34:22 (29,820)	
Goulding, Mark	5:14:29 (26,330)	
Goumri, Abderrahim	2:07:44 (2)	
Goundry, Andrew C	3:40:53 (5,343)	
Goupille, Thierry	4:02:10 (9,638)	
Gourd, Jacob R.	4:45:41 (19,989)	
Gournay, Kevin J.	3:35:38 (4,504)	
Goux, Fabrice	5:15:59 (26,654)	
Goveia, Gavin A.	4:36:07 (17,563)	
Gow, Andie F	6:41:03 (34,690)	
Gow, Chris	4:09:05 (10,971)	
Gower, Kevin A	5:09:18 (25,333)	
Gower, Nicholas J	3:02:36 (1,032)	
Gower, Simon N	4:42:25 (19,156)	
Gower, Stephen D	5:43:08 (30,952)	
Gowers, Ian J	3:55:53 (8,204)	
Gowing, Peter J.	4:12:48 (11,789)	
Gowing, Richard J	4:12:15 (11,670)	
Goy, William	5:18:34 (27,175)	
Goyder, Nicholas P	4:43:54 (19,509)	
Graber, Patrick	4:03:05 (9,799)	
Grace, Daniel	3:43:23 (5,751)	
Grace, Gavin	5:30:56 (29,286)	
Grace, John	5:08:56 (25,269)	
Grace, Mike	4:12:17 (11,681)	
Grace, Philip	4:51:24 (21,343)	
Gradden, Michael D	4:01:13 (9,462)	
Grady, Leslie	4:09:25 (11,053)	
Grafton, Mathew J	4:44:34 (19,705)	
Graggaber, Johann	3:19:45 (2,460)	
Graham, Barry M	5:22:44 (27,896)	
Graham, Carl A	4:20:55 (13,833)	
Graham, Carl M	5:00:12 (23,551)	
Graham, David C	3:29:04 (3,583)	
Graham, David I	4:32:19 (16,630)	
Graham, David T	6:26:05 (34,173)	
Graham, Dean W	4:42:33 (19,190)	
Graham, Ian	4:40:16 (18,594)	
Graham, James M	4:44:05 (19,560)	
Graham, John A	4:42:21 (19,139)	
Graham, Keith R	5:19:06 (27,267)	
Graham, Mark A	6:15:57 (33,680)	
Graham, Mark R	2:56:08 (619)	
Graham, Martin	4:39:47 (18,483)	
Graham, Matthew P	3:55:40 (8,155)	
Graham, Michael J	4:21:22 (13,926)	
Graham, Michael R.	3:17:26 (2,221)	
Graham, Neil C	4:46:12 (20,107)	
Graham, Paul W	4:00:28 (9,303)	
Graham, Peter W	5:25:18 (28,320)	
Graham, Russell	4:05:55 (10,332)	
Graham, Stuart	3:30:00 (3,719)	
Graham, Tom G	5:02:16 (23,982)	
Graham, Warren V	4:27:49 (15,543)	
Graham, William	4:17:12 (12,853)	
Grainger, Adrian P	3:38:02 (4,837)	
Gramson, Mark J	6:10:34 (33,342)	
Grande, Jean Pierre	3:31:04 (3,843)	
Grandison, Rowen D	3:28:35 (3,502)	
Grandy, Mark	4:11:55 (11,596)	
Granfield, Keith M	4:28:01 (15,592)	
Grange, Ian V	4:05:16 (10,197)	
Grange, Robert P	4:43:07 (19,324)	
Granger, Clive	4:21:01 (13,857)	
Grant, Alexander	5:00:11 (23,547)	
Grant, Allan	4:17:26 (12,921)	
Grant, Allen	4:29:49 (16,095)	
Grant, Andrew N	5:08:05 (25,110)	
Grant, Antonio B	2:36:19 (89)	
Grant, David J	5:05:36 (24,619)	
Grant, Elliott	4:53:34 (21,904)	
Grant, Eugene	5:51:27 (31,822)	
Grant, Eugene J	2:45:19 (248)	
Grant, Gavin S	4:53:12 (21,810)	
Grant, James R	4:04:31 (10,059)	
Grant, Jamie N	5:13:56 (26,217)	
Grant, Jonathan P	3:13:04 (1,824)	
Grant, Kevin M	3:51:16 (7,199)	
Grant, Mark S	4:47:00 (20,280)	
Grant, Matthew J	3:42:16 (5,565)	
Grant, Mick J	3:59:45 (9,152)	
Grant, Nigel J	2:54:14 (527)	
Grant, Paul	4:42:33 (19,190)	
Grant, Paul	6:07:25 (33,125)	
Grant, Peter	4:09:33 (11,085)	
Grant, Peter	4:59:13 (23,314)	
Grant, Stewart M	5:14:56 (26,435)	
Grant, Stuart J	6:10:26 (33,330)	
Grant, Tony	4:02:06 (9,622)	
Grantham, James	3:23:25 (2,842)	
Grantham, Richard	5:06:44 (24,826)	
Graversen, Lars B	4:48:46 (20,711)	
Graves, Christopher A	4:37:58 (17,999)	
Graves, Phillip	4:53:42 (21,942)	
Gravis, Craig B	4:38:56 (18,265)	
Gray, Adam N	3:19:09 (2,409)	
Gray, Alan	4:40:27 (18,640)	
Gray, Andrew C	3:09:54 (1,548)	
Gray, Andrew N	3:52:19 (7,437)	
Gray, Andrew R	4:28:39 (15,773)	
Gray, Anthony D	3:25:08 (3,035)	
Gray, Benjamin R	5:23:31 (28,013)	
Gray, Brian A	4:30:06 (16,174)	
Gray, Bryan S	4:52:13 (21,546)	
Gray, Colin T	4:38:20 (18,106)	
Gray, Crispin N	4:30:54 (16,335)	
Gray, David C	3:28:42 (3,524)	
Gray, Duncan J	4:13:36 (11,996)	
Gray, Frank T	5:00:43 (23,664)	
Gray, James C	4:29:02 (15,865)	
Gray, John A	4:29:31 (16,013)	
Gray, John L	4:39:25 (18,394)	
Gray, Jonathan M	4:30:54 (16,335)	
Gray, Keith A	5:53:28 (32,004)	
Gray, Kelvin D	4:03:46 (9,919)	
Gray, Lindsay	4:22:17 (14,148)	
Gray, Matthew B	4:44:34 (19,705)	
Gray, Patrick J	5:41:17 (30,739)	
Gray, Paul	3:57:17 (8,549)	
Gray, Paul	4:13:41 (12,014)	
Gray, Paul C	5:24:27 (28,175)	
Gray, Paul R	3:46:21 (6,227)	
Gray, Peter	5:04:44 (24,455)	
Gray, Richard	3:27:25 (3,345)	
Gray, Shane G	2:52:19 (456)	
Gray, Simon C	4:53:00 (21,756)	
Gray, Simon J	4:44:06 (19,563)	
Gray, Stephen R.	4:31:13 (16,410)	
Gray, Steven A	5:40:35 (30,662)	
Gray, Steven J.	5:35:38 (30,003)	
Gray, Toby	5:14:10 (26,262)	
Grayshon, Lee A	3:25:48 (3,100)	
Graysmark, Robin S	4:47:23 (20,379)	
Graziani, Alessandro	4:34:06 (17,050)	
Graziani, Rodolfo	4:49:58 (20,986)	
Grazioli, Claudio	4:14:35 (12,224)	
Greaney, Stuart F.	3:31:10 (3,858)	
Greatorex, Brett	5:06:14 (24,749)	
Greaves, Mark F.	2:57:33 (713)	
Greaves, Paul	4:07:00 (10,575)	
Greaves, Philip A	5:08:27 (25,180)	
Greedy, Philip	4:20:33 (13,742)	
Greeenberg, Glenn R	7:18:19 (35,372)	
Green, Alan D	3:59:21 (9,053)	
Green, Alan E.	4:35:06 (17,298)	
Green, Alan P	7:06:07 (35,220)	
Green, Andrew	3:57:51 (8,680)	
Green, Andrew	4:52:05 (21,509)	
Green, Andrew D	5:08:12 (25,139)	
Green, Andrew J	2:42:21 (185)	
Green, Andrew J	3:32:35 (4,082)	
Green, Andy S	3:43:09 (5,714)	
Green, Brian M	2:54:55 (575)	
Green, Christopher S	4:30:37 (16,284)	
Green, Daniel J	4:42:44 (19,238)	
Green, David C	3:40:48 (5,321)	
Green, David C	4:16:09 (12,609)	
Green, David D	5:08:39 (25,217)	
Green, David J	3:57:52 (8,689)	
Green, David J	6:18:16 (33,789)	
Green, David P	4:13:52 (12,056)	
Green, Eric	3:02:56 (1,045)	
Green, Gareth J	4:25:55 (15,037)	
Green, Gary	3:58:49 (8,913)	
Green, Howard J	3:57:23 (8,577)	
Green, James P	6:30:43 (34,347)	
Green, James R	4:24:36 (14,727)	
Green, Jeremy A	5:50:37 (31,735)	
Green, John	4:32:25 (16,647)	
Green, John K	3:04:33 (1,135)	
Green, Johnny	4:55:11 (22,311)	
Green, Jonathan P	6:50:28 (34,944)	
Green, Leo P	4:46:42 (20,216)	
Green, Mark A	4:40:28 (18,644)	
Green, Matthew J	3:29:47 (3,686)	
Green, Michael	4:10:14 (11,212)	
Green, Michael D	3:50:26 (7,027)	
Green, Michael D	5:40:57 (30,700)	
Green, Michael G	3:27:19 (3,328)	
Green, Michael R	3:26:58 (3,272)	
Green, Michael R	3:47:23 (6,405)	
Green, Michael T	5:41:10 (30,724)	
Green, Mick	3:11:04 (1,638)	
Green, Mickey	4:41:06 (18,811)	
Green, Nigel M	4:25:36 (14,970)	
Green, Patrick M	3:11:02 (1,635)	
Green, Paul	3:47:46 (6,492)	
Green, Peter	5:37:41 (30,258)	
Green, Peter W	4:56:21 (22,602)	
Green, Richard A	4:05:38 (10,273)	
Green, Richard A	4:24:22 (14,669)	
Green, Rob	4:19:41 (13,504)	
Green, Robert J	3:54:12 (7,839)	
Green, Robert J	4:28:49 (15,814)	
Green, Robert T	7:33:00 (35,518)	
Green, Spencer J	4:51:58 (21,477)	
Green, Steven L	3:26:54 (3,258)	
Green, Stuart A	4:58:08 (23,060)	
Green, Thomas S	3:20:06 (2,506)	
Green, Timothy	4:32:02 (16,565)	
Green, Toby	5:11:54 (25,834)	
Green, Tony	6:36:47 (34,569)	
Green, William A	6:36:15 (34,550)	
Green, Winston E	5:04:58 (24,512)	
Greene, David A	6:55:43 (35,050)	
Greener, John M	4:01:53 (9,584)	
Greenfield, David A	4:22:26 (14,181)	
Greenfield, Philip	4:23:15 (14,388)	
Greenfield, Sam J	5:10:23 (25,552)	
Greenfield, Thomas M	5:10:24 (25,560)	
Greenhalgh, Andrew F	4:16:20 (12,654)	
Greenhalgh, Clifford	4:50:58 (21,233)	
Greenhalgh, John D	3:58:37 (8,857)	
Greenhalgh, Mark A	4:59:03 (23,272)	
Greenham, David H	4:44:35 (19,712)	
Greenham, Peter	4:56:33 (22,643)	
Greenhough, Anthony	3:52:14 (7,416)	
Greenhous, Richard V	4:43:20 (19,390)	
Greenhouse, David J	4:32:40 (16,709)	
Greening, Barry J	5:16:08 (26,691)	
Greenland, Richard D	4:27:53 (15,558)	
Greenleaf, Keith M	6:46:22 (34,839)	
Greenough, Craig M	3:13:15 (1,848)	
Greenslade, David	5:29:19 (29,043)	
Greenslade, Tim	4:30:51 (16,324)	
Greenslade, Tim N	6:14:44 (33,595)	

Greenwood, Adie 3:39:07 (5,038)
Greenwood, Andrew J 3:35:50 (4,526)
Greenwood, Gareth J 4:10:41 (11,310)
Greenwood, Ian J 7:08:18 (35,251)
Greenwood, Jon B 3:56:33 (8,374)
Greenwood, Paul B 4:23:10 (14,369)
Greer, James 5:30:24 (29,200)
Greer, Ryan 3:45:39 (6,125)
Greet, Mark A 2:58:00 (746)
Greet, Wayne A 3:42:52 (5,661)
Gregg, Paul 2:49:33 (360)
Gregg, Sean A 3:19:58 (2,490)
Gregg, Simon M 4:14:55 (12,302)
Greggs, Michael A 4:34:26 (17,131)
Gregor, Daniel M 4:29:09 (15,898)
Gregory, Bryan P 5:22:10 (27,804)
Gregory, Christopher J 5:57:52 (32,397)
Gregory, David H 4:16:21 (12,660)
Gregory, Ian D 4:03:52 (9,939)
Gregory, Jeff P 3:41:13 (5,401)
Gregory, Kevin 4:29:40 (16,058)
Gregory, Kevin C 5:26:02 (28,463)
Gregory, Mark 4:43:57 (19,520)
Gregory, Mark A 5:03:25 (24,221)
Gregory, Mark J 3:25:40 (3,085)
Gregory, Mark S 5:29:59 (29,129)
Gregory, Mark T 5:08:09 (25,126)
Gregory, Neil G 3:39:21 (5,073)
Gregory, Nicholas A 3:08:10 (1,403)
Gregory, Nicholas J 4:06:44 (10,509)
Gregory, Nick J 4:43:20 (19,390)
Gregory, Paul F 2:44:08 (218)
Gregory, Stewart J 2:35:59 (83)
Gregory, Stuart R 6:22:57 (34,040)
Gregson, David 4:40:54 (18,760)
Gregson, Michael J 4:44:13 (19,604)
Gregson, Warren A 3:24:16 (2,935)
Greig, Stuart 4:36:17 (17,606)
Grena, Fabrizio 3:47:11 (6,375)
Grender-Jones, Maxwell D 4:34:47 (17,218)
Gresham-Cooke, Gerald N 4:23:50 (14,525)
Gresswell, David J 3:16:16 (2,102)
Greve, Sander 3:14:24 (1,933)
Grew, Neil G 4:24:51 (14,797)
Grew, Stephen B 5:54:08 (32,066)
Grewal, Guy 3:43:06 (5,707)
Grey, Garry 3:45:01 (6,029)
Grey, William M 3:27:34 (3,359)
Gribben, Iain 5:19:22 (27,318)
Gribbon, John P 4:13:13 (11,883)
Gribbon, Luke P 4:14:17 (12,165)
Grice, Michael A 5:23:26 (27,997)
Grice, Zippy 2:56:30 (633)
Grieve, Alan J 4:22:32 (14,213)
Grieve, Craig W 4:17:34 (12,969)
Grieve, Graham D 3:48:45 (6,678)
Griffin, Andrew J 4:56:35 (22,656)
Griffin, Andrew P 5:06:43 (24,822)
Griffin, Gareth P 3:53:40 (7,721)
Griffin, Ian 3:33:46 (4,235)
Griffin, Ian C 4:42:39 (19,215)
Griffin, John E 5:54:28 (32,107)
Griffin, John F 3:02:09 (1,012)
Griffin, Kenneth M 4:36:55 (17,771)
Griffin, Kurt 4:11:19 (11,452)
Griffin, Michael J 7:41:57 (35,581)
Griffin, Paul J 5:09:07 (25,298)
Griffin, Peter L 4:00:08 (9,234)
Griffin, Roger F 3:39:13 (5,048)
Griffin, Simon C 2:59:08 (835)
Griffin, Stephen 4:27:07 (15,357)
Griffin, Steven M 4:51:25 (21,348)
Griffin-Davies, Neil R 5:49:13 (31,604)
Griffith, Aaron D 4:20:18 (13,679)
Griffith, Jackson E 3:50:06 (6,962)
Griffith, John O 5:02:54 (24,108)
Griffith-Jones, Freddie N 5:29:07 (28,998)
Griffiths, Alan 4:53:12 (21,810)
Griffiths, Alan P 3:53:23 (7,660)
Griffiths, Alan T 5:12:08 (25,879)
Griffiths, Alistair J 4:36:26 (17,649)
Griffiths, Andrew 4:13:11 (11,874)
Griffiths, Andrew J 3:43:09 (5,714)
Griffiths, Andrew J 5:17:53 (27,025)
Griffiths, Barrie W 3:07:42 (1,360)
Griffiths, Barry 3:49:35 (6,848)
Griffiths, Barry 5:03:55 (24,312)
Griffiths, Craig P 4:26:37 (15,214)
Griffiths, Dave J 4:04:32 (10,062)
Griffiths, David A 4:17:25 (12,914)
Griffiths, David P 4:11:21 (11,459)
Griffiths, Gareth D 3:50:42 (7,078)
Griffiths, Graeme D 3:14:31 (1,943)
Griffiths, James S 4:53:19 (21,842)
Griffiths, Jonathan P 4:40:10 (18,573)
Griffiths, Keith D 3:50:30 (7,044)
Griffiths, Keith D 4:51:26 (21,352)
Griffiths, Mark D 4:10:24 (11,248)
Griffiths, Michael J 4:10:07 (11,186)
Griffiths, Mike 4:05:31 (10,241)
Griffiths, Mike J 3:48:50 (6,694)
Griffiths, Neil T 4:43:14 (19,349)
Griffiths, Paul 4:25:06 (14,848)
Griffiths, Paul 4:39:02 (18,293)
Griffiths, Paul W 3:19:56 (2,487)
Griffiths, Peter 3:31:34 (3,919)
Griffiths, Richard 4:37:14 (17,826)
Griffiths, Richard J 3:08:22 (1,421)
Griffiths, Robert E 4:53:09 (21,797)
Griffiths, Thomas A 6:16:52 (33,727)
Griffiths, Thomas P 4:06:45 (10,513)
Griffiths, William T 6:33:22 (34,451)
Griffon, Vincent 3:40:24 (5,248)
Grifi, Gianluca 4:14:22 (12,180)
Grigg, Alan 5:28:33 (28,910)
Grigg, Jonathan W 3:55:17 (8,074)
Griggs, Jeremy 3:51:56 (7,351)
Grigor, Alexander C 3:41:29 (5,443)
Grillo, Ennio 3:30:00 (3,719)
Grimaldi, Pasquale 3:56:46 (8,423)
Grimer, Nicholas P 2:49:30 (359)
Grimes, James L 4:06:57 (10,558)
Grimmett, Andy N 4:38:24 (18,126)
Grimsey, William 3:31:27 (3,898)
Grimshaw, Grahame D 3:51:01 (7,142)
Grindell, Philip 5:04:16 (24,370)
Grindu, Louis 4:43:13 (19,343)
Grinnell, Laurence C 4:37:25 (17,870)
Grint, Lee S 6:40:09 (34,669)
Grisley, Chris D 3:57:13 (8,533)
Grisoni, Jack M 4:35:10 (17,316)
Grist, Roger 3:42:05 (5,534)
Grlica, Vladimir F 4:09:08 (10,986)
Grocott, Tony E 4:04:52 (10,125)
Groenewald, Andrew L 4:08:28 (10,866)
Groke, Michael C 4:58:25 (23,136)
Gronow, Richard T 4:34:35 (17,169)
Gronqvist, Robert 4:16:06 (12,596)
Groom, Alex 4:02:11 (9,642)
Groom, Steven 3:41:19 (5,415)
Groombridge, Nicholas 7:07:21 (35,236)
Groombridge, Paul 3:37:41 (4,773)
Grossbard, David M 4:55:59 (22,508)
Grosso, Giulio G 4:42:11 (19,089)
Grosvenor, Howard P 3:28:34 (3,501)
Groussard, Patrice 4:22:17 (14,148)
Grout, Andrew D 4:54:26 (22,132)
Grout, Nic P 5:26:38 (28,560)
Grove, Darren 3:32:56 (4,129)
Grove, Martyn T 6:21:16 (33,966)
Grove, Richard C 7:07:59 (35,245)
Grover, Rob J 5:31:08 (29,327)
Groves, Benjamin J 3:57:42 (8,654)
Groves, David J 5:03:43 (24,273)
Groves, Jonathan A 4:27:47 (15,538)
Groves, Kelvin 4:46:18 (20,127)
Groves, Mark R 3:59:24 (9,068)
Groves, Paul M 4:46:59 (20,274)
Groves, Peter J 4:47:14 (20,340)
Groves, Ricky 5:22:29 (27,844)
Grubb, Andrew D 3:13:38 (1,869)
Grubb, Thomas R 3:33:24 (4,194)
Grubb, Timothy J 4:18:39 (13,252)
Gruben, Jorge 4:46:22 (20,149)
Gruber, Alex B 5:09:57 (25,463)
Gruber, Frank 4:12:55 (11,809)
Grubjerg, Andreas 4:15:42 (12,486)
Grueneberg, Ingo 3:25:59 (3,123)
Grumbridge, Michael G 4:46:15 (20,115)
Grummet, Paul J 4:56:37 (22,665)
Grundy, Kristian M 4:52:49 (21,706)
Grundy, Paul M 4:37:51 (17,969)
Grundy, Paul W 6:08:15 (33,191)
Gtillis, Thomas 4:14:45 (12,261)
Gualdi, Giuseppe 3:39:28 (5,100)
Guard, Andrew J 4:19:50 (13,555)
Guarnieri, Paul J 5:41:11 (30,726)
Guatterini, Renato 3:40:27 (5,253)
Gubbins, Matthew J 5:17:33 (26,969)
Gubbins, Michael I 4:26:47 (15,260)
Gubel, Ekkehard W 4:05:37 (10,268)
Guccione, Edward J 4:18:12 (13,124)
Gudgin, Paul M 3:58:45 (8,897)
Gudka, Piyush 3:46:33 (6,257)
Guedes, Pedro 3:37:30 (4,752)
Gueneron, Jacques 3:26:28 (3,194)
Gueorguiev, Krasse N 3:47:36 (6,447)
Guerard, Stuart N 5:26:57 (28,617)
Guerra, Carlos 3:05:04 (1,167)
Guerra, Enricomaria 4:22:41 (14,253)
Guerrero, José A 3:06:34 (1,276)
Guest, Andrew I 4:52:45 (21,681)
Guest, Andy 5:27:50 (28,767)
Guest, Arron S 5:47:10 (31,365)
Guest, Craig S 5:47:11 (31,368)
Guest, Glyn 3:33:07 (4,156)
Guest, Ian S 4:27:24 (15,448)
Guest, Martin N 4:04:12 (10,006)
Guest, Paul A 3:10:39 (1,607)
Guest, Richard M 4:14:51 (12,278)
Guest, Robert J 4:43:09 (19,330)
Guevara, Miguel 3:02:29 (1,026)
Guezzar, Abdelrhani 3:47:54 (6,512)
Guida, Michael S 3:56:32 (8,369)
Guidotti, Sergio 5:41:52 (30,816)
Guignard, Arnaud D 3:26:56 (3,265)
Guile, Simon G 4:48:18 (20,605)
Guillamet, Daniel R 5:32:21 (29,503)
Guillamet, Martial P 4:49:19 (20,842)
Guillaume, Roland 4:11:45 (11,558)
Guimaraes, Francisco E 4:29:22 (15,964)
Guimard, Dominique 4:17:53 (13,038)
Guinan, Paul E 2:37:11 (100)
Guinane, Simon J 4:16:33 (12,704)
Guise, Alexander P 3:51:48 (7,315)
Guiseley, Andrew 3:14:54 (1,984)
Guivarc'h, Stephane 4:15:01 (12,328)
Guiver, Edward P 4:06:07 (10,376)
Guiver, William 4:06:26 (10,450)
Gujudhur, Vladimir 6:01:31 (32,720)
Gulc, Peter 3:07:20 (1,337)
Gull, William E 4:41:40 (18,958)
Gullbrandsson, Jan V 3:54:28 (7,897)
Gullis, Michael A 3:29:48 (3,688)
Gulliver, David 4:26:26 (15,170)
Gumley, Bruce 3:39:15 (5,055)
Gummer, Andrew J 4:20:14 (13,660)
Gummery, Ian 4:22:32 (14,213)
Gunaratnam, David R 4:17:41 (12,992)
Gunby, Peter F 4:19:52 (13,563)
Gundersen, Steinar 3:47:35 (6,441)
Guner, David 3:31:22 (3,887)
Gunn, Adam D 5:13:42 (26,166)
Gunn, Andrew N 4:53:28 (21,883)
Gunn, Graham 3:55:01 (8,011)
Gunn, Mark L 5:18:42 (27,199)
Gunnell, James W 5:09:31 (25,375)
Gunning, Simon M 3:24:25 (2,949)
Gunther, Stephen T 4:13:39 (12,007)
Guomunosson, Jorunnour S 4:51:06 (21,266)
Gupta, John 4:40:10 (18,573)
Gurd, Richard 2:56:59 (673)
Gurdag, Huseyin 5:56:28 (32,282)
Gurden, Dean C 5:29:08 (29,005)
Gurden, Matthew J 4:26:06 (15,074)
Gurr, Stuart 3:35:19 (4,457)
Gurteen, Lee 6:34:39 (34,480)
Gussoni, Carlo 4:48:18 (20,605)
Gustasab, Abbas 5:51:33 (31,833)

Gustavsson, Daniel B....4:21:25 (13,942)
Gutbrod, Hubert....4:07:10 (10,601)
Guthrie, Eugene J....7:47:10 (35,609)
Guthrie, Greg....5:28:55 (28,971)
Gutierrez, Carlos A....5:16:52 (26,829)
Gutjahr, Lothar....5:54:43 (32,118)
Gutridge, Stephen J....4:21:34 (13,978)
Guy, Graham....4:49:44 (20,940)
Guy, Kerry C....4:54:14 (22,085)
Guy, Robert J....4:00:12 (9,250)
Guy, William....4:12:58 (11,822)
Guyan, Paul R....4:08:24 (10,848)
Guyatt, Robert J....5:10:32 (25,584)
Guyll, Christopher....4:57:20 (22,870)
Guyte, Kristian....4:50:03 (21,007)
Gwenter, Matthew J....4:42:10 (19,082)
Gwilliam, David J....3:47:51 (6,503)
Gwilliam, David J....4:02:14 (9,659)
Gwilliam, Steven J....4:48:05 (20,549)
Gwyn, Graeme....4:34:55 (17,250)
Gwyther, Michael I....4:46:31 (20,185)
Gyliason, Kjartan....4:05:50 (10,314)
Gymer, Alex W....4:34:33 (17,159)
Gyte, Barry G....3:02:14 (1,014)
Haas, Otto....2:53:14 (479)
Haas, Timothy E....3:38:13 (4,871)
Haberl, Andreas....3:41:38 (5,460)
Haberlin, Keith J....3:59:57 (9,198)
Hack, Damian G....5:53:21 (31,993)
Hackenberger, Raimund....3:42:31 (5,599)
Hackett, Wayne I....4:58:31 (23,153)
Hackforth, Clive C....3:44:15 (5,896)
Hackland, Andrew S....4:52:14 (21,552)
Hackney, Thomas D....4:27:35 (15,488)
Hadaway, Mark D....3:39:29 (5,104)
Haddad, Mish....5:17:19 (26,922)
Hadden, Matthew....3:38:36 (4,939)
Haddock, Paul A....5:27:10 (28,654)
Haddrell, Roger....3:24:29 (2,954)
Haddy, Marcus....6:11:02 (33,372)
Haden, Matthew D....4:22:59 (14,331)
Haden, Stuart T....4:17:45 (13,010)
Hadfield, Andrew M....4:56:50 (22,728)
Hadfield, Peter....4:46:17 (20,120)
Hadi, Benjamin....6:06:04 (33,054)
Hadland, Jeremy R....3:51:55 (7,342)
Hadley, Christian L....4:09:02 (10,956)
Hadley, Ian P....5:12:20 (25,929)
Hadley, Nicholas J....4:53:09 (21,797)
Hadley, Peter E....3:39:28 (5,100)
Hadley, Ricky....5:25:13 (28,308)
Hadlow, Edward J....3:40:33 (5,278)
Hadnutt, Antony M....4:09:19 (11,034)
Hadwen, Nick....4:22:09 (14,116)
Haeffner, Christopher H....3:58:20 (8,793)
Haese, Peter M....4:29:08 (15,895)
Haffenden, Michael....3:55:07 (8,035)
Hagemann, Carl....4:45:55 (20,040)
Hagemo, Jostein S....3:33:49 (4,238)
Hagen, Hugo....4:53:18 (21,840)
Hagen, Oeivind Ravn....5:00:32 (23,621)
Hagen, Othmar....3:38:14 (4,873)
Haggarty, Scot I....4:09:35 (11,092)
Hagman, Martin G....3:38:25 (4,904)
Hague, Jack W....4:45:49 (20,010)
Hague, Thomas....4:59:14 (23,319)
Haigh, Jason....3:27:49 (3,387)
Haigh, Matthew R....3:59:13 (9,017)
Haigh, Michael D....4:20:24 (13,707)
Haigh, Paul D....6:04:11 (32,900)
Haigh, Paul R....4:56:11 (22,559)
Haigh, Philip A....3:43:13 (5,723)
Haigh, Robert R....5:27:09 (28,646)
Haigh, Stewart....5:16:04 (26,674)
Hails, Philip J....2:38:50 (122)
Haimes, Eliot B....3:21:59 (2,705)
Hain, Ingo....3:06:47 (1,296)
Haine, Ronald P....5:16:50 (26,815)
Haines, Adrian R....3:29:33 (3,657)
Haines, Ben J....3:49:59 (6,934)
Haines, Duncan....3:56:12 (8,274)
Haines, Mark S....4:37:15 (17,831)
Haines, Michael A....3:33:20 (4,184)
Haines, Stephen....3:34:31 (4,345)
Haining, Colin W....4:02:27 (9,690)
Haining, William....3:54:45 (7,953)
Hains, Kevin I....3:54:50 (7,970)
Hainsworth, Stephen M....3:49:11 (6,767)
Hajdu, Vojtech....2:56:25 (627)
Hajji, Amin....4:28:12 (15,646)
Hald, Jesper....4:56:17 (22,582)
Hale, Adrian J....7:04:24 (35,196)
Hale, David J....3:38:14 (4,873)
Hale, David M....4:27:56 (15,567)
Hale, Lee C....4:22:01 (14,089)
Hale, Michael A....4:52:34 (21,629)
Hale, Ross A....3:31:30 (3,911)
Haleem, Malik....5:10:57 (25,656)
Hales, Andrew M....4:24:14 (14,638)
Hales, Colin S....4:45:29 (19,946)
Hales, Daniel S....4:52:18 (21,568)
Hales, Edward J....4:28:32 (15,738)
Hales, Matthew....4:10:36 (11,287)
Hales, Shane....6:16:06 (33,686)
Haley, Andrew....3:59:10 (9,003)
Haley, Nik....4:40:42 (18,702)
Halfacree, Andrew J....3:52:18 (7,434)
Halford, David....3:44:53 (6,007)
Halfpenny, Stuart J....5:14:45 (26,396)
Hall, Adrian W....4:19:21 (13,420)
Hall, Alex....3:14:56 (1,985)
Hall, Andrew....4:20:15 (13,665)
Hall, Andrew K....4:04:36 (10,077)
Hall, Andrew M....4:25:53 (15,032)
Hall, Andrew R....5:15:26 (26,548)
Hall, Andrew W....4:50:44 (21,172)
Hall, Anthony M....4:27:07 (15,357)
Hall, Arnold W....7:33:56 (35,526)
Hall, Bengt....4:03:47 (9,924)
Hall, Bruce J....2:58:45 (808)
Hall, Carl....3:59:34 (9,111)
Hall, Charles R....4:13:58 (12,089)
Hall, Christopher G....4:25:27 (14,934)
Hall, Christopher J....3:39:44 (5,148)
Hall, Damon....4:50:07 (21,026)
Hall, Daniel S....4:56:04 (22,528)
Hall, David A....4:01:04 (9,429)
Hall, David W....3:07:03 (1,314)
Hall, Dominic J....3:50:18 (6,998)
Hall, Elvis....3:56:10 (8,267)
Hall, Frederick J....4:25:04 (14,837)
Hall, Gareth....4:09:45 (11,123)
Hall, Gary L....2:56:05 (615)
Hall, Geoffrey A....4:36:07 (17,563)
Hall, Graeme A....3:03:27 (1,073)
Hall, Harry....5:20:16 (27,470)
Hall, James A....4:24:22 (14,669)
Hall, John....3:48:03 (6,533)
Hall, Jonathan C....5:06:24 (24,769)
Hall, Jonathan D....3:12:22 (1,763)
Hall, Kevin D....5:59:37 (32,552)
Hall, Kieran D....5:32:02 (29,463)
Hall, Kieron L....4:42:39 (19,215)
Hall, Leon R....4:27:09 (15,366)
Hall, Leslie....5:13:39 (26,150)
Hall, Mark D....4:24:05 (14,593)
Hall, Mark N....2:59:14 (842)
Hall, Michael....4:17:45 (13,010)
Hall, Michael....4:28:57 (15,846)
Hall, Michael I....3:54:05 (7,812)
Hall, Michael R....4:48:58 (20,757)
Hall, Mike....2:54:23 (539)
Hall, Mike....4:14:39 (12,247)
Hall, Patrick D....4:14:37 (12,235)
Hall, Pete D....5:35:17 (29,951)
Hall, Peter....4:50:03 (21,007)
Hall, Peter L....4:32:09 (16,598)
Hall, Philip M....4:41:12 (18,841)
Hall, Philip M....5:24:31 (28,184)
Hall, Phillip J....4:22:48 (14,286)
Hall, Richard A....3:34:43 (4,366)
Hall, Rob W....2:46:37 (275)
Hall, Robert F....2:56:49 (661)
Hall, Russell C....2:56:52 (663)
Hall, Ryan....2:08:24 (7)
Hall, Samuel....3:56:05 (8,244)
Hall, Scott D....5:01:32 (23,835)
Hall, Simon....3:26:53 (3,254)
Hall, Simon C....4:21:07 (13,878)
Hall, Simon P....3:59:53 (9,178)
Hall, William L....5:04:49 (24,472)
Hallac, Toby E....3:51:00 (7,139)
Hallam, Andrew W....3:37:33 (4,760)
Hallam, John R....4:55:06 (22,289)
Hallam, Jonathan A....3:54:53 (7,982)
Hallam, Simon P....3:45:28 (6,092)
Hallas, Steve J....2:45:24 (249)
Halliday, Edward M....4:26:50 (15,275)
Halligan, James K....3:13:03 (1,823)
Hallissey, Martin....3:16:20 (2,108)
Halliwell, Grant L....3:56:45 (8,420)
Halliwell, John K....3:19:49 (2,469)
Halloran, Kieran E....3:03:47 (1,091)
Hallos, Richard J....3:34:54 (4,395)
Halls, Mark A....3:08:15 (1,413)
Halls, Paul G....5:51:33 (31,833)
Halls, Terry....5:08:22 (25,165)
Halls, Tim E....4:58:12 (23,076)
Halmi, Gabor....3:51:33 (7,266)
Halpern, Mick....4:21:52 (14,055)
Halsall, Dean....5:54:22 (32,089)
Halsey, Chris....5:40:59 (30,705)
Halsey, Michael W....5:34:51 (29,894)
Halstead, Geoff N....4:34:25 (17,118)
Halstead, Paul F....3:49:44 (6,881)
Halverson, Michael J....5:49:36 (31,638)
Halvey, James J....4:39:15 (18,351)
Halvey, Martin....2:50:22 (383)
Ham, Clive....4:13:31 (11,969)
Hamblen, Stephen J....5:31:24 (29,366)
Hambleton, Stephen W....4:33:06 (16,810)
Hamblett, Paul A....2:59:37 (870)
Hamblin, Paul M....3:59:03 (8,972)
Hambling, Stephen J....6:01:12 (32,697)
Hambling, Stuart I....4:08:04 (10,782)
Hambright, Ross....5:29:43 (29,097)
Hamburger, Neil S....4:31:18 (16,423)
Hamer, Christopher....6:03:51 (32,878)
Hamer, Luke....4:41:48 (18,995)
Hamer, Steve G....3:50:16 (6,991)
Hamerston, Gerald J....4:36:33 (17,681)
Hamid, Imran J....6:30:20 (34,335)
Hamill, Shaun....3:34:31 (4,345)
Hamilton, Alastair I....5:48:17 (31,503)
Hamilton, Alastair M....3:31:18 (3,877)
Hamilton, Andrew....4:01:04 (9,429)
Hamilton, Anthony P....4:35:33 (17,415)
Hamilton, Bob....3:33:01 (4,140)
Hamilton, Brian R....4:06:25 (10,445)
Hamilton, Craig....3:57:37 (8,629)
Hamilton, David I....4:57:31 (22,907)
Hamilton, Edward S....3:32:21 (4,051)
Hamilton, Graham M....3:12:10 (1,746)
Hamilton, Henrik W....3:59:44 (9,149)
Hamilton, James P....4:09:01 (10,954)
Hamilton, John....4:57:42 (22,956)
Hamilton, Joseph B....3:59:09 (9,000)
Hamilton, Mark....3:14:48 (1,968)
Hamilton, Nick....5:35:34 (29,989)
Hamilton, Nigel M....4:48:13 (20,582)
Hamilton, Robert A....4:00:43 (9,360)
Hamilton, Robert J....3:46:00 (6,178)
Hamilton, Rod T....3:26:08 (3,146)
Hamilton-Gould, Henry....4:25:07 (14,852)
Hamlet, Colin....3:42:58 (5,682)
Hamling, Mark....3:35:45 (4,519)
Hamlyn, Peter J....5:19:24 (27,319)
Hammel, Matthew T....4:51:18 (21,315)
Hamment, Jamie A....4:44:44 (19,753)
Hammersley, Jon....3:36:49 (4,659)
Hammersley, Mathew D....5:44:15 (31,073)
Hammerton, Steve L....4:15:38 (12,472)
Hammett, Jim I....5:25:50 (28,431)
Hammond, Andrew P....3:55:25 (8,109)
Hammond, Brendan W....4:52:50 (21,711)
Hammond, Gareth J....4:57:21 (22,875)
Hammond, John K....4:22:04 (14,102)
Hammond, Jon M....4:49:33 (20,900)
Hammond, Mark T....4:11:35 (11,518)

Hammond, Paul A	4:15:10	(12,360)
Hammond, Richard	4:15:58	(12,551)
Hammond, Robert J	5:39:04	(30,459)
Hamon, Patrick M	3:15:15	(2,016)
Hampartsumian, Charles	4:12:15	(11,670)
Hampel, Simon M	5:01:53	(23,909)
Hampshire, Graeme R	4:42:12	(19,095)
Hampshire, James J	3:28:57	(3,565)
Hampshire, Stephen J	4:29:53	(16,118)
Hampson, Danny M	4:52:44	(21,677)
Hampton, Erik C	3:55:36	(8,138)
Hampton, Graeme W	6:10:06	(33,311)
Hampton, Ian	4:40:44	(18,706)
Hampton, James I	5:21:10	(27,626)
Hampton, Michael J	4:50:21	(21,080)
Hampton, Ray	3:32:58	(4,134)
Hampton, Vincent	5:22:35	(27,873)
Hams, Steven P	4:47:43	(20,459)
Hamsher, Mark W	5:01:18	(23,794)
Hamson, Peter J	4:18:26	(13,190)
Hanafin, Denis	6:01:08	(32,691)
Hanania, Edward C	4:14:53	(12,292)
Hancock, Alan C	4:01:44	(9,555)
Hancock, Anthony	3:33:06	(4,154)
Hancock, Charles C	4:04:04	(9,978)
Hancock, David	4:12:24	(11,701)
Hancock, Matthew E	5:25:56	(28,447)
Hancock, Neil E	3:52:59	(7,564)
Hancock, Paul J	3:27:24	(3,341)
Hancox, Karl	3:32:02	(3,993)
Hancox, Michael J	4:22:36	(14,230)
Hand, David R	4:38:07	(18,045)
Hand, Michael	3:36:41	(4,640)
Hand, Richard	4:36:38	(17,700)
Handasyde Dick, Oli	4:17:56	(13,052)
Handley, Christopher J	5:02:00	(23,934)
Handley, Graham	4:20:28	(13,724)
Handley, Jerome F	4:24:56	(14,809)
Handley, Mark S	5:02:13	(23,971)
Handley, Matthew D	6:03:06	(32,827)
Handley, Nicholas	4:18:12	(13,124)
Handley, William M	3:57:22	(8,570)
Handlgruber, Peter	3:52:13	(7,411)
Hands, Richard S	4:30:57	(16,344)
Handy, Lionel P	3:19:52	(2,475)
Hanifan, Gary L	6:35:07	(34,503)
Hankins, Simon D	4:54:16	(22,095)
Hankins, Tristan V	7:12:14	(35,308)
Hanks, William	5:15:54	(26,643)
Hanley, Richard F	4:13:22	(11,926)
Hanley, Richard M	6:01:27	(32,714)
Hanlon, Patrick J	4:34:09	(17,062)
Hanlow, Stephen H	4:30:26	(16,242)
Hann, Kevin P	5:33:36	(29,703)
Hanna, Des A	4:22:03	(14,097)
Hanna, Joshua J	3:40:54	(5,347)
Hanna, Liam J	3:30:28	(3,782)
Hanna, Mark	4:11:44	(11,554)
Hannaford, Andrew R	4:08:10	(10,799)
Hannaghan, Paul	4:28:21	(15,687)
Hannah, Brian W	5:27:28	(28,707)
Hannah, Errick	3:54:11	(7,835)
Hannan, Michael	5:58:25	(32,461)
Hannath, Jeff	7:29:16	(35,475)
Hannaway, Paul	5:54:59	(32,147)
Hannigan, John	5:06:35	(24,795)
Hannington, Warren	3:15:48	(2,061)
Hansard, Larry W	5:18:46	(27,207)
Hanscomb, John W	4:35:41	(17,456)
Hansen, Daniel I	4:43:44	(19,470)
Hansen, Erik	4:53:20	(21,845)
Hansen, Jason	4:19:06	(13,355)
Hansen, Keir T	3:43:13	(5,723)
Hansen, Olou H	4:33:47	(16,987)
Hansen, Paul	3:27:45	(3,380)
Hansen, Paul S	3:30:11	(3,746)
Hansford, Adrian N	4:04:03	(9,974)
Hansford, Alex D	5:10:04	(25,495)
Hansford, James A	4:11:39	(11,537)
Hanson, Carl	4:39:57	(18,527)
Hanson, Edward J	4:09:07	(10,979)
Hanson, Eric S	5:21:23	(27,673)
Hanson, Lee S	5:48:27	(31,521)
Hanson, Michael E	4:07:02	(10,580)
Hanson, Peter	5:08:12	(25,139)
Hanwell, Tim E	3:57:39	(8,639)
Haoudi, Abdelhak	3:40:08	(5,206)
Happe, Guido	3:47:23	(6,405)
Happe, Joe R	4:10:40	(11,307)
Harbage, David A	7:02:12	(35,163)
Harber, Mark R	4:55:57	(22,502)
Harber, Peter A	4:25:34	(14,962)
Harbon, Richard I	3:17:33	(2,233)
Harbour, Jason V	3:01:10	(969)
Harbron, Christopher G	3:22:24	(2,739)
Harbrow, Andrew J	5:39:29	(30,523)
Hardaker, Christopher D	4:15:58	(12,551)
Hardaker, Steve	3:34:15	(4,302)
Hardcastle, Graham S	4:18:20	(13,159)
Harden, Laurence J	6:22:38	(34,030)
Harder, Johan A	4:14:47	(12,267)
Hardie, David A	4:56:52	(22,739)
Hardie, Michel R	4:02:56	(9,773)
Hardie, Robert	4:56:52	(22,739)
Hardie, Stewart	3:55:30	(8,117)
Hardiman, Gareth E	4:28:07	(15,626)
Harding, Colin A	5:26:48	(28,587)
Harding, Evan J	4:12:24	(11,701)
Harding, Harold P	4:45:40	(19,985)
Harding, Jason P	3:18:02	(2,284)
Harding, Jonathan F	4:27:51	(15,554)
Harding, Leslie P	5:26:44	(28,581)
Harding, Nicholas H	5:25:26	(28,351)
Harding, Robert M	4:33:35	(16,930)
Harding, Roger J	5:41:19	(30,744)
Hardingham, Nicholas	3:16:07	(2,092)
Hardisty, Michael	4:41:35	(18,944)
Hardman, David	5:57:09	(32,345)
Hardman, Gareth P	3:13:12	(1,840)
Hardman, Hugo	4:17:20	(12,887)
Hardman, Keith T	5:02:19	(23,993)
Hardman, Roger	4:23:34	(14,463)
Hards, Stephen J	3:33:40	(4,224)
Hardwicke, Humphrey	4:12:39	(11,751)
Hardwidge, Stephen P	5:00:04	(23,520)
Hardy, John C	4:28:31	(15,730)
Hardy, Jonathan S	5:13:30	(26,124)
Hardy, Nicholas R	5:27:58	(28,789)
Hardy, Philip	4:14:27	(12,198)
Hardy, Philip J	5:05:39	(24,627)
Hardy, Richard J	4:07:41	(10,700)
Hardy, Russell	3:38:43	(4,960)
Hare, Julian C	5:28:19	(28,871)
Hare, Philip M	3:54:39	(7,934)
Hare, Robert M	5:05:20	(24,558)
Hares, Colin R	4:46:50	(20,235)
Haresign, Martin	4:54:28	(22,139)
Harffey, Craig B	6:00:57	(32,665)
Harfield, Patrick D	6:41:44	(34,710)
Harfield, Phillip D	3:32:56	(4,129)
Harfield, Stephen P	6:41:44	(34,710)
Harford, David J	5:18:42	(27,199)
Harford, William J	3:54:35	(7,917)
Hargreavbes, Tim R	4:56:56	(22,759)
Hargreaves, Billy F	4:12:03	(11,621)
Hargreaves, Gary D	6:31:34	(34,385)
Hargreaves, John S	3:22:49	(2,780)
Hargreaves, Michael S	5:34:53	(29,900)
Hargreaves, Paul G	5:22:01	(27,784)
Hargreaves, Paul S	6:42:31	(34,736)
Hargreaves, Richard M	5:25:32	(28,376)
Harison-Church, John N	3:45:36	(6,113)
Harkens, Stephen S	3:01:07	(964)
Harkin, Derek A	3:39:13	(5,048)
Harknett, Stephen	3:55:46	(8,178)
Harkus, Gavin M	2:54:47	(568)
Harle, Deacon	5:23:28	(28,004)
Harley, Andrew K	4:36:08	(17,567)
Harley, Colin P	4:10:48	(11,327)
Harley, Michael J	3:42:11	(5,549)
Harlow, Daniel S	3:56:06	(8,247)
Harlow, Derek V	4:33:28	(16,906)
Harlow, Dominic C	3:42:47	(5,643)
Harman, Gary R	3:34:10	(4,290)
Harman, Guy D	3:46:21	(6,227)
Harman, Lee J	4:09:08	(10,986)
Harman, Matthew I	4:42:16	(19,117)
Harman, Steven J	4:29:38	(16,048)
Harmer, Charles R	4:19:20	(13,412)
Harmer, Jonathan P	3:05:19	(1,185)
Harmer, Nigel D	4:11:01	(11,371)
Harmsworth, Mark	4:44:37	(19,720)
Harnett, Mark E	3:45:52	(6,157)
Harnett, Paul R	3:14:57	(1,988)
Harnett, Peter S	4:19:38	(13,491)
Harney, Brian	3:40:43	(5,304)
Harney, Mark	3:33:05	(4,150)
Harper, Colin J	3:50:53	(7,111)
Harper, Jeffrey F	2:50:17	(380)
Harper, John	4:30:32	(16,261)
Harper, Matthew	3:26:05	(3,140)
Harper, Richard N	4:01:27	(9,506)
Harper, Robert A	4:31:54	(16,542)
Harper, Simon R	4:32:33	(16,675)
Harper, Steven	5:34:59	(29,911)
Harper, Steven D	4:42:40	(19,219)
Harper, Steven P	3:49:56	(6,923)
Harquevaux, Benjamin	3:19:26	(2,431)
Harradine, Rob D	5:45:02	(31,157)
Harrap, Paul R	4:19:24	(13,431)
Harries, Owen D	3:03:27	(1,073)
Harries, Richard W	5:10:00	(25,477)
Harriman, Scott	4:47:29	(20,401)
Harrington, David J	4:51:13	(21,292)
Harrington, John F	4:34:48	(17,223)
Harrington, Patrick	4:54:08	(22,054)
Harrington, Paul	4:33:09	(16,823)
Harrington, Steven G	3:38:25	(4,904)
Harris, Alex S	3:41:01	(5,369)
Harris, Andrew C	4:03:02	(9,791)
Harris, Andrew J	4:56:50	(22,728)
Harris, Andrew P	4:57:14	(22,828)
Harris, Andrew T	5:03:43	(24,273)
Harris, Benjamin L	4:54:04	(22,033)
Harris, Benjamin M	3:46:08	(6,200)
Harris, Christopher W	4:18:20	(13,159)
Harris, Danny P	4:37:38	(17,918)
Harris, Darrell L	5:36:37	(30,127)
Harris, David M	5:16:26	(26,746)
Harris, Desmon J	4:35:33	(17,415)
Harris, Geraint L	5:07:29	(24,995)
Harris, Giles	2:56:40	(649)
Harris, Howard A	4:51:05	(21,262)
Harris, Jason	2:57:45	(725)
Harris, Jeff R	4:26:06	(15,074)
Harris, Keith J	5:01:00	(23,725)
Harris, Kevin D	3:23:53	(2,894)
Harris, Liam A	7:10:00	(35,271)
Harris, Mark A	4:17:41	(12,992)
Harris, Mark D	3:38:22	(4,897)
Harris, Mark D	5:09:01	(25,281)
Harris, Mark D	5:18:40	(27,192)
Harris, Mark E	3:59:53	(9,178)
Harris, Martin	4:35:49	(17,491)
Harris, Matthew C	3:33:30	(4,203)
Harris, Michael I	4:11:46	(11,563)
Harris, Norman J	4:46:27	(20,166)
Harris, Paul	3:56:55	(8,458)
Harris, Paul	4:12:52	(11,801)
Harris, Paul	4:28:57	(15,846)
Harris, Paul	5:36:16	(30,077)
Harris, Paul A	3:49:48	(6,897)
Harris, Paul D	3:04:09	(1,109)
Harris, Peter R	4:55:06	(22,289)
Harris, Philip J	3:42:18	(5,570)
Harris, Phillip I	5:01:57	(23,922)
Harris, Richard A	5:21:54	(27,774)
Harris, Richard A	5:59:37	(32,552)
Harris, Richard P	4:39:19	(18,368)
Harris, Robert B	4:55:08	(22,298)
Harris, Robert J	3:02:00	(1,003)

LONDON MARATHON

Harris, Robert T 4:17:58 (13,064)
Harris, Rodney 3:52:02 (7,370)
Harris, Scott L 5:06:45 (24,831)
Harris, Simon D 3:20:22 (2,536)
Harris, Simon P 5:16:31 (26,759)
Harris, Steven C 3:57:25 (8,584)
Harris, Stewart I 3:39:58 (5,183)
Harris, Terry D 3:59:02 (8,965)
Harris, Tony D 5:10:36 (25,594)
Harris, William G 3:13:37 (1,866)
Harrison, Adrian J 4:21:49 (14,036)
Harrison, Alexander M 4:33:05 (16,806)
Harrison, Andrew E 3:52:09 (7,400)
Harrison, Andrew J 2:38:35 (118)
Harrison, Christpher C 4:21:18 (13,911)
Harrison, Danny B 4:23:52 (14,536)
Harrison, Darren K 5:36:04 (30,057)
Harrison, David A 3:24:28 (2,952)
Harrison, David A 4:16:32 (12,702)
Harrison, David R 3:31:05 (3,846)
Harrison, Derek J 3:12:48 (1,808)
Harrison, Graham J 4:33:43 (16,970)
Harrison, Graham S 3:32:03 (3,995)
Harrison, Ian 5:26:39 (28,566)
Harrison, James D 3:10:30 (1,595)
Harrison, James H 3:36:27 (4,605)
Harrison, Jonathan C 3:45:15 (6,056)
Harrison, Leslie S 4:29:58 (16,139)
Harrison, Mark A 5:55:36 (32,201)
Harrison, Mark R 4:38:00 (18,011)
Harrison, Matt 3:15:51 (2,068)
Harrison, Michael D 4:18:16 (13,137)
Harrison, Nick 4:06:51 (10,540)
Harrison, Oliver J 3:47:35 (6,441)
Harrison, Paul 6:06:23 (33,074)
Harrison, Paul M 4:48:58 (20,757)
Harrison, Richard P 2:58:27 (787)
Harrison, Richard P 4:12:22 (11,693)
Harrison, Rob M 2:56:23 (625)
Harrison, Simon 4:56:23 (22,609)
Harrison, Stephen C 5:15:36 (26,586)
Harrison, Stephen J 4:55:44 (22,440)
Harrison, Steve 3:20:14 (2,522)
Harrison, Steven 4:21:17 (13,909)
Harrison, Thomas C 3:08:26 (1,426)
Harrison, Tom 4:32:02 (16,565)
Harrison, Trevor L 4:29:00 (15,856)
Harrisson, Stuart E 4:07:08 (10,597)
Harrod, Simon G 5:38:10 (30,329)
Harrold, Christopher H 5:18:42 (27,199)
Harrold, John C 3:51:03 (7,145)
Harrold, Martin R 4:07:51 (10,737)
Harrop, Simon M 3:47:53 (6,509)
Harrow, Martin D 3:54:16 (7,861)
Harrower, Andrew G 5:58:21 (32,453)
Harrup, Ian G 4:46:20 (20,135)
Harry, Ian D 4:29:16 (15,930)
Harry, Richard D 2:57:47 (731)
Hart, Al 2:33:30 (56)
Hart, Andrew D 3:01:38 (989)
Hart, Anthony 3:55:51 (8,195)
Hart, Antony J 4:06:30 (10,468)
Hart, Craig A 4:06:57 (10,558)
Hart, Daniel A 3:33:10 (4,165)
Hart, David W 3:03:04 (1,054)
Hart, James M 3:54:11 (7,835)
Hart, John D 4:57:35 (22,926)
Hart, Josh P 3:27:02 (3,288)
Hart, Malcolm 4:50:31 (21,129)
Hart, Mark A 3:48:06 (6,543)
Hart, Matthew 4:40:38 (18,685)
Hart, Nigel G 4:21:20 (13,918)
Hart, Peter J 3:15:35 (2,034)
Hart, Sam R 3:17:19 (2,205)
Hart, Stuart P 5:22:05 (27,794)
Hart, Timothy P 4:34:38 (17,186)
Harte, David M 3:17:51 (2,266)
Harte, John P 4:22:02 (14,095)
Harte, Tony 3:48:25 (6,598)
Harten, Sven P 3:40:22 (5,246)
Hartery, Paul A 4:42:48 (19,255)
Hart-George, Rad 3:10:04 (1,564)
Hartigan, Matthew 4:35:10 (17,316)
Hartley, Alan P 5:18:04 (27,071)
Hartley, Allan 4:02:58 (9,779)
Hartley, Benjamin E 4:35:58 (17,527)
Hartley, Chris 3:47:26 (6,417)
Hartley, Ian M 6:10:30 (33,335)
Hartley, Jonathan P 3:34:26 (4,334)
Hartley, Marcus E 4:29:31 (16,013)
Hartley, Mathew J 5:08:42 (25,226)
Hartley, Robert P 4:57:46 (22,973)
Hartley, Scott L 4:22:13 (14,131)
Hartley, Steve 5:46:20 (31,295)
Hartley, Steve 6:04:46 (32,940)
Hartmayer, Horst 4:23:57 (14,555)
Hartnell, Stephen T 3:59:41 (9,136)
Hartnett, Peter J 4:15:57 (12,543)
Hartshorne, Damien L 4:30:00 (16,148)
Hartwell, David K 2:50:58 (406)
Hartwell, Greg 4:14:00 (12,096)
Harvey, Adrian M 5:06:09 (24,726)
Harvey, Alexander 3:52:41 (7,497)
Harvey, Clive 4:46:05 (20,073)
Harvey, Clive S 3:53:18 (7,641)
Harvey, Damian A 3:35:12 (4,436)
Harvey, Dan 4:16:41 (12,733)
Harvey, Daniel J 4:39:08 (18,314)
Harvey, David G 4:59:37 (23,417)
Harvey, Derek J 5:00:22 (23,592)
Harvey, Elliott C 4:49:29 (20,885)
Harvey, Gary S 4:24:10 (14,622)
Harvey, Ian H 3:30:04 (3,729)
Harvey, John 3:16:16 (2,102)
Harvey, Kevin 3:09:11 (1,485)
Harvey, Kevin R 3:51:34 (7,269)
Harvey, Mark J 5:29:34 (29,078)
Harvey, Mike 4:52:35 (21,635)
Harvey, Paul D 5:50:39 (31,744)
Harvey, Peter J 3:33:17 (4,176)
Harvey, Philip C 3:56:07 (8,254)
Harvey, Philip J 4:57:14 (22,828)
Harvey, Richard P 5:26:30 (28,544)
Harvey, Richard R 3:46:42 (6,283)
Harvey, Terry 5:21:16 (27,650)
Harvie, Gavin B 4:11:53 (11,588)
Harvie, Robin G 3:35:51 (4,528)
Harwood, Bryan 5:54:41 (32,117)
Harwood, Justin J 5:02:21 (24,001)
Harwood, Mark 4:44:14 (19,611)
Harwood, Paul R 5:42:01 (30,830)
Hary, Alain 3:16:54 (2,172)
Haselden, Adrian M 6:13:04 (33,494)
Hasell, Luke 3:13:44 (1,878)
Hasenbalg, Bernhard 3:23:52 (2,888)
Hasler, Andrew C 4:35:33 (17,415)
Hasler, Paul G 2:29:11 (36)
Haslett, Francis P 6:41:17 (34,699)
Haslett, James M 4:44:19 (19,626)
Haslop, Peter 4:10:32 (11,274)
Hassall, Andrew C 4:32:21 (16,636)
Hassall, Simon A 2:46:16 (267)
Hassan, Osman 6:49:52 (34,925)
Hassan Masoudi, Omed M 5:04:00 (24,327)
Hassell, Des 4:00:48 (9,372)
Hassett, Daniel 4:07:33 (10,662)
Hassett, Gerry 4:39:59 (18,533)
Hasson, Gavin 3:56:21 (8,319)
Hastie, David I 3:36:05 (4,554)
Hastie, David R 5:18:02 (27,064)
Hastie, Jonathan E 5:18:02 (27,064)
Hastings, Brian A 4:11:42 (11,550)
Hastings, Darren A 4:50:52 (21,210)
Hastings, Roger D 5:36:26 (30,103)
Hastings, Terence A 5:08:02 (25,101)
Haswell, Robert R 5:31:07 (29,320)
Haswell, Stephen 3:36:59 (4,682)
Hatch, Murray J 4:44:25 (19,654)
Hatch, Steven B 5:30:31 (29,224)
Hatchard, Anthony D 3:09:50 (1,542)
Hatcliffe, Richard E 5:57:48 (32,392)
Hatfield, Alexander J 4:10:45 (11,318)
Hatfield, Paul 4:59:31 (23,390)
Hatfield, Rob J 3:33:20 (4,184)
Hatfield, Stephen 4:54:27 (22,137)
Hathaway, Barry D 4:13:48 (12,043)
Hathaway, Mark D 4:57:39 (22,948)
Hatherell, Andrew M 5:31:20 (29,349)
Hatherill, Jason 6:49:27 (34,918)
Hatherley, David W 6:05:46 (33,029)
Hatton, Ben J 5:25:02 (28,279)
Hatton, Ian 3:40:03 (5,198)
Hatton, James M 5:41:23 (30,756)
Hatton, Keith 6:03:37 (32,861)
Hatton, Stephen J 3:33:26 (4,199)
Haubenthal, Manfred 5:14:57 (26,439)
Haudeck, Bernhard 6:03:57 (32,883)
Hauer, Randolph N 5:37:36 (30,246)
Haughan, Don R 6:04:23 (32,909)
Haughey, Duncan J 3:21:34 (2,658)
Haughey, John F 3:56:06 (8,247)
Haughey, Ted J 4:48:20 (20,620)
Haughton, Colin T 3:31:30 (3,911)
Haughton, Warren 5:37:52 (30,281)
Hautbois, Christopher 3:17:26 (2,221)
Havard, Michael 3:27:26 (3,347)
Havelock, John W 4:44:47 (19,772)
Havenhand, David C 3:28:32 (3,494)
Havercroft, Andrew R 3:28:02 (3,411)
Haverson, Quinton 5:36:10 (30,064)
Hawcroft, Matthew K 2:56:58 (672)
Hawes, Adam 5:05:47 (24,656)
Hawes, Andrew J 4:56:45 (22,706)
Hawes, Paul 3:48:16 (6,568)
Hawes, Pete 4:29:22 (15,964)
Hawke, Aubrey J 5:32:34 (29,545)
Hawker, Kyle P 4:52:11 (21,537)
Hawker, Martin 5:21:03 (27,612)
Hawker, Simon R 3:06:23 (1,261)
Hawkes, Richard D 3:36:53 (4,672)
Hawkes, Simon T 5:25:21 (28,330)
Hawkins, Andrew R 4:46:20 (20,135)
Hawkins, David H 4:35:31 (17,407)
Hawkins, David P 4:28:16 (15,662)
Hawkins, Graeme 3:32:02 (3,993)
Hawkins, Jeff J 4:11:40 (11,542)
Hawkins, Jim 6:37:02 (34,583)
Hawkins, Julian A 5:40:44 (30,675)
Hawkins, Matthew D 4:40:06 (18,556)
Hawkins, Raymond C 6:24:07 (34,085)
Hawkins, Shaun 4:00:09 (9,238)
Hawkins, Stephen 3:35:59 (4,545)
Hawkins, Steven 4:32:49 (16,744)
Hawkins, Stuart 5:21:10 (27,626)
Hawkins, Thomas L 5:22:29 (27,844)
Hawkins, Timothy D 5:17:08 (26,884)
Hawkins, William A 4:22:27 (14,184)
Hawkshaw-Burn, Charles 4:22:42 (14,258)
Hawksworth, Max A 4:42:12 (19,095)
Hawley, Graham 4:04:08 (9,991)
Hawley, Terry J 3:58:21 (8,796)
Hawse, Robert J 3:50:56 (7,123)
Hawthorn, Christopher A 3:58:50 (8,921)
Hawthorne, Edward 4:42:18 (19,123)
Hawthorne, Michael E 4:00:25 (9,297)
Hay, Benjamin T 5:07:55 (25,080)
Hay, John L 4:02:35 (9,705)
Hay, Stuart G 3:20:44 (2,580)
Hayburn, Ian 3:09:04 (1,472)
Haycock, Christopher A 5:10:06 (25,506)
Haycock, Nick R 5:40:14 (30,617)
Haycock, Richard G 5:26:02 (28,463)
Hayden, Alan C 4:41:11 (18,836)
Hayden, Barry E 4:40:13 (18,581)
Hayden, Chris J 5:11:51 (25,824)
Hayden, Darrin P 4:28:03 (15,608)
Hayden, Gareth L 4:26:36 (15,212)
Hayden, John E 4:54:22 (22,114)
Hayden, Peter H 5:59:16 (32,534)
Haydock, Jonathan E 4:52:50 (21,711)
Hayer, Karlwinder S 3:07:17 (1,332)
Hayes, Alan T 4:26:33 (15,205)
Hayes, Barry M 4:58:41 (23,186)
Hayes, Brian A 7:07:22 (35,237)
Hayes, Damian P 4:39:58 (18,531)
Hayes, Jack 5:05:03 (24,520)
Hayes, John J 3:52:42 (7,503)
Hayes, Jonathan M 4:57:14 (22,828)
Hayes, Lee P 6:26:02 (34,171)

Hayes, Lewis	6:25:57 (34,162)	
Hayes, Mark A	4:04:04 (9,978)	
Hayes, Michael A	3:42:07 (5,540)	
Hayes, Michael G	3:37:25 (4,739)	
Hayes, Nicholas W	5:50:30 (31,727)	
Hayes, Peter J	4:59:19 (23,341)	
Hayes, Rob	3:54:24 (7,883)	
Hayes, Roger B	2:51:44 (430)	
Hayes, Roy M	4:40:59 (18,780)	
Hayes, Shaun P	4:12:22 (11,693)	
Hayes, Simon	5:09:56 (25,457)	
Hayes, Stephen A	4:40:45 (18,714)	
Haylock, Ian D	4:26:49 (15,270)	
Hayman, Thomas	5:53:27 (32,000)	
Haymes, Anthony S	4:17:18 (12,877)	
Haynes, John M	4:16:31 (12,700)	
Haynes, Les	4:20:18 (13,679)	
Haynes, Martin R	5:34:22 (29,820)	
Haynes, Paul	4:28:57 (15,846)	
Haynes, Richard E	3:38:53 (4,995)	
Haynes, Russell J	3:43:46 (5,822)	
Haynes, Stuart M	5:20:25 (27,497)	
Haynes-Oliver, Simon	5:21:21 (27,666)	
Hayre, Sukhbir S	4:50:43 (21,171)	
Hays, Ian T	4:18:47 (13,281)	
Hays, Tim	4:10:56 (11,358)	
Haysom, Jim	5:21:41 (27,731)	
Hayter, Quinton N	5:31:37 (29,389)	
Hayton, Nick	5:32:30 (29,525)	
Hayton, Paul	4:17:28 (12,932)	
Hayward, Michael J	4:30:30 (16,257)	
Hayward, Mike	4:55:58 (22,506)	
Haywood, Christopher K	4:25:44 (15,002)	
Haywood, Geoffrey	5:24:40 (28,212)	
Haywood, Kevin	4:19:18 (13,405)	
Haywood, Nicholas	6:08:34 (33,210)	
Haywood, Tim R	4:32:02 (16,565)	
Hazard, Mark	6:03:31 (32,852)	
Hazel, Lee D	4:49:53 (20,970)	
Hazell, Christopher J	4:07:41 (10,700)	
Hazell, Peter L	4:06:40 (10,494)	
Head, Christopher	4:31:46 (16,520)	
Head, Gary J	4:37:32 (17,897)	
Head, John P	6:08:20 (33,195)	
Head, Jonathan	4:13:36 (11,996)	
Head, Jonathan M	3:52:02 (7,370)	
Head, Julian P	3:58:07 (8,746)	
Head, Keith J	5:33:27 (29,672)	
Head, Marcus N	4:09:06 (10,973)	
Head, Martyn	4:24:07 (14,603)	
Head, Peter J	5:49:36 (31,638)	
Head, Stephen P	4:50:27 (21,109)	
Head, Tom R	3:55:36 (8,138)	
Headon, David L	2:49:41 (366)	
Headridge, Keith D	3:55:56 (8,214)	
Heal, Steven J	5:13:42 (26,166)	
Heale, Gareth A	4:50:19 (21,070)	
Heale, George S	4:52:55 (21,730)	
Heale, Simon	3:47:02 (6,352)	
Healeas, Andrew J	5:24:07 (28,126)	
Healeas, Gavin A	5:24:07 (28,126)	
Healeas, Jason C	5:24:07 (28,126)	
Healey, James	3:44:17 (5,900)	
Healey, Paul A	5:18:27 (27,155)	
Healey, Timothy J	3:54:35 (7,917)	
Healey, William T	5:05:30 (24,602)	
Healy, Christopher	3:45:50 (6,154)	
Healy, Martin	6:12:49 (33,481)	
Healy, Peter J	4:19:27 (13,446)	
Heaman, Giles D	3:32:08 (4,017)	
Heaney, Ciaran O	4:02:26 (9,687)	
Heap, Clive R	4:20:34 (13,745)	
Heap, Jonathan	3:36:32 (4,617)	
Heap, Michael	4:40:19 (18,610)	
Heap, Michael A	2:56:52 (663)	
Heapy, Terence	4:49:05 (20,789)	
Heard, Michael J	4:54:20 (22,106)	
Hearn, Andrew D	3:50:50 (7,102)	
Hearn, Barry M	4:35:40 (17,446)	
Hearn, Kevan	4:52:37 (21,649)	
Hearn, Robert C	5:17:44 (27,007)	
Hearn, Shaun P	4:27:35 (15,488)	
Hearn, Stephen T	4:20:10 (13,645)	

Hearnden, Philip J	4:47:25 (20,387)	
Hearne, Matthew F	4:06:14 (10,399)	
Heaselgrave, Daryl R	4:58:15 (23,089)	
Heasman, John P	4:06:28 (10,458)	
Heath, Alasdair D	6:06:20 (33,069)	
Heath, Andrew J	5:17:59 (27,052)	
Heath, Chris P	5:03:18 (24,191)	
Heath, Frederick C	3:37:42 (4,778)	
Heath, John A	4:21:19 (13,914)	
Heath, Marc D	4:13:11 (11,874)	
Heath, Paul	5:39:02 (30,454)	
Heath, Rob D	4:32:38 (16,701)	
Heaton, David	4:22:54 (14,309)	
Heaton, Roy	5:08:54 (25,265)	
Heaton-Renshaw, George	3:53:52 (7,757)	
Heaven, Matthew P	4:11:10 (11,417)	
Heaver, Michael J	5:15:22 (26,535)	
Hebden, Nick S	4:11:09 (11,413)	
Hebden, Roderick G	4:59:46 (23,448)	
Heber, Andrew J	3:58:10 (8,750)	
Heck, Chris J	3:42:12 (5,554)	
Hecking, Matt B	3:20:52 (2,593)	
Hector, Robert	3:51:59 (7,363)	
Hector, Stephen H	4:57:27 (22,896)	
Hedegaard Nielsen, Lars	6:33:20 (34,450)	
Hedger, Graham	3:24:53 (3,008)	
Hedger, Mark C	3:39:24 (5,087)	
Hedger, Michael E	6:18:28 (33,805)	
Hedges, Robert D	3:28:58 (3,569)	
Hedgethorne, Peter J	4:42:47 (19,251)	
Hedley, George	5:03:02 (24,135)	
Heeks, Lewis C	4:18:43 (13,269)	
Heelas, Jeremy N	5:12:49 (26,001)	
Heeley, David G	3:43:05 (5,704)	
Heeley, Paul	2:59:12 (840)	
Heenderson, Desmond G	5:27:51 (28,771)	
Heezen, Pedro	5:04:15 (24,363)	
Hefferman, Terry	4:33:59 (17,030)	
Heffield, Scott	4:38:24 (18,126)	
Hegarty, Gerard F	4:39:11 (18,329)	
Hegarty, Hugo	3:14:56 (1,985)	
Hegarty, Jack	4:02:57 (9,774)	
Hegarty, Sean A	5:09:29 (25,367)	
Hegen, Erwin	4:00:26 (9,300)	
Hehir, Gerry	3:58:26 (8,816)	
Heidenreich, Nicholas	4:25:47 (15,015)	
Heider, Norbert	4:12:27 (11,713)	
Heighley, Stephen T	5:55:50 (32,221)	
Heijmans, Hans	4:25:43 (14,998)	
Heine, Ralf	4:03:32 (9,874)	
Heinig, Mikael	4:57:30 (22,904)	
Heiron, Andrew G	4:38:55 (18,258)	
Heley, Robert W	4:44:00 (19,538)	
Helfrick, Garry L	5:36:07 (30,062)	
Helgason, Petur	3:26:00 (3,127)	
Hellawell, Peter J	3:27:46 (3,383)	
Hellebreckers, Casper J	3:59:45 (9,152)	
Hellen, David J	4:57:44 (22,966)	
Hellman, Bernt A	5:03:42 (24,271)	
Hellmers, Christopher L	3:23:44 (2,870)	
Helm, Ian	3:55:18 (8,077)	
Helm, Jonathan	4:08:28 (10,866)	
Helps, David	4:09:59 (11,162)	
Helps, Michael W	5:59:44 (32,559)	
Hely, Chris P	5:00:45 (23,676)	
Hember, Rob C	4:39:56 (18,520)	
Hemingway, Maurice	3:46:49 (6,307)	
Hemingway, Neil R	4:47:22 (20,374)	
Heminway, Chris	5:10:01 (25,486)	
Hemmings, George W	5:42:45 (30,902)	
Hemmings, Lance R	3:18:03 (2,288)	
Hemphill, Stephen J	5:07:58 (25,088)	
Hemson, Robert A	6:04:57 (32,959)	
Henchy, Dan J	3:21:57 (2,702)	
Henderson, Alan J	5:27:00 (28,619)	
Henderson, Andrew N	2:57:54 (740)	
Henderson, Brian S	4:23:39 (14,477)	
Henderson, David	4:17:21 (12,895)	
Henderson, David G	3:04:57 (1,160)	
Henderson, Desmond M	4:13:30 (11,963)	
Henderson, Gordon D	5:11:04 (25,679)	
Henderson, Ian N	3:57:38 (8,634)	
Henderson, Jay	5:14:05 (26,243)	

Henderson, Johanna	6:31:10 (34,367)	
Henderson, John J	5:06:41 (24,811)	
Henderson, Mark	5:41:56 (30,824)	
Henderson, Mark	5:45:17 (31,180)	
Henderson, Mark J	4:20:32 (13,738)	
Henderson, Michael B	3:40:52 (5,337)	
Henderson, Neil C	5:22:33 (27,868)	
Henderson, Stuart J	5:00:21 (23,587)	
Henderson, Tristan J	4:03:13 (9,822)	
Henderson, William John C	5:11:04 (25,679)	
Hendra, Kevin P	5:40:40 (30,670)	
Hendry, John S	3:50:08 (6,967)	
Hendry, Robert S	3:25:59 (3,123)	
Heney, Kenneth J	2:53:44 (510)	
Henigan, Steven J	4:13:28 (11,951)	
Henkel, Nils	3:48:23 (6,587)	
Henley, Steve P	4:35:11 (17,323)	
Henley, Wayne D	4:11:36 (11,527)	
Hennessey, Brian	2:49:48 (370)	
Hennessy, Philip	3:01:35 (987)	
Hennessy, Robert	6:06:15 (33,064)	
Henney, Sean	4:35:13 (17,338)	
Henney, Valerie A	5:04:20 (24,385)	
Henningsen, Michael	4:32:05 (16,578)	
Henry, Derek	4:40:25 (18,634)	
Henry, Leon A	4:20:37 (13,758)	
Henry, Michael	3:24:46 (2,993)	
Henry, Nigel J	3:46:18 (6,219)	
Hensby, Kenneth	5:14:19 (26,294)	
Hensby, Paul A	3:00:43 (941)	
Henshaw, Lee	5:16:02 (26,671)	
Henshaw, Paul A	3:51:59 (7,363)	
Henson, Alistair R	4:31:53 (16,540)	
Henwood, David B	6:02:20 (32,772)	
Henwood, Phillip W	4:21:28 (13,957)	
Henzell, Nick C	3:31:32 (3,915)	
Henzies, Justin	4:12:15 (11,670)	
Hepworth, Ian	5:04:22 (24,397)	
Hepworth, Ian D	3:57:24 (8,581)	
Hepworth, Richard V	4:40:44 (18,706)	
Hepworth, Robert A	3:58:11 (8,755)	
Herald, Mark J	4:23:48 (14,517)	
Herarle, Adrian D	3:48:20 (6,580)	
Herbert, Ashley J	5:04:03 (24,336)	
Herbert, David R	4:05:24 (10,224)	
Herbert, Edward B	4:30:26 (16,242)	
Herbert, Jason	4:59:12 (23,308)	
Herbert, Jonathan N	3:55:41 (8,161)	
Herbert, Lee R	4:33:56 (17,016)	
Herbert, Matthew C	3:05:30 (1,201)	
Herbert, Neal	5:04:06 (24,345)	
Herbert, Nicholas G	4:55:25 (22,368)	
Herbert, Raymond L	7:18:24 (35,375)	
Herbert, Richard C	6:05:29 (33,002)	
Herbert, Thomas V	6:07:41 (33,141)	
Herbertson, Nathan C	6:01:41 (32,732)	
Hercules, Tyrone A	4:54:50 (22,234)	
Herd, Darren G	4:54:17 (22,099)	
Herd, Jonathan J	4:20:06 (13,624)	
Herd, William A	4:20:19 (13,686)	
Herdman, Allan	3:11:48 (1,701)	
Herdman, Christopher	3:45:03 (6,032)	
Heritage, Mick	4:13:06 (11,859)	
Herlihy, Mark	6:14:09 (33,560)	
Hermans, Carl R	3:24:50 (2,999)	
Hermo, Bertin	4:33:31 (16,916)	
Hermon, Steven M	3:56:58 (8,473)	
Hermsen, Henk	3:46:31 (6,249)	
Hernandez, Francisco J	3:05:50 (1,225)	
Hernandez, César	6:41:18 (34,701)	
Herod, Darren	4:12:40 (11,761)	
Heron, Chris D	4:16:03 (12,582)	
Heron, Iain R	3:34:50 (4,384)	
Heron, James	3:15:37 (2,040)	
Heron, Philip	5:37:50 (30,274)	
Heron, Robert C	5:14:29 (26,330)	
Herridge, Neil	4:06:16 (10,409)	
Herring, Anthony R	3:59:40 (9,131)	
Herring, Denis	6:21:29 (33,981)	
Herring, Jonathan I	2:53:32 (496)	
Herring, Richard L	3:17:52 (2,268)	
Herrington, Richard C	3:28:23 (3,460)	
Herriott, Marc C	4:43:07 (19,324)	

Herrity, David	4:39:09 (18,320)	
Hershkowitz, Jesse	3:42:02 (5,527)	
Hertz, Daniel A	4:28:18 (15,672)	
Hertz, Philip L	4:39:37 (18,443)	
Hesketh, Barnaby A	4:51:40 (21,412)	
Hesketh, Ben H	4:32:12 (16,609)	
Hesketh, Tony J	3:32:55 (4,126)	
Heslop, Garry	4:46:39 (20,208)	
Heslop, Mark	3:51:11 (7,182)	
Heslop, Stuart	4:51:03 (21,255)	
Hesse, Carsten	4:47:50 (20,489)	
Hesselschwerdt, Stefan	3:56:51 (8,444)	
Hetherington, Julian M	4:53:16 (21,828)	
Hetherington, Paul A	3:59:10 (9,003)	
Hetherlington, Andrew J	4:21:35 (13,980)	
Hett, Jonathan P	5:21:17 (27,652)	
Hewer, David E	5:10:55 (25,648)	
Hewett, Arron	5:52:28 (31,917)	
Hewings, Robert M	4:20:53 (13,827)	
Hewison, Andrew R	4:21:42 (14,003)	
Hewitt, Bryan J	6:45:28 (34,809)	
Hewitt, David J	4:56:57 (22,763)	
Hewitt, James M	4:23:40 (14,484)	
Hewitt, Michael D	3:28:06 (3,420)	
Hewitt, Phil G	3:20:25 (2,547)	
Hewitt, Richard G	3:54:44 (7,949)	
Hewitt, Simon	3:19:07 (2,405)	
Hewitt, Thomas	4:23:49 (14,518)	
Hewson, Anthony J	3:42:46 (5,637)	
Hexter, Paul A	5:32:05 (29,469)	
Hey, Jonathan D	5:05:44 (24,642)	
Hey, Michael-James	4:11:18 (11,448)	
Hey, Perry	6:14:36 (33,585)	
Heyes, Neil E	5:49:24 (31,620)	
Heyes, Ryan D	4:25:37 (14,973)	
Heys, Brian	3:53:39 (7,717)	
Heys, Jeremy R	4:57:18 (22,854)	
Heys, Simon R	3:11:30 (1,673)	
Heys, Stuart J	5:52:07 (31,885)	
Heywood, Dave R	5:34:47 (29,884)	
Heywood, Simon V	4:30:43 (16,295)	
Heyworth, Paul R	4:06:54 (10,552)	
Hibberd, Duncan S	5:09:07 (25,298)	
Hibberd, Matthew D	2:59:19 (849)	
Hibberd, Roy G	4:57:36 (22,932)	
Hibbert, Jon-Paul R	3:52:04 (7,386)	
Hibbs, David R	5:17:21 (26,927)	
Hick, Gareth D	5:31:51 (29,427)	
Hickey, Patrick	3:26:36 (3,206)	
Hickish, Joseph R	3:40:44 (5,306)	
Hickish, Tamas F	3:26:38 (3,212)	
Hickley, Matthew E	4:30:42 (16,294)	
Hickman, Andrew J	5:22:33 (27,868)	
Hickman, Ian D	5:11:38 (25,784)	
Hickman, James D	4:52:59 (21,749)	
Hickman, Michael G	4:13:22 (11,926)	
Hickman, Michael J	3:26:00 (3,127)	
Hickman, Paul	5:43:11 (30,960)	
Hickman, Paul D	5:17:50 (27,013)	
Hickmott, Patrick E	3:56:39 (8,393)	
Hicks, Anthony J	3:31:56 (3,980)	
Hicks, Barry M	4:58:21 (23,119)	
Hicks, Brian D	5:19:58 (27,420)	
Hicks, Chris	4:36:17 (17,606)	
Hicks, Guy M	5:37:56 (30,291)	
Hicks, Jonathan A	5:09:38 (25,400)	
Hicks, Michael	5:33:18 (29,644)	
Hicks, Murray	4:52:55 (21,730)	
Hicks, Paul	3:41:42 (5,471)	
Hicks, Ronald C	4:19:51 (13,559)	
Hicks, Thomas C	3:56:27 (8,346)	
Hicks, Timothy W	3:38:15 (4,877)	
Hidary, Murray	4:11:21 (11,459)	
Hide, Carlton	3:00:53 (948)	
Hide, George	2:38:50 (122)	
Hider, Ian	3:28:46 (3,534)	
Hieber, Ben G	3:07:52 (1,375)	
Hienkens, Ralph	4:40:03 (18,545)	
Higgin, Ryan P	3:40:51 (5,335)	
Higginbotham, Gary L	5:37:01 (30,172)	
Higgins, Adrian J	3:39:48 (5,157)	
Higgins, Antony J	4:21:53 (14,060)	
Higgins, Bernard	3:30:09 (3,742)	

Higgins, Daniel J	2:44:43 (233)	
Higgins, David S	4:56:52 (22,739)	
Higgins, Eamon P	4:34:13 (17,079)	
Higgins, Leo G	4:43:54 (19,509)	
Higgins, Malcolm	3:31:56 (3,980)	
Higgins, Matthew R	6:11:53 (33,418)	
Higgins, Peter	3:46:48 (6,305)	
Higgins, Robert I	4:41:53 (19,016)	
Higgins, Steven J	4:40:37 (18,682)	
Higgins, Stuart M	5:17:19 (26,922)	
Higginson, George	5:11:11 (25,698)	
Higginson, Liam T	4:15:08 (12,351)	
Higgs, David W	3:39:35 (5,121)	
Higgs, Gary A	5:06:56 (24,865)	
Higgs, Mark A	3:43:28 (5,770)	
Higgs, Matthew J	5:11:20 (25,730)	
Higgs, Nicholas B	5:16:50 (26,815)	
Higgs, Philip A	3:23:38 (2,861)	
Higgs, Simon J	4:16:14 (12,630)	
Higgs, Terence A	4:04:34 (10,071)	
High, Charles	5:00:19 (23,581)	
Highfield, Colin R	3:08:44 (1,447)	
Highfield, Mark	4:10:05 (11,180)	
Hight, Christopher M	5:24:12 (28,137)	
Higlett, Kevin R	5:47:16 (31,378)	
Higney, Matthew L	4:15:35 (12,456)	
Higson, David	6:20:37 (33,931)	
Higton, Paul	4:57:54 (23,010)	
Hilbery, Graham J	3:41:58 (5,511)	
Hilder, Ian J	4:06:51 (10,540)	
Hilders, Cornelis	4:40:03 (18,545)	
Hildesley, Simon H	4:33:11 (16,838)	
Hildrew, Ross G	3:59:05 (8,981)	
Hildyard, Michael L	3:40:44 (5,306)	
Hiles, Paul A	4:44:27 (19,663)	
Hiley, Paul	3:42:53 (5,665)	
Hill, Adam S	4:36:03 (17,547)	
Hill, Adrian	3:46:45 (6,291)	
Hill, Amos R	5:20:22 (27,488)	
Hill, Andrew J	4:11:57 (11,603)	
Hill, Carwyn M	3:48:32 (6,630)	
Hill, Christian A	5:16:28 (26,751)	
Hill, Christian J	4:58:45 (23,196)	
Hill, Christopher J	5:55:10 (32,163)	
Hill, Colin D	3:48:16 (6,568)	
Hill, Dave L	5:04:27 (24,411)	
Hill, Dave M	3:13:37 (1,866)	
Hill, David	5:29:32 (29,074)	
Hill, David J	4:35:16 (17,353)	
Hill, Dominic C	5:25:48 (28,425)	
Hill, Edward C	3:47:40 (6,468)	
Hill, Fraser	4:04:50 (10,120)	
Hill, Gary M	5:18:04 (27,071)	
Hill, Gavin H	4:15:07 (12,345)	
Hill, Guy D	3:06:24 (1,263)	
Hill, John	4:49:27 (20,874)	
Hill, Jonathon A	4:18:49 (13,287)	
Hill, Justin B	3:18:14 (2,315)	
Hill, Kenneth A	5:49:50 (31,664)	
Hill, Kevin	3:48:06 (6,543)	
Hill, Lee W	4:05:05 (10,160)	
Hill, Mark A	3:38:33 (4,929)	
Hill, Mark I	5:21:45 (27,741)	
Hill, Martin J	3:29:19 (3,620)	
Hill, Martin T	4:11:23 (11,470)	
Hill, Michael	5:15:43 (26,610)	
Hill, Paul E	4:26:15 (15,120)	
Hill, Peter J	3:25:31 (3,067)	
Hill, Raymond	3:12:46 (1,806)	
Hill, Richard E	5:11:14 (25,709)	
Hill, Roger P	4:24:21 (14,665)	
Hill, Scot J	3:31:47 (3,950)	
Hill, Simon J	4:53:47 (21,962)	
Hill, Simon P	5:14:32 (26,344)	
Hill, Stephen	5:10:25 (25,561)	
Hill, Stephen A	5:03:53 (24,305)	
Hill, Stephen D	4:59:11 (23,302)	
Hill, Steve	3:49:24 (6,808)	
Hill, Steven G	4:45:25 (19,927)	
Hill, Steven R	3:23:28 (2,849)	
Hill, Stuart C	4:26:21 (15,146)	
Hill, Tim J	4:43:02 (19,304)	
Hill, Tommy J	4:08:24 (10,848)	

Hill, Walter J	3:11:07 (1,644)	
Hillam, Mathew	5:18:55 (27,235)	
Hillary, Ian	6:02:47 (32,807)	
Hillary, Matthew A	3:00:12 (907)	
Hilliard, David J	5:31:10 (29,330)	
Hillier, Adam I	5:30:42 (29,257)	
Hillier, Nigel G	3:49:42 (6,872)	
Hillier, Thomas J	3:40:34 (5,283)	
Hillman, Mark W	4:18:25 (13,181)	
Hillman, Peter	2:51:00 (410)	
Hills, Adam S	3:31:28 (3,905)	
Hills, Christopher J	6:30:03 (34,328)	
Hills, Daniel J	3:14:39 (1,960)	
Hills, Graham J	4:55:25 (22,368)	
Hills, James D	4:19:57 (13,589)	
Hills, Jason R	5:09:39 (25,404)	
Hills, Joseph D	4:35:10 (17,316)	
Hills, Matthew J	3:31:09 (3,855)	
Hills, Matthew J	4:55:09 (22,305)	
Hills, Peter B	6:07:43 (33,146)	
Hills, Richard D	6:23:05 (34,042)	
Hills, Simon M	4:14:09 (12,128)	
Hills, Stuart	4:11:59 (11,608)	
Hills, Tom	4:54:23 (22,117)	
Hills, Wayne	4:29:18 (15,941)	
Hills, Zachary	3:37:28 (4,747)	
Hilton, Clifford J	3:55:14 (8,064)	
Hilton, David	5:19:09 (27,280)	
Hilton, Dominic	3:02:08 (1,008)	
Hilton, James E	3:48:05 (6,539)	
Hilton, John	3:41:18 (5,411)	
Hilton, Oliver J	3:04:18 (1,121)	
Hilton, Paul	4:20:08 (13,637)	
Hinchelwood, Richard G	5:55:43 (32,210)	
Hind, Andy M	4:33:57 (17,024)	
Hind, Grame M	4:41:48 (18,995)	
Hind, Jamie	4:36:37 (17,696)	
Hinde, Rogers	5:30:34 (29,230)	
Hinder, Gavin A	4:58:30 (23,151)	
Hindley, David J	3:52:11 (7,406)	
Hindley, Mark C	2:59:37 (870)	
Hinds, Andrew P	3:59:33 (9,108)	
Hine, Toby R	5:00:24 (23,598)	
Hines, Ian M	4:28:49 (15,814)	
Hines, Russell	4:49:35 (20,912)	
Hines, Shane J	3:49:44 (6,881)	
Hines, Stuart C	4:19:49 (13,544)	
Hines-Randle, Andrew W Jnr	6:34:15 (34,469)	
Hinett, Karl J	4:50:39 (21,158)	
Hinton, Ben W	4:47:00 (20,280)	
Hinton, Geoffrey P	4:28:08 (15,629)	
Hinton, Lee S	4:17:06 (12,830)	
Hinton, Matthew H	3:42:09 (5,545)	
Hinton, Thomas H	5:07:54 (25,077)	
Hiorns, Andrew J	3:41:54 (5,498)	
Hiorns, Stephen R	3:10:47 (1,613)	
Hipp, Thomas K	3:46:17 (6,216)	
Hipperson, Rodney A	4:27:14 (15,400)	
Hirani, Bhavesh	4:56:26 (22,602)	
Hircock, Shaun D	5:55:23 (32,182)	
Hird, Ian	3:26:54 (3,258)	
Hirons, Steve	3:15:36 (2,038)	
Hirrell, Martin	3:21:51 (2,690)	
Hirsch, Dean	4:55:50 (22,468)	
Hirsch, Richard A	4:30:46 (16,308)	
Hirst, John	5:33:17 (29,641)	
Hirst, Kelvin P	4:52:02 (21,492)	
Hirst, Richard D	4:34:59 (17,268)	
Hirst, Russell J	5:51:10 (31,791)	
Hirtle, Thilo	4:13:05 (11,853)	
Hitch, Oliver J	3:50:28 (7,039)	
Hitchcock, David	4:36:52 (17,758)	
Hitchcock, Stephen J	4:33:06 (16,810)	
Hitchcroft, Nicholas J	4:03:19 (9,835)	
Hitchens, Richard J	4:11:49 (11,573)	
Hitchins, Christopher E	4:03:49 (9,930)	
Hithersay, Simon M	3:46:25 (6,240)	
Hives, Lionel	4:58:18 (23,103)	
Hoad, Gary J	4:10:30 (11,268)	
Hoad, Ian A	3:41:06 (5,382)	
Hoad, Ian P	4:18:49 (13,287)	
Hoad, Mark	3:31:32 (3,915)	
Hoad, Stephen	3:36:12 (4,570)	

Hoadley, Jeffrey T......3:57:51 (8,680)
Hoang, David......4:31:04 (16,368)
Hoare, James......3:59:37 (9,123)
Hoare, Leonard......6:48:17 (34,893)
Hoare, Raymond......4:14:37 (12,235)
Hoare, Ronald H......4:53:41 (21,937)
Hoban, Liam C......4:31:26 (16,447)
Hobart, Gary S......5:21:49 (27,758)
Hobbs, Andrew......3:04:38 (1,140)
Hobbs, Daniel J......7:01:24 (35,150)
Hobbs, David......4:09:57 (11,156)
Hobbs, John......4:34:32 (17,156)
Hobbs, Jonathan M......3:00:18 (917)
Hobbs, Mark H......3:53:57 (7,779)
Hobbs, Matt P......4:48:15 (20,592)
Hobbs, Mike J......3:08:10 (1,403)
Hobbs, Paul......4:58:11 (23,070)
Hobbs, Robert S......4:40:35 (18,678)
Hobbs, Stephen D......4:44:41 (19,740)
Hobbs, Stephen M......3:51:50 (7,324)
Hobin, Mark J......3:15:20 (2,022)
Hobson, Alex R......3:57:11 (8,520)
Hobson, Geophrey......6:17:06 (33,737)
Hobson, Harry......6:19:30 (33,860)
Hobson, Iain M......4:45:51 (20,020)
Hobson, Jonathan G......4:09:49 (11,129)
Hobson, Kevin M......5:54:48 (32,125)
Hobson, Leslie J......4:43:28 (19,409)
Hobson, Richard C......4:09:49 (11,129)
Hobson, Robert D......3:48:42 (6,666)
Hobson, Simon A......4:49:52 (20,968)
Hobson, Simon P......5:25:53 (28,439)
Hockett, Michael T......3:48:58 (6,723)
Hockey, Martin I......3:56:02 (8,231)
Hocking, Julian......4:21:24 (13,939)
Hocking, Steve......5:41:00 (30,708)
Hocking, Zack......4:06:47 (10,526)
Hockley, Stephen R......3:35:18 (4,449)
Hoddell, David L......3:07:40 (1,356)
Hodey, Matthew R......4:21:35 (13,980)
Hodge, Brian M......5:14:00 (26,228)
Hodge, Ian......3:32:59 (4,136)
Hodge, Ian R......5:38:38 (30,402)
Hodge, Jonathan......4:33:55 (17,011)
Hodge, Matthew J......3:54:53 (7,982)
Hodge, Paul......5:21:34 (27,705)
Hodge, Robert G......3:44:05 (5,878)
Hodge, Steve......5:01:03 (23,739)
Hodge, Tony G......3:51:26 (7,240)
Hodges, Darren P......4:22:19 (14,157)
Hodges, James A......4:35:43 (17,463)
Hodges, James E......4:19:27 (13,446)
Hodges, Marlon J......6:46:46 (34,850)
Hodges, Nick B......2:54:23 (539)
Hodges, Simon C......3:23:38 (2,861)
Hodgetts, Peter C......6:28:28 (34,265)
Hodgin, Justin A......5:47:35 (31,413)
Hodgkinson, Matt......3:42:00 (5,522)
Hodgkinson, Thomas D......5:08:17 (25,152)
Hodgkiss, Ian J......4:59:09 (23,297)
Hodgskiss, Callen A......3:14:21 (1,928)
Hodgson, Alan......4:32:24 (16,644)
Hodgson, Andrew......5:01:28 (23,823)
Hodgson, Andy W......3:51:03 (7,145)
Hodgson, Barnaby P......3:56:32 (8,369)
Hodgson, Christopher L......3:08:38 (1,439)
Hodgson, Christopher P......3:10:37 (1,603)
Hodgson, David J......3:59:02 (8,965)
Hodgson, Jeff......6:48:48 (34,905)
Hodgson, Mark A......5:03:18 (24,191)
Hodgson, Matthew......3:26:43 (3,227)
Hodgson, Philip......5:45:32 (31,212)
Hodgson, Robin G......6:34:56 (34,495)
Hodgson, Russell J......3:30:43 (3,808)
Hodgson, Shaun B......6:44:01 (34,772)
Hodgson, Tony......4:37:56 (17,989)
Hodkins, Norman......5:43:40 (31,009)
Hodkinson, Mark A......4:37:44 (17,946)
Hodson, David......3:23:18 (2,832)
Hodson, James A......4:41:17 (18,858)
Hodson, James R......4:39:00 (18,283)
Hoegh, Soren......4:14:46 (12,264)
Hoenle, Martin......4:35:45 (17,473)
Hoennecke, Markus......4:23:07 (14,358)
Hoeper, Hanno......3:29:09 (3,596)
Hoermann, Peter E......4:05:39 (10,277)
Hoerner, Pascal A......3:28:53 (3,553)
Hoey, Kenneth......3:43:04 (5,701)
Hoey, Michael A......3:14:11 (1,910)
Hoey, Paul F......4:38:12 (18,058)
Hofeling, Kirk......4:45:19 (19,908)
Hoffmeister, Marc......3:33:21 (4,187)
Hofmann, Kurt......3:39:24 (5,087)
Hogan, Graham S......2:57:51 (736)
Hogan, James......3:51:56 (7,351)
Hogan, Paul J......4:04:44 (10,100)
Hogan, Stuart......4:53:53 (21,985)
Hogarth, Paul M......5:07:15 (24,942)
Hogben, Paul C......3:48:12 (6,561)
Hogbin, Timothy P......3:08:44 (1,447)
Hogdson, Angus J......3:32:05 (4,004)
Hogg, Douglas C......4:37:43 (17,942)
Hogg, Michael N......3:48:27 (6,608)
Hogg, Paul R......5:07:04 (24,902)
Hogg, Percy......4:46:12 (20,107)
Hogg, Richard J......3:14:36 (1,952)
Hoile, Kevin P......4:59:11 (23,302)
Hoiom, Runar......2:26:23 (27)
Hokin, Robert S......5:58:45 (32,488)
Holberton, Peter D......4:54:29 (22,145)
Holborn, Adrian......3:58:31 (8,842)
Holbrook, Adam J......4:18:55 (13,313)
Holbrook, Bill......4:30:55 (16,339)
Holbrook, Mark A......5:34:37 (29,865)
Holbrook, Philip P......3:50:10 (6,971)
Holburn, Simon J......4:41:54 (19,017)
Holcombe, Andrew P......5:54:53 (32,135)
Holcroft, Allan......5:14:47 (26,403)
Holcroft, Glyn M......3:35:29 (4,479)
Holda, Bartlomiej H......3:09:49 (1,540)
Holdaway, Leslie B......4:36:43 (17,718)
Holdcroft, Leslie D......2:56:03 (612)
Holdcroft, Stephen J......3:04:14 (1,114)
Holden, Andrew J......5:35:14 (29,948)
Holden, Bernard L......6:17:28 (33,746)
Holden, Brian......5:11:41 (25,790)
Holden, Chris......5:09:30 (25,371)
Holden, Clive J......4:32:36 (16,690)
Holden, David F......3:38:02 (4,837)
Holden, David R......4:11:23 (11,470)
Holden, Frank......5:12:51 (26,008)
Holden, Gary J......4:10:11 (11,201)
Holden, Gary L......5:20:01 (27,428)
Holden, John......4:34:29 (17,143)
Holden, Mark......5:09:42 (25,415)
Holden, Maurice D......4:50:29 (21,116)
Holden, Peter J......4:52:24 (21,597)
Holden, Stephen......3:55:44 (8,171)
Holden, Wayne......3:50:45 (7,087)
Holden, William K......4:38:05 (18,035)
Holden-Brown, Nicholas S......4:02:43 (9,733)
Holder, David P......4:27:03 (15,339)
Holder, Godfrey......6:14:17 (33,568)
Holder, John......4:16:02 (12,575)
Holder, John M......3:39:21 (5,073)
Holder, Julian T......4:07:40 (10,695)
Holder, Keith M......4:34:39 (17,191)
Holdich, Stephen N......5:37:11 (30,195)
Holdsworth, Andrew S......3:59:36 (9,119)
Holdsworth, Ivan L......3:29:16 (3,611)
Holdway, John......3:48:59 (6,729)
Holford, Simon D......4:44:01 (19,542)
Holgate, Martin N......4:47:03 (20,299)
Holl, James D......3:36:34 (4,621)
Holland, Adam J......3:02:37 (1,033)
Holland, Alex......4:10:56 (11,358)
Holland, Alistair P......4:43:02 (19,304)
Holland, Brian......3:26:09 (3,149)
Holland, Chris......4:36:36 (17,692)
Holland, Gregg......5:49:29 (31,624)
Holland, James A......3:25:43 (3,092)
Holland, James A......4:59:26 (23,359)
Holland, John D......3:12:55 (1,815)
Holland, Jonathan D......3:42:42 (5,627)
Holland, Oliver A......5:25:25 (28,346)
Holland, Olivier D......4:16:46 (12,755)
Holland, Paul E......4:24:22 (14,669)
Holland, Pete......5:38:20 (30,364)
Hollands, Mark T......2:40:26 (147)
Hollands, Paul......3:17:01 (2,180)
Holley, Andrew J......3:46:47 (6,301)
Holley, Paul S......2:52:03 (443)
Hollick, Steve P......5:43:40 (31,009)
Hollick, Warren D......6:37:42 (34,595)
Holliday, Andy......5:00:56 (23,715)
Holliday, David S......3:37:48 (4,788)
Holliday, Paul W......4:17:13 (12,860)
Hollier, Matthew E......3:55:01 (8,011)
Holligan, Michael D......4:18:24 (13,174)
Hollingsworth, Noel S......3:35:56 (4,540)
Hollingworth, Mark W......3:34:22 (4,326)
Hollingworth, Richard A......5:23:50 (28,084)
Hollinshead, Christopher D......2:57:51 (736)
Hollioake, Adam......6:50:16 (34,938)
Hollioake, John F......6:50:16 (34,938)
Hollis, Keith L......4:06:31 (10,469)
Hollis, Paul......4:05:24 (10,224)
Hollis, Stephen M......4:22:50 (14,295)
Holloway, Andrew P......4:46:20 (20,135)
Holloway, Donald......3:55:03 (8,019)
Holloway, Edward W......4:19:18 (13,405)
Holloway, Nicholas F......4:55:08 (22,298)
Holloway, Stephen......4:33:26 (16,899)
Hollowood, Ben......4:44:22 (19,639)
Hollyoak, David G......3:36:20 (4,592)
Hollywood, Bernie P......4:41:33 (18,939)
Holman, Darrell......4:08:51 (10,933)
Holman, Thomas H......4:33:18 (16,867)
Holme, David J......5:17:44 (27,007)
Holmes, Andrew......3:59:29 (9,091)
Holmes, Benjamin R......3:32:29 (4,065)
Holmes, Craig......5:18:42 (27,199)
Holmes, Daniel......4:22:48 (14,286)
Holmes, Daniel S......3:35:21 (4,460)
Holmes, Darren......5:23:45 (28,063)
Holmes, David......3:45:36 (6,113)
Holmes, David A......5:40:16 (30,622)
Holmes, David I......4:58:20 (23,115)
Holmes, David J......4:11:55 (11,596)
Holmes, David J......4:15:30 (12,442)
Holmes, David W......3:56:29 (8,355)
Holmes, Dennis......3:47:23 (6,405)
Holmes, Derrick W......4:03:12 (9,818)
Holmes, Gary......3:59:02 (8,965)
Holmes, John H......3:33:13 (4,168)
Holmes, Jon......4:00:15 (9,263)
Holmes, Karl......5:57:18 (32,352)
Holmes, Mark......4:20:17 (13,674)
Holmes, Martin D......3:39:34 (5,119)
Holmes, Mike T......2:51:43 (429)
Holmes, Nicholas I......4:48:59 (20,765)
Holmes, Nicholas M......2:56:46 (658)
Holmes, Nick J......3:40:28 (5,257)
Holmes, Nigel D......3:58:43 (8,887)
Holmes, Paul......4:38:00 (18,011)
Holmes, Paul M......4:20:04 (13,618)
Holmes, Richard A......3:30:21 (3,775)
Holmes, Robert W......5:28:59 (28,979)
Holmes, Russell J......4:22:11 (14,121)
Holmes, Scott P......4:22:31 (14,209)
Holmes, Seth H......3:56:46 (8,423)
Holmes, Stephen......5:34:01 (29,764)
Holmes, Trevor R......4:26:29 (15,184)
Holohan, Tom......4:15:46 (12,501)
Holroyd, Alan J......4:54:44 (22,207)
Holst, Neil......3:40:18 (5,231)
Holt, David G......5:37:39 (30,255)
Holt, David J......4:27:11 (15,381)
Holt, Jacob E......4:00:23 (9,287)
Holt, John F......4:16:45 (12,751)
Holt, Jonathan D......4:18:10 (13,112)
Holt, Julian D......3:48:13 (6,565)
Holt, Martin J......3:53:11 (7,610)
Holt, Nick......3:31:23 (3,888)
Holt, Richard A......4:39:10 (18,324)
Holt, Robert G......5:13:18 (26,088)
Holt, Robin A......3:54:55 (7,992)
Holt, Roy S......5:15:14 (26,507)
Holt, Stephen......3:44:16 (5,898)

Holt, Tim C	5:00:48	(23,689)
Holt, Timothy R	5:15:14	(26,507)
Holthuis, John	4:40:18	(18,603)
Holtom, Geoffrey	4:41:20	(18,869)
Holtom, Keith	5:11:18	(25,719)
Holton, Adam	3:30:29	(3,785)
Holton, David W	3:38:27	(4,913)
Holy, Kristian J	5:13:41	(26,161)
Holyoak, Michael	3:36:54	(4,676)
Holyoak, Michael J	3:08:19	(1,417)
Holyoak, Stuart E	4:00:44	(9,363)
Holzinger, Erik H	3:34:38	(4,356)
Homan, Carl J	6:25:06	(34,133)
Homer, James W	5:02:39	(24,066)
Homer, Mark R	3:18:34	(2,348)
Homer, Paul R	4:01:11	(9,457)
Homewood, Christopher P	5:48:39	(31,539)
Homewood, Gordon A	4:59:38	(23,419)
Hommel-Hansen, Thomas	3:32:35	(4,082)
Hone, Eddie	3:42:46	(5,637)
Honegger, Othmar	3:11:43	(1,697)
Hones, Stephen	3:15:43	(2,051)
Honey, Michael J	6:12:16	(33,441)
Honey, Richard P	5:36:23	(30,095)
Honeyman, David	5:50:28	(31,725)
Honeywood, Ian	4:29:37	(16,042)
Honeywood, Ian A	4:50:14	(21,055)
Honeywood, Philip C	3:34:30	(4,340)
Honnor, Ian C	3:25:19	(3,046)
Honsel, Ralf	4:36:44	(17,723)
Hoo, Jonathan C	3:33:39	(4,222)
Hood, David I	3:53:38	(7,713)
Hood, Paul	3:06:21	(1,257)
Hood, Richard	4:57:48	(22,986)
Hood, Thomas S	4:15:46	(12,501)
Hook, John C	3:46:59	(6,342)
Hook, Myles	4:43:58	(19,527)
Hook, Simon L	4:44:56	(19,815)
Hooke, Andrew P	6:11:16	(33,388)
Hooker, Paul A	3:28:41	(3,520)
Hooley, Andrew P	3:30:28	(3,782)
Hooley, Neil	5:52:44	(31,944)
Hoomans, Guido	4:24:05	(14,593)
Hooper, Christopher S	3:35:15	(4,443)
Hooper, Craig J	4:37:50	(17,965)
Hooper, Duncan M	4:39:19	(18,368)
Hooper, Graham	5:18:48	(27,214)
Hooper, Gregg P	3:05:40	(1,213)
Hooper, Martin	3:43:58	(5,862)
Hooper, Martin	4:23:00	(14,334)
Hooper, Martin J	3:50:18	(6,998)
Hooper, Nicholas J	3:15:50	(2,064)
Hooper, Oliver J	3:56:12	(8,274)
Hooper, Paul	3:47:31	(6,432)
Hooper, Paul D	4:37:24	(17,862)
Hooper, Pete L	5:03:08	(24,156)
Hooper, Rowan	2:43:03	(199)
Hooper, William W	4:33:36	(16,938)
Hooton, Michael A	5:56:30	(32,289)
Hooton, Nick P	4:26:32	(15,201)
Hopcraft, Christopher D	4:26:18	(15,130)
Hopcraft, Robert J	3:42:23	(5,581).
Hope, Alex	2:44:00	(215)
Hope, Gary J	2:38:49	(121)
Hope, Lee C	6:29:41	(34,317)
Hope, Paul H	6:09:09	(33,246)
Hope, Robert J	4:31:37	(16,490)
Hope-Gill, James P	4:51:28	(21,363)
Hopewell, Stefan J	4:43:07	(19,324)
Hopgood, Martin A	4:21:44	(14,012)
Hopkins, Bruce A	4:06:12	(10,396)
Hopkins, Chris	3:54:50	(7,970)
Hopkins, Gabriel	4:20:20	(13,691)
Hopkins, Gareth J	3:21:53	(2,693)
Hopkins, Greg	4:00:17	(9,269)
Hopkins, Howard L	3:49:50	(6,904)
Hopkins, James T	5:29:12	(29,023)
Hopkins, Jason A	5:29:11	(29,018)
Hopkins, John	4:55:44	(22,440)
Hopkins, Jonathan A	3:59:00	(8,960)
Hopkins, Lee J	6:08:48	(33,226)
Hopkins, Martin J	5:12:41	(25,983)
Hopkins, Martin P	5:25:38	(28,391)
Hopkins, Michael	5:46:34	(31,317)
Hopkins, Michael D	3:28:54	(3,558)
Hopkins, Michael D	3:45:06	(6,037)
Hopkins, Paul M	5:33:30	(29,682)
Hopkins, Peter R	5:46:50	(31,339)
Hopkins, Richard D	5:22:54	(27,921)
Hopkins, Robert	3:31:35	(3,925)
Hopkins, Simon P	5:46:50	(31,339)
Hopkins, Stephen A	3:49:09	(6,758)
Hopkins, Stuart D	2:55:30	(592)
Hopkinson, Christopher A	4:00:05	(9,224)
Hopkinson, David G	4:23:49	(14,518)
Hopkinson, Neil D	3:28:02	(3,411)
Hopkinson, Timothy	4:42:34	(19,195)
Hopla, Robert W	5:10:38	(25,604)
Hopper, Andrew P	5:50:08	(31,684)
Hopper, Peter	3:11:04	(1,638)
Hopps, Benjamin W	3:47:33	(6,436)
Hopps, Peter W	3:29:09	(3,596)
Hopton, Tim P	4:44:30	(19,681)
Hopwood, Craig	4:43:28	(19,409)
Hopwood, John	4:05:38	(10,273)
Horbatiuk, Kevin G	4:39:03	(18,299)
Horbury, Julian	3:47:30	(6,424)
Hordern, Chris	4:10:45	(11,318)
Hordley, Jeff	3:57:38	(8,634)
Hordon, David W	4:44:24	(19,649)
Hore, Kevin J	6:12:41	(33,472)
Horel, Jean Marie	3:51:10	(7,177)
Hori, Kenji	7:21:29	(35,400)
Horkan, Tom F	3:50:26	(7,027)
Horn, Andrew	4:52:59	(21,749)
Horn, Andrew P	4:01:06	(9,436)
Horn, Colin M	4:35:25	(17,386)
Horn, Duncan R	3:34:27	(4,338)
Horn, Jeff	5:31:39	(29,395)
Horn, Leo	4:27:10	(15,375)
Horn, Peter B	4:24:14	(14,638)
Horn, Steven M	5:13:42	(26,166)
Horn, Stuart C	4:38:57	(18,274)
Hornblower, Christopher J	6:00:21	(32,609)
Hornby, Simon	3:14:58	(1,991)
Horne, Andrew	5:17:38	(26,987)
Horne, Gary	4:11:15	(11,438)
Horne, Louis	4:23:11	(14,374)
Horne, Martin P	4:51:24	(21,343)
Horner, Richard W	4:52:48	(21,700)
Horner, Warren C	5:51:55	(31,866)
Hornigold, David C	4:23:27	(14,432)
Hornsby, Graham R	3:45:11	(6,065)
Hornsey, David G	4:27:02	(15,331)
Hornsey, Michael G	3:32:43	(4,097)
Hornsey, Mike D	4:16:16	(12,639)
Hornshaw, Aleck E	5:36:17	(30,080)
Horrell, Charlie E	4:32:12	(16,609)
Horrex, James R	4:06:41	(10,497)
Horridge, Chris R	3:54:36	(7,921)
Horrigan, Michael	4:23:47	(14,508)
Horrocks, Paul A	4:15:09	(12,357)
Horrocks, Peter	3:58:58	(8,954)
Horry, Geoff A	4:22:35	(14,224)
Horsfall, Christopher	3:54:37	(7,925)
Horsley, Andrew J	3:58:14	(8,772)
Horsnell, Richard	5:43:05	(30,944)
Horton, Clive	3:57:59	(8,718)
Horton, Colin N	3:31:27	(3,898)
Horton, David L	5:15:13	(26,505)
Horton, James R	3:37:35	(4,764)
Horton, Jeremy K	5:03:17	(24,189)
Horton, Nicholas B	2:57:23	(701)
Horton, Peter H	3:15:50	(2,064)
Horton, Robert H	4:39:59	(18,533)
Horton, Robert J	3:49:57	(6,927)
Horwood, Alan H	5:17:36	(26,980)
Horwood, Mike J	3:47:12	(6,377)
Hosford, Scott	3:47:30	(6,424)
Hosie, John J	3:17:22	(2,212)
Hosie, Nick	4:05:36	(10,265)
Hosker, Michael P	4:48:12	(20,578)
Hosking, Simon D	4:44:54	(19,810)
Hoskins, Phil	3:52:05	(7,389)
Hoskyn, John D	5:37:51	(30,279)
Hosmer, Mark	4:38:23	(18,122)
Hossain, Syed	5:16:16	(26,717)
Hossepian Junior, Arnaldo	3:49:34	(6,846)
Hossick, Ian M	5:59:53	(32,566)
Hostachy, Franck	2:50:02	(378)
Hotchins, Gordon I	4:50:07	(21,026)
Hotchkiss, David B	4:45:51	(20,020)
Houdayer, Bernard	4:26:44	(15,245)
Houden, Jon	3:41:00	(5,365)
Hough, Andrew J	4:44:32	(19,697)
Hough, Philip	4:08:43	(10,911)
Hough, Richard I	4:03:36	(9,886)
Hough, Steven J	3:13:04	(1,824)
Houghton, David J	5:57:22	(32,360)
Houghton, Greg L	3:32:49	(4,110)
Houghton, Marc	5:15:00	(26,449)
Houghton, Paul V	4:49:07	(20,798)
Houghton, Philip D	4:22:55	(14,313)
Houghton, Robin J	2:39:18	(129)
Houghton, Stephen	4:56:58	(22,768)
Houghton, Stephen J	3:43:14	(5,727)
Houghton, Toby J	3:48:05	(6,539)
Houliston, Austin	4:47:01	(20,286)
Houlston, Howard S	3:02:21	(1,019)
Houlston, Philip E	4:39:07	(18,310)
Hoult, Nigel S	3:32:17	(4,044)
Hoult, Spencer G	5:19:50	(27,399)
Houlton, Matthew	3:22:22	(2,734)
Houlton, Nicholas J	2:36:58	(99)
Hounslow, Ian C	3:46:06	(6,196)
Hourseau, Pascal	4:52:05	(21,509)
House, David O	5:22:30	(27,854)
House, Dean C	3:18:07	(2,298)
House, Matt J	4:22:17	(14,148)
Housman, Christopher D	3:39:50	(5,164)
Houston, Andrew R	4:38:46	(18,220)
Houston, Darren L	4:27:56	(15,567)
Houston, Ian	4:38:45	(18,212)
Houweling, Bastiaan	5:07:14	(24,938)
Hovery, Gary S	5:08:09	(25,126)
How, Nicholas M	4:29:40	(16,058)
Howard, Alan M	3:58:46	(8,903)
Howard, Allan D	4:54:57	(22,257)
Howard, Andrew J	3:52:35	(7,480)
Howard, Andrw S	3:51:48	(7,315)
Howard, Andy D	5:17:10	(26,886)
Howard, Charles D	3:26:56	(3,265)
Howard, David R	4:30:32	(16,261)
Howard, Gavin M	4:35:08	(17,310)
Howard, James E	4:21:02	(13,860)
Howard, James P	3:51:22	(7,213)
Howard, Jason A	3:15:10	(2,010)
Howard, John N	4:24:55	(14,804)
Howard, Julian	4:41:48	(18,995)
Howard, Karl A	4:27:40	(15,509)
Howard, Paul J	3:53:24	(7,668)
Howard, Philip E	3:24:36	(2,969)
Howard, Richard P	4:09:49	(11,129)
Howard, Simon M	4:15:41	(12,487)
Howard, Stephen	3:48:51	(6,696)
Howard, Stephen C	3:14:45	(1,965)
Howard, Stephen P	5:02:19	(23,993)
Howarth, Alastair G	4:39:34	(18,427)
Howarth, James	4:51:19	(21,321)
Howarth, Raymond	4:25:53	(15,032)
Howarth, Raymond P	3:16:15	(2,099)
Howarth, Thomas D	3:51:32	(7,262)
Howarth, Tim S	3:23:38	(2,861)
Howat, Paul	4:41:09	(18,828)
Howden, Gary	4:23:02	(14,340)
Howe, David I	6:16:23	(33,711)
Howe, David T	4:48:42	(20,697)
Howe, Glen E	3:20:08	(2,509)
Howe, John	6:29:07	(34,288)
Howe, Martin L	4:28:17	(15,666)
Howe, Robert L	4:22:03	(14,097)
Howe, Simon C	4:16:03	(12,582)
Howe, Steven J	4:21:57	(14,077)
Howe, Tim	4:30:25	(16,237)
Howel, Stuart	3:26:07	(3,143)
Howell, Andrew K	5:06:02	(24,698)
Howell, Charles A	5:14:39	(26,373)
Howell, Christopher E	7:09:20	(35,264)
Howell, Graham	3:29:04	(3,583)

Howell, Jonathan V 3:49:36 (6,851)
Howell, Malcolm 3:50:00 (6,942)
Howell, Mark 4:39:41 (18,462)
Howell, Robert D 5:31:06 (29,317)
Howell, Scott 3:01:09 (966)
Howells, Benjamin M 4:04:10 (10,000)
Howells, Colin M 5:07:22 (24,970)
Howells, David C 3:23:09 (2,815)
Howells, Gareth J 4:54:05 (22,037)
Howells, Mark D 5:27:35 (28,728)
Howes, Alan D 5:33:24 (29,664)
Howes, Bradley A 5:13:45 (26,178)
Howes, Sean 4:15:59 (12,558)
Howick, Stuart R 4:07:53 (10,742)
Howitt, Andrew C 4:03:49 (9,930)
Howland, Kenneth 5:16:40 (26,784)
Howlett, Aaron W 6:09:47 (33,290)
Howlett, Vincent D 5:19:14 (27,297)
Howley, Vincent I 3:14:32 (1,947)
Howorth, Aaron J 3:48:53 (6,700)
Howram, Martin 4:52:44 (21,677)
Hows, Gavin J 3:11:42 (1,696)
Howson, Andrew J 3:04:14 (1,114)
Howson, Luke J 3:05:37 (1,210)
Howson, Peter J 5:14:06 (26,247)
Hoy, Christopher D 5:29:15 (29,034)
Hoy, Stuart C 4:29:27 (15,993)
Hoyland, Richard J 3:37:24 (4,737)
Hoyle, Jason P 5:08:09 (25,126)
Hoyle, Mark J 5:11:20 (25,730)
Hoyle, Michael G 4:40:29 (18,654)
Hoyle, Nick 5:00:59 (23,722)
Hoyle, Raymond J 6:35:49 (34,531)
Hreidarsson, Kristinn O 3:41:48 (5,484)
Htompson, Steve N 5:09:41 (25,411)
Huang, Yan 5:24:21 (28,164)
Hubbard, John W 3:42:58 (5,682)
Hubbard, Jonathan G 3:28:32 (3,494)
Hubbard, Nick 4:34:15 (17,088)
Hubble, Peter L 5:21:33 (27,701)
Huber, Helmut 3:33:14 (4,171)
Hubert, François-Xavier 3:45:38 (6,122)
Huck, Ernest F 3:32:01 (3,990)
Huckell, Victor F 5:15:27 (26,553)
Hucker, Martin I 4:50:16 (21,061)
Huckett, James 5:37:20 (30,219)
Huckle, Alan P 3:21:37 (2,663)
Huckle, Julian T 3:18:53 (2,377)
Hucklesby, Tony 3:45:15 (6,056)
Hudd, Daniel 4:31:11 (16,401)
Huddle, Andrew V 4:26:29 (15,184)
Huddleston, Mark 3:20:04 (2,503)
Hudson, Andrew S 3:26:56 (3,265)
Hudson, Craig A 5:09:11 (25,313)
Hudson, Dale 4:09:11 (11,002)
Hudson, Damian R 4:31:58 (16,554)
Hudson, Guy 4:13:43 (12,022)
Hudson, James R 4:31:58 (16,554)
Hudson, John W 5:17:28 (26,951)
Hudson, Kenneth 3:54:01 (7,794)
Hudson, Mat J 4:58:49 (23,211)
Hudson, Michael J 5:13:00 (26,048)
Hudson, Paul R 7:27:16 (35,452)
Hudson, Richard A 3:25:12 (3,038)
Hudson, Simon R 5:40:14 (30,617)
Hudson, Thomas 4:35:16 (17,353)
Hudson, Tim J 4:49:25 (20,864)
Hudspith, John E 3:02:30 (1,029)
Huggett, Ross 4:50:35 (21,145)
Huggill, Samuel A 5:51:17 (31,806)
Huggins, Terence 5:49:35 (31,636)
Huggon, Philip 5:36:12 (30,072)
Hughes, Adam J 5:13:14 (26,084)
Hughes, Adam P 3:41:54 (5,498)
Hughes, Adrian C 5:17:51 (27,018)
Hughes, Aled W 5:27:52 (28,773)
Hughes, Alexander P 5:32:28 (29,518)
Hughes, Aneirin M 5:35:54 (30,038)
Hughes, Ceri 4:15:45 (12,495)
Hughes, Ceri D 4:25:46 (15,009)
Hughes, Chris B 4:34:42 (17,203)
Hughes, Colin R 3:46:43 (6,287)
Hughes, Darren 4:17:30 (12,947)
Hughes, Darren R 3:59:20 (9,050)
Hughes, David A 3:14:22 (1,931)
Hughes, David G 5:48:29 (31,522)
Hughes, David M 4:14:22 (12,180)
Hughes, David R 3:07:04 (1,318)
Hughes, Dean 2:58:24 (781)
Hughes, Frank D 3:27:36 (3,362)
Hughes, Frazer 6:27:12 (34,218)
Hughes, Frederick J 3:53:46 (7,742)
Hughes, Geraint 2:59:54 (893)
Hughes, Graham D 4:08:34 (10,882)
Hughes, Ian R 5:05:33 (24,612)
Hughes, James A 5:09:25 (25,358)
Hughes, James J 6:00:31 (32,626)
Hughes, John A 5:38:10 (30,329)
Hughes, John K 5:37:24 (30,229)
Hughes, Keith 3:18:26 (2,337)
Hughes, Kenneth G 4:02:57 (9,774)
Hughes, Leslie 3:41:16 (5,405)
Hughes, Martin A 5:03:09 (24,160)
Hughes, Matt 3:20:31 (2,558)
Hughes, Nicholas 3:36:00 (4,550)
Hughes, Oliver J 4:47:34 (20,426)
Hughes, Peter G 3:55:07 (8,035)
Hughes, Peter R 5:09:14 (25,323)
Hughes, Peter T 5:25:23 (28,335)
Hughes, Richard G 5:07:39 (25,027)
Hughes, Richard J 4:23:26 (14,427)
Hughes, Richard T 3:47:12 (6,377)
Hughes, Ronald R 5:49:32 (31,631)
Hughes, Simon G 5:16:05 (26,680)
Hughes, Simon P 3:10:47 (1,613)
Hughes, Simon R 4:50:35 (21,145)
Hughes, Steffan 3:39:32 (5,113)
Hughes, Stephen 5:43:01 (30,936)
Hughes, Stephen 5:45:32 (31,212)
Hughes, Stephen R 4:30:43 (16,295)
Hughes, Wayne 5:16:23 (26,733)
Hughes, William A 4:18:56 (13,314)
Hugues, Xavier 3:29:49 (3,691)
Hulbert, Dan A 3:44:08 (5,884)
Hulbert, Simon A 3:40:50 (5,329)
Hulcoop, Simon P 4:48:54 (20,745)
Hulcoop, Stephen V 4:44:10 (19,587)
Hulin, Gareth D 5:23:57 (28,101)
Hulin, Vincent 3:50:46 (7,091)
Hull, Daniel J 6:45:28 (34,809)
Hull, Jeremy P 3:48:01 (6,529)
Hull, Jonathan A 3:52:02 (7,370)
Hull, Keith 3:35:09 (4,431)
Hull, Martin 3:43:29 (5,776)
Hull, Michael 4:30:51 (16,324)
Hull, Neil 4:37:07 (17,811)
Hull, Peter E 6:13:32 (33,523)
Hull, Richard T 6:21:41 (33,985)
Hull, Stephen C 5:01:26 (23,820)
Hulland, Tom 4:09:13 (11,010)
Hulley, Andrew R 4:47:45 (20,470)
Hulley, Michael S 3:35:54 (4,537)
Hulme, David 7:36:49 (35,543)
Hulme, John 5:09:07 (25,298)
Hulme, Simon J 4:28:17 (15,666)
Hulse, Christopher J 3:26:54 (3,258)
Hulsing, Egbert H 4:43:58 (19,527)
Hume, Christopher J 4:01:53 (9,584)
Hume, James S 3:55:09 (8,044)
Hume, Richard M 4:06:08 (10,380)
Humes, Richard A 3:28:59 (3,575)
Hummerson, Jonathan J 5:29:08 (29,005)
Hummersone, Christopher 3:49:58 (6,932)
Humphrey, Christopher 6:26:06 (34,175)
Humphrey, Tom J 3:37:04 (4,697)
Humphreys, Alastair J 2:58:25 (782)
Humphreys, Christopher E 4:47:16 (20,347)
Humphreys, Neal 2:51:22 (422)
Humphreys, Peter 3:45:11 (6,047)
Humphreys, Rhona M 6:50:31 (34,947)
Humphreys, Thomas M 5:20:42 (27,555)
Humphries, Anthony J 3:43:48 (5,829)
Humphries, Dan J 5:12:25 (25,942)
Humphries, John W 4:08:36 (10,893)
Humphries, Jonathan P 5:03:46 (24,284)
Humphries, Martin 6:07:20 (33,121)
Humphries, Nick P 6:08:35 (33,211)
Humphries, Stuart 5:13:49 (26,194)
Humphry, Nicholas J 4:57:42 (22,956)
Humphryes, Kevin S 4:35:45 (17,473)
Humzah, Dowshan 4:54:42 (22,198)
Hund, Michael 3:47:38 (6,460)
Hunjan, Sanjay 5:18:05 (27,074)
Hunt, Alan J 3:48:55 (6,709)
Hunt, Andrew 5:47:16 (31,378)
Hunt, Andy J 4:46:58 (20,269)
Hunt, Anthony C 4:02:09 (9,630)
Hunt, Benjamin D 5:19:31 (27,344)
Hunt, Christopher P 3:41:04 (5,374)
Hunt, Darryl J 5:02:31 (24,045)
Hunt, George J 4:10:21 (11,236)
Hunt, Graham 4:06:59 (10,572)
Hunt, Graham D 6:07:34 (33,133)
Hunt, Gregory P 6:13:29 (33,518)
Hunt, Ian H 5:09:49 (25,434)
Hunt, Jeremy J 4:23:41 (14,488)
Hunt, John H 6:15:50 (33,673)
Hunt, Jon 4:39:21 (18,381)
Hunt, Kirk H 4:49:40 (20,930)
Hunt, Lee 5:36:33 (30,118)
Hunt, Marcus 5:22:04 (27,789)
Hunt, Mark J 5:44:55 (31,142)
Hunt, Michael E 3:01:06 (963)
Hunt, Paul N 4:29:14 (15,924)
Hunt, Philip C 5:16:24 (26,736)
Hunt, Richard H 6:07:44 (33,152)
Hunt, Richard J 5:04:46 (24,460)
Hunt, Shane P 3:16:06 (2,089)
Hunt, Simon A 3:19:51 (2,473)
Hunt, Simon F 3:55:15 (8,067)
Hunt, Simon P 5:29:47 (29,107)
Hunt, Stephen R 5:14:35 (26,359)
Hunt, Stephen J 4:12:02 (11,619)
Hunt, Steve B 4:47:56 (20,512)
Hunt, Terry D 6:09:28 (33,268)
Hunt, Tom 5:13:52 (26,206)
Hunt, Tom F 5:03:35 (24,251)
Hunter, Aitken 4:23:33 (14,459)
Hunter, Douglas 4:56:48 (22,715)
Hunter, Edward C 5:19:10 (27,283)
Hunter, Graham A 4:57:05 (22,792)
Hunter, Harry W 4:01:05 (9,434)
Hunter, James A 4:50:42 (21,168)
Hunter, Jon M 4:13:57 (12,084)
Hunter, Ken G 4:16:59 (12,813)
Hunter, Liam 3:48:10 (6,557)
Hunter, Pete J 4:27:29 (15,467)
Hunter, Richard I 5:19:10 (27,283)
Hunter, Simon J 4:54:34 (22,158)
Hunter, Stephen J 3:20:30 (2,553)
Hunter-Rice, Richard 6:06:13 (33,062)
Huntley, David C 3:45:46 (6,142)
Huntley, Neil 4:33:02 (16,795)
Huntley, Nicholas J 4:23:10 (14,369)
Hunton, Chris 3:37:46 (4,784)
Hurditch, Bert R 5:51:04 (31,782)
Hurdle, Richard J 3:56:04 (8,240)
Hurford, Mike J 3:07:22 (1,340)
Hurley, Joe 3:35:32 (4,490)
Hurley, Michael P 6:18:37 (33,812)
Hurley, Russell 5:11:44 (25,799)
Hurley, Steve D 3:36:19 (4,589)
Hurley, Thomas 4:30:04 (16,165)
Hurran, Chris J 4:52:31 (21,618)
Hurrell, Colin A 5:45:52 (31,243)
Hurrell, Ian E 5:48:38 (31,535)
Hurrell, Tim A 4:40:54 (18,760)
Hurren, Mark A 4:36:08 (17,567)
Hursey, Brian 5:32:38 (29,557)
Hurst, Alan 5:13:35 (26,135)
Hurst, Anthony 5:06:51 (24,854)
Hurst, David 2:50:21 (381)
Hurst, David 6:15:02 (33,616)
Hurst, Jamie 5:48:50 (31,567)
Hurst, Kevin J 4:48:44 (20,706)
Hurst, Tim J 5:54:36 (32,113)
Hurworth, Mark L 4:32:43 (16,720)
Husbands, James R 4:26:11 (15,091)
Husby, Dag S 4:52:21 (21,583)

Hussain, Abul	4:50:34 (21,139)	
Hussain, Mohibul	7:04:29 (35,199)	
Hussain, Nazir	5:24:52 (28,256)	
Hussain, Tariq	3:56:50 (8,439)	
Hussain, Zabeer	7:02:09 (35,162)	
Hussein, Samir	4:51:17 (21,307)	
Hussey, Adrian H	5:21:02 (27,609)	
Hussey, Paul	4:44:32 (19,697)	
Hutchen, Tim R	4:19:47 (13,539)	
Hutchence, Tim G	3:53:28 (7,681)	
Hutcheson, Adam	4:41:02 (18,797)	
Hutcheson, Christopher F	5:26:21 (28,521)	
Hutchin, Anthony D	3:13:07 (1,828)	
Hutchings, David	4:00:44 (9,363)	
Hutchings, James W	3:43:02 (5,697)	
Hutchings, Mark	4:54:03 (22,031)	
Hutchings, Mark A	4:22:34 (14,219)	
Hutchins, Leon J	4:40:40 (18,694)	
Hutchins, Michael A	3:49:56 (6,923)	
Hutchins, Steven R	3:38:29 (4,917)	
Hutchinson, Andrew L	4:19:56 (13,582)	
Hutchinson, Brett G	3:28:32 (3,494)	
Hutchinson, Dave A	4:58:50 (23,216)	
Hutchinson, David J	4:55:52 (22,479)	
Hutchinson, James	4:20:49 (13,807)	
Hutchinson, Malcolm D	5:23:26 (27,997)	
Hutchinson, Mark E	3:32:09 (4,024)	
Hutchinson, Paul	5:15:18 (26,525)	
Hutchinson, Peter R	3:58:13 (8,769)	
Hutchinson, Robert B	4:56:09 (22,550)	
Hutchison, Adam C	6:18:20 (33,792)	
Hutchison, Mark P	4:45:28 (19,938)	
Hutchison, Paul R	4:00:22 (9,283)	
Hutchison, Tom P	3:02:30 (1,029)	
Hutt, Alsadair	3:07:09 (1,321)	
Hutt, Gregory N	5:14:58 (26,444)	
Hutton, Eddie G	5:23:18 (27,976)	
Hutton, Jason A	6:10:43 (33,349)	
Hutton, John A	4:28:51 (15,822)	
Hutton, Kenneth M	3:28:32 (3,494)	
Hutton, Owen M	5:15:08 (26,486)	
Huxley, Gareth J	2:55:54 (608)	
Hyam, Stephen J	4:20:47 (13,792)	
Hyams, Peter A	4:11:59 (11,608)	
Hyatt, Gary F	3:57:47 (8,671)	
Hyatt, James	3:59:21 (9,053)	
Hyatt, Tim J	3:56:50 (8,439)	
Hyde, Andrew L	5:39:31 (30,533)	
Hyde, Gordon E	6:18:47 (33,823)	
Hyde, James E	5:06:43 (24,822)	
Hyde, Jasper E	4:24:32 (14,712)	
Hyde, Matthew E	3:13:11 (1,836)	
Hyde, Patrick A	4:13:16 (11,899)	
Hyde, Richard S	4:31:45 (16,517)	
Hyde, Robert J	4:44:24 (19,649)	
Hyde-Smith, Brent R	4:41:01 (18,794)	
Hyland, Andy	3:40:14 (5,220)	
Hyland, Martin	4:14:13 (12,141)	
Hyldmo, Terje	3:54:27 (7,893)	
Hylton, Neville	3:55:25 (8,109)	
Hyman, Dave A	3:21:17 (2,633)	
Hyoms, Mark C	4:21:56 (14,073)	
Hyson, Stuart J	4:50:23 (21,093)	
Hyvonen, Mauri	4:35:32 (17,410)	
Iaciofano, Antonio	5:55:33 (32,196)	
Ianson, Thomas P	6:01:02 (32,679)	
Iapicca, Mario	3:47:41 (6,473)	
Iball, John K	4:09:56 (11,155)	
Ibbots, Ian R	3:19:47 (2,464)	
Ibbotson, David J	3:10:58 (1,628)	
Ibbs, Robert J	3:37:14 (4,716)	
Ibnabdeljalil, Nacer	3:35:22 (4,465)	
Ibrahim, Sharief	3:21:53 (2,693)	
Ichihashi, Masakuni	4:34:41 (17,201)	
Icke, Jordan P	4:25:05 (14,842)	
Iddles, Brent W	6:24:15 (34,090)	
Ide, Gillan	4:40:17 (18,597)	
Ide, Stephen W	4:20:52 (13,822)	
Ikoli, Tandy	4:57:19 (22,860)	
Ikram, Tan	5:42:12 (30,847)	
Iles, Andrew P	3:49:28 (6,821)	
Iles, Spencer J	4:09:27 (11,063)	
Iley, Paul	4:57:34 (22,919)	

Illing, Paul	3:12:05 (1,738)	
Illingworth, Colin J	5:18:36 (27,180)	
Illingworth, Simon	4:29:59 (16,146)	
Illman, Bradley W	3:26:37 (3,211)	
Illman, Keith J	3:26:35 (3,204)	
Ilott, Martin C	5:11:34 (25,773)	
Ilott, Paul J	2:44:38 (230)	
Ilsley, Mark D	4:53:37 (21,919)	
Imber, Charles J	4:57:07 (22,800)	
Imberg, Petri	2:59:44 (881)	
Imeri, Fadil	3:30:38 (3,798)	
Imhoff, Martyn J	5:42:47 (30,904)	
Imperadore, Giuseppe	4:11:19 (11,452)	
Imrie, William R	4:52:08 (21,521)	
Ince, Paul J	4:47:58 (20,525)	
Inchley, Andrew B	3:12:21 (1,761)	
Incostante, Emanuele	3:39:26 (5,095)	
Infante, Felice	4:42:27 (19,164)	
Ingall-Tombs, Stuart M	3:49:09 (6,758)	
Ingelbrechtsen, Bo	3:54:38 (7,930)	
Ingham, Alex	3:35:20 (4,458)	
Ingham, Lee	4:35:47 (17,483)	
Ingham, Mark A	4:16:55 (12,792)	
Ingham, Robert J	5:26:18 (28,511)	
Ingle, Mark J	4:14:16 (12,157)	
Ingle, Phil J	4:39:11 (18,329)	
Ingle, Philip M	3:12:02 (1,734)	
Ingle, Richard J	5:33:44 (29,719)	
Ingledew, Niel	3:31:06 (3,850)	
Ingman, Marcus	3:13:36 (1,865)	
Ingoe, Phil E	3:18:36 (2,352)	
Ingram, Alistair	4:37:39 (17,922)	
Ingram, Michael R	4:47:32 (20,417)	
Ingram, Neal G	6:50:27 (34,943)	
Ingram, Tommy	3:14:52 (1,975)	
Inker, Gareth L	3:48:44 (6,674)	
Inman, Benedict J	5:15:08 (26,486)	
Inman, Gary J	4:26:24 (15,161)	
Inman, Stuart L	4:49:44 (20,940)	
Innes, Andrew P	4:36:40 (17,708)	
Innes, Garrard	6:00:57 (32,665)	
Innis, Marlon	6:47:32 (34,872)	
Insua, José	3:34:50 (4,384)	
Inwards, Richard J	4:40:10 (18,573)	
Ioannides, Marios T	5:28:02 (28,805)	
Ioannou, John	5:49:30 (31,626)	
Iqbal, Omar	3:46:38 (6,272)	
Irchad, Abdelmounaim	4:30:24 (16,234)	
Ireland, Mark	4:49:50 (20,959)	
Irish, John C	3:07:40 (1,356)	
Irons, David J	5:07:45 (25,044)	
Irons, Nicholas J	5:16:49 (26,808)	
Ironside, Fraser M	5:01:23 (23,811)	
Irvine, Andrew C	4:00:59 (9,417)	
Irvine, Angus	5:55:14 (32,167)	
Irvine, Angus D	3:54:46 (7,957)	
Irvine, Bobbie	3:44:33 (5,949)	
Irvine, Craig S	5:38:19 (30,362)	
Irvine, James E	2:54:32 (549)	
Irvine, Jon P	5:11:50 (25,820)	
Irvine, Robert N	3:24:36 (2,969)	
Irvine, Stuart D	3:37:01 (4,689)	
Irving, Jeremy J	3:43:42 (5,811)	
Irving, Mark	4:44:00 (19,538)	
Irving, Richard J	5:41:08 (30,721)	
Irving, William G	4:30:59 (16,349)	
Irwin, Laurie E	3:37:51 (4,799)	
Irwin, Lee J	5:37:13 (30,199)	
Isaac, Colin A	4:36:05 (17,553)	
Isaac, David T	5:24:13 (28,140)	
Isaac, Vincent	3:31:10 (3,858)	
Isaacs, David W	4:25:58 (15,049)	
Isaacs, Jason	4:12:38 (11,748)	
Isaacs, John	5:01:09 (23,761)	
Isaacson, Mark	5:04:46 (24,460)	
Isbell, Gary M	4:42:46 (19,246)	
Isbell, Richard J	5:01:52 (23,905)	
Isconte, Patrick	3:06:44 (1,292)	
Islam, Faisal	5:44:46 (31,125)	
Islam, Masum I	5:51:43 (31,848)	
Isles, Bruce	3:59:53 (9,178)	
Isola, Marco	5:07:36 (25,019)	
Isom, Neil	3:21:09 (2,617)	

Israel, James D	3:39:22 (5,079)	
Issatt, Howard T	3:39:51 (5,167)	
Isted, Jonathan I	4:48:35 (20,666)	
Iuliano, Domenico	3:56:08 (8,259)	
Ivatt, Mike J	4:20:14 (13,660)	
Ive, Martin J	3:11:48 (1,701)	
Ivens, Derek M	3:08:20 (1,419)	
Ivers, Michael A	4:38:43 (18,205)	
Iversen, Gunnar	5:12:18 (25,923)	
Iversen, Gunvald-Andreas	4:49:00 (20,769)	
Iverson, Keith A	4:22:42 (14,258)	
Ives, Philip E	5:24:41 (28,217)	
Ives, Roger V	4:59:02 (23,264)	
Ives, Stuart J	2:58:15 (766)	
Iveson, William J	4:42:30 (19,178)	
Ivory, Graham J	3:06:47 (1,296)	
Ivory, Kenneth J	3:14:57 (1,988)	
Iwens, Peter	3:51:25 (7,231)	
Izod, Stuart G	4:53:58 (22,012)	
Izzidien, Ali	4:00:22 (9,283)	
Jabbitt, Andrew	4:35:40 (17,446)	
Jabbour, Richard J	4:22:54 (14,309)	
Jabour, Stephen J	3:57:34 (8,615)	
Jack, Alan G	5:07:21 (24,967)	
Jack, Cameron	3:42:46 (5,637)	
Jack, Ian A	4:23:27 (14,432)	
Jack, James	4:49:10 (20,813)	
Jack, Robert A	4:56:36 (22,662)	
Jack, Rodney M	5:53:19 (31,989)	
Jack, Tom E	4:04:05 (9,983)	
Jackaman, Paul	4:10:53 (11,345)	
Jackett, Mark	3:40:53 (5,343)	
Jackman, Marcus I	5:21:38 (27,717)	
Jackman, Neil W	5:55:31 (32,194)	
Jackman, Paul	4:58:46 (23,198)	
Jacks, Andrew E	5:21:53 (27,772)	
Jackson, Alan	3:30:05 (3,731)	
Jackson, Alan C	5:14:33 (26,350)	
Jackson, Andrew	2:34:31 (70)	
Jackson, Andrew G	4:46:17 (20,120)	
Jackson, Andrew G	4:51:57 (21,474)	
Jackson, Andrew M	3:22:02 (2,710)	
Jackson, Anthony B	2:37:41 (106)	
Jackson, Barry	4:24:44 (14,756)	
Jackson, Christopher E	4:05:34 (10,256)	
Jackson, Colin	3:29:59 (3,717)	
Jackson, Colin E	3:51:37 (7,279)	
Jackson, Colin J	4:44:21 (19,635)	
Jackson, Daniel M	4:03:24 (9,850)	
Jackson, David G	4:53:06 (21,779)	
Jackson, David R	4:30:34 (16,274)	
Jackson, Derek	3:22:18 (2,727)	
Jackson, Edward J	5:08:06 (25,112)	
Jackson, George D	3:08:52 (1,455)	
Jackson, Ian	5:56:24 (32,278)	
Jackson, John P	5:04:50 (24,476)	
Jackson, Kevin J	3:25:23 (3,053)	
Jackson, Lee	5:50:17 (31,701)	
Jackson, Luke	3:05:24 (1,193)	
Jackson, Martyn R	4:05:26 (10,228)	
Jackson, Matthew J	3:11:02 (1,635)	
Jackson, Michael G	4:02:14 (9,659)	
Jackson, Mick E	4:26:14 (15,114)	
Jackson, Neil	2:49:02 (345)	
Jackson, Nigel G	4:15:37 (12,468)	
Jackson, Paul B	3:31:46 (3,947)	
Jackson, Paul T	4:11:15 (11,438)	
Jackson, Philip A	4:08:34 (10,882)	
Jackson, Philip M	4:31:17 (16,419)	
Jackson, Robert	5:01:32 (23,835)	
Jackson, Robert P	4:52:37 (21,649)	
Jackson, Russell B	5:32:12 (29,483)	
Jackson, Simon	3:21:38 (2,667)	
Jackson, Simon W	3:46:31 (6,249)	
Jackson, Stephen R	5:39:15 (30,482)	
Jackson, Steve J	3:11:56 (1,719)	
Jackson, Steven R	4:26:40 (15,231)	
Jackson, Stuart	3:00:24 (924)	
Jackson, Tim F	4:37:50 (17,965)	
Jackson, Tom A	3:51:31 (7,259)	
Jackson, Vincent A	5:09:00 (25,280)	
Jackson-Graham, Bradley	5:18:33 (27,173)	
Jacob, Kevin M	3:20:45 (2,583)	

Joddrell, Peter	4:29:29 (15,998)	
Joergensen, Erik S	5:33:57 (29,754)	
Joergensen, Jakob Milling	3:17:56 (2,282)	
Jogi, Narottam	5:19:54 (27,409)	
Johal, Kulwant S	4:08:01 (10,769)	
Johal, Manpreet S	5:15:39 (26,593)	
Johannesen, Stein H	4:27:33 (15,477)	
Johannessen, Jacob L	4:40:11 (18,578)	
Johansen, Mark J	5:44:59 (31,152)	
Johansson, Ake	5:17:51 (27,018)	
Johansson, Kent	4:15:56 (12,538)	
Johansson, Lars O	4:13:08 (11,865)	
Johansson, Roger	4:19:13 (13,379)	
John, Andrew R	4:00:21 (9,278)	
John, Chris	4:27:23 (15,442)	
John, Christopher	7:29:43 (35,494)	
John, Gareth M	4:51:34 (21,387)	
John, Paul C	3:19:42 (2,453)	
Johns, Alexander C	4:35:40 (17,446)	
Johns, Dominic P	6:00:27 (32,616)	
Johns, Matthew	5:02:00 (23,934)	
Johnsdton, Andrew I	4:09:41 (11,113)	
Johnson, Aaron R	4:51:55 (21,469)	
Johnson, Alan	3:29:26 (3,640)	
Johnson, Allan	4:59:33 (23,399)	
Johnson, Andrew	4:47:43 (20,459)	
Johnson, Andrew C	3:59:56 (9,193)	
Johnson, Andrew D	5:46:12 (31,283)	
Johnson, Andrew E	3:55:40 (8,155)	
Johnson, Andrew K	4:00:30 (9,311)	
Johnson, Andrew S	4:03:23 (9,846)	
Johnson, Andy R	4:43:06 (19,318)	
Johnson, Anthony C	3:36:32 (4,617)	
Johnson, Baden J	4:39:40 (18,454)	
Johnson, Cameron	3:08:55 (1,460)	
Johnson, Chris A	5:09:10 (25,306)	
Johnson, Christopher P	3:54:30 (7,905)	
Johnson, Colin N	3:55:40 (8,155)	
Johnson, Colm M	4:15:45 (12,495)	
Johnson, Darren W	3:26:19 (3,177)	
Johnson, David	3:48:16 (6,568)	
Johnson, David P	5:19:36 (27,360)	
Johnson, Dean	4:23:42 (14,490)	
Johnson, Duncan S	4:49:48 (20,955)	
Johnson, Fraser A	3:26:55 (3,261)	
Johnson, Gary	4:20:51 (13,817)	
Johnson, Gavin R	3:36:49 (4,659)	
Johnson, Gerald C	4:45:15 (19,893)	
Johnson, Gerard	4:09:15 (11,017)	
Johnson, Gerry	5:26:01 (28,458)	
Johnson, Jake	5:55:39 (32,207)	
Johnson, James I	5:36:33 (30,118)	
Johnson, James R	5:01:32 (23,835)	
Johnson, James W	4:21:51 (14,049)	
Johnson, Joe J	3:17:06 (2,190)	
Johnson, John R	5:16:56 (26,848)	
Johnson, Keefe D	4:48:09 (20,563)	
Johnson, Kevin	4:25:43 (14,998)	
Johnson, Lee	4:05:41 (10,286)	
Johnson, Lee A	4:11:03 (11,383)	
Johnson, Lee B	5:28:51 (28,957)	
Johnson, Lee J	4:48:54 (20,745)	
Johnson, Mark A	4:45:03 (19,852)	
Johnson, Mark R	5:46:48 (31,334)	
Johnson, Michael	5:02:18 (23,988)	
Johnson, Michael J	2:39:31 (136)	
Johnson, Myles A	3:24:29 (2,954)	
Johnson, Neil	4:08:10 (10,799)	
Johnson, Neil J	5:07:33 (25,010)	
Johnson, Nicholas	4:22:06 (14,109)	
Johnson, Paul	5:58:16 (32,438)	
Johnson, Paul W	4:21:20 (13,918)	
Johnson, Pete G	4:26:33 (15,205)	
Johnson, Peter	4:16:10 (12,612)	
Johnson, Peter M	3:40:48 (5,321)	
Johnson, Ray D	3:59:58 (9,201)	
Johnson, Richard	4:18:10 (13,112)	
Johnson, Richard M	3:43:25 (5,756)	
Johnson, Robert J	5:22:52 (27,916)	
Johnson, Robert P	3:15:47 (2,057)	
Johnson, Simon P	3:57:56 (8,705)	
Johnson, Sophie	5:19:05 (27,262)	
Johnson, Stephen A	5:34:30 (29,851)	
Johnson, Steve M	5:13:41 (26,161)	
Johnson, Steven D	4:42:30 (19,178)	
Johnson, Thomas	5:19:19 (27,313)	
Johnson, Thomas M	5:22:52 (27,916)	
Johnson, Tony	3:13:39 (1,871)	
Johnson, Tony M	5:01:03 (23,739)	
Johnstoln, Anthony	5:28:16 (28,855)	
Johnston, Colin	4:57:12 (22,821)	
Johnston, Craig W	3:51:00 (7,139)	
Johnston, Daren J	3:34:51 (4,387)	
Johnston, Dylan	4:28:30 (15,726)	
Johnston, Finlay	4:07:48 (10,724)	
Johnston, Gordon A	3:40:35 (5,284)	
Johnston, Iain	5:12:47 (25,998)	
Johnston, James A	5:03:47 (24,288)	
Johnston, Mark	3:01:45 (995)	
Johnston, Martin	5:10:47 (25,625)	
Johnston, Philip R	5:01:33 (23,843)	
Johnston, Richard A	4:12:11 (11,653)	
Johnston, Richard R	4:42:15 (19,110)	
Johnston, Simon J	4:10:37 (11,292)	
Johnstone, Douglas	3:20:56 (2,603)	
Johnstone, Iain R	4:19:27 (13,446)	
Johnstone, Peter H	3:30:33 (3,794)	
Johnstone, Roderick	3:07:24 (1,345)	
Jol, Onno	4:34:13 (17,079)	
Joliffe, Tim J	4:45:10 (19,876)	
Jollie, David M	4:24:16 (14,647)	
Jolliffe, Ian T	3:40:24 (5,248)	
Jolly, Raymond T	7:02:24 (35,166)	
Jolly, Steve D	3:49:46 (6,886)	
Joly, Robin B	4:36:45 (17,732)	
Joncoux, Benoit	3:59:17 (9,037)	
Joneja, Hemant	5:41:43 (30,798)	
Jones, Adam M	3:37:43 (4,779)	
Jones, Adrian	4:01:40 (9,545)	
Jones, Alan	4:32:20 (16,634)	
Jones, Alastair	4:51:55 (21,469)	
Jones, Allan S	2:47:41 (303)	
Jones, Andi	2:17:49 (10)	
Jones, Andrew F	4:26:11 (15,091)	
Jones, Andrew I	4:50:30 (21,120)	
Jones, Andrew M	2:52:09 (449)	
Jones, Andrew M	5:05:33 (24,612)	
Jones, Andrew S	5:26:44 (28,581)	
Jones, Andrew W	4:09:31 (11,078)	
Jones, Andy P	4:24:39 (14,735)	
Jones, Anthony	5:23:30 (28,010)	
Jones, Anthony M	4:21:39 (13,995)	
Jones, Anthony S	5:11:00 (25,665)	
Jones, Ben	4:47:39 (20,441)	
Jones, Ben P	4:36:59 (17,783)	
Jones, Bernard	3:57:01 (8,486)	
Jones, Berwyn P	4:50:40 (21,159)	
Jones, Brad D	3:40:25 (5,250)	
Jones, Brian	5:12:08 (25,879)	
Jones, Bruce A	3:49:28 (6,821)	
Jones, Cerith W	5:39:12 (30,477)	
Jones, Chris	4:53:45 (21,951)	
Jones, Chris P	4:04:23 (10,035)	
Jones, Christopher C	4:50:34 (21,139)	
Jones, Christopher D	3:44:04 (5,875)	
Jones, Christopher D	4:44:08 (19,571)	
Jones, Christopher H	5:04:47 (24,464)	
Jones, Christopher L	4:29:10 (15,900)	
Jones, Christopher L	5:14:55 (26,432)	
Jones, Colin	4:25:37 (14,973)	
Jones, Colin	5:32:31 (29,533)	
Jones, Colin B	5:03:21 (24,204)	
Jones, Colin D	4:43:06 (19,318)	
Jones, Colin F	5:14:32 (26,344)	
Jones, Colin W	3:32:05 (4,004)	
Jones, Cyril	4:38:04 (18,028)	
Jones, Daniel	4:36:49 (17,747)	
Jones, Daniel G	4:04:59 (10,141)	
Jones, Daniel G	4:31:40 (16,500)	
Jones, Darren G	5:20:58 (27,601)	
Jones, Darren J	5:34:28 (29,843)	
Jones, Dave	4:57:52 (23,002)	
Jones, David	3:34:15 (4,302)	
Jones, David A	3:28:05 (3,416)	
Jones, David A	4:19:04 (13,343)	
Jones, David A	4:30:49 (16,317)	
Jones, David B	3:52:37 (7,483)	
Jones, David G	4:59:27 (23,363)	
Jones, David J	4:31:54 (16,542)	
Jones, David P	5:12:20 (25,929)	
Jones, David T	3:47:30 (6,424)	
Jones, David W	4:56:41 (22,694)	
Jones, Dennis R	5:16:53 (26,835)	
Jones, Derek N	4:12:39 (11,751)	
Jones, Derwyn H	4:57:40 (22,951)	
Jones, Duncan	5:44:26 (31,085)	
Jones, Dylan W	3:22:37 (2,757)	
Jones, Francis D	5:01:25 (23,815)	
Jones, Frichard M	3:57:59 (8,718)	
Jones, Gareth	4:29:48 (16,090)	
Jones, Gareth	5:52:34 (31,924)	
Jones, Gareth D	5:48:47 (31,559)	
Jones, Gareth M	5:21:34 (27,705)	
Jones, Garry	5:35:11 (29,938)	
Jones, Garry D	4:00:37 (9,337)	
Jones, Gary D	5:33:06 (29,620)	
Jones, Gary P	3:59:10 (9,003)	
Jones, George	6:06:48 (33,095)	
Jones, George C	5:21:45 (27,741)	
Jones, George H	6:42:44 (34,742)	
Jones, Geraint D	5:12:03 (25,865)	
Jones, Glyn	3:40:30 (5,266)	
Jones, Glyn D	5:48:55 (31,575)	
Jones, Glyndwr	4:44:10 (19,587)	
Jones, Graham G	4:06:20 (10,422)	
Jones, Grahame	7:29:14 (35,471)	
Jones, Howard N	3:47:56 (6,516)	
Jones, Howard R	4:19:21 (13,420)	
Jones, Huw	3:09:12 (1,490)	
Jones, Huw	4:26:51 (15,280)	
Jones, Ian	4:50:24 (21,097)	
Jones, Ian H	3:44:51 (5,999)	
Jones, Iestyn	4:49:45 (20,943)	
Jones, James P	3:55:43 (8,169)	
Jones, Jerome	4:49:28 (20,882)	
Jones, John	3:30:32 (3,790)	
Jones, John	5:57:57 (32,409)	
Jones, John B	4:49:19 (20,842)	
Jones, John C	5:18:55 (27,235)	
Jones, Jonathan P	4:15:35 (12,456)	
Jones, Josh H	4:31:40 (16,500)	
Jones, Keith G	3:43:53 (5,846)	
Jones, Kelvyn	3:13:01 (1,820)	
Jones, Kenneth I	5:17:11 (26,891)	
Jones, Kevin	5:33:53 (29,742)	
Jones, Kevin E	6:41:17 (34,699)	
Jones, Lloyd B	3:43:17 (5,734)	
Jones, Malcolm	4:38:40 (18,188)	
Jones, Marcus	5:32:12 (29,483)	
Jones, Marcus L	3:50:20 (7,008)	
Jones, Mark	4:28:12 (15,646)	
Jones, Mark A	7:29:25 (35,484)	
Jones, Mark B	5:53:54 (32,046)	
Jones, Mark R	4:48:06 (20,552)	
Jones, Mark S	3:34:32 (4,347)	
Jones, Martin G	4:27:04 (15,345)	
Jones, Matthew M	5:50:36 (31,732)	
Jones, Matthew T	5:54:27 (32,103)	
Jones, Meirion	5:26:22 (28,524)	
Jones, Michael	4:51:25 (21,348)	
Jones, Michael C	4:33:02 (16,795)	
Jones, Michael D	3:14:37 (1,956)	
Jones, Michael J	4:43:39 (19,452)	
Jones, Michael L	4:44:01 (19,542)	
Jones, Michael N	3:22:46 (2,773)	
Jones, Nathan T	5:25:26 (28,351)	
Jones, Neil	3:33:09 (4,161)	
Jones, Neil	4:34:37 (17,181)	
Jones, Neil A	4:29:44 (16,070)	
Jones, Neil G	5:25:39 (28,396)	
Jones, Neil R	3:18:43 (2,361)	
Jones, Neil R	4:09:12 (11,007)	
Jones, Nicholas D	3:55:33 (8,126)	
Jones, Nicholas R	4:35:27 (17,389)	
Jones, Nigel F	3:52:07 (7,395)	
Jones, Nigel L	4:36:14 (17,592)	
Jones, Oliver	2:55:36 (597)	
Jones, Patrick	4:33:19 (16,876)	
Jones, Patrick M	3:59:53 (9,178)	

Jones, Paul	4:55:02 (22,271)	
Jones, Paul	5:01:32 (23,835)	
Jones, Paul A	4:39:27 (18,404)	
Jones, Paul B	4:52:30 (21,612)	
Jones, Paul H	4:29:07 (15,893)	
Jones, Paul M	4:22:45 (14,272)	
Jones, Peter	3:58:56 (8,947)	
Jones, Peter C	4:34:22 (17,109)	
Jones, Peter L	4:00:48 (9,372)	
Jones, Philip M	5:24:13 (28,140)	
Jones, Quentin N	3:26:44 (3,229)	
Jones, Ralph W	4:19:38 (13,491)	
Jones, Rhodri L	3:32:05 (4,004)	
Jones, Richard A	3:45:36 (6,113)	
Jones, Richard E	3:34:36 (4,355)	
Jones, Richard G	5:14:46 (26,400)	
Jones, Richard L	2:54:33 (551)	
Jones, Richard L	5:06:38 (24,806)	
Jones, Richard M	3:40:42 (5,302)	
Jones, Richard M	4:05:48 (10,309)	
Jones, Richard P	4:40:54 (18,760)	
Jones, Richard R	5:42:08 (30,839)	
Jones, Robert A	3:31:46 (3,947)	
Jones, Robert A	4:19:55 (13,578)	
Jones, Robert D	5:20:20 (27,482)	
Jones, Robert K	6:11:04 (33,374)	
Jones, Robert P	3:31:55 (3,976)	
Jones, Robin W	5:01:47 (23,886)	
Jones, Roger T	4:41:50 (19,005)	
Jones, Ross M	5:10:00 (25,477)	
Jones, Rowland W	4:34:47 (17,218)	
Jones, Scott	4:37:45 (17,948)	
Jones, Scott K	5:33:57 (29,754)	
Jones, Sean L	5:20:09 (27,447)	
Jones, Sean W	5:01:18 (23,794)	
Jones, Simon	3:17:19 (2,205)	
Jones, Simon A	4:20:42 (13,775)	
Jones, Simon B	5:08:24 (25,174)	
Jones, Simon N	4:38:55 (18,258)	
Jones, Simon P	5:50:37 (31,735)	
Jones, Steffan	4:09:36 (11,095)	
Jones, Stephen	3:23:05 (2,804)	
Jones, Stephen	4:21:02 (13,860)	
Jones, Stephen A	4:43:15 (19,355)	
Jones, Stephen C	5:12:37 (25,970)	
Jones, Stephen P	3:53:18 (7,641)	
Jones, Steve	4:32:07 (16,584)	
Jones, Steven I	2:48:43 (335)	
Jones, Stuart D	3:48:34 (6,640)	
Jones, Tegryn D	5:14:55 (26,432)	
Jones, Terry M	4:19:42 (13,510)	
Jones, Thomas H	5:27:11 (28,658)	
Jones, Tim	3:12:08 (1,744)	
Jones, Tim I	3:17:36 (2,239)	
Jones, Tim J	5:03:12 (24,173)	
Jones, Timothy A	4:29:45 (16,075)	
Jones, Toby W	5:11:02 (25,675)	
Jones, Vincent M	5:07:12 (24,929)	
Jones, William K	3:53:50 (7,752)	
Jones, William M	4:47:16 (20,347)	
Jones, William R	4:11:04 (11,390)	
Jones-Davies, Aled L	4:26:47 (15,260)	
Jooste, Conrad G	4:02:30 (9,699)	
Jopling, Edward H	3:15:33 (2,032)	
Jordan, Andrew P	4:21:23 (13,933)	
Jordan, Anthony M	3:20:01 (2,500)	
Jordan, Christopher R	2:47:57 (307)	
Jordan, Jason L	6:37:29 (34,591)	
Jordan, John P	5:25:54 (28,443)	
Jordan, Jonathan	4:13:00 (11,827)	
Jordan, Justin L	4:52:15 (21,556)	
Jordan, Mark	4:19:20 (13,412)	
Jordan, Mark A	3:49:06 (6,751)	
Jordan, Mark D	4:28:23 (15,695)	
Jordan, Mark R	5:06:21 (24,760)	
Jordan, Nicholas P	4:44:39 (19,727)	
Jordan, Nick H	3:22:07 (2,716)	
Jordan, Nigel R	7:14:58 (35,346)	
Jordan, Percy A	6:18:28 (33,805)	
Jordan, Simon K	3:59:20 (9,050)	
Jordan, Tom N	5:06:49 (24,844)	
Jordan, Vincent	4:57:12 (22,821)	
Jordorson, David J	4:32:07 (16,584)	

Joseph, Adam J	5:13:52 (26,206)	
Joseph, Antone	3:34:41 (4,364)	
Joseph, Bernard	3:04:21 (1,123)	
Joseph, Gareth L	5:10:13 (25,528)	
Joseph, Patrick M	3:58:06 (8,743)	
Joseph, Sony	4:53:57 (22,006)	
Joseph, Vincent D	4:33:59 (17,030)	
Josephidou, Marios	4:40:28 (18,644)	
Josephs, Merrick	4:30:24 (16,234)	
Joslin, Gary	4:21:52 (14,055)	
Joslyn, Tim	5:00:12 (23,551)	
Joss, Norman J	5:23:47 (28,075)	
Josty, Daniel C	5:23:15 (27,970)	
Joughin, Nick	4:38:47 (18,226)	
Joules, Keith	2:53:31 (495)	
Jourdain, Loic	4:17:49 (13,028)	
Jourdain, Mike E	4:04:50 (10,120)	
Jourdam, Antonio M	2:38:55 (124)	
Jowett, Mark I	5:23:23 (27,988)	
Joy, Danny	4:14:00 (12,096)	
Joyce, Alistair W	4:17:27 (12,927)	
Joyce, Dave R	5:46:29 (31,309)	
Joyce, David C	5:23:14 (27,966)	
Joyce, Dominic H	4:23:25 (14,421)	
Joyce, Gareth J	6:01:09 (32,694)	
Joyce, Ian P	4:48:58 (20,757)	
Joyce, Michael A	6:16:13 (33,698)	
Joyce, Phil	3:13:06 (1,827)	
Joyner, Lewis M	3:58:02 (8,734)	
Joynes, David	3:26:13 (3,159)	
Joynson, David	3:49:50 (6,904)	
Joynson, Mark	3:06:49 (1,301)	
Joynson, Richard A	5:55:51 (32,224)	
Joynson, Robert	4:53:45 (21,951)	
Jrewinnard, Mark P	5:20:34 (27,534)	
Judd, Darren P	3:43:54 (5,850)	
Jude, Tim S	4:41:15 (18,851)	
Judge, Ciaran C	6:07:20 (33,121)	
Judge, James C	5:21:46 (27,748)	
Judge, Oliver	5:21:12 (27,633)	
Juett, Michael E	6:39:20 (34,652)	
Jugg, Andy L	5:38:16 (30,350)	
Jugg, Trevor D	5:38:16 (30,350)	
Jukes, Chris J	4:14:15 (12,152)	
Jukes, Daman	3:45:45 (6,139)	
Julien, Kelvin S	5:21:18 (27,657)	
Julyan, Martin K	5:14:58 (26,444)	
Junerby, Goran	3:47:47 (6,495)	
Jung, Michael	4:17:01 (12,819)	
Juniper, Gavin S	4:56:08 (22,543)	
Juravich, Nicholas A	2:53:15 (481)	
Juson, Phillip E	6:15:49 (33,672)	
Justice, Sean	4:54:23 (22,117)	
Juszczak, Wlodzimierz	3:09:18 (1,502)	
Kabbaj, Mohamed	3:46:35 (6,267)	
Kabbaj, Samir	4:07:49 (10,730)	
Kaczmarczyk, Wacek	5:44:33 (31,099)	
Kading, Jan P	3:59:52 (9,173)	
Kadir, Wan A	5:01:43 (23,871)	
Kadiwar, Kantilal M	7:16:31 (35,358)	
Kadobinskyj, Peter	3:36:21 (4,594)	
Kaempfer, Matthias	6:10:14 (33,323)	
Kaess, Herman	3:54:06 (7,820)	
Kahn, Sebastien	3:00:23 (922)	
Kahrs, Gerd-Diedrich	4:15:28 (12,435)	
Kainth, Ranjiet	3:09:32 (1,519)	
Kaiser, Nicholas	2:58:08 (757)	
Kaisser, Michael	3:34:48 (4,283)	
Kalavannan, Kanthamourthy	6:15:30 (33,651)	
Kalek, Dean M	5:14:42 (26,381)	
Kamalanathan, Selladurai	5:53:03 (31,968)	
Kamallakharan, Bala M	4:08:10 (10,799)	
Kamatani, Toru	4:20:44 (13,780)	
Kan, Alan K	5:45:55 (31,246)	
Kan, Peter	3:50:12 (6,974)	
Kane, John	5:07:04 (24,902)	
Kane, John P	3:26:38 (3,212)	
Kane, Jonathan J	3:34:30 (4,340)	
Kane, Keith	3:51:36 (7,277)	
Kane, Kevan R	4:13:21 (11,921)	
Kanga, Dominic R	3:36:06 (4,557)	
Kanga, Russ H	5:13:40 (26,157)	
Kanji, Mohamed	4:54:06 (22,041)	

Kankelborg, Henrik J	3:57:15 (8,542)	
Kanolik, Paul T	4:07:53 (10,742)	
Kansagra, Deepak M	4:57:01 (22,779)	
Kantarjian, Berj A	5:07:03 (24,896)	
Kanyua, John G	4:29:13 (15,915)	
Kaou, Samir N	5:55:23 (32,182)	
Kapoor, Kieran S	3:48:58 (6,723)	
Kapoor, Neil	2:45:56 (259)	
Kapsalis, Stavros A	4:31:05 (16,374)	
Kapur, Ashish	5:26:13 (28,495)	
Kara, Altaf	5:09:26 (25,362)	
Karall, Andreas	2:41:56 (179)	
Karavis, Graeme L	3:34:22 (4,326)	
Karby, Michael T	4:26:44 (15,245)	
Karim, Abdul	4:45:10 (19,876)	
Karim, Kesser A	5:45:45 (31,234)	
Karlsson, Johann	3:19:10 (2,411)	
Karp, Phil	4:32:06 (16,581)	
Karthikeyan, Sanju	5:20:33 (27,531)	
Kasmir, Daniel	5:43:24 (30,984)	
Kat, Gregory	3:52:28 (7,462)	
Katasi, Steve	4:26:31 (15,197)	
Kato, Hiroshi	5:49:24 (31,620)	
Katz, Jeremy	4:26:45 (15,249)	
Kavanagh, Rod	5:07:26 (24,984)	
Kavanagh, Ronan	4:51:57 (21,474)	
Kavanagh, Terence W	7:05:36 (35,210)	
Kawczynski, Daniel	5:45:28 (31,203)	
Kay, Benjamin J	3:37:35 (4,764)	
Kay, Danny	4:08:16 (10,829)	
Kay, Martin J	3:47:19 (6,394)	
Kay, Matthew S	2:53:08 (475)	
Kay, Neil J	4:18:41 (13,259)	
Kay, Peter	3:57:12 (8,528)	
Kay, Richard M	4:38:23 (18,122)	
Kay, Thomas W	5:40:55 (30,698)	
Kaye, Ian	5:27:56 (28,784)	
Kaygorodtsev, Georgy	3:49:15 (6,790)	
Kayley, Chris P	4:52:01 (21,489)	
Kayman, Simon J	4:51:52 (21,459)	
Kazalbash, Imran M	4:43:49 (19,482)	
Kazalbash, Kamran M	5:34:17 (29,811)	
Kazimierski, Michael	2:54:07 (523)	
Keal, Robert J	2:34:39 (71)	
Keane, David	5:25:12 (28,302)	
Keane, Denis	4:14:59 (12,318)	
Keane, Jim	3:45:41 (6,132)	
Keane, Patrick C	3:47:15 (6,387)	
Keane, Patrick F	4:37:45 (17,948)	
Keane, Peter T	4:11:16 (11,444)	
Keane, Vincent	4:29:29 (15,998)	
Kearney, Edward M	4:03:34 (9,880)	
Kearney, Peter J	3:30:13 (3,750)	
Kearney, Robert	3:58:37 (8,857)	
Kearns, Adrian	3:02:51 (1,042)	
Kearns, Julian	4:30:03 (16,159)	
Keary, Duncan R	5:35:13 (29,944)	
Keasey, Damion	4:26:45 (15,249)	
Keast, Jon R	2:45:15 (245)	
Keast, Timothy P	3:24:05 (2,918)	
Keast, Wayne B	4:21:07 (13,878)	
Keating, Daniel	3:26:19 (3,177)	
Keating, Joseph	5:59:42 (32,557)	
Keating, Michael J	3:47:22 (6,401)	
Keay, Stephen	5:24:39 (28,207)	
Keayes, Donald N	4:46:01 (20,062)	
Kee, Philip	6:14:42 (33,590)	
Keeble, Adrian D	4:51:32 (21,376)	
Keeble, Ian R	2:48:12 (320)	
Keeble, James	4:35:44 (17,470)	
Keeble, John R	4:49:32 (20,897)	
Keegan, David J	4:23:19 (14,402)	
Keegan, Joseph	7:19:58 (35,387)	
Keegan, Luke	4:03:52 (9,939)	
Keegan, Mark	5:18:11 (27,098)	
Keegan, Martin E	3:50:56 (7,123)	
Keel, Anthony	5:13:46 (26,183)	
Keelan, Peter	5:35:22 (29,962)	
Keeley, Anthony J	3:48:35 (6,642)	
Keeling, Geoff	4:50:22 (21,087)	
Keem, Nicholas I	4:43:18 (19,372)	
Keen, Andrew	4:51:11 (21,281)	
Keen, Graham A	4:06:15 (10,405)	

Keen, Howard S 4:38:30 (18,153)
Keen, James T 3:55:09 (8,044)
Keen, Richard A 3:56:20 (8,314)
Keen, Stuart J 4:06:06 (10,370)
Keenaghan, Shaun N 3:51:11 (7,182)
Keenan, Brian 4:14:52 (12,284)
Keenan, Dean J 4:41:31 (18,927)
Keenan, Ian 4:10:21 (11,236)
Keenan, John W 5:55:31 (32,194)
Keenan, Noel F 3:35:52 (4,533)
Keenan, Timothy J 5:39:31 (30,533)
Keene, Dominic P 5:31:21 (29,351)
Keenleyside, Piers B 3:53:08 (7,602)
Keeshan, Matthew 3:43:21 (5,746)
Keet, Wayne L 4:03:40 (9,896)
Kehoe, Noel 5:05:27 (24,588)
Kehoe, Robert 4:39:41 (18,462)
Keill, Robert J 5:48:54 (31,572)
Keilloh, Richard J 5:47:40 (31,426)
Keilty, Russell 3:17:35 (2,237)
Keitch, Arthur 6:21:53 (33,991)
Keith, Bruce R 5:00:31 (23,617)
Keldi, Said 4:37:37 (17,914)
Kelf, Jason R 3:35:32 (4,490)
Kelf, Jon 3:44:21 (5,920)
Kelf, Paul D 5:34:25 (29,833)
Kell, Richard J 3:49:57 (6,927)
Kell, Stephen M 3:59:22 (9,061)
Kelleher, Peter 3:16:22 (2,112)
Kelleher, Stephen J 3:27:27 (3,350)
Keller, Mathew J 2:59:29 (861)
Keller, Nicholas F 3:46:14 (6,213)
Kellett, Gary K 3:29:45 (3,679)
Kelley, Christopher M 4:53:13 (21,818)
Kelley, David C 4:30:46 (16,308)
Kelley, Dean R 4:29:21 (15,956)
Kellie, David L 3:55:20 (8,088)
Kelliher, Paul J 3:44:51 (5,999)
Kelliher, Simon W 3:43:26 (5,761)
Kellner, Thomas C 2:54:39 (555)
Kelly, Andrew M 4:24:06 (14,598)
Kelly, Andrew P 4:07:51 (10,737)
Kelly, Ben L 7:08:44 (35,257)
Kelly, Christopher J 3:41:26 (5,434)
Kelly, Christopher T 3:07:33 (1,352)
Kelly, Conall F 4:10:23 (11,244)
Kelly, David 3:56:46 (8,423)
Kelly, David A 3:40:52 (5,337)
Kelly, Dean L 5:06:23 (24,764)
Kelly, Dominic J 2:56:35 (644)
Kelly, Gavin R 3:54:45 (7,953)
Kelly, Glenn S 5:51:07 (31,788)
Kelly, Hamish S 3:49:25 (6,815)
Kelly, Jack A 5:00:37 (23,639)
Kelly, James 3:59:52 (9,173)
Kelly, James 4:13:31 (11,969)
Kelly, James D 3:45:41 (6,132)
Kelly, James W 5:12:52 (26,014)
Kelly, John G 5:20:28 (27,508)
Kelly, John T 4:53:43 (21,948)
Kelly, Julian T 3:27:10 (3,305)
Kelly, Liam P 4:57:01 (22,779)
Kelly, Liam T 4:44:30 (19,681)
Kelly, Marcus 5:29:40 (29,093)
Kelly, Martin A 5:02:19 (23,993)
Kelly, Michael 3:24:40 (2,980)
Kelly, Michael 5:53:38 (32,024)
Kelly, Myles 4:23:01 (14,337)
Kelly, Neill J 4:25:18 (14,894)
Kelly, Noel G 5:02:18 (23,988)
Kelly, Paul C 3:34:49 (4,381)
Kelly, Paul D 5:45:48 (31,239)
Kelly, Paul J 4:07:37 (10,684)
Kelly, Peter 4:21:49 (14,036)
Kelly, Peter J 3:53:13 (7,626)
Kelly, Philip J 4:31:34 (16,475)
Kelly, Philip J 4:52:36 (21,642)
Kelly, Robert H 5:23:02 (27,941)
Kelly, Sean E 5:47:17 (31,381)
Kelly, Simon M 3:43:30 (5,779)
Kelly, Stephen J 3:31:10 (3,858)
Kelly, Stephen P 5:01:09 (23,761)
Kelly, Steve C 3:26:44 (3,229)
Kelly, Tim C 3:40:30 (5,266)
Kelly, Tom G 5:28:37 (28,923)
Kelly, Tony B 5:10:09 (25,517)
Kelman, Bob M 6:30:35 (34,345)
Kelsey, Bruce S 5:53:04 (31,969)
Kelsey, Chris P 4:48:48 (20,722)
Kelsey, David W 4:18:26 (13,190)
Kelsey, Howard W 4:10:45 (11,318)
Kelsey, Stephen B 5:06:14 (24,749)
Kelso, William 3:47:22 (6,401)
Kelson, Rod 3:20:39 (2,572)
Kelvey-Brown, Jonathan L 3:38:56 (5,002)
Kelway, Gary P 4:33:24 (16,892)
Kember, Julian J 4:37:26 (17,874)
Kemble-Diaz, William 5:18:52 (27,226)
Kemp, Albert L 3:36:17 (4,585)
Kemp, Andrew W 5:37:14 (30,203)
Kemp, Benjamin J 2:53:36 (501)
Kemp, Christopher A 4:06:11 (10,390)
Kemp, Christopher J 4:32:53 (16,762)
Kemp, James A 5:57:53 (32,402)
Kemp, Jon M 3:06:35 (1,278)
Kemp, Jonathan 5:57:26 (32,365)
Kemp, Stephen J 4:13:08 (11,865)
Kemp, Stephen W 3:44:15 (5,896)
Kempson, Bill 5:16:04 (26,674)
Kempton, Richard M 5:03:06 (24,146)
Kench, Dan S 3:51:24 (7,225)
Kenchington, Chris J 3:11:37 (1,686)
Kendall, Leon A 4:20:38 (13,764)
Kendall, Matthew S 3:50:03 (6,955)
Kendall, Michael 4:13:17 (11,905)
Kendall, Michael S 4:48:06 (20,552)
Kendall, Philip 4:03:14 (9,824)
Kendall, Rowland W 4:06:33 (10,476)
Kendle, Richard J 5:36:04 (30,057)
Kendon, Michael C 4:07:15 (10,613)
Kendrew, Michael P 4:06:23 (10,435)
Kendrick, Alastair 5:26:56 (28,614)
Kendrick, Christopher A 5:10:23 (25,552)
Kendrick, Ian R 5:58:06 (32,420)
Kendrick, Philip 2:54:16 (530)
Kendrick, Shane C 5:43:00 (30,934)
Kenealy, Andrew 6:06:38 (33,086)
Kenley, Jeremy 5:44:05 (31,052)
Kennair, Jonathan M 5:12:08 (25,879)
Kennard, David 4:01:11 (9,457)
Kennedy, Andrew 6:10:51 (33,355)
Kennedy, Andrew J 4:58:38 (23,176)
Kennedy, Andrew M 5:34:29 (29,845)
Kennedy, Anthony R 3:41:21 (5,418)
Kennedy, Daniel T 6:07:08 (33,114)
Kennedy, Ian D 4:55:56 (22,499)
Kennedy, James P 5:25:26 (28,351)
Kennedy, Les 3:41:17 (5,408)
Kennedy, Mark A 4:45:23 (19,922)
Kennedy, Neil 3:37:26 (4,741)
Kennedy, Patrick J 6:00:55 (32,659)
Kennedy, Paul J 4:49:22 (20,853)
Kennedy, Paul J 6:08:17 (33,193)
Kennedy, Peter A 3:46:16 (6,214)
Kennedy, Peter D 3:52:44 (7,511)
Kennedy, Scott H 2:54:19 (533)
Kennelly, Edmond T 4:56:01 (22,519)
Kennelly, Mike V 5:33:16 (29,640)
Kennerdale, Casdar 4:04:16 (10,017)
Kennerknecht, Guenter 5:41:57 (30,825)
Kennett, Steffan A 2:43:29 (207)
Kenny, Anthony G 5:33:30 (29,682)
Kenny, Barry A 5:24:15 (28,148)
Kenny, Ed M 3:42:49 (5,650)
Kenny, Jack 3:58:45 (8,897)
Kenny, Richard E 4:43:49 (19,482)
Kenny, Sasha 4:08:35 (10,888)
Kensett, Mark P 4:38:51 (18,244)
Kensett, Martin J 4:04:45 (10,103)
Kensington, Nick D 3:06:58 (1,306)
Kent, Christopher J 3:59:13 (9,017)
Kent, David T 4:14:26 (12,194)
Kent, Justin G 4:37:43 (17,942)
Kent, Matthew 4:58:04 (23,050)
Kent, Mike 4:15:22 (12,411)
Kent, Nicolas L 4:34:12 (17,076)
Kent, Nigel D 4:09:26 (11,057)
Kenway, Michael 4:33:11 (16,838)
Kenworthy, Paul 3:30:00 (3,719)
Kenwright, Mike J 4:39:49 (18,490)
Kenyon, Craig 4:52:04 (21,503)
Kenyon, Craig P 4:08:14 (10,821)
Kenyon, Stephen 3:14:53 (1,978)
Kenyon, Thomas 6:15:45 (33,667)
Kenyon-Muir, Nick 2:54:22 (537)
Keogh, Craig 6:31:26 (34,379)
Keogh, Denis 5:06:50 (24,850)
Keogh, Paul E 6:08:28 (33,201)
Keown, Gary J 3:31:30 (3,911)
Keown, Will E 3:42:12 (5,554)
Kerai, Sanjay 4:56:31 (22,635)
Kerfoot, Mark J 4:50:51 (21,204)
Kerley, Andrew 5:11:51 (25,824)
Kern, Marcus 3:57:18 (8,556)
Kernn, Uwe 3:10:10 (1,578)
Kerper, Warren 3:51:46 (7,311)
Kerr, Christopher C 6:28:18 (34,256)
Kerr, Christopher J 4:33:07 (16,816)
Kerr, Darren 5:43:25 (30,985)
Kerr, Duncan A 3:36:36 (4,628)
Kerr, Duncan A 4:05:52 (10,322)
Kerr, Edward 5:07:43 (25,038)
Kerr, James 3:53:20 (7,655)
Kerr, James C 4:55:43 (22,433)
Kerr, Jason 5:43:25 (30,985)
Kerr, John 4:04:42 (10,090)
Kerr, Martin 6:12:38 (33,465)
Kerr, Nicholas S 4:55:14 (22,325)
Kerr, Paul S 3:18:34 (2,348)
Kerr, Richard M 5:10:55 (25,648)
Kerridge, Peter 5:02:15 (23,980)
Kerrigan, Charles P 3:29:54 (3,704)
Kerrigan, Mike 6:01:00 (32,671)
Kerry, Patrick J 4:58:20 (23,115)
Kersey, Gary P 4:56:08 (22,543)
Kersh, Jonathan C 5:39:45 (30,565)
Kershaw, Christopher D 4:02:12 (9,646)
Kershaw, Craig 4:04:45 (10,103)
Kershaw, David A 3:33:56 (4,258)
Kershaw, Nicholas J 3:57:29 (8,597)
Kershaw, Richard D 4:19:06 (13,355)
Kerslake, Geoffrey R 4:59:24 (23,352)
Kerton, Christopher 5:32:27 (29,516)
Kerwick, Anthony 4:58:01 (23,039)
Kesby, Phillips D 5:46:27 (31,306)
Keshwala, Jay 5:03:35 (24,251)
Keskitalo, Juha M 3:07:20 (1,337)
Keskitalo, Mikko 3:17:33 (2,233)
Kesley, Russell D 5:06:44 (24,826)
Kessler, Peter 5:00:08 (23,532)
Kester, John E 4:13:53 (12,062)
Kesterton, Steven A 5:03:39 (24,266)
Kestle, Michael J 3:10:35 (1,600)
Kesy, Jean-Pierre 3:25:31 (3,067)
Ketley, Peter 3:54:37 (7,925)
Ketley, Thomas 4:48:11 (20,573)
Kettle, James R 5:21:08 (27,621)
Kettlewell, Andrew M 5:45:59 (31,256)
Kettle-Williams, Adam 3:38:47 (4,971)
Keveren, Dean 6:29:58 (34,323)
Kevill, Russell J 4:02:29 (9,694)
Kewell, Gareth J 5:23:37 (28,033)
Key, Raymond J 4:24:58 (14,817)
Keyne, Jonathan 6:05:40 (33,021)
Keys, Nicholas 2:42:12 (182)
Keys, Stephen G 3:26:44 (3,229)
Keywood, Paul A 3:40:19 (5,236)
Keywood, Stephen J 2:55:08 (582)
Keyworth, Antony J 3:53:51 (7,753)
Khadga, Kabindra 6:40:14 (34,673)
Khan, Amanullah 5:14:15 (26,283)

Khan, Anjum B....4:27:11 (15,381)
Khan, Imran M....5:48:58 (31,580)
Khan, Kash....5:28:56 (28,974)
Khan, Mark A....5:51:25 (31,816)
Khan, Maruf....7:12:07 (35,305)
Khan, Shakeel I....6:30:02 (34,327)
Khan, Sherali J....4:31:00 (16,354)
Khan, Tariq S....4:51:03 (21,255)
Khan, Waheed....3:27:19 (3,328)
Khan, Wasim....5:40:16 (30,622)
Khandelwal, Ajay K....5:55:33 (32,196)
Khenniche, Madjid....5:39:22 (30,502)
Khimasia, Mehul M....5:39:38 (30,549)
Khinda, Nav S....4:28:53 (15,828)
Khodabukus, Andrew F....6:28:36 (34,269)
Khoo, Boo-Hock....4:08:36 (10,893)
Khoo, Jonathan....5:38:25 (30,374)
Kibblewhite, Michael....4:49:58 (20,986)
Kibby, Paul M....3:58:28 (8,832)
Kidd, Andrew J....4:54:44 (22,207)
Kidd, James B....4:38:04 (18,028)
Kidd, Mattehw S....4:44:48 (19,780)
Kidd, Michael J....3:17:42 (2,253)
Kidney, Roger A....4:56:37 (22,665)
Kielty, Michael....5:50:13 (31,696)
Kiely, Jason....5:09:40 (25,407)
Kiersey, Raymond R....5:51:37 (31,839)
Kiko, Al....5:53:31 (32,012)
Kilbourn, Sean R....4:47:01 (20,286)
Kilby, Andrew N....4:32:23 (16,642)
Kilby, Robert E....3:58:54 (8,941)
Kilgallon, Paul....4:55:14 (22,325)
Kilgannon, Martin J....4:03:42 (9,902)
Kilgarriff, Patrick H....4:18:41 (13,259)
Kilkenny, Kevin J....3:53:20 (7,655)
Kilkenny, Mark J....5:00:37 (23,639)
Killeen, Patrick J....4:01:22 (9,492)
Killick, John C....5:43:37 (31,003)
Kilminster, Kevin J....5:29:44 (29,100)
Kilshaw, Brad D....4:16:43 (12,741)
Kim, Alan N....5:25:55 (28,446)
Kim, Tae Wan....3:49:35 (6,848)
Kim, Walter S....4:11:10 (11,417)
Kimber, John R....3:01:59 (1,002)
Kimber, Nicholas....3:52:39 (7,489)
Kimberley, Lee J....5:06:23 (24,764)
Kimble, Mark P....5:25:58 (28,451)
Kimmins, Simon B....5:23:32 (28,018)
Kina, Antonio M....5:22:30 (27,854)
Kinahan, Kieran M....4:16:51 (12,772)
Kinane, Joseph....4:04:46 (10,106)
Kinch, Markus B....4:01:01 (9,423)
Kinchen, John E....4:06:15 (10,405)
Kind, David J....3:28:58 (3,569)
King, Adam....4:11:40 (11,542)
King, Alan....3:48:57 (6,717)
King, Andrew J....4:41:22 (18,879)
King, Andy....4:55:27 (22,377)
King, Anthony W....4:48:18 (20,605)
King, Christopher C....4:47:06 (20,313)
King, Damian M....5:38:52 (30,436)
King, Daniel W....5:36:24 (30,097)
King, Dave....3:29:24 (3,635)
King, David A....3:57:45 (8,665)
King, David G....5:17:30 (26,958)
King, David J....4:25:30 (14,945)
King, David M....3:18:22 (2,331)
King, David P....4:28:53 (15,828)
King, Edward J....4:12:08 (11,639)
King, Edward S....3:26:13 (3,159)
King, Gary....4:16:28 (12,692)
King, Gary R....4:03:01 (9,789)
King, Graham R....3:55:11 (8,053)
King, Gregory B....4:05:09 (10,175)
King, James S....5:04:16 (24,370)
King, James T....3:15:59 (2,078)
King, Jason J....5:22:34 (27,870)
King, Jeff....5:45:07 (31,169)
King, Jeremy....4:27:24 (15,448)
King, Jonathan D....4:40:39 (18,687)
King, Jonathan J....5:07:22 (24,970)
King, Justin P....4:38:51 (18,244)
King, Larry G....4:22:28 (14,190)
King, Leslie J....5:22:20 (27,825)
King, Llewellyn J....3:55:38 (8,146)
King, Malcolm J....5:34:24 (29,827)
King, Martin S....3:31:44 (3,944)
King, Martin S....5:02:16 (23,982)
King, Mathew....4:00:12 (9,250)
King, Mathew....4:43:51 (19,497)
King, Matthew G....3:51:02 (7,144)
King, Michael....6:49:06 (34,914)
King, Michael E....4:51:45 (21,429)
King, Neil D....3:37:57 (4,819)
King, Nicholas J....4:06:08 (10,380)
King, Nicholas J....4:18:05 (13,091)
King, Norman P....5:43:06 (30,947)
King, Peter....4:00:51 (9,386)
King, Peter S....4:38:01 (18,015)
King, Philip....4:45:54 (20,033)
King, Philip....7:00:22 (35,133)
King, Richard....4:27:10 (15,375)
King, Richard....5:17:26 (26,944)
King, Richard A....5:32:54 (29,589)
King, Robert S....4:42:23 (19,146)
King, Robin J....4:22:20 (14,162)
King, Scott O....4:42:15 (19,110)
King, Simon....4:30:55 (16,339)
King, Simon D....4:30:00 (16,148)
King, Stephen P....4:30:30 (16,257)
King, Stephen R....3:30:09 (3,742)
King, Steven A....3:11:46 (1,699)
King, Steven J....5:04:39 (24,438)
King, Thomas....4:18:07 (13,103)
King, Timothy A....5:30:35 (29,232)
King, Tommy....4:38:35 (18,170)
Kingaby, Joseph....4:37:14 (17,826)
Kingham, Leslie W....5:07:28 (24,991)
Kingsford, Rob S....4:06:17 (10,414)
Kingston, Andrew M....5:50:36 (31,732)
Kingston, Anthony P....4:05:07 (10,165)
Kingston, Samuel....3:45:37 (6,120)
Kingston, Stephen R....5:14:47 (26,403)
Kingston-Lee, Matthew F....2:59:45 (882)
Kingwill, William....3:51:14 (7,194)
Kinloch, Charles....5:01:32 (23,835)
Kinnaird, Alan J....5:32:19 (29,498)
Kinoshita, Naoya....6:10:52 (33,358)
Kinross, James M....4:25:31 (14,949)
Kinsella, Nigel P....5:25:13 (28,308)
Kinsella, Sean P....4:37:11 (17,820)
Kinsey, Nicholas J....2:43:40 (208)
Kinsey, Peter....4:16:38 (12,723)
Kinsey, Richard J....5:23:34 (28,024)
Kinsiona, Ives S....3:56:24 (8,334)
Kinson, Simon P....3:08:08 (1,400)
Kioufi, Niazy....5:59:08 (32,518)
Kipisz, Steven M....4:07:31 (10,655)
Kirby, Alan D....4:35:24 (17,382)
Kirby, Andrew J....3:07:37 (1,354)
Kirby, Graham L....3:26:59 (3,278)
Kirby, Gregory J....4:43:24 (19,400)
Kirby, Guy M....4:28:27 (15,715)
Kirby, James M....5:40:33 (30,658)
Kirby, Mark R....3:16:52 (2,165)
Kirby, Michael A....3:51:40 (7,288)
Kirby, Neil A....4:31:01 (16,357)
Kirby, Neil R....5:23:30 (28,010)
Kirby, Nick J....3:56:02 (8,231)
Kirby, Shane....4:43:19 (19,383)
Kirchner, Harald....5:37:57 (30,295)
Kirk, Elliott....3:56:09 (8,265)
Kirk, Lindsay R....5:53:13 (31,979)
Kirk, Michael J....5:56:17 (32,264)
Kirk, Nick....4:44:30 (19,681)
Kirk, Peter D....4:18:30 (13,211)
Kirk, Stephan....5:57:16 (32,350)
Kirkby, Darron M....5:44:04 (31,049)
Kirkby, Leonard....4:41:33 (18,939)
Kirkby, Simon....3:53:12 (7,618)
Kirkdale, Brian G....3:38:39 (4,949)
Kirkham, Adie....4:55:33 (22,404)
Kirkham, Adrian J....4:53:03 (21,762)
Kirkham, Allan D....4:49:26 (20,867)
Kirkham, Gareth....5:47:03 (31,359)
Kirkham, John G....4:16:53 (12,778)
Kirkham, Liam D....4:31:09 (16,396)
Kirkham, Richard....4:05:37 (10,268)
Kirkhope, Peter J....4:24:50 (14,793)
Kirkland, James W....5:25:17 (28,318)
Kirkman, Oliver D....4:47:04 (20,305)
Kirkpatrick, Mark A....5:04:13 (24,359)
Kirk-Wilson, Ed J....3:04:46 (1,146)
Kirkwood, Felix....6:28:30 (34,267)
Kirman, Ben J....4:30:41 (16,292)
Kirrage-De-Hond, Michael A....7:48:50 (35,614)
Kirschner, Andrew....3:54:05 (7,812)
Kirston, Paul M....4:36:11 (17,576)
Kirtley, Paul....4:12:09 (11,644)
Kirton, Douglas L....4:41:05 (18,807)
Kirton, Rowan A....3:53:17 (7,638)
Kirton, Simon R....3:48:43 (6,672)
Kisbee, Murray P....3:32:25 (4,056)
Kitchen, Jay....4:16:27 (12,688)
Kitchen, Jonathan J....5:20:47 (27,572)
Kitchen, Michael C....4:24:30 (14,704)
Kitchen, Neil D....3:59:30 (9,094)
Kitchener, William M....4:40:32 (18,662)
Kitchenham, Ian....5:27:09 (28,646)
Kitcher, David....2:57:15 (694)
Kitching, Darren....4:17:26 (12,921)
Kitching, Ian D....2:55:13 (585)
Kitching, Kevin R....5:28:02 (28,805)
Kitching, Peter A....5:28:02 (28,805)
Kitromilides, Alex S....3:38:35 (4,937)
Kitson, Terry C....5:43:23 (30,982)
Kitt, Matthew....5:50:11 (31,691)
Kittler, Robert L....5:56:31 (32,290)
Kitts, Andrew D....4:26:04 (15,069)
Kitts, Stephen....4:24:05 (14,593)
Klaassen, Jan....4:54:10 (22,069)
Klaiber, Mark....4:17:19 (12,880)
Klammert, Rainer....3:30:00 (3,719)
Klass, Benjamin R....5:04:47 (24,464)
Klatt, Andreas....5:23:28 (28,004)
Kleiboer, Lambertus A....3:57:54 (8,698)
Kleinman, Martin P....6:09:26 (33,264)
Klenerman, Paul....4:45:51 (20,020)
Klesser, Dean....5:02:55 (24,111)
Klietsch, Detlef....4:43:36 (19,440)
Klimach, Otto E....4:06:53 (10,547)
Klingenschmid, Robert J....3:55:56 (8,214)
Kloet, Gareth J....4:16:27 (12,688)
Knapman, Derek E....5:10:15 (25,534)
Knapman, Phillip....4:21:16 (13,905)
Knapp, Kevin J....4:41:08 (18,823)
Knapp, Nigel J....6:36:32 (34,559)
Knappett, Michael....3:16:59 (2,177)
Kneale, Barry J....4:27:18 (15,425)
Kneebone, Craig....3:50:47 (7,094)
Kneeshaw, Paul....4:19:34 (13,471)
Kneller, Stephen T....4:24:44 (14,756)
Knibbs, Alan A....4:30:03 (16,159)
Knight, Adrian....3:43:25 (5,756)
Knight, Andy J....5:34:29 (29,845)
Knight, Antony J....4:13:13 (11,883)
Knight, Ashley P....4:53:54 (21,991)
Knight, Ben C....3:57:09 (8,511)
Knight, Bruce....4:57:58 (23,025)
Knight, Casey....6:27:47 (34,245)
Knight, Colin....3:56:49 (8,435)
Knight, David....4:33:45 (16,978)
Knight, David A....2:40:46 (153)
Knight, David L....3:57:22 (8,570)
Knight, David M....3:18:11 (2,309)
Knight, David P....4:38:59 (18,280)
Knight, Geoffrey P....2:39:18 (129)
Knight, James....6:20:46 (33,937)
Knight, James A....3:57:28 (8,594)
Knight, Kevin L....5:20:46 (27,567)
Knight, Lindsay C....4:46:34 (20,191)
Knight, Malcolm J....3:48:30 (6,619)
Knight, Mark C....4:33:57 (17,024)
Knight, Martin K....5:00:00 (23,503)
Knight, Matthew W....5:13:04 (26,058)
Knight, Michael J....4:24:06 (14,598)
Knight, Paul A....5:17:23 (26,937)
Knight, Philip....3:54:15 (7,855)
Knight, Richard....8:08:54 (35,655)

Knight, Russell J 4:49:38 (20,923)
Knight, Steven J 4:59:01 (23,259)
Knight, Terry R 5:31:47 (29,415)
Knight, Thomas 4:52:47 (21,689)
Knight, Timothy J 5:44:07 (31,059)
Knight-Markiegi, Adam 4:13:55 (12,073)
Knighton, Adrian 4:30:59 (16,349)
Knighton, Ian 5:42:24 (30,867)
Knights, Jim 5:22:57 (27,931)
Knights, Matthew J 3:34:54 (4,395)
Knights, Thomas J 5:15:17 (26,520)
Knights-Branch, Chris A 4:27:42 (15,519)
Knopik, Stanislaw D 2:55:02 (579)
Knopp, David A 3:38:39 (4,949)
Knopp, Simon A 3:28:13 (3,435)
Knott, David H 4:05:32 (10,245)
Knott, Geoff P 3:44:18 (5,905)
Knott, Jonathan P 3:44:18 (5,905)
Knott, Paul 4:18:32 (13,221)
Knott, Peter J 4:42:50 (19,264)
Knott, Shane 4:27:10 (15,375)
Knowler, Phil J 8:03:04 (35,646)
Knowles, Andrew M 3:42:15 (5,561)
Knowles, Charles H 3:21:51 (2,690)
Knowles, John W 5:17:14 (26,904)
Knowles, Mark D 4:23:09 (14,366)
Knowles, Matthew J 3:44:47 (5,991)
Knowles, Michael P 4:43:11 (19,337)
Knowles, Neil J 5:17:14 (26,904)
Knowles, Patrick I 4:59:23 (23,350)
Knowles, Richard G 4:20:52 (13,822)
Knowles, Roy F 4:52:34 (21,629)
Knox, Douglas J 4:34:19 (17,098)
Knox, Robbie 5:33:08 (29,624)
Knudsen, Sebastian 4:05:04 (10,156)
Koampah, Kris K 5:02:33 (24,051)
Kocen, Peter H 5:04:45 (24,457)
Kohner, Olivier 4:01:01 (9,423)
Kojcinovic, Philip M 5:45:59 (31,256)
Kojodjojo, Pipin 5:03:56 (24,314)
Kolk, Uwe 4:18:43 (13,269)
Kolly, Sven 3:07:13 (1,329)
Kolodzies, Jerzy 9:12:08 (35,695)
Kong, Rick 4:06:24 (10,439)
Konstantinidis, Marios 4:49:28 (20,882)
Koo, Richard W 4:14:52 (12,284)
Koornhof, Hendrik J 4:34:14 (17,085)
Kopp, Michal 4:41:24 (18,889)
Kormornick, Lawrence 4:11:09 (11,413)
Koroscik, Karl K 5:42:12 (30,847)
Korten, Christopher J 4:18:01 (13,080)
Korten, Robert 4:53:47 (21,962)
Kosaka, Yoshiharu 4:53:07 (21,784)
Kothe, Noel 5:01:50 (23,897)
Kotze, Chris 3:27:00 (3,281)
Koulakis, David 5:11:20 (25,730)
Kouvaros, Menicos I 5:50:17 (31,701)
Kovacs, Alexander 3:56:57 (8,466)
Kovacs, James 2:40:37 (150)
Kovats, Steven L 3:00:00 (900)
Kowalski, Andrzej M 3:55:26 (8,112)
Krainock, Peter 4:35:14 (17,343)
Kramer, Robert E 6:07:58 (33,167)
Krasnikov, Gennadi 4:39:31 (18,418)
Kratz, Philip R 5:58:29 (32,467)
Krautzberger, Michael 3:08:00 (1,389)
Krebs, Renaud 4:10:26 (11,253)
Kreett, Michael C 4:42:06 (19,064)
Krijn, Willem A 5:13:48 (26,190)
Kristensen, Peder N 4:20:47 (13,792)
Kristofcar, Alexander 3:30:16 (3,759)
Krivacs, James 5:28:42 (28,933)
Kroencke, Wilhelm 4:31:11 (16,401)
Krosnar, Thomas 3:51:49 (7,318)
Krug, Florian Hl 2:52:45 (468)
Kruise, Dirk 4:19:20 (13,412)
Krumins, John 3:58:22 (8,800)
Kubicki, Jean Luc 4:27:43 (15,524)
Kuczynski, Stuart A 4:14:00 (12,096)
Kudlacik, Richard 4:37:42 (17,937)
Kuen, Ra Hyve 4:35:52 (17,502)
Kugler, Guenther 4:55:55 (22,493)
Kuhl, William H 4:37:40 (17,926)
Kuhn, Ralph P 4:35:34 (17,421)
Kuhnel, Michael J 5:29:16 (29,036)
Kuhrt, Douglas V 5:23:41 (28,048)
Kullar, Hardeep S 3:42:56 (5,675)
Kullar, Paul A 5:39:29 (30,523)
Kumar, Ashok 5:19:01 (27,251)
Kumar, Peter 4:58:01 (23,039)
Kumihashi, Hideaki 5:04:51 (24,487)
Kummer, Martin 5:22:19 (27,822)
Kumra, Sudhir 5:16:19 (26,724)
Kunz, Korbinian 4:07:32 (10,658)
Kurtulus, Ersun N 4:41:56 (19,026)
Kurunathan, Ramesh 5:34:55 (29,904)
Kutner, Christian A 3:36:50 (4,665)
Kuznetsov, Petr 3:29:32 (3,652)
Kvassheim, Einar 4:09:11 (11,002)
Kwakman, Dick 3:21:46 (2,682)
Kydd, David A 5:24:45 (28,230)
Kyle, Peter 4:30:32 (16,261)
Kyle, Tom 4:31:37 (16,490)
Kyriacou, Peter 4:35:40 (17,446)
Kyriacou, Simon N 4:49:04 (20,783)
Kyriakides, Lakis S 5:30:36 (29,235)
Kyritsis, Nick 5:04:49 (24,472)
Kyte, David J 6:44:51 (34,798)
Laab-Garia, Gabriel 3:51:08 (7,168)
Laad, Hiten P 4:09:11 (11,002)
Labatut, Jean-Marc 4:26:59 (15,321)
Labbe, Reny 3:35:41 (4,511)
Labirua-Iturburu, Unai 4:18:28 (13,201)
Labrie, Alexandre 4:04:46 (10,106)
Labrooy, Jason P 4:14:03 (12,112)
Labruzzo, Antonio 4:17:06 (12,830)
Labuschagne, Pieter 4:13:13 (11,883)
Labuschagne, Timothy J 4:00:09 (9,238)
Lacaille, Laurent 3:29:45 (3,679)
Lacaz, Thierry 3:37:23 (4,730)
Lacey, Adam S 5:01:11 (23,768)
Lacey, Alan 5:06:51 (24,854)
Lacey, Ben W 3:50:58 (7,131)
Lacey, Douglas N 4:27:18 (15,425)
Lacey, Drewe W 5:09:11 (25,313)
Lacey, John 5:34:42 (29,874)
Lacey, Kenneth 5:27:13 (28,667)
Lacey, Mark D 2:54:15 (528)
Lacey, Sean P 5:36:27 (30,107)
Lacey, Tom A 4:40:14 (18,585)
Lack, Richard A 3:08:40 (1,442)
Lack, Stuart G 4:09:30 (11,072)
Lacroix, Henri 5:38:17 (30,359)
Lacy, David 4:49:58 (20,986)
Ladanowski, John D 3:39:10 (5,043)
Ladd, Joe 3:56:44 (8,415)
Ladd, Julian A 3:34:22 (4,326)
Laden, Ron 4:55:11 (22,311)
Ladlow, Peter 5:15:17 (26,520)
Lafford, Damon J 4:13:27 (11,947)
Lafleche, Trevor 4:11:41 (11,547)
Lagnado, Max 3:08:13 (1,409)
Lagrou, Yves 3:32:44 (4,098)
Lahimar, Abderrahim 3:15:00 (1,995)
Lahjou, Mustapha 3:00:14 (911)
Lahlou, Abdeljalil 4:26:06 (15,074)
Lai, Eubenh 5:51:15 (31,801)
Lai, Simon 5:02:23 (24,010)
Lai, Simon C 5:20:27 (27,504)
Laidlaw, James C 4:35:12 (17,333)
Laing, Bruce R 4:16:54 (12,785)
Laing, Charlie A 4:43:27 (19,407)
Laing, David J 2:54:31 (547)
Laing, Derrick A 3:24:14 (2,933)
Laing, Robert 3:44:13 (5,892)
Lainsbury, Raymond J 4:16:02 (12,575)
Laird, Allister 4:05:35 (10,262)
Laird, Eoin 5:09:03 (25,285)
Laird, James A 3:39:12 (5,046)
Lake, Carl J 2:57:37 (716)
Lake, Danny 2:56:12 (622)
Lake, John 4:49:25 (20,864)
Lake, Martin A 5:52:52 (31,956)
Lake, Michael W 6:47:15 (34,868)
Lake, Oliver J 3:57:18 (8,556)
Lake, Philip N 4:16:04 (12,585)
Lake, Richard 4:23:23 (14,415)
Lake, Richard J 5:02:58 (24,116)
Lake, Simon S 4:12:40 (11,761)
Lake, Stephen J 4:29:01 (15,861)
Lake, Steve R 4:14:20 (12,173)
Lakeland, Andrew J 3:20:54 (2,597)
Laker, Stephen A 4:13:02 (11,840)
Lakey, Daniel J 4:18:28 (13,201)
Lalande, Christophe 3:50:48 (7,095)
Lalanne, Bertrand 4:06:16 (10,409)
Lally, Kevin W 3:31:46 (3,947)
Lally, Mark 4:28:45 (15,799)
Lamb, Craig R 4:23:15 (14,388)
Lamb, David 4:37:48 (17,955)
Lamb, Ian S 3:10:16 (1,583)
Lamb, Jason F 4:34:51 (17,236)
Lamb, Jeremy 3:40:08 (5,206)
Lamb, Julian K 4:16:18 (12,650)
Lamb, Ken D 3:47:38 (6,460)
Lamb, Michael J 4:01:35 (9,533)
Lamb, Michael L 4:46:05 (20,073)
Lamb, Michael P 4:56:55 (22,753)
Lamb, Richard 3:55:16 (8,070)
Lamb, Shaun C 3:02:41 (1,036)
Lamb, Spencer L 5:17:03 (26,868)
Lamb, Tilden R 5:14:48 (26,409)
Lambden, Murray M 2:58:19 (773)
Lambe, Gareth J 3:34:34 (4,351)
Lamberg, Ben 7:16:05 (35,353)
Lambert, Allan T 6:00:12 (32,595)
Lambert, Christopher I 4:40:20 (18,615)
Lambert, Daniel P 4:03:15 (9,828)
Lambert, David M 5:37:16 (30,210)
Lambert, Guy R 3:05:50 (1,225)
Lambert, Ian D 6:07:43 (33,146)
Lambert, James E 4:21:00 (13,853)
Lambert, Jon P 4:54:17 (22,099)
Lambert, Karl 4:04:54 (10,129)
Lambert, Mark P 4:54:47 (22,223)
Lambert, Matthew J 5:16:44 (26,794)
Lambert, Nigel K 5:13:43 (26,172)
Lambert, Richard C 4:25:31 (14,949)
Lambert, Stephen A 4:53:31 (21,892)
Lambillion-Jameson, Peter W 3:19:40 (2,450)
Lambley, Stephen W 4:57:33 (22,914)
Lambourn, Guy 4:58:38 (23,176)
Lambourne, Ryan P 4:35:55 (17,519)
Lambrick, Geoff J 4:29:56 (16,128)
Lambrou, Antonis 5:16:24 (26,736)
Lambrou, Tony 4:48:55 (20,750)
Lam-Hing, Jean-Marc J 5:09:01 (25,281)
Laming, Andrew 4:30:54 (16,335)
Lamkin, David S 4:35:31 (17,407)
Lamkin, Simon 3:53:18 (7,641)
Lammali, Aziouz 3:31:50 (3,959)
Lammas, Edward 3:29:57 (3,709)
Lammy, Simon P 5:14:02 (26,235)
Lamont, Alistair J 3:46:38 (6,272)
Lamont, Jack O 4:19:14 (13,387)
Lamont, Jason 5:40:37 (30,665)
Lampe, Peter 6:08:12 (33,186)
Lamprecht, Sean A 5:11:48 (25,813)
Lancaster, Christopher P 4:26:22 (15,149)
Lancaster, Matthew D 4:36:56 (17,774)
Lancaster, Philip A 4:20:25 (13,714)
Lance, Ian S 4:32:18 (16,627)
Land, Christopher J 4:29:23 (15,971)
Land, Jack 3:05:34 (1,206)
Landells, Stephen H 5:10:57 (25,656)
Lander, David J 3:28:18 (3,449)
Lander, Noel F 2:54:44 (564)
Lander, William I 5:45:44 (31,231)
Landers, Michael V 5:47:36 (31,414)
Landless, Martin C 4:43:51 (19,497)
Landon, Christopher P 5:09:59 (25,473)
Landon, Guy W 3:01:43 (992)
Landon, Mark 3:45:35 (6,111)
Landon, Neil 4:18:04 (13,088)
Landrock, Graham J 7:16:02 (35,352)
Landymore, Roderick W 4:04:32 (10,062)
Lane, Adrian S 4:01:20 (9,486)
Lane, Andrew F 5:28:50 (28,956)
Lane, Anthony W 3:06:24 (1,263)

Lane, Carl Frederick 3:16:40 (2,141)
Lane, Chris 5:28:02 (28,805)
Lane, David J 2:58:31 (790)
Lane, David J 4:29:43 (16,064)
Lane, Gary R 4:31:33 (16,471)
Lane, John C 4:59:13 (23,314)
Lane, Lewis S 4:38:17 (18,084)
Lane, Luke 4:25:05 (14,842)
Lane, Matt 3:59:48 (9,162)
Lane, Michael 5:00:33 (23,624)
Lane, Michael A 3:48:45 (6,678)
Lane, Michael J 2:46:27 (272)
Lane, Michael P 4:10:21 (11,236)
Lane, Nathaniel R 2:40:21 (146)
Lane, Nicholas D 4:27:05 (15,350)
Lane, Philip E 6:42:40 (34,740)
Lane, Ronald F 3:52:14 (7,416)
Lang, Alfred J 5:51:55 (31,866)
Lang, Ben 2:51:18 (419)
Lang, David M 4:04:09 (9,994)
Lang, Mark S 5:21:13 (27,637)
Langborne, John D 6:08:41 (33,217)
Langdon, Ben 4:03:55 (9,950)
Langdon, Dean M 4:18:51 (13,296)
Langdon, Jeremy 3:41:41 (5,466)
Langdon, Miles D 4:31:56 (16,551)
Langdown, Stephen J 5:04:42 (24,448)
Langdown, Thomas 4:38:54 (18,254)
Lange, Eric W 5:33:55 (29,750)
Langfield, Richard R 4:27:20 (15,431)
Langford, Darren L 5:23:59 (28,105)
Langham, Dale E 4:57:19 (22,860)
Langham, Richard 5:28:34 (28,913)
Langholz, Peter 5:07:03 (24,896)
Langley, Colin 2:50:24 (386)
Langley, Kelly P 5:07:33 (25,010)
Langlois, Pascal X 3:48:20 (6,580)
Langly-Smith, Anthony G 4:13:28 (11,951)
Langridge, James D 4:36:23 (17,637)
Langrish, Ray J 5:28:15 (28,849)
Langton, Harry C 3:29:19 (3,620)
Langton, John S 3:27:43 (3,375)
Langton, Richard J 6:25:49 (34,160)
Laniado, Salomon 4:47:34 (20,426)
Lanier, Romain 3:27:38 (3,365)
Lanigan, Stuart 4:13:54 (12,068)
Lanjri, Alex 5:00:12 (23,551)
Lannen, Stephen 4:28:17 (15,666)
Lanning, Tony J 5:13:26 (26,110)
Lansdown, Christopher B 5:25:18 (28,320)
Lansell, Mark H 4:15:41 (12,480)
Lantsbery, Jonathan D 4:06:13 (10,398)
Laoudi, Merzouk 4:11:53 (11,588)
Lapins, Terry D 3:45:59 (6,176)
Lappin, Noel G 6:03:31 (32,852)
Laqua, Markus 4:18:41 (13,259)
Larder, Darren M 3:18:58 (2,389)
Large, David E 4:49:18 (20,838)
Large, Paul 3:35:02 (4,413)
Large, Phillip H 3:25:54 (3,115)
Large, Steven G 2:58:15 (766)
Larkam, Douglas J 5:26:44 (28,581)
Larke, Joseph 3:56:30 (8,360)
Larkin, James A 6:05:54 (33,035)
Larking, James W 4:29:26 (15,986)
Larmour, James D 4:21:56 (14,073)
Laroin, James W 4:44:04 (19,556)
Larose, Andrew D 4:54:39 (22,185)
Larrenduche, Christopher 3:16:05 (2,087)
Larrs, Philip A 4:55:10 (22,309)
Larsen, Dennis 3:53:29 (7,683)
Larsen, Soren 5:47:24 (31,399)
Larsen, Torben Steen 4:16:10 (12,612)
Larson, Greger C 4:53:12 (21,810)
Larsson, Charles A 4:36:06 (17,560)
Larter, Stewart 4:16:18 (12,650)
Lartey, Lawrence 5:03:13 (24,176)
Lascelles, Martin C 3:11:37 (1,686)
Lashmar, Anthony 2:36:55 (98)
Laslett, Philip D 5:38:33 (30,388)
Lassbeck, David 4:16:21 (12,660)
Lassbeck, Holger 4:14:35 (12,224)
Last, Shane W 3:59:26 (9,075)
Laszcz, Jean-François 5:15:30 (26,563)
Latham, Andrew S 6:04:34 (32,921)
Latham, Philip M 5:18:38 (27,187)
Latham, Stan F 4:28:42 (15,789)
Lathion, Philippe 4:13:39 (12,007)
Lathwell, Simon G 3:09:59 (1,557)
Latif, Haroon 4:17:44 (13,006)
Latimer, Adam G 4:50:38 (21,155)
Latner, Alexander J 5:09:39 (25,404)
Latorre, Antonio B 5:35:22 (29,962)
La-Touche, Clement N 5:10:51 (25,633)
Latteman, Mark R 4:31:09 (16,396)
Latter, Darren J 3:49:49 (6,899)
Lattimer, Iain D 4:46:34 (20,191)
Lau, Cheung 5:53:53 (32,042)
Lau, Mike R 4:08:11 (10,808)
Lau, Sie 4:48:17 (20,597)
Laubis, Hans P 4:49:05 (20,789)
Laudato, Adriano 4:10:50 (11,335)
Laughton, Christopher A 4:54:26 (22,132)
Laughton, Douglas E 4:37:04 (17,801)
Laughton, Michael J 4:14:35 (12,224)
Launchbury, Richard A 6:28:55 (34,282)
Launder, Gavin Q 4:54:05 (22,037)
Laundy, Peter 4:22:52 (14,303)
Laurence, Garry E 4:51:05 (21,262)
Laurent, Thierry 5:54:52 (32,133)
Laurent, Thomas 3:27:43 (3,375)
Laurie, Steven 3:10:10 (1,578)
Laustsen, Neils Jakob 3:22:20 (2,730)
Lautch, Peter M 4:49:43 (20,936)
Lavan, Michael J 4:07:39 (10,690)
Lavan, Nicholas 3:40:36 (5,286)
Lavan, Roderick M 4:54:41 (22,194)
Lavelle, Dominic 5:05:43 (24,639)
Laver, Graham K 3:40:31 (5,273)
Laver, Simon 3:14:28 (1,938)
Laver, Toby B 2:54:39 (555)
Laverrie, Cedryc 4:03:26 (9,856)
Lavers, Roderick J 3:09:56 (1,551)
Laverty, Hugh 4:07:39 (10,690)
Laverty, Sean 3:06:31 (1,272)
Lavery, Alexander 5:26:48 (28,587)
Lavery, Andrew 5:55:09 (32,159)
Lavery, James A 5:33:20 (29,653)
Lavin, Malcolm T 3:49:11 (6,767)
Lavino, James 4:20:15 (13,665)
Law, Alan 4:34:46 (17,215)
Law, Andrew P 4:36:32 (17,677)
Law, Chris A 6:54:52 (35,031)
Law, Christopher N 3:32:54 (4,123)
Law, Kevin 3:17:03 (2,186)
Law, Michael B 4:42:06 (19,064)
Law, Michael J 4:31:32 (16,466)
Law, Rob 4:17:28 (12,932)
Law, Simon N 3:06:26 (1,268)
Law, Tin-Kin 4:31:42 (16,509)
Lawes, Robert S 3:58:37 (8,857)
Lawford, Nicholas. N 4:44:13 (19,604)
Lawlor, Michael 4:36:19 (17,614)
Lawne, James J 3:32:29 (4,065)
Lawrance, Michael E 5:31:33 (29,383)
Lawrence, C 3:13:23 (1,856)
Lawrence, Chris D 6:07:48 (33,156)
Lawrence, Christopher T 4:06:48 (10,530)
Lawrence, Craig S 4:48:06 (20,552)
Lawrence, Daniel W 5:40:09 (30,611)
Lawrence, Graham 7:05:45 (35,215)
Lawrence, Ian A 4:48:10 (20,566)
Lawrence, James W 4:02:52 (9,763)
Lawrence, Keith 6:13:09 (33,500)
Lawrence, Martyn A 5:18:35 (27,178)
Lawrence, Matt E 3:48:42 (6,666)
Lawrence, Michael-John 3:40:14 (5,220)
Lawrence, Richard N 3:55:14 (8,064)
Lawrence, Robert F 6:00:03 (32,585)
Lawrence, Scott 4:45:11 (19,884)
Lawrence, Scott M 5:28:06 (28,818)
Lawrence, Simon 5:08:46 (25,237)
Lawrence, Thomas D 4:46:07 (20,086)
Lawrey, Timothy J 4:42:35 (19,203)
Lawrie, David E 3:58:29 (8,838)
Lawrie, David J 5:31:44 (29,410)
Laws, Derek W 3:55:53 (8,204)
Laws, Frank S 4:41:49 (19,001)
Lawson, Bill 4:54:14 (22,085)
Lawson, David A 3:28:52 (3,550)
Lawson, Guy 4:09:41 (11,113)
Lawson, Ian J 3:28:54 (3,558)
Lawson, James D 4:03:47 (9,924)
Lawson, Neal 4:56:39 (22,679)
Lawson, Sam 3:58:26 (8,816)
Lawson, Steve A 4:59:16 (23,332)
Lawton, Bryan W 3:15:01 (1,999)
Lawton, James P 3:44:53 (6,007)
Lawton, Matt 3:03:33 (1,081)
Lawton, Matthew J 5:01:11 (23,768)
Lawton, Michael J 4:52:54 (21,727)
Lawton, Nicholas E 4:33:01 (16,791)
Lawton, Peter L 3:54:58 (8,003)
Lawton, Steven J 3:33:56 (4,258)
Lay, Jeremy M 4:46:47 (20,227)
Lay, Peter A 3:48:56 (6,712)
Laybourne, Alexander C 6:17:10 (33,739)
Laycock, Grant 3:56:59 (8,476)
Layland, Clive A 5:18:26 (27,148)
Layland, David M 4:44:59 (19,833)
Layton, Shaun 3:26:35 (3,204)
Layton, Stephen A 5:29:45 (29,103)
Lazarevic, Andrew 6:57:55 (35,092)
Lazarus, Mark 4:51:21 (21,332)
Lazarus, Tobias J 5:01:41 (23,865)
Lazenby, John R 5:35:31 (29,976)
Lazenby, Peter A 5:35:31 (29,976)
Lazzaro, Arianna 6:28:50 (34,277)
Le Breton, Timothy S 3:38:43 (4,960)
Le Cordeur, James 4:00:23 (9,287)
Le Couteur, James N 3:54:47 (7,958)
Le Jaouen, Eric C 5:37:28 (30,233)
Le Lann, Franck 3:24:45 (2,992)
Le Leroux, Florian 5:34:50 (29,892)
Le Roux, Marc 3:54:06 (7,820)
Le Vailly, Pierre M 6:57:34 (35,084)
Lea, Benjamin J 6:15:27 (33,644)
Lea, Colin 3:41:48 (5,484)
Lea, Jeffrey H 4:27:24 (15,448)
Lea, John L 3:43:47 (5,826)
Lea, Joseff 5:06:30 (24,784)
Leach, Darren R 4:18:18 (13,149)
Leach, Darren S 3:50:27 (7,029)
Leach, David A 5:34:15 (29,803)
Leach, Robert 3:26:48 (3,240)
Leach, Robin T 4:40:46 (18,722)
Leach, Rocky N 3:39:35 (5,121)
Leader, David A 3:59:19 (9,045)
Leaf, Simon L 4:59:50 (23,463)
Leafe, Jonathan G 5:11:52 (25,827)
Leahy, Paul D 4:25:40 (14,992)
Leahy, Richard P 3:33:30 (4,203)
Leak, Andrew S 6:07:38 (33,138)
Leake, David S 4:16:17 (12,644)
Leary, Mark 3:51:21 (7,209)
Leary, Paul A 4:26:57 (15,312)
Leary-Joyce, John S 5:15:23 (26,540)
Leat, Ashley J 4:47:23 (20,379)
Leather, Giles M 4:35:19 (17,363)
Leatherbarrow, Charles K 3:53:02 (7,577)
Leatherbarrow, Nicholas M 4:32:36 (16,690)
Leatherland, Paul 4:02:14 (9,659)
Leathers, Raymond D 5:12:26 (25,945)
Leathley, Nicholas 3:34:43 (4,366)
Leaworthy, Kristian J 4:14:47 (12,267)
Leber, Philippe R 3:16:36 (2,134)
Leblanc, Patrick 4:01:07 (9,439)
Lebold, John W 6:17:28 (33,746)
Lebon, Richard S 3:29:46 (3,682)
Leborgne, Olivier 4:06:45 (10,513)
Lebreton, Bernard 4:43:24 (19,400)
Leckerman, Antony G 4:26:16 (15,123)
Lecoq, Jean-Yves 4:17:53 (13,038)
Leddington, Stephen R 5:16:15 (26,711)
Lederer, Chris G 4:15:39 (12,474)
Ledger, Charles 4:22:38 (14,241)
Ledsam, Charles E 4:52:04 (21,503)
Leduc, Didier F 3:51:07 (7,161)
Ledwidge, Alan 5:09:30 (25,371)

Lee, Alex R 5:21:47 (27,751)
Lee, Andrew 5:13:46 (26,183)
Lee, Andrew J 5:30:26 (29,205)
Lee, Anthony 3:58:55 (8,942)
Lee, Anthony C 5:12:55 (26,026)
Lee, Bobby 3:57:11 (8,520)
Lee, Brett S 4:20:52 (13,822)
Lee, Brian J 5:35:55 (30,043)
Lee, Charles G 4:11:01 (11,371)
Lee, Chris 6:46:48 (34,851)
Lee, Christopher D 6:10:11 (33,316)
Lee, Colin B 3:27:17 (3,323)
Lee, Daniel 3:52:09 (7,400)
Lee, David 3:22:55 (2,788)
Lee, David 5:33:06 (29,620)
Lee, David E 5:16:59 (26,855)
Lee, David M 6:29:36 (34,312)
Lee, David P 3:36:45 (4,654)
Lee, Ewehoe 4:56:40 (22,686)
Lee, Hae Seung 4:11:21 (11,459)
Lee, James W 4:37:37 (17,914)
Lee, Jason S 5:19:20 (27,316)
Lee, Jeremy R 4:46:01 (20,062)
Lee, John C 4:13:52 (12,056)
Lee, Jonathan M 4:31:11 (16,401)
Lee, Kevin 4:43:14 (19,349)
Lee, Kin-Hung Alec 4:22:28 (14,190)
Lee, Kwok H 3:33:44 (4,231)
Lee, Marcus 4:55:54 (22,487)
Lee, Marcus T 4:21:27 (13,952)
Lee, Matthew J 4:38:26 (18,134)
Lee, Michael I 3:56:19 (8,307)
Lee, Nicholas 3:36:39 (4,634)
Lee, Nigel 3:35:36 (4,499)
Lee, Peter R 4:10:55 (11,352)
Lee, Peter W 7:19:59 (35,388)
Lee, Philip 4:30:08 (16,182)
Lee, Richard 3:12:01 (1,729)
Lee, Richard 4:29:20 (15,947)
Lee, Richard 4:53:17 (21,831)
Lee, Richard C 4:05:22 (10,212)
Lee, Rob J 4:02:15 (9,664)
Lee, Robert A 4:48:49 (20,725)
Lee, Robert S 4:53:14 (21,822)
Lee, Royston A 4:56:21 (22,602)
Lee, Stuart 5:39:39 (30,551)
Lee, William E 4:48:49 (20,725)
Leeburn, Robin E 3:51:41 (7,290)
Leech, Benedict 3:44:30 (5,942)
Leech, David R 4:37:37 (17,914)
Leech, Simon A 5:18:56 (27,239)
Leech, Terry 3:19:36 (2,443)
Leegwater, Sander 3:42:05 (5,534)
Leek, Jonathan 4:38:42 (18,201)
Leek, Shawn J 5:08:06 (25,112)
Leeks, Clinton E 3:47:10 (6,373)
Leeks, Shane 4:24:55 (14,804)
Leeming, John D 4:28:00 (15,586)
Leeper, Christopher P 4:25:13 (14,879)
Leeper, Patrick 5:06:00 (24,694)
Lees, Andy A 4:36:21 (17,626)
Lees, Chris A 3:23:12 (2,823)
Lees, Keith A 5:56:26 (32,280)
Lees, Toby J 4:28:01 (15,592)
Leeuwerik, Hans 4:47:23 (20,379)
Leforestier, Ludovic 3:59:12 (9,011)
Legendre, François 3:52:39 (7,489)
Legg, Andrew J 3:56:03 (8,235)
Legg, Daniel H 3:53:04 (7,582)
Legg, Graeme R 3:54:16 (7,861)
Legg, Jonathan A 4:09:24 (11,048)
Legg, Richard T 4:55:22 (22,353)
Legg, Timothy J 4:56:55 (22,753)
Legge, Jonathan M 6:22:57 (34,040)
Leglerc, Valere 3:17:14 (2,201)
Legrand, Ghislain 4:12:46 (11,780)
Legresley, Edward M 3:47:37 (6,454)
Legros, Eric 3:55:54 (8,208)
Le-Guehennec, Gerard 5:00:30 (23,613)
Leguy, Didier 4:31:01 (16,357)
Lehmann, Antoine 3:13:52 (1,890)
Leigh, Andrew R 4:37:24 (17,862)
Leigh, David R 5:54:20 (32,086)

Leigh, Graham 4:29:49 (16,095)
Leigh, Jon 3:32:03 (3,995)
Leigh, Nick 5:11:06 (25,687)
Leightell, Chris 4:21:36 (13,985)
Leighton, Daniel 6:12:07 (33,434)
Leitch, Thomas J 3:21:32 (2,655)
Leite, Fernando 3:38:05 (4,850)
Leith, Clifford W 3:16:06 (2,089)
Leith, William A 7:48:53 (35,615)
Leiton, Marco A 4:40:10 (18,573)

Lel, Martin 2:07:41 (1)

Lelliott, Stephen 3:12:17 (1,756)
Lemanski, Stuart L 3:22:45 (2,769)
Lemon, David J 3:17:22 (2,212)
Lemon, Jamie C 5:09:19 (25,336)
Lemon, Mark E 4:52:09 (21,527)
Lemon, Peter 3:39:39 (5,135)
Lemon, Thomas G 4:28:48 (15,811)
Lenane, Brian 4:58:47 (23,202)
Leng, Robert 5:33:37 (29,705)
Lenihan, Kevin G 3:08:43 (1,446)
Lennock, Mark J 4:50:51 (21,204)
Lennon, Brad O 4:40:22 (18,624)
Lennon, Chris 5:51:15 (31,801)
Lennon, Clifford 4:50:55 (21,221)
Lennon, James P 4:00:58 (9,411)
Lennon, Niall D 4:09:36 (11,095)
Lenton, Richard P 4:47:34 (20,426)
Leon, Ariel V 5:13:12 (26,080)
Leonard, Adrian H 5:02:23 (24,010)
Leonard, David J 5:08:58 (25,276)
Leonard, Paul 3:35:55 (4,538)
Leonard, Paul F 3:58:37 (8,857)
Leonard, Stephen P 4:26:03 (15,066)
Leonardi, Roberto 4:42:54 (19,281)
Leone Ganado, Timothy 4:43:38 (19,448)
Leong, Swee H 5:23:07 (27,951)
Lepage, Beniot 5:29:20 (29,047)
Leparoux, Alain 4:07:56 (10,758)
Leparoux, Patrick R 3:31:51 (3,963)
Leppard, James E 4:33:27 (16,900)
Leppard, Robert A 4:27:39 (15,501)
Leppard, Robert K 7:42:09 (35,585)

Lepper, Leslie A 3:34:46 (4,371)
Lequime, Georges D 4:05:07 (10,165)
Lerner, Michel N 3:17:42 (2,253)
Leroux, Eric 3:14:12 (1,914)
Leroy, Jason S 4:03:57 (9,958)
Leroy, Philippe 4:45:19 (19,908)
Lesiau, Ori 5:00:54 (23,709)
Leslie, David T 4:22:11 (14,121)
Leslie, Mark P 5:19:28 (27,330)
Leslie, William J 4:50:30 (21,120)
Leslie-Smith, Paul A 3:41:23 (5,425)
Lessa Neto, Mandel 4:45:57 (20,050)
Lessel, Bruce 5:21:06 (27,618)
Lesser, Dean G 7:02:40 (35,171)
Lester, Gareth C 4:06:44 (10,509)
Lester, Ricard 4:28:23 (15,695)
Lester, Roy E 5:47:17 (31,381)
Letchworth, Nicholas T 3:37:10 (4,708)
Lethaby, Raymond J 4:55:43 (22,433)
Lettice, Alan 3:35:31 (4,486)
Letton, David 4:32:10 (16,599)
Leungsangnam, Carl P 5:31:54 (29,433)
Levai, Jean-Paul 5:46:38 (31,321)
Levasseur, Eric 4:39:32 (18,421)
Levasseur, Olivier 3:43:36 (5,800)
Levene, Paul 3:49:40 (6,862)
Levenstein, Ben M 4:42:44 (19,238)
Leveque, Bernard 3:59:31 (9,097)
Leverton, Steven 2:51:49 (433)
Leveson, Joseph M 4:07:39 (10,690)
Levi, David W 4:30:51 (16,324)
Levick, John W 3:19:55 (2,483)
Levine, Luke H 3:40:20 (5,240)
Levinson, Oliver T 6:17:39 (33,762)
Levitt, Martyn J 4:50:34 (21,139)
Levitz, Michael D 5:31:47 (29,415)
Levy, Alejandro 5:28:08 (28,826)
Levy, Daniel 4:07:21 (10,626)
Levy, Dave J 4:03:56 (9,956)
Levy, Jamie P 5:41:18 (30,740)
Levy, Martin G 5:29:09 (29,011)
Levy, Paul A 4:40:39 (18,687)
Levy, Robert M 4:06:09 (10,383)
Lewer, Aidan P 4:04:09 (9,994)
Lewi, Daniel 4:49:55 (20,976)
Lewin, Bernard 5:35:04 (29,922)
Lewin, Danzel C 3:45:33 (6,103)
Lewin, Michael 4:50:06 (21,023)
Lewin, Michael R 4:39:39 (18,449)
Lewin, Robert A 4:07:51 (10,737)
Lewis, Adrian 4:19:55 (13,578)
Lewis, Alan 5:07:20 (24,965)
Lewis, Alan E 3:09:21 (1,505)
Lewis, Alex J 4:54:36 (22,172)
Lewis, Anthony 5:22:50 (27,912)
Lewis, Barry J 4:52:42 (21,668)
Lewis, Christopher C 4:26:58 (15,314)
Lewis, Clive 5:11:20 (25,730)
Lewis, Daniel 2:40:36 (149)
Lewis, Darren J 2:58:18 (772)
Lewis, David A 4:14:03 (12,112)
Lewis, David E 4:07:23 (10,633)
Lewis, David J 4:19:58 (13,594)
Lewis, David M 4:12:37 (11,743)
Lewis, Dunbar H 4:57:45 (22,970)
Lewis, Gary S 3:52:58 (7,557)
Lewis, Gavin M 4:58:17 (23,098)
Lewis, Giles R 5:09:43 (25,419)
Lewis, Graham D 4:33:41 (16,955)
Lewis, Ian M 5:34:32 (29,856)
Lewis, Jake R 4:19:18 (13,405)
Lewis, James 5:21:10 (27,626)
Lewis, James H 4:22:24 (14,176)
Lewis, James M 3:16:56 (2,173)
Lewis, James R 3:54:58 (8,003)
Lewis, John D 3:40:14 (5,220)
Lewis, Kevin 3:36:55 (4,677)
Lewis, Lee 4:19:01 (13,330)
Lewis, Leonard J 4:43:29 (19,413)
Lewis, Mark D 4:37:21 (17,848)
Lewis, Matthew 5:09:22 (25,344)
Lewis, Michael 6:52:50 (34,988)
Lewis, Michael J 7:33:00 (35,518)

Lewis, Neil 5:20:17 (27,472)
Lewis, Paul D 4:28:10 (15,640)
Lewis, Rhodri P 4:32:54 (16,763)
Lewis, Richard 5:32:30 (29,525)
Lewis, Richard A 7:01:53 (35,155)
Lewis, Richard J............................5:38:52 (30,436)
Lewis, Robert O.............................5:44:13 (31,067)
Lewis, Robert R 3:55:01 (8,011)
Lewis, Simon 3:03:00 (1,049)
Lewis, Stephen A............................4:00:05 (9,224)
Lewis, Steven J 6:08:43 (33,220)
Lewis, Tim 2:46:47 (278)
Lewis, Tim D...................................3:58:49 (8,913)
Lewis, Trevor A..............................4:06:36 (10,486)
Lewis, Vasco 5:10:35 (25,591)
Lewis Webb, L 3:37:38 (4,768)
Lewis-Jones, Mark..........................3:45:11 (6,047)
Lewisman, Hagan...........................3:26:57 (3,270)
Lewis-Russell, Mark........................5:28:20 (28,877)
Lewtas, Jeffrey R 4:30:05 (16,170)
Ley, Graham J 4:49:20 (20,849)
Ley, Stephen 4:48:19 (20,613)
Leybourne, David M 4:52:48 (21,700)
Leyenda, Manuel.............................3:43:30 (5,779)
Leys, Calum P..................................4:34:19 (17,098)
Lichtenthaeler, Stefan 3:11:36 (1,680)
Lichtenthaler, Jurgen.....................5:07:07 (24,912)
Liddell, Simon J 5:24:58 (28,266)
Liddle, Malcolm 5:02:45 (24,084)
Liddle, Stuart J 4:37:26 (17,874)
Lidgate, Simon C 4:42:25 (19,156)
Lidgate Taylor, Steven P................2:57:54 (740)
Lie-A-Cheong, Leonard 4:02:43 (9,733)
Liebenberg, Louis...........................3:52:02 (7,370)
Liebenberg, Marius.........................6:42:12 (34,728)
Liggat, Steven 3:31:01 (3,840)
Light, Darren T 5:16:54 (26,840)
Light, Richard D 4:27:34 (15,480)
Lightfoot, Alan T 3:12:50 (1,811)
Lightfoot, Ian 6:12:47 (33,478)
Lightfoot, John S.............................6:41:04 (34,691)
Lightman, Shaun 5:54:22 (32,089)
Liljeberg, Hakan E..........................5:06:39 (24,809)
Liljestrom, Lars O 3:23:14 (2,826)
Lill, Gary..3:43:01 (5,694)
Lillevik, Oyvind 3:07:03 (1,314)
Lilley, Stephen D.............................5:41:12 (30,728)
Lilley, Thomas J 3:38:50 (4,983)
Lilley, Tim..3:58:41 (8,880)
Lilley, Tony 5:22:00 (27,782)
Lillie, Joseph D 6:32:24 (34,421)
Lillywhite, Dominic L 4:33:54 (17,007)
Lim, Eng B.......................................4:51:46 (21,430)
Lima, Jorge......................................3:46:29 (6,247)
Lima, Paulo 3:37:20 (4,725)
Limmer, David R 4:48:02 (20,541)
Limo, Felix 2:07:47 (3)
Linares, Eduardo 3:28:17 (3,445)
Lincoln, Aaron S 3:44:43 (5,983)
Lincoln, Andrew C..........................4:30:14 (16,202)
Lincoln, David W 5:08:19 (25,158)
Lincoln, Gary J 3:44:10 (5,888)
Lincoln, Tim W................................6:01:25 (32,713)
Lind, Michael 3:56:01 (8,228)
Lindbolm, Stefan 4:01:47 (9,564)
Lindebotten, John...........................3:17:00 (2,179)
Lindesay, Andrew D 7:14:35 (35,341)
Lindley, James M 4:01:01 (9,423)
Lindley, Mark 5:51:46 (31,852)
Lindop, Nigel K...............................4:43:09 (19,330)
Lindsay, David 2:48:11 (319)
Lindsay, David N 5:49:00 (31,586)
Lindsay, Robert G............................4:52:43 (21,673)
Lindsay, Steven J 3:58:37 (8,857)
Lindsay, Stuart A 4:38:19 (18,101)
Lindsay, Vaughan E.........................3:11:39 (1,691)
Lindsay, William R...........................5:20:31 (27,522)
Line, Ian 4:06:45 (10,513)
Line, Martin J 5:11:45 (25,800)
Linehan, Kevin P.............................3:10:00 (1,559)
Lines, Derek C.................................2:42:49 (195)
Lines, Edward T 4:00:08 (9,234)
Lines, George 4:36:31 (17,671)
Lines, John R...................................4:59:57 (23,490)
Lines, Michael 4:50:45 (21,177)
Lines, Nicholas G 4:35:43 (17,463)
Lines, Richard R..............................3:46:22 (6,231)
Lines, Trevor P 6:59:04 (35,111)
Lines, William J 3:31:18 (3,877)
Ling, Alexander E............................4:13:28 (11,951)
Ling, Daniel.....................................2:57:09 (686)
Ling, Kevin P 5:13:42 (26,166)
Ling, Peter R 4:47:21 (20,370)
Lingard, John 3:11:36 (1,680)
Linkison, Charles W........................3:59:26 (9,075)
Linkson, Gavin M............................4:41:32 (18,932)
Linlay, Michael S 3:30:55 (3,831)
Linner, Jens 3:08:11 (1,408)
Linney, Mark D................................4:10:10 (11,196)
Linsell, Robin 6:49:31 (34,920)
Linsell, Shane W 4:36:50 (17,752)
Linstead, Michael D 5:52:55 (31,961)
Linton, Charles H 3:27:30 (3,356)
Linton, Nick 6:46:56 (34,856)
Linton, Thomas D............................4:13:01 (11,833)
Lintott, Wayne D 3:54:52 (7,978)
Lipinski, Kai S..................................3:40:39 (5,290)
Lipscomb, Scott...............................3:58:38 (8,867)
Lipscombe, Peter 5:34:36 (29,861)
Lipszyc, Uri......................................3:23:35 (2,857)
Liptrott, Mark..................................5:19:10 (27,283)
Lisgarten, Philip B 4:39:25 (18,394)
Lisi, Daniel.......................................3:59:19 (9,045)
Lisle, Richard A...............................3:28:07 (3,422)
Lister, Andrew R..............................4:42:09 (19,076)
Lister, Daniel E................................3:39:24 (5,087)
Lister, Darron 3:59:00 (8,960)
Lister, Ewart G................................3:38:17 (4,885)
Lister, Kevin....................................6:46:06 (34,832)
Lister, Robert C 4:29:05 (15,880)
Litchfield, Andrew J........................3:41:19 (5,415)
Litchfield, Steven 3:49:29 (6,827)
Lithgow, Simon M...........................3:37:51 (4,799)
Littke, Vincent.................................3:50:27 (7,029)
Little, Craig.....................................5:47:55 (31,454)
Little, Craig B 3:46:13 (6,207)
Little, Duncan B..............................4:22:01 (14,089)
Little, Graeme 4:33:51 (17,002)
Little, Ian 4:42:49 (19,260)
Little, Ian K.....................................3:15:38 (2,043)
Little, Jonathan R............................4:40:27 (18,640)
Little, Oliver R................................5:04:22 (24,397)
Little, Robert 4:46:50 (20,235)
Little, Tom 4:29:42 (16,062)
Little, Tony N 4:15:36 (12,460)
Littleboy, Daniel.............................6:42:11 (34,726)
Littleboy, Sam D.............................6:19:17 (33,853)
Littlechild, Justin P 2:55:16 (586)
Littlecott, Stephen R.......................3:51:26 (7,240)
Littlejohn, Andrew J........................5:56:22 (32,272)
Littlejohn, Robert E........................4:22:29 (14,202)
Littler, Frank H 4:02:22 (9,679)
Littler, Stephen T............................2:33:07 (54)
Littlewood, Mike H 4:39:49 (18,490)
Litvin, Norman P.............................2:57:35 (715)
Liu, Benjamin..................................3:29:04 (3,583)
Liu, Hin Yan 5:44:08 (31,060)
Liva, Anthony J................................4:12:57 (11,819)
Livermore, Ben J 4:04:26 (10,045)
Livesey, Ian F 3:44:19 (5,908)
Livings, Ben 4:25:51 (15,025)
Livingstone, David 3:10:05 (1,569)
Livingstone, Guy 4:05:19 (10,206)
Ljungkvist, Bengt A.........................4:03:02 (9,791)
Llagostera, Marc..............................6:20:36 (33,928)
Llamas, Javier G...............................5:35:44 (30,016)
Llewellyn, Andrew...........................4:24:03 (14,585)
Llewellyn, Stephen..........................7:12:44 (35,313)
Llewellyn, Terence P 4:59:00 (23,253)
Llewellyn, William M 4:24:36 (14,727)
Llewleyn, Robert W.........................4:29:24 (15,976)
Lloyd, David R.................................4:53:46 (21,956)
Lloyd, Gareth 4:10:11 (11,201)
Lloyd, Gareth P 3:36:42 (4,646)
Lloyd, Gerwyn 5:33:59 (29,756)
Lloyd, John A 3:48:30 (6,619)
Lloyd, John P...................................5:17:29 (26,956)
Lloyd, Luke J 4:51:07 (21,271)
Lloyd, Mark 3:56:16 (8,290)
Lloyd, Martin P 3:13:52 (1,890)
Lloyd, Matthew L 6:01:32 (32,721)
Lloyd, Peter 5:54:18 (32,080)
Lloyd, Peter D 3:08:03 (1,395)
Lloyd, Peter J 5:30:58 (29,288)
Lloyd, Phil 3:25:17 (3,042)
Lloyd, Phillip E...............................4:56:21 (22,602)
Lloyd, Richard A 4:04:16 (10,017)
Lloyd, Richard T 3:18:02 (2,284)
Lloyd, Robert D..............................3:32:31 (4,074)
Lloyd, Robin 3:53:59 (7,790)
Lloyd Owen, Tom O 4:48:22 (20,628)
Loader, Ian C...................................4:51:09 (21,278)
Loader, Nick....................................5:16:19 (26,724)
Lobb, Antony L 6:03:09 (32,831)
Lobo, Leon 4:38:27 (18,138)
Lochmann, Thomas.........................2:49:36 (362)
Lock, Brian S...................................4:32:55 (16,768)
Lock, Craig N 4:38:44 (18,208)
Lock, David S...................................4:25:57 (15,043)
Lock, David S...................................5:41:21 (30,748)
Lock, Gary 5:28:39 (28,928)
Lock, Richard B 5:31:13 (29,337)
Lock, Shaun M 3:00:42 (940)
Locke, Dean 7:34:39 (35,531)
Locke, Gary K..................................4:40:45 (18,714)
Locke, Martin P...............................6:05:27 (32,994)
Locke, Matthew...............................4:22:44 (14,268)
Lockett, Ben D 5:07:15 (24,942)
Lockett, Patrick 3:05:13 (1,175)
Lockett, Philip J...............................5:00:00 (23,503)
Lockey, Alistair J 2:41:00 (157)
Lockhart, Keith M...........................5:55:01 (32,150)
Lockhart, Malcolm C 3:43:33 (5,792)
Lockhart Smith, Alistair M 4:37:14 (17,826)
Lockie, Christopher.........................4:43:53 (19,505)
Lockley, Paul M 4:51:43 (21,424)
Lockwood, Paul R 4:42:03 (19,054)
Lockwood-Cowell, Stuart J..............4:54:09 (22,062)
Lockyer, Paul A................................3:41:18 (5,411)
Lockyer-Stevens, Noel.....................4:01:13 (9,462)
Loddo, Arthur J...............................3:46:42 (6,283)
Loder-Symonds, James R 5:08:36 (25,205)
Lodge, Carl A 5:32:32 (29,539)
Lodge, Christopher D......................4:12:42 (11,768)
Lodge, Steve 4:39:15 (18,351)
Loewe, Andreas...............................3:40:28 (5,257)
Lofgren, Gunnar S 4:19:56 (13,582)
Lofino, Gianfranco 4:06:10 (10,385)
Lofthouse, Nick...............................5:20:02 (27,429)
Logan, John.....................................4:31:02 (16,364)
Logan, Neil A 5:34:29 (29,845)
Logan, Robert M.............................4:42:21 (19,139)
Logie, Peter W.................................5:39:04 (30,459)
Loguancio, Sam 3:31:51 (3,963)
Logue, Alan 4:35:00 (17,270)
Loh, Tom 4:45:24 (19,925)
Lohier, Stephane J 3:33:34 (4,209)
Loizou, Christopher.........................2:58:06 (755)
Loizou, James P...............................3:43:31 (5,783)
Lok, Jospeh......................................4:26:22 (15,149)
Lok, Mike...5:59:17 (32,536)
Lomas, Gary P 4:34:49 (17,225)
Lomas, Jim S....................................4:20:24 (13,707)
Lomas, Peter....................................4:27:08 (15,365)
Lomas, Richard J..............................3:16:22 (2,112)
Lomas, Roger 3:51:03 (7,145)
Lomas, Stephen D............................4:21:06 (13,874)
Lomas-Brown, Richard E 3:04:15 (1,117)
Lomax, Peter 5:32:07 (29,470)
Lombard, David J.............................3:20:24 (2,542)
Lonardi, Mario 5:10:41 (25,610)
Londesbrough, Jim 2:59:50 (889)
Lonergan, Alan 4:15:04 (12,336)
Long, Brian M 5:09:56 (25,457)
Long, Daniel P 5:18:20 (27,133)
Long, Douglas A...............................4:01:16 (9,474)
Long, Edward..................................3:43:01 (5,694)
Long, James A 3:55:39 (8,150)
Long, Justin N 5:00:11 (23,547)

Name	Time (Position)
Long, Martin K.	5:05:32 (24,609)
Long, Oliver	4:47:05 (20,308)
Long, Ryan J	6:43:14 (34,756)
Longbottom, Barry	5:40:51 (30,689)
Longfield, Richard W	4:25:48 (15,018)
Longhurst, Martin J	3:12:55 (1,815)
Longland, Ian M	4:09:55 (11,153)
Longley, Robert C	6:05:53 (33,033)
Longman, Michael P	4:48:01 (20,535)
Longstaff, Martyn	4:56:53 (22,743)
Longstaff, Tony	4:54:38 (22,179)
Longthorn, Alan	5:35:22 (29,962)
Longthorne, Keith M	4:29:32 (16,025)
Longthorpe, Andrew J	3:19:00 (2,392)
Longthorpe, Simon	2:56:45 (655)
Longueville, Jacques	4:22:59 (14,331)
Lonsdale, Shaun	4:58:21 (23,119)
Looney, Richard M	3:31:25 (3,892)
Loose, Simon D	3:55:24 (8,105)
Lopez, Armando J	5:10:01 (25,486)
Lopez, Javier	2:51:59 (438)
Lopez, Rob	4:21:36 (13,985)
Lopfe, Theophill	3:50:37 (7,059)
Lorberg, Stuart I	3:24:49 (2,997)
Lorch, David W	5:22:54 (27,921)
Lord, Alistair P	5:07:30 (24,999)
Lord, Chris	4:26:38 (15,218)
Lord, Michael	3:14:11 (1,910)
Lord, Steven T	3:10:54 (1,623)
Lordi, Tommaso	4:34:03 (17,039)
Lorenzi, Ugo	3:53:23 (7,660)
Lores-Penalver, Frank A	5:41:40 (30,791)
Lorimer, Raymond	4:40:09 (18,566)
Lorkin, James P	5:34:11 (29,791)
Lorkin, Paul J	5:13:45 (26,178)
Lornie, Richard	4:32:28 (16,652)
Lorre, Joris	5:15:31 (26,567)
Lorriman, Anthony J	3:53:23 (7,660)
Lorriman, Steve	4:19:35 (13,479)
Losavio, Giacomo	4:05:08 (10,169)
Lotinga, Nicholas A	5:06:25 (24,772)
Lotter, François	5:10:46 (25,621)
Louden, Adrian R	4:50:49 (21,196)
Louden, Marc S	5:04:52 (24,492)
Lough, Thomas	4:45:40 (19,985)
Loughman, John S	6:04:01 (32,890)
Loughnane, Simon P	3:05:52 (1,227)
Loughrey, Peter	4:22:09 (14,116)
Lound, Charles A	2:43:04 (200)
Louth, Shaun M	5:32:09 (29,475)
Louw, Willem P	4:41:04 (18,803)
Love, Adam	5:09:34 (25,391)
Love, Christopher C	5:48:20 (31,512)
Love, Jason D	4:08:10 (10,799)
Love, Nick J	5:27:59 (28,794)
Loveday, Glyn	3:05:07 (1,170)
Lovegrove, Geoffrey	4:50:51 (21,204)
Lovegrove, Guy	5:16:06 (26,683)
Loveland, Andrew T	4:38:11 (18,057)
Loveless, Paul V	4:27:02 (15,331)
Lovell, David J	4:11:55 (11,596)
Lovell, Joseph F	4:15:47 (12,507)
Lovell, Max H	5:22:15 (27,816)
Lovelock, Richard C	3:23:10 (2,819)
Loveridge, David R	3:56:29 (8,355)
Loveridge, Trevor J	4:49:59 (20,990)
Lovett, Andrew V	5:53:29 (32,007)
Lovett, Ashley	4:07:34 (10,672)
Lovett, Jamie	4:36:22 (17,629)
Lovett, Paul	3:36:16 (4,582)
Lovick, Andrew J	4:48:16 (20,595)
Lovidge, Leslie J	4:22:16 (14,142)
Low, Li Chun	3:17:36 (2,239)
Low, Mathew	5:03:35 (24,251)
Low, Richard G	4:34:27 (17,135)
Low, Roger L	3:38:33 (4,929)
Low, Scott A	4:19:52 (13,563)
Low, Stephen A	2:58:22 (777)
Low, Stephen J	5:03:35 (24,251)
Lowdell, George D	4:20:22 (13,700)
Lowe, Aaron C	3:58:14 (8,772)
Lowe, Alexander V	3:56:37 (8,385)
Lowe, Alistair J	3:52:20 (7,440)
Lowe, Andrew J	4:22:29 (14,202)
Lowe, Andrew M	3:52:38 (7,485)
Lowe, Edward W	4:43:50 (19,489)
Lowe, Gary M	5:43:44 (31,017)
Lowe, Graham P	5:36:16 (30,077)
Lowe, Guy J	3:48:22 (6,585)
Lowe, Ian	3:50:04 (6,957)
Lowe, Neal M	5:23:27 (28,001)
Lowe, Paul	5:25:54 (28,443)
Lowe, Robert J	4:15:26 (12,426)
Lowe, Simon J	3:25:20 (3,047)
Lowe, Steven P	5:10:40 (25,608)
Lowe, Stuart R	4:12:05 (11,628)
Lower, Rob W	3:42:58 (5,682)
Lowes, Andrew	3:16:33 (2,130)
Lowman, David M	4:59:02 (23,264)
Lown, Kevin A	4:37:50 (17,965)
Lowne, Alan S	3:55:50 (8,190)
Lowrie, James	2:59:02 (827)
Lowry, Christopher T	4:07:05 (10,592)
Lowry, Colin C	5:07:18 (24,956)
Lowry, Jason	4:53:03 (21,762)
Lowry, Neil	7:02:32 (35,169)
Lowson, Frederick J	4:46:38 (20,204)
Lowson, Richard J	2:50:59 (408)
Lowther, Adrian	2:38:58 (125)
Loxton, James W	3:49:10 (6,761)
Loxton, Paul A	3:56:27 (8,346)
Loy, Alan M	4:02:48 (9,753)
Loydall, John E	4:49:45 (20,943)
Loyen, Frans S	3:40:53 (5,343)
Loynes, Chris J	4:53:46 (21,956)
Lubos, Winfried	6:28:53 (34,281)
Luby, Michael A	6:41:23 (34,702)
Luca, Max	4:24:55 (14,804)
Lucas, Adam O	3:43:26 (5,761)
Lucas, Bernard S	3:41:58 (5,511)
Lucas, Jonathan D	4:59:45 (23,443)
Lucas, Lenny C	5:54:50 (32,127)
Lucas, Marc R	3:34:52 (4,390)
Lucas, Mark J	4:16:26 (12,681)
Lucas, Mark R	5:05:53 (24,672)
Lucas, Martin	3:11:27 (1,667)
Lucas, Matthew D	4:33:48 (16,991)
Lucas, Michael	5:21:05 (27,615)
Lucas, Mike	5:13:07 (26,065)
Lucas, Paul M	4:25:21 (14,907)
Lucas, Paul R	6:20:48 (33,939)
Lucitt, Stewart A	4:50:01 (20,998)
Lucitt-Rees, Samuel D	4:50:01 (20,998)
Luck, Jamie D	3:27:22 (3,336)
Luck, Martin J	5:50:38 (31,739)
Luck, Roger A	5:14:07 (26,251)
Luck, Ronald W	4:46:53 (20,247)
Luckhurst, Anthony P	5:28:39 (28,928)
Luckhurst, Jon A	3:38:53 (4,995)
Luckhurst, Simon	3:45:39 (6,125)
Ludlam, Chris D	4:30:43 (16,295)
Ludlow, Michael K	4:49:11 (20,817)
Ludwig, Dirk	4:24:17 (14,651)
Ludwigsen, Harald	4:01:07 (9,439)
Luetchford, Peter J	4:49:15 (20,830)
Luff, Bradley I	6:12:27 (33,456)
Luff, Christopher I	6:12:27 (33,456)
Luffman, Daniel R	4:19:34 (13,471)
Luigi Penco, Vittorio	3:30:28 (3,782)
Luke, Philip S	4:09:18 (11,031)
Lumsden, Ian	4:41:24 (18,889)
Lumsden, William	4:25:33 (14,955)
Lunardi, Michele	3:17:03 (2,186)
Lund, David A	5:21:22 (27,667)
Lund, Philip	3:59:28 (9,087)
Lund, Simon	3:10:59 (1,630)
Lund, Trevor B	3:40:20 (5,240)
Lunde, Orjan	2:20:21 (12)
Lundie, Matthew J	4:36:38 (17,700)
Lundy, Andrew P	3:31:42 (3,942)
Lunelli, Adriano	4:16:46 (12,755)
Lunn, Andrew P	3:58:15 (8,780)
Lunn, Gary J	3:06:41 (1,286)
Lunn, Peter	3:59:56 (9,193)
Lunt, Geoffrey	4:51:55 (21,469)
Lunt, John	5:03:06 (24,146)
Luong, Hien V	4:13:25 (11,940)
Luppi, Claudio	3:40:28 (5,257)
Lupton, Ronan T	4:20:28 (13,724)
Lush, Martin K	4:15:18 (12,395)
Lush, Mike	5:27:24 (28,697)
Luton, Brad H	4:08:29 (10,868)
Luton, James T	4:03:25 (9,852)
Luton, Sam	3:06:24 (1,263)
Lux, Jakob	4:05:46 (10,300)
Luxford, Peter A	4:24:48 (14,777)
Luxton, David P	4:47:20 (20,367)
Luxton, Martin J	4:04:38 (10,080)
Luya, Jason S	5:04:57 (24,511)
Lyall, Graham C	3:08:10 (1,403)
Lyburn, Iain D	4:19:58 (13,594)
Lydall, Ben A	3:56:31 (8,364)
Lydiate, Christopher	5:07:03 (24,896)
Lydon, Paul K	7:06:27 (35,229)
Lydon, Peter J	4:37:27 (17,883)
Lydri, Simon	3:29:58 (3,714)
Lygate, David K	4:06:42 (10,502)
Lyle, David	4:28:39 (15,773)
Lynas, Matthew N	2:37:14 (101)
Lynas, Stewart	2:59:18 (847)
Lynch, Benjamin J	5:37:08 (30,189)
Lynch, Christopher G	4:44:23 (19,645)
Lynch, Darren	5:08:08 (25,122)
Lynch, David S	3:27:32 (3,357)
Lynch, Edward M	4:48:07 (20,555)
Lynch, Elliott L	4:41:10 (18,831)
Lynch, Foster M	3:48:59 (6,729)
Lynch, Fred	3:22:56 (2,789)
Lynch, James P	4:24:05 (14,593)
Lynch, Jim E	5:52:05 (31,878)
Lynch, John	4:24:01 (14,576)
Lynch, John E	4:09:38 (11,101)
Lynch, Matthew J	4:12:28 (11,715)
Lynch, Michael V	4:28:18 (15,672)
Lynch, Neil	4:55:20 (22,346)
Lynch, Paul M	4:10:20 (11,233)
Lynch, Paul S	6:34:58 (34,497)
Lynch, Robert J	3:59:19 (9,045)
Lynch, Robert M	6:02:47 (32,807)
Lynch, Stephen	5:01:12 (23,773)
Lynch, Timothy C	3:23:43 (2,868)
Lynch, Warren M	2:35:35 (78)
Lyne, Andrew G	3:20:24 (2,542)
Lyne, Eliot	2:49:50 (371)
Lyness, Matthew P	4:24:50 (14,793)
Lyng, James G	4:22:29 (14,202)
Lynham, Robert G	3:35:08 (4,427)
Lynn, Jeff	3:08:36 (1,437)
Lynn, Stuart W	4:44:57 (19,820)
Lynn, Tony	3:06:11 (1,245)
Lynn, Warren J	3:53:29 (7,683)
Lyon, John	4:57:44 (22,966)
Lyon, Max C	5:01:52 (23,905)
Lyon, Paul J	3:41:50 (5,491)
Lyon, Roger	6:31:20 (34,373)
Lyons, Alan S	4:18:52 (13,302)
Lyons, Dale R	5:25:38 (28,391)
Lyons, James M	3:32:50 (4,111)
Lyons, Kevin O	3:44:29 (5,937)
Lyons, Lee M	4:25:11 (14,867)
Lyons, Matthew W	3:41:35 (5,454)
Lyons, Stephen L	4:36:33 (17,681)
Lyons, Tim J	5:57:19 (32,354)
Lyons, Timothy	4:55:54 (22,487)
Lysons, Mark	4:58:48 (23,206)
Maag, Felix	3:57:14 (8,539)
Maas, Benjamin A	3:06:10 (1,244)
Mabbott, Alex	4:01:53 (9,584)
Mabey, Chris E	4:19:40 (13,499)
Macadie, William E	5:13:33 (26,131)
MacAllan, Ray	4:35:50 (17,497)
Macarthur, Ian R	6:35:41 (34,527)
Macarthur, John D	5:03:53 (24,305)
Macartney, Simon I	5:13:12 (26,080)
MacAskill, Andy	2:36:08 (85)
Macaulay, Fritz T	5:32:24 (29,508)
Macaulay, Ian	4:58:44 (23,193)
Macaulay, John R	4:08:47 (10,920)
Macauley, James I	4:59:25 (23,354)

Macbeth, Kenneth D	2:58:54 (816)	
MacCormac, Oscar J	6:15:52 (33,674)	
MacDavid, Stephen J	5:37:08 (30,189)	
Macdonald, Adam	4:19:02 (13,335)	
Macdonald, Alexander J	3:56:26 (8,338)	
Macdonald, Calum	5:04:45 (24,457)	
Macdonald, Charles J	4:01:06 (9,436)	
Macdonald, Colin N	5:33:25 (29,667)	
Macdonald, David M	2:56:54 (666)	
Macdonald, George A	4:29:31 (16,013)	
Macdonald, Gordon W	4:24:36 (14,727)	
Macdonald, Graeme B	4:39:43 (18,466)	
Macdonald, Greg	2:44:57 (238)	
Macdonald, Harry	5:08:30 (25,188)	
Macdonald, Jonathan	6:20:19 (33,907)	
Macdonald, Keith W	3:41:26 (5,434)	
Macdonald, Keith W	4:52:46 (21,685)	
Macdonald, Robert	4:21:52 (14,055)	
Macdonald, Roddy J	4:22:22 (14,167)	
Macdonald, Ross J	4:50:58 (21,233)	
Macdonald, Steve S	5:06:13 (24,744)	
Macdonald, Stewart F	2:28:39 (34)	
Macdonald-Brown, James G	4:37:21 (17,848)	
MacDougall, Gary A	5:18:21 (27,135)	
MacDougall, Ian D	2:58:13 (762)	
Mace, Simon J	3:01:43 (992)	
MacEnhill, Damian P	3:04:52 (1,150)	
Macer, Dugald S	5:04:01 (24,328)	
Macey, Mark R	5:29:20 (29,047)	
Macey, Terence J	4:14:03 (12,112)	
MacFadyen, Angus	7:14:00 (35,334)	
Macfarlane, Brian S	3:30:10 (3,744)	
Macfarlane, Fraser B	5:23:25 (27,992)	
Macfarlane, Paul G	4:56:24 (22,613)	
Macfarlane, Richard J	4:44:28 (19,670)	
Macfarlane, Stuart M	4:47:24 (20,385)	
MacGregor, Alistaire	4:44:35 (19,712)	
MacGregor, Calum D	4:15:10 (12,360)	
MacGregor, John C	3:45:25 (6,086)	
MacGregor, Simon G	4:18:35 (13,234)	
MacGregor, Stuart A	3:54:30 (7,905)	
Machado, Manuel P	3:24:33 (2,964)	
Machida, Yoshihiro	4:54:28 (22,139)	
Machin, Geoffrey A	4:17:38 (12,982)	
Macintosh, Max B	4:00:51 (9,386)	
Macintyre, Ivan G	7:52:57 (35,632)	
Mack, Darren R	2:55:20 (589)	
Mack, Keith J	3:35:41 (4,511)	
Mack, Stephen	4:35:47 (17,483)	
Mack, Timothy A	3:54:29 (7,899)	
Mackaness, Matthew G	4:10:50 (11,335)	
Mackay, Andrew	4:29:48 (16,090)	
Mackay, Brian W	4:15:36 (12,460)	
Mackay, David H	5:28:44 (28,936)	
Mackay, Graeme	3:31:53 (3,969)	
Mackay, Ian	2:51:50 (434)	
Mackay, John A	3:21:22 (2,637)	
Mackay, Michael	3:16:53 (2,169)	
Mackay, Mike	3:46:53 (6,318)	
Mackay, Ross W	4:50:55 (21,221)	
Macken, Robert T	5:21:39 (27,726)	
Mackender, Troy A	4:08:05 (10,787)	
Mackenzie, Adrian B	4:29:50 (16,101)	
Mackenzie, Alexander J	3:26:59 (3,278)	
Mackenzie, Andrew V	6:20:16 (33,903)	
Mackenzie, Gordon D	4:05:00 (10,143)	
Mackenzie, James W	4:44:31 (19,692)	
Mackenzie, Jason	3:20:52 (2,593)	
Mackenzie, Matthew R	4:06:53 (10,547)	
Mackenzie, Robin K	3:26:47 (3,236)	
Mackenzie, Stuart D	4:22:42 (14,258)	
Mackervoy, Stephen M	4:31:35 (16,481)	
Mackey, Richard	3:57:36 (8,624)	
Mackie, Craig	5:13:31 (26,126)	
Mackness, Anthony S	3:20:08 (2,509)	
Mackworth Gee, Alistair	4:44:40 (19,734)	
MacLachlan, Michael C	4:38:20 (18,106)	
MacLachlan, Neil	3:10:19 (1,588)	
MacLagan, Ross A	5:18:05 (27,074)	
Maclaren, Donald B	3:10:16 (1,583)	
Maclean, Christopher G	4:56:51 (22,735)	
Maclean, Colin W	4:52:09 (21,527)	
Maclean, Fergus R	2:35:11 (72)	
Maclean, Matthew E	5:14:42 (26,381)	
Maclean, Rod A	4:51:46 (21,430)	
MacLennean, William	5:14:54 (26,428)	
Macleod, Andrew J	3:41:29 (5,443)	
Macleod, Angus	4:54:23 (22,117)	
Macleod, Daniel L	4:18:45 (13,276)	
Macleod, Dougals G	4:49:37 (20,920)	
Macleod, Iain J	4:29:50 (16,101)	
Macleod, Michael H	4:40:54 (18,760)	
Macmillan, Stuart	4:36:16 (17,602)	
MacNamara, James J	4:44:09 (19,579)	
MacNamara, Paul	3:35:58 (4,544)	
MacNaughton, Robert M	4:06:03 (10,361)	
MacNeil, Ewen K	4:13:29 (11,956)	
MacNiallais, Donncha P	4:41:47 (18,989)	
MacNish Porter, James A	6:05:41 (33,022)	
MacPhail, Scott H	4:01:48 (9,568)	
Macpherson, Alan A	3:04:55 (1,155)	
MacQuarrie, Hugh	4:28:28 (15,720)	
MacQueen, Anthony N	3:35:47 (4,521)	
MacQueen, Ian M	5:28:38 (28,926)	
Macrae, Duncan J	2:34:04 (63)	
Macrae, Scott	5:11:35 (25,778)	
Macro, Anthony J	5:32:46 (29,571)	
Macrosson, Ker G	3:52:44 (7,511)	
MacTavish, Scott L	4:40:35 (18,678)	
Madarbux, Rahim	3:54:10 (7,833)	
Maddams, Andrew J	3:51:41 (7,290)	
Maddams, Roger J	5:17:28 (26,951)	
Madden, Peter	3:59:54 (9,185)	
Madders, Craig P	5:13:32 (26,129)	
Maddison, David	3:55:33 (8,126)	
Maddison, Michael S	3:26:52 (3,251)	
Maddison, Peter J	3:47:59 (6,522)	
Maddock, Andrew J	5:52:25 (31,912)	
Maddock, Raymonde	3:32:47 (4,102)	
Maddocks, Jordan	3:09:35 (1,522)	
Maddocks, Terry	4:31:17 (16,419)	
Maddy, John D	3:53:07 (7,594)	
Mader, Reinhard	4:19:20 (13,412)	
Madge, Anthony C	3:18:13 (2,314)	
Madge, Daniel	7:32:56 (35,515)	
Madrazo Pintado, Roberto	3:39:35 (5,121)	
Madrazo Rosas, Federico	3:43:55 (5,852)	
Madsen, Ben R	3:14:16 (1,921)	
Madsen, Harald G	5:20:15 (27,467)	
Madsen, John Leth	3:40:44 (5,306)	
Maecker, Otto	5:39:36 (30,545)	
Maeno, Shoji	3:43:18 (5,739)	
Mafham, Paul J	4:50:01 (20,998)	
Magang, Thola	4:36:56 (17,774)	
Magdzinski, Tom M	4:29:07 (15,893)	
Magee, James P	4:26:25 (15,164)	
Maggs, Keith A	4:57:11 (22,819)	
Maggs, Nigel J	3:56:11 (8,270)	
Maggs, Simon	3:18:46 (2,364)	
Magill, John A	3:49:50 (6,904)	
Magnusson, Jan	3:28:50 (3,545)	
Magoffin, Hamish R	3:41:52 (5,497)	
Maguire, Luke T	5:49:47 (31,659)	
Maguire, Michael	4:23:54 (14,544)	
Maguire, Paul M	5:49:47 (31,659)	
Maguire, Trevor A	3:03:44 (1,088)	
Maher, Alastair J	3:36:01 (4,551)	
Maher, Andrew J	4:28:13 (15,649)	
Maher, Christopher J	3:33:13 (4,168)	
Maher, Paul J	4:45:44 (19,996)	
Maheswaran, Shanmuga S	5:44:40 (31,119)	
Maheswaran, Tim	5:20:48 (27,573)	
Mahfoor, Alam	5:13:29 (26,120)	
Mahmood, Arshad	4:57:00 (22,772)	
Mahmood, Talat T	5:11:54 (25,834)	
Mahmut, Paul J	5:13:49 (26,194)	
Mahoney, Anthony J	4:37:42 (17,917)	
Mahoney, Clive	4:42:44 (19,238)	
Mahoney, James	4:13:28 (11,951)	
Mahoney, Luke	5:08:45 (25,234)	
Mahoney, Mark	5:25:17 (28,318)	
Mahoney, Matt	3:21:28 (2,646)	
Mahoney, Paul	4:11:25 (11,478)	
Mahoney, Philip C	4:51:05 (21,262)	
Mahoney, Tom S	4:17:58 (13,064)	
Mahsoudi, Bruno E	3:24:39 (2,977)	
Maidment, Malcolm A	5:47:01 (31,356)	
Maidment, Mike E	4:54:02 (22,029)	
Main, Iain D	6:12:41 (33,472)	
Main, Peter	3:41:55 (5,504)	
Mainstone, Stephen D	3:54:13 (7,843)	
Mainwaring, Rupert W	4:20:16 (13,670)	
Mair, Alastair R	4:09:01 (10,954)	
Mair, Ian W	3:49:45 (6,884)	
Mairs, Graham	3:26:55 (3,261)	
Mairs, Stuart	6:16:10 (33,692)	
Major, Anthony J	5:18:19 (27,128)	
Major, Jason S	3:28:55 (3,561)	
Major, Paul	6:17:43 (33,766)	
Makepeace, Alan D	4:16:15 (12,634)	
Makewell, Adam S	5:38:44 (30,422)	
Makin, Andy	5:29:35 (29,082)	
Makin, Frank H	3:41:22 (5,421)	
Makin, Paul	5:03:00 (24,121)	
Makings, Philip C	3:19:01 (2,394)	
Makker, Tarun	4:22:21 (14,164)	
Makoku, Ivan K	4:45:30 (19,952)	
Makuwa, Bill	3:13:41 (1,872)	
Mal, Firouz	3:58:55 (8,942)	
Mal, Neema M	3:57:57 (8,708)	
Malcharek, Mark J	4:47:26 (20,389)	
Malcolm, Andy J	6:11:04 (33,374)	
Malcolmson, Philip	4:20:47 (13,792)	
Male, Tony K	5:40:05 (30,605)	
Malecot, Jean	3:52:28 (7,462)	
Maleedy, Christian A	4:18:22 (13,165)	
Maleguri, Giuseppe	5:07:32 (25,007)	
Maley, Matthew	5:32:19 (29,498)	
Malham, Kevin J	5:14:46 (26,400)	
Malherbe, Isak J	5:15:28 (26,556)	
Malherbe, Stephen P	4:28:58 (15,852)	
Mali, Jarkko J	4:18:31 (13,217)	
Malik, Muhammad T	7:41:23 (35,576)	
Malin, Robert M	3:28:49 (3,541)	
Malin, Stephen A	4:23:19 (14,402)	
Malinki, Daniel	5:49:37 (31,642)	
Malins, Alastair	4:52:02 (21,492)	
Malkin, Nicholas J	4:48:01 (20,535)	
Malkin, Paul	3:59:03 (8,972)	
Mallen, Garry C	4:22:01 (14,089)	
Mallen, James L	7:02:18 (35,164)	
Mallet, Karl A	5:33:37 (29,705)	
Mallet, Sebastien	4:44:28 (19,670)	
Mallett, Stephen J	3:54:04 (7,806)	
Mallett, William A	5:36:00 (30,048)	
Mallinson, Conrad	4:36:41 (17,714)	
Mallinson, Matthew	4:18:37 (13,245)	
Mallinson, Richard	4:08:19 (10,835)	
Mallison, Duncan	3:39:06 (5,033)	
Mallon, Paul A	4:21:39 (13,995)	
Mallory, David J	4:38:40 (18,188)	
Malmontet, Gilbert J	3:52:05 (7,389)	
Malmqvist, Tony	3:21:19 (2,636)	
Malone, Gary	6:09:42 (33,285)	
Malone, James R	4:56:40 (22,686)	
Malone, Kevin I	5:00:21 (23,587)	
Malone, Lawrence	3:38:28 (4,915)	
Maloney, Liam E	3:33:37 (4,217)	
Maloney, Mark J	4:29:45 (16,075)	
Malsom, Dominic J	3:38:02 (4,837)	
Malsom, Dominic M	3:41:56 (5,507)	
Malyon, Tony	5:43:45 (31,019)	
Malysse, Geert	5:18:51 (27,221)	
Malyszek, Wulf	3:30:16 (3,759)	
Manceau, Luc	4:21:22 (13,926)	
Mancer, Jez	2:50:59 (408)	
Manchester, Iain D	4:51:25 (21,348)	
Mancuso, Angelo	3:53:19 (7,648)	
Mancuso, Filippo	4:58:11 (23,070)	
Mancuso, Riccardo	4:11:16 (11,444)	
Mander, David	5:33:07 (29,622)	
Mandray, Phillippe	3:11:55 (1,718)	
Mandrou, Christian	3:09:28 (1,513)	
Manek, Ronak	5:26:00 (28,455)	
Manford, James	4:44:09 (19,570)	
Manfredi, Andrea	3:37:41 (4,773)	
Manger, Garth S	4:27:04 (15,345)	
Mangion, Ted F	4:58:42 (23,189)	
Manheim, Shlomo	5:00:34 (23,629)	

Manir-Jolley, Mohammed............3:11:27 (1,667)
Manley, Simon J............4:16:43 (12,741)
Mann, Alan S............3:56:51 (8,444)
Mann, Andrew P............4:35:53 (17,508)
Mann, Craig............3:15:35 (2,034)
Mann, Dave K............4:07:57 (10,760)
Mann, Dean............3:20:05 (2,505)
Mann, Fergus............4:01:36 (9,535)
Mann, Julian............2:43:49 (209)
Mann, Lee J............4:28:05 (15,616)
Mann, Mark............5:05:09 (24,536)
Mann, Peter C............2:57:54 (740)
Mann, Steve............4:46:56 (20,262)
Mann, Stuart H............3:37:44 (4,780)
Mann, Thomas J............4:40:30 (18,659)
Mann, Tom J............5:24:38 (28,204)
Manna, Angelo............2:53:57 (519)
Manners, Philip B............5:37:09 (30,192)
Manning, Charles B............4:55:19 (22,341)
Manning, Jason............3:23:29 (2,851)
Manning, John R............3:47:44 (6,486)
Manning, Joseph A............4:27:24 (15,448)
Manning, Julian H............3:00:53 (948)
Manning, Paul............4:15:41 (12,480)
Manning, Paul P............3:14:48 (1,968)
Manning, Richard R............6:01:20 (32,706)
Manning, Robert P............4:34:06 (17,050)
Manning, Roger A............4:38:44 (18,208)
Manning, Stephen............4:46:20 (20,135)
Manning, Timothy T............5:23:48 (28,079)
Mannion, Christopher M............6:16:06 (33,686)
Mannix, Robert P............3:46:59 (6,342)
Manolescu, Nicolae S............5:42:29 (30,877)
Manouelides, Christophe............3:38:56 (5,002)
Mansbirdge, Anthony............7:29:33 (35,490)
Mansell, Christopher............6:01:01 (32,675)
Mansell, Peter............4:19:24 (13,431)
Mansell, Robert J............5:09:18 (25,333)
Mansfield, Brian A............4:36:52 (17,758)
Mansfield, Christopher C............5:06:56 (24,865)
Mansfield, Christopher D............3:54:57 (8,000)
Mansfield, Grant............4:59:33 (23,399)
Mansfield, Iain W............3:38:54 (4,998)
Mansfield, Michael R............4:42:28 (19,171)
Mansfield, Michael S............3:15:10 (2,010)
Mansfield, Philip M............5:24:50 (28,243)
Mansfield, Richard J............5:11:12 (25,703)
Mansfield, Ron............5:46:21 (31,298)
Mansfield, Stephen P............4:26:23 (15,155)
Mansi, Andrew J............3:23:09 (2,815)
Manson, David J............3:44:05 (5,878)
Manson, James............3:51:06 (7,160)
Manson, Peter............4:25:06 (14,848)
Mansoor, Shahid............5:52:10 (31,889)
Mantel, David G............4:27:15 (15,407)
Manton, Christopher J............4:38:05 (18,035)
Manuel, Philip R............4:14:34 (12,222)
Manze, David P............5:55:16 (32,170)
Manzi, Marcello............4:37:37 (17,914)
Manzini, David............3:26:11 (3,155)
Maoakes, David P............4:53:38 (21,924)
Mapes, Neil A............4:36:09 (17,571)
Maraia, Antonio............3:43:25 (5,756)
Marais, Charel P............4:17:51 (13,032)
Marais, Ernest J............4:07:32 (10,658)
Marais, Wessel............4:35:33 (17,415)
Marangoni, Andrea E............5:48:38 (31,535)
Marc, Mewis............4:39:36 (18,437)
Marcar, Rik M............4:16:15 (12,634)
Marcato, Germano............5:46:33 (31,313)
Marcato, Stefano............3:57:31 (8,602)
Marcelle, Nick P............4:18:28 (13,201)
March, Steve P............3:13:21 (1,854)
March, Steven D............3:22:56 (2,789)
Marchand, Paul J............3:55:33 (8,126)
Marchant, Nigel F............4:31:54 (16,542)
Marchant, Ross F............4:01:09 (9,452)
Marchant, Simon............4:03:28 (9,860)
Marchesi, Ernesto............3:11:39 (1,691)
Marcinkowski, Dariusz............5:39:20 (30,494)
Marcucci, Paolo............4:31:23 (16,441)
Marek, Robert K............4:46:09 (20,092)
Marghani, Essam M............5:59:09 (32,520)
Margolis, Geoffrey A............4:38:20 (18,106)
Margossian, Arnaud N............3:53:54 (7,765)
Mariani, Stefano............5:44:03 (31,048)
Mariault, Louis............4:19:46 (13,532)
Marie, Antonio............5:25:23 (28,335)
Marigliano, Arturo............4:00:12 (9,250)
Maris, Pantelis............5:29:39 (29,091)
Marjeram, Neil B............4:24:57 (14,814)
Markham, Alexander D............5:09:15 (25,326)
Markham, Dean............4:24:17 (14,651)
Markham, Jack G............4:55:49 (22,461)
Marklew, Steve............2:52:07 (446)
Markley, Nick D............4:24:07 (14,603)
Marks, David C............5:06:36 (24,798)
Marks, John-Paul F............4:59:50 (23,463)
Marks, Paul............4:15:50 (12,518)
Marks, Paul E............5:55:28 (32,188)
Marks, Paul W............4:24:03 (14,585)
Marks, Stuart A............3:36:19 (4,589)
Markwick, David C............4:31:12 (16,407)
Marland, Edward J............3:55:40 (8,155)
Marley, Nigel R............2:58:02 (749)
Marlow, Giles D............4:40:59 (18,780)
Marlow, Paul............4:41:55 (19,020)
Marlow, Paul C............3:53:12 (7,618)
Marner, Oliver J............5:02:45 (24,084)
Marotta, Ciro............4:10:36 (11,287)
Marquand, Ben G............4:42:52 (19,273)
Marques, David............3:23:04 (2,803)
Marquez, Axel I............4:52:04 (21,503)
Marr, Irvine............3:44:28 (5,936)
Marr, Peter C............3:42:51 (5,657)
Marr, Richard A............5:35:35 (29,992)
Marrero, Jorge L............5:26:27 (28,539)
Marriage, Paul S............5:57:36 (32,376)
Marriage, Sampson J............4:19:36 (13,486)
Marriott, Andrew C............4:34:00 (17,034)
Marriott, Brian C............4:48:12 (20,578)
Marriott, Craig............4:01:55 (9,591)
Marriott, David P............4:50:44 (21,172)
Marriott, James J............4:28:35 (15,754)
Marriott, Kevin J............4:37:36 (17,911)
Marriott, Richard J............3:30:42 (3,806)
Marriott, Robert............4:30:51 (16,324)
Marrow, Robert M............7:24:10 (35,426)
Marrs, Nicholas............3:32:05 (4,004)
Marsan, David A............4:02:44 (9,740)
Marsden, John............5:15:56 (26,648)
Marsden, John G............4:20:10 (13,645)
Marsden, Paul J............5:08:32 (25,193)
Marsden, Peter K............3:38:58 (5,009)
Marseglia, Pasquale............2:51:45 (431)
Marsh, Adrian N............3:05:41 (1,216)
Marsh, Daniel J............5:39:30 (30,530)
Marsh, Darren L............5:33:51 (29,737)
Marsh, David J............4:17:06 (12,830)
Marsh, Jim............5:03:51 (24,298)
Marsh, Jonathan N............4:03:22 (9,844)
Marsh, Julian A............4:19:49 (13,544)
Marsh, Nigel............3:58:39 (8,871)
Marsh, Patrick C............4:16:43 (12,741)
Marsh, Paul C............4:11:49 (11,573)
Marsh, Philip D............5:21:16 (27,650)
Marsh, Ryan............4:40:04 (18,549)
Marsh, Simon J............3:50:56 (7,123)
Marsh, Stephen J............5:01:15 (23,785)
Marsh, Steven J............4:09:40 (11,108)
Marsh, Thomas J............5:09:51 (25,439)
Marsh, Timothy W............3:29:50 (3,695)
Marshall, Andrew............3:22:21 (2,732)
Marshall, Andrew............7:29:24 (35,482)
Marshall, Andrew J............3:55:08 (8,039)
Marshall, Brent............4:40:51 (18,747)
Marshall, Cameron A............4:42:00 (19,038)
Marshall, Damon L............5:35:07 (29,929)
Marshall, Daniel J............4:47:35 (20,432)
Marshall, Daniel P............5:19:06 (27,267)
Marshall, Giles R............4:34:49 (17,225)
Marshall, Ian T............3:26:25 (3,189)
Marshall, James............4:22:47 (14,281)
Marshall, James A............6:01:06 (32,684)
Marshall, Jim N............3:56:40 (8,396)
Marshall, John............6:18:35 (33,810)
Marshall, Jonathan P............4:02:17 (9,667)
Marshall, Julian E............4:23:39 (14,477)
Marshall, Keith R............4:42:34 (19,195)
Marshall, Kevin J............3:11:01 (1,633)
Marshall, Matthew............4:06:21 (10,423)
Marshall, Michael............5:54:19 (32,082)
Marshall, Niall G............3:44:19 (5,908)
Marshall, Norman H............4:48:53 (20,740)
Marshall, Paul D............4:24:46 (14,771)
Marshall, Peter............4:43:30 (19,414)
Marshall, Simon P............3:54:38 (7,930)
Marshall, Stanley T............3:58:05 (8,738)
Marshall, Steven............4:20:02 (13,606)
Marsil, Jean-Claude............4:17:53 (13,038)
Marsland, Philip............4:33:39 (16,947)
Marsland, Steve J............4:37:57 (17,993)
Marston, Michael E............5:52:41 (31,937)
Marston, Richard I............5:52:36 (31,927)
Martell, Paul M............5:19:40 (27,369)
Martin, Adrian P............3:29:47 (3,686)
Martin, Alex............6:29:16 (34,297)
Martin, Alistair D............3:58:03 (8,735)
Martin, Andrew E............5:23:04 (27,945)
Martin, Andrew J............6:00:56 (32,661)
Martin, Andrew R............4:08:21 (10,842)
Martin, Andrew T............4:34:25 (17,118)
Martin, Christopher J............3:28:36 (3,505)
Martin, Colin J............4:21:18 (13,911)
Martin, Corin R............5:46:14 (31,287)
Martin, Darran J............5:59:26 (32,548)
Martin, David............5:09:11 (25,313)
Martin, David J............4:15:44 (12,491)
Martin, David R............4:48:17 (20,597)
Martin, Dean P............5:03:15 (24,182)
Martin, Denzil............4:19:49 (13,544)
Martin, Geoffrey C............4:52:04 (21,503)
Martin, Gerard P............4:35:35 (17,427)
Martin, Giles............4:51:19 (21,321)
Martin, Guy............6:33:03 (34,439)
Martin, Hugh W............4:20:06 (13,624)
Martin, Iain A............3:28:52 (3,550)
Martin, Ian R............5:22:15 (27,816)
Martin, James H............5:03:11 (24,170)
Martin, Jeffrey M............4:41:05 (18,807)
Martin, Jim............4:50:47 (21,189)
Martin, John A............5:22:43 (27,892)
Martin, Kenny............5:14:13 (26,270)
Martin, Kevin R............3:39:43 (5,146)
Martin, Matthew B............5:30:20 (29,190)
Martin, Mike............5:01:33 (23,843)
Martin, Neil J............3:55:55 (8,212)
Martin, Paul............3:48:45 (6,678)
Martin, Paul D............4:10:29 (11,261)
Martin, Paul J............4:09:33 (11,085)
Martin, Peter J............4:20:04 (13,618)
Martin, Philip A............3:14:53 (1,978)
Martin, Philip L............3:00:49 (944)
Martin, Richard............5:51:36 (31,837)
Martin, Rick J............3:50:49 (7,101)
Martin, Serge............3:19:36 (2,443)
Martin, Shane............5:14:49 (26,410)
Martin, Simon D............5:05:41 (24,631)
Martin, Steven............4:31:19 (16,428)
Martin, Thomas J............3:26:15 (3,166)
Martin, Tim J............4:36:59 (17,783)
Martin, Toby............4:55:59 (22,508)
Martin, Troy A............4:02:03 (9,612)
Martinelli, Louis............3:58:05 (8,738)
Martinez, Antonio J............3:47:52 (6,504)
Martinez, Candido............4:23:22 (14,411)
Martinez, Daniel............3:58:17 (8,786)
Martinez, Luis J............4:36:39 (17,704)
Martinez Diez, Miguel Angel............3:39:44 (5,148)
Martinez-Calcerrada, Luis............4:00:17 (9,269)
Martini, Franck M............3:56:00 (8,226)
Martini, Patrick G............4:01:38 (9,539)
Martins, Joao............5:12:23 (25,936)
Martin-Smith, Albert............6:09:01 (33,239)
Martin-Smith, Nick A............5:22:50 (27,912)
Martland, Raymond J............3:53:00 (7,570)
Martyn, Daniel............4:38:36 (18,177)
Martyn, Nicholas A............2:27:11 (30)
Maru, Tony C............3:12:16 (1,754)

Maruzzi, Lino 5:26:40 (28,571)
Marven, Roger A 4:47:11 (20,331)
Marwick, Clyde 2:55:39 (599)
Maryan, David E 5:33:19 (29,649)
Maryan, Michael E 5:33:19 (29,649)
Mas, Julien L 3:39:00 (5,017)
Masaba, Luke W 5:11:29 (25,750)
Masefield, Aaron C 5:32:54 (29,589)
Masefield, Andrew R 3:41:23 (5,425)
Masefield, Dean A 4:59:13 (23,314)
Masefield, Ian A 4:33:51 (17,002)
Masetti, Sandro 5:41:37 (30,781)
Masey, John S 5:09:24 (25,353)
Mashford, Graham H 6:14:23 (33,574)
Mashford, Roger 5:27:22 (28,688)
Mashford, Steve J 6:14:23 (33,574)
Mashru, Kanesh 5:23:45 (28,063)
Maske, Ulf 4:26:09 (15,084)
Maskell, Stuart A 7:14:34 (35,339)
Maslen, Andy M 4:26:19 (15,136)
Maslen, Jonathan H 6:04:56 (32,957)
Maslin, Mark 4:44:46 (19,763)
Mason, Andrea 3:34:07 (4,281)
Mason, Andrew C 4:39:19 (18,368)
Mason, Brendan 4:23:37 (14,470)
Mason, Charles 3:12:31 (1,778)
Mason, Chris J 5:35:43 (30,013)
Mason, Christopher 5:10:19 (25,540)
Mason, Christopher J 3:25:50 (3,103)
Mason, Dale J 6:05:32 (33,008)
Mason, Daniel 4:19:14 (13,387)
Mason, David E 6:09:50 (33,293)
Mason, Duncan A 3:52:24 (7,451)
Mason, Lee 4:57:08 (22,805)
Mason, Martin A 4:42:30 (19,178)
Mason, Matthew 5:41:52 (30,816)
Mason, Michael J 3:40:56 (5,353)
Mason, Paul 4:57:10 (22,811)
Mason, Peter 3:48:52 (6,697)
Mason, Peter A 4:47:33 (20,422)
Mason, Peter J 3:52:03 (7,378)
Mason, Thomas R 4:03:53 (9,945)
Mason, Tim J 5:47:39 (31,422)
Mason, Toby K 4:57:35 (22,926)
Massara, Nicholas A 3:17:53 (2,272)
Massey, Adrian P 3:22:20 (2,730)
Massey, Daniel E 6:26:00 (34,164)
Massey, Kevin 4:55:33 (22,404)
Massey, Stephen 3:21:55 (2,698)
Massey, Stuart A 4:38:17 (18,084)
Masson, Gilbert 4:46:49 (20,232)
Masson, Jim 4:41:01 (18,794)
Masterman, Andrew 3:08:36 (1,437)
Masters, Daniel J 4:40:22 (18,624)
Masters, David J 5:23:36 (28,029)
Masters, Lee B 4:06:48 (10,530)
Masters, Sam P 4:40:44 (18,706)
Masterson, James P 5:09:58 (25,469)
Mastrogiacomi, Angelo 5:18:52 (27,226)
Matalon, Joel D 4:00:22 (9,283)
Matcham, Derek J 3:28:09 (3,424)
Materne, Markus 4:53:30 (21,885)
Materne, Philippe R 5:04:39 (24,438)
Materne, Wolfgang 5:59:09 (32,520)
Matharu, Jagjivan S 4:52:39 (21,656)
Mathe, James E 5:27:10 (28,654)
Mathe, Jean Yves A 3:16:18 (2,104)
Mathebula, Ndumiso G 5:01:50 (23,897)
Mather, Peter 4:26:44 (15,245)
Mathers, Dale 3:25:41 (3,086)
Mathews, Andrew C 5:41:07 (30,718)
Mathieson, James E 4:10:00 (11,166)
Mathis, Armin 2:59:06 (832)
Mathurin, Mark A 5:16:27 (26,749)
Matin, Shamu 6:11:42 (33,408)
Matisonn, Shaun 3:45:21 (6,072)
Mativat, Fabrice 4:56:05 (22,532)
Matley, Kenny J 4:47:44 (20,464)
Matlock, Kevin M 4:55:33 (22,404)
Matrone, Vincenzo 5:49:03 (31,591)
Matson, Alistair G 3:37:57 (4,819)
Matsui, Keiichiro 5:50:48 (31,758)
Matsumura, Susmu 4:51:49 (21,440)
Matthai, Clarence C 5:08:12 (25,139)
Matthams, David J 4:45:29 (19,946)
Matthew, Paul 4:26:28 (15,179)
Matthews, Adrian S 5:19:10 (27,283)
Matthews, Andrew 5:39:29 (30,523)
Matthews, Andrew J 4:14:57 (12,311)
Matthews, Christopher 4:15:13 (12,370)
Matthews, Christopher J 3:49:34 (6,846)
Matthews, David 4:12:55 (11,809)
Matthews, David W 4:54:16 (22,095)
Matthews, Elis A 5:50:12 (31,693)
Matthews, Gair R 3:26:08 (3,146)
Matthews, Gareth R 3:21:48 (2,685)
Matthews, Hamilton I 5:25:15 (28,315)
Matthews, Hefin 3:23:06 (2,810)
Matthews, Ian R 3:39:04 (5,027)
Matthews, James D 3:44:26 (5,928)
Matthews, James H 4:02:24 (9,682)
Matthews, Jeffrey A 3:17:09 (2,195)
Matthews, Joe 6:45:32 (34,812)
Matthews, John S 4:44:09 (19,579)
Matthews, Johnny R 3:24:52 (3,006)
Matthews, Martin 2:35:40 (81)
Matthews, Paul 3:36:42 (4,646)
Matthews, Paul D 3:53:41 (7,725)
Matthews, Paul R 4:39:00 (18,283)
Matthews, Paul S 4:41:29 (18,915)
Matthews, Peter I 3:50:20 (7,008)
Matthews, Philip N 3:56:41 (8,399)
Matthews, Robert W 4:35:58 (17,527)
Matthews, Sean 2:59:59 (899)
Matthews, Shaun 5:25:51 (28,435)
Matthews, Stephen D 6:13:30 (33,519)
Matthews, Stuart 3:55:54 (8,208)
Matthews, Thomas 3:04:17 (1,119)
Mattingly, Roger A 5:01:32 (23,835)
Mattis, Darryn M 5:58:39 (32,482)
Mattison, Michael J 5:15:09 (26,490)
Mattison, Simon 4:34:40 (17,196)
Mattock, Robert A 4:56:00 (22,517)
Mattocks-Maxwell, Rickardo F 6:52:31 (34,983)
Mattson, Tony R 3:26:15 (3,166)
Mattsson, Bengt 4:52:31 (21,618)
Matyus-Flynn, Scott M 5:58:37 (32,477)
Mauck, Klaus-Dieter 4:23:37 (14,470)
Maude, Francis 4:41:07 (18,817)
Maull, Robert 4:11:39 (11,537)
Maurizi, Massimo 3:30:08 (3,740)
Maury, Neil 4:27:45 (15,533)
Maw, Richard G 3:11:48 (1,701)
Maw, Tim 4:34:46 (17,215)
Mawdsley, Alan G 3:31:10 (3,858)
Mawer, Roger 4:29:26 (15,986)
Maxfield, Simon P 5:12:31 (25,956)
Maxton, Drummond A 5:25:37 (28,390)
Maxwell, Andrew D 5:51:24 (31,815)
Maxwell, Graham 4:09:22 (11,044)
Maxwell, Greg W 3:30:31 (3,788)
Maxwell, Henry 3:54:05 (7,812)
Maxwell, John G 4:08:59 (10,948)
Maxwell, Paul 5:50:27 (31,722)
Maxwell, Paul P 3:25:05 (3,028)
May, Adrian 4:54:47 (22,223)
May, Andrew J 3:21:44 (2,677)
May, Andrew P 4:48:44 (20,706)
May, Andy 4:46:58 (20,269)
May, Daniel G 5:33:45 (29,722)
May, Danny J 4:13:02 (11,840)
May, David 4:05:02 (10,150)
May, James E 6:19:36 (33,868)
May, John C 5:17:26 (26,944)
May, Jonathan E 3:50:03 (6,955)
May, Kevin 3:04:19 (1,122)
May, Mark J 4:23:47 (14,508)
May, Peter 4:17:57 (13,058)

LONDON MARATHON

May, Ross A 5:03:23 (24,213)
May, Stephen J 4:14:32 (12,211)
May, Steven E 5:14:22 (26,305)
May, Tom 3:26:18 (3,176)
May, Vincent J 3:27:26 (3,347)
Mayall, Philip 3:50:27 (7,029)
Mayer, Charles R 4:40:10 (18,573)
Mayger, Boris 4:47:06 (20,313)
Mayhew, John D 4:26:16 (15,123)
Mayhew, Jonathan E 4:33:01 (16,791)
Mayhew, Roy 6:31:38 (34,388)
Mayhew, Simon M 5:02:53 (24,102)
Maynar, Javier 3:38:41 (4,954)
Maynard, Graham L 3:24:16 (2,935)
Maynard, James L 4:32:11 (16,604)
Maynard, Peter J 7:05:17 (35,207)
Maynard, Steven 4:45:31 (19,954)
Mayo, Garry J 5:04:21 (24,390)
Mayo, Philip I 3:17:02 (2,183)
Mayoh, Paul 4:54:33 (22,154)
Mayor, Gines E 3:51:50 (7,324)
Mays, Robert A 4:27:17 (15,416)
Mayson, Howard J 4:18:36 (13,240)
Mayson, Michael 5:21:43 (27,734)
Maywood, Paul C 7:23:44 (35,422)
Maze, Lee 4:24:15 (14,643)
Mazur, first name unknown 4:05:46 (10,300)
Mazur, Lukasz A 5:16:14 (26,706)
Mazza, Gordon P 4:16:00 (12,562)
Mazzola, Fernando 3:48:42 (6,666)
Mazzone, Tony 4:55:50 (22,468)
M'bengue, Aboubacar 3:33:07 (4,156)
McAdam, Bobby C 5:09:45 (25,425)
McAdam, Duncan S 4:08:04 (10,782)
McAdam, Sean J 4:59:41 (23,427)
McAfee, William A 5:07:19 (24,960)
McAleenan, John 3:20:52 (2,593)
McAleer, Jason J 4:38:20 (18,106)
McAlister, Joseph 2:27:10 (29)
McAllister, Andrew P 5:19:26 (27,326)
McAllister, Darren J 2:58:02 (749)
McAllister, Gordon 3:40:52 (5,337)
McAllister, James A 6:21:23 (33,975)
McAllister, John D 6:02:35 (32,790)
McAllister, Williams A 4:04:57 (10,135)
McArdle, Philip G 4:34:21 (17,104)
McArthur, Keith J 3:35:06 (4,420)
McArthur, Robert 4:00:47 (9,369)
McAsey, Adrian 3:47:01 (6,350)
McAteer, Paul A 5:39:09 (30,470)
McAuley, Damian 2:46:57 (284)
McAuley, Roddy M 6:31:21 (34,374)
McAuslan-Crine, Simon F 5:47:12 (31,371)
McAvoy, Richard 4:22:43 (14,264)
McBride, Hugh A 7:03:37 (35,185)
McBride, Iain A 3:35:21 (4,460)
McBride, Martin G 3:26:36 (3,206)
McBride, Michael P 3:27:14 (3,318)
McBride, Neil 4:47:39 (20,441)
McBrown, Philip 4:21:31 (13,971)
McBurney, Sean L 4:52:08 (21,521)
McCabe, Andrew 6:05:00 (32,963)
McCabe, Dan 6:35:23 (34,518)
McCabe, David C 5:13:24 (26,102)
McCabe, Gerry 4:02:02 (9,608)
McCabe, Michael E 3:00:49 (944)
McCabe, Phil 4:29:22 (15,964)
McCabe, Terence P 4:01:57 (9,594)
McCaffrey, Robert J 3:30:48 (3,820)
McCahill, Jonathan J 3:25:54 (3,115)
McCall, Laurence M 4:40:37 (18,682)
McCall, Robert 3:27:12 (3,309)
McCallion, Seamus M 3:16:19 (2,105)
McCandless, James 5:26:13 (28,495)
McCandless, Paul J 4:27:12 (15,387)
McCann, Christopher J 4:42:10 (19,082)
McCann, Gerard J 4:54:35 (22,168)
McCann, James 5:44:04 (31,049)
McCann, John D 3:51:41 (7,290)
McCann, John F 3:56:41 (8,399)
McCann, John G 5:42:08 (30,839)
McCann, Michael 4:08:12 (10,811)
McCann, Michael 4:40:26 (18,638)

McCann, Paul......................4:00:25 (9,297)
McCartan, Stephen 5:12:16 (25,915)
McCarter, Domonic 2:41:30 (167)
McCarthy, Bernard.................7:27:51 (35,455)
McCarthy, Bernard J 5:30:55 (29,282)
McCarthy, Ciaran 5:20:46 (27,567)
McCarthy, Craig A..................5:05:28 (24,595)
McCarthy, Damon L..................5:39:06 (30,463)
McCarthy, Daniel K 4:45:54 (20,033)
McCarthy, Dean J 5:52:36 (31,927)
McCarthy, Des J 3:41:43 (5,472)
McCarthy, Gregory J..................5:47:41 (31,427)
McCarthy, Ian A 5:25:13 (28,308)
McCarthy, Ian J..................4:45:09 (19,870)
McCarthy, Ian S 4:43:53 (19,505)
McCarthy, James A 4:52:36 (21,642)
McCarthy, James D 4:24:47 (14,773)
McCarthy, Keith D..................5:41:04 (30,714)
McCarthy, Patrick 5:17:33 (26,969)
McCarthy, Paul A..................5:13:47 (26,186)
McCarthy, Paul J..................5:30:24 (29,200)
McCarthy, Peter J 4:43:37 (19,444)
McCarthy, Richard W..................5:39:39 (30,551)
McCarthy, Scott P..................6:13:55 (33,543)
McCarthy, Sean G..................3:28:44 (3,529)
McCarthy, Tim A..................4:50:34 (21,139)
McCarthy, Timothy 4:01:32 (9,518)
McCauley, David T 3:53:40 (7,721)
McCavana, Dermot P 4:29:57 (16,134)
McClay, Richard G 5:01:13 (23,776)
McClean, Colin G..................4:07:09 (10,600)
McClean, Mike 4:38:18 (18,093)
McCleery, Andrew G 4:18:07 (13,103)
McClellan, Steve F..................5:29:51 (29,114)
McClelland, Paul B 3:11:56 (1,719)
McClorry, Paul..................4:33:24 (16,892)
McCloud, Neil 4:23:39 (14,477)
McCloud, Victor A 4:29:11 (15,906)
McCloy, Ciaran 4:15:50 (12,518)
McClumpha, William C 5:27:29 (28,710)
McCluney, Michael J 4:00:10 (9,242)
McClung, Edward 5:10:43 (25,612)
McClure, Conor R..................4:20:51 (13,817)
McClure, Gary R..................4:25:35 (14,963)
McClure, Greg M 3:00:24 (924)
McClure, Steven 3:39:52 (5,171)
McCluskey, Andrew P..................3:24:12 (2,929)
McCluskey, Shaun 4:50:50 (21,200)
McCluskie, Kristen 4:19:10 (13,370)
McClutchie, Mike 4:16:35 (12,712)
McComb, Michael S..................3:14:49 (1,971)
McCombie, Gregor 3:20:24 (2,542)
McCombie, Stuart..................3:27:09 (3,302)
McConnachie, Iain 4:58:08 (23,060)
McConnell, Barry..................3:00:50 (947)
McConnell, Stephen A 3:46:25 (6,240)
McConochie, Andrew 3:39:25 (5,093)
McConville, John P 3:17:43 (2,259)
McCormack, Brendan..................6:05:18 (32,985)
McCormack, Cormac J..................4:25:33 (14,955)
McCormack, David 4:26:28 (15,179)
McCormack, Dermot 4:41:55 (19,020)
McCormack, Garry A 4:59:11 (23,302)
McCormack, James R 4:22:58 (14,322)
McCormack, Matthew J 7:02:04 (35,159)
McCormack, Stephen 4:46:25 (20,157)
McCormack, Wayne P..................6:59:06 (35,113)
McCormick, Andrew B 3:29:03 (3,581)
McCormick, Andrew D 6:05:43 (33,023)
McCormick, Martin..................4:15:25 (12,421)
McCormick, Peter 4:07:29 (10,647)
McCosker-Smith, James R..................4:44:17 (19,621)
McCowen, James W..................3:18:54 (2,381)
McCoy, Andrew J..................2:45:03 (242)
McCoy, Colin 4:59:40 (23,425)
McCoy, David T 3:33:18 (4,179)
McCoy, Edward J 5:28:47 (28,950)
McCoy, Robin E..................3:29:20 (3,625)
McCracken, Andrew G..................4:05:22 (10,212)
McCrae, James A 5:02:36 (24,057)
McCrea, Richard C..................3:32:16 (4,040)
McCreadie, John 5:56:23 (32,276)
McCready, David A..................6:10:11 (33,316)

McCreton, Josh L 5:07:44 (25,042)
McCrone, Paul R..................3:29:26 (3,640)
McCrory, Denis 5:25:19 (28,323)
McCrory, Finn M..................3:17:27 (2,226)
McCrossin, Paul A..................2:54:53 (573)
McCudden, Paul J..................3:49:02 (6,740)
McCullagh, Colin 4:19:23 (13,427)
McCullen, Sam 3:59:21 (9,053)
McCullie, Alec 4:53:26 (21,876)
McCulloch, Aaron 5:14:08 (26,253)
McCulloch, Gary 6:16:15 (33,701)
McCulloch, Jonathan B 3:44:39 (5,967)
McCulloch, William S 4:49:01 (20,771)
McCurrie, Mark T 5:31:23 (29,359)
McCurry, Stephen 3:56:20 (8,314)
McCusker, Eamonn P 4:01:15 (9,470)
McCutcheon, Andrew W 5:32:39 (29,560)
McDade, Norman 5:20:13 (27,459)
McDaid, Gerard 4:52:31 (21,618)
McDerment, Leslie J 3:17:27 (2,226)
McDermid, Paul 4:02:13 (9,652)
McDermott, Dennis P 4:45:35 (19,962)
McDermott, Emilio B..................3:49:06 (6,751)
McDermott, Gregory J 3:12:00 (1,727)
McDermott, Nigel 4:11:31 (11,505)
McDiarmid, Grear C 5:10:50 (25,631)
McDonagh, Luke 5:27:09 (28,646)
McDonald, Alan 3:16:53 (2,169)
McDonald, Colin 5:15:42 (26,602)
McDonald, Don 3:44:20 (5,916)
McDonald, Gordon A 4:28:28 (15,720)
McDonald, John 5:56:28 (32,282)
McDonald, John D 4:26:05 (15,070)
McDonald, Kevin P 6:00:43 (32,639)
McDonald, Maurice G 5:24:45 (28,230)
McDonald, Miles K..................4:09:58 (11,159)
McDonald, Peter 3:23:47 (2,876)
McDonald, Philip F 3:46:25 (6,240)
McDonald, Robert 3:40:45 (5,310)
McDonald, Sean 4:04:56 (10,133)
McDonald, Simon 4:18:32 (13,221)
McDonald, Stephen G 5:51:12 (31,796)
McDonald, Stephen P..................3:51:37 (7,279)
McDonald, Terry J..................4:15:55 (12,533)
McDonald-Liggins, Anthony N ...4:38:04 (18,028)
McDonnell, first name unknown 4:32:05 (16,578)
McDonnell, Terence P 5:23:02 (27,941)
McDonough, Robert K 3:34:48 (4,379)
McDougal, Richard J..................4:22:51 (14,301)
McDougall, Grant R..................4:49:22 (20,853)
McDowall, Alan S 4:00:40 (9,349)
McDowall, Ewan J..................4:55:00 (22,264)
McDowell, Robert W..................4:20:12 (13,655)
McEaughey, Paul D 5:16:12 (26,700)
McElligott, Matthew D..................4:23:12 (14,379)
McElwee, Stephen P 3:58:39 (8,871)
McEntaggart, Eamonn A 7:08:19 (35,252)
McEntee, Colin 4:34:32 (17,156)
McEntee, Scott 4:15:43 (12,487)
McEntee, Sean 3:13:43 (1,876)
McEvilly, Ian 3:46:09 (6,203)
McEvoy, Antony..................5:00:16 (23,568)
McEvoy, Gavin P 6:03:39 (32,866)
McEvoy, Julian S 5:37:37 (30,250)
McEvoy, Michael S..................4:56:36 (22,662)
McEwan, David J 4:43:58 (19,527)
McEwan, Joe 4:29:00 (15,856)
McEwan, Robert..................3:00:59 (959)
McEwing, David..................3:49:58 (6,932)
McFadden, Anthony 4:13:57 (12,084)
McFadden, Jay 5:20:55 (27,593)
McFadden, Kevin 6:34:02 (34,467)
McFadden, Kieran C..................7:21:55 (35,405)
McFadden, Paul L..................3:26:42 (3,223)
McFadzean, Angus 3:56:12 (8,274)
McFarlane, James W..................3:36:17 (4,585)
McFarlane, John..................2:22:18 (17)
McFarlane, William 6:34:45 (34,484)
McFeeters, Mark D..................4:26:57 (15,312)
McGaffney, Brendan N 6:25:43 (34,156)
McGarty, Eddy A..................5:37:53 (30,285)
McGarvey, Kevin 5:04:04 (24,337)
McGee, Aidan P 6:20:27 (33,918)

McGee, Michael G 4:49:27 (20,874)
McGeoch, Mick..................2:57:02 (680)
McGeorge, Lee..................6:25:04 (34,130)
McGeown, Michael H 3:30:20 (3,771)
McGhee, James A 3:50:13 (6,977)
McGill, Colin A..................2:44:08 (218)
McGill, Trevor A..................3:24:18 (2,941)
McGilloway, Paul 3:57:20 (8,561)
McGilloway, Paula 3:57:20 (8,561)
McGinley, Ciaran 5:19:55 (27,412)
McGivern, Jeremy 4:16:54 (12,785)
McGivern, Kieran 4:58:50 (23,216)
McGivern, Mike B 4:44:46 (19,763)
McGlachie, Steven M 4:26:24 (15,161)
McGlade, Anthony 3:56:30 (8,360)
McGlasson, John R..................4:29:24 (15,976)
McGlennon, David L 3:58:50 (8,921)
McGoldick, Michael J..................3:58:23 (8,805)
McGoldrick, Andy 4:11:16 (11,444)
McGonagle, John 4:11:03 (11,383)
McGonnell, John 4:32:50 (16,748)
McGough, Kevin S 4:23:45 (14,502)
McGoun, Neil A 3:15:07 (2,006)
McGovern, Aidan 4:12:40 (11,761)
McGowan, Brian P 4:26:59 (15,321)
McGowan, first name unknown ..5:26:12 (28,491)
McGowan, John J 4:28:07 (15,626)
McGowan, Michael 3:43:43 (5,816)
McGowan, Robert J 5:33:46 (29,726)
McGown, Joe F 5:47:15 (31,375)
McGraine, Jon D 4:31:36 (16,484)
McGrath, Adam J 4:04:17 (10,022)
McGrath, Daniel 4:42:05 (19,060)
McGrath, Dennis J 5:23:57 (28,101)
McGrave, Larry R 5:12:58 (26,039)
McGreary, Anthony T 5:20:48 (27,573)
McGregor, Campbell 4:12:36 (11,737)
McGregor, Dan 6:20:59 (33,950)
McGregor, Emma 4:44:19 (19,626)
McGregor, Gordon R 2:48:06 (313)
McGregor, Graeme D 4:21:32 (13,973)
McGregor, Nigel A 4:50:12 (21,045)
McGregor, Paul D 4:56:13 (22,570)
McGregor, Peter 4:20:22 (13,700)
McGregor, Ronin T 4:19:28 (13,457)
McGregor, Scott A 3:08:18 (1,415)
McGuigan, James D 5:41:14 (30,735)
McGuigan, Mick 3:32:08 (4,017)
McGuinness, Harold 4:46:32 (20,187)
McGuinness, Martin M 5:13:07 (26,065)
McGuinness, Nicky 2:29:03 (35)
McGuinness, Pat..................4:17:22 (12,897)
McGuinness, Paul..................4:11:41 (11,547)
McGuinness, Steve M 5:31:42 (29,406)
McGuire, Aron T..................4:33:43 (16,970)
McGuire, Robert G 5:22:30 (27,854)
McGuirk, Finn 4:34:03 (17,039)
McGuirk, Richard B..................3:26:41 (3,221)
McGurk, Paul 3:40:59 (5,361)
McGurn, James A 4:17:46 (13,015)
McHugh, Bryan 4:24:27 (14,695)
McHugh, Derek F 5:31:38 (29,393)
McHugh, Graham 5:31:39 (29,395)
McIlhargey, Neil D 3:32:22 (4,054)
McIlwee, Ian 2:45:15 (245)
McInerney, John J 6:38:34 (34,622)
McInerney, Michael C..................4:37:57 (17,993)
McInerney, Paul A..................3:38:49 (4,978)
McInnes, Andrew R..................3:28:09 (3,424)
McInnes, James M 3:11:06 (1,642)
McInnes, John J..................5:00:55 (23,712)
McInness, Stuart A 2:54:12 (525)
McIntosh, Andrew D..................4:15:30 (12,442)
McIntosh, Christopher G 4:10:14 (11,212)
McIntosh, Graeme 4:19:43 (13,515)
McIntosh, Malcolm 4:19:04 (13,343)
McIntyre, Alan 5:53:34 (32,017)
McIntyre, David N..................3:53:09 (7,603)
McIntyre, Niall M 3:42:31 (5,599)
McIntyre, Ruairdh B 4:18:21 (13,163)
McIntyre, Tim 3:51:04 (7,154)
McIver, Christopher J..................2:54:22 (537)
McIver, Duncan 5:05:25 (24,577)

McIvor, Aaron 3:07:54 (1,383)
McIvor, Paul 5:05:08 (24,532)
McIvor, Peter 3:49:30 (6,832)
McKavanagh, Peter A 4:18:35 (13,234)
McKay, Albert K 4:53:48 (21,964)
McKay, Daniel D 4:38:14 (18,064)
McKay, Douglas J 4:26:00 (15,058)
McKay, James I 5:50:10 (31,687)
McKay, Mark P 4:04:25 (10,041)
McKay, Neil W 3:46:18 (6,219)
McKay, Stuart K 4:48:29 (20,643)
McKechnie, James D 4:35:28 (17,397)
McKee, Alexander J 3:53:54 (7,765)
McKee, Jamie M 4:08:54 (10,943)
McKeeman, Andrew P 3:44:19 (5,908)
McKeeney, Paul 3:42:43 (5,632)
McKell, Laurence E 5:10:09 (25,517)
McKellar, James R 4:28:01 (15,592)
McKellar, Quinton A 4:25:01 (14,829)
McKenna, Michael A 3:45:07 (6,038)
McKenna, Michael P 3:23:05 (2,804)
McKenna, Paul F 5:33:00 (29,605)
McKenna, Paul J 5:23:49 (28,083)
McKenna, Richard C 5:31:08 (29,327)
McKenna, Scott D 3:21:59 (2,705)
McKenzie, Alan J 4:07:48 (10,724)
McKenzie, Duncan 3:51:32 (7,262)
McKenzie, Graham 4:55:09 (22,305)
McKenzie, Ian R 4:00:01 (9,211)
McKenzie, Simon J 2:59:53 (891)
McKenzie, Stuart 4:11:25 (11,478)
McKenzie, Stuart 4:20:10 (13,645)
McKenzie-Cook, Scott 3:58:35 (8,853)
McKeown, Ciaran F 4:01:19 (9,480)
McKeown, Des M 3:24:43 (2,989)
McKeown, James P 5:09:19 (25,336)
McKeown, Jeremy P 4:20:10 (13,645)
McKeown, John C 5:16:11 (26,697)
McKeown, Peter F 3:36:23 (4,599)
McKevitt, David 4:38:22 (18,117)
McKevitt, Lee 4:55:51 (22,475)
McKie, Mick 6:36:38 (34,563)
McKinlay, John T 4:22:32 (14,213)
McKinney, Cormac 4:59:31 (23,390)
McKinney, James E 3:13:34 (1,878)
McKinney, Patrick J 4:25:13 (14,879)
McKinstrie, James H 3:55:36 (8,138)
McKinstry, Lee J 5:27:45 (28,754)
McKirdy, Gordon J 5:16:49 (26,808)
McKnight, Cecil R 5:27:52 (28,773)
McKnight, Peter J 2:46:55 (281)
McKnight, Steven 4:33:11 (16,838)
McLachlan, John C 4:45:41 (19,989)
McLachlan, Neil M 4:55:12 (22,318)
McLardy, Daniel K 5:15:00 (26,449)
McLaren, David J 5:35:03 (29,920)
McLaren, Guy N 3:03:28 (1,076)
McLaren, James 3:38:02 (4,837)
McLaren, Neil M 3:45:16 (6,062)
McLaren, Peter L 4:42:22 (19,145)
McLaren, Scott 4:44:20 (19,630)
McLauchlan, Richard J 3:37:47 (4,786)
McLaughlin, Clifton J 4:34:18 (17,094)
McLaughlin, Eugene 6:45:04 (34,801)
McLaughlin, Gerald 6:03:57 (32,883)
McLaughlin, Ianek S 3:20:47 (2,586)
McLaughlin, Jonathan 4:11:14 (11,433)
McLaughlin, Paul A 5:15:59 (26,654)
McLaughlin, Philip 5:23:12 (27,958)
McLaughlin, Stephen 3:48:46 (6,682)
McLaughlin, Tim 5:35:18 (29,953)
McLean, Andrew 3:09:49 (1,540)
McLean, Angus D 5:07:13 (24,934)
McLean, Christopher S 4:36:06 (17,560)
McLean, Darryl G 4:47:03 (20,299)
McLean, David A 3:21:48 (2,685)
McLean, Gary C 3:35:52 (4,533)
McLean, Henry 3:58:11 (8,755)
McLean, Ian R 4:23:07 (14,358)
McLean, Paul 5:15:28 (26,556)
McLean, Sean A 7:37:23 (35,548)
McLean, Steve 5:25:01 (28,272)
McLean, Trevor 6:05:58 (33,044)

McLean-Reid, David J 4:39:28 (18,410)
McLellan, Kevin 5:04:18 (24,377)
McLelland, Stephen 6:42:36 (34,738)
McLelland, Steve 4:06:29 (10,463)
McLening, Marc-Stuart 4:33:31 (16,916)
McLeod, Alastair D 3:33:04 (4,148)
McLeod, Alexander 4:29:45 (16,075)
McLeod, Andrew J 3:10:41 (1,608)
McLoughlin, Chris M 4:26:11 (15,091)
McLoughlin, John 3:47:37 (6,454)
McLoughlin, Paul A 4:34:33 (17,159)
McLoughlin, Ted 3:28:13 (3,435)
McLucky, Garwin 4:18:19 (13,155)
McMahon, Brian K 5:09:04 (25,289)
McMahon, Michael J 4:55:23 (22,361)
McMahon, Paul 3:47:50 (6,501)
McManamon, Gerald 4:54:53 (22,241)
McManamon, Martin 5:40:28 (30,648)
McManmon, Pascal J 4:47:50 (20,489)
McManus, Anthony T 5:40:20 (30,633)
McManus, Graham F 4:47:27 (20,394)
McManus, James M 4:28:56 (15,842)
McManus, John 4:57:12 (22,821)
McManus, Keith A 4:52:40 (21,659)
McManus, Matt 5:37:08 (30,189)
McManus, Simon 4:33:40 (16,952)
McMaster, Aaron S 4:44:14 (19,611)
McMaster, Andrew D 4:16:49 (12,765)
McMellon, Andrew P 4:36:33 (17,681)
McMenamin, John G 4:25:51 (15,025)
McMonagle, Christopher 4:00:50 (9,384)
McMonagle, Noel 4:21:45 (14,019)
McMongale, Roger 5:03:15 (24,182)
McMullan, Gordon J 3:50:57 (7,127)
McMullan, Michael 4:53:36 (21,913)
McMullan, John 4:07:16 (10,616)
McMyler, Sean A 2:58:01 (747)
McNab, David P 3:37:35 (4,764)
McNair, Martin A 4:54:25 (22,128)
McNally, David P 4:39:55 (18,514)
McNally, James W 4:10:26 (11,253)
McNally, Mark 3:20:22 (2,536)
McNamara, Edward S 5:03:10 (24,166)
McNamara, Mario P 3:06:50 (1,302)
McNamara, Paul A 4:05:48 (10,309)
McNeely, Darren 2:41:38 (170)
McNeill, Alan 3:54:05 (7,812)
McNeill, Andrew S 2:36:50 (95)
McNeill, Andy 3:34:55 (4,400)
McNeill, Andy C 6:09:31 (33,272)
McNeill, Billy 3:41:22 (5,421)
McNeill, Brian T 4:19:53 (13,569)
McNeill, Rory C 4:22:27 (14,184)
McNeill, Stuart M 3:55:35 (8,133)
McNeill, Stuart T 5:06:35 (24,795)
McNelis, Robin N 3:02:46 (1,040)
McNicholas, Michael G 4:49:58 (20,986)
McNicol, Alistair L 3:32:12 (4,030)
McNight, Stefan 6:01:06 (32,684)
McNill, Alasdair 5:05:49 (24,657)
McNulty, Dermot 4:58:42 (23,189)
McPaul, Robert 4:19:27 (13,446)
McPeake, Francis B 3:51:29 (7,250)
McPhail, Colin D 4:11:15 (11,438)
McPhee, Justin 3:40:40 (5,293)
McQue, Aidan 4:25:38 (14,977)
McQuillan, Darryl R 4:14:31 (12,207)
McQuistan, Carl R 3:32:11 (4,028)
McRobert, Chris A 4:26:29 (15,184)
McShane, Dessie C 3:08:32 (1,433)
McStrafick, Ross 3:10:31 (1,596)
McSweeney, Brian G 4:57:16 (22,839)
McTigue, Paul 3:25:36 (3,076)
McVey, John P 4:33:09 (16,823)
McVie, Rob J 4:20:30 (13,732)
McWalter, Noel R 4:02:18 (9,668)
McWilliam, David C 4:28:02 (15,602)
McWilliams, Brendan F 6:09:12 (33,248)
McWilliams, Thomas 2:54:25 (541)
Meacham, Anthony 4:33:29 (16,909)
Meacham, Anthony J 4:19:04 (13,343)
Meacher, Barrington 5:18:07 (27,084)
Meacher, Roseanne L 5:18:17 (27,117)

Meacock, David G 3:19:45 (2,460)
Mead, Adrian M 3:13:44 (1,878)
Mead, Andrew J 4:22:47 (14,281)
Mead, Ben 5:34:12 (29,796)
Mead, Daniel P 5:17:14 (26,904)
Mead, Howard I 3:35:49 (4,525)
Mead, Kevin 4:52:46 (21,685)
Mead, Kym A 4:38:35 (18,170)
Mead, Peter A 4:07:39 (10,690)
Mead, Simon P 4:18:37 (13,245)
Mead, Stuart 4:13:25 (11,940)
Meade, Gareth 4:25:06 (14,848)
Meadows, Christopher S 4:49:11 (20,817)
Meadows, Craig M 5:04:41 (24,445)
Meadows, Ralph A 3:50:01 (6,948)
Meadows, William P 5:43:13 (30,964)
Meads, Neil 5:16:24 (26,736)
Meads, Paul G 4:33:44 (16,976)
Meagor, David R 4:02:28 (9,692)
Meagor, Lucas 4:27:17 (15,416)
Meakes, Timothy G 4:33:07 (16,816)
Meakin, Billy 3:46:44 (6,289)
Meakin, Brian R 4:03:02 (9,791)
Meakins, Chris 6:37:45 (34,596)
Mean, Richard J 4:37:00 (17,786)
Mean, Scott 3:06:42 (1,288)
Mean, Tim C 3:43:30 (5,779)
Mearns, Peter J 5:53:58 (32,051)
Mears, David F 3:49:05 (6,747)
Mears, Ian 5:04:19 (24,379)
Mears, Kristian P 5:30:05 (29,159)
Measham, Hayden H 4:11:54 (11,594)
Meban, Robert 5:19:02 (27,252)
Meckel, Jans N 3:26:12 (3,157)
Medcalf, Justin B 4:59:57 (23,490)
Medhurst, James R 6:16:59 (33,732)
Medhurst, Steve 4:39:19 (18,368)
Medley, Philip K 4:58:42 (23,189)
Medway, Jim S 4:20:40 (13,768)
Mee, Douglas 3:50:16 (6,991)
Meech, Victor D 5:16:37 (26,773)
Meehan, David J 3:43:07 (5,711)
Meehan, Paul A 4:34:09 (17,062)
Meehan, Ray 5:00:47 (23,683)
Meehan, Scott A 4:40:17 (18,597)
Meehan, Tony 4:52:56 (21,735)
Meek, Kevin J 5:07:45 (25,044)
Meekcoms, Dean C 5:06:12 (24,741)
Mees, Ruedinger W 5:03:14 (24,178)
Meese, Geert 3:47:26 (6,410)
Meeten, Craig 4:06:43 (10,507)
Megarrell, Andrew 4:51:57 (21,474)
Meggs, Timothy W 4:54:39 (22,185)
Meggy, Charles W 4:50:03 (21,007)
Meghjee, Ashif 3:09:06 (1,477)
Meguer, Jean-Xavier 4:33:27 (16,900)
Mehat, Raminder 3:54:59 (8,006)
Meheust, David 3:05:11 (1,173)
Mehta, Bhavin 6:10:57 (33,365)
Mehta, Paresh 4:27:30 (15,469)
Meier, Robert P 4:04:33 (10,067)
Meignan, Eric 4:15:59 (12,558)
Meiklejohn, Graham K 4:56:11 (22,559)
Meki, Muhammad 4:31:33 (16,471)
Melay, Steve J 6:13:39 (33,533)
Melchior, Szymon 3:32:21 (4,051)
Melchor, José 3:21:31 (2,651)
Meldon, Paul 4:12:36 (11,737)
Meldrum, David P 4:39:36 (18,437)
Meldrum, Patrick K 3:21:25 (2,641)
Melia, Michael J 4:54:54 (22,246)
Melis, Paul 5:19:33 (27,348)
Mella, Luca 4:11:46 (11,563)
Meller, David 2:52:07 (446)
Meller, Paul G 5:05:29 (24,600)
Mellerick, Raphael G 6:05:26 (32,991)
Mellett, Pete 5:32:52 (29,588)
Melley, Simon J 5:04:40 (24,443)
Melling, Kevin S 4:21:06 (13,874)
Melling, Phil J 3:43:48 (5,829)
Melling, Steven W 4:55:20 (22,346)
Mellish, Gary L 4:59:11 (23,302)
Mellish, Joseph J 5:41:04 (30,714)

Mellon, James	6:55:04	(35,036)
Mellon, Mark L	3:26:50	(3,247)
Mellor, Mike	3:44:36	(5,959)
Mellor, Nicholas	4:32:39	(16,706)
Mellor, Paul	4:38:17	(18,084)
Mellor, Robert L	4:41:10	(18,831)
Mellor, Tom	2:59:29	(861)
Mellors, Benjamin T	4:26:14	(15,114)
Melody, David	4:32:37	(16,695)
Melrose, Graham R	3:48:10	(6,557)
Melville, Colin M	3:44:00	(5,867)
Melville, Gavin R	4:18:22	(13,165)
Melville, Toby	3:21:53	(2,693)
Melvin, Lindsay V	4:27:17	(15,416)
Menard, Karl J	3:02:54	(1,044)
Mendenhall, Ross	4:37:44	(17,946)
Mendes Da Costa, Tim	4:00:27	(9,301)
Mendez, Allan C	5:58:54	(32,497)
Menditta, Peter G	4:37:40	(17,926)
Mendonca, Paulo R	4:02:11	(9,642)
Mendoza, Juan L	4:04:37	(10,078)
Mendoza, Lorenzo A	3:43:49	(5,834)
Menegazzo, Andrea	4:29:44	(16,070)
Mengin, Andreas	4:11:49	(11,573)
Menon, Gop	5:39:32	(30,535)
Mentiply, Iain	6:07:37	(33,137)
Mepham, Derek C	4:12:33	(11,729)
Mercer, David G	4:30:51	(16,324)
Mercer, James	6:47:38	(34,875)
Mercer, Philip S	4:56:51	(22,735)
Mercer, Simon N	3:33:40	(4,224)
Mercer, Timothy I	4:13:47	(12,040)
Merchant, David M	4:25:11	(14,867)
Merckel, Bob	5:59:19	(32,539)
Meredith, Alexander D	5:13:48	(26,190)
Meredith, Roy	4:09:52	(11,141)
Meredith, Simon S	2:48:09	(316)
Meredith, Steve	5:07:19	(24,960)
Meredith, Thomas D	5:04:37	(24,432)
Meredith, Tim D	4:41:10	(18,831)
Merer, Ewan R	4:42:27	(19,164)
Merkle, Franz	4:31:49	(16,530)
Merlin, Ben H	3:50:20	(7,008)
Merola, Toni	4:12:31	(11,726)
Merrey, Stephen W	6:34:29	(34,473)
Merrick, Brian	4:03:59	(9,963)
Merrick, Peter D	5:42:13	(30,852)
Merrick, Phil T	3:58:22	(8,800)
Merritt, Anthony E	3:57:27	(8,590)
Merritt, Matthew R	3:57:14	(8,539)
Merron, Bernard J	3:17:42	(2,253)
Merry, James	5:52:50	(31,953)
Merry, Philip L	5:00:36	(23,634)
Merry, Russell A	5:58:16	(32,438)
Merry, Scott C	4:37:00	(17,786)
Mersmann, Hans H	5:18:23	(27,144)
Meryon, Angus J	3:38:43	(4,960)
Mesney, Peter M	4:29:29	(15,998)
Messenger, Mark	3:54:09	(7,829)
Messenger, Simon E	4:56:37	(22,665)
Messer, Robin P	3:49:13	(6,779)
Messick, William C	5:06:45	(24,831)
Metcafe, Leonard	4:50:12	(21,045)
Metcalf, Alan E	2:56:33	(639)
Metcalf, Craig	3:15:44	(2,052)
Metcalf, John D	4:11:40	(11,542)
Metcalf, Michael	6:09:26	(33,264)
Metcalf, Peter C	3:13:09	(1,831)
Metcalfe, Barry	3:14:53	(1,978)
Metcalfe, Benjamin L	4:17:07	(12,833)
Metcalfe, Tim C	3:18:25	(2,336)
Metcalfe, Tom H	5:19:33	(27,348)
Metherall, Glenn D	5:34:23	(29,824)
Metson, Leslie P	5:08:02	(25,101)
Metson, Nicholas R	3:54:52	(7,978)
Metzgen, Fred	5:25:23	(28,335)
Meusinger, Reinhard	3:24:43	(2,989)
Mewse, Dale L	4:20:18	(13,679)
Mewse, Nicholas J	4:06:16	(10,409)
Meyburg, Gordon	6:09:31	(33,272)
Meyer, Matthew	6:00:44	(32,642)
Meyler, Sean D	3:26:47	(3,236)
Mezzetti, Edward A	3:57:27	(8,590)
Micallef, Carlos	3:45:14	(6,054)
Michael, Dennis	3:53:54	(7,765)
Michael, Tony G	3:49:26	(6,818)
Michaelwaite, Alastair J	3:58:55	(8,942)
Michaut, Dominique	3:30:54	(3,827)
Michaux, Fabrice	3:17:17	(2,204)
Miche, Eric P	5:06:50	(24,850)
Michel, Antoine	4:53:42	(21,942)
Michel, Gerard	4:05:52	(10,322)
Michel, Ludovic	4:30:49	(16,317)
Michell, Edward G	4:13:05	(11,853)
Michelsen, Tore	3:05:25	(1,195)
Michie, Jamie	4:23:28	(14,440)
Mickleburgh, Trevor J	4:27:09	(15,366)
Micklethwaite, Marc	4:12:16	(11,677)
Middlebrook, Ian	3:14:12	(1,914)
Middlemiss, Peter	3:25:59	(3,123)
Middleton, Chistopher	4:21:48	(14,033)
Middleton, Kevan	4:22:13	(14,131)
Middleton, Mark T	4:29:20	(15,947)
Middleton, Neil M	3:54:02	(7,799)
Middleton, Simon	4:09:03	(10,966)
Middleton, William S	4:11:46	(11,563)
Midgley, James W	2:59:22	(851)
Midgley, Keith	3:17:45	(2,260)
Midgley, Martin N	3:13:09	(1,831)
Midwinter, Dale	3:52:17	(7,429)
Midwinter, Jeremy T	4:36:56	(17,774)
Midwood, Howard C	4:20:48	(13,799)
Mifsud, Stephen M	4:01:56	(9,592)
Mihdidin, Yashraj	3:29:36	(3,660)
Mikelas, Trevor	4:07:19	(10,621)
Mikhailides, Solon	5:30:19	(29,185)
Mikkelsen, Vidar	3:22:35	(2,754)
Milam, Darren	4:34:44	(17,211)
Milan, Chris M	3:43:48	(5,829)
Milbourn, Gervase M	4:36:30	(17,664)
Milburn, Ian W	3:43:23	(5,751)
Milburn, Mark W	5:57:44	(32,387)
Milburn, Neil	5:12:44	(25,990)
Milburn, Rick G	4:47:54	(20,505)
Miles, Albert J	5:15:02	(26,464)
Miles, Andy K	4:15:44	(12,491)
Miles, Carl	3:48:19	(6,578)
Miles, Christopher T	4:57:17	(22,847)
Miles, Daniel F	4:46:13	(20,110)
Miles, Mark	2:24:20	(22)
Miles, Paul G	4:27:56	(15,567)
Miles, Paul W	3:07:10	(1,323)
Miles, Peter M	5:34:25	(29,833)
Miles, Phillip A	3:58:10	(8,750)
Miles, Phillip R	3:05:23	(1,191)
Miles, Sebastian	3:54:16	(7,861)
Milgate, Darren	4:13:55	(12,073)
Millar, Ben G	3:48:09	(6,553)
Millar, Eldon N	3:58:12	(8,760)
Millar, James	3:59:55	(9,188)
Millard, Christopher J	2:59:34	(867)
Millard, Duncan R	4:10:49	(11,332)
Millard, Iain	5:31:42	(29,406)
Millard, Jeremy R	4:18:06	(13,094)
Millard, Leigh A	3:20:23	(2,540)
Millard-Beer, Matthew W	4:50:31	(21,129)
Miller, Adam J	3:13:48	(1,883)
Miller, Alastair R	3:34:33	(4,348)
Miller, Amos	5:00:47	(23,683)
Miller, Andrew J	4:52:37	(21,649)
Miller, Andrew W	3:49:11	(6,767)
Miller, Bryan J	4:59:53	(23,470)
Miller, Chris R	4:09:19	(11,034)
Miller, Christopher	4:19:09	(13,367)
Miller, Christopher D	5:11:59	(25,852)
Miller, Christopher P	5:11:29	(25,750)
Miller, Craig J	4:06:22	(10,429)
Miller, Daniel	4:01:33	(9,521)
Miller, Daniel H	5:19:02	(27,252)
Miller, Darren L	3:13:55	(1,894)
Miller, David A	5:50:26	(31,720)
Miller, David J	3:38:04	(4,846)
Miller, David P	6:00:02	(32,582)
Miller, Garth	3:58:52	(8,934)
Miller, Gary	4:59:18	(23,340)
Miller, Gavin P	4:16:39	(12,726)
Miller, Glenn	4:47:23	(20,379)
Miller, Gordon P	5:35:36	(29,996)
Miller, Graeme	3:18:10	(2,306)
Miller, Graham F	3:41:54	(5,498)
Miller, James I	4:38:43	(18,205)
Miller, Jeremy S	7:11:20	(35,293)
Miller, Joseph A	4:11:39	(11,537)
Miller, Keith R	4:18:24	(13,174)
Miller, Lee	4:05:09	(10,175)
Miller, Les D	5:51:50	(31,858)
Miller, Michael J	3:50:22	(7,014)
Miller, Paul	2:58:27	(787)
Miller, Peter	3:20:18	(2,530)
Miller, Peter J	4:20:46	(13,790)
Miller, Richard C	5:04:38	(24,434)
Miller, Roy	5:18:33	(27,173)
Miller, Roy	6:07:12	(33,118)
Miller, Simon A	5:00:08	(23,532)
Miller, Stephen	7:11:20	(35,293)
Miller, Stephen M	5:16:27	(26,749)
Miller, Steven	2:36:51	(97)
Miller, Steven M	5:12:46	(25,994)
Miller, Tom	4:11:34	(11,512)
Miller, William J	4:28:15	(15,657)
Millership, Stephen J	6:32:04	(34,410)
Millichamp, James J	7:11:08	(35,291)
Millichamp, Roger D	7:11:08	(35,291)
Milligan, Andrew R	4:29:13	(15,915)
Milligan, Graham	4:41:57	(19,028)
Milligan, Ken	5:07:10	(24,918)
Milligan, Stuart R	5:32:33	(29,542)
Millington, Garry	5:01:47	(23,886)
Millington, James S	4:33:52	(17,005)
Millington, Robert H	4:39:38	(18,445)
Millington, Stuart J	7:06:20	(35,225)
Millman, Dominic	4:58:49	(23,211)
Millman, Geoffrey S	5:57:38	(32,377)
Millman, Robin	5:12:47	(25,998)
Millns, Tom J	3:45:09	(6,041)
Mills, Andrew D	4:05:25	(10,226)
Mills, Andrew D	5:03:26	(24,224)
Mills, Brian	4:25:27	(14,934)
Mills, Christopher P	4:42:21	(19,139)
Mills, Craig	4:14:42	(12,257)
Mills, Dean A	6:36:53	(34,577)
Mills, Ewan	4:54:51	(22,237)
Mills, Gary R	7:06:00	(35,219)
Mills, Jeremy	4:36:05	(17,553)
Mills, Jonathan C	5:50:36	(31,732)
Mills, Lee E	5:39:18	(30,490)
Mills, Mark J	5:06:42	(24,817)
Mills, Matthew P	5:21:22	(27,667)
Mills, Nathanael L	4:12:20	(11,687)
Mills, Nicholas	4:28:03	(15,608)
Mills, Philip	4:47:38	(20,438)
Mills, Richie	5:51:04	(31,782)
Mills, Robert M	3:46:03	(6,186)
Mills, Robin	5:03:33	(24,246)
Mills, Simon	4:47:56	(20,512)
Mills, Stephen J	3:42:11	(5,549)
Mills, Steve J	4:40:28	(18,644)
Mills, Steve J	5:14:09	(26,257)
Mills, Steven W	4:18:49	(13,287)
Mills, Stewart N	5:23:13	(27,961)
Mills, Stuart A	3:21:50	(2,689)
Millsom, Tony	5:58:28	(32,465)
Millward, Graham E	4:11:27	(11,490)
Millward, Piers D	3:12:16	(1,754)
Millward, Richard B	5:00:40	(23,650)
Millward, Simon A	7:10:26	(35,275)
Millward, Stephen J	2:48:44	(336)
Millwood, Nigel W	5:21:27	(27,687)
Milmoe, Michael	3:46:57	(6,335)
Milne, Alex	4:55:48	(22,455)
Milne, Andrew S	4:31:38	(16,495)
Milne, Kevin B	4:09:02	(10,956)
Milne, Nicholas C	5:10:12	(25,526)
Milne, Stephen	3:49:24	(6,808)
Milner, Alexander M	4:20:10	(13,645)
Milner, Colin	4:25:01	(14,829)
Milnes, Alistair L	4:48:13	(20,582)
Milnes, Christopher J	4:10:14	(11,212)
Milnes, Richard W	4:38:22	(18,117)

Milnthorpe, Paul A 5:18:59 (27,248)	Mladek, Alexander J 5:02:29 (24,033)	Moorby, Thomas E.....4:14:16 (12,157)
Milone, Carmelo 3:46:01 (6,182)	Mo, Lab K.....4:45:37 (19,970)	Moore, Adrian P.....3:56:13 (8,279)
Mils, Nathan E.....3:13:11 (1,836)	Moat, Darren E.....3:25:03 (3,025)	Moore, Andrew.....4:07:38 (10,686)
Milsom, Francis.....6:48:20 (34,895)	Moate, Simon R.....4:57:46 (22,973)	Moore, Andrew J.....4:14:51 (12,278)
Milson, Damian.....5:30:25 (29,204)	Moate, Toby J.....4:07:49 (10,730)	Moore, Anthony J.....4:19:18 (13,405)
Milson, Paul J.....3:37:39 (4,770)	Mochan, Martin.....3:44:38 (5,964)	Moore, Ashley.....4:34:11 (17,072)
Milton, David J 4:16:29 (12,695)	Mocharrafie, Bassan.....5:11:43 (25,793)	Moore, Ben.....4:26:53 (15,288)
Milton, David R.....3:58:12 (8,760)	Mocillo Aixela, Alfonso.....4:36:16 (17,602)	Moore, Charles D.....5:05:42 (24,637)
Milton, Johnny S.....4:28:04 (15,614)	Modaher, Jasvir Singh.....6:07:50 (33,157)	Moore, Christopher.....6:09:41 (33,284)
Milton, Paul J.....5:20:40 (27,550)	Modaher, Tejinder S.....6:00:43 (32,639)	Moore, Christopher E.....4:33:10 (16,830)
Minerva, Paolo.....3:29:50 (3,695)	Moden, Ian.....6:53:29 (35,006)	Moore, Daniel C.....4:39:50 (18,494)
Mingay, Simon.....3:12:15 (1,750)	Moe Omrdberg, Markus 3:18:12 (2,310)	Moore, David G.....2:55:37 (598)
Minhall, Martin P.....4:24:13 (14,634)	Moerch, Atle.....4:42:27 (19,164)	Moore, David J.....3:58:16 (8,783)
Minhas, Pardip S.....4:18:47 (13,281)	Moffatt, Jason.....4:53:26 (21,876)	Moore, Gary A.....4:23:13 (14,383)
Minihane, Ross W.....3:52:56 (7,551)	Moffatt, Peter G.....6:05:38 (33,018)	Moore, Gary C.....5:10:50 (25,631)
Minnis, Barrie A.....6:19:38 (33,872)	Moffitt, Deane.....4:29:35 (16,034)	Moore, Gary N.....4:00:41 (9,354)
Minnis, Mark.....4:46:17 (20,120)	Mogelinski, Jerome M.....4:57:53 (23,006)	Moore, Geoffrey.....6:02:10 (32,758)
Minns, Phillip I.....5:27:04 (28,631)	Moggan, Frank M.....4:39:25 (18,394)	Moore, Gerrard T.....4:13:35 (11,990)
Minogue, James A 6:39:42 (34,667)	Moggia, Gianni.....3:06:48 (1,298)	Moore, Graham S.....2:58:45 (808)
Minotti, Virginio.....4:19:56 (13,582)	Moggridge, Jonathan D 4:31:37 (16,490)	Moore, Hugo C.....4:34:57 (17,257)
Minta, Anthony J.....5:39:40 (30,554)	Mogridge, Chris.....4:37:52 (17,974)	Moore, Ian P.....4:26:17 (15,127)
Minton, Rob J.....2:53:40 (504)	Mogridge, Russ.....3:37:06 (4,700)	Moore, James A 3:55:17 (8,074)
Miquel, Ramon.....5:46:40 (31,325)	Mohamed, Jamal.....2:41:48 (176)	Moore, James S.....4:50:25 (21,104)
Mir, Rahim.....3:31:48 (3,954)	Mohan, Bernard P.....5:33:51 (29,737)	Moore, Jed D.....5:05:03 (24,520)
Mirams, Jeremy E.....3:33:16 (4,174)	Mohrle, Tim O.....4:10:58 (11,362)	Moore, Jimmy C.....4:56:56 (22,759)
Miranda, Luis A.....3:26:38 (3,212)	Moineau, Philippe.....4:18:09 (13,108)	Moore, John W.....5:32:58 (29,601)
Miranda, Maurizio.....3:54:41 (7,940)	Moinier, Gilles.....4:02:42 (9,729)	Moore, Julian P.....3:28:46 (3,534)
Mirando, Sanjiv.....4:36:37 (17,696)	Moir, Barry R.....3:48:08 (6,550)	Moore, Karl D.....2:57:51 (736)
Misje, Roar.....3:03:57 (1,102)	Moir, Richard J.....4:36:20 (17,621)	Moore, Lee R.....4:20:03 (13,611)
Miskell, Adrian.....4:46:55 (20,257)	Moisey, Richard.....4:39:04 (18,302)	Moore, Lee R.....5:02:37 (24,060)
Misselbrook, Allen K.....3:57:00 (8,482)	Moisley, Mark P.....4:52:34 (21,629)	Moore, Marcus D 4:41:10 (18,831)
Missions, David W.....5:36:50 (30,153)	Mole, David.....4:40:40 (18,694)	Moore, Melwyn J.....5:15:11 (26,495)
Misson, Trev.....3:08:48 (1,450)	Mole, Robert A.....3:37:51 (4,799)	Moore, Michael K.....3:27:04 (3,293)
Mistry, Ashwin.....5:57:24 (32,363)	Mole, Stuart.....3:40:00 (5,189)	Moore, Nick J.....3:39:05 (5,030)
Mistry, Harshad N 6:24:39 (34,114)	Molesworth, Tony.....4:35:15 (17,348)	Moore, Nigel J.....5:47:44 (31,435)
Mistry, Hitesh S.....3:53:45 (7,738)	Moller, Marcus.....4:22:13 (14,131)	Moore, Paul A.....3:03:07 (1,056)
Mistry, Jayesh.....4:48:39 (20,679)	Mollison, Adrian J.....4:29:24 (15,976)	Moore, Peter G.....6:06:50 (33,098)
Mistry, Shashikant M.....6:40:38 (34,680)	Molloy, John M.....3:23:52 (2,888)	Moore, Philip.....5:09:52 (25,444)
Mitchell, Alex T.....5:36:06 (30,060)	Molloy, Wayne.....4:19:07 (13,359)	Moore, Richard J.....3:48:58 (6,723)
Mitchell, Andrew R.....5:01:37 (23,856)	Moloney, Ryan.....5:36:01 (30,050)	Moore, Richard J.....4:22:28 (14,190)
Mitchell, Binney.....3:09:17 (1,500)	Moloney, Tim.....3:29:17 (3,614)	Moore, Richard P.....3:22:44 (2,766)
Mitchell, Cheyne.....4:54:23 (22,117)	Molyneux, Paul M.....2:36:03 (84)	Moore, Richard W.....5:33:38 (29,708)
Mitchell, Christopher W.....4:35:15 (17,348)	Molyneux, Thomas.....3:23:56 (2,898)	Moore, Robert C.....3:51:25 (7,231)
Mitchell, Daniel L.....3:09:41 (1,531)	Monaghan, Edmund J 4:47:13 (20,337)	Moore, Ross M.....4:39:53 (18,504)
Mitchell, Danny.....6:04:44 (32,936)	Monaghan, Gary D.....4:53:46 (21,956)	Moore, Scott S.....5:00:45 (23,676)
Mitchell, David.....5:07:42 (25,033)	Monehen, Colin J.....4:40:53 (18,755)	Moore, Sean P.....3:59:04 (8,976)
Mitchell, David J.....6:08:55 (33,233)	Money, Antony H.....3:59:15 (9,027)	Moore, Shaun T.....7:22:18 (35,410)
Mitchell, George E.....6:01:01 (32,675)	Monger, Desmond L.....4:30:09 (16,188)	Moore, Simon G.....4:36:58 (17,779)
Mitchell, Glen I.....3:54:33 (7,911)	Monk, Geoff.....4:54:10 (22,069)	Moore, Simon J.....5:16:22 (26,730)
Mitchell, Greig A.....4:08:19 (10,835)	Monk, Harold.....4:18:12 (13,124)	Moore, Stephen J.....4:46:05 (20,073)
Mitchell, Henry.....5:10:10 (25,522)	Monk, Howard.....4:41:35 (18,944)	Moore, Stephen J.....5:35:08 (29,934)
Mitchell, Hugh S.....4:11:40 (11,542)	Monk, Ian R.....5:05:41 (24,631)	Moore, Stuart.....3:59:55 (9,188)
Mitchell, James C 4:16:49 (12,765)	Monk, Jonathan P 3:08:30 (1,432)	Moore, Stuart.....4:29:20 (15,947)
Mitchell, James K.....3:52:18 (7,434)	Monk, Lewis M.....4:09:28 (11,066)	Moore, Tony P.....3:26:49 (3,244)
Mitchell, Jason M.....4:31:10 (16,398)	Monk, Michael J.....5:07:31 (25,004)	Moore, Trevor E.....4:43:57 (19,520)
Mitchell, Jeremy D.....4:41:21 (18,875)	Monks, Christopher S.....4:52:01 (21,489)	Moore, Trevor J.....3:17:19 (2,205)
Mitchell, John L.....5:43:58 (31,033)	Monks, Gavin S.....2:52:17 (455)	Moore, Warren J.....4:44:48 (19,780)
Mitchell, Jonathan.....5:00:26 (23,603)	Monopoli, Francesco 3:11:36 (1,680)	Moores, Kerry.....5:00:51 (23,696)
Mitchell, Jonathan D.....3:38:51 (4,988)	Montague, Peter A 6:58:24 (35,098)	Moores, Philip G.....4:52:32 (21,623)
Mitchell, Justin A.....2:53:40 (504)	Montaque, Peter A.....5:37:02 (30,175)	Moorhouse, Dominic J.....5:17:17 (26,915)
Mitchell, Keith.....4:38:47 (18,226)	Monteil, Patrice.....4:15:45 (12,495)	Moorhouse, Edward J 3:40:25 (5,250)
Mitchell, Kieron J.....3:20:57 (2,608)	Monteith, Joseph S.....5:37:26 (30,231)	Moorhouse, Graham L 3:18:47 (2,368)
Mitchell, Matthew B.....5:52:10 (31,889)	Monteith, Steven.....6:31:43 (34,392)	Moorhouse, Jon.....4:29:39 (16,056)
Mitchell, Neil R.....5:24:40 (28,212)	Monteith, William J.....6:50:57 (34,955)	Moorley, Christopher J 6:13:22 (33,511)
Mitchall, Nicholas L.....4:16:00 (12,562)	Montet, John.....4:17:24 (12,908)	Morales, Alexandre J.....3:40:33 (5,278)
Mitchell, Paul D.....4:23:59 (14,566)	Montgomery, John W.....4:07:00 (10,575)	Morales, Alfonso.....3:56:27 (8,346)
Mitchell, Paul R.....3:07:01 (1,309)	Moodie, Richard P.....4:16:05 (12,589)	Moran, Chris.....4:46:42 (20,216)
Mitchell, Richard M.....4:04:16 (10,017)	Moody, Adrian J.....6:54:59 (35,034)	Moran, David.....3:20:35 (2,567)
Mitchell, Robert G 5:10:28 (25,571)	Moody, Antony.....4:20:03 (13,611)	Moran, Dennis.....3:30:13 (3,750)
Mitchell, Robert J.....3:25:30 (3,063)	Moody, Chris.....5:43:58 (31,033)	Moran, Frank.....4:56:09 (22,550)
Mitchell, Robin.....4:56:11 (22,559)	Moody, Luke W 5:24:41 (28,217)	Moran, Ian L.....3:14:22 (1,931)
Mitchell, Sam A.....4:00:04 (9,221)	Moody, William.....4:06:25 (10,445)	Moran, James M 4:07:24 (10,634)
Mitchell, Scott J.....5:02:11 (23,967)	Moon, Chris.....5:13:50 (26,197)	Moran, Michael A 4:12:37 (11,743)
Mitchell, Simon J.....4:07:33 (10,662)	Moon, Daniel S 4:07:29 (10,647)	Moran, Paschal P.....3:36:08 (4,562)
Mitchelmore, Philip J.....5:45:32 (31,212)	Moon, David W 5:28:28 (28,896)	Moran, Patrick A.....3:57:18 (8,556)
Mitchelson, Andy J.....3:40:41 (5,299)	Moon, James K.....2:59:07 (833)	Moran, Peter.....6:04:41 (32,932)
Mitcheson, Adrian R.....4:53:27 (21,881)	Mooney, Alex T 5:13:39 (26,150)	Moran, Robert J.....3:32:48 (4,109)
Mitchla, Zuber.....3:36:49 (4,659)	Mooney, Andrew N 3:08:15 (1,413)	Moran, Robin.....4:15:39 (12,474)
Mitchley, Paul.....4:57:23 (22,883)	Mooney, Colin J.....3:14:53 (1,978)	Moran, Stephen.....5:16:24 (26,736)
Mitterle, Mathias.....5:21:49 (27,758)	Mooney, Francis.....3:43:31 (5,783)	Morant, William A.....4:48:30 (20,647)
Mixter, Alex J.....4:58:09 (23,063)	Mooney, Patrick J.....4:36:02 (17,544)	Morante, Yann.....4:27:21 (15,433)
Miyachi, Katsunori.....3:19:59 (2,493)	Mooney, Robert P.....6:18:47 (33,823)	Morar, Vikram.....5:31:14 (29,339)
Mjelstad, Ragnar Arve.....2:45:05 (244)	Moor, James W 3:40:49 (5,324)	Moratinos, José Luis.....4:31:57 (16,552)

Mordue, Alan J 5:04:48 (24,467)
Mordue, Stefan J 4:03:11 (9,813)
Moreau, Lionel 3:23:45 (2,872)
Morel, Vincent 5:29:07 (28,998)
Moreland, Jonathan M 4:43:51 (19,497)
More-Molyneux, Michael G 6:30:03 (34,328)
Morenan, Justin 5:10:54 (25,643)
Moreso, Marc 3:41:35 (5,454)
Moreton, Lloyd 6:40:27 (34,677)
Moreton, Michael A 7:01:01 (35,146)
Morez, Spencer H 3:59:52 (9,173)
Morfey, Michael J 5:22:40 (27,885)
Morgan, Alan J 4:51:47 (21,434)
Morgan, Andrew 4:27:34 (15,480)
Morgan, Andrew A 5:27:44 (28,751)
Morgan, Andrew R 4:49:54 (20,974)
Morgan, Anthony 6:18:24 (33,797)
Morgan, Ceri 4:13:21 (11,921)
Morgan, Charles J 3:39:50 (5,164)
Morgan, Chris 4:19:09 (13,367)
Morgan, Christopher H 4:14:03 (12,112)
Morgan, Christopher J 5:39:20 (30,494)
Morgan, Christopher L 3:43:19 (5,742)
Morgan, Darren M 4:28:31 (15,730)
Morgan, David 5:38:10 (30,329)
Morgan, David B 3:22:11 (2,720)
Morgan, David M 4:17:19 (12,880)
Morgan, David M 5:13:54 (26,211)
Morgan, David R 4:58:36 (23,166)
Morgan, Emyr W 3:37:12 (4,712)
Morgan, Gareth D 4:38:10 (18,055)
Morgan, Gareth J 2:56:43 (651)
Morgan, Glen A 3:19:55 (2,483)
Morgan, Graeme J 4:03:25 (9,852)
Morgan, Graham J 6:11:04 (33,374)
Morgan, Howard 4:33:22 (16,884)
Morgan, Ian R 4:33:39 (16,947)
Morgan, John D 4:06:57 (10,558)
Morgan, John S 4:25:43 (14,998)
Morgan, Lester J 4:59:14 (23,319)
Morgan, Matthew J 4:57:34 (22,919)
Morgan, Michael 5:14:38 (26,369)
Morgan, Nathan G 4:30:06 (16,174)
Morgan, Nicholas 4:34:06 (17,050)
Morgan, Nicholas G 3:57:11 (8,520)
Morgan, Nicholas V 4:08:18 (10,833)
Morgan, Peter 5:30:09 (29,168)
Morgan, Peter D 5:51:17 (31,806)
Morgan, Philip 4:11:04 (11,390)
Morgan, Philip J 4:04:01 (9,969)
Morgan, Richard A 5:34:37 (29,865)
Morgan, Richard J 4:45:22 (19,920)
Morgan, Richard K 3:32:03 (3,995)
Morgan, Robert P 4:15:08 (12,351)
Morgan, Roger L 3:47:21 (6,397)
Morgan, Russell J 5:09:33 (25,384)
Morgan, Simon A 5:44:06 (31,057)
Morgan, Simon L 3:49:42 (6,872)
Morgan, Steven A 4:29:11 (15,906)
Morgan, Steven R 3:28:49 (3,541)
Morgan, Thomas J 5:53:59 (32,052)
Morgan, Wayne S 4:41:36 (18,948)
Morgan, Wesley J 3:50:02 (6,951)
Morgan Locke, Nathan 3:46:32 (6,254)
Morgan-Harvey, Piers 4:34:40 (17,196)
Morgans, Colin M 8:32:47 (35,679)
Morgatroyd, Matthew D 4:57:15 (22,834)
Morgetroyd, Richard 3:17:42 (2,253)
Moriarty, Brendan M 3:33:06 (4,154)
Moriarty, Neil M 3:18:48 (2,369)
Moriarty, Richard J 4:09:04 (10,969)
Moriaty, Stephen 5:34:43 (29,877)
Morimoto, Kojiro 4:23:24 (14,418)
Morison, Stuart 4:22:46 (14,279)
Morlacci, Patrizio 3:18:03 (2,288)
Morley, Bryan 3:37:23 (4,730)
Morley, Chris M 4:22:36 (14,230)
Morley, Colin J 4:20:48 (13,799)
Morley, Darren L 4:56:02 (22,522)
Morley, Don 5:18:03 (27,068)
Morley, Duncan 5:25:34 (28,382)
Morley, Michael J 3:15:29 (2,028)
Morley, Phil A 3:05:15 (1,180)
Morley, Philip E 4:01:19 (9,480)
Morley, Richard 5:02:14 (23,974)
Morley, Roger T 4:17:34 (12,969)
Morley, Simon J 4:44:42 (19,744)
Morley, Steve L 6:03:47 (32,873)
Morley, Stuart 6:11:59 (33,427)
Morling, Matt J 4:36:13 (17,585)
Morony, Michael 4:37:17 (17,838)
Morrall, Alexander 3:28:24 (3,462)
Morrall, James S 4:42:35 (19,203)
Morrell, Aubrey L 3:27:58 (3,403)
Morrin, Cyril J 5:09:56 (25,457)
Morrin, Damian J 4:00:19 (9,275)
Morris, Alan 4:49:17 (20,836)
Morris, Andrew 3:56:13 (8,279)
Morris, Andrew J 5:23:21 (27,984)
Morris, Anthony J 4:01:58 (9,597)
Morris, Antony T 6:12:38 (33,465)
Morris, Carl 5:07:12 (24,929)
Morris, Chris J 3:06:58 (1,306)
Morris, Christopher 4:39:06 (18,306)
Morris, Christopher 5:27:29 (28,710)
Morris, David E 4:27:57 (15,571)
Morris, David L 4:17:08 (12,837)
Morris, Dean G 4:16:24 (12,670)
Morris, Dereck J 4:11:50 (11,578)
Morris, Edmund A 4:18:38 (13,250)
Morris, Glyn E 3:40:52 (5,337)
Morris, Grant 5:51:40 (31,844)
Morris, Greg 4:05:09 (10,175)
Morris, Gregory D 4:40:33 (18,666)
Morris, Ian 4:40:50 (18,740)
Morris, Ian 4:43:18 (19,372)
Morris, Iestyn 5:17:23 (26,937)
Morris, James S 2:55:32 (596)
Morris, Jeffery 3:37:40 (4,772)
Morris, Jonathan R 3:23:43 (2,868)
Morris, Mark 3:29:51 (3,699)
Morris, Mark 5:29:24 (29,057)
Morris, Neil C 4:28:59 (15,854)
Morris, Paul 6:01:46 (32,739)
Morris, Paul 6:45:19 (34,805)
Morris, Pete H 4:27:11 (15,381)
Morris, Peter F 5:58:38 (32,481)
Morris, Peter I 6:00:01 (32,576)
Morris, Richard G 3:54:53 (7,982)
Morris, Richard P 3:18:09 (2,304)
Morris, Robert P 5:37:38 (30,252)
Morris, Ryan M 3:37:11 (4,711)
Morris, Sheridan J 3:22:44 (2,766)
Morris, Stephen J 3:48:20 (6,580)
Morris, Stephen L 5:12:30 (25,951)
Morris, Trevor H 2:59:07 (833)
Morrish, Stuart R 3:23:25 (2,842)
Morrison, Alexander W 4:12:09 (11,644)
Morrison, Andrew C 4:17:14 (12,861)
Morrison, Angus 5:07:18 (24,956)
Morrison, Barry 3:52:51 (7,536)
Morrison, Christopher F 2:51:25 (423)
Morrison, Colin D 3:50:20 (7,008)
Morrison, David J 4:53:39 (21,927)
Morrison, Derek J 3:57:58 (8,712)
Morrison, Dougal 4:54:14 (22,085)
Morrison, George 3:37:44 (4,780)
Morrison, Kevin 3:36:59 (4,682)
Morrison, Sid 3:44:34 (5,951)
Morrison, Stewart B 4:10:28 (11,258)
Morrissey, Ian 3:54:23 (7,880)
Morrissey, John P 4:11:50 (11,578)
Morrone, Salvatore 3:52:29 (7,464)
Morrow, Nicholas E 2:54:20 (535)
Morrow, Stephen N 7:10:46 (35,282)
Morse, Lee R 4:16:06 (12,596)
Morse, Robert J 5:03:00 (24,121)
Morsley, John 5:16:17 (26,719)
Mort, Allan D 5:29:24 (29,057)
Mort, Stephen I 4:36:03 (17,547)
Mort, Stephen W 3:56:16 (8,290)
Mortazavi, Mahmood 4:45:13 (19,890)
Mortensen, Michael C 3:37:28 (4,747)
Mortimer, Andrew P 4:13:07 (11,860)
Mortimer, Andy D 6:23:14 (34,045)
Mortimer, Carl C 6:34:49 (34,488)
Mortimer, Robert W 3:26:43 (3,227)
Mortimer, Steven P 5:24:53 (28,257)
Mortimer, Timothy M 4:06:57 (10,558)
Mortimer-Ford, Matthew D 4:16:45 (12,751)
Morton, Andy 5:31:02 (29,302)
Morton, Brian 5:12:51 (26,008)
Morton, Charles I 5:02:20 (23,998)
Morton, Chris I 3:49:12 (6,774)
Morton, Colin 5:38:31 (30,384)
Morton, Gary E 3:53:58 (7,785)
Morton, Iain A 4:01:23 (9,494)
Morton, Ian P 5:34:41 (29,872)
Morton, John S 3:46:07 (6,198)
Morton, Nicholas T 4:58:29 (23,149)
Morton, Richard F 3:10:51 (1,618)
Morton, Ricky 6:41:37 (34,705)
Morton, Scot S 4:24:44 (14,756)
Morton, Simon R 3:52:45 (7,515)
Morton, Steven J 2:56:41 (650)
Morton-Jones, Ian 6:56:41 (35,066)
Mortonson, Neil S 5:45:19 (31,185)
Morvan, Sebastien 4:25:35 (14,963)
Morwood, David W 2:34:08 (66)
Moscatelli, Stefano 4:32:35 (16,686)
Moscuzza, Franco 4:33:15 (16,857)
Moseley, James C 4:17:22 (12,897)
Moseley, Simon 3:15:36 (2,038)
Moser, Daniel 3:43:29 (5,776)
Mosiadz, Miroslaw 4:44:20 (19,630)
Mosley, Paul G 5:54:54 (32,139)
Moss, Ashley J 5:05:21 (24,564)
Moss, Benjamin I 3:28:29 (3,483)
Moss, Brandon J 5:25:08 (28,292)
Moss, Gavin P 3:24:16 (2,935)
Moss, Gerrard A 4:11:15 (11,438)
Moss, James I 3:19:53 (2,478)
Moss, Jonathan R 4:57:19 (22,860)
Moss, Moddy J 3:56:57 (8,466)
Moss, Nicholas C 4:18:39 (13,252)
Moss, Stuart B 5:56:12 (32,255)
Moss, Trevor D 4:15:57 (12,543)
Moss, Trevor G 3:31:49 (3,957)
Mostert, Jacobus A 6:29:48 (34,320)
Mothersole, Jason 5:01:09 (23,761)
Motson, Arran 4:20:02 (13,606)
Motson, Nicholas E 3:56:04 (8,240)
Mott, Anthony J 5:21:38 (27,717)
Mott, Keith 5:23:12 (27,958)
Mott, Shane 4:02:48 (9,753)
Motte, David W 3:34:09 (4,286)
Motteram, Michael C 4:09:34 (11,090)
Mottram, Patrick G 4:06:56 (10,557)
Mottram, Richard S 6:27:13 (34,222)
Mottram-Jones, Robert C 3:41:02 (5,370)
Moughton, Peter T 4:31:28 (16,457)
Mould, Rex 4:51:42 (21,423)
Moulder, David R 3:45:47 (6,145)
Moulding, Jonathan H 4:16:36 (12,716)
Moulds, Charlton L 3:39:45 (5,152)
Moule, John 4:52:59 (21,749)
Moulla, Mustapha 3:55:39 (8,150)
Moulsdale, Michael C 5:26:02 (28,463)
Moulton, Stephen D 4:12:37 (11,743)
Mound, David G 5:28:10 (28,832)
Mountain, Joe 5:42:24 (30,867)
Mountcastle, Chris 5:42:03 (30,833)
Mountfield, David 4:49:39 (20,926)
Mountford, Glenn 3:57:05 (8,497)
Mountford, Peter A 4:44:05 (19,560)
Mountjoy, Roger 5:09:19 (25,336)
Mountjoy-Row, Brian 4:05:11 (10,184)
Moura, Jean-Gabiel 3:51:22 (7,213)
Moura, Jorge 4:00:23 (9,287)
Mousdale, Anthony 3:20:08 (2,509)
Mowat, Joanathan B 5:54:21 (32,088)
Mower, Jeremy H 3:03:48 (1,093)
Mowle, Lee C 2:59:05 (830)
Mowling, Michael A 5:01:21 (23,803)
Moxon, David S 3:43:21 (5,746)
Moxon, Stephen 5:33:18 (29,644)
Moyes, David R 4:28:33 (15,745)
Moyle, Steven 4:42:00 (19,038)
Moyser, Shaun 5:31:11 (29,333)

Muakuku Masela, Pelayo 6:30:47 (34,353)
Mucklow, John S..........................4:22:00 (14,087)
Mucklow, Stuart E 4:52:23 (21,595)
Mudawi, Ahmed...........................5:20:08 (27,444)
Muddu, Ajay K.............................4:34:57 (17,257)
Mudge, Ian D 3:36:15 (4,579)
Mudimu, Collen 3:47:30 (6,424)
Muduroglu, Alper 4:44:15 (19,615)
Muehlhausen, Karl-Heinz............4:46:18 (20,127)
Muehlthaler, Paul M 5:41:01 (30,710)
Mueller, Peter H...........................6:49:52 (34,925)
Mueller, Volker............................5:09:22 (25,344)
Mueller-Schaudt, Brigitte S 4:09:50 (11,134)
Muenkel, Helge S.........................3:56:58 (8,473)
Muffler, Markus R 3:32:45 (4,101)
Muggleton, Carl D 4:57:14 (22,828)
Mughal, Muntzer 4:56:20 (22,598)
Mughal, Shakir M.........................4:09:03 (10,966)
Mugliston, David P 4:26:11 (15,091)
Muhill, Robert M 6:43:51 (34,767)
Muino, José M 5:35:46 (30,018)
Muir, Cameron J...........................5:32:07 (29,470)
Muir, David 6:38:30 (34,621)
Muir, Jonathan R..........................3:19:26 (2,431)
Muir, Malcolm J............................2:53:33 (497)
Muir, Michael J.............................3:46:49 (6,307)
Muir, Ronald A.............................4:57:02 (22,782)
Muir, Ross L..................................4:18:19 (13,155)
Muirhead, Nigel D 4:49:16 (20,831)
Muizer, Dick 5:02:40 (24,069)
Mujica, Mikel................................2:38:15 (112)
Mulcahy, Graeme 4:16:08 (12,604)
Mulcahy, Rory M 3:23:50 (2,882)
Mulder, Jacco A 4:33:46 (16,983)
Mulder, Jan-Maarten 4:57:09 (22,809)
Muldon, Kevin M 5:19:28 (27,330)
Muldoon, David M 5:13:26 (26,110)
Mulgrew, Gerry C 5:19:28 (27,330)
Mulhall, Craig R............................5:25:12 (28,302)
Mulholland, Damian.....................3:38:19 (4,889)
Mulholland, David T.....................5:12:43 (25,988)
Mulholland, Harry 3:04:11 (1,112)
Mulholland, James W...................4:16:20 (12,654)
Mulholland, Kevin R.....................5:11:53 (25,832)
Mulholland, Michael 6:23:50 (34,067)
Mulindwa, Steve 5:44:52 (31,136)
Mulkerrins, Sean 4:21:58 (14,080)
Mullan, Paul 3:50:58 (7,131)
Mullan, Terry J 5:14:43 (26,389)
Mullaney, Daniel J........................7:43:56 (35,594)
Mullaney, David L 4:25:29 (14,944)
Mullany, David..............................4:32:30 (16,662)
Mullarkey, Peter J 3:26:17 (3,172)
Mullen, Paul A..............................4:17:48 (13,023)
Mullen, Vincent P 4:26:13 (15,105)
Muller, Helgaard...........................5:16:53 (26,835)
Muller, Mirko 5:43:09 (30,954)
Mullery, Peter J.............................3:11:29 (1,672)
Mulley, Ian W................................6:50:46 (34,952)
Mulligan, Ciaran J.........................4:10:39 (11,300)
Mulligan, Paul E............................3:51:21 (7,209)
Mullins, James P............................4:31:43 (16,511)
Mullins, Jamie M 4:06:42 (10,502)
Mullins, Paul A 3:52:47 (7,520)
Mullins, Sean M.............................5:57:52 (32,397)
Mullish, Elliot D 3:33:52 (4,247)
Mulroy, Joseph S...........................4:03:12 (9,818)
Mulvenna, Stephen.......................3:04:41 (1,142)
Mumberson, James 4:14:12 (12,138)
Mumford, Kieron M......................4:20:37 (13,758)
Munday, Andrew D 5:05:15 (24,549)
Munday, Bob 5:33:30 (29,682)
Munday, Clifford 5:20:38 (27,545)
Munday, David A 5:07:21 (24,967)
Munday, David R 7:12:17 (35,309)
Munday, James 4:45:20 (19,914)
Munday, Simon E..........................3:57:22 (8,570)
Munday, Timothy G 3:51:13 (7,191)
Mundy, Andrew S 4:58:36 (23,166)
Mundy, James 4:02:01 (9,605)
Mundy, Robert..............................4:39:41 (18,462)
Munford, Andy..............................4:25:44 (15,002)
Mungroo, Jashal............................5:36:30 (30,114)

Munn, Nigel S 5:20:29 (27,513)
Munns, Brian.................................3:14:13 (1,916)
Munro, Cameron D 3:49:28 (6,821)
Munro, Jonathan C........................4:15:57 (12,543)
Munro, Kenneth 5:45:21 (31,187)
Munro, Neil....................................3:37:05 (4,698)
Munro, Neil G 4:12:15 (11,670)
Munro, Neil R 5:04:51 (24,487)
Munroe, Andy J 3:44:03 (5,873)
Munroe, Mark A.............................3:47:42 (6,478)
Munroe, Patrick 5:01:10 (23,766)
Munt, Kevin N 3:54:12 (7,839)
Murch, Andrew J 4:44:08 (19,571)
Murdey, Ian D................................2:56:05 (615)
Murdoch, Graeme A......................3:27:20 (3,330)
Murdoch, Keith M 4:21:32 (13,973)
Murdoch, Steven J.........................2:53:19 (485)
Mureithi, David M.........................5:08:41 (25,220)
Murfitt, Jody S 5:26:20 (28,516)
Murgatroyd, Kevin 5:21:14 (27,643)
Murguia, Ramon 3:19:12 (2,414)
Murphy, Andrew P 4:08:30 (10,871)
Murphy, Bradley............................2:55:11 (583)
Murphy, Brendan..........................4:59:35 (23,407)
Murphy, Brian J.............................4:16:14 (12,630)
Murphy, Chris P 5:06:43 (24,822)
Murphy, Colin 3:34:25 (4,330)
Murphy, Darren.............................3:42:45 (5,635)
Murphy, Darren J 5:06:02 (24,698)
Murphy, Denis J.............................4:48:04 (20,547)
Murphy, Dermot P 4:11:24 (11,474)
Murphy, Gerry M..........................4:00:17 (9,269)
Murphy, John C.............................4:06:19 (10,421)
Murphy, John C.............................4:58:25 (23,136)
Murphy, John M 3:54:51 (7,975)
Murphy, John P 3:23:36 (2,858)
Murphy, Kevin J.............................2:43:58 (214)
Murphy, Kieran C..........................3:06:32 (1,274)
Murphy, Luke.................................3:50:54 (7,115)
Murphy, Marcus A.........................4:29:46 (16,080)
Murphy, Mark................................4:02:25 (9,685)
Murphy, Martin 5:01:30 (23,829)
Murphy, Martin P..........................4:55:03 (22,274)
Murphy, Neil..................................4:52:40 (21,659)
Murphy, Niall.................................4:28:20 (15,680)
Murphy, Paul S 5:27:39 (28,736)
Murphy, Paul W.............................4:27:41 (15,512)
Murphy, Peter J 3:39:36 (5,128)
Murphy, Roy 3:48:27 (6,608)
Murphy, Stephen...........................4:29:38 (16,048)
Murphy, Stephen D........................4:16:20 (12,654)
Murphy, Timo P 5:11:59 (25,852)
Murphy, Tony 5:03:43 (24,273)
Murphy, Tony J..............................7:46:43 (35,607)
Murphy, Vincent J 4:28:02 (15,602)
Murphy, William J 3:14:27 (1,936)
Murphy-Sullivan, Stephen J 4:04:03 (9,974)
Murphyu, Eddie T..........................7:13:17 (35,327)
Murray, Alan..................................5:32:13 (29,485)
Murray, Alasdair 3:47:31 (6,432)
Murray, Andrew D 4:29:46 (16,080)
Murray, Barry G.............................5:01:08 (23,759)
Murray, Conor J.............................3:16:15 (2,099)
Murray, Daniel C...........................5:16:01 (26,669)
Murray, David J..............................3:26:19 (3,177)
Murray, David J..............................3:30:34 (3,796)
Murray, David J..............................4:13:04 (11,850)
Murray, Eoghan P 5:25:26 (28,351)
Murray, Frank................................4:11:50 (11,578)
Murray, Gordon 5:35:49 (30,025)
Murray, Graeme 4:07:11 (10,606)
Murray, James I..............................3:14:31 (1,943)
Murray, Joe S 4:33:41 (16,955)
Murray, John S...............................4:24:59 (14,818)
Murray, Jonathan J 3:11:27 (1,667)
Murray, Julian................................4:14:58 (12,313)
Murray, Malcolm P.........................4:19:17 (13,403)
Murray, Neil R 7:23:37 (35,421)
Murray, Paul 4:18:51 (13,296)
Murray, Peter J...............................4:37:32 (17,897)
Murray, Peter N..............................5:29:56 (29,124)
Murray, Philip J 4:40:33 (18,666)
Murray, Richard J 5:25:38 (28,391)

Murray, Stephen J 5:09:55 (25,453)
Murray, Stephen S.........................4:54:34 (22,158)
Murray, Thomas J..........................5:12:52 (26,014)
Murray, Thomas W.........................4:48:17 (20,597)
Mursell, John W 3:43:20 (5,744)
Murtagh, Peter M..........................2:41:41 (171)
Murthwaite, Robert J 5:05:32 (24,609)
Musa, Gbadebo O 5:39:48 (30,572)
Muse, Alan G..................................6:00:01 (32,576)
Musgrove, Eric W 3:35:20 (4,458)
Musgrove, Leigh D.........................4:42:21 (19,139)
Musselle, Paul................................4:49:01 (20,771)
Musselwhite, Andrew 4:35:30 (17,401)
Musson, Anthony R........................5:10:46 (25,621)
Mustafa, Daoud 2:28:29 (32)
Muster, René 4:08:35 (10,888)
Musty, Mark J 3:04:49 (1,149)
Muttoni, Antonio 4:11:16 (11,444)
Muxlow, Lee T................................3:58:42 (8,882)
Mwinga, Nchimunya......................5:40:04 (30,601)
Myers, Ian S 4:59:25 (23,354)
Myers, James..................................4:22:58 (14,322)
Myers, Mark L................................3:48:30 (6,619)
Myers, Robert K.............................5:37:36 (30,246)
Myers, Roger F 3:45:48 (6,149)
Myers, Terry A 4:56:15 (22,577)
Myerscough, Steve.........................2:58:57 (820)
Myland Osman, Neil M..................4:24:02 (14,580)
Myttion, Duncan 4:21:06 (13,874)
Mytton, Steven S............................3:47:50 (6,501)
Nabarro, Mike M............................4:38:08 (18,047)
Nadal, Matthew 4:17:17 (12,871)
Nadali, Michele..............................2:47:17 (291)
Nadin, Paul J 4:59:40 (23,425)
Nadin, Steve 3:54:08 (7,823)
Nagar, Nico....................................4:53:03 (21,762)
Nagarajan, Mahesh 6:37:34 (34,593)
Nagel, Roger D...............................3:57:02 (8,487)
Nagle, Paul 4:22:22 (14,167)
Nagra, Kanwaljit S 5:02:21 (24,001)
Nair, Sanil......................................6:27:32 (34,233)
Naish, Keith D 5:26:48 (28,587)
Nakamura, Kazutoshi.....................6:38:19 (34,617)
Nakazawa, Yasukazu 4:54:49 (22,229)
Nancarrow, James...........................4:32:59 (16,780)
Nanton, Carl D...............................3:32:21 (4,051)
Napthine, Paul K............................4:34:14 (17,085)
Nardi, Alessandro...........................5:12:29 (25,949)
Narducci, Fausto 3:42:56 (5,675)
Narel, Slawomir Paul 4:43:16 (19,363)
Narinesingh, Gareth 3:54:01 (7,794)
Naseem, Muhammad S....................4:42:35 (19,203)
Nash, David E 4:33:41 (16,955)
Nash, Dean G 4:24:08 (14,610)
Nash, Gary J...................................5:12:50 (26,005)
Nash, James E.................................5:26:11 (28,487)
Nash, James W................................6:18:27 (33,802)
Nash, Jonathan...............................4:22:48 (14,286)
Nash, Mark J...................................4:15:49 (12,511)
Nash, Michael A 5:47:17 (31,381)
Nash, Patrick J................................6:00:02 (32,582)
Nash, Paul S....................................3:53:11 (7,610)
Nash, Peter S 3:23:00 (2,796)
Nash, Simon P 3:21:32 (2,655)
Nash, Steve 5:16:41 (26,787)
Nash, Steven R................................4:28:33 (15,745)
Nash, Tim C....................................4:23:09 (14,366)
Nasryth-Miller, Dominic 4:25:54 (15,035)
Natali, Paul E.................................3:38:10 (4,865)
Nathan, Jorgen 3:54:47 (7,958)
Nathan, Joseph A 4:26:02 (15,064)
Nation, Richard..............................3:59:39 (9,129)
Natkiel, Alastair.............................4:11:35 (11,518)
Natoli, Gianfranco 4:28:24 (15,703)
Nattrass, Roy..................................5:32:29 (29,520)
Naude, Ignatius..............................4:39:32 (18,421)
Nauerth, Werner 3:27:24 (3,341)
Naughton, Peter..............................4:58:55 (23,230)
Naulleau, Remy A 3:29:04 (3,583)
Nauth-Misir, Rohan R 5:24:54 (28,261)
Navarro, Gregorio...........................4:02:10 (9,638)
Nayager, Preven..............................5:54:50 (32,127)
Nayler, Stephen M..........................4:11:06 (11,397)

Naylor, Dave G............3:31:28 (3,905)
Naylor, Gary............3:47:16 (6,389)
Naylor, Glen A............4:38:56 (18,265)
Naylor, Graham M............3:54:36 (7,921)
Naylor, Howard K............4:18:41 (13,259)
Nazeri, Kaspar............3:52:17 (7,429)
Neads, Kevin M............3:18:05 (2,295)
Neal, David C............3:25:42 (3,088)
Neal, Gregory G............4:55:15 (22,331)
Neal, Luke D............5:11:32 (25,763)
Neal, Martin J............4:36:27 (17,653)
Neal, Nigel P............4:13:31 (11,969)
Neal, Steve M............3:46:32 (6,254)
Neal, Thomas K............5:13:53 (26,209)
Neal, Tom D............4:57:02 (22,782)
Neal, Trevor J............6:15:29 (33,648)
Neale, Andrew J............5:05:56 (24,684)
Neale, David A............4:39:14 (18,345)
Neale, Nathan L............5:12:17 (25,917)
Neale, Steven B............4:09:39 (11,103)
Neale, Warren C............4:03:48 (9,927)
Nealon, Nick M............4:16:06 (12,596)
Neary, Dave............4:13:24 (11,936)
Neary, Gary M............5:36:42 (30,134)
Neath, Kevin............3:13:48 (1,883)
Nedjar, Magli............4:24:28 (14,698)
Needham, Ben............3:33:50 (4,241)
Needham, James............4:18:54 (13,306)
Needham, Joseph R............4:45:07 (19,863)
Needham, Michael J............4:24:43 (14,753)
Needham, Russell J............5:10:07 (25,509)
Needleman, Ian G............3:26:48 (3,240)
Neep, Andrew B............3:59:05 (8,981)
Neeson, Patrick J............4:07:00 (10,575)
Negre, Guilhen............4:15:05 (12,338)
Neidhart, Klaus............4:08:30 (10,871)
Neil, Martin L............4:15:09 (12,357)
Neild, Michael............5:09:27 (25,365)
Neill, David G............5:41:58 (30,827)
Neill, Peter P............5:18:59 (27,248)
Neilly, Mark............3:50:05 (6,960)
Neilson, Richard W............3:51:09 (7,171)
Nejat, Nejat N............4:38:41 (18,195)
Nellessen, Ernst............4:36:52 (17,758)
Nellins, Christopher T............3:18:57 (2,385)
Nellis, Joseph G............4:15:51 (12,526)
Nelson, Chris J............4:43:18 (19,372)
Nelson, Darren............3:52:07 (7,395)
Nelson, Gordon............4:35:48 (17,487)
Nelson, James J............4:27:14 (15,400)
Nelson, Jamie R............6:01:06 (32,684)
Nelson, John E............4:20:36 (13,752)
Nelson, Luke A............4:28:01 (15,592)
Nelson, Paul............5:25:43 (28,411)
Nelson, Paul S............3:28:15 (3,438)
Nelson, Peter C............4:11:22 (11,466)
Nelson, Tom............4:43:03 (19,306)
Nelson, William............4:54:20 (22,106)
Neocleous, Richard R............4:51:35 (21,392)
Nery, Simon J............3:55:42 (8,164)
Nesbit, Simon T............5:48:49 (31,562)
Nesbitt, Clive............4:57:45 (22,970)
Nessling, Mark A............4:48:41 (20,689)
Nester, Michael J............2:47:18 (294)
Neto, Luis M............4:16:55 (12,792)
Nettleford, Clive............4:49:51 (20,965)
Neuberg, Alain............3:46:45 (6,291)
Neuberger, Oliver............3:55:40 (8,155)
Neve, John R............4:06:52 (10,544)
Nevett, Geoffrey L............5:54:28 (32,107)
Nevill, Mark G............5:45:05 (31,163)
Nevill, Pete............3:29:50 (3,695)
Neville, Jan............6:24:58 (34,122)
Neville, Paul R............4:47:01 (20,286)
Nevzat, Aren............3:50:48 (7,095)
New, Michael J............3:19:22 (2,425)
New, Stephen B............4:27:58 (15,578)
Newall, Oliver J............4:18:41 (13,259)
Newbery, Mark............5:20:13 (27,459)
Newbold, Kevin J............4:34:58 (17,263)
Newbould, Andrew J............3:12:00 (1,727)
Newbury, Duncan J............3:47:35 (6,441)
Newbury, James............4:32:59 (16,780)

Newbury, Richard A............3:50:37 (7,059)
Newby, Christopher J............2:54:19 (533)
Newby, Scott J............6:15:05 (33,621)
Newcombe, Sean B............5:15:13 (26,505)
Newcombe, Tom............4:51:06 (21,266)
Newcome, Alexander C............3:29:50 (3,695)
Newell, Christopher M............3:55:09 (8,044)
Newell, Joe............5:01:38 (23,860)
Newell, Julian A............3:00:15 (913)
Newell, Mark S............4:03:10 (9,810)
Newell, Paul............3:25:00 (3,019)
Newell, Terry............6:44:19 (34,784)
Newey, Adam M............6:04:35 (32,923)
Newey, Jonathan P............3:04:56 (1,156)
Newey, Roy............7:04:24 (35,196)
Newham, Peter............3:12:17 (1,756)
Newhill, Lewis S............4:20:37 (13,758)
Newill, Stephen P............5:25:06 (28,289)
Newing, Andrew P............3:35:27 (4,478)
Newington-Bridges, Charles S.....4:48:18 (20,605)
Newins, Mathew D............4:05:45 (10,297)
Newitt, Mark W............4:36:55 (17,771)
Newland, David J............3:44:55 (6,015)
Newland, John H............5:56:53 (32,325)
Newman, Benjamin............4:28:12 (15,646)
Newman, Bernard S............6:17:36 (33,758)
Newman, David C............4:37:12 (17,823)
Newman, David J............5:19:33 (27,348)
Newman, Dominic J............4:47:53 (20,502)
Newman, Eddie............3:10:58 (1,628)
Newman, Gregory S............5:04:50 (24,476)
Newman, Ian............5:28:04 (28,812)
Newman, James A............4:22:50 (14,295)
Newman, Jonathan D............5:27:26 (28,702)
Newman, Karl............4:02:36 (9,708)
Newman, Paul S............3:12:24 (1,766)
Newman, Perry L............5:29:35 (29,082)
Newman, Peter J............5:54:19 (32,082)
Newman, Roberto............4:31:58 (16,554)
Newman, Roger............4:14:30 (12,204)
Newman, Ross............5:31:26 (29,371)
Newman, Steven J............5:20:46 (27,567)
Newman, Stuart E............4:55:41 (22,423)
Newman, Tom P............3:53:19 (7,648)
Newnham, Andrew R............4:11:46 (11,563)
Newnham, Matthew T............5:01:43 (23,871)
Newnham, Robin P............3:28:54 (3,558)
Newsham, Andrew............4:06:53 (10,547)
Newsham, John V............4:39:11 (18,329)
Newsome, Peter............3:59:04 (8,976)
Newstead, Louis G............5:23:41 (28,048)
Newstone, David............3:36:41 (4,640)
Newton, Eddy J............4:10:05 (11,180)
Newton, Harry J............4:00:45 (9,365)
Newton, Jack D............5:21:35 (27,709)
Newton, Lee............3:56:51 (8,444)
Newton, Maritn............3:02:59 (1,046)
Newton, Paul............4:37:53 (17,977)
Newton, Paul............5:45:44 (31,231)
Newton, Richard J............5:15:31 (26,567)
Newton, Richard M............5:17:39 (26,992)
Newton, Simon R............4:02:16 (9,665)
Newton, Stuart J............3:50:27 (7,029)
Newton Lee, Andy............4:45:00 (19,836)
Neys, Kristof............3:27:42 (3,373)
Ng, Chun W............4:00:19 (9,275)
Ng, Silky N............5:20:43 (27,557)
Nguimfack, Alain............2:48:12 (320)
Nguyen, Tuan P............6:38:46 (34,630)
Niblett, James R............4:35:52 (17,502)
Niblock, Andrew C............4:09:36 (11,095)
Niblock, Barry............5:58:22 (32,455)
Nice, Matthew A............4:07:16 (10,616)
Nicel, John M............4:08:14 (10,821)
Nicell, Patrick J............3:23:51 (2,886)
Nichol, David W............4:33:35 (16,930)
Nicholas, Adam K............3:50:06 (6,962)
Nicholas, Kevin M............3:59:28 (9,087)
Nicholas, Stephen............6:13:20 (33,510)
Nicholls, Andrew P............5:10:32 (25,584)
Nicholls, Andrew S............3:16:53 (2,169)
Nicholls, Anthony R............3:08:41 (1,444)
Nicholls, David W............3:55:59 (8,221)

Nicholls, Gareth............5:17:48 (27,011)
Nicholls, Gary R............5:14:34 (26,354)
Nicholls, Ian W............5:59:04 (32,513)
Nicholls, Jimmy............5:47:10 (31,365)
Nicholls, Keith A............5:03:24 (24,218)
Nicholls, Kenneth E............4:46:00 (20,061)
Nicholls, Martin J............5:31:07 (29,320)
Nicholls, Michael J............4:40:18 (18,603)
Nicholls, Paul K............5:59:11 (32,526)
Nicholls, Peter............4:46:46 (20,224)
Nicholls, Phil T............4:39:19 (18,368)
Nicholls, Richard D............4:20:09 (13,643)
Nichols, Alistair M............4:31:40 (16,500)
Nichols, Carl A............5:18:27 (27,155)
Nichols, Charles E............4:41:31 (18,927)
Nichols, James............4:56:06 (22,535)
Nichols, John D............3:45:07 (6,038)
Nichols, Michael............2:51:10 (416)
Nichols, Robert J............4:08:08 (10,794)
Nicholson, Alexander D............4:38:00 (18,011)
Nicholson, Andrew R............4:43:13 (19,343)
Nicholson, Angus............5:22:58 (27,932)
Nicholson, Dean............4:51:17 (21,307)
Nicholson, Dennis............7:29:29 (35,488)
Nicholson, Ian R............4:05:33 (10,250)
Nicholson, Jeremy M............4:18:59 (13,325)
Nicholson, Kevin............4:47:11 (20,331)
Nicholson, Luke A............4:40:54 (18,760)
Nicholson, Richard D............3:11:20 (1,657)
Nicholson, Ryan M............4:20:08 (13,637)
Nicholson, Timothy C............4:19:04 (13,343)
Nickless, Jeremy............4:05:27 (10,232)
Nicklin, John............5:23:25 (27,992)
Nicol, Edward............4:52:24 (21,597)
Nicol, Tim............4:59:41 (23,427)
Nicoli, Giuseppe............3:09:22 (1,506)
Nicolle, Richard J............4:51:31 (21,371)
Nicolson, Christian............2:31:52 (50)
Niederhuefner, Reiner............3:54:48 (7,962)
Nield, David J............3:20:20 (2,533)
Nielsen, Patrick W............3:54:04 (7,806)
Nielsen-Mazewski, Paul S............3:09:20 (1,503)
Niemann, Martin K............5:28:05 (28,815)
Nier, Jean-Philippe............3:35:30 (4,480)
Niewald, Ralf............4:55:36 (22,410)
Nightingale, Andrew J............5:45:58 (31,253)
Nightingale, David............4:00:58 (9,411)
Nightingale, John R............5:30:02 (29,147)
Nightingale, Mark J............3:26:45 (3,233)
Nightingale, Peter J............5:27:09 (28,646)
Nightingale, Tim B............3:29:38 (3,665)
Nigri, Ailar............2:58:37 (801)
Nijhawan, Anil............6:39:30 (34,655)
Nikolajsen, Ole............4:29:54 (16,121)
Nikolaou, Achilleas............6:25:11 (34,135)
Nikolic, Marko............4:29:44 (16,070)
Nikolich, Michael B............5:21:15 (27,644)
Nilsson, Jakob............2:52:08 (448)
Nilsson, Jan-Olof............3:02:02 (1,005)
Nilsson, Martin K............4:20:19 (13,686)
Nimmo, Steven G............3:06:25 (1,266)
Nisbett, Mark P............5:18:48 (27,214)
Nissen, Holger............5:10:54 (25,643)
Nitsch, Bob J............4:18:24 (13,174)
Nix, Kevin J............6:05:14 (32,977)
Nixon, Christopher F............4:40:44 (18,706)
Nixon, Mark A............4:12:43 (11,770)
Nkereuwen, Etibensi B............3:58:49 (8,913)
Noad, Peter J............3:39:41 (5,141)
Nobbs, Graham J............4:06:03 (10,361)
Nobbs, Stephen............5:20:44 (27,560)
Noble, Ian............6:02:14 (32,769)
Noble, John R............5:55:34 (32,199)
Noble, Mark A............6:01:58 (32,750)
Noble, Michael J............4:31:44 (16,515)
Noble, Robert J............5:04:56 (24,506)
Noble, Stephen J............3:59:26 (9,075)
Nock, Andrew C............4:30:20 (16,223)
Nock, Graham S............3:21:17 (2,633)
Nockels, David J............4:37:10 (17,817)
Nodari, Alessandro............3:23:14 (2,826)
Noden, Nicholas D............5:34:35 (29,860)
Noel-Johnson, Dominic C............4:10:37 (11,292)

Nolan, Barry J....4:49:13 (20,824)
Nolan, Francis S....6:04:40 (32,929)
Nolan, Frank....3:39:19 (5,067)
Nolan, Mark....4:50:17 (21,067)
Nolan, Richard K....3:17:02 (2,183)
Nolan, Thomas....5:00:36 (23,634)
Nonders, Henk P....4:53:39 (21,927)
Noon, Chris....5:16:12 (26,700)
Noore, Graeme J....3:52:34 (7,476)
Norbury, Antony....4:25:37 (14,973)
Nordgaard, Haavard....2:46:07 (262)
Nordli, Jan R....5:56:08 (32,250)
Norman, Alistair J....5:11:11 (25,698)
Norman, Andrew C....4:29:29 (15,998)
Norman, Kevin R....5:47:55 (31,454)
Norman, Peter J....4:21:08 (13,882)
Norman, Stephen J....4:14:36 (12,230)
Normand, Peter J....3:49:46 (6,886)
Normoyle, Trevor F....4:34:24 (17,114)
Norridge, Christopher....3:49:28 (6,821)
Norrie, Peter A....4:55:29 (22,389)
Norrington, Andrew P....5:07:10 (24,918)
Norris, Chris J....4:21:31 (13,971)
Norris, James A....4:22:04 (14,102)
Norris, John F....4:00:54 (9,399)
Norris, Jon R....4:05:19 (10,206)
Norris, Justin J....4:52:41 (21,662)
Norris, Leigh J....4:56:17 (22,582)
Norris, Paul M....4:18:04 (13,088)
Norris, Peter J....2:52:13 (452)
Norris, Philip....3:16:30 (2,128)
Norris, Robert J....5:19:33 (27,348)
Norriss, Brent T....3:47:20 (6,396)
North, Colin W....4:27:11 (15,381)
North, Glenn R....2:48:45 (337)
North, Ian K....4:26:55 (15,299)
North, Neil P....5:02:33 (24,051)
North, Paul R....4:48:41 (20,689)
North, Ryan P....4:56:14 (22,575)
North, Shaun R....2:54:09 (524)
North, Steffan J....2:31:39 (47)
Northall, David J....4:54:00 (22,022)
Northcott, Adrian P....3:42:12 (5,554)
Northcott, Roy....4:46:56 (20,262)
Northcott, Stephen J....3:32:56 (4,129)
Northfield, Ian J....4:48:25 (20,636)
Northmore, Andrew B....3:33:02 (4,141)
Northover, Martin J....4:57:48 (22,986)
Northy-Baker, Luke T....4:44:06 (19,563)
Nortima, Einar....3:36:23 (4,599)
Norton, Andrew R....4:48:10 (20,566)
Norton, Colin J....3:53:55 (7,769)
Norton, David R....4:00:03 (9,216)
Norton, Howard J....3:55:37 (8,143)
Norton, James P....4:15:07 (12,345)
Norton, Jerry P....5:04:28 (24,417)
Norton, John R....5:21:27 (27,687)
Norton, Jonathan F....3:50:44 (7,084)
Norton, Kenn....5:40:18 (30,627)
Norton, Nigel R....4:32:51 (16,755)
Norton, Oliver J....4:11:13 (11,430)
Norton, Paul F....5:25:57 (28,448)
Norton-Smith, Julian R....4:18:24 (13,174)
Norville, Keith J....4:24:51 (14,797)
Noshib, Hassan M....4:51:27 (21,356)
Nossel, Craig J....4:24:06 (14,598)
Nothanagel, Hayden B....5:26:03 (28,468)
Notley, Richard M....4:28:33 (15,745)
Notridge, Gavin L....5:34:20 (29,815)
Nott, Robert A....3:43:05 (5,704)
Notton, Christopher J....4:43:04 (19,310)
Nouillan, Bill....4:52:39 (21,656)
Noun, Anthony....3:33:35 (4,210)
Novais, José....3:30:18 (3,763)
Novis, Bob A....3:05:46 (1,224)
Nowacki, Wies....3:37:19 (4,724)
Noyce, Rob J....4:56:17 (22,582)
Ntuli, Dumisani T....5:17:17 (26,915)
Ntulume, Kezron E....5:27:11 (28,658)
Nu, Aqasa....4:45:14 (19,891)
Nugent, Brian A....4:29:23 (15,971)
Nugent, Paul....3:21:15 (2,628)
Nughes, Salvatore....5:05:45 (24,650)
Nugus, John P....2:56:59 (673)
Nundy, Stephen J....3:44:44 (5,984)
Nunn, Christopher R....3:19:03 (2,397)
Nunn, Jason R....4:59:20 (23,344)
Nunn, Peter E....5:50:16 (31,699)
Nunn, Terry....4:06:33 (10,476)
Nunn, Thomas W....4:17:28 (12,932)
Nuno Dias, Silva....3:06:04 (1,237)
Nurney, Andrew....4:24:49 (14,785)
Nurrish, David L....4:01:39 (9,543)
Nurse, Ian A....2:29:51 (40)
Nussey, Mark....3:57:22 (8,570)
Nuti, Renato....4:00:49 (9,378)
Nutley, Philip C....5:17:54 (27,031)
Nutt, Matthew R....2:57:43 (721)
Nutt, Robert....4:43:45 (19,471)
Nuttal, Peter E....4:59:33 (23,399)
Nuttall, John B....2:57:26 (705)
Nuttall, Luke J....3:15:13 (2,014)
Nuttall, Roger....4:41:14 (18,848)
Nuttall, Stephen G....3:57:41 (8,649)
Nutter, Eric....4:40:56 (18,772)
Nutter, Keith E....5:55:44 (32,211)
Nutter, Matthew J....5:55:55 (32,229)
Nutton, David....3:24:12 (2,929)
Nutton, Jonathan....4:04:33 (10,067)
Nye, Alexanderr C....4:00:18 (9,273)
Nye, Daniel A....4:59:32 (23,396)
Nye, Derek J....5:06:23 (24,764)
Nye, John....5:53:40 (32,026)
Nye, Steven J....4:46:25 (20,157)
Oakes, Mark A....4:26:25 (15,164)
Oakley, Alan....5:33:28 (29,675)
Oakley, Scott D....4:52:05 (21,509)
Oakley, Stephen T....6:44:01 (34,772)
Oates, John J....4:24:57 (14,814)
Oates, Trevor G....3:24:17 (2,939)
Oatham, Philip N....3:56:04 (8,240)
Oatley, Andrew A....5:04:17 (24,376)
Obelkevich, Dave....4:43:33 (19,426)
Obeng, Edward A....6:06:33 (33,082)
Oberle, Bertrand....4:07:30 (10,651)
O'Boyle, Jeff M....5:21:37 (27,715)
O'Bree, Michael W....4:54:36 (22,172)
O'Brien, Andrew J....6:17:05 (33,735)
O'Brien, David J....6:27:39 (34,240)
O'Brien, Declan J....5:22:10 (27,804)
O'Brien, Derek M....5:30:09 (29,168)
O'Brien, Greg....3:51:12 (7,189)
O'Brien, John G....3:50:15 (6,984)
O'Brien, Kevin....5:30:09 (29,168)
O'Brien, Kieran A....2:59:01 (825)
O'Brien, Mark....4:27:55 (15,563)
O'Brien, Martin I....4:58:19 (23,109)
O'Brien, Michael....4:59:54 (23,475)
O'Brien, Nigel D....5:09:35 (25,395)
O'Brien, Patrick J....5:45:22 (31,188)
O'Brien, Peter....5:26:25 (28,534)
O'Brien, Phillip....4:07:27 (10,644)
O'Brien, Richard J....4:31:00 (16,354)
O'Brien, Sean....3:56:27 (8,346)
O'Callaghan, James....2:58:45 (808)
O'Callaghan, Stephen T....4:09:39 (11,103)
O'Carroll, David....5:53:53 (32,042)
O'Carroll, Franklin O....4:00:21 (9,278)
Ochiltree, Ian....4:19:51 (13,559)
Ochs, Martin J....4:07:04 (10,587)
Ockwell, Ian R....5:25:45 (28,417)
Ocleirigh, Tiarnan....3:32:50 (4,111)
O'Connell, Desmond S....4:41:44 (18,969)
O'Connell, Eoin....2:35:34 (77)
O'Connell, Paul....4:54:34 (22,158)
O'Connell, Philip L....3:48:46 (6,682)
O'Connell, Simon....5:41:21 (30,748)
O'Connor, Aidan....3:52:03 (7,378)
O'Connor, Alan J....4:50:29 (21,116)
O'Connor, Calvin....4:11:38 (11,536)
O'Connor, David....5:33:04 (29,612)
O'Connor, Ian J....5:01:58 (23,929)
O'Connor, James T....5:10:00 (25,477)
O'Connor, Jason....3:17:55 (2,277)
O'Connor, John....4:46:52 (20,243)
O'Connor, Kevin....4:37:43 (17,942)
O'Connor, Kevin....5:00:22 (23,592)
O'Connor, Michael A....3:20:51 (2,591)
O'Connor, Niall J....3:32:16 (4,040)
O'Connor, Ray....3:59:17 (9,037)
O'Connor, Rory....4:22:23 (14,170)
O'Connor, Shane....3:17:26 (2,221)
O'Connor, William J....4:10:21 (11,236)
Octavio, Pantaleo....4:16:05 (12,589)
Oddie, William M....3:52:58 (7,557)
Oddy, James....4:46:24 (20,155)
Odele, Peter....6:22:15 (34,009)
Odell, Michael E....2:51:21 (421)
Odey, Loyd J....4:36:58 (17,779)
Odgers, Ian....4:11:07 (11,401)
O'Donnell, Brian....3:27:00 (3,281)
O'Donnell, Chris M....4:43:18 (19,372)
O'Donnell, Craig A....3:58:56 (8,947)
O'Donnell, Gary....3:20:48 (2,588)
O'Donnell, Gary J....3:43:32 (5,787)
O'Donnell, Julian E....5:32:04 (29,467)
O'Donnell, Kevin....5:22:44 (27,896)
O'Donnell, Kevin G....5:08:17 (25,152)
O'Donnell, Liam....5:15:39 (26,593)
O'Donnell, Paul V....3:03:05 (1,055)
O'Donnell, Stephen P....5:31:05 (29,312)
O'Donnellan, Colm....4:53:06 (21,779)
O'Donoghue, Barry....4:30:02 (16,155)
O'Donoghue, David J....3:42:46 (5,637)
O'Donoghue, Mark....4:03:26 (9,856)
O'Donoghue, Paul A....4:26:33 (15,205)
O'Donoghue, Thomas....3:18:28 (2,340)
O'Donovan, Timothy....3:39:26 (5,095)
O'Dowd, Noel P....2:55:53 (606)
O'Driscoll, Barry....3:30:43 (3,808)
O'Durand, Franklin....4:45:56 (20,042)
Odusanwo, Toyin....5:09:31 (25,375)
O'Dwyer, Daragh H....4:56:47 (22,710)
O'Dwyer, David S....4:07:53 (10,742)
O'Dwyer, Michael C....5:56:20 (32,269)
Oekland, Oeystein....3:51:22 (7,213)
Oelschlagger, Reinhard....4:41:23 (18,884)
O'Farrell, Vincent G....6:09:32 (33,275)
Offin, Michael G....5:27:21 (28,686)
Ofori, Nicholas....5:11:50 (25,820)
Ogbonna, Joseph C....5:41:27 (30,762)
Ogden, David....4:51:34 (21,387)
Ogden, David M....2:57:50 (733)
Ogierman, Andrew....5:21:38 (27,717)
Ogilvie, Douglas....6:35:18 (34,512)
Ogilvie, John A....4:28:55 (15,838)
Ogilvie, Paul N....4:34:29 (17,143)
Ogilvie Smals, Toby A....4:20:31 (13,736)
Ogle, Michael D....4:41:30 (18,920)
Ogle, Wesley T....5:48:39 (31,539)
Oglesby, Mark C....3:51:46 (7,311)
Ogne, Bjarne....5:16:55 (26,845)
O'Gorman, Timothy J....4:59:12 (23,308)
Ogostinetto, Gianfranco....4:23:27 (14,432)
O'Grady, Ashley....4:53:21 (21,848)
O'Grady, Eugene P....6:25:01 (34,125)
O'Grady, Paul....4:01:33 (9,521)
O'Grady, Sean....4:04:31 (10,059)
O'Grady, Thomas A....3:32:18 (4,047)
Ogun, Abi A....4:52:17 (21,566)
Ogunsanlu, Ayo O....4:23:47 (14,508)
O'Hagan, Fintan....4:30:00 (16,148)
O'Halloran, Lee P....5:14:43 (26,389)
O'Hanlon, Marcus C....5:12:42 (25,985)
O'Hanlon, Philip G....8:28:46 (35,676)
Ohar, Zeeshan....5:10:01 (25,486)
O'Hara, Stephen H....6:47:14 (34,867)
O'Hare, Alfred....4:36:54 (17,768)
O'Hare, Brendan J....4:39:13 (18,340)
O'Hare, Brian....5:30:30 (29,222)
O'Hare, James B....4:59:07 (23,292)
O'Hare, John P....4:44:03 (19,552)
O'Hare, Michael P....6:14:17 (33,568)
O'Hea, Allan J....4:52:05 (21,509)
Ohlhoff, Hermanus J....5:12:46 (25,994)
Ohlson, James A....3:51:09 (7,171)
Ohlson, Tim....5:04:50 (24,476)
Ojeda, Idelfonso F....5:33:59 (29,756)
Okae, Masazumi....4:53:36 (21,913)

Okano, Kiichiro	3:58:50	(8,921)
O'Keefe, Michael P	4:47:05	(20,308)
O'Keeffe, David A	5:34:29	(29,845)
O'Keeffe, David P	6:04:54	(32,950)
O'Keeffe, James B	5:08:06	(25,112)
O'Keeffe, Luke D	6:04:54	(32,950)
Okey, Daniel N	4:09:18	(11,031)
Okhrimenko, Ihor	3:59:40	(9,131)
Okoth, Nicholas O	6:51:59	(34,973)
Okubo, Kenji	4:44:58	(19,828)
Okuzaki, Yoshio	4:39:43	(18,466)
O'Ladide, Marc	5:26:34	(28,552)
Olafsson, Bergthor	3:00:27	(928)
Olafsson, David	4:12:56	(11,817)
Olaleye, Richard	4:15:10	(12,360)
Olavarria, Edvardo	3:18:44	(2,362)
Olbrisch, Jan	3:53:11	(7,610)
Olchawa, Piotr	3:24:41	(2,984)
Old, George	3:47:58	(6,520)
Oldendoerp, Horst	4:01:24	(9,499)
Oldfield, Alexander	3:14:24	(1,933)
Oldfield, Christopher J	3:57:53	(8,693)
Oldfield, Francis L	6:02:55	(32,817)
Oldfield, James V	5:48:45	(31,557)
Oldfield, Mark	5:40:19	(30,630)
Oldfield, Philip N	6:16:21	(33,709)
Oldfield, Richard	6:50:38	(34,949)
Oldfield, Richard T	4:59:29	(23,379)
Oldfield, Robert G	4:09:02	(10,956)
Oldroyd, Stuart J	4:48:18	(20,605)
Oleara, Gearoid	5:27:11	(28,658)
O'Leary, Jerome	3:52:48	(7,524)
O'Leary, Jim A	4:56:44	(22,702)
O'Leary, Patrick	4:56:35	(22,656)
O'Leary, Steven J	5:08:52	(25,256)
Olesen, Morten K	4:47:56	(20,512)
Oliphant, Benjamin E	6:19:11	(33,848)
Oliphant, Crawford	3:02:59	(1,046)
Oliphant, Matthew J	4:20:01	(13,602)
Oliveira, Jorge	3:27:04	(3,293)
Oliveira, Junio	2:42:42	(192)
Oliver, Adam P	5:16:37	(26,773)
Oliver, Andrew J	4:47:52	(20,494)
Oliver, Archie	7:06:44	(35,232)
Oliver, Brian E	3:54:13	(7,843)
Oliver, Danny	3:33:50	(4,241)
Oliver, David C	4:46:50	(20,235)
Oliver, Earl J	5:43:28	(30,990)
Oliver, Gareth I	3:44:19	(5,908)
Oliver, Gary D	5:00:27	(23,607)
Oliver, Geoff J	3:34:46	(4,371)
Oliver, James R	4:11:55	(11,596)
Oliver, Jean-Luc D	4:06:55	(10,554)
Oliver, Martin R	4:39:13	(18,340)
Oliver, Raife M	5:20:54	(27,587)
Oliver, Ralph M	4:24:49	(14,785)
Oliver, Rowan L	3:53:07	(7,594)
Oliver, Stephen J	5:49:15	(31,610)
Olivier, François	3:33:49	(4,238)
Olivieri, Massimo	5:09:22	(25,344)
Ollerton, Paul	3:54:07	(7,822)
Olliffe, Peter	4:34:52	(17,240)
Olmedo, Francisco J	2:49:56	(374)
Olney, Benjamin J	4:15:00	(12,325)
Olomu, Dayo	6:31:12	(34,370)
O'Loughlin, Pat F	5:14:42	(26,381)
O'Loughlin, Stephen J	5:14:39	(26,373)
O'Loughlin, Timothy O	3:43:52	(5,838)
O'Loughlin, Trevor	5:25:41	(28,402)
Olubaji, Abdul O	5:38:51	(30,435)
Olver, Charles R	3:56:19	(8,307)
O'Mahoney, Bernard P	7:01:34	(35,151)
O'Mahoney, Kevin P	4:59:12	(23,308)
O'Mahony, Jer M	3:57:14	(8,539)
O'Mahony, Noel P	3:27:46	(3,383)
Omar, Said T	3:11:23	(1,663)
O'Mara, Peter	3:57:42	(8,654)
Omar-Basha, Alexander	4:47:17	(20,357)
Omeara, David P	4:19:01	(13,330)
Omeara, Philip	4:08:17	(10,831)
Omuilleoir, Mairtin	4:23:04	(14,348)
Omurchu, Daithi G	4:05:48	(10,309)
O'Neill, Adam A	4:25:46	(15,009)
O'Neill, Douglas	3:49:13	(6,779)
O'Neill, Eamonn	2:49:38	(364)
O'Neill, Gerry G	5:01:33	(23,843)
O'Neill, Jevon	3:38:42	(4,956)
O'Neill, John A	3:24:01	(2,905)
O'Neill, John P	4:40:28	(18,644)
O'Neill, Kevin	4:09:10	(10,997)
O'Neill, Liam	3:57:36	(8,624)
O'Neill, Mark A	3:51:03	(7,145)
O'Neill, Martin G	5:56:14	(32,259)
O'Neill, Patrick	4:33:43	(16,970)
O'Neill, Patrick N	5:13:33	(26,131)
O'Neill, Peter J	4:24:00	(14,571)
O'Neill, Simon	3:51:24	(7,225)
O'Neill, Steve	5:14:52	(26,422)
Ong, Juling	4:59:01	(23,259)
Ong, Soon Seng	2:51:01	(413)
Ong, Stephen	4:59:01	(23,259)
Onslon, Richard E	4:13:49	(12,048)
Ooi, Adrian	5:39:10	(30,472)
Ooi, Arron L	5:39:09	(30,470)
Oosthuizen, Wessel	5:08:16	(25,151)
Openshaw, Jasmin M	5:14:52	(26,422)
Openshaw, Justin M	4:24:15	(14,643)
O'Phelan, Richard H	5:56:08	(32,250)
Or Kam Fat, Patrick N	5:28:22	(28,882)
Oram, William J	4:17:43	(13,002)
Orama, Antti	3:22:17	(2,725)
Orange, Jon	2:37:52	(108)
Orange, Tom J	3:11:51	(1,708)
Orbinson, Alexander	5:12:51	(26,008)
Orbrien, Bernard	4:14:55	(12,302)
Orchard, Stephen R	3:55:53	(8,204)
Orchard, Thomas J	5:11:56	(25,842)
Ord, Kevin B	4:16:54	(12,785)
Orefice, Michael J	5:59:22	(32,542)
O'Reilly, Bob	3:57:33	(8,610)
O'Reilly, Fintan	4:23:11	(14,374)
O'Reilly, John	5:10:05	(25,501)
O'Reilly, John P	4:06:06	(10,370)
O'Reilly, John Paul	5:05:41	(24,631)
Orford, Martin I	4:24:29	(14,701)
Organ, James E	3:59:16	(9,034)
Orhiunu, Wilson E	6:27:50	(34,246)
O'Riley, Dominic	3:42:55	(5,672)
Orlando, Antonio	5:15:40	(26,599)
Orloff, Simon M	4:05:55	(10,332)
Orme, Peter	3:31:29	(3,910)
Orme, Richard D	3:34:46	(4,371)
Ormerod, Kevin	4:19:49	(13,544)
Ormesher, Andrew	4:19:07	(13,359)
Ormiston, Chris J	4:37:49	(17,960)
Ormiston, Paul A	3:57:04	(8,494)
Ormiston, Simon J	4:24:53	(14,801)
Ormond, John M	5:32:07	(29,470)
Ormond, Michael E	5:34:05	(29,777)
O'Rourke, Kevin J	5:00:24	(23,598)
O'Rourke, Martin D	4:46:28	(20,170)
Orpwood, Nicholas S	3:44:11	(5,890)
Orr, Craig A	4:05:45	(10,297)
Orr, Robert	3:46:19	(6,222)
Orr Ewing, Robert C	3:51:07	(7,161)
Orrell, Mark	4:04:04	(9,978)
Orrell, Mark D	5:22:03	(27,788)
Orrom, James	4:35:20	(17,368)
Ortiz, Elmer A	4:15:35	(12,456)
Osbiston, Alan G	4:25:21	(14,907)
Osborn, Alexander	4:29:37	(16,042)
Osborn, Andrew J	5:33:48	(29,731)
Osborn, Leo B	3:43:33	(5,792)
Osborn, Mark E	4:17:01	(12,819)
Osborn, Matthew N	4:36:23	(17,637)
Osborn, Robert	5:18:42	(27,199)
Osborne, Adam M	2:36:29	(91)
Osborne, Andrew	3:48:32	(6,630)
Osborne, Christopher A	4:43:35	(19,437)
Osborne, Colin	4:45:11	(19,884)
Osborne, Colin J	5:19:34	(27,353)
Osborne, David A	5:38:00	(30,303)
Osborne, Graham	4:52:08	(21,521)
Osborne, Jamie	4:51:23	(21,339)
Osborne, Jarrod S	3:31:06	(3,850)
Osborne, Michael J	5:28:35	(28,914)
Osborne, Scott S	5:21:18	(27,657)
O'Seaghdha, Diarmuid	2:34:12	(67)
Osenton, Clive F	4:49:22	(20,853)
Osgood, Neil R	5:20:30	(27,517)
Osgood, Patrick T	3:48:30	(6,619)
O'Shaughnessy, Mark J	6:40:20	(34,674)
O'Shea, David J	4:05:40	(10,280)
O'Shea, John	3:23:15	(2,829)
O'Shea, John	4:36:43	(17,718)
O'Shea, John A	3:40:02	(5,195)
O'Shea, John M	3:13:57	(1,899)
O'Shea, Keld F	5:25:36	(28,389)
O'Shea, Kelvin A	5:35:30	(29,974)
O'Shea, Sean M	3:59:17	(9,037)
Osman, Paul M	3:56:01	(8,228)
Osman, Rick	4:13:00	(11,827)
Osmand, Alan	5:04:52	(24,492)
Ost, Philip	4:39:27	(18,404)
Osta, Massimo	4:04:24	(10,038)
Osteruann, Lothar	4:35:58	(17,527)
Ostler, Nicholas D	3:51:29	(7,250)
O'Sulivan, Michael A	4:04:03	(9,974)
O'Sullivan, Gerard N	3:29:29	(3,646)
O'Sullivan, John	3:39:55	(5,177)
O'Sullivan, Kevin J	3:36:15	(4,579)
O'Sullivan, Lewis C	4:44:27	(19,663)
O'Sullivan, Michael G	5:30:03	(29,152)
O'Sullivan, Michael P	3:20:22	(2,536)
O'Sullivan, Rikki J	5:44:00	(31,042)
Oswald, David M	5:42:57	(30,928)
Oswald, Richard A	4:05:20	(10,210)
Ota, Hiroyuki	4:53:08	(21,788)
Othen, Andy	4:19:08	(13,365)
Othen, Dean	5:36:38	(30,131)
Otkay, Emirali	5:25:18	(28,320)
Ottaway, Andrew	5:01:07	(23,755)
Ottaway, William J	5:12:21	(25,931)
Otten, Steven	4:10:51	(11,340)
Otter, Ian J	5:27:37	(28,732)
Otter, Simon T	4:38:58	(18,277)
Otty, Mark D	3:12:36	(1,789)
Ough, Anthony J	4:18:01	(13,080)
Oughton, Simon A	5:11:51	(25,824)
Outen, Sarah D	4:49:19	(20,842)
Ovenden, Jonathan	4:54:26	(22,132)
Over, Richard P	4:24:00	(14,571)
Overall, Robert I	4:22:51	(14,301)
Overberg, Siobhan M	4:11:31	(11,505)
Overman, David	4:11:56	(11,601)
Overney, Simon	5:37:22	(30,227)
Overy, Mike F	5:07:05	(24,905)
Ovington, Neil J	3:07:52	(1,375)
Owen, Andrew	4:17:25	(12,914)
Owen, Andrew	4:56:01	(22,519)
Owen, Chris A	3:40:48	(5,321)
Owen, Christopher	4:03:39	(9,891)
Owen, Colin M	3:57:37	(8,629)
Owen, David A	4:16:12	(12,621)
Owen, Eugene	3:49:20	(6,800)
Owen, Gareth E	4:32:21	(16,636)
Owen, John	4:51:40	(21,412)
Owen, John	5:16:10	(26,692)
Owen, John S	3:58:14	(8,772)
Owen, Kevin P	4:24:44	(14,756)
Owen, Lloyd S	5:21:50	(27,626)
Owen, Mark R	3:34:27	(4,338)
Owen, Martin J	3:24:29	(2,954)
Owen, Paul A	5:12:51	(26,008)
Owen, Philip A	5:18:28	(27,158)
Owen, Royden	5:01:58	(23,929)
Owen, Simon D	4:38:24	(18,126)
Owen, Steven R	3:55:52	(8,200)
Owen, Timothy H	5:34:00	(29,762)
Owen, Toby	3:47:43	(6,482)
Owen, Wayne C	3:25:34	(3,073)
Owens, John	6:18:51	(33,825)
Owens, John D	5:12:10	(25,892)
Owens, Kevin P	5:36:27	(30,107)
Owens, Nicholas J	4:56:30	(22,633)
Owens, Russell	4:47:58	(20,525)
Owens, Simon J	4:00:24	(9,293)
Oxberry, Paul	5:38:39	(30,409)
Oxbrow, Dave	4:49:24	(20,861)

Oxley, Chris 4:27:03 (15,339)
Oxley, Matthew D 4:51:34 (21,387)
Oxley, Philip M 4:10:02 (11,173)
Oxley, Simon 3:26:23 (3,184)
Oxley, Simon J 5:31:21 (29,351)
Oxley, Tim D 5:43:56 (31,029)
Oyston, Peter 4:19:20 (13,412)
Ozguven, Tevfik O 5:39:25 (30,510)
Ozturk, Bilal 5:30:02 (29,147)
Ozturk, Osman G 5:29:03 (28,992)
Pabla, Gursharnjit 5:16:38 (26,778)
Pace, David A 5:15:39 (26,593)
Pace, Michael J 3:59:46 (9,158)
Pace, Richard D 5:48:31 (31,524)
Pace, Richard J 3:04:17 (1,119)
Pace, Vincenzo 3:34:57 (4,403)
Pacey, Darren M 2:59:18 (847)
Packard, Christopher J 4:16:29 (12,695)
Packer, Gary E 5:20:52 (27,585)
Packer, Malcolm P 3:01:54 (999)
Packham, Mandy J 5:27:09 (28,646)
Packham, Terry S 4:48:08 (20,560)
Padden, Damian A 5:40:01 (30,592)
Padden, Eamonn Joseph 6:54:24 (35,025)
Paddison, Simon W 5:02:54 (24,108)
Paddock, Steven A 2:57:17 (698)
Paddon, David T 3:27:54 (3,396)
Paddon, Guy 4:00:42 (9,358)
Padfield, David 4:50:30 (21,120)
Padfield, Tim M 4:09:02 (10,956)
Padington, Mark A 5:30:40 (29,246)
Padmore, Kevin A 4:55:01 (22,267)
Padovan, Nicholas C 5:15:05 (26,478)
Page, Aaron J 3:51:54 (7,337)
Page, Aarron L 5:22:23 (27,831)
Page, Andrew C 4:10:36 (11,287)
Page, Andy R 3:23:23 (2,839)
Page, Danny 4:45:05 (19,857)
Page, David B 5:40:30 (30,654)
Page, David J 4:32:49 (16,744)
Page, Derek J 3:24:02 (2,909)
Page, Gary B 3:51:03 (7,145)
Page, Gordon R 6:23:24 (34,051)
Page, Ian W 5:10:19 (25,540)
Page, Jeremy L 4:23:30 (14,444)
Page, Mark A 6:32:45 (34,431)
Page, Martyn A 5:30:28 (29,216)
Page, Matthew 4:33:42 (16,962)
Page, Neal S 3:17:04 (2,189)
Page, Nigel D 4:24:12 (14,630)
Page, Nigel P 7:16:17 (35,355)
Page, Simon G 4:56:25 (22,616)
Page, Stephen J 3:38:52 (4,992)
Page, Steven D 5:42:09 (30,841)
Page, William S 4:40:46 (18,722)
Page-Dove, Max J 4:43:43 (19,466)
Pagerie, Thierry H 3:31:13 (3,868)
Paget, Jamie 4:58:49 (23,211)
Paget, Simon J 4:36:13 (17,585)
Paglino, Ciro 3:48:05 (6,539)
Paice, Graham B 4:05:21 (10,211)
Paice, Jonathan B 4:38:09 (18,051)
Paige, Graham J 4:10:48 (11,327)
Pain, David C 5:17:13 (26,900)
Pain, Malcolm 4:38:28 (18,140)
Paine, Julian 4:04:07 (9,989)
Paine, Malcolm A 3:15:45 (2,055)
Painter, Ian P 3:38:08 (4,860)
Painter, James A 3:39:04 (5,027)
Painter, Mark C 5:25:24 (28,341)
Painter, Michael N 4:54:53 (22,241)
Painter, Mike A 6:00:09 (32,592)
Paiva De Brito, Edvaldo 5:55:00 (32,149)
Pakey, John 4:22:09 (14,116)
Pakrington, Russell C 2:58:14 (764)
Palethorpe, Christopher 4:41:59 (19,033)
Paley, Stuart J 3:40:39 (5,290)
Palfery-Smith, James D 5:49:22 (31,616)
Palfrey, Daryl B 3:34:52 (4,390)
Palfrey, Ian A 5:20:58 (27,601)
Paliy, Alexey 3:58:58 (8,954)
Palladinetti, Fabrizio 3:08:56 (1,464)
Pallott, Patrick M 4:58:15 (23,089)

LONDON MARATHON

Palmer, Ben C 3:17:59 (2,283)
Palmer, Carl D 5:10:46 (25,621)
Palmer, Charles T 5:04:15 (24,363)
Palmer, Daniel 4:53:24 (21,862)
Palmer, Garry 2:57:41 (719)
Palmer, Graeme 5:00:16 (23,568)
Palmer, Ian S 4:57:42 (22,956)
Palmer, James 6:06:40 (33,088)
Palmer, Jeff E 3:57:53 (8,693)
Palmer, Justin M 4:37:51 (17,969)
Palmer, Kelvin J 3:22:43 (2,765)
Palmer, Kenneth L 3:32:27 (4,059)
Palmer, Michael 3:19:55 (2,483)
Palmer, Nigel D 5:28:29 (28,900)
Palmer, Richard 4:01:09 (9,452)
Palmer, Richard C 4:36:28 (17,657)
Palmer, Rod H 4:17:43 (13,002)
Palmer, Sam N 4:08:38 (10,900)
Palmer, Steven 5:18:47 (27,212)
Palmer, Stuart N 3:59:50 (9,167)
Palmer, Terry J 5:10:52 (25,639)
Palmer, Thomas J 4:51:52 (21,459)
Palmer, William R 3:43:16 (5,731)
Palmner, Matthew S 5:44:54 (31,139)
Palombella, Andrew N 3:27:22 (3,336)
Palterman, Stephen 5:20:32 (27,530)
Pamidighantam, Sreeram 5:05:06 (24,527)
Pamplin, John E 4:39:21 (18,381)
Panchal, Bharat J 5:31:57 (29,439)
Panchaud, Pascal 3:50:38 (7,062)
Panchen, Matthew N 5:39:43 (30,560)
Pancutt, Carl 5:49:12 (31,603)
Pandit, Steph J 5:31:44 (29,410)
Panesar, Harpal 4:24:48 (14,777)
Pankhania, Mahendra M 7:32:18 (35,510)
Pannell, Len J 4:25:26 (14,931)
Pannell, Mark A 5:42:31 (30,882)
Pannell, Scott L 5:39:29 (30,523)
Pannell, Toby J 4:51:07 (21,271)
Pant, Muktesh 5:19:05 (27,262)
Panter, John A 4:56:32 (22,640)
Panzert, Hartmut 4:20:37 (13,758)
Paolucci, Giustino 5:50:39 (31,744)
Papaioannou, Alexander 4:51:23 (21,339)
Pape, Robert 4:26:15 (15,120)
Papia, Dominick J 5:02:34 (24,055)
Papot, Yves 4:06:42 (10,502)
Papworth, Colin 5:16:28 (26,751)
Papworth, Michael J 6:09:07 (33,243)
Papworth, Nicholas 5:20:57 (27,598)
Paquet, Ulrich 2:56:45 (655)
Paramo, Miguel 3:15:01 (1,999)
Paramor, Joshua K 5:51:12 (31,796)
Paramore, Ian 2:48:23 (325)
Paranandi, Rajeev 3:36:12 (4,570)
Paratte, René 4:11:59 (11,608)
Parcell, Benjamin S 6:42:05 (34,723)
Parcell, Glen D 5:11:01 (25,671)
Pardo, Salvatore 3:28:09 (3,424)
Pares, John E 2:43:06 (201)
Parfitt, Mark 3:29:31 (3,650)
Parfitt, Martin J 4:22:11 (14,121)
Pargeter, Matthew J 4:30:43 (16,295)
Park, David 5:25:40 (28,398)
Park, Jeff A 4:52:43 (21,673)
Park, Michael J 3:48:03 (6,533)
Parke, Iain M 3:39:33 (5,118)
Parke, Kevin D 4:18:54 (13,306)
Parker, Brian S 4:52:52 (21,717)
Parker, Carl W 4:17:00 (12,814)
Parker, Chris F 2:56:48 (660)
Parker, Christopher J 3:30:39 (3,803)
Parker, Christopher S 4:54:55 (22,250)
Parker, Daniel M 3:28:37 (3,507)
Parker, Daniel S 4:33:35 (16,930)
Parker, David J 3:05:45 (1,222)
Parker, Graham J 6:03:37 (32,861)
Parker, James L 4:29:29 (15,998)
Parker, James L 5:11:08 (25,696)
Parker, James P 5:06:49 (24,844)
Parker, Jeremy 5:19:34 (27,353)
Parker, Jonathan R 3:38:36 (4,939)
Parker, Louis J 4:11:12 (11,427)
Parker, Matthew J 3:41:50 (5,491)
Parker, Mel T 2:59:27 (860)
Parker, Michael G 4:28:08 (15,629)
Parker, Miles I 5:29:11 (29,018)
Parker, Philip G 4:34:31 (17,154)
Parker, Richard 3:02:39 (1,035)
Parker, Robert 4:42:59 (19,291)
Parker, Robert B 4:40:09 (18,566)
Parker, Robert E 4:00:28 (9,303)
Parker, Robert J 4:28:28 (15,720)
Parker, Rodney J 3:55:35 (8,133)
Parker, Ronnie T 4:49:18 (20,838)
Parker, Stephen 3:22:52 (2,785)
Parker, Terence R 4:33:23 (16,890)
Parker, Terence T 5:07:19 (24,960)
Parker, Thomas D 5:09:57 (25,463)
Parker, William J 3:07:53 (1,379)
Parkes, Alastair J 5:00:06 (23,524)
Parkes, Brandon L 3:26:26 (3,190)
Parkes, George 2:58:11 (760)
Parkes, Guy R 5:29:00 (28,984)
Parkes, Laurence V 4:09:27 (11,063)
Parkes, Richard F 3:59:25 (9,073)
Parkin, James M 5:15:21 (26,531)
Parkin, Richard 5:31:55 (29,436)
Parkins, Stephen J 4:31:14 (16,411)
Parkinson, Alastair 6:41:42 (34,707)
Parkinson, Anthony G 5:41:32 (30,774)
Parkinson, Chris J 5:04:01 (24,328)
Parkinson, David A 4:05:17 (10,202)
Parkinson, David L 4:49:08 (20,803)
Parkinson, Fraser N 5:03:52 (24,301)
Parkinson, Jon J 3:09:13 (1,494)
Parkinson, Terence 3:14:36 (1,952)
Parkman, Daniel J 3:47:52 (6,504)
Parks, Jason S 4:22:12 (14,128)
Parks, Nick 3:25:31 (3,067)
Parks, Shaun 3:45:04 (6,033)
Parmar, Dilip 5:24:36 (28,199)
Parmar, Jayesh S 6:07:43 (33,146)
Parmar, Kamlesh 6:12:14 (33,437)
Parmar, Paul 4:46:16 (20,118)
Parmenter, Robert A 4:39:50 (18,494)
Parmiter, Thomas M 5:06:08 (24,723)
Parnaby, David 5:42:55 (30,924)
Parr, Harold E 4:09:40 (11,108)
Parr, Matthew J 3:33:02 (4,141)
Parr, Richard 5:03:26 (24,224)
Parrish, James 4:57:41 (22,954)
Parrish, Michael. P 4:22:28 (14,190)
Parrish, Robin A 5:32:47 (29,574)
Parrott, Mark 5:20:03 (27,430)
Parrott, Nick M 4:00:36 (9,330)
Parry, Adrian D 6:39:32 (34,657)
Parry, Colin R 5:17:12 (26,895)
Parry, David J 4:00:30 (9,311)
Parry, Doug 4:44:53 (19,803)
Parry, Duncan G 5:26:34 (28,552)
Parry, Karl G 4:11:36 (11,527)
Parry, Lindsay E 4:05:58 (10,348)
Parry, Malcolm 3:55:37 (8,143)
Parry, Peter J 3:19:50 (2,471)
Parry, Philip E 2:36:34 (92)
Parry, Phillip C 5:38:38 (30,402)
Parry, Steven R 4:06:27 (10,454)
Parry, Stuart P 5:27:50 (28,767)
Parry, William 4:28:35 (15,754)
Parske, Stephen 5:18:25 (27,146)
Parsley, Elvis I 2:50:55 (404)
Parsonage, Gareth J 5:09:53 (25,449)
Parsonage, John G 3:43:35 (5,797)
Parsonage, John R 4:07:08 (10,597)
Parsons, Andrew D 5:15:36 (26,586)
Parsons, Andrew R 3:13:46 (1,882)
Parsons, Ashley J 5:18:28 (27,158)

Parsons, Christopher J.....5:30:48 (29,264)
Parsons, Damon.....5:49:03 (31,591)
Parsons, David.....4:03:59 (9,963)
Parsons, David.....4:10:22 (11,240)
Parsons, David C.....5:42:17 (30,860)
Parsons, David R.....3:52:01 (7,366)
Parsons, Garry.....3:18:18 (2,325)
Parsons, Ian C.....4:47:54 (20,505)
Parsons, Julian G.....4:53:42 (21,942)
Parsons, Laurence M.....5:37:55 (30,290)
Parsons, Marc R.....5:41:31 (30,770)
Parsons, Matthew P.....4:02:05 (9,617)
Parsons, Michael E.....4:55:45 (22,444)
Parsons, Nick G.....4:55:49 (22,461)
Parsons, Paul.....6:14:14 (33,565)
Parsons, Roger.....3:57:38 (8,634)
Parsons, Stephen.....4:33:49 (16,995)
Partington, David A.....3:37:31 (4,754)
Partner, David.....4:40:47 (18,728)
Partner, Nicholas.....4:58:11 (23,070)
Partridge, Alan R.....4:55:54 (22,487)
Partridge, Andrew N.....5:36:21 (30,093)
Partridge, Anthony W.....4:17:19 (12,880)
Partridge, Simon.....5:07:53 (25,073)
Partridge, Simon D.....3:27:13 (3,312)
Paschalides, Ambrosios X.....6:53:15 (34,999)
Pascoe, Daniel J.....5:25:40 (28,398)
Pascoe, Edward.....6:04:46 (32,940)
Pascoe, Guy.....4:06:39 (10,491)
Pascoe, Matthew J.....3:18:57 (2,385)
Pascoe, Richard C.....3:18:52 (2,374)
Pascoe, Shaun W.....4:34:06 (17,050)
Pascoe, Stephen J.....4:00:27 (9,301)
Pasha, Tariq.....7:00:53 (35,145)
Pask, Jonathan M.....4:40:18 (18,603)
Pask, Martyn A.....6:07:31 (33,131)
Paskins, Paul N.....3:40:50 (5,329)
Pasquale, Michelino.....4:02:11 (9,642)
Passemier, Philippe A.....4:40:26 (18,638)
Passingham, Leonard J.....2:46:56 (282)
Passirani, Arcangelo.....3:59:11 (9,008)
Passley, Patrick D.....7:32:48 (35,513)
Passmore, David S.....5:09:05 (25,291)
Passmore, Jerome.....4:06:10 (10,385)
Pasturel, Pierre.....2:41:21 (161)
Patching, Daniel R.....4:05:48 (10,309)
Patel, Ajay.....4:14:53 (12,292)
Patel, Bharat.....4:31:14 (16,411)
Patel, Bhupendrabhai.....3:47:38 (6,460)
Patel, Brijesh R.....5:41:19 (30,744)
Patel, Deep.....5:43:13 (30,964)
Patel, Deepesh R.....4:29:31 (16,013)
Patel, Dhruve H.....4:25:44 (15,002)
Patel, Ghansham D.....5:21:29 (27,694)
Patel, Hiren R.....5:24:00 (28,107)
Patel, Jayesh K.....5:50:58 (31,771)
Patel, Kalpesh.....4:51:12 (21,286)
Patel, Kalpesh.....5:52:08 (31,886)
Patel, Kamlesh.....5:19:43 (27,376)
Patel, Kamlesh K.....3:50:00 (6,942)
Patel, Kiran D.....5:11:06 (25,687)
Patel, Mitul H.....4:45:52 (20,024)
Patel, Nehal S.....4:29:31 (16,013)
Patel, Paresh.....3:57:05 (8,497)
Patel, Praful A.....5:36:53 (30,161)
Patel, Raj.....5:09:46 (25,430)
Patel, Rohit.....5:58:39 (32,482)
Patel, Saagar J.....5:02:29 (24,033)
Patel, Sajid.....4:12:06 (11,630)
Patel, Sandip.....4:35:48 (17,487)
Patel, Shivlal H.....5:12:23 (25,936)
Patel, Sirish J.....5:08:56 (25,269)
Patel, Vinod M.....4:32:35 (16,686)
Patel, Vipin.....4:42:42 (19,230)
Patel, Vishal.....5:39:57 (30,580)
Patenall, Simon C.....3:57:21 (8,567)
Paterlini, Fabrizio.....4:09:59 (11,162)
Paterson, David J.....4:34:52 (17,240)
Paterson, Graham.....4:13:48 (12,043)
Paterson, Nathan.....5:08:51 (25,251)
Paterson, Robert.....4:59:19 (23,341)
Paterson, Stephen.....8:02:06 (35,645)
Paterson, Stephen J.....2:50:26 (389)
Paterson, Stephen J.....4:44:13 (19,604)
Paterson, Stuart H.....5:12:39 (25,974)
Pates, Jeremy N.....3:55:18 (8,077)
Pathak, Jay.....5:12:22 (25,933)
Pathak, Sanjay.....5:30:26 (29,205)
Pather, Rubin.....4:28:31 (15,730)
Pathmanathan, Kangesu.....7:16:11 (35,354)
Patman, James.....5:35:02 (29,918)
Patman, Simon B.....5:03:55 (24,312)
Paton, Alastair.....5:27:00 (28,619)
Paton, Colin G.....2:40:07 (142)
Paton, Damian.....4:20:34 (13,745)
Paton, Philip S.....3:38:46 (4,969)
Paton, Rikki.....5:32:26 (29,514)
Patrick, Aaron.....4:12:04 (11,624)
Patrick, David.....4:15:56 (12,538)
Patrick, Iain P.....6:00:52 (32,653)
Patrick, Nicholas A.....4:46:19 (20,130)
Patrick, Noel M.....6:43:08 (34,753)
Patrick, Stanley.....4:38:34 (18,168)
Patrizio, Di Toria.....4:10:25 (11,252)
Patten, Francis D.....5:03:15 (24,182)
Patten, Richard B.....4:27:39 (15,501)
Patterson, Andrew.....5:18:46 (27,207)
Patterson, Andrew L.....3:26:40 (3,217)
Patterson, Benjamin J.....3:50:29 (7,042)
Patterson, Dean K.....4:46:29 (20,174)
Patterson, Grant A.....4:33:35 (16,930)
Patterson, Michael J.....5:33:45 (29,722)
Patterson, Michael R.....6:09:53 (33,299)
Patterson, Stephen.....4:10:08 (11,190)
Pattinson, Richard J.....2:36:48 (94)
Pattison, Graham.....4:37:24 (17,862)
Pattison, Guy P.....4:20:19 (13,686)
Pattison, Mark R.....5:01:12 (23,773)
Patwardhan, Mahesh V.....5:05:37 (24,621)
Paul, Adrian M.....4:36:38 (17,700)
Paul, Alex R.....3:59:27 (9,083)
Paul, Andrew J.....3:47:06 (6,364)
Paul, Chris D.....4:35:52 (17,502)
Paul, David W.....4:49:21 (20,852)
Paul, Emerson R.....4:06:40 (10,494)
Paul, Raymond J.....4:42:12 (19,095)
Paul, Richard.....3:43:28 (5,770)
Paul, Robert.....5:04:48 (24,467)
Paul, Robert J.....6:29:19 (34,299)
Paul, Rupert B.....3:26:36 (3,206)
Paul Florence, Grant I.....3:09:55 (1,550)
Paule, Arnaud.....4:15:55 (12,533)
Pauley, George D.....3:06:42 (1,288)
Paull, Stephen J.....4:59:51 (23,467)
Paulo, Antonello.....3:45:33 (6,103)
Pauls, Wolfgang.....4:38:08 (18,047)
Paulson, Darryll A.....4:08:23 (10,846)
Pavey, Philip D.....4:14:53 (12,292)
Pavia, Francesco.....3:54:00 (7,792)
Pavitt, Peter.....4:35:38 (17,436)
Pawlett, Mark.....4:26:43 (15,242)
Pawson, Daniel.....4:41:30 (18,920)
Paxman, Eric.....3:01:34 (986)
Paxman, Josh M.....5:47:51 (31,444)
Pay, Dominic J.....4:17:51 (13,032)
Paya, Patrick.....3:17:38 (2,242)
Paydon, Marc B.....4:12:06 (11,630)
Paymen, Stijn A.....4:25:41 (14,993)
Payn, Daniel J.....4:26:56 (15,307)
Payne, Alastair W.....2:53:28 (494)
Payne, Andrew.....3:37:56 (4,814)
Payne, Andrew.....5:00:59 (23,722)
Payne, Andrew M.....4:11:35 (11,518)
Payne, Anthony.....3:24:04 (2,915)
Payne, Barry J.....4:55:36 (22,410)
Payne, Benjamin J.....5:52:04 (31,876)
Payne, Bradley M.....3:50:53 (7,111)
Payne, Chirstopher W.....5:21:49 (27,758)
Payne, Christopher M.....5:11:31 (25,759)
Payne, Darren.....4:35:40 (17,446)
Payne, Darren J.....4:58:15 (23,089)
Payne, David A.....4:37:26 (17,874)
Payne, David J.....5:14:30 (26,334)
Payne, Garry P.....2:39:31 (136)
Payne, Gary F.....5:05:21 (24,564)
Payne, Graeme M.....4:00:39 (9,345)
Payne, Greg A.....4:17:28 (12,932)
Payne, James N.....5:33:05 (29,617)
Payne, James R.....4:41:07 (18,817)
Payne, Keith J.....5:06:59 (24,876)
Payne, Kevin L.....6:22:22 (34,017)
Payne, Leonard A.....8:02:02 (35,643)
Payne, Lisa A.....5:16:28 (26,751)
Payne, Mathew.....3:39:28 (5,100)
Payne, Matthew R.....3:50:02 (6,951)
Payne, Michael T.....6:00:40 (32,637)
Payne, Neil J.....3:54:41 (7,940)
Payne, Nick J.....4:22:41 (14,253)
Payne, Philip.....4:33:46 (16,983)
Payne, Richard J.....4:56:39 (22,679)
Payne, Richard S.....5:55:53 (32,227)
Payne, Robert.....3:49:05 (6,747)
Payne, Robert A.....4:55:36 (22,410)
Payne, Robert R.....3:33:53 (4,250)
Payne, Stephen.....6:38:28 (34,620)
Payne, Tim.....4:41:00 (18,791)
Paynter, David I.....3:49:59 (6,934)
Payton, Scott J.....4:38:05 (18,035)
Peace, Andrew S.....2:37:18 (102)
Peace, Anthony J.....4:40:18 (18,603)
Peace, Michael S.....3:57:27 (8,590)
Peach, Tony M.....3:53:05 (7,587)
Peachey, Mike.....3:25:54 (3,115)
Peacock, Carl J.....5:34:05 (29,777)
Peacock, Christopher.....4:16:45 (12,751)
Peacock, John.....5:08:10 (25,131)
Peacock, Kim C.....5:34:17 (29,811)
Peacock, Mark R.....4:34:27 (17,135)
Peacock, Michael J.....4:57:57 (23,022)
Peacock, Simon L.....4:19:30 (13,460)
Peacock, Trevor.....4:08:16 (10,829)
Pead, Mark S.....4:05:39 (10,277)
Peak, Daniel.....3:42:06 (5,538)
Peake, Andrew A.....5:25:00 (28,269)
Peake, Stan E.....4:24:49 (14,785)
Peaock, Darren.....4:39:48 (18,488)
Pearce, Andrew R.....3:54:49 (7,965)
Pearce, Andrew W.....3:59:45 (9,152)
Pearce, Antony.....5:01:57 (23,922)
Pearce, David A.....3:01:16 (973)
Pearce, David S.....4:40:59 (18,780)
Pearce, Gary R.....4:36:44 (17,723)
Pearce, Gavin J.....4:25:41 (14,993)
Pearce, Graham.....5:07:53 (25,073)
Pearce, Ian P.....4:33:17 (16,863)
Pearce, Keith G.....4:26:13 (15,105)
Pearce, Matthew D.....4:50:01 (20,998)
Pearce, Matthew S.....4:19:29 (13,458)
Pearce, Michael W.....4:40:54 (18,760)
Pearce, Paul.....6:19:35 (33,866)
Pearce, Paul R.....3:56:41 (8,399)
Pearce, Richard A.....4:16:00 (12,562)
Pearce, Richard J.....4:06:05 (10,367)
Pearce, Robert E.....4:04:12 (10,006)
Pearce, Steve.....4:56:10 (22,555)
Pearce, Steve J.....4:15:17 (12,391)
Pearce, Steven J.....5:58:25 (32,461)
Pearce, Stuatr J.....4:32:32 (16,672)
Pearce, Todd.....4:45:04 (19,856)
Pearce, William S.....4:27:45 (15,533)
Pearl, Kenneth J.....6:01:22 (32,710)
Pearman, Adrian C.....5:36:52 (30,159)
Pearman, Matthew.....5:19:57 (27,417)
Pearman, Nicholas W.....5:03:51 (24,298)
Pearn, Mark W.....3:56:59 (8,476)
Pears, Bryan M.....3:35:05 (4,417)
Pearse, David K.....3:53:56 (7,775)
Pearse, Gary.....3:09:38 (1,525)
Pearse, Justin M.....4:16:24 (12,670)
Pearson, Andrew A.....4:13:32 (11,980)
Pearson, Andrew J.....3:17:07 (2,192)
Pearson, Andrew J.....4:44:47 (19,772)
Pearson, Andrew J.....4:50:11 (21,042)
Pearson, Anthony.....3:54:15 (7,855)
Pearson, Charles J.....5:25:54 (28,443)
Pearson, Charlie L.....2:46:57 (284)
Pearson, Christopher J.....3:34:39 (4,358)
Pearson, Daniel.....4:54:14 (22,085)
Pearson, David.....4:30:19 (16,218)

Pearson, David S....3:44:27 (5,933)
Pearson, Don....3:22:57 (2,793)
Pearson, Gary....3:53:30 (7,689)
Pearson, Hugh A....3:07:04 (1,318)
Pearson, John E....4:06:28 (10,458)
Pearson, John H....3:53:43 (7,733)
Pearson, Lee A....4:57:38 (22,939)
Pearson, Richard D....4:38:17 (18,084)
Pearson, Robert A....4:27:29 (15,467)
Pearson, Robert D....5:12:58 (26,039)
Pearson, Toby S....2:44:27 (227)
Pearsons, Phil N....4:02:10 (9,638)
Peart, Daniel J....4:37:55 (17,986)
Peart, David....3:51:49 (7,318)
Pease, Steven A....4:13:30 (11,963)
Peasgood, David M....3:49:40 (6,862)
Peat, James....4:05:59 (10,350)
Peatfield, Tristan....5:18:09 (27,091)
Peciulis, Ed....4:22:53 (14,308)
Peck, Andrew R....4:35:24 (17,382)
Peckitt, Simon M....3:23:41 (2,867)
Pecorari, Claudio....5:21:24 (27,680)
Peddeer, David M....3:45:32 (6,097)
Peddie, Neil A....5:16:52 (26,829)
Peddie, Steven A....2:58:42 (806)
Pedersen, Mogens....4:54:39 (22,185)
Pedley, Daniel J....4:13:42 (12,018)
Pedley, Martin J....6:06:09 (33,060)
Pedras, Rui M....4:17:10 (12,845)
Pedrini, Didier....3:38:37 (4,943)
Peebles, Hugo....5:21:49 (27,758)
Peebles, Keith A....4:24:09 (14,618)
Peek, Martin....6:00:25 (32,614)
Peel, Anthony....4:09:36 (11,095)
Peel, Christoher J....3:53:01 (7,573)
Peel, David G....4:00:03 (9,216)
Peel, David J....4:51:11 (21,281)
Peel, Mike....4:30:32 (16,261)
Peel, Stephen W....5:38:31 (30,384)
Peers, Gareth....4:56:22 (22,606)
Peers, Richard W....3:54:33 (7,911)
Peers, Robert J....4:22:04 (14,102)
Peers, Wayne V....5:10:14 (25,530)
Peet, David S....5:09:42 (25,415)
Peevor, Robert F....3:57:57 (8,708)
Pegg, Jonathan C....4:29:03 (15,867)
Pegler, Adrian M....4:34:03 (17,039)
Pegler, Graham N....5:28:03 (28,810)
Pegrum, Nigel....3:23:39 (2,864)
Peleszok, Matthew....5:17:56 (27,037)
Pell, David J....5:07:53 (25,073)
Pell, Gary M....4:58:29 (23,149)
Pellew, Alex....3:45:58 (6,174)
Pelling, Derek M....5:43:05 (30,944)
Peltier, Andrew....5:10:47 (25,625)
Peltor, Edward....2:58:36 (797)
Pemberton, Alan R....3:36:16 (4,582)
Pemberton, William J....4:27:16 (15,411)
Pembroke, John P....3:19:05 (2,401)
Penaluna, Karl S....3:59:24 (9,068)
Penaranda, Fernando....4:10:17 (11,226)
Pendlebury, Christopher J....3:42:55 (5,672)
Pendleton, Ray....4:56:20 (22,598)
Pendrick, Graham....3:56:37 (8,385)
Pendrill, James C....2:54:32 (549)
Penfold, Christopher....5:07:22 (24,970)
Penfold, Miles A....3:18:46 (2,364)
Penfold, Mungo....3:53:42 (7,728)
Penfold, Robert A....5:28:03 (28,810)
Penfold, Robert J....6:01:17 (32,703)
Penhale, Bruce....3:49:31 (6,836)
Penka, Wolfgang....3:59:30 (9,094)
Penman, Jeffrey J....5:36:10 (30,064)
Penman, Robert M....5:08:34 (25,197)
Penn, Gregory....3:07:22 (1,340)
Penn, Jeremy J....4:42:50 (19,264)
Penn, Russell....3:59:45 (9,152)
Penn, Timothy E....4:54:18 (22,101)
Pennell, Ian J....4:46:17 (20,120)
Penney, Andrew D....2:48:57 (344)
Penney, Andrew M....4:15:41 (12,480)
Penney, Michael W....4:54:59 (22,261)
Penney, Paul J....4:57:37 (22,936)
Pennicott, James....3:17:01 (2,180)
Pennington, David....4:49:16 (20,831)
Pennington, David C....4:13:30 (11,963)
Pennington, John....5:22:44 (27,896)
Pennington, Mark....4:29:38 (16,048)
Pennington, Michael J....3:21:27 (2,644)
Pennington, Robert....4:25:57 (15,043)
Penny, Brian W....2:50:55 (404)
Penny, Justin V....4:36:30 (17,664)
Penny, Ray G....4:20:28 (13,724)
Penny Smith, Simon....4:49:59 (20,990)
Pennycook, Dave....4:11:34 (11,512)
Penswick, Stuart P....5:56:12 (32,255)
Penta, Vincenzo....4:47:15 (20,345)
Pentecost, Rickard A....5:21:24 (27,680)
Pentin, Richard P....3:26:14 (3,163)
Pentner, Joe....3:55:51 (8,195)
Penwarden, Nigel C....4:01:44 (9,555)
Pepels, Willebrorous R....3:50:48 (7,095)
Pepin, Nick....4:16:39 (12,726)
Pepper, David....3:47:29 (6,423)
Pepper, John R....4:17:12 (12,853)
Pepperell, John....5:49:56 (31,670)
Percey, Steven J....4:13:22 (11,926)
Percival, Deon L....3:59:37 (9,123)
Percival, Thomas....3:39:23 (5,082)
Percival-Smith, Paul E....3:27:27 (3,350)
Percy, Robin J....4:42:02 (19,047)
Pere, Sebastien....4:12:06 (11,630)
Perego, Stefano....4:07:49 (10,730)
Pereira, Ashley....4:42:08 (19,073)
Pereira, Luis J....5:05:28 (24,595)
Pereira, Stephen....5:18:21 (27,135)
Pereira Da Costa, José P....3:59:44 (9,149)
Perez, Antonio....3:16:23 (2,116)
Perez, Jesus Manuel....4:24:03 (14,585)
Perez, John....3:37:37 (4,767)
Perez, Luis....4:01:40 (9,545)
Perez, Richard M....5:04:48 (24,467)
Perfect, Martin J....5:53:27 (32,000)
Pergola, Luca G....5:03:25 (24,221)
Perin, Ivan....3:16:48 (2,158)
Perini, Gino....4:42:28 (19,171)
Perini, Giovanni....4:13:35 (11,990)
Perkin, Simon L....3:38:27 (4,913)
Perkins, Chris R....4:02:01 (9,605)
Perkins, John D....6:38:16 (34,616)
Perkins, Mark R....3:50:09 (6,969)
Perkins, Martyn....3:15:58 (2,076)
Perkins, Matthew D....4:56:03 (22,526)
Perkins, Tom W....3:36:43 (4,650)
Perks, Tony....5:05:28 (24,595)
Peros, Paul....4:11:05 (11,393)
Perrault, Adrien....3:12:32 (1,782)
Perrault, Gilles....2:54:30 (545)
Perrett, Royden W....3:40:55 (5,351)
Perrett, William P....5:38:15 (30,342)
Perrie, James A....3:56:09 (8,265)
Perriello, Andrea....3:45:23 (6,079)
Perrin, David B....4:07:57 (10,760)
Perrin, Gabriel....3:58:56 (8,947)
Perrin, Kevin....4:38:38 (18,183)
Perrott, Anthony M....3:30:04 (3,729)
Perrucci, Pietro....4:44:57 (19,820)
Perry, Ben....4:31:31 (16,463)
Perry, Daniel H....4:18:31 (13,217)
Perry, David....5:48:51 (31,568)
Perry, Giles C....4:52:56 (21,735)
Perry, James....4:57:47 (22,983)
Perry, Jonathan....4:50:46 (21,183)
Perry, Mark T....3:13:57 (1,899)
Perry, Matthew S....4:07:42 (10,704)
Perry, Richard C....4:56:40 (22,686)
Perry, Simon....5:57:05 (32,341)
Perry, Simon C....5:25:26 (28,351)
Perry, Simon W....3:50:32 (7,046)
Perry, Stephen E....4:33:19 (16,876)
Perry, Steve....5:59:04 (32,513)
Perryman, Andrew I....5:07:13 (24,934)
Perryman, Andrew S....5:08:01 (25,099)
Perryman, Graham....3:28:06 (3,420)
Persson, Per E....4:14:32 (12,211)
Pert, Jeremy....4:26:27 (15,176)
Pescod, Daniel....3:10:08 (1,574)
Peskett, Malcolm J....3:50:15 (6,984)
Peskett, Paul J....4:08:24 (10,848)
Pesquero, Gary D....3:08:09 (1,401)
Pessok, Ben....3:32:18 (4,047)
Pessok, Ben....4:26:43 (15,242)
Pester, Paul D....3:54:15 (7,855)
Petagna, Marco....4:14:54 (12,297)
Petch, Christopher J....3:19:51 (2,473)
Peters, Daniel....5:47:19 (31,392)
Peters, Gary R....4:14:01 (12,101)
Peters, Iain J....5:40:43 (30,673)
Peters, James....3:43:30 (5,779)
Peters, Keith G....4:51:49 (21,440)
Peters, Lee M....4:29:20 (15,947)
Peters, Lyle....3:54:26 (7,889)
Peters, Michael....3:52:45 (7,515)
Peterson, Richard J....3:11:45 (1,698)
Petit, Alain H....3:19:50 (2,471)
Petite, Keith S....4:34:00 (17,034)
Petith, Howard C....5:40:51 (30,689)
Petrides, John G....6:25:26 (34,145)
Petrie, James C....5:54:16 (32,078)
Petrozzi, Franco T....5:21:41 (27,731)
Petruso, Tony....3:55:19 (8,085)
Petry, Dirk....3:50:36 (7,054)
Pettefar, David C....6:13:57 (33,548)
Pettengell, Lee B....5:32:56 (29,597)
Petter, James C....4:14:29 (12,200)
Pettet, David A....4:40:48 (18,733)
Pettifer, Edward B....5:57:22 (32,360)
Pettifer, John S....4:46:33 (20,190)
Pettigrew, Andrew D....5:05:33 (24,612)
Pettit, Daniel S....3:53:51 (7,753)
Pettit, Mark S....4:14:51 (12,278)
Pettit, Simon....4:51:32 (21,376)
Pettitt, Martin J....4:40:40 (18,694)
Pettitt, Nathan....5:11:05 (25,682)
Pettitt, Nick....3:42:37 (5,611)
Pettitt, Simon P....3:35:31 (4,486)
Peuker, Martin....5:38:53 (30,439)
Pezic, Stanko N....4:09:07 (10,979)
Pfeffer, Jerome....4:41:20 (18,869)
Pfeifer, Sandy A....3:26:26 (3,190)
Phamba, Loic....4:35:08 (17,310)
Pharoah, Andrew F....3:36:11 (4,568)
Pheasant, Colin R....4:41:55 (19,020)
Phelan, Chris....2:54:15 (528)
Phelan, James D....6:10:11 (33,316)
Phelan, Jim F....3:34:40 (4,361)
Phelan, Joseph....4:55:50 (22,468)
Phelan, Mark....5:23:59 (28,105)
Phelps, Nigel A....4:13:41 (12,014)
Philip, Daryl R....2:57:29 (708)
Philip, John D....5:42:10 (30,844)
Philip, Simon J....4:48:49 (20,725)
Philippe, Fleury....6:13:00 (33,490)
Philippides, Tristan....3:46:56 (6,332)
Philippou, Stefanos....3:56:17 (8,297)
Philips, Julian....4:18:48 (13,286)
Philips, Scot....4:49:11 (20,817)
Phillipps, Graham....5:07:09 (24,915)
Phillips, Alan....7:00:38 (35,140)
Phillips, Andrew J....3:57:27 (8,590)
Phillips, Andrew J....4:25:13 (14,879)
Phillips, Anthony J....4:31:48 (16,527)
Phillips, Ben S....3:53:19 (7,648)
Phillips, Brian P....5:36:25 (30,101)
Phillips, Bryan R....5:00:07 (23,526)
Phillips, Christopher J....4:09:25 (11,053)
Phillips, Colin....5:44:38 (31,116)
Phillips, Darren....4:00:14 (9,261)
Phillips, David H....4:19:15 (13,395)
Phillips, David M....4:28:58 (15,852)
Phillips, Gavin S....3:47:09 (6,370)
Phillips, George....4:34:30 (17,148)
Phillips, Graeme C....5:09:56 (25,457)
Phillips, Greg S....4:47:27 (20,394)
Phillips, Henry....8:38:09 (35,680)
Phillips, Iain J....4:45:18 (19,905)
Phillips, Ian D....4:42:10 (19,082)
Phillips, James....4:44:35 (19,712)
Phillips, James A....5:23:31 (28,013)

Phillips, James W 6:35:19 (34,514)
Phillips, John D 3:56:34 (8,376)
Phillips, Larry L 4:40:54 (18,760)
Phillips, Lee M 3:53:30 (7,689)
Phillips, Leonard J 4:08:00 (10,767)
Phillips, Mark I 5:19:31 (27,344)
Phillips, Mark J 3:50:13 (6,977)
Phillips, Matthew 6:36:47 (34,569)
Phillips, Neil C 5:54:25 (32,099)
Phillips, Paul G 4:22:40 (14,248)
Phillips, Richard H 2:55:25 (590)
Phillips, Richard N 4:46:05 (20,073)
Phillips, Rob 2:44:07 (217)
Phillips, Roger 5:01:30 (23,829)
Phillips, Roger S 3:51:01 (7,142)
Phillips, Simon 5:36:26 (30,103)
Phillips, Simon B 5:16:29 (26,755)
Phillips, Simon R 4:41:52 (19,013)
Phillips, Terence G 4:31:41 (16,504)
Phillips, Terry M 4:42:46 (19,246)
Phillips, Tomas E 4:56:17 (22,582)
Phillips, Trevor 4:23:31 (14,451)
Phillips, Trevor 5:32:30 (29,525)
Phillipson, Ian M 5:02:27 (24,026)
Phillis, Richard G 3:51:55 (7,342)
Philp, Bruce M 4:59:46 (23,448)
Philp, Dean J 5:31:01 (29,298)
Philp, Russell P 4:17:20 (12,887)
Philpot, Dave 5:58:55 (32,498)
Philpot, David S 3:15:44 (2,052)
Philpott, Mark A 3:49:25 (6,815)
Philpott, Matthew J 4:30:53 (16,334)
Philpott, Ryan 4:21:08 (13,882)
Philpotts, Dennis L 4:49:04 (20,783)
Philpotts, Robert G 3:42:35 (5,608)
Philps, Stuart C 5:14:10 (26,262)
Phipps, Kevin M 4:34:20 (17,101)
Phoenix, Ian 4:03:17 (9,832)
Phoenix, Mike 5:11:14 (25,709)
Phull, Gurvinder 6:05:31 (33,006)
Picatto, Mirto 3:32:55 (4,126)
Piccavet, Luc 3:38:49 (4,978)
Pick, David 5:05:37 (24,621)
Pickard, Mark J 3:56:26 (8,338)
Pickavance, John P 4:52:52 (21,717)
Pickering, Derrick J 5:33:43 (29,715)
Pickering, Ian D 4:28:23 (15,695)
Pickering, James L 4:37:51 (17,969)
Pickering, James R 5:41:39 (30,787)
Pickering, Steven D 3:38:39 (4,949)
Pickersgill, Richard M 5:33:22 (29,660)
Pickett, Ian 3:29:25 (3,637)
Pickett, James R 3:22:45 (2,769)
Pickford, Christopher A 5:17:57 (27,041)
Pickford, David C 4:37:51 (17,969)
Pickford, Tony 6:18:59 (33,836)
Pickles, Damieon H 4:43:42 (19,463)
Pickles, Martin A 3:52:52 (7,537)
Pickles, Mike 4:06:04 (10,364)
Pickthall, Chris 3:57:39 (8,639)
Pickup, David 5:01:57 (23,922)
Pickup, John M 4:09:00 (10,949)
Pickup, Simon 6:14:31 (33,581)
Picquet, Rodolphe 3:54:14 (7,848)
Picton, Colin D 5:03:26 (24,224)
Pidgeon, Nicholas H 3:46:23 (6,233)
Pidgeon, Philip J 5:58:14 (32,434)
Pidgeon, Simon J 5:38:43 (30,420)
Pidgeon, Steve T 5:26:56 (28,614)
Pie, Carl B 4:29:20 (15,947)
Pierce, Ben J 3:39:20 (5,071)
Pierce, Giles A 4:12:40 (11,761)
Pierce, Lee J 5:18:22 (27,140)
Piercy, Richard 5:08:38 (25,213)
Piercy, Timothy J 4:51:41 (21,419)
Pierpoint, Richard 4:23:57 (14,555)
Piers, Milton R 5:48:58 (31,580)
Piersall, Anthony C 5:12:53 (26,019)
Pierson, David W 4:39:46 (18,476)
Pierson, Michael N 6:09:27 (33,267)
Pieterse, Vlam G 5:10:23 (25,552)
Piette, Jean 4:43:56 (19,517)
Piewtrafesa, Leonardo 5:20:05 (27,435)
Piga, Salvatore 4:30:04 (16,165)
Pigford, Mark 3:04:30 (1,131)
Piggott, Jonathan D 5:15:39 (26,593)
Pighills, Stephen G 5:20:12 (27,457)
Pigott, Alan M 4:17:57 (13,058)
Pigott, Richard J 4:11:48 (11,570)
Pigott, Timothy M 3:30:51 (3,825)
Pigozzi, Giorgio 4:30:38 (16,285)
Pigram, Matthew D 4:59:28 (23,369)
Pike, Andrew R 3:28:15 (3,438)
Pike, Chris 5:29:36 (29,088)
Pike, David 3:38:20 (4,892)
Pike, David J 4:40:00 (18,538)
Pike, Graham J 4:21:21 (13,923)
Pike, Karl N 5:51:02 (31,774)
Pike, Oliver S 4:20:19 (13,686)
Pike, Timothy D 4:37:59 (18,003)
Pilbeam, David M 5:13:44 (26,174)
Pilch, Richard F 4:14:26 (12,194)
Pilch, Tony 4:10:55 (11,352)
Pilcher, Martin K 3:54:32 (7,909)
Pilgrim, Adam J 5:46:48 (31,334)
Pilgrim, Matthew 4:49:20 (20,849)
Pilgrim, Rufus J 4:59:56 (23,484)
Piliszczuk, Thomas A 3:57:05 (8,497)
Pilkington, Adrian 3:14:16 (1,921)
Pilkington, Andrew W 5:13:19 (26,091)
Pill, Stephen J 4:21:54 (14,066)
Pillar, Andrew C 4:16:00 (12,562)
Pillau, Ulrich 4:51:07 (21,271)
Pilling, Paul M 3:45:35 (6,111)
Pillinger, Chris 5:15:04 (26,475)
Pillinger, Karl S 5:26:11 (28,487)
Piludu, Nicola 4:20:49 (13,807)
Pim, Jonathan J 4:11:15 (11,438)
Pimazzoni, Carlo 4:54:38 (22,179)
Pimlott, David L 4:36:51 (17,754)
Pimpaneau, Remy B 3:28:20 (3,454)
Pinate, Robert E 4:59:50 (23,463)
Pinches, Joss 3:05:21 (1,188)
Pinckney, James C 5:31:18 (29,344)
Pincock, Andy J 3:52:48 (7,524)
Pinder, George 3:25:30 (3,063)
Pineiro-Varela, Roberto 3:59:21 (9,053)
Ping, Darren J 3:55:44 (8,171)
Pingel, Soenke 4:16:48 (12,762)
Pini, Alberto 2:39:21 (132)
Pink, Neil M 6:38:37 (34,623)
Pinkham, Christopher G 4:19:56 (13,582)
Pinner, Richard E 5:56:29 (32,285)
Pinnick, David 4:16:12 (12,621)
Pinniger, Anthony R 4:34:56 (17,253)
Pinnock, Nick W 4:33:36 (16,938)
Pino, Esteban R 3:52:59 (7,564)
Pinson, Anthony W 3:51:24 (7,225)
Pinto, George M 5:28:13 (28,840)
Pinto, José C 4:17:33 (12,961)
Pinto Cardoso, Gongalo R 3:33:31 (4,205)
Piotrowski, Henryk B 2:44:09 (220)
Pipe, Simon T 4:36:22 (17,629)
Piper, Daniel W 5:53:31 (32,012)
Piper, Maurice A 3:39:31 (5,109)
Piper, Simon M 3:31:09 (3,855)
Pirelli, Sabino 2:48:49 (339)
Pires, Artur F 3:01:16 (973)
Pires, Daniel 3:38:51 (4,988)
Pires, Kenneth G 7:10:33 (35,278)
Pirie, Andrew 3:51:10 (7,177)
Pirie, Grant 5:15:17 (26,520)
Pirotti, Antonio 3:14:21 (1,928)
Pirozzi, Giuseppe 4:51:03 (21,255)
Pirzer, Berhard 3:42:50 (5,654)
Pisal, Narendra 5:05:37 (24,621)
Pisaneschi, Joel 3:38:58 (5,009)
Pisani, Giovanni 3:24:51 (3,002)
Pistidda, Angelo 5:51:36 (31,837)
Pistidda, David 4:15:47 (12,507)
Pisu, Silvestro 3:30:34 (3,796)
Pitchell, Ian 3:24:34 (2,967)
Pitcher, Jason 3:19:39 (2,448)
Pitchforth, Nikolai S 2:56:01 (610)
Pitchley, Danny C 4:18:32 (13,221)
Pitchley, Percy 5:07:57 (25,086)
Pite, Benjamin L 3:14:09 (1,906)
Pithers, Stephen E 5:14:36 (26,362)
Pitkin, Brian H 4:45:19 (19,908)
Pitt, Arron J 3:48:31 (6,625)
Pitt, Rhys A 3:40:50 (5,329)
Pitt, Stephen J 4:51:01 (21,244)
Pitt, William 4:13:04 (11,850)
Pittaway, Mark 2:51:36 (425)
Pittaway, Simon J 4:52:09 (21,527)
Pittock, André R 3:29:38 (3,665)
Pitts, Andrew S 2:59:26 (857)
Pitts, Colin P 3:57:00 (8,482)
Pitts, David L 4:39:43 (18,466)
Pitts, Roger C 4:35:17 (17,356)
Pitts, Simon M 3:48:57 (6,717)
Pitt-Watson, David J 4:43:17 (19,367)
Pitzer, Guenmter 4:40:01 (18,539)
Pizii, Tony 5:09:33 (25,384)
Plant, Andrew J 7:12:24 (35,311)
Plant, David J 4:39:24 (18,389)
Plaskett, Gary R 5:31:40 (29,399)
Plastow, Ricci G 3:54:36 (7,921)
Platt, Austin 4:26:45 (15,249)
Platt, Gary A 3:32:29 (4,065)
Platt, Ian 4:23:08 (14,362)
Platt, John 4:09:45 (11,123)
Platt, Mark R 4:18:04 (13,088)
Platt, Martin C 3:15:02 (2,001)
Platt, Paul D 3:49:01 (6,738)
Platt, Terence R 4:51:06 (21,266)
Platte, David M 5:31:15 (29,341)
Platten, David 4:17:58 (13,064)
Platteuw, Lionel Y 4:19:22 (13,424)
Platts, Tom N 3:37:56 (4,814)
Playdon, Andrew 4:42:36 (19,207)
Player, Phil K 5:05:20 (24,558)
Playford-Smith, Terry R 5:30:32 (29,227)
Plaza, Luis 4:59:43 (23,436)
Pledger, Alan G 5:22:22 (27,829)
Pledger, Shane A 5:04:59 (24,515)
Pledger, Stephen P 3:40:54 (5,347)
Plemper, Mark 4:52:31 (21,618)
Plester, Russell J 4:24:14 (14,638)
Plew, Richard B 3:29:42 (3,675)
Plimmer, Daniel J 6:11:59 (33,427)
Plimmer, Phillip J 5:44:30 (31,094)
Plowman, Ian A 6:11:07 (33,378)
Plowman, Robin 5:17:39 (26,992)
Pluck, Ricky J 3:33:09 (4,161)
Plumb, Giles J 3:17:55 (2,277)
Plumb, Steven J 4:07:06 (10,594)
Plumer, Keith 3:02:08 (1,008)
Plumley, Barry K 5:23:26 (27,997)
Plummer, Bradley C 3:59:00 (8,960)
Plummer, Richard K 4:42:59 (19,291)
Plumridge, Neil J 3:00:13 (910)
Plunkett, Mark 3:34:08 (4,283)
Plunkett, Steve K 4:31:43 (16,511)
Pockley, Michael J 3:58:44 (8,893)
Pocklington, Mark S 5:24:28 (28,178)
Pocock, Andrew J 4:18:05 (13,091)
Pocock, Mark J 4:04:04 (9,978)
Pocock, Matthew 4:20:28 (13,724)
Pocock, Michael J 3:37:53 (4,805)
Pogas, Joaquim 4:10:24 (11,248)
Pogose, Robert P 5:18:10 (27,096)
Pohlmann, Wolfgang 4:20:54 (13,829)
Poinok, Sathit 4:50:04 (21,016)
Poinot, Patrick 3:34:14 (4,300)
Pointer, Bren P 3:23:18 (2,832)
Pointet, David A 4:47:52 (20,494)
Pointon, Philip 5:42:49 (30,915)
Poleyn, Steven 3:06:03 (1,235)
Pollard, Anthony G 3:11:40 (1,695)
Pollard, Darren P 4:06:18 (10,417)
Pollard, Ivan 5:12:39 (25,974)
Pollard, Lee D 4:21:22 (13,926)
Pollard, Matthew N 3:46:41 (6,280)
Pollen, Alexander C 4:13:51 (12,053)
Pollen, Richard J 4:17:07 (12,833)
Polley, Richard 5:04:59 (24,515)
Pollitt, Alastair J 3:56:37 (8,385)
Pollock, Jeremy R 2:57:17 (698)

Pollock, Neil A..............3:46:41 (6,280)
Pollock, Nicholas S..............3:04:59 (1,161)
Polywka, Mario 5:40:55 (30,698)
Ponchelle, Jerome P 4:55:11 (22,311)
Pond, Chris R 3:56:19 (8,307)
Poneskis, Kevin D 3:54:45 (7,953)
Ponsford, Michael..............4:48:31 (20,651)
Ponsford, Richard 4:05:54 (10,331)
Ponte, Pietro..............5:28:17 (28,858)
Pontin, Mark W 4:48:50 (20,729)
Ponting, Matthew D 2:59:01 (825)
Poo Campos, Maximo..............4:15:37 (12,468)
Poole, Andrew J..............5:41:15 (30,736)
Poole, Ben 3:34:17 (4,312)
Poole, Brian C 3:47:36 (6,447)
Poole, Colin 5:02:18 (23,988)
Poole, James 4:42:20 (19,129)
Poole, John R 3:53:48 (7,744)
Poole, Ken 4:47:34 (20,426)
Poole, Mark J 3:38:34 (4,934)
Poole, Michael..............3:44:29 (5,937)
Poole, Richard T 5:40:26 (30,644)
Pooley, Martin J..............4:12:50 (11,795)
Poots, Timothy S 3:53:13 (7,626)
Pope, Andrew 3:36:33 (4,620)
Pope, Bob 3:36:26 (4,604)
Pope, Dennis M 3:50:15 (6,984)
Pope, Ed 4:11:51 (11,585)
Pope, Michael R 5:02:52 (24,099)
Pope, Nicholas 5:41:27 (30,762)
Pope, Robert A..............2:42:32 (190)
Pope, Robin 4:29:21 (15,956)
Pope, Roger 6:18:51 (33,825)
Pope, Rupert V..............5:03:14 (24,178)
Pope, Timothy S 4:05:50 (10,314)
Popham, Anthony 5:02:40 (24,069)
Popkin, Jeffrey S..............4:52:15 (21,556)
Popplewell, Alex H 5:22:29 (27,844)
Portch, Darren M..............4:49:04 (20,783)
Porteous, Henry J..............3:42:40 (5,622)
Porteous, Robert S 5:11:52 (25,827)
Porter, Adam L..............5:36:26 (30,103)
Porter, Alan 4:30:36 (16,280)
Porter, Craig 4:51:29 (21,368)
Porter, Danny M..............4:26:39 (15,223)
Porter, David C 5:58:34 (32,471)
Porter, Ian D 4:12:06 (11,630)
Porter, James D 5:34:16 (29,806)
Porter, James J 5:03:22 (24,208)
Porter, John 4:31:37 (16,490)
Porter, Justin W 4:55:27 (22,377)
Porter, Keith D 5:28:00 (28,799)
Porter, Robert J 5:10:55 (25,648)
Porter, Stuart 3:45:51 (6,156)
Porter, Thomas C 5:28:46 (28,946)
Portero Garcia, Daniel 3:07:59 (1,388)
Portnoi, Peter 3:56:10 (8,267)
Portsmouth, Nicholas J..............4:49:28 (20,882)
Portus, James O 4:45:57 (20,050)
Portus, Tony..............3:06:48 (1,298)
Pose, José 3:57:17 (8,549)
Posner, Andy..............4:49:16 (20,831)
Posner, Rupert T 4:02:29 (9,694)
Postlethwaite, James D 5:06:44 (24,826)
Postma, Maarten J 5:23:36 (28,205)
Potash, Steven 5:05:08 (24,532)
Potashnick, Luke B 4:57:16 (22,839)
Potiwal, Sukhdev S 5:52:47 (31,947)
Potten, James H..............3:37:56 (4,814)
Potten, Mattehw 3:22:01 (2,708)
Potter, Adrian 4:29:25 (15,980)
Potter, David C 4:27:10 (15,375)
Potter, Gary T R..............5:40:50 (30,684)
Potter, Graham M 4:09:54 (11,152)
Potter, Greg I 5:37:48 (30,270)
Potter, John 4:45:26 (19,930)
Potter, Jon N 4:09:15 (11,017)
Potter, Jonothan J..............4:14:30 (12,204)
Potter, Keith 4:44:46 (19,763)
Potter, Mark J 3:17:23 (2,216)
Potter, Michael 5:26:54 (28,610)
Potter, Nicholas J..............4:08:48 (10,923)
Potter, Peter B 4:27:59 (15,582)

Potter, Steven..............4:28:36 (15,761)
Potticary, Simon 4:16:55 (12,792)
Pottinger, Gavin J 5:57:51 (32,395)
Pottinger, Timothy..............4:10:00 (11,166)
Pottle, Christopher L..............4:25:00 (14,820)
Pottle, Richard J..............4:25:00 (14,820)
Pottorff, Daniel 4:35:43 (17,463)
Potts, Colin I..............2:39:32 (139)
Potts, Edward M 4:34:01 (17,036)
Potts, Jonathan 4:48:27 (20,639)
Potts, Russell..............4:51:50 (21,450)
Potts, Stuart C 6:39:04 (34,643)
Poulain, Jean Marc..............3:57:21 (8,567)
Poulain, John S..............4:32:31 (16,667)
Poulter, Christopher 4:49:37 (20,920)
Poulter, Darren 3:54:16 (7,861)
Poulter, Gary..............2:56:57 (670)
Poulter, Matthew J..............4:18:18 (13,149)
Poulton, Paul 4:49:10 (20,813)
Pound, Anthony S..............3:19:12 (2,414)
Pound, Bill J 5:06:36 (24,798)
Pouteau, Alain 3:35:05 (4,417)
Powell, Aleaxander J 4:59:57 (23,490)
Powell, Alex 4:52:53 (21,721)
Powell, Andrew K 5:19:05 (27,262)
Powell, Barry 4:41:24 (18,889)
Powell, Chris T 5:59:58 (32,570)
Powell, Darren B 4:28:53 (15,828)
Powell, David W 5:29:30 (29,070)
Powell, James G 4:07:37 (10,684)
Powell, John..............4:51:26 (21,352)
Powell, John..............5:28:13 (28,840)
Powell, Jonathan G 4:36:14 (17,592)
Powell, Keith..............4:09:07 (10,979)
Powell, Mark D 4:15:27 (12,432)
Powell, Mark H 3:52:41 (7,497)
Powell, Martin J..............4:02:43 (9,733)
Powell, Matthew W..............4:50:45 (21,177)
Powell, Melvyn J 5:11:32 (25,763)
Powell, Michael T 4:35:00 (17,270)
Powell, Mike J 5:05:25 (24,577)
Powell, Nick J..............4:50:29 (21,116)
Powell, Osian D 4:13:21 (11,921)
Powell, Richard F 4:42:08 (19,073)
Powell, Robert T 3:59:15 (9,027)
Powell, Simon..............4:03:11 (9,813)
Powell, Simon C 2:38:10 (110)
Powell, Simon D 6:34:49 (34,488)
Powell, Simon J 4:37:23 (17,855)
Powell, Stephen T 4:58:46 (23,198)
Powell, Steve..............5:11:42 (25,791)
Powell, Steve D 4:42:51 (19,270)
Powell, Terry R 4:19:14 (13,387)
Powell, William J 4:48:41 (20,689)
Powis, David R..............4:03:06 (9,801)
Powles, Frederick R..............5:12:56 (26,027)
Powles, James A 5:10:14 (25,530)
Powley, James..............5:51:05 (31,784)
Pownall, Lee J 3:48:31 (6,625)
Powrie, Richard..............6:02:36 (32,793)
Poynton, Robert..............5:57:33 (32,374)
Poyser, Simon 4:27:32 (15,475)
Pozsgai, Conrad..............4:26:54 (15,296)
Prangle, Christopher P 4:50:21 (21,080)
Pranzas, Soenke 4:34:43 (17,206)
Praschl, Markus J..............3:24:20 (2,942)
Pratt, Barry 5:00:41 (23,652)
Pratt, Christopher M..............3:21:15 (2,628)
Pratt, Derek R..............3:27:00 (3,281)
Pratt, Malcolm J..............3:47:43 (6,482)
Praud, Stephane..............3:09:01 (1,470)
Praudi, Marco 5:01:18 (23,794)
Precious, John M..............4:33:35 (16,930)
Preda, Angelo Franco 4:22:16 (14,142)
Preece, Clive L..............4:36:51 (17,754)
Preece, Dave J..............3:43:26 (5,761)
Preece, David J 3:36:53 (4,672)
Prendergast, Dominic..............4:49:22 (20,853)
Prendergast, Eamon M..............4:24:24 (14,681)
Prentice, Neil P 3:41:18 (5,411)
Prescher, Joerg 3:26:46 (3,234)
Prescott, David P 5:22:30 (27,854)
Prescott, Graeme..............3:57:23 (8,577)

Prescott, James G 4:07:40 (10,695)
Prescott, Kevin..............5:11:05 (25,682)
Press, James S 3:04:59 (1,161)
Press, Matthew J 5:45:37 (31,219)
Press, Stephen B..............3:42:50 (5,654)
Preston, Andrew L 3:57:00 (8,482)
Preston, Bamber R 4:46:12 (20,107)
Preston, Kevin B 4:34:12 (17,076)
Preston, Leigh P 4:54:21 (22,112)
Preston, Paul E 3:24:27 (2,951)
Preston, Paul M 4:48:31 (20,651)
Preston, Peter J..............5:01:14 (23,782)
Preston, Richard A..............5:43:39 (31,007)
Preston, Robert J 5:25:47 (28,421)
Preston, Terry..............4:35:03 (17,285)
Preston, Thomas A..............4:05:01 (10,147)
Preston, Thomas E..............3:07:43 (1,364)
Preston, Timothy J 4:46:56 (20,262)
Pretsell, Barry C 4:01:08 (9,444)
Previero, Michele 4:33:32 (16,924)
Prewer, Michael 4:44:27 (19,663)
Price, Andrew..............5:40:20 (30,633)
Price, Benjamin D 5:55:22 (32,180)
Price, Carl 2:55:18 (587)
Price, Dan 3:48:04 (6,535)
Price, Darren C 4:33:30 (16,911)
Price, Dave I 4:56:19 (22,590)
Price, Dave J 2:57:53 (739)
Price, David..............4:45:01 (19,842)
Price, Iain D 4:52:47 (21,689)
Price, Ian 3:20:50 (2,589)
Price, Ian M 4:27:57 (15,571)
Price, Ian R 3:11:52 (1,711)
Price, James 3:25:01 (3,022)
Price, Jamie S 4:21:42 (14,003)
Price, Jeremy C 4:25:23 (14,918)
Price, Jonathan B 5:05:14 (24,547)
Price, Leonard F 7:28:53 (35,462)
Price, Luke J 5:00:25 (23,601)
Price, Malcolm 4:16:55 (12,792)
Price, Matt J 3:47:42 (6,478)
Price, Matthew J 4:32:07 (16,584)
Price, Melvyn 5:19:37 (27,362)
Price, Michael 4:57:59 (23,032)
Price, Michael T 4:52:26 (21,604)
Price, Owen C 5:27:04 (28,631)
Price, Paul..............5:14:42 (26,381)
Price, Paul E 4:57:10 (22,811)
Price, Paul T 5:22:56 (27,929)
Price, Rodney G 4:31:06 (16,381)
Price, Shane..............6:11:34 (33,401)
Price, Timothy C 4:40:46 (18,722)
Prichard, Dafydd L 4:38:05 (18,035)
Prichard, Spencer R..............5:24:34 (28,192)
Prickett, Clive A..............4:14:20 (12,173)
Priday, Roger 5:30:10 (29,172)
Pride, Will 5:02:30 (24,040)
Prideaux, Michael 3:55:12 (8,058)
Pridham, Tom H 4:29:22 (15,964)
Priest, Andrew C..............3:55:59 (8,221)
Priest, James G..............3:58:05 (8,738)
Priest, Richard C 4:27:14 (15,400)
Priest, Thomas M 5:30:46 (29,262)
Priestley, Alan 5:03:04 (24,140)
Priestley, David A..............4:14:38 (12,242)
Priestley, David R..............4:12:29 (11,718)
Priestley, Derek R 5:33:29 (29,678)
Priestley, Jamie 4:55:06 (22,289)
Priestley, Michael D..............6:14:02 (33,555)
Prigmore, Sean A 4:24:07 (14,603)
Prime, David D 4:57:03 (22,786)
Prince, Kevin J..............5:11:24 (25,741)
Pringle, Benedict M 4:56:37 (22,665)
Pringle, Neil A..............3:16:57 (2,175)
Pringle, Paul G 4:08:47 (10,920)
Pringle, Steven J 4:39:14 (18,345)
Prinsloo, Neville 3:33:44 (4,231)
Prior, Ben 4:50:00 (20,997)
Prior, David N 3:17:49 (2,264)
Prior, Matt 3:55:20 (8,088)
Prior, Robbie 5:07:45 (25,044)
Prior, Stephen D..............5:45:01 (31,156)
Prior, Stephen J 5:19:38 (27,365)

Prior, Stuart J 5:17:03 (26,868)
Prior, Tom J 4:49:39 (20,926)
Priscott, Neil G 5:34:08 (29,786)
Priscott, Philip J 4:20:35 (13,749)
Pritchard, Benjamin H 5:13:19 (26,091)
Pritchard, David J 5:11:56 (25,842)
Pritchard, Graham J 3:05:29 (1,199)
Pritchard, Oli I 4:06:45 (10,513)
Pritchard, Paul J 5:46:17 (31,291)
Pritchard, Simon G 3:20:53 (2,596)
Pritchett, Andrew N 4:50:26 (21,107)
Pritchett, Mark 4:12:04 (11,624)
Procter, Ben W 3:44:14 (5,894)
Procter, Jonathan G 5:44:05 (31,052)
Procter, Michael A 4:19:50 (13,555)
Procter, Russell 3:29:09 (3,596)
Proctor, Dean M 3:46:33 (6,257)
Proctor, Mark 7:11:38 (35,299)
Proctor, Richard J 4:05:34 (10,256)
Proctor, Simon J 3:48:40 (6,659)
Prod'homme, Stephane 4:08:38 (10,900)
Profeta, Eugen C 3:53:55 (7,769)
Proffitt, Jeremy C 5:01:35 (23,851)
Proffitt-White, John W 4:39:14 (18,345)
Proietti, Roberto F 4:09:27 (11,063)
Pronk, Wouter 4:42:46 (19,246)
Prosser, Jonathan D 5:08:30 (25,188)
Prosser, Mark A 6:48:59 (34,911)
Prosser, Matthew 3:49:37 (6,854)
Prosser, Robert C 3:52:15 (7,421)
Protani, Nikoli 5:28:09 (28,828)
Protheau, Alain 4:16:41 (12,733)
Prothero, Robert A 3:21:41 (2,674)
Proud, David 3:18:05 (2,295)
Proudley, Gavin J 3:14:57 (1,988)
Proudlock, James H 4:20:21 (13,697)
Proudlove, Michael J 4:28:37 (15,765)
Proust, Gaetan 4:48:17 (20,597)
Proven, Mike J 2:49:16 (353)
Provost, J François 3:42:44 (5,633)
Prowse, David M 5:06:07 (24,718)
Prowse, Philip 4:12:05 (11,628)
Prudham, Joseph P 3:51:08 (7,168)
Pruneda, Pedro T 4:17:16 (12,866)
Pryce, Andrew J 4:00:43 (9,360)
Pryce, Charles A 4:33:59 (17,030)
Pryde, Graham 4:06:57 (10,558)
Pryke, Andrew M 4:33:25 (16,895)
Pryke, Timothy P 4:33:38 (16,944)
Pryke, William 3:58:25 (8,812)
Pryor, Keith P 4:42:35 (19,203)
Pryor, Thomas P 3:49:31 (6,836)
Prythian, Jamie 4:38:02 (18,022)
Przyniczka, Piotr C 4:34:38 (17,186)
Pticher, Jason J 4:13:55 (12,073)
Pucci, Gennard 6:21:22 (33,973)
Puckett, Ian C 5:17:59 (27,052)
Puddick, Julian U 3:41:04 (5,374)
Puddifant, Jon D 4:42:15 (19,110)
Puddy, Alexander W 4:38:09 (18,051)
Pudney, Nicholas P 4:11:34 (11,512)
Puegner, Stephan 4:47:09 (20,322)
Pugh, Adiran E 3:46:34 (6,263)
Pugh, Andrew 4:08:37 (10,898)
Pugh, Andrew R 4:12:25 (11,705)
Pugh, David J 4:37:41 (17,933)
Pugh, Eddie 5:40:20 (30,633)
Pugh, Graham K 3:49:41 (6,868)
Pugh, Jamie 4:18:12 (13,124)
Pugh, John D 4:06:41 (10,497)
Pugh, Marc 3:59:54 (9,185)
Pugh, Mitch 3:59:03 (8,972)
Pugh, Neil D 4:46:16 (20,118)
Pugh, Richard 3:58:30 (8,841)
Pugh, Roderick M 3:14:09 (1,906)
Pugh, Tom D 4:45:21 (19,917)
Puglisi Maraja, Sergio 4:11:18 (11,448)
Pugsley, Richard J 4:49:03 (20,777)
Puiggari, German 3:30:46 (3,815)
Pulfer, Anthony C 5:07:29 (24,995)
Pulford, Peter E 4:40:49 (18,737)
Pulford, Tom G 5:41:15 (30,736)
Pulham, Andrew D 4:46:51 (20,239)
Pulido, Luis E 4:23:50 (14,525)
Pullen, Bob F 5:09:22 (25,344)
Pullen, Graham 4:33:08 (16,821)
Pullen, James E 5:08:48 (25,242)
Pullen, Keith L 5:42:00 (30,829)
Pullen, Leslie C 5:10:45 (25,617)
Pullen, Tim J 3:38:51 (4,988)
Pullen, Tom 4:59:21 (23,345)
Pullinger, Richard M 3:26:09 (3,149)
Pullinger, Tom A 5:45:02 (31,157)
Pullman, Mark G 6:00:00 (32,574)
Pulman, Jon J 4:06:05 (10,367)
Pumfleet, Jon P 5:07:14 (24,938)
Pumpel, Paolo 3:50:51 (7,107)
Pun, Krishna 3:57:39 (8,639)
Punch, Julian E 4:18:13 (13,129)
Purchase, Garry 4:44:27 (19,663)
Purdon, Nicholas T 4:25:00 (14,820)
Purkiss-McEndoo, Shaun 2:53:18 (483)
Purnell, Colin 4:27:42 (15,519)
Purnell, David 4:19:11 (13,374)
Purnell, Ian G 4:36:27 (17,653)
Purser, Antony G 4:11:43 (11,552)
Pursey, Ashley J 4:58:04 (23,050)
Pursey, Nigel T 5:37:33 (30,240)
Purvis, Darrell A 6:35:28 (34,521)
Purvis, Darren M 2:43:24 (205)
Purvis, Keith 2:57:43 (721)
Pussard, Marc L 6:14:09 (33,560)
Pusztai, Arpad 3:03:21 (1,069)
Putnam, Neil 5:02:05 (23,947)
Puttick, Michael B 5:09:10 (25,306)
Puttkammer, Andrei 4:51:03 (21,255)
Puttock, Clifford G 5:53:32 (32,015)
Pyck, Michael 4:17:00 (12,814)
Pycroft, Harry E 6:20:35 (33,926)
Pye, Alan E 3:14:21 (1,928)
Pye, George A 6:27:08 (34,214)
Pye, James W 5:01:00 (23,725)
Pye, Jonathan R 5:08:07 (25,118)
Pym, Benjamin T 5:36:51 (30,156)
Pyne, Daniel T 2:58:25 (782)
Pyne, Steven R 4:04:11 (10,002)
Pyne-O'Donnell, Sean D 3:54:45 (7,953)
Pyott, Bruce F 4:15:59 (12,558)
Qadar, Shabab 5:56:42 (32,308)
Qadri, Emile 3:49:40 (6,862)
Quarella, Daniele 3:03:57 (1,102)
Quaresma, Sergio P 3:29:46 (3,682)
Quartermaine, Richard A 4:21:28 (13,957)
Quartly, Leonard S 4:16:53 (12,778)
Quattromini, Gianriccardo 4:14:56 (12,306)
Quayle, Roger 4:18:59 (13,325)
Quelch, Steven R 5:44:23 (31,083)
Quenet, Tony 4:06:02 (10,355)
Quennell, Richard G 3:26:03 (3,135)
Quest, Jonathan D 3:05:39 (1,212)
Qugley, Damien 3:12:24 (1,766)
Quick, Andrew R 4:19:35 (13,479)
Quick, James H 3:14:10 (1,908)
Quigley, E Matthew 5:23:03 (27,944)
Quigley, Philip A 5:42:57 (30,928)
Quilter, John 4:36:53 (17,763)
Quin, Stephen 4:51:26 (21,352)
Quinby, Richard N 3:50:32 (7,046)
Quince, Mark G 3:53:23 (7,660)
Quiney, Nial F 4:23:13 (14,383)
Quinlan, Gavin R 5:47:52 (31,446)
Quinlan, Rikki 4:36:10 (17,572)
Quinlivan, Mike 5:30:03 (29,152)
Quinn, Bradley J 4:33:00 (16,785)
Quinn, Daniel J 3:19:58 (2,490)
Quinn, Dennis F 5:31:02 (29,302)
Quinn, Eamonn A 6:56:12 (35,057)
Quinn, Gerald I 4:53:39 (21,927)
Quinn, Greg 3:44:10 (5,888)
Quinn, James E 3:30:14 (3,753)
Quinn, John E 3:53:26 (7,673)
Quinn, Kevin 2:46:19 (269)
Quinn, Malcolm K 5:25:52 (28,437)
Quinn, Paul 4:58:23 (23,129)
Quinn, William A 4:09:07 (10,979)
Quinney, Michael G 6:11:14 (33,384)
Quintanar, Sergio 3:42:33 (5,604)
Quiza, Reycardo 5:32:04 (29,467)
Quraishi, Naveedulislam 5:26:16 (28,503)
Rabbetts, Mark A 3:34:11 (4,291)
Rabener, Nicolas 3:38:49 (4,978)
Rabin, Nicholas P 3:41:58 (5,511)
Rabin-Boutin, Dominique 3:18:16 (2,323)
Rabjohns, Peter 3:17:30 (2,231)
Raboldt, Marco 4:11:31 (11,505)
Rabourdin, Bruno 5:33:46 (29,726)
Raby, Simon D 3:45:47 (6,145)
Race, Andrew A 4:53:17 (21,831)
Race, George 4:54:34 (22,158)
Race, Julian F 5:20:43 (27,557)
Race, Timothy M 4:46:51 (20,239)
Rach, Nihar B 6:58:39 (35,101)
Rackham, Andrew 3:35:18 (4,449)
Rackham, Craig I 4:59:17 (23,335)
Rackham, Nigel D 2:41:47 (175)
Radaelli, Giuseppe 4:28:35 (15,754)
Radbourne, Mathew 3:10:54 (1,623)
Radcliffe, Richard 3:44:00 (5,867)
Radhakrishnan, Nerukav V 5:09:12 (25,320)
Radici, Jay 4:08:49 (10,924)
Radley, Adam D 5:28:25 (28,891)
Radley, Craig C 5:02:45 (24,084)
Radley, Lee 4:05:32 (10,245)
Radmann, Christopher H 4:52:59 (21,749)
Radovanovic, Andrew 3:46:21 (6,227)
Rae, Ewan G 4:50:46 (21,183)
Rae, Ian W 5:46:16 (31,289)
Rae, Simon J 3:56:02 (8,231)
Rae, Stuart 5:20:44 (27,560)
Raeburn, David J 4:53:24 (21,862)
Rafiq-Craske, Matthew R 4:16:26 (12,681)
Ragg, David 4:21:33 (13,977)
Raggi, Lorenzo 2:48:18 (323)
Ragless, Ben 3:56:44 (8,415)
Ragus, Marek 4:15:02 (12,332)
Ragus, Ryszard 4:53:14 (21,822)
Rahman, Alinoor 4:23:28 (14,440)
Rahman, Emdad 7:17:40 (35,366)
Rahman, Jahad 4:37:35 (17,906)
Rai, Kam 6:28:48 (34,275)
Rai, Sundeep S 5:27:59 (28,794)
Railton, William L 3:30:06 (3,736)
Rainbow, Steven 6:35:16 (34,511)
Raine, Andrew T 4:17:32 (12,956)
Raine, Andy D 4:35:12 (17,333)
Raines, Matthew L 3:59:26 (9,075)
Rainsby, Ian H 4:19:32 (13,467)
Raisbeck, Gordon 4:11:49 (11,573)
Rajaratnam, Rathan 3:47:09 (6,370)
Rakusen, Philip 4:59:59 (23,501)
Ralfe, Philip 4:12:47 (11,786)
Ralley, Daniel 4:07:45 (10,712)
Ralley, James 4:32:57 (16,773)
Ralph, Andrew J 3:48:26 (6,604)
Ralph, James K 4:14:13 (12,141)
Ralph, John 4:51:36 (21,398)
Ralph, Mark 3:51:41 (7,290)
Ralston, Simon T 5:16:11 (26,697)
Ralton, Paul J 3:09:52 (1,544)
Ramaala, Hendrick 2:07:56 (5)
Ramage, Alan 2:34:00 (62)
Ramage, Phillip J 4:34:39 (17,191)
Ramage, Robert E 5:33:00 (29,605)
Ramakrishna, Suresha 6:33:03 (34,439)
Ramanaharan, Venugopal 4:28:46 (15,807)
Ramanauskas, Stephen 5:10:52 (25,639)
Rambaud, Bernard M 4:13:58 (12,089)
Rambie, Richard 4:00:46 (9,368)
Rameshon, Murugiah 3:05:15 (1,180)
Ramirez, Raul 4:20:52 (13,822)
Ramirez, Ruben G 4:00:41 (9,354)
Ramnath, Errol R 3:49:49 (6,899)
Ramon, Marco A 6:16:29 (33,717)
Ramos, Mannie F 3:51:34 (7,269)
Ramos, Paul 5:48:52 (31,569)
Rampelt, Jerome T 5:51:03 (31,779)
Rampersad, Neil A 4:53:48 (21,964)
Rampling, Peter 4:23:36 (14,467)
Ramsay, Andrew C 5:19:32 (27,347)

Ramsay, Ciaran O 5:38:34 (30,390)
Ramsay, Gordon 4:20:11 (13,653)
Ramsay, Jonathan R 3:17:53 (2,272)
Ramsay, Matthew D 5:32:25 (29,511)
Ramsay, Nicholas J 4:26:08 (15,081)
Ramsay, Stephen J 4:34:52 (17,240)
Ramsdale, Ian M 3:39:52 (5,171)
Ramsdale, Peter A 4:23:21 (14,408)
Ramsden, Adam 4:13:15 (11,896)
Ramsden, Andrew W 5:16:05 (26,680)
Ramsden, James M 4:26:14 (15,114)
Ramsey, Andrew D 6:21:36 (33,984)
Ramsey, John S 5:56:00 (32,240)
Ramsey, Nichoals G 4:23:51 (14,530)
Ramsey, Philip L 3:33:03 (4,146)
Ramsey, Stuart 5:39:30 (30,530)
Ramsey Smith, David 3:48:37 (6,648)
Rand, Keith W 4:28:45 (15,799)
Randall, Adrian H 5:32:10 (29,477)
Randall, David 5:08:41 (25,220)
Randall, Edward C 5:16:51 (26,820)
Randall, Matthew 3:55:03 (8,019)
Randall, Steve M 4:35:39 (17,440)
Randall, Timothy S 4:57:21 (22,875)
Randell, Steven B 4:39:30 (18,415)
Randeree, Hoosen D 3:42:53 (5,665)
Randfield, Graham 4:27:09 (15,366)
Randhawa, Kuldip S 3:48:59 (6,729)
Randle, Keith 5:27:14 (28,669)
Randles, Stephen 4:26:01 (15,061)
Randu, Alexandre 3:46:34 (6,263)
Ranganathan, Arjuna 4:51:19 (21,321)
Rangecroft, Mike 4:58:54 (23,227)
Ranger, Terry E 3:32:37 (4,086)
Rankin, Nicholas D 3:15:53 (2,071)
Rann, James P 3:53:16 (7,634)
Ranscombe, Norman G 5:40:50 (30,684)
Ransley, Laurence D 4:49:11 (20,817)
Ransom, Jeremy C 2:58:30 (789)
Ransome, Andrew G 4:56:47 (22,710)
Ransome, Simon 3:55:18 (8,077)
Ranson, Ashleigh V 3:33:44 (4,231)
Ranson, Stuart J 4:38:01 (18,015)
Rant, Robert J 4:57:25 (22,889)
Rantanikunen, Markus J 4:53:09 (21,797)
Rantell, David A 2:48:06 (313)
Rantell, Matt J 4:44:39 (19,727)
Raphael, Michael 4:55:19 (22,341)
Raphael, Michael J 6:16:53 (33,729)
Rapley, David 5:39:42 (30,558)
Rapley, David J 5:41:33 (30,776)
Rasburn, Steven 5:15:10 (26,493)
Rasey, Jason R 4:49:23 (20,858)
Rashid, Nasir 5:17:57 (27,041)
Rashid, Riaz 4:43:50 (19,489)
Rasmussen, Tore 3:38:05 (4,850)
Rastelli, Roberto 5:21:15 (27,644)
Ratchford, Carl J 6:03:14 (32,834)
Ratcliffe, Andrew 3:44:25 (5,926)
Ratcliffe, David J 4:24:35 (14,722)
Ratcliffe, George 3:18:07 (2,298)
Ratcliffe, Jim 3:46:55 (6,327)
Ratcliffe, Jonathan D 4:15:56 (12,538)
Ratcliffe, Jonathan P 2:52:28 (458)
Ratcliffe, Mark 5:18:07 (27,084)
Ratcliffe, Neil 4:22:19 (14,157)
Ratcliffe, Neil T 4:32:38 (16,701)
Rathbone, Colin E 3:06:20 (1,255)
Rattan, Mandeep S 5:30:00 (29,137)
Raubenheimer, Hendrik J 3:29:26 (3,640)
Rault, Thierry 4:41:00 (18,791)
Rauscher, Franz 4:37:22 (17,852)
Raveh, Doron 4:26:46 (15,255)
Raveiser, Georg 6:13:52 (33,540)
Raven, Gareth 2:23:27 (18)
Ravenhall, Paul M 5:39:02 (30,454)
Ravey, Barry-Leslie L 7:33:33 (35,522)
Rawes, Christopher W 5:12:54 (26,022)
Rawes, David J 3:53:09 (7,603)
Rawlence, Nigel J 4:51:24 (21,343)
Rawlings, Dean F 5:47:59 (31,464)
Rawlings, Keith C 4:29:27 (15,993)
Rawlings, Len 5:15:59 (26,654)
Rawlings, Stephen G 4:21:16 (13,905)
Rawlingson-Plant, Matt 3:39:16 (5,060)
Rawlins, Gary 6:58:44 (35,104)
Rawlins, John D 4:47:31 (20,413)
Rawlins, John W 3:54:22 (7,879)
Rawlins, Steven C 4:57:18 (22,854)
Rawlinson, John M 3:45:10 (6,044)
Rawlinson, Tony 4:57:20 (22,870)
Rawnsley, Richard 4:49:03 (20,777)
Rawson, Stephen 4:34:33 (17,159)
Ray, Duncan 5:09:10 (25,306)
Ray, Graham N 5:12:14 (25,904)
Ray, Ian 5:59:14 (32,531)
Ray, Pascal 4:46:21 (20,144)
Ray, Paul B 4:45:56 (20,042)
Ray, Spencer 5:08:10 (25,131)
Ray, Wesley 4:27:41 (15,512)
Rayfield, David W 3:08:06 (1,397)
Rayment, Christopher P 3:49:18 (6,796)
Raymond, Byron J 3:00:37 (937)
Raymond, Joad 3:03:26 (1,071)
Raymond, Paul 4:18:10 (13,112)
Raynaud, Jean-Michel 3:10:41 (1,608)
Raynaud, Martine 4:45:16 (19,896)
Rayner, Andrew 4:34:35 (17,169)
Rayner, Gary R 3:05:34 (1,206)
Rayner, Graeme J 4:20:16 (13,670)
Rayner, Julian A 3:49:16 (6,792)
Rayner, Kieran J 5:21:29 (27,694)
Rayner, Luke 3:49:17 (6,795)
Rayner, Paul R 4:16:25 (12,678)
Rayner, Peter 3:46:52 (6,314)
Rayner, Sean 5:15:20 (26,529)
Rayner, Steve H 6:29:19 (34,299)
Rayner, Trevor D 3:19:14 (2,419)
Raynes, Douglas C 4:22:27 (14,184)
Raynor, Andrew P 4:27:37 (15,493)
Raynor, Maurice P 4:38:56 (18,265)
Raynor, Tony 3:30:29 (3,785)
Raynsford, Jody 4:46:38 (20,204)
Rayson, Christopher M 4:31:30 (16,461)
Raza, Benjamin J 3:41:38 (5,460)
Rea, Anthony W 4:15:58 (12,551)
Rea, Keith W 4:50:52 (21,210)
Rea, Martin 2:58:55 (817)
Rea, Matthew 3:50:13 (6,977)
Rea, Michael 6:09:15 (33,250)
Rea, Robert 6:09:15 (33,250)
Rea, Terence J 4:27:16 (15,411)
Reach, Simon 4:18:16 (13,137)
Read, Adrian 3:35:18 (4,449)
Read, Anthony G 5:15:01 (26,456)
Read, Chris M 4:06:35 (10,482)
Read, David N 5:25:13 (28,308)
Read, Dean D 5:00:00 (23,503)
Read, Douglas E 7:22:10 (35,408)
Read, James M 3:31:34 (3,919)
Read, Jason S 4:21:50 (14,044)
Read, Kevin R 6:11:20 (33,394)
Read, Martyn J 4:52:15 (21,556)
Read, Mike W 3:23:49 (2,879)
Read, Nicholas W 3:55:49 (8,187)
Read, Niki L 5:33:27 (29,672)
Read, Pat 4:34:58 (17,263)
Read, Peter B 3:27:13 (3,312)
Read, Philip L 5:30:53 (29,277)
Read, Simon A 3:54:00 (7,792)
Read, Trevor 5:53:36 (32,022)
Reader, Paul T 4:27:28 (15,464)
Reading, Gary B 5:39:23 (30,505)
Readings, Thomas 6:41:25 (34,703)
Readman, Ben 3:43:41 (5,809)
Readman, Darren 4:21:45 (14,019)
Readrer, Alistair W 3:59:15 (9,027)
Ready, Charles F 5:33:02 (29,610)
Ready, Thomas 5:09:56 (25,457)
Real Del Sarte, Raphael 3:19:48 (2,466)
Reams, Benjamin D 4:51:22 (21,334)
Reason, Andrew J 4:02:16 (9,665)
Reay, Kenneth S 5:17:21 (26,927)
Reay, Tim 4:24:54 (14,803)
Reay, Tim J 4:29:05 (15,880)
Reay-Jones, Nicholas H 3:48:04 (6,535)
Reay-Jones, Simon H 4:09:26 (11,057)
Rebellato, Mario 6:09:01 (33,239)
Reber, Dominic C 3:58:12 (8,760)
Rebodos, Lee M 3:11:54 (1,714)
Reboul, Kevin P 3:20:47 (2,586)
Reburn, William J 2:55:42 (600)
Recalde, Oscar 3:32:11 (4,028)
Recchia, Christopher J 4:43:25 (19,404)
Reck, Lyell 3:20:41 (2,575)
Reckless, Mark J 3:23:58 (2,902)
Record, Matthew C 3:40:02 (5,195)
Reda, Pietro 3:40:49 (5,324)
Redding, Andrew J 2:44:39 (231)
Redding, Chris 4:31:12 (16,407)
Reddy, Bruno 5:35:33 (29,984)
Reddy, Ugan 5:21:56 (27,776)
Redfearn, Graham I 5:36:31 (30,117)
Redfern, Richard J 4:27:53 (15,558)
Redfern, Samuel A 3:38:42 (4,956)
Redford, Albert R 7:36:49 (35,543)
Redgate, David H 5:10:27 (25,566)
Redgrove, Nicholas J 4:31:42 (16,509)
Redhead, Roland B 6:07:58 (33,167)
Redman, Gary S 4:40:09 (18,566)
Redman, Nigel 4:40:54 (18,760)
Redmayne, Mark N 3:23:26 (2,845)
Redmond, John J 3:43:06 (5,707)
Redondo, José 6:03:32 (32,856)
Redpath, David W 4:09:14 (11,014)
Redsell, Maurice 5:47:18 (31,386)
Redshaw, Jonathan M 3:39:21 (5,073)
Redshaw, Simon 3:34:12 (4,293)
Redwood, Derek S 5:23:37 (28,033)
Redwood, Michael E 4:45:58 (20,054)
Reece, William 3:20:30 (2,553)
Reed, Adam J 4:29:25 (15,980)
Reed, Alan 3:33:28 (4,201)
Reed, Charles W 5:00:59 (23,722)
Reed, David R 2:44:13 (221)
Reed, Declan A 2:52:48 (471)
Reed, Duncan J 4:26:13 (15,105)
Reed, Graham J 5:11:17 (25,714)
Reed, Harvey Q 5:27:33 (28,719)
Reed, James 5:07:32 (25,007)
Reed, Jamie 7:27:02 (35,447)
Reed, Malcolm 5:17:02 (26,863)
Reed, Martin 4:39:17 (18,357)
Reed, Martin 5:59:10 (32,523)
Reed, Matthew G 3:33:39 (4,222)
Reed, Michael J 4:47:49 (20,482)
Reed, Peter A 6:07:00 (33,106)
Reed, Philip R 5:05:50 (24,659)
Reed, Steve 4:44:42 (19,744)
Reed, Stuart R 4:03:00 (9,785)
Reedman, David J 5:39:26 (30,514)
Reekie, Harry J 5:05:21 (24,564)
Rees, Bryan D 4:40:39 (18,687)
Rees, Colin D 5:30:38 (29,241)
Rees, Colin J 3:43:24 (5,754)
Rees, Gary B 6:58:53 (35,109)
Rees, Grant N 4:10:46 (11,322)
Rees, Malcolm T 7:50:23 (35,619)
Rees, Mark 4:26:58 (15,314)
Rees, Mark 5:12:19 (25,926)
Rees, Matt 3:29:24 (3,635)
Rees, Michael J 3:26:04 (3,136)
Rees, Mike 5:34:43 (29,877)
Rees, Peter P 4:13:43 (12,022)
Rees, Philip W 3:31:15 (3,872)
Rees, Stuart R 4:42:30 (19,178)
Reese, Jim 4:47:34 (20,426)
Reese, Timothy C 4:33:00 (16,785)
Reeve, Adrian D 6:14:46 (33,598)
Reeve, David M 4:26:55 (15,299)
Reeve, Nicholas P 5:05:27 (24,588)
Reeve, Steven M 3:01:02 (961)
Reeve, Victor L 5:28:19 (28,871)
Reeve, Warren 4:18:51 (13,296)
Reevell, John 3:46:08 (6,200)
Reeves, Andrew B 2:41:21 (161)
Reeves, Andrew W 5:29:33 (29,076)
Reeves, Barry G 5:24:42 (28,219)
Reeves, Gavin J 4:17:46 (13,015)

Reeves, Matt S..............5:44:12 (31,064)
Reeves, Melvin..............5:30:46 (29,262)
Reeves, Paul C..............5:17:19 (26,922)
Reeves, Philip L..............4:56:07 (22,540)
Reeves, Steve..............3:13:24 (1,858)
Reeves, Stuart N..............2:53:24 (489)
Regan, James..............4:43:48 (19,478)
Regan, Matthew P..............4:22:28 (14,190)
Regan, Paul R..............5:34:53 (29,900)
Regan, Peter L..............5:20:19 (27,479)
Regent, Nazaire R..............4:21:03 (13,862)
Rehman, Kamran A..............5:28:19 (28,871)
Rehn, Lars R..............4:34:36 (17,177)
Reibold, Michael..............5:14:14 (26,278)
Reichardt, Christian..............3:46:59 (6,342)
Reid, Adam P..............3:56:05 (8,244)
Reid, Andrew P..............4:46:47 (20,227)
Reid, David M..............4:58:48 (23,206)
Reid, Donald D..............3:41:02 (5,370)
Reid, Donald W..............3:51:37 (7,279)
Reid, Gavin..............2:51:54 (436)
Reid, Gavin..............3:21:40 (2,673)
Reid, George..............4:22:03 (14,097)
Reid, Ian..............4:01:46 (9,562)
Reid, Ian D..............2:54:41 (558)
Reid, Jasper T..............5:08:24 (25,174)
Reid, John R..............5:50:20 (31,709)
Reid, John R..............5:52:27 (31,915)
Reid, Karl..............3:32:09 (4,024)
Reid, Martin A..............3:54:24 (7,883)
Reid, Nicholas I..............3:05:43 (1,218)
Reid, Paul A..............4:48:13 (20,582)
Reid, Rupert J..............4:33:43 (16,970)
Reid, Stephen W..............4:38:39 (18,185)
Reid, Steven J..............3:04:56 (1,156)
Reid, Thomas..............4:01:24 (9,499)
Reid, Timothy J..............3:59:15 (9,027)
Reidy, Padraig G..............4:35:39 (17,440)
Reidy, Scott P..............4:26:17 (15,127)
Reif, Christian..............3:40:45 (5,310)
Reiffer, Ian S..............4:02:21 (9,677)
Reilly, Christopher S..............5:31:57 (29,439)
Reilly, Gerry..............4:21:49 (14,036)
Reilly, John..............5:52:36 (31,927)
Reilly, Leon..............4:48:58 (20,757)
Reilly, Michael W..............4:29:17 (15,934)
Reilly, Patrick S..............4:16:09 (12,609)
Reilly, Paul J..............3:48:35 (6,642)
Reilly, Philip J..............3:40:30 (5,266)
Reilly, Stephen J..............3:31:27 (3,898)
Reilly, Thomas S..............4:26:29 (15,184)
Reiser, René..............4:03:39 (9,891)
Reiss, Bjoern..............2:56:08 (619)
Rej, Edward R..............4:18:26 (13,190)
Remblance, Harry..............4:38:16 (18,077)
Remblance, Perry..............4:41:28 (18,910)
Remigio, Adriano..............4:58:17 (23,098)
Remnant, Neil A..............5:31:26 (29,371)
Remoriquet, Regis..............5:18:09 (27,091)
Renak, Daniel J..............5:34:24 (29,827)
Renaud, Yves..............4:11:00 (11,369)
Renault, Neil..............2:23:44 (19)
Renault, Sergio..............4:17:11 (12,848)
Rendall, Julian I..............2:34:06 (65)
Rendall, Mike J..............4:33:02 (16,795)
Rendell, Graham..............4:17:20 (12,887)
Rendell, Richard..............3:40:20 (5,240)
Rendell-Read, Steven I..............4:00:35 (9,327)
Rengert, Paul M..............4:51:01 (21,244)
Renkema, Cornelis..............4:06:25 (10,445)
Renner, Tilo..............3:45:23 (6,079)
Rennie, Allain..............5:30:23 (29,197)
Rennie, David J..............3:45:42 (6,136)
Rennie, Gavin A..............3:45:48 (6,149)
Rennie, Jamie S..............4:35:27 (17,389)
Rennie, Michael J..............4:27:41 (15,512)
Rennison, David C..............4:45:28 (19,938)
Rennison, Mark..............3:13:51 (1,888)
Rens, Keith R..............3:51:11 (7,182)
Renshaw, Alan..............3:48:00 (6,526)
Renshaw, Ben..............5:07:51 (25,068)
Renshaw, Dominic I..............5:00:38 (23,645)
Renstrom, Nicolai..............4:58:39 (23,180)

Renstrom, Preben..............4:58:28 (23,148)
Renton, Hamish..............3:57:38 (8,634)
Reppold, Hans-Juergen..............4:40:04 (18,549)
Resnick, Brian L..............5:06:59 (24,876)
Reuben, Nigel..............4:03:28 (9,860)
Revans, Mark A..............5:22:55 (27,926)
Revell, Laurence J..............5:04:12 (24,357)
Revell, Paul S..............5:14:31 (26,341)
Revell, Peter A..............5:07:56 (25,082)
Revell, Thomas A..............3:56:03 (8,235)
Revenault, Didier..............4:06:23 (10,435)
Revill, Craig I..............4:59:34 (23,404)
Rew, Simon D..............3:50:53 (7,111)
Rex, Eddie A..............3:33:09 (4,161)
Reyes, Pedro J..............4:44:30 (19,681)
Reyes-Aldasoro, Gerardo..............3:20:15 (2,523)
Reynecke, Walter..............4:59:22 (23,347)
Reynolds, Andrew M..............3:10:37 (1,603)
Reynolds, Daniel J..............5:45:41 (31,223)
Reynolds, Daniel L..............5:40:21 (30,637)
Reynolds, Graham..............3:32:32 (4,076)
Reynolds, Ivor M..............4:07:55 (10,755)
Reynolds, James G..............2:57:50 (733)
Reynolds, John..............5:40:51 (30,689)
Reynolds, John A..............5:01:45 (23,880)
Reynolds, Jonathan L..............3:57:46 (8,667)
Reynolds, Lee M..............4:03:14 (9,824)
Reynolds, Mark..............3:18:03 (2,288)
Reynolds, Mark G..............2:58:47 (812)
Reynolds, Markus..............3:24:52 (3,006)
Reynolds, Matthew J..............3:29:55 (3,705)
Reynolds, Paul..............2:46:14 (264)
Reynolds, Paul K..............4:19:31 (13,463)
Reynolds, Paul R..............3:24:13 (2,932)
Reynolds, Peter..............4:17:04 (12,825)
Reynolds, Peter..............4:56:27 (22,627)
Reynolds, Simon..............4:46:45 (20,221)
Reynolds, Stephen J..............4:20:57 (13,840)
Reynolds, Steven J..............6:35:30 (34,524)
Reynolds, Thomas A..............4:19:20 (13,412)
Reynolds, Tony M..............4:09:36 (11,095)
Rhead, Robert J..............4:14:13 (12,141)
Rhimes, Godfrey H..............2:50:22 (383)
Rhoades, Tony M..............4:18:54 (13,306)
Rhodes, Benjamin A..............4:35:15 (17,348)
Rhodes, Lee A..............4:03:44 (9,911)
Rhodes, Malcolm S..............4:50:10 (21,039)
Rhodes, Philip J..............4:42:00 (19,038)
Rhodes, Steven..............4:28:03 (15,608)
Rhodes, Stewart..............3:29:37 (3,663)
Riccardo, Ruscitti..............3:27:38 (3,365)
Rice, Joseph J..............3:58:25 (8,812)
Rice, Martin J..............3:26:36 (3,206)
Rice, Nicholas..............5:00:22 (23,592)
Rice, Scott M..............3:10:08 (1,574)
Rice, Thomas I..............5:06:07 (24,718)
Rich, Andrew J..............5:37:21 (30,226)
Rich, Lee W..............4:03:09 (9,808)
Richard, Alain..............4:40:27 (18,640)
Richards, Alistair H..............3:20:11 (2,517)
Richards, Andrew..............4:10:12 (11,205)
Richards, Anthony D..............5:25:26 (28,351)
Richards, Anthony J..............6:20:49 (33,941)
Richards, Arwel W..............4:56:59 (22,770)
Richards, Clive J..............2:48:22 (324)
Richards, Craig J..............4:21:12 (13,897)
Richards, David..............4:00:40 (9,349)
Richards, David..............6:02:26 (32,781)
Richards, David A..............4:47:34 (20,426)
Richards, Gary J..............5:44:34 (31,104)
Richards, Geraint H..............5:34:07 (29,784)
Richards, Gideon B..............5:33:24 (29,664)
Richards, Gordon..............3:24:50 (2,999)
Richards, Ian E..............3:29:51 (3,699)
Richards, Jon D..............3:53:35 (7,705)
Richards, Julian E..............4:39:46 (18,476)
Richards, Mark..............3:33:52 (4,247)
Richards, Michael D..............3:31:40 (3,936)
Richards, Neil A..............5:38:11 (30,333)
Richards, Peter T..............6:15:27 (33,644)
Richards, Philip H..............3:52:53 (7,540)
Richards, Robert E..............5:13:46 (26,183)
Richards, Selwyn C..............3:40:47 (5,318)

Richards, Simon D..............5:53:19 (31,989)
Richards, Stephen G..............4:27:57 (15,571)
Richards, Tom..............4:39:11 (18,329)
Richards, Tom..............4:49:07 (20,798)
Richardson, Andrew G..............6:03:12 (32,832)
Richardson, Andrew L..............3:46:45 (6,291)
Richardson, Chuck..............3:46:27 (6,246)
Richardson, Clive..............3:29:23 (3,633)
Richardson, Colin..............3:11:36 (1,680)
Richardson, Colin I..............4:33:30 (16,911)
Richardson, Duncan R..............3:37:28 (4,747)
Richardson, Eamonn P..............3:54:24 (7,883)
Richardson, Geoff L..............4:57:58 (23,025)
Richardson, George W..............4:42:09 (19,076)
Richardson, Hilary L..............4:33:42 (16,962)
Richardson, Jeremy..............3:31:03 (3,842)
Richardson, Kenneth P..............3:45:00 (6,028)
Richardson, Kevin J..............5:52:18 (31,902)
Richardson, Mark A..............5:45:42 (31,228)
Richardson, Mark D..............3:30:53 (3,826)
Richardson, Mark H..............5:32:02 (29,463)
Richardson, Martin P..............4:11:15 (11,558)
Richardson, Michael..............5:11:33 (25,769)
Richardson, Neil..............4:04:18 (10,025)
Richardson, Neil G..............4:48:27 (20,639)
Richardson, Nicholas..............5:27:08 (28,644)
Richardson, Nigel G..............4:00:47 (9,369)
Richardson, Paul..............4:16:36 (12,716)
Richardson, Paul J..............4:36:39 (17,704)
Richardson, Paul W..............5:16:22 (26,730)
Richardson, Simon J..............6:16:10 (33,692)
Richardson, Simons C..............3:05:00 (1,163)
Richardson, Stephen P..............4:39:36 (18,437)
Richardson, Steven..............3:59:47 (9,160)
Richardson, Terry J..............5:58:11 (32,430)
Richardson, Thomas D..............4:38:50 (18,242)
Richardson, Tom D..............3:23:08 (2,814)
Richardson-Perks, Tim R..............3:16:39 (2,138)
Richer, Paul G..............4:45:54 (20,033)
Riches, Chris..............3:54:40 (7,937)
Riches, Mark C..............2:50:37 (397)
Riches, Simon J..............5:56:47 (32,318)
Riches, Steven J..............6:22:24 (34,020)
Richman, David..............4:53:08 (21,788)
Richman, Gary..............5:42:48 (30,909)
Richmond, David F..............3:12:33 (1,785)
Richmond, Kenny..............2:33:45 (59)
Richter, Holger..............4:01:24 (9,499)
Rickard, Graham K..............4:48:11 (20,573)
Ricker, Christoph..............3:50:19 (7,003)
Ricketts, Robert L..............4:57:37 (22,936)
Rickey, Charles H..............4:37:14 (17,826)
Riddaway, Robert..............4:21:23 (13,933)
Riddell, Lachlan..............3:44:42 (5,978)
Riddick, Karl N..............3:06:38 (1,283)
Riddiford, Magnus O..............4:11:23 (11,470)
Riddington, Bruce..............4:04:43 (10,095)
Riddle, John M..............5:45:49 (31,240)
Riddle, Steven..............4:41:48 (18,995)
Riddoch, Andy J..............3:07:12 (1,328)
Rider, Julian..............4:01:34 (9,529)
Ridgeway, Paul B..............3:23:50 (2,882)
Ridgewell, Stanley A..............4:49:48 (20,955)
Ridgway, John..............4:55:08 (22,298)
Ridgway, Mark C..............2:47:58 (298)
Ridler, Nigel..............4:08:53 (10,940)
Ridley, Bill..............3:05:13 (1,175)
Ridley, David J..............3:54:16 (7,861)
Ridley, Jake..............5:08:00 (25,093)
Ridley, Jason..............4:07:54 (10,748)
Ridley, Stephen C..............3:50:50 (7,102)
Ridout, John P..............3:23:19 (2,834)
Ridout, Tony..............4:47:08 (20,321)
Riedel, Konrad..............4:21:46 (14,025)
Riefler, Oliver H..............2:55:49 (604)
Riego, Rodrigo..............5:17:41 (26,998)
Riemer, Michael S..............3:48:07 (6,547)
Rigg, Nigel K..............3:27:08 (3,300)
Rigolet, José..............4:03:53 (9,945)
Rijpstra, Eelke S..............4:08:12 (10,811)
Rikkelman, Joop..............5:22:26 (27,839)
Riley, Cameron G..............4:17:47 (13,019)
Riley, Christopher J..............2:35:47 (82)

Riley, Colin A 5:48:41 (31,550)
Riley, Damian 3:59:04 (8,976)
Riley, George S 4:18:06 (13,094)
Riley, Kenneth 5:01:09 (23,761)
Riley, Mark J 4:30:56 (16,343)
Riley, Matthew C 4:49:25 (20,864)
Riley, Michael A 5:00:40 (23,650)
Riley, Neal 5:14:37 (26,365)
Riley, Patrick 3:19:02 (2,395)
Riley, Sam J 4:57:08 (22,805)
Riley, Tim D 3:36:04 (4,552)
Riley, Trevor I 3:49:55 (6,921)
Riley, William N 3:39:22 (5,079)
Rimmer, Tim 4:39:38 (18,445)
Rimondi, Giuseppe 3:45:50 (6,154)
Rinaldi, Andrew J 4:27:12 (15,387)
Rindlisbacher, Daniel 3:07:53 (1,379)
Ring, Christopher 4:02:02 (9,608)
Ringrose, Colin D 3:40:58 (5,359)
Rink, Marcus J 4:38:46 (18,220)
Rints, Richard E 4:50:38 (21,155)
Riolfi, Rossano 4:41:25 (18,896)
Riordan, Joseph G 5:32:13 (29,485)
Riordan, Peter 4:59:55 (23,479)
Ripley, Michael S 4:46:29 (20,174)
Ripping, David P 5:19:25 (27,324)
Rippon, Peter E 3:43:16 (5,731)
Rippon, William 4:43:43 (19,466)
Rising, Stuart 4:29:51 (16,110)
Risk, Ralph T 5:07:26 (24,984)
Risley, Darrey S 4:33:06 (16,810)
Rist, Philip J 4:03:11 (9,813)
Ritchie, James L 4:39:55 (18,514)
Ritchie, Neil 5:24:30 (28,183)
Ritchie, Paul W 6:05:24 (32,988)
Rithamer, Torben 4:50:22 (21,087)
Ritschard, Thomas 3:04:28 (1,127)
Ritter, Gordon J 5:04:58 (24,512)
Rivers, Terry M 3:39:32 (5,113)
Riverts, Tony 4:39:25 (18,394)
Riviere, Serge 3:58:18 (8,789)
Rivington, James H 4:25:27 (14,934)
Rixon, Paul A 5:11:37 (25,780)
Rizzi, Giancarlo 5:19:44 (27,379)
Roach, Dave J 4:23:51 (14,530)
Roach, John 5:08:57 (25,273)
Roach, William M 4:02:34 (9,704)
Robb, Andy J 3:50:17 (6,995)
Robb, Russell J 4:52:47 (21,689)
Robbie, Nicholas 3:59:45 (9,152)
Robbins, Jason C 4:54:10 (22,069)
Robbins, Keith G 5:49:35 (31,636)
Robbins, Matthew P 4:53:49 (21,972)
Robbins, Paul 3:52:13 (7,411)
Robbins, Stuart 4:12:38 (11,748)
Robe, Michel 3:37:54 (4,806)
Roberston, Derek 6:44:16 (34,782)
Robert, Iain A 2:45:03 (242)
Roberts, Alan F 3:36:20 (4,592)
Roberts, Alex J 4:56:05 (22,532)
Roberts, Alun H 5:15:01 (26,456)
Roberts, Andrew 4:09:55 (11,153)
Roberts, Andrew F 5:20:26 (27,501)
Roberts, Andrew J 3:36:51 (4,667)
Roberts, Andrew J 3:38:41 (4,954)
Roberts, Anthony P 4:19:54 (13,574)
Roberts, Benjamin J 4:17:50 (13,029)
Roberts, Chris A 3:35:23 (4,467)
Roberts, Chris W 3:39:04 (5,027)
Roberts, Craig H 4:59:25 (23,354)
Roberts, David A 4:13:34 (11,986)
Roberts, David B 4:20:25 (13,714)
Roberts, David L 3:34:08 (4,283)
Roberts, David W 5:02:36 (24,057)
Roberts, David W 5:36:58 (30,168)
Roberts, David W 5:46:35 (31,319)
Roberts, Edward C 4:26:55 (15,299)
Roberts, Gareth P 4:24:08 (14,610)
Roberts, Glyn C 4:22:13 (14,131)
Roberts, Graeme 4:20:56 (13,838)
Roberts, Haydn C 4:45:01 (19,842)
Roberts, Howard S 5:43:46 (31,021)
Roberts, Huntley J 4:12:23 (11,697)
Roberts, Huw 4:22:54 (14,309)
Roberts, Ian D 5:06:34 (24,791)
Roberts, Ian W 3:30:44 (3,813)
Roberts, James W 4:50:31 (21,129)
Roberts, Jason 4:00:53 (9,393)
Roberts, John E 5:22:28 (27,842)
Roberts, Kerry J 2:51:40 (427)
Roberts, Konrad P 4:12:00 (11,613)
Roberts, Luke S 3:15:49 (2,063)
Roberts, Malcolm 3:27:20 (3,330)
Roberts, Matt 4:21:22 (13,926)
Roberts, Matt J 4:09:45 (11,123)
Roberts, Nicholas G 5:11:40 (25,788)
Roberts, Paul 4:21:18 (13,911)
Roberts, Pete J 5:29:09 (29,011)
Roberts, Peter T 4:36:00 (17,534)
Roberts, Peter W 4:13:54 (12,068)
Roberts, Phil T 4:07:02 (10,580)
Roberts, Russell W 5:20:38 (27,545)
Roberts, Simon 3:39:35 (5,121)
Roberts, Simon A 3:27:22 (3,336)
Roberts, Simon D 4:47:18 (20,359)
Roberts, Steve J 3:28:24 (3,462)
Roberts, Stewart M 4:54:28 (22,139)
Roberts, Trevor 4:48:56 (20,752)
Roberts, Vincent C 5:01:33 (23,843)
Roberts, William J 4:56:49 (22,719)
Robertshaw, Jason S 3:44:59 (6,025)
Robertshaw, Philip 4:26:18 (15,130)
Robertshaw, Tom 2:58:21 (775)
Robertson, Alex W 4:53:12 (21,810)
Robertson, Colin M 5:37:03 (30,177)
Robertson, Frank C 4:57:01 (22,779)
Robertson, Iain 5:24:28 (28,178)
Robertson, Iain D 3:44:35 (5,955)
Robertson, Ian H 3:32:28 (4,063)
Robertson, John B 6:01:06 (32,684)
Robertson, John R 2:53:40 (504)
Robertson, Keith J 3:44:35 (5,955)
Robertson, Kevin R 3:39:19 (5,067)
Robertson, Michael P 4:25:10 (14,862)
Robertson, Neil D 4:50:10 (21,039)
Robertson, Paul 2:57:14 (693)
Robertson, Peter C 4:08:33 (10,879)
Robertson, Richard 6:25:29 (34,147)
Robertson, Robin 3:54:05 (7,812)
Robertson, Stewart D 3:28:24 (3,462)
Robey, Chris J 5:02:23 (24,010)
Robins, Alex G 3:36:56 (4,680)
Robins, George 5:58:21 (32,453)
Robins, Stuart 3:50:45 (7,087)
Robinson, Adam J 4:39:53 (18,504)
Robinson, Alan S 5:52:23 (31,909)
Robinson, Alex 3:24:08 (2,925)
Robinson, Alexander 6:25:04 (34,130)
Robinson, Andrew 4:06:02 (10,355)
Robinson, Andrew M 6:05:06 (32,972)
Robinson, Andrew N 3:17:41 (2,250)
Robinson, Barry J 4:27:25 (15,454)
Robinson, Christopher D 5:18:36 (27,180)
Robinson, Clive R 3:58:45 (8,897)
Robinson, Dan 2:14:14 (9)
Robinson, Daniel L 3:24:05 (2,918)
Robinson, Darren 3:58:12 (8,760)
Robinson, David J 4:01:52 (9,581)
Robinson, David J 5:51:11 (31,793)
Robinson, David K 3:15:09 (2,009)
Robinson, David M 4:01:22 (9,492)
Robinson, David P 7:27:20 (35,453)
Robinson, Frank W 5:29:24 (29,057)
Robinson, Fred D 3:41:58 (5,511)
Robinson, Geoffrey C 5:29:35 (29,082)
Robinson, George 3:05:32 (1,205)
Robinson, James E 6:47:15 (34,868)
Robinson, James S 4:00:05 (9,224)
Robinson, Jonathan D 4:58:36 (23,166)
Robinson, Jonathan J 4:16:44 (12,748)
Robinson, Joseph E 5:38:16 (30,350)
Robinson, Lee 4:47:00 (20,280)
Robinson, Mark A 5:04:42 (24,448)
Robinson, Martin R 3:53:56 (7,775)
Robinson, Matthew I 5:39:15 (30,482)
Robinson, Michael J 5:38:48 (30,431)
Robinson, Neil S 6:03:23 (32,845)
Robinson, Nick 4:39:17 (18,357)
Robinson, Oliver 4:42:28 (19,171)
Robinson, Owne 5:28:22 (28,882)
Robinson, Patrick A 5:29:45 (29,103)
Robinson, Paul 4:59:03 (23,272)
Robinson, Paul A 4:15:10 (12,360)
Robinson, Peter 3:44:42 (5,978)
Robinson, Peter J 5:55:56 (32,232)
Robinson, Peter N 6:04:24 (32,911)
Robinson, Raymond G 4:33:01 (16,791)
Robinson, Richard 4:47:58 (20,525)
Robinson, Richard 5:21:32 (27,700)
Robinson, Simon 3:53:27 (7,677)
Robinson, Simon 4:52:13 (21,546)
Robinson, Simon A 4:21:08 (13,882)
Robinson, Simon E 5:16:57 (26,850)
Robinson, Steve S 4:51:58 (21,477)
Robinson, Stewart N 4:13:45 (12,030)
Robinson, Thomas 5:34:36 (29,861)
Robinson, Tom M 5:59:10 (32,523)
Robinson, Victor 5:50:30 (31,727)
Robinson, Victor C 5:22:44 (27,896)
Robinson, William M 3:25:52 (3,108)
Robinson-Marshall, Stuart A 4:33:35 (16,930)
Robiot, Jocelyn 3:59:58 (9,201)
Robjohns, Graham 4:26:05 (15,070)
Robley, Neil 5:21:38 (27,717)
Roborgh, Dominic L 4:35:22 (17,375)
Robotham, Simon J 5:19:30 (27,337)
Robson, Colin E 5:28:29 (28,900)
Robson, Dale 5:43:20 (30,976)
Robson, Garry 7:29:22 (35,479)
Robson, Graham D 3:53:28 (7,681)
Robson, Henry R 5:52:52 (31,956)
Robson, John E 3:48:57 (6,717)
Robson, Mark 4:21:25 (13,942)
Robson, Phillip A 4:28:57 (15,846)
Robson, Robert J 6:04:40 (32,929)
Robson, Stephen M 3:31:24 (3,890)
Robson, Terry R 4:52:49 (21,706)
Rocchi, Jonthon S 3:44:58 (6,023)
Rochard, Marc J 3:28:30 (3,485)
Roche, Alan R 4:19:04 (13,343)
Roche, Brendan J 3:55:03 (8,019)
Roche, James A 4:20:17 (13,674)
Roche, Paul M 5:44:14 (31,069)
Rock, Ian T 4:13:23 (11,933)
Rockett, Peter J 5:58:50 (32,492)
Rockey, Alan J 5:09:31 (25,375)
Rockley, Trevor S 3:51:55 (7,342)
Rodd, Antony J 4:41:27 (18,902)
Rodda, Philip F 3:49:21 (6,805)
Roddan, John R 5:55:06 (32,155)
Roden, Scot 4:41:28 (18,910)
Roderick, Kevin 4:22:05 (14,105)
Rodewald, Dag 4:10:10 (11,196)
Rodger, Jody S 3:18:04 (2,291)
Rodger, Peter S 3:26:24 (3,186)
Rodgers, Christopher F 4:05:05 (10,160)
Rodgers, Paul J 4:39:34 (18,427)
Rodgers, Stephen 4:03:06 (9,801)
Rodney, David J 4:16:26 (12,681)
Rodrigues, Mervyn A 3:34:35 (4,352)
Rodriguez, José L 2:48:24 (328)
Rodriguez, Juan 4:04:25 (10,041)
Rodui, Benjamin 3:40:46 (5,312)
Rodwell, Lee 4:15:15 (12,376)
Rodwell, Paul W 4:39:03 (18,299)
Roe, David N 3:26:56 (3,265)
Roe, John 5:59:53 (32,566)
Roebuck, Tony P 4:16:17 (12,644)
Roedel, Paul 5:38:50 (30,434)
Roeder, Bernd 4:33:42 (16,962)
Roel, Craig 4:30:14 (16,202)
Roepke, Wilfried 4:28:27 (15,715)
Roesler, Thomas 3:59:08 (8,992)
Roets, Lourens 4:30:40 (16,290)
Roffey, David 4:48:20 (20,620)
Roffey, Tery A 5:21:09 (27,624)
Rog, Martin J 4:22:55 (14,313)
Rogan, Gary P 5:30:04 (29,155)
Roger, David 3:36:56 (4,680)

Rogers, Adrian M	5:17:27 (26,948)	
Rogers, Andrew J	5:11:32 (25,763)	
Rogers, Andy J	4:47:37 (20,435)	
Rogers, Benjamin	4:40:36 (18,680)	
Rogers, Christian M	3:54:44 (7,949)	
Rogers, Christopher K	4:14:16 (12,157)	
Rogers, Daryl J	4:41:23 (18,884)	
Rogers, David	3:56:11 (8,270)	
Rogers, David A	5:09:16 (25,328)	
Rogers, Dominic	3:32:13 (4,032)	
Rogers, Ed J	6:07:54 (33,161)	
Rogers, George E	6:00:16 (32,600)	
Rogers, Ian J	3:50:07 (6,964)	
Rogers, Jeremy	2:42:24 (187)	
Rogers, Jim	6:53:10 (34,996)	
Rogers, John E	5:06:07 (24,718)	
Rogers, Mark B	3:50:00 (6,942)	
Rogers, Mark J	2:57:11 (689)	
Rogers, Matthew A	4:42:26 (19,163)	
Rogers, Michael S	4:12:31 (11,726)	
Rogers, Nick P	4:00:38 (9,342)	
Rogers, Paul	4:35:16 (17,353)	
Rogers, Paul A	5:24:38 (28,204)	
Rogers, Paul B	4:15:44 (12,491)	
Rogers, Philip A	3:16:48 (2,158)	
Rogers, Sean C	3:18:37 (2,354)	
Rogers, Simon P	4:53:39 (21,927)	
Rogers, Stephen	5:27:37 (28,732)	
Rogers, Steven	4:36:01 (17,540)	
Rogers, Stuart J	5:56:26 (32,280)	
Rogers, Stuart M	4:48:43 (20,700)	
Rogers, Timothy M	5:50:03 (31,681)	
Rogers, William E	3:49:57 (6,927)	
Rogerson, Ian D	4:49:04 (20,783)	
Rogerson, Keith E	6:04:20 (32,906)	
Rohde, Allan	3:17:13 (2,198)	
Roi, Piercarlo	5:47:26 (31,403)	
Rokenson, Gary	4:46:56 (20,262)	
Roker, Phil J	3:45:16 (6,062)	
Rolf, Gavin P	4:44:08 (19,571)	
Rolfe, Alan T	4:06:35 (10,482)	
Rolfe, John W	5:58:34 (32,471)	
Rolfe, Les J	3:49:29 (6,827)	
Rolfe, Michael A	3:01:20 (977)	
Rolfe, Michael J	5:56:03 (32,242)	
Rollason, Christopher S	4:35:38 (17,436)	
Rollason, Stephen G	4:35:47 (17,483)	
Roller, John N	4:45:02 (19,848)	
Rollings, Adrian J	3:50:59 (7,135)	
Rollings, Jamie	4:02:20 (9,676)	
Rollinson, Peter	6:08:07 (33,181)	
Rolph, Patrick J	4:58:14 (23,085)	
Roman, Fred	5:36:12 (30,072)	
Rome, Paul	5:55:37 (32,202)	
Romeijn, Ron	4:53:50 (21,975)	
Romero, Adolfo	3:43:31 (5,783)	
Romero, Gustavo	4:33:42 (16,962)	
Romo, Christophe	3:59:26 (9,075)	
Romo, David	4:47:16 (20,347)	
Ronald, Mark	5:29:24 (29,057)	
Rondepierre, Philippe A	4:13:32 (11,980)	
Rones, Kare	3:38:48 (4,973)	
Ronnan, Andrew	5:18:09 (27,091)	
Rood, Matt	5:08:14 (25,147)	
Rook, Spencer J	2:59:39 (875)	
Rooke, Nigel G	6:03:15 (32,836)	
Rooke, Steven J	3:38:05 (4,850)	
Rooney, Tom	4:36:36 (17,692)	
Root, Philip J	5:48:52 (31,569)	
Roper, James	3:52:56 (7,551)	
Roper, Luke J	3:52:57 (7,554)	
Roper, Martin J	4:57:16 (22,839)	
Roper, Simon	5:05:43 (24,639)	
Roper, Stephen C	5:18:32 (27,169)	
Roper, Steve R	5:18:41 (27,196)	
Rosagro, Danny	4:12:43 (11,770)	
Rosak, Anthony R	2:51:00 (410)	
Rosamond, Damon	4:38:23 (18,122)	
Rosbergen, Wilem	4:09:20 (11,039)	
Rosbrook, Simon J	4:15:05 (12,338)	
Roscoe, Adam I	4:39:51 (18,498)	
Rose, Adam M	4:04:52 (10,125)	
Rose, Alex	3:28:09 (3,424)	
Rose, Alun M	4:05:09 (10,175)	
Rose, Andrew D	5:07:23 (24,975)	
Rose, Benjamin J	4:15:59 (12,558)	
Rose, Chris	3:52:54 (7,544)	
Rose, Daniel J	3:54:48 (7,962)	
Rose, Daniel R	5:55:16 (32,170)	
Rose, David	4:16:24 (12,670)	
Rose, Dean	4:44:15 (19,615)	
Rose, Duncan	4:21:30 (13,967)	
Rose, Harvey D	2:47:28 (298)	
Rose, Ian P	4:22:42 (14,258)	
Rose, Johnathan W	4:30:01 (16,151)	
Rose, Kevin	4:02:18 (9,668)	
Rose, Mark R	4:09:02 (10,956)	
Rose, Martin	3:41:27 (5,440)	
Rose, Michael J	4:55:44 (22,440)	
Rose, Paul J	2:47:02 (286)	
Rose, Peter	5:13:03 (26,056)	
Rose, Sean A	2:48:03 (311)	
Rosemont, Jonathan D	5:11:58 (25,848)	
Rosen, Hugh D	4:04:14 (10,013)	
Rosen, Simon N	5:04:56 (24,506)	
Rosenbach, Jonathan T	3:27:17 (3,323)	
Rosendale, Philip J	6:34:29 (34,473)	
Rosenfeld, David J	4:31:49 (16,530)	
Rosen-Nash, William A	5:37:33 (30,240)	
Rosenquist, Fredrik	4:09:00 (10,949)	
Rosenstein, Andrew	4:19:24 (13,431)	
Rosenthal, Nicholas B	4:12:03 (11,621)	
Rosewell, David Z	4:36:29 (17,659)	
Rosie, Bill	4:32:34 (16,681)	
Rosland, Frode	3:14:52 (1,975)	
Rosling, David J	4:52:11 (21,537)	
Ross, Aaron	6:18:42 (33,818)	
Ross, Barry J	4:12:25 (11,705)	
Ross, Brian T	4:22:01 (14,089)	
Ross, David	3:06:11 (1,245)	
Ross, David I	5:03:06 (24,146)	
Ross, Iain D	5:29:33 (29,076)	
Ross, James M	3:43:25 (5,756)	
Ross, Jim	3:56:03 (8,235)	
Ross, Mark J	4:02:12 (9,646)	
Ross, Nicholas E	4:23:37 (14,470)	
Ross, Philip A	3:55:37 (8,143)	
Ross, Rick P	6:09:52 (33,297)	
Ross, Robert P	5:18:55 (27,235)	
Ross, Stuart B	3:37:29 (4,751)	
Rossall, Stephen G	3:40:58 (5,359)	
Rossell, Steve	4:49:47 (20,951)	
Rosser, David R	4:51:02 (21,248)	
Rossi, Andrea	3:58:10 (8,750)	
Rossi, Paolo	3:58:11 (8,755)	
Rossi, Sergio	4:20:11 (13,653)	
Rossiter, Martin R	3:23:48 (2,878)	
Rossiter, Philippe R	4:26:08 (15,081)	
Rosso, Francesco	4:21:38 (13,994)	
Rosso, Michele	4:06:48 (10,530)	
Rossouw, Noel A	3:31:53 (3,969)	
Rotbart, Robert A	4:08:31 (10,877)	
Roth, Carel	4:47:10 (20,328)	
Roth, Georg	4:25:47 (15,015)	
Roth, Markus	4:18:05 (13,091)	
Rotherham, Matthew	4:52:46 (21,685)	
Rothery, Brendan	3:06:40 (1,285)	
Rothery, Ian M	4:26:46 (15,255)	
Rothman, Mark D	4:29:42 (16,062)	
Rothwell, Alan	5:09:09 (25,304)	
Rothwell, Colin	3:06:19 (1,252)	
Rotondo, Cosimo	4:40:05 (18,552)	
Rotondo, Luigi	4:10:00 (11,166)	
Rought, Craig	4:28:26 (15,709)	
Roulson, Nathan J	3:39:13 (5,048)	
Roulstone, Colin J	4:00:50 (9,384)	
Round, Derrick J	4:38:35 (18,170)	
Round, Philip H	6:37:11 (34,586)	
Rounthwaite, George E	3:54:21 (7,877)	
Rourke, Martin A	3:41:41 (5,466)	
Rourke, Simon M	3:36:17 (4,585)	
Rous, Simon	4:14:32 (12,211)	
Rouse, Adam J	3:01:33 (985)	
Rouse, Anthony L	4:35:37 (17,434)	
Rouse, Christopher	5:13:35 (26,135)	
Rouse, Michael J	5:02:07 (23,954)	
Rouse, Richard	5:14:27 (26,321)	
Rouse, Stephen	3:15:00 (1,995)	
Rousell, Lee T	5:32:25 (29,511)	
Rousseau, Benjamin	4:00:51 (9,386)	
Rousseau, Frederic	4:41:09 (18,828)	
Rousseau, Jean-Pierre	4:32:51 (16,755)	
Rousseau, Nicolas	4:20:42 (13,775)	
Rousseau, Stanislas	3:13:07 (1,828)	
Roussel, Alain	4:31:29 (16,460)	
Routledge, George	5:37:24 (30,229)	
Routledge, Ian	4:57:05 (22,792)	
Routledge, Oliver	4:08:04 (10,782)	
Routledge, Richard J	4:20:04 (13,618)	
Routledge, Sam J	3:53:55 (7,769)	
Roux, Michel A	3:31:39 (3,935)	
Roux, Philippe	3:29:36 (3,660)	
Rowan, Paul J	6:03:49 (32,875)	
Rowden, Jon	4:27:28 (15,464)	
Rowe, Alan P	5:30:31 (29,224)	
Rowe, Alex R	2:43:56 (212)	
Rowe, David Q	4:18:57 (13,319)	
Rowe, David W	2:56:43 (651)	
Rowe, Davied L	6:03:35 (32,860)	
Rowe, Ian W	5:42:57 (30,928)	
Rowe, Kim	3:58:16 (8,783)	
Rowe, Simon J	3:21:11 (2,622)	
Rowell, Ben	4:34:20 (17,101)	
Rowland, Andrew J	2:50:33 (394)	
Rowland, Brice M	4:41:42 (18,966)	
Rowland, Colin M	5:33:00 (29,605)	
Rowland, Colin P	5:49:14 (31,605)	
Rowland, Ian	2:59:38 (874)	
Rowland, Ian C	4:24:23 (14,675)	
Rowland, Lawrence G	3:42:51 (5,657)	
Rowland, Matt F	5:26:06 (28,474)	
Rowland, Michael J	5:51:37 (31,839)	
Rowland, Robert A	2:57:31 (711)	
Rowland, Stewart	4:54:26 (22,132)	
Rowland, Stuart J	5:39:27 (30,518)	
Rowlands, Clive P	4:35:22 (17,375)	
Rowlands, David	3:56:32 (8,369)	
Rowlands, Marc N	4:04:50 (10,120)	
Rowles, Christopher I	4:18:39 (13,252)	
Rowles, Guy F	4:13:30 (11,963)	
Rowley, Benjamin P	4:09:30 (11,072)	
Rowley, Chris R	4:22:14 (14,137)	
Rowley, Liam J	4:02:13 (9,652)	
Rowley, Michael D	4:34:08 (17,060)	
Rowley, Simon P	4:34:09 (17,062)	
Rowling, Matthew J	4:46:15 (20,115)	
Rowlinson, Paul	6:04:58 (32,960)	
Rowlinson, Paul D	4:46:30 (20,178)	
Rowney, Stuart J	4:13:04 (11,850)	
Rowse, Andrew	4:43:48 (19,478)	
Rowswell, Huw R	4:11:26 (11,486)	
Roxburgh, Alexis	3:49:50 (6,904)	
Roy, Partha	5:03:33 (24,246)	
Roy, Philippe G	4:03:26 (9,856)	
Roy, Shaibal S	6:46:11 (34,835)	
Roy, Steev M	5:17:27 (26,948)	
Royle, Anthony D	4:43:14 (19,349)	
Royston, Christopher S	4:10:39 (11,300)	
Royston, Josh	3:18:02 (2,284)	
Rozalen Martinez, José M	4:07:34 (10,672)	
Rozemeijer, Steven	4:29:13 (15,915)	
Ruales, Jorge A	3:38:10 (4,865)	
Rubenstein, Brian	4:42:37 (19,211)	
Rubly, Bradley N	5:06:51 (24,854)	
Rubner, Matthias	3:09:10 (1,483)	
Ruby, Mark	5:50:20 (31,709)	
Rucklidge, Paul	5:08:41 (25,220)	
Rudall, David C	3:33:53 (4,250)	
Rudd, Andrew N	3:43:42 (5,811)	
Rudd, Darran C	3:09:27 (1,512)	
Rudd, David M	4:28:31 (15,730)	
Rudd, Ian N	4:22:40 (14,248)	
Rudd, Martin R	4:24:20 (14,660)	
Rudder, Simon L	4:19:13 (13,379)	
Ruddock, Jonathan P	4:51:43 (21,424)	
Ruddock, Norman E	4:46:32 (20,187)	
Rudge, David P	4:50:19 (21,070)	
Rudge, Stephen P	6:03:50 (32,876)	
Rudkin, Tony P	4:53:59 (22,016)	

Rudland, Lee	3:33:36 (4,213)
Rudling, Robert J	5:36:53 (30,161)
Rudnick, Errol	3:57:57 (8,708)
Rudolph, Guy R	4:16:33 (12,704)
Ruebner, Frank	4:15:00 (12,325)
Ruff, Elliot M	4:13:56 (12,079)
Ruff, Juergen	5:08:14 (25,147)
Ruffell, Andrew	3:20:54 (2,597)
Ruffell, Richard H	3:21:06 (2,615)
Ruffle, Steve	4:24:28 (14,698)
Ruffo, Giorgio	5:14:01 (26,231)
Rugg, Vincent C	4:43:19 (19,383)
Ruhen, Peter M	4:32:39 (16,706)
Rui, Alberto	6:14:51 (33,604)
Ruia, Alok	4:20:23 (13,704)
Ruia, Sunil	6:13:13 (33,505)
Ruiz, Antonio	5:20:54 (27,587)
Ruiz, César	4:03:19 (9,835)
Ruiz, Ernesto	4:13:38 (12,004)
Ruiz, Francisco	3:26:16 (3,169)
Ruiz Anitua, Javier A	4:55:31 (22,395)
Rule, Ally D	4:06:52 (10,544)
Rule, Brian R	4:18:42 (13,264)
Rule, Chris M	4:08:44 (10,914)
Rule, David	4:55:04 (22,282)
Rule, Graham P	6:13:38 (33,531)
Rumbelow, Nick A	3:08:34 (1,435)
Rumble, Ryan M	5:50:55 (31,765)
Rumbles, Allan C	3:55:41 (8,161)
Rumney, Darren M	3:17:27 (2,226)
Rumsey, Stephen	4:46:06 (20,082)
Runciman, Lee R	3:54:53 (7,982)
Rundle, Michael	4:27:35 (15,488)
Rundle, Simon D	4:39:49 (18,490)
Runyard, Steven	4:13:11 (11,874)
Rupert, Max	3:52:31 (7,470)
Rusby, Timothy N	4:42:34 (19,195)
Rush, Jason P	4:32:47 (16,735)
Rush, Michael F	5:15:22 (26,535)
Rushbrooke, James W	4:28:20 (15,680)
Rushby, Dean	4:11:59 (11,608)
Rushby, Ian J	4:49:30 (20,889)
Rushden, Max P	5:25:26 (28,351)
Rushton, Paul	4:16:17 (12,644)
Rushton, Robert J	5:28:22 (28,882)
Russ, Graham M	2:46:38 (276)
Russell, Alex	4:13:23 (11,933)
Russell, Andrew W	4:04:24 (10,038)
Russell, Andy	5:29:37 (29,090)
Russell, Brian	4:32:44 (16,724)
Russell, Christopher J	5:04:28 (24,417)
Russell, Colin D	5:04:16 (24,370)
Russell, Craig R	5:11:52 (25,827)
Russell, David C	5:19:42 (27,373)
Russell, George	3:20:09 (2,512)
Russell, Ian C	4:03:35 (9,883)
Russell, Ian D	3:25:53 (3,112)
Russell, James A	4:07:20 (10,623)
Russell, John A	4:31:27 (16,451)
Russell, John R	2:59:48 (886)
Russell, John R	3:43:29 (5,776)
Russell, Joseph G	4:55:06 (22,289)
Russell, Mark	4:20:58 (13,845)
Russell, Mark	4:34:47 (17,218)
Russell, Mark	5:27:51 (28,771)
Russell, Mike	4:51:52 (21,459)
Russell, Nigel D	3:10:04 (1,564)
Russell, Nigel P	6:00:34 (32,629)
Russell, Oliver M	5:20:10 (27,449)
Russell, Paul D	4:54:42 (22,198)
Russell, Peter J	2:50:21 (381)
Russell, Phillip	3:15:41 (2,046)
Russell, Richard J	3:55:53 (8,204)
Russell, Shaune D	3:10:19 (1,588)
Russell, Simon M	4:34:27 (17,135)
Russell, Stephen C	4:01:38 (9,539)
Russell, Stephen F	3:20:43 (2,579)
Russell, Will	6:43:59 (34,771)
Russell, William E	3:57:16 (8,547)
Russon, Ben	4:12:40 (11,761)
Rust, Christopher W	4:48:10 (20,566)
Rutherford, Mark A	5:52:32 (31,921)
Rutherford, Paul A	3:41:33 (5,448)

Rutherford, Simon	2:48:37 (332)
Rutherford, Simon	4:02:13 (9,652)
Rutherford, Simon R	4:24:48 (14,777)
Rutherford, Stephen	6:28:21 (34,258)
Rutherford, Tim J	4:45:16 (19,896)
Rutland, Matthew J	5:19:08 (27,276)
Rutt, Tom F	3:44:39 (5,967)
Rutter, Paul	3:26:42 (3,223)
Rutter, Peter L	3:53:06 (7,591)
Rutter, Phil	4:03:59 (9,963)
Rutterford, Darren P	3:57:09 (8,511)
Ryall, Ben	2:53:24 (489)
Ryalls, Terry J	3:40:19 (5,236)
Ryan, Aiden F	4:41:52 (19,013)
Ryan, Chris	3:51:45 (7,305)
Ryan, Clifford J	5:14:36 (26,362)
Ryan, Duncan C	3:51:25 (7,231)
Ryan, John M	5:28:53 (28,963)
Ryan, Jon	5:24:06 (28,122)
Ryan, Liam P	3:58:01 (8,728)
Ryan, Matthew T	4:51:37 (21,402)
Ryan, Noel P	4:55:20 (22,346)
Ryan, Paul B	5:25:19 (28,323)
Ryan, Paul J	3:51:43 (7,297)
Ryan, Peter J	3:56:07 (8,254)
Ryan, Richard V	5:49:33 (31,633)
Ryan, Robert G	3:41:09 (5,389)
Ryan, Sean L	3:49:10 (6,761)
Ryan, Will	5:23:41 (28,048)
Rybak, Martin P	4:59:42 (23,433)
Rycroft, Matthew P	5:19:50 (27,399)
Ryder, Darren L	4:34:10 (17,069)
Ryder, Mark J	3:58:09 (8,749)
Rye, Joseph M	2:40:30 (148)
Ryffel, Markus	3:07:10 (1,323)
Ryles, David J	5:14:49 (26,410)
Ryles, Nicholas D	3:28:30 (3,485)
Ryman, Paul	6:28:40 (34,272)
Rymer, Timothy S	3:58:15 (8,780)
Ryznar, Matthew K	5:52:47 (31,947)
Sacande, Moctar	4:37:41 (17,933)
Sadler, Alan	5:28:18 (28,865)
Sadler, Dan	4:21:04 (13,864)
Sadler, Dominic P	7:31:15 (35,504)
Sadr, Amir	5:27:23 (28,691)
Saffer, Daniel	4:27:17 (15,416)
Sagaseta, Pedro	3:38:25 (4,904)
Sage, David J	4:50:41 (21,164)
Saggers, Adam B	5:51:29 (31,829)
Saggers, Martin S	4:13:22 (11,926)
Saggs, Mark	5:02:59 (24,119)
Saha, Saku N	6:00:51 (32,650)
Sahar, Alon	4:09:17 (11,024)
Sahman, Dave	5:00:26 (23,603)
Sahodree, Mike	5:22:01 (27,784)
Sahota, Gurmit	4:48:51 (20,732)
Said, Peter	5:08:13 (25,144)
Said, Said A	4:20:24 (13,707)
Sainio, Harry O	3:27:43 (3,375)
Sainsbury, Donald A	7:29:26 (35,485)
Sainty, Christopher J	4:06:41 (10,497)
Sakhrani, Benedict	3:40:11 (5,213)
Sakpoba, Alex	5:40:58 (30,702)
Salazar, Joseph H	4:32:12 (16,609)
Salde, Edward P	4:42:23 (19,146)
Sale, Nick J	3:10:09 (1,577)
Saleem, Adam	4:50:53 (21,213)
Salem, Jonathan M	4:45:48 (20,007)
Salem, Murtaza K	4:10:52 (11,341)
Sales, Alexander D	3:50:24 (7,020)
Sales, Roberto	3:12:27 (1,774)
Sales, Roger J	4:28:09 (15,635)
Saliba, Fouad H	4:28:55 (15,838)
Salih, Mustafa	3:15:26 (2,026)
Salisbury, Christian R	5:26:13 (28,495)
Salisbury, David B	3:53:40 (7,721)
Salisbury, David J	5:05:16 (24,552)
Salisbury, Jon R	4:19:54 (13,574)
Salisbury, Thomas	5:23:51 (28,085)
Sallows, Alan N	3:41:59 (5,518)
Salmon, Daniel J	3:48:23 (6,587)
Salmon, Jon	3:53:57 (7,779)
Salmon, Michael J	3:36:27 (4,605)

Salmons, Jonathan M	4:14:01 (12,101)
Salmons, Malcolm D	5:06:56 (24,865)
Salomone, Samuel D	3:57:17 (8,549)
Salt, Colin	5:09:39 (25,404)
Salt, Jeff B	4:35:53 (17,508)
Salt, Jonathan R	5:17:14 (26,904)
Salt, Martin	4:50:38 (21,155)
Salt, Neil B	5:17:14 (26,904)
Salt, Stephen A	4:38:17 (18,084)
Salter, Chris J	3:40:35 (5,284)
Salter, Dan P	2:56:54 (666)
Salter, Ian G	3:48:44 (6,674)
Salter, Michael P	3:23:07 (2,812)
Salter, Robert S	3:22:17 (2,725)
Saltmarsh, Geoffrey W	6:36:03 (34,537)
Saltrick, Chris	4:31:47 (16,522)
Salva, Daniel	4:34:18 (17,094)
Salvador, Bruno C	3:08:00 (1,389)
Salvatore, John D	4:15:16 (12,383)
Salzburg, Karsetn	4:03:55 (9,950)
Sam, Nemonique	4:30:11 (16,192)
Samarasinghe, Roshan S	5:23:06 (27,948)
Sambridge, John	3:06:20 (1,255)
Sambrook, Gregory	4:39:06 (18,306)
Sami, Noureddine	3:19:19 (2,422)
Samkin, James P	5:03:17 (24,189)
Sampey, Philip C	5:33:52 (29,739)
Sample, Timothy M	4:48:32 (20,656)
Sampson, Mark R	5:41:38 (30,784)
Sampson, Nicholas P	5:11:55 (25,838)
Sampson, Stuart	4:46:41 (20,212)
Samra, Harjap S	3:45:36 (6,113)
Sams, Ron A	5:39:34 (30,541)
Samson, Douglas W	4:10:50 (11,335)
Samson, Thomas J	5:40:43 (30,673)
Samubcini, Mario	3:42:13 (5,558)
Samuel, Joshua W	4:39:22 (18,385)
Samuel, Nicolas	3:45:32 (6,097)
Samuels, Paul S	5:46:49 (31,337)
Samuels, Stephen	4:32:00 (16,560)
Samuels, Steve	3:46:33 (6,257)
San Martin, Bartolome	3:26:17 (3,172)
Sananes, Isaac M	6:04:59 (32,961)
Sanchez, Ramon	4:16:38 (12,723)
Sancroft-Baker, Robert	4:24:48 (14,777)
Sanctuary, Nigel L	5:23:37 (28,033)
Sandall, Michael J	5:21:47 (27,751)
Sandalls, Steve	3:41:27 (5,440)
Sandeman, Donald	3:22:21 (2,732)
Sander, Mark A	3:29:19 (3,620)
Sander, Peter	5:03:33 (24,246)
Sanders, Clive	5:25:26 (28,351)
Sanders, Daniel R	3:58:39 (8,871)
Sanders, Gerald K	4:11:50 (11,578)
Sanders, Graham	4:46:05 (20,073)
Sanders, Keith M	4:18:17 (13,142)
Sanders, Kim	4:59:55 (23,479)
Sanders, Mark D	6:15:21 (33,637)
Sanders, Martin	2:42:31 (189)
Sanders, Matthew I	5:25:45 (28,417)
Sanders, Paul C	4:41:36 (18,948)
Sanders, Philip M	3:04:56 (1,156)
Sanders, Richard	5:17:53 (27,025)
Sanders, Richard I	6:15:46 (33,669)
Sanderson, Andrew C	5:38:09 (30,325)
Sanderson, Andrew J	5:21:33 (27,701)
Sanderson, Brett M	6:24:27 (34,097)
Sanderson, David S	3:19:33 (2,439)
Sanderson, Ian	3:47:56 (6,516)
Sanderson, Michael	3:47:43 (6,482)
Sanderson, Nicholas J	4:40:49 (18,737)
Sanderson, Nicholas M	3:39:51 (5,167)
Sanderson, Paul A	5:00:16 (23,568)
Sanderson, Paul J	2:57:39 (718)
Sanderson, Richard G	4:28:09 (15,635)
Sanderson, Richard G	5:37:14 (30,203)
Sanderson, Terence	4:45:02 (19,848)
Sanderson, Terry M	4:29:41 (16,060)
Sandford, Ashley J	6:00:30 (32,622)
Sandham, John M	5:17:56 (27,037)
Sandham, Nicholas P	6:13:34 (33,527)
Sandhu, Amanjeet	5:14:26 (26,318)
Sandhu, Dilbag Singh	5:50:12 (31,693)

Sandhu, Ranjeet S....4:43:04 (19,310)
Sandom, Geoff C....6:50:55 (34,954)
Sandoval, Luis J....3:58:24 (8,809)
Sandry, Paul J....4:27:24 (15,448)
Sands, Andrew....6:15:20 (33,636)
Sandy, Ben N....4:33:18 (16,867)
Sanford, Andrew G....4:30:08 (16,182)
Sanford, Gary M....5:24:07 (28,126)
Sanford, Roger....6:10:18 (33,327)
Sanger, Glenn D....4:46:20 (20,135)
Sanger, Martin W....6:01:04 (32,682)
Sanger, Philip B....2:39:24 (134)
Sanger, Stuart J....6:08:33 (33,209)
Sangera, Mo....4:03:29 (9,866)
Sangha, Amo....3:53:58 (7,785)
Sangha, Jagtar....4:54:48 (22,227)
Sanghera, Jas....3:39:31 (5,109)
Sanghera, Kirn K....5:07:30 (24,999)
Sanghera, Lember S....6:37:48 (34,598)
Sangiorgi, Gustavo....3:36:44 (4,651)
Sankey, Mark H....3:12:26 (1,771)
Sansom, Chris J....4:01:10 (9,456)
Sansom, Trevor M....4:30:32 (16,261)
Sansome, Paul E....4:47:33 (20,422)
Sansone, Ugo....3:40:15 (5,225)
Santais, Christophe....4:29:57 (16,134)
Santais, Frederic....4:08:40 (10,905)
Santamaria, Paul....4:35:27 (17,389)
Santos, Sergio F....2:45:39 (255)
Santos, Waldir....3:51:23 (7,221)
Saouli, Mood....5:43:21 (30,981)
Saounatsos, Emmanuel....5:28:19 (28,871)
Sapey, Andrew T....5:10:09 (25,517)
Saraiva, Artur S....4:25:46 (15,009)
Sarapionov, Volodymyr....4:17:38 (12,982)
Sarcevic, Milan....5:21:23 (27,673)
Sardina, Franck....3:32:59 (4,136)
Sargeant, Ben....4:55:46 (22,450)
Sargeant, Malcolm C....4:56:40 (22,686)
Sargent, David G....3:05:11 (1,173)
Sargent, Keith B....5:03:56 (24,314)
Sargent, Richard....4:57:33 (22,914)
Sargent, Rob....3:39:20 (5,071)
Sarnari, Federico....4:05:40 (10,280)
Sarson, Peter....2:59:15 (844)
Sarti, Matthew....4:40:09 (18,566)
Sassone, Joseph S....4:12:46 (11,780)
Saterlay, Andrew J....5:11:17 (25,714)
Satireyo, Luigi....3:25:01 (3,022)
Sattler, Wolfgang....4:41:29 (18,915)
Sauer, Ulrich....4:04:00 (9,967)
Sault, Carl S....4:27:09 (15,366)
Saunders, Andrew....5:18:47 (27,212)
Saunders, Andrew T....4:01:35 (9,533)
Saunders, Bernard A....6:24:15 (34,090)
Saunders, David P....4:35:43 (17,463)
Saunders, Garry....3:43:52 (5,838)
Saunders, Jamie E....5:00:51 (23,696)
Saunders, Jason W....4:50:22 (21,087)
Saunders, John....3:53:04 (7,582)
Saunders, Julian A....4:43:18 (19,372)
Saunders, Justin....5:12:01 (25,858)
Saunders, Malcolm J....4:15:37 (12,468)
Saunders, Mark....4:19:49 (13,544)
Saunders, Mark A....4:34:48 (17,223)
Saunders, Mark P....5:34:54 (29,903)
Saunders, Matthew....7:45:58 (35,603)
Saunders, Nick B....3:52:54 (7,544)
Saunders, Roger W....3:42:28 (5,593)
Saunders, Rowan G....3:20:16 (2,527)
Saunders, Ryan L....4:37:02 (17,795)
Saunders, Stephen....4:10:52 (11,341)
Saunderson, Eric M....5:01:24 (23,814)
Saunderson, Paul R....4:43:28 (19,409)
Sauvageot, Lauren....5:07:39 (25,027)
Sauve, Paul....4:27:57 (15,571)
Savage, Anthony M....3:49:30 (6,832)
Savage, Bryn....4:36:53 (17,763)
Savage, Damien K....4:01:33 (9,521)
Savage, Jamie M....3:36:32 (4,617)
Savage, Mark A....4:17:30 (12,947)
Savage, Miles T....5:03:56 (24,314)
Savage, Paul....3:48:08 (6,550)
Savage, Regan N....3:24:56 (3,012)
Savery, Andrew J....2:37:57 (109)
Savery, Ernie J....5:26:02 (28,463)
Savill, Peter M....3:35:56 (4,540)
Saville, Dennis....4:42:36 (19,207)
Saville, Oliver J....3:42:11 (5,549)
Saville, Philip....3:28:28 (3,477)
Savin, James R....4:45:43 (19,993)
Savoy, Hubert M....4:28:39 (15,773)
Sawbridge, Mark T....4:53:27 (21,881)
Sawbridge, Thomas H....3:15:41 (2,046)
Sawell, Neil G....6:03:03 (32,822)
Sawford, Matthew A....4:34:35 (17,169)
Sawtell, Edward P....4:32:10 (16,599)
Sawyer, Craig G....6:09:28 (33,268)
Sawyer, Lee J....4:55:03 (22,274)
Sawyer, Paul D....4:55:03 (22,274)
Saxel, Mark R....5:13:37 (26,145)
Sayer, Darren R....6:08:56 (33,234)
Sayer, Richard....4:39:55 (18,514)
Sayer, Stuart J....4:11:02 (11,380)
Sayers, Julian A....4:47:57 (20,520)
Sayle, Roger B....3:41:59 (5,518)
Saywell, Stephen H....5:26:06 (28,474)
Sborgia, Franco....5:32:47 (29,574)
Scaife, Nick F....4:55:38 (22,415)
Scales, Mark R....5:19:53 (27,405)
Scanlan, Bernard A....4:45:19 (19,908)
Scanlan, Desmond H....4:04:42 (10,090)
Scanlan, Oliver....4:40:58 (18,777)
Scanlon, John....4:48:13 (20,582)
Scanlon, John P....3:58:55 (8,942)
Scanlon, Paul J....4:56:12 (22,564)
Scanlon, Peter J....4:26:05 (15,070)
Scanlon, Rodney S....4:15:27 (12,432)
Scanlon, Sean T....5:21:04 (27,614)
Scantlin, Matt J....5:48:14 (31,494)
Scarborough, John....5:23:18 (27,976)
Scarborough, Linton J....3:16:03 (2,085)
Scarcia, Gianluca....2:46:56 (282)
Scarff, Richard J....5:14:13 (26,270)
Scarrott, Lea P....4:39:42 (18,465)
Scarrow, Dan H....3:31:05 (3,846)
Scarrow, Richard....4:05:10 (10,179)
Schaefer, Karl J....4:01:44 (9,555)
Schaefer, Lothar....4:32:34 (16,681)
Schaer, Heinz....5:07:05 (24,905)
Schaerer, Juerg....5:23:53 (28,090)
Schaetti, Alfred....4:16:19 (12,653)
Schafer, Wolfgang....3:51:45 (7,305)
Schapira, Paul S....4:29:25 (15,980)
Schappelle, James....3:46:42 (6,283)
Schechter, Alexander....4:42:43 (19,233)
Scheer, Andrew D....3:55:51 (8,195)
Scheibe, Frank....4:38:08 (18,047)
Schenk, Kurt S....4:58:25 (23,136)
Schiffer-Harte, Benjamin G....4:21:05 (13,868)
Schindewolf, Stephan....4:28:34 (15,753)
Schippel, John E....6:29:03 (34,286)
Schirato, Sergio R....4:08:09 (10,796)
Schleip, Nicolai J....4:25:19 (14,898)
Schmid, Carl....4:43:39 (19,452)
Schmitz, Michael....6:28:50 (34,277)
Schneider, Michael F....4:22:25 (14,179)
Schneider, Nick....6:58:44 (35,104)
Schneiter, Jean-Marc....4:18:06 (13,094)
Schoenbach, Roland....2:55:06 (581)
Schoenberg, Timm....4:17:57 (13,058)
Schofield, Alan....4:09:08 (10,986)
Schofield, Craig....4:53:57 (22,006)
Schofield, Darren M....5:07:25 (24,980)
Schofield, Dominic....6:18:24 (33,797)
Schofield, Graham....3:53:01 (7,573)
Schofield, Ian A....4:25:21 (14,907)
Schofield, Nigel A....4:24:01 (14,576)
Schofield, Peter N....4:16:10 (12,612)
Schofield, William R....5:22:18 (27,820)
Schokman, Tony J....5:36:43 (30,135)
Scholefield, Robert D....5:04:07 (24,347)
Scholfield, Michael....4:36:58 (17,779)
Scholte, Paul....2:58:35 (794)
Schonhofer, Hartmut....3:51:40 (7,288)
Schooling, Robert J....3:39:32 (5,113)
Schott, Ralf....4:17:05 (12,828)
Schreder, Emmanuel....4:19:24 (13,431)
Schreder, Hughes....3:00:19 (918)
Schreefel, Henry D....4:56:14 (22,575)
Schroeder, Martin....4:19:12 (13,375)
Schubert, Dave J....3:03:16 (1,064)
Schubnel, Pascal....3:20:54 (2,597)
Schulte, Lutz....4:10:29 (11,261)
Schulz, Hans-Detlev....4:51:33 (21,383)
Schumacher, Stefan....3:34:01 (4,270)
Schumm, Gerhard....4:03:58 (9,960)
Schuster, Juergen....4:27:55 (15,563)
Schuy, Tim O....4:16:54 (12,785)
Schwanengel, Wito....5:46:48 (31,334)
Schwarte, Jorg....5:13:11 (26,077)
Schwarte, Wolfgang H....5:13:12 (26,080)
Schwartz, Jeremy S....4:04:32 (10,062)
Schwartz, John N....4:14:04 (12,118)
Schwartz, Steven J....3:21:24 (2,639)
Schwarz, Daniel M....3:28:58 (3,569)
Schweinberger, Bernhard....5:06:58 (24,873)
Schwendl, Herbert....3:49:33 (6,842)
Schwer, Billy....4:56:28 (22,628)
Schwiebert, Klaus....5:38:41 (30,412)
Schwindack, Martin....3:33:28 (4,201)
Schwoerke, Michael....5:26:14 (28,500)
Schwyter, Philippe....3:26:14 (3,163)
Scibor-Kaminski, Jan....4:09:06 (10,973)
Sciscione, Giuseppe....3:29:06 (3,591)
Sciver, Richard J....3:51:27 (7,243)
Scobie, Duncan H....2:56:31 (635)
Scoffin, Robert F....6:12:35 (33,463)
Scopes, Ian P....4:29:19 (15,943)
Scorey, Christopher K....5:57:42 (32,384)
Scorey, James R....5:27:33 (28,719)
Scorthorne, Richard J....5:27:26 (28,702)
Scotford, James R....3:20:31 (2,558)
Scott, Alan M....6:05:21 (32,987)
Scott, Alister....3:59:14 (9,021)
Scott, Andrew J....4:51:19 (21,321)
Scott, Angus....4:44:52 (19,797)
Scott, Antony W....4:45:28 (19,938)
Scott, Christopher A....4:56:17 (22,582)
Scott, Clive R....4:23:18 (14,399)
Scott, Crispin R....3:51:39 (7,285)
Scott, Daniel J....4:58:37 (23,171)
Scott, David C....4:57:15 (22,834)
Scott, Dean K....6:17:34 (33,757)
Scott, Dominic L....4:02:05 (9,617)
Scott, Douglas F....3:52:29 (7,464)
Scott, Eoin....4:16:41 (12,733)
Scott, Fraser W....4:41:51 (19,010)
Scott, Gareth....4:25:04 (14,837)
Scott, Geoffrey W....3:14:14 (1,918)
Scott, George....5:06:25 (24,772)
Scott, Gregory J....4:56:49 (22,719)
Scott, Ian....3:13:55 (1,894)
Scott, Ian A....5:38:08 (30,322)
Scott, Ian T....4:15:07 (12,345)
Scott, James A....2:57:59 (744)
Scott, James C....4:26:11 (15,091)
Scott, Jim A....3:39:17 (5,061)
Scott, John R....4:17:16 (12,866)
Scott, Kenneth D....4:56:06 (22,535)
Scott, Kevin....4:09:06 (10,973)
Scott, Kieran A....4:34:35 (17,169)
Scott, Lee John....5:50:20 (31,709)
Scott, Mark A....5:50:09 (31,685)
Scott, Mark T....5:48:36 (31,533)
Scott, Martin....5:26:31 (28,545)
Scott, Michael A....3:49:59 (6,934)
Scott, Michael K....4:56:42 (22,696)
Scott, Michael R....5:59:02 (32,509)
Scott, Nicholas G....3:08:14 (1,410)
Scott, Oliver....4:05:16 (10,197)
Scott, Oliver J....4:41:50 (19,005)
Scott, Philip I....4:52:18 (21,568)
Scott, Richard....4:37:03 (17,796)
Scott, Richard J....6:21:44 (33,986)
Scott, Robert D....4:26:40 (15,231)
Scott, Robin G....5:10:33 (25,586)
Scott, Robin H....3:13:02 (1,821)
Scott, Rod....4:00:40 (9,349)

Scott, Stephen J....4:42:13 (19,101)
Scott, Steven A....4:25:39 (14,985)
Scott, Stewart A....4:19:22 (13,424)
Scott, Stuart J....3:23:50 (2,882)
Scott, Timothy J....5:12:07 (25,874)
Scott, Tom....3:44:19 (5,908)
Scott-Priestley, Simon C....4:28:46 (15,807)
Scotts, Roger G....5:20:31 (27,522)
Scourfield, Adam J....4:13:15 (11,896)
Scrase, Paul M....4:46:58 (20,269)
Scrimgeour, Owen J....4:03:45 (9,916)
Scriven, Andrew J....7:21:10 (35,398)
Scriven, Harvey W....3:19:32 (2,437)
Scrivener, Aaron....5:27:27 (28,704)
Scrivener, Chris....2:58:04 (753)
Scrivener, Keith A....4:52:30 (21,612)
Scrivener, Russell J....5:06:35 (24,795)
Scrivens, Justin....4:46:41 (20,212)
Scroggie, John R....4:05:27 (10,232)
Scroggins, Jeremy J....3:41:55 (5,504)
Scroop, Richard....3:37:56 (4,814)
Scrowston, Michael G....3:31:24 (3,890)
Scrutoon, Neil....3:01:31 (984)
Scudder, David M....5:16:06 (26,683)
Sculland, Jonathan P....3:46:24 (6,237)
Scully, Alban F....3:27:29 (3,353)
Scutt, Oliver....4:48:40 (20,682)
Scyner, Mark A....4:20:27 (13,719)
Seaborn, Gary....4:16:50 (12,770)
Seabourne, Ben....4:55:54 (22,487)
Seago, Mark D....4:55:27 (22,377)
Sealey, George....6:28:23 (34,262)
Sealey, Joe H....6:28:22 (34,260)
Sealey, Robert J....5:58:42 (32,484)
Sealy, David G....4:16:56 (12,798)
Seaman, Carl....5:01:19 (23,798)
Seaman, Oliver R....4:57:34 (22,919)
Seaman, Thomas P....5:47:17 (31,381)
Sear, Stephen A....3:42:42 (5,627)
Searl, Nicholas P....3:35:26 (4,474)
Searle, Alex B....5:03:06 (24,146)
Searle, Michael A....4:22:36 (14,230)
Searle, Paul....4:01:40 (9,545)
Searle, Stephen G....4:52:36 (21,642)
Sears, André J....5:12:11 (25,895)
Sears, Derek J....4:11:35 (11,518)
Seaton, Adam....5:39:07 (30,469)
Seaton, Gary D....4:48:54 (20,745)
Seaton, Joseph E....4:10:30 (11,268)
Seaton, Kieran B....4:13:31 (11,969)
Seaton, Simon D....2:48:32 (330)
Seaton, Steven A....4:30:21 (16,227)
Seddon, Andrew....5:25:47 (28,421)
Seddon, Jeff....3:07:47 (1,369)
Seddon, Patrick....3:56:21 (8,319)
Seddon, Paul....3:43:52 (5,838)
Seddon-Brown, Les W....4:30:52 (16,332)
Sedge, Martyn J....2:58:35 (794)
Sedgemore, Edward H....4:46:17 (20,120)
Sedgwick, Glenn C....4:46:26 (20,164)
Sedgwick, John....4:34:33 (17,159)
Sedgwick, Robert....5:12:59 (26,046)
Sedlmeier, Gregor N....2:50:00 (377)
Sedman, Lloyd V....3:24:32 (2,958)
Sedman, Nigel H....3:26:53 (3,254)
Seed, James....4:29:56 (16,128)
Seeger, Frank....3:42:00 (5,522)
Seelandt, Frank....3:43:52 (5,838)
Seelochan, David S....3:52:49 (7,531)
Seely, Robert W....6:22:37 (34,028)
Seffens, Andrew V....3:58:21 (8,796)
Segall, Alan M....4:33:04 (16,803)
Seguret, Benoit....3:55:48 (8,185)
Sehdev, Om Parkash....4:58:25 (23,136)
Seiger, Darin G....4:24:18 (14,654)
Seiler, Norbert....5:13:36 (26,141)
Selby, Ben P....4:21:48 (14,033)
Selby, Ian S....5:16:42 (26,789)
Selby, Mark....4:34:43 (17,206)
Selby, Mark J....5:08:44 (25,232)
Selby, Paul....4:19:35 (13,479)
Self, Simon J....5:00:29 (23,610)
Selfe, Christopher P....4:13:42 (12,018)
Sell, James W....4:05:17 (10,202)
Sellers, Martin D....5:34:01 (29,764)
Sellers, Patrick E....4:24:21 (14,665)
Sellers, Scott....4:22:28 (14,190)
Sellick, Phil....4:33:12 (16,846)
Selsby, Paul....5:26:16 (28,503)
Selves, Stephen J....4:45:56 (20,042)
Selway, Matthew R....4:13:52 (12,056)
Semmence, Philip J....3:45:16 (6,062)
Semple, John....4:41:31 (18,927)
Semple, Paul S....5:31:58 (29,444)
Senaddou-Idrissi, Chakir....6:29:04 (34,287)
Sendall, Richard H....4:56:46 (22,708)
Sendon-Smith, Manuel A....6:18:27 (33,802)
Sendra, Laurent....2:56:45 (655)
Senior, Paul A....3:57:35 (8,619)
Senior, Timothy J....5:18:12 (27,103)
Senkiw, Walter....5:15:01 (26,456)
Senner, David H....6:27:14 (34,225)
Sequeira, Edgar....3:25:45 (3,096)
Sequeira, Ryan D....3:48:04 (6,535)
Serjeant, James....4:48:36 (20,669)
Serle, Adam G....4:52:08 (21,521)
Serle, Adrian M....5:22:07 (27,797)
Serna, Hugo....5:31:14 (29,339)
Serocold, Charles E....4:55:23 (22,361)
Serrano, Angel....3:50:04 (6,957)
Serroukh, Redouane....4:21:09 (13,889)
Servaes, Michael J....5:16:07 (26,687)
Seth, Grant S....4:34:51 (17,236)
Seth, Stephen J....4:01:08 (9,444)
Setters, Chris M....3:51:39 (7,285)
Settimi, Giovanni....4:04:13 (10,010)
Settle, Richard J....3:41:47 (5,482)
Severein, Pieter D....4:10:16 (11,222)
Severimo, Maurizio....4:45:21 (19,917)
Severs, Jonathan....4:55:29 (22,389)
Sevint, Philippe....3:59:32 (9,104)
Seward, Colin E....4:03:21 (9,840)
Seward, James A....4:33:39 (16,947)
Sewell, Andrew P....3:14:49 (1,971)
Sewell, Dan J....3:44:48 (5,994)
Sewter, Lance....4:31:47 (16,522)
Sexton, Christopher P....3:46:51 (6,311)
Sexton, Christopher P....6:35:08 (34,505)
Sexton, David H....3:07:42 (1,360)
Sexton, Philip....6:17:36 (33,758)
Seymour, David J....4:25:10 (14,862)
Seymour, Derek G....4:38:55 (18,258)
Seymour, Ian....5:11:04 (25,679)
Seymour, Kenny T....6:07:10 (33,116)
Seymour, Michael J....5:40:29 (30,650)
Seymour, Thomas W....4:02:36 (9,708)
Sfelagis, Andoni....5:07:11 (24,926)
Sgamma, Pasqualino....3:07:36 (1,353)
Shabbir, Adeef....6:29:20 (34,302)
Shackleton, Peter....5:16:35 (26,769)
Shadbolt, Glenn M....3:58:13 (8,769)
Shaddick, Ross E....3:00:57 (954)
Shafier, Lawrence E....3:39:24 (5,087)
Shafiq, Shehryar F....4:53:03 (21,762)
Shah, Akshay A....5:18:51 (27,221)
Shah, Anuj S....4:44:44 (19,753)
Shah, Dilan P....7:22:52 (35,414)
Shah, Jatin K....4:28:14 (15,653)
Shah, Jitendra N....3:49:57 (6,927)
Shah, Kavi....4:43:36 (19,440)
Shah, Mitul V....4:30:02 (16,155)
Shah, Neil N....6:11:14 (33,384)
Shah, Paras D....5:29:13 (29,027)
Shah, Priyesh S....4:51:38 (21,406)
Shah, Sanjeev....5:07:01 (24,887)
Shah, Vishal....5:15:06 (26,479)
Shaikh, Nadeem....3:16:19 (2,105)
Shakespeare, Gwidion T....4:13:14 (11,889)
Shakespeare, Simon J....3:28:26 (3,468)
Shalchi, Zaid....5:16:22 (26,730)
Shalders, Michael D....3:48:04 (6,535)
Shaler, Nigel....4:02:09 (9,630)
Shaller, Gary....5:11:18 (25,719)
Shanahan, Gregory K....4:46:01 (20,062)
Shanahan, Leon....7:00:42 (35,141)
Shand, Alan J....3:44:38 (5,964)
Shandley, Adrian P....4:08:47 (10,920)
Shane, David C....4:19:13 (13,379)
Shanks, Stephen M....2:50:46 (401)
Shanley, Alan R....3:14:15 (1,919)
Shannon, Daniel C....4:21:09 (13,889)
Shannon, David P....4:25:59 (15,054)
Shannon, Gary J....5:29:15 (29,034)
Shannon, Robert....4:25:00 (14,820)
Shannon, Ronald D....3:33:10 (4,165)
Shapcott, Michael....6:03:21 (32,841)
Shapland, Christopher L....3:57:40 (8,646)
Shardlow, Richard A....2:59:17 (846)
Share, Adrian W....4:22:38 (14,241)
Share, Richard P....3:30:54 (3,827)
Shariff, Faisal....5:37:31 (30,238)
Sharkett, Spencer....4:38:01 (18,015)
Sharkey, Thomas J....4:37:08 (17,813)
Sharma, Bhasker....4:47:56 (20,512)
Sharma, Munish M....6:12:52 (33,485)
Sharma, Nick....5:28:17 (28,858)
Sharma, Rajiv....5:53:47 (32,033)
Sharma, Sanjai....3:10:00 (1,559)
Sharma, Veeresh K....5:56:37 (32,300)
Sharman, Alan....4:03:44 (9,911)
Sharman, Ben T....3:46:06 (6,196)
Sharman, Ian M....2:57:44 (724)
Sharman, Kevin J....2:54:40 (557)
Sharp, Andrew C....4:43:52 (19,503)
Sharp, Andrew M....3:54:48 (7,962)
Sharp, Chris B....4:00:42 (9,358)
Sharp, Jeremy....3:21:58 (2,704)
Sharp, Marcus....3:33:58 (4,266)
Sharp, Mick....5:13:50 (26,197)
Sharp, Nick....6:47:57 (34,887)
Sharp, Nigel P....4:12:30 (11,721)
Sharp, Richard J....5:10:36 (25,594)
Sharp, Robin D....4:25:35 (14,963)
Sharp, Russell P....3:47:33 (6,436)
Sharp, Stephen C....4:50:54 (21,217)
Sharp, Trevor....4:09:26 (11,057)
Sharpe, Anthony C....4:27:31 (15,473)
Sharpe, Christopher A....4:16:43 (12,741)
Sharpe, Darren....2:57:01 (679)
Sharpe, David W....5:10:27 (25,566)
Sharpe, Michael A....4:27:07 (15,357)
Sharpe, Robert J....4:35:00 (17,270)
Sharples, Matthew....4:37:49 (17,960)
Sharples, Richard W....3:50:18 (6,998)
Sharrock, Kieran....4:18:10 (13,112)
Sharrod, Martin....5:52:25 (31,912)
Shaw, Adam J....4:52:12 (21,541)
Shaw, Andrew D....4:18:43 (13,269)
Shaw, Anthony T....4:09:12 (11,007)
Shaw, Colin E....4:31:23 (16,441)
Shaw, David....4:47:13 (20,337)
Shaw, David A....3:24:07 (2,922)
Shaw, Dean P....4:37:59 (18,003)
Shaw, Gary J....3:02:29 (1,026)
Shaw, Jonathan P....4:20:55 (13,833)
Shaw, Mark J....7:10:55 (35,288)
Shaw, Martyn P....3:45:07 (6,038)
Shaw, Neil....4:56:01 (22,519)
Shaw, Neil M....3:55:59 (8,221)
Shaw, Paul B....5:54:40 (32,116)
Shaw, Paul F....4:44:11 (19,594)
Shaw, Peter E....3:17:21 (2,211)
Shaw, Robert....3:52:48 (7,524)
Shaw, Robert....5:39:51 (30,575)
Shaw, Robert D....4:05:55 (10,332)
Shawcroft, Graham P....4:11:07 (11,401)
Shaylor, Neil....4:45:35 (19,962)
Shayshutt, Daniel....4:59:59 (23,501)
Sheard, Bryan A....4:14:50 (12,273)
Sheard, Colin....4:11:08 (11,407)
Sheard, Nicholas A....3:37:57 (4,819)
Shearer, Anthony I....4:06:24 (10,439)
Shearer, Ben....3:02:16 (1,015)
Shearer, Richard J....2:42:13 (183)
Shearer, Rob....3:43:28 (5,770)
Shearing, Philip R....6:01:01 (32,675)
Shearing, Stephen G....4:15:24 (12,418)
Shea-Simonds, Duncan R....2:56:25 (627)
Sheath, Adrian G....5:48:18 (31,505)

Shedden, Piers P 3:39:40 (5,138)
Sheehan, Andrew 4:52:56 (21,735)
Sheehan, Eamon J 4:51:54 (21,466)
Sheehan, Jody W 3:41:54 (5,498)
Sheehan, Michael D 4:11:29 (11,496)
Sheehan, Philip W 4:13:55 (12,073)
Sheehan, Timothy G 3:53:39 (7,717)
Sheelan, Liam A 4:49:47 (20,951)
Sheen, Graham 4:29:11 (15,906)
Sheen, Mark R 4:25:28 (14,940)
Sheeran, Benjamin J 5:20:45 (27,565)
Sheeran, Christopher M 5:41:23 (30,756)
Sheeran, Frank 5:20:28 (27,508)
Shegog, Andrew 3:35:33 (4,495)
Sheikh, Anwar 6:31:12 (34,370)
Sheil, John 4:30:47 (16,313)
Sheil, Peter M 5:28:51 (28,957)
Sheils, Liam A 3:18:54 (2,381)
Sheldon, Bryan 4:48:18 (20,605)
Sheldon, Chris J 5:31:00 (29,294)
Sheldon, Mark 4:36:05 (17,553)
Sheldon, Mike D 4:00:12 (9,250)
Sheldon, Paul E 4:43:09 (19,330)
Sheldon, Robert A 4:37:26 (17,874)
Sheldrake, Jonathan G 5:06:45 (24,831)
Shellard, Neil T 4:20:48 (13,799)
Shelly, Glenn 3:53:23 (7,660)
Shelton, Daniel M 4:55:27 (22,377)
Shelton, Edward F 3:51:35 (7,274)
Shelton, James T 5:04:39 (24,438)
Shenton, Simon 5:41:43 (30,798)
Shephard, Duncan P 6:48:42 (34,902)
Shepherd, Alex J 4:34:29 (17,143)
Shepherd, Ben 3:58:53 (8,938)
Shepherd, Chris R 4:08:37 (10,898)
Shepherd, Dave 5:22:05 (27,794)
Shepherd, David M 5:23:13 (27,961)
Shepherd, James A 5:34:48 (29,886)
Shepherd, Lee M 3:42:41 (5,625)
Shepherd, Mark A 4:20:54 (13,829)
Shepherd, Mark D 4:32:29 (16,657)
Shepherd, Matthew W 3:22:37 (2,757)
Shepherd, Steven 5:18:51 (27,221)
Shepherd, Stuart 4:22:35 (14,224)
Shepley, Chris A 4:46:10 (20,095)
Sheppard, Bill 4:15:46 (12,501)
Sheppard, Christopher R 5:40:03 (30,598)
Sheppard, David J 3:49:49 (6,899)
Sheppard, James M 4:16:42 (12,738)
Sheppard, Jay W 6:21:26 (33,978)
Sheppard, John A 5:09:22 (25,344)
Sheppard, Leon G 4:05:35 (10,262)
Sheppard, Richard P 4:34:13 (17,079)
Sheppard, Simon L 4:39:12 (18,335)
Sher, David S 4:41:45 (18,975)
Sherchan, Manoj 5:08:21 (25,162)
Shergil, Mandip 5:48:11 (31,486)
Shergold, Robert 5:17:21 (26,927)
Sheridan, Gavin 5:47:48 (31,438)
Sheridan, Mark C 6:14:58 (33,611)
Sheridan, Pat 3:39:28 (5,100)
Sheridan, Robert W 5:07:50 (25,066)
Sherley, Paul S 4:57:00 (22,772)
Sherlock, Joe 4:50:03 (21,007)
Sherman, Jason L 4:59:13 (23,314)
Sherman, Julian M 3:11:49 (1,705)
Shermer, Duncan J 3:41:44 (5,474)
Sherratt, Craig D 4:45:38 (19,977)
Sherratt, James 3:12:43 (1,799)
Sherriff, Mark D 2:56:55 (668)
Sherriff, Michael J 5:01:51 (23,902)
Sherrington, Peter E 4:58:00 (23,036)
Sherrington, Richard A 4:58:26 (23,143)
Sherrington, Simon M 5:11:39 (25,786)
Shervington, Michael W 6:01:06 (32,684)
Sherwin, Graham B 6:35:02 (34,500)
Sherwin, James C 4:37:29 (17,889)
Sherwin, James W 4:45:17 (19,900)
Sherwood, Edward J 3:16:47 (2,156)
Sherwood, Nicky N 5:35:13 (29,944)
Sherwood, Roland E 4:55:41 (22,423)
Sheshuryak, Sergey 3:59:16 (9,034)
Shevki, Ian J 5:32:57 (29,599)
Sheward, Neil 3:35:06 (4,420)
Sheyers, Johan E 3:43:18 (5,739)
Shiel, Peter 3:52:42 (7,503)
Shield, Jerry M 3:05:23 (1,191)
Shields, Alan C 4:52:42 (21,668)
Shields, Dominic J 3:46:21 (6,227)
Shields, Graeme D 3:49:40 (6,862)
Shields, Michael G 6:26:16 (34,187)
Shields, Paul A 5:04:50 (24,476)
Shiels, Robin E 4:02:39 (9,719)
Shimada, Shigeharu 3:33:45 (4,234)
Shimell, Matthew J 5:45:55 (31,246)
Shimizu, Yoichi 4:18:58 (13,323)
Shinn, Richard 4:22:15 (14,141)
Shinton, Ed 3:58:23 (8,805)
Shipley, Adrian J 4:19:43 (13,515)
Shipley, David H 5:33:39 (29,709)
Shipley, Gareth E 3:40:54 (5,347)
Shipton, Kevin R 4:58:55 (23,230)
Shipton, Neil R 5:07:31 (25,004)
Shipway, Richard M 2:57:46 (727)
Shirakawa, Masaki 5:37:20 (30,219)
Shiraki, Shinichiro 4:23:30 (14,444)
Shirley, Damian D 2:54:41 (558)
Shirley, Gerald L 4:58:24 (23,134)
Shirley, Stephen C 5:21:38 (27,717)
Shirreff, Simon 4:38:45 (18,212)
Shokunbi, Debo 3:47:05 (6,361)
Sholl, William H 4:30:44 (16,303)
Shore, Joe 3:57:44 (8,660)
Shore, Justin M 4:32:06 (16,581)
Shorley, Giles R 3:35:39 (4,505)
Shorrock, Adrian 3:05:28 (1,198)
Shorrock, Christopher 4:36:22 (17,629)
Short, Arthur V 4:29:21 (15,956)
Short, Kevin 3:27:04 (3,293)
Short, Martin 5:12:14 (25,904)
Short, Michael D 3:55:34 (8,131)
Short, Steven 4:55:16 (22,333)
Shorter, Benjamin J 4:59:32 (23,396)
Shorter, Christopher S 4:30:57 (16,344)
Shorter, Lee 6:04:55 (32,956)
Shortland, Tony 5:02:05 (23,947)
Shortley, Tom 5:03:23 (24,213)
Shotbolt, Adrian W 3:51:51 (7,327)
Shott, James M 4:45:10 (19,876)
Shoubridge, Paul M 4:55:48 (22,455)
Shoulders, Antony W 3:51:55 (7,342)
Shoults, Will C 4:07:43 (10,708)
Shraga, Nicholas 3:49:47 (6,894)
Shrager, Ed W 4:46:30 (20,178)
Shreeves, Benjamin 4:33:30 (16,911)
Shrimplin, Stephen J 4:09:19 (11,034)
Shrimpton, Benjamin J 3:23:02 (2,799)
Shropshire, Mark C 3:45:28 (6,092)
Shuck, Steve P 3:28:28 (3,477)
Shugart III, Thomas H 4:08:19 (10,835)
Shuker, Richard J 3:33:57 (4,264)
Shulver, Elliot 5:26:34 (28,552)
Shulver, Roderick L 5:49:33 (31,633)
Shurlock, Matthew P 3:32:51 (4,115)
Shury, Dean 3:49:11 (6,767)
Shutt, Alexander D 4:42:34 (19,195)
Shutt, Martin 5:15:49 (26,626)
Shuttle, Jamie R 4:11:30 (11,501)
Shuttleworth, Andrew 3:34:35 (4,352)
Shuttleworth, Greg 3:05:30 (1,201)
Shuttleworth, Nigel W 4:44:31 (19,692)
Shyjka, Michael G 4:23:44 (14,497)
Sibaev, Ruslan D 5:42:50 (30,919)
Sibellas, Patrick 3:39:17 (5,061)
Sibley, Trevor J 5:02:14 (23,974)
Sibun, Jonathan A 5:11:40 (25,788)
Sica, Ademir A 4:25:21 (14,907)
Sicard, Thierry 3:10:13 (1,580)
Siciliano, Oronzo 3:26:10 (3,153)
Sidders, Andrew J 4:38:50 (18,242)
Sidders, Stuart J 5:06:42 (24,817)
Siddiq, Sajid 5:29:31 (29,073)
Siddle, Paul A 3:01:09 (966)
Siddons, Barrie J 4:42:33 (19,190)
Sidebotham, John P 2:55:30 (592)
Sidher, Sunil D 4:12:50 (11,795)
Sidi-Moussa, Abdelkader K 3:30:07 (3,737)
Sidnick, Darren L 4:32:29 (16,657)
Sidwell, Gary M 6:11:46 (33,412)
Sidwell, Mark L 4:20:03 (13,611)
Sieberg, Christoph H 4:23:04 (14,348)
Siedel, Mirko 3:12:07 (1,742)
Sieff, Richard M 4:15:25 (12,421)
Siegerink, André 4:28:36 (15,761)
Sifield, Michael D 5:44:28 (31,087)
Signerin, François-Xavier 4:02:43 (9,733)
Signes, Yves 4:57:52 (23,002)
Sihdu, Simon 4:26:38 (15,218)
Sihdu, Solomon 3:51:04 (7,154)
Siklos, Jonathan A 3:37:08 (4,705)
Silberzahn, Tobias 3:53:12 (7,618)
Silcock, David 7:26:53 (35,446)
Silcock, Graham 4:53:26 (21,876)
Silcock, Peter D 3:45:43 (6,137)
Silk, James 3:31:41 (3,939)
Silk, Jonathan H 3:53:16 (7,634)
Silk, Michael P 4:09:46 (11,126)
Sille, Richard A 3:57:47 (8,671)
Sills, Ian E 2:56:31 (635)
Silva, Geraldino 3:59:36 (9,119)
Silver, Andrew C 3:04:12 (1,113)
Silverberg, Antony N 3:40:08 (5,206)
Silverman, Tom 4:29:36 (16,040)
Silversides, Nick 5:19:29 (27,334)
Silverton, Ross L 4:55:08 (22,298)
Silvester, Adam 6:14:51 (33,604)
Silvester, Brian W 3:21:03 (2,614)
Silvester, Robin A 4:17:50 (13,029)
Silvestre, Robert J 5:38:33 (30,388)
Silvestri, Giuliano F 5:45:19 (31,185)
Silvey, Norman 5:21:15 (27,644)
Sim, Paul 4:37:53 (17,977)
Sim, Richard A 4:15:49 (12,511)
Sime, Neil G 3:58:44 (8,893)
Simeone, Francesco 4:07:54 (10,748)
Simkin, Dave 4:17:09 (12,842)
Simkins, Paul J 6:30:37 (34,346)
Simmonds, David T 6:35:29 (34,522)
Simmonds, Gareth P 5:15:47 (26,621)
Simmonds, Ian D 3:22:45 (2,769)
Simmonds, Michael J 4:48:15 (20,592)
Simmonds, Neil A 4:57:06 (22,798)
Simmonds, Paul 6:06:54 (33,104)
Simmonds, Paul A 4:50:09 (21,034)
Simmonds, Thomas 3:56:59 (8,476)
Simmons, Andrew J 4:22:49 (14,290)
Simmons, Cyril H 7:29:03 (35,465)
Simmons, David S 5:13:48 (26,190)
Simmons, Graham R 4:25:58 (15,049)
Simmons, James S 4:36:38 (17,700)
Simmons, Michael J 3:58:52 (8,934)
Simmons, Neale 5:35:21 (29,957)
Simmons, Nolan A 5:13:25 (26,106)
Simmons, Paul D 5:28:46 (28,946)
Simmons, Ralph 5:19:03 (27,255)
Simmons, Scott 4:53:37 (21,919)
Simmons, Tony D 3:32:01 (3,990)
Simms, Lee P 4:05:27 (10,232)
Simms, Mark G 5:17:43 (27,002)
Simms, Mark P 3:14:13 (1,916)
Simms, Michael E 5:08:13 (25,144)
Simms, Stuart A 4:41:32 (18,932)
Simon, Gilles 4:36:21 (17,626)
Simon, Joel 4:14:16 (12,157)
Simon, Paul F 4:38:25 (18,131)
Simon, Stephane 3:30:05 (3,731)
Simon, Thierry 3:37:59 (4,828)
Simonazzi, Fabio 3:28:19 (3,452)
Simons, Gareth F 4:34:10 (17,069)
Simons, Malcolm 5:04:39 (24,438)
Simons, Paul R 3:13:42 (1,875)
Simons, Richard A 5:45:22 (31,188)
Simpkin, Ian G 3:49:36 (6,851)
Simpkins, Lee 4:48:48 (20,722)
Simpson, Alexander J 4:28:09 (15,635)
Simpson, Andrew 3:42:01 (5,525)
Simpson, Andrew H 4:56:33 (22,643)
Simpson, Andrew J 5:13:23 (26,096)
Simpson, Andrew M 6:14:22 (33,572)

Simpson, Christopher N	5:26:06 (28,474)	
Simpson, David	4:33:11 (16,838)	
Simpson, Gerry M	4:27:22 (15,436)	
Simpson, Graeme S	4:53:36 (21,913)	
Simpson, Greg F	3:00:33 (934)	
Simpson, Joe	5:45:58 (31,253)	
Simpson, John H	6:17:32 (33,753)	
Simpson, Keith A	4:21:47 (14,031)	
Simpson, Kenneth J	4:58:51 (23,218)	
Simpson, Mark J	5:19:56 (27,416)	
Simpson, Matt S	4:21:05 (13,868)	
Simpson, Matthew	6:15:13 (33,630)	
Simpson, Neil	5:12:30 (25,951)	
Simpson, Raymond C	3:49:52 (6,911)	
Simpson, Richard J	5:06:23 (24,764)	
Simpson, Robert	5:24:19 (28,160)	
Simpson, Robert J	3:58:05 (8,738)	
Simpson, Robert R	3:49:59 (6,934)	
Simpson, Timothy S	4:01:32 (9,518)	
Simpson, William G	3:55:06 (8,033)	
Simpson, William R	3:41:41 (5,466)	
Sims, Andrew J	4:32:52 (16,758)	
Sims, Chris	4:04:57 (10,135)	
Sims, David A	5:58:56 (32,502)	
Sims, James V	5:44:08 (31,060)	
Sims, Nicholas J	4:15:43 (12,487)	
Sims, Paul R	4:40:45 (18,714)	
Sinclair, Adrian L	3:31:41 (3,939)	
Sinclair, Andrew	3:29:00 (3,577)	
Sinclair, David M	5:14:42 (26,381)	
Sinclair, Doug	4:21:04 (13,864)	
Sinclair, James D	4:57:09 (22,809)	
Sinclair, James W	5:03:28 (24,230)	
Sinclair, John C	4:14:52 (12,284)	
Sinclair, Malcolm	3:04:52 (1,150)	
Sinclair, Nicholas	4:35:49 (17,491)	
Sinclair, Nigel P	3:49:46 (6,886)	
Sinclair, Paul A	4:13:37 (11,999)	
Sinclair, Richard P	5:58:19 (32,445)	
Sincock, Stephen M	2:53:27 (493)	
Sinfield, Colin D	4:51:51 (21,453)	
Sinfield, Matthew S	3:31:56 (3,980)	
Singh, Amarprit	4:03:42 (9,902)	
Singh, George G	4:37:39 (17,922)	
Singh, Harjit	4:03:30 (9,869)	
Singh, Harmander	5:22:30 (27,854)	
Singh, Jagjit J	4:58:33 (23,159)	
Singh, Makhan	4:55:00 (22,264)	
Singh, Malkiat	8:06:52 (35,652)	
Singh, Manjinder	4:32:34 (14,219)	
Singh, Manjit	4:03:28 (9,860)	
Singh, Manjit	4:22:36 (14,230)	
Singh, Parmjit	5:46:12 (31,283)	
Singh, Raghbir	5:19:14 (27,297)	
Singh, Simon	4:44:19 (19,626)	
Singh, Sukhjinder	5:41:11 (30,726)	
Singh, Tarsem	5:21:25 (27,685)	
Singh Dehl, Gurmal	2:57:24 (703)	
Singleton, Jonathan M	5:05:27 (24,588)	
Singleton, Steve D	5:16:49 (26,808)	
Sinha, Amrendra K	4:33:14 (16,854)	
Sinha, Ian	5:16:35 (26,769)	
Sinha, Rajesh C	6:47:06 (34,861)	
Sinker, Andrew B	4:04:23 (10,035)	
Sinnott, David	4:08:44 (10,914)	
Sinnott, Matt A	2:59:24 (854)	
Sinnott, Stephen P	2:57:10 (687)	
Sinthofen, Juergen	3:59:59 (9,205)	
Sinton, Charles F	4:48:20 (20,620)	
Sinton, Ed	4:18:17 (13,142)	
Sinton, Jeremy	4:15:47 (12,507)	
Sinton, Mark	3:58:35 (8,853)	
Sirakovsky, Susan L	3:52:34 (7,476)	
Sironi, Mauro	5:24:25 (28,174)	
Sirs, Nicholas J	2:49:58 (376)	
Sisson, Guy	5:08:27 (25,180)	
Sisson, William G	4:19:27 (13,446)	
Sitotaw, Alemayehu	2:36:41 (93)	
Sitt, Isaac	4:26:06 (15,074)	
Siu, Alan Y	3:31:56 (3,980)	
Sivyer, Stephen	5:40:30 (30,654)	
Sizeland, Tim J	3:32:08 (4,017)	
Sizer, Guy M	4:34:25 (17,118)	

Skansberg, Erik	4:19:49 (13,544)	
Skates, Clark V	5:01:17 (23,789)	
Skeate, Denis R	4:53:58 (22,012)	
Skehan, Douglas	4:03:13 (9,822)	
Skelding, Matthew C	5:25:25 (28,346)	
Skelly, Mark A	3:48:01 (6,529)	
Skelly, Timothy J	4:39:47 (18,483)	
Skelton, Alexander J	4:01:47 (9,564)	
Skelton, John	3:23:52 (2,888)	
Skelton, Steve	5:04:18 (24,377)	
Skerratt, Clark I	3:15:04 (2,003)	
Skerratt, Paul	3:56:06 (8,247)	
Skerry, Jon E	4:35:00 (17,270)	
Skidmore, Jonathan	3:28:27 (3,471)	
Skidmore, Paul	4:35:27 (17,389)	
Skilton, Guy H	4:42:02 (19,047)	
Skilton, Hayden J	4:07:10 (10,601)	
Skingley, Neil J	5:00:35 (23,631)	
Skinkis, Michael F	4:36:05 (17,553)	
Skinner, Adam R	4:38:56 (18,265)	
Skinner, Darryl E	4:53:05 (21,771)	
Skinner, Greg J	4:19:35 (13,479)	
Skinner, Joseph	5:41:47 (30,807)	
Skinner, Mark A	4:06:16 (10,409)	
Skinner, Miles D	3:06:03 (1,235)	
Skipworth, Julian	3:54:18 (7,872)	
Skizas, Nikos	5:17:37 (26,984)	
Skjerven, Eivind	5:27:09 (28,646)	
Skoczylas, Jean-Paul B	5:30:04 (29,155)	
Skorubskas, Andriv	2:56:43 (651)	
Skott, Jakob	2:58:38 (803)	
Skoulding, Alan G	4:23:47 (14,508)	
Skriver, Bjarke	3:14:58 (1,991)	
Skrzypecki, Anthony S	3:25:50 (3,103)	
Skyrme, Andrew	4:10:39 (11,300)	
Skyrme, Benjamin M	3:40:33 (5,278)	
Skyrme, Jeremy M	4:40:51 (18,747)	
Slack, John A	4:07:49 (10,730)	
Slade, Bernard P	5:14:32 (26,344)	
Slade, Glen	3:15:15 (2,016)	
Slade, Paul J	6:08:04 (33,176)	
Slade, Richard J	4:05:16 (10,197)	
Slade, Steven L	6:10:54 (33,361)	
Slagel, Craig A	5:15:14 (26,507)	
Slagel, Dean	5:15:14 (26,507)	
Slater, Adam D	4:58:38 (23,176)	
Slater, Ben	5:49:09 (31,599)	
Slater, Darren	3:55:30 (8,117)	
Slater, John P	4:49:33 (20,900)	
Slater, Martin F	5:24:32 (28,186)	
Slater, Neil	3:37:57 (4,819)	
Slater, Paul A	3:39:54 (5,175)	
Slater, Paul N	3:06:06 (1,239)	
Slater, Philip H	3:51:57 (7,356)	
Slatery, Sean E	7:39:45 (35,560)	
Slatter, Anthony J	4:02:47 (9,747)	
Slaughter, James D	3:43:57 (5,856)	
Slaughter, John N	4:15:16 (12,383)	
Sleath, Michael J	4:22:31 (14,209)	
Sleeman, Marcus	4:53:53 (21,985)	
Sleep, Anthony R	5:43:32 (30,995)	
Sleep, Tim R	4:06:15 (10,405)	
Sleigh, Michael J	6:12:31 (33,461)	
Slessor, Anthony	3:38:14 (4,873)	
Sletten, Helge	3:35:18 (4,449)	
Slimane, Karim D	3:54:24 (7,883)	
Slinger, John A	3:09:24 (1,510)	
Slinn, Gregory J	5:35:37 (30,000)	
Sloan, Ben D	4:18:47 (13,281)	
Sloan, Harry	3:16:40 (2,141)	
Sloan, Tomas P	3:13:45 (1,881)	
Sloley, Robert J	3:12:06 (1,740)	
Slootweg, Dirk	4:14:53 (12,292)	
Sloss, Philip A	4:32:46 (16,729)	
Slow, Jonathan M	3:41:24 (5,428)	
Sluman, John A	4:09:09 (10,993)	
Slutter, Ben	4:47:57 (20,520)	
Sly, Andy	3:02:12 (1,013)	
Smale, Ian N	3:42:52 (5,661)	
Small, Alexander D	5:23:37 (28,033)	
Small, Martin J	3:52:54 (7,544)	
Small, Matthew	4:51:16 (21,300)	
Small, Richard J	3:27:27 (3,350)	

Smallbone, Simon M	5:26:00 (28,455)	
Smalley, Jamie	3:04:31 (1,133)	
Smalley, Philip J	4:51:43 (21,424)	
Smallman, Chris C	3:22:30 (2,747)	
Smallman, Philip P	4:23:26 (14,427)	
Smalls, Allen	2:44:52 (237)	
Smallwood, Andrew W	3:13:14 (1,845)	
Smart, Adrian J	4:46:14 (20,113)	
Smart, Andrew B	3:25:37 (3,079)	
Smart, Andrew D	3:25:29 (3,061)	
Smart, Christopher L	3:51:09 (7,171)	
Smart, Darren I	3:35:36 (4,499)	
Smart, David	4:56:54 (22,749)	
Smart, Ian L	4:01:32 (9,518)	
Smart, Kevin A	3:46:05 (6,193)	
Smart, Sam D	4:25:42 (14,997)	
Smeddle, Jeremy H	4:41:08 (18,823)	
Smedley, Jack I	5:42:48 (30,909)	
Smedley, Mark	4:41:43 (18,968)	
Smedley, Stephen M	3:46:54 (6,321)	
Smee, Grahame J	4:51:41 (21,419)	
Smelik, Marc	4:58:47 (23,202)	
Smethurst, Mike	3:30:49 (3,824)	
Smiddy, Francis O	4:25:32 (14,952)	
Smillie, Paul	5:16:49 (26,808)	
Smit, Jason	4:35:01 (17,278)	
Smith, Adam A	4:05:00 (10,143)	
Smith, Adam G	4:56:18 (22,588)	
Smith, Adam P	4:37:38 (17,918)	
Smith, Alan H	3:58:01 (8,728)	
Smith, Alan W	4:12:56 (11,817)	
Smith, Alex E	3:32:16 (4,040)	
Smith, Alex N	5:09:03 (25,285)	
Smith, Andrew	4:24:36 (14,727)	
Smith, Andrew	4:36:10 (17,572)	
Smith, Andrew C	4:01:13 (9,462)	
Smith, Andrew J	3:08:38 (1,439)	
Smith, Andrew J	3:09:56 (1,551)	
Smith, Andrew J	4:02:08 (9,626)	
Smith, Andrew J	4:36:30 (17,664)	
Smith, Andrew L	3:52:02 (7,370)	
Smith, Andrew M	3:25:53 (3,112)	
Smith, Andy	3:49:29 (6,827)	
Smith, Andy D	3:53:23 (7,660)	
Smith, Anthony J	2:51:56 (437)	
Smith, Anthony P	4:13:57 (12,084)	
Smith, Anthony R	4:36:24 (17,640)	
Smith, Antony P	3:59:41 (9,136)	
Smith, Barry	5:51:37 (31,839)	
Smith, Ben	3:38:07 (4,857)	
Smith, Ben R	6:10:33 (33,339)	
Smith, Benjamin E	5:41:12 (30,728)	
Smith, Bill	3:20:09 (2,512)	
Smith, Bradley M	6:07:41 (33,141)	
Smith, Brett	3:54:04 (7,806)	
Smith, Brian	5:25:50 (28,431)	
Smith, Brian G	6:17:27 (33,745)	
Smith, Brian W	5:17:28 (26,951)	
Smith, Carl L	4:20:09 (13,643)	
Smith, Chris	5:07:11 (24,926)	
Smith, Chris David	5:11:19 (25,726)	
Smith, Christopher	4:06:55 (10,554)	
Smith, Christopher A	4:36:21 (17,626)	
Smith, Christopher C	4:28:27 (15,715)	
Smith, Christopher J	4:42:32 (19,187)	
Smith, Christopher R	5:54:46 (32,120)	
Smith, Clive	7:29:22 (35,479)	
Smith, Clive G	3:20:15 (2,523)	
Smith, Colin	5:04:19 (24,379)	
Smith, Colin	5:43:04 (30,942)	
Smith, Colin J	7:40:27 (35,563)	
Smith, Colin S	4:48:24 (20,633)	
Smith, Craig	3:54:32 (7,909)	
Smith, Craig	5:13:42 (26,166)	
Smith, Craig A	4:33:48 (16,991)	
Smith, Craig P	3:43:40 (5,807)	
Smith, Daniel J	3:00:02 (902)	
Smith, Daniel J	4:29:38 (16,048)	
Smith, Daniels J	5:28:22 (28,882)	
Smith, Darren	5:00:12 (23,551)	
Smith, Darren	5:55:09 (32,159)	
Smith, Darren C	4:31:41 (16,504)	
Smith, Darren K	4:17:09 (12,842)	

LONDON MARATHON, 2007: MALE RUNNERS 889

Smith, David 3:55:51 (8,195)
Smith, David 4:42:50 (19,264)
Smith, David 5:00:14 (23,560)
Smith, David 5:20:29 (27,513)
Smith, David A 4:13:35 (11,990)
Smith, David A 5:37:51 (30,279)
Smith, David G 4:02:13 (9,652)
Smith, David I 3:54:53 (7,982)
Smith, David J 3:54:16 (7,861)
Smith, David J 5:10:14 (25,530)
Smith, David J 5:23:48 (28,079)
Smith, David K 4:02:02 (9,608)
Smith, David K 6:36:50 (34,572)
Smith, David L 4:44:11 (19,594)
Smith, David M 2:50:32 (393)
Smith, David M 3:48:32 (6,630)
Smith, David P 5:56:45 (32,315)
Smith, Dean 4:16:25 (12,678)
Smith, Dean G 4:52:06 (21,518)
Smith, Dean O 4:29:03 (15,867)
Smith, Derek N 3:44:22 (5,921)
Smith, Desmond J 5:47:42 (31,430)
Smith, Donald J 6:10:33 (33,339)
Smith, Donald M 5:41:41 (30,793)
Smith, Donald R 4:38:24 (18,126)
Smith, Douglas J 4:52:23 (21,595)
Smith, Duncan I 5:47:42 (31,430)
Smith, Edward J 4:44:51 (19,791)
Smith, Edwin J 3:47:16 (6,389)
Smith, Garry M 5:31:07 (29,320)
Smith, Garry N 5:43:55 (31,028)
Smith, Garth A 6:10:28 (33,332)
Smith, Gary 4:23:36 (14,467)
Smith, Gary 5:28:15 (28,849)
Smith, Gary J 6:09:28 (33,268)
Smith, Gary S 4:36:27 (17,653)
Smith, Gary S 4:49:24 (20,861)
Smith, Gavin M 4:56:31 (22,635)
Smith, Gerry J 4:31:54 (16,542)
Smith, Giles R 3:52:21 (7,444)
Smith, Gordon A 3:32:39 (4,091)
Smith, Graeme D 5:33:21 (29,657)
Smith, Graham G 4:23:31 (14,451)
Smith, Graham J 5:54:02 (32,055)
Smith, Guy O 4:04:47 (10,110)
Smith, Howard 3:48:17 (6,575)
Smith, Howard J 4:00:17 (9,269)
Smith, Ian A 5:01:32 (23,835)
Smith, Ian A 5:11:58 (25,848)
Smith, Ian D 4:00:55 (9,402)
Smith, Ian D 4:49:36 (20,919)
Smith, Ian D 5:25:25 (28,346)
Smith, Ian M 3:15:00 (1,995)
Smith, Jake T 4:59:55 (23,479)
Smith, James C 3:59:31 (9,097)
Smith, James L 3:55:03 (8,019)
Smith, James P 4:19:52 (13,563)
Smith, Jason M 5:38:12 (30,336)
Smith, Jason M 7:40:56 (35,568)
Smith, Jeffrey O 5:55:50 (32,221)
Smith, Jeremy 5:05:32 (24,609)
Smith, Jeremy C 6:12:30 (33,459)
Smith, Jeremy P 3:25:02 (3,024)
Smith, Jim 5:16:50 (26,815)
Smith, John 5:47:08 (31,362)
Smith, John D 4:13:46 (12,035)
Smith, John J 3:03:56 (1,101)
Smith, John M 4:37:04 (17,801)
Smith, John P 4:17:11 (12,848)
Smith, Jonathan C 4:37:27 (17,883)
Smith, Jonathan D 4:57:04 (22,788)
Smith, Jonathan P 5:17:05 (26,875)
Smith, Jonathan P 5:28:58 (28,978)
Smith, Jordan S 5:20:51 (27,581)
Smith, Julian L 4:43:01 (19,300)
Smith, Justin P 5:48:55 (31,575)
Smith, Karl 5:36:45 (30,138)
Smith, Keith A 3:20:29 (2,552)
Smith, Keith G 4:45:57 (20,050)
Smith, Keith J 4:01:00 (9,420)
Smith, Kenny D 5:35:30 (29,974)
Smith, Kerr W 4:47:29 (20,401)
Smith, Kevin 4:43:33 (19,426)
Smith, Kevin J 3:50:09 (6,969)
Smith, Kevin J 4:24:46 (14,771)
Smith, Kevin J 5:12:27 (25,946)
Smith, Kevin R 5:04:26 (24,407)
Smith, Lawrence G 4:38:45 (18,212)
Smith, Lee 6:20:52 (33,944)
Smith, Les 5:39:45 (30,565)
Smith, Luke C 4:54:06 (22,041)
Smith, Luke W 4:34:35 (17,169)
Smith, Malcolm R 3:55:19 (8,085)
Smith, Mark 4:23:57 (14,555)
Smith, Mark A 3:49:44 (6,881)
Smith, Mark A 4:13:34 (11,986)
Smith, Mark A 4:46:56 (20,262)
Smith, Mark A 5:28:33 (28,910)
Smith, Mark A 5:31:19 (29,347)
Smith, Mark B 4:51:40 (21,412)
Smith, Mark D 4:10:55 (11,352)
Smith, Mark D 4:39:16 (18,355)
Smith, Mark J 6:22:29 (34,022)
Smith, Mark N 5:18:34 (27,175)
Smith, Mark S 4:27:18 (15,425)
Smith, Martin 3:46:57 (6,335)
Smith, Martin B 4:24:25 (14,685)
Smith, Martin J 3:04:54 (1,154)
Smith, Mathew P 4:00:39 (9,345)
Smith, Matt A 5:30:06 (29,161)
Smith, Matthew J 5:54:14 (32,073)
Smith, Matthew D 3:52:39 (7,489)
Smith, Matthew D 4:49:53 (20,970)
Smith, Matthew E 3:48:28 (6,612)
Smith, Michael D 3:44:08 (5,884)
Smith, Michael J 2:28:36 (33)
Smith, Michael J 3:12:03 (1,736)
Smith, Michael J 3:56:20 (8,314)
Smith, Michael J 4:55:25 (22,368)
Smith, Michael M 4:12:55 (11,809)
Smith, Mike 4:59:06 (23,287)
Smith, Nathan D 3:58:52 (8,934)
Smith, Nathan R 3:31:12 (3,865)
Smith, Nathan T 3:22:14 (2,722)
Smith, Nathan W 4:33:32 (16,924)
Smith, Neil 3:29:51 (3,699)
Smith, Neil A 4:57:46 (22,973)
Smith, Neil C 4:44:42 (19,744)
Smith, Neil G 6:45:48 (34,820)
Smith, Nicholas 3:47:40 (6,468)
Smith, Nicholas C 5:18:46 (27,207)
Smith, Nicholas G 6:11:25 (33,396)
Smith, Nicholas J 3:53:43 (7,733)
Smith, Nigel A 3:50:38 (7,062)
Smith, Nigel B 4:19:48 (13,542)
Smith, Nigel H 4:20:15 (13,665)
Smith, Oliver H 4:50:37 (21,154)
Smith, Patrick E 5:21:05 (27,615)
Smith, Patrick J 4:58:57 (23,241)
Smith, Paul 4:23:19 (14,402)
Smith, Paul 5:16:24 (26,736)
Smith, Paul 6:03:28 (32,850)
Smith, Paul 6:05:29 (33,002)
Smith, Paul A 3:29:46 (3,682)
Smith, Paul D 3:48:22 (6,585)
Smith, Paul D 5:22:38 (27,880)
Smith, Paul E 4:11:06 (11,397)
Smith, Paul E 4:25:16 (14,889)
Smith, Paul E 5:34:25 (29,833)
Smith, Paul T 4:32:57 (16,773)
Smith, Paul T 6:05:57 (33,041)
Smith, Peter 4:45:36 (19,967)
Smith, Peter A 6:41:07 (34,696)
Smith, Peter C 3:56:56 (8,461)
Smith, Peter J 3:53:10 (7,608)
Smith, Peter M 4:16:17 (12,644)
Smith, Peter M 6:03:22 (32,842)
Smith, Peter W 5:02:25 (24,021)
Smith, Philip 5:51:26 (31,818)
Smith, Philip A 3:03:25 (1,070)
Smith, Philip N 5:00:28 (23,608)
Smith, Piers D 5:09:25 (25,358)
Smith, Richard 3:20:41 (2,575)
Smith, Richard 4:29:52 (16,115)
Smith, Richard 4:31:21 (16,436)
Smith, Richard 4:55:47 (22,453)
Smith, Richard A 4:40:18 (18,603)
Smith, Richard G 3:54:26 (7,889)
Smith, Richard J 5:34:06 (29,780)
Smith, Richard L 5:18:00 (27,058)
Smith, Richard N 3:08:25 (1,423)
Smith, Richard S 3:59:48 (9,162)
Smith, Richard W 4:07:17 (10,619)
Smith, Ricky L 5:04:19 (24,379)
Smith, Rob 5:26:21 (28,521)
Smith, Rob 5:28:24 (28,888)
Smith, Robert A 3:08:14 (1,410)
Smith, Robert B 3:42:54 (5,669)
Smith, Robert D 4:52:19 (21,576)
Smith, Robert H 6:02:26 (32,781)
Smith, Robert J 3:34:16 (4,309)
Smith, Robert M 4:02:57 (9,774)
Smith, Robert M 5:37:56 (30,291)
Smith, Rod 4:13:29 (11,956)
Smith, Rod W 5:01:57 (23,922)
Smith, Roger 5:53:13 (31,979)
Smith, Rory O 3:41:10 (5,390)
Smith, Roy C 3:25:20 (3,047)
Smith, Royston 3:41:24 (5,428)
Smith, Russell H 3:37:32 (4,757)
Smith, Russell I 4:37:20 (17,847)
Smith, Russell I 4:52:27 (21,607)
Smith, Russell J 4:27:44 (15,529)
Smith, Sam 3:37:41 (4,773)
Smith, Sam J 6:46:55 (34,855)
Smith, Scott P 3:59:19 (9,045)
Smith, Scott P 4:58:31 (23,153)
Smith, Sean 2:53:54 (517)
Smith, Sean D 4:15:46 (12,501)
Smith, Sean G 4:00:33 (9,322)
Smith, Shaun M 5:33:53 (29,742)
Smith, Simon M 3:34:53 (4,392)
Smith, Simon W 4:08:43 (10,911)
Smith, Stephen 4:25:31 (14,949)
Smith, Stephen 4:39:17 (18,357)
Smith, Stephen 5:17:43 (27,002)
Smith, Stephen A 4:55:14 (22,325)
Smith, Stephen A 5:28:35 (28,914)
Smith, Stephen H 4:31:02 (16,364)
Smith, Stephen J 5:24:42 (28,219)
Smith, Stephen M 4:58:40 (23,183)
Smith, Steve 3:18:06 (2,297)
Smith, Steve 7:29:11 (35,470)
Smith, Steve A 4:06:28 (10,458)
Smith, Steve C 3:28:30 (3,485)
Smith, Steven 3:19:04 (2,399)
Smith, Steven 4:26:09 (15,084)
Smith, Steven M 5:12:35 (25,965)
Smith, Stewart A 3:44:23 (5,922)
Smith, Stuart 4:35:41 (17,456)
Smith, Stuart D 4:40:09 (18,566)
Smith, Stuart W 5:28:11 (28,836)
Smith, Susan J 5:01:57 (23,922)
Smith, Terence 4:46:04 (20,072)
Smith, Terry A 4:24:48 (14,777)
Smith, Thomas A 4:46:21 (20,144)
Smith, Thomas D 3:47:53 (6,509)
Smith, Tim P 5:19:04 (27,259)
Smith, Toby N 4:44:11 (19,594)
Smith, Toby P 4:39:46 (18,476)
Smith, Tom 3:51:30 (7,256)
Smith, Tony R 4:24:32 (14,712)
Smith, Trevor 4:48:19 (20,613)
Smith, Trevor J 5:28:44 (28,936)
Smith, Troy A 4:56:19 (22,590)
Smith, Tyrone G 4:21:24 (13,939)
Smith, Vincent 4:52:30 (21,612)
Smith, Vincent F 4:15:07 (12,345)
Smith, Warren 5:44:13 (31,067)
Smith, Wayne J 4:22:12 (14,128)

Smith, Wayne M 5:05:27 (24,588)
Smithers, Stuart M 6:47:50 (34,883)
Smithey, John 5:27:28 (28,707)
Smithson, Martin J 4:55:49 (22,461)
Smuts, Paul G 3:54:20 (7,875)
Smyth, Alistair G 3:10:16 (1,583)
Smyth, Andrew T 4:12:53 (11,803)
Smyth, David A 3:10:07 (1,573)
Smyth, David A 3:48:39 (6,656)
Smyth, Justin P 4:09:16 (11,020)
Smyth, Michael S 3:43:48 (5,829)
Smyth, Stephen 6:20:20 (33,909)
Smythe, Stephen J 2:46:47 (278)
Smythe, Steve 2:51:40 (427)
Snaith, David M 3:22:52 (2,785)
Snead, Martin P 4:14:36 (12,230)
Sneary, Lawrence W 5:45:16 (31,179)
Sneezum, Patrick 5:16:31 (26,759)
Snelgrove, William R 3:25:23 (3,053)
Snell, Anthony D 5:32:46 (29,571)
Snell, Philip E 3:32:50 (4,111)
Snell, Trevor W 7:12:52 (35,319)
Snelling-Colyer, Nigel 5:17:20 (26,925)
Snelson, Bryn D 4:16:49 (12,765)
Sneyd, David J 4:52:48 (21,700)
Sneyd, Russell 5:13:44 (26,174)
Snoddy, Paul 5:21:43 (27,734)
Snook, Gareth 4:26:51 (15,280)
Snook, Steven R 3:30:43 (3,808)
Snorrason, Adalsteinn 3:56:16 (8,290)
Snow, David R 4:37:54 (17,981)
Snow, Dean 5:31:10 (29,330)
Snow, Robert 5:34:38 (29,867)
Snowden, Ben I 5:23:41 (28,048)
Snowden, Christopher W 4:05:28 (10,236)
Snowden, Craig I 5:40:04 (30,601)
Snowden, David H 3:26:53 (3,254)
Snowden, Thomas J 4:26:39 (15,223)
Snowdon, David R 4:55:57 (22,502)
Snowdon, James P 3:23:14 (2,826)
Snowling, Ian K 4:50:16 (21,061)
Snoxall, Jonathan D 3:51:34 (7,269)
Snyth, Ciaran M 6:44:48 (34,795)
Soanes, John D 5:52:19 (31,904)
Soardo, Simone 4:52:26 (21,604)
Sockett, Sam 4:32:33 (16,675)
Soddy, Richard A 4:41:44 (18,969)
Soderberg, Lars 4:41:10 (18,831)
Soeda, Ken 5:10:19 (25,540)
Soeiro, Fernando A 4:46:45 (20,221)
Soelberg, Lars K 3:43:26 (5,761)
Sohal, Achhar Sinksh 5:44:58 (31,150)
Solakian, Yann-Gael 4:06:45 (10,513)
Solanki, Harshad 5:09:07 (25,298)
Solari, Tim J 5:23:57 (28,101)
Solheim, Erik M 4:03:50 (9,935)
Solieman, Samuel E 3:32:07 (4,013)
Soliveres, Serge 4:38:35 (18,170)
Solomon, David B 5:25:02 (28,279)
Solomon, Nicholas J 4:03:17 (9,832)
Solomon, Nissim D 5:28:01 (28,801)
Soltysik, Andrew 3:09:50 (1,542)
Somerfield, Christopher D 3:48:25 (6,598)
Somerville, Alan 5:01:57 (23,922)
Somerville, Derek 3:05:25 (1,195)
Somerville, Joe 7:01:55 (35,156)
Sommerfeld, Thimo L 2:59:29 (861)
Sommerlad, Michael J 7:11:59 (35,304)
Sommerville, James A 7:02:49 (35,172)
Sonneved, Erik 4:57:51 (22,998)
Soon, Julian 5:11:17 (25,714)
Soper, Keith G 5:05:59 (24,691)
Soper, Paul A 4:54:06 (22,041)
Soraf, David G 4:46:10 (20,095)
Sordam, Andreauw M 3:52:39 (7,489)
Sorel, Didier 6:13:22 (33,511)
Sorenti, Chris J 5:00:56 (23,715)
Sorgeloos, Guido F 4:13:29 (11,956)
Sorimachi, Kenjiro 5:42:59 (30,933)
Sorrell, Jason E 5:06:02 (24,698)
Sorrie, Paul D 2:38:16 (114)
Soto, Claudio 4:05:15 (10,193)
Soubra, Roudi 5:18:46 (27,207)
Soudain, Maximillian C 4:45:00 (19,836)
Soukup, Karl 4:28:16 (15,662)
Soulsby, Martin 3:58:42 (8,882)
South, Clifford R 4:43:11 (19,337)
Southall, Ben I 3:56:43 (8,411)
Southall, Paul C 3:39:24 (5,087)
Southall, Roger 5:12:17 (25,917)
Southam, Anthony 3:44:42 (5,978)
Southam, Christopher 2:41:15 (159)
Southby, David 3:23:34 (2,855)
Southee, Richard J 6:02:51 (32,811)
Southerton, Michael 4:56:12 (22,564)
Southgate, Mark D 5:20:30 (27,517)
Southgate, Mathew J 4:54:31 (22,149)
Southgate, Oliver P 4:56:55 (22,753)
Southgate, Ross W 5:09:57 (25,463)
Southwell, Geoffrey C 6:01:08 (32,691)
Southwell, Ian J 5:13:48 (26,190)
Southwood, Robin M 5:08:34 (25,197)
Southworth, Richard H 5:22:10 (27,804)
Southwould, Richard W 5:08:17 (25,152)
Sovegjarto, Pete 4:28:35 (15,754)
Sowden, Richard J 3:42:57 (5,677)
Sowerby, Adrian R 3:10:29 (1,594)
Soya, Koichi 3:51:34 (7,269)
Spaczek, Hubert 4:26:12 (15,102)
Spain, Martin J 4:52:10 (21,533)
Spall, Jonathan D 4:01:52 (9,581)
Spall, Stephen 3:48:57 (6,717)
Spanos, Kirstin A 4:58:58 (23,244)
Sparey, Guy J 5:57:26 (32,365)
Spargo, Peter J 4:36:31 (17,671)
Spark, Graham 4:49:19 (20,842)
Sparkes, Stephen 5:34:55 (29,904)
Sparks, Barry 5:18:03 (27,068)
Sparks, David M 3:59:02 (8,965)
Sparks, Ian A 3:17:01 (2,180)
Sparling, Gari 4:34:50 (17,234)
Sparrow, Andrew 5:39:25 (30,510)
Sparrow, Ian M 4:31:07 (16,386)
Sparrow, Roger L 4:44:17 (19,621)
Spashett, Matthew 4:32:25 (16,647)
Spavin, Carl J 4:57:48 (22,986)
Speake, Andrew I 5:47:29 (31,407)
Speake, Malcolm D 4:22:38 (14,241)
Speake, William J 2:33:59 (61)
Speakman, Gary S 7:10:07 (35,273)
Speakman, Gary T 4:56:40 (22,686)
Speakman, Peter R 4:36:46 (17,737)
Spearing, Warwick S 3:56:53 (8,452)
Spearman, Rod 6:11:00 (33,368)
Spearpoint, Robert S 4:28:39 (15,773)
Spears, Tony 4:38:09 (18,051)
Speck, Gary 5:28:35 (28,914)
Specterman, David B 5:21:50 (27,762)
Speechley, Simon A 5:13:53 (26,209)
Speed, Andrew P 3:48:59 (6,729)
Speed, Christopher A 3:26:04 (3,136)
Speed, David J 5:05:26 (24,584)
Speed, Mark F 3:52:12 (7,409)
Speers, Gary A 3:56:53 (8,452)
Speight, David A 4:59:17 (23,335)
Speight, Mark A 5:12:17 (25,917)
Speller, Martin D 3:21:10 (2,618)
Spelman, Nigel D 4:15:28 (12,435)
Spelman, Peter J 3:31:47 (3,950)
Spence, Shaun A 4:17:56 (13,052)
Spence, Trevor J 4:51:40 (21,412)
Spencer, Andrew M 3:05:31 (1,203)
Spencer, Clive C 3:29:19 (3,620)
Spencer, Darren 3:07:49 (1,370)
Spencer, David 3:32:13 (4,032)
Spencer, David E 3:39:48 (5,157)
Spencer, David J 4:37:34 (17,902)
Spencer, Harry B 4:15:22 (12,411)
Spencer, Ian H 3:50:13 (6,977)
Spencer, Jamie P 5:53:00 (31,962)
Spencer, Jeremy A 3:25:14 (3,040)
Spencer, Joe M 5:01:21 (23,803)
Spencer, Jonathan P 3:48:07 (6,547)
Spencer, Martin 5:01:21 (23,803)
Spencer, Matthew W 5:04:34 (24,427)
Spencer, Neil J 5:08:44 (25,232)
Spencer, Philip B 5:14:47 (26,403)
Spencer, Richard D 4:21:58 (14,080)
Spencer, Richard J 5:20:49 (27,577)
Spencer, Robert J 4:59:46 (23,448)
Spencer, Ryan M 5:13:36 (26,141)
Spencer, Stephen A 4:51:39 (21,409)
Spencer-Perkins, Michael D 6:10:41 (33,347)
Spendley, Matthew 4:19:31 (13,463)
Sperrey, Michael J 5:21:15 (27,644)
Spiceley, Paul D 3:21:36 (2,660)
Spiegelberg, Maximilian 3:49:41 (6,868)
Spieler, Peter 4:20:35 (13,749)
Spielmann, Rolf P 4:31:06 (16,381)
Spiers, Adam B 4:38:44 (18,208)
Spiers, Roger 4:01:19 (9,480)
Spillner, Joerg 3:38:59 (5,012)
Spindler, Peter 3:58:37 (8,857)
Spink, Christopher J 4:20:51 (13,817)
Spinks, Jeremy 3:33:43 (4,228)
Spiro, Joseph A 4:13:00 (11,827)
Spiteri, Thomas R 4:53:07 (21,784)
Spohner, Lothar E 4:28:05 (15,616)
Spooner, Martin 5:43:29 (30,992)
Spooner, Maurice 4:15:56 (12,538)
Spooner, Paul G 4:37:26 (17,874)
Spragg, Christian M 4:30:57 (16,344)
Spratt, Matthew 4:28:01 (15,592)
Spratt, Oliver P 3:55:49 (8,187)
Spreadborough, David C 6:12:51 (33,482)
Spreadbury, Ray 4:28:53 (15,828)
Spriggs, Andrew J 4:29:16 (15,930)
Spriggs, Chris J 4:08:27 (10,862)
Spriggs, Peter J 3:53:12 (7,618)
Spring, David 3:31:04 (3,843)
Spring, William J 4:48:49 (20,725)
Springall, Darryl P 3:20:27 (2,549)
Springall, Edward 3:45:12 (6,052)
Springell, Ryan P 3:43:00 (5,692)
Springer, Gideon L 3:44:52 (6,004)
Springers, Marcellus A 3:33:23 (4,193)
Springett, Lee A 5:01:35 (23,851)
Springett, Steven J 4:00:13 (9,259)
Springett, Toby 4:31:07 (16,386)
Springett, Tony 5:43:14 (30,966)
Sprinks, David A 6:26:48 (34,205)
Sprott, Yodi G 3:57:29 (8,597)
Sprowson, Hugh 4:41:18 (18,862)
Sprules, Christopher F 3:24:32 (2,958)
Sprules, Michael R 4:12:33 (11,729)
Spruzs, Michael 4:40:44 (18,706)
Spry, Jason M 4:29:38 (16,048)
Spurgeon, Tony W 5:03:52 (24,301)
Spurle, Tony S 4:56:54 (22,749)
Spurling, Scott 3:50:16 (6,991)
Spurr, James C 4:28:01 (15,592)
Spurr, Mike 5:00:41 (23,652)
Spurr, Tim J 4:08:09 (10,796)
Spurrier, Jack B 4:19:59 (13,599)
Spurrier, Peter D 5:23:06 (27,948)
Spychal, Carl G 4:13:34 (11,986)
Squaillea, Maurizio 4:33:23 (16,890)
Squibb, Robert D 3:45:24 (6,084)
Squire, Anthony J 3:08:29 (1,430)
Squires, Kevin N 3:12:01 (1,729)
Squires, Troy 3:53:29 (7,683)
Squirrell, David H 5:57:30 (32,368)
St Clair, Richard 3:06:19 (1,252)
St Clair Roberts, John 4:03:30 (9,869)
St Croix, Dennis C 4:26:23 (15,155)
St John, Anthony 3:58:42 (8,882)
St John, Jeremy A 5:38:41 (30,412)
St Pierre, James E 4:02:09 (9,630)
Staas, Kersten 4:35:56 (17,523)
Stabile, Debbie 5:03:27 (24,229)
Stacey, Andrew 4:15:57 (12,543)
Stacey, Brett E 4:53:33 (21,901)
Stacey, Jim 4:38:28 (18,140)
Stacey, Mark R 4:26:56 (15,307)
Stacey, Michael W 3:19:36 (2,443)
Stacey, Neil R 4:33:55 (17,011)
Stacey, Paul A 4:55:45 (22,444)
Stacey, Robin 5:07:56 (25,082)
Stacey, Steve J 4:15:16 (12,383)

Stack, Nick J....4:57:22 (22,881)
Stackhouse, Daniel W....5:14:27 (26,321)
Staddon, Luke J....4:59:15 (23,327)
Stadler, Helmut....4:16:57 (12,806)
Stafford, John F....5:29:21 (29,051)
Stafford, Paul A....4:50:02 (21,003)
Stafford, Thomas M....5:13:58 (26,224)
Stafford, Tommy....5:02:41 (24,074)
Stafilopatis, Alex....4:34:01 (17,036)
Staiano, Mario....6:33:05 (34,442)
Stainer, Jamie K....5:14:49 (26,410)
Stainer, Peter....2:45:44 (257)
Staines, Toby N....3:39:14 (5,053)
Stainthorpe, Ian....3:05:01 (1,165)
Stainthorpe, Michael K....4:10:32 (11,274)
Stainton, Andrew....4:26:48 (15,267)
Staithe, Peter....5:17:52 (27,022)
Stalker, Alan....6:04:00 (32,889)
Stalker, Howard J....5:19:57 (27,417)
Stalley, Christopher D....5:49:51 (31,667)
Stamford, John....5:30:53 (29,277)
Stammers, Andrew J....3:54:03 (7,803)
Stammers, Mark....4:44:46 (19,763)
Stamper, John T....4:22:34 (14,219)
Stamper, Nicholas J....3:24:01 (2,905)
Stanbury, Kevin J....4:45:58 (20,054)
Stancliffe, Tom....5:56:37 (32,300)
Standen, Neil....4:27:31 (15,473)
Standfast, David J....4:17:25 (12,914)
Standing, Joseph F....3:48:28 (6,612)
Standing, Robett D....5:32:35 (29,547)
Standley, James K....5:25:45 (28,417)
Stanford, James R....5:03:31 (24,240)
Stanforth, David B....3:58:38 (8,867)
Stanger, Michael J....4:00:57 (9,409)
Stanham, Gareth P....5:40:23 (30,638)
Stanhope, Richard C....3:51:43 (7,297)
Stanier, Keith....4:55:39 (22,418)
Stanier, Raymond....3:00:40 (939)
Staniforth, Adam J....4:15:26 (12,426)
Stanley, Andrew....4:18:11 (13,121)
Stanley, Christopher J....4:43:13 (19,343)
Stanley, David A....3:25:37 (3,079)
Stanley, Ian R....4:08:53 (10,940)
Stanley, Peter J....4:12:27 (11,713)
Stanley, Shaun....4:19:26 (13,440)
Stannett, Charlie....4:49:08 (20,803)
Stansfield, Sion E....4:05:57 (10,342)
Stanton, Andrew D....5:07:48 (25,058)
Stanton, Gary....6:05:49 (33,032)
Stanton, Geoff R....4:20:45 (13,784)
Stanton, Ian D....3:26:53 (3,254)
Stanton, Jamie L....4:49:34 (20,908)
Stanton, Neil....4:30:19 (16,218)
Stanton, Richard J....5:15:47 (26,621)
Stanway, Robert W....4:29:48 (16,090)
Stanworth, Tom M....4:33:55 (17,011)
Stapley, Gregg W....3:39:31 (5,109)
Stapley, Matthew J....4:27:39 (15,501)
Stapley, Phillip D....6:18:38 (33,815)
Starbrook, Samuel J....6:04:56 (32,957)
Starbuck, Robert....4:58:16 (23,093)
Starfield, Marc O....5:33:30 (29,682)
Stark, Peter....3:54:41 (7,940)
Stark, Stephen....3:12:45 (1,802)
Stark, Stuart M....4:09:15 (11,017)
Stark Toller, Simon D....3:22:59 (2,794)
Starkey, Andrew J....3:44:09 (5,887)
Starkey, Ian J....6:02:37 (32,794)
Starkey, Simon C....5:24:16 (28,151)
Starkey, Trevor J....4:46:11 (20,104)
Starling, Andrew J....4:21:16 (13,905)
Starling, Barrie....4:17:33 (12,961)
Starling, John A....4:22:14 (14,137)
Starr, Robert P....4:35:28 (17,397)
Start, David R....5:42:20 (30,864)
Starz, Dirk-Juergen....5:23:41 (28,048)
Starz, Mariusz....4:18:56 (13,314)
Stather-Lodge, Jason A....4:54:57 (22,257)
Statter, Ian G....3:58:05 (8,738)
Staunton, John C....5:13:01 (26,052)
Staunton, Michael....4:44:31 (19,692)
Staut, Jan....3:34:12 (4,293)
Stavenuiter, Kees J....4:18:06 (13,094)
Stawman, Colin....5:28:46 (28,946)
Stayt, Paul....3:57:26 (8,588)
Stayton, Jonathan R....4:01:23 (9,494)
Stead, Edward J....3:35:51 (4,528)
Stead, Mark G....5:39:19 (30,493)
Stearn, Martyn K....4:13:35 (11,990)
Stecher, Hans....3:14:20 (1,927)
Stedman, Sam J....3:37:08 (4,705)
Steed, Mark S....4:16:10 (12,612)
Steel, Angus M....3:36:52 (4,669)
Steel, Ian S....4:08:02 (10,774)
Steel, Martin....3:27:41 (3,370)
Steel, William D....5:22:36 (27,875)
Steele, Andrew T....5:33:55 (29,750)
Steele, David P....4:44:58 (19,828)
Steele, Kristian N....4:19:19 (13,410)
Steele, Roger....3:46:58 (6,338)
Steele, Stuart....4:35:53 (17,508)
Steels, Mark....4:51:41 (21,419)
Steer, Anthony D....5:17:33 (26,969)
Steer, James S....3:32:57 (4,133)
Steer, Steven J....5:05:41 (24,631)
Steere, Brian....4:33:11 (16,838)
Steers, Paul J....4:32:50 (16,748)
Steeves, Mark D....5:12:02 (25,861)
Steger, Mark....4:01:04 (9,429)
Steggle, Paul....4:32:46 (16,729)
Stein, Jonathan P....5:32:40 (29,561)
Stein, Peter J....3:11:54 (1,714)
Steinbicker, Michael....4:01:24 (9,499)
Steinfurth, Sven....5:57:17 (32,351)
Steinmann, Didier....3:57:16 (8,547)
Stelfox, Andrew....3:52:24 (7,451)
Stell, Patrick T....5:16:39 (26,781)
Stembridge, Andrew....3:47:21 (6,397)
Stennett, James J....5:39:47 (30,570)
Stenning, James....4:18:18 (13,149)
Stenson, Jules A....4:36:41 (17,714)
Stenson, Michael J....5:00:18 (23,575)
Step, Gavin P....5:42:41 (30,892)
Stephen, Patrick J....4:26:56 (15,307)
Stephens, Adrian J....4:57:56 (23,014)
Stephens, Alan....5:24:27 (28,175)
Stephens, Christopher J....3:03:43 (1,087)
Stephens, Clifford....4:50:24 (21,097)
Stephens, Daniel M....4:45:46 (20,001)
Stephens, David M....4:02:36 (9,708)
Stephens, Edward J....4:29:05 (15,880)
Stephens, George A....5:23:08 (27,953)
Stephens, George H....3:01:24 (980)
Stephens, Graham C....2:47:16 (290)
Stephens, Jon....5:50:38 (31,739)
Stephens, Joshua J....5:09:11 (25,313)
Stephens, Keith J....6:18:54 (33,833)
Stephens, Mark J....3:35:51 (4,528)
Stephens, Raymond....5:05:50 (24,659)
Stephens, Richard J....4:38:17 (18,084)
Stephens, Trevor N....5:40:17 (30,626)
Stephenson, Andrew J....4:40:53 (18,755)
Stephenson, Charlie D....3:56:28 (8,352)
Stephenson, Ian R....4:35:55 (17,519)
Stephenson, James P....3:34:58 (4,406)
Stephenson, Jason....5:33:28 (29,675)
Stephenson, Philip....5:14:23 (26,308)
Stepien, Zenon....2:57:49 (732)
Steptoe, Colin F....2:41:41 (171)
Steptoe, Karl J....5:48:39 (31,539)
Stern, Jaroslav....4:21:28 (13,957)
Sterritt, Robert J....3:45:36 (6,113)
Steven, Roy....3:33:49 (4,238)
Stevenhaagen, Pieter J....4:09:44 (11,120)
Stevens, Alan N....3:59:21 (9,053)
Stevens, Andrew....4:40:14 (18,585)
Stevens, Andrew D....3:58:33 (8,849)
Stevens, Anthony....5:16:10 (26,692)
Stevens, Brian A....3:36:30 (4,609)
Stevens, Conrad....4:39:24 (18,389)
Stevens, Dominic M....4:53:13 (21,818)
Stevens, Edward J....4:53:08 (21,788)
Stevens, Gareth....4:59:02 (23,264)
Stevens, Gary D....4:33:35 (16,930)
Stevens, Gary S....7:43:08 (35,589)
Stevens, Greg J....6:27:36 (34,237)
Stevens, Greg P....2:44:05 (216)
Stevens, Greg R....4:17:04 (12,825)
Stevens, Ian....6:09:15 (33,250)
Stevens, Ian P....5:34:47 (29,884)
Stevens, Mark L....5:02:15 (23,980)
Stevens, Mark R....5:07:03 (24,896)
Stevens, Martin J....2:50:44 (400)
Stevens, Neil A....4:49:40 (20,930)
Stevens, Paul E....5:22:06 (27,796)
Stevens, Pelham C....5:04:50 (24,476)
Stevens, Phil G....4:21:10 (13,894)
Stevens, Phillip J....4:02:35 (9,705)
Stevens, Richard....4:21:35 (13,980)
Stevens, Robert C....4:08:25 (10,856)
Stevens, Shaun I....6:56:21 (35,059)
Stevens, Simon....4:32:43 (16,720)
Stevens, Thomas L....5:02:38 (24,065)
Stevens, Tony W....5:03:59 (24,322)
Stevenson, Alistair S....4:14:37 (12,235)
Stevenson, Andrew....4:23:25 (14,421)
Stevenson, Andrew D....3:23:55 (2,896)
Stevenson, Antony M....5:41:21 (30,748)
Stevenson, Clive....4:12:48 (11,789)
Stevenson, Giles....5:26:49 (28,593)
Stevenson, Ian....5:43:44 (31,017)
Stevenson, Michael J....3:36:49 (4,659)
Stevenson, Neil J....5:40:05 (30,605)
Stevenson, Nigel W....4:05:25 (10,226)
Stevenson, Robert....4:53:23 (21,854)
Stevick, Joseph....2:53:48 (513)
Stevignon, Maxime....3:44:47 (5,991)
Stew, John M....4:38:18 (18,093)
Steward, James J....5:23:53 (28,090)
Steward, Jonathan A....5:12:51 (26,008)
Stewardson, Stephen M....4:47:19 (20,365)
Stewart, Alexander J....5:47:11 (31,368)
Stewart, Andrew....6:23:24 (34,051)
Stewart, Charlie....5:34:38 (29,867)
Stewart, Christopher T....3:53:55 (7,769)
Stewart, Conal R....3:59:03 (8,972)
Stewart, Damon M....4:09:59 (11,162)
Stewart, David C....4:10:29 (11,261)
Stewart, Duncan J....3:11:39 (1,691)
Stewart, George....4:03:11 (9,813)
Stewart, Gordon R....5:41:38 (30,784)
Stewart, Ian....4:21:01 (13,857)
Stewart, Ian....4:42:51 (19,270)
Stewart, Jay W....3:49:20 (6,800)
Stewart, Kevin....4:22:36 (14,230)
Stewart, Kevin D....4:20:24 (13,707)
Stewart, Mark C....2:59:14 (842)
Stewart, Mark S....5:50:40 (31,747)
Stewart, Owen P....4:28:39 (15,773)
Stewart, Philip A....5:16:51 (26,820)
Stewart, Philip D....4:08:40 (10,905)
Stewart, Richard M....4:12:21 (11,690)
Stewart, Robert A....3:36:12 (4,570)
Stewart, Ronald A....5:17:38 (26,987)
Stewart, Tim D....3:22:37 (2,757)
Stewart, Wayne....3:58:49 (8,913)
Stgewart, Alan W....3:57:44 (8,660)
St-Hill, Allan J....5:21:31 (27,698)
Stick, Carl R....4:17:10 (12,845)
Stickells, Jonathan R....5:56:32 (32,292)
Stickland, Paul A....4:05:46 (10,300)
Stickley, John F....6:42:05 (34,723)
Stidolph, Richard A....4:23:04 (14,348)
Stidwill, Nicolas A....3:53:03 (7,580)
Stiff, Dudley K....5:52:48 (31,949)
Stiff, Michael....3:09:16 (1,499)
Stigner, Simon J....4:19:40 (13,499)
Stiles, Andy D....3:29:11 (3,602)
Still, Colin J....3:25:06 (3,030)
Still, Stuart J....4:40:50 (18,740)
Stimpson, Andrew J....5:43:09 (30,954)
Stimpson, Jason....5:09:11 (25,313)
Stinchcombe, Nigel S....3:37:48 (4,788)
Stirling, Fraser T....4:51:46 (21,430)
Stirling, Hugh....5:51:59 (31,871)
Stoakley, Robin E....4:31:14 (16,411)
Stoat, Antony D....3:53:01 (7,573)
Stoate, Howard G....4:46:29 (20,174)

Stock, Barry G 4:01:42 (9,551)
Stock, Mark P 3:16:32 (2,129)
Stock, Nicholas S 3:45:47 (6,145)
Stockdale, Andrew 4:11:10 (11,417)
Stockdale, David A 5:12:19 (25,926)
Stockdale, Desmond 5:08:29 (25,185)
Stockdale, Peter C 3:16:45 (2,152)
Stocken, Robin J 4:10:22 (11,240)
Stocker, John L 5:18:40 (27,192)
Stocking, David 3:43:23 (5,751)
Stocks, Richard 4:33:00 (16,785)
Stocks, Terry E 4:55:41 (22,423)
Stockton, Ben W 4:32:48 (16,740)
Stockwell, Mark R 4:40:23 (18,628)
Stockwin, Matthew 5:30:17 (29,181)
Stoddard, Mark 3:17:39 (2,248)
Stoddart, Daniel F 4:37:23 (17,855)
Stoddart, Noel T 4:41:58 (19,031)
Stoddart, Paul D 5:53:30 (32,008)
Stoffel, Nicholas A 4:27:20 (15,431)
Stoffell, David P 4:55:05 (22,285)
Stoffels, Johan R 4:11:03 (11,383)
Stoker, Anthony C 5:54:51 (32,130)
Stoker, Michael 3:04:29 (1,129)
Stoker, Paul A 5:06:45 (24,831)
Stokes, Barry 4:31:46 (16,520)
Stokes, Christopher A 2:42:13 (183)
Stokes, Craig M 5:12:08 (25,879)
Stokes, David K 4:54:42 (22,198)
Stokes, Dylan D 4:36:16 (17,602)
Stokes, Gavin J 3:55:05 (8,026)
Stokes, Graeme L 3:42:41 (5,625)
Stokes, Graham B 4:45:01 (19,842)
Stokes, Mark 5:15:50 (26,628)
Stokes, Michael 4:50:23 (21,093)
Stokes, Simon J 4:10:41 (11,310)
Stokes, Wayne J 3:43:53 (5,846)
Stone, Anthony C 4:44:47 (19,772)
Stone, Avid M 2:42:25 (188)
Stone, Barry 5:11:01 (25,671)
Stone, Ben J 4:35:25 (17,386)
Stone, Chris 3:03:11 (1,059)
Stone, Christian A 5:04:09 (24,350)
Stone, Christopher H 3:49:55 (6,921)
Stone, Daniel C 4:19:41 (13,504)
Stone, David F 5:17:12 (26,895)
Stone, David J 5:04:56 (24,506)
Stone, Derek C 2:52:40 (466)
Stone, Desmond 5:33:31 (29,688)
Stone, Jon 5:28:53 (28,963)
Stone, Kenneth 4:43:00 (19,297)
Stone, Kevin R 3:38:52 (4,992)
Stone, Michael H 5:14:11 (26,265)
Stone, Paul D 5:07:27 (24,989)
Stone, Philip 5:57:19 (32,354)
Stone, Roger 3:23:31 (2,852)
Stone, Simon 5:33:31 (29,688)
Stone, Stefan P 3:31:09 (3,855)
Stone, Timothy A 3:36:55 (4,677)
Stone, Timothy J 4:56:08 (22,543)
Stoneley, Jonathan R 5:20:13 (27,459)
Stoner, Simon 4:55:12 (22,318)
Stones, Darren G 4:03:21 (9,840)
Stones, Joel D 3:50:36 (7,054)
Stones, Philip L 4:58:19 (23,109)
Stones, Simon 7:26:39 (35,440)
Stoney, Jarrod P 4:18:30 (13,211)
Stoop, Nick M 4:09:53 (11,147)
Stoop, Piers W 5:28:18 (28,865)
Stopard, Nigel 3:24:57 (3,015)
Stopforth, Steven 4:18:30 (13,211)
Stopher, Jed 5:34:42 (29,874)
Stopher, Kelvin P 4:13:14 (11,889)
Storer, Daniel F 5:28:14 (28,846)
Storey, Miles 5:01:53 (23,909)
Storey, Richard H 4:02:52 (9,763)
Storey, Tom J 6:11:58 (33,424)
Storey, Will M 4:06:46 (10,521)
Storie, Ryan 4:53:51 (21,977)
Stork, Robert F 4:28:08 (15,629)
Storrie, Martin J 3:59:20 (9,050)
Story, Anthony A 6:18:57 (33,835)
Story, Thomas R 4:06:37 (10,489)
Stothard, Peter 4:22:24 (14,176)
Stothard, Simon J 3:50:55 (7,120)
Stott, Chris 5:12:24 (25,940)
Stott, Mark G 3:37:02 (4,695)
Stout, Andrew J 4:48:25 (20,636)
Stout, Brian R 2:58:09 (759)
Stow, Derek C 5:16:33 (26,767)
Stowell, David 5:35:46 (30,018)
Stowell, Michael 3:49:07 (6,754)
Strachan, David 4:26:11 (15,091)
Strachan, Stuart 4:02:12 (9,646)
Strain, David C 4:33:10 (16,830)
Strain, Justin 4:13:39 (12,007)
Straker, David J 3:18:39 (2,356)
Straker, Simon J 3:56:08 (8,259)
Stramer, Brian 3:02:29 (1,026)
Strand, Neil 4:30:28 (16,250)
Strange, Jon 5:36:11 (30,069)
Strange, Matthew T 4:30:51 (16,324)
Strange, Peter C 4:51:08 (21,275)
Strange, Peter D 4:26:44 (15,245)
Strange, Peter J 4:51:38 (21,406)
Stratford, John R 5:55:34 (32,199)
Strathearn, Daniel M 4:03:16 (9,830)
Stratton, David I 3:40:07 (5,204)
Stratton, Garry D 3:29:41 (3,671)
Stratton, Robert. J 4:13:05 (11,853)
Straughan, Ross E 4:06:14 (10,399)
Straw, David 5:27:04 (28,631)
Straw, Jonathan J 3:33:56 (4,258)
Strawbridge, James 4:57:46 (22,973)
Straziota, Pasquale 4:38:20 (18,106)
Streatfeild, Richard G 4:16:10 (12,612)
Stredwick, Mark 3:26:58 (3,272)
Street, Ian C 4:18:56 (13,314)
Street, James 3:24:50 (2,999)
Street, Jon W 3:57:13 (8,533)
Street, Liberty V 4:31:20 (16,432)
Street, Paul 4:23:07 (14,358)
Street, Paul A 3:58:51 (8,930)
Streeter, Daryl C 4:34:04 (17,043)
Streeter, Gareth B 6:10:17 (33,325)
Stretch, Gary 5:41:45 (30,804)
Stretch, Steven 5:55:02 (32,151)
Stretton, James D 5:14:42 (26,381)
Stretton, Neil W 4:06:29 (10,463)
Strickland, David 6:42:35 (34,737)
Strickland, Steven W 4:13:07 (11,860)
Strickland, Thomas W 3:23:02 (2,799)
Strimer, Marco 4:20:49 (13,807)
Stringer, David A 3:27:53 (3,394)
Stringer, Ian M 5:42:09 (30,841)
Stringer, Nicholas S 4:39:21 (18,381)
Stringfellow, Andrew J 4:46:37 (20,202)
Strohbach, Wolfgang 4:41:11 (18,836)
Strong, Craig P 4:36:00 (17,534)
Strong, Nigel G 4:44:33 (19,703)
Stroud, Andrew P 4:34:01 (17,036)
Stroud, Ben 3:11:50 (1,707)
Stroud, Tom 4:34:27 (17,135)
Strudwick, Andrew P 4:50:20 (21,075)
Strudwick, Peter J 3:57:58 (8,712)
Struggl, Andreas 3:40:37 (5,287)
Strugnell, Mark A 5:35:40 (30,009)
Strutt, Barry J 4:54:55 (22,250)
Stryczek, John J 3:29:32 (3,652)
Strydom, Grant A 5:22:59 (27,936)
Strydon, Nelis 5:17:16 (26,912)
Stua, William 3:52:24 (7,451)
Stuart, Keith M 6:11:25 (33,396)
Stuart, Malcolm M 4:16:30 (12,698)
Stuart, Peter G 4:41:36 (18,948)
Stuart-Leach, Christopher 3:56:47 (8,428)
Stubbings, Darren 6:20:24 (33,913)
Stubbings, Martin 5:15:19 (26,528)
Stubbs, Adrian K 4:34:03 (17,039)
Stubbs, Daniel A 6:25:35 (34,151)
Stubbs, Gareth W 3:29:48 (3,688)
Stubbs, James L 4:31:17 (16,419)
Stubbs, Neil 5:32:25 (29,511)
Stubbs, Nicholas J 3:59:02 (8,965)
Stubbs, Paul A 5:22:32 (27,862)
Stubbs, Tim B 3:43:47 (5,826)
Studd, Neil 5:16:51 (26,820)
Studley, John G 4:17:56 (13,052)
Studwell, David J 3:32:41 (4,094)
Stuehmeier, Joerg 4:00:56 (9,405)
Stuempel, Frank 4:15:50 (12,518)
Stukas, Paul 3:57:19 (8,559)
Stummel, Henning F 4:13:20 (11,917)
Stumpf, Stefan 4:38:06 (18,040)
Stumpf, William O 4:54:37 (22,177)
Sturdy, Christopher S 5:06:56 (24,865)
Sturdy, Jonathan R 5:26:49 (28,593)
Sturges, Joshua A 5:02:33 (24,051)
Sturgess, Gavin O 4:59:07 (23,292)
Sturgess, Phillip J 4:06:33 (10,476)
Sturgess, Robert A 4:36:12 (17,581)
Sturgess, Simon P 5:05:30 (24,602)
Sturla, Timothy S 4:52:07 (21,519)
Sturm, Wolfgang F 4:42:58 (19,290)
Sturman, Darren L 4:55:43 (22,433)
Stutchbury, James M 6:29:26 (34,306)
Stvenson, Michael H 4:43:36 (19,440)
Styles, Elliot 5:40:11 (30,616)
Styles, Paul A 6:21:18 (33,971)
Stylianou, Andrew A 3:47:53 (6,509)
Stylianou, Pantelis 5:20:40 (27,550)
Stylo, Adam W 5:14:13 (26,270)
Such, Stephen D 3:19:58 (2,490)
Suchet, Rob 3:37:00 (4,686)
Sudbury, Nicholas D 4:27:40 (15,509)
Suff, Maxwell P 3:13:56 (1,897)
Sugarhood, Paul A 3:33:53 (4,250)
Sugden, Ben H 2:53:55 (518)
Sugden, Jason J 4:33:55 (17,011)
Sugden, Neil J 4:56:12 (22,564)
Sugg, Elliott J 5:02:05 (23,947)
Suggett, Lee B 8:18:41 (35,666)
Sughayer, Najeeb 4:44:08 (19,571)
Sujimoto, Daisuke 3:17:52 (2,268)
Suleman, Aarif 4:49:06 (20,796)
Suleman, Karim 5:48:49 (31,562)
Sulley, Andrew F 4:54:09 (22,062)
Sullivan, Daniel J 4:21:08 (13,882)
Sullivan, David J 7:18:33 (35,377)
Sullivan, Daviean R 6:48:18 (34,894)
Sullivan, Dieter L 5:37:06 (30,181)
Sullivan, James P 5:06:44 (24,826)
Sullivan, John C 5:25:44 (28,413)
Sullivan, Liam P 5:38:16 (30,350)
Sullivan, Mark J 4:30:06 (16,174)
Sullivan, Neil C 4:38:15 (18,068)
Sullivan, Patrick J 4:36:28 (17,657)
Sullivan, Paul J 4:18:16 (13,137)
Sullivan, Rob 5:18:05 (27,074)
Sullivan, Stuart C 6:05:43 (33,023)
Sullivan, Tomas J 5:44:33 (31,099)
Sully, Keith 4:38:29 (18,146)
Sulman, Keith B 5:54:07 (32,065)
Sum, Nick 5:11:49 (25,817)
Sumboo, Dev 7:04:52 (35,201)
Summerfield, Richard 3:35:21 (4,460)
Summers, Andrew J 4:00:15 (9,263)
Summers, Derek G 4:51:49 (21,440)
Summers, Martin A 3:28:04 (3,414)
Summers, Ryan 5:57:55 (32,406)
Summers, Stephen P 4:15:24 (12,418)
Summerskill, Andrew D 3:56:50 (8,439)
Summerton, John 6:44:48 (34,795)
Summerton, Phillip A 4:01:14 (9,466)
Sumner, Clifford 5:28:53 (28,963)
Sumner, Daniel G 4:17:14 (12,861)
Sumner, Joseph 3:31:10 (3,858)
Sumner, Marc D 4:54:04 (22,033)
Sumner, Timothy D 5:29:52 (29,117)
Sumpton, Christopher A 5:31:30 (29,377)
Sunderland, Darren L 6:25:33 (34,150)
Sundstrup, Henrik 4:33:56 (17,016)
Sundvik, Harri H 3:56:41 (8,399)
Sunner, Pavitar S 5:22:25 (27,836)
Sunye Sotomayor, Javier 5:09:45 (25,425)
Suorkdal, Bjoern 3:14:16 (1,921)
Supple, Kevin S 4:57:35 (22,926)
Supple, Martin L 4:57:35 (22,926)
Surcouf, Raoul 4:29:17 (15,934)

Surfield, Christopher	3:54:15 (7,855)	
Surget, Jacky	3:43:09 (5,714)	
Surplice, Andy N	3:49:24 (6,808)	
Surratt, Robert W	5:16:54 (26,840)	
Surridge, Andrew	4:15:40 (12,478)	
Surry, Dominic	4:22:05 (14,105)	
Sussex, John S.	5:27:06 (28,638)	
Sustins, Gordon C	4:28:23 (15,695)	
Sutcliffe, Alistair P	4:37:01 (17,793)	
Sutcliffe, Nigel	5:16:12 (26,700)	
Suter, John P	5:35:49 (30,025)	
Suter, Paul R	4:40:55 (18,768)	
Sutherland, David J	4:20:27 (13,719)	
Sutherland, Graham	4:29:29 (15,998)	
Sutherland, Graham T	3:48:24 (6,595)	
Sutherland, Leslie	4:50:55 (21,221)	
Sutton, Andrew C	3:31:54 (3,972)	
Sutton, Darren	4:25:45 (15,006)	
Sutton, Graham M	5:44:46 (31,125)	
Sutton, Ian J	3:47:36 (6,447)	
Sutton, John D	3:53:09 (7,603)	
Sutton, Jonathan L	3:25:37 (3,079)	
Sutton, Kevin J	5:29:00 (28,984)	
Sutton, Malcolm J	4:19:45 (13,524)	
Sutton, Martin C	4:19:13 (13,379)	
Sutton, Nigel D	4:59:36 (23,412)	
Sutton, Paul A	5:45:24 (31,192)	
Sutton, Philip M	4:44:10 (19,587)	
Sutton, Reece	4:30:32 (16,261)	
Sutton, Richard A	4:14:05 (12,120)	
Sutton, Richard A	4:17:38 (12,982)	
Sutton, Richard J	4:33:12 (16,846)	
Sutton, Robert D	4:05:31 (10,241)	
Sutton, Shaun J	4:27:18 (15,425)	
Svanberg, Mikael	3:37:50 (4,794)	
Sveen, Halvor	3:03:03 (1,053)	
Svendsen, David	4:39:27 (18,404)	
Svensson, Benet-Ake	4:28:31 (15,730)	
Swadling, Michael P	5:08:10 (25,131)	
Swain, Benjamin J	4:58:13 (23,080)	
Swain, Chris	4:06:45 (10,513)	
Swain, Gavin J	4:26:47 (15,260)	
Swain, Russell J	5:51:05 (31,784)	
Swain, Tom M	4:46:35 (20,196)	
Swaine, Alan	4:59:04 (23,277)	
Swaine, Michael	4:32:30 (16,662)	
Swainson, David J	4:15:29 (12,439)	
Swainson, Mike J	5:15:24 (26,544)	
Swales, Darren	4:02:49 (9,757)	
Swallow, Craig P	4:19:59 (13,599)	
Swallow, Phillip	4:00:31 (9,314)	
Swallow, Robert S	5:29:07 (28,998)	
Swallow, Thomas W	3:28:45 (3,531)	
Swan, Alan	3:22:10 (2,719)	
Swan, Charles T	3:58:23 (8,805)	
Swan, Kim R	4:09:13 (11,010)	
Swan, Robert C	5:48:07 (31,481)	
Swan, Toby W	4:46:42 (20,216)	
Swanepoel, Anthony	3:51:38 (7,283)	
Swanepoel, Peter M	3:52:49 (7,531)	
Swanevelder, Justiaan L	3:59:06 (8,988)	
Swann, David	4:28:08 (15,629)	
Swann, David J	3:29:03 (3,581)	
Swann, Graham A	4:47:47 (20,478)	
Swann, Roger	3:58:50 (8,921)	
Swannell, Ian J	3:50:42 (7,078)	
Swanson, Lorraine	6:25:06 (34,133)	
Swanton, Paul N	2:48:07 (315)	
Swarbrick, Joe	3:28:30 (3,485)	
Swarbrick, Michael	3:50:24 (7,020)	
Swarbrick, Michael	4:54:20 (22,106)	
Swart, Nico	3:16:35 (2,132)	
Swash, Kevin R	4:18:57 (13,319)	
Swatton, Neville R	3:26:17 (3,172)	
Swayne, Richard P	5:08:52 (25,256)	
Sweeney, Andrew	3:43:42 (5,811)	
Sweeney, Andrew J	4:58:22 (23,124)	
Sweeney, Derek F	4:06:58 (10,566)	
Sweeney, Iain J	5:17:33 (26,969)	
Sweeney, John	5:48:14 (31,494)	
Sweeney, John J	4:27:25 (15,454)	
Sweeney, Jonathan D	4:38:35 (18,170)	
Sweeney, Mark	4:45:51 (20,020)	
Sweeney, Michael A	4:04:20 (10,030)	
Sweeney, Paul	5:26:33 (28,548)	
Sweeney, Paul A	3:59:57 (9,198)	
Sweeney, Paul D	4:58:53 (23,224)	
Sweeney, Simon	3:56:57 (8,466)	
Sweet, David P	3:14:31 (1,943)	
Sweet, Michael C	6:39:14 (34,648)	
Sweet, William H	3:27:12 (3,309)	
Sweetingham, Craig W	4:45:06 (19,861)	
Sweetlove, Malcolm	3:38:26 (4,908)	
Sweetman, David A	5:04:21 (24,390)	
Sweetman, Jeff M	5:16:50 (26,815)	
Swift, Andrew	3:22:15 (2,723)	
Swift, Carl A	4:45:25 (19,927)	
Swift, Chris J	4:18:27 (13,196)	
Swift, Derek A	4:18:24 (13,174)	
Swift, Derrick J	3:21:16 (2,631)	
Swift, Edward	3:55:10 (8,051)	
Swift, Gary P	5:04:49 (24,472)	
Swift, James M	5:15:56 (26,648)	
Swift, Lee J	4:24:38 (14,734)	
Swift, Simeon A	3:54:38 (7,930)	
Swift, William H	4:36:48 (17,740)	
Swindells, Paul	4:21:13 (13,899)	
Swinden, Mark	4:10:48 (11,327)	
Swords, Jon	3:52:16 (7,425)	
Sycamore, Paul C	6:00:36 (32,630)	
Syers, Graham E	3:11:34 (1,676)	
Sykes, Adam	3:53:05 (7,587)	
Sykes, Glenn	4:05:44 (10,295)	
Sykes, Julian P	3:35:18 (4,449)	
Sykes, Paul D	5:04:41 (24,445)	
Syme, David	4:31:06 (16,381)	
Symeou, Joseph A	4:36:14 (17,592)	
Symeou, Nicos	4:36:14 (17,592)	
Symes, Robert	3:31:41 (3,939)	
Symms, Nigel J	5:18:54 (27,234)	
Symonds, Barrie J	3:24:47 (2,994)	
Symons, David W	3:58:37 (8,857)	
Symons, Marcus F	4:39:17 (18,357)	
Symons, Nicholas J	5:37:30 (30,235)	
Synge, Timothy	4:25:28 (14,940)	
Syrett, Jason K	3:35:04 (4,415)	
Syrett, Paul J	4:33:01 (16,791)	
Systad, Espen	3:37:27 (4,745)	
Szilagyi, Laszlo	3:27:57 (3,402)	
Szilard, Gabor	3:22:40 (2,763)	
Szkwarok, Stefan	4:01:51 (9,578)	
Szynaka, Stefan	5:11:11 (25,698)	
Taberner, Matt P	3:05:29 (1,199)	
Tabib, Daniel H	3:25:46 (3,097)	
Tabor, Paul A	4:08:11 (10,808)	
Tack, Ian R	3:16:01 (2,080)	
Tackley, Adam R	4:18:37 (13,245)	
Taft, David A	6:18:43 (33,819)	
Taft, Michael	4:44:44 (19,753)	
Tager, Alejandro	4:53:25 (21,868)	
Taggart, Ian	3:22:36 (2,755)	
Taggart, Mark J	5:36:25 (30,101)	
Tahitu, Ronald F	4:53:12 (21,810)	
Tain, Daniel R	5:25:20 (28,327)	
Tainsh, Robert	5:45:26 (31,195)	
Tait, Alan S	2:58:14 (764)	
Tait, Ian	2:59:48 (886)	
Tait, John S	6:32:06 (34,412)	
Tait, Oliver T	4:49:04 (20,783)	
Tait, Richard A	3:05:40 (1,213)	
Taiwo, Ayo	4:04:49 (10,116)	
Talamantes-Silva, Jesus	5:25:09 (28,297)	
Talbot, Adrian M	7:29:48 (35,495)	
Talbot, Colin A	3:24:36 (2,969)	
Talbot, Edward C	4:39:39 (18,449)	
Talbot, Richard J	3:51:21 (7,209)	
Talbot, Sean V	3:55:49 (8,187)	
Talbot, Simon C	4:27:58 (15,578)	
Talbot, Wilf	5:32:00 (29,451)	
Taller, Gabor	4:21:49 (14,036)	
Tallier, Alain J	4:45:17 (19,900)	
Tallis, Steven W	4:52:48 (21,700)	
Tallott, Giles	4:27:44 (15,529)	
Talmage, Alan J	5:38:16 (30,350)	
Talowarn, Louis M	3:47:55 (6,514)	
Tamada, Katsutaka	5:04:19 (24,379)	
Tamang, Saran	3:47:49 (6,499)	
Tambling, Daniel P	4:10:16 (11,222)	
Tambour, Torbjorn	3:23:46 (2,875)	
Tame, Ian D	5:33:31 (29,688)	
Tame, Kevin M	4:12:08 (11,639)	
Tameza, Florian	4:20:10 (13,645)	
Tamoni, Daniele	3:02:46 (1,040)	
Tan, Joon Y	4:38:45 (18,212)	
Tanaka, Hideharu	4:40:51 (18,747)	
Tanara, Alexandre	4:07:04 (10,587)	
Tandy, Simon P	5:49:45 (31,653)	
Tang, Simon	5:29:55 (29,120)	
Tanini, Andrea	4:53:48 (21,964)	
Tann, Edmund J	3:53:45 (7,738)	
Tann, Simon C	4:28:52 (15,825)	
Tanner, Adrian G	2:47:17 (291)	
Tanner, Ian D	3:42:09 (5,545)	
Tanner, Jonathan E	3:40:32 (5,276)	
Tanner, Joseph R	4:46:55 (20,257)	
Tanner, Keith E	4:41:05 (18,807)	
Tanner, Martin J	4:47:49 (20,482)	
Tanner, Thomas	3:28:32 (3,494)	
Tannian, Mark	3:39:06 (5,033)	
Tant, Mark D	4:45:15 (19,893)	
Tapley, John	3:22:37 (2,757)	
Taplin, Alan J	4:36:29 (17,659)	
Taplin, Derek R	4:32:40 (16,709)	
Taplin, Steve P	3:15:40 (2,045)	
Tapp, Ashley R	4:28:35 (15,754)	
Tapp, Edward J	3:56:27 (8,346)	
Tappenden, Robert E	4:16:33 (12,704)	
Tapper, Paul	3:45:47 (6,145)	
Tappin, Nick D	4:49:27 (20,874)	
Taranik, Dan	8:19:03 (35,667)	
Tarcea, Florian E	5:27:10 (28,654)	
Tarcsai, Laszlo	3:18:15 (2,319)	
Tardivo, Sylvain	3:28:51 (3,547)	
Tarleton, Michael P	5:29:30 (29,070)	
Tarnai, Tibor	4:31:19 (16,428)	
Tarpey, Patrick M	4:48:55 (20,750)	
Tarplee, Simon R	3:00:20 (919)	
Tarr, Gary P	3:49:40 (6,862)	
Tarragano, Joe	4:27:59 (15,582)	
Tarragona-Fiol, Tony	5:29:13 (29,027)	
Tarrant, Andrew R	4:03:41 (9,901)	
Tarrant, Dominic	4:36:48 (17,740)	
Tarrant, Nick G	5:54:33 (32,110)	
Tarrant, Thomas S	4:10:46 (11,322)	
Tarrant, Tony C	4:16:01 (12,570)	
Tarratt, Christopher S	3:53:34 (7,702)	
Tassi, Francesco	3:51:54 (7,337)	
Tate, Andrew R	3:34:39 (4,358)	
Tate, Gabriel J	4:51:12 (21,286)	
Tate, Kevin	5:13:50 (26,197)	
Tate, Paul A	3:49:06 (6,751)	
Tate, Stephen R	4:57:23 (22,883)	
Tatman, James C	5:15:38 (26,590)	
Tattersall, Michael J	4:17:19 (12,880)	
Tattersall, Neil	4:44:09 (19,579)	
Tattley, James	4:16:58 (12,808)	
Tatum, Mark	5:52:38 (31,934)	
Taunton-Burnet, William D	5:40:58 (30,702)	
Taut, Thomas	4:41:17 (18,858)	
Tavano, Vincenzo	5:10:56 (25,654)	
Tavarone, Michael A	5:02:19 (23,993)	
Tavernaro, Sandro	4:24:21 (14,665)	
Taverner, Mark V	5:11:47 (25,808)	
Taverner, Philip J	5:13:55 (26,213)	
Tavernor, Jack	4:30:27 (16,246)	
Taviner, Nick	3:58:12 (8,760)	
Tayabali, Asad	5:33:22 (29,660)	
Tayfur, Hasan	4:36:40 (17,708)	
Taylor, Adam	3:09:10 (1,483)	
Taylor, Adrian P	4:11:29 (11,496)	
Taylor, Alan	3:32:50 (4,111)	
Taylor, Andrew E	4:35:06 (17,298)	
Taylor, Andrew J	5:46:33 (31,313)	
Taylor, Andrew P	3:46:39 (6,276)	
Taylor, Andrew P	3:56:32 (8,369)	
Taylor, Andrew P	4:03:21 (9,840)	
Taylor, Andrew S	3:49:38 (6,858)	
Taylor, Benjamin N	5:35:52 (30,033)	
Taylor, Bob	4:27:32 (15,475)	

Thomas, Peter 3:11:09 (1,645)
Thomas, Phillip G 3:56:59 (8,476)
Thomas, Richard 5:22:10 (27,804)
Thomas, Richard C 3:09:38 (1,525)
Thomas, Richard L 4:31:25 (16,444)
Thomas, Richard P 3:55:33 (8,126)
Thomas, Robert D 4:53:32 (21,894)
Thomas, Robert K 5:09:44 (25,422)
Thomas, Robert M 3:50:43 (7,082)
Thomas, Russell 3:30:05 (3,731)
Thomas, Shaun 3:55:57 (8,217)
Thomas, Simon H 5:10:08 (25,513)
Thomas, Simon M 4:02:12 (9,646)
Thomas, Stephen 2:45:18 (247)
Thomas, Stephen G 4:42:17 (19,121)
Thomas, Stephen J 4:21:51 (14,049)
Thomas, Steven P 4:03:55 (9,950)
Thomas, Stuart W 4:34:30 (17,148)
Thomas, Teifion B 3:38:22 (4,897)
Thomas, Trevor J 5:56:35 (32,299)
Thomas, Wade 3:46:08 (6,200)
Thomas, Wayne 5:32:37 (29,551)
Thomas, Will 5:04:33 (24,425)
Thomason, Francis L 4:06:51 (10,540)
Thomassin, Mathias 3:17:41 (2,250)
Thomlinson, James 4:11:50 (11,578)
Thompson, Adam W 4:10:32 (11,274)
Thompson, Alan 6:19:10 (33,847)
Thompson, Alan B 4:16:52 (12,775)
Thompson, Alastair J 4:17:55 (13,047)
Thompson, Alex R 3:27:17 (3,323)
Thompson, Alexander J 4:01:29 (9,512)
Thompson, Andrew 3:50:50 (7,102)
Thompson, Andrew 3:57:50 (8,677)
Thompson, Andrew D 2:53:41 (508)
Thompson, Ashley 3:42:23 (5,581)
Thompson, Ben 4:12:00 (11,613)
Thompson, Chrstopher 5:18:15 (27,113)
Thompson, Daniel 6:29:37 (34,313)
Thompson, David 3:58:27 (8,822)
Thompson, David 5:06:05 (24,710)
Thompson, David 5:17:57 (27,041)
Thompson, David A 4:11:08 (11,407)
Thompson, David M 2:54:04 (521)
Thompson, David M 3:03:32 (1,079)
Thompson, David R 4:50:05 (21,020)
Thompson, David S 4:40:25 (18,634)
Thompson, Gregg A 5:13:28 (26,116)
Thompson, Guy R 4:05:03 (10,153)
Thompson, Ian J 3:19:35 (2,441)
Thompson, James J 3:13:52 (1,890)
Thompson, James O 5:19:27 (27,327)
Thompson, John 5:45:24 (31,192)
Thompson, John P 4:36:12 (17,581)
Thompson, Joshua A 3:41:06 (5,382)
Thompson, Keith N 3:25:56 (3,120)
Thompson, Kevin E 4:55:37 (22,414)
Thompson, Mark 4:43:47 (19,476)
Thompson, Melvyn R 4:57:05 (22,792)
Thompson, Michael E 4:34:52 (17,240)
Thompson, Michael G 5:04:08 (24,348)
Thompson, Michael J 3:40:07 (5,204)
Thompson, Nathan 5:19:52 (27,402)
Thompson, Nicholas J 4:14:40 (12,249)
Thompson, Nigel P 2:39:34 (140)
Thompson, Paul 2:31:47 (48)
Thompson, Paul 5:34:14 (29,801)
Thompson, Paul D 6:28:37 (34,270)
Thompson, Paul R 4:59:45 (23,443)
Thompson, Peter A 5:54:31 (32,109)
Thompson, Phillip J 3:38:00 (4,830)
Thompson, Richard A 3:04:53 (1,152)
Thompson, Robert 4:22:00 (14,087)
Thompson, Scott 4:35:21 (17,372)
Thompson, Scott G 3:56:03 (8,235)
Thompson, Stephen N 5:37:34 (30,242)
Thompson, Steven 6:26:18 (34,188)
Thompson, Stuart 3:06:55 (1,305)
Thompson, Stuart A 4:27:49 (15,543)
Thompson, Stuart W 5:02:23 (24,010)
Thompson, Timothy T 4:35:07 (17,303)
Thompson, Trevor G 4:33:18 (16,867)
Thompson, William 6:08:18 (33,194)
Thompson-Dredge, Owen 3:56:42 (8,406)
Thoms, Derek F 4:15:36 (12,460)
Thomsen, Anders 4:32:06 (16,581)
Thomsen, Morten 5:11:03 (25,676)
Thomson, Alex J 4:13:14 (11,889)
Thomson, Andrew J 4:11:08 (11,407)
Thomson, Blair 3:25:04 (3,027)
Thomson, David 4:41:15 (18,851)
Thomson, David B 2:45:45 (258)
Thomson, David W 4:06:44 (10,509)
Thomson, Douglas 5:08:33 (25,195)
Thomson, Graeme 5:58:20 (32,451)
Thomson, Gregory D 4:45:27 (19,934)
Thomson, Keith R 5:29:10 (29,017)
Thomson, Mark 4:54:28 (22,139)
Thomson, Mark J 4:29:50 (16,101)
Thomson, Martin D 5:14:09 (26,257)
Thomson, Martin P 3:12:15 (1,750)
Thomson, Michael A 3:16:02 (2,081)
Thomson, Neil C 4:40:52 (18,752)
Thomson, Paul D 3:29:33 (3,657)
Thomson, Robert 4:55:46 (22,450)
Thomson, Stephen 3:07:20 (1,337)
Thomson, Steven 4:19:07 (13,359)
Thorell, Johan 4:16:45 (12,751)
Thoren, Bjorn 4:19:03 (13,337)
Thorgood, George A 6:23:23 (34,049)
Thorley, Matthew S 5:31:31 (29,378)
Thorman, Darren W 5:33:17 (29,641)
Thorn, Jake P 5:07:00 (24,883)
Thorn, Richard I 2:44:40 (232)
Thornby, David G 4:09:17 (11,024)
Thorne, Andrew 5:21:23 (27,673)
Thorne, Colin 5:25:24 (28,341)
Thorne, Kevin M 4:53:05 (21,771)
Thorne, Rob 5:03:09 (24,160)
Thorne, Robin M 4:14:51 (12,278)
Thorne, Stephen J 4:48:02 (20,541)
Thorneloe, Guy R 3:08:55 (1,460)
Thorner, Roddy G 4:25:27 (14,934)
Thorneton-Field, Matthew 5:31:12 (29,335)
Thornewell, Piers B 5:29:18 (29,039)
Thorneycroft, Martin P 3:12:05 (1,738)
Thornhill, Francis J 4:17:48 (13,023)
Thornhill, Ric 4:24:07 (14,603)
Thornton, Craig C 4:20:16 (13,670)
Thornton, Dean A 3:20:55 (2,600)
Thornton, James O 3:51:43 (7,297)
Thornton, Jeff 3:24:56 (3,012)
Thornton, John 5:19:13 (27,295)
Thornton, Keith J 3:16:19 (2,105)
Thornton, Lee 5:13:14 (26,084)
Thornton, Stanley 4:56:11 (22,559)
Thorpe, Jason 5:13:00 (26,048)
Thorpe, Julian R 3:56:15 (8,286)
Thorpe, Martyn 4:13:58 (12,089)
Thorpe, Nick 4:06:28 (10,458)
Thorpe, Oliver 5:03:47 (24,288)
Thorpe, Paul J 3:51:18 (7,202)
Thorsen, Philip 3:33:58 (4,266)
Thrale, Daniel P 4:20:57 (13,840)
Thranberend, Klaus 4:28:16 (15,662)
Thraves, Jon M 3:10:20 (1,591)
Threadgold, Robert 5:02:24 (24,018)
Threadgold, Robin J 3:15:20 (2,022)
Threlkeld, Alex J 3:58:55 (8,942)
Thresh, Brian 5:07:23 (24,975)
Thrift, Jonathan M 3:40:19 (5,236)
Throssell, Stephen 3:09:11 (1,485)
Thrower, David F 3:05:53 (1,228)
Thubisi, Kabelo M 5:18:02 (27,064)
Thumwood, Michael E 4:55:04 (22,282)
Thun-Ho-Henstein, Christian 4:36:13 (17,585)
Thurgood, Hugh A 4:20:08 (13,637)
Thurgood, Joe V 4:20:08 (13,637)
Thurley, Adam 5:09:43 (25,419)
Thurlwell, Jonathan R 4:11:27 (11,490)
Thurman, Simon W 4:20:31 (13,736)
Thurtle, Gary D 4:31:04 (16,368)
Thury, Juergen 5:13:23 (26,096)
Thushyanthan, Vivekanathan 4:51:16 (21,300)
Thuy, Wim 3:46:46 (6,296)
Tibbitts, Peter 3:43:31 (5,783)
Tibbles, David S 6:24:12 (34,087)
Tibbles, Mark W 3:31:37 (3,931)
Tickner, Paul 4:53:11 (21,804)
Tickner, Richard D 5:22:02 (27,786)
Tickner, Tony J 4:47:16 (20,347)
Tidder, Anthony R 4:21:09 (13,889)
Tidiman, Steve 3:12:40 (1,795)
Tidury, Colin E 5:54:18 (32,080)
Tidy, Gary D 4:19:57 (13,589)
Tiengo, Renzo 4:20:02 (13,606)
Tierney, Trevor D 4:08:35 (10,888)
Tietz, Karl 3:22:28 (2,744)
Tietze, Andrews 3:29:52 (3,702)
Tijerina, Mentor 4:54:59 (22,261)
Tilbrook, Christopher J 2:59:09 (837)
Tilbrook, David J 5:02:14 (23,974)
Tiley, Daniel A 4:24:25 (14,685)
Tilke, Warren 4:03:07 (9,804)
Till, Matthew J 4:21:00 (13,853)
Tillbrooke, Tony 4:38:16 (18,077)
Tiller, Mathew D 4:21:55 (14,069)
Tiller, Roger E 5:50:49 (31,759)
Tiller, Russell N 5:31:41 (29,402)
Tillery, Paul 4:25:20 (14,904)
Tilley, Anthony J 4:54:10 (22,069)
Tilley, Duncan E 6:29:18 (34,298)
Tilley, Ian R 5:20:46 (27,567)
Tilley, Jason 3:07:58 (1,385)
Tillyer, Bryan 4:05:53 (10,327)
Tillyer, Dave W 5:52:16 (31,899)
Tillyer, David J 3:38:38 (4,945)
Tilt, Ralph L 3:38:04 (4,846)
Timbrell, Wayne J 4:29:03 (15,867)
Timlin, John P 4:31:11 (16,401)
Timlin, Shane M 5:11:24 (25,741)
Timmins, Adrian 2:51:00 (410)
Timmins, Gary D 4:39:10 (18,324)
Timmins, Rodney J 4:17:42 (12,996)
Timmis, Charles E 3:26:04 (3,136)
Timmis, Craig S 5:24:49 (28,240)
Timms, Anthony R 4:07:36 (10,680)
Timms, Russell J 3:49:10 (6,761)
Timms, Terence W 3:07:40 (1,356)
Timoney, Wayne 4:54:06 (22,041)
Timothy, Kevin M 5:42:47 (30,904)
Timson, Richard 3:27:17 (3,323)
Tindall, Dave W 5:01:39 (23,862)
Tindall, Simon R 4:42:40 (19,219)
Tindall, Thomas J 3:40:28 (5,257)
Tindill, Troy 4:24:49 (14,785)
Tindle, Robert J 5:28:06 (28,818)
Tingey, Nigel J 5:14:45 (26,396)
Tink, Andy E 4:28:03 (15,608)
Tinker, Antony A 4:04:33 (10,067)
Tinniswood, Russell 4:30:28 (16,250)
Tinsley, David 4:00:31 (9,314)
Tinsley, Ian D 4:00:41 (9,354)
Tinton, Glen W 4:45:40 (19,985)
Tinworth, Mark S 5:17:58 (27,049)
Tiplady, David R 3:30:43 (3,808)
Tipper, Robert L 5:05:50 (24,659)
Tippet, Simon J 5:06:06 (24,712)
Tippett, Graham 3:57:43 (8,657)
Tippins, Jason N 6:00:30 (32,622)
Tipton, Andrew K 3:35:31 (4,486)
Tissier, Dominique 4:05:22 (10,212)
Titchener, John B 4:23:54 (14,544)
Titcombe, Anthony W 3:52:03 (7,378)
Titcombe, Michael D 4:26:53 (15,288)
Titheridge, Alex P 3:53:02 (7,577)
Titley, Marcus M 4:16:35 (12,712)
Titley, Sam 4:41:45 (18,975)
Titmus, Gregg 4:23:31 (14,451)
Tittle, Dave J 4:00:32 (9,318)
Tivnan, Brian E 5:10:21 (25,548)
To, Ken 4:34:28 (17,141)
Tobin, David J 4:58:07 (23,058)
Tobin, Michael V 4:30:29 (16,254)
Tobisawa, Ikkei 6:19:49 (33,881)
Toby, Jackson 3:50:31 (7,045)
Tocknell, Paul D 4:30:29 (16,254)
Tod, Raymond J 5:43:40 (31,009)
Todd, David W 3:57:04 (8,494)

Todd, Ian	4:19:58 (13,594)	
Todd, James H	3:50:27 (7,029)	
Todd, John B	3:05:55 (1,229)	
Todd, Michael	6:10:23 (33,329)	
Todd, Robert B	5:17:57 (27,041)	
Todd, Stephen A	5:50:47 (31,756)	
Todd-Dunning, Chris J	4:23:51 (14,530)	
Toft, Michael D	5:28:16 (28,855)	
Tofte, Matt H	6:43:44 (34,765)	
Togwell, Jamie T	4:42:43 (19,233)	
Tolcher, Michael C	4:40:08 (18,565)	
Tole, Richard P	4:44:13 (19,604)	
Toleman, Martin J	5:56:28 (32,282)	
Tolfrey, Neil	3:21:45 (2,680)	
Tolhurst, Lee A	3:11:05 (1,640)	
Toll, Alexander J	3:01:09 (966)	
Toller, James W	4:10:37 (11,292)	
Tollet, Paul	4:11:57 (11,603)	
Tolley, Andrew P	4:18:34 (13,230)	
Tolley, Stuart A	4:19:39 (13,494)	
Tolley, Tom W	4:34:57 (17,257)	
Tolliday, Clive W	4:57:00 (22,772)	
Tollner, Kenneth I	3:45:20 (6,070)	
Tolman, Brian C	5:44:30 (31,094)	
Tomalin, Ian D	5:55:45 (32,213)	
Tomasome, Michele R	3:33:35 (4,210)	
Tomassi, Nick	3:31:49 (3,957)	
Tomaszewski, Peter	4:15:50 (12,518)	
Tombling, Anthony	5:33:08 (29,624)	
Tombs, Jonathan M	3:38:50 (4,983)	
Tomkins, Nicholas A	3:46:58 (6,338)	
Tomkins, Paul J	3:49:18 (6,796)	
Tomkins, Stephen P	4:22:43 (14,264)	
Tomlin, David L	2:52:01 (440)	
Tomlinson, Andrew M	3:55:32 (8,121)	
Tomlinson, Dennis J	3:29:38 (3,665)	
Tomlinson, Fred	7:34:36 (35,530)	
Tomlinson, Ian M	4:19:42 (13,510)	
Tomlinson, James E	4:15:36 (12,460)	
Tomlinson, Jeremy S	2:48:25 (329)	
Tomlinson, John	3:07:53 (1,379)	
Tomlinson, Lee M	2:53:35 (499)	
Tomlinson, Mark W	3:17:25 (2,219)	
Tomlinson, Michael	3:28:11 (3,432)	
Tomlinson, Mick P	4:29:26 (15,986)	
Tomlinson, Paul	5:39:24 (30,507)	
Tompsett, Rory J	5:37:04 (30,179)	
Tompson, Stephen R	4:33:28 (16,906)	
Toms, David A	4:35:19 (17,363)	
Toms, Lee W	3:59:31 (9,097)	
Tondini, Nicola	4:15:21 (12,406)	
Toner, Neil	3:54:23 (7,880)	
Tongue, Steven R	5:01:17 (23,789)	
Tonkin, Craig	3:34:20 (4,322)	
Tonks, Alan	6:12:25 (33,452)	
Toogood, James J	5:48:03 (31,472)	
Toone, Richard S	4:12:55 (11,809)	
Tootell, Simon P	3:37:22 (4,728)	
Tootill, Ian	4:57:58 (23,025)	
Tooze, Matthew D	4:15:34 (12,453)	
Topiwala, Hinesh	3:45:26 (6,088)	
Topliffe, David R	4:47:02 (20,295)	
Topp, Simon R	5:06:04 (24,707)	
Topper, Steve	3:49:10 (6,761)	
Topping, Bill	4:14:38 (12,242)	
Toquero, Lawrence	4:15:23 (12,416)	
Torija, Carlos	3:10:04 (1,564)	
Torija, José	2:56:13 (623)	
Torley, John	8:56:06 (35,689)	
Torpie, Gordon M	3:26:21 (3,180)	
Torr, Joseph W	3:57:44 (8,660)	
Torr, Peter M	3:25:26 (3,056)	
Torrens, Jamie C	4:12:18 (11,685)	
Torrens, Pip	3:47:39 (6,466)	
Torres, Angel	5:06:13 (24,744)	
Tosin, Mirko	4:39:51 (18,498)	
Tossell, Stewart	4:29:12 (15,914)	
Toth, Robert	4:40:07 (18,560)	
Tothill, Michael D	3:24:24 (2,948)	
Tottenham, Hugh L	3:33:47 (4,236)	
Toupin, Claude	4:11:55 (11,596)	
Toury, Didier	4:21:15 (13,903)	
Tout, John G	6:14:34 (33,583)	
Tovey, Neil P	4:52:35 (21,635)	
Tovey, Stephen C	3:30:29 (3,785)	
Towart, Gavin	4:00:07 (9,230)	
Towell, Jason O	6:31:33 (34,384)	
Towell, Shaun A	4:22:46 (14,279)	
Tower, Scott B	5:41:30 (30,769)	
Towers, Andy	3:52:41 (7,497)	
Towers, Paul D	3:27:25 (3,345)	
Towler, Mike W	5:38:42 (30,417)	
Towler, Stewart J	3:39:05 (5,030)	
Town, Jamie C	3:52:30 (7,468)	
Towner, Justin R	3:45:36 (6,113)	
Townley, Richard M	4:57:38 (22,939)	
Towns, Justin	5:15:23 (26,540)	
Townsend, David	6:20:21 (33,911)	
Townsend, Gerald E	3:47:14 (6,384)	
Townsend, John	3:57:17 (8,549)	
Townsend, Martin B	3:24:23 (2,947)	
Townsend, Philip M	3:23:32 (2,853)	
Townsend, Terence N	3:51:25 (7,231)	
Townshend, Neil W	4:13:46 (12,035)	
Townson, Lyndon L	5:11:20 (25,730)	
Towse, Kevin	6:25:12 (34,136)	
Toy, Jonathon F	4:25:26 (14,931)	
Toyne, Adam C	3:16:28 (2,124)	
Toynton, James D	3:34:04 (4,276)	
Tozer, Don P	4:55:30 (22,393)	
Tozer, Shaun A	2:52:59 (474)	
Trabanino, Herbert	2:55:42 (600)	
Tracey, Dave	5:14:36 (26,362)	
Tracey, Francis J	3:28:30 (3,485)	
Tracey, Phillip A	4:13:07 (11,860)	
Trafford, Graham S	4:57:21 (22,875)	
Trailor, Lee J	5:51:10 (31,791)	
Trampe, Ralph	4:47:39 (20,441)	
Trant, Mike M	4:13:01 (11,833)	
Tranter, Paul	3:06:19 (1,252)	
Trask, Philip A	6:12:00 (33,429)	
Trathen, Mark	4:55:11 (22,311)	
Travaglini, Donatello	6:25:26 (34,145)	
Travers, Don	2:49:34 (361)	
Travers, Rob C	4:33:30 (16,911)	
Travis, Neil	4:35:43 (17,463)	
Travitzky, Benjamin	5:24:51 (28,250)	
Traynor, Mark R	4:41:11 (18,836)	
Treacy, Nigel K	3:58:12 (8,760)	
Treadwell, Neil	4:15:09 (12,357)	
Treadwell, Paul D	4:13:25 (11,940)	
Treadwell, Robert W	3:40:52 (5,337)	
Treanor, Edward F	5:25:11 (28,300)	
Treasure, Guy D	3:37:55 (4,809)	
Trebilcock, Mark C	3:28:17 (3,445)	
Tredant, Adrian S	4:47:40 (20,449)	
Tredger, Charles R	5:31:52 (29,429)	
Tredger, Robert S	5:48:10 (31,484)	
Tree, Peter J	4:56:44 (22,702)	
Treen, Martin D	5:22:30 (27,854)	
Trees, Steven D	4:23:16 (14,393)	
Tregear, Colin	3:57:52 (8,689)	
Treherne, Jonathan S	4:34:19 (17,098)	
Treneman, Brian P	6:35:33 (34,525)	
Trenkel, Daniel J	5:12:06 (25,870)	
Trennery, David S	4:30:02 (16,155)	
Trent, Dean	6:06:51 (33,100)	
Treppass, Alexander P	5:14:59 (26,447)	
Trevelyan, Adrian	3:32:33 (4,079)	
Trevelyan, Oliver W	4:26:37 (15,214)	
Trevilcock, Norman A	4:56:47 (22,710)	
Trevor, Jon	5:36:34 (30,120)	
Tribe, Barrie J	4:50:35 (21,145)	
Trick, Mark	4:57:25 (22,889)	
Tricker, Scott J	4:21:03 (13,862)	
Trickett, Philip. J	3:39:46 (5,154)	
Trieb, Manfred	3:55:11 (8,053)	
Trigg, Christopher	5:04:02 (24,332)	
Trigg, Robert W	5:16:46 (26,800)	
Trighet, Piette	3:47:32 (6,435)	
Trigwell, Stuart J	3:12:47 (1,807)	
Trim, Nick L	5:31:53 (29,431)	
Trimarco, Victor	4:55:42 (22,429)	
Trimble, Gareth	4:15:12 (12,368)	
Trimemr, Benjamin J	4:53:45 (21,951)	
Trimnell, Terance L	4:57:24 (22,887)	
Trinnaman, Neil	4:04:27 (10,049)	
Tripp, Peter H	4:11:11 (11,424)	
Tristram, Joe J	3:49:25 (6,815)	
Tritta, Ben P	6:04:15 (32,902)	
Trivedi, Naresh	4:59:53 (23,470)	
Trivedi, Prateesh M	5:31:58 (29,444)	
Trivero, Baptiste	4:06:26 (10,450)	
Troca, Joao	3:56:36 (8,381)	
Trodahl, Jostein	3:18:14 (2,315)	
Trodd, Daniel G	5:58:34 (32,471)	
Trodd, Ron C	5:15:14 (26,507)	
Trofimczuk, Darren T	5:57:00 (32,331)	
Troke, Robert	4:19:06 (13,355)	
Tromans, Stuart J	2:56:10 (621)	
Trory, John A	4:03:09 (9,808)	
Trotter, Bruce	4:42:33 (19,190)	
Trotter, Ian	3:23:03 (2,801)	
Troughton, Wayne E	4:20:12 (13,655)	
Troup, Michael G	3:17:38 (2,242)	
Trout, Stephen D	3:38:29 (4,917)	
Trowbridge, Tony T	4:16:05 (12,589)	
Trowell, David E	4:49:09 (20,807)	
Trower, Paul J	3:48:37 (6,648)	
Trowles, Colin	4:39:02 (18,293)	
Trowsdale, John	4:52:19 (21,576)	
Trowsdale, Paul J	3:31:53 (3,969)	
Troy, Joe N	5:23:22 (27,987)	
Trudgen, Russell C	4:35:01 (17,278)	
Trudgill, Graham J	4:19:50 (13,555)	
Truelove, Michael J	4:38:10 (18,055)	
Trueman, Philip A	5:25:19 (28,323)	
Truepenny, David J	3:05:14 (1,178)	
Truesdale, Nevin J	4:05:23 (10,221)	
Truman, Chris P	5:08:43 (25,229)	
Truman, Daniel J	3:38:29 (4,917)	
Truman, David J	4:38:25 (18,131)	
Truman, Jason M	4:33:18 (16,867)	
Trumper, Mark	5:38:27 (30,379)	
Trunkfield, Dale M	5:02:51 (24,095)	
Truscott, Malcolm S	3:42:37 (5,611)	
Trussell, Stephen M	3:00:24 (924)	
Trussler, Ian R	3:52:25 (7,455)	
Trusty, Paul A	5:13:35 (26,135)	
Truter, René	4:44:28 (19,670)	
Trygve, Tveter	3:21:36 (2,660)	
Tsang, Francis F	4:32:32 (16,672)	
Tsang, Simon	4:53:24 (21,862)	
Tschopp, Marcel	2:26:56 (28)	
Tsouvallaris, Christopher S	5:43:19 (30,975)	
Tsouvallaris, Peter	6:32:28 (34,422)	
Tsyrklevich, Eugene	5:50:58 (31,771)	
Ttouli, Peter	6:09:18 (33,256)	
Tubb, Anthony A	5:19:18 (27,310)	
Tubman, Keith A	5:10:34 (25,589)	
Tucci, Maurisio	3:24:37 (2,972)	
Tuck, Michael	4:56:44 (22,702)	
Tucker, Alan S	4:44:35 (19,712)	
Tucker, Andrew J	5:20:34 (27,534)	
Tucker, Christopher J	5:15:54 (26,643)	
Tucker, Gareth J	4:01:19 (9,480)	
Tucker, Graham J	3:39:34 (5,119)	
Tucker, Guy A	6:29:12 (34,291)	
Tucker, Lee	4:41:19 (18,867)	
Tucker, Lucy	5:03:08 (24,156)	
Tucker, Matthew E	3:58:21 (8,796)	
Tucker, Phillip	3:27:18 (3,327)	
Tucker, Sam J	4:11:34 (11,512)	
Tucker, Samuel	4:28:36 (15,761)	
Tucker, Stephen R	5:29:08 (29,005)	
Tuckett, Mark A	3:54:41 (7,940)	
Tuckey, Antony S	7:07:39 (35,242)	
Tuddenham, Robin J	2:41:42 (173)	
Tuffs, Nicholas J	4:37:34 (17,902)	
Tufnell, Raoul F	3:36:21 (4,594)	
Tufts, Mark J	4:23:12 (14,379)	
Tuite, James F	3:09:56 (1,551)	
Tullett, Adam K	3:24:07 (2,922)	
Tulley, Darren R	4:13:57 (12,084)	
Tulloch, Kevin J	3:19:02 (2,395)	
Tully, Adam	5:32:00 (29,451)	
Tully, Sean W	4:43:33 (19,426)	
Tumber, Justin	5:00:32 (23,621)	
Tumuluri, Krishna	4:24:55 (14,804)	

LONDON MARATHON

Vandenbol, Ben G	5:31:57	(29,439)
Vandepoel, Piet B	5:23:25	(27,992)
Vanjak, Denis P	4:18:34	(13,230)
Vankempen, Daniel L	4:27:11	(15,381)
Vanmarcke, Philippe F	4:19:20	(13,412)
Vann, Stuart K	5:46:18	(31,292)
Vannucci, Leonardo	3:16:45	(2,152)
Vanrenen, Daniel N	4:50:10	(21,039)
Vansteenkiste, Koenraad H	4:22:50	(14,295)
Varden, Mark G	2:57:46	(727)
Varley, Andrew E	6:03:30	(32,851)
Varley, Ian	6:09:25	(33,262)
Varley, Nicholas J	4:27:03	(15,339)
Varley, Peter R	5:07:38	(25,025)
Varney, James	5:31:45	(29,414)
Varrenti, Berardino	4:15:56	(12,538)
Varry, Olivier	3:28:25	(3,466)
Varry, Philippe	4:31:22	(16,438)
Vary, Gary G	4:42:31	(19,185)
Vasallo, Juan I	6:14:43	(33,593)
Vasapollo, Giuseppe	4:38:56	(18,265)
Vass, Simon O	3:31:12	(3,865)
Vaudin, David	3:42:53	(5,665)
Vaudin, John N	4:18:25	(13,181)
Vaudin, Mark	5:00:18	(23,575)
Vaudrey, Graham E	4:28:43	(15,792)
Vaudrey, James	3:09:14	(1,496)
Vaughan, Andrew J	5:03:44	(24,276)
Vaughan, Bryan J	4:25:19	(14,898)
Vaughan, Dan	3:14:47	(1,966)
Vaughan, Daniel J	3:42:39	(5,618)
Vaughan, David N	5:00:14	(23,560)
Vaughan, Frankie H	4:14:46	(12,264)
Vaughan, Gareth D	4:50:08	(21,030)
Vaughan, Gary R	5:17:21	(26,927)
Vaughan, Graham	4:50:30	(21,120)
Vaughan, Matthew D	5:43:14	(30,966)
Vaughan, Richard	5:07:47	(25,054)
Vaughan, Steven J	3:48:33	(6,637)
Vaz, David P	3:11:01	(1,633)
Vazzoler, Andrea	3:51:11	(7,182)
Veale, Peter R	5:21:35	(27,709)
Veasey, Dominick J	3:36:41	(4,640)
Vecina, Jesus	4:54:07	(22,048)
Veen, Stuart W	3:34:12	(4,293)
Veenhuijsen, Johan	4:49:09	(20,807)
Veghini, Massimo	4:09:49	(11,129)
Veillard, Pierre	3:52:17	(7,429)
Veitch, Paul J	2:59:37	(870)
Vekaria, Arvind	7:41:24	(35,578)
Vekaria, Pritam	5:32:15	(29,491)
Vekic, John	5:01:10	(23,766)
Vekria, Bhanuprasad N	6:25:01	(34,125)
Vekria, Harilal N	3:31:12	(3,865)
Velasco, Angel	3:29:20	(3,625)
Vella, Simon P	4:52:57	(21,742)
Velleman, Adam J	4:49:34	(20,908)
Velluet, Pete J	3:43:32	(5,787)
Veloso, Manuel	3:49:49	(6,899)
Venables, Benjamin J	3:41:15	(5,402)
Venditto, Luca	4:56:23	(22,609)
Venekas, Antoine L	4:58:55	(23,230)
Venn, Geoffrey G	3:50:19	(7,003)
Venn, William A	4:44:46	(19,763)
Venner, Adam N	4:38:15	(18,068)
Venning, John W	3:31:34	(3,919)
Venning, Jonathan C	3:30:19	(3,767)
Venning, Mark	5:14:54	(26,428)
Ventora, Carlos	6:14:51	(33,604)
Ventress, Michael F	6:01:11	(32,695)
Vercoe, Rik J	5:07:30	(24,999)
Verde, Nick	4:10:28	(11,255)
Vere, Derek	5:28:55	(28,971)
Vereker, Edward	3:30:38	(3,798)
Vergauwe, Philippe L	3:12:39	(1,792)
Vergo, René	2:52:32	(460)
Verheijen, Wil	5:05:51	(24,665)
Verhulst, Georges	4:44:27	(19,663)
Verity, Lee R	5:12:49	(26,001)
Verity, Sean P	5:17:52	(27,022)
Verlaque, Raymond J	4:24:15	(14,643)
Verma, Manish	5:47:17	(31,381)
Vermaak, Christian	5:17:34	(26,974)

Verna, Alfredo	3:28:04	(3,414)
Vernau, David	3:22:47	(2,774)
Vernazza, Robert W	6:48:31	(34,900)
Vernon, Alan R	5:24:48	(28,238)
Vernon, Christopher R	5:20:16	(27,470)
Vernon, Darren L	3:17:03	(2,186)
Vernon, Mike	4:56:38	(22,672)
Verrall, Paul M	5:06:04	(24,707)
Verry, Richard	4:37:21	(17,848)
Verwey, Mark H	4:14:02	(12,106)
Vesey, Derek	3:21:54	(2,696)
Vespucci, Fernando	3:47:56	(6,516)
Vesterdal, Johan E	3:19:23	(2,428)
Vesty, Tony D	3:43:55	(5,852)
Vetaas, Terje	5:46:54	(31,344)
Vetaas, Tony	4:11:01	(11,371)
Veysey, James H	3:15:47	(2,057)
Viaene, Luc E	3:55:20	(8,088)
Vialatte, Hubert	4:48:21	(20,625)
Vialls, Ronald	3:46:37	(6,271)
Vian, Andrew S	3:33:57	(4,264)
Vianello, Didier	2:41:55	(178)
Vianello, Nerino	4:57:08	(22,805)
Vicenzi, Giorgio	3:30:19	(3,767)
Vickerage, John A	4:55:54	(22,487)
Vickers, Bernard	3:00:58	(957)
Vickers, Colin	4:44:44	(19,753)
Vickers, Steve	5:23:37	(28,033)
Vickers, Wayne J	5:52:49	(31,951)
Vickers, Wayne M	3:04:53	(1,152)
Vickers-Jones, Giles	5:14:05	(26,243)
Vickery, Anthony S	5:44:37	(31,111)
Victor, David	3:59:51	(9,171)
Victor, David M	3:44:29	(5,937)
Vidion, Neil R	4:44:42	(19,744)
Viegas, Frank S	5:14:24	(26,312)
Vieira, Antonio	4:07:27	(10,644)
Vighier, Florian	3:46:54	(6,321)
Vilar, Rui	4:10:52	(11,341)
Villa, Mario	2:49:40	(365)
Villa, Roberto	5:08:03	(25,105)
Villani, Luigi	4:38:29	(18,146)
Villars, Philip	5:26:52	(28,602)
Villaverde, Eduardo	3:19:48	(2,466)
Vince, Stuart	5:13:07	(26,065)
Vincent, David G	5:17:39	(26,992)
Vincent, James I	5:07:41	(25,031)
Vincent, James R	3:40:55	(5,351)
Vincent, Leroy	4:15:38	(12,472)
Vincent, Mark D	4:50:53	(21,213)
Vincent, Menu	2:39:49	(141)
Vincent, Michael T	5:45:30	(31,209)
Vincent, Ronald E	5:03:21	(24,204)
Vincenzo Salzano, Ernesto	4:00:00	(9,208)
Vinciguerra, Giuseppe	4:35:32	(17,410)
Vinegrad, Michael	3:12:11	(1,747)
Vines, Edward P	4:44:43	(19,750)
Vines, Mark	4:04:57	(10,135)
Vines, Matthew I	5:23:20	(27,982)
Vines, Paul	3:29:52	(3,702)
Vint, David D	3:54:11	(7,835)
Vinter, Ian R	6:01:45	(32,737)
Viquez Rojas, Rafael Angel	3:43:15	(5,729)
Virk, Jaswant S	5:40:53	(30,693)
Virton, Emeric P	3:00:23	(922)
Vishan, Ibrahim	5:43:32	(30,995)
Vishnubala, Dane A	4:09:05	(10,971)
Visockis, Antoon	5:23:44	(28,059)
Vitse, Eric	4:26:40	(15,231)
Vitteaut, Gerard	3:52:06	(7,392)
Vitty, Martyn J	4:23:15	(14,388)
Viviani, Ernesto	4:30:43	(16,295)
Voakes, Kris	4:09:24	(11,048)
Voce, Robert E	4:14:36	(12,230)
Vogel, Philippe R	4:35:20	(17,368)

Vogel, William G	3:43:26	(5,761)
Vogelzang, Barnabas H	4:38:56	(18,265)
Vohra, Ravinder S	4:37:19	(17,845)
Voigtlander, Darren C	3:48:44	(6,674)
Voland, Mario	3:12:31	(1,778)
Volken, Urs	3:59:05	(8,981)
Vollentine, Brian	3:49:10	(6,761)
Voller, Philip	3:17:38	(2,242)
Volonte, Ezio	3:53:26	(7,673)
Volpe, Nicholas	4:57:32	(22,911)
Volpi, Oliviero	3:42:08	(5,543)
Volvak, Oleksandr	4:22:58	(14,322)
Von Allmen, Friedrich	3:46:02	(6,185)
Von Beck, Eckart	5:57:04	(32,337)
Von Kumberg, Wolf J	4:35:54	(17,515)
Vonier, Willy	3:51:26	(7,240)
Voralia, Liladhar G	5:11:36	(25,779)
Vorres, Dimitri	3:18:18	(2,325)
Vos, Ashley C	5:02:41	(24,074)
Voskuhl, Justin B	4:41:30	(18,920)
Vossenaar, Franciscus P	3:28:17	(3,445)
Vothknecht, Heiko	5:07:53	(25,073)
Vouillamoz, Shile	2:55:50	(605)
Vout, Tony R	4:22:03	(14,097)
Vowell, Darrin L	4:42:07	(19,071)
Vowles, Michael J	6:31:37	(34,387)
Vrind, Hans J	5:56:18	(32,266)
Vuaillat, Bernard	5:14:41	(26,379)
Vukusic, Tomislav	4:48:43	(20,700)
Vye, Nicholas A	5:25:25	(28,346)
Vymeris, Alex	4:01:19	(9,480)
Waby, Andrew I	4:29:53	(16,118)
Wachenje, Benjamin	5:14:35	(26,359)
Waddell, Douglas R	3:53:01	(7,573)
Waddingham, Jon P	4:47:05	(20,308)
Waddington, David	3:27:16	(3,320)
Waddington, Michael P	7:27:11	(35,451)
Waddington, Neil	5:03:00	(24,121)
Waddington, Nick	4:53:12	(21,810)
Waddington, Nigel H	4:01:20	(9,486)
Waddington, Phil	5:30:24	(29,200)
Waddy, Antony	5:25:12	(28,302)
Wade, Daniel J	3:42:22	(5,579)
Wade, Ian	4:08:04	(10,782)
Wade, James A	3:30:01	(3,725)
Wade, Peter	3:35:10	(4,433)
Wade, Rex A	5:24:29	(28,181)
Wade, Robert H	4:29:52	(16,115)
Wade, Ronald	3:45:34	(6,107)
Wade, William M	4:28:09	(15,635)
Wadey, Graham P	3:55:00	(8,009)
Wadey, Ian D	3:25:16	(3,041)
Wadley, John M	4:48:09	(20,563)
Wadley, Mark J	3:52:16	(7,425)
Wadsworth, Adrian M	3:35:14	(4,438)
Wadsworth, John E	2:56:23	(625)
Waelti, Philippe	6:29:23	(34,304)
Waggett, Steven R	5:10:19	(25,540)
Waghorn, Arthur M	5:55:06	(32,155)
Waghorn, Howard	4:16:35	(12,712)
Waghorn, Philip R	5:00:44	(23,670)
Wagner, Kurt	3:48:23	(6,587)
Wagner, Marcus	4:54:38	(22,179)
Wagstaff, Jonathan	4:06:02	(10,355)
Wagstaff, Simon	5:00:21	(23,587)
Wahl, Max O	3:17:38	(2,242)
Wain, Chris	3:58:36	(8,856)
Wain, Simon N	3:44:39	(5,967)
Wain, Terry	6:07:13	(33,119)
Wainewright, David M	5:17:56	(27,037)
Wainhouse, Owen	5:37:56	(30,291)
Wainwright, Gordon L	6:33:31	(34,454)
Wainwright, Jack	4:56:26	(22,622)
Wainwright, John	4:35:43	(17,463)
Wainwright, Michael F	6:21:51	(33,990)
Wainwright, Robert T	5:02:06	(23,953)
Wainwright, Thomas	3:56:39	(8,393)
Waite, Howard	3:22:47	(2,774)
Waite, James D	2:57:23	(701)
Waite, Mark	3:16:49	(2,161)
Waite, Russ	5:29:12	(29,023)
Wake, Adam N	3:28:36	(3,505)
Wake, Simon C	3:47:45	(6,488)

Wake, Stephen P 5:44:37 (31,111)
Wakefield, Andrew 5:51:52 (31,861)
Wakefield, Anthony 3:48:55 (6,709)
Wakefield, Iain S 3:49:33 (6,842)
Wakefield, Mark 5:42:49 (30,915)
Wakefield, Paul M 4:21:30 (13,967)
Wakefield, Robin 5:06:22 (24,762)
Wakeford, Stephen 3:42:36 (5,610)
Wakeham, Michael B 5:08:37 (25,212)
Wakelen, Kevin H 4:11:26 (11,486)
Wakely, Clive J 5:16:30 (26,757)
Wakem, Michael J 5:03:06 (24,146)
Wakeman, Robert 6:21:46 (33,987)
Wakenell, Craig W 5:35:23 (29,965)
Wakenshaw, Trevor 3:59:12 (9,011)
Waker, Stuart M 5:38:15 (30,342)
Wakerley, Nick 4:32:29 (16,657)
Walbank, Paul R 4:45:36 (19,967)
Walby, Chris 3:59:50 (9,167)
Walden, Adam J 5:15:30 (26,563)
Walder, Ben M 4:48:29 (20,643)
Walding, Stuart M 4:19:56 (13,582)
Waldron-Lynch, Tom 3:05:08 (1,171)
Wales, Christopher 3:29:22 (3,629)
Wales, Stephen P 5:34:52 (29,896)
Walford, Alastair M 3:07:22 (1,340)
Walford, Matthew 5:10:05 (25,501)
Walia, Steven 3:59:35 (9,114)
Walkden, Johnny R 3:53:53 (7,761)
Walker, Adam 4:15:57 (12,543)
Walker, Adam 4:17:30 (12,947)
Walker, Andrew D 4:57:12 (22,821)
Walker, Andrew M 3:36:14 (4,577)
Walker, Andrew P 4:20:06 (13,624)
Walker, Andrew S 4:59:33 (23,399)
Walker, Andy J 5:44:53 (31,138)
Walker, Angus C 4:35:45 (17,473)
Walker, Barry J 5:17:31 (26,960)
Walker, Ben 4:12:46 (11,780)
Walker, Brian 5:24:21 (28,164)
Walker, Callum J 5:12:41 (25,983)
Walker, Christopher 4:43:35 (19,437)
Walker, Clive 5:38:38 (30,402)
Walker, Craig M 3:01:39 (990)
Walker, Daniel M 3:35:01 (4,411)
Walker, David 4:49:18 (20,838)
Walker, David B 4:17:58 (13,064)
Walker, David F 5:17:16 (26,912)
Walker, David J 4:09:52 (11,141)
Walker, David P 3:09:39 (1,529)
Walker, Derek A 3:00:30 (931)
Walker, Derek M 3:48:10 (6,557)
Walker, Derry J 3:16:47 (2,156)
Walker, Edward C 6:48:58 (34,910)
Walker, Garry 5:26:12 (28,491)
Walker, Gary 4:19:14 (13,387)
Walker, Gary J 3:49:42 (6,872)
Walker, Geoffrey R 4:43:35 (19,437)
Walker, Iain 4:11:46 (11,563)
Walker, James 6:00:58 (32,669)
Walker, John W 4:35:13 (17,338)
Walker, Kevin A 5:14:30 (26,334)
Walker, Lee D 4:36:49 (17,747)
Walker, Marc P 6:16:24 (33,712)
Walker, Mark D 3:00:20 (919)
Walker, Martin J 3:24:32 (2,958)
Walker, Martin W 4:08:34 (10,882)
Walker, Michael 4:34:47 (17,218)
Walker, Mick A 5:08:53 (25,261)
Walker, Neil 5:01:44 (23,878)
Walker, Neil A 5:00:42 (23,661)
Walker, Paul 3:47:35 (6,441)
Walker, Paul 4:18:50 (13,291)
Walker, Paul 4:41:23 (18,884)
Walker, Paul 4:49:31 (20,892)
Walker, Paul S 4:26:14 (15,114)
Walker, Peter D 5:22:48 (27,907)
Walker, Phillip A 4:56:20 (22,598)
Walker, Phillip C 5:26:25 (28,534)
Walker, Robert L 4:35:40 (17,446)
Walker, Scott J 4:18:54 (13,306)
Walker, Simon 4:32:04 (16,574)
Walker, Simon 5:24:21 (28,164)
Walker, Stephen 4:08:13 (10,816)
Walker, Stephen J 4:43:57 (19,520)
Walker, Steve 4:54:28 (22,139)
Walker, Stewart 4:40:32 (18,662)
Walker, Stewart J 3:38:15 (4,877)
Walker, Stuart D 3:23:50 (2,882)
Walker, Thomas J 3:26:13 (3,159)
Walker, Tim 4:23:27 (14,432)
Walker, Tim 4:46:38 (20,204)
Walker, Tony P 5:09:24 (25,353)
Walker, Vincent S 5:48:48 (31,561)
Walker, Will 4:29:13 (15,915)
Walker-Reed, Roger 3:53:32 (7,696)
Walkington, Michael D 5:04:27 (24,411)
Walkinshaw, Paul 4:59:04 (23,277)
Wall, Ian T 3:12:38 (1,791)
Wall, Ivan 3:31:23 (3,888)
Wall, Ivan 3:56:45 (8,420)
Wall, Michael D 5:41:13 (30,731)
Wall, Richard J 4:22:34 (14,219)
Wallace, Adam R 6:20:29 (33,920)
Wallace, Alistair 4:22:28 (14,190)
Wallace, Bob 3:36:37 (4,629)
Wallace, David 3:40:29 (5,261)
Wallace, David 4:51:21 (21,332)
Wallace, David M 5:04:27 (24,411)
Wallace, Garry J 4:46:50 (20,235)
Wallace, Iain 4:03:42 (9,902)
Wallace, James 4:28:27 (15,715)
Wallace, James T 3:52:36 (7,482)
Wallace, Jim 3:04:14 (1,114)
Wallace, John M 3:40:27 (5,253)
Wallace, Jonathan M 4:55:11 (22,311)
Wallace, Mark 4:24:55 (14,804)
Wallace, Martyn E 4:42:31 (19,185)
Wallace, Melvin 3:14:18 (1,925)
Wallace, Michael J 4:25:01 (14,829)
Wallace, Steve M 4:09:53 (11,147)
Wallace, Tony J 4:10:57 (11,361)
Walland, John 5:42:37 (30,889)
Wallbank, Peter J 5:04:01 (24,328)
Waller, Andrew D 5:26:17 (28,510)
Waller, Bevan A 6:16:24 (33,712)
Waller, Douglas W 4:20:26 (13,717)
Waller, James 4:04:01 (9,969)
Waller, Robert J 4:17:52 (13,034)
Wallhead, Nicholas J 4:31:10 (16,398)
Wallin, Ulf 3:58:31 (8,842)
Walling, Kevin D 4:37:54 (17,981)
Wallington, Andrew J 4:21:44 (14,012)
Wallington, Darren J 4:32:15 (16,620)
Wallington, Steven C 4:33:41 (16,955)
Wallis, Colin 3:39:14 (5,053)
Wallis, George W 3:55:24 (8,105)
Wallis, Ian P 5:03:24 (24,218)
Wallis, John M 3:00:12 (907)
Wallis, Neil 5:19:19 (27,313)
Wallis, Paul J 4:58:19 (23,109)
Wallis, Philip J 3:59:54 (9,185)
Wallis-Smith, Simon P 4:00:45 (9,365)
Wallsgrove, Ian C 4:26:22 (15,149)
Walmsley, Alastair 3:12:45 (1,802)
Walmsley, Dave M 2:43:02 (198)
Walmsley, Dennis G 2:46:17 (268)
Walmsley, Paul 5:13:40 (26,157)
Walne, Jason G 4:29:11 (15,906)
Walper, Gerhard 4:00:36 (9,330)
Walpole, Chris I 4:49:35 (20,912)
Walpole, David B 4:07:38 (10,686)
Wals, Adrian 4:08:57 (10,945)
Walsgrove, John D 3:03:26 (1,071)
Walsh, Andrew D 3:41:11 (5,396)
Walsh, Andrew J 5:29:02 (28,990)
Walsh, Andrew P 4:39:22 (18,385)
Walsh, Brian J 3:02:23 (1,020)
Walsh, Carl 5:16:15 (26,711)
Walsh, Colin N 4:20:53 (13,827)
Walsh, Daniel M 3:13:48 (1,883)
Walsh, David 4:00:24 (9,293)
Walsh, Dominic A 4:55:21 (22,349)
Walsh, Frank 6:09:23 (33,261)
Walsh, James 4:10:14 (11,212)
Walsh, John 4:37:12 (17,823)
Walsh, Michael J 4:38:28 (18,140)
Walsh, Nicholas J 3:12:29 (1,776)
Walsh, Phillip I 3:37:41 (4,773)
Walsh, Raymond F 3:57:46 (8,667)
Walsh, Richard S 3:19:24 (2,429)
Walsh, Robert M 3:54:57 (8,000)
Walsh, Simon 5:00:16 (23,568)
Walsh, Steven 4:44:42 (19,744)
Walsh, Stewart P 4:26:00 (15,058)
Walsham, James M 3:20:10 (2,515)
Walshe, Donal P 5:34:16 (29,806)
Walshe, Sean E 4:51:18 (21,315)
Walsmley, Davcid J 5:58:56 (32,502)
Walter, Morten 3:54:47 (7,958)
Walter, Stephen M 4:19:47 (13,539)
Walters, Andrew 5:56:47 (32,318)
Walters, Chris 3:45:39 (6,125)
Walters, David 4:05:08 (10,169)
Walters, Ed J 3:41:12 (5,398)
Walters, Gyp M 3:39:21 (5,073)
Walters, Humphrey J 4:53:02 (21,760)
Walters, Ian P 3:58:47 (8,906)
Walters, Martin J 3:58:22 (8,800)
Walters, Matt L 3:57:32 (8,606)
Walters, Morgan 2:54:20 (535)
Walters, Peter D 3:46:30 (6,248)
Walters, Tom J 4:24:40 (14,739)
Walton, Ewan T 3:39:23 (5,082)
Walton, Frank 4:44:47 (19,772)
Walton, Ian 4:40:39 (18,687)
Walton, James A 5:16:01 (26,669)
Walton, James M 5:19:30 (27,337)
Walton, Jim P 4:26:28 (15,179)
Walton, Mark P 3:39:26 (5,095)
Walton, Michael A 4:29:06 (15,888)
Walton, Richard J 4:16:17 (12,644)
Walton, Sam 4:40:46 (18,722)
Walton, Simon P 6:23:52 (34,069)
Walton, Tim J 3:52:23 (7,448)
Wandasiewicz, Nelson 3:43:08 (5,713)
Wanless, Aiden C 4:18:17 (13,142)
Want, Mark A 4:47:01 (20,286)
Waplington, James D 4:38:05 (18,035)
Warby, Tony J 6:15:29 (33,648)
Ward, Alan J 4:39:35 (18,433)
Ward, Chris 3:31:04 (3,843)
Ward, Christopher A 5:18:14 (27,109)
Ward, Darren T 4:55:27 (22,377)
Ward, David J 3:09:45 (1,536)
Ward, Derek 5:56:37 (32,300)
Ward, Gary C 3:57:32 (8,606)
Ward, Gary N 4:14:24 (12,189)
Ward, Ian A 5:48:04 (31,476)
Ward, Ian J 3:06:00 (1,233)
Ward, John 3:43:34 (5,796)
Ward, Jonathan D 3:58:32 (8,846)
Ward, Jonathan D 4:55:23 (22,361)
Ward, Joseph M 4:14:37 (12,235)
Ward, Julian L 3:28:33 (3,499)
Ward, Kevin 5:28:10 (28,832)
Ward, Mark 3:35:30 (4,480)
Ward, Martin 4:35:14 (17,343)
Ward, Matthew I 4:10:10 (11,196)
Ward, Michael 3:41:43 (5,472)
Ward, Michael R 4:48:14 (20,586)
Ward, Nigel P 3:50:58 (7,131)
Ward, Patrick J 3:22:34 (2,753)
Ward, Philip 4:52:12 (21,541)
Ward, Philip R 4:53:35 (21,909)
Ward, Robert 5:14:37 (26,365)
Ward, Robert A 4:44:59 (19,833)
Ward, Robert G 5:25:44 (28,413)
Ward, Simon L 3:58:50 (8,921)
Ward, Stephen 4:51:36 (21,398)
Ward, Steven J 5:56:22 (32,272)
Ward, Stewart 4:35:32 (17,410)
Ward, Stuart J 4:30:13 (16,201)
Wardell, Chris 3:53:07 (7,594)
Wardell, Dave A 3:59:38 (9,127)
Wardlaw, Robert G 3:50:38 (7,062)
Wardley, Robin 4:48:51 (20,732)
Wardrop, Alan 3:34:51 (4,387)
Wardrop-Szilagyi, Allan C 3:32:09 (4,024)

Weber, Joseph	4:17:01	(12,819)
Weber, Martin A	5:00:24	(23,598)
Weber, Tobias	4:03:00	(9,785)
Webner, Andreas	3:47:40	(6,468)
Webster, Andrew	4:23:11	(14,374)
Webster, Andrew P	4:42:43	(19,233)
Webster, Cedric	5:51:41	(31,845)
Webster, Christopher R	6:23:43	(34,064)
Webster, David	3:39:37	(5,131)
Webster, Gary	5:00:01	(23,508)
Webster, Gilbert	5:21:40	(27,729)
Webster, Graeme J	4:40:33	(18,666)
Webster, James M	5:18:11	(27,098)
Webster, John	4:30:39	(16,286)
Webster, Jon	3:49:54	(6,918)
Webster, Jonathan H	5:39:13	(30,479)
Webster, Mark T	4:11:13	(11,430)
Webster, Nicholas G	4:02:57	(9,774)
Webster, Paul A	4:29:47	(16,087)
Webster, Paul A	4:39:01	(18,288)
Webster, Paul J	3:05:13	(1,175)
Webster, Robert H	4:33:32	(16,924)
Webster, Ross P	4:44:13	(19,604)
Webster, Simon C	4:05:56	(10,338)
Webster, Stuart M	4:38:48	(18,234)
Wedderburn-Maxwell, Matthew C	4:58:19	(23,109)
Wederell, Graham A	4:29:29	(15,998)
Wedge, Iain D	3:08:49	(1,451)
Wedge, Sean	4:28:44	(15,796)
Wedgwood, Stuart T	4:55:43	(22,433)
Wedlock, Keith	5:22:37	(27,879)
Wedlock, Michael T	3:56:43	(8,411)
Weedall, Gary	4:03:24	(9,850)
Weeden, Charlie	6:45:04	(34,801)
Weeden, Daniel	4:12:55	(11,809)
Weedon, Jonathan J	4:31:47	(16,522)
Weeks, Andrew	4:41:51	(19,010)
Weeks, Andrew P	4:23:47	(14,508)
Weeks, Antony N	4:48:22	(20,628)
Weeks, David	4:33:08	(16,821)
Weeks, David J	4:08:17	(10,831)
Weeks, John L	4:05:52	(10,322)
Weeks, Michael J	4:29:49	(16,095)
Weeks, Michael R	2:53:12	(477)
Weeks, Neil M	5:33:54	(29,747)
Weeks, Richard	6:30:29	(34,340)
Weetman, Stephen G	2:35:33	(76)
Wehner, Oliver	4:11:32	(11,508)
Wehrle, Stephen R	5:12:45	(25,992)
Weichart, Anthony W	3:45:24	(6,084)
Weigall, James A	4:15:51	(12,526)
Weighell, Robert D	3:51:57	(7,356)
Weight, Mark A	3:49:53	(6,914)
Weill-Raynal, David M	3:25:32	(3,071)
Weiner, Mark A	4:34:57	(17,257)
Weiner, Philip A	5:02:57	(24,114)
Weir, Andrew A	5:28:32	(28,907)
Weir, Andrew P	2:30:22	(42)
Weir, Gareth D	5:38:36	(30,398)
Weir, Michael H	3:21:28	(2,646)
Weir, Richard S	4:52:22	(21,589)
Weir, Robert S	5:01:56	(23,920)
Weisleder, Rodney	3:49:54	(6,918)
Weissenborn, Norbert	4:57:37	(22,936)
Weissgerber, Frank E	3:58:28	(8,832)
Welbury, James H	3:48:00	(6,526)
Welch, Dick	5:26:08	(28,479)
Welch, Joseph S	3:46:04	(6,189)
Welch, Peter J	4:23:29	(14,442)
Welch, Philip	4:00:48	(9,372)
Welch, Terry G	3:30:40	(3,804)
Welchman, Alan	4:22:28	(14,190)
Weldin, Phil C	4:27:43	(15,524)
Welfare, Bruce	6:00:38	(32,635)
Welham, Bryn J	4:21:55	(14,069)
Welham, Glenn D	4:28:57	(15,846)
Welland, David P	4:55:48	(22,455)
Weller, Christopher D	4:59:28	(23,369)
Weller, Geoffrey C	3:45:57	(6,171)
Wellings, Duncan	5:43:58	(31,033)
Wells, Alan M	5:09:55	(25,453)
Wells, Anthony T	5:21:51	(27,766)
Wells, Ben	3:52:12	(7,409)
Wells, Brian R	5:11:00	(25,665)
Wells, Christopher H	5:37:18	(30,213)
Wells, Colin J	5:12:57	(26,033)
Wells, Craig L	4:31:39	(16,497)
Wells, David G	2:53:49	(515)
Wells, David P	3:38:04	(4,846)
Wells, Duncan	3:38:01	(4,833)
Wells, Ivor	5:49:36	(31,638)
Wells, Jody	3:17:41	(2,250)
Wells, Mark A	4:45:40	(19,985)
Wells, Mark E	4:34:09	(17,062)
Wells, Michael D	4:37:11	(17,820)
Wells, Michael J	5:19:14	(27,297)
Wells, Mike E	4:33:56	(17,016)
Wells, Paul D	3:38:28	(4,915)
Wells, Reuben O	4:39:10	(18,324)
Wells, Robert P	3:51:29	(7,250)
Wells, Steven W	5:46:11	(31,281)
Wells, Trevor A	4:14:58	(12,313)
Wells, Trevor G	3:34:01	(4,270)
Welsh, Barry G	3:57:02	(8,487)
Welsh, Christopher J	3:46:51	(6,311)
Welsh, Gavin A	2:44:59	(241)
Welsh, Philip J	3:39:08	(5,039)
Welton, Paul W	5:17:33	(26,969)
Welton, Peter M	5:29:16	(29,036)
Welton, Tim	4:29:50	(16,101)
Wembridge, Mark R	3:41:15	(5,402)
Wemyss, Rory J	6:38:06	(34,610)
Wendling, Michael E	3:57:40	(8,646)
Wenlock, Keith	5:32:37	(29,551)
Wenlock, Tony	3:50:27	(7,029)
Wenman, David R	5:16:26	(26,746)
Wens, Dirk	5:11:24	(25,741)
Wentink, Derk J	4:39:33	(18,424)
Wenton, Timothy	4:24:18	(14,654)
Wentworth, Alfred	6:03:34	(32,857)
Wentzel, Jaco	4:06:25	(10,445)
Werder, Marc	5:39:23	(30,505)
Werenne, Olivier E	5:25:13	(28,308)
Werner, Karl D	6:04:35	(32,923)
Werner, Karl H	5:38:38	(30,402)
Werrett, Graham J	3:19:29	(2,436)
Wesborp, Dimitri	3:38:30	(4,922)
Wescomb, Christopher P	3:17:52	(2,268)
Wescott, Richard M	4:30:08	(16,182)
Wesley, Neil R	5:02:30	(24,040)
Wessinghage, Thomas	3:07:10	(1,323)
Wesson, Antony W	2:59:16	(845)
West, Adam M	4:54:00	(22,022)
West, Alan	6:04:37	(32,926)
West, Andrew J	4:05:26	(10,228)
West, Andrew M	5:02:10	(23,964)
West, Brogan	4:13:45	(12,030)
West, Clive R	3:05:43	(1,218)
West, Colin	2:55:11	(583)
West, Darren	5:42:55	(30,924)
West, Dave A	3:57:32	(8,606)
West, Dean T	5:08:07	(25,118)
West, Dean T	5:39:58	(30,584)
West, James D	4:10:38	(11,296)
West, Kenneth J	4:01:33	(9,521)
West, Matt S	7:30:27	(35,498)
West, Michael J	5:16:25	(26,742)
West, Paul D	4:31:04	(16,368)
West, Stephen P	4:05:51	(10,319)
West, Steve	5:40:40	(30,670)
West, Steven S	4:27:42	(15,519)
Westbrook, Matthew J	3:53:09	(7,603)
Westcott, Richard	4:03:54	(9,948)
Westelaken, Gaby	5:13:45	(26,178)
Western, Ashley J	4:19:10	(13,370)
Western, Ian M	3:07:09	(1,321)
Western, John	5:55:14	(32,167)
Westgate, Andrew M	5:21:02	(27,609)
Westgate, Mark A	5:13:15	(26,086)
Westhead, Terence A	3:44:40	(5,972)
Westlake, Mark L	3:43:17	(5,734)
Westlake, Peter J	4:26:13	(15,105)
Westley, Gareth R	4:45:27	(19,934)
Weston, Asher J	4:27:22	(15,436)
Weston, Daniel J	3:01:36	(988)
Weston, Martin C	3:21:10	(2,618)
Weston, Robert A	4:24:09	(14,618)
Westren, Paul	4:18:06	(13,094)
Westrop, Russell	6:59:27	(35,120)
Westwood, Jamie I	3:03:39	(1,085)
Westwood, Jason D	3:07:23	(1,343)
Westwood, Scott	5:00:23	(23,595)
Wetheridge, Darren S	4:17:22	(12,897)
Wetherill, Gary	5:15:02	(26,464)
Whale, Christopher A	4:30:31	(16,260)
Whalley, Adrian H	3:54:57	(8,000)
Whalley, Simon	4:00:10	(9,242)
Whalley, Steve	3:45:39	(6,125)
Wharfe, Ben J	5:10:07	(25,509)
Wharton, David J	4:24:42	(14,747)
Wharton, James P	5:36:21	(30,093)
Wharton, Nick J	3:42:23	(5,581)
Wharton, Stephen L	3:45:48	(6,149)
Whatton, Andrew J	4:52:05	(21,509)
Wheatcroft, Christopher J	6:05:27	(32,994)
Wheatcroft, Kevin C	4:07:33	(10,662)
Wheater, John	4:21:23	(13,933)
Wheatley, David	4:07:45	(10,712)
Wheatley, James M	4:21:27	(13,952)
Wheatley, John B	4:47:32	(20,417)
Wheatley, Jon	3:32:44	(4,098)
Wheatley, Richard M	4:37:03	(17,796)
Wheatman, Sacha M	4:41:46	(18,983)
Wheeldon, Gary	5:07:57	(25,086)
Wheeldon, Paul A	5:07:42	(25,033)
Wheeler, Daniel W	3:07:16	(1,331)
Wheeler, Ian J	3:29:21	(3,627)
Wheeler, Jeremy J	5:15:02	(26,464)
Wheeler, Mark E	4:22:36	(14,230)
Wheeler, Mark T	4:52:12	(21,541)
Wheeler, Michael A	3:16:56	(2,173)
Wheeler, Michael N	4:51:02	(21,248)
Wheeler, Nicholas N	6:01:22	(32,710)
Wheeler, Patrick	4:01:19	(9,480)
Wheeler, Robert A	5:15:41	(26,600)
Wheeler, Roy L	5:36:20	(30,092)
Wheeler, Simon W	5:06:42	(24,817)
Wheeler, Stephen J	6:49:59	(34,928)
Wheeler, Steven P	5:20:38	(27,545)
Wheeler, Sydney J	5:37:20	(30,219)
Wheeler, Thomas L	4:08:05	(10,787)
Wheeler, Timothy R	3:38:45	(4,967)
Wheen, Stephen D	4:55:08	(22,298)
Whelan, Andrew M	4:44:01	(19,542)
Whelan, Michael J	3:22:31	(2,749)
Whelan, Ryan P	5:17:05	(26,875)
Wheten, Andrew R	3:42:49	(5,650)
Whetherly, Alan	6:46:12	(34,838)
Whetter, Richard S	4:43:54	(19,509)
Whetter, Robert G	5:12:56	(26,027)
Whewell, Sean	3:45:21	(6,072)
Whickman, David E	3:57:44	(8,660)
Whiffen, David P	4:29:35	(16,034)
Whiffin, James L	4:22:49	(14,290)
Whiffin, Toby	5:05:50	(24,659)
While, Adrian	5:43:59	(31,039)
Whiley, Graham L	6:35:02	(34,500)
Whincup, Tony R	4:17:22	(12,897)
Whinham, Charles	6:13:51	(33,539)
Whipp, Peter F	5:11:20	(25,730)
Whipp, Sean C	5:27:22	(28,688)
Whitaker, Adrian P	4:19:12	(13,375)
Whitaker, Paul	4:59:26	(23,359)
Whitby, Stephen	5:03:38	(24,263)
Whitby-Samways, Greg	4:39:07	(18,310)
Whitcombe, Christopher J	4:02:51	(9,760)
Whitcombe, Tim T	4:07:10	(10,601)
White, Adam	4:41:17	(18,858)
White, Alec A	3:53:45	(7,738)
White, Alex	3:55:58	(8,219)
White, Andrew J	3:37:55	(4,809)
White, Andrew M	5:09:30	(25,371)
White, Andy	4:47:56	(20,512)
White, Andy R	4:16:24	(12,670)
White, Anthony	4:47:52	(20,494)
White, Benjamin	4:49:05	(20,789)
White, Benjamin T	5:21:23	(27,673)
White, Brian J	3:59:38	(9,127)
White, Charlie L	4:52:18	(21,568)

White, Christopher R....3:46:41 (6,280)
White, Colin R....4:42:51 (19,270)
White, Craig A....3:42:57 (5,677)
White, Craig A....5:36:27 (30,107)
White, Daniel J....5:01:46 (23,885)
White, Daniel W....4:54:22 (22,114)
White, Darren W....3:31:52 (3,967)
White, David....4:01:46 (9,562)
White, David....4:15:13 (12,370)
White, David D....4:29:55 (16,123)
White, David R....3:54:02 (7,799)
White, Derek G....5:45:28 (31,203)
White, Douglas M....5:53:21 (31,993)
White, Edward J....3:25:22 (3,052)
White, Geoff D....4:34:09 (17,062)
White, Ian....5:53:21 (31,993)
White, Ian P....4:29:20 (15,947)
White, James R....4:26:53 (15,288)
White, Jason H....4:28:21 (15,687)
White, John....6:00:04 (32,587)
White, John A....4:19:43 (13,515)
White, John D....3:29:17 (3,614)
White, John L....6:03:54 (32,879)
White, John R....4:36:22 (17,629)
White, Jonathan H....4:17:23 (12,904)
White, Joseph A....4:57:35 (22,926)
White, Keith R....3:55:02 (8,015)
White, Kevin M....6:00:36 (32,630)
White, Kevin M....7:08:36 (35,255)
White, Louis....5:00:18 (23,575)
White, Luke....6:06:40 (33,088)
White, Malcolm J....3:55:04 (8,025)
White, Mark....3:15:11 (2,013)
White, Mark....3:49:45 (6,884)
White, Mark A....3:45:53 (6,161)
White, Martin....5:00:15 (23,563)
White, Martin D....4:09:13 (11,010)
White, Matt....4:35:05 (17,291)
White, Michael C....3:56:37 (8,385)
White, Michael E....3:55:44 (8,171)
White, Michael G....5:16:24 (26,736)
White, Mike P....2:54:46 (566)
White, Nick G....4:02:22 (9,679)
White, Nick S....4:57:04 (22,788)
White, Paul A....3:36:11 (4,568)
White, Paul A....5:05:24 (24,573)
White, Paul M....3:24:10 (2,927)
White, Peter A....5:54:10 (32,069)
White, Philip....5:02:29 (24,033)
White, Philip....5:41:25 (30,759)
White, Philip D....4:58:07 (23,058)
White, Richard J....4:30:05 (16,170)
White, Robert....4:21:50 (14,044)
White, Robert J....3:59:31 (9,097)
White, Robert R....5:01:01 (23,732)
White, Robin....6:06:39 (33,087)
White, Roland G....4:21:43 (14,009)
White, Simon....3:53:31 (7,694)
White, Stuart G....4:37:18 (17,843)
White, Terence....5:04:05 (24,340)
White, Toby J....5:15:42 (26,602)
White, William H....4:25:18 (14,894)
Whitefield, Adam B....5:05:44 (24,642)
Whitefield, Giles E....4:19:49 (13,544)
Whitefield, Rupert H....4:04:26 (10,045)
Whitefoot, Oliver....5:19:35 (27,357)
Whitehead, Mark....4:20:26 (13,717)
Whitehead, Martyn J....4:52:43 (21,673)
Whitehead, Michael R....3:09:43 (1,533)
Whitehead, Paul A....4:39:34 (18,427)
Whitehead, Peter....5:57:31 (32,371)
Whitehead, Richard....3:52:58 (7,557)
Whitehead, Simon....4:27:55 (15,563)
Whitehead, Thomas....4:49:50 (20,959)
Whitehead, Thomas D....4:24:16 (14,647)
Whitehouse, Andrew J....5:44:50 (31,134)
Whitehouse, Darren....3:59:43 (9,144)
Whitehouse, Matthew W....4:52:54 (21,727)
Whitehouse, Michael A....5:29:43 (29,097)
Whitehouse, Mick....4:04:25 (10,041)
Whitehouse, Neil R....4:31:25 (16,444)
Whitelaw, Sandy....5:09:59 (25,473)
Whitelegg, Mathew J....5:08:29 (25,185)
Whiteley, Jonathan....4:54:09 (22,062)
Whiteley, Nigel P....3:59:02 (8,965)
Whiteley, Stephen P....4:12:39 (11,751)
Whitelock, James G....3:58:22 (8,800)
Whitelock, Neil P....3:52:20 (7,440)
Whiteman, Anthony W....5:45:18 (31,182)
Whiteman, Oliver R....4:23:24 (14,418)
Whitfield, Adam....3:55:13 (8,061)
Whitfield, Karl J....4:29:01 (15,861)
Whitfield, Matthew....3:13:34 (1,863)
Whiting, Andrew....4:06:35 (10,482)
Whiting, David C....5:24:00 (28,107)
Whiting, Glen A....5:04:25 (24,405)
Whiting, Richard....5:19:30 (27,337)
Whitley, Neil C....5:16:37 (26,773)
Whitley, Steve J....3:29:32 (3,652)
Whitlock, David R....4:41:07 (18,817)
Whitlock, Tony R....3:20:33 (2,562)
Whitmarsh, Jim F....4:04:29 (10,054)
Whitmore, Ivon E....3:12:32 (1,782)
Whitmore, James R....5:36:49 (30,150)
Whitmore, Kris....4:07:51 (10,737)
Whitmore, Mathew A....4:11:33 (11,510)
Whitmore, Paul T....5:29:01 (28,988)
Whitney, Neil D....5:39:33 (30,538)
Whittaker, Anthony J....4:55:22 (22,353)
Whittaker, Ben....3:51:32 (7,262)
Whittaker, Dean....5:04:05 (24,340)
Whittaker, James D....4:52:27 (21,607)
Whittaker, John S....4:49:02 (20,774)
Whittaker, Paul....6:15:42 (33,661)
Whittaker, Peter....4:05:17 (10,202)
Whittaker, Philip J....4:13:11 (11,874)
Whittaker, Samuel J....3:06:21 (1,257)
Whittell, Brian....4:21:22 (13,926)
Whittell, Stuart K....4:14:26 (12,194)
Whitting, Charlie....3:06:21 (1,257)
Whittingham, Andrew J....3:33:00 (4,138)
Whittington, Aaron....5:58:11 (32,430)
Whittington, David H....6:15:08 (33,627)
Whittington, Russell....3:00:59 (959)
Whittle, Rusty M....5:28:37 (28,923)
Whittley, Shane....3:57:53 (8,693)
Whittock, Miles....5:24:53 (28,257)
Whitton, Peter R....5:42:57 (30,928)
Whitty, Maurice W....3:10:47 (1,613)
Whitworth, Bill J....4:15:55 (12,533)
Whitworth, Nicholas C....5:09:06 (25,295)
Whybrow, Nikki....4:41:04 (18,803)
Whyment, Andrew D....5:30:36 (29,235)
Whyte, Michael....5:13:18 (26,088)
Whyte, Steven R....5:18:22 (27,140)
Whytock, Andrew G....4:37:34 (17,902)
Wibaux, Max....4:20:44 (13,780)
Wick, Darren....4:48:52 (20,736)
Wickenden, Anthony....5:14:52 (26,422)
Wickenden, Sephen....4:40:45 (18,714)
Wickert, Keith F....4:43:16 (19,363)
Wickham, Ian....3:49:30 (6,832)
Wicks, Gavin C....4:27:16 (15,411)
Wicks, Jonathan R....3:20:28 (2,551)
Wicks, Marc....4:52:19 (21,576)
Wicks, Nathan....4:07:15 (10,613)
Wicks, Ryan....5:13:04 (26,058)
Widdison, Richard....4:38:20 (18,106)
Widdows, Terence....4:44:15 (19,615)
Widdowson, Nigel....4:15:25 (12,421)
Widelski, Gregg P....3:58:31 (8,842)
Widiwardhono, Aryo....6:31:03 (34,364)
Wield, Christopher....5:10:53 (25,641)
Wiesenberg, Nathan....5:00:39 (23,648)
Wiesner, Carsten....3:17:32 (2,232)
Wigaard, Espen....3:02:43 (1,038)
Wigbout, Rod....4:24:39 (14,735)
Wigens, John....3:51:33 (7,266)
Wiggans, Andy K....3:40:12 (5,217)
Wiggins, Ashley W....5:35:32 (29,980)
Wiggins, Derek A....4:49:01 (20,771)
Wiggins, Michael....3:17:39 (2,248)
Wiggins, Robert C....3:05:34 (1,206)
Wiggins, Simon P....3:49:14 (6,788)
Wiggins, Stephen M....4:36:34 (17,686)
Wightwick, Jonathan G....4:39:26 (18,400)
Wigley, Timothy J....2:53:44 (510)
Wigmore, Darren C....3:00:27 (928)
Wigmore, Nick I....2:58:17 (770)
Wigzell, Edward W....4:12:52 (11,801)
Wiiliams, Dewi....3:26:36 (3,206)
Wikeley, Adrian....5:10:48 (25,628)
Wikeley, Matthew R....4:58:03 (23,045)
Wilberforce, Gary....4:20:20 (13,691)
Wilbur, Duncan....3:51:45 (7,305)
Wilby, Guy D....5:25:25 (28,346)
Wilcock, Martin....2:56:35 (644)
Wilcock, Nigel H....5:00:00 (23,503)
Wilcox, Alan....3:49:19 (6,799)
Wilcox, Brett E....4:36:39 (17,704)
Wilcox, Glenn G....3:55:23 (8,102)
Wild, David A....7:03:44 (35,186)
Wild, Richard....2:53:42 (509)
Wild, Ron W....4:41:06 (18,811)
Wild, Stuart B....5:46:07 (31,275)
Wilde, Aaron....5:27:57 (28,786)
Wilde, Anthony....5:10:51 (25,633)
Wilde, Mark D....5:47:23 (31,396)
Wilde, Michael S....4:24:08 (14,610)
Wilderoder, Brian K....5:34:49 (29,889)
Wilderspin, Richard J....5:12:30 (25,951)
Wildey, Shaun T....4:34:42 (17,203)
Wilding, Nick....6:10:10 (33,315)
Wilding, Ravin....4:07:36 (10,680)
Wilding, Steve J....5:32:00 (29,451)
Wildisen, Greg J....3:32:35 (4,082)
Wildman, Alistair J....3:44:54 (6,013)
Wildman, Anthony....5:32:29 (29,520)
Wildman, Paul A....4:10:58 (11,362)
Wileman, Paul....4:57:27 (22,896)
Wileman, Ryan....4:02:59 (9,781)
Wiles, Andrew E....4:23:55 (14,547)
Wiles, Andrew J....4:23:08 (14,362)
Wilgoss, Andy J....4:22:30 (14,205)
Wiliams, Brian....5:22:58 (27,932)
Wiliams, Paul M....3:43:55 (5,852)
Wiliams, Ronnie....5:27:07 (28,640)
Wiliams, Wesley D....6:34:46 (34,485)
Wilkerson, Paul J....3:44:27 (5,933)
Wilkes, Alan P....4:37:16 (17,834)
Wilkes, Andrew C....4:18:10 (13,112)
Wilkes, Anthony N....3:18:30 (2,343)
Wilkes, Don M....4:26:58 (15,314)
Wilkes, Morris....5:30:32 (29,227)
Wilkes, Neil H....4:11:22 (11,466)
Wilkes, Paul....3:55:50 (8,190)
Wilkes, Roger J....4:50:52 (21,210)
Wilkie, Peter....4:51:31 (21,371)
Wilkie, Stuart H....3:20:24 (2,542)
Wilkie, Thomas A....5:30:51 (29,270)
Wilkins, Gavin....6:53:01 (34,993)
Wilkins, John....3:28:33 (3,499)
Wilkins, Paul....4:33:12 (16,846)
Wilkins, Robert....5:16:00 (26,662)
Wilkins, Simon....4:27:27 (15,460)
Wilkins, Tom J....4:20:36 (13,752)
Wilkins, Ty C....4:33:27 (16,900)
Wilkinson, Adam....4:49:26 (20,867)
Wilkinson, Ben....4:07:11 (10,606)
Wilkinson, Ben D....4:48:31 (20,651)
Wilkinson, Daniel A....4:51:13 (21,292)
Wilkinson, David R....3:31:54 (3,972)
Wilkinson, Edward M....3:54:53 (7,982)
Wilkinson, Graham....4:56:31 (22,635)
Wilkinson, Graham A....3:33:25 (4,198)
Wilkinson, Ian J....4:01:45 (9,561)
Wilkinson, James M....3:39:27 (5,098)
Wilkinson, Jeffrey K....4:20:20 (13,691)
Wilkinson, Keith H....5:14:19 (26,294)
Wilkinson, Lee....4:52:47 (21,689)
Wilkinson, Matthew J....5:37:06 (30,181)
Wilkinson, Matthew L....4:26:26 (15,170)
Wilkinson, Michael....6:53:20 (35,000)
Wilkinson, Michael B....4:41:50 (19,005)
Wilkinson, Nigel J....3:54:05 (7,812)
Wilkinson, Paul....5:44:29 (31,092)
Wilkinson, Scott....4:54:13 (22,081)
Wilkinson, Sean D....4:00:49 (9,378)
Wilkinson, Stephen....4:18:10 (13,112)

Wilkinson, Stephen A.....4:02:26 (9,687)
Wilkinson, Steven M.....3:11:48 (1,701)
Wilkinson, Stewart M.....4:34:33 (17,159)
Wilkinson, Stuart M.....4:00:32 (9,318)
Wilkinsoon, Ron.....5:17:36 (26,980)
Willard, Adrian.....3:58:32 (8,846)
Willard, James A.....4:03:02 (9,791)
Willatgamuwa, Don S.....5:15:44 (26,612)
Willcock, Andrew P.....4:06:03 (10,361)
Willcock, James M.....4:08:03 (10,778)
Willcocks, Sydney G.....4:48:38 (20,676)
Willcox, Ian G.....4:29:30 (16,007)
Willcox, Kevan.....5:34:17 (29,811)
Willday, Trevor J.....5:48:54 (31,572)
Willer, Joseph.....4:13:24 (11,936)
Willerton, Andy.....3:54:19 (7,874)
Willerton, Neville A.....5:01:04 (23,745)
Willett, Raymond A.....4:55:38 (22,415)
Willetts, Andrew J.....5:26:19 (28,512)
Willetts, Colin G.....3:21:26 (2,643)
Willetts, John M.....5:31:23 (29,359)
Willey, Martin J.....3:40:38 (5,289)
Williams, Adam B.....5:23:16 (27,973)
Williams, Alex.....5:17:01 (26,861)
Williams, Andrew.....4:53:54 (21,991)
Williams, Andrew H.....5:26:50 (28,597)
Williams, Andrew K.....4:27:52 (15,556)
Williams, Andrew P.....4:17:46 (13,015)
Williams, Andrew S.....5:14:55 (26,432)
Williams, Andy.....5:03:01 (24,129)
Williams, Anthony.....3:51:08 (7,168)
Williams, Anthony A.....4:04:06 (9,985)
Williams, Anthony S.....4:03:29 (9,866)
Williams, Arthur C.....6:19:22 (33,856)
Williams, Benjamin J.....4:14:57 (12,311)
Williams, Brian H.....3:38:10 (4,865)
Williams, Chris J.....5:12:22 (25,933)
Williams, Christopher.....5:36:18 (30,082)
Williams, Clive T.....5:00:13 (23,557)
Williams, Colin C.....4:07:27 (10,644)
Williams, Coningsby R.....3:52:07 (7,395)
Williams, Dafydd W.....3:24:54 (3,009)
Williams, Dai A.....4:06:34 (10,480)
Williams, Damian.....3:25:35 (3,074)
Williams, Daniel H.....4:15:05 (12,338)
Williams, Darren P.....2:54:03 (520)
Williams, Daryl M.....5:30:15 (29,180)
Williams, David.....4:35:53 (17,508)
Williams, David A.....4:54:12 (22,079)
Williams, David A.....5:00:32 (23,621)
Williams, David D.....5:25:34 (28,382)
Williams, David F.....6:45:50 (34,825)
Williams, David J.....3:16:20 (2,108)
Williams, David J.....4:55:25 (22,368)
Williams, David K.....5:39:37 (30,546)
Williams, David T.....4:49:27 (20,874)
Williams, David W.....5:46:46 (31,330)
Williams, Dean.....5:43:56 (31,029)
Williams, Dennis S.....5:24:22 (28,168)
Williams, Dominic J.....5:03:14 (24,178)
Williams, Dominic M.....5:34:39 (29,870)
Williams, Edward P.....3:40:46 (5,312)
Williams, Edwin L.....4:01:29 (9,512)
Williams, Gareth.....4:36:25 (17,644)
Williams, Gareth I.....3:54:14 (7,848)
Williams, Gary.....5:20:07 (27,440)
Williams, Gary C.....4:16:26 (12,681)
Williams, Gary M.....4:22:57 (14,319)
Williams, George.....3:32:10 (4,027)
Williams, Glenn.....6:05:02 (32,965)
Williams, Glyn.....4:44:30 (19,681)
Williams, Glyn C.....3:52:58 (7,557)
Williams, Graham.....4:36:11 (17,576)
Williams, Gregory T.....5:21:13 (27,637)
Williams, Haydn J.....3:21:32 (2,655)
Williams, Howard B.....4:59:54 (23,475)
Williams, Howard M.....4:01:17 (9,477)
Williams, Huw G.....6:01:52 (32,744)
Williams, Hywel G.....4:55:48 (22,455)
Williams, Iain.....3:15:38 (2,043)
Williams, Iwan W.....3:20:56 (2,603)
Williams, Jack S.....4:15:58 (12,551)
Williams, James.....5:47:54 (31,449)
Williams, James D.....5:09:43 (25,419)
Williams, Jim R.....4:36:08 (17,567)
Williams, John.....4:09:35 (11,092)
Williams, John.....4:34:25 (17,118)
Williams, John D.....4:17:37 (12,981)
Williams, John D.....5:11:42 (25,791)
Williams, John G.....6:34:24 (34,472)
Williams, Jonathan D.....3:19:52 (2,475)
Williams, Jonathan D.....4:25:15 (14,884)
Williams, Jonathan N.....4:23:10 (14,369)
Williams, Joseph K.....4:12:16 (11,677)
Williams, Joseph S.....5:01:21 (23,803)
Williams, Julian.....3:36:37 (4,629)
Williams, Keith E.....3:31:35 (3,925)
Williams, Kevin H.....4:04:48 (10,114)
Williams, Leon S.....3:19:35 (2,441)
Williams, Luke R.....3:59:44 (9,149)
Williams, Mark.....4:01:21 (9,490)
Williams, Mark H.....5:17:53 (27,025)
Williams, Mark K.....4:04:08 (9,991)
Williams, Mark L.....3:24:37 (2,972)
Williams, Mark R.....4:16:34 (12,708)
Williams, Mark R.....5:47:18 (31,386)
Williams, Martin C.....5:16:42 (26,789)
Williams, Matthew.....4:23:06 (14,355)
Williams, Matthew.....4:39:07 (18,310)
Williams, Matthew A.....6:45:49 (34,822)
Williams, Matthew B.....3:58:07 (8,746)
Williams, Matthew D.....5:14:03 (26,239)
Williams, Matthew I.....4:06:50 (10,537)
Williams, Michael.....4:44:58 (19,828)
Williams, Mike G.....4:08:10 (10,799)
Williams, Nathan.....6:14:00 (33,554)
Williams, Nefyn.....4:48:41 (20,689)
Williams, Neil.....4:02:12 (9,646)
Williams, Neil J.....3:32:19 (4,050)
Williams, Neil J.....3:47:42 (6,478)
Williams, Neil R.....4:05:05 (10,160)
Williams, Nigel.....4:14:17 (12,165)
Williams, Nigel P.....4:33:16 (16,862)
Williams, Noel A.....4:27:49 (15,543)
Williams, Owen T.....5:29:46 (29,105)
Williams, Paul.....4:36:14 (17,592)
Williams, Paul D.....4:37:23 (17,855)
Williams, Paul E.....3:40:03 (5,198)
Williams, Paul J.....5:00:44 (23,670)
Williams, Paul M.....3:30:32 (3,790)
Williams, Paul M.....4:05:42 (10,291)
Williams, Paul R.....5:33:48 (29,731)
Williams, Peter C.....3:57:13 (8,533)
Williams, Peter E.....3:30:14 (3,753)
Williams, Peter F.....3:55:02 (8,015)
Williams, Peter G.....3:32:07 (4,013)
Williams, Peter R.....5:06:54 (24,861)
Williams, Philip R.....5:07:23 (24,975)
Williams, Ray G.....4:38:41 (18,195)
Williams, Rhodri.....4:17:48 (13,023)
Williams, Rhys J.....4:04:11 (10,002)
Williams, Richard.....3:55:16 (8,070)
Williams, Richard.....5:01:27 (23,821)
Williams, Richard J.....4:28:49 (15,814)
Williams, Richard J.....5:28:02 (28,805)
Williams, Richard L.....5:09:42 (25,415)
Williams, Robert B.....5:03:22 (24,208)
Williams, Roger B.....4:26:26 (15,170)
Williams, Ross D.....5:14:30 (26,334)
Williams, Russell.....3:59:01 (8,964)
Williams, Sam E.....4:48:46 (20,711)
Williams, Samuel J.....4:19:38 (13,491)
Williams, Scott.....6:26:42 (34,200)
Williams, Scott R.....5:47:57 (31,462)
Williams, Simon K.....5:03:44 (24,276)
Williams, Simon P.....3:30:14 (3,753)
Williams, Stanley.....3:27:00 (3,281)
Williams, Stephen.....4:34:40 (17,196)
Williams, Stephen A.....4:45:56 (20,042)
Williams, Stephen D.....5:19:55 (27,412)
Williams, Stephen G.....4:12:10 (11,650)
Williams, Stephen P.....5:51:32 (31,831)
Williams, Steven D.....3:53:42 (7,728)
Williams, Steven Y.....3:05:16 (1,182)
Williams, Thomas.....4:15:53 (12,531)
Williams, Thomas A.....2:59:23 (852)
Williams, Tim J.....4:48:41 (20,689)
Williams, Timothy.....6:00:52 (32,653)
Williams, Tony R.....4:54:40 (22,190)
Williams-Gunn, Andrew.....3:54:34 (7,914)
Williamson, Andrew.....5:46:05 (31,271)
Williamson, Anthony M.....6:29:51 (34,322)
Williamson, David.....6:02:53 (32,813)
Williamson, James.....7:32:00 (35,508)
Williamson, James A.....4:24:16 (14,647)
Williamson, James I.....3:46:59 (6,342)
Williamson, Karl A.....4:10:20 (11,233)
Williamson, Mark.....5:01:57 (23,922)
Williamson, Matt C.....2:44:15 (222)
Williamson, Neil G.....4:34:55 (17,250)
Williamson, Neil R.....5:55:56 (32,232)
Williamson, Peter.....4:02:21 (9,677)
Williamson, Richard E.....5:18:41 (27,196)
Williamson, Robin D.....3:52:04 (7,386)
Williamson, Sam R.....2:47:20 (295)
Williamson, Stephen W.....2:49:43 (367)
Williamson, Steve.....3:17:28 (2,230)
Williamson, Steven W.....4:13:18 (11,909)
Williamson, Toby D.....5:48:03 (31,472)
Willicott, Mark.....3:53:10 (7,608)
Willis, Andrew D.....6:36:17 (34,551)
Willis, Andrew M.....3:46:38 (6,272)
Willis, Andrew M.....7:14:47 (35,344)
Willis, Brian A.....4:38:17 (18,084)
Willis, Bryan J.....3:34:11 (4,291)
Willis, Chris A.....7:14:47 (35,344)
Willis, Craig A.....5:16:55 (26,845)
Willis, David.....5:46:35 (31,319)
Willis, Gary S.....3:20:55 (2,600)
Willis, John D.....5:27:35 (28,728)
Willis, Lloyd M.....4:31:16 (16,416)
Willis, Mark C.....4:15:15 (12,376)
Willis, Martin.....5:12:32 (25,957)
Willis, Matthew J.....2:56:35 (644)
Willis, Michael.....4:04:49 (10,116)
Willis, Paul J.....5:22:45 (27,902)
Willis, Simeon.....3:48:12 (6,561)
Willis, Spencer A.....4:10:26 (11,253)
Willis, Stephen J.....3:42:26 (5,589)
Willis, Tony N.....4:53:56 (22,000)
Willmitt, William J.....4:26:13 (15,105)
Willmott, Adam E.....4:23:44 (14,497)
Willmott, Daniel J.....5:24:33 (28,188)
Willmott, Gary J.....4:44:40 (19,734)
Willmott, John A.....4:08:33 (10,879)
Willmott, Jon J.....4:53:17 (21,831)
Willmott, Martin G.....4:08:05 (10,787)
Wills, Andrew.....5:16:04 (26,674)
Wills, Dixe.....4:23:56 (14,549)
Wills, Tony.....4:55:27 (22,377)
Willsher, Anthony J.....4:10:24 (11,248)
Willson, Tim.....3:58:35 (8,853)
Wilmot, Andrew H.....3:40:17 (5,227)
Wilmot, Michael D.....5:15:45 (26,618)
Wilmot, Oliver R.....4:57:00 (22,772)
Wilmshurst, Andrew P.....2:55:31 (594)
Wilsher, Amos.....6:19:31 (33,861)
Wilsher, Peter B.....4:57:38 (22,939)
Wilsher, Philip J.....4:32:14 (16,616)
Wilson, Adrian A.....5:08:25 (25,176)
Wilson, Adrian M.....5:27:00 (28,619)
Wilson, Alan A.....5:44:55 (31,142)
Wilson, Alex.....5:04:55 (24,504)
Wilson, Alexander H.....3:27:03 (3,290)
Wilson, Andrew.....5:23:36 (28,029)
Wilson, Andrew P.....4:22:56 (14,317)
Wilson, Anthony G.....6:01:58 (32,750)
Wilson, Anthony R.....4:41:49 (19,001)
Wilson, Barry N.....3:02:59 (1,046)
Wilson, Bernard J.....4:53:25 (21,868)
Wilson, Billy J.....3:38:42 (4,956)
Wilson, Chris D.....3:50:55 (7,120)
Wilson, Christopher A.....3:55:03 (8,019)
Wilson, Christopher D.....5:16:31 (26,759)
Wilson, Christopher J.....4:11:35 (11,518)
Wilson, Christopher L.....4:12:45 (11,775)
Wilson, Colin.....4:20:27 (13,719)
Wilson, Damian R.....3:32:17 (4,044)
Wilson, Daniel.....5:51:23 (31,814)

Wilson, Daren M	4:44:57	(19,820)
Wilson, Darren M	4:41:27	(18,902)
Wilson, David C	3:56:59	(8,476)
Wilson, David H	3:10:25	(1,593)
Wilson, David J	6:21:59	(33,993)
Wilson, Donough	6:50:58	(34,956)
Wilson, Fraser J	2:48:09	(316)
Wilson, Gareth E	2:52:23	(457)
Wilson, Gary	4:34:20	(17,101)
Wilson, Gary J	4:31:51	(16,537)
Wilson, Geoffrey	3:32:29	(4,065)
Wilson, George W	4:25:59	(15,054)
Wilson, Glenn C	3:14:38	(1,958)
Wilson, Graeme S	2:33:40	(57)
Wilson, Gregory A	2:48:53	(342)
Wilson, Gregory J	4:29:21	(15,956)
Wilson, Hugh D	3:36:51	(4,667)
Wilson, Iain L	3:58:42	(8,882)
Wilson, Ian J	4:21:19	(13,914)
Wilson, Ian R	4:20:58	(13,845)
Wilson, James	5:35:38	(30,003)
Wilson, James	6:28:21	(34,258)
Wilson, Jamie R	5:56:04	(32,244)
Wilson, John W	3:42:01	(5,525)
Wilson, Keith R	4:02:42	(9,729)
Wilson, Kenneth J	5:05:37	(24,621)
Wilson, Lee R	4:05:47	(10,304)
Wilson, Mark R	4:51:47	(21,434)
Wilson, Matt	4:13:20	(11,917)
Wilson, Michael G	3:53:13	(7,626)
Wilson, Nicholas C	3:13:12	(1,840)
Wilson, Nicholas M	3:16:14	(2,097)
Wilson, Nicholas T	4:16:21	(12,660)
Wilson, Nick	4:46:34	(20,191)
Wilson, Paul A	5:51:13	(31,798)
Wilson, Paul J	3:32:18	(4,047)
Wilson, Paul M	5:34:51	(29,894)
Wilson, Paul S	4:57:19	(22,860)
Wilson, Philip L	3:29:11	(3,602)
Wilson, Rhydderch	3:43:59	(5,865)
Wilson, Richard	5:40:38	(30,668)
Wilson, Richard A	7:35:58	(35,539)
Wilson, Richard J	3:13:38	(1,869)
Wilson, Robert	2:47:06	(287)
Wilson, Robert J	3:48:56	(6,712)
Wilson, Robin H	4:55:22	(22,353)
Wilson, Rory J	5:30:12	(29,177)
Wilson, Simon H	3:24:32	(2,958)
Wilson, Steve	5:10:51	(25,633)
Wilson, Stewart J	3:51:09	(7,171)
Wilson, Terry	4:22:58	(14,322)
Wilson, Thomas A	3:40:39	(5,290)
Wilson, Thomas A	6:14:46	(33,598)
Wilson, Timothy GA	3:49:13	(6,779)
Wilson, Tony	4:07:30	(10,651)
Wilson, Tony D	4:42:36	(19,207)
Wiltcher, David M	5:40:10	(30,614)
Wilton, David C	4:40:21	(18,618)
Wilton, Graham G	2:49:47	(368)
Wiltshire, Alex	5:23:17	(27,974)
Wiltshire, Craig J	5:09:19	(25,336)
Wiltshire, Jeremy	4:10:49	(11,332)
Wiltshire, John R	4:28:22	(15,689)
Wiltshire, Jon I	4:26:07	(15,080)
Wimbush, Paul D	4:00:25	(9,297)
Wimphen, Gilles	3:35:14	(4,438)
Wimshurst, Thomas H	3:04:02	(1,107)
Winch, Dean D	3:56:21	(8,319)
Winch, Jason P	6:04:54	(32,950)
Winch, Martin J	4:13:01	(11,833)
Winchester, Kenneth R	4:52:47	(21,689)
Windass, Alastair J	4:01:33	(9,521)
Winder, David J	3:12:02	(1,734)
Winder, Robert W	7:12:09	(35,306)
Windle, Daron K	4:40:34	(18,673)
Windsor, Colin G	4:26:32	(15,201)
Winfield, Stephen D	4:38:52	(18,246)
Winfield, Stephen J	4:02:54	(9,767)
Winfield, Stuart D	4:14:41	(12,253)
Wing, Matt	4:52:57	(21,742)
Wing, Stephen	6:06:24	(33,076)
Wingate, Carl E	5:07:10	(24,918)
Wingfield, Simon J	6:18:21	(33,793)

Wingrove, Chris J	5:25:01	(28,272)
Winkley, Don	3:59:34	(9,111)
Winning, Gary	5:29:00	(28,984)
Winsbury, Mark W	3:48:41	(6,663)
Winslade, James C	4:06:21	(10,423)
Winsland, Derek	4:28:05	(15,616)
Winslow, Michael P	4:01:36	(9,535)
Winsor, Ian R	4:21:51	(14,049)
Winstanley, Brian	4:29:30	(16,007)
Winston, Alan	4:48:41	(20,689)
Winston, Blake	5:00:44	(23,670)
Winstone, Nick	4:28:41	(15,781)
Winter, Andrew J	6:02:11	(32,761)
Winter, Eric B	4:34:49	(17,225)
Winter, Joerg C	3:51:49	(7,318)
Winter, Martin	4:00:47	(9,369)
Winter, Richard A	4:24:12	(14,630)
Winter, Richard C	5:43:07	(30,949)
Winterflood, David	4:29:05	(15,880)
Winterflood, Simon	5:13:10	(26,075)
Winters, John T	4:28:26	(15,709)
Wintle, David M	3:14:11	(1,910)
Wintle, George W	4:44:03	(19,552)
Wipp, Jonathan P	5:47:27	(31,405)
Wisbey, Simon J	4:05:55	(10,332)
Wisdom, Martin J	3:45:46	(6,142)
Wise, Chris A	3:42:28	(5,593)
Wise, Daniel	3:57:39	(8,639)
Wise, David J	4:03:46	(9,919)
Wise, Glyn	5:02:44	(24,083)
Wise, Jason	4:21:49	(14,036)
Wise, John	3:13:14	(1,845)
Wise, Larry M	4:48:17	(20,597)
Wise, Matthew J	4:48:50	(20,729)
Wiseman, Derek	4:10:24	(11,248)
Witcomb, Mark D	5:20:08	(27,444)
Witheat, Charles G	5:09:03	(25,285)
Withers, David G	4:14:59	(12,318)
Withers, Julian J	4:36:19	(17,614)
Withers, Philip J	5:02:48	(24,088)
Withers, Thomas J	4:14:37	(12,235)
Withers Green, Jeremy	4:40:05	(18,552)
Withey, Bernard	5:24:24	(28,172)
Withington, Michael S	4:05:31	(10,241)
Withington, Terry	5:35:34	(29,989)
Witschard, Remy P	4:15:29	(12,439)
Witt, Jonathan J	4:33:27	(16,900)
Wittering, Mark A	3:08:26	(1,426)
Wizard, Danny N	3:15:58	(2,076)
Wodzianski, Juliusz V	4:38:25	(18,131)
Wohlgemuth, Glenn	6:53:38	(35,010)
Wojcio, Michael D	5:24:21	(28,164)
Wolfendale, Stewart	4:06:02	(10,355)
Wolfenden, Matthew	5:19:49	(27,396)
Wolff, David A	4:37:34	(17,902)
Wolke, Achim	4:07:57	(10,760)
Wolking, Dominikus	4:29:35	(16,034)
Wolliscroft, Michael P	4:15:43	(12,487)
Wollwinder, Erwin	3:56:51	(8,444)
Wolovitz, Lionel	3:36:30	(4,609)
Wolton, Peter H	4:25:22	(14,913)
Womack, Douglas E	4:50:21	(21,080)
Womack, Mark R	4:01:09	(9,452)
Wombell, Alan	4:57:19	(22,860)
Wombell, Michael	4:42:25	(19,156)
Womersley, Martyn G	4:17:09	(12,842)
Wong, Alvin F	5:34:58	(29,910)
Wong, Baldwin	4:09:32	(11,080)
Wong, Chi H	4:30:08	(16,182)
Wong, Foo Yuen	3:52:33	(7,473)
Wong, Justin X	4:02:08	(9,626)
Wong, Mark C	5:00:41	(23,652)
Wong, Michael	4:23:34	(14,463)
Wong, Terence	5:22:32	(27,862)
Wong, Wai K	4:52:49	(21,706)
Woo, Daniel V	4:40:37	(18,682)
Wood, Alan G	4:25:06	(14,848)
Wood, Benjamin C	4:53:59	(22,016)
Wood, Bernard J	4:14:19	(12,172)
Wood, Brian E	4:22:31	(14,209)
Wood, Chris	3:57:25	(8,584)
Wood, Chris J	3:54:44	(7,949)
Wood, Christopher J	4:08:05	(10,787)

Wood, Christopher J	4:19:45	(13,524)
Wood, Clive R	5:02:01	(23,938)
Wood, Colin	3:51:43	(7,297)
Wood, Daniel D	4:10:26	(11,253)
Wood, Dave	4:46:02	(20,067)
Wood, David A	3:36:42	(4,646)
Wood, David A	4:12:51	(11,799)
Wood, David J	5:52:50	(31,953)
Wood, David M	3:44:08	(5,884)
Wood, David T	4:13:51	(12,053)
Wood, Douglas G	3:28:26	(3,468)
Wood, Gareth D	3:16:04	(2,086)
Wood, Gordon	5:29:59	(29,129)
Wood, Graham R	4:23:41	(14,488)
Wood, Halvor	4:27:24	(15,448)
Wood, Ian D	3:04:36	(1,138)
Wood, Ian S	5:26:41	(28,574)
Wood, James M	4:07:14	(10,611)
Wood, Jeremy C	6:29:38	(34,315)
Wood, Joseph D	3:26:24	(3,186)
Wood, Kevin	6:10:52	(33,358)
Wood, Kevin G	4:35:44	(17,470)
Wood, Kevin M	3:53:07	(7,594)
Wood, Marc L	4:20:03	(13,611)
Wood, Mark T	3:26:46	(3,234)
Wood, Martin C	5:41:31	(30,770)
Wood, Martin I	3:07:42	(1,360)
Wood, Matthew C	4:08:52	(10,937)
Wood, Nicholas	5:24:44	(28,224)
Wood, Nick G	4:56:37	(22,665)
Wood, Nick K	3:39:47	(5,155)
Wood, Nigel T	4:06:50	(10,537)
Wood, Paul J	2:54:43	(562)
Wood, Peter C	4:17:08	(12,837)
Wood, Peter J	4:44:10	(19,587)
Wood, Peter M	5:17:54	(27,031)
Wood, Philip J	4:05:51	(10,319)
Wood, Reece H	3:01:56	(1,001)
Wood, Richard C	3:25:43	(3,092)
Wood, Stephen J	4:49:48	(20,955)
Wood, Stephen J	5:31:38	(29,393)
Wood, Stephen M	3:28:44	(3,529)
Wood, Steven	4:09:10	(10,997)
Wood, Thomas J	3:16:52	(2,165)
Wood, Vic	4:46:10	(20,095)
Woodall, Brian E	4:28:33	(15,745)
Woodards, Simon K	5:09:17	(25,330)
Woodburn, Geoffrey	5:21:45	(27,741)
Woodburn, Peter J	2:43:16	(203)
Woodcock, Stephen	3:57:06	(8,502)
Wooderson, Andrew D	4:25:23	(14,918)
Woodford, Dominic P	4:34:39	(17,191)
Woodgate, Paul J	3:41:33	(5,448)
Woodhall, Richard A	5:15:29	(26,560)
Woodhall, William H	5:17:35	(26,976)
Woodhams, Richard M	4:12:46	(11,780)
Woodhead, Stephen R	4:27:12	(15,387)
Woodhill, Nicholas J	5:24:44	(28,224)
Woodhouse, Christopher N	3:42:37	(5,611)
Woodhouse, Nigel A	4:22:58	(14,322)
Woodhouse, Richard K	6:22:05	(33,999)
Wooding, Peter D	4:09:52	(11,141)
Woodland, Alistair S	4:12:46	(11,780)
Woodland, Nathan C	3:48:40	(6,659)
Woodley, David W	4:15:01	(12,328)
Woodley, Laurence	5:14:39	(26,373)
Woodman, Mark J	2:39:27	(135)
Woodman, Philip C	3:29:13	(3,605)
Woodroffe, Ian	4:55:29	(22,389)
Woodroof, Alan R	4:41:31	(18,927)
Woodroof, Neil D	3:57:53	(8,693)
Woodrow, Andrew M	3:14:29	(1,941)
Woodrow, William J	4:57:07	(22,800)
Woods, Alec T	2:53:48	(513)
Woods, Alex M	4:29:41	(16,060)
Woods, Christopher T	5:17:38	(26,987)
Woods, George H	4:56:23	(22,609)
Woods, Guy N	5:05:24	(24,573)
Woods, Jonathan P	4:06:57	(10,558)
Woods, Kevin	3:58:49	(8,913)
Woods, Lee M	3:16:40	(2,141)
Woods, Leslie S	5:08:14	(25,147)
Woods, Martin J	4:44:12	(19,602)

LONDON MARATHON, 2007: MALE RUNNERS 905

Woods, Matthew W	4:33:18	(16,867)
Woods, Michael A	3:35:00	(4,409)
Woods, Philip R	3:22:56	(2,789)
Woods, Roger K	4:15:21	(12,406)
Woods, William B	4:43:00	(19,297)
Woodsmith, Jonathan D	3:52:06	(7,392)
Woodthorpe, Timothy J	2:43:20	(204)
Woodward, Aaron R	5:14:53	(26,426)
Woodward, Henry A	5:49:30	(31,626)
Woodward, Jason B	5:08:49	(25,244)
Woodward, Kevin J	4:19:45	(13,524)
Woodward, Mark N	3:53:00	(7,570)
Woodward, Michael	5:15:28	(26,556)
Woodward, Simon D	5:08:28	(25,182)
Woodward, Simon P	3:29:16	(3,611)
Woodward, Tristan D	4:30:29	(16,254)
Woodworth, James P	4:54:48	(22,227)
Woodyatt, Paul	3:10:04	(1,564)
Wookey, Paul	5:08:11	(25,136)
Wooldridge, John P	4:36:00	(17,534)
Woolf, Michael S	4:17:35	(12,975)
Woolford, Andrew J	4:26:01	(15,061)
Woolford, Jeremy W	6:09:31	(33,272)
Woolgrove, David R	5:39:12	(30,477)
Woolham, Craig	5:44:37	(31,111)
Woollard, James L	3:55:14	(8,064)
Woollatt, Simon T	4:37:06	(17,810)
Woolley, Karl A	5:06:07	(24,718)
Woolley, Michael	5:34:59	(29,911)
Woolley, Peter J	4:37:27	(17,883)
Woolley, Ricky	3:55:21	(8,093)
Woolley, Robert	2:53:40	(504)
Woollon, Andy	4:11:34	(11,512)
Woolman, Paul L	4:53:07	(21,784)
Woolmer, Alastair J	3:36:16	(4,582)
Woolnough, Paul D	4:30:04	(16,165)
Woolridge, Stephen J	4:27:53	(15,558)
Woolstenholmes, Peter L	4:56:16	(22,580)
Woosey, Mark	5:19:03	(27,255)
Wootton, Antony S	5:25:32	(28,376)
Wootton, David J	4:08:15	(10,826)
Wootton, Neil K	4:37:42	(17,937)
Wootton, Richard D	4:26:54	(15,296)
Wootton, Terence E	5:25:33	(28,379)
Worboys, Nick	3:01:04	(962)
Wore, Andrew D	4:27:19	(15,429)
Worman, Anthony R	3:56:58	(8,473)
Worn, Steven	4:23:37	(14,470)
Worrall, Michael	5:20:31	(27,522)
Worricker, Russell	5:56:49	(32,321)
Worrow, Jeff J	4:39:03	(18,299)
Worsdell, Philip	4:36:55	(17,771)
Worsell, David P	5:19:11	(27,290)
Worsley, Adam R	5:15:12	(26,500)
Worsley, Christopher J	4:37:39	(17,922)
Worsley, Simon D	4:17:35	(12,975)
Worster, Kevin P	4:07:34	(10,672)
Worster, Paul D	4:27:19	(15,429)
Wort, Peter M	4:36:25	(17,644)
Wort, Steven S	3:06:38	(1,283)
Worth, Glenn J	5:28:49	(28,954)
Worthington, John A	2:47:10	(289)
Worthington, Luke	3:01:18	(975)
Worthington, Paul L	5:11:25	(25,744)
Wortley, John F	5:30:38	(29,241)
Worton, Chris	4:05:13	(10,187)
Wostenholm, Anthony C	4:18:25	(13,181)
Wotton, David A	3:39:42	(5,143)
Wotton, George	5:28:36	(28,918)
Wotton, Kevin M	3:04:56	(1,156)
Wotton, Stephen J	4:44:17	(19,621)
Wragg, Andrew	3:53:12	(7,618)
Wrake, Kevin	4:07:45	(10,712)
Wrapson, Chip	3:48:32	(6,630)
Wray, Darren L	4:46:55	(20,257)
Wray, Paul G	4:49:18	(20,838)
Wreglesworth, Craig S	6:12:24	(33,449)
Wren, Steven	5:07:09	(24,915)
Wrench, James R	3:09:22	(1,506)
Wrenn, Laurence P	5:39:22	(30,502)
Wrenn, Philip J	5:35:21	(29,957)
Wrey, Eddie G	3:48:36	(6,645)
Wright, Adrian P	4:57:46	(22,973)
Wright, Adrian P	5:37:07	(30,184)
Wright, Alan E	3:29:57	(3,709)
Wright, Andrew	3:49:24	(6,808)
Wright, Andrew J	4:19:01	(13,330)
Wright, Andy	5:19:24	(27,319)
Wright, Chris W	4:39:05	(18,303)
Wright, Christopher J	4:40:59	(18,780)
Wright, Craig	4:14:51	(12,278)
Wright, David	2:36:10	(86)
Wright, David	5:14:15	(26,283)
Wright, David A	5:28:37	(28,923)
Wright, David A	5:40:47	(30,680)
Wright, David B	4:21:07	(13,878)
Wright, David C	3:48:09	(6,553)
Wright, David J	3:35:35	(4,497)
Wright, David J	5:36:15	(30,076)
Wright, David P	3:54:27	(7,893)
Wright, Derek	3:44:34	(5,951)
Wright, Gary	3:12:57	(1,818)
Wright, Gary	5:38:25	(30,374)
Wright, Geoffrey	5:18:19	(27,128)
Wright, Graham S	6:46:50	(34,852)
Wright, Ian	5:05:52	(24,666)
Wright, James	3:46:33	(6,257)
Wright, James A	5:50:47	(31,756)
Wright, James H	3:42:07	(5,540)
Wright, James H	5:14:35	(26,359)
Wright, James N	4:46:17	(20,120)
Wright, Jamie A	4:11:13	(11,430)
Wright, Jim J	4:52:41	(21,662)
Wright, Joff M	4:41:48	(18,995)
Wright, John J	4:42:28	(19,171)
Wright, John P	3:33:52	(4,247)
Wright, Joseph T	4:31:04	(16,368)
Wright, Kevin J	4:46:52	(20,243)
Wright, Kevin L	4:43:07	(19,324)
Wright, Kevin R	4:05:40	(10,280)
Wright, Lee W	4:58:55	(23,230)
Wright, Mark	4:25:46	(15,009)
Wright, Mark A	3:30:10	(3,744)
Wright, Martin	4:24:40	(14,739)
Wright, Michael A	4:53:38	(21,924)
Wright, Michael P	5:42:50	(30,919)
Wright, Neil	4:44:57	(19,820)
Wright, Nicholas	4:23:52	(14,536)
Wright, Nigel	5:24:33	(28,188)
Wright, Owen D	3:36:13	(4,574)
Wright, Paul	4:35:20	(17,368)
Wright, Paul A	4:40:42	(18,702)
Wright, Paul D	5:01:45	(23,880)
Wright, Paul M	5:20:13	(27,459)
Wright, Peter	3:57:12	(8,528)
Wright, Peter	4:23:57	(14,555)
Wright, Philip	3:50:34	(7,050)
Wright, Richard E	5:14:39	(26,373)
Wright, Richard K	5:26:48	(28,587)
Wright, Rollo A	3:48:55	(6,709)
Wright, Simon	5:15:15	(26,513)
Wright, Stephen	4:35:24	(17,382)
Wright, Stephen A	4:40:38	(18,685)
Wright, Stephen G	4:44:25	(19,654)
Wright, Stephen J	3:06:25	(1,266)
Wright, Steve J	4:33:02	(16,795)
Wright, Terence J	5:46:38	(31,321)
Wright, Thomas D	4:32:35	(16,686)
Wright, Tom	3:56:36	(8,381)
Wrighton, James P	5:25:26	(28,351)
Wriglesworth, David H	5:13:54	(26,211)
Wriglesworth, John	3:11:54	(1,714)
Wrigley, Russell	4:07:03	(10,586)
Wrintmore, Gary	5:19:54	(27,409)
Wroblewskki, Steve J	3:48:09	(6,553)
Wroe, Stephen A	4:14:13	(12,141)
Wroe, Stephen O	5:02:43	(24,079)
Wroth, James J	5:03:40	(24,269)
Wuermli, Sam	3:22:23	(2,736)
Wwoonton-Pink, Justin D	6:25:19	(34,141)
Wyatt, Andrew A	4:18:50	(13,291)
Wyatt, Cliff L	3:44:19	(5,908)
Wyatt, Darren S	3:29:08	(3,593)
Wyatt, Gary P	3:31:21	(3,885)
Wyatt, Keith M	4:44:17	(19,621)
Wyatt, Michael J	5:26:23	(28,529)
Wyatt, Neil S	4:45:56	(20,042)
Wyatt, Norman	6:25:57	(34,162)
Wyatt, Paul	3:03:14	(1,063)
Wyatt, Simon M	3:56:30	(8,360)
Wyeth, Michael	4:14:59	(12,318)
Wyldbore, Mark	3:05:24	(1,193)
Wyler, Peter	4:34:30	(17,148)
Wyles, Chris	3:13:49	(1,886)
Wylie, David R	3:20:20	(2,533)
Wylie, Guy	4:38:41	(18,195)
Wylie, Stephen F	5:02:24	(24,018)
Wyllie, Stuart	4:44:26	(19,660)
Wyn Pugh, Dylan D	4:24:05	(14,593)
Wynn, Eddie L	5:05:13	(24,545)
Wynne, Colin	4:32:14	(16,616)
Wynne, Gronwy	6:36:05	(34,539)
Wynter Bee, Peter F	5:30:06	(29,161)
Wyse, Barry D	4:03:27	(9,859)
Wysocki, Richard	4:21:59	(14,085)
Wysocki-Jones, Simon J	5:09:03	(25,285)
Wyss, Stephen P	4:20:54	(13,829)
Xenophontos, Chris	4:23:25	(14,421)
Xerri, Richard J	2:46:11	(263)
Xu, Zhenjun	3:37:07	(4,704)
Yabandzhiev, Tsvyatko	4:31:31	(16,463)
Yacomine, Anthony J	4:34:29	(17,143)
Yadave, Rush L	4:08:19	(10,835)
Yajnik, Sanjiv	4:04:09	(9,994)
Yamaki, Masatoshi	4:53:54	(21,991)
Yan, Larry O	3:16:46	(2,155)
Yandell, Lawrence D	4:19:35	(13,479)
Yap, Wooi Huen	4:01:50	(9,574)
Yard, Chris	3:55:13	(8,061)
Yardley, Graham	4:53:35	(21,909)
Yardley-Rees, Guy P	3:26:00	(3,127)
Yarker, Kit	4:37:25	(17,870)
Yarlett, Peter C	4:53:25	(21,868)
Yasumatsu, Kazuhiko	4:31:50	(16,533)
Yates, Andrew F	3:01:15	(972)
Yates, Clifford R	5:16:16	(26,717)
Yates, Ian R	4:55:03	(22,274)
Yates, Jonathan	3:46:26	(6,244)
Yates, Mark	4:51:49	(21,440)
Yau, Jason C	4:09:09	(10,993)
Yau, Raymond	4:34:49	(17,225)
Yazaki, Etsuro	3:18:16	(2,323)
Yeaman, Derek	6:24:44	(34,119)
Yearwood, Nicholas A	4:35:13	(17,338)
Yeates, Chris E	4:22:30	(14,205)
Yelding, Steven R	5:54:55	(32,142)
Yeoman, Paul J	4:14:52	(12,284)
Yeomans, Jason	5:23:40	(28,044)
Yeomans, Lawrence J	3:55:50	(8,190)
Yeomans, Richard J	5:39:17	(30,489)
Yeung, Stephen	4:57:45	(22,970)
Yexley, John	5:36:30	(30,114)
Yianni, John	4:07:20	(10,623)
Yilmaz, Timothy	5:02:14	(23,974)
Yip, Ching S	5:07:23	(24,975)
Yip, David	5:52:48	(31,949)
York, David J	5:28:17	(28,858)
York, Philip A	4:15:07	(12,345)
York, Richard J	5:25:13	(28,308)
York, Stewart	4:41:27	(18,902)
Yorke-Long, Marcus J	4:56:34	(22,647)
Youens, James A	4:26:29	(15,184)
Youl, Andrew T	4:23:58	(14,562)
Youmans, Christopher	4:13:54	(12,068)
Young, Alan	4:40:33	(18,666)
Young, Alastair J	3:40:57	(5,356)
Young, Alexander D	5:21:28	(27,691)
Young, Barnaby E	3:19:20	(2,423)
Young, Ben J	3:38:02	(4,837)
Young, Bob	6:06:36	(33,084)

Young, Chris D 3:07:42 (1,360)
Young, Christopher J 3:19:12 (2,414)
Young, Colin S 3:56:46 (8,423)
Young, Darren J 6:25:12 (34,136)
Young, Gary R 4:36:11 (17,576)
Young, George E 5:38:24 (30,370)
Young, Harvey T 4:43:39 (19,452)
Young, Ian W 4:15:53 (12,531)
Young, Jason M 4:44:56 (19,815)
Young, Jason M 5:55:09 (32,159)
Young, Keith L 5:04:06 (24,345)
Young, Mark A 5:03:11 (24,170)
Young, Martin C 3:57:19 (8,559)
Young, Matthew 5:59:44 (32,559)
Young, Matthew I 3:47:10 (6,373)
Young, Michael M 3:44:29 (5,937)
Young, Michael P 6:45:03 (34,800)
Young, Murray V 7:09:30 (35,266)
Young, Patrick G 3:46:18 (6,219)
Young, Paul N 4:39:13 (18,340)
Young, Philip A 4:29:13 (15,915)
Young, Philip D 5:47:56 (31,459)
Young, Richard 3:48:24 (6,595)
Young, Richard L 4:59:58 (23,497)
Young, Robin 3:38:04 (4,846)
Young, Rodney 3:59:04 (8,976)
Young, Roger G 4:59:31 (23,390)
Young, Russell 2:51:25 (423)
Young, Scott 5:01:47 (23,886)
Young, Simon E 4:54:27 (22,137)
Young, Simon M 3:37:31 (4,754)
Young, Stephen 5:41:41 (30,793)
Young, Truc 3:21:38 (2,667)
Youngman, James D 4:36:12 (17,581)
Yuill, Charles L 5:08:57 (25,273)
Yuill, Ian G 3:04:45 (1,145)
Zabaleta, Koldo 4:14:15 (12,152)
Zabicki, Frederic J 3:19:36 (2,443)
Zajackowski, Jan 5:02:52 (24,099)
Zaman, Arif O 3:53:21 (7,658)
Zaman, Nadim G 5:25:26 (28,351)
Zambaux, Pierre 3:51:54 (7,337)
Zammit, Arthur F 3:29:41 (3,671)
Zammuto, Stefano N 5:06:49 (24,844)
Zanelli, Alessio 3:37:26 (4,741)
Zanelli, Gary N 3:48:35 (6,642)
Zanobini, Enrico 4:23:25 (14,421)
Zanon, Paul 4:35:27 (17,389)
Zanotti, Paolo 4:11:24 (11,474)
Zardini, Max 4:16:58 (12,808)
Zarzuela De Pedro, Adolfo 3:17:48 (2,262)
Zasadzki, Victor 4:23:27 (14,432)
Zavoli, Primo 4:52:05 (21,509)
Zdeba, John R 4:10:02 (11,173)
Zdebik, Peter J 3:37:57 (4,819)
Zech, Manfred 4:12:54 (11,806)
Zechner, Bernhard 5:24:59 (28,267)
Zehner, Ralf 3:57:04 (8,494)
Zehnpfennig, Theo 3:42:13 (5,558)
Zeidman, Moshe 6:17:58 (33,777)
Zelei, Zsolt 3:39:21 (5,073)
Zelmat, Abel 3:55:17 (8,074)
Zelmat, Jean Marc 3:20:00 (2,497)
Zeman, Jakub 4:52:47 (21,689)
Zemontas, Paul 4:50:25 (21,104)
Zeru, Goitom 3:25:27 (3,059)
Zeyssolff, Olivier 3:13:55 (1,894)
Ziegenhorn, Stephan 4:33:20 (16,879)
Zietsman, Warren G 4:22:50 (14,295)
Zillig, Peter D 4:03:49 (9,930)
Zimmerman, Mark A 5:15:43 (26,610)
Zimmermann, Urs W 4:32:50 (16,748)
Zingg, Christian 3:09:57 (1,554)
Zinn, Simon 4:05:37 (10,268)
Zissis, Akis 5:23:47 (28,075)
Zoller, Gary J 3:17:36 (2,239)
Zucker, Andrew 6:26:02 (34,171)
Zuliani, Davide 3:55:07 (8,035)
Zumino, Nicholas 5:07:10 (24,918)
Zurawlin, Paul A 3:50:36 (7,054)
Zwart, Arie J 5:07:16 (24,947)
Zykov, Andrey 4:22:13 (14,131)

FEMALE RUNNERS

Abbott, Joanne L 6:18:51 (33,825)
Abbott, Sarah A 5:22:13 (27,815)
Abbott, Tracey C 6:36:53 (34,577)
Abbs, Wendy M 5:36:18 (30,082)
Abedi, Kaz 5:01:06 (23,751)
Abela, Cheryl 4:44:02 (19,548)
Abercrombie, Caroline 6:40:50 (34,683)
Abitova, Inga 2:34:25 (69)
Ablett, Ann P 5:24:15 (28,148)
Abraham, Beverley D 4:10:01 (11,171)
Abraham, Hayley G 4:19:14 (13,387)
Abrahams, Jane E 6:01:56 (32,748)
Abrahams, Natalie M 4:18:10 (13,112)
Ackerman, Angela 5:24:40 (28,212)
Ackland, Susan C 6:05:28 (32,999)
Acton, Michele L 5:23:25 (27,992)
Adams, Alison J 5:58:03 (32,417)
Adams, Claire 3:55:39 (8,150)
Adams, Elizabeth 3:51:58 (7,359)
Adams, Jackie H 5:14:00 (26,228)
Adams, Jane E 6:13:04 (33,494)
Adams, Jeanette E 6:36:14 (34,549)
Adams, Jennifer L 5:47:56 (31,459)
Adams, Rebecca R 3:55:20 (8,088)
Adams, Samantha J 4:26:31 (15,197)
Adams, Sarah K 7:00:37 (35,139)
Adams, Stephanie L 4:53:23 (21,854)
Adams, Wendy F 6:40:50 (34,683)
Adamson, Tracy J 4:27:16 (15,411)
Adcock, Rosemary A 5:07:51 (25,068)
Addis, Beatrice E 5:55:33 (32,196)
Addison, Bernadette M 5:11:37 (25,780)
Addison, Sophie J 5:16:05 (26,680)
Addison, Susan 5:08:26 (25,179)
Adere, Berhane 2:39:11 (128)
Adie, Gemma L 5:15:06 (26,479)
Adlum, Jane 4:44:13 (19,604)
Adshead, Jennifer R 5:23:00 (27,939)
Aeugle, Sonja 3:56:49 (8,435)
Affleck, Katie L 4:47:24 (20,385)
Afzal, Sadia 7:50:19 (35,618)
Aghanti, Julie I 6:09:59 (33,303)
Ahl, Lucie 3:18:28 (2,340)
Ahmad, Tazeen 4:40:44 (18,706)
Ahmed, Shehneela J 5:39:13 (30,479)
Aigbirhio, Az A 4:51:51 (21,453)
Aiken, Susan 5:29:34 (29,078)
Ainscough, Nicola E 4:54:43 (22,204)
Ainslie, Caroline M 7:23:20 (35,418)
Ainslie, Jane L 5:24:53 (28,257)
Ainsworth, Laura J 4:20:49 (13,807)
Aitchison, Edda I 5:00:19 (23,581)
Aitchison, Elise M 4:54:41 (22,194)
Aitchison, Pauline A 4:16:26 (12,681)
Aitken, Jayne A 5:13:18 (26,088)
Akhanoba, Bernadine D 6:17:42 (33,765)
Akhtar, Kally 4:45:29 (19,946)
Akintayo, Michel 7:24:52 (35,430)
Akkerhuys, Zahra T 6:31:52 (34,399)
Al Na'ama, Yasmin 4:49:59 (20,990)
Al-Ani, Patricia M 5:17:43 (27,002)
Albutt, Beverley J 4:30:39 (16,286)
Alcock, Julie M 6:22:52 (34,038)
Alden, Pauline B 6:32:05 (34,411)
Alder, Clare H 7:02:19 (35,165)
Alder, Joanne L 3:53:35 (7,705)
Alder, Louise B 6:07:30 (33,130)
Alderman, Pauline M 4:53:22 (21,850)
Aldous, Lucy G 4:10:18 (11,228)
Aldridge, Bridget 6:27:12 (34,218)
Aldridge, Jacqueline 5:35:15 (29,949)
Aldridge, Katherine S 3:35:11 (4,434)
Alessandro, Theresa K 6:05:55 (33,039)
Alexander, Alison 6:05:19 (32,986)
Alexander, Lesley 4:49:09 (20,807)
Alexander, Rachel H 4:38:15 (18,068)
Alexander, Samantha 5:02:29 (24,033)
Alexander, Storme E 4:17:00 (12,814)
Alexandrou, Tracey A 3:31:14 (3,871)
Alfieri, Rosa 3:17:09 (2,195)
Alford, Sara 4:31:11 (16,401)
Ali, Samira 6:03:45 (32,872)

Aliane, Jane L 4:43:09 (19,330)
Allan, Dotty 4:17:29 (12,940)
Allan, Elizabeth A 4:12:24 (11,701)
Allanson, Carolyn A 5:17:34 (26,974)
Allberry, Sian H 4:29:45 (16,075)
Allcorn, Gaye E 5:45:57 (31,249)
Allen, Amanda 4:36:48 (17,740)
Allen, Charlotte L 6:01:53 (32,746)
Allen, Claire D 5:25:57 (28,448)
Allen, Clare E 4:51:49 (21,440)
Allen, Debbie B 7:43:47 (35,593)
Allen, Deborah S 6:12:24 (33,449)
Allen, Dionne 5:04:35 (24,430)
Allen, Elizabeth L 5:52:23 (31,909)
Allen, Heather 3:53:00 (7,570)
Allen, Helen E 4:55:26 (22,372)
Allen, Joy 4:07:33 (10,662)
Allen, Katie M 4:36:19 (17,614)
Allen, Louise M 5:09:55 (25,453)
Allen, Lucy 5:17:13 (26,900)
Allen, Melanie L 4:21:53 (14,060)
Allen, Michelle J 4:08:02 (10,774)
Allen, Patricia 4:44:29 (19,677)
Allen, Patricia A 6:08:42 (33,218)
Allen, Rachel 5:07:27 (24,989)
Allen, Stacey M 5:38:47 (30,426)
Allen, Tanya S 5:09:30 (25,371)
Allen, Valerie J 5:06:18 (24,757)
Allis, Sinead A 4:28:20 (15,680)
Allison, Louise E 4:36:22 (17,629)
Allsobrook, Debbie A 5:26:52 (28,602)
Allsop, Ann 5:39:13 (30,479)
Allsopp, Lucy V 5:28:06 (28,818)
Allum, Tammie J 4:41:45 (18,975)
Almond, Katherine M 5:06:59 (24,876)
Alston, Heather M 4:03:48 (9,927)
Alston, Lisa C 5:38:42 (30,417)
Altamura, Lydia E 6:33:12 (34,444)
Alves De Sousa, Sarah J 4:25:11 (14,867)
Amaral, Denise F 5:23:33 (28,021)
Amend, Samantha 3:07:01 (1,309)
Amery, Sarah E 5:09:50 (25,438)
Amery, Suzanne T 4:32:33 (16,675)
Ames, Sally E 5:31:48 (29,419)
Amies, Kate R 3:55:11 (8,053)
Amson-Orth, Karyn 4:44:11 (19,594)
Amy, Beverley A 5:53:13 (31,979)
Anders, Lisamarie A 5:19:34 (27,353)
Andersen, Birgitte 4:10:48 (11,327)
Anderson, Amanda 6:51:12 (34,961)
Anderson, Elizabeth R 4:13:17 (11,905)
Anderson, Gail J 6:05:05 (32,970)
Anderson, Gemma 3:52:20 (7,440)
Anderson, Isobel E 4:28:38 (15,768)
Anderson, Jacqui 4:54:52 (22,238)
Anderson, Jennie 6:52:57 (34,989)
Anderson, Jill 3:50:54 (7,115)
Anderson, Karen M 5:21:12 (27,633)
Anderson, Katharine M 3:53:19 (7,648)
Anderson, Katy M 3:32:08 (4,017)
Anderson, Kirsty E 3:43:15 (5,729)
Anderson, Louisa E 4:18:03 (13,086)
Anderson, Lynn 4:46:44 (20,220)
Anderson, Margaret J 6:13:50 (33,537)
Anderson, Penny J 5:20:31 (27,522)
Anderson, Sarah M 4:42:19 (19,126)
Anderson, Shirley H 3:32:31 (4,074)
Andersson, Anne C 3:43:46 (5,822)
Anderton, Karen A 5:28:12 (28,838)
Andow, Teresa Z 4:33:10 (16,830)
Andrade-Brown, Fiona J 4:36:45 (17,732)
Andrew, Angela L 5:41:57 (30,825)
Andrew, Beth L 3:04:28 (1,127)
Andrew, Jane A 4:33:56 (17,016)
Andrew, Lucy M 5:41:18 (30,740)
Andrews, Amanda J 5:16:23 (26,733)
Andrews, Angela 4:46:31 (20,185)
Andrews, Angela A 4:11:07 (11,401)
Andrews, Carly H 3:40:31 (5,273)
Andrews, Chris E 4:16:15 (12,634)
Andrews, Faye 5:52:02 (31,874)
Andrews, Hilary 6:38:15 (34,615)
Andrews, Jo 4:44:23 (19,645)

Andrews, Maureen	6:28:47 (34,274)	
Andrews, Sandra D	4:23:10 (14,369)	
Andrews, Sarah L	5:10:08 (25,513)	
Andrews, Susan J	5:57:44 (32,387)	
Andrzejewski, Jacek	4:33:15 (16,857)	
Angel, Melanie R	4:33:49 (16,995)	
Angell, Harriet	5:27:11 (28,658)	
Angilley, Jane	5:34:04 (29,775)	
Angilley, Jayne	3:47:36 (6,447)	
Anglim, Tara L	4:43:49 (19,482)	
Angove, Emma K.	4:41:20 (18,869)	
Angus, Georgina	5:29:42 (29,095)	
Angus, Susan	4:14:51 (12,278)	
Ankarett, Helen	4:07:33 (10,662)	
Anki, Farida	4:16:00 (12,562)	
Annals, Jackie L	4:55:47 (22,453)	
Anner, Kerry	5:12:00 (25,856)	
Ansell, Natalia O	3:42:32 (5,602)	
Anselm, Jessie D	5:06:43 (24,822)	
Anstee, Jessica	3:54:52 (7,978)	
Anstey, Liz	6:37:37 (34,594)	
Anstey, Victoria C	4:00:58 (9,411)	
Antell, Helen O	4:25:19 (14,898)	
Anthony, Shirley A	6:15:03 (33,618)	
Antinora, Laurlelyn A	3:24:39 (2,977)	
Antolik, Olivia C.	4:15:16 (12,383)	
Antoniou, Angela	7:08:16 (35,250)	
Antoniou, Georgina	7:28:57 (35,463)	
Antram, Nicola A	5:03:49 (24,294)	
Apollo-Schubert, Winnie	5:33:52 (29,739)	
Appleton, Patricia A	6:07:10 (33,116)	
Appleyard, Christine A	4:48:34 (20,663)	
Applin, Deborah	5:29:04 (28,994)	
Applin, Susan I	5:33:59 (29,756)	
April, Merrill	3:41:28 (5,442)	
Arbon, Jemma D	6:50:19 (34,940)	
Arbuckle, Andrena	6:21:17 (33,967)	
Arbuckle, Kirsten J	6:15:08 (33,627)	
Arbuthnot, Suzanne K	3:35:30 (4,480)	
Arcand, Meg	4:57:26 (22,893)	
Arceo, Lori A	5:38:24 (30,370)	
Archbold, Karen J	4:28:09 (15,635)	
Archbutt, Rachel	7:39:13 (35,556)	
Archer, Isobel K.	5:54:33 (32,110)	
Archer, Jan	7:34:00 (35,527)	
Archer, Kathey	5:36:23 (30,095)	
Archer, Maureen A	5:20:19 (27,479)	
Archer, Natalie	6:17:29 (33,748)	
Ardouin, Sandra J	7:18:03 (35,370)	
Arguile, Julie L	3:57:00 (8,482)	
Armer, Sarah K.	4:49:02 (20,774)	
Armitage, Jacqueline A	7:45:41 (35,601)	
Armitage, Rachel G	4:21:37 (13,992)	
Armour, Elaine	3:43:33 (5,792)	
Armour, Nancy R.	4:23:29 (14,442)	
Armstrong, Donna L	3:45:23 (6,079)	
Armstrong, Elaine	4:18:30 (13,211)	
Armstrong, Esaula D	4:47:40 (20,449)	
Armstrong, Greta P	3:49:05 (6,747)	
Armstrong, Marie L	5:14:51 (26,419)	
Armstrong, Rosemary F	4:28:11 (15,645)	
Armstrong-Smith, Linsey K	4:18:29 (13,208)	
Arnold, Fiona M	3:52:14 (7,416)	
Arnold, Hannah	3:34:20 (4,322)	
Arnold, Tracey	6:20:13 (33,900)	
Arnold-Masters, Katrina L	6:00:57 (32,665)	
Arnold-Pepper, Chrissie J	4:27:47 (15,538)	
Arnott, Clare E	4:17:32 (12,956)	
Arrowsmith, Jacqueline R	4:21:21 (13,923)	
Ash, Lorna	5:54:47 (32,122)	
Ash, Nicola K.	5:15:39 (26,593)	
Ashburn, Susan A	5:40:50 (30,684)	
Ashcroft, Cynthia	4:33:48 (16,991)	
Ashdown, Sophie R	6:06:30 (33,079)	
Ashe, Debby	4:24:30 (14,704)	
Ashford, Rachel L	4:20:07 (13,629)	
Ashford-Smith, Paulette D	5:06:41 (24,811)	
Ash-Huynh, Jane L	5:38:16 (30,350)	
Ashkettle, Charlotte L	4:32:25 (16,647)	
Ashley, Linda H	4:13:59 (12,094)	
Ashpole, Emma L	5:35:01 (29,916)	
Ashton, Anne E	4:56:36 (22,662)	
Ashton, Devon R	5:19:24 (27,319)	

Ashton, Helen C	4:54:54 (22,246)	
Ashton, Karen C	5:26:25 (28,534)	
Ashton-Rigby, Lee C	5:10:00 (25,477)	
Ashurst, Catherine M	4:24:09 (14,618)	
Ashwall, Sophie H	4:52:55 (21,730)	
Ashworth, Elizabeth J	7:16:53 (35,359)	
Askew, Kerry M	5:49:30 (31,626)	
Asmi, Saadia	9:58:54 (35,698)	
Aspinall, Sheila	4:32:17 (16,625)	
Asplin, Nicola L	5:26:40 (28,571)	
Asquith, Emma	5:44:34 (31,104)	
Asquith, Karlie D	5:41:37 (30,781)	
Assen, Sarah	6:26:48 (34,205)	
Astrom, Anna I	5:39:51 (30,575)	
Atkins, Helen L	5:07:13 (24,934)	
Atkins, Marie	4:31:05 (16,374)	
Atkins, Rebecca J	4:17:41 (12,992)	
Atkinson, Alison J	4:26:31 (15,197)	
Atkinson, Catherine H	4:30:11 (16,192)	
Atkinson, Denise	5:17:50 (27,013)	
Atkinson, Ellen J	5:48:21 (31,515)	
Atkinson, Rebecca	4:34:18 (17,094)	
Atkinson, Rebecca	6:09:34 (33,279)	
Atkinson, Sue	5:33:31 (29,688)	
Attenborough, Joanne M	5:00:09 (23,535)	
Attenborough, Lisa A	4:36:15 (17,599)	
Attenborough, Rebecca	4:57:33 (22,914)	
Attride, Ruth N	4:42:06 (19,064)	
Attwell, Christine E	4:26:21 (15,146)	
Attwell, Susannah K	3:40:40 (5,293)	
Attwood, Sue M	4:27:15 (15,407)	
Aubert, Collette	4:46:46 (20,224)	
Aubrey, Ami	4:42:12 (19,095)	
Auger, Martine	5:03:29 (24,235)	
Augustus, Diane R	4:25:46 (15,009)	
Auld, Deborah A	6:50:01 (34,930)	
Auld, Katherine M	5:15:24 (26,544)	
Aus Der Fuenten, Karen	3:09:53 (1,546)	
Aussenberg, Glenda J	7:41:05 (35,571)	
Austin, Alison K.	5:27:58 (28,789)	
Austin, Allison M	4:53:13 (21,818)	
Austin, Angela M	4:33:27 (16,900)	
Austin, Anna C	5:20:13 (27,459)	
Austin, Jennifer A	4:39:28 (18,410)	
Austin, Maria A	6:05:45 (33,026)	
Austin, Melissa L	5:34:44 (29,877)	
Austin, Patricia I	5:12:57 (26,033)	
Austin, Rebecca J	4:50:23 (21,093)	
Austin, Rose M	7:18:18 (35,371)	
Austin, Teresa	6:23:29 (34,054)	
Avery, Amanda	3:20:23 (2,540)	
Avgousti, Melanie C	5:34:44 (29,881)	
Ayliff, Andrea	5:39:58 (30,584)	
Ayling, Alissa K	4:48:37 (20,674)	
Aylmer, Sarah J	3:51:25 (7,231)	
Aylott, Caroline V	4:50:16 (21,061)	
Aylward, Mary	8:06:57 (35,653)	
Aylward, Sinead M	5:05:56 (24,684)	
Ayres, Sarah	5:46:33 (31,313)	
Ayscough, Ursula J	3:32:03 (3,995)	
Babajide, Vivian A	4:45:38 (19,977)	
Babb, Kim M	5:12:38 (25,971)	
Baber, Sophie E	4:19:45 (13,524)	
Babington, Amanda J	5:22:50 (27,912)	
Bachert, Ina H	5:29:41 (29,094)	
Bach-Petersen, Kitsten	4:43:12 (19,341)	
Backhouse, Victoria J	4:25:45 (15,006)	
Backstrand, Lena	5:00:03 (23,517)	
Bacon, Marie L	5:42:44 (30,898)	
Badcock, Janine	5:00:41 (23,652)	
Badger, Susan J	5:13:39 (26,150)	
Badham, Charlotte L	5:17:40 (26,997)	
Baertschi, Rahel	4:18:44 (13,273)	
Bage, Dawn L	5:18:18 (27,124)	
Baggaley, Elizabeth J	5:07:16 (24,947)	
Baggaley, Marie	6:16:21 (33,709)	
Baggs, Julia C.	4:26:25 (15,164)	
Bagley, Sarah E	4:17:25 (12,914)	
Bagnall, Michelle A	6:00:13 (32,597)	
Bahaijoub, Leila	4:59:47 (23,456)	
Baierl, Penelope	3:57:09 (8,511)	
Baikie, Charlie H	5:39:37 (30,546)	
Bailey, Angela	5:18:57 (27,242)	

Bailey, Brandi	4:06:14 (10,399)	
Bailey, Carina	5:56:50 (32,322)	
Bailey, Charlotte E.	4:31:05 (16,374)	
Bailey, Clare L	5:44:34 (31,104)	
Bailey, Donna M	5:38:04 (30,312)	
Bailey, Emma C	5:19:12 (27,292)	
Bailey, Fiona	4:11:19 (11,452)	
Bailey, Fiona K.	3:31:11 (3,864)	
Bailey, Georgina A	5:13:09 (26,071)	
Bailey, Joanna G	5:07:36 (25,019)	
Bailey, Laura N	5:34:46 (29,883)	
Bailey, Margaret A	5:01:51 (23,902)	
Bailey, Marie	4:55:16 (22,333)	
Bailey, Rhiannon L	5:46:06 (31,272)	
Bailey, Ruth E	4:50:49 (21,196)	
Bailey, Ruth H	5:29:46 (29,105)	
Bailey, Sarah E	3:48:48 (6,687)	
Bailey, Sheila M	4:04:43 (10,095)	
Bailey, Shelia G	8:09:41 (35,657)	
Bailey, Sheralee N	5:20:21 (27,485)	
Bailey, Tina L	3:16:40 (2,141)	
Bailey, Victoria L	5:21:08 (27,621)	
Bailie, Clare	4:41:51 (19,010)	
Bain, Clare	5:09:17 (25,330)	
Bainbridge, Laura A	4:29:11 (15,906)	
Bainbridge, Wendy E	5:26:55 (28,612)	
Baines, Michelle N	6:15:10 (33,629)	
Baird, Gillian L	4:55:26 (22,372)	
Baird, Jill	5:53:10 (31,976)	
Baird, Sarah K	3:55:18 (8,077)	
Bajaj, Yogita	4:06:06 (10,370)	
Baker, Amanda J	7:29:03 (35,465)	
Baker, Angela M	4:17:02 (12,822)	
Baker, Bridget D	3:14:28 (1,938)	
Baker, Cathy J	4:21:23 (13,933)	
Baker, Denise J	5:43:20 (30,976)	
Baker, Elizabeth C.	5:02:50 (24,093)	
Baker, Hannah E	4:59:51 (23,467)	
Baker, Joss	7:43:04 (35,588)	
Baker, Kirstin J	3:57:55 (8,702)	
Baker, Michelle	5:20:51 (27,581)	
Baker, Rachel	5:26:02 (28,463)	
Baker, Ruth E	5:01:41 (23,865)	
Baker, Susan B	5:17:17 (26,915)	
Baker, Teresa	6:05:57 (33,041)	
Bakewell, Penny A	5:40:57 (30,700)	
Balcombe, Karen	4:03:55 (9,950)	
Balding, Angela	5:09:45 (25,425)	
Baldry, Gillian R	4:15:25 (12,421)	
Baldwin, Debra J	4:32:46 (16,703)	
Baldwin, Jayne L	3:34:25 (4,330)	
Bale, Debbie E	5:17:51 (27,018)	
Bale, Debbie J	4:43:53 (19,505)	
Balfour, Jacky L	3:57:05 (8,497)	
Ball, Janet E	3:55:54 (8,268)	
Ballantyne, Zoe S	4:21:23 (13,933)	
Ballard, Lisa M	4:03:15 (9,828)	
Ballardie, Danielle G.	3:51:52 (7,330)	
Balmer, Joanne M	7:08:11 (35,247)	
Bamford, Catherine	7:39:37 (35,557)	
Bampton, Pauline J	4:28:38 (15,768)	
Banbury, Helen J	4:08:39 (10,903)	
Bancroft, Michelle A	5:55:25 (32,184)	
Banerjee, Tina B	4:36:12 (17,581)	
Banham, Kate	5:15:01 (26,456)	
Banks, Angela L	3:31:57 (3,985)	
Banks, Faye M	2:56:34 (641)	
Banks, Sarah J	4:39:59 (18,533)	
Banks, Sharon D	4:31:34 (16,475)	
Bannister, Roselyn	4:18:58 (13,323)	
Bannon, Barbara A	3:58:49 (8,913)	
Bannon, Bozena M	7:06:53 (35,234)	
Bannon, Clare G	4:12:45 (11,775)	
Bannon, Linda C	4:42:48 (19,255)	
Bannon, Victoria J	5:23:46 (28,071)	
Banszky, Elaine C	3:51:49 (7,318)	
Bant, Linda	6:12:46 (33,477)	
Banyard, Sarah	5:31:57 (29,439)	
Bara, Nicole	4:20:58 (13,845)	
Baran, Maria	5:29:20 (29,047)	
Baranowski, Maria	5:21:17 (27,652)	
Barber, Alyce E	7:33:53 (35,525)	
Barber, Cecily A	3:40:54 (5,347)	

Barber, Charlotte L 5:21:39 (27,726)
Barber, Elizabeth M 4:33:41 (16,955)
Barber, Lucy 5:38:53 (30,439)
Barber, Lynne E 5:13:38 (26,146)
Barber, Rosemary 6:18:52 (33,828)
Barber, Sarah 4:22:19 (14,157)
Barber, Shirley 7:44:05 (35,597)
Barber, Zoe E 3:42:15 (5,561)
Barbosa, Olga 4:28:30 (15,726)
Barboza, Felicia 3:34:22 (4,326)
Barclay, Jessica E 5:09:13 (25,321)
Bardsley, Sarah L 4:27:43 (15,524)
Barfoot, Alayne M 7:00:27 (35,135)
Bargetto, Vanya 5:22:10 (27,804)
Barker, Anna B 3:52:27 (7,461)
Barker, Carmel M 3:41:24 (5,428)
Barker, Charlotte J 4:38:47 (18,226)
Barker, Colette L 4:37:28 (17,887)
Barker, Elizabeth 5:07:05 (24,905)
Barker, Emma E 5:50:24 (31,717)
Barker, Helen L 5:21:22 (27,667)
Barker, Jackie J 3:38:36 (4,939)
Barker, Karen T 4:26:53 (15,288)
Barker, Margaret 4:03:37 (9,889)
Barker, Nikki 4:32:39 (16,706)
Barker, Paula 4:32:34 (16,681)
Barker, Rosamund A 3:11:17 (1,652)
Barker, Sally-Jo 4:52:53 (21,721)
Barker, Sarah 5:11:33 (25,769)
Barker, Stephanie 5:43:17 (30,969)
Barker, Susan J 4:43:19 (19,383)
Barksby, Justine 6:12:51 (33,482)
Barley, Julie A 3:08:55 (1,460)
Barley, Marie R 4:29:20 (15,947)
Barlow, Hazel G 5:51:27 (31,822)
Barlow, Sally 4:26:23 (15,155)
Barlow, Susan T 4:09:07 (10,979)
Barlow, Vanessa T 4:33:14 (16,854)
Barltrop, Melissa M 4:52:19 (21,576)
Barnaby, Tracey A 5:42:35 (30,885)
Barnard, Helen K 4:26:48 (15,267)
Barnard, Kirsty M 5:49:45 (31,653)
Barnes, Anna V 4:34:21 (17,104)
Barnes, Carol 5:57:22 (32,360)
Barnes, Christine 5:38:04 (30,312)
Barnes, Ellie 3:38:54 (4,998)
Barnes, Jane 4:17:16 (12,866)
Barnes, Joanne 5:37:18 (30,213)
Barnes, Marina A 5:05:24 (24,573)
Barnes, Sue E 3:42:32 (5,602)
Barnes, Victoria M 4:41:04 (18,803)
Barnes, Wendy A 3:39:21 (5,073)
Barnes, Yvonne W 5:36:00 (30,048)
Barnet, Gemma L 6:33:50 (34,459)
Barnett, Helen R 5:43:53 (31,027)
Barnett, Kirsty G 3:29:42 (3,675)
Barnett, Pamela M 5:44:55 (31,142)
Barnett, Zoe A 6:19:50 (33,882)
Barnfield, Emma J 4:56:08 (22,543)
Barnfield, Shirley A 6:02:43 (32,800)
Baron, Lorraine A 4:24:32 (14,712)
Barone, Barbara 3:45:23 (6,079)
Barr, Janice E 6:14:45 (33,596)
Barr, Julie D 5:21:30 (27,697)
Barras, Nicky J 4:39:22 (18,385)
Barrass, Sandra 5:52:17 (31,900)
Barren, Clare J 5:12:42 (25,985)
Barrett, Caroline 4:44:53 (19,803)
Barrett, Dharam 7:48:15 (35,612)
Barrett, Lisa F 6:27:12 (34,218)
Barrett, Tina 6:10:51 (33,355)
Barrett, Vanessa L 4:35:30 (17,401)
Barrett, Victoria A 5:33:52 (29,739)
Barron, Jill 3:53:51 (7,753)
Barron, Leigh 4:21:24 (13,939)
Barron, Teresa 5:22:12 (27,813)
Barrow, Cara L 4:34:30 (17,148)
Barrow-Green, June E 3:32:33 (4,079)
Barry, Emma A 4:34:30 (17,148)
Barry, Lorraine K 5:28:40 (28,931)
Barter, Laura M 4:35:11 (17,323)
Bartlett, Cheryl P 5:43:58 (31,033)
Bartlett, Lisa 4:17:55 (13,047)
Barton, Catherine 4:37:00 (17,786)
Barton, Joanna L 4:46:34 (20,191)
Barton, Sophie J 5:32:43 (29,567)
Barton, Tamsyn S 4:33:22 (16,884)
Barton-Nicol, Sandra V 4:10:42 (11,313)
Bartram, Stella A 5:08:36 (25,205)
Barulis, Victoria J 6:10:17 (33,325)
Barwell, Lorraine P 4:53:20 (21,845)
Bass, Catherine 5:06:15 (24,753)
Bass, Michelle 8:23:04 (35,672)
Bass, Yvette L 4:32:37 (16,695)
Bassett, Sarah J 5:17:14 (26,904)
Bassett, Thomas W 5:43:39 (31,007)
Bassil, Anna K 4:36:05 (17,553)
Basson, Vanessa M 3:54:03 (7,803)
Bastable, Melanie A 6:19:31 (33,861)
Batchelor, Eleanor M 5:19:37 (27,362)
Batchelor, Elizabeth C 3:57:46 (8,667)
Batchelor, Helen E 5:20:00 (27,424)
Bate, Felicity A 5:19:05 (27,262)
Bate, June M 5:25:12 (28,302)
Bateman, Victoria 4:39:47 (18,483)
Bates, Angela M 6:13:33 (33,525)
Bates, Claire L 3:28:16 (3,442)
Bates, Dawn 4:19:34 (13,471)
Bates, Fiona H 5:12:56 (26,027)
Bates, Gabrielle N 6:04:53 (32,948)
Bates, Gillian M 5:31:31 (29,378)
Bates, Karen F 5:58:02 (32,416)
Bates, Katherine J 4:10:30 (11,268)
Bates, Wendy J 4:56:35 (22,656)
Bateson, Marie L 4:36:22 (17,629)
Bath, Ann C 4:03:08 (9,806)
Bath, Doreen A 4:51:25 (21,348)
Batson, Natasha I 4:44:47 (19,772)
Batt, Dulcie E 4:14:32 (12,211)
Batt, Katherine M 4:38:27 (18,138)
Battell, Rebecca L 4:48:31 (20,651)
Batten, Carina M 5:28:20 (28,877)
Battershell, Sarah K 4:24:08 (14,610)
Battista, Katherine A 6:03:08 (32,829)
Battle, Nicola J 4:47:39 (20,441)
Battson, Elaine C 3:49:59 (6,934)
Bauckham, Nicky J 5:22:48 (27,907)
Baulch, Gillian B 5:20:44 (27,560)
Baulderstone, Kathrine R 5:02:04 (23,946)
Baum, Chloe A 6:45:49 (34,822)
Baumann, Margaretha 2:58:36 (797)
Bax, Amy J 5:37:41 (30,258)
Baxter, Catherine 5:41:10 (30,724)
Baxter, Heather J 5:05:40 (24,628)
Baxter, Kathleen C 6:44:30 (34,787)
Baxter, Rebecca M 3:54:41 (7,940)
Baxter, Wendy S 4:38:57 (18,274)
Baxter, Zoe 5:27:46 (28,758)
Baylis, Kerri A 6:00:57 (32,665)
Bayliss, Emma J 4:00:21 (9,278)
Baynes, Lana S 5:27:22 (28,688)
Bazany-Taylor, Alexandra S 7:40:40 (35,564)
Beacham, Emily 4:18:09 (13,108)
Beacham, Sharon 6:39:21 (34,653)
Beadle, Emma L 4:39:46 (18,476)
Beadle, Suzanne 4:54:32 (22,150)
Beagrie, Lynn 4:53:42 (21,942)
Beal, Lynne 5:01:13 (23,776)
Beale, Nicola J 4:36:45 (17,732)
Beale, Nina N 5:06:21 (24,760)
Bean, Susan N 5:58:16 (32,438)
Beaney, Lisa A 5:10:43 (25,612)
Bear, Angie 4:16:24 (12,670)
Beardmore, Lisa J 5:17:42 (27,000)
Bearman, Ruth C 6:39:37 (34,660)
Beattie, Victoria J 4:11:58 (11,607)
Beatty, Claire 6:16:13 (33,698)
Beaumont, Katherine M 6:14:18 (33,570)
Beavan, Faye 5:34:25 (29,833)
Beaven, Diane K 4:20:19 (13,686)
Bebbington, Amanda D 6:01:08 (32,691)
Bebbington, Lisa 5:13:55 (26,213)
Beck, Emma L 6:10:44 (33,351)
Beck, Josephine K 3:54:29 (7,899)
Becker, Lucy J 6:29:49 (34,321)
Beckingham, Emma 5:38:10 (30,329)
Beckwith, Julie L 4:19:15 (13,395)
Beddis, Gail D 5:10:11 (25,525)
Beddow, Charlotte L 6:13:49 (33,536)
Bedford, Hannah F 3:56:57 (8,466)
Bedford, Rachel L 6:10:11 (33,316)
Beebee, Alice J 5:07:14 (24,938)
Beech, Gemma 5:33:12 (29,634)
Beech, Jane L 3:39:06 (5,033)
Beech, Tessa 4:25:14 (14,882)
Beecham, Helen C 4:10:39 (11,300)
Beecher, Lesley 5:53:45 (32,031)
Beecroft, Janet 4:29:34 (16,031)
Beer, Amelia E 3:56:41 (8,399)
Beerling, Julie A 5:43:23 (30,982)
Beeson, Semirah 3:39:15 (5,055)
Beetram, Julia 5:18:27 (27,155)
Beever, Helen J 4:46:55 (20,257)
Beevers, Clare L 4:34:15 (17,088)
Begg, Tracy W 3:44:17 (5,900)
Begley, Jayne L 5:58:55 (32,498)
Behan, Julie A 5:12:15 (25,911)
Behm, Monica E 6:06:21 (33,071)
Bekenn, Jenny 4:28:39 (15,773)
Belam, Wendy 4:38:07 (18,045)
Belcher, Belinda K 4:49:12 (20,821)
Belfield, Kerry M 4:11:47 (11,568)
Belford, Charlotte A 4:41:37 (18,952)
Belfrage, Rachael S 5:31:03 (29,307)
Bell, Alice M 4:18:00 (13,074)
Bell, Alison 4:05:22 (10,212)
Bell, Amelia A 6:13:35 (33,529)
Bell, Carla C 4:19:25 (13,436)
Bell, Emily 6:05:02 (32,965)
Bell, Emily J 5:46:14 (31,287)
Bell, Jacqui D 4:17:32 (12,956)
Bell, Janet A 5:54:48 (32,125)
Bell, Kate M 3:27:50 (3,388)
Bell, Lily E 8:22:09 (35,671)
Bell, Linda J 4:53:16 (21,828)
Bell, Mandy 5:11:18 (25,719)
Bell, Natasha J 4:42:13 (19,101)
Bell, Patrina M 4:25:19 (14,898)
Bell, Samantha 4:38:33 (18,163)
Bell, Tina 6:11:56 (33,421)
Bell, Zoe 3:46:13 (6,207)
Bellamy, Amy J 4:47:56 (20,512)
Bellamy, Laura L 5:22:39 (27,882)
Bellingham, Susan J 7:12:09 (35,306)
Belmonte, Ana M 5:47:41 (31,427)
Belsham, Katie A 5:08:13 (25,144)
Belsom, Natasha J 3:40:20 (5,240)
Beltoft Neilsen, Pia 5:11:03 (25,676)
Belyavin, Julia R 3:07:32 (1,350)
Bem Haim, Sabine 6:21:35 (33,983)
Bending, Laura C 4:54:14 (22,085)
Benfield, Nila C 4:45:50 (20,019)
Benfield, Rebecca 6:15:28 (33,647)
Benjamin, Carli L 5:35:21 (29,957)
Benjamin, Ermine C 5:03:16 (24,185)
Benjamin, Floella 5:51:39 (31,843)
Benjamin, Jennifer Jane 6:08:32 (33,206)
Bennadi, Denise H 6:32:47 (34,435)
Bennett, Alison C 4:50:05 (21,020)
Bennett, Andrea M 4:12:58 (11,822)
Bennett, Anne-Marie 5:16:51 (26,820)
Bennett, Carolyn T 6:03:44 (32,871)
Bennett, Charlotte E 6:26:08 (34,178)
Bennett, Elettra T 5:26:00 (28,455)
Bennett, Emma 6:38:04 (34,609)
Bennett, Georgina E 3:30:56 (3,833)
Bennett, Johanna K 5:28:11 (28,836)
Bennett, Keeley F 6:28:33 (34,268)
Bennett, Lisa J 3:37:48 (4,788)
Bennett, Lizzy C 4:47:22 (20,374)
Bennett, Magda K 3:55:21 (8,093)
Bennett, Maxine M 4:39:47 (18,483)
Bennett, Natalie D 5:57:06 (32,342)
Bennett, Paula E 5:50:01 (31,677)
Bennett, Rachel C 5:00:08 (23,532)
Bennett, Sarah 3:41:54 (5,498)
Bennett, Sarah J 6:00:24 (32,611)
Bennett, Sophie J 4:40:25 (18,634)
Bennett, Victoria E 4:39:56 (18,520)

Bourn, Sally L.................5:57:53 (32,402)
Bourne, Anna J.................4:44:52 (19,797)
Bourne, Naomi A.................3:29:45 (3,679)
Bourne, Susan M.................6:54:12 (35,023)
Bourqui, Stephanie.................3:57:58 (8,712)
Bouston, Sarah J.................4:15:19 (12,401)
Boutell, Clare-Louise.................3:36:53 (4,672)
Bowden, Annie M.................3:29:10 (3,600)
Bowen, Jo.................4:30:27 (16,246)
Bowen, Kirsty.................3:42:25 (5,587)
Bowen, Laura J.................5:52:08 (31,886)
Bowen, Michelle A.................3:43:10 (5,720)
Bowen Rees, Mary V.................3:18:04 (2,291)
Bower, Elizabeth.................5:07:51 (25,068)
Bower, Hilary.................6:02:18 (32,771)
Bowers, Debbie E.................4:33:39 (16,947)
Bowers, Heather A.................6:20:17 (33,904)
Bowers, Katharine J.................5:05:27 (24,588)
Bowers, Mary E.................4:34:06 (17,050)
Bowers, Samantha K.................4:08:34 (10,882)
Bowers, Sandra.................3:13:14 (1,845)
Bowie, Sarah P.................4:46:22 (20,149)
Bowlas, Rachel L.................5:16:37 (26,773)
Bowler, Karen J.................4:35:59 (17,532)
Bowles, Joanne.................5:15:26 (26,548)
Bowling, Mary.................6:11:58 (33,424)
Bowman, Jennie.................3:28:27 (3,471)
Bowman, Sharon A.................4:50:55 (21,221)
Bown, Rachel H.................3:52:21 (7,444)
Bowron, Mary E.................4:43:50 (19,489)
Bowthorpe-Weller, Clare L.................7:01:49 (35,154)
Bowyer, Philippa J.................4:50:53 (21,213)
Box, Judith.................3:51:14 (7,194)
Boxall, Fiona.................4:51:38 (21,406)
Boxus, Laurence.................3:55:20 (8,088)
Boyce, Aisling V.................5:20:31 (27,522)
Boyce, Fiona J.................6:18:53 (33,831)
Boyce, Sarah K.................4:27:39 (15,501)
Boyd, Heather M.................5:32:09 (29,475)
Boyd, Judith.................4:10:47 (11,324)
Boyd, Julie A.................3:57:31 (8,602)
Boyd, Julie K.................4:48:12 (20,578)
Boyd, Lucy B.................3:56:37 (8,385)
Boyd Heudebourck, Sarah M.................5:30:45 (29,260)
Boylan, Jan V.................3:47:24 (6,410)
Boyle, Brenda M.................4:38:46 (18,220)
Boyle, Holly.................6:32:36 (34,426)
Boyt, Laura E.................5:20:40 (27,550)
Bracebridge, Claire E.................4:15:39 (12,474)
Bracewell, Margaret A.................4:41:12 (18,841)
Bradberry, Belinda H.................3:18:58 (2,389)
Bradbury, Helen M.................4:43:58 (19,527)
Braddick, Sue J.................5:28:35 (28,914)
Braddins, Louise E.................6:20:36 (33,928)
Bradford, Joanne.................4:30:09 (16,188)
Bradford, Katie J.................5:02:12 (23,970)
Bradford, Sue.................4:00:33 (9,322)
Bradgate, Maggi.................5:38:41 (30,412)
Bradley, Amanda J.................5:01:33 (23,843)
Bradley, Bonnie K.................4:17:11 (12,848)
Bradley, Emma C.................5:00:20 (23,586)
Bradley, Emma F.................8:23:59 (35,673)
Bradley, Emma M.................3:01:25 (981)
Bradley, Fleur M.................6:24:00 (34,079)
Bradley, Jane E.................4:36:24 (17,640)
Bradley, Jean.................5:02:27 (24,026)
Bradley, Julie.................6:51:19 (34,965)
Bradley, Julie C.................4:47:21 (20,370)
Bradley, Katherine S.................5:35:29 (29,972)
Bradley, Rosanna.................7:07:43 (35,243)
Bradley, Sandra.................6:25:55 (34,161)
Bradley, Sarah.................4:14:45 (12,261)
Bradley, Sarah J.................4:16:17 (12,644)
Bradley, Vicky.................5:45:31 (31,210)
Bradley-Roberts, Susan.................5:55:16 (32,170)
Bradshaw, Ann.................5:41:04 (30,714)
Bradshaw, Geraldine I.................5:45:41 (31,223)
Bradshaw, Helen M.................5:29:56 (29,124)
Bradshaw, Sarah.................4:57:34 (22,919)
Bradshaw, Tracey A.................4:40:19 (18,610)
Brady, Claire R.................4:57:28 (22,900)
Brady, Emma.................4:55:52 (22,479)
Brady, Niamh N.................4:51:32 (21,376)

Brady, Sandra M.................4:28:02 (15,602)

Brady, Vanessa M.................4:32:38 (16,701)

As runners gathered, stretching and donning costumes, a St John's volunteer was easing tension making us laugh. There were superheroes, a rhino and an astronaut to name a few; then the announcement to make our way to the start. I waited, listening to a favourite track, playing it over until I crossed the line. I felt calm and confident. It was hot. I found my pace and settled down; on to Tower Bridge, Docklands, and then on to the Highway and Embankment. The showers were refreshing though not great for a photo finish! I passed Big Ben and knew the end was near. The crowd shouted my name; those last few hundred yards were tough! I raised my arms to cross the finish. Amazing! What an experience.

Braeger, Louise.................4:59:14 (23,319)
Braillard, Ella L.................4:26:16 (15,123)
Brain, Carla E.................5:34:13 (29,799)
Braine, Elizabeth.................5:24:35 (28,196)
Braithwaite, Susan.................5:34:24 (29,827)
Bramley, Nicola J.................3:41:10 (5,390)
Brandon, Victoria K.................5:38:16 (30,350)
Brandrick, Gillian A.................5:22:34 (27,870)
Brandt, Karen R.................4:28:31 (15,730)
Brannan, Anne.................7:16:22 (35,356)
Brannan, Gail.................4:11:36 (11,527)
Bransfield, Paula M.................6:35:03 (34,502)
Branson, Tracey.................5:56:50 (32,322)
Branton, Leanne B.................6:34:47 (34,487)
Branyik, Cornelia.................4:45:20 (19,914)
Brassfield, Emily M.................3:39:48 (5,157)
Brawchett, Emma E.................4:51:19 (21,321)
Bray, Cecilia.................5:18:48 (27,214)
Bray, Gill F.................6:32:45 (34,431)
Bray, Joanna L.................5:37:59 (30,298)
Bray, Sandra J.................5:33:48 (29,731)
Brazier, Karen P.................4:52:34 (21,629)
Breagan, Heidi B.................4:28:28 (15,720)
Breakspeare, Hayley.................3:34:51 (4,387)
Brearley, Cari J.................5:52:43 (31,941)

Breathwick, Jo-Ann M.................6:34:55 (34,494)
Breden, Donna A.................6:27:58 (34,251)
Bredenkamp, Lorett E.................6:28:28 (34,265)
Breed, Wendy J.................3:31:25 (3,892)
Breeden, Laura.................6:46:07 (34,833)
Breen, Louise A.................4:57:32 (22,911)
Breen, Rosanna L.................4:35:58 (17,527)
Bremner, Jane S.................3:23:20 (2,837)
Brendolan, Alessandra.................4:00:54 (9,399)
Brennan, Julia F.................4:11:03 (11,383)
Brennan, Naomi.................6:13:26 (33,515)
Brennan, Nicky.................5:53:49 (32,034)
Brennan, Nicola.................5:31:39 (29,395)
Brennan, Sharon.................3:27:20 (3,330)
Brennan-Wright, Nicola J.................4:30:28 (16,250)
Brenner, Sachiko.................6:15:59 (33,682)
Brenni, Pietro M.................3:31:15 (3,872)
Brenot, Ghislaine S.................5:16:53 (26,835)
Brenton, Sarah J.................4:18:11 (13,121)
Brett, Elizabeth J.................6:30:45 (34,348)
Brett, Jo.................5:42:22 (30,866)
Brett, Rebecca J.................6:36:39 (34,564)
Brett, Sophie D.................5:33:21 (29,657)
Brettie, Doris.................4:34:36 (17,177)
Brew, Elizabeth A.................4:44:10 (19,587)
Brewer, Georgina R.................5:04:26 (24,407)
Brewer, Kate N.................5:15:59 (26,654)
Brewis, Linda M.................4:12:11 (11,653)
Brewster, Karen J.................4:25:19 (14,898)
Brewster, Vanessa M.................4:51:11 (21,281)
Brice, Fiona H.................6:20:46 (33,937)
Brickwood, Elizabeth R.................5:10:41 (25,610)
Bricoca, Sonali.................5:05:43 (24,639)
Bridge, Katherine E.................5:20:28 (27,508)
Bridge, Kathy.................6:02:39 (32,797)
Bridger, Kirsty L.................6:42:17 (34,730)
Bridges, Elizabeth L.................5:51:02 (31,774)
Bridges, Joanna M.................6:20:48 (33,939)
Bridges, Valerie P.................5:24:47 (28,234)
Bridgwater, Sandra.................4:48:40 (20,682)
Brierley, Deborah K.................4:42:44 (19,238)
Briggs, Camilla.................3:14:04 (1,901)
Briggs, Helen L.................3:59:26 (9,075)
Briggs, Kathryn J.................4:55:38 (22,415)
Brightman, Eugenie M.................4:34:23 (17,111)
Brightman, Pat A.................5:58:16 (32,438)
Brightmore, Emma.................5:36:12 (30,072)
Brighton, Susan L.................3:48:58 (6,723)
Brightwell, Emma.................4:58:23 (23,129)
Bringlow, Véronique M.................3:16:43 (2,150)
Brinsdon, Nicola J.................5:45:39 (31,220)
Briscoe, Emma C.................5:57:25 (32,364)
Bristow, Mary.................5:10:27 (25,566)
Bristow Tyler, Linda.................5:47:43 (31,434)
Britt, Caroline A.................4:55:51 (22,475)
Britton, Judith C.................3:51:17 (7,200)
Britton, Toni.................3:52:11 (7,406)
Britton, Vanessa C.................4:33:31 (16,916)
Britton-Hall, Caroline L.................5:42:02 (30,832)
Broadhead, Jennifer.................4:47:01 (20,286)
Broadway, Lynn D.................4:54:34 (22,158)
Brocard, Pierrette.................4:12:01 (11,617)
Brock, Sarah J.................6:50:28 (34,944)
Brock, Victoria E.................6:23:57 (34,075)
Brockhurst, Christine.................4:45:01 (19,842)
Brocklebank, Ella.................4:42:24 (19,152)
Brocklehurst, Jaine J.................3:26:16 (3,169)
Broda, Krysia B.................4:17:32 (12,956)
Brodie, Beverley A.................6:19:16 (33,852)
Brogan, Caroline M.................4:30:39 (16,286)
Brogden, Sara E.................5:57:53 (32,402)
Brognoli, Simona.................4:42:03 (19,054)
Brolly, Emma.................6:57:01 (35,072)
Bromley, Julie A.................4:45:21 (19,917)
Brook, Angela K.................5:22:32 (27,832)
Brooke, Jennifer M.................5:48:44 (31,556)
Brooke, Sallie N.................5:05:26 (24,584)
Brooker, Fiona C.................4:02:37 (9,716)
Brookes, Debbie T.................5:27:23 (28,691)
Brookes, Keeley J.................4:19:49 (13,544)
Brookhouse, Jane C.................4:56:42 (22,696)
Brooking, Yvonne E.................5:19:07 (27,271)
Brooks, Amy L.................5:41:31 (30,770)

Brooks, Emma C	4:57:22 (22,881)	
Brooks, Emma J	5:01:36 (23,854)	
Brooks, Josie F	6:03:54 (32,879)	
Brooks, Julia E	4:42:05 (19,060)	
Brooks, Keelie A	3:54:59 (8,006)	
Brooks, Kimberley L	4:38:24 (18,126)	
Brooks, Krista M	6:15:00 (33,614)	
Brooks, Linda M	5:06:38 (24,806)	
Brooks, Michelle C	4:43:15 (19,355)	
Brooksbank, Anna	4:50:36 (21,151)	
Brooksbank, Carol A	8:19:51 (35,668)	
Broom, Deborah	5:25:01 (28,272)	
Broom, Linda J	3:52:52 (7,537)	
Broome, Catherine J	4:10:32 (11,274)	
Broome, Joanna F	6:02:58 (32,819)	
Broome, Sara E	4:54:24 (22,123)	
Brosnan, Jacqueline V	4:50:40 (21,159)	
Broster, Linsey J	4:20:57 (13,840)	
Broughton, Andrea C	4:29:32 (16,025)	
Broughton, Georgina M	6:38:54 (34,633)	
Broughton, Jocelyn M	5:19:48 (27,392)	
Brown, Alison E	3:57:22 (8,570)	
Brown, Angela H	4:14:12 (12,138)	
Brown, Angela K	7:24:53 (35,431)	
Brown, Anne	5:59:59 (32,573)	
Brown, Barbara M	6:01:28 (32,717)	
Brown, Carrie	5:40:16 (30,622)	
Brown, Catherine	4:33:17 (16,863)	
Brown, Catherine J	4:45:58 (20,054)	
Brown, Cheryl M	4:20:54 (13,829)	
Brown, Claire	5:28:28 (28,896)	
Brown, Debra J	5:47:12 (31,371)	
Brown, Diana V	4:44:55 (19,812)	
Brown, Eleanor M	5:30:48 (29,264)	
Brown, Fiona L	4:14:29 (12,200)	
Brown, Francis H	4:48:02 (20,541)	
Brown, Helen E	3:55:59 (8,221)	
Brown, Helen E	4:24:48 (14,777)	
Brown, Janet H	3:36:41 (4,640)	
Brown, Jennifer D	4:07:25 (10,636)	
Brown, Jenny E	4:49:03 (20,777)	
Brown, Joanne	5:37:14 (30,203)	
Brown, Johanna E	4:51:17 (21,307)	
Brown, Judy	3:51:54 (7,337)	
Brown, Julie	4:28:10 (15,640)	
Brown, Julie M	3:56:57 (8,466)	
Brown, Karen	5:34:13 (29,799)	
Brown, Karen T	5:31:59 (29,448)	
Brown, Kathleen	4:59:44 (23,440)	
Brown, Kathryn J	5:33:43 (29,715)	
Brown, Kerry A	5:54:05 (32,060)	
Brown, Kirsty F	5:04:51 (24,487)	
Brown, Kirsty L	5:08:41 (25,220)	
Brown, Kirsty P	4:49:56 (20,980)	
Brown, Lindsay J	4:42:34 (19,195)	
Brown, Louise J	5:35:43 (30,013)	
Brown, Lynsey V	5:42:48 (30,909)	
Brown, Mandy S	4:10:43 (11,316)	
Brown, Margaret M	5:19:18 (27,310)	
Brown, Mary B	4:49:43 (20,936)	
Brown, Mina	4:26:25 (15,164)	
Brown, Nicola C	5:34:49 (29,889)	
Brown, Nicola E	5:00:57 (23,719)	
Brown, Rebecca L	5:24:47 (28,234)	
Brown, Rhona M	3:44:06 (5,881)	
Brown, Rosalind	5:59:09 (32,520)	
Brown, Sarah A	4:32:02 (16,565)	
Brown, Sue	3:45:55 (6,166)	
Brown, Susan A	4:53:39 (21,927)	
Brown, Susan C	5:57:57 (32,409)	
Brown, Tania M	4:52:25 (21,600)	
Brown, Tracey A	5:08:06 (25,112)	
Brown, Tracy A	5:35:02 (29,918)	
Brown, Victoria	3:52:14 (7,416)	
Brown, Wendy J	4:18:12 (13,124)	
Browne, Gabrielle	3:58:38 (8,867)	
Browning, Barbara	3:41:03 (5,372)	
Browning, Gina M	6:07:42 (33,145)	
Browning, Jackie E	4:54:46 (22,216)	
Brownlee, Charlotte A	6:02:31 (32,787)	
Brownsdon, Kizzy	5:10:20 (25,546)	
Brownsell, Catherine	4:25:58 (15,049)	
Brox, Astrid	4:24:32 (14,712)	

Bruce, Charlotte C	4:17:58 (13,064)	
Bruce, Elizabeth A	4:41:55 (19,020)	
Bruce, Jacqui A	5:11:47 (25,808)	
Bruce, Sarah	7:35:16 (35,534)	
Bruce-Feijen, Tineke	4:18:45 (13,276)	
Bruckshaw, Jenny N	5:31:05 (29,312)	
Brueck, Katrin	3:55:21 (8,093)	
Bruff, Karen J	3:42:19 (5,572)	
Brumwell, Susan E	3:40:04 (5,200)	
Brunner, Carol A	4:47:23 (20,379)	
Brussels, Linzi M	5:40:20 (30,633)	
Bruzinski, Lind-Jean	5:49:41 (31,647)	
Bryan, Hannah J	4:39:50 (18,494)	
Bryan, Joanne M	4:42:54 (19,281)	
Bryant, Carol	5:07:03 (24,896)	
Bryant, Celia P	4:34:28 (17,141)	
Bryant, Jennifer A	3:52:50 (7,534)	
Bryant, Joanna E	4:05:49 (10,313)	
Bryant, Margaret E	4:49:41 (20,932)	
Bryant, Nicola	4:23:23 (14,415)	
Bryant, Susan A	7:03:53 (35,190)	
Bryant, Zoe	6:04:08 (32,898)	
Bryson, Nicola S	4:02:09 (9,630)	
Bryson, Renea	7:17:29 (35,363)	
Buchanan, Ingrid J	5:00:44 (23,670)	
Buck, Maxine A	5:12:38 (25,971)	
Buckhorn, Susan A	5:19:09 (27,280)	
Buckingham, Fiona	4:08:13 (10,816)	
Buckingham, Kathleen C	4:06:08 (10,380)	
Buckley, Belinda G	5:20:00 (27,424)	
Buckley, Jo C	3:51:53 (7,335)	
Buckley, Kelly E	4:37:01 (17,793)	
Buckley, Natasha K	3:37:18 (4,722)	
Buckley, Sharon	5:07:26 (24,984)	
Buckley, Victoria	4:03:43 (9,908)	
Buckman, Kirsten J	5:34:01 (29,764)	
Budby, Josephine A	5:39:18 (30,490)	
Budd, Vivien K	6:27:58 (34,251)	
Buenfeld, Gina	4:10:00 (11,166)	
Bueno-Lopez, Ofelia	5:06:56 (24,865)	
Buerdsell, Rebecca F	5:53:01 (31,965)	
Buffini, Lauren	3:58:14 (8,772)	
Bufton, Teresa J	4:09:30 (11,072)	
Bugden, Christine	7:21:52 (35,401)	
Bugeja, Karen P	4:39:26 (18,400)	
Buick Lovegrove, Penelope	7:45:57 (35,602)	
Buila, Natalie D	6:13:31 (33,522)	
Bula, Deborah A	4:35:18 (17,359)	
Bulak, Fay N	6:15:16 (33,632)	
Bulkeley, Bayly J	3:26:47 (3,236)	
Bull, Claire L	4:01:53 (9,584)	
Bullen, Emma C	5:10:54 (25,643)	
Buller, Rachel L	3:40:01 (5,192)	
Bullivant, Sharon	6:03:39 (32,866)	
Bullock, Amanda J	5:37:13 (30,199)	
Bullock, Sarah R	5:06:10 (24,729)	
Bulmer, Lesley J	7:39:11 (35,555)	
Bulock, Janet M	5:46:51 (31,342)	
Bunbury, Victoria E	5:31:00 (29,294)	
Bunch, Iona S	4:39:01 (18,288)	
Bundy, Lucy J	5:07:22 (24,970)	
Bunten, Susan E	4:08:10 (10,799)	
Bunting, Katie S	5:14:44 (26,393)	
Burbage, Sue	5:06:09 (24,726)	
Burbidge, Sarah	4:20:18 (13,679)	
Burdett, Jennie T	4:04:18 (10,025)	
Burdett, Melanie	4:27:02 (15,331)	
Burdon, Lynne C	6:38:59 (34,638)	
Burge, Frances	3:35:05 (4,417)	
Burge, Jill P	4:31:38 (16,495)	
Burger, Estelle	5:08:08 (25,122)	
Burgess, Annette	3:32:44 (4,098)	
Burgess, Catherine	4:00:37 (9,337)	
Burgess, Claire	4:09:19 (11,034)	
Burgess, Nicola	4:41:47 (18,989)	
Burgess, Rosemary	4:12:30 (11,721)	
Burke, Ailbhe M	4:17:17 (12,871)	
Burke, Catherine E	4:54:39 (22,185)	
Burke, Ebony	6:29:37 (34,313)	
Burke, Eileen	4:46:53 (20,247)	
Burke, Melanie	2:52:52 (472)	
Burke, Morag B	5:07:25 (24,980)	
Burkitt, Hilary	4:13:44 (12,026)	

Burkmar, Juliette M	4:09:32 (11,080)	
Burles, Julie A	6:50:30 (34,946)	
Burley, Caroline L	3:46:00 (6,178)	
Burley, Justine	3:59:06 (8,988)	
Burley, Megan J	3:58:27 (8,822)	
Burman, Jayne	5:34:10 (29,788)	
Burnell, Ceri L	3:38:43 (4,960)	
Burnell, Gillian	4:40:59 (18,780)	
Burnell, Linda R	5:33:18 (29,644)	
Burner, Alexandra S	5:48:23 (31,516)	
Burnett, Carole-Anne	5:12:36 (25,967)	
Burnett, Patricia	5:55:03 (32,154)	
Burnett, Wendy	5:11:29 (25,750)	
Burnett-Hall, Clare M	4:53:08 (21,788)	
Burnley, Hannah	4:43:10 (19,336)	
Burns, Elisabeth A	5:37:07 (30,184)	
Burns, Hannah E	4:11:30 (11,501)	
Burns, Hazel J	3:21:55 (2,698)	
Burns, Joanna K	5:25:03 (28,283)	
Burns, Laura	5:37:54 (30,287)	
Burnside, Kirstie A	6:56:37 (35,065)	
Burow, Linda J	5:20:54 (27,587)	
Burr, Katherine L	4:27:21 (15,433)	
Burrage, Carolyn A	5:40:15 (30,621)	
Burrett, Sally	5:30:04 (29,155)	
Burridge, Jane	4:33:27 (16,900)	
Burrow, Rachel L	4:59:00 (23,253)	
Burrows, Anita L	5:32:01 (29,459)	
Burrows, Christopher	4:16:40 (12,729)	
Burrows, Elaine M	4:43:55 (19,514)	
Burrows, Janet F	4:19:13 (13,379)	
Burrows, Karen B	4:41:50 (19,005)	
Burrows, Karen J	4:35:27 (17,389)	
Burrows, Maggie J	5:52:29 (31,918)	
Burrows, Mora J	4:43:01 (19,300)	
Burston, Judy	4:53:46 (21,956)	
Burt, Charlie C	4:46:18 (20,127)	
Burt, Coral L	6:07:36 (33,136)	
Burt, Victoria L	6:27:55 (34,249)	
Burton, Christine J	5:02:29 (24,033)	
Burton, Diane E	6:07:26 (33,127)	
Burton, Dionne	5:43:58 (31,033)	
Burton, Kate	7:41:03 (35,569)	
Burton, Tina	7:34:40 (35,532)	
Burton-Hopkins, Abigail E	5:24:34 (28,192)	
Burville, Claire E	4:24:30 (14,704)	
Bury, Alison J	5:32:13 (29,485)	
Bury, Anna E	6:31:28 (34,382)	
Buse, Siglinde	5:14:57 (26,439)	
Bush, Alison J	6:18:07 (33,783)	
Bushell, Claire L	5:58:31 (32,469)	
Bushnell, Julie-Ann	4:32:19 (16,630)	
Bussell, Anna C	6:08:02 (33,171)	
Bussell, Fiona	4:02:30 (9,699)	
Busser, Celeste F	5:25:45 (28,417)	
Butcher, Catherine L	4:02:47 (9,747)	
Butcher, Lucy E	5:21:02 (27,609)	
Butcher, Susan E	5:53:20 (31,991)	
Butland, Orlanda C	3:33:14 (4,171)	
Butler, Alice B	4:02:00 (9,604)	
Butler, Deb S	7:06:15 (35,222)	
Butler, Gail C	4:39:00 (18,283)	
Butler, Gemma	4:32:48 (16,740)	
Butler, Helen E	4:07:41 (10,700)	
Butler, Jenna L	6:40:10 (34,670)	
Butler, Judith K	5:12:56 (26,027)	
Butler, Louise M	6:13:58 (33,550)	
Butler, Lucy	4:52:13 (21,546)	
Butler, Sandra J	5:23:28 (28,004)	
Butler, Sarah	3:25:41 (3,086)	
Butler, Susan J	4:30:07 (16,177)	
Butt, Carmel D	4:25:10 (14,862)	
Butterfield, Caroline A	8:11:05 (35,660)	
Butterworth, Claire	4:34:59 (17,268)	
Butterworth, Myra	5:05:42 (24,637)	
Butterworth, Natasha	5:33:46 (29,726)	
Buttery, Davina M	5:17:56 (27,037)	
Button, Claire L	4:32:16 (16,672)	
Buxton, Helen L	4:03:25 (9,852)	
Buxton, Helen R	5:26:31 (28,545)	
Buzzard, Michelle J	3:44:04 (5,875)	
Bye, Natasha J	4:52:12 (21,541)	
Byng-Maddick, Zillah E	4:39:11 (18,329)	

Byrne, Cathy ...5:41:53 (30,819)
Byrne, Charlotte B ...5:20:55 (27,593)
Byrne, Dara B ...5:18:43 (27,206)
Byrne, Kerry L ...5:11:54 (25,834)
Byrne, Laura E ...4:27:58 (15,578)
Byrne, Niamh M ...4:22:52 (14,303)
Byrne, Sharon ...4:07:48 (10,724)
Byrne, Sue N. ...3:53:30 (7,689)
Byrom, Jenny M ...5:15:06 (26,479)
Byrom, Lynda G ...5:46:03 (31,266)
Caballero, Jane M ...5:03:10 (24,166)
Cable, Sally E ...4:39:14 (18,345)
Cabourne, Penny ...5:30:41 (29,251)
Caddick, Eleanor R ...5:07:47 (25,054)
Caffari, Dee ...7:23:59 (35,424)
Cafferrey, Annette M ...4:26:52 (15,285)
Cahill, Elizabeth A ...3:47:12 (6,377)
Cahill, Ruth M ...5:05:30 (24,602)
Cahill, Sinead E ...5:16:51 (26,820)
Caillet, Patricia ...4:08:08 (10,794)
Cain, Helen R ...4:35:11 (17,323)
Cain, Sandra ...4:40:52 (18,752)
Cain, Sharen ...5:17:06 (26,877)
Cain, Susan P ...4:18:28 (13,201)
Caira, Trudy ...5:22:43 (27,892)
Cakebread, Julie A ...5:36:50 (30,153)
Caldeira, Concy M ...4:55:48 (22,455)
Caldeira, Maria Teresa M ...4:52:02 (21,492)
Calder, Alexandra G ...5:21:38 (27,717)
Calder, Helen L ...5:01:21 (23,803)
Calder, Susan E ...7:05:40 (35,211)
Caldwell, Carol A ...4:20:29 (13,729)
Caldwell, Helen J ...4:47:30 (20,407)
Caldwell, Jane E ...4:32:56 (16,771)
Calesky, Vicky A ...5:31:48 (29,419)
Callaghan, Jacqui L ...3:54:28 (7,897)
Callaghan, Katie E ...4:12:58 (11,822)
Callender, Claire M ...5:41:13 (30,731)
Calliste, Gillian L ...5:03:33 (24,246)
Callow, Melanie E ...5:47:25 (31,400)
Calver, Sarah J ...3:46:58 (6,338)
Calvert, Katie ...7:38:00 (35,552)
Calvo, Vania S ...3:59:16 (9,034)
Cambridge, Lucy C ...4:24:08 (14,610)
Cameron, Fiona ...4:05:23 (10,221)
Cameron, Jo R ...5:20:44 (27,560)
Cameron, Karen M ...3:35:17 (4,445)
Cameron-Doe, Julie M ...4:25:27 (14,934)
Camfield, Olwen C ...5:06:59 (24,876)
Campbell, Anna E ...4:29:15 (15,926)
Campbell, Emma J ...5:49:21 (31,615)
Campbell, Ilidia M ...4:13:58 (12,089)
Campbell, Joanna K ...5:11:43 (25,793)
Campbell, Kathryn ...4:28:52 (15,825)
Campbell, Melissa R ...4:38:16 (18,077)
Campbell, Michelle ...4:25:33 (14,955)
Campbell, Miranda ...5:27:47 (28,759)
Campbell, Sonia J ...5:24:13 (28,140)
Campbell, Susan C ...6:08:13 (33,187)
Campbell-Hunter, Ester ...5:34:17 (29,811)
Campey, Melanie A ...5:18:58 (27,247)
Campion, Alison M ...4:26:22 (15,149)
Campion, Jane ...3:27:36 (3,362)
Campofiore, Gail G ...6:06:16 (33,065)
Candido, Elizeth M ...6:38:56 (34,634)
Cane, Nicola E ...5:31:11 (29,333)
Cane, Susan ...5:00:01 (23,508)
Caney, Pauline J ...4:29:17 (15,934)
Canham, Janine S ...5:48:10 (31,484)
Cann, Sally E ...4:14:52 (12,284)
Cannell, Lucy C ...3:56:25 (8,336)
Cannell, Susan H ...6:11:48 (33,414)
Canning, Amanda J ...5:15:12 (26,500)
Canning, Katie E ...4:25:35 (14,963)
Cantillon, Julie ...5:36:30 (30,114)
Cantle, Samantha J ...6:16:07 (33,689)
Canty, Jenny ...4:35:36 (17,431)
Cape, Lindsey A ...5:55:42 (32,209)
Capel, Sarah R ...4:32:54 (16,763)
Caporaso, Julie ...6:02:09 (32,757)
Capper, Suzan E ...5:39:02 (30,454)
Caps, Marylou ...5:13:40 (26,157)
Capstick, Christine A ...4:44:57 (19,820)

Capstick, Dianna E ...4:01:13 (9,462)
Capstick, Dorothy M ...5:24:50 (28,243)
Capsuto, Tara L ...4:49:39 (20,926)
Cardno-Strachan, Gillian ...3:32:17 (4,044)
Cardy, Christine ...4:10:53 (11,345)
Careddu, Giuseppina ...7:30:54 (35,500)
Carew-Robinson, Katie D ...4:13:56 (12,079)
Carey, Fiona ...4:31:17 (16,419)
Carey, Kelly J ...5:44:16 (31,075)
Carey, Michelle E ...4:25:47 (15,015)
Cariss, Helen L ...5:59:33 (32,551)
Carley, Rachel ...5:29:34 (29,078)
Carley, Wendy ...3:48:54 (6,703)
Carlin, Annette K ...3:37:32 (4,757)
Carlisle, Helen A ...6:23:31 (34,057)
Carmichael, Isabella ...4:22:03 (14,097)
Carney, Ann ...4:48:01 (20,535)
Carney, Sarah L ...7:37:19 (35,547)
Carpenter, Angela A ...6:38:45 (34,628)
Carpenter, Christine M ...4:52:14 (21,552)
Carpenter, Melissa ...4:55:18 (22,338)
Carpenter, Sarah K ...6:09:30 (33,271)
Carr, Claire J ...6:24:33 (34,103)
Carr, Eileen M ...4:59:04 (23,277)
Carr, Emma L ...5:21:23 (27,673)
Carr, Hazel ...5:20:19 (27,479)
Carr, Laura E ...5:00:35 (23,631)
Carr, Louise M ...4:46:17 (20,120)
Carr, Noreen M ...5:07:17 (24,951)
Carr, Sarah L ...6:24:33 (34,103)
Carr, Sylvia ...7:13:07 (35,325)
Carr, Tanya H ...4:22:28 (14,190)
Carrapato, Maria J ...4:42:55 (19,285)
Carre, Paula L ...4:48:54 (20,745)
Carrick, Marie J ...4:23:08 (14,362)
Carrick, Nicki J ...5:27:33 (28,719)
Carrig, Rita ...5:32:51 (29,585)
Carrigg, Tania D ...5:05:11 (24,541)
Carrington, Annie M ...3:46:35 (6,267)
Carrington, Gaynor J ...5:50:20 (31,709)
Carrington, Lucy R ...4:00:16 (9,266)
Carritt, Joanna ...3:13:51 (1,888)
Carroll, Belinda ...4:25:35 (14,963)
Carroll, Tilghman ...4:41:12 (18,841)
Carroll, Zoe L ...6:39:41 (34,664)
Carruthers, Sheila ...4:18:28 (13,201)
Carson, Cassandra J ...3:20:30 (2,553)
Carson, Hayley ...4:47:27 (20,394)
Carson, Roger P ...4:19:27 (13,446)
Carter, Angela J ...4:53:03 (21,762)
Carter, Caroline A ...5:29:11 (29,018)
Carter, Charlotte E ...4:45:30 (19,952)
Carter, Cheryl ...3:45:17 (6,065)
Carter, Christopher G ...3:59:56 (9,193)
Carter, Clare L ...4:01:59 (9,600)
Carter, Dawn ...4:59:14 (23,319)
Carter, Elaine V ...5:18:07 (27,084)
Carter, Gillian M ...4:16:52 (12,775)
Carter, Helen S ...5:29:35 (29,082)
Carter, Jacqueline A ...4:27:48 (15,541)
Carter, Keri M ...6:25:35 (34,151)
Carter, Louise E ...5:33:34 (29,698)
Carter, Nicola ...3:26:33 (3,201)
Carter, Nicola M ...4:11:35 (11,518)
Carter, Rachel ...5:09:58 (25,469)
Carter, Rebecca G ...4:53:23 (21,854)
Carter, Sarah ...6:04:21 (32,907)
Carter, Suzanne L ...5:32:32 (29,539)
Carter, Tina L ...6:14:29 (33,577)
Carter, Victoria A ...4:47:45 (20,470)
Carter, Victoria E ...4:18:52 (13,302)
Cartledge, Gabrielle C ...4:17:26 (12,921)
Cartlidge, Holly ...4:18:29 (13,208)
Cartmell, Caroline M ...4:06:29 (10,463)
Cartwright, Susan J ...4:49:33 (20,900)
Cartwright, Tracey ...6:01:27 (32,714)
Caruana, Gail J ...5:36:19 (30,088)
Carver, Alison J ...5:13:26 (26,110)
Casagne, Catherine ...4:40:40 (18,694)
Caseley, Julie A ...4:18:16 (13,137)
Casey, Ann M ...7:27:58 (35,457)
Casey, Cicely M ...5:53:30 (32,008)
Casey, Diane B ...7:04:14 (35,192)

Casey, Frances C ...5:34:42 (29,874)
Casey, Julie ...6:19:18 (33,854)
Casha, Daniela ...3:49:51 (6,908)
Cashman, Sarah ...5:34:01 (29,764)
Cashmore, Ann L ...4:29:34 (16,031)
Cashmore, Emma N ...4:48:32 (20,656)
Cassamally, Laura ...5:23:35 (28,026)
Cassells, Joanna M ...6:16:02 (33,685)
Casserly, Julia M ...5:14:13 (26,270)
Cassey, Joanna ...4:30:14 (16,202)
Cassey, Vanessa J ...3:47:08 (6,369)
Cassidy, Marina J ...7:05:51 (35,216)
Cast, Jacqueline L ...5:27:30 (28,712)
Castellane, Daniele ...4:56:57 (22,763)
Castle, Jennifer ...4:08:14 (10,821)
Castle, Rosemary A ...4:47:13 (20,337)
Castle, Susan ...4:56:55 (22,753)
Castro, Maria L ...5:32:27 (29,516)
Castro, Sandra W ...6:00:47 (32,643)
Catchpole, Paula ...4:41:22 (18,879)
Catchpole, Sarah J ...4:20:32 (13,738)
Cater, Janet ...6:50:20 (34,941)
Catford, Sarah L ...4:52:16 (21,565)
Cathie, Helen ...4:53:11 (21,804)
Catley, Alison ...4:42:40 (19,219)
Catlin, Jennifer A ...5:01:13 (23,776)
Cattell, Sy ...3:33:37 (4,217)
Catterson, Christine A ...3:49:42 (6,872)
Cauldwell, Sophia K ...4:17:31 (12,951)
Caulfield, Sarah ...4:37:04 (17,801)
Caulfield, Vanda ...3:32:38 (4,088)
Caunter, Janice N ...3:54:30 (7,905)
Causer, Joanna E ...4:37:00 (17,786)
Cavanagh, Kwendy S ...4:04:09 (9,994)
Cavarzan, Tisiana ...4:30:27 (16,246)
Cave, Sonia C ...5:10:30 (25,578)
Caven, Alexandra J ...3:21:56 (2,700)
Caven, Hannah ...5:29:23 (29,054)
Cawley, Jacqueline ...6:35:45 (34,530)
Cawtherley, Sian C ...4:24:08 (14,610)
Ccarelli, Annamaria ...3:44:30 (5,942)
Celis, Bianca V ...4:38:53 (18,251)
Cerveny, Gretchen ...3:38:33 (4,929)
Chabrol, Benedicte ...5:39:57 (30,580)
Chaffer, Oonagh C ...4:37:04 (17,801)
Chaffer, Peter ...3:09:08 (1,481)
Chaffey, Lorraine A ...4:45:39 (19,983)
Chahal, Kulvinder ...6:09:09 (33,246)
Chahal, Kulvinder K ...7:38:06 (35,553)
Chai, Kuy Youb ...5:00:52 (23,704)
Chalkley, Denise ...5:08:51 (25,251)
Chalmers, Nicki L ...5:34:43 (29,877)
Chamberlain, Anne ...6:24:38 (34,113)
Chambers, Gill ...4:14:55 (12,302)
Chambers, Keeley A ...5:04:51 (24,487)
Chambers, Marcia C ...6:18:03 (33,780)
Chambers, Margaret M ...6:52:57 (34,989)
Chambers, Sophie ...5:08:35 (25,201)
Champetier, Brigitte ...5:37:59 (30,298)
Champney, Christine M ...5:52:44 (31,944)
Chan, Christina Y ...4:53:46 (21,956)
Chan, Emma ...6:05:26 (32,991)
Chan, Ling K ...4:21:49 (14,036)
Chana, Raj K ...5:01:04 (23,745)
Chana, Rupinder K ...4:42:17 (19,121)
Chandelle, Helen C ...5:20:07 (27,440)
Chandler, Clare J ...6:04:50 (32,946)
Chandler, Pauline ...3:57:17 (8,549)
Chandler, Stephanie E ...4:42:40 (19,219)
Chandler, Trudi ...5:49:23 (31,619)
Chaney, Jacqueline C ...5:40:54 (30,695)
Chantry, Laura ...4:58:18 (23,103)
Chaplin, Elizabeth ...5:24:06 (28,122)
Chaplin, Zara K ...5:11:31 (25,759)
Chaplin-Armer, Toni ...4:25:22 (14,913)
Chapman, Cynthia M ...4:27:12 (15,387)
Chapman, Denise A ...3:30:17 (3,762)
Chapman, Emma L ...4:49:35 (20,912)
Chapman, Jane C ...5:09:19 (25,336)
Chapman, Janie ...3:33:43 (4,228)
Chapman, Joanna ...7:40:49 (35,566)
Chapman, Joanne D ...4:58:23 (23,129)
Chapman, Karen ...5:39:29 (30,523)

Chapman, Katharine M.............5:17:14 (26,904)
Chapman, Katie E.............3:11:20 (1,657)
Chapman, Lee.............4:54:19 (22,104)
Chapman, Pamela K.............4:00:09 (9,238)
Chapman, Rosemary.............6:03:15 (32,836)
Chapman, Sarah L.............4:23:02 (14,340)
Chappell, Jane P.............3:16:41 (2,147)
Charalambous, Pat.............4:37:04 (17,801)
Chard, Andrea P.............4:58:09 (23,063)
Charles, Lisa A.............4:46:43 (20,219)
Charlett, Pauline A.............4:40:06 (18,556)
Charlton, Ailsa J.............5:01:55 (23,916)
Charlton, Louise.............5:24:59 (28,267)
Charnley, Caroline.............3:59:47 (9,160)
Charrington, Susie J.............4:02:06 (9,622)
Charters, Tracey L.............5:10:47 (25,625)
Chase, Alison J.............4:12:43 (11,770)
Chase, Tina K.............3:35:21 (4,460)
Chatterton, Kathryn.............4:22:07 (14,110)
Chatwin, Rachel M.............3:16:23 (2,116)
Chaudhri, Sarah E.............4:06:39 (10,491)
Chaudhry, Bina.............5:16:46 (26,800)
Chaudhry, Karen A.............5:42:05 (30,836)
Chaundy, Alison J.............5:01:03 (23,739)
Chavasse, Diane M.............5:17:18 (26,920)
Chedzoy, Claire S.............5:28:09 (28,828)
Cheeseman, Mairead C.............7:23:50 (35,423)
Cheeseman, Pauline M.............7:24:45 (35,428)
Cheesley, Amanda J.............6:47:24 (34,870)
Cheetham, Simon.............4:51:58 (21,477)
Chelmick, Sophie J.............5:00:18 (23,575)
Chemin, Martine.............4:50:25 (21,104)
Chenel, Claire.............4:16:13 (12,627)
Cheng-Echevarria, Ann.............4:15:05 (12,338)
Cheriton, Ginny.............5:43:51 (31,025)
Cheshire, Alison R.............5:24:05 (28,120)
Chesney, Lisa B.............5:35:55 (30,043)
Chessell, Alison L.............5:39:28 (30,521)
Chessum, Deborah S.............4:53:15 (21,825)
Chesterton, Hayley.............4:05:22 (10,212)
Chestnutt, Sarah A.............4:19:49 (13,544)
Chevassut, Alison.............5:20:11 (27,453)
Chew, Shelby.............3:44:49 (5,995)
Cheyne, Emma R.............5:03:06 (24,146)
Chick, Amanda K.............5:09:31 (25,375)
Chicken, Sian.............4:13:17 (11,905)
Chidson, Valerie J.............6:23:42 (34,062)
Chigariro, Moira.............5:44:56 (31,147)
Chigwedere, Terry Z.............4:50:14 (21,055)
Child, Jennifer C.............5:15:29 (26,560)
Childs, Stacy A.............5:26:36 (28,557)
Chillery, Leah.............4:44:39 (19,727)
Chillet, Mary P.............5:42:53 (30,923)
Chillingworth, Grace E.............3:23:36 (2,858)
Chilton, Katie L.............4:48:19 (20,613)
Chilton, Lucy E.............5:03:22 (24,208)
Chinn, Joanne.............5:01:31 (23,833)
Chinwala, Yasmine.............6:17:58 (33,777)
Chipperfield, Tamsin E.............3:42:46 (5,637)
Chiswell, Stephanie A.............4:31:36 (16,484)
Chitson, Jade A.............4:59:00 (23,253)
Chitty, James A.............5:09:29 (25,367)
Chitty, Kacey E.............4:44:09 (19,579)
Chiu, Miliyun.............4:53:22 (21,850)
Chivers, Ann E.............5:48:58 (31,580)
Chivers, Charlotte.............5:11:19 (25,726)
Chivers, Laura F.............5:11:19 (25,726)
Chivers, Samantha J.............4:39:02 (18,293)
Chomka, Krysia.............4:41:02 (18,797)
Choonos, Stephanie D.............5:31:34 (29,384)
Chowdhury, Tanya J.............3:58:32 (8,846)
Christensen, Alison.............7:48:15 (35,612)
Christian, Victoria.............4:52:13 (21,546)
Christie, Caroline M.............5:26:49 (28,593)
Christie, Ceri A.............6:09:45 (33,289)
Christie, Erica M.............3:15:21 (2,024)
Christie, Jill.............3:21:37 (2,663)
Christie, Nathalie.............3:20:20 (2,533)
Christopher, Helen.............5:15:00 (26,449)
Christy, Tracey J.............3:40:20 (5,240)
Chryss, Jennifer.............6:34:46 (34,485)
Chumber, Asha R.............6:30:45 (34,348)
Chung, Julie.............5:23:54 (28,093)

Chunxiu, Zhou.............2:20:38 (14)

Zhou Chunxiu (born 15 November 1978 in Jiangsu, China) was the first Chinese winner of the women's race at the London Marathon in a time of 2:20:38. She won bronze in the marathon at the 2008 Olympics in Beijing, and competed at the 2004 Olympics, finishing the marathon in 33rd place. Zhou is the daughter of farmers in one of the poorest provinces in China. Despite these humble beginnings, Britain's Chinese community flocked to London for the Marathon to support her. Chinese community leaders hosted a post-race party in the capital attended by the cultural attaché from the London embassy. Zhou reportedly runs between 120 and 190 miles a week in two or three training sessions.

Chupp, Teresa.............5:52:09 (31,888)
Church, Gemma L.............6:05:25 (32,990)
Church, Moya A.............4:41:44 (18,969)
Churchill, Carly J.............4:29:01 (15,861)
Churchill, Lesley J.............5:07:02 (24,892)
Churchill, Margaret.............5:58:27 (32,464)
Churnin, Anna.............7:21:59 (35,406)
Ciaiola, Maria.............6:24:29 (34,098)
Ciampa, Julia G.............3:39:42 (5,143)
Ciapryna, Natalia.............5:33:26 (29,671)
Cichocki, Clare M.............4:21:22 (13,926)
Cioffi, Danielle.............5:32:51 (29,585)
Cipolat, Corinne.............4:35:07 (17,303)
Clague, Louise.............4:36:18 (17,612)
Clampin, Shelley J.............7:26:49 (35,443)
Clanachan, Ann.............4:09:50 (11,134)
Clancy, Chrissie.............4:03:23 (9,846)
Clancy, Lara R.............4:53:22 (21,850)
Clapton, Pauline M.............4:48:39 (20,679)
Clare, Susanne.............3:46:07 (6,198)
Clargo, Andrea M.............4:34:56 (17,253)
Clark, Adele.............4:23:11 (14,374)
Clark, Billie.............3:59:32 (9,104)
Clark, Brigitte.............4:43:42 (19,463)
Clark, Dawn.............3:46:52 (6,314)
Clark, Emma R.............6:19:54 (33,885)
Clark, Fiona E.............5:00:47 (23,683)
Clark, Fiona H.............4:58:16 (23,093)
Clark, Heather S.............5:04:12 (24,357)
Clark, Helen E.............3:53:49 (7,746)
Clark, Jill.............4:07:54 (10,748)
Clark, Jo H.............3:38:15 (4,877)
Clark, Joanne A.............4:47:15 (20,345)
Clark, Juliet R.............4:18:23 (13,170)
Clark, Katrina E.............5:57:49 (32,393)
Clark, Lindsey A.............4:00:59 (9,417)
Clark, Lucy J.............5:15:02 (26,464)
Clark, Maureen A.............5:53:17 (31,984)
Clark, Melissa.............5:40:28 (30,648)
Clark, Patricia A.............8:44:36 (35,684)
Clark, Rachel L.............5:03:16 (24,185)
Clark, Sarah J.............5:08:34 (25,197)
Clark, Sue.............5:44:33 (31,099)
Clark, Vicki C.............5:02:05 (23,947)
Clark, Wendy A.............4:20:35 (13,749)
Clark, Wendy M.............6:10:51 (33,355)
Clark, Zoe A.............4:03:35 (9,883)
Clarke, Ailsa C.............4:08:26 (10,859)
Clarke, Alison F.............6:00:08 (32,589)
Clarke, Angela.............6:31:58 (34,405)
Clarke, Angela M.............4:34:17 (17,093)
Clarke, Anna L.............4:37:10 (17,817)
Clarke, Anne E.............7:55:10 (35,633)
Clarke, Annette J.............3:32:13 (4,032)
Clarke, Ashlee P.............6:57:43 (35,087)
Clarke, Claire M.............4:56:53 (22,743)
Clarke, Constanze A.............4:49:09 (20,807)
Clarke, Corinne I.............3:36:22 (4,598)
Clarke, Debbie E.............3:53:53 (7,761)
Clarke, Eleanor R.............4:03:50 (9,935)
Clarke, Erika L.............4:31:43 (16,511)
Clarke, Jacqueline S.............4:20:58 (13,845)
Clarke, Jenny S.............6:41:39 (34,706)
Clarke, Julia.............4:28:46 (15,807)
Clarke, Katharine E.............3:51:36 (7,277)
Clarke, Lesley.............3:39:42 (5,143)
Clarke, Louise M.............7:04:26 (35,198)
Clarke, Maxine G.............5:15:50 (26,628)
Clarke, Melissa J.............5:48:19 (31,509)
Clarke, Michelle M.............3:42:50 (5,654)
Clarke, Natacha D.............4:27:28 (15,464)
Clarke, Natalie A.............5:55:57 (32,236)
Clarke, Pamela.............5:03:29 (24,235)
Clarke, Penny.............5:37:18 (30,213)
Clarke, Samantha M.............4:08:21 (10,842)
Clarke, Tina J.............4:19:01 (13,330)
Clarke, Tracy J.............6:31:22 (34,376)
Clarke, Victoria J.............5:56:42 (32,308)
Clarke Noble, Désirée A.............3:41:50 (5,491)
Clarkson, Alan.............3:26:21 (3,180)
Clarkson, Emily R.............5:06:03 (24,702)
Clarkson, Joanne.............5:12:36 (25,967)
Clarkson, Linda P.............3:16:48 (2,158)
Clarkson, Louise J.............4:03:10 (9,810)
Clarkson, Suzanne.............4:18:23 (13,170)
Clatworthy, Patricia.............5:54:15 (32,077)
Clay, Gemma A.............5:02:27 (24,026)
Clay, Mary L.............4:19:27 (13,446)
Clay, Nicola K.............2:46:25 (270)
Clay, Rachael E.............5:46:54 (31,344)
Claydon, Lisa J.............6:14:51 (33,604)
Clayton, Carolanne.............6:10:13 (33,322)
Clayton, Claire M.............4:45:09 (19,870)
Clayton, Denise.............4:38:45 (18,212)
Clayton, Francesca M.............5:23:28 (28,004)
Clayton, Jacqueline M.............3:57:55 (8,702)
Clayton, Julie A.............4:44:34 (19,705)
Clayton, Lucy.............3:48:09 (6,553)
Clayton, Susan L.............4:37:26 (17,874)
Clayton-Drabble, Susan.............4:39:31 (18,418)
Cleary, Catherine M.............5:12:13 (25,901)
Cleary, Jane M.............5:10:23 (25,552)
Cleary, Marianne.............5:02:51 (24,095)
Cleary, Vivien A.............6:23:25 (34,053)
Cleathero, Claire L.............3:20:35 (2,567)
Cleaver, Margaret.............4:44:11 (19,594)
Clegg, Andrea.............6:16:17 (33,702)
Clegg, Gill.............4:12:45 (11,775)
Clegram, Julie E.............4:58:33 (23,159)
Cleland, Diane.............4:23:44 (14,497)
Clemens, Linda A.............5:04:26 (24,407)
Clements, Katie E.............4:55:43 (22,433)
Clements, Michelle C.............3:47:07 (6,368)
Clements, Pauline.............5:35:13 (29,944)

Clements, Sarah	5:10:40 (25,608)	
Clementson, Emma J	5:44:56 (31,147)	
Clenshaw, Sarah	4:42:20 (19,129)	
Clews, Sarah L	5:17:37 (26,984)	
Clibbon, Lara	5:07:06 (24,909)	
Cliff, Jill M	3:27:33 (3,358)	
Clifford, Debbie A	5:05:35 (24,617)	
Clifford, Erin	5:42:11 (30,846)	
Clifford, Lizzie J	3:02:25 (1,021)	
Clift, Deborah R	3:47:41 (6,473)	
Clifton, June	5:14:45 (26,396)	
Clifton, Lynne I	5:14:25 (26,314)	
Clifton, Lynsey M	5:05:44 (24,642)	
Clinch, Agnes M	4:01:08 (9,444)	
Clinch, Georgina	3:52:05 (7,389)	
Clingham, Gillian	4:58:53 (23,224)	
Clink, Jenny	4:18:42 (13,264)	
Clinton, Jacqueline W	4:41:28 (18,910)	
Clinton, Jane	4:03:00 (9,785)	
Clish, Clare	6:13:28 (33,517)	
Cloke, Yvie M	4:43:32 (19,421)	
Close, Lindsay	5:07:32 (25,007)	
Cloudesley, Rachel E	5:39:20 (30,494)	
Clough, Judith S	5:06:59 (24,876)	
Clubbe, Jayne	4:30:32 (16,261)	
Cluett, Anna L	6:19:39 (33,874)	
Clugston, Paula	7:20:43 (35,394)	
Cluitt, Sonia	4:19:44 (13,520)	
Clutton, Hayley L	4:23:10 (14,369)	
Coates, Emma L	4:27:38 (15,498)	
Coates, Lauren V	4:46:23 (20,151)	
Coates, Zoe H	3:29:28 (3,643)	
Coats, Nichola A	5:36:54 (30,165)	
Cobbold, Marie D	5:48:19 (31,509)	
Cobby, Janet A	4:01:51 (9,578)	
Cobley, Rachel J	5:56:06 (32,246)	
Cochrane, Eleanor J	5:10:08 (25,513)	
Cockerell, Diana	4:53:56 (22,000)	
Codling, Marian J	6:01:19 (32,704)	
Codrington, Emma L	6:16:29 (33,717)	
Coe, Jane E	6:14:13 (33,564)	
Coello, Soledad	4:40:28 (18,644)	
Coetzee, Irma	4:25:28 (14,940)	
Coffin, Maureen A	5:48:59 (31,584)	
Coghlan, Lin M	6:48:55 (34,909)	
Coghlin, Susan M	4:39:36 (18,437)	
Cohen, Debbie	8:09:18 (35,656)	
Cohen, Nicola J	4:25:41 (14,993)	
Cohen, Robina L	6:17:50 (33,772)	
Coker, Rachel B	4:29:17 (15,934)	
Colbert, Jill P	3:37:17 (4,721)	
Colbert, Sarah J	3:51:52 (7,330)	
Colbourne, Tracy A	5:33:32 (29,693)	
Colbridge, Ruth	5:21:58 (27,777)	
Coldrick, Ginastein S	5:08:52 (25,256)	
Coldwell, Polly	4:29:08 (15,895)	
Cole, Barbara	4:17:02 (12,822)	
Cole, Dawn	5:13:29 (26,120)	
Cole, Julie	4:45:05 (19,857)	
Cole, Rachel A	5:55:18 (32,176)	
Cole, Stephanie L	5:28:18 (28,865)	
Colebrook, Catherine M	6:58:43 (35,103)	
Coleman, Hayley C	6:46:52 (34,853)	
Coleman, Heidi L	3:04:34 (1,136)	
Coleman, Jaclyn L	6:55:45 (35,051)	
Coleman, Lucinda M	6:06:09 (33,060)	
Coles, Debi G	4:00:53 (9,393)	
Collard, Andrea L	5:42:30 (30,878)	
Collard, Monica J	6:15:18 (33,633)	
Collas, Christine	7:29:04 (35,467)	
Collett, Joanna	5:20:04 (27,433)	
Colley, Rachael S	4:54:45 (22,212)	
Colley, Rachel E	3:51:55 (7,342)	
Collier, Lucy B	6:41:04 (34,691)	
Collingbine, Jennie	6:19:33 (33,865)	
Collings, Cathy M	3:51:12 (7,189)	
Collins, Amy C	4:08:19 (10,835)	
Collins, Claire	5:45:26 (31,195)	
Collins, Claire M	6:03:24 (32,846)	
Collins, Emma A	5:59:25 (32,545)	
Collins, Leigh	6:16:17 (33,702)	
Collins, Michelle A	4:58:14 (23,085)	
Collins, Peri D	4:13:17 (11,905)	
Collins, Rosie A	5:25:42 (28,406)	
Collins, Sarah M	6:24:17 (34,093)	
Collins, Susan	6:57:08 (35,077)	
Collins, Victoria	5:40:59 (30,705)	
Collinson, Libby	4:25:07 (14,852)	
Collinson, Nicola S	6:01:36 (32,728)	
Collis, Helen	4:57:21 (22,875)	
Collyer, Lucy	5:29:12 (29,023)	
Colman, Jill M	4:40:05 (18,552)	
Colman, Judith M	5:57:40 (32,379)	
Colquhoun, Shirley J	3:39:08 (5,039)	
Coltart, Iona C	4:06:39 (10,491)	
Colton, Martine A	8:54:55 (35,688)	
Colville, Valerie J	5:18:26 (27,148)	
Colvin, Harriet A	5:04:11 (24,355)	
Colwell, Catherine M	4:27:30 (15,469)	
Combellack, Frances M	5:18:11 (27,098)	
Comben, Elizabeth A	5:37:38 (30,252)	
Combine, Jacqueline	4:32:31 (16,667)	
Comerford, Anna	4:23:39 (14,477)	
Comins, Penny C	4:04:15 (10,014)	
Commander, Ruth F	5:48:57 (31,578)	
Commins, Sarah K	4:07:35 (10,676)	
Comyns, Claire	4:30:12 (16,196)	
Conaghan, Maria U	3:19:37 (2,447)	
Concannon, Joanne	3:59:15 (9,027)	
Conceicao, Maria	3:23:45 (2,872)	
Coney, Deborah C	3:34:12 (4,293)	
Coney, Diane J	3:32:01 (3,990)	
Congiu, Gabriella	4:27:34 (15,480)	
Conn, Joanna E	4:02:40 (9,722)	
Conneely, Janet E	4:38:06 (18,040)	
Connell, Keeley W	3:59:56 (9,193)	
Connell, Moira	4:23:52 (14,536)	
Connery, Julie	6:33:58 (34,465)	
Connolly, Gemma C	4:35:23 (17,380)	
Connolly, Jennifer	5:04:19 (24,379)	
Connolly, Leann	5:23:48 (28,079)	
Connolly, Sarah F	5:50:38 (31,739)	
Connor, Emma	5:43:12 (30,961)	
Connor, Jill M	4:39:54 (18,508)	
Connor, Lynda M	4:08:02 (10,774)	
Constable, Sarah L	6:35:08 (34,505)	
Constance, Paddy J	3:58:19 (8,790)	
Conte, Franca	5:28:19 (28,871)	
Convert, Danielle A	4:42:06 (19,064)	
Convery, Roey E	5:03:49 (24,294)	
Conway, Anne	5:27:33 (28,719)	
Conway, Anneli F	5:17:50 (27,013)	
Conway, Caroline S	6:20:26 (33,916)	
Conway, Laura C	6:43:02 (34,751)	
Conway, Liz	8:04:51 (35,649)	
Conway, Marie C	5:53:49 (32,034)	
Conway, Paula L	5:21:28 (27,691)	
Coogan, Juliann M	4:33:57 (17,024)	
Cooil, Jan M	3:50:54 (7,115)	
Cook, Anne E	4:42:05 (19,060)	
Cook, Claire	4:48:35 (20,666)	
Cook, Elaine S	4:59:38 (23,419)	
Cook, Elizabeth L	5:01:48 (23,892)	
Cook, Gemma A	5:34:05 (29,777)	
Cook, Helen S	4:03:45 (9,916)	
Cook, Jennifer M	5:20:25 (27,497)	
Cook, Joanne E	5:07:33 (25,010)	
Cook, Laura A	4:53:17 (21,831)	
Cook, Lesley M	6:10:16 (33,324)	
Cook, Lindsay C	5:28:46 (28,946)	
Cook, Mandy E	5:15:03 (26,472)	
Cook, Nicola J	6:32:33 (34,425)	
Cook, Rachel J	3:12:21 (1,761)	
Cook, Ruth H	4:53:52 (21,980)	
Cook, Sarah A	4:40:59 (18,780)	
Cook, Shirley K	5:50:11 (31,691)	
Cook, Siobhan N	4:36:35 (17,689)	
Cook, Susan M	4:33:55 (17,011)	
Cook, Tonia M	3:55:46 (8,178)	
Cook, Wendy J	4:38:55 (18,258)	
Cooke, Annabel E	7:27:21 (35,454)	
Cooke, Joanne	4:47:12 (20,334)	
Cooke-Hurle, Jo	6:26:52 (34,208)	
Coole, Alison M	3:52:22 (7,446)	
Cooley, Charlotte E	4:52:56 (21,735)	
Coombs, Hannah K	3:40:04 (5,200)	
Coombs, Rachel J	4:28:06 (15,623)	
Coonan, Caren	3:24:22 (2,946)	
Cooper, Alison	3:31:27 (3,898)	
Cooper, Alison J	4:48:05 (20,549)	
Cooper, Anne	4:09:41 (11,113)	
Cooper, Cheryl L	7:46:03 (35,606)	
Cooper, Claire	5:12:14 (25,904)	
Cooper, Elaine D	4:15:41 (12,480)	
Cooper, Elizabeth A	4:53:57 (22,006)	
Cooper, Elizabeth H	5:37:50 (30,274)	
Cooper, Heidi	4:45:54 (20,033)	
Cooper, Holly J	3:53:48 (7,744)	
Cooper, Judith A	5:43:59 (31,039)	
Cooper, Julie A	5:20:11 (27,453)	
Cooper, Lindsey J	4:31:01 (16,357)	
Cooper, Lisanne	4:03:34 (9,880)	
Cooper, Louise J	3:08:18 (1,415)	
Cooper, Louise J	4:25:10 (14,862)	
Cooper, Michelle S	6:00:47 (32,643)	
Cooper, Michelle V	6:29:41 (34,317)	
Cooper, Nicola F	5:06:33 (24,790)	
Cooper, Sally A	4:39:44 (18,471)	
Cooper, Sally L	5:13:51 (26,204)	
Cooper, Sue	4:33:22 (16,884)	
Cooper, Theresa M	5:20:53 (27,586)	
Cooper, Tracey S	5:36:43 (30,135)	
Cooper, Victoria S	4:15:36 (12,460)	
Cooper, Wendy A	4:27:39 (15,501)	
Cope, Catherine L	6:15:04 (33,620)	
Cope, Wendy A	4:51:01 (21,244)	
Copeland, Katie	4:57:03 (22,786)	
Copeland, Kay	5:03:18 (24,191)	
Copland, Lisa L	4:27:38 (15,498)	
Copps, Vivienne T	4:39:40 (18,454)	
Copse, Georgina M	6:45:24 (34,808)	
Copsey-Blake, Debbie	5:32:17 (29,494)	
Copson, Angela	3:57:15 (8,542)	
Corbett, Niamh C	4:44:31 (19,692)	
Corbett, Tanya M	5:35:49 (30,025)	
Corbin, Francine	4:32:30 (16,662)	
Corby, Cathy N	7:41:09 (35,573)	
Corcut, Sarah M	3:59:56 (9,193)	
Cordell, Mavis A	5:41:27 (30,762)	
Cordery, Jane C	4:56:53 (22,743)	
Cordingley, Frank J	3:13:10 (1,834)	
Cordingley, Jacqueline A	3:54:02 (7,799)	
Cordwell, Lisa A	5:30:52 (29,274)	
Cornell, Katie E	5:14:58 (26,444)	
Corner, Susie J	6:13:57 (33,548)	
Corney, Susan C	4:54:36 (22,172)	
Cornish, Clare M	3:58:33 (8,849)	
Cornwell, Laura L	5:00:50 (23,693)	
Cornwell, Michelle	4:23:30 (14,444)	
Cornwell, Naomi	6:34:39 (34,480)	
Corper, Johanna S	4:30:30 (16,257)	
Corr, Madeleine	5:02:56 (24,113)	
Corral, Laura V	4:56:09 (22,550)	
Corrie, Sharon	5:46:25 (31,302)	
Corrigan, Beverley A	5:15:04 (26,475)	
Corsini, Susan J	3:38:20 (4,892)	
Cosnard, Claudie	4:59:27 (23,363)	
Coss, Katie	4:52:13 (21,546)	
Cossington, Kay D	5:18:02 (27,064)	
Costello, Bernie	4:35:18 (17,359)	
Costello, Dee	5:50:14 (31,697)	
Coster, Lorraine A	6:22:02 (33,996)	
Costiff, Christine	3:25:49 (3,102)	
Costigan, Leone M	4:21:42 (14,003)	
Cottam, Ruth	4:40:06 (18,556)	
Cotter, Ruth D	5:12:08 (25,879)	
Cotterill, Fiona	3:34:26 (4,334)	
Cotton, Katherine A	4:13:53 (12,062)	
Cotton, Kim R	8:07:11 (35,654)	
Cotton, Tracy R	5:40:44 (30,675)	
Cottrell, Emily M	5:58:11 (32,430)	
Cottrell, Kay	3:55:56 (8,214)	
Cottrell, Michelle L	5:27:48 (28,761)	
Coughlan, Amanda	4:05:31 (10,241)	
Coughlan, Sharon B	5:02:16 (23,982)	
Coughlin, Nicole M	4:06:58 (10,566)	
Coulbert, Julie A	3:56:18 (8,304)	
Coull, Zoe C	4:42:06 (19,064)	
Coultart, Sarah J	4:34:41 (17,201)	

Coulter, Jenny 6:05:15 (32,978)
Coulter, Nicola J 6:11:21 (33,395)
Coulter, Rebecca M 4:41:41 (18,964)
Coundley, Helen C 4:15:10 (12,360)
Courage, Lindsey J 2:59:26 (857)
Couratier, Juliette M 5:06:22 (24,762)
Court, Mariette 4:57:46 (22,973)
Court, Michelle C 6:36:08 (34,542)
Courtney, Eleanor L 5:36:47 (30,145)
Courtney, Emma L 4:53:17 (21,831)
Courtney, Polly E 3:56:53 (8,452)
Courtney, Sylvia 6:24:31 (34,101)
Cousen, Sharon L 3:48:30 (6,619)
Cousin, Kate J 4:23:47 (14,508)
Cousin, Monica B 4:51:08 (21,275)
Cousins, Alison 4:58:11 (23,070)
Cousins, Anne 5:30:30 (29,222)
Cousins, Annie J 4:31:35 (16,481)
Coutts, Ann 5:59:15 (32,532)
Couturier, Lucille 4:44:24 (19,649)
Cove, Hayley J 5:27:11 (28,658)
Covey, Jenny M 4:13:14 (11,889)
Cowan, Eleanor F 4:19:53 (13,569)
Cowan, Rebecca M 4:38:49 (18,239)
Cowan, Rosie E 5:08:07 (25,118)
Cowburn, Louise H 4:51:46 (21,430)
Cowdery, Rosalind M 4:49:23 (20,858)
Cowen, Annie 5:25:29 (28,367)
Cowie, Lesley P 5:07:59 (25,091)
Cowie, Stephanie 5:52:37 (31,931)
Cowking, Marilyn L 3:47:30 (6,424)
Cowley, Beth 4:38:15 (18,068)
Cowley, Laura J 2:48:46 (338)
Cowley, Melissa L 4:30:12 (16,196)
Cowling, Gert T 4:40:59 (18,780)
Cowling, Michelle 5:23:14 (27,966)
Cowman, Sharon 5:03:36 (24,258)
Cowne, Pauline J 6:11:15 (33,387)
Cowsill, Elaine 4:04:43 (10,095)
Cox, Claudia L 5:27:45 (28,754)
Cox, Elizabeth A 5:48:59 (31,584)
Cox, Katy 7:29:39 (35,492)
Cox, Laura 4:47:09 (20,322)
Cox, Lisa M 4:12:12 (11,655)
Cox, Louise J 6:57:29 (35,081)
Cox, Lucy J 5:04:54 (24,501)
Cox, Nicolanne S 5:16:00 (26,662)
Cox, Sally A 4:45:35 (19,962)
Cox, Sarah 5:05:44 (24,642)
Cox, Sarah J 7:09:44 (35,268)
Cox, Victoria A 4:42:39 (19,215)
Coyne, Glenis V 4:42:40 (19,219)
Coyne, Johanna J 4:41:58 (19,031)
Coyne, Sharon A 3:11:06 (1,642)
Crabb, Mary 4:20:45 (13,784)
Crabb, Sarah L 4:06:47 (10,526)
Crabtree, Amy R 4:29:35 (16,034)
Crabtree, Linda C 4:29:18 (15,941)
Cradock, Claire L 5:29:14 (29,031)
Craig, Charlotte J 4:12:54 (11,806)
Craig, Elizabeth S 4:29:58 (16,139)
Craig, Pamela 5:07:26 (24,984)
Craig, Rebecca E 5:58:56 (32,502)
Craig, Yvonne C 6:20:17 (33,904)
Craigie, Louise 4:10:37 (11,292)
Craik, Carolyn J 3:58:10 (8,750)
Craker, Tracey E 5:04:52 (24,492)
Cramp, Christine 5:22:56 (27,929)
Crampin, Sophie 3:53:45 (7,738)
Crane, Meggie S 4:54:09 (22,062)
Cranmer, Marijana 4:44:37 (19,720)
Cranwell, Patricia S 3:57:39 (8,639)
Craven, Ruth D 4:44:51 (19,791)
Crawford, Elizabeth H 3:10:13 (1,580)
Crawford, Emmalyn F 4:45:47 (20,006)
Crawford, Kathryn R 4:35:00 (17,270)
Crawford, Rebecca J 3:55:02 (8,015)
Crawley, Jane E 4:52:00 (21,486)
Crawley, Natasha S 4:59:36 (23,412)
Crawshaw, Veronica R 5:20:36 (27,541)
Cream, Tania J 3:32:07 (4,013)
Creaney, Nicola 4:58:48 (23,206)
Crease, Hermione J 4:43:30 (19,414)
Creed, Gemma 4:31:05 (16,374)
Creed, Jo Anne J 4:32:46 (16,729)
Creed, Joanna S 4:14:52 (12,284)
Creed, Julie J 5:16:58 (26,852)
Creegan, Gina M 4:08:46 (10,916)
Crement, Sandra 4:53:53 (21,985)
Cremin, Sharon E 4:40:39 (18,687)
Cresswell, Fiona V 5:06:03 (24,702)
Crews, Sharon 4:17:30 (12,947)
Crick, Anette 4:13:16 (11,899)
Crick, Joy 4:14:11 (12,134)
Crideford, Freda M 4:54:03 (22,031)
Crighton, Melanie A 5:11:30 (25,756)
Crilley, Kathy 6:08:03 (33,175)
Cringle, Tara L 5:28:53 (28,963)
Crisford, Sarah 5:19:34 (27,353)
Crispin, Darla M 5:24:06 (28,122)
Crispin, Georgina 4:39:34 (18,427)
Critchley, Joanne L 5:31:01 (29,298)
Critchlow, Anna E 2:59:43 (879)
Crocker, Jessica J 4:23:47 (14,508)
Crocker, Rosemarie J 4:34:38 (17,186)
Crockett, Lindsey 5:21:43 (27,734)
Crockett, Phillipa M 4:37:00 (17,786)
Crofts, Judy 7:17:55 (35,368)
Crofts, Tanya E 4:00:40 (9,349)
Croggon, Lorraine 4:53:02 (21,760)
Croke, Nicola 5:51:03 (31,779)
Croker, Rhona M 3:35:48 (4,523)
Crompton, Barbara A 5:33:18 (29,644)
Crompton, Sue J 4:26:37 (15,214)
Cromwell, Carrie L 4:36:22 (17,629)
Cron, Nina L 6:12:06 (33,432)
Cronan, Kim M 3:23:09 (2,815)
Cronin, Claire M 4:52:56 (21,735)
Cronin, Marianne 5:38:15 (30,342)
Cronin-Jones, Susan 5:42:04 (30,834)
Crook, Alison 5:02:10 (23,964)
Crooks, Nicky L 6:45:47 (34,819)
Croome, Rachael A 5:04:42 (24,448)
Croot, Sarah E 4:33:00 (16,785)
Crosbie, Beverley A 5:48:11 (31,486)
Crosbie Dawson, Lucy C 4:34:05 (17,046)
Crosby, Laura E 5:08:51 (25,251)
Crosby, Louise 4:22:33 (14,217)
Crosier, Joanna K 3:51:28 (7,246)
Cross, Catherine A 4:27:41 (15,512)
Cross, Claire L 5:17:39 (26,992)
Cross, Denise 3:53:52 (7,757)
Cross, Jillian L 4:38:17 (18,084)
Cross, Louise 5:57:52 (32,397)
Cross, Selina C 5:30:51 (29,270)
Cross, Valerie 5:52:52 (31,956)
Cross, Wendy J 5:26:13 (28,495)
Crossley, Katherine A 5:50:00 (31,675)
Crossley, Mandy E 5:50:46 (31,753)
Crosswell, Elizabeth 4:28:18 (15,672)
Crosswell, Margaret E 4:35:04 (17,288)
Croton, Catherine C 7:19:45 (35,383)
Crouch, Nicola J 5:40:50 (30,684)
Crouch, Sara M 6:23:20 (34,046)
Crowder, Cora 3:42:26 (5,589)
Crowe, Fidelma J 4:01:59 (9,600)
Crowe, Katherine R 4:02:57 (9,774)
Crowfoot, Sarah E 5:33:23 (29,663)
Crowhurst, Paula 4:47:59 (20,531)
Crowley, Hazel M 4:21:29 (13,963)
Crowson, Michelle S 5:14:44 (26,393)
Crowther, Ann 4:59:08 (23,295)
Crowther, Jane E 4:37:28 (17,887)
Croxford, Tracie 3:18:52 (2,374)
Croxson, Louise H 3:49:46 (6,886)
Cruickshank, Jacqueline 4:40:34 (18,673)
Crump, Gail A 4:24:04 (14,592)
Cruse, Sharon A 5:07:58 (25,088)
Cryer, Jackie A 4:10:33 (11,281)
Crystal, Lucy H 5:20:17 (27,472)
Csupa, Andrea 5:05:28 (24,595)
Cuchillo, Eva 4:14:56 (12,306)
Cudmore, Angela J 4:51:35 (21,392)
Cuffe, Josephine M 4:53:14 (21,822)
Cull, Désirée A 4:12:50 (11,795)
Cullard, Talitha E 6:16:31 (33,719)
Cullen, Deborah K 5:39:43 (30,560)
Cullen, Elizabeth 4:46:53 (20,247)
Cullen, Jane 6:40:57 (34,688)
Cullen, Virginia A 5:43:03 (30,938)
Cullum, Gail P 3:58:27 (8,822)
Culver, Victoria L 4:27:01 (15,326)
Cumine, Susan A 4:53:19 (21,842)
Cumming, Jade B 4:18:06 (13,094)
Cummings, Naomi S 5:32:56 (29,597)
Cummins, Linda D 3:12:15 (1,750)
Cunliffe, Helena C 5:29:59 (29,129)
Cunliffe, Jayne E 5:31:23 (29,359)
Cunliffe, Rachel E 4:21:05 (13,868)
Cunner, Terri-Ann 4:53:57 (22,006)
Cunningham, Astrid C 4:41:16 (18,855)
Cunningham, Hannah V 3:27:44 (3,378)
Cunningham, Hilary A 5:29:55 (29,120)
Cunningham, Julia M 5:48:40 (31,547)
Cunningham, Veronica 5:38:57 (30,445)
Curley, Nicola A 4:29:35 (16,034)
Curran, Beverley J 5:34:31 (29,853)
Curran, Joan 4:49:30 (20,889)
Curran, Sarah T 3:54:50 (7,970)
Currey, Jo 4:43:34 (19,434)
Currie, Alexandra V 4:13:28 (11,951)
Currie, Gillian T 6:20:09 (33,893)
Currie, Rachael 3:21:10 (2,618)
Currie, Victoria J 5:05:07 (24,530)
Curry, Julia R 4:25:07 (14,852)
Curry, Stefanie 3:54:14 (7,848)
Curtin, Emily J 4:23:53 (14,540)
Curtis, Joanna H 4:03:14 (9,824)
Curtis, Lucy C 4:07:25 (10,636)
Curtis, Nadine 5:40:24 (30,640)
Curtis, Sarah-Jane 3:49:39 (6,861)
Curtis-Evans, Kate L 5:39:32 (30,535)
Custance, Lucie J 3:42:39 (5,618)
Custis, Kate E 3:48:38 (6,654)
Cuthbert, Verna J 3:59:14 (9,021)
Cutland, Deborah L 6:02:41 (32,799)
Cutler, Penny M 3:34:33 (4,348)
Cutler, Sarah 3:52:03 (7,378)
Cutmore, Sara L 4:22:21 (14,164)
Cutner, Christine J 4:01:41 (9,549)
Cutress, Kaye A 5:49:16 (31,612)
Cutting, Donna M 4:39:07 (18,310)
Czartoryski, Tamara L 6:50:38 (34,949)
Czifra, Aniko 4:37:40 (17,926)
Czuczman, Linda 5:11:50 (25,820)
Czyzak-Dannenbaun, Peggy S 6:04:26 (32,914)
Dable, Kristy M 4:49:42 (20,935)
Dack, Anne E 4:35:34 (17,421)
Dack, Faye 5:17:54 (27,031)
Dacosta, Marva 5:58:19 (32,445)
Dadd, Charlotte S 3:48:25 (6,598)
Dadd, Jackie 4:29:32 (16,025)
Dadey, Teresa F 5:25:08 (28,292)
Dadoun, Lucy S 4:21:05 (13,868)
Dagg, Alice 3:45:18 (6,068)
Dagless, Karren 6:46:23 (34,840)
Dagless, Lynne P 5:48:54 (31,572)
Daives, Helen A 4:10:18 (11,228)
Dakin, Fiona A 4:14:17 (12,165)
Dale, Alison V 5:26:27 (28,539)
Dale, Amy E 3:03:28 (1,076)
Dale, Jacqui A 6:31:53 (34,400)
Dale, Louise M 5:31:54 (29,433)
Dale, Nicola I 4:31:12 (16,407)
Dale, Samantha L 5:00:10 (23,541)
Dale, Sue I 3:42:57 (5,677)
D'Alessandro, Jalanie 3:53:29 (7,683)
Daley, Lesley R 5:27:30 (28,712)
Daley, Loretta E 3:56:51 (8,444)
Daley, Stephanie J 3:44:51 (5,999)
Daligan, Sally C 6:59:12 (35,116)
Dalingwater, Jeanette 3:25:00 (3,019)
Daly, Andrea L 4:40:13 (18,581)
Daly, Christine H 5:44:40 (31,119)
Daly, Elizabeth 4:03:36 (9,886)
Daly, Gwen 4:13:31 (11,969)
Daly, Heather C 3:44:59 (6,025)
Daly, Jacqueline 6:00:14 (32,599)
Daly, Maria F 5:42:21 (30,865)

Daly, Teresa B 6:32:44 (34,429)
D'Amone, Marilena 4:26:29 (15,184)
Damonsing, Charlotte A 6:19:35 (33,866)
Danaher, Claire M 6:13:08 (33,498)
Dance, Helen 4:33:12 (16,846)
Dance, Ruth 3:38:56 (5,002)
Daniel, Alix L 4:49:31 (20,892)
Daniel, Dusanka 4:59:30 (23,384)
Daniel, Kay 5:14:18 (26,292)
Daniel, Marged L 6:49:00 (34,913)
Daniel, Nicola N 7:36:52 (35,546)
Daniells, Sally J 7:42:04 (35,583)
Daniels, Emma 5:43:36 (31,001)
Daniels, Marie-Anne R 3:54:34 (7,914)
Daniels, Natalie A 6:31:05 (34,365)
Dannunzio-Green, Norma 4:41:40 (18,958)
Dansey, Susanne E 5:54:04 (32,058)
Dansie, Suzanne 5:37:00 (30,171)
Dany, Alazard 4:39:27 (18,404)
Danziger, Verity H 5:48:24 (31,517)
Darbon, Nathalie M 3:31:56 (3,980)
Darby, Sarah L 7:04:16 (35,194)
Darcy, Anna M 4:08:05 (10,787)
Darke, Tracy A 3:29:58 (3,714)
Darlington, Catherine E 5:02:53 (24,102)
Darlington, Jode M 6:07:34 (33,133)
Darlow, Natalie J 4:13:48 (12,043)
D'Artista, Daniela 5:32:48 (29,578)
Darvill, Sarah A 6:44:04 (34,774)
Darvill, Sian N 5:10:19 (25,540)
Darwen, Carole Ann 8:43:53 (35,683)
Darwin, Jennifer 6:04:44 (32,936)
Darwood, Joanne 3:39:25 (5,093)
Dasilva, Kate J 4:59:12 (23,308)
Davenport, Victoria 4:54:09 (22,062)
Davey, Antionette M 6:16:50 (33,725)
Davey, Bridget B 3:33:53 (4,250)
Davey, Elizabeth 4:29:28 (15,997)
Davey, Heather J 5:06:55 (24,864)
Davey, Jean 4:19:03 (13,337)
Davey, Sue M 5:53:27 (32,000)
Davey, Tracey 4:11:20 (11,456)
David, Anna 3:28:21 (3,457)
David-John, Jean C 5:34:31 (29,853)
Davidson, Anne A 3:32:07 (4,013)
Davidson, Anne D 4:14:17 (12,165)
Davidson, Karen 4:28:43 (15,792)
Davidson, Karen 5:12:52 (26,014)
Davidson, Margaret A 4:34:12 (17,076)
Davie, Claudine L 4:29:25 (15,980)
Davies, Alison 5:42:47 (30,904)
Davies, Angela J 6:32:03 (34,409)
Davies, Bente 7:33:33 (35,522)
Davies, Carla N 4:19:39 (13,494)
Davies, Carol-Ann 3:34:59 (4,407)
Davies, Cate 6:19:38 (33,872)
Davies, Ceri-Anne 3:24:58 (3,016)
Davies, Christine A 6:38:38 (34,624)
Davies, Debra L 5:43:03 (30,938)
Davies, Elin H 5:19:15 (27,303)
Davies, Emma 6:39:33 (34,658)
Davies, Hannah G 5:00:42 (23,661)
Davies, Hayley M 6:38:03 (34,608)
Davies, Hazel L 4:43:37 (19,444)
Davies, Jean 4:46:09 (20,092)
Davies, Jennifer 4:53:17 (21,831)
Davies, Jessica C 4:55:21 (22,349)
Davies, Joanne 9:03:05 (35,692)
Davies, Josephine 4:33:56 (17,016)
Davies, Julie P 6:39:08 (34,645)
Davies, Kasie B 4:16:56 (12,798)
Davies, Kim L 5:42:17 (30,860)
Davies, Kim N 4:56:50 (22,728)
Davies, Lisa M 6:21:07 (33,962)
Davies, Lucy 4:32:45 (16,726)
Davies, Lucy V 3:29:17 (3,614)
Davies, Lyn A 4:33:42 (16,962)
Davies, Natalie 4:00:28 (9,303)
Davies, Olwen E 4:44:19 (19,626)
Davies, Rachel M 3:56:42 (8,406)
Davies, Samantha 4:33:29 (16,909)
Davies, Samantha J 6:36:02 (34,536)
Davies, Sara N 4:44:03 (19,552)
Davies, Sarah E 5:53:40 (32,026)
Davies, Sheila E 6:04:39 (32,927)
Davies, Susan J 5:18:13 (27,108)
Davies, Tara C 3:57:17 (8,549)
Davies, Valerie J 6:17:26 (33,743)
Davies, Victoria R 6:28:25 (34,264)
Davies, Yolande 4:23:18 (14,399)
Davies, Yvonne M 3:52:43 (7,506)
Davies, Zoe M 6:00:16 (32,600)
Davila, Justine R 4:46:54 (20,254)
Davis, Abigail A 5:35:53 (30,035)
Davis, Dawn Y 5:38:19 (30,362)
Davis, Denise 6:13:58 (33,550)
Davis, Emma L 4:02:36 (9,708)
Davis, Gillian A 6:01:48 (32,742)
Davis, Harriet J 4:21:19 (13,914)
Davis, Helen M 5:01:37 (23,856)
Davis, Jane 6:37:07 (34,584)
Davis, Julie D 5:38:12 (30,336)
Davis, Karen E 4:28:00 (15,586)
Davis, Katherine A 3:18:51 (2,371)
Davis, Kathleen M 5:15:31 (26,567)
Davis, Kerry 5:15:11 (26,495)
Davis, Lucie J 4:32:34 (16,681)
Davis, Lydia 3:23:06 (2,810)
Davis, Maria 5:54:22 (32,089)
Davis, Mary J 4:57:58 (23,025)
Davis, Natalie A 5:12:06 (25,870)
Davis, Rebecca J 4:17:25 (12,914)
Davis, Sophie 5:11:47 (25,808)
Davison, Julie A 4:25:00 (14,820)
Davison, Paula 6:13:59 (33,553)
Davison, Penny 4:19:31 (13,463)
Dawe, Lucy K 6:12:39 (33,467)
Dawes, Jane W 5:37:36 (30,246)
Dawes, Rachel M 5:35:49 (30,025)
Dawes-Clark, Sarah L 6:02:10 (32,758)
Dawett, Sunita 4:05:56 (10,338)
Dawkins, Debbie 4:53:32 (21,894)
Dawkins, Justine C 4:59:27 (23,363)
Dawkins, Pauline D 6:08:43 (33,220)
Dawson, Anne 5:36:19 (30,088)
Dawson, Annie C 5:09:47 (25,431)
Dawson, Chrissie A 5:33:18 (29,644)
Dawson, Debra A 6:58:45 (35,107)
Dawson, Elizabeth 5:31:31 (29,378)
Dawson, Heather V 4:03:44 (9,911)
Dawson, Joanna M 4:51:50 (21,450)
Dawson, Mandy C 3:51:48 (7,315)
Dawson, Nadia E 4:56:39 (22,679)
Dawson, Paula J 4:25:16 (14,889)
Day, Elizabeth A 3:48:34 (6,640)
Day, Fiona C 5:27:48 (28,761)
Day, Gillian M 5:13:22 (26,094)
Day, Jackelyn 5:59:03 (32,511)
Day, Natasha 3:52:57 (7,554)
Day, Nina V 4:16:40 (12,729)
Day, Symone T 5:54:37 (32,115)
Day, Wendy E 5:35:35 (29,992)
Day, Wendy L 7:22:17 (35,409)
Daykin, Alison 5:30:36 (29,235)
De Barra, Deirdre 4:16:08 (12,604)
De Bono, Naz 4:44:41 (19,740)
De Cothi, Elizabeth 3:49:47 (6,894)
De Koning, Fleur 5:32:00 (29,451)
De La Porte, Joanne K 5:10:06 (25,506)
De Lissandri, Giulietta H 5:36:03 (30,056)
De Marwicz, Marie A 6:18:59 (33,836)
De Min, Martine A 3:52:40 (7,494)
De Rosa, Clara 4:45:16 (19,896)
De Souza Gomes, Toya 4:14:24 (12,189)
De Vos, Sarah M 5:55:50 (32,221)
De Wit, Andri 4:30:40 (16,290)
Dean, Claire 4:53:32 (21,894)
Dean, Claire L 4:45:09 (19,870)
Dean, Lauren J 4:06:27 (10,454)
Dean, Lucinda G 5:03:32 (24,243)
Dean, Melanie R 4:47:17 (20,357)
Dean, Susan J 6:14:08 (33,559)
Dean, Suzanne C 4:38:26 (18,134)
Dean, Suzanne E 6:00:01 (32,576)
Deans, Deborah A 4:39:43 (18,466)
Deans, Victoria L 5:09:13 (25,321)
Dear, Louise C 3:59:35 (9,114)
Deasy, Mary-Ann 3:56:31 (8,364)
Decker, Helen J 2:56:36 (647)
Decristofaro, Antonietta 6:24:30 (34,100)
Dedman, Anna 4:48:32 (20,656)
Dedow, Christina 4:36:51 (17,754)
Deegan, Julie 3:14:36 (1,952)
Deeprose, Gail L 4:27:05 (15,350)
Deer, Julie 4:58:21 (23,119)
Deering, Pauline D 5:39:22 (30,502)
Deery, Anny C 4:14:59 (12,318)
Deeson, Fleur P 5:13:15 (26,086)
Degenhard, Clare E 6:26:10 (34,180)
Deheeger, Audrey 6:02:46 (32,805)
Deighton, Helen J 4:18:00 (13,074)
Deiss, Erika 3:56:51 (8,444)
Delaney, Dolores 5:27:02 (28,625)
Delany, Helen L 4:04:59 (10,141)
De-Lapeyre, Rose-Marie 4:30:22 (16,229)
Delay, Jeanine A 4:34:11 (17,072)
Delderfield, Diane L 4:59:28 (23,369)
Dell, Patricia 6:54:46 (35,030)
Dell, Sally J 3:58:58 (8,954)
Deller, Jane E 5:18:30 (27,164)
Dellow, Katherine 5:32:40 (29,561)
Dembitz, Sarah 6:17:57 (33,775)
Dempsey, Deirdre 4:55:51 (22,475)
Dempster, Anna M 4:39:25 (18,394)
Dempster, Ellen M 5:11:56 (25,842)
Dempster, Tina M 5:08:36 (25,205)
Denby, Lucinda 4:30:46 (16,308)
Denby-Ashe, Daniela J 4:11:21 (11,459)
Deneys, Lies 4:26:45 (15,249)
Denneth, Nadine E 5:03:06 (24,146)
Denning, Terri A 5:09:48 (25,433)
Dennis, Ann 5:09:05 (25,291)
Dennis, Anne-Marie 5:59:01 (32,507)
Dennis, Beth A 5:32:55 (29,594)
Dennis, Caroline C 5:17:43 (27,002)
Dennis, Christine J 6:31:21 (34,374)
Dennis, Darren 6:02:44 (32,801)
Dennison, Andrea M 3:02:26 (1,024)
Dennison, Mikaila D 7:40:06 (35,561)
Denny, Christina M 5:11:29 (25,750)
Dent, Emma G 5:41:07 (30,718)
Dent, Hilary M 3:59:09 (9,000)
Dent, Verity 4:53:46 (21,956)
Denton, Charlotte 3:59:05 (8,981)
Denton, Nicola D 6:07:43 (33,146)
Denyer, Brigitte 5:29:27 (29,065)
De-Oliveira, Maria 5:07:18 (24,956)
Derain, Laura 5:30:41 (29,251)
Derbyshire, Angie 4:49:54 (20,974)
Desai, Sangeeta 4:44:08 (19,571)
Desborough, Valerie C 4:11:10 (11,417)
Deslandes, Kate 5:09:24 (25,353)
Desmond, Bridget C 5:13:58 (26,224)
Despotovic, Jelena 4:38:41 (18,195)
Dethick, Lisa A 3:49:31 (6,836)
Deutsch, Naomi S 5:30:07 (29,165)
Devery, Michelle K 6:23:56 (34,073)
Devine, Andrea 5:00:15 (23,563)
Devine, Lucinda M 5:23:56 (28,097)
Devine, Sally A 4:22:47 (14,281)
Dewar, Paula A 4:00:51 (9,386)
Dewberry, Michelle L 4:33:20 (16,879)
Dewhirst, Lesley 4:23:59 (14,566)
Dewick, Nicola A 5:01:47 (23,886)
Dexter, Ashleigh C 5:30:28 (29,216)
Dhupelia, Suni R 3:00:17 (915)
Di Benedetto, Angela 4:23:32 (14,456)
Dibble, Deborah L 3:45:57 (6,171)
Dibble, Sandra M 4:58:23 (23,129)
Dibbs, Juliet C 4:41:31 (18,927)
Dick, Eleanor M 3:26:00 (3,127)
Dick, Jennifer 3:09:45 (1,536)
Dick, Kerry 4:37:59 (18,003)
Dick, Patricia A 3:44:26 (5,928)
Dickens, Jayne 3:12:26 (1,771)
Dickie, Anna 4:18:32 (13,221)
Dickinson, Carol J 4:34:25 (17,118)
Dickinson, Janet E 4:29:51 (16,110)
Dickinson, Lesley A 5:07:29 (24,995)

Dickinson, Shantha C 3:31:21 (3,885)
Dickinson, Timasin K 4:55:27 (22,377)
Dickson, Catherine A 5:23:37 (28,033)
Dickson, Fern 4:56:22 (22,606)
Didwell, Dawn L 5:47:31 (31,410)
Dieulafait, Dominique 4:34:37 (17,181)
Difallah, Malika 3:29:30 (3,649)
Dilley, Claire 5:45:28 (31,203)
Dillon, Hazel D 5:53:31 (32,012)
Dillon, Helen M 5:28:57 (28,975)
Dillon, Jo 4:07:30 (10,651)
Dilnot, Angelika 5:07:54 (25,077)
Dilworth, Sarah L 5:45:28 (31,203)
Dines, Sarah E 4:40:18 (18,603)
Ding, Lorraine A 4:37:40 (17,926)
Ding, Tara 4:03:52 (9,939)
Disney, Glennys 3:21:42 (2,675)
Diss, Jacqueline A 5:42:26 (30,874)
Divers, Leander L 6:03:19 (32,839)
Dix, Katie L 5:31:40 (29,399)
Dixon, Chantelle E 5:14:23 (26,308)
Dixon, Elise 5:58:50 (32,492)
Dixon, Fiona J 3:43:43 (5,816)
Dixon, Michelle J 5:39:24 (30,507)
Dixon, Patricia M 4:55:55 (22,493)
Dixon, Rachel J 4:20:57 (13,840)
Dixon, Sharon 3:14:52 (1,975)
Dixon, Tracey 4:53:22 (21,850)
Dixon, Tracey 5:07:10 (24,918)
Do Adro Quinteiro, Silvia 4:11:45 (11,558)
Dobbie, Janet 5:12:51 (26,008)
Dobbie, Shona H 4:49:50 (20,959)
Dobbs, Helen 6:34:07 (34,468)
Dobby, Sarah 3:50:25 (7,024)
Dobson, Joanne M 4:54:09 (22,062)
Dobson, Katie 6:07:56 (33,164)
Dobson, Rachel 3:47:19 (6,394)
Dobson, Sally 6:07:56 (33,164)
Docker, Sarah J 7:02:57 (35,174)
Dockerhill, Jackie A 4:13:05 (11,853)
Dockering, Kelly 5:24:04 (28,116)
Dockwray, Karen D 5:37:52 (30,281)
Dodd, Alison J 5:53:42 (32,028)
Dodd, Belinda M 4:03:40 (9,896)
Dodd, Joanne E 5:18:06 (27,081)
Doddington, Denise A 3:36:07 (4,561)
Dodds, Beatrice M 6:08:28 (33,201)
Dodds, Fiona A 6:33:13 (34,446)
Doe, Trudy R 6:29:12 (34,291)
Dogherty, Carol 7:51:37 (35,625)
Doherty, Kathryn 5:15:11 (26,495)
Doherty, Kay 6:16:56 (33,730)
Doherty, Susannah J 7:12:59 (35,322)
Dolan, Anita M 5:00:10 (23,541)
Dolan, Gina C 5:00:10 (23,541)
Dolphin, Jill M 5:29:06 (28,997)
Dominguez, Anna L 5:20:54 (27,587)
Don, Georgina K 4:37:42 (17,937)
Donaghy, Alison M 3:56:15 (8,286)
Donaghy, Chris 7:06:21 (35,226)
Donald, Julie 3:31:20 (3,881)
Donaldson, Nicole A 6:22:22 (34,017)
Donaldson, Rosemary J 3:59:55 (9,188)
Donaldson, Sue M 5:02:05 (23,947)
Donbavand, Nicky 5:29:19 (29,043)
Donker, Larissa 5:18:18 (27,124)
Donkin, Carrie A 7:14:39 (35,342)
Donnelley, Laura K 5:10:37 (25,599)
Donnelly, Ann M 6:30:06 (34,332)
Donnelly, Katie A 5:21:10 (27,626)
Donnelly, Susan C 6:16:19 (33,707)
Donoghue, Ashley E 4:33:31 (16,916)
Donoghue, Susan E 3:32:38 (4,088)
Donoho, Kelly J 5:09:49 (25,434)
Donovan, Renate J 5:06:24 (24,769)
Donta, Helen 2:40:42 (152)
Doody, Daphne A 6:24:31 (34,101)
Doogan, Mary 6:24:41 (34,116)
Dooley, Alison L 5:53:34 (32,017)
Dooley, Caroline E 5:15:45 (26,618)
Dooley, Lauren C 5:21:18 (27,657)
Dooley, Michelle C 5:28:48 (28,952)
Dooley, Sharon M 5:35:34 (29,989)
Doradoux, Claire 3:47:59 (6,522)
Doran, Elyse 4:16:12 (12,621)
Doran, Natalie M 4:57:29 (22,903)
Doran, Susan L 5:05:56 (24,684)
Doran, Victoria E 5:48:05 (31,477)
Dore, Anna K 4:13:48 (12,043)
Dorey, Claire A 5:04:48 (24,467)
Dorey, Natalie 5:29:12 (29,023)
Dorrell, Patricia A 4:18:37 (13,245)
Dorrity, Miriam 4:19:42 (13,510)
Dossett, Sarah 3:54:15 (7,855)
Dossin, Teresinha J 5:23:48 (28,079)
Doucette, Krista E 4:36:10 (17,572)
Dougall, Annie K 3:50:15 (6,984)
Dougall, Lynne 5:26:22 (28,524)
Douglas, Brondwyn M 6:11:51 (33,417)
Douglas, Helen R 3:52:08 (7,398)
Douglas, Susan J 7:08:49 (35,259)
Douglas, Veronica S 5:45:15 (31,177)
Douglas, Zoe 5:36:48 (30,148)
Douglass, Fiona E 4:25:39 (14,985)
Doulton, Lindsay M 4:00:23 (9,287)
Dove, Katie B 4:12:57 (11,819)
Doven, Emma J 4:27:30 (15,469)
Down, Caroline L 5:19:38 (27,365)
Down, Domonique 5:30:02 (29,147)
Downer, Aimée S 4:45:10 (19,876)
Downes, Elizabeth N 4:36:36 (17,692)
Downes, Leo V 5:09:14 (25,323)
Downes, Wendy A 5:59:04 (32,513)
Downey, Faye 4:09:00 (10,949)
Downey, Gillian M 6:47:06 (34,861)
Downham, Lynsey 5:36:45 (30,138)
Downie, Lauren 5:28:32 (28,907)
Downie, Leah 4:50:47 (21,189)
Downing, Anne 4:59:30 (23,384)
Downing, Becky C 4:03:39 (9,891)
Downs, Gabrielle A 3:43:53 (5,846)
Dowse, Daisy E 5:32:35 (29,547)
Dowty, Clare 4:58:53 (23,224)
Doy, Lindsay E 3:52:38 (7,485)
Doyle, Alison M 6:44:11 (34,780)
Doyle, Carly V 7:35:06 (35,533)
Doyle, Carole C 4:59:54 (23,475)
Doyle, Michelle A 6:29:39 (34,316)
Doyle, Sheila M 5:22:41 (27,889)
Doyle, Siobhan 4:18:26 (13,190)
Drahos, Veronika B 3:33:58 (4,266)
Drake, Dawn A 3:49:12 (6,774)
Drake, Joanne L 5:15:42 (26,602)
Drake, Julie E 3:48:12 (6,561)
Dransfield, Elspeth H 5:30:29 (29,218)
Draper, Eleanor N 4:24:45 (14,767)
Draper, Julie E 4:40:29 (18,654)
Draper, Michelle 5:53:49 (32,034)
Draper, Sarah V 5:47:56 (31,459)
Drayton, Diane 5:34:23 (29,824)
Drew, Ceri V 3:55:05 (8,026)
Drew, Helen J 6:02:45 (32,802)
Drewe, Kerrie M 4:55:40 (22,421)
Driscoll, Jean M 5:00:15 (23,563)
Driscoll-Bennett, Julia A 4:05:52 (10,322)
Driver, Kathi 3:59:48 (9,162)
Drljaca-Chandler, Angelina 4:28:45 (15,799)
Droog, Sarah J 5:38:38 (30,402)
Drought, Lucinda B 4:27:23 (15,442)
Druce, Lauren C 6:05:15 (32,978)
Drummond, Heidi L 5:58:35 (32,475)
Drury, Joanne 5:23:51 (28,085)
Drury, Judith 5:47:49 (31,442)
Du Plessis, Louise 4:13:20 (11,917)
Du Plessis, Sonja A 5:11:55 (25,838)
Du Preez, Maxine 4:12:08 (11,639)
Du Sautuy, Shani Ram 5:35:37 (30,000)
Du Toit, Yvette E 6:21:22 (33,973)
Duckstein, Nina 4:58:18 (23,103)
Duckworth, Avril Mary M 3:42:26 (5,589)
Duckworth, Ruth E 4:47:57 (20,520)
Duddridge, Abbi C 5:13:50 (26,197)
Dudfield, Cathy J 4:11:19 (11,452)
Dudin, Elizabeth M 4:15:02 (12,332)
Dudley, Emer B 3:32:56 (4,129)
Dudley, Joanne J 6:15:32 (33,653)
Duerden, Tanya A 6:44:31 (34,789)
Duff, Leesa 3:43:39 (5,805)
Duff, Zoe R 5:11:07 (25,693)
Duffield, Denise T 5:54:59 (32,147)
Duffy, Gill 4:49:51 (20,965)
Duffy, Lindsay C 5:04:15 (24,363)
Duffy, Michelle 7:23:00 (35,415)
Duffy, Nicola 7:38:08 (35,554)
Dufty, Lisa M 3:55:32 (8,121)
Dugdale, Hannah L 4:52:50 (21,711)
Dugdale, Ruth J 5:41:55 (30,822)
Duggal, Sheila P 4:31:18 (16,423)
Duggan, Andrea 4:54:36 (22,172)
Duggan, Lisa M 4:28:23 (15,695)
Duggin, Lisa J 5:36:18 (30,082)
Duggleby, Kay 4:48:14 (20,586)
Dugourd, Catherine 5:03:52 (24,301)
Duke, Lisa 4:13:32 (11,980)
Dukes, Suzie L 5:03:20 (24,202)
Dumas Roques, Mireille T 4:37:59 (18,003)
Dumba, Reenie N 5:06:46 (24,837)
Dumbleton, Emma Jayne 4:34:11 (17,072)
Dumbrill, Elizabeth A 5:51:45 (31,850)
Dumolo, Karen F 6:31:01 (34,363)
Dumonteil, Natasha L 4:56:43 (22,700)
Dunbar, Elisa S 4:47:14 (20,340)
Dunbar, Janet 3:16:35 (2,132)
Dunbar, Sarah L 4:58:13 (23,080)
Duncan, Abigail 4:30:19 (16,218)
Duncan, Annette 5:10:43 (25,612)
Duncan, Catriona M 4:31:47 (16,522)
Duncan, Jennifer R 4:52:59 (21,749)
Duncker, Caryn L 5:27:19 (28,682)
Dundas, Gemma 4:37:48 (17,955)
Dungworth, Jo-Ann L 6:13:08 (33,498)
Dunley, Laura A 5:24:03 (28,114)
Dunlop, Kirstie 3:39:15 (5,055)
Dunlop, Paul 3:30:05 (3,731)
Dunmall, Carmel M 5:06:00 (24,694)
Dunn, Angela K 4:14:59 (12,318)
Dunn, Fiona L 4:35:12 (17,333)
Dunn, Julie E 4:16:15 (12,634)
Dunn, Nicola L 5:50:17 (31,701)
Dunn, Stephen G 4:55:06 (22,289)
Dunne, Clare C 5:19:35 (27,357)
Dunnett, Anne M 7:21:54 (35,402)
Dunning, Angela M 6:27:11 (34,216)
Dunnings, Zoe M 5:32:41 (29,565)
Dunstan, Gill 6:34:33 (34,478)
Dunthorne, Leah K 4:24:35 (14,722)
Dupain, Emma L 4:16:52 (12,775)
Dupe, Françoise 4:10:23 (11,244)
Dupont, Beatrice 4:42:06 (19,064)
Dupont, Christiane 4:49:29 (20,885)
Duran, Pilar 4:25:33 (14,955)
Durden, Hannah C 4:36:22 (17,629)
Durham, Kathryn L 5:02:25 (24,021)
Durham, Lee C 6:36:37 (34,562)
Durkan, Lydia M 4:55:34 (22,408)
Durkin, Una 5:44:35 (31,109)
Durn, Carol 5:06:11 (24,734)
Durnin, Aine M 4:38:48 (18,234)
Duroe, Fiona 4:27:03 (15,339)
Durrant, Hilary J 5:29:59 (29,129)
Dushey, Joy M 3:25:57 (3,121)
Dussaux, Anne 4:07:36 (10,680)
Dutton, Bronwyn M 6:01:20 (32,706)
Dwyer, Sabina M 4:12:28 (11,715)
Dwyer, Sarah E 4:24:35 (14,722)
Dyde, Rosalind H 4:51:49 (21,440)
Dye, Kate L 4:43:23 (19,399)
Dyer, Liza 4:13:44 (12,026)
Dyker, Rachel 3:45:15 (6,056)
Dykers, Joy 4:24:01 (14,576)
Dymond, Penni C 3:44:34 (5,951)
Dymore-Brown, Linda S 4:33:49 (16,995)
Dyson-Laurie, Shirley A 3:47:01 (6,350)
Dyus, Kerry A 5:02:23 (24,010)
Dzialdow, Resi 4:28:49 (15,814)
Dzurcaninova, Ludmila 6:04:17 (32,903)
Eagling, Natasha 5:31:39 (29,395)
Eakins, Victoria K 4:40:17 (18,597)
Eames, Genienne 6:02:50 (32,810)

Eames, Susan E....4:17:36 (12,979)
Earl, Jacqueline A....6:54:07 (35,021)
Earl, Victoria....6:05:32 (33,008)
Earnshaw, Angela J....4:21:52 (14,055)
Earnshaw, Dawn....5:13:23 (26,096)
Easingwood-Wilson, Sarah A....4:24:24 (14,681)
Easom, Annette J....5:02:16 (23,982)
Easson, Georgina....6:00:28 (32,618)
East, Janet....6:22:20 (34,014)
East, Jennifer A....6:22:20 (34,014)
East, Julia E....5:30:55 (29,282)
Eastbury, Justine A....4:16:35 (12,712)
Eastland, Diane M....4:05:41 (10,286)
Eastland, Sharon J....5:22:40 (27,885)
Eastman, Jo....4:56:35 (22,656)
Eastwood, Kim Y....5:45:05 (31,163)
Eastwood, Mandy C....4:44:23 (19,645)
Eaton, Caroline C....5:16:25 (26,742)
Eaton, Lindsay A....6:05:24 (32,988)
Eaton, Naomi A....3:40:17 (5,227)
Eaton, Sandra....6:00:50 (32,648)
Eaton, Vikki L....5:22:00 (27,782)
Eaton, Zoe....4:17:36 (12,979)
Ebberson, Charlene V....5:18:18 (27,124)
Ebberson, Elisa....7:28:47 (35,461)
Eccles, Karen A....3:50:53 (7,111)
Eccles, Rachael....5:32:55 (29,594)
Eckersley, Fiona J....5:41:51 (30,814)
Eckersley, Helen M....5:36:47 (30,145)
Eckersley, Jody A....4:01:54 (9,589)
Economou, Androulla....6:53:22 (35,001)
Eddicott, Helen A....6:04:02 (32,892)
Edeam, Catherine M....4:03:23 (9,846)
Edelmann, Diana M....4:58:20 (23,115)
Edelsten, Marika E....4:04:16 (10,017)
Edgecombe, Louise K....5:19:47 (27,388)
Edgerley, Wendy N....4:49:59 (20,990)
Edis, Sally-Anne E....5:31:52 (29,429)
Edmends, Holly C....6:41:04 (34,691)
Edmonds, Lisa J....6:11:35 (33,403)
Edmonds, Nicola....5:06:24 (24,769)
Edmonds Nicholson, Alison....5:01:01 (23,732)
Edmondson, Patricia M....4:03:02 (9,791)
Edmondson, Rowena M....3:54:08 (7,823)
Edsell, Jane C....5:20:05 (27,435)
Edward, Susan A....4:57:28 (22,900)
Edwardes, Nicola C....6:50:13 (34,935)
Edwards, Aimie C....4:57:52 (23,002)
Edwards, Alice V....3:47:39 (6,466)
Edwards, Ami C....6:16:11 (33,695)
Edwards, Anna M....5:27:27 (28,704)
Edwards, Anne-Marie....4:19:26 (13,440)
Edwards, Christine E....8:21:55 (35,670)
Edwards, Claire J....4:33:00 (16,785)
Edwards, Claire L....6:43:09 (34,754)
Edwards, Felicity G....6:28:52 (34,280)
Edwards, Hermione C....5:18:55 (27,235)
Edwards, Jenny L....5:06:26 (24,778)
Edwards, Joanne K....4:01:14 (9,466)
Edwards, Karen L....5:05:08 (24,532)
Edwards, Lianne L....5:02:39 (24,066)
Edwards, Louise C....4:32:13 (16,613)
Edwards, Mary A....4:10:52 (11,341)
Edwards, Nadja U....6:53:07 (34,995)
Edwards, Natalie J....4:38:54 (18,254)
Edwards, Natalie P....5:39:21 (30,499)
Edwards, Natalie R....3:55:22 (8,099)
Edwards, Nicola R....3:20:07 (2,508)
Edwards, Olivia G....4:22:35 (14,224)
Edwards, Penny....3:10:53 (1,620)
Edwards, Polly A....5:05:55 (24,682)
Edwards, Sara A....5:18:22 (27,140)
Edwards, Sarah J....5:51:06 (31,786)
Edwards, Sharon....6:02:21 (32,774)
Edwards, Susan E....4:26:56 (15,307)
Edwards, Traci....4:16:42 (12,738)
Edwards, Vivienne A....5:50:22 (31,716)
Edwardson, Jane A....3:39:59 (5,185)
Edwards-Pulman, Susan E....6:05:54 (33,035)
Eeles, Monica M....5:15:02 (26,464)
Eggett, Heather....5:38:04 (30,312)
Eggleton, Jacqueline A....6:16:01 (33,684)
Ehrenberg, Margaret....3:57:52 (8,689)
Eilerts De Haan, Carin G....4:06:36 (10,486)
Ek, Marie-Louise....4:36:26 (17,649)
El Filali, Youssef....3:29:11 (3,602)
Elakkad, Nadia....5:22:55 (27,926)
Elcock, Lorna J....5:11:59 (25,852)
Elcome, Lorraine L....6:35:21 (34,516)
Eldridge, Katie A....4:53:49 (21,972)
Elkington, Amanda T....3:47:45 (6,488)
Elks, Teresa M....5:57:47 (32,390)
Ellender, Michelle A....6:51:26 (34,967)
Ellerton, Joanne M....3:28:27 (3,471)
Elliot, Bridget....4:00:06 (9,229)
Elliot, Katharine....3:55:39 (8,150)
Elliot, Katherine G....5:26:43 (28,580)
Elliott, Christine M....5:08:06 (25,112)
Elliott, Dawn....5:36:06 (30,060)
Elliott, Gillian D....4:42:30 (19,178)
Elliott, Jenny A....6:15:19 (33,634)
Elliott, Joanne L....4:57:06 (22,798)
Elliott, Kate R....4:51:22 (21,334)
Elliott, Penelope A....4:18:34 (13,230)
Elliott, Vanessa....5:03:49 (24,294)
Ellis, Donna....4:35:14 (17,343)
Ellis, Kathryn N....5:01:45 (23,880)
Ellis, Martine E....7:01:39 (35,152)
Ellis, Michele....6:47:06 (34,861)
Ellis, Rebecca E....4:11:14 (11,433)
Ellison, Corinne E....6:19:36 (33,868)
Ellison, Jane....4:14:31 (12,207)
Ellwood, Lisa J....5:28:00 (28,799)
El-Mariesh, Abi F....7:00:03 (35,123)
Elmore, Lynda A....5:57:42 (32,384)
Elphick, Nicola A....6:52:13 (34,979)
Elsden, Lorraine....3:58:43 (8,887)
Elsdon, Celia A....4:40:53 (18,755)
Elsdon, Claire L....4:45:44 (19,996)
Elstub, Gill E....5:33:09 (29,627)
Elvin, Charlotte L....4:47:06 (20,313)
Elvin, Jackie....5:25:41 (28,402)
Elwick, Kirsty L....5:32:37 (29,551)
Embling, Alison R....6:46:03 (34,829)
Emerson, Jennifer G....6:45:46 (34,817)
Emery, Carol A....3:35:14 (4,438)
Emery, Claire M....4:52:10 (21,533)
Emery, Tracey A....6:02:12 (32,766)
Eminsang, Barbara....8:47:06 (35,685)
Emmerson, Beatrice....5:39:05 (30,461)
Emsley, Victoria L....3:50:17 (6,995)
Enard, Julia....3:57:52 (8,689)
Eneas, Tiffany....4:31:27 (16,451)
Engdahl, Elin....3:12:53 (1,813)
Engel, Barbara....4:53:32 (21,894)
Engel, Louise E....4:35:34 (17,421)
Engelbracht, Gesa....3:54:56 (7,995)
Engels, Janine....4:22:55 (14,313)
England-Hall, Suzanne....4:47:40 (20,449)
English, Leanne C....5:24:34 (28,192)
English, Tara J....6:06:01 (33,052)
Enhard, Suanne....3:29:22 (3,629)
Ennis, Marie F....4:35:18 (17,359)
Ennis, Sallie J....3:55:31 (8,120)
Erasmus, Kathleen....4:56:38 (22,672)
Erasnus, Christie J....3:55:18 (8,077)
Erdas, Emanuela....3:43:58 (5,862)
Erdozain, Sophia K....4:33:10 (16,830)
Ericksen, Karen....5:42:16 (30,858)
Ernoult, Irene....5:04:28 (24,417)
Erritt, Amanda G....4:31:06 (16,381)
Ervin, Philippa....5:05:20 (24,558)
Escrie, Kimberley L....4:03:48 (9,927)
Espasandin, Maria D....6:00:43 (32,639)
Essex, Gemma L....5:41:22 (30,754)
Essex, Jessica R....4:26:39 (15,223)
Esslemont, Susan M....5:49:02 (31,589)
Esslinger, Frauke B....4:02:03 (9,612)
Esteem, Samantha E....6:17:29 (33,748)
Etchells, Katy J....5:08:19 (25,158)
Etheridge, Lee H....3:38:59 (5,012)
Etheridge, Michelle A....5:05:21 (24,564)
Etherington, Karen F....5:40:54 (30,695)
Ettridge, Madeleine A....5:25:29 (28,367)
Eude, Celina A....4:56:46 (22,708)
Eungblut, Hannah V....5:22:39 (27,882)
Euwe, Suzanne....4:41:44 (18,969)
Evans, Angela M....3:00:14 (911)
Evans, Angharad....5:35:48 (30,022)
Evans, Ann....5:15:08 (26,486)
Evans, Anne....4:19:59 (13,599)
Evans, Caroline....4:26:27 (15,176)
Evans, Caroline....5:25:19 (28,323)
Evans, Catrin E....3:59:13 (9,017)
Evans, Claire....4:13:33 (11,984)
Evans, Delyth A....4:47:29 (20,401)
Evans, Fleur L....4:42:55 (19,285)
Evans, Gemma E....5:05:44 (24,642)
Evans, Hannah K....6:34:36 (34,479)
Evans, Heidi....4:18:13 (13,129)
Evans, Jaimie C....5:26:32 (28,547)
Evans, Jane E....5:03:37 (24,261)
Evans, Jane M....5:17:59 (27,052)
Evans, Janet M....5:58:18 (32,444)
Evans, Joan M....6:50:04 (34,933)
Evans, Joanna C....3:37:54 (4,806)
Evans, Julia A....5:10:23 (25,552)
Evans, Julie A....5:02:27 (24,026)
Evans, Karen L....6:00:37 (32,632)
Evans, Kathryn L....7:04:14 (35,192)
Evans, Laura J....3:29:22 (3,629)
Evans, Laura J....5:59:24 (32,544)
Evans, Laura J....7:57:16 (35,637)
Evans, Linda S....4:56:41 (22,694)
Evans, Lisa J....5:25:08 (28,292)
Evans, Maureen H....5:21:46 (27,748)
Evans, Rachel G....4:57:16 (22,839)
Evans, Rachel J....5:02:25 (24,021)
Evans, Rachel M....4:50:24 (21,097)
Evans, Roz J....6:07:41 (33,141)
Evans, Samantha....5:39:33 (30,538)
Evans, Sara....4:46:27 (20,166)
Evans, Sarah J....5:44:47 (31,127)
Evans, Shirley A....5:05:03 (24,520)
Evans, Sian E....6:28:49 (34,276)
Evans, Tina J....7:13:51 (35,333)
Evans, Tracey L....5:31:37 (29,389)
Evans, Tricia G....4:51:33 (21,383)
Evelyn, Christine E....5:45:06 (31,167)
Evennett, Helen C....5:57:21 (32,359)
Everall, Vicky L....6:08:45 (33,223)
Everest, Frances J....5:26:52 (28,602)
Everett, Hazel L....6:33:25 (34,452)
Everett, Julie....5:32:31 (29,533)
Everett, Julie A....5:39:05 (30,461)
Everett, Kathyrn S....4:54:08 (22,054)
Everington, Chrissie....6:35:01 (34,499)
Everson, Angela....6:23:55 (34,072)
Eves, Celina....5:02:54 (24,108)
Ewen, Elizabeth K....4:51:27 (21,356)
Ewing, Katherine E....5:15:33 (26,577)
Exall, Annina T....4:56:19 (22,590)
Eyes, Elizabeth....5:45:05 (31,163)
Eyo, Karen....4:57:36 (22,932)
Ezard, Jacqueline....5:14:19 (26,294)
Eze, Uju....3:55:24 (8,105)
Facktor, Michelle....4:13:19 (11,912)
Fader, Naoko....4:43:05 (19,315)
Faes, Madeleine....4:43:50 (19,489)
Fagan, Helena M....5:23:12 (27,958)
Fagan, Jacinta P....5:55:12 (32,165)
Fagan, Miriam J....6:01:34 (32,726)
Fagan, Rachel E....3:12:45 (1,802)
Fahey, Rachael M....4:59:56 (23,484)
Fairbairn, Rosalind N....4:20:41 (13,773)
Fairbanks, Denise M....3:32:39 (4,091)
Fairclough, Julie....5:00:37 (23,639)
Fairclough, Julie....5:22:32 (27,862)
Fairclough, Susan A....4:46:24 (20,155)
Fairhall, Victoria....3:03:13 (1,061)
Fairhurst, Maggie L....3:49:59 (6,934)
Fairlamb, Paula....6:30:49 (34,356)
Fairlamb, Vivien R....5:41:43 (30,798)
Fairley, Donna....6:31:42 (34,390)
Fairman, Louise....5:01:47 (23,886)
Fairs, Elizabeth J....4:46:58 (20,269)
Fairs, Jeanne M....4:57:47 (22,983)
Fairs, Stephanie R....4:47:44 (20,464)
Falcus, Elaine C....4:34:18 (17,094)

Fallon, Michele A	5:27:11 (28,658)
Fallon, Rosalind M	4:39:40 (18,454)
Falsini, Helen	4:39:16 (18,355)
Fanning, Gabrielle J	5:09:33 (25,384)
Fanning, Jane L	3:28:00 (3,407)
Fanning, Louise K	5:09:33 (25,384)
Farbridge, Nicola L	4:26:41 (15,238)
Farley, Claire E	3:41:51 (5,496)
Farley, Joanne	5:14:47 (26,403)
Farman, Michelle C	3:26:47 (3,236)
Farmer, Kathryn J	4:14:01 (12,101)
Farmer, Katie J	6:06:43 (33,091)
Farnell, Helley	4:57:59 (23,032)
Farquhar, Helen M	4:14:32 (12,211)
Farrall, Ali	3:29:04 (3,583)
Farrant, Catriona M	5:48:33 (31,528)
Farrar, Julie	5:24:39 (28,207)
Farrar, Victoria T	5:27:18 (28,677)
Farrell, Ann	4:32:27 (16,651)
Farrell, Denise H	5:14:47 (26,403)
Farrell, Heather J	4:41:25 (18,896)
Farrell, Helen E	6:32:59 (34,438)
Farrell, Lisa	5:20:31 (27,522)
Farrell, Mo M	4:45:17 (19,900)
Farrell, Rosie P	4:29:17 (15,934)
Farren, Joanna M	7:01:23 (35,149)
Farrow, Elaine M	5:44:02 (31,046)
Farrow, Heidi	5:22:36 (27,875)
Farrow, Joanna E	3:54:20 (7,875)
Farrow, Sharon B	4:38:33 (18,163)
Farrugia, Claire	5:03:02 (24,135)
Fashoni, Kelly L	5:05:53 (24,672)
Fasja, Olga L	3:57:13 (8,533)
Fathers, Katharine E	5:54:46 (32,120)
Faucher, Penny	5:12:15 (25,911)
Faulkner, Chloe	4:12:48 (11,789)
Faulkner, Jodie M	4:06:06 (10,370)
Faulkner, Nicola	4:52:18 (21,568)
Faux, Valerie	5:10:28 (25,571)
Fawcett, Paula	5:22:36 (27,875)
Fawcett, Trudy J	3:03:37 (1,084)
Fawcett, Vanessa C	3:20:02 (2,501)
Fawzy, Sandra	6:31:45 (34,393)
Fay, Josephine	4:50:09 (21,034)
Fay, Victoria J	6:09:32 (33,275)
Fearn, Margaret A	4:20:40 (13,768)
Fearn, Sharon E	3:44:32 (5,947)
Fearne, Katy L	5:16:10 (26,692)
Fearnside, Maureen F	5:27:23 (28,691)
Featherstone, Holly	5:21:19 (27,660)
Feaver, Adele	6:43:58 (34,769)
Fedrick, Jane	4:16:40 (12,729)
Fee, Helen	4:53:25 (21,868)
Feeney, Mary	5:45:47 (31,236)
Feeney, Stephanie	4:35:45 (17,473)
Feiner, Maria	3:28:57 (3,565)
Feldberg, Emily J	4:52:57 (21,742)
Felden, Sylvie	5:40:03 (30,598)
Felice Pace, Claire	4:54:29 (22,145)
Fell, Carol S	5:23:24 (27,990)
Fellowes, Janet L	3:48:52 (6,697)
Fellows, Joanne E	4:26:20 (15,142)
Feltham, Denise	5:48:18 (31,505)
Felton, Ann R	4:49:33 (20,900)
Felton, Emma J	5:43:41 (31,013)
Fenkoe, Natalia A	5:05:30 (24,602)
Fenn, Maggie L	3:47:52 (6,504)
Fenner, Christine	6:53:26 (35,003)
Fenton, Kelly K	5:33:13 (29,636)
Fenton, Sarah J	4:02:39 (9,719)
Fenwick, Rebecca H	4:47:41 (20,454)
Fereday, Abbie C	4:20:20 (13,691)
Feretti, Sabrina	4:20:07 (13,629)
Ferguson, Christine	3:41:59 (5,518)
Ferguson, Claire	4:43:09 (19,330)
Ferguson, Eliza C	4:59:04 (23,277)
Ferguson, Lindsay K	4:07:17 (10,619)
Ferguson, Naomi L	3:45:33 (6,103)
Ferguson, Naomi M	5:20:26 (27,501)
Ferguson, Neesha	4:47:40 (20,449)
Ferguson, Rachel L	4:48:59 (20,765)
Ferguson, Ruth	5:33:17 (29,641)
Ferman-Moore, Lucy	4:58:31 (23,153)

Fernando, Nisha P	4:54:53 (22,241)
Fernendez Garita, Maria Lucia	3:58:43 (8,887)
Ferraby, Rachel L	5:19:58 (27,420)
Ferrari, Elena	4:29:46 (16,080)
Ferrari Ellis, Caroline D	5:07:30 (24,999)
Ferrin, Karine	4:16:53 (12,778)
Ferris, Kate	4:43:18 (19,372)
Ferris, Pam	6:04:49 (32,945)
Ferry, Emma	4:53:26 (21,876)
Fewell, Helen D	4:20:47 (13,792)
Ffrench, Anja E	4:13:59 (12,094)
Fiander, Zoe	4:44:06 (19,563)
Fiarbairn, Fraser G	4:08:56 (10,944)
Fidge, Ann E	5:03:04 (24,140)
Field, Angela M	5:17:43 (27,002)
Field, Carolyn J	5:30:09 (29,168)
Field, Claire	6:53:46 (35,015)
Field, Juliana L	5:35:15 (29,949)
Field, Tanya	4:42:15 (19,110)
Fielder, Jodie A	3:13:54 (1,893)
Fifield, Helen M	3:27:45 (3,380)
Fillery, Ann C	5:53:38 (32,024)
Finbow, Linda A	4:15:55 (12,533)
Finch, Cerian C	4:09:39 (11,103)
Finch, Emma C	5:15:15 (26,513)
Finch, Hannah	4:47:41 (20,454)
Finch, Jennifer L	6:13:26 (33,515)
Finch, Joanne E	5:19:13 (27,295)
Finch, Katy L	4:10:39 (11,300)
Fincham, Clare A	4:53:18 (21,840)
Findel-Hawkins, Lisa J	5:17:26 (26,944)
Findlay, Celia A	3:38:20 (4,892)
Findlay, Emma	4:56:29 (22,631)
Findon, Elaine	5:43:38 (31,005)
Findon, Natalie J	4:58:39 (23,180)
Fink, Angela	3:33:08 (4,158)
Finkle, Toni M	6:54:41 (35,028)
Finlay, Helen M	5:54:26 (32,102)
Finlay, Lisa	3:39:01 (5,021)
Finlay, Robin C	5:25:49 (28,429)
Finlayson, Victoria	4:55:13 (22,323)
Finn, Anna K	4:42:03 (19,054)
Finn, Claire F	5:46:49 (31,337)
Finney, Gemma C	4:35:03 (17,285)
Finnimore, Dianne Y	5:10:19 (25,540)
Finning, Nikki	5:13:25 (26,106)
Firmager, Carolyn	4:16:05 (12,589)
Firth, Gemma V	4:03:28 (9,860)
Firth, Mel	4:51:31 (21,371)
Fischer, Carmen	4:29:26 (15,986)
Fisher, Ann Louise	5:40:33 (30,658)
Fisher, Clare D	5:57:59 (32,412)
Fisher, Julie	3:55:42 (8,164)
Fisher, Karen L	7:08:25 (35,254)
Fisher, Louise	4:14:38 (12,242)
Fisher, Naomi E	3:53:32 (7,696)
Fishlocke, Hannah F	4:02:10 (9,638)
Fishwick, Jane C	4:50:45 (21,177)
Fisk, Karen E	4:33:28 (16,906)
Fitchie, Catherine	7:52:29 (35,627)
Fitt, Suzy	3:24:04 (2,915)
Fitzgerald, Jillian M	4:35:23 (17,380)
Fitzgerald, Pola	5:04:13 (24,359)
Fitzgerald, Rebecca M	4:57:07 (22,800)
Fitzgerald, Samantha J	4:52:24 (21,597)
Fitzharris, Ruth C	5:19:29 (27,334)
Fitzsimmons, Catherine M	5:16:15 (26,711)
Fitzsimmons, Cherry E	4:07:07 (10,595)
Fjelle, Amy L	5:34:27 (29,841)
Flanagan, Anne F	3:12:04 (1,737)
Flanagan, Helen	5:50:56 (31,766)
Flannery, Julia	4:01:59 (9,600)
Flannigan, Teresa J	5:38:34 (30,390)
Flavell, Margaret A	5:14:31 (26,341)
Fleming, Ashleigh	5:03:04 (24,140)
Fleming, Clare L	4:31:01 (16,357)
Fleming, Julia T	6:57:07 (35,075)
Fleming, Louise	6:03:34 (32,857)
Fleming, Lucy C	5:25:09 (28,297)
Fleming, Sarah E	4:15:46 (12,501)
Fleming, Susan A	5:31:54 (29,433)
Fleming, Zoe	2:57:59 (744)
Fletcher, Anna L	4:04:02 (9,973)

Fletcher, Elizabeth	5:24:24 (28,172)
Fletcher, Helen M	4:07:45 (10,712)
Fletcher, Holly A	6:16:50 (33,725)
Fletcher, Jane R	5:11:11 (25,698)
Fletcher, Laura J	4:39:56 (18,520)
Fletcher, Monica J	4:46:13 (20,110)
Fletcher, Natalie J	7:29:06 (35,469)
Fletcher, Pat	4:31:28 (16,457)
Fletcher, Samantha J	4:02:39 (9,719)
Fletcher, Sarah E	5:08:36 (25,205)
Flett, Tracey D	5:15:15 (26,513)
Flexman, Annette K	5:19:33 (27,348)
Flintoff, Andrea S	5:08:30 (25,188)
Flokenes, Linda	5:12:45 (25,992)
Flood, Petring	4:39:20 (18,379)
Florentin, Marie-Françoise	3:56:34 (8,376)
Floro, Lia	4:03:43 (9,908)
Flower, Emma L	3:56:16 (8,290)
Floyd, Tracey L	5:18:40 (27,192)
Flury, Joanna C	3:37:48 (4,788)
Flynn, Belinda J	8:13:29 (35,665)
Flynn-Samuels, Mary B	4:44:25 (19,654)
Foddis, Giorgia	5:25:33 (28,379)
Fogden, Emma	4:07:34 (10,672)
Folan, Cheryl K	6:57:49 (35,090)
Foley, Andri	6:36:59 (34,582)
Foley, Helen S	7:08:22 (35,253)
Foley, Katherine E	6:00:58 (32,669)
Foley Lawless, Annelouise	5:08:12 (25,139)
Folman, Lisa-Marie	5:14:49 (26,410)
Fonnereau, Julia	4:10:14 (11,212)
Fonseca, Cristiana S	3:50:18 (6,998)
Fontaine, Marie C	4:01:42 (9,551)
Foord, Cassandra	5:33:55 (29,750)
Foran, Gilian P	4:44:50 (19,789)
Forbes, Linda A	5:58:10 (32,429)
Forbes, Sandra K	5:57:55 (32,406)
Ford, Ali	5:21:54 (27,774)
Ford, Amy L	5:48:39 (31,539)
Ford, Denise M	3:57:39 (8,639)
Ford, Jenny E	4:14:09 (12,128)
Ford, Joanne L	5:56:29 (32,285)
Ford, Julie C	4:30:08 (16,182)
Ford, Katie A	4:32:52 (16,758)
Ford, Kim M	4:39:40 (18,454)
Ford, Sarah F	4:19:40 (13,499)
Ford, Tove	7:00:11 (35,129)
Ford, Verity E	4:40:12 (18,580)
Forde, Bridget	5:41:41 (30,793)
Forde, Vanessa B	5:55:18 (32,376)
Fordwoh-Smyth, Simone	6:23:31 (34,057)
Foreman, Clare V	4:08:36 (10,893)
Forrest, Ginny	5:33:34 (29,698)
Forrest, Jacqueline E	7:40:21 (35,562)
Forrest, Jane	3:52:15 (7,421)
Forrest, Kirsty A	4:46:49 (20,232)
Forshaw, Alison T	5:16:15 (26,711)
Forster, Nicola E	6:38:56 (34,634)
Forster, Sharon C	6:13:58 (33,550)
Forster, Vicky L	5:38:41 (30,412)
Forsyth, Kelly M	4:19:53 (13,569)
Fortescue, Alison M	4:28:38 (15,768)
Forth, Judi M	4:49:03 (20,777)
Forth, Tamara J	4:48:57 (20,754)
Fortune, Carole M	3:25:38 (3,082)
Forward, Hazel J	6:05:27 (32,994)
Fossey, Emily S	5:54:54 (32,139)
Fossey, Janine E	5:31:47 (29,415)
Foster, Caroline L	6:01:32 (32,721)
Foster, Deborah F	5:36:01 (30,050)
Foster, Hazel J	4:55:43 (22,433)
Foster, Joanne	5:54:53 (32,135)
Foster, Nicola M	4:17:05 (12,828)
Foster, Rosalind C	4:11:21 (11,459)
Foster, Solange	5:18:29 (27,163)
Fotheringham, Lisa S	4:41:49 (19,001)
Foulds, Annette M	4:21:53 (14,060)
Foulds, Claire L	5:16:44 (26,704)
Foulds, Katherine A	7:21:54 (35,402)
Foundling-Hawker, Heather R	2:54:56 (576)
Fountain, Michelle T	5:01:04 (23,745)
Fournier, Rocio Q	4:46:10 (20,095)
Fowler, Ann	6:47:58 (34,888)

Fowler, Claire.....................3:30:56 (3,833)
Fowler, Claire E 3:44:40 (5,972)
Fowler, Janet......................5:14:45 (26,396)
Fowler, Kay........................3:17:16 (2,203)
Fowler, Olly V 5:55:30 (32,192)
Fowler, Shirley M...............5:33:20 (29,653)
Fowles, Nicola L.................4:50:23 (21,093)
Fox, Catherine M................3:56:51 (8,444)
Fox, Catherine S.................4:40:50 (18,740)
Fox, Gillian........................5:11:45 (25,800)
Fox, Helen J.......................5:03:32 (24,243)
Fox, Judy D........................5:42:30 (30,878)
Fox, Kate............................6:05:58 (33,044)
Fox, Linda A.......................4:45:52 (20,024)
Fox, Mary C.......................6:12:26 (33,453)
Fox, Sue.............................5:14:03 (26,239)
Fox, Sue J...........................4:48:35 (20,666)
Fox, Sylvana.......................7:15:51 (35,350)
Foxon, Clare E 5:54:19 (32,082)
Foy, Linda..........................5:28:31 (28,903)
Foyster, Mandy L................3:36:42 (4,646)
Frampton, Marion P 4:43:37 (19,444)
France, Sharon 6:34:52 (34,492)
Francioli-Charmoilla, Nathalie....5:45:00 (31,154)
Francis, Abby......................5:13:07 (26,065)
Francis, Andrea K...............3:43:26 (5,761)
Francis, Anna L...................3:40:32 (5,276)
Francis, Barbara A..............5:12:11 (25,895)
Francis, Denise L.................5:57:41 (32,382)
Francis, Jacqueline M..........5:10:00 (25,477)
Francis, Jacqui...................4:58:14 (23,085)
Francis, James D.................4:39:19 (18,368)
Francis, Jen.........................3:45:23 (6,079)
Francis, Lesley A.................5:11:06 (25,687)
Francis, Lorna.....................4:23:56 (14,549)
Francis, Nicola J 4:05:56 (10,338)
Francis, Sarah L..................4:23:49 (14,518)
Francis, Teresa....................5:20:43 (27,557)
Francke, Hilary R 5:13:56 (26,217)
Frank, Flora.......................6:05:59 (33,049)
Frank, Graziella..................4:33:31 (16,916)
Frankland, Heather A..........4:30:44 (16,303)
Frankland, Sharon 4:45:12 (19,887)
Franklin, Anna M................5:11:19 (25,726)
Franklin, Melanie A 4:56:24 (22,613)
Franklin, Sarah J 6:03:24 (32,846)
Franks, Eleanor J................4:05:15 (10,193)
Fransella, Sarah L...............4:37:59 (18,003)
Fraser, Carolyn F 5:40:26 (30,644)
Fraser-Betts, Elizabeth A 4:54:35 (22,168)
Frazer, Donna M 3:49:03 (6,743)
Freebairn, Claire B..............6:08:57 (33,235)
Freegard, Emilia..................5:03:21 (24,204)
Freeland, Julie R 4:18:50 (13,291)
Freeman, Heather................5:08:17 (25,152)
Freeman, Judy E..................4:22:42 (14,258)
Freeman, Shirley.................5:49:24 (31,620)
Freeman, Sue......................5:49:37 (31,642)
Freestone, Caroline M 5:57:49 (32,393)
Fremond, Dominique 4:45:08 (19,867)
French, Amanda..................3:56:07 (8,254)
French, Annette E................4:42:02 (19,047)
French, Katie......................4:44:07 (19,568)
French, Margaret A..............4:19:15 (13,395)
French, Rebecca C 3:58:45 (8,897)
French, Stephanie J 3:38:56 (5,002)
French, Yvonne A................5:09:06 (25,295)
Frenken, Hildegard 4:34:49 (17,225)
Freshwater, Dawn S 5:14:50 (26,415)
Freston, Claire E 5:31:05 (29,312)
Fretschl, Julia M 5:22:29 (27,844)
Frettingham, Debbie............5:56:44 (32,313)
Fretwell, Susannah L............4:48:15 (20,592)
Frewer, Julia 3:54:42 (7,945)
Frewin, Elaine D..................4:48:24 (20,633)
Friday, Abbie......................4:32:08 (16,591)
Friden, Ellinor A 5:30:27 (29,210)
Friel, Kelly L 4:56:04 (22,528)
Friend, Jenny N 3:47:09 (6,370)
Frisby, Tracy A 4:50:46 (21,183)
Fronzoni, Monica 5:19:27 (27,327)
Frost, Amanda J..................6:05:02 (32,965)
Frost, Andrea E...................3:40:17 (5,227)

Frost, Andrea L 5:44:34 (31,104)
Frost, Barbara M.................6:53:59 (35,020)
Frost, Hilda........................4:41:22 (18,879)
Frostick, Deborah................4:08:12 (10,811)
Froud, Helen K 5:16:32 (26,763)
Froud, Jennifer....................4:50:22 (21,087)
Frroku, Donna M 6:10:55 (33,362)
Frudd, Jenna L....................5:28:23 (28,887)
Fry, Jacqui D.......................4:07:43 (10,708)
Fry, Jaine F.........................6:08:42 (33,218)
Fry, Karen L........................4:26:46 (15,255)
Fry, Samantha L 4:19:46 (13,532)
Frydas, Anju.......................4:35:00 (17,270)
Fryer, Natalie L...................3:38:05 (4,850)
Fudge, Natalie L..................4:18:27 (13,196)
Fuhrmann, Andrea 5:00:33 (23,624)
Fulgoni, Nadia....................5:24:43 (28,222)
Fullalove, Mary T 4:17:11 (12,848)
Fullarton, Ailsa 6:03:15 (32,836)
Fuller, Ann E......................3:36:35 (4,625)
Fuller, Catherine J 3:55:51 (8,195)
Fuller, Jade E......................5:30:21 (29,194)
Fuller, Susan J.....................4:36:19 (17,614)
Fulmine, Anna L..................3:51:07 (7,161)
Fulton, Caroline..................4:29:24 (15,976)
Funaho, Michiko.................8:12:10 (35,663)
Fung, Rosie Y......................5:41:44 (30,802)
Furbank, Valerie A 6:01:27 (32,714)
Furlong, Paula M.................5:39:45 (30,565)
Furlong, Tammy J................3:31:55 (3,976)
Furmage, Alaine M 4:34:38 (17,186)
Furnell, Amanda L...............5:15:14 (26,507)
Furness, Debbie L................5:29:04 (28,994)
Furness, Madeleine A 4:55:53 (22,483)
Fursman, Rachel 4:16:04 (12,585)
Furze, Helen J 3:33:33 (4,208)
Fustos, Tunde 5:44:55 (31,142)
Futcher, Sarah 5:15:01 (26,456)
Gabbarelli, Jennifer R..........4:37:41 (17,933)

Gable, Candy E....................5:44:37 (31,111)

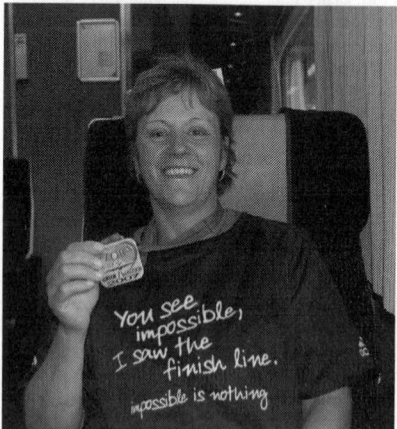

Candy Gable has run the London Marathon three times now. Candy raised over £3,000 in 2000 with the proceeds split 50/50 between Guiseley Senior Citizens Association and Macmillan Cancer Support. Pete Dominey was Candy's inspirational trainer. In 2002 Candy ran for the Bobby Moore 1966 fund and after donating £1,966 to this charity the remainder of nearly £1,000 also went to Guiseley Senior Citizens. Candy also ran the 2007 Marathon. Was that her last one? Probably not!

Gadd, Maxine J....................5:31:01 (29,298)
Gadgil, Anjana R 3:42:13 (5,558)
Gaff, Jennifer......................5:19:55 (27,412)
Gaffing, Denise....................5:32:13 (29,485)
Gage, Kelly-Jo 5:32:00 (29,451)
Gagiano, Zunett 4:33:56 (17,016)
Gaiger, Dee L......................5:30:54 (29,279)

Gaile, Rhonda 4:32:35 (16,686)
Gaillardde Laubenque, Teresa J...3:20:03 (2,502)
Gain, Sarah L......................4:58:39 (23,180)
Galbraith, Helen L...............4:15:19 (12,401)
Gale, Jill E..........................4:38:33 (18,163)
Gall, Lorna P 4:45:31 (19,954)
Gallacher, Christine 4:40:58 (18,777)
Gallacher, Julie E.................4:59:14 (23,319)
Gallagher, Elizabeth Z 7:14:25 (35,338)
Gallagher, Felicity V 4:35:17 (17,356)
Gallagher, Joan G................6:43:47 (34,766)
Gallagher, Natalie 5:36:19 (30,088)
Gallaugher, Ruth E 3:53:41 (7,725)
Gallego, Paula C..................6:48:21 (34,896)
Gallen, Kathleen 5:50:29 (31,726)
Galli, Guendalina 6:45:38 (34,815)
Gallien, Emmanuelle 4:27:02 (15,331)
Galloway, Alison J 4:58:58 (23,244)
Gallup-Black, Adria 4:00:56 (9,405)
Galvin, Alice 4:44:49 (19,784)
Galvin, Gurbaksho 4:59:29 (23,379)
Gambaro, Paola...................5:07:15 (24,942)
Gamble, Deborah J 5:00:30 (23,613)
Gamez, Kate S 6:17:19 (33,741)
Gammon, Nicola J................5:00:02 (23,512)
Gammon, Rita M 6:24:00 (34,079)
Gander, Kaye......................6:18:19 (33,790)
Gannon, Lisa M...................3:54:14 (7,848)
Gannon, Sharon K 3:20:06 (2,506)
Gappy, Tina L 3:33:24 (4,194)
Garcia, Paula Jane 5:03:13 (24,176)
Garcia, Paula Maria 4:15:03 (12,334)
Garciarguelles, Susana.........4:26:54 (15,296)
Gardener, Dawn S 4:36:11 (17,576)
Gardener, Sue E 3:22:22 (2,734)
Gardiner, Christina 5:36:35 (30,123)
Gardiner, Jackie..................6:35:57 (34,534)
Gardiner, Lisa J...................5:34:52 (29,896)
Gardiner, Sandra E 5:54:47 (32,122)
Gardner, Deborah................5:17:35 (26,976)
Gardner, Julie.....................5:29:16 (29,036)
Gardner, Julie A 4:31:32 (16,466)
Gardner, Julie R 5:57:55 (32,406)
Gardner, Kate E...................4:52:07 (21,519)
Gardner, Rachel E................4:04:38 (10,080)
Gardner, Sandra..................5:19:00 (27,250)
Gardner, Tracy....................8:54:12 (35,687)
Gardner-Hall, Sarah J..........4:26:45 (15,249)
Garner, Gemma E 5:11:20 (25,730)
Garner, Helen L...................5:27:53 (28,776)
Garner, Joanne R 6:32:52 (34,437)
Garnett, Hilary J 5:59:37 (32,552)
Garnett, Kathleen 4:30:36 (16,280)
Garney, Marianne................4:50:04 (21,016)
Garraghty, Helen E 8:10:15 (35,659)
Garrard, Anna E..................4:15:36 (12,460)
Garrett, Barbara E...............5:32:37 (29,551)
Garrett, Kirsty M.................6:07:53 (33,159)
Garrett, Sarah 5:02:52 (24,099)
Garrido, Kathleen P 4:13:08 (11,865)
Garrod, Beverley J 6:41:42 (34,707)
Garside, Sally-Ann 5:03:47 (24,288)
Garside, Theresa M..............4:56:54 (22,749)
Garth, Jenny.......................4:34:38 (17,186)
Garthsore, Elizabeth S 5:05:54 (24,679)
Garton, Elaine 5:36:01 (30,050)
Gartry, Laura N 4:21:25 (13,942)
Garwood, Gemma S 4:57:04 (22,788)
Gascoigne, Julie..................3:45:55 (6,116)
Gaskell, Sophie....................3:21:34 (2,658)
Gates, Caroline M 5:14:15 (26,283)
Gates, Jane S.......................5:53:18 (31,986)
Gatherer, Amanda J 4:40:29 (18,654)
Gaucheron Land, Ruth..........5:45:27 (31,201)
Gauci, Benny 4:09:44 (11,120)
Gaunt, Suzanne...................5:46:18 (31,292)
Gauvin, Sarah 3:59:43 (9,144)
Gaveniciakova, Anna............7:00:07 (35,125)
Gavin, Suzanne J 5:15:49 (26,626)
Gaweda, Barbara 5:04:21 (24,390)
Gawman, Susan M................5:27:30 (28,712)
Gay, Carina A......................3:54:04 (7,806)
Gay, Karen A.......................5:25:00 (28,269)

Gay, Kate 5:12:56 (26,027)
Gay, Suzanne C.................6:05:30 (33,004)
Gaylor, Barbara A..............4:30:05 (16,170)
Gaynor, Irene M................3:26:34 (3,203)
Gaywood, Shelley L.............4:27:02 (15,331)
Gazzard, Lesley................4:33:12 (16,846)
Gearing, Elizabeth R...........5:23:33 (28,021)
Geary, Natalie.................4:40:59 (18,780)
Geddes, Sarah..................3:48:27 (6,608)
Geddes, Tina M.................6:53:50 (35,017)
Gedge, Karen...................5:27:23 (28,691)
Gee, Belinda...................5:44:28 (31,087)
Gee, Donna E...................5:43:35 (31,000)
Gee, Julie.....................5:47:54 (31,449)
Gee, Natalie A.................3:56:14 (8,284)
Gee, Samantha M................5:20:31 (27,522)
Gee, Sarah R...................3:03:53 (1,099)
Geeson-Orsgood, Sarah E........4:26:31 (15,197)
Geldard, Lisa J................6:29:12 (34,291)
Gelder, Emily J................3:18:42 (2,359)
Gelsthorpe, Lora J.............4:30:23 (16,232)
Gemmill, Joanna C..............4:31:32 (16,466)
Genovesa, Michelle J...........5:41:39 (30,787)
Gent, Joanne C.................3:45:14 (6,054)
Gent, Sarah A..................6:22:33 (34,024)
Gentle, Rebecca L..............5:51:20 (31,810)
George, Clare..................5:54:27 (32,103)
George, Elinor E...............7:43:58 (35,596)
George, Jennifer S.............5:56:31 (32,290)
George, Joanne.................6:03:48 (32,874)
George, Vicky..................4:47:58 (20,525)
Georgelin, Catherine...........3:59:08 (8,992)
Gerbe, Denise..................5:45:47 (31,236)
Gerhan, Deborah M..............4:39:45 (18,475)
German, Kelly..................5:31:16 (29,342)
Gessey, Joanne.................5:17:02 (26,863)
Gethin-Jones, Sian M...........5:59:18 (32,538)
Gettins, Lucy A................3:44:39 (5,967)
Ghant, Debbie J................4:35:28 (17,397)
Giambastiani Rapp, Alicia......4:47:01 (20,286)
Giauna, Stephanie J............5:39:10 (30,472)
Gibb, Penny....................7:23:31 (35,420)
Gibbins, Deborah K.............3:50:15 (6,984)
Gibbins, Emma..................4:06:47 (10,526)
Gibbon, Nadine.................5:19:44 (27,379)
Gibbons, Catherine M...........4:14:47 (12,267)
Gibbons, Gillian...............4:19:14 (13,387)
Gibbons, Linford M.............3:41:39 (5,463)
Gibbons, Rachel K..............4:37:15 (17,831)
Gibbs, Anita M.................4:16:46 (12,755)
Gibbs, Carole E................4:26:19 (15,136)
Gibbs, Victoria F..............5:07:42 (25,033)
Gibbs, Victoria L..............5:17:31 (26,960)
Giblin, Michelle L.............5:47:39 (31,422)
Gibney, Win M..................6:14:46 (33,598)
Gibson, Beverley J.............3:07:25 (1,346)
Gibson, Carol..................4:45:14 (19,891)
Gibson, Caroline M.............4:54:15 (22,093)
Gibson, Carolyn................4:48:58 (20,757)
Gibson, Cheryl.................5:38:57 (30,445)
Gibson, Deborah C..............4:29:31 (16,013)
Gibson, Hazel..................3:41:05 (5,378)
Gibson, Janet..................4:43:05 (19,315)
Gibson, Julie..................4:54:14 (22,085)
Gibson, Julie D................5:34:26 (29,839)
Gibson, Lorraine...............5:35:53 (30,035)
Gibson, Louise.................4:13:19 (11,912)
Gibson, Louise R...............5:07:43 (25,038)
Gibson, Lydia J................4:45:49 (20,010)
Gibson, Michelle D.............4:59:30 (23,384)
Gibson, Shirley R..............4:07:02 (10,580)
Gicquel, Claudie...............4:38:21 (18,113)
Gifford, Anne..................5:32:35 (29,547)
Gigg, Denise M.................5:53:28 (32,004)
Gigg, Louise A.................5:47:47 (31,437)
Gil, Candida J.................4:06:29 (10,463)
Gilbert, Diane T...............5:31:18 (29,344)
Gilbert, Ellen J...............6:20:50 (33,942)
Gilbert, Leanne................6:02:58 (32,819)
Gilbert, Lindsay J.............6:19:11 (33,848)
Gilbert, Sally A...............3:17:47 (2,261)
Gilbert, Sally A...............5:12:49 (26,001)
Gilbert, Sue...................6:45:36 (34,814)

Gilbey, Elizabeth..............4:55:08 (22,298)
Gilbride, Breege...............6:16:33 (33,720)
Gilder, Juliet R...............7:00:10 (35,126)
Gildon, Phoebe Y...............4:39:19 (18,368)
Giles, Susan B.................6:02:21 (32,774)
Giles-Brown, Kerry.............6:13:55 (33,543)
Gilham, Wendy A................5:04:33 (24,425)
Gilhooley, Karen...............5:19:42 (27,373)
Gilkes, Pauline D..............4:41:46 (18,983)
Gill, Diana M..................4:36:04 (17,549)
Gill, Dilbinder K..............5:20:26 (27,501)
Gill, Gillian..................5:25:34 (28,382)
Gill, Jasbir K.................6:33:15 (34,449)
Gill, Jen M....................6:04:05 (32,893)
Gill, Nicola J.................6:03:55 (32,881)
Gill, Samantha J...............5:39:59 (30,590)
Gill, Sara.....................4:55:18 (22,338)
Gill, Wendy L..................4:39:57 (18,527)
Gillam, Sally E................4:04:04 (9,978)
Gillespie, Emer C..............4:38:16 (18,077)
Gillett, Julie A...............6:48:53 (34,908)
Gillett, Karrie L..............4:47:31 (20,413)
Gillham, Rosie M...............5:31:23 (29,359)
Gillie, Leanne.................5:45:49 (31,240)
Gillman, Katherine A...........3:52:16 (7,425)
Gillot, Claire.................5:38:58 (30,448)
Gills, Michelle................3:42:19 (5,572)
Gilman, Fiona J................5:29:21 (29,051)
Gilmartin, Charlotte H.........4:10:29 (11,261)
Gilmartin, Penny...............4:16:21 (12,660)
Gilmore, Jane E................5:26:38 (28,560)
Gilpin, Jasmine E..............6:28:00 (34,253)
Gilsenan, Danielle.............4:45:46 (20,001)
Gimber, Sophie C...............4:56:32 (22,640)
Gingell, Lynne A...............5:00:16 (23,568)
Gipson, Jessica................6:09:20 (33,258)
Given, Kim T...................5:41:28 (30,767)
Gladman, Katie L...............5:20:48 (27,573)
Gladman, Kirsty................4:53:50 (21,975)
Gladwell-Hunt, Justine S.......5:51:54 (31,864)
Glanville, Clare S.............6:04:24 (32,911)
Glass, Casilda M...............4:20:47 (13,792)
Glass, Michelle R..............5:19:15 (27,303)
Glass, Rebecca K...............4:44:52 (19,797)
Glavan, Cornelia...............4:59:29 (23,379)
Glavina, Claire M..............4:24:03 (14,585)
Glaze, Jane....................5:06:34 (24,791)
Gleed, Gillian.................4:12:14 (11,666)
Gleeson, Julia M...............3:56:42 (8,406)
Glen, Fiona....................5:39:02 (30,454)
Glibbery, Angela B.............6:13:09 (33,500)
Glorioso, Carmela..............4:21:01 (13,857)
Glover, Alice C................5:07:56 (25,082)
Glover, Cat E..................4:19:36 (13,486)
Glover, Louise M...............4:51:12 (21,286)
Glover, Sarah J................4:34:49 (17,225)
Glynn, Lorna M.................4:45:02 (19,848)
Goatham, Claire................3:56:56 (8,461)
Gobey, Tracey E................5:13:23 (26,096)
Godber, Emma J.................4:48:10 (20,566)
Goddard, Claire................6:31:24 (34,378)
Goddard, Elizabeth J...........5:49:05 (31,594)
Goddard, Henrietta M...........5:01:21 (23,803)
Goddard, Laura A...............5:36:11 (30,069)
Godden, Caryl..................6:24:14 (34,088)
Godfrey, Louise J..............4:05:50 (10,314)
Godfrey, Patricia..............6:39:31 (34,656)
Godfrey, Wendy A...............4:08:00 (10,767)
Godsmark, Nia E................5:25:40 (28,398)
Goedeke, Maren.................4:58:03 (23,045)
Goggin, Natasha................3:45:38 (6,122)
Goillot, Christiane M..........4:22:11 (14,121)
Gold, Lorna....................4:23:53 (14,540)
Gold, Tania L..................4:57:18 (22,854)
Goldener, Christa..............4:06:06 (10,370)
Goldie, Samantha...............5:48:14 (31,494)
Golding, Katherine E...........4:49:53 (20,970)
Goldman, Emma J................6:19:09 (33,846)
Goldsmith, Alexandra J.........5:24:37 (28,200)
Goldsmith, Karly S.............6:11:42 (33,408)
Goldsmith, Sarah L.............3:58:33 (8,849)
Golsby, Carol J................4:40:48 (18,733)
Golunska, Nicola...............3:54:59 (8,006)

Gomm, Christine H..............5:44:31 (31,097)
Goncalves, Anna P..............4:25:02 (14,834)
Gonzalez, Samantha J...........6:52:00 (34,974)
Gonzalez Sanchez, Susana.......3:19:55 (2,483)
Gooch, Kimberly E..............5:14:25 (26,314)
Goodall, Diane.................5:54:23 (32,095)
Goodburn, Elizabeth A..........5:37:39 (30,255)
Goodburn, Sandra F.............6:05:54 (33,035)
Goode, Lisa C..................4:09:17 (11,024)
Goode, Valerie J...............4:23:47 (14,508)
Goodenough, Jenny..............5:16:19 (26,724)
Goodfellow, Suzanne............4:17:41 (12,992)
Gooding, Dionne L..............7:50:29 (35,620)
Gooding, Emma J................5:15:34 (26,579)
Gooding, Laura E...............7:50:29 (35,620)
Goodman, Lesley M..............4:40:20 (18,615)
Goodman, Sylvia J..............4:32:58 (16,777)
Goodrich, June.................6:58:20 (35,097)
Goodrick, Gail.................4:51:32 (21,376)
Goodson, Alexis P..............6:12:35 (33,463)
Goodwill, Jo M.................5:54:22 (32,089)
Goosen, Mia C..................6:36:56 (34,580)
Goosens, Anja..................6:15:44 (33,665)
Gordon, Amy S..................6:14:14 (33,565)
Gordon, Annabel C..............5:04:13 (24,359)
Gordon, Anne S.................6:33:58 (34,465)
Gordon, Claire.................3:00:48 (943)
Gordon, Elizabeth J............4:54:32 (22,150)
Gordon, Gwen G.................6:26:32 (34,193)
Gordon, Katie..................4:42:33 (19,190)
Gordon, Laura A................5:18:01 (27,060)
Gordon, Laura R................5:35:38 (30,003)
Gordon, Zoe....................4:57:39 (22,948)
Gordon Lennox, Flora L.........3:54:51 (7,975)
Gore, Alison M.................3:38:07 (4,857)
Gore, Brighde..................5:36:27 (30,107)
Gore, Kathleen A...............6:37:56 (34,603)
Goris, Nesya E.................5:04:15 (24,363)
Gorman, Barbara................5:47:55 (31,454)
Gorman, Jane...................4:42:41 (19,227)
Gorman, Jennie.................4:10:58 (11,362)
Gorrie, Annabel J..............4:04:18 (10,025)
Gorringe, Susan J..............4:50:24 (21,097)
Gorry, Sally A.................4:42:28 (19,171)
Gorton, Diane..................6:12:41 (33,472)
Gosling, Fiona A...............4:27:13 (15,396)
Gosling, Joanne C..............4:52:44 (21,677)
Gosling, Matilda A.............4:40:34 (18,673)
Goss, Breda M..................4:37:07 (17,811)
Gossage, Lucy A................3:38:24 (4,902)
Gothberg-Venter, Jessica S.....6:19:54 (33,885)
Gotschi, Tina E................4:29:17 (15,934)
Goucher, Bethan R..............4:20:33 (13,742)
Goudie, Alice P................4:10:59 (11,365)
Goudie, Angela H...............6:49:59 (34,928)
Gough, Beverley J..............4:11:36 (11,527)
Gough, Bridget I...............5:24:06 (28,122)
Gough, Kerry...................6:59:07 (35,114)
Gough, Louise..................4:51:16 (21,300)
Gough, Teresa..................5:28:27 (28,895)
Gouiffes, Cathy................4:16:41 (12,733)
Gould, Ann L...................5:39:58 (30,584)
Gould, Chloe A.................4:30:50 (16,320)
Gould, Lara....................4:30:49 (16,317)
Gould, Sarah E.................5:59:31 (32,550)
Gould, Sarah-Jane M............6:25:43 (34,156)
Gould, Sharon R................4:43:31 (19,419)
Gould, Yvonne B................6:15:06 (33,642)
Goulding, Alison E.............5:57:03 (32,336)
Goulty, Alison E...............5:27:12 (28,666)
Gourves, Raphaelle.............4:35:40 (17,446)
Gow, Jessica L.................6:41:10 (34,690)
Gower, Hayley..................4:57:49 (22,991)
Gower, Katy....................4:00:24 (9,293)
Gowling, Linda M...............6:14:39 (33,588)
Graaf, Melanie M...............4:54:44 (22,207)
Grace, Adina E.................6:48:29 (34,899)
Gradwell, Emma J...............4:12:35 (11,734)
Grady, Sarah...................4:26:13 (15,105)
Graham, Alison M...............4:44:22 (19,639)
Graham, Alison M...............5:32:44 (29,569)
Graham, Emma-Jane L............5:14:08 (26,253)

Graham, Georgina 4:27:17 (15,416)
Graham, Jane R 4:24:07 (14,603)
Graham, Jennifer M 4:56:51 (22,735)
Graham, Julia M 4:04:42 (10,090)
Graham, Justine S 7:13:04 (35,324)
Graham, Ruth 5:15:53 (26,638)
Graham, Sarah L 5:51:59 (31,871)
Graham, Sharon L 4:41:01 (18,794)
Graham, Shirley F 5:27:17 (28,675)
Graham, Susan E 3:54:35 (7,917)
Graham Jones, Zoe L 4:50:30 (21,120)
Grahamslaw, Margaret 5:18:26 (27,148)
Grainger, Joanne E 4:02:13 (9,652)
Grainger, Michele 4:14:41 (12,253)
Grainger, Sarah 4:24:20 (14,660)
Graley, Joanne T 4:42:59 (19,291)
Granfield, Paula M 4:28:01 (15,592)
Granger, Dawn E 6:36:52 (34,575)
Granger, Julie A 6:05:02 (32,965)
Grant, Denise A 6:07:26 (33,127)
Grant, Karen M 4:19:33 (13,469)
Grant, Pamela C 4:08:49 (10,924)
Grant, Samantha E 4:10:04 (11,179)
Grant, Sarah 5:54:53 (32,135)
Grant, Sheila 5:11:59 (25,852)
Grant, Susan P 4:05:37 (10,268)
Grasso, Gina 6:06:13 (33,062)
Grave, Linda M 3:51:28 (7,246)
Graver, Catherine L 4:48:58 (20,757)

Graves, Lucinda J 3:24:54 (3,009)

This was my first ever marathon and it was far too hot for me. Made the mistake of taking on board too much water and ended up in the loo three times. However, not a bad time for a marathon virgin! I raised over £2,500 for Asthma UK. Decided I needed to run it again in 2008 without the loo stops!

Graves, Susan J 5:05:12 (24,543)
Gravestock, Mary-Lou 4:33:06 (16,810)
Gravis, Karen H 6:04:24 (32,911)
Gray, Alex L 4:46:34 (20,191)
Gray, Amanda L 3:21:48 (2,685)
Gray, Caroline 4:28:13 (15,649)
Gray, Elizabeth 6:08:06 (33,180)
Gray, Faye 6:15:03 (33,618)
Gray, Gillian 5:35:11 (29,938)
Gray, Gillian A 4:19:05 (13,350)
Gray, Karen A 5:22:54 (27,921)
Gray, Karen A 5:23:21 (27,984)
Gray, Kate 4:53:52 (21,980)
Gray, Kaye A 5:24:27 (28,175)
Gray, Rosaire P 3:58:21 (8,796)
Graylen, Maria A 5:12:00 (25,856)
Graysmark, Claire F 5:33:44 (29,719)
Grayson, Susan T 3:59:37 (9,123)
Greaney, Lisa 3:53:23 (7,660)
Greatrix, Emma L 3:36:45 (4,654)
Greaves, Caroline A 6:35:21 (34,516)
Greaves, Elena J 4:43:33 (19,426)
Greaves, Elizabeth R 5:26:54 (28,610)
Greaves, Sarah A 5:23:26 (27,997)
Greaves, Tracey 3:53:11 (7,610)
Greco, Maria Raffalla 4:14:35 (12,224)
Green, Aleksandra C 4:31:07 (16,386)
Green, Amy A 4:42:41 (19,227)
Green, Anna C 4:32:43 (16,720)
Green, Anna L 6:18:22 (33,795)
Green, Anne 6:32:28 (34,422)
Green, Caroline M 4:39:14 (18,345)
Green, Caroline S 4:44:22 (19,639)
Green, Chloe 5:56:23 (32,276)
Green, Claire M 4:33:45 (16,978)
Green, Denise M 4:40:44 (18,706)
Green, Diana M 6:20:36 (33,928)
Green, Elizabeth A 6:24:22 (34,094)
Green, Gail 4:31:18 (16,423)
Green, Heather C 5:43:18 (30,972)
Green, Helen S 4:54:34 (22,158)
Green, Jackie 5:19:40 (27,369)
Green, Jacqueline L 3:46:54 (6,321)
Green, Janet E 4:13:11 (11,874)
Green, Katrina 5:22:45 (27,902)
Green, Laura C 5:22:24 (27,833)
Green, Laura L 7:52:50 (35,628)
Green, Mary B 5:10:36 (25,594)
Green, Nicola 4:48:47 (20,717)
Green, Nicola S 4:45:10 (19,876)
Green, Pauline 4:50:31 (21,129)
Green, Rhian 5:30:19 (29,185)
Green, Sara J 4:40:56 (18,772)
Green, Sarah J 4:26:29 (15,184)
Green, Susan M 4:07:45 (10,712)
Green, Vivienne P 5:37:43 (30,263)
Greenacre, Louisa 3:32:53 (4,118)
Greenall, Vicki A 3:15:15 (2,016)
Greenburg, Elizabeth A 4:40:48 (18,733)
Greene, Margaret A 4:28:20 (15,680)
Greene, Rosemary A 6:55:42 (35,049)
Greener, Liat 4:21:09 (13,889)
Greenfield, Claire E 5:56:06 (32,246)
Greenfield, Jane E 5:30:54 (29,279)
Greenhalgh, Christy A 4:59:34 (23,404)
Greenhalgh, Helen J 6:39:59 (34,668)
Greenhalgh, Rebecca A 7:01:56 (35,157)
Greenhalgh-Harvey, Grace C 3:15:33 (2,032)
Greenidge, Tara 4:51:17 (21,307)
Greenleaf, Caroline M 5:38:35 (30,397)
Greenough, Emma M 4:52:15 (21,556)
Greenspan, Emily 5:02:59 (24,119)
Greenway, Tanya J 4:25:38 (14,977)
Greenwood, Claire L 4:59:54 (23,475)
Greenwood, Judith S 5:49:39 (31,644)
Greenwood, Laura M 5:56:44 (32,313)
Greer, Patricia 3:32:38 (4,088)
Greer, Sarah N 4:32:54 (16,763)
Greer, Sharon 5:30:24 (29,200)
Greer, Tracey 6:16:59 (33,732)
Greeves, Catherine L 5:08:15 (25,150)
Gregory, Ali M 4:52:56 (21,735)
Gregory, Allison K 5:15:44 (26,612)
Gregory, Elizabeth D 3:50:24 (7,020)
Gregory, Kate L 5:06:41 (24,811)
Gregory, Lisa J 4:38:09 (18,051)
Gregory, Nicola 4:52:08 (21,521)
Gregory, Sarah L 3:42:58 (5,682)
Gregory, Simone A 5:24:02 (28,110)
Gregson, Charlotte K 4:34:22 (17,109)
Gregson, Liz 5:15:11 (26,495)
Gregurec, Julia 4:39:08 (18,314)
Grehan, Monica 5:27:35 (28,728)
Greiller, Dawn M 4:21:28 (13,957)
Grenside, Emma J 6:48:59 (34,911)
Grewal, Pritika 5:27:32 (28,716)
Grewal Fry, Rajinder 6:14:40 (33,589)
Greyling, Annabelle 5:28:17 (28,858)
Gribben, Lorraine 3:33:19 (4,183)
Grice, Annie E 4:53:10 (21,801)
Grieg, Camilla M 3:06:27 (1,270)
Griesel, Karen 5:11:28 (25,749)
Grieve, Catherine 5:02:23 (24,010)
Griffin, Alison 3:50:32 (7,046)
Griffin, Anna R 5:56:12 (32,255)
Griffin, Chanese 3:40:47 (5,318)
Griffin, Rachelle L 4:33:54 (17,007)
Griffith, Becky L 3:40:11 (5,213)
Griffith, Helen O 5:49:07 (31,597)
Griffiths, Aileen M 5:23:29 (28,009)
Griffiths, Andrea M 5:30:01 (29,144)
Griffiths, Anne R 5:06:31 (24,786)
Griffiths, Evelyn 4:57:58 (23,025)
Griffiths, Hannah R 4:15:10 (12,360)
Griffiths, Jane 4:44:14 (19,611)
Griffiths, Joanna 5:24:37 (28,200)
Griffiths, Joanna B 5:28:15 (28,849)
Griffiths, Lesley 6:26:12 (34,182)
Griffiths, Margot 4:59:21 (23,345)
Griffiths, Nadine S 5:50:37 (31,735)
Griffiths, Nicola E 5:33:13 (29,636)
Griffiths, Rhian 4:57:19 (22,860)
Griffiths, Sally C 3:57:34 (8,615)
Griffiths, Sandra 8:04:17 (35,648)
Grigg, Veronica 4:13:16 (11,899)
Griggs, Jill E 4:32:42 (16,716)
Grigor, Sarah L 4:37:40 (17,926)
Grigoriou, Elina 5:33:54 (29,747)
Grillo, Egizia 3:37:32 (4,757)
Grimes, Sadie A 5:12:43 (25,988)
Grimshaw, Maxine C 5:30:29 (29,218)
Grindley, Jenny 3:34:15 (4,302)
Grindu, Christiane 4:39:19 (18,368)
Grist, Tina D 4:41:45 (18,975)
Grobler, Gina E 5:29:59 (29,129)
Groeneveld, Eva 4:10:45 (11,318)
Grogan, Angela M 5:18:31 (27,167)
Gromski, Katie E 4:44:35 (19,712)
Groner, Lieselotte 4:59:16 (23,332)
Grosse, Petra 5:34:36 (29,861)
Grosvenor, Emma C 3:23:39 (2,864)
Grout, Carol E 4:41:45 (18,975)
Grout, Jackie A 4:12:30 (11,721)
Grove, Deborah 5:05:59 (24,691)
Grover, Rebecca K 4:52:47 (21,689)
Grover, Tarminder K 4:18:16 (13,137)
Groves, Brigitte 5:03:10 (24,166)
Groves, Emma L 4:58:31 (23,153)
Groves, Katherine H 5:08:52 (25,256)
Groves, Kathleen 6:20:50 (33,942)
Groves, Sarah 7:23:07 (35,416)
Grubb, Penny J 5:29:07 (28,998)
Gruenbaum, Tandi A 3:53:16 (7,634)
Grumbridge, Zoe 5:25:48 (28,425)
Grundy, Amy E 4:20:18 (13,679)
Grylls, Samantha 4:29:44 (16,070)
Grzelak, Bozena 4:43:17 (19,367)
Guard, Maureen 5:24:19 (28,160)
Gudgeon, Thea K 3:17:55 (2,277)
Guess, Sophie E 4:56:49 (22,719)
Guest, Caroline B 4:13:27 (11,947)
Guillemin, Alison 4:39:46 (18,476)
Guimard, Edith 4:17:54 (13,043)
Gulati, Madhuri 4:52:49 (21,706)
Gulley, Christy L 5:35:26 (29,968)
Gulson, Christabel P 5:54:14 (32,073)
Gumbrill, Emma J 5:31:25 (29,367)
Gundle, Joanna L 3:47:12 (6,377)
Gundry, Jacqueline A 3:56:33 (8,374)
Gunn, Cathy M 4:54:34 (22,158)
Gunn, Geraldine C 4:24:19 (14,658)
Gunn, Nichola L 5:37:27 (30,232)

Gunnell, Sally J 3:50:40 (7,071)

Gurr, Tracey S.............5:12:57 (26,033)
Gusmaroli, Danielle.............4:45:15 (19,893)
Gut, Eva.............4:16:54 (12,785)
Gutensohn, April D.............4:08:01 (10,769)
Gutierrez, Marie-Christine.............4:03:01 (9,789)
Guy, Evie E.............4:58:13 (23,080)
Guy, Linda.............6:12:15 (33,439)
Gwaderi, Razia.............7:06:14 (35,221)
Gwilliam, Rachel C.............4:11:05 (11,393)
Gwilliams, Bernadette K.............5:08:18 (25,157)
Hack, Chris A.............6:35:11 (34,508)
Hack, Justine.............4:05:33 (10,250)
Hacker, Lisa C.............4:34:06 (17,050)
Hackett, Karen.............5:24:47 (28,234)
Hackney, Georgina A.............4:18:29 (13,208)
Haddad, Jane.............4:19:04 (13,343)
Haddrick, Gaynor.............5:55:28 (32,188)
Hadfield, Deborah J.............4:44:14 (19,611)
Hadgraft, Eleanor T.............5:22:49 (27,909)
Hadland, Sarah C.............3:56:22 (8,324)
Hadler, Lucy J.............3:19:04 (2,399)
Hadley, Ann-Marie.............5:48:52 (31,569)
Hadley, Glynis F.............4:53:09 (21,797)
Hadley, Rebecca S.............5:46:00 (31,259)
Haggan, Nicoli A.............5:10:43 (25,612)
Haggarty, Elaine.............5:34:06 (29,780)
Hague, Carrie A.............3:57:08 (8,508)
Hague, Theresa A.............6:04:43 (32,934)
Haigh, Ann.............4:26:29 (15,184)
Haigh, Jane.............5:01:20 (23,799)
Haigh, Rosalind.............5:26:04 (28,470)
Hailey, Dee.............4:06:46 (10,521)
Haines, Amanda.............6:12:24 (33,449)
Haines, Francesca L.............5:16:06 (26,683)
Haines, Lesley.............3:13:16 (1,849)
Haines, Maria.............4:24:26 (14,691)
Haines, Michelle J.............7:37:49 (35,551)
Haines-Jones, Nicola A.............3:54:37 (7,925)
Halbauer, Ann W.............5:19:49 (27,396)
Halden, Sophie K.............4:41:21 (18,875)
Hale, Lisa C.............3:26:58 (3,272)
Hale, Lucy H.............4:20:24 (13,707)
Hale, Nicola J.............3:53:02 (7,577)
Hales, Brenda J.............4:35:40 (17,446)
Hales, Elizabeth J.............5:51:09 (31,789)
Hales, Elizabeth S.............3:25:51 (3,106)
Hales, Rebecca A.............4:53:41 (21,937)
Halfacree, Sheri L.............4:12:20 (11,687)
Halfhead, Harriet L.............4:16:31 (12,700)
Halford, Sally E.............6:15:02 (33,616)
Halfpenny, Claire L.............6:04:14 (32,901)
Halfpenny, Fiona J.............4:36:48 (17,740)
Hall, Abigail J.............5:43:40 (31,009)
Hall, Ailsa J.............4:03:25 (9,852)
Hall, Amber.............5:03:00 (24,121)
Hall, Amelia.............3:15:25 (2,025)
Hall, Barbara A.............7:41:08 (35,572)
Hall, Beverley J.............6:18:11 (33,787)
Hall, Caroline A.............3:55:12 (8,058)
Hall, Catherine A.............4:28:16 (15,662)
Hall, Christine J.............5:14:33 (26,350)
Hall, Deborah A.............3:52:19 (7,437)
Hall, Elizabeth M.............5:34:21 (29,817)
Hall, Emma.............5:44:52 (31,136)
Hall, Gillian M.............5:54:08 (32,066)
Hall, Jill.............5:24:32 (28,186)
Hall, Juliette.............4:16:51 (12,772)
Hall, Katy J.............5:09:18 (25,333)
Hall, Martha A.............3:24:16 (2,935)
Hall, Renée D.............5:50:35 (31,731)
Hall, Sarah.............4:01:23 (9,494)
Hallam, Lisa J.............4:36:14 (17,592)
Hallas, Sam J.............5:02:55 (24,111)
Hallett, Carol.............5:09:52 (25,444)
Halliburton, Sharon.............3:45:31 (6,096)
Halliwell, Sian M.............4:33:11 (16,838)
Halls, Charlotte W.............5:14:34 (26,354)
Halls, Kersti A.............4:47:33 (20,422)
Hallur, Gowri.............5:00:31 (23,617)
Halsey, Jennifer L.............6:32:50 (34,436)
Halstead, Victoria L.............4:07:26 (10,641)
Hambleton, Karen.............4:17:47 (13,019)
Hamblett, Linda E.............5:44:51 (31,135)

Hamburger, Lauren D.............5:37:16 (30,210)
Hamer-Davies, Elizabeth A.............5:03:04 (24,140)
Hamilton, Calire L.............4:42:14 (19,107)
Hamilton, Carol.............5:20:28 (27,508)
Hamilton, Deborah N.............3:45:25 (6,086)
Hamilton, Georgina.............5:08:51 (25,251)
Hamilton, Janine.............4:04:53 (10,127)
Hamilton, Lucy A.............3:27:10 (3,305)
Hamilton, Sarah-Jane.............5:13:35 (26,135)
Hamlett, Alison.............4:21:51 (14,049)
Hammerson, Samantha J.............5:38:34 (30,390)
Hammett, Susan J.............6:17:40 (33,764)
Hammon, Caroline A.............5:05:35 (24,617)
Hammond, Deborah J.............4:59:38 (23,419)
Hammond, Frances.............4:36:04 (17,549)
Hammond, Kate.............5:55:55 (32,229)
Hammond, Louise.............5:01:17 (23,789)
Hampshire, Fay.............5:50:17 (31,701)
Hampton, Fiona M.............6:26:20 (34,190)
Hampton, Ruth H.............6:29:58 (34,323)
Hampton-Jones, Linda M.............4:23:15 (14,388)
Hamson, Clare L.............3:39:32 (5,113)
Hamson, Julie C.............5:42:12 (30,847)
Hamu, Ella.............6:05:27 (32,994)
Han, Susanna.............5:46:55 (31,348)
Hanaway, Michelle C.............5:11:16 (25,712)
Hancock, Elizabeth M.............4:29:37 (16,042)
Hancock, Naomi J.............5:37:35 (30,245)
Hancock, Sioned.............5:42:09 (30,841)
Hancock, Vivienne K.............5:33:19 (29,649)
Handisyde, Linda K.............5:56:41 (32,306)
Handyside, Bethan S.............5:24:16 (28,151)
Hanford, Julia.............5:26:53 (28,607)
Hanken, Jacqueline V.............5:00:52 (23,704)
Hankin, Yvonne E.............5:12:10 (25,892)
Hanks, Julie.............3:59:43 (9,144)
Hanley, Pat J.............4:24:33 (14,717)
Hannaford, Janet E.............5:19:35 (27,357)
Hansen, Fay T.............5:17:03 (26,868)
Hanson, Anna.............6:51:29 (34,969)
Hanson, Kristiina.............4:43:30 (19,414)
Hanson, Nicola J.............5:33:35 (29,700)
Hanwell, Alison L.............6:28:37 (34,270)
Haq, Soraya.............5:07:41 (25,031)
Haran, Kalea J.............5:29:25 (29,061)
Harbon, Emily.............4:52:17 (21,566)
Hardie, Sheona K.............6:07:53 (33,159)
Harding, Caroline A.............4:09:59 (11,162)
Harding, Claire J.............4:18:59 (13,325)
Harding, Joanne.............6:59:14 (35,117)
Harding, Nancy J.............3:55:12 (8,058)
Harding, Sharon J.............5:48:01 (31,468)
Harding, Wendy J.............4:38:57 (18,274)
Hardman, Annette L.............4:28:18 (15,672)
Hardman, Christine E.............4:17:23 (12,904)
Hardman, Joy.............4:29:50 (16,101)
Hardman, Nicola.............5:52:15 (31,898)
Hardman, Rachael M.............3:54:13 (7,843)
Hardy, Anne.............5:22:24 (27,833)
Hardy, Catherine E.............4:45:27 (19,934)
Hardy, Gill.............4:08:24 (10,848)
Hardy, Karen M.............5:05:14 (24,547)
Hardy, Pamela J.............5:27:58 (28,789)
Hare, Caroline L.............5:37:15 (30,209)
Hare Duke, Hilary.............3:39:51 (5,167)
Hargadon, Sue E.............4:40:19 (18,610)
Hargie, Patricia G.............5:36:29 (30,111)
Hargrave, Emma L.............3:37:01 (4,689)
Hargrave, Louise S.............4:39:11 (18,329)
Hargreaves, Claire.............5:25:03 (28,283)
Hari, Anushka M.............4:48:30 (20,647)
Harkin, Karen L.............4:52:40 (21,659)
Harkins, Sally.............4:48:29 (20,643)
Harland, Julie E.............5:41:19 (30,744)
Harland, Rachel C.............3:21:29 (2,649)
Harling, Sally L.............6:44:43 (34,794)
Harlow, Beverley.............4:47:27 (20,394)
Harmer, Fran.............7:13:41 (35,329)
Harmer, Samantha V.............4:43:58 (19,217)
Harmon, Laura J.............6:37:17 (34,588)
Harnden, Fiona S.............5:47:10 (31,365)
Harne, Vicky R.............4:14:14 (12,149)
Harper, Alison J.............4:11:44 (11,554)

Harper, Katie N.............4:50:18 (21,068)
Harper, Louise A.............3:56:17 (8,297)
Harper, Pauline A.............5:09:51 (25,439)
Harper, Suzanne.............4:53:52 (21,980)
Harps, Lindsey A.............5:44:05 (31,052)
Harries, Claire L.............6:03:37 (32,861)
Harries, Elaine A.............5:42:44 (30,898)
Harries, Michelle D.............6:47:48 (34,881)
Harrington, Angela M.............5:19:16 (27,306)
Harrington, Ann.............5:18:52 (27,226)
Harrington, Joanne K.............5:15:59 (26,654)
Harrington, Kylie M.............5:09:33 (25,384)
Harrington, Michelle.............7:08:13 (35,249)
Harris, Abi.............6:15:33 (33,655)
Harris, Carli.............4:51:50 (21,450)
Harris, Charlotte M.............3:35:06 (4,420)
Harris, Claire.............4:43:19 (19,383)
Harris, Denise.............3:39:57 (5,181)
Harris, Heather.............4:07:21 (10,626)
Harris, Jacqueline M.............4:57:14 (22,828)
Harris, Jane E.............3:58:24 (8,809)
Harris, Janice A.............6:02:20 (32,772)
Harris, Jennifer L.............6:10:28 (33,332)
Harris, Joan K.............4:16:58 (12,808)
Harris, Kathy.............4:35:15 (17,348)
Harris, Kimberley.............6:03:59 (32,887)
Harris, Louise E.............4:18:36 (13,240)
Harris, Margaret J.............5:20:36 (27,541)
Harris, Marion W.............5:06:38 (24,806)
Harris, Naomi L.............4:38:45 (18,212)
Harris, Nicola J.............5:27:32 (28,716)
Harris, Rachel.............5:15:20 (26,529)
Harris, Rebecca.............3:42:37 (5,611)
Harris, Sally-Ann.............6:56:24 (35,060)
Harris, Samantha J.............3:35:06 (4,420)
Harris, Shirley M.............4:46:11 (20,104)
Harris, Stacey L.............5:58:15 (32,435)
Harris, Tina Marie.............4:26:05 (15,070)
Harris, Vikki.............4:51:49 (21,440)
Harrison, Carina L.............7:04:50 (35,200)
Harrison, Charlotte E.............3:32:53 (4,118)
Harrison, Clare.............5:52:34 (31,924)
Harrison, Gill M.............3:30:43 (3,808)
Harrison, Jackie.............6:04:44 (32,936)
Harrison, Jodie E.............4:12:46 (11,780)
Harrison, Karen.............3:34:55 (4,400)
Harrison, Karen E.............3:59:23 (9,065)
Harrison, Katherine L.............3:50:15 (6,984)
Harrison, Michelle L.............5:14:22 (26,305)
Harrison, Ruth L.............4:55:00 (22,264)
Harrison, Samantha J.............3:46:16 (6,214)
Harrison, Stephanie.............5:09:36 (25,398)
Harrison, Susanna J.............3:08:40 (1,442)
Harrold, Valerie A.............4:44:30 (19,681)
Harrop, Bernadette L.............3:33:03 (4,146)
Harrop, Katie L.............5:33:10 (29,629)
Harrop, Louise M.............4:59:45 (23,443)
Harrowby, Jenny.............5:47:32 (31,411)
Harsant, Jan A.............5:40:24 (30,640)
Hart, Alice.............3:57:46 (8,667)
Hart, Emma J.............4:03:19 (9,835)
Hart, Frances E.............6:22:11 (34,005)
Hart, Harriet B.............3:20:22 (2,536)
Hart, Jackie.............5:28:14 (28,846)
Hart, Jacqueline.............7:08:05 (35,244)
Hart, Jody.............5:48:41 (31,550)
Hart, Judith.............7:51:38 (35,626)
Hart, Tracey A.............6:24:00 (34,079)
Hartas, Jane.............5:16:47 (26,802)
Hartley, Alison C.............4:00:00 (9,208)
Hartley, Joanne.............5:10:16 (25,536)
Hartley, Karen A.............5:45:03 (31,160)
Hartley, Maureen.............4:32:48 (16,740)
Hartman, Annabelle.............5:23:32 (28,018)
Hartnack, Annett.............3:26:09 (3,149)
Hartnett, Jennifer L.............3:55:05 (8,026)
Hartnoll, Samantha J.............6:19:41 (33,877)
Hartwell, Jacqueline M.............3:21:38 (2,667)
Hartwell, Justine.............5:26:16 (28,503)
Hartwright, Caryl E.............4:11:25 (11,478)
Harvey, Abigail.............5:11:45 (25,800)
Harvey, Carol.............5:19:46 (27,386)
Harvey, Julia J.............4:53:45 (21,951)

Harvey, Lisa A....4:42:01 (19,043)
Harvey, Louise A....6:25:23 (34,144)
Harvey, Melissa J....5:05:12 (24,543)
Harvey, Sarah E....4:50:57 (21,230)
Harvey, Stephanie....6:50:15 (34,937)
Harvey-Wells, Nicki....5:46:23 (31,300)
Harwood, Lesley....6:18:26 (33,801)
Haskell, Devena....7:29:15 (35,472)
Haskins, Wendy M....6:31:53 (34,400)
Haslam, Joanne....3:31:47 (3,950)
Haslam, Johanna J....5:03:44 (24,276)
Haslam, Lucy E....6:28:58 (34,284)
Haslam, Nicola J....4:08:24 (10,848)
Hassan-Hicks, Anne....6:56:10 (35,056)
Hassan-Hicks, Lora....5:27:59 (28,794)
Hassell, Patricia A....5:30:19 (29,185)
Hassell, Paula S....4:03:56 (9,956)
Hassett, Rebecca....5:09:54 (25,451)
Hasslacher, Charlotte R....4:33:42 (16,962)
Hatch, Louise E....5:21:34 (27,705)
Hatch, Samantha K....5:24:28 (28,178)
Hatchard, Bryony E....5:04:15 (24,363)
Hatcher, Jessica J....3:38:03 (4,843)
Hatcher, Kerry-Anne....5:32:11 (29,480)
Hathaway, Daphne L....5:59:08 (32,518)
Hattam, Sarah A....4:54:44 (22,207)
Hatton, Gillian M....5:45:57 (31,249)
Hatton, Margaret....6:25:15 (34,140)
Haughan, Anne....6:04:23 (32,909)
Havers, Elizabeth....6:33:50 (34,459)
Haviland, Clare....5:02:28 (24,032)
Hawke, Anthea L....4:22:13 (14,131)
Hawken, Jessica L....3:55:46 (8,178)
Hawken, Valerie E....5:47:42 (31,430)
Hawker, Lesley C....5:25:50 (28,431)
Hawker, Liz....2:47:55 (306)
Hawker, Vicky L....4:14:23 (12,183)
Hawkes, Melanie....5:07:17 (24,951)
Hawkins, Annys....5:01:13 (23,776)
Hawkins, Emma L....4:57:31 (22,907)
Hawkins, Gaynor L....6:00:53 (32,657)
Hawkins, Georgia D....6:16:11 (33,695)
Hawkins, Gill C....6:22:19 (34,012)
Hawkins, Jacqueline....4:33:41 (16,955)
Hawkins, Laura....3:51:43 (7,297)
Hawkins, Phillipa J....6:26:53 (34,209)
Hawkins, Tilly....7:52:55 (35,631)
Hawkins, Vicky J....4:09:13 (11,010)
Hawley, Astrid....4:55:56 (22,499)
Hawley, Gillian....4:47:49 (20,482)
Haworth, Emma C....4:00:08 (9,234)
Hay, Anne E....3:43:16 (5,731)
Hay, Ruth....4:58:13 (23,080)
Hay, Stephanie L....5:40:18 (30,627)
Haycock, Patrick M....6:05:46 (33,029)
Hayden, Debbie....5:09:29 (25,367)
Hayden, Juliet S....6:11:35 (33,403)
Hayes, Becky....4:39:56 (18,520)
Hayes, Carla....4:27:39 (15,501)
Hayes, Carol A....4:44:56 (19,815)
Hayes, Eranga....5:42:12 (30,847)
Hayes, Joanne....4:37:47 (17,953)
Hayes, Lizzy A....4:54:21 (22,112)
Hayes, Michelle J....6:09:38 (33,281)
Hayes, Sophie E....5:06:10 (24,729)
Hayes-Gill, Claire S....3:26:07 (3,143)
Hayhow, Prunella V....3:29:18 (3,618)
Hayhurst, Kathryn D....4:05:34 (10,256)
Hayles, Laura....5:17:10 (26,886)
Hayles, Linda M....4:03:16 (9,830)
Haylett, Ainslie....3:42:17 (5,566)
Hayne, Rachel H....4:37:21 (17,848)
Haynes, Fiona A....4:06:15 (10,405)
Haynes, Janine....4:50:08 (21,030)
Haynes, Lisa C....4:56:23 (22,609)
Haynes, Sarah J....5:26:51 (28,599)
Haynes, Susan A....4:28:06 (15,623)
Hayter, Joanne E....5:31:37 (29,389)
Hayter, Lucy S....5:20:33 (27,531)
Hayter, Patsy M....4:46:28 (20,170)
Hayward, Angelika....5:35:50 (30,030)
Hayward, Lizzie....5:09:45 (25,425)
Hayward, Rachel L....5:07:26 (24,984)
Hayward, Rebecca F....3:49:13 (6,779)
Haywood, Diane....3:30:33 (3,794)
Haywood, Fiona L....6:08:35 (33,211)
Hazard, Elizabeth A....6:03:31 (32,852)
Hazell, Clair L....6:38:02 (34,607)
Hazell, Renée A....6:54:39 (35,026)
Hazlehurst, Anna C....5:25:49 (28,429)
Hazlehurt, Lyndsay J....5:23:39 (28,040)
Hazzard, Susan....4:04:22 (10,032)
Hdgson, Louise E....5:22:44 (27,896)
Head, Claire-Anne....4:25:38 (14,977)
Head, Jean L....6:08:22 (33,196)
Head, Laura....4:53:41 (21,937)
Heald, Rebecca J....6:13:50 (33,537)
Healey, Beverley J....4:21:57 (14,077)
Healey, Jill C....4:14:29 (12,200)
Healey, Julie....5:30:06 (29,161)
Healy, Joanne L....4:10:38 (11,296)
Healy, Stephanie....6:23:10 (34,043)
Heaney, Jude....6:20:10 (33,895)
Heap, Catherine....4:54:25 (22,128)
Heard, Nicola....5:37:18 (30,213)
Heard, Rachel D....5:29:58 (29,128)
Hearn, Amy L....3:42:19 (5,572)
Hearn, Jacqueline M....5:31:32 (29,382)
Hearn, Kathy....4:39:17 (18,357)
Heath, Bridget A....4:49:02 (20,774)
Heath, Lisa....5:34:12 (29,796)
Heath, Lucy A....4:22:12 (14,128)
Heath, Pippa....4:31:05 (16,374)
Heath, Sheryl L....3:28:31 (3,490)
Heathcote, Selina....4:41:23 (18,884)
Heaton, Christine....3:59:41 (9,136)
Heaton, Mathilde M....2:54:56 (576)
Heaver, Melanie J....5:15:21 (26,531)
Heaviside, Karen M....3:07:17 (1,332)
Hedberg, Maj....5:23:20 (27,982)
Hedges, Anita E....3:59:32 (9,104)
Hedges, June....4:01:54 (9,589)
Hedges, Michelle....5:32:07 (29,470)
Hedges, Trudy A....5:41:55 (30,822)
Hedley-Lewis, Penelope A....4:10:30 (11,268)
Heeley, Lesley M....4:57:27 (22,896)
Hefferan, Penelope J....4:56:21 (22,602)
Hegarty, Kerri....5:14:57 (26,439)
Heij, Henny....6:06:47 (33,094)
Heimann, Amy C....5:40:39 (30,669)
Heliwell, Brenda L....6:02:22 (32,777)
Hellier, Alison J....4:11:33 (11,510)
Hellisen, Signe....4:04:58 (10,139)
Helliwell, Fay....4:58:16 (23,093)
Helliwell, Helen L....5:26:14 (28,500)
Helliwell, Rebecca A....4:34:10 (17,069)
Helps, Dawn P....5:59:44 (32,559)
Helsby, Genevieve....4:06:32 (10,471)
Helweg-Larsen, Gillian....4:32:04 (16,574)
Heminsley, Caroline F....3:35:37 (4,501)
Hemming, Caroline....3:14:47 (1,966)
Hemsworth, Marion V....4:07:56 (10,758)
Hemworth, Caroline....3:36:30 (4,609)
Henderson, Caroline....6:06:21 (33,071)
Henderson, Jane....4:17:23 (12,904)
Henderson, Jane A....4:49:48 (20,955)
Henderson, Lesley A....5:55:49 (32,219)
Henderson, Lesley C....5:03:30 (24,239)
Henderson, Linda....5:37:57 (30,295)
Henderson, Lorraine A....4:34:43 (17,206)
Henderson, Noreen B....4:21:25 (13,942)
Henderson, Sarah L....6:10:47 (33,353)
Hendricks, Beverley D....5:01:11 (23,768)
Hendrie, Susan D....6:04:05 (32,893)
Henman, Jill....5:06:50 (24,850)
Hennessey-Ford, Kelly L....6:00:29 (32,620)
Hennigan, Emma M....5:10:04 (25,495)
Henriksen, Christina....4:59:16 (23,332)
Henry, Alice G....5:10:45 (25,617)
Henry, Fredricka T....4:09:53 (11,147)
Henry, Sophie C....5:10:45 (25,617)
Henry, Victoria A....6:39:01 (34,639)
Henshall, Bethan S....6:21:17 (33,967)
Henshall, Sian....6:21:17 (33,967)
Henson, Victoria A....5:02:14 (23,974)
Heppell, Sarah J....5:20:36 (27,541)
Heppelthwaite, Shauna M....5:18:34 (27,175)
Hepton, Vikki A....5:08:46 (25,237)
Herald, Tracey M....7:24:50 (35,429)
Herbert, Alison E....4:05:07 (10,165)
Herbert, Jayne....4:45:58 (20,054)
Herbert, Niki L....5:45:05 (31,163)
Herft, Laura E....5:42:07 (30,838)
Hermida, Maria C....4:54:00 (22,022)
Herod, Emma....5:17:27 (26,948)
Herrero-Martinez, Erica....4:59:58 (23,497)
Herriman, Emma L....5:01:43 (23,871)
Herring, Patricia M....6:58:13 (35,094)
Herring, Valerie J....4:40:13 (18,581)
Hersey, Rebecca L....6:51:13 (34,962)
Heryet, Nicole....4:07:54 (10,748)
Heseltine, Elizabeth R....5:06:49 (24,844)
Hesketh, Joanne....3:36:48 (4,657)
Heslip, Andrea L....4:18:45 (13,276)
Hessey, Charlotte....5:51:16 (31,804)
Hess-Long, Elaine L....7:03:01 (35,176)
Hester, Amanda S....3:28:17 (3,445)
Hettle, Elizabeth C....5:12:39 (25,974)
Hewer, Susan E....5:50:06 (31,683)
Hewett, Lydia A....4:06:24 (10,439)
Hewett, Pascale M....5:11:31 (25,759)
Hewitt, Caroline J....3:00:22 (921)
Hewitt, Catherine E....3:10:49 (1,617)
Hewitt, Chantal B....6:38:47 (34,631)
Hewitt, Kirsty J....5:04:09 (24,350)
Hewitt, Sally A....4:31:45 (16,517)
Hewlett, Vicki....4:54:50 (22,234)
Hewlin, Tiffany O....6:00:12 (32,595)
Hewson, Tara....6:00:01 (32,576)
Hewstone, Clare M....5:58:25 (32,461)
Heycock, Carol....3:37:23 (4,730)
Heydecker, Deirdre A....3:39:15 (5,055)
Heywood, Elizabeth K....4:43:58 (19,527)
Heywood, Nicola J....4:30:08 (16,182)
Heywood, Pippa....4:43:33 (19,426)
Hibberd, Stephanie E....6:27:46 (34,244)
Hibbs, Angela E....2:59:54 (893)
Hibbs, Philippa B....5:45:07 (31,169)
Hickey, Angela M....5:42:44 (30,898)
Hickey, Charlotte L....4:39:36 (18,437)
Hickey, Claire M....8:38:33 (35,681)
Hickey, Lynn J....5:10:33 (25,586)
Hickie, Alison J....4:41:30 (18,920)
Hickingbotham, Margaret A....5:09:45 (25,425)
Hickling, Tina M....5:40:09 (30,611)
Hickman, Breeda M....3:44:58 (6,023)
Hickman, Janet....6:53:45 (35,014)
Hickman, Julia C....4:59:29 (23,379)
Hickman, Lesley J....5:42:25 (30,871)
Hicks, Cheryl K....7:32:59 (35,516)
Hicks, Julie A....5:47:50 (31,443)
Hicks, Karen J....4:32:29 (16,657)
Hicks, Patricia A....5:42:30 (30,878)
Hickson, Julie....4:23:26 (14,427)
Hier, Diane R....3:21:44 (2,677)
Higginbottom, Denise A....5:09:29 (25,367)
Higginbottom, Wendy E....3:23:24 (2,841)
Higgins, Anita....4:56:25 (22,616)
Higgins, Carolyn M....5:22:29 (27,844)
Higgins, Cynthia R....4:00:12 (9,250)
Higgins, Elizabeth....4:56:42 (22,696)
Higgins, Julie....6:26:43 (34,201)
Higgins, Tessa R....6:01:39 (32,730)
Higginson, Michelle....5:11:11 (25,698)
Highgate, Cath J....4:03:46 (9,919)
Higlett, Joanna M....4:57:38 (22,939)
Higson, Susan M....5:37:44 (30,266)
Hilbery, Hannah....5:38:23 (30,367)
Hili, Carmen....3:07:32 (1,350)
Hill, Amanda C....5:02:19 (23,993)
Hill, Carole J....4:34:57 (17,257)
Hill, Cheryl W....3:56:13 (8,279)
Hill, Clare Y....4:36:00 (17,534)
Hill, Deborah....3:55:18 (8,077)
Hill, Deborah J....5:23:40 (28,044)
Hill, Fiona J....6:00:24 (32,611)
Hill, Heather R....3:50:44 (7,084)
Hill, Jacqueline A....5:48:55 (31,575)
Hill, Janet M....4:23:05 (14,354)

Hill, Jessica 6:29:46 (34,319)
Hill, Katherine J 3:42:46 (5,637)
Hill, Laura 4:14:58 (12,313)
Hill, Linzi J 5:51:37 (31,839)
Hill, Lorna 6:52:15 (34,980)
Hill, Louise C 5:25:53 (28,439)
Hill, Morna S 4:47:26 (20,389)
Hill, Paula K 3:22:49 (2,780)
Hill, Pauline 5:54:51 (32,130)
Hill, Rachael F 5:52:22 (31,907)
Hill, Rachel S 5:08:12 (25,139)
Hill, Suzannah M 5:30:20 (29,190)
Hill, Suzanne 5:51:26 (31,818)
Hill, Tracy J 4:50:36 (21,151)
Hilliard, Sarah J 4:55:05 (22,285)
Hillier, Ann B 3:44:46 (5,989)
Hillier, Rebecca A 5:40:45 (30,679)
Hillier, Trudi J 3:52:34 (7,476)
Hillis, Joanne L 6:23:33 (34,059)
Hillman, Donna S 3:06:36 (1,279)
Hillman, Jill 4:53:32 (21,894)
Hills, Diana 5:28:10 (28,832)
Hills, Jennifer B 5:00:09 (23,535)
Hills, Linda K 5:13:21 (26,093)
Hills, Lynne M 4:54:13 (22,081)
Hilman, Paula K 4:36:01 (17,540)
Hilson, Linda M 6:43:37 (34,762)
Hilton, Lindsay 5:10:01 (25,486)
Hincks, Kerry 5:11:37 (25,780)
Hindhaugh, Julia A 7:33:29 (35,521)
Hindley, Emma J 3:53:57 (7,779)
Hindley, Jo C 4:40:49 (18,737)
Hinds, Alison 5:24:16 (28,151)
Hine, Sophie I 3:35:46 (4,520)
Hines, Emma L 4:28:49 (15,814)
Hinman, Angela K 4:42:34 (19,195)
Hinns, Marina J 4:37:23 (17,855)
Hinton, Amy F 3:49:02 (6,740)
Hinton, Jessica L 4:01:09 (9,452)
Hinxman, Kathryn E 3:58:12 (8,760)
Hird, Linda D 4:02:36 (9,708)
Hire, Caroline V 5:44:48 (31,128)
Hiroko, Minami 4:28:35 (15,754)
Hirons, Louise A 5:17:06 (26,877)
Hirotsuna, Shoko 6:14:58 (33,611)
Hirst, Lucy C 4:27:34 (15,480)
Hirst, Wendy J 5:24:44 (28,224)
Hiscock, Karli M 6:37:56 (34,603)
Hiscocks, Lucy 5:41:38 (30,784)
Hitchcox, Susan L 4:11:53 (11,588)
Hitchens, Wietske 3:59:17 (9,037)
Ho, Olivia 3:56:22 (8,324)
Ho, Saphire 3:33:58 (4,266)
Hoare, Carol A 4:53:41 (21,937)
Hoare, Gemma P 4:45:18 (19,905)
Hoareau, Juliette R 5:00:23 (23,595)
Hobb, Sarah E 7:00:47 (35,143)
Hobbs, Angie L 5:22:25 (27,836)
Hobbs, Diana M 4:38:45 (18,212)
Hobday, Jacqueline 4:16:07 (12,602)
Hobin, Carolyne M 4:13:31 (11,969)
Hoborough, Hazel J 4:41:18 (18,862)
Hobson, Claire L 4:45:45 (19,998)
Hobson, Emma M 4:11:23 (11,470)
Hobson, Melanie 3:57:11 (8,520)
Hockley, Aimée L 5:51:18 (31,808)
Hockley, Anna M 3:36:27 (4,605)
Hockley, Debra L 4:04:17 (10,022)
Hockney, Karen 4:52:08 (21,521)
Hodder, Rebecca 3:24:28 (2,952)
Hodgen, Kathryn C 6:26:00 (34,164)
Hodges, Caroline A 5:24:04 (28,116)
Hodges, Joanna 6:34:29 (34,473)
Hodgetts, Josie 3:34:14 (4,300)
Hodgson, Diane 5:36:19 (30,088)
Hodgson, Rachel 4:16:16 (12,639)
Hodkinson, Gemma D 6:27:38 (34,238)
Hodnett, Maria 6:18:37 (33,812)
Hodnett, Nicola A 5:54:03 (32,057)
Hodson, Amelia J 5:00:38 (23,645)
Hodson, Lucy C 5:27:02 (28,625)
Hodson, Sarah C 5:33:53 (29,742)
Hoeben, Sohja 4:05:55 (10,332)

Hoets, Belinda L 5:18:17 (27,117)
Hoffman, Angela C 4:25:17 (14,893)
Hoffman, Stella 6:15:53 (33,675)
Hogan, Caroline L 5:57:01 (32,333)
Hogan, Heather J 4:52:52 (21,717)
Hogan, Katherine A 5:00:51 (23,696)
Hogan, Rebecca L 4:49:50 (20,959)
Hogg, Janet E 5:00:41 (23,652)
Hogg, Natalie M 6:12:26 (33,453)
Hoggarth, Alison J 4:33:22 (16,884)
Hoglova, Katarina 4:19:46 (13,532)
Hoigaard, Christine E 4:40:31 (18,660)
Hojskov, Lise 5:04:38 (24,434)
Holassie, Antoinette 4:37:49 (17,960)
Holden, Heather J 4:15:16 (12,383)
Holden, Marie B 5:03:22 (24,208)
Holden, Roberta F 3:40:57 (5,356)
Holden, Tracey D 4:29:38 (16,048)
Holden, Vivienne A 5:42:30 (30,878)
Holden-Gill, Ursula 3:57:34 (8,615)
Holden-Peters, Ana 5:18:26 (27,148)
Holder, Kate S 6:08:45 (33,223)
Holding, Dawn N 4:04:37 (10,078)
Holding, Elizabeth A 5:19:08 (27,276)
Holdsworth, Ruth 5:16:39 (26,781)
Holes, Gillian M 6:21:26 (33,978)
Holl, Emily 5:39:37 (30,546)
Hollak, Severina G 3:51:24 (7,225)
Hollamby, Nicola J 5:10:02 (25,492)
Holland, Kim 3:55:40 (8,155)
Holland, Kirsty M 6:13:33 (33,525)
Holland, Marie 3:59:53 (9,178)
Holland, Susan M 4:34:37 (17,181)
Holland, Victoria S 4:10:05 (11,180)
Hollands, Emma L 4:18:47 (13,281)
Hollenberg, Antje 4:51:23 (21,339)
Holliman, Debbie J 5:22:38 (27,880)
Hollingsworth, Juliet L 5:55:56 (32,232)
Hollingsworth, Nadine L ...4:50:12 (21,045)
Hollington, Rachel 5:57:57 (32,409)
Hollingworth, Gemma E ...6:20:17 (33,904)
Hollins, Annick 4:30:44 (16,303)
Hollins, Teresa A 3:53:07 (7,594)
Holloway-Guilfoyle, Tracy ...2:56:03 (612)
Holloway-Vine, Diane L 5:02:37 (24,060)
Holmes, Alison C 4:53:15 (21,825)
Holmes, Andrea 5:49:15 (31,610)
Holmes, Corina T 4:18:25 (13,181)
Holmes, Elizabeth J 5:58:46 (32,489)
Holmes, Emily J 3:24:58 (3,016)
Holmes, Jane E 5:10:00 (25,477)
Holmes, Kelly S 3:48:06 (6,543)
Holmes, Linda C 4:49:20 (20,849)
Holmes, Rachael 3:55:23 (8,102)
Holmes, Teresa 5:06:49 (24,844)
Holmes, Tracy 3:42:40 (5,622)
Holohan, Caroline A 7:47:54 (35,610)
Holohan, Kim E 5:34:23 (29,824)
Holroyd, Carla A 4:23:30 (14,444)
Holroyd, Caroline E 5:21:50 (27,762)
Holt, Denise 5:56:14 (32,259)
Holt, Genevieve C 5:38:47 (30,426)
Holt, Jane 5:24:54 (28,261)
Holt, Jessica A 5:41:28 (30,767)
Holt, Saba G 3:28:27 (3,471)
Holt, Tina 5:24:50 (28,243)
Holyoake, Joanne 4:31:07 (16,386)
Homan, Catherine M 6:47:33 (34,873)
Home, Lynda A 4:10:29 (11,261)
Homer, Britta 3:42:19 (5,572)
Honderd Ev Krijn, Alie 6:06:36 (33,084)
Hone, Jenny 5:20:20 (27,482)
Honeyman, Lucy 4:23:58 (14,562)
Honour, Alison M 4:23:57 (14,555)
Honsel, Martina 4:36:44 (17,723)
Hood, Andrea M 3:46:13 (6,207)
Hood-Leeder, Nina 5:18:39 (27,189)
Hook, Rebecca L 5:13:02 (26,054)
Hool, Sue E 3:00:36 (936)
Hoon, Kim Young 3:44:50 (5,997)
Hooper, Bonnie J 4:33:36 (16,938)
Hooper, Joanne L 4:50:49 (21,196)
Hooper, Nicola J 4:13:43 (12,022)

Hooper, Sheila 5:21:20 (27,663)
Hooton, Jacqueline T 5:00:21 (23,587)
Hope, Helen E 4:15:31 (12,445)
Hope, Lindsay B 6:00:55 (32,659)
Hope-Gill, Julia S 4:51:28 (21,363)
Hopegood, Karen J 5:13:50 (26,197)
Hopewell, Sarah J 4:42:20 (19,129)
Hopewell, Valerie 6:14:47 (33,601)
Hopgood, Jo L 4:44:25 (19,654)
Hopkins, Alison C 3:07:10 (1,323)
Hopkins, Jill A 4:48:19 (20,613)
Hopkins, Kelly A 6:48:42 (34,902)
Hopkins, Loretta M 6:24:34 (34,109)
Hoppe, Ceri 4:19:25 (13,436)
Hoppe, Gisela 3:41:34 (5,451)
Horden, Teresa A 5:19:47 (27,388)
Hordern, Fern 4:49:27 (20,874)
Hore, Angela 6:12:41 (33,472)
Horgan, Joanne L 4:48:41 (20,689)
Horler, Emma C 4:55:39 (22,418)
Horman, Tracey A 6:57:31 (35,083)
Horn, Kerry F 5:51:49 (31,857)
Horne, Pauline E 5:03:21 (24,204)
Horner, Angela 5:19:48 (27,392)
Horner, Nicola 4:59:28 (23,369)
Hornigold, Rachael E 4:13:29 (11,956)
Hornshaw, Melanie A 5:20:22 (27,488)
Horsburgh, Joanne L 5:14:19 (26,294)
Horsley, Laura 5:36:45 (30,138)
Horsman, Beverly A 5:21:17 (27,652)
Horta-Osorio, Ana C 4:16:56 (12,798)
Horton, Jacquelyn 5:29:59 (29,129)
Horton, Lindsay J 4:28:41 (15,781)
Horton, Sarah 5:04:50 (24,476)
Horton, Sarah J 3:55:50 (8,190)
Horton, Sarah J 5:08:04 (25,108)
Hoskins, Ginette L 4:51:16 (21,300)
Hosmer De Zuniga, Sarah ...4:29:11 (15,906)
Hossick, Ceridwen 5:59:52 (32,565)
Houden, Aase 3:41:00 (5,365)
Hougego, Lydia J 5:35:13 (29,944)
Houghton, Helena A 4:57:10 (22,811)
Houghton, Joanne M 3:47:41 (6,473)
Houghton, Teresa E 6:49:12 (34,917)
Houlding, Helen M 3:51:03 (7,145)
Houldsworth, Zoey S 4:09:33 (11,085)
Hounslow, Cheryl J 3:46:13 (6,207)
Houpeau, Martine 4:40:16 (18,594)
House, Clare L 4:23:14 (14,385)
Houseman, Rachael H 3:19:07 (2,405)
Houston, Catherine M 4:36:48 (17,740)
Houston, Sarah 3:34:15 (4,302)
Hovan, Marta 4:42:20 (19,129)
Hovanessian, Harriet C 5:19:17 (27,308)
Howard, Alice T 5:48:01 (31,468)
Howard, Annette 7:09:07 (35,262)
Howard, Beverley P 4:50:06 (21,023)
Howard, Christine E 3:56:17 (8,297)
Howard, Hazel 4:35:46 (17,480)
Howard, Helen F 5:50:27 (31,722)
Howard, Jo 5:50:17 (31,701)
Howard, Louisa 5:03:12 (24,173)
Howard, Lucy I 4:17:17 (12,871)
Howard, Rachel L 4:18:07 (13,103)
Howard, Sarah E 5:54:02 (32,055)
Howarth, Angela 4:16:13 (12,627)
Howe, Angela D 2:49:57 (375)
Howe, Cheryl T 4:47:53 (20,502)
Howe, Lindsay R 4:33:05 (16,806)
Howe, Maryanne 3:10:55 (1,625)
Howell, Camilla J 4:18:03 (13,086)
Howell, Catherine F 5:37:09 (30,192)
Howell, Vivien J 6:50:03 (34,931)
Howells, Catherine L 5:14:30 (26,334)
Howells, Leanne 5:38:04 (30,312)
Howes, Lucy 4:57:17 (22,847)
Howie, Ruth J 4:30:04 (16,165)
Howkins, Catherine V 4:10:34 (11,283)
Howlett, Donna M 5:50:04 (31,682)
Howman, Emily V 5:48:35 (31,531)
Howse, June A 5:52:13 (31,895)
Howting, Sharyn 5:38:15 (30,342)
Hubbard, Denise A 5:53:51 (32,038)

Hubbard, Penelope J	4:16:54 (12,785)	
Hubbard, Rachel	6:24:01 (34,082)	
Hubbick, Joanne S	5:04:19 (24,379)	
Huckle, Sarah E	3:37:16 (4,720)	
Hudson, Claire A	3:38:29 (4,917)	
Hudson, Jackie C	5:06:20 (24,759)	
Hudson, Kym	4:06:22 (10,429)	
Hudson, Lynn	4:27:36 (15,491)	
Hudson, Melanie A	5:16:30 (26,757)	
Hudson, Steph	6:15:26 (33,643)	
Huff, Zoe L	5:18:11 (27,098)	
Hufton, Elizabeth J	5:16:25 (26,742)	
Huggett, Bridget M	5:54:24 (32,097)	
Huggett, Sylvia A	3:50:14 (6,983)	
Hughes, Allison E	5:13:55 (26,213)	
Hughes, Angela H	5:24:45 (28,230)	
Hughes, Claire	5:40:33 (30,658)	
Hughes, Claire T	6:32:40 (34,428)	
Hughes, Desiree M	5:33:45 (29,722)	
Hughes, Elaine J	6:12:20 (33,447)	
Hughes, Helen E	3:52:02 (7,370)	
Hughes, Jane	6:10:56 (33,363)	
Hughes, Karys	6:01:13 (32,699)	
Hughes, Katharine	3:51:03 (7,145)	
Hughes, Kathyrn A	6:54:08 (35,022)	
Hughes, Liz	4:44:40 (19,734)	
Hughes, Louise D	6:41:04 (34,691)	
Hughes, Lucy M	5:48:24 (31,517)	
Hughes, Nicola	5:59:07 (32,517)	
Hughes, Nicola A	7:57:57 (35,638)	
Hughes, Rebecca	5:09:25 (25,358)	
Hughes, Rebecca	7:27:59 (35,458)	
Hughes, Ruth M	3:59:14 (9,021)	
Hughes, Shona	3:28:27 (3,471)	
Hughes, Sinead B	4:45:17 (19,900)	
Hughes, Suki	4:02:29 (9,694)	
Hughes, Susan J	6:04:29 (32,917)	
Hughes, Yolanda M	5:07:48 (25,058)	
Hughes, Zoe J	4:57:16 (22,839)	
Hugh-Jones, Pia S	5:00:51 (23,696)	
Hull, Gemma D	4:42:00 (19,038)	
Hull, Margaret	4:57:55 (23,012)	
Humby, Gina A	5:44:49 (31,132)	
Hume, Emmy	4:12:39 (11,751)	
Hume, Shirley	3:39:06 (5,033)	
Humphrey, Amanda M	5:24:38 (28,204)	
Humphreys, Claire	5:46:28 (31,308)	
Humphreys, Kerry A	5:14:02 (26,235)	
Humphries, Mary M	5:16:17 (26,719)	
Humphries, Sharon T	5:28:45 (28,941)	
Humphry, Claire E	5:56:24 (32,278)	
Humpidge, Kath	4:09:53 (11,147)	
Hundrieser, Stephanie A	4:57:15 (22,834)	
Hung, Kitty S	5:13:01 (26,052)	
Hung, Ton Yee	6:34:58 (34,497)	
Hunpleby, Sarah J	5:50:01 (31,677)	
Hunt, Caoimhe B	3:19:42 (2,453)	
Hunt, Daisy	6:35:55 (34,533)	
Hunt, Elizabeth A	5:54:04 (32,058)	
Hunt, Gail	5:16:23 (26,733)	
Hunt, Helen D	5:08:38 (25,213)	
Hunt, Jayne	5:06:12 (24,741)	
Hunt, Laura	4:38:15 (18,068)	
Hunt, Natalie A	5:09:07 (25,298)	
Hunt, Nicola J	3:45:11 (6,047)	
Hunt, Sarah L	6:30:04 (34,331)	
Hunt, Sharon G	5:12:36 (25,967)	
Hunt, Sonia L	4:48:00 (20,533)	
Hunt, Theresa G	5:24:18 (28,157)	
Hunt, Tracey F	5:28:06 (28,818)	
Hunt, Tracy	5:35:38 (30,003)	
Hunter, Ann M	6:02:24 (32,778)	
Hunter, Caroline A	5:23:35 (28,026)	
Hunter, Hazel C	3:47:48 (6,496)	
Hunter, Kimberley J	6:12:04 (33,430)	
Hunter, Marsha J	5:13:56 (26,217)	
Hunter, Martyn	4:39:08 (18,314)	
Hunter, Rachel S	3:59:09 (9,000)	
Hunter, Susanne	4:57:34 (22,919)	
Huntley-James, Sian E	5:18:05 (27,074)	
Hurd, Tracey	5:33:04 (29,612)	
Hurley, Joanna E	5:22:34 (27,870)	
Hurley, Joanne M	3:45:44 (6,138)	

Hurley, Nicola	5:29:20 (29,047)	
Hurrell, Karen A	4:54:01 (22,028)	
Hurst, Deborah A	5:00:57 (23,719)	
Hurst, Donna M	4:47:06 (20,313)	
Husbands, Melissa J	4:50:24 (21,097)	
Huse, Geraldine C	3:52:14 (7,416)	
Huseein, Suzanne	7:45:30 (35,600)	
Hussain, Afshan	5:20:35 (27,538)	
Hussain, Yasmeen	3:45:45 (6,139)	
Hussey, Bryony S	5:39:29 (30,523)	
Hussey, Deborah	5:09:40 (25,407)	
Hussey, Lisa M	3:25:39 (3,083)	
Hüsseyin, Çiğdem E	5:53:09 (31,974)	
Hustler, Carol A	6:10:39 (33,345)	
Hustwick, Hilary A	5:05:22 (24,572)	
Hutchens, Sarah E	5:38:15 (30,342)	
Hutchings, Clare B	4:42:46 (19,246)	
Hutchings, Kate	5:07:42 (25,033)	
Hutchings, Rebecca	5:26:01 (28,458)	
Hutchinson, Deborah J	3:54:17 (7,870)	
Hutchinson, Jennifer	5:03:09 (24,160)	
Hutchinson, Katy L	5:09:05 (25,291)	
Hutchinson, Sally	5:39:15 (30,482)	
Hutchinson, Samantha E	3:23:34 (2,855)	
Hutchinson, Sophie J	4:51:30 (21,370)	
Hutton, Ceri S	5:09:51 (25,439)	
Hutton, Chloe	5:31:06 (29,317)	
Hutton, Kristi	3:22:16 (2,724)	
Huws, Ceirios	6:06:52 (33,101)	
Huxtable, Emily M	5:35:35 (29,992)	
Huxtable, Gail	4:23:39 (14,477)	
Huynh, Ai	4:45:35 (19,962)	
Hyam, Lee	5:45:28 (31,203)	
Hyatt, Jenny C	4:21:53 (14,060)	
Hyde, Alison C	6:22:43 (34,033)	
Hyde, Jodie	5:12:58 (26,039)	
Hyland, Emma J	4:17:53 (13,038)	
Hylton, Denise C	5:29:36 (29,088)	
Hylton, Millie A	5:35:48 (30,022)	
Hyne, Joanna	4:22:40 (14,248)	
Iannelli, Sarah L	3:03:49 (1,096)	
Ibberson, Jill	4:11:05 (11,393)	
Ibbotson, Rachel	3:58:06 (8,743)	
Ibell, Emma L	3:27:10 (3,305)	
Ibrahimi, Fatema S	4:27:03 (15,339)	
Ihle-Hansen, Hege M	4:13:31 (11,969)	
Ilelaboye, Kemi	5:48:15 (31,498)	
Iles, Karen A	5:43:17 (30,969)	
Iles, Lesley	6:19:44 (33,879)	
Iles, Patricia A	6:26:00 (34,164)	
Illing, Glenda	3:29:32 (3,652)	
Illingworth, Barbara J	4:52:51 (21,715)	
Ilsley, Stephanie J	3:54:29 (7,899)	
Imafidon, Bisi	4:02:47 (9,747)	
Imperadore, Ada	5:41:34 (30,778)	
Imrie, Claire E	3:16:25 (2,119)	
Inch, Christine A	3:37:52 (4,802)	
Inches, Christine J	5:57:52 (32,397)	
Ingham, Amelia M	6:11:02 (33,372)	
Ingham, Elizabeth C	5:11:21 (25,738)	
Ingham, Janine H	4:17:42 (12,996)	
Ingle, Natasha A	6:43:43 (34,764)	
Ingledew, Georgina J	4:08:51 (10,933)	
Ingram, Sarah M	4:59:45 (23,443)	
Ingrao, Stefanie	4:59:42 (23,433)	
Innes, Laura M	5:01:07 (23,755)	
Inness, Vicky L	3:38:44 (4,965)	
Ioannou, Angela M	4:23:50 (14,525)	
Irani, Hana	6:23:45 (34,066)	
Ireland, Jayne E	5:20:03 (27,430)	
Irvine, Amelia	5:25:00 (28,269)	
Irving, Susan C	3:43:42 (5,811)	
Irwin, Angela I	3:57:02 (8,487)	
Irwin, Catherine C	4:41:54 (19,017)	
Irwin, Rachel	5:45:03 (31,160)	
Isaac, Jane	5:50:16 (31,699)	
Ison, Margaret	7:11:46 (35,301)	
Ivall, Justine N	4:56:25 (22,616)	
Ivantsoff, Mariana J	4:24:43 (14,753)	
Iverson, Stacey J	3:49:24 (6,808)	
Ives, Lesley G	5:29:55 (29,120)	
Jabeen, Farkhanda	7:21:54 (35,402)	
Jablkowska, Miki	5:45:17 (31,180)	

Jack, Catherine L	6:47:03 (34,860)	
Jack, Nicola	4:30:52 (16,332)	
Jack, Sheena C	3:45:34 (6,107)	
Jack, Tanya L	4:00:12 (9,250)	
Jacks, Annette F	5:21:53 (27,772)	
Jackson, Anna C	5:01:02 (23,736)	
Jackson, Anne	3:49:20 (6,800)	
Jackson, Ava	4:02:45 (9,742)	
Jackson, Charlotte R	5:26:39 (28,566)	
Jackson, Deborah	5:41:35 (30,779)	
Jackson, Deborah I	4:56:49 (22,719)	
Jackson, Denise	5:47:18 (31,386)	
Jackson, Emma J	5:27:44 (28,751)	
Jackson, Emma L	6:00:37 (32,632)	
Jackson, Glen P	3:57:33 (8,610)	
Jackson, Hayley S	5:06:25 (24,772)	
Jackson, Jayne	5:08:00 (25,093)	
Jackson, Karen E	4:33:03 (16,802)	
Jackson, Katie E	5:55:16 (32,170)	
Jackson, Kirsten	3:01:20 (977)	
Jackson, Lucy	4:53:06 (21,779)	
Jackson, Rachel M	4:33:13 (16,852)	
Jackson, Ruth	4:57:39 (22,948)	
Jackson, Sandre D	3:45:32 (6,097)	
Jackson, Wendy	6:11:57 (33,422)	
Jackson-Leach, Rachel J	4:50:53 (21,213)	
Jackson-Stops, Henrietta	4:48:37 (20,674)	
Jacobs, Jennifer E	4:09:49 (11,129)	
Jacobs, Kate	3:11:12 (1,648)	
Jacobs, Nicole	5:22:11 (27,811)	
Jacq, Rachel	3:43:20 (5,744)	
Jagger, Amy	5:06:34 (24,791)	
Jagger, Joanne	4:14:00 (12,096)	
Jaggs, Sarah E	5:09:52 (25,444)	
Jago, Lisa	6:34:21 (34,470)	
Jagus, Nicola J	6:03:07 (32,828)	
Jakich, Lee	4:26:55 (15,299)	
Jakobsson, Claire E	5:02:31 (24,045)	
James, Alice-Rose	6:26:01 (34,169)	
James, Cherry I	4:58:59 (23,250)	
James, Dawn H	4:54:08 (22,054)	
James, Debbie M	3:38:50 (4,983)	
James, Helen	4:48:38 (20,676)	
James, Helen E	3:19:59 (2,493)	
James, Jennifer E	4:29:20 (15,947)	
James, Joanne	5:48:41 (31,550)	
James, Julie	5:48:11 (31,486)	
James, Lisa M	4:13:13 (11,883)	
James, Louisa	4:18:06 (13,094)	
James, Rebecca T	4:11:37 (11,533)	
James, Sharon L	6:08:28 (33,201)	
James, Susan M	3:29:14 (3,607)	
James, Victoria T	4:52:00 (21,486)	
Jameson-Till, Fiona K	6:57:35 (35,085)	
James-Rogers, Kimberley	5:39:11 (30,475)	
Jamieson, Cristin F	3:52:26 (7,459)	
Jamieson, Georgina K	3:43:48 (5,829)	
Jamieson, Linsey A	6:47:29 (34,871)	
Jamieson, Sandra M	5:29:59 (29,129)	
Jamieson, Sheila	4:46:10 (20,095)	
Janke, Kristin	5:34:41 (29,872)	
Jaramillo, Mayerlin	4:31:30 (16,461)	
Jardine, Sandie L	6:08:02 (33,171)	
Jarrett-Kerr, Alice S	5:25:04 (28,285)	
Jarvis, Alison J	5:45:22 (31,188)	
Jarvis, Hannah	5:50:17 (31,701)	
Jarvis, Jackie L	3:30:58 (3,836)	
Jarvis, Jacqueline L	3:55:52 (8,200)	
Jarvis, Justine	6:39:29 (34,654)	
Jarvis, Kate	4:40:43 (18,704)	
Jarvis, Loraine	7:14:22 (35,336)	
Jarvis, Sylvia M	4:50:20 (21,075)	
Jarvis, Tracie H	5:26:07 (28,477)	
Jaureguy, Valerie	4:44:11 (19,594)	
Jayawardena, Crishi	5:07:19 (24,960)	
Jeakins, Kimberley S	5:30:03 (29,152)	
Jefferies, Clare J	5:14:25 (26,314)	
Jefferies, Erica F	4:47:38 (20,438)	
Jefferies, Linda	4:24:03 (14,585)	
Jefferies, Sarah	4:54:07 (22,048)	
Jefferson, Holly R	4:35:08 (17,310)	
Jefferson, Sarah E	3:49:29 (6,827)	
Jeffery, Diana	5:10:05 (25,501)	

Jeffery, Hannah C	5:56:48	(32,320)
Jeffery, Louise	5:54:17	(32,079)
Jeffrey, Della J	5:18:38	(27,187)
Jeffrey, Laura R	4:54:16	(22,095)
Jeffrey, Lynne C	4:38:03	(18,024)
Jeffrey, Melissa F	4:46:13	(20,110)
Jeffrey, Rebecca G	5:01:34	(23,848)
Jeffries, Amber	5:35:01	(29,916)
Jeffries, Sarah J	5:33:04	(29,612)
Jeffs, Catherine E	6:31:57	(34,404)
Jeffs, Chris K	3:58:19	(8,790)
Jeggo, Georgina	4:25:00	(14,820)
Jelley, Diana M	4:20:06	(13,624)
Jenkin, Emma L	4:06:11	(10,390)
Jenkins, Caroline J	5:47:23	(31,396)
Jenkins, Catherine A	3:41:16	(5,405)
Jenkins, Clare	4:37:00	(17,786)
Jenkins, Greta	4:15:01	(12,328)
Jenkins, Helen	3:51:29	(7,250)
Jenkins, Sandra M	4:02:55	(9,771)
Jenkins, Wendy	5:26:21	(28,521)
Jenkinson, Claire A	4:43:14	(19,349)
Jenkinson, Clare E	5:03:58	(24,318)
Jenkinson, Karen A	6:21:05	(33,959)
Jenkinson, Katherine	5:39:35	(30,543)
Jenks, Jennifer C	3:48:23	(6,587)
Jenner, Laura	4:32:03	(16,569)
Jenner, Lizzie	4:28:15	(15,657)
Jennings, Grace E	5:01:35	(23,851)
Jennings, Helen P	6:59:14	(35,117)
Jennings, Kim M	5:34:24	(29,827)
Jennings, Linda A	5:22:26	(27,839)
Jennings, Samantha M	4:38:16	(18,077)
Jennings, Sylvia M	5:55:25	(32,184)
Jennings, Val	3:58:25	(8,812)
Jennison, Lucy A	5:29:19	(29,043)
Jenson, Rachel S	5:03:25	(24,221)
Jepson, Anna L	4:12:09	(11,644)
Jepson, Sarah F	4:52:05	(21,509)
Jermey, Meg	6:20:31	(33,922)
Jersild, Helle	3:38:32	(4,926)
Jeschny, Joan	3:44:44	(5,984)
Jesson, Samantha	5:25:47	(28,421)
Jesson-Heslin, Maree	3:14:31	(1,943)
Jessup, Alison M	6:17:02	(33,734)
Jessup, Wendy E	5:22:41	(27,889)
Jevons, Laura K	4:01:58	(9,597)
Jewell, Jenny R	5:24:13	(28,140)
Jewett, Melanie K	3:41:19	(5,415)
Jewiss, Emma J	5:17:11	(26,891)
Jeyes, Charlotte G	7:05:41	(35,212)
Jhappan, Shauna M	4:26:19	(15,136)
Jobey, Julie E	5:01:03	(23,739)
Jobling, Margaret	4:46:05	(20,073)
Jobson, Amber J	6:54:39	(35,026)
Jobson, Diane	3:33:18	(4,179)
Jobson, Hazel	4:38:02	(18,022)
Jocelyn, Sarah L	4:47:49	(20,482)
Johannesen, Maren E	4:35:58	(17,527)
Johannsdottir, Vilborg	4:56:40	(22,686)
John, Ebony R	5:04:28	(24,417)
John, Lorraine L	4:22:41	(14,253)
John, Rhiannon W	5:26:10	(28,483)
Johnn, Caroline V	3:29:04	(3,583)
Johns, Julie A	4:34:44	(17,211)
Johns, Rebecca C	3:43:14	(5,727)
Johns, Shirley	4:56:00	(22,517)
Johnson, Anne	5:16:56	(26,848)
Johnson, Benita	2:29:47	(39)
Johnson, Claire A	3:18:42	(2,359)
Johnson, Debra A	3:48:26	(6,604)
Johnson, Elizabeth A	4:11:05	(11,393)
Johnson, Georgina	4:44:48	(19,780)
Johnson, Heather C	4:42:50	(19,264)
Johnson, Jean A	4:13:22	(11,926)
Johnson, Kirstin F	4:15:16	(12,383)
Johnson, Louise	6:17:06	(33,737)
Johnson, Nisha	5:08:08	(25,122)
Johnson, Paula	6:10:02	(33,308)
Johnson, Riona	6:10:32	(33,338)
Johnson, Sarah E	6:56:41	(35,066)
Johnson, Sohpie A	5:26:25	(28,534)
Johnson, Sophie L	4:54:49	(22,229)
Johnson, Treena	3:04:41	(1,142)
Johnston, Amanda J	5:57:19	(32,354)
Johnston, Carron	4:14:35	(12,224)
Johnston, Catehrine	5:46:08	(31,278)
Johnston, Deborah	6:00:22	(32,610)
Johnston, Helen M	6:12:16	(33,441)
Johnston, Jennifer	5:45:26	(31,195)
Johnston, Loraine	4:50:44	(21,172)
Johnston, Lorna T	5:49:14	(31,605)
Johnston, Lynn	5:25:40	(28,398)
Johnston, Sarah L	4:50:31	(21,129)
Johnstone, Charlotte	5:15:38	(26,590)
Johnstone, Helen J	4:56:55	(22,753)
Johnstone, Melanie	4:00:53	(9,393)
Johnstone, Tracey J	4:47:07	(20,317)
Jones, Adele	4:39:55	(18,514)
Jones, Alison T	4:57:56	(23,014)
Jones, Almon A	4:30:21	(16,227)
Jones, Amanda	4:14:08	(12,125)
Jones, Amanda J	4:12:12	(11,655)
Jones, Amanda T	5:27:43	(28,747)
Jones, Amy E	5:41:01	(30,710)
Jones, Anita J	3:51:56	(7,351)
Jones, Ann Merle	6:18:45	(33,822)
Jones, Belinda J	4:27:07	(15,357)
Jones, Bethan	4:49:46	(20,947)
Jones, Bethan R	5:44:41	(31,122)
Jones, Bev D	5:42:35	(30,885)
Jones, Carole	4:09:25	(11,053)
Jones, Carole A	5:44:28	(31,087)
Jones, Catherine M	4:16:46	(12,755)
Jones, Christine D	4:28:13	(15,649)
Jones, Claire J	4:47:29	(20,401)
Jones, Daphne L	4:28:55	(15,838)
Jones, Debbie	3:56:19	(8,307)
Jones, Debbie A	4:16:55	(12,792)
Jones, Deirdre A	6:01:42	(32,734)
Jones, Dianne P	5:14:05	(26,243)
Jones, Dionne	3:53:56	(7,775)
Jones, Edwina S	6:20:06	(33,892)
Jones, Elaine C	5:46:47	(31,332)
Jones, Eleri W	4:51:03	(21,255)
Jones, Enfys A	3:51:07	(7,161)
Jones, Erica L	4:32:42	(16,716)
Jones, Faye L	5:30:38	(29,241)
Jones, Gemma	5:39:01	(30,452)
Jones, Gwenan L	4:09:29	(11,068)
Jones, Gwyneth	5:33:01	(29,609)
Jones, Helen	4:32:37	(16,695)
Jones, Helen D	4:19:34	(13,471)
Jones, Helen E	5:13:45	(26,178)
Jones, Imogen B	5:14:01	(26,231)
Jones, Jane	5:31:34	(29,384)
Jones, Janet L	6:01:12	(32,697)
Jones, Janice A	3:20:04	(2,503)
Jones, Julia A	3:37:57	(4,819)
Jones, Julia M	6:39:37	(34,660)
Jones, Julie	5:39:18	(30,490)
Jones, Kate E	3:53:07	(7,594)
Jones, Katherine E	4:53:11	(21,804)
Jones, Kirstie	5:59:17	(32,536)
Jones, Kirsty A	4:44:55	(19,812)
Jones, Kyle E	4:08:12	(10,811)
Jones, Lauren	4:29:31	(16,013)
Jones, Lesley A	4:30:32	(16,261)
Jones, Lesley A	4:47:07	(20,317)
Jones, Linda M	6:31:42	(34,390)
Jones, Louise A	6:21:21	(33,972)
Jones, Louise D	5:32:17	(29,494)
Jones, Louise F	5:46:01	(31,261)
Jones, Lynn M	5:40:06	(30,607)
Jones, Marie C	4:59:10	(23,299)
Jones, Michael D	5:26:56	(28,614)
Jones, Nanette K	5:25:47	(28,421)
Jones, Nina L	4:20:28	(13,724)
Jones, Patricia	4:47:16	(20,347)
Jones, Rebecca	5:54:55	(32,142)
Jones, Rebecca L	4:34:34	(17,166)
Jones, Rhian	4:40:01	(18,539)
Jones, Rosemary A	4:57:53	(23,006)
Jones, Sally A	6:16:10	(33,692)
Jones, Sandra J	4:55:46	(22,450)
Jones, Sarah L	6:44:59	(34,799)
Jones, Sarah M	4:09:07	(10,979)
Jones, Sharon L	4:30:15	(16,210)
Jones, Shirley A	5:48:43	(31,554)
Jones, Sian M	5:22:29	(27,844)
Jones, Tina	3:59:53	(9,178)
Jones, Tracy J	3:33:24	(4,194)
Jones, Uanna L	7:00:13	(35,130)
Jones, Victoria H	3:51:00	(7,139)
Jones, Yvonne	4:11:25	(11,478)
Jones, Yvonne I	3:35:08	(4,427)
Jones-Reading, Rebecca F	4:53:08	(21,788)
Jongsma, Kirsten E	3:45:57	(6,171)
Jonsson, Agneta	3:19:44	(2,459)
Jonsson, Linda	3:18:22	(2,331)
Jordan, Angela J	5:12:33	(25,959)
Jordan, Catherine	4:18:27	(13,196)
Jordan, Deidre V	5:01:07	(23,755)
Jordan, Helena M	5:12:08	(25,879)
Jordan, Julia S	5:33:11	(29,632)
Jordan, Orla A	5:11:34	(25,773)
Jordan, Rachel A	4:45:46	(20,001)
Jordansen, Karin I	3:30:38	(3,798)
Joseph, Jini	5:39:16	(30,487)
Joseph, Naomi	5:24:51	(28,250)
Jourdain, Wendy	5:06:03	(24,702)
Jowett, Faye L	4:20:04	(13,618)
Jowman, Sarah L	4:12:13	(11,662)
Joyce, Katie E	5:49:45	(31,653)
Joyce, Lesley	6:04:54	(32,950)
Joyce, Lisa A	4:58:58	(23,244)
Joyner, Anna-Jean D	4:59:03	(23,272)
Joynson, Seonaid	5:30:40	(29,246)
Juchau, Nathalie G	4:20:22	(13,700)
Judd, Joanne E	5:46:27	(31,306)
Judd, Laura	4:56:34	(22,647)
Judd, Susanne E	4:44:11	(19,594)
Judson, Fiona A	4:52:04	(21,503)
Jukes, Helen F	3:50:28	(7,039)
Jukes, Naomi L	4:31:07	(16,386)
Jukes, Victoria A	5:22:04	(27,789)
Julian, Gladys A	7:06:33	(35,230)
Julier, Sian L	5:48:12	(31,490)
Junanto, Angela K	5:54:13	(32,070)
Junnila, Anna P	3:33:51	(4,243)
Jury, Carol-Anne S	7:35:44	(35,538)
Kaba, Sasha	4:13:07	(11,860)
Kacedan, Alyson	5:59:11	(32,526)
Kadic, Hollie L	7:23:23	(35,419)
Kah, Sylvia A	3:54:09	(7,829)
Kahrs, Birgit	4:15:28	(12,435)
Kaker, Mariam	5:20:17	(27,472)
Kaldor, Ellen P	4:24:09	(14,618)
Kalek, Claire	5:14:42	(26,381)
Kallaway, Felicite J	4:37:16	(17,834)
Kalsi, Hardeep K	6:32:14	(34,418)
Kaminski, Ann	7:34:19	(35,529)
Kampz, Jemma	5:44:33	(31,099)
Kamvari, Anousha	6:00:16	(32,600)
Kanan, Rhonda J	6:26:12	(34,182)
Kanbi, Kalpana L	7:13:45	(35,331)
Kanczula, Antonia	4:42:56	(19,287)
Kane, Aine T	3:43:56	(5,855)
Kane, Michelle	7:17:47	(35,367)
Kanu, Gloria	5:22:11	(27,811)
Kanyari-Noghaddan, Catherine	6:00:16	(32,600)
Kaputin, Elspeth M	4:15:27	(12,432)
Karkaletsos, Zoe L	4:06:00	(10,351)
Karlsen, Marit	3:53:15	(7,633)
Karolczak, Ewa	5:11:46	(25,805)
Kary, Nicola A	4:24:20	(14,660)
Kasowska, Renata	4:17:29	(12,940)
Kavanagh, Sheila E	4:25:51	(15,025)
Kavanagh, Susan J	6:20:32	(33,923)
Kay, Annabel J	4:43:38	(19,448)
Kay, Frances E	5:11:18	(25,719)
Kay, Rebecca J	4:37:54	(17,981)
Kay, Sally B	4:32:22	(16,640)
Kay, Wendy	5:55:37	(32,202)
Kay, Zelda M	4:55:59	(22,508)
Kayani, Rachael J	5:11:53	(25,832)
Kayser, Anne	4:00:21	(9,278)
Kayser, Fenella K	5:40:01	(30,592)
Kayum, Elene S	5:26:10	(28,483)

Ke, Allyson J 4:39:28 (18,410)
Keane, Jacinta 4:17:42 (12,996)
Keane, Susie M 5:17:58 (27,049)
Kearley, Vivienne T 5:30:45 (29,260)
Kearney, Emma J 5:37:18 (30,213)
Kearney, Lesley E 4:17:32 (12,956)
Kearns, Joan F 4:37:46 (17,951)
Kearns, Lindsay E 4:16:53 (12,778)
Kearns, Pamela R 5:05:44 (24,642)
Keast, Sheelagh A 6:08:36 (33,213)
Keat, Claire 4:35:46 (17,480)
Keats, Nikki D 6:35:19 (34,514)
Keavney, Jacqueline S 3:24:09 (2,926)
Keck, Michaela 4:44:58 (19,828)
Keeble, Deborah A 5:04:20 (24,385)
Keegan, Karen 4:08:42 (10,910)
Keegan, Kerry Ann 5:15:15 (26,513)
Keene, Alison T 5:41:26 (30,760)
Keenleyside, Kathryn S 5:46:53 (31,343)
Keet Marsh, Lorayne M 4:00:48 (9,372)
Keevill, Heather K 4:53:33 (21,901)
Keith, Caroline M 5:06:44 (24,826)
Keith, Jane E 4:11:37 (11,533)
Kelland, Kate 3:40:40 (5,293)
Kellar, Helen J 4:21:53 (14,060)
Kelleher, Catherine 5:24:02 (28,110)
Kellie, Samantha C 5:11:34 (25,773)
Kelly, Claire E 4:54:35 (22,168)
Kelly, Deborah M 5:39:21 (30,499)
Kelly, Deirdre E 4:23:06 (14,355)
Kelly, Elaine 6:10:46 (33,352)
Kelly, Emma 5:27:59 (28,794)
Kelly, Gemma 4:52:36 (21,642)
Kelly, Karen 7:06:15 (35,222)
Kelly, Kate M 4:18:57 (13,319)
Kelly, Leigh S 5:43:48 (31,022)
Kelly, Mary H 6:09:53 (33,299)
Kelly, Maureen 5:34:03 (29,774)
Kelly, Rachel L 5:03:31 (24,240)
Kelly, Roni 6:19:52 (33,884)
Kelly, Samantha G 4:44:04 (19,556)
Kelly, Sarah J 4:26:51 (15,280)
Kelly, Susan M 5:15:31 (26,567)
Kelman, Lucy 4:01:34 (9,529)
Kelsey, Debbie C 4:52:22 (21,589)
Kelsey, Elaine M 4:24:40 (14,739)
Kelsey, Gita M 4:54:10 (22,069)
Kelsey, Jo R 2:47:59 (308)
Kelvey-Brown, Denise 3:46:00 (6,178)
Kember, Deborah L 6:10:01 (33,305)
Kemp, Ann E 5:32:26 (29,514)
Kemp, Erica 6:40:45 (34,681)
Kemp, Helen A 6:08:28 (33,201)
Kemp, Jessica L 4:17:14 (12,861)
Kemp, Lynsay 6:02:01 (32,753)
Kemp, Valerie 3:55:30 (8,117)
Kempster, Jackie 4:56:37 (22,665)
Kendall, Gillian A 5:16:48 (26,805)
Kendall, Jessica S 5:14:57 (26,439)
Kendall, Nicola S 5:19:47 (27,388)
Kendallwoods, Sacha L 4:58:22 (23,124)
Kenden, Fran 4:14:56 (12,306)
Kennard, Ruth 5:57:51 (32,395)
Kennedy, Carole 4:34:25 (17,118)
Kennedy, Caroline A 4:58:56 (23,238)
Kennedy, Eileen M 5:40:59 (30,705)
Kennedy, Linda 4:16:41 (12,733)
Kennedy, Lindsey D 5:49:07 (31,597)
Kennedy, Lucy V 4:44:17 (19,621)
Kennedy, Sheila 5:07:10 (24,918)
Kennedy, Susan 4:04:11 (10,002)
Kennedy, Tracey G 5:10:57 (25,656)
Kennedy, Tracy A 4:40:51 (18,747)
Kennedy, Wendy E 4:55:51 (22,475)
Kennerson, Shirley P 4:05:52 (10,322)
Kennett, Elizabeth J 3:25:08 (3,035)
Kennett, Hannah J 6:03:58 (32,885)
Kenny, Abigail 5:08:39 (25,217)
Kenny, Aida A 3:44:57 (6,021)
Kenny, Lisa C 5:09:58 (25,469)
Kenny, Louise C 5:44:33 (31,099)
Kensett, Helen G 4:14:45 (12,261)
Kent, Heather 4:31:34 (16,475)

LONDON MARATHON

Kent, Karen 5:49:10 (31,601)
Kent, Leanne 4:28:00 (15,586)
Kent, Lisa M 5:16:36 (26,771)
Kent, Terina J 6:57:39 (35,086)
Kent, Veronica 6:18:54 (33,833)
Kenth, Jasvinder 6:52:00 (34,974)
Kenwright, Dawn L 3:21:24 (2,639)
Kenyon, Jane 6:45:14 (34,803)
Kenyon, Sarah 3:33:36 (4,213)
Keogh, Debbie 5:38:53 (30,439)
Kepper, Roberta 5:30:10 (29,172)
Ker, Aileen F 7:28:06 (35,459)
Kerbel, Naomi A 4:44:06 (19,563)
Kerby-Collins, Elizabeth A 3:48:11 (6,560)
Kerr, Alison C 6:19:13 (33,851)
Kerr, Amy L 5:14:51 (26,419)
Kerr, Angela 4:06:02 (10,355)
Kerr, Mary 3:58:28 (8,832)
Kerr, Rachel J 3:57:58 (8,712)
Kerrigan, Colette M 4:51:12 (21,286)
Kerrison, Lois E 3:45:46 (6,142)
Kerry, Katharine E 5:18:57 (27,242)
Kershaw, Harriet E 5:52:37 (31,931)
Kershaw, Vicky L 6:30:06 (34,332)
Kersting, Brenda E 5:53:57 (32,048)
Kerwick, Zoe 4:58:01 (23,039)
Keshwara, Anjana 6:58:32 (35,099)
Kett-Brodie, Juli M 4:27:42 (15,519)
Kettle, Gillian A 5:57:18 (32,352)
Kettless, Karen J 5:47:08 (31,362)
Kewell, Charlotte S 4:21:37 (13,992)
Key, Cherry 4:27:57 (15,571)
Keyte, Jennifer C 5:04:50 (24,476)
Keyworth, Nicky J 5:19:47 (27,388)
Keyzor, Elaine C 6:39:14 (34,648)
Khan, Fariha 6:46:33 (34,845)
Khan, Shanaz B 6:06:08 (33,059)
Khideja, Nazmeen 7:01:56 (35,157)
Khoshnevis, Heather 3:34:56 (4,402)
Khouri, Carla L 4:17:31 (12,951)
Khoury, Nadia C 5:44:05 (31,052)
Khutti, Rakhi 4:54:13 (22,081)
Kidd, Bethany H 5:32:51 (29,585)
Kidd, Debbie 5:13:35 (26,135)
Kidd, Gillian 3:42:10 (5,547)
Kidd, Sophie L 6:43:42 (34,763)
Kienert, Paula J 5:38:47 (30,426)
Kiernan, Kirsten A 6:34:22 (34,471)
Kift, Joanne E 6:44:16 (34,782)
Kiggundu, Victoria K 6:25:02 (34,127)
Kightly, Emma 4:48:52 (20,736)
Kilbey, Naemi 5:39:39 (30,551)
Kilgannon, Nicola J 7:04:23 (35,195)
Kilgore, Amanda 5:07:12 (24,929)
Kilgour, Kirsteen 4:07:59 (10,764)
Killeen, Elizabeth J 4:17:24 (12,908)
Killen, Andrea J 4:57:48 (22,986)
Killingback, Sarah 6:16:07 (33,689)
Killip, Liz 3:53:21 (7,658)
Kim, Young Ok 6:25:29 (34,147)
Kimani, Monica M 4:34:39 (17,191)
Kimura, Maki 3:50:29 (7,042)
Kinch, Brenda E 4:34:11 (17,072)
Kinchin, Barbara A 5:51:02 (31,774)
Kinder, Mary A 4:46:20 (20,135)
Kinder, Penny 4:53:05 (21,771)
Kindred, Alys R 4:36:37 (17,696)
King, Angela C 4:35:55 (17,519)
King, Anna 4:15:30 (12,442)
King, Bonnie M 5:47:12 (31,371)
King, Chris A 3:16:59 (2,177)
King, Christine 5:38:34 (30,390)
King, Elizabeth K 5:57:33 (32,374)
King, Emma 5:08:11 (25,136)
King, Fiona M 5:32:28 (29,518)
King, Jacqueline 5:45:18 (31,182)
King, Judith D 5:25:57 (28,448)
King, Julia 4:06:29 (10,463)
King, Karen A 5:16:38 (26,778)
King, Karen A 6:52:38 (34,984)
King, Kathryn 5:09:33 (25,384)
King, Linda I 6:03:43 (32,869)
King, Louise A 6:15:47 (33,670)
King, Lucy 4:34:58 (17,263)
King, Melanie E 7:26:28 (35,439)
King, Nadine M 6:18:07 (33,783)
King, Nicky L 3:54:38 (7,930)
King, Philippa J 4:54:38 (22,179)
King, Ruth D 6:18:43 (33,819)
King, Sally 4:31:20 (16,432)
King, Sarah 4:45:05 (19,857)
King, Sarah E 4:25:15 (14,884)
King, Sarah J 5:33:30 (29,682)
King, Sarah L 6:22:43 (34,033)
King, Sheila 4:20:48 (13,799)
King, Wendy 3:07:17 (1,332)
King, Yvonne 3:51:28 (7,246)
Kingdom, Liz 6:11:47 (33,413)
Kingdon, Fiona J 3:44:55 (6,015)
Kingdon, Rebecca J 4:05:08 (10,169)
Kinge, Katherine S 5:20:35 (27,538)
Kingsnorth, Rebecca 5:40:10 (30,614)
Kingston, Alison L 3:28:48 (3,539)
Kingston, Sarah L 3:22:27 (2,743)
Kingwell, Catherine L 5:04:16 (24,370)
Kinnear, Marlo Z 4:25:41 (14,993)
Kinnunen, Tarja K 3:36:10 (4,566)
Kinsell, Catherine E 4:19:35 (13,479)
Kinsella, Sarah 4:42:11 (19,089)
Kinsella Frost, Carol 4:06:48 (10,530)
Kinsey, Kathryn L 4:05:47 (10,304)
Kinsley, Amanda L 4:17:47 (13,019)
Kinson, Jennifer A 4:45:41 (19,989)
Kiplagat, Lornah 2:24:46 (23)
Kipling, Liz 3:20:11 (2,517)
Kippax, Elizabeth M 5:06:09 (24,726)
Kiralyfi, Carole A 5:12:03 (25,865)
Kirby, Alysia 4:12:42 (11,768)
Kirk, Deborah J 6:16:06 (33,686)
Kirk, Emma J 4:21:42 (14,003)
Kirk, Gretchen 5:18:32 (27,169)
Kirk, Noel E 4:24:44 (14,756)
Kirk, Sally 4:15:49 (12,511)
Kirkby, Rachel 5:09:26 (25,362)
Kirkham, Myshola 3:12:25 (1,770)
Kirkwood, Victoria I 5:51:50 (31,858)
Kirley, Sandra 5:15:42 (26,602)
Kirreh, Karen 4:56:34 (22,647)
Kirwan, Cathryn D 5:50:12 (31,693)
Kirwan, Ita 4:11:22 (11,466)
Kishida, Kazumi 6:31:41 (34,389)
Kisler, Jill E 3:52:48 (7,524)
Kitchen, Diane B 4:09:22 (11,044)
Kitchener, Tracey S 4:58:55 (23,230)
Kitchingham, Helen S 6:58:51 (35,108)
Kite, Carole A 5:10:23 (25,552)
Kjaeraard, Lonnie H 3:22:51 (2,783)
Kjartansdottir, Sigrun 5:12:58 (26,039)
Kjerstad, Torunn Anita 4:25:00 (14,820)
Klaassen, Jessica J 5:10:26 (25,563)
Kleijwegt, Anne I 4:38:53 (18,251)
Klier, Birgit 4:35:06 (17,298)
Klimczak, Anna E 3:37:23 (4,730)
Klincke, Victoria M 4:23:02 (14,340)
Klug, Katja 4:36:57 (17,778)
Knass, Jenny E 3:04:15 (1,117)
Knee, Wendy E 5:08:56 (25,269)
Knell, Kathie E 4:13:47 (12,040)
Knell, Matthew 4:29:33 (16,028)
Knell, Nicola J 5:02:03 (23,943)
Knight, Alexandra S 4:29:15 (15,926)
Knight, Caroline S 5:18:48 (27,214)
Knight, Colette S 5:08:53 (25,261)
Knight, Dawn 5:07:33 (25,010)
Knight, Helen S 4:33:54 (17,007)
Knight, Jill 5:03:44 (24,276)
Knight, Kate 6:53:12 (34,998)
Knight, Linsey D 5:03:14 (24,178)

Knight, Lisa 4:44:43 (19,750)
Knight, Lucy J 6:54:59 (35,034)
Knight-Adams, Olivia 3:49:01 (6,738)
Knighton, Julie 5:32:14 (29,490)
Knighton, Karen 4:06:52 (10,544)
Knights, Angharad S 5:49:49 (31,662)
Knights, Bethan M 5:47:53 (31,448)
Knights, Candice 3:28:43 (3,527)
Knights, Diana 4:39:17 (18,357)
Knights, Diane 4:14:23 (12,183)
Knights, Julia C 5:39:01 (30,452)
Knock, Yvonne C 4:38:40 (18,188)
Knopp, Rosalind J 4:04:43 (10,095)
Knott, Katie F 4:44:30 (19,681)
Knott, Laura L 4:51:36 (21,398)
Knott, Susan H 4:02:19 (9,671)
Knowlden, Tina M 4:21:44 (14,012)
Knowles, Gillian 7:36:48 (35,541)
Knowles, Hannah V 4:50:40 (21,159)
Knowles, Juliet S 3:08:59 (1,468)
Knowles, Rebecca 4:43:59 (19,535)
Knox, Dawn C 4:49:12 (20,821)
Knox, Sarah L 4:35:01 (17,278)
Konchesky, Sarah J 7:30:26 (35,497)
Kondza, Amra 6:01:00 (32,671)
Kortum, Debby M 4:56:19 (22,590)
Kosa, Katalin 5:00:05 (23,522)
Kosa, Victoria A 5:51:20 (31,810)
Kosgei, Salina 2:24:13 (21)
Kosicka-Knox, Ania 4:28:38 (15,768)
Kosten, Becky 4:41:29 (18,915)
Kotwinski, Anna L 3:39:51 (5,167)
Kraftaite, Asta 4:18:23 (13,170)
Kralj, Lucy G 4:48:42 (20,697)
Kramer, Fabri 5:04:38 (24,434)
Kraus, Ursula 5:25:34 (28,382)
Krawec, Natalka Z 4:47:48 (20,481)
Kreupl, Petra 4:35:06 (17,298)
Krishnan, Priya 4:15:50 (12,518)
Kristensen, Karina 5:21:40 (27,729)
Kristiansen, Lara 3:30:21 (3,775)
Krivacs, Victoria 5:28:42 (28,933)
Krollig, Sharon J 5:13:47 (26,186)
Kuan, Ann 4:46:45 (20,221)
Kubis, Sylwia 5:07:16 (24,947)
Kullar, Jane 5:50:25 (31,718)
Kumi, Adwoa K 4:55:49 (22,461)
Kuritko, Christina P 4:37:12 (17,823)
Kurzawski, Amylu 5:53:21 (31,993)
Kutner, Sara 4:11:48 (11,570)
Kwiatkowski, Laura 5:10:02 (25,492)
Kyriacou, Kat 4:41:13 (18,844)
Kyte, Jennifer 3:54:09 (7,829)
Laban, Chrissie 4:47:05 (20,308)
Labed, Sylvia 5:16:15 (26,711)
Lacayo, Hollie A 7:36:49 (35,543)
Lacey, Amanda C 5:36:24 (30,097)
Lacey, Gill M 5:13:35 (26,135)
Lacey, Kim 4:56:33 (22,643)
Lacey, Liz 6:07:02 (33,109)
Lacey, Sarah J 4:51:19 (21,321)
Lacrosse, Martha 5:20:49 (27,577)
Ladlow, Samantha 5:15:34 (26,579)
Ladwa, Radhika 6:57:22 (35,080)
Laforet, Kate 3:19:18 (2,421)
Lafosse, Geves C 5:15:07 (26,484)
Laguarda, Lisa K 4:55:11 (22,311)
Laidler, Alison J 4:51:08 (21,275)
Lainchbury, Lianne M 6:00:00 (32,574)
Laing, Catriona H 4:13:51 (12,053)
Laing, Elizabeth S 4:48:46 (20,711)
Laing, Janet 4:31:36 (16,484)
Laing, Jo 3:34:47 (4,377)
Lainsbury, Kelly-Anne 4:46:40 (20,210)
Laithwaite, Gill 2:48:32 (330)
Lake, Samantha J 4:15:47 (12,507)
Laking, Sophie P 4:50:30 (21,120)
Lam, Man-Yee 4:58:26 (23,143)
Lamb, Harriet 3:51:04 (7,154)
Lamb, Rebecca A 5:51:02 (31,774)
Lamb, Virginia M 5:01:31 (23,833)
Lambert, Jennie L 5:15:53 (26,638)
Lambert, Marie L 5:33:43 (29,715)
Lambert, Sue Q 4:00:12 (9,250)
Lambert, Vicky 4:38:26 (18,134)
Lamble, Nicole V 5:47:54 (31,449)
Lamerton, Dawn E 4:57:23 (22,883)
Laming, Aimée B 4:23:22 (14,411)
Lamont, Amy 4:19:15 (13,395)
Lampa, Wendy J 4:49:19 (20,842)
Lamport, Sarah J 8:01:58 (35,642)
Lanaway, Claire M 4:45:38 (19,977)
Lancaster, Jane M 4:41:41 (18,964)
Lander, Joanne L 4:16:32 (12,702)
Lander, Kerry 5:27:35 (28,728)
Lane, Dawn M 4:43:26 (19,405)
Lane, Samantha L 4:35:19 (17,363)
Lane, Suzanne E 4:50:40 (21,159)
Laney, Lynne M 7:41:13 (35,575)
Lang, Carla 5:22:44 (27,896)
Lang-Andersen, Nicolette 4:47:26 (20,389)
Lange, Janna 4:51:06 (21,266)
Lange, Ulrike 3:29:44 (3,678)
Langeberg, Ilonka 3:24:02 (2,909)
Langfield, Jacqueline A 3:44:56 (6,017)
Langford, Sarah L 5:41:07 (30,718)
Langham, Charlotte R 4:09:35 (11,092)
Langham, Katrina S 4:57:19 (22,860)
Langley, Irene A 6:37:50 (34,599)
Langston, Victoria J 4:16:37 (12,720)
Langton, Jane E 5:27:41 (28,739)
Lanigan, Sue 4:39:55 (18,514)
Lankertis, Vicky A 4:44:45 (19,758)
Lannon, Fiona J 4:55:14 (22,325)
Lansley, Sarah 5:59:37 (32,552)
Lansley, Victoria E 6:57:02 (35,073)
Larard-Davies, Emma L 6:27:42 (34,241)
Large, Alexandra E 5:02:32 (24,048)
Large, Andrea L 4:06:23 (10,435)
Larkham, Jenny H 5:40:49 (30,683)
Larkin, Valerie 4:49:59 (20,990)
Larner, Judy A 4:55:24 (22,366)
Larrabure-Garacco, Monica V 6:11:26 (33,398)
Larrad, Denise 6:17:26 (33,743)
Larsen, Angela E 5:15:12 (26,500)
Lartey, Amy Urmila 4:47:00 (20,280)
Lashua, Jennifer 3:18:14 (2,315)
Latham, Emma A 4:30:18 (16,216)
Latham, Tracy M 3:57:13 (8,533)
Lathion, Liliane 4:27:00 (15,324)
Lattanzio, Silvana 4:50:27 (21,109)
Latter, Elizabeth V 4:57:47 (22,983)
Lattey, Alison J 5:43:00 (30,934)
Lau, Ava K 4:46:06 (20,082)
Lauenborg, Karen 6:13:56 (33,545)
Laughton, Sarah E 4:14:07 (12,124)
Laundon, Emma F 6:04:17 (32,903)
Laundon, Lara 6:04:17 (32,903)
Laurence, India 5:38:09 (30,325)
Laurens, Barb 5:03:16 (24,185)
Laurens, Kristin R 4:45:29 (19,946)
Laurenson, Francesca 5:51:48 (31,855)
Lavan, Janette E 5:12:21 (25,931)
Lavelle, Christina M 5:01:06 (23,751)
Lavelle, Jane 4:49:26 (20,867)
Lavery, Ouida G 4:20:17 (13,674)
Lavery, Victoria L 6:10:31 (33,336)
Law, Barbara D 4:18:37 (13,245)
Law, Christine M 6:12:11 (33,436)
Law, Melanie J 4:06:27 (10,454)
Lawhead, Emily R 4:05:36 (10,265)
Lawless, Joanna 5:32:55 (29,594)
Lawrence, Emily J 3:40:49 (5,324)
Lawrence, Emily J 6:01:28 (32,717)
Lawrence, Felicity R 5:40:09 (30,611)
Lawrence, Helen 2:55:19 (588)
Lawrence, Helen M 4:45:29 (19,946)
Lawrence, Joy 7:10:21 (35,274)
Lawrence, Julie 5:13:08 (26,069)
Lawrence, Julie P 6:55:18 (35,042)
Lawrence, Kirsten A 5:12:17 (25,917)
Lawrence, Louise 4:23:17 (14,397)
Lawrence, Penny L 4:51:35 (21,392)
Lawrence, Rachael M 3:08:55 (1,460)
Lawrence, Telina J 5:45:10 (31,173)
Lawrence, Vanessa V 6:34:50 (34,491)
Lawrie, Karen A 5:31:44 (29,410)
Laws, Amy 5:13:56 (26,217)
Lawson, Emma 5:14:20 (26,300)
Lawson, Helen D 6:06:06 (33,056)
Lawson, Katie R 3:55:35 (8,133)
Lawson, Michelle L 7:07:33 (35,241)
Lawson, Sandra A 6:26:51 (34,207)
Lawson, Sarah 4:19:49 (13,544)
Lawson, Val J 5:30:56 (29,286)
Lawton, Tasha G 4:55:32 (22,401)
Lawton, Teresita 5:48:19 (31,509)
Laxton, Caroline E 5:40:24 (30,640)
Laxton, Gemma C 5:40:24 (30,640)
Laythorpe, Kathleen M 5:17:38 (26,987)
Layton-Hannam, Louise A 4:16:48 (12,762)
Layzell, Caroline L 4:26:27 (15,176)
Lazell, Marguerite A 3:13:28 (1,861)
Le Bras, Lenaig A 4:23:37 (14,470)
Le Cocq, Heather D 5:10:26 (25,563)
Le Fort, Clare E 5:05:00 (24,517)
Lea, Joanne R 5:48:12 (31,490)
Lea, Pauline E 5:03:07 (24,153)
Leach, Jude E 5:42:24 (30,867)
Leach, Melanie J 4:56:50 (22,728)
Leach, Michelle 3:43:26 (5,761)
Leach, Sarah E 5:46:23 (31,300)
Learmond, Katriona J 4:06:18 (10,417)
Leask, Annette B 4:24:03 (14,585)
Leask, Helen E 5:13:58 (26,224)
Leathes, Jenny 5:00:21 (23,587)
Leblanc, Yolande 4:01:08 (9,444)
Le-Calvez, Caroline 4:05:27 (10,232)
Lechner, Andrea 4:19:14 (13,387)
Ledbury, Sarah L 4:42:40 (19,219)
Ledgard, Penny J 4:24:26 (14,691)
Ledger, Elaine 6:41:09 (34,697)
Lee, Angela 7:20:00 (35,389)
Lee, Anne 3:44:17 (5,900)
Lee, Carolyn 4:00:05 (9,224)
Lee, Clare 4:32:10 (16,599)
Lee, Diane 4:05:15 (10,193)
Lee, Fiona H 4:25:24 (14,927)
Lee, Jay E 5:34:11 (29,791)
Lee, Jim Soon 6:21:29 (33,981)
Lee, Josephine 6:20:38 (33,934)
Lee, Julie S 4:42:20 (19,129)
Lee, Lean P 5:31:01 (29,298)
Lee, Lisa J 5:07:43 (25,038)
Lee, Melissa E 4:14:35 (12,224)
Lee, Natasha J 5:04:37 (24,432)
Lee, Rachel 5:35:09 (29,936)
Lee, Ruth C 4:13:58 (12,089)
Lee, Soo Kil 5:12:25 (25,942)
Lee, Stephanie M 3:45:38 (6,122)
Lee, Susannah 3:34:09 (4,286)
Lee, Wendy Y 4:19:05 (13,350)
Lee-Browne, Nicola J 4:14:10 (12,130)
Leecy, Jean M 6:27:53 (34,247)
Leedom, Kira A 5:05:10 (24,538)
Leek, Katy L 5:25:24 (28,341)
Leek, Sheena H 4:57:56 (23,014)
Leeson, Catherine M 3:58:26 (8,816)
Leeson, Yvonne 3:42:52 (5,661)
Lefevre, Chantal J 3:53:24 (7,668)
Lefevre, Marianne 4:26:55 (15,299)
Legg, Charlotte H 4:19:02 (13,335)
Legg, Karrena A 6:10:41 (33,347)
Legg, Kim A 5:56:29 (32,285)
Legg, Natalie 6:18:39 (33,816)
Leggat, Claire L 5:33:49 (29,734)
Leguen De Lacroix, Philippa C 4:26:19 (15,136)
Leguy, Monique 4:59:27 (23,363)
Lehain, Janet 4:45:03 (19,852)
Leigh-Pemberton, Catarina E 4:59:39 (23,423)
Leighton, Michelle J 3:42:00 (5,522)
Leijenhorst, Jany G 5:12:14 (25,904)
Leiper, Karen J 6:32:37 (34,427)
Leitch, Jessica R 2:58:11 (760)
Lemon, Katy J 6:46:04 (34,830)
Lenaghan, Moira 4:20:49 (13,807)
Leng, Jennifer M 5:15:00 (26,449)
Lennon, Caroline A 4:35:11 (17,323)
Lennon, Jacqueline A 5:21:36 (27,712)

Lennon, Myanna N 3:00:17 (915)
Leonard, Angela J 3:49:42 (6,872)
Leonera, Carol M 5:43:12 (30,961)
Leosawasthiphong, Emily 6:23:10 (34,043)
Lepillier, Collette A 5:21:01 (27,605)
Leppard, Julie D 4:44:41 (19,740)
Lesley, Bonnie J 5:03:35 (24,251)
Lesley, Georgina 5:31:58 (29,444)
Letham, Anneka J 5:13:47 (26,186)
Letts, Rachel J 4:11:50 (11,578)
Leung, Kem 5:10:22 (25,549)
Levai, Valerie 3:49:52 (6,911)
Lever, Jennie L 5:01:11 (23,768)
Levinson, Jacqueline E 5:21:27 (27,687)
Levison, Karen 4:40:15 (18,589)
Levitt, Victoria S 5:01:48 (23,892)
Levoir, Judi 4:11:43 (11,552)
Levy, Fiona 4:06:14 (10,399)
Levy, Wendy 6:32:11 (34,416)
Lewington, Barbara E 5:17:17 (26,915)
Lewis, Belinda A 4:01:23 (9,494)
Lewis, Carol A 6:00:16 (32,600)
Lewis, Caroline J 4:43:16 (19,363)
Lewis, Claire D 5:08:08 (25,122)
Lewis, Clare F 6:11:17 (33,391)
Lewis, Deb 5:46:06 (31,272)
Lewis, Elaine F 6:05:58 (33,044)
Lewis, Elizabeth A 4:58:03 (23,045)
Lewis, Emma 4:23:51 (14,530)
Lewis, Emma S 4:07:42 (10,704)
Lewis, Hannah C 4:12:57 (11,819)
Lewis, Hannah J 4:22:23 (14,170)
Lewis, Jacqueline 5:48:12 (31,490)
Lewis, Jane 5:28:14 (28,846)
Lewis, Jennifer C 4:49:31 (20,892)
Lewis, Joanna 4:12:12 (11,655)
Lewis, Joanne 7:12:46 (35,316)
Lewis, Julie A 4:43:33 (19,426)
Lewis, Karen L 4:42:53 (19,278)
Lewis, Kim E 5:19:18 (27,310)
Lewis, Melanie J 4:23:23 (14,415)
Lewis, Sarah J 6:12:39 (33,467)
Lewis, Sarah R 4:57:31 (22,907)
Lewis, Sharon M 5:24:47 (28,234)
Lewis, Sophie L 4:54:23 (22,117)
Lewis, Susan K 4:59:17 (23,335)
Lewis, Susan P 5:27:43 (28,747)
Lewis, Valerie J 5:01:47 (23,886)
Lewis, Victoria J 4:27:23 (15,442)
Lewis Wright, Angela I 6:29:08 (34,289)
Lewis-Aburn, Michelle A 5:52:44 (31,944)
Lewtas, Susanne A 3:51:23 (7,221)
Li, Harfun 6:29:30 (34,308)
Li, Jing 4:52:05 (21,509)
Li, Karen 5:26:33 (28,548)
Liardet, Caroline A 3:58:04 (8,737)
Lickman, Clare J 5:20:04 (27,433)
Liddiard, Cat 4:56:02 (22,522)
Liddle, Amanda C 5:25:51 (28,435)
Liddle, Samantha L 4:32:29 (16,657)
Lidford, Laura M 4:17:19 (12,880)
Lidgard, Toni 5:35:32 (29,980)
Lidster, Becky J 5:31:10 (29,330)
Lie, Annette J 4:54:46 (22,216)
Liebenberg, Melony E 3:51:58 (7,359)
Light, Fiona E 3:53:17 (7,638)
Lightfoot, Christine C 3:48:07 (6,547)
Lightman, Sarah J 5:47:01 (31,356)
Liley, Clare E 4:30:23 (16,232)
Lilley, Cheryl L 6:11:29 (33,399)
Lilley, Hannah R 5:01:49 (23,894)
Lilley, Helen C 4:13:02 (11,840)
Lillistone, Christine 5:15:22 (26,535)
Limb, Tracy D 6:33:57 (34,464)
Limbrick, Ceri 5:18:41 (27,196)
Linard, Kirsty A 4:26:17 (15,127)
Lincoln, Anastasia 5:09:35 (25,395)
Lincoln, Vanessa 5:18:56 (27,239)
Lincoln, Victoria M 4:07:33 (10,662)
Lind, Elizabeth C 4:49:32 (20,897)
Linden, Suzette 3:57:51 (8,680)
Lindenfield, Susannah G 5:14:50 (26,415)
Linder, Barbara 5:17:42 (27,000)
Lindsay, Judy 5:09:08 (25,303)
Lindsay, Kerry 5:13:09 (26,071)
Lindsey Colton, Robyn E 4:56:12 (22,564)
Lindsey-Clark, Helen M 4:39:38 (18,445)
Lindstedt, Rose C 4:35:48 (17,487)
Lindstrom, Veronica 4:50:58 (21,233)
Lineham, Rachel S 6:07:26 (33,127)
Lines, Emma 3:51:15 (7,197)
Lines, Janet 6:59:04 (35,111)
Lines, Teresa J 4:32:11 (16,604)
Linford, Amy J 3:44:51 (5,999)
Linley, Sara J 5:22:15 (27,816)
Linnell, Linda M 5:32:58 (29,601)
Linney, Rachel W 4:51:20 (21,328)
Linwood, Joanna K 4:52:37 (21,649)
Lipede, Kehinde F 4:38:49 (18,239)
Liptrot, Claire P 5:13:09 (26,071)
Liptrot, Katherine 4:47:23 (20,379)
Liptrott, Katrina J 6:06:52 (33,101)
Lishman, Tracy L 4:16:01 (12,570)
Lisney, Lisa M 5:13:29 (26,120)
Lister, Emma-Jane 4:13:03 (11,847)
Lister, Evelyne 4:44:02 (19,548)
Lister, Jessica A 5:10:55 (25,648)
Lister, Leigh F 5:05:16 (24,552)
Litchfield, Sarah 4:41:17 (18,858)
Little, Gina M 4:44:21 (19,635)
Little, Kate A 4:23:39 (14,477)
Little, Louise M 3:32:06 (4,011)
Little, Rachael J 4:19:47 (13,539)
Littlechild, Karen E 4:00:07 (9,230)
Littlehales, Victoria E 4:28:22 (15,689)
Littler, Mary T 5:22:36 (27,875)
Liu, Michelle 3:41:23 (5,425)
Livermore, Sarah S 5:19:53 (27,405)
Livesey, Abigail J 3:58:56 (8,947)
Livesey, Alison P 5:48:40 (31,547)
Livesey, Emma 4:49:07 (20,798)
Livesey, Karen G 5:14:01 (26,231)
Livingstone, Claire 5:20:20 (27,482)
Livingstone, Jane E 7:34:12 (35,528)
Ljubojevic, Angelica 4:17:12 (12,853)
Lloyd, Caroline 5:01:50 (23,897)
Lloyd, Claire 5:13:26 (26,110)
Lloyd, Donna E 4:32:34 (16,681)
Lloyd, Emma J 5:06:58 (24,873)
Lloyd, Helen A 4:19:45 (13,524)
Lloyd, Helen A 4:20:02 (13,606)
Lloyd, Janet E 4:32:50 (16,748)
Lloyd, Nicole 4:03:28 (9,860)
Lloyd, Philippa R 6:29:14 (34,295)
Lloyd, Rachel J 5:02:18 (23,988)
Lloyd, Rebecca E 5:04:55 (24,504)
Lloyd Roberts, Chrisi 5:31:26 (29,371)
Lloyd-Thomas, Katherine S 5:27:03 (28,628)
Loach, Kate 3:35:11 (4,434)
Local, Michelle 5:04:20 (24,385)
Lock, Claire A 5:01:55 (23,916)
Lock, Claire J 4:12:20 (11,687)
Lock, Gillian 6:11:16 (33,388)
Lock, Kate 4:22:11 (14,121)
Lock, Lynne 4:18:00 (13,074)
Lock, Michelle A 5:37:20 (30,219)
Lockett, Susannah M 4:57:20 (22,870)
Lockhart, Maria 4:59:45 (23,443)
Lockhart-Gregg, Jennifer 4:43:19 (19,383)
Lockhart-Mummery, Clare E 3:23:26 (2,845)
Lockwood, Linda A 4:21:44 (14,012)
Lockwood, Lyn W 5:35:07 (29,929)
Lockwood, Ruth 5:55:14 (32,167)
Lockyer, Janice 4:21:25 (13,942)
Lodder, Veronica 5:38:22 (30,365)
Loder, Philippa J 4:54:46 (22,216)
Loftus, Helen 4:45:31 (19,954)
Logan, Caroline 6:10:43 (33,349)
Logan, Caroline A 5:29:21 (29,051)
Logan, Caroline J 5:40:31 (30,656)
Logue, Nicola 4:15:25 (12,421)
Lohan, Sharon T 5:16:14 (26,706)
Lomas, Hayley 4:08:13 (10,816)
Lomas, Sarah 3:19:22 (2,425)
Lomasney, Fiona J 5:17:07 (26,882)
Lomax, Jayne D 4:25:24 (14,927)
London, Joanna 4:06:58 (10,566)
Long, Ann 5:50:43 (31,749)
Long, Cheryl 4:54:46 (22,216)
Long, Christine 5:50:43 (31,749)
Long, Jacqueline C 6:39:41 (34,664)
Long, Kristopher D 3:51:25 (7,231)
Long, Mandy M 5:00:10 (23,541)
Long, Suzanne L 5:28:17 (28,858)
Longden, Lorraine L 4:26:51 (15,280)
Longhurst, Claire J 5:13:31 (26,126)
Longhurst, Emma L 5:34:12 (29,796)
Longhurst, Hayley 6:18:53 (33,831)
Longley, Elaine L 6:09:38 (33,281)
Longman, Sarah 5:41:37 (30,781)
Longstaff, Leeann E 6:25:43 (34,156)
Longstreet, Katie R 5:31:40 (29,399)
Lonsdale, Becky 6:08:54 (33,231)
Lonsdale, Edwina 4:42:42 (19,230)
Lonsdale, Rachel E 4:17:33 (12,961)
Loosemore, Kathryn M 4:42:01 (19,043)
Lopez, Angie 5:14:38 (26,369)
Lopez, Gillian P 4:02:59 (9,781)
Lopez, Maria D 5:37:07 (30,184)
Lord, Carol A 4:43:37 (19,444)
Lord, Terrina 6:36:00 (34,535)
Lorimer, Sarah E 6:12:04 (33,430)
Lorkins, Christina L 4:59:48 (23,459)
Lorraine, Veronica B 5:21:45 (27,741)
Losnedal, Heidi E 5:12:46 (25,994)
Lotter, Cecilia M 5:10:46 (25,621)
Loubser, Rona C 3:09:46 (1,538)
Loughridge, Clare 3:53:58 (7,785)
Louw, Edwina C 6:12:20 (33,447)
Lovage, Shivanii C 5:19:06 (27,267)
Lovatt, Nina 6:19:05 (33,842)
Love, Catherine 5:31:47 (29,415)
Love, Jacqueline L 5:09:34 (25,391)
Loveday, Annette S 5:00:36 (23,634)
Lovegrove, Fay 5:20:17 (27,472)
Lovejoy, Annabelle C 3:41:36 (5,457)
Lovell, Sally J 3:30:16 (3,759)
Lovell, Theresa A 3:48:38 (6,654)
Lovell, Yvonne 7:08:55 (35,261)
Lovell-Knight, Jade A 5:38:34 (30,390)
Lovelock, Victoria E 4:30:32 (16,261)
Loveridge, Catherine A 5:44:31 (31,097)
Lovett, Valerie 7:31:59 (35,507)
Low, Alexandra D 4:46:54 (20,254)
Low, Carolyn M 4:47:49 (20,482)
Low, Helen J 5:40:33 (30,658)
Low, Jacqueline E 6:01:30 (32,719)
Lowdon, Rachel 3:28:37 (3,507)
Lowe, Andrea H 4:18:54 (13,306)
Lowe, Caroline E 4:38:04 (18,028)
Lowe, Christina J 5:15:01 (26,456)
Lowe, Denise 5:16:51 (26,820)
Lowe, Jaki 6:08:47 (33,225)
Lowe, Janine L 3:31:47 (3,950)
Lowe, Kim 3:49:20 (6,800)
Lowe, Maria T 3:18:53 (2,377)
Lowe, Rachel M 4:45:37 (19,970)
Lowe, Stephanie J 4:29:19 (15,943)
Lowe, Vicki A 3:53:31 (7,694)
Lowe, Wendy 5:00:09 (23,535)
Lowes, Bernadette L 7:03:21 (35,179)
Lowman, Sarah A 4:05:46 (10,300)
Lowne, Hilary R 5:18:36 (27,180)
Lu, Peilan 5:49:14 (31,605)
Lua, Suet H 4:54:49 (22,229)
Lubbersen, Esther M 4:32:11 (16,604)
Lucas, Anne 4:55:18 (22,338)
Lucas, Faieeza 4:50:16 (21,061)
Lucas, Sara J 4:20:52 (13,822)
Lucas, Susan M 3:51:31 (7,259)
Luck, Nicola J 5:50:38 (31,739)
Lucy, Samantha 4:44:45 (19,758)
Ludnow, Anna L 5:07:11 (24,926)
Lund, Helen J 5:36:17 (30,080)
Lundie, Sonja 5:48:05 (31,477)
Lunt, Rozanne E 7:50:29 (35,620)
Lush, Vicky F 5:28:01 (28,801)
Lusty, Elizabeth R 3:55:11 (8,053)
Luu, Nichola 5:30:41 (29,251)

Name	Time (Position)
Luxford, Louise R	6:29:29 (34,307)
Luxton, Jane N	4:01:14 (9,466)
Lyall, Fiona M	4:07:53 (10,742)
Lydall, Denise J	5:10:27 (25,566)
Lyddy, Sylvia	6:26:09 (34,179)
Lyle, Susan V	4:12:37 (11,743)
Lynch, Emma J	5:11:55 (25,838)
Lynch, Marianne	4:31:27 (16,451)
Lynch, Susan	5:44:28 (31,087)
Lynn, Wendy J	6:00:27 (32,616)
Lyon, Andrée	5:03:46 (24,284)
Lyons, Alexandra C	5:00:36 (23,634)
Lyons, Sarah A	6:17:43 (33,766)
Lysme, Kristin S	3:41:10 (5,390)
Maag, Ana	3:08:27 (1,428)
Mabb, Samantha J	5:36:04 (30,057)
Mabley, Melissa N	4:51:17 (21,307)
MacAdie, Diana	7:56:25 (35,636)
Macarthy, Alison E	5:33:56 (29,753)
Macarthy, Sophie L	5:46:16 (31,289)
Macartney, Catherine J	6:17:57 (33,775)
MacAskill, Jane L	4:59:06 (23,287)
Macaulay, Janine	5:19:20 (27,316)
Macaulay, Sheila M	4:53:33 (21,901)
MacCabe, Gillian	5:15:57 (26,650)
MacCafferty, Marian D	5:39:15 (30,482)
MacCallum, Lucy J	5:10:57 (25,656)
MacCrimmon, Shirlee	4:35:53 (17,508)
Macdonald, Alison	3:43:51 (5,836)
Macdonald, Fiona M	4:53:28 (21,883)
Macdonald, Genevieve C	4:59:12 (23,308)
Macdonald, Laura M	5:51:53 (31,863)
Macdonald, Patricia	5:45:34 (31,216)
Macdonald, Roberta N	5:26:03 (28,468)
Macdonald, Sally A	3:50:07 (6,964)
Macduff, Fiona L	4:48:05 (20,549)
Mace, Tina L	5:25:08 (28,292)
MacEanruig, Heather C	4:24:59 (14,818)
Macfarlane, Veronica	5:52:18 (31,902)
MacGillivray, Alice L	5:33:04 (29,612)
MacGregor, Elissa	4:49:27 (20,874)
MacGregor, Sue M	3:52:20 (7,440)
Machin, Donna L	4:38:13 (18,062)
Macintosh, Katie E	8:54:11 (35,686)
Macintyre, Posy	5:02:43 (24,079)
MacIver, Isabel	5:32:24 (29,508)
Mack, Anne M	5:14:27 (26,321)
Mackaness, Sarah J	5:27:02 (28,625)
Mackay, Julia D	5:23:15 (27,970)
Mackenzie, Kaeti A	2:50:28 (391)
Mackey, Barbara	4:29:17 (15,934)
Mackie, Katrina L	5:30:01 (29,144)
Mackintosh, Megan	4:38:28 (18,140)
Mackworth Gee, Nicola C	5:56:19 (32,268)
Maclean, Fiona	8:11:11 (35,661)
Maclean, Rachel	4:29:21 (15,956)
MacLeary, Rebekah	4:12:39 (11,751)
Macleod, Helen	4:15:33 (12,450)
Macleod, Kathleen	4:25:54 (15,035)
Macmillan, Georgia T	4:37:57 (17,993)
Macmillan, Gilly	5:43:33 (30,997)
MacPhail, Georgie	4:46:25 (20,157)
MacPhail, Shelly S	3:46:38 (6,272)
Macpherson, Jane A	5:34:24 (29,827)
Macrae, Sue A	6:30:56 (34,361)
Madden, Fiona J	6:06:42 (33,090)
Madders, Rachel C	4:10:54 (11,351)
Maddock, Sheila E	3:53:11 (7,610)
Maddocks, Jennifer H	3:50:39 (7,066)
Maddox, Gretchen	4:23:33 (14,459)
Maddox, Karan	4:24:18 (14,654)
Madeley, Alison C	5:12:34 (25,961)
Maden, Deborah N	4:23:47 (14,508)
Mader, Ursula	4:57:17 (22,847)
Madge, Tricia A	4:54:42 (22,198)
Maestre, Rosa	4:58:37 (23,171)
Magang, Bonang M	5:41:50 (30,811)
Magennis, Janice A	4:48:19 (20,613)
Magnani, Helen E	5:00:37 (23,639)
Magness, Teresa M	6:14:55 (33,609)
Magnotti, Jodi L	4:55:03 (22,274)
Magnusdottir, Brynhildur	5:21:43 (27,734)
Magrath, Sharon L	5:06:41 (24,811)
Maguire, Fiona E	3:53:27 (7,677)
Maguire, Hazel J	5:27:57 (28,786)
Maguire, Sarah	3:23:54 (2,895)
Mahen, Philippa J	4:27:49 (15,543)
Mahiques, Philippa M	6:00:20 (32,608)
Maidmen, Annemarie	4:27:23 (15,442)
Maidment, Marilyn F	4:04:35 (10,074)
Maidment, Tanya A	4:54:02 (22,029)
Maier, Janet E	3:59:27 (9,083)
Maillard Porte, Nathalie	4:14:40 (12,249)
Mainard, Joanne C	4:11:07 (11,401)
Maingi, Deborah	3:50:25 (7,024)
Mainwaring, Joanne E	3:25:52 (3,108)
Maisey, Margaret	6:01:00 (32,671)
Maisey, Rebecca L	4:55:11 (22,311)
Maison, Margaret C	5:00:30 (23,613)
Maitland, Fiona M	3:50:02 (6,951)
Maitland, Julie	4:28:56 (15,842)
Maitland, Wendy	4:26:28 (15,179)
Majgaard, Ann B	4:01:20 (9,486)
Majithia, Roshni	5:44:11 (31,063)
Major, Helen K	6:17:44 (33,769)
Majtanova, Miriam	5:02:58 (24,116)
Majumdar, Anita	4:58:59 (23,250)
Makin, Cheryl L	4:29:33 (16,028)
Makowska, Jolanta	3:39:10 (5,043)
Male, Ruth E	4:52:22 (21,589)
Malin, Frances C	3:27:52 (3,390)
Malin, Victoria	5:17:28 (26,951)
Malir, Sarah A	3:12:06 (1,740)
Malkinson, Caroline S	3:52:59 (7,564)
Mallen, Eloise K	6:08:04 (33,176)
Mallender, Jacqueline A	5:38:16 (30,350)
Mallery, Lynne	5:55:47 (32,217)
Mallett, Lean J	4:00:51 (9,386)
Mallett, Sally L	6:31:28 (34,382)
Mallorie, Charlotte J	3:25:07 (3,033)
Malone, Ann M	4:04:32 (10,062)
Malone, Paulette	4:59:06 (23,287)
Malone, Tania	4:59:46 (23,448)
Maloney, Barbara L	6:18:25 (33,800)
Maloney, Margaret M	3:40:11 (5,213)
Maloney, Shona M	4:50:12 (21,045)
Maltby, Bridget A	4:38:40 (18,188)
Maltby, Gemma L	5:33:59 (29,756)
Maltby, Hannah K	5:13:39 (26,150)
Maltby, Louise A	4:38:40 (18,188)
Maltby, Nicola J	5:54:22 (32,089)
Maltby, Sarah L	4:43:45 (19,471)
Malzburg, Regina	5:08:38 (25,213)
Mandelman, Mariah J	3:28:43 (3,527)
Manghi, Barbara	4:11:04 (11,390)
Manir-Jolley, Lynn H	4:17:54 (13,043)
Manley, Katherine	5:52:49 (31,951)
Manly, Rita	4:13:34 (11,986)
Mann, Amanda	4:26:41 (15,238)
Mann, Hilary J	6:05:03 (32,969)
Mann, Melanie A	4:04:15 (10,014)
Mann, Pauline J	5:36:02 (30,054)
Mann, Rosalind	4:02:29 (9,694)
Mann, Sharanjit K	6:01:33 (32,724)
Manning, Caroline	5:46:29 (31,309)
Manning, Jane M	4:14:03 (12,112)
Manning, Josephine	5:59:22 (32,542)
Manning, Karen S	3:58:27 (8,822)
Manning, Pamela	6:24:09 (34,086)
Manning, Stacy	4:45:34 (19,961)
Manning, Susan A	4:27:30 (15,469)
Mannion, Deirbhle	4:21:19 (13,914)
Mannoukas, Barbara A	5:53:20 (31,991)
Manouelides, Adeline	5:37:14 (30,203)
Manrique, Anne L	4:36:46 (17,737)
Mansbridge, Kaye	2:56:27 (629)
Mansbridge, Rebecca M	7:29:33 (35,490)
Mansfield, Frances S	5:03:24 (24,218)
Mansfield, Lynn S	3:57:15 (8,542)
Mansfield, Wendy E	5:42:31 (30,882)
Manson, Heather H	4:56:13 (22,570)
Mansourpour, Mandy M	5:16:44 (26,794)
Manthorpe, Hana J	4:37:05 (17,809)
Manthorpe, Jane	4:03:33 (9,878)
Mantle, Debbie	5:21:13 (27,637)
Mapala, Grace	6:47:08 (34,864)
Maples, Marion J	4:32:48 (16,740)
March, Katherine J	3:16:39 (2,138)
March, Shirley A	7:09:12 (35,263)
Marchant, Carmen L	3:25:44 (3,094)
Marchant, Christine	4:33:06 (16,810)
Marchant, Judy C	3:59:05 (8,981)
Marchant, Kate A	4:35:30 (17,401)
Marchant, Sarah M	5:46:11 (31,281)
Mardania, Nilam	5:34:16 (29,806)
Mardon, Philippa F	4:00:38 (9,342)
Maresca, Alessia	5:13:25 (26,106)
Margaillan, Helen J	3:45:21 (6,072)
Marietta, Anna	3:54:44 (7,949)
Maris, Alison	4:18:25 (13,181)
Mark, Carolyn	4:56:38 (22,672)
Markett, Lianne E	6:39:13 (34,647)
Markham, Hannah M	4:34:34 (17,166)
Markland, Kate	4:38:22 (18,117)
Marks, Adele	6:02:11 (32,761)
Marks, Erica L	6:13:11 (33,503)
Marks, Hayley M	6:26:38 (34,197)
Marks, Leander G	4:28:53 (15,828)
Markwick, Joanne	5:27:42 (28,744)
Marler, Janice	6:04:44 (32,936)
Marlow, Amanda E	4:45:38 (19,977)
Marrero-Blanco, Sheeyla	6:33:52 (34,462)
Marriage, Isabel M	4:28:56 (15,842)
Marriott, Catherine T	4:25:16 (14,889)
Marriott, Helen	4:12:36 (11,737)
Marriott, Katherine L	4:30:32 (16,261)
Marriott, Rosemary S	3:44:56 (6,017)
Marsden, Christine L	5:10:04 (25,495)
Marsden, Helen R	5:53:45 (32,031)
Marsden, Joanna G	3:20:31 (2,558)
Marsden, Lauren	3:57:25 (8,584)
Marsden-Jones, Catherine A	4:41:02 (18,797)
Marsh, Angela H	5:23:24 (27,990)
Marsh, Catherine A	4:48:33 (20,661)
Marsh, Clare J	5:30:54 (29,279)
Marsh, Clare L	5:39:27 (30,518)
Marsh, Glenda	5:03:48 (24,292)
Marsh, Sara E	4:27:41 (15,512)
Marsh, Susan	5:07:44 (25,042)
Marshall, Catriona F	4:10:38 (11,296)
Marshall, Cerri A	5:30:52 (29,274)
Marshall, Claire L	6:35:23 (34,518)
Marshall, Dawn	4:21:27 (13,952)
Marshall, Deborah	4:38:37 (18,181)
Marshall, Emma V	4:33:38 (16,944)
Marshall, Heather	4:14:50 (12,273)
Marshall, Jill	5:25:08 (28,292)
Marshall, Joanna	5:10:38 (25,604)
Marshall, Judith R	4:34:49 (17,225)
Marshall, Julia M	4:22:45 (14,272)
Marshall, Lia	3:44:14 (5,894)
Marshall, Lucy J	4:08:31 (10,877)
Marshall, Martine E	3:41:07 (5,384)
Marshall, Nina J	5:06:51 (24,854)
Marshall, Rebecca C	5:11:47 (25,808)
Marshall, Sarah E	5:03:38 (24,263)
Marshall, Sharon	5:15:06 (26,479)
Marshall, Sheila M	3:58:40 (8,877)
Martens, Hannah	4:59:47 (23,456)
Martin, Anna J	5:28:36 (28,918)
Martin, Anna K	4:29:43 (16,064)
Martin, Clare E	3:18:31 (2,345)
Martin, Deborah R	7:10:52 (35,284)
Martin, Elsie	5:52:42 (31,940)
Martin, Emma C	6:25:03 (34,124)
Martin, Frances G	5:35:19 (29,955)
Martin, Gillian P	6:12:26 (33,453)
Martin, Isobel	4:10:01 (11,171)
Martin, Jenny A	4:38:12 (18,058)
Martin, Joanne	4:13:07 (11,860)
Martin, Kathryn S	4:12:13 (11,662)
Martin, Katie G	5:16:49 (26,808)
Martin, Milly-May	4:35:10 (17,316)
Martin, Nicola L	4:54:53 (22,241)
Martin, Rebecca A	4:32:50 (16,748)
Martin, Rebecca L	4:54:56 (22,254)
Martin, Rosie L	5:22:25 (27,836)
Martin, Ruth	4:56:19 (22,590)
Martin, Samantha J	4:37:29 (17,889)

Martin, Sarah J	4:21:49 (14,036)	
Martin, Sarah L	6:31:53 (34,400)	
Martin, Stephanie	5:20:25 (27,497)	
Martin, Tracey A	4:09:20 (11,039)	
Martin, Victoria L	5:10:09 (25,517)	
Martin, Zoe K	3:54:25 (7,887)	
Martin, Zoe L	4:35:10 (17,316)	
Martindale, Jo C	5:14:08 (26,253)	
Martindale, Kate	3:43:28 (5,770)	
Martindale, Sandra	4:00:48 (9,372)	
Martinelli, Andrea M	4:35:51 (17,499)	
Martin-Elliston, Paulette A	6:45:54 (34,826)	
Martins, Marketa	4:27:12 (15,387)	
Martyn, Erica L	6:35:18 (34,512)	
Martyn, Maria C	5:33:41 (29,711)	
Maruyama, Chieko	5:40:47 (30,680)	
Marvel, Alison J	4:03:23 (9,846)	
Mascall, Jacqueline A	5:47:39 (31,422)	
Mascart, Deborah	5:22:45 (27,902)	
Masciulli, Arianna	4:02:32 (9,703)	
Mason, Alice	5:16:03 (26,672)	
Mason, Alison J	5:20:54 (27,587)	
Mason, Angharad E	3:39:30 (5,107)	
Mason, Carol J	6:50:03 (34,931)	
Mason, Claire L	5:39:25 (30,510)	
Mason, Dawn	4:51:32 (21,376)	
Mason, Denise	5:41:00 (30,708)	
Mason, Gayle A	4:50:58 (21,233)	
Mason, Helen C	4:37:56 (17,989)	
Mason, Joanna E	4:59:15 (23,327)	
Mason, Katie A	4:38:22 (18,117)	
Mason, Lindsay	5:53:57 (32,048)	
Mason, Natalie M	5:53:53 (32,042)	
Mason, Sarah J	6:05:31 (33,006)	
Mason, Soraua N	5:07:07 (24,912)	
Mason, Stephanie R	6:52:00 (34,974)	
Mason, Tracey L	6:52:48 (34,986)	
Mason, Wendy	7:26:51 (35,445)	
Massey, Beth F	3:15:56 (2,074)	
Massey, Kara J	3:34:16 (4,309)	
Massey, Nikki J	5:13:28 (26,116)	
Massey, Sarah A	5:46:30 (31,311)	
Massey, Theresa J	4:32:56 (16,771)	
Masson, Kim C	3:02:03 (1,006)	
Masson, Paula M	4:41:24 (18,889)	
Masterman, Julie	3:32:29 (4,065)	
Masters, Anne	5:08:00 (25,093)	
Masters, Jane A	4:39:12 (18,335)	
Mataria, Memuna	3:33:47 (4,236)	
Mateboer, Wimke	5:18:17 (27,117)	
Mathen, Lucy C	3:52:57 (7,554)	
Mather, Carol A	6:03:22 (32,842)	
Mather, Karen	6:30:23 (34,336)	
Mather, Samantha A	5:36:44 (30,137)	
Mathers, Denise	3:42:05 (5,534)	
Matheson, Michaela	5:07:39 (25,027)	
Matheson, Patricia E	3:52:01 (7,366)	
Mathias, Jayne L	5:25:06 (28,289)	
Mathias, Tanya	4:42:23 (19,146)	
Mathieson, Emma L	5:12:25 (25,942)	
Mathison, Camilla T	3:28:20 (3,454)	
Matkovich, Jenna K	4:45:06 (19,861)	
Matlib, Nahreen	6:51:17 (34,964)	
Matlock, Rosemary	4:59:28 (23,369)	
Matt, Esther R	3:39:27 (5,098)	
Mattey, Elayne M	4:50:18 (21,068)	
Matthee, Yvonne	5:17:46 (27,010)	
Matthew, Sarah J	5:36:53 (30,161)	
Matthews, Ann R	4:40:55 (18,768)	
Matthews, Claire M	4:25:16 (14,889)	
Matthews, Denise	3:55:25 (8,109)	
Matthews, Elizabeth G	4:05:57 (10,342)	
Matthews, Gail	5:16:37 (26,773)	
Matthews, Hayley V	6:04:47 (32,942)	
Matthews, Hazel L	5:13:05 (26,060)	
Matthews, Jeane H	6:13:30 (33,519)	
Matthews, Joanna L	6:26:25 (34,191)	
Matthews, Joanne	4:02:09 (9,630)	
Matthews, Letitia A	4:17:28 (12,932)	
Matthews, Nicola D	3:59:25 (9,073)	
Matthews, Nila	3:58:14 (8,772)	
Matthews, Rachel L	4:44:09 (19,579)	
Matthews, Sasha	4:44:15 (19,615)	
Matthews, Susan J	4:43:41 (19,459)	
Matthews, Susie J	5:13:31 (26,126)	
Mauchlen, Helene	5:06:16 (24,754)	
Maughan, Lynne	3:28:51 (3,547)	
Maughan, Natalie A	4:38:01 (18,015)	
Mauloni, Mandy L	4:39:37 (18,443)	
Maurice, Tory	4:11:52 (11,587)	
Mavromihales, Victoria L	4:36:41 (17,714)	
Maw, Anne	5:06:06 (24,712)	
Maw, Georgie H	4:50:16 (21,061)	
Mawdsley, Caroline M	5:12:49 (26,001)	
Mawdsley, Kelley S	4:39:59 (18,533)	
Mawer, Lisa M	3:00:30 (931)	
Mawhinney, Abigail C	6:21:12 (33,965)	
Mawson, Katie M	4:47:58 (20,525)	
Maxton, Pauline J	5:05:06 (24,527)	
Maxwell, Dawn	4:48:31 (20,651)	
Maxwell-Macdonald, Rebecca L	6:46:43 (34,849)	
May, Angela	6:26:01 (34,169)	
May, Hannah E	4:42:01 (19,043)	
May, Jackie J	5:06:02 (24,698)	
May, Jill	3:56:19 (8,307)	
May, Lucy J	6:09:00 (33,237)	
May, Penelope J	4:29:43 (16,064)	
May, Rebecca L	6:21:25 (33,977)	
Maybin, Jenny R	5:01:49 (23,894)	
Maycock, Fiona J	3:39:24 (5,087)	
Mayer, Lucy	3:41:39 (5,463)	
Mayers, Nicola L	4:02:05 (9,617)	
Mayes, Laura E	5:10:01 (25,486)	
Maynard, Jean A	7:13:07 (35,325)	
Maynard, Rebecca L	5:41:21 (30,748)	
Mayne, Nicola L	3:47:02 (6,352)	
Mayne, Victoria J	4:37:29 (17,889)	
Maythay, Kathryn F	5:15:02 (26,464)	
Mazdon, Lucy E	5:04:05 (24,340)	
Mazey, Katharine	4:25:12 (14,875)	
Maziere, Angela M	3:59:40 (9,131)	
Mazur, Jacqui A	5:39:06 (30,463)	
Mazza, Lucia	5:10:56 (25,654)	
McAdam, Nicola J	3:57:37 (8,629)	
McAfee, Alison E	5:27:24 (28,697)	
McAlindon, Antonia E	5:23:18 (27,976)	
McAllister, Clodagh M	5:04:53 (24,496)	
McAllister, Fiona R	5:01:15 (23,785)	
McAllister, Joanne L	6:21:23 (33,975)	
McAndrew, Claire M	4:58:46 (23,198)	
McAndrew, Nancy	5:35:44 (30,016)	
McAndrew, Nell	5:35:43 (30,013)	
McArthur, Erica	4:12:35 (11,734)	
McArthur, Lucie-Jane	3:52:03 (7,378)	
McAteer, Pippa J	5:41:32 (30,774)	
McBeth, Maria T	5:05:54 (24,679)	
McBlane, Kate E	4:41:57 (19,028)	
McBride, Margaret A	3:59:10 (9,003)	
McBrien, Kate M	4:35:19 (17,363)	
McCabe, Emma J	4:22:16 (14,142)	
McCabe, Jane	6:35:23 (34,518)	
McCabe, Julia A	6:53:33 (35,008)	
McCabe, Maureen A	6:11:39 (33,407)	
McCabe, Rosalind L	4:55:59 (22,508)	
McCafferty, Garry D	4:27:17 (15,416)	
McCaffrey, Annika B	6:34:29 (34,473)	
McCall, Julie	4:18:33 (13,228)	
McCall, Kerry	4:23:39 (14,477)	
McCallion, Carmel	7:27:06 (35,449)	
McCallum, Carolanne	4:58:33 (23,159)	
McCann, Elaine L	4:54:35 (22,168)	
McCarney, Maureen	4:24:11 (14,627)	
McCarron, Louise P	6:38:56 (34,634)	
McCarthy, Christine	3:08:10 (1,403)	
McCarthy, Dee M	4:21:14 (13,901)	
McCarthy, Hilary A	4:11:25 (11,478)	
McCarthy, Jane	4:43:15 (19,355)	
McCarthy, Lisa	5:11:48 (25,813)	
McCarthy, Mary	4:15:18 (12,395)	
McCarthy, Sarah A	3:36:08 (4,562)	
McCarthy, Su	4:01:07 (9,439)	
McCarthy, Victoria	4:49:30 (20,889)	
McCartney, Abigail	3:26:31 (3,198)	
McCartney, Joyce	5:16:00 (26,662)	
McCauley, Katherine M	4:29:56 (16,128)	
McCauley, Treena	5:02:21 (24,001)	
McCayna, Debbie S	5:16:11 (26,697)	
McClary, Samantha A	3:58:43 (8,887)	
McCluskie, Caroline E	4:00:56 (9,405)	
McCole, Selina I	3:42:11 (5,549)	
McColgan, Liz	2:50:38 (399)	
McComb, Christina	4:42:18 (19,123)	
McComb, Elaine E	4:50:54 (21,217)	
McComb, Tessa G	4:40:15 (18,589)	
McConnachie, Caroline	4:28:02 (15,602)	
McConnell, Anita R	5:00:15 (23,563)	
McConville, Tracy E	6:55:50 (35,052)	
McCormack, Caren M	5:35:54 (30,038)	
McCormack, Cerys S	6:05:16 (32,981)	
McCormack, Elaine A	6:12:58 (33,489)	
McCormack, Georgina L	5:47:16 (31,378)	
McCormick, Sheree A	4:07:29 (10,647)	
McCourt, Maureen F	5:00:50 (23,693)	
McCracken, Morag	3:30:58 (3,836)	
McCreedy, Claire E	3:25:50 (3,103)	
McCrow, Kathleen L	4:44:34 (19,705)	
McCullagh, Valerie	5:52:05 (31,878)	
McCulley, Brenda	5:32:02 (29,463)	
McCulloch, Ellyn S	5:00:18 (23,575)	
McCulloch, Susan	6:02:54 (32,815)	
McDermott, Claire	5:00:13 (23,557)	
McDermott, Karen E	4:26:21 (15,146)	
McDermott, Patricia M	7:22:51 (35,413)	
McDonagh, Nicki A	4:27:17 (15,416)	
McDonald, Claire	4:17:24 (12,908)	
McDonald, Harriet S	4:43:53 (19,505)	
McDonald, Jacqui	4:04:50 (10,120)	
McDonald, Kristal	3:45:04 (6,033)	
McDonald, Nakia G	5:44:54 (31,139)	
McDonald, Susan	3:06:09 (1,242)	
McDonald-Hamilton, Heather	4:44:44 (19,753)	
McDonnell, Caroline	4:53:54 (21,991)	
McDonnell, Claire F	3:59:55 (9,188)	
McDonnell, Karen D	5:10:04 (25,495)	
McDonough, Annie	3:29:42 (3,675)	
McDougall, Fiona	4:17:52 (13,034)	
McDowall, Sarah J	4:02:24 (9,682)	
McDowell, Eileen	7:19:57 (35,386)	
McElhinney, Siobhan	4:13:22 (11,926)	
McEniery, Carmel M	3:56:17 (8,297)	
McEntee, Kelly	5:22:04 (27,789)	
McEwan, Paula J	6:13:19 (33,509)	
McFadden, Florence	6:21:02 (33,953)	
McFadden, Frances	3:36:35 (4,625)	
McFadden, Miriam A	3:58:01 (8,728)	
McFadyen, Rachael	4:21:53 (14,060)	
McFall, Josie	6:56:06 (35,054)	
McFarlane, Isabel	5:45:25 (31,194)	
McFarlane, Jessica M	5:26:27 (28,539)	
McGall, Ashleigh C	5:24:43 (28,222)	
McGann, Geraldine M	4:35:32 (17,410)	
McGarry, Yvonne C	3:26:17 (3,172)	
McGeachie, Gemma	4:38:19 (18,101)	
McGee, Tamala L	5:03:01 (24,129)	
McGeehan, Oliver	3:13:17 (1,851)	
McGeorge, Julie	4:21:48 (14,033)	
McGivern, Pauline M	4:56:10 (22,555)	
McGonigle, Emma	5:21:01 (27,605)	
McGowan, Christine H	6:23:30 (34,055)	
McGowan, Lindsay J	4:10:47 (11,324)	
McGrath, Elizabeth	6:35:08 (34,505)	
McGrath, Erin	5:29:00 (28,984)	
McGrath, Jacqueline C	4:46:59 (20,274)	
McGrath, Maria J	5:17:04 (26,871)	
McGreevy, Adele M	3:43:33 (5,792)	
McGregor, Helena	7:10:52 (35,284)	
McGregor-Macdonald, Athene	4:21:45 (14,019)	
McGuffin, Madeleine J	5:22:08 (27,800)	
McGuigan, Elizabeth	5:48:00 (31,466)	
McGuire, Christina M	4:17:48 (13,023)	
McGuire, Clare A	5:14:06 (26,247)	
McGuire, Donna M	4:50:47 (21,189)	
McGuire, Mary C	6:07:24 (33,123)	
McGuire, Sharon	3:30:25 (3,779)	
McHard, Liz	5:13:25 (26,106)	
McHardy, Susan E	5:20:22 (27,488)	
McHugh, Sharon	3:40:23 (5,247)	
McIlroy, Sara A	4:38:26 (18,134)	
McInnes, Caroline	4:57:00 (22,772)	

McIntosh, Francesca K 6:20:52 (33,944)
McIntosh, Heather M 5:02:00 (23,934)
McIntosh, Shona 2:54:04 (521)
McIntyre, Jane M 6:19:50 (33,882)
McKain, Kathryn L 5:38:07 (30,319)
McKain, Shirley G 5:38:07 (30,319)
McKay, Joanne K 4:13:00 (11,827)
McKay, Kirsty E 5:21:48 (27,756)
McKay, Val E 4:06:28 (10,458)
McKeand, Sadie A 4:40:28 (18,644)
McKechnie, Marie L 5:01:36 (23,854)
McKee, Elaine 5:42:41 (30,892)
McKee, Natalie A 4:35:35 (17,427)
McKenna, Angela 4:35:05 (17,291)
McKenna, Bronwyn 6:30:55 (34,360)
McKenna, Charlotte J 4:09:43 (11,119)
McKenna, Gillian 4:26:26 (15,170)
McKenna, Sara L 5:17:58 (27,049)
McKenzie, Clare 3:47:59 (6,522)
McKenzie, Frances 6:24:26 (34,096)
McKenzie, Jill 4:53:23 (21,854)
McKenzie, Nicola L 5:16:00 (26,662)
McKeown, Sarah 4:39:02 (18,293)
McKernan, Brenda 4:24:49 (14,785)
McKernan, Phyllis 6:57:07 (35,075)
McKernan, Steven J 6:45:19 (34,805)
McKevitt, Una F 4:56:15 (22,577)
McKibbin, Julie 4:34:25 (17,118)
McKinney, Emma L 5:14:49 (26,410)
McKinnon, Amanda J 5:07:52 (25,072)
McKinnon, Kate M 3:31:17 (3,876)
McKirdy, Nicola S 5:16:49 (26,808)
McKnight, Rebecca H 5:40:44 (30,675)
McLafferty, Margaret 5:29:13 (29,027)
McLaren, Anne-Marie 5:05:18 (24,557)
McLaren, Valerie J 4:51:59 (21,483)
McLaughlin, Alison M 4:40:21 (18,618)
McLaughlin, Jane 5:37:30 (30,235)
McLaughlin, Alison E 6:12:07 (33,434)
McLean, Anna J 5:33:36 (29,703)
McLean, Rebecca L 3:42:42 (5,627)
McLellan, Gillian 5:43:37 (31,003)
McLeman, Jane L 4:11:59 (11,608)
McLeod, Jacqueline 5:58:46 (32,489)
McLoughlin, Rebecca M 3:46:56 (6,332)
McMahon, Kathy M 5:27:50 (28,767)
McMahon, Lora J 5:29:32 (29,074)
McMahon, Theresa A 4:43:36 (19,440)
McManus, Gabrielle F 6:01:33 (32,724)
McManus, Vivienne L 4:43:03 (19,306)
McMaster, Jill 4:26:49 (15,270)
McMaster, Katharine J 6:21:17 (33,967)
McMaster, Rachel 5:35:59 (30,046)
McMeekin, Karen C 5:38:36 (30,398)
McMichael, Laine 4:27:50 (15,552)
McMillen, Barbara A 5:43:10 (30,957)
McMorran, Melissa J 5:09:40 (25,407)
McMullin, Rebecca 4:43:24 (19,400)
McMurtrie, May J 6:14:29 (33,577)
McMurtrie, Valerie M 6:14:29 (33,577)
McNair, Helen-Marie 5:23:44 (28,059)
McNally, Caroline J 4:23:15 (14,388)
McNally, Sharon L 3:47:25 (6,413)
McNamara, Catherine J 4:21:04 (13,864)
McNamara, Sarah L 6:55:05 (35,038)
McNamee, Louise 5:19:30 (27,337)
McNay, Jane 4:50:06 (21,023)
McNeil, Brenda 7:00:10 (35,126)
McNeill, Sandra I 5:43:12 (30,961)
McNicol, Georgia S 3:26:52 (3,251)
McNicol, Rebekah A 5:17:35 (26,976)
McNiff, Mary A 5:45:02 (31,157)
McNulty, Lucy J 4:27:43 (15,524)
McPartlan, Ruth A 4:38:42 (18,201)
McPartland, Katie M 4:55:23 (22,361)
McQuade, Colette 4:59:02 (23,264)
McQuaid, Victoria K 4:46:08 (20,090)
McQuoid, Claire S 6:28:23 (34,262)
McRory, Helen M 4:55:59 (22,508)
McRow, Rebecca J 5:52:23 (31,909)
McWilliam, Kate H 4:22:43 (14,264)
McWilliams, Jo K 3:59:08 (8,992)
McWilliams, Rosalind C 5:43:08 (30,952)
McWilliams, Sarah C 4:44:40 (19,734)
Mead, Nell K 5:16:19 (26,724)
Meade, Ruselle K 6:09:51 (33,295)
Meade, Sarah L 4:30:07 (16,177)
Meaning, Tracey J 5:15:30 (26,563)
Mearing-Smith, Cecilia T 4:21:26 (13,947)
Mears, Hazel L 3:53:49 (7,746)
Medcalf, Louise 3:49:03 (6,743)
Medhurst, Kate L 6:33:46 (34,457)
Meek, Catherine 6:13:01 (33,492)
Meek-Welsh, Beverley 4:48:53 (20,740)
Meer, Anna E 6:16:11 (33,695)
Meeran, Deirdre 6:15:53 (33,675)
Mehnert, Uschi 5:45:53 (31,244)
Mehraban, Ziba 5:40:23 (30,638)
Mehta, Neena 6:02:45 (32,802)
Mehta, Tina 6:40:58 (34,689)
Meier, Sonja S 3:56:36 (8,381)
Meikle, Geraldine M 6:01:34 (32,726)
Meiklejohn, Janice G 5:30:51 (29,270)
Melia, Linda 4:38:18 (18,093)
Meller, Eira 4:52:03 (21,499)
Melling, Alexia 4:56:03 (22,526)
Mellin-Olsen, Jannicke 3:45:53 (6,161)
Mellows, Katie E 4:28:45 (15,799)
Melmoe, Victoria A 5:32:02 (29,463)
Melville, Christine 5:53:26 (31,998)
Melville, Susan M 7:33:45 (35,524)
Melvin, Anna L 4:06:41 (10,497)
Melvin, Helen M 4:15:11 (12,367)
Mendes, Telma M 4:19:39 (13,494)
Mendoza, Lisa 4:46:30 (20,178)
Mengin, Marianne 5:41:43 (30,798)
Mennell, Sarah 4:11:12 (11,427)
Menzies, Issy 2:56:04 (614)
Mercado Torres, Yolanda 2:44:58 (240)
Mercer, Laura J 6:13:07 (33,496)
Mercer, Marrianne L 4:52:48 (21,700)
Mercer, Rachel 5:24:50 (28,243)
Mercer, Ruth J 4:04:27 (10,049)
Mercer-Leach, Lisa A 5:13:44 (26,174)
Mercer-Rees, Alixandra E 5:15:52 (26,634)
Merchant, Sarah J 5:21:34 (27,705)
Mercken, Yvette 3:39:37 (5,131)
Mercy, Jane E 5:20:34 (27,534)
Meredith, Jean 5:34:02 (29,771)
Meredith, Julie 5:03:47 (24,288)
Merkin, Eleanor K 4:59:38 (23,419)
Mermet, Nicole M 5:06:10 (24,729)
Merriman, Claire L 4:02:38 (9,718)
Merryweather, Marilyn 5:19:04 (27,259)
Mesher, Clare M 6:44:32 (34,790)
Messenger, Claire E 3:30:11 (3,746)
Metcalf, Julia 5:45:26 (31,195)
Metcalf, Kate E 4:41:02 (18,797)
Metcalf, Tracey 4:06:57 (10,558)
Metcalf, Valerie M 3:20:00 (2,497)
Metcalfe, Claire T 5:02:32 (24,048)
Metcalfe, Margaret R 4:17:28 (12,932)
Mew, Maureen Z 4:52:38 (21,655)
Mewis, Jenny J 6:06:02 (33,053)
Meyer, Sheryl K 5:22:22 (27,829)
Mian, Ameera 5:48:58 (31,580)
Michaelides, Clare L 7:19:52 (35,385)
Michael-Ives, Adrienne A 5:36:52 (30,159)
Michau, Samantha D 4:13:23 (11,933)
Michel, Debbie 4:48:28 (20,642)
Michelitsch, Verema B 6:39:33 (34,658)
Michie, Annabel N 4:41:25 (18,896)
Mickleburgh, Joy L 6:41:57 (34,715)
Middle, Georgina S 3:53:42 (7,728)
Middleburgh, Lorraine 6:11:57 (33,422)
Middleton, Angela D 5:29:27 (29,065)
Middleton, Julie A 4:33:43 (16,970)
Middleton, Margaret M 4:54:34 (22,158)
Middleton, Marion R 4:19:35 (13,479)
Middleton, Susannah J 4:52:15 (21,556)
Middleton Pink, Amy J 5:34:11 (29,791)
Middleton-Hockin, Caroline J 4:53:30 (21,885)
Middleweek, Lucy M 4:48:57 (20,754)
Midgley, Nicola 3:57:43 (8,657)
Midgley, Sandra 4:30:25 (16,237)
Midwood, Wyn V 6:05:33 (33,012)
Mieczakowski, Anna 5:23:46 (28,071)
Miell-Ingram, Wendy K 3:31:51 (3,963)
Mihaylova, Milka 2:44:35 (228)
Mikhael, Joanna R 4:50:20 (21,075)
Milani, Bianca 4:46:59 (20,274)
Milatova, Lucia 5:55:26 (32,187)
Milbourn, Helen F 5:24:14 (28,147)
Milburn, Sophie A 3:39:02 (5,023)
Milelr, Francesca 4:43:17 (19,367)
Miles, Beverly J 4:16:12 (12,621)
Miles, Chloe E 4:28:23 (15,695)
Miles, Emma L 5:47:38 (31,420)
Miles, Helen 3:55:27 (8,113)
Miles, Holly 4:59:35 (23,407)
Miles, Jenny 5:56:46 (32,316)
Miles, Victoria R 4:54:45 (22,212)
Miles-Young, Sarah 4:49:06 (20,796)
Millane, Aine 5:41:48 (30,809)
Millar, Gillian M 3:39:58 (5,183)
Millar, Hilary 3:21:27 (2,644)
Millar, Jen 4:53:21 (21,848)
Millard, Helena M 4:49:07 (20,798)
Miller, Amy J 5:17:36 (26,980)
Miller, Carol A 3:51:07 (7,161)
Miller, Caroline L 3:39:52 (5,171)
Miller, Christine 5:24:29 (28,181)
Miller, Claire L 5:01:03 (23,739)
Miller, Debbie J 5:23:47 (28,075)
Miller, Guy J 5:48:06 (31,479)
Miller, Irene J 4:01:05 (9,434)
Miller, Jayne E 5:38:06 (30,318)
Miller, Laura J 4:34:53 (17,244)
Miller, Mary 5:17:59 (27,052)
Miller, Nicola J 5:10:55 (25,648)
Miller, Sarahamanda L 5:49:33 (31,633)
Miller, Stephanie J 3:57:24 (8,581)
Miller, Tracey 4:52:21 (21,583)
Miller-Bakewell, Julia J 5:42:55 (30,924)
Millership, Julie 5:43:17 (30,969)
Milligan, Felicity A 5:32:33 (29,542)
Milligan, Jessica E 4:14:23 (12,183)
Millman, Natalie L 4:27:55 (15,563)
Mills, Ann P 4:59:04 (23,277)
Mills, Caroline A 4:36:17 (17,606)
Mills, Claire 5:20:21 (27,485)
Mills, Deborah A 5:38:05 (30,317)
Mills, Diana H 3:43:22 (5,749)
Mills, Esther 5:34:28 (29,843)
Mills, Francesca L 5:35:36 (29,996)
Mills, Georgina E 6:06:20 (33,069)
Mills, Julia A 4:09:08 (10,986)
Mills, Lorraine 4:38:36 (18,177)
Mills, Patsy A 5:33:33 (29,696)
Mills, Sarah J 5:17:32 (26,964)
Mills, Yvonne P 5:06:37 (24,801)
Millson, Carrie H 3:11:25 (1,664)
Millward, Holly C 4:01:39 (9,543)
Milne, Juliet N 4:50:11 (21,042)
Milne, Sandra J 3:49:24 (6,808)
Milne, Sarah E 4:05:16 (10,197)
Milne, Sarah E 4:46:59 (20,274)
Milner, Lisa M 7:02:06 (35,160)
Milsom, Elizabeth V 4:34:32 (17,156)
Mimpress, Chloe A 6:39:39 (34,663)
Mingay, Karen 5:09:55 (25,453)
Minshall, Patricia D 6:13:01 (33,492)
Minter, Lisa H 6:14:59 (33,613)
Mischka, Rita 7:03:26 (35,182)
Missions, Alice C 3:51:27 (7,243)
Mistri, Reena 6:08:04 (33,176)
Mitcham, Tarida J 5:15:03 (26,472)
Mitchell, Alison A 6:01:01 (32,675)
Mitchell, Amanda J 5:02:57 (24,114)
Mitchell, Avril C 5:27:25 (28,699)
Mitchell, Christine 4:53:51 (21,977)
Mitchell, Elizabeth C 5:10:31 (25,580)
Mitchell, Elizabeth R 4:34:23 (17,111)
Mitchell, Emma V 4:34:04 (17,043)
Mitchell, Esther J 5:38:04 (30,312)
Mitchell, Gill 5:30:00 (29,137)
Mitchell, Heather M 4:24:14 (14,638)
Mitchell, Jackie A 5:26:38 (28,560)
Mitchell, Karen 5:02:29 (24,033)

Mitchell, Kate 5:24:03 (28,114)
Mitchell, Katherine 4:02:46 (9,745)
Mitchell, Kathryn E 6:01:02 (32,679)
Mitchell, Kathryn L 6:21:05 (33,959)
Mitchell, Katie A 5:11:00 (25,665)
Mitchell, Kim 4:50:04 (21,016)
Mitchell, Laura J 5:02:46 (24,087)
Mitchell, Lauren J 4:18:25 (13,181)
Mitchell, Lindsey J 4:57:44 (22,966)
Mitchell, Lisa 4:35:37 (17,434)
Mitchell, Samantha E 4:42:47 (19,251)
Mitchell, Sarah A 4:00:04 (9,221)
Mitchell, Tracy 3:25:48 (3,100)
Mitchell, Tracy L 4:59:47 (23,456)
Mitchinson, Kirsten A 5:14:29 (26,330)
Mitham, Lisa S 4:04:34 (10,071)
Mitra, Meena 4:51:53 (21,463)
Mitterle, Antje 4:28:24 (15,703)
Miura, Shizuko 5:14:50 (26,415)
Mizen, Angela 5:45:09 (31,172)
Moate, Sabra 4:57:46 (22,973)
Mobbs, Justine G 5:26:39 (28,566)
Mocatta, Stephanie C 4:37:38 (17,918)
Moden, Diane 6:53:29 (35,006)
Moffat, Cheryl L 4:01:15 (9,470)
Moffat, Rosie A 5:26:25 (28,534)
Moffatt, Fiona H 3:35:07 (4,425)
Moffatt, Hannah L 5:37:22 (30,227)
Moffatt, Tarryn L 4:10:11 (11,201)
Mogensen, Karin 4:44:53 (19,803)
Mogg, Lisa J 4:23:27 (14,432)
Moggan, Adele J 5:24:54 (28,261)
Mogridge, Katy 4:57:20 (22,870)
Mogridge, Tracey A 7:03:31 (35,183)
Mohan, Ann-Marie 4:30:14 (16,202)
Mohan, Grainne B 5:02:13 (23,971)
Moir, Karen 4:35:54 (17,515)
Moir, Laura A 4:10:30 (11,268)
Moisander, Jennifer L 4:21:36 (13,985)
Mole, Patricia L 4:46:11 (20,104)
Moller, Margot 5:48:15 (31,498)
Molloy, Stephanie 4:23:59 (14,566)
Moloney, Jennifer M 3:29:56 (3,707)
Molyneaux, Jo 3:38:14 (4,873)
Molyneux, Nadia 5:36:18 (30,082)
Monaghan, Cherie M 5:03:58 (24,318)
Monaghan, Joanna 5:59:58 (32,570)
Monahan, Sian E 2:56:28 (631)
Monk, Caroline A 4:40:32 (18,662)
Monk, Samantha L 4:26:58 (15,314)
Monks, Kay 6:27:55 (34,249)
Monks, Nicola E 5:41:47 (30,807)
Monks, Patricia 3:39:23 (5,082)
Montague, Eleanor 4:55:59 (22,508)
Montgomery, Maggie C 9:14:23 (35,696)
Monti, Kim E 4:52:45 (21,681)
Moodie, Clemmie 3:49:48 (6,897)
Moodie, Lynne M 4:15:58 (12,551)
Moodie, Rachel L 4:17:42 (12,996)
Moodien, Esme 4:28:25 (15,707)
Moody, Alison J 4:29:10 (15,900)
Moody, Dawn K 4:19:30 (13,460)
Moody, Laura K 5:32:16 (29,492)
Moody, Patricia M 4:29:23 (15,971)
Moody, Shilo A 4:48:09 (20,563)
Mooney, Catrina 4:10:55 (11,352)
Mooney, Nicholle C 4:17:34 (12,969)
Mooney, Rosemary 5:16:49 (26,808)
Moorcroft, Tiffany A 3:57:17 (8,549)
Moore, Anne M 5:56:13 (32,258)
Moore, Astrid 6:15:00 (33,614)
Moore, Catherine A 6:20:12 (33,896)
Moore, Elizabeth A 5:07:46 (25,052)
Moore, Georgina 4:21:46 (14,025)
Moore, Jacey E 5:39:21 (30,499)
Moore, Jennifer 3:00:03 (903)
Moore, Julie E 4:48:56 (20,752)
Moore, Katie L 5:44:09 (31,062)
Moore, Kirsty H 4:10:36 (11,287)
Moore, Kristina M 4:51:18 (21,315)
Moore, Louise A 5:11:48 (25,813)
Moore, Lucinda 4:02:51 (9,760)
Moore, Lyndsey L 3:49:11 (6,767)
Moore, Nancy 4:22:36 (14,230)
Moore, Nicola 3:51:25 (7,231)
Moore, Rachel A 5:35:29 (29,972)
Moore, Rosalind S 4:38:36 (18,177)
Moore, Tracy A 8:09:51 (35,658)
Moore Fitzgerald, Lindsey 4:35:14 (17,343)
Moores, Helen L 4:53:30 (21,885)
Moores, Laura 5:54:13 (32,070)
Moores, Sarah E 3:38:56 (5,002)
Moorman, Annette 5:02:49 (24,089)
Moralejo, Gabriela 4:59:24 (23,352)
Morales, Nora 4:09:12 (11,007)
Morales, Sarah E 4:10:43 (11,316)
Moran, Rebecca J 4:41:48 (18,995)
Moran, Stella A 6:20:21 (33,911)
Mordecai, Jeannie C 5:04:42 (24,448)
Morden, Emily 7:18:45 (35,379)
Moreau, Linda R 3:36:38 (4,632)
Moreau, Nathalie C 3:11:25 (1,664)
More-Molyneux, Sarah 6:30:03 (34,328)
Moreton, Claire N 4:36:59 (17,783)
Moreton, Jennifer H 6:40:27 (34,677)
Morgan, Alison E 3:21:36 (2,660)
Morgan, Amanda 4:06:14 (10,399)
Morgan, Andrea C 6:11:50 (33,415)
Morgan, Carole A 4:04:09 (9,994)
Morgan, Christine G 4:53:53 (21,985)
Morgan, Christine H 5:52:17 (31,900)
Morgan, Diana H 4:26:38 (15,218)
Morgan, Gemma 4:30:34 (16,274)
Morgan, Helen 5:38:38 (30,402)
Morgan, Jayne A 4:20:02 (13,606)
Morgan, Julia 7:50:29 (35,620)
Morgan, Julie 5:04:48 (24,467)
Morgan, Karen A 4:52:18 (21,568)
Morgan, Kay E 6:20:15 (33,901)
Morgan, Kelly 3:26:23 (3,184)
Morgan, Lesley P 5:52:05 (31,878)
Morgan, Lon 4:13:31 (11,969)
Morgan, Lynette C 6:32:00 (34,408)
Morgan, Sarah A 4:59:41 (23,427)
Morgan, Sonia J 4:47:26 (20,389)
Morgan, Susan E 5:03:01 (24,129)
Morgan, Trish A 4:47:18 (20,359)
Morgan, Valerie 5:48:25 (31,519)
Morgans, Claire L 4:32:03 (16,569)
Morgans, Natalie C 6:24:16 (34,092)
Mori, Kate 4:34:21 (17,104)
Morison, Isabel A 4:22:47 (14,281)
Morley, Angela D 4:14:50 (12,273)
Morley, Catherine L 5:13:47 (26,186)
Morley, Christine E 6:11:16 (33,388)
Morley, Emma J 4:09:22 (11,044)
Morley, Jayne L 5:48:43 (31,554)
Morris, Carole 3:54:09 (7,829)
Morris, Carole E 5:19:28 (27,330)
Morris, Cheryl C 6:11:30 (33,400)
Morris, Christiane M 5:11:57 (25,846)
Morris, Claire L 3:59:27 (9,083)
Morris, Colette M 5:07:42 (25,033)
Morris, Colette M 5:18:39 (27,189)
Morris, Elaine L 7:11:07 (35,290)
Morris, Elizabeth R 5:41:45 (30,804)
Morris, Gemma L 5:12:12 (25,897)
Morris, Janet R 5:46:34 (31,317)
Morris, Jen C 5:37:38 (30,252)
Morris, June 5:16:54 (26,840)
Morris, Karen 5:25:42 (28,406)
Morris, Karen A 5:25:42 (28,406)
Morris, Karen L 4:00:43 (9,360)
Morris, Kirsten A 5:48:39 (31,539)
Morris, Linda S 4:14:11 (12,134)
Morris, Margaret A 3:59:18 (9,043)
Morris, Phillippa L 3:09:12 (1,490)
Morris, Sarah A 4:22:08 (14,112)

LONDON MARATHON

Morris, Ursula M 4:17:08 (12,837)
Morrison, Amy E 4:34:36 (17,177)
Morrison, Cecilia A 4:11:03 (11,383)
Morrison, Lindsay 5:00:43 (23,664)
Morrison, Moira L 5:07:35 (25,017)
Morrissey, Julie A 4:55:50 (22,468)
Morrow, Cathie R 4:58:11 (23,070)
Morse, Julia E 4:51:49 (21,440)
Mort, Helen R 3:25:47 (3,099)
Mort, Samantha 6:08:14 (33,189)
Mortensen, Rikke 6:51:44 (34,972)
Mortimer, Ceri E 5:00:41 (23,652)
Mortimer, Hilary J 5:33:45 (29,722)
Mortimer, Julie 4:55:33 (22,404)
Mortimer-Ford, Zoe L 4:57:16 (22,839)
Mortlock, Brenda D 5:33:35 (29,700)
Morton, Alison J 4:55:59 (22,508)
Morton, Frances 5:58:09 (32,428)
Morton, Jacqueline A 3:36:04 (4,552)
Morton, Joanna L 5:03:18 (24,191)
Morton, Lisa 5:04:27 (24,411)
Morton, Lisa C 5:01:02 (23,736)
Morton, Lorna J 4:53:15 (21,825)
Morton, Lydia P 5:53:00 (31,962)
Morton, Meredith G 4:30:47 (16,313)
Moruzzi, Christine A 3:56:04 (8,240)
Mosedale, Emily A 4:47:09 (20,322)
Moseley, Alexandra R 6:45:48 (34,820)
Moseley, Elizabeth J 4:22:45 (14,272)
Moses, Joanna 5:19:10 (27,283)
Mosley, Helen G 5:54:55 (32,142)
Moss, Gwen M 5:26:24 (28,531)
Moss, Jennifer A 4:24:07 (14,603)
Moss, Linda J 5:42:15 (30,857)
Mossman, Bernadette 4:11:34 (11,512)
Mostert, Natalie N 4:20:55 (13,833)
Mostyn, Shelley J 6:15:21 (33,637)
Motoi, Tomi E 4:29:31 (16,013)
Motson, Sarah E 5:35:12 (29,940)
Mottier, Raymonde 4:40:27 (18,640)
Mottley, Bev A 5:00:09 (23,535)
Mottram, Elizabeth C 6:27:13 (34,222)
Mould, Frances J 6:10:03 (33,309)
Mould, Toni-Jayne 6:13:34 (33,527)
Moulden, Adeline 4:37:03 (17,796)
Moullin, Alison M 7:25:28 (35,434)
Mounsey, Philippa H 4:16:51 (12,772)
Mount, Felicity J 5:32:11 (29,480)
Mountain, Claire E 4:28:32 (15,738)
Mountain, Helen R 4:42:54 (19,281)
Mountain, Janine 5:36:37 (30,127)
Mounteney, Helen 4:41:28 (18,910)
Mountford, Sarah E 6:00:19 (32,607)
Mountfort, Helen J 4:12:22 (11,693)
Mourelle, Cristina 5:28:09 (28,828)
Mowat, Nicky 3:38:52 (4,992)
Mowbray, Elizabeth M 5:10:59 (25,662)
Mowlam, Bethany J 5:33:25 (29,667)
Mowles, Rebecca L 5:39:38 (30,549)
Moxey, Alison T 4:34:57 (17,257)
Moyle, Avril J 4:36:52 (17,758)
Moyler, Joanne K 4:42:42 (19,230)
Moyse, Catherine S 4:36:20 (17,621)
Moyse, Tracy O 4:38:00 (18,011)
Muckle, Jessica C 5:08:36 (25,205)
Muenzer, Ursula 4:17:34 (12,969)
Mugford, Nicola T 5:21:47 (27,751)
Muino, Stacey V 5:35:46 (30,018)
Muir, Julie Ann 4:50:08 (21,030)
Muir, Shelagh R 4:02:29 (9,694)
Muirhead, Elaine 4:07:59 (10,764)
Mulcahy, Pauline V 6:09:32 (33,275)
Mulhall, Helen J 3:20:09 (2,512)
Mulhern, Lisa M 5:34:02 (29,771)
Mulholland, Karen 5:04:24 (24,403)
Mulholland, Sharon L 6:02:12 (32,766)
Mullan, Lucia M 5:01:00 (23,725)
Mullenger, Clare 3:31:34 (3,919)
Muller, Nicola A 5:27:41 (28,739)
Mulley, Rebecca J 4:29:00 (15,856)
Mulley, Sarah 6:50:46 (34,952)
Mulligan, Samantha 3:57:25 (8,584)
Mullineux, Nikki 5:17:54 (27,031)

Mullins, Karen A	4:05:42 (10,291)
Mullins, Monica	5:17:04 (26,871)
Mullins, Nicola	5:17:00 (26,858)
Mulraine-Simkin, Rebecca J	4:48:20 (20,620)
Mumbray, Nicola	5:03:46 (24,284)
Mumford, Jane A	4:40:14 (18,585)
Mumford, Joanne L	3:21:12 (2,626)
Munday, Kay M	5:33:30 (29,682)
Munday, Mandy	5:47:19 (31,392)
Munday, Sarah L	4:15:15 (12,376)
Mundy, Suzanne J	5:08:28 (25,182)
Munn, Flavia	4:09:24 (11,048)
Munro, Patricia A	3:30:00 (3,719)
Munro, Sarah J	6:22:01 (33,995)
Munroe, Jo	4:56:08 (22,543)
Munroe, Lynsey	3:41:37 (5,458)
Munrow, Julia J	5:28:28 (28,896)
Munton, Karen A	5:09:10 (25,306)
Muraro, Paola	5:40:04 (30,601)
Murchie, Shonagh	5:19:16 (27,306)
Murdock, Adele	4:15:08 (12,351)
Murfitt, Sarah E	3:55:39 (8,150)
Murphy, Amber K	4:10:03 (11,176)
Murphy, Carol A	4:36:10 (17,572)
Murphy, Clodagh M	5:39:58 (30,584)
Murphy, Eimear	4:21:17 (13,909)
Murphy, Elizabeth	4:30:43 (16,295)
Murphy, Emma C	4:44:28 (19,670)
Murphy, Eve	4:44:53 (19,803)
Murphy, Gemma B	2:50:34 (395)
Murphy, Jackie	4:49:41 (20,932)
Murphy, Jennifer A	6:51:05 (34,958)
Murphy, Julia M	6:20:01 (33,891)
Murphy, Kerrie A	5:18:06 (27,081)
Murphy, Lucy J	5:43:16 (30,968)
Murphy, Margaret D	5:46:59 (31,352)
Murphy, Maureen T	5:15:51 (26,630)
Murphy, Megan A	4:10:59 (11,365)
Murphy, Michelle	6:15:43 (33,663)
Murphy, Philippa C	4:21:13 (13,899)
Murphy, Rebecca F	4:20:49 (13,807)
Murphy, Sarah J	3:18:51 (2,371)
Murphy, Sharon A	3:06:00 (1,233)
Murphy, Sue	5:41:13 (30,731)
Murphy, Susan L	5:42:41 (30,892)
Murray, Carys	4:38:47 (18,226)
Murray, Catriona S	4:54:07 (22,048)
Murray, Celia J	6:18:29 (33,808)
Murray, Clare A	3:49:11 (6,767)
Murray, Heather	4:26:24 (15,161)
Murray, Jane P	4:29:21 (15,956)
Murray, Mary	7:03:21 (35,179)
Murray, Maxine A	5:44:57 (31,149)
Murray, Petra L	5:29:27 (29,065)
Murray, Sara L	5:28:29 (28,900)
Murray-Bruce, Alexandra A	5:51:22 (31,813)
Murrihy, Vanessa J	4:59:57 (23,490)
Murtagh, Kathryn M	4:17:22 (12,897)
Murzell, Anna E	5:19:14 (27,297)
Muscas, Adriana	5:31:16 (29,342)
Musetti, Catherine M	4:04:28 (10,052)
Musgrave-Brown, Esther	4:32:25 (16,647)
Musisi, Hannah K	5:13:49 (26,194)
Mussio, Simona	5:39:41 (30,555)
Mustafa, Hatice	5:40:01 (30,592)
Muster, Monica	5:36:46 (30,144)
Mutersbaugh, Julie Anne	4:53:30 (21,885)
Muzellec, Christine	4:49:09 (20,807)
Mylles, Laura	6:44:36 (34,793)
Mytton, Rowena R	5:49:40 (31,645)
Nadine, Fleury-Voquet	6:13:00 (33,490)
Nagelkerke, Jane B	5:37:43 (30,263)
Naidoo, Vinesha	5:07:12 (24,929)
Naing, Claire L	3:57:07 (8,504)
Nairn, Fionn	3:12:30 (1,777)
Naish, Edna	7:45:14 (35,598)
Naish, Joanne H	5:15:01 (26,456)
Napier, Deborah K	3:18:36 (2,352)
Napper, Jodi D	5:33:32 (29,693)
Narang, Asheila	6:05:27 (32,994)
Nash, Doireann	4:09:30 (11,072)
Nash, Sarah	4:08:15 (10,826)
Nash, Stephanie V	5:45:34 (31,216)

Nash, Susan W	5:12:32 (25,957)
Nathan, Jane C	4:12:39 (11,751)
Nathan, Kylie A	6:11:00 (33,368)
Nathan, Laura S	5:08:51 (25,251)
Nathanielsz, Pauline E	5:59:58 (32,570)
Natoli, Courtney B	5:29:57 (29,127)
Natoli, Karen	2:48:23 (325)
Natschowny, Clare J	6:00:11 (32,594)
Naude, Karen P	3:43:41 (5,809)
Naudi, Jacqueline	6:31:26 (34,379)
Nauman, Zoe	5:49:44 (31,649)
Naylor, Arabella M	5:49:48 (31,661)
Neal, Elizabeth C	4:47:37 (20,435)
Neal, Helen L	4:25:39 (14,985)
Neal, Kelli J	5:15:44 (26,612)
Neal, Nikki H	3:05:00 (1,163)
Neal, Stefany	5:51:42 (31,846)
Neale, Julie A	5:41:53 (30,819)
Neale, Mandy	4:13:05 (11,853)
Neale, Tamsin R	3:40:49 (5,324)
Neary, Helen P	4:07:55 (10,755)
Neave, Fiona	5:20:30 (27,517)
Neave, Sandra M	4:22:58 (14,322)
Nedimovic, Summer N	5:55:59 (32,239)
Needham, Jane A	4:20:17 (13,674)
Needham, Jayne S	7:10:33 (35,278)
Needham, Maria I	4:21:46 (14,025)
Neely, Julia M	5:47:29 (31,407)
Negreira, Isabel C	4:43:04 (19,310)
Neidhold, Andrea	4:40:47 (18,728)
Neill, Debra L	6:45:54 (34,826)
Neilson, Carrie A	4:43:15 (19,355)
Neilson, Julie M	4:38:12 (18,058)
Neligan, Fiona	4:45:33 (19,960)
Nellessen, Martina	4:36:52 (17,758)
Nelson, Beth E	5:24:02 (28,110)
Nelson, Francesca	3:50:36 (7,054)
Nelson, Katie	6:05:58 (33,044)
Nelson, Kim F	3:46:36 (6,270)
Nelson, Louise E	6:22:41 (34,032)
Nelson, Louise E	7:42:24 (35,586)
Nelson, Maxine	7:11:33 (35,297)
Nelson, Sandra J	4:29:26 (15,986)
Nemtzov, Denise	5:42:17 (30,860)
Neogleous, Julia	4:51:35 (21,392)
Nerva, Anne R	5:44:38 (31,116)
Nethercott, Heather A	4:21:30 (13,967)
Neuberger, Francesca	5:12:23 (25,936)
Neville, Fiona S	4:57:38 (22,939)
Neville, Liz	3:48:31 (6,625)
Nevin, Gillian M	5:21:17 (27,652)
New, Kim E	4:11:24 (11,474)
Newark, Kim C	4:15:43 (12,487)
Newark, Louise A	5:07:06 (24,909)
Newberry, Dorothy	4:36:44 (17,723)
Newbery, Polly J	3:36:15 (4,579)
Newbery, Tara J	4:13:01 (11,833)
Newbon, Rebecca A	5:58:22 (32,455)
Newby, Nancy	5:44:16 (31,075)
Newcomb, Madeleine M	5:49:53 (31,669)
Newcombe, Colette L	5:03:59 (24,322)
Newcombe, Louise M	4:04:46 (10,106)
Newell, Caroline	5:37:06 (30,181)
Newell, Emma	5:03:39 (24,266)
Newell, Rebecca J	4:35:34 (17,421)
Newing, Lisa M	2:58:36 (797)
Newington-Bridges, Lucinda M	4:48:17 (20,597)
Newland, Anna M	5:01:04 (23,745)
Newling, Hope	4:52:41 (21,662)
Newman, Anne-Marie	5:35:09 (29,936)
Newman, Claire L	4:26:49 (15,270)
Newman, Holly	4:24:00 (14,571)
Newman, Jo	6:19:05 (33,842)
Newman, Kate L	5:54:54 (32,139)
Newman, Tracey	4:29:46 (16,080)
Newman, Veronica S	5:18:57 (27,242)
Newnham, Rebecca K	5:22:23 (27,831)
Newsome, Julia D	5:42:47 (30,904)
Newson, Marian E	5:45:22 (31,188)
Newson, Susan A	4:29:04 (15,875)
Newstead, Johanne	3:48:17 (6,575)
Newth, Kim E	6:51:36 (34,970)
Newton, Sally	4:24:49 (14,785)

Newton, Stacey A	3:31:07 (3,853)
Newton Dunn, Carolyn	6:14:42 (33,590)
Ng, Elin	4:32:41 (16,715)
Ng, Yeelan	5:04:45 (24,457)
Ngeow, Teresa	5:00:48 (23,689)
Niccol, Katy A	4:59:46 (23,448)
Nichol, Janette E	4:54:23 (22,117)
Nicholas, Charlotte R	4:17:46 (13,015)
Nicholas, Hannah M	4:06:31 (10,469)
Nicholas, Juliet C	4:48:10 (20,566)
Nicholas, Katie L	6:23:42 (34,062)
Nicholls, Alison	3:53:53 (7,761)
Nicholls, Alison H	7:18:45 (35,379)
Nicholls, Clare L	4:13:16 (11,899)
Nicholls, Kirsty	5:00:07 (23,526)
Nicholls, Sara L	8:20:58 (35,669)
Nicholls, Sarah L	4:03:58 (9,960)
Nicholls, Susan A	5:31:41 (29,402)
Nicholls, Yvonne L	4:08:46 (10,916)
Nichols, Jane E	6:00:48 (32,645)
Nichols, Maggie J	4:37:25 (17,870)
Nichols, Sarah	5:08:36 (25,205)
Nicholson, Andrea	4:53:10 (21,801)
Nicholson, Clare M	3:32:47 (4,102)
Nicholson, Margaret A	7:52:51 (35,629)
Nick, Bettina	4:03:59 (9,963)
Nicol, Anne	5:57:00 (32,331)
Nicol, Doris G	6:55:06 (35,039)
Nicol, Joanna M	4:05:22 (10,212)
Nicol, Julie	4:32:08 (16,591)
Nicol, Melanie J	5:43:56 (31,029)
Nicol, Nicola A	4:41:25 (18,896)
Nicol, Paula M	4:05:00 (10,143)
Nicoll, Elizabeth A	4:10:49 (11,332)
Nicoll, Lucy J	3:49:38 (6,858)
Nicols, Victoria L	5:55:54 (32,228)
Nielsen, Wendy	4:24:02 (14,580)
Niewczasinski, Jane M	4:29:36 (16,040)
Nightingale, Laura	4:34:25 (17,118)
Nightingale, Rebecca J	7:10:41 (35,281)
Nimmo, Elizabeth D	4:30:32 (16,261)
Nissen, Jnga	5:10:54 (25,643)
Nissen, Sharon A	5:24:33 (28,188)
Niven, Sarah E	5:52:06 (31,881)
Nixon, Rachel J	4:26:13 (15,105)
Nizzola, Verna A	5:43:07 (30,949)
Noake, Alyson J	3:44:19 (5,908)
Noakes, Deborah A	4:44:22 (19,639)
Nobbs, Stefania	5:29:53 (29,118)
Nobelen, Marijke C	5:12:15 (25,911)
Noble, Eileen R	5:30:00 (29,137)
Noble, Imelda P	5:09:20 (25,342)
Noble, Linda	3:39:36 (5,128)
Noble, Nicola	5:33:03 (29,611)
Nobles, Margaret	4:34:51 (17,236)
Nobrega, Vanessa J	3:59:43 (9,144)
Nock, Victoria J	5:27:05 (28,637)
Noel, Maureen	3:44:40 (5,972)
Nogami, Geraldine	4:56:53 (22,743)
Nolan, Christina M	4:54:15 (22,093)
Nolan, Elizabeth S	6:04:40 (32,929)
Nolan, Sarah L	6:41:58 (34,716)
Noone, Joanne L	5:06:01 (24,696)
Noone, Sophie	5:49:00 (31,586)
Norden, Claire M	5:31:25 (29,367)
Nordin, Breege J	3:20:10 (2,515)
Noris, Paola	4:44:21 (19,635)
Norman, Alison L	5:13:52 (26,206)
Norman, Carmen A	5:21:25 (27,685)
Norman, Chloe S	7:08:49 (35,259)
Norman, Jill T	4:21:41 (13,999)
Norman, Julia F	4:10:28 (11,258)
Norris, Christine B	4:50:42 (21,168)
Norris, Emma L	4:07:08 (10,597)
Norris, Janet	5:32:58 (29,601)
Norris, Katherine	4:25:57 (15,043)
Norris, Louise J	4:38:06 (18,040)
Norris, Patricia	5:42:35 (30,885)
Norrish, Donna M	3:58:59 (8,959)
Norry, Rita M	5:07:04 (24,902)
North, Amanda J	6:37:58 (34,606)
North, Heather J	3:33:36 (4,213)
North, Louise E	5:07:01 (24,887)

Northage, Kirsty N....4:38:48 (18,234)
Northey, Joanna L....4:53:23 (21,854)
Northey, Teresa J....4:02:55 (9,771)
Northridge, Tanya E....5:06:03 (24,702)
Northwood, Emma....4:31:54 (16,542)
Norton, Emma S....5:48:49 (31,562)
Norton, Samuel E....4:24:41 (14,745)
Norton, Sheila M....4:35:50 (17,497)
Norwood, Carol A....5:14:13 (26,270)
Notton, Sarah C....4:44:05 (19,560)
Nowell, Stella H....4:01:12 (9,459)
Nowobilski, Susan....5:18:36 (27,180)
Noyce, Stephanie J....3:36:40 (4,637)
Nugent, Mandy....5:22:43 (27,892)
Nunn, Charlotte E....5:17:59 (27,052)
Nunn, Gill A....3:52:39 (7,489)
Nunn, Natalie....4:58:00 (23,036)
Nunnerley-Hood, Lorena E....6:23:41 (34,061)
Nutbeam, Vanessa C....4:51:02 (21,248)
Nutburn, Jennifer A....6:03:34 (32,857)
Nutt, Charlotte S....6:05:38 (33,018)
Nutt, Tracey L....5:32:00 (29,451)
Nutter, Christine A....5:25:01 (28,272)
Nutter, Glenys....5:53:00 (31,962)
Nwagboso, Thelma N....5:09:09 (25,304)
Oakden, Rachel....4:57:38 (22,939)
Oakes, Anne....4:39:24 (18,389)
Oakes, Zoe L....5:15:22 (26,535)
Oakley, Gemma D....5:26:27 (28,539)
Oakley, Janet....5:08:50 (25,247)
Oakley, Suzan E....5:53:35 (32,020)
Oakman, Tara....5:28:09 (28,828)
Obertell, Joanne E....4:22:08 (14,112)
O'Boyle, Barbara J....4:19:54 (13,574)
O'Boyle, Hazel....6:23:57 (34,075)
O'Brien, Eve M....4:01:15 (9,470)
O'Brien, Jane J....6:02:39 (32,797)
O'Brien, Joanne....4:13:31 (11,969)
O'Brien, Katherine L....4:57:48 (22,986)
O'Brien, Kathryn H....4:46:59 (20,274)
O'Brien, Tina Y....4:53:04 (21,769)
O'Brien, Wendy K....5:33:33 (29,696)
O'Brien, Yesmin....4:57:33 (22,914)
O'Bryan, Louisa R....3:28:31 (3,490)
O'Callaghan, Jennifer....4:10:48 (11,327)
O'Callaghan, Jennifer A....6:24:41 (34,116)
O'Callaghan, Susan....6:19:21 (33,855)
O'Carroll, Anne E....5:53:53 (32,042)
Ockendon, Barbara J....5:06:11 (24,734)
O'Connell, Alison....4:31:31 (16,463)
O'Connell, Jennifer....3:48:54 (6,703)
O'Connell, Sophie J....6:35:15 (34,510)
O'Connell, Sue E....4:46:20 (20,135)
O'Connor, Carolyn A....4:52:28 (21,609)
O'Connor, Catherine A....5:12:24 (25,940)
O'Connor, Fiona M....4:06:36 (10,486)
O'Connor, Helen L....4:23:14 (14,385)
O'Connor, Jennifer....4:20:45 (13,784)
O'Connor, Katy D....5:06:10 (24,729)
O'Connor, Rachel E....4:12:10 (11,650)
Odell, Elizabeth M....5:31:44 (29,410)
Oderuth, Nashreen B....6:01:39 (32,730)
Odlin, Rebecca M....4:43:59 (19,535)
Odonkor, Georgina J....7:02:49 (35,172)
O'Donnell, Aodheen....5:17:22 (26,935)
O'Donnell, Helen....3:31:59 (3,989)
O'Donnell, Teresa J....4:46:30 (20,178)
O'Donoghue, Terri A....4:46:48 (20,229)
O'Donoghue, Tracey A....4:29:51 (16,110)
O'Driscoll, Bronwen E....6:58:34 (35,100)
O'Duffy, Libby K....3:27:02 (3,288)
O'Dwyer, Julie A....4:43:33 (19,426)
O'Dwyer, Valerie J....5:43:09 (30,954)
Ody, Victoria H....6:09:38 (33,281)
Oestmann, Meike....4:06:45 (10,513)
O'Farrell, Alison....5:03:54 (24,310)
Offer, Caroline V....4:50:45 (21,177)
Offredi, Doreen....7:42:03 (35,582)
O'Flynn, Kate....4:38:14 (18,064)
Ogden, Caroline....3:58:20 (8,793)
Ogden, Catherine E....4:52:39 (21,656)
Ogle, Katherine E....4:41:30 (18,920)
O'Grady, Annie L....5:56:34 (32,296)
O'Grady, Clare S....3:43:42 (5,811)
Ogundimu, Tola A....6:28:05 (34,255)
O'Hagan, Collette M....4:56:50 (22,728)
Ohaka, Gesella....4:47:18 (20,359)
O'Halloran, Neasa....4:10:55 (11,352)
O'Hanlon, Denise S....4:18:28 (13,201)
O'Hanlon, Janine B....8:28:49 (35,677)
O'Hara, Dawn C....5:08:58 (25,276)
O'Hara, Karen M....3:53:49 (7,746)
O'Hara, Katherine M....4:20:24 (13,707)
O'Hare, Marie-Thérèse....6:14:16 (33,567)
O'Hara, Michelle E....4:07:40 (10,695)
O'Hare, Carol....4:04:42 (10,090)
Ohlsson, Solveig....4:07:33 (10,662)
Oiller, Donna....6:42:03 (34,721)
Oja, Claire M....3:46:26 (6,244)
Okafor, Mandi N....6:59:21 (35,119)
O'Kane, Karen D....3:55:09 (8,044)
Oke, Elizabeth....6:08:01 (33,170)
O'Keefe, Debbie L....6:36:25 (34,554)
O'Keefe, Lisa A....5:47:20 (31,394)
O'Keefe, Patricia A....3:43:37 (5,801)
Okelve, Eunice V....5:44:15 (31,073)
Okennedy, Eretia....4:29:06 (15,888)
Okoye, Ginika S....5:57:31 (32,371)
Okwu, Antonia S....3:34:04 (4,276)
Olazabal Forcen, Gabriela....3:58:27 (8,822)
Olazabal Forcen, Sara....4:35:04 (17,288)
Oldershaw, Beth A....5:11:06 (25,687)
Oldershaw, Tina J....3:02:41 (1,036)
Oldfield, Julie C....6:50:38 (34,949)
Oldfield, Juliette A....3:41:38 (5,460)
Oldham, Michelle....3:26:10 (3,153)
Oldham, Nicola S....3:26:15 (3,166)
Oldman, Nicola M....3:49:12 (6,774)
Oldroyd, Sue....4:37:48 (17,955)
Olds, Denise....4:47:19 (20,365)
Olive, Philippa....4:28:06 (15,623)
Oliver, Barbara....5:06:13 (24,744)
Oliver, Deborah K....3:59:53 (9,178)
Oliver, Donna L....3:51:25 (7,231)
Oliver, Katie....4:17:10 (12,845)
Oliver, Natasha F....5:03:10 (24,166)
Ollis, Jan R....5:00:29 (23,610)
Olney, Yvonne....4:35:10 (17,316)
Olsson, Maria....7:05:41 (35,212)
O'Malley, Susan A....4:57:46 (22,973)
Ombler, Sharon L....4:30:26 (16,242)
O'Meara, Shannon M....4:50:31 (21,129)
O'Neill, Anne J....5:34:50 (29,892)
O'Neill, Claire M....5:01:39 (23,862)
O'Neill, Jane E....6:27:11 (34,216)
O'Neill, Nyree L....4:25:33 (14,955)
O'Neill, Patricia A....4:02:25 (9,685)
Onions, Joanne H....5:57:15 (32,349)
Open, Sarah A....6:46:33 (34,845)
Oprey, Karen D....6:43:25 (34,759)
Opute, Anne E....4:57:34 (22,919)
Oram, Audrey T....5:45:44 (31,231)
Orange, Heather M....6:26:44 (34,203)
Orange, Sally J....4:08:13 (10,816)
Orban, Mary Bridget....4:24:33 (14,717)
Orchard, Kimberley A....3:43:32 (5,787)
Ord, Louise M....5:52:27 (31,915)
Ordoyno, Sarah L....4:47:31 (20,413)
O'Regan, Aisling C....4:29:45 (16,075)
O'Regan, Angela K....4:41:38 (18,955)
O'Regan, Maire....6:20:12 (33,896)
O'Reilly, Claire K....4:29:00 (15,856)
O'Reilly, Jean....5:24:40 (28,212)
O'Reilly, Jessica M....6:00:24 (32,611)
Organ, Karen....5:27:04 (28,631)
Oriet, Daniela C....4:17:27 (12,927)
O'Riordan, Helen C....3:30:19 (3,767)
Orme, Sarah A....4:18:06 (13,094)
Orme, Vivienne A....5:01:44 (23,878)
Ormond, Lindsey R....4:12:10 (11,650)
Ornsby, Nadine C....5:56:09 (32,253)
Orr, Jennifer A....5:29:25 (29,061)
Orr, Sally F....3:49:43 (6,879)
Orrells, Caroline....5:12:53 (26,019)
Orridge, Harriet G....5:15:12 (26,500)
Orth, Barbara....3:41:26 (5,434)
Osborn, Deborah A....5:19:54 (27,409)
Osborn, Kirsty....5:38:39 (30,409)
Osborn, Lucie....4:44:21 (19,635)
Osborne, Fiona L....4:39:01 (18,288)
Osborne, Janette....4:51:17 (21,307)
Osborne, Kathleen A....4:22:17 (14,148)
Osborne, Kathy....5:14:30 (26,334)
Osborne, Tim J....5:00:00 (23,503)
Oseman, Carol....5:42:25 (30,871)
O'Shaughnessy, Kirsty R....6:40:20 (34,674)
O'Shaughnessy, Linda A....4:00:29 (9,308)
O'Shaughnessy, Teresa J....5:25:02 (28,279)
O'Shea, Lindsay....4:45:18 (19,905)
Osmand, Kerry L....5:04:52 (24,492)
Osmani, Fatima....4:57:17 (22,847)
Osmond, Wendy J....5:05:36 (24,619)
Ostojic, Vera....4:20:13 (13,659)
Ostrykiewicz, Marta E....4:20:40 (13,768)
O'Sullivan, Catherine....5:47:23 (31,396)
O'Sullivan, Kate M....4:17:26 (12,921)
O'Sullivan, Maureen N....5:44:34 (31,104)
O'Sullivan, Tracy....6:28:57 (34,283)
Otache, Joy....4:44:54 (19,810)
Otley, Deborah....4:26:36 (15,212)
O'Tool, Natasha M....5:01:45 (23,880)
O'Toole, Julie J....5:27:16 (28,672)
O'Toole, Karen P....4:32:38 (16,701)
Otte, Jessica F....6:43:29 (34,760)
Otter, Suzanne....5:38:37 (30,400)
Ottogalli, Franca....7:12:22 (35,310)
Outhwaite, Wendy H....4:39:33 (18,424)
Ov, Sarah....5:34:04 (29,775)
Ovenden, Shelley J....5:57:13 (32,347)
Overton, Helen F....4:55:28 (22,386)
Ovington, Debra A....4:28:49 (15,814)
Owen, Bernadette A....4:11:35 (11,518)
Owen, Carly L....5:35:26 (29,968)
Owen, Cindy....4:01:25 (9,503)
Owen, Elsbeth J....4:54:07 (22,048)
Owen, Lucy E....4:33:22 (16,884)
Owen, Lyn....5:18:40 (27,192)
Owen, Mary B....3:11:19 (1,656)
Owen, Samantha J....4:30:44 (16,303)
Owen, Victoria J....5:05:45 (24,650)
Owens, Cherokee R....6:18:52 (33,828)
Owens, Emma....4:23:32 (14,456)
Owens, Kate L....5:46:40 (31,325)
Owens, Morgyn....4:57:26 (22,893)
Owens, Rebecca A....7:12:55 (35,320)
Owens, Rosemary....5:36:26 (30,103)
Owens, Susan A....4:31:25 (16,444)
Ozanne, Lindsay J....4:16:34 (12,708)
Pacey, Sadie....8:13:28 (35,664)
Packer, Jane E....5:48:32 (31,526)
Paddock, Rachel L....4:48:50 (20,729)
Paddon, Alison M....5:04:05 (24,340)
Page, Adele S....5:42:48 (30,909)
Page, Amy....5:16:14 (26,706)
Page, Clare V....3:17:38 (2,242)
Page, Hayley....4:29:48 (16,090)
Page, Jeane....4:26:39 (15,223)
Page, Joanne....4:56:39 (22,679)
Page, Lisa....5:00:33 (23,624)
Page, Louise....4:49:33 (20,900)
Page, Paula J....4:29:02 (15,865)
Page, Sian L....8:05:43 (35,650)
Page, Tina L....5:06:48 (24,841)
Paget, Janie....4:45:52 (20,024)
Paige, Helen....4:36:29 (17,659)
Pain, Ruth....4:29:00 (15,856)
Paine, Helen A....4:46:53 (20,247)
Painter, Lindsay C....4:50:12 (21,045)
Pallen, Clare E....5:27:48 (28,761)
Pallipet, Victoria L....3:55:06 (8,033)
Palmer, Carol L....4:36:06 (17,560)
Palmer, Hayley L....3:41:15 (5,402)
Palmer, Janine E....5:47:11 (31,368)
Palmer, Jocelyn W....5:10:43 (25,612)
Palmer, Julia....3:12:26 (1,771)
Palmer, Michelle....4:39:05 (18,303)
Palmer, Orlene....5:58:15 (32,435)
Palmer, Siobhan M....3:58:39 (8,871)
Palmieri, Giulia....4:02:46 (9,745)

Palombo, Sonja C....4:35:00 (17,270)
Palumbo, Amber T....5:07:19 (24,960)
Pamplin, Diane R....3:41:44 (5,474)
Panayiotou, Vicky J....4:04:40 (10,088)
Pantaleon, Nicole E....6:01:57 (32,749)
Panum, Tina I....4:53:30 (21,885)
Paonessa, Carla....4:11:30 (11,501)
Pape, Catherine L....5:02:05 (23,947)
Pape, Dawn....4:48:12 (20,578)
Papple, Jennifer E....5:14:34 (26,354)
Papuga, Katrina....6:21:01 (33,952)
Parcell, Diane L....4:47:55 (20,509)
Parcell, Michelle C....6:42:05 (34,723)
Paredes, Eva....6:11:18 (33,393)
Paremain, Gillian A....4:51:20 (21,328)
Paretchan, Julie....5:20:12 (27,457)
Parfitt, Dena B....2:59:05 (830)
Parfoot, Katie....3:18:15 (2,319)
Parfrey, Sonja K....5:26:10 (28,483)
Paris, Anna N....4:43:54 (19,509)
Parish, Natalie....4:28:17 (15,666)
Park, Karen....4:08:15 (10,826)
Parkash, Vanesha V....4:08:41 (10,907)
Parker, Camilla H....4:17:38 (12,982)
Parker, Debbie L....4:09:52 (11,141)
Parker, Elizabeth A....5:16:39 (26,781)
Parker, Emma J....4:59:36 (23,412)
Parker, Fiona J....5:58:23 (32,458)
Parker, Helen M....4:33:15 (16,857)
Parker, Janet E....5:07:06 (24,909)
Parker, Julia A....4:15:55 (12,533)
Parker, Kirsty M....4:07:49 (10,730)
Parker, Lisa J....4:21:42 (14,003)
Parker, Lucie V....4:34:49 (17,225)
Parker, Rachel C....5:14:56 (26,435)
Parker, Sabina....5:18:52 (27,226)
Parker, Sioban C....3:50:12 (6,974)
Parker, Susan H....5:37:41 (30,258)
Parker, Susan W....7:15:45 (35,348)
Parker, Sylvia-Anne....5:00:54 (23,709)
Parker, Tarnya....4:35:39 (17,440)
Parker McKibbin, Shelagh....5:49:44 (31,649)
Parkes, Linda J....3:17:25 (2,219)
Parkes, Samantha....7:05:41 (35,212)
Parkes, Sarah A....6:41:59 (34,719)
Parkes, Sarah J....4:52:30 (21,612)
Parkin, Sarah....5:37:13 (30,199)
Parkinson, Barbara....4:11:41 (11,547)
Parkinson, Bridget S....4:29:30 (16,007)
Parkinson, Helen A....3:00:43 (941)
Parkinson, Jacqueline S....5:16:00 (26,662)
Parkinson, Katharine R....4:11:37 (11,533)
Parkinson, Miranda K....4:47:39 (20,441)
Parks, Marianne....5:18:52 (27,226)
Parle, Shirley Y....6:05:13 (32,976)
Parmiter, Ceri L....5:18:52 (27,226)
Parnell, Sarah L....5:18:31 (27,167)
Parnham, Sarah....5:34:21 (29,817)
Parratt, Susie....6:21:27 (33,980)
Parry, Bethan J....4:47:18 (20,359)
Parry, Beverly A....4:19:34 (13,471)
Parry, Cathy M....7:00:49 (35,144)
Parry, Lisa A....5:51:44 (31,849)
Parry, Louise H....4:49:26 (20,867)
Parry, Tracey A....5:39:15 (30,482)
Parry, Wendy C....5:58:15 (32,435)
Parsley, Sue....5:34:20 (29,815)
Parsons, Alexandra G....5:11:07 (25,693)
Parsons, Alice E....4:15:49 (12,511)
Parsons, Della....5:18:26 (27,148)
Parsons, Elizabeth J....5:34:57 (29,907)
Parsons, Karla M....3:56:43 (8,411)
Parsons, Katherine Z....4:43:32 (19,421)
Parsons, Laura C....4:08:30 (10,871)
Parsons, Maxine....5:58:00 (32,415)
Parsons, Sandra I....4:17:08 (12,837)
Parsons, Sarah J....4:18:31 (13,217)
Partner, Caroline D....6:09:19 (33,257)
Parton, Clare....4:34:06 (17,050)
Partridge, Amanda-Jane....4:41:20 (18,869)
Partridge, Brenna J....5:52:37 (31,931)
Partridge, Emma L....3:22:04 (2,711)
Pascall, Nina T....3:51:03 (7,145)
Pascoe, Angela....5:25:41 (28,402)
Pascoe, Bridget M....5:34:53 (29,900)
Pashley, Nicola F....4:58:37 (23,171)
Passi, Lina....6:55:27 (35,047)
Passingham, Charlotte L....5:18:14 (27,109)
Patchett, Nicola A....4:59:15 (23,327)
Patching, Katrina J....4:35:21 (17,372)
Patel, Dharmista....4:56:06 (22,535)
Patel, Gina....6:14:31 (33,581)
Patel, Pratiksha K....5:50:10 (31,687)
Patel, Saijal....5:26:08 (28,479)
Patel, Sheel....4:40:16 (18,594)
Patel, Vanisha K....6:11:45 (33,411)
Patenon, Vanessa S....5:58:08 (32,426)
Paterson, Harriet....4:09:34 (11,090)
Paterson, Kirsty....6:00:29 (32,620)
Paterson, Shelley....3:58:45 (8,897)
Paterson, Susan....4:40:04 (18,549)
Paterson, Susan....4:49:12 (20,821)
Paterson, Tracy C....4:37:03 (17,796)
Pates, Cathy....5:13:29 (26,120)
Patmore, Tracey....6:36:40 (34,565)
Paton, Abigail....4:10:32 (11,274)
Paton, Elizabeth A....5:15:03 (26,472)
Paton, Hilda C....5:07:00 (24,883)
Paton, Karen R....3:46:13 (6,207)
Patrick, Anne....5:20:28 (27,508)
Patterson, Jane....3:56:48 (8,431)
Patterson, Karen....3:57:20 (8,561)
Patterson, Marjet W....3:42:02 (5,527)
Patterson, Rachel A....6:10:04 (33,310)
Patterson-Kelly, Wizzy J....5:01:25 (23,815)
Pattinson, Amanda L....4:14:08 (12,125)
Pattison, Michelle J....5:05:04 (24,525)
Paul, Carol....4:15:01 (12,328)
Paul, Caroline M....6:24:33 (34,103)
Paul, Gabriele....4:05:33 (10,250)
Pauletto, Francesca....5:27:50 (28,767)
Pauli, Astrid....4:05:23 (10,221)
Paulin, Ruth M....4:44:01 (19,542)
Paull, Irene H....4:45:10 (19,876)
Paver, Barbara I....5:33:12 (29,634)
Pawson, Amy....6:01:13 (32,699)
Payne, Daphne....5:28:10 (28,832)
Payne, Elaine....4:09:50 (11,134)
Payne, Francesca....5:27:07 (28,640)
Payne, Jenny S....5:03:01 (24,129)
Payne, Jo....6:42:00 (34,720)
Payne, Katie A....4:58:32 (23,157)
Payne, Marietjie....4:42:14 (19,107)
Payne, Rachel M....4:08:22 (10,845)
Payne, Susan M....4:13:48 (12,043)
Peace, Angela....3:33:31 (4,205)
Peace, Frances M....5:05:52 (24,666)
Peace, Mandy J....3:48:23 (6,587)
Peach, Nichola E....5:15:59 (26,654)
Peacock, Kieron....4:08:13 (10,816)
Peacock, Laura M....3:56:24 (8,334)
Pealling, Jenny A....4:57:04 (22,788)
Pearce, Alison J....5:52:34 (31,924)
Pearce, Jo....5:06:26 (24,778)
Pearce, Julia A....4:08:30 (10,871)
Pearce, Julia S....5:24:57 (28,265)
Pearce, Katie A....3:39:00 (5,017)
Pearce, Katie L....5:30:35 (29,232)
Pearce, Louise A....4:38:53 (18,251)
Pearcy, Karen....4:37:38 (17,918)
Peard, Emma-Jayne....4:51:16 (21,300)
Pearson, Ali....6:02:11 (32,761)
Pearson, Alison K....5:14:03 (26,239)
Pearson, Andrea....3:59:14 (9,021)
Pearson, Debra....5:12:01 (25,858)
Pearson, Elizabeth A....4:41:02 (18,797)
Pearson, Helen J....3:18:07 (2,298)
Pearson, Jayne....5:52:14 (31,897)
Pearson, Jennifer A....4:29:52 (16,115)
Pearson, Joanna....4:14:33 (12,219)
Pearson, Paula E....5:02:27 (24,026)
Pearson, Rachel....4:39:36 (18,437)
Pearson, Rachel A....5:08:01 (25,099)
Pearson, Rebecca M....5:10:00 (25,477)
Pearson, Sara A....4:58:47 (23,202)
Pearson, Sarah E....3:52:54 (7,544)
Pearson, Sarah L....4:38:21 (18,113)
Pearson, Susan J....5:09:57 (25,463)
Pearson, Wendy....6:26:00 (34,164)
Peasgood, Teresa J....3:44:44 (5,984)
Peate, Stephanie D....4:15:36 (12,460)
Peatfield, Kim....4:44:09 (19,579)
Peck, Gemma M....3:47:40 (6,468)
Peck, Janet M....5:08:53 (25,261)
Peck, Rita....4:17:43 (13,002)
Peckett, Catherine....4:44:08 (19,571)
Pedersen, Beth A....5:08:25 (25,176)
Pederzolli, Amanda T....4:05:51 (10,319)
Pedley, Teresa A....5:22:46 (27,905)
Peel, Zoe C....4:47:42 (20,457)
Pegg, Catherine....5:37:50 (30,274)
Pegler, Evi J....5:51:29 (31,829)
Pelosi, Bonnie....4:37:24 (17,862)
Peltier, Martine....4:42:25 (19,156)
Penalver, Ruth....7:10:26 (35,275)
Pender, Jane L....4:01:31 (9,516)
Pendered, Jane E....4:26:23 (15,155)
Pendleton, Clare L....6:31:53 (34,400)
Pene, Monique....5:38:29 (30,381)
Penfold, Amanda C....4:20:34 (13,745)
Penfold, Claire L....6:51:21 (34,966)
Penfold-Strauss, Deborah....7:11:02 (35,289)
Pengelley, Emma E....4:44:01 (19,542)
Penistan, Patricia....4:22:08 (14,112)
Pennell, Christine....4:38:14 (18,064)
Pennington, Samantha F....6:02:54 (32,815)
Penny, Helen L....4:09:02 (10,956)
Pennycook, Sarah D....4:20:20 (13,691)
Penrose, Janet M....4:45:28 (19,938)
Penrose, Katie P....3:44:01 (5,870)
Pepper, Debbie....4:22:41 (14,253)
Pepper, Shae E....6:16:52 (33,727)
Peraud, Marcia C....5:07:36 (25,019)
Perbellini, Alessandra....4:21:39 (13,995)
Percival, Juliet S....4:47:40 (20,449)
Percox, Lisa J....4:05:10 (10,179)
Percy, Sharon L....3:56:28 (8,352)
Pered, Alison....5:37:07 (30,184)
Perez, Andrea M....5:29:34 (29,078)
Perger, Rosa....4:18:17 (13,142)
Perham, Tracy E....5:21:38 (27,717)
Perrett, Shirley J....5:20:07 (27,440)
Perrimans, Jacqueline A....4:43:18 (19,372)
Perry, Amanda J....4:24:45 (14,767)
Perry, Deborah A....4:35:11 (17,323)
Perry, Emma C....4:47:44 (20,464)
Perry, Gillian....5:17:10 (26,886)
Perry, Lucy M....5:22:49 (27,909)
Perry, Mandy J....4:09:58 (11,159)
Perry, Natasha C....7:00:19 (35,132)
Perry, Samantha....4:21:44 (14,012)
Perry, Sarah....3:57:22 (8,570)
Perry, Susy A....3:29:55 (3,705)
Perry, Victoria A....2:54:29 (543)
Perryman, Sarah A....4:59:27 (23,363)
Peruzzi, Cristina M....5:57:02 (32,335)
Perveen, Rahat....5:30:26 (29,205)
Pescood, Helen S....4:55:19 (22,341)
Pesonen, Senja M....5:29:08 (29,005)
Petch, Emma J....4:41:49 (19,001)
Petein, Hajley C....6:18:40 (33,817)
Peters, Danielle....4:53:48 (21,964)
Peters, Joanne M....5:29:11 (29,018)
Peters, Lynn....5:25:23 (28,335)
Peters, Pamela T....4:57:59 (23,032)
Petersen, Grethe L....3:28:01 (3,409)
Petersen, Mette F....4:58:41 (23,186)
Petrie, Jane....4:25:30 (14,945)
Pett, Domini B....5:33:35 (29,700)
Pettit, Elisa E....4:38:16 (18,077)
Pettit, Kayleigh L....5:58:03 (32,417)
Petts, Jill....5:14:11 (26,265)
Peywot, Catherine....4:26:18 (15,130)
Phaka, Kate M....5:44:54 (31,139)
Phelps, Johanna E....4:47:32 (20,417)
Philbrick, Leah K....4:46:30 (20,178)
Phillips, Anita....6:21:02 (33,953)
Phillips, Anna J....3:14:48 (1,968)
Phillips, Anne M....4:48:14 (20,586)

Phillips, Carole	3:27:26 (3,347)	
Phillips, Catherine R	5:41:22 (30,754)	
Phillips, Clare	3:04:29 (1,129)	
Phillips, Debra A	4:25:32 (14,952)	
Phillips, Diane K	4:43:30 (19,414)	
Phillips, Gillian E	3:46:05 (6,193)	
Phillips, Helen L	5:21:19 (27,660)	
Phillips, Julie	6:23:36 (34,060)	
Phillips, Julie E	5:25:26 (28,351)	
Phillips, Juliet	5:53:55 (32,047)	
Phillips, Karen J	5:22:59 (27,936)	
Phillips, Lisa	4:30:12 (16,196)	
Phillips, Lisa A	5:43:03 (30,938)	
Phillips, Lynn	6:43:19 (34,758)	
Phillips, Marina M	6:22:19 (34,012)	
Phillips, Meg J	5:09:32 (25,381)	
Phillips, Morag	6:20:57 (33,948)	
Phillips, Olivia	5:51:28 (31,827)	
Phillips, Raelynn M	6:40:37 (34,679)	
Phillips, Ruth E	3:50:19 (7,003)	
Phillips, Samantha J	6:36:06 (34,540)	
Phillips, Sarah J	6:36:47 (34,569)	
Phillips, Sarah L	5:31:22 (29,355)	
Phillips, Sue	3:49:00 (6,736)	
Phillips, Tamara	4:47:54 (20,505)	
Phillips, Tanya D	6:22:09 (34,002)	
Philpott, Alex L	3:48:36 (6,645)	
Philpott, Anne M	5:16:52 (26,829)	
Philpott, Helen E	5:02:23 (24,010)	
Philpott, Kathryn A	5:07:01 (24,887)	
Phin, Catriona M	3:43:09 (5,714)	
Phipps, Anna C	5:04:25 (24,405)	
Phipps, Catriona M	5:33:41 (29,711)	
Phipps, Elaine M	3:07:49 (1,370)	
Pianka, Stephanie E	4:50:46 (21,183)	
Piattella, Marina	3:27:08 (3,300)	
Pichelski, Lorraine	4:26:49 (15,270)	
Pichler, Silke C	3:10:55 (1,625)	
Pick, Alison K	4:40:03 (18,545)	
Pickard, Kathryn M	4:34:39 (17,191)	
Pickering, Anna H	5:26:46 (28,586)	
Pickering, Lisa A	4:23:24 (14,418)	
Pickering, Sylvia E	7:02:08 (35,161)	
Pickett, Laura T	5:55:18 (32,176)	
Pickford, Alison L	4:25:39 (14,985)	
Pickles, Karen	3:23:45 (2,872)	
Picksley, Mary L	3:37:55 (4,809)	
Pickup, Andrea L	3:18:53 (2,377)	
Pickup, Helen	5:22:29 (27,844)	
Pidler, Jill C	7:08:41 (35,256)	
Pierce, Clara	5:01:55 (23,916)	
Pike, Emma R	5:08:43 (25,229)	
Pike, Zoe M	2:59:47 (884)	
Pilborough, Stephanie T	5:58:22 (32,455)	
Pilgrim, Janet M	5:39:06 (30,463)	
Pilgrim, Mary J	5:06:14 (24,749)	
Pilkington, Helen	5:05:41 (24,631)	
Pilkington, Terrie	5:48:47 (31,559)	
Pilling, Anne M	5:24:50 (28,243)	
Pimm, Louse M	5:24:07 (28,126)	
Pinborough, Claire M	5:44:28 (31,087)	
Pinch, Carole A	5:31:50 (29,424)	
Pinchbeck, Kathryn A	5:35:31 (29,976)	
Pindoria, Sophie C	5:16:00 (26,662)	
Ping Guimaraes, Cheng H	5:10:36 (25,594)	
Pinkerton, Joanne	5:26:24 (28,531)	
Pinkney, Jessica	4:32:24 (16,644)	
Pinnegar, Sally J	3:56:17 (8,297)	
Piper, Beverley A	4:33:49 (16,995)	
Pires, Rachel E	6:15:59 (33,682)	
Pirie, Eleanor F	6:13:07 (33,496)	
Pirie, Jane	5:17:11 (26,891)	
Pirie, Theresa Y	7:04:52 (35,201)	
Pirovano, Monica	4:29:25 (15,980)	
Pisaneschi, Nadine	5:43:20 (30,976)	
Pisani, Andea L	5:36:47 (30,145)	
Pisapia, Jacqueline	6:19:05 (33,842)	
Pitcher, Cherie E	6:49:52 (34,925)	
Pithie, Jane L	4:34:24 (17,114)	
Pitkin, Alison J	4:45:19 (19,908)	
Pitkin, Tracy	4:37:57 (17,993)	
Pitman, Sophie J	7:58:34 (35,639)	
Pitt, Maresa E	3:34:12 (4,293)	
Pittman, Nicola J	6:42:41 (34,741)	
Pitts, Alyson C	5:18:12 (27,103)	
Pizer, Rebecca B	6:22:07 (34,001)	
Plane, Alexandra L	3:53:24 (7,668)	
Plane, Joanna	4:52:35 (21,635)	
Plante, Nadia M	5:29:43 (29,097)	
Platt, Karen D	4:29:50 (16,101)	
Platts, Emma L	4:07:02 (10,580)	
Playford, Marie B	4:11:56 (11,601)	
Playle, Marion E	4:54:20 (22,106)	
Pleasence, Caroline	4:09:02 (10,956)	
Ploszaj, Jennifer M	4:51:55 (21,469)	
Plowman, Kay L	6:25:30 (34,149)	
Pluke, Rebecca H	4:24:07 (14,603)	
Plume, Jennifer L	6:18:07 (33,783)	
Plume, Susanna K	5:04:46 (24,460)	
Plumley, Helen	4:58:03 (23,045)	
Plumley, Sally A	5:43:48 (31,022)	
Plumridge, Juile	5:19:24 (27,319)	
Plutek, Nathalie	4:22:24 (14,176)	
Pocock, Ella L	5:58:06 (32,420)	
Pocock, Laura A	5:09:40 (25,407)	
Poelijoe, Jill L	5:05:53 (24,672)	
Poggher, Rachel	4:55:50 (22,468)	
Points, Lucy K	4:38:30 (18,153)	
Pokarier, Amanda L	3:56:55 (8,458)	
Polden, Katie	6:11:12 (33,382)	
Pollard, Abigail M	5:31:56 (29,437)	
Pollard, Kate	4:47:20 (20,367)	
Pollard, Kelly J	5:10:04 (25,495)	
Pollard, Linda S	4:27:09 (15,366)	
Pollard, Rosemary M	4:39:54 (18,508)	
Pollen, Isabel	4:42:56 (19,287)	
Pollitt, John	4:09:30 (11,072)	
Pollock, Felicity S	4:34:34 (17,166)	
Pomeroy, Linda C	4:01:17 (9,477)	
Pomeroy, Louise S	5:06:05 (24,710)	
Pomfret, Mary M	6:10:08 (33,314)	
Pomgranc, Lisa H	4:15:32 (12,448)	
Pond, Elizabeth A	4:53:23 (21,854)	
Ponticaccia, Josiane	4:36:20 (17,621)	
Pook, Lisa A	4:04:25 (10,041)	
Pook, Tanya J	3:58:39 (8,871)	
Poole, Judith M	5:38:02 (30,308)	
Poole, Louise A	4:09:10 (10,997)	
Poole, Louise E	5:27:55 (28,781)	
Poole, Nardia D	3:40:09 (5,209)	
Pooler, Sophie A	4:51:01 (21,244)	
Pooley, Kelly E	3:45:54 (6,163)	
Pooley, Miriam J	6:22:36 (34,026)	
Pope, Jennifer	4:43:38 (19,448)	
Pope, Karen M	5:30:08 (29,167)	
Pope, Lucy H	6:00:04 (32,587)	
Pope, Sarah	4:17:07 (12,833)	
Popham, Lorraine H	4:54:08 (22,054)	
Pople, Melanie J	4:08:10 (10,799)	
Porlier, Christine	4:53:11 (21,804)	
Porter, Christine M	5:14:12 (26,267)	
Porter, Gertrud F	4:10:05 (11,180)	
Porter, Laura J	5:45:41 (31,223)	
Porter, Lynette A	3:04:31 (1,133)	
Porter, Sarah	4:44:36 (19,718)	
Porter, Zoe G	3:38:24 (4,902)	
Porthouse, Hayley L	4:57:31 (22,907)	
Potter, Alex J	3:38:37 (4,943)	
Potter, Ann F	5:19:07 (27,271)	
Potter, Dawn T	4:42:25 (19,156)	
Potter, Janet	3:31:28 (3,905)	
Potter, Laura	5:39:48 (30,572)	
Potter, Rachel	4:53:25 (21,868)	
Potter, Rachel L	5:20:09 (27,447)	
Potter, Sarah L	4:37:04 (17,801)	
Potts, Katherine L	5:25:43 (28,411)	
Potts, Lorraine	5:37:07 (30,184)	
Poulain, Clare C	5:11:48 (25,813)	
Poulter, Justine C	4:34:49 (17,225)	
Poulter, Michelle S	5:42:35 (30,885)	
Poulton, Hannah	5:58:04 (32,419)	
Poulton, Lynda J	7:01:14 (35,148)	
Poulton, Patricia A	5:10:39 (25,607)	
Pountney, Helen J	4:48:52 (20,736)	
Povey, Laura J	5:01:58 (23,929)	
Powell, Claire L	5:13:39 (26,150)	
Powell, Dawn	4:12:50 (11,795)	
Powell, Emma R	4:48:52 (20,736)	
Powell, Jan	7:06:26 (35,228)	
Powell, Karen A	5:11:39 (25,786)	
Powell, Linda R	4:53:40 (21,933)	
Powell, Lucy F	5:16:51 (26,820)	
Powell, Paula M	4:36:35 (17,689)	
Powell, Pauline P	2:52:47 (470)	
Powell, Vikki	4:52:00 (21,486)	
Powell-Wileman, Penny P	6:15:39 (33,659)	
Power, Suzanna C	4:32:05 (16,578)	
Poynter, Lisa J	6:24:14 (34,088)	
Poynton, Linda M	5:49:57 (31,671)	
Pozzi-Gurung, Helen O	4:13:31 (11,969)	
Prance, Carole	3:52:53 (7,540)	
Prasad, Naomi U	5:00:07 (23,526)	
Pratt, Kate	6:00:09 (32,592)	
Precious, Sally	4:47:01 (20,286)	
Preece, Hazel B	5:31:02 (29,302)	
Preece, Ruth	5:44:40 (31,119)	
Preen, Jane L	3:07:52 (1,375)	
Prentice, Caroline A	4:27:25 (15,454)	
Prentice, Michelle	5:35:59 (30,046)	
Prescod, Christine	5:45:41 (31,223)	
Prescott, Jennifer H	4:21:10 (13,894)	
Presske, Steffi	4:35:34 (17,421)	
Preston, Emma M	6:10:11 (33,316)	
Preston, Janet	6:05:53 (33,033)	
Preston, Kelly E	3:36:46 (4,656)	
Preston, Paula	6:22:13 (34,008)	
Pretty, Jacqueline S	5:34:21 (29,817)	
Pretty, Sadie K	5:05:45 (24,650)	
Prettyman, Marie-Claire	4:19:01 (13,330)	
Price, Amy	7:33:05 (35,520)	
Price, Clare	6:27:12 (34,218)	
Price, Deborah J	4:55:09 (22,305)	
Price, Emma C	4:43:50 (19,489)	
Price, Heather A	6:32:19 (34,420)	
Price, Jacqueline A	5:25:15 (28,315)	
Price, Jane	5:49:45 (31,653)	
Price, Joanne E	3:50:24 (7,020)	
Price, Julie	4:23:25 (14,421)	
Price, Kelly M	4:56:50 (22,728)	
Price, Lee M	4:16:13 (12,627)	
Price, Lorraine A	5:12:58 (26,039)	
Price, Louise C	6:23:30 (34,055)	
Price, Nina K	4:00:49 (9,378)	
Price, Ruth	5:20:03 (27,430)	
Price, Sarah	4:48:58 (20,757)	
Price, Sarah	4:57:05 (22,792)	
Price, Sarah-Jane	5:49:50 (31,664)	
Price, Susan J	5:40:54 (30,695)	
Price-Davies, Rachel M	4:28:37 (15,765)	
Priddle, Elisabeth A	5:32:42 (29,566)	
Priechenfried, Julia	4:38:04 (18,028)	
Priest, Caroline M	4:44:52 (19,797)	
Priest, Sharon J	6:44:05 (34,776)	
Priestley, Vanessa	5:17:16 (26,912)	
Prime, Laura J	5:18:32 (27,169)	
Prince, Debbie J	4:12:16 (11,667)	
Prince, Edna C	5:22:04 (27,789)	
Prince, Sarah J	5:24:39 (28,207)	
Pring, Charlene D	4:43:34 (19,434)	
Prins, Angela	4:53:40 (21,933)	
Prior, Alex	5:55:40 (32,208)	
Prior, Emma M	4:51:11 (21,281)	
Prior, Harriet S	4:13:45 (12,030)	
Prior, Judy	4:19:05 (13,350)	
Prior, Michelle J	4:16:01 (12,570)	
Prior, Tracey	3:35:39 (4,505)	
Priscott, Anne	5:24:18 (28,157)	
Pritchard, Helen M	4:28:26 (15,709)	
Pritchard-Gordon, Amy A	6:16:26 (33,715)	
Pritchett, Julie	5:00:44 (23,670)	
Probert, Jayne	6:10:26 (33,330)	
Probert, Katherine M	3:56:22 (8,324)	
Procter, Helena J	5:29:14 (29,031)	
Proctor, Gina L	5:07:56 (25,082)	
Proctor, Julia A	3:44:26 (5,928)	
Profir, Diana	5:01:16 (23,787)	
Prosper, Helen R	4:29:16 (15,930)	
Prosser, Claire A	4:22:58 (14,322)	
Prosser, Linda M	4:54:33 (22,154)	

Prosser, Michelle L 5:38:47 (30,426)
Provan, Fiona L 5:20:57 (27,598)
Pruden, Ann 4:53:01 (21,758)
Prus, Susannah R 4:05:40 (10,280)
Pryce-Tidd, Jane C 4:49:03 (20,777)
Pryke, Melanie J 3:51:50 (7,324)
Pryke, Sara A 5:41:16 (30,738)
Prymakokska, Barbara 4:58:36 (23,166)
Pucillo, Maria Carla 6:06:50 (33,098)
Puech, Brenda 4:00:36 (9,330)
Puffett, Angela J 4:32:45 (16,726)
Pugh, Emilie I 4:28:18 (15,672)
Pugh, Gillian E 3:37:06 (4,700)
Pulford, Alice 5:26:49 (28,593)
Pulford, Nina 4:48:21 (20,625)
Pullinger, Claire D 5:10:54 (25,643)
Pumford, Suzanne G 5:33:13 (29,636)
Punton, Gillian S 4:56:59 (22,770)
Purdy, Vivienne L 4:59:43 (23,436)
Purnell, Nichola L 7:30:45 (35,499)
Pusey, Claire L 3:02:37 (1,033)
Pussard, Gail V 6:14:10 (33,563)
Putnam, Amber K 4:36:15 (17,599)
Pycroft, Joy S 6:20:35 (33,926)
Pye, Jacqueline P 5:11:29 (25,750)
Pye, Margaret M 4:44:46 (19,763)
Pyke, Joanna L 5:49:50 (31,664)
Pyke, Lisa 4:46:19 (20,130)
Pyke, Yvonne 6:19:40 (33,876)
Pyne, Deborah 6:59:07 (35,114)
Pyne, Janet L 5:32:31 (29,533)
Qcamley, Camilla S 5:52:12 (31,893)
Qualtrough, Michele 5:42:49 (30,915)
Quazi, Jacqueline M 5:27:18 (28,677)
Queen, Lisa A 5:20:35 (27,538)
Quek, Ai Ling 4:38:45 (18,212)
Quick, Emma L 6:22:35 (34,025)
Quin, Catherine J 4:05:33 (10,250)
Quine, Jeanette M 4:26:18 (15,130)
Quine, Lynne 5:13:38 (26,146)
Quinn, Brigid M 4:44:53 (19,803)
Quinn, John B 5:34:07 (29,784)
Quinn, Louise 4:11:07 (11,401)
Quinn, Molly M 3:51:56 (7,351)
Quinn, Tara L 4:58:30 (23,151)
Quinn, Thirza J 5:25:31 (28,375)
Quinney, Emily J 5:55:02 (32,151)
Quinsee, Marianne 5:45:39 (31,220)
Quinton, Eileen R 4:51:40 (21,412)
Quittner, Joanne 4:09:26 (11,057)
Qureshi, Asma 7:28:18 (35,460)
Raaijmakers, Monique M 3:28:58 (3,569)
Rabindra, Gayathri 4:59:32 (23,396)
Rabindrakumar, Geethanjali 4:42:54 (19,281)
Raby, Beth A 5:22:53 (27,918)
Rach, Sabrina 4:53:53 (21,985)
Radcliffe, Jannette S 5:32:36 (29,550)
Radford, Joy C 3:28:31 (3,490)
Radley, Brooke L 4:53:48 (21,964)
Radley, Krystina 5:50:51 (31,763)
Rae, Jane E 4:24:00 (14,571)
Rae, Laura 5:49:32 (31,631)
Raeside, Karen J 4:52:15 (21,556)
Raffell, Jane L 3:11:14 (1,649)
Ragg, Monica E 4:29:47 (16,087)
Rahbek, Helle 4:36:45 (17,732)
Rahman, Huma 3:31:40 (3,936)
Rahman, Taharim 5:07:45 (25,044)
Raidy, Davina J 3:35:07 (4,425)
Rainbird, Claire L 4:06:53 (10,547)
Rainbow, Julie 4:09:14 (11,014)
Raine, Barbara A 4:52:11 (21,537)
Rainer-Seath, Julie F 6:22:11 (34,005)
Rainey, Linda V 6:42:04 (34,722)
Rainey, Melanie 7:09:54 (35,270)
Raja, Catherine M 5:30:42 (29,257)
Rajput, Toni 5:18:06 (27,081)
Ralph, Barbara 3:24:01 (2,905)
Ralph, Helen F 4:06:53 (10,547)
Ralph, Tracy A 7:23:18 (35,417)
Ramage, Caroline L 5:08:22 (25,165)
Ramage, Shiona M 4:24:45 (14,767)
Rambridge, Melissa M 4:50:30 (21,120)
Ramon, Jane 6:06:23 (33,074)
Ramos, Lorraine M 5:39:32 (30,535)
Rampling, Laura E 4:25:28 (14,940)
Ramsay, Dianne 5:46:20 (31,295)
Ramsay, Hannah S 5:43:07 (30,949)
Ramsay, Yasmin O 4:51:24 (21,343)
Ramsden, Jane 4:22:16 (14,142)
Ramsden, Thalia Rose 6:28:51 (34,279)
Ramsey, Cayetana E 4:50:58 (21,233)
Ramsey, Deborah A 6:08:31 (33,205)
Ramsey, Helen J 5:51:03 (31,779)
Ramsey Smith, Sarah 3:48:37 (6,648)
Rance, Bunty L 4:31:02 (16,364)
Randall, Bernice M 3:50:01 (6,948)
Randall, Zoe 4:20:36 (13,752)
Randell, Louise M 5:45:14 (31,175)
Randells, Jane M 8:43:26 (35,682)
Ranford, Lucia E 6:38:14 (34,614)
Rankin, Alison W 4:58:35 (23,164)
Ranson, Pauline F 5:14:54 (26,428)
Rantanikunen, Helena T 5:10:03 (25,494)
Raphael, Amanda J 4:25:38 (14,977)
Rapley, Emma J 5:41:33 (30,776)
Rapley, Jean S 4:30:36 (16,280)
Rascher, Yvonne 4:49:46 (20,947)
Rashid, Shahina 5:09:44 (25,422)
Rastelli, Osanna 4:13:35 (11,990)
Ratcliffe, Alison J 5:12:42 (25,985)
Ratcliffe, Georgina 4:22:16 (14,142)
Ratcliffe, Tracy J 4:54:52 (22,238)
Rattu, Beneesha 6:13:30 (33,519)
Raven, Jackie 6:02:24 (32,778)
Raven, Sharon 4:49:26 (20,867)
Ravenhall, Sally G 5:52:13 (31,895)
Ravenhill, Natalie 4:29:16 (15,930)
Ravic, Rebecca J 4:17:22 (12,897)
Rawson, Amanda J 3:32:03 (3,995)
Ray, Alison M 5:16:04 (26,674)
Ray, Joanna R 5:31:21 (29,351)
Rayment, Heather A 4:48:43 (20,700)
Raymond, Jennifer L 4:22:45 (14,272)
Raymond, Joanne M 5:26:19 (28,512)
Rayneard, Keirsten 3:41:04 (5,374)
Rayner, Andrea J 4:50:04 (21,016)
Rayner, Laura J 4:52:18 (21,568)
Rayner, Marion R 3:40:29 (5,261)
Rayner, Ruth J 4:18:44 (13,273)
Raynor, Claire G 4:49:56 (20,980)
Raynor, Zoe 4:54:41 (22,194)
Razzolini, Ilaria 4:41:32 (18,932)
Razzolini, Serena 4:41:32 (18,932)
Rea, Jane A 6:03:04 (32,826)
Rea, Norma 4:13:10 (11,871)
Reach, Lucy E 3:57:40 (8,646)
Read, Helen B 4:40:59 (18,780)
Read, Louise B 3:52:47 (7,520)
Read, Marian E 5:55:16 (32,170)
Read, Michelle A 4:43:50 (19,489)
Read, Natalie C 5:06:03 (24,702)
Read, Nicola A 4:50:51 (21,204)
Read, Philippa S 5:04:34 (24,427)
Read, Sonya 6:52:08 (34,978)
Read, Tracy C 5:04:39 (24,438)
Reade, Kirsty E 3:57:32 (8,606)
Reading, Barbara 4:35:49 (17,491)
Readman, Penny J 4:36:32 (17,677)
Readman, Tamzin C 4:06:59 (10,572)
Ready, Deborah J 4:03:58 (9,960)
Reagan, Helen A 3:56:11 (8,270)
Reaney, Shirley 6:15:45 (33,667)
Reanney, Georgia K 4:35:57 (17,524)
Reaper, Beckie 5:31:22 (29,355)
Reay, Sarah Jane 6:52:48 (34,986)
Recchia, Frances 5:04:49 (24,472)
Record, Wendy H 4:23:19 (14,402)
Rector, Sarah L 6:11:14 (33,384)
Redding, Rebecca J 4:07:33 (10,662)
Reddy, Siobhan A 3:59:12 (9,011)
Redgrave, Ann 7:29:04 (35,467)
Redman, Lisa J 4:50:32 (21,138)
Redmayne, Jacqueline 3:51:11 (7,182)
Redmile, Karen E 6:57:20 (35,079)
Redmond, Amy E 3:53:07 (7,594)
Redmond, Anna 5:38:49 (30,433)
Redmond, Deborah J 4:30:39 (16,286)
Redmore, Lisa 6:21:06 (33,961)
Redpath, Janet M 4:56:34 (22,647)
Reed, Annabelle J 5:26:13 (28,495)
Reed, Laura A 6:18:59 (33,836)
Reed, Lois A 4:29:03 (15,867)
Reed, Lucille A 4:23:12 (14,379)
Reed, Moira J 6:07:00 (33,106)
Reed, Sandra R 6:19:02 (33,840)
Rees, Anne-Marie L 4:01:34 (9,529)
Rees, Heather F 7:03:10 (35,177)
Rees, Janis M 6:53:22 (35,001)
Rees, Kelly A 6:13:48 (33,535)
Rees, Lisa E 4:36:45 (17,732)
Rees, Mark G 5:11:32 (25,763)
Rees, Michelle J 5:26:51 (28,599)
Rees, Nichola L 7:32:59 (35,516)
Rees, Penelope A 4:55:41 (22,423)
Rees, Rhiannon 4:38:46 (18,220)
Reeve, Emma 4:08:50 (10,928)
Reeve, Lesley 5:35:08 (29,934)
Reeve, Maria T 5:30:48 (29,264)
Reeves, Alice 4:53:25 (21,868)
Reeves, Catherine A 5:44:12 (31,064)
Reeves, Emily E 5:38:26 (30,378)
Reeves, Julie A 3:46:22 (6,231)
Reeves, Rosalind R 4:25:45 (15,006)
Reeves, Thelma 6:24:59 (34,123)
Refson, Nicole 5:07:01 (24,887)
Regan, Coleen C 3:51:37 (7,279)
Regan, Connie F 5:15:27 (26,553)
Regine, Verdier 4:22:27 (14,184)
Reglar, Kate 5:35:21 (29,957)
Rehbein, Colleen N 4:43:30 (19,414)
Reich, Arlene R 7:31:05 (35,503)
Reid, Carol A 3:30:11 (3,746)
Reid, Gillian M 5:38:34 (30,390)
Reid, Helen L 4:18:50 (13,291)
Reid, Jacqueline E 5:17:11 (26,891)
Reid, Kathy M 6:25:42 (34,154)
Reid, Margaret M 5:06:06 (24,712)
Reid, Stephanie J 4:37:17 (17,838)
Reid, Teresa M 7:18:20 (35,373)
Reid, Toni 5:14:23 (26,308)
Reif, Brigitte 4:47:57 (20,520)
Reiff, Jemma L 6:12:16 (33,441)
Reilly, Amanda J 5:01:45 (23,880)
Reilly, Cynthia A 5:58:46 (32,489)
Reilly, Samantha J 4:42:30 (19,178)
Reiser, Sandra 4:43:21 (19,394)
Reis-Wilmart, Laurence 4:10:59 (11,365)
Renfer, Fionuala 3:54:08 (7,823)
Rennie, Caroline G 4:51:31 (21,371)
Rennie, Felicity C 3:50:40 (7,071)
Rennolds, Laura L 5:53:32 (32,015)
Revett, Jill T 4:17:43 (13,002)
Revill, Julia 4:35:57 (17,524)
Reynecke, Marinda 4:59:22 (23,347)
Reynolds, Abigail M 4:17:29 (12,940)
Reynolds, Emma H 4:52:48 (21,700)
Reynolds, Emma L 7:05:08 (35,206)
Reynolds, Emma V 5:10:37 (25,599)
Reynolds, Frances M 4:24:23 (14,675)
Reynolds, Janet L 5:51:14 (31,799)
Reynolds, Julie M 3:51:49 (7,318)
Reynolds, Lee 4:33:37 (16,942)
Reynolds, Leigh 4:24:40 (14,739)
Reynolds, Maria H 5:41:41 (30,793)
Reynolds, Marie 3:59:57 (9,198)
Reynolds, Rachael 4:40:53 (18,755)
Reynolds, Rachel 4:00:55 (9,402)
Reynolds, Sandra J 3:19:05 (2,401)
Rhodes, Caroline A 3:59:17 (9,037)
Rhodes, Cathy A 4:45:42 (19,992)
Rhodes, Deborah A 3:36:44 (4,651)
Rhodes, Gillian L 5:58:30 (32,468)
Rhodes, Jacqueline S 5:17:26 (26,944)
Rhymes, Natasha A 3:48:45 (6,678)
Rhys, Nicola 3:54:17 (7,870)
Rhys-Gill, Emma L 5:26:16 (28,503)
Rice, Juliet S 4:32:21 (16,636)
Rice, Margaret 4:45:53 (20,029)

Rich, Sue L 4:52:57 (21,742)
Richard, Lil G 4:51:51 (21,453)
Richards, Caroline M 7:11:27 (35,295)
Richards, Caryl E 4:14:33 (12,219)
Richards, Deborah R 4:28:48 (15,811)
Richards, Denise 6:44:06 (34,778)
Richards, Elizabeth A 5:21:38 (27,717)
Richards, Haren 4:12:39 (11,751)
Richards, Jane 6:24:33 (34,103)
Richards, Katie 5:10:33 (25,586)
Richards, Mary 4:06:17 (10,414)
Richards, Nicole 5:17:17 (26,915)
Richards, Ruth G 4:13:21 (11,921)
Richardson, Alyson J 3:41:35 (5,454)
Richardson, Helen E 6:07:38 (33,138)
Richardson, Karen E 4:58:56 (23,238)
Richardson, Melanie C 4:48:07 (20,555)
Richardson, Penny A 4:57:58 (23,025)
Richardson, Rachel A 5:43:18 (30,972)
Richardson, Susan L 5:57:04 (32,337)
Richards-Warren, Sara J 5:28:57 (28,975)
Richey, Kelly L 4:38:18 (18,093)
Richmond, Andrea 4:31:47 (16,522)
Richmond, Denise 5:34:56 (29,906)
Richmond, Karen J 5:02:11 (23,967)
Richmond, Louise A 4:58:43 (23,192)
Richmond, Louise A 5:41:50 (30,811)
Richmond, Mandy K 3:58:56 (8,947)
Richmond, Nicola J 3:56:56 (8,461)
Rickard, Donna 4:21:57 (14,077)
Rickard, Lisa D 5:25:53 (28,439)
Rickett, Leanne 5:19:43 (27,376)
Ricketts, Deborah R 5:04:35 (24,430)
Rickey, Angela J 4:37:14 (17,826)
Riddell, Grainne 3:38:03 (4,843)
Riddle, Kayley M 4:37:43 (17,942)
Ridehalgh, Sarah E 3:22:48 (2,777)
Rideout, Amanda 5:03:22 (24,208)
Rideout, Becky J 6:20:52 (33,944)
Ridge, Julia P 4:18:33 (13,228)
Ridgley, Clare L 4:48:17 (20,597)
Ridgley, Julie R 3:40:12 (5,217)
Ridgway, Frances 3:43:06 (5,707)
Ridings, Susan A 4:50:21 (21,080)
Ridler, Suzie J 4:47:11 (20,331)
Ridnell, Katie A 6:46:11 (34,835)
Ridout, Linda B 5:30:00 (29,137)
Ridout, Sarah M 4:20:44 (13,780)
Rigal, Christine 4:00:16 (9,266)
Rigby, Rachael L 4:40:14 (18,585)
Rigney, Hansi 4:16:06 (12,596)
Riley, Adele L 4:36:31 (17,671)
Riley, Belinda J 4:28:41 (15,781)
Riley, Debra M 5:24:20 (28,163)
Riley, Donna R 3:43:28 (5,770)
Riley, Michelle A 4:59:48 (23,459)
Riley, Nicola D 5:56:37 (32,300)
Riley-Jordan, Christine 4:23:32 (14,456)
Rimmer, Dawn I 5:13:39 (26,150)
Rimmington, Maria 5:34:00 (29,762)
Ringer, Samantha C 7:43:18 (35,590)
Ringham, Gypsy R 4:07:10 (10,601)
Riordan, Pamela 5:32:54 (29,589)
Riseborough, Catharine 4:54:58 (22,260)
Riseborough, Jaqueline A 7:55:46 (35,635)
Riseley, Katie A 3:55:38 (8,146)
Ritchie, Hazel A 4:51:35 (21,392)
Ritchie, Kate E 4:49:19 (20,842)
Ritchie, Nicola D 4:17:56 (13,052)
Rivers, Anna M 5:09:52 (25,444)
Rivers, Katherine M 4:29:49 (16,095)
Rivlin, Adrienne J 4:42:40 (19,219)
Roach, Denise V 3:57:30 (8,600)
Roake, Jane E 4:55:57 (22,502)
Roake, Karen N 4:09:39 (11,103)
Robb, Allison 5:02:21 (24,001)
Robb, Nicola 4:48:53 (20,740)
Robbins, Diane E 5:31:25 (29,367)
Robbins, Helen F 4:46:06 (20,082)
Robbins, Patricia 4:58:27 (23,147)
Robbins, Sarah C 4:27:12 (15,387)
Robboy, Anita W 5:14:00 (26,228)
Robert, Vanessa L 4:05:13 (10,187)
Roberts, Alison L 4:32:01 (16,562)
Roberts, Andrea E 3:15:16 (2,019)
Roberts, Angela 4:47:26 (20,389)
Roberts, Annette 4:10:13 (11,209)
Roberts, Carole M 3:54:11 (7,835)
Roberts, Claire 4:31:21 (16,436)
Roberts, Corrie 4:17:56 (13,052)
Roberts, Debbie 5:20:24 (27,496)
Roberts, Dee R 4:49:37 (20,920)
Roberts, Dominique M 6:14:37 (33,586)
Roberts, Elsie T 3:42:45 (5,635)
Roberts, Esther A 4:13:05 (11,853)
Roberts, Glenda 3:53:57 (7,779)
Roberts, Hannah L 4:12:49 (11,793)
Roberts, Hayley A 4:48:58 (20,757)
Roberts, Jacqueline L 3:49:37 (6,854)
Roberts, Janine J 5:04:21 (24,390)
Roberts, Karen R 5:42:49 (30,915)
Roberts, Karina A 9:01:49 (35,691)
Roberts, Katherine S 3:26:13 (3,159)
Roberts, Lindy D 5:44:49 (31,132)
Roberts, Lydia 4:58:05 (23,054)
Roberts, Mary G 5:58:37 (32,477)
Roberts, Melanie J 4:02:04 (9,616)
Roberts, Michelle 3:48:23 (6,587)
Roberts, Nicola J 6:04:30 (32,919)
Roberts, Paula A 5:31:50 (29,424)
Roberts, Raceh E 6:09:17 (33,253)
Roberts, Rachel C 5:04:16 (24,370)
Roberts, Rhian L 7:39:42 (35,559)
Roberts, Sally A 5:55:51 (32,224)
Roberts, Sarah J 4:09:08 (10,986)
Roberts, Sheila 5:18:21 (27,135)
Roberts, Stacy B 5:16:45 (26,798)
Roberts, Veronica A 4:56:34 (22,647)
Robertson, Abigail K 4:50:16 (21,061)
Robertson, Carolyn F 5:42:47 (30,904)
Robertson, Clare E 3:53:30 (7,689)
Robertson, Iona 3:18:18 (2,325)
Robertson, Isabel 5:15:35 (26,582)
Robertson, Jennifer 6:36:19 (34,552)
Robertson, Joanne M 4:36:24 (17,640)
Robertson, Lindsay F 6:10:52 (33,358)
Robertson, Moira C 6:18:08 (33,786)
Robertson-Tawse, Karen A 5:23:39 (28,040)
Robins, Amanda P 6:10:57 (33,365)
Robins, Mia 5:29:23 (29,054)
Robins, Samantha 5:25:44 (28,413)
Robinson, Carol 5:49:30 (31,626)
Robinson, Christine P 5:42:13 (30,852)
Robinson, Cordelia A 3:39:49 (5,163)
Robinson, Deborah M 3:35:32 (4,490)
Robinson, Deena S 5:11:00 (25,665)
Robinson, Donagh M 6:21:03 (33,956)
Robinson, Emily H 3:58:17 (8,786)
Robinson, Emma L 4:13:10 (11,871)
Robinson, Fiona C 3:41:56 (5,507)
Robinson, Isla J 3:49:03 (6,743)
Robinson, Joanne N 5:44:58 (31,150)
Robinson, Joy 4:57:53 (23,006)
Robinson, Julie A 3:56:06 (8,247)
Robinson, Karen 6:32:11 (34,416)
Robinson, Karen A 4:06:57 (10,558)
Robinson, Katharine M 4:52:52 (21,717)
Robinson, Kay H 5:55:49 (32,219)
Robinson, Liza G 5:34:32 (29,856)
Robinson, Louise A 7:21:05 (35,397)
Robinson, Louise S 5:13:41 (26,161)
Robinson, Mandy 5:22:12 (27,813)
Robinson, Nikki J 5:45:58 (31,253)
Robinson, Paula R 3:52:13 (7,411)
Robinson, Rebecca A 3:32:30 (4,073)
Robinson, Sally L 5:05:21 (24,564)
Robinson, Samantha J 4:04:23 (10,035)
Robinson, Sue 4:31:32 (16,466)
Robinson, Susan J 4:17:59 (13,072)
Robinson, Tracy M 5:55:45 (32,213)
Robjohns, Karen S 5:18:26 (27,148)
Robson, Clare L 7:14:34 (35,339)
Robson, Dany L 3:37:24 (4,737)
Robson, Dawn E 4:16:44 (12,748)
Robson, Jane 5:11:30 (25,756)
Robson, Janie E 7:17:55 (35,368)
Robson, Joanne P 4:16:20 (12,654)
Robson, Patricia A 6:47:50 (34,883)
Robson, Trish 3:24:49 (2,997)
Roby, Rachael A 6:12:40 (33,469)
Rochard, Annyvonne L 4:07:45 (10,712)
Roche, Alison D 4:26:39 (15,223)
Roche, Charlotte L 5:26:20 (28,516)
Roche, Claudine 5:02:22 (24,008)
Roche, Elizabeth 5:44:14 (31,069)
Rochez, Hazel M 4:48:45 (20,708)
Rochford, Eleanor M 5:21:10 (27,626)
Rockey, Katrina C 4:39:49 (18,490)
Rockliffe, Jacqueline M 3:07:45 (1,367)
Roddick, Dimah 4:07:11 (10,606)
Rodger, Louise V 5:12:02 (25,861)
Rodger, Suzanne M 4:20:07 (13,629)
Rodseth, Anthea 3:53:57 (7,779)
Rodway, Feyi 6:41:50 (34,714)
Roehreke, Yuki 5:45:27 (31,201)
Roehrle, Madelaine 3:34:45 (4,368)
Roffe-Silvester, Alice L 3:33:17 (4,176)
Rogers, Caroline M 4:53:59 (22,016)
Rogers, Caron 4:53:23 (21,854)
Rogers, Jennifer L 4:56:28 (22,628)
Rogers, Joanne 4:34:24 (17,114)
Rogers, Lauren 4:58:22 (23,124)
Rogers, Linda A 3:59:30 (9,094)
Rogers, Pamela M 6:04:01 (32,890)
Rogers, Patricia M 4:42:20 (19,129)
Rogerson, Donna M 3:50:54 (7,115)
Roggenstein, Eva S 3:53:03 (7,580)
Rolfe, Sally A 4:59:10 (23,299)
Rolland, Beatrice 4:30:02 (16,155)
Rollings, Jacquelyn T 4:04:38 (10,080)
Rollinson, Sally A 6:08:07 (33,181)
Rolph, Claire L 5:39:26 (30,514)
Rolph, Dawn 4:12:55 (11,809)
Romaine, Kimberly K 4:03:12 (9,818)
Romanos, Mary H 4:59:48 (23,459)
Romecin, Lindsay H 3:48:33 (6,637)
Ronaldson, Emma L 6:05:26 (32,991)
Rook, Alexandria J 6:28:02 (34,254)
Rooney, Jacqueline A 5:32:24 (29,508)
Rooney, Louise 4:45:28 (19,938)
Rooney, Samantha E 6:02:25 (32,780)
Rooney, Sarah 4:59:36 (23,412)
Rooney, Sharron D 5:25:39 (28,396)
Roper, Helen 4:30:32 (16,261)
Rorke, Claire L 4:42:16 (19,117)
Rosa, Marie-France 4:20:45 (13,784)
Rosales, Ana M 5:22:59 (27,936)
Rose, Andrea 5:58:36 (32,476)
Rose, Caroline 5:42:25 (30,871)
Rose, Dina R 5:35:54 (30,038)
Rose, Jane E 6:20:12 (33,896)
Rose, Joanna K 4:28:43 (15,792)
Rose, Joanne V 4:47:07 (20,317)
Rose, Julie 5:07:25 (24,980)
Rose, Shirley 6:39:02 (34,640)
Rose-Quirie, Alison J 3:56:26 (8,338)
Rosewarne, Kim 5:56:56 (32,327)
Ross, Catherine 5:09:11 (25,313)
Ross, Emily J 6:04:39 (32,927)
Ross, Fiona F 4:30:03 (16,159)
Ross, Frances M 4:24:35 (14,722)
Ross, Marianne E 6:56:32 (35,062)
Ross, Tina 6:08:10 (33,184)
Ross Russell, Fiona 3:11:33 (1,675)
Rossall, Sue 5:50:44 (31,752)
Rossi, Pascale 5:40:47 (30,680)
Rossi, Stefania 5:11:33 (25,769)
Rossi, Valeria 6:48:51 (34,907)
Rossouw, Julie A 4:09:40 (11,108)
Roth, Kirsten 4:08:52 (10,937)
Rothwell, Tania 5:26:11 (28,487)
Roudette, Lisa 5:18:25 (27,146)
Roumilhac, Jocelyne M 5:08:11 (25,136)
Rounsevell, Jessica K 5:04:51 (24,487)
Rouse, Fiona B 6:56:06 (35,054)
Rouse, Janice J 5:07:02 (24,892)
Rouse, Judy H 4:00:10 (9,242)
Routledge, Olivia J 4:50:34 (21,139)
Rowan, Frances A 6:12:28 (33,458)

Rowbotham, Emily C	4:30:35 (16,276)	
Rowden, Lisa D	4:59:56 (23,484)	
Rowe, Catherine A	4:49:41 (20,932)	
Rowe, Catherine D	4:35:11 (17,323)	
Rowe, Diane	4:57:20 (22,870)	
Rowe, Elizabeth A	4:23:40 (14,484)	
Rowe, Emily J	4:43:52 (19,503)	
Rowe, Joy	4:27:41 (15,512)	
Rowe, Juliet	3:12:01 (1,729)	
Rowe, Vanessa C	4:37:51 (17,969)	
Rowell, Marianne C	4:23:46 (14,505)	
Rowland, Carole	6:35:07 (34,503)	
Rowland, Emily L	5:07:22 (24,970)	
Rowland, Jude A	6:05:45 (33,026)	
Rowland, Leah	5:37:10 (30,194)	
Rowland, Ronina P	3:40:31 (5,273)	
Rowbold, Sarah A	6:56:46 (35,068)	
Rowlands, Alison N	4:44:12 (19,602)	
Rowlands, Angela	4:43:55 (19,514)	
Rowlands, Angela M	5:21:01 (27,605)	
Rowlands, Catherine J	5:10:23 (25,552)	
Rowlands, Helen M	5:43:52 (31,026)	
Rowlands, Sophie	6:01:59 (32,752)	
Rowlands-Wong, Christina P	5:26:05 (28,472)	
Rowles, Juliet	6:20:37 (33,931)	
Rowling, Julie	6:31:09 (34,366)	
Rowlinson, Helen E	5:31:00 (29,294)	
Rowntree, Karen	4:29:26 (15,986)	
Rowswell, Kathryn M	4:48:51 (20,732)	
Roy, Diane	3:30:18 (3,763)	
Ruaro, Bruna	5:31:36 (29,388)	
Rubenstein, Terry	4:42:36 (19,207)	
Ruby, Kay E	5:49:18 (31,614)	
Rudaz, Katie D	3:33:00 (4,138)	
Rudd, Bee J	5:07:43 (25,038)	
Rudd, Donna	4:47:03 (20,299)	
Rudd, Nicola S	7:35:32 (35,537)	
Ruderman, Louisa J	3:07:38 (1,355)	
Rudge, Gina	6:03:50 (32,876)	
Rudkins, Lorna J	5:47:42 (31,430)	
Rudland, Deborah	5:27:34 (28,726)	
Rudman, Bernadette	5:12:10 (25,892)	
Ruest, Martha	5:01:41 (23,865)	
Ruff, Susan E	4:57:49 (22,991)	
Rugg, Joanna	5:24:54 (28,261)	
Ruggles, Nicola L	4:42:44 (19,238)	
Ruks, Mandy	5:25:01 (28,272)	
Rule, Jennifer J	4:47:39 (20,441)	
Rumbold, Naomi	4:26:29 (15,184)	
Rumins, Tanya H	5:38:02 (30,308)	
Rusby, Linda A	4:57:32 (22,911)	
Ruscuklic, Brooke	4:14:16 (12,157)	
Rushby, Sonia M	4:01:23 (9,494)	
Rushton, Michelle	3:30:08 (3,740)	
Rushton, Victoria E	5:09:16 (25,328)	
Rushworth, Elaine	5:30:41 (29,251)	
Rusling, Barbara	3:46:51 (6,311)	
Russ, Julie M	4:29:30 (16,007)	
Russell, Alex	4:53:24 (21,862)	
Russell, Brenda D	4:57:56 (23,014)	
Russell, Catharine F	5:02:10 (23,964)	
Russell, Cathryn S	6:02:33 (32,789)	
Russell, Danielle L	6:05:08 (32,973)	
Russell, Emma	5:27:53 (28,776)	
Russell, Janet	6:33:51 (34,461)	
Russell, Julie M	5:07:31 (25,004)	
Russell, Lisa T	4:42:59 (19,291)	
Russell, Rachel C	3:50:37 (7,059)	
Russell, Rebecca	4:51:49 (21,440)	
Russell, Sophie C	3:52:13 (7,411)	
Russell, Tina M	5:37:59 (30,298)	
Russell, Vikki M	5:18:42 (27,199)	
Rusyn, Linda	5:01:28 (23,823)	
Ruta, Julie F	4:42:40 (19,219)	
Rutherford, Carolyn M	7:27:57 (35,456)	
Rutherford, Julia	3:51:18 (7,202)	
Rutherford, Karen M	4:39:27 (18,404)	
Rutherford, Pam	4:20:44 (13,780)	
Ruthven, Stephanie	4:24:20 (14,660)	
Rutter, Alison J	6:58:16 (35,095)	
Ryan, Anne T	5:41:39 (30,787)	
Ryan, Claire	4:56:48 (22,715)	
Ryan, Claire	5:11:21 (25,738)	

Ryan, Dorothea E	4:31:27 (16,451)	
Ryan, Elizabeth M	6:10:00 (33,304)	
Ryan, Fiona H	8:03:30 (35,647)	
Ryan, Geraldine	5:29:48 (29,110)	
Ryan, Julie	4:53:30 (21,885)	
Ryan, Leslie A	6:24:05 (34,084)	
Ryan, Rhian	6:03:24 (32,846)	
Rychtrmocova, Alena	4:36:44 (17,723)	
Ryde, Michaela L	4:23:45 (14,502)	
Ryder, Helen S	3:36:31 (4,616)	
Ryder, Ros S	3:46:11 (6,205)	
Rydland, Mona	3:28:11 (3,432)	
Ryland, Emma J	4:37:55 (17,986)	
Rytchalov, Joanna	4:29:05 (15,880)	
Saddler-Young, Leanne	5:02:51 (24,095)	
Sadler, Caroline A	5:40:19 (30,630)	
Sadler, Kay	4:23:44 (14,497)	
Safa, Mersedeh	5:55:38 (32,204)	
Saines, Caroline	4:09:29 (11,068)	
Saint, Debbie M	3:58:01 (8,728)	
Saint, Elizabeth J	4:53:34 (21,904)	
Saldo, Antonella	5:38:14 (30,340)	
Sale, Sally	6:34:43 (34,482)	
Sale, Susan A	4:41:45 (18,975)	
Sales, Elizabeth J	4:18:49 (13,287)	
Saliba, Myrna	4:03:10 (9,810)	
Salisbury, Michelle	5:14:43 (26,389)	
Salkeld, Anne E	6:48:06 (34,890)	
Salley, Joanne	4:12:39 (11,751)	
Salmon, Amelia J	5:05:20 (24,558)	
Salmon, Catherine J	5:25:59 (28,453)	
Salmon, Elizabeth	6:47:08 (34,864)	
Salmon, Emily	5:10:38 (25,604)	
Salmon, Victoria R	5:04:58 (24,512)	
Salt, Annie	6:01:38 (32,729)	
Salter, Nicola J	4:56:48 (22,715)	
Salvisberg, Erica	4:39:31 (18,418)	
Salway, Jill	4:04:03 (9,974)	
Salzmann, Liliane	4:56:07 (22,540)	
Sammer-Englert, Hiltrud	4:06:00 (10,351)	
Sampson, Philippa L	5:38:41 (30,412)	
Sams, Sarah M	5:50:17 (31,701)	
Sams, Sharon	4:38:55 (18,258)	
Samson, Denise	5:17:06 (26,877)	
Samson, Rachel M	4:42:20 (19,129)	
Samuelson-Dean, Katie M	3:27:22 (3,336)	
Samways, Carol A	5:22:04 (27,789)	
Sandell, Pennie S	4:06:16 (10,409)	
Sanders, Bethany E	5:02:49 (24,089)	
Sanders, Caroline	4:24:23 (14,675)	
Sanders, Elizabeth J	6:04:59 (32,961)	
Sanders, Lucinda E	5:02:49 (24,089)	
Sanders, Stephanie A	4:21:46 (14,025)	
Sanders-Hewett, Rebecca F	5:29:28 (29,069)	
Sanderson, Julie L	5:08:46 (25,237)	
Sanderson, Zoe M	4:05:45 (10,297)	
Sandford, Elizabeth J	3:40:30 (5,266)	
Sandford, Gillian	6:00:30 (32,622)	
Sandiford, Frances M	5:04:08 (24,348)	
Sandilands, Julie	4:20:25 (13,714)	
Sandilands, Marietta M	5:11:26 (25,746)	
Sands, Helen E	5:24:51 (28,250)	
Sands, Tim J	5:10:59 (25,662)	
Sankey, Adele C	7:12:46 (35,316)	
Sanna, Maria Adele	4:29:50 (16,101)	
Sapey, Jayne E	4:33:05 (16,806)	
Sarai, Satpal	5:35:31 (29,976)	
Sardina, Annie	5:54:22 (32,089)	
Sargeant, Wendy E	4:54:29 (22,145)	
Sargent, Rebecca C	5:17:00 (26,858)	
Sargent, Ylarna L	5:24:40 (28,212)	
Sargent Wong, Suzanne	5:22:31 (27,860)	
Satgunasingam, Yamna J	5:12:07 (25,874)	
Saul, Bernadette B	5:20:49 (27,577)	
Saul, Jodie P	8:30:05 (35,678)	
Saul, Nikki A	7:05:24 (35,208)	
Saunders, Ann R	4:29:23 (15,971)	
Saunders, Clare M	4:24:51 (14,797)	
Saunders, Hannah L	5:34:39 (29,870)	
Saunders, Jamie Lee	4:53:40 (21,933)	
Saunders, Jane	7:45:58 (35,603)	
Saunders, Juliet E	4:33:18 (16,867)	
Saunders, Linda D	5:21:24 (27,680)	

Saunders, Linda K	7:28:59 (35,464)	
Saunders, Nadine	5:18:12 (27,103)	
Saunt, Tonia E	4:23:22 (14,411)	
Savage, Emma	5:03:59 (24,322)	
Savage, Melissa M	4:58:25 (23,136)	
Savjani, Nisha J	6:44:04 (34,774)	
Sawyer, Helen	4:27:01 (15,326)	
Sawyer, Olivia	5:21:17 (27,652)	
Saxon, Lesley	5:40:27 (30,646)	
Say, Shelly L	5:10:12 (25,526)	
Sayer, Katie	4:13:44 (12,026)	
Scadding, Kristianne L	5:01:42 (23,869)	
Scahill, Helen L	5:19:44 (27,379)	
Scale, Barbara A	6:43:34 (34,761)	
Scammell, Amy K	6:46:23 (34,840)	
Scammell, Emily H	6:46:24 (34,842)	
Scanlon, Trudy A	5:25:12 (28,302)	
Scarborough, Sara	5:58:33 (32,470)	
Scarisbrick, Jane	4:17:44 (13,006)	
Scarrott, Yvonne C	3:25:52 (3,108)	
Scarth, Anna M	5:21:27 (27,687)	
Scatchard, Bernadette M	4:39:44 (18,471)	
Sceeny, Claire E	5:34:11 (29,791)	
Schadschneider, Sabine	4:49:38 (20,923)	
Schaer, Regina	4:55:16 (22,333)	
Schaerer, Patricia	3:53:09 (7,603)	
Schafer, Alexandra	6:12:14 (33,437)	
Schafer, Birgit	5:14:56 (26,435)	
Schellekens, Patricia	4:11:01 (11,371)	
Schickhoff-Brown, Claire E	4:54:43 (22,204)	
Schier, Peggy A	4:57:51 (22,998)	
Schiess, Fabienne	4:48:39 (20,679)	
Schmid, Erika R	3:25:36 (3,076)	
Schmidt, Elke	2:47:09 (288)	
Schmidt, Sandra H	3:38:11 (4,870)	
Schneider, Natasha M	6:58:44 (35,104)	
Schoenbach, Sandra	3:34:59 (4,407)	
Schoepp, Melanie J	4:15:03 (12,334)	
Schofield, Alice M	4:35:21 (17,372)	
Schofield, Claire E	3:27:01 (3,286)	
Schofield, Sarah J	4:48:19 (20,613)	
Scholes, Lee T	5:10:29 (25,574)	
Scholten, Arleen P	4:00:24 (9,293)	
Schrapel, Alison J	6:16:17 (33,702)	
Schroeder, Eva	4:36:24 (17,640)	
Schroeter, Kate A	4:55:43 (22,433)	
Schuberth, Tess	4:40:43 (18,704)	
Schuller, Lynne	4:38:58 (18,277)	
Schulz, Ursula G	3:41:18 (5,411)	
Schwab, Correna	5:36:55 (30,166)	
Schwarz, Marion	4:07:48 (10,724)	
Schweizer, Kathryn P	4:48:02 (20,541)	
Schwerdtfeger, Kylie	5:31:23 (29,359)	
Scorer, Sally L	4:35:30 (17,401)	
Scotchford, Janet	3:52:13 (7,411)	
Scott, Abi	4:57:15 (22,834)	
Scott, Alison C	4:51:02 (21,248)	
Scott, Amanda	6:28:20 (34,257)	
Scott, Amy R	5:12:57 (26,033)	
Scott, Angela G	4:42:37 (19,211)	
Scott, Carol M	4:39:08 (18,314)	
Scott, Catriona C	5:11:03 (25,676)	
Scott, Debbie A	5:13:51 (26,204)	
Scott, Elaine M	6:58:08 (35,093)	
Scott, Hannah J	5:33:54 (29,747)	
Scott, Helen	5:01:00 (23,725)	
Scott, Helen M	5:49:05 (31,594)	
Scott, Jane E	4:01:20 (9,486)	
Scott, Kelly Y	5:59:02 (32,509)	
Scott, Kimberleigh K	5:05:17 (24,555)	
Scott, Kirsty	5:12:54 (26,022)	
Scott, Laura-Lee	5:37:36 (30,246)	
Scott, Linda M	5:07:28 (24,991)	
Scott, Margaret	5:22:54 (27,921)	
Scott, Myrna L	4:58:40 (23,183)	
Scott, Penny	4:11:10 (11,417)	
Scott, Polly K	4:03:14 (9,824)	
Scott, Rachel J	3:56:21 (8,319)	
Scott, Rosemarie D	4:16:46 (12,755)	
Scott, Sally D	4:23:20 (14,407)	
Scott, Sally L	3:24:15 (2,934)	
Scott, Sarah J	5:15:44 (26,612)	
Scott, Sarah K	4:56:49 (22,719)	

Scott, Sheila	7:11:45 (35,300)	
Scott, Susan P	5:36:24 (30,097)	
Scott, Wendy A	3:10:31 (1,596)	
Scott, Yvonne F	5:03:35 (24,251)	
Scotter, Kate	4:02:59 (9,781)	
Scott-Lewis, Jenna B	7:13:25 (35,328)	
Scrafton, Gaynor D	4:51:05 (21,262)	
Scrase, Linda E	4:55:01 (22,267)	
Scroggs, Josephine A	3:59:11 (9,008)	
Scully, Rebecca C	6:41:58 (34,716)	
Seaborne, Becci N	4:58:18 (23,103)	
Seabrook, Patricia H	5:22:08 (27,800)	
Seager, Jill A	5:14:29 (26,330)	
Seager, Lise A	5:24:22 (28,168)	
Seal, Janine	5:03:18 (24,191)	
Sealey, Samantha C	5:39:44 (30,564)	
Seaman, Lucy A	4:52:18 (21,568)	
Searle, Kerry-Ann	6:36:52 (34,575)	
Seaton, Naomi	4:37:59 (18,003)	
Sedda, Chaiara	3:57:59 (8,718)	
Sedda, Roberta	4:26:15 (15,120)	
Seddon, Suzannah L	4:50:55 (21,221)	
Sefton, Emma A	4:37:54 (17,981)	
Segal, Laura	6:12:48 (33,480)	
Segal, Michael	7:18:22 (35,374)	
Sekhon, Amanpreet	7:11:46 (35,301)	
Sekulin, Jenny L	6:24:29 (34,098)	
Selby, Elizabeth A	4:53:36 (21,913)	
Selby, Kathryn A	5:58:42 (32,484)	
Selby, Tricia M	4:25:59 (15,054)	
Sell, Merran R	4:27:43 (15,524)	
Sellar, Julia M	3:58:00 (8,725)	
Sellard, Lesley J	4:54:19 (22,104)	
Selman, Katharine E	4:48:45 (20,708)	
Selves, Julie A	6:58:55 (35,110)	
Semaine, Kelly	6:37:17 (34,588)	
Sembhi, Satvinder K	6:03:02 (32,821)	
Semikin, Allison K	5:34:29 (29,845)	
Semple, Denise A	7:09:21 (35,265)	
Semple, Ruth S	4:48:11 (20,573)	
Senior, Gill V	3:38:03 (4,843)	
Senior, Gina L	5:06:48 (24,841)	
Senior, Kelly M	6:04:06 (32,895)	
Senner, Patricia L	5:41:24 (30,758)	
Serocold, Caroline	7:21:21 (35,399)	
Serruys, Birgit	4:52:41 (21,662)	
Seton, Sarah	5:50:01 (31,677)	
Settle, Allison D	5:28:45 (28,941)	
Settle, Clare R	3:16:20 (2,108)	
Settle, Dianne	5:08:23 (25,172)	
Seward, Caroline J	4:26:14 (15,114)	
Sewell, Anna	3:56:44 (8,415)	
Sewell, Carina L	3:52:55 (7,549)	
Sewell, Melaine J	3:57:13 (8,533)	
Sexton, Penelope H	4:41:28 (18,910)	
Seymour, Allison	5:47:15 (31,375)	
Seymour, Angela L	5:02:09 (23,961)	
Seymour, Annmarie	4:05:01 (10,147)	
Seymour, Charlotte	5:00:11 (23,547)	
Seymour, Heather L	4:31:44 (16,515)	
Seymour, Jackie S	6:20:57 (33,948)	
Seymour, Karen	5:16:58 (26,852)	
Seymour, Miranda F	3:59:35 (9,114)	
Seymour, Natalie	5:10:58 (25,660)	
Sforza, Sandra	4:15:32 (12,448)	
Shadbolt, Veronica M	3:35:06 (4,420)	
Shah, Deepa	7:41:04 (35,570)	
Shah, Kirti	4:52:25 (21,600)	
Shah, Panna M	4:15:50 (12,518)	
Shah, Shila	4:52:19 (21,576)	
Shandbolt, Rebecca E	4:25:55 (15,037)	
Shanley, Suzy J	4:46:21 (20,144)	
Shannon, Carole	4:24:25 (14,685)	
Shannon, Clare L	4:55:45 (22,444)	
Shapps, Belinda	4:51:35 (21,392)	
Sharkey, Hayley D	5:05:33 (24,612)	
Sharland, Sharon L	3:44:49 (5,995)	
Sharman, Charlotte A	3:54:14 (7,848)	
Sharman, Deborah	6:26:37 (34,196)	
Sharman, Suzanne C	3:24:11 (2,928)	
Sharp, Lisa C	5:48:18 (31,505)	
Sharp, Nicola	5:28:13 (28,840)	
Sharp, Phillippa R	6:39:03 (34,641)	

Sharp, Rebecca L	4:19:26 (13,440)	
Sharp, Sherley A	5:50:21 (31,715)	
Sharpe, Anthea L	3:35:15 (4,443)	
Sharpe, Deborah M	5:51:47 (31,854)	
Sharpe, Linda	6:21:02 (33,953)	
Sharpe, Rebecca A	5:28:15 (28,849)	
Sharpe, Toni J	7:00:13 (35,130)	
Sharrod, Sandra	5:08:31 (25,191)	
Shave, Donna E	5:39:26 (30,514)	
Shaw, Carol E	4:25:09 (14,859)	
Shaw, Caroline M	4:37:04 (17,801)	
Shaw, Deborah A	3:36:41 (4,640)	
Shaw, Diane R	4:55:35 (22,409)	
Shaw, Fiona	5:06:26 (24,778)	
Shaw, Helene L	4:35:44 (17,470)	
Shaw, Janet E	4:21:12 (13,897)	
Shaw, Juliette M	4:34:33 (17,159)	
Shaw, Kerry	5:27:28 (28,707)	
Shaw, Margaret R	6:55:10 (35,040)	
Shaw, Sue	5:30:55 (29,282)	
Shaw, Tanya J	3:14:33 (1,949)	
Shaw, Tracey	6:30:30 (34,341)	
Shawe, Diane J	5:08:04 (25,108)	
Shayler, Donna	6:24:41 (34,116)	
Shea, Samantha L	5:00:44 (23,670)	
Sheahan, Sarah L	3:53:40 (7,721)	
Shearer, Jennifer F	4:48:29 (20,643)	
Shearing, Vanessa F	5:12:16 (25,915)	
Shea-Simonds, Claire	3:48:53 (6,700)	
Sheath, Emily R	4:58:23 (23,129)	
Sheehan, Belinda M	3:59:33 (9,108)	
Sheehan, Sheila M	6:33:09 (34,443)	
Sheen, Alice M	5:56:33 (32,294)	
Sheen, Toni R	5:58:51 (32,495)	
Sheldon, Sheena F	5:46:03 (31,266)	
Shelley, Jo	4:02:08 (9,626)	
Shelley, Louise A	5:46:21 (31,298)	
Shelley, Prue A	4:31:36 (16,484)	
Shelton-Smith, Katie	6:14:38 (33,587)	
Shennan, Lisa C	5:48:45 (31,557)	
Shepherd, Amanda	4:32:20 (16,634)	
Shepherd, Jacqueline	5:00:37 (23,639)	
Shepherd, Jennifer M	4:16:29 (12,695)	
Shepherd, Jet Jon	3:22:33 (2,752)	
Shepherd, Sarah	4:05:04 (10,156)	
Shepherd, Sarah L	6:26:55 (34,210)	
Sheppard, Katharine A	4:47:04 (20,305)	
Sheppard, Sharron L	4:12:55 (11,809)	
Sheppard-Jones, Victoria L	5:00:28 (23,608)	
Sheppey, Sallanne	4:43:46 (19,475)	
Sherbourne, Amy L	4:44:07 (19,568)	
Sherlock, Fiona J	5:01:23 (23,811)	
Sherlock, Susan J	5:50:50 (31,762)	
Sherman-Weldon, Jodie	4:59:13 (23,314)	
Sherrard, Polly J	5:16:12 (26,700)	
Sherridan, Angela	5:49:09 (31,599)	
Sherry, Charlotte E	5:03:28 (24,230)	
Sherwood, Katie E	3:35:18 (4,449)	
Sherwood, Kelly K	5:35:12 (29,940)	
Sherwood-Smith, Joanne	6:55:17 (35,041)	
Shettlesworth, Charlotte S	4:18:39 (13,252)	
Sheward, Victoria E	3:56:32 (8,369)	
Shields, Clare S	4:47:31 (20,413)	
Shields, Diane C	4:09:52 (11,141)	
Shields, Julie	3:59:50 (9,167)	
Shields, Julie	5:04:50 (24,476)	
Shields, Polly	5:29:19 (29,043)	
Shimizu, Yoko	8:11:51 (35,662)	
Shimmin, Diane	4:13:16 (11,899)	
Shipley, Deborah	5:33:39 (29,709)	
Shipp, Amanda K	5:18:01 (27,060)	
Shippey, Susan M	5:02:07 (23,954)	
Shipulina, Alexandra V	4:29:05 (15,880)	
Shirley, Kellie	5:21:15 (27,644)	
Shone, Carol M	7:20:43 (35,394)	
Short, Amber	4:05:22 (10,212)	
Short, Deborah R	5:04:02 (24,332)	
Short, Fiona E	4:57:35 (22,926)	
Short, Suzanne T	4:41:47 (18,989)	
Shorten, Laison M	5:02:49 (24,089)	
Shortley, Kate	5:03:23 (24,213)	
Shortt, Jemma E	5:24:35 (28,196)	

Shotter, Elizabeth A	6:22:22 (34,017)	
Shouls, Susanna C	5:32:30 (29,525)	
Shout, Maria M	5:05:50 (24,659)	
Shrubsole, Clair	3:39:53 (5,174)	
Shubotham, Christine A	4:50:54 (21,217)	
Shufflebottom, Tracy	4:41:44 (18,969)	
Shugart, Shari F	5:42:01 (30,830)	
Shurrock, Claire	5:33:41 (29,711)	
Siba, Lea F	5:51:11 (31,793)	
Sibbald, Blanche	4:59:25 (23,354)	
Sibilla, Julia S	5:09:41 (25,411)	
Sibley, Michelle P	6:12:42 (33,476)	
Sibun, Clare D	4:51:18 (21,315)	
Sicard, Marie L	5:15:31 (26,567)	
Siddall, Melanie	4:11:11 (11,424)	
Sidhwa, Ruki V	3:53:37 (7,709)	
Sieloff, Cheryl J	6:30:25 (34,338)	
Sienkewitz, Nichola	4:28:59 (15,854)	
Siggs, Melanie	4:32:49 (16,744)	
Siklos, Tabitha R	5:24:39 (28,207)	
Silverman, Ruth H	3:43:05 (5,704)	
Silverwood, Emma	3:48:02 (6,532)	
Silvester, Kathryn A	6:57:29 (35,081)	
Sim, Jacqueline	5:16:15 (26,711)	
Sim, Susan M	4:43:16 (19,363)	
Simeon, Helga L	5:25:30 (28,372)	
Simington, Naomi L	5:02:40 (24,069)	
Simmonds, Rebecca J	6:44:05 (34,776)	
Simmonds, Sarah L	4:24:49 (14,785)	
Simmons, Carmel	3:46:31 (6,249)	
Simmons, Eleanor K	3:46:55 (6,327)	
Simmons, Kathy	3:39:40 (5,138)	
Simmons, Lucinda J	3:59:07 (8,990)	
Simmons, Lyn	5:06:37 (24,801)	
Simmons, Rebecca	3:44:53 (6,007)	
Simms, Cheryl R	6:46:56 (34,856)	
Simms, Helen M	5:10:34 (25,589)	
Simpkin, Lorna S	4:49:43 (20,936)	
Simpson, Faith	5:12:30 (25,951)	
Simpson, Liz	4:28:57 (15,846)	
Simpson, Sarah E	4:27:17 (15,416)	
Simpson, Shona R	4:34:21 (17,104)	
Simpson, Toni L	5:09:11 (25,313)	
Sims, Ann C	7:15:46 (35,349)	
Sims, Anne E	5:06:10 (24,729)	
Sims, Claire	5:34:38 (29,867)	
Sims, Gillian	5:35:21 (29,957)	
Sims, Jenny C	5:56:34 (32,296)	
Sims, Luci	6:42:53 (34,746)	
Sims, Rosie G	3:40:40 (5,293)	
Sims, Sarah A	6:14:35 (33,584)	
Sims, Vicky J	4:30:47 (16,313)	
Sinclair, Laura J	4:18:25 (13,181)	
Sinclair, Lynne A	4:16:47 (12,760)	
Sinclair, Zoe E	5:52:41 (31,937)	
Sincock, Kathleen M	3:02:28 (1,025)	
Sinden, Amanda K	5:55:29 (32,190)	
Singer, Jo L	3:23:05 (2,804)	
Singer, Michelle	4:20:42 (13,775)	
Singleton, Janet L	6:38:47 (34,631)	
Singleton, Louisa J	4:30:25 (16,237)	
Sinkinson, Susan J	6:47:43 (34,878)	
Sinnett, Ann E	3:07:56 (1,384)	
Sipidias, Christine	4:08:14 (10,821)	
Sishu, Herdip K	4:09:40 (11,108)	
Sitt, Jennifer	3:42:57 (5,677)	
Sittampalam, Mara J	5:05:21 (24,564)	
Siveyer, Nicola J	4:31:34 (16,475)	
Sjoo, Solweig	5:30:36 (29,235)	
Skae, Kathleen	5:24:31 (28,184)	
Skaith, Karen M	6:26:38 (34,197)	
Skapoullis, Debra	6:29:21 (34,303)	
Skehan, Marcelle W	4:05:43 (10,293)	
Skelcher, Catherine A	6:48:24 (34,847)	
Skelton, Katie V	4:40:19 (18,610)	
Skelton, Xaviera M	5:58:53 (32,496)	
Skews, Tina	5:01:06 (23,751)	
Skidmore, Flora	3:19:47 (2,464)	
Skidmore, Kate M	4:39:28 (18,410)	
Skilbeck, Emma V	4:58:51 (23,218)	
Skilton, Fiona E	5:40:36 (30,664)	
Skinner, Julia D	5:37:37 (30,250)	
Skivington, Karen	5:57:19 (32,354)	

Skivington, Sharon L	3:43:45 (5,820)	
Sklenar, Charlotte A	3:41:17 (5,408)	
Slack, Philippa	4:14:54 (12,297)	
Slade, Catherine	4:29:22 (15,964)	
Slade, Elizabeth S	5:31:41 (29,402)	
Slade, Karen E	5:38:30 (30,382)	
Slade, Sarah	5:13:56 (26,217)	
Slamon, Lynne	4:47:43 (20,459)	
Slater, Alison J	5:54:47 (32,122)	
Slater, Crystal G	5:00:09 (23,535)	
Slater, Gillian A	4:39:18 (18,364)	
Slater, Lisa C	5:31:05 (29,312)	
Slater, Lucie	5:01:55 (23,916)	
Slater, Margaret M	4:24:36 (14,727)	
Slater, Ruth V	5:12:12 (25,897)	
Slavin, Tracy	5:33:44 (29,719)	
Slaymaker, Dorte	4:10:09 (11,194)	
Sleath, Elaine	5:34:06 (29,780)	
Sleator, Karen	7:00:36 (35,138)	
Sledge, Charlotte E	4:48:32 (20,656)	
Slee, Olivia A	3:32:53 (4,118)	
Sligar, Sally L	4:17:19 (12,880)	
Slinn, Michelle E	4:52:30 (21,612)	
Slinn, Patricia M	4:48:11 (20,573)	
Sloan, Fiona R	5:55:30 (32,192)	
Sloan, Lichu W	5:08:52 (25,256)	
Sloane, Nicola	5:06:48 (24,841)	
Slocombe, Hazel	7:41:25 (35,579)	
Sloman, Helen M	4:20:47 (13,792)	
Sloper, Charlene V	6:15:43 (33,663)	
Sloss, Ruth E	3:47:42 (6,478)	
Smale, Dee	3:01:07 (964)	
Small, Christina	4:56:44 (22,702)	
Small, Emma K	4:57:17 (22,847)	
Small, Helen A	4:34:36 (17,177)	
Small, Rachel E	4:45:03 (19,852)	
Smallman, Peta C	6:03:38 (32,865)	
Smallwood, Victoria B	5:08:07 (25,118)	
Smart, Ann P	3:54:53 (7,982)	
Smart, Claire M	6:18:06 (33,782)	
Smart, Judith	6:18:19 (33,790)	
Smedley, Dawn E	5:59:57 (32,569)	
Smedley, Dionne	5:53:51 (32,038)	
Smee, Carolyn J	9:03:24 (35,693)	
Smee, Katharine	3:37:00 (4,686)	
Smeeton, Valerie M	6:29:31 (34,309)	
Smillie, Carolyn H	5:49:14 (31,605)	
Smillie, Lesley H	4:46:10 (20,095)	
Smillie, Susan	5:49:14 (31,605)	
Smith, Alexandra M	3:45:49 (6,153)	
Smith, Amanda	4:49:32 (20,897)	
Smith, Amy L	3:27:13 (3,312)	
Smith, Andrea	6:45:40 (34,816)	
Smith, Anna	4:58:02 (23,043)	
Smith, Anna M	4:27:07 (15,357)	
Smith, Annette D	5:25:44 (28,413)	
Smith, Barbara A	5:31:50 (29,424)	
Smith, Barbara S	6:54:54 (35,032)	
Smith, Bathsheba R	4:37:56 (17,989)	
Smith, Bernadette M	3:45:54 (6,163)	
Smith, Caroline	6:41:49 (34,712)	
Smith, Caroline	6:42:54 (34,747)	
Smith, Caroline M	4:30:01 (16,151)	
Smith, Catherine	3:57:24 (8,581)	
Smith, Catherine M	5:12:22 (25,933)	
Smith, Chantal	4:39:10 (18,324)	
Smith, Charlene V	4:52:15 (21,556)	
Smith, Charlotte V	5:38:09 (30,325)	
Smith, Cindy J	4:23:22 (14,411)	
Smith, Claire C	6:11:55 (33,419)	
Smith, Claire L	6:19:24 (33,857)	
Smith, Clarissa L	4:59:17 (23,335)	
Smith, Corin B	5:38:59 (30,450)	
Smith, Debbie	3:42:35 (5,608)	
Smith, Deborah	4:27:42 (15,519)	
Smith, Elaine G	4:24:56 (14,809)	
Smith, Elizabeth A	5:48:12 (31,490)	
Smith, Emily	4:27:26 (15,458)	
Smith, Emma C	3:56:07 (8,254)	
Smith, Emma-Louise F	4:25:11 (14,867)	
Smith, Esra	4:18:06 (13,094)	
Smith, Fay K	4:59:53 (23,470)	
Smith, Gemma	4:41:29 (18,915)	
Smith, Gemma L	5:31:18 (29,344)	
Smith, Gemma R	5:00:31 (23,617)	
Smith, Ginette	4:08:03 (10,778)	
Smith, Hannah L	4:56:06 (22,535)	
Smith, Harriet	4:23:36 (14,467)	
Smith, Hazel D	4:54:53 (22,241)	
Smith, Heather	3:53:52 (7,757)	
Smith, Heather S	5:28:44 (28,936)	
Smith, Heila M	4:11:39 (11,537)	
Smith, Helen L	5:21:59 (27,778)	
Smith, Helen M	4:50:30 (21,120)	
Smith, Helen M	4:54:00 (22,022)	
Smith, Helen M	6:11:43 (33,410)	
Smith, Jaclyn E	4:38:15 (18,068)	
Smith, Jeanette M	4:55:44 (22,440)	
Smith, Jennie A	5:17:02 (26,863)	
Smith, Jill	4:51:36 (21,398)	
Smith, Joanne	4:16:27 (12,688)	
Smith, Jodie	3:46:50 (6,310)	
Smith, Jullie	5:41:06 (30,717)	
Smith, Karen	5:56:43 (32,312)	
Smith, Karen	5:57:52 (32,397)	
Smith, Karren	4:17:29 (12,940)	
Smith, Katharine	5:26:16 (28,503)	
Smith, Kathleen N	6:53:44 (35,013)	
Smith, Kathy L	7:05:56 (35,218)	
Smith, Katrina C	6:20:37 (33,931)	
Smith, Kristina G	5:33:09 (29,627)	
Smith, Lesley H	4:20:45 (13,697)	
Smith, Linden C	4:05:33 (10,250)	
Smith, Lisa A	5:27:04 (28,631)	
Smith, Liz	4:15:58 (12,551)	
Smith, Liz A	3:48:56 (6,712)	
Smith, Lorna A	4:42:13 (19,101)	
Smith, Lorna M	4:19:20 (13,412)	
Smith, Lorraine	5:01:01 (23,732)	
Smith, Margaret L	5:27:23 (28,691)	
Smith, Maria	5:14:16 (26,286)	
Smith, Maria T	4:27:00 (15,324)	
Smith, Marilyn J	5:49:40 (31,645)	
Smith, Naomi	5:49:31 (31,630)	
Smith, Naomi L	4:31:20 (16,432)	
Smith, Natalie	4:44:13 (19,604)	
Smith, Nickola A	5:05:54 (24,679)	
Smith, Nicky G	6:40:50 (34,683)	
Smith, Norma F	3:55:28 (8,114)	
Smith, Pamela A	4:45:22 (19,920)	
Smith, Paula J	5:01:52 (23,905)	
Smith, Penny	6:08:40 (33,216)	
Smith, Philippa K	4:52:22 (21,589)	
Smith, Philomena	4:08:10 (10,799)	
Smith, Ruth H	5:19:08 (27,276)	
Smith, Sally	4:43:58 (19,527)	
Smith, Sally A	5:27:58 (28,789)	
Smith, Samantha J	3:58:12 (8,760)	
Smith, Sandra J	4:59:00 (23,253)	
Smith, Shantelle S	3:59:21 (9,053)	
Smith, Sharon E	4:40:55 (18,768)	
Smith, Sian	7:40:55 (35,567)	
Smith, Sophie A	4:38:19 (18,101)	
Smith, Sue A	6:38:13 (34,613)	
Smith, Susan	5:13:11 (26,077)	
Smith, Suzie A	5:59:10 (32,523)	
Smith, Tamsin A	4:40:15 (18,589)	
Smith, Tanya C	7:20:07 (35,390)	
Smith, Tina	5:19:37 (27,362)	
Smith, Zoe H	4:56:15 (22,577)	
Smith, Zoe M	5:03:52 (24,301)	
Smith-Hamblin, Alison M	5:15:26 (26,548)	
Smitten, Jennifer	5:11:46 (25,805)	
Smoker, Sally R	3:44:34 (5,951)	
Smyth, Anne E	4:07:48 (10,724)	
Smyth, Cara A	5:22:07 (27,797)	
Smyth, Catherine C	7:12:45 (35,314)	
Smyth, Christina	6:44:48 (34,795)	
Smyth, Helen A	7:12:46 (35,316)	
Smyth, Michelle M	7:12:45 (35,314)	
Snary, Lisa C	4:47:41 (20,454)	
Sneezum, Beverley E	4:51:51 (21,453)	
Snell, Jacqui L	5:46:02 (31,263)	
Snell, Jenny C	5:46:02 (31,263)	
Snellgrove, Kirste L	5:17:12 (26,895)	
Snelling, Jean E	5:23:13 (27,961)	
Snelson, Ann	5:30:29 (29,218)	
Snippe, Marjolein	3:46:20 (6,225)	
Snoek, Tamsin	5:04:21 (24,390)	
Snook, Suzanne E	3:26:44 (3,229)	
Snow, Alice F	4:16:20 (12,654)	
Snoxall, Charlotte E	5:13:30 (26,124)	
Snyder, Susan S	4:49:19 (20,842)	
Soar, Susan R	4:28:13 (15,649)	
Soden, Lucy	5:38:01 (30,306)	
Soeiro, Vania M	5:49:06 (31,596)	
Sohm, Jennifer G	4:45:02 (19,848)	
Solah, Gabriela	3:17:53 (2,272)	
Solheim, Trude	5:03:08 (24,156)	
Solloway, Juliana F	3:59:40 (9,131)	
Solomon, Larissa R	5:16:54 (26,840)	
Somervaille, Katherine E	5:51:27 (31,822)	
Somerville, Tracey	5:37:34 (30,242)	
Song, Wei	5:28:18 (28,865)	
Sonneveld Hoencamp, Joke G	4:57:51 (22,998)	
Soobratty, Melissa	5:06:29 (24,783)	
Sooerquist, Petra M	4:18:22 (13,165)	
Sorrell, Amy F	6:01:32 (32,721)	
Sotheby, Angela	4:08:07 (10,792)	
Southerden, Isabel C	5:08:59 (25,278)	
Southway, Janice A	4:00:58 (9,411)	
Sowden, Charlotte F	4:17:12 (12,853)	
Sowerby, Catharine	4:28:03 (15,608)	
Sowter, Elizabeth M	3:38:22 (4,897)	
Spacey, Emma L	7:26:39 (35,440)	
Spaczek, Sylvie	4:22:28 (14,190)	
Spano, Alessandra	7:30:55 (35,501)	
Spanton, Angela M	6:18:22 (33,795)	
Sparham, Michele	6:22:30 (34,023)	
Sparkes, Pauline E	5:39:54 (30,579)	
Sparks, Katharine	5:00:15 (23,563)	
Sparks, Nicola J	4:37:18 (17,843)	
Sparling, Clare M	4:40:53 (18,755)	
Sparrow, Gillian L	4:27:23 (15,442)	
Sparrow, Samantha G	5:01:37 (23,856)	
Spatz, Angela F	4:18:32 (13,221)	
Spaull, Sally	6:49:44 (34,923)	
Speakman, Unity J	4:44:39 (19,727)	
Spearing, Natalie	4:16:58 (12,808)	
Spearman, Helen C	5:29:42 (29,095)	
Spedding, Elaine J	4:39:34 (18,427)	
Speight, Gail S	6:05:15 (32,978)	
Speller, Nicola C	4:16:04 (12,585)	
Spence, Laura E	3:37:55 (4,809)	
Spence, Pamela H	5:44:06 (31,057)	
Spence, Sally C	5:08:35 (25,201)	
Spencer, Anna L	4:58:14 (23,085)	
Spencer, Collette M	4:23:25 (14,421)	
Spencer, Jayne P	4:28:48 (15,811)	
Spencer, Katherine W	4:24:45 (14,767)	
Spencer, Michelle	5:28:13 (28,840)	
Spencer, Naomi J	3:59:00 (8,960)	
Spencer, Sally A	3:24:12 (2,929)	
Spencer, Sally H	4:49:09 (20,807)	
Spencer, Tania	5:13:36 (26,141)	
Spencer, Victoria J	4:30:17 (16,215)	
Spender, Sophie C	4:37:55 (17,988)	
Sperring, Lucy T	5:59:03 (32,511)	
Spicer, Lisa J	4:32:08 (16,591)	
Spierings, Rickie	4:54:54 (22,246)	
Spies, Gloudien M	4:01:33 (9,521)	
Spindler-Niemann, Hannelore	4:22:50 (14,295)	
Spittle, Julia A	4:53:51 (21,977)	
Spivey, Whitney J	3:59:22 (9,061)	
Spong, Carole	3:48:28 (6,612)	
Spong, Sue	3:25:35 (3,074)	
Sporton, Dennie	4:41:38 (18,955)	
Spotswood, Fiona M	3:52:22 (7,446)	
Spouse, Kelly J	4:36:40 (17,708)	
Sprenkels-Bontje, Paula	4:12:03 (11,621)	
Sprigings, Ann D	4:04:06 (9,985)	
Springthorpe, Andrea	4:59:26 (23,359)	
Sprules, Tracey	6:27:00 (34,212)	
Spurgin, Deborah J	5:10:13 (25,528)	
Spurr, Sarah J	6:09:51 (33,295)	
Spurr, Tess	5:00:41 (23,652)	
Squires, Annabel	4:28:32 (15,738)	
St John Webster, Alice	5:18:09 (27,091)	
St Vicent Welch, Caitlin H	4:16:12 (12,621)	

Stacey, Helen....6:45:34 (34,813)
Stacey, Judith C....3:55:38 (8,146)
Stacey, Julia....4:46:35 (20,196)
Stacey, Victoria....5:07:03 (24,896)
Stafford, Ceri E....4:43:06 (19,318)
Stafford, Fay....4:56:35 (22,656)
Stafford, Helen L....4:57:43 (22,963)
Stagg, Joanne E....5:00:51 (23,696)
Stainer, Rachel C....4:17:18 (12,877)
Staines, Linda....3:19:28 (2,435)
Stainforth, Emma....5:17:00 (26,858)
Stamp, Rose J....5:00:07 (23,526)
Stamper, Linda....3:32:15 (4,038)
Stanbrough, Michelle....6:14:52 (33,608)
Standen, Lesley M....4:56:22 (22,606)
Standley, Cara L....5:38:24 (30,370)
Standring, Debbie....4:21:29 (13,963)
Stanford, Helen V....4:54:06 (22,041)
Stanger, Alex J....4:22:27 (14,184)
Stanger, Samantha P....5:28:59 (28,979)
Stanhope, Ann E....4:17:48 (13,023)
Stanhope, Rachel C....4:54:08 (22,054)
Staniforth, Kerry A....4:33:09 (16,823)
Stanislaw, Katrina A....4:55:31 (22,395)
Stanley, Anamaria....5:49:57 (31,671)
Stannard, Helen M....5:52:06 (31,881)
Stansfield, Jane E....5:24:11 (28,135)
Stanton, Emma A....4:33:36 (16,938)
Stanton, Natalie D....5:15:25 (26,546)
Stanton, Nicola S....3:51:19 (7,206)
Stanton, Sandra....5:47:48 (31,438)
Stanton, Tracy A....5:23:39 (28,040)
Stanwyck, Michelle E....6:28:22 (34,260)
Stanyard, Philippa J....3:44:53 (6,007)
Stanyer, Nicola....4:33:38 (16,944)
Staples, Phillippa L....5:19:44 (27,379)
Stapleton, Rachel E....4:25:30 (14,945)
Starbuck, Helen J....4:33:59 (17,030)
Stares, Diane B....4:03:22 (9,844)
Stark, Andrea P....6:00:30 (32,622)
Starkey, Vanessa A....5:11:01 (25,671)
Star-Stone, Fi....7:32:49 (35,514)
Statham, Hannah L....4:44:56 (19,815)
Statham, Maxine....6:19:56 (33,888)
Staud, Sylvie....3:44:33 (5,949)
Staunton, Louise J....3:36:39 (4,634)
Staunton, Rebecca L....4:23:02 (14,340)
Stavisky, Jenny H....6:05:45 (33,026)
Steans, Hannah....5:48:20 (31,512)
Steans, Jean....6:20:38 (33,934)
Stearn, Michelle L....5:03:58 (24,318)
Stedman, Beverly J....6:15:15 (33,631)
Stedman, Jane L....4:40:01 (18,539)
Steed, Christina....4:17:28 (12,932)
Steed, Maureen E....5:25:34 (28,382)
Steed, Shelley....4:41:23 (18,884)
Steel, Louise J....4:47:22 (20,374)
Steele, Heather J....5:24:13 (28,140)
Steele, Julie....4:04:06 (9,985)
Steenson, Janet....4:11:27 (11,490)
Steer, Deborah A....2:55:05 (580)
Steeves, Dawn....5:14:09 (26,257)
Stein, Chantal....4:46:05 (20,073)
Stein, Julia....4:45:01 (19,842)
Stein, Kate....4:38:31 (18,157)
Steinberg, Danielle S....3:33:15 (4,173)
Stenner, Sue C....4:56:04 (22,528)
Stephen, Catherine....3:52:49 (7,531)
Stephens, Adele F....5:21:07 (27,620)
Stephens, Johanna....5:59:12 (32,529)
Stephens, Nicola C....5:30:55 (29,282)
Stephens, Phillippa G....3:05:17 (1,183)
Stephens, Victoria C....4:49:04 (20,783)
Stephenson, Judith....6:46:25 (34,843)
Stephenson, Judith M....4:43:55 (19,514)
Stephenson, Kim....3:14:35 (1,951)
Steptoe, Charlotte F....3:34:45 (4,368)
Sterba, Gemma L....5:53:05 (31,970)
Stevens, Amanda L....5:34:25 (29,833)
Stevens, Annabel M....5:40:14 (30,617)
Stevens, Corrina....3:28:28 (3,477)
Stevens, Emily V....5:00:12 (23,551)
Stevens, Gillian....3:34:49 (4,381)
Stevens, Jo....3:59:41 (9,136)
Stevens, Kim....4:35:49 (17,491)
Stevens, Laura A....5:13:11 (26,077)
Stevens, Patricia A....4:42:34 (19,195)
Stevens, Penelope J....5:00:49 (23,692)
Stevens, Rebecca H....4:11:25 (11,478)
Stevens, Sian R....4:47:16 (20,347)
Stevens, Sue....5:38:15 (30,342)
Stevens, Zoe L....4:50:07 (21,026)
Stevenson, Catriona E....4:28:52 (15,825)
Stevenson, Gemma K....4:34:13 (17,079)
Stevenson, Kathleen R....5:40:06 (30,607)
Stevenson, Lorraine....5:03:00 (24,121)
Stevenson, Louise M....4:10:53 (11,345)
Steward, Claire E....3:35:14 (4,438)
Stewart, Alice B....4:15:22 (12,411)
Stewart, Beverley....5:47:20 (31,394)
Stewart, Corah B....6:00:41 (32,638)
Stewart, Emma E....5:38:00 (30,303)
Stewart, Jacqueline....4:38:28 (18,140)
Stewart, Jennie....7:03:49 (35,188)
Stewart, Julie....3:48:32 (6,630)
Stewart, Lauren....4:32:28 (16,652)
Stewart, Lindsay M....6:16:19 (33,707)
Stewart, Lindsey M....4:26:55 (15,299)
Stewart, Louise....5:59:19 (32,539)
Stewart, Pamela C....4:32:03 (16,569)
Stewart, Sophie....4:42:46 (19,246)
Stewart, Susan A....4:17:25 (12,914)
Stewart-Daters, Jane V....6:33:13 (34,446)
Stibbs, Helen J....3:51:49 (7,318)
Stiles, Helen M....5:19:57 (27,417)
Still, Paula N....4:23:34 (14,463)
Stilling, Trine E....4:33:25 (16,895)
Stimson, Juliet....4:52:02 (21,492)
Stirling, Susan L....5:05:25 (24,577)
Stockdale, Pamela C....4:57:49 (22,991)
Stocken, Janet L....4:52:41 (21,662)
Stoddart, Elisabeth E....4:39:46 (18,476)
Stoker, Carla M....5:41:59 (30,828)
Stokes, Elizabeth P....4:40:33 (18,666)
Stokes, Jo-Ann E....4:49:27 (20,874)
Stokes, Margaret G....5:12:46 (25,994)
Stokes, Tracey L....4:59:35 (23,407)
Stokley, Maria A....5:29:09 (29,011)
Stokoe, Vicki K....4:27:49 (15,543)
Stone, Elaine M....6:04:43 (32,934)
Stone, Gill....5:23:41 (28,048)
Stone, Helena....5:02:32 (24,048)
Stone, Joanne C....5:36:37 (30,127)
Stone, Karen L....6:07:14 (33,120)
Stone, Kate J....4:13:29 (11,956)
Stone, Leanne....5:51:02 (31,774)
Stone, Marie L....4:12:23 (11,697)
Stone, Sarah L....5:14:23 (26,308)
Stone, Veronica A....4:52:03 (21,499)
Stoner, Carrie L....7:10:00 (35,271)
Stones, Caroline M....4:58:18 (23,103)
Stones, Janine A....3:29:01 (3,579)
Stones, Judith A....4:50:24 (21,097)
Stopford, Anne L....4:35:07 (17,303)
Storer, Elizabeth C....6:01:24 (32,712)
Storer, Joanne H....5:46:01 (31,261)
Storey, Katherine....3:57:51 (8,680)
Storey, Pamela....6:36:12 (34,543)
Storr, Ann....5:23:08 (27,953)
Stothard, Adele L....5:02:37 (24,060)
Stott, Sarah L....4:18:27 (13,196)
Stout, Caroline P....3:52:34 (7,476)
Stovell, Elizabeth....4:55:42 (22,429)
Stracey, Serena P....4:30:35 (16,276)
Straderick, Amanda....5:28:01 (28,801)
Strain, Catherina....4:32:47 (16,735)
Strang Steel, Meriel I....4:07:25 (10,636)
Stratford, Angela R....4:34:43 (17,206)
Stratford, Karen J....7:41:44 (35,580)
Strawbridge, Kay....4:55:41 (22,423)
Stredwick, Marian S....5:19:41 (27,372)
Street, Charlotte K....6:26:43 (34,201)
Street, Stephanie A....4:30:26 (16,242)
Stretton, Jackie M....4:57:42 (22,956)
Strickland, Nicola J....4:52:05 (21,509)
Stringer, Jennifer J....6:29:14 (34,295)
Strong, Claire....4:00:28 (9,303)
Strong, Julia E....4:53:05 (21,771)
Strotton, Claire....5:34:02 (29,771)
Stroud, Sian J....3:53:38 (7,713)
Stroud, Verity A....4:48:46 (20,711)
Strouts, Fiona....3:23:09 (2,815)
Stuart, Helen M....2:53:38 (502)
Stuart, Kate M....5:20:31 (27,522)
Stuart, Peter....3:27:06 (3,298)
Stubbins, Amanda E....4:18:51 (13,296)
Stubbs, Amanda P....4:45:00 (19,836)
Stubbs, Elizabeth R....5:23:52 (28,088)
Stubbs, Emily....5:33:31 (29,688)
Stubbs, Moira E....6:01:13 (32,699)
Stubbs, Sally J....3:35:40 (4,508)
Stuller, Martina....4:35:30 (17,401)
Sturdy, Cheryl....5:06:56 (24,865)
Sturgeon, Natalie....4:44:49 (19,784)
Sturgess, Stella....4:56:52 (22,739)
Sturt Taylor, Xanthe M....5:47:55 (31,454)
Sturtivant, Justine L....6:10:31 (33,336)
Sturzaker, Jane R....4:21:50 (14,044)
Stvenson, Carly....6:48:46 (34,904)
Styles, Brenda R....6:02:46 (32,805)
Styring, Zoe Y....5:23:27 (28,001)
Suchet, Katherine....4:40:19 (18,610)
Suff, Julie A....4:19:52 (13,563)
Sugden, Ingrid....5:20:05 (27,435)
Sugden, Jean E....4:55:32 (22,401)
Sugg, Tracey E....4:14:38 (12,242)
Sugiyama, Chiyomi....6:51:36 (34,970)
Sullivan, Allana C....4:37:53 (17,977)
Sullivan, Carmel M....3:32:03 (3,995)
Sullivan, Donna....4:52:03 (21,499)
Sullivan, Gemma N....5:05:56 (24,684)
Sullivan, Helen J....5:26:53 (28,607)
Sullivan, Ruth M....4:06:22 (10,429)
Summerfield, Georgina....4:58:54 (23,227)
Summers, Amy V....6:32:46 (34,434)
Summers, Francine N....4:46:25 (20,157)
Summers, Jane A....4:12:55 (11,809)
Summers, Joanne T....6:14:09 (33,560)
Summers, Melanie J....4:53:11 (21,804)
Sumner, Alexandra J....5:27:52 (28,773)
Sumsion, Suzie L....6:04:54 (32,950)
Sund, Berit....4:30:46 (16,308)
Sunderland, Louise M....4:45:12 (19,887)
Sunderland, Martina E....5:28:26 (28,894)
Sunderland, Rachel E....4:55:22 (22,353)
Surtees, Lydia C....5:28:59 (28,979)
Surti, Jay....5:36:18 (30,082)
Susans, Nicola D....3:10:38 (1,606)
Susskind-Sacks, Bat-Zion....5:50:56 (31,766)
Sutcliffe, Alison C....4:20:05 (13,622)
Sutcliffe, Deborah....6:38:19 (34,617)
Sutcliffe, Denise J....5:02:13 (23,971)
Sutcliffe, Elaine....4:27:13 (15,396)
Sutcliffe, Katy J....5:11:45 (25,800)
Sutcliffe, Laura F....4:49:44 (20,940)
Suter, Pamela....4:58:54 (23,227)
Sutherland, Emma J....5:38:53 (30,439)
Sutherland, Fiona H....3:53:35 (7,705)
Sutherland, Isabel M....3:36:13 (4,574)
Sutherland, Megan....4:47:32 (20,417)
Suttle, Haley A....4:23:01 (14,337)
Sutton, Bronwyn....5:44:00 (31,042)
Sutton, Claire I....3:40:19 (5,236)
Sutton, Jacqueline....4:51:09 (21,278)
Sutton, Juantia L....5:53:13 (31,979)
Sutton, Laura J....4:35:03 (17,285)
Sutton, Lisa B....3:48:42 (6,666)
Sutton, Margarette M....6:30:46 (34,351)
Sutton, Tracy H....4:42:30 (19,178)
Suzia, Sakira K....5:06:32 (24,789)
Suzuki, Sachiko....5:48:06 (31,479)
Suzuki, Tomi....6:23:44 (34,065)
Svarovsky, Patricia....4:38:52 (18,246)
Swallow, Nicola J....5:17:39 (26,992)
Swan, Eileen M....5:16:40 (26,784)
Swan, Nicole....4:27:53 (15,558)
Swan, Sarah J....3:17:22 (2,212)
Swan, Suzanne E....5:52:33 (31,923)
Swani, Lynn M....3:41:16 (5,405)

Swann, Carol J	4:56:38 (22,672)	
Swanson, Katherine M	3:18:41 (2,358)	
Swaysland, Sarah L	3:39:35 (5,121)	
Sweet, Jennifer	4:27:27 (15,460)	
Sweeting, Alison J	7:06:15 (35,222)	
Swift, Claire L	5:55:56 (32,232)	
Swift, Claire M	4:17:22 (12,897)	
Swift, Jessica	5:42:10 (30,844)	
Swift, Victoria J	6:14:47 (33,601)	
Swift MBE, Joy A	7:31:42 (35,506)	
Swinbank, Jane	5:15:18 (26,525)	
Swinburne, Barbara C	6:29:34 (34,310)	
Swindell, Jennifer	4:27:25 (15,454)	
Swinnerton, Shelagh A	5:05:30 (24,602)	
Swords, Georgia R	5:15:26 (26,548)	
Syed, Nelofer	4:11:26 (11,486)	
Sygrove, Alexandra B	7:07:24 (35,239)	
Sykes, Jean	6:35:44 (34,529)	
Sykes, Judi F	3:55:05 (8,026)	
Sykes, Yvonne	4:46:20 (20,135)	
Symmons, Samantha E	6:05:34 (33,013)	
Symonds, Cerys	6:57:46 (35,088)	
Symonds, Claire B	4:18:36 (13,240)	
Symonds, Karen A	4:29:26 (15,986)	
Symonds, Keeley L	5:28:17 (28,858)	
Symonds, Lisa J	4:13:02 (11,840)	
Symons, Amy M	4:40:50 (18,740)	
Symons, Rebecca E	4:25:05 (14,842)	
Synnott-Wells, Marie	3:08:25 (1,423)	
Synott, Claire L	4:32:40 (16,709)	
Sythes, Teresa	7:27:05 (35,448)	
Szabo, Szuzsanna	4:54:25 (22,128)	
Szafarczyk, Joanna M	4:11:10 (11,417)	
Szonyi, Julia E	4:41:14 (18,848)	
Szulc, Linda	5:34:57 (29,907)	
Taccori, Serena	4:27:34 (15,480)	
Tadd, Cheryl	5:37:50 (30,274)	
Tagg, Susan G	3:43:52 (5,838)	
Tailby, Helen D	3:45:15 (6,056)	
Tait, Rosie E	5:54:06 (32,063)	
Taiwo, Ayo	5:44:19 (31,079)	
Talbot, Julie	5:02:08 (23,956)	
Talbot, Nora E	5:31:57 (29,439)	
Talbot, Sandra D	6:07:39 (33,140)	
Talbot-Rosner, Victoria H	3:59:12 (9,011)	
Tallett, Ceridwen J	5:27:41 (28,739)	
Tam, Emily W	4:11:48 (11,570)	
Tammen, Constance C	3:15:41 (2,046)	
Tan, Xiaohe L	5:37:32 (30,239)	
Tang, Dawn W	4:47:43 (20,459)	
Tanis-Greff, Kathryn A	4:45:46 (20,001)	
Tanna, Neha	5:08:45 (25,234)	
Tanner, Abbie L	5:48:03 (31,472)	
Tanner, Claire J	5:51:46 (31,852)	
Tanner, Louise M	5:31:23 (29,359)	
Tapley, Julie	4:11:53 (11,588)	
Tapley, Nicola K	5:48:49 (31,562)	
Tapper, Gissel M	5:11:32 (25,763)	
Tarant, Antje	4:29:50 (16,101)	
Tarkow-Reinisch, Lili R	5:03:53 (24,305)	
Tarmey, Patricia	5:47:48 (31,438)	
Tarr, Sharon	5:26:36 (28,557)	
Tarrach, Chevaun M	3:24:48 (2,996)	
Tarrach, Zoe C	3:30:38 (3,798)	
Tarring, Caroline R	4:53:12 (21,810)	
Tarry, Beverley H	4:36:08 (17,567)	
Tarver, Melissa J	5:10:23 (25,552)	
Tasker, Kathleen J	5:03:02 (24,135)	
Tassell, Katie	4:04:46 (10,106)	
Taswell, Ann Marie	3:35:40 (4,508)	
Tatam, Margaret	6:42:23 (34,733)	
Tatem, Lisa C	5:28:06 (28,818)	
Tatnall, Christine B	4:45:29 (19,946)	
Taub, Alia	5:40:41 (30,672)	
Taut, Andrea	4:58:17 (23,098)	
Tavares, Ivone	4:31:35 (16,481)	
Taylor, Ailsa J	4:52:59 (21,749)	
Taylor, Alana R	4:42:37 (19,211)	
Taylor, Alexandra C	4:22:57 (14,319)	
Taylor, Amanda C	7:25:56 (35,436)	
Taylor, Amanda J	5:51:06 (31,786)	
Taylor, Anna X	4:59:28 (23,369)	
Taylor, Annette L	4:57:15 (22,834)	

Taylor, Annette M	5:07:28 (24,991)	
Taylor, Caroline	6:00:17 (32,605)	
Taylor, Claire	4:46:14 (20,113)	
Taylor, Corinna	6:13:16 (33,507)	
Taylor, Dawn J	6:20:00 (33,890)	
Taylor, Eleanor	5:27:21 (28,686)	
Taylor, Eleanor J	4:46:02 (20,067)	
Taylor, Elizabeth A	5:38:14 (30,340)	
Taylor, Emma	5:25:59 (28,453)	
Taylor, Evey L	5:47:12 (31,371)	
Taylor, Fiona J	6:38:58 (34,637)	
Taylor, Gemma J	6:36:56 (34,580)	
Taylor, Georgina	4:51:34 (21,387)	
Taylor, Glenda K	6:56:47 (35,069)	
Taylor, Hazel	5:47:18 (31,386)	
Taylor, Helen	5:44:48 (31,128)	
Taylor, Hilary M	6:36:50 (34,572)	
Taylor, Jennifer S	5:38:58 (30,448)	
Taylor, Jennifer V	5:32:11 (29,480)	
Taylor, Joanne	3:38:17 (4,885)	
Taylor, Johanna	3:48:54 (6,703)	
Taylor, Judy A	5:11:20 (25,730)	
Taylor, Julie K	4:53:59 (22,016)	
Taylor, Karen P	3:54:42 (7,945)	
Taylor, Karen S	6:49:11 (34,916)	
Taylor, Kate	5:34:01 (29,764)	
Taylor, Katharine E	4:01:44 (9,555)	
Taylor, Leila	4:38:12 (18,058)	
Taylor, Louise	3:56:39 (8,393)	
Taylor, Lucy A	5:34:01 (29,764)	
Taylor, Marianne C	5:18:20 (27,133)	
Taylor, Melissa J	6:07:35 (33,135)	
Taylor, Michelle	4:59:44 (23,440)	
Taylor, Natalie	5:43:03 (30,938)	
Taylor, Nicole J	5:11:49 (25,817)	
Taylor, Paula B	5:24:35 (28,196)	
Taylor, Rachel H	5:00:48 (23,689)	
Taylor, Sara	5:03:09 (24,160)	
Taylor, Sarah J	5:44:48 (31,128)	
Taylor, Sarah L	3:59:14 (9,021)	
Taylor, Sharon A	4:50:03 (21,007)	
Taylor, Sharon L	4:13:21 (11,921)	
Taylor, Simone K	5:28:18 (28,865)	
Taylor, Stephanie A	5:57:01 (32,333)	
Taylor, Susan S	6:36:24 (34,553)	
Taylor, Susann M	4:49:03 (20,777)	
Taylor, Suzanne E	5:50:33 (31,730)	
Taylor, Tracey	4:30:24 (16,234)	
Taylor, Trish	4:58:03 (23,045)	
Taylor, Yvonne	5:20:23 (27,494)	
Taylor-Walker, Caroline R	5:05:25 (24,577)	
Taylor-Walker, Valerie J	6:10:01 (33,305)	
Teague, Emily K	5:25:02 (28,279)	
Teare, Jayne E	3:33:02 (4,141)	
Teasdale, Helen F	4:25:21 (14,907)	
Tebbett, Lorraine	5:38:38 (30,402)	
Tebbey, Kate J	5:00:25 (23,601)	
Teenan, Elizabeth A	6:08:16 (33,192)	
Tees, Caroline	4:26:22 (15,149)	
Teesdale, Nikki J	6:39:16 (34,650)	
Tekchandani, Myfanwy F	4:02:36 (9,708)	
Telco, Diana H	5:13:57 (26,222)	
Telfer Brunton, Fiona L	4:26:03 (15,066)	
Telford, Angela	3:36:05 (4,554)	
Telford, Eileen J	4:04:24 (10,038)	
Temple, Anna C	7:35:21 (35,535)	
Tennant, Maggie B	5:08:09 (25,126)	
Teper, Julia L	6:00:03 (32,585)	
Terrill, Jessica H	3:51:42 (7,296)	
Terry, Dawn S	5:23:58 (28,104)	
Testa, Lesley J	5:54:20 (32,086)	
Testo, Sue L	4:09:21 (11,041)	
Tetlow, Gemma C	4:55:07 (22,296)	
Teynie, Claire	4:05:34 (10,256)	
Thacker, Helen	5:38:45 (30,423)	
Thacker, Sarah L	4:32:11 (16,604)	
Thakur, Hema	5:53:59 (32,052)	
Thatcher, Sarah L	4:19:41 (13,504)	
Thawley, Louise	5:15:35 (26,582)	
Thawley, Rebecca	5:27:53 (28,776)	
Theobald, Louisa A	5:29:50 (29,112)	
Thewlis-Smith, Corrina M	4:50:55 (21,221)	

Thiebe, Liz A	5:09:57 (25,463)	
Thiele, Hiltrudis	5:27:45 (28,754)	
Thierens, Elizabeth	6:23:21 (34,048)	
Thierry, Christel M	4:52:45 (21,681)	
Thin, Joanne M	4:15:22 (12,411)	
Thio, Johanna M	4:41:33 (18,939)	
Thoeni, Elenoreelisabeth	4:35:30 (17,401)	
Thomas, Ann	2:57:29 (708)	
Thomas, Anne	5:41:26 (30,760)	
Thomas, Beverley	5:27:41 (28,739)	
Thomas, Catherine H	4:02:02 (9,608)	
Thomas, Ceri	5:55:52 (32,226)	
Thomas, Deborah	3:18:57 (2,385)	
Thomas, Deborah J	5:27:06 (28,638)	
Thomas, Dee L	5:27:38 (28,734)	
Thomas, Emma	5:58:37 (32,477)	
Thomas, Emma C	4:51:48 (21,439)	
Thomas, Gail R	5:01:41 (23,865)	
Thomas, Geraldine	4:46:23 (20,151)	
Thomas, Helen M	4:37:35 (17,906)	
Thomas, Jeanette	3:58:49 (8,913)	
Thomas, Jill R	4:31:59 (16,557)	
Thomas, Jo C	4:35:47 (17,483)	
Thomas, Joanne K	6:15:23 (33,641)	
Thomas, Katherine M	4:19:57 (13,589)	
Thomas, Kerian	4:15:18 (12,395)	
Thomas, Leanne	5:25:48 (28,425)	
Thomas, Linda M	5:30:19 (29,185)	
Thomas, Louise	4:28:33 (15,745)	
Thomas, Natalie B	3:47:30 (6,424)	
Thomas, Nunette	5:56:40 (32,305)	
Thomas, Patricia D	3:49:13 (6,779)	
Thomas, Pauline R	4:44:57 (19,820)	
Thomas, Rachael C	4:20:15 (13,665)	
Thomas, Rachel K	4:43:50 (19,489)	
Thomas, Rose	4:49:16 (20,831)	
Thomas, Sheryl E	3:38:22 (4,897)	
Thomas, Victoria F	4:33:25 (16,895)	
Thomas, Wendy	6:18:36 (33,811)	
Thomas, Whitni M	4:10:15 (11,220)	
Thomasson, Linda J	4:37:54 (17,981)	
Thomas-Wright, Joanna M	5:40:02 (30,595)	
Thombs, Alison J	4:32:50 (16,748)	
Thompson, Adele M	4:19:43 (13,515)	
Thompson, Alison C	4:51:24 (21,343)	
Thompson, Caroline	4:35:08 (17,310)	
Thompson, Chancy L	5:13:28 (26,116)	
Thompson, Charlotte A	4:03:53 (9,945)	
Thompson, Charlotte L	6:47:43 (34,878)	
Thompson, Clare J	4:31:59 (16,557)	
Thompson, Donna D	4:57:30 (22,904)	
Thompson, Elizabeth K	4:25:03 (14,836)	
Thompson, Emily	4:16:43 (12,741)	
Thompson, Fiona T	5:39:06 (30,463)	
Thompson, Gemma E	4:20:40 (13,768)	
Thompson, Janet	4:48:30 (20,647)	
Thompson, Joanna C	4:39:52 (18,500)	
Thompson, Karen	3:57:59 (8,718)	
Thompson, Katie J	4:54:33 (22,154)	
Thompson, Linda C	5:07:18 (24,956)	
Thompson, Lisa J	5:27:18 (28,677)	
Thompson, Louise	4:52:41 (21,662)	
Thompson, Lynne P	5:35:04 (29,922)	
Thompson, Margaret	5:22:02 (27,786)	
Thompson, Marjorie P	4:52:25 (21,660)	
Thompson, Sarah Jane	4:27:49 (15,543)	
Thompson, Sarah L	5:04:16 (24,370)	
Thompson, Stephanie	5:18:26 (27,148)	
Thompson, Tracey	4:38:54 (18,254)	
Thomsen, Kirsten	5:00:03 (23,517)	
Thomson, Catherine	4:33:42 (16,962)	
Thomson, Jackie P	4:12:13 (11,662)	
Thomson, Jo	5:17:13 (26,900)	
Thomson, Julia M	3:48:20 (6,580)	
Thomson, Katie	5:30:38 (29,241)	
Thomson, Kerry A	5:20:05 (27,435)	
Thomson, Lorraine V	6:27:53 (34,247)	
Thomson, Nicola J	4:58:40 (23,183)	
Thomson, Pamela	4:29:31 (16,013)	
Thomson, Tracey L	6:23:53 (34,071)	
Thorkelsoottir, Hlin	3:52:59 (7,564)	
Thorn, Georgina L	5:10:00 (25,477)	
Thorn, Pauline M	5:28:38 (28,926)	

Thorne, Catherine A 4:21:20 (13,918)
Thorne, Christine 4:14:11 (12,134)
Thorner, Sophie H....................6:27:31 (34,232)
Thorneycroft, Katy E................4:55:45 (22,444)
Thornton, Eirian......................5:10:04 (25,495)
Thornton, Jane M.....................5:20:22 (27,488)
Thornton, Rachel......................4:56:49 (22,719)
Thornton, Tracey......................4:55:49 (22,461)
Thorpe, Emma J........................5:12:29 (25,949)
Thorpe, Gemma........................5:50:37 (31,735)
Thorstrand, Kat.......................4:19:23 (13,427)
Thoua, Nora M.........................3:59:55 (9,188)
Thrift, Jessica A 4:53:17 (21,831)
Thrower, Kristina 4:51:32 (21,376)
Thurgood, Clare L....................3:27:40 (3,368)
Thurland, Abigail L 4:33:31 (16,916)
Thurling, Kate E.......................5:26:29 (28,543)
Thwaites, Claire J....................4:19:25 (13,436)
Thyne, Virginia R......................4:48:48 (20,722)
Tibbatts, Joanne......................3:53:05 (7,587)
Tibbetts, Anna-Liese H 4:18:35 (13,234)
Tidd, Megan M.........................5:28:47 (28,950)
Tierney, Elaine........................4:16:25 (12,678)
Tierney, Jill............................4:23:45 (14,502)
Tilbury, Camilla........................5:26:22 (28,524)
Tiley, Kristen L........................4:48:47 (20,717)
Tiley, Leanne M.......................4:12:51 (11,799)
Tiley, Philippa H 4:24:24 (14,681)
Till, Joanna............................5:32:37 (29,551)
Tillett, Natalie J......................5:02:26 (24,024)
Tilley, Jackie...........................7:20:21 (35,392)
Tilly, Helen............................5:54:53 (32,135)
Timbrell, Amanda J 5:34:44 (29,881)
Timbrell, Shelley K 6:36:25 (34,554)
Timmins, Lucy C.....................6:08:13 (33,187)
Timmis, Emily J.......................3:54:50 (7,970)
Timms, Louise C......................4:59:02 (23,264)
Tingey, Morag M......................6:41:33 (34,704)
Tinker, Lucie A........................4:15:50 (12,518)
Tinning, Sue...........................4:22:34 (14,219)
Tinsley-Marshall, Sarah R 6:43:58 (34,769)
Tipton, Jacqueline S 7:07:16 (35,235)
Titley, Tracey K.......................5:00:47 (23,683)
Titmuss, Karen 6:29:19 (34,299)
Toby, Julia K...........................3:50:42 (7,078)
Todd, Lindsey C......................5:17:50 (27,013)
Todd, Lisa J...........................4:26:51 (15,280)
Todd, Sonja............................4:37:23 (17,855)
Todd, Yvette E........................4:59:55 (23,479)
Toft, Ingrid J..........................5:15:25 (26,546)
Tointon, Kara 7:21:59 (35,406)
Tokairin, Mika.........................3:20:16 (2,527)
Tole, Ellie C............................4:17:31 (12,951)
Tolman, Michelle L...................5:44:30 (31,094)
Tomasz, Courtney H 6:15:37 (33,658)
Tombs, Gail............................3:58:45 (8,897)
Tomescu-Dita, Constantina 2:23:55 (20)
Tomeu, Jeannie M....................3:47:15 (6,387)
Tomic, Olga............................4:57:19 (22,860)
Tomkins, Angela 4:59:46 (23,448)
Tomkins, Josephine L 5:30:20 (29,190)
Tomkins, Paula A 3:56:45 (8,420)
Tomlins, Louise M....................5:26:38 (28,560)
Tomlinson, Kate 4:50:15 (21,060)
Tomlinson, Laura.....................5:37:44 (30,266)
Tomlinson, Lorraine D 5:09:15 (25,326)
Tomlinson, Victoria A................4:53:36 (21,913)
Tompkins, Elaine 5:26:35 (28,555)
Tompkins, Helen M 4:22:42 (14,258)
Toms, Faye 3:57:20 (8,561)
Toms, Sharron 4:14:10 (12,130)
Tong, Anne-Marie 5:44:05 (31,052)
Tong, Lydia J 4:00:22 (9,283)
Tonkin, Jane E.........................5:33:10 (29,629)
Tonkin, Joanne........................4:59:41 (23,427)
Tonkin, Sarah J........................5:49:58 (31,674)
Toogood, Rachel A....................4:15:19 (12,401)
Tooth, Joy M 6:49:51 (34,924)
Tooth, Charlene J.....................6:03:03 (32,822)
Topp, Vanessa J.......................4:20:07 (13,629)
Topper, Claire L.......................5:01:17 (23,789)
Torgersen, Jenny L...................4:13:46 (12,035)
Torrens, Lorna A......................4:40:33 (18,666)

Torri, Mirca 4:21:45 (14,019)
Tourish, Siobhan......................5:01:00 (23,725)
Tourlamain, Monica 6:22:09 (34,002)
Tovari, Szofia A........................6:01:52 (32,744)
Towers, Julie A.........................3:47:03 (6,355)
Towerton, Kate 3:35:56 (4,540)
Towey, Claire E........................5:18:17 (27,117)
Townend, Helen A 3:40:50 (5,329)
Townend, Laura 6:58:41 (35,102)
Townend, Rachael L 6:01:21 (32,708)
Towner, Susan K 4:50:34 (21,139)
Towns, Jill M 5:28:54 (28,970)
Towns, Sharron 3:59:40 (9,131)
Townsend, Lucy.......................5:36:58 (30,168)
Townsend, Rebecca..................5:18:51 (27,221)
Towse, Grace...........................6:25:12 (34,136)
Tozer, Nicola M........................4:28:29 (15,725)
Tracey, Sian P 4:59:34 (23,404)
Traiger, Elizabeth A..................5:51:32 (31,831)
Traill, Elizabeth 6:19:04 (33,841)
Trant, Linda J 5:32:00 (29,451)
Travers, Kate M........................5:34:36 (29,861)
Travers, Kimberley L 3:49:24 (6,808)
Traylen, Nicola G 5:09:05 (25,291)
Trayling, Denise J 4:07:20 (10,623)
Trdant, Anna M........................6:10:21 (33,328)
Treadwell, Lorraine F 3:50:19 (7,003)
Treadwell, Rosalind A 4:06:58 (10,566)
Treanor, Jennifer......................6:53:38 (35,010)
Treece, Lisa C 5:35:35 (29,992)
Tremaine, Tina D......................4:08:46 (10,916)
Tremonti, Joanne L...................3:53:37 (7,709)
Tremud, Olga...........................4:41:03 (18,802)
Treneman, Angela J 6:35:33 (34,525)
Trevaskis, Brigid 5:07:48 (25,058)
Trevaskis, Janet M....................4:05:15 (10,193)
Trevena, Niki M........................3:51:51 (7,327)
Trevor-Jones, Suzanne C............4:53:53 (21,985)
Trick, Lisa 4:59:12 (23,308)
Trickett, Caroline 6:36:04 (34,538)
Trickett, Faye C........................4:22:01 (14,089)
Trigell, Alison J........................6:30:47 (34,353)
Trigg, Michelle M......................4:12:24 (11,701)
Tritton, Mo P...........................6:26:14 (34,186)
Trivedi, Seema G......................5:50:38 (31,739)
Trivett, Gina............................5:38:30 (30,382)
Trkulja, Clare A 6:05:08 (32,973)
Trotman, Mandy J 5:33:19 (29,649)
Trotman, Rebecca A..................4:29:22 (15,964)
Trotter, Louise A 4:16:03 (12,582)
Trought, Nicola A......................4:49:56 (20,980)
Trowbridge, Catherine M 4:53:42 (21,942)
Trowsdale, Katie V....................3:45:34 (6,107)
Truelove, Ruth F.......................5:15:31 (26,567)
Truman, Delyth W.....................4:28:30 (15,726)
Trumper, Michele J 3:58:37 (8,857)
Trusch, Sharon L......................3:56:15 (8,286)
Trypronides, Andrea..................6:30:49 (34,356)
Trywhitt-Drake, Rosemary J 6:56:28 (35,061)
Tuck, Ida E.............................4:57:25 (22,889)
Tuck, Julia M 3:28:16 (3,442)
Tucker, Gillian 6:12:54 (33,487)
Tucker, Jessica M 4:08:43 (10,911)
Tucker, Natalie J.......................5:39:06 (30,463)
Tucker, Sarra L........................5:04:46 (24,460)
Tudball, Laura F.......................5:09:19 (25,336)
Tudor-Williams, Polly.................5:16:26 (26,746)
Tuite, Samantha.......................5:11:58 (25,848)
Tull, Andrea............................5:18:05 (27,074)
Tullis, Caroline 4:35:38 (17,436)
Tully, Helen M 5:01:02 (23,736)
Tummons, Sharon L 5:07:13 (24,934)
Tun, Mya M.............................5:16:50 (26,815)
Tunley, Alison J........................4:33:21 (16,883)
Tunnard, Fleur 4:17:20 (12,887)
Tunnicliffe, Helen.....................5:37:04 (30,179)
Tunstall, Rebecca K..................4:14:18 (12,169)
Tuoyo, Tosan 5:30:59 (29,291)
Turk, Elizabeth J.......................3:42:28 (5,593)
Turkington, Helen R..................4:32:47 (16,735)
Turley, Christina R 5:19:04 (27,259)
Turley, Frances M 4:59:25 (23,354)
Turner, Caroline M 4:18:26 (13,190)

Turner, Corinne 5:00:06 (23,524)
Turner, Desley 6:55:31 (35,048)
Turner, Donna L.......................4:08:24 (10,848)
Turner, Fleur M 5:36:10 (30,064)
Turner, Hilary..........................5:18:50 (27,219)
Turner, Jane D.........................5:24:11 (28,135)
Turner, Janet C........................5:35:27 (29,971)
Turner, Katie L.........................5:53:57 (32,048)
Turner, Rebecca 4:11:03 (11,383)
Turner, Ruth P.........................4:13:01 (11,833)
Turner, Teresa M......................5:54:58 (32,146)
Turner, Victoria E......................4:57:46 (22,973)
Turner, Yvonne A......................3:58:48 (8,910)
Turner-Smith, Alison S...............5:21:46 (27,748)
Turquet, Francesca I 5:20:15 (27,467)
Turrell, Nancy M 4:36:29 (17,659)
Turton, Fiona 5:46:47 (31,332)
Turton, Helen..........................3:22:18 (2,727)
Tuson, Caroline L 5:09:38 (25,400)
Tutin, Angela M 4:17:18 (12,877)
Tuton, Maria S.........................4:29:06 (15,888)
Tuttle, Patricia A.......................4:43:32 (19,421)
Tweddell, Susan.......................5:15:28 (26,556)
Tweedie, Juliette H....................4:22:39 (14,246)
Tween, Emma J........................5:34:24 (29,827)
Twelvetree, Yvonne..................3:43:13 (5,723)
Twiner, Jill.............................5:38:07 (30,319)
Twitchin, Katherine 4:22:57 (14,319)
Twizell, Hayley K......................5:18:52 (27,226)
Twomey, Emma V......................4:27:33 (15,477)

Twyman, Lucy M 5:32:43 (29,567)

It was one of the hottest Marathons. The water
supplies were running out along the route and
in desperation I resorted to pouring half empty
discarded bottles of water, thrown down to the
ground, over my head. The feeling of the water
running through my hair and down my face was
magical, particularly since I hit the 'wall' early and
every painful step was becoming a real effort. The
crowds were fantastic and although it was my worst
official finish time, seeing my parents cheering me
on at Birdcage Walk and running down The Mall
brought a smile to my face, knowing that I had
raised funds for the charity Changing Faces.

Tydeman, Louise E....5:20:44 (27,560)
Tye, Sophie A....5:07:36 (25,019)
Tyers, Sarah J....4:26:56 (15,307)
Tyler, Amy....4:53:20 (21,845)
Tyler, Anthony....3:16:26 (2,121)
Tyler, Jacky A....3:27:13 (3,312)
Tyler, Karen M....6:36:13 (34,546)
Tyler, Michelle A....6:17:47 (33,771)
Tyler, Rona L....6:40:24 (34,676)
Tyler, Rosemary A....5:11:13 (25,706)
Tyler, Ruth R....5:12:52 (26,014)
Tyler, Sarah E....4:18:54 (13,306)
Tymen, Laurence....5:00:57 (23,719)
Tyrrell, Claire....4:45:09 (19,870)
Tyrrell, Jill P....5:20:51 (27,581)
Tyrrell, Karryn L....7:43:23 (35,591)
Tyrrell, Nichola J....4:26:47 (15,260)
Tyrrell, Nicola D....3:18:10 (2,306)
Tyson, Pauline....4:53:13 (21,818)
Tyson-Bloor, Adel J....4:38:42 (18,201)
Tytler, Kathryn M....5:04:31 (24,422)
Ubierna, Maria L....3:18:53 (2,377)
Uchoa, Marcia S....6:27:24 (34,227)
Uglow, Lyndsey S....4:22:22 (14,167)
Uglow, Miriam H....4:47:22 (20,374)
Uglow, Nicola J....5:40:29 (30,650)
Ujvari, Lesley C....4:09:40 (11,108)
Underwood, Danielle A....4:15:18 (12,395)
Underwood, Susan R....5:14:42 (26,381)
Uppal, Karen....5:30:19 (29,185)
Upsdell, Alexandra M....6:17:50 (33,772)
Upton, Alexandra....3:56:44 (8,415)
Uras, Caterina....4:56:10 (22,555)
Urban, Wendy H....3:10:37 (1,603)
Urbany, Marijana....4:06:54 (10,552)
Urwin, Katy P....4:05:02 (10,150)
Urwin-Mann, Sarah L....3:10:59 (1,630)
Usher, Tanya I....3:44:17 (5,900)
Vacher, Sam A....3:53:11 (7,610)
Vakilpour, Janet....4:24:16 (14,647)
Valapinee, Anick M....3:24:58 (3,016)
Valdes, Frances E....5:55:16 (32,170)
Vallance, Lita D....5:29:11 (29,018)
Vallier, Christine....4:42:09 (19,076)
Van Aardt, Emily....3:56:55 (8,458)
Van Der Does, Mary....5:36:34 (30,120)
Van Der Graaf, Tina J....4:34:26 (17,131)
Van Der Merwe, Christelle....3:39:55 (5,177)
Van Der Ryst, Elna....4:37:31 (17,892)
Van Der Tas, Marlie....3:49:30 (6,832)
Van Deventer, Anna....4:35:39 (17,440)
Van Dijk, Suzan M....5:56:06 (32,246)
Van Herreweghe, Inge....5:39:06 (30,463)
Van Huyssteen, Sue A....4:02:43 (9,733)
Van Mil, Anita....3:38:38 (4,945)
Van Rompaey, Anna M....6:32:06 (34,412)
Van Rooyen, Elzare....4:26:53 (15,288)
Van Stek-The, Martine....4:31:39 (16,497)
Van Stry, Jennifer L....5:27:33 (28,719)
Van Summeren, Maria....3:52:44 (7,511)
Van Vuuren, Anita....7:07:24 (35,239)
Van Zyl, Hetsie....3:53:57 (7,779)
Vanderplank, Kathryn J....5:45:00 (31,154)
Vanegas, Clara E....5:43:06 (30,947)
Vango, Jeannette K....4:35:51 (17,499)
Vanhala, Lisa C....4:30:10 (16,191)
Varley, Kim....5:20:58 (27,601)
Varley, Paula A....4:04:45 (10,103)
Varney, Suzanne G....5:15:37 (26,589)
Varsani, Harsha V....5:32:54 (29,589)
Vartiainen, Maria K....4:34:13 (17,079)
Vasey, Ann C....4:37:52 (17,974)
Vasquez, Martha V....5:13:43 (26,172)
Vaughan, Caroline L....4:48:23 (20,631)
Vaughan, Diane E....3:56:37 (8,385)
Vaughan, Grethe....4:49:24 (20,861)
Vaughan, Jane....6:15:39 (33,659)
Vaughan, Lynsey S....4:23:38 (14,476)
Vaughan, Sarah....4:58:37 (23,171)
Vaughan, Tamsin C....5:28:18 (28,865)
Veal, Leanna R....3:45:36 (6,113)
Veal, Leanne M....6:31:27 (34,381)
Veingard, Tanya A....4:48:03 (20,546)
Velasco, Maribel....6:16:44 (33,723)
Vella, Keryn T....4:47:03 (20,299)
Velzeboer, Freya E....5:43:20 (30,976)
Venekas, Hilary R....4:59:23 (23,350)
Venter, Sarah L....4:27:46 (15,535)
Ventress, Katie A....6:01:11 (32,695)
Ventura, Marisa....4:04:50 (10,120)
Verbruggen, Anne-Marie F....4:01:51 (9,578)
Verde Nieto, Diana....4:13:03 (11,847)
Verduijn, Marjanne....3:42:08 (5,543)
Vernazza, Patricia....3:53:34 (7,702)
Vernet, Isabelle....4:13:13 (11,883)
Verney, Helen M....5:22:53 (27,918)
Vernon, Elizabeth H....7:03:53 (35,190)
Vernon, Susan J....5:53:51 (32,038)
Verrek, Ilona K....5:12:06 (25,870)
Verrill, Freda....4:02:13 (9,652)
Verspeelt, Efvelyne J....4:51:22 (21,334)
Verstappen, Ingrid J....4:12:06 (11,630)
Vesty, Sue....4:24:00 (14,571)
Vian, Stephanie K....4:09:19 (11,034)
Viccars, Kerry G....6:39:38 (34,662)
Vick, Jane....4:53:48 (21,964)
Vickers, Jane E....5:13:44 (26,174)
Vickers, Lisa M....4:26:30 (15,195)
Vickers, Sarah....4:03:42 (9,902)
Vickers, Stacey J....5:38:57 (30,445)
Vickerstaff, Lucy M....4:32:42 (16,716)
Vickery, Pauline A....5:21:38 (27,717)
Victor, Christina R....4:54:06 (22,041)
Vielvoye, Eileen D....6:03:14 (32,834)
Vignudelli, Daniela....4:26:28 (15,179)
Vinall, Janice....5:22:42 (27,891)
Vinall, Lucie E....4:06:27 (10,454)
Vince, Debbie K....6:18:02 (33,779)
Vincent, Jacqueline....5:42:50 (30,919)
Vincent, Louise N....4:30:14 (16,202)
Vincent, Nadia G....5:33:53 (29,742)
Vine, Rachel L....5:31:51 (29,427)
Vines, Andrea J....3:47:21 (6,397)
Vinten, Jackie L....3:58:50 (8,921)
Vinter, Carol....5:43:33 (30,997)
Virgin, Suzy....4:48:53 (20,740)
Visser, Paula A....4:26:40 (15,231)
Vivekananthan, Uma....4:39:14 (18,345)
Vivian, Katherine A....3:20:24 (2,542)
Vogiatzis, Anna....5:57:30 (32,368)
Volkert, Jana....5:17:52 (27,022)
Volland, Helen E....4:15:33 (12,450)
Voquet-Tragin, Isabelle....5:17:18 (26,920)
Vose, Madeleine....5:51:59 (31,871)
Vowels, Helen J....5:18:32 (27,169)
Waddilove, Johanna D....3:47:35 (6,441)
Wade, Hayley J....5:00:43 (23,664)
Wadforth, Cath....3:53:42 (7,728)
Wadge, Samantha J....6:13:09 (33,500)
Wadsworth, Natasha J....4:57:18 (22,854)
Wadsworth, Tracey....5:34:31 (29,853)
Wadsworth, Wendy J....4:42:59 (19,291)
Wagstaff, Nina E....3:17:13 (2,198)
Wainer, Jennifer K....4:43:22 (19,397)
Wainner, Carolyn A....6:27:16 (34,226)
Wainwright, Catherine....4:07:44 (10,710)
Wait, Debra E....3:14:44 (1,963)
Waite, Alison....4:42:49 (19,260)
Waite, Gail....4:59:50 (23,463)
Waite, Helen....6:03:43 (32,869)
Waite, Sandra N....4:23:49 (14,518)
Wakefield, Caroline W....3:16:22 (2,112)
Wakefield, Sarah-Jane....6:06:48 (33,095)
Wakefield, Sonia....5:54:27 (32,103)
Wakeford, Helen M....6:13:32 (33,523)
Wakeling, Nicola S....4:54:33 (22,154)
Waker, Karen S....7:12:31 (35,312)
Wake-Smith, Sarah M....5:12:53 (26,019)
Walas, Monika M....5:59:15 (32,532)
Walbridge, Fiona K....4:43:43 (19,466)
Walbrin, Sarah V....5:54:05 (32,060)
Walczak, Josephine A....5:37:43 (30,263)
Walden, Jodie M....5:04:23 (24,399)
Waldoch, Lorraine M....3:49:41 (6,868)
Waldron, Kate A....4:42:02 (19,047)
Walford, Teresa....4:49:38 (20,923)
Walker, Abigail V....3:40:29 (5,261)
Walker, Allison J....4:44:47 (19,772)
Walker, Caroline J....3:50:39 (7,066)
Walker, Clare J....4:30:58 (16,347)
Walker, Donna M....6:05:17 (32,984)
Walker, Ellen M....8:02:04 (35,644)
Walker, Emma....5:39:57 (30,580)
Walker, Helen K....5:57:27 (32,367)
Walker, Helen M....4:10:39 (11,300)
Walker, Hilary....3:54:01 (7,794)
Walker, Jane S....5:00:02 (23,512)
Walker, Jayne Louise....5:16:04 (26,674)
Walker, Jennifer L....5:02:17 (23,987)
Walker, Jill F....4:14:21 (12,175)
Walker, Joanne C....5:40:50 (30,684)
Walker, Julie D....5:54:09 (32,068)
Walker, Katherine....3:53:05 (7,587)
Walker, Laura A....5:15:55 (26,647)
Walker, Laura-Jane....6:38:43 (34,626)
Walker, Lindsay....4:07:55 (10,755)
Walker, Lisa....4:46:38 (20,204)
Walker, Lou....4:23:18 (14,399)
Walker, Pauline A....5:00:43 (23,664)
Walker, Rosemary I....5:53:30 (32,008)
Walker, Sarah L....3:33:54 (4,254)
Walker, Susan F....3:55:16 (8,070)
Walker, Theresa A....5:26:12 (28,491)
Walker, Tracey....5:53:16 (31,983)
Walker, Valerie H....5:32:22 (29,504)
Walker-Leach, Jenny C....4:32:12 (16,609)
Walkinshaw, Stephanie J....4:56:17 (22,582)
Wall, Alison M....5:42:17 (30,860)
Wall, Amy....5:23:18 (27,976)
Wall, Helen R....6:46:56 (34,856)
Wall, Michala C....3:28:47 (3,537)
Wall, Nikkie A....4:49:05 (20,789)
Wall, Pamela H....4:50:45 (21,177)
Wall, Rebecca J....3:35:50 (4,526)
Wallace, Anna....3:19:12 (2,414)
Wallace, Bastien L....6:05:36 (33,016)
Wallace, Carol....5:18:17 (27,117)
Wallace, Gina S....5:46:13 (31,285)
Wallace, Jennifer....7:06:52 (35,233)
Wallace, Jennifer J....4:38:41 (18,195)
Wallace, Sarah....6:11:37 (33,406)
Wallace, Susan....5:03:26 (24,224)
Wallace, Susan M....5:01:25 (23,815)
Wallace, Susan M....5:15:53 (26,638)
Wallbridge, Sarah M....5:27:32 (28,716)
Wallen, Brigid E....4:00:01 (9,211)
Waller, Teresa A....5:13:06 (26,063)
Wallin, Susanne....4:27:51 (15,554)
Wallington, Hannah....4:26:40 (15,231)
Walliss, Eleanor E....5:08:22 (25,165)
Walls, Margaret-Catriona....4:34:25 (17,118)
Wallwork, Catherine A....6:21:47 (33,988)
Walmsley, Elsie M....5:13:41 (26,161)
Walmsley, Louisa K....5:28:51 (28,957)
Walpole, Jan....4:37:23 (17,855)
Walpole, Mary....5:14:40 (26,377)
Walpole, Tracy J....5:07:45 (25,044)
Walsh, Belinda M....4:54:47 (22,223)
Walsh, Caroline E....3:07:10 (1,323)
Walsh, Gillian L....7:46:58 (35,608)
Walsh, Jess....4:06:32 (10,471)
Walsh, Jillian R....3:50:54 (7,115)
Walsh, Peta L....6:10:01 (33,305)
Walsh, Victoria L....5:16:54 (26,840)
Walsh, Victoria R....5:16:10 (26,692)
Walter, Angela J....4:44:24 (19,649)
Walters, Joan M....4:45:26 (19,930)
Walters, Kathryn....4:12:34 (11,731)
Walters, Sherryl A....5:14:16 (26,286)
Walters, Susan-Lynn....4:19:03 (13,337)
Walton, Alice E....5:57:30 (32,368)
Walton, Barbara H....5:15:00 (26,449)
Walton, Elizabeth A....5:24:04 (28,116)
Walton, Frances E....5:30:27 (29,210)
Walton, Jan D....5:06:46 (24,837)
Walton, Kirsten A....3:57:33 (8,610)
Walton, Laura J....4:13:37 (11,999)
Walton, Linda....3:25:31 (3,067)
Walton, Lisa A....5:51:45 (31,850)

Walton, Ruth H	5:26:01 (28,458)	
Walton-Peile, Michala	5:16:21 (26,729)	
Wami, Gete	2:21:45 (16)	
Wands, Susan E	4:21:07 (13,878)	
Wanklyn, Ann	6:35:29 (34,522)	
Want, Victoria A	5:35:54 (30,038)	
Waple, Karen A	4:54:36 (22,172)	
Ward, Anna L	4:35:38 (17,436)	
Ward, Carol P	5:46:59 (31,352)	
Ward, Cressida E	4:43:06 (19,318)	
Ward, Jessica C	3:52:19 (7,437)	
Ward, Joanna E	3:52:15 (7,421)	
Ward, Karen E	6:57:51 (35,091)	
Ward, Katie	4:00:32 (9,318)	
Ward, Linda D	4:20:51 (13,817)	
Ward, Linda N	5:11:43 (25,793)	
Ward, Margaret J	5:28:55 (28,971)	
Ward, Mary V	4:49:57 (20,984)	
Ward, Rachel A	3:35:26 (4,474)	
Ward, Rachel V	5:21:42 (27,733)	
Ward, Sara A	5:34:09 (29,787)	
Ward, Stella	4:41:46 (18,983)	
Ward, Tina D	6:29:25 (34,305)	
Ward, Tracy L	4:40:15 (18,589)	
Ward, Victoria J	5:55:09 (32,159)	
Warden, Sarah J	4:36:53 (17,763)	
Wardman, Sarah E	4:07:44 (10,710)	
Wares, Harriet L	4:12:22 (11,693)	
Warham, Jennifer A	4:48:01 (20,535)	
Warhurst, Helen	4:48:46 (20,711)	
Waring, Gabrielle M	4:14:13 (12,141)	
Waring, Judith R	5:05:46 (24,655)	
Warne, Catherine P	4:05:26 (10,228)	
Warne, Paula J	4:06:22 (10,429)	
Warner, Anne	4:46:25 (20,157)	
Warner, Anne	5:49:29 (31,624)	
Warner, Claire L	3:13:22 (1,855)	
Warner, Denise C	4:56:19 (22,590)	
Warner, Julie	4:56:19 (22,590)	
Warner, Rhona F	5:58:20 (32,451)	
Warner, Sarah L	4:19:45 (13,524)	
Warren, Alison J	5:52:52 (31,956)	
Warren, Claire M	5:05:30 (24,602)	
Warren, Gail	5:35:48 (30,022)	
Warren, Gail B	5:19:15 (27,303)	
Warren, Julie	4:46:35 (20,196)	
Warren, Karen A	5:56:57 (32,329)	
Warren, Lee W	5:44:21 (31,081)	
Warren, Sara D	4:56:55 (22,753)	
Warren, Sarah	4:56:08 (22,543)	
Warrener, Della	5:25:24 (28,341)	
Warrick, Asha	3:46:53 (6,318)	
Warrick, Stephanie M	4:41:46 (18,983)	
Warrillow, Sara J	6:01:19 (32,704)	
Warrington, Katie	5:33:47 (29,730)	
Warrington, Sarah M	4:42:15 (19,110)	
Warwick, Cathy	6:40:51 (34,686)	
Warwick, Sarah J	5:20:33 (27,531)	
Warwicker, Sarah J	5:31:26 (29,371)	
Wasmeier, Christina	3:28:53 (3,553)	
Wass, Victoria	6:16:07 (33,689)	
Wasyliw, Antoinette	4:22:08 (14,112)	
Watchorn, Nicola J	5:34:06 (29,780)	
Watchorn Rice, Ruth F	3:11:21 (1,659)	
Waterfield, Melanie L	7:15:55 (35,351)	
Waterhouse, Cassy	5:06:06 (24,712)	
Waterman, Isobel S	4:58:32 (23,157)	
Waters, Anne-Marie	4:22:49 (14,290)	
Waters, Bel A	4:01:49 (9,572)	
Waters, Jane S	5:54:27 (32,103)	
Waterworth, Claire	4:58:16 (23,093)	
Watkins, Kersten	4:55:50 (22,468)	
Watkins, Rachel	4:14:36 (12,230)	
Watkins, Sarah L	4:53:32 (21,894)	
Watkins, Shirley J	5:55:02 (32,151)	
Watkins, Tanya S	4:53:05 (21,771)	
Watkinson, Katie	7:06:43 (35,231)	
Watson, Ally	5:50:40 (31,747)	
Watson, Anna K	4:53:30 (21,885)	
Watson, Christina M	4:18:19 (13,155)	
Watson, Claire P	5:17:44 (27,007)	
Watson, Denise M	5:04:23 (24,399)	
Watson, Edwina M	5:12:38 (25,971)	

Watson, Jacqueline D	6:23:56 (34,073)	
Watson, Jane	4:12:26 (11,710)	
Watson, Jodie G	4:27:46 (15,535)	
Watson, Julie K	4:18:26 (13,190)	
Watson, Laura	6:36:41 (34,567)	
Watson, Maggi C	3:53:29 (7,683)	
Watson, Tracey	5:18:19 (27,128)	
Watt, Fiona	4:59:06 (23,287)	
Watt, Fiona E	4:40:47 (18,728)	
Watt, Sarah A	5:09:57 (25,463)	
Watts, Francesca A	4:31:19 (16,428)	
Watts, Jenny S	6:53:56 (35,019)	
Watts, Lucy	5:46:42 (31,328)	
Watts, Nicola A	3:35:42 (4,514)	
Watts, Rebecca	4:41:04 (18,803)	
Watts, Sarah	5:07:15 (24,942)	
Way, Nicky J	3:43:26 (5,761)	
Waymark, Leanne	4:24:33 (14,717)	
Wayt, Clare J	4:39:39 (18,449)	
Weatherall, Gayle M	4:36:41 (17,714)	
Weatherill, Joanna R	4:18:23 (13,170)	
Weatherley, Karen	5:58:55 (32,498)	
Weaver, Patricia A	5:16:14 (26,706)	
Weaver, Sara J	4:40:15 (23,119)	
Weaver, Susan	5:06:34 (24,791)	
Webb, Claire L	4:47:44 (20,464)	
Webb, Dani K	5:18:16 (27,116)	
Webb, Felicity R	5:12:39 (25,974)	
Webb, Gaynor N	4:24:25 (14,685)	
Webb, Heather	6:42:48 (34,745)	
Webb, Jason	4:47:44 (20,464)	
Webb, Joelle	5:25:21 (28,330)	
Webb, Judith	4:32:10 (16,599)	
Webb, Karla	4:46:05 (20,073)	
Webb, Lauren E	4:27:12 (15,387)	
Webb, Lucy	4:31:45 (16,517)	
Webb, Lynn	3:51:41 (7,290)	
Webb, Shelley M	4:12:00 (11,613)	
Webber, Claire A	6:52:21 (34,981)	
Webber, Clare A	5:46:59 (31,352)	
Webber, Janet V	6:14:42 (33,590)	
Webber, Lucy H	6:41:49 (34,712)	
Webber, Sarah	4:54:13 (22,081)	
Webling, Barbara	5:39:46 (30,569)	
Webster, Catherine A	5:19:31 (27,344)	
Webster, Emma L	4:43:47 (19,476)	
Webster, Hannah J	5:01:30 (23,829)	
Webster, Julia A	4:58:06 (23,056)	
Webster, Kathie C	4:07:41 (10,700)	
Webster, Katy M	2:52:05 (444)	
Webster, Kelly	6:38:45 (34,628)	
Weeden, Annabel M	4:35:53 (17,508)	
Weeden, Susan M	5:28:39 (28,928)	
Weekes, Bridgit	4:00:31 (9,314)	
Weeks, Angela P	6:02:35 (32,790)	
Weeks, Honeysuckle	3:57:08 (8,508)	
Weeks, Jess	5:20:18 (27,477)	
Weetman, Anne	5:29:05 (28,996)	
Weetman, Helen J	6:16:13 (33,698)	
Wegrzynek, Kate	5:53:01 (31,965)	
Wehbe, Angeline	3:34:30 (4,340)	
Wehrenberg, Frauke	3:59:05 (8,981)	
Wei, Hui Y	5:25:38 (28,391)	
Wei, Karen A	4:04:01 (9,969)	
Weidenmueller, Gudrun	4:47:52 (20,494)	
Weight, Catherine S	4:26:52 (15,285)	
Weightman, Joanne L	5:35:56 (30,045)	
Weissenborn, Myriam	4:57:38 (22,939)	
Welander, Birgitta	6:01:02 (32,679)	
Welbourne, Terri	4:26:06 (15,074)	
Welbury, Dominique B	6:06:16 (33,065)	
Welch, Alex	5:30:05 (29,159)	
Welch, Louise A	4:09:26 (11,057)	
Welch, Maree	4:05:53 (10,327)	
Welfare, Claudia	6:00:39 (32,636)	
Welham, Lisa J	4:25:55 (15,037)	
Welham, Lyn M	6:13:56 (33,545)	
Weller, Ruth E	4:43:49 (19,482)	
Wellman, Sarah J	5:08:50 (25,247)	
Wells, Fiona J	5:18:51 (27,221)	
Wells, Karen J	5:34:52 (29,896)	
Wells, Lindsay E	5:21:13 (27,637)	
Wells, Lorraine	4:50:02 (21,003)	

Wells, Lyn F	5:21:51 (27,766)	
Wells, Sharon N	4:30:41 (16,292)	
Wells, Sophie J	4:40:09 (18,566)	
Wells, Susan A	5:21:03 (27,612)	
Wells, Tanya M	4:27:34 (15,480)	
Wells, Victoria F	5:41:21 (30,748)	
Welsby, Jacinta S	6:07:47 (33,155)	
Welsby, Pauline A	4:00:11 (9,247)	
Welsh, Christine J	4:14:31 (12,207)	
Welsh, Fiona	5:04:02 (24,332)	
Wemyss, Molly V	5:22:17 (27,819)	
Wengradt, Jean	5:30:59 (29,291)	
Wenman, Debbie C	3:38:46 (4,969)	
Wensley, Helen R	3:49:35 (6,848)	
Werth, Suzanne Y	4:56:31 (22,635)	
Wescott, Sandra A	3:57:02 (8,487)	
Wessel, Alexandra J	5:15:21 (26,531)	
West, Andrée	5:52:06 (31,881)	
West, Anita	5:21:52 (27,769)	
West, Diane	5:52:20 (31,905)	
West, Lorraine M	5:14:02 (26,235)	
West, Susan M	7:39:40 (35,558)	
West, Tracey J	3:10:18 (1,587)	
Westcott, Miranda J	4:19:45 (13,524)	
Westell, Polly A	6:27:05 (34,213)	
Westgate, Lesley	4:32:57 (16,773)	
Westhead, Jo	5:45:12 (31,174)	
Westlake, Mandy	3:18:04 (2,291)	
Westlake, Suzanne S	4:35:07 (17,303)	
Westle, Sue J	5:06:31 (24,786)	
Weston, Denise	3:38:48 (4,973)	
Weston, Helen	5:15:32 (26,575)	
Weston, Jane M	5:49:26 (31,623)	
Weston, Judith D	5:36:51 (30,156)	
Weston, Natasha T	4:32:36 (16,690)	
Weston, Sally	5:37:20 (30,219)	
Westra, Gerda	3:59:04 (8,976)	
Westwood, Emma	6:08:54 (33,231)	
Wetherall, Kathy M	5:19:48 (27,392)	
Wexner, Abigail	4:31:24 (16,443)	
Weymouth, Susan A	6:49:33 (34,922)	
Whang, Bonnie B	4:50:41 (21,164)	
Wharam, Hilary M	4:57:17 (22,847)	
Wharton, Emma L	3:26:42 (3,223)	
Wharton, Joanna L	5:15:18 (26,525)	
Wharton, Sarah J	5:48:39 (31,539)	
Whatling, Kerry L	5:08:02 (25,101)	
Whatling, Nicky	6:01:13 (32,699)	
Wheatley, André A	4:28:49 (15,814)	
Wheatley, Kate J	4:02:03 (9,612)	
Wheatley, Kerry M	6:33:27 (34,453)	
Wheatley, Rachel	4:20:01 (13,602)	
Wheeler, Amanda H	5:20:22 (27,488)	
Wheeler, Jennifer A	5:33:21 (29,657)	
Wheeler, Sharon L	5:18:14 (27,109)	
Whelan, Collette	4:47:46 (20,475)	
Whelan, Suzanne M	4:55:12 (22,318)	
Whelband, Bernadette	5:11:37 (25,780)	
Whichello, Kathryn J	5:17:36 (26,980)	
Whidburn, Amy G	4:37:52 (17,974)	
Whiley, Louise J	4:59:00 (23,253)	
Whish, Adrianna M	6:18:14 (33,788)	
Whitaker, Catherine M	5:04:50 (24,476)	
Whitaker, Emma K	5:51:52 (31,861)	
Whitaker, Ffreuer H	4:55:45 (22,444)	
Whitby, Katherine A	4:58:55 (23,230)	
White, Belinda H	4:00:53 (9,393)	
White, Cheryl L	5:15:51 (26,630)	
White, Debbie	4:34:53 (17,244)	
White, Denise J	7:42:04 (35,583)	
White, Elaine	5:08:35 (25,201)	
White, Jane L	3:22:32 (2,750)	
White, Jo	4:53:55 (21,997)	
White, Joanna L	3:50:34 (7,050)	
White, Katherine	5:11:31 (25,759)	
White, Katy A	4:26:19 (15,136)	
White, Kay	5:20:11 (27,453)	
White, Lorraine K	5:21:11 (27,631)	
White, Pamela L	4:11:01 (11,317)	
White, Patricia Y	5:19:12 (27,292)	
White, Reagan J	5:41:13 (30,731)	
White, Suzanne J	5:18:14 (27,109)	
White, Sylvia	4:32:54 (16,763)	

White, Ursula C 3:56:06 (8,247)
White, Victoria E 5:17:13 (26,900)
Whiteford, Anna K 4:50:56 (21,227)
Whitehead, Frederika C 5:55:13 (32,166)
Whitehead, Sharon 4:39:01 (18,288)
Whitehead-Waterlow, Amy 2:53:34 (498)
Whitehurst, Louise M 4:33:33 (16,928)
Whitehurst, Tracy 3:57:23 (8,577)
Whitelaw, Jodie 3:52:25 (7,455)
Whitelaw, Julianne C 4:57:10 (22,811)
Whiteley, Amy E 3:56:22 (8,324)
Whiteley, Melanie J 4:05:57 (10,342)
Whiteley, Susan 5:44:36 (31,110)
Whitelock, Nikki G 4:34:16 (17,091)
Whitelock, Vicky L 4:32:31 (16,667)
Whitelocks, Laura J 6:36:32 (34,559)
Whitestone, Joanne D 4:44:43 (19,750)
Whitfield, Aimée L 6:14:05 (33,557)
Whitfield, Vivienne 6:14:05 (33,557)
Whitford, Gemma 4:22:54 (14,309)
Whitham, Aliciia R 3:51:19 (7,206)
Whitham, Margaret M 4:28:14 (15,653)
Whitham, Vivien A 5:14:51 (26,419)
Whitiing, Layla L 6:25:05 (34,132)
Whiting, Elizabeth 3:27:45 (3,380)
Whiting, Zoe 5:23:14 (27,966)
Whitman, Maureen P 5:27:25 (28,699)
Whitman, Sally 5:27:38 (28,734)
Whitmore, Alexandra E 5:36:49 (30,150)
Whitmore, Lauren N 4:07:54 (10,748)
Whitnall, Lynn K 4:53:38 (21,924)
Whittaker, Jo 6:39:41 (34,664)
Whittaker, Linda 6:17:30 (33,751)
Whittaker, Lynn 4:55:53 (22,483)
Whittaker, Rachel C 5:16:51 (26,820)
Whittingham, Jenny S 5:13:42 (26,166)
Whittle, Anna E 4:41:55 (19,020)
Whittle, Debbie 5:12:13 (25,901)
Whittle, Sally A 4:36:13 (17,585)
Whitton, Kate S 5:42:58 (30,932)
Whitworth, Claire L 5:33:13 (29,636)
Whyley, Abigail J 5:55:06 (32,155)
Whyte, Geraldine J 5:15:47 (26,621)
Whyte, Kerry A 6:04:47 (32,942)
Whyte, Louise M 4:32:01 (16,562)
Whythe, Maria 7:17:25 (35,362)
Whythe, Maureen E 7:17:24 (35,361)
Wickens, Jennifer 5:08:35 (25,201)
Wickham, Sharon A 4:24:13 (14,634)
Wickham, Sue L 5:56:51 (32,324)
Wicks, Terry J 5:05:27 (24,588)
Widman, Gabriella 6:29:59 (34,325)
Wieland, Barbara 5:08:55 (25,266)
Wienand, Beverley A 5:24:08 (28,131)
Wiener, Nikki C 3:33:21 (4,187)
Wiffen, Philippa 4:02:30 (9,699)
Wiggett, Nina R 3:21:01 (2,612)
Wiggins, Kim 6:07:57 (33,166)
Wiggins, Rena 6:33:13 (34,446)
Wiggins, Samantha G 5:35:32 (29,980)
Wigley, Emma J 5:16:51 (26,820)
Wikner, Anne 5:53:09 (31,974)
Wilby, Betty A 5:44:02 (31,046)
Wilby, Joanne C 5:00:33 (23,624)
Wilcox, Denise B 4:22:37 (14,240)
Wild, Christine 4:44:56 (19,815)
Wild, Jane 3:55:47 (8,183)
Wild, Lisa D 6:47:39 (34,877)
Wild, Sian L 5:41:41 (30,793)
Wild, Vivien E 7:03:44 (35,186)
Wilders, Beverley 4:26:09 (15,084)
Wilding, Catherine M 2:49:07 (348)
Wileman, Sarah 3:37:27 (4,745)
Wiliams, Sarah L 3:56:08 (8,259)
Wiliamson, Libby S 4:11:11 (11,424)
Wilk, Jennifer L 4:41:32 (18,932)
Wilkes, Olivia J 5:56:32 (32,292)
Wilkes, Pamela S 5:07:10 (24,918)
Wilkie, Gillian M 5:08:03 (25,105)
Wilkie, Josephine H 3:59:52 (9,173)
Wilkin, Penny 4:17:58 (13,064)
Wilkins, Gayle 4:17:42 (12,996)
Wilkins, Mary 4:32:47 (16,735)
Wilkinson, Dorothy A 3:19:22 (2,425)
Wilkinson, Helen L 3:43:43 (5,816)
Wilkinson, Holly 3:06:43 (1,290)
Wilkinson, Jennifer 5:23:42 (28,055)
Wilkinson, Joy L 3:53:59 (7,790)
Wilkinson, Lisa 3:38:48 (4,973)
Wilkinson, Mandy A 5:31:07 (29,320)
Wilkinson, Pauline A 6:57:48 (35,089)
Wilks, Claire 6:26:10 (34,180)
Wilks, Clarissa 4:35:12 (17,333)
Willbond, Andrea F 4:52:42 (21,668)
Willems, Katya 5:04:04 (24,337)
Willetts, Joanne M 5:28:24 (28,888)
Willey, Lisa A 5:46:56 (31,351)
Willgrass, Kate E 6:48:40 (34,901)
Williams, Alexandra M 5:47:18 (31,386)
Williams, Alexandra S 4:34:42 (17,203)
Williams, Angela J 4:08:10 (10,799)
Williams, Anita 5:45:56 (31,248)
Williams, Beverley A 6:29:09 (34,290)
Williams, Carol 4:49:35 (20,912)
Williams, Carol F 5:30:59 (29,291)
Williams, Caroline 4:09:08 (10,986)
Williams, Caroline C 5:52:26 (31,914)
Williams, Caroline E 5:27:30 (28,712)
Williams, Cathryn E 5:19:12 (27,292)
Williams, Charlotte A 3:44:45 (5,987)
Williams, Claire L 4:45:49 (20,010)
Williams, Corinne E 6:04:22 (32,908)
Williams, Delyth N 5:32:30 (29,525)
Williams, Denise E 4:25:39 (14,985)
Williams, Elizabeth N 5:15:54 (26,643)
Williams, Emily 4:42:10 (19,082)
Williams, Emma L 3:43:58 (5,862)
Williams, Emma L 5:14:32 (26,344)
Williams, Enfys M 6:16:56 (33,730)
Williams, Ffion 4:29:31 (16,013)
Williams, Frances 4:15:17 (12,391)
Williams, Gail A 3:31:28 (3,905)
Williams, Gaynor 6:19:27 (33,858)
Williams, Geraldine 5:17:53 (27,025)
Williams, Gwenndolyn A 6:05:35 (33,015)
Williams, Hannah K 4:38:29 (18,146)
Williams, Hayley 4:33:14 (16,854)
Williams, Hilary 4:55:58 (22,506)
Williams, Jane C 4:53:07 (21,784)
Williams, Jayne M 3:19:15 (2,420)
Williams, Jennfer A 4:52:32 (21,623)
Williams, Joanne 4:07:26 (10,641)
Williams, Karen J 5:53:02 (31,967)
Williams, Karen P 6:45:56 (34,828)
Williams, Kate E 4:42:27 (19,164)
Williams, Kate R 6:40:11 (34,671)
Williams, Katie O 5:08:57 (25,273)
Williams, Kim 4:45:24 (19,925)
Williams, Leasa J 5:36:16 (30,077)
Williams, Linda A 4:58:59 (23,250)
Williams, Lindsey 5:15:02 (26,464)
Williams, Lisa B 4:24:42 (14,747)
Williams, Lisa K 4:50:48 (21,195)
Williams, Lisa K 5:51:15 (31,801)
Williams, Lucy R 6:05:54 (33,035)
Williams, Lyn M 5:28:59 (28,979)
Williams, Lynne A 6:05:34 (33,013)
Williams, Margaret 4:48:42 (20,697)
Williams, Margaret O 5:25:34 (28,382)
Williams, Mary B 3:40:40 (5,293)
Williams, Maureen 7:02:27 (35,167)
Williams, Maureen M 5:09:02 (25,283)
Williams, Mel C 4:19:23 (13,427)
Williams, Michelle L 4:44:16 (19,619)
Williams, Nancy H 4:05:28 (10,236)
Williams, Natalie A 6:00:18 (32,606)
Williams, Nicola J 5:23:52 (28,088)
Williams, Patricia M 5:01:06 (23,751)
Williams, Philippa 5:37:20 (30,219)
Williams, Rebecca L 4:46:25 (20,157)
Williams, Sarah A 3:13:25 (1,859)
Williams, Sarah A 5:19:53 (27,405)
Williams, Shirley A 5:28:41 (28,932)
Williams, Silifa 4:47:27 (20,394)
Williams, Sophie A 5:29:07 (28,998)
Williams, Susan E 4:29:38 (16,048)
Williams, Teresa K 3:39:54 (5,175)
Williams, Tracey A 4:41:50 (19,005)
Williams, Tracy A 4:05:08 (10,169)
Williams, Victoria G 5:21:43 (27,734)
Williamson, Catherine 4:25:23 (14,918)
Williamson, Jemma L 4:19:21 (13,420)
Williamson, Julia F 4:25:38 (14,977)
Williamson, Philomena R 4:45:32 (19,958)
Williamson, Tessa F 4:05:32 (10,245)
Williamson, Verleta A 5:00:46 (23,680)
Williamson, Zelda 4:24:08 (14,610)
Willis, Caroline A 5:27:34 (28,726)
Willis, Debra J 4:28:32 (15,738)
Willis, Gaynor C 4:54:00 (22,022)
Willis, Georgina L 4:17:24 (12,908)
Willis, Julia S 4:49:46 (20,947)
Willis, Laura H 4:20:33 (13,742)
Willis, Lesley S 4:21:05 (13,868)
Willmington, Lesley A 4:46:10 (20,095)
Willmont, Joanna F 5:35:26 (29,968)
Willmott, Terri 4:34:27 (17,135)
Willocks-Watts, Michelle S 4:25:57 (15,043)
Willocott, Anne-Marie 4:02:40 (9,722)
Willoughby, Kate M 6:38:10 (34,611)
Wills, Amy T 4:38:23 (18,122)
Wills, Denise J 4:58:52 (23,223)
Wills, Tanya S 6:35:41 (34,527)
Willson, Samantha J 5:19:07 (27,271)
Wilsher, Andrea 4:13:53 (12,062)
Wilsher, Rachael M 3:55:58 (8,219)
Wilson, Alison 4:01:01 (9,423)
Wilson, Anne 4:15:13 (12,370)
Wilson, Antonia 5:39:20 (30,494)
Wilson, Antonia M 4:56:42 (22,696)
Wilson, Bernadette 6:10:11 (33,316)
Wilson, Bridget D 6:18:24 (33,797)
Wilson, Carly M 5:26:20 (28,516)
Wilson, Carolyn 4:46:27 (20,166)
Wilson, Claire 5:59:27 (32,549)
Wilson, Claire L 4:07:49 (10,730)
Wilson, Elizabeth H 4:31:11 (16,401)
Wilson, Esme I 3:47:37 (6,454)
Wilson, Fiona M 5:37:49 (30,273)
Wilson, Gemma C 4:08:36 (10,893)
Wilson, Heather J 5:33:05 (29,617)
Wilson, Heidi J 2:57:43 (721)
Wilson, Heidi S 5:30:31 (29,224)
Wilson, Irene A 5:03:45 (24,282)
Wilson, Jacqueline L 3:16:25 (2,119)
Wilson, Janice M 3:51:45 (7,305)
Wilson, Joanna L 5:20:23 (27,494)
Wilson, Joanne C 3:22:28 (2,744)
Wilson, Jules D 5:43:18 (30,972)
Wilson, Kathryn M 5:17:21 (26,927)
Wilson, Laura A 3:38:56 (5,002)
Wilson, Lisa 5:09:51 (25,439)
Wilson, Louise H 5:25:26 (28,351)
Wilson, Luclinda S 3:27:16 (3,320)
Wilson, Mandy 6:59:51 (35,122)
Wilson, Mandy J 4:47:35 (20,432)
Wilson, Marie M 5:28:22 (28,882)
Wilson, Mary A 6:31:34 (34,385)
Wilson, Michelle L 5:31:04 (29,311)
Wilson, Nicola A 3:43:22 (5,749)
Wilson, Nicola M 5:35:36 (29,996)
Wilson, Patricia M 3:54:12 (7,839)
Wilson, Peta J 4:03:54 (9,948)
Wilson, Phylly 5:16:59 (26,855)
Wilson, Rachael J 4:15:18 (12,395)
Wilson, Sarah L 3:35:02 (4,413)
Wilson, Stacey L 4:23:07 (14,358)
Wilson, Susan 4:19:30 (13,460)
Wilson, Susie H 4:34:26 (17,131)
Wilson, Ursula R 4:06:10 (10,385)

Wilson, Veronica G	6:50:59	(34,957)
Wiltshire, Clare L	6:18:28	(33,805)
Winder, Laura F	4:48:14	(20,586)
Winders, Catherine F	4:45:09	(19,870)
Windle, Sarah L	6:26:56	(34,211)
Wines, Gillian A	4:34:44	(17,211)
Winfield, Alice L	4:03:55	(9,950)
Winfrey, Jane H	5:34:33	(29,858)
Wing, Julie A	5:15:39	(26,593)
Wing, Sarah M	5:33:00	(29,605)
Wingfield, Zoe E	4:38:38	(18,183)
Wingrave, Rachael R	6:22:09	(34,002)
Winkfield, Hazel	6:56:50	(35,071)
Winn, Heidi N	3:29:56	(3,707)
Winser, Charlotte C	5:41:21	(30,748)
Winslow, Michelle	5:26:41	(28,574)
Winstone, Sarah L	5:47:59	(31,464)
Winter, Louise D	4:59:35	(23,407)
Winter, Victoria C	3:57:02	(8,487)
Winterson, Victoria	3:42:51	(5,657)
Winton, Christiane	4:48:00	(20,533)
Winwood, Nicola J	5:15:27	(26,553)
Wise, Claire	7:07:53	(35,244)
Wise, Gaye S	5:46:25	(31,302)
Wise, Susan M	7:11:31	(35,296)
Wisehall, Alicia C	6:13:23	(33,514)
Wiseman, Joanne	6:19:58	(33,889)
Wishart, Sara M	6:51:06	(34,959)
Wisxe, Paula M	5:40:27	(30,646)
Witcomb, Francesca	3:40:46	(5,312)
Witcombe, Julia M	5:03:31	(24,240)
Witham, Angela	4:24:35	(14,722)
Witham, Nondyebo G	6:22:02	(33,996)
Withe, Sharon M	5:51:11	(31,793)
Withers, Janette	3:54:37	(7,925)
Withers, Pamela R	3:58:56	(8,947)
Withey, Sarah J	4:47:21	(20,370)
Witt, Helen	4:00:11	(9,247)
Witt, Raj	4:16:42	(12,738)
Witts, Katherine J	5:20:10	(27,449)
Wixey, Denise E	5:39:48	(30,572)
Woffenden, Eleanor J	5:26:48	(28,587)
Wohanka, Oonagh	3:56:47	(8,428)
Wohlgemuth, Alison A	6:53:39	(35,012)
Wojna, Joanna M	4:19:46	(13,532)
Wollaston, Sandra J	4:51:20	(21,328)
Wolliscroft, Rachel L	4:46:28	(20,170)
Wolstenholme, Donna M	4:29:20	(15,947)
Wolstenholme, Hazel	4:33:50	(17,001)
Wolstenholme, Susan A	4:08:27	(10,862)
Wolstenholme, Susie L	5:28:05	(28,815)
Wong, Kimberley	6:27:10	(34,215)
Wong, Mable	3:37:59	(4,828)
Wong, Mailee	4:24:20	(14,660)
Wong, Marie	5:00:34	(23,629)
Wong, Mavis	4:56:39	(22,679)
Wong, Nicola	4:20:07	(13,629)
Wong, Patsy	4:13:39	(12,007)
Wong, Serena W	5:03:19	(24,197)
Wong, Suzie	4:20:36	(13,752)
Wong, Wendy	6:09:25	(33,262)
Wood, Amanda J	4:12:58	(11,822)
Wood, Barbara J	3:39:31	(5,109)
Wood, Carol A	7:45:21	(35,599)
Wood, Caroline L	5:23:45	(28,063)
Wood, Ger	5:34:59	(29,911)
Wood, Jacquie F	6:34:44	(34,483)
Wood, Jenni B	5:11:26	(25,746)
Wood, Jenny C	4:54:24	(22,123)
Wood, Joanna L	4:20:29	(13,729)
Wood, Joanne L	5:04:44	(24,455)
Wood, Katie F	4:56:49	(22,719)
Wood, Kerrie J	3:06:32	(1,274)
Wood, Linda J	4:31:41	(16,504)
Wood, Lorna J	5:58:59	(32,506)
Wood, Louise G	6:17:43	(33,766)
Wood, Lucie J	4:56:49	(22,719)
Wood, Margaret	3:46:23	(6,233)
Wood, Maria L	5:44:48	(31,128)
Wood, Penny O	4:38:55	(18,258)
Wood, Rachael L	6:13:13	(33,505)
Wood, Rachel A	4:13:27	(11,947)
Wood, Rachel H	3:35:59	(4,545)
Wood, Rebekah L	3:52:48	(7,524)
Wood, Stephanie J	4:44:50	(19,789)
Woodall, Sallianne	4:59:36	(23,412)
Woodbridge, Krystal F	5:37:11	(30,195)
Woodhouse, Ann E	6:22:05	(33,999)
Woodhouse, Janet M	4:19:13	(13,379)
Woodhouse, Wendy J	4:16:14	(12,630)
Woodley, Christine A	5:17:04	(26,871)
Woodman, Carol	3:50:40	(7,071)
Woodroffe, Amanda	4:57:26	(22,893)
Woods, Abigail L	3:26:04	(3,136)
Woods, Bonnie	4:50:31	(21,129)
Woods, Carol A	7:00:27	(35,135)
Woods, Catherine M	4:43:54	(19,509)
Woods, Katharine	5:41:40	(30,791)
Woodward, Allison J	7:55:20	(35,634)
Woodward, Lesley	3:56:44	(8,415)
Woodyatt, Lucie E	3:31:52	(3,967)
Woof, Kathryn A	4:12:58	(11,822)
Wooldridge, Hayley	4:54:04	(22,033)
Wooley, Theresa	2:58:13	(762)
Woolfson, Jennifer H	3:53:26	(7,673)
Woolgar, Allyson G	5:32:31	(29,533)
Woollard, Claire	3:55:42	(8,164)
Woollard, Harriet	4:26:34	(15,210)
Wooller, Diane E	4:12:34	(11,731)
Wooller, Sue L	4:14:13	(12,141)
Woolley, Janice L	4:30:11	(16,192)
Woolley, Kelly	5:47:54	(31,449)
Woolley, Mailynne	6:12:17	(33,446)
Woolley, Sophie J	6:09:34	(33,279)
Woonton-Pink, Patricia M	6:25:19	(34,141)
Woosey, Nicola	5:28:36	(28,918)
Wooster, Stella E	4:47:14	(20,340)
Wootton, Imogen E	4:52:21	(21,583)
Wopling, Katie V	4:42:21	(19,139)
Worden, Maxine C	3:31:20	(3,881)
Workman, Hayley	5:02:24	(24,018)
Worley, Rachel M	4:22:38	(14,241)
Wormald, Abbie J	4:39:57	(18,527)
Worms, Kerry J	4:42:47	(19,251)
Worrall, Julie	5:38:48	(30,431)
Worrall, Marie L	4:29:58	(16,139)
Worrall, Tamlyn G	4:57:38	(22,939)
Worrell, Laura N	6:07:31	(33,131)
Worsfold, Shirley A	4:35:07	(17,303)
Worster, Vicky L	3:50:34	(7,050)
Worth, Maria J	4:29:04	(15,875)
Worthington, Lindsey	6:08:49	(33,227)
Wortley, Helen J	6:02:55	(32,817)
Wotherspoon, Donna	6:38:10	(34,611)
Wotherspoon, Jane D	3:29:48	(3,688)
Wotherspoon, Lesley A	5:48:15	(31,498)
Wouda, Sharon L	4:09:06	(10,973)
Wozniak, Hannah C	6:13:16	(33,507)
Wratten, Katie L	4:58:09	(23,063)
Wray, Lisa	3:56:50	(8,439)
Wray, Shelley A	4:19:04	(13,343)
Wren, Ali R	3:56:06	(8,247)
Wren, Alyson K	4:56:13	(22,570)
Wren, Sam L	4:47:33	(20,422)
Wrenn, Emma J	5:20:29	(27,513)
Wrenn, Sara	5:56:08	(32,250)
Wrigglesworth, Julia R	3:47:25	(6,413)
Wrigglesworth, Vivien E	5:30:02	(29,147)
Wright, Alice M	3:52:06	(7,392)
Wright, Annabel C	5:38:12	(30,336)
Wright, Emma A	5:36:35	(30,123)
Wright, Fiona	3:58:51	(8,930)
Wright, Gemma F	5:00:07	(23,526)
Wright, Heather V	5:20:30	(27,517)
Wright, Joanna V	5:11:52	(25,827)
Wright, Joanne L	5:12:57	(26,033)
Wright, Julia	5:14:38	(26,369)
Wright, Julia T	6:17:36	(33,758)
Wright, Kate	3:39:02	(5,023)
Wright, Kate	4:25:15	(14,884)
Wright, Margaret M	5:36:49	(30,150)
Wright, Nichola J	5:40:51	(30,689)
Wright, Nicola J	4:09:02	(10,956)
Wright, Pamela M	5:37:48	(30,270)
Wright, Paula	4:44:32	(19,697)
Wright, Sally L	5:42:48	(30,909)
Wright, Sarah J	6:01:21	(32,708)
Wright, Sherry A	4:28:31	(15,730)
Wright, Tracey L	5:16:19	(26,724)
Wright, Vicki	4:28:00	(15,586)
Wright-Morris, Kate A	5:47:25	(31,400)
Wright-Whyte, Kelda S	5:58:16	(32,438)
Wrigley, Camilla M	5:05:37	(24,621)
Wrigley, Karen J	5:30:20	(29,190)
Wroe, Caitlin J	5:11:27	(25,748)
Wulkan, Nancy	4:59:15	(23,327)
Wyatt, Felicity A	5:50:31	(31,729)
Wyatt, Fiona C	5:18:21	(27,135)
Wyatt, Jane E	5:13:38	(26,146)
Wyatt, Margaret A	5:27:43	(28,747)
Wyatt, Rachel E	3:49:15	(6,790)
Wyer, Karen P	3:47:03	(6,355)
Wyer, Natalie A	3:42:23	(5,581)
Wyke, Yvonne D	3:14:41	(1,961)
Wyld, Olivia F	4:25:11	(14,867)
Wylde, Lyanne S	4:49:17	(20,836)
Wyngard, Clare E	3:46:40	(6,277)
Wynn, Elizabeth J	3:00:04	(905)
Yamauchi, Mara	2:25:41	(26)
Yan, Mary	4:17:47	(13,019)
Yardley, Susan M	5:50:02	(31,680)
Yarwood, Natasha	5:05:53	(24,672)
Yates, Alison S	4:28:05	(15,616)
Yates, Catherine M	3:40:43	(5,304)
Yates, Ceri E	5:32:17	(29,494)
Yates, Gill	4:53:10	(21,801)
Yates, Nicola L	5:18:36	(27,180)
Yates, Rachel E	4:02:12	(9,646)
Yates, Sarah E	3:21:12	(2,626)
Yates, Suzanne	4:55:03	(22,274)
Yeadon, Anna L	5:04:20	(24,385)
Yearley, Lesley C	4:22:14	(14,137)
Yeldham, Anne E	4:35:14	(17,343)
Yelling, Liz	2:30:44	(44)
Yendell, Anne E	4:07:15	(10,613)
Yendley, Susan E	4:02:05	(9,617)
Yeoell, Jeanette	5:14:02	(26,235)
Yeoell, Shelley L	5:14:01	(26,231)
Yeomans, Melanie D	5:10:37	(25,599)
Yeomans, Shelagh M	5:19:44	(27,379)
Yeung, Karen	4:53:03	(21,762)
Yewer, Kelly L	7:03:13	(35,178)
Yewman, Karen P	4:05:07	(10,165)
Yoe, Jenny	4:45:37	(19,970)
Yoloye, Opeyemi	7:43:56	(35,594)
York, Amanda J	5:16:48	(26,805)
Yorke, Karen D	4:13:44	(12,026)
Yorke-Long, Lucy E	4:56:34	(22,647)
Younan, Marleine	3:40:33	(5,278)
Young, Andrea	4:59:49	(23,462)
Young, Angela B	4:36:07	(17,563)
Young, Anna J	4:14:56	(12,306)
Young, Catherine F	3:37:10	(4,708)
Young, Christine A	4:42:11	(19,089)
Young, Claire	4:27:49	(15,543)
Young, Frances	4:42:01	(19,043)
Young, Gemma L	5:11:01	(25,671)
Young, George A	3:51:55	(7,342)
Young, Helen L	6:02:02	(32,754)
Young, Hilary	3:37:13	(4,713)
Young, Holly	5:21:59	(27,778)
Young, Jane	5:36:18	(30,082)
Young, Katherine E	5:39:30	(30,530)
Young, Lisa	5:51:28	(31,827)
Young, Lorna G	5:20:40	(27,550)
Young, Louise E	6:44:30	(34,787)
Young, Lucy M	5:30:26	(29,205)
Young, Melissa E	6:25:13	(34,139)
Young, Michelle A	4:58:58	(23,244)
Young, Nicola J	4:29:23	(15,971)
Young, Rhoda	4:16:53	(12,778)
Young, Sarah	4:12:06	(11,630)
Young, Sarah M	4:36:30	(17,664)
Young, Vicki	4:42:23	(19,146)
Young, Zoe A	5:29:18	(29,039)
Younghusband, Monica M	4:13:18	(11,909)
Yu, Susan W	6:11:09	(33,380)
Yuill, Chris	4:13:55	(12,073)
Zahalkova, Katerina	5:48:38	(31,535)

Zahl, Margaret E 5:25:41 (28,402)
Zahringer, Amanda J..................3:57:47 (8,671)
Zainul-Abidin, Suraya 5:11:17 (25,714)
Zanda, Federica............................4:31:50 (16,533)
Zanoletti, Doris 4:11:35 (11,518)
Zarpanely, Renée.........................4:28:54 (15,835)
Zdebik, Rose.................................4:15:08 (12,351)
Zeineldine, Ranya 5:14:17 (26,288)
Zemankova, Iva 4:52:54 (21,727)
Zemke, Suzanne..........................4:59:28 (23,369)
Zentner, Heike 5:02:11 (23,967)
Zernadji, Sonia............................5:10:29 (25,574)
Zimmerman, Debbie A...............4:54:28 (22,139)
Zouppas, Margarite.....................4:54:43 (22,204)
Zuiderveen, Anneloes.................5:18:08 (27,089)
Zuiderwijk Van Hal, Marion.......5:16:03 (26,672)
Zurawliw, Susan R.......................4:25:33 (14,955)
Zuschlag, Daniela........................3:55:11 (8,053)

WHEELCHAIR ENTRANTS

Adepitan, Ade 2:31:55 (20)
Alldis, Brian 1:44:31 (6)
Allen, Geoff...................................2:22:26 (16)
Baker, Gary 2:20:27 (14)
Cassell, Ric....................................3:05:08 (26)
Cheek, Andrew............................1:58:14 (9)
Derwin, Steve...............................3:39:23 (31)
Downing, Peter............................2:56:52 (24)
Erwin, Darrell...............................3:17:53 (28)
Fearnley, Kurt...............................1:30:50 (2)
Forde, Jerry...................................3:23:43 (30)
Golightly, Andy............................3:15:00 (27)
Holliday, Rob................................2:29:03 (18)
Hussain, Iftakhar.........................2:17:04 (13)
Marten, Michael..........................3:22:18 (29)
Martin, Butch 2:20:28 (15)
Mendoza, Saul 1:33:46 (3)
Phillips, Wayne 2:15:49 (12)
Piercy, Sarah 2:41:18 (22)
Porcellato, Francesca 1:59:46 (10)
Qadir, Shaho 7:46:49 (32)
Rea, Paul.......................................2:05:07 (11)
Stone, Douglas 2:49:55 (23)
Tan, William 2:26:32 (17)

Marathon firsts

Wheelchair athletes made their first appearance in the London Marathon in 1983. Tanni Grey-Thompson won the women's wheelchair event six times, for the first time in 1992. The training matches that of any elite athlete. David Weir, who took Double Gold at the Beijing Paralympics, says: 'Each racer has a different disability and way of sitting. I hold my hand like a fist. Mind you, one knuckle is bigger than the other because I had blisters for years.' Shelly Woods, who won the women's wheelchair title in 2007, says: 'I train six days a week, doing 80 to 120 miles weekly, and I'm in the gym twice a week. Wheelchairs are light and they're built to go fast – we get up to speeds of 20 or 30 mph. They can cost up to £3,000.'

Telford, Mark 1:54:18 (8)
Turner, James 2:30:31 (19)
Van Dyk, Ernst.............................1:33:46 (4)
Ward, Kevin 2:41:14 (21)
Weir, David 1:30:49 (1)

Woods, Shelly 1:50:40 (7)

Shelly Woods of Britain, (born 4 June 1986) had her first London Marathon breakthrough in 2005, when she was only 18, as she battled the title-holder, Italian Francesca Porcellato, right to the line and was only beaten by 3 seconds. She also beat the six-time London winner Tanni Grey-Thompson into third place. Woods was second again in the London 2006, but the following year she realised her potential winning in 1:50:40. She achieved British wheelchair records at 800m, 1500m, 5000m, and the marathon. At the 2008 Paralympics in Beijing, Woods won bronze in the 5000m Wheelchair final, having originally been awarded silver. A controversial protest arising from six athletes crashing in the final straight led to the race being re-staged four days later. Woods became paralysed from the waist down when she fell out of a tree aged 11. Woods is from Blackpool and works part-time in the leisure department for her council's Sports Development Department.

Yasuoka, Choke 1:33:50 (5)
Young, Derek................................3:00:48 (25)

The 2008 London Marathon

The London Marathon in 2008 marked 100 years since the marathon was fixed at the classic distance of 26 miles 385 yards. On show was a team from Capri, Italy – all dressed as Dorando Pietri, who was first over the finish line in the 1908 London Olympic Marathon.

Dorando was later disqualified for receiving assistance, but the gold cup that had been presented to him by Queen Alexandra had been flown to London for the Marathon Expo. The anniversary was commemorated by a book, *The Marathon Makers*, and a banquet given at Windsor Castle attended by the Queen, Prince Philip and the Princess Royal.

The Italian team, dressed as Dorando, had stiff competition to capture the public's imagination from Masai warriors and a man, Buster Martin, who claimed to be 101 years old.

Six Masai warriors from northern Tanzania came dressed in elaborate costumes of head-dresses, shields, jewellery and shoes freshly cut from old car tyres. They were raising money to build a clean water well for their home village back in Africa and they delighted the crowds by singing and dancing their way around the marathon – while Buster Martin appeared confused about his age.

Favourite Martin Lel from Kenya won the men's race for the third time in one of the quickest marathons in history. He followed the world record pace for 20 miles but somehow found enough energy for a wonderful sprint finish.

The Kenyan proved again that he has the strongest finish in marathon racing as he broke his personal best by over a minute. In only his second marathon, Wanjiru finished second in 2:05:24, knocking 75 seconds from his personal best, while Abderrahim Goumri was third in 2:05:30, a massive 2 minutes 14 seconds inside his previous

best. Britain's Dan Robinson finished thirteenth in 2:13:10, again a new personal best by 43 seconds.

Irina Mikitenko, 35, won the women's race in 2:24:14 beating Ethiopian favourites Gete Wami and Berhane Adere and lowering her personal best by 37 seconds.

The conditions were calm and sunny when the race began, but in the closing stages rain and a fierce wind made the going tough. Mikitenko became the first German winner in London since Katrin Dorre took the third of her trio of titles in 1994. The 37-year-old Zakharova finished second with 2:24:39, while Wami overcame a dramatic fall at 30km to finish third in 2:25:37.

British athlete Liz Yelling finished ninth in 2:28:33, some 4 minutes behind the winner. She set a personal best by 2 minutes and booked a ticket to Bejing with Britain's Olympic team for the 2008 Olympic Games in China.

In the men's wheelchair race, Britain's David Weir became the first male athlete to win three titles in a row in 1:33:56 after a fierce battle with six other competitors over the final 300 metres. Australia's Kurt Fearnley finished second, as he did the previous year, with France's Denis Lemeunier only fractionally behind in third.

Sandra Graf of Switzerland smashed the course record in the women's wheelchair race, winning in 1:48:04. This was more than a minute faster than the time set by the Swede Monica Wetterstrom in 1997. Graf finished some 4 minutes clear of the American Amanda McGrory (1:51:58), with Briton Shelly Woods a distant third in 2:01.59.

British wheelchair athlete Shaho Qadir drew huge applause from the crowd when he got out of his wheelchair a few yards short of the line, pushed it across, and then pulled himself over the finish on his hands.

At one point the marathon took a detour after reports of a gas leak at a pub near the halfway

point. The race switched from one carriageway of the road to the other for about 200 yards on the Highway, near Tower Bridge. The pub was quickly taped off by police but a subsequent inspection saw the course restored to its original route.

The man who claimed to be 101, 'Buster' Martin, was much heralded in the press as the oldest man to complete the course. But as he hobbled his way through some ten hours plus in the London drizzle, his true history started to unfold. The Guinness Book of World Records refused to verify Buster's claim to be 101 and correspondence between senior officials at the organisation revealed that Guinness had evidence that in 2008 Buster Martin was a mere spring chicken of 94.

Explanation of placing system

Each London Marathon year in this register is divided up into four categories: first, a summary of the **Elite Athletes**, containing names (last, first) and times (hours : minutes : seconds) of the top 50 male runners, top 50 female runners, top 3 male and top 2 female wheelchair entrants; then **Male Runners, Female Runners** and **Wheelchair Entrants**. These last three sections display the individual names and times of *every* entrant, including elite athletes, alphabetically and with their overall finishing position in that year's Marathon displayed in brackets alongside.

Some entrants have chosen to enhance past London Marathon entries with photos and recollections online at **www.aubreybooks.com**. Please visit the website to find out more about appearing in future editions.

Top 50 male runners

Lel, Martin	2:05:15
Wanjiru, Samuel	2:05:24
Goumri, Abderrahim	2:05:30
Mutai, Emmanuel	2:06:15
Hall, Ryan	2:06:17
Merga, Deriba	2:06:38
Kifle, Yonas	2:08:51
Limo, Felix	2:10:35
Sokolov, Aleksey	2:11:41
Ramaala, Hendrick	2:11:44
Kibet, Luke	2:12:25
Baldini, Stefano	2:13:06
Robinson, Dan	2:13:10
Letherby, Andrew	2:13:50
Kassap, Danny	2:15:20
Abyu, Tomas	2:15:49
Kiplagat, Richard	2:17:34
Riley, Pete	2:18:21
Lambert, Toby	2:18:40
Johnson, Chad	2:18:49
Guerra, Silvio	2:19:03
Gardiner, Richie	2:20:28
Costley, Phil	2:20:40
Osterlund, Kristoffer	2:21:41
Skinner, Kevin	2:22:41
Tucker, Peter R	2:23:12
McFarlane, John	2:23:17
Carroll, Michael J	2:23:30
Bilton, Darran E	2:23:49
Birchall, Christopher T	2:23:58
Bateson, Steven	2:24:01
Vermeesch, Pieter	2:24:23
Lane, Nathaniel R	2:24:46
Galan, Ivan	2:24:55
Littler, Stephen T	2:25:21
Williams, Jesse J	2:25:43

ELITE ATHLETES

Frost, Jonathan	2:26:16
Edwards, Orlando	2:26:48
Sumpter, James P	2:27:04
Chisholm, Neil S	2:27:47
Heywood, Kevin J	2:27:57
Martelletti, Paul V	2:28:13
Galpin, Peter C	2:28:38
Boucher, Michael B	2:28:46
Bannister, Dominic	2:28:52
Murphy, Bernard	2:29:00
Robertson, Kevin J	2:29:03
Cockerell, William	2:29:12
Fox, Stuart	2:29:13
Mussett, Adrian N	2:29:20

Top 50 female runners

Mikitenko, Irina	2:24:14
Zakharova, Svetlana	2:24:39
Wami, Gete	2:25:37
Kosgei, Salina	2:26:30
Petrova, Ludmila	2:26:45
Ait Salem, Souad	2:27:41
Adere, Berhane	2:27:42
Dita, Constantina	2:27:45
Yelling, Liz	2:28:33
Pirtea, Adriana	2:28:52
Skvortsova, Silvia	2:29:11
Haining, Hayley	2:29:18
Weightman, Lisa	2:32:32
Sun, Weiwei	2:36:34
Hasell, Lucy	2:40:31
Donta, Helen	2:41:10
Partridge, Susan	2:41:40
Fawke, Kim	2:42:08
Gardner, Louise	2:45:00
Whitehead, Amy	2:45:38
Woodvine, Andrea	2:45:49

McIntosh, Shona	2:47:38
Decker, Helen J	2:47:43
Salt, Adela M	2:48:23
Cowley, Laura J	2:48:25
Brown, Kate V	2:49:21
Hartney, Liz E	2:49:24
Winter, Sara C	2:49:56
Briggs, Ruth G	2:50:20
Gibson, Claire	2:50:30
Howe, Angela D	2:51:02
Martin, Clare E	2:51:08
Gee, Sarah R	2:51:16
Knight, Victoria	2:51:35
Stradling, Sarah	2:51:48
Swaney, Fleur C	2:51:52
Wright, Megan F	2:52:44
Swan, Sarah J	2:52:55
Webster, Katy	2:53:39
Clark, Tamsin L	2:54:02
Mustat, Lara	2:54:35
Rosenthal, Gaby O	2:54:42
Gooderham, Emma L	2:54:51
Fawcett, Trudy J	2:55:00
Perry, Victoria A	2:55:08
Thomas, Ann	2:55:16
Grima, Claire M	2:55:36
Coslett, Deborah S	2:55:47
Letherby, Meg	2:55:50
Pike, Zoe M	2:56:26

Top 3 male and top 2 female wheelchair entrants

Weir, David	1:33:56
Fearnley, Kurt	1:34:00
Lemeunier, Denis	1:34:01
Graf, Sandra	1:48:04
McGrory, Amanda	1:51:58

MALE RUNNERS

Abas, Rabie 3:46:56 (8,093)
Abbas, Ahmed C 5:08:37 (27,917)
Abbasi, Naveed S 5:44:50 (31,752)
Abbate, Michael A 3:42:29 (7,137)
Abbey, Nick J 3:49:13 (8,632)
Abbitt, Philip E 4:49:54 (24,575)
Abbott, Benjamin T 5:19:24 (29,337)
Abbott, Graham S 4:24:52 (18,233)
Abbott, Laurence 4:04:49 (13,004)
Abbott, Matthew T 3:39:33 (6,551)
Abbott, Phil A 3:16:20 (2,795)
Abbott, Simon T 5:49:33 (32,089)
Abbraccio, Tino 3:59:32 (11,683)
Abdalla, Zein 4:15:08 (15,605)
Abeal, Dean N 4:16:53 (16,054)
Abedeen, Bobby Z 5:00:47 (26,756)
Abel, Christopher J 4:14:59 (15,553)
Abel, Clive E 5:16:24 (28,981)
Abel, Lawrence J 3:09:32 (1,945)
Abel, Richard K 4:49:23 (24,456)
Ab-Elwyn, Rhys 2:54:59 (748)
Abercrombie, Paul A 4:02:03 (12,376)
Aberdour, George E 3:51:11 (9,096)
Ablett, Justin 5:28:37 (30,335)
Ablett, Martin C 4:57:08 (26,115)
Abouzied, Matthew 3:27:34 (4,372)
Abraham, John 5:11:01 (28,278)
Abraham, Philip I 3:34:48 (5,664)
Abrahams, Robert S 4:00:14 (11,905)
Abrahams, Timothy O 4:24:29 (18,137)
Abram, Barry E 3:13:38 (2,408)
Abram, Charles H 3:13:25 (2,388)
Abram, Ron R 5:10:23 (28,204)
Abrha, Asmelash 2:44:37 (318)
Abrons, Andrew 4:30:03 (19,646)
Absolon, James A 3:17:26 (2,924)
Abt, Grant A 4:31:41 (20,074)
Abyu, Tomas 2:15:49 (16)
Acid, Rab 3:41:09 (6,859)
Ackerley, John 3:51:39 (9,211)
Ackroyd, Patrick 3:53:05 (9,602)
Ackroyd, Stephen J 4:18:11 (16,399)
Acton, Andrew 4:21:37 (17,341)
Acton, Mark 4:18:46 (16,565)
Adamopoulos, Elias 5:29:43 (30,449)
Adams, Andrew J 4:41:15 (22,498)
Adams, Antony J 4:49:24 (24,457)
Adams, Christopher J 3:25:38 (4,041)
Adams, Colin J 3:48:53 (8,549)
Adams, Daniel P 4:20:37 (17,068)
Adams, Daniel R 3:56:30 (10,626)
Adams, Douglas V 4:31:01 (19,887)
Adams, Ewan 3:42:10 (7,061)
Adams, Gary D 5:03:07 (27,119)
Adams, Ian 3:50:50 (9,014)
Adams, James C 3:50:31 (8,931)
Adams, James L 4:25:42 (18,444)
Adams, Jason 4:07:38 (13,684)
Adams, John E 5:16:54 (29,042)
Adams, John R 6:03:37 (32,872)
Adams, Keith J 3:33:17 (5,436)
Adams, Kevin J 3:28:38 (4,587)
Adams, Lee 4:22:40 (17,639)
Adams, Mark W 4:53:04 (25,289)
Adams, Matthew J 3:42:58 (7,227)
Adams, Michael 3:21:58 (3,487)
Adams, Mike D 4:03:42 (12,765)
Adams, Oliver L 4:06:13 (13,333)
Adams, Paul A 5:21:25 (29,549)
Adams, Paul N 3:47:52 (8,319)
Adams, Paul R 4:17:35 (16,244)
Adams, Peter F 6:49:59 (34,075)
Adams, Richard 4:50:53 (24,818)
Adams, Robert 4:42:21 (22,763)
Adams, Ronald E 2:36:34 (139)
Adams, Stephen A 4:14:15 (15,383)
Adamson, Harry 4:34:50 (20,918)
Adamson, Jim 3:21:14 (3,389)
Adamson, Stuart 4:20:08 (16,920)
Adamu, Abdul 5:49:43 (32,102)
Adan, Andrew N 5:48:20 (31,996)
Adcock, Richard 4:06:18 (13,355)
Addis, Jon P 4:27:43 (19,002)
Addis, Stefano 3:04:49 (1,504)
Addison, Blair L 4:44:05 (23,200)
Addison, Owen 4:40:04 (22,198)
Addison, Tony G 4:43:38 (23,080)
Addrison, Martin K 3:58:04 (11,136)
Adedeji, Matthew 5:54:35 (32,433)
Adekanye, Michael 4:34:58 (20,962)
Adekoya, Anthony D 3:36:51 (6,029)
Adenbui, Akin 5:13:35 (28,619)
Adey, Des D 3:34:30 (5,623)
Adissa, Jalal 3:30:26 (4,960)
Adkins, Paul D 4:15:55 (15,811)
Adkins, Peter J 3:32:22 (5,293)
Adlam, Michael J 3:57:44 (11,029)
Adlard, Simon C 3:29:34 (4,792)
Adlem, Matthew J 4:27:53 (19,058)
Adlington, Ben 3:17:53 (2,973)
Adnitt, Robert I 3:20:26 (3,282)
Adofo, Samuel 5:31:09 (30,577)
Adolff, Philipp Y 3:49:21 (8,666)
Adriaenssens, Jan H 4:04:06 (12,846)
Adriaenssews, Stefan J 3:39:36 (6,558)
Adrian, Stephan 3:25:02 (3,937)
Adriano, Laudato 4:02:46 (12,556)
Aeby, Pascal L 3:21:57 (3,483)
Affleck, Michael V 3:35:29 (5,788)
Afifi, Russell W 3:24:15 (3,811)
Afolabi, Oladapo 3:48:51 (8,539)
Afshar, Dan 3:22:10 (3,507)
Agar, Rob S 4:46:19 (23,745)
Agar, Simon 3:57:11 (10,858)
Agarini, Jean-Pierre 3:42:09 (7,057)
Agbo, Celestine 4:12:51 (14,992)
Ager, Stephen 3:04:07 (1,457)
Aggar, Martin R 4:43:35 (23,075)
Agmon, Gil H 4:26:10 (18,579)
Agnew, Todd 4:48:42 (24,290)
Agona, Andrew W 3:12:18 (2,248)
Agostini, Richard G 3:59:58 (11,842)
Agran, Alex 3:50:07 (8,847)
Agrusta, Domenico E 3:49:14 (8,637)
Agyemang, Kojo 5:22:57 (29,696)
Ahearn, Robert 5:16:30 (28,992)
Aherne, Shane 3:30:41 (4,997)
Ahier, Phil B 3:05:22 (1,545)
Ahmed, Ataul Q 4:27:23 (18,928)
Ahmed, Maher 5:29:28 (30,420)
Ahmed, Shamin 3:36:24 (5,950)
Ahrens, Mark J 4:24:41 (18,192)
Ahuja, Anand S 5:53:14 (32,355)
Ainge, Philip 3:43:24 (7,323)
Ainger, Matthew R 4:05:24 (13,146)
Ainscow, Edward K 3:06:45 (1,661)
Ainsley, Matthew J 4:44:00 (23,180)
Ainsley, Sam E 3:17:11 (2,885)
Ainslie, Paul 3:12:12 (2,235)
Ainsworth-Smith, Richard 4:33:07 (20,461)
Aird, Haydn J 3:37:44 (6,206)
Airey, Andy D 5:29:53 (30,464)
Aitchison, Alan 5:21:18 (29,536)
Aitken, Angus C 4:00:10 (11,886)
Aitken, Clive 4:01:38 (12,275)
Aitken, Edward J 3:59:26 (11,646)
Aitken, Jamie 4:20:17 (16,971)
Aitken, John M 3:12:30 (2,266)
Aitken, Jonathan G 3:56:27 (10,616)
Aitken, Neil E 2:44:40 (320)
Aitken, Nigel J 3:45:37 (7,817)
Aitken-Davies, William J 4:13:46 (15,243)
Akehurst, Brian 3:35:54 (5,859)
Akenhead, David 5:49:30 (32,086)
Akerman, Nick 3:27:34 (4,372)
Akers, Carl 4:38:03 (21,724)
Akers, Neil 4:08:30 (13,909)
Akhtar, Khurram 4:17:40 (16,268)
Akhurst, Graeme A 3:43:17 (7,303)
Akinbile, Victor 4:58:59 (26,474)
Akiyama, Takeshi 3:21:29 (3,423)
Akpojaro, Princeton 3:32:29 (5,320)
Al Quraishi, Assaf 4:24:12 (18,050)
Alain, Castaing 3:15:02 (2,635)
Alasen, Peter 4:27:21 (18,916)
Albeker, Feras 5:00:05 (26,653)
Albers-Brough, Stefan 4:54:30 (25,581)
Alberti, Marno 4:28:34 (19,280)
Albiero, Alessandro 3:44:30 (7,553)
Albury, Adrian T 3:58:12 (11,190)
Albutt, John W 4:35:19 (21,062)
Alcaix, Vincent 4:12:45 (14,974)
Alcock, David 3:34:46 (5,656)
Alcock, John 3:51:14 (9,105)
Alcock, Paul 3:00:32 (1,204)
Alcock, Stephen R 4:21:24 (17,275)
Alcock, Stephen R 4:47:12 (23,961)
Alden, Jeremy D 4:46:55 (23,888)
Alderin, Filip 3:28:05 (4,477)
Alderman, Wulston 4:45:27 (23,529)
Alderson, Dale A 4:40:57 (22,423)
Alderson, David C 3:03:24 (1,412)
Alderson, Paul M 3:38:47 (6,405)
Alderson, Steven A 4:19:16 (16,693)
Alderton, Colin N 4:20:38 (17,074)
Aldred, Mark K 4:07:00 (13,518)
Aldred, Peter 4:30:32 (19,758)
Aldus, Graham 5:29:33 (30,429)
Aldworth, David 4:44:27 (23,286)
Alexander, Bret 4:08:08 (13,810)
Alexander, Charlie 4:25:29 (18,388)
Alexander, Mark I 4:34:36 (20,845)
Alexander, Matthew J 3:07:57 (1,786)
Alexander, Mike P 4:28:29 (19,256)
Alexander, Ratan 3:37:45 (6,210)
Alexander, Sebastian 5:04:27 (27,316)
Alexiou, Alexander S 4:16:12 (15,874)
Al-Falah, Oliver J 5:37:51 (31,182)
Alfaro, Carlos E 4:43:06 (22,962)
Alford, Stephen P 3:49:59 (8,821)
Ali, Altan H 3:45:54 (7,879)
Ali, Malik 4:48:11 (24,179)
Ali, Moshin 4:13:49 (15,254)
Ali, Nazim 4:42:04 (22,689)
Ali, Shahib M 4:32:32 (20,311)
Ali, Tariq 3:38:41 (6,386)
Ali Noor, Ilyaas 6:25:29 (33,562)
Ali Noor, Sehar I 4:54:39 (25,609)
Al-Juzi, Nidal 5:58:34 (32,673)
Alkhub, Mohammed H 3:45:18 (7,755)
Allali, Hicham 4:49:56 (24,587)
Allan, Christopher T 4:48:00 (24,148)
Allan, Crawford 3:36:22 (5,945)
Allan, John 4:13:01 (15,037)
Allan, John J 4:14:03 (15,320)
Allan, Rory D 4:11:28 (14,665)
Allan, Ross S 4:17:32 (16,232)
Allan, Simon R 3:10:29 (2,038)
Allan, Stephen 5:17:49 (29,157)
Allanach, Benjamin C 4:20:59 (17,177)
Allard, Claude 4:24:17 (18,077)
Allard, Charles J Jnr 3:10:46 (2,074)
Allaway, Dean A 4:16:16 (15,895)
Allder, Greg T 7:25:28 (34,430)
Allee, Aaron R 4:30:29 (19,740)
Allee, Ivor L 5:13:41 (28,633)
Allegritti, Fabrizio 5:16:24 (28,981)
Allen, Andrew E 3:58:09 (11,163)
Allen, Andrew N 4:41:59 (22,667)
Allen, Carl S 3:56:19 (10,568)
Allen, Chris P 3:17:26 (2,924)
Allen, Christopher 3:19:20 (3,140)
Allen, Christopher O 4:44:19 (23,260)
Allen, Clive 4:29:09 (19,439)
Allen, Craig D 4:34:52 (20,931)
Allen, Daren P 4:07:34 (13,658)
Allen, David W 3:43:54 (7,441)
Allen, Dean 4:14:53 (15,530)
Allen, Gavin P 3:40:59 (6,820)
Allen, Gavin R 3:16:22 (2,798)
Allen, James M 4:29:35 (19,537)
Allen, James N 2:48:22 (438)
Allen, James S 4:22:09 (17,482)
Allen, Joe 5:10:55 (28,268)
Allen, Keith 4:44:02 (23,190)
Allen, Kristian W 4:00:03 (11,863)
Allen, Lee M 5:53:21 (32,365)
Allen, Malcolm G 3:31:01 (5,055)

Allen, Michael 3:53:26 (9,702)
Allen, Michael G 4:38:23 (21,796)
Allen, Michael J 4:26:48 (18,753)
Allen, Oliver J 4:52:16 (25,096)
Allen, Paul M 3:02:11 (1,320)
Allen, Paul R 3:38:05 (6,281)
Allen, Paul R 4:52:00 (25,042)
Allen, Philip J 3:59:55 (11,825)
Allen, Richard S 4:13:16 (15,105)
Allen, Stephen J 5:44:15 (31,690)
Allen, Steve P 3:32:43 (5,346)
Allen, Stuart J 4:08:30 (13,909)
Allen, Terry C 5:26:38 (30,114)
Allen, Tim P 3:32:23 (5,296)
Allen, Tim P 4:00:17 (11,921)
Allenby, Steven 4:53:01 (25,275)
Allen-Shirtcliffe, Keith S 3:28:06 (4,481)
Allford, Simon J 3:32:47 (5,360)
Allgoewer, Dietegen 4:18:35 (16,526)
Allibone, Richard M 3:57:04 (10,816)
Allingham, Daniel 4:58:57 (26,466)
Allingham, Richard 4:35:25 (21,088)
Allison, Gary M 4:26:16 (18,601)
Allison, Jason C 2:54:04 (699)
Allison, Malcolm J 6:39:59 (33,881)
Allison, Paul R 6:00:54 (32,775)
Allison, Tim 3:43:19 (7,311)
Allitt, Paul F 5:58:10 (32,647)
Allman, Alexander P 5:47:24 (31,944)
Allon, Clive 4:40:41 (22,346)
Allpass, Sam R 2:58:15 (972)
Allsop, Ian A 5:24:05 (29,816)
Allsop, Paul 4:23:33 (17,883)
Allsop, Tmothy K 2:51:09 (559)
Allsopp, Craig 3:30:00 (4,885)
Allton, Christopher R 3:14:49 (2,610)
Allum, Andrew M 3:45:36 (7,814)
Allum, Paul T 4:53:31 (25,379)
Allwright, Darren P 4:05:34 (13,193)
Allwright, Nic J 4:22:37 (17,622)
Alm, Jonathan 3:17:01 (2,864)
Al-Mawlawi, Ali 5:29:10 (30,394)
Almond, Liam P 3:41:46 (6,983)
Almond, Martin P 4:22:21 (17,531)
Almond, Stuart 4:12:38 (14,954)
Alsford, Michael J 3:51:16 (9,113)
Al-Shakarchi, Mohamed 3:50:39 (8,974)
Alsop, Doug A 3:16:04 (2,760)
Alsos, Bjorn 3:18:24 (3,031)
Alston, David G 4:10:41 (14,457)
Alston, Richard 3:38:21 (6,327)
Altman, James S 5:53:41 (32,385)
Altman, John 5:18:36 (29,242)
Altman, Jonas 5:43:32 (31,610)
Alton, Gregg 3:29:17 (4,735)
Alvarado Corpus, Armando 3:41:00 (6,824)
Alvarez, Manuel 3:36:22 (5,945)
Alvarez Aldean, Javier 3:40:03 (6,649)
Alves, Carols 3:52:01 (9,305)
Alwash, Craig 3:05:30 (1,553)
Alwin, Philip 4:10:16 (14,356)
Amagata, Hiroshi 5:31:37 (30,624)
Amatt, Robert 4:17:36 (16,250)
Ambery, William D 3:38:06 (6,287)
Amblat, Jean-Pascal 3:03:19 (1,403)
Ambrose, Mark S 3:26:39 (4,218)
Ambrose, Richard P 4:44:50 (23,380)
Ambrose, Simon 4:27:22 (18,924)
Ambrose, Steve T 4:00:23 (11,944)
Ambrosi, Simon O 3:28:13 (4,508)
Ambrosio, Antonio 3:35:03 (5,711)
Amendola, Antonio 5:15:18 (28,850)
Amer, Tarik 3:59:04 (11,511)
Amery, Richard 4:10:48 (14,492)
Amies, Matthew 3:34:33 (5,627)
Amin, Kapil 6:42:16 (33,916)
Amin, Pankaj R 5:36:36 (31,090)
Amla, Ismail 4:07:33 (13,653)
Ammirati, Alfonso 4:34:17 (20,774)
Amoah, Richard 5:16:40 (29,016)
Amoils, Matthew 3:29:39 (4,809)
Amoo, Paul J 4:26:28 (18,654)
Amoo-Bediako, Michael K 4:12:36 (14,950)
Amooquaye, Eno 5:00:30 (26,707)
Amor, Ross 5:08:36 (27,912)
Amos, Chris J 3:30:06 (4,906)
Amos, Graham 5:38:33 (31,226)
Amos, Hugo J 4:09:48 (14,251)
Amos, John 3:44:44 (7,617)
Amos, Mark 3:10:54 (2,089)
Amos, Nigel S 4:31:32 (20,032)
Amos, Nikki A 5:09:19 (28,014)
Amos, Peter 3:35:25 (5,780)
Ampola, Lucio 3:59:27 (11,656)
Amroliwala, Feroze F 5:58:31 (32,669)
Anceschi, Myles G 4:16:06 (15,857)
Anciaux, Jean-Marie 3:42:14 (7,076)
Andena, Gianluca 4:02:42 (12,542)
Anderluung, Rikard 3:36:47 (6,012)
Andersen, Bernard W 4:02:36 (12,513)
Anderson, Adrian E 5:03:18 (27,154)
Anderson, Alan T 4:59:15 (26,523)
Anderson, Andy M 3:55:29 (10,335)
Anderson, Brian P 3:29:21 (4,751)
Anderson, Daniel J 2:41:10 (221)
Anderson, Evan 4:58:09 (26,315)
Anderson, Fraser 3:58:51 (11,440)
Anderson, Gareth J 3:35:56 (5,865)
Anderson, Garth 5:22:19 (29,643)
Anderson, George 4:08:07 (13,801)
Anderson, Gordon 4:18:10 (16,393)
Anderson, Gregory D 6:04:06 (32,891)
Anderson, Ian 3:52:46 (9,495)
Anderson, Ian M 5:00:34 (26,712)
Anderson, Ian P 3:56:17 (10,557)
Anderson, Ian S 2:41:48 (239)
Anderson, James R 4:41:29 (22,553)
Anderson, Jamie R 2:55:01 (752)
Anderson, John 3:48:56 (8,565)
Anderson, John S 4:17:33 (16,236)
Anderson, John W 3:28:06 (4,481)
Anderson, Joseph E 5:04:36 (27,342)
Anderson, Lee J 4:26:04 (18,558)
Anderson, Mark T 4:05:37 (13,202)
Anderson, Martin J 4:04:28 (12,926)
Anderson, Mick J 5:09:45 (28,107)
Anderson, Nicholas 4:40:52 (22,395)
Anderson, Niel G 3:38:36 (6,369)
Anderson, Peter M 3:31:40 (5,161)
Anderson, Richard D 3:51:04 (9,068)
Anderson, Richard J 3:33:09 (5,410)
Anderson, Richard W 4:25:57 (18,519)
Anderson, Roger 5:44:23 (31,711)
Anderson, Roy 4:56:31 (25,973)
Anderson, Simon F 3:22:47 (3,607)
Anderson, Stephen J 4:45:35 (23,555)
Anderson, Stuart G 4:21:48 (17,406)
Anderson, Tim J 4:41:27 (22,546)
Anderson, Tony 3:52:40 (9,472)
Anderson, William 4:06:35 (13,420)
Andersson, Mattias 4:03:43 (12,771)
Andersson, Mikael 3:27:23 (4,346)
Anderton, James P 4:01:31 (12,247)
Anderton, Rupert J 5:07:23 (27,749)
Andrade-Claros, Ivar 4:26:44 (18,738)
Andrasch, Ruediger 4:25:59 (18,531)
Andrea, Michael 3:51:50 (9,254)
Andrew, Chris J 3:32:16 (5,271)
Andrew, Clive 3:33:06 (5,400)
Andrew, Kevin J 3:25:55 (4,091)
Andrew, Nicholas P 4:10:21 (14,376)
Andrew, Ross 5:19:45 (29,385)
Andrews, Ben H 4:56:17 (25,930)
Andrews, Brian 3:56:33 (10,646)
Andrews, David C 3:48:30 (8,466)
Andrews, David P 5:09:08 (27,988)
Andrews, Gary F 3:53:35 (9,737)
Andrews, Henry T 3:04:38 (1,491)
Andrews, Jason 3:38:51 (6,420)
Andrews, John A 3:19:42 (3,191)
Andrews, Marcus L 4:37:40 (21,634)
Andrews, Mark 5:05:04 (27,412)
Andrews, Mark V 3:15:15 (2,664)
Andrews, Michael J 4:46:35 (23,793)
Andrews, Micky 5:21:12 (29,523)
Andrews, Nicholas 4:27:18 (18,906)
Andrews, Noel J 4:59:29 (26,561)
Andrews, Paul 4:20:27 (17,011)
Andrews, Paul J 3:13:43 (2,424)
Andrews, Paul S 6:06:02 (32,974)
Andrews, Paul T 4:16:33 (15,971)
Andrews, Paul T 4:43:28 (23,035)
Andrews, Philip 3:27:54 (4,439)
Andrews, Phillip 4:38:49 (21,919)
Andrews, Ricky 5:41:48 (31,487)
Andrews, Roger 5:17:25 (29,111)
Andrews, Stephen M 3:38:17 (6,314)
Andrews, Stuart N 4:02:11 (12,413)
Andrews, Terry 4:31:35 (20,050)
Andrieu, Roger 4:23:07 (17,757)
Anelay, Lance E 5:13:24 (28,595)
Angel, Richard J 3:27:14 (4,323)
Angel Avila, Juan M 3:33:34 (5,484)
Angell, Keith E 5:53:19 (32,361)
Angell, Vaughan P 4:11:03 (14,559)
Angilley, David 3:00:44 (1,220)
Anglin, Morris 5:28:20 (30,308)
Angold, Christopher F 5:23:12 (29,716)
Angove, Mark J 3:30:28 (4,965)
Angus, Bob 4:21:49 (17,409)
Angus, Nigel L 4:30:42 (19,800)
Angus, Stephen 4:40:55 (22,410)
Angus, Steve 3:01:34 (1,280)
Anholm, Matthew C 3:29:21 (4,751)
Ankers, Brendan T 7:18:09 (34,384)
Annable, Stuart J 3:40:53 (6,802)
Annable, Tom 2:50:37 (540)
Annand, Nathan J 4:51:00 (24,844)
Annegarn, Michael 4:09:54 (14,278)
Anrude, Edward W 3:43:20 (7,315)
Ansari, Asif S 6:40:21 (33,890)
Ansell, Robert S 4:21:12 (17,225)
Anson, Alan J 5:38:53 (31,254)
Anson, Malcolm 3:08:39 (1,846)
Anstee, Matthew 3:38:48 (6,410)
Anstee, Nick J 4:15:55 (15,811)
Anthony, Ian J 3:00:36 (1,212)
Anthony, James K 4:07:21 (13,603)
Anthony, Mike 3:55:56 (10,473)
Antoiniotti, Bruno 4:20:36 (17,061)
Anton, John 4:21:27 (17,292)
Antonelos, Evaggelos 3:07:53 (1,776)
Antongiulio, Luca 3:36:47 (6,012)
Antonio, Ernesto 3:53:21 (9,677)
Antonsen, Cristoffer 3:36:57 (6,050)
Antscherl, Robert J 3:44:52 (7,648)
Anzalichi, Steve 4:43:05 (22,954)
Apperley, Hugh C 3:13:53 (2,447)
Apperley, Ian J 3:18:23 (3,030)
Appiah, Louis L 5:58:52 (32,690)
Appleby, Alan 3:02:35 (1,351)
Appleby, Luke P 4:10:22 (14,381)
Appleby, Richard J 4:50:30 (24,715)
Appleby, Rod J 3:48:29 (8,460)
Applegate, Jeffrey 3:57:26 (10,939)
Appleing, David N 3:43:40 (7,383)
Appleton, Andrew D 3:24:49 (3,892)
Appleton, Darren 5:19:11 (29,313)
Appleton, Ian 4:18:48 (16,572)
Appleton, Mark J 4:08:14 (13,839)
Appletree, Richard M 4:03:27 (12,715)
Applewhite, Ben P 4:15:05 (15,594)
Applin, Kerry J 4:49:18 (24,431)
Apps, Nicholas J 3:48:24 (8,440)
Apted, Brian G 5:14:24 (28,732)
Arain, Jibran 4:07:35 (13,666)
Arandelovic, Milan M 3:59:40 (11,741)
Aranguren, Santiago 4:36:13 (21,301)
Arbuthnott, Giles 4:43:22 (23,018)
Arcasenza, Claudio 2:56:09 (815)
Archer, Andrew W 4:23:53 (17,958)
Archer, Mark J 3:00:24 (1,195)
Archer, Michael J 4:03:44 (12,777)
Archer, Orville 4:06:50 (13,482)
Archer, Paul 2:48:09 (428)
Archer, Paul A 4:30:45 (19,816)
Archer, Richard 5:18:43 (29,255)
Archer, Steven W 4:01:20 (12,196)
Archer, Tony W 3:18:47 (3,073)

Archibald, Andrew	3:53:41 (9,764)	
Archibald, Paul S	4:51:48 (25,003)	
Ardin, James C	2:54:40 (726)	
Arenhold, Kevin	4:00:10 (11,886)	
Argyle, Christopher D	4:40:42 (22,353)	
Argyle, Dennis C	3:07:21 (1,717)	
Arias, José M	4:14:01 (15,310)	
Arico, Rodolfo	4:16:28 (15,954)	
Arif, Ikram	4:47:08 (23,940)	
Arif, Saleem	5:26:48 (30,126)	
Aris, David L	5:00:17 (26,681)	
Arkell, Robin J	3:47:50 (8,306)	
Arkle, Sid	5:10:54 (28,267)	
Arkwright, Paul	3:49:53 (8,794)	
Arlt, Bernhard	4:11:21 (14,633)	
Armellini, Armando A	5:24:34 (29,865)	
Armitage, Mark	2:53:42 (675)	
Armitage, Mark E	3:48:31 (8,469)	
Armson, Phil	5:53:04 (32,345)	
Armstrong, Martin	5:27:45 (30,232)	
Armstrong, Adrian J	4:14:05 (15,331)	
Armstrong, Benjamin J	4:03:08 (12,639)	
Armstrong, Christopher	4:02:23 (12,473)	
Armstrong, David E	5:47:17 (31,931)	
Armstrong, John	2:55:50 (796)	
Armstrong, Kevin L	3:37:38 (6,191)	
Armstrong, Nigel J	2:53:19 (656)	
Armstrong, Robert D	4:35:54 (21,211)	
Armstrong, Robert J	3:17:01 (2,864)	
Armstrong, Stephen	2:59:03 (1,064)	
Armstrong-Jones, Peregrine	4:34:10 (20,746)	
Arneil, Russell	4:15:45 (15,768)	
Arnold, Adrian T	3:41:15 (6,884)	
Arnold, Andy	3:57:05 (10,829)	
Arnold, Benjamin J	4:00:28 (11,965)	
Arnold, Dave	3:09:24 (1,927)	
Arnold, David S	4:05:40 (13,216)	
Arnold, Gerald	3:38:01 (6,263)	
Arnold, Pascal	3:29:44 (4,831)	
Arnold, Rainer	3:37:54 (6,240)	
Arnold, Richard D	3:55:08 (10,246)	
Arnold, Roland A	4:50:28 (24,703)	
Arnott, Robert J	8:40:20 (34,576)	
Arnsby, Brian K	4:02:28 (12,491)	
Aron, Narcis	3:46:55 (8,088)	
Arpaia, Gabriel	3:33:57 (5,542)	
Arregger, Andreas	3:15:50 (2,734)	
Arrowsmith, James	4:03:20 (12,685)	
Arrowsmith, Lee	3:44:06 (7,474)	
Arrowsmith, Len	4:32:44 (20,355)	
Arrowsmith, Mark A	3:02:32 (1,343)	
Arrowsmith, Paul	3:44:22 (7,527)	
Arroyo, Javier	3:07:45 (1,760)	
Arthur, Damian J	4:05:37 (13,202)	
Arthur, David	3:30:18 (4,939)	
Arthur, John	3:27:58 (4,453)	
Arthur, Nigel A	3:51:37 (9,203)	
Artigas, Francisco	3:40:09 (6,663)	
Artist, Steven	3:18:11 (3,007)	
Artley, Philip	3:50:07 (8,847)	
Arundel, John	4:26:04 (18,558)	
Arundel, Michael J	4:11:22 (14,638)	
Arup, Martin	4:25:04 (18,278)	
Arup, Michael	4:25:04 (18,278)	
Arzul, Michel	3:53:16 (9,653)	
Ascham, Wallace P	3:58:17 (11,208)	
Aseginolaza Munoz, Jon	4:47:43 (24,074)	
Asghar, Adam K	3:30:23 (4,950)	
Ash, Gareth	3:47:01 (8,113)	
Ash, Nicholas D	4:28:29 (19,256)	
Ash, Peter D	3:22:11 (3,509)	
Ash, Will	2:58:36 (1,018)	
Ashbee, Nicholas P	3:46:17 (7,948)	
Ashburn, Justin P	3:44:32 (7,558)	
Ashby, Charles E	3:14:30 (2,546)	
Ashby, Edward	4:19:52 (16,853)	
Ashby, John F	5:02:22 (27,018)	
Ashby, Jonathan	4:31:54 (20,141)	
Ashby, Mark	3:07:51 (1,771)	
Ashby, Mike J	2:57:22 (901)	
Ashcroft, Keith R	6:42:55 (33,939)	
Ashcroft, Paul	4:31:55 (20,144)	
Ashcroft, Paul R	3:59:42 (11,750)	
Ashdown, Anthony E	6:00:07 (32,744)	
Ashdown, David J	4:22:29 (17,575)	
Ashdown, Stephen D	5:43:20 (31,596)	
Ashenden, Simon V	4:35:25 (21,088)	
Ashfield, Thomas A	3:46:13 (7,930)	
Ashford, Justin M	3:54:32 (10,045)	
Ashley, Jonathan H	2:54:03 (696)	
Ashley, Jonathan M	4:04:14 (12,871)	
Ashley, Jonathan P	3:34:57 (5,694)	
Ashley, Mark	5:14:06 (28,686)	
Ashley, Philip	4:14:57 (15,544)	
Ashley, Richard C	4:18:17 (16,429)	
Ashley, Richard J	5:39:50 (31,316)	
Ashley Cantello, William	4:09:16 (14,108)	
Ashley-Cooper, Nicholas	3:20:16 (3,260)	
Ashman, Joe	3:18:20 (3,023)	
Ashman, Richard A	4:44:04 (23,195)	
Ashman, Rod J	4:54:07 (25,504)	
Ashman, Roy	4:11:29 (14,674)	
Ashmead, Gareth	4:41:26 (22,541)	
Ashmore, Andrew	4:23:00 (17,728)	
Ashmore, Michael A	3:47:00 (8,108)	
Ashmore, Terry C	3:53:59 (9,869)	
Ashover, John R	4:37:51 (21,683)	
Ashraf, Muhammad	3:59:02 (11,499)	
Ashton, Carl A	4:25:30 (18,397)	
Ashton, David	3:59:52 (11,807)	
Ashton, Jason W	3:59:42 (11,750)	
Ashton, Jeffrey	3:52:55 (9,544)	
Ashton, Neil	3:15:22 (2,686)	
Ashton, Nigel P	3:59:57 (11,836)	
Ashton, Philip J	4:59:17 (26,529)	
Ashton, Stefan J	4:20:24 (16,997)	
Ashton, Timothy J	4:17:56 (16,332)	
Ashurst, Clive	3:29:49 (4,843)	
Ashurst, Stephen	3:40:19 (6,692)	
Ashwell, Ian J	5:00:22 (26,688)	
Ashwell, Simon G	3:31:10 (5,070)	
Ashwood, Nicolas	3:57:22 (10,913)	
Ashworth, Andy	3:24:09 (3,798)	
Ashworth, John	4:21:04 (17,202)	
Ashworth, Luke	3:34:29 (5,619)	
Ashworth, Michael W	5:52:00 (32,291)	
Ashworth, Tom	4:20:01 (16,890)	
Ask, Richard	5:11:58 (28,405)	
Askew, Andy M	4:57:29 (26,182)	
Askew, Duncan J	4:13:43 (15,230)	
Askew, Mark S	3:45:03 (7,697)	
Askey, Michael	4:23:59 (17,987)	
Askin, Ciaran G	3:54:23 (9,987)	
Asp, Martin	2:58:20 (982)	
Aspin, Jamie G	2:58:25 (995)	
Aspinall, Kyle M	4:44:38 (23,332)	
Aspinall, Nathan E	2:35:45 (125)	
Aspinall, Richard C	5:04:08 (27,268)	
Assarsson, Bengt A	4:48:59 (24,370)	
Asseo, David	3:20:02 (3,230)	
Astbury, Paul R	4:28:08 (19,142)	
Astell, Trevor K	4:01:28 (12,232)	
Astill, Bryan	3:06:01 (1,597)	
Astill, Keith A	4:11:59 (14,806)	
Astin, Stephen	3:38:01 (6,263)	
Astle, Paul M	4:31:16 (19,952)	
Astle, Thomas W	2:59:15 (1,091)	
Aston, Andrew	2:54:58 (745)	
Aston, Christopher	3:18:08 (2,998)	
Aston, Darran	3:07:49 (1,767)	
Aston, Jeffrey R	3:36:37 (5,983)	
Aston, Jeremy P	3:53:34 (9,732)	
Aston, Martin R	4:35:41 (21,164)	
Aston, Peter G	4:02:45 (12,553)	
Aston-Odonovan, Marc A	4:09:53 (14,276)	
Atherton, Andy J	3:40:35 (6,743)	
Atherton, Derek J	3:56:20 (10,573)	
Atherton, Graham	4:16:48 (16,038)	
Atherton, John	4:09:42 (14,228)	
Atherton, Joseph J	3:58:25 (11,268)	
Atherton, Lawrence J	4:31:17 (19,961)	
Atherton, Mark R	4:12:19 (14,887)	
Atherton, Nicholas W	5:41:28 (31,462)	
Athreya, Kannan	3:58:42 (11,374)	
Atkin, Douglas K	3:57:04 (10,816)	
Atkin, James	4:33:13 (20,485)	
Atkin, Nick M	4:19:03 (16,639)	
Atkin, Rob J	2:37:44 (162)	
Atkin, Robert	4:54:12 (25,519)	
Atkin, Steven	5:17:27 (29,119)	
Atkins, David M	5:10:42 (28,236)	
Atkins, Gary J	4:27:05 (18,834)	
Atkins, Karl J	4:29:03 (19,412)	
Atkins, Malcolm A	3:52:43 (9,484)	
Atkins, Mark	4:35:13 (21,035)	
Atkins, Matthew J	3:56:40 (10,680)	
Atkins, Michael K	5:14:18 (28,722)	
Atkins, Nicholas C	4:48:43 (24,298)	
Atkins, Peter	3:59:39 (11,734)	
Atkins, Rowan	3:58:07 (11,151)	
Atkins, Ryan	4:25:22 (18,359)	
Atkins, Ryan M	4:23:32 (17,875)	
Atkins, Simon M	3:58:21 (11,248)	
Atkins, Timothy M	3:57:13 (10,868)	
Atkinson, Adam E	5:32:51 (30,734)	
Atkinson, Andrew	5:01:43 (26,916)	
Atkinson, Bill	4:09:41 (14,220)	
Atkinson, Colin C	3:29:04 (4,682)	
Atkinson, David J	3:54:21 (9,974)	
Atkinson, Euan E	3:47:32 (8,227)	
Atkinson, Ian C	5:03:11 (27,130)	
Atkinson, Ian J	3:51:02 (9,058)	
Atkinson, Jason	3:19:35 (3,175)	
Atkinson, John N	4:38:41 (21,880)	
Atkinson, John S	4:18:25 (16,470)	
Atkinson, Lee J	4:46:11 (23,709)	
Atkinson, Paul S	4:32:31 (20,307)	
Atkinson, Steven	3:47:01 (8,113)	
Atlee, Paul	5:45:14 (31,778)	
Attard, Robert G	2:38:33 (177)	
Attelsey, Philip J	4:34:15 (20,768)	
Atter, Mike J	3:38:50 (6,415)	
Attree, Bruce T	3:56:22 (10,582)	
Attridge, Warren J	4:36:04 (21,258)	
Attwood, Alexander G	4:58:23 (26,357)	
Attwood, Clive	3:20:40 (3,315)	
Attwood, Donald K	4:57:37 (26,213)	
Attwood, Howard M	4:47:43 (24,074)	
Attwood, James	4:35:46 (21,184)	
Atwell, Phil	3:53:21 (9,677)	
Aubert, Fabrice	3:58:20 (11,236)	
Aubin, Yves-Fabrice	4:16:42 (16,010)	
Auchterlonie, Allen J	5:33:03 (30,754)	
Audenshaw, Tony	3:01:55 (1,306)	
Auger, Chris	4:05:46 (13,235)	
Auger, John-Paul	4:10:31 (14,415)	
Aughney, James P	3:14:28 (2,541)	
Aughterson, Anthony J	4:10:32 (14,418)	
Augschoell, Hansjoerg	3:19:07 (3,110)	
Aukland, Stein M	3:29:23 (4,760)	
Auld, Doug J	3:47:12 (8,154)	
Aury, Pierre	3:06:49 (1,664)	
Ausland, Jarle	3:22:46 (3,604)	
Austen, Andy	4:41:09 (22,475)	
Austen, David J	4:23:04 (17,744)	
Austen, Michael J	5:39:00 (31,262)	
Austin, Christopher W	3:47:43 (8,282)	
Austin, Danny	4:12:27 (14,917)	
Austin, Dean	4:08:20 (13,864)	
Austin, Derek G	3:53:47 (9,800)	
Austin, Henry D	4:37:24 (21,574)	
Austin, Ian C	4:51:43 (24,991)	
Austin, Jonathan L	4:42:20 (22,761)	
Austin, Matt	3:41:16 (6,891)	
Austin, Nicholas J	4:15:49 (15,786)	
Austin, Paul	6:10:22 (33,127)	
Austin, Ray J	4:07:55 (13,758)	
Austin, Russell J	3:59:44 (11,759)	
Avard, Martin J	3:54:00 (9,873)	
Avenell, Keith A	5:34:58 (30,937)	
Avery, Joseph A	3:14:42 (2,591)	
Avery, Mark N	4:31:28 (20,017)	
Avery, Thomas P	3:03:25 (1,414)	
Aves, Clayton A	3:15:32 (2,705)	
Avis, Sean	3:50:02 (8,830)	
Aviss, Tim	4:57:04 (26,098)	
Avoscan, Philippe	2:58:15 (972)	
Awobode, Olusiji O	5:49:54 (32,113)	
Awofadeju, Robert	4:24:58 (18,256)	

Awogboro, Olukayode F 5:03:49 (27,230)
Axon, Terry 3:29:50 (4,847)
Axon, Tim E 5:00:03 (26,643)
Ayala, Gustavo 3:30:44 (5,007)
Ayerst, Michael T 4:03:27 (12,715)
Aylen, Joseph L 4:11:40 (14,726)
Ayling, Samuel 3:02:04 (1,313)
Aylott, Wayne T 3:41:20 (6,902)
Aymen, Turul A 4:49:20 (24,442)
Aynsley, Graham D 4:53:49 (25,446)
Ayorinde, Ayodeji 6:45:17 (33,984)
Ayre, Paul 4:47:38 (24,050)
Ayres, Alan 3:04:01 (1,449)
Ayres, Alan 4:02:13 (12,420)
Ayres, Jon 3:24:24 (3,828)
Ayres, Kevin 4:07:55 (13,758)
Ayres, Maximillian 3:44:46 (7,626)
Ayres, Terry B 3:38:01 (6,263)
Ayscough, Matt C 3:58:49 (11,426)
Ayton, Paul R 3:55:52 (10,457)
Azdad, Abel 3:53:54 (9,836)
Azeem, Shahid 5:42:35 (31,535)
Babar, Rehan 6:03:13 (32,855)
Babington, Duncan 3:40:12 (6,673)
Babynec, Wayne A 4:08:16 (13,845)
Bacchini, Rocco 3:54:17 (9,954)
Bach, Alisdair 5:15:18 (28,850)
Bache, Christopher A 4:17:24 (16,190)
Baci, Arber 2:43:17 (276)
Baci, Perparim 3:56:51 (10,743)
Back, Adam R 3:58:45 (11,389)
Backus, Thomas W 3:55:28 (10,331)
Bacon, Clive 4:10:37 (14,440)
Bacon, Guy T 3:53:02 (9,586)
Bacon, John P 4:35:13 (21,035)
Bacon, Lee S 4:48:27 (24,238)
Bacon, Martin S 3:00:04 (1,173)
Bacon, Nick A 6:29:47 (33,649)
Bacon, Peter H 5:25:55 (30,025)
Bacon, Robert A 4:23:11 (17,778)
Bacon, Steven 4:26:00 (18,538)
Bacon, Steven P 5:09:58 (28,139)
Baczkowski, Karol 3:08:24 (1,828)
Badcock, David B 4:23:44 (17,922)
Badcock, Fraser 3:59:49 (11,789)
Badcott, Nicholas D 4:07:13 (13,582)
Baddeley, Matthew 3:31:27 (5,123)
Badenhorst, Heinrich 3:12:30 (2,266)
Bader, Ronald 3:40:06 (6,656)
Badger, Jonathan 3:18:16 (3,012)
Badgery, Stephen 2:59:38 (1,133)
Badh, Jas S 4:18:38 (16,541)
Badillo, José 4:23:40 (17,908)
Badman, Keith A 4:14:10 (15,357)
Badr, Ishmail 3:10:36 (2,054)
Badusche, Walter 5:33:58 (30,831)
Baenziger, Walter 4:29:17 (19,467)
Baerlocher, Christian 3:59:30 (11,676)
Bagagli, Robertino 3:58:07 (11,151)
Bagdady, Lee 5:02:17 (27,003)
Baggaley, Clive R 3:27:45 (4,408)
Baggs, Len 4:28:16 (19,194)
Baggs, Stewart A 4:17:09 (16,140)
Bagguley, Michael J 4:31:12 (19,938)
Bagnall, Stewart 5:49:17 (32,073)
Bagoban, Mitesh 3:55:11 (10,261)
Bagshaw, Martin 4:34:55 (20,940)
Baguley, John S 4:41:40 (22,608)
Bagwell, David 4:28:50 (19,360)
Bahia, Randeep 5:09:27 (28,036)
Bailess, Thomas D 3:48:41 (8,507)
Bailey, Adrian J 3:44:29 (7,549)
Bailey, Alastair M 3:07:52 (1,774)
Bailey, Alyn H 4:27:46 (19,011)
Bailey, Andreas N 6:15:50 (33,289)
Bailey, Andrew J 4:14:57 (15,544)
Bailey, Andrew L 5:06:07 (27,571)
Bailey, Anthony J 3:54:24 (9,994)
Bailey, Anthony J 5:34:01 (30,839)
Bailey, Ashman 4:42:35 (22,827)
Bailey, Bart J 3:48:27 (8,453)
Bailey, Brian P 3:30:16 (4,935)
Bailey, Chris S 4:13:31 (15,164)
Bailey, Darren J 3:59:54 (11,818)
Bailey, David A 3:40:50 (6,789)
Bailey, David D 3:37:16 (6,118)
Bailey, Derek A 5:34:59 (30,940)
Bailey, Edmund 3:08:24 (1,828)
Bailey, Frank J 3:48:52 (8,544)
Bailey, Guy M 4:25:53 (18,507)
Bailey, Ian 3:10:50 (2,081)
Bailey, Ian M 4:28:54 (19,378)
Bailey, Jonathan P 6:12:06 (33,171)
Bailey, Keith W 5:39:16 (31,282)
Bailey, Mark A 4:45:39 (23,572)
Bailey, Mark J 4:50:13 (24,644)
Bailey, Martin 3:24:50 (3,897)
Bailey, Michael 5:14:14 (28,710)
Bailey, Mike C 5:26:04 (30,042)
Bailey, Nigel D 3:44:51 (7,642)
Bailey, Peter 5:35:00 (30,941)
Bailey, Peter S 4:29:11 (19,447)
Bailey, Russell M 3:20:56 (3,348)
Bailey, Ryan J 4:11:57 (14,791)
Bailey, Simon R 3:04:55 (1,511)
Bailey, Stephen 4:29:19 (19,477)
Bailey, Steve 4:28:43 (19,318)
Bailey, Steve T 5:31:56 (30,651)
Bailey, Steven P 5:25:00 (29,914)
Bailey, Stuart G 3:50:13 (8,876)
Bailey, Thomas W 4:56:46 (26,019)
Bailey, Thomas W 5:12:25 (28,452)
Bailey, Toby 4:09:03 (14,056)
Bailie, Fergus R 4:21:56 (17,435)
Baillie, Andrew J 4:32:54 (20,401)
Baillie, Angus R 4:32:53 (20,397)
Baillie, Doug A 4:28:32 (19,274)
Bain, Charles E 4:06:02 (13,297)
Bain, Chris C 4:01:06 (12,136)
Bainbridge, Daniel J 3:52:46 (9,495)
Bainbridge, James 4:00:54 (12,080)
Bainbridge, Michael S 5:51:14 (32,233)
Baines, Michael 4:02:00 (12,363)
Baines, Michael A 3:25:25 (3,997)
Baines, Peter L 4:42:23 (22,770)
Baines, Peter W 3:36:58 (6,058)
Baines, Sam J 4:41:23 (22,531)
Bains, Narinder S 3:54:01 (9,878)
Bains, Pav S 6:27:15 (33,606)
Bains, Richard W 3:48:07 (8,380)
Baird, James 5:22:04 (29,606)
Bajwa, Jaguar 5:03:39 (27,202)
Bajwa, Prabhjot S 4:23:43 (17,920)
Bakehouse, Adam 3:52:28 (9,426)
Baker, Adam J 4:06:47 (13,471)
Baker, Adrian M 5:09:27 (28,036)
Baker, Andrew 5:42:06 (31,511)
Baker, Andrew R 2:55:25 (772)
Baker, Andrew W 3:29:56 (4,873)
Baker, Brian 3:21:10 (3,381)
Baker, Carl 2:59:34 (1,124)
Baker, Christopher C 3:49:56 (8,808)
Baker, Clive A 2:52:46 (625)
Baker, Daniel L 4:07:53 (13,745)
Baker, David C 4:29:41 (19,564)
Baker, Dean W 5:34:28 (30,882)
Baker, Edward 6:03:23 (32,861)
Baker, Gary J 4:54:52 (25,669)
Baker, Gary L 3:57:03 (10,811)
Baker, Gary P 3:10:58 (2,094)
Baker, Gavin T 4:59:04 (26,491)
Baker, Ian B 3:37:26 (6,156)
Baker, James 3:47:12 (8,154)
Baker, Jason G 4:33:11 (20,475)
Baker, Joss C 7:29:30 (34,453)
Baker, Julian D 2:37:20 (151)
Baker, Keith 5:54:56 (32,454)
Baker, Marcus D 3:31:43 (5,173)
Baker, Mark 3:09:19 (1,922)
Baker, Martin 3:47:32 (8,227)
Baker, Martin 4:09:08 (14,069)
Baker, Matthew 3:43:51 (7,424)
Baker, Neil A 4:10:05 (14,313)
Baker, Newar 4:33:47 (20,658)
Baker, Nick 2:37:59 (168)
Baker, Nick M 3:29:46 (4,838)
Baker, Oliver H 4:31:51 (20,123)
Baker, Patrick 4:01:47 (12,313)
Baker, Richard H 3:44:54 (7,656)
Baker, Richard I 4:30:01 (19,639)
Baker, Richard P 4:58:42 (26,420)
Baker, Simon D 4:12:04 (14,830)
Baker, Stephen 5:03:14 (27,138)
Baker, Stephen B 4:19:00 (16,625)
Baker, Stephen R 3:51:52 (9,265)
Baker, Tim J 4:32:44 (20,355)
Baker, Timothy A 4:13:48 (15,252)
Baker, Toby S 4:32:32 (20,311)
Baker, Tony 4:13:46 (15,243)
Bakewell, Anthony E 4:43:18 (23,001)
Bakker, John 5:38:21 (31,217)
Bakrania, Mehul 3:54:40 (10,089)
Balaam, Ian C 4:00:48 (12,056)
Balboni, Flavio 5:24:08 (29,823)
Baldacci, Matthew 3:31:30 (5,127)
Balderson, Paul S 3:37:27 (6,159)
Balding, Terence S 4:10:50 (14,503)
Baldini, Stefano 2:13:06 (12)
Baldock, Robert J 3:36:15 (5,923)
Baldry, Stephen J 4:16:15 (15,892)
Baldursson, Johannes 3:49:48 (8,773)
Baldwin, Anthony M 4:22:29 (17,575)
Baldwin, Eric M 5:04:21 (27,303)
Baldwin, John N 4:05:41 (13,218)
Baldwin, Kurt J 4:04:07 (12,848)
Baldwin, Michael J 4:23:55 (17,968)
Baldwin, Paul J 4:42:56 (22,915)
Baldwin, Robert J 6:01:44 (32,809)
Baldwin, Stuart D 4:20:09 (16,928)
Bale, Mons 2:45:57 (358)
Bale, Robert C 3:16:04 (2,760)
Bale, Simon M 3:05:49 (1,583)
Bales, John R 4:11:08 (14,581)
Bales, Stephen C 5:00:44 (26,747)
Balestrin, Dick 5:07:45 (27,805)
Balfour, David 5:20:00 (29,411)
Balfour, Justin D 3:39:49 (6,600)
Balfour, Leslie J 5:11:45 (28,376)
Balfour, Richard 3:43:45 (7,400)
Balfour, Robert H 6:30:35 (33,673)
Balfourth, Winston R 3:13:52 (2,444)
Balharrie, Gordon A 3:24:22 (3,826)
Ball, Adam F 4:27:47 (19,017)
Ball, Andrew 2:56:30 (842)
Ball, Daniel W 4:21:59 (17,449)
Ball, Douglas 5:09:42 (28,094)
Ball, Kristopher W 5:17:53 (29,165)
Ball, Martin J 3:02:47 (1,361)
Ball, Russell N 4:08:34 (13,931)
Ball, Wayne M 4:45:46 (23,611)
Ballam, Paul 3:47:04 (8,125)
Ballantyne, Ross R 4:06:49 (13,476)
Ballard, Ashley J 3:49:30 (8,701)
Ballard, David E 4:52:15 (25,091)
Ballard, Martin D 5:24:59 (29,910)
Ballard, Stuart 4:44:19 (23,260)
Ballard, William F 5:00:53 (26,776)
Ballett, Leighton C 3:23:50 (3,745)
Ballinger, Anthony C 3:29:01 (4,678)
Ballinger, Chris J 4:11:02 (14,551)
Ballinger, Paul 3:17:31 (2,934)
Balmer, Jon R 3:31:52 (5,193)
Balmer, Martin R 5:31:35 (30,622)
Balshaw, Carl C 4:25:02 (18,271)
Balsom, Daniel 4:29:34 (19,529)
Balteskard, Birger 4:17:34 (16,238)
Balthazard, Philippe 3:03:29 (1,417)
Bamber, Dean R 5:46:26 (31,875)
Bamber, Ian J 3:09:33 (1,948)
Bambini, Luca 3:46:10 (7,922)
Bambury, Richard J 4:26:34 (18,685)
Bamelis, Koen H 4:05:00 (13,050)
Bamford, Andrew J 4:28:20 (19,217)
Bamford, Ian M 5:00:53 (26,776)
Bamford, Paul J 4:29:21 (19,489)
Bamforth, Gary L 4:05:11 (13,093)
Bammant, Philip 4:30:39 (19,785)
Bampton, Nicholas K 3:57:42 (11,017)
Bance, Matt 4:25:47 (18,473)

Bancroft, Ian R 3:37:28 (6,167)
Bandy, Clive R 3:19:43 (3,195)
Banerjee, James 5:56:17 (32,543)
Banerjee, Somen R 5:47:59 (31,977)
Banfield, Alistair P 3:41:25 (6,920)
Banfield, David 4:29:11 (19,447)
Bangs, Gary C 3:26:34 (4,198)
Bangs, Neil G 3:26:34 (4,198)
Banham, Joseph 4:04:16 (12,880)
Banister, Karl R 4:36:31 (21,372)
Bankes, William N 4:32:30 (20,300)
Banks, Arron F 6:45:26 (33,988)
Banks, Chris 5:06:07 (27,571)
Banks, Martin P 4:09:16 (14,108)
Banks, Michael J 7:49:17 (34,506)
Banks, Roy 4:05:35 (13,198)
Banks, Stephen 4:55:30 (25,783)
Banks, Tom A 3:41:20 (6,902)
Banks, Wayne P 3:59:25 (11,639)
Bannatyne, Tom 4:20:50 (17,133)
Banner, Charles 3:14:11 (2,497)
Banner, John D 4:47:15 (23,969)
Bannerman, Alastair G 4:30:33 (19,764)
Bannerman, Keith 3:50:53 (9,023)
Bannister, David J 4:18:28 (16,486)
Bannister, Dominic 2:28:52 (54)
Bannister, Paul 5:51:43 (32,270)
Bannister, Peter D 3:51:16 (9,113)
Bannister, Peter J 4:41:04 (22,450)
Bannister, Warren 5:40:37 (31,384)
Banno, Giancarlo 5:02:58 (27,105)
Barabato, Claudio 3:11:26 (2,140)
Barbaro Sant, Douglas 3:48:35 (8,483)
Barber, Andy P 4:23:32 (17,875)
Barber, David A 3:27:45 (4,408)
Barber, Ian B 3:54:04 (9,894)
Barber, Kenneth J 4:36:41 (21,415)
Barber, Kevin P 3:50:04 (8,837)
Barber, Kyle 3:11:45 (2,181)
Barber, Matthew 4:25:59 (18,531)
Barber, Nick C 4:56:32 (25,977)
Barber, Paul J 4:03:14 (12,665)
Barber, Phillip A 3:52:33 (9,444)
Barber, Richard 4:26:26 (18,641)
Barber, Robert D 4:16:10 (15,868)
Barbour, Hamish M 3:18:57 (3,094)
Barbour, Richard N 4:10:22 (14,381)
Barbrooke, Adrian R 3:30:29 (4,968)
Barbugian, Renzo 2:49:15 (473)
Barclay, Alan 4:08:01 (13,774)
Barclay, Andrew K 4:03:29 (12,722)
Barclay, Greig I 4:38:40 (21,871)
Barclay, Ian S 5:44:42 (31,738)
Barclay, Paul 3:09:53 (1,978)
Barclay, Simon 3:27:16 (4,325)
Barclay, Tom H 4:22:34 (17,601)
Bardell, Peter J 5:58:56 (32,692)
Bardsley, Adam 3:44:46 (7,626)
Bareham, Robert E 4:36:09 (21,280)
Barfield, Richard T 4:40:32 (22,316)
Barfoot, Anthony I 3:45:10 (7,719)
Barford, Stuart 3:41:39 (6,959)
Barge, Alistair D 4:27:54 (19,065)
Bargh, Robert 4:28:29 (19,256)
Barham, Andrew C 5:13:44 (28,641)
Barham, Andy J 6:06:02 (32,974)
Barham, Jeffrey P 4:25:01 (18,266)
Barham, Jonathan M 4:24:54 (18,241)
Barillon, Gilles R 3:48:25 (8,447)
Barkatali, Raza 4:26:09 (18,574)
Barke, Chris P 4:58:59 (26,474)
Barker, Carl A 3:50:02 (8,830)
Barker, Christopher H 4:57:19 (26,145)
Barker, Dave A 4:08:20 (13,864)
Barker, David R 4:43:50 (23,132)
Barker, Edward P 2:53:37 (668)
Barker, Hugh P 4:05:46 (13,235)
Barker, Kent J 3:18:27 (3,042)
Barker, Kevin 4:56:18 (25,931)
Barker, Matthew J 3:53:55 (9,839)
Barker, Matthew P 5:59:22 (32,705)
Barker, Michael 4:37:14 (21,534)
Barker, Nigel S 4:42:15 (22,742)
Barker, Ralph 3:00:47 (1,223)
Barker, Roger F 3:29:59 (4,882)
Barker, Ryan 2:45:31 (350)
Barker, Thomas A 3:59:43 (11,756)
Barker, Tom A 4:04:51 (13,011)
Barker, Vernon I 3:34:24 (5,605)
Barker, Warren T 4:38:15 (21,767)
Barkes, Tom R 3:49:11 (8,622)
Barkoski, Victor 3:24:15 (3,811)
Barkway, Symon P 4:43:33 (23,064)
Barley, Clive 4:39:39 (22,108)
Barley, Richard 3:43:33 (7,355)
Barlow, Alexander P 3:59:07 (11,535)
Barlow, Andrew J 3:41:48 (6,991)
Barlow, David 4:17:35 (16,244)
Barlow, Kevin W 3:08:42 (1,851)
Barlow, Paul M 3:15:58 (2,752)
Barlow, Simon R 4:25:45 (18,463)
Barlow, Stephen T 3:10:39 (2,060)
Barltrop, Verne 3:24:05 (3,790)
Barnard, Alan 3:44:45 (7,622)
Barnard, Andrew R 4:19:11 (16,675)
Barnard, Edward M 3:23:26 (3,699)
Barnard, Graeme R 5:45:06 (31,774)
Barnard, James J 5:15:39 (28,899)
Barnard, John 4:31:04 (19,900)
Barnard, Luke 4:30:12 (19,678)
Barnard, Russell 4:47:23 (24,004)
Barnard, Steven B 4:20:50 (17,133)
Barnes, Alexander G 3:24:33 (3,855)
Barnes, Alexander H 3:52:33 (9,444)
Barnes, Arthur J 3:24:49 (3,892)
Barnes, Brian 4:46:45 (23,838)
Barnes, Christopher J 4:30:43 (19,806)
Barnes, Christopher M 3:50:38 (8,968)
Barnes, Clinton C 3:39:08 (6,456)
Barnes, Daniel L 5:35:25 (30,969)
Barnes, David W 3:55:39 (10,389)
Barnes, Edward 3:52:27 (9,423)
Barnes, Garry R 4:37:31 (21,597)
Barnes, Graeme R 3:28:22 (4,531)
Barnes, James A 3:56:29 (10,623)
Barnes, James R 5:43:52 (31,639)
Barnes, Mark J 4:26:26 (18,641)
Barnes, Matt T 4:49:03 (24,386)
Barnes, Matthew 4:40:23 (22,282)
Barnes, Mick 3:12:52 (2,314)
Barnes, Nigel 3:02:06 (1,315)
Barnes, Paul A 3:07:51 (1,771)
Barnes, Paul R 5:23:43 (29,768)
Barnes, Peter D 5:06:43 (27,655)
Barnes, Roy J 3:38:40 (6,382)
Barnes, Simon A 4:16:42 (16,010)
Barnes, Simon P 2:57:37 (912)
Barnes, Thomas J 3:14:02 (2,470)
Barnes, Tim 4:15:11 (15,613)
Barnes, Tristan G 4:22:22 (17,542)
Barnett, Chris J 4:37:38 (21,625)
Barnett, Garry J 3:53:42 (9,771)
Barnett, Graham J 4:45:07 (23,438)
Barnett, Jonathan R 4:00:02 (11,860)
Barnett, Murray W 4:53:51 (25,454)
Barnett, Nicholas J 4:26:26 (18,641)
Barnett, Nick 4:08:17 (13,849)
Barnett, Paul 5:12:45 (28,502)
Barnett, Peter E 3:57:20 (10,906)
Barnett, Philip A 3:40:44 (6,765)
Barnett, Stewart H 3:59:56 (11,831)
Barnett-Connolly, Michael A 5:44:58 (31,761)
Barni, Marco 4:01:44 (12,302)
Barnwell, Scott A 3:34:40 (5,638)
Barnwell, Tony L 4:07:35 (13,666)
Baroa Tornavaca, Juan A 4:04:33 (12,939)
Baron, Ashworth 4:32:49 (20,377)
Baron, Germain 3:57:55 (11,094)
Baron, Louis 4:58:00 (26,281)
Baron, Michael E 3:55:33 (10,354)
Baronio, Roberto 3:20:12 (3,249)
Barot, Surendra P 7:14:34 (34,362)
Barough, Michael J 4:30:52 (19,855)
Barr, Adam W 3:41:35 (6,952)
Barr, Dave A 3:29:43 (4,824)
Barr, David M 3:27:44 (4,405)
Barr, Robert 3:41:23 (6,913)
Barr, Roger 2:49:25 (486)
Barr, Travers R 3:26:22 (4,169)
Barracchia, Salvatore 3:33:33 (5,483)
Barrance, Tony 4:46:36 (23,799)
Barrand, James 3:07:54 (1,778)
Barrass, Barnaby J 2:54:12 (710)
Barrass, Daniel J 4:18:23 (16,458)
Barrass, Simon 4:20:47 (17,118)
Barratt, Clinton D 3:47:04 (8,125)
Barrell, Justin 4:17:53 (16,321)
Barrell, Richard J 4:32:40 (20,340)
Barrell, Stuart 4:11:44 (14,740)
Barrett, Alan 3:41:52 (7,008)
Barrett, Anthony 5:45:01 (31,770)
Barrett, Craig A 3:39:27 (6,526)
Barrett, David R 4:36:34 (21,384)
Barrett, Francis M 3:32:20 (5,286)
Barrett, Gordon D 3:15:00 (2,627)
Barrett, Gregg S 3:59:28 (11,662)
Barrett, James 5:37:21 (31,145)
Barrett, Jonathan 5:00:02 (26,638)
Barrett, Kevin A 3:59:36 (11,714)
Barrett, Mark A 6:30:40 (33,677)
Barrett, Michael 4:00:58 (12,105)
Barrett, Mike A 4:36:48 (21,444)
Barrett, Paul W 3:56:10 (10,530)
Barrett, Peter 3:48:38 (8,496)
Barretto Ko, Percival 4:31:58 (20,164)
Barrie, Euan 3:21:09 (3,378)
Barrie, James A 4:11:48 (14,753)
Barrigon, Mario 4:28:27 (19,247)
Barron, Christopher 4:18:00 (16,345)
Barron, Daniel 4:19:07 (16,660)
Barron, Ernest 6:20:58 (33,426)
Barron, Paul D 4:34:14 (20,765)
Barron, Paul T 3:25:57 (4,099)
Barron, Peter 3:35:39 (5,824)
Barros, Paulino R 5:02:12 (26,991)
Barrow, Keith 5:36:06 (31,042)
Barrow, Paul 5:44:49 (31,750)
Barrow, Paul J 3:48:50 (8,534)
Barrowman, Michael S 3:58:09 (11,163)
Barrows, Darren J 3:15:28 (2,699)
Barrs, Gary E 4:37:58 (21,708)
Barry, Andrew 4:29:43 (19,568)
Barry, Andrew J 3:19:37 (3,178)
Barry, David 6:09:49 (33,111)
Barry, John 4:09:23 (14,139)
Barry, Patrick J 5:57:10 (32,587)
Barry, Sean J 3:38:23 (6,336)
Barsby, David R 3:42:07 (7,051)
Barter, Ian P 4:55:57 (25,871)
Barter, Phil E 3:22:21 (3,541)
Bartholomew, David 4:28:40 (19,303)
Bartholomew, David 4:42:14 (22,736)
Bartkowiak, Dariusz 3:11:52 (2,194)
Bartle, Robert M 4:22:46 (17,661)
Bartle, Stephen 4:43:11 (22,978)
Bartlett, Andrew W 4:35:05 (21,005)
Bartlett, David K 4:13:07 (15,067)
Bartlett, David P 3:58:41 (11,369)
Bartlett, Edwin H 4:42:16 (22,746)
Bartlett, Martin 4:02:01 (12,368)
Bartlett, Paul D 5:14:42 (28,775)
Bartlett, Paul R 3:59:21 (11,613)
Bartlett, Paul R 5:36:12 (31,052)
Bartlett, Richard G 6:36:17 (33,797)
Bartlett, Robert K 4:46:48 (23,854)
Bartlett, Stephen W 5:13:52 (28,658)
Bartlett, Tom 3:32:08 (5,248)
Bartley, David J 3:55:50 (10,446)
Bartley, Lee A 4:19:34 (16,775)
Bartley, Michael F 4:49:08 (24,403)
Bartley, Paul 4:43:13 (22,985)
Bartman, Nick M 3:55:01 (10,201)
Barton, Alan J 4:39:05 (21,999)
Barton, Alex E 5:51:53 (32,281)
Barton, Charlie H 3:52:55 (9,544)
Barton, David 4:38:21 (21,790)
Barton, Liam A 4:12:25 (14,910)
Barton, Patrick J 3:53:44 (9,783)
Barton, Robert 5:18:05 (29,188)

Barton, Robert L 4:51:20 (24,910)
Barton-Smith, Colin 4:31:51 (20,123)
Bartram, Ian J 3:45:44 (7,840)
Bartrip, Lee 4:05:08 (13,080)
Barwick, Paul 5:30:34 (30,534)
Barwise, Tony 4:04:17 (12,882)
Bas, José M 3:39:37 (6,561)
Basak, Saikat K 4:25:41 (18,438)
Basham, Leslie J 3:59:32 (11,683)
Bashford, Gary 3:49:50 (8,778)
Bashford, Graham 5:12:47 (28,512)
Baskott, John W 4:42:13 (22,732)
Bass, Andrew P 2:46:30 (374)
Bass, Anthony W 5:59:31 (32,717)
Bass, Christopher C 3:45:02 (7,691)
Bass, Christopher G 5:51:46 (32,274)
Bass, Iain N 3:48:18 (8,424)
Bass, Richard E 2:58:28 (1,004)
Bassett, Peter J 5:27:48 (30,236)
Bassetto, Rogerio 4:51:38 (24,973)
Bassi, Gian-Paolo 3:38:08 (6,292)
Bassi, Michele 3:41:27 (6,924)
Bassom, David G 5:04:22 (27,307)
Bastable, Mark L 4:10:41 (14,457)
Baston, Andrew 3:52:18 (9,386)
Baston, Gareth J 4:15:02 (15,574)
Bastow, Michael I 3:39:04 (6,447)
Batchelor, Daniel 5:05:45 (27,516)
Batchelor, Jonathan M 4:20:23 (16,990)
Batchford, Daniel R 5:23:53 (29,787)
Bate, David K 3:25:40 (4,046)
Bate, David L 3:17:14 (2,892)
Bate, Neil 4:37:42 (21,643)
Bateman, Danny A 4:35:14 (21,039)
Bateman, Jack 4:03:18 (12,681)
Bateman, Jeremy D 3:00:15 (1,184)
Bateman, Jonathan S 3:01:55 (1,306)
Bateman, Nicholas 3:23:15 (3,668)
Bateman, Phillip W 3:51:45 (9,238)
Bateman, Rory L 4:06:06 (13,313)
Bater, Christopher 4:14:59 (15,553)
Bates, Andrew J 4:51:27 (24,930)
Bates, Anthony S 3:56:14 (10,545)
Bates, Dean 3:47:28 (8,215)
Bates, Jon 4:29:06 (19,420)
Bates, Joseph 7:10:36 (34,326)
Bates, Kevin P 5:24:32 (29,861)
Bates, Matthew J 3:48:46 (8,525)
Bates, Steven P 5:49:48 (32,106)
Bates, Toby J 5:18:50 (29,265)
Bates, Trevor 4:51:58 (25,036)
Bateson, Nathaniel A 4:54:56 (25,683)
Bateson, Steven 2:24:01 (31)
Batey, Alan W 3:56:47 (10,724)
Batey, Richard 3:49:03 (8,592)
Bath, Mike J 3:41:11 (6,866)
Batho, Charles W 3:57:50 (11,071)
Batley, Lloyd E 4:34:01 (20,699)
Batrick, Lee 4:47:56 (24,132)
Batt, James C 4:23:57 (17,978)
Batteauw, Philipe M 3:17:21 (2,911)
Batten, Paul R 3:46:48 (8,059)
Batterbee, Paul 5:46:06 (31,842)
Batterby, Chris D 4:37:09 (21,514)
Batterham, Richard J 3:09:45 (1,965)
Battersby, John A 3:44:12 (7,494)
Battersby, Richard M 3:56:59 (10,788)
Batterton, Daniel T 3:52:58 (9,560)
Batth, Sukhjeet S 4:07:41 (13,694)
Battle, Richard J 4:45:17 (23,492)
Batty, Alex J 4:55:27 (25,775)
Batty, Darren R 6:42:39 (33,931)
Batty, Jonathan 5:18:44 (29,258)
Batty, Paul J 5:55:07 (32,470)
Bauer, Terence 3:58:57 (11,473)
Baughan, Mark 4:52:38 (25,180)
Baulch, James 2:43:04 (268)
Baum, Paul M 4:51:36 (24,960)
Baumann, Didier 3:28:56 (4,650)
Baumann, Florian 3:33:11 (5,416)
Baumann, Roman 4:23:43 (17,920)
Baumgart, Jaromir J 5:56:28 (32,555)
Baumlin, Yves 4:08:31 (13,919)
Baun, John B 5:10:45 (28,241)
Baur, Bruno 4:14:45 (15,508)
Bausor, Neil T 3:56:14 (10,545)
Bautista-Parra, Fernando 4:47:56 (24,132)
Bawden, Simon N 4:19:14 (16,685)
Bax, Chris M 5:41:31 (31,467)
Bax, Nick 4:52:48 (25,222)
Baxendale, James L 4:02:36 (12,513)
Baxendale, Sam 3:44:42 (7,604)
Baxendale, Toby D 3:22:11 (3,509)
Baxi, Naimish 4:05:44 (13,230)
Baxter, David E 4:21:23 (17,270)
Baxter, Duncan R 4:20:33 (17,043)
Baxter, Eric G 3:29:46 (4,838)
Baxter, Glenn A 4:35:48 (21,195)
Baxter, Greg 2:44:12 (301)
Baxter, Harry R 6:32:56 (33,722)
Baxter, John 4:49:32 (24,484)
Baxter, Nick A 3:58:26 (11,276)
Baxter, Noel C 3:44:39 (7,593)
Baxter, Robert J 4:27:31 (18,953)
Baybutt, James N 3:24:04 (3,788)
Bayes, Jonathan 4:07:53 (13,745)
Bayes, Peter 5:31:28 (30,611)
Bayley, David A 3:43:45 (7,400)
Bayley, Keith 6:45:58 (34,004)
Bayley, Tom 3:54:07 (9,909)
Bayley-Dainton, Stuart J 3:26:33 (4,192)
Baylie, Richard 4:54:50 (25,657)
Baylin Larios, Carlos 3:44:38 (7,587)
Bayliss, Daniel S 4:54:03 (25,492)
Bayliss, Michael C 3:52:30 (9,433)
Bayliss, Paul A 5:34:17 (30,863)
Bayman, Richard J 3:48:55 (8,559)
Bazance, Max W 2:50:00 (513)
Bazley, Phillip C 4:27:48 (19,022)
Bazzy, Richard S 3:34:06 (5,564)
Beacall, Reginald N 4:00:22 (11,941)
Beacham, Ian R 4:30:05 (19,650)
Beacroft, Mark 4:39:23 (22,061)
Beacroft, Robert C 4:04:26 (12,918)
Beadell, Conrad V 4:10:39 (14,451)
Beadle, David 3:02:15 (1,326)
Beadle, Jamie R 4:01:38 (12,275)
Beagley, Andrew C 5:37:22 (31,147)
Beagley, Mark H 3:12:52 (2,314)
Beaken, Christopher G 4:12:09 (14,852)
Beale, Darren G 4:47:06 (23,930)
Beale, Fraser B 5:25:59 (30,034)
Beale, Miles G 3:39:17 (6,494)
Beale, Nicholas C 4:28:18 (19,207)
Beale, Phillip J 4:25:44 (18,456)
Bealey, Adam S 4:54:56 (25,683)
Beaman, Richard A 3:56:00 (10,491)
Beames, Michael 5:08:25 (27,879)
Beamish, Andrew J 3:30:26 (4,960)
Beamish, David 5:27:22 (30,189)
Beamish, Ian C 3:30:54 (5,039)
Beamiss, Graham A 3:36:00 (5,882)
Bean, Andrew J 4:29:00 (19,399)
Bean, Martyn 3:13:49 (2,438)
Beaney, Chris 3:55:00 (10,195)
Beany, Captain 5:46:25 (31,872)
Beard, David P 4:43:15 (22,994)
Beard, Graham D 3:23:51 (3,749)
Beard, Peter 4:47:11 (23,955)
Beard, Stephen G 4:11:38 (14,712)
Beardmore, Anthony 4:02:57 (12,598)
Beardmore, Roger C 3:12:13 (2,236)
Beardshaw, Mark R 4:52:28 (25,136)
Beardwell, Dominic 4:49:47 (24,552)
Bearley, Paul 9:25:51 (34,583)
Bearman, Jamie R 3:55:43 (10,409)
Beasley, Adam D 3:37:34 (6,176)
Beasley, Christopher A 3:44:56 (7,665)
Beasley, David C 5:51:37 (32,262)
Beasley, Glen 4:14:27 (15,436)
Beasley, Paul 4:07:55 (13,758)
Beathe, Carl J 3:12:02 (2,214)
Beaton, Alex J 3:39:28 (6,531)
Beaton, Paul W 3:27:46 (4,412)
Beattie, Brian 3:39:39 (6,565)
Beattie, David I 3:15:51 (2,737)
Beattie, Michael J 3:06:36 (1,644)
Beatty, Clive W 5:25:07 (29,941)
Beatty, Stephan C 3:39:37 (6,561)
Beauchamp, Simon 4:59:23 (26,543)
Beaumont, Angus 3:58:32 (11,310)
Beaumont, Neil 5:44:11 (31,685)
Beaumont, Richard 3:39:25 (6,522)
Beaumont, Steve 4:48:55 (24,350)
Beaumont, Steven M 5:14:56 (28,810)
Beaux, Jean-François 3:42:25 (7,120)
Beavan, Carl 5:27:23 (30,191)
Beaven, Graeme J 4:33:20 (20,523)
Beaver, Michael L 4:14:58 (15,548)
Beaver, Thomas E 4:50:26 (24,694)
Beavis, Joey 3:47:46 (8,289)
Beazer, Derek G 5:21:49 (29,589)
Bebbington, Richard K 4:03:56 (12,812)
Becerra, Mario E 4:57:53 (26,259)
Becher, Paul 4:41:00 (22,437)
Beck, Carsten M 4:07:21 (13,603)
Beck, Richard P 4:23:25 (17,842)
Beckenkamp, Axel 4:56:19 (25,934)
Becker, Howard 7:34:02 (34,468)
Becker, Joseph 4:30:36 (19,775)
Becker, Oliver 3:36:23 (5,948)
Beckett, Kelvin W 4:06:20 (13,362)
Beckett, Mark C 4:31:22 (19,983)
Bedder, Stephen R 3:31:45 (5,179)
Beddis, Graham 4:54:50 (25,657)
Bedem Van Den, Gerardus E 3:01:53 (1,302)
Bedford, Grahaam J 4:20:33 (17,043)
Bedford, Matthew 3:28:37 (4,583)
Bedford, Richard 4:48:38 (24,277)
Bedgery, Andrew J 4:41:46 (22,622)
Bedington, Terence J 3:27:46 (4,412)
Bednall, Michael 5:20:23 (29,451)
Bedward, Paul 3:55:36 (10,371)
Bedwell, Mick 3:32:13 (5,263)
Bedwell, Peter R 4:08:56 (14,026)
Bee, Alexander J 4:45:37 (23,567)
Bee, Anthony J 4:45:38 (23,569)
Beech, Michael G 4:44:51 (23,385)
Beech, Ross M 4:53:35 (25,398)
Beecham, George 6:30:00 (33,658)
Beecham, Mat J 5:14:37 (28,764)
Beecher, Daniel J 3:57:06 (10,835)
Beecroft, David 2:58:44 (1,034)
Beeden, Paul 5:19:35 (29,369)
Beedie, Keith 3:08:05 (1,798)
Beer, James M 5:50:24 (32,163)
Beer, Simon A 4:55:44 (25,827)
Beer, Stephen 3:37:53 (6,235)
Beesley, Paul J 3:58:54 (11,458)
Beesley, Peter J 5:52:04 (32,292)
Beeson, Nigel A 4:51:01 (24,847)
Beeston, James E 3:28:41 (4,600)
Beeton, James 3:25:04 (3,941)
Beevers, James 3:57:10 (10,856)
Beevor, Richard 3:31:58 (5,217)
Beggs, William K 3:44:37 (7,582)
Begiristain, Enaut 4:47:45 (24,088)
Begley, Christopher J 3:48:18 (8,424)
Begley, Simon G 3:48:29 (8,460)
Behan, Kenneth J 3:05:01 (1,520)
Beheshti, Payam 3:49:50 (8,778)
Beilby, Owen R 2:35:46 (126)
Beirne, Robert J 4:46:41 (23,823)
Beische, Eric 3:59:22 (11,622)
Beisel, Wolfgang 3:55:05 (10,225)
Bejon, Pascal 3:32:36 (5,334)
Belallam, Said 3:52:35 (9,452)
Belamendia Huarte, Inaki 2:59:19 (1,100)
Beland, Paul 4:04:27 (12,919)
Belassie, Simon D 3:50:23 (8,910)
Belchamber, Scott 6:04:46 (32,914)
Belcher, John 5:21:47 (29,585)
Belcher, Paul F 3:01:24 (1,269)
Bell, Andy 6:21:56 (33,461)
Bell, Archie J 5:03:32 (27,189)
Bell, Chris 4:46:48 (23,854)
Bell, Christopher J 4:01:23 (12,210)
Bell, Craig J 2:57:48 (931)
Bell, David J 3:16:23 (2,801)

Bell, Duncan E	5:24:55 (29,907)	
Bell, Geoffrey D	4:36:50 (21,449)	
Bell, Gordon	4:54:16 (25,536)	
Bell, Graham A	3:12:06 (2,224)	
Bell, Jack	3:37:47 (6,212)	
Bell, Jonathan	4:50:41 (24,762)	
Bell, Jonathan N	3:51:34 (9,188)	
Bell, Joseph	5:15:36 (28,889)	
Bell, Keith A	4:37:43 (21,644)	
Bell, Kevin J	4:42:07 (22,701)	
Bell, Martin	3:56:35 (10,657)	
Bell, Martin G	4:14:05 (15,331)	
Bell, Martyn	4:03:57 (12,820)	
Bell, Michael B	4:42:43 (22,858)	
Bell, Nicholas P	3:59:26 (11,646)	
Bell, Patrick D	4:09:36 (14,200)	
Bell, Peter	5:20:47 (29,482)	
Bell, Robert G	4:02:00 (12,363)	
Bell, Simon	4:11:52 (14,772)	
Bell, Stephen	3:44:41 (7,597)	
Bell, Timothy F	3:57:56 (11,098)	
Bellacosa, Maurizio	4:44:21 (23,265)	
Bellamy, Darren N	4:43:03 (22,944)	
Bellamy, Edward J	3:10:04 (1,995)	
Bellamy, Richard J	2:41:03 (216)	
Bellenger, James F	4:03:48 (12,788)	
Bellicini, Andrea	3:59:12 (11,562)	
Bellis, Deryn S	3:04:48 (1,503)	
Bello, Aurelio M	4:15:58 (15,828)	
Bellotti, Lee	3:47:50 (8,306)	
Bellutti, Stefano	3:28:39 (4,592)	
Bellworthy, Douglas P	7:09:17 (34,308)	
Belmokhtar, Omar	3:19:14 (3,125)	
Belmont, Anthony J	4:13:38 (15,198)	
Belson, Simon J	5:11:21 (28,313)	
Belton, Christopher C	3:29:28 (4,774)	
Beltran, Armando	3:25:49 (4,070)	
Beltran, Yannick	3:59:38 (11,724)	
Bembridge, Simon	4:18:09 (16,386)	
Ben Ismail, Maaouia	3:05:30 (1,553)	
Ben-Brahem, Daoud	4:11:37 (14,706)	
Bence, Christopher G	4:28:12 (19,171)	
Bendall, Mark	2:40:29 (204)	
Bendle, Simon J	4:01:06 (12,136)	
Benfield, Philip	3:32:25 (5,304)	
Benfredj, Sacha M	3:53:11 (9,635)	
Bengtsson, Jonas	3:04:44 (1,499)	
Benham, Kevin D	3:15:11 (2,651)	
Benini, Luca	2:57:37 (912)	
Benjamin, Alister C	4:22:48 (17,668)	
Benjamin, Daniel	4:00:42 (12,034)	
Benjamin, Michael A	3:53:09 (9,620)	
Benjamin, Trevor G	3:56:51 (10,743)	
Benke, Graham N	4:28:40 (19,303)	
Benkirane, Driss	3:52:36 (9,454)	
Benn, Christopher S	4:05:19 (13,125)	
Ben-Nathan, Marc I	4:27:36 (18,979)	
Bennett, Adam M	3:51:20 (9,132)	
Bennett, Adrian	4:02:44 (12,550)	
Bennett, Andrew D	4:28:40 (19,303)	
Bennett, Ashley C	4:08:38 (13,950)	
Bennett, Barry J	5:11:47 (28,383)	
Bennett, Ben D	2:34:27 (106)	
Bennett, Bill	3:17:57 (2,981)	
Bennett, Brian	4:53:02 (25,280)	
Bennett, Cameron J	3:00:45 (1,222)	
Bennett, Christopher F	3:18:45 (3,071)	
Bennett, Christopher J	4:01:34 (12,259)	
Bennett, Colin F	4:16:24 (15,932)	
Bennett, Craig	3:59:12 (11,562)	
Bennett, Daniel	4:30:07 (19,660)	
Bennett, Darren M	5:09:38 (28,079)	
Bennett, David	3:19:48 (3,207)	
Bennett, David	3:54:02 (9,882)	
Bennett, David	4:10:09 (14,325)	
Bennett, David A	3:59:21 (11,613)	
Bennett, David M	4:05:18 (13,121)	
Bennett, James	4:20:08 (16,920)	
Bennett, John	4:41:34 (22,570)	
Bennett, Marc	4:47:42 (24,068)	
Bennett, Mark A	4:32:15 (20,243)	
Bennett, Michael J	3:49:40 (8,736)	
Bennett, Nick	3:45:34 (7,806)	
Bennett, Nick J	3:23:14 (3,667)	
Bennett, Peter M	4:18:29 (16,491)	
Bennett, Raymond	3:53:21 (9,677)	
Bennett, Robert C	4:55:54 (25,859)	
Bennett, Robert J	4:18:20 (16,443)	
Bennett, Scott	3:56:00 (10,491)	
Bennett, Simeon	3:06:49 (1,664)	
Bennett, Simon	5:50:17 (32,153)	
Bennett, Simon J	3:25:54 (4,085)	
Bennett, Stephen	4:35:18 (21,056)	
Bennett, Stephen G	4:37:56 (21,699)	
Bennetts, David	4:24:14 (18,063)	
Bennetts, Steve	3:43:18 (7,306)	
Benning, Joe T	3:29:16 (4,730)	
Bennis, Just H	3:45:40 (7,830)	
Bennon, Paul	4:21:42 (17,374)	
Benorads, Abdelkader	2:51:44 (582)	
Bensetti, Abdelkader	4:00:15 (11,909)	
Benskin, Ian D	3:02:51 (1,366)	
Benson, Bruce B	3:36:08 (5,903)	
Benson, Colin	3:23:00 (3,636)	
Benson, Dan	5:01:10 (26,821)	
Benson, Daniel	5:14:00 (28,674)	
Benson, David J	4:41:16 (22,501)	
Benson, Ian C	3:07:55 (1,780)	
Benson, Jonathan J	4:57:17 (26,139)	
Benson, Kenneth	4:44:40 (23,341)	
Benson, Kevin B	4:47:15 (23,969)	
Benson, Lee	5:30:12 (30,498)	
Benstead, Robin J	3:38:21 (6,327)	
Bensted, Duncan I	4:11:52 (14,772)	
Benstock, Brian R	3:43:18 (7,306)	
Bent, Alan	3:34:03 (5,557)	
Bentham, Ian S	6:29:55 (33,655)	
Bentley, Adrian L	3:50:36 (8,955)	
Bentley, Alex J	4:12:28 (14,920)	
Bentley, Daniel S	4:20:51 (17,138)	
Bentley, Ian R	4:27:29 (18,950)	
Bentley, John S	3:38:27 (6,350)	
Bentley, Jon E	3:46:36 (8,024)	
Bentley, Justin	3:24:03 (3,785)	
Bentley, Mark	3:19:57 (3,221)	
Bentley, Mike	3:39:54 (6,616)	
Bentley, Neil D	3:44:55 (7,660)	
Bentley, Paul D	5:53:37 (32,383)	
Bentley, Phil J	3:34:47 (5,659)	
Bentley, Robert W	4:15:37 (15,734)	
Bentley, Stuart	4:50:54 (24,824)	
Bentley, Tom	4:38:19 (21,786)	
Benton, Jack	5:32:23 (30,691)	
Berdelou, Michel L	4:08:00 (13,772)	
Bere, Adam T	4:36:12 (21,296)	
Berenblut, Benjamin	4:25:49 (18,487)	
Beresford, John P	3:35:57 (5,869)	
Beresford, Martin P	3:53:06 (9,607)	
Beresford, Ross J	5:32:55 (30,739)	
Beresford, Simon C	5:44:32 (31,724)	
Beretta, Marco	3:08:41 (1,849)	
Berg, James M	4:27:16 (18,896)	
Bergamin, Markus	4:06:44 (13,459)	
Berger, David R	3:47:34 (8,239)	
Bergh, Gregory	5:02:13 (26,994)	
Berghauser, Ulrich	3:52:03 (9,318)	
Bergin, Patrick M	4:38:13 (21,759)	
Bergmeier, Tim	3:48:12 (8,400)	
Bergomi, Giulio	3:44:43 (7,610)	
Bergonzoni, Massimiliano	3:17:16 (2,898)	
Berman, Gavin B	3:43:25 (7,327)	
Bermody, Brian J	5:09:31 (28,054)	
Bernaez, Alfredo	3:30:46 (5,015)	
Bernard, Cyril	3:34:32 (5,625)	
Bernardelli, Paolo	3:53:20 (9,673)	
Bernardi, Mark O	3:43:53 (7,434)	
Bernstein, Nathan H	4:29:03 (19,412)	
Berntsen, Bent O	2:47:10 (394)	
Berradi, Mostpha	4:09:36 (14,200)	
Berrett, Andrew S	4:20:10 (16,936)	
Berrett, Shaun	3:49:18 (8,650)	
Berrill, Lee	3:07:54 (1,778)	
Berrisford, Richard A	4:44:59 (23,409)	
Berry, Charles R	3:56:25 (10,602)	
Berry, Christopher D	5:54:24 (32,427)	
Berry, David	6:01:50 (32,816)	
Berry, David J	4:37:47 (21,663)	
Berry, Gearoid P	4:04:37 (12,960)	
Berry, Grant R	4:38:45 (21,898)	
Berry, Ian J	2:55:12 (763)	
Berry, Jamie M	3:45:33 (7,800)	
Berry, Jason	3:12:44 (2,294)	
Berry, John	3:38:04 (6,277)	
Berry, Mark	2:55:52 (770)	
Berry, Matthew	4:27:56 (19,078)	
Berry, Paul J	4:32:47 (20,372)	
Berry, Paul R	3:04:09 (1,462)	
Berry, Richard L	4:09:14 (14,097)	
Berry, Stephen F	5:45:48 (31,820)	
Berry, Stephen J	4:01:20 (12,196)	
Berry, Thomas	4:07:05 (13,539)	
Berry, Timothy C	5:53:55 (32,400)	
Berryman, Guy	3:59:36 (11,714)	
Berryman, Mark A	3:46:39 (8,031)	
Bertazzoli, Serafino	3:51:07 (9,078)	
Berthold, Richard	3:31:41 (5,166)	
Bertolani, Piero	3:42:21 (7,105)	
Berton, Enrico	4:01:57 (12,348)	
Bertone, Paolo	4:08:16 (13,845)	
Bertran Diaz, Joan	4:02:37 (12,520)	
Bertrand, Alejandro	3:43:10 (7,281)	
Bertrand, Jacques	4:13:50 (15,258)	
Bertrand, Patrice O	3:23:04 (3,646)	
Bertschin, Keith	3:52:42 (9,479)	
Bertucci, Claudio	3:58:41 (11,369)	
Beruffi, Silvano	4:24:01 (18,000)	
Best, Adam R	4:43:08 (22,968)	
Best, Benjamin D	5:17:05 (29,075)	
Best, Chris	5:05:09 (27,427)	
Best, Craig G	5:36:08 (31,046)	
Best, Darren C	4:51:12 (24,880)	
Best, David	5:50:44 (32,192)	
Best, David C	4:13:02 (15,045)	
Best, Michael J	3:16:24 (2,804)	
Best, Nigel C	4:59:34 (26,568)	
Besuijen, Marius	3:22:31 (3,570)	
Beswick, Mike	3:56:42 (10,690)	
Beszant, Chris D	4:21:01 (17,188)	
Bethell, Mark A	3:29:57 (4,879)	
Betteridge, Anthony F	6:14:58 (33,267)	
Betteridge, Karl J	4:26:03 (18,552)	
Betteridge, Philip	3:44:15 (7,502)	
Bettey, Stephen J	3:59:33 (11,688)	
Betti, Stefano	3:46:55 (8,088)	
Bettney, Jamie D	4:43:00 (22,926)	
Betts, Christopher N	4:27:34 (18,967)	
Betts, James A	4:45:41 (23,577)	
Betts, Lee	4:11:13 (14,610)	
Betts, Liam J	5:54:14 (32,420)	
Betts, Robert	3:50:53 (9,023)	
Betts, Samuel	4:33:25 (20,550)	
Betts, Simon	5:12:32 (28,468)	
Bettsworth, Richard G	2:56:14 (827)	
Beurier, Stefan	3:52:30 (9,433)	
Beurnez, Jean-Michel	3:32:42 (5,345)	
Beutter, Ralph M	4:25:54 (18,509)	
Bevan, Alexander J	3:26:39 (4,218)	
Bevan, David A	4:14:02 (15,316)	
Bevan, James	4:46:10 (23,707)	
Bevan, Jonathan N	5:53:29 (32,374)	
Bevan, Kristian J	4:54:50 (25,657)	
Bevan, Matthew	3:54:56 (10,175)	
Bevan, Neil	3:07:44 (1,757)	
Bevan, Nick	4:10:32 (14,418)	
Bevan, Stephen J	3:31:36 (5,151)	
Bevan, Steve	3:42:45 (7,185)	
Beveridge, Cameron S	3:28:18 (4,518)	
Beverley, Michael	4:02:26 (12,483)	
Bevil, Robert G	4:14:04 (15,326)	
Bevis, Luke E	4:54:13 (25,525)	
Bewsher, Nigel P	4:07:15 (13,588)	
Beyer, Paul K	3:51:54 (9,276)	
Beynon, David	5:13:54 (28,663)	
Bezance, Tom M	3:36:27 (5,956)	
Bezodis, Mark S	4:52:41 (25,196)	
Bhagavathula, Shashi	5:35:51 (31,014)	
Bhailok, Adam	8:31:57 (34,568)	
Bhakar, Balvinder	5:07:37 (27,785)	
Bhakar, Surinder S	4:37:23 (21,569)	

Bhatt, Aneil K 4:42:49 (22,880)
Bhatti, Jumshad H 7:21:18 (34,405)
Bhumber, Satbinder S 6:49:04 (34,054)
Bianchi, Gilbert 2:57:56 (941)
Bianco, Emilio 2:58:04 (956)
Bibani, Alex 3:44:20 (7,519)
Bibby, Gary J 4:09:09 (14,073)
Bibby, Paul A 4:14:24 (15,424)
Bickers, Michael A 3:25:06 (3,947)
Bickerton, Michael 4:14:59 (15,553)
Bickley, Jonathan R 4:07:27 (13,627)
Bicknell, Andrew K 3:57:30 (10,953)
Bicknell, Marcus 3:44:47 (7,631)
Bicknell, Richard J 3:24:54 (3,909)
Bidault, David 3:07:16 (1,705)
Biddis, Mark G 4:32:22 (20,264)
Biddlscombe, Peter W 4:36:59 (21,482)
Biddulph, Brett A 4:47:25 (24,006)
Biddulph, Daniel E 4:32:27 (20,282)
Biddulph, Robert A 4:32:27 (20,282)
Bide, Nicholas 4:06:30 (13,400)
Bidnell, Andrew P 4:31:49 (20,112)
Bidois, Richard J 3:15:20 (2,680)
Bidwell, Colin F 4:56:59 (26,071)
Bidwell, Stephen H 4:48:31 (24,255)
Bie, Andrew J 5:12:57 (28,540)
Bielderman, Erik 3:58:15 (11,198)
Bienkowski, Stephen 4:52:13 (25,084)
Bieris, Stan 4:03:45 (12,782)
Biggar, Alister J 3:18:25 (3,034)
Biggart, Douglas 4:25:17 (18,336)
Biggin, Charles R 4:59:06 (26,493)
Biggin, Matthew J 3:30:47 (5,017)
Biggins, Andy 3:28:27 (4,552)
Biggs, Andrew J 3:38:08 (6,292)
Biggs, Gerard M 6:17:38 (33,343)
Biggs, Mark J 3:30:04 (4,900)
Biggs, Nicholas J 4:37:31 (21,597)
Biggs, Robert 3:46:15 (7,940)
Bigl, Manfred 4:42:52 (22,897)
Bigmore, Paul T 4:01:45 (12,306)
Bihannic, Arnaud 3:08:41 (1,849)
Bijl, Henk 6:12:08 (33,173)
Bilboe, Ian H 4:06:29 (13,395)
Bilke, David C 3:44:11 (7,489)
Bill, Simon D 6:49:05 (34,055)
Billard, Dominique P 3:15:52 (2,744)
Billes, René 3:44:35 (7,574)
Billing, Mike 3:11:19 (2,129)
Billingham, David P 3:05:25 (1,549)
Billingham, Huw W 4:12:58 (15,021)
Billinghurst, Antony 3:47:51 (8,313)
Billinghurst, Michael 3:59:00 (11,489)
Billington, Geoff 4:04:17 (12,882)
Billington, James A 5:55:11 (32,476)
Billson, Jeremy P 4:23:05 (17,750)
Billson, Patrick J 5:27:42 (30,227)
Bilsby, Roger 5:20:16 (29,435)
Bilton, Darran E 2:23:49 (29)
Bilton, John 4:09:25 (14,147)
Bindman, Adam 4:25:24 (18,367)
Bindra, Amrit P 5:30:39 (30,542)
Binet, Ben 3:47:26 (8,205)
Bing, Steven J 3:38:40 (6,382)
Bingham, Hugh M 2:51:59 (593)
Bingham, Iain S 4:15:41 (15,742)
Bingham, James L 3:46:56 (8,093)
Bingham, Raymond 4:29:17 (19,467)
Bingham, Stuart J 3:51:10 (9,089)
Bingley, Kenneth 4:38:50 (21,924)
Binnie, David 4:46:16 (23,733)
Binnington, Tim J 3:46:09 (7,919)
Binns, Neil W 3:33:05 (5,397)
Binuya, Julius 5:05:34 (27,491)
Bir, Claude R 3:32:46 (5,355)
Biraud, Jim 3:42:29 (7,137)
Birbeck, John R 4:37:20 (21,557)
Birch, Alex C 3:51:49 (9,252)
Birch, Christopher J 3:59:52 (11,807)
Birch, David 3:15:50 (2,734)
Birch, Mark 3:52:35 (9,452)
Birch, Robert E 4:09:51 (14,262)
Birch, Sean 3:40:26 (6,726)
Birch, Tim D 3:46:20 (7,960)
Birchall, Christopher T 2:23:58 (30)
Birchall, Clayton 4:29:41 (19,564)
Birchall, Edward 3:58:36 (11,336)
Birchall, James C 3:39:10 (6,467)
Bircher, David J 4:48:42 (24,290)
Birchmore, Mark S 4:40:27 (22,298)
Bird, Andrew P 3:18:48 (3,074)
Bird, Colin C 5:50:24 (32,163)
Bird, Conrad 3:58:29 (11,295)
Bird, David J 3:05:24 (1,547)
Bird, David J 4:55:52 (25,851)
Bird, David W 4:28:17 (19,199)
Bird, Gavin D 3:00:38 (1,213)
Bird, James A 7:20:49 (34,401)
Bird, Jamie E 3:14:35 (2,566)
Bird, John 4:46:17 (23,739)
Bird, Matthew 3:45:00 (7,681)
Bird, Matthew J 3:49:30 (8,701)
Bird, Paul A 2:58:56 (1,056)
Bird, Phil 3:38:13 (6,303)
Bird, Simon 4:24:14 (18,063)
Bird, Tom R 3:35:33 (5,800)
Bird, Vincent J 4:49:18 (24,431)
Birdsey, Ian M 4:25:06 (18,288)
Birgisson, Jon O 4:28:28 (19,252)
Biris, Ioannis A 3:41:09 (6,859)
Birkenhead, Thomas 5:58:22 (32,659)
Birkens, John B 3:31:56 (5,208)
Birkett, Charlie N 4:40:32 (22,316)
Birkett, Frederick 5:10:19 (28,195)
Birkett, Peter 3:57:53 (11,085)
Birkett, Robert E 4:54:32 (25,586)
Birkholm, Jon 5:24:40 (29,875)
Birkin, David A 4:37:31 (21,597)
Birkinshaw, Andrew D 3:47:33 (8,235)
Birkinshaw, Dan E 3:15:22 (2,686)
Birks, David L 3:33:01 (5,388)
Birleson, John A 4:30:01 (19,639)
Birney, James C 4:16:11 (15,871)
Birnie, Andrew E 2:54:01 (693)
Birot, Jean Luc 3:58:30 (11,298)
Birrane, Paul A 3:25:21 (3,988)
Birts, Thomas C 5:03:25 (27,167)
Birtwistle, Adam J 3:56:41 (10,684)
Bisby, David 4:00:15 (11,909)
Biscomb, Geoffrey C 3:26:03 (4,113)
Bisdee, Trevor T 5:43:52 (31,639)
Bisgaard, Sean 5:15:37 (28,892)
Bishop, James I 3:27:59 (4,456)
Bishop, John T 4:36:35 (21,388)
Bishop, Mark A 5:01:02 (26,803)
Bishop, Mark J 4:10:59 (14,542)
Bishop, Murray C 4:45:11 (23,462)
Bishop, Peter I 4:20:40 (17,084)
Bishop, Tim P 3:56:40 (10,680)
Bisoglio, Maurizio 4:49:32 (24,484)
Biss, Colin J 5:39:54 (31,325)
Bisschop, Murray 4:34:58 (20,962)
Bissell, Jason 4:08:43 (13,973)
Bisset, Ian A 4:12:31 (14,931)
Bissett, Mark E 4:14:51 (15,523)
Bissett, Richard 4:39:47 (22,150)
Bissoli, Franco G 3:03:07 (1,382)
Bittermann, Rolf 4:53:37 (25,404)
Bjerga, Morten 4:16:56 (16,070)
Bjoersdorff, Tomas L 3:46:55 (8,088)
Blaber, Jamie 5:15:01 (28,821)
Black, Alistair M 4:26:57 (18,798)
Black, Ben 3:59:21 (11,613)
Black, David A 4:09:34 (14,195)
Black, Douglas P 5:11:10 (28,289)
Black, Douglas S 4:47:09 (23,947)
Black, Elliott N 5:24:25 (29,849)
Black, Fraser M 4:58:03 (26,293)
Black, Graham P 3:57:48 (11,061)
Black, Ian P 3:37:34 (6,176)
Black, Martin J 3:45:12 (7,728)
Black, Michael J 4:38:37 (21,861)
Black, Richard L 4:19:57 (16,874)
Black, Robert 5:31:55 (30,648)
Black, Robert H 3:40:13 (6,676)
Black, Ross K 3:53:14 (9,644)
Black, Roy 4:29:50 (19,594)
Black, Stephen 3:18:54 (3,086)
Blackburn, Bradley J 6:12:00 (33,165)
Blackburn, Chris 5:23:08 (29,712)
Blackburn, David 3:38:19 (6,319)
Blackburn, David 3:45:44 (7,840)
Blackburn, Gavin J 4:12:45 (14,974)
Blackburn, Graham M 3:06:23 (1,634)
Blackburn, Ian 3:53:23 (9,693)
Blackburn, Simon A 4:21:38 (17,350)
Blacker, Anthony 4:54:32 (25,586)
Blackmore, Daniel C 4:16:49 (16,041)
Blackmore, Michael T 2:33:11 (98)
Blackstock, Murray J 4:31:34 (20,046)
Blackwell, Christian M 3:29:09 (4,703)
Blackwell, Colin 4:22:20 (17,527)
Blackwell, Gary S 5:32:40 (30,718)
Blackwell, Paul A 3:58:37 (11,341)
Blackwell, Tim W 4:52:55 (25,258)
Blackwood, Justin 4:24:48 (18,218)
Bladen, Alan J 4:54:51 (25,664)
Bladen, Sion A 5:03:35 (27,196)
Bladt, Ulrich 4:54:35 (25,599)
Blair, Christopher 4:57:29 (26,182)
Blair, James T 3:56:17 (10,557)
Blair, Jason H 3:51:55 (9,282)
Blaize, Andy J 2:52:07 (599)
Blaize, Cuthbert 4:48:47 (24,315)
Blaize-Smith, Matthew S 4:13:22 (15,132)
Blake, Alan G 3:32:17 (5,276)
Blake, Arthur F 3:37:23 (6,140)
Blake, Benjamin D 5:01:05 (26,807)
Blake, Edward M 2:46:08 (365)
Blake, John 3:34:22 (5,601)
Blake, Kevin 4:18:25 (16,470)
Blake, Kevin C 3:49:22 (8,668)
Blake, Paul D 3:24:31 (3,850)
Blakelock, Peter 4:08:06 (13,789)
Blakemore, Jim F 4:49:42 (24,534)
Blampied, Peter T 4:10:29 (14,406)
Blanc, François 5:07:14 (27,728)
Blanchard, David 3:51:01 (9,052)
Blanchard, Emmanuel F 4:03:59 (12,827)
Blanchard, Eric 3:25:34 (4,025)
Blanchard, Luke 4:00:25 (11,951)
Blanche, Paul M 3:14:39 (2,580)
Blancke, Michel 4:32:10 (20,215)
Bland, Jonathan A 5:18:00 (29,181)
Bland, Philip A 4:16:47 (16,029)
Blaney, Jonathan M 2:57:12 (887)
Blanford, Richard M 3:26:09 (4,130)
Blantz, Andrew 4:30:03 (19,646)
Blaquiere, Ronnie 5:05:47 (27,519)
Blaquiere, Timothy 4:17:45 (16,294)
Blaskett, Neil 4:23:12 (17,786)
Blatchford, Barry-John 6:02:44 (32,843)
Blatchford, Ian K 4:01:49 (12,322)
Blatchford, Ricky J 3:25:14 (3,967)
Blaylock, Matthew R 3:49:54 (8,800)
Blaylock, Stuart K 4:37:40 (21,634)
Bleach, Paul A 2:41:23 (230)
Bledman-Alleyne, James O 5:43:52 (31,639)
Blencowe, Rupert D 5:03:15 (27,141)
Blenkinsop, Bob M 4:50:05 (24,621)
Blewett, Hender 4:44:43 (23,349)
Blewitt, Tim A 4:35:01 (20,988)
Blick, Stephen C 4:33:24 (20,540)
Bligh, Peter 3:51:57 (9,287)
Blinkhorn, David 5:01:15 (26,834)
Blinkhorn, Sean 4:34:05 (20,720)
Blinman, Leigh S 4:38:55 (21,948)
Bliss, Keith M 4:24:27 (18,128)
Bliss, Paul R 4:03:23 (12,695)
Blizzard, Sean A 4:31:29 (20,022)
Bloemers, Tom A 4:05:17 (13,120)
Blogg, Kieran M 3:26:41 (4,228)
Blois, Richard H 7:31:17 (34,461)
Blokland, Jacobus A 4:39:11 (22,022)
Blomley, Greg 3:53:22 (9,687)
Blondel, Benoit A 2:49:08 (469)
Bloomer, Alan S 3:23:27 (3,701)
Bloomer, James W 3:39:08 (6,456)
Bloomfield, Brian S 5:09:51 (28,125)

Bloomfield, Colin F....4:06:13 (13,333)
Bloomfield, Mitchell A....5:56:32 (32,558)
Bloomfield, Stephen J....6:24:03 (33,519)
Bloor, Jon....4:32:35 (20,318)
Bloor, Kenneth....3:44:49 (7,635)
Bloor, Richard A....3:04:55 (1,511)
Bloore, Alastair....4:58:27 (26,370)
Bloquet, Pascal L....3:18:54 (3,086)
Blore, Richard M....4:38:44 (21,893)
Bloss, Richard J....3:34:28 (5,617)
Blount, David J....3:30:29 (4,968)
Blowers, Chris D....4:14:09 (15,354)
Blowes, Benjamin D....2:52:25 (614)
Bloxham, Christie B....3:22:46 (3,604)
Bloxham, Clive....4:43:36 (23,077)
Bloxham, Matthew E....3:48:26 (8,451)
Bloxham, Roy W....3:57:15 (10,877)
Bloxsome, Iain M....3:39:09 (6,462)
Bluck, Andrew P....4:45:53 (23,642)
Bluck, Gavin W....3:38:03 (6,274)
Blum, Richard G....5:25:45 (30,007)
Blumenow, Warren....4:42:29 (22,800)
Blundell, Edward P....4:28:12 (19,171)
Blunnie, Simon....6:24:31 (33,533)
Blurton, Andrew L....5:14:41 (28,772)
Blurton, James R....4:14:51 (15,523)
Blyth, Kevin....2:58:18 (979)
Blyth, Paul J....4:05:12 (13,098)
Boalch, Simon J....6:42:35 (33,927)
Boam, Ady J....5:01:01 (26,798)
Board, Tim....4:11:08 (14,581)
Boardley, Ian....2:56:50 (861)
Boardley, John T....5:02:31 (27,043)
Boardman, Daniel J....4:19:26 (16,735)
Boardman, John....3:45:35 (7,808)
Boardman, Keith....2:49:30 (491)
Boardman, Liam J....3:47:05 (8,130)
Boase, Duncan K....4:29:10 (19,444)
Boatman, Jack W....4:05:07 (13,074)
Bobadilla, Oscar E....4:32:38 (20,331)
Bobbins, Thomas A....3:31:33 (5,141)
Boddy, Michael J....3:35:11 (5,735)
Boddy, Tim....3:59:10 (11,548)
Boden, Alex D....3:29:36 (4,800)
Boden, Matthew D....4:05:06 (13,069)
Boden, Robert....4:31:47 (20,097)
Bodenham, Ciaran D....5:08:02 (27,828)
Bodini, Claudio....4:53:46 (25,432)
Bodley-Scott, Sam....3:55:05 (10,225)
Bodmer, Uwe....2:54:03 (696)
Bodson, Bertrand....3:19:31 (3,167)
Boehm, Stefan....3:46:54 (8,083)
Boeke, Thies....4:06:10 (13,328)
Boex, Rupert....4:37:38 (21,625)
Bogdon, Horst....4:33:43 (20,639)
Boggi, Daniel....4:45:34 (23,551)
Boggia, Graham....4:40:54 (22,402)
Bogoevski, Sasho....4:45:36 (23,563)
Bogush, Jeremy H....4:15:19 (15,642)
Bohe, Olaf....2:49:29 (490)
Bohling, Jolyon K....5:07:56 (27,817)
Bohn, Wayne M....4:08:56 (14,026)
Boisgard, Jacky J....4:01:43 (12,299)
Bolam, John P....4:59:04 (26,491)
Boland, Dean C....5:16:49 (29,033)
Boland, Reinhard A....5:15:03 (28,827)
Bolas, Dave....3:09:26 (1,934)
Bolcskei, Tibor....4:52:53 (25,247)
Bolland, Stephen....4:07:04 (13,534)
Bolledi, Ettore....4:47:08 (23,940)
Bolster, Eric G....3:24:47 (3,885)
Bolt, Sean W....3:28:23 (4,534)
Bolton, Ashley J....3:41:29 (6,938)
Bolton, David J....5:09:13 (27,999)
Bolton, Lawrence A....7:55:55 (34,526)
Bolton, Neil M....4:28:17 (19,199)
Bolwell, Jeremy....4:24:41 (18,192)
Bom, Michiel J....4:47:25 (24,006)
Bonaccolta, Carmelo....4:00:40 (12,024)
Bonacina, Giuseppe....3:58:01 (11,122)
Bonaretti, Franco....4:41:40 (22,608)
Bonavita, Luca....5:05:55 (27,536)
Bond, Andrew....4:47:52 (24,109)
Bond, Christopher....4:03:01 (12,611)
Bond, David S....4:00:55 (12,086)
Bond, Edward R....3:11:55 (2,199)
Bond, Francis D....3:12:52 (2,314)
Bond, Leon P....4:13:16 (15,105)
Bond, Mark G....4:22:26 (17,560)
Bond, Martin A....4:27:48 (19,022)
Bond, Michael G....5:09:31 (28,054)
Bond, Michael J....2:50:20 (523)
Bond, Rickey....5:47:21 (31,937)
Bond, Stephen....4:25:46 (18,468)
Bond, Stephen A....4:01:18 (12,184)
Bond, Stewart A....3:17:41 (2,953)
Bone, Andy G....3:03:19 (1,403)
Bone, Christian A....4:44:29 (23,297)
Bone, Krister....3:43:56 (7,446)
Bone, Lawrence R....5:04:47 (27,370)
Bonelli, Anthony S....3:29:17 (4,735)
Bones, Colin G....3:57:07 (10,842)
Bonetti, Vittorio....3:52:14 (9,370)
Boni, Fausto....3:37:36 (6,183)
Boniface, Andrew....4:30:46 (19,823)
Boniface, Lee....3:42:10 (7,061)
Bonifacio, Riccardo A....5:41:42 (31,480)
Bonner, Ian....5:15:18 (28,850)
Bonner, Mark L....5:37:00 (31,119)
Bonner, Matt C....4:12:32 (14,936)
Bonner, Neil....3:45:14 (7,736)
Bonnet, Daniel....3:59:26 (11,646)
Bonney, Kevin....5:37:26 (31,151)
Bonnor-Moris, Richard....3:58:46 (11,397)
Bonollo, Livio R....5:51:25 (32,243)
Bonora, Liam....5:14:40 (28,770)
Bonsall, Nicholas S....3:31:23 (5,112)
Bonson, Robert W....3:27:21 (4,344)
Bontoft, Alan....3:12:28 (2,262)
Bonwick, Peter....5:26:11 (30,056)
Boocock, Scott A....4:21:21 (17,259)
Booker, Matthew G....4:20:50 (17,133)
Booker, Paul....4:25:28 (18,386)
Boom, Gary....4:06:15 (13,346)
Boomer, Andrew M....4:22:39 (17,631)
Boon, Clive A....5:37:24 (31,150)
Boon, Cornelis P....3:38:37 (6,374)
Boon, Dominic R....3:46:37 (8,025)
Boon, Richard....4:24:21 (18,094)
Boon, Richard J....7:14:13 (34,355)
Boon, Robert....3:07:43 (1,753)
Boon, Robert L....4:18:08 (16,383)
Boora, Rajinder....5:07:09 (27,713)
Boorman, William....7:47:18 (34,502)
Booroff, Paul....5:19:45 (29,385)
Booth, Darren B....5:08:58 (27,965)
Booth, Jonathan....4:47:14 (23,967)
Booth, Mark....3:29:42 (4,819)
Booth, Roger....2:58:19 (981)
Booth, Simon M....4:26:49 (18,761)
Booth, Stephen G....2:54:07 (702)
Booth, Tom....3:24:40 (3,863)
Booth, Vincent A....2:53:37 (668)
Booth, William L....3:44:27 (7,543)
Boothroyd, Bobby....3:14:10 (2,494)
Boothroyd, Colin P....4:40:03 (22,193)
Booty, Graham....3:14:28 (2,541)
Bopp, James....4:55:43 (25,821)
Bord, Daniel....5:10:01 (28,147)
Bordas Lopez, Ricardo....3:21:16 (3,397)
Bordet, Marc....4:30:32 (19,758)
Bordiss, John....4:31:42 (20,082)
Boreham, Martin J....4:25:37 (18,416)
Borensztejn, Marc....4:02:08 (12,396)
Borg, Lewis....4:32:54 (20,401)
Borg, Thomas....4:00:20 (11,933)
Borgund, Ole J....4:02:57 (12,598)
Borkett, Keith M....4:15:12 (15,618)
Borland, David L....4:24:42 (18,194)
Borland, John A....5:21:01 (29,497)
Borley, Harry....4:37:32 (21,600)
Borman, Christopher D....4:21:55 (17,430)
Borner, Colin S....4:02:10 (12,409)
Borrer, Tristan....4:43:46 (23,113)
Borrett, Brian C....4:21:23 (17,270)
Borrett, James N....3:24:03 (3,785)
Borrett, Keith G....4:49:37 (24,507)
Borwell, Kevin....4:26:39 (18,706)
Borysko, Robert....4:53:53 (25,456)
Boscawen, William....4:06:25 (13,375)
Bosch, Ulf....3:06:57 (1,680)
Bosch Canas, Marc....4:46:47 (23,849)
Bosley, Philip M....4:22:30 (17,582)
Bosman, Andrew D....3:45:08 (7,713)
Bossi, Maurizio....4:50:13 (24,644)
Bosson, Paul J....2:52:45 (624)
Bostock, Marc....3:59:58 (11,842)
Bostock, Nigel B....2:58:35 (1,017)
Boston, Terence P....3:36:01 (5,885)
Bostrow, Anders....3:28:10 (4,502)
Boswell, Graham....3:23:33 (3,714)
Boswell, Guy M....3:23:20 (3,682)
Boswell, Robert J....5:50:56 (32,205)
Botella, Antoine....4:47:01 (23,915)
Botfield, Glyn J....4:21:33 (17,319)
Botfield, Howard T....8:09:45 (34,546)
Botnen, Tore....4:54:12 (25,519)
Bott, Ian W....4:12:31 (14,931)
Bottomley, Edward A....7:06:27 (34,278)
Bottomley, Ian J....4:02:53 (12,581)
Bottomley, Simon J....4:15:16 (15,632)
Bottomley, Steve....3:50:57 (9,036)
Boucher, Ian T....5:11:51 (28,391)
Boucher, Michael B....2:28:46 (53)
Boucher, Stuart C....4:54:51 (25,664)
Bouda, Christopher M....4:25:49 (18,487)
Bouet, Gilles....3:20:28 (3,289)
Boughton, Neil C....4:31:58 (20,164)
Boukeroui, Djamel....3:12:21 (2,251)
Bould, Paul G....4:02:15 (12,430)
Boulden, Lee D....4:00:52 (12,074)
Boulet, Pascal....2:56:18 (832)
Boulter, Neil....3:55:30 (10,343)
Boulting, Ned....3:45:47 (7,853)
Boulton, Christopher P....5:11:29 (28,331)
Boulton, Shane A....5:00:48 (26,761)
Boulton, Stewart R....4:28:59 (19,397)
Boumechka, Kabbour....5:04:53 (27,382)
Bouquet, Regis....3:08:54 (1,867)
Bourdarias, Clement....4:19:22 (16,718)
Bourde, Marc P....5:48:26 (32,006)
Bourgain, Christian....3:15:49 (2,730)
Bourgeay, Michel....4:13:26 (15,145)
Bourke, Adrian T....3:34:14 (5,580)
Bourke, Mark A....3:41:27 (6,924)
Bourke, Shaun....3:18:10 (3,005)
Bourke, Stephen J....3:17:58 (2,984)
Bourman, Charles D....4:32:59 (20,427)
Bourn, David J....4:15:11 (15,613)
Bourne, Alan L....5:13:33 (28,615)
Bourne, Gareth A....4:02:21 (12,460)
Bourne, Jonathan E....4:43:55 (23,156)
Bourne, Michael....3:51:17 (9,120)
Bourne, Paul....5:21:43 (29,581)
Bourne, Richard L....4:41:27 (22,546)
Bournes, Michael J....4:18:21 (16,446)
Bourse, Eric....4:19:57 (16,874)
Bousfield, Richard S....3:58:07 (11,151)
Bouvrot, Jean-Michel....4:48:11 (24,179)
Bouzahar, Yousef....3:49:02 (8,587)
Bovet, Jerome....6:10:53 (33,137)
Bowal, Paul....4:15:06 (15,600)
Bowcher, Adrian P....3:47:13 (8,161)
Bowden, Andrew....4:33:42 (20,635)
Bowden, George A....4:28:45 (19,327)
Bowden, John C....4:21:40 (17,364)
Bowden, John R....3:38:52 (6,423)
Bowden, Mathew G....4:34:08 (20,733)
Bowden, Peter J....4:39:49 (22,155)
Bowden, Simon....3:53:18 (9,661)
Bowder, Jonathan M....3:43:37 (7,370)
Bowell, Clive R....4:25:54 (18,509)
Bowen, Andy....3:17:05 (2,870)
Bowen, David C....4:53:20 (25,337)
Bowen, James K....2:56:31 (843)
Bowen, Matthew S....4:27:13 (18,880)
Bowen, Paul E....3:57:43 (11,023)
Bowen, Phillip....3:33:55 (5,534)
Bowen, Simon J....3:21:56 (3,479)

Bower, Andrew 3:29:49 (4,843)
Bower, Chris L 4:17:09 (16,140)
Bowers, Gerald I 5:13:55 (28,664)
Bowers, Jared P 5:00:38 (26,725)
Bowers, Stephen T 5:55:24 (32,493)
Bowes, Kevin 4:11:08 (14,581)
Bowes, Michael 4:45:19 (23,497)
Bowker, Richard 3:49:06 (8,601)
Bowles, Neil A 3:35:18 (5,756)
Bowles, Richard 6:06:01 (32,972)
Bowles, Rob G 3:57:18 (10,890)
Bowles, Stephen J 3:29:25 (4,766)
Bowley, Spencer J 4:37:43 (21,644)
Bowmaker, Jonathan J 5:17:25 (29,111)
Bowman, James 4:08:27 (13,895)
Bowman, John 5:29:25 (30,414)
Bown, Alistair E 4:49:24 (24,457)
Bown, Russell 5:15:05 (28,832)
Bowring, Hugh R 4:28:08 (19,142)
Bowring, Scyld 3:38:18 (6,318)
Bowser, Phillip R 4:36:11 (21,289)
Box, Adam J 3:45:11 (7,724)
Box, Christopher J 4:09:43 (14,233)
Boxall, Mark 4:10:08 (14,320)
Boxall-Hunt, Bruce 5:43:52 (31,639)
Boxford, Stephen H 5:19:24 (29,337)
Boxley, Keith W 4:01:06 (12,136)
Boxshall, Peter J 3:22:40 (3,596)
Boyall, Tim J 3:37:35 (6,180)
Boyce, John Christopher J 5:52:07 (32,296)
Boyce, Richard J 5:02:26 (27,031)
Boyce-Pendleton, Stuart 4:38:04 (21,729)
Boyd, Andrew B 4:51:54 (25,023)
Boyd, Billy 4:45:08 (23,444)
Boyd, Derek 4:42:11 (22,715)
Boyd, John Paul 4:25:58 (18,524)
Boyd, John S 4:57:28 (26,177)
Boyd, Steven P 3:48:36 (8,489)
Boyd, Timothy 3:57:41 (11,006)
Boyes, Andrew 3:24:24 (3,828)
Boyks, Gunter 4:36:52 (21,454)
Boyle, George M 4:13:25 (15,138)
Boyle, James 5:00:51 (26,773)
Boyle, Jay E 5:09:35 (28,068)
Boyle, Kelvin 6:34:37 (33,766)
Boyle, Matthew J 4:12:29 (14,928)
Boyle, Simon J 3:54:35 (10,065)
Boyles, Matthew G 4:29:26 (19,503)
Boyter, Gavin 3:17:44 (2,957)
Boza, Christian 2:51:43 (581)
Boza, Max 2:55:29 (777)
Bozzini, Luca 3:34:49 (5,669)
Bracchetti, Guido 3:19:28 (3,158)
Bracken, Michael 4:52:53 (25,247)
Brackley, Graham H 3:20:55 (3,343)
Brackstone, Robert L 4:21:35 (17,332)
Bradbury, Andrew P 4:36:06 (21,268)
Bradbury, Guy W 4:03:07 (12,635)
Bradbury, Miles A 4:07:07 (13,549)
Bradbury, Steven P 4:07:19 (13,599)
Braddy, Christopher A 5:27:39 (30,218)
Brades, Keith J 4:44:12 (23,229)
Bradfield, Ian N 3:47:20 (8,181)
Bradford, Chris J 4:05:43 (13,226)
Bradford, David 3:03:20 (1,406)
Bradford, Matt S 3:06:11 (1,616)
Brading, Neil T 3:59:34 (11,696)
Bradley, Alan 6:08:53 (33,078)
Bradley, Barry J 3:53:00 (9,572)
Bradley, David M 3:36:46 (6,005)
Bradley, Ian 3:59:04 (11,511)
Bradley, Ian 5:01:40 (26,906)
Bradley, Jack 3:59:10 (11,548)
Bradley, Jeremy R 3:59:04 (11,511)
Bradley, John T 3:49:34 (8,711)
Bradley, Julian 5:20:16 (29,435)
Bradley, Mark 3:32:01 (5,228)
Bradley, Mark 4:19:03 (16,639)
Bradley, Mark J 4:15:40 (15,739)
Bradley, Mark P 5:12:05 (28,417)
Bradley, Mark S 3:56:26 (10,605)
Bradley, Matthew J 4:14:26 (15,432)
Bradley, Philip A 3:05:55 (1,589)
Bradley, Richard J 4:14:36 (15,470)
Bradley, Robert J 4:27:27 (18,941)
Bradley, Roger D 4:51:53 (25,020)
Bradley, Scott 2:38:38 (178)
Bradley, Tony J 3:44:51 (7,642)
Bradley-Barnard, Harry 4:13:19 (15,122)
Bradnam, Stephen E 3:13:44 (2,426)
Bradshaw, Allan 5:46:18 (31,861)
Bradshaw, Ben 4:35:07 (21,016)
Bradshaw, Christopher A 3:29:52 (4,857)
Bradshaw, Eric G 4:26:06 (18,566)
Bradshaw, John L 4:21:01 (17,188)
Bradshaw, Mark A 5:06:26 (27,620)
Brady, Bryan T 4:23:06 (17,754)
Brady, Edward P 4:07:14 (13,586)
Brady, Harold J 6:19:23 (33,385)
Brady, John C 3:31:13 (5,082)
Brady, Luke 4:36:19 (21,328)
Brady, Luke 4:43:29 (23,044)
Brady, Richard 5:31:01 (30,569)
Brady, Scott M 4:09:14 (14,097)
Brady, Stephen W 4:03:29 (12,722)
Bragalli, Nicola 4:03:06 (12,629)
Braglewicz, Gresh Z 4:44:00 (23,180)
Braglewicz, Jan L 4:26:41 (18,716)
Braham, Barry J 4:31:51 (20,123)
Braidwood, Billy G 3:06:01 (1,597)
Brain, Douglas H 3:43:37 (7,370)
Brain, Robert E 4:14:40 (15,487)
Braithwaite, Daniel 4:32:51 (20,388)
Braithwaite, Henry R 5:18:41 (29,252)
Braithwaite, Lee A 3:58:34 (11,326)
Braley, Mark P 2:47:41 (409)
Bramall, Hugh A 3:43:29 (7,342)
Brambles, Neil 3:25:33 (4,020)
Bramley, Daryl M 5:15:03 (28,827)
Bramley, Neil J 5:26:48 (30,126)
Bramley, Stuart W 4:21:59 (17,449)
Bramley, Wayne 3:01:17 (1,259)
Brammer, Paul 5:13:40 (28,631)
Bramwell, Richard J 4:27:09 (18,858)
Branch, James 3:53:10 (9,629)
Branch, Stuart 3:33:30 (5,474)
Branciari, Federico 4:40:58 (22,425)
Brand, Joel D 3:02:33 (1,347)
Brand, Philip 4:30:35 (19,770)
Brandon, Daniel M 5:13:48 (28,648)
Brandon, Dean 4:05:52 (13,260)
Brandon, John 5:13:48 (28,648)
Brandt, Oliver 3:59:13 (11,568)
Brann, Richard J 4:39:51 (22,161)
Brannlaund, Ian N 4:38:13 (21,759)
Brant, Matthew 6:05:46 (32,965)
Brant, Raymond P 3:56:55 (10,768)
Brant, William M 3:36:57 (6,050)
Branton, Spencer C 3:58:47 (11,406)
Brassington, Jonathan C 3:53:57 (9,854)
Bratchell, Roger T 4:10:03 (14,305)
Bratt, Christopher J 3:20:32 (3,295)
Bratt, Stephen P 3:58:48 (11,416)
Braude, Jonathan H 5:52:11 (32,299)
Bravo, Ferdinand 4:31:58 (20,164)
Brawn, Glenn J 4:38:40 (21,871)
Bray, Barry 4:08:49 (13,993)
Bray, Matthew R 6:17:00 (33,323)
Bray, Michael A 4:43:23 (23,023)
Bray, Paul 5:13:45 (28,646)
Bray, Vivian F 3:51:07 (9,078)
Braybrook, Colin A 3:14:19 (2,521)
Braybrook, Mark H 4:52:26 (25,130)
Braybrook, Mark W 3:01:15 (1,257)
Braybrooke, Barry 4:02:00 (12,363)
Brayn, Warren P 4:56:34 (25,985)
Brayne, Christopher 4:01:42 (12,295)
Brazier, Ian P 4:14:03 (15,320)
Brazier, Paul N 4:12:45 (14,974)
Brazier, Russell 4:59:21 (26,538)
Brazier, Tony M 3:44:23 (7,530)
Breach, Steve D 3:38:46 (6,402)
Breadmore, Nigel D 3:38:57 (6,433)
Breagan, Steven D 4:32:35 (20,318)
Brearley, Michael 2:58:23 (992)
Brearley, Stephen 4:41:08 (22,472)
Brearley, Tom S 3:56:38 (10,674)
Breda, Errol 5:24:18 (29,838)
Breen, Christopher M 3:36:21 (5,938)
Breen, Derek 2:50:11 (517)
Breen, Ronan A 2:44:21 (306)
Breen, Sebastian 5:17:48 (29,155)
Brehaut, Matthew 3:45:16 (7,745)
Brehe, Michael 3:11:30 (2,150)
Brena, Pierino 5:11:56 (28,402)
Brench, Darren E 3:39:32 (6,545)
Brenkley, Stephen J 7:15:44 (34,371)
Brennan, Anthony 4:54:00 (25,485)
Brennan, Daniel 4:50:42 (24,766)
Brennan, James C 3:47:43 (8,282)

Brennan, Joe C 5:38:08 (31,199)

It started well in the sunshine, then, 4 miles in, my calf muscle 'popped'. I hobbled for the next 16 miles, it started to rain and I walked the last 6 miles in the wet and cold, managing to finish in 5hrs 38mins. Loved every minute of it and am doing it again in 2011!

Brennan, Michael J 4:16:33 (15,971)
Brennan, Peter J 4:19:15 (16,688)
Brenne, John 3:48:09 (8,391)
Brent, Charles J 2:57:20 (899)
Brent, Robert J 5:58:07 (32,644)
Brentnall, Matthew 3:47:55 (8,329)
Brereton, Christopher J 5:16:39 (29,013)
Brereton, Simon J 5:30:48 (30,553)
Bresler, Andrew E 4:47:36 (24,044)
Breslin, Darren 3:45:11 (7,724)
Breslin, John 3:33:52 (5,528)
Breslin, John A 3:22:23 (3,544)
Bresnahan, Danny 4:06:57 (13,504)
Bresnen, Stephen W 4:12:13 (14,864)
Bressamin, Emilio Giorgio 3:53:41 (9,764)
Bressington, Darrell C 3:48:28 (8,454)
Breteau, Michael 3:00:58 (1,240)
Brett, David 4:03:15 (12,670)
Brett, Stephen 3:35:57 (5,869)
Brett, Thomas R 4:47:10 (23,949)
Brew, Mark I 4:22:48 (17,668)
Brewer, Damian M 3:55:09 (10,251)
Brewer, Jeff 5:23:21 (29,731)
Brewer, John 3:59:54 (11,818)
Brewer, John R 3:28:10 (4,502)
Brewer, John S 4:34:10 (20,746)
Brewer, Julian A 3:37:01 (6,067)
Brewer, Nick D 3:57:18 (10,890)
Brewer, Richard J 3:56:35 (10,657)
Brewer, Roger G 4:25:29 (18,388)
Brewitt, Jonathan K 4:24:55 (18,245)
Brewster, Gary A 7:05:13 (34,264)
Brewster, Graham J 5:49:12 (32,067)
Brewster, Matthew J 4:37:47 (21,663)
Breydin, Patrick 5:17:32 (29,132)
Breze, Nathan J 4:03:30 (12,727)
Brichard, Jean-Noel 5:05:04 (27,412)
Brickle, Simon V 4:23:11 (17,778)
Bridge, John D 3:14:12 (2,498)
Bridge, Martin K 4:24:32 (18,155)
Bridgeland, Michael J 2:46:59 (386)
Bridger, Mark 5:05:35 (27,495)
Bridger, Michael J 3:21:33 (3,428)
Bridges, Anthony M 2:49:49 (501)
Bridges, Barry 3:56:34 (10,650)
Bridges, David 4:31:08 (19,919)
Bridges, Graham R 5:00:42 (26,737)
Bridges, Jason D 4:36:11 (21,289)
Bridges, Myles 4:25:54 (18,509)
Bridges, Paul T 4:37:15 (21,538)
Bridges, Russell T 3:18:00 (2,986)
Bridgewater, Keith 4:27:55 (19,071)
Bridgman, Lee 4:26:37 (18,700)
Bridgman, Lewis J 3:40:06 (6,656)
Bridgwater, Chris 5:07:22 (27,747)
Briere, Dominique 3:20:58 (3,357)
Briggs, Andrew J 5:38:48 (31,248)

Briggs, Eric 5:51:41 (32,266)
Briggs, Gareth 2:40:43 (209)
Briggs, Martin P 4:42:19 (22,758)
Briggs, Michael J 4:38:48 (21,912)
Briggs, Stephen W....5:03:44 (27,213)
Briggs, William 8:02:43 (34,534)
Bright, Andrew A 4:15:44 (15,763)
Bright, Nick 4:33:53 (20,680)
Bright, Simon J....4:08:53 (14,014)
Brighton, Mark....3:15:07 (2,643)
Brightwell, Simon L 3:01:35 (1,281)
Brillouet, Bernard....4:13:16 (15,105)
Brillouet, Franck 3:10:23 (2,028)
Brim, Christian....4:35:34 (21,122)
Brin, Wilfried....3:48:36 (8,489)
Brindle, Phill 3:43:47 (7,411)
Brindley, Gary E 4:43:40 (23,095)
Brine, Danny R....4:36:19 (21,328)
Brinkley, Paul A....4:42:06 (22,695)
Brinkman, Stephen....3:47:38 (8,263)
Brinton, Henry G....4:06:38 (13,436)
Brinton, Nicholas J....4:07:08 (13,553)
Briody, Ben B....3:48:16 (8,418)
Brisco, Douglas A....2:50:20 (523)
Briscoe, Noel A....3:38:05 (6,281)
Briscomb, Sean....3:40:13 (6,676)
Brisland, Ian M....3:59:58 (11,842)
Bristow, Rick E....4:17:26 (16,200)
Britt, Anthony J 4:52:53 (25,247)
Britt, Paul A....3:31:14 (5,087)
Brittain, James M....4:27:50 (19,033)
Brittain, Paul M 5:00:47 (26,756)
Brittain, Richard D....3:11:18 (2,127)
Britten, Bill 4:12:18 (14,885)
Britten, Richard 4:54:43 (25,627)
Britton, Ben J....5:09:24 (28,028)
Britton, Philip L 4:47:35 (24,038)
Brizziarelli, Dario 3:22:37 (3,588)
Broadbent, Clive G....5:23:12 (29,716)
Broadbent, David J....4:15:05 (15,594)
Broadbent, Richard A....7:06:15 (34,274)

Broadbent, Steven S....4:28:06 (19,130)

2010 saw the completion of my 21st consecutive London Marathon. One of my more memorable years was 2008 when I raised £4,500 for Cancer Care running from Land's End to London. A marathon a day for 14 days. After running London I cycled 900 miles to John O'Groats via Britain's 3 highest peaks.

Broadhead, Andrew R 5:04:27 (27,316)
Broadhurst, Jeff M....4:20:34 (17,050)
Brobin, James M....4:48:25 (24,227)
Brock, Barry O 3:22:24 (3,549)
Brockett, Simon 4:06:46 (13,466)
Brockington, Martin J....5:16:23 (28,979)
Brocklehurst, Christopher....4:07:10 (13,568)
Brocklehurst, Christopher J 3:15:48 (2,729)
Brocklesby, Keith A 4:14:34 (15,464)
Broderick, Derek....5:19:09 (29,309)
Broderick, Steven J....5:23:55 (29,794)
Brodie, Mark C....3:42:59 (7,233)
Brodie, Nick P 4:59:36 (26,574)
Brodie, Steve J 3:53:42 (9,771)
Brodrick, James A 4:16:34 (15,975)
Brodrick, Michael D....4:27:03 (18,828)
Brodziak, Andy....2:50:56 (550)
Brogden, Adam J....4:26:46 (18,745)
Brogden, Richard....3:59:41 (11,746)
Brolly, Chris 3:39:44 (6,582)
Brolly, Sean....4:29:32 (19,524)
Bromilow, Phillip....4:20:45 (17,103)
Bromley, Alec E 4:38:08 (21,747)
Bromley, Mark....4:05:42 (13,222)
Bromley, Nigel G....4:13:52 (15,266)
Bromwich, Steven F 4:34:38 (20,855)
Bromwich, Stuart J 4:15:43 (15,752)
Brook, Ashley 3:16:10 (2,770)
Brook, Daniel C....4:21:41 (17,368)
Brook, David J 3:54:57 (10,179)
Brook, Matt J 3:55:31 (10,346)
Brook, Matthew R 4:42:25 (22,784)
Brook, Peter 4:02:25 (12,479)
Brook, Simon G....3:43:56 (7,446)
Brooke, Craig D 3:26:39 (4,218)
Brooke, David....4:15:19 (15,642)
Brooke, Martin....3:50:03 (8,834)
Brooker, Martin....5:20:25 (29,456)
Brooker, Nick 4:58:35 (26,395)
Brookes, Andrew W 4:06:42 (13,451)
Brookes, Malcolm J....4:06:43 (13,455)
Brookes, Mark....4:56:49 (26,029)
Brookes, Nick A....4:30:02 (19,643)
Brookes, Paul A....4:22:35 (17,611)
Brookes, Richard A 3:44:32 (7,558)
Brookes, Stuart A 5:51:31 (32,250)
Brookes, Tim 4:07:37 (13,677)
Brooking, Gary A 4:23:24 (17,838)
Brooking, Paul J 3:10:21 (2,022)
Brookner, Luke 3:42:32 (7,142)
Brooks, Adrian 4:45:34 (23,551)
Brooks, Adrian C....4:23:59 (17,987)
Brooks, Alec....4:55:26 (25,770)
Brooks, Alex D 2:40:33 (206)
Brooks, Anthony D....5:50:43 (32,190)
Brooks, Arthur J 4:11:20 (14,632)
Brooks, Ashley....4:01:14 (12,170)
Brooks, Barry....5:59:45 (32,728)
Brooks, Cameron M....2:57:40 (917)
Brooks, Charles V....5:58:01 (32,632)
Brooks, Christopher....4:21:25 (17,284)
Brooks, David J 3:35:02 (5,708)
Brooks, Graham L....4:53:44 (25,422)
Brooks, Graham L....5:55:05 (32,468)
Brooks, Michael G....4:02:58 (12,602)
Brooks, Paul J 3:57:52 (11,079)
Brooks, Paul K....3:38:23 (6,336)
Brooks, Paul N....3:36:09 (5,907)
Brooks, Paul S 3:51:21 (9,141)
Brooks, Paul T....3:51:01 (9,052)
Brooks, Richard D....3:44:59 (7,676)
Brooks, Steve J 3:40:23 (6,711)
Brooks, Steve J 4:23:58 (17,981)
Brooks, Stuart....5:32:03 (30,667)
Broom, Tim J....4:33:19 (20,516)
Broomberg, Jonathan 4:04:21 (12,905)
Broome, Craig A 5:53:16 (32,356)
Broomhead, Adam....4:18:40 (16,546)
Brosnan, Reece 6:20:51 (33,421)
Broster, Richard 4:02:53 (12,581)
Broster, Richard B....4:29:54 (19,606)
Brotherhood, Alan....5:27:51 (30,246)
Brotherton, Anthony C....4:45:15 (23,481)

Brouet Philippe, Philippe....4:30:52 (19,855)
Brough, Dickon M 2:41:18 (228)
Brough, Jon R....3:11:38 (2,166)
Broughton, Alan 2:59:14 (1,090)
Broughton, Bob C....6:03:42 (32,876)
Broughton, Richard A 5:11:26 (28,323)
Broughton, Richard F....6:13:04 (33,213)
Browett, Rupert....4:13:12 (15,081)
Brown, Aaron Rhys 6:25:23 (33,559)
Brown, Aidan T 2:57:55 (938)
Brown, Ainsley P 5:44:31 (31,723)
Brown, Alan....4:03:43 (12,771)
Brown, Alasdair 3:43:52 (7,430)
Brown, Andrew C....4:48:11 (24,179)
Brown, Andrew D....5:56:12 (32,537)
Brown, Andrew J 4:31:58 (20,164)
Brown, Andrew M 3:54:00 (9,873)
Brown, Anthony S 5:47:11 (31,926)
Brown, Benjamin T....4:24:14 (18,063)
Brown, Bruce M 4:28:42 (19,313)
Brown, Chris....3:52:51 (9,522)
Brown, Chris....5:43:53 (31,660)
Brown, Chris G....5:21:19 (29,538)
Brown, Christopher 3:50:49 (9,009)
Brown, Christopher D 4:21:38 (17,350)
Brown, Christopher S 4:26:32 (18,673)
Brown, Colin J 4:48:50 (24,328)
Brown, Dan J 4:20:37 (17,068)
Brown, Daniel....4:43:05 (22,954)
Brown, Daniel P 4:30:51 (19,850)
Brown, Daren 4:03:38 (12,755)
Brown, Darren....4:14:14 (15,377)
Brown, Dave 4:39:03 (21,988)
Brown, David....3:55:33 (10,354)
Brown, David....4:31:07 (19,915)
Brown, David....5:46:37 (31,886)
Brown, David A 4:50:00 (24,604)
Brown, David P....4:13:54 (15,279)
Brown, David R 4:48:00 (24,148)
Brown, Derek 2:36:06 (134)
Brown, Derek 3:57:41 (11,006)
Brown, Dexter R....4:58:58 (26,468)
Brown, Dominic A....3:47:03 (8,122)
Brown, Elliot C 4:10:16 (14,356)
Brown, Francis H 4:37:28 (21,588)
Brown, Gary....4:28:01 (19,103)
Brown, Gary....4:32:33 (20,314)
Brown, Gavin J....3:32:03 (5,234)
Brown, Geoff M....4:28:39 (19,302)
Brown, Geoffrey C....5:10:15 (28,183)
Brown, Glenn A....4:47:19 (23,989)
Brown, Gordon 3:43:19 (7,311)
Brown, Graham....4:14:40 (15,487)
Brown, Gregor....4:07:26 (13,625)
Brown, Henry....3:44:56 (7,665)
Brown, Hugh....4:12:57 (15,017)
Brown, Iain 4:33:12 (20,482)
Brown, Ian 3:26:18 (4,154)
Brown, Ian S 4:40:40 (22,341)
Brown, James F....5:38:00 (31,193)
Brown, James H....3:10:24 (2,030)
Brown, Jason....5:29:32 (30,426)
Brown, John J 3:23:12 (3,663)
Brown, John P 3:45:19 (7,761)
Brown, Justin G 4:41:41 (22,613)
Brown, Kale W....4:15:30 (15,704)
Brown, Keith....3:37:27 (6,159)
Brown, Keith A 3:54:38 (10,082)
Brown, Kevin 3:22:23 (3,544)
Brown, Kevin 6:47:25 (34,029)
Brown, Kevin A....3:03:45 (1,435)
Brown, Lloyd J....5:24:35 (29,867)
Brown, Martin 3:46:26 (7,988)
Brown, Matthew C....4:25:16 (18,330)
Brown, Matthew F 3:33:28 (5,467)
Brown, Matthew P 4:20:35 (17,055)
Brown, Matthew S 3:57:45 (11,039)
Brown, Matthew T....4:20:29 (17,020)
Brown, Michael 5:12:20 (28,439)
Brown, Mick 6:17:08 (33,324)
Brown, Neil W....4:29:48 (19,588)
Brown, Owen....3:46:52 (8,074)
Brown, Paul D 4:07:09 (13,563)

Brown, Paul R 4:13:16 (15,105)
Brown, Peter 5:00:08 (26,659)
Brown, Peter D 4:24:36 (18,170)
Brown, Peter M 4:54:06 (25,497)
Brown, Peter N 5:39:01 (31,263)
Brown, Ray 3:54:29 (10,022)
Brown, Raymond P 3:42:58 (7,227)
Brown, Richard E 4:49:43 (24,537)
Brown, Richard I 3:42:26 (7,124)
Brown, Robert 4:37:39 (21,630)
Brown, Robert J 3:18:16 (3,012)
Brown, Robert J 3:29:50 (4,847)
Brown, Robert L 3:39:31 (6,540)
Brown, Robert P 4:21:50 (17,411)
Brown, Robert S 3:55:48 (10,437)
Brown, Roger 3:40:12 (6,673)
Brown, Roger J 4:40:54 (22,402)
Brown, Rory 3:09:11 (1,906)
Brown, Roy V 4:03:19 (12,683)
Brown, Russell M 3:59:26 (11,646)
Brown, Scott A 4:38:16 (21,770)
Brown, Simon A 4:55:39 (25,814)
Brown, Simon D 3:57:33 (10,969)
Brown, Simon J 4:54:06 (25,497)
Brown, Simon W 4:03:59 (12,827)
Brown, Stephen 6:12:58 (33,209)
Brown, Stephen J 3:49:01 (8,585)
Brown, Steven R 4:41:36 (22,581)
Brown, Stuart 4:56:02 (25,881)
Brown, Stuart C 3:29:21 (4,751)
Brown, Stuart R 3:26:40 (4,224)
Brown, Timothy D 3:33:39 (5,495)
Brown, Timothy D 5:16:03 (28,943)
Brown, Tom E 3:37:47 (6,212)
Brown, Tony 4:22:32 (17,594)
Brown, Tony A 3:31:58 (5,217)
Brown, Urel S 4:38:43 (21,890)
Brown, Will 4:04:45 (12,994)
Brown, William 8:21:00 (34,559)
Brown, Alexander Snr 4:35:09 (21,020)
Browne, Arthur J 4:22:21 (17,531)
Browne, Christopher 4:08:06 (13,789)
Browne, Dean L 4:25:18 (18,341)
Browne, Derek S 7:53:49 (34,519)
Browne, James A 4:03:43 (12,771)
Browne, Justin P 4:37:35 (21,613)
Browne, Martin 3:27:24 (4,349)
Browne, Martin L 3:43:37 (7,370)
Browne, Patrick N 3:35:23 (5,772)
Browne, Simon M 4:40:32 (22,316)
Brownhill, Jason 3:50:53 (9,023)
Browning, Allen J 5:30:17 (30,506)
Browning, David C 4:33:33 (20,591)
Brownsdon, James E 5:11:56 (28,402)
Brownsword, Christopher 3:59:04 (11,511)
Bruce, Alan C 4:29:13 (19,455)
Bruce, Alec D 4:38:17 (21,775)
Bruce, Andrew J 4:18:29 (16,491)
Bruce, David 4:37:45 (21,652)
Bruce, Dugald A 4:34:49 (20,908)
Bruce, John 4:44:21 (23,265)
Bruce, John A 4:23:27 (17,856)
Bruce, Jonathan P 4:46:25 (23,762)
Bruce, Robert 4:19:30 (16,757)
Bruce, Thomas 4:10:14 (14,349)
Brueckiner, Bernd 4:15:47 (15,780)
Bruene, Matthias H 5:09:13 (27,999)
Bruford, Edward C 4:19:40 (16,804)
Bruinaars, Bartholomeus 4:40:15 (22,245)
Brun, Christian 4:20:40 (17,084)
Bruna, Nelson M 3:30:23 (4,950)
Brunjes, Andrew J 3:52:55 (9,544)
Brunker, Niall H 3:55:32 (10,350)
Brunning, James J 2:48:09 (428)
Brunning, Nigel P 3:54:55 (10,170)
Bruno, David C 3:43:21 (7,317)
Bruns, Emil 4:20:46 (17,112)
Brunskill, Andrew W 4:46:41 (23,823)
Brunskill, Kevin 3:54:54 (10,160)
Brunt, Ybo G 4:18:21 (16,446)
Brunyee, John S 3:52:31 (9,437)
Brush, Paul 4:48:25 (24,227)
Bruskin, Alexander 2:46:11 (366)

Bryan, Adrian C 3:27:48 (4,421)
Bryan, Bobby 4:11:04 (14,563)
Bryan, Gordon C 5:48:16 (31,994)
Bryan, Jerry S 3:03:54 (1,442)
Bryan, John B 6:59:44 (34,205)
Bryan, Nigel 2:59:41 (1,139)
Bryan, Paul T 3:31:56 (5,208)
Bryan, Timothy A 4:54:55 (25,676)
Bryant, Alexander B 5:04:58 (27,394)
Bryant, Ben L 4:41:00 (22,437)
Bryant, Chris 3:35:58 (5,875)
Bryant, Darren S 4:59:29 (26,561)
Bryant, John 5:50:37 (32,180)
Bryant, John W 5:15:26 (28,872)
Bryant, Jonathan P 3:58:16 (11,203)
Bryant, Oliver R 3:57:08 (10,847)
Bryant, Richard J 3:54:33 (10,052)
Bryant, Robert J 4:17:23 (16,186)
Bryant, Stewart R 3:14:38 (2,575)
Bryant, William G 5:15:26 (28,872)
Bryars, Richard 3:00:48 (1,225)
Bryce, Alastair K 4:06:37 (13,433)
Bryning, John D 3:47:33 (8,235)
Bryson, Kenneth M 3:18:46 (3,072)
Bubb, Nick J 4:25:29 (18,388)
Buchan, Andrew 3:08:01 (1,793)
Buchan, David S 3:26:47 (4,246)
Buchan, Steven 3:42:47 (7,194)
Buchanan, Andrew 3:52:13 (9,363)
Buchanan, Ben J 4:34:40 (20,865)
Buchanan, James B 5:42:04 (31,503)
Buchanan, Mark K 3:41:20 (6,902)
Bucher, Eckhard W 4:59:39 (26,584)
Buck, Andrew 3:04:14 (1,470)
Buck, Christopher G 5:02:08 (26,977)
Buck, David 4:07:09 (13,563)
Buck, Derek C 5:31:23 (30,601)
Buck, Paul 5:02:11 (26,985)
Buck, Samuel R 4:10:11 (14,335)
Bucken Ham, Lindsay A 4:41:39 (22,598)
Buckett, Les 4:50:30 (24,715)
Buckham, Paul 3:06:17 (1,624)
Buckingham, Andrew P 4:38:41 (21,880)
Buckingham, Graham L 3:29:16 (4,730)
Buckingham, Richard 3:56:41 (10,684)
Buckland, Adam S 3:54:36 (10,071)
Buckland, Andrew M 4:59:36 (26,574)
Buckland, Paul 3:56:31 (10,629)
Buckland, Trevor 5:58:21 (32,658)
Buckle, David 4:22:45 (17,659)
Buckle, Jim 3:37:56 (6,246)
Buckle, Michael G 3:53:47 (9,800)
Buckle, Stephen 4:34:33 (20,834)
Buckley, Andrew G 3:56:04 (10,507)
Buckley, Brian W 3:16:40 (2,831)
Buckley, Carlo G 4:06:29 (13,395)
Buckley, Colin 3:38:40 (6,382)
Buckley, Dean 4:37:40 (21,634)
Buckley, Mark 4:35:26 (21,094)
Buckley, Matthew 5:00:36 (26,718)
Buckley, Peter J 3:45:16 (7,745)
Buckley, Robert P 3:57:36 (10,977)
Buckley, Ronnie 5:15:19 (28,855)
Buckley, Stephen M 5:50:09 (32,142)
Buckley, Terence P 5:29:49 (30,459)
Buckman, Richard J 3:59:23 (11,626)
Bucknall, Clive 3:46:26 (7,988)
Bucknall, David E 3:27:26 (4,357)
Buckner, Jason D 4:56:41 (26,001)
Buckney, Edward W 3:26:32 (4,191)
Budd, Michael J 4:48:42 (24,290)
Budden, Craig D 6:51:09 (34,093)
Budge, Keith J 5:17:19 (29,098)
Budge, Kurt R 3:54:46 (10,118)
Budge, Paul 4:36:47 (21,437)

LONDON MARATHON

Buehl, Matthias 3:29:34 (4,792)
Buehrs, Ralf 4:15:26 (15,684)
Buenrostro, Ernesto 3:50:35 (8,949)
Buffham, Peter E 5:33:55 (30,826)
Buffoni, Marco 3:47:47 (8,293)
Bufton, Daniel 4:01:17 (12,178)
Bufton, Richard J 3:43:11 (7,283)
Bugby, Antony R 5:28:54 (30,366)
Bugden, Robin 3:15:02 (2,635)
Buggy, Michael W 5:47:20 (31,934)
Buglass, Thomas 6:42:14 (33,914)
Buick, Jason 4:30:31 (19,749)
Buick, Jim 4:59:09 (26,500)
Buisson, Stephane 4:03:22 (12,689)
Bulaitis, Peter A 3:37:55 (6,242)
Bulgarelli, Giovanni 4:51:17 (24,898)
Bulgin, Bruce G 5:02:42 (27,064)
Bull, Andrew 5:19:30 (29,354)
Bull, Christopher A 5:04:40 (27,352)
Bull, Ian P 4:10:37 (14,440)
Bull, Jonathan C 4:01:22 (12,202)
Bull, Martin J 4:59:56 (26,622)
Bull, Martyn G 7:17:35 (34,380)
Bull, Ross 7:41:10 (34,485)
Bull, Steve R 4:05:33 (13,189)
Bullard, Nicholas M 3:20:27 (3,286)
Bullas, Julian E 4:36:50 (21,449)
Bullen, Colin R 4:04:08 (12,852)
Bullen, Matt P 3:57:32 (10,964)
Bullen, Timothy F 6:38:22 (33,854)
Buller, Anthony T 5:24:47 (29,885)
Bulley, David A 3:11:54 (2,198)
Bulley, Jason 3:36:49 (6,024)
Bullimore, Simon 4:34:27 (20,811)
Bullivant, Paul 4:24:09 (18,033)
Bullock, Dan R 4:43:41 (23,098)
Bullock, David G 3:42:58 (7,227)
Bullock, Paul D 5:07:13 (27,722)
Bullock, Peter S 3:51:02 (9,058)
Bullock, Richard S 3:15:30 (2,701)
Bullock, Terry 3:00:53 (1,231)
Bulmer, Ian S 4:34:35 (20,839)
Bulmer, Kevin 4:28:11 (19,164)
Bulmer, Richard 4:00:06 (11,876)
Bulst, Sebastian S 3:45:48 (7,858)
Bult, Robert A 4:37:52 (21,688)
Bultz, Peter 5:04:46 (27,367)
Bumfrey, Stephen 6:14:45 (33,263)
Bumstead, Stephen S 4:24:07 (18,023)
Bunbury, Anthony 3:50:35 (8,949)
Bunday, Simon P 4:14:19 (15,401)
Bundy, Philip 4:40:14 (22,242)
Bungay, Graham C 2:49:50 (502)
Bungay, Matt 6:01:45 (32,812)
Bungey, St John J 4:35:25 (21,088)
Bunker, Brian C 5:57:20 (32,596)
Bunn, Peter L 3:25:46 (4,065)
Bunn, Richard 3:40:32 (6,740)
Bunn, Sean R 3:27:53 (4,436)
Bunn, Tim M 3:59:16 (11,585)
Bunner, Colin 3:10:53 (2,086)
Bunnett, Graham R 3:26:23 (4,171)
Bunning, Richard 5:02:26 (27,031)
Bunston, Michael J 3:19:27 (3,154)
Bunting, Daniel J 4:50:00 (24,604)
Bunting, Gary 4:32:30 (20,300)
Bunting, Simon J 4:16:32 (15,969)
Bunting, William C 5:28:13 (30,296)
Bunyan, David M 4:08:39 (13,955)
Bunyan, Robert G 3:33:37 (5,493)
Bunyard, Nicholas 3:24:17 (3,815)
Bura, John D 5:33:28 (30,783)
Burbidge, Joshua R 3:46:15 (7,940)
Burbidge, Wayne 5:59:30 (32,716)
Burborough, Peter F 3:35:15 (5,747)
Burch, Dean R 4:54:26 (25,569)
Burch, Robert 5:47:00 (31,908)
Burchall, Nicholas P 4:12:34 (14,944)
Burchell, Neil R 4:35:06 (21,011)
Burchett, Rainer H 4:12:23 (14,904)
Burchill, Peter M 3:59:17 (11,590)
Burchnall, Nicholas 3:09:09 (1,901)
Burden, Andrew R 5:00:06 (26,654)

Burden, Keith M 3:15:59 (2,753)
Burden, Phil R.....................4:19:13 (16,680)
Burden, Simon D 3:27:43 (4,402)
Burden, Steven J...................3:29:51 (4,849)
Burdett, David G 3:56:01 (10,498)
Burdett, John W 5:58:04 (32,636)
Burdon, Brian 4:46:48 (23,854)
Burdon, David 5:20:06 (29,418)
Burfoot, Peter D..................3:22:53 (3,622)
Burge, Edward R 5:04:29 (27,326)
Burger, Adam J 3:54:29 (10,022)
Burger, Carl M....................5:58:45 (32,685)
Burger, Primarius 4:08:01 (13,774)
Burger, Theuns M 4:09:58 (14,291)
Burgess, Andrew R 4:13:20 (15,126)
Burgess, David J..................4:07:30 (13,640)
Burgess, David P..................6:25:28 (33,561)
Burgess, Dean 4:05:11 (13,093)
Burgess, Graham T 4:07:57 (13,765)
Burgess, John F 4:10:31 (14,415)
Burgess, Justin 4:19:41 (16,811)
Burgess, Ken 3:13:06 (2,346)
Burgess, Lee J 3:48:59 (8,576)
Burgess, Michael 4:27:51 (19,040)
Burgess, Michael B..............3:09:01 (1,885)
Burgess, Michael J...............3:36:54 (6,038)
Burgess, Paul 4:05:54 (13,266)
Burgess, Phil 4:32:46 (20,367)
Burgess, Rae J 4:09:51 (14,262)
Burgess, Simon 3:13:40 (2,416)
Burgess, Stephen J 5:23:20 (29,730)
Burgess, Timothy J 4:43:50 (23,132)
Burghgraef, Hielke 3:48:24 (8,440)
Burgin, Brian 3:27:41 (4,395)
Burgon, Andy P 5:00:51 (26,773)
Burgoyne, Chris 2:58:03 (954)
Burgoyne, Robert S.............4:29:37 (19,544)
Burke, Darren M 4:54:58 (25,694)
Burke, David 3:00:54 (1,235)
Burke, Dermot M 3:31:30 (5,127)
Burke, Des 4:55:50 (25,842)
Burke, Geoffrey P 4:07:56 (13,762)
Burke, Iain A 4:20:38 (17,074)
Burke, James......................5:28:40 (30,341)
Burke, James M 4:23:22 (17,835)
Burke, Jonjo 3:40:58 (6,819)
Burke, Kevin 3:20:51 (3,336)
Burke, Martin J 3:38:34 (6,365)
Burke, Michael 5:08:07 (27,834)
Burke, Neil 3:33:48 (5,518)
Burke, Peter D 3:09:26 (1,934)
Burke, Steve 4:04:57 (13,038)
Burke, Terence J 3:53:43 (9,775)
Burkinshaw, John 4:45:45 (23,606)
Burks, Michael P 4:13:44 (15,233)
Burlace, Paul 5:13:48 (28,648)
Burlats, Eric 4:06:57 (13,504)
Burleigh, Philip J................3:13:39 (2,413)
Burley, David A 5:06:55 (27,687)
Burley, Matthew G 4:00:55 (12,086)
Burley, Simon 4:52:37 (25,174)
Burliston, Paul 4:34:56 (20,949)
Burman, James E 4:14:23 (15,418)
Burman, Justin P 3:49:15 (8,644)
Burmeister, Daniel P 3:37:28 (6,167)
Burn, Steven 4:13:07 (15,067)
Burne, Richard....................3:45:00 (7,681)
Burnett, Allan R 4:19:53 (16,855)
Burnett, Christopher 4:10:52 (14,514)
Burnett, Joe 3:26:54 (4,261)
Burnett, Thomas S 4:27:01 (18,818)
Burnham, John C..................4:32:31 (20,307)
Burnham, Paul S 4:13:39 (15,203)
Burningham, Leo J 3:18:54 (3,086)
Burniston, Mark 3:59:08 (11,540)
Burns, Ben 4:42:48 (22,877)
Burns, Christopher M 4:52:06 (25,064)
Burns, Craig.......................4:34:55 (20,940)
Burns, Craig D 4:01:47 (12,313)
Burns, Daniel 3:52:47 (9,499)
Burns, Francis 5:21:03 (29,501)
Burns, Garry 4:20:16 (16,966)
Burns, John F 4:15:23 (15,663)

Burns, Lee R......................4:13:14 (15,096)
Burns, Phillip W 3:32:16 (5,271)
Burns, Robert E...................3:58:17 (11,208)
Burns, Robert J....................3:32:06 (5,245)

Burns, Simon J 4:15:58 (15,828)

My seventh London Marathon and the wettest.
Even worse for my little fan club: my wife Denise,
Mum and Dad, Joan and Jim who got soaked
cheering me on. My favourite part of the course is
Embankment. Running down that long road in the
final few miles with thousands of people screaming
at you to keep going is just so emotional. Turning
right at Westminster Bridge, through Parliament
Square into Birdcage Walk and the final mile and
the tears of pain and joy flow freely down my face.
Pass Buckingham Palace, one final turn into The
Mall, I can see the red tarmac and up ahead the
finish line. Hands held aloft as I step over the line.
I've done it, I've finished. What an achievement.

Burnside, William 3:42:43 (7,175)
Burr, Christopher P.............4:02:09 (12,404)
Burr, William J 4:38:50 (21,924)
Burrage, Adam S 5:05:20 (27,446)
Burreddu, Andrea................2:58:46 (1,037)
Burrell, Stuart M 3:57:39 (10,995)
Burridge, John E 4:33:03 (20,442)
Burridge, Michael J.............5:59:02 (32,696)
Burridge, Paul 4:16:49 (16,041)
Burrill, Thomas I................4:07:25 (13,618)
Burrluck, Andrew G............4:23:35 (17,890)
Burrows, Alan D 3:31:38 (5,158)
Burrows, Andrew 4:37:34 (21,606)
Burrows, Christopher P 5:18:52 (29,273)
Burrows, James E................4:02:35 (12,511)
Burrows, Jonathan M 5:29:14 (30,401)
Burrows, Richard E..............3:43:58 (7,452)
Burrows, Simon G 4:22:34 (17,601)
Burrows, Steve P 3:40:02 (6,646)
Burslem, Paul 2:59:59 (1,166)
Burt, Alistair J 4:39:17 (22,043)
Burt, Daniel R 3:56:39 (10,677)
Burt, Nicholas J 3:23:55 (3,767)
Burt, Sam R 4:00:56 (12,096)
Burt, Stephen R 6:56:00 (34,166)
Burton, Adrian 4:17:37 (16,255)
Burton, Andrew 4:23:45 (17,929)
Burton, Andrew J 3:30:32 (4,978)
Burton, Daniel 4:13:03 (15,050)
Burton, Daniel P 4:40:59 (22,431)

Burton, David......................4:02:22 (12,469)
Burton, David......................4:12:15 (14,873)
Burton, Gareth C.................4:28:44 (19,321)
Burton, Gareth J..................4:20:51 (17,138)
Burton, Gavin M.................3:26:18 (4,154)
Burton, Grahame D 4:33:04 (20,448)
Burton, James D 4:38:58 (21,967)
Burton, John.......................3:07:18 (1,711)
Burton, John L 3:29:30 (4,782)
Burton, John R 4:27:48 (19,022)
Burton, Jon A 3:58:37 (11,341)
Burton, Kenny 5:39:59 (31,333)
Burton, Kevin J 3:49:14 (8,637)
Burton, Mark C 4:37:18 (21,550)
Burton, Paul A 3:35:43 (5,834)
Burton, Paul M 3:58:45 (11,389)
Burton, Philip M 4:41:16 (22,501)
Burton, Richard A................4:39:09 (22,018)
Burton, Shaun S 3:56:41 (10,684)
Burton, Stuart N 2:34:34 (107)
Burton, Tim D 3:18:09 (3,002)
Burvill, Richard J.................3:52:06 (9,337)
Bury, Robert D 3:45:10 (7,719)
Busbridge, Kerry 6:42:36 (33,928)
Busby, Michael J 4:42:23 (22,770)
Busch, Graham 3:24:45 (3,878)
Bush, Daniel A....................3:56:46 (10,714)
Bush, James 4:33:45 (20,649)
Bush, Mark A 3:06:20 (1,631)
Bush, Nigel L 3:44:36 (7,577)
Bush, William G 5:17:03 (29,068)
Bushby, Ray 3:16:01 (2,755)
Bushell, David 4:00:31 (11,978)
Busk, Cris 3:56:31 (10,629)
Buss, Anthony R 5:54:40 (32,437)
Bussey, Steven C 4:19:13 (16,680)
Bustard, James.....................5:33:03 (30,754)
Buswell, Andrew W 4:59:52 (26,613)
Buswell, Andy M 3:23:25 (3,694)
Butcher, Alan R 4:42:49 (22,880)
Butcher, Alexander 6:58:52 (34,195)
Butcher, Antony 5:21:37 (29,571)
Butcher, Darryl...................4:56:56 (26,063)
Butcher, Duncan E 5:28:11 (30,290)
Butcher, Gary 2:50:24 (531)
Butcher, Geoffrey C 3:28:02 (4,467)
Butcher, James....................3:29:37 (4,803)
Butcher, Jeremy J 3:39:56 (6,623)
Butcher, Philip J..................4:17:59 (16,343)
Butland, Jonathan................4:36:47 (21,437)
Butler, Adam 4:52:13 (25,084)
Butler, Adrian W 3:29:04 (4,682)
Butler, Alan J 2:51:17 (563)
Butler, Andrew J 2:55:10 (760)
Butler, Andrew P 4:06:22 (13,366)
Butler, Bruce C 3:54:29 (10,022)
Butler, Chris 2:46:16 (370)
Butler, Daniel 5:51:33 (32,256)
Butler, David G 5:13:12 (28,571)
Butler, James T 4:48:32 (24,258)
Butler, Jeffrey.....................2:58:50 (1,045)
Butler, Mark 4:01:00 (12,112)
Butler, Matthew 3:40:25 (6,723)
Butler, Matthew P 4:30:25 (19,724)
Butler, Michael D 4:34:59 (20,974)
Butler, Nigel J 4:11:02 (14,551)
Butler, Paul A 4:02:54 (12,585)
Butler, Phil M 5:41:34 (31,471)
Butler, Philip A 6:52:16 (34,117)
Butler, Rob A 3:27:47 (4,416)
Butler, Robert A 3:09:18 (1,918)
Butler, Ross S 3:45:23 (7,769)
Butler, Steven 4:15:26 (15,684)
Butler, Steven C 3:43:20 (7,315)
Butt, Nadeem 3:49:40 (8,736)
Butterfield, Robert...............3:50:27 (8,920)
Butterlin, Marc B 4:14:44 (15,502)
Butters, Mark A 5:05:35 (27,495)
Butters, Martin A 5:23:24 (29,734)
Butterworth, Thomas F.........4:21:22 (17,261)
Button, Thomas A.................3:24:24 (3,828)
Button, Tim 3:52:37 (9,461)
Butwell, Darren M 4:01:09 (12,148)

Buxton, David H 4:03:35 (12,742)
Buxton, Kevin 2:48:00 (422)
Buxton, Thomas Y 3:33:17 (5,436)
Bycroft, Colin R 5:15:32 (28,885)
Bye, Alan F 3:33:54 (5,532)
Bye, Benjamin G 4:35:04 (20,998)
Bye, David E 4:23:27 (17,856)
Byerley, Andrew L 3:14:38 (2,575)
Byers, Martin J 4:13:18 (15,116)
Byers, Richard J 3:07:09 (1,694)
Byfield, Andrew E 4:00:41 (12,029)
Byford, Graham A 3:34:48 (5,664)
Byford, Marc A 4:23:59 (17,987)
Bygrave, Stephen J 3:44:47 (7,631)
Byhurst, Stuart 4:39:05 (21,999)
Byran, Johan N 4:37:06 (21,506)
Byrne, Anthony W 4:51:08 (24,868)
Byrne, Brendan 4:53:33 (25,387)
Byrne, Carl P 5:48:24 (32,002)
Byrne, Damien 4:42:50 (22,884)
Byrne, David A 2:47:28 (401)
Byrne, Mark J 2:56:37 (850)
Byrne, Philip 3:38:09 (6,296)
Byrne, Robert 4:24:14 (18,063)
Byrnes, Edward M 4:40:11 (22,235)
Byrom, Christopher E 4:58:57 (26,466)
Byrom, Matthew W 3:16:06 (2,766)
Byron, Tim 4:28:45 (19,327)
Bywater, Andrew W 3:33:35 (5,486)
Bywater, Charles E 4:42:42 (22,851)
Bywater, Craig M 4:37:09 (21,514)
Byworth, first name unknown 3:39:20 (6,503)
Caba, Marcel 3:57:23 (10,919)
Cabeca, Nuno J 3:39:48 (6,597)
Cabiran, Alain 3:16:17 (2,785)
Cable, Paul A 3:37:59 (6,260)
Cable, Stephen D 3:41:22 (6,911)
Cable, Stephen J 2:53:43 (676)
Cabrera, Francisco 3:49:11 (8,622)
Cadbury, Rupert J 3:55:06 (10,233)
Caddy, Andy 4:19:24 (16,723)
Caddy, Dave J 2:43:46 (285)
Cade, Jason J 4:44:26 (23,283)
Cadman, Richard J 4:02:19 (12,450)
Cadogan, Paul D 3:45:15 (7,741)
Cadogan, Tom 3:31:24 (5,116)
Cadwallader, Roger 5:03:48 (27,225)
Cafferkey, Stephen 4:26:35 (18,690)
Caffrey, Steve 3:40:11 (6,669)
Cahill, Adam E 4:23:21 (17,831)
Cahill, Michael L 4:53:30 (25,376)
Cahill, Richard L 4:19:18 (16,704)
Cahill, Shane D 4:55:04 (25,711)
Cahill, Stephen C 5:28:05 (30,276)
Cahn, Nicholas T 4:26:50 (18,765)
Cailloux, Olivier 4:01:17 (12,178)
Cain, Paul D 3:52:47 (9,499)
Cain, Peter M 4:19:16 (16,693)
Cain, Steve 5:39:50 (31,316)
Cairnie, Peter E 3:44:04 (7,465)
Cairns, Andrew W 4:51:15 (24,893)
Cairns, David 4:37:21 (21,560)
Cairns, Jarrod A 5:19:39 (29,380)
Cairns, Stuart R 3:31:14 (5,087)
Caironi, Davide P 4:26:06 (18,566)
Cake, Phil J 2:45:33 (351)
Calabrese, Danilo 3:42:43 (7,175)
Calcraft, Robert 3:47:10 (8,142)
Calcutt, Philip D 5:19:49 (29,390)
Caldarera, Roberto 3:49:40 (8,736)
Calder-Smith, Benjamin J 5:32:33 (30,704)
Caldo, Giuseppe 3:05:45 (1,577)
Caldwell, Barry 4:20:01 (16,890)
Calero, Angel 2:32:38 (93)
Caley, Lee P 4:34:24 (20,799)
Calicchia, Luciano 4:11:26 (14,656)
Callaghan, Adam T 4:31:14 (19,945)
Callaghan, Adrian 2:56:53 (864)
Callaghan, Harry 4:02:15 (12,430)
Callaghan, Mark 4:02:27 (12,488)
Callaghan, Matt 4:35:42 (21,168)
Callaghan, Paul 4:17:00 (16,095)
Callaghan, Peter E 3:20:56 (3,348)
Callan, Brian A 4:07:37 (13,677)
Callan, Mark J 3:49:08 (8,611)
Callanan, Denis B 4:43:18 (23,001)
Callanan, Kevin M 4:31:48 (20,103)
Callanan, Mike M 5:32:00 (30,662)
Callanan, Richard J 4:34:21 (20,785)
Callas, Didier 3:43:30 (7,345)
Callaway, Keith 5:14:02 (28,677)
Caller, John D 4:56:27 (25,957)
Caller, Mark J 5:10:17 (28,186)
Callesen, Jacob D 4:13:57 (15,286)
Callini, Franco 3:41:40 (6,961)
Callister, Ian D 5:00:55 (26,782)
Callow, Adam B 4:50:24 (24,684)
Callow, James S 3:36:10 (5,912)
Calmonson, Byron 3:41:23 (6,913)
Calnan, Thomas 3:28:21 (4,528)
Caltagirone, Antonio 4:42:07 (22,701)
Calthrop, Ben C 3:35:30 (5,791)
Calverley, Adam R 6:05:43 (32,963)
Calvert, John G 3:10:27 (2,035)
Calvert, Jonathan R 3:28:35 (4,574)
Calvert, Philip 4:33:40 (20,629)
Calvert-Jones, James P 3:22:32 (3,574)
Calves, Heberto J 4:01:36 (12,272)
Cameron, Andrew J 4:29:18 (19,472)
Cameron, Angus J 3:26:22 (4,169)
Cameron, John L 5:45:28 (31,801)
Cameron, Neil 4:37:05 (21,503)
Camfield, Bryan 2:53:20 (657)
Camley, Mark 4:36:31 (21,372)
Camm, Darryl 6:42:16 (33,916)
Camoccio, Tony 6:18:17 (33,363)
Camon, Gilles 4:02:33 (12,506)
Camp, Anthony 4:10:13 (14,340)
Camp, Paul 5:27:14 (30,168)
Camp, Paul J 4:04:19 (12,893)
Campanini, James 3:52:22 (9,401)
Campbell, Alex 4:09:54 (14,278)
Campbell, Andrew 3:58:59 (11,481)
Campbell, Andrew A 4:37:47 (21,663)
Campbell, Brian A 3:49:51 (8,786)
Campbell, Brian J 3:26:14 (4,142)
Campbell, Chris 4:19:16 (16,693)
Campbell, Daniel 4:20:46 (17,112)
Campbell, Donald J 3:20:13 (3,253)
Campbell, Ewan J 5:30:12 (30,498)
Campbell, Geoff 2:54:35 (723)
Campbell, Graeme T 3:58:48 (11,416)
Campbell, Hew D 5:17:03 (29,068)
Campbell, Iain A 3:33:14 (5,426)
Campbell, Ian P 3:08:58 (1,878)
Campbell, James D 3:33:40 (5,501)
Campbell, James P 4:00:35 (11,998)
Campbell, Kenneth O 4:04:21 (12,905)
Campbell, Khalil 4:44:34 (23,313)
Campbell, Lee J 4:07:07 (13,549)
Campbell, Logan J 3:26:28 (4,182)
Campbell, Mark F 4:00:03 (11,863)
Campbell, Martin 4:20:06 (16,913)
Campbell, Nathan J 3:08:56 (1,869)
Campbell, Niall 3:52:52 (9,526)
Campbell, Niall 4:52:28 (25,136)
Campbell, Robert K 3:11:09 (2,110)
Campbell, Rory G 4:02:38 (12,530)
Campbell, Stephen D 3:59:34 (11,696)
Campion, James P 3:44:50 (7,639)
Campion, Mark A 2:49:23 (483)
Campion, Stephen 3:12:28 (2,262)
Campione, Francesco 4:51:54 (25,023)
Campolmi, Giovanni 3:25:59 (4,103)
Campos, Leonardo T 3:05:37 (1,562)
Canacott, John A 4:09:27 (14,156)
Cander, Raymond M 4:20:08 (16,920)
Candrea, Simion 3:55:51 (10,452)
Candy, Martyn J 4:26:08 (18,571)
Candy, Steven 4:27:09 (18,858)
Cane, Oliver 4:00:48 (12,056)
Cane, Peter S 3:53:05 (9,602)
Canenti, Roberto 4:26:21 (18,621)
Caney, David O 4:16:39 (15,997)
Canham, Paul A 3:19:08 (3,112)
Canham, Ray D 4:06:32 (13,412)
Cann, Andrew 4:23:20 (17,825)
Cann, Gary J 4:24:19 (18,084)
Cann, Stephen P 5:57:36 (32,609)
Cann, Stuart W 5:55:08 (32,471)
Cannell, Mark 4:13:01 (15,037)
Canning, Mark 4:09:29 (14,165)
Canning, Peter I 4:21:12 (17,225)
Canning, Robert 4:58:01 (26,284)
Canning, Terence 4:39:01 (21,975)
Cannon, Alan J 5:27:20 (30,184)
Cannon, Eoin F 3:37:31 (6,174)
Cannon, Gary 4:11:25 (14,650)
Cannon, James 3:50:49 (9,009)
Cannon, John 4:41:47 (22,628)
Cannon, Peter 4:10:37 (14,440)
Cannon, Russell G 3:10:53 (2,086)
Canobbio, Giuseppe 3:10:06 (1,998)
Canonica, Gianni 4:07:56 (13,762)
Cansfield, Christopher C 6:02:03 (32,823)
Cansfield, Nicholas 5:28:16 (30,301)
Cant, Chris W 4:38:17 (21,775)
Capelin-Jones, Kevin S 4:45:07 (23,438)
Capell, Geoff 4:39:55 (22,170)
Capell, Marcus A 5:11:58 (28,405)
Caplen, Stephen G 3:40:55 (6,807)
Caplice, Jason A 4:35:38 (21,148)
Capogrosso, Sergio 3:47:36 (8,251)
Capon, Ian H 5:44:19 (31,698)
Capon, Malcolm K 4:25:09 (18,306)
Capp, Ross M 3:58:52 (11,444)
Capper, Christopher D 3:55:53 (10,462)
Capper, Colin G 4:08:26 (13,890)
Capper, Paul A 5:18:11 (29,196)
Capponi, Massimo 5:16:24 (28,981)
Capps, Chris S 4:09:01 (14,045)
Cappuccio, Peter 3:50:20 (8,897)
Carabott, Francis A 4:28:31 (19,268)
Carameli, Alfredo 4:22:08 (17,476)
Carbery, Stephen J 4:22:06 (17,471)
Carcasona Garcia, Alfonso 3:42:06 (7,049)
Cardani, David J 3:34:56 (5,691)
Cardew, James 3:33:44 (5,512)
Cardon, Daniel M 4:50:15 (24,656)
Carelli, Alessandro 3:19:31 (3,167)
Carelsen, Lukas 4:57:42 (26,230)
Carey, John P 4:53:25 (25,354)
Carey, Ken 4:18:59 (16,620)
Carey, Kevin 3:57:26 (10,939)
Carfrae, Peter 4:38:04 (21,729)
Cargill, David S 6:44:37 (33,969)
Carleysmith, William G 3:54:53 (10,150)
Carlile, Nicholas D 4:23:37 (17,897)
Carlin, Hugh 4:34:43 (20,883)
Carlin, Paul G 4:24:58 (18,256)
Carlock, Cuauhtemoc 3:55:00 (10,195)
Carlotti, Sandro 3:42:20 (7,100)
Carlson, David 4:59:22 (26,540)
Carlsson, Leif G 3:37:21 (6,130)
Carlucci, Sergio 3:26:53 (4,259)
Carmichael, Jeremy R 3:25:21 (3,988)
Carmody, Paul R 3:30:45 (5,012)
Carnan, Paul B 4:14:24 (15,424)
Carnelley, Lee S 4:25:58 (18,524)
Carnet, Michel 5:57:02 (32,582)
Carol, Riel 3:54:47 (10,121)
Carolan, Patrick J 3:08:34 (1,843)
Carolan, Thomas J 4:12:24 (14,907)
Carpenter, Christopher J 5:12:51 (28,525)
Carpenter, Clive T 4:47:29 (24,020)
Carpenter, Colin B 5:47:07 (31,917)
Carpenter, Gareth K 3:55:02 (10,210)
Carpenter, Julien 3:58:43 (11,382)
Carpenter, Lee M 5:25:16 (29,959)
Carpenter, Michael 4:45:14 (23,473)
Carpenter, Nicholas J 5:01:34 (26,883)
Carpenter, William T 4:29:48 (19,588)
Carr, Barry J 5:01:03 (26,806)
Carr, Billy J 4:31:33 (20,039)
Carr, Graham E 4:30:27 (19,735)
Carr, Malcolm A 5:23:35 (29,756)
Carr, Martin G 4:19:49 (16,838)
Carr, Matthew J 3:43:34 (7,357)
Carr, Matthew J 4:20:32 (17,040)

Carr, Mike J	4:07:16 (13,591)	Cartwright, Spencer	4:45:47 (23,617)	Cave, Merfyn	4:14:44 (15,502)
Carr, Paul	4:24:40 (18,186)	Cartwright, Stephen	3:59:55 (11,825)	Cavender, Paul	4:50:55 (24,826)
Carr, Philip J	4:48:00 (24,148)	Carty, Damien N	5:24:11 (29,826)	Cavero, Felipe	5:16:13 (28,961)
Carr, Phillip	3:25:28 (4,007)	Carver, John	3:31:31 (5,135)	Cawkwell, Andrew A	5:25:01 (29,915)
Carr, Robert	3:12:18 (2,248)	Cary, Nicolas G	4:03:43 (12,771)	Cawood, Kevin R	4:43:13 (22,985)
Carr, Ronan	4:45:46 (23,611)	Caryesford, Christopher	4:10:46 (14,485)	Cawston, Derek	5:29:06 (30,387)
Carr, Toby J	4:24:17 (18,077)	Casarini, Lauro	4:50:46 (24,787)	Cawte, Martin I	3:49:02 (8,587)
Carradice, Darren P	5:08:25 (27,879)	Casasbuenas, Juan	3:20:27 (3,286)	Cawthorne, Timothy J	4:15:52 (15,801)
Carrasco, Asier	3:16:27 (2,808)	Casasbuenas, Pablo	5:06:14 (27,588)	Cayre, Bruno	3:56:46 (10,714)
Carre, Christopher J	2:48:32 (449)	Casavant, Christian J	6:00:32 (32,761)	Cecil, Rupert	4:28:05 (19,125)
Carre, François C	3:33:36 (5,491)	Casburn, Nick	3:13:18 (2,373)	Cecilla Cervera, Javier	3:42:27 (7,130)
Carrea, Michael	3:41:05 (6,841)	Case, Benjamin M	4:34:02 (20,705)	Cederstrom, Jan B	3:38:10 (6,298)
Carrere, Dominique	3:39:12 (6,473)	Caselton, John D	4:56:05 (25,889)	Celestine, Glen K	3:47:59 (8,345)
Carrier, Gary	5:31:53 (30,645)	Casey, Dan J	4:19:40 (16,804)	Cerre, Marco	3:37:37 (6,189)
Carrigy, John F	4:50:29 (24,708)	Casey, David J	4:11:37 (14,706)	Cerullo, Italo	4:48:49 (24,324)
Carrington, Alex G	3:42:04 (7,042)	Casey, John M	5:54:09 (32,415)	Cerullo, Mario	4:46:14 (23,723)
Carrington, Guy M	4:20:55 (17,157)	Casey, Michael A	3:56:52 (10,749)	Cha, Bruce Y	3:53:39 (9,755)
Carrington, James A	4:13:18 (15,116)	Casey, Michael G	5:23:17 (29,724)	Chaban, Taras	4:10:26 (14,395)
Carrodus, Paul S	4:04:27 (12,919)	Casey, Michael P	3:25:02 (3,937)	Chabrelie, Pierre L	3:14:34 (2,563)
Carroll, Alan T	5:42:50 (31,559)	Casey, Stephen C	4:38:26 (21,811)	Chabrol, Jean	5:34:57 (30,934)
Carroll, Bernard J	4:25:44 (18,456)	Cash, Adam J	3:23:50 (3,745)	Chadwick, Ben	3:53:35 (9,737)
Carroll, Daniel	4:48:27 (24,238)	Cash, Danny	5:17:32 (29,132)	Chadwick, Ben	4:18:58 (16,618)
Carroll, Mark M	4:02:24 (12,476)	Cash, Ian	3:59:20 (11,610)	Chadwick, Jeffrey M	2:52:51 (634)
Carroll, Michael J	2:23:30 (28)	Cash, Lee	4:53:13 (25,318)	Chaffe, Gary A	4:33:51 (20,671)
Carroll, Michael J	4:25:24 (18,367)	Cashman, Gerard P	5:36:02 (31,035)	Chaffer, Peter	3:01:18 (1,263)
Carroll, Patrick	6:02:23 (32,829)	Cashmore, Paul C	4:03:09 (12,641)	Chaffey, Martin D	4:07:41 (13,694)
Carroll, Paul	4:04:32 (12,937)	Casidy, Declan A	3:25:49 (4,070)	Chahal, Manjinder S	4:40:20 (22,269)
Carroll, Raymond L	4:57:24 (26,166)	Cason, Christopher J	3:37:10 (6,096)	Chahid, Basidi	3:45:42 (7,836)
Carroll, Sean	4:04:22 (12,909)	Cass, John E	4:43:01 (22,933)	Chalencon, François	3:35:47 (5,841)
Carroll, Sean M	4:00:33 (11,987)	Cass, Jonathan L	3:28:57 (4,657)	Chalk, David R	5:01:29 (26,868)
Carroll, Steven D	4:22:56 (17,710)	Cassanelli, Andrea	3:55:52 (5,858)	Chalk, Jason A	3:33:10 (5,413)
Carroll, Stuart P	3:00:26 (1,198)	Casserley, Billy	2:55:35 (780)	Chalker, James	4:49:38 (24,514)
Carroll, Thomas W	3:39:10 (6,467)	Casserley, Robert W	3:08:08 (1,807)	Chalkley, Nicholas S	4:08:24 (13,882)
Carrott, Greg P	5:31:16 (30,593)	Casserley, Tom M	2:52:11 (602)	Challa, Aditya	5:11:11 (28,294)
Carruthers, Paul M	4:06:28 (13,390)	Cassidy, Anthony	5:09:38 (28,079)	Challis, Kevin D	3:38:02 (6,268)
Carsberg, Simon P	3:50:22 (8,907)	Cassidy, Declan M	4:36:52 (21,454)	Challis, Leigh J	4:10:41 (14,457)
Carson, Brian C	4:36:52 (21,454)	Cassidy, Dermot	4:56:53 (26,047)	Challis, Matthew P	4:43:52 (23,146)
Carson, Graham R	4:17:43 (16,284)	Cassidy, Frederick M	4:33:35 (20,601)	Challis, Paul D	6:28:48 (33,636)
Carson, Matthew M	5:43:36 (31,614)	Cassidy, Jonathan	3:54:15 (9,943)	Challis, Ross	5:51:00 (32,208)
Cartailler, Mathias	2:52:06 (598)	Cassidy, Robin P	4:18:25 (16,470)	Challis, Shaun W	3:30:40 (4,993)
Carter, Alexander W	3:40:51 (6,793)	Cassidy, Sean R	4:02:56 (12,592)	Chalmers, Alexander J	4:54:00 (25,485)
Carter, Alun J	3:20:05 (3,233)	Castaldo, Paul	3:33:34 (5,484)	Chalmers, Dave A	3:41:51 (7,001)
Carter, Andrew D	3:33:48 (5,518)	Caster, Brian W	4:21:58 (17,445)	Chalmers, Hugh A	3:40:49 (6,784)
Carter, Andrew S	2:56:13 (822)	Castille, Bernard	3:34:07 (5,567)	Chaloner, Andrew	6:27:13 (33,605)
Carter, Anthony L	4:25:13 (18,323)	Castle, John A	2:45:02 (334)	Chamberlain, Brian	4:15:18 (15,639)
Carter, Ben L	3:59:18 (11,595)	Castle, Kevin A	4:33:55 (20,686)	Chamberlain, Ed G	3:41:12 (6,873)
Carter, Colin R	5:01:59 (26,954)	Castle, Simon S	5:06:25 (27,617)	Chamberlain, James	5:23:34 (29,753)
Carter, Daren D	4:10:58 (14,537)	Castle, Toby A	3:24:18 (3,817)	Chamberlain, Jeremy N	3:48:30 (8,466)
Carter, Dave A	2:33:21 (99)	Castleman, James S	4:11:03 (14,559)	Chamberlain, Kevin C	4:24:01 (18,000)
Carter, Dominic J	4:58:26 (26,366)	Castricum, Nico	3:19:34 (3,172)	Chamberlain, Mark A	4:48:03 (24,159)
Carter, Graeme P	4:38:58 (21,967)	Castro Pardo, David	3:33:56 (5,539)	Chamberlain, Mark J	4:00:05 (11,873)
Carter, Graham S	3:26:10 (4,132)	Caswell, James W	3:39:17 (6,494)	Chamberlain, Michael D	3:09:32 (1,945)
Carter, Jake	4:38:41 (21,880)	Caswell, Jonathan M	4:42:27 (22,790)	Chamberlain, Roger B	5:40:14 (31,356)
Carter, John E	4:09:00 (14,041)	Catalano, Carlo	4:10:43 (14,467)	Chambers, Alan	3:46:37 (8,025)
Carter, Jonathan M	4:17:49 (16,311)	Catanach, David	3:51:52 (9,265)	Chambers, Andrew T	3:49:54 (8,800)
Carter, Keith A	3:45:22 (7,767)	Catchpole, Christopher R	3:19:05 (3,105)	Chambers, Carl A	3:48:32 (8,473)
Carter, Kevin P	5:05:06 (27,418)	Cater, James S	3:10:52 (2,084)	Chambers, Carl J	3:55:59 (10,488)
Carter, Mark	3:47:23 (8,193)	Catherall, Mark L	5:28:01 (30,268)	Chambers, David A	4:57:37 (26,213)
Carter, Michael	4:02:39 (12,533)	Catlett, Andrew C	4:11:23 (14,640)	Chambers, David P	3:30:09 (4,917)
Carter, Nic J	4:49:39 (24,521)	Catmull, Jeremy	3:14:13 (2,504)	Chambers, Guy	3:31:57 (5,215)
Carter, Paul J	3:03:24 (1,412)	Catmull, Julian A	2:58:29 (1,006)	Chambers, Jamie O	4:58:37 (26,403)
Carter, Paul J	5:12:38 (28,475)	Caton, Philip M	5:21:17 (29,534)	Chambers, Lindley	4:20:37 (17,068)
Carter, Peter E	3:28:48 (4,624)	Catt, Christopher	3:02:38 (1,355)	Chambers, Mark	3:44:15 (7,502)
Carter, Phil C	5:25:52 (30,016)	Catt, Edward R	4:21:33 (17,319)	Chambers, Mark B	4:04:36 (12,949)
Carter, Rob N	5:21:41 (29,577)	Cattaneo, Germano	3:17:51 (2,969)	Chambers, Richard E	4:29:47 (19,581)
Carter, Robin	6:44:18 (33,964)	Cattell, Michael J	6:56:04 (34,168)	Chambers, Vincent	6:40:11 (33,886)
Carter, Ross	5:40:45 (31,395)	Catterall, Paul G	4:06:30 (13,400)	Champion, David	3:21:58 (3,487)
Carter, Samuel J	3:20:44 (3,322)	Catterfeld, John	4:37:21 (21,560)	Champion, Mark S	2:56:05 (811)
Carter, Stephen	5:57:53 (32,625)	Cattermole, Glen A	5:43:14 (31,592)	Champion, Stuart M	3:42:33 (7,145)
Carter, Stephen J	4:16:40 (16,005)	Cattley, Paul S	4:28:54 (19,378)	Champlois, Jerome	3:08:52 (1,865)
Carter, Steven	5:10:20 (28,196)	Caulder, Graham A	3:24:24 (3,828)	Chan, Edmond	3:45:18 (7,755)
Carter, Tim R	4:27:26 (18,939)	Cauldwell, Matthew	3:49:54 (8,800)	Chan, Edmond	5:07:00 (27,694)
Carter, Tom M	4:12:14 (14,868)	Caulfield, Michael	4:49:59 (24,597)	Chan, Heego	4:06:25 (13,375)
Cartin, John J	3:18:01 (2,989)	Cauli, Andrea	3:58:20 (11,236)	Chan, Nicholas	4:00:02 (11,860)
Cartledge, Andrew J	6:44:38 (33,971)	Causey, Mark J	3:39:56 (6,623)	Chan, Peter G	2:45:27 (349)
Cartledge, Ben	3:13:15 (2,364)	Causton, Ian C	4:43:09 (22,971)	Chan, Tim P	4:27:46 (19,011)
Carton, Kenneth H	3:44:50 (7,639)	Cautick, Ravi M	4:59:09 (26,500)	Chana, Jaswant S	4:43:15 (22,994)
Cartwright, Alan R	5:28:11 (30,290)	Cavagnaro, Felipe	3:23:44 (3,734)	Chanagasubbay, Darren C	5:46:50 (31,901)
Cartwright, Benjamin N	3:54:56 (10,175)	Cavalli, Giorgio	4:28:43 (19,318)	Chancelier, Didier	4:44:16 (23,248)
Cartwright, Chris A	3:27:09 (4,304)	Cavallo, Carlo	3:26:02 (4,109)	Chandak, Akhil	4:35:24 (21,082)
Cartwright, Edward	3:55:47 (10,429)	Cavanagh, Martyn J	4:17:01 (16,100)	Chandarana, Neel	5:42:37 (31,537)
Cartwright, Edward A	3:30:58 (5,052)	Cavanagh, Sean A	4:07:36 (13,670)	Chandler, Karl G	3:09:01 (1,885)
Cartwright, Matthew W	4:24:33 (18,159)	Cavazza, Gianluca	4:23:09 (17,766)	Chandler, Michael J	4:53:50 (25,449)

Chandler, Paul....4:56:51 (26,036)
Chandler, Stephen J....4:27:23 (18,928)
Chandley, Paul J....4:07:36 (13,670)
Chandrasekhar, Prithviraj....5:35:47 (31,004)
Chanin, Jean-Marc....3:56:31 (10,629)
Chant, Ian R....3:00:58 (1,240)
Chantrey, Justin N....4:26:40 (18,712)
Chantry, Matthew C....4:53:26 (25,358)
Chaplin, Andrew J....4:50:40 (24,759)
Chaplin, David G....4:27:42 (18,997)
Chaplin, David I....2:57:56 (941)
Chaplin, Richard....3:40:23 (6,711)
Chapman, Andrew J....3:38:45 (6,401)
Chapman, Anthony C....4:51:25 (24,925)
Chapman, Barrie E....5:02:14 (26,997)
Chapman, Christopher....4:17:55 (16,329)
Chapman, David J....3:19:29 (3,165)
Chapman, David P....3:52:36 (9,454)
Chapman, Derek....5:13:36 (28,622)
Chapman, Gary D....4:53:33 (25,387)
Chapman, James....3:12:04 (2,218)
Chapman, John....3:03:09 (1,385)
Chapman, Karl J....3:54:41 (10,097)
Chapman, Kenneth J....4:31:42 (20,082)
Chapman, Mark....4:58:41 (26,417)
Chapman, Mark R....3:14:46 (2,600)
Chapman, Martyn T....4:28:22 (19,229)
Chapman, Neil W....3:49:25 (8,679)
Chapman, Nik....4:58:32 (26,380)
Chapman, Oliver V....3:30:49 (5,024)
Chapman, Paul....4:04:53 (13,019)
Chapman, Reg M....3:08:49 (1,857)
Chapman, Richard....3:31:13 (5,082)
Chapman, Scott....4:57:44 (26,234)
Chapman, Simon....4:28:48 (19,349)
Chapman, Simon F....3:27:34 (4,372)
Chapman, Simon N....5:04:14 (27,285)
Chapoulie, Philippe....4:13:20 (15,126)
Chappell, Darren R....3:15:41 (2,716)
Chappell, David R....5:46:14 (31,856)
Chappell, Jason C....3:22:28 (3,560)
Chapple, Andrew T....2:59:07 (1,075)
Chapple, Robin J....4:01:34 (12,259)
Chapple, Stephen D....3:19:41 (3,188)
Charalambous, Chris....4:54:19 (25,542)
Charaoui, Said....4:42:06 (22,695)
Chard, Ken R....3:11:00 (2,097)
Charles, Gregory G....3:06:24 (1,637)
Charles, Jonathan P....3:53:00 (9,572)
Charles, Lee M....4:48:57 (24,359)
Charles, Peter C....3:35:20 (5,760)
Charlesworth, John....3:57:05 (10,829)
Charlesworth, Martin....3:53:34 (9,732)
Charlesworth, Paul....3:12:59 (2,333)
Charleton, Barry....4:36:25 (21,352)
Charlton, Adam R....3:42:45 (7,185)
Charlton, Eamonn....4:07:42 (13,698)
Charlton, Karl....4:45:02 (23,417)
Charlton, Martin J....3:51:40 (9,220)
Charman, Dan....3:14:50 (2,612)
Charnley, Edward J....3:43:57 (7,449)
Charnley, Joe....3:11:59 (2,204)
Charnock, Graham H....4:09:15 (14,104)
Charnock, Nicholas S....4:10:42 (14,462)
Chart, Robert J....3:12:45 (2,295)
Charters, Paul W....3:58:03 (11,131)
Charvat, Franz....3:41:11 (6,866)
Chastel, Olivier....3:36:41 (5,995)
Chatburn, Dean P....4:13:42 (15,225)
Chater, Thomas P....3:31:46 (5,183)
Chatfield, Martin K....4:03:50 (12,794)
Chattell, Steven A....2:55:37 (783)
Chatterton, Richard S....3:50:48 (9,008)
Chaudhuri, Sanjit....6:21:06 (33,432)
Chauhan, Chetan S....4:44:14 (23,237)
Chavda, Dilip A....6:15:14 (33,273)
Chavez, Alvaro....3:27:56 (4,449)
Chaytor, Stephen....5:50:56 (32,205)
Chaytow, Ben K....3:34:03 (5,557)
Cheal, Ben J....3:11:53 (2,196)
Cheaveau, James....4:19:08 (16,663)
Cheaveau, Matthew E....4:10:54 (14,522)
Checchia, Frank....2:55:14 (765)
Checkley, Mark R....3:35:49 (5,850)
Chedd, Paul D....4:19:32 (16,768)
Chedzoy, Andrew....4:37:30 (21,592)
Cheek, Simon A....3:44:59 (7,676)
Cheema, Barinderjit S....6:16:42 (33,317)
Cheeseman, Ray D....4:38:47 (21,908)
Cheesman, Charles R....4:47:01 (23,915)
Cheesman, Clifford D....4:37:01 (21,490)
Cheesman, David A....6:17:53 (33,353)
Cheetham, Gregg E....5:12:40 (28,480)
Cheetham, Robert S....3:40:01 (6,641)
Cheetham, Ronnie A....4:20:53 (17,147)
Chell, Ian M....3:13:11 (2,357)
Chell, Matthew P....3:35:16 (5,752)
Chen, Lei....4:02:35 (12,511)
Chequer, Jonathan P....3:32:27 (5,309)
Cherix, Stephane....4:43:18 (23,001)
Cherqaoui, Nouredding....2:42:28 (254)
Cherry, Christopher S....4:57:08 (26,115)
Cherry, James G....4:01:25 (12,220)
Cherry, Jason....4:18:15 (16,413)
Cherry, Michael J....3:54:22 (9,978)
Cherry, Robert M....4:00:01 (11,857)
Cheshire, Geoffrey M....3:20:07 (3,236)
Chessis, Lewis A....5:00:34 (26,712)
Chester, Martin G....2:59:38 (1,133)
Chestney, Jon....3:03:49 (1,439)
Chesvassut, Timothy J....4:05:38 (13,206)
Chettle, Richard....4:45:16 (23,487)
Chetty, Devanand....4:04:14 (12,871)
Cheung, Dickie J....4:05:34 (13,193)
Cheung, Jonathan....4:30:09 (19,667)
Chevalier, Laurent A....4:51:12 (24,880)
Cheverton, James A....4:04:01 (12,838)
Chevin, Robert W....4:44:29 (23,297)
Chewter, David....5:03:16 (27,143)
Chiaramonte, Ivan....3:20:38 (3,310)
Chichester, Rory A....4:10:48 (14,492)
Chico, Ben P....4:24:17 (18,077)
Chidgey, Nigel J....4:16:44 (16,013)
Chidlow, Darren P....5:11:50 (28,390)
Chierico, Gilbert....4:20:42 (17,095)
Chilcott, Darren....3:52:49 (9,506)
Chilcott, Peter....4:59:45 (26,600)
Child, David A....2:42:26 (253)
Child, Nicholas P....5:21:24 (29,546)
Childerhouse, Paul....4:30:41 (19,795)
Childs, John....5:25:34 (29,993)
Childs, Matthew C....5:15:19 (28,855)
Childs, Paul A....3:18:00 (2,986)
Childs, Samuel J....3:39:02 (6,443)
Childs, Steven P....5:16:00 (28,936)
Chiles, Matthew....3:14:02 (2,470)
Chilton, Christopher J....3:17:28 (2,930)
Chilvers, Simon R....4:43:31 (23,054)
Chilvers, Steven R....4:15:21 (15,652)
Chinn, Rodney D....4:43:45 (23,111)
Chipeur, Gerald D....5:18:46 (29,261)
Chipot, Guy....3:49:28 (8,694)
Chippendale, Kevin R....4:34:34 (20,836)
Chisholm, Barry-John....3:19:46 (3,203)
Chisholm, Neil S....2:27:47 (48)
Chisholm, Paul R....3:42:03 (7,038)
Chislett, David W....3:21:45 (3,454)
Chislett, Nick C....3:07:39 (1,747)
Chittell, Christopher....5:05:12 (27,434)
Chittenden, Paul....4:17:40 (16,268)
Chittick, David G....4:55:28 (25,777)
Chitty, Bryan....3:51:13 (9,101)
Chitty, Gavyn D....5:14:01 (28,675)
Chivers, Greg....4:34:45 (20,891)
Chivers, John....7:19:43 (34,393)
Chivers, Richard....3:43:43 (7,391)
Chivers, Steven A....4:16:48 (16,038)
Chiweshenga, Aubrey T....4:16:57 (16,074)
Chmara, Edward Z....5:03:07 (27,119)
Chmielewski, Kevan J....4:18:19 (16,440)
Chong, Shao Foong....3:45:50 (7,867)
Chopra, Munish....6:47:01 (34,019)
Chorley, Martin....3:05:30 (1,553)
Chorlton, Matthew R....3:20:26 (3,282)
Choudhury, Mahdi N....4:01:41 (12,289)
Choules, David....3:17:11 (2,885)
Chow, Paul J....3:44:24 (7,534)
Chow, Richard J....4:47:50 (24,102)
Chowdhry, Mark T....4:17:24 (16,190)
Chowdhury, Mikail M....5:28:27 (30,317)
Chowdhury, Mudasser H....4:45:26 (23,524)
Christian, Darold....3:49:14 (8,637)
Christiansen, Lars....4:27:40 (18,990)
Christiansen, Oliver....4:27:56 (19,078)
Christie, David....3:59:35 (11,705)
Christie, Emlyn D....2:42:38 (257)
Christie, Liam C....6:19:15 (33,382)
Christie, Martin D....4:15:45 (15,768)
Christie, Sandy....3:14:48 (2,607)
Christie, Stephen J....4:08:25 (13,887)
Christmas, Richard A....4:13:18 (15,116)
Christopher, Laurent....3:33:10 (5,413)
Christopher, Rob J....4:22:15 (17,509)
Christopherson, Ian A....4:37:16 (21,539)
Christy, Mark....4:32:50 (20,383)
Chritchlow, Philip....2:32:30 (89)
Chrysostomou, Vasos....4:07:51 (13,730)
Chu, Justin....4:41:33 (22,565)
Chudasama, Vijay H....4:54:43 (25,627)
Chudzynski, Richard A....5:13:10 (28,564)
Chumbley, Matthew J....3:34:18 (5,588)
Church, Bryan T....3:58:25 (11,268)
Church, Colin W....3:56:50 (10,738)
Church, Gary A....3:34:53 (5,682)
Church, James S....4:26:50 (18,765)
Church, John W....3:50:08 (8,854)
Church, Leigh D....4:16:35 (15,980)
Church, William J....3:26:40 (4,224)
Churchard, Brian E....3:39:20 (6,503)
Churchard, Neil....4:30:50 (19,843)
Churcher, Greg D....4:52:30 (25,146)
Churchill, Adam....4:14:58 (15,548)
Churchill, Mark J....4:06:58 (13,508)
Churchill, Stephen J....5:54:53 (32,451)
Churchouse, John H....3:57:24 (10,928)
Churton, Mark A....3:44:19 (7,518)
Chuter, Charles S....3:21:22 (3,412)
Cilia, Charles....2:31:58 (85)
Cima, Edward....3:59:06 (11,527)
Cima, Keith H....4:02:29 (12,494)
Cimalley, Jason....4:45:08 (23,444)
Cincotta, Bernard....5:09:23 (28,026)
Cioci, Gaetano....3:36:13 (5,916)
Cioffi, Andrew....4:32:24 (20,268)
Clabby, Robert....5:18:40 (29,249)
Clack, Paul C....4:57:57 (26,271)
Clack, Paul R....4:02:31 (12,499)
Clacy, John....4:05:53 (13,262)
Claessens, Thomas A....3:22:56 (3,626)
Clague, Mark W....2:53:15 (652)
Clancy, Robert....3:43:48 (7,414)
Clapp, Matthew N....2:35:12 (113)
Clapton, Roland A....4:43:45 (23,111)
Clare, Simon J....5:14:16 (28,717)
Clarehugh, Mark....2:37:13 (150)
Claremont-Davies, Mathew P....4:30:51 (19,850)
Claret, Jacques....3:40:20 (6,695)
Claris, Clifton....3:34:26 (5,610)
Clark, Alan L....5:21:31 (29,558)
Clark, Alastair T....4:11:19 (14,631)
Clark, Alex G....3:56:22 (10,582)
Clark, Andrew M....5:30:25 (30,518)
Clark, Anthony....4:28:37 (19,296)
Clark, Antony A....4:45:57 (23,661)
Clark, Billy....3:13:48 (2,436)
Clark, Brent J....4:50:15 (24,656)
Clark, Daniel E....5:20:45 (29,479)
Clark, Darren A....3:48:29 (8,460)
Clark, Darren J....4:58:42 (26,420)
Clark, Darrin....4:40:16 (22,249)
Clark, David....5:45:14 (31,778)
Clark, David A....3:11:40 (2,170)
Clark, David G....4:19:30 (16,757)
Clark, David H....3:37:49 (6,219)
Clark, David R....4:40:59 (22,431)
Clark, David V....4:30:52 (19,855)
Clark, Derek J....3:24:24 (3,828)
Clark, Derek W....4:24:06 (18,019)
Clark, Duncan J....4:14:00 (15,302)

Clark, Frank H.	4:23:05 (17,750)	
Clark, Gareth C	4:27:06 (18,843)	
Clark, Geoffrey R	5:33:03 (30,754)	
Clark, Gordon D	4:14:37 (15,472)	
Clark, Graham S	3:07:43 (1,753)	
Clark, Jamie C	4:42:16 (22,746)	
Clark, Jason	4:19:05 (16,651)	
Clark, Jeffrey L	3:26:38 (4,213)	
Clark, John	2:44:35 (315)	
Clark, John	4:49:02 (24,381)	
Clark, Joseph T	3:12:40 (2,282)	
Clark, Lee J	4:08:39 (13,955)	
Clark, Lee J	4:58:02 (26,289)	
Clark, Liam	4:03:54 (12,804)	
Clark, Lloyd G	3:56:47 (10,724)	
Clark, Lorenzo B	4:06:39 (13,441)	
Clark, Mark D	3:43:04 (7,255)	
Clark, Martyn S	5:01:23 (26,858)	
Clark, Michael	3:39:09 (6,462)	
Clark, Neil E	4:31:05 (19,906)	
Clark, Niall D	4:03:32 (12,734)	
Clark, Oliver T	4:53:22 (25,344)	
Clark, Paul W	3:24:54 (3,909)	
Clark, Peter D	4:53:49 (25,446)	
Clark, Richard H	3:35:26 (5,783)	
Clark, Richard J	4:29:28 (19,513)	
Clark, Richard J	4:44:46 (23,358)	
Clark, Richard N	4:40:00 (22,183)	
Clark, Rob G	3:37:38 (6,191)	
Clark, Robert	4:11:27 (14,662)	
Clark, Robert G	7:31:15 (34,460)	
Clark, Rupert J	4:50:33 (24,733)	
Clark, Simon D	5:14:24 (28,732)	
Clark, Simon F	5:24:36 (29,868)	
Clark, Stephen	4:48:16 (24,196)	
Clark, Stephen A	4:18:04 (16,361)	
Clark, Steven V	3:40:06 (6,656)	
Clark, Stuart W	5:10:21 (28,198)	
Clark, Tim	5:23:13 (29,719)	
Clark, William	3:53:09 (9,620)	
Clarke, Adam	5:11:15 (28,301)	
Clarke, Andrew T	3:11:03 (2,101)	
Clarke, Chris	3:20:47 (3,329)	
Clarke, Christopher	3:56:51 (10,743)	
Clarke, Craig H	3:55:50 (10,446)	
Clarke, Dave A	3:59:03 (11,507)	
Clarke, David	3:13:41 (2,419)	
Clarke, David E	4:26:03 (18,552)	
Clarke, David L	3:55:01 (10,201)	
Clarke, Gary	4:18:34 (16,519)	
Clarke, Gary A	4:18:35 (16,526)	
Clarke, Gavin D	7:05:45 (34,271)	
Clarke, Harry	5:16:38 (29,011)	
Clarke, Ian J	3:39:16 (6,490)	
Clarke, James D	3:13:54 (2,453)	
Clarke, Jez	5:12:20 (28,439)	
Clarke, John	3:21:53 (3,470)	
Clarke, John B	5:23:31 (29,746)	
Clarke, John F	6:12:23 (33,181)	
Clarke, Jonathan J	3:46:40 (8,035)	
Clarke, Kenneth C	4:17:16 (16,166)	
Clarke, Kevin J	7:20:09 (34,397)	
Clarke, Michael D	5:24:07 (29,822)	
Clarke, Michael F	3:41:02 (6,834)	
Clarke, Michael J	6:42:27 (33,919)	
Clarke, Michael P	4:35:05 (21,005)	
Clarke, Michael W	5:55:01 (32,461)	
Clarke, Mick	3:41:10 (6,865)	
Clarke, Nick	3:56:37 (10,669)	
Clarke, Nigel	5:15:11 (28,843)	
Clarke, Patrick J	3:25:57 (4,099)	
Clarke, Phillip J	4:28:29 (19,256)	
Clarke, Piers	5:19:30 (29,354)	
Clarke, Richard A	3:22:52 (3,617)	
Clarke, Richard J	4:11:18 (14,626)	
Clarke, Robert	3:49:20 (8,659)	
Clarke, Robert	6:06:16 (32,995)	
Clarke, Robert M	6:18:00 (33,357)	
Clarke, Robert V	3:51:40 (9,220)	
Clarke, Ryan H	5:00:46 (26,755)	
Clarke, Samuel J	3:31:40 (5,161)	
Clarke, Shane J	4:12:35 (14,948)	
Clarke, Simon D	4:21:39 (17,357)	
Clarke, Simon O	4:37:18 (21,550)	
Clarke, Stephen	5:06:47 (27,664)	
Clarke, Stephen F	3:56:53 (10,756)	
Clarke, Stephen J	4:00:36 (12,004)	
Clarke, Stephen M	3:47:46 (8,289)	
Clarke, Steve	3:18:26 (3,036)	
Clarke, Stuart	4:19:55 (16,864)	
Clarke, Stuart R	4:51:09 (24,870)	
Clarke, Thomas	4:32:47 (20,372)	
Clarke, Tony J	4:05:20 (13,133)	
Clarke, Warren P	3:55:03 (10,216)	
Clarkson, Alan	3:08:57 (1,872)	
Clarkson, Graham	2:55:41 (786)	
Clarkson, Peter D	4:15:37 (15,734)	
Clarkson, Richard J	3:46:53 (8,078)	
Clarkson, Stuart M	5:09:31 (28,054)	
Classen, Carl A	3:27:37 (4,383)	
Clatworthy, Tim J	3:03:11 (1,390)	
Clausen, Jake	4:03:14 (12,665)	
Clavin, Neil G	4:11:48 (14,753)	
Clawson, Mark	3:40:20 (6,695)	
Clay, Andrew D	4:51:33 (24,947)	
Clay, Andrew J	4:43:14 (22,990)	
Clay, Brad	3:03:16 (1,398)	
Clay, Christopher	3:32:35 (5,330)	
Clay, Henry	3:37:21 (6,130)	
Clayden, Steven R	4:15:50 (15,792)	
Claydon, Andrew C	3:50:04 (8,837)	
Claydon, Matthew B	3:39:17 (6,494)	
Claydon, Nick F	6:09:56 (33,114)	
Clayton, Christopher J	4:15:28 (15,693)	
Clayton, Dan	4:26:48 (18,753)	
Clayton, Ian	5:43:11 (31,585)	
Clayton, James E	5:43:11 (31,585)	
Clayton, James S	5:29:43 (30,449)	
Clayton, Paul	4:33:57 (20,691)	
Clayton, Rob T	3:41:11 (6,866)	
Clayton, Robert	3:35:26 (5,783)	
Clayton, Robert J	4:21:38 (17,350)	
Clayton, Robin C	5:17:43 (29,142)	
Cleary, Christopher F	2:59:01 (1,061)	
Cleave, Richard J	3:57:31 (10,960)	
Cleaver, Jim	4:27:34 (18,967)	
Cleaver, Stephen P	4:27:12 (18,871)	
Clee, Adrian P	4:21:57 (17,442)	
Clegg, Kevin A	4:46:59 (23,904)	
Clegg, Mark	4:09:33 (14,188)	
Cleghorn, Douglas M	6:27:08 (33,603)	
Cleghorn, Shaun M	3:38:22 (6,334)	
Cleland, Jonathan B	3:57:06 (10,835)	
Clelland, Craig	3:14:06 (2,484)	
Clement, Paul	3:48:55 (8,559)	
Clemente, Nuno M	3:39:45 (6,591)	
Clements, Andrew C	3:27:29 (4,360)	
Clements, Andrew P	4:44:37 (23,330)	
Clements, Andrew P	5:14:58 (28,815)	
Clements, Edward G	3:01:11 (1,253)	
Clements, Graham	3:52:26 (9,421)	
Clements, Harry M	3:43:32 (7,350)	
Clements, Ian	4:04:55 (13,031)	
Clements, Martin	3:20:23 (3,276)	
Clements, Martin R	4:14:23 (15,418)	
Clements, Peter	3:57:37 (10,987)	
Clements, Stephen G	3:59:25 (11,639)	
Clements, Trevor W	3:12:22 (2,255)	
Clemo, Philip J	4:22:26 (17,560)	
Clemson, Mark	4:20:31 (17,032)	
Clemson, Matt	3:46:06 (7,905)	
Clerkin, Stephen J	3:35:48 (5,848)	
Cleveland, Kevin	5:25:55 (30,025)	
Cleveland, Trevor	3:23:59 (3,779)	
Cleverly, Joseph T	4:12:38 (14,954)	
Clews, Paul R	4:22:30 (17,582)	
Clews, William	3:08:18 (1,821)	
Clidas, John W	3:45:41 (7,831)	
Cliff, Simon	6:00:46 (32,767)	
Cliffe, Dan J	3:55:33 (10,354)	
Cliffe, James W	4:27:50 (19,033)	
Clifford, Alexander	4:56:06 (25,892)	
Clifford, John R	4:24:12 (18,050)	
Clifford, Robin P	2:51:39 (579)	
Clifford, Stephen	3:38:30 (6,359)	
Clifford, Stephen J	3:26:05 (4,119)	
Clift, Paul	3:37:44 (6,206)	
Clifton, Matthew J	3:42:11 (7,068)	
Clifton, Michael	3:29:32 (4,788)	
Clifton, Russell	3:46:24 (7,979)	
Clifton, Tony J	3:59:13 (11,568)	
Cline, Michael P	4:21:37 (17,341)	
Cline-Bailey, William	3:36:55 (6,041)	
Clinton, Barry J	5:52:32 (32,316)	
Clinton, Michael A	4:04:17 (12,882)	
Clinton, Peter	3:51:45 (9,238)	
Clissold, Cole	3:19:41 (3,188)	
Cloke, Simon J	4:24:57 (18,249)	
Cloney, Justin	3:54:15 (9,943)	
Clooney, Brendan	4:02:29 (12,494)	
Close, Ashley J	4:53:22 (25,344)	
Close, Geoffrey R	4:26:20 (18,619)	
Closs, Stephen G	3:30:10 (4,919)	
Clothier, Philip E	4:01:52 (12,329)	
Clough, Jeremy	4:19:25 (16,728)	
Clough, Robin D	3:28:01 (4,462)	
Clough, Stephen J	6:15:31 (33,278)	
Clough, Trevor	2:51:00 (552)	
Clout, David A	4:17:58 (16,338)	
Clow, Daniel D	3:59:58 (11,842)	
Clowes, Stuart G	4:06:53 (13,492)	
Clowser, James	4:04:49 (13,004)	
Clubb, Stuart A	4:58:40 (26,410)	
Clucas, Paul	4:22:44 (17,654)	
Cluness, Benjamin J	4:48:30 (24,252)	
Clusker, Dean	3:45:09 (7,715)	
Clutterbuck, Barnaby T	4:28:15 (19,191)	
Clutterbuck, Jason	4:13:58 (15,292)	
Clutterbuck, Richard	3:22:25 (3,553)	
Clutton, Andrew E	4:17:46 (16,298)	
Clyde, Ivor	5:45:59 (31,831)	
Clyne, Adam S	5:02:20 (27,009)	
Clyne, Jon R	4:19:35 (16,777)	
Clyne, Mark R	5:02:20 (27,009)	
Coady, James V	4:13:58 (15,292)	
Coady, Michael P	5:44:19 (31,698)	
Coaker, Stephen J	4:25:27 (18,382)	
Coales, David J	2:53:13 (651)	
Coates, Brian W	3:06:36 (1,644)	
Coates, Graeme J	4:29:49 (19,591)	
Coates, James A	3:09:40 (1,960)	
Coates, James D	3:41:24 (6,916)	
Coates, John	5:27:00 (30,144)	
Coates, John T	4:37:48 (21,671)	
Coates, Jonathon L	3:28:49 (4,629)	
Coates, Mark	3:08:53 (1,866)	
Coates, Martin A	4:23:18 (17,816)	
Coates, Martin R	4:03:01 (12,611)	
Coates, Stephen	6:23:56 (33,516)	
Cobb, James L	4:10:14 (14,349)	
Cobb, Mark C	3:55:21 (10,298)	
Cobb, Richard J	5:14:42 (28,775)	
Cobb, Robert J	4:13:30 (15,159)	
Cobbold, Alex J	3:42:40 (7,168)	
Cobbold, Ryan J	4:35:03 (20,996)	
Cobill, Sebastian C	3:32:11 (5,259)	
Cobley, Lee W	4:44:11 (23,224)	
Coche, Yves	3:44:46 (7,626)	
Cochran, Gary J	4:29:11 (19,447)	
Cochrane, Adam	5:44:20 (31,701)	
Cochrane, Jason I	3:58:10 (11,174)	
Cock, Darren	3:58:29 (11,295)	
Cock, Malcolm	3:38:21 (6,327)	
Cockbain, Richard I	2:54:47 (734)	
Cockbill, Brett	4:45:30 (23,539)	
Cocker, Paul A	3:43:54 (7,441)	
Cockerell, William	2:29:12 (59)	
Cockerill, Tobias	5:03:20 (27,160)	
Cocking, Sam	5:14:58 (28,815)	
Cockings, Rob C	3:04:16 (1,472)	
Cocklin, James	4:41:07 (22,467)	
Cocklin, John J	4:32:35 (20,318)	
Cocklin, Matthew	4:58:28 (26,371)	
Cockman, Bob P	5:56:10 (32,533)	
Cockram, Kevin J	3:39:47 (6,594)	
Cockrell, Nigel B	3:54:02 (9,882)	
Cocksedge, Mark J	3:31:54 (5,198)	
Cocksedge, Richard J	4:15:54 (15,807)	
Cockshott, Alex J	5:33:25 (30,781)	

Cockshott, David L....3:37:27 (6,159)
Cockshott, Richard....4:08:07 (13,801)
Codd, Peter J....5:25:13 (29,951)
Codgbrook, Richard M....3:50:15 (8,884)
Coe, Damian J....5:37:08 (31,125)
Coe, Richard A....3:40:50 (6,789)
Coe, Steven M....4:49:55 (24,583)
Coetzee, Deon C....3:11:53 (2,196)
Coffey, Paul J....6:02:57 (32,847)
Coffey, Scott R....4:23:31 (17,872)
Coffin, Malcolm F....4:53:12 (25,316)
Coggan, Ben D....4:18:52 (16,589)
Coggan, Thomas M....4:18:52 (16,589)
Coghill, Chris....3:39:32 (6,545)
Cogill, James H....3:44:23 (7,530)
Cohen, Adrian N....6:03:28 (32,863)
Cohen, David B....4:19:09 (16,667)
Cohen, Howard....3:19:20 (3,140)
Cohen, Ronald....5:01:22 (26,854)
Cohen, Stefan K....2:55:52 (800)
Cohen-Price, Daniel L....6:21:22 (33,439)
Cohring, John P....5:29:25 (30,414)
Coker, Ben M....4:35:17 (21,051)
Coker, Neil R....6:45:36 (33,993)
Colbert, Dave....3:34:26 (5,610)
Colbert, Desmond....2:59:37 (1,131)
Colbert, Stuart N....3:09:28 (1,938)
Colbourne, Steve I....3:00:14 (1,181)
Colby, Chris D....3:57:24 (10,928)
Colclough, Liam T....4:57:32 (26,194)
Colcough, David....6:39:56 (33,877)
Coldman, Tim R....3:33:42 (5,506)
Coldwell, Michael R....3:55:45 (10,422)
Coldwell, Steve....4:45:27 (23,529)
Cole, Alan....3:53:17 (9,657)
Cole, Andrew G....4:42:50 (22,884)
Cole, Andrew J....4:04:19 (12,893)
Cole, Brian....3:04:32 (1,487)
Cole, Brian....5:13:26 (28,602)
Cole, Jonathan D....3:21:28 (3,421)
Cole, Justin M....3:59:21 (11,613)
Cole, Michael G....3:55:21 (10,298)
Cole, Nathan J....4:00:51 (12,068)
Cole, Nicholas A....3:06:18 (1,626)
Cole, Paul....4:55:41 (25,817)
Cole, Paul....5:19:51 (29,396)
Cole, Paul T....3:57:30 (10,953)
Cole, Peter B....6:35:10 (33,774)
Cole, Ray J....2:51:46 (583)
Cole, Richard G....4:38:14 (21,762)
Cole, Stephen H....4:09:24 (14,141)
Cole, Stephen J....5:14:21 (28,729)
Cole, Terence J....4:23:15 (17,797)
Cole, Terry M....3:41:56 (7,015)
Colegate, Andrew....2:44:58 (329)
Colehan, Timothy E....4:25:16 (18,330)
Coleman, Adam B....4:51:14 (24,887)
Coleman, Fergus....3:19:19 (3,137)
Coleman, George E....5:16:31 (28,997)
Coleman, Glenn R....5:48:37 (32,022)
Coleman, Jamie C....3:57:27 (10,942)
Coleman, Jason E....4:52:43 (25,203)
Coleman, Martin R....4:49:10 (24,409)
Coleman, Michael....3:16:28 (2,810)
Coleman, Paul....4:22:05 (17,466)
Coleman, Paul....4:47:07 (23,935)
Coleman, Paul J....5:34:00 (30,836)
Coleman, Phillip M....4:58:40 (26,410)
Coleman, Richard S....4:22:59 (17,722)
Coleman, Stuart R....3:25:55 (4,091)
Coles, Barry J....4:46:32 (23,785)
Coles, Christian J....4:24:43 (18,199)
Coles, Christopher L....3:48:11 (8,395)
Coles, Clive A....4:05:19 (13,125)
Coles, George....4:06:46 (13,466)
Coles, Louis F....3:19:05 (3,105)
Coles, Michael....4:11:18 (14,626)
Coles, Nick J....3:52:37 (9,461)
Coles, Richard....4:23:37 (17,897)
Coles, Simon....5:18:55 (29,280)
Coles, Terence G....3:41:30 (6,940)
Coletti, Francesco....3:49:57 (8,814)
Coley, David H....5:18:12 (29,198)
Coley, Mark D....4:20:14 (16,957)
Colgate, Lee M....4:33:23 (20,537)
Colhoun, David R....3:33:30 (5,474)
Coll, Joe....5:01:11 (26,824)
Colla, Joseph A....4:26:33 (18,679)
Collard, Dominic P....3:37:22 (6,137)
Collard, John....4:05:04 (13,062)
Collard, Samuel W....4:28:28 (19,252)
Collazos, Alex....4:37:39 (21,630)
Colledge, Mark....4:48:45 (24,307)
Collenette, John P....4:12:08 (14,843)
Collerton, Liam....3:43:05 (7,263)
Collett, George W....4:48:53 (24,342)
Colley, Jeffrey M....6:04:42 (32,912)
Colley, John W....4:40:56 (22,418)
Colley, Martin A....4:22:36 (17,613)
Colley, Peter A....5:36:03 (31,037)
Collier, Darren W....3:27:20 (4,342)
Collier, David S....2:58:30 (1,009)
Collier, Ian R....6:24:57 (33,548)
Collier, Jamie....6:03:45 (32,878)
Collier, Lee P....5:09:11 (27,992)
Collier, Paul E....3:22:18 (3,532)
Collin, Frederick S....4:28:05 (19,125)
Collin, Michael P....3:07:00 (1,682)
Collington, Robert F....3:31:23 (5,112)
Collingwood, Mark A....3:24:21 (3,823)
Collingwood, Paul S....2:58:40 (1,028)
Collingwood, Pete....3:37:24 (6,149)
Collins, Andrew J....5:17:18 (29,096)
Collins, Andy....2:43:02 (266)
Collins, Barry....4:44:11 (23,224)
Collins, Christopher....5:34:04 (30,842)
Collins, Daryl B....3:30:27 (4,962)
Collins, David....3:16:24 (2,804)
Collins, Gary....4:05:28 (13,168)
Collins, Grahame F....3:54:42 (10,102)
Collins, Greg E....3:59:45 (11,766)
Collins, John J....4:17:28 (16,211)
Collins, Lance K....4:34:59 (20,974)
Collins, Louis....4:50:44 (24,774)
Collins, Mark....3:41:35 (6,952)
Collins, Mark....4:50:38 (24,752)
Collins, Martin A....3:02:16 (1,327)
Collins, Maurice S....3:03:26 (1,415)
Collins, Michael....3:48:28 (8,454)
Collins, Michael J....5:26:44 (30,120)
Collins, Mick P....5:03:16 (27,143)
Collins, Nigel....4:28:21 (19,223)
Collins, Nigel....4:45:19 (23,497)
Collins, Paul....4:43:28 (23,035)
Collins, Paul J....3:00:54 (1,235)
Collins, Phil J....4:33:50 (20,667)
Collins, Phillip M....3:17:52 (2,971)
Collins, Raymond L....6:10:29 (33,131)
Collins, Robert C....5:15:37 (28,892)
Collins, Robert L....4:25:37 (18,416)
Collins, Sean W....3:28:36 (4,580)
Collins, Simon....4:18:53 (16,595)
Collins, Simon L....3:16:22 (2,798)
Collins, Stephen....2:57:33 (909)
Collins, Stuart....3:52:59 (9,566)
Collins, Stuart J....3:19:38 (3,183)
Collins, Terry M....6:14:10 (33,248)
Collinson, Anthony....3:15:34 (2,710)
Collinson, Chris....3:39:55 (6,619)
Collinson, Gareth A....4:23:10 (17,770)
Collinson, Sean....5:36:47 (31,101)
Collinson, Stephen C....4:26:55 (18,790)
Collis, Ben C....4:30:58 (19,875)
Collis, Stephen....4:46:29 (23,774)
Collishaw, James....4:07:47 (13,711)
Collison, Brian G....4:47:40 (24,059)
Collisson, Steve J....4:17:23 (16,186)
Collom, Robert I....3:48:15 (8,414)
Colls, Stewart C....3:36:17 (5,929)
Collyer, Chris S....4:00:07 (11,879)
Collyer, William L....4:14:39 (15,482)
Colman, Paul M....3:34:19 (5,590)
Colman, Stanley H....4:57:28 (26,177)
Colmer, Adam M....4:56:21 (25,940)
Colmer, Douglas J....4:15:30 (15,704)
Colombarini, Rino....4:05:19 (13,125)
Colombo, Guiseppe....4:27:17 (18,900)
Colombo, Marco Giuseppe....3:46:13 (7,930)
Colpaert, Alexander....4:32:16 (20,245)
Colquhoun, Stephen....4:26:34 (18,685)
Colton, Jason P....4:46:55 (23,888)
Colton, Thomas....4:29:15 (19,463)
Colver, Phillip M....4:22:13 (17,503)
Colwell, Stephen J....4:35:00 (20,982)
Coman, Brian D....6:05:43 (32,963)
Comeau, Darren E....3:39:39 (6,565)
Comish, Roger P....4:28:42 (19,313)
Common, Robert F....3:36:29 (5,966)
Comport, David J....3:58:33 (11,317)
Compton, John....4:45:35 (23,555)
Compton, Steve C....3:30:29 (4,968)
Compton, Toby....5:35:31 (30,979)
Conboy, Sean P....3:59:50 (11,797)
Concar, Simon D....4:57:36 (26,209)
Condolo, Danilo L....5:01:16 (26,837)
Condon, Dave T....3:58:00 (11,116)
Condon, David B....4:20:34 (17,050)
Condon, Richard....3:05:05 (1,526)
Condron, Chris J....3:42:09 (7,057)
Conduit-Smith, Luke B....4:32:38 (20,331)
Conetta, Robert....5:09:30 (28,048)
Coney, James R....6:09:44 (33,110)
Congdon, Andrew J....3:32:23 (5,296)
Congdon, Lee S....4:40:26 (22,294)
Congdon, Marc....3:51:50 (9,254)
Coning, Darren R....2:58:03 (954)
Coningham, Jason M....4:26:23 (18,629)
Conlan, Paul J....4:08:23 (13,876)
Conley, Neil M....3:55:00 (10,195)
Conlon, Kevan....4:25:52 (18,502)
Conlon, Michael....3:11:00 (2,097)
Conn, Gavin....4:05:32 (13,185)
Connearn, Dale....3:25:45 (4,061)
Connell, Anthony....5:08:43 (27,932)
Connell, Brian A....3:57:41 (11,006)
Connell, Charles P....4:33:13 (20,485)
Connell, Christopher....4:21:28 (17,293)
Connell, Darrel....3:38:31 (6,361)
Connell, Richard J....4:11:24 (14,648)
Connery, Matthew B....4:48:31 (24,255)
Connery, Neil E....3:58:43 (11,382)
Conniffe, Matthew J....5:36:51 (31,107)
Connolly, David A....4:09:44 (14,239)
Connolly, David M....3:30:20 (4,944)
Connolly, Declan B....4:04:41 (12,979)
Connolly, Edward J....3:29:11 (4,713)
Connolly, Gary....3:43:24 (7,323)
Connolly, Jamie....3:37:57 (6,252)
Connolly, Joseph E....5:53:44 (32,390)
Connolly, Kevin J....4:10:33 (14,423)
Connolly, Mark J....3:16:43 (2,837)
Connolly, Ray....4:02:34 (12,508)
Connolly, Sean F....4:23:56 (17,975)
Connolly, Simon....3:56:46 (10,714)
Connon, James M....3:04:32 (1,487)
Connop, Lee....4:52:51 (25,234)
Connor, Chris....4:30:12 (19,678)
Connor, David....2:33:35 (100)
Connor, Dennis....3:30:03 (4,895)
Connor, Edward....4:16:27 (15,949)
Connor, Lee D....4:38:58 (21,967)
Connor, Ray O....3:41:14 (6,883)
Connor, Simon P....4:44:08 (23,211)
Conoley, Michael P....4:31:41 (20,074)
Conoplia, Sasha....2:51:19 (565)
Conotti, Emilio F....4:29:44 (19,575)
Conradson, David J....2:59:29 (1,117)
Conridge, Philip N....3:36:57 (6,050)
Conron, Nick....3:39:30 (6,534)
Conry, John....4:55:48 (25,840)
Consani, Marco P....2:48:19 (435)
Consani, Paul C....3:36:02 (5,888)
Constable, Jonathan P....3:59:40 (11,741)
Constant, Jean-Paul....5:13:21 (28,583)
Constantine, Stan....5:48:14 (31,992)
Constantinou, Andreas....6:06:09 (32,988)
Constantis, Chris....6:34:08 (33,753)
Contable, Adrian J....3:38:48 (6,410)
Contessi, Leandro....2:53:11 (650)

Contoli, Piercarlo....3:50:39 (8,974)
Contractor, Bhadresh R....4:46:59 (23,904)
Contreras, Demetrio....4:00:33 (11,987)
Contreras, Raul....4:26:52 (18,781)
Conway, Ben....4:26:30 (18,667)
Conway, Rod....5:35:27 (30,970)
Conway, Steven A....3:59:24 (11,633)
Conway, Stewart D....3:24:08 (3,796)
Conway, Tony T....3:17:08 (2,876)
Conyers, Daniel....4:52:39 (25,185)
Cook, Adrian C....3:47:35 (8,243)
Cook, Craig M....3:52:56 (9,549)
Cook, Danny....4:18:02 (16,352)
Cook, Danny M....5:16:35 (29,004)
Cook, Dave J....4:29:47 (19,581)
Cook, David....4:10:07 (14,318)
Cook, David J....3:01:43 (1,291)
Cook, David S....3:13:48 (2,436)
Cook, Desmond J....4:43:28 (23,035)
Cook, Douglas G....3:50:44 (8,996)
Cook, Gary J....2:59:05 (1,070)
Cook, Ian J....4:11:35 (14,702)
Cook, James G....4:22:23 (17,547)
Cook, Jason M....4:42:37 (22,836)
Cook, Jeremy J....4:57:53 (26,259)
Cook, John B....3:53:44 (9,783)
Cook, Jon J....4:16:14 (15,888)
Cook, Keith A....3:33:39 (5,495)
Cook, Kristopher M....3:41:15 (6,884)
Cook, Leonard J....4:36:59 (21,482)
Cook, Malcolm J....4:09:12 (14,088)
Cook, Nicholas....4:41:22 (22,526)
Cook, Nigel A....3:12:57 (2,329)
Cook, Nigel V....3:41:15 (6,884)
Cook, Peter....3:12:08 (2,226)
Cook, Richard J....3:59:05 (11,521)
Cook, Richard P....4:44:25 (23,276)
Cook, Stephen....3:20:41 (3,319)
Cook, Tim....5:43:05 (31,576)
Cook, Timothy P....2:59:05 (1,070)
Cooke, Adam J....4:11:08 (14,581)
Cooke, Anthony P....3:55:48 (10,437)
Cooke, Brian H....4:52:45 (25,211)
Cooke, Bruce....3:21:43 (3,447)
Cooke, Bryan....3:55:44 (10,418)
Cooke, David....3:51:49 (9,252)
Cooke, David G....3:36:04 (5,892)
Cooke, Gary J....3:47:03 (8,122)
Cooke, James B....3:50:59 (9,042)
Cooke, Jason L....7:31:57 (34,463)
Cooke, John A....4:24:01 (18,000)
Cooke, Jordan J....3:54:39 (10,086)
Cooke, Mike R....4:01:30 (12,241)
Cooke, Neil D....4:26:53 (18,784)
Cooke, Nigel....3:50:32 (8,937)
Cooke, Patrick....3:58:57 (11,473)
Cooke, Peter J....5:28:10 (30,285)
Cooke, Tim....3:21:13 (3,386)
Cooknell, Andrew J....3:54:15 (9,943)
Cooksey, Andrew P....3:58:03 (11,131)
Cookson, Noel....4:08:25 (13,887)
Coombe, Duncan D....3:55:36 (10,371)
Coombe, Glenn C....3:57:18 (10,890)
Coomber, Danny R....4:41:29 (22,553)
Coombes, Anthony W....5:16:13 (28,961)
Coombes, Barry A....4:41:57 (22,663)
Coombes, Matthew G....4:28:36 (19,289)
Coombs, David T....4:57:15 (26,135)
Coombs, Neil M....6:52:02 (34,111)
Coombs, Roger R....5:05:20 (27,446)
Coombs, Stephen J....5:09:02 (27,975)
Cooney, Andrew S....3:39:33 (6,551)
Cooper, Aaron C....3:31:44 (5,178)
Cooper, Andrew C....5:19:41 (29,383)
Cooper, Ben....3:27:50 (4,428)
Cooper, Dana K....4:05:08 (13,080)
Cooper, David....3:27:42 (4,396)
Cooper, David A....2:51:33 (574)
Cooper, David J....4:20:15 (16,962)
Cooper, Dean J....4:13:29 (15,154)
Cooper, Douglas N....3:07:35 (1,740)
Cooper, Gareth....3:53:45 (9,791)
Cooper, Gary....4:42:22 (22,766)
Cooper, Gary L....4:23:45 (17,929)
Cooper, Giles E....3:41:29 (6,938)
Cooper, Glenn....3:07:35 (1,740)
Cooper, Ian P....3:25:24 (3,993)
Cooper, Ian T....4:38:07 (21,743)
Cooper, James D....3:07:01 (1,685)
Cooper, James R....4:15:43 (15,752)
Cooper, Jonathan E....3:34:46 (5,656)
Cooper, Keith....5:07:01 (27,698)
Cooper, Kurt....5:06:06 (27,568)
Cooper, Lee S....4:45:44 (23,598)
Cooper, Marc....5:01:19 (26,842)
Cooper, Mark....6:03:33 (32,870)
Cooper, Mark J....4:43:06 (22,962)
Cooper, Michael....3:11:03 (2,101)
Cooper, Michael J....3:07:19 (1,713)
Cooper, Nicholas G....2:54:40 (726)
Cooper, Nicholas R....4:22:21 (17,531)
Cooper, Nigel E....4:44:23 (23,274)
Cooper, Nigel P....3:56:35 (10,657)
Cooper, Paul N....4:13:35 (15,184)
Cooper, Peter J....3:58:35 (11,331)
Cooper, Philip J....2:49:17 (476)
Cooper, Richard J....3:48:46 (8,525)
Cooper, Ricky M....4:22:25 (17,555)
Cooper, Robert....4:54:34 (25,593)
Cooper, Ryan S....4:15:48 (15,783)
Cooper, Simon J....3:59:56 (11,831)
Cooper, Stephen J....3:25:01 (3,935)
Cooper, Tony....5:49:55 (32,115)
Coopey, Simon J....4:11:09 (14,590)
Coote, Mark R....4:30:37 (19,780)
Coote, Oliver B....4:09:54 (14,278)
Copas, Nicholas....3:15:12 (2,654)
Cope, David A....4:31:24 (19,995)
Cope, Gareth R....4:53:02 (25,280)
Cope, Trevor A....4:22:53 (17,698)
Copeland, Alexander....3:35:21 (5,764)
Copeland, John....6:43:33 (33,949)
Copeland, Terry R....3:46:38 (8,028)
Copestake, Jeremy C....4:45:10 (23,456)
Copland, Adrian....5:16:14 (28,964)
Copland, Andy....3:39:27 (6,526)
Copland, Gavin R....4:14:18 (15,398)
Coppin, Russell C....3:57:49 (11,066)
Copping, Michael S....5:01:48 (26,929)
Copping, Nathan M....4:27:35 (18,974)
Coppinger, Eugene....3:14:28 (2,541)
Copsey, Nicholas R....4:04:37 (12,960)
Copsey, Peter D....4:07:52 (13,739)
Cora Decunto, Adrian....3:39:39 (6,565)
Corberand, Pascal....3:13:00 (2,334)
Corbett, Brian D....3:29:22 (4,758)
Corbett, David D....4:55:40 (25,815)
Corbett, James B....4:09:38 (14,209)
Corbett, Phillip J....3:28:50 (4,633)
Corbishley-Forbes, Wayne....5:44:18 (31,697)
Corbo, Michele A....5:19:29 (29,352)
Corbould, Clive....6:02:57 (32,847)
Corbould, Graham T....5:54:51 (32,448)
Corbould, Jason P....4:08:45 (13,980)
Corbridge, Michael....4:39:33 (22,090)
Corby, Colin D....4:57:48 (26,249)
Corby, Matthew T....3:06:41 (1,654)
Corcoran, Chris....3:15:27 (2,694)
Corcoran, Cornelius....3:20:34 (3,302)
Corcoran, John M....4:04:00 (12,833)
Cordell, Roger....4:38:57 (21,961)
Corden, James M....2:52:50 (633)
Corden-Lloyd, Alistair J....4:55:56 (25,867)
Corden-Lloyd, Warwick R....4:18:33 (16,513)
Corder, Christopher C....5:08:37 (27,917)
Cordery, James....4:01:39 (12,281)
Cordiner-Barton, Mark J....5:29:32 (30,426)
Cording, James....4:45:26 (23,524)
Cording, Stephen J....4:45:26 (23,524)
Cordingley, Frank J....3:05:18 (1,537)
Cordingley, Mark A....3:25:49 (4,070)
Cordingley, Simon N....5:45:42 (31,814)
Cordle, George....3:28:00 (4,459)
Cordova, Edison....4:16:12 (15,874)
Cordwell, James P....2:49:39 (496)
Corfield, Ben....4:31:08 (19,919)
Corfield, John W....4:49:53 (24,569)
Cork, Gary J....4:38:39 (21,868)
Corker, Richard....3:51:45 (9,238)
Corless, David....3:34:13 (5,579)
Corless, Iain P....4:19:49 (16,838)
Corless, Ian....3:33:12 (5,421)
Corless, Paul....2:57:01 (872)
Corlett, John B....4:02:03 (12,376)
Corn, Jonathan G....3:49:28 (8,694)
Cornacchlone, Domenico W....5:23:37 (29,761)
Cornelis, Rudi....4:10:47 (14,488)
Cornelius, Leon C....5:03:16 (27,143)
Cornelius, Paul....3:52:37 (9,461)
Cornelius, Tristan D....4:02:50 (12,574)
Cornell, Matthew....5:28:49 (30,351)
Cornell, Timothy B....4:20:09 (16,928)
Corner, Christopher J....4:47:47 (24,098)
Corner, Ian....3:14:30 (2,546)
Cornewall-Walker, James O....3:53:00 (9,572)
Corney, Robert A....4:12:12 (14,860)
Cornfield, Geoffrey C....4:21:42 (17,374)
Cornford, Adrian....3:14:48 (2,607)
Cornford, Pete....3:16:57 (2,856)
Cornhill, Max....4:00:51 (12,068)
Cornic, Francis....4:07:10 (13,568)
Cornic, Michel....4:22:36 (17,613)
Cornick, David J....3:56:55 (10,768)
Cornick, Ian A....4:10:05 (14,313)
Cornock, David E....3:17:36 (2,942)
Cornock, Ian J....5:02:10 (26,980)
Corns, Ian....4:34:38 (20,855)
Cornwall, Michael D....3:29:15 (4,725)
Cornwell, Christopher P....3:05:21 (1,544)
Cornwell, David....4:56:54 (26,052)
Corr, Martin G....4:27:38 (18,984)
Corr, Thomas P....3:57:48 (11,061)
Corradini, Fabio....3:31:07 (5,064)
Correia, Bernardo....4:21:22 (17,261)
Correia, Rui....4:21:22 (17,261)
Corriente, Manuel E....3:15:32 (2,705)
Corrigan, Michael J....4:16:58 (16,082)
Corrigan, Patrik J....3:37:57 (6,252)
Corringham, Barry G....4:06:22 (13,366)
Corsi, Gary....4:47:41 (24,064)
Corstorphine, Iain A....4:27:27 (18,941)
Cortese, Guiseppe....4:40:46 (22,372)
Corvin, Darach J....5:36:18 (31,064)
Cosco, Antonio....5:20:33 (29,471)
Cosentino, Yves....3:26:10 (4,132)
Cossar, Anthony J....3:53:22 (9,687)
Costa, Michael R....3:58:36 (11,336)
Costain, Michael G....3:47:57 (8,338)
Costas, Barry P....3:27:35 (4,376)
Costas, Paul....3:24:32 (3,853)
Costello, Colin J....3:43:25 (7,327)
Costello, John F....3:15:54 (2,747)
Costello, Kevin....4:15:07 (15,603)
Costello, Patrick....4:22:16 (17,514)
Costello, Robert J....3:36:15 (5,923)
Costello, Stephen....3:51:20 (9,132)
Costello, Terrance P....4:49:32 (24,484)
Coster, Ian C....4:53:42 (25,417)
Costley, Phil....2:20:40 (23)
Coter, Steven M....4:33:33 (20,591)
Cottam, Lee T....4:28:08 (19,142)
Cotter, Barry N....3:58:37 (11,341)
Cotter, Ian J....3:00:30 (1,201)
Cotterell, Owen M....3:28:41 (4,600)
Cotterill, Phil J....4:26:26 (18,641)
Cottle, James H....3:33:01 (5,388)
Cottle, Richard....3:10:06 (1,998)
Cottle, Simon W....3:22:00 (3,491)
Cotton, Andrew....5:01:11 (26,824)
Cotton, Anthony E....3:57:41 (11,006)
Cotton, Chris....4:29:40 (19,557)
Cotton, Darrel C....3:22:58 (3,631)
Cotton, Jeremy D....4:26:48 (18,753)
Cotton, Michael A....4:05:20 (13,133)
Cotton, Paul D....6:34:56 (33,771)
Cottrell, Dale L....3:39:51 (6,609)
Cottrell, Steven J....3:27:52 (4,434)
Cotzias, Constantin M....3:08:06 (1,803)
Couallier, Richard....4:18:32 (16,508)

Couchman, Neil R 4:59:26 (26,550)
Couchman, Paul M 4:23:42 (17,914)
Coughlan, Charlie 3:06:03 (1,603)
Coughlan, Thomas J 3:11:16 (2,121)
Couldridge, Paul J 2:41:26 (231)
Couling, Steven 3:47:25 (8,202)
Coulson, Bryan 4:33:05 (20,452)
Coulson, Clint P 3:53:05 (9,602)
Coulson, Clive W 4:09:14 (14,097)
Coulson, James R 4:05:16 (13,113)
Coulson, Jeffrey 3:52:39 (9,470)
Coulson, Mark J 5:56:34 (32,561)
Coulson, Phil 2:34:37 (108)
Coulson, Stephen H 4:11:33 (14,693)
Coulson, Tom 4:35:36 (21,137)
Coulson, Wayne A 3:12:30 (2,266)
Coulter, Barry A 3:20:18 (3,266)
Coulter, Graham 5:00:04 (26,648)
Coulter, Leon 4:12:52 (14,996)
Coulthard, Garry 4:07:57 (13,765)
Counihan, Paul 3:52:54 (9,536)
Coupe, Benjamin J 4:36:58 (21,480)
Coupe, Michael F 3:41:51 (7,001)
Coupland, Glynn D 4:47:25 (24,006)
Coupland, John M 4:37:14 (21,534)
Coupland, Krishan J 5:28:09 (30,283)
Coupland, Paul D 5:02:57 (27,104)
Course, David M 4:22:50 (17,679)
Court, Alan R 3:14:13 (2,504)
Court, Simon J 5:33:08 (30,763)
Court, Steve 3:21:05 (3,371)
Courtenay, Tim W 3:59:19 (11,602)
Courtenay-Evans, Tom D 4:09:38 (14,209)
Courtier, Michael 4:08:42 (13,969)
Courtier, Robert S 5:08:15 (27,849)
Courtney, John 5:27:50 (30,242)
Courtney, Max M 5:27:51 (30,246)
Courtney, Paul R 4:05:43 (13,226)
Courtney, Trevor A 4:30:10 (19,671)
Cousens, Charles L 4:45:38 (23,569)
Cousins, Gavin 3:42:12 (7,071)
Cousins, James 4:11:55 (14,784)
Cousins, Nicholas J 2:49:13 (471)
Cousins, Roger N 4:17:11 (16,153)
Coutant, Eric 4:01:20 (12,196)
Coutelle, Oliver 4:12:03 (14,824)
Covell, Andrew D 4:04:45 (12,994)
Cowan, Andrew 4:18:46 (16,565)
Cowan, Christopher J 4:48:56 (24,354)
Cowan, David J 3:36:09 (5,907)
Cowan, Nick 4:06:16 (13,352)
Cowan, Russell N 4:42:24 (22,780)
Cowcher, Paul 3:36:51 (6,029)
Cowdrill, Andrew 4:24:00 (17,994)
Cowdrill, Gary T 4:23:59 (17,987)
Cowdy, Daniel P 4:05:52 (13,260)
Cowell, Antony J 3:14:38 (2,575)
Cowell, Dean 4:18:15 (16,413)
Cowell, Kevin S 4:05:36 (13,201)
Cowell, Mark 5:39:58 (31,330)
Cowell, Martin F 3:47:32 (8,227)
Cowell, Nick C 3:59:26 (11,646)
Cowie, James 4:18:33 (16,513)
Cowie, James 6:26:42 (33,590)
Cowie, Wayne D 4:25:34 (18,408)
Cowland, Brian 5:00:55 (26,782)
Cowlard, David 3:49:05 (8,599)
Cowley, John 4:02:23 (12,473)
Cowley, Keith F 3:10:49 (2,078)
Cowley, Simon 3:56:46 (10,714)
Cowling, Peter C 4:21:43 (17,380)
Cowlishaw, Matthew E 5:06:15 (27,591)
Cowlishaw, Steven G 3:10:30 (2,041)
Cox, Adrian N 3:47:02 (8,120)
Cox, Alan D 4:11:30 (14,679)
Cox, Alistair N 4:51:38 (24,973)
Cox, Allan 5:04:31 (27,329)
Cox, Andrew P 3:23:41 (3,725)
Cox, Andrew T 3:57:24 (10,928)
Cox, Brian L 4:16:16 (15,895)
Cox, Christopher S 4:08:50 (14,001)
Cox, Darren 3:31:33 (5,141)
Cox, David 3:55:09 (10,251)
Cox, David L 3:44:07 (7,476)
Cox, Humphrey 3:40:18 (6,691)
Cox, Ian M 4:21:36 (17,334)
Cox, James 5:22:05 (29,612)
Cox, John W 4:01:11 (12,159)
Cox, Justin A 2:56:05 (811)
Cox, Kevin I 3:14:43 (2,594)
Cox, Mark M 3:31:20 (5,105)
Cox, Michael 4:25:54 (18,509)
Cox, Neil P 3:53:18 (9,661)
Cox, Nick E 4:00:09 (11,883)
Cox, Oliver S 3:29:15 (4,725)
Cox, Paul 4:55:10 (25,726)
Cox, Richard 5:13:12 (28,571)
Cox, Richard V 3:36:46 (6,005)
Cox, Stephen 3:44:14 (7,496)
Cox, Steven 4:46:30 (23,777)
Cox, Steven W 5:02:26 (27,031)
Cox, Stewart J 2:55:44 (791)
Cox, Stuart W 4:33:18 (20,511)
Coxhead, Mark A 3:52:22 (9,401)
Coxon, Christopher A 4:05:53 (13,262)
Coxsedge, Benjamin J 5:10:07 (28,164)
Coxshall, Andrew D 2:59:30 (1,118)
Coyle, Danny J 4:00:29 (11,969)
Coyle, James R 3:58:30 (11,298)
Coyle, Mark A 4:40:04 (22,198)
Coyle, Mark F 3:57:21 (10,910)
Coyle, Michael J 5:11:43 (28,369)
Coyne, Craig M 4:22:08 (17,476)
Coyne, Martyn P 3:57:43 (11,023)
Cozens, Christopher 5:07:07 (27,706)
Crabb, Bobby 4:48:25 (24,227)
Crabb, Kieron N 5:55:47 (32,509)
Crabtree, Ian P 3:10:27 (2,035)
Crabtree, Mark 3:00:34 (1,209)
Crabtree, Paul 4:04:50 (13,007)
Crabtree, Tom R 3:42:10 (7,061)
Cracknell, Andrew D 2:48:12 (431)
Cracknell, James 2:59:11 (1,083)
Cradden, Brendan 3:35:12 (5,737)
Craddock, Dean 4:20:51 (17,138)
Crafford, Pieter 3:36:39 (5,988)
Craft, Mark T 4:49:53 (24,569)
Cragg, Andrew C 4:29:10 (19,444)
Cragg, Kevin 3:56:18 (10,565)
Cragg, Philip R 4:54:46 (25,642)
Cragg, Richard N 4:24:31 (18,147)
Cragg, Stephen 4:25:00 (18,264)
Cragg, Stuart J 2:48:51 (458)
Crahart, Lee J 4:15:12 (15,618)
Craig, Andrew T 3:25:18 (3,978)
Craig, Darren 4:37:50 (21,679)
Craig, Edward D 3:57:51 (11,075)
Craig, Gerard 2:51:51 (587)
Craig, Jonathan J 4:25:13 (18,323)
Craig, Michael 2:52:28 (616)
Craig, Oliver D 3:59:19 (11,602)
Craig, Robert S 4:06:28 (13,390)
Craig, Scott 5:12:34 (28,470)
Craig, Simon 4:41:06 (22,460)
Craig, Stevie 4:54:22 (25,553)
Craige, Robert L 4:06:40 (13,446)
Crail, Richard 5:02:35 (27,048)
Crampton, Colin P 4:15:50 (15,792)
Crampton, Ian 2:30:40 (80)
Crampton, Peter 4:28:26 (19,243)
Cran, Alexander N 3:01:54 (1,305)
Crandley, Royston B 5:41:32 (31,468)
Crandon, David 4:19:53 (16,855)
Crane, Andrew R 5:10:11 (28,171)
Crane, Carl L 3:22:49 (3,612)
Crane, James B 3:54:36 (10,071)
Crane, Mark 3:02:08 (1,318)
Crane, Melvin I 4:52:52 (25,241)

LONDON MARATHON

Crane, Michael A 5:00:41 (26,733)
Crane, Richard C 4:20:16 (16,966)
Crane, Robert 4:01:58 (12,353)
Crane, Stephen 3:53:16 (9,653)
Crane, Terence V 4:48:47 (24,315)
Crane, Tim 4:29:07 (19,428)
Crane, William T 3:24:51 (3,899)
Cranfield, Steven D 3:41:04 (6,840)
Crangle, Robert 3:41:05 (6,841)
Crann, Richard 3:53:14 (9,644)
Crannage, Jonathan 3:45:35 (7,808)
Cranwell, Mark A 2:59:39 (1,135)
Cratchley, Neil 4:02:09 (12,404)
Craven, Alan 5:05:53 (27,529)
Craven, Martin 4:20:08 (16,920)
Craven, Tim P 4:11:29 (14,674)
Craw, Gavin J 5:00:07 (26,657)
Crawford, Colin 3:17:26 (2,924)
Crawford, Damian 3:16:40 (2,831)
Crawford, James A 3:53:08 (9,615)
Crawford, Mark D 4:18:50 (16,582)
Crawford, Paul 4:07:49 (13,720)
Crawford, Paul 4:41:35 (22,575)
Crawford, Peter A 3:59:24 (11,633)
Crawford, Robert K 4:17:03 (16,108)
Crawford-Taylor, Adam P 5:32:00 (30,662)
Crawley, David G 5:08:02 (27,828)
Craxton, Alistair J 3:49:20 (8,659)
Crayston, David 2:57:46 (927)
Craze, Lee 5:27:41 (30,224)
Creamer, Marcus J 4:38:14 (21,762)
Creaney-Birch, Neil S 5:27:56 (30,257)
Crease, Gregory B 5:27:40 (30,220)
Creasey, Daniel 4:42:11 (22,715)
Creasey, John F 6:59:18 (34,203)
Cree, Ed 4:47:38 (24,050)
Creed, Gary D 5:06:07 (27,571)
Creffield, Ken 4:24:10 (18,039)
Creighton, Jim 4:11:25 (14,650)
Crellin, Mark A 3:51:07 (9,078)
Cremin, James 5:38:54 (31,255)
Crespi, Alessandro 3:17:00 (2,863)
Cresser, Henry S 4:17:04 (16,112)
Cressman, David E 4:51:09 (24,870)
Cresswell, Dennis T 5:59:31 (32,717)
Cresswell, Paul E 5:17:47 (29,154)
Cresswell, Richard J 3:58:42 (11,374)
Cresswell, Robin 3:42:08 (7,054)
Cresswell, Steve J 3:34:43 (5,648)
Creswell, Andrew S 3:24:08 (3,796)
Creus Pardina, Ramon 4:28:07 (19,137)
Crew, Danny E 3:51:54 (9,276)
Crew, Nathan 4:15:40 (15,739)
Crews, Jon E 3:11:40 (2,170)
Cribier, Guillaume J 2:37:24 (154)
Crichton, Jamie 3:36:30 (5,969)
Crick, Steve J 4:09:37 (14,204)
Crighton, Colin G 4:43:58 (23,172)
Crighton, Matthew D 3:32:09 (5,253)
Crighton, Timothy P 4:47:52 (24,109)
Crinnion, Richard J 4:27:50 (19,033)
Cripps, Paul A 6:01:57 (32,820)
Cripps, Peter G 4:03:06 (12,629)
Crisford, Simon G 4:56:59 (26,071)
Crisp, Charles P 4:49:54 (24,575)
Crisp, Clive A 3:27:30 (4,363)
Crisp, Gordon D 5:38:12 (31,207)
Crisp, John C 5:12:17 (28,432)
Crispin, Stuart J 4:20:46 (17,112)
Critchley, Mark A 4:04:23 (12,912)
Critchley, Paul M 3:59:51 (11,802)
Croasdale, Mark J 2:32:31 (90)
Crocker, Rob W 3:58:15 (11,198)
Crocker, Russell P 4:32:38 (20,331)
Crocket, Graham 3:08:50 (1,860)
Crockett, Mark S 4:55:55 (25,864)
Croese, Eduard W 4:13:02 (15,045)
Croft, Lee D 3:58:03 (11,131)
Croft, Stephen J 3:50:07 (8,847)
Croker, Robert J 3:39:15 (6,483)
Cromarty, Michael 4:13:35 (15,184)
Crompton, Martin J 5:05:54 (27,532)
Crompton, Neil W 2:42:55 (262)

Crone, Michael J 5:13:07 (28,558)
Crone, Paul G 4:52:08 (25,070)
Crone, Stuart D 3:25:24 (3,993)
Cronin, Alfred P 3:19:42 (3,191)
Cronin, Arun D 3:29:24 (4,763)
Cronin, David A 3:55:18 (10,289)
Cronin, Iain D 5:07:39 (27,791)
Cronin, Jonathan 4:13:26 (15,145)
Crook, Andrew P 4:20:47 (17,118)
Crook, Andrew S 5:05:29 (27,472)
Crook, David 3:34:03 (5,557)
Crook, Graham 5:21:56 (29,594)
Crook, Jonathan S 2:44:13 (302)
Crook, Michael J 4:04:01 (12,838)
Crook, Paul A 4:25:59 (18,531)
Crook, Ross 4:09:07 (14,065)
Crook, Steve 4:15:10 (15,610)
Crook, Tony L 4:25:11 (18,318)
Crookall, Jonathan M 3:36:52 (6,033)
Cropton, Jason G 3:27:59 (4,456)
Crorkin, James P 5:42:37 (31,537)
Crosby, David J 3:59:05 (11,521)
Crosby, Luke O 4:15:33 (15,718)
Cross, Andrew R 4:56:21 (25,940)
Cross, Ben R 4:12:28 (14,920)
Cross, Dean 3:14:54 (2,617)
Cross, John 4:11:49 (14,761)
Cross, Martin 5:15:57 (28,931)
Cross, Martin J 3:49:10 (8,619)
Cross, Matt R 3:23:52 (3,755)
Cross, Paul J 4:45:59 (23,671)
Cross, Peter 3:23:28 (3,704)
Cross, Peter 5:38:47 (31,244)
Cross, Philip J 2:52:03 (597)
Cross, Rog 3:45:18 (7,755)
Cross, Shane P 4:03:36 (12,748)
Cross, Simon J 4:02:06 (12,389)
Crossan, Mark A 3:30:00 (4,885)
Crosse, Matthew P 2:56:34 (846)
Crossfield, Leon M 3:54:04 (9,894)
Crossland, Brian C 4:12:12 (14,860)
Crossland, Tom T 3:35:58 (5,875)
Crossley, Mark R 4:18:09 (16,386)
Croston, Matthew L 4:22:12 (17,495)
Crouch, Alan J 5:51:42 (32,268)
Crouch, Oliver T 4:04:30 (12,931)
Crouch, Paul 5:35:02 (30,944)
Crouch, Robert J 3:49:13 (8,632)
Croucher, Graham J 4:38:50 (21,924)
Crouchman, Marc 4:28:00 (19,099)
Crouchman, Paul A 4:41:49 (22,641)
Crouchman, Robert J 4:30:19 (19,702)
Crous, Steyn S 3:42:17 (7,090)
Crouzet, Philippe J 3:23:17 (3,673)
Crow, Andrew P 4:11:26 (14,656)
Crow, Barry W 4:11:47 (14,745)
Crow, Jolyon N 3:49:47 (8,769)
Crow, Justin R 3:49:46 (8,764)
Crowder, Neil 3:42:51 (7,205)
Crowe, Norman L 5:57:46 (32,618)
Crowe, Thomas 5:42:37 (31,537)
Crowe, Wayne 4:00:03 (11,863)
Crowhurst, Keith A 4:30:53 (19,863)
Crowhurst, Paul J 4:03:13 (12,658)
Crowley, Arron 4:16:03 (15,849)
Crowley, Gregory S 3:14:36 (2,567)
Crowley, Phillip J 4:32:03 (20,184)
Crowley, Stuart A 5:30:34 (30,534)
Crowley, Vincent 3:46:07 (7,911)
Crownshaw, Terry W 7:08:34 (34,298)
Crowshaw, Darren J 3:40:36 (6,744)
Crowson, James M 4:05:45 (13,232)
Crowson, Kevin W 4:02:10 (12,409)
Crowther, George S 4:02:05 (12,382)
Crowther, Jon 4:16:26 (15,942)
Crowther, Julian G 2:52:11 (602)
Crozier, Peter 3:22:47 (3,607)
Crozier, Rob 4:12:46 (14,981)
Crudgington, Tommy G 3:42:25 (7,120)
Cruickshank, Angus 4:47:16 (23,976)
Cruickshank, Brian 2:44:42 (322)
Cruickshank, George A 4:38:55 (21,948)
Cruise, Benedict J 4:32:02 (20,181)
Cruise, Paul S 4:42:07 (22,701)
Cruise, Richard 4:37:05 (21,503)
Crummack, Ian J 4:13:35 (15,184)
Crump, Stephen L 4:45:22 (23,503)
Cruse, Peter 3:04:49 (1,504)
Crutchley, Philip R 4:45:23 (23,506)
Cruttenden, Duncan 3:18:51 (3,079)
Cruwys, Simon J 6:16:30 (33,308)
Cruz Garcia, Armando 5:16:42 (29,019)
Cubbon, Henry 4:04:13 (12,866)
Cubitt, David 4:28:25 (19,238)
Cuddeford, Paul M 4:00:53 (12,077)
Cuesta, Felipe P 4:38:15 (21,767)
Cuffe, Anthony 4:33:19 (20,516)
Cuffe, John G 5:25:17 (29,961)
Cugini, Patrick 3:53:47 (9,800)
Cull, Clem P 5:32:39 (30,715)
Cull, Matthew 3:35:59 (5,881)
Cull, Michael 4:03:49 (12,792)
Cullen, Alasdair T 5:03:47 (27,222)
Cullen, Andrew D 4:27:15 (18,890)
Cullen, Martin J 3:41:52 (7,008)
Cullern, Doug A 4:31:04 (19,900)
Culligan, Stephen E 3:01:24 (1,269)
Culliney, Kevin J 4:56:39 (25,992)
Culling, Stephen C 4:16:49 (16,041)
Cullingworth, Ian M 3:22:13 (3,519)
Cullum, Ian D 4:47:11 (23,955)
Cullwick, Michael J 4:26:16 (18,601)
Cully, Robert 4:18:40 (16,546)
Culmer, Mark P 4:39:24 (22,063)
Culshaw, Edmund 4:27:58 (19,088)
Culshaw, Tim 3:29:16 (4,730)
Culverwell, Steven 4:03:29 (12,722)
Culwin, Fintan 5:50:15 (32,149)
Cumberbatch, Ashley 5:27:44 (30,229)
Cumberbatch, Lee 4:34:11 (20,752)
Cumine, Colin 4:50:38 (24,752)
Cumming, Iain 3:14:32 (2,556)
Cummings, Arthur B 5:12:51 (28,525)
Cummings, Efe B 4:23:16 (17,804)
Cummings, Glenworth 6:12:20 (33,180)
Cummings, Matthew A 3:21:02 (3,366)
Cummings, Oliver M 3:14:04 (2,479)
Cummings, Trevor S 3:24:17 (3,815)
Cummins, Mark C 3:59:22 (11,622)
Cummins, Michael A 4:33:38 (20,618)
Cummins, Rob H 4:13:49 (15,254)
Cummins, Steven J 3:10:38 (2,057)
Cummins, Timothy D 3:58:27 (11,282)
Cunha, Sergio M 3:57:02 (10,805)
Cunliffe, Guy D 3:16:23 (2,801)
Cunnah, Carl 6:27:04 (33,601)
Cunniffe, Matthew P 6:13:25 (33,224)
Cunniffe, Michael T 6:13:26 (33,225)
Cunningham, Barney 4:20:57 (17,164)
Cunningham, Harry A 3:40:15 (6,684)
Cunningham, Ian 6:08:40 (33,071)
Cunningham, James 3:42:04 (7,042)
Cunningham, James P 4:06:55 (13,496)
Cunningham, Jim D 3:55:52 (10,457)
Cunningham, Martin A 3:41:33 (6,949)
Cunningham, Michael A 2:52:12 (604)
Cunningham, Michael R 3:46:47 (8,056)
Cunningham, Nick A 4:29:28 (19,513)
Cunningham, Peter F 4:35:57 (21,228)
Cunningham, Peter T 6:56:47 (34,180)
Cunningham, Philip P 2:54:59 (748)
Cunningham, Rick 4:34:49 (20,908)
Cunningham, Robert T 4:55:57 (25,871)
Cunningham, Stuart J 2:45:55 (357)
Cunningham, Thomas 4:42:57 (22,920)
Cupitt, Matthew R 3:31:58 (5,217)
Curd, Robert S 5:33:57 (30,829)
Curley, Dermot 2:57:08 (880)
Curley, Garry A 5:50:23 (32,162)
Curphey, Paul T 3:09:11 (1,906)
Curr, Brian 4:30:39 (19,785)
Curran, Kevin 5:06:34 (27,633)
Curran, Len S 4:54:50 (25,657)
Curran, Mathew 4:15:42 (15,745)
Curran, Matthew J 5:42:58 (31,567)
Curran, Michael 5:11:23 (28,315)
Curran, Paul N 3:54:54 (10,160)
Curran, Philip P 3:36:46 (6,005)
Curran, Phillipe 4:20:29 (17,020)
Curran, William R 3:00:48 (1,225)
Currell, John 9:44:29 (34,585)
Currell, Kevin 4:07:05 (13,539)
Currie, Glenn 4:15:28 (15,693)
Curry, James C 3:54:52 (10,144)
Curtis, Adam 4:33:03 (20,442)
Curtis, Daniel J 3:53:45 (9,791)
Curtis, David L 3:35:47 (5,841)
Curtis, David L 4:35:04 (20,998)
Curtis, Graham 4:20:30 (17,028)
Curtis, James R 3:10:08 (2,002)
Curtis, Jason 4:54:36 (25,600)
Curtis, John R 3:23:43 (3,729)
Curtis, Matthew J 3:53:50 (9,824)
Curtis, Matthew J 4:00:15 (11,909)
Curtis, Nicholas G 4:26:26 (18,641)
Curtis, Paul F 2:48:00 (422)
Curtis, Steven A 3:23:16 (3,669)
Curtis, Timothy 6:32:55 (33,720)
Curwen, Paul 4:00:23 (11,944)
Curzon, Matt J 4:54:46 (25,642)
Cusack, David M 3:26:24 (4,173)
Cusack, Eric G 3:49:07 (8,606)
Cusack, Mark A 3:33:29 (5,472)
Cushing, George S 3:52:36 (9,454)
Cussans, Phil G 4:26:47 (18,750)
Cusson, Fabrice D 3:13:55 (2,454)
Custance, Ian E 5:14:12 (28,704)
Cutbill, Ron D 4:35:52 (21,205)
Cutbush, Chris A 4:17:10 (16,147)
Cuthbertson, Paul 3:43:53 (7,434)
Cutter, Clayton J 4:44:59 (23,409)
Cuttill, Gordon 4:07:42 (13,698)
Cutting, Gary 4:32:07 (20,204)
Cutts, Richard 4:00:10 (11,886)
Cuzens, Tim R 3:53:57 (9,854)
Czaja, Alan J 3:40:10 (6,666)
Czernuszka, Edward A 4:07:58 (13,767)
Da Paixao, Johnny 4:28:11 (19,164)
Da Silva, Deolor 4:25:36 (18,413)
Dable, Paul T 3:58:19 (11,226)
Dace, Laurence T 4:21:48 (17,406)
Dacey, Patrick W 4:16:19 (15,907)
Dacosta, Joseph 5:50:02 (32,128)
Dada, Mohamed 4:17:38 (16,258)
Dadd, Joshua 5:01:40 (26,906)
Dadd, Michael L 4:40:39 (22,337)
D'Addese, Carmelo A 4:50:44 (24,774)
Dadds, Gary N 5:12:48 (28,514)
Dadge, Nigel G 4:38:38 (21,864)
Dadzie, Frederick B 4:18:48 (16,572)
Daffin, Ashley 4:00:49 (12,062)
Dagul, Robert A 4:09:45 (14,242)
Dahanayake, Kit 4:55:30 (25,783)
Daher, Mostafa 4:35:13 (21,035)
Dahl, Jesper 6:59:51 (34,209)
Dahlberg, Peder 5:43:39 (31,623)
Daines, Michael 3:46:40 (8,035)
Daines, Paul J 3:57:18 (10,890)
Dainty, Andrew H 4:03:05 (12,627)
Daish, Sam G 3:33:01 (5,388)
Dal Cero, Marco 3:44:18 (7,515)
Dale, Adrian B 3:21:57 (3,483)
Dale, Ady J 3:39:56 (6,623)
Dale, Alex 4:18:59 (16,620)
Dale, Chris D 4:11:41 (14,729)
Dale, Graham T 4:29:11 (19,447)
Dale, Ingolf 4:47:22 (24,001)
Dale, John 3:50:47 (9,006)
Dale, Jonathan B 2:51:25 (569)
Dale, Nick 3:09:18 (1,918)
Dale, Phil S 5:28:28 (30,319)
Dale, Stephen G 3:19:56 (3,219)
Dale, Steven G 5:25:46 (30,008)
Dales, Donovan 4:41:33 (22,565)
Dales, Robert R 5:50:06 (32,135)
D'Alessio, Giovanni 3:44:21 (7,522)
Daley, Andrew J 5:29:52 (30,463)
Daley, Bruce 5:58:43 (32,682)
Daley, Paul D 3:39:18 (6,499)

Daley, Sam 3:24:20 (3,820)
Dalgarno, Mark F 3:32:37 (5,336)
Dallard, Steve 3:58:55 (11,460)
Dallas, Gordon C 3:51:46 (9,241)
Dalley, Robert J 3:55:56 (10,473)
Dalmas, Gilbert 4:17:08 (16,135)
Dalton, James R 3:29:10 (4,707)
Dalton, Jason C 5:02:37 (27,053)
Dalton, Paul W 4:33:27 (20,562)
Dalton, Stephen W 4:26:59 (18,809)
Dalton, William N 5:34:22 (30,872)
Dalton-Moore, Charles J 4:30:22 (19,717)
Daly, Bryan C 5:57:16 (32,591)
Daly, Chris 4:01:18 (12,184)
Daly, Francis 4:11:02 (14,551)
Daly, Hugh D 3:51:09 (9,086)
Daly, Neil R 3:51:02 (9,058)
Daly, Peter 4:25:02 (18,271)
Dalziel, Julian A 3:32:51 (5,371)
D'Amato, Andy 4:17:30 (16,220)
Dambry, Thibaut 3:49:32 (8,706)
Dameno, Luigi 3:23:51 (3,749)
Damerell, Neil M 3:28:13 (4,508)
Damette, Yves 4:24:58 (18,256)
Dampney, Hugh 4:13:55 (15,283)
Danaher, James D 3:42:55 (7,214)
Danaher, Kieran J 4:08:06 (13,789)
Danber, William K 3:44:05 (7,470)
Danbury, David W 5:02:24 (27,027)
Dance, Andrew 3:33:23 (5,449)
Danciger, Simon L 3:12:16 (2,245)
Dando, Richard L 3:15:51 (2,737)
Dane, Barnaby P 3:28:13 (4,508)
Daneels, Thomas 3:50:44 (8,996)
Daneshvar, Ahrash J 4:54:50 (25,657)
Danesi, Mark J 4:41:49 (22,641)
Dangla, Philippe L 3:55:37 (10,379)
Dani, Tushar 7:02:22 (34,235)
Daniel, Angus 4:44:48 (23,367)
Daniel, Raymond A 4:32:30 (20,300)
Daniele-Brewer, Steve P 4:48:07 (24,169)
Daniels, Alan 3:29:27 (4,772)
Daniels, Andrew R 5:57:42 (32,614)
Daniels, Danny 5:00:38 (26,725)
Daniels, David J 3:19:28 (3,158)
Daniels, Ian 4:56:11 (25,910)
Daniels, Mike 4:56:26 (25,953)
Daniels, Paul 3:06:02 (1,600)
Daniels, Paul 3:55:07 (10,241)
Daniels, Paul 4:06:54 (13,493)
Daniels, Paul B 4:30:09 (19,667)
Daniels, Phil 4:49:11 (24,410)
Daniels, Stephen P 3:16:59 (2,861)
Daniels, Thomas C 5:33:48 (30,814)
Danielsen, Staale 3:14:15 (2,509)
Daniju, Michael 5:33:45 (30,807)
Danks, Peter R 4:56:56 (26,063)
Danks, Simon J 3:14:46 (2,600)
Dann, Mitchell 3:26:25 (4,175)
Dann, Neil R 3:15:30 (2,701)
Dann, Peter 4:17:25 (16,195)
Dannan, Stephen 3:57:29 (10,948)
Dansey, Mathew T 5:22:40 (29,675)
Danton, Marc P 4:54:26 (25,569)
Danzey, Mark S 3:29:30 (4,782)
Dapra, Frederic 3:03:57 (1,445)
Darby, Matthew J 3:38:20 (6,321)
Darby, Richard A 4:33:06 (20,457)
Darbyshire, Phillip B 2:36:05 (132)
Darcy, Paul 3:56:26 (10,605)
D'Arcy, Adrian 3:49:15 (8,644)
Dark, David E 4:51:26 (24,928)
Dark, Jeremy M 4:24:08 (18,029)
Darke, Adam 3:43:38 (7,373)
Darler, Stephen J 4:22:24 (17,551)
Darley, Edward P 4:09:33 (14,188)
Darling, Don F 3:53:21 (9,677)
Darling, Nicholas P 5:55:05 (32,468)
Darling, Steven M 3:45:17 (7,752)
Darnell, Peter F 4:28:36 (19,289)
Darnell, Robert J 5:19:10 (29,311)
Darragh, James 4:28:54 (19,378)
Darroch, Nick C 4:05:48 (13,246)
Dart, Ian 3:15:57 (2,751)
Dart, Kenneth R 3:42:18 (7,094)
Darton, David 3:47:33 (8,235)
Dash, Jonathan P 3:51:12 (9,099)
Dashper, Wayne R 2:36:05 (132)
Datardina, Azim S 5:11:48 (28,385)
Dattani, Dilip 3:03:14 (1,395)
Daubignard, Xavier 4:40:06 (22,213)
Daude, Helder H 3:53:50 (9,824)
Dauge, Christophe 4:12:33 (14,940)
Daugherty, Duane W 3:13:59 (2,463)
Dauncey, William 3:40:57 (6,815)
Dauver, Robert 3:37:11 (6,098)
Davenport, Malcolm C 3:59:09 (11,544)
Davenport, Mark 4:42:53 (22,901)
Davenport, Matt G 4:25:22 (18,359)
Davey, Aaron J 5:02:11 (26,985)
Davey, Alan J 4:49:04 (24,388)
Davey, Arren J 4:07:03 (13,531)
Davey, Craig 2:58:36 (1,018)
Davey, Howard R 3:25:50 (4,075)
Davey, Ian 5:11:39 (28,354)
Davey, Ian P 3:56:26 (10,605)
Davey, Jack R 4:05:33 (13,189)
Davey, Kristian S 3:37:57 (6,252)
Davey, Michael J 4:42:15 (22,742)
Davey, Mo M 5:41:33 (31,470)
Davey, Paul 4:10:10 (14,328)
Davey, Paul K 6:05:04 (32,931)
Davey, Peter W 7:03:01 (34,243)
Davey, Sam 3:48:30 (8,466)
Davey, Thomas W 4:00:17 (11,921)
David, Carol A 5:02:29 (27,041)
Davidson, Andrew J 4:28:41 (19,310)
Davidson, Colin M 4:48:51 (24,333)
Davidson, David W 5:49:26 (32,081)
Davidson, John G 4:40:10 (22,229)
Davidson, Kenneth G 3:06:22 (1,632)
Davidson, Len 3:36:46 (6,005)
Davidson, Mark W 3:38:20 (6,321)
Davidson, Matthew T 4:19:47 (16,832)
Davidson, Steven A 5:39:11 (31,273)
Davidson, Stuart 4:58:55 (26,459)
Davie, Michael G 4:21:43 (17,380)
Davie, Tim D 3:10:22 (2,027)
Davies, Adam H 4:37:49 (21,675)
Davies, Adrian H 5:17:25 (29,111)
Davies, Alexander J 4:25:06 (18,288)
Davies, Andrew L 2:52:59 (639)
Davies, Ben 4:47:53 (24,120)
Davies, Ben 4:55:54 (25,859)
Davies, Brian C 4:00:34 (11,994)
Davies, Chris 4:14:18 (15,398)
Davies, Clive T 3:14:06 (2,484)
Davies, Conrad C 4:12:20 (14,892)
Davies, Dalis G 3:46:17 (7,948)
Davies, David 4:42:51 (22,892)
Davies, David 5:01:01 (26,798)
Davies, Dylan H 4:43:24 (23,026)
Davies, Fred H 3:53:14 (9,644)
Davies, Gareth 4:45:44 (23,598)
Davies, Gareth H 4:31:01 (19,887)
Davies, Gareth I 5:48:36 (32,021)
Davies, Gareth R 4:04:45 (12,994)
Davies, Gavin R 2:50:51 (547)
Davies, Geoff J 4:40:36 (22,330)
Davies, Graham M 3:49:26 (8,681)
Davies, Haydn 5:22:37 (29,672)
Davies, Haydn 6:43:45 (33,955)
Davies, Huw 4:30:44 (19,811)
Davies, Hywel J 3:50:18 (8,896)
Davies, Ian 3:14:39 (2,580)
Davies, Ian J 3:34:50 (5,676)
Davies, Ioan 3:55:41 (10,399)
Davies, James E 2:48:40 (453)
Davies, James E 3:29:18 (4,739)
Davies, James S 4:17:57 (16,334)
Davies, Jason L 3:27:15 (4,324)
Davies, Jim 4:50:12 (24,643)
Davies, John C 4:38:35 (21,855)
Davies, John F 4:47:27 (24,011)
Davies, Julian 4:06:28 (13,390)
Davies, Kasie B 3:47:11 (8,149)
Davies, Keith 3:48:11 (8,395)
Davies, Keith J 2:56:13 (822)
Davies, Kevin 5:02:38 (27,055)
Davies, Kevin J 2:58:47 (1,038)
Davies, Kevin M 3:56:53 (10,756)
Davies, Lee J 5:38:44 (31,242)
Davies, Lee M 4:30:12 (19,678)
Davies, Leighton E 4:20:38 (17,074)
Davies, Lyndon H 3:53:15 (9,649)
Davies, Mark C 3:07:12 (1,698)
Davies, Mark C 3:31:26 (5,122)
Davies, Mark W 5:29:54 (30,466)
Davies, Martin 5:04:56 (27,387)
Davies, Martin L 3:23:05 (3,651)
Davies, Martin V 3:08:10 (1,811)
Davies, Mathew D 5:50:53 (32,201)
Davies, Matthew 5:43:04 (31,575)
Davies, Matthew R 4:48:55 (24,350)
Davies, Max 3:32:20 (5,286)
Davies, Michael H 4:20:37 (17,068)
Davies, Michael J 4:08:05 (13,784)
Davies, Michael J 5:42:54 (31,561)
Davies, Nick 3:44:56 (7,665)
Davies, Nick M 4:52:25 (25,127)
Davies, Nick S 3:11:21 (2,132)
Davies, Oliver R 3:25:44 (4,058)
Davies, Oliver S 3:52:13 (9,363)
Davies, Paul A 2:50:21 (528)
Davies, Paul J 3:53:46 (9,796)
Davies, Peter 5:09:07 (27,984)
Davies, Peter J 3:43:25 (7,327)
Davies, Peter J 3:44:30 (7,553)
Davies, Phil J 3:25:00 (3,930)
Davies, Philip N 4:42:36 (22,832)
Davies, Rhys G 4:32:59 (20,427)
Davies, Richard 4:01:58 (12,353)
Davies, Richard 4:14:29 (15,446)
Davies, Richard 5:00:49 (26,769)
Davies, Richard L 5:48:22 (32,000)
Davies, Robert 5:34:55 (30,932)
Davies, Robert W 5:59:18 (32,704)
Davies, Robin D 4:28:29 (19,256)
Davies, Roger P 4:55:47 (25,836)
Davies, Sam J 4:15:03 (15,579)
Davies, Simon L 3:47:15 (8,169)
Davies, Stephen 4:15:42 (15,745)
Davies, Stephen C 2:50:30 (536)
Davies, Stephen H 4:01:06 (12,136)
Davies, Stephen J 3:15:10 (2,649)
Davies, Thomas G 3:15:01 (2,634)
Davies, Thomas R 3:05:15 (1,534)
Davies, Timothy C 4:22:15 (17,509)
Davies, Tony M 5:38:07 (31,197)
Davini, Antonio 5:17:15 (29,090)
Davis, Adam 4:01:10 (12,156)
Davis, Andrew M 4:03:24 (12,700)
Davis, Andrew R 3:03:02 (1,375)
Davis, Barry 4:45:57 (23,661)
Davis, Ben 4:44:49 (23,375)
Davis, Brian 4:04:14 (12,871)
Davis, Brian K 4:12:50 (14,988)
Davis, Charles 3:10:09 (2,006)
Davis, Chris 6:42:06 (33,913)
Davis, Christopher 3:52:03 (9,318)
Davis, Daniel F 3:37:40 (6,197)
Davis, Ewen 3:33:17 (5,436)
Davis, Francis 4:33:43 (20,639)
Davis, Iain C 4:10:15 (14,351)
Davis, Ian H 2:47:08 (392)
Davis, James R 5:15:43 (28,908)
Davis, John E 3:55:51 (10,452)
Davis, Jonathan M 4:11:54 (14,778)
Davis, Justin 5:38:25 (31,221)
Davis, Kristian J 3:39:20 (6,503)
Davis, Mark A 3:04:51 (1,507)
Davis, Mark E 3:59:30 (11,676)
Davis, Martin 6:39:59 (33,881)
Davis, Martin B 3:19:22 (3,146)
Davis, Martin J 2:50:41 (543)
Davis, Nicholas G 2:53:50 (681)
Davis, Paul 3:29:49 (4,843)
Davis, Paul A 7:36:41 (34,475)
Davis, Paul W 2:50:25 (533)

Davis, Peter A 3:40:56 (6,811)
Davis, Richard M 3:08:25 (1,831)
Davis, Richard M 3:52:01 (9,305)
Davis, Robert J 3:14:09 (2,492)
Davis, Ross G 3:59:56 (11,831)
Davis, Sean 6:21:05 (33,431)
Davis, Simon J 3:43:26 (7,332)
Davis, Simon M 3:52:38 (9,468)
Davis, Stephen D 3:46:08 (7,916)
Davis, Stephen M 3:52:05 (9,327)
Davis, Stephen P 4:22:58 (17,719)
Davis, Tom 4:14:02 (15,316)
Davis, Trevor 4:04:58 (13,042)
Davison, Andrew S 4:04:40 (12,972)
Davison, Lee 5:13:30 (28,608)
Davison, Max 3:42:52 (7,210)
Davison, Neil A 2:35:37 (122)
Davison, Patrick 4:15:03 (15,579)
Davison, Scott H 4:13:38 (15,198)
Davitt, James R 4:59:38 (26,582)
Davy, Martin S 5:36:19 (31,067)
Davy, P-J 5:36:19 (31,067)
Davy, Simon 4:31:56 (20,147)
Daw, Philip J 3:32:43 (5,346)
Dawe, Andrew M 3:26:57 (4,271)
Dawe, James 4:17:32 (16,232)
Dawes, Ian P 4:40:42 (22,353)
Dawes, Michael E 4:06:29 (13,395)
Dawes, Paul W 3:22:28 (3,560)
Dawkins, Colin 4:04:58 (13,042)
Dawson, Alan R 3:13:31 (2,396)
Dawson, Bernard J 3:59:52 (11,807)
Dawson, Christopher D 3:12:27 (2,260)
Dawson, Christopher R 3:26:33 (4,192)
Dawson, Gavin J 4:41:50 (22,647)
Dawson, Geoff 3:34:15 (5,584)
Dawson, John 5:44:32 (31,724)
Dawson, Kevin J 3:50:21 (8,900)
Dawson, Lee 3:50:31 (8,931)
Dawson, Martin 4:19:50 (16,842)
Dawson, Matthew J 4:20:36 (17,061)
Dawson, Philip B 3:17:32 (2,935)
Dawson, Philip J 3:44:15 (7,502)
Dawson, Richard A 4:15:51 (15,795)
Dawson, Robert B 6:35:24 (33,784)
Dawson, Stevie 4:51:36 (24,960)
Dawson, Vincent M 4:51:19 (24,909)
Day, Adam 3:44:03 (7,463)
Day, Andrew R 4:31:37 (20,056)
Day, Ashley B 3:02:39 (1,357)
Day, Colin J 3:43:03 (7,248)
Day, David C 3:54:08 (9,915)
Day, Ian 2:46:36 (377)
Day, Joseph J 4:06:42 (13,451)
Day, Julian E 3:58:20 (11,236)
Day, Kevin G 5:39:16 (31,282)
Day, Mark 5:57:47 (32,619)
Day, Matthew J 4:58:09 (26,315)
Day, Richard J 3:41:41 (6,964)
Day, Richard J 4:14:04 (15,326)
Day, Richard N 4:22:39 (17,631)
Day, Stephen M 6:26:55 (33,597)
Day, Toby G 3:31:07 (5,064)
Days, Anthony G 5:06:58 (27,692)
De Baere, Paul 3:28:09 (4,498)
De Beer, Zach J 3:35:02 (5,708)
De Belder, Daniel L 3:42:57 (7,223)
De Bisschop, Ivo 3:49:52 (8,791)
De Boise, Matthew J 4:36:17 (21,320)
De Bono, Carl 4:43:39 (23,088)
De Bosredon, Jean Paul F 4:12:56 (15,011)
De Bruijn, Walter R 4:29:45 (19,578)
De Bruin, Andreas N 4:20:45 (17,103)
De Bruyne, Izaak 2:48:13 (433)
De Chazal, Oscar 3:33:41 (5,504)
De Cock, Christian E 4:16:57 (16,074)
De Cock, Frederic G 3:49:51 (8,786)
De Croos, Douglas J 4:57:57 (26,271)
De Fanis, Alberto 2:59:23 (1,108)
De Fazio, Domenico 3:48:23 (8,437)
De Groot, Benedict C 3:45:46 (7,849)
De Groot, Sebastian 4:05:18 (13,121)
De Jong, Gerard 3:25:11 (3,959)
De Keyzer, Herman J 5:36:44 (31,097)
De La Hey, Johnny D 3:08:42 (1,851)
De Laeter, Sietse 4:11:05 (14,571)
De Luca, Paolo A 3:14:22 (2,526)
De Man, Laurens J 3:24:40 (3,863)
De Marchi, Renato 3:23:00 (3,636)
De Martin, Stephen 4:12:33 (14,940)
De Montfort, Guy 4:38:08 (21,747)
De Mowbray, Richard M 4:10:09 (14,325)
De Quidt, Andy C 3:58:06 (11,142)
De Rienzo, Roberto 4:32:59 (20,427)
De Silva, Suresh P 4:38:34 (21,849)
De Souza, Peter 5:25:06 (29,936)
De Vengoechea, Felipe 4:24:37 (18,175)
De Vent, Ruud 5:02:24 (27,027)
De Vere Moss, Christopher C 5:11:10 (28,289)
De Vignemont, Gilles 4:39:03 (21,988)
De Vrind, Hans M 6:38:08 (33,844)
De Vroeg, Eric 4:05:19 (13,125)
Deacon, Ross M 4:49:11 (24,410)
Deadfield, Tony 4:51:42 (24,985)
Deadman, Scott 5:43:16 (31,594)
Deadman, Sean A 4:08:54 (14,018)
Deahl, Nicholas A 3:52:25 (9,415)
Deakin, Lee 4:59:14 (26,522)
Deakin, Rob 4:10:44 (14,475)
Deal, James 5:06:46 (27,660)
Deal, Stuart 4:53:28 (25,364)
Dean, Barnaby L 3:58:45 (11,389)
Dean, David E 3:32:27 (5,309)
Dean, Gary 3:01:36 (1,283)
Dean, Gary 5:08:23 (27,871)
Dean, Gary J 5:44:16 (31,693)
Dean, Glyn P 5:44:16 (31,693)
Dean, Justin 3:40:23 (6,711)
Dean, Mark R 3:39:36 (6,558)
Dean, Martin J 5:19:27 (29,346)
Dean, Michael R 3:10:11 (2,010)
Dean, Paul D 5:54:03 (32,411)
Dean, Peter A 3:47:45 (8,286)
Dean, Russell J 4:18:40 (16,546)
Dean, Stuart 4:43:05 (22,954)
Dean, Thomas P 4:14:21 (15,410)
Deane, Leo J 4:13:53 (15,273)
Deans, Frank 5:01:49 (26,932)
Deans, Nick 3:40:22 (6,708)
Dear, Andrew J 5:27:36 (30,209)
Dear, Richard A 4:06:13 (13,333)
Dear, Stephen 4:38:03 (21,724)
Dear, Steve C 3:25:42 (4,049)
Deardon, Ray R 7:48:51 (34,505)
Dearnley, Adam 5:04:08 (27,268)
Dearsley, Tony P 3:51:07 (9,078)
Deason, Davd 3:39:28 (6,531)
Deasy, James L 3:56:54 (10,762)
Debatisse, Jean-François 4:05:12 (13,098)
Debboudt, Mario 3:19:28 (3,158)
Debling, David H 4:19:10 (16,673)
Decair, Thomas W 7:12:03 (34,343)
Decambre, Phillip 6:05:21 (32,937)
Decote, Pierre B 3:21:55 (3,475)
Dee, Kobie J 5:49:54 (32,113)
Deen, Paul J 4:09:26 (14,151)
Deeny, Simon J 3:43:27 (7,335)
Deer, William B 4:11:13 (14,610)
Dees, Craig R 4:00:44 (12,043)
Degeneve, Fabrice 4:47:44 (24,080)
Degrange, Julien 3:36:04 (5,892)
Deidda, Giuseppe 4:07:54 (13,753)
Dekas, Ioannis 4:55:28 (25,777)
De-Kisshazy, Peter R 3:54:40 (10,089)
Del Gobbo, Gino 3:58:34 (11,326)
Del Pino Ruano, Juan 3:42:15 (7,081)
Del Val Perez, Juan 3:44:20 (7,519)
Del Valle, Fernando 2:29:46 (71)
Del Valle Garrido, Manuel 3:40:12 (6,673)
Del Vecchio, Aurelio 4:09:50 (14,259)
Delagrange, Herve 5:03:08 (27,123)
Delahoy, Trevor R 3:43:39 (7,378)
Delaisse, Bernard F 3:53:44 (9,783)
Delaney, James 3:35:12 (5,737)
Delaney, Joseph P 4:52:32 (25,154)
Delaney, Lee D 4:40:19 (22,262)
Delaney, Sean J 4:25:42 (18,444)
Delaney, Shaun M 5:28:44 (30,346)
Delangle, Florent 3:25:35 (4,029)
Delbrouck, Christian F 3:59:33 (11,688)
De-Lempdes, Michel 3:22:54 (3,624)
Delgado Medina, Ruben D 3:35:47 (5,841)
Delgaty, Neil J 4:21:45 (17,389)
Dell, Graeme J 4:22:05 (17,466)
Della Torre, Elvio 3:42:31 (7,141)
Dellavedova, Michel 3:22:05 (3,501)
Delneri, Gabriele 3:34:43 (5,648)
Delooze, Gary A 4:38:34 (21,849)
Delph, Paul S 4:52:57 (25,259)
Del-Vecchio, Jerome 4:09:42 (14,228)
Del-Vecchio, Patrick 3:09:42 (1,961)
Demarco, David 4:15:38 (15,737)
Demetriou, Peter M 4:27:15 (18,890)
Demin, Soren 5:26:30 (30,098)
Deminier, Loic 4:04:54 (13,021)
Demirel, Murat 4:31:22 (19,983)
Denee, Hugo A 4:07:49 (13,720)
Denham, Brian R 3:39:19 (6,501)
Denham, Lee W 4:39:50 (22,157)
Denham, Paul T 3:21:30 (3,426)
Denham, Toby N 3:32:54 (5,373)
Denis, Roberto 4:56:30 (25,971)
Denmel, Michael 4:22:38 (17,627)
Denn, Simon R 3:20:56 (3,348)
Denney, Mark 3:48:05 (8,368)
Dennis, Anthony M 4:23:30 (17,867)
Dennis, Jason L 4:40:48 (22,379)
Dennis, Matthew J 4:05:23 (13,140)
Dennis, Matthew R 5:30:10 (30,493)
Dennis, Paul 3:56:56 (10,774)
Dennis, Paul A 3:14:12 (2,498)
Dennis, Paul J 3:03:38 (1,426)
Dennis, Paul M 5:25:19 (29,968)
Dennis, Robert A 5:22:06 (29,614)
Dennis, Spencer C 3:34:26 (5,610)
Dennis, Steven P 5:25:17 (29,961)
Dennison, Michael 5:17:08 (29,080)
Dennison, Nicholas J 4:48:51 (24,333)
Dennison, Paul J 4:25:12 (18,321)
Denny, Jason R 4:36:20 (21,334)
Denny, Jonny A 5:30:11 (30,496)
Denny, Lynden 5:37:07 (31,123)
Denny, Michael J 5:03:25 (27,167)
Denny, Stephen D 4:05:25 (13,153)
Dent, Darren 4:11:43 (14,739)
Dent, David R 3:46:25 (7,984)
Denton, Roger S 2:59:37 (1,131)
Denyer, James E 3:32:38 (5,338)
Denyer, John F 3:33:25 (5,457)
Denyer, William 4:00:30 (11,975)
Deol, Jaswant S 3:39:15 (6,483)
Deotto, Marco 3:15:00 (2,627)
De-Poorter, Eric 2:46:48 (382)
Derbyshire, David 4:13:39 (15,203)
Derbyshire, Martin 5:10:51 (28,260)
Derbyshire, Russell J 2:59:36 (1,129)
Derbyshire, Stephen J 4:58:37 (26,403)
Derdau, Christian 4:58:11 (26,323)
Derdau, Gunther 4:58:13 (26,328)
Dering, David 3:48:14 (8,407)
Derrett, Joe 3:31:45 (5,179)
Derrett, Keith J 4:12:57 (15,017)
Derrett, Robin 4:28:36 (19,289)
Derrick, Ian M 4:11:50 (14,765)
Derrick, Stuart 4:49:39 (24,521)
Derry, Mark 3:03:36 (1,425)
Dervish, Tolga 6:38:04 (33,842)
Desai, Bhavik 3:57:44 (11,029)
Desborough, Simon J 4:11:06 (14,578)
Deschrevel, Gaetan 3:33:48 (5,518)
Desentis, Arturo 4:30:26 (19,728)
Desmond, Colin B 3:51:53 (9,271)
Desmond, Paul 4:47:52 (24,109)
Desmond, Stephen 4:04:33 (12,939)
Desouza, Michael J 5:43:24 (31,600)
Despic, John S 3:28:06 (4,481)
Desprats, Guy 4:56:25 (25,951)
Dessioux, Jean François 4:24:07 (18,023)
Deuchar, James A 4:24:00 (17,994)

Deunf, Philippe 5:11:46 (28,379)
Devereaux, John 4:50:55 (24,826)
Deverell, Adrian E 4:43:13 (22,985)
Devereux, James W 3:55:56 (10,473)
Deverson, Grahame M 3:59:51 (11,802)
Devile, Simon 3:47:16 (8,172)
Deville, Christophe 3:47:51 (8,313)
Devine, Andrew T 3:22:25 (3,553)
Devine, Paul D 3:44:42 (7,604)
Devine, Ron 4:35:36 (21,137)
Devitt, Martin R 4:07:36 (13,670)
Devitt, Russell 4:05:56 (13,275)
Devlin, Brendan J 3:38:50 (6,415)
Devlin, Mike M 4:26:02 (18,548)
Devlin, Paul D 4:18:03 (16,354)
Devonish, Anthony 4:57:34 (26,199)
Dew, Simon J 2:56:11 (819)
Dewar, Will 3:17:21 (2,911)
Dewey, Martin A 4:27:32 (18,960)
Dexter, Colin G 5:52:11 (32,299)
Dexter, Jonathan N 6:31:01 (33,685)
Dexter Smith, Michael J 4:21:33 (17,319)
Dey, Andrew J 4:05:46 (13,235)
Dhaliwal, Jagdeep 3:31:11 (5,073)
Dhami, Gurdip 4:48:47 (24,315)
Dhariwal, Navraj S 4:26:47 (18,750)
Dhesi, Surjit 3:23:17 (3,673)
Dhillon, Myles P 4:25:55 (18,513)
Dhoat, Jasjeet S 4:58:04 (26,297)
Dhuhulow, Abdifatah 3:14:40 (2,583)
Di Ck, Michael J 3:36:00 (5,882)
Di Liberto, Lorenzo 3:16:54 (2,852)
Di Mascio, Corrado 4:52:30 (25,146)
Di Prospero, Daniele 3:53:49 (9,815)
Di Ruzza, Martin 3:42:48 (7,197)
Di Salvo, Dino 4:20:28 (17,015)
Diagana, Stephane 2:56:13 (822)
Diamond, Jim 4:52:18 (25,104)
Diamond, Samuel P 3:26:13 (4,139)
Diana, Aldo 5:57:13 (32,589)
Diarcy, Andrew 5:57:43 (32,617)
Dias, Luis 5:14:54 (28,806)
Dias, Roberto P 3:14:00 (2,466)
Diaz Olmo, Jesus 4:03:06 (12,629)
Diazzi, Giorgio 4:06:22 (13,366)
Dibaba, Siraj 3:54:32 (10,045)
Dibb Fuller, Jason P 3:33:40 (5,501)
Dibben, Francis R 5:09:03 (27,976)
Di-Bella, Jonathan 5:21:42 (29,578)
Dick, Alistair 3:10:47 (2,075)
Dick, Robert T 2:58:20 (982)
Dickens, Peter 4:44:28 (23,294)
Dicker, David 3:17:34 (2,937)
Dickie, Peter C 5:15:02 (28,826)
Dickinson, Anthony J 3:43:13 (7,290)
Dickinson, Christopher R 5:24:06 (29,817)
Dickinson, David J 4:40:07 (22,215)
Dickinson, Duncan 4:52:57 (25,259)
Dickinson, Kelvin B 4:16:41 (16,009)
Dickinson, Mark 2:35:48 (127)
Dickinson, Mark 5:25:21 (29,973)
Dickinson, Mark T 4:49:59 (24,597)
Dickinson, Ralph W 3:36:52 (6,033)
Dickinson, Richard 3:27:30 (4,363)
Dickinson, Russell 4:27:05 (18,834)
Dickmann, Volker 5:05:10 (27,431)
Dicks, Christopher M 4:34:04 (20,712)
Dicks, Philip L 5:19:10 (29,311)
Dickson, Alan R 3:25:06 (3,947)
Dickson, Christopher M 3:31:18 (5,100)
Dickson, James 4:55:02 (25,706)
Dickson, Kevin G 3:54:38 (10,082)
Dickson, Matthew J 5:29:08 (30,389)
Dickson, Paul 4:06:42 (13,451)
Didaoui, Tarek 5:26:19 (30,073)
Diddams, Greg 3:09:35 (1,950)
Dides, Simon 4:16:47 (16,029)
Didier, Carfanton 3:46:46 (8,054)
Diesinger, Aloys 3:58:52 (11,444)
Dietz, Carl 3:51:42 (9,229)
Digby, Adrian J 4:38:16 (21,770)
Digby, Julian E 3:42:07 (7,051)
Digby-Baker, Hugh J 4:36:29 (21,364)
Digernes, Marton 4:00:13 (11,901)
Diggens, Carl E 4:37:00 (21,485)
Diggens, Karl R 4:29:58 (19,625)
Dignan, Robert 5:06:42 (27,652)
Digwa, Gurmukh S 4:12:16 (14,879)
Dilasser, Olivier 3:44:34 (7,569)
Dilaudo, Stephen H 3:54:15 (9,943)
Dilks, Justin M 3:41:32 (6,945)
Dillet, Alain 3:37:16 (6,118)
Dilley, Sean 4:52:27 (25,134)
Dillon, Greg 6:20:01 (33,395)
Dillon, Mark T 5:11:45 (28,376)
Dillon, Oliver 3:37:36 (6,183)
Dilworth, Joseph R 5:03:33 (27,191)
Dilworth, Robby A 4:31:56 (20,147)
Dimbleby, Peter J 2:42:17 (249)
Dimelow, Geoffrey 3:39:52 (6,612)
Dimelow, Glenn C 3:25:42 (4,049)
Dimmock, Chris P 3:47:01 (8,113)
Dimond, Keith J 6:24:37 (33,536)
Dimond, Martyn D 5:51:32 (32,253)
Dineley, Mark 4:08:46 (13,985)
Dingle, Nick B 4:09:15 (14,104)
Dingley, Graham J 3:14:12 (2,498)
Dingley, Paul 3:39:29 (6,533)
Dingwall, Basil 5:17:43 (29,142)
Dingwall, Mark S 3:47:16 (8,172)
Dinn, Anthony J 3:56:19 (10,568)
Dinsdale, Ewan A 3:29:00 (4,669)
Dionisio, Tiago B 4:02:21 (12,460)
Dipple, Peter H 5:11:31 (28,333)
Disson, John P 4:12:19 (14,887)
Ditcham, Robert J 3:56:36 (10,663)
Ditton, Jamie R 4:02:14 (12,423)
Ditz, Johannes 3:27:11 (4,310)
Dix, Greg H 5:31:53 (30,645)
Dix, Peter G 5:08:33 (27,904)
Dix, Phil M 5:24:32 (29,861)
Dix, Philip J 3:48:45 (8,521)
Dixon, Andrew 3:57:24 (10,928)
Dixon, Andrew J 3:28:56 (4,650)
Dixon, Ben 3:32:02 (5,233)
Dixon, Christopher 4:57:53 (26,259)
Dixon, Clem 2:44:43 (323)
Dixon, Craig L 3:23:51 (3,749)
Dixon, David 3:15:20 (2,680)
Dixon, Garry J 2:36:20 (136)
Dixon, Gary 4:40:16 (22,249)
Dixon, George D 4:17:53 (16,321)
Dixon, Gordon M 2:44:03 (294)
Dixon, Ian H 3:19:28 (3,158)
Dixon, Kent 3:25:13 (3,962)
Dixon, Kevin A 4:04:31 (12,934)
Dixon, Mark E 5:26:20 (30,077)
Dixon, Mark H 5:16:36 (29,007)
Dixon, Mark R 4:00:06 (11,876)
Dixon, Mark S 5:00:29 (26,704)
Dixon, Michael P 6:11:26 (33,154)
Dixon, Neil A 3:30:00 (4,885)
Dixon, Paul A 3:54:08 (9,915)
Dixon, Rob 3:31:30 (5,127)
Dixon, Robert S 3:21:20 (3,408)
Dixon, Rupert 4:55:54 (25,859)
Dixon, Sam J 4:38:27 (21,818)
Dixon, Steve 4:33:31 (20,579)
Dixon, Thomas C 4:18:32 (16,508)
Dixon, Trevor J 2:43:50 (287)
Djaouk, Samir 4:20:30 (17,028)
D'Netto, Matthew J 3:36:55 (6,041)
Dobbie, David R 3:54:42 (10,102)
Dobbins, Lee C 3:40:44 (6,765)
Dobbs, Andrew R 3:35:58 (5,875)
Dobbs, Patrick A 3:31:54 (5,198)
Dobbs, Simon C 2:49:09 (470)
Dobby, Andrew M 2:54:04 (699)
Dobek, Jonathan 4:13:33 (15,172)
Dobrzinsky, Manfred 3:33:35 (5,486)
Dobson, Christopher J 4:05:44 (13,230)
Dobson, Jay 4:16:44 (16,013)
Dobson, John 4:20:50 (17,133)
Dobson, Jonathan J 3:51:31 (9,176)
Dobson, Luke A 4:52:44 (25,207)
Dobson, Nicholas J 4:53:47 (25,437)
Dobson, Nigel J 5:02:01 (26,960)
Dobson, Philip 4:18:07 (16,374)
Dobson, Raymond 4:24:42 (18,194)
Dobson, Richard 3:53:01 (9,582)
Docherty, John H 6:56:56 (34,182)
Dockar, Andrew D 3:43:43 (7,391)
Dockerill, Steven C 3:32:46 (5,355)
Docking, Steve J 3:44:08 (7,480)
Dodd, Andrew K 3:20:38 (3,310)
Dodd, Gavin R 3:57:04 (10,816)
Dodd, Kevin A 4:17:57 (16,334)
Dodd, Michael G 3:58:53 (11,451)
Dodd, Rowan 5:23:02 (29,701)
Dodd, Simon P 4:38:46 (21,902)
Dodd, Stephen J 5:25:57 (30,030)
Dodds, Alastair 4:28:46 (19,335)
Dodds, Duncan M 4:47:44 (24,080)
Dodds, Jeffrey 4:18:17 (16,429)
Dodds, Kirk 4:04:00 (12,833)
Dodes, Mark 4:31:16 (19,952)
Dodson, Edward C 3:53:46 (9,796)
Dodsworth, Peter A 4:48:29 (24,243)
Doe, Don G 3:11:47 (2,187)
Doggett, James A 5:41:22 (31,447)
Dogra, Ray 5:40:40 (31,388)
Doherty, Anthony 4:38:47 (21,908)
Doherty, Ciaran M 4:39:00 (21,974)
Doherty, Daniel 4:50:25 (24,688)
Doherty, Declan P 4:28:27 (19,247)
Doherty, Dominic 4:39:01 (21,975)
Doherty, James H 6:55:30 (34,161)
Doherty, John A 3:20:17 (3,263)
Doherty, Peter 3:54:37 (10,078)
Doherty, Tom A 3:32:30 (5,322)
Doktor, Bernd 4:37:57 (21,704)
Dolan, Keith M 4:37:27 (21,585)
Dolan, Mark 4:25:42 (18,444)
Dolan, Peter 3:12:16 (2,245)
Dolan, Robert 3:14:30 (2,546)
Dolan, Robert 3:21:09 (3,378)
Dolben, Ian P 5:27:38 (30,216)
Dolden, Gerry S 4:35:48 (21,195)
Dolinar, Robert 4:24:21 (18,094)
Dolle, Gaston A 4:35:49 (21,197)
Dollin, Paul 3:58:43 (11,382)
Dollman, Peter J 5:14:01 (28,675)
Dolman, Glen R 5:15:37 (28,892)
Dolphin, James H 3:01:45 (1,292)
Dolphin, Nicholas A 3:52:52 (9,526)
Domaille, Colin P 4:06:44 (13,459)
Doman, Anthony J 4:56:52 (26,040)
Domart, Pierre 4:00:00 (11,853)
Dome, Andrew J 3:45:24 (7,774)
Domercq, Pascal 4:13:22 (15,132)
Domingo Corpas, Juan 3:44:49 (7,635)
Dominguez de la Maza, Manuel 3:58:22 (11,251)
Dominguez Martin, Jon 4:27:58 (19,088)
Dommett, Paul M 3:30:31 (4,974)
Dommett, Robert A 6:35:51 (33,792)
Domoney, Nigel R 5:07:35 (27,778)
Domoney, Richard M 3:55:43 (10,409)
Don, Robert M 3:33:32 (5,480)
Donaghey, Jamie M 3:25:54 (4,085)
Donaghy, Nigel 6:08:27 (33,063)
Donald, Callum 3:29:51 (4,849)
Donald, Gary 4:13:13 (15,091)
Donald, Michael J 4:16:55 (16,065)
Donald, Paul 3:49:19 (8,653)
Donald, Steven S 3:53:16 (9,653)
Donaldson, Andrew S 3:51:29 (9,173)
Donaldson, Anthony 4:30:34 (19,766)
Donaldson, Craig E 4:07:01 (13,522)
Donaldson, Graham M 3:17:52 (2,971)
Donaldson, Jamie P 4:33:41 (20,633)
Donaldson, William M 3:30:53 (5,035)
Donegan, David 5:25:12 (29,948)
Donelan, Raymond 5:23:38 (29,762)
Donn, Robert A 3:36:56 (6,047)
Donnachie, Jason 5:53:04 (32,345)
Donnan, Graeme E 3:40:10 (6,666)
Donnellan, Anthony M 4:50:03 (24,613)
Donnellan, Craig 5:53:44 (32,390)
Donnelly, Adam S 4:15:34 (15,720)

Donnelly, David	4:31:59 (20,169)	
Donnelly, George C	3:19:11 (3,116)	
Donnelly, Gerard M	4:02:59 (12,606)	
Donnelly, Michael	3:26:00 (4,107)	
Donoghue, Anthony	7:02:08 (34,233)	
Donoghue, Steven P	3:45:24 (7,774)	
Donohoe, Francis B	5:24:54 (29,905)	
Donovan, Clive	3:30:11 (4,922)	
Donovan, John	3:59:35 (11,705)	
Donovan, Patrick J	4:03:22 (12,689)	
Donovan, Richard	4:47:11 (23,955)	
Donovan, Robby	5:50:45 (32,194)	
Donovan, Robert G	4:30:44 (19,811)	
Doodson, Gary J	3:31:36 (5,151)	
Doody, Mark	3:59:54 (11,818)	
Dooey, John D	2:54:09 (705)	
Dook, Hadrian T	3:34:09 (5,571)	
Doolan, Gary E	5:24:03 (29,814)	
Doolan, Michael J	5:02:46 (27,076)	
Doole, Robert G	4:51:34 (24,950)	
Dooley, Anthony B	5:27:30 (30,201)	
Dooley, Dermot K	5:04:42 (27,359)	
Dooley, Michael S	2:40:46 (210)	
Dooley, Simon A	5:20:53 (29,487)	
Dooling, Colin M	4:06:25 (13,375)	
Doolittle, Anthony I	3:04:56 (1,517)	
Door, Timothy J	5:38:08 (31,199)	
Dopierala, Francis	4:45:10 (23,456)	
Dopierala, Loic	5:36:25 (31,073)	
Doran, John	4:16:30 (15,959)	
Doran, Martin	3:38:20 (6,321)	
Doran, Matt	4:56:28 (25,963)	
Doran, Nathan	3:31:28 (5,124)	
Doran, Steve J	5:40:32 (31,378)	
Doran, Tim	2:36:39 (142)	
Dorazio, Humbert	4:48:46 (24,312)	
Dorean, Sean D	4:06:30 (13,400)	
Doree, Stuart	4:34:32 (20,829)	
Dorey, Paul R	5:51:20 (32,239)	
Dorgan, Andrew	4:52:50 (25,229)	
Doris, William J	3:41:56 (7,015)	
Dorling, Alan R	5:37:44 (31,173)	
Dorman, Brian J	4:22:39 (17,631)	
Dorman, Stuart	3:53:55 (9,839)	
Dorn, Mat P	4:21:46 (17,398)	
Dornan, Mark A	3:10:01 (1,989)	
Dorney, Mike	4:40:21 (22,275)	
Dorrington, Mark	4:29:43 (19,568)	
Dorward, Neil L	3:00:53 (1,231)	
Dos Reis Barros, Mario J	3:52:02 (9,314)	
Doshi, Rajen A	4:14:21 (15,410)	
Double, Graham H	5:40:59 (31,411)	
Dougherty, John P	4:21:06 (17,206)	
Doughty, Garry	4:13:41 (15,218)	
Doughty, Jason R	5:01:13 (26,829)	
Douglas, Alan	3:44:49 (7,635)	
Douglas, Andrew	3:21:54 (3,473)	
Douglas, James A	2:59:49 (1,151)	
Douglas, Keith	3:47:39 (8,270)	
Douglas, Keith S	4:39:26 (22,071)	
Douglas, Neil	2:39:39 (191)	
Douglas, Neil A	2:51:16 (560)	
Douglas, Paul D	2:58:21 (987)	
Douglas, Scott	3:50:36 (8,955)	
Douglas, Stephen G	4:20:22 (16,988)	
Douglass, Chippy	3:24:58 (3,921)	
Douheret, David	4:44:30 (23,303)	
Dourlen, Jean-Marie	3:11:18 (2,127)	
Doust, Peter	5:47:31 (31,952)	
Doutreleau, Stephane L	3:12:48 (2,306)	
Dove, Christopher W	4:31:25 (20,004)	
Dove, Paul J	4:47:42 (24,068)	
Dove, Peter W	4:40:18 (22,257)	
Dover, Nicholas S	4:01:40 (12,285)	
Dovey, Ivan E	3:45:23 (7,769)	
Dovey, Spencer R	6:20:24 (33,405)	
Dow, Gordon J	4:32:21 (20,263)	
Dow, Peter J	3:13:09 (2,352)	
Dowd, Christopher P	4:52:13 (25,084)	
Dowd, John	5:00:48 (26,761)	
Dowden, Andrew P	4:58:43 (26,427)	
Dowden, Derek B	3:41:50 (6,996)	
Dowden, Sean M	3:57:59 (11,109)	
Dowding, Dan	4:09:01 (14,045)	
Dowdle, David M	3:38:08 (6,292)	
Dowdle, Ian J	5:26:19 (30,073)	
Dowland, Nicholas D	4:19:38 (16,790)	
Dowler, John J	4:10:03 (14,305)	
Dowling, Andrew J	4:23:45 (17,929)	
Dowling, David	4:03:42 (12,765)	
Dowling, Eugene	4:03:31 (12,732)	
Dowling, Lee	3:51:46 (9,241)	
Down, Gary	4:46:10 (23,707)	
Down, Joel	4:29:16 (19,464)	
Downer, Neil A	3:50:06 (8,844)	
Downes, Oliver T	4:05:56 (13,275)	
Downes, Tony	3:47:54 (8,326)	
Downey, Jamal	5:34:37 (30,897)	
Downey, James	6:07:49 (33,039)	
Downey, Kevin	5:25:37 (29,997)	
Downham, James	4:27:08 (18,851)	
Downie, Garry	4:52:34 (25,161)	
Downing, Andy	4:28:20 (19,217)	
Downs, Peter	3:42:37 (7,155)	
Downs, Richard H	4:06:58 (13,508)	
Downs, Robert H	2:41:48 (239)	
Dowse, Peter M	4:41:24 (22,534)	
Dowse, Raymond	3:52:01 (9,305)	
Dowsett, Kevin R	3:54:48 (10,125)	
Dowsett, Michael	5:25:25 (29,981)	
Dowsett, Peter C	3:53:18 (9,661)	
Dowson, John R	4:07:09 (13,563)	
Doyle, Adrian	4:35:21 (21,068)	
Doyle, Alastair K	3:05:27 (1,551)	
Doyle, Christopher J	4:51:15 (24,893)	
Doyle, Geoffrey E	3:00:48 (1,225)	
Doyle, Ian E	3:13:49 (2,438)	
Doyle, James	4:26:43 (18,731)	
Doyle, James H	3:51:10 (9,089)	
Doyle, John	4:15:09 (15,607)	
Doyle, John B	3:50:23 (8,910)	
Doyle, Mark J	3:23:01 (3,641)	
Doyle, Patrick D	2:58:24 (993)	
Doyle, Philip L	4:24:36 (18,170)	
Doyle, Ronan	3:59:18 (11,595)	
Drabble, Mark	5:19:34 (29,367)	
Drabwell, Lee S	4:24:37 (18,175)	
Drage, Tom W	4:02:46 (12,556)	
Drake, Alexander Y	4:56:28 (25,963)	
Drake, Brendan J	3:23:51 (3,749)	
Drake, Kevin J	5:48:38 (32,023)	
Drake, Tom R	5:48:38 (32,023)	
Draper, Dennis W	4:23:12 (17,786)	
Draper, Edward J	4:10:34 (14,428)	
Draper, Ian	4:25:58 (18,524)	
Draper, Martin J	5:17:15 (29,090)	
Dray, Rudi	3:22:47 (3,607)	
Draycott, Mark R	4:24:23 (18,106)	
Dreau, Lionel A	5:56:08 (32,529)	
Dredge, Robert	3:46:43 (8,042)	
Dreher, Markus	3:38:28 (6,352)	
Dresemann, Gregor	3:54:53 (10,150)	
Drever, Jonathan G	4:07:16 (13,591)	
Drew, Christopher	4:23:28 (17,862)	
Drew, David	4:16:38 (15,989)	
Drew, Peter	3:38:12 (6,301)	
Drew, Steve C	3:50:11 (8,866)	
Drewe, Martin	3:55:09 (10,251)	
Dring, Philip W	3:47:41 (8,276)	
Drinkwater, James R	4:36:07 (21,276)	
Driscoll, John W	3:47:20 (8,181)	
Driscoll, Matt	6:00:22 (32,753)	
Driscoll, Neil	4:16:14 (15,888)	
Driscoll, Sean P	3:27:08 (4,301)	
Driscoll, Steve	5:05:32 (27,487)	
Driver, Andrew P	3:25:37 (4,039)	
Drummond, Alan	3:29:23 (4,760)	
Drummond, Christopher J	4:44:51 (23,385)	
Drummond, Daniel	4:20:37 (17,068)	
Drury, Antony	5:55:31 (32,504)	
Drury, David J	3:28:39 (4,592)	
Drury, Ian P	5:17:04 (29,074)	
Drury, Richard	4:31:28 (20,017)	
Dry, Peter F	3:45:03 (7,697)	
Dryden, Steven	4:06:36 (13,428)	
Dryland, Keith	4:20:25 (17,003)	
Du, Dafydd	4:14:37 (15,472)	
Du Plessis, Thomas	3:52:02 (9,314)	
Du Toit, Hendrik	3:13:20 (2,377)	
Duarte, Juanluis	3:53:56 (9,849)	
Dubie, Guy R	3:23:42 (3,726)	
Dublish, Shashank	4:41:36 (22,581)	
Dubuisson, Abbey	4:50:59 (24,839)	
Duck, Philip	2:57:40 (917)	
Duck, Tony	4:01:14 (12,170)	
Duckitt, Jack N	3:52:44 (9,490)	
Duckworth, Kevin	2:46:22 (372)	
Ducros, Adrian P	3:46:24 (7,979)	
Dudbridge, Frank	2:44:30 (311)	
Duddy, Gerard H	2:54:06 (701)	
Duddy, Paul	3:54:40 (10,089)	
Dude, Viesturs	2:53:01 (644)	
Dudfield, Stuart K	3:34:29 (5,619)	
Dudik, Thade K	3:28:15 (4,513)	
Dudley, Dennis C	3:44:44 (7,617)	
Dudley, Peter J	4:38:32 (21,831)	
Dudman, Neil A	5:20:22 (29,446)	
Dufeu, Jacques	4:17:30 (16,220)	
Duff, Craig	4:05:06 (13,069)	
Duff, Robert J	4:54:17 (25,539)	
Duff, Thomas H	3:57:47 (11,053)	
Duffell, Craig	4:31:56 (20,147)	
Duffell, Craig S	4:17:35 (16,244)	
Duffield, Andrew J	4:48:39 (24,282)	
Duffield, Gary G	4:21:26 (17,286)	
Duffield, Geoff	6:18:24 (33,369)	
Duffin, Mark S	4:03:15 (12,670)	
Duffus, John A	4:08:10 (13,825)	
Duffus, Richard L	3:59:25 (11,639)	
Duffy, Andrew D	3:11:16 (2,121)	
Duffy, Anthony P	4:30:02 (19,643)	
Duffy, Christopher D	4:43:42 (23,102)	
Duffy, Dean	3:58:37 (11,341)	
Duffy, Jim	4:10:16 (14,356)	
Duffy, Laurence B	3:05:47 (1,580)	
Duffy, Luke J	4:53:36 (25,400)	
Duffy, Michael J	3:28:58 (4,659)	
Duffy, Patrick J	4:04:41 (12,979)	
Duffy, Paul	3:56:13 (10,540)	
Duffy, Robert M	4:45:26 (23,524)	
Dufrane, Jean-Jacques M	4:17:02 (16,104)	
Duggan, Kevin J	4:13:54 (15,279)	
Duggan, Michael T	4:57:23 (26,161)	
Duggan, Robin J	3:33:04 (5,394)	
Duivenvoorden, Johannes	5:17:49 (29,157)	
Duke, Carsten	3:26:43 (4,234)	
Dulake, Neil S	3:53:51 (9,831)	
Dullehan, Michael F	4:05:27 (13,161)	
Dulson, Richard	3:56:10 (10,530)	
Dumas, Christopher	3:35:37 (5,815)	
Dumas, Emile	2:48:05 (426)	
Dumas, Fabrice	3:21:18 (3,402)	
Dumbell, James C	4:01:07 (12,141)	
Duna, Ron B	3:44:09 (7,482)	
Dunajko, Adam C	2:54:01 (693)	
Dunbar, Ross J	3:22:04 (3,499)	
Duncan, Christopher S	4:49:05 (24,392)	
Duncan, George B	5:11:28 (28,328)	
Duncan, Graeme	6:55:37 (34,164)	
Duncan, James A	4:01:16 (12,177)	
Duncan, Mark G	3:14:25 (2,533)	
Duncan, Richard A	3:23:26 (3,699)	
Duncan, Richard R	5:55:12 (32,478)	
Duncan, Tony	4:11:31 (14,686)	
Duncan-King, Oliver	3:51:11 (9,096)	
Duncton, Ross	5:12:05 (28,417)	
Dunford, Paul J	6:08:02 (33,043)	
Dunford, Stephen C	3:37:27 (6,159)	
Dungate, Christopher	4:15:47 (15,780)	
Dungworth, David C	3:57:32 (10,964)	
Dunk, Shaun	4:23:35 (17,890)	
Dunkin, Christopher J	5:21:00 (29,495)	
Dunkin, Stephen C	6:19:49 (33,393)	
Dunkley, Chris S	4:24:56 (18,248)	
Dunkley, Kerry	3:20:52 (3,337)	
Dunkley, Paul	4:15:11 (15,613)	
Dunkley, Timothy J	5:26:28 (30,093)	
Dunlea, Brian C	4:25:22 (18,359)	
Dunleavy, Daniel W	4:34:25 (20,804)	

Dunleavy, Michael 4:34:25 (20,804)
Dunlop, Paul 3:18:39 (3,061)
Dunlop, Wayne A 4:44:57 (23,402)
Dunn, Aaron J 5:25:02 (29,920)
Dunn, Andrew S 4:48:59 (24,370)
Dunn, Barrie 3:08:11 (1,813)
Dunn, Chris 4:40:04 (22,198)
Dunn, Colin R 4:30:31 (19,749)
Dunn, Geoffrey A 4:19:38 (16,790)
Dunn, George W 2:58:47 (1,038)
Dunn, Jamie L 4:41:35 (22,575)
Dunn, Martin H 4:45:15 (23,481)
Dunn, Norman F 4:18:15 (16,413)
Dunn, Peter M 4:06:21 (13,364)
Dunn, Philip J 4:01:50 (12,324)
Dunn, Robert 3:40:01 (6,641)
Dunn, Roger W 4:23:24 (17,838)
Dunn, Stephen L 5:11:20 (28,312)
Dunn, Thomas M 3:58:22 (11,251)
Dunn, Tim 3:53:19 (9,667)
Dunn, William A 4:10:49 (14,498)
Dunne, Gerard M 3:57:13 (10,868)
Dunne, Kevin 3:38:13 (6,303)
Dunne, Leigh J 4:10:34 (14,428)
Dunnett, Keith 4:20:19 (16,979)
Dunnill, Philip A 3:51:22 (9,147)
Dunning, Thomas W 3:38:26 (6,347)
Dunn-Parrant, Glenn D 2:59:13 (1,087)
Dunn-Veale, Christopher J 5:39:32 (31,300)
Dunscombe, Guy C 3:11:32 (2,153)
Dunscombe, Mark 3:05:43 (1,575)
Dunsdon, Robert J 4:03:23 (12,695)
Dunsire, Magnus F 3:40:00 (6,638)
Dunstall, Dave 3:11:13 (2,116)
Dunstan, Andrew G 5:03:28 (27,177)
Dunstone, Nicholas A 4:16:23 (15,927)
Dunton, Nicholas J 4:44:17 (23,252)
Dupain, Nigel C 4:33:35 (20,601)
Dupey, Stephen 5:54:38 (32,435)
Duprez, Denis 5:26:23 (30,086)
Durance, Richard 3:58:11 (11,182)
Durante, Fabrizio 4:11:27 (14,662)
Durden, Gary J 3:39:44 (6,582)
Durham, Michael C 5:08:50 (27,947)
Durham, Neil J 4:44:27 (23,286)
Durkan, John J 3:43:26 (7,332)
Durkin, Jacob A 4:58:05 (26,301)
Durnford, John A 3:19:42 (3,191)
Durnford, Tony 6:09:17 (33,090)
Durrant, Carlton R 3:58:22 (11,251)
Durrant, Ian P 2:45:13 (340)
Durrant, Jeremy 3:45:14 (7,736)
Durrant, Wayne L 3:22:45 (3,601)
Durst, Michael B 3:35:34 (5,806)
Durston Smith, Simon E 3:43:03 (7,248)
Dury, Mark J 3:40:17 (6,688)
Duschz, Martin 4:02:34 (12,508)
Dustan, Rob D 4:53:01 (25,275)
Duton, Patrick 2:59:03 (1,064)
Dutton, Allan H 3:59:21 (11,613)
Dutton, David E 6:36:52 (33,819)
Dutton, Gavin M 3:36:59 (6,061)
Dutton, Kevin J 3:55:33 (10,354)
Dutton, Richard J 4:36:09 (21,280)
Dutton, Timothy N 3:39:51 (6,609)
Duval, Michel 3:58:44 (11,387)
Duval, Yves 3:33:09 (5,410)
Duxbury, Robert A 3:25:50 (4,075)
Dvorak, Martin 4:21:43 (17,380)
Dwatson, Peter D 3:50:25 (8,913)
Dwyer, Andrew 3:25:05 (3,945)
Dwyer, Christopher M 3:18:51 (3,079)
Dwyer, Sean 4:14:16 (15,387)
Dy, Anderson 6:54:46 (34,149)
Dyble, Craig S 4:44:45 (23,357)
Dyckes, John J 3:12:46 (2,298)
Dye, Michael 4:23:44 (17,922)
Dye, Richard J 3:33:32 (5,480)
Dyer, Adrian J 4:12:51 (14,992)
Dyer, Alistair M 3:57:27 (10,942)
Dyer, Andrew 4:14:01 (15,310)
Dyer, Andrew C 4:58:54 (26,455)
Dyer, Ben A 4:15:26 (15,684)
Dyer, Dale G 5:09:18 (28,009)
Dyer, Jason T 4:57:01 (26,084)
Dyer, Kevin P 4:32:25 (20,273)
Dyke, Alan J 4:29:07 (19,428)
Dyke, Paul 4:26:46 (18,745)
Dymond, Graeme H 3:46:06 (7,905)
Dymond, Steve J 4:22:41 (17,645)
Dyson, Graham 3:40:04 (6,653)
Dyson, Lee 3:45:49 (7,863)
Dziedziczak, Frederic 3:13:08 (2,351)
Eade, Darren J 4:17:51 (16,315)
Eaden, Ken 4:33:14 (20,488)
Eaglestone, William 4:40:55 (22,410)
Eales, Darryl C 4:45:23 (23,506)
Eales, Paul T 4:50:30 (24,715)
Ealham, Paul 5:48:09 (31,986)
Eames, Chris 4:34:56 (20,949)
Eames, Matthew D 5:25:24 (29,979)
Eames, Michael 5:23:24 (29,734)
Earey, Richard A 5:45:17 (31,784)
Earl, Adam R 4:12:08 (14,843)
Earl, Anthony C 3:56:35 (10,657)
Earl, David W 4:19:25 (16,728)
Earl, Derek W 4:17:05 (16,119)
Earl, Martin J 3:47:56 (8,335)
Earley, David M 3:33:08 (5,407)
Earley, Simon 3:12:29 (2,264)
Earnshaw, Paul F 3:52:31 (9,437)
Earthy, Paul S 3:41:59 (7,022)
Earthy, Robert R 4:10:44 (14,475)
Easmon, Charlie J 5:28:03 (30,273)
Easson, James M 2:57:12 (887)
East, Graeme P 4:40:31 (22,313)
East, John 4:11:25 (14,650)
East, Jon P 4:55:10 (25,726)
East, Lloyd J 3:50:17 (8,890)
East, Steven G 3:41:40 (6,961)
Eastaff, John 4:37:09 (21,514)
Eastgate, John P 4:22:51 (17,686)
Eastham, Barry 4:03:51 (12,797)
Eastham, Robert E 4:20:00 (16,884)
Eastman, Carsten C 5:59:22 (32,705)
Eastman, John 3:23:04 (3,646)
Easton, Daniel T 3:29:06 (4,693)
Easton, Richard J 3:32:16 (5,271)
Eastwood, Paul M 2:58:48 (1,042)
Easy, Jason L 3:44:43 (7,610)
Eato, Gary R 4:22:44 (17,654)
Eaton, Andrew L 4:34:40 (20,865)
Eaton, Ben W 3:51:50 (9,254)
Eaton, Dom 3:41:28 (6,932)
Eaton, Guy R 4:14:00 (15,302)
Eaton, James M 3:07:15 (1,700)
Eaton, James R 4:52:00 (25,042)
Eaton, Ken C 5:55:10 (32,473)
Eaton, Matthew 3:58:45 (11,389)
Eaton, Michael 3:54:28 (10,013)
Eaton, Paul 3:48:24 (8,440)
Eaton, Paul A 3:35:56 (5,865)
Eaton, Richard A 4:00:21 (11,937)
Eaton, Robert J 5:20:44 (29,478)
Eaton, Simon A 3:18:13 (3,011)
Eaton, Simon M 3:59:07 (11,535)
Eaton, Stephen D 5:49:46 (32,104)
Eatough, Bob J 4:12:05 (14,835)
Eavers, Christopher J 3:18:39 (3,061)
Eaves, Stephen M 4:35:18 (21,056)
Ebdon, Mark A 3:51:05 (9,072)
Ebert, Bernd 4:20:18 (16,975)
Ebrahim Nanji, Mehaboob E 4:43:51 (23,141)
Eccles, Henry 3:42:15 (7,081)
Eccles, Jonathan A 6:12:34 (33,189)
Eccles, Michael 5:04:41 (27,354)
Eccleshare, William 4:05:49 (13,249)
Echeverria, Andrés 3:28:45 (4,613)
Eckersley, Fergus J 4:47:00 (23,910)
Eckersley, Jonathan P 4:25:05 (18,285)
Eckersley, William 4:46:59 (23,904)
Ecollan, Patrick 4:07:51 (13,730)
Eddelbuettel, Dirk 3:24:41 (3,867)
Eddie, Adam G 3:42:51 (7,205)
Eddleston, Mike J 3:10:44 (2,067)
Eddy, Simon J 4:23:11 (17,778)
Eden, Paul A 3:54:33 (10,052)
Edet, Danny 4:18:04 (16,361)
Edgar, Martin 4:11:08 (14,581)
Edgar, Simon F 4:22:24 (17,551)
Edgar, Stephen 3:22:01 (3,493)
Edge, Gary B 4:36:44 (21,423)
Edge, Michael A 5:11:09 (28,287)
Edgell, Andrew L 3:29:00 (4,669)
Edgeworth, Brett I 3:20:23 (3,276)
Edginton, Tony 4:24:42 (18,194)
Edgley, Jonathon E 3:13:45 (2,429)
Ediker, Simon C 4:37:56 (21,699)
Edland, Jonas 4:27:15 (18,890)
Edmond, Colin M 5:02:58 (27,105)
Edmond, Graham 4:50:33 (24,733)
Edmond, Michael J 3:59:35 (11,705)
Edmonds, Christopher J 3:56:06 (10,514)
Edmonds, Gavin 2:55:14 (765)
Edmonds, Paul R 4:59:22 (26,540)
Edmondson, Dominic J 3:46:21 (7,965)
Edmondson, Michael J 3:47:28 (8,215)
Edmondson, Peter 3:52:08 (9,348)
Edmondson, Peter 5:15:25 (28,868)
Edmunds, Chris J 4:03:34 (12,736)
Edney, Jonathan 3:36:36 (5,981)
Edridge, Norman F 3:58:48 (11,416)
Edward, William R 3:14:00 (2,466)
Edwards, Alan 4:23:36 (17,894)
Edwards, Alan R 5:34:32 (30,888)
Edwards, Alexander D 4:28:47 (19,343)
Edwards, Andrew L 4:22:39 (17,631)
Edwards, Andrew N 4:33:22 (20,533)
Edwards, Aynsley 4:06:51 (13,484)
Edwards, Barry 4:36:03 (21,251)
Edwards, Ben K 4:53:10 (25,310)
Edwards, Chris 4:32:24 (20,268)
Edwards, Colin 3:59:50 (11,797)
Edwards, Craig 3:55:47 (10,429)
Edwards, Daniel 4:15:30 (15,704)
Edwards, Daniel J 4:20:54 (17,152)
Edwards, Daniel P 5:22:31 (29,664)
Edwards, Danny 4:40:33 (22,319)
Edwards, Darren M 3:53:43 (9,775)
Edwards, Darren P 3:54:52 (10,144)
Edwards, David 3:55:16 (10,279)
Edwards, David C 3:52:59 (9,566)
Edwards, David F 3:19:46 (3,203)
Edwards, David J 7:31:04 (34,459)
Edwards, Duncan J 4:10:38 (14,449)
Edwards, Edward E 4:15:44 (15,763)
Edwards, Francis D 5:04:34 (27,338)
Edwards, Gareth D 3:37:12 (6,105)
Edwards, Gregory S 5:18:56 (29,282)
Edwards, Haydn J 5:45:20 (31,790)
Edwards, Hugh G 5:46:25 (31,872)
Edwards, Ian L 3:33:12 (5,421)
Edwards, Ian P 3:47:47 (8,293)
Edwards, James 4:30:14 (19,687)
Edwards, James M 3:02:22 (1,336)
Edwards, Jason 4:43:08 (22,968)
Edwards, Jason C 4:45:39 (23,572)
Edwards, Kenneth D 3:53:43 (9,775)
Edwards, Malcolm J 3:52:24 (9,412)
Edwards, Marc D 4:10:01 (14,299)
Edwards, Mark 2:59:24 (1,111)
Edwards, Mark A 4:02:56 (12,592)
Edwards, Matthew A 4:55:58 (25,874)
Edwards, Micki 4:10:37 (14,440)
Edwards, Neil 4:13:01 (15,037)
Edwards, Neil A 3:49:04 (8,593)
Edwards, Neil A 4:03:56 (12,812)
Edwards, Orlando 2:26:48 (43)
Edwards, Paul 5:11:43 (28,369)
Edwards, Paul 5:58:55 (32,691)
Edwards, Paul D 4:47:34 (24,033)
Edwards, Paul J 4:34:32 (20,829)
Edwards, Paul T 4:22:26 (17,560)
Edwards, Peter R 3:43:17 (7,303)
Edwards, Phillip J 5:14:28 (28,736)
Edwards, Richard B 5:06:59 (27,693)
Edwards, Richard C 3:42:35 (7,150)
Edwards, Richard H 4:06:51 (13,484)
Edwards, Robert 4:26:01 (18,544)

Edwards, Robert C	3:10:17 (2,016)	
Edwards, Robert T	4:30:17 (19,694)	
Edwards, Steve	3:02:35 (1,351)	
Edwards, Thomas	5:14:19 (28,726)	
Edwards, Thomas D	4:48:55 (24,350)	
Edwardson, William	5:04:19 (27,294)	
Edwin, Jay	3:26:25 (4,175)	
Efstratiou, Stratos	4:08:05 (13,784)	
Efthimiou, Panikos	3:54:46 (10,118)	
Egan, Conor T	3:49:18 (8,650)	
Egan, Daniel A	4:13:51 (15,259)	
Egan, David J	4:27:55 (19,071)	
Egan, Declan J	3:29:23 (4,760)	
Egan, Richard J	4:01:18 (12,184)	
Egbe, Tony S	4:16:11 (15,871)	
Egeland, Frode	2:51:34 (576)	
Egelie, Eduard C	3:04:29 (1,482)	
Egerton, Charles R	7:31:51 (34,462)	
Egerton, James	3:47:53 (8,321)	
Eggenhuizen, Frederikus M	4:04:54 (13,021)	
Eggett, Christopher J	3:37:20 (6,128)	
Eggett, Tim J	3:59:18 (11,595)	
Eggleton, Paul	4:06:55 (13,496)	
Eglington, Michael J	4:31:23 (19,991)	
Egua, Andrea	4:26:00 (18,538)	
Eguiguren, Alberto	4:06:29 (13,395)	
Ehren, Gary R	4:16:52 (16,049)	
Einchcomb, Nicholas P	3:23:21 (3,685)	
Eisma, Han	4:27:59 (19,096)	
El Fakir, Mounir	4:15:56 (15,819)	
El Maghraby, Ahmed	5:04:50 (27,372)	
El Mrah, Said	3:45:14 (7,736)	
Elam, Tom	3:48:52 (8,544)	
El-Atribi, Omar	3:13:31 (2,396)	
Elder, Brian M	5:15:01 (28,821)	
Eldon, Simon	3:48:13 (8,403)	
Eldred, Nick	3:54:28 (10,013)	
Eldred, Peter	4:13:19 (15,122)	
Eldridge, Leigh A	4:49:57 (24,591)	
Eldridge, Peter J	4:51:38 (24,973)	
Eley, Allan	4:00:36 (12,004)	
Eley, David C	4:23:32 (17,875)	
Elghannani, Abdelilah	4:19:15 (16,688)	
Elgohary, Mostafa A	5:34:57 (30,934)	
Elia, Charlie	6:16:20 (33,302)	
Elia, Nicholas	5:03:43 (27,209)	
Eliot, Henry H	3:42:22 (7,111)	
Elkan, Stephen	4:15:04 (15,584)	
Elkerton, William J	3:46:17 (7,948)	
Elkhadraoui, Aziz	4:43:37 (23,078)	
Elkins, George R	4:14:34 (15,464)	
Ellacott, Tom M	2:34:53 (111)	
Ellerby, Roger K	3:13:50 (2,441)	
Ellerton, Stephen	3:17:30 (2,932)	
Ellett, Ryan	3:31:43 (5,173)	
Ellice, William A	3:50:59 (9,042)	
Ellingford, David	4:52:58 (25,264)	
Ellingham, Chris W	5:17:25 (29,111)	
Ellingham, Jason C	5:04:44 (27,364)	
Elliot, Kevin	4:19:15 (16,688)	
Elliott, Brendon M	3:43:24 (7,323)	
Elliott, Christopher M	4:41:41 (22,613)	
Elliott, Corin C	3:51:28 (9,169)	
Elliott, Daren P	4:07:33 (13,653)	
Elliott, David	5:16:59 (29,060)	
Elliott, David W	4:30:21 (19,712)	
Elliott, David W	5:00:40 (26,730)	
Elliott, Gareth	5:08:20 (27,860)	
Elliott, Garry J	5:05:39 (27,504)	
Elliott, Gavin B	3:40:20 (6,695)	
Elliott, Giles P	4:03:53 (12,802)	
Elliott, Joe V	3:01:53 (1,302)	
Elliott, Jonathan R	4:50:56 (24,829)	
Elliott, Kenneth	4:31:01 (19,887)	
Elliott, Kevin M	4:41:08 (22,472)	
Elliott, Mark C	3:17:20 (2,905)	
Elliott, Peter G	4:21:45 (17,389)	
Elliott, Robert A	4:54:48 (25,649)	
Elliott, Russell P	4:23:25 (17,842)	
Elliott, Timothy	4:37:21 (21,560)	
Elliott, Tom J	3:54:33 (10,052)	
Ellis, Barnaby	4:15:20 (15,646)	
Ellis, Christopher M	3:48:07 (8,380)	
Ellis, David	3:59:30 (11,676)	
Ellis, David A	3:26:18 (4,154)	
Ellis, David A	4:46:46 (23,845)	
Ellis, David C	4:39:15 (22,039)	
Ellis, Dominic C	5:40:29 (31,373)	
Ellis, Garry E	4:30:28 (19,738)	
Ellis, James A	2:46:27 (373)	
Ellis, James W	5:42:02 (31,500)	
Ellis, John	5:31:39 (30,627)	
Ellis, Jon W	3:29:56 (4,873)	
Ellis, Jonathan N	7:20:29 (34,398)	
Ellis, Mark	7:48:10 (34,504)	
Ellis, Mark A	4:21:56 (17,435)	
Ellis, Michael	3:24:27 (3,837)	
Ellis, Michael W	4:36:55 (21,471)	
Ellis, Mike	3:56:46 (10,714)	
Ellis, Myles P	4:51:41 (24,982)	
Ellis, Ralph	4:41:05 (22,452)	
Ellis, Richard F	4:21:12 (17,225)	
Ellis, Richard J	4:13:21 (15,130)	
Ellis, Richard J	4:48:29 (24,243)	
Ellis, Robert J	2:59:23 (1,108)	
Ellis, Russell J	4:08:25 (13,887)	
Ellis, Samuel J	5:23:57 (29,799)	
Ellis, Simon	4:15:03 (15,579)	
Ellis, Simon	4:40:07 (22,215)	
Ellis, Steve P	3:27:44 (4,405)	
Ellis, Stuart	3:40:54 (6,804)	
Ellis, Tim	2:44:17 (304)	
Ellis, Tim H	3:02:18 (1,329)	
Ellis, Vince	3:12:00 (2,205)	
Ellison, Hugh F	4:56:38 (25,990)	
Ellison, Mark W	4:04:54 (13,021)	
Ellison-Burns, Simon J	4:07:11 (13,575)	
Ellmore, Daniel J	3:31:51 (5,191)	
Ellsbury, Mark	3:52:31 (9,437)	
Ellson, Donald A	5:12:40 (28,480)	
Ellson, Robert H	3:29:35 (4,795)	
Ellwood, Ian J	4:13:38 (15,198)	
Ellwood, Tim	3:17:25 (2,920)	
Elmer, John	5:36:47 (31,101)	
Elms, Allan W	3:35:57 (5,869)	
Elms, Michael R	4:08:08 (13,810)	
Elms, Philip M	4:19:37 (16,787)	
Elphick, Ian	3:54:56 (10,175)	
Elsawy, Magdy H	3:59:02 (11,499)	
Elsby, Dominic A	2:41:11 (224)	
Elsdon, Damian	3:58:17 (11,208)	
Elsen, Sam	4:37:45 (21,652)	
Elsmore, Nigel R	3:25:42 (4,049)	
Elsmore Dodsworth, John	5:03:20 (27,160)	
Elsom, David J	3:51:08 (9,084)	
Elsome, Tim G	4:42:12 (22,723)	
Elson, Jason L	3:44:29 (7,549)	
El-Sour, Allen	3:29:05 (4,688)	
Elsworth, Stephen	3:39:51 (6,609)	
Elvidge, Dean M	4:33:43 (20,639)	
Elvidge, Matt D	4:45:25 (23,517)	
Elvin, James J	3:41:27 (6,924)	
Elwell, Anthony J	5:20:42 (29,476)	
Elwell, Greg	2:57:10 (884)	
Elwick, Peter M	5:05:31 (27,479)	
Elworthy, Stephen J	4:30:47 (19,828)	
Emanuel, Thomas A	5:07:33 (27,774)	
Emanuel, Wayne	5:34:46 (30,909)	
Emberton, James	3:58:17 (11,208)	
Embleton, Dennis	4:24:47 (18,210)	
Embleton, Eddie T	4:43:20 (23,012)	
Emerson, Zachary D	3:34:42 (5,645)	
Emerton, Steven J	3:13:09 (2,352)	
Emery, Alan	4:16:25 (15,938)	
Emery, Michael P	5:08:47 (27,943)	
Emery, Nathan J	4:51:43 (24,991)	
Emery, Peter K	3:40:14 (6,681)	
Emery, Richard O	4:20:03 (16,904)	
Emery, Robert P	4:34:20 (20,781)	
Emin, Zeki	4:31:28 (20,017)	
Eminson, Richard B	8:17:02 (34,555)	
Emirali, Kenan	3:33:25 (5,457)	
Emirali, Orbay	4:25:22 (18,359)	
Emirali, Ozzy	4:31:53 (20,135)	
Emmanuel, Marc	4:57:50 (26,251)	
Emmanuel, Richard	5:12:04 (28,416)	
Emmerson, Bob	4:32:50 (20,383)	
Emmerson, David J	3:56:26 (10,605)	
Emmerson, Jeffrey	4:35:28 (21,104)	
Emmert, Thomas	4:40:09 (22,226)	
Emmerton, Kevin J	3:32:54 (5,373)	
Emmett, Martin G	4:01:01 (12,114)	
Emmett, Robert	4:50:16 (24,661)	
Emms-Clements, Simon	5:56:20 (32,550)	
Empson, Robert J	5:36:02 (31,035)	
Emptage, Tristan P	3:59:51 (11,802)	
Emsden, Gavin	3:46:19 (7,956)	
Emsley, Paul G	4:02:55 (12,588)	
Emson, Oliver	5:08:38 (27,921)	
Enders, David J	3:54:23 (9,987)	
Endo, Yashiro	3:46:56 (8,093)	
Engdahl, Lars-Ake	2:56:53 (864)	
Engelhardt, Uwe	4:19:48 (16,835)	
Engelsen, Stanley S	4:47:34 (24,033)	
England, Andrew M	3:58:27 (11,282)	
England, Kevin P	5:22:17 (29,636)	
Englefield, Bruce	4:58:22 (26,354)	
Engulu, Ednard O	5:09:41 (28,088)	
Ennals, Brad T	4:09:45 (14,242)	
Ennis, Keith	3:27:03 (4,286)	
Enstone, Robin W	3:39:57 (6,628)	
Enticknap, Andrew	3:57:29 (10,948)	
Enticott, Jack	5:10:27 (28,213)	
Entwistle, James	4:10:56 (14,531)	
Entwistle, Peter R	3:07:40 (1,749)	
Enville, Paul	6:31:47 (33,699)	
Eperon, Alastair D	3:33:52 (5,528)	
Eppleston, James J	3:47:49 (8,303)	
Epps, Terry A	3:07:17 (1,707)	
Epps, Wade	4:28:44 (19,321)	
Epsom, Joseph	5:02:56 (27,102)	
Erb-Satullo, Nathaniel L	2:46:37 (378)	
Ergas, Alfredo	3:51:34 (9,188)	
Eriksson, Duncan	5:15:25 (28,868)	
Eriksson, Peter	5:14:56 (28,810)	
Errejon, Carlos	4:50:17 (24,663)	
Errington, David J	4:25:25 (18,373)	
Errington, John	3:20:11 (3,245)	
Erritt, Andrew M	3:35:55 (5,862)	
Erwin, Patrick	5:20:30 (29,465)	
Escott, Samuel	4:11:12 (14,607)	
Escott, Steve D	4:53:03 (25,286)	
Eshelby, Mark S	4:11:04 (14,563)	
Esler, Colin N	4:14:57 (15,544)	
Espino Lledo, Guillermo M	3:40:20 (6,695)	
Espinosa, Juan G	3:16:44 (2,841)	
Espinosa, Thierry V	3:16:01 (2,755)	
Esplin, Ron M	5:30:23 (30,514)	
Essa, Andrew	4:15:43 (15,752)	
Essex, Francis-John	4:21:59 (17,449)	
Essex, Simon J	4:44:26 (23,283)	
Essigman, Martin N	3:38:23 (6,336)	
Esson, Stephen G	4:20:02 (16,899)	
Estall, Jim H	4:07:50 (13,725)	
Etchells, Craig W	5:23:08 (29,712)	
Etchenou, Arnaud	4:17:11 (16,153)	
Etherington, James A	3:28:22 (4,531)	
Etherington, Mark J	3:29:20 (4,744)	
Etty, Peter G	5:58:01 (32,632)	
Etzrodt, Frank-Ulrich	4:59:48 (26,609)	
Euden, Jamie R	3:26:52 (4,256)	
Euler Huerta, Guillermo	5:09:15 (28,004)	
Evans, Adam L	4:55:44 (25,827)	
Evans, Alexandre C	3:31:53 (5,195)	
Evans, Alun T	3:17:08 (2,876)	
Evans, Andrew M	4:26:14 (18,590)	
Evans, Andrew N	3:39:32 (6,545)	
Evans, Andrew R	3:48:40 (8,504)	
Evans, Barrie J	4:03:50 (12,794)	
Evans, Benjamin J	4:22:44 (17,654)	
Evans, Christopher J	3:29:43 (4,824)	
Evans, Christopher J	3:57:59 (11,109)	
Evans, Daniel	2:48:46 (455)	
Evans, Daniel M	4:13:45 (15,240)	
Evans, Daniel R	2:43:01 (265)	
Evans, Daniel S	2:57:09 (882)	
Evans, Daren J	4:53:21 (25,343)	
Evans, David F	4:16:19 (15,907)	
Evans, Dominic	3:49:20 (8,659)	

Evans, Douglas K 5:12:27 (28,453)
Evans, Edwin 3:36:07 (5,901)
Evans, Elfyn 6:25:57 (33,575)
Evans, Frank C 3:58:17 (11,208)
Evans, Gareth J 3:09:04 (1,890)
Evans, Gavin 4:58:42 (26,420)
Evans, Gavin M 2:52:14 (606)
Evans, Gerald H 3:26:48 (4,248)
Evans, Greg J 3:34:25 (5,607)
Evans, Guy 4:18:20 (16,443)
Evans, Gwyn W 3:29:28 (4,774)
Evans, Harford 3:27:28 (4,359)
Evans, Ian S 4:32:19 (20,255)
Evans, James R 3:45:33 (7,800)
Evans, Jeff M 3:44:31 (7,555)
Evans, Jeffrey 4:24:51 (18,229)
Evans, John 3:51:40 (9,220)
Evans, John 4:01:43 (12,299)
Evans, Jonathan M 3:49:45 (8,758)
Evans, Kevin J 4:36:11 (21,289)
Evans, Kyle D 3:41:50 (6,996)
Evans, Lee J 5:58:11 (32,650)
Evans, Lloyd H 3:49:46 (8,764)
Evans, Marc T 2:54:59 (748)
Evans, Mark 4:02:32 (12,503)
Evans, Mark 4:47:38 (24,050)
Evans, Mark 4:52:03 (25,056)
Evans, Mark A 3:54:35 (10,065)
Evans, Mark A 5:44:20 (31,701)
Evans, Mark J 4:57:19 (26,145)
Evans, Matt T 5:44:15 (31,690)
Evans, Matthew J 3:56:54 (10,762)
Evans, Matthew W 3:42:34 (7,147)
Evans, Matthew W 5:07:16 (27,733)
Evans, Meirion R 4:28:20 (19,217)
Evans, Michael 4:54:23 (25,558)
Evans, Michael J 3:52:22 (9,401)
Evans, Neil D 5:41:01 (31,417)
Evans, Nick 3:43:32 (7,350)
Evans, Noel S 3:47:50 (8,306)
Evans, Owen 5:40:26 (31,368)
Evans, Pascal J 2:58:41 (1,030)
Evans, Paul 3:51:28 (9,169)
Evans, Paul 4:11:37 (14,706)
Evans, Paul A 3:25:45 (4,061)
Evans, Paul D 3:37:58 (6,257)
Evans, Peter R 3:44:34 (7,569)
Evans, Philip J 3:29:15 (4,725)
Evans, Ray 5:15:42 (28,905)
Evans, Raymond E 6:13:46 (33,237)
Evans, Richard L 4:01:46 (12,312)
Evans, Richard M 4:20:56 (17,159)
Evans, Robert 3:57:12 (10,862)
Evans, Robert A 4:56:33 (25,980)
Evans, Robert M 4:18:39 (16,542)
Evans, Roland D 4:41:27 (22,546)
Evans, Scott 2:56:15 (828)
Evans, Shane 4:09:55 (14,283)
Evans, Stephen J 3:58:23 (11,256)
Evans, Stephen L 3:59:20 (11,610)
Evans, Steve 4:44:14 (23,237)
Evans, Stuart J 3:49:24 (8,674)
Evans, Timothy M 3:35:34 (5,806)
Evans, William 3:35:21 (5,764)
Evatt, Geoffrey W 4:24:10 (18,039)
Evatt, Simon T 4:33:34 (20,597)
Eve, Brian 5:23:39 (29,763)
Evenden, Mark A 4:33:34 (20,597)
Evennett, Nicholas J 3:43:31 (7,348)
Everard, Alan J 4:21:10 (17,216)
Everard, Roger P 3:16:39 (2,828)
Everest, Keith 3:52:31 (9,437)
Everett, Barry 4:39:13 (22,034)
Everett, Jerry 3:02:11 (1,320)
Everson, Peter F 4:24:57 (18,249)
Eves, Colin E 4:19:48 (16,835)
Eves, Gregory W 3:57:09 (10,852)
Eves, James 3:57:58 (11,106)
Eveson, Robert W 3:42:50 (7,201)
Evgen, Ivanc 4:17:28 (16,211)
Evin, Philippe 3:58:20 (11,236)
Ewart, Michael D 3:41:46 (6,983)
Ewart, Tim 4:32:37 (20,329)

A royal race

The London Marathon was the first to be run over 26 miles 385 yards. During the 1908 London Olympics the planned route was 26 miles, from Windsor Castle to the stadium at the White City in Shepherd's Bush, London. But the race organisers added 385 yards to ensure that the finish line was beneath the Royal Box. On a fearsomely hot day, the leader Dorando Pietri collapsed five times and was disqualified for receiving assistance. The gold medal was given to Johnny Hayes from the USA, but Queen Alexandra presented Dorando with a gold cup for the 'pluck' he had shown in crossing the line first. Bookies and promoters thirsted for a rematch and we have been stuck with the distance of 26 miles 385 yards ever since.

Ewbank, Tim D 5:04:14 (27,285)
Ewen, Colin 3:58:25 (11,268)
Ewence, Martin W 5:42:34 (31,534)
Ewin, Alexander D 3:18:00 (2,986)
Ewin, Mark J 4:00:40 (12,024)
Ewing, Tom 4:26:56 (18,793)
Ewington, Simon J 4:07:19 (13,599)
Ewins, Chris 4:34:01 (20,699)
Exall, Ian 3:55:26 (10,316)
Exall, Mark E 4:28:53 (19,371)
Exton, Gareth J 4:44:11 (23,224)
Eycken, Renoit 3:53:16 (9,653)
Eyes, Neil C 4:27:08 (18,851)
Eyles, George P 3:23:23 (3,689)
Eyre, Anthony J 4:45:27 (23,529)
Eyre, Christopher R 4:55:51 (25,848)
Eyre, Douglas 4:36:44 (21,423)
Eyre, Graham 4:44:18 (23,256)
Eyre, Ian 4:10:50 (14,503)
Eyre, Torbjorn K 5:26:15 (30,064)
Ezard, Ollie 4:11:06 (14,578)
Ezard, Paul 3:26:15 (4,145)
Ezickson, Elan 5:03:13 (27,137)
Ezquerro Adan, Jesus 3:54:49 (10,131)
Eztala Aldosoro, Anartz 4:47:46 (24,093)
Faaij, Johannes A 4:50:53 (24,818)
Fackrell, David W 3:17:25 (2,920)
Fadden, Alastair J 3:01:29 (1,277)
Fagan, Kevin J 3:34:57 (5,694)
Fagan, Paul W 3:40:41 (6,756)
Fagg, Tom W 3:54:25 (9,998)
Faherty, Liam D 5:01:29 (26,868)
Fahey, Christian 4:30:20 (19,706)
Fahrenheim, Robert M 3:58:26 (11,276)
Fahy, Liam A 4:15:40 (15,739)
Faichen, Andy D 4:28:00 (19,099)
Fair, Edward P 4:50:14 (24,650)
Fair, Michael J 4:01:12 (12,165)
Fairbairn, James A 4:03:24 (12,700)
Fairbairn, James A 4:55:26 (25,770)
Fairbairn, Stuart J 5:21:02 (29,500)
Fairbrother, George 3:59:18 (11,595)
Fairbrother, Mark 4:54:33 (25,591)
Fairclough, John 4:12:51 (14,992)
Fairclough, Neil R 4:16:28 (15,954)
Fairclough, Thomas 3:47:23 (8,193)
Fairhall, Mark 3:40:21 (6,704)
Fairhurst, Robin 4:25:16 (18,330)

Fairhurst, Russell L 3:23:24 (3,690)
Fairlie, Kenneth W 3:43:53 (7,434)
Fairlie, Peter 4:50:29 (24,708)
Fairweather, Henry 5:44:56 (31,758)
Fairweather, Trevor W 4:18:24 (16,464)
Fairweather, Walter H 5:26:11 (30,056)
Fais, Pier Claudio 3:53:37 (9,747)
Faithfull, Paul 5:12:55 (28,534)
Falcon Munoz, Tomas 4:15:51 (15,795)
Falconer, Angus 3:31:14 (5,087)
Falcus, Brett M 3:49:44 (8,756)
Falkiner, Alan P 6:02:29 (32,833)
Falkner, Tobias 4:23:32 (17,875)
Fallman, Ian P 4:19:50 (16,842)
Fallon, Domhnall S 4:27:33 (18,964)
Fallon, Michael C 7:25:55 (34,434)
Fallows, David 3:53:12 (9,640)
Fallows, Michael L 6:04:21 (32,905)
Fan, Toby 3:51:10 (9,089)
Fanetti, Pierluigi 3:57:13 (10,868)
Fannin, Trevor J 3:50:37 (8,961)
Fanning, Alastair S 3:38:25 (6,344)
Fanning, Carl P 5:11:39 (28,354)
Fanning, Richard D 2:57:32 (907)
Faraaz, Mohammed 4:40:54 (22,402)
Faragher, Ian 4:04:12 (12,864)
Farber, Bruce F 4:09:54 (14,278)
Farber, David J 3:49:52 (8,791)
Farber, Richard 5:38:29 (31,225)
Farcas, David 3:15:18 (2,674)
Fardey, Nick 4:42:20 (22,761)
Fardini, Alexander S 4:34:17 (20,774)
Fargnoli, Eric 4:22:52 (17,691)
Farley, Adam M 4:03:11 (12,649)
Farlow, Stuart 5:45:15 (31,781)
Farmer, Darren D 5:07:39 (27,791)
Farmer, Dean A 4:33:49 (20,665)
Farmer, Dennis C 6:10:11 (33,122)
Farmer, George 5:06:29 (27,625)
Farmer, Paul S 4:12:27 (14,917)
Farmer, Robert C 4:11:48 (14,753)
Farmer, Robert J 5:47:17 (31,931)
Farmer, Stuart M 3:18:27 (3,042)
Farnan, Stuart 4:10:17 (14,365)
Farnell, Mark A 2:55:22 (770)
Farneti, Stefano 3:30:21 (4,947)
Farnham, Bill F 4:31:09 (19,923)
Farnham, Lyndon J 4:29:02 (19,408)
Farnsworth, Graham R 3:16:59 (2,861)
Faroppa, Richard J 3:51:14 (9,105)
Farquhar, Richard D 4:24:06 (18,019)
Farquharson, Andrew J 2:51:30 (572)
Farquharson, Stuart A 4:38:26 (21,811)
Farrant, Nick M 5:36:40 (31,094)
Farrar, David I 3:58:49 (11,426)
Farrar, Robin A 4:35:27 (21,098)
Farre José, Carlos 3:15:17 (2,669)
Farrell, Bernard 3:56:38 (10,674)
Farrell, David 4:35:49 (21,197)
Farrell, David D 4:43:34 (23,070)
Farrell, Mark S 5:12:56 (28,537)
Farrell, Paul 3:50:27 (8,920)
Farrell, Paul S 3:51:54 (9,276)
Farrelly, Brian P 4:05:27 (13,161)
Farrelly, Kevin V 4:42:37 (22,836)
Farrelly, Martin P 4:08:36 (13,942)
Farren, David M 6:24:33 (33,535)
Farrer, Richard A 4:12:21 (14,895)
Farrier, David 4:03:12 (12,654)
Farrimond, Jonathan Mawdsley M 6:26:05 (33,582)
Farrington, Des 3:51:54 (9,276)
Farrington, Gary J 4:27:55 (19,071)
Farrington, Neil T 6:10:16 (33,125)
Farrington, Stephen J 3:44:53 (7,654)
Farrow, Edward T 4:10:26 (14,395)
Farrow, Mark J 2:52:08 (600)
Farrow, Michael 3:54:36 (10,071)
Farrow, Neil B 4:15:38 (15,737)
Farrow, Peter J 4:05:10 (13,089)
Farrugia, Nathan 3:54:48 (10,125)
Farthing, Tim 4:08:38 (13,950)
Fasel, Roland 3:59:51 (11,802)
Fassnidge, Matthew J 4:27:18 (18,906)

Fauconnier, Gerard	4:16:24 (15,932)	
Faul, Ian D	6:08:51 (33,077)	
Faulder, Peter	3:40:02 (6,646)	
Faulkner, Donald N	4:25:37 (18,416)	
Faulkner, Jonathan H	4:01:22 (12,202)	
Faulkner, Kevin M	3:45:26 (7,780)	
Faulkner, Richard A	6:15:55 (33,291)	
Faulkner, Richard S	4:37:24 (21,514)	
Faulkner, Simon P	3:36:28 (5,961)	
Faulkner, Stephen J	5:04:15 (27,288)	
Fauser, Hermann	3:37:25 (6,154)	
Fautz, Harald	4:08:37 (13,946)	
Faux, Eric	3:22:42 (3,598)	
Faver, Steven G	4:32:28 (20,288)	
Favreau, Serge	3:52:29 (9,428)	
Fawbert, David T	5:19:26 (29,344)	
Fawcett, Dean H	3:40:43 (6,761)	
Fawcett, Hugh T	4:28:21 (19,223)	
Fawcett, Neil R	4:01:39 (12,281)	
Fawcett, Nick	4:48:46 (24,312)	
Fawcett, Paul	5:56:53 (32,577)	
Fawcett, Stuart R	3:42:50 (7,201)	
Fayers, Alex	5:55:28 (32,500)	
Fayers, David S	5:45:25 (31,795)	
Fazzi, Umberto	6:22:47 (33,482)	
Feander, Chris N	5:33:10 (30,765)	
Fear, Richard H	4:56:29 (25,967)	
Fear, Ross M	4:37:08 (21,512)	
Fearn, Adrian M	3:43:28 (7,337)	
Fearn, Terry	4:10:48 (14,492)	
Fearnley, Andrew	4:35:47 (21,190)	
Fearnley, David A	3:09:11 (1,906)	
Fearns, Neil A	4:29:22 (19,494)	
Fearon, Corrie	4:34:51 (20,925)	
Feather, Michael J	4:23:49 (17,943)	
Featherstone, James M	3:21:14 (3,389)	
Featherstone, John P	4:21:40 (17,364)	
Featherstone, Richard J	3:41:45 (6,977)	
Feaver, John	3:41:32 (6,945)	
Feeney, Sean	4:29:49 (19,591)	
Fel, Georges	4:41:32 (22,562)	
Feldman, Brian R	3:49:20 (8,659)	
Felgate, Leon	4:22:58 (17,719)	
Felice Pace, Patrick	4:17:31 (16,227)	
Felix, Wolfgang	4:15:18 (15,639)	
Fell, David	3:53:10 (9,629)	
Fell, Stuart P	5:16:53 (29,040)	
Feller, Sam	4:27:41 (18,994)	
Fellows, Andy	3:48:14 (8,407)	
Fellows, Dominic P	3:18:37 (3,057)	
Fellows, Paul	4:54:16 (25,536)	
Fellows, Stephen E	5:11:36 (28,346)	
Fels, Lee	4:46:45 (23,838)	
Fels, Marc	4:53:22 (25,344)	
Felstead, Alec I	3:57:15 (10,877)	
Felter, Christian T	4:44:55 (23,397)	
Feltham, Barry	4:29:58 (19,625)	
Felton, Ben J	4:03:54 (12,804)	
Felton, David J	3:13:37 (2,407)	
Felton, Mark J	4:53:04 (25,289)	
Felton, Richard J	4:28:17 (19,199)	
Felus, Clement	4:22:26 (17,560)	
Fender, Tom H	3:34:25 (5,607)	
Fendley, David J	5:41:09 (31,426)	
Fenn, David T	6:38:56 (33,864)	
Fenn, Geoff	3:46:35 (8,020)	
Fenn, Mark M	4:43:05 (22,954)	
Fenn, Richard A	3:52:21 (9,396)	
Fennell, David	3:48:45 (8,521)	
Fennell, Steve D	4:45:47 (23,617)	
Fenney, Eric	3:43:30 (7,345)	
Fentham Fletcher, Simon	4:24:19 (18,084)	
Fenton, Andrew P	5:07:35 (27,778)	
Fenton, Graham D	3:10:12 (2,011)	
Fenton, Jeffrey A	3:56:42 (10,690)	
Fenton, Nick	5:38:41 (31,239)	
Fenton, Paul E	4:08:43 (13,973)	
Fenwick, Charlie W	3:52:15 (9,375)	
Fenwick, John	3:35:30 (5,791)	
Fenwick, Paul	4:48:36 (24,271)	
Fenwick, William G	5:08:56 (27,961)	
Fereday, David H	5:42:12 (31,516)	
Ferel, Dieter H	4:09:20 (14,127)	

Ferera, Leon	6:31:02 (33,686)	
Ferguson, Charles	4:22:25 (17,555)	
Ferguson, Christopher J	4:39:46 (22,148)	
Ferguson, Gavin	3:48:23 (8,437)	
Ferguson, Ian C	4:49:16 (24,425)	
Ferguson, Jonathan S	2:35:30 (121)	
Ferguson, Paul A	4:40:17 (22,254)	
Ferguson, Raymond G	3:30:01 (4,888)	
Ferguson, Scott	3:02:10 (1,319)	
Fergusson, Bryan W	5:35:07 (30,951)	
Fergusson, Ian R	4:34:10 (20,746)	
Ferlito, Gianluca	3:39:37 (6,561)	
Fernandes, Joaquim J	5:23:04 (29,706)	
Fernandes, Joe	4:23:39 (17,905)	
Fernandes, José M	3:37:52 (6,230)	
Fernandez, Philippe	3:13:45 (2,429)	
Fernandez, Ramon	4:19:59 (16,882)	
Fernandez Vega, Luis E	3:16:57 (2,856)	
Fernandez-Combarro, Luis	3:35:12 (5,737)	
Fernandez-Miranda, Ignacio	3:35:12 (5,737)	
Fernez, Jean-Marc	3:35:16 (5,752)	
Fernez, Pascal	3:07:51 (1,771)	
Ferns, Gerard	4:52:37 (25,174)	
Ferrao, José M	5:15:45 (28,914)	
Ferraro, Fabrizio	3:31:31 (5,135)	
Ferraro, Julian D	2:41:32 (234)	
Ferreira, Carlos J	3:30:53 (5,035)	
Ferreira, Jacobus A	3:29:10 (4,707)	
Ferreira, Luisfilipe S	4:57:39 (26,220)	
Ferrell, Mark J	4:44:15 (23,241)	
Ferretti, Paolo	4:59:06 (26,493)	
Ferriday, Ernie	5:01:50 (26,934)	
Ferris, Christopher	3:56:46 (10,714)	
Ferris, David P	3:56:15 (10,552)	
Ferris, Martin R	4:34:13 (20,760)	
Ferris, Stewart	5:10:01 (28,147)	
Ferris, Thomas W	4:01:52 (12,329)	
Ferron, Shaun A	3:31:32 (5,137)	
Ferrrari, Fabrizio	4:45:32 (23,547)	
Ferry, Alexandra	6:37:02 (33,823)	
Fether, Harold R	4:39:29 (22,076)	
Feuchter, Marcel	4:38:09 (21,750)	
Few, Robert	4:34:58 (20,962)	
Fhima, Meyer	4:42:13 (22,732)	
Fiddes, David J	3:39:57 (6,628)	
Fiddis, Richard W	3:59:27 (11,656)	
Fiddler, Lee J	5:28:52 (30,360)	
Fiddy, Simon E	4:20:29 (17,020)	
Fidler, Nick	3:03:04 (1,379)	
Fiebig, Dante S	3:57:49 (11,066)	
Field, Andrew E	3:16:29 (2,814)	
Field, Dean J	5:39:52 (31,322)	
Field, Geoffrey	3:59:17 (11,590)	
Field, Jason	4:23:08 (17,760)	
Field, Richard M	4:34:28 (20,816)	
Field, Robert M	4:38:26 (21,811)	
Field, Steve	3:25:53 (4,083)	
Field, Thomas W	4:36:53 (21,461)	
Fielden, Christopher D	4:43:20 (23,012)	
Fielden, Matthew	3:37:49 (6,219)	
Fielder, Colin	3:54:21 (9,974)	
Fielder, Henry	4:58:44 (26,432)	
Fielding, Ian L	4:47:42 (24,068)	
Fields, Brian O	3:41:20 (6,902)	
Fields, Paul	4:35:36 (21,137)	
Fieldsend, Jonathan F	4:42:56 (22,915)	
Fieldwick, Lee	3:38:10 (6,298)	
Figg, Benjamin D	4:37:46 (21,659)	
Figg, Dale R	5:19:53 (29,402)	
Figg, Joseph J	4:46:49 (23,863)	
Figg, Timothy T	4:50:53 (24,818)	
Figgins, William A	4:49:59 (24,597)	
Figueiras, Marcelo R	3:54:03 (9,887)	
Fila, Marco	3:09:46 (1,967)	
Filby, Adam	5:43:52 (31,639)	
Filby, Raymond G	5:43:52 (31,639)	
Filby, Richard J	4:28:26 (19,243)	
Fillmore, Andrew J	4:22:17 (17,517)	
Filloux, Alain	3:26:49 (4,249)	
Finch, Andrew G	5:17:36 (29,137)	
Finch, Bobby	4:50:14 (24,650)	
Finch, Jason T	4:45:03 (23,423)	
Finch, John	4:55:34 (25,792)	

Finch, John R	4:30:25 (19,724)	
Finch, Peter L	3:36:04 (5,892)	
Finch, Ronnie	4:27:48 (19,022)	
Finch, Simon K	3:25:19 (3,982)	
Fincher, Lachlan A	3:56:59 (10,788)	
Findlay, Adam D	5:21:06 (29,509)	
Findlay, David	4:41:00 (22,437)	
Findlay, Gordon	2:58:50 (1,045)	
Findlay, Paul A	4:35:51 (21,203)	
Fine, Martin H	3:52:14 (9,370)	
Finegan, Timothy	4:11:25 (14,650)	
Finegold, Jason E	5:18:43 (29,255)	
Fines, David A	3:27:58 (4,453)	
Finill, Chris T	2:48:18 (434)	
Finlay, Adrian	3:55:26 (10,316)	
Finlay, David C	4:48:19 (24,212)	
Finlay, Jack A	3:48:02 (8,358)	
Finlay, Michael	3:22:11 (3,509)	
Finlayson-Green, Jordan	4:07:34 (13,658)	
Finn, Allan G	4:23:51 (17,953)	
Finn, Graham R	4:57:29 (26,182)	
Finn, James A	3:49:56 (8,808)	
Finn, Peter J	3:49:56 (8,808)	
Finn, Russell	4:41:50 (22,647)	
Finn, Sean	3:33:25 (5,457)	
Finn, Stephen P	4:38:06 (21,740)	
Finnerty, Mark J	5:09:19 (28,014)	
Finney, Colin	3:14:54 (2,617)	
Finney, Giles R	4:16:27 (15,949)	
Finney, John R	4:25:55 (18,513)	
Fiore, Dominic P	3:34:49 (5,669)	
Fiore, Maurizio	4:22:49 (17,676)	
Fiori, Giuseppe Fabio	3:29:32 (4,788)	
Fiorini, Francesco	3:32:01 (5,228)	
Firetto, Andrew J	3:57:50 (11,071)	
Firmstone, Michael	4:08:12 (13,829)	
Firouzi, Mazeyar	2:47:50 (416)	
Firth, David A	4:57:04 (26,098)	
Firth, David J	3:25:17 (3,976)	
Firth, Edward	4:32:29 (20,293)	
Firth, Oliver M	3:22:32 (3,574)	
Firth, Richard	5:22:17 (29,636)	
Firth, Simon	4:56:16 (25,927)	
Fischer, Jurgen	4:35:06 (21,011)	
Fischer, Markus G	5:07:18 (27,739)	
Fish, Gary Edd	5:05:54 (27,532)	
Fish, Jonathan P	3:05:58 (1,594)	
Fisher, Andrew	4:34:59 (20,974)	
Fisher, Anthony P	7:43:04 (34,490)	
Fisher, Ben	3:59:01 (11,496)	
Fisher, Christopher	3:37:11 (6,098)	
Fisher, Christopher	5:46:37 (31,886)	
Fisher, Gary M	4:21:37 (17,341)	
Fisher, Geoffrey R	4:04:37 (12,960)	
Fisher, John	4:13:04 (15,054)	
Fisher, Malcolm D	3:08:51 (1,863)	
Fisher, Mark	4:38:27 (21,818)	
Fisher, Martyn R	4:12:14 (14,868)	
Fisher, Paul B	4:30:26 (19,728)	
Fisher, Scott E	4:46:51 (23,874)	
Fisher, Simon M	3:25:48 (4,069)	
Fisher, Simon W	3:26:57 (4,271)	
Fisher, Steve P	4:14:38 (15,478)	
Fisher, Stewart R	4:45:42 (23,585)	
Fisher, Stuart B	5:02:06 (26,967)	
Fisher, Tony	3:52:50 (9,514)	
Fisher, William E	4:36:45 (21,429)	
Fishlock, Andy B	4:50:02 (24,608)	
Fishlock, David J	4:15:05 (15,594)	
Fishman, David M	4:58:11 (26,323)	
Fitch, David F	2:58:10 (964)	
Fitch, Edd	4:05:30 (13,178)	
Fitch, Ian R	4:27:07 (18,847)	
Fitchett, James R	4:19:38 (16,790)	
Fitsall, Trevor J	4:53:29 (25,368)	
Fitt, Graham	4:47:13 (23,963)	
Fittock, Paul J	2:54:15 (712)	
Fitzgerald, Jerome E	4:02:23 (12,473)	
Fitzgerald, John A	3:26:56 (4,268)	
Fitzgerald, Mark A	3:59:47 (11,774)	
Fitzgerald, Mark J	3:59:42 (11,750)	
Fitzgerald, Michael R	6:08:31 (33,068)	
Fitzgerald, Terence P	4:23:33 (17,883)	

Fitzgibbon, Francis	4:01:54	(12,340)
Fitzherbert, Richard G	4:11:47	(14,745)
Fitzherbert, Rory B	3:40:19	(6,692)
Fitzjohn, Graeme E	3:12:31	(2,272)
Fitzmaurice, David	4:34:49	(20,908)
Fitzpatrick, Ben	6:38:11	(33,849)
Fitzpatrick, Ian	4:26:56	(18,793)
Fitzpatrick, Jason	4:22:09	(17,482)
Fitzpatrick, John	5:20:30	(29,465)
Fitzpatrick, N	4:36:21	(21,336)
Fitzpatrick, Peter G	4:24:25	(18,114)
Fitzsimmons, Keith M	4:34:47	(20,904)
Fitzsimmons, Keith W	5:22:22	(29,646)
Fjelldal, Jens C	4:36:18	(21,324)
Flack, Adam C	4:55:26	(25,770)
Flack, Colin	5:06:04	(27,564)
Flade, Peter	4:49:25	(24,462)
Flanagan, Brian	3:42:45	(7,185)
Flanagan, Graham	3:57:25	(10,935)
Flanagan, Thomas B	3:27:48	(4,421)
Flanders, John	4:58:35	(26,395)
Flannery, David J	3:54:15	(9,943)
Flannery, John P	3:26:02	(4,109)
Flannigan, Anthony	4:15:22	(15,655)
Flannigan, Kevin J	4:33:25	(20,550)
Flather, Edward J	4:54:56	(25,683)
Flatt, Christopher J	3:27:48	(4,421)
Flavell, Allan D	3:45:50	(7,867)
Flaxman, John J	5:04:10	(27,276)
Flecknoe, Daniel	5:16:11	(28,957)
Fleetwood, Daniel	4:01:01	(12,114)
Flello, Carl	4:23:42	(17,914)
Fleming, Ben	4:18:30	(16,497)
Fleming, John A	4:03:26	(12,712)
Fleming, Martyn	4:55:50	(25,842)
Fleming, Matthew V	3:54:22	(9,978)
Fleming, Oliver S	3:52:53	(9,532)
Fleming, Paul A	2:55:01	(752)
Fleming, Roy	5:24:32	(29,861)
Fleming, Timothy J	3:24:58	(3,921)
Fleming-Gale, Jacob T	3:10:50	(2,081)
Flesch, Christoph M	3:35:58	(5,875)
Flesher, Roy	3:12:30	(2,266)
Fletcher, Andy J	3:48:32	(8,473)
Fletcher, Colin J	2:57:19	(898)
Fletcher, Colin W	4:18:12	(16,403)
Fletcher, Eddie	3:05:57	(1,593)
Fletcher, Graham	3:32:33	(5,327)
Fletcher, Graham N	5:20:27	(29,460)
Fletcher, Henry C	3:29:51	(4,849)
Fletcher, James S	4:13:42	(15,225)
Fletcher, Jonathan P	3:53:33	(9,726)
Fletcher, Marcus	4:49:35	(24,498)
Fletcher, Mark	3:30:51	(5,029)
Fletcher, Mark P	4:08:05	(13,784)
Fletcher, Matthew J	3:59:36	(11,714)
Fletcher, Michael J	5:10:14	(28,180)
Fletcher, Neil B	4:51:14	(24,887)
Fletcher, Patrick J	3:53:02	(9,586)
Fletcher, Paul A	3:33:51	(5,526)
Fletcher, Paul D	3:37:04	(6,074)
Fletcher, Robert	4:31:51	(20,123)
Fletcher, Robin	3:22:44	(3,599)
Fletcher, Simon M	4:27:50	(19,033)
Fletcher, Steven E	3:55:16	(10,279)
Fletcher, Tony	4:53:49	(25,446)
Flick, Anthony	3:52:22	(9,401)
Flinders, Ian	3:51:57	(9,287)
Flint, Mark A	3:46:35	(8,020)
Flint, Robert	3:47:16	(8,172)
Flint, Steven	3:58:42	(11,374)
Flint, Stuart J	4:23:53	(17,958)
Flint, Thomas P	3:07:06	(1,689)
Flitney, Paul	4:08:13	(13,833)
Flockhart, Kevin R	5:22:17	(29,636)
Flood, Donal	3:26:33	(4,192)
Flood, Matthew E	4:27:40	(18,990)
Flores, Armando	5:53:22	(32,366)
Flores, Juan A	5:01:09	(26,818)
Floresta, Attilio	3:30:31	(4,974)
Flower, Mark	4:53:39	(25,410)
Flower, Michael D	3:42:30	(7,140)
Flowers, Mark A	3:43:32	(7,350)

Floyd, Chris G	3:23:35	(3,716)
Floyd, Mark R	5:28:29	(30,320)
Fluhme, Ulrich	2:37:27	(157)
Flynn, Jamie J	3:24:58	(3,921)
Flynn, John	5:46:08	(31,845)
Flynn, John M	3:18:28	(3,045)
Flynn, John R	3:47:50	(8,306)
Flynn, Keith	5:17:19	(29,098)
Flynn, Michael P	5:04:46	(27,367)
Flynn, Steven	4:26:41	(18,716)
Foale, Adam P	4:41:13	(22,493)
Foddy, Matthew D	3:04:27	(1,481)
Foden, John E	3:44:59	(7,676)
Foden, Neil	5:12:44	(28,501)
Fogerty, David	4:10:47	(14,488)
Fogerty, Simon J	3:57:52	(11,079)
Fogg, Brian	3:57:54	(11,091)

Fogle, Ben	4:04:29	(12,928)

Fohim, Juvoyr	4:18:24	(16,464)
Foirest, Mickael	2:59:06	(1,073)
Foley, David O	5:36:44	(31,097)
Foley, Gary M	4:46:09	(23,700)
Foley, James	5:25:04	(29,926)
Foley, James J	4:45:58	(23,665)
Foley, John	3:35:32	(5,798)
Folker, Mark T	4:04:54	(13,021)
Follan, Michael G	3:27:38	(4,384)
Folland, Mike	3:44:31	(7,555)
Folland, Nick A	3:52:00	(9,301)
Folley, Sam D	4:36:06	(21,268)
Follows, Dominic	3:56:44	(10,702)
Folwell, John A	4:27:52	(19,051)
Fontana, Luigi	3:33:58	(5,543)
Fonteijn, Tino	3:41:31	(6,943)
Fonteneau, Nicolas	4:12:31	(14,931)
Fontenoy, Claude	4:27:51	(19,040)
Foong, Thomas	4:14:21	(15,410)
Foord, Andrew R	3:27:02	(4,284)
Foord, Roger J	4:21:37	(17,341)
Foot, Michael F	4:00:39	(12,017)
Foot, Peter G	5:30:11	(30,496)
Foote, Simon J	3:55:47	(10,429)
Forbes, Angus S	4:19:57	(16,874)
Forbes, Christopher L	3:14:50	(2,612)
Forbes, Jeremy J	5:05:55	(27,536)
Forbes, Justin	4:08:55	(14,022)
Forbes, Matthew T	4:33:43	(20,639)
Forbes, Steve	2:54:31	(722)
Forbes, Stuart A	3:04:21	(1,475)

Forbes, Thomas	4:07:34	(13,658)
Ford, Adam J	3:26:33	(4,192)
Ford, Alexander C	4:30:20	(19,706)
Ford, Christopher J	4:16:27	(15,949)
Ford, Christopher M	4:06:28	(13,390)
Ford, David	5:55:13	(32,480)
Ford, Dean R	5:00:41	(26,733)
Ford, Graham	3:57:54	(11,091)
Ford, Graham N	4:04:19	(12,893)
Ford, John	3:33:09	(5,410)
Ford, Martin C	3:14:38	(2,575)
Ford, Martin G	4:17:25	(16,195)
Ford, Matthew L	3:33:00	(5,387)
Ford, Matthew R	3:33:14	(5,426)
Ford, Michael S	3:46:35	(8,020)
Ford, Neil A	4:06:55	(13,496)
Ford, Peter F	3:43:51	(7,424)
Ford, Peter S	5:20:40	(29,475)
Ford, Richard	4:38:56	(21,954)
Ford, Richard L	4:44:16	(23,248)
Ford, Robert	4:44:35	(23,315)
Ford, Robert A	3:33:11	(5,416)
Ford, Robert A	3:47:27	(8,212)
Ford, Simon P	3:15:12	(2,654)
Forder, Michael P	3:48:42	(8,514)
Fordyce, Bruce	3:47:32	(8,227)
Forecast, Allen B	4:11:24	(14,648)
Foreman, John M	4:27:12	(18,871)
Foreman, Paul	4:15:25	(15,676)
Foreman, Peter S	3:52:06	(9,337)
Foreman, Timothy F	3:25:59	(4,103)
Fores, Shaun	3:50:12	(4,924)
Forey, Austin	4:29:18	(19,472)
Forey, Simon	5:01:32	(26,876)
Forkin, Harry	4:40:11	(22,235)
Formstone, Martin D	3:10:09	(2,006)
Forrest, Darryl T	5:00:59	(26,792)
Forrest, Ian M	3:10:38	(2,057)
Forrest, Richard P	3:54:17	(9,954)
Forrest, Rick	4:16:24	(15,932)
Forrest, Robin D	4:41:33	(22,565)
Forrest, Stephen A	4:06:09	(13,326)
Forrester, Andrew	4:43:33	(23,064)
Forrester, Andrew P	4:24:48	(18,218)
Forrester, Edward P	3:52:36	(9,454)
Forrester, Gary M	3:18:31	(3,050)
Forrester, Liam	6:35:10	(33,774)
Forrester, Paul	5:50:01	(32,123)
Forrester, Peter J	4:11:38	(14,712)
Forsdike, Mark A	4:42:18	(22,755)
Forsell, Thomas E	3:23:19	(3,679)
Forshaw, Antony P	5:51:09	(32,218)
Forshaw, Stephen D	4:28:12	(19,171)
Forster, Adrian J	4:45:53	(23,642)
Forster, David M	4:08:16	(13,845)
Forster, John L	3:50:17	(8,890)
Forster, Mark	4:33:33	(20,591)
Forster, Richard	3:45:21	(7,765)
Forster, Stephen P	4:31:06	(19,910)
Forsyth, Andrew C	3:46:48	(8,059)
Forsyth, Nicholas S	4:11:23	(14,640)
Forsyth, Richard J	3:54:26	(10,006)
Forsyth, Rory	3:17:30	(2,932)
Forte, Franco	3:02:42	(1,358)
Forte, Phil	3:29:37	(4,803)
Forton, Christopher J	4:17:44	(16,291)
Fortun, Phil J	3:41:38	(6,956)
Fortune, David J	3:59:47	(11,774)
Fortune, Tom R	3:44:44	(7,617)
Fortuny Fillo, Pol	3:16:14	(2,780)
Forwood, Nick	4:34:09	(20,739)
Fosbrooke, Geoffrey P	4:26:08	(18,571)
Foskett, Geoffrey I	4:09:19	(14,122)
Foskett, Graham P	4:41:05	(22,452)
Fossey, Chris	4:06:26	(13,381)
Fossey, Joe E	3:30:48	(5,022)
Foster, Andrew	3:59:55	(11,825)
Foster, Christopher	4:58:37	(26,403)
Foster, David	4:44:35	(23,315)
Foster, David M	4:10:21	(14,376)
Foster, Gavin R	5:03:29	(27,181)
Foster, Gerard S	4:35:57	(21,228)
Foster, Graeme	4:40:27	(22,298)

Foster, Graham J	3:45:14 (7,736)	Francis, David	5:13:24 (28,595)	French, Neil	3:50:37 (8,961)
Foster, James	5:33:48 (30,814)	Francis, Gareth	3:21:46 (3,456)	French, Neil J	3:57:18 (10,890)
Foster, James A	4:53:28 (25,364)	Francis, Ian N	4:08:12 (13,829)	French, Paul	3:22:03 (3,497)
Foster, Kevin J	4:13:14 (15,096)	Francis, Ira	5:03:48 (27,225)	French, Paul	4:46:50 (23,867)
Foster, Kevin R	4:24:10 (18,039)	Francis, Mark A	3:13:25 (2,388)	French, Peter A	4:46:50 (23,867)
Foster, Kristopher A	5:26:39 (30,116)	Francis, Nicholas J	4:52:11 (25,078)	French, Richard A	3:06:49 (1,664)
Foster, Lee S	5:00:59 (26,792)	Francis, Paul J	5:15:55 (28,926)	French, Stephen E	4:08:13 (13,833)
Foster, Mark	5:27:02 (30,148)	Francis, Richard C	4:18:33 (16,513)	Fretz, Willi	4:41:29 (22,553)
Foster, Neil A	4:47:10 (23,949)	Francis, Richard J	3:34:56 (5,691)	Freuler, Niklaus K	4:45:09 (23,452)
Foster, Paul L	3:37:47 (6,212)	Francis, Robin A	4:17:31 (16,227)	Freyd, Mark	4:58:11 (26,323)
Foster, Robert P	3:19:05 (3,105)	Francis, Stephen A	3:56:56 (10,774)	Fricke, Simon G	3:15:31 (2,703)
Foster, Roger	5:00:49 (26,769)	Francis, Trevor B	4:26:48 (18,753)	Friday, Benjamin J	4:28:14 (19,188)
Foster, Roy	6:23:06 (33,494)	François, Elvis	4:43:04 (22,948)	Fried, Bertrand	5:29:21 (30,409)
Foster, Simon L	4:34:06 (20,725)	François, Pierre-Yves	4:11:57 (14,791)	Friedlander, Edward A	3:32:50 (5,367)
Foster, Stephen J	3:58:39 (11,357)	François, Yvio	2:53:40 (672)	Friedrich, Volker	3:21:16 (3,397)
Foster, Stephen M	3:43:28 (7,337)	Frank, Charlie N	4:00:25 (11,951)	Friel, Robert N	4:20:13 (16,951)
Foster, Steven M	3:59:47 (11,774)	Frank, Glen D	4:28:24 (19,232)	Friel, Simon J	4:34:43 (20,883)
Foster, Tim A	3:55:18 (10,289)	Frank, Wayne	3:51:27 (9,164)	Friend, Brian S	3:14:51 (2,614)
Foster, Tim J	4:53:39 (25,410)	Frankinet, Pierre H	2:58:43 (1,032)	Fright, Matthew P	4:52:54 (25,256)
Foster, Will	3:49:39 (8,731)	Frankland, Brad A	5:31:12 (30,585)	Friis, Kentaro	3:40:51 (6,793)
Fosteryvold, Joseph J	6:04:51 (32,918)	Franklin, Andrew	5:28:47 (30,348)	Frith, Andrew J	3:48:33 (8,479)
Fotherby, Kenneth J	3:20:39 (3,313)	Franklin, Edward	4:22:51 (17,686)	Frith, Andy	3:43:01 (7,243)
Fothergill, Wayne A	4:23:11 (17,778)	Franklin, John A	6:16:06 (33,296)	Froderberg, Bjorn O	3:56:09 (10,528)
Fouche, Philip N	4:44:02 (23,190)	Franklin, Kelvin	4:52:06 (25,064)	Froggatt, Richard	4:14:25 (15,429)
Foucras, Sebastien	3:01:57 (1,309)	Franklin, Leslie	4:32:17 (20,249)	Frogley, George C	5:52:51 (32,331)
Foulds, John	3:41:50 (6,996)	Franklin, Mark R	3:58:18 (11,219)	Frost, Andrew	3:59:48 (11,782)
Foulger, Martin	4:35:39 (21,152)	Franklin, Nicholas A	5:32:14 (30,677)	Frost, Andrew J	4:51:46 (25,000)
Foulkes, Chris A	4:01:03 (12,121)	Franklin, Richard C	4:42:38 (22,840)	Frost, David M	3:15:37 (2,712)
Foulkes, Llifon A	3:26:36 (4,206)	Franklin, Thomas W	3:36:56 (6,047)	Frost, Graeme T	3:28:41 (4,600)
Foure, Gilles A	4:32:20 (20,260)	Franks, David A	3:19:58 (3,223)	Frost, Iain	3:51:50 (9,254)
Fournet, Serge	4:32:56 (20,415)	Franks, Robert	4:02:20 (12,454)	Frost, Jonathan	2:26:16 (40)
Foweather, Liam R	3:46:13 (7,930)	Franks, Simon P	4:02:00 (12,363)	Frost, Jonathan H	4:25:58 (18,524)
Fowell, Mark A	3:02:52 (1,368)	Frankson, Clive A	4:43:01 (22,933)	Frost, Kevin D	3:49:43 (8,752)
Fowkes, Joseph A	5:49:52 (32,109)	Frankton, Andrew	3:57:37 (10,987)	Frost, Kevin P	4:12:42 (14,962)
Fowler, Alex	4:04:35 (12,947)	Franzoni, Mauro	3:58:31 (11,306)	Frost, Martin J	2:51:22 (567)
Fowler, Charlie N	4:20:34 (17,050)	Fraquelli, Andrea	2:54:56 (743)	Frost, Miles P	5:00:17 (26,681)
Fowler, Craig A	3:03:03 (1,377)	Fraser, Elliot	3:36:15 (5,923)	Frost, Morten	3:59:37 (11,720)
Fowler, David J	4:53:05 (25,293)	Fraser, Jack	3:37:33 (6,175)	Frost, Paul S	4:36:06 (21,268)
Fowler, Jonathon S	5:22:04 (29,606)	Fraser, Leslie E	5:26:18 (30,071)	Frost, Peter A	3:47:08 (8,138)
Fowler, Keith	4:23:41 (17,910)	Fraser, Matthew	5:23:57 (29,799)	Frost, Richard A	4:07:16 (13,591)
Fowler, Kevin V	2:59:51 (1,155)	Fraser, Matthew J	4:20:45 (17,103)	Frost, Richard A	4:26:26 (18,641)
Fowler, Mark C	3:33:11 (5,416)	Fraser, Stuart C	3:50:09 (8,859)	Frost, Rodney F	3:56:32 (10,639)
Fowler, Matthew	3:00:30 (1,201)	Fraser, Tony S	3:29:26 (4,770)	Frost, Stephen T	6:33:20 (33,731)
Fowler, Matthew D	2:52:49 (632)	Frattini, Alberto	4:37:37 (21,621)	Frostick, Carl S	4:34:27 (20,811)
Fowler, Richard	4:42:21 (22,763)	Fray, Martin D	3:05:38 (1,565)	Froud, Michael	3:28:51 (4,635)
Fowler, Rob N	4:39:03 (21,988)	Frayne, Anthony	5:19:24 (29,337)	Froude, Gregory P	4:01:01 (12,114)
Fowler, Steve P	3:38:52 (6,423)	Frazer, Anthony	4:22:02 (17,459)	Froydenlund, Paul F	3:32:08 (5,248)
Fowler, Tom G	3:09:46 (1,967)	Frazer, Matthew	4:22:03 (17,460)	Fry, Edward J	3:40:57 (6,815)
Fowles, Matthew J	4:54:44 (25,632)	Fredon, Eric	3:48:59 (8,576)	Fry, Malcolm M	4:33:16 (20,496)
Fox, Barrie	3:31:33 (5,141)	Freedman, Ben M	4:19:05 (16,651)	Frydman, Eric	3:16:34 (2,820)
Fox, Brian T	3:09:19 (1,922)	Freedman, Paul	6:31:59 (33,702)	Fryer, Anthony R	4:17:28 (16,211)
Fox, Darren	3:56:49 (10,730)	Freel, Christopher J	3:39:21 (6,509)	Fryer, John	3:16:43 (2,837)
Fox, James	4:09:24 (14,141)	Freeman, Alan	4:15:21 (15,652)	Fryer, Laurence W	4:20:57 (17,164)
Fox, James M	4:14:26 (15,432)	Freeman, Andi R	5:04:34 (27,338)	Fryer, Simon M	4:34:12 (20,758)
Fox, James W	4:50:28 (24,703)	Freeman, Anthony W	4:48:26 (24,233)	Fryer, Stephen J	3:06:12 (1,618)
Fox, James R	3:56:51 (10,743)	Freeman, Colin W	3:02:31 (1,342)	Fu, Raymond	6:45:48 (34,001)
Fox, Jonathan R	5:01:51 (26,936)	Freeman, David J	4:32:35 (20,318)	Fuchs, Michael	3:38:15 (6,308)
Fox, Justian C	4:35:57 (21,228)	Freeman, Dennis G	3:47:49 (8,303)	Fuggle, Tony J	4:58:33 (26,386)
Fox, Malcolm	5:50:53 (32,201)	Freeman, Edward	4:48:06 (24,162)	Fuggles, John	5:08:57 (27,962)
Fox, Mike	5:20:22 (29,446)	Freeman, James T	3:05:18 (1,537)	Fulberg, Paul	4:06:15 (13,346)
Fox, Simon I	4:27:17 (18,900)	Freeman, John	4:28:08 (19,142)	Fulcher, Chris J	3:04:23 (1,477)
Fox, Stevan	4:38:35 (21,855)	Freeman, John F	5:04:41 (27,354)	Fulford, Charles J	3:47:20 (8,181)
Fox, Stuart	2:29:13 (60)	Freeman, Kevin C	3:29:51 (4,849)	Fulford-Talbot, James L	3:55:13 (10,269)
Fox, Terry J	3:49:50 (8,778)	Freeman, Patrick	5:46:10 (31,849)	Fullbrook, Richard	4:01:04 (12,128)
Fox, Thomas	3:45:33 (7,800)	Freeman, Peter A	5:24:06 (29,817)	Fuller, Alexander G	4:00:53 (12,077)
Fox, Thomas G	3:51:10 (9,089)	Freeman, Simon B	3:14:36 (2,567)	Fuller, Andrew	4:13:44 (15,233)
Fox, Thomas S	4:08:28 (13,901)	Freeman, Tom M	3:56:07 (10,516)	Fuller, Andrew T	4:39:30 (22,080)
Fox, Thomas W	3:59:26 (11,646)	Freeman, Walter L	4:58:55 (26,459)	Fuller, Chris	4:16:23 (15,927)
Foxall, Peter L	3:17:40 (2,948)	Freer, Anthony B	5:08:59 (27,967)	Fuller, John R	3:23:24 (3,690)
Foy, David C	5:31:34 (30,617)	Freer, David M	4:12:24 (14,907)	Fuller, Mark	5:29:24 (30,411)
Foyle, Christopher N	4:37:52 (21,688)	Freer, Mark S	3:59:02 (11,499)	Fuller, Martin G	2:47:38 (406)
Foyle, Edward F	5:28:53 (30,364)	Freer, Mathew H	4:25:29 (18,388)	Fuller, Nicholas	4:57:27 (26,173)
Fraga, David	3:51:07 (9,078)	Freese, Leon	4:32:03 (20,184)	Fuller, Paul	3:55:11 (10,261)
Fraioli, Mariano	3:25:29 (4,010)	Freeston, Paul B	3:33:54 (5,532)	Fuller, Peter J	4:35:16 (21,048)
Franca, Julio	3:47:28 (8,215)	Freestone, Oliver	3:31:29 (5,126)	Fuller, Richard N	3:13:15 (2,364)
Francavilla, Tommaso	3:55:33 (10,354)	Frega, Javier	2:56:36 (849)	Fuller, Robert J	4:31:04 (19,900)
France, Colin	3:15:26 (2,693)	Freire, Idilio	3:50:26 (8,916)	Fuller, Sean	4:11:33 (14,693)
Franchi, Carlo	2:54:58 (745)	Frempong, Peter	5:14:51 (28,794)	Fuller, Will S	4:43:51 (23,141)
Franciosi, Giancarlo	5:46:36 (31,884)	French, Andrew	4:21:46 (17,398)	Fuller, William R	3:23:42 (3,726)
Francis, Alistair L	4:26:26 (18,641)	French, Charles M	4:08:41 (13,965)	Fulton, Colin	4:56:26 (25,953)
Francis, Andrew F	4:58:05 (26,301)	French, Chris	3:16:10 (2,770)	Fung, Harry H	4:41:25 (22,537)
Francis, Chris	4:25:20 (18,352)	French, Freddie A	4:56:16 (25,927)	Fung, Ming	4:21:34 (17,328)
Francis, David	4:00:21 (11,937)	French, Karl D	4:35:49 (21,197)	Funk, Jason	3:58:08 (11,157)

Funnell, Simon I 5:26:21 (30,082)
Funnell, Tim 4:01:35 (12,267)
Furber, Jeremy D 4:04:55 (13,031)
Furber, Stuart 4:27:57 (19,081)
Furey, Dara E 2:57:03 (877)
Furey, Jake 4:01:55 (12,343)
Furley, Andrew 3:22:19 (3,536)
Furlow, Nick E 6:30:53 (33,684)
Furness, Chris B 3:35:27 (5,785)
Furniss, Henry W 3:50:00 (8,824)
Furnival, Andrew 3:51:37 (9,203)
Furnivall, Robert L 6:40:26 (33,892)
Furse, Darren 4:35:20 (21,064)
Furse, Jonathan M 5:51:13 (32,228)
Furukawa, Mitsuaki 3:44:21 (7,522)
Furze, Richard 4:35:20 (21,064)
Furzer, Paul M 3:51:52 (9,265)
Fuss, Heiko 3:28:42 (4,606)
Fussien, Marc P 3:20:55 (3,343)
Fuszard, Mark A 4:55:04 (25,711)
Futers, Justin P 3:42:28 (7,134)
Futrell, Rodney 3:53:31 (9,715)
Futter, Luke V 4:24:19 (18,084)
Futtit, Mike 4:12:55 (15,007)
Fyall, Drummond 5:13:44 (28,641)
Fyfe, Angus G 4:02:51 (12,577)
Fyshe, Henry 4:50:50 (24,801)
Gabb, Graham R 3:46:32 (8,011)
Gabbi, Carlo 3:58:10 (11,174)
Gabriel, Roland 3:17:08 (2,876)
Gabrielsen, Stian 4:31:12 (19,938)
Gadd, Adam 4:51:00 (24,844)
Gadd, Ian M 4:56:09 (25,903)
Gade, Jorn 4:00:49 (12,062)
Gadeke, Jason R 4:56:33 (25,980)
Gadgil, Devendra V 6:43:40 (33,954)
Gadsden, Marc J 3:14:16 (2,513)
Gaertner, Dominik 4:07:24 (13,612)
Gaffney, Marcus J 5:11:44 (28,374)
Gafoor, Graeme D 5:47:14 (31,929)
Gagan, Adam 3:56:59 (10,788)
Gage, Matthew T 4:47:26 (24,009)
Gager, George W 4:34:52 (20,931)
Gager, Terry C 4:02:47 (12,561)
Gaile, Thomas P 2:48:57 (462)
Gailhac, Philippe 4:40:41 (22,346)
Gailland, Serge 2:54:14 (711)
Gaillemin, Oliver S 3:23:06 (3,654)
Gaitely, Mark C 4:06:49 (13,476)
Galan, Ivan 2:24:55 (36)
Galbraith, Scott 3:51:55 (9,282)
Gale, Andrew M 4:06:04 (13,305)
Gale, Benjamin 4:01:57 (12,348)
Gale, David 4:58:16 (26,338)
Gale, Joseph C 3:38:21 (6,327)
Gale, Melvyn G 5:36:53 (31,110)
Gale, Simon 4:39:44 (22,137)
Galentino, Giuliano 3:52:19 (9,392)
Gale-Ward, Lloyd E 3:36:47 (6,012)
Galimberti, Andrea 5:01:32 (26,876)
Galiunas, Michael D 3:28:26 (4,545)
Gall, Scott A 3:29:39 (4,809)
Gallacher, Daniel J 5:12:41 (28,489)
Gallacher, Russell S 3:39:49 (6,600)
Gallagher, Andy 5:35:28 (30,973)
Gallagher, Christian J 4:26:42 (18,723)
Gallagher, David S 4:26:42 (18,723)
Gallagher, Finbarr 3:16:39 (2,828)
Gallagher, Harvey 4:08:54 (14,018)
Gallagher, Martin D 3:08:12 (1,814)
Gallagher, Michael 4:36:14 (21,308)
Gallagher, Michael A 2:54:11 (708)
Gallagher, Nick 3:25:11 (3,959)
Gallagher, Oliver M 3:44:05 (7,470)
Gallagher, Patrick J 3:29:21 (4,751)
Gallagher, Paul 4:58:16 (26,338)
Gallagher, Peter A 4:30:51 (19,850)
Gallagher, Shane G 4:09:26 (14,151)
Gallagher, Spencer 4:11:40 (14,726)
Gallagher, Tony C 4:31:09 (19,923)
Gallanagh, Peter 2:55:34 (779)
Gallen, Brendan 3:41:34 (6,951)
Gallen, Gerrard A 5:00:22 (26,688)
Galler, Leon A 4:08:42 (13,969)
Gallerani, Stefano 4:09:27 (14,156)
Galley, Brian 3:53:32 (9,719)
Galley, Junior 2:56:16 (830)
Gallimore, David 4:00:35 (11,998)
Gallivan, John F 7:13:51 (34,352)
Gallo, Simon J 5:42:45 (31,554)
Galpin, John T 4:05:56 (13,275)
Galpin, Peter C 2:28:38 (52)
Galvao-Rogers, John P 5:05:23 (27,458)
Gambarini, Edward J 4:31:25 (20,004)
Gamble, Ben P 3:26:16 (4,148)
Gamble, Iain 4:51:38 (24,973)
Gamble, Steven 4:32:06 (20,197)
Game, Barry 4:16:15 (15,892)
Game, Kevin J 2:58:30 (1,009)
Gami, Manji 4:54:55 (25,676)
Gammage, Tom J 3:44:53 (7,654)
Gammie, Scott M 4:28:04 (19,118)
Gammon, Adrian 4:21:07 (17,208)
Gammon, Vincent J 3:55:29 (10,335)
Gan, Andrew J 3:49:50 (8,778)
Ganbury, David P 3:56:57 (10,779)
Gandhi, Shirish 3:39:01 (6,440)
Gandini, Carlo 3:39:47 (6,594)
Gandon, Andrew J 4:15:55 (15,811)
Gandy, Ray D 4:46:49 (23,863)
Gane, Jeremy 3:57:13 (10,868)
Ganivet, Joffrey 3:56:43 (10,699)
Gannon, David E 6:22:20 (33,468)
Gannon, Richard 3:26:42 (4,231)
Gannon, Richard J 2:46:58 (385)
Gannon, Stephen C 3:55:32 (10,350)
Gant, Andrew J 4:40:21 (22,275)
Gant, Matthew J 3:46:15 (7,940)
Ganthi, Kiran Kumar R 4:55:05 (25,715)
Garaasen, Gar 5:51:49 (32,276)
Garavaglia, Andrea 2:56:57 (868)
Garbett, Danny 4:26:15 (18,595)
Garcia, Adolfo 3:03:57 (1,445)
Garcia, Carlos 3:13:42 (2,422)
Garcia, David 3:03:34 (1,421)
Garcia, Frederic 3:32:39 (5,340)
Garcia, Guillermo 4:39:50 (22,157)
Garcia, José M 3:56:55 (10,768)
Garcia, Julian 3:21:01 (3,362)
Garcia, Pascal 3:55:24 (10,313)
Garcia, Richard 5:01:59 (26,954)
Garcia, Tony 4:01:05 (12,132)
Garcia Velez, José C 4:23:50 (17,946)
Gard, Merlin 6:53:55 (34,135)
Gardelli, Paride 2:52:08 (600)
Garden, Andrew S 5:31:30 (30,614)
Garden, Scott 4:51:34 (24,950)
Gardener, Ben W 6:58:24 (34,193)
Gardener, Geoff T 4:49:09 (24,408)
Gardener, Nigel 3:52:12 (9,360)
Gardener, Toby O 6:58:24 (34,193)
Gardes, Thierry P 3:24:20 (3,820)
Gardiner, Colin F 4:09:30 (14,174)
Gardiner, Gary 3:55:23 (10,309)
Gardiner, John P 4:17:43 (16,284)
Gardiner, Kevin L 3:46:15 (7,940)
Gardiner, Richie 2:20:28 (22)
Gardiner, Thomas 4:58:56 (26,464)
Gardiner, Wesley 7:01:52 (34,229)
Gardiner, Will R 5:46:00 (31,834)
Gardner, Alex D 3:58:38 (11,351)
Gardner, Chris 4:49:01 (24,376)
Gardner, Clive D 3:58:53 (11,451)
Gardner, Darren 4:53:06 (25,295)
Gardner, Douglas C 5:16:43 (29,020)
Gardner, Giles L 3:56:26 (10,605)
Gardner, Joe D 4:26:09 (18,574)
Gardner, Joshua 4:58:34 (26,390)
Gardner, Leighton J 3:11:44 (2,179)
Gardner, Neal T 4:39:18 (22,049)
Gardner, Nick A 4:47:16 (23,976)
Gardner, Paul A 4:27:14 (18,883)
Gardner, Ronald S 4:45:08 (23,444)
Gardner, Rupert 4:05:30 (13,178)
Gardner, Wayne A 3:34:47 (5,659)
Gardner-Browne, Ellis 4:36:28 (21,361)
Gare, Adrian 4:33:32 (20,586)
Gargallo Renom, Eduardo 3:04:31 (1,485)
Gargaro, Steven 4:39:25 (22,069)
Gargaro, Vincent 5:09:30 (28,048)
Garland, Lee R 3:07:23 (1,722)
Garner, James B 4:31:32 (20,032)
Garner, James P 4:06:08 (13,322)
Garner, Michael 6:05:21 (32,937)
Garner, Paul D 3:13:55 (2,454)
Garner, Phillip J 3:40:13 (6,676)
Garnett, Mark S 4:18:27 (16,479)
Garnham, Piers C 3:48:06 (8,374)
Garnier, Patrick 4:18:59 (16,620)
Garrad, Marcel H 3:34:08 (5,568)
Garrad, Nicholas 5:31:08 (30,574)
Garrard, Terence D 5:56:53 (32,577)
Garratt, Mark 2:43:27 (280)
Garrett, Andrew T 3:34:54 (5,685)
Garrett, Benjamin J 3:35:03 (5,711)
Garrett, Martin A 3:52:01 (9,305)
Garrett, Michael A 3:09:37 (1,952)
Garrett, Nicholas 4:10:25 (14,391)
Garrett, Robert P 4:22:53 (17,698)
Garrigos, Jean Claude 4:34:11 (20,752)
Garrison, Robert 5:01:55 (26,946)
Garrity, Martin J 4:31:41 (20,074)
Garrood, Steve J 3:52:05 (9,327)
Garside, Steve 5:37:16 (31,136)
Garth, Alan J 5:33:18 (30,773)
Garthwaite, William T 4:26:19 (18,613)
Gartland, David M 6:48:12 (34,039)
Gartshore, Andrew 3:54:28 (10,013)
Garuti, Enrico 4:01:29 (12,237)
Garvey, Michael J 5:38:19 (31,216)
Garvey, Sean R 5:57:16 (32,591)
Garvey, Stephen 3:07:20 (1,716)
Garwood, James 3:26:29 (4,186)
Garzelli, Gianpiero 5:13:06 (28,556)
Gascoigne, Ian V 4:28:40 (19,303)
Gascoigne, Tim 3:07:15 (1,700)
Gascoyne, Dennis 4:20:54 (17,152)
Gaskarth, Andrew 3:02:21 (1,334)
Gaskell, Dave J 4:52:35 (25,166)
Gaskell, Harry 3:56:15 (10,552)
Gaskell, Tom J 3:56:00 (10,491)
Gasson, Antony R 4:50:21 (24,676)
Gasson, James L 4:25:58 (18,524)
Gateley, Peter J 4:08:06 (13,789)
Gately, John 3:50:17 (8,890)
Gately, Peter M 3:46:54 (8,083)
Gatens, John R 4:18:47 (16,567)
Gatens, Lawrence 2:58:13 (969)
Gates, Andrew S 3:42:37 (7,155)
Gates, Cathal A 4:46:52 (23,876)
Gates, Gary A 3:29:19 (4,743)
Gates, Justin R 4:00:18 (11,926)
Gath, David A 3:52:37 (9,461)
Gatrell, Christopher A 4:42:36 (22,832)
Gatto, Morris L 5:38:35 (31,227)
Gaudry, Jean-Michel 3:53:35 (9,737)
Gaughan, Martin P 3:12:01 (2,210)
Gaul, Stephen G 4:31:25 (20,004)
Gauld, Jethro G 4:00:00 (11,853)
Gaulder, Nicholas R 3:52:22 (9,401)
Gault, Steve 4:33:10 (20,473)
Gaunt, Martin 2:35:56 (130)
Gaunt, Mike 5:26:21 (30,082)
Gaunt, Oliver 4:26:24 (18,635)
Gaunt, Steve J 3:47:48 (8,296)
Gaunt, Trevor 4:55:03 (25,709)
Gautama, Govind 5:41:23 (31,452)
Gauvin, David 3:38:30 (6,359)
Gava, Christian 3:27:24 (4,349)
Gavaldon Rosas, Wenceslao 4:16:13 (15,882)
Gavan, Peter 4:51:21 (24,915)
Gavin, John 4:16:55 (16,065)
Gavin, Liam 5:36:13 (31,054)
Gavin, Oliver B 3:09:31 (1,942)
Gavin, Patrick J 5:14:07 (28,691)
Gawane, Mahendra D 7:44:37 (34,494)
Gawne, Richard A 4:43:28 (23,035)
Gay, Samuel 5:12:19 (28,435)
Gayler, James 3:48:31 (8,469)

Gaynor, Julian 2:57:00 (871)
Gaywood, Andi 5:39:11 (31,273)
Gaze, Nicholas C 4:14:05 (15,331)
Gaziano, Tony M 4:31:10 (19,928)
Gazzard, Alan J 4:33:26 (20,556)
Gazzelloni, Marco 3:26:01 (4,108)
Gear, Allan R 3:53:35 (9,737)
Gearing, Daniel L 3:24:27 (3,837)
Geary, Nigel 4:20:08 (16,920)
Geary, Stewart A 3:47:34 (8,239)
Geddes, Ian J 3:55:16 (10,279)
Geddes, John 4:01:25 (12,220)
Geddes, Readford R 5:14:52 (28,797)
Gedye, Michael W 3:56:08 (10,522)
Gee, Christopher W 4:35:22 (21,072)
Gee, David 5:43:06 (31,579)
Gee, Raymond 4:12:50 (14,988)
Gee, Wayne B 5:17:46 (29,150)
Gee, William J 4:45:29 (23,536)
Geen, Peter 4:48:24 (24,225)
Geering, Rupert E 5:22:18 (29,642)
Geeson, Andrew L 5:26:18 (30,071)
Gefen, Ben 4:40:40 (22,341)
Gehrig, Roman 2:33:46 (102)
Gehrke, Christopher M 4:09:18 (14,118)
Gehrmann, Wolfgang 4:45:08 (23,444)
Geiger, Christopher 4:58:07 (26,310)
Geitner, Joseph J 3:00:55 (1,238)
Geland, Pascal 3:44:27 (7,543)
Gelder, Andrew 4:57:47 (26,245)
Gelderd, Steven P 3:49:32 (8,706)
Gell, Colin 2:34:38 (109)
Geloen, Jean-Marc 3:43:15 (7,296)
Gelson, Stephen C 4:27:05 (18,834)
Gemma, Yoshikazu 6:33:47 (33,742)
Gemming, Logan 3:16:09 (2,768)
Genc, Ufuk 4:16:47 (16,029)
Gencel, Laurent 3:58:02 (11,130)
Genge, Bernard J 3:07:00 (1,682)
Gennery, Michael J 3:58:30 (11,298)
Genovesi, Athos 4:04:52 (13,015)
Gentchev, Vess G 4:43:33 (23,064)
Genter, Heinz-Peter 4:20:06 (16,913)
Gentilli, Hugo T 5:23:32 (29,749)
Gentle, Christopher R 3:07:56 (1,785)
Gentzler, Ryan C 3:14:03 (2,474)
George, Ajith P 4:29:19 (19,477)
George, Andrew D 4:15:27 (15,692)
George, Benjamin 3:20:32 (3,295)
George, Chris 3:28:04 (4,473)
George, David P 3:23:53 (3,758)
George, Derek 3:08:58 (1,878)
George, Iain P 4:24:16 (18,073)
George, Ian J 6:32:16 (33,710)
George, John F 4:23:09 (17,766)
George, Mark 3:17:13 (2,889)
George, Mark 3:28:27 (4,552)
George, Martin J 2:54:43 (730)
George, Martin P 4:04:33 (12,939)
George, Matthias 4:37:16 (21,539)
George, Nicholas J 4:04:05 (12,844)
George, Ronald 4:23:25 (17,842)
George, Thomas A 3:50:57 (9,036)
George, Trevor J 3:59:27 (11,656)
George, Zane M 4:01:28 (12,232)
Georgii, Michael G 4:11:07 (14,580)
Georgiou, George A 4:43:12 (22,982)
Georgiou, Marios A 3:40:13 (6,676)
Georgiou, Yiannis 4:16:20 (15,915)
Geraghty, Jason W 5:10:03 (28,153)
Gerhardt, Daniel T 4:52:51 (25,234)
Gerling, Rolf 4:50:31 (24,722)
Germain, David 6:01:54 (32,817)
Germain, Guy M 3:52:38 (9,468)
German, Peter M 4:00:05 (11,873)
Germann, Rico 2:49:26 (487)
Gerrard, Andrew 4:02:26 (12,483)
Gerrish, Benjamin S 6:12:16 (33,178)
Gerritsen, Rolf 4:27:24 (18,932)
Gersching, Erwin 5:32:22 (30,689)
Gerstner, Josef 4:35:05 (21,005)
Gerty, David W 3:43:50 (7,419)
Gething, Colin J 4:41:05 (22,452)
Gewald, Thomas 4:32:44 (20,355)
Ghaffarian, Medi 3:54:20 (9,968)
Ghatora, Amritral 4:42:52 (22,897)
Ghelardini, Massimo 4:33:00 (20,431)
Ghezzi, Giampiero 3:37:42 (6,201)
Ghoorun, Nigel M 3:46:07 (7,911)
Ghorashi, Rahim 4:59:28 (26,555)
Giacche, Robert 6:44:24 (33,967)
Giacobino, Luc 4:17:15 (16,165)
Giammalva, Giuseppe 4:34:42 (20,876)
Giampaoli, Jorge A 5:21:22 (29,543)
Giani, Michel P 2:52:40 (622)
Gibb, Martin C 4:23:10 (17,770)
Gibb, Robin J 4:09:12 (14,088)
Gibb, Stephen 3:52:16 (9,380)
Gibbard, Adrian B 3:13:38 (2,408)
Gibbens, Paul S 4:10:13 (14,340)
Gibbins, Martin T 5:15:58 (28,932)
Gibbon, John 4:53:25 (25,354)
Gibbon, Jonathan H 4:26:13 (18,585)
Gibbons, Michael P 3:12:47 (2,302)
Gibbons, Nigel F 3:55:43 (10,409)
Gibbons, Stephen 3:02:28 (1,339)
Gibbs, Alan 3:42:22 (7,111)
Gibbs, Ben L 3:29:06 (4,693)
Gibbs, Christopher J 5:52:46 (32,326)
Gibbs, David 3:39:15 (6,483)
Gibbs, Donald 4:34:41 (20,870)
Gibbs, Marcus J 3:16:53 (2,851)
Gibbs, Martin 4:12:05 (14,835)
Gibbs, Peter 3:55:27 (10,323)
Giborski, Gordie 3:27:40 (4,392)
Gibson, Adam 3:57:04 (10,816)
Gibson, Ali 3:57:04 (10,816)
Gibson, Andrew R 4:14:54 (15,536)
Gibson, Andrew R 4:16:10 (15,868)
Gibson, David M 4:07:54 (13,753)
Gibson, Finley J 4:33:43 (20,639)
Gibson, Giles 3:48:28 (8,454)
Gibson, Guy R 4:51:32 (24,944)
Gibson, John D 4:30:16 (19,691)
Gibson, Kevin R 4:50:03 (24,613)
Gibson, Neal M 3:10:39 (2,060)
Gibson, Oliver 2:44:06 (296)
Gibson, Patrick M 4:00:09 (11,883)
Gibson, Peter L 4:36:12 (21,296)
Gibson, Scott J 4:24:34 (18,164)
Gibson, Timothy M 3:15:46 (2,725)
Gibson, William D 3:34:19 (5,590)
Gifford, Alan P 4:13:05 (15,063)
Gifford, Andrew 4:21:33 (17,319)
Gigg, Martin A 4:47:17 (23,983)
Giglio, Roberto 4:25:48 (18,482)
Gikas, Panagiotis D 5:15:54 (28,921)
Gil, Carlos M 4:52:36 (25,169)
Gil Morales, Alfonso 3:44:47 (7,631)
Gilbank, Daniel 3:33:26 (5,461)
Gilbank, Paul 4:34:48 (20,907)
Gilbert, Anthony J 6:12:15 (33,176)
Gilbert, Anthony W 4:41:22 (22,526)
Gilbert, David L 3:48:18 (8,424)
Gilbert, Edward J 3:35:17 (5,754)
Gilbert, Jonathan P 4:15:08 (15,605)
Gilbert, Kevin A 3:51:41 (9,226)
Gilbert, Peter D 3:56:27 (10,616)
Gilbert, Ralph R 3:38:17 (6,314)
Gilbert, Sean W 4:33:42 (20,635)
Gilbert, Simon M 3:11:38 (2,166)
Gilbert, Will R 4:24:22 (18,098)
Gilbertson, John P 3:45:44 (7,840)
Gilbertson, Kenneth 4:18:27 (16,479)
Gilbertson, Paul E 4:43:56 (23,162)
Gilbody, Cap Jon 5:26:09 (30,048)
Gilbourne, James 5:59:05 (32,699)
Gilby, Daniel S 3:59:11 (11,554)

LONDON MARATHON

Gilby, Pete R 3:59:14 (11,574)
Gilchrist, David J 4:06:22 (13,366)
Gilchrist, Tyrone 5:08:46 (27,942)
Giles, David W 3:52:03 (9,318)
Giles, Jonathan M 5:07:17 (27,736)
Giles, Martin R 3:05:50 (1,584)
Giles, Steven J 4:44:48 (23,367)
Giles, Terry 4:41:26 (22,541)
Gilfillan, Dean 3:27:19 (4,336)
Gilhespy, Jonathan M 5:31:55 (30,648)
Gilkes, Alex W 4:54:51 (25,664)
Gilkes, Michael 3:11:50 (2,193)
Gill, Amarjit 5:56:55 (32,579)
Gill, David R 3:36:53 (6,036)
Gill, David T 3:53:48 (9,808)
Gill, Jeffrey I 4:49:16 (24,425)
Gill, John 3:57:51 (11,075)
Gill, Matthew R 5:37:44 (31,173)
Gill, Michael 4:21:26 (17,286)
Gill, Michael B 3:33:55 (5,534)
Gill, Nicholas J 3:24:51 (3,899)
Gill, Paul D 4:04:25 (12,916)
Gill, Paul J 5:56:19 (32,547)
Gill, Peter 4:46:53 (23,880)
Gill, Richard 3:56:50 (10,738)
Gill, Simon 3:49:29 (8,696)
Gill, Stevan S 4:31:33 (20,039)
Gill, Steve 3:53:41 (9,764)
Gillan, John A 4:13:25 (15,138)
Gillan, Kevin 5:06:09 (27,576)
Gillard, Barry 4:22:34 (17,601)
Gillard, Claude 3:32:35 (5,330)
Gillard, Colin 4:09:57 (14,287)
Gillard, Mathew 4:12:59 (15,027)
Gillard, Vernon M 3:28:46 (4,618)
Gillert, Daniel J 3:43:03 (7,248)
Gilles, Dean H 3:52:37 (9,461)
Gillespie, Andrew J 3:48:54 (8,557)
Gillespie, Bill 4:22:50 (17,679)
Gillespie, Keith A 4:32:03 (20,184)
Gillespie, Mark T 4:13:40 (15,213)
Gillespie, Nathan R 4:08:39 (13,955)
Gillespie, Neil J 5:30:58 (30,563)
Gillespie, Peter R 3:23:52 (3,755)
Gillett, Alex 5:01:44 (26,921)
Gillett, Andy L 3:51:33 (9,182)
Gillett, Charles 4:07:49 (13,720)
Gillett, Daniel J 2:56:26 (838)
Gillett, Dean H 4:40:05 (22,209)
Gillett, Richard 5:40:17 (31,359)
Gilley, Mark J 3:25:13 (3,962)
Gillham, Richard J 4:42:13 (22,732)
Gillham, Thomas J 4:42:14 (22,736)
Gilliam, Andrew 5:41:03 (31,421)
Gillibrand, Christian S 3:06:52 (1,670)
Gillies, Andrew S 3:28:18 (4,518)
Gillies, Calum P 3:55:09 (10,251)
Gillies, Carl 6:13:47 (33,239)
Gillies, Stuart 3:55:13 (10,269)
Gillies, William S 3:54:25 (9,998)
Gilligan, David W 4:33:46 (20,653)
Gilligan, Jack D 4:33:46 (20,653)
Gilling, Jonathan C 2:43:53 (290)
Gillingham, John M 3:18:53 (3,084)
Gillman, Chris 4:47:43 (24,074)
Gillman, David R 4:02:19 (12,450)
Gillmore, Ricky 4:06:58 (13,508)
Gillooly, Jamie 5:24:16 (29,835)
Gillooly, Timothy J 5:23:32 (29,749)
Gillson, Steve P 3:23:46 (3,736)
Gillson, Steven J 4:48:35 (24,268)
Gilmour, Duncan N 3:27:49 (4,426)
Gilmour, Keith M 3:36:18 (5,933)
Gilroy, Francis J 4:32:27 (20,282)
Gilroy, Robert 2:30:34 (79)
Gilson, John 5:21:06 (29,509)
Gilyatt, Richard J 4:17:01 (16,100)
Ginman, Anthony 5:44:40 (31,734)
Ginnaw, Colin 5:06:54 (27,682)
Giordano, Pasquale 4:28:41 (19,310)
Giorgino, Mauro 3:50:41 (8,985)
Giovetti, Vittorio 3:33:59 (5,545)
Girard, Stephane 4:00:09 (11,883)

Girling, Ricky E	4:09:44	(14,239)
Girolami, Stefano I	5:29:10	(30,394)
Gisbey, Joseph P	5:09:11	(27,992)
Gisin, Rainer	3:27:30	(4,363)
Gissing, Barry J	5:40:38	(31,386)
Githui, Davidson M	5:42:40	(31,545)
Gittus, Colin M	4:28:26	(19,243)
Giugliano, Alessio	4:25:12	(18,321)
Giusto, Valerio	5:03:44	(27,213)
Gladman, David J	4:06:14	(13,341)
Gladwell, Mark	3:51:35	(9,191)
Gladwin, James	4:13:54	(15,279)
Glasby, Keith M	4:23:15	(17,797)
Glasgon, Douglas	4:18:19	(16,440)
Glasgow, Philip D	5:23:35	(29,756)
Glass, Garry	3:55:31	(10,346)
Glass, John E	4:12:01	(14,814)
Glass, Jonathan M	3:29:25	(4,766)
Glass, Rafi	5:21:03	(29,501)
Glass, Stephen	4:14:27	(15,436)
Glassford, Richard	5:24:24	(29,847)
Glastonbury, Simon	4:47:16	(23,976)
Glauser, Alfred	4:26:48	(18,753)
Glavin, James A	5:07:23	(27,749)
Glazebrook, Jamie D	4:38:04	(21,729)
Glazer, Anthony H	4:25:38	(18,422)
Gleadall, Owen	5:29:54	(30,466)
Gleave, Martin	4:06:00	(13,291)
Gledhill, Mark	4:20:11	(16,940)
Gleeson, David	4:05:15	(13,110)
Glen, Alasdair	4:08:43	(13,973)
Glen, Andrew	3:08:31	(1,840)
Glen, Andrew	5:34:05	(30,843)
Glen, Christopher I	3:42:58	(7,227)
Glendining, Daniel	3:52:29	(9,428)
Glendinning, Tom B	3:25:55	(4,091)
Glenn, Felix	4:10:17	(14,365)
Glenn, Nathaniel M	2:58:25	(995)
Glennon, Liam A	4:27:05	(18,834)
Glew, David W	4:48:09	(24,176)
Glew, Steve	3:58:18	(11,219)
Glick, James	4:14:54	(15,536)
Glockner, Dennis	4:08:19	(13,857)
Glova, Aziz	5:06:09	(27,576)
Glover, Adrian D	4:17:22	(16,184)
Glover, Alan C	4:10:42	(14,462)
Glover, Brian R	4:57:57	(26,271)
Glover, Gary C	4:25:46	(18,468)
Glover, Ian G	4:10:10	(14,328)
Glover, James D	4:33:36	(20,609)
Glover, Mike J	4:16:46	(16,023)
Glover, Paul	4:36:28	(21,361)
Glover, Richard P	3:48:35	(8,483)
Glover, Stuart C	5:13:12	(28,571)
Glyde, Stuart K	4:17:51	(16,315)
Godbee, Peter	3:53:15	(9,649)
Godber, Duncan E	3:10:49	(2,078)
Godbold, Jamie T	4:52:50	(25,229)
Goddard, Alan J	4:25:22	(18,359)
Goddard, Craig J	4:15:10	(15,610)
Goddard, James M	3:36:29	(5,966)
Goddard, Joe S	3:42:41	(7,170)
Goddard, Matt	4:06:07	(13,318)
Goddard, Matthew	3:21:35	(3,430)
Goddard, Matthew T	5:28:15	(30,300)
Goddard, Paul T	4:53:08	(25,303)
Goddard, Russell M	3:21:35	(3,430)
Godden, John	4:28:36	(19,289)
Godding, Jonathan	5:29:58	(30,477)
Godet, Steve	4:04:40	(12,972)
Godfray, Tim	5:11:13	(28,297)
Godfrey, David J	6:46:09	(34,007)
Godfrey, David R	4:42:46	(22,868)
Godfrey, James	5:56:00	(32,521)
Godfrey, Paul J	3:28:44	(4,609)
Godfrey, Peter	5:28:16	(30,301)
Godison-Powell, Jordan T	5:07:37	(27,785)
Godley, Simon	5:10:35	(28,228)
Godsall, Matt	4:35:04	(20,998)
Godsell, Joe	3:14:47	(2,606)
Godwin, Martin T	3:30:31	(4,974)
Goetzinger, Christer L	4:10:25	(14,391)
Gofers, Paul	4:29:22	(19,494)

Goff, Graham D	4:55:34	(25,792)
Goffe, James R	3:25:55	(4,091)
Gohil, Farouk	3:45:41	(7,831)
Gohil, Rajen V	6:02:43	(32,842)
Gold, Adam	4:12:21	(14,895)
Gold, Jeremy A	2:48:53	(459)
Gold, Lawrence F	4:01:12	(12,165)
Goldberg, Michael	5:36:27	(31,076)
Golding, Andrew	3:54:07	(9,909)
Golding, Clive	3:31:21	(5,109)
Golding, Daniel J	2:29:51	(73)
Golding, David A	3:45:02	(7,691)
Golding, Vincent P	4:03:11	(12,649)
Goldman, Paul D	4:53:08	(25,303)
Goldsack, Stuart	5:17:09	(29,084)
Goldsby, Cameron	4:42:37	(22,836)
Goldsmith, Andrew J	5:07:13	(27,722)
Goldsmith, Christopher R	3:56:30	(10,626)
Goldsmith, Mark R	5:03:30	(27,183)
Goldsmith, Stuart G	3:28:35	(4,574)
Goldsmith, Tim	4:30:39	(19,785)
Goldstein, Jonathan	4:16:13	(15,882)
Goldstein, Simon L	3:37:37	(6,189)
Goldsworthy, John	4:52:24	(25,123)
Goligher, William N	4:13:12	(15,081)
Golland, Clive R	4:36:53	(21,461)
Golledge, Clive G	4:00:46	(12,050)
Golton, Ian	5:31:56	(30,651)
Gomez, Antonio	3:39:05	(6,450)
Gomez, Ernest J	4:41:21	(22,524)
Gomez, Luis E	4:33:35	(20,601)
Gomez, Luis F	2:49:50	(502)
Gomez, Marcos S	3:07:21	(1,717)
Gomez, Mario	3:36:58	(6,058)
Gompertz, Gary G	5:20:03	(29,415)
Gompertz, Henry	4:14:31	(15,453)
Gonde, Chris E	3:57:17	(10,887)
Goniszewski, Jan	6:05:21	(32,937)
Gonnella, Josh	4:18:08	(16,383)
Gonsalves, Raphael N	6:30:12	(33,665)
Gonsalves, Victor	4:27:18	(18,906)
Gonzalez, David	2:53:25	(660)
Gonzalez, Jorge	3:01:47	(1,296)
Gonzalez, Jorge	3:46:19	(7,956)
Gonzalez, Paul J	4:08:16	(13,845)
Gonzalez, Victor	3:22:35	(3,583)
Gonzalez Longaray, Eduardo	3:35:00	(5,703)
Gonzalez Perez, Juan M	3:40:03	(6,649)
Gooch-Smith, Nigel A	4:44:14	(23,237)
Good, Christopher R	3:27:09	(4,304)
Good, Michael E	4:14:10	(15,357)
Good, Patrick J	3:47:15	(8,169)
Good, Richard S	3:53:40	(9,758)
Gooda, Andrew H	2:56:24	(837)
Goodacre, Robert I	3:27:24	(4,349)
Goodall, Adrian J	3:53:37	(9,747)
Goodall, Gareth J	4:01:41	(12,289)
Goodall, Stuart J	4:28:41	(19,310)
Goodall, Warwick J	4:25:39	(18,429)
Goodayle, Robert J	4:35:35	(21,129)
Goodbun, Mark J	3:46:42	(8,039)
Goodchild, Julian P	4:27:36	(18,979)
Goode, Philip	2:58:47	(1,038)
Goode, Tom A	6:00:08	(32,745)
Gooderick, Bob L	5:24:15	(29,834)
Goodeve, Andrew	5:12:38	(28,475)
Goodfellow, Edward	3:56:05	(10,511)
Goodfield, Paul	3:59:11	(11,554)
Goodger, Dean E	5:25:13	(29,951)
Goodhew, Rob C	5:57:42	(32,614)
Gooding, James H	3:29:54	(4,867)
Gooding, Michael J	2:52:25	(614)
Gooding, Paul	2:59:54	(1,158)
Goodland, Jonathan N	2:49:02	(465)
Goodlet, Robin T	3:55:16	(10,279)
Goodley, Simon	5:05:41	(27,508)
Goodliffe, Paul	4:52:43	(25,203)
Goodman, Colin E	3:39:59	(6,636)
Goodman, David	5:33:51	(30,820)
Goodman, Jon	3:58:09	(11,163)
Goodman, Paul J	4:20:13	(16,951)
Goodreid, Ian C	3:14:54	(2,617)
Goodridge, Mark	2:40:49	(212)

Goodridge, Michael S	4:38:18	(21,781)
Goodridge, Stephen P	5:41:15	(31,440)
Goodship, Richard D	4:31:49	(20,112)
Goodson, Benjamin J	5:59:52	(32,732)
Goodwin, Julian	2:57:54	(936)
Goodwin, Kevin	3:53:56	(9,849)
Goodwin, Mark	4:07:48	(13,714)
Goodwin, Mark I	3:16:18	(2,788)
Goodwin, Neil R	4:06:15	(13,346)
Goodwin, Nicki	5:37:58	(31,192)
Goodwin, Paul O	4:06:26	(13,381)
Goodwin, Philip C	4:53:01	(25,275)
Goodwin, Simon J	4:33:17	(20,504)
Goodwin, Stephen H	3:30:40	(4,993)
Goodwin, Steven	5:50:22	(32,160)
Goodwin, Sydney C	5:35:28	(30,973)
Goodwin, Wayne	4:05:12	(13,098)
Goonan, Graeme K	4:09:14	(14,097)
Goonery, Jason T	5:04:29	(27,326)
Gord, Terry Lee	3:54:14	(9,936)
Gordon, Adrian T	3:53:34	(9,732)
Gordon, Alasdair J	5:04:57	(27,390)
Gordon, Garron	3:23:01	(3,641)
Gordon, Ian R	4:29:49	(19,591)
Gordon, Jeffrey	4:46:41	(23,823)
Gordon, Martin T	3:53:17	(9,657)
Gordon, Rob M	4:23:30	(17,867)
Gordon, Stephen	2:59:42	(1,141)
Gordon, William S	4:04:24	(12,915)
Gordon-Williams, Richard M	5:14:32	(28,745)
Gore, Adrian	4:01:32	(12,251)
Gore, Jeremy	4:07:45	(13,707)
Gore, Stephen	3:49:09	(8,615)
Goree, Nicholas	5:07:52	(27,812)
Goring, Domonic	3:43:18	(7,306)
Goring, Jasper	4:41:17	(22,509)
Gorman, Brian R	4:56:02	(25,881)
Gorman, Malachi	4:25:29	(18,388)
Gorman, Martin J	2:57:57	(943)
Gorman, Paul	5:23:25	(29,736)
Gorman, Robert	3:32:00	(5,225)
Gorman, Tom	4:17:44	(16,291)
Gornall, Robert	2:43:33	(282)
Gorringe, Tom H	4:43:58	(23,172)
Gorry, Kevin	4:51:48	(25,003)
Gorse, Christopher A	3:59:04	(11,511)
Gorton, Peter	4:58:17	(26,341)
Gorvett, Darren P	3:10:40	(2,062)
Gosbee, Norman	4:14:16	(15,387)
Goslett, Dominic M	4:54:39	(25,609)
Gosling, Adam P	3:43:39	(7,378)
Gosling, Christopher P	4:22:52	(17,691)
Gosling, Ian	3:12:05	(2,221)
Gosling, Simon R	5:02:00	(26,958)
Gosney, Edward J	5:21:32	(29,560)
Gosney, Paul	3:43:04	(7,255)
Goss, John	4:27:20	(18,914)
Goss, Paul D	3:40:45	(6,772)
Goss-Custard, John D	4:27:11	(18,868)
Gothard, Maxwell	6:42:49	(33,936)
Gotke, Peter E	4:02:12	(12,417)
Gotting, Wayne I	4:34:51	(20,925)
Goudime, Michael	4:24:39	(18,181)
Gough, Andy	4:19:58	(16,880)
Gough, James	5:17:36	(29,107)
Gough, Jonathan M	4:35:00	(20,982)
Gough, Kevin P	3:39:11	(6,469)
Gough, Mike	3:44:43	(7,610)
Gough, Peter D	4:56:24	(25,949)
Gough, Peter W	4:35:00	(20,982)
Gough, Robert A	4:40:55	(22,410)
Goulbourn, Mark A	4:17:28	(16,211)
Gould, Andrew J	4:06:37	(13,433)
Gould, Bruce K	7:14:28	(34,358)
Gould, Chris D	5:01:42	(26,913)
Gould, Edward	3:55:33	(10,354)
Gould, Jeffrey S	7:14:28	(34,358)
Gould, Martin	3:09:59	(1,987)
Gould, Matthew	3:51:12	(9,099)
Gould, Norman S	7:14:27	(34,357)
Gould, Peter	4:27:21	(18,916)
Gould, Timothy J	4:57:17	(26,139)
Gouldburn, Sean	5:09:00	(27,971)

Goulding, Mark..........................3:46:55 (8,088)
Goulding, Neil C..........................5:58:24 (32,663)
Goulding, Ronnie D..................5:49:19 (32,077)

Goumri, Abderrahim................2:05:30 (3)

Gouranton, Gustave...................3:53:24 (9,696)
Gourley, Ian J..........................5:01:35 (26,887)
Gournay, Kevin J.....................3:49:35 (8,715)
Gow, Chris.............................4:57:51 (26,252)
Goward, Mark T.......................4:29:29 (19,516)
Gowen, Neil R.........................4:47:07 (23,935)
Gowen, Richard.......................2:37:41 (161)
Gower, Anthony J.....................5:21:10 (29,516)
Gower, Ian J..........................3:45:52 (7,873)
Gower, Mark A.........................3:25:25 (3,997)
Gower, Mark J.........................3:35:14 (5,745)
Gower, Richard C......................4:26:57 (18,798)
Gower, Stuart D.......................4:38:57 (21,961)
Gowers, John R........................4:49:26 (24,464)
Gowers, Matt R........................4:05:03 (13,060)
Gowrie-Smith, Lachlan I.............3:59:14 (11,574)
Goy, Nick J...........................4:19:40 (16,804)
Goy, William D........................4:47:12 (23,961)
Goymer, David B.......................3:25:39 (4,044)
Gozzoli, Luca.........................2:43:52 (289)
Grace, Andrew.........................4:15:20 (15,646)
Grace, Colin..........................3:32:05 (5,239)
Grace, Steve..........................4:50:37 (24,749)
Gracey, Guy...........................3:35:45 (5,838)
Gracia, Mark..........................4:00:26 (11,957)
Gracie, Nick J........................2:58:47 (1,038)
Gradden, Michael D...................3:52:15 (9,375)
Grafham, Richard P....................4:34:06 (20,725)
Grafton, Christopher J...............4:43:16 (22,994)
Graham, Alan..........................4:41:38 (22,593)
Graham, Alex..........................4:29:03 (19,412)
Graham, Andrew G......................5:23:26 (29,741)
Graham, Bill..........................3:20:22 (3,274)
Graham, Carl..........................5:10:30 (28,217)
Graham, Charles F.....................3:33:32 (5,480)
Graham, David L.......................4:57:45 (26,237)
Graham, Geoff J.......................4:48:50 (24,328)
Graham, Guy J.........................3:53:06 (9,607)
Graham, Hugh..........................4:09:19 (14,122)
Graham, Ian A.........................3:06:02 (1,600)
Graham, Jonty.........................3:25:27 (4,002)
Graham, Mark R........................2:58:01 (951)
Graham, Martin J......................6:03:54 (32,884)
Graham, Paul M........................3:16:37 (2,823)

Graham, Peter M.......................4:42:43 (22,858)
Graham, Ray K.........................4:07:03 (13,531)
Graham, Richard N.....................4:38:15 (21,767)
Graham, Scott J.......................5:15:56 (28,929)
Graham, Steven J......................4:20:53 (17,147)
Graham, Stuart........................3:27:47 (4,416)
Graham, Warren V......................4:33:47 (20,658)
Graham-Dobson, Glen...................4:43:26 (23,031)
Grain, Tom............................4:28:19 (19,213)
Grainger, Jonathan E..................4:26:21 (18,621)
Grainger, Martin R....................4:58:09 (26,315)
Grainger, Robert P....................3:21:56 (3,479)
Grainger, Stuart......................6:06:40 (33,008)
Granado, Thierry......................4:44:11 (23,224)
Granados, David J.....................4:11:53 (14,776)
Granahan, Jim.........................3:23:58 (3,774)
Grandison, Julian M...................4:12:47 (14,984)
Grandison, Rowen......................3:28:20 (4,523)
Grandy, Mark..........................3:36:17 (5,929)
Graney, Thomas M......................5:16:30 (28,992)
Grange, Ian V.........................4:04:47 (12,999)
Grange, Maurice.......................5:14:35 (28,757)
Granier, Stephen......................3:14:34 (2,563)
Granneman, John M.....................5:20:30 (29,465)
Grant, Andrew.........................5:18:33 (29,234)
Grant, Antonio B......................2:32:58 (96)
Grant, Derrick A......................6:33:23 (33,734)
Grant, Ian............................5:15:09 (28,839)
Grant, Jeremy J.......................4:13:47 (15,248)
Grant, Mark S.........................4:20:47 (17,118)
Grant, Matthew........................3:37:12 (6,105)
Grant, Neil...........................4:11:18 (14,626)
Grant, Neil...........................5:06:14 (27,588)
Grant, Paul...........................5:06:17 (27,599)
Grant, Paul A.........................4:53:09 (25,307)
Grant, Peter..........................4:42:19 (22,758)
Grant, Peter F........................5:16:14 (28,964)
Grant, Ross I.........................5:39:53 (31,324)
Grant, Simon R........................3:12:36 (2,276)
Grantham, James.......................3:08:57 (1,872)
Grantham, Richard.....................5:02:34 (27,047)
Granville, Sean.......................4:26:18 (18,610)
Grasselli, Massimo....................4:08:30 (13,909)
Gravells, John........................4:07:13 (13,582)
Graves, Derek R.......................3:48:12 (8,400)
Graves, Howard........................4:01:14 (12,170)
Gravis, Craig B.......................4:49:18 (24,431)
Gray, Alan............................3:50:13 (8,876)
Gray, Allan J.........................5:06:40 (27,647)
Gray, Andrew C........................3:01:26 (1,276)
Gray, Andrew J........................4:16:12 (15,874)
Gray, Andrew W........................4:11:53 (14,776)
Gray, Anthony D.......................3:16:38 (2,825)
Gray, Chad R..........................4:14:24 (15,424)
Gray, Christopher D...................4:00:04 (11,867)
Gray, Christopher I...................5:38:26 (31,223)
Gray, Colin R.........................3:05:25 (1,549)
Gray, Daniel J........................4:36:08 (21,278)
Gray, David R.........................3:58:06 (11,142)
Gray, Duncan..........................4:36:53 (21,461)
Gray, Duncan J........................4:20:33 (17,043)
Gray, Gavin M.........................4:08:14 (13,839)
Gray, James E.........................4:53:33 (25,387)
Gray, Jason M.........................4:49:14 (24,420)
Gray, Jim.............................5:05:39 (27,504)
Gray, John............................4:53:06 (25,295)
Gray, John A..........................4:13:11 (15,080)
Gray, John C..........................3:46:48 (8,059)
Gray, John D..........................4:41:56 (22,658)
Gray, Kelvin D........................3:34:47 (5,659)
Gray, Lee M...........................5:22:41 (29,676)
Gray, Lewis D.........................3:56:54 (10,762)
Gray, Marc............................3:47:12 (8,154)
Gray, Nicholas J......................4:34:42 (20,876)
Gray, Oliver..........................4:41:34 (22,570)
Gray, Patrick.........................4:36:54 (21,464)
Gray, Peter...........................4:43:53 (23,148)
Gray, Peter D.........................3:00:33 (1,207)
Gray, Robert J........................4:50:43 (24,770)
Gray, Robert R........................3:52:57 (9,553)
Gray, Robert T........................4:01:23 (12,210)
Gray, Robin J.........................6:25:30 (33,564)
Gray, Simon...........................3:17:07 (2,873)

Gray, Simon...........................4:40:19 (22,262)
Gray, Simon J.........................4:19:54 (16,861)
Gray, Stephen C.......................5:23:36 (29,760)
Gray, Stephen J.......................6:01:46 (32,813)
Gray, Steve C.........................3:38:13 (6,303)
Gray, Todd C..........................3:46:22 (7,971)
Grayson, Matthew M....................4:59:00 (26,477)
Grealy, Michael J.....................3:35:39 (5,824)
Greany, Liam..........................4:11:41 (14,729)
Greasby, Jonathan C...................3:31:14 (5,087)
Greasley, John D......................4:09:22 (14,136)
Greaves, Andrew T.....................5:19:51 (29,396)
Greaves, Arthur H.....................5:33:07 (30,761)
Greaves, Ian R........................5:04:53 (27,382)
Greaves, Mark F.......................3:15:42 (2,719)
Grecian, Peter J......................3:57:18 (10,890)
Green, Adam M.........................4:26:47 (18,750)
Green, Adrian B.......................4:34:05 (20,720)
Green, Alan D.........................3:15:22 (2,686)
Green, Alexander R....................4:45:13 (23,469)
Green, Andrew.........................4:06:03 (13,301)
Green, Andrew J.......................2:36:09 (135)
Green, Andrew J.......................5:48:28 (32,009)
Green, Andrew R.......................4:54:39 (25,609)
Green, Andrew S.......................3:16:57 (2,856)
Green, Andrew S.......................4:42:36 (22,832)
Green, Andy...........................5:05:03 (27,409)
Green, Andy J.........................3:52:51 (9,522)
Green, Aubrey J.......................4:07:11 (13,575)
Green, Brian..........................2:52:46 (625)
Green, Chris..........................6:13:38 (33,233)
Green, Colin..........................3:51:00 (9,046)
Green, Daniel.........................4:49:49 (24,555)
Green, Daniel.........................6:56:08 (34,172)
Green, Darren M.......................4:23:27 (17,856)
Green, David..........................4:42:14 (22,736)
Green, David J........................3:26:54 (4,261)
Green, David P........................3:44:52 (7,648)
Green, Errol L........................5:20:56 (29,492)
Green, James..........................3:35:13 (5,744)
Green, James A........................3:59:58 (11,842)
Green, James O........................4:05:56 (13,275)
Green, James P........................6:38:30 (33,859)
Green, James W........................4:39:47 (22,150)
Green, Jeremy A.......................4:29:53 (19,605)
Green, Jim............................3:56:22 (10,582)
Green, John J.........................4:05:12 (13,098)
Green, John K.........................2:53:02 (645)
Green, Jon P..........................4:34:24 (20,799)
Green, Jonathon M.....................4:23:02 (17,737)
Green, Kevin P........................4:14:27 (15,436)
Green, Kevin R........................3:23:39 (3,721)
Green, Laurence.......................4:04:43 (12,989)
Green, Lucas..........................3:31:24 (5,116)
Green, Mark C.........................4:24:28 (18,133)
Green, Martin A.......................4:43:48 (23,122)
Green, Martin H.......................3:21:52 (3,467)
Green, Michael D......................4:28:24 (19,232)
Green, Michael G......................3:24:30 (3,848)
Green, Mick...........................3:05:46 (1,579)
Green, Mike R.........................4:52:51 (25,234)
Green, Neil D.........................5:13:23 (28,592)
Green, Nicky L........................5:12:49 (28,518)
Green, Nigel..........................4:35:14 (21,039)
Green, Norman J.......................4:22:39 (17,631)
Green, Paul...........................3:01:37 (1,286)
Green, Paul T.........................3:33:16 (5,434)
Green, Richard A......................3:52:17 (9,384)
Green, Robert J.......................3:45:12 (7,728)
Green, Robert J.......................4:45:49 (23,626)
Green, Robert T.......................4:58:17 (26,341)
Green, Roddy P........................4:41:49 (22,641)
Green, Ryan L.........................4:51:28 (24,934)
Green, Sam............................4:36:05 (21,263)
Green, Sean S.........................5:48:12 (31,990)
Green, Shayne A.......................4:19:39 (16,797)
Green, Simon..........................5:15:47 (28,916)
Green, Simon R........................5:19:13 (29,317)
Green, William........................2:57:33 (909)
Green, William J......................4:38:57 (21,961)
Green, William W......................4:02:24 (12,476)
Greenall, Jack E......................6:08:28 (33,064)
Greenall, Toby P......................3:56:01 (10,498)

Greenaway, Stephen B	4:24:40 (18,186)	
Greenbank, Martin	3:43:44 (7,396)	
Greene, Alan	5:10:24 (28,208)	
Greene, Richard J	4:33:33 (20,591)	
Greener, Clinton L	3:53:09 (9,620)	
Greenfield, Sam J	4:02:27 (12,488)	
Greenhalgh, Clifford	4:33:31 (20,579)	
Greenhalgh, James S	4:07:06 (13,545)	
Greenhalgh, Stephen C	4:30:52 (19,855)	
Greenhill, Michael A	5:49:52 (32,109)	
Greenhough, Karl	4:40:04 (22,198)	
Greening, Robert C	4:29:18 (19,472)	
Greenland, Edward C	3:21:19 (3,406)	
Greenland, Richard D	3:44:05 (7,470)	
Greenleaf, Andrew H	2:29:47 (72)	
Greenleaf, Daniel	4:09:08 (14,069)	
Greenlees, John F	5:44:07 (31,676)	
Greenshields, Thomas J	5:26:33 (30,108)	
Greensides, William J	4:03:44 (12,777)	
Greensill, Mark I	3:52:43 (9,484)	
Greenslade, Christopher W	4:30:19 (19,702)	
Greenslade, Daevid V	4:40:45 (22,367)	
Greenslade, Danny P	3:19:37 (3,178)	
Greenstein, David	3:35:38 (5,821)	
Greenwood, Alan	4:49:20 (24,442)	
Greenwood, Andrew M	4:46:05 (23,685)	
Greenwood, Chris O	4:28:12 (19,171)	
Greenwood, Gareth J	3:12:46 (2,298)	
Greenwood, Peter	5:04:07 (27,265)	
Greenwood, Richard J	4:10:10 (14,328)	
Greenwood, Robert W	4:55:33 (25,791)	
Greenwood, Stuart G	4:35:52 (21,205)	
Greer, James T	5:03:12 (27,131)	
Greer, Ryan	3:34:52 (5,680)	
Greer, Samuel J	3:56:25 (10,602)	
Greet, Mark A	2:55:43 (790)	
Greeves, Dominic	4:19:33 (16,774)	
Gregg, Martin	5:03:55 (27,244)	
Gregg, William S	3:55:03 (10,216)	
Gregor, Zdenek J	3:59:04 (11,511)	
Gregory, Alex J	5:21:43 (29,581)	
Gregory, Bryan P	4:15:53 (15,804)	
Gregory, David	5:23:18 (29,725)	
Gregory, David A	3:11:11 (2,113)	
Gregory, James	4:48:14 (24,189)	
Gregory, John A	3:54:53 (10,150)	
Gregory, Jonathan P	4:23:56 (17,975)	
Gregory, Kevin C	4:00:10 (11,886)	
Gregory, Mark J	3:00:18 (1,186)	
Gregory, Mark T	4:19:57 (16,874)	
Gregory, Morris R	5:18:36 (29,242)	
Gregory, Nicholas A	3:22:34 (3,579)	
Gregory, Nigel	5:01:56 (26,948)	
Gregory, Paul A	4:16:34 (15,975)	
Gregory, Paul F	2:43:46 (285)	
Gregory, Paul R	4:04:19 (12,893)	
Gregory, Stephen J	4:02:31 (12,499)	
Gregory, Timothy J	4:05:14 (13,109)	
Gregson, Andrew P	4:11:41 (14,729)	
Gregson, John N	3:59:31 (11,680)	
Gregson, Paul	5:01:14 (26,832)	
Greif, Stephen	6:21:02 (33,430)	
Gresswell, David J	3:36:08 (5,903)	
Gresty, Paul J	3:14:25 (2,533)	
Grethe, Robert	5:53:42 (32,386)	
Gretton, Adam C	4:37:09 (21,514)	
Grevatt, Lee	3:59:14 (11,574)	
Grew, Adam D	3:23:37 (3,717)	
Grew, William R	4:45:52 (23,637)	
Grewar, John C	4:01:29 (12,237)	
Grewer, Craig M	3:35:20 (5,760)	
Greybrook, Matthew R	6:26:31 (33,586)	
Greyling, Bester	3:55:19 (10,292)	
Gribben, George A	5:31:07 (30,573)	
Gribble, Ian	4:18:34 (16,519)	
Grice, Andrew D	6:11:20 (33,149)	
Grice, Christian	4:39:41 (22,122)	
Grice, David T	4:56:34 (25,985)	
Grice, Zippy	2:48:11 (430)	
Grier, Nick C	4:21:31 (17,312)	
Grierson, Douglas	4:41:10 (22,478)	
Grierson, Rocky	5:24:41 (29,876)	
Grieshaber, Simon T	3:52:02 (9,314)	

Grieshammer, Thomas	5:23:01 (29,699)	
Grieve, Steven	3:43:00 (7,239)	
Grieves, Mark	4:19:44 (16,821)	
Grieveson, Richard W	3:58:52 (11,444)	
Griffin, Garry	4:45:45 (23,606)	
Griffin, Ian C	4:15:28 (15,693)	
Griffin, Michael	7:45:52 (34,499)	
Griffin, Peter L	3:41:13 (6,878)	
Griffin, Richard F	4:21:45 (17,389)	
Griffin, Roger F	3:43:44 (7,396)	
Griffin, Simon C	3:03:13 (1,393)	
Griffin, Steven M	4:28:01 (19,103)	
Griffin, Thomas G	2:57:42 (921)	
Griffin, Timothy R	3:29:14 (4,721)	
Griffin-Davies, Neil R	5:49:55 (32,115)	
Griffith, Stephen	3:39:30 (6,534)	
Griffiths, Adam L	3:56:22 (10,582)	
Griffiths, Adam O	3:30:01 (4,888)	
Griffiths, Alan P	3:28:26 (4,545)	
Griffiths, Alan T	4:40:59 (22,431)	
Griffiths, Andrew J	5:50:18 (32,155)	
Griffiths, Barrie W	2:51:01 (555)	
Griffiths, Barry	4:35:47 (21,190)	
Griffiths, Brian A	3:28:58 (4,659)	
Griffiths, Bryn	4:44:38 (23,332)	
Griffiths, Colin	4:33:16 (20,496)	
Griffiths, David	4:21:36 (17,334)	
Griffiths, David	4:32:06 (20,197)	
Griffiths, David F	4:08:39 (13,955)	
Griffiths, David J	3:27:54 (4,439)	
Griffiths, Gareth S	5:00:03 (26,643)	
Griffiths, Jonathan M	5:34:55 (30,932)	
Griffiths, Julian R	5:29:29 (30,424)	
Griffiths, Keith	3:24:56 (3,916)	
Griffiths, Mark P	4:16:04 (15,853)	
Griffiths, Matthew R	3:11:00 (2,097)	
Griffiths, Matthew S	3:37:13 (6,107)	
Griffiths, Neville	3:23:21 (3,685)	
Griffiths, Nicholas	7:06:54 (34,283)	
Griffiths, Nicholas D	4:06:45 (13,462)	
Griffiths, Nigel P	4:10:43 (14,467)	
Griffiths, Owain P	3:54:10 (9,924)	
Griffiths, Paul R	3:53:47 (9,800)	
Griffiths, Paul W	3:08:54 (1,867)	
Griffiths, Peter	3:28:07 (4,491)	
Griffiths, Peter J	4:54:13 (25,525)	
Griffiths, Phillip N	4:20:48 (17,127)	
Griffiths, Richard	4:25:51 (18,496)	
Griffiths, Steven D	5:19:29 (29,352)	
Grigg, Jeremy S	3:42:02 (7,035)	
Griggs, Simon J	5:09:16 (28,005)	
Griggs, Stephen	4:36:04 (21,258)	
Grigoleit, Peter M	3:12:47 (2,302)	
Grigolin, Ivan	2:57:55 (938)	
Grime, Christopher J	3:58:20 (11,236)	
Grimes, Anthony J	4:06:36 (13,428)	
Grimes, Philip J	4:03:36 (12,748)	
Grimley, Chris R	3:30:18 (4,939)	
Grimsey, John	4:06:54 (13,493)	
Grimsey, Mark	3:59:55 (11,825)	
Grimsey, William	3:53:21 (9,677)	
Grimshaw, Graham D	4:21:09 (17,213)	
Grimshaw, Michael A	4:25:41 (18,438)	
Grimwade, Doug R	3:28:11 (4,505)	
Grimwood, Graham A	4:17:09 (16,140)	
Grimwood, Peter K	4:34:51 (20,925)	
Grindley, Nick G	4:17:31 (16,227)	
Grindu, Louis	4:39:37 (22,100)	
Grinsdale, Tim	3:12:17 (2,247)	
Grint, Lee S	5:16:57 (29,053)	
Grinyer, Alan A	5:40:59 (31,411)	
Grist, Matthew R	4:46:21 (23,752)	
Grist, Roger W	3:26:57 (4,271)	
Gritschneder, Konrad	5:02:20 (27,009)	
Grizzell, Carl	5:30:01 (30,480)	
Grobler, Daniel F	4:51:56 (25,028)	
Grocott, Adrian	5:43:52 (31,639)	
Grocott, Ian F	3:50:45 (8,998)	
Grocott, Tony E	3:54:02 (9,882)	
Grogut, Nicholas R	4:40:48 (22,379)	
Gronow, Richard M	3:51:42 (9,229)	
Groocock, Mike J	3:39:14 (6,482)	
Groom, Lloyd J	4:33:24 (20,540)	

Groom, Nicholas S	3:25:10 (3,957)	
Gross, Frank	3:02:26 (1,338)	
Gross, Johann	4:16:34 (15,975)	
Grosso, Giulio G	3:56:18 (10,565)	
Grosvenor, Sean B	2:58:09 (961)	
Groujean, René	5:32:55 (30,739)	
Grout, Alan C	4:30:58 (19,875)	
Grout, Paul J	5:06:43 (27,655)	
Grout, Steve R	3:25:04 (3,941)	
Grove, Christopher	4:03:44 (12,777)	
Grove, Shaun D	4:03:30 (12,727)	
Grover, David D	4:42:26 (22,786)	
Grover, Nick A	4:18:07 (16,374)	
Groves, Gary R	4:07:02 (13,527)	
Groves, Patrick	4:38:41 (21,880)	
Groves, Peter J	4:24:44 (18,201)	
Groves, William R	4:59:07 (26,496)	
Grubb, Ian W	4:19:19 (16,707)	
Grubb, Julian R	3:15:00 (2,627)	
Gruber, Rudolf	4:03:40 (12,761)	
Grude, Kjell E	3:43:40 (7,383)	
Grueber, Jean-Paul	4:07:30 (13,640)	
Gruenbacher, Gerald A	3:29:09 (4,703)	
Grummell, Oliver C	3:36:02 (5,888)	
Grundy, Michael S	5:21:13 (29,525)	
Grundy, Nigel R	4:15:57 (15,823)	
Grunewald, Ralf J	4:31:46 (20,091)	
Grunwald, Thomas S	4:11:36 (14,704)	
Gruter, Jan	4:45:50 (23,629)	
Grygiel, Jayson	3:59:06 (11,527)	
Grylls, Charlie	5:26:19 (30,073)	
Guard, Michael G	3:18:17 (3,016)	
Gubanski, Martin	3:50:58 (9,040)	
Gudgin, Terence E	7:09:32 (34,314)	
Gudissa, Atoma	2:54:07 (702)	
Gudka, Piyush	3:32:46 (5,355)	
Guequierre, John	3:27:24 (4,349)	
Gueraud, Christophe L	3:56:19 (10,568)	
Guerin, Yann	4:49:40 (24,525)	
Guerinot, Thierry	3:45:06 (7,709)	
Guerra, Silvio	2:19:03 (21)	
Guerra Crespo, Carlos	2:50:33 (539)	
Guerra Montanez, Luis Henrique	4:34:39 (20,863)	
Guest, Andrew	4:50:02 (24,608)	
Guest, Christopher M	3:52:54 (9,536)	
Guest, Ian J	5:12:02 (28,411)	
Guest, Ian S	4:22:47 (17,666)	
Guest, Ross I	3:25:06 (3,947)	
Guest, Thomas J	4:18:34 (16,519)	
Guglielmetti, Nicola	3:46:53 (8,078)	
Guilera Navarro, Eduardo	3:35:01 (5,706)	
Guillerm, Jean Marc	3:07:52 (1,774)	
Guimah, Sam	5:24:51 (29,900)	
Guinchard, Marcel A	3:55:05 (10,225)	
Guiseley, Andrew	2:53:46 (679)	
Guiseppe, Ciucci	5:39:19 (31,287)	
Gulc, Peter	3:19:40 (3,186)	
Guler, Caner G	4:28:25 (19,238)	
Gulich, Thomas J	3:06:17 (1,624)	
Gullick, John	4:27:49 (19,030)	
Gulliver, Andrew	6:54:52 (34,151)	
Gullu, Ibrahim	3:58:30 (11,298)	
Gumble, Raymond	6:13:17 (33,218)	
Gumbleton, Michael J	3:53:59 (5,545)	
Gundry, Sean C	4:30:08 (19,663)	
Gunn, David J	4:30:50 (19,843)	
Gunn, Graham	5:20:56 (29,492)	
Gunn, John A	4:02:49 (12,569)	
Gunn, Peter R	3:10:35 (2,053)	
Gunnell, Julian M	5:13:42 (28,635)	
Gunning, Simon M	3:39:11 (6,469)	
Gunstone, Douglas W	3:37:48 (6,217)	
Guo, Weisi	5:57:47 (32,619)	
Gupta, Anil K	9:59:58 (34,590)	
Gurney, Jonathan E	3:32:19 (5,281)	
Gurney, Jonathan R	3:45:28 (7,786)	
Gurney, Lawrence	3:16:17 (2,785)	
Gurney, Matthew J	4:29:08 (19,434)	
Gurr, David A	5:06:14 (27,588)	
Gurr, Raymond J	5:02:53 (27,094)	
Gurria, Angel	4:06:28 (13,390)	
Gush, Mike H	3:59:27 (11,656)	
Gussey, Andrew	3:58:36 (11,336)	

Gustausson, Marcus	4:10:37 (14,440)	
Gustave, David T	5:34:37 (30,897)	
Gusterson, Jeremy P	2:59:46 (1,148)	
Guthrie, Duncan	3:24:42 (3,870)	
Gutierrez Saez, Pedro M	3:47:01 (8,113)	
Guttenplan, Don D	4:19:05 (16,651)	
Guttman, Richard W	6:48:22 (34,043)	
Gutzan, Peter	4:23:34 (17,888)	
Guveya, John	3:33:12 (5,421)	
Guy, Andrew C	5:04:12 (27,280)	
Guy, Ben J	4:39:39 (22,108)	
Guy, James	4:37:53 (21,693)	
Guy, Jean Michel	3:23:04 (3,646)	
Guy, Paul H	4:35:56 (21,220)	
Guy, Steven	3:55:53 (10,462)	
Guy, William R	3:14:43 (2,594)	
Guyver, Neil	3:49:50 (8,778)	
Guzman, Fernando	3:00:53 (1,231)	
Gwilliam, David J	4:33:38 (20,618)	
Gwilliam, Steven J	4:29:59 (19,631)	
Gwynn, Peter J	4:41:22 (22,526)	
Gwyther, Andrew G	3:13:52 (2,444)	
Gyakyi, Gordon A	4:27:37 (18,983)	
Gylfason, Johann	2:47:26 (399)	
Gyte, Barry G	3:14:46 (2,600)	
Haak, Rick	3:38:04 (6,277)	
Haas, Marc D	4:25:43 (18,453)	
Haase, Mark P	5:19:59 (29,410)	
Habgood, Hayden	5:28:04 (30,275)	
Hack, Claudius	2:48:53 (459)	
Hacker, Glyn R	4:54:34 (25,593)	
Hacker, Peter J	4:18:10 (16,393)	
Hackett, Peter J	4:56:08 (25,900)	
Hackett, Simon J	3:34:10 (5,573)	
Hackett, Wayne I	4:02:01 (12,368)	
Hacking, Guy C	3:08:08 (1,807)	
Haddad, Fares S	3:44:56 (7,665)	
Hadden, James W	4:27:03 (18,828)	
Haddington, Jason N	4:19:36 (16,781)	
Haddon, Peter A	4:45:13 (23,469)	
Haddon, Phil P	3:17:17 (2,901)	
Haddow, Ross	5:53:02 (32,339)	
Haddrell, Jon G	6:09:58 (33,115)	
Haddrell, Michael	5:34:47 (30,914)	
Haddrell, Paul D	5:38:10 (31,205)	
Haddrell, Rod R	3:43:34 (7,357)	
Haddrell, Roger	3:06:06 (1,606)	
Haden, Tony F	2:57:17 (895)	
Hadfield, Andrew M	4:46:26 (23,765)	
Hadfield, Christopher	5:47:00 (31,908)	
Hadfield, Mark	4:32:34 (20,315)	
Hadfield, Michael J	5:17:48 (29,155)	
Hadfield, Tom D	2:50:06 (516)	
Hadgraft, Peter R	4:38:32 (21,831)	
Hadl, Johann	4:17:17 (16,170)	
Hadland, Richard J	7:02:42 (34,237)	
Hadleigh, Nigel	4:14:07 (15,340)	
Hadley, Daniel	4:35:31 (21,112)	
Hadley, Ian P	5:02:23 (27,021)	
Hadley, Peter E	3:43:26 (7,332)	
Hadlow, Hugo F	3:57:23 (10,919)	
Hadrava, Lee	4:49:56 (24,587)	
Haenel, Michael A	4:22:58 (17,719)	
Haenen, Gregory	4:53:44 (25,422)	
Haffaf, Samy	3:46:50 (8,068)	
Haffey, Anthony T	4:38:03 (21,724)	
Hagan, Keith	3:40:52 (6,800)	
Hagen, Oeivind Ravn	4:50:29 (24,708)	
Hager, Sean	3:52:15 (9,375)	
Hagg, Lennart	4:09:10 (14,077)	
Haggag, Hossam	5:34:58 (30,937)	
Haggart, David A	3:12:09 (2,227)	
Haggarty, Peter	4:28:59 (19,397)	
Haggarty, Scot I	3:51:17 (9,120)	
Haggqvist, Tony	3:40:21 (6,704)	
Hagio, Kohei	5:51:28 (32,247)	
Hagland, Gary	5:05:36 (27,498)	
Hahnel, Mario	3:05:20 (1,540)	
Hahnen, Ulrich	4:02:42 (12,542)	
Haigh, Gavin R	4:08:06 (13,789)	
Haigh, Joel	4:54:02 (25,489)	
Haigh, Martin J	4:12:53 (15,002)	
Haigh, Nicholas S	4:52:24 (25,123)	

Haigh, Phillip	3:29:09 (4,703)	
Haigh, Tim J	4:01:05 (12,132)	
Hails, Philip J	2:41:18 (228)	
Hails, Stephen	3:46:06 (7,905)	
Hain, Ingo	3:07:48 (1,765)	
Haines, Anthony J	4:07:37 (13,677)	
Haines, Ian J	3:58:42 (11,374)	
Haines, Joey	4:54:30 (25,581)	
Haines, Mark S	3:47:00 (8,108)	
Haines, Michael A	3:02:38 (1,355)	
Haines, Stephen	4:14:47 (15,512)	
Haines, Timothy J	4:13:03 (15,050)	
Haining, Benjamin	4:36:42 (21,418)	
Hainsworth, Keith A	5:23:14 (29,722)	
Hainsworth, Paul J	3:11:47 (2,187)	
Haire, Oliver J	4:45:12 (23,465)	
Haiselden, Step C	4:47:46 (24,093)	
Halcombe, Anthony S	5:20:55 (29,488)	
Haldane, Nick O	3:48:57 (8,567)	
Hale, Darryl T	3:02:48 (1,363)	
Hale, Duncan J	4:15:19 (15,642)	
Hale, John	5:11:13 (28,297)	
Hale, Kenneth	3:55:29 (10,335)	
Hale, Ross A	3:26:41 (4,228)	
Hale, Tony G	4:00:51 (12,068)	
Hales, Daniel S	4:13:04 (15,054)	
Hales, Matthew	4:19:45 (16,825)	
Halestrap, Gary	4:18:04 (16,361)	
Haley, Andrew P	4:24:24 (18,111)	
Haley, Justin	6:23:27 (33,502)	
Halfacree, Graham C	3:49:46 (8,764)	
Halford, David J	3:10:04 (1,995)	
Halford, Glynn	3:51:09 (9,086)	
Halil, Russell M	4:33:35 (20,601)	
Hall, Alexander	3:07:43 (1,753)	
Hall, Alistair M	4:02:21 (12,460)	
Hall, Andrew M	5:06:00 (27,552)	
Hall, Andrew W	4:31:10 (19,928)	
Hall, Anthony	3:43:50 (7,419)	
Hall, Ben	4:44:00 (23,180)	
Hall, Brian	5:25:16 (29,959)	
Hall, Brian M	3:32:21 (5,291)	
Hall, Carl N	3:33:20 (5,445)	
Hall, Chris J	4:09:29 (14,165)	
Hall, Chris J	4:24:21 (18,094)	
Hall, Christopher	4:12:58 (15,021)	
Hall, Christopher G	4:15:36 (15,730)	
Hall, Christopher J	3:37:23 (6,140)	
Hall, Christopher J	3:57:19 (10,902)	
Hall, Christopher S	4:11:02 (14,551)	
Hall, David	3:45:35 (7,808)	
Hall, David W	2:58:22 (989)	
Hall, Derek J	4:19:39 (16,797)	
Hall, Dominic J	3:46:28 (8,001)	
Hall, Doug J	4:51:29 (24,935)	
Hall, Gary	3:48:05 (8,368)	
Hall, Gary	4:30:59 (19,878)	
Hall, Gavin	5:38:21 (31,217)	
Hall, Geoffrey	5:04:27 (27,316)	
Hall, Geoffrey A	4:28:07 (19,137)	
Hall, Giles J	3:49:06 (8,601)	
Hall, Ian D	3:41:08 (6,856)	
Hall, James A	3:49:33 (8,709)	
Hall, Jamie	3:29:19 (4,743)	
Hall, Jason	4:44:44 (23,352)	
Hall, Jeremy J	4:24:47 (18,210)	
Hall, John	3:37:30 (6,170)	
Hall, Jonathan C	4:02:21 (12,460)	
Hall, Jonathan D	3:06:50 (1,667)	
Hall, Jonathan L	3:27:30 (4,363)	
Hall, Ken	4:37:40 (21,634)	
Hall, Kev R	4:34:38 (20,855)	
Hall, Leon R	4:30:28 (19,738)	
Hall, Leslie	5:10:26 (28,212)	
Hall, Marc J	4:38:05 (21,736)	
Hall, Mark	3:27:04 (4,291)	
Hall, Mark	4:45:53 (23,642)	
Hall, Martin K	3:30:23 (4,950)	
Hall, Matthew	3:29:51 (4,849)	
Hall, Matthew	3:32:54 (5,373)	
Hall, Matthew D	4:41:47 (22,628)	
Hall, Matthew S	4:01:19 (12,192)	
Hall, Michael J	3:29:41 (4,817)	

Hall, Michael R	4:28:24 (19,232)	
Hall, Micheal C	4:22:21 (17,531)	
Hall, Mike	4:09:22 (14,136)	
Hall, Peter	4:21:12 (17,225)	
Hall, Peter	5:20:57 (29,494)	
Hall, Peter L	4:23:42 (17,914)	
Hall, Philip M	4:35:01 (20,988)	
Hall, Phillip S	6:43:26 (33,947)	
Hall, Richard A	3:02:34 (1,348)	
Hall, Richard J	4:20:23 (16,990)	
Hall, Richard W	3:40:55 (6,807)	
Hall, Rob W	3:07:30 (1,732)	
Hall, Robert J	4:46:50 (23,867)	
Hall, Robert W	4:22:38 (17,627)	
Hall, Ross P	4:59:55 (26,619)	
Hall, Russell	6:42:31 (33,923)	
Hall, Ryan	2:06:17 (5)	
Hall, Scott	4:39:19 (22,055)	
Hall, Scott D	4:12:24 (14,907)	
Hall, Simon	4:23:04 (17,744)	
Hall, Stephen	3:42:54 (7,213)	
Hall, Stephen R	3:42:32 (7,142)	
Hall, William	3:53:08 (9,615)	
Hallam, Chris	5:01:06 (26,811)	
Hallam, Simon P	3:42:27 (7,130)	
Hallard, Luke M	4:25:09 (18,306)	
Hallaways, Timothy	4:25:26 (18,377)	
Hallet, Jean François	4:08:19 (13,857)	
Hallett, Kevin J	3:42:24 (7,116)	
Hallett, Ross	3:04:01 (1,449)	
Hallett, Stephen	4:38:32 (21,831)	
Hallgrimsson, Kari	3:38:40 (6,382)	
Halliday, Michael P	4:45:16 (23,487)	
Halliday, Neil	2:45:57 (358)	
Halliday, William A	4:16:50 (16,047)	
Hallifax, Eoin J	4:12:10 (14,816)	
Halligan, James K	3:08:28 (1,834)	
Halligan, Lee P	3:48:53 (8,549)	
Halligan, William	5:38:18 (31,213)	
Hallissey, Martin	3:00:01 (1,171)	
Halliwell, Andrew J	3:58:08 (11,157)	
Halliwell, John K	3:13:53 (2,447)	
Halloran, Kieran	2:59:17 (1,096)	
Halloran, Michael J	4:26:23 (18,629)	
Hallos, Richard J	3:17:56 (2,979)	
Halls, Mark A	3:12:40 (2,282)	
Halmshaw, Nigel P	4:18:08 (16,383)	
Halpin, Alex J	2:59:27 (1,114)	
Halsall, Dean	5:49:34 (32,090)	
Halsey, Peter	4:27:41 (18,994)	
Halsey, Stephen J	3:12:13 (2,236)	
Halstead Cleak, Derek A	3:49:04 (8,593)	
Halter, Martin E	4:16:21 (15,922)	
Halton, Jason A	4:36:13 (21,301)	
Halton, Ray	4:01:09 (12,148)	
Halvey, Martin	2:45:58 (360)	
Hamblett, Steven B	5:58:37 (32,678)	
Hambly, Darren A	5:32:50 (30,730)	
Hambly, Darren P	4:55:20 (25,753)	
Hambsch, Joerg	4:19:39 (16,797)	
Hamed, Khalid J	3:43:07 (7,271)	
Hamer, David R	3:22:16 (3,526)	
Hamer, Scott	4:08:07 (13,801)	
Hamill, Craig J	5:06:49 (27,668)	
Hamilton, Alastair L	4:23:18 (17,816)	
Hamilton, Allan	3:40:57 (6,815)	
Hamilton, Andrew J	3:45:48 (7,858)	
Hamilton, Craig	3:50:28 (8,924)	
Hamilton, Edward J	4:13:04 (15,054)	
Hamilton, Graham M	3:13:41 (2,419)	
Hamilton, James J	3:56:46 (10,714)	
Hamilton, James R	3:17:39 (2,946)	
Hamilton, Keith W	3:55:20 (10,295)	
Hamilton, Liam	3:30:08 (4,912)	
Hamilton, Nick J	3:10:40 (2,062)	
Hamilton, Richard N	4:59:21 (26,538)	
Hamilton, Robert J	3:51:26 (9,162)	
Hamilton, Rod	3:22:01 (3,493)	
Hamilton, Ross M	3:56:49 (10,730)	
Hamilton, Simon	4:14:19 (15,401)	
Hamilton, Stuart	4:20:59 (17,177)	
Hamilton, Timothy G	3:50:40 (8,980)	
Hamilton, William	3:49:02 (8,587)	

Hamilton-Bruce, Vincent P 4:24:28 (18,133)
Hamilton-Gould, Henry 4:08:54 (14,018)
Hamit, Josh 4:27:39 (18,986)
Hamlyn, Andy J 3:47:48 (8,296)
Hamlyn, Peter J 5:11:44 (28,374)
Hamment, Michael G 4:48:33 (24,262)
Hammersley, Mark A 4:00:45 (12,047)
Hammick, Paul 3:41:11 (6,866)
Hammon, Alexander P 4:20:39 (17,080)
Hammond, Dan 4:26:11 (18,582)
Hammond, Daniel J 3:36:55 (6,041)
Hammond, Gary 4:37:20 (21,557)
Hammond, Greg W 4:32:12 (20,225)
Hammond, Harry D 3:54:37 (10,078)
Hammond, James R 4:17:38 (16,258)
Hammond, Jason R 5:22:11 (29,623)
Hammond, Keith 4:17:28 (16,211)
Hammond, Luke 4:41:54 (22,652)
Hammond, Mike P 4:24:39 (18,181)
Hammond, Nicky 3:25:36 (4,037)
Hammond, Paul R 4:46:38 (23,807)
Hammond, Paul S 3:39:23 (6,516)
Hammond, Richard 4:03:20 (12,685)
Hammond, Robert J 4:43:55 (23,156)
Hammoud, Tarek 5:34:54 (30,929)
Hamon, Olivier 3:02:32 (1,343)
Hamoudi, Feras 4:43:48 (23,122)
Hamp, Jonathan 4:20:02 (16,899)
Hampsey, Hugh 4:29:20 (19,481)
Hampson, Benjamin T 3:54:48 (10,125)
Hampson, Jonathan W 3:25:08 (3,955)
Hampton, Anthony N 3:39:44 (6,582)
Hampton, Jonathan C 3:51:43 (9,233)
Hampton, Neil G 3:59:18 (11,595)
Hampton, Ray 3:47:22 (8,189)
Hams, Steven P 4:27:53 (19,058)
Hamsher, Mark W 4:43:52 (23,146)
Hanbury, James 4:14:23 (15,418)
Hancock, Charlie T 3:30:39 (4,991)
Hancock, David 5:55:47 (32,509)
Hancock, Derek A 3:47:32 (8,227)
Hancock, Derek J 5:27:39 (30,218)
Hancock, Duncan W 4:02:37 (12,520)
Hancock, Hartley J 4:21:09 (17,213)
Hancock, Ian 4:54:51 (25,664)
Hancock, Jeremy 5:43:52 (31,639)
Hancock, Jonathan B 3:22:30 (3,564)
Hancock, Keith G 5:27:47 (30,234)
Hancock, Oliver J 4:06:06 (13,313)
Hancock, Oliver K 5:27:47 (30,234)
Hancock, Richard 5:14:20 (28,727)
Hancock, Simon J 3:07:58 (1,787)
Hancock, Tim 4:19:28 (16,743)
Hancox, Grenville R 4:36:21 (21,336)
Hancox, John R 3:57:50 (11,071)
Hancox, Karl A 3:25:44 (4,058)
Hancox, Rob G 3:42:20 (7,100)
Hand, Dominic W 5:42:43 (31,551)
Hand, Michael 3:15:14 (2,660)
Hand, Simon 3:50:26 (8,916)
Hand, Stuart 6:09:41 (33,104)
Handelaar, Greg J 4:45:51 (23,633)
Handley, Graham P 4:02:19 (12,450)
Handley, Simon J 3:00:50 (1,229)
Hando, Nick A 3:20:53 (3,341)
Hands, Stuart 4:24:08 (18,029)
Handy, Graham S 4:12:04 (14,830)
Hankinson, Neil 3:44:11 (7,489)
Hanks, Colin 3:55:11 (10,261)
Hanley, Michael J 5:07:24 (27,753)
Hanlon, John 3:59:06 (11,527)
Hanlon, John F 6:39:05 (33,867)
Hanlon, John M 4:04:13 (12,866)
Hann, David R 4:11:47 (14,745)
Hanna, Mark 4:02:43 (12,547)
Hanna, Paul M 4:31:48 (20,103)
Hannaford, Martyn J 3:58:48 (11,416)
Hannah, David S 5:47:09 (31,922)
Hannah, Philip I 4:42:32 (22,816)
Hannah, Tom 3:27:18 (4,332)
Hannam, Paul J 5:09:11 (27,992)
Hannant, Peter G 4:50:27 (24,697)
Hannaway, Paul B 5:59:27 (32,714)
Hanney, Scott 3:57:38 (10,990)
Hannington, Warren 3:04:23 (1,477)
Hannington-Smith, David S 4:17:58 (16,338)
Hannon, Gerard F 4:28:01 (19,103)
Hannon, Jason P 4:27:52 (19,051)
Hannon, Martin J 4:29:54 (19,606)
Hannon, Peter J 3:49:39 (8,731)
Hanratty, Andrew J 3:53:41 (9,764)
Hanscomb, John W 4:46:37 (23,801)
Hansen, Henning S 4:01:24 (12,217)
Hansen, Iain 4:08:07 (13,801)
Hansen, Michael S 4:07:13 (13,582)
Hansen, Paul 3:07:55 (1,780)
Hansen, Paul S 3:38:04 (6,277)
Hansen, Thornsten 2:58:15 (972)
Hansford, David J 4:49:54 (24,575)
Hanson, Carl 4:58:43 (26,427)
Hanson, David 4:43:18 (23,001)
Hanson, David J 3:21:26 (3,417)
Hanson, James 4:30:41 (19,795)
Hanson, Michael E 3:37:39 (6,196)
Hanson, Ross H 4:17:25 (16,195)
Hanson, Stephen K 3:34:43 (5,648)
Hansson, Magnus 2:37:34 (159)
Happe, Joe 3:33:28 (5,467)
Happs, David J 5:02:21 (27,014)
Haraldsen, Anders 3:58:33 (11,317)
Harari, Isaac 5:21:20 (29,540)
Harber, Mark R 3:26:46 (4,242)
Harber, Martin 5:07:21 (27,743)
Harbon, Christopher P 3:44:45 (7,622)
Harborow, Adam J 3:04:29 (1,482)
Harbour, John 4:25:26 (18,377)
Harchese, James T 5:45:01 (31,770)
Hardacre, Richard J 5:40:15 (31,357)
Hardcastle, Graham S 3:53:49 (9,815)
Hardcastle, Richard P 3:45:35 (7,808)
Harden, Ryan 4:10:29 (14,406)
Hardiman, Dawson J 3:25:18 (3,978)
Hardiman, Dominic 4:09:29 (14,165)
Harding, Andrew J 5:56:16 (32,542)
Harding, Colin 5:47:02 (31,914)
Harding, Ian 5:27:49 (30,239)
Harding, Jason P 3:22:52 (3,617)
Harding, Jonathan F 4:17:17 (16,170)
Harding, Keir 4:39:12 (22,027)
Harding, Mark A 4:09:06 (14,063)
Harding, Michael T 3:50:09 (8,859)
Harding, Norman W 5:50:16 (32,152)
Harding, Steve 5:11:33 (28,341)
Harding, Stuart S 4:09:57 (14,287)
Hardisty, Dan 5:21:22 (29,543)
Hardisty, Michael 4:16:55 (16,065)
Hardman, Paul 3:10:08 (2,002)
Hardman, Paul A 5:00:02 (26,638)
Hardwick, Bjorn J 3:44:07 (7,476)
Hardwick, David W 3:59:48 (11,782)
Hardwick, Kevin A 5:16:39 (29,013)
Hardwick, Philip R 5:25:32 (29,989)
Hardy, Andrew 3:39:48 (6,597)
Hardy, Andrew C 3:59:49 (11,789)
Hardy, Danny 3:33:24 (5,451)
Hardy, John G 3:37:53 (6,235)
Hardy, Jonathan M 3:36:55 (6,041)
Hardy, Roy W 5:15:21 (28,860)
Hare, Michael J 5:46:05 (31,840)
Hare, Stephen A 4:28:37 (19,296)
Hare, William 5:18:50 (29,265)
Harel, Maryan B 3:28:54 (4,644)
Haresign, Martin 4:34:38 (20,855)
Haresnape, Alan J 3:47:29 (8,219)
Haresnape, Charles 4:34:49 (20,908)
Harfield, Patrick D 6:18:18 (33,366)
Harfield, Stephen P 6:18:18 (33,366)
Hargrave, David 3:31:36 (5,151)
Hargreaves, John S 3:31:56 (5,208)
Hargreaves, Jon 4:52:36 (25,169)
Hargreaves, Luke 6:21:51 (33,458)
Hargreaves, Michael S 5:09:48 (28,114)
Haria, Dilesh P 4:20:28 (17,015)
Harianto, Irwan 3:48:35 (8,483)
Harison, Matthew 4:16:13 (15,882)
Harji, Sameer 3:44:41 (7,597)
Harkin, Derek 3:21:26 (3,417)
Harkin, James R 4:41:56 (22,658)
Harkness, Andrew 3:52:32 (9,442)
Harkus, Gavin M 2:45:00 (331)
Harkus, Nathan H 4:57:51 (26,252)
Harland, Andrew N 3:55:39 (10,389)
Harland, Jason 3:32:26 (5,308)
Harland, Joe R 4:57:16 (26,137)
Harle, Jamie 4:46:48 (23,854)
Harley, Andrew 4:15:32 (15,715)
Harley, Colin P 3:22:47 (3,607)
Harley, Darren J 3:10:24 (2,030)
Harman, Alan 3:58:42 (11,374)
Harman, Gary R 3:46:33 (8,013)
Harman, Jamie 3:44:45 (7,622)
Harman, Matthew P 4:18:48 (16,572)
Harman, Timothy M 3:27:42 (4,396)
Harmer, Richard J 5:03:51 (27,235)
Harmsworth, Neil R 4:44:44 (23,352)
Harmsworth, Patrick M 4:00:55 (12,086)
Harmsworth, Terry 4:08:26 (13,890)
Harness, James M 3:31:55 (5,203)
Harnett, Dennis 3:09:39 (1,958)
Harnett, Peter S 3:26:50 (4,250)
Harney, Mark 3:09:25 (1,930)
Harper, Andrew M 3:30:01 (4,888)
Harper, Andrew P 5:10:38 (28,234)
Harper, Chris R 4:37:12 (21,526)
Harper, Giles E 4:28:31 (19,268)
Harper, Graeme W 5:33:52 (30,823)
Harper, Iain 4:43:29 (23,044)
Harper, Peter A 3:07:55 (1,780)
Harper, Richard P 4:21:03 (17,197)
Harper, Theo 2:58:12 (968)
Harper, Tim 4:53:20 (25,337)
Harper, Tom S 4:50:45 (24,782)
Harpham, Peter 4:42:49 (22,880)
Harpoutlian, Cyril 4:07:45 (13,707)
Harpum, Robert 4:24:19 (18,084)
Harradence, Oliver 2:32:51 (95)
Harrap, Mark D 5:02:11 (26,985)
Harrap, Paul R 3:40:36 (6,744)
Harries, Owen D 2:50:24 (531)
Harries, Richard W 4:38:18 (21,781)
Harries, Stuart P 3:15:14 (2,660)
Harrigan, Christopher 4:28:20 (19,217)
Harriman, David J 4:41:11 (22,484)
Harrington, Alexander 4:20:57 (17,164)
Harrington, John 4:00:37 (12,010)
Harrington, Liam 4:21:26 (17,286)
Harrington, Mathew F 3:23:29 (3,706)
Harrington, Richard 3:34:14 (5,580)
Harrington, Scott M 3:04:55 (1,511)
Harrington, Stephen A 6:03:50 (32,881)
Harris, Alex C 4:35:06 (21,011)
Harris, Ben 4:07:01 (13,522)
Harris, Ben 4:11:21 (14,633)
Harris, Bret D 5:12:48 (28,514)
Harris, Christopher L 4:40:43 (22,360)
Harris, Colin 5:31:12 (30,585)
Harris, David I 4:52:40 (25,190)
Harris, David J 4:37:35 (21,613)
Harris, Dennis 5:56:18 (32,545)
Harris, Dominic 3:46:25 (7,984)
Harris, Dominic 4:15:01 (15,568)
Harris, George P 3:42:04 (7,042)
Harris, Giles 2:51:46 (583)
Harris, Ian A 4:16:39 (15,997)
Harris, Ian A 4:38:52 (21,934)
Harris, Ian G 4:34:52 (20,931)
Harris, Jake 4:27:55 (19,071)
Harris, James 4:08:38 (13,950)
Harris, James A 5:20:04 (29,417)
Harris, Jason 2:50:56 (550)
Harris, Joshua D 4:26:09 (18,574)
Harris, Kieren A 6:33:31 (33,738)
Harris, Lance D 3:07:53 (1,776)
Harris, Lee M 4:01:17 (12,178)
Harris, Mark 5:05:09 (27,427)
Harris, Mark E 4:31:30 (20,026)
Harris, Matthew D 5:06:23 (27,611)
Harris, Michael 2:55:05 (756)
Harris, Neil 4:58:34 (26,390)

Harris, Neil A 4:19:42 (16,814)
Harris, Neil P 5:12:12 (28,427)
Harris, Neville W 3:50:07 (8,847)
Harris, Nigel 5:05:34 (27,491)
Harris, Nigel D 3:31:16 (5,095)
Harris, Paul 3:50:16 (8,887)
Harris, Paul 4:39:05 (21,999)
Harris, Paul 5:24:19 (29,841)
Harris, Paul A 4:58:49 (26,440)
Harris, Paul A 5:14:14 (28,710)
Harris, Paul D 3:36:09 (5,907)
Harris, Peter C 3:26:02 (4,109)
Harris, Phillip J 3:57:44 (11,029)
Harris, Raymond A 4:04:59 (13,046)
Harris, Reg 4:07:45 (13,707)
Harris, Rhys 5:54:00 (32,404)
Harris, Richard 4:13:16 (15,105)
Harris, Richard 4:24:33 (18,159)
Harris, Richard D 4:09:52 (14,271)
Harris, Richard J 3:42:29 (7,137)
Harris, Richard J 4:09:37 (14,204)
Harris, Robb 3:51:39 (9,211)
Harris, Robin 4:28:49 (19,351)
Harris, Ronald M 5:28:01 (30,268)
Harris, Ryan 4:56:26 (25,953)
Harris, Shaun P 4:41:49 (22,641)
Harris, Simon D 3:43:09 (7,276)
Harris, Steven L 4:33:28 (20,567)
Harris, Steven M 5:16:24 (28,981)
Harris, Stewart 3:28:03 (4,471)
Harris, William G 2:56:11 (819)
Harrison, Andrew E 3:54:29 (10,022)
Harrison, Chad 5:45:00 (31,769)
Harrison, Clive H 4:54:13 (25,525)
Harrison, Craig 4:44:09 (23,214)
Harrison, David A 4:07:41 (13,694)
Harrison, David M 4:31:50 (20,120)
Harrison, Derek J 3:10:59 (2,095)
Harrison, Derek W 3:35:15 (5,747)
Harrison, Gary P 3:27:39 (4,387)
Harrison, Iain M 3:01:36 (1,283)
Harrison, Jacob 3:39:49 (6,600)
Harrison, Jason T 3:48:32 (8,473)
Harrison, Jeremy P 3:59:17 (11,590)
Harrison, Kenneth 4:43:57 (23,169)
Harrison, Martyn A 4:27:19 (18,911)
Harrison, Matt 3:04:58 (1,518)
Harrison, Matthew P 4:39:39 (22,108)
Harrison, Nicholas 4:15:20 (15,646)
Harrison, Paul 5:20:24 (29,454)
Harrison, Paul A 3:08:04 (1,797)
Harrison, Paul D 3:43:22 (7,319)
Harrison, Philip A 5:10:53 (28,263)
Harrison, Philip D 3:58:38 (11,351)
Harrison, Philip L 4:35:27 (21,098)
Harrison, Richard P 2:55:02 (755)
Harrison, Robert M 2:55:50 (796)
Harrison, Sam B 5:32:31 (30,701)
Harrison, Simon W 3:24:54 (3,909)
Harrison, Stephen J 4:00:27 (11,960)
Harrison, Timothy 5:24:42 (29,877)
Harrison, Timothy C 3:42:28 (7,134)
Harrison, Tom 4:26:02 (18,548)
Harrison, William 4:42:07 (22,701)
Harrisson, James T 3:51:16 (9,113)
Harrod, Matthew A 6:20:54 (33,422)
Harrold, Bruce 2:56:54 (867)
Harrold, John C 3:28:07 (4,491)
Harrold, Julian D 3:29:18 (4,739)
Harrold, Mark P 4:34:15 (20,768)
Harrow, Martin D 3:32:08 (5,248)
Harry, Michael P 4:57:01 (26,084)
Harry, Richard 2:55:06 (757)
Hart, Adam G 5:12:45 (28,502)
Hart, Andrew T 4:58:07 (26,310)
Hart, Antony J 3:34:40 (5,638)
Hart, David T 4:04:16 (12,880)
Hart, David W 2:59:19 (1,100)
Hart, David W 4:31:06 (19,910)
Hart, Gordon 4:08:37 (13,946)
Hart, Graeme A 5:49:41 (32,100)
Hart, Graham A 4:34:40 (20,865)
Hart, Gregory P 3:41:06 (6,846)
Hart, James 3:05:38 (1,565)
Hart, Mark A 3:58:49 (11,426)
Hart, Matthew J 4:20:53 (17,147)
Hart, Nigel 3:53:58 (9,863)
Hart, Paul M 2:42:55 (262)
Hart, Simon 3:02:58 (1,371)
Hart, Toby 3:04:04 (1,452)
Harte, David M 3:01:22 (1,267)
Harte, James 3:50:46 (9,002)
Harte, John P 4:29:39 (19,551)
Harten, Kieran 4:09:27 (14,156)
Hartevelt, Peter L 5:42:41 (31,547)
Hartin, John 3:17:18 (2,904)
Hartland, Christopher C 3:23:19 (3,679)
Hartland, Ian E 4:36:31 (21,372)
Hartley, Allan 3:21:25 (3,415)
Hartley, Andrew N 2:46:59 (386)
Hartley, Ben S 4:16:36 (15,984)
Hartley, Geoffrey H 4:53:46 (25,432)
Hartley, Jonathan A 4:29:32 (19,524)
Hartley, Richard A 3:46:01 (7,891)
Hartley, Steve 4:09:18 (14,118)
Hartley, Steve 4:12:19 (14,887)
Hartley, Thomas W 3:09:12 (1,909)
Hartley, Timothy D 6:32:08 (33,705)
Hartmann, Elmar 4:25:47 (18,473)
Hartnett, Chris D 3:51:59 (9,297)
Hartop, James W 2:47:49 (415)
Hartshorn, Paul 4:09:48 (14,251)
Harvey, Alan P 4:24:48 (18,218)
Harvey, Barry 3:44:51 (7,642)
Harvey, Clive S 3:20:21 (3,272)
Harvey, David N 4:56:45 (26,013)
Harvey, Edward M 4:18:04 (16,361)
Harvey, Glen 3:57:15 (10,877)
Harvey, Glenn 5:12:19 (28,435)
Harvey, Ian M 3:21:21 (3,410)
Harvey, Jonathan H 3:16:15 (2,781)
Harvey, Joseph C 4:41:12 (22,488)
Harvey, Kevin R 3:26:56 (4,268)
Harvey, Luke A 3:21:01 (3,362)
Harvey, Matthew J 2:52:00 (595)
Harvey, Paul 4:48:15 (24,190)
Harvey, Phil C 4:38:50 (21,924)
Harvey, Richard 4:26:00 (18,538)
Harvey, Richard R 3:41:49 (6,994)
Harvey, Shane 3:47:35 (8,243)
Harvey, Stephen R 3:58:20 (11,236)
Harvie, Gavin 3:19:28 (3,158)
Harward, Darren P 6:21:30 (33,445)
Harward, Mark P 6:25:25 (33,560)
Harwood, Adrian N 3:44:00 (7,456)
Harwood, Andrew J 4:00:56 (12,096)
Hasegawa, Eiichi 4:40:35 (22,325)
Hasell, Ian R 4:53:18 (25,332)
Haskey, John T 2:57:33 (909)
Haskey-Jones, James R 3:17:40 (2,948)
Haskins, David R 3:39:13 (6,477)
Haslam, Paul 3:12:29 (2,264)
Hasler, Ralph 4:52:40 (25,190)
Haslett, Francis P 6:30:15 (33,666)
Haslop, Peter 3:53:26 (9,702)
Haspels, Joost 4:12:59 (15,027)
Hassall, Glyn R 4:28:46 (19,335)
Hassan, Anas 4:43:38 (23,080)
Hassan, Medhat 5:19:16 (29,327)
Hassan, Nejmi 4:31:45 (20,088)
Hassan, William W 3:53:49 (9,815)
Hassani, Said 2:47:07 (391)
Hassell, Desmond J 4:02:42 (12,542)
Hassett, Daniel 3:35:00 (5,703)
Hassett, Darren M 6:43:28 (33,948)
Hassett, Magnus J 4:11:10 (14,597)
Hasson, Peter F 3:50:00 (8,824)
Hastie, David R 3:56:26 (10,605)
Hastie, Greg 2:42:30 (255)
Hastilow, Sean P 4:22:54 (17,703)
Hastings, Brian F 5:41:02 (31,418)
Hastings, Mark R 5:32:44 (30,720)
Hastings, Rob 4:53:27 (25,360)
Hastings, Roger D 4:47:17 (23,983)
Hastings, Terence A 4:40:04 (22,198)
Hasuk, Gregor 4:01:08 (12,145)
Hatcher, Adrian G 3:59:42 (11,750)
Hatchett, Michael J 3:29:34 (4,792)
Hateley, Adam L 6:38:03 (33,841)
Hatfield, Alexander J 4:06:45 (13,462)
Hatfield, Robert J 3:36:30 (5,969)
Hatfield, Stephen 4:03:55 (12,807)
Hathaway, Carl A 3:29:37 (4,803)
Hathaway, Neil J 3:47:13 (8,161)
Hatherley, Ben W 4:10:24 (14,388)
Hatley, Mark S 4:07:25 (13,618)
Hatt, Daniel J 3:52:18 (9,386)
Hatto, David M 4:16:59 (16,088)
Hatton, Jeff 3:54:10 (9,924)
Hatton, John C 3:58:33 (11,317)
Hatton, Mark B 4:08:07 (13,801)
Hatton, Michael 2:40:00 (198)
Hatton, Paul 3:58:28 (11,290)
Hattori, Shinichi 4:52:31 (25,151)
Hatvany, Alan P 3:13:31 (2,396)
Hatzis, Philip 3:11:26 (2,140)
Hauck, Brian 3:22:15 (3,524)
Haucke, Albrecht 4:43:32 (23,059)
Haughn, Eric C 4:34:30 (20,822)
Haughton, Colin T 3:23:01 (3,641)
Haupt, Simon P 4:32:13 (20,233)
Hausner, Sven 3:16:24 (2,804)
Haust, Wilhelm M 3:47:35 (8,243)
Hautzinger, Gerhard 4:06:31 (13,407)
Havill, Neil S 4:09:09 (14,073)
Hawcroft, Richard J 4:58:22 (26,354)
Hawes, Ian M 5:40:07 (31,341)
Hawke, Robin 5:51:13 (32,228)
Hawker, Kevin R 2:41:29 (233)
Hawker, Marc H 3:28:54 (4,644)
Hawker, Mark K 3:14:15 (2,509)
Hawkes, Anthony J 3:57:52 (11,079)
Hawkes, Elliot L 4:44:35 (23,315)
Hawkes, Fraser T 5:57:38 (32,611)
Hawkes, Martin 4:25:43 (18,453)
Hawkes, Simon T 5:02:56 (27,102)
Hawking, Oliver C 3:53:00 (9,572)
Hawkins, Alistair J 3:46:34 (8,018)
Hawkins, Carl J 6:47:38 (34,030)
Hawkins, Graeme 3:14:26 (2,536)
Hawkins, Graham D 3:32:09 (5,253)
Hawkins, James P 4:18:50 (16,582)
Hawkins, Jeff J 4:11:39 (14,719)
Hawkins, Martin S 3:09:35 (1,950)
Hawkins, Paul 3:24:52 (3,905)
Hawkins, Pete 3:33:14 (5,426)
Hawkins, Ross A 6:13:02 (33,212)
Hawkins, Russell P 4:24:14 (18,063)
Hawkins, Thomas J 4:00:59 (12,110)
Hawkins, Timothy J 2:39:08 (184)
Hawkins, William A 4:10:34 (14,428)
Hawley, Graham 4:15:03 (15,579)
Hawliczek, Edward J 3:39:12 (6,473)
Hawliczek, Simon E 3:56:34 (10,650)
Haworth, Ben R 5:28:56 (30,371)
Haworth, Daniel N 3:18:26 (3,036)
Haworth, John 3:52:56 (9,549)
Haworth, Trevor D 4:46:19 (23,745)
Hawthorn, Daniel 4:12:03 (14,824)
Hawthorne, Michael J 4:02:36 (12,513)
Hay, Andrew W 3:30:03 (4,895)
Hay, Fraser T 5:23:53 (29,787)
Hay, Graeme 4:25:58 (18,524)
Hay, Nathan B 3:46:59 (8,104)
Hay, Paul N 3:18:33 (3,052)
Hay, Simon J 3:21:29 (3,423)
Hayashi, Yoshinori 3:42:01 (7,031)
Hayat, Faisal 4:48:56 (24,354)
Hayday, Nick T 4:18:37 (16,538)
Hayden, Paul G 4:34:05 (20,720)
Haye, Denis 4:36:48 (21,444)
Hayer, Jaswinder S 3:27:43 (4,402)
Hayes, Barry M 4:18:18 (16,434)
Hayes, Ben 6:00:37 (32,764)
Hayes, Bernard A 8:05:25 (34,537)
Hayes, Brian 3:09:00 (1,883)
Hayes, Christopher 4:37:35 (21,613)
Hayes, Dan 3:44:02 (7,461)
Hayes, David 4:41:25 (22,537)

Hayes, Dennis 3:48:14 (8,407)
Hayes, James 2:59:25 (1,112)
Hayes, Jonathan P 3:30:14 (4,933)
Hayes, Lee 6:10:07 (33,121)
Hayes, Lee J 4:38:33 (21,842)
Hayes, Mike 5:24:50 (29,893)
Hayes, Paul 5:17:30 (29,126)
Hayes, Paul M 2:53:31 (663)
Hayes, Peter J 4:14:34 (15,464)
Hayes, Richard N 3:17:09 (2,880)
Hayes, Richard S 3:24:31 (3,850)
Hayes, Roger B 3:36:50 (6,026)
Hayes, Simon 5:52:15 (32,305)
Hayes, Tony 3:42:36 (7,153)
Haygarth, Richard K 3:56:55 (10,768)
Hayler, Ian C 3:42:57 (7,223)
Hayley, Alec 4:40:05 (22,209)
Hayllar, Crispin F 3:58:34 (11,326)
Haylock, Ian D 3:53:37 (9,747)
Haylock, Keith J 4:18:42 (16,552)
Hayman, Mark 3:34:43 (5,648)
Hayman-Joyce, Nicholas P 4:47:38 (24,050)
Hayne, Ian R 3:52:13 (9,363)
Hayne, Robert 3:53:07 (9,611)
Haynes, Anton C 4:12:16 (14,879)
Haynes, Darren P 3:58:20 (11,236)
Haynes, Greg G 4:14:04 (15,326)
Haynes, Iain M 3:48:01 (8,355)
Haynes, James R 3:42:16 (7,087)
Haynes, Jonathan K 3:47:12 (8,154)
Haynes, Kevin M 3:37:23 (6,140)
Haynes, Oliver F 3:36:57 (6,050)
Haynes, Richard 3:08:31 (1,840)
Haynes, Roy 6:18:17 (33,363)
Haynes, Steven G 3:55:46 (10,425)
Hayter, Richard J 5:08:03 (27,831)
Hayter, Sam 4:33:39 (20,622)
Hayter, Steven C 4:38:33 (21,842)
Hayton, David M 3:22:36 (3,584)
Hayton, Thomas D 5:12:46 (28,508)
Hayward, Adrian 3:35:47 (5,841)
Hayward, Alexander D 4:45:08 (23,444)
Hayward, Antony M 3:32:50 (5,367)
Hayward, Byron I 4:24:45 (18,205)
Hayward, Christopher 5:23:54 (29,792)
Hayward, Michael J 5:58:17 (32,654)
Hayward, Mike 3:50:41 (8,985)
Hayward, Roger V 4:39:01 (21,975)
Haywood, Dexter 3:42:26 (7,124)
Haywood, Roy 5:39:30 (31,296)
Haywood, Steve 4:50:28 (24,703)
Hazard, John R 3:21:48 (3,458)
Hazel, Neil G 4:37:34 (21,606)
Hazel, Simon R 3:16:00 (2,754)
Hazelden, David J 4:27:42 (18,997)
Hazeldene, Richard A 3:47:12 (8,154)
Hazell, Andrew J 4:27:05 (18,834)
Hazell, Graham 5:02:41 (27,062)
Hazell, Peter L 3:57:39 (10,995)
Hazell, Wayne D 3:56:29 (10,623)
Hazlewood, Paul F 5:08:48 (27,946)
Hazlewood, Peter R 4:22:36 (17,613)
Head, Christopher S 4:27:07 (18,847)
Head, John P 5:46:22 (31,867)
Head, Julian P 3:48:00 (8,351)
Head, Leigh 3:00:38 (1,213)
Head, Lionel 4:27:06 (18,843)
Head, Marcus 4:02:07 (12,392)
Head, Richard J 4:18:01 (16,348)
Head, Stuart R 3:28:42 (4,606)
Headley, Stephen R 3:51:59 (9,297)
Headon, David L 3:54:37 (10,078)
Heaford, Jamie L 3:41:47 (6,988)
Heal, Tom 3:54:45 (10,114)
Heale, James M 3:50:43 (8,994)
Heale, Timothy M 4:35:50 (21,200)
Healey, James 3:58:53 (11,451)
Healey, John 7:01:50 (34,228)
Healey, Phil W 4:20:13 (16,951)
Healy, Andrew 3:56:06 (10,514)
Healy, Christopher M 3:46:47 (8,056)
Healy, James M 4:54:28 (25,575)
Healy, Kevin 3:27:10 (4,308)
Heap, Clive R 4:27:15 (18,890)
Heap, Michael 3:32:27 (5,309)
Heap, Richard J 3:26:50 (4,250)
Heaps, Stephen J 4:16:00 (15,837)
Heard, David H 3:26:37 (4,209)
Heard, Mark 2:43:02 (266)
Hearn, Clive D 3:48:16 (8,418)
Hearn, Derek 4:39:04 (21,994)
Hearn, Kevin S 4:42:30 (22,810)
Hearn, Martin J 5:06:31 (27,627)
Hearne, Matthew F 3:51:00 (9,046)
Hearne, William C 3:41:53 (7,012)
Heartford, Damian D 5:41:44 (31,482)
Heaslewood, Adam 4:12:42 (14,962)
Heasman, David A 3:51:18 (9,123)
Heath, Brenhan 4:19:19 (16,707)
Heath, Frederick C 3:29:43 (4,824)
Heath, Gary 4:05:12 (13,098)
Heath, James L 4:49:54 (24,575)
Heath, Roger 4:26:51 (18,773)
Heath, Terry S 5:10:53 (28,263)
Heath, Will 4:06:29 (13,395)
Heather, Adam J 5:10:21 (28,198)
Heather, Richard G 4:25:29 (18,388)
Heaton, Geoffrey 3:50:17 (8,890)
Heaver, Dan 3:51:52 (9,265)
Hebbes, Christopher P 3:39:05 (6,450)
Hebden, Nicholas S 3:44:06 (7,474)
Hecher, Kurt 3:48:38 (8,496)
Heck, Jochen 5:00:58 (26,791)
Heckford, John W 3:42:46 (7,190)
Heckscher, Ben D 4:16:52 (16,049)
Hector, Stuart R 4:44:36 (23,321)
Heddon, Anthony P 5:09:59 (28,144)
Hedge, Jonpaul 4:46:09 (23,700)
Hedger, Douglas J 5:14:12 (28,704)
Hedger, Graham 3:06:03 (1,603)
Hedges, Robert 3:25:35 (4,029)
Hedgethorne, Peter J 4:17:12 (16,157)
Hedin, Joakim 4:17:06 (16,122)
Hedin, Jonas 4:17:06 (16,122)
Hedley, Chris A 4:09:16 (14,108)
Hedley, Michael S 4:56:04 (25,888)
Hedley, Tristan 3:56:00 (10,491)
Hedman, Peter 4:06:42 (13,451)
Hedmann, Lindsay M 3:48:05 (8,368)
Heeks, Paul J 5:18:27 (29,220)
Heeley, Dave G 5:23:35 (29,756)
Heffell, Joseph 4:13:34 (15,181)
Hefferan, Rob 3:55:29 (10,335)
Hefferman, Toby 4:05:31 (13,182)
Heffron, Colin 4:38:26 (21,811)
Hefni, Mohamed 5:05:22 (27,454)
Hegarty, David J 5:14:09 (28,694)
Hegarty, Hugo 3:20:35 (3,305)
Hegarty, Terry J 4:48:37 (24,274)
Hegelstad, Eivind 3:27:12 (4,313)
Heger, Marco 3:50:35 (8,949)
Hegesippe, Mickael 2:47:17 (397)
Heggie, Donald W 5:45:07 (31,775)
Hegi, Christoph 3:09:17 (1,916)
Heide, Wolfgang 3:55:04 (10,222)
Heidelberger, Klaus 3:11:07 (2,107)
Heighley, Stephen T 5:23:25 (29,736)
Heikel, Paul C 3:43:35 (7,363)
Heimdal, Arne 3:44:38 (7,587)
Heininger, Bernhard 4:00:36 (12,004)
Heisinger, Klaus D 3:28:32 (4,566)
Heler, Philip J 3:37:30 (6,170)
Helfon, Alfredo 3:29:56 (4,873)
Helgason, Gudmundur 4:53:29 (25,368)
Heliiwell, Peter J 3:50:54 (9,028)
Helland, Ronny 4:52:52 (25,241)
Hellard, David 3:05:45 (1,577)
Heller, Douglas P 2:54:54 (740)
Hellgren, Jan E 5:21:24 (29,546)
Helliwell, Matthew 5:21:30 (29,555)
Helliwell, Paul 2:48:02 (425)
Hellmers, Christopher L 3:15:13 (2,656)
Hellyer, Patrick 3:28:46 (4,618)
Helm, Simon J 4:53:14 (25,322)
Helme, Mark 3:29:53 (4,862)
Helmer, Jamie 2:49:14 (472)
Helps, David 3:27:46 (4,412)
Helstrip, Seth L 3:59:49 (11,789)
Heming, Tim 3:22:01 (3,493)
Heminsley, William 4:06:30 (13,400)
Hemming, Gary 3:32:24 (5,300)
Hemming, Michael P 4:51:55 (25,026)
Hemming, Neil 4:08:33 (13,927)
Hemming, Sean 4:40:00 (22,183)
Hemmings, Dave E 5:47:23 (31,941)
Hemmings, Jason P 5:17:07 (29,077)
Hemmings, Thomas E 3:54:31 (10,040)
Hempstead, Charles N 4:04:40 (12,972)
Hemson, Robert A 5:50:19 (32,157)
Henderson, Andrew T 3:25:45 (4,061)
Henderson, Bernard J 3:57:53 (11,085)
Henderson, Christopher D 3:58:59 (11,481)
Henderson, Danny 5:34:43 (30,906)
Henderson, David G 2:49:22 (481)
Henderson, Garry 3:40:54 (6,804)
Henderson, James 5:35:56 (31,025)
Henderson, Jason 3:06:52 (1,670)
Henderson, Jay 4:38:34 (21,849)
Henderson, Jon R 5:30:05 (30,483)
Henderson, Kyle M 3:55:59 (10,488)
Henderson, Martn 4:48:53 (24,342)
Henderson, Neil C 5:09:13 (27,999)
Henderson, Rhys K 3:18:17 (3,016)
Henderson, Rob A 5:15:21 (28,860)
Henderson, Ryan 4:40:37 (22,334)
Henderson, Steve 5:17:20 (29,100)
Henderson, Stuart 4:31:00 (19,882)
Henderson, Stuart 4:42:14 (22,736)
Hendriksen, Danny 4:03:42 (12,765)
Hendry, David C 4:39:45 (22,146)
Heney, Kenneth J 3:07:15 (1,700)
Henley, Wayne D 3:18:42 (3,064)
Henly, Jonathan D 4:18:22 (16,452)
Hennegan, Peter A 5:10:25 (28,211)
Hennemann, Peter 4:16:57 (16,074)
Henness, David 4:41:29 (22,553)
Hennessy, Huw C 3:49:45 (8,758)
Hennessy, Keith T 4:58:34 (26,390)
Henney, Sean 4:19:55 (16,864)
Henni, Abderrahman 3:11:16 (2,121)
Henni, Djilali 2:41:46 (238)
Hennings, Stephen J 4:10:37 (14,440)
Henningsen, Michael 3:31:33 (5,141)
Henriques, Wayne W 4:27:56 (19,078)
Henry, Derek 4:13:37 (15,191)
Henry, Matthew J 4:53:59 (25,478)
Henry, Michael G 5:16:30 (28,992)
Henry, Nigel J 3:37:08 (6,086)
Henshaw, Paul A 4:06:58 (13,508)
Hentze, Matthias W 3:48:53 (8,549)
Henville, Andrew 4:01:48 (12,317)
Henwood, Christian J 3:34:25 (5,607)
Henwood, Phillip W 4:08:36 (13,942)
Henzell, Nick C 3:15:45 (2,722)
Hepburn, Gerard S 4:00:14 (11,905)
Heppell, Robert G 3:57:41 (11,006)
Hepple, Jason N 5:24:19 (29,841)
Hepworth, Charles D 3:37:05 (6,078)
Hepworth, Ian D 4:11:55 (14,784)
Herbert, Andrew C 3:55:21 (10,298)
Herbert, Cled 4:27:46 (19,011)
Herbert, Guy G 4:15:48 (15,783)
Herbert, Martyn 6:34:49 (33,769)
Herbert, Matthew C 3:18:20 (3,023)
Herbert, Neil M 4:13:20 (15,126)
Herbert, Raymond L 7:03:12 (34,245)
Herbert, Richard C 5:40:07 (31,341)
Herbert, Simon J 5:21:11 (29,521)
Herbertson, James A 4:14:42 (15,495)
Hercules, Tyrone A 4:27:45 (19,009)
Hergeirsson, Grimur 3:28:45 (4,613)
Hermans, Carl R 3:12:14 (2,243)
Hernandez, Jamie L 5:19:53 (29,402)
Herod, Kevin 5:22:24 (29,650)
Heron, David G 4:41:42 (22,616)
Heron, James R 3:03:02 (1,375)
Heron, Zigmond 4:37:32 (21,600)
Heronneau, Gilles N 4:17:02 (16,104)
Heronneau, Jean B 4:23:38 (17,900)

Herring, Michael J	5:33:43 (30,801)
Herringshaw, Robin M	5:08:34 (27,906)
Herrington, David A	3:28:05 (4,477)
Herriot, Stuart W	3:46:44 (8,045)
Herrod, Ian N	4:00:49 (12,062)
Herron, Iain S	4:41:19 (22,518)
Herron, Piers S	4:02:48 (12,565)
Hershaw, Neil	3:47:09 (8,140)
Hertz, Daniel A	3:59:25 (11,639)
Herzog, Klaus H	4:35:35 (21,129)
Hesford, Robert K	4:20:45 (17,103)
Hesketh, Benjamin W	4:00:07 (11,879)
Heslop, Garry	4:09:29 (14,165)
Hesse, Olaf	3:53:09 (9,620)
Hession, Wayne M	4:21:54 (17,422)
Heteau, Arnaud	4:53:36 (25,400)
Hetherington, Chris	5:56:30 (32,557)
Hetherington, Martin H	4:27:10 (18,866)
Hetherington, Paul A	3:54:38 (10,082)
Hewett, Kelvin E	4:46:59 (23,904)
Hewitson, Robert A	4:03:20 (12,685)
Hewitt, Andrew J	6:06:57 (33,016)
Hewitt, Antony G	4:58:04 (26,297)
Hewitt, David	4:29:40 (19,557)
Hewitt, Lee S	5:38:08 (31,199)
Hewitt, Leslie D	4:28:14 (19,188)
Hewitt, Michael	5:13:09 (28,563)
Hewitt, Phil G	3:32:05 (5,239)
Hewitt, Samuel J	3:41:28 (6,932)
Hewitt, Simon	3:27:13 (4,315)
Hewlett, Ian M	3:51:24 (9,152)
Hewlett, Kevin	5:42:56 (31,566)
Hewlett, Ryan	4:30:41 (19,795)
Hewson, Anthony J	3:46:26 (7,988)
Hewson, Kevin M	4:20:12 (16,942)
Hey, Michael	3:50:10 (8,863)
Hey, Michael J	3:58:38 (11,351)
Heycock, Robert W	4:34:44 (20,886)
Heyes, Edmund	3:52:33 (9,444)
Heyhirst, Chris J	4:46:50 (23,867)
Heyl, Dawid P	3:39:15 (6,483)
Heymer, Matthew S	4:34:18 (20,776)
Heys, Simon R	3:27:16 (4,325)
Heys, Tom W	4:30:56 (19,873)
Heyvaerts, Stijn	4:34:46 (20,897)
Heywood, Kevin J	2:27:57 (49)
Heywood, Matthew W	3:29:59 (4,882)
Hiatt, David	3:36:26 (5,954)
Hibberd, Roy G	4:34:44 (20,886)
Hibbert, Andrew I	4:53:59 (25,478)
Hibbert, Steven D	4:13:08 (15,071)
Hibbs, Sam	4:06:56 (13,501)
Hickenbotham, Peter T	3:48:40 (8,504)
Hickey, Christopher J	5:09:06 (27,981)
Hickey, Colm F	4:44:07 (23,206)
Hickey, Paul Y	5:19:16 (29,327)
Hickey, Stuart W	4:35:22 (21,072)
Hickish, Tamas F	3:16:17 (2,785)
Hickling, Graham M	4:06:08 (13,322)
Hickling, Phill	4:40:27 (22,298)
Hickling, Phillip J	4:34:59 (20,974)
Hickman, Andy J	3:32:15 (5,267)
Hickman, Dean	4:59:17 (26,529)
Hickman, Michael J	3:52:21 (9,396)
Hickman, Oliver	3:58:56 (11,468)
Hickman, Paul	4:02:26 (12,483)
Hickman, Philip G	3:47:37 (8,257)
Hickman, Stephen P	3:46:15 (7,940)
Hickmott, Andy	3:40:44 (6,765)
Hicks, Adrian T	4:12:58 (15,021)
Hicks, David J	4:43:48 (23,122)
Hicks, Michael P	5:41:07 (31,424)
Hicks, Norman	4:05:56 (13,275)
Hicks, Paul	3:39:54 (6,616)
Hicks, Tom M	5:15:01 (28,821)
Hide, Carlton	2:55:38 (784)
Hide, George	2:37:52 (164)
Hide, Will	4:49:50 (24,556)
Hieber, Ben G	2:55:58 (806)
Hield, Mark S	3:59:02 (11,499)
Higgin-Jones, Peter	4:10:21 (14,376)
Higgins, Adrian J	3:31:15 (5,092)
Higgins, Andrew	3:40:07 (6,660)

Higgins, Andrew J	5:31:04 (30,572)
Higgins, Daniel J	2:39:41 (193)
Higgins, Jeremy R	4:00:38 (12,013)
Higgins, Kevin G	3:39:42 (6,576)
Higgins, Patrick J	3:49:24 (8,674)
Higgs, Andrew D	5:46:44 (31,897)
Higgs, Andrew D	5:53:48 (32,393)
Higgs, David J	4:26:39 (18,706)
Higgs, Matthew	5:09:49 (28,117)
Higgs, Philip G	4:57:49 (26,250)
Higgs, Terence A	3:47:32 (8,227)
Highfield, Colin R	3:15:14 (2,660)
Highfield, Mark	4:05:04 (13,062)
Hignell, David A	4:40:23 (22,282)
Higson, Martin	5:23:47 (29,779)
Higson, Paul	4:23:35 (17,890)
Higton, Mark C	4:44:51 (23,385)
Hilaire, John M	4:02:39 (12,533)
Hildebrandt, Charles R	3:27:47 (4,416)
Hildenbrandt, Erich	4:17:07 (16,128)
Hilditch, Peter T	5:13:58 (28,670)
Hiles, Paul A	4:12:08 (14,843)
Hiley, Paul	2:59:54 (1,158)
Hilkowitz, Robert	4:50:45 (24,782)
Hill, Alec J	3:59:38 (11,724)
Hill, Andrew	4:31:22 (19,983)
Hill, Andrew D	3:45:57 (7,883)
Hill, Andrew J	4:21:01 (17,188)
Hill, Anthony W	5:09:00 (27,971)
Hill, Brett	4:07:31 (13,645)
Hill, Brian	5:48:54 (32,041)
Hill, Chris	3:52:03 (9,318)
Hill, Chris	4:30:15 (19,690)
Hill, Christopher C	4:52:17 (25,101)
Hill, David R	4:26:23 (18,629)
Hill, Edward C	3:48:34 (8,482)
Hill, Fraser	3:45:12 (7,728)
Hill, Gary M	4:50:32 (24,727)
Hill, Graham	3:54:06 (9,903)
Hill, Iain G	4:07:46 (13,710)
Hill, Jeremy P	6:07:43 (33,034)
Hill, Julian	4:21:54 (17,422)
Hill, Julian	4:58:24 (26,361)
Hill, Kenneth	2:59:49 (1,151)
Hill, Martin T	3:55:47 (10,429)
Hill, Matthew	4:49:31 (24,478)
Hill, Michael J	5:13:27 (28,603)
Hill, Michael V	3:24:28 (3,840)
Hill, Nicholas	3:43:18 (7,306)
Hill, Nigel L	4:24:59 (18,259)
Hill, Patrick A	3:38:44 (6,396)
Hill, Paul	5:33:32 (30,788)
Hill, Paul D	4:13:46 (15,243)
Hill, Paul W	3:44:16 (7,505)
Hill, Raymond	3:02:05 (1,314)
Hill, Roger M	3:48:24 (8,440)
Hill, Simon C	3:05:42 (1,573)
Hill, Simon J	3:08:29 (1,837)
Hill, Stephen J	4:02:41 (12,540)
Hill, Stephen T	4:14:00 (15,302)
Hill, Stuart P	3:17:26 (2,924)
Hill, Tim J	4:56:54 (26,052)
Hill, Timothy	3:59:28 (11,662)
Hill, Walter J	3:03:10 (1,389)
Hillary, Matthew	2:59:59 (1,166)
Hillery, Simon G	5:30:26 (30,520)
Hilliage, Neil J	4:44:51 (23,385)
Hilliard, David J	4:51:18 (24,905)
Hillier, Neil E	3:03:07 (1,382)
Hillier, Nigel G	3:28:07 (4,491)
Hillis, Tom P	4:45:31 (23,541)
Hillman, Mark R	5:42:18 (31,521)
Hillman, Paul	4:18:10 (16,393)
Hills, Adam S	3:14:10 (2,494)
Hills, Jason R	6:35:33 (33,787)
Hills, Martin P	4:30:18 (19,698)
Hills, Steven G	4:34:55 (20,940)
Hills, Trevor D	4:50:48 (24,795)
Hills, Vernon J	4:15:42 (15,745)
Hills, Wayne	3:58:01 (11,122)
Hillyer, Stuart D	5:00:04 (26,648)
Hilmer, Bengt Ove	4:48:06 (24,162)
Hilton, Jon-Paul C	2:55:25 (772)

Hilton, Mark	5:46:33 (31,882)
Hilton, Martin	4:00:04 (11,867)
Hilton, Michael G	4:23:49 (17,943)
Hilton, Russ A	4:42:26 (22,786)
Hilton, Stephen	3:08:49 (1,857)
Hilton, Travis A	4:19:24 (16,723)
Hinchelwood, Richard	5:14:29 (28,738)
Hincks, Tim	3:50:57 (9,036)
Hind, Andy	4:53:37 (25,404)
Hind, Neil D	5:11:57 (28,404)
Hindell, James G	4:36:39 (21,402)
Hindes, Michael P	4:34:34 (20,836)
Hindley, David J	3:57:42 (11,017)
Hindocha, Amit S	4:46:33 (23,789)
Hinds, Carlos	5:56:10 (32,533)
Hinds, David B	4:02:08 (12,396)
Hine, Adrian J	3:48:55 (8,559)
Hiner, Mike J	4:49:01 (24,376)
Hines, Richard L	3:29:51 (4,849)
Hingston, Joe	3:43:45 (7,400)
Hinks, Peter	4:43:55 (23,156)
Hinnells, Duncan	4:52:39 (25,185)
Hinns, Kevin	3:04:43 (1,496)
Hinsley, Jeff	4:20:29 (17,020)
Hinson, Damien	4:29:34 (19,529)
Hinson, Robert	4:41:18 (22,513)
Hinton, Paul A	4:35:27 (21,098)
Hinz, Ludwig	4:39:06 (22,005)
Hiorns, Steve R	2:59:08 (1,077)
Hiorth, Erling	4:27:24 (18,932)
Hipkin, John W	4:32:29 (20,293)
Hipkiss, Adrian M	4:15:31 (15,711)
Hipp, Gerhard	3:37:11 (6,098)
Hirani, Narendra R	3:31:43 (5,173)
Hird, Kean H	4:36:46 (21,434)
Hirons, Gary R	4:46:02 (23,678)
Hirons, Nicholas	5:06:50 (27,672)
Hirrell, John P	4:22:38 (17,627)
Hirschorn, Logis	5:25:50 (30,013)
Hirst, David A	4:05:41 (13,218)
Hirst, John	5:37:33 (31,158)
Hirst, Paul J	3:48:06 (8,374)
Hirst, Russell J	6:06:09 (32,988)
Hiscock, Jonathan N	2:39:02 (182)
Hitchcock, Paul W	4:19:25 (16,728)
Hitchcock, Simon J	5:17:46 (29,150)
Hitchens, Nicholas J	3:53:20 (9,673)
Hitching, Ian	4:55:21 (25,757)
Hitchings, Andrew M	4:49:52 (24,564)
Hixson, Richard C	4:49:45 (24,543)
Hizzey, Robert J	3:47:40 (8,273)
Hlobo, Rampeoane	4:42:46 (22,868)
Ho, Simon	4:00:35 (11,998)
Hoad, Mark	3:21:12 (3,384)
Hoadley, James	3:39:58 (6,635)
Hoar, Alan G	6:24:46 (33,542)
Hoar, Francis J	3:30:22 (4,949)
Hoare, Christopher J	5:07:00 (27,694)
Hoare, Ian P	2:56:13 (822)
Hoare, John W	4:48:37 (24,274)
Hoare, Philip	4:00:39 (12,017)
Hoath, Mark	4:16:39 (15,997)
Hoban, Neil W	4:01:18 (12,184)
Hobbis, Stuart	4:29:57 (19,621)
Hobbs, Ben	4:15:13 (15,682)
Hobbs, Chris G	3:20:55 (3,343)
Hobbs, Chris M	4:02:12 (12,417)
Hobbs, Daniel P	3:15:56 (2,749)
Hobbs, Jonathan M	2:53:16 (655)
Hobbs, Mark S	3:12:51 (2,312)
Hobbs, Matthew I	4:13:56 (15,285)
Hobbs, Michael J	3:30:43 (5,002)
Hobbs, Peter B	3:56:45 (10,708)
Hobbs, Robert S	5:13:33 (28,615)
Hobbs, Roger P	3:19:09 (3,113)
Hobbs, Stephen M	3:20:11 (3,245)
Hobbs, Terry J	6:04:08 (32,892)
Hobday, Barry V	4:06:59 (13,514)
Hobday, Michael E	3:25:34 (4,025)
Hobden, David B	5:37:45 (31,175)
Hobson, Charles J	5:24:00 (29,806)
Hobson, Christian J	4:13:51 (15,259)
Hobson, Kevin M	6:02:10 (32,826)

Hobson, Philip A.	5:39:57 (31,327)	
Hobson, Robert G.	3:57:24 (10,928)	
Hockley, Ryan J	4:52:28 (25,136)	
Hodder, Shaun	3:45:17 (7,752)	
Hoddinott, Jake	4:31:01 (19,887)	
Hodge, Kenneth	4:19:16 (16,693)	
Hodge, Matthew J	3:46:21 (7,965)	
Hodge, Richard F.	3:30:13 (4,927)	
Hodge, Steve	4:33:38 (20,618)	
Hodges, Matthew D	4:38:29 (21,828)	
Hodges, Nick	2:37:23 (152)	
Hodges, Peter T	2:53:33 (664)	
Hodges, Simon C	3:44:42 (7,604)	
Hodgins, David C	2:53:30 (662)	
Hodgkin, Christopher J	3:39:35 (6,556)	
Hodgkins, Andrew R	3:50:50 (9,014)	
Hodgkinson, David J	4:11:21 (14,633)	
Hodgkinson, Robin S	4:15:47 (15,780)	
Hodgkiss, Ian J	4:21:01 (17,188)	
Hodgson, Adam	5:18:18 (29,208)	
Hodgson, Andrew	3:07:44 (1,757)	
Hodgson, Andrew	3:37:50 (6,224)	
Hodgson, Duncan	3:32:45 (5,353)	
Hodgson, Duncan L	4:58:20 (26,348)	
Hodgson, Grant L	5:24:34 (29,865)	
Hodgson, John	6:33:30 (33,737)	
Hodgson, Lee	4:29:09 (19,439)	
Hodgson, Michael I	4:25:17 (18,336)	
Hodgson, Timothy D	5:37:21 (31,145)	
Hodgson, Tom A	3:13:22 (2,383)	
Hodgson, Tony	3:25:50 (4,075)	
Hodkinson, Paul A	5:14:21 (28,729)	
Hodkinson, Robin I	3:21:58 (3,487)	
Hodkinson, Thomas R	5:53:17 (32,357)	
Hodson, Anthony B	5:09:36 (28,072)	
Hodson, Steven L	4:45:44 (23,598)	
Hodson, Tony	3:51:16 (9,113)	
Hoe, Bryan P	5:00:23 (26,692)	
Hoeflinger, Peter	5:41:09 (31,426)	
Hoehn, Christian	3:31:55 (5,203)	
Hoelzl, Andreas	3:28:44 (4,609)	
Hoem, Jan Willy	3:35:21 (5,764)	
Hoey, Kenneth	3:20:11 (3,245)	
Hoey, Paul	4:08:49 (13,993)	
Hoffelner, James C	4:53:29 (25,368)	
Hoffman, James C	3:03:17 (1,400)	
Hoffman, Mark E	4:11:47 (14,745)	
Hoffman, Thomas J	5:05:21 (27,450)	
Hofmann, Raymond	3:30:24 (4,954)	
Hogan, Andrew	4:53:13 (25,318)	
Hogan, Gary	5:09:46 (28,109)	
Hogan, Graham S	2:53:57 (690)	
Hogan, James	3:38:21 (6,327)	
Hogan, Michael J	3:15:09 (2,647)	
Hogan, Michael P	4:33:26 (20,556)	
Hogan, Paul	3:52:31 (9,437)	
Hogarth, Paul M	4:01:33 (12,255)	
Hogarth, Thomas J	4:10:43 (14,467)	
Hogarty, Frank M	4:42:53 (22,901)	
Hogben, David A	5:14:15 (28,713)	
Hogg, Andrew N	5:12:30 (28,464)	
Hogg, Douglas R	5:04:59 (27,397)	
Hogg, Michael J	4:27:00 (18,812)	
Hogg, Paul R	3:26:17 (4,150)	
Hogg, Philip J	3:49:30 (8,701)	
Hogg, Richard J	3:23:40 (3,722)	
Hogg, Roland M	4:30:46 (19,823)	
Hohmann, Lee A	3:57:41 (11,006)	
Holah, Daniel J	4:03:56 (12,812)	
Holborn, Adrian	3:36:28 (5,961)	
Holby, David J	6:43:15 (33,945)	
Holcroft, Clyde M	5:01:23 (26,858)	
Holda, Bartlomiej	3:03:21 (1,407)	
Holdaway, Les B	4:31:07 (19,915)	
Holdcroft, Philip J	2:57:46 (927)	
Holdcroft, Philip J	3:51:52 (9,265)	
Holden, Alan	5:14:03 (28,679)	
Holden, Brian	4:50:14 (24,650)	
Holden, Christopher D	3:18:33 (3,052)	
Holden, Christopher J	4:16:17 (15,901)	
Holden, David F	3:25:18 (3,978)	
Holden, David R	3:41:17 (6,894)	
Holden, Frank	4:49:41 (24,529)	
Holden, Jed	4:04:29 (12,928)	
Holden, John	4:18:34 (16,519)	
Holden, Mark	3:40:26 (6,726)	
Holden, Mark A	3:57:44 (11,029)	
Holden, Matt	2:57:32 (907)	
Holden, Richard	5:24:58 (29,909)	
Holden, Russell	4:18:01 (16,348)	
Holding, Kingsley C	4:31:11 (19,934)	
Holdstock, Brian	4:05:46 (13,235)	
Holdstock, Donald J	3:57:39 (10,995)	
Holdsworth, Mark P	3:47:22 (8,189)	
Holdsworth, Michael Y	5:02:48 (27,082)	
Holdsworth, Ralph J	4:14:43 (15,499)	
Holdsworth, Trevor P	5:48:25 (32,004)	
Holdway, Gideon D	3:56:31 (10,629)	
Hole, Gordon	4:34:07 (20,731)	
Hole, Graham J	3:54:20 (9,968)	
Hole, Steve	3:50:41 (8,985)	
Hole, Wayne D	4:13:51 (15,259)	
Holierhoek, Robert	4:20:23 (16,990)	
Holland, Al	4:27:44 (19,005)	
Holland, Alex J	3:30:38 (4,989)	
Holland, Alistair D	4:18:33 (16,513)	
Holland, Andy M	3:45:21 (7,765)	
Holland, Ashley P	4:55:51 (25,848)	
Holland, Craig	4:36:44 (21,423)	
Holland, David C	3:40:29 (6,731)	
Holland, John D	2:59:13 (1,087)	
Holland, John M	4:48:13 (24,188)	
Holland, Jonathan J	4:11:33 (14,693)	
Holland, Leigh M	4:10:56 (14,531)	
Holland, Mark	3:58:22 (11,251)	
Holland, Mark E	3:36:13 (5,916)	
Holland, Mark J	6:55:39 (34,165)	
Holland, Michael S	3:49:15 (8,644)	
Holland, Oliver A	3:38:24 (6,339)	
Holland, Richard E	3:31:36 (5,151)	
Holland, Steven	4:26:34 (18,685)	
Holland, Warren A	4:10:23 (14,384)	
Hollard, Christopher	4:08:59 (14,036)	
Hollebone, Ryan	5:35:11 (30,954)	
Hollemeersch, Stijn	4:02:11 (12,413)	
Holleran, Clive	3:10:19 (2,020)	
Hollick, Warren	5:15:10 (28,842)	
Holliday, Alex	4:13:12 (15,081)	
Holliday, Stuart	4:11:57 (14,791)	
Holliday, Tom M	4:05:55 (13,270)	
Hollidge, Tommy J	4:29:31 (19,519)	
Hollinger, Mark N	3:52:48 (9,505)	
Hollingshead, Paul	3:34:08 (5,568)	
Hollingsworth, Kristian	3:52:07 (9,345)	
Hollingsworth, Richard	4:39:07 (22,008)	
Hollingsworth, Terry	5:23:28 (29,745)	
Hollingsworth, Timothy D	3:47:36 (8,251)	
Hollingworth, Mark W	3:27:55 (4,448)	
Hollins, Gary J	4:59:12 (26,516)	
Hollinshead, Christopher D	2:40:58 (213)	
Hollinshead, Mark	4:01:02 (12,118)	
Hollis, Ashley S	2:48:34 (452)	
Hollis, Barry S	4:21:58 (17,445)	
Hollis, Jonathan S	4:10:36 (14,433)	
Hollis, Sam J	3:13:25 (2,388)	
Holloway, Peter R	5:31:55 (30,648)	
Hollowell, Michael D	4:55:06 (25,718)	
Hollywood, Bernie P	5:05:37 (27,502)	
Holman, David P	4:21:22 (17,261)	
Holman, James C	4:26:18 (18,610)	
Holman, Tom O	4:01:52 (12,329)	
Holme, Olly J	3:49:23 (8,671)	
Holmes, Adam	3:26:45 (4,240)	
Holmes, Alex	6:35:49 (33,790)	
Holmes, Barry	5:26:08 (30,047)	
Holmes, Christian	3:48:57 (8,567)	
Holmes, Colin	3:35:29 (5,788)	
Holmes, Darrell	5:07:57 (27,819)	
Holmes, Darren	5:16:01 (28,938)	
Holmes, David M	5:08:33 (27,904)	
Holmes, Elton D	4:44:10 (23,219)	
Holmes, Gavin	6:21:50 (33,454)	
Holmes, George V	4:23:10 (17,770)	
Holmes, Graeme R	4:20:31 (17,032)	
Holmes, Ian H	3:14:14 (2,507)	
Holmes, James M	4:11:39 (14,719)	
Holmes, John	6:29:01 (33,638)	
Holmes, Jonathan M	4:05:10 (13,089)	
Holmes, Mark	4:49:13 (24,417)	
Holmes, Nicholas M	2:53:41 (674)	
Holmes, Paul	4:40:04 (22,198)	
Holmes, Peter B	4:09:43 (14,233)	
Holmes, Richard J	3:41:40 (6,961)	
Holmes, Russell J	3:46:15 (7,940)	
Holmes, Sorrel B	4:09:39 (14,215)	
Holohan, Martin D	4:18:15 (16,413)	
Holohan, Tom J	3:55:29 (10,335)	
Holroyd, Brandon	3:22:16 (3,526)	
Holt, Aidan	4:13:41 (15,218)	
Holt, Chris	4:23:27 (17,856)	
Holt, Daniel C	3:53:58 (9,863)	
Holt, Nicholas J	4:23:15 (17,797)	
Holt, Patrick D	3:58:17 (11,208)	
Holt, Roy S	4:19:20 (16,711)	
Holt, Tim	4:24:27 (18,128)	
Holton, Simon J	4:31:49 (20,112)	
Holyoak, Michael J	3:09:02 (1,887)	
Holyoak, Stuart E	3:18:03 (2,991)	
Homan, Tom	4:06:46 (13,466)	
Homer, Mark A	3:44:46 (7,626)	
Homeyard, Lee J	4:29:09 (19,439)	
Homolatsch, Georg	4:30:35 (19,770)	
Honan, Dean G	4:33:35 (20,601)	
Honey, Matthew J	4:18:15 (16,603)	
Honey, Richard	4:58:55 (26,459)	
Honeyball, Willie	3:40:53 (6,802)	
Honeyfield, James R	4:42:52 (22,897)	
Honeyman, Gary	5:01:34 (26,883)	
Honeyman, Richard N	4:44:58 (23,406)	
Honnor, Ian C	3:23:01 (3,641)	
Hooban, Matt	4:45:14 (23,473)	
Hood, Andrew R	3:31:10 (5,070)	
Hood, Anthony J	4:34:43 (20,883)	
Hood, Graeme	3:55:34 (10,365)	
Hood, Jonathan	4:01:34 (12,259)	
Hood, Jonathan	4:43:29 (23,044)	
Hood, Paul	2:59:04 (1,068)	
Hooft, Patrick	3:32:19 (5,281)	
Hook, David J	5:19:51 (29,396)	
Hook, Jeremy D	3:49:42 (8,746)	
Hook, Philip F	3:46:29 (8,004)	
Hook, Simon	4:53:13 (25,318)	
Hook, Trevor L	3:12:13 (2,236)	
Hooker, Andrew	4:26:14 (18,590)	
Hooker, Christopher G	3:58:17 (11,208)	
Hooker, Malcolm J	4:27:13 (18,880)	
Hooker, Michael D	3:48:10 (8,392)	
Hoolahan, Roy M	4:14:53 (15,530)	
Hooles, Michael A	7:14:08 (34,354)	
Hooper, Graham	5:46:59 (31,907)	
Hooper, Marcus P	3:45:16 (7,745)	
Hooper, Martin	3:22:56 (3,626)	
Hooper, Michael J	4:50:57 (24,834)	
Hooper, Nicholas J	3:02:03 (1,311)	
Hooper, Paul D	3:19:20 (3,140)	
Hooper, Paul W	3:30:02 (4,893)	
Hooper, Ronald L	5:01:19 (26,842)	
Hooper, Samuel H	4:21:30 (17,308)	
Hooper, Scott	3:50:10 (8,863)	
Hooper, Tony	3:17:13 (2,889)	
Hooton, Paul	3:57:38 (10,990)	
Hope, Alan C	3:48:48 (8,531)	
Hope, Alex	2:43:54 (291)	
Hope, Gary G	2:35:38 (123)	
Hope, Lee C	6:23:56 (33,516)	
Hope, Peter W	5:29:56 (30,472)	
Hope, Robert R	4:24:45 (18,205)	
Hope, Stuart M	4:23:16 (17,804)	
Hopegood, James	4:45:55 (23,657)	
Hopes, Ben	3:46:50 (8,068)	
Hopfner, Witiko	4:48:48 (24,320)	
Hopkins, Alun J	3:12:21 (2,251)	
Hopkins, Andy	3:42:02 (7,035)	
Hopkins, Christopher J	4:12:57 (15,017)	
Hopkins, Graham A	4:03:52 (12,801)	
Hopkins, Greg	3:45:02 (7,691)	
Hopkins, Mark S	4:59:25 (26,548)	
Hopkins, Martin J	4:16:30 (15,959)	
Hopkins, Mick A	4:39:54 (22,166)	

Hopkins, Rhys W 4:29:16 (19,464)
Hopkins, Stuart D 2:48:19 (435)
Hopkinson, Giles H 3:32:18 (5,278)
Hopkinson, Maxwell J 4:01:35 (12,267)
Hopkinson, Tom 3:23:04 (3,646)
Hopper, Nicholas J 4:07:08 (13,553)
Hopps, Peter W 3:33:42 (5,506)
Hopton, Ioian 5:16:01 (28,938)
Hopwell, Tim 4:19:11 (16,675)
Horan, David J 3:13:40 (2,416)
Hordley, Jeff 3:40:59 (6,820)
Horgan, John 4:48:30 (24,252)
Horler, Mark 5:30:04 (30,482)
Horler, Steven C 4:42:01 (22,676)
Horn, Colin M 4:44:44 (23,352)
Horn, Steven M 4:18:36 (16,534)
Hornby, Fraser 4:41:35 (22,575)
Horncastle, Kevin C 4:04:39 (12,968)
Horne, Andrew 5:45:41 (31,813)
Horne, Andrew C 4:29:21 (19,489)
Horne, Bruce A 3:46:53 (8,078)
Horne, David J 4:13:07 (15,067)
Horne, Louis A 4:26:57 (18,798)
Horne, Louis J 3:39:32 (6,545)
Horne, Nigel C 6:44:04 (33,960)
Horne, Ross F 4:15:22 (15,655)
Horne, Stephen J 4:08:46 (13,985)
Horne, Timothy J 3:33:03 (5,391)
Horner, Jeremy P 3:47:46 (8,289)
Horner, Justin 3:52:49 (9,506)
Horner, Raymond D 3:21:05 (3,371)
Hornsby, Danny 4:31:57 (20,159)
Hornung, Oliver 4:48:05 (24,161)
Horridge, Chris R 3:42:15 (7,081)
Horridge, Dean 5:30:57 (30,560)
Horridge, Mark 5:30:58 (30,563)
Horrocks, David M 3:23:48 (3,737)
Horrocks, John 4:35:20 (21,064)
Horrocks, Richard 3:43:13 (7,290)
Horrocks, Rodney J 4:00:14 (11,905)
Horsley, David R 4:20:02 (16,899)
Horsley, Richard P 4:35:42 (21,168)
Horsman, Joseph 3:41:15 (6,884)
Horsman, Stephen 4:56:43 (26,010)
Horta, Nuno C 4:12:00 (14,812)
Horton, Andrew R 4:19:29 (16,750)
Horton, Clive 3:15:03 (2,638)
Horton, David L 4:44:43 (23,349)
Horton, James C 4:32:05 (20,192)
Horton, Lee 4:21:33 (17,319)
Horton, Michael E 3:33:23 (5,449)
Horton, Peter H 3:11:11 (2,113)
Horton, Richard 4:31:21 (19,978)
Horton, Rob 4:10:36 (14,433)
Horton, Robert M 5:31:13 (30,590)
Horton, Russell 5:14:51 (28,794)
Horton, Simon 3:16:43 (2,837)
Horton, Stephen O 4:30:23 (19,719)
Horton, Tod 3:26:40 (4,224)
Horwood, David 4:14:50 (15,520)
Horwood, Mike J 3:45:01 (7,688)
Hosey, Declan J 4:35:13 (21,035)
Hosken, Simon 4:18:03 (16,354)
Hoskin, Jeremy D 3:52:28 (9,426)
Hoskin, Michael 3:33:07 (5,401)
Hoskins, Andrew 4:07:48 (13,714)
Hoskins, Neil 4:19:32 (16,768)
Hosler, John A 4:36:03 (21,251)
Hosley, Ian D 3:29:33 (4,790)
Hossick, Ian M 4:16:19 (15,907)
Hostin, Ludovic 3:46:07 (7,911)
Houben, Alexander 3:53:32 (9,719)
Houben, Rein M 3:22:16 (3,526)
Houchin, Anthony M 4:50:41 (24,762)
Houden, Jon 3:28:47 (4,621)
Hough, Andrew 3:40:07 (6,660)
Hough, Daniel J 5:32:13 (30,673)
Hough, John 6:47:12 (34,024)
Hough, Martin G 3:04:08 (1,460)
Hough, Tim M 3:54:35 (10,065)
Houghton, Greg 3:22:26 (3,555)
Houghton, Jonathan D 3:50:04 (8,837)
Houghton, Mark A 3:09:28 (1,938)
Houghton, Philip D 4:24:33 (18,159)
Houghton, Robin J 3:42:21 (7,105)
Houghton, Simon J 4:21:24 (17,275)
Houlder, Peter J 4:35:56 (21,220)
Houlford, Rodney 6:51:35 (34,104)
Houlgrave, Paul 4:34:45 (20,891)
Houlihan-Burne, David 3:33:21 (5,447)
Houlot, Geoffroy M 3:30:21 (4,947)
Houlot, Vincent N 3:22:48 (3,611)
Houlpen, Grant P 4:43:30 (23,049)
Hoult, Spencer G 3:57:31 (10,960)
Houlton, Nicholas J 2:38:31 (176)
Hourseau, Pascal 5:28:19 (30,305)
House, Derek J 4:07:08 (13,553)
House, Matt J 3:55:47 (10,429)
House, Trent A 3:41:01 (6,829)
Household, Richard 4:04:02 (12,841)
Housham, Kevin J 4:01:21 (12,200)
Houston, Jamie 5:41:18 (31,442)
Houtby, John F 4:42:11 (22,715)
Hovington, Chris 4:44:00 (23,180)
Howard, Andrew S 3:32:01 (5,228)
Howard, Ben R 3:27:34 (4,372)
Howard, Charles 5:52:32 (32,316)
Howard, Christopher J 3:37:35 (6,180)
Howard, Dave 4:00:51 (12,068)
Howard, Edward J 4:33:40 (20,629)
Howard, Graham W 4:32:29 (20,293)
Howard, Martin J 3:56:57 (10,779)
Howard, Michael B 3:31:52 (5,193)
Howard, Paul J 3:34:01 (5,550)
Howard, Phil 3:11:31 (2,151)
Howard, Phillip J 6:37:55 (33,839)
Howard, Stephen C 3:26:15 (4,145)
Howard, Stewart O 4:05:27 (13,161)
Howard, Thomas W 3:33:56 (5,539)
Howarth, Chris 4:03:24 (12,700)
Howarth, Mark 4:23:00 (17,728)
Howarth, Mark A 3:53:43 (9,775)
Howarth, Raymond 4:37:02 (21,494)
Howarth, Raymond P 3:24:20 (3,820)
Howarth, Richard J 2:52:58 (638)
Howarth, Thomas J 3:24:39 (3,862)
Howat, Gordon 3:56:26 (10,605)
Howden, Daniel S 3:28:06 (4,481)
Howden, David R 6:20:40 (33,414)
Howdon, Michael 4:33:24 (20,540)
Howe, Andrew J 4:08:02 (13,778)
Howe, Bradley 4:01:07 (12,141)
Howe, Darren S 5:49:43 (32,102)
Howe, Gary 3:05:20 (1,540)
Howe, Grahame T 3:52:09 (9,350)
Howe, James E 5:03:50 (27,234)
Howe, Kevin 4:10:21 (14,376)
Howe, Reece K 3:28:38 (4,587)
Howe, Robert L 4:40:56 (22,418)
Howe, Steve 5:44:05 (31,673)
Howe, Steven 3:52:06 (9,337)
Howe, Stewart L 5:02:09 (26,978)
Howe, Stewart T 3:38:55 (6,430)
Howell, Andrew K 4:43:50 (23,132)
Howell, Brendan J 4:18:22 (16,452)
Howell, Christopher E 7:02:04 (34,232)
Howell, Dan 4:03:34 (12,736)
Howell, David 4:01:47 (12,313)
Howell, Duncan M 4:10:43 (14,467)
Howell, Ken F 3:32:09 (5,253)
Howell, Matthew 4:39:04 (21,994)
Howell, Matthew A 3:57:11 (10,858)
Howell, Peter J 3:39:39 (6,565)
Howell, Scott 5:46:46 (31,899)
Howell, Scott J 3:06:08 (1,609)
Howell, Sebastian E 3:11:29 (2,149)
Howells, Ben 4:31:51 (20,123)
Howells, David C 3:30:28 (4,965)
Howells, Gareth J 4:21:39 (17,357)
Howells, Gareth P 5:45:28 (31,801)
Howells, Malcolm 3:23:32 (3,711)
Howells, Phillip B 4:14:17 (15,392)
Howes, Colin T 3:41:45 (6,977)
Howes, Jeremy 4:47:00 (23,910)
Howes, Matthew D 3:05:58 (1,594)
Howes, Ross 5:14:17 (28,719)
Howes, William J 3:39:08 (6,456)
Howey, Christopher A 4:26:26 (18,641)
Howie, Duncan 4:11:33 (14,693)
Howkins, Alex J 5:20:19 (29,440)
Howlader, Hasib R 4:45:26 (23,524)
Howles, Chris 3:59:45 (11,766)
Howlett, Aaron 5:50:09 (32,142)
Howlett, Kevin C 3:31:09 (5,067)
Howley, Vincent 3:12:22 (2,255)
Howram, Martin 3:51:50 (9,254)
Howse, Christopher M 3:19:13 (3,122)
Howsham, John P 3:31:34 (5,149)
Hoy, David A 3:54:35 (10,065)
Hoye, Kenneth C 2:56:44 (858)
Hoyle, Raymond J 7:22:04 (34,410)
Hoyles, Thomas F 5:53:43 (32,388)
Hoyos Ascencio, Luis 4:24:01 (18,000)
Hrabe, Mick 4:32:38 (20,331)
Hrekow, Benjamin J 4:44:02 (23,190)
Htomas, Nick E 3:29:21 (4,751)
Htomas, Nigel R 4:19:56 (16,868)
Hua, Van Hung 5:30:12 (30,498)
Huang, Wenlong 4:42:56 (22,915)
Hubbard, David J 4:19:22 (16,718)
Hubbard, Tim C 3:31:42 (5,169)
Hubbard, Trevor M 4:38:27 (21,818)
Huber, Craig M 4:33:17 (20,504)
Huber, Simon I 3:46:52 (8,074)
Huberman, Paul L 4:06:30 (13,400)
Hubert, Bart 4:56:30 (25,971)
Hubert, Dan 3:44:38 (7,587)
Hubert, Steven S 3:53:45 (9,791)
Huck, Ernest F 3:30:31 (4,974)
Hucker, Ian 4:38:51 (21,929)
Hucker, Kevin D 3:34:53 (5,682)
Hucker, Mark 3:09:38 (1,955)
Hucker, Nicholas A 3:53:36 (9,743)
Huckle, Alan P 3:19:13 (3,122)
Huckle, Philip L 3:47:26 (8,205)
Hucklesby, Tony 3:16:20 (2,795)
Hudd, Timothy J 4:35:33 (21,116)
Huddart, Andrew J 4:22:30 (17,582)
Huddleston, Guy 4:14:32 (15,460)
Hudson, Alex P 5:06:47 (27,664)
Hudson, Andrew 5:08:26 (27,884)
Hudson, Brian D 4:42:04 (22,689)
Hudson, Colin D 4:36:14 (21,308)
Hudson, John W 4:29:26 (19,503)
Hudson, Mark 5:04:07 (27,265)
Hudson, Martin J 5:46:22 (31,867)
Hudson, Michael J 4:28:58 (19,393)
Hudson, Pat 3:15:08 (2,646)
Hudson, Paul A 4:51:59 (25,040)
Hudson, Paul R 4:11:28 (14,665)
Hudson, Sam 5:16:39 (29,013)
Hudson, Simon R 5:04:29 (27,326)
Hudson-Evans, Christian J 5:28:23 (30,310)
Hudspith, John E 2:58:51 (1,047)
Huebner, Fred 4:27:35 (18,974)
Huepe, Hugo 4:16:38 (15,989)
Huett, Colin J 5:08:31 (27,899)
Huges, Oliver J 4:23:44 (17,922)
Huggett, Nicholas 4:28:32 (19,274)
Huggett, Tarkon E 4:22:55 (17,706)
Huggins, Nick T 4:36:35 (21,388)
Huggins, Richard 3:40:39 (6,749)
Hughes, Adrian J 5:44:12 (31,687)
Hughes, Alan J 3:40:54 (6,804)
Hughes, Alastair S 3:38:42 (6,391)
Hughes, Chris 4:35:47 (21,190)
Hughes, Craig J 4:38:51 (21,929)
Hughes, Daniel 4:11:02 (14,551)
Hughes, Daniel 5:07:29 (27,762)
Hughes, Darren A 3:40:55 (6,807)
Hughes, Dave 3:08:40 (1,848)
Hughes, David 7:46:28 (34,500)
Hughes, Dean 3:31:56 (5,208)
Hughes, Dean A 4:45:02 (23,417)
Hughes, Frank D 3:19:36 (3,177)
Hughes, Gareth J 4:53:56 (25,468)
Hughes, Gavin 5:07:57 (27,819)
Hughes, Ian 2:56:53 (864)
Hughes, James 5:27:50 (30,242)

Hughes, Jamie R.	4:20:01 (16,890)	
Hughes, John	6:17:50 (33,350)	
Hughes, John G.	3:58:31 (11,306)	
Hughes, John R.	4:22:19 (17,524)	
Hughes, Jon	5:57:24 (32,601)	
Hughes, Jonathan	4:38:17 (21,775)	
Hughes, Justin	5:20:23 (29,451)	
Hughes, Ken	3:49:39 (8,731)	
Hughes, Kevin A.	4:32:17 (20,249)	
Hughes, Leonard M.	3:13:11 (2,357)	
Hughes, Mark	3:34:08 (5,568)	
Hughes, Mark A.	3:56:37 (10,669)	
Hughes, Mark A.	4:00:41 (12,029)	
Hughes, Mark A.	4:44:20 (23,264)	
Hughes, Martin J.	4:05:23 (13,140)	
Hughes, Martin J.	5:41:30 (31,466)	
Hughes, Michael	4:51:40 (24,980)	
Hughes, Nicholas J.	4:47:52 (24,109)	
Hughes, Nicholas P.	3:27:29 (4,360)	
Hughes, Paul D.	4:04:51 (13,011)	
Hughes, Paul M.	4:52:52 (25,241)	
Hughes, Philip J.	5:11:35 (28,343)	
Hughes, Richard	4:23:21 (17,831)	
Hughes, Richard J.	4:17:36 (16,250)	
Hughes, Robin	3:56:16 (10,555)	
Hughes, Russell D.	4:47:18 (23,986)	
Hughes, Sean	4:44:47 (23,365)	
Hughes, Sean M.	5:11:00 (28,275)	
Hughes, Simon	5:20:19 (29,440)	
Hughes, Simon P.	2:59:45 (1,146)	
Hughes, Stephen F.	3:21:15 (3,395)	
Hughes, Stephen J.	4:25:19 (18,348)	
Hugill, Shane J.	3:39:01 (6,440)	
Hugonnet, Blaise	3:50:28 (8,924)	
Huhges, Dorian G.	3:45:33 (7,800)	
Huille, Alexandre.	3:37:43 (6,203)	
Huille, Matthieu	3:36:03 (5,890)	
Hulbert, Martin	3:27:17 (4,330)	
Hulbert, Thomas H.	4:06:35 (13,420)	
Hulcoop, Stephen V	4:57:18 (26,142)	
Hulett, Carl S.	3:01:14 (1,255)	
Hull, Alan	4:48:16 (24,196)	
Hull, David	4:56:40 (25,995)	
Hull, Keith	3:19:04 (3,103)	
Hull, Mark J.	3:36:06 (5,898)	
Hull, Richard	5:56:14 (32,540)	
Hulland, Paul	6:01:27 (32,794)	
Hully, Peter	4:40:17 (22,254)	
Hulme, Ben P.	4:17:51 (16,315)	
Hulme, David	7:03:12 (34,245)	
Hulme, John	4:31:29 (20,022)	
Hulme, Thomas A.	3:55:03 (10,216)	
Hulse, Christopher T	3:14:24 (2,531)	
Hulsmann, Daniel	5:09:54 (28,131)	
Hume, James D	4:43:03 (22,944)	
Hummerson, Jonathan J.	4:39:42 (22,130)	
Humphrey, Keith C.	3:06:09 (1,612)	
Humphrey, Nicholas T	5:40:27 (31,372)	
Humphrey, Simon I	4:14:53 (15,530)	
Humphrey, Thomas	3:50:16 (8,887)	
Humphreys, Daniel P.	4:20:27 (17,011)	
Humphreys, Jake	4:54:34 (25,593)	
Humphreys, Tony	3:53:48 (9,808)	
Humphries, Martin J.	4:32:36 (20,327)	
Humphries, Paul	3:28:35 (4,574)	
Humphries, Paul R	2:49:27 (488)	
Humphries, Stephen	4:34:56 (20,949)	
Hunjan, Sanjay	4:59:22 (26,540)	
Hunnybun, Shaun D.	4:22:12 (17,495)	
Hunot, Jonathan	4:05:56 (13,275)	
Hunt, Anthony C.	4:00:55 (12,086)	
Hunt, Ben A	3:53:07 (9,611)	
Hunt, Bill	5:08:28 (27,888)	
Hunt, Christopher P	3:10:54 (2,089)	
Hunt, Colin M	3:53:58 (9,863)	
Hunt, Craig	3:05:01 (1,520)	
Hunt, Edward P.	5:11:19 (28,309)	
Hunt, Henry N	4:10:10 (14,328)	
Hunt, James C	4:32:27 (20,282)	
Hunt, Lee	4:27:52 (19,051)	
Hunt, Lee M	5:05:33 (27,489)	
Hunt, Matt	3:07:15 (1,700)	
Hunt, Matt S	2:59:21 (1,104)	
Hunt, Matthew	4:00:54 (12,080)	
Hunt, Neil	4:54:46 (25,642)	
Hunt, Peter J	4:13:12 (15,081)	
Hunt, Peter S	5:03:18 (27,154)	
Hunt, Robbie	5:20:19 (29,440)	
Hunt, Robert	4:16:00 (15,837)	
Hunt, Scott	4:11:09 (14,590)	
Hunt, Sean	3:34:56 (5,691)	
Hunt, Shane P	3:00:25 (1,196)	
Hunt, Stephen	4:37:08 (21,512)	
Hunt, Stephen J	3:55:57 (10,477)	
Hunt, Steve B	7:25:33 (34,431)	
Hunt, Steve P.	3:12:53 (2,318)	
Hunt, Tim	3:24:37 (3,860)	
Hunt, Wayne	4:24:24 (18,111)	
Hunter, Alan W	4:17:17 (16,170)	
Hunter, Andrew M	3:40:57 (6,815)	
Hunter, Daniel J	3:25:07 (3,954)	
Hunter, Gareth J	3:29:47 (4,840)	
Hunter, John	3:56:21 (10,577)	
Hunter, Martin W	4:06:24 (13,373)	
Hunter, Scott	5:37:08 (31,125)	
Hunter, Simon D	4:42:35 (22,827)	
Hunter, Tony	3:08:56 (1,869)	
Huntley, Neil	4:32:05 (20,192)	
Hurd, Ashley	4:33:05 (20,452)	
Huret, Claude	3:22:52 (3,617)	
Hurford, Mike J.	3:01:35 (1,281)	
Hurfurt, Gareth J	3:39:35 (6,556)	
Hurhges, Matt D.	3:18:59 (3,097)	
Hurley, Arthur G	3:36:38 (5,984)	
Hurley, Christopher R	4:29:55 (19,613)	
Hurley, Joe	3:01:12 (1,254)	
Hurley, Russell	4:56:19 (25,934)	
Hurn, Paul A	3:55:39 (10,389)	
Hurrell, Geoff	3:22:58 (3,631)	
Hurrell, Mark J	3:09:30 (1,941)	
Hurren, Mark A.	3:59:26 (11,646)	
Hurst, Alan	4:52:47 (25,217)	
Hurst, David	3:50:40 (8,980)	
Hurst, David	6:42:24 (33,918)	
Hurst, David A.	4:28:55 (19,383)	
Hurst, Gary A.	5:30:58 (30,563)	
Hurst, Ian	4:46:17 (23,739)	
Hurstfield, Christopher S	4:17:18 (16,175)	
Hurtado, Carlos.	3:26:36 (4,206)	
Hurtley, Charles	4:38:25 (21,805)	
Hurton, Colin N.	3:34:38 (5,634)	
Husband, Ian S.	3:11:43 (2,176)	
Huse, David M.	5:10:04 (28,158)	
Hussain, Abid	5:26:48 (30,126)	
Hussain, Moklul	4:38:07 (21,743)	
Hussain, Nazir	5:17:45 (29,148)	
Hussain, Tareen	5:39:51 (31,320)	
Hussell, Ben M	5:06:13 (27,585)	
Hussey, Alexander D	2:53:35 (667)	
Hussey, Dennis A.	3:59:51 (11,802)	
Hussey, Joseph	4:19:03 (16,639)	
Hussey, Nick J	5:02:43 (27,068)	
Hussey, Paul	4:08:17 (13,849)	
Hussey, William	4:21:06 (17,206)	
Hussey, William K.	3:27:38 (4,384)	
Hutchen, Timothy R.	3:49:19 (8,653)	
Hutcheon, Dave	4:34:37 (20,849)	
Hutcheon, Adam	4:22:01 (17,457)	
Hutcheson, Christopher F.	4:28:30 (19,264)	
Hutcheson, Luke J	3:54:16 (9,950)	
Hutcheson, Mark M.	3:00:25 (1,196)	
Hutcheson, Michael R	3:59:25 (11,639)	
Hutchings, Richard G	4:50:09 (24,633)	
Hutchinson, Ben	3:54:50 (10,139)	
Hutchinson, Brett G	3:27:10 (4,308)	
Hutchinson, Chris J	4:51:34 (24,950)	
Hutchinson, G Brian.	3:22:13 (3,519)	
Hutchinson, Ian N	3:49:47 (8,769)	
Hutchinson, James	4:09:27 (14,156)	
Hutchinson, Lloyd	5:24:27 (29,853)	
Hutchinson, Peter R	4:07:56 (13,762)	
Hutchison, Iain J	5:35:33 (30,981)	
Hutchison, Michael.	5:35:48 (31,009)	
Hutchison, Robert B	5:35:47 (31,004)	
Hutchison, Scott R	3:24:57 (3,920)	
Hutter, Nicholas J.	4:26:54 (18,786)	
Huttley, Peter.	3:53:00 (9,572)	
Hutton, Charles D	3:14:02 (2,470)	
Hutton, Colin M.	4:29:25 (19,502)	
Hutton, Dean	4:43:39 (23,088)	
Hutton, Nicholas W	4:01:23 (12,210)	
Huus, Howell C	3:40:44 (6,765)	
Huxley, Andrew.	3:50:11 (8,866)	
Huxley, Gareth J	2:48:24 (441)	
Huxstep, Charles N.	3:46:59 (8,104)	
Hyatt, Gary F	3:55:21 (10,298)	
Hyatt-Williams, Tristan.	5:01:39 (26,901)	
Hyde, Ian	5:01:45 (26,924)	
Hyde, Jon C	4:24:39 (18,181)	
Hyde, Richard T.	3:10:30 (2,041)	
Hyde-Blake, Gavin	6:45:11 (33,982)	
Hyder, Malcolm C	3:22:49 (3,612)	
Hyde-Smith, Oliver	3:05:37 (1,562)	
Hynd, Mike	4:54:55 (25,676)	
Hynes, Andrew R.	3:40:56 (6,811)	
Hynne, Bjoernar	3:28:38 (4,587)	
Ibarra, Javier	4:27:34 (18,967)	
Ibba, Silvestro	4:29:04 (19,417)	
Ibbett, Neal A	4:02:56 (12,592)	
Ibbotson-Ducker, Andrew S.	4:01:22 (12,202)	
Ibison, Garry.	3:51:26 (9,162)	
Ibiza, José	3:29:53 (4,862)	
Ibrahim, Jaf.	4:12:32 (14,936)	
Ide, Philip J.	3:12:54 (2,325)	
Idowu, Fidelis	3:56:28 (10,619)	
Igbokwe, Geoff G	4:19:01 (16,633)	
Ikie, Victor O	4:48:45 (24,307)	
Iles-Smith, Peter C	5:33:35 (30,793)	
Iley, Paul	4:59:34 (26,568)	
Illingworth, Colin J	4:45:54 (23,651)	
Illingworth, Miles J.	4:23:12 (17,786)	
Ilott, James	5:13:24 (28,595)	
Ilsley, Mark D	4:51:24 (24,924)	
Ilsley, Nigel	5:47:24 (31,944)	
Imam, Hisham	4:44:54 (23,395)	
Imberg, Petri M	3:00:16 (1,185)	
Imehli, Mohamed	3:18:38 (3,059)	
Imeson, Michael D	3:55:08 (10,246)	
Impallomeni, Tom	4:29:02 (19,408)	
Impey, Robert J.	4:33:27 (20,562)	
Imrie, Gavin A	3:56:53 (10,756)	
Ince, Carl S	4:37:40 (21,634)	
Ince, Mark G.	3:17:20 (2,905)	
Ind, Andrew J	3:06:45 (1,661)	
Ind, Stephen B	3:40:40 (6,751)	
India Navarro, Francisco J	3:29:30 (4,782)	
Ing, John L	3:42:50 (7,201)	
Ingels, Peter.	4:11:47 (14,745)	
Ingham, Lee	4:08:34 (13,931)	
Ingham, Mark R	4:33:12 (20,482)	
Ingham, Paul J.	3:48:26 (8,451)	
Ingham, Troy J.	3:50:55 (9,032)	
Ingle, Philip M	3:13:21 (2,381)	
Ingleby, David S.	4:13:40 (15,213)	
Ingledew, Neil.	3:21:55 (3,475)	
Ingles, Richard D	5:36:03 (31,037)	
Ingleson, Martin S.	3:10:23 (2,028)	
Inglis, David	5:13:21 (28,583)	
Inglis, John	3:27:40 (4,392)	
Inglis, Stuart J	3:40:29 (6,731)	
Ingram, Alexander G	4:33:23 (20,537)	
Ingram, Anthony	4:43:22 (23,018)	
Ingram, Gareth P	5:02:07 (26,974)	
Ingram, Michael J	3:58:33 (11,317)	
Ingram, Michael W	4:26:25 (18,639)	
Ingram, Nicholas J	4:26:24 (18,635)	
Ingrouille, Scott M	3:52:24 (9,412)	
Ings, Ross A	3:22:58 (3,631)	
Ings, Russell	4:22:08 (17,476)	
Ing-Simmons, Christopher H.	3:58:00 (11,116)	
Inman, Ben J	4:07:01 (13,522)	
Inman, Matthew P.	3:29:12 (4,714)	
Inman, Tom W	3:27:19 (4,336)	
Innes, Iain	3:58:24 (11,261)	
Innes, Richard G	3:48:02 (8,358)	
Innis, Marlon	5:37:31 (31,154)	
Inskip, Alan	6:34:08 (33,753)	
Inwood, Graham J	6:04:59 (32,924)	
Ioannou, John	4:36:01 (21,246)	

Ioannou, John M....4:58:32 (26,380)
Iparragirre, Asier....3:29:10 (4,707)
Iredale, Nigel....4:30:42 (19,800)
Ireland, Alasdair R....3:33:41 (5,504)
Ireland, Ian....4:35:56 (21,220)
Irisawa, Masahiro....4:34:02 (20,705)
Irish, Steve....4:26:36 (18,695)
Irlam, Jim C....3:20:00 (3,227)
Irons, Andrew J....4:09:55 (14,283)
Irons, Graham....3:18:58 (3,095)
Irons, Matthew....4:18:43 (16,556)
Irvine, Duncan S....3:26:37 (4,209)
Irvine, James....3:27:49 (4,426)
Irvine, Robert N....3:26:29 (4,186)
Irvine, Thomas W....3:44:50 (7,639)
Irvine Brown, Richard....3:48:35 (8,483)
Irving, Christopher M....4:57:57 (26,271)
Isaac, Vincent....3:26:54 (4,261)
Isaacs, Andrew J....3:42:43 (7,175)
Isaacs, Jonny....3:56:44 (10,702)
Isaacs, Mark....4:40:07 (22,215)
Isconte, Patrick....2:57:16 (893)
Iseke, Hans....3:38:31 (6,361)
Isely, Robert E....3:44:11 (7,489)
Isherwood, Jonathan R....4:34:49 (20,908)
Isherwood, Mark A....5:42:02 (31,500)
Isherwood, Roger D....4:50:09 (24,633)
Islam, Sayeed Z....3:47:30 (8,223)
Isle, Matthew J....3:33:55 (5,534)
Isman, Renaud....4:42:46 (22,868)
Isnardi, Tino....3:40:20 (6,695)
Issroff, Anthony....3:58:45 (11,389)
Ithell, Mark....5:54:09 (32,415)
Itkin, Simon E....4:16:59 (16,088)
Iuliano, Domenico....3:51:50 (9,254)
Ive, Martin J....3:07:24 (1,725)
Ivens, Derek M....3:15:49 (2,730)
Iversen Tiller, Bjorn....3:21:00 (3,360)
Ives, Colin....5:57:27 (32,604)
Ives, Kevin M....3:56:49 (10,730)
Ivins, Matthew....5:07:12 (27,719)
Ivory, Anthony M....3:28:37 (4,583)
Ivory, Julian....4:03:14 (12,665)
Ivory, Kenneth J....2:58:53 (1,053)
Iwegbu, Charles....6:44:21 (33,966)
Iwlliams, David G....4:50:13 (24,644)
Jaber, Jaber A....7:21:42 (34,407)
Jack, Angus R....4:53:19 (25,335)
Jack, Keith M....5:01:30 (26,871)
Jack, Michael J....3:50:50 (9,014)
Jack, Peter....3:59:39 (11,734)
Jack, Rodney....6:12:26 (33,186)
Jackaman, Robert....2:46:00 (362)
Jacki, Swen H....3:53:35 (9,737)
Jackman, Marcus I....4:41:48 (22,637)
Jackman, Stephen P....3:39:07 (6,454)
Jackson, Adrian G....4:53:33 (25,387)
Jackson, Alfred....4:11:52 (14,772)
Jackson, Andrew....2:51:57 (592)
Jackson, Anthony B....2:37:24 (154)
Jackson, Anthony C....2:49:46 (499)
Jackson, Anthony R....2:37:26 (156)
Jackson, Ben....4:24:30 (18,143)
Jackson, Charlie P....4:07:29 (13,636)
Jackson, Chris....3:49:27 (8,686)
Jackson, Christian....4:58:52 (26,446)
Jackson, Darren A....4:21:42 (17,374)
Jackson, David....4:20:05 (16,908)
Jackson, David G....4:19:17 (16,701)
Jackson, David J....5:25:42 (30,003)
Jackson, Dominic H....4:16:54 (16,061)
Jackson, Duncan M....3:56:20 (10,573)
Jackson, Howard....4:16:57 (16,074)
Jackson, Ian C....4:47:08 (23,940)
Jackson, Joe....4:44:41 (23,342)
Jackson, Kevin A....3:53:48 (9,808)
Jackson, Kevin J....3:24:28 (3,840)
Jackson, Laurence G....3:28:47 (4,621)
Jackson, Lee G....5:23:11 (29,715)
Jackson, Lee R....3:02:11 (1,320)
Jackson, Leslie....4:33:24 (20,540)
Jackson, Mark P....5:22:23 (29,649)
Jackson, Martyn R....4:17:24 (16,190)
Jackson, Mathew I....4:37:04 (21,499)
Jackson, Neil....2:46:15 (368)
Jackson, Neil....3:35:04 (5,713)
Jackson, Neil....4:18:39 (16,542)
Jackson, Neil....4:22:52 (17,691)
Jackson, Nick M....3:50:11 (8,866)
Jackson, Nigel G....4:08:26 (13,890)
Jackson, Paul....5:13:36 (28,622)
Jackson, Paul J....4:31:17 (19,961)
Jackson, Paul B....3:06:54 (1,675)
Jackson, Paul P....5:33:20 (30,777)
Jackson, Paul T....3:48:14 (8,407)
Jackson, Pete....4:50:25 (24,688)
Jackson, Peter N....4:46:41 (23,823)
Jackson, Richard N....5:11:10 (28,289)
Jackson, Robert E....4:02:31 (12,499)
Jackson, Simon M....4:52:04 (25,059)
Jackson, Simon W....3:25:33 (4,020)
Jackson, Simon W....3:51:57 (9,287)
Jackson, Stephen R....5:10:11 (28,171)
Jackson, Steven....4:42:53 (22,901)
Jackson, Stewart W....5:31:33 (30,615)
Jackson, Sydney I....4:12:22 (14,900)
Jackson, Tim....3:26:16 (4,148)
Jackson, Tim D....5:43:12 (31,587)
Jaco, Matthew J....4:08:30 (13,909)
Jacob, James....4:24:25 (18,114)
Jacobs, Alan....4:06:35 (13,420)
Jacobs, Colin B....3:23:17 (3,673)
Jacobs, Darrel W....5:05:43 (27,512)
Jacobs, Darrell M....4:03:01 (12,611)
Jacobs, Doug....4:52:32 (25,154)
Jacobs, Lee....3:23:43 (3,729)
Jacobs, Mark....4:41:34 (22,570)
Jacobs, Nick E....3:19:12 (3,120)
Jacobs, Paul....3:35:56 (5,865)
Jacobs, Ricki....4:24:09 (18,033)
Jacobs, Robert E....3:07:46 (1,763)
Jacobsen, Roger....4:56:07 (25,898)
Jacobson, Brett....3:31:30 (5,127)
Jacoto, Marcelo....4:14:48 (15,515)
Jacques, Marc....2:54:00 (692)
Jacques, William....4:38:11 (21,752)
Jaenisch, Frank....3:28:35 (4,574)
Jaffa, Adam K....3:52:22 (9,401)
Jaffe, Peter S....3:31:19 (5,102)
Jagger, Mark C....3:16:30 (2,816)
Jagger, Martyn K....4:47:15 (23,969)
Jagger, Tom....3:32:22 (5,293)
Jagiello, Jakub M....4:40:25 (22,290)
Jago, Stephen J....4:19:42 (16,814)
Jagpal, Navdeep S....6:38:11 (33,849)
Jagutpal, Previn....5:28:56 (30,371)
Jahans, Stephen D....4:43:56 (23,162)
Jaime, Ricardo....3:01:36 (1,283)
Jain, Manish....5:06:41 (27,650)
Jakic, Marko....4:12:07 (14,840)
Jakobs, Juergen....5:09:07 (27,984)
Jallo, Abdul A....4:21:51 (17,412)
Jalloh, Amadu A....2:47:50 (416)
Jama, Ibrahim A....5:50:07 (32,138)
Jamalullail, Syed Haizam....6:25:30 (33,564)
James, Adam....5:36:52 (31,108)
James, Adam L....4:50:30 (24,715)
James, Alistair....6:38:59 (33,865)
James, Alun....4:21:57 (17,442)
James, Alun....6:09:24 (33,094)
James, Brian....3:43:04 (7,255)
James, Brian A....5:31:56 (30,651)
James, Colin....2:52:59 (639)
James, David....3:35:04 (5,713)
James, David C....4:30:52 (19,855)
James, Gareth R....3:28:51 (4,635)
James, Hamish E....4:42:03 (22,683)
James, Ian M....4:11:26 (14,656)
James, Jay....4:44:52 (23,391)
James, John W....3:15:44 (2,720)
James, Keith M....3:52:49 (9,506)
James, Keith R....4:19:05 (16,651)
James, Mark D....3:43:01 (7,243)
James, Matthew R....4:25:10 (18,310)
James, Neil A....4:50:28 (24,703)
James, Oliver D....4:14:19 (15,401)
James, Owen....3:14:30 (2,546)
James, Paul....3:57:38 (10,990)
James, Paul L....4:28:24 (19,232)
James, Philip L....4:38:56 (21,954)
James, Richard M....3:58:51 (11,440)
James, Robert S....2:38:27 (175)
James, Russell J....3:53:32 (9,719)
James, Ryan P....3:40:37 (6,746)
James, Simon A....2:45:04 (336)
James, Steven....3:18:51 (3,079)
James, Vincent....5:29:09 (30,392)
Jameson, Tom I....4:16:29 (15,957)
Jameson, William G....6:36:43 (33,813)
Jamieson, Mark J....4:15:46 (15,774)
Jamieson, Robin L....3:53:56 (9,849)
Jandu, Rendeep....6:27:32 (33,613)
Jane, Christopher J....4:16:58 (16,082)
Jane, Sonnie-Lee G....5:33:48 (30,814)
Janes, Mark I....4:01:09 (12,148)
Janes, Michael R....4:59:36 (26,574)
Janes, Paul E....3:13:53 (2,447)
Janiaud, Pascal....3:12:53 (2,318)
Janikiewicz, Andrew S....4:37:53 (21,693)
Janikiewicz, Dougie J....4:00:13 (11,901)
Janion, Pierre....3:56:59 (10,788)
Janjuha, Sohail A....4:00:56 (12,096)
Jankowiak, Maciej....4:09:00 (14,041)
Jansen, Graham....3:55:39 (10,389)
Jansen, Raf R....3:26:12 (4,138)
Janssen, Willem....4:39:41 (22,122)
Janssens, Alistair....4:50:07 (24,625)
Jany, Chris H....4:28:09 (19,151)
Janz, Henry....7:25:22 (34,428)
Jarad, Anthony....5:42:54 (31,561)
Jaramillo Aguado, Carlos....2:59:22 (1,106)
Jardine, William L....5:37:35 (31,161)
Jarman, Charles K....4:18:16 (16,421)
Jarman, Derek I....5:56:43 (32,567)
Jarman, Nick D....4:02:04 (12,378)
Jarman, Rhys....4:50:58 (24,837)
Jarosz, Adam R....4:05:05 (13,067)
Jarred, Robert A....4:37:37 (21,621)
Jarrey, Christopher D....6:16:35 (33,314)
Jarvill, Chris....4:00:15 (11,909)
Jarvis, Andrew G....4:07:23 (13,608)
Jarvis, Dean W....3:48:43 (8,517)
Jarvis, Ian....4:33:28 (20,567)
Jarvis, Ian J....5:43:16 (31,594)
Jarvis, Justin....3:59:39 (11,734)
Jarvis, Mark....3:23:33 (3,714)
Jarvis, Paul....4:20:31 (17,032)
Jarvis, Robert A....5:52:04 (32,292)
Jarvis, Steve....4:05:08 (13,080)
Jarvis, Tony....5:59:51 (32,731)
Jashapara, Dipak....6:43:51 (33,956)
Jasinevicius, Mindaugas....4:50:34 (24,740)
Jasper, Richard E....3:58:37 (11,341)
Jassani, Yassar....5:30:46 (30,552)
Jaubert, Fabrice....4:03:30 (12,727)
Jauncey, Lee....4:11:10 (14,597)
Jaunich, Volker....4:07:24 (13,612)
Jaunin, Marc-Henri....2:37:59 (168)
Javed, Tariq....4:50:25 (24,688)
Javens, Barrie....4:50:14 (24,650)
Javicoli, Gerard....4:35:14 (21,039)
Jawor, Paul A....4:36:54 (21,464)
Jaworski, Edward Z....4:53:45 (25,426)
Jawse Van Rensburg, Petrus J....3:24:41 (3,867)
Jay, Stephen A....3:47:20 (8,181)
Jeacock, Simon E....4:17:04 (16,112)
Jeal, Paul A....3:48:21 (8,431)
Jean-Claude, Rotiel....4:37:47 (21,663)
Jean-Jacques, Pierre-Yves....4:17:00 (16,095)
Jean-Paul, Desmond....4:18:41 (16,550)
Jeans, Paul D....3:45:16 (7,745)
Jebb, David A....3:46:12 (7,927)
Jeffcoat, Mark....4:18:43 (16,556)
Jefferies, Christopher....2:58:20 (982)
Jefferies, Mark J....3:26:19 (4,161)
Jeffery, Daniel J....4:51:34 (24,950)
Jeffery, David L....3:04:09 (1,462)
Jeffery, Graham K....5:47:29 (31,951)
Jeffery, Kevin....5:59:41 (32,725)

Jeffery, Michael............4:34:55 (20,940)
Jeffery, Mike P 4:30:53 (19,863)
Jefferys, Luke D 3:39:45 (6,591)
Jefford, Mark 3:07:30 (1,732)
Jeffrey, Dan M 3:34:39 (5,635)
Jeffrey, John 4:47:35 (24,038)
Jeffrey, Tom 3:47:19 (8,180)
Jeffreys, John 3:42:24 (7,116)
Jeffreys, Karl R 3:44:16 (7,505)
Jeffries, Gary S 3:12:13 (2,236)
Jeffries, John L 4:11:48 (14,753)
Jeffries, Kevin J 3:07:45 (1,760)
Jeffs, Mark R 3:50:42 (8,990)
Jefska, David A............4:28:09 (19,151)
Jehring, David E 4:41:47 (22,628)
Jehu, Gareth E............3:32:15 (5,267)
Jelfs, Richard W............3:36:59 (6,061)
Jelley, Craig M 4:07:27 (13,627)
Jelley, Nick 3:57:45 (11,039)
Jellicoe, George N............4:42:17 (22,752)
Jemini, Enrico 3:22:30 (3,564)
Jendrysik, Dieter-Wilhelm............3:20:36 (3,307)
Jenkin, Daniel L 2:47:36 (404)
Jenkins, Andrew 3:51:20 (9,132)
Jenkins, Carl M 3:13:09 (2,352)
Jenkins, Christopher 3:56:37 (10,669)
Jenkins, Christopher 4:56:27 (25,957)
Jenkins, Clifford I............5:22:19 (29,643)
Jenkins, Colin 4:28:31 (19,268)
Jenkins, Dagan 5:20:15 (29,434)
Jenkins, David............4:40:58 (22,425)
Jenkins, David P 4:27:53 (19,058)
Jenkins, David W 4:25:25 (18,373)
Jenkins, Gareth A............3:58:58 (11,478)
Jenkins, Gareth J 4:54:32 (25,586)
Jenkins, Gareth S............2:52:12 (604)
Jenkins, Gary L 5:13:11 (28,569)
Jenkins, Geraint H 3:42:49 (7,198)
Jenkins, Gordon S............6:32:22 (33,711)
Jenkins, Graeme J 3:24:46 (3,882)
Jenkins, Huw R............4:17:43 (16,284)
Jenkins, Huw W 3:05:03 (1,524)
Jenkins, John R............6:12:23 (33,181)
Jenkins, Jonathan M............4:34:08 (20,733)
Jenkins, Michael D 4:04:45 (12,994)
Jenkins, Michael J............5:25:56 (30,029)
Jenkins, Neil D 3:54:18 (9,960)
Jenkins, Paul D 4:15:57 (15,823)
Jenkins, Paul D 6:32:22 (33,711)
Jenkins, Paul J............3:17:40 (2,948)
Jenkins, Peter H 5:40:12 (31,353)
Jenkins, Rob M 3:57:18 (10,890)
Jenkins, Robert............3:48:00 (8,351)
Jenkins, Robert A 4:08:09 (13,817)
Jenkins, Robert E 4:39:12 (22,027)
Jenkins, Robert W 5:15:44 (28,910)
Jenkins, Ron 3:03:23 (1,410)
Jenkins, Simon D............4:11:49 (14,761)
Jenkins, Stephen P 3:49:44 (8,756)
Jenkins, Terry 4:19:31 (16,765)
Jenkins, Timothy............5:23:43 (29,768)
Jenkins, William A............5:27:46 (30,233)
Jenkins, William E............3:15:07 (2,643)
Jenkinson, Damian F 4:18:48 (16,752)
Jenkinson, Gary J............3:58:10 (11,174)
Jenkinson, Mark G 4:45:31 (23,541)
Jenkisn, Darren K............4:06:38 (13,436)
Jenks, Andrew............4:59:28 (26,555)
Jenner, Adam 3:43:28 (7,337)
Jenner, David B 5:19:23 (29,336)
Jenner, Graham A 4:28:56 (19,386)
Jenner, Jack V 3:24:41 (3,867)
Jenner, Jo J 3:39:03 (6,445)
Jennings, Andrew J............4:55:20 (25,753)
Jennings, Barrie C............3:58:59 (11,481)
Jennings, Daryl P 5:13:24 (28,595)
Jennings, David A............5:10:47 (28,248)
Jennings, George C............4:56:36 (25,987)
Jennings, Joe............8:13:39 (34,550)
Jennings, Ken 4:54:42 (25,623)
Jennings, Lee R............4:25:30 (18,397)
Jennings, Nigel L............3:11:41 (2,173)
Jennings, Richard S............3:29:09 (4,703)

Jennings, Roy............5:45:08 (31,776)
Jennings, Shaun 5:03:35 (27,196)
Jennings, Stewart............5:02:35 (27,048)
Jennison, Wesley A............5:30:19 (30,509)
Jenny, Christian 3:01:07 (1,249)
Jensen, Anders 4:53:28 (25,364)
Jensen, Bent 3:22:16 (3,526)
Jensen, Jan 3:31:32 (5,137)
Jensen, Ken A 5:48:33 (32,016)
Jensen, Lloyd A 5:53:05 (32,347)
Jensen, Peter............5:00:16 (26,679)
Jepps, Russell A 4:19:45 (16,825)
Jepson, John C............4:00:28 (11,965)
Jereissati, Demetrio 4:38:49 (21,919)
Jerez Florez, Reinaldo............4:23:17 (17,813)
Jerman, Toby A............4:46:09 (23,700)
Jervis, Graham D 5:46:03 (31,839)
Jerwood, Matthew J............4:32:01 (20,177)
Jess, Michael J............4:47:06 (23,930)
Jessa, Uwe 4:15:58 (15,828)
Jessop, Martin T 4:16:07 (15,858)
Jessup, Clive A 3:35:40 (5,827)
Jest, Andrew N............3:54:44 (10,108)
Jethwa, Dharmendra............4:53:00 (25,269)
Jeudy, Bruno 3:08:05 (1,798)
Jewell, Malcolm R............4:59:07 (26,496)
Jewell, Martin R............3:07:10 (1,696)
Jewett, Barry W 5:39:17 (31,285)
Jewkes, Richard S 3:01:01 (1,244)
Jex, Matthew S 4:53:45 (25,426)
Jimenez, Agustin 5:17:20 (29,100)
Jishi, Hass............5:25:40 (30,002)
Job, Alun T 4:28:20 (19,217)
Jobling, David I 4:41:59 (22,667)
Johal, Gurpal S 5:56:46 (32,569)
Johal, Jaymini............4:03:24 (12,700)
Johannes, Vanderendt 4:47:41 (24,064)
Johannesen, Stein H............4:06:33 (13,415)
Johansson, Bjorn E............6:51:03 (34,091)
Johansson, Jan A 4:22:57 (17,716)
Johansson, Martin 4:39:12 (22,027)
John, Andrew J............3:40:20 (6,695)
John, Christopher 4:02:12 (12,417)
John, Christopher 5:19:54 (29,404)
John, David 3:59:21 (11,613)
John, Duncan 5:57:58 (32,629)
John, Gareth R............5:19:04 (29,298)
John, Gilbert G............4:25:57 (18,519)
John, Lewis D 5:08:24 (27,876)
John, Paul............3:58:39 (11,357)
John, Richard C............3:17:46 (2,960)
John, Steven W 4:09:10 (14,077)
John, William P 4:54:58 (25,694)
Johns, Douglas A 5:05:28 (27,467)
Johns, Douglas E 4:16:59 (16,088)
Johns, Gavin P 4:00:29 (11,969)
Johns, Michael A 4:33:45 (20,649)
Johnson, Andrew C............4:06:02 (13,297)
Johnson, Andrew E 3:55:49 (10,440)
Johnson, Andrew R 5:14:11 (28,700)
Johnson, Anthony C............3:40:59 (6,820)
Johnson, Carl A 4:09:14 (14,097)
Johnson, Chad............2:18:49 (20)
Johnson, Christopher 4:11:48 (14,753)
Johnson, Christopher M............4:29:37 (19,544)
Johnson, Clive I............5:07:33 (27,774)
Johnson, Corun R 4:21:49 (17,409)
Johnson, Cory A 5:09:31 (28,054)
Johnson, Darren............4:05:25 (13,153)
Johnson, Darren J 4:41:06 (22,460)
Johnson, David............6:35:23 (33,783)
Johnson, David B............4:04:11 (12,859)
Johnson, Enda M 2:50:49 (544)
Johnson, Eric 4:40:03 (22,193)
Johnson, Gary............4:38:54 (21,941)
Johnson, Geoffrey J............6:23:52 (33,511)
Johnson, Gerald C............4:31:02 (19,893)
Johnson, Gerry 4:57:25 (26,168)
Johnson, Glenn 4:36:18 (21,324)
Johnson, Guy J............5:00:15 (26,676)
Johnson, Harry S............5:34:50 (30,922)
Johnson, Ian 5:38:47 (31,244)
Johnson, Ian S 4:40:55 (22,410)

Johnson, John D............3:19:14 (3,125)
Johnson, John N............4:04:58 (13,042)
Johnson, Jonathan 3:44:57 (7,672)
Johnson, Kevin 4:10:26 (14,395)
Johnson, Kevin C............5:57:09 (32,585)
Johnson, Kevin L............3:44:35 (7,574)
Johnson, Kirk 4:26:41 (18,716)
Johnson, Liam 4:28:56 (19,386)
Johnson, Martin A............3:29:36 (4,800)
Johnson, Martin M............5:04:27 (27,316)
Johnson, Matthew H............4:24:09 (18,033)
Johnson, Michael A............4:18:55 (16,603)
Johnson, Michael J............3:55:28 (10,331)
Johnson, Michael O............4:38:21 (21,790)
Johnson, Mike 6:55:17 (34,156)
Johnson, Neil............4:18:34 (16,519)
Johnson, Nicholas D 5:38:45 (31,243)
Johnson, Paul 3:12:55 (2,326)
Johnson, Paul T............3:28:38 (4,587)
Johnson, Paul T............4:22:41 (17,645)
Johnson, Paul W............3:14:04 (2,479)
Johnson, Peter............3:50:39 (8,974)
Johnson, Ray D 3:42:50 (7,201)
Johnson, Raymond............6:23:07 (33,495)
Johnson, Richard............4:49:51 (24,562)
Johnson, Richard J............5:46:17 (31,860)
Johnson, Richard M 3:44:16 (7,505)
Johnson, Robert............4:26:41 (18,716)
Johnson, Robert P 3:11:17 (2,125)
Johnson, Stephen A 4:00:31 (11,978)
Johnson, Steven C............5:49:04 (32,059)
Johnson, Stuart J 4:26:56 (18,793)
Johnson, Tony 2:57:15 (892)
Johnson, Tony M 4:19:19 (16,707)
Johnson, Walter D 5:55:00 (32,460)
Johnson, Warwick............4:32:59 (20,427)
Johnsson, Fred 4:04:23 (12,912)
Johnston, David............4:02:08 (12,396)
Johnston, Andrew G............3:53:47 (9,800)
Johnston, Andrew J............3:54:58 (10,184)
Johnston, Greame D 5:01:29 (26,868)
Johnston, John H 4:28:46 (19,335)
Johnston, Kevin D 3:48:51 (8,539)
Johnston, Lea M 4:03:14 (12,665)
Johnston, Magnus D 4:25:49 (18,487)
Johnston, Mark C............3:30:57 (5,046)
Johnston, Mark T 3:34:52 (5,680)
Johnston, Martin P............4:11:37 (14,706)
Johnston, Neal K............2:58:29 (1,006)
Johnston, Paul A 3:07:22 (1,720)
Johnston, Philip R............4:47:16 (23,976)
Johnston, Richard N 5:01:24 (26,863)
Johnston, Robert D 3:55:36 (10,371)
Johnston, Robin A............4:17:38 (16,258)
Johnston, Scott 4:18:55 (16,603)
Johnston, Scott P 3:41:08 (6,856)
Johnston, Simon J 4:45:42 (23,585)
Johnston, Stuart F 4:10:36 (14,433)
Johnstone, Darren 4:26:19 (18,613)
Johnstone, Tom............3:39:31 (6,540)
Johnstone-Robertson, Graeme C ..4:05:23 (13,140)
Joiner, Leigh 5:01:39 (26,901)
Joint, Andrew J 4:39:03 (21,988)
Jolliffe, Jeff............5:25:18 (29,965)
Jolly, Alan 4:09:01 (14,045)
Jolly, Gareth R 4:32:22 (20,264)
Jolly, Steve D 3:47:22 (8,189)
Joly, Olivier C............4:24:09 (18,033)
Jones, Adam O 4:23:45 (17,929)
Jones, Adrian B 6:14:20 (33,255)
Jones, Adrian J............3:05:02 (1,523)
Jones, Alan R 3:50:13 (8,876)
Jones, Allan S............2:38:09 (170)
Jones, Andrew C............3:35:30 (5,791)
Jones, Andrew D............3:49:57 (8,814)
Jones, Andrew F 5:00:51 (26,773)
Jones, Andrew J............3:35:24 (5,775)
Jones, Andrew R 5:14:06 (28,686)
Jones, Andy............2:53:37 (668)
Jones, Andy............4:01:26 (12,224)
Jones, Andy P 2:38:14 (172)
Jones, Andy R 4:34:50 (20,918)
Jones, Anthony A 4:45:16 (23,487)

Jones, Anthony D	4:36:15 (21,312)	
Jones, Anthony S	4:07:23 (13,608)	
Jones, Antony M	4:48:52 (24,335)	
Jones, Arwell W	3:23:40 (3,722)	
Jones, Barrie J	3:23:20 (3,682)	
Jones, Barry J	5:06:17 (27,599)	
Jones, Ben	4:20:42 (17,095)	
Jones, Ben	4:32:44 (20,355)	
Jones, Benjamin L	5:12:34 (28,470)	
Jones, Benjamin M	3:48:19 (8,427)	
Jones, Bernard	5:06:15 (27,591)	
Jones, Breckon K	4:50:11 (24,640)	
Jones, Brian	5:19:04 (29,298)	
Jones, Brian P	3:57:45 (11,039)	
Jones, Chris	3:47:29 (8,219)	
Jones, Chris N	4:46:18 (23,742)	
Jones, Christophe G	4:20:29 (17,020)	
Jones, Christopher D	4:22:10 (17,486)	
Jones, Christopher J	5:45:51 (31,825)	
Jones, Christopher S	3:44:16 (7,505)	
Jones, Colin	5:40:05 (31,337)	
Jones, Colin	6:19:26 (33,387)	
Jones, Craig	4:57:01 (26,084)	
Jones, Dafydd	4:32:46 (20,367)	
Jones, Dai H	5:44:27 (31,718)	
Jones, Daniel J	5:12:40 (28,480)	
Jones, Daniel S	4:10:00 (14,298)	
Jones, Darren J	2:45:15 (341)	
Jones, Darren L	4:01:59 (12,358)	
Jones, Dave	3:57:50 (11,071)	
Jones, David	2:56:03 (809)	
Jones, David	3:59:23 (11,626)	
Jones, David	4:18:55 (16,603)	
Jones, David	4:38:40 (21,871)	
Jones, David	4:42:00 (22,673)	
Jones, David A	3:58:46 (11,397)	
Jones, David A	4:45:04 (23,426)	
Jones, David B	3:51:06 (9,075)	
Jones, David G	5:48:11 (31,989)	
Jones, David H	3:46:13 (7,930)	
Jones, David J	4:35:27 (21,098)	
Jones, David L	6:09:42 (33,107)	
Jones, David M	4:29:38 (19,547)	
Jones, David S	3:44:55 (7,660)	
Jones, Dominic E	4:26:43 (18,731)	
Jones, Dryden G	5:54:57 (32,456)	
Jones, Emyr W	5:04:46 (27,367)	
Jones, Francis A	4:44:00 (23,180)	
Jones, Gareth	4:09:41 (14,220)	
Jones, Gareth	4:27:55 (19,071)	
Jones, Gareth J	4:07:28 (13,633)	
Jones, Gareth L	5:55:04 (32,465)	
Jones, Gareth M	4:12:20 (14,892)	
Jones, Garry	5:14:50 (28,788)	
Jones, Gary A	4:08:35 (13,937)	
Jones, Gary E	4:51:14 (24,887)	
Jones, Gavin M	4:02:14 (12,423)	
Jones, Glyn D	4:46:31 (23,781)	
Jones, Glyn R	3:38:01 (6,263)	
Jones, Glynn T	5:08:55 (27,955)	
Jones, Graham M	6:41:45 (33,905)	
Jones, Greg	4:12:12 (14,860)	
Jones, Gruffydd R	3:28:56 (4,650)	
Jones, Ian G	5:28:10 (30,285)	
Jones, Ian J	4:18:49 (16,579)	
Jones, Jeffrey	5:08:03 (27,831)	
Jones, Jimmie L	3:24:29 (3,845)	
Jones, Joe W	4:56:59 (26,071)	
Jones, John	3:26:34 (4,198)	
Jones, John	4:33:27 (20,562)	
Jones, John A	5:25:20 (29,970)	
Jones, John D	3:26:17 (4,150)	
Jones, John H	4:08:10 (13,825)	
Jones, Johnny C	4:16:20 (15,915)	
Jones, Josh	4:13:27 (15,149)	
Jones, Keith G	3:27:40 (4,392)	
Jones, Keith N	4:20:05 (16,908)	
Jones, Kenneth G	4:49:58 (24,594)	
Jones, Kenneth I	4:39:38 (22,104)	
Jones, Kevin P	4:48:29 (24,243)	
Jones, Lawrence W	3:59:53 (11,813)	
Jones, Lee M	3:48:02 (8,358)	
Jones, Lee R	4:32:40 (20,340)	
Jones, Malcolm	4:21:24 (17,275)	
Jones, Marc R	4:57:04 (26,098)	
Jones, Mark A	4:21:11 (17,220)	
Jones, Mark B	4:32:40 (20,340)	
Jones, Mark P	5:24:18 (29,838)	
Jones, Martin	4:04:42 (12,985)	
Jones, Martin D	4:39:05 (21,999)	
Jones, Matthew C	3:48:04 (8,365)	
Jones, Matthew D	4:41:40 (22,608)	
Jones, Matthew G	4:02:45 (12,553)	
Jones, Matthew J	3:35:04 (5,713)	
Jones, Meirion	5:21:05 (29,506)	
Jones, Michael	3:41:15 (6,884)	
Jones, Michael	3:56:45 (10,708)	
Jones, Michael A	4:54:12 (25,519)	
Jones, Michael C	4:59:17 (26,529)	
Jones, Michael D	2:55:10 (760)	
Jones, Michael E	4:41:39 (22,598)	
Jones, Michael J	4:23:54 (17,963)	
Jones, Milton P	4:19:24 (16,723)	
Jones, Morgan T	3:35:41 (5,829)	
Jones, Nathan	3:38:24 (6,339)	
Jones, Neil	3:53:55 (9,839)	
Jones, Neil	4:46:21 (23,752)	
Jones, Neil	5:23:52 (29,784)	
Jones, Neil D	4:17:41 (16,276)	
Jones, Nicholas C	4:23:02 (17,737)	
Jones, Nick	3:03:49 (1,439)	
Jones, Nigel D	3:06:08 (1,609)	
Jones, Nigel F	3:03:19 (1,403)	
Jones, Nigel H	4:16:37 (15,987)	
Jones, Noel H	3:49:53 (8,794)	
Jones, Norman	5:08:30 (27,896)	
Jones, Oliver	2:57:43 (924)	
Jones, Oliver A	3:50:20 (8,897)	
Jones, Owain C	2:51:00 (552)	
Jones, Owen M	3:47:13 (8,161)	
Jones, Patrick M	3:52:52 (9,526)	
Jones, Paul	4:31:56 (20,147)	
Jones, Paul	4:57:00 (26,080)	
Jones, Paul	6:13:26 (33,225)	
Jones, Paul A	4:02:11 (12,413)	
Jones, Paul D	3:38:05 (6,281)	
Jones, Peter A	3:54:10 (9,924)	
Jones, Peter K	3:32:27 (5,309)	
Jones, Peter R	3:56:21 (10,577)	
Jones, Peter S	4:35:15 (21,046)	
Jones, Philip	3:56:21 (10,577)	
Jones, Ralph	4:06:40 (13,446)	
Jones, Ralph W	5:16:02 (28,941)	
Jones, Ray	4:41:28 (22,551)	
Jones, Richard A	3:10:05 (1,997)	
Jones, Richard A	6:16:43 (33,318)	
Jones, Richard D	6:28:36 (33,633)	
Jones, Richard L	3:31:32 (5,137)	
Jones, Richard L	4:13:58 (15,292)	
Jones, Richard M	3:25:25 (3,997)	
Jones, Richard P	4:28:44 (19,321)	
Jones, Rob	3:50:45 (8,998)	
Jones, Rob	4:19:32 (16,768)	
Jones, Robert	4:19:43 (16,818)	
Jones, Robert A	4:46:36 (23,799)	
Jones, Robert P	5:43:52 (31,639)	
Jones, Robin	3:11:25 (2,137)	
Jones, Roger	5:52:57 (32,335)	
Jones, Roland R	4:32:45 (20,363)	
Jones, Rue	3:50:37 (8,961)	
Jones, Russell B	3:14:46 (2,600)	
Jones, Russell P	4:26:31 (18,671)	
Jones, Sean W	5:30:21 (30,511)	
Jones, Shaun	4:54:37 (25,603)	
Jones, Simon	3:59:38 (11,724)	
Jones, Simon	4:19:20 (16,711)	
Jones, Simon	4:26:03 (18,552)	
Jones, Simon C	3:13:14 (2,363)	
Jones, Simon F	3:48:56 (8,565)	
Jones, Simon M	4:53:15 (25,325)	
Jones, Stephen	2:54:10 (706)	
Jones, Stephen	3:38:50 (6,415)	
Jones, Stephen D	4:29:01 (19,402)	
Jones, Stephen J	3:47:01 (8,113)	
Jones, Steve	4:59:11 (26,512)	
Jones, Steve N	3:07:18 (1,711)	
Jones, Steve R	4:42:03 (22,683)	
Jones, Steve R	5:15:21 (28,860)	
Jones, Steven R	3:38:47 (6,405)	
Jones, Stuart J	4:48:38 (24,277)	
Jones, Tegid R	3:06:32 (1,641)	
Jones, Terence	3:59:58 (11,662)	
Jones, Tim P	3:15:21 (2,685)	
Jones, Timothy A	3:12:14 (2,243)	
Jones, Trevor	4:46:13 (23,717)	
Jones, Wayne P	4:03:35 (12,742)	
Jonsson, Lars	4:41:38 (22,593)	
Jooste, Conrad G	3:41:09 (6,859)	
Jopling, Edward H	2:58:34 (1,016)	
Jopling, Stevie J	5:16:54 (29,042)	
Jordan, Andrew	3:58:11 (11,182)	
Jordan, Andy	3:43:51 (7,424)	
Jordan, Ben C	4:52:30 (25,146)	
Jordan, Christopher R	2:37:56 (167)	
Jordan, Kevin	3:45:33 (7,800)	
Jordan, Mark	3:55:25 (10,315)	
Jordan, Mark C	5:34:49 (30,919)	
Jordan, Martin J	3:28:09 (4,498)	
Jordan, Mike J	4:30:37 (19,780)	
Jordan, Miles J	4:24:13 (18,056)	
Jordan, Paul W	5:10:59 (28,273)	
Jordan, Peter A	3:58:31 (11,306)	
Jordan, Phil	3:32:17 (5,276)	
Jordan, Richard	4:08:52 (14,010)	
Jordan, Richard M	5:59:57 (32,738)	
Jorge, Alexandre	3:24:46 (3,882)	
Jorgensen, Leo V	3:14:21 (2,525)	
Joseph, Darren	4:19:30 (16,757)	
Joseph, Koster	2:35:27 (119)	
Joseph, Lance	4:08:00 (13,772)	
Joseph, Peter F	3:39:20 (6,503)	
Joseph, Vincent D	4:14:01 (15,310)	
Josephs, Merrick L	3:24:49 (3,892)	
Joshi, Dhruv R	3:59:04 (11,511)	
Joshi, Hiten	4:55:29 (25,780)	
Joslin, Gary	3:47:48 (8,296)	
Joslin, Ian R	3:14:12 (2,498)	
Joules, Keith	2:48:55 (461)	
Jour, Rodiger	4:58:13 (26,328)	
Jourdain, Flavien	3:18:24 (3,031)	
Jovanovic, Nebojsa	4:54:13 (25,525)	
Jowett, Chris J	3:56:37 (10,669)	
Joy, Rob	2:29:40 (67)	
Joyce, Alistair W	3:43:29 (7,342)	
Joyce, David C	5:00:18 (26,683)	
Joyce, Dominic H	4:26:32 (18,673)	
Joyce, Dominic P	3:32:39 (5,340)	
Joyce, Gary R	3:41:06 (6,846)	
Joyce, James	3:54:59 (10,191)	
Joyce, Michael	3:27:50 (4,428)	
Joyce, Richard	4:47:02 (23,918)	
Joyce, Stephen	3:34:42 (5,645)	
Joyce, William D	3:54:34 (10,060)	
Joynt, Chris	5:19:25 (29,342)	
Juckes, Ian T	3:53:22 (9,687)	
Judd, Harry	3:52:58 (9,560)	
Judd, Michael	3:18:20 (3,023)	
Judd, Mike	3:14:59 (2,626)	
Judd, Paul A	4:50:29 (24,708)	
Judge, Bruce G	2:39:43 (194)	
Judge, Conrad V	5:27:07 (30,159)	
Judge, Oliver O	4:30:50 (19,843)	
Judge, Stephen	4:30:50 (19,843)	
Juffs, Charles	4:18:27 (16,479)	
Juge, Alain	3:42:18 (7,094)	
Jugnarain, Pravin	4:04:13 (12,866)	
Jukes, Clive	5:12:43 (28,500)	
Jukes, Jeremy D	4:11:21 (14,633)	
Jukes, Shaun	4:06:35 (13,420)	
Julca, Alex	4:34:37 (20,849)	
Julien, James W	7:11:18 (34,333)	
Jump, Graham	4:40:48 (22,379)	
Jung, John	4:32:49 (20,377)	
Junge, Micki	2:59:17 (1,096)	
Juniper, Adam	2:44:40 (320)	
Jupe, Stephen J	5:04:34 (27,338)	
Juravich, Nicholas A	2:59:34 (1,124)	
Jurgens, Mark J	5:11:41 (28,362)	
Jury, Tim J	3:56:11 (10,533)	

Just, Gerald	2:45:59 (361)	
Jutsum, Edward J	4:23:06 (17,754)	
Juupaluoma, Jarmo	4:03:37 (12,751)	
Kadhim, Robert A	5:38:48 (31,248)	
Kadiwar, Kantilal M	7:27:39 (34,443)	
Kaempfer, Matthias	5:55:10 (32,473)	
Kaess, Hermann	3:46:45 (8,050)	
Kafi, Ali	3:27:04 (4,291)	
Kahlon, Tarlok S	5:40:35 (31,382)	
Kahn, David	4:56:12 (25,916)	
Kainth, Ranjiet	3:17:37 (2,943)	
Kaiser, Neil	3:46:56 (8,093)	
Kaiser, Nick	3:13:04 (2,343)	
Kakoullis, Panos K	3:45:52 (7,873)	
Kalaitzakis, Zacharias	4:36:16 (21,315)	
Kalaker, Raymond J	4:05:13 (13,105)	
Kallenberg, Albert	4:22:23 (17,547)	
Kalm, Benjamin	3:23:56 (3,770)	
Kalsi, Nirmal S	5:01:20 (26,847)	
Kalton, Alan G	4:34:51 (20,925)	
Kaminski, Marek	3:41:17 (6,894)	
Kan, Alan	5:26:52 (30,138)	
Kanbriss, Housam	6:01:39 (32,799)	
Kandela, Matt P	4:15:25 (15,676)	
Kane, Graeme	4:11:08 (14,581)	
Kane, Jonathan	3:25:45 (4,061)	
Kane, Jonathan	4:56:54 (26,052)	
Kane, Jonathan J	3:24:51 (3,899)	
Kane, Stephen	4:31:10 (19,928)	
Kang, Ajmer S	5:50:42 (32,189)	
Kang, Roger S	5:29:16 (30,405)	
Kanji, Mohamed	4:53:09 (25,307)	
Kanner, Edward	3:41:07 (6,851)	
Kantsedikas, Ilia A	4:15:19 (15,642)	
Kanu, Emeka	6:31:24 (33,691)	
Kanyamibwa, Jean-Yves H	4:30:29 (19,740)	
Kapadia, Praful	4:49:19 (24,436)	
Kapoor, Neil	4:16:44 (16,013)	
Kara, Zaahid	3:59:55 (11,825)	
Karachiwalla, Hanif	4:13:15 (15,098)	
Karatzas, Panagiotis	4:35:36 (21,137)	
Karia, Kishan M	6:34:27 (33,762)	
Karim, Malik	5:27:31 (30,203)	
Karling, David	4:29:39 (19,551)	
Karn, Robin J	2:42:09 (245)	
Karp, Eric	3:31:51 (5,191)	
Karrlein, Wolfgang M	5:16:51 (29,036)	
Kashima, Manabu	4:15:01 (15,568)	
Kasper, Benjamin R	4:14:15 (15,383)	
Kass, Mark L	2:50:03 (514)	
Kassam, Azim	4:01:19 (12,192)	
Kassap, Danny	2:15:20 (15)	
Kassebohm, Martin	3:50:55 (9,032)	
Kassell, Tom	3:38:05 (6,281)	
Kassim, Adam	4:14:15 (15,383)	
Katechia, Bhagesh C	3:43:49 (7,416)	
Kathmann, Christoph	5:00:59 (26,792)	
Katsimpas, George	5:33:32 (30,788)	
Kattouche, Farid	4:28:52 (19,367)	
Kauders, Magnus	5:21:43 (29,581)	
Kavanagh, John M	3:47:20 (8,181)	
Kavanagh, Mel W	4:02:42 (12,542)	
Kavanagh, Michael A	4:20:23 (16,990)	
Kavanagh, Steven	4:29:24 (19,500)	
Kavanagh, Thomas	4:47:58 (24,139)	
Kawabata, Daisuke	2:52:33 (618)	
Kawakami, Mashiro	4:07:51 (13,730)	
Kawczynski, Michael J	4:39:08 (22,011)	
Kawoh, John	4:06:33 (13,415)	
Kay, Ben R	3:53:02 (9,586)	
Kay, Benjamin	3:27:21 (4,344)	
Kay, David J	3:18:54 (3,086)	
Kay, John H	2:47:48 (414)	
Kay, Mark W	5:00:25 (26,696)	
Kay, Martin A	4:08:36 (13,942)	
Kay, Matthew S	2:44:14 (303)	
Kay, Peter R	5:34:09 (30,849)	
Kay, Robert	3:49:38 (8,728)	
Kay, Tim	4:26:28 (18,654)	
Kaye, Darren M	4:50:07 (24,625)	
Kaye, David R	4:45:47 (23,617)	
Kaye, Paul P	4:44:07 (23,206)	
Kazmi, Ahsan	6:01:56 (32,818)	
Keall, Stephen	4:14:08 (15,347)	
Kean, Roger	4:30:08 (19,663)	
Keane, Anthony	4:08:30 (13,909)	
Keane, Jim	3:31:12 (5,076)	
Keaney, Dominic	5:54:12 (32,418)	
Kear, Simon E	3:59:42 (11,750)	
Kearney, John B	3:44:18 (7,515)	
Kearns, Adrian	2:56:32 (845)	
Kearns, James A	4:23:55 (17,968)	
Kearns, John G	3:08:26 (1,832)	
Kearns, Jonathan	4:51:42 (24,985)	
Kearns, Simon J	3:12:02 (2,214)	
Kearse, James W	3:41:23 (6,913)	
Keast, Jason	3:49:14 (8,637)	
Keast, Jon R	2:39:40 (192)	
Keast, Mark	3:55:26 (10,316)	
Keast, Richard L	3:54:54 (10,160)	
Keates, John	3:49:39 (8,731)	
Keates, Lester T	4:20:25 (17,003)	
Keatina, Niall J	3:44:57 (7,672)	
Keating, Dermot J	3:52:34 (9,448)	
Keating, Mark A	3:59:28 (11,662)	
Keating, Nick M	3:59:33 (11,688)	
Keating, Paul N	4:52:15 (25,091)	
Keating, Ronan	3:59:44 (11,759)	
Keating, Stephen C	6:42:41 (33,932)	
Keay, Francis	4:21:16 (17,244)	
Keay, Stephen	4:12:56 (15,011)	
Keayes, Donald N	5:14:17 (28,719)	
Kebler, Thomas	3:55:06 (10,233)	
Kedney, Gary J	3:34:41 (5,641)	
Kee, Howard W	3:04:04 (1,452)	
Kee, Robert J	4:28:52 (19,367)	
Keeble, Colin T	6:44:15 (33,962)	
Keeble, Ian R	2:52:57 (636)	
Keech, Paul A	3:25:43 (4,057)	
Keech, Tony	3:57:54 (11,091)	
Keefe, Daniel R	4:12:08 (14,843)	
Keegan, Andy J	3:37:56 (6,246)	
Keegan, Brian D	4:42:34 (22,823)	
Keegan, Glen C	3:45:29 (7,790)	
Keegan, Joseph	5:51:26 (32,245)	
Keegan, Nicholas J	5:30:31 (30,528)	
Keeler, Paul	3:36:57 (6,050)	
Keeley, Daniel J	3:38:34 (6,365)	
Keeley, James W	4:07:10 (13,568)	
Keeley, Rupert G	3:52:25 (9,415)	
Keeling, Geoff	4:43:44 (23,108)	
Keen, Alan	4:08:31 (13,919)	
Keen, Andy	4:48:57 (24,359)	
Keen, Howard S	5:01:42 (26,913)	
Keen, Kevin	4:43:33 (23,064)	
Keen, Mark P	6:26:04 (33,581)	
Keen, Michael G	3:48:08 (8,385)	
Keenan, Ben J	5:26:48 (30,126)	
Keenan, David C	4:29:40 (19,557)	
Keenan, Frank E	4:13:33 (15,172)	
Keenan, Iain D	5:29:47 (30,456)	
Keenan, Simon M	5:42:42 (31,548)	
Keenan, Thomas S	4:04:35 (12,947)	
Keep, David J	3:42:37 (7,155)	
Keep, Trevor	3:09:10 (1,903)	
Kefford, Andrew D	3:40:39 (6,749)	
Kehoe, Michael N	5:41:06 (31,422)	
Kehoe, Michael T	3:08:28 (1,834)	
Kehoe, Niall	3:53:10 (9,629)	
Keigher, James	3:29:00 (4,669)	
Keiller, Robert	5:39:02 (31,265)	
Keiller, Roderick G	4:51:43 (24,991)	
Keilty, Paul	4:39:33 (22,090)	
Keilty, Russell J	3:13:38 (2,408)	
Keily, Lee	2:56:12 (821)	
Keith, Andrew	4:39:40 (22,114)	
Kejser, Niels	4:32:14 (20,238)	
Kekana, Malose	3:59:37 (11,720)	
Kelk, Mark	5:06:38 (27,642)	
Kelleher, Cornelius G	3:23:48 (3,737)	
Keller, Dieter P	3:25:24 (3,993)	
Kellett, Neil A	3:54:28 (10,013)	
Kellett, Steve	3:57:36 (10,977)	
Kelley, Chris M	4:24:52 (18,233)	
Kelley, John	4:31:16 (19,952)	
Kelley, Sean D	5:16:02 (28,941)	
Kellock, Rob O	4:03:48 (12,788)	
Kellond, David C	5:08:45 (27,937)	
Kells, John T	3:23:28 (3,704)	
Kelly, Alan W	3:54:27 (10,008)	
Kelly, Brian	5:03:28 (27,177)	
Kelly, Brian R	3:48:11 (8,395)	
Kelly, Brian V	3:17:37 (2,943)	
Kelly, Christopher T	3:14:23 (2,528)	
Kelly, Daniel P	4:31:48 (20,103)	
Kelly, Dermot T	5:08:21 (27,865)	
Kelly, Fergal	4:23:49 (17,943)	
Kelly, Graham E	3:50:31 (8,931)	
Kelly, Hugh G	4:22:12 (17,495)	
Kelly, James M	3:54:03 (9,887)	
Kelly, Jim	4:52:51 (25,234)	
Kelly, John	4:08:39 (13,955)	
Kelly, John A	3:31:48 (5,187)	
Kelly, John A	4:35:55 (21,217)	
Kelly, Justin L	2:42:45 (260)	
Kelly, Kevin P	3:24:29 (3,845)	
Kelly, Lee	4:29:01 (19,402)	
Kelly, Lee J	3:45:46 (7,849)	
Kelly, Michael J	3:31:59 (5,223)	
Kelly, Michael T	4:26:19 (18,613)	
Kelly, Neil	3:56:36 (10,663)	
Kelly, Paul J	3:42:59 (7,233)	
Kelly, Phillip J	4:52:51 (25,234)	
Kelly, Richard J	3:46:25 (7,984)	
Kelly, Robert T	3:44:27 (7,543)	
Kelly, Ronan	3:59:16 (11,585)	
Kelly, Sean	5:50:49 (32,198)	
Kelly, Sean F	4:31:24 (19,995)	
Kelly, Simon J	5:10:44 (28,238)	
Kelly, Stephen J	4:53:06 (25,295)	
Kelly, Stephen P	4:49:43 (24,537)	
Kelly, Thomas M	5:08:11 (27,841)	
Kelly, Tim C	3:18:21 (3,028)	
Kelly, Toby B	4:52:53 (25,247)	
Kelly, William T	4:25:48 (18,482)	
Kelsey, David W	3:57:12 (10,862)	
Kelsey, Howard W	4:20:02 (16,899)	
Kelsey, Stephen B	4:38:47 (21,908)	
Kelshaw, Jaymie L	4:30:36 (19,775)	
Kelson, Rod	3:57:44 (11,029)	
Kelty, Paul A	5:24:47 (29,885)	
Kember, Julian J	4:11:01 (14,547)	
Kemish, Gary N	3:27:35 (4,376)	
Kemp, Craig I	5:21:04 (29,503)	
Kemp, David J	4:28:35 (19,284)	
Kemp, Graham	4:14:29 (15,446)	
Kemp, Graham B	4:48:25 (24,227)	
Kemp, Jonathan R	3:20:48 (3,331)	
Kemp, Kevin	5:06:50 (27,672)	
Kemp, Mark A	5:01:52 (26,940)	
Kemp, Michael T	5:14:25 (28,734)	
Kemp, Philip G	4:25:51 (18,496)	
Kemp, Robert	3:59:05 (11,521)	
Kemp, Steven J	5:22:00 (29,600)	
Kemperink, Jeroen	3:28:21 (4,528)	
Kempson, Gary	5:11:53 (28,395)	
Kempster, Neil R	5:18:37 (29,245)	
Kempton, Andrew J	4:42:23 (22,770)	
Kenchington, Christopher J	3:17:23 (2,918)	
Kendall, Ian J	4:28:07 (19,137)	
Kendall, Kevin	3:59:33 (11,688)	
Kendall, Paul O	4:53:27 (25,360)	
Kendall, Philip C	4:23:13 (17,792)	
Kendall, Simon P	4:02:37 (12,520)	
Kendra, Alan T	3:28:36 (4,580)	
Kendrick, Alastair	4:50:59 (24,839)	
Kendrick, Christopher A	4:40:37 (22,334)	
Kendrick, John E	4:45:08 (23,444)	
Kendrick, Philip	2:49:57 (510)	
Kendrick, Simon T	4:58:24 (26,361)	
Kendrick, Stewart	6:28:45 (33,635)	
Kenington, Richard J	4:04:54 (13,021)	
Kenn, Christopher W	4:43:00 (22,926)	
Kennard, Barnaby J	3:23:24 (3,690)	
Kennard, David A	3:47:18 (8,177)	
Kennard, Martin R	2:37:38 (160)	
Kennedy, Anthony R	3:26:55 (4,266)	
Kennedy, Donald E	2:47:23 (398)	
Kennedy, George	3:09:24 (1,927)	

Kirkelund, Vagn 2:59:54 (1,158)
Kirkham, Gareth 4:56:03 (25,885)
Kirkham, Richard A 4:54:25 (25,564)
Kirkland, Anthony 3:50:37 (8,961)
Kirkman, Andrew J 4:33:39 (20,622)
Kirkman, Jeremy 3:18:08 (2,998)
Kirkman, Simon J 4:36:40 (21,409)
Kirk-Wilson, Ed J 3:12:21 (2,251)
Kirk-Wilson, William A 3:05:07 (1,527)
Kirleis, Thor 2:59:33 (1,119)
Kirsch, Jens 3:37:09 (6,088)
Kirschner, Uwe 3:00:58 (1,240)
Kirtland, James L 5:47:28 (31,950)
Kirtley, Michael J 4:52:38 (25,180)
Kirtley, Paul 4:10:47 (14,488)
Kirton, John E 4:09:46 (14,247)
Kirwan, Eric M 4:30:17 (19,694)
Kirwan, John 3:57:14 (10,876)
Kisbee, Murray P 3:25:59 (4,103)
Kisler, Jonathan D 4:10:36 (14,433)
Kiszow, Stephen R 4:23:27 (17,856)
Kitchen, Dave A 3:55:15 (10,275)
Kitchen, Jason 3:52:42 (9,479)
Kitchen, Steven P 4:13:29 (15,154)
Kitchener, Darran D 5:10:47 (28,248)
Kitcher, David 3:01:22 (1,267)
Kitcher, Stephen M 4:30:42 (19,800)
Kitching, Barrie 3:47:59 (8,345)
Kitching, Gordon 4:49:57 (24,591)
Kitching, Ian C 3:21:04 (3,368)
Kitching, Jamie C 3:58:32 (11,310)
Kite, Jonathan S 4:45:28 (23,534)
Kitney, Steve J 2:57:10 (884)
Kitromilides, Alex S 2:55:27 (774)
Kitson, Andrew M 4:09:41 (14,220)
Kitson, John N 4:37:10 (21,518)
Kitson-Smith, Anthony 4:07:24 (13,612)
Kittappa, Adam P 4:19:27 (16,739)
Kittle, Ian D 3:16:10 (2,770)
Kitts, Stephen 3:57:02 (10,805)
Kiuna, Ngugi 3:59:24 (11,633)
Klaber, Robert E 4:22:46 (17,661)
Klein, Ben 3:51:38 (9,206)
Klein, Jason R 4:49:13 (24,417)
Klein, Joseph 3:55:13 (10,269)
Klein, Thilo 2:53:52 (683)
Kleinman, Martin 4:46:16 (23,733)
Klemke, Carl-Heinz 4:31:16 (19,952)
Klenerman, Paul 3:54:22 (9,978)
Kletter, Evan S 5:14:12 (28,704)
Klingemeier, Peter-Jasef 4:49:29 (24,471)
Klingenschmid, Robert J 3:54:27 (10,008)
Klink, Ralf 3:41:36 (6,955)
Klopper, David J 4:06:13 (13,333)
Kloster, Ivar 3:33:46 (5,516)
Klube, Mario 4:00:28 (11,965)
Kluth, Andrew 3:59:32 (11,683)
Knab, Heiner 4:37:48 (21,671)
Knab, Timothy J 4:20:12 (16,942)
Knackstedt, Scott F 2:36:31 (138)
Knapman, Barrie 4:11:47 (14,745)
Knapp, Mark D 3:00:41 (1,216)
Knapp, Markus 4:32:25 (20,273)
Knappett, Michael D 3:09:04 (1,890)
Kneale, Barry 3:58:18 (11,219)
Kneebone, Craig 3:46:49 (8,066)
Knell, Nigel 4:02:01 (12,368)
Knibbs, Alec V 6:19:40 (33,389)
Knight, Andrew J 3:45:04 (7,700)
Knight, Brian 6:32:36 (33,717)
Knight, Bruce W 5:10:22 (28,201)
Knight, Danny R 4:51:03 (24,855)
Knight, David L 3:57:56 (11,098)
Knight, Geoffrey P 2:39:06 (183)
Knight, Graham D 3:49:09 (8,615)
Knight, Ian J 3:22:29 (3,562)
Knight, Jason 4:21:54 (17,422)
Knight, John 3:14:09 (2,492)
Knight, John 5:49:03 (32,057)
Knight, John P 4:42:03 (22,683)
Knight, Lee R 4:06:22 (13,366)
Knight, Malcolm J 3:43:21 (7,317)
Knight, Peter C 4:36:54 (21,464)
Knight, Peter E 3:40:29 (6,731)
Knight, Roger 4:53:06 (25,295)
Knight, Simon D 4:30:26 (19,728)
Knight, Steven P 5:34:41 (30,905)
Knight, Stuart 3:51:25 (9,157)
Knight, Stuart A 3:23:53 (3,758)
Knight, Timothy M 4:08:19 (13,857)
Knights, John I 3:23:48 (3,737)
Knights, Stephen J 4:00:41 (12,029)
Knoth, Carsten 3:57:30 (10,953)
Knott, Chris R 5:25:39 (30,000)
Knott, Christopher J 6:07:45 (33,036)
Knott, Peter J 4:12:46 (14,981)
Knott, Shane 4:28:09 (19,151)
Knowlden, Alex J 5:14:11 (28,700)
Knowles, Adam D 4:04:00 (12,833)
Knowles, Andrew M 3:31:02 (5,058)
Knowles, David 4:34:16 (20,771)
Knowles, Martyn 3:40:45 (6,772)
Knowles, Patrick I 5:47:41 (31,960)
Knowles, Paul W 2:58:57 (1,058)
Knowles, Simon 3:11:15 (2,120)
Knowles, Stephen P 3:51:21 (9,141)
Knox, Andrew 3:39:24 (6,519)
Knox, Bryan 4:07:09 (13,563)
Knox, Ian C 4:22:45 (17,659)
Kobayashi, Hideo 4:46:38 (23,807)
Kocan, Camil 4:00:28 (11,965)
Kodjie, Erik A 3:51:36 (9,196)
Koehler, Martin 2:48:48 (457)
Koekemoer, Johan G 4:24:14 (18,063)
Koerfgen, Stephan 4:12:02 (14,816)
Kofmel, Willy 3:54:32 (10,045)
Koh, Lin H 5:27:12 (30,164)
Kohler, Philip R 5:12:08 (28,422)
Kohlmann, Jan-Caspar 3:27:51 (4,432)
Kolar, Kumar 4:27:16 (18,896)
Kolator, Rainer 4:09:01 (14,045)
Kolb, Alexander 4:23:16 (17,804)
Kolb, Johannes M 4:26:16 (18,601)
Kolesnikow, Mark C 3:56:40 (10,680)
Kollberger, Simon D 4:35:21 (21,068)
Kolloen, Edmund 4:40:47 (22,376)
Komduur, Anton 4:11:13 (14,610)
Kong, Matthew W 4:46:39 (23,814)
Konopka, Thomas 4:36:16 (21,315)
Konstadakopoylos, Panos 4:48:42 (24,290)
Koornhof, Hendrik J 4:10:55 (14,527)
Korlevic, Robert 3:25:54 (4,085)
Korsen, Olav 5:09:48 (28,114)
Korten, Chris J 3:55:01 (10,201)
Korten, Robert 4:24:13 (18,056)
Koshy, Sam G 4:44:32 (23,310)
Koska, Alexander 2:56:38 (851)
Koster, Johan 4:41:11 (22,235)
Kotecha, Deepak 6:27:43 (33,618)
Kothari, Dipesh P 4:16:46 (16,023)
Kotik, Romain 4:21:52 (17,415)
Kotinkaduwe, Ranil P 4:22:55 (17,706)
Koto, Wempy 4:53:11 (25,314)
Kotze, Johan M 3:48:55 (8,559)
Kotze, Nicholas M 3:31:38 (5,158)
Kouyoumbjian, Richard 3:53:44 (9,783)
Kovach, Robert 4:57:14 (26,132)
Kovacs, James 2:29:32 (65)
Kovats, Steven L 3:00:43 (1,218)
Kovijanich, Dan J 3:59:02 (11,499)
Kovoory, Appi R 4:37:47 (21,663)
Kowalenko, Steve P 3:07:55 (1,780)
Kowaleski, Joseph R 4:24:32 (18,155)
Kowalski, Marek 5:25:57 (30,030)
Kral, Paul 3:52:18 (9,386)
Kraler, Alex 4:46:28 (23,769)
Kraolemeas, George A 3:33:03 (5,391)
Kraska, Tadeusz 4:05:46 (13,235)
Krauhaus, Carl A 4:51:23 (24,921)
Krauss, Martin A 6:29:39 (33,648)
Krebs, Helmut 3:28:51 (4,635)
Krebs, Steve P 6:13:34 (33,230)
Kremer, John 3:29:14 (4,721)
Kreuter, Reiner 3:49:53 (8,794)
Kriesche, Wolfgang 4:46:37 (23,801)
Krige, Willem A 4:25:03 (18,275)
Krishnamurthy, Arun K 4:02:15 (12,430)
Kristal, Doron C 3:32:40 (5,342)
Kristensen, Finn 5:32:13 (30,673)
Kristensen, Jan 3:46:43 (8,042)
Krivacs, James K 4:42:12 (22,723)
Kroenike, Wilhelm 4:16:40 (16,005)
Krom, Norman 4:14:48 (15,515)
Kronberg, Espen A 4:59:15 (26,523)
Kroon, Martijn 4:08:10 (13,825)
Kropach, Jared A 4:52:06 (25,064)
Kruelkeberg, Christian 3:51:18 (9,123)
Krug, Michael 4:05:48 (13,246)
Kruger, Hermann B 3:18:08 (2,998)
Kruiderink, Anton W 3:31:06 (5,063)
Krumins, John 3:41:22 (6,911)
Kruszynski, Carl 3:45:12 (7,728)
Kuaran, Axel 5:30:19 (30,509)
Kuchergin, Oleksandr 6:10:58 (33,141)
Kufluk, Kenneth P 4:58:59 (26,474)
Kuhnel, Michael J 4:26:29 (18,662)
Kuijlaars, Joost 3:22:37 (3,588)
Kukoda, Stephen 4:11:09 (14,590)
Kulahcigil, Tolga 5:51:50 (32,278)
Kumar, Ashok 4:55:34 (25,792)
Kumar, Sanjay 4:32:05 (20,192)
Kumpf, Matthias 5:15:31 (28,882)
Kung, Lau 4:41:38 (22,593)
Kuntara, Walter 3:12:34 (2,274)
Kurukulasooriya, Anil 4:21:10 (17,216)
Kurzreiter, Werner 4:20:14 (16,957)
Kutner, Christian A 3:27:00 (4,281)
Kuzhin, Stephane M 3:01:00 (1,243)
Kvalvaagnes, Ronny 6:53:13 (34,126)
Kveiborg, Thomas B 3:31:15 (5,092)
Kwaskowski, Martin 4:30:38 (19,783)
Kwiatkowski, Carl A 4:29:31 (19,519)
Kyd, Laurence D 4:39:44 (22,137)
Kyle, Chris 2:59:59 (1,166)
Kynaston, Mark 4:54:56 (25,683)
Kynaston, Matthew J 3:41:16 (6,891)
Kynaston, Neil 5:55:31 (32,504)
Kyriacou, Peter 4:06:39 (13,441)
La Fratta, Charles F 4:08:42 (13,969)
La Mattina, Benjamin 4:32:25 (20,273)
Laab-Garia, Gabriel 3:47:10 (8,142)
Laad, Hiten P 4:09:49 (14,257)
Laarss, Michael 4:28:49 (19,351)
Labbe, Benoit 3:23:50 (3,745)
Labia, Natale B 4:17:06 (16,122)
Labuschagne, Timothy J 4:37:50 (21,679)
Lacaille, Yves 4:09:17 (14,112)
Lacey, Allan J 5:55:17 (32,485)
Lacey, Charles P 5:44:25 (31,713)
Lacey, James M 3:50:39 (8,974)
Lach, Alexandre 3:12:41 (2,288)
Lack, Stuart 3:54:13 (9,932)
Lackey, Peter J 3:50:38 (8,968)
Lacroze, Yves 4:41:17 (22,509)
Lacy, Charles A 4:09:32 (14,183)
Lad, Mahesh 6:20:34 (33,410)
Ladbury, James 4:39:19 (22,055)
Ladd, Andrew R 4:21:11 (17,220)
Ladd, Joe 3:26:02 (4,109)
Ladell, Donald P 6:32:15 (33,708)
Ladlow, Stephen M 4:41:47 (22,628)
Ladwa, Rakesh 4:27:34 (18,967)
Laffan, Matt 4:52:12 (25,083)
Lafferty, Neil R 3:26:57 (4,271)
Lafleche, Trevor 3:59:29 (11,668)
Lagache, Henri 3:21:42 (3,446)
Lagnado, Max 3:03:05 (1,380)
Lahiry, Varge 5:58:36 (32,676)
Lai, Lai 5:28:39 (30,338)
Laidlaw, Jack R 3:57:57 (11,102)
Laikin, Richard E 5:00:25 (26,696)
Laing, David J 2:40:14 (201)
Lainsbury, Martin P 4:43:51 (23,141)
Laishley, Matthew J 3:24:48 (3,888)
Laisney, Duncan J 4:10:25 (14,391)
Laithwaite, David H 3:59:16 (11,585)
Laitt, Andrew R 4:21:33 (17,319)
Lake, David 3:26:37 (4,209)
Lake, Oliver J 3:38:51 (6,420)

Lake, Richard J	5:29:10 (30,394)	
Lake, Simon S	3:49:07 (8,606)	
Lake, Steve R	3:50:21 (8,900)	
Laker, Stephen A	3:03:41 (1,429)	
Lakes, Sebastian	3:22:27 (3,557)	
Lakey, Jack	4:02:47 (12,561)	
Lakhani, Kiran	4:15:07 (15,603)	
Laking, Steve	4:19:50 (16,842)	
Lalau, Michel K	3:34:28 (5,617)	
Lall, Andrew	4:29:13 (19,455)	
Lalley, Michael	3:50:36 (8,955)	
Lally, Dermot S	4:13:34 (15,181)	
Lally, Kevin W	3:18:26 (3,036)	
Lally, Michael J	3:26:18 (4,154)	
Lam, Ryan S	4:31:04 (19,900)	
Lamagna, Armando	3:30:27 (4,962)	
Lamata, Ferran	4:25:06 (18,288)	
Lamb, Christopher	5:06:44 (27,657)	
Lamb, David	4:53:34 (25,392)	
Lamb, Jason F	4:17:39 (16,265)	
Lamb, Jeremy	3:55:22 (10,304)	
Lamb, Jonathan D	4:25:06 (18,288)	
Lamb, Ken D	3:32:12 (5,260)	
Lamb, Phillip	5:41:47 (31,485)	
Lamb, Richard A	4:15:18 (15,639)	
Lamb, Robert A	4:45:38 (23,569)	
Lamb, Simon P	4:34:39 (20,863)	
Lamb, Spencer	4:40:51 (22,393)	
Lamb, William I	4:50:31 (24,722)	
Lambarth, Brian D	3:55:17 (10,286)	
Lambden, Keith S	3:51:36 (9,196)	
Lambden, Murray M	3:09:52 (1,977)	
Lambert, Daniel	3:58:24 (11,261)	
Lambert, Dean E	4:01:27 (12,230)	
Lambert, Edouard J	4:05:16 (13,113)	
Lambert, Gabriel J	4:17:16 (16,166)	
Lambert, Heath J	3:17:21 (2,911)	
Lambert, Ian	5:17:29 (29,123)	
Lambert, Ian L	3:22:52 (3,617)	
Lambert, James E	3:58:25 (11,268)	
Lambert, John D	4:06:54 (13,493)	
Lambert, John E	4:55:13 (25,732)	
Lambert, Keith E	4:46:31 (23,781)	
Lambert, Kevin J	4:40:35 (22,325)	
Lambert, Matthew K	4:15:43 (15,752)	
Lambert, Michael	3:59:00 (11,489)	
Lambert, Philip	3:58:49 (11,426)	
Lambert, Toby	2:18:40 (19)	
Lambouroud, Alban	3:24:31 (3,850)	
Lambrou, Tony	6:32:55 (33,720)	
Lamford, Russell M	6:13:52 (33,240)	
Lamhang, Ben	5:42:05 (31,507)	
Lami, Grant A	4:10:26 (14,395)	
Lammali, Aziouz	3:23:22 (3,687)	
Lammas, Edward	3:47:24 (8,197)	
Lamond, Mike B	4:46:43 (23,833)	
Lamont, James P	3:58:57 (11,473)	
Lancashire, Craig R	4:42:34 (22,823)	
Lancaster, Darren S	3:59:45 (11,766)	
Lancaster, Garry S	4:10:30 (14,409)	
Lancaster, Michael	3:42:59 (7,233)	
Lancaster, Philip A	4:06:11 (13,329)	
Lancelot, Adam	6:22:55 (33,489)	
Lancet, Gary P	5:00:14 (26,672)	
Lander, Mark	4:22:52 (17,691)	
Lander, Mark P	3:40:44 (6,765)	
Landers, Richard	5:51:11 (32,223)	
Landles, Simon J	3:54:07 (9,909)	
Landucci, Tim L	3:47:54 (8,326)	
Landy, Mark D	2:52:46 (625)	
Lane, Andrew	4:08:23 (13,876)	
Lane, Andrew G	3:26:11 (4,136)	
Lane, Andy S	5:05:27 (27,464)	
Lane, Garth	4:53:05 (25,293)	
Lane, Graham R	3:57:13 (10,868)	
Lane, Martin	3:54:34 (10,060)	
Lane, Matt	3:43:53 (7,434)	
Lane, Michael J	2:46:18 (371)	
Lane, Nathaniel R	2:24:46 (35)	
Lane, Norman	3:30:14 (4,933)	
Lane, Richard	4:12:49 (14,986)	
Lane, Ronald F	3:53:02 (9,586)	
Lane, William	4:00:48 (12,056)	
Lanfant, Joel	3:59:21 (11,613)	
Lang, Ben	2:45:15 (341)	
Lang, Colin J	3:28:27 (4,552)	
Lang, David M	4:38:45 (21,898)	
Lang, Grant L	3:37:21 (6,130)	
Lang, Helmut	3:20:34 (3,302)	
Lang, John N	4:54:07 (25,504)	
Lang, Pascal	4:11:52 (14,772)	
Lang, Shaun	4:45:23 (23,506)	
Lang, Stephen G	4:27:51 (19,040)	
Lang, Steven	6:15:38 (33,283)	
Langa Hontoria, Juan J	3:50:21 (8,900)	
Langan, Kevin A	2:56:42 (856)	
Langbein, Jochen	4:39:28 (22,074)	
Langdon, Ben	3:50:17 (8,890)	
Langdon, Jeremy	3:28:58 (4,659)	
Langdon, Tom N	3:27:35 (4,376)	
Langdown, Thomas G	4:09:30 (14,174)	
Lange, Knud	3:57:08 (10,847)	
Langer, George K	5:37:22 (31,147)	
Langford, David	4:31:28 (20,017)	
Langford, Karl	3:58:35 (11,331)	
Langholz, Peter	5:22:51 (29,690)	
Langley, Colin	2:58:15 (972)	
Langley, Peter G	3:53:55 (9,839)	
Langley, Peter J	3:31:30 (5,127)	
Langley, Robert F	3:05:09 (1,529)	
Langley, Toby R	3:58:48 (11,416)	
Langman, Phil	5:12:02 (28,411)	
Langmore, Jack W	4:25:08 (18,302)	
Langridge, Adrian B	3:21:45 (3,454)	
Langridge, George D	4:56:36 (25,987)	
Langridge, James P	3:01:47 (1,296)	
Langridge, John R	3:57:41 (11,006)	
Langridge, Sam	5:10:46 (28,243)	
Langridge Brown, Gary M	3:41:03 (6,838)	
Langrish, Ray J	5:26:02 (30,039)	
Langrishe, Thomas	5:11:32 (28,339)	
Langton, Daniel G	3:54:44 (10,108)	
Langton, Martin	4:43:44 (23,108)	
Langton, Michael S	5:30:42 (30,548)	
Langton, Paul F	4:11:02 (14,551)	
Langton, Philip D	4:22:21 (17,531)	
Langton, Richard	4:58:19 (26,346)	
Langton, Will	4:17:21 (16,182)	
Lanham, James P	4:03:56 (12,812)	
Lanning, Alexis D	4:00:44 (12,043)	
Lannon, Adam	4:11:10 (14,597)	
Lansdell, Andrew M	3:13:46 (2,431)	
Lansdowne, Paul S	4:21:00 (17,182)	
L'Anson, Anthony	5:28:05 (30,276)	
Lantorp, Bo	4:26:50 (18,765)	
Laporte, Thierry J	3:54:31 (10,040)	
Lappage, Michael	5:34:34 (30,892)	
Lappin, Clifford G	6:08:55 (33,079)	
Lappin, Noel G	3:46:54 (8,083)	
Lapthorne, Nigel J	5:48:20 (31,996)	
Lara, David	4:23:39 (17,905)	
Lara, Horacio	3:35:24 (5,775)	
Larcombe, Derek R	5:18:51 (29,270)	
Large, Barnaby R	4:34:57 (20,957)	
Large, Phillip H	3:04:06 (1,454)	
Large, Steven G	2:55:50 (796)	
Large, Steven J	4:45:53 (23,642)	
Lari, Francesco	3:29:55 (4,870)	
Larken, Jonathan J	3:58:01 (11,122)	
Larkin, David A	4:30:13 (19,683)	
Larkin, James A	5:37:35 (31,161)	
Larkin, Neil J	3:36:47 (6,012)	
Larman, Toby J	3:36:01 (5,885)	
Larmer, Darren	5:14:23 (28,731)	
Larmour, James D	3:39:16 (6,490)	
Larn Jones, Theodore S	4:16:07 (15,858)	
Larner, James	4:49:53 (24,569)	
Larner, Martin D	4:35:03 (20,996)	
Laroussi, Alexandre	3:29:52 (4,857)	
Larrington, Michael J	4:44:48 (23,367)	
Larroucau, Mark J	3:28:27 (4,552)	
Larrs, Philip	5:15:13 (28,846)	
Larsen, Allan S	5:34:40 (30,903)	
Larsen, Atle	3:27:13 (4,315)	
Larsen, Jan Magne	4:42:51 (22,892)	
Larsen, Morten L	4:01:30 (12,241)	
Larsen, Svein K	3:50:34 (8,944)	
Larsson, Jorgen	3:41:45 (6,977)	
Larvin, Tim D	4:01:56 (12,345)	
Lasfargues, Francis A	3:52:25 (9,415)	
Lashbrook, Alan	4:49:43 (24,537)	
Lashmar, Anthony P	2:51:24 (568)	
Lassagne, Franck	3:19:46 (3,203)	
Lasslett, Matthew J	4:41:32 (22,562)	
Last, Antony S	5:28:42 (30,344)	
Latham, Colin J	4:45:07 (23,438)	
Latham, Steven G	3:13:38 (2,408)	
Lathwell, Simon G	3:14:17 (2,516)	
Latif, Rooman	4:50:20 (24,673)	
Latner, Richard	3:57:30 (10,953)	
Latour, Alain	3:38:36 (6,369)	
Latta, Archie J	5:04:38 (27,351)	
Latter, Peter E	5:14:18 (28,722)	
Lau, Boris W	3:50:10 (8,863)	
Lau, Sie L	4:04:10 (12,856)	
Lauder, Rod D	4:28:10 (19,159)	
Laufer, Oren	4:23:16 (17,804)	
Lauga, Philippe	3:25:00 (3,930)	
Laurance, Stephen J	4:51:25 (24,925)	
Laurie, Ian R	4:13:30 (15,159)	
Laurs, Alex	5:41:09 (31,426)	
Lautizi, Claudio	3:28:39 (4,592)	
Laval, Sean A	4:10:08 (14,320)	
Lavan, Michael J	3:53:58 (9,863)	
Lavell, Richard P	4:25:42 (18,444)	
Laver, Arnold E	3:26:35 (4,202)	
Laver, Graham K	3:29:04 (4,682)	
Laver, Matt	4:32:42 (20,348)	
Laver, Toby B	3:04:29 (1,482)	
Lavers, Stephen R	3:20:43 (3,321)	
Laverty, Sean A	2:59:19 (1,100)	
Lavery, Gareth G	4:18:14 (16,409)	
Lavery, Greg J	3:09:53 (1,978)	
Lavin, Paddy	4:29:07 (19,428)	
Lavino, James	3:57:09 (10,852)	
Law, Albert	3:44:40 (7,595)	
Law, Andrew J	4:46:03 (23,682)	
Law, Andrew P	4:21:36 (17,334)	
Law, David J	6:10:53 (33,137)	
Law, James	3:34:11 (5,575)	
Law, Mark A	3:00:32 (1,204)	
Law, Philip A	3:15:00 (2,627)	
Law, Simon N	2:59:20 (1,103)	
Lawan, Joshua	4:19:14 (16,685)	
Lawes, Leslie	5:37:22 (31,147)	
Lawes, Robert S	4:00:40 (12,024)	
Lawler, Daniel	3:53:47 (9,800)	
Lawler, Tim J	3:51:39 (9,211)	
Lawley, Matthew N	5:50:40 (32,182)	
Lawley, Steven G	3:38:03 (6,274)	
Lawlor, Colin R	3:51:17 (9,120)	
Lawlor, Eoin	4:27:10 (18,866)	
Lawlor, James M	5:33:39 (30,794)	
Lawlor, Keith	4:16:57 (16,074)	
Lawlor, Kevin	4:23:02 (17,737)	
Lawlor, Paul A	3:12:22 (2,255)	
Lawlor, Sean	3:38:49 (6,414)	
Lawrance, Dominic J	3:46:01 (7,891)	
Lawrance, Richard S	3:15:03 (2,638)	
Lawrence, Alan D	4:22:26 (17,560)	
Lawrence, Andrew D	4:15:22 (15,655)	
Lawrence, Ben S	4:20:36 (17,061)	
Lawrence, David	3:52:11 (9,356)	
Lawrence, Dean	4:00:50 (12,066)	
Lawrence, Francis S	5:30:07 (30,489)	
Lawrence, Ian P	4:44:07 (23,206)	
Lawrence, James K	4:44:41 (23,342)	
Lawrence, Marc T	7:18:06 (34,383)	
Lawrence, Michael A	6:21:24 (33,441)	
Lawrence, Nigel E	4:13:44 (15,233)	
Lawrence, Richard G	4:34:31 (20,824)	
Lawrence, Steve	3:59:36 (11,714)	
Lawrence, Tim	3:25:53 (4,083)	
Lawrenson, Matthew P	4:27:18 (18,906)	
Lawrie, Dennis M	5:02:06 (26,967)	
Lawrie, Stewart K	4:00:01 (11,857)	
Laws, Christopher	5:46:08 (31,845)	
Laws, Robert D	5:35:17 (30,958)	
Lawson, Ben	4:20:25 (17,003)	

Lawson, Christopher 4:07:40 (13,692)
Lawson, David 3:55:46 (10,425)
Lawson, David A 4:20:33 (17,043)
Lawson, George 4:59:33 (26,565)
Lawson, Guy 3:56:34 (10,650)
Lawson, Ian J 3:08:43 (1,854)
Lawson, Ian S 4:05:13 (13,105)
Lawson, Mark S 4:41:26 (22,541)
Lawson, Robert W 4:14:19 (15,401)
Lawson, Simon 4:49:17 (24,429)
Lawson, Steve 4:24:28 (18,133)
Lawson, Steven 4:08:35 (13,937)
Lawson, Tom G 4:42:49 (22,880)
Lawton, Bryan W 3:12:53 (2,318)
Lawton, James A 3:31:55 (5,203)
Lawton, Nicholas E 4:08:50 (14,001)
Lawton, Peter J 4:44:48 (23,367)
Lawty, Roger 3:09:03 (1,888)
Lay, James 4:09:17 (14,112)
Lay, Stuart C 4:13:12 (15,081)
Laycock, James P 4:08:23 (13,876)
Layet, Christopher 3:51:15 (9,109)
Laylee, Graham 4:19:28 (16,743)
Layman, Ralph 5:18:59 (29,287)
Layton, Brian 4:13:42 (15,225)
Layzell, Peter M 4:12:10 (14,855)
Layzell, Stuart 3:51:40 (9,220)
Lazaro, Enrique 4:38:24 (21,800)
Lazaro Valero, Juan C 5:01:05 (26,807)
Lazell, Luke A 3:15:05 (2,641)
Lazell, Richard J 2:50:53 (549)
Lazzarini, Francesco 3:13:15 (2,364)
Le, Franck 5:19:38 (29,377)
Le Berre, Jean-Yves 3:21:14 (3,389)
Le Bihan, Brieuc 4:52:02 (25,052)
Le Bihan, Jean-Pierre 4:43:25 (23,028)
Le Bosquet, Charles 4:09:19 (14,122)
Le Bras, Philippe 4:16:35 (15,980)
Le Geyt, André P 3:28:20 (4,523)
Le Good, Graham P 3:14:04 (2,479)
Le Henaff, Loic 4:38:51 (21,929)
Le Jeanne, Paul T 3:58:07 (11,151)
Le Jeanne, Pierre C 2:58:44 (1,034)
Le Pennec, Dominique 3:05:19 (1,539)
Le Petit, David 4:34:42 (20,876)
Le Poidevin, Paul C 4:37:22 (21,565)
Le Roux, Eric 3:55:36 (10,371)
Lea, Chris M 5:13:58 (28,670)
Lea, Christopher E 4:56:45 (26,013)
Lea, Martin A 3:12:23 (2,258)
Leabeater, James F 3:42:09 (7,057)
Leach, Benjamin R 4:07:53 (13,745)
Leach, Christopher S 4:34:56 (20,949)
Leach, Craig J 3:55:31 (10,346)
Leach, Gavin J 6:05:38 (32,961)
Leach, Mark A 4:09:22 (14,136)
Leach, Oliver J 3:24:26 (3,835)
Leach, Richard J 5:00:48 (26,761)
Leadbetter, Derek 4:17:00 (16,095)
Leahy, Anthony M 4:17:17 (16,170)
Leahy, Cliff J 5:14:43 (28,777)
Leak, Peter M 5:58:07 (32,644)
Leake, David S 3:50:33 (8,941)
Lear, Michael J 6:48:13 (34,040)
Learmouth, Terry D 3:40:09 (6,663)
Learner, Huw 5:35:17 (30,958)
Leary Joyce, John S 4:37:20 (21,557)
Leask, Andrew W 3:53:49 (9,815)
Leat, Christopher J 3:34:16 (5,586)
Leathers, Ray 5:34:47 (30,914)
Leathers, Richard L 4:24:09 (18,033)
Leaver, Benjamin 4:33:48 (20,661)
Leaver, Michael T 3:40:50 (6,789)
Lebby, Adrian B 4:17:47 (16,300)
Le-Bec, Gilbert 3:30:47 (5,017)
Leblanc, Mark 4:33:35 (20,601)
Leblond, Joel 3:22:39 (3,593)
Leblond, Laurent 4:33:31 (20,579)
Lech, Charles 3:37:26 (6,156)
Leckie, Bill 5:57:25 (32,602)
Lecossier, Emile 4:16:31 (15,965)
Leder, Florian P 4:02:46 (12,556)
Ledesma Muniz, Antonio 3:35:21 (5,764)
Ledger, Charles 4:04:41 (12,979)
Ledger, Russell D 5:23:18 (29,725)
Ledwidge, Alan 4:14:27 (15,436)
Lee, Andrew 3:51:58 (9,291)
Lee, Brett 3:44:20 (7,519)
Lee, Chris 3:17:15 (2,894)
Lee, Daniel M 5:22:48 (29,685)
Lee, Daniel W 4:39:41 (22,122)
Lee, Gareth J 3:42:38 (7,160)
Lee, Jason C 5:37:26 (31,151)
Lee, Jason N 4:23:14 (17,794)
Lee, John 3:57:21 (10,910)
Lee, John 3:59:39 (11,734)
Lee, John M 3:59:05 (11,521)
Lee, Julian 4:23:14 (17,794)
Lee, Leslie J 4:23:54 (17,963)
Lee, Marcus T 3:43:41 (7,386)
Lee, Michael A 3:11:37 (2,164)
Lee, Nicolas R 2:58:31 (1,012)
Lee, Paul A 3:22:53 (3,622)
Lee, Paul P 3:27:38 (4,384)
Lee, Peter G 2:51:06 (557)
Lee, Peter J 3:36:28 (5,961)
Lee, Richard 3:36:21 (5,938)
Lee, Richard J 4:55:18 (25,749)
Lee, Ricky 3:46:24 (7,979)
Lee, Robert S 4:55:52 (25,851)
Lee, Simon 3:48:07 (8,380)
Lee, Spencer J 3:51:04 (9,068)
Lee, Stephen A 4:41:10 (22,478)
Lee, Steven J 5:28:26 (30,315)
Lee, Stuart 3:48:52 (8,544)
Lee, Victor 5:32:29 (30,700)
Lee Miller, Jonny 3:01:40 (1,287)
Lee Tan, Chris C 3:53:25 (9,700)
Leece, Terence 3:50:11 (8,866)
Leech, David E 4:19:16 (16,693)
Leek, Robert I 4:41:19 (22,518)
Leek, Shawn J 4:18:27 (16,479)
Leek, Steven 3:58:47 (11,406)
Leeke, Jason 4:23:15 (17,797)
Lee-Majors, Christian 6:09:05 (33,083)
Lees, Christopher 4:05:16 (13,113)
Lees, Martin A 4:54:26 (25,569)
Lees-Jones, Dylan A 4:59:53 (26,615)
Leeson, John P 5:12:23 (28,448)
Leeson, Tom D 5:12:23 (28,448)
Legendre, Stephane 2:50:31 (538)
Legg, Garry A 3:47:58 (8,341)
Legg, Mark 3:58:49 (11,426)
Legg, Michael D 3:11:58 (2,202)
Leggate, Jody R 3:54:49 (10,131)
Leggett, Adam J 6:02:07 (32,825)
Leggett, John 4:04:55 (13,031)
Le-Gleut, Philippe 4:05:40 (13,216)
Legrand, Ghislain 3:55:01 (10,201)
Legrove, Ian R 4:20:43 (17,100)
Lehal, John S 5:11:17 (28,307)
Le-Hir, Patrice 3:51:18 (9,123)
Lehman, David J 4:19:55 (16,864)
Lehmann-Tolkmitt, Bardo 5:06:48 (27,666)
Leiber, Christof 3:36:44 (6,001)
Leidman, Konstantin 5:23:45 (29,775)
Leigh, Adrian P 4:32:01 (20,177)
Leigh, Adrian P 5:14:18 (28,722)
Leigh, Alex 4:52:40 (25,190)
Leigh, Andrew J 3:42:53 (7,211)
Leigh, Christopher W 3:46:01 (7,891)
Leigh, David P 3:57:37 (10,987)
Leigh, David R 5:21:42 (29,578)
Leigh, Ian S 3:23:09 (3,657)
Leigh, Kevin S 5:37:41 (31,166)
Leigh, Philip 3:05:35 (1,561)
Leigh, Vincent R 3:32:30 (5,322)
Leighfield, Stephen P 3:54:17 (9,954)
Leighton, Allan L 5:55:27 (32,497)
Leighton, Alun P 3:54:22 (9,978)
Leighton, Mike 3:51:24 (9,152)
Leighton, Neil 3:45:20 (7,762)
Leighton, Robert G 3:42:16 (7,087)
Leighton-Crawford, Henry 4:52:58 (25,264)
Leitch, Derek 3:09:04 (1,890)
Leith, Wynne A 3:30:57 (5,046)
Lel, Martin 2:05:15 (1)
Lemambot Mbele, Willy Hugues 4:53:10 (25,310)
Lemanski, Stuart L 3:12:20 (2,250)
Lemay, Richard 3:57:06 (10,835)
Lemin, Mike J 3:56:22 (10,582)
Lemming, Mark M 4:00:36 (12,004)
Le-Moignic, Thierry 3:39:00 (6,437)
Lemon, Daniel R 4:45:13 (23,469)
Lemon, Darren M 4:45:11 (23,462)
Lemon, Edward 3:37:14 (6,109)
Lemon, Peter J 3:11:52 (2,194)
Lemos, Tiago 4:30:53 (19,863)
Lenehan, Gerard J 3:05:53 (1,588)
Lenehan, Toby 4:45:12 (23,465)
Lenihan, Keith J 4:22:29 (17,575)
Lenihan, Kevin G 3:07:50 (1,769)
Lennard, Andrew 3:37:15 (6,114)
Lennock, Mark J 4:06:59 (13,514)
Lennox, Timothy J 3:26:47 (4,246)
Lenoir, Gerard 3:27:18 (4,332)
Leo, Simon F 5:22:04 (29,606)
Leon, Clement 6:46:55 (34,015)
Leonard, Andrew J 5:26:31 (30,101)
Leonard, Mark J 5:13:59 (28,672)
Leonard, Paul 4:12:26 (14,914)
Leonard, Simon 3:26:51 (4,253)
Leone, Pasqualino 3:59:11 (11,554)
Lepine, Steven R 4:33:06 (20,457)
Lepper, Leslie A 3:26:11 (4,136)
Lequite, Didier 3:23:38 (3,720)
Lerman, Antony 4:32:49 (20,377)
Leroy, Robert W 5:49:38 (32,095)
Lerwill, Ben J 4:00:46 (12,050)
Lescot, Philippe 4:26:27 (18,651)
Lesiak, Craig A 3:58:32 (11,310)
Leslau, Ori 4:05:38 (13,206)
Lesley, Robin 4:43:15 (22,994)
Leslie, David 6:01:23 (32,792)
Leslie, Marc P 5:23:13 (29,719)
Leslie, Mark 3:53:34 (9,732)
Leslie, Richard P 3:25:13 (3,962)
Leslie Melville, Jake 4:55:43 (25,821)
Lessard, Ghislain 3:34:27 (5,615)
Lessell, James S 4:25:38 (18,422)
Lessware, Edward P 4:35:40 (21,157)
Lester, Brad 4:54:07 (25,504)
Lester, Martin D 6:08:44 (33,072)
Lester, Paul D 2:51:53 (589)
Lester, Richard D 4:14:05 (15,331)
Lester, Roy E 5:01:36 (26,896)
Lesti, Attila 2:57:31 (905)
Le-Strat, Jean 4:29:20 (19,481)
Letford, John 3:26:26 (4,178)
Lethaby, Raymond J 4:54:04 (25,493)
Letherby, Andrew 2:13:50 (14)
Letheren, Mark 4:34:41 (20,870)
Letts, Anthony W 3:04:40 (1,493)
Leuenberger, Michael 3:10:54 (2,089)
Leutert, Christoe 4:08:48 (13,992)
Levens, Nicholas B 5:40:34 (31,381)
Levenstein, Allan 3:59:29 (11,668)
Lever, Alexander Z 3:59:59 (11,850)
Lever, John 5:00:48 (26,761)
Leverett, Clive E 4:43:48 (23,122)
Leverett, Michael J 3:48:11 (8,395)
Leveritt, Stephen R 4:16:02 (15,845)
Levermore, Gary A 3:34:15 (5,584)
Leversuch, Robert 5:21:48 (29,588)
Levett, Mark 5:34:00 (30,836)
Levine, Pascal 4:14:49 (15,518)
Levitan, Tamir 4:06:24 (13,373)
Levitton, James M 5:35:27 (30,970)
Levitz, Michael 4:15:02 (15,574)
Levy, Elliot 5:05:52 (27,525)
Levy, Paul 3:31:20 (5,105)
Levy, Simon J 3:35:15 (5,747)
Lewes, James H 3:27:00 (4,281)
Lewi, Daniel 5:09:04 (27,979)
Lewi, Matthew 5:09:03 (27,976)
Lewin, Gary S 5:27:18 (30,180)
Lewis, Andrew C 4:18:53 (16,595)
Lewis, Andy 3:13:52 (2,444)
Lewis, Andy J 4:29:12 (19,453)

Lewis, Anthony R 3:56:31 (10,629)
Lewis, Ben 4:33:33 (20,591)
Lewis, Ben 5:07:46 (27,806)
Lewis, Brandon 5:32:08 (30,671)
Lewis, Colin 3:29:08 (4,700)
Lewis, Craig M 4:35:35 (21,129)
Lewis, Daniel 5:22:22 (29,646)
Lewis, Daniel M 4:39:03 (21,988)
Lewis, David C 5:07:11 (27,716)
Lewis, David G 4:01:43 (12,299)
Lewis, David J 3:34:14 (5,580)
Lewis, David J 4:18:07 (16,374)
Lewis, David P 4:26:51 (18,773)
Lewis, Dunbar H 5:28:50 (30,353)
Lewis, Francis M 3:59:32 (11,683)
Lewis, Gil 4:27:51 (19,040)
Lewis, Graham 4:18:16 (16,421)
Lewis, Graham F 4:20:59 (17,177)
Lewis, Graham M 4:15:11 (15,613)
Lewis, Hugh T 4:01:59 (12,358)
Lewis, Ian M 5:00:01 (26,637)
Lewis, Jason F 4:01:52 (12,329)
Lewis, John 4:30:00 (19,636)
Lewis, John D 3:50:27 (8,920)
Lewis, Jordan 5:58:37 (32,678)
Lewis, Julian D 3:30:08 (4,912)
Lewis, Julian P 3:03:03 (1,377)
Lewis, Karl 4:57:34 (26,199)
Lewis, Ken 5:55:52 (32,515)
Lewis, Kenneth B 4:26:52 (18,781)
Lewis, Leighton C 5:04:32 (27,333)
Lewis, Leonard J 4:20:18 (16,975)
Lewis, Mark 4:48:43 (24,298)
Lewis, Mark J 3:11:32 (2,153)
Lewis, Mark S 3:57:32 (10,964)
Lewis, Martin G 2:34:03 (104)
Lewis, Martin W 5:43:27 (31,606)
Lewis, Matthew D 3:59:13 (11,568)
Lewis, Matthew K 3:42:43 (7,175)
Lewis, Michael J 3:56:48 (10,727)
Lewis, Michael P 4:31:16 (19,952)
Lewis, Neil J 4:01:54 (12,340)
Lewis, Owen 5:23:59 (29,803)
Lewis, Paul A 2:49:38 (495)
Lewis, Paul G 5:13:48 (28,648)
Lewis, Paul J 4:01:29 (12,237)
Lewis, Peter J 6:47:40 (34,031)
Lewis, Phil A 4:00:29 (11,969)
Lewis, Rhodri P 4:45:58 (23,665)
Lewis, Richard W 5:39:17 (31,285)
Lewis, Ryan M 4:23:12 (17,786)
Lewis, Stefan E 4:29:55 (19,613)
Lewis, Tim 4:38:47 (21,908)
Lewis, Tim J 3:27:13 (4,315)
Lewis, Timothy D 4:15:04 (15,584)
Lewis, Trevor A 3:05:43 (1,575)
Lewis-Jones, Peter J 4:15:56 (15,819)
Lewisman, Hagan 3:31:30 (5,127)
Lewison, Jeremy R 4:42:05 (22,692)
Lewis-Russell, Mark A 5:04:01 (27,255)
Lewkowicz, Nicholas M 4:22:56 (17,710)
Lewsey, David G 5:05:11 (27,433)
Lewton, Sean A 3:41:00 (6,824)
Leyenda, Manuel 3:32:32 (5,325)
Leyland, Jim 5:56:24 (32,553)
Leyland, Simon J 3:51:16 (9,113)
Leyssene, Vincent 3:50:31 (8,931)
L'Hopital, Thibaut 3:16:25 (2,807)
Li, Jun 5:41:50 (31,489)
Li, Victor 4:45:27 (23,529)
Li, Xin 4:40:44 (22,364)
Li Calzi, Rocco 4:42:12 (22,723)
Li Fook, Donald 4:58:13 (26,328)
Licata, Gaetano 3:22:17 (3,530)
Licht, Floris 4:30:26 (19,728)
Liddle, Andy A 3:10:24 (2,030)
Lidgate-Taylor, Steven P 2:52:48 (630)
Liegeois, Serge 4:09:02 (14,050)
Liet, Philippe L 3:35:05 (5,723)
Ligabue, Roberto 3:54:14 (9,936)
Liggat, Steven 3:29:00 (4,669)
Light, Barry J 3:28:49 (4,629)
Light, David G 4:43:06 (22,962)
Light, Dominic P 3:37:09 (6,088)
Light, Ian J 5:35:46 (31,003)
Light, Jon M 3:24:36 (3,857)
Light, Marc 4:43:05 (22,954)
Light, Paul L 5:14:32 (28,745)
Light, Richard D 4:04:27 (12,919)
Lightfoot, Andrew R 4:59:46 (26,606)
Liguori, Pietro 2:59:35 (1,127)
Liiv, Owen A 5:05:31 (27,479)
Lilja, Peter E 4:52:29 (25,143)
Lilley, Gordon 5:26:55 (30,140)
Lilley, Samuel E 4:01:17 (12,178)
Lillico, Jim 3:48:52 (8,544)
Lillywhite, James A 4:26:00 (18,538)
Lima, Reagan 4:49:38 (24,514)
Limbert, Mark J 4:20:45 (17,103)
Limehouse, Gary A 5:33:00 (30,749)
Limo, Felix 2:10:35 (8)
Linathan, Julian 3:17:10 (2,884)
Lincoln, Andrew 3:42:15 (7,081)
Lincoln, Eliot 2:58:51 (1,047)
Lindahl, Johan 3:00:53 (1,231)
Lindebotten, John 3:37:30 (6,170)
Lindemann, Thomas 5:01:00 (26,796)
Lindenmeyer, Ruediger 5:22:03 (29,604)
Lindo, Murray 5:40:50 (31,401)
Lindop, Tim 2:47:50 (416)
Lindsay, Andrew J 4:32:28 (20,288)
Lindsay, Brian 5:09:19 (28,014)
Lindsay, David N 5:35:34 (30,983)
Lindsay, Don 4:11:27 (14,662)
Lindsay, John 4:15:26 (15,684)
Lindsay, John 4:53:00 (25,269)
Lindsay, John C 4:55:50 (25,842)
Lindsay, Nigel M 3:53:09 (9,620)
Lindsay, Simon D 3:55:54 (10,465)
Lindsay, Steven W 3:54:44 (10,108)
Lindsay, Vaughan E 3:36:41 (5,995)
Lindsey-Clark, Matthew P 4:05:16 (13,113)
Line, Darrell 4:12:40 (14,958)
Line, Ian 3:38:16 (6,312)
Linehan, Kevin P 2:57:03 (877)
Lines, Edward 4:58:30 (26,375)
Ling, Robert 4:42:11 (22,715)
Lingard, John 3:52:37 (9,461)
Lingard, Richard 4:20:48 (17,127)
Lingis, Nicholas 4:51:36 (24,960)
Link, Simon J 2:43:56 (292)
Linkenbach, Alexander 3:52:54 (9,536)
Linn, Mark 4:22:22 (17,542)
Linnane, Neil 4:47:52 (24,109)
Linnane, Paul S 5:08:58 (27,965)
Linnett, Ian C 4:08:13 (13,833)
Linton, Martin 4:29:08 (19,434)
Linton, Stephen P 4:27:00 (18,812)
Lintott, Edward J 3:58:52 (11,444)
Liogier, Christian 3:48:47 (8,529)
Lipka, Lawrence A 5:42:02 (31,500)
Lippi, Francesco 3:35:33 (5,800)
Lippiett, Thomas P 4:15:55 (15,811)
Lipsch, René M 3:16:38 (2,825)
Lipscomb, David 3:29:41 (4,817)
Lipscomb, Scott 3:51:31 (9,176)
Lipscombe, Sam J 4:06:33 (13,415)
Lipshaw, Danny 4:08:06 (13,789)
Lipshaw, Simon C 4:08:06 (13,789)
Liptrot, John F 3:13:35 (2,404)
Lisk, Harold E 6:54:09 (34,139)
Lisk, Rodney T 4:23:16 (17,804)
Lisle, Richard A 3:20:44 (3,322)
Lister, Adam 4:24:47 (18,210)
Lister, Andrew 3:28:44 (4,609)
Lister, Darron 4:11:33 (14,693)
Lister, Kevin 4:56:59 (26,071)
Lister, Pete J 5:40:59 (31,411)
Litherland, Ross B 3:11:47 (2,187)
Little, Ian K 2:57:43 (924)
Little, Kelvin T 4:28:15 (19,191)
Little, Martin R 3:51:53 (9,271)
Little, Paul J 3:27:46 (4,412)
Little, Rupert J 3:50:09 (8,859)
Little, Simon C 4:19:08 (16,663)
Littlechild, Joseph E 3:49:24 (8,674)
Littlechild, Justin P 3:02:49 (1,364)
Littlejohn, Matthew S 3:24:58 (3,921)
Littlejohn, Robert E 3:54:49 (10,131)
Littlejohns, Alan W 3:35:21 (5,764)
Littler, Darren M 6:12:33 (33,188)
Littler, Stephen T 2:25:21 (37)
Littlewood, Mike H 4:24:22 (18,098)
Litton, Toby J 3:35:43 (5,834)
Litvin, Norman P 2:59:28 (1,116)
Litwin, Kevin 4:49:32 (24,484)
Livermore, Robert F 4:51:09 (24,870)
Livesey, Richard I 5:45:18 (31,785)
Livingston, Thomas J 4:12:20 (14,892)
Livingstone-Learmont, Max 3:28:33 (4,569)
Livsey, Richard E 5:12:42 (28,494)
Lizarraga Perez, Mikel 3:50:45 (8,998)
Lkinkenberg, Ross H 4:46:39 (23,814)
Llagostera, Marc 4:52:39 (25,185)
Llewellyn, Clive 3:46:53 (8,078)
Llewellyn, Paul 3:12:11 (2,231)
Llewellyn, William M 4:15:01 (15,568)
Lloyd, Adrian C 3:25:56 (4,097)
Lloyd, Adrian E 3:50:17 (8,890)
Lloyd, Alastair M 3:37:04 (6,074)
Lloyd, Benjamin P 4:04:12 (12,864)
Lloyd, Julian F 4:01:18 (12,184)
Lloyd, Kevin 4:24:34 (18,164)
Lloyd, Matthew 4:46:44 (23,836)
Lloyd, Peter D 3:18:36 (3,056)
Lloyd, Richard C 4:13:36 (15,187)
Lloyd, Robin 3:46:28 (8,001)
Lloyd, Thomas M 4:03:39 (12,758)
Lloyd, Thomas P 6:30:33 (33,672)
Lloyd, Tom 3:36:42 (5,999)
Lloyd, Tom 4:27:31 (18,953)
Lloyd Owen, Edward 6:25:53 (33,573)
Loader, Guy 3:51:35 (9,191)
Loadman, Neil 4:45:50 (23,629)
Loakes, Martin S 4:27:22 (18,924)
Lobb, Ian K 4:48:21 (24,216)
Lobb, Kevin M 3:32:08 (5,248)
Lobb, Matt R 3:31:17 (5,098)
Lobb, Peregrine A 4:13:02 (15,045)
Lobina, Alberto 4:48:02 (24,157)
Lobina, Paolo 3:43:47 (7,411)
Lobley, David P 4:07:19 (13,599)
Loccock, Ian A 5:39:14 (31,279)
Lochtie, Angus A 2:59:23 (1,108)
Lock, Barry 4:24:49 (18,221)
Lock, Christopher M 5:09:12 (27,996)
Lock, Dan 4:41:59 (22,667)
Lock, Darren 3:27:23 (4,346)
Lock, David 2:58:28 (1,004)
Lock, David S 5:51:08 (32,217)
Lock, Ian K 4:48:52 (24,335)
Lock, Leslie K 3:25:42 (4,049)
Lock, Ricky 4:01:12 (12,165)
Locke, David J 4:23:58 (17,981)
Locke, Mark A 5:44:09 (31,678)
Locke, William J 3:51:02 (9,058)
Locker, Darren 4:36:24 (21,344)
Lockett, Gary J 5:15:21 (28,860)
Lockett, Patrick 3:09:54 (1,982)
Lockey, Alistair J 2:35:39 (124)
Lockie, David A 5:08:30 (27,896)
Lockington, Andrew 5:19:46 (29,387)
Lockley, Darren 3:42:26 (7,124)
Lockwood, Leslie 5:58:04 (32,636)
Lockwood, Paul R 4:06:50 (13,482)
Lockwood, Simon R 4:29:39 (19,551)
Lockwood-Cowell, Stuart 4:31:55 (20,144)
Lockyear, Kevin R 3:38:02 (6,268)
Lockyer, Anthony R 4:27:05 (18,834)
Lockyer, Philip M 3:03:57 (1,445)
Locock, Martin R 4:46:45 (23,838)
Loder, Adam 3:24:13 (3,806)
Loder, Austin 3:48:41 (8,507)
Loder, Mark 4:09:50 (14,259)
Lodge, Derek H 3:27:03 (4,286)
Lodge, Gareth A 4:59:27 (26,551)
Lodge, John C 3:35:33 (5,800)
Lodge, Paul D 4:44:36 (23,321)
Lodge, Philip M 4:44:57 (23,402)

Lodge, Steve 4:05:11 (13,093)
Lodge, Stuart 3:24:51 (3,899)
Lodi, Paolo 2:58:20 (982)
Loeffler, Reinhold 4:26:57 (18,798)
Loftus, Kevin J 3:19:51 (3,212)
Logan, Gregory D 5:05:05 (27,414)
Logan, Liam P 5:24:50 (29,893)
Logan, Ross E 4:53:14 (25,322)
Logan, Stuart 3:12:21 (2,251)
Loi, Giuseppe 3:54:46 (10,118)
Loizou, Christopher 2:59:27 (1,114)
Lok, Joseph 3:46:18 (7,952)
Lomans, Franciscus P 4:10:58 (14,537)
Lomas, Bryan G 2:47:00 (388)
Lomas, Gary 3:59:12 (11,562)
Lomas, Ian 4:42:12 (22,723)
Lomas, Jim S 4:05:29 (13,172)
Lomas, Roger 3:34:39 (5,635)
Lomas, T 4:36:09 (21,280)
Lombard, Declan F 4:35:00 (20,982)
Lombardo, Mauro 4:23:46 (17,937)
London, Gavin J 3:55:14 (10,273)
Lonergan, John W 3:01:24 (1,269)
Long, Charles I 4:06:38 (13,436)
Long, Charles J 4:19:50 (16,842)
Long, David J 4:09:26 (14,151)
Long, Gavin P 3:27:25 (4,354)
Long, Keith A 5:48:56 (32,046)
Long, Matthew 5:09:27 (28,036)
Long, Neil B 3:51:20 (9,132)
Long, Neil I 3:59:21 (11,613)
Long, Steve 4:33:44 (20,647)
Long, Stuart G 4:50:36 (24,746)
Long, Thomas M 3:34:49 (5,669)
Long, Tim 4:05:47 (13,243)
Long, Trevor 5:27:17 (30,176)
Longhorn, Dave 3:36:39 (5,988)
Longhurst, Adam 5:28:39 (30,338)
Longley, Adam S 4:13:39 (15,203)
Longley, Robert C 4:49:45 (24,543)
Longman, Christopher 4:35:56 (21,220)
Longmire, Anthony 4:58:40 (26,410)
Longmuir, Andrew A 3:37:09 (6,088)
Longoni, Emanuele 4:37:13 (21,531)
Longoni, Paolo 3:35:58 (5,875)

Longster, Philip J 5:04:02 (27,256)

My daughter, Hope, was born in 2007 with Down's Syndrome and a hole in the heart. So running for the Down's Heart Group made the day all the more worthwhile. This was my third London Marathon and dedicated to Hope. Thinking of her spurred me on to complete the course in quite difficult conditions!

Longthorp, Andrew 4:35:05 (21,005)
Lonnroth, Johnny-Stefan 2:53:52 (683)
Lonsdale, Andrew M 4:29:56 (19,617)
Lonsdale, Christopher 4:07:37 (13,677)
Loo, Hon Ming 4:35:26 (21,094)
Loom, Jason 5:02:06 (26,967)
Loomes, Kevin A 4:08:31 (13,919)
Loosemore, David H 3:58:32 (11,310)
Lopez, Gabriel 3:57:59 (11,109)
Lopez, Gabriel 4:25:04 (18,278)
Lopez, Hector G 5:33:44 (30,803)
Lopez Fernandez, Francisco J 3:09:43 (1,963)
Lopez-Cruz, Daniel 4:02:16 (12,436)
Lord, Christopher I 4:26:05 (18,564)
Lord, David A 3:09:50 (1,975)
Lord, Derek 3:29:05 (4,688)
Lord, Richard J 5:34:12 (30,858)
Lorente Iranzo, Manuel I 2:57:50 (932)
Lorentz, Christian 5:09:50 (28,123)
Lorenz, Michael P 4:30:31 (19,749)
Lorenzo Muradas, Francisco J 4:38:59 (21,971)
Lorgat, Zakir 5:29:42 (30,445)
Lorig, Milton L 3:44:28 (7,547)
Lorimer, Stephen J 5:44:20 (31,701)
Lorkin, David J 3:52:29 (9,428)
Lornie, Richard 4:09:51 (14,262)
Lorusso, Domenico 4:24:07 (18,023)
Lott, Andrew 3:39:16 (6,490)
Lotz, Paul E 3:54:45 (10,114)
Loucaides, George 2:53:28 (661)
Louch, Colin A 4:05:27 (13,161)
Loudon, David 4:03:59 (12,827)
Lough, Nigel D 6:20:10 (33,399)
Loughlan, Joseph 4:54:54 (25,673)
Loughlin, Kenny W 3:14:08 (2,489)
Loughlin, Tim 3:29:00 (4,669)
Loughman, Richard 4:25:35 (18,411)
Loughnane, Martin C 3:08:05 (1,798)
Loughran, Nicholas A 3:50:35 (8,949)
Lound, Charles A 2:44:03 (294)
Lound-Keast, Joe 3:51:52 (9,265)
Louw, Bertus J 3:38:28 (6,352)
Lovatt, Adam 5:04:12 (27,280)
Love, Christopher C 5:05:28 (27,467)
Loveday, Richard M 4:23:42 (17,914)
Lovegrove, Paul D 3:30:47 (5,017)
Lovegrove, Thomas S 4:42:57 (22,920)
Lovell, Christopher J 4:11:35 (14,702)
Lovell, Guy 4:39:10 (22,020)
Lovell, John C 4:31:32 (20,032)
Lovell, Michael A 2:45:20 (344)
Lovell, Peter R 3:19:15 (3,128)
Lovell, Robert D 4:26:17 (18,605)
Lovell, Ross P 4:19:28 (16,743)
Lovelock, Charles 5:42:58 (31,567)
Lovelock, David J 4:12:59 (15,027)
Lovelock, Trevor J 3:35:07 (5,726)
Loveridge, Paul J 3:41:59 (7,022)
Loveridge, Trevor J 4:59:39 (26,584)
Lovering, Ian P 4:32:10 (20,215)
Lovesey, Neil R 3:29:54 (4,867)
Lovett, Lee 4:00:50 (12,066)
Lovick, Christopher 4:07:11 (13,575)
Lovick, Paul J 3:50:12 (8,873)
Lovidge, Leslie J 3:36:47 (6,012)
Low, Colin I 6:04:41 (32,911)
Low, Dominic 4:41:39 (22,598)
Low, Joshua S 3:20:37 (3,309)
Low, Nicholas 4:33:56 (20,689)
Low, Richard G 4:12:54 (15,005)
Low, Roger L 3:47:04 (8,125)
Low, Steven D 3:18:17 (3,016)
Low, Tony M 4:45:53 (23,642)
Lowde, Antony S 3:36:21 (5,938)
Lowde, Kim R 3:38:44 (6,396)
Lowden, Chris D 4:54:56 (25,683)
Lowe, Andrew M 3:34:11 (5,575)
Lowe, Anthony S 5:14:52 (28,797)
Lowe, Daniel W 5:14:15 (28,713)
Lowe, David 4:26:16 (18,601)
Lowe, Gareth 4:25:47 (18,473)
Lowe, Gary M 4:05:28 (13,168)
Lowe, Graham P 5:43:24 (31,600)
Lowe, Jake 3:18:29 (3,047)
Lowe, James D 4:57:19 (26,145)
Lowe, Liam P 4:17:23 (16,186)
Lowe, Matthew J 4:07:03 (13,531)
Lowe, Richard S 4:17:46 (16,298)
Lowe, Rick 5:11:49 (28,387)
Lowe, Simon J 3:12:37 (2,279)
Lower, Rob W 3:22:34 (3,579)
Lowery, Tony 4:33:16 (20,496)
Lowes, Andrew 3:22:08 (3,505)
Lownie, Mark 4:56:55 (26,060)
Lowrie, Scott M 5:22:33 (29,669)
Lowry, Daniel 4:58:23 (26,357)
Lowry, Hugo G 3:49:13 (8,632)
Lowson, Richard J 2:42:06 (243)
Lowther, Keith A 3:09:37 (1,952)
Lowther, Paul D 4:56:48 (26,025)
Loy, Martin 3:05:33 (1,558)
Loydall, Mark A 5:32:58 (30,744)
Luard, David 3:53:45 (9,791)
Lubbe, Waldie 3:44:59 (7,676)
Luca, Luiz Alberto O 3:45:16 (7,745)
Lucas, Alan 3:43:36 (7,366)
Lucas, Chris P 3:54:41 (10,097)
Lucas, Christopher 3:28:04 (4,473)
Lucas, Graham C 4:58:44 (26,432)
Lucas, Marc 3:09:20 (1,924)
Lucas, Mark 4:44:01 (23,188)
Lucas, Matthew J 5:28:29 (30,320)
Lucas, Michael J 4:48:29 (24,243)
Lucas, Mike G 4:49:19 (24,436)
Lucas, Peter 3:47:14 (8,165)
Lucas, Rick 3:55:36 (10,371)
Luciani, Gianfranco 4:00:19 (11,929)
Lucker, Alan 3:21:58 (3,487)
Luckhurst, Anthony P 4:49:04 (24,388)
Luckman, Neil E 6:21:24 (33,441)
Ludlow-Palafox, Carlos 4:49:54 (24,575)
Ludman, Ian T 3:43:11 (7,283)
Lui, Stephen L 5:58:44 (32,683)
Luiten, Anthony M 4:44:16 (23,248)
Luke, Theo 4:30:13 (19,683)
Lumaca, Silverio 3:27:25 (4,354)
Lumb, Christopher J 4:28:58 (19,393)
Lumber, Nigel R 3:06:44 (1,660)
Lumley, Matthew 3:53:00 (9,572)
Lumley, Paul 4:04:34 (12,942)
Lumsden, William 4:26:18 (18,610)
Lund, Geoffrey D 4:09:00 (14,041)
Lund, Matthew 3:30:57 (5,046)
Lund, Simon 3:14:36 (2,567)
Lundemose, Anker 4:24:31 (18,147)
Lundie, Blair A 4:49:51 (24,562)
Lundie, Matthew J 4:14:07 (15,340)
Lunn, Chris J 3:32:07 (5,246)
Lunn, Ian 5:06:54 (27,682)
Lunn, Mark 3:46:21 (7,965)
Lunn, Peter 3:31:23 (5,112)
Lunt, Geoffrey 4:32:14 (20,238)
Lunt, Stephen J 4:12:51 (14,992)
Lunzer, Josef 3:32:15 (5,267)
Luong, Hien V 3:49:31 (8,704)
Lupi, Stefano 4:15:37 (15,734)
Lurcott, Richard P 4:25:31 (18,402)
Lush, Martin K 3:49:12 (8,627)
Lushington, Henry R 3:52:59 (9,566)
Luther, Robert 5:33:45 (30,807)
Lutkin, Max 3:47:12 (8,154)
Lutman-Pauc, Sam 4:29:54 (19,606)
Luton, David 4:54:12 (25,519)
Lutz, Oliver 4:02:17 (12,444)
Luxon, Keith 3:09:57 (1,984)
Luzio, Gian 5:13:06 (28,556)
Lyall, Graham C 3:06:54 (1,675)
Lycett, Paul J 5:28:51 (30,358)
Lyle, Ewan A 3:41:18 (6,899)
Lynall, Richard 4:40:27 (22,298)
Lynam, Jason 4:23:59 (17,987)
Lynam, Robert G 3:21:19 (3,406)
Lynch, Andrew J 3:55:38 (10,382)
Lynch, Brian D 3:20:12 (3,249)
Lynch, Bryan A 3:42:10 (7,061)
Lynch, Daniel J 5:20:13 (29,431)
Lynch, Darren 4:54:54 (25,673)
Lynch, Donald T 5:09:55 (28,132)
Lynch, Fred 2:58:38 (1,022)
Lynch, Raymond M 5:58:23 (32,661)
Lynch, Richard J 4:45:46 (23,611)
Lynch, Robert J 3:47:57 (8,338)
Lynch, Simon 4:08:39 (13,955)
Lynch, Simon N 4:47:04 (23,923)
Lynch, Steven R 3:55:58 (10,483)
Lynch, Terry J 4:41:02 (22,445)
Lyndon, Andrew S 6:00:03 (32,741)
Lyne, Andrew G 2:50:22 (529)
Lyne, Graham A 4:12:37 (14,953)
Lyne, Steven G 3:49:57 (8,814)
Lyness, Alex M 4:05:10 (13,089)
Lynn, Jeff 3:30:55 (5,041)
Lynn, Matthew 4:18:13 (16,405)
Lynn, Simon 4:17:52 (16,318)
Lynn, Stuart W 3:30:51 (5,029)
Lynock, Mark 3:43:49 (7,416)
Lyon, Andrew W 4:16:07 (15,858)
Lyon, Daniel 4:12:08 (14,843)
Lyon, David G 5:19:25 (29,342)
Lyon, John H 3:56:44 (10,702)
Lyon, Nigel 3:43:45 (7,400)

Lyon, Paul A	5:01:35 (26,887)	
Lyon, Roger J	5:08:27 (27,886)	
Lyonnet, Gerard	4:07:50 (13,725)	
Lyons, Andrew	2:33:55 (103)	
Lyons, Barnaby T	4:43:09 (22,971)	
Lyons, Dale	5:18:17 (29,206)	
Lyons, Denys	3:21:53 (3,470)	
Lyons, Gary S	3:52:10 (9,351)	
Lyons, Kevin O	3:31:49 (5,189)	
Lyons, Mark A	4:30:52 (19,855)	
Lyons, Matthew	5:24:50 (29,893)	
Lyons, Michael E	4:54:19 (25,542)	
Lyons, Stuart	5:37:09 (31,127)	
Lyrsholt, Frederik H	3:12:00 (2,205)	
Lyttle, John	4:45:53 (23,642)	
Lyubenov, Radi A	3:24:54 (3,909)	
Ma, Ruoyi	4:04:50 (13,007)	
Maan, Mark	3:54:52 (10,144)	
Mabbutt, Steven D	4:47:45 (24,088)	
Mabey, Christopher P	5:44:58 (31,761)	
Mabey, Peter F	3:17:15 (2,894)	
Mabire, Leon	2:49:33 (493)	
Maby, Richard W	6:00:54 (32,775)	
Mac, Steve	4:15:04 (15,584)	
MacAlister, Angus J	3:18:32 (3,051)	
MacAllan, Ray	4:16:40 (16,005)	
MacAninch, Cal	4:00:33 (11,987)	
Macarthur, Robert J	4:27:43 (19,002)	
MacAskill, Andy	2:41:10 (221)	
MacAskill, Day N	4:25:01 (18,266)	
MacAskill, John R	3:24:58 (3,921)	
Macaulay, Martin	3:55:20 (10,295)	
Macaulay, William	4:33:29 (20,572)	
Maccarrone, Franck	3:42:12 (7,071)	
Mac Con Iomaire, Ronan	4:27:55 (19,071)	
MacCormac, Oscar J	4:33:28 (20,567)	
Macdonald, Alasdair J	4:47:40 (24,059)	
Macdonald, Alistair K	3:58:46 (11,397)	
Macdonald, Charles J	3:42:01 (7,031)	
Macdonald, David M	2:53:56 (689)	
Macdonald, Gordon D	4:42:29 (22,800)	
Macdonald, Gordon N	3:56:36 (10,663)	
Macdonald, Ian M	3:46:29 (8,004)	
Macdonald, Jay	5:55:51 (32,512)	
Macdonald, John R	3:34:23 (5,603)	
Macdonald, Mark J	4:17:08 (16,135)	
Macdonald, Rob S	4:56:48 (26,025)	
Macdonald, Scott R	4:12:02 (14,816)	
Macdonald, Stephen G	5:43:52 (31,639)	
Macdonald-Jones, Glenn L	3:05:13 (1,531)	
MacDougall, Ian D	2:39:35 (189)	
Mace, Will N	4:04:58 (13,042)	
MacEnhill, Damian P	3:08:08 (1,807)	
Macey, David P	4:16:49 (16,041)	
Macey, Mark R	5:06:26 (27,620)	
Macey, Robert F	5:11:15 (28,301)	
Macey, Terence J	4:30:45 (19,816)	
Macfarlane, Angus J	5:29:10 (30,394)	
MacGregor, Callum	5:00:21 (26,687)	
MacGregor, James G	5:28:38 (30,337)	
MacGregor, Jim K	4:49:24 (24,457)	
Machado, Fernando	5:00:36 (26,718)	
Machell, Phill K	5:32:31 (30,701)	
Machin, Paul J	3:27:35 (4,376)	
Machray, Simon M	4:18:48 (16,572)	
Macintyre, Paul J	4:03:11 (12,649)	
MacIver, Allan P	6:11:49 (33,160)	
Mack, Christiaan M	3:58:53 (11,451)	
Mack, Daniel	4:51:30 (24,940)	
Mack, Darren R	2:57:59 (947)	
Mack, Martin W	3:14:33 (2,559)	
Mack, Peter R	3:14:31 (2,554)	
Mack, Stephen	4:15:23 (15,663)	
Mackay, Andrew C	4:31:28 (20,017)	
Mackay, Derek	5:35:47 (31,004)	
Mackay, Graeme	3:07:07 (1,691)	
Mackay, Iain	6:04:18 (32,903)	
Mackay, Jason S	4:57:28 (26,177)	
Mackay, Nicholas	3:49:53 (8,794)	
MacKeaggan, Kevin	4:15:53 (15,804)	
Mackenzie, Adam N	4:42:08 (22,709)	
Mackenzie, Adrian B	4:06:44 (13,459)	
Mackenzie, Brian	2:58:25 (995)	

Mackenzie, Nick P	3:05:48 (1,581)	
Mackenzie, Robert E	3:28:25 (4,538)	
Mackenzie, Robin K	3:25:42 (4,049)	
Mackey, Paul	4:50:18 (24,667)	
Mackey, Richard	4:13:00 (15,034)	
Mackie, Ian G	5:39:44 (31,313)	
MacKinnon, Ewen	4:21:46 (17,398)	
Mackintosh, Angus P	4:43:34 (23,070)	
Mackley, Daniel J	4:03:12 (12,654)	
MacKonochie, Robin H	4:57:10 (26,119)	
Mackrill, Colin	4:02:08 (12,396)	
MacLachlan, Neil	2:55:13 (764)	
Maclaren, Donald B	3:05:40 (1,567)	
MacLaurin, Toby J	5:50:41 (32,185)	
Maclean, Alan	5:30:34 (30,534)	
Maclean, Fraser W	3:55:39 (10,389)	
Maclean, Graham A	5:14:39 (28,768)	
Maclean, John	3:10:52 (2,084)	
Maclean, Philip	4:02:05 (12,382)	
Maclean, Quentin J	3:12:00 (2,205)	
Maclean, Richard A	4:46:15 (23,727)	
Maclean, Richard G	5:34:17 (30,863)	
Maclean, Robert D	4:17:40 (16,268)	
Maclean, Ross C	4:26:24 (18,635)	
Maclean, Spencer L	3:52:43 (9,484)	
Macleod, Douglas R	4:42:43 (22,858)	
Macleod, James R	3:39:44 (6,582)	
Macleod, Marco M	4:21:39 (17,357)	
Mac Manus, Paul	3:25:55 (4,091)	
Macmillan, Douglas T	5:23:25 (29,736)	
Macmillan, Fergus N	3:49:29 (8,696)	
Macmillan, Neil A	3:57:12 (10,862)	
Macmillan, Paul	4:46:16 (23,733)	
Macmillan, Robert	4:47:35 (24,038)	
MacNamara, James J	4:07:59 (13,770)	
MacNaught, Alister	3:59:40 (11,741)	
MacNiven, Philip J	5:29:28 (30,420)	
Macoustra, Andrew	3:12:50 (2,310)	
Macpherson, Alan A	3:02:07 (1,317)	
MacQueen, Ian	5:16:06 (28,946)	
Macro, Anthony J	4:52:34 (25,161)	
Macro, Kevin	5:29:43 (30,449)	
Macrow, Timothy	5:22:45 (29,681)	
MacSephney, Scott A	2:58:10 (964)	
MacSporran, Alasdair D	4:04:59 (13,046)	
Mac Taggart, Scott W	5:38:36 (31,229)	
MacVicar, William	4:09:24 (14,141)	
Madarbux, Rahim	3:41:46 (6,983)	
Madden, Liam J	4:44:12 (23,229)	
Madden, Peter V	4:39:16 (22,040)	
Madden, Pierce	4:16:55 (16,065)	
Madden, Scott	4:26:01 (18,544)	
Madden, Will F	4:58:20 (26,348)	
Maddison, Ian	5:07:16 (27,733)	
Maddock, Laurence J	4:25:19 (18,348)	
Madelin, Gary	3:40:51 (6,793)	
Madges, Mark	4:50:09 (24,633)	
Madigan, Sean	5:51:53 (32,281)	
Madjarevic, Mark	4:29:35 (19,537)	
Madlani, Vivek	4:36:21 (21,336)	
Madle, John R	5:25:12 (29,948)	
Madoc-Jones, Steven R	4:36:36 (21,393)	
Maeda, Malcolm	4:16:39 (15,997)	
Maes, Emiel	3:32:18 (5,278)	
Magee, Damian G	3:52:58 (9,560)	
Maggs, Nigel J	3:32:32 (5,325)	
Maggs, Robert	3:26:28 (4,182)	
Maggs, Simon D	3:04:25 (1,511)	
Magill, Bruce A	3:57:27 (10,942)	
Magill, John A	3:31:37 (5,156)	
Maginnis, Rob	4:27:15 (18,890)	
Magni, Paolo	4:33:39 (20,622)	
Magnus, Thomas H	3:48:44 (8,520)	
Magnusson, Thomas S	4:30:21 (19,712)	
Magudia, Manoj	4:44:06 (23,202)	
Maguire, Adam	4:53:20 (25,337)	
Maguire, Allan P	4:34:18 (20,776)	
Maguire, David A	4:01:25 (12,220)	
Maguire, Mark	3:45:44 (7,840)	
Maguire, Michael	5:01:50 (26,934)	
Maguire, Ross J	4:35:39 (21,152)	
Maguire, Samuel J	4:35:15 (21,046)	
Maguire, Terence J	6:45:19 (33,986)	

Maguire, Trevor A	2:59:55 (1,161)	
Mahajan, Rakesh	6:06:03 (32,978)	
Mahal, Malkit	5:41:28 (31,462)	
Mahal, Rajiv	4:25:20 (18,352)	
Maher, David D	3:44:55 (7,660)	
Maher, Derek P	4:25:40 (18,434)	
Mahgiub, Hisham	3:33:38 (5,494)	
Mahmood, Arshad	4:25:41 (18,438)	
Mahobah, Dominique	3:13:43 (2,424)	
Mahon, Peter J	4:14:12 (15,367)	
Mahoney, Chris P	4:25:38 (18,422)	
Mahoney, Terry M	4:28:02 (19,113)	
Mahsoudi, Bruno E	3:25:33 (4,020)	
Maia, Samaroni S	4:27:03 (18,828)	
Maidlow, Ian S	4:46:35 (23,793)	
Maidment, Charles G	4:12:47 (14,984)	
Maidment, Paul C	4:26:28 (18,654)	
Maier, Sven	3:13:18 (2,373)	
Main, Vincent	3:22:57 (3,628)	
Mainwaring, Robert	4:05:48 (13,246)	
Maione, Tony	6:32:11 (33,706)	
Mairs, Graham	3:06:06 (1,606)	
Mairs, Stuart	4:39:02 (21,981)	
Maish, Gavin P	5:25:04 (29,926)	
Maita, Junichi	5:26:14 (30,063)	
Maitland Smith, Gavin N	4:14:05 (15,331)	
Maitland-Wood, David J	4:16:44 (16,013)	
Maitre-D'Hotel, Claude	3:50:39 (8,974)	
Majer, Raymond V	4:28:25 (19,238)	
Majid, Waseem	4:22:08 (17,476)	
Major, Louis	5:14:53 (28,801)	
Major, Paul	2:48:26 (444)	
Major, Philip J	4:42:16 (22,746)	
Makepeace-Taylor, James	3:59:59 (11,850)	
Makin, Andy J	5:12:30 (28,464)	
Makin, Paul	4:51:09 (24,870)	
Maknana, Pritesh H	5:50:08 (32,140)	
Makuwa, Bill M	2:42:52 (261)	
Mal, Firduz	3:36:11 (5,914)	
Mal, Nader S	3:37:22 (6,137)	
Malcolm, Jonathan	5:10:58 (28,272)	
Malcolm, Peter	3:56:35 (10,657)	
Malde, Svein	3:55:11 (10,261)	
Male, Les	4:28:40 (19,303)	
Male, Nick	4:25:31 (18,402)	
Maleedy, Christian A	3:53:57 (9,854)	
Maleh, Lewis	4:12:41 (14,960)	
Malekkou, Constantine	5:31:01 (30,569)	
Males, Antz R	4:16:26 (15,942)	
Malessa, Rolf	4:14:20 (15,406)	
Malhotra, Chhavi	6:52:05 (34,113)	
Malhotra, Jay	4:49:45 (24,543)	
Malik, Ijaz	6:49:38 (34,071)	
Malik, Mal	5:30:59 (30,567)	
Malin, Richard A	2:47:10 (394)	
Malins, Alastair	4:45:52 (23,637)	
Malins, Dominic P	3:28:28 (4,558)	
Maliphant, Wayne	5:45:20 (31,790)	
Mall, Jonathan	4:13:10 (15,076)	
Mallard, Lee J	4:04:42 (12,985)	
Mallen, James P	3:30:47 (5,017)	
Mallen, Max	4:08:15 (13,842)	
Malley, Gregory P	3:51:37 (9,203)	
Mallinson, Chris	3:13:47 (2,434)	
Mallon, David	3:55:37 (10,379)	
Mallon, Guy R	4:24:54 (18,241)	
Mallory, Paul	4:15:22 (15,655)	
Mallott, Lee	3:39:12 (6,473)	
Malloy, Duncan	3:08:59 (1,881)	
Malone, Ben	4:50:51 (24,805)	
Malone, Edward	3:52:52 (9,526)	
Malone, Kenny	4:39:16 (22,040)	
Malone, Kevin	4:04:42 (12,985)	
Malone, Lawrence J	3:22:51 (3,616)	
Maloney, Justin H	5:31:08 (30,574)	
Maloney, Nathan M	4:17:28 (16,211)	
Malough, Peter M	5:36:55 (31,115)	
Malpas, Jamie	5:29:01 (30,379)	
Malpass, Timothy J	3:20:26 (3,282)	
Malski, Adam M	3:22:23 (3,544)	
Maltby, Paul T	5:51:14 (32,233)	
Maltman, Mark	4:40:56 (22,418)	
Mameli, Sergio	3:55:46 (10,425)	

Mamenia, Mohamed....................2:59:46 (1,148)
Mamnani, Suresh H....................6:00:50 (32,770)
Man, Sang Y....................5:41:25 (31,459)
Manam, Ajay K....................5:32:33 (30,704)
Manby, Christopher P....................3:54:35 (10,065)
Mance, Peter E....................4:37:52 (21,688)
Mancini, John....................5:36:41 (31,095)
Mancuso, Filippo....................4:30:32 (19,758)
Mander, Peter V....................4:19:03 (16,639)
Mandikos, James....................4:31:57 (20,159)
Manel Nunes Alves, Martins V....3:44:36 (7,577)
Manfredi, Luciano Antonio........3:26:17 (4,150)
Mangion, Ted....................4:25:16 (18,330)
Mangnall, Christopher....................4:37:57 (21,704)
Mani, Simon....................3:00:22 (1,192)
Mankee, Grant....................3:10:48 (2,077)
Manktelow, Stuart J....................3:15:22 (2,686)
Manley, Craig M....................4:24:21 (18,094)
Manlove, Richard J....................4:47:19 (23,989)
Mann, Ben C....................3:58:39 (11,357)
Mann, Bhupinder S....................6:25:17 (33,552)
Mann, Chris B....................4:23:46 (17,937)
Mann, Christopher D....................4:10:37 (14,440)
Mann, Craig....................3:09:57 (1,984)
Mann, Dave K....................4:00:17 (11,921)
Mann, David....................5:14:16 (28,717)
Mann, John M....................5:46:05 (31,840)
Mann, Jonathan R....................4:53:20 (25,337)
Mann, Julian....................2:35:54 (128)
Mann, Nigel D....................3:41:38 (6,956)
Mann, Patrick K....................3:11:34 (2,158)
Mann, Perry....................3:59:01 (11,496)
Mann, Philip....................3:11:13 (2,116)
Mann, Stuart H....................3:15:20 (2,680)
Mann, Stuart I....................5:19:02 (29,296)
Mann, Tim C....................4:53:24 (25,351)
Manners, James....................2:50:15 (520)
Mannhold, Oliver....................2:59:07 (1,075)
Manning, Andrew J....................3:51:56 (9,285)
Manning, David R....................4:57:35 (26,208)
Manning, Edward J....................3:31:25 (5,120)
Manning, Jason I....................3:13:16 (2,368)
Manning, John R....................4:28:04 (19,118)
Manning, Julian H....................2:51:49 (586)
Manning, Paul J....................3:12:11 (2,231)
Manning, Robert J....................4:15:59 (15,832)
Mannion, Daniel....................3:24:29 (3,845)
Mannion, Kevin....................5:19:26 (29,344)
Mannix, Robert P....................4:08:49 (13,993)
Manns, Robbie H....................4:27:07 (18,847)
Manoli, Dino....................6:09:52 (33,112)
Mansbridge, Adam J....................4:11:50 (14,765)
Mansell, John B....................4:26:22 (18,627)
Mansell, Steve D....................4:32:28 (20,288)
Manser, Lee J....................3:44:33 (7,563)
Mansergh, Andrew C....................3:07:17 (1,707)
Mansfield, David S....................3:28:59 (4,665)
Mansfield, Derek L....................4:23:19 (17,820)
Mansfield, Ian P....................5:01:13 (26,829)
Mansfield, John F....................5:07:55 (27,816)
Mansfield, Mike S....................2:49:32 (492)
Mansfield, Ron....................5:34:01 (30,839)
Mansfield, Trevor A....................3:58:42 (11,374)
Mansfield, William A....................3:55:49 (10,440)
Manship, Philip A....................4:11:00 (14,543)
Mansi, Andrew J....................3:10:18 (2,018)
Mansi, Dominic A....................4:36:10 (21,284)
Mansilla, Mario H....................4:51:55 (25,026)
Mantle, David S....................3:10:34 (2,052)
Mantle, Glenn J....................4:24:17 (18,077)
Manton, Leigh....................4:41:16 (22,501)
Manwaring, Simon G....................3:36:47 (6,012)
Manwaring, Stephen L....................3:41:01 (6,829)
Manzetti, Alessandro....................3:39:27 (6,526)
Manzi, Lee....................4:11:37 (14,706)
Mapes, Neil A....................4:28:17 (19,199)
Maplestone, Gary K....................4:39:01 (21,975)
Mapp, Ian S....................4:21:04 (17,202)
Mapson, Andy....................5:27:23 (30,191)
Maquillen, Gordon J....................5:29:48 (30,457)
Mara, James M....................6:31:43 (33,697)
Marangos, Nick....................4:08:09 (13,817)
Maranzano, Marco F....................4:45:16 (23,487)
Marcelle, Nicholas P....................4:10:22 (14,381)
March, Jamie G....................4:08:34 (13,931)
March, Neil E....................4:47:30 (24,021)
Marchand, Paul J....................3:38:57 (6,433)
Marchant, Paul....................2:33:01 (97)
Marchetti, Sergio....................3:29:42 (4,819)
Marenghi, Peter J....................3:48:21 (8,431)
Maresta, Paolo....................4:08:53 (14,014)
Marfell, Ian J....................4:17:07 (16,128)
Margerison, Craig C....................4:55:08 (25,723)
Margulies, Daniel A....................3:47:34 (8,239)
Mariani, Massimiliano....................4:32:00 (20,173)
Marinelli, Alessio....................5:04:36 (27,342)
Mariottino, Fabio....................3:10:42 (2,065)
Maris, David H....................3:48:59 (8,576)
Maritn, James R....................4:27:46 (19,011)
Markham, Joel....................5:46:22 (31,867)
Markham, Mattthew C....................5:20:50 (29,484)
Markland, John K....................3:45:02 (7,691)
Marklew, Steve....................2:43:06 (269)
Marks, Jon....................5:29:54 (30,466)
Marks, Jonathan G....................4:21:24 (17,275)
Marks, Roger....................4:44:46 (23,358)
Marks, Russ....................4:38:25 (21,805)
Marks, Stuart A....................3:29:19 (4,743)
Markwell, Nicholas J....................3:44:04 (7,465)
Marletta, Giuseppe....................4:11:32 (14,687)
Marley, Liam....................3:29:53 (4,862)
Marley, Nigel R....................2:36:57 (147)
Marlow, Jeff J....................3:45:17 (7,752)
Marlow, Mark W....................4:50:27 (24,697)
Marlow, Paul....................4:15:24 (15,670)
Marlow, Paul C....................4:11:56 (14,788)
Marlow, Simon J....................4:21:39 (17,357)
Marner, Barry S....................6:42:42 (33,934)
Marno, Edward C....................5:20:11 (29,425)
Marnoch, Adam....................3:37:03 (6,071)
Marns, Neil J....................5:36:54 (31,112)
Maros, Gael....................3:39:42 (6,576)
Marquand, Ben....................4:21:07 (17,208)
Marques da Silva, Eloi A....................3:45:38 (7,822)
Marr, Robert....................3:34:48 (5,664)
Marrai, Sandro....................2:59:33 (1,119)
Marriott, Duncan....................4:46:07 (23,693)
Marriott, Paul....................4:17:11 (16,153)
Marriott, Richard J....................2:58:33 (1,014)
Marriott-Reynolds, Anthony E.....4:34:41 (20,870)
Marryat, Christian E....................5:02:15 (26,999)
Marsden, Andrew....................5:15:28 (28,878)
Marsden, Bruce R....................3:04:21 (1,475)
Marsden, Christopher N....................4:22:05 (17,466)
Marsden, Philip....................3:16:02 (2,758)
Marsden, Richard D....................4:49:28 (24,469)
Marsden, Stephen J....................4:18:30 (16,497)
Marsh, Adrian N....................3:10:44 (2,067)
Marsh, Anthony P....................3:34:03 (5,557)
Marsh, Clive F....................4:54:50 (25,657)
Marsh, Danny....................3:40:28 (6,729)
Marsh, David J....................4:06:25 (13,375)
Marsh, David J....................4:45:42 (23,585)
Marsh, Duncan G....................4:08:34 (13,931)
Marsh, Jason....................4:19:36 (16,781)
Marsh, Jim F....................4:18:13 (16,405)
Marsh, Paul D....................4:44:17 (23,252)
Marsh, Paul G....................3:18:56 (3,092)
Marsh, Richard....................4:34:28 (20,816)
Marsh, Stephen J....................4:13:47 (15,248)
Marsh, Timothy W....................3:37:41 (6,199)
Marshall, Andrew....................3:00:19 (1,189)
Marshall, Anthony J....................4:57:30 (26,188)
Marshall, Ben A....................4:39:54 (22,166)
Marshall, Carl D....................5:43:00 (31,572)
Marshall, Craig S....................5:11:35 (28,343)
Marshall, Daniel J....................4:05:28 (13,168)
Marshall, Gary....................4:13:58 (15,292)
Marshall, Ian A....................5:31:33 (30,615)
Marshall, Ian M....................3:13:30 (2,395)
Marshall, John....................3:55:00 (10,195)
Marshall, John D....................4:40:18 (22,257)
Marshall, Johnathan....................4:34:44 (20,886)
Marshall, Joseph A....................4:10:32 (14,418)
Marshall, Kevin J....................3:30:25 (4,955)
Marshall, Kevin J....................4:04:54 (13,021)
Marshall, Kris....................4:38:34 (21,849)
Marshall, Lee H....................3:22:11 (3,509)
Marshall, Nicholas S....................3:49:07 (8,606)
Marshall, Paul F....................3:41:42 (6,968)
Marshall, Paul R....................4:04:11 (12,859)
Marshall, Peter D....................5:07:27 (27,760)
Marshall, Philip G....................3:59:58 (11,842)
Marshall, Ray C....................3:57:27 (10,942)
Marshall, Ray W....................4:22:36 (17,613)
Marshall, Robert....................3:32:05 (5,239)
Marshall, Simon P....................4:20:24 (16,997)
Marshall, Stephen....................2:50:51 (547)
Marshall, Tom....................3:00:35 (1,211)
Marshall, Vinny....................4:00:34 (11,994)
Marshall, Wayne....................6:06:02 (32,974)
Marshall-Stevens, Gary J....................3:46:23 (7,975)
Marshman, Adrian J....................3:42:43 (7,175)
Marsland, Steve J....................4:06:05 (13,309)
Marson, Peter P....................4:02:15 (12,430)
Marston, Tim R....................4:50:42 (24,766)
Marta, Massimiliano....................3:40:51 (6,793)
Martell, Simon D....................5:27:59 (30,264)
Martelletti, Paul V....................2:28:13 (50)
Martens, James....................4:49:38 (24,514)
Martensson, Max M....................3:30:57 (5,046)
Martin, Adrian....................4:25:25 (18,373)
Martin, Allan C....................5:04:32 (27,333)
Martin, Andrew E....................4:50:11 (24,640)
Martin, Andrew J....................4:26:56 (18,793)
Martin, Andrew M....................3:59:02 (11,499)
Martin, Andrew R....................3:52:42 (9,479)
Martin, Andrew W....................7:51:50 (34,516)
Martin, Andy....................4:32:12 (20,225)
Martin, Benjamin L....................5:03:27 (27,175)
Martin, Charles W....................3:58:05 (11,137)
Martin, Chris N....................3:40:45 (6,772)
Martin, Christopher....................5:02:10 (26,980)
Martin, Ciaran L....................3:20:17 (3,263)
Martin, Colin L....................5:08:14 (27,847)
Martin, Daniel....................4:36:26 (21,355)
Martin, David L....................4:15:51 (15,795)
Martin, David T....................4:12:22 (14,900)
Martin, Ed T....................3:48:23 (8,437)
Martin, Enrique....................2:30:11 (76)
Martin, Ernest C....................4:25:49 (18,487)
Martin, Eusebio....................4:04:54 (13,021)
Martin, Geoff C....................4:55:57 (25,871)
Martin, George H....................4:09:38 (14,209)
Martin, Gerard X....................4:33:16 (20,496)
Martin, Grant....................5:16:33 (29,001)
Martin, Guy H....................4:33:31 (20,579)
Martin, Harry C....................3:52:16 (9,380)
Martin, Henry F....................3:25:31 (4,017)
Martin, James T....................3:55:28 (10,331)
Martin, Jamie....................3:17:57 (2,981)
Martin, Jean....................4:18:44 (16,562)
Martin, Jim....................5:05:29 (27,472)
Martin, Joward....................4:08:15 (13,842)
Martin, Karl J....................4:17:56 (16,332)
Martin, Ken J....................3:50:52 (9,019)
Martin, Kenneth J....................3:44:22 (7,527)
Martin, Kevin R....................3:19:00 (3,100)
Martin, Larry N....................4:10:26 (14,395)
Martin, Lee M....................2:55:06 (757)
Martin, Mark A....................3:41:11 (6,866)
Martin, Matthew....................3:17:54 (2,974)
Martin, Matthew....................5:12:46 (28,508)
Martin, Michael C....................3:25:42 (4,049)
Martin, Michael D....................4:51:10 (24,875)
Martin, Nathan....................5:19:15 (29,323)
Martin, Neil J....................4:28:09 (19,151)
Martin, Neil P....................3:23:40 (3,722)
Martin, Paul....................3:00:11 (1,177)
Martin, Paul....................5:24:50 (29,893)
Martin, Paul E....................4:31:38 (20,063)
Martin, Paul R....................4:34:58 (20,962)
Martin, Peter H....................3:45:26 (7,780)
Martin, Peter J....................6:29:18 (33,643)
Martin, Philip....................4:15:43 (15,752)
Martin, Phillip....................3:54:05 (9,899)
Martin, Richard G....................4:06:31 (13,407)
Martin, Richard I....................4:43:28 (23,035)
Martin, Rick J....................3:07:49 (1,767)

Martin, Sean 3:34:57 (5,694)
Martin, Sean C 4:27:48 (19,022)
Martin, Simon A 3:03:16 (1,398)
Martin, Simon P 5:17:12 (29,088)
Martin, Stephen C 3:55:58 (10,483)
Martin, Thomas T 3:57:36 (10,977)
Martin, Vernon L 5:54:18 (32,426)
Martin, Victor O 4:39:59 (22,181)
Martin, William 2:41:08 (218)
Martin, Yannick 3:43:09 (7,276)
Martindale, Mark R 4:23:15 (17,797)
Martin-Dye, Ben 2:54:03 (696)
Martineau, Adrian 3:57:23 (10,919)
Martinelli, Claudio 4:53:59 (25,478)
Martinelli, Sandro 3:10:53 (2,086)
Martinez, Carlos 3:41:45 (6,977)
Martinez, Diego 3:24:45 (3,878)
Martinez, Gabriel 3:34:05 (5,561)
Martinez Diez, Miguel Angel 3:39:30 (6,534)
Martinez Lopez, Francisco 3:44:36 (7,577)
Martinez Martin, Arturo 4:04:06 (12,846)
Martini, Silvio 3:07:15 (1,700)
Martins, Antonio M 3:13:15 (2,364)
Martinsen, Sverre 3:14:14 (2,507)
Martin-Smith, Kollyn P 3:17:27 (2,928)
Martinson, Travis R 5:20:24 (29,454)
Martinuzzi, Stephan 4:32:56 (20,415)
Martland, Raymond J 3:42:06 (7,049)
Martyn, Daniel 3:57:35 (10,974)
Martyn, James G 3:35:28 (5,787)
Martyn, Nicholas A 2:41:36 (236)
Marum, Raymond J 4:21:54 (17,422)
Marven, Nigel A 4:03:54 (12,804)
Marven, Roger A 4:35:16 (21,048)
Marvin, Roger P 4:19:39 (16,797)
Marvinsson, Helgi K 4:17:26 (16,200)
Marwood, Richard 3:23:57 (3,772)
Mary, Philippe 4:20:15 (16,962)
Marzari, Stefano 3:27:30 (4,363)
Marzocchini, Serge 3:45:00 (7,681)
Mascall, Bruce 4:00:15 (11,909)
Maskell, Robert J 5:18:54 (29,277)
Maskell, Scott 5:25:06 (29,936)
Maskens, David C 4:00:29 (11,969)
Maslin, Paul J 4:52:11 (25,078)
Mason, Anthony D 6:06:19 (32,998)
Mason, Benjamin R 3:49:37 (8,724)
Mason, Christopher J 6:44:05 (33,961)
Mason, Dale J 4:56:12 (25,916)
Mason, Edward G 3:53:18 (9,661)
Mason, James H 3:08:06 (1,803)
Mason, John 6:25:35 (33,567)
Mason, John B 5:44:37 (31,731)
Mason, Keith 4:20:53 (17,147)
Mason, Marc 3:07:35 (1,740)
Mason, Paul A 3:08:16 (1,818)
Mason, Paul J 3:39:25 (6,522)
Mason, Peter 5:22:32 (29,667)
Mason, Richard 5:30:05 (30,483)
Mason, Ross M 4:17:58 (16,338)
Mason, Scott M 4:28:02 (19,113)
Mason, Spencer S 4:52:20 (25,110)
Mason, Stephen 3:36:39 (5,988)
Mason, Stuart G 5:45:19 (31,786)
Mason, Thomas 4:17:38 (16,258)
Mason, Toby K 4:09:40 (14,216)
Massa, Gennaro 3:28:26 (4,545)
Massen, Nigel A 4:36:15 (21,312)
Massey, Adrian P 3:18:30 (3,048)
Massey, Antony G 4:57:06 (26,108)
Massey, Brynnen D 3:24:53 (3,907)
Massey, Kevin T 4:40:18 (22,257)
Massey, Richard 5:46:14 (31,856)
Massey, Stephen J 3:46:08 (7,916)
Massie-Taylor, Simon E 3:54:57 (10,179)
Massingham, Darren 4:01:45 (12,306)
Masson, Philip 4:59:03 (26,485)
Mast, Robert J 3:02:43 (1,359)
Masters, Antony P 4:38:32 (21,831)
Masters, Trevor 4:47:54 (24,123)
Masterson, John G 3:48:24 (8,440)
Masterson, Jonathan D 4:32:54 (20,401)
Masterson, Michael J 3:25:30 (4,015)
Masterson, Paul 3:45:57 (7,883)
Maston, Francis L 3:49:40 (8,736)
Mastracco, Angelo 3:00:39 (1,215)
Mate, Abhijit 4:39:41 (22,122)
Mateus, Paul 6:53:33 (34,131)
Matharoo, Tajinder S 4:56:09 (25,903)
Matharu, Ishvinder S 5:47:51 (31,970)
Mather, Alec J 5:52:20 (32,308)
Mather, Andrew 4:46:03 (23,682)
Mather, Barry 5:34:26 (30,877)
Mather, Colin 5:54:48 (32,445)
Mather, Jeffrey 4:14:08 (15,347)
Mathers, Dale 2:57:42 (921)
Mathers, Derek A 3:18:52 (3,083)
Mathers, Ian C 3:54:30 (10,034)
Matheson, Andrew J 4:25:57 (18,519)
Mathew, Kim 4:17:03 (16,108)
Mathias, Jason J 4:10:16 (14,356)
Mathie, James P 3:54:00 (9,873)
Mathieson, Derek 4:57:12 (26,124)
Mathieson, Eddie O 3:13:57 (2,460)
Mathieson, Neil M 4:08:45 (13,980)
Mathys, Beat 3:46:56 (8,093)
Matijuk, Stephen M 5:37:43 (31,170)
Matisonn, Shaun 3:37:52 (6,230)
Matkin, Roger N 5:35:16 (30,956)
Maton, Nick 4:21:18 (17,254)
Matsiko, Sheck K 6:24:41 (33,538)
Matson, Andrew M 4:23:25 (17,842)
Matt, Peter 5:00:41 (26,733)
Matteucci, Giulio 3:35:31 (5,795)
Matthams, David J 4:09:29 (14,165)
Matthewman, David T 4:24:14 (18,063)
Matthews, Alexander W 3:59:28 (11,662)
Matthews, Andrew J 3:58:27 (11,282)
Matthews, Andrew R 3:56:32 (10,639)
Matthews, Chris S 3:47:36 (8,251)
Matthews, David 4:23:36 (17,894)
Matthews, David J 4:38:23 (21,796)
Matthews, Dene J 4:04:27 (12,919)
Matthews, Gregory J 3:25:35 (4,029)
Matthews, Hefin 3:21:04 (3,368)
Matthews, Jeff A 3:17:02 (2,867)
Matthews, Joe 6:02:06 (32,824)
Matthews, Nick 5:07:08 (27,711)
Matthews, Paul A 3:19:26 (3,151)
Matthews, Roy 4:41:48 (22,637)
Matthews, Sean 3:45:47 (7,853)
Matthews, Stuart J 3:23:43 (3,729)
Matthinson, John J 5:30:32 (30,530)
Matthws, James H 3:33:28 (5,467)
Mattia, Clayton 5:05:26 (27,462)
Mattison, Michael J 3:14:08 (2,489)
Mauger, Nicholas 4:20:54 (17,152)
Mauger, Simon P 4:32:44 (20,355)
Maughan, Simon T 5:35:17 (30,958)
Mauldon, Kenni P 4:23:19 (17,820)
Mauldridge, Oliver C 3:17:54 (2,974)
Maume, Michael 3:53:12 (9,640)
Maund, Graham 4:54:15 (25,534)
Maund, William S 4:23:29 (17,864)
Maunder Taylor, William 5:52:33 (32,319)
Maunders, David P 4:49:19 (24,436)
Maundrell, David F 4:34:45 (20,891)
Mauree, Alex V 4:02:20 (12,454)
Maurice-Jones, Mark N 4:00:02 (11,860)
Maury, Neil 3:24:09 (3,798)
Mavor, Alastair J 4:11:08 (14,581)
Mawdsley, Owen 3:46:27 (7,997)
Mawer, Roger 5:13:04 (28,552)
Maxen, Hayden K 5:05:44 (27,514)
Maxfield, Steve P 4:36:24 (21,344)
Maxwell, Andrew P 4:01:03 (12,121)
Maxwell, Bryce 3:37:00 (6,065)
Maxwell, Feliim J 3:14:42 (2,591)
Maxwell, James 3:59:03 (11,507)
Maxwell, John 5:08:00 (27,825)
Maxwell, Joseph J 4:54:14 (25,531)
Maxwell, Marcus D 2:47:50 (416)
Maxwell, Paul 5:04:42 (27,359)
Maxwell, Rowan C 4:48:54 (24,346)
Maxwell, Simon A 3:45:38 (7,822)
Maxwell-Holroyd, Paul 3:34:48 (5,664)
May, Adam J 4:28:45 (19,327)
May, Adrain A 3:54:19 (9,963)
May, Andy 4:05:34 (13,193)
May, Colin 4:10:49 (14,498)
May, David 3:40:25 (6,723)
May, David J 5:03:53 (27,238)
May, Douglas S 5:30:26 (30,520)
May, Gavin R 2:57:30 (904)
May, Jeremy S 3:42:55 (7,214)
May, Jon 6:45:28 (33,989)
May, Kev 2:56:29 (841)
May, Mike 4:20:39 (17,080)
May, Neil A 4:18:31 (16,503)
May, Richard D 4:05:07 (13,074)
May, Stephen J 3:58:46 (11,397)
May, Stuart A 3:58:08 (11,157)
May, Timothy J 5:23:43 (29,768)
May, Toby M 5:42:12 (31,516)
May, Tom 3:14:57 (2,624)
Maycock, Peter C 5:02:43 (27,068)
Maye, John P 3:12:13 (2,236)
Mayers, Richard A 3:58:21 (11,248)
Mayes, Craig M 4:11:14 (14,615)
Mayes, Tim M 3:28:02 (4,467)
Mayes, Warren O 6:12:02 (33,167)
Mayles, Gregg A 4:00:45 (12,047)
Maynard, Alan M 4:21:10 (17,216)
Maynard, Chris B 4:03:55 (12,807)
Maynard, Graham L 3:06:54 (1,675)
Maynard, Kenny 5:57:13 (32,589)
Maynard, Paul M 5:13:21 (28,583)
Maynard, Peter 5:05:53 (27,529)
Maynard, Richard S 3:56:30 (10,626)
Maynard, Simon J 4:01:42 (12,295)
Mayneord, Richard W 4:25:26 (18,377)
Mayo, Mark J 6:14:44 (33,260)
Mayo, Paul N 4:15:15 (15,629)
Mayo, Philip I 3:13:50 (2,441)
Mayo, Stuart 4:31:31 (20,027)
Mayo, Tom R 6:14:44 (33,260)
Mayor, Lawson 6:15:40 (33,285)
Mayor, William 6:15:40 (33,285)
Mays, Kevin 4:25:09 (18,306)
Mayson, Howard J 3:58:49 (11,426)
Maywood, Graham P 4:47:00 (23,910)
Maziere, Frederic 4:56:40 (25,995)
Mazio, Andrea 4:07:54 (13,753)
Mazoyer, Thierry 2:53:02 (645)
Mazur, first name unknown 3:51:41 (9,226)
Mazzolini, Fabio 3:38:54 (6,427)
McAdam, Paul P 4:08:24 (13,882)
McAfee, Clive T 3:55:47 (10,429)
McAleavey, John H 4:55:32 (25,786)
McAleavey, Martin J 5:07:23 (27,749)
McAleece, Neil R 4:12:42 (14,962)
McAleenan, John 3:19:27 (3,154)
McAleese, James K 4:39:01 (21,975)
McAleese, Lyle 4:02:42 (12,542)
McAlister, Gary 4:44:56 (23,400)
McAlister, Gerard K 3:27:52 (4,434)
McAlister, Henry 3:43:44 (7,396)
McAllen, Jonathan 3:46:06 (7,905)
McAllion, Neil D 4:59:18 (26,534)
McAllister, Richard C 5:17:21 (29,103)
McAllister, William 3:58:18 (11,219)
McAllister-Williams, Hamish 3:14:23 (2,528)
McAnaney, Justin K 4:40:40 (22,341)
McAndrew, Ian M 5:57:20 (32,596)
McArdle, Joseph 4:52:33 (25,156)
McAree, Will R 3:20:47 (3,329)
McArthur, Alastair H 4:05:34 (13,193)
McAslan, Alastair 4:49:34 (24,495)
McAuliffe, Andrew P 3:17:01 (2,864)
McAvinue, Darren L 3:21:06 (3,374)
McAvoy, Richard 4:07:51 (13,730)
McAvoy, Scott 3:57:56 (11,098)
McAvoy, Stephen 3:58:47 (11,406)
McBride, Alistair 4:09:33 (14,188)
McBride, Andy 4:28:12 (19,171)
McBride, Bernard J 4:43:18 (23,001)
McBride, Kevin N 5:53:23 (32,367)
McBride, Martin J 3:24:02 (3,783)
McBride, Michael P 3:16:39 (2,828)

McBride, Scott	3:53:21 (9,677)
McCabe, David	4:39:28 (22,074)
McCabe, Gerard	6:36:28 (33,802)
McCabe, Mark A	5:17:31 (29,129)
McCabe, Michael E	3:02:34 (1,348)
McCabe, Philip E	5:17:30 (29,126)
McCafferty, Garry D	3:43:50 (7,419)
McCafferty, Thomas S	4:40:43 (22,360)
McCaffery, Stephen A	3:33:07 (5,401)
McCaffrey, Andrew	5:11:27 (28,326)
McCaffrey, Sean T	6:59:03 (34,198)
McCahill, Patrick G	5:35:04 (30,948)
McCallion, Seamus M	3:14:36 (2,567)
McCallum, Alistair	4:02:48 (12,565)
McCallum, Kenny M	3:58:01 (11,122)
McCallum, Neil R	4:07:34 (13,658)
McCallum, Stephen	4:14:12 (15,367)
McCandless, Mark	3:56:12 (10,538)
McCann, Gerard J	3:11:33 (2,156)
McCann, Henry	4:42:30 (22,810)
McCann, John D	3:44:16 (7,505)
McCann, John F	4:08:55 (14,022)
McCann, Michael	4:20:32 (17,040)
McCann, Patrick O	5:29:22 (30,410)
McCann, Paul J	3:49:27 (8,686)
McCann, Philip	4:56:24 (25,949)
McCann, Terry	4:32:04 (20,190)
McCarron, Paul C	4:15:34 (15,720)
McCarter, Dominic	2:43:15 (274)
McCarthy, Anthony J	3:58:39 (11,357)
McCarthy, Bernard J	5:03:28 (27,177)
McCarthy, Charles John	3:00:32 (1,204)
McCarthy, Charles N	4:47:34 (24,033)
McCarthy, David A	4:10:05 (14,313)
McCarthy, Dean P	3:56:03 (10,503)
McCarthy, Hugh J	4:33:49 (20,665)
McCarthy, James A	4:29:31 (19,519)
McCarthy, Keith D	5:17:31 (29,129)
McCarthy, Michael R	4:47:22 (24,001)
McCarthy, Paul F	5:06:49 (27,668)
McCarthy, Paul J	4:37:46 (21,659)
McCarthy, Richard J	3:52:50 (9,514)
McCarthy, Thomas F	4:21:53 (17,419)
McCartney, John	4:58:15 (26,335)
McCartney, Stephen J	5:17:44 (29,145)
McCarty, Scott V	4:28:50 (19,360)
McCauley, Edward A	7:05:14 (34,266)
McCausland, Dan H	4:59:43 (26,594)
McCavera, Kevin P	4:36:02 (21,250)
McCawley, Gary J	4:35:43 (21,171)
McClean, Ian P	3:54:16 (9,950)
McCleave, Jamie	4:31:07 (19,915)
McClelland, Michael B	3:19:49 (3,210)
McClelland, Paul B	3:04:09 (1,462)
McClorry, Paul	3:50:22 (8,907)
McCloud, Victor A	3:58:40 (11,364)
McCloy, Mark G	3:45:15 (7,741)
McCloy, Michael J	3:30:10 (4,919)
McClure, Greg M	2:58:21 (987)
McCluskie, Kristen	3:54:48 (10,125)
McClymont, Ewan R	3:56:53 (10,756)
McColl, Ewen M	2:54:27 (718)
McCombe, Stuart R	3:54:55 (10,170)
McComish, James L	3:55:22 (10,304)
McComisky, Daniel	3:54:14 (9,936)
McConnel, Rob J	4:02:31 (12,499)
McConnell, Barry	2:59:15 (1,091)
McConnell, Ross	4:05:29 (13,172)
McConnell, Simon P	4:28:51 (19,366)
McConnell, Stewart T	3:52:07 (9,345)
McConochie, Andrew	3:19:39 (3,185)
McConville, Alastair C	3:26:34 (4,198)
McConville, Kevin	3:56:00 (10,491)
McCool, Peter J	3:57:45 (11,039)
McCoombes, Andrew L	4:07:32 (13,650)
McCormac, Rupert	3:37:49 (6,219)
McCormack, Ben	2:57:17 (895)
McCormack, Dan	2:57:16 (893)
McCormack, David P	3:48:05 (8,368)
McCormack, Dean	4:47:42 (24,068)
McCormack, Dominic J	4:17:35 (16,244)
McCormack, Gavin	4:11:28 (14,665)
McCormack, Wayne P	7:38:04 (34,478)

McCormick, Andrew B	4:27:58 (19,088)
McCormick, Andrew D	4:30:06 (19,656)
McCormick, Chris J	2:58:08 (959)
McCourt, George	2:58:27 (1,002)
McCoy, Gerard M	3:36:55 (6,041)
McCoy, Kenneth M	2:37:27 (157)
McCoy, Kevin M	5:06:15 (27,591)
McCoy, Robin E	3:04:46 (1,502)
McCrabbe, Clyde J	3:51:39 (9,211)
McCready, Colin	4:41:32 (22,562)
McCrimmon, Ian	4:44:46 (23,358)
McCrindle, Mark	4:48:52 (24,335)
McCrobb, Gary	4:47:41 (24,064)
McCrossin, Paul A	2:52:16 (608)
McCubbing, Mark R	4:47:33 (24,029)
McCulloch, Duane D	3:52:27 (9,423)
McCulloch, Gary	3:45:20 (7,762)
McCulloch, William S	4:58:39 (26,409)
McCullough, Darren K	4:24:12 (18,050)
McCullough, John	4:35:50 (21,200)
McCullough, Patrick J	4:12:19 (14,887)
McCullough, Stephen	3:23:16 (3,669)
McCusker, Niall F	3:26:56 (4,268)
McDaid, Neil J	4:17:13 (16,159)
McDaid, Trevor A	3:28:45 (4,613)
McDerment, Leslie J	3:13:44 (2,426)
McDermott, Dennis	4:13:41 (15,218)
McDermott, Emilio B	3:58:12 (11,190)
McDermott, Jonathan D	4:16:25 (15,938)
McDermott, Kevan P	4:10:15 (14,351)
McDermott, Sean P	3:12:36 (2,276)
McDermott, Thomas R	3:43:22 (7,319)
McDermott, Trevor J	4:00:53 (12,077)
McDiarmid, David B	4:56:18 (25,931)
McDicken, Scott	4:45:52 (23,637)
McDonagh, Luke	3:29:51 (4,849)
McDonald, Andrew E	4:14:37 (15,472)
McDonald, Daniel W	3:39:46 (6,593)
McDonald, Jamie T	5:26:47 (30,122)
McDonald, John	4:25:23 (18,364)
McDonald, John	5:01:09 (26,818)
McDonald, Lawrence A	3:16:45 (2,842)
McDonald, Matt J	4:44:50 (23,380)
McDonald, Maurice G	5:33:14 (30,769)
McDonald, Nathan A	4:59:17 (26,529)
McDonald, Paul M	6:30:15 (33,666)
McDonald, Peter	3:15:49 (2,730)
McDonald, Peter H	3:21:38 (3,438)
McDonald, Scott	3:59:00 (11,489)
McDonald, Scott K	3:57:55 (11,094)
McDonald, Stephen P	3:43:49 (7,416)
McDonald, Will E	4:33:08 (20,468)
McDonald-Liggins, Anthony N	4:32:35 (20,318)
McDonnell, Christopher B	3:23:55 (3,767)
McDonnell, Kieran P	3:38:43 (6,394)
McDonnell, Rory	3:57:39 (10,995)
McDonough, Matthew S	4:51:36 (24,960)
McDonough, Robert J	4:08:27 (13,895)
McDougal, Richard J	3:51:13 (9,101)
McDougall, Jeremy	4:38:11 (21,752)
McDowell, William J	4:34:42 (20,876)
McEachern, John G	4:18:22 (16,452)
McElhatton, Nic	4:48:59 (24,370)
McElhinney, Paul	3:24:44 (3,877)
McElwaine, Frederick H	4:43:56 (23,162)
McEntaggart, Eamonn A	6:33:23 (33,734)
McEntee, Ken	3:24:19 (3,819)
McEntee, John	3:11:06 (2,105)
McEnteggart, Brian T	4:23:23 (18,132)
McEuen, James S	3:37:04 (6,074)
McEvoy, Richard K	4:39:43 (22,133)
McEvoy, Sean M	4:45:00 (23,412)
McEwan, Christopher	4:49:37 (24,507)
McEwan, Kieren R	6:00:23 (32,754)
McEwan, Raymond N	5:45:58 (31,829)
McEwan, Robert	3:03:13 (1,393)
McEwan, Robert S	5:07:14 (27,728)
McEwan, Stephen J	4:59:41 (26,591)
McEwen, Andrew	3:57:06 (10,835)
McEwen, Ross D	4:13:18 (15,116)
McFadden, Harry	4:49:38 (24,514)
McFadden, Kieran C	7:13:24 (34,350)
McFadden, Paul C	4:12:44 (14,969)

McFadzean, Angus	3:40:29 (6,731)
McFarland, Andrew	6:55:27 (34,160)
McFarlane, Jamie	3:00:44 (1,220)
McFarlane, John	2:23:17 (27)
McFarlane, Paul M	4:00:04 (11,867)
McFaul, Daniel C	4:53:46 (25,432)
McFerran, Robert	3:57:24 (10,928)
McGaffney, Brendan N	4:43:19 (23,007)
McGann, Mark A	4:55:46 (25,831)
McGarr, Anthony	3:50:57 (9,036)
McGarva, Adrian	2:42:57 (264)
McGeady, David P	3:23:19 (3,679)
McGee, Craig A	4:28:01 (19,103)
McGee, James	4:29:30 (19,517)
McGeehan, Dominic	4:49:21 (24,451)
McGeever, Patrick D	2:42:16 (247)
McGeoch, Gregg A	4:59:06 (26,493)
McGhee, Andrew W	3:26:46 (4,242)
McGill, Colin A	2:39:54 (197)
McGillan, David P	4:34:21 (20,785)
McGinley, Dolan J	4:49:56 (24,587)
McGinley, Mark D	4:27:59 (19,096)
McGinn, John A	4:10:30 (14,409)
McGinty, Martyn J	4:02:18 (12,446)
McGinty, Samuel D	4:45:01 (23,416)
McGivern, Ian J	4:27:31 (18,953)
McGlade, David	4:08:52 (14,010)
McGlashan, Alex	3:29:13 (4,718)
McGlennon, David L	3:54:33 (10,052)
McGloin, Ray	3:51:21 (9,141)
McGoldrick, Joseph G	4:11:59 (14,806)
McGough, Liam	5:27:18 (30,180)
McGovern, Carl P	4:05:10 (13,089)
McGovern, Peter A	6:12:28 (33,187)
McGovern, Terence (Tez) C	3:02:55 (1,370)
McGowan, Glen	3:29:44 (4,831)
McGowan, Joe M	5:03:48 (27,225)
McGowan, Julian P	3:00:42 (1,217)
McGowan, Michael J	4:38:00 (21,716)
McGowan, Ronnie	4:56:42 (26,007)
McGrail, Steven T	5:44:46 (31,743)
McGraine, Jon D	3:58:55 (11,460)
McGranaghan, Sean H	4:15:57 (15,823)
McGrath, Christopher J	3:40:41 (6,756)
McGrath, Daniel R	3:13:07 (2,348)
McGrath, David	3:18:41 (3,063)
McGrath, Kevin P	3:33:10 (5,413)
McGrath, Nicholas J	4:19:56 (16,868)
McGraw, Anthony E	3:39:27 (6,526)
McGread, Michael P	3:25:10 (3,957)
McGreevy, Liam	3:58:40 (11,364)
McGregor, Dan E	5:43:55 (31,665)
McGregor, David K	2:40:04 (199)
McGregor, Ronin T	3:41:32 (6,945)
McGrory, Michael J	4:27:59 (19,096)
McGrory, Paul	5:25:02 (29,920)
McGuffie, Andy	3:13:01 (2,336)
McGuigan, Anthony J	4:54:08 (25,512)
McGuigan, Sean C	3:49:19 (8,653)
McGuigan, Sean T	4:08:41 (13,965)
McGuinness, David R	4:51:39 (24,978)
McGuinness, John J	3:43:51 (7,424)
McGuinness, Jonathan O	4:51:39 (24,978)
McGuire, Lee	5:42:38 (31,541)
McGuire, Robert J	5:07:59 (27,843)
McGuire, Stewart P	3:26:41 (4,228)
McGuirk, Simon	3:39:53 (6,614)
McGurn, James A	4:35:56 (21,220)
McHale, Richard	4:09:29 (14,165)
McHugh, Dan	3:28:37 (4,583)
McHugh, Derek F	4:40:22 (22,279)
McHugh, Noel	3:29:43 (4,824)
McIlwee, Ian	2:48:21 (437)
McInerney, Michael A	3:53:43 (9,775)
McInman, Victor M	3:47:53 (8,321)
McInnes, Stuart A	2:48:12 (431)
McIntosh, Christopher G	4:01:40 (12,285)
McIntosh, Kevin J	4:34:35 (20,839)
McIntyre, John R	4:58:51 (26,443)
McIntyre, Neil A	4:12:14 (14,868)
McIntyre, Tim J	3:13:20 (2,377)
McIntyre-Pell, Andrew G	4:00:16 (11,917)
McIver, Alan M	5:06:51 (27,675)

McIver, Andrew F	3:33:05 (5,397)	
McIver, Duncan	3:06:18 (1,626)	
McIvor, Aaron	3:35:10 (5,734)	
McJennett, Tom	3:57:25 (10,935)	
McKay, Craig	4:17:54 (16,324)	
McKay, Douglas J	3:35:38 (5,821)	
McKay, John C	4:05:24 (13,146)	
McKay, Paul W	3:31:11 (5,073)	
McKay, William J	5:57:47 (32,619)	
McKechnie, Gary	3:42:03 (7,038)	
McKechnie, Ian A	5:48:43 (32,027)	
McKechnie, Ronnie	4:02:32 (12,503)	
McKee, Alex J	3:43:13 (7,290)	
McKee, Ray	4:35:18 (21,056)	
McKellar, James R	4:53:54 (25,464)	
McKenna, Martin H	3:55:20 (10,295)	
McKenna, Michael	3:39:02 (6,443)	
McKenna, Michael P	3:06:04 (1,605)	
McKenney, Walter K	5:35:54 (31,020)	
McKenning, Matthew J	3:32:07 (5,246)	
McKenzie, Alan	5:06:36 (27,636)	
McKenzie, James M	3:41:43 (6,969)	
McKenzie, Leith D	4:36:49 (21,447)	
McKenzie, Manfred C	4:20:31 (17,032)	
McKeown, Des M	3:17:06 (2,871)	
McKeown, Jeremy P	3:47:05 (8,130)	
McKeown, Michael	3:35:35 (5,812)	
McKeown, Peter F	3:28:06 (4,481)	
McKernan, Ail J	4:42:08 (22,709)	
McKernan, Bernard V	4:48:53 (24,342)	
McKernan, John J	3:17:08 (2,876)	
McKernan, Michael J	7:09:22 (34,310)	
McKerral, Calum S	3:14:52 (2,616)	
McKeverne, Anselm J	3:31:12 (5,076)	
McKevitt, Vincent D	4:01:22 (12,202)	
McKie, Richard	4:30:46 (19,823)	
McKinlay, Jason	5:13:21 (28,583)	
McKinlay, John C	3:29:33 (4,790)	
McKinlay, Robert J	3:15:13 (2,656)	
McKinna, Jeremy	3:37:09 (6,088)	
McKinney, Conor	4:57:29 (26,182)	
McKinney, Cormac	5:37:52 (31,184)	
McKinstrie, James H	3:56:26 (10,605)	
McKinstry, Danny	3:58:59 (11,481)	
McKirdy, Gordon	7:25:37 (34,433)	
McKnight, A	6:22:48 (33,483)	
McKnight, Andrew J	4:15:02 (15,574)	
McLachlan, Graham A	4:47:34 (24,033)	
McLachlan, Stuart A	4:16:54 (16,061)	
McLane, Andy J	4:43:56 (23,162)	
McLaren, Alan	6:32:04 (33,704)	
McLaren, Alec C	3:26:39 (4,218)	
McLaren, Bruce J	3:36:32 (5,974)	
McLaren, Guy N	3:36:57 (6,050)	
McLaren, James C	3:17:25 (2,920)	
McLaren, Lawrence	6:45:45 (33,999)	
McLaren, Peter L	4:50:24 (24,684)	
McLauchlan, Julian	3:49:57 (8,814)	
McLaughlin, Andrew	3:18:26 (3,036)	
McLaughlin, Brian J	3:53:57 (9,854)	
McLaughlin, David M	5:17:46 (29,150)	
McLaughlin, Paul M	3:05:33 (1,558)	
McLaughlin, Peter T	3:38:41 (6,386)	
McLaughlin, Philip	5:14:15 (28,713)	
McLaughlin, Stephen B	5:41:58 (31,495)	
McLaughlin, Stuart E	5:22:25 (29,654)	
McLean, Adam L	3:38:15 (6,308)	
McLean, Craig R	4:28:09 (19,151)	
McLean, Darryl	4:28:06 (19,130)	
McLean, Grant A	2:36:24 (137)	
McLean, Henry	4:28:49 (19,351)	
McLean, Ian	3:44:24 (7,534)	
McLean, Ian A	4:14:00 (15,302)	
McLean, Jeff B	3:29:24 (4,763)	
McLean, Kevin J	3:34:53 (5,682)	
McLean, Nicholas J	4:58:50 (26,442)	
McLean, Paul	5:07:28 (27,761)	
McLeavey, Lewis J	5:09:43 (28,097)	
McLeish, David M	3:57:21 (10,910)	
McLellan, Kevin	6:06:27 (33,001)	
McLelland, Steve	3:49:14 (8,637)	
McLeod, Adam C	4:56:57 (26,065)	
McLeod, Alastair	3:25:05 (3,945)	
McLeod, Alexander	4:14:02 (15,316)	
McLeod, Miles D	4:46:31 (23,781)	
McLeod, Neil J	3:44:08 (7,480)	
McLeod Roberts, Luke B	4:36:38 (21,399)	
McLoughlin, Stephen	5:10:30 (28,217)	
McMahon, Brian K	4:41:07 (22,467)	
McMahon, Gavin	4:03:37 (12,751)	
McMahon, Graham R	4:03:27 (12,715)	
McMahon, Michael	4:12:44 (14,969)	
McMahon, Toby S	3:10:44 (2,067)	
McMann, Brian	3:38:48 (6,410)	
McManus, Duncan M	4:12:27 (14,917)	
McManus, John	4:16:09 (15,863)	
McManus, Mark A	7:01:31 (34,222)	
McManus, Matt	4:03:15 (12,670)	
McMaster, Philip J	4:06:39 (13,441)	
McMellon, Nicholas D	3:23:51 (3,749)	
McMillan, Craig	3:53:01 (9,582)	
McMillan, David D	3:05:20 (1,540)	
McMillan, Graham	3:41:43 (6,969)	
McMillan, Mark D	3:57:44 (11,029)	
McMillan, Robert	4:01:23 (12,210)	
McMonagle, Brian P	3:10:12 (2,011)	
McMonagle, Noel	3:52:10 (9,351)	
McMorrow, James	5:51:01 (32,211)	
McMullen, John A	3:49:45 (8,758)	
McMurray, Tony	5:40:08 (31,347)	
McMurray, Trent	4:44:47 (23,365)	
McMurtrie, David L	4:31:03 (19,896)	
McMyler, Sean A	2:49:16 (474)	
McNab, Alex L	6:21:49 (33,452)	
McNab, David P	3:27:59 (4,456)	
McNab, Robert	5:15:04 (28,830)	
McNab, Robert D	4:11:01 (14,547)	
McNabb, Cormac	4:32:12 (20,225)	
McNaboe, Philip S	5:34:54 (30,929)	
McNally, David P	4:06:02 (13,297)	
McNally, David W	3:50:42 (8,990)	
McNamara, Christopher J	4:55:07 (25,721)	
McNamara, John T	3:46:04 (7,902)	
McNamara, Stuart J	5:29:50 (30,460)	
McNamara, Timothy J	4:55:18 (25,749)	
McNeil, Andrew S	2:36:38 (141)	
McNeil, Piers D	4:11:23 (14,640)	
McNeill, Andrew	3:50:34 (8,944)	
McNeilly, John J	3:24:25 (3,833)	
McNelis, Matthew J	4:02:14 (12,423)	
McNelis, Robin N	2:53:53 (686)	
McNulty, John	4:45:54 (23,651)	
McParlin, Peter J	4:51:36 (24,960)	
McPartlan, Paul	6:31:55 (33,701)	
McPartland, Ben J	4:20:08 (16,920)	
McPaul, Robert	3:46:59 (8,104)	
McPhee, Norman B	4:39:44 (22,137)	
McPherson, André S	6:16:43 (33,318)	
McPherson, George A	2:59:08 (1,077)	
McPherson, Hugh A	3:58:09 (11,163)	
McPherson, Wayne K	3:58:06 (11,142)	
McPhillips, Kevin R	3:42:32 (7,142)	
McQuade, David	4:51:53 (25,020)	
McQuaid, Dermot J	5:51:43 (32,270)	
McQualter, Jon F	3:58:46 (11,397)	
McQueen, Daniel	4:26:35 (18,690)	
McQueen, Dave	4:40:20 (22,269)	
McQueen, Steven	5:47:01 (31,911)	
McQuillan, Andrew	4:05:02 (13,057)	
McQuistan, Carl R	3:35:41 (5,829)	
McRae, David D	4:31:17 (19,961)	
McReadie, Ian S	5:08:23 (27,871)	
McShane, Dessie C	3:06:41 (1,654)	
McShane, Gareth M	4:57:47 (26,245)	
McShane, James C	5:16:55 (29,047)	
McShane, Michael J	4:30:43 (19,806)	
McSweeney, Christopher P	4:15:42 (15,745)	
McSweeney, James S	4:26:43 (18,731)	
McSweeney, Timothy P	3:44:33 (7,563)	
McSweeney, Aidan P	4:03:56 (12,812)	
McTasney, Kevin P	4:39:44 (22,137)	
McTernan, Christopher S	3:56:05 (10,511)	
McTigue, Joseph	3:48:50 (8,534)	
McVey, Anthony J	3:32:58 (5,383)	
McVey, Geoff P	4:13:46 (15,243)	
McVey, Michael L	6:50:51 (34,089)	
McVickers, Declan J	5:20:38 (29,473)	
McVinish, Andrew	4:49:34 (24,495)	
McWatt, Roy B	4:14:31 (15,453)	
McWilliam, Colin J	4:37:45 (21,652)	
McWilliams, Brian	4:26:21 (18,621)	
Meacham, Edward	5:57:19 (32,595)	
Meachem, John A	3:49:10 (8,619)	
Mead, Adrian M	3:21:52 (3,467)	
Mead, Glenn J	4:31:25 (20,004)	
Mead, Peter A	4:01:26 (12,224)	
Meade, Ian D	3:57:04 (10,816)	
Meadowcroft, Ian C	2:52:14 (606)	
Meadows, Clive	5:43:10 (31,583)	
Meadows, Paul	4:49:18 (24,431)	
Meads, Jason R	5:53:26 (32,371)	
Meager, John B	3:46:05 (7,903)	
Meagher, Mark T	4:56:58 (26,069)	
Meakin, Ben R	4:02:01 (12,368)	
Meakin, Billy	3:42:16 (7,087)	
Meakin, Thomas	4:19:47 (16,832)	
Meakins, Che P	3:57:47 (11,053)	
Meakins, Christopher G	5:13:23 (28,592)	
Mealing, Jonathan W	3:54:17 (9,954)	
Meanwell, David	3:15:41 (2,716)	
Meardon, Kevin E	2:58:39 (1,026)	
Meares, Chris	3:57:23 (10,919)	
Mears, Aaron J	4:11:28 (14,665)	
Mears, Stewart	4:11:57 (14,791)	
Meddings, Kevin J	4:25:07 (18,296)	
Medici, Marco	3:58:09 (11,163)	
Medina, José R	3:32:18 (5,278)	
Medina, Pablo A	2:50:39 (541)	
Medina Gonzalez, Lorenzo J	5:00:55 (26,782)	
Medlen, Stuart	3:55:08 (10,246)	
Medley, Leighton J	3:27:19 (4,336)	
Medlock, Scott	4:27:14 (18,883)	
Mee, Douglas	3:51:07 (9,078)	
Mee, Paul	3:18:27 (3,042)	
Mee, Steve	4:33:17 (20,504)	
Meehan, David J	3:29:48 (4,842)	
Meek, Allan D	3:41:27 (6,924)	
Meek, Jon M	3:20:48 (3,331)	
Meer, Bart V	4:21:29 (17,300)	
Meghjee, Ashif	3:06:36 (1,644)	
Megilley, Grahame	4:38:41 (21,880)	
Mehling, Markus	4:26:43 (18,731)	
Mehmet, John	4:54:19 (25,542)	
Mehta, Paresh	5:17:45 (29,148)	
Meier, Robert P	3:46:45 (8,050)	
Meile, Markus	4:08:09 (13,817)	
Mein, William	6:14:14 (33,250)	
Melbourne, Ed R	3:11:42 (2,174)	
Melbourne, Harry R	4:39:24 (22,063)	
Melbourne, Joseph F	4:23:51 (17,953)	
Meldrum, James D	2:37:23 (152)	
Meldrum, Peter W	5:00:09 (26,661)	
Mele, Giuseppe	5:09:56 (28,135)	
Melet, François	2:58:38 (1,022)	
Melgaard, Nicholas	4:28:08 (19,142)	
Melhuish, Stuart A	4:21:39 (17,357)	
Melia, Christian E	4:57:54 (26,263)	
Melia, Michael J	4:32:38 (20,331)	
Melin, Lars	2:56:21 (835)	
Meller, David	2:50:20 (523)	
Melling, Philip	2:40:22 (202)	
Melling, Stewart A	3:37:21 (6,130)	
Mello, Michael D	3:42:13 (7,075)	
Mellon, James	6:06:28 (33,002)	
Mellon, Michael	5:32:25 (30,696)	
Mellor, Adrian J	3:03:52 (1,441)	
Mellor, Clive P	4:41:06 (22,460)	
Mellor, Jonathan P	4:33:05 (20,452)	
Mellor, Nicholas	4:05:41 (13,218)	
Mellor, Philip D	3:58:47 (11,406)	
Melloy, Scott	3:59:57 (11,836)	
Melmoth, Oliver J	4:17:10 (16,147)	
Melville, Alvin F	4:57:13 (26,127)	
Melville, Gavin R	3:11:37 (2,164)	
Menard, Patrice	3:12:13 (2,236)	
Mendelssohn, Daniel F	4:58:04 (26,297)	
Mendes Da Costa, Niall	5:13:57 (28,668)	
Menewe, Desmond	4:47:35 (24,038)	
Menga, David	4:45:06 (23,434)	

Menham, Paul C 4:18:31 (16,503)
Mennem, Ben A 3:52:04 (9,324)
Menouer, Abdelkader 2:49:53 (505)
Menozzi, Guido 2:46:35 (376)
Menschel, Jens 3:25:25 (3,997)
Mentis, Konstantin 4:21:28 (17,293)
Menzies, Alistair J 4:29:18 (19,472)
Mepstead, Sid 4:16:45 (16,020)
Meraviglia, Nicola 4:27:09 (18,858)
Mercader Nieto, Jorge 4:02:04 (12,378)
Mercer, Anthony 5:55:02 (32,463)
Mercer, Ian J 3:30:13 (4,927)
Mercer, Joseph 5:07:38 (27,788)
Mercer, Paul 4:56:59 (26,071)
Mercer, Simon N 3:22:07 (3,503)
Merchant, David M 4:09:34 (14,195)
Merchant, Simon P 4:25:10 (18,310)
Merchant, Wez D 4:47:33 (24,029)
Merga, Deriba 2:06:38 (6)
Mergay, Peter 4:56:14 (25,924)
Merigot, Mark 4:14:11 (15,363)
Merino Del Valle, Cipriano 3:56:01 (10,498)
Merlatti, Andrea 3:54:14 (9,936)
Merley, Christian 4:10:30 (14,409)
Merlotti, Francesco 4:50:48 (24,795)
Merrick, Dean 3:44:27 (7,543)
Merrick, Paul 3:14:30 (2,546)
Merricks, Joe 5:05:33 (27,489)
Merrill, Simon R 4:51:12 (24,880)
Merritt, David 5:59:24 (32,708)
Merriweather, Richard J 4:22:48 (17,668)
Merron, Bernard J 3:13:12 (2,359)
Merry, Andy G 3:41:21 (6,906)
Merry, Roger 4:13:10 (15,076)
Merryweather, John M 4:56:01 (25,879)
Mertin, Friedrich 6:18:08 (33,358)
Merwood, Simon D 3:00:00 (1,169)
Meskini, Mohamed 3:02:19 (1,331)
Mesplomb, Jean-Luc 3:26:28 (4,182)
Messenger, Mark 3:30:20 (4,944)
Messenger, Richard G 6:20:54 (33,422)
Messer, David 4:22:46 (17,661)
Messinger, William T 3:51:02 (9,058)
Metcalf, Andrew S 4:26:14 (18,590)
Metcalf, Craig 3:01:24 (1,269)
Metcalf, David 4:42:42 (22,851)
Metcalf, Hugh 4:13:57 (15,286)
Metcalf, Lester 6:18:38 (33,373)
Metcalf, Peter C 3:11:14 (2,119)
Metcalfe, James S 2:59:10 (1,080)
Metcalfe, John C 4:44:27 (23,286)
Metchear, Kevin J 5:04:15 (27,288)
Metham, David W 4:01:58 (12,353)
Metson, Leslie P 5:33:09 (30,764)
Metson, Nicholas R 3:07:30 (1,732)
Metzler, Manuel 4:21:42 (17,374)
Meuldijk, Gieljam 3:41:00 (6,824)
Meulhaupt, Juergen 4:18:58 (16,618)
Meurs-Gerken, Michael 4:32:00 (20,173)
Mewse, Dale L 3:53:28 (9,705)
Meyers, Philip J 5:32:51 (30,734)
Meyrick, Andrew P 4:25:29 (18,388)
Mezzatesta, Shane 4:00:38 (12,013)
Mezzetti, Edward A 3:11:26 (2,140)
Miah, Koyes 6:25:12 (33,551)
Miah, Moksud 5:13:22 (28,588)
Miah, Sanu 4:22:19 (17,524)
Miah, Simon 4:26:54 (18,786)
Micallef, José L 3:55:30 (10,343)
Michael, Alex L 4:37:32 (21,600)
Michael, Nicholas 4:27:36 (18,979)
Michael, Steven 4:35:08 (21,017)
Michalias, Andy 5:32:14 (30,677)
Micheal, Sim 5:59:01 (32,694)
Michelena, Santos E 3:56:29 (10,623)
Micheli, Carlo 3:22:41 (3,597)
Micklefield, Jon D 3:30:48 (5,022)
Micklethwaite, Ian 3:32:25 (5,304)
Micklewright, Colin 5:01:23 (26,858)
Middlemass, Andrew 4:13:08 (15,071)
Middleton, Clifford B 4:52:50 (25,229)
Middleton, Craig G 5:07:42 (27,797)
Middleton, David J 3:34:49 (5,669)
Middleton, Hugo R 4:10:44 (14,475)
Middleton, Ian C 5:52:30 (32,315)
Middleton, James A 3:02:28 (1,339)
Middleton, Jim 5:01:00 (26,796)
Middleton, Mark T 4:10:40 (14,455)
Middleton, Nicholas R 3:50:41 (8,985)
Middleton, Thomas E 3:57:47 (11,053)
Midgley, Mark S 3:21:13 (3,386)
Mielgo Hernandez, Juan J 4:18:32 (16,508)
Miesen, Marcel 3:58:43 (11,382)
Mifsud-Ellul, Paul 4:40:11 (22,235)
Mikellides, Andreas 3:53:49 (9,815)
Milan, Chris M 3:34:43 (5,648)
Miles, Andrew J 3:56:20 (10,573)
Miles, Anthony I 5:32:57 (30,743)
Miles, Anthony J 6:43:38 (33,951)
Miles, Carl 3:31:12 (5,076)
Miles, Christopher S 3:15:24 (2,691)
Miles, Christopher T 4:49:31 (24,478)
Miles, David M 3:07:19 (1,713)
Miles, Dominic J 3:20:18 (3,266)
Miles, Graham R 3:06:10 (1,614)
Miles, Kevin D 4:04:57 (13,038)
Miles, Laurence 2:41:07 (217)
Miles, Nicholas 4:13:41 (15,218)
Miles, Nick 3:25:06 (3,947)
Miles, Paul J 3:57:43 (11,023)
Miles, Paul W 3:00:18 (1,186)
Miles, Sebastian 4:13:42 (15,225)
Millar, Craig E 5:06:08 (27,575)
Millar, Gavin 3:52:50 (9,514)
Millar, Gordon N 5:30:25 (30,518)
Millard, Christopher G 4:01:35 (12,267)
Millard, Christopher J 2:58:00 (948)
Millard, Duncan R 4:14:13 (15,373)
Millard, Iain 5:53:51 (32,395)
Millard, Mark P 3:50:21 (8,900)
Millard, Simon R 4:58:42 (26,420)
Millbank, Andy M 3:18:42 (3,064)
Miller, Adrian D 3:44:37 (7,582)
Miller, Andrew 6:08:16 (33,056)
Miller, Andrew T 5:12:45 (28,502)
Miller, Carl W 4:04:41 (12,979)
Miller, Christopher P 4:32:11 (20,223)
Miller, Claire 4:07:27 (13,627)
Miller, David I 4:46:22 (23,755)
Miller, David M 3:45:20 (7,762)
Miller, Edward P 4:13:58 (15,292)
Miller, Garth 5:23:34 (29,753)
Miller, Graeme 3:08:10 (1,811)
Miller, Graham F 3:42:53 (7,211)
Miller, Ian D 3:14:04 (2,479)
Miller, James 3:31:22 (5,111)
Miller, James E 3:55:11 (10,261)
Miller, James G 4:09:20 (14,127)
Miller, Joe 4:32:58 (20,424)
Miller, John D 3:46:54 (8,083)
Miller, Kenneth W 3:55:50 (10,446)
Miller, Kevin T 5:28:58 (30,375)
Miller, Lee 3:46:40 (8,035)
Miller, Matthew R 5:51:11 (32,223)
Miller, Paul 2:40:28 (203)
Miller, Peter 3:15:14 (2,660)
Miller, Ross 5:44:36 (31,728)
Miller, Roy F 5:22:06 (29,614)
Miller, Thomas 5:14:31 (28,741)
Miller, Tim 4:27:39 (18,986)
Millican, Christopher 4:46:05 (23,685)
Millican, Graham J 3:01:51 (1,301)
Millican, Keith M 4:46:15 (23,727)
Millington, Allan J 3:58:27 (11,282)
Millington, James S 4:21:01 (17,188)
Millington, John 4:46:25 (23,762)
Millington, Matthew A 5:19:38 (29,377)
Millington, Nicholas J 4:36:13 (21,301)
Millington, Robert H 4:46:37 (23,801)
Milller, David 5:48:53 (32,039)
Millman, Dom 4:18:55 (16,603)
Millman, Robin 4:33:50 (20,667)
Millns, Gary K 3:46:43 (8,042)
Millns, Tom J 3:26:54 (4,261)
Millray, Roger 4:34:35 (20,839)
Mills, Aaron P 5:15:39 (28,899)
Mills, Barnaby T 4:14:15 (15,383)
Mills, Chris J 4:51:40 (24,980)
Mills, Craig J 4:41:58 (22,666)
Mills, Daniel R 3:44:33 (7,563)
Mills, Freddie J 5:23:01 (29,699)
Mills, Gareth 4:16:02 (15,845)
Mills, Julius R 4:29:48 (19,588)
Mills, Kevin D 3:28:06 (4,481)
Mills, Mark J 4:25:48 (18,482)
Mills, Oliver L 4:18:48 (16,572)
Mills, Paul 4:46:25 (23,762)
Mills, Peter 4:37:39 (21,630)
Mills, Richard W 5:15:54 (28,921)
Mills, Robert A 3:25:34 (4,025)
Mills, Roger 5:31:58 (30,661)
Mills, Shaun 4:25:46 (18,468)
Mills, Shaun J 3:13:03 (2,341)
Mills, Simon P 3:53:28 (9,705)
Mills, Steve J 5:14:12 (28,704)
Mills, Steven W 3:48:53 (8,549)
Mills, Stuart 3:17:14 (2,892)
Mills, Tim W 4:24:25 (18,114)
Millward, Michael P 4:36:13 (21,301)
Millward, Neil J 4:21:28 (17,293)
Millward, Stephen N 4:02:39 (12,533)
Milmine, Matthew S 3:35:51 (5,855)
Milmoe, Michael 3:54:57 (10,179)
Milne, Alex 4:39:33 (22,090)
Milne, Alexander J 3:30:20 (4,944)
Milne, Andrew 5:02:10 (26,980)
Milne, Gary B 5:14:29 (28,738)
Milne, James J 4:06:35 (13,420)
Milne, Jeremy A 3:46:01 (7,891)
Milne, Mikki G 4:27:14 (18,883)
Milne, Stephen R 4:33:25 (20,550)
Milner, Alistair 4:24:01 (18,000)
Milner, Iain A 4:38:24 (21,800)
Milner, James R 5:05:28 (27,467)
Milner, Mark 4:48:19 (24,212)
Milner, Simon 6:05:05 (32,932)
Milses, John 5:25:03 (29,924)
Milsom, Mark 3:57:12 (10,862)
Milsom, Michael P 3:25:36 (4,037)
Milstead, Robert G 3:19:54 (3,215)
Milton, Dean 4:31:56 (20,147)
Milton, John S 6:24:29 (33,532)
Milton, Paul J 4:27:47 (19,017)
Milwain, Kevin I 5:06:03 (27,560)
Milz, Volker 4:04:07 (12,848)
Minas, Charilaos P 6:56:05 (34,169)
Mindel, Morris J 5:36:26 (31,075)
Ming, Stewart A 4:49:47 (24,552)
Mingay, Simon 3:05:04 (1,525)
Minguella Morales, Marc 3:29:28 (4,774)
Minhas, Pardip Singh S 4:30:20 (19,706)
Minnaar, Stefan 4:29:21 (19,489)
Minns, Phillip I 3:30:49 (5,024)
Minogue, James 6:29:03 (33,639)
Minshall, Andrew C 4:52:17 (25,101)
Minshull, Paul 3:45:29 (7,790)
Minson, Paul 4:22:56 (17,710)
Minter, John R 7:02:39 (34,236)
Minty, Kevin J 2:50:28 (535)
Miralles, José 3:59:11 (11,554)
Mirjan, Razzak 3:23:43 (3,729)
Mironchik, Roman 4:56:40 (25,995)
Misa, Gavan 4:31:21 (19,978)
Misani, Patrizio 4:37:22 (21,565)
Miscali, Gianluca 3:56:08 (10,522)
Miscera, Alessio 4:58:58 (26,468)
Missingham, Andrew D 3:52:47 (9,499)
Missions, William M 3:49:49 (8,774)
Mistorini, Francesco 4:31:47 (20,097)
Mistretta, Gaetano 3:55:33 (10,354)
Mistri, John 5:40:17 (31,359)
Mistry, Jayanti 4:48:26 (24,233)
Mistry, Mayur L 6:56:18 (34,174)
Mistry, Mukesh 4:34:03 (20,711)
Mistry, Prashant 6:30:01 (33,659)
Mistry, Sanjay N 4:31:01 (19,887)
Mistry, Shashikant M 6:19:12 (33,380)
Mistry, Shashikant V 5:08:59 (27,967)
Mitcham, David J 3:38:47 (6,405)

Mitchell, Andrew D	4:49:57 (24,591)	
Mitchell, Andrew M	3:32:05 (5,239)	
Mitchell, Barry W	4:08:35 (13,937)	
Mitchell, Bernie J	4:47:39 (24,057)	
Mitchell, Bruce R	3:22:58 (3,631)	
Mitchell, Christopher S	5:46:40 (31,892)	
Mitchell, Colin M	5:30:15 (30,502)	
Mitchell, David	3:53:13 (9,643)	
Mitchell, David J	4:52:23 (25,121)	
Mitchell, David J	6:53:24 (34,129)	
Mitchell, David R	3:58:43 (11,382)	
Mitchell, David R	4:51:03 (24,855)	
Mitchell, David S	4:18:16 (16,421)	
Mitchell, Edward O	3:08:50 (1,860)	
Mitchell, Ian B	4:50:19 (24,670)	
Mitchell, James	4:07:16 (13,591)	
Mitchell, James B	5:14:58 (28,815)	
Mitchell, John L	5:40:47 (31,397)	
Mitchell, Justin A	2:44:10 (299)	
Mitchell, Matthew J	3:54:53 (10,150)	
Mitchell, Nicholas J	3:44:29 (7,549)	
Mitchell, Paul A	5:47:12 (31,928)	
Mitchell, Paul R	2:44:31 (312)	
Mitchell, Peter A	4:01:51 (12,327)	
Mitchell, Rchard J	4:52:29 (25,143)	
Mitchell, Rob	4:50:10 (24,637)	
Mitchell, Robert J	3:11:17 (2,125)	
Mitchell, Samuel T	3:39:22 (6,512)	
Mitchell, Simon J	3:42:47 (7,194)	
Mitchell, Steve	3:12:38 (2,280)	
Mitchell, Steven	5:07:04 (27,702)	
Mitchell, Timothy P	4:36:32 (21,378)	
Mitcheson, Adrian R	4:49:28 (24,469)	
Mitchinson, Mark	5:24:45 (29,881)	
Mitchley, Paul	3:55:35 (10,367)	
Mitropapas, Constantinos	4:21:28 (17,293)	
Mitton, Charles N	3:56:44 (10,702)	
Mitton, Jamie A	4:01:02 (12,118)	
Mitton, Thomas E	5:34:36 (30,896)	
Miyaji, Yoichiro	4:36:06 (21,268)	
Mizen, Ricki	3:57:04 (10,816)	
Moaby, Malcolm D	3:57:59 (11,109)	
Moate, Toby J	4:16:52 (16,049)	
Mobbs, Chris J	4:57:11 (26,122)	
Moberly, James P	4:48:56 (24,354)	
Mocevic, Blazenko	4:20:01 (16,890)	
Mocquard, Pascal	3:34:01 (5,550)	
Modaher, Jasvir S	5:41:29 (31,465)	
Modde, André	4:00:47 (12,054)	
Moerk, Michael	3:01:45 (1,292)	
Moffat, Peter	3:31:20 (5,105)	
Moffat, Stephen H	2:58:27 (1,002)	
Moffatt, Graham D	2:59:41 (1,139)	
Moffett, Christopher J	6:07:55 (33,041)	
Moffett, David J	4:03:44 (12,777)	
Moffett, James S	4:25:43 (18,453)	
Moga, Frederic	3:30:57 (5,046)	
Mogensen, Knud	5:26:29 (30,095)	
Mogford, Philip B	5:11:27 (28,326)	
Moggan, Frank M	4:11:57 (14,791)	
Mogridge, Chris	5:11:01 (28,278)	
Mohamed, Jeremy	4:13:46 (15,243)	
Mohaupt, Jorg	4:07:15 (13,588)	
Mohle, Holger	3:17:17 (2,901)	
Moir, Richard J	3:57:00 (10,796)	
Mokuena, Mikail	4:24:35 (18,166)	
Mole, Robert A	3:14:20 (2,524)	
Mole, Rufus H	4:00:32 (11,982)	
Moles, Chris	3:56:20 (10,573)	
Molesworth, Tony	3:53:03 (9,593)	
Molinari, Andrea F	4:42:53 (22,901)	
Molineris, Mauro	3:16:11 (2,773)	
Moll, Simon T	4:36:19 (21,328)	
Mollart, Nicholas E	3:57:42 (11,017)	
Moller Jensen, Per	4:09:25 (14,147)	
Mollett, Nathan	4:24:45 (18,205)	
Mollison, John A	4:03:31 (12,732)	
Molloy, Anthony P	5:21:10 (29,516)	
Molloy, John M	3:26:24 (4,173)	
Molnar, Csaba	3:20:31 (3,293)	
Moloney, Kevin	5:08:16 (27,853)	
Moloney, Simon J	4:00:12 (11,897)	
Molony, David	3:33:15 (5,432)	
Molony, Neil	3:51:39 (9,211)	
Molyneux, Allan R	4:56:52 (26,040)	
Molyneux, Graham J	3:06:02 (1,600)	
Molyneux, Paul M	2:31:56 (84)	
Molyneux, Simon G	4:20:47 (17,118)	
Monaghan, Robert L	5:09:24 (28,028)	
Monighan, Andrew	4:56:06 (25,892)	
Monk, Harold	4:01:38 (12,275)	
Monk, Howard C	4:10:49 (14,498)	
Monk, Ian P	5:00:47 (26,756)	
Monks, Christopher O	5:26:57 (30,141)	
Monks, Simon J	5:11:40 (28,359)	
Monnicendam, Giles C	2:51:33 (574)	
Monnoyer, Gaspard	4:15:43 (15,752)	
Monro-Davies, Ben	4:10:50 (14,503)	
Monsch, Jeam-Marie	3:21:11 (3,383)	
Monsen, Espen Osvold	5:57:18 (32,594)	
Montagu Pollock, Thomas G	4:49:40 (24,525)	
Montague, Peter A	7:57:39 (34,529)	
Montalbano, Aurelio	4:14:47 (15,512)	
Montanari, Enrique Carlos	3:58:40 (11,364)	
Montano Monge, Manuel	3:26:59 (4,277)	
Montanus, Kees	3:16:04 (2,760)	
Montero, Mario	3:27:13 (4,315)	
Montes Ramos, Albaro V	5:20:38 (29,473)	
Montgomerie, Richard R	4:14:10 (15,357)	
Montgomery, Arthur D	5:47:23 (31,941)	
Montgomery, Gerard	3:26:03 (4,113)	
Montgomery, John W	3:59:12 (11,562)	
Montgomery, Michael J	4:39:09 (22,018)	
Montgomery, Richard R	4:32:08 (20,208)	
Montini, Roberto	4:01:11 (12,159)	
Moody, Colin A	3:05:14 (1,533)	
Moody, Daniel E	4:16:36 (15,984)	
Moody, Robert J	4:55:24 (25,767)	
Moody, William E	4:35:58 (21,238)	
Moohan, Michael J	5:07:00 (27,694)	
Moon, Arny	3:56:58 (10,781)	
Moon, Chris	4:11:44 (14,740)	
Mooney, Colin J	4:41:16 (22,501)	
Moor, Avishai D	4:50:47 (24,793)	
Moor, Gary	4:28:32 (19,274)	
Moorcroft, David R	4:53:53 (25,456)	
Moore, Andrew J	3:46:39 (8,031)	
Moore, Andrew M	3:22:13 (3,519)	
Moore, Andrew P	4:00:35 (11,998)	
Moore, Andrew P	5:14:04 (28,683)	
Moore, Ben A	4:34:11 (20,752)	
Moore, Benjamin	4:43:00 (22,926)	
Moore, Carl R	4:49:55 (24,583)	
Moore, Christopher	4:25:26 (18,377)	
Moore, Christopher J	4:14:52 (15,527)	
Moore, Colin D	3:33:31 (5,476)	
Moore, Colin D	4:14:37 (15,472)	
Moore, David M	4:55:32 (25,786)	
Moore, Derek S	4:32:42 (20,348)	
Moore, Derrick	4:52:53 (25,247)	
Moore, Frederic C	3:57:11 (10,858)	
Moore, George M	4:55:05 (25,715)	
Moore, Gerard	4:13:41 (15,218)	
Moore, Graham S	3:03:42 (1,430)	
Moore, Gregory I	3:47:05 (8,130)	
Moore, James	5:09:27 (28,036)	
Moore, James D	4:21:26 (17,286)	
Moore, James P	3:54:18 (9,960)	
Moore, Jimmy	4:55:55 (25,864)	
Moore, John	4:31:21 (19,978)	
Moore, John D	3:41:41 (6,988)	
Moore, Joseph A	3:46:02 (7,896)	
Moore, Justin M	3:14:51 (2,614)	
Moore, Karl D	2:48:31 (448)	
Moore, Ken A	5:43:37 (31,618)	
Moore, Lee R	4:38:38 (21,864)	
Moore, Martin C	4:41:54 (22,652)	
Moore, Melwyn J	4:02:58 (12,602)	
Moore, Michael J	3:27:23 (4,346)	
Moore, Michael R	3:23:27 (3,701)	
Moore, Mick J	4:34:09 (20,739)	
Moore, Nigel J	5:27:36 (30,209)	
Moore, Paul A	2:47:08 (392)	
Moore, Paul R	4:08:18 (13,853)	
Moore, Philip	4:08:54 (14,018)	
Moore, Richard C	3:06:16 (1,623)	
Moore, Richard J	3:50:42 (8,990)	
Moore, Richard P	3:23:32 (3,711)	
Moore, Robert G	4:11:44 (14,740)	
Moore, Scott A	4:22:31 (17,591)	
Moore, Sean G	4:57:13 (26,127)	
Moore, Simon	3:49:52 (8,791)	
Moore, Simon P	3:45:05 (7,704)	
Moore, Thomas L	3:24:15 (3,811)	
Moore, Timothy J	3:53:50 (9,824)	
Moore, Trevor A	3:09:12 (1,909)	
Moore, Trevor E	4:00:42 (12,034)	
Moores, David J	5:01:22 (26,854)	
Moores, Mark J	3:54:44 (10,108)	
Moores, Rob	4:34:19 (20,779)	
Moorhouse, Andrew D	4:05:00 (13,050)	
Mooris, Gregory E	4:14:59 (15,553)	
Moos, Chris J	3:37:38 (6,191)	
Moralee, Alastair	3:48:21 (8,431)	
Morales, Alex J	3:19:20 (3,140)	
Morales Vallejo, Julian	4:06:03 (13,301)	
Moran, David	3:07:17 (1,707)	
Moran, Hugh L	3:46:38 (8,028)	
Moran, John D	3:49:38 (8,728)	
Moran, Nicholas J	3:31:59 (5,223)	
Moran, Paschal P	3:28:04 (4,473)	
Moran, Richard F	3:53:03 (9,593)	
Moran, Robin	4:09:14 (14,097)	
Morati, Pierino	4:29:51 (19,600)	
Moreira, José Avelino B	4:40:50 (22,389)	
Moreno, José L	3:40:51 (6,793)	
Moretto, Gerardo	4:45:40 (23,576)	
Morfey, Michael J	5:46:52 (31,902)	
Morford, Richard J	3:41:51 (7,001)	
Morgan, Andrew	3:55:06 (10,233)	
Morgan, Arwell T	4:54:49 (25,653)	
Morgan, Charles J	3:09:25 (1,930)	
Morgan, Christopher J	4:05:01 (13,053)	
Morgan, Christopher L	3:28:00 (4,459)	
Morgan, David	4:28:01 (19,103)	
Morgan, David	4:50:24 (24,684)	
Morgan, David	5:01:05 (26,807)	
Morgan, David G	3:55:02 (10,210)	
Morgan, David J	4:28:35 (19,284)	
Morgan, David R	3:14:33 (2,559)	
Morgan, David R	5:05:31 (27,479)	
Morgan, Gavin J	4:23:04 (17,744)	
Morgan, James S	4:07:25 (13,618)	
Morgan, Jonny	3:42:36 (7,153)	
Morgan, Lee	4:19:00 (16,625)	
Morgan, Lee T	4:43:53 (23,148)	
Morgan, Michael	5:03:12 (27,131)	
Morgan, Neil V	3:20:14 (3,256)	
Morgan, Neill F	5:20:20 (29,444)	
Morgan, Nicholas A	3:58:09 (11,163)	
Morgan, Oliver G	3:55:43 (10,409)	
Morgan, Paul	3:48:55 (8,559)	
Morgan, Ray E	5:03:05 (27,115)	
Morgan, Rhys C	3:58:42 (11,374)	
Morgan, Rob C	4:02:13 (12,420)	
Morgan, Robert J	3:07:50 (1,769)	
Morgan, Ross W	3:30:51 (5,029)	
Morgan, Sean	3:28:27 (4,552)	
Morgan, Stacey J	2:44:37 (318)	
Morgan, Steve	4:13:13 (15,091)	
Morgan, Steve J	3:45:38 (7,822)	
Morgan, Steven A	4:37:47 (21,663)	
Morgan, Thomas G	4:12:52 (14,996)	
Morgan, Tim	3:35:41 (5,829)	
Morgan, Toby C	3:56:25 (10,602)	
Morgan, William	4:13:58 (15,292)	
Morgetroyd, Richard	3:08:29 (1,837)	
Moriarty, Mark C	4:30:44 (19,811)	
Moriarty, Richard	4:16:16 (15,895)	
Moriarty, Sean B	3:57:24 (10,928)	
Morin, Denis P	3:33:17 (5,436)	
Morini, Antonio	4:41:39 (22,598)	
Morison, Chris	4:21:28 (17,293)	
Morisset, Jean-Paul	3:16:28 (2,810)	
Morley, Alex J	4:09:37 (14,204)	
Morley, Benjamin P	4:43:11 (22,978)	
Morley, Craig S	3:28:56 (4,650)	
Morley, Daren	4:09:07 (14,065)	
Morley, Darren L	4:20:52 (17,144)	

Morley, David J....3:47:29 (8,219)
Morley, Dean....3:06:50 (1,667)
Morley, James R....3:23:56 (3,770)
Morley, Paul....3:54:27 (10,008)
Morley, Phil A....2:59:49 (1,151)
Morling, Russell J....3:25:20 (3,984)
Moroney, Alan J....4:05:08 (13,080)
Moroney, Mark....4:03:57 (12,820)
Morphett, Keith S....4:12:08 (14,843)
Morrall, Alexander....3:14:40 (2,583)
Morreale, Austin....5:06:26 (27,620)
Morreale, Paz....5:20:45 (29,479)
Morrell, David J....3:47:59 (8,345)
Morrell, Ian D....4:20:26 (17,008)
Morrin, Cyril....5:45:53 (31,827)
Morris, Aaron....4:37:02 (21,494)
Morris, Adam S....3:59:00 (11,489)
Morris, Alan D....4:14:04 (15,326)
Morris, Alun H....3:55:30 (10,343)
Morris, Andrew D....5:23:04 (29,706)
Morris, Andrew M....3:53:10 (9,629)
Morris, Andrew R....4:47:32 (24,026)
Morris, Andy....3:57:06 (10,835)
Morris, Anthony....4:23:02 (17,737)
Morris, Ashley J....3:39:21 (6,509)
Morris, Brendon....5:01:09 (26,818)
Morris, Brian....4:47:06 (23,930)
Morris, Chris J....2:54:46 (733)
Morris, Colin....3:47:35 (8,243)
Morris, Colin R....4:13:29 (15,154)
Morris, Darren....4:01:40 (12,285)
Morris, Dave J....4:35:40 (21,157)
Morris, David C....4:45:04 (23,426)
Morris, David G....5:01:54 (26,944)
Morris, David M....4:42:47 (22,874)
Morris, David T....4:57:34 (26,199)
Morris, George E....4:26:58 (18,806)
Morris, Glyn E....3:23:11 (3,661)
Morris, Guy....4:02:00 (12,363)
Morris, Ian P....5:10:28 (28,215)
Morris, James....3:59:52 (11,807)
Morris, James....5:58:16 (32,653)
Morris, James I....3:56:24 (10,598)
Morris, James S....2:46:56 (384)
Morris, Jonathan D....3:21:04 (3,368)
Morris, Keneth....3:43:54 (7,441)
Morris, Kevin S....5:01:22 (26,854)
Morris, Lee....6:25:50 (33,571)
Morris, Luke....3:51:28 (9,169)
Morris, Mark....3:19:19 (3,137)
Morris, Mark....5:43:01 (31,573)
Morris, Mark N....4:38:09 (21,750)
Morris, Paul....4:31:15 (19,950)
Morris, Paul W....3:17:50 (2,965)
Morris, Peter I....5:10:14 (28,180)
Morris, Philip J....3:30:57 (5,046)
Morris, Richard....4:00:46 (12,050)
Morris, Richard G....3:42:59 (7,233)
Morris, Robert A....5:40:30 (31,375)
Morris, Robert H....3:47:06 (8,134)
Morris, Robert P....5:01:32 (26,876)
Morris, Robert W....2:51:16 (560)
Morris, Ryan M....3:21:55 (3,475)
Morris, Simon P....4:33:36 (20,609)
Morris, Thomas A....3:55:15 (10,275)
Morris, Trevor H....3:12:41 (2,288)
Morrish, Stuart R....3:20:46 (3,327)
Morrison, Angus....4:52:41 (25,196)
Morrison, Benjamin L....3:54:19 (9,963)
Morrison, David A....4:21:11 (17,220)
Morrison, Graham....3:34:12 (5,577)
Morrison, Shane A....4:29:39 (19,551)
Morrison, Sidney....3:45:47 (7,853)
Morrison, Stewart B....3:58:32 (11,310)
Morrison-Smith, Nicholas A....3:28:56 (4,650)
Morrisroe, Alexander....4:50:52 (24,812)
Morriss, Aaran G....4:27:57 (19,081)
Morrow, Andrew J....3:41:45 (6,977)
Morrow, Nicholas E....2:45:06 (337)
Morse, Neil J....3:52:50 (9,514)
Morse, Peter....5:30:06 (30,486)
Morsley, John H....3:28:51 (4,635)
Morsley, Magnus C....4:03:51 (12,797)

Morson, Myles G....5:11:42 (28,367)
Morte, Carl....4:05:56 (13,275)
Mortimer, Alan B....5:15:54 (28,921)
Mortimer, Christopher....5:09:40 (28,086)
Mortimer, Ian A....4:46:30 (23,777)
Mortimer, John....5:28:58 (30,375)
Mortimer, John G....4:34:05 (20,720)
Mortimer, Simon H....5:16:47 (29,030)
Mortimer, Simon T....2:51:00 (552)
Mortlock, Andrew E....4:40:19 (22,262)
Mortlock, David S....4:36:23 (21,342)
Morton, Andrew D....4:29:58 (19,625)
Morton, Brian G....5:00:54 (26,779)
Morton, Colin....5:00:42 (26,737)
Morton, James....3:59:10 (11,548)
Morton, Mitchell R....5:10:33 (28,221)
Morton, Peter H....4:56:41 (26,001)
Morton, Steven J....2:57:21 (900)
Morton, Steven M....4:00:57 (12,102)
Moruzzi, Marco....3:44:57 (7,672)
Morwood, David W....2:36:57 (147)
Mosca, Francesco....4:16:59 (16,088)
Mosedale, Wayne W....3:32:34 (5,328)
Moseley, Alan....3:23:54 (3,764)
Moseley, Simon....2:57:39 (915)
Moses, Rob....3:27:33 (4,371)
Moss, Andrew R....4:21:00 (17,182)
Moss, Darren P....5:18:19 (29,209)
Moss, Dave T....5:44:33 (31,726)
Moss, Gary T....3:40:55 (6,807)
Moss, Gerrard A....3:39:39 (6,565)
Moss, Ian D....5:08:50 (27,947)
Moss, John R....4:44:35 (23,315)
Moss, Moddy J....4:13:12 (15,081)
Moss, Paul A....4:42:11 (22,715)
Moss, Robert M....3:44:54 (7,656)
Moss, Stephen D....4:07:52 (13,739)
Moss, Tony....5:40:46 (31,396)
Mossman, Alan....4:42:50 (22,884)
Mossop, Andrew E....3:58:56 (11,468)
Mota Pereira, Antonio Sergio L....3:58:21 (11,248)
Mothe, Christian....3:15:00 (2,627)
Motley, David G....3:43:39 (7,378)
Motley, Philip E....3:48:15 (8,414)
Mott, Oliver J....4:03:55 (12,807)
Mott, Paul R....3:47:31 (8,225)
Mottey, Michel....4:11:34 (14,700)
Mottola, Aurelio....3:55:04 (10,222)
Mouafiq, Mbarek....3:43:02 (7,246)
Mouffok, Amine....3:35:11 (5,735)
Mould, Andrew R....4:36:27 (21,358)
Mould, David G....4:00:39 (12,017)
Moulder, David R....3:17:11 (2,885)
Moulder, Duncan J....3:52:47 (9,499)
Moulsdale, Jonathan M....4:19:04 (16,647)
Moulson, Stuart C....3:37:52 (6,230)
Moulton, Paul D....4:55:01 (25,705)
Mound, David G....5:44:46 (31,743)
Mounsey, Paul J....3:21:05 (3,371)
Mountford, Nicholas W....4:05:49 (13,249)
Mountford, Rob S....5:49:58 (32,118)
Mountjoy, Roger....4:42:42 (22,851)
Mouritzen, Jesper T....3:20:08 (3,239)
Moutchiev, Pavel....4:16:46 (16,023)
Moutoussamy, Florent....3:33:29 (5,472)
Mouzer, Robert....3:19:16 (3,130)
Mower, Melvin....3:29:08 (4,700)
Mowle, Chris B....2:45:18 (343)
Mowle, Lee L....3:02:03 (1,311)
Mowlem, Matthew C....4:15:54 (15,807)
Moxon, Howard....4:15:25 (15,676)
Moy, Jason....4:25:07 (18,296)
Moyes, Peter D....4:44:18 (23,256)
Moyles, Phillip....3:40:23 (6,711)
Moynihan, Benjamin R....4:50:46 (24,787)
Moyse, Gary P....4:14:22 (15,415)
Mucklow, Stuart E....4:34:35 (20,839)
Mudd, Thomas C....5:03:53 (27,238)
Mudimu, Collen....3:01:42 (1,289)
Mueller, Patrick....4:53:56 (25,468)
Muffett, Paul J....3:33:17 (5,436)
Mughal, Muntzer....4:29:58 (19,625)
Muil, John H....4:53:28 (25,364)

Muinos Pantin, Iago....3:24:48 (3,888)
Muir, Alasdair....3:50:02 (8,830)
Muir, Alex W....3:28:00 (4,459)
Muir, Andrew S....4:32:54 (20,401)
Muir, David....4:29:54 (19,606)
Muir, Fraser J....5:24:59 (29,910)
Muir, Graham M....3:47:29 (8,219)
Muir, Jonathan....5:06:30 (27,626)
Muir, Malcolm J....2:46:53 (383)
Muir, Peter D....5:51:13 (32,228)
Muir, Tim R....3:57:39 (10,995)
Muirhead, Graeme A....3:31:13 (5,082)
Muirhead Smith, Andrew....4:22:34 (17,601)
Muiryan, Danny....4:09:32 (14,183)
Mukhtar, Bashir M....3:55:01 (10,201)
Mulcahy, Brian....3:45:18 (7,755)
Mulcahy, Peter W....4:08:03 (13,780)
Muldoon, Gerald....4:21:58 (17,445)
Mulhall, Patrick B....4:51:42 (24,985)
Mulholland, Brian J....4:56:41 (26,001)
Mulholland, Damian....3:05:55 (1,589)
Mulholland, Michael J....5:53:51 (32,395)
Mulindwa, Steve....5:49:07 (32,061)
Mulla, Shoeb....5:34:07 (30,846)
Mullane, Steve....4:24:29 (18,137)
Mullard, Tom E....5:25:10 (29,945)
Mullarkey, Chris....4:50:47 (24,793)
Mullen, Michael....4:01:29 (12,237)
Mullen, Peter J....4:28:01 (19,103)
Muller, Richard A....5:07:14 (27,728)
Muller, Thomas....3:35:12 (5,737)
Mullery, Peter J....3:16:18 (2,788)
Mullett, James S....3:55:54 (10,465)
Mulley, Ian W....5:39:50 (31,316)
Mulley, John W....4:22:07 (17,474)
Mullin, Daniel E....5:54:01 (32,408)
Mullin, John....5:20:25 (29,456)
Mullineux, Andrew....3:30:01 (4,888)
Mullins, Jason....4:53:09 (25,307)
Mullins, Paul A....3:49:55 (8,804)
Mullins, Samm....9:59:58 (34,590)
Mulock, Michael L....5:44:40 (31,734)
Mulry, Ian....4:24:19 (18,084)
Mumford, Mark....4:54:38 (25,606)
Munasinghe, Indumina C....4:31:22 (19,983)
Munday, David A....5:05:26 (27,462)
Munday, Philip J....3:59:29 (11,668)
Mundie, Philip J....4:17:48 (16,305)
Munds, Mike P....3:45:03 (7,697)
Mundy, James....3:28:45 (4,613)
Mundy, James A....4:22:48 (17,668)
Mundy, Robert J....4:33:16 (20,496)
Mungovan, James....3:49:27 (8,686)
Munim, Abdul....7:08:53 (34,301)
Muniz, Mannuel....4:50:25 (24,688)
Muniz-Morell, Carlos....4:13:15 (15,098)
Munn, Anthony W....4:05:38 (13,206)
Munn, Gavin....6:50:43 (34,086)
Munns, Brian....3:54:44 (10,108)
Munro, David A....3:07:45 (1,760)
Munro, Jonathan C....3:59:57 (11,836)
Munroe, Anthony V....4:58:26 (26,366)
Munroe, Mark A....4:33:29 (20,572)
Munson, John P....4:46:04 (23,684)
Muradas Bertolo, Manuel....3:53:40 (9,758)
Muratani, Masafumi....4:27:03 (18,828)
Murchison, Andrew....3:18:54 (3,086)
Murdoch, Graeme A....3:14:42 (2,591)
Murdoch, Robert F....3:25:52 (4,081)
Murdoch, Steven J....3:03:00 (1,372)
Mureithi, David M....4:23:25 (17,842)
Murless, Keith J....4:18:55 (16,603)
Murphy, Alan J....7:40:36 (34,483)
Murphy, Andrew D....4:11:58 (14,801)
Murphy, Andrew J....3:36:47 (6,012)
Murphy, Anthony C....4:24:40 (18,186)
Murphy, Anthony J....4:20:00 (16,884)
Murphy, Ben....4:10:36 (14,433)
Murphy, Ben....4:41:12 (22,488)
Murphy, Bernard....2:29:00 (56)
Murphy, Brendan....4:48:15 (24,190)
Murphy, Brian....4:32:30 (20,300)
Murphy, Brian P....4:33:34 (20,597)

Murphy, Chris P 4:15:43 (15,752)
Murphy, Christian 3:35:31 (5,795)
Murphy, Daniel P 4:17:08 (16,135)
Murphy, David 5:29:33 (30,429)
Murphy, David J 4:22:36 (17,613)
Murphy, Edmond J 4:00:48 (12,056)
Murphy, Gerry M 3:51:23 (9,149)
Murphy, Jack 3:58:45 (11,389)
Murphy, John A 4:20:19 (16,979)
Murphy, John C 3:58:46 (11,397)
Murphy, John E 3:38:26 (6,347)
Murphy, Justin S 4:14:27 (15,436)
Murphy, Kieran C 3:05:12 (1,530)
Murphy, Lee 3:31:18 (5,100)
Murphy, Lee D 4:06:57 (13,504)
Murphy, Martin 4:03:44 (12,777)
Murphy, Nicholas J 5:47:09 (31,922)
Murphy, Paul S 3:56:24 (10,598)
Murphy, Paul W 3:51:24 (9,152)
Murphy, Paul W 4:19:55 (16,864)
Murphy, Peter J 3:29:35 (4,795)
Murphy, Ray D 6:06:29 (33,004)
Murphy, Stephen 5:12:40 (28,480)
Murphy, Steve W 5:03:53 (27,238)
Murray, Allen A 3:44:09 (7,482)
Murray, Andrew C 3:37:14 (6,109)
Murray, Bruce A 4:01:42 (12,295)
Murray, Chris J 3:28:57 (4,657)
Murray, Daniel C 4:29:43 (19,568)
Murray, David 3:59:09 (11,544)
Murray, David J 4:07:50 (13,725)
Murray, Dean C 5:06:39 (27,645)
Murray, Dominic 4:27:58 (19,088)
Murray, Eoghan 3:38:24 (6,339)
Murray, Francis 4:08:21 (13,869)
Murray, Hamish R 3:31:04 (5,060)
Murray, Iain 3:09:45 (1,965)
Murray, Iain P 4:04:38 (12,967)
Murray, John 3:50:25 (8,913)
Murray, John S 3:29:13 (4,718)
Murray, Julian J 3:59:54 (11,818)
Murray, Leon 4:36:39 (21,402)
Murray, Michael R 3:56:11 (10,533)
Murray, Neil A 3:05:13 (1,531)
Murray, Neil A 3:58:37 (11,341)
Murray, Rob 4:04:17 (12,882)
Murray, Robert R 3:52:41 (9,476)
Murray, Scott 4:02:16 (12,436)
Murray, Scott 4:13:39 (15,203)
Murray, Stuart 4:39:46 (22,148)
Murray, Thomas D 2:59:10 (1,080)
Murrell, Gregg R 4:52:06 (25,064)
Murrell, Nick 3:50:16 (8,887)
Murrell, Richard D 4:13:33 (15,172)
Murrish, Darren P 4:14:00 (15,302)
Murry, Adam 5:27:40 (30,220)
Murtagh, Dominic A 3:58:09 (11,163)
Murtagh, Simon R 4:34:02 (20,705)
Murtagh, Stephen J 2:59:57 (1,164)
Murton, Alexander P 6:23:26 (33,500)
Muschamp, David J 4:20:02 (16,899)
Muschietti, Dino 3:15:46 (2,725)
Musgrave Brown, Christopher 5:00:03 (26,643)
Musgrove, Alistair M 4:05:45 (13,232)
Musgrove, Ian 3:55:08 (10,246)
Musgrove, Phil J 5:14:15 (28,713)
Mushtaq, Wasim 5:35:03 (30,946)
Musk, Ryan L 5:11:37 (28,348)
Musker, Robert F 4:11:29 (14,674)
Mussellle, Robert J 4:35:02 (20,992)
Musselwhite, James D 3:58:47 (11,406)
Mussett, Adrian N 2:29:20 (62)
Mussett, Nick C 3:57:49 (11,066)
Mussett, Stephen 4:46:09 (23,700)
Musson, Anthony R 4:43:41 (23,098)
Musumeci, Andrea 4:35:05 (21,005)
Mutai, Emmanuel 2:06:15 (4)
Mutch, George M 4:33:16 (20,496)
Mutsaers, Adrian R 3:26:39 (4,218)
Muyuka, Stephen H 5:48:35 (32,019)
Muzzi, Claudio 3:22:24 (3,549)
Mwandia, Nicholas K 4:54:24 (25,560)
Myatt, Alister J 4:13:21 (15,130)
Myatt, John P 4:48:54 (24,346)
Mycock, Gareth J 3:23:04 (3,646)
Myers, Bob 4:39:37 (22,100)
Myers, Charles V 2:55:48 (795)
Myers, Jonathan B 4:46:28 (23,769)
Myers, Peter 4:58:01 (26,284)
Myers, Richard C 4:52:38 (25,180)
Myers, Terence J 4:27:14 (18,883)
Myerscough, Steve V 2:58:14 (970)
Myhill, Andrew 4:41:57 (22,663)
Myhill, Ian 4:02:43 (12,547)
Myhill, James T 3:30:13 (4,927)
Myhill, Jonathan P 4:15:45 (15,768)
Myhill, Robert 4:18:21 (16,446)
Myhre, Stephen J 4:18:16 (16,421)
Myles, Patrick T 5:08:57 (27,962)
Nackel, Karsten 4:18:29 (16,491)
Nagai, Hisashi 2:56:16 (830)
Nagar, Nico 5:20:23 (29,451)
Nagata, Masato 4:15:51 (15,795)
Nagel, Philipp 3:22:29 (3,562)
Nagel, Richard T 5:06:55 (27,687)
Nagel, Robert 4:15:26 (15,684)
Nagele, Christian E 4:05:26 (13,158)
Nagle, Paul J 4:14:23 (15,418)
Nagler, Stuart M 4:54:49 (25,653)
Naidoo, Kebsi R 5:43:50 (31,636)
Naidoo, Suresh 7:18:14 (34,385)
Naish, David W 4:17:37 (16,255)
Najurally, Nashir A 3:19:17 (3,134)
Nakano, Kunihiko 4:42:02 (22,680)
Nakrani, Mansukh 5:25:22 (29,974)
Nalder, David J 3:32:47 (5,360)
Naman, Colin 4:30:36 (19,775)
Nametz, John E 5:58:25 (32,665)
Nanavati, Mayur 4:31:29 (20,022)
Nance, David J 3:44:36 (7,577)
Nankivell, Philip L 3:19:18 (3,135)
Nannini, Marco Fabio 4:28:42 (19,313)
Nanopoulos, Constantinos 4:10:30 (14,409)
Nanton, Carl D 3:09:25 (1,930)
Napthine, Tim M 4:05:18 (13,121)
Naranjo, Jorge I 3:14:30 (2,546)
Naranjo Motta, Rafael 4:22:40 (17,639)
Narcisi, Eric 2:46:38 (379)
Narel, Slawomir P 3:45:32 (7,797)
Narey, Daniel 4:32:44 (20,355)
Narnett, Anthony P 4:06:34 (13,418)
Nascimento, Joad M 3:34:35 (5,629)
Nash, Daniel T 5:13:42 (28,635)
Nash, Gary J 4:57:23 (26,161)
Nash, Gary T 4:53:55 (25,467)
Nash, Jonathan 3:59:35 (11,705)
Nash, Lee 3:58:06 (11,142)
Nash, Mark 3:52:11 (9,356)
Nash, Ralph A 3:45:37 (7,817)
Nash, Rupert 3:15:37 (2,712)
Nash, Tony 5:14:57 (28,813)
Nason, Christopher J 5:28:29 (30,320)
Natali, Paul E 3:53:04 (9,596)
Nathan, Alan 5:47:22 (31,939)
Nathan, Joel S 3:59:23 (11,626)
Nathan, Joseph A 3:53:36 (9,743)
Nathan, Robert 4:55:44 (25,827)
Nation, Andrew 6:03:29 (32,865)
Natoli, Stephen M 2:51:18 (564)
Naude, Gysbertus 3:47:41 (8,276)
Naughton, Christopher E 4:05:01 (13,053)
Naumann, Volker 4:01:57 (12,348)
Navesey, Ged 4:05:11 (13,093)
Navrady, Jeremy L 3:48:28 (8,454)
Nayler, Darren W 5:33:42 (30,798)
Naylor, Dave G 3:19:16 (3,130)
Naylor, Glen A 4:24:31 (18,147)
Naylor, James A 4:21:08 (17,211)
Naylor, William 4:16:13 (15,882)
Neads, Kevin M 3:12:11 (2,231)
Neal, Michael J 4:17:54 (16,324)
Neal, Trevor J 4:57:39 (26,220)
Neale, Grahame A 4:27:02 (18,824)
Neale, Philip S 3:57:12 (10,862)
Neale, Robert J 4:20:57 (17,164)
Neale, Simon M 3:37:14 (6,109)
Nealon, Paul J 3:57:48 (11,061)
Nealon, William 4:15:24 (15,670)
Neasham, David 4:17:04 (16,112)
Neath, Andrew P 4:28:42 (19,313)
Neath, Kevin 2:59:33 (1,119)
Nebiolo, Patrick 3:36:25 (5,952)
Nederby, Nikolaj H 3:46:33 (8,013)
Nee, Michael 4:27:28 (18,946)
Nee, Thomas 3:42:01 (7,031)
Needham, Andrew 4:11:42 (14,733)
Needham, Andrew J 4:05:33 (13,189)
Needham, Paul J 4:08:32 (13,925)
Needham, Stephen D 4:19:39 (16,797)
Needle, Simon P 6:36:42 (33,812)
Neer, Christopher 3:54:03 (9,887)
Neeson, Patrick J 3:52:46 (9,495)
Negrerie, Sebastien 3:38:56 (6,431)
Negus, Abel 5:11:41 (28,362)
Neil, Alexander D 4:28:55 (19,383)
Neil, Martin L 3:49:00 (8,579)
Neil, Patrick 4:47:46 (24,093)
Neill, Francis J 3:10:45 (2,073)
Neilson, Edward 3:18:54 (3,086)
Nel, Leroy Garet 4:00:51 (12,068)
Neligan, Andrew 4:02:36 (12,513)
Nelis, Paul P 3:49:11 (8,622)
Nellis, Joe G 4:20:57 (17,164)
Nelson, Blair R 5:31:17 (30,594)
Nelson, Cliff G 4:46:48 (23,854)
Nelson, Craig M 4:00:27 (11,960)
Nelson, Daniel M 4:25:44 (18,456)
Nelson, Darren 3:28:58 (4,659)
Nelson, Darren T 3:57:05 (10,829)
Nelson, Gordon 3:57:29 (10,948)
Nelson, Ian P 4:06:36 (13,428)
Nelson, James 3:55:39 (10,389)
Nelson, James J 4:03:28 (12,720)
Nelson, James T 4:13:51 (15,259)
Nelson, John 3:44:52 (7,648)
Nelson, Keith J 4:15:23 (15,663)
Nelson, Mark J 4:45:36 (23,563)
Nelson, Michael J 4:28:18 (19,207)
Nelson, Roger P 4:20:57 (17,164)
Nenjerama, Paul 4:40:39 (22,337)
Neocleous, Richard 4:47:27 (24,011)
Neri, Gian Luca 3:38:54 (6,427)
Nerozzi, Fabrizio 3:51:42 (9,229)
Nery, Simon J 4:09:11 (14,085)
Nesbit, John A 4:34:31 (20,824)
Nesbitt, Adrian F 4:51:22 (24,919)
Nesbitt, Darren L 5:58:23 (32,661)
Nesom, Andrew M 3:06:36 (1,644)
Nesset, Thomas F 4:26:51 (18,773)
Nessling, Mark A 4:22:20 (17,527)
Neto, Pedro 3:47:40 (8,273)
Netti, Paul 4:51:29 (24,935)
Neubauer, Alexander 3:57:00 (10,796)
Neugebauer, Gerald P 3:19:24 (3,149)
Neuhaeuser, Guido 3:31:41 (5,166)
Neuman, Robert 3:54:29 (10,022)
Neumann, David J 3:45:05 (7,704)
Neumann, Gunther 4:24:32 (18,155)
Neumann, Wolfgang M 4:23:11 (17,778)
Nevelos, Paul D 4:00:22 (11,941)
Neville, Aaron 3:57:43 (11,023)
Neville, Michael J 2:57:28 (902)
Nevin, Austin F 3:49:31 (8,704)
Nevison, David S 5:35:03 (30,946)
Nevola, Venturino R 3:11:05 (2,104)
New, Andrew 5:22:54 (29,692)
New, Michael J 3:09:58 (1,986)
Newall, Mark R 4:29:04 (19,417)
Newberry, Christopher D 4:44:36 (23,321)
Newbery, Mark 4:54:07 (25,504)
Newbrook, Ralph 3:39:49 (6,600)
Newbury, John S 3:14:41 (2,587)
Newby, Gavin 4:00:06 (11,876)
Newby, Paul 4:14:53 (15,530)
Newell, Alan J 5:45:19 (31,786)
Newell, Bob 3:14:06 (2,484)
Newell, David 5:05:08 (27,425)
Newell, David M 5:36:50 (31,106)
Newell, John P 4:38:14 (21,762)

Newell, Mark S 3:55:52 (10,457)
Newell, Terry E 8:16:04 (34,552)
Newens, Mark S 3:43:25 (7,327)
Newey, Benjamin 3:57:52 (11,079)
Newing, Rod A 4:43:34 (23,070)
Newins, Mathew D 3:30:17 (4,937)
Newland, Conal T 3:17:07 (2,873)
Newland, David J 3:50:06 (8,844)
Newland, Deryck K 3:46:52 (8,074)
Newland, Rob A 5:08:40 (27,924)
Newland, Sean D 3:11:47 (2,187)
Newman, Daniel 3:33:48 (5,518)
Newman, David J 4:58:32 (26,380)
Newman, Duane 4:11:54 (14,778)
Newman, James A 3:52:32 (9,442)
Newman, Kris 5:05:15 (27,442)
Newman, Matthew J 5:26:32 (30,106)
Newman, Matthew J 5:31:57 (30,657)
Newman, Matthew W 4:16:20 (15,915)
Newman, Neville J 4:15:23 (15,663)
Newman, Nicholas G 3:28:51 (4,635)
Newman, Nick J 4:30:08 (19,663)
Newman, Patrick J 5:41:22 (31,447)
Newman, Paul 3:53:40 (9,758)
Newman, Paul M 3:39:37 (6,561)
Newman, Robert C 4:36:41 (21,415)
Newman, Steven 3:18:17 (3,016)
Newman, Tom P 3:21:16 (3,397)
Newman, Tony D 5:38:36 (31,229)
Newman, Wayne A 4:43:17 (23,000)
Newman-Lomax, Mark 5:16:01 (28,938)
Newmark, Brooks 5:37:15 (31,135)
Newnham, Andrew M 3:59:47 (11,774)
Newsham, David 3:46:19 (7,956)
Newsham, David A 5:26:27 (30,092)
Newsome, Peter 3:07:01 (1,685)
Newson-Smith, Piers G 3:39:12 (6,473)
Newstead, Steven 3:30:30 (4,971)
Newton, Darren A 3:29:17 (4,735)
Newton, Harry J 3:52:30 (9,433)
Newton, Jed 4:55:13 (25,732)
Newton, Jeremy 4:45:53 (23,642)
Newton, John E 4:52:48 (25,222)
Newton, Mark 4:15:49 (15,786)
Newton, Mark S 3:31:58 (5,217)
Newton, Ross 3:45:48 (7,858)
Newton, Simon 2:39:45 (195)
Newton, Simon M 4:08:19 (13,857)
Newton, Simon R 4:05:23 (13,140)
Newton, Stephen A 5:19:06 (29,303)
Newton, WM 3:11:24 (2,136)
Newton-Lee, Andy 3:35:58 (5,875)
Ng, Jason H 4:25:44 (18,456)
Nguyen, Huu-Hong-Vu 4:46:20 (23,750)
Nice, Matthew A 3:45:45 (7,845)
Nicel, John M 3:43:43 (7,391)
Nichol, David W 3:45:49 (7,863)
Nichol, Ian J 3:40:56 (6,811)
Nichol, Ky P 3:06:01 (1,597)
Nichol, Robert W 3:54:51 (10,143)
Nicholas, Adam K 3:31:30 (5,127)
Nicholas, Barry 4:28:35 (19,284)
Nicholas, David J 4:18:24 (16,464)
Nicholas, Gary 9:44:30 (34,586)
Nicholas, Guy 4:12:13 (14,864)
Nicholas, Guy 4:14:11 (15,363)
Nicholas, Kevin 4:58:36 (26,400)
Nicholl, Arthur J 4:33:03 (20,442)
Nicholl, James A 4:37:14 (21,534)
Nicholls, Alexander H 5:01:19 (26,842)
Nicholls, Andrew J 4:56:23 (25,945)
Nicholls, Andrew P 4:27:09 (18,858)
Nicholls, Daniel R 4:31:33 (20,039)
Nicholls, David 3:23:24 (3,690)
Nicholls, David J 3:50:51 (9,017)
Nicholls, Gary S 4:01:19 (12,192)
Nicholls, Ian K 4:41:14 (22,496)
Nicholls, James E 5:49:36 (32,092)
Nicholls, Jonathan S 5:18:54 (29,277)
Nicholls, Keith A 5:18:34 (29,238)
Nicholls, Mark A 3:49:15 (8,644)
Nicholls, Michael A 3:57:23 (10,919)
Nicholls, Michael J 3:48:06 (8,374)
Nicholls, Nicholas Z 4:56:11 (25,910)
Nicholls, Paul 4:09:20 (14,127)
Nicholls, Paul J 3:52:06 (9,337)
Nicholls, Paul W 4:10:49 (14,498)
Nicholls, Peter J 3:43:36 (7,366)
Nichols, John D 3:37:43 (6,203)
Nichols, Michael 3:45:00 (7,681)
Nicholson, Andrew 4:42:50 (22,884)
Nicholson, Angus 5:40:12 (31,353)
Nicholson, Chris 3:49:27 (8,686)
Nicholson, Dean 4:51:05 (24,862)
Nicholson, Dylan 4:48:06 (24,162)
Nicholson, James 4:47:11 (23,955)
Nicholson, Jason 3:47:14 (8,165)
Nicholson, Mark 3:20:30 (3,291)
Nicholson, Nick E 5:54:58 (32,457)
Nicholson, Stuart H 3:07:47 (1,764)
Nicklas, Carl D 4:04:34 (12,942)
Nickol, Mark D 4:51:18 (24,905)
Nickson, David A 5:25:10 (29,945)
Nicol, Alister 3:07:21 (1,717)
Nicol, Craig A 6:08:12 (33,052)
Nicol, Lindsay 4:46:38 (23,807)
Nicolas, Michel C 4:38:33 (21,842)
Nicoli, Enrico 3:51:18 (9,123)
Nicoll, Chris 2:41:08 (218)
Nicoll, Paul A 3:21:43 (3,447)
Nicolle, Philip R 3:41:17 (6,894)
Nielsen, Erik P 4:50:21 (24,676)
Nielsen, Jan 3:32:57 (5,380)
Nielsen, Patrick 3:53:21 (9,677)
Niepceron, Claude 3:43:27 (7,335)
Niesen, Claus 4:35:38 (21,148)
Nieuwenhuijs, Hugo 5:41:06 (31,422)
Nightingale, Colin S 5:08:20 (27,860)
Nightingale, David 3:25:33 (4,020)
Nightingale, Kevin T 4:46:58 (23,900)
Nightingale, Steven G 4:46:09 (23,700)
Nightingale, Thomas 8:39:11 (34,574)
Nihei, Katsuyoshi 3:56:58 (10,781)
Nihouarn, Yannick 4:16:29 (15,957)
Nijs, Dirk 3:26:03 (4,113)
Nikolich, Michael B 3:59:40 (11,741)
Nilbett, Daryl C 5:10:07 (28,164)
Nilsson, Hans 2:58:26 (999)
Nimmick, Christopher R 5:18:39 (29,247)
Nimmo, Steven G 2:59:06 (1,073)
Niranjan, Nathan 4:24:31 (18,147)
Nisbet, Angus R 5:50:48 (32,196)
Nisbet, Jack 3:12:56 (2,328)
Nivoix, Pierre 4:00:12 (11,897)
Nixon, Barry 3:37:23 (6,140)
Nixon, Marcellus 3:13:56 (2,457)
Nixon, Paul 3:14:55 (2,621)
Nixon, Philip R 3:51:32 (9,179)
Njie, Chris 4:51:37 (24,969)
Noack, Carl J 4:21:42 (17,374)
Noad, Stephen J 3:50:12 (8,873)
Noad, Trevor 4:28:14 (19,188)
Noble, Christopher J 4:45:44 (23,598)
Noble, Darren 5:19:36 (29,374)
Noble, Ian 4:02:36 (12,513)
Noble, Matthew D 3:17:16 (2,898)
Noble, Peter S 3:59:47 (11,774)
Nock, Graham S 3:11:26 (2,140)
Nockels, David J 3:33:24 (5,451)
Noe, Andreas 3:27:54 (4,439)
Noel, Vernon L 6:56:01 (34,167)
Noe-Nordberg, Markus 3:11:38 (2,166)
Nolan, Brian T 3:38:53 (6,425)
Nolan, David 3:09:08 (1,900)
Nolan, Matthew J 3:56:31 (10,629)
Nolan, Matthew J 4:56:50 (26,033)
Nolan, Paul D 6:46:56 (34,017)
Nolan, William P 4:07:16 (13,591)
Nonaas, Georg K 4:21:46 (17,398)
Noon, Adrian 4:26:44 (18,738)
Noon, Ian A 4:17:40 (16,268)
Noonan, Andrew J 4:35:58 (21,238)
Noot, Gareth P 3:27:12 (4,313)
Norbury, Antony 3:57:06 (10,835)
Norbury, Julian P 4:09:03 (14,056)
Norcross, Mark S 4:09:33 (14,188)
Nordestedt, Jakob 3:46:18 (7,952)
Nordlinder, Jan 2:52:47 (629)
Norfolk, David 3:37:44 (6,206)
Norfolk, Paul D 4:39:18 (22,049)
Norman, Anthony J 3:13:03 (2,341)
Norman, Daniel G 2:40:07 (200)
Norman, Eward F 3:44:18 (7,515)
Norman, Jon 4:31:42 (20,082)
Norman, Max 4:18:30 (16,497)
Norman, Richard G 3:50:34 (8,944)
Norman, Russell A 3:48:57 (8,567)
Normand, Peter J 3:42:42 (7,172)
Normoyle, Trevor F 3:48:51 (8,539)
Norridge, Christopher 3:40:23 (6,711)
Norrie, David S 3:44:37 (7,582)
Norrington, Matthew 4:46:32 (23,785)
Norris, Eli D 4:35:36 (21,137)
Norris, Gary 4:53:29 (25,368)
Norris, James A 4:19:45 (16,825)
Norris, James W 5:04:26 (27,312)
Norris, Jon 3:49:49 (8,774)
Norris, Martin J 3:54:37 (10,078)
Norris, Philip M 4:30:42 (19,800)
Norris, Santino 4:50:21 (24,676)
Norris, Stuart B 4:16:31 (15,965)
Northcote, Andrew 4:57:42 (26,230)
Northcott, Roy 3:56:49 (10,730)
North-Matthiassen, Craig 5:36:20 (31,070)
Northover, Martin J 3:53:26 (9,702)
Norton, Alan R 6:13:35 (33,231)
Norton, Andrew R 3:44:49 (7,635)
Norton, Chris 4:20:04 (16,905)
Norton, Craig 5:00:43 (26,742)
Norton, Gary P 5:26:07 (30,046)
Norton, James P 4:08:08 (13,810)
Norton, Jonathan F 3:42:45 (7,185)
Norton, Jonathan R 4:09:36 (14,200)
Norton, Richard 3:50:08 (8,854)
Norton, Simon N 5:46:29 (31,877)
Norwood, Mark 4:24:51 (18,229)
Noseda, Vittorio 3:12:51 (2,312)
Notley, Andrew J 3:43:43 (7,391)
Notley, Nigel J 2:59:02 (1,062)
Notley, Richard M 4:13:00 (15,034)
Nott, Jon R 3:58:35 (11,331)
Nottingham, Duncan 3:58:19 (11,226)
Nottingham, Jeremy L 4:00:07 (11,879)
Nouillan, Bill 4:54:19 (25,542)
Novak, Ben 6:09:05 (33,083)
Novak, Steven A 4:31:22 (19,983)
Novelli, Alberto 3:16:47 (2,843)
Nowak, Krzysztof 5:15:47 (28,916)
Nowak, Tad J 3:47:36 (8,251)
Nowicki, Matthew P 4:40:28 (22,304)
Noy, Amiram 3:44:10 (7,485)
Noyce, Darren M 4:49:27 (24,466)
Nucci, Andrea 3:52:13 (9,363)
Nugent, Ashley J 5:54:02 (32,409)
Nugent, Daniel R 5:24:08 (29,823)
Nugent, Paul 3:12:53 (2,318)
Nugus, John P 2:53:06 (647)
Nunes, Luis M 3:26:53 (4,259)
Nunn, Peter E 5:35:18 (30,962)
Nunn, Sarah 5:56:09 (32,530)
Nunn, Thomas W 4:13:18 (15,116)
Nunn, Timothy R 4:23:07 (17,757)
Nunziata, Salvatore 3:33:11 (5,416)
Nurrish, David L 3:59:59 (11,850)
Nursey, James S 4:43:48 (23,122)
Nutbrown, Kieron J 4:06:51 (13,484)
Nutburn, Keith W 5:26:31 (30,101)
Nute, Dominic L 4:37:41 (21,641)
Nuti, Giuseppe 4:44:07 (23,206)
Nutt, Matthew R 2:56:01 (807)
Nuttall, James 4:11:39 (14,719)
Nuttall, Luke J 3:05:33 (1,558)
Nuttall, Peter E 4:20:14 (16,957)
Nutter, Matthew 4:12:41 (14,960)
Nutton, David E 3:09:31 (1,942)
Nutton, Jonathan 3:45:01 (7,688)
Nyasamo, Stephen O 5:11:23 (28,315)
Nye, Alan D 4:17:23 (16,186)
Nye, John 5:40:40 (31,388)

Nye, Keith 5:18:30 (29,227)
Nyegaard, Bo S 4:31:46 (20,091)
Nygren, Thomas W 4:00:04 (11,867)
Nyhan, David 4:53:00 (25,269)
Nykolyszyn, Andy 5:42:16 (31,519)
Nykolyszyn, Roman M 4:10:09 (14,325)
Nyland, Paul 3:02:21 (1,334)
Nyman, Samuel R 4:50:46 (24,787)
Oakes, Gary 4:11:30 (14,679)
Oakes, Matthew 4:44:36 (23,321)
Oakes, Wayne 3:18:12 (3,008)
Oakley, Kevin G 3:20:14 (3,256)
Oakley, Paul H 3:59:25 (11,639)
Oakley, Philip S 4:06:06 (13,313)
Oakley, Simon I 4:37:49 (21,675)
Oates, Richard 4:07:43 (13,702)
Oates, Stephen M 4:58:47 (26,439)
Oates, Todd 2:48:58 (464)
Oatham, Phil 3:18:09 (3,002)
O'Beirne, Gerry B 3:26:06 (4,125)
Oberhauser, Christopher P 5:59:16 (32,703)
Obitz, Willi 4:41:28 (22,551)
O'Boyle, Christopher C 4:35:21 (21,068)
O'Brien, Adrian G 3:57:19 (10,902)
O'Brien, Alexander 4:43:00 (22,926)
O'Brien, Anthony S 4:57:40 (26,225)
O'Brien, Brian 5:56:51 (32,572)
O'Brien, Chris R 3:59:03 (11,507)
O'Brien, David J 3:29:39 (4,809)
O'Brien, Declan P 3:27:18 (4,332)
O'Brien, Derek M 5:03:09 (27,126)
O'Brien, Fegal M 5:56:52 (32,576)
O'Brien, James G 3:40:14 (6,681)
O'Brien, Kevin 4:35:18 (21,056)
O'Brien, Mark 3:27:39 (4,387)
O'Brien, Mike J 4:11:37 (14,706)
O'Brien, Neil J 5:37:31 (31,154)
O'Brien, Neil T 4:25:47 (18,473)
O'Brien, Tim J 4:40:46 (22,372)
O'Brien, Tony 4:20:15 (16,962)
O'Brien, Wayne 4:15:20 (15,646)
O'Callaghan, Daniel A 4:29:30 (19,517)
O'Callaghan, James M 4:10:58 (14,537)
Ochsenfeld, Guenter 3:45:24 (7,774)
Ockelton, Darren 4:06:30 (13,400)
Ockwell, Christopher J 4:21:28 (17,293)
Ockwell, Gregory J 4:14:11 (15,363)
Ockwell, Miles G 4:14:11 (15,363)
Ockwell, Timothy W 3:31:39 (5,160)
Ocleirigh, Tiarnan 3:08:58 (1,878)
O'Clery, David T 4:29:43 (19,568)
O'Connell, Daniel 3:31:01 (5,055)
O'Connell, Daniel M 5:00:14 (26,672)
O'Connell, Eoin G 2:34:07 (105)
O'Connell, Finbarr 6:07:05 (33,023)
O'Connell, Jimmy J 3:48:58 (8,572)
O'Connell, Kevin A 3:29:06 (4,693)
O'Connor, Andrew G 3:47:01 (8,113)
O'Connor, Anthony 2:54:08 (704)
O'Connor, Brendan 5:22:28 (29,660)
O'Connor, Colin R 4:32:43 (20,351)
O'Connor, Daniel F 3:31:12 (5,076)
O'Connor, David 4:57:59 (26,278)
O'Connor, Dominic F 3:49:29 (8,696)
O'Connor, Dwyer M 5:03:44 (27,213)
O'Connor, Frank 4:44:22 (23,271)
O'Connor, Harry J 6:14:18 (33,253)
O'Connor, James T 5:22:04 (29,606)
O'Connor, John 3:57:53 (11,085)
O'Connor, Michael A 3:03:40 (1,428)
O'Connor, Richard 3:41:44 (6,974)
O'Connor, Rory 4:11:11 (14,604)
O'Connor, Ruairi G 4:23:11 (17,778)
O'Connor, Ruairi S 3:27:50 (4,428)
O'Connor, Shane 3:10:59 (2,095)
O'Connor, Steven 4:28:12 (19,171)
O'Connor, Terry 4:36:10 (21,284)
O'Connor, William J 4:33:18 (20,511)
Oddy, Simon P 3:53:55 (9,839)
Odell, Michael E 2:49:56 (507)
Oderin, Kim W 4:24:36 (18,170)
Odgers, David H 4:48:01 (24,154)
O'Doherty, Martin 3:29:51 (4,849)
Odong, Simon 5:43:52 (31,639)
O'Donnell, Kieron O 3:04:44 (1,499)
O'Donnell, Sean 4:37:38 (21,625)
O'Donoghue, Ricky 3:56:28 (10,619)
O'Donoghue, Thomas 3:10:50 (2,081)
O'Donovan, Barry 5:06:41 (27,650)
O'Donovan, Fergal 5:46:30 (31,879)
O'Donovan, Jim 3:19:07 (3,110)
Odowd, Philip A 5:13:27 (28,603)
Odutola, Benjamin 4:34:19 (20,779)
Odzioba, Andrzej 4:22:56 (17,710)
Oetzel, Roland K 3:48:08 (8,385)
Oeygarden, Rolf T 3:50:46 (9,002)
Offord, Matthew J 3:57:36 (10,977)
O'Flaherty, Steve 4:23:42 (17,914)
Ogborn, Steve D 3:07:01 (1,685)
Ogden, James G 7:01:05 (34,213)
Ogden, Mike 3:27:03 (4,286)
Ogden, Paul C 5:44:04 (31,670)
Ogden, Peter J 4:48:33 (24,262)
Ogden, Robert 3:49:36 (8,719)
Ogilvie, Stuart M 4:46:42 (23,829)
Ogle, Nigel A 4:19:28 (16,743)
Ogne, Baard T 4:32:58 (20,424)
Ogne, Bjarne Oerjan 4:13:31 (15,164)
Ogne, Espen 5:25:22 (29,974)
Ogne, Hans S 4:36:50 (21,449)
Ognedal, Tormod 4:13:57 (15,286)
O'Gorman, Brian J 5:37:56 (31,188)
O'Gorman, Eugene D 3:43:19 (7,311)
O'Grady, Ashley 3:58:29 (11,295)
O'Grady, Gavin W 3:59:10 (11,548)
O'Grady, Geoff V 3:33:07 (5,401)
O'Grady, Vinny C 3:28:52 (4,641)
Ogun, Abi A 4:26:43 (18,731)
Oh, Philip 5:12:45 (28,502)
O'Hagan, Michael L 3:43:08 (7,273)
O'Halloran, Stephen 2:49:53 (505)
O'Hara, Andy W 5:54:16 (32,423)
O'Hara, Christopher A 4:02:32 (12,503)
O'Hara, Gary 4:07:05 (13,539)
O'Hara, Simon D 4:21:45 (17,389)
O'Hara, Stephen 5:27:04 (30,149)
O'Hare, Mark 4:12:13 (14,864)
O'Hare, Mark C 4:28:22 (19,229)
Ohlenschlager, Ross 4:16:53 (16,054)
Ohlsson, Fredrik 4:32:54 (20,401)
Ohr, Steinar P 3:37:30 (6,170)
Ojeda, Idelfonso 5:18:30 (29,227)
O'Kane, Patrick 4:12:53 (15,002)
O'Kane, Peter J 4:05:24 (13,146)
O'Kane, Sean 4:28:08 (19,142)
O'Kane, Sean M 4:11:51 (14,769)
O'Keefe, David 5:44:49 (31,750)
O'Keefe, Jason D 5:04:55 (27,385)
O'Keefe, Joe E 4:55:10 (25,726)
O'Keefe, Michael P 3:56:32 (10,639)
O'Keefe, Sean 3:43:48 (7,414)
O'Keefe, Steven 7:12:04 (34,344)
O'Keeffe, David A 6:54:33 (34,147)
O'Keeffe, Jeremiah J 4:07:30 (13,640)
O'Keeffe, Jonathan P 4:09:51 (14,262)
O'Keeffe, Peter 5:27:38 (30,216)
O'Keeffe, Sean 3:11:45 (2,181)
O'Kelly, Rich D 3:48:41 (8,507)
Okkerse, James R 4:43:49 (23,128)
Okotie, Simon M 3:33:04 (5,394)
Okseniuk, Derek 4:52:40 (25,190)
Okuliar, Boris N 5:20:03 (29,415)
Olaribigbe, Robert M 4:39:01 (21,975)
Olchawa, Piotr 3:29:27 (4,772)
Old, John 3:38:07 (6,289)
Oldbury, James E 4:31:53 (20,135)
Olden, Andrew M 3:52:59 (9,566)
Oldfield, Christopher J 4:25:15 (18,328)
Oldfield, David J 4:42:22 (22,766)
Oldfield, James 5:05:28 (27,467)
Oldfield, Mark 5:41:50 (31,489)
Oldfield, Richard 4:56:50 (26,033)
Oldfield, Richard 5:05:29 (27,472)
Oldham, Daniel A 3:14:30 (2,546)
Oldham, James M 4:17:07 (16,128)
Oldham, Jon 3:57:20 (10,906)
Olds, Joe 3:45:35 (7,808)
Olds, Peter J 3:10:32 (2,048)
Oldstein, Howard L 5:37:48 (31,179)
O'Leary, Aaron D 4:28:00 (19,099)
O'Leary, Alex 4:12:10 (14,855)
O'Leary, Bryan K 3:40:42 (6,760)
O'Leary, James A 4:41:34 (22,570)
O'Leary, Paul M 3:45:57 (7,883)
Olesen, Kasper J 3:53:55 (9,839)
Olins, Benjamin G 5:06:32 (27,629)
Oliphant, Mark J 3:27:54 (4,439)
Oliphant, Robert A 5:05:27 (27,464)
Olive, Enric 4:41:16 (22,501)
Olive, Richard T 3:29:16 (4,730)
Oliveira, Pedro 3:30:51 (5,029)
Olivella Puyol, Jorge 3:17:54 (2,974)
Oliver, Carlton J 4:01:09 (12,148)
Oliver, Christopher 4:31:48 (20,103)
Oliver, Darren J 4:47:44 (24,080)
Oliver, Dave M 4:53:23 (25,348)
Oliver, David W 3:58:30 (11,298)
Oliver, Eddie A 5:21:19 (29,538)
Oliver, Gary 6:03:53 (32,883)
Oliver, Geoffrey J 3:32:25 (5,304)
Oliver, James R 3:56:07 (10,516)
Oliver, Jonathan D 3:56:17 (10,557)
Oliver, Keith 5:16:08 (28,950)
Oliver, Luke S 2:39:27 (188)
Oliver, Michael 4:32:34 (20,315)
Oliver, Paul J 3:48:24 (8,440)
Oliver, Peter H 4:48:07 (24,169)
Oliver, Richard D 5:07:26 (27,758)
Oliver, Stephen R 3:41:21 (6,906)
Olivetto, Artino 3:36:41 (5,995)
Ollerenshaw, Mark 3:48:45 (8,521)
Olley, Richard 6:03:56 (32,886)
Olliffe, Peter W 4:18:21 (16,446)
Olomu, Dayo 6:41:55 (33,909)
O'Loughlin, Jason D 5:17:03 (29,068)
Olsen, Mark J 4:50:51 (24,805)
O'Mahony, Jer M 3:37:36 (6,183)
O'Mahony, John G 3:53:53 (9,833)
O'Mahony, Tadhg C 3:45:46 (7,849)
O'Malley, Brian 6:20:26 (33,406)
O'Malley, Gerard J 3:42:21 (7,105)
O'Malley, Graham D 5:41:09 (31,426)
O'Malley, John 4:01:39 (12,281)
O'Malley, Marc D 4:10:06 (14,317)
O'Mathuna, Fiachra 4:31:10 (19,928)
O'Neill, Conan J 4:02:05 (12,382)
O'Neill, Donal J 4:43:31 (23,054)
O'Neill, James 4:10:15 (14,351)
O'Neill, Kevin F 3:42:03 (7,038)
O'Neill, Kevin J 3:47:44 (8,285)
O'Neill, Kevin P 4:22:23 (17,547)
O'Neill, Mark A 3:51:53 (9,271)
O'Neill, Mathew B 4:02:26 (12,483)
O'Neill, Melvin B 4:40:53 (22,398)
O'Neill, Michael A 4:34:56 (20,949)
O'Neill, Michael J 4:46:54 (23,885)
O'Neill, Michael M 3:59:53 (11,813)
O'Neill, Patrick 4:34:08 (20,733)
O'Neill, Paul M 4:33:35 (20,601)
O'Neill, RP 4:51:42 (24,985)
O'Neill, Robert 4:11:49 (14,761)
O'Neill, Stephen J 4:22:51 (17,686)
O'Neill, Vincent 3:55:03 (10,216)
Onigbanjo, Ade 5:16:56 (29,051)
Onions, Terence R 3:54:23 (9,987)
Onions, Tom N 3:29:42 (4,819)
Onita, Tommy 4:15:06 (15,600)
Onobu, Masanori 5:14:50 (28,788)
Onslow, Richard E 4:31:41 (20,074)
Onwuchekwa, Elekwa K 4:36:16 (21,315)
Oo, Tun 5:16:15 (28,967)
Oosthuizen, Mark 4:42:12 (22,723)
Openshaw, Martin J 5:10:56 (28,270)
Openshaw, Thomas K 3:59:30 (11,676)
Opie, Giles J 4:08:33 (13,927)
Opie, Justin G 4:49:26 (24,464)
Opsanger, Einar 4:00:56 (12,096)
Or Kam Fat, Patrick N 5:13:00 (28,546)
Orbell, Ian D 5:13:51 (28,655)

Orchard, Andrew J....................3:52:58 (9,560)
Orchard, Mark J.......................3:54:58 (10,184)
Orchard, Thomas J....................4:03:15 (12,670)
Orde, Gavin R...........................4:34:02 (20,705)
Orde, Hugh S............................4:05:55 (13,270)
O'Regan, Christopher O............5:12:05 (28,417)
O'Regan, John A.......................4:21:22 (17,261)
O'Regan, Terry M......................3:47:49 (8,303)
O'Reilly, Brendan E...................4:08:05 (13,784)
O'Reilly, Cormac.......................3:32:44 (5,351)
O'Reilly, Frank..........................5:42:33 (31,533)
O'Reilly, John...........................4:27:48 (19,022)
O'Reilly, John A.......................4:09:41 (14,220)
O'Reilly, John P........................3:40:48 (6,780)
O'Reilly, Jonathan.....................3:50:40 (8,980)
O'Reilly, Paddy J.......................4:03:17 (12,679)
O'Reilly, Jim..............................3:47:55 (8,329)
O'Reilly, Stephen F...................3:49:51 (8,786)
Orfanos, John............................5:50:04 (32,132)
Organ, Adrian C.........................3:36:50 (6,026)
Oriol Perez, Narciso..................4:00:29 (11,969)
O'Riordan, Dermot.....................4:53:07 (25,301)
Orlowski, Andrew G...................3:36:28 (5,961)
Ormerod, James P......................3:51:58 (9,291)
Ormond, John M........................5:17:08 (29,080)
Ormond, Patrick H.....................4:12:28 (14,920)
Ormston, Neil............................3:32:15 (5,267)
Ornstein, Kenneth G..................4:31:14 (19,945)
O'Rourke, Kevin........................4:45:32 (23,547)
Orozco, Gerardo........................3:32:54 (5,373)
Orr, Andrew B............................2:57:57 (943)
Orr, Billy....................................3:10:06 (1,998)
Orr, James P..............................4:23:20 (17,825)
Orr, Jamie..................................4:47:26 (24,009)
Orr, Nicholas P..........................5:11:00 (28,275)
Orr, Stuart A..............................4:30:20 (19,706)
Orr, Toby A................................4:16:20 (15,915)
Orrock, Duncan J.......................3:30:04 (4,900)
Orsman, Philip E........................4:16:13 (15,882)
Ortega Gutierrez, Miguel...........3:46:24 (7,979)
Ortenstein, Michael...................3:37:25 (6,154)
Ortiz Cobo, Javier......................3:40:02 (6,646)
Orton, Sebastian G....................4:21:24 (17,275)
Ortu, Umberto............................3:14:27 (2,540)
Osayogie, Dean..........................4:48:25 (24,227)
Osbiston, Alan G........................4:06:27 (13,386)
Osborn, Roger............................3:44:31 (7,555)
Osborne, Adam M.......................2:37:09 (149)
Osborne, Colin J.........................4:19:24 (16,723)
Osborne, David G.......................4:52:37 (25,174)
Osborne, Douglas.......................4:38:41 (21,880)
Osborne, Ian...............................2:58:38 (1,022)
Osborne, Matthew W...................3:49:42 (8,746)
Osborne, Michael A....................3:01:06 (1,248)
Osborne, Paul L..........................4:56:58 (26,069)
Osborne, Remi............................4:11:04 (14,563)
Osbourne, Nigel S.......................3:56:42 (10,690)
O'Seaghdha, Diarmuid D.............2:29:23 (63)
Osgathorp, David........................3:59:35 (11,705)
Osgood, David C.........................5:16:12 (28,959)
Osgood, Roger.............................3:50:28 (8,924)
O'Shaughnessy, John B...............3:36:13 (5,916)
O'Shea, Denis F...........................4:28:17 (19,199)
O'Shea, Jason..............................5:51:45 (32,272)
O'Shea, John A............................3:14:03 (2,474)
Osias, Brian C..............................3:24:12 (3,804)
Osinowo, Remi A.........................3:34:59 (5,700)
Osman, Adib.................................3:34:32 (5,625)
Osmond, Philip R.........................6:33:35 (33,739)
Osmond, Robin.............................4:24:14 (18,063)
Osseiran, Abdullah......................6:01:22 (32,791)
Ostergaard, Lars..........................3:31:12 (5,076)
Ostergaard, Ole............................3:31:13 (5,082)
Osterlund, Kristoffer....................2:21:41 (24)
Ostermann, Alex..........................4:02:50 (12,574)
Ostinelli, John..............................4:09:10 (14,077)
O'Sullivan, Brendan.....................3:55:11 (10,261)
O'Sullivan, Christopher M...........4:13:39 (15,203)
O'Sullivan, Hugh R......................4:35:46 (21,184)
O'Sullivan, John P.......................3:39:33 (6,551)
O'Sullivan, Lochlan......................4:03:09 (12,641)
O'Sullivan, Martin R....................3:47:10 (8,142)
O'Sullivan, Michael J...................3:52:11 (9,356)
O'Sullivan, Michael P..................3:12:40 (2,282)
O'Sullivan, Neil M........................4:08:17 (13,849)
O'Sullivan, Owen..........................4:01:35 (12,267)
O'Sullivan, Paul E........................3:37:17 (6,122)
O'Sullivan, Richard J...................2:43:09 (273)
Oswald, James R...........................4:32:55 (20,411)
Otchie, Andrew..............................4:44:31 (23,307)
Othen, Andy...................................3:54:29 (10,022)
Otkay, Emir....................................5:13:50 (28,654)
O'Toole, Sean.................................5:08:36 (27,912)
Ottaway, Sean................................3:38:20 (6,321)
Otte, Bernd.....................................4:43:23 (23,023)
Otten, Richard J.............................3:41:49 (6,994)
Otten, Steven P..............................3:48:08 (8,385)
Otter, Neville L...............................5:17:54 (29,168)
Otty, Neil A.....................................3:58:03 (11,131)
Otty, Timothy J...............................2:58:30 (1,009)
Otunla, Afolabi O...........................6:06:15 (32,994)
Oubibi, Mohamed............................3:42:44 (7,181)
Oudghiri, Driss................................3:22:12 (3,514)
Outram, Matt D...............................4:55:17 (25,747)
Outten, Lee M..................................4:34:46 (20,897)
Outtersides, Christopher J............3:26:42 (4,231)
Ouzman, Nicholas W......................6:40:53 (33,898)
Overall, Robert I.............................4:14:00 (15,302)
Overby, Martin D.............................4:54:29 (25,577)
Overy, John I...................................4:23:55 (17,968)
Owen, Alun J...................................5:04:34 (27,338)
Owen, Andy M.................................5:38:58 (31,259)
Owen, Carl M...................................4:38:44 (21,893)
Owen, David J..................................4:56:19 (25,934)
Owen, Dewi W..................................4:36:47 (21,437)
Owen, Matthew J.............................4:17:06 (16,122)
Owen, Philip.....................................4:47:55 (24,126)
Owen, Richard R..............................5:14:44 (28,778)
Owen, Rob L.....................................6:23:21 (33,498)
Owen, Robert T................................3:47:09 (8,140)
Owen, Roy V.....................................4:49:54 (24,575)
Owen, Thomas J...............................3:27:20 (4,342)
Owen, Wayne C................................3:57:36 (10,977)
Owens, David...................................4:47:02 (23,918)
Owens, David H................................3:15:44 (2,720)
Owens, Gareth A..............................5:48:03 (31,981)
Owens, Ian R....................................6:16:27 (33,307)
Owens, John D..................................5:09:19 (28,014)
Owens, Nicholas J............................5:21:04 (29,503)
Oxborough, Steven..........................3:52:22 (9,401)
Oxbrough, James L...........................4:15:21 (15,652)
Oxford, Keith....................................4:31:36 (20,054)
Oxley, David T..................................3:17:51 (2,969)
Oxley, Philip.....................................4:01:41 (12,289)
Oxley, Scott A..................................3:35:07 (5,726)
Oxley, William..................................4:26:28 (18,654)
Oxtoby, Mark A................................4:35:23 (21,079)
Oyling, Lars......................................4:17:54 (16,324)
Oza, Hitesh.......................................5:20:22 (29,446)
Ozanne, André C..............................2:59:12 (1,086)
Ozols, Nathan A................................3:21:50 (3,462)
Pace, Mark F.....................................4:09:11 (14,085)
Pace, Michael J.................................3:24:18 (3,817)
Pacey, Andy M..................................3:22:12 (3,514)
Pacheco, Manuel A...........................5:02:15 (26,999)
Pacini, Massimo................................4:18:51 (16,587)
Packer, Adam....................................3:59:53 (11,813)
Packer, Leigh J..................................2:46:30 (374)
Packer, Malcolm P............................2:57:39 (915)
Packham, Daniel...............................4:23:33 (17,883)
Packwood, Clive R............................6:58:58 (34,196)
Packwood, Wayne.............................4:04:59 (13,046)
Paddick, Brian L...............................4:52:33 (25,156)
Paddison, Chris................................4:43:32 (23,059)
Paddon, Guy......................................3:35:47 (5,841)
Paddon, Neil B..................................3:21:37 (3,437)
Padfield, Cameron K.........................4:13:54 (15,279)
Padfield, Tim M.................................3:38:25 (6,344)
Padhiar, Raj......................................4:58:43 (26,427)
Padley, Benjamin J............................4:34:50 (20,918)
Page, Ben W.....................................5:30:24 (30,516)
Page, Bill..4:12:10 (14,855)
Page, David B...................................4:52:21 (25,113)
Page, Gary B.....................................3:34:20 (5,594)
Page, James D...................................3:58:46 (11,397)
Page, Kevin..4:09:10 (14,077)
Page, Kevin R.....................................4:39:25 (22,069)
Page, Michael G.................................3:27:09 (4,304)
Page, Nicholas J.................................6:43:53 (33,958)
Page, Nick..4:38:21 (21,790)
Page, Stephen C.................................3:52:57 (9,553)
Pages, Didier......................................3:46:40 (8,035)
Paice, Jonathan B...............................4:25:18 (18,341)
Pain, Michael W.................................3:10:33 (2,050)
Pain, Stephen M.................................3:30:09 (4,917)
Paine, Colin..4:12:22 (14,900)
Paine, William A.................................7:44:40 (34,495)
Painter, Daniel C.................................3:38:17 (6,314)
Painter, Gary..5:17:01 (29,064)
Painter, Gary J.....................................4:10:54 (14,522)
Painter, Richard D...............................5:17:01 (29,064)
Paintin, Edward J.................................4:11:23 (14,640)
Pairman, John.......................................3:30:37 (4,988)
Pairman, Steven....................................3:25:42 (4,049)
Paisley, Graham W...............................4:05:12 (13,098)
Paisley, Nicholas J................................4:05:32 (13,185)
Paiva de Brito, Edvaldo........................4:51:02 (24,852)
Pajak, Stan...4:08:29 (13,905)
Pakenham, Dermot P.............................5:25:59 (30,034)
Palacio, Laurie G...................................4:52:28 (25,136)
Palairet, Ben..3:14:15 (2,509)
Palethorpe, Christopher........................4:03:59 (12,827)
Palfreyman, Paul....................................6:49:35 (34,070)
Palij, Michael I.......................................3:58:54 (11,458)
Palikiras, Andreas...................................3:46:23 (7,975)
Pallant, Edward K...................................5:48:33 (32,016)
Pallant, Richard G..................................5:21:40 (29,575)
Palluault, Stephane O.............................4:07:08 (13,553)
Palmer, Andrew G...................................3:23:06 (3,654)
Palmer, Charles T....................................4:24:36 (18,170)
Palmer, David M......................................4:03:10 (12,644)
Palmer, Edwin G......................................4:26:51 (18,773)
Palmer, Fergus N.....................................3:41:59 (7,022)
Palmer, Graeme K....................................5:07:30 (27,766)
Palmer, James L.......................................3:59:06 (11,527)
Palmer, Jeremy...3:45:31 (7,795)
Palmer, John D...9:48:59 (34,587)
Palmer, Kenneth L....................................3:44:45 (7,622)
Palmer, Mark L..3:30:35 (4,985)
Palmer, Mark S..4:01:38 (12,275)
Palmer, Matt J...4:21:00 (17,182)
Palmer, Richard...3:04:07 (1,457)
Palmer, Robert D......................................4:11:28 (14,665)
Palmer, Roger W.......................................3:28:40 (4,596)
Palmer, Stephen L.....................................3:47:11 (8,149)
Palmer, Steve..4:07:31 (13,645)
Palmer, Terry J..4:34:46 (20,897)
Palmiere, Christian....................................4:09:51 (14,262)
Palmulli, Giuseppe.....................................4:42:11 (22,715)
Paltridge, Thomas J...................................3:31:41 (5,166)
Pambakian, Naz H......................................5:44:47 (31,747)
Pambianchi, Gianni....................................4:50:03 (24,613)
Panayi, Philip..3:57:20 (10,906)
Pancaldi, Matthew C..................................4:32:37 (20,329)
Panesar, Talvinder S...................................4:43:30 (23,049)
Panetta, Roland...5:13:02 (28,547)
Pangbourne, Neil C.....................................4:32:29 (20,293)
Pankhurst, Garry..3:56:14 (10,545)
Pankhurst, Sean M.......................................3:52:50 (9,514)
Pankiewicz, Stephan....................................4:15:26 (15,684)
Panter, Kevin A..4:36:54 (21,464)
Panting, Stephen J..4:02:21 (12,460)
Pantlin, Andrew W..4:49:35 (24,498)
Pantlin, Tim..4:05:19 (13,125)
Pantling, Robert..5:04:43 (27,363)
Pape, Andrew B...4:25:10 (18,310)
Paquet, Ulrich..2:54:27 (718)
Paragreen, Norman J.....................................6:05:00 (32,926)
Paramor, Jon..3:42:39 (7,164)
Pardon, Andrew...4:23:26 (17,852)
Parello, Salvatore...3:24:46 (3,882)
Parfitt, James M..3:04:34 (1,489)
Parfitt, Jeremy A...4:19:09 (16,667)
Parfitt, Scott T..3:02:47 (1,361)
Parfitt, Tim S..3:39:09 (6,462)
Parham, John S...4:52:00 (25,042)
Parham, Martin I..3:47:38 (8,263)
Parish, Dave..3:18:35 (3,055)
Park, Andrew D..4:47:33 (24,029)

Park, Ben J	5:41:09 (31,426)
Park, David P	3:31:55 (5,203)
Park, Gregor J	3:29:57 (4,879)
Park, Kenneth	5:44:21 (31,706)
Park, Oliver	3:41:12 (6,873)
Park, Robert J	3:48:01 (8,355)
Park, Stuart	3:30:41 (4,997)
Parke, Kevin D	3:57:17 (10,887)
Parke, Simon C	3:24:40 (3,863)
Parker, Aaron	4:10:13 (14,340)
Parker, Adrian B	4:03:13 (12,658)
Parker, Adrian J	3:59:02 (11,499)
Parker, Andrew P	4:55:29 (25,780)
Parker, Benjamin C	3:30:56 (5,044)
Parker, Christopher F	2:45:22 (346)
Parker, Colin W	3:55:47 (10,429)
Parker, David J	3:29:04 (4,682)
Parker, David M	5:19:33 (29,366)
Parker, David S	5:02:20 (27,009)
Parker, Denny C	5:15:28 (28,878)
Parker, Eliot	4:08:19 (13,857)
Parker, Gerry	4:41:39 (22,598)
Parker, Howard	6:09:08 (33,086)
Parker, Ian	4:14:05 (15,331)
Parker, Ian D	4:11:48 (14,753)
Parker, Ian J	3:04:06 (1,454)
Parker, James L	4:21:15 (17,236)
Parker, Jeremy D	4:51:06 (24,864)
Parker, Kevin S	4:01:09 (12,148)
Parker, Lee M	4:49:11 (24,410)
Parker, Mike	3:42:15 (7,081)
Parker, Miles J	4:59:11 (26,512)
Parker, Nigel R	3:30:11 (4,922)
Parker, Rhys W	4:17:24 (16,190)
Parker, Richard A	4:16:47 (16,029)
Parker, Robert	3:58:25 (11,268)
Parker, Robert B	4:26:51 (18,773)
Parker, Robert B	4:33:32 (20,586)
Parker, Robert G	4:35:45 (21,177)
Parker, Sean	4:37:28 (21,588)
Parker, Stephen	3:10:49 (2,078)
Parker, Steven J	4:49:32 (24,484)
Parker, Terence T	5:40:29 (31,373)
Parker, Tom R	5:06:15 (27,591)
Parker, W	2:58:49 (1,044)
Parkes, Brandon L	3:07:28 (1,730)
Parkes, Duncan R	3:43:31 (7,348)
Parkes, George	3:54:03 (9,887)
Parkes, Jeff R	4:12:03 (14,824)
Parkes, Matthew E	4:15:25 (15,676)
Parkes, Michael J	4:26:33 (18,679)
Parkes, Robert	6:51:12 (34,097)
Parkin, Graham D	3:40:21 (6,704)
Parkin, Rob	4:04:17 (12,882)
Parkin, Rupert J	4:31:16 (19,952)
Parkin, Shaun M	2:58:26 (999)
Parkin, Thomas B	5:12:48 (28,514)
Parkington, David	2:59:17 (1,096)
Parkins, Steve J	4:10:01 (14,299)
Parkinson, Andrew	3:44:04 (7,465)
Parkinson, Benjamin S	4:03:42 (12,765)
Parkinson, James M	4:10:04 (14,310)
Parmar, Paul	4:21:17 (17,249)
Parmeggiani, Piero	3:37:44 (6,206)
Parmentelat, Jean-Philippe	3:35:48 (5,848)
Parmenter, Chris	4:42:38 (22,840)
Parmiter, Thomas M	4:41:44 (22,619)
Parmley, Philip	3:55:41 (10,399)
Parncutt, Andrew J	4:48:44 (24,303)
Parnell, Adam	4:24:17 (18,077)
Parnell, Gareth A	4:29:02 (19,408)
Parnham, Alan T	4:08:27 (13,895)
Parnham, Jeremy F	5:08:32 (27,903)
Parodi, Gonzalo	3:26:08 (4,127)
Parr, Billy	3:48:10 (8,392)
Parr, James	4:44:26 (23,283)
Parr, John R	3:42:56 (7,218)
Parr, Mark	4:47:16 (23,976)
Parr, Matthew J	3:22:23 (3,544)
Parrack, Chris J	4:14:52 (15,527)
Parrish, James	5:27:27 (30,199)
Parrott, John G	3:29:40 (4,816)
Parrott, Mykel C	4:54:41 (25,618)
Parry, Alister R	3:41:24 (6,916)
Parry, Chris S	4:15:29 (15,702)
Parry, Christopher D	3:27:53 (4,436)
Parry, David	3:44:10 (7,485)
Parry, David C	4:52:19 (25,107)
Parry, David J	3:17:38 (2,945)
Parry, Eddie	4:30:09 (19,667)
Parry, Guy	3:35:08 (5,729)
Parry, Ian	3:42:44 (7,181)
Parry, Jonathan R	4:11:49 (14,761)
Parry, Karl G	3:38:37 (6,374)
Parry, Lee K	4:13:44 (15,233)
Parry, Lindsay E	3:47:02 (8,120)
Parry, Malcolm	4:04:22 (12,909)
Parry, Malcolm J	4:12:56 (15,011)
Parry, Peter	3:21:23 (3,413)
Parry, Phillip J	4:51:03 (24,855)
Parry, Robert G	3:18:34 (3,054)
Parry, Robin W	3:56:39 (10,677)
Parry, Ross W	4:52:38 (25,180)
Parry, Stephen G	3:54:59 (10,191)
Parry, William	4:38:50 (21,924)
Parsley, Elvis I	2:48:07 (427)
Parsonage, Liam	4:58:33 (26,386)
Parsons, Adam	3:42:58 (7,227)
Parsons, Andrew A	5:25:47 (30,010)
Parsons, Andrew D	4:54:32 (25,586)
Parsons, Andy	4:08:18 (13,853)
Parsons, David R	4:06:22 (13,366)
Parsons, Garry	3:24:48 (3,888)
Parsons, James S	3:52:54 (9,536)
Parsons, John	3:34:55 (5,688)
Parsons, Joseph	3:35:08 (5,729)
Parsons, Matt	4:45:55 (23,657)
Parsons, Matthew R	4:36:26 (21,355)
Parsons, Michael D	4:11:01 (14,547)
Parsons, Nigel R	3:47:50 (8,306)
Parsons, Richard B	5:01:01 (26,798)
Parsons, Robert	4:26:15 (18,595)
Parsons, Ron H	6:38:27 (33,856)
Parsons, Simon	4:28:30 (19,264)
Parsons, Stephen	4:19:47 (16,832)
Parsons, Stephen	5:35:42 (30,999)
Parsons, Tim D	3:52:49 (9,506)
Parsons, Tom	3:56:56 (10,774)
Partington, Chris R	5:47:10 (31,925)
Partington, Jorden A	3:57:51 (11,075)
Partington, Lee	5:06:19 (27,605)
Parton, David J	4:27:00 (18,812)
Partridge, Andrew W	6:13:41 (33,236)
Partridge, Anthony W	3:41:50 (6,996)
Partridge, Ben	2:49:39 (496)
Partridge, Colin	4:01:23 (12,210)
Partridge, David A	4:38:25 (21,805)
Partridge, James S	4:20:16 (16,966)
Partridge, Keith G	3:18:50 (3,078)
Pascal, Bois	3:29:19 (4,743)
Paschalis, Haris A	4:36:22 (21,339)
Pascoe, Barry	4:23:05 (17,750)
Pascoe, Christian J	3:28:55 (4,648)
Pascoe, Shaun W	4:26:45 (18,743)
Pascolini, Luca	3:37:55 (6,242)
Pask, Howard	5:05:08 (27,425)
Pask, Jonathan M	4:33:07 (20,461)
Pask, Mike R	2:57:08 (880)
Pass, Andrew S	4:40:58 (22,425)
Pass, Terry M	3:53:31 (9,715)
Passatempi, Maurizio	4:26:50 (18,765)
Passey, Andrew J	4:53:58 (25,474)
Passingham, Keith W	4:18:04 (16,361)
Passoni, Giordano	4:08:38 (13,950)
Pastore, Michel	4:23:30 (17,867)
Pastorini, Giancarlo	3:53:42 (9,771)
Pasutti, Manfred	3:55:05 (10,225)
Patching, Daniel R	3:29:06 (4,693)
Patching, Lewis J	3:50:37 (8,961)
Patel, Abhik P	4:38:07 (21,743)
Patel, Ajay	4:13:52 (15,266)
Patel, Ameet	4:19:08 (16,663)
Patel, Amit	5:26:20 (30,077)
Patel, Ashok K	3:22:32 (3,574)
Patel, Atul S	4:32:58 (20,424)
Patel, Balwant K	5:13:37 (28,628)
Patel, Bhupendrabhai	3:51:20 (9,132)
Patel, Dharmesh	4:38:11 (21,752)
Patel, Dinesh	4:20:09 (16,928)
Patel, Ghansham	4:25:44 (18,456)
Patel, Hitesh	4:40:07 (22,215)
Patel, Hitesh	5:52:04 (32,292)
Patel, Jeetesh V	4:42:41 (22,850)
Patel, Jitesh	5:30:41 (30,544)
Patel, Ketan	4:32:02 (20,181)
Patel, Kevai M	5:23:26 (29,741)
Patel, Kiran D	4:50:44 (24,774)
Patel, Nalin G	4:46:17 (23,739)
Patel, Neal	5:18:03 (29,186)
Patel, Neel	4:58:05 (26,301)
Patel, Ramesh M	5:15:36 (28,889)
Patel, Ronak	4:45:41 (23,577)
Patel, Sage	3:46:51 (8,071)
Patel, Sanjay	4:59:54 (26,617)
Patel, Sanjay	6:25:57 (33,575)
Patel, Shivlal H	4:33:54 (20,684)
Patel, Sunil K	4:39:40 (22,114)
Patel, Tapan	4:45:24 (23,510)
Patel, Umesh M	4:46:50 (23,867)
Patel, Vijay K	4:33:16 (20,496)
Patel, Vinod J	6:36:33 (33,808)
Patel, Vipin	4:32:27 (20,282)
Patel, Yogesh	5:16:27 (28,989)
Pateman, Mark	4:45:54 (23,651)
Paterson, Duncan J	3:56:33 (10,646)
Paterson, George L	4:16:16 (15,895)
Paterson, James M	3:43:53 (7,434)
Paterson, Keith	3:32:08 (5,248)
Patience, Kevin S	4:10:23 (14,384)
Patil, Vijay	4:58:38 (26,408)
Paton, Colin G	2:38:53 (180)
Paton, James R	3:36:01 (5,885)
Paton, Luke K	4:10:11 (14,335)
Patrizi, Giuseppe	4:51:52 (25,017)
Patten, David E	5:19:54 (29,404)
Patten, Kevin A	4:42:53 (22,901)
Patterson, Angus A	3:19:10 (3,115)
Patterson, David G	4:46:48 (23,854)
Patterson, Dean K	4:19:29 (16,750)
Patterson, Jay L	4:27:21 (18,916)
Patterson, John	3:14:01 (2,468)
Patterson, Mark	4:26:04 (18,558)
Patterson, Neil	3:55:19 (10,292)
Patterson, Nigel	3:41:03 (6,838)
Patterson, Robert W	4:15:12 (15,618)
Pattison, Andrew M	4:40:57 (22,423)
Pattison, Glen A	4:37:46 (21,659)
Pattison, Ian	3:59:11 (11,554)
Pattison, Martyn R	3:27:05 (4,296)
Pattison, Matt J	4:00:21 (11,937)
Patwardhan, Mahesh	4:38:05 (21,736)
Paul, Alexander R	3:55:06 (10,233)
Paul, David	3:58:11 (11,182)
Paul, Martin G	4:15:35 (15,724)
Paul, Philippe J	4:31:09 (19,923)
Paul, Robert H	4:37:05 (21,503)
Paul, Sunjay K	5:38:35 (31,227)
Paul Florence, Grant I	2:57:13 (889)
Paull, Stephen F	3:24:47 (3,885)
Paulson, John	2:58:55 (1,055)
Pawar, Manjit	4:27:44 (19,005)
Pawsey, Christian O	3:58:26 (11,276)
Pawson, Mark D	7:47:55 (34,503)
Paxman, Eric J	3:00:27 (1,199)
Paxton, Will	3:55:38 (10,382)
Paydon, Marc B	3:52:15 (9,375)
Payen, Patrick	3:25:42 (4,049)
Payne, Adam C	4:22:32 (17,594)
Payne, Alastair W	2:45:02 (334)
Payne, Anthony	3:22:21 (3,541)
Payne, Benjamin T	3:04:43 (1,496)
Payne, Garry P	2:37:46 (163)
Payne, Gary F	5:06:25 (27,617)
Payne, Ian	4:23:44 (17,922)
Payne, Joe	5:03:59 (27,249)
Payne, Joel M	3:27:27 (4,358)
Payne, John L	2:54:43 (730)
Payne, Jonathan	4:41:31 (22,560)
Payne, Julian	4:08:26 (13,890)

Payne, Julian 4:36:30 (21,368)
Payne, Julian L 4:28:50 (19,360)
Payne, Mark A 5:14:10 (28,697)
Payne, Martin C 3:56:10 (10,530)
Payne, Mathew 3:24:07 (3,792)
Payne, Matthew Robert R 3:48:06 (8,374)
Payne, Michael 5:26:10 (30,052)
Payne, Michael J 4:19:07 (16,660)
Payne, Neil T 4:05:49 (13,249)
Payne, Robert A 3:58:51 (11,440)
Payne, Russ 2:58:07 (958)
Payne, Stephen K 4:14:44 (15,502)
Payne, Thomas W 3:27:29 (4,360)
Peace, Ian D 5:39:58 (31,330)
Peace, Michael S 3:25:35 (4,029)
Peach, Simon R 5:00:11 (26,665)
Peach, Tony M 3:27:13 (4,315)
Peacher, Ricky C 2:58:18 (979)
Peachey, David 5:00:14 (26,672)
Peachey, Michael 3:35:34 (5,806)
Peachey, Michael 4:55:29 (25,780)
Peacock, Christopher 3:26:14 (4,142)
Peacock, Damian P 3:58:36 (11,336)
Peacock, Daniel 4:43:13 (22,985)
Peacock, John 5:06:00 (27,552)
Peacock, Lenny 3:47:35 (8,243)
Peacock, Michael J 4:39:17 (22,043)
Peak, James M 4:45:08 (23,444)
Peake, Malcolm 4:28:37 (19,296)
Pearce, Andrew S 3:04:35 (1,490)
Pearce, Chris J 5:53:08 (32,349)
Pearce, Craig 4:42:34 (22,823)
Pearce, Gareth 4:37:16 (21,539)
Pearce, Geoff 7:04:17 (34,258)
Pearce, James S 4:40:23 (22,282)
Pearce, Jonathan 5:59:24 (32,708)
Pearce, Kelvyn J 3:27:19 (4,336)
Pearce, Lance 4:50:02 (24,608)
Pearce, Leon 3:55:45 (10,422)
Pearce, Mark J 4:29:09 (19,439)
Pearce, Martin 4:56:53 (26,047)
Pearce, Max 4:52:20 (25,110)
Pearce, Richard 6:09:41 (33,104)
Pearce, Richard J 3:38:42 (6,391)
Pearce, Robert E 4:00:25 (11,951)
Pearce, Robert L 3:34:26 (5,610)
Pearce, Sean L 4:03:42 (12,765)
Pearce, Stephen G 3:54:47 (10,121)
Pearce, Stephen P 3:29:16 (4,730)
Pearce, Steve J 4:00:20 (11,933)
Pearce, William S 4:29:32 (19,524)
Pearce-Molland, Ivan J 3:50:26 (8,916)
Pearch, Sam S 5:14:41 (28,772)
Pearcy, Michael C 4:04:27 (12,919)
Pearman, Adrian C 5:05:13 (27,437)
Pearman, Lee C 5:13:12 (28,571)
Pearn, Martin M 4:45:41 (23,577)
Pears, Richard 3:56:24 (10,598)
Pearse, Justin M 4:13:37 (15,191)
Pearse, Tom N 3:21:10 (3,381)
Pearson, Andrew 3:45:02 (7,691)
Pearson, Andrew J 4:38:04 (21,729)
Pearson, Anthony M 3:56:31 (10,629)
Pearson, Charles L 2:43:51 (288)
Pearson, David B 4:44:09 (23,214)
Pearson, Gavin 6:52:43 (34,122)
Pearson, Graham A 4:24:13 (18,056)
Pearson, Hayden R 3:52:22 (9,401)
Pearson, Hugh A 3:11:36 (2,162)
Pearson, Jamie 3:39:49 (6,600)
Pearson, John E 4:09:07 (14,065)
Pearson, Kevin C 3:45:41 (7,831)
Pearson, Mark 7:34:10 (34,470)
Pearson, Michael D 4:13:36 (15,187)
Pearson, Michael J 4:12:03 (14,824)
Pearson, Toby S 2:42:21 (250)
Pearsons, Mat 3:29:53 (4,862)
Pearsons, Phil N 4:13:29 (15,154)
Peart, Ben R 3:46:13 (7,930)
Peasnell, James J 4:01:32 (12,251)
Peat, James 3:40:00 (6,638)
Peatfield, Carl D 3:29:02 (4,679)
Pech, Simon J 4:45:12 (23,465)

Peck, Andrew J 4:04:49 (13,004)
Peck, Ian L 5:36:00 (31,028)
Peck, Robert J 4:15:24 (15,670)
Peck, Simon J 2:55:01 (752)
Peck, Thomas 3:54:22 (9,978)
Peckett, Mark G 3:23:25 (3,694)
Peckham, Robert J 6:00:08 (32,745)
Pecoraro, Antonio 2:55:36 (781)
Pedder, Carl W 3:52:36 (9,454)
Pedder, Mark J 4:38:48 (21,912)
Pedder-Smith, Stephen M 3:41:52 (7,008)
Peddie, Neil 4:35:47 (21,190)
Peddle, Mark 3:42:59 (7,233)
Pedlar, Charlie 3:01:16 (1,258)
Pedroni, Marco 4:41:17 (22,509)
Pee, Kevin N 4:31:56 (20,147)
Peel, David G 3:28:51 (4,635)
Peel, David J 4:17:42 (16,281)
Peel, Jonathan 4:36:54 (21,464)
Peel, Marcus C 4:27:58 (19,088)
Peel, Mike 4:12:28 (14,920)
Peers, Alan 5:03:07 (27,119)
Peers, Richard 4:00:11 (11,894)
Peers, Richard 5:20:55 (29,488)
Peers, Robert A 4:57:01 (26,084)
Pegg, Geoffrey H 4:36:15 (21,312)
Pegg, Jonathan C 4:07:01 (13,522)
Pegg, Martyn 4:22:51 (17,686)
Peirce, Gary B 3:43:38 (7,373)
Pekk, Tonu 3:10:07 (2,001)
Pelaud, Philippe 3:52:39 (9,470)
Peled, Asaf 4:32:42 (20,348)
Pellatt, Neville J 5:17:03 (29,068)
Pelle, Cyril 3:05:16 (1,535)
Pellegrini, Andrea 4:17:33 (16,236)
Pellissier, Stephane 4:18:57 (16,616)
Pellizzaro, Paolo Mario 4:02:15 (12,430)
Peltor, Edward 2:57:10 (884)
Peluso, Pietro 2:48:57 (462)
Pemberton, Anthony 5:17:32 (29,132)
Pemberton, Gareth J 3:12:42 (2,291)
Pemberton, Leo C 3:58:17 (11,208)
Pemberton, Stephen N 3:38:22 (6,334)
Pembery, Graham 4:02:49 (12,569)
Pemble, Colin 3:12:01 (2,210)
Pembroke, John P 3:06:07 (1,608)
Pendlebury, Richard A 3:21:56 (3,479)
Penfold, Keith J 4:59:50 (26,612)
Pengelly, Andrew J 3:16:28 (2,810)
Penman, Jeffrey D 4:25:16 (18,330)
Penman, Jeffrey T 5:11:46 (28,379)
Penman, Stuart T 3:27:54 (4,439)
Penn, Nicholas J 4:22:23 (17,547)
Pennetier, Pascal 3:13:05 (2,345)
Penney, Sam G 5:23:51 (29,783)
Penneycard, Matt J 4:08:20 (13,864)
Pennicott, Derek J 3:42:57 (7,223)
Pennington, Lee 5:44:52 (31,755)
Pennington, Michael J 3:13:02 (2,338)
Pennington, Noel D 5:08:31 (27,899)
Penny, Chris 4:12:45 (14,974)
Penny, Matthew J 3:28:32 (4,566)
Penrose, Charlie T 3:50:33 (8,941)
Penrose, Richard B 5:20:13 (29,431)
Penrose, Ronald K 3:25:27 (4,002)
Pentland, Bob 3:07:36 (1,744)
Pentland, Chris M 3:51:56 (9,285)
Pepes, Peter S 3:37:00 (6,065)
Peppard, Brent 5:24:52 (29,902)
Pepper, David 3:29:18 (4,739)
Pepper, Grahame S 4:19:13 (16,680)
Pepper, Robert A 4:11:09 (14,590)
Pepper, Thomas D 4:29:43 (19,568)
Pepperday, Anthony 3:47:37 (8,257)
Peral, Renato P 3:58:13 (11,196)
Perarnau, Joan 3:28:40 (4,596)
Percival, Deon 4:01:33 (12,255)
Percival, Martin R 3:59:26 (11,646)
Percival-Smith, Paul E 3:31:45 (5,179)
Percy, Matthew S 3:29:07 (4,697)
Perego, Stefano 3:27:39 (4,387)
Pereira Veiga, David 4:19:03 (16,639)
Perello Roca, Jordi 3:53:05 (9,602)

Perera, Jorge C 4:30:53 (19,863)
Perera-Sweetman, Martin J 4:07:38 (13,684)
Peresson, Ben M 3:57:45 (11,039)
Perez de la Fuenta, Manuel 3:22:12 (3,514)
Perez Orquin, Andrés 4:45:57 (23,661)
Perez-Montejano, Paul 5:16:20 (28,973)
Perhab, Willibald 3:18:58 (3,095)
Perkin, Sam J 4:00:42 (12,034)
Perkins, Andrew F 3:57:08 (10,847)
Perkins, Christopher J 4:18:17 (16,429)
Perkins, James D 3:49:36 (8,719)
Perkins, Mark G 3:29:35 (4,795)
Perkins, Matthew J 3:12:00 (2,205)
Perkins, Michael P 4:38:32 (21,831)
Perkins, Simon N 3:28:39 (4,592)
Perkins, Stuart 4:32:49 (20,377)
Perkins, Tim J 3:48:36 (8,489)
Perkins, Tom W 3:12:01 (2,210)
Perks, Benjamin 4:26:36 (18,695)
Perlin, Michael S 5:31:09 (30,577)
Perlmutter, Antony 4:14:08 (15,347)
Peroni, Gianluca 3:42:21 (7,105)
Perovic, Srdjan 4:43:07 (22,967)
Perowne, Matthew 4:59:27 (26,551)
Perrett, Michael 4:16:59 (16,088)
Perrett, Michael S 4:32:50 (20,383)
Perrez, Jean-Paul 3:28:11 (4,505)
Perridge, Ed 4:52:36 (25,169)
Perrin, Andrew F 4:55:18 (25,749)
Perrin, Dan J 3:54:54 (10,160)
Perrin, Marc 3:58:36 (11,336)
Perrin, Stephen R 3:13:27 (2,394)
Perring, David A 3:59:31 (11,680)
Perrott, Nathan 3:57:11 (10,858)
Perry, Ben 3:44:32 (7,558)
Perry, David 6:34:23 (33,758)
Perry, Dean S 4:34:50 (20,918)
Perry, Greg N 4:53:57 (25,472)
Perry, John F 4:37:04 (21,499)
Perry, Luke B 5:03:03 (27,111)
Perry, Mark 3:07:34 (1,738)
Perry, Mark A 3:50:51 (9,017)
Perry, Neil A 3:53:32 (9,719)
Perry, Neil S 3:14:33 (2,559)
Perry, Nicholas 4:08:57 (14,032)
Perry, Paul 2:43:18 (277)
Perry, Ryan R 3:43:07 (7,271)
Perry, Steve 4:50:49 (24,799)
Perry, Steven M 4:43:51 (23,141)
Perry, Thomas E 3:53:57 (9,854)
Perryman, Adrian 4:31:20 (19,975)
Perryman, David G 4:28:19 (19,213)
Perryman, Graham 3:36:10 (5,912)
Perryman-Best, Nevil J 4:24:22 (18,098)
Persse, Alexander W 5:29:28 (30,420)
Persson, Anders 3:20:13 (3,253)
Pertini, Mark A 5:35:37 (30,991)
Perugia, Edward J 4:12:53 (15,002)
Perversi, Pablo 4:19:30 (16,757)
Pescod, Daniel 3:01:21 (1,266)
Pesek, Martin 3:34:43 (5,648)
Pestridge, Mark V 3:31:16 (5,095)
Petchey, Dave R 4:43:38 (23,080)
Peter, Christopher F 3:53:48 (9,808)
Peter, Gareth J 4:16:53 (16,054)
Peters, Darren 4:09:10 (14,077)
Peters, Geoffrey C 3:07:35 (1,740)
Peters, John R 4:53:45 (25,426)
Peters, Marc A 5:48:00 (31,978)
Peters, Rich M 4:05:05 (13,067)
Petersen, Finn T 4:09:35 (14,198)
Peterson, Calum H 3:53:04 (9,596)
Peterson, Garth D 3:11:45 (2,181)
Peterson, Gregor R 4:24:13 (18,056)
Petersons, Edijs 3:42:08 (7,054)
Petit, Jeremy R 4:54:36 (25,600)
Petrak, Daniel K 3:44:04 (7,465)
Petreni, Enzo Giuseppe 6:26:45 (33,591)
Petri, Johan 3:19:27 (3,154)
Petri, Rickard 5:04:05 (27,261)
Petrides, George 6:19:23 (33,385)
Petrie, Derek J 3:15:20 (2,680)
Petrie, Grant S 4:02:05 (12,382)

Petrie, Richard	3:51:35 (9,191)	
Petruso, Tony	3:39:13 (6,477)	
Pettet, David A	5:37:41 (31,166)	
Pettifer, John	4:31:18 (19,968)	
Pettigrew, Andrew D	5:10:41 (28,235)	
Pettigrove, Jason M	4:58:58 (26,468)	
Pettit, Andy T	3:52:03 (9,318)	
Pettit, James E	5:34:40 (30,903)	
Pettitt, Alan	3:31:40 (5,161)	
Petty, Michael	3:48:03 (8,363)	
Petty, Richard J	3:07:34 (1,738)	
Petty-Mayor, Mark E	3:34:45 (5,654)	
Petyt, Joe	4:44:36 (23,321)	
Pewter, Joshua W	3:19:44 (3,197)	
Pewtner, Joe P	3:34:21 (5,598)	
Peynichou, Bruno	4:15:09 (15,607)	
Pfaller, Franco	4:22:11 (17,492)	
Pfeifer, Werner	3:30:45 (5,012)	
Pfeiffer, Carl J	3:51:59 (9,297)	
Pfendler, Emile	3:53:25 (9,700)	
Phan, Michael	4:01:30 (12,241)	
Phare, James A	4:01:09 (12,148)	
Phelan, Brian P	3:21:26 (3,417)	
Phelan, William P	3:39:09 (6,462)	
Phelps, David J	4:14:50 (15,520)	
Phelps, Rhys W	3:55:43 (10,409)	
Phelps, Stephen E	3:39:49 (6,600)	
Phelps, Stephen J	4:31:20 (19,975)	
Phelps, Thomas	4:11:28 (14,665)	
Pheplow, Michael	4:10:33 (14,423)	
Philbin, John-Mark	4:36:20 (21,334)	
Philcox, Ian J	4:03:17 (12,679)	
Philip, David	2:52:16 (608)	
Philip, Jamie	3:23:13 (3,665)	
Philip, Paul John J	4:53:45 (25,426)	
Philip, Peter J	5:19:30 (29,354)	
Philipps, Euan J	4:19:12 (16,679)	
Philipps, Will	4:22:59 (17,722)	
Phillips, Adam G	4:33:18 (20,511)	
Phillips, Alan	4:44:15 (23,241)	
Phillips, Alec W	5:06:19 (27,605)	
Phillips, Alex	3:32:48 (5,363)	
Phillips, Andrew J	4:58:51 (26,443)	
Phillips, Anthony M	4:23:25 (17,842)	
Phillips, Ben	3:39:21 (6,509)	
Phillips, Brian	4:40:10 (22,229)	
Phillips, Christopher J	4:00:58 (12,105)	
Phillips, Christopher J	4:25:53 (18,507)	
Phillips, Craig W	5:56:17 (32,543)	
Phillips, Darren	5:01:21 (26,849)	
Phillips, Daryl J	4:44:06 (23,202)	
Phillips, David A	3:22:04 (3,499)	
Phillips, David M	4:36:29 (21,364)	
Phillips, Dean R	4:47:08 (23,940)	
Phillips, Glenn H	4:16:54 (16,061)	
Phillips, Graeme C	4:51:36 (24,960)	
Phillips, Greg S	4:20:45 (17,103)	
Phillips, Hedley S	4:21:41 (17,368)	
Phillips, Ian J	3:58:19 (11,226)	
Phillips, Ian J	6:11:20 (33,149)	
Phillips, James G	3:53:54 (9,836)	
Phillips, James P	4:19:05 (16,651)	
Phillips, John	3:57:40 (11,001)	
Phillips, John N	4:07:23 (13,608)	
Phillips, John S	3:41:07 (6,851)	
Phillips, Leonard J	3:38:07 (6,289)	
Phillips, Mark H	3:53:44 (9,783)	
Phillips, Mark I	4:02:08 (12,396)	
Phillips, Mark I	5:08:22 (27,868)	
Phillips, Matthew	5:09:44 (28,103)	
Phillips, Michael H	5:54:00 (32,404)	
Phillips, Nick J	5:38:02 (31,195)	
Phillips, Nick R	3:20:32 (3,295)	
Phillips, Paul	3:57:00 (10,796)	
Phillips, Pete	3:51:33 (9,182)	
Phillips, Peter	3:46:02 (7,896)	
Phillips, Peter	4:17:34 (16,238)	
Phillips, Rawle M	5:23:43 (29,768)	
Phillips, Rhodri P	3:17:50 (2,965)	
Phillips, Richard	3:54:36 (10,071)	
Phillips, Rob	2:47:50 (416)	
Phillips, Robin	4:07:05 (13,539)	
Phillips, Stephen R	4:49:30 (24,474)	

Phillips, Steven	4:05:56 (13,275)	
Phillips, Steven T	5:10:36 (28,232)	
Phillips, Tim	4:10:33 (14,423)	
Phillips, Timothy W	3:54:40 (10,089)	
Phillips, Tomas	5:08:47 (27,943)	
Phillips, Tony P	4:18:05 (16,368)	
Phillips, Trevor	3:55:07 (10,241)	
Phillips, Will	4:52:11 (25,078)	
Phillis, Richard G	3:39:50 (6,607)	
Philllips, Mervyn R	3:44:43 (7,610)	
Phillpot, Ian	5:33:13 (30,768)	
Phillpot, Timothy S	4:00:43 (12,039)	
Phillpott, Thomas	5:35:55 (31,023)	
Philo, Mark R	3:25:29 (4,010)	
Philp, Russell	4:07:39 (13,689)	
Philpot, Saul T	4:45:27 (23,529)	
Philpott, Ivan P	4:03:06 (12,629)	
Philpott, Ryan	3:54:43 (10,105)	
Philpotts, Robert	3:28:30 (4,562)	
Phipp, Rob	4:06:45 (13,462)	
Phippen, Peter	5:05:07 (27,423)	
Phipps, Kevin M	3:58:11 (11,182)	
Phipps, Mark	3:38:34 (6,365)	
Phiri, Ackson	5:06:24 (27,614)	
Phiri, Martin	4:49:59 (24,597)	
Phoenix, Andrew	4:12:26 (14,914)	
Phoenix, Ian	4:22:30 (17,582)	
Phoenix, Mike B	4:53:48 (25,440)	
Phull, Gurvinder	5:09:12 (27,996)	
Phythian, Jamie	4:02:48 (12,565)	
Picchioni, Alessandro	2:53:45 (678)	
Piccone, Mark A	3:20:21 (3,272)	
Pichl, Jan	2:29:42 (68)	
Pickard, Mark J	3:44:40 (7,595)	
Pickering, Antony	5:32:45 (30,723)	
Pickering, David	4:33:45 (20,649)	
Pickering, Derrick J	5:34:00 (30,836)	
Pickering, Ian D	5:12:09 (28,423)	
Pickering, Mark C	4:40:53 (22,398)	
Pickering, Steven D	3:25:57 (4,099)	
Pickett, Anthony R	4:21:03 (17,197)	
Pickett, Kenneth G	5:35:28 (30,973)	
Pickford, Andy J	3:06:30 (1,639)	
Pickford, Chris A	4:40:16 (22,249)	
Pickford, Paul J	4:43:43 (23,106)	
Pickles, Roger G	5:08:55 (27,955)	
Pickthall, Christopher	3:37:58 (6,257)	
Pickup, Ian	4:17:10 (16,147)	
Pickup, Jeffrey	3:17:47 (2,961)	
Pickup, Lewis C	3:49:14 (8,637)	
Pickup, Oliver J	3:48:50 (8,534)	
Pickup, Stephen I	3:29:39 (4,809)	
Picton, Graham	2:58:22 (989)	
Picton, Graham	6:16:11 (33,299)	
Pidd, Jamie	5:26:20 (30,077)	
Piejos, Franck S	3:49:07 (8,606)	
Pierce, Mark	5:31:36 (30,623)	
Piercy, Gareth L	4:02:51 (12,577)	
Piercy, Stephen	5:18:32 (29,232)	
Pierson, Matthew	2:34:53 (111)	
Piertroni, Danny R	4:10:16 (14,356)	
Pietquin, Jean-Jierre	4:26:17 (18,605)	
Piggott, Darren M	5:18:30 (29,227)	
Pigott, Richard G	3:19:34 (3,172)	
Pihema, Kenneth V	3:45:09 (7,715)	
Pike, Alan K	4:29:04 (19,417)	
Pike, Andrew	6:37:36 (33,831)	
Pike, Daniel P	4:01:39 (12,281)	
Pike, Darren M	4:31:24 (19,995)	
Pike, David	3:23:50 (3,745)	
Pike, David W	3:06:37 (1,649)	
Pike, Jason	4:02:25 (12,479)	
Pike, Oliver Simon	3:53:11 (9,635)	
Pike, Richard D	4:08:12 (13,829)	
Pilch, Matthew J	4:17:32 (16,232)	
Pilgrim, Matthew	4:58:26 (26,366)	
Pilgrim, Melvyn	7:02:52 (34,238)	
Pilgrim, Rufus J	4:40:52 (22,395)	
Pilkington, Mark A	6:38:32 (33,861)	
Pilkington, Rory I	3:55:17 (10,286)	
Pillar, Andrew C	3:48:35 (8,483)	
Pilling, Dan	3:58:55 (11,460)	
Pilling, Paul M	3:16:47 (2,843)	

Pilling, Robert R	4:09:43 (14,233)	
Pillinger, Jonathan M	3:48:02 (8,358)	
Pillow, Michel	4:04:13 (12,866)	
Pilot, Colin	3:54:49 (10,131)	
Pim, Brian	3:40:40 (6,751)	
Pinault, Denis	4:02:24 (12,476)	
Pincay Macias, Rolando R	4:38:03 (21,724)	
Pinchen, James	5:08:23 (27,871)	
Pinchin, Philip G	5:01:36 (26,896)	
Pinder, Nicholas G	3:58:30 (11,298)	
Pinder, Richard M	3:42:46 (7,190)	
Pinfield, Ben	3:32:19 (5,281)	
Pinheiro Gonsalves, José J	3:17:43 (2,956)	
Pink, Daniel J	4:54:07 (25,504)	
Pinney, Mark R	6:06:03 (32,978)	
Pinnick, David	4:12:32 (14,936)	
Pinnion, Clive R	2:57:14 (890)	
Pinnock, Stephen M	4:20:49 (17,130)	
Pino Pardal, Alfredo	4:00:15 (11,909)	
Pinon, Bernard G	3:25:00 (3,930)	
Pinori, Mauro	3:47:15 (8,169)	
Pinson, Christopher J	4:33:02 (20,439)	
Pintado, Juan C	4:37:00 (21,485)	
Piper, Damian	4:09:41 (14,220)	
Piper, Daniel F	5:01:35 (26,887)	
Piper, Daniel W	5:28:50 (30,353)	
Piper, David J	4:11:22 (14,638)	
Piper, Michael	4:13:04 (15,054)	
Piper, Paul J	5:27:50 (30,242)	
Piper, Simon M	3:13:35 (2,404)	
Piper, Thomas J	4:12:58 (15,021)	
Pirali, Franco	4:29:51 (19,600)	
Pires, Daniel	4:08:24 (13,882)	
Pires, José	4:33:46 (20,653)	
Pires, Julio	4:01:22 (12,202)	
Pirozzolo, Mario	5:35:40 (30,994)	
Pisal, Narendra	3:54:32 (10,045)	
Pisolkar, Bob	3:56:17 (10,557)	
Pispa, Jussi E	3:26:05 (4,119)	
Pistilli, Stefano	3:24:43 (3,872)	
Pitchell, Ian	3:25:51 (4,080)	
Piterzak, John	3:18:37 (3,057)	
Pitfield, Tim B	3:39:18 (6,499)	
Pithers, Daniel	5:01:08 (26,816)	
Pitkethly, Rob J	3:36:19 (5,935)	
Pitkin, Mark	4:13:37 (15,191)	
Pitson, Stephen C	4:27:04 (18,832)	
Pitt, Alan	3:05:29 (1,552)	
Pitt, Chris J	4:25:01 (18,266)	
Pitt, Clive J	5:02:27 (27,036)	
Pitt, Graham R	5:27:26 (30,196)	
Pittini, Dario	4:16:52 (16,049)	
Pittman, Andrew R	2:57:53 (934)	
Place, Paul M	4:53:29 (25,368)	
Plaistowe, Richard	4:11:04 (14,563)	
Planner, Don	6:49:59 (34,075)	
Plant, Darren	5:00:43 (26,742)	
Plant, John F	4:42:29 (22,800)	
Plant, Richard	4:40:54 (22,402)	
Plant, Selwyn	4:00:37 (12,010)	
Plaskett, Gary R	5:10:48 (28,250)	
Platt, Andrew C	4:23:10 (17,770)	
Platt, Charlie	4:37:45 (21,652)	
Platt, Gary A	3:14:45 (2,598)	
Platt, James	3:55:06 (10,233)	
Platt, Matthew S	4:35:58 (21,238)	
Platt, Paul D	4:09:48 (14,251)	
Platts, Stephen D	4:16:09 (15,863)	
Playdon, Vincent	3:36:09 (5,907)	
Player, Alex M	4:46:38 (23,807)	
Player, Mark R	5:10:04 (28,158)	
Playford-Smith, Terry R	6:18:26 (33,370)	
Please, Toby W	4:55:11 (25,730)	
Pledger, Ian P	3:57:46 (11,049)	
Pledger, Philip I	3:44:00 (7,456)	
Plenderleith, Scott M	4:25:42 (18,444)	
Plester, Russell J	3:24:21 (3,823)	
Plews, Andrew P	3:46:44 (8,045)	
Pleydell-Bovverie, Edward R	6:22:46 (33,481)	
Plimmer, Peter S	3:33:36 (5,491)	
Ploner, Kurt	2:44:53 (326)	
Plowman, Barry	3:19:48 (3,207)	
Pluchinotta, Alessandro	4:20:46 (17,112)	

Pluke, Matthew H.	3:57:34 (10,971)	
Plumb, Stephen T	5:07:23 (27,749)	
Plumb, Steven J	4:20:19 (16,979)	
Plumbley, Andrew I.	4:52:59 (25,268)	
Plumbly, Edward G.	4:09:07 (14,065)	
Plumer, Keith	3:09:26 (1,934)	
Plummer, Daniel	4:42:06 (22,695)	
Plummer, Matthew R	4:20:46 (17,112)	
Plummer, Nick	4:17:19 (16,179)	
Plummer, Tim S	5:24:29 (29,857)	
Plump, Brent	3:20:08 (3,239)	
Plumridge, Stuart D	4:11:30 (14,679)	
Plumstead, Pat	3:11:57 (2,201)	
Plumtree, Jonathan	3:41:18 (6,899)	
Plunkett, David P	4:42:42 (22,851)	
Plunkett, Mark	3:22:01 (3,493)	
Plunkett, Richard	3:35:21 (5,764)	
Poade, Matthew J	4:46:12 (23,714)	
Pocas, Joaquim	3:55:02 (10,210)	
Pochat, Jean-Luc	3:12:47 (2,302)	
Pocknell, Leon P	4:28:11 (19,164)	
Pockney, Timothy E	4:07:08 (13,553)	
Pocock, John W	3:20:57 (3,354)	
Pocock, Mark J	3:45:44 (7,840)	
Pocock, Michael J	3:14:34 (2,563)	
Podbury, Alexander J	3:42:08 (7,054)	
Podemsky, Gary J	4:48:12 (24,205)	
Podoba, Jacek T	3:34:59 (5,700)	
Poggio, Mario	4:26:54 (18,786)	
Pohle, Christian	4:37:43 (21,644)	
Pointon, Matthew C	3:05:37 (1,562)	
Poke, Matthew L	4:37:02 (21,494)	
Pokoj, Jack S	3:58:00 (11,116)	
Polak, William A	4:33:04 (20,448)	
Pole, Michael I	3:40:38 (6,747)	
Poli, Guido	4:20:38 (17,074)	
Poll, Graham	4:19:38 (16,790)	
Pollard, Anthony G	3:03:09 (1,385)	
Pollard, Gary J	3:44:00 (7,456)	
Pollard, Ian F	2:55:53 (802)	
Pollard, Philip P	3:27:05 (4,296)	
Pollard, Simon R	4:09:48 (14,251)	
Pollard, Tim J	3:37:13 (6,107)	
Pollen, Andrew F	3:23:00 (3,636)	
Pollett, Derek J	4:05:49 (13,249)	
Polley, Keith A	5:17:22 (29,104)	
Pollitt, Martyn D	3:08:09 (1,810)	
Pollock, Conor J	3:09:07 (1,897)	
Pollock, David J	3:35:05 (5,723)	
Pollock, Jeremy R	2:46:39 (380)	
Pollock, Nicholas S	2:57:17 (895)	
Pollock, Wayne B	4:06:04 (13,305)	
Polman, Paul	3:53:14 (9,644)	
Pomford, Carl D	4:52:43 (25,203)	
Pomfret, Graham L	3:22:54 (3,624)	
Pomphrey, Chris J	4:16:20 (15,915)	
Ponchelle, Jerome R	3:49:23 (8,671)	
Pond, Andrew J	3:51:08 (9,084)	
Pond, Christopher M	3:37:27 (6,159)	
Pond, Nick C	5:14:03 (28,679)	
Pond, Stephen S	4:17:24 (16,190)	
Pons, Andy	4:49:31 (24,478)	
Ponsford, Robert J	3:48:33 (8,479)	
Ponzini, Paul	3:57:18 (10,890)	
Pook, Michael S	3:24:16 (3,814)	
Pool, Robert C	4:12:15 (14,873)	
Poole, Alan R	4:43:11 (22,978)	
Poole, Dale A	4:34:36 (20,845)	
Poole, Greg W	3:52:47 (9,499)	
Poole, James	7:21:13 (34,403)	
Poole, John R	3:24:09 (3,798)	
Poole, Matthew M	3:57:13 (10,868)	
Poot, Richard J	5:01:10 (26,821)	
Poots, Timothy S	3:48:32 (8,473)	
Pope, Christopher S	4:40:52 (22,395)	
Pope, Dave	6:24:20 (33,526)	
Pope, James W	4:26:28 (18,654)	
Pope, Richard D	4:42:29 (22,800)	
Pope, Robert A	2:44:34 (313)	
Pope, Robin	4:06:32 (13,412)	
Pope, Roger	5:19:37 (29,375)	
Popham, Andrew H	4:08:40 (13,961)	
Poppe, Lucien	3:27:48 (4,421)	
Poppett, Craig J	5:00:39 (26,728)	
Popplestone, Alan	4:05:01 (13,053)	
Pordum, Chris	3:58:08 (11,157)	
Porritt, Jim	4:13:57 (15,286)	
Portanier, Daniel E.	3:59:36 (11,714)	
Portavella Pallas, Carles	3:34:42 (5,645)	
Portelli, Kellinu J	4:36:14 (21,308)	
Porteous, Henry J	3:14:03 (2,474)	
Porteous, Robert	4:48:06 (24,162)	
Porter, Ben J	4:09:27 (14,156)	
Porter, Bryan A	4:19:25 (16,728)	
Porter, David R	4:03:41 (12,763)	
Porter, James S	4:51:57 (25,031)	
Porter, John G	4:22:27 (17,568)	
Porter, Liam C	4:43:59 (23,177)	
Porter, Mitchell	4:50:33 (24,733)	
Porter, Patrick W	3:55:43 (10,409)	
Porter, Phillip A	4:28:00 (19,099)	
Porter, Richard L	3:45:53 (7,877)	
Porter, Stephen J	4:16:30 (15,959)	
Porter, Tim	4:08:59 (14,036)	
Porter, Wayne	4:59:41 (26,591)	
Porthouse, Stephen G	4:24:06 (18,019)	
Portlock, Peter	5:01:33 (26,880)	
Portmann, Reto	3:09:06 (1,894)	
Portwain, Christopher T	5:42:49 (31,556)	
Posey, Bryn	5:50:40 (32,182)	
Posner, Michael	4:31:23 (19,991)	
Posnett, John J	4:52:57 (25,259)	
Poss, Steven K	5:06:54 (27,682)	
Posselt, Clive D	4:13:18 (15,116)	
Post, Richard	3:42:35 (7,150)	
Postgate, James W	4:21:30 (17,308)	
Postill, Daniel	4:08:47 (13,990)	
Postill, Mark	5:33:03 (30,754)	
Postlethwaite, James D	4:13:52 (15,266)	
Potash, Steven	5:42:21 (31,526)	
Potier, Bernard	3:39:44 (6,582)	
Potten, Matthew J	3:17:55 (2,977)	
Potter, Adrian J	4:08:49 (13,993)	
Potter, Alan	4:19:53 (16,855)	
Potter, Christopher	3:31:46 (5,183)	
Potter, Clifford	5:18:40 (29,249)	
Potter, Dean	5:58:31 (32,669)	
Potter, Howard	5:04:32 (27,333)	
Potter, John H	4:38:54 (21,941)	
Potter, Kevin	3:53:40 (9,758)	
Potter, Matthew C	4:03:15 (12,670)	
Potter, Neil	3:33:14 (5,426)	
Potter, Nicholas J	3:56:54 (10,762)	
Potter, Oliver J	4:14:03 (15,320)	
Potter, Richard G	4:25:11 (18,318)	
Potter, Richard J	4:50:07 (24,625)	
Potter, Richard T	5:54:17 (32,424)	
Potter, Stephen J	4:20:25 (17,003)	
Potts, Andrew D	4:28:04 (19,118)	
Potts, Anthony E	4:15:28 (15,693)	
Potts, Colin I	2:32:35 (92)	
Potts, David E	6:20:47 (33,418)	
Potts, Ed	4:10:29 (14,406)	
Potts, Ian R	5:24:36 (29,868)	
Potts, Richard M	4:16:33 (15,971)	
Potts, Steven	4:04:07 (12,848)	
Potts, Tony	5:06:40 (27,647)	
Pouget, Henri P	3:11:00 (2,097)	
Poulsom, Michael W	5:11:48 (28,385)	
Poulton, David J	4:51:08 (24,868)	
Pounder, Nicholas	3:41:43 (6,969)	
Povall, Tim J	4:57:39 (26,220)	
Povey, Kevin R	4:55:15 (25,742)	
Povinelli, Raymond A	3:53:22 (9,687)	
Pow, Jordan D	4:52:58 (25,264)	
Powdthavee, Nattavudh	4:25:18 (18,341)	
Powell, Alan J	4:34:04 (20,712)	
Powell, Andrew K	4:54:40 (25,615)	
Powell, Anthony L	2:56:09 (815)	
Powell, Barry	4:31:57 (20,159)	
Powell, Chris J	4:38:49 (21,919)	
Powell, Christopher	6:06:56 (33,014)	
Powell, Greg A	5:19:30 (29,354)	
Powell, Gregg J	3:30:44 (5,007)	
Powell, Jeff R	3:20:57 (3,354)	
Powell, John E	4:52:48 (25,222)	
Powell, Jonathan G	3:58:33 (11,317)	
Powell, Lloyd	3:53:00 (9,572)	
Powell, Matthew D	4:18:13 (16,405)	
Powell, Nathan C	3:08:07 (1,806)	
Powell, Nicholas	5:25:42 (30,003)	
Powell, Peter W	3:57:40 (11,001)	
Powell, Philip D	3:09:59 (1,987)	
Powell, Rhys D	4:23:08 (17,760)	
Powell, Richard	3:31:11 (5,073)	
Powell, Richard	4:37:13 (21,531)	
Powell, Simon J	3:58:49 (11,426)	
Powell, Simson C	2:30:04 (75)	
Powell, Steve J	5:15:37 (28,892)	
Powell, Tony P	3:54:55 (10,170)	
Powell-Chandler, Andrew	4:04:43 (12,989)	
Powell-Jackson, Simon	4:15:50 (15,792)	
Power, Andrew D	4:31:44 (20,087)	
Power, Gary	3:54:20 (9,968)	
Power, Rolf G	3:16:33 (2,819)	
Power-Ryce, Patrick	5:43:41 (31,626)	
Powles, Derek A	3:30:33 (4,981)	
Powles, James A	4:53:27 (25,360)	
Powles, Richard J	3:49:55 (8,804)	
Powling, Mark A	5:41:22 (31,447)	
Pownall, Paul D	3:37:09 (6,088)	
Powney, Simon	3:31:54 (5,198)	
Poyner, Vincent	4:19:35 (16,777)	
Poynter, Michael R	2:42:22 (252)	
Poyser, Tom	3:18:02 (2,990)	
Prado Blogg, Pablo	4:13:17 (15,112)	
Praill, Jason L	3:31:43 (5,173)	
Praill, John	4:29:19 (19,477)	
Pratizzoli, Alberto	3:35:56 (5,865)	
Pratt, Andrew J	5:06:00 (27,552)	
Pratt, Chris	3:25:26 (4,001)	
Pratt, Gary	3:48:37 (8,493)	
Pratt, Martin	4:54:44 (25,632)	
Preece, Clive L	4:22:05 (17,466)	
Preece, David J	3:31:05 (5,062)	
Premzl, Ales	4:07:25 (13,618)	
Prendergast, Paul M	5:38:41 (31,239)	
Prendergast, Raman	5:05:47 (27,519)	
Prentice, Stuart N	3:22:27 (3,557)	
Prescott, Neil J	3:19:37 (3,178)	
Prescott, Richard W	4:42:36 (22,832)	
Prescott, Stephen	4:32:19 (20,255)	
Presley, Mark A	5:44:56 (31,758)	
Press, Richard D	3:38:39 (6,379)	
Prest, Michael S	4:47:58 (24,139)	
Prest, Simon O	4:21:24 (17,275)	
Prestidge, Alistair T	4:14:17 (15,392)	
Prestidge, Caspar	3:04:50 (1,506)	
Preston, Alistair L	3:57:34 (10,971)	
Preston, Bamber R	3:00:19 (1,189)	
Preston, Chris B	5:31:26 (30,606)	
Preston, Daniel	4:01:08 (12,145)	
Preston, Darren	4:03:24 (12,700)	
Preston, Guy	4:45:15 (23,481)	
Preston, James R	5:08:40 (27,924)	
Preston, Jonathan A	5:25:54 (30,021)	
Preston, Marc A	5:36:34 (31,087)	
Preston, Mark A	3:39:41 (6,572)	
Preston, Michael	4:57:01 (26,084)	
Preston, Paul E	3:09:10 (1,903)	
Preston, Paul R	5:07:22 (27,747)	
Preston, Richard A	5:32:38 (30,713)	
Preston, Ryan M	4:02:07 (12,392)	
Preston, Steven M	5:09:29 (28,044)	
Prestwood, Mark A	2:46:15 (368)	
Presutti, Francesco	3:15:27 (2,694)	
Pretsell, Barry C	3:45:09 (7,715)	
Pretty, Graham	4:49:08 (24,403)	
Prettyman, Richard J	3:57:35 (10,974)	
Prevett, Ian R	5:29:32 (30,426)	
Prevost, Philippe	4:22:37 (17,622)	
Prew, Robert	5:33:00 (30,749)	
Price, Aled	4:11:40 (14,726)	
Price, Andy J	4:29:14 (19,459)	
Price, Bob G	5:49:27 (32,083)	
Price, Carl	2:52:39 (620)	
Price, Christopher	3:44:34 (7,569)	
Price, Colin M	4:09:28 (14,162)	
Price, David P	5:01:17 (26,838)	

Price, Gareth D 4:57:54 (26,263)
Price, Ian R 3:22:36 (3,584)
Price, James 3:07:14 (1,699)
Price, James N 5:18:53 (29,274)
Price, Jamie 4:22:47 (17,666)
Price, Keith 4:04:36 (12,949)
Price, Mark H 4:35:37 (21,145)
Price, Martin G 3:10:19 (2,020)
Price, Nigel T 3:59:35 (11,705)
Price, Richard 3:20:48 (3,331)
Price, Robert 4:55:52 (25,851)
Price, Robert J 6:08:03 (33,044)
Price, Robin M 3:44:23 (7,530)
Price, Stephen D 3:24:38 (3,861)
Price, Stephen G 2:47:27 (400)
Price, Stephen J 2:58:56 (1,056)
Price, Stuart N 5:04:56 (27,387)
Price, Tim R 2:39:23 (187)
Price, Timothy C 4:51:36 (24,960)
Prichard, Andrew J 4:38:55 (21,948)
Prichard, Euan D 4:13:32 (15,169)
Prichard, Michael J 3:59:34 (11,696)
Prichard, Tom 4:50:50 (24,801)
Prickett, Clive A 4:27:08 (18,851)
Priday, James A 4:46:11 (23,709)
Priday, Nicholas C 3:26:04 (4,118)
Priddle, Darren J 3:43:09 (7,276)
Priddy, David P 3:26:43 (4,234)
Priddy, Roger I 4:57:32 (26,194)
Priddy, Samuel 4:57:31 (26,190)
Pride, Michael 4:08:32 (13,925)
Priest, David S 4:11:16 (14,620)
Priest, Samuel J 4:30:00 (19,636)
Priestley, Chris 3:47:41 (8,276)
Priestley, Malcolm 4:56:41 (26,001)
Priestley, Steve G 4:10:16 (14,356)
Prieto, José L 3:04:55 (1,511)
Prietzel, Christopher H 3:37:56 (6,246)
Primarlol, George P 5:28:11 (30,290)
Prime, Chris J 5:01:19 (26,842)
Prime, David D 4:26:15 (18,595)
Prince, Kevin J 4:34:52 (20,931)
Prince, Martin A 6:30:03 (33,661)
Pring, Richard A 4:50:53 (24,818)
Pringle, Neil 3:04:55 (1,511)
Pringle, Simon R 4:17:36 (16,250)
Prins, Gysbertus P 3:57:23 (10,919)
Prior, Oli 3:56:36 (10,663)
Prior, Richard M 6:06:30 (33,005)
Prior, Rod 5:26:13 (30,060)
Prior, Tom J 4:22:56 (17,710)
Prior, Tomas 3:52:16 (9,380)
Prisco, Marcelo 3:28:41 (4,600)
Pritchard, David W 3:57:44 (11,029)
Pritchard, Edward W 4:04:00 (12,833)
Pritchard, Gary 5:01:11 (26,824)
Pritchard, Graham J 2:52:39 (620)
Pritchard, Keith 4:43:10 (22,975)
Pritchard, Lee J 3:55:38 (10,382)
Pritchard, Roger 5:17:26 (29,117)
Pritchard, Rory T 3:37:27 (6,159)
Prochazka, Ivo 4:10:45 (14,483)
Procter, Neil 4:07:59 (13,770)
Procter, Ryan 3:36:46 (6,005)
Proctor, David A 3:11:13 (2,116)
Proctor, Dominic A 5:01:30 (26,871)
Proctor, Mark 4:45:37 (23,567)
Proctor, Robert M 4:11:50 (14,765)
Proctor, Roger J 5:27:50 (30,242)
Profanter, Helmuth 4:15:36 (15,730)
Proffitt-White, John W 4:18:01 (16,348)
Proietti, Roberto F 4:37:10 (21,518)
Prosperi, Giorgio 4:20:31 (17,032)
Prosperi, Mauro 5:02:58 (27,105)
Prospero, Fabrizio 3:38:44 (6,396)
Prosser, Marc A 6:34:25 (33,761)
Prosser, Robert C 3:10:36 (2,054)
Prothero, Robert A 3:13:59 (2,463)
Prothon, Jacques 4:31:27 (20,014)
Proudfoot, Alan 3:09:53 (1,978)
Proust, Michel 3:35:51 (5,855)
Prout, Ryan 2:49:16 (474)
Prowse, Barrie K 4:10:08 (14,320)
Prudham, Joseph P 4:01:15 (12,174)
Pruene, Dietmar 5:00:59 (26,792)
Prunier, Thierry 3:51:47 (9,245)
Pruscino, Michael J 3:57:01 (10,802)
Pryce, Andrew G 4:32:39 (20,339)
Pryce, David W 3:03:23 (1,410)
Pryce, Jonathan C 4:49:32 (24,484)
Pryce, Simon P 3:32:35 (5,330)
Pryke, Andrew M 3:49:23 (8,671)
Pryke, Justin I 5:45:26 (31,797)
Pryke, Nicholas J 3:52:45 (9,493)
Pryke, Russell N 3:57:22 (10,913)
Pryke, Will M 4:11:10 (14,597)
Pryke-Smith, Mike D 4:21:29 (17,300)
Prytherch, David S 4:19:20 (16,711)
Puch, Jody P 4:16:26 (15,942)
Pudsey, David J 3:57:02 (10,805)
Pudsey-Dawson, Christopher E 4:04:19 (12,893)
Puech, Philippe 4:57:38 (26,219)
Puentes-Puertas, Juan-Alberto 5:05:02 (27,406)
Puerta, François 4:48:43 (24,298)
Pugh, Christopher J 4:12:02 (14,816)
Pugh, Gary A 4:35:10 (21,024)
Pugh, Gerwyn A 3:46:39 (8,031)
Pugh, Harvey 4:22:50 (17,679)
Pugh, Ian C 3:35:55 (5,862)
Pugh, Marc 3:52:54 (9,536)
Pugh, Patrick F 3:10:44 (2,067)
Pugh, Roderick M 3:23:43 (3,729)
Pugh, Simon C 5:46:39 (31,891)
Pugh, Thomas D 4:22:46 (17,661)
Pugi, Leonardo 5:09:41 (28,088)
Pulford, Tom G 5:30:10 (30,493)
Pull, Matthew R 4:25:41 (18,438)
Pullan, John K 3:53:29 (9,709)
Pullen, Bob F 4:21:16 (17,244)
Pullen, Huw 3:40:11 (6,669)
Pullen, Leslie C 4:56:44 (26,012)
Pullman, David 4:31:17 (19,961)
Pulver, Tristan 3:42:28 (7,134)
Pumfleet, Jon P 4:20:54 (17,152)
Pummell, Antony D 3:57:00 (10,796)
Punch, Julian E 4:04:30 (12,931)
Punchard, Neil T 3:51:11 (9,096)
Punter, Michael A 4:38:05 (21,736)
Punter, Steve T 3:45:32 (7,797)
Purcell, Peter A 5:15:22 (28,867)
Purchase, Alan D 3:58:16 (11,203)
Purchase, Garry 4:29:47 (19,581)
Purdie, Craig A 4:15:26 (15,684)
Purdom, Lee D 3:59:13 (11,568)
Purdon, Jason T 3:10:31 (2,045)
Purdy, Alan T 2:59:02 (1,062)
Purdy, Paul M 5:43:52 (31,639)
Purkiss, Michael T 5:40:05 (31,337)
Purkiss-McEndoo, Shaun 2:49:20 (479)
Purnell, Andrew G 4:26:54 (18,786)
Purnell, David S 3:54:21 (9,974)
Purser, Kevin 4:36:43 (21,421)
Purser, Nicholas J 3:33:17 (5,436)
Purser, Richard J 4:17:53 (16,321)
Purton, Simon C 3:46:11 (7,924)
Purvey, Alan 4:36:16 (21,315)
Purvis, Andrew 4:20:19 (16,979)
Purvis, Darren M 2:43:24 (279)
Purvis, Duncan 3:29:28 (4,774)
Purvis, Keith 2:52:59 (639)
Putman, John R 6:07:38 (33,032)
Puts, Johannes J 5:15:29 (28,880)
Puttkammer, Andrei 4:52:36 (25,169)
Puttock, Clifford G 3:42:34 (7,147)
Puzone, Massimo 4:46:39 (23,814)
Pye, Alan E 3:03:33 (1,420)
Pye, Geoff M 4:13:16 (15,105)
Pye, Roy F 4:32:32 (20,311)
Pye, Shaw D 2:51:53 (589)
Pyecroft, Matthew A 3:34:27 (5,615)
Pym, Edward C 5:12:39 (28,477)
Pymm, Mark F 3:51:18 (9,123)
Pyne, Daniel T 2:58:15 (972)
Pyne, Michael 4:28:57 (19,390)
Pyne, Steven 3:38:48 (6,410)
Pyrah, Jeff G 2:35:54 (128)
Python, Olivier G 4:20:30 (17,028)
Qazi, Mehboob 4:20:45 (17,103)
Quaid, Alan D 5:33:23 (30,779)
Quane, Andrew P 6:37:15 (33,825)
Quant, Daniel 4:07:04 (13,534)
Quantrill, Clive A 3:35:12 (5,737)
Quantrill, Richard J 2:54:10 (706)
Quaramby, Oliver 5:48:45 (32,031)
Quaye, Humphrey O 6:47:09 (34,023)
Quelch, Steven R 5:26:26 (30,090)
Quentin, Niki 3:20:08 (3,239)
Querrec, Gilles 4:38:20 (21,787)
Querstret, John P 2:58:57 (1,058)
Quest, Jonathan D 3:12:05 (2,221)
Quigley, Anthony 5:15:12 (28,845)
Quigley, Jonathan M 4:23:51 (17,953)
Quigley, Paul 5:28:54 (30,366)
Quigley, Philip A 5:14:32 (28,745)
Quillevere, Bernard 3:10:44 (2,067)
Quilter, Tom A 3:13:07 (2,348)
Quin, Stephen D 4:18:32 (16,508)
Quin, Thomas H 5:27:24 (30,195)
Quince, Mark G 3:45:58 (7,887)
Quinlan, Lee S 4:33:45 (20,649)
Quinlivan, Michael J 4:23:50 (17,946)
Quinn, Brian T 4:51:01 (24,847)
Quinn, Charles 5:05:58 (27,544)
Quinn, Eamon 6:49:21 (34,067)
Quinn, Edward S 4:43:42 (23,102)
Quinn, James R 4:29:41 (19,564)
Quinn, John E 3:39:00 (6,437)
Quinn, Michael G 4:10:26 (14,395)
Quinn, Niall D 3:33:17 (5,436)
Quinn, Peter 4:52:08 (25,070)
Quinn, Simon 4:47:51 (24,106)
Quinn, Thomas S 3:11:34 (2,158)
Quintal, Raymond 5:38:56 (31,256)
Quintana, Luis 3:10:21 (2,022)
Quinton, Nicholas O 4:25:10 (18,310)
Quirk, Paul A 4:03:26 (12,712)
Qvist-Sorensen, Per 3:46:02 (7,896)
Rabatin, Arthur 4:21:56 (17,435)
Rabbetts, Mark A 2:47:36 (404)
Rabey, Derrick A 3:20:13 (3,253)
Rabin, Nicholas P 3:16:27 (2,808)
Rabjohns, Peter 2:54:51 (737)
Raboldt, Marco 4:13:41 (15,218)
Rabone, Martin J 4:12:22 (14,900)
Race, Gavin 3:29:36 (4,800)
Race, Matthew J 4:13:12 (15,081)
Race, Philip S 4:54:47 (25,647)
Rach, Thomas 3:45:52 (7,873)
Racher, Brett A 3:57:42 (11,017)
Racke, Trevor J 4:03:22 (12,689)
Rackham, Nigel D 2:36:55 (146)
Racktoo, Andrew J 6:00:50 (32,770)
Racle, François 3:19:49 (3,210)
Racussen, Jonathan 3:41:27 (6,924)
Radbourne, Michael L 5:49:39 (32,096)
Radcliffe, Richard 3:19:37 (3,178)
Radford, Ian 3:50:15 (8,884)
Radford, Martin F 4:01:22 (12,202)
Radford, Tim P 4:43:05 (22,954)
Radley, Adam D 5:14:55 (28,808)
Radley, Kris J 5:19:32 (29,365)
Radley, Lee 3:50:08 (8,854)
Radnedge, Simon 4:17:18 (16,175)
Rae, Ian 4:49:41 (24,529)
Rae, Ian A 3:14:43 (2,594)
Ragazzini, Maurizio 4:13:17 (15,112)
Rai, Gurpreet 3:38:35 (6,368)
Rai, Mandeep S 5:06:10 (27,580)
Raimondi, Franco 3:57:47 (11,053)
Rainbow, Stephen M 3:20:48 (3,331)
Rainer, James R 4:02:37 (12,520)
Rainey, Ira 4:12:07 (14,840)
Rainford, Bruce A 2:58:08 (959)
Rainsford, Michael A 3:30:49 (5,024)
Rainsforth, Chris J 4:47:38 (24,050)
Rajan, Saradhi 3:50:00 (8,824)
Rajapakse, Jovan A 6:25:51 (33,572)
Raker, Dan J 3:52:13 (9,363)
Rakusen, Lloyd 4:39:35 (22,096)

Rakusen, Philip 4:34:57 (20,957)
Ralf, Paul A 4:49:36 (24,503)
Ralley, Paul D 3:52:20 (9,394)
Ralph, David T 4:05:31 (13,182)
Ralton, Paul J 3:11:16 (2,121)
Ramaala, Hendrick 2:11:44 (10)
Ramakrishna, Harish 3:34:48 (5,664)
Ramakrishna, Suresha 6:00:37 (32,764)
Rameau, Gerard 3:24:56 (3,916)
Ramirez Aznar, Ivan 3:32:24 (5,300)
Ramirez Jara, Constantino 4:36:05 (21,263)
Ramsay, Adam D 3:41:46 (6,983)
Ramsay, Ben P 4:17:06 (16,122)

Ramsay, Gordon 3:45:41 (7,831)

Ramsay, Ian B 3:48:51 (8,539)
Ramsay, Ramsay M 2:43:31 (281)
Ramsay, Steven A 3:24:42 (3,870)
Ramsdale, Ian M 3:25:16 (3,974)
Ramsden, Andy 4:31:36 (20,054)
Ramsden, Mark L 4:39:33 (22,090)
Ramsden, Neil A 4:07:04 (13,534)
Ramsden, Simon L 3:27:13 (4,315)
Ramsell, Chris D 2:56:41 (854)
Ramsell, Ian R 4:15:22 (15,655)
Ramsey, Gavin 4:09:24 (14,141)
Ramsey, James T 4:02:44 (12,550)
Ramsey, Julian 5:13:48 (28,648)
Ramsey, Mark W 3:56:47 (10,724)
Ramsey, Nicholas G 3:38:57 (6,433)
Ramsey Smith, David 3:33:07 (5,401)
Rance, John P 3:49:36 (8,719)
Rance, Keith J 4:03:49 (12,792)
Rance, Peter J 4:13:39 (15,203)
Rand, Steven 2:58:44 (1,034)
Randall, Andrew R 3:16:57 (2,856)
Randall, David 3:19:32 (3,169)
Randall, Edward C 4:59:24 (26,545)
Randall, James 4:09:50 (14,259)
Randall, Lucian T 4:15:57 (15,823)
Randall, Tim M 4:06:58 (13,508)
Randell, Tony M 2:52:59 (639)
Randeree, Hoosen 4:02:37 (12,520)
Randhawa, Kuldip S 3:42:12 (7,071)
Randhawa, Pirtpal S 5:05:14 (27,439)
Randhawa, Raj 4:45:50 (23,629)
Randles, Malcolm P 4:27:29 (18,950)
Randles, Stephen 4:15:20 (15,646)
Randles, Thomas M 2:53:23 (659)
Ranford, Brett T 3:35:39 (5,824)
Rankin, David J 4:28:48 (19,349)
Rankin, Eeyin 4:55:53 (25,854)
Rankin, Richard 6:37:31 (33,830)
Ransome, Tom 4:09:45 (14,242)
Ranson, Ashleigh V 4:03:10 (12,644)
Rao, Prasad G 5:40:37 (31,384)
Rapana, Luigi 3:17:21 (2,911)
Raper, Gareth D 4:54:06 (25,497)
Raphael, Michael 6:26:59 (33,598)
Rapin, Philippe 3:43:06 (7,266)
Rapson, Gregory P 4:47:04 (23,923)
Raquin, Olivier 4:07:15 (13,588)
Rasey, Jason M 4:16:53 (16,054)
Rashid, Sammy N 3:37:06 (6,081)
Rasmussen, Graeme P 2:39:20 (185)
Rastall, Ollie 3:24:14 (3,809)
Rasul, Emdad 5:03:23 (27,166)
Ratcliffe, Andrew 5:11:12 (28,295)
Ratcliffe, Andy P 4:42:50 (22,884)
Ratcliffe, George 3:13:22 (2,383)
Ratcliffe, James A 3:43:04 (7,255)
Ratcliffe, Jonathan P 2:56:20 (834)
Ratcliffe, Paul 3:27:54 (4,439)
Ratcliffe, Sam 4:22:10 (17,486)
Ratcliffe, Simon 4:16:09 (15,863)
Ratcliffe, Steven M 3:23:31 (3,709)
Ratcliffe, Timothy 3:52:29 (9,428)
Rathee, Sudhanshu 4:22:40 (17,639)
Ratheram, Jonathan M 3:23:12 (3,663)
Rato, Luis M 3:56:08 (10,522)
Rattee, James V 3:41:28 (6,932)
Ravaglia, Luca 3:47:37 (8,257)
Ravasio, Massimiliano 3:02:19 (1,331)
Ravazzani, Sergio 4:24:42 (18,194)
Raven, Jack M 4:56:09 (25,903)
Raven, Jonathan D 3:56:41 (10,684)
Raven, Kristan M 4:30:29 (19,740)
Raven, Timothy C 3:09:32 (1,945)
Ravenscroft, Simon 3:20:12 (3,249)
Ravine, James B 3:58:37 (11,341)
Rawes, David J 3:43:57 (7,449)
Rawling, Simon 3:41:09 (6,859)
Rawlings, Jonathan G 3:19:55 (3,218)
Rawlins, Enrique 4:02:14 (12,423)
Rawlinson, Alan 4:08:40 (13,961)
Rawlinson, John M 3:25:50 (4,075)
Rawlinson, Lee 4:43:38 (23,080)
Rawlinson, Robert J 4:41:26 (22,541)
Rawson, Christopher P 6:09:05 (33,083)
Rawsthorne, Matthew I 4:45:25 (23,517)
Ray, Matthew 2:37:54 (165)
Ray, Robert E 3:40:23 (6,711)
Ray, Shaun 5:32:55 (30,739)
Ray, Simon J 4:17:43 (16,284)
Raybould, Ed 3:07:59 (1,788)
Raybould, Will 3:10:28 (2,037)
Rayers, Jonathan M 4:32:24 (20,268)
Rayers, Matt R 4:30:13 (19,683)
Rayfield, David W 2:57:01 (872)
Rayment, Ewan 4:21:13 (17,231)
Raymond, Joad 3:45:47 (7,853)
Raymond-Barker, William F 5:59:14 (32,702)
Raynaud, Gilles 4:27:51 (19,040)
Rayner, Alastair J 3:05:51 (1,585)
Rayner, Andrew 4:24:07 (18,023)
Rayner, David A 3:18:26 (3,036)
Rayner, Gary R 3:00:48 (1,225)
Rayner, Graeme J 5:23:55 (29,794)
Rayner, Jeremy C 4:49:08 (24,403)
Rayner, Peter 3:14:23 (2,528)
Rayner, Richard P 3:43:12 (7,288)
Rayner, Thomas A 4:26:30 (18,667)
Raynes, Andrew 3:44:38 (7,587)
Raynes, David 4:14:47 (15,512)
Raynor, John D 3:19:42 (3,191)
Raynor, Lloyd J 4:04:37 (12,960)
Raynor, Richard T 4:13:33 (15,172)
Rea, Martin 2:59:10 (1,080)
Rea, Matthew 4:05:39 (13,213)
Rea, Tony 3:46:03 (7,899)
Read, Adrian 3:26:50 (4,250)
Read, Anthony 5:25:27 (29,985)
Read, Chris J 4:29:01 (19,402)
Read, Chris J 5:18:35 (29,239)
Read, Daniel J 3:26:58 (4,276)
Read, James H 3:28:02 (4,467)
Read, Jason S 3:41:55 (7,013)
Read, John V 4:02:22 (12,469)
Read, Kevin M 3:12:50 (2,310)
Read, Kevin R 6:30:16 (33,669)
Read, Mark E 4:29:08 (19,434)
Read, Niki L 4:29:31 (19,519)
Read, Simon A 4:23:33 (17,883)
Read, Stephen J 5:26:20 (30,077)
Read, Stuart M 4:18:07 (16,374)
Reade, Alan J 3:07:24 (1,725)
Reade, John A 5:09:04 (27,979)
Reader, Frank R 6:35:21 (33,782)
Reader, Paul T 4:12:54 (15,005)
Reader, Robert D 4:41:57 (22,663)
Readfearn, Paul 4:05:57 (13,285)
Reading, David J 4:38:16 (21,770)
Reading, Duncan J 3:49:41 (8,743)
Reading, Gary B 5:24:45 (29,881)
Reading, Paul J 3:57:26 (10,939)
Reading, Sean A 4:53:22 (25,344)
Readman, Benjamin G 3:42:01 (7,031)
Readman, Darren 4:06:11 (13,329)
Real-del-Sarte, Raphael 3:19:44 (3,197)
Reardon, Jim P 4:12:45 (14,974)
Rebecchini, Nicolo 3:08:57 (1,872)
Rebeiro, Mark E 4:55:41 (25,817)
Reber, Daniel 3:21:50 (3,462)
Reccagni, Stefano 4:11:39 (14,719)
Redden, Phil 2:47:45 (413)
Redding, Andrew J 2:44:36 (317)
Redfern, Simon 3:30:08 (4,912)
Redfern, Stuart T 3:42:37 (7,155)
Redford, Roy 7:37:38 (34,477)
Redgwell, Adam J 4:27:02 (18,824)
Redman, Gary 4:39:37 (22,100)
Redman, Thomas 4:39:38 (22,104)
Redmond, Ciaran M 6:01:24 (32,793)
Redvers, David J 3:10:29 (2,038)
Redwood, Simon 4:31:10 (19,928)
Reece, Andrew 4:35:55 (21,217)
Reece, Mark 3:43:58 (7,452)
Reece, Trevor G 3:53:24 (9,696)
Reed, David 4:07:02 (13,527)
Reed, John R 4:27:34 (18,967)
Reed, Mark K 4:02:47 (12,561)
Reed, Mark L 4:55:28 (25,777)
Reed, Michael G 5:38:15 (31,210)
Reed, Michael J 4:42:35 (22,827)
Reed, Robert J 4:21:37 (17,341)
Reed, Steven J 4:42:07 (22,701)
Reed, Stewart 4:17:30 (16,220)
Reed, William 3:13:46 (2,431)
Reeder, Anthony A 4:02:13 (12,420)
Reedy, Matthew S 2:59:13 (1,087)
Rees, Alan 3:41:21 (6,906)
Rees, Andrew 4:24:22 (18,098)
Rees, Bryan 4:28:07 (19,137)
Rees, Chris J 3:32:56 (5,378)
Rees, Christopher O 5:57:38 (32,611)
Rees, Colin J 3:29:42 (4,819)
Rees, David 5:23:53 (29,787)
Rees, Gary 4:38:38 (21,864)
Rees, Ian W 4:38:24 (21,800)
Rees, James W 4:44:12 (23,229)
Rees, John 5:12:50 (28,520)
Rees, Jonathan 3:30:19 (4,942)
Rees, Matt 3:21:06 (3,374)
Rees, Mike 5:37:38 (31,163)
Rees, Paul 4:50:31 (24,722)
Rees, Paul J 3:48:38 (8,496)
Rees, Philip A 3:26:36 (4,206)
Rees, Stephen J 4:07:33 (13,653)
Rees, Steven C 2:39:46 (196)
Rees, Stuart S 3:56:44 (10,702)
Reese, Tim 3:31:10 (5,070)
Rees-Hughes, David W 3:28:25 (4,538)
Rees-Jones, Glyn G 4:36:24 (21,344)
Reeve, Christopher A 4:43:57 (23,169)
Reeve, David M 4:56:19 (25,934)

Reeve, Matthew R....3:43:05 (7,263)
Reeve, Peter A....3:35:33 (5,800)
Reeve, Robert....4:03:38 (12,755)
Reeve, Stuart....4:30:16 (19,691)
Reeves, Andrew B....2:44:25 (309)
Reeves, Charles....4:33:46 (20,653)
Reeves, Christopher D....4:13:39 (15,203)
Reeves, David....4:23:45 (17,929)
Reeves, Gavin J....3:39:44 (6,582)
Reeves, Matt....3:45:18 (7,755)
Reeves, Matthew....4:35:54 (21,211)
Reeves, Michael J....4:35:09 (21,020)
Reeves, Paul A....5:33:27 (30,782)
Reeves, Stephen....3:40:52 (6,800)
Reeves, Stephen M....6:12:04 (33,168)
Reeves, Stuart N....2:56:59 (870)
Refaie, Ramsay R....3:57:47 (11,053)
Refstie, Erlend....4:35:00 (20,982)
Regan, Callum J....3:57:46 (11,049)
Regan, Peter M....5:24:48 (29,887)
Regnault, Christian....4:31:26 (20,010)
Regulski, Brett R....4:25:21 (18,355)
Rehman, Bobby....5:22:31 (29,664)
Rehn, Lars F....3:30:19 (4,942)
Reid, Andrew....2:54:56 (743)
Reid, Andrew....3:58:46 (11,397)
Reid, Benjamin J....3:42:38 (7,160)
Reid, Brian....5:25:19 (29,968)
Reid, Christopher....3:52:24 (9,412)
Reid, Clive S....4:16:51 (16,048)
Reid, Craig A....3:19:26 (3,151)
Reid, Douglas....3:30:34 (4,983)
Reid, Gary J....4:03:28 (12,720)
Reid, Gavin....3:13:46 (2,431)
Reid, Gavin J....2:53:15 (652)
Reid, George A....4:19:41 (16,811)
Reid, Graham R....3:49:54 (8,800)
Reid, Iain....5:55:26 (32,494)
Reid, Ian....3:13:47 (2,434)
Reid, Ian D....2:44:56 (328)
Reid, Jamie....2:41:28 (232)
Reid, Kris D....4:31:34 (20,046)
Reid, Maurice J....3:17:22 (2,916)
Reid, Neil D....3:42:22 (7,111)
Reid, Nicholas I....2:48:32 (449)
Reid, Nick J....3:42:38 (7,160)
Reid, Philip....3:35:27 (5,785)
Reid, Rob E....4:06:01 (13,294)
Reid, Stephen W....4:32:30 (20,300)
Reid, Steven J....2:49:58 (512)
Reid, Stuart D....3:20:31 (3,293)
Reid, Thomas K....3:23:20 (3,682)
Reid, Thomas W....4:40:10 (22,229)
Reid, Tristan M....7:04:50 (34,259)
Reidy, Matthew J....4:14:40 (15,487)
Reilly, Damien....4:10:26 (14,395)
Reilly, David G....3:13:56 (2,457)
Reilly, Lewis S....5:10:02 (28,150)
Reilly, Peter....5:23:40 (29,764)
Reilly, Peter A....4:25:40 (18,434)
Reiner, Donald J....5:37:47 (31,176)
Reis e Sa, Pedro....3:33:28 (5,467)
Reising, Marcel....4:55:38 (25,810)
Reith, Phillip C....3:54:04 (9,894)
Relf, Jon L....4:53:59 (25,478)
Relf, Neil D....5:34:20 (30,869)
Rendall, Andrew G....3:34:50 (5,676)
Rendall, Duncan L....4:41:55 (22,657)
Rendall, Julian....2:29:25 (64)
Rendall, Mike J....4:04:52 (13,015)
Rendell, John G....4:56:45 (26,013)
Rendle, Nicholas....4:19:50 (16,842)
Rennie, Allan....3:38:51 (6,420)
Rennie, Gavin A....3:23:51 (3,749)
Rennie, Keith J....3:54:12 (9,931)
Renny, Steven W....3:04:41 (1,494)
Renphrey, Tom A....3:36:47 (6,012)
Renshaw, Arthur W....4:04:09 (12,854)
Renshaw, Ben....4:55:42 (25,820)
Renshaw, Paul....4:00:39 (12,017)
Reppesgaard, Harald....4:37:25 (21,578)
Reppesgaard, Oeystein R....3:41:02 (6,834)
Resnick, Brian....4:55:37 (25,803)
Restrucci, Karl A....5:21:47 (29,585)
Reulland, Loic....3:44:25 (7,539)
Reuter, Markus....3:42:11 (7,068)
Reveley, Adam N....4:14:43 (15,499)
Revell, Craig J....5:25:06 (29,936)
Revell, David C....5:04:37 (27,348)
Revell, Kevin....3:00:19 (1,189)
Revie, William A....3:43:42 (7,387)
Revill, Craig I....4:50:06 (24,623)
Revill, Keith J....5:31:26 (30,606)
Revington, Nick....4:25:38 (18,422)
Revuelta, Paul D....5:59:42 (32,726)
Rey, Simon C....3:55:43 (10,409)
Reyes, Pedro Jesus....5:15:31 (28,882)
Reynal, Franck....4:02:26 (12,483)
Reynolds, Adam....4:38:53 (21,937)
Reynolds, Andrew K....4:17:16 (16,166)
Reynolds, Anthony L....3:53:50 (9,824)
Reynolds, Bryan M....3:50:14 (8,880)
Reynolds, Gavin A....3:15:51 (2,737)
Reynolds, Gavin J....3:28:28 (4,558)
Reynolds, Guy J....5:16:08 (28,950)
Reynolds, Jason P....5:00:56 (26,787)
Reynolds, John A....3:57:32 (10,964)
Reynolds, Jonathan....3:45:41 (7,831)
Reynolds, Kevin P....3:46:12 (7,927)
Reynolds, Mark A....3:42:11 (7,068)
Reynolds, Mark G....2:54:23 (715)
Reynolds, Matt D....4:36:25 (21,352)
Reynolds, Nathan M....4:07:33 (13,653)
Reynolds, Nigel....3:36:45 (6,003)
Reynolds, Paul....3:00:10 (1,175)
Reynolds, Paul....3:28:05 (4,477)
Reynolds, Paul....3:29:00 (4,669)
Reynolds, Paul K....3:59:41 (11,746)
Reynolds, Peter....4:40:54 (22,402)
Reynolds, Richard H....5:26:37 (30,112)
Reynolds, Simon....4:27:50 (19,033)
Reynolds, Steven....3:39:24 (6,519)
Reynolds, Thomas W....3:56:23 (10,594)
Reynolds, Tim D....7:07:20 (34,286)
Reynolds, Toby S....4:00:31 (11,978)
Rhodes, Andrew B....5:18:54 (29,277)
Rhodes, Gary S....5:20:19 (29,440)
Rhodes, Ian....4:20:37 (17,068)
Rhodes, Jonathan M....5:35:44 (31,002)
Rhodes, Karl D....6:22:19 (33,467)
Rhodes, Peter....4:19:41 (16,811)
Rhodes, Stephen D....3:34:20 (5,594)
Rhodes-Smith, Jonathan....4:28:35 (19,284)
Rhys-Davies, Stephen....4:20:58 (17,174)
Ribbits, Daniel S....5:08:37 (27,917)
Ribchester, Rob....4:15:25 (15,676)
Ribeiro, Rui....4:41:33 (22,565)
Ribton, Nicholas....4:07:48 (13,714)
Ricci, Arnaud....3:58:56 (11,468)
Rice, Daniel M....4:51:49 (25,010)
Rice, Frederick J....4:00:30 (11,975)
Rice, Martin....4:51:20 (24,910)
Rice, Nicholas I....3:37:03 (6,071)
Rice, Paul....4:23:12 (17,786)
Rice, Scott M....2:56:26 (838)
Rice, Sebastian J....3:37:50 (6,224)
Rice, Tim E....5:24:50 (29,893)
Rice, Tim S....4:58:10 (26,320)
Rice, Tom....4:17:09 (16,140)
Rich, Andrew J....5:19:27 (29,346)
Rich, Jonathan E....3:26:21 (4,167)
Rich, Nicholas A....4:29:03 (19,412)
Rich, Pat....3:17:40 (2,948)
Rich, Steve J....3:57:36 (10,977)
Richards, Andrew C....4:16:31 (15,965)
Richards, Anthony J....5:56:37 (32,563)
Richards, Arwel W....3:46:31 (8,009)
Richards, Christopher J....6:39:36 (33,875)
Richards, Clive J....2:46:06 (364)
Richards, David....3:45:45 (7,845)
Richards, David P....6:13:20 (33,222)
Richards, Douglas....4:52:08 (25,070)
Richards, James H....3:56:36 (10,663)
Richards, John....4:25:36 (18,413)
Richards, John E....4:50:21 (24,676)
Richards, Jon D....3:55:41 (10,399)
Richards, Jonathan M....4:01:26 (12,224)
Richards, Jonathan T....3:25:22 (3,990)
Richards, Marcus P....4:10:54 (14,522)
Richards, Michael D....3:15:19 (2,678)
Richards, Mike....4:46:42 (23,829)
Richards, Neil A....3:07:32 (1,736)
Richards, Neil M....3:53:59 (9,869)
Richards, Nigel J....4:57:52 (26,255)
Richards, Paul S....4:06:49 (13,476)
Richards, Peter....5:35:00 (30,941)
Richards, Peter W....4:51:01 (24,847)
Richards, Scott....4:34:08 (20,733)
Richards, Simon L....5:24:02 (29,812)
Richards, Tom....4:25:36 (18,413)
Richards, Tony....4:35:42 (21,168)
Richardson, Alan....3:43:46 (7,408)
Richardson, Andrew R....4:45:43 (23,592)
Richardson, Andrew S....4:43:14 (22,990)
Richardson, Colin B....3:58:47 (11,406)
Richardson, Darren....4:49:59 (24,597)
Richardson, David I....3:36:47 (6,012)
Richardson, Dean....3:58:48 (11,416)
Richardson, Eamonn P....3:45:01 (7,688)
Richardson, Geoff D....4:54:43 (25,627)
Richardson, Graeme S....5:07:43 (27,802)
Richardson, Hilary L....4:46:15 (23,727)
Richardson, James G....4:06:15 (13,346)
Richardson, Jonathan M....3:44:41 (7,597)
Richardson, Joseph P....5:07:36 (27,782)
Richardson, Julian....2:53:50 (681)
Richardson, Kevin J....4:12:21 (14,895)
Richardson, Kevin R....4:41:40 (22,608)
Richardson, Lee....4:17:27 (16,205)
Richardson, Liam A....3:01:17 (1,259)
Richardson, Matthew G....4:02:16 (12,436)
Richardson, Matthew J....5:34:58 (30,937)
Richardson, Matthew T....4:16:56 (16,070)
Richardson, Neil D....5:59:24 (32,708)
Richardson, Paul W....5:02:54 (27,098)
Richardson, Philip....3:27:42 (4,396)
Richardson, Philip M....4:39:32 (22,085)
Richardson, Simon C....2:56:52 (863)
Richardson, Stephen J....4:32:11 (20,223)
Richardson, Steven....3:37:34 (6,176)
Richardson-Perks, Tim R....3:14:31 (2,554)
Richer, Glenn J....4:51:03 (24,855)
Richer, Paul G....4:31:52 (20,130)
Richert, Jean-Claude....3:26:55 (4,266)
Riches, Andrew J....3:47:21 (8,187)
Riches, Christopher D....4:21:03 (17,197)
Riches, Mark C....3:00:18 (1,186)
Richman, Aryeh....5:33:48 (30,814)
Richman, David J....4:24:53 (18,238)
Richmond, Colin....4:16:26 (15,942)
Richmond, Graham K....4:01:41 (12,289)
Richmond, Kenny....2:29:53 (74)
Richmond, Mark....3:26:08 (4,127)
Rickard, Neville....3:12:13 (2,236)
Rickards, Lee R....3:56:58 (10,781)
Rickertsen, Maik....4:24:01 (18,000)
Ricketts, Jack D....4:41:18 (22,513)
Ricketts, James A....3:37:16 (6,118)
Rickey, Benedict E....4:32:52 (20,392)
Rickus, Michael S....3:48:41 (8,507)
Rickwood, Simon L....4:09:17 (14,112)
Riddick, Karl N....3:13:31 (2,396)
Riddington, Bruce....3:50:46 (9,002)
Riddle, Martin....4:08:49 (13,993)
Riddle, Steven....4:21:15 (17,236)
Riddoch, Neil....3:34:59 (5,700)
Ridehalgh, Anthony I....4:20:09 (16,928)
Rideout, James S....3:11:34 (2,158)
Rider, Richard....6:23:54 (33,514)
Ridgeway, Paul B....3:09:38 (1,955)
Ridgway, Timothy C....4:01:23 (12,210)
Ridgwell, Oliver J....5:21:16 (29,530)
Ridler, Nigel....3:54:54 (10,160)
Ridley, Donald....5:03:45 (27,219)
Ridley, Jason....3:49:55 (8,804)
Ridsdale, Brian....6:12:04 (33,168)
Ridsdale, Dan....4:00:19 (11,929)
Ridsdale, Geoff....3:21:36 (3,434)
Ridsdale, Neil....5:01:02 (26,803)

Ridsdale, Tom N....3:22:12 (3,514)
Riedlinger, Csaba 3:57:52 (11,079)
Riefler, Oliver H....2:47:31 (402)
Rielander, Ian....4:47:52 (24,109)
Rigarlsford, Giles A....3:37:54 (6,240)
Rigby, Ian....4:26:50 (18,765)
Rigby, Oliver J....3:43:06 (7,266)
Rigby, Russel L....4:16:18 (15,903)
Rigby, Thomas F....3:48:39 (8,500)
Rigden, Tom I....4:50:00 (24,604)
Rigg, Nigel K....3:11:26 (2,140)
Riggens, Stephen G....4:42:33 (22,820)
Righetto, Marco....3:58:20 (11,236)
Riley, Benjamin....5:08:21 (27,865)
Riley, Christopher J....4:56:27 (25,957)
Riley, John A....4:54:15 (25,534)
Riley, Joseph L....4:21:22 (17,261)
Riley, Matthew G....4:29:55 (19,613)
Riley, Neal....4:27:00 (18,812)
Riley, Patrick....3:01:09 (1,252)
Riley, Pete....2:18:21 (18)
Riley, Richard P....3:14:33 (2,559)
Riley-Jordan, Peter B....4:35:39 (21,152)
Riminton, Robert....4:34:24 (20,799)
Rimmer, Michael....3:32:46 (5,355)
Rimmer, Paul W....4:32:52 (20,392)
Rimmer, Shaun A....5:27:57 (30,259)
Rinderknecht, Paul....3:39:57 (6,628)
Ring, Chris....3:53:53 (9,833)
Ringrose, Colin D....3:41:51 (7,001)
Ringshaw, Matthew J....5:28:14 (30,297)
Riordan, Doninic J....4:01:02 (12,118)
Ripa di Meana, Aimone....3:35:19 (5,757)
Ririe, David B....3:42:37 (7,155)
Risby, Brendan P....5:01:43 (26,916)
Riseborough, Andrew J....4:25:59 (18,531)
Risidore, Anthony....5:31:40 (30,631)
Risley-Duhrsen, Thomas R....3:52:07 (9,345)
Ritchie, Gavin J....5:06:15 (27,591)
Ritchie, Mark....3:53:00 (9,572)
Ritchie, Neil....3:08:00 (1,790)
Ritchie, Roderick J....3:41:02 (6,834)
Ritchie, Will R....3:11:19 (2,129)
Ritter, Gordon....4:21:12 (17,225)
Rius, Sebastien....4:58:05 (26,301)
Rivas May, Marco....3:19:00 (3,100)
Riverain, Eric T....4:17:34 (16,238)
Riverain, Pacal R....4:27:12 (18,871)
Rivers, Brian....3:40:22 (6,708)
Rivers, Terry M....3:36:34 (5,978)
Rivers, Timothy J....3:40:11 (6,669)
Rix, Matthew C....5:09:41 (28,088)
Rix, Michael W....2:56:44 (858)
Rixon, Karl D....3:22:31 (3,570)
Rizzo, Francesco....4:56:13 (25,919)
Rizzo Gomez, César H....3:35:08 (5,729)
Roach, Chris L....6:11:04 (33,143)
Roach, Christopher J....3:30:25 (4,955)
Roach, John....5:00:26 (26,700)
Roake, Simon....4:03:12 (12,654)
Roan, Alan R....4:47:40 (24,059)
Roarty, John J....5:11:23 (28,315)
Roarty, Paul J....2:43:08 (272)
Roast, Paul H....5:29:30 (30,425)
Robb, Andrew....3:52:01 (9,305)
Robb, Tim....4:45:44 (23,598)
Robbins, Andrew....2:44:28 (310)
Robbins, Conrad....4:57:04 (26,098)
Robbins, Darren J....4:50:19 (24,670)
Robbins, Jon P....4:14:01 (15,310)
Robbins, Jonathan G....3:38:38 (6,377)
Robbins, Philip J....3:49:11 (8,622)
Robbins, Richard W....3:08:06 (1,803)
Robbins, Stephen P....4:44:48 (23,367)
Robbins, Stuart....3:38:47 (6,405)
Robbins Cherry, Jos....5:05:27 (27,464)
Rober, Gustav A....4:13:39 (15,203)
Roberson, Paul....2:49:27 (488)
Robers-Thomson, Harold J....3:59:33 (11,688)
Robert, Alan J....4:52:31 (25,151)
Robert, Iain A....2:54:58 (745)
Roberts, Alan....5:49:02 (32,056)
Roberts, Alan F....3:42:55 (7,214)
Roberts, Andrew F....4:56:33 (25,980)
Roberts, Andrew J....3:35:06 (5,725)
Roberts, Barry J....3:45:04 (7,700)
Roberts, Barry J....5:18:33 (29,234)
Roberts, Christopher J....6:05:51 (32,968)
Roberts, Clive B....3:57:29 (10,948)
Roberts, Daniel M....4:13:33 (15,172)
Roberts, Darren....4:50:31 (24,722)
Roberts, David....3:23:53 (3,758)
Roberts, David B....4:14:28 (15,443)
Roberts, David G....4:20:00 (16,884)
Roberts, David L....4:39:11 (22,022)
Roberts, David W....5:26:24 (30,088)
Roberts, Emlyn G....4:24:59 (18,259)
Roberts, Emyr M....2:50:50 (545)
Roberts, Gareth....4:30:45 (19,816)
Roberts, Glyn....4:20:41 (17,089)
Roberts, Graham....4:34:36 (20,845)
Roberts, Hugh C....3:38:05 (6,281)
Roberts, Ian....3:51:19 (9,130)
Roberts, Ioan W....4:13:32 (15,169)
Roberts, James L....3:18:38 (3,059)
Roberts, James L....4:19:18 (16,704)
Roberts, James S....2:53:44 (677)
Roberts, John....2:54:24 (717)
Roberts, Kevin G....4:47:15 (23,969)
Roberts, Kristian A....4:03:30 (12,727)
Roberts, Luke D....3:52:43 (9,484)
Roberts, Mark....3:50:02 (8,830)
Roberts, Mark H....2:32:08 (86)
Roberts, Mark J....5:17:24 (29,109)
Roberts, Martin S....3:51:09 (9,086)
Roberts, Matthew A....3:25:34 (4,025)
Roberts, Neil....5:30:54 (30,557)
Roberts, Neil R....5:18:42 (29,253)
Roberts, Nicholas....5:11:16 (28,305)
Roberts, Nigel D....5:26:47 (30,122)
Roberts, Paul....4:18:18 (16,434)
Roberts, Paul A....4:04:37 (12,960)
Roberts, Paul E....4:25:41 (18,438)
Roberts, Peter A....4:47:44 (24,080)
Roberts, Peter T....4:20:10 (16,936)
Roberts, Peter W....4:03:07 (12,635)
Roberts, Philip J....4:23:52 (17,957)
Roberts, Richard....3:18:03 (2,991)
Roberts, Stephen J....4:46:58 (23,900)
Roberts, Stephen S....4:48:56 (24,354)
Roberts, Stephen W....3:25:16 (3,974)
Roberts, Steve....3:23:52 (3,755)
Roberts, Steven J....4:22:52 (17,691)
Roberts, Stewart....4:34:38 (20,855)
Roberts, Tom....5:33:51 (30,820)
Roberts, Vincent J....4:16:57 (16,074)
Roberts, William G....4:45:16 (23,487)
Roberts, Wyn....4:46:13 (23,717)
Robertshaw, Keith....2:45:20 (344)
Robertshaw, Tom....3:01:48 (1,299)
Robertson, Colin....3:40:34 (6,741)
Robertson, Craig....4:26:50 (18,765)
Robertson, Craig....4:34:45 (20,891)
Robertson, Gary S....4:12:59 (15,027)
Robertson, George A....4:35:17 (21,051)
Robertson, Gordon....3:59:16 (11,585)
Robertson, Grant A....4:05:29 (13,172)
Robertson, Greg....4:14:12 (15,367)
Robertson, Ian D....3:18:12 (3,008)
Robertson, Ian M....3:29:10 (4,707)
Robertson, Jim....4:56:53 (26,047)
Robertson, Jim F....3:39:42 (6,576)
Robertson, Joedy R....5:10:02 (28,150)
Robertson, John R....2:47:39 (408)
Robertson, Kevin J....2:29:03 (57)
Robertson, Lee L....6:21:35 (33,447)
Robertson, Neil R....4:59:11 (26,512)
Robertson, Neil W....5:21:32 (29,560)
Robertson, Paul....4:02:37 (12,520)
Robertson, Paul....4:23:16 (17,804)
Robertson, Roderick E....4:11:14 (14,615)
Robertson, Simon M....3:44:05 (7,470)
Robertson, Stuart J....4:42:38 (22,840)
Robertson, Thomas....4:56:53 (26,047)
Robertson, Thomas I....2:57:01 (872)
Robins, Ian N....3:34:20 (5,594)
Robins, Paul....4:12:02 (14,816)
Robins, Steve....3:37:35 (6,180)
Robins, William T....3:56:49 (10,730)
Robinson, Alexander....4:22:10 (17,486)
Robinson, Andy P....3:18:03 (2,991)
Robinson, Barry I....4:30:47 (19,828)
Robinson, Barry J....3:55:50 (10,446)
Robinson, Brett....3:23:29 (3,706)
Robinson, Chris M....4:03:03 (12,620)
Robinson, Dale....3:53:33 (9,726)
Robinson, Dan....2:13:10 (13)
Robinson, Daniel....5:03:12 (27,131)
Robinson, Daniel J....4:36:47 (21,437)
Robinson, Daniel V....3:01:07 (1,249)
Robinson, David....5:07:29 (27,762)
Robinson, David A....2:57:37 (912)
Robinson, David G....3:59:44 (11,759)
Robinson, David J....3:30:30 (4,971)
Robinson, David K....3:06:51 (1,669)
Robinson, David N....4:19:04 (16,647)
Robinson, Edward....4:21:18 (17,254)
Robinson, Elliott C....5:10:13 (28,178)
Robinson, Frank W....4:55:47 (25,836)
Robinson, Graham D....3:45:57 (7,883)
Robinson, Ian C....4:52:33 (25,156)
Robinson, Islay....5:34:24 (30,874)
Robinson, James N....3:07:22 (1,720)
Robinson, John L....4:27:14 (18,883)
Robinson, Jonathan....5:02:42 (27,064)
Robinson, Jonathan J....3:37:49 (6,219)
Robinson, Kevin J....5:43:21 (31,597)
Robinson, Lee....4:21:17 (17,249)
Robinson, Luke W....3:39:39 (6,565)
Robinson, Mark....4:14:13 (15,373)
Robinson, Mark A....4:25:03 (18,275)
Robinson, Matthew....3:28:25 (4,538)
Robinson, Michael E....4:44:30 (23,303)
Robinson, Michael R....3:35:24 (5,775)
Robinson, Nicholas D....3:49:04 (8,593)
Robinson, Nicholas V....4:30:18 (19,698)
Robinson, Nick C....4:41:06 (22,460)
Robinson, Owain B....3:28:48 (4,624)
Robinson, Paul....4:17:41 (16,276)
Robinson, Paul....4:50:54 (24,824)
Robinson, Paul H....3:34:57 (5,694)
Robinson, Paul M....3:42:33 (7,145)
Robinson, Paul M....5:24:01 (29,808)
Robinson, Peter A....4:39:54 (22,166)
Robinson, Peter J....3:56:42 (10,690)
Robinson, Peter K....4:46:33 (23,789)
Robinson, Phillip M....3:50:30 (8,929)
Robinson, Raymond G....3:47:04 (8,125)
Robinson, Richard B....3:47:14 (8,165)
Robinson, Richard C....4:49:33 (24,491)
Robinson, Roger T....4:53:02 (25,280)
Robinson, Sam A....4:22:50 (17,679)
Robinson, Scott....3:47:36 (8,251)
Robinson, Stewart N....3:34:14 (5,580)
Robinson, Thomas....4:42:32 (22,816)
Robinson, Tom....4:09:19 (14,122)
Robinson, Tom....5:53:51 (32,395)
Robiot, Jocelyn....4:44:15 (23,241)
Robiot, Olivier....4:44:15 (23,241)
Robles, Jorge....5:19:30 (29,354)
Roblin, Mark....4:44:41 (23,342)
Robling, Mark R....5:32:53 (30,737)
Robson, Colin E....5:48:28 (32,009)
Robson, Daniel J....4:16:58 (16,082)
Robson, Dean....3:58:08 (11,157)
Robson, Denreigh....4:25:38 (18,422)
Robson, John A....4:52:37 (25,174)
Robson, John N....3:55:26 (10,316)
Robson, Mark D....4:41:54 (22,652)
Robson, Rich....4:45:58 (23,665)
Robson, Richard....3:58:50 (11,436)
Roby, Neil S....4:11:30 (14,679)
Roccas, Emmanuel J....4:58:46 (26,436)
Rocchelli, Mario....3:45:13 (7,733)
Roche, Angus A....3:47:45 (8,286)
Roche, Chris....4:43:42 (23,102)
Roche, Chris N....4:19:43 (16,818)
Roche, Francis....4:13:38 (15,198)
Roche, Maxwell....3:17:27 (2,928)

Roche, Paul D.	7:05:02 (34,262)	
Roche, Stephen	6:37:50 (33,838)	
Rodaway, Keith	5:21:13 (29,525)	
Roden, Andrew J	4:09:52 (14,271)	
Roden, Scott	4:42:15 (22,742)	
Rodero Nunez, José R.	3:41:56 (7,015)	
Rodger, Andy	4:53:27 (25,360)	
Rodger, Graeme	5:05:38 (27,503)	
Rodger, Mark D	4:20:21 (16,985)	
Rodgers, Ian G	3:20:56 (3,348)	
Rodgers, James	4:11:51 (14,769)	
Rodgers, Malcolm	4:16:34 (15,975)	
Rodgers, Martin C	4:31:33 (20,039)	
Rodgers, Samuel	4:20:15 (16,962)	
Rodgers, Sean	4:38:02 (21,721)	
Rodier, Christophe	3:40:47 (6,778)	
Rodourn, Paul R	3:04:15 (1,471)	
Rodrigues, Jean-Christophe E	3:39:26 (6,525)	
Rodrigues, Mervyn A	3:31:09 (5,067)	
Rodrigues, Stephen G	4:16:12 (15,874)	
Rodriguez, Antonio C	4:01:58 (12,353)	
Rodriguez, Wuilliams	3:30:52 (5,033)	
Rodriguez-Torres, Jorge	6:15:38 (33,283)	
Rodway, Jeffrey D	3:54:36 (10,071)	
Rodwell, Peter J	4:06:43 (13,455)	
Roe, Damon S	6:14:05 (33,243)	
Roe, James C	3:52:22 (9,401)	
Roe, Philip	3:44:58 (7,675)	
Roe, Richard R	4:11:14 (14,615)	
Roebuck, Mark J	5:00:54 (26,779)	
Roelandt, Michel	5:48:28 (32,009)	
Roelofse, Natale C	3:52:16 (9,380)	
Roets, Michael	3:47:41 (8,276)	
Roff, Keith G	4:16:07 (15,858)	
Roffey, Terry A	3:55:57 (10,477)	
Rogan, Chris J	5:39:12 (31,277)	
Rogers, Christopher J	3:51:46 (9,241)	
Rogers, Colin A	4:20:23 (16,990)	
Rogers, Craig D	4:26:13 (18,585)	
Rogers, Daniel S	4:43:50 (23,132)	
Rogers, David A	5:12:45 (28,502)	
Rogers, David G	3:58:57 (11,473)	
Rogers, Dennis	4:34:08 (20,733)	
Rogers, Graham	3:44:16 (7,505)	
Rogers, Grahame P	6:07:20 (33,029)	
Rogers, Ian	3:59:19 (11,602)	
Rogers, Ian M	4:36:35 (21,388)	
Rogers, Joel H	4:37:32 (21,600)	
Rogers, Keith F	5:27:26 (30,196)	
Rogers, Lee E	4:48:03 (24,159)	
Rogers, Mark	4:23:19 (17,820)	
Rogers, Mark J	5:36:11 (31,051)	
Rogers, Nick	4:16:30 (15,959)	
Rogers, Nigel M	3:33:51 (5,526)	
Rogers, Paul G	3:34:49 (5,669)	
Rogers, Peter	2:53:52 (683)	
Rogers, Peter J	3:52:57 (9,553)	
Rogers, Philip A	3:12:09 (2,227)	
Rogers, Roy T	6:49:12 (34,061)	
Rogers, Sean C	3:17:21 (2,911)	
Rogers, Simon P	4:20:00 (16,884)	
Rogers, Stephen P	3:35:47 (5,841)	
Rogers, Steven	4:35:45 (21,177)	
Rogers, Stuart J	5:28:39 (30,338)	
Rogerson, Ian D	4:32:13 (20,233)	
Rogerson, Keith E	5:15:21 (28,860)	
Rogerson, Nigel	3:09:46 (1,967)	
Rojas-Giraldo, Carlos A	5:16:58 (29,058)	
Roles, Matthew P	5:41:23 (31,452)	
Rolfe, John	4:32:48 (20,374)	
Rolfe, Les J	3:18:30 (3,048)	
Rolfe, Tim	4:28:09 (19,151)	
Roma, Nicola	4:33:51 (20,671)	
Roman, José F	3:49:08 (8,611)	
Roman Pino, Juan C	5:12:29 (28,461)	
Romano, Antonio	3:39:57 (6,628)	
Romanowski, Perry T	3:35:36 (5,813)	
Ronaldson, Simon B	4:05:07 (13,074)	
Ronayne, Ian M	2:59:55 (1,161)	
Ronchetti, Nicola	3:02:32 (1,343)	
Ronen, Rami	4:15:31 (15,711)	
Ronksley, Andrew M	5:08:01 (27,827)	
Ronnan, Andrew	5:10:48 (28,250)	
Rooke, Nathan J	3:59:47 (11,774)	
Rooke, Steven J	3:17:17 (2,901)	
Rooney, Frank S	3:05:24 (1,547)	
Rooney, Robert W	4:12:02 (14,816)	
Roost, Ben	4:07:55 (13,758)	
Rootjes, Kees M	2:59:36 (1,129)	
Roper, Daniel E	3:53:12 (9,640)	
Roper, David	4:53:37 (25,404)	
Roper, Edward B	5:33:32 (30,788)	
Roper, Giles T	4:21:37 (17,341)	
Roper, Goy	2:57:02 (875)	
Roper, Ian	5:08:08 (27,836)	
Roper, James R	3:44:33 (7,563)	
Roper, Jon	3:43:50 (7,419)	
Roper, Martin J	4:42:12 (22,723)	
Roper, Miles	4:07:25 (13,618)	
Roper, Peter L	5:16:14 (28,964)	
Roper, Tom	4:28:12 (19,171)	
Ros Camara, Federico	2:54:36 (725)	
Rosak, Anthony R	2:51:31 (573)	
Rosam, Jason	6:37:08 (33,824)	
Roscoe, Andrei P	4:24:15 (18,072)	
Roscoe, Daren R	3:42:26 (7,124)	
Rose, Alistair M	3:42:10 (7,061)	
Rose, Andrew M	4:53:38 (25,408)	
Rose, Anthony J	4:30:09 (19,667)	
Rose, Ben	4:02:20 (12,454)	
Rose, Chris	4:53:17 (25,329)	
Rose, David	5:01:33 (26,880)	
Rose, David A	3:04:09 (1,462)	
Rose, David J	5:01:53 (26,942)	
Rose, David M	4:01:26 (12,224)	
Rose, Glyn R	5:17:02 (29,066)	
Rose, Ian	4:43:28 (23,035)	
Rose, James B	5:24:19 (29,841)	
Rose, James D	4:47:20 (23,996)	
Rose, Martin D	3:33:44 (5,512)	
Rose, Nathan C	3:54:30 (10,034)	
Rose, Nick J	6:01:44 (32,809)	
Rose, Paul J	2:44:22 (307)	
Rose, Philip	3:44:14 (7,496)	
Rose, Philip J	4:02:17 (12,444)	
Rose, Richard	4:13:38 (15,198)	
Rose, Stuart	4:02:55 (12,588)	
Rose, Tom J	4:47:14 (23,967)	
Roseborne, Nicholas	4:10:44 (14,475)	
Rosell, Martin J	4:03:35 (12,742)	
Rosenbach, Jonathan T	3:08:03 (1,795)	
Rosenbach, Lee S	3:54:24 (9,994)	
Rosenbach, Philip W	3:57:02 (10,805)	
Rosenbaum, Josh S	3:56:09 (10,528)	
Rosenberg, Stuart	5:02:51 (27,086)	
Rosendale, Philip J	5:56:03 (32,525)	
Roseneeld, David J	3:54:24 (9,994)	
Rosenstein, Andrew P	3:55:32 (10,350)	
Rosenstrom, Jan	3:46:20 (7,960)	
Rosie, Andrew M	3:37:06 (6,081)	
Rosier, Bendit F	2:54:19 (713)	
Rosinski, Zbigniew	3:20:07 (3,236)	
Ross, Alasdair R	4:31:53 (20,135)	
Ross, Alastair W	4:10:33 (14,423)	
Ross, Andy	4:18:05 (16,368)	
Ross, Anthony	5:39:54 (31,325)	
Ross, David P	3:35:43 (5,834)	
Ross, George	4:40:01 (22,186)	
Ross, George J	4:47:36 (24,044)	
Ross, Graeme C	4:22:12 (17,495)	
Ross, Jim F	3:30:38 (4,989)	
Ross, Joe A	4:35:29 (21,108)	
Ross, Mark J	4:08:13 (13,833)	
Ross, Michael E	6:15:29 (33,275)	
Ross, Simon J	4:31:58 (20,164)	
Ross, Stuart B	3:47:32 (8,227)	
Ross Gower, Sam	3:51:01 (9,052)	
Rossall, Stephen G	3:55:34 (10,365)	
Rosser, David R	5:19:51 (29,396)	
Rosser, Stephen J	4:07:10 (13,568)	
Rosset, Michel	3:59:28 (11,662)	
Ross-Gardner, Paul A	5:25:15 (29,958)	
Rossi, Armand	3:28:20 (4,523)	
Rossi, Stefano	4:12:17 (14,881)	
Rossington, Gary	4:06:36 (13,428)	
Rossiter, Andrew C	3:55:50 (10,446)	
Rossiter, Daniel J	3:41:16 (6,891)	
Rostance, Philip	4:15:56 (15,819)	
Rostern, Paul	3:13:02 (2,338)	
Roth, Alexander	3:35:15 (5,747)	
Rothe, Carsten	3:14:39 (2,580)	
Rotheram, Nicholas P	3:36:16 (5,927)	
Rothery, Paul	4:35:01 (20,988)	
Rothwell, Alex C	3:42:26 (7,124)	
Rothwell, Simon J	3:13:21 (2,381)	
Rotondo, Giuseppe	5:22:48 (29,685)	
Rottenburg, Alexander T	5:27:20 (30,184)	
Rouffy, Cedric	3:12:04 (2,318)	
Roughton, Mark A	4:07:21 (13,603)	
Roumen, Frans J	4:04:52 (13,015)	
Rounce, Phil	4:48:01 (24,154)	
Round, Anton	3:35:22 (5,771)	
Round, Derek T	4:50:32 (24,727)	
Round, Matt A	3:30:06 (4,906)	
Round, Stephen J	3:09:06 (1,894)	
Roure, Patrick	3:26:35 (4,202)	
Rourke, Simon M	3:47:28 (8,215)	
Rouse, Andrew	5:14:31 (28,741)	
Rouse, Stephen	3:49:36 (8,719)	
Rousselot, Swany	3:31:20 (5,105)	
Rousset, Pierre	3:39:47 (6,594)	
Routex, Jean Paul	4:34:09 (20,739)	
Routledge, George	5:48:51 (32,037)	
Routley, Luke J	4:58:36 (26,400)	
Roux, Jean-Marc	3:32:43 (5,346)	
Roux, Michel	3:28:27 (4,552)	
Rovelli, Benito	4:37:21 (21,560)	
Row, Ian P	5:26:36 (30,110)	
Rowan, Matthew	3:20:32 (3,295)	
Rowbotham, Neil	4:44:44 (23,352)	
Rowden, David J	3:03:46 (1,436)	
Rowe, Aaron	3:47:32 (8,227)	
Rowe, Alex R	2:51:29 (570)	
Rowe, Andrew J	3:51:18 (9,123)	
Rowe, Christopher J	4:49:59 (24,597)	
Rowe, Clifford G	5:31:14 (30,592)	
Rowe, Dave	4:52:14 (25,090)	
Rowe, David	3:35:20 (5,760)	
Rowe, David J	3:40:38 (6,747)	
Rowe, David P	3:53:33 (9,726)	
Rowe, Ian T	3:19:06 (3,109)	
Rowe, James S	5:42:51 (31,560)	
Rowe, John A	3:52:05 (9,327)	
Rowe, Michael S	4:36:32 (21,378)	
Rowe, Peter M	3:53:32 (9,719)	
Rowe, Philip	4:23:51 (17,953)	
Rowe, Raymond	5:42:04 (31,503)	
Rowe, Robin M	4:04:03 (12,843)	
Rowe, Simon J	3:11:06 (2,105)	
Rowe, Tim N	3:47:39 (8,270)	
Rowell, Barry M	4:44:24 (23,275)	
Rowell, Ben	3:59:10 (11,548)	
Rowett, James A	3:21:57 (3,483)	
Rowland, Andrew J	2:54:20 (714)	
Rowland, Colin P	5:09:55 (28,132)	
Rowland, Ian	2:54:53 (739)	
Rowland, Michael J	5:44:59 (31,766)	
Rowland, Robert A	2:49:06 (468)	
Rowland, Stewart	5:13:29 (28,607)	
Rowland-Jones, John R	4:59:37 (26,579)	
Rowlands, Dan J	2:58:01 (951)	
Rowlands, David	6:28:20 (33,630)	
Rowlands, David A	3:53:44 (9,783)	
Rowlands, Glenn N	4:26:33 (18,679)	
Rowlands, Kevin	4:14:38 (15,478)	
Rowlands, Peter F	4:47:53 (24,120)	
Rowlandson, Mark N	4:28:28 (19,252)	
Rowlands-Roberts, Matthew S	4:15:45 (15,768)	
Rowley, Chris R	3:58:50 (11,436)	
Rowley, Colin	5:14:06 (28,686)	
Rowley, John R	3:30:36 (4,986)	
Rowley, Paul	3:25:47 (4,067)	
Rowley, Richard J	2:51:39 (579)	
Rowlinson, Paul A	3:38:21 (6,327)	
Rowlinson, Paul D	4:13:49 (15,254)	
Rowney, Stuart J	3:58:57 (11,473)	
Rowson, David A	4:11:00 (14,543)	
Roxburgh, Oliver	4:23:44 (17,922)	
Roy, Steve M	4:22:17 (17,517)	

Roy, Zachary W....4:16:47 (16,029)
Royden, Barry M....2:37:55 (166)
Royer, Gerd....3:35:21 (5,764)
Royle, Neil G....4:29:35 (19,537)
Royle, Timothy J....6:02:54 (32,845)
Ruane, Milo....4:06:57 (13,504)
Ruane, Sean....4:16:35 (15,980)
Rubio Beloqui, Juan B....3:15:16 (2,667)
Rucklidge, Paul....4:56:29 (25,967)
Rudd, Ian N....4:13:45 (15,240)
Ruddock, James I....4:24:13 (18,056)
Ruddock, Matthew J....5:25:54 (30,021)
Ruddy, Mark....5:42:25 (31,528)
Rudge, Anthony L....4:26:23 (18,629)
Rudgyard, Iain D....5:07:38 (27,788)
Rudkin, Kevin P....4:07:48 (13,714)
Rudman, Jason M....2:53:20 (657)
Rufer, Rolf....4:29:31 (19,519)
Ruff, Craig M....4:44:48 (23,367)
Ruff, Keith P....3:46:03 (7,899)
Ruffell, Andrew....3:25:14 (3,967)
Ruffell, Richard H....3:24:03 (3,785)
Ruffle, Ged....3:18:16 (3,012)
Ruffle, Steve....5:00:35 (26,716)
Ruffley, Mike....5:19:38 (29,377)
Rugg, Tom C....4:12:28 (14,920)
Ruggeri, Pietgiorgio....3:52:13 (9,363)
Ruggeri, Theirry J....3:52:15 (9,375)
Ruggiero, Pasquale....3:38:37 (6,374)
Ruiz D Bustillo Pont, Juan....3:40:10 (6,666)
Rule, Graham P....6:06:56 (33,014)
Rumbelow, Nick A....3:06:42 (1,656)
Rumble, Simon J....5:05:42 (27,511)
Rumbold, John L....3:13:55 (2,454)
Rumney, Brian E....6:22:48 (33,483)
Rumsey, Steve....4:27:25 (18,936)
Runarsson, Gudbjartur....6:01:12 (32,786)
Runciman, Edward R....6:19:46 (33,391)
Runciman, Lee R....4:11:55 (14,784)
Runtz, Stephen J....4:00:29 (11,969)
Ruocco, Michael J....4:08:21 (13,869)
Rusch, Daniel....2:52:57 (636)
Rushmer, Gary....3:15:15 (2,664)
Rushton, Ian C....4:02:09 (12,404)
Russ, Andrew J....5:10:53 (28,263)
Russ, Peter A....5:43:23 (31,599)
Russel, John A....4:20:53 (17,147)
Russell, Alex....3:51:19 (9,130)
Russell, Alex M....3:59:13 (11,568)
Russell, Alfie....4:38:54 (21,941)
Russell, Andrew P....3:46:26 (7,988)
Russell, Andrew R....4:00:43 (12,039)
Russell, Andrew W....4:30:19 (19,702)
Russell, Andy D....4:40:20 (22,269)
Russell, Clive J....3:11:42 (2,174)
Russell, David J....4:20:32 (17,040)
Russell, David P....4:39:08 (22,011)
Russell, Gareth W....5:25:23 (29,976)
Russell, George....3:16:09 (2,768)
Russell, Iain D....4:51:20 (24,910)
Russell, Ian P....4:51:04 (24,860)
Russell, James....6:36:51 (33,818)
Russell, John....5:13:02 (28,547)
Russell, John R....3:26:10 (4,132)
Russell, John W....3:27:42 (4,396)
Russell, Keith J....2:46:14 (367)
Russell, Kevin J....4:19:07 (16,660)
Russell, Mark....5:02:10 (26,980)
Russell, Mark K....4:28:10 (19,159)
Russell, Michael....3:39:44 (6,582)
Russell, Michael....4:44:10 (23,219)
Russell, Mike....4:10:56 (14,531)
Russell, Nigel P....4:20:41 (17,089)
Russell, Paul....4:23:06 (17,754)
Russell, Ryan....4:04:01 (12,838)
Russell, Shaune D....3:07:43 (1,753)
Russell, Simon M....4:20:39 (17,080)
Russell, Tim D....4:26:17 (18,605)
Russell, William....4:23:46 (17,937)
Russo, Salvatore....4:10:16 (14,356)
Russon, Christopher L....3:37:08 (6,086)
Rustichelli, Maurizio....4:41:39 (22,598)
Ruston, Stuart R....3:33:58 (5,543)
Rusyn, Stephen....3:38:38 (6,377)
Ruthe, Ben....2:52:46 (625)
Ruthenberg, Juergen P....5:23:57 (29,799)
Rutley, Andrew....4:04:17 (12,882)
Rutt, Carl....3:52:21 (9,396)
Rutter, Arnaud....4:28:36 (19,289)
Rutter, Graeme A....4:01:55 (12,343)
Rutter, Jon....3:41:19 (6,901)
Rutter, Mark P....5:01:07 (26,814)
Rutter, Michael F....4:12:42 (14,962)
Rutter, Neil E....4:14:29 (15,446)
Rutter, Paul....3:21:48 (3,458)
Rutter, Thomas....4:37:16 (21,539)
Rutterford, Alan J....4:31:46 (20,091)
Ryall, Samuel....2:45:24 (347)
Ryan, Alan....5:06:37 (27,638)
Ryan, Andrew....4:42:06 (22,695)
Ryan, Andrew J....4:08:30 (13,909)
Ryan, Anthony F....6:05:27 (32,947)
Ryan, Damian M....3:20:38 (3,310)
Ryan, Declan....4:27:27 (18,941)
Ryan, Gerry M....5:08:16 (27,853)
Ryan, James C....4:51:15 (24,893)
Ryan, John C....4:01:44 (12,302)
Ryan, Jonathan P....4:21:32 (17,315)
Ryan, Michael J....4:01:18 (12,184)
Ryan, Michael J....4:22:14 (17,506)
Ryan, Neil....4:13:52 (15,266)
Ryan, Nick P....4:12:59 (15,027)
Ryan, Paul B....4:57:52 (26,255)
Ryan, Peter P....5:50:05 (32,134)
Ryan, Richard J....3:24:22 (3,826)
Ryan, Robert J....5:13:03 (28,550)
Ryan, Shane....4:23:59 (17,987)
Ryan, Stephen....4:46:09 (23,700)
Ryan, Thomas....4:30:59 (19,878)
Rybka, Karsten....2:57:54 (936)
Ryder, Clive S....3:20:56 (3,348)
Ryder, David A....3:41:13 (6,878)
Ryder, Peter C....2:52:24 (613)
Ryder, Steve....4:04:56 (13,035)
Rye, Andrew E....3:00:43 (1,218)
Rye, Jonathan P....5:32:42 (30,719)
Rye, Joseph M....2:44:58 (329)
Ryffel, Markus....3:53:32 (9,719)
Rylatt, Matt N....3:30:40 (4,993)
Ryles, Nicholas D....3:34:19 (5,590)
Ryman, Paul....6:27:18 (33,607)
Rysdale, Andrew....4:53:47 (25,437)
Rysdale, Edward J....3:45:34 (7,806)
Sabey, Darren....4:25:02 (18,271)
Sabey, David....4:13:19 (15,122)
Sabharwal, Hari H....3:41:43 (6,969)
Sabino, Giacomo....4:10:32 (14,418)
Sabino, Nuno....4:47:04 (23,923)
Sabir, Waqar S....6:06:31 (33,006)
Sachse, Matthias....3:36:29 (5,966)
Sacks, Steven E....4:52:16 (25,096)
Sadigh, Parviz L....4:27:21 (18,916)
Sadler, David....5:07:40 (27,794)
Sadler, Duncan T....3:18:03 (2,991)
Sadler, Kevin....4:56:06 (25,892)
Sadler, Michael....3:22:18 (3,532)
Sadler, Steve....3:45:18 (7,755)
Sadohree, Mike....5:32:04 (30,670)
Sadrian, Luke A....3:16:34 (2,820)
Saevarsson, Birgir....2:38:10 (171)
Saffery, Graham P....4:23:30 (17,867)
Sagar, Richard M....5:04:41 (27,354)
Sage, Gary L....3:25:31 (4,017)
Saggers, Chris P....4:41:17 (22,509)
Saggers, Mark J....2:55:42 (787)
Saggu, Gurpreet S....5:41:59 (31,496)
Sahman, Dave I....4:42:12 (22,723)
Saill, Anthony D....3:54:34 (10,060)
Sainsbury, Timothy J....5:34:14 (30,861)
Saint Onge, John E....4:44:36 (23,321)
Saitas, Jeffrey A....3:27:57 (4,452)
Sakamoto, Ezio....4:43:38 (23,080)
Saker, Andrew M....4:38:56 (21,954)
Sakpoba, Alex....5:33:58 (30,831)
Salam, Abdul....3:31:25 (5,120)
Salame Calderon, Francisco....3:01:08 (1,251)
Salaris, Antonio F....2:41:14 (226)
Salawu, Adebambo....6:14:34 (33,259)
Sale, Antonio....4:18:43 (16,556)
Sale, Nicholas J....2:57:46 (927)
Sale, Stewart L....4:47:28 (24,015)
Salem, Paul A....3:59:17 (11,590)
Sales, Darren M....4:11:05 (14,571)
Sales, Martin S....3:40:13 (6,676)
Sales, Mike R....5:36:09 (31,048)
Salih, Salih....5:34:52 (30,925)
Salinas, Victor....3:30:28 (4,965)
Salinn, Faisal....4:48:58 (24,366)
Salisbury, Andrew J....3:28:41 (4,600)
Salisbury, James R....4:54:39 (25,609)
Sallnow, Andy J....3:29:35 (4,795)
Salmon, Jonathan....3:46:27 (7,997)
Salmon, Jonathan E....3:55:35 (10,367)
Salmon, Michael J....3:49:09 (8,615)
Salmon, Oliver....4:58:53 (26,450)
Salmon, Richard J....4:07:53 (13,745)
Salmon, Stephen J....3:28:01 (4,462)
Salome-Bentley, Simon....5:31:26 (30,606)
Salovaara, Ransu....4:19:45 (16,825)
Salt, Thomas E....3:30:04 (4,900)
Salter, Anthony J....3:40:47 (6,778)
Salter, Christopher M....5:12:19 (28,435)
Salter, Ian G....3:39:54 (6,616)
Salter, Robert S....3:08:59 (1,881)
Salthouse, Mark....3:36:06 (5,898)
Salton, Wesley S....4:45:10 (23,456)
Samani, Hicham....3:28:09 (4,498)
Sami, Selchouk....3:18:43 (3,066)
Samkin, James P....4:10:02 (14,303)
Sammons, Robert F....4:47:35 (24,038)
Sampaio, Adriano....4:11:45 (14,744)
Sampasivamoorthy, Aijieenthan....5:09:29 (28,044)
Sample, Edward C....5:40:33 (31,380)
Sampson, James....3:16:30 (2,816)
Sampson, Martin....3:16:41 (2,833)
Sampson, Stuart....4:26:52 (18,781)
Samra, Harjap S....3:41:12 (6,873)
Sams, Mark G....4:32:03 (20,184)
Samson, Andrew M....3:54:53 (10,150)
Samson, Douglas W....3:49:49 (8,774)
Samson, Owen W....4:23:26 (17,852)
Samson, Paul A....4:23:02 (17,737)
Samuel, Anthony G....4:06:14 (13,341)
Samuel, Harry J....4:59:10 (26,506)
Samuel, Jonathan P....3:58:41 (11,369)
Samuel, Nicholas M....3:44:14 (7,496)
Samuel, Rob E....2:40:42 (208)
Samuels, Lionel E....4:18:09 (16,386)
Samwell, Ben Gerhardus....4:24:26 (18,122)
San Sampiero, Florencio....5:58:25 (32,665)
Sanabria, Mariano....2:56:07 (813)
Sanchez, Eduardo A....5:43:25 (31,602)
Sanchez, Timote....3:50:08 (8,854)
Sanchez Pardo, Pedro....3:42:39 (7,164)
Sandel, Chris E....3:56:50 (10,738)
Sandel, Rob....4:13:44 (15,233)
Sandercock, Graham M....4:11:18 (14,626)
Sanders, Chay M....3:53:19 (9,667)
Sanders, Gary A....4:36:04 (21,258)
Sanders, Jake C....4:05:21 (13,136)
Sanders, Jonathan P....4:53:19 (25,335)
Sanders, Keith....3:11:46 (2,186)
Sanders, Leslie W....3:53:09 (9,620)
Sanders, Martin....2:29:33 (66)
Sanders, Oliver M....3:26:19 (4,161)
Sanders, Paul....3:54:54 (10,160)
Sanders, Richard....4:13:15 (15,098)
Sanders, Sean....3:59:49 (11,789)
Sanderson, Andrew C....5:39:38 (31,309)
Sanderson, Brian J....3:53:37 (9,747)
Sanderson, Mark C....4:52:18 (25,104)
Sanderson, Martin....4:32:41 (20,345)
Sanderson, Paul....4:49:55 (24,583)
Sanderson, Terence....4:33:02 (20,439)
Sanderson, Tom D....3:25:29 (4,010)
Sandford, Nicky S....4:13:26 (15,145)
Sandford, Richard P....4:19:58 (16,880)
Sandford-Hart, John....6:47:57 (34,036)
Sandham, David A....3:14:56 (2,622)

Sandison, Peter T 4:29:00 (19,399)
Sandison, Richard 4:56:25 (25,951)
Sandler, Akiva L 3:43:12 (7,288)
Sandom, Neil J 3:50:14 (8,880)
Sandry, Paul J 5:59:07 (32,700)
Saner, René 3:05:17 (1,536)
Sangha, Charanjit 4:44:39 (23,338)
Sanghera, Kirn K 4:48:50 (24,328)
Sanghera, Lember S 6:34:05 (33,750)
Sangster, Ewan J 4:17:40 (16,268)
Sangster, James 4:34:34 (20,836)
Sangsue, Bernard 6:10:52 (33,136)
Sankey, David J 5:00:29 (26,704)
Sansom, Rupert 3:57:43 (11,023)
Santamaria, Paul 4:22:53 (17,698)
Santini, Renato 3:51:00 (9,046)
Santoni, Alessandro 4:24:30 (18,143)
Santos, Lester 3:57:13 (10,868)
Sanzy, Bruno 4:08:33 (13,927)
Sao Pedro, Aires 2:58:09 (961)
Saouli, Mood 4:52:07 (25,069)
Sarai, Satwinder 4:32:26 (20,280)
Sarapuk, Krzysztof 2:35:17 (116)
Sargant, Antony J 4:38:55 (21,948)
Sargant, Nick J 5:00:00 (26,633)
Sargeant, Jonathan D 3:04:08 (1,460)
Sargeant, Laurence E 3:28:08 (4,496)
Sargeant, Malcolm C 4:44:27 (23,286)
Sargeant, Marc J 4:06:55 (13,496)
Sargeant, Robert 3:16:05 (2,765)
Sargeaunt-Thomson, Tristan J 3:43:45 (7,400)
Sargent, Craig P 4:09:35 (14,198)
Sargent, David G 4:56:52 (26,040)
Sargent, Ian 4:25:19 (18,348)
Sargent, Nicholas D 4:26:45 (18,743)
Sargent, Ryan S 4:08:30 (13,909)
Sargisson, Stuart 5:51:53 (32,281)
Sarjent, Bruce M 3:55:26 (10,316)
Sarret, Jean-Claude 4:34:01 (20,699)
Sarson, Peter 3:05:41 (1,570)
Sartorato, Paolo 3:58:20 (11,236)
Saso, Srdjan 4:47:03 (23,920)
Sasso, Mauro 3:07:38 (1,745)
Satake, Shigeru 4:56:00 (25,877)
Satapathy, Sarthak 5:33:04 (30,759)
Satchwell, Andrew 3:57:08 (10,847)
Sato, Fumitoshi 5:51:11 (32,223)
Sato, Hideo 6:39:57 (33,879)
Satterly, Charles A 5:05:14 (27,439)
Satterly, James A 4:43:29 (23,044)
Sauer, Hans J 4:08:17 (13,849)
Sauer, Uli 3:39:30 (6,534)
Sauka, Thomas A 3:25:06 (3,947)
Saunders, Andrew 5:06:37 (27,638)
Saunders, Andrew J 5:34:54 (30,929)
Saunders, Charles 4:14:03 (15,320)
Saunders, Daniel T 5:01:23 (26,858)
Saunders, David A 2:52:18 (612)
Saunders, David A 4:12:02 (14,816)
Saunders, Graheme 3:40:00 (6,638)
Saunders, Ian 3:59:58 (11,842)
Saunders, Leon C 4:23:16 (17,804)
Saunders, Marc 3:18:44 (3,069)
Saunders, Mark A 4:16:56 (16,070)
Saunders, Martin D 5:24:37 (29,870)
Saunders, Murray J 3:56:14 (10,545)
Saunders, Paul 4:32:51 (20,388)
Saunders, Peter J 3:34:02 (5,555)
Saunders, Richard 3:09:17 (1,916)
Saunders, Ross G 4:31:24 (19,995)
Saunders, Stephen 3:50:45 (8,998)
Saunders, Stephen J 4:46:33 (23,789)
Saunders, Tony 3:16:01 (2,755)
Saunderson, Eric M 4:45:00 (23,412)
Sauvetre, Jean Michel 3:28:23 (4,534)
Savage, Andrew G 3:48:54 (8,557)
Savage, Anthony K 4:26:46 (18,745)
Savage, Anthony M 3:18:48 (3,074)
Savage, Benjamin D 4:00:03 (11,863)
Savage, James G 4:06:20 (13,362)
Savage, James R 4:42:28 (22,793)
Savage, James S 2:33:42 (101)
Savage, Malcolm B 3:26:52 (4,256)
Savage, Paul R 3:39:55 (6,619)
Savage, Tim J 6:28:58 (33,637)
Saviana, Ezequiel 4:49:30 (24,474)
Savidge, Nicholas 3:50:01 (8,829)
Savill, David C 3:38:20 (6,321)
Savill, Keith D 3:58:52 (11,444)
Savill, Neil 2:58:37 (1,020)
Savill, Stuart D 5:14:56 (28,810)
Saville, Dennis W 4:15:33 (15,718)
Saville, Gary M 4:18:10 (16,393)
Saville, Graham 4:11:04 (14,563)
Saville, James E 5:40:56 (31,408)
Savills, Michael G 5:13:07 (28,558)
Sawa, Peter F 4:51:58 (25,036)
Sawdon, Jon C 5:00:20 (26,686)
Sawdon, Neville J 3:19:32 (3,169)
Sawer, Martin 3:47:18 (8,177)
Sawford, Steven 4:05:46 (13,235)
Sawko, Peter W 4:14:20 (15,406)
Sawley, Paul 4:00:18 (11,926)
Sawyer, David J 3:59:56 (11,831)
Sayani, Yusufali F 8:06:04 (34,540)
Sayer, John L 6:09:40 (33,103)
Sayers, Brian A 4:08:09 (13,817)
Sayers, Julian A 4:20:12 (16,942)
Sayers, Matthew T 3:19:43 (3,195)
Sayward, William 4:58:32 (26,380)
Saywell, Matthew E 4:30:51 (19,850)
Sbuttoni, Paolo 4:08:12 (13,829)
Scadeng, Andrew 5:06:04 (27,564)
Scaldini, Daniele 4:33:01 (20,434)
Scales, Alex J 4:51:36 (24,960)
Scales, Thomas D 3:26:39 (4,218)
Scally, Kevin 4:51:34 (24,950)
Scanlan, Ronan J 4:34:41 (20,870)
Scanlon, Andrew 3:50:04 (8,837)
Scanlon, Sean T 4:58:20 (26,348)
Scarborough, Dean K 5:20:10 (29,422)
Scarborough, Linton J 3:07:39 (1,747)
Scard, Andrew 3:21:52 (3,467)
Scarfe, Geoff 4:06:17 (13,354)
Scargill, Nigel 5:52:33 (32,319)
Scarlett, Laurence S 3:02:50 (1,365)
Scarperi, Robert 3:42:18 (7,094)
Scarratt, Alan J 3:37:11 (6,098)
Scarr-Hall, Ian 6:26:36 (33,588)
Scarrott, Alistair J 4:27:51 (19,040)
Scarrott, Lee P 4:37:34 (21,606)
Schaefer, Wolfgang 3:45:04 (7,700)
Schaerer, Juerg 5:05:59 (27,547)
Schaper, Philipp 3:44:26 (7,542)
Scharff, Christopher 4:25:08 (18,302)
Schatz, Michael 3:57:03 (10,811)
Scheer, Andrew D 3:47:17 (8,176)
Schenkel, Erik 4:00:17 (11,921)
Schiavi, Massimo 3:55:29 (10,335)
Schiavina, Vittorio 3:32:20 (5,286)
Schiavottiello, Vincenzo 3:03:42 (1,430)
Schilling, William F 3:59:26 (11,646)
Schindler, Gernod 3:51:04 (9,068)
Schippel, John E 6:01:41 (32,802)
Schirmbrand, Norbert 3:55:43 (10,409)
Schittone, Joe 3:46:16 (7,946)
Schless, John 3:54:34 (10,060)
Schlitz, Mark 3:31:43 (5,173)
Schlosser, Roderik A 3:31:03 (5,059)
Schlotz, Wolff 3:39:56 (6,623)
Schmidt, Mike S 4:40:04 (22,198)
Schmidt, Volker 4:54:48 (25,649)
Schmidt-Soltau, Nils S 4:54:47 (25,647)
Schmidt-Soltau, Peer 3:54:58 (10,184)
Schmunk, Sascha 4:01:03 (12,121)
Schneider, Dietmar 4:07:32 (13,650)
Schneyderberg, Frank 3:13:13 (2,360)
Schoenfeld, Gary H 3:52:42 (9,479)
Schofield, James 2:45:12 (339)
Schofield, John P 5:20:25 (29,456)
Schofield, Mark S 4:12:58 (15,021)
Schofield, Michael 3:56:35 (10,657)
Schofield, Michael 5:08:10 (27,839)
Schofield, Nicholas P 4:18:31 (16,503)
Schofield, Paul J 4:54:41 (25,618)
Schofield, Robert A 4:14:08 (15,347)
Scholer, Dieter 4:52:02 (25,052)
Scholes, George J 5:44:17 (31,695)
Scholey, Mark L 4:24:47 (18,210)
Scholle, Uwe 3:58:01 (11,122)
Scholte, Paul 2:51:56 (591)
Scholtz, Richard B 4:22:43 (17,653)
Scholz, Guenther 4:11:58 (14,801)
Schooling, Robert 3:23:18 (3,678)
Schoonderwoerd, Petrus B 6:00:53 (32,773)
Schrauwen, Stepham 4:11:05 (14,571)
Schreder, Hughes 3:04:09 (1,462)
Schrefler, Wolfgang 3:29:07 (4,697)
Schubert, Peter 2:56:18 (832)
Schubnel, Pascal 5:10:51 (28,260)
Schulz, Alexander 3:24:11 (3,802)
Schumann, Paul 2:53:53 (686)
Schwab, August 3:11:10 (2,111)
Schwab, Hubert 3:26:52 (4,256)
Schwartz, Jeremy S 3:33:22 (5,448)
Schwartz, Karl-Heinz 4:55:53 (25,854)
Schwarz, Bastian 4:55:53 (25,854)
Schwarz, David B 3:27:53 (4,436)
Schwarz, Dieter 4:12:10 (14,855)
Schweiss, Michael 3:07:08 (1,692)
Schwinger, Denis 3:25:38 (4,041)
Sciba, Craig P 4:25:02 (18,271)
Sciuto, Conceto 3:30:13 (4,927)
Sciver, Richard J 3:24:32 (3,853)
Scodellard, Franco 4:12:15 (14,873)
Scoggins, Dean A 4:07:18 (13,597)
Scoggins, Peter R 4:20:07 (16,917)
Scollo, Paolao 4:39:55 (22,170)
Scorer, Allan H 3:46:20 (7,960)
Scorey, Nicholas 4:54:48 (25,649)
Scotney, James J 3:19:21 (3,144)
Scott, Alan F 5:22:17 (29,636)
Scott, Alex 4:00:31 (11,978)
Scott, Andrew 3:42:44 (7,181)
Scott, Andrew 5:16:26 (28,987)
Scott, Angus 4:40:11 (22,235)
Scott, Anthony J 5:59:52 (32,732)
Scott, Benjamin J 4:43:56 (23,162)
Scott, Cameron T 3:02:51 (1,366)
Scott, Danny A 2:59:44 (1,145)
Scott, David R 4:28:31 (19,268)
Scott, Gareth 4:15:49 (15,786)
Scott, Ian 3:24:14 (3,809)
Scott, James M 3:52:50 (9,514)
Scott, Jason 5:45:37 (31,807)
Scott, Kalvin 4:59:03 (26,485)
Scott, Kenny 4:07:37 (13,677)
Scott, Kevin 4:01:38 (12,275)
Scott, Mark C 5:10:59 (28,273)
Scott, Michael A 3:29:20 (4,747)
Scott, Michael K 5:01:43 (26,916)
Scott, Nathan 4:17:40 (16,268)
Scott, Nathan S 4:35:59 (21,241)
Scott, Neil 4:46:15 (23,727)
Scott, Neil S 2:59:16 (1,094)
Scott, Paul 4:35:11 (21,029)
Scott, Peter D 4:22:09 (17,482)
Scott, Peter S 4:53:23 (25,348)
Scott, Philip J 5:02:07 (26,974)
Scott, Richard 4:31:31 (20,027)
Scott, Richard A 3:07:26 (1,727)
Scott, Richard M 8:05:39 (34,539)
Scott, Richard S 4:21:00 (17,182)
Scott, Robin G 4:08:07 (13,801)
Scott, Robin H 3:06:39 (1,651)
Scott, Russell 4:23:32 (17,875)
Scott, Stephen M 3:48:00 (8,351)
Scott, Stephen M 4:25:50 (18,491)
Scott, Stewart 5:31:18 (30,596)
Scott, Stewart P 3:55:41 (10,399)
Scott, Stuart D 5:33:59 (30,833)
Scott, Thomas C 3:15:13 (2,656)
Scott, Tom 4:22:06 (17,471)
Scott, Tom E 4:16:49 (16,041)
Scott, Wayne L 4:49:54 (24,575)
Scott Cowley, Orlando 3:36:48 (6,021)
Scott-Douglas, Christopher 4:03:24 (12,700)
Scotting, Ian P 5:39:58 (31,330)
Scoular, Oliver W 3:20:56 (3,348)

Scovell, Keith 4:36:37 (21,396)
Scragg, Jem 3:28:56 (4,650)
Scragg, Terence M 5:25:51 (30,015)
Scraggs, Nick J 4:32:12 (20,225)
Scrase, Daniel G 4:36:54 (21,464)
Scrase, Scott 4:45:25 (23,517)
Scrase, William G 4:39:21 (22,059)
Scrimgeour, Andrew J 4:14:29 (15,446)
Scripps, Terry A 5:27:22 (30,189)
Scrivener, Chris 2:55:52 (800)
Scrivener, Paul W 3:29:12 (4,714)
Scroop, Richard 3:41:26 (6,922)
Scudder, Darren 4:29:57 (19,621)
Scullion, David 5:24:48 (29,887)
Seabourne, Ben 3:51:39 (9,211)
Seaden, Paul 3:55:24 (10,313)
Seal, Matt I 5:44:09 (31,678)
Sealby, Matthew 3:19:44 (3,197)
Seale, Stephen G 3:23:37 (3,717)
Seaman, Michael A 5:49:15 (32,071)
Seaman, Paul 3:37:58 (6,257)
Seaman, Phillip W 4:59:43 (26,594)
Searby, Thomas A 2:59:16 (1,094)
Searle, Kevin M 3:42:10 (7,061)
Searle, Mark 4:22:10 (17,486)
Searle, Richard C 4:23:58 (17,981)
Sear-Mayes, David J 4:27:17 (18,900)
Sears, Richard J 3:53:22 (9,687)
Seaton, Mark I 5:21:49 (29,589)
Seaton, Robert A 4:37:45 (21,652)
Seaton, Steven 4:20:33 (17,043)
Seatter, Anton M 4:01:17 (12,178)
Sebastian, Peter A 4:56:29 (25,967)
Secnik, Drago 3:54:30 (10,034)
Seddon, Andrew 5:07:06 (27,704)
Seddon, Dwaine P 4:25:23 (18,364)
Seddon, Jonathan F 4:10:49 (14,498)
Seddon, Marvin 4:59:27 (26,551)
Seddon, Paul 3:37:14 (6,109)
Sedge, Martyn J 2:58:51 (1,047)
Sedge, Stephano 3:49:20 (8,659)
Sedgmond, Andrew M 3:51:36 (9,196)
Sedgwick, Glenn C 4:36:40 (21,409)
Sedgwick, John 3:51:36 (9,196)
Sedman, Nigel H 3:13:20 (2,377)
Seed, Andy D 3:48:28 (8,454)
Seedat, Yahya Y 3:29:26 (4,770)
Seehra, Jatinder S 4:50:42 (24,766)
Seekings, James E 4:11:28 (14,665)
Seelandt, Frank 3:36:21 (5,938)
Seeley, Andrew 3:54:52 (10,144)
Seeley, David 4:03:11 (12,649)
Seelochan, David 3:39:31 (6,540)
Seffens, Andrew V 4:00:20 (11,933)
Segade Vieito, Roque 4:15:42 (15,745)
Segaller, Tim M 4:48:16 (24,196)
Segerslatt, Sten 4:21:43 (17,380)
Seggie, David J 6:23:23 (33,499)
Seib, Ron J 4:21:52 (17,415)
Seivewright, Andrew 3:47:14 (8,165)
Sekito, Byoji 3:46:58 (8,102)
Selby, Aaron H 4:27:04 (18,832)
Selby, Mark 4:34:23 (20,794)
Selby, Paul 3:28:59 (4,665)
Selby, Phillip H 4:33:26 (20,556)
Selck, Juergen 4:11:34 (14,700)
Self, Richard J 3:11:44 (2,179)
Seligman, Peter A 3:35:38 (5,821)
Sell, Richard E 3:54:52 (10,144)
Sellars, Robin T 5:22:07 (29,616)
Sellay, Abdul 4:34:40 (20,865)
Sellers, Malcolm 4:45:39 (23,572)
Sellwood, Gary J 4:07:29 (13,636)
Selves, Stephen J 4:28:17 (19,199)
Selway, Richard P 3:36:14 (5,919)
Selwood, Keith 3:16:19 (2,791)
Sen, Ruben 5:30:10 (30,493)
Senda, Kenzo 5:27:53 (30,251)
Senft, Gerhard 4:02:16 (12,436)
Senior, Andrew P 3:35:00 (5,703)
Senior, John T 3:48:04 (8,365)
Senior, Stephen P 3:19:28 (3,158)
Sennett, Paul W 6:08:26 (33,062)

Sentenac, Didier D 3:43:15 (7,296)
Sentenac, Philippe 3:47:25 (8,202)
Sephton, Richard 3:31:23 (5,112)
Sepulveda, Luis-Fernando 2:56:02 (808)
Sequeira, Edgar 3:14:22 (2,526)
Sercombe, Alistair 5:45:42 (31,814)
Seres, Adam 3:52:20 (9,394)
Serge, Jolly 4:31:39 (20,067)
Serra Cabanas, Josep 4:59:25 (26,548)
Serra Hernandez, Francisco 5:17:28 (29,121)
Serrano Baylin, Francisco M 3:19:25 (3,150)
Serrano Ceballos, Angel 3:55:41 (10,399)
Servent, Jeff J 4:42:03 (22,683)
Serventich, Daniel 3:54:05 (9,899)
Servini, Dominic J 5:20:09 (29,421)
Sesto Novas, Juan Luis 5:00:35 (26,716)
Sethard-Wright, Matthew G 5:16:40 (29,016)
Setrem, Mark 4:30:10 (19,671)
Severs, Jonathan R 4:21:29 (17,300)
Sevilla, Carlos 3:20:14 (3,256)
Sewell, Jonathan B 5:27:52 (30,250)
Sewell, Michae 3:21:50 (3,462)
Sewell, Michael B 4:34:58 (20,962)
Sewell, Nigel J 3:24:13 (3,806)
Sewell, Stuart J 4:20:05 (16,908)
Sewter, Lance 4:21:59 (17,449)
Sexton, Bernie 4:06:35 (13,420)
Sexton, Chris P 6:48:56 (34,049)
Sexton, David H 3:11:36 (2,162)
Sexton, Michael E 3:23:58 (3,774)
Sexton, Neil B 4:08:36 (13,942)
Sexton, Patrick J 4:53:11 (25,314)
Sexton, Richard A 3:46:57 (8,100)
Seymour, Ben 4:22:50 (17,679)
Seymour, Brian R 5:04:54 (27,384)
Seymour, Christopher J 3:44:51 (7,642)
Seymour, James D 3:50:21 (8,900)
Seymour, Paul F 4:42:16 (22,746)
Seymour, Philip 4:51:48 (25,003)
Shackleford, Mark J 4:44:48 (23,367)
Shackleford, Nicholas 4:16:00 (15,837)
Shaddick, Nigel 5:30:57 (30,560)
Shaddock, John 4:01:31 (12,247)
Shadick, James J 4:24:33 (18,159)
Shadrack, Graham 5:04:52 (27,381)
Shafier, Lawrence E 3:05:41 (1,570)
Shah, Amit 5:36:53 (31,110)
Shah, Harish 4:50:41 (24,762)
Shah, Harshad 5:51:13 (32,228)
Shah, Kalpesh 5:46:32 (31,881)
Shah, Kaushik 4:44:04 (23,195)
Shah, Kirtan 5:34:32 (30,888)
Shah, Meenesh 5:23:50 (29,781)
Shah, Nicholas 3:49:58 (8,819)
Shah, Niraj 4:29:27 (19,508)
Shah, Pratik 4:09:17 (14,112)
Shah, Rajesh 4:10:42 (14,462)
Shah, Rakesh 4:03:29 (12,722)
Shah, Rashmi 5:19:06 (29,303)
Shah, Shirish L 5:19:02 (29,296)
Shah, Sujan 4:28:45 (19,327)
Shakespeare, David W 4:14:27 (15,436)
Shakespeare, Gwidion T 3:55:57 (10,477)
Shakespeare, Jack 3:41:57 (7,018)
Shakespeare, Simon 6:48:34 (34,046)
Shakespeare, Wayne K 4:09:52 (14,271)
Shakoor, Arsalan 6:03:29 (32,865)
Shaler, Nigel 3:40:48 (6,780)
Shallis, Paul C 5:26:03 (30,040)
Shammas, David J 5:48:43 (32,027)
Shanahan, Greg 4:33:07 (20,461)
Shand, Alan J 3:41:45 (6,977)
Shand, Andrew 4:26:41 (18,716)
Shandley, Adrian P 3:50:38 (8,968)
Shane, David C 4:00:26 (11,957)
Shanks, Stephen M 2:44:07 (297)
Shann, Harry 3:26:57 (4,271)
Shannon, Andrew M 3:46:21 (7,965)
Shannon, Gary J 4:28:50 (19,360)
Shannon, Martin P 4:09:09 (14,073)
Shannon, William A 4:36:07 (21,276)
Shapland, Mark 3:42:25 (7,120)
Shapleski, David J 4:05:54 (13,266)

Shardlow, Richard A 2:52:48 (630)
Shardlow, Robert 4:31:33 (20,039)
Sharie, Norman A 3:47:16 (8,172)
Sharkey, Jon D 2:38:57 (181)
Sharkey, Thomas J 4:37:19 (21,554)
Sharland, Richard J 3:04:07 (1,457)
Sharma, Dhan 4:42:06 (22,695)
Sharma, Sanjai 2:58:22 (989)
Sharma, Sunil 4:46:59 (23,904)
Sharma, Varun 7:30:44 (34,458)
Sharman, Alan 3:28:26 (4,545)
Sharman, Ben 3:40:29 (6,731)
Sharman, Craig J 3:56:04 (10,507)
Sharman, David C 4:01:42 (12,295)
Sharman, Ian 3:12:27 (2,260)
Sharman, Neil M 4:15:46 (15,774)
Sharman, Tim 3:40:43 (6,761)
Sharp, Andrew 4:07:53 (13,745)
Sharp, Ed A 4:35:23 (21,079)
Sharp, John 3:56:14 (10,545)
Sharp, Mark 5:16:59 (29,060)
Sharp, Matt 3:50:06 (8,844)
Sharp, Michael 3:27:16 (4,325)
Sharp, Steve 4:23:54 (17,963)
Sharp, Stuart C 4:54:00 (25,485)
Sharpe, Anthony C 4:26:42 (18,723)
Sharpe, Christopher 3:31:53 (5,195)
Sharpe, Damien R 4:27:51 (19,040)
Sharpe, Darren 3:14:07 (2,488)
Sharpe, David W 5:20:28 (29,462)
Sharpe, Tony 3:26:25 (4,175)
Sharples, Jonathan M 5:02:29 (27,041)
Sharran, Nasser 5:07:51 (27,810)
Sharrock, James L 4:51:23 (24,921)
Sharrod, Martin 5:36:01 (31,033)
Shaughnessy, Gary P 4:32:14 (20,238)
Shaw, Adam J 5:15:40 (28,902)
Shaw, Alastair 4:08:07 (13,801)
Shaw, Andrew 4:10:48 (14,492)
Shaw, Andrew S 4:21:17 (17,249)
Shaw, Clayton Scott 3:57:07 (10,842)
Shaw, Colin E 4:00:47 (12,054)
Shaw, David 4:14:05 (15,331)
Shaw, Edward D 4:01:04 (12,128)
Shaw, Gary 3:31:24 (5,116)
Shaw, Jeremy D 4:09:26 (14,151)
Shaw, Lee A 4:30:39 (19,785)
Shaw, Leslie J 4:54:02 (25,489)
Shaw, Michael R 3:52:23 (9,410)
Shaw, Neil M 3:47:24 (8,197)
Shaw, Nick 4:50:07 (24,625)
Shaw, Paul 3:32:12 (5,260)
Shaw, Paul A 4:27:34 (18,967)
Shaw, Paul D 3:30:52 (5,033)
Shaw, Paul F 4:47:55 (24,126)
Shaw, Peter E 3:12:41 (2,288)
Shaw, Peter J 4:05:02 (13,057)
Shaw, Richard 4:03:15 (12,670)
Shaw, Richard F 3:21:35 (3,430)
Shaw, Robert 3:50:30 (8,929)
Shaw, Robert 5:28:26 (30,315)
Shaw, Steven 3:53:01 (9,582)
Shaw, Steven L 5:01:53 (26,942)
Shaw, Stuart A 2:52:17 (610)
Shawyer, Peter J 3:49:12 (8,627)
Shead, David 4:48:50 (24,328)
Sheard, Bryan A 3:58:40 (11,364)
Shearer, Andrew J 3:28:48 (4,624)
Shearer, Ben 2:57:41 (919)
Shearer, Graham J 4:05:22 (13,139)
Shearer, Nic 3:27:04 (4,291)
Shearer, Richard J 2:44:54 (327)
Shearing, Nicholas J 3:31:56 (5,208)
Shears, Brian R 4:38:13 (21,759)
Shears, Joseph H 6:12:48 (33,200)
Shearwood, Adam 4:18:06 (16,371)
Sheasby, Craig S 4:23:41 (17,910)
Sheath, Kevin J 5:06:17 (27,599)
Sheehan, Bobby B 3:57:38 (10,990)
Sheehan, Eric J 5:54:59 (32,458)
Sheehan, John-Paol 4:21:36 (17,334)
Sheehan, Martin 2:44:47 (324)
Sheehan, Martin J 6:21:38 (33,450)

Sheehan, Nicholas P	4:52:23	(25,121)
Sheen, Richard	3:43:53	(7,434)
Sheen, William G	4:34:13	(20,760)
Sheffield, Andy D	4:23:57	(17,978)
Sheffield, John	4:01:38	(12,275)
Sheffield, Richard J	3:37:23	(6,140)
Sheil, John	4:16:35	(15,980)
Shek, Robin	3:22:18	(3,532)
Shelbourn, Stuart M	5:15:42	(28,905)
Sheldon, Mark	5:44:46	(31,743)
Sheldon, Robert A	3:53:33	(9,726)
Sheldon, Tim	4:26:36	(18,695)
Shelley, Alastair C	4:42:00	(22,673)
Shelley, Andrew T	4:27:58	(19,088)
Shelley, James C	4:47:52	(24,109)
Shelley, Richard N	2:59:25	(1,112)
Shelley, Robin	3:53:37	(9,747)
Shelling, Andrew J	3:29:54	(4,867)
Shelton, Charles R	3:22:20	(3,538)
Shelton, Richard J	3:54:26	(10,006)
Shelton-Smith, Kevin C	2:50:18	(521)
Sheperd, Dean	4:12:52	(14,996)
Shephard, Mark S	4:08:45	(13,980)
Shepheard, Nicholas S	3:14:36	(2,567)
Shepherd, Adam R	6:59:26	(34,204)
Shepherd, Andrew P	4:35:19	(21,062)
Shepherd, Ben	3:47:35	(8,243)
Shepherd, Brett	4:35:54	(21,211)
Shepherd, Christopher J	2:55:55	(805)
Shepherd, David	3:58:10	(11,174)
Shepherd, David J	3:18:24	(3,031)
Shepherd, John	6:00:28	(32,757)
Shepherd, John	6:02:27	(32,832)
Shepherd, Keith	3:52:01	(9,305)
Shepherd, Lloyd M	4:46:43	(23,833)
Shepherd, Mark A	2:43:07	(270)
Shepherd, Mark A	4:23:21	(17,831)
Shepherd, Max R	4:01:22	(12,202)
Shepherd, Michael D	3:36:14	(5,919)
Shepherd, Michael T	5:01:13	(26,829)
Shepherd, Robert N	4:27:47	(19,017)
Shepherd, Tom J	3:08:02	(1,794)
Sheppard, Andrew J	4:24:25	(18,114)
Sheppard, David J	3:47:00	(8,108)
Sheppard, David W	3:42:40	(7,168)
Sheppard, Jay	4:40:40	(22,341)
Sheppard, Jonathan N	6:44:20	(33,965)
Sheppard, Justin D	4:58:29	(26,373)
Sheppard, Quinton J	4:01:54	(12,340)
Sheppard, Richard P	4:07:35	(13,666)
Sheppard, Spencer R	4:39:23	(22,061)
Sheppard, Steven H	6:17:09	(33,329)
Sheppard, Tomas J	3:45:25	(7,778)
Shepperd, Nicholas J	2:58:54	(1,054)
Shepperson, Malcolm C	3:53:43	(9,775)
Shepperson, Mark A	4:57:18	(26,142)
Sheridan, John	4:58:42	(26,420)
Sheridan, Paul J	3:28:31	(4,565)
Sheridan, Philip	3:06:31	(1,640)
Sheriff, Finley C	4:14:13	(15,373)
Sheriff, Paul N	3:49:00	(8,579)
Sherling, Adrian M	4:33:52	(20,676)
Sherlock, Joseph	4:28:17	(19,199)
Sherman, Julian M	3:15:17	(2,669)
Sherman, Marc D	4:52:01	(25,048)
Sherman MBE, David	4:17:38	(16,258)
Shermer, Warren B	5:25:14	(29,954)
Sherrard, Dion G	5:15:08	(28,836)
Sherratt, James	3:27:45	(4,408)
Sherratt, Stephen A	4:42:35	(22,827)
Sherriff, Mark D	2:48:32	(449)
Sherrington, Gareth J	4:22:36	(17,613)
Sherry, Robin	4:13:15	(15,098)
Sherwen, Peter J	5:00:57	(26,790)
Sherwin, Andrew C	4:01:18	(12,184)
Sherwin, James C	4:20:56	(17,159)
Sherwood, Charles N	3:21:36	(3,434)
Sherwood, Christopher A	3:53:04	(9,596)
Shew, Brian L	5:12:40	(28,480)
Shewan, Neil	4:21:54	(17,422)
Shewbridge, Paul L	4:20:36	(17,061)
Shiani, Ajay	4:27:47	(19,017)
Shickell, Matt J	3:41:06	(6,846)
Shiekh, Naveed A	6:29:57	(33,657)
Shield, Jerry M	3:08:38	(1,845)
Shields, Andrew J	3:09:39	(1,958)
Shields, Dominic J	3:45:00	(7,681)
Shields, Michael	6:32:54	(33,719)
Shiggins, Brian T	4:47:20	(23,996)
Shilleto, Simon J	4:18:30	(16,497)
Shillinglaw, Tom E	4:35:45	(21,177)
Shimabukuro, Tsutomu	6:57:42	(34,185)
Shine, Francis	5:38:15	(31,210)
Shingler, Jason	4:50:27	(24,697)
Shinn, Andrew D	3:09:56	(1,983)
Shino, Hiroaki	4:21:03	(17,197)
Shipley, Gareth E	3:17:40	(2,948)
Shipley, Peter D	3:57:22	(10,913)
Shipman, Ryan	3:20:17	(3,263)
Shipman, Stephen J	6:10:21	(33,126)
Shipton, Matthew D	3:27:07	(4,299)
Shires, Paul M	4:42:54	(22,907)
Shirley, Damian D	2:55:42	(787)
Shirley, Peter J	3:10:56	(2,093)
Shirotani, Michihiro	4:42:55	(22,912)
Shively, Bill	2:54:48	(735)
Shkurka, Mike P	3:58:47	(11,406)
Shnaa, Baker	4:10:40	(14,455)
Shneor, Cheshin	3:32:45	(5,353)
Sholl, William H	4:31:52	(20,130)
Shone, Matt C	2:29:44	(69)
Shore, Alex M	5:21:14	(29,527)
Shore, Martyn A	5:27:41	(30,224)
Short, Christopher D	3:49:25	(8,679)
Short, Eddie	4:13:40	(15,213)
Short, Gary J	5:24:19	(29,841)
Short, Kevin	3:10:13	(2,013)
Shortall, Martin P	3:25:22	(3,990)
Shorten, Neil J	3:32:27	(5,309)
Shotton, Richard A	3:51:33	(9,182)
Shraga, Nicholas	4:03:00	(12,609)
Shreeve, Norman	3:13:39	(2,413)
Shrimpton, Anthony	3:59:34	(11,696)
Shrimpton, Dan J	2:53:34	(666)
Shropshire, Jake	3:39:44	(6,582)
Shrourou, Tareq Y	4:08:07	(13,801)
Shrubsole, Duncan	4:57:00	(26,080)
Shuck, Stephen P	3:13:53	(2,447)
Shuckford, Mark J	4:01:15	(12,174)
Shufflebottom, Kevin J	4:17:31	(16,227)
Shuler, David W	5:07:35	(27,778)
Shuriah, Horace	4:10:48	(14,492)
Shurmer, Jason R	3:58:05	(11,137)
Shute, Rupert N	2:48:28	(445)
Shutt, Peter D	4:37:40	(21,634)
Sian, Jaspal	4:00:00	(11,853)
Sibley, William J	5:15:08	(28,836)
Sice, Richard	5:15:53	(28,920)
Sicilia, Gero	5:47:32	(31,953)
Sicurella, Aldo	4:34:36	(20,845)
Siddall, Stephen C	4:19:35	(16,777)
Siddans, Richard S	4:47:10	(23,949)
Sidders, Andrew J	3:53:37	(9,747)
Siddle, Paul A	2:52:17	(610)
Siddle, Sumeet S	4:58:32	(26,380)
Siddons, Barrie J	4:47:19	(23,989)
Sidebotham, John P	2:56:46	(860)
Siderfin, Justin F	3:28:01	(4,462)
Sidgwick, Paul R	5:27:04	(30,149)
Sidik, Osman G	4:40:08	(22,221)
Sidlin, Richard	3:29:02	(4,679)
Sidnick, Darren L	3:23:29	(3,706)
Sidonio, David M	4:25:30	(18,397)
Siegel, Robert	3:54:29	(10,022)
Siegfried, Edward J	3:01:11	(1,265)
Siegler, Konrad	3:19:45	(3,200)
Sieling, Richard D	4:32:19	(20,255)
Sieppi, Niclas	3:43:13	(7,290)
Sierra, Victor	3:14:41	(2,587)
Sigalas, Evangelos	4:19:10	(16,673)
Signorelli, David A	4:36:10	(21,284)
Signori, Saverio	2:59:43	(1,142)
Sigurjonsson, Gudjon A	3:59:39	(11,734)
Sigvaldason, Simon	3:29:57	(4,879)
Silcock, Christopher W	4:18:00	(16,345)
Silcock, Peter D	3:45:10	(7,719)
Silk, Benjamin C	4:27:36	(18,979)
Silk, Dominic J	4:22:21	(17,531)
Silk, James	3:14:56	(2,622)
Silk, Jonathan C	4:56:19	(25,907)
Silk, Michael P	3:51:44	(9,236)
Sillett, Graham M	4:04:27	(12,919)
Sillince, Alan	4:13:52	(15,266)
Silva, Paulo Ricardo L	4:37:58	(21,708)
Silver, Carl	3:01:14	(1,255)
Silver, Michael I	3:49:40	(8,736)
Silverman, Barry	5:52:46	(32,326)
Silvestre, Carles	3:30:27	(4,962)
Silvey, Melvin J	3:06:09	(1,612)
Silvia, Gugloo H	3:53:18	(9,661)
Sim, Andrew	3:37:38	(6,191)
Sim, Chris	3:47:22	(8,189)
Simcox, Mark N	3:11:20	(2,131)
Simcox, Paul A	4:45:06	(23,434)
Sime, Andrew J	4:15:54	(15,807)
Simei, Gianluca	3:26:05	(4,119)
Simister, Graham R	3:37:19	(6,126)
Simkins, Christopher J	5:11:28	(28,328)
Simkins, Paul F	4:42:53	(22,901)
Simmelink, Victor I	2:51:34	(576)
Simmonds, Gareth P	4:27:12	(18,871)
Simmonds, Kevin	6:12:15	(33,176)
Simmonds, Luke R	4:23:57	(17,978)
Simmonds, Martin	3:42:20	(7,100)
Simmonds, Neil	3:46:06	(7,905)
Simmonds, Paul A	5:08:28	(27,888)
Simmonds, Richard	3:39:20	(6,503)
Simmonds, Roger E	3:47:42	(8,280)
Simmonds, Ronald	4:23:01	(17,733)
Simmons, Christopher	4:15:55	(15,811)
Simmons, James A	3:44:07	(7,476)
Simmons, James S	4:22:12	(17,495)
Simmons, Keith D	4:39:18	(22,049)
Simmons, Kevin J	3:51:53	(9,271)
Simmons, Luke	5:30:45	(30,550)
Simmons, Mark	4:33:20	(20,523)
Simmons, Michael J	4:07:37	(13,677)
Simmons, Paul H	3:49:06	(8,601)
Simmons, Peter	3:49:10	(8,619)
Simms, Mark P	3:08:14	(1,815)
Simnett, Ben J	3:32:43	(5,346)
Simon, Claude	2:57:41	(919)
Simon, Jacky	3:11:25	(2,137)
Simon, Michael	4:45:19	(23,497)
Simon, Paul F	4:10:58	(14,521)
Simon, Yvonnick	3:25:14	(3,967)
Simons, Malcolm	4:22:24	(17,551)
Simons, Paul R	3:16:13	(2,778)
Simonsen, Peter	3:59:23	(11,626)
Simpkin, Daniel P	4:37:16	(21,539)
Simpkins, Ryan	4:36:05	(21,263)
Simpson, Alan	4:28:04	(19,118)
Simpson, Alastair	4:01:03	(12,121)
Simpson, Andrew	5:41:24	(31,455)
Simpson, Andrew J	4:46:47	(23,849)
Simpson, Ben	4:58:07	(26,310)
Simpson, Brian E	5:47:44	(31,961)
Simpson, Colin	3:16:04	(2,760)
Simpson, Colin	4:39:08	(22,011)
Simpson, Daniel E	5:21:12	(29,523)
Simpson, Darryl F	3:57:01	(10,802)
Simpson, David E	3:42:04	(7,042)
Simpson, Dennis A	4:34:24	(20,799)
Simpson, Derek B	3:25:14	(3,967)
Simpson, Duncan	4:37:19	(21,554)
Simpson, Edward A	4:30:34	(19,766)
Simpson, Gordon A	3:56:51	(10,743)
Simpson, James	4:01:34	(12,259)
Simpson, Jason	2:31:38	(82)
Simpson, Keith A	4:11:10	(14,597)
Simpson, Malcolm	4:50:26	(24,694)
Simpson, Nicky J	4:33:19	(20,516)
Simpson, Paul A	4:54:09	(25,513)
Simpson, Peter	3:03:35	(1,422)
Simpson, Peter	4:39:44	(22,137)
Simpson, Peter J	3:22:45	(3,601)
Simpson, Richard H	4:40:35	(22,325)
Simpson, Richard J	4:19:56	(16,868)
Simpson, Robert J	3:48:07	(8,380)

Simpson, Robert R....3:44:04 (7,465)
Simpson, Stephen P....4:52:57 (25,259)
Simpson, William....3:58:18 (11,219)
Simpson Gee, Will J....3:52:18 (9,386)
Simpson-Foster, Matthew T....4:26:40 (18,712)
Sims, Andrew H....3:10:03 (1,993)
Sims, Matthew D....3:37:59 (6,260)
Sims, Michael R....3:49:50 (8,778)
Sinclair, Gareth....4:19:15 (16,688)
Sinclair, Graeme....4:17:38 (16,258)
Sinclair, Graeme....4:49:53 (24,569)
Sinclair, Malcolm....2:59:11 (1,083)
Sinclair, Mike J....4:17:47 (16,300)
Sinclair, Simon....4:07:38 (13,684)
Sinclair, Terence F....3:12:48 (2,306)
Sinclair, Thomas S....3:40:06 (6,656)
Sinden, Darryl P....4:26:51 (18,773)
Sinfield, Matthew S....3:28:49 (4,629)
Singer, Gary F....4:31:37 (20,056)
Singer, Jamie J....6:42:14 (33,914)
Singer, Stuart....3:49:12 (8,627)
Singer, William A....4:58:45 (26,435)
Singh, Ashish....6:17:29 (33,335)
Singh, Baldev....4:29:06 (19,420)
Singh, George G....4:17:13 (16,159)
Singh, Gurlal S....3:55:22 (10,304)
Singh, Gurpritpal....4:18:29 (16,491)
Singh, Harjit....4:59:23 (26,543)
Singh, Harmander....9:59:57 (34,589)
Singh, Jagjit....4:33:40 (20,629)
Singh, Joginder....4:11:12 (14,607)
Singh, Makhan....4:44:39 (23,338)
Singh, Malkiat....8:54:31 (34,579)
Singh, Manjit....3:51:28 (9,169)
Singh, Manminder....4:44:38 (23,332)
Singh, Ojesh L....5:46:15 (31,858)
Singh, Page....5:39:31 (31,298)
Singh, Prabh S....5:22:34 (29,671)
Singh, Raghbir....5:12:46 (28,508)
Singh, Rashpal....4:49:50 (24,556)
Singh, Rob H....5:20:14 (29,433)
Singh, Samson....5:27:26 (30,196)
Singh, Steve....4:03:47 (12,785)
Singh Lotay, Mirmal....9:59:58 (34,590)
Singh Parmar, Manjinder....5:02:12 (26,991)
Singhal, Anuj....5:25:07 (29,941)
Single, Peter....3:26:18 (4,154)
Singleton, Adam D....4:47:05 (23,929)
Singleton, Andrew J....5:34:17 (30,863)
Singleton, Jonathan M....4:58:11 (26,323)
Singleton, Joshua M....5:00:34 (26,712)
Singleton, Luke D....4:05:57 (13,285)
Singleton, Mark D....4:16:47 (16,029)
Singleton, Martin J....5:16:18 (28,971)
Singleton, Phillip C....4:55:46 (25,831)
Sinnoot, Colin E....3:40:15 (6,684)
Sinnott, David....4:18:52 (16,589)
Sinnott, Matt A....3:04:59 (1,519)
Sinnott, Philip J....4:40:55 (22,410)
Sinnott, Russell....4:33:17 (20,504)
Sint-Nicolaas, Marcel....4:33:28 (20,567)
Sinton, Robert J....4:04:19 (12,893)
Siou, Vincent....2:50:23 (530)
Sirdefield, Stephen....3:31:21 (5,109)
Sirs, Nicholas J....2:53:33 (664)
Sito, Pasquale....3:43:56 (7,446)
Sittington, Geoffrey....3:31:40 (5,161)
Siva Subramaniam, K....5:03:40 (27,204)
Siviter, Roger....4:13:17 (15,112)
Sjolund, Martin P....3:24:43 (3,872)
Skali, Moulay....3:59:41 (11,746)
Skan, Matthew....4:20:04 (16,905)
Skarbek, Sacha J....3:29:20 (4,747)
Skayman, Patrick W....5:19:24 (29,337)
Skeeles, Damian....5:37:34 (31,159)
Skeen, Robert M....3:36:56 (6,047)
Skeet, Martin W....3:14:46 (2,600)
Skeggs, Steven R....4:11:23 (14,640)
Skehan, John D....3:47:48 (8,296)
Skelland, Christopher....3:13:40 (2,416)
Skelton, David....4:30:49 (19,838)
Skelton, John....4:05:23 (13,140)
Skelton, Simon....3:37:56 (6,246)
Skelton, Timothy M....4:14:39 (15,482)
Skeoch, James....4:38:08 (21,747)
Skerratt, Clark I....3:06:18 (1,626)
Skerritt, Paul....5:14:09 (28,694)
Sketch, Mike....4:59:46 (26,606)
Sketchley, Norman P....4:02:52 (12,579)
Skevington, Timothy M....3:42:00 (7,028)
Skidmore, David N....3:59:05 (11,521)
Skidmore, Jonathan....2:57:02 (875)
Skillett, Nick J....4:19:51 (16,850)
Skilton, Martin J....3:52:26 (9,421)
Skinner, Gregory V....4:41:46 (22,622)
Skinner, James E....3:58:48 (11,416)
Skinner, John P....4:26:48 (18,753)
Skinner, Kevin....2:22:41 (25)
Skinner, Stephen N....3:48:25 (8,447)
Skipp, Asa J....4:39:40 (22,114)
Skippen, Steven D....7:13:26 (34,351)
Skipper, David L....4:06:13 (13,333)
Skipwith, Julian....4:15:12 (15,618)
Skipworth, Paul J....4:30:18 (19,698)
Skivington, Alan M....4:53:14 (25,322)
Skivington, Brian D....4:24:23 (18,106)
Skriczka, James R....4:08:52 (14,010)
Skulnick, Paul....4:35:25 (21,088)
Slack, Rupert A....4:14:07 (15,340)
Slack, William J....4:23:12 (17,786)
Slade, Duncan P....4:47:38 (24,050)
Slade, Glen J....3:09:10 (1,903)
Slade, Jonathan W....5:27:59 (30,264)
Slade, Matt C....4:26:06 (18,566)
Slade, Paul....5:40:59 (31,411)
Slade, Rob M....4:04:39 (12,968)
Slade, Robert....4:59:45 (26,600)
Slager, John....4:16:01 (15,842)
Slama, Alain....3:19:38 (3,183)
Slark-Hollis, Trevor J....5:31:39 (30,627)
Slate, Richard J....4:55:38 (25,810)
Slater, Andrew....4:03:53 (12,802)
Slater, Andy....6:18:26 (33,370)
Slater, Ben T....3:54:58 (10,184)
Slater, Chris....4:36:42 (21,418)
Slater, Frederick J....4:13:49 (15,254)
Slater, Gregg R....3:51:14 (9,105)
Slater, John S....4:25:04 (18,278)
Slater, Leonard G....3:09:37 (1,952)
Slater, Neil....3:31:45 (5,179)
Slater, Peter E....4:45:31 (23,541)
Slatford, Andrew....4:16:04 (15,853)
Slator, Clive....3:46:14 (7,936)
Slatter, Keith A....5:04:23 (27,308)
Slaughter, Daniel....4:05:33 (13,189)
Slaughter, James D....3:37:20 (6,128)
Slaughter, John....4:17:08 (16,135)
Slavin, Laurence M....5:27:04 (30,149)
Sleat, Dylan....5:08:23 (27,871)
Sledmore, Simon J....3:45:12 (7,728)
Sleight, Matthew....4:19:19 (16,707)
Slessor, Neil G....5:16:54 (29,042)
Slinger, John A....3:10:03 (1,993)
Slinn, Gregory J....5:06:00 (27,552)
Slinn, Les F....3:37:27 (6,159)
Slinn, Simon J....4:06:07 (13,318)
Sliwerski, Trevor Z....5:13:36 (28,622)
Sloan, Harry....3:13:25 (2,388)
Sloan, James R....3:42:27 (7,130)
Sloan, Jonathan A....5:00:30 (26,707)
Sloan, Seamus....4:07:05 (13,539)
Sloan, Tomas P....3:06:58 (1,681)
Sloley, Robert J....3:09:48 (1,971)
Sloman, Gary....4:00:54 (12,080)
Sloope, Tom M....3:37:18 (6,125)
Sloot, William G....3:58:15 (11,198)
Sly, Andrew W....4:02:43 (12,547)
Sly, Andy....2:59:15 (1,091)
Slysz, Geoffrey P....3:12:46 (2,298)
Smadja, Alain....4:04:59 (13,046)
Smailes, Paul....4:09:38 (14,209)
Smale, Nigel J....4:18:10 (16,393)
Smale, Tristan W....4:08:57 (14,032)
Small, Christopher W....4:11:13 (14,610)
Small, Jonathan S....4:43:41 (23,098)
Small, Matthew D....3:44:41 (7,597)
Small, Peter....4:45:41 (23,577)
Small, Steve....4:06:31 (13,407)
Smallbone, Simon M....4:31:09 (19,923)
Smalley, Antony W....5:00:06 (26,654)
Smalley, Scott....4:40:02 (22,189)
Smallman, Graham H....4:43:30 (23,049)
Smallwood, Harry J....4:44:09 (23,214)
Smallwood, Ollie J....4:16:53 (16,054)
Smardon, Gregory P....5:27:08 (30,161)
Smart, Albert C....4:33:24 (20,540)
Smart, Christopher R....4:27:09 (18,858)
Smart, Darren I....3:43:40 (7,383)
Smart, Lord....4:57:29 (26,182)
Smart, Matthew N....4:23:50 (17,946)
Smart, Simon J....4:01:28 (12,232)
Smears, Richard....9:03:59 (34,582)
Smeath, David J....3:13:26 (2,393)
Smee, Tim....3:14:17 (2,516)
Smellie, David C....4:41:00 (22,437)
Smiles, Paul W....4:38:00 (21,716)
Smillie, Robert A....4:37:35 (21,613)
Smit, Ben-Burt J....4:16:16 (15,895)
Smit, Cobus....4:50:43 (24,770)
Smith, Alan....4:01:52 (12,329)
Smith, Alex....4:52:22 (25,118)
Smith, Andrew....3:48:08 (8,385)
Smith, Andrew....4:30:47 (19,828)
Smith, Andrew....5:53:10 (32,350)
Smith, Andrew A....3:44:52 (7,648)
Smith, Andrew B....3:29:45 (4,836)
Smith, Andrew C....4:29:34 (19,529)
Smith, Andrew C....5:51:35 (32,261)
Smith, Andrew E....4:36:26 (21,355)
Smith, Andrew J....3:05:31 (1,557)
Smith, Andrew J....3:13:31 (2,396)
Smith, Andrew J....3:21:14 (3,389)
Smith, Andrew K....3:16:11 (2,773)
Smith, Andrew M....4:18:54 (16,599)
Smith, Andrew M....4:37:34 (21,606)
Smith, Andrew M....4:57:55 (26,268)
Smith, Andrew S....4:08:42 (13,969)
Smith, Andrew V....4:38:32 (21,831)
Smith, Andy J....3:50:03 (8,834)
Smith, Anthony....4:13:58 (15,292)
Smith, Anthony K....3:54:02 (9,882)
Smith, Anthony L....4:37:59 (21,711)
Smith, Anthony R....4:26:11 (18,582)
Smith, Barrie J....6:34:05 (33,750)
Smith, Ben....3:25:27 (4,002)
Smith, Ben W....4:47:56 (24,132)
Smith, Bill....3:20:52 (3,337)
Smith, Bill E....4:29:32 (19,524)
Smith, Bradley A....5:55:27 (32,497)
Smith, Brian....4:47:44 (24,080)
Smith, Brian K....4:51:47 (25,001)
Smith, Bryan S....4:40:42 (22,353)
Smith, Cameron A....3:06:08 (1,609)
Smith, Charles A....4:09:23 (14,139)
Smith, Charley D....5:46:02 (31,838)
Smith, Chris....4:11:48 (14,753)
Smith, Chris J....4:31:17 (19,961)
Smith, Chris P....4:36:32 (21,378)
Smith, Chris R....5:14:33 (28,752)
Smith, Christopher A....4:01:58 (12,353)
Smith, Christopher A....4:11:32 (14,687)
Smith, Christopher J....4:01:37 (12,273)
Smith, Christopher J....4:10:39 (14,451)
Smith, Christopher M....3:20:30 (3,291)
Smith, Clive S....3:16:04 (2,760)
Smith, Colin R....3:58:01 (11,122)
Smith, Craig A....3:55:39 (10,389)
Smith, Dale....4:03:56 (12,812)
Smith, Dale A....4:18:24 (16,464)
Smith, Daniel....3:55:41 (10,399)
Smith, Daniel S....3:55:07 (10,241)
Smith, Darren....4:03:05 (12,627)
Smith, Darren D....4:12:42 (14,962)
Smith, Darren M....4:39:44 (22,137)
Smith, David....3:49:12 (8,627)
Smith, David....4:11:15 (14,618)
Smith, David....4:36:24 (21,344)
Smith, David A....4:05:42 (13,222)
Smith, David B....3:24:55 (3,914)

Name	Time (Position)
Smith, David C	4:01:41 (12,289)
Smith, David C	5:00:12 (26,666)
Smith, David G	3:50:20 (8,897)
Smith, David J	5:43:52 (31,639)
Smith, Dean	4:46:55 (23,888)
Smith, Dean G	5:40:30 (31,375)
Smith, Derek A	5:11:35 (28,343)
Smith, Derek G	3:27:56 (4,449)
Smith, Derek R	4:02:59 (12,606)
Smith, Derek R	4:43:38 (23,080)
Smith, Derek W	5:37:01 (31,120)
Smith, Edward	4:33:59 (20,696)
Smith, Edward G	3:16:12 (2,776)
Smith, Frederick	7:15:17 (34,366)
Smith, Gary	3:30:13 (4,927)
Smith, Gary A	4:34:59 (20,974)
Smith, Gary T	4:57:05 (26,104)
Smith, George A	4:56:21 (25,940)
Smith, Gerald S	3:15:07 (2,643)
Smith, Gerry C	3:08:21 (1,826)
Smith, Glenn G	3:44:41 (7,597)
Smith, Gordon A	3:01:33 (1,279)
Smith, Graham P	4:01:34 (12,259)
Smith, Greg	3:59:04 (11,511)
Smith, Guy C	3:43:35 (7,363)
Smith, Harry J	4:02:15 (12,430)
Smith, Hayden R	5:19:35 (29,369)
Smith, Haydn G	3:43:00 (7,239)
Smith, Howard G	4:21:10 (17,216)
Smith, Iain	3:32:25 (5,304)
Smith, Ian	2:56:35 (847)
Smith, Ian	4:33:29 (20,572)
Smith, Ian	5:13:19 (28,580)
Smith, Ian J	4:28:57 (19,390)
Smith, Ian M	3:03:44 (1,434)
Smith, Ian R	4:28:07 (19,137)
Smith, J Edward K	6:33:18 (33,729)
Smith, James A	4:44:39 (23,338)
Smith, James D	5:34:11 (30,854)
Smith, James G	4:36:56 (21,474)
Smith, Jamie K	3:40:14 (6,681)
Smith, Jamie K	6:26:30 (33,585)
Smith, Jeremy	5:43:05 (31,576)
Smith, Jeremy P	3:15:04 (2,640)
Smith, John C	5:04:50 (27,372)
Smith, John G	4:33:27 (20,562)
Smith, Jon M	5:25:39 (30,000)
Smith, Jonathan	4:45:21 (23,502)
Smith, Jonathan	4:52:15 (25,091)
Smith, Jonathan M	3:53:57 (9,854)
Smith, Jonathan P	4:32:31 (20,307)
Smith, Josh T	4:08:19 (13,857)
Smith, Karl R	4:10:34 (14,428)
Smith, Keith A	3:26:23 (4,171)
Smith, Keith A	4:12:33 (14,940)
Smith, Kempley M	3:21:09 (3,378)
Smith, Kenny D	5:44:21 (31,706)
Smith, Kevin D	5:41:59 (31,496)
Smith, Kevin J	4:09:33 (14,188)
Smith, Lee	3:29:04 (4,682)
Smith, Lee G	2:48:30 (447)
Smith, Leigh A	5:03:05 (27,115)
Smith, Luke O	4:13:13 (15,091)
Smith, Malcolm	5:02:14 (26,997)
Smith, Malcolm	5:09:41 (28,088)
Smith, Malcolm C	4:15:05 (15,594)
Smith, Mark	4:40:55 (22,410)
Smith, Mark A	3:51:01 (9,052)
Smith, Mark A	4:00:43 (12,039)
Smith, Mark A	4:20:34 (17,050)
Smith, Mark A	5:42:42 (31,548)
Smith, Mark D	4:35:18 (21,056)
Smith, Mark G	4:05:39 (13,213)
Smith, Mark J	4:10:31 (14,415)
Smith, Mark J	6:06:46 (33,011)
Smith, Mark P	4:26:10 (18,579)
Smith, Martin A	4:01:32 (12,251)
Smith, Martin J	2:56:42 (856)
Smith, Martin J	3:59:57 (11,836)
Smith, Martin J	4:48:16 (24,196)
Smith, Martin J	5:34:38 (30,900)
Smith, Martyn D	5:48:08 (31,984)
Smith, Matt	5:32:33 (30,704)
Smith, Matthew	4:02:30 (12,497)
Smith, Matthew D	3:41:55 (7,013)
Smith, Matthew D	3:56:23 (10,594)
Smith, Matthew W	3:57:56 (11,098)
Smith, Michael	4:18:42 (16,552)
Smith, Michael D	5:00:53 (26,776)
Smith, Michael J	2:31:24 (81)
Smith, Michael J	3:06:12 (1,618)
Smith, Michael J	4:15:14 (15,626)
Smith, Michael J	4:41:06 (22,460)
Smith, Michael W	4:40:50 (22,389)
Smith, Mike	3:24:58 (3,921)
Smith, Mike	3:35:40 (5,827)
Smith, Mike	4:59:10 (26,506)
Smith, Nathan	3:52:34 (9,448)
Smith, Neil C	4:11:00 (14,543)
Smith, Neville	4:53:48 (25,440)
Smith, Nicholas	4:20:45 (17,103)
Smith, Nicholas C	4:11:05 (14,571)
Smith, Nicholas J	3:51:44 (9,236)
Smith, Nicholas N	4:19:44 (16,821)
Smith, Nicholas P	4:32:51 (20,388)
Smith, Nicholas R	4:28:53 (19,371)
Smith, Nick	4:10:53 (14,516)
Smith, Nick W	4:15:54 (15,807)
Smith, Nigel B	3:47:27 (8,212)
Smith, Oliver	5:43:30 (31,607)
Smith, Patrick J	4:06:04 (13,305)
Smith, Paul	4:21:16 (17,244)
Smith, Paul	5:02:50 (27,085)
Smith, Paul	5:18:32 (29,232)
Smith, Paul D	5:17:54 (29,168)
Smith, Paul J	4:02:40 (12,538)
Smith, Pete	4:48:57 (24,359)
Smith, Peter	4:13:04 (15,054)
Smith, Peter A	3:24:27 (3,837)
Smith, Peter J	3:16:38 (2,825)
Smith, Peter J	4:11:39 (14,719)
Smith, Peter M	3:51:48 (9,248)
Smith, Phil A	5:00:44 (26,747)
Smith, Phil R	5:18:31 (29,231)
Smith, Philip	4:31:17 (19,961)
Smith, Philip A	3:00:34 (1,209)
Smith, Philip J	4:14:56 (15,540)
Smith, Philip M	3:02:12 (1,324)
Smith, Philip M	5:31:34 (30,617)
Smith, Richard	3:10:01 (1,989)
Smith, Richard A	3:40:48 (6,780)
Smith, Richard A	5:20:55 (29,488)
Smith, Richard C	3:56:21 (10,577)
Smith, Richard D	4:38:11 (21,752)
Smith, Richard F	3:50:59 (9,042)
Smith, Richard F	4:25:47 (18,473)
Smith, Richard I	5:58:03 (32,634)
Smith, Richard N	2:58:43 (1,032)
Smith, Robert	3:48:10 (8,392)
Smith, Robert	5:14:45 (28,781)
Smith, Robert J	3:49:45 (8,758)
Smith, Robert L	5:55:12 (32,478)
Smith, Robert M	3:11:27 (2,145)
Smith, Robert W	4:28:28 (19,252)
Smith, Roger A	4:15:14 (15,626)
Smith, Ross H	3:50:38 (8,968)
Smith, Rupert C	3:48:46 (8,525)
Smith, Russell H	3:35:33 (5,800)
Smith, Ryan P	4:24:54 (18,241)
Smith, Sebastian	4:42:04 (22,689)
Smith, Simon A	4:00:33 (11,987)
Smith, Simon A	4:33:03 (20,442)
Smith, Simon C	4:01:47 (12,313)
Smith, Simon P	5:09:27 (28,036)
Smith, Stephen	4:33:40 (23,095)
Smith, Stephen	5:38:18 (31,213)
Smith, Stephen J	6:17:28 (33,334)
Smith, Stephen L	5:16:21 (28,976)
Smith, Stephen R	3:53:31 (9,715)
Smith, Steve A	6:29:53 (33,653)
Smith, Steve J	3:15:18 (2,674)
Smith, Steve R	3:08:30 (1,839)
Smith, Steven A	5:05:30 (27,476)
Smith, Steven J	4:11:57 (14,791)
Smith, Stuart	2:56:09 (815)
Smith, Stuart A	4:27:48 (19,022)
Smith, Stuart I	7:15:05 (34,365)
Smith, Stuart W	4:44:49 (23,375)
Smith, Terry A	4:05:03 (13,060)
Smith, Timothy	3:57:17 (10,887)
Smith, Timothy C	4:00:27 (11,960)
Smith, Timothy D	4:46:11 (23,709)
Smith, Tom R	5:20:08 (29,419)
Smith, Tony D	4:19:03 (16,639)
Smith, Trevor	4:39:27 (22,073)
Smith, Trevor C	6:47:23 (34,028)
Smith, Trevor J	4:18:53 (16,595)
Smith, Uriah B	6:36:30 (33,805)
Smith, Warren L	5:24:01 (29,808)
Smith, William	5:37:49 (31,181)
Smith, William G	4:24:06 (18,019)
Smith, William H	3:53:07 (9,611)
Smitham, David L	3:46:33 (8,013)
Smithers, Andy J	4:17:45 (16,294)
Smithers, Richard J	3:47:59 (8,345)
Smithers, Stuart M	6:17:38 (33,343)
Smithey, John	4:35:39 (21,152)
Smith-Maxwell, Edward J	3:47:35 (8,243)
Smoult, Robin M	3:00:01 (1,171)
Smout, Martin J	4:48:52 (24,335)
Smussi, Sandro	4:03:13 (12,658)
Smyth, Alistair G	3:19:28 (3,158)
Smyth, Barry	4:39:18 (22,049)
Smyth, Ben A	3:29:59 (4,882)
Smyth, Brett	3:57:02 (10,805)
Smyth, David	6:27:35 (33,615)
Smyth, John H	2:53:54 (688)
Smyth, Jonny P	4:17:04 (16,112)
Smyth, Kevin A	3:17:09 (2,880)
Smyth, Louis	4:28:50 (19,360)
Smyth, Nathaniel J	4:17:05 (16,119)
Smyth, Nicholas B	3:45:10 (7,719)
Smyth, Patrick E	6:20:19 (33,404)
Smyth, Rory	4:10:36 (14,433)
Smythe, Stephen	2:43:40 (284)
Snailum, Gary P	3:54:31 (10,040)
Snaith, David M	3:20:45 (3,326)
Snaith, Thomas	3:42:57 (7,223)
Snead, Martin P	4:19:00 (16,625)
Sneddon, Alan T	5:50:06 (32,135)
Sneezum, Patrick	5:01:30 (26,871)
Snelgrove, Richard A	3:44:25 (7,539)
Snelgrove, William R	3:15:51 (2,737)
Snell, Andrew J	4:50:06 (24,623)
Snell, Andrew J	4:58:17 (26,341)
Snell, Daniel B	3:43:18 (7,306)
Snell, Phillip	4:58:17 (26,341)
Snelling, Michael	4:30:40 (19,791)
Snider, Craig B	4:03:03 (12,620)
Snodgrass, Ryan	3:19:12 (3,120)
Snook, Glenn R	4:41:36 (22,581)
Snook, Philip	7:06:52 (34,282)
Snow, Andrew	5:44:13 (31,688)
Snowden, Chris	3:40:24 (6,718)
Snowdon, Benjamin I	4:59:13 (26,520)
Sobey, Kieron J	3:58:19 (11,226)
Soderberg, Phillip	4:20:59 (17,177)
Soegaard-Hansen, Jan	3:56:42 (10,690)
Soekeland, Georg	4:18:20 (16,443)
Soervaag, Reidar	4:52:52 (25,241)
Sokhal, Kulvinder	3:57:41 (11,006)
Sokolov, Aleksey	2:11:41 (9)
Sola, Barthelemy	4:16:30 (15,959)
Sola, Miguel	3:20:05 (3,233)
Solanki, Vinay	4:47:39 (24,057)
Solari, Christophe M	3:39:25 (6,522)
Solbes, Marc F	3:29:31 (4,787)
Sole, James H	4:47:32 (24,026)
Sole, Joe	4:13:05 (15,063)
Sole, Paul	4:01:26 (12,224)
Solly, Gary	4:36:05 (21,263)
Solomon, Chris	5:34:46 (30,909)
Solomon, David B	5:04:55 (27,385)
Solomon, Tom	2:42:13 (246)
Solomons, Darren P	6:28:19 (33,629)
Solon, Francisco C	4:54:29 (25,577)
Solsona, Oscar	4:25:06 (18,288)
Soltysik, Andrew	2:59:57 (1,164)
Soma, Chhotu	5:45:26 (31,797)

Somerfield, Christopher D 3:53:45 (9,791)
Somers, Michael 5:09:20 (28,019)
Somersall, David A 3:09:51 (1,976)
Somerville, Gerald F 8:27:57 (34,564)
Sommavilla, Yves 3:15:11 (2,651)
Sommer, Carl 2:42:21 (250)
Sommers, Robertus 3:46:20 (7,960)
Sommerville, Bart 4:41:07 (22,467)
Sones, Kye E 5:34:10 (30,852)
Sonley, Garth W 5:44:25 (31,713)
Sonnenstein, Keith 5:03:46 (27,221)
Sonnery-Cottet, Damien 3:44:56 (7,665)
Soon, Yew C 4:33:36 (20,609)
Soper, Matthew P 4:31:37 (20,056)
Soper, Steven A 4:05:35 (13,198)
Sorby, Robert C 3:42:43 (7,175)
Sorensen, Jorgen M 3:59:33 (11,688)
Sorensen, Per L 4:31:48 (20,103)
Sorensen, Robert S 4:09:19 (14,122)
Sorley, Scott 4:20:06 (16,913)
Sorrentino, Lawrence D 3:36:07 (5,901)
Sorted, Simon 3:28:15 (4,513)
Soto, Thierry 4:05:58 (13,289)
Sotos Garcia, José L 3:21:56 (3,479)
Souden, Alex J 3:30:39 (4,991)
Soul, John P 3:36:46 (6,005)
Soulsby, Tom 5:04:11 (27,279)
Soum, Laurent 3:47:56 (8,335)
Soussan, Henry C 4:30:48 (19,833)
Soutar, Gavin 3:12:42 (2,291)
South, Clifford R 4:15:49 (15,786)
South, William 4:23:42 (17,914)
Southam, Christopher 2:34:48 (110)
Southby, David P 3:12:40 (2,282)
Southern, Anthony C 4:13:36 (15,187)
Southgate, David C 3:49:43 (8,752)
Southgate, John 5:18:02 (29,185)
Southgate, Mathew J 5:11:25 (28,320)
Southin, Barney S 2:35:20 (117)
Southward, Will 4:15:22 (15,655)
Southwell, Anthony M 3:54:19 (9,963)
Southworth, Dominic A 3:35:34 (5,806)
Southworth, Jonathan P 4:43:10 (22,975)
Sowden, Jonathan P 4:23:08 (17,760)
Sowler, Jamie 4:26:23 (18,629)
Sowler, Jonathan G 4:42:40 (22,846)
Spalton, Phil N 4:26:24 (18,635)
Spangler, Alan M 3:58:55 (11,460)
Spano, Nicolo 3:11:43 (2,176)
Sparano, Ciro 4:25:56 (18,517)
Sparey, Darryl 4:49:20 (24,442)
Sparkes, Steve 4:29:34 (19,529)
Sparks, Ian A 2:59:49 (1,151)
Sparks, Jason L 4:49:13 (24,417)
Sparrey, Graham M 3:02:34 (1,348)
Sparrey, Ian G 4:39:04 (21,994)
Spary, Adrian 4:33:09 (20,470)
Spatz, Ian D 4:08:51 (14,006)
Speak, Andrew 3:03:29 (1,417)
Speake, Malcolm D 5:09:31 (28,054)
Speake, William J 2:36:03 (131)
Speakman, James I 4:12:00 (14,812)
Speakman, Paul D 4:20:12 (16,942)
Spear, Jonathan R 3:40:28 (6,729)
Spear, Mark T 3:49:46 (8,764)
Speare, Adam 4:36:40 (21,409)
Spearpoint, Nicholas J 4:14:58 (15,548)
Speck, Adam B 3:06:39 (1,651)
Speck, Dennis 2:59:03 (1,064)
Speed, Christopher A 3:44:52 (7,648)
Speed, David G 4:22:12 (17,495)
Speed, Fergus 4:55:37 (25,803)
Speed, Morley W 3:38:03 (6,274)
Speight, Dennis N 3:47:04 (8,125)
Speiser, Thomas M 4:24:22 (18,098)
Spells, Simon G 4:07:34 (13,658)
Spence, Derek M 3:57:27 (10,942)
Spence, Gary J 4:58:40 (26,410)
Spence, James M 5:55:57 (32,518)
Spence, Shaun A 3:53:46 (9,796)
Spence, Tony 4:55:16 (25,745)
Spencer, Adrian 3:21:49 (3,460)
Spencer, Andrew M 3:03:05 (1,380)
Spencer, Anthony P 3:30:25 (4,955)
Spencer, Anthony W 3:49:05 (8,599)
Spencer, Daniel I 3:27:05 (4,296)
Spencer, David P 2:44:51 (325)
Spencer, Dennis 5:12:41 (28,489)
Spencer, Ian H 3:29:13 (4,718)
Spencer, James S 4:50:24 (24,684)
Spencer, Jeff 4:37:30 (21,592)
Spencer, Jeremy A 3:05:30 (1,553)
Spencer, Jonathan P 3:31:54 (5,198)
Spencer, Mark N 5:28:02 (30,270)
Spencer, Martyn J 6:00:59 (32,779)
Spencer, Neil C 5:26:47 (30,122)
Spencer, Nicholas R 3:40:49 (6,784)
Spencer, Phil 4:50:58 (24,837)
Spencer, Phil J 3:34:49 (5,669)
Spencer, Richard D 4:09:42 (14,228)
Spencer, Russell J 4:55:15 (25,742)
Spencer, Ryan M 3:14:30 (2,546)
Spencer, Sion J 5:04:36 (27,342)
Spencer, Stuart 3:09:06 (1,894)
Spencer, Timothy J 5:04:36 (27,342)
Spencer, Will 3:50:42 (8,990)
Spencer-Perkins, Michael D 5:00:13 (26,667)
Spens, Michael C 3:54:04 (9,894)
Spensley, Martin J 4:44:15 (23,241)
Speroni, Cristian 5:22:27 (29,657)
Sperring, Mark E 6:22:26 (33,472)
Spianzze, Luciano 3:37:55 (6,242)
Spicer, Derek A 5:32:47 (30,727)
Spicer, Graham F 4:40:35 (22,325)
Spicer, John E 5:12:42 (28,494)
Spicer, Roger A 5:35:18 (30,962)
Spielmann, Horst 5:30:29 (30,525)
Spielmann, Rolf P 4:21:56 (17,435)
Spiers, Adam M 4:21:40 (17,364)
Spiga, Marcello 3:59:27 (11,656)
Spiller, Gerald W 5:29:35 (30,435)
Spilsted, Martin 4:53:40 (25,413)
Spilsted, Nathan 3:58:06 (11,142)
Spindler, Paul 6:17:08 (33,324)
Spink, Adam J 3:39:06 (6,452)
Spinks, Lee E 4:56:31 (25,973)
Spiteri, Emmanuel O 3:50:09 (8,859)
Spittle, Tony 3:57:19 (10,902)
Splain, Mark A 4:30:24 (19,723)
Spoerer, Peter A 4:57:21 (26,152)
Spooner, Darren 3:21:49 (3,460)
Spooner, Jonathan E 3:34:33 (5,627)
Spooner, Richard 5:08:45 (27,937)
Spooner, Richard S 4:07:44 (13,704)
Spotswood, Michael 4:41:35 (22,575)
Spouse, Andrew D 4:23:14 (17,794)
Spouse, Antony J 4:22:00 (17,455)
Spouse, Iain 3:36:33 (5,975)
Spraggett, Simon J 4:33:24 (20,540)
Spraggs, Gerald E 5:00:23 (26,692)
Sprague, Andrew I 4:12:55 (15,007)
Spratt, Graham K 6:03:18 (32,859)
Spratt, Norman S 2:58:33 (1,014)
Spreadborough, Ashley J 3:52:33 (9,444)
Spreadbury, Leroy 5:00:15 (26,676)
Spring, Fred J 4:33:39 (20,622)
Springett, Peter 3:32:23 (5,296)
Springthorpe, Nigel 4:42:27 (22,790)
Sprosen, Bruce I 5:38:43 (31,241)
Sprosen, Tim 3:17:03 (2,869)
Sproston, Sam 4:11:17 (14,622)
Spruell, Robin J 4:11:10 (14,597)
Sprules, Anthony 3:00:47 (1,223)
Sprules, Christopher F 3:17:58 (2,984)
Spurgeon, Jeremy C 4:55:35 (25,797)
Spurr, Tim J 3:43:23 (7,321)
Spurrell, David 5:09:27 (28,036)
Squibb, Westley J 5:18:13 (29,200)
Srikandakumar, Anton 5:01:51 (26,936)
Srikanthan, Karthikan A 4:00:55 (12,086)
Srinivasan, Makaram S 5:22:15 (29,633)
St Aubyn, Charles H 4:09:12 (14,088)
St Clair, Richard 3:09:14 (1,914)
St Croix, Dennis C 4:18:24 (16,464)
St Pierre, James E 3:53:11 (9,635)
Stace, Edward 4:18:11 (16,399)
Stacey, Mark 5:16:12 (28,959)
Stacey, Nigel 4:23:10 (17,770)
Stacey, Paul A 3:08:57 (1,872)
Stacey, Robin D 4:46:37 (23,801)
Stacey, Steve J 3:52:13 (9,363)
Stach, Richard 3:37:07 (6,084)
Stack, Christopher J 3:48:05 (8,368)
Stacy, Gary W 5:02:36 (27,052)
Staddon, Andrew D 5:58:42 (32,681)
Staffan, James M 5:56:12 (32,537)
Stafford, Anthony T 3:58:09 (11,163)
Stafford, John F 3:28:33 (4,569)
Stafford, Patrick G 3:39:22 (6,512)
Stafford, Thomas A 3:43:43 (7,391)
Stafford, Thomas M 4:51:35 (24,958)
Stagg, Hugo H 4:39:37 (22,100)
Stagg, Steven 4:24:31 (18,147)
Staggs, Robert 4:36:24 (21,344)
Staggs, Robert J 4:07:00 (13,518)
Stainbank, Warner D 3:58:49 (11,426)
Stainer, Peter 2:54:23 (715)
Staines, Toby N 2:59:52 (1,156)
Stallard, Lee R 4:01:45 (12,306)
Stallard, Philip 4:11:38 (14,712)
Stalley, Andrew C 3:11:23 (2,135)
Stalley, Derek R 4:48:38 (24,277)
Stamford, John E 5:58:36 (32,676)
Stamler, John 3:37:10 (6,096)
Stammers, James 4:16:38 (15,989)
Stamp, David E 3:21:40 (3,441)
Stanborough, Darren J 4:58:37 (26,403)
Stanborough, Ryan J 4:10:34 (14,428)
Stanbrook, Anton D 6:37:49 (33,837)
Stanbrook, Bob 3:55:29 (10,335)
Standen, Jason K 4:07:34 (13,658)
Standen, Michael W 4:25:29 (18,388)
Standen, Neil R 3:36:04 (5,892)
Standen McDougal, James S 3:43:06 (7,266)
Standfast, David J 4:07:10 (13,568)
Standing, Robert 4:28:37 (19,296)
Standley, Glen M 4:23:45 (17,929)
Stanford, Jonathan P 4:30:27 (19,735)
Stanger, Mike J 3:45:36 (7,814)
Stanger, Sean J 3:26:27 (4,179)
Stanier, Keith 4:05:37 (13,202)
Stanier, Raymond 2:53:59 (691)
Staniforth, Phil 3:43:53 (7,434)
Staniforth, Ryan P 4:06:21 (13,364)
Staniland, Anthony 3:33:12 (5,421)
Staniland, Paul 5:39:06 (31,270)
Stanish, Jeremy B 4:53:33 (25,387)
Stanius, Fredrik 3:28:41 (4,600)
Stanley, Christopher M 5:33:07 (30,761)
Stanley, Clem 4:59:09 (26,500)
Stanley, Darren 5:34:02 (30,841)
Stanley, Marc 4:56:53 (26,047)
Stanley, Roger 3:49:53 (8,794)
Stannard, Alex J 4:34:20 (20,781)
Stannard, John 4:21:33 (17,319)
Stannard, Paul L 3:24:59 (3,929)
Stannett, Charlie 4:51:29 (24,935)
Stannett, Steve M 5:21:06 (29,509)
Stansfield, Hamilton A 4:33:56 (20,689)
Stansfield, Peter 3:36:17 (5,929)
Stansfield, Steve L 4:41:39 (22,598)
Stanton, Martin 4:35:02 (20,992)
Staples, Mark 4:53:29 (25,368)
Staples, Robert A 3:56:36 (10,663)
Stapley, Gregg W 3:29:04 (4,682)
Stapley, Jim O 3:07:31 (1,735)
Stapley, Matthew J 4:13:43 (15,230)
Starbrook, Samuel J 4:46:02 (23,678)
Stares, David M 4:28:12 (19,171)
Stark, Adam D 4:35:17 (21,051)
Stark, Fraser 3:42:51 (7,205)
Stark, Sam 3:26:18 (4,154)
Stark, Stephen 3:12:01 (2,210)
Stark, Warren 4:32:51 (20,388)
Starkie, Timothy M 5:43:36 (31,614)
Starks, Gordon C 4:09:21 (14,134)
Starling, Barrie 4:14:14 (15,377)
Starns, Ben A 5:29:19 (30,408)
Starr, Adam 4:29:26 (19,503)

Statham, Jason K	2:58:11 (966)	
Statham, Malcolm J	3:27:24 (4,349)	
Statham, Neil F	4:33:51 (20,671)	
Staton, Oliver N	5:14:55 (28,808)	
Statter, Ian G	3:49:42 (8,746)	
Staveley, Andy J	3:00:08 (1,174)	
Stavenuiter, Kees	3:54:01 (9,878)	
Staves, Trevor	4:40:10 (22,229)	
Stavrinides, Chris	4:10:04 (14,310)	
Stawowski, Peter	3:49:45 (8,758)	
Stead, Colin	3:29:29 (4,780)	
Stead, Edward J	3:29:30 (4,782)	
Stead, Jonathan P	2:42:43 (259)	
Stead, Nigel	4:38:52 (21,934)	
Steadman, Jon G	3:41:25 (6,920)	
Steadman, Mark R	3:51:38 (9,206)	
Steadman, Robert J	3:36:06 (5,898)	
Steadman, Terry	3:33:55 (5,534)	
Stearn, Martyn K	3:48:15 (8,414)	
Steatham, James	3:58:20 (11,236)	
Stecher, Thomas	2:59:43 (1,142)	
Steeet, Graeme P	3:20:40 (3,315)	
Steel, John R	4:33:39 (20,622)	
Steel, Marc L	5:19:06 (29,303)	
Steel, Mark I	3:46:46 (8,054)	
Steel, Martin	3:16:12 (2,776)	
Steel, Spencer	4:34:14 (20,765)	
Steele, André A	6:43:13 (33,944)	
Steele, Andrew T	5:26:47 (30,122)	
Steele, Chris	4:49:03 (24,386)	
Steele, Christopher D	3:50:40 (8,980)	
Steele, John A	4:11:54 (14,778)	
Steele, Julian D	3:36:23 (5,948)	
Steele, Michael A	3:54:15 (9,943)	
Steele, Roy N	3:32:05 (5,239)	
Steele, Wayne	4:16:20 (15,915)	
Steels, Robin	3:54:06 (9,903)	
Steeples, Trevor M	3:46:05 (7,903)	
Stefanelli, Moreno	3:30:44 (5,007)	
Stefanowski, Robert	3:37:51 (6,227)	
Steggles, Daniel J	4:06:45 (13,462)	
Stegmann, Richard	4:26:29 (18,662)	
Stehr, Peter	4:37:16 (21,539)	
Stein, Bill	4:00:08 (11,882)	
Steinacher, Wolfgang	3:59:48 (11,782)	
Steinbock, Mike P	4:30:30 (19,744)	
Stendall, Chris A	5:18:22 (29,214)	
Stene, Jak	3:56:32 (10,639)	
Steneker, Robert J	3:54:59 (10,191)	
Stengel, Kai	4:31:56 (20,147)	
Stenhouse, Jamieson M	4:31:11 (19,934)	
Stenning, Gavin B	4:08:52 (14,010)	
Stenson, Ian J	4:22:57 (17,716)	
Stenson, Michael	4:48:34 (24,265)	
Stephant, Jacques	3:33:56 (5,539)	
Stephen, Richard P	4:30:12 (19,678)	
Stephen, Stuart B	4:39:58 (22,175)	
Stephens, Andrew	3:51:54 (9,276)	
Stephens, David	5:35:23 (30,967)	
Stephens, Fergus	3:56:00 (10,491)	
Stephens, Garry A	4:29:03 (19,412)	
Stephens, Graham C	2:47:41 (409)	
Stephens, John	4:00:48 (12,056)	
Stephens, John	4:36:44 (21,423)	
Stephens, Keith J	6:05:26 (32,945)	
Stephens, Paul J	6:05:26 (32,945)	
Stephens, Peter J	4:36:06 (21,268)	
Stephens, Timothy W	6:18:12 (33,361)	
Stephens, Toby C	5:31:34 (30,617)	
Stephens, Todd M	3:53:48 (9,808)	
Stephens, Tony	4:32:38 (20,331)	
Stephens, Tony	4:46:06 (23,689)	
Stephenson, Andrew J	5:43:36 (31,614)	
Stephenson, Charlie	3:51:33 (9,182)	
Stephenson, Darren	4:21:29 (17,300)	
Stephenson, Jack C	4:21:31 (17,312)	
Stephenson, Jeffrey B	3:30:44 (5,007)	
Stephenson, Mathew S	2:54:43 (730)	
Stephenson, Philip	3:34:40 (5,638)	
Stephenson, Thomas	4:08:51 (14,006)	
Stepler, Jeff	3:26:28 (4,182)	
Stepler, Paul W	3:36:14 (5,919)	
Stepniewski, Robert	5:12:40 (28,480)	

Steptoe, Colin F	2:45:10 (338)	
Sterling, Gerald M	3:50:56 (9,035)	
Sternkopf, Stefan	2:56:31 (843)	
Sterry, Andrew G	3:58:26 (11,276)	
Sterry-Macdonald, George W	3:34:05 (5,561)	
Steuernagel, Curt	3:58:00 (11,116)	
Stevens, Alan D	4:43:47 (23,119)	
Stevens, Andrew G	3:46:37 (8,025)	
Stevens, Andrew J	4:09:30 (14,174)	
Stevens, Anthony	5:09:56 (28,135)	
Stevens, Bernard E	4:36:11 (21,289)	
Stevens, Brian A	3:29:56 (4,873)	
Stevens, Craig J	5:25:29 (29,986)	
Stevens, Daniel J	4:21:37 (17,341)	
Stevens, David	6:30:28 (33,671)	
Stevens, Gary S	6:39:02 (33,866)	
Stevens, Gavin R	2:32:26 (88)	
Stevens, Kevin	4:47:15 (23,969)	
Stevens, Mark F	4:21:55 (17,430)	
Stevens, Martin J	2:55:47 (793)	
Stevens, Nicholas H	3:00:54 (1,235)	
Stevens, Paul	3:48:41 (8,507)	
Stevens, Paul R	5:23:56 (29,798)	
Stevens, Peter R	3:36:58 (6,058)	
Stevens, Robert	3:26:35 (4,202)	
Stevens, Roy	3:46:19 (7,956)	
Stevens, Will G	5:29:39 (30,442)	
Stevens-Olsen, Andy	3:40:41 (6,756)	
Stevenson, Antony M	4:45:49 (23,626)	
Stevenson, Charles D	4:57:44 (26,234)	
Stevenson, Huw J	4:59:02 (26,482)	
Stevenson, Iain J	4:27:31 (18,953)	
Stevenson, Laurence E	4:22:34 (17,601)	
Stevenson, Matthew D	3:17:48 (2,963)	
Stevenson, William C	4:50:07 (24,625)	
Stevick, Joseph W	2:48:01 (424)	
Steward, Andrew	4:15:34 (15,720)	
Steward, Jonathan A	4:33:30 (20,577)	
Steward, Marlon G	5:46:09 (31,848)	
Steward, Paul	5:54:08 (32,414)	
Stewart, Alex	4:14:58 (15,548)	
Stewart, Alexander J	5:37:34 (31,159)	
Stewart, Barry A	3:11:47 (2,187)	
Stewart, Conal D	3:45:59 (7,888)	
Stewart, Gary	4:03:33 (12,735)	
Stewart, Gary M	3:38:53 (6,425)	
Stewart, George	2:40:46 (210)	
Stewart, Gordon K	5:40:54 (31,404)	
Stewart, Iain	4:10:25 (14,391)	
Stewart, Iain	4:34:29 (20,820)	
Stewart, James D	5:01:49 (26,932)	
Stewart, James M	5:23:04 (29,706)	
Stewart, Jay W	3:54:07 (9,909)	
Stewart, Kenneth G	3:42:39 (7,164)	
Stewart, Kevin O	4:24:57 (18,249)	
Stewart, Mark	3:33:55 (5,534)	
Stewart, Nick	4:07:27 (13,627)	
Stewart, Robert A	3:30:45 (5,012)	
Stewart, Robin	4:08:45 (13,980)	
Stewart, Ryan J	3:01:24 (1,269)	
Stewart, Steven	5:26:49 (30,132)	
Stewart, Taylor R	4:25:48 (18,482)	
Stewart, Thomas	5:32:03 (30,667)	
Stewart, Tim	3:54:57 (10,179)	
Stick, Carl R	4:12:55 (15,007)	
Stickelbrucks, Tim	4:12:34 (14,944)	
Stiff, Clive	3:18:20 (3,023)	
Stiff, Michael J	3:05:40 (1,567)	
Stiffin, Rob	4:14:27 (15,436)	
Stiles, Andrew D	3:14:16 (2,513)	
Stiles, Joseph H	3:45:08 (7,713)	
Stiles, Robert D	4:24:51 (18,229)	
Still, Nathan	3:51:25 (9,157)	
Still, Sam	4:01:30 (12,241)	
Still, Stuart J	3:47:03 (8,122)	
Stillwell, Timothy P	3:55:05 (10,225)	
Stinchcombe, Nigel S	3:22:36 (3,584)	
Stippig, Bernaard	4:08:10 (13,825)	
Stirling, Andy J	4:31:06 (19,910)	
Stirling, Fraser T	4:10:44 (14,475)	
Stirrup, Paul G	3:31:24 (5,116)	
Stoat, Antony D	3:42:17 (7,090)	
Stocchero, Daniel M	4:20:01 (16,890)	

Stock, Christopher	4:57:41 (26,228)	
Stock, Philip A	3:35:50 (5,852)	
Stock, Tim	2:58:42 (1,031)	
Stock, Timothy	6:00:33 (32,762)	
Stock, Tobias W	3:55:35 (10,367)	
Stock, William E	4:52:49 (25,227)	
Stockdale, Peter C	3:06:23 (1,634)	
Stocker, Bryan	3:56:22 (10,582)	
Stocker, Jim	3:51:15 (9,109)	
Stocker, John	4:36:39 (21,402)	
Stocker, Paul	4:15:03 (15,579)	
Stockford, Michael J	4:48:22 (24,218)	
Stockley, Jamie M	3:51:36 (9,196)	
Stockreisser, Patrick J	3:24:06 (3,791)	
Stocks, Michael A	2:41:32 (234)	
Stocks, Robert E	3:17:34 (2,937)	
Stockton, Mark	3:46:58 (8,102)	
Stockton, Nigel	4:16:38 (15,989)	
Stofberg, Nicholas H	5:46:18 (31,861)	
Stoffell, Christopher D	4:56:06 (25,892)	
Stoker, Brian	4:57:45 (26,237)	
Stoker, Hendrik S	4:02:06 (12,389)	
Stoker, Robert J	4:00:24 (11,948)	
Stokes, Clifford R	4:07:19 (13,599)	
Stokes, Ian W	4:14:56 (15,540)	
Stokes, Michael	4:38:02 (21,721)	
Stokes, Michael K	4:48:37 (24,274)	
Stokes, Mike E	3:49:39 (8,731)	
Stokes, Wayne J	3:30:18 (4,939)	
Stoll, Eddie	8:04:20 (34,536)	
Stone, Andy	4:51:11 (24,878)	
Stone, David M	2:38:49 (179)	
Stone, Desmond G	5:04:05 (27,261)	
Stone, Gab	3:59:13 (11,568)	
Stone, Gerald	6:23:14 (33,496)	
Stone, Guy C	4:17:07 (16,128)	
Stone, Ian A	4:51:29 (24,935)	
Stone, Judson	4:39:36 (22,099)	
Stone, Kevin P	4:49:52 (24,564)	
Stone, Mark	3:31:16 (5,095)	
Stone, Mat	3:57:34 (10,971)	
Stone, Patrick C	3:59:50 (11,797)	
Stone, Peter	5:38:37 (31,231)	
Stone, Rory	4:30:57 (19,874)	
Stone, Sam	4:34:52 (20,931)	
Stone, Simon	5:29:08 (30,389)	
Stone, Simon N	4:35:09 (21,020)	
Stone, Stefan P	3:08:18 (1,821)	
Stone, Steven D	4:24:25 (18,114)	
Stone, Stuart J	3:25:33 (4,020)	
Stoneham, Stuart	3:50:35 (8,949)	
Stonehouse, David	5:10:06 (28,163)	
Stoneley, Andrew	3:55:23 (10,309)	
Stoneley, Paul A	3:17:48 (2,963)	
Stones, Chris	4:09:58 (14,291)	
Stoodley, Lee	4:26:49 (18,761)	
Stopher, Andy M	4:04:51 (13,011)	
Stopher, Bradley	4:43:49 (23,128)	
Stopher, Jay P	4:49:19 (24,436)	
Stopher, Jed	4:52:58 (25,264)	
Storer, Sam	3:56:58 (10,781)	
Storey, Daniel	4:06:46 (13,466)	
Storey, John A	5:30:23 (30,514)	
Storey, John E	4:25:48 (18,482)	
Storey, Liam M	3:53:30 (9,711)	
Storey, Matthew H	3:39:13 (6,477)	
Storey, Simon M	3:55:26 (10,316)	
Storey, Steven B	4:04:25 (12,916)	
Stork, Robert F	4:18:23 (16,458)	
Storr, Francis	4:53:29 (25,368)	
Story, Sam O	3:31:42 (5,169)	
Story, Tom	4:27:33 (18,964)	
Stott, Chris	4:47:04 (23,923)	
Stott, Nic M	4:17:48 (16,305)	
Stott, Robin	5:27:57 (30,259)	
Stotter, Nelo L	3:08:42 (1,851)	
Stout, Robert W	4:29:40 (19,557)	
Stovell, Tim C	5:11:43 (28,369)	
Stovold, Jack	3:21:03 (3,367)	
Straathof, Jacobus	4:30:49 (19,825)	
Strachan, David	4:14:33 (15,462)	
Strachan, Grant F	4:06:01 (13,294)	
Stradis, Andreas	3:09:53 (1,978)	

Sykes, David I....5:52:48 (32,330)
Sykes, Duncan....4:13:31 (15,164)
Sykes, Jonathan....4:15:01 (15,568)
Sykes, Peter J....3:55:32 (10,350)
Symeou, Nicos....4:28:11 (19,164)
Symes, Nicholas C....4:04:19 (12,893)
Symington, Neil....5:17:44 (29,145)
Symmonds, Mark....3:42:27 (7,130)
Symonds, Callum M....4:10:39 (14,451)
Symonds, Malcolm A....4:27:42 (18,997)
Symons, Chris C....3:33:08 (5,407)
Symons, David S....2:35:14 (115)
Symons, Tony....3:05:48 (1,581)
Synge, Timothy P....3:53:23 (9,693)
Synnott, Anthony....4:36:49 (21,447)
Syred, Mark T....3:41:17 (6,894)
Syrett, Jason K....3:18:10 (3,005)
Systad, Espen....3:28:26 (4,545)
Szcepura, Matthew J....3:42:15 (7,081)
Szerezla, Sean P....4:26:19 (18,613)
Szkolar, Ivor J....5:44:44 (31,741)
Szpak, Mike A....4:49:42 (24,534)
Szumera, Piotr....5:45:42 (31,814)
Tabb, Nigel F....4:37:07 (21,510)
Tabley, Keith A....3:01:41 (1,288)
Tabner, Reuben F....3:59:17 (11,590)
Taboulet, Stephane....5:09:58 (28,139)
Tack, Joe E....4:59:45 (26,600)
Tackley, Adam....5:29:53 (30,464)
Tadesse, Wondwosen W....4:14:25 (15,429)
Tadie, Alexis J....3:12:47 (2,302)
Tagg, Graham....2:55:30 (778)
Tague, Andrew R....4:19:39 (16,797)
Tailor, Dennis....4:38:06 (21,740)
Tailor, Raj....5:46:37 (31,886)
Tait, David J....4:37:07 (21,510)
Tait, Ian....2:58:17 (978)
Takano, Hideo....4:07:24 (13,612)
Talamonti, Carlo....4:56:32 (25,977)
Talbot, Adrian....5:25:05 (29,933)
Talbot, Colin A....3:27:16 (4,325)
Talbot, Jack....3:36:53 (6,036)
Talbot, Kevin P....3:37:36 (6,183)
Talbot, Richard....4:48:42 (24,290)
Tallott, Giles....3:54:17 (9,954)
Talone, Americo....4:20:29 (17,020)
Tam, Man L....3:37:01 (6,067)
Tamang, Pemba L....3:50:31 (8,931)
Tame, David J....3:06:32 (1,641)
Tampkins, Neil D....3:55:01 (10,201)
Tamura, Hideaki....5:10:44 (28,238)
Tan, Eric....5:46:08 (31,845)
Tan, Joon Y....4:12:40 (14,958)
Tanchel, Trevor M....5:35:17 (30,958)
Tandy, Simon P....5:48:07 (31,983)
Tang, Dennis Yew Siang....3:32:28 (5,318)
Tang, Johnny C....3:29:14 (4,721)
Tang, Kiy Hong....4:08:53 (14,014)
Tanker, Peter N....3:28:32 (4,566)
Tanner, Jean-Paul....5:15:09 (28,839)
Tanner, Keith E....4:09:29 (14,165)
Tanner, Nicholas J....4:26:39 (18,706)
Tanner, Peter R....4:33:53 (20,680)
Tanner, Steve R....3:03:57 (1,445)
Tansley, Gavin P....4:29:27 (19,508)
Tant, Mark....4:21:56 (17,435)
Tapley, Matthew S....4:33:58 (20,693)
Tapley, Peter D....4:51:31 (24,941)
Tapley, Simon C....4:36:31 (21,372)
Taplin, Derek R....4:14:25 (15,429)
Tapp, Edward S....3:42:17 (7,090)
Tappenden, Ben Z....3:55:57 (10,477)
Tappenden, Christopher P....3:40:31 (6,738)
Tappenden, Rob E....4:21:17 (17,249)
Tappin, Andrew P....3:49:19 (8,653)
Tappin, David C....5:05:21 (27,450)
Tapping, Jason P....4:46:35 (23,793)
Tardon Fernandez, Juan....3:35:57 (5,869)
Targett, Paul A....3:22:12 (3,514)
Tarleton, Michael....5:18:16 (29,204)
Tarpey, Christopher M....3:15:54 (2,747)
Tarpey, Jonathan A....4:21:56 (17,435)
Tarplee, Simon R....2:59:35 (1,127)
Tarrant, Dominic....5:02:33 (27,045)
Tarrier, Peter I....3:07:00 (1,682)
Tarsey, David J....3:50:39 (8,974)
Tarter, Alex....3:51:27 (9,164)
Tasker, Adam D....3:41:41 (6,964)
Tasker, Frederick....4:06:52 (13,490)
Tate, Alexander J....2:45:52 (356)
Tate, Kevin....4:17:13 (16,159)
Tate, Max....3:55:27 (10,323)
Tate, Steve J....3:23:49 (3,742)
Tatham, Joe P....4:22:13 (17,503)
Tattersall, Leon....3:47:25 (8,202)
Tattersdill, Steve....5:04:57 (27,390)
Tattershall, David G....4:13:22 (15,132)
Tatum, Matthew J....4:47:50 (24,102)
Tatum, Steven J....4:40:41 (22,346)
Tavares, Spencer C....3:56:52 (10,749)
Taverner, Patrick R....4:52:34 (25,161)
Tawse, James J....3:54:00 (9,873)
Tayeb, Rawand....2:41:15 (227)
Tayler, Andrew D....3:51:43 (9,233)
Tayler, Martin J....4:24:02 (18,007)
Taylor, Alex....4:15:34 (15,720)
Taylor, Andrew....4:46:13 (23,717)
Taylor, Andrew I....4:02:52 (12,579)
Taylor, Andrew J....3:34:47 (5,659)
Taylor, Andrew P....3:52:23 (9,410)
Taylor, Arron....3:59:48 (11,782)
Taylor, Ashley D....4:03:03 (12,620)
Taylor, Ben....4:27:22 (18,924)
Taylor, Charles G....3:59:45 (11,766)
Taylor, Chas....3:39:22 (6,512)
Taylor, Chris....3:55:27 (10,323)
Taylor, Chris....4:52:41 (25,196)
Taylor, Chris M....5:03:16 (27,143)
Taylor, Chris P....3:46:47 (8,056)
Taylor, Colin D....4:02:09 (12,404)
Taylor, Colin D....5:15:32 (28,885)
Taylor, Colin S....5:40:03 (31,336)
Taylor, David A....3:28:49 (4,629)
Taylor, David G....5:40:10 (31,351)
Taylor, David I....4:25:51 (18,496)
Taylor, David J....3:55:02 (10,210)
Taylor, David M....5:37:32 (31,157)
Taylor, David S....3:57:47 (11,053)
Taylor, Dean M....4:30:21 (19,712)
Taylor, Donald G....3:47:37 (8,257)
Taylor, Duncan A....5:17:26 (29,117)
Taylor, Duncan P....4:59:12 (26,516)
Taylor, Eric....3:13:18 (2,373)
Taylor, Evan....3:19:52 (3,213)
Taylor, Garry J....3:30:17 (4,937)
Taylor, Gary....3:39:36 (6,558)
Taylor, Gary A....3:41:41 (6,964)
Taylor, Gary S....3:59:44 (11,759)
Taylor, Geoffrey S....4:22:57 (17,716)
Taylor, George K....2:43:15 (274)
Taylor, Gerry....4:10:53 (14,516)
Taylor, Glen....4:04:44 (12,992)
Taylor, Glenn C....3:38:41 (6,386)
Taylor, Graham C....3:01:17 (1,259)
Taylor, Gregory D....4:37:12 (21,526)
Taylor, Hamish M....3:49:24 (8,674)
Taylor, Ian....5:32:56 (30,742)
Taylor, Ian K....3:00:10 (1,175)
Taylor, Ian R....4:46:59 (23,904)
Taylor, James....4:31:19 (19,972)
Taylor, James W....2:58:59 (1,060)
Taylor, Jeffrey T....4:40:45 (22,367)
Taylor, Jeremy P....4:51:21 (24,915)
Taylor, John....3:22:20 (3,538)
Taylor, John....3:23:32 (3,711)
Taylor, John....4:14:46 (15,510)
Taylor, John C....3:41:21 (6,906)
Taylor, John G....4:07:44 (13,704)
Taylor, John V....4:35:09 (21,020)
Taylor, Karl J....3:43:04 (7,255)
Taylor, Keith....3:55:02 (10,210)
Taylor, Keith E....4:18:04 (16,361)
Taylor, Keith R....3:47:10 (8,142)
Taylor, Kenneth M....4:44:49 (23,375)
Taylor, Kevin....4:12:25 (14,910)
Taylor, Kevin....5:16:53 (29,040)
Taylor, Kevin J....4:59:35 (26,570)
Taylor, Lee G....6:27:05 (33,602)
Taylor, Mark....4:26:55 (18,790)
Taylor, Mark....5:13:35 (28,619)
Taylor, Mark C....4:20:34 (17,050)
Taylor, Mark E....3:41:26 (6,922)
Taylor, Mark J....6:03:22 (32,860)
Taylor, Mark N....3:47:48 (8,296)
Taylor, Martin....6:52:33 (34,119)
Taylor, Matthew J....3:18:59 (3,097)
Taylor, Matthew J....4:06:40 (13,446)
Taylor, Matthew P....3:47:26 (8,205)
Taylor, Michael J....3:33:53 (5,530)
Taylor, Michael J....3:57:41 (11,006)
Taylor, Mike....5:42:18 (31,521)
Taylor, Neil R....4:19:32 (16,768)
Taylor, Nigel A....5:14:36 (28,759)
Taylor, Nigel R....3:32:14 (5,266)
Taylor, Paul....4:52:27 (25,134)
Taylor, Paul J....4:52:04 (25,059)
Taylor, Paul J....6:35:30 (33,785)
Taylor, Paul L....3:16:19 (2,791)
Taylor, Paul R....4:54:27 (25,574)
Taylor, Peter A....5:42:39 (31,544)
Taylor, Peter I....5:35:42 (30,999)
Taylor, Philip C....3:43:54 (7,441)
Taylor, Philip C....5:31:21 (30,599)
Taylor, Philip J....4:25:55 (18,513)
Taylor, Richard....3:26:30 (4,188)
Taylor, Richard S....4:45:14 (23,473)
Taylor, Rob....5:20:00 (29,411)
Taylor, Robert M....4:54:21 (25,549)
Taylor, Ryan D....4:20:29 (17,020)
Taylor, Sam J....3:25:41 (4,048)
Taylor, Scott A....3:43:35 (7,363)
Taylor, Scott G....3:56:33 (10,646)
Taylor, Simon....3:53:53 (9,833)
Taylor, Simon B....3:01:53 (1,302)
Taylor, Simon G....3:58:09 (11,163)
Taylor, Stephen J....3:17:28 (2,930)
Taylor, Stephen K....4:50:36 (24,746)
Taylor, Stuart....3:55:16 (10,279)
Taylor, Tracy....4:20:00 (16,884)
Taylor, Trevor B....3:20:53 (3,341)
Taylor, Zachary....4:58:56 (26,464)
Taylorson, Simon L....3:24:21 (3,823)
Teague, William J....3:59:12 (11,562)
Teale, Lea M....4:09:30 (14,174)
Teale, Russell....4:01:33 (12,255)
Teale, Simon....4:53:59 (25,478)
Tearle, John D....3:59:48 (11,782)
Teasdale, David....3:54:56 (10,175)
Tebbutt, Adam L....4:58:11 (26,323)
Tebbutt, Gary D....3:55:33 (10,354)
Tebbutt, Stuart J....4:13:41 (15,218)
Tedder, Kevin....4:13:27 (15,149)
Tee, Paul H....3:36:33 (5,975)
Teece, Philip R....3:03:11 (1,390)
Teer, Robert L....3:54:29 (10,022)
Teevan, Pete....3:32:27 (5,309)
Tegg, Jonathan R....4:49:02 (24,381)
Teillol, Dominique....3:28:40 (4,596)
Teixeira, Pedro....3:02:37 (1,354)
Tejero, Christophe....2:47:31 (402)
Teji, Shalinder....3:15:24 (2,691)
Telfer, George M....4:23:01 (17,733)
Telford, Alexander J....5:21:10 (29,516)
Telford, Colin S....4:05:50 (13,254)
Telford-Reed, Nicholas J....4:27:31 (18,953)
Temerlies, Simon....3:54:16 (9,950)
Temple, Paul....5:16:51 (29,036)
Temple, Stephen V....4:17:42 (16,281)
Templeman, Andrew J....4:14:54 (15,536)
Templer, Mark....3:13:53 (2,447)
Templeton, James....4:10:18 (14,369)
Templeton, Stephen P....3:54:28 (10,013)
Temporal, Justin I....4:05:04 (13,062)
Ten Bosch, Eric....3:45:07 (7,711)
Ten Have, Antonius....3:16:48 (2,847)
Ten Have, Eric S....3:08:28 (1,834)
Tennant, John....3:14:41 (2,587)
Tennant, Mark D....4:23:55 (17,968)
Tennyson, Mark....2:47:05 (389)

Tennyson, Mark S	3:51:48 (9,248)	
Teran, Manlio	4:16:24 (15,932)	
Terblanche, Etienne	4:30:02 (19,643)	
Terceno, José J	4:06:27 (13,386)	
Terel, Jacques	5:16:50 (29,035)	
Terheege, Robert	5:50:57 (32,207)	
Terlecki, Jozef	4:28:37 (19,296)	
Terrell, Andrew M	3:29:17 (4,735)	
Terry, Andrew L	4:44:00 (23,180)	
Terry, Colin D	4:08:04 (13,781)	
Terry, Guy M	6:04:38 (32,909)	
Terry, James E	4:12:13 (14,864)	
Terry, Martin	3:03:43 (1,432)	
Terry, Paul D	5:40:49 (31,399)	
Terry, Tom W	3:28:11 (4,505)	
Tesch, Thomas	3:53:11 (9,635)	
Tesson, Yves	4:03:06 (12,629)	
Testa, Mario	3:48:52 (8,544)	
Tester, Dominic V	4:28:10 (19,159)	
Tester, Michel C	5:01:59 (26,954)	
Testolina, Luca	3:58:55 (11,460)	
Teston, Davy	3:39:57 (6,628)	
Tether, Jonathan	4:31:46 (20,091)	
Tetrel, Gilbert	4:11:36 (14,704)	
Tettambel, Johann	3:47:58 (8,341)	
Teverini, Luke	3:29:56 (4,873)	
Thacker, Rob M	3:30:32 (4,978)	
Thackeray, Richard P	3:08:00 (1,790)	
Thackery, Carl E	3:03:09 (1,385)	
Thackway, Alexander J	4:54:31 (25,585)	
Thain, Steven	4:25:47 (18,473)	
Thake, James	4:15:46 (15,774)	
Thakore, Ash	4:52:05 (25,062)	
Thakore, Kirit	5:19:12 (29,315)	
Thakur, Khushal C	4:22:19 (17,524)	
Thaler, David	4:25:46 (18,468)	
Thapa, Benjamin	5:03:36 (27,198)	
Tharratt, James D	4:32:17 (20,249)	
Thatcher, Andrew	5:44:21 (31,706)	
Thatcher, Gary M	4:45:59 (23,671)	
Thatcher, Steven B	4:07:53 (13,745)	
Thaw, George T	4:53:04 (25,289)	
Theaker, Darren I	3:59:55 (11,825)	
Theobald, Andy J	4:12:55 (15,007)	
Theobold, Nigel G	3:57:01 (10,802)	
Theophanous, Chris M	4:52:25 (25,127)	
Thevenot, Yves	3:47:01 (8,113)	
Thews, Peter	5:42:38 (31,541)	
Thexton, David	3:26:59 (4,277)	
Thickbroom, Stacy P	3:57:59 (11,109)	
Thiele, Michael	4:27:12 (18,871)	
Thiersdebar, Jean Claude	4:04:10 (12,856)	
Thies, Juergen	3:43:34 (7,357)	
Thillmann, Helmut	3:27:47 (4,416)	
Thimmegowda, Hanume	6:01:07 (32,784)	
Thirkettle, Gary C	4:18:42 (16,552)	
Thirkettle, Nicholas G	3:54:41 (10,097)	
Thirsk, Michael	4:11:57 (14,791)	
Thoday, Corin L	3:29:21 (4,751)	
Thoennes, Walter	3:23:59 (3,779)	
Thom, Alistair J	4:16:00 (15,837)	
Thom, Matthew P	3:27:04 (4,291)	
Thomas, Adam	3:55:33 (10,354)	
Thomas, Adrien	3:49:20 (8,659)	
Thomas, Alan J	4:52:40 (25,190)	
Thomas, Allan	3:45:45 (7,845)	
Thomas, Andrew	3:27:58 (4,453)	
Thomas, Andrew	4:07:31 (13,645)	
Thomas, Andrew K	3:07:33 (1,737)	
Thomas, Andrew R	4:10:11 (14,335)	
Thomas, Anthony	3:42:51 (7,205)	
Thomas, Anthony M	4:11:08 (14,581)	
Thomas, Bob	4:53:24 (25,351)	
Thomas, Bryan P	3:59:15 (11,583)	
Thomas, Carwyn	2:48:40 (453)	
Thomas, Christopher P	3:49:29 (8,696)	
Thomas, Clive	3:17:07 (2,873)	
Thomas, Clive W	3:32:10 (5,257)	
Thomas, Colin	4:51:45 (24,999)	
Thomas, Daniel R	5:06:23 (27,611)	
Thomas, Daniel R	5:18:08 (29,191)	
Thomas, Darren M	5:05:12 (27,434)	
Thomas, David A	4:31:09 (19,923)	

Thomas, David I	4:00:40 (12,024)
Thomas, David M	5:41:27 (31,461)
Thomas, Dean A	3:29:38 (4,808)
Thomas, Desmond G	4:22:50 (17,679)
Thomas, Dieter L	4:56:39 (25,992)
Thomas, Edward C	5:01:18 (26,841)
Thomas, Eric J	3:22:30 (3,564)
Thomas, Gary	3:42:55 (7,214)
Thomas, Gary J	3:33:48 (5,518)
Thomas, Gavin	3:42:09 (7,057)
Thomas, Gavin	3:51:15 (9,109)
Thomas, Geoff	4:28:47 (19,343)
Thomas, Geraint S	3:58:52 (11,444)
Thomas, Glen	5:17:20 (29,100)
Thomas, Gordon	5:09:46 (28,109)
Thomas, Graham R	3:24:07 (3,792)
Thomas, Grahame G	3:33:24 (5,451)
Thomas, Grant G	5:26:42 (30,119)
Thomas, Henry J	3:12:55 (2,326)
Thomas, Huw	3:35:54 (5,859)
Thomas, Huw	4:48:15 (24,190)
Thomas, James M	3:43:36 (7,366)
Thomas, John	4:38:25 (21,805)
Thomas, Jonathan	4:18:21 (16,446)
Thomas, Joseph	5:16:30 (28,992)
Thomas, Kevin P	4:44:25 (23,276)
Thomas, Laurence	5:08:25 (27,879)
Thomas, Lloyd	7:03:37 (34,247)
Thomas, Luke	4:52:25 (25,127)
Thomas, Marc A	3:52:37 (9,461)
Thomas, Mark C	3:51:59 (9,297)
Thomas, Mark R	4:56:22 (25,944)
Thomas, Matthew J	4:28:12 (19,171)
Thomas, Michael	4:28:19 (19,213)
Thomas, Michael	4:35:20 (21,064)
Thomas, Michael G	4:43:53 (23,148)
Thomas, Neil	4:00:56 (12,096)
Thomas, Neil E	4:07:25 (13,618)
Thomas, Nicholas P	3:57:22 (10,913)
Thomas, Nigel	4:02:22 (12,469)
Thomas, Paul	5:10:35 (28,228)
Thomas, Paul D	3:33:26 (5,461)
Thomas, Paul D	3:36:20 (5,937)
Thomas, Paul I	4:02:20 (12,454)
Thomas, Peter	3:47:24 (8,197)
Thomas, Rainer	2:57:09 (882)
Thomas, Raymond P	3:34:41 (5,641)
Thomas, Richard	3:33:47 (5,517)
Thomas, Richard	3:48:47 (8,529)
Thomas, Richard	4:14:22 (15,415)
Thomas, Richard C	2:58:48 (1,042)
Thomas, Richard L	4:15:29 (15,702)
Thomas, Richard M	2:58:00 (948)
Thomas, Robin	3:57:08 (10,847)
Thomas, Ron J	5:19:14 (29,319)
Thomas, Sam	3:41:48 (6,991)
Thomas, Shaun D	4:03:24 (12,700)
Thomas, Simon A	3:59:24 (11,633)
Thomas, Simon H	5:08:25 (27,879)
Thomas, Stephen	2:49:52 (504)
Thomas, Stephen	2:57:46 (927)
Thomas, Stephen G	4:40:30 (22,310)
Thomas, Stephen J	4:20:12 (16,942)
Thomas, Steven A	4:56:51 (26,036)
Thomason, Francis L	4:22:07 (17,474)
Thomassin, Mathias	2:47:06 (390)
Thompson, Alex	4:44:04 (23,195)
Thompson, Andrew J	2:58:26 (999)
Thompson, Andrew J	4:08:08 (13,810)
Thompson, Ashley G	5:06:49 (27,668)
Thompson, Barry S	2:58:39 (1,026)
Thompson, Carl A	3:01:46 (1,295)
Thompson, Christopher J	3:50:55 (9,032)
Thompson, Colin W	3:37:55 (6,242)
Thompson, Craig J	4:09:06 (14,063)
Thompson, Daniel J	5:17:29 (29,123)
Thompson, David	3:51:05 (9,072)
Thompson, David	3:56:42 (10,690)
Thompson, David	5:01:32 (26,876)
Thompson, David J	3:14:32 (2,556)
Thompson, David M	2:42:37 (256)
Thompson, David M	2:57:57 (943)
Thompson, David P	3:10:09 (2,006)

Thompson, Gary J	5:11:40 (28,359)
Thompson, Graham	4:39:26 (22,071)
Thompson, Grant P	3:59:08 (11,540)
Thompson, Ian P	4:54:45 (25,638)
Thompson, James D	6:12:06 (33,171)
Thompson, Jonathan P	4:07:47 (13,711)
Thompson, Joseph	4:58:37 (26,403)
Thompson, Joseph A	3:17:42 (2,954)
Thompson, Kent R	4:51:13 (24,884)
Thompson, Kevin	3:49:13 (8,632)
Thompson, Kevin	3:57:57 (11,102)
Thompson, Kevin E	4:33:29 (20,572)
Thompson, Lee	4:58:23 (26,357)
Thompson, Lee D	4:16:12 (15,874)
Thompson, Mark	4:17:49 (16,311)
Thompson, Mark D	4:24:52 (18,233)
Thompson, Mark L	3:33:35 (5,486)
Thompson, Matt E	4:16:44 (16,013)
Thompson, Matthew G	4:53:50 (25,449)
Thompson, Melvyn R	4:43:30 (23,049)
Thompson, Michael	4:18:29 (16,491)
Thompson, Michael J	3:28:07 (4,491)
Thompson, Michael O	3:49:37 (8,724)
Thompson, Miles C	4:55:47 (25,836)
Thompson, Nigel	5:28:30 (30,323)
Thompson, Nigel P	2:41:09 (220)
Thompson, Paul A	3:34:55 (5,688)
Thompson, Phil I	4:35:53 (21,209)
Thompson, Phillip J	3:23:57 (3,772)
Thompson, Ralph	4:18:23 (16,458)
Thompson, Richard J	3:26:42 (4,231)
Thompson, Rob	3:04:52 (1,508)
Thompson, Robert E	3:30:44 (5,007)
Thompson, Steven N	4:39:12 (22,027)
Thompson, Stewart C	4:49:29 (24,471)
Thompson, Stuart J	3:20:11 (3,245)
Thompson, Tony	3:03:09 (1,385)
Thompson, Trevor G	4:36:46 (21,434)
Thompson, Trevor N	6:05:51 (32,968)
Thompson, Victor M	4:10:50 (14,503)
Thomson, Alex	3:54:40 (10,089)
Thomson, Craig R	4:59:28 (26,555)
Thomson, David B	6:20:58 (33,426)
Thomson, David W	5:04:28 (27,322)
Thomson, Graeme D	4:26:59 (18,809)
Thomson, Graeme J	3:51:02 (9,058)
Thomson, James P	4:41:29 (22,553)
Thomson, Richard I	4:14:07 (15,340)
Thomson, Stephen	3:07:09 (1,694)
Thomson, Steven	5:04:28 (27,322)
Thomson, Stuart	3:28:53 (4,643)
Thomson, Toby J	4:13:07 (15,067)
Thordarson, Stefan	3:18:17 (3,016)
Thorell, Johan	3:46:20 (7,960)
Thoren, Bjorn	5:03:42 (27,208)
Thorn, Mike A	3:38:19 (6,319)
Thorn, Steven	3:54:39 (10,086)
Thorne, Alex M	3:59:14 (11,574)
Thorne, Andrew M	4:25:04 (18,278)
Thorne, Andrew N	3:59:22 (11,622)
Thorne, Colin	5:11:28 (28,328)
Thorne, Liam M	4:59:57 (26,627)
Thorne, Rob	5:43:52 (31,639)
Thorne, Scott	5:18:08 (29,191)
Thorneloe, Guy R	2:58:52 (1,052)
Thorner, Roddy	4:31:49 (20,112)
Thornett, Lee R	7:21:00 (34,402)
Thorneycroft, Richard J	3:55:22 (10,304)
Thorn-Gent, Leo S	5:31:47 (30,639)
Thornley, David E	4:14:32 (15,460)
Thornton, Alex D	3:35:17 (5,754)
Thornton, Clifford	3:12:02 (2,214)
Thornton, Craig C	4:20:08 (16,920)
Thornton, David A	5:34:08 (30,848)
Thornton, Edwrd H	3:51:38 (9,206)
Thornton, James	5:25:01 (29,915)
Thornton, Simon R	2:56:40 (852)
Thornton, Stanley	5:19:47 (29,388)
Thornton-Jones, Timothy	5:04:31 (27,329)
Thorogood, Keith S	4:00:19 (11,929)
Thorp, Jeremy	5:14:49 (28,786)
Thorp, Samuel	3:54:48 (10,125)
Thorpe, David W	5:16:25 (28,985)

Thorpe, John....5:51:54 (32,284)
Thorpe, John M....2:56:13 (822)
Thorpe, Matt....4:37:19 (21,554)
Thorpe, Michael....5:15:18 (28,850)
Thorpe, Nicky....6:18:48 (33,375)
Thorpe, Paul J....3:32:59 (5,385)
Thorpe, Robert M....4:44:02 (23,190)
Thorpe, Roger....6:14:59 (33,268)
Thorsell, Jorgen E....2:54:50 (736)
Thorup, Klaus M....4:00:12 (11,897)
Thouless, Gavin....3:59:29 (11,668)
Thrasher, Danny....3:16:47 (2,843)
Threadgold, Stephen J....3:03:18 (1,402)
Threadgould, Michael D....4:55:05 (25,715)
Thring, Ashley D....5:13:59 (28,672)
Throop, Christopher J....4:15:55 (15,811)
Throssell, Stephen....2:59:33 (1,119)
Thrower, Andrew M....5:13:48 (28,648)
Thrower, Michael A....5:45:39 (31,812)
Thrush, Alastair J....3:54:53 (10,150)
Thubron, Neil A....3:06:43 (1,659)
Thunegard, Olof....2:35:13 (114)
Thurgood, Geoffrey A....6:37:40 (33,835)
Thurgood, Hugh A....4:21:15 (17,236)
Thurgood, Joe V....4:21:15 (17,236)
Thursby Pelham, Brian E....3:51:13 (9,101)
Thushyanthan, Vivekananthan....4:14:56 (15,540)
Thwaite, Philip A....4:18:09 (16,386)
Tibbles, David M....4:03:19 (12,683)
Tibbs, Christopher....4:50:48 (24,795)
Tickle, Stephen....4:42:50 (22,884)
Tickner, Paul....4:39:20 (22,057)
Tickner, Richard D....5:06:21 (27,610)
Tickner, Tony J....4:53:51 (25,454)
Tidd, Gary....5:06:50 (27,672)
Tidder, Robert....5:09:37 (28,075)
Tidiman, Daniel....6:28:14 (33,628)
Tidiman, Thomas....3:58:11 (11,182)
Tidswell, Daniel....4:55:36 (25,801)
Tiensa, Simon....4:16:59 (16,088)
Tierney, Christopher P....4:09:25 (14,147)
Tierney, Kristian J....3:03:46 (1,436)
Tierney, Stephen....4:44:38 (23,332)
Tietz, Karl....3:28:02 (4,467)
Tighe, John P....4:09:43 (14,233)
Tighe, Martyn....5:47:51 (31,970)
Tighe, Raymond....4:53:02 (25,280)
Tigneres, Marc....4:02:08 (12,396)
Tilbrook, Christopher J....2:50:14 (519)
Tilbury, Neil A....3:24:45 (3,878)
Tilby, Graham P....4:13:27 (15,149)
Tilcock, Trevor J....5:09:00 (27,971)
Tillard, Jean Pierre....3:53:49 (9,815)
Tillbrooke, Tony....4:31:16 (19,952)
Tiller, Nicholas B....3:34:57 (5,694)
Tillery, Andrew J....3:09:38 (1,955)
Tillery, Paul....4:33:17 (20,504)
Tilley, Andrew....3:58:07 (11,151)
Tilley, Clive....4:19:20 (16,711)
Tilley, David....4:23:36 (17,894)
Tilley, David K....4:42:26 (22,786)
Tilley, Ian R....4:56:20 (25,939)
Tilling, Rich....4:17:57 (16,334)
Tillotson, John....3:44:42 (7,604)
Tillott, Neil D....2:55:28 (775)
Tilly, Alan J....4:18:47 (16,567)
Tillyer, Bryan....3:39:15 (6,483)
Tilson, Scott A....3:12:58 (2,330)
Tilson, Steve....4:48:23 (24,222)
Timas, Trevor....4:15:01 (15,568)
Timbrell, Jonathan T....4:57:57 (26,271)
Timbrell, Simon C....4:29:59 (19,631)
Timeneys, Ricky....4:26:04 (18,558)
Timm, Owen N....4:55:43 (25,821)
Timmins, Adrian....2:43:34 (283)
Timms, Giles M....3:08:18 (1,821)
Timms, Richard V....4:52:01 (25,048)
Timpson, Anthony E....4:24:35 (18,166)
Timuri, Farhad....5:27:08 (30,161)
Tindall, Dave....4:55:06 (25,718)
Tindle, William....4:28:34 (19,280)
Tinegate, Geoff....4:01:59 (12,358)
Tinker, Antony A....3:46:51 (8,071)
Tinline, David P....4:35:32 (21,113)
Tinline, Robert J....4:05:38 (13,206)
Tinney, Adam J....4:08:24 (13,882)
Tinoco, Gerardo....4:34:24 (20,799)
Tinton, Glen W....4:34:52 (20,931)
Tippen, Ian....5:09:42 (28,094)
Tippet, Simon J....4:27:51 (19,040)
Tippett, Graham....3:49:00 (8,579)
Tipping, Paul A....4:19:29 (16,750)
Tipple, Derek J....4:29:52 (19,604)
Tisner Madrid, Mariano....3:27:16 (4,325)
Titchener, Frank....5:26:10 (30,052)
Titchmarsh, Ben....4:31:40 (20,071)
Tite, Julian C....3:53:21 (9,677)
Titmuss, Julian F....4:43:49 (23,128)
Tizard, Michael V....3:54:00 (9,873)
To, Ken....3:59:36 (11,714)
Toates, Nigel D....3:41:59 (7,022)
Tobias, Patrick....3:53:11 (9,635)
Tobin, Dominick L....4:52:39 (25,185)
Tobin, Mark P....3:27:51 (4,432)
Tobin, Mark R....4:05:26 (13,158)
Tobin, Paul J....6:52:05 (34,113)
Tocknell, Paul D....4:00:32 (11,982)
Tod, Jonathan....2:56:07 (813)
Tod, Simon....3:58:07 (11,151)
Todd, David S....4:29:55 (19,613)
Todd, John B....3:00:22 (1,192)
Todd, Matthew R....5:44:33 (31,726)
Todd, Paul....2:41:12 (225)
Todd, Richard....4:16:36 (15,984)
Todd, Stephen....3:14:49 (2,610)
Tofts, Kenneth F....5:43:56 (31,667)
Tokley, Shaun....4:33:43 (20,639)
Tolchard, Edward....3:13:25 (2,388)
Tole, Richard P....4:28:46 (19,335)
Toll, Alex J....2:55:21 (768)
Tollner, Kit....3:29:18 (4,739)
Tomaschett, Martin....3:57:18 (10,890)
Tomasini, Giuseppe....4:23:50 (17,946)
Tomasoni, Valentino....3:51:51 (9,261)
Tomassoli, Gianfranco....4:14:59 (15,553)
Tombazis, James G....5:50:28 (32,170)
Tomblin, Kristian J....4:26:56 (18,793)
Tombs, Jonathan M....3:47:52 (8,319)
Tomkins, Andrew J....3:26:13 (4,139)
Tomkins, Christopher D....3:26:27 (4,179)
Tomkins, Fred....4:57:34 (26,199)
Tomkins, Paul J....4:07:41 (13,694)
Tomlin, James R....4:09:20 (14,127)
Tomlinson, Dean L....4:44:19 (23,260)
Tomlinson, Frederick G....7:26:13 (34,437)
Tomlinson, Howard C....5:06:02 (27,559)
Tomlinson, Ian D....4:09:21 (14,134)
Tomlinson, James....2:44:10 (299)
Tomlinson, Jeremy S....3:01:42 (1,289)
Tomlinson, John....3:01:18 (1,263)
Tomlinson, Mark W....3:02:19 (1,331)
Tomlinson, Michael....4:28:44 (19,321)
Tomlinson, Robert C....4:42:23 (22,770)
Tommey, Jonathan....5:44:42 (31,738)
Tompkins, Martin B....5:22:24 (29,650)
Tompson, Brian J....3:48:39 (8,500)
Toms, David A....4:20:12 (16,942)
Tomsett, Peter L....4:33:36 (20,609)
Tomter, Jorn....4:17:09 (16,140)
Tonetto, Giancarlo....4:04:20 (12,901)
Tongue, Steven R....4:19:40 (16,804)
Tonkes, Remco E....5:07:18 (27,739)
Tonkin, Craig....3:24:09 (3,798)
Tonks, Barry....4:49:58 (24,594)
Tonner, Ian S....4:37:01 (21,490)
Tononi, Aldo....3:29:21 (4,751)
Tonstad, Per K....3:57:31 (10,960)
Toogood, Mark S....4:22:22 (17,542)
Tooley, Frank A....3:53:30 (9,711)
Toombs, Paul F....3:54:28 (10,013)
Toomey, Benjamin L....5:53:02 (32,339)
Toomey, Chris I....3:59:24 (11,633)
Toon, Paul....5:45:44 (31,818)
Toothill, Michael....3:46:13 (7,930)
Toothill, Richard J....4:52:00 (25,042)
Tootill, Tan M....3:53:04 (9,596)
Topp, Craig R....4:01:23 (12,210)
Toppani, Daniel....3:22:10 (3,507)
Topper, Steve....3:36:21 (5,938)
Topping, Brian J....4:36:39 (21,402)
Topping, Gordon J....4:26:58 (18,806)
Topping, Mark C....6:17:30 (33,336)
Topping, Troy....3:14:46 (2,600)
Torrance, Christopher J....5:14:18 (28,722)
Torrejon Pascual, Ismael....3:20:57 (3,354)
Tort Nieto, Jordi....4:02:37 (12,520)
Torz, Malcolm....4:13:59 (15,300)
Toscano, Matthew....3:09:00 (1,883)
Tosdevin, Leslie....4:17:04 (16,112)
Tosh, John....3:44:21 (7,522)
Tosley, Geoff W....5:37:53 (31,186)
Tossell, Stewart....4:16:44 (16,013)
Totty, Patrick....3:57:44 (11,029)
Touchart, Michel....3:30:56 (5,044)
Toumazis, Tom....4:21:54 (17,422)
Tourlamain, Stanley R....5:47:24 (31,944)
Tourle, David E....4:12:46 (14,981)
Toussenel, Stephane....3:13:13 (2,360)
Tovell, Kenneth J....3:38:14 (6,307)
Tovey, Austin....3:52:55 (9,544)
Tovey, Simon....3:49:26 (8,681)
Towell, Clive M....4:41:10 (22,478)
Towell, Shaun A....3:50:35 (8,949)
Towers, Gareth....4:09:59 (14,296)
Towlson, Carl D....3:27:39 (4,387)
Townhill, Steven H....4:05:47 (13,243)
Townsend, Ben C....4:54:57 (25,693)
Townsend, Daniel E....4:49:30 (24,474)
Townsend, James D....4:59:12 (26,516)
Townsend, Martin B....3:09:21 (1,925)
Townsend, Matthew....5:07:30 (27,766)
Townsend, Michael E....4:48:25 (24,227)
Townsend, Philip M....3:11:08 (2,108)
Townsend, Richard L....4:49:59 (24,597)
Townsend, Ross....4:53:41 (25,415)
Townsend-Rose, James D....4:05:08 (13,080)
Townson, Matthew....3:51:29 (9,173)
Toye, Anthony....3:54:33 (10,052)
Toye, Francis....4:27:09 (18,858)
Tozer, Shaun A....2:48:22 (438)
Tracey, Craig P....5:39:34 (31,304)
Tracey, Dave....4:22:13 (17,503)
Tracey, Graham R....3:05:41 (1,570)
Tracey, Ian R....4:05:15 (13,110)
Tracey, John T....3:39:15 (6,483)
Trafford, Richard L....3:31:12 (5,076)
Trainer, Matthew P....3:39:34 (6,555)
Tran, Quan....3:14:12 (2,498)
Tranter, Joss....3:45:13 (7,733)
Tranter, Robin....5:14:58 (28,815)
Tranter, Stephen....3:48:00 (8,351)
Trask, Philip A....5:42:15 (31,518)
Trathan, Philip N....4:31:27 (20,014)
Travers, Alex....3:49:21 (8,666)
Travers, Ralph W....4:41:45 (22,620)
Travis, Andrew J....3:23:42 (3,726)
Treadwell, Mark....3:36:44 (6,001)
Treadwell, Mark A....3:06:13 (1,620)
Treadwell, Neil....4:19:04 (16,647)
Treanor, Eddie....4:27:13 (18,880)
Trebble, Richard J....5:12:24 (28,450)
Trebilcock, Michael N....3:39:11 (6,469)
Trebilcock, Norman A....4:47:46 (24,093)
Tredaniel, Claude....4:40:58 (22,425)
Tredant, Adrian S....4:20:56 (17,159)
Tredget, Andrew D....4:11:01 (14,547)
Tredler, Daniel....4:48:52 (24,335)
Treece, Francis G....5:17:43 (29,142)
Treen, Martin D....3:57:35 (10,974)
Treffler, Richard M....4:48:16 (24,196)
Tregellas, Simon J....7:17:48 (34,382)
Tregidga, Robert W....4:46:45 (23,838)
Trehearn, Jonathan....3:06:42 (1,656)
Treiber, Martin....4:14:07 (15,340)
Treille, Christian L....3:52:21 (9,396)
Tremain, Anthony F....4:41:11 (22,484)
Tremante Tescione, Andrea....4:40:36 (22,330)
Tremblet, Stephan....3:04:20 (1,474)
Tremellen, Richard M....3:50:13 (8,876)

Trendall, Jamie E 3:47:37 (8,257)
Trennery, David S 4:57:34 (26,199)
Treppass, Andrew R 5:04:45 (27,365)
Tresadern, Philip A 4:36:58 (21,480)
Trethewey, Martin P 4:15:24 (15,670)
Trevarthen, Mark 3:45:28 (7,786)
Trevenna, Steven G 3:56:31 (10,629)
Trevor, Kevin J 4:28:53 (19,371)
Trevorrow, Thomas L 4:47:46 (24,093)
Tribe, Adam J 3:04:39 (1,492)
Trick, Mark J 4:35:28 (21,104)
Trickett, Jeremy W 4:30:14 (19,687)
Trickett, Neil 4:08:41 (13,965)
Trickett, Philip J 3:37:17 (6,122)
Tricklebank, Joseph 6:03:15 (32,858)
Trigg, James J 4:21:12 (17,225)
Trigger, Mark E 3:55:38 (10,382)
Triggs, Alan L 3:40:29 (6,731)
Trigwell, Stuart J 2:49:03 (467)
Trimmer, Simon T 3:40:09 (6,663)
Tripodi, Renzo 5:03:49 (27,230)
Tripp, Michael D 4:10:08 (14,320)
Tritscher, Herbert 3:18:56 (3,092)
Trivedi, Deven 4:54:04 (25,493)
Trivedi, Naresh 4:21:58 (17,445)
Trivett, Fraser 5:49:07 (32,061)
Trocherie, Patrice 3:31:33 (5,141)
Trocki, Jan Z 4:45:09 (23,452)
Trodden, John E 4:47:00 (23,910)
Trory, John A 3:42:00 (7,028)
Trotman, Luke B 5:15:58 (28,932)
Trotman, Stephen H 4:10:52 (14,514)
Trott, Jeremy C 3:53:55 (9,839)
Trott, Wayne L 4:36:50 (21,449)
Trotta, Pierluigi 3:32:31 (5,324)
Trotter, James W 2:57:55 (938)
Troubridge, Paul 3:58:39 (11,357)
Trouverie, Thierry 2:41:50 (241)
Trow, Paul A 4:37:16 (21,539)
Trowbridge, Tony 3:48:20 (8,429)
Trowsdale, John 4:44:15 (23,241)
Troy, David C 4:24:12 (18,050)
Truan, Steven 3:57:43 (11,023)
Trudgill, Graham J 4:21:45 (17,389)
Trueman, Ian 4:44:31 (23,307)
Trueman, Malcolm J 4:43:13 (22,985)
Trueman, Mark 4:23:05 (17,750)
Trueman, Neil C 6:16:19 (33,301)
Trujillo, Carlos 3:26:37 (4,209)
Trunkfield, Dale M 3:41:28 (6,932)
Truran, Martin G 3:19:27 (3,154)
Truss, Daniel J 3:59:19 (11,602)
Trussler, Mark J 3:19:14 (3,125)
Trusty, Sam 3:48:11 (8,395)
Tsang, Philip M 3:30:07 (4,909)
Tse, Ping C 3:20:10 (3,244)
Tsede, Emmanuel 3:21:27 (3,420)
Tselentis, Paul 4:23:29 (17,864)
Tsering, Lobsang 5:02:58 (27,105)
Tu, Wenbin 4:14:20 (15,406)
Tucci, Marco 4:39:32 (22,085)
Tuck, Kevin 7:00:33 (34,211)
Tucker, Alan S 4:46:28 (23,769)
Tucker, Andrew 5:12:24 (28,450)
Tucker, Andy J 2:57:50 (932)
Tucker, Darren 4:46:15 (23,727)
Tucker, Gareth J 3:54:31 (10,040)
Tucker, Graham J 3:12:53 (2,318)
Tucker, Nik C 3:58:20 (11,236)
Tucker, Paul W 5:50:40 (32,182)
Tucker, Peter R 2:23:12 (26)
Tucker, Simon P 3:32:00 (5,225)
Tuckwood, Graham 4:46:23 (23,759)
Tuddenham, Robin 2:36:52 (145)
Tudge, Scott 3:28:30 (4,562)
Tudor, Erryl N 5:01:48 (26,929)
Tudor, Steve J 3:17:06 (2,871)
Tudor, Tony 4:45:43 (23,592)
Tuffnell, Dennis 4:08:26 (13,890)
Tugwood, Clive J 3:45:32 (7,797)
Tuithof, Hennie 3:59:34 (11,696)
Tukacs, Laszlo 3:57:44 (11,029)
Tulip, Alan 4:07:35 (13,666)
Tullett, Peter 3:34:23 (5,603)
Tulloch, Alexander R 3:49:58 (8,819)
Tulloch, Kevin J 3:24:28 (3,840)
Tully, Perry 4:51:35 (24,958)
Tumane, Rakesh 5:12:49 (28,518)
Tumber, David 3:44:03 (7,463)
Tumber, Justin 4:47:40 (24,059)
Tumlty, Owen 4:25:47 (18,473)
Tune, Christopher 4:27:57 (19,081)
Tune, Michael K 2:49:18 (477)
Tune, Mick G 3:41:15 (6,884)
Tunkel, Daniel 5:21:06 (29,509)
Tunstall, Shaun 4:02:06 (12,389)
Tuppen, Alexander R 3:45:56 (7,880)
Tuppen, Darren J 4:06:11 (13,329)
Tupper, Gareth 3:45:47 (7,853)
Tupynamba, Rodrigo C 3:33:27 (5,464)
Turan, Turan T 4:37:00 (21,485)
Turbitt, Martin 4:21:39 (17,357)
Turkington, David P 3:48:04 (8,365)
Turkington, Richard 2:32:45 (94)
Turley, John H 5:02:55 (27,100)
Turnbull, Alexander B 3:50:53 (9,023)
Turnbull, Andrew T 3:09:12 (1,909)
Turnbull, David R 2:32:10 (87)
Turnbull, Gary J 5:29:37 (30,437)
Turnbull, John N 4:53:24 (25,351)
Turnbull, Keith 3:50:22 (8,907)
Turnbull, Martin 4:17:07 (16,128)
Turnbull, Neil H 4:28:50 (19,360)
Turnbull, Peter R 4:57:18 (26,142)
Turnbull, Richard M 4:54:42 (25,623)
Turnbull, Robert M 4:39:02 (21,981)
Turnbull, Sean G 4:12:39 (14,956)
Turnbull, William J 4:20:58 (17,174)
Turner, Andrew J 3:16:42 (2,835)
Turner, Andrew J 4:51:21 (24,915)
Turner, Andrew J 4:59:27 (26,551)
Turner, Andrew K 3:18:08 (2,998)
Turner, Barry 4:47:19 (23,989)
Turner, Ben G 4:57:10 (26,119)
Turner, Benjamin 4:52:06 (25,064)
Turner, Carl J 3:33:07 (5,401)
Turner, Dave J 3:22:23 (3,544)
Turner, David 5:09:29 (28,044)
Turner, David A 4:20:35 (17,055)
Turner, David J 3:28:16 (4,515)
Turner, David J 6:13:38 (33,233)
Turner, Eduardo 3:29:08 (4,700)
Turner, Gareth 6:49:43 (34,072)
Turner, Graham 4:56:49 (26,029)
Turner, Hugh 5:20:20 (29,444)
Turner, Iaian J 6:23:47 (33,509)
Turner, Iain A 4:37:01 (21,490)
Turner, Ian J 5:07:31 (27,769)
Turner, Ian M 4:10:16 (14,356)
Turner, James A 6:13:36 (33,232)
Turner, James P 3:44:51 (7,642)
Turner, Jamie M 3:08:35 (1,844)
Turner, Lee R 2:49:36 (494)
Turner, Mark 4:34:26 (20,808)
Turner, Matthew J 4:48:28 (24,240)
Turner, Matthew W 3:26:10 (4,132)
Turner, Michael S 3:02:16 (1,327)
Turner, Pablo 3:30:53 (5,035)
Turner, Patrick L 3:52:10 (9,351)
Turner, Paul 4:01:09 (12,148)
Turner, Paul J 4:54:28 (25,575)
Turner, Peter I 4:29:16 (19,464)
Turner, Philip K 4:46:21 (23,752)
Turner, Roberto 3:18:25 (3,034)
Turner, Sam 4:55:40 (25,815)
Turner, Sam 5:15:09 (28,839)
Turner, Sean A 4:51:10 (24,875)
Turner, Simon A 3:51:47 (9,245)
Turner, Steven G 5:25:20 (29,970)
Turner, Steven P 4:47:34 (24,033)
Turner, Stuart G 5:08:13 (27,845)
Turner, Tomas F 4:26:09 (18,574)
Turner-Stockham, Clive J 5:07:32 (27,771)
Turney, Michael P 3:02:14 (1,325)
Turone, Calogero D 5:16:48 (29,032)
Turpin, Ian M 4:30:42 (19,800)
Turpin, Mark R 6:14:53 (33,266)
Turpin, Wayne A 5:01:43 (26,916)
Turrini, Fabrizio 3:32:44 (5,351)
Turton, Paul A 4:10:15 (14,351)
Tustin, Bayley J 3:24:36 (3,857)
Tutt, Kevin B 3:58:32 (11,310)
Tveter, Lars K 3:17:42 (2,954)
Tweeddale, Eoin K 4:35:38 (21,148)
Tweeddale, Richard W 4:21:42 (17,374)
Twine, Mark E 5:47:07 (31,917)
Twinem, Richard J 4:46:49 (23,863)
Twinley, Jason A 5:27:37 (30,214)
Twiselton, Christopher J 4:17:03 (16,108)
Twissell, Adrian 3:22:30 (3,564)
Twombley, Andrew 3:54:23 (9,987)
Twose, Gary R 4:35:43 (21,171)
Twum-Ampofo, Mark K 3:30:08 (4,912)
Twyford, Alan J 3:57:06 (10,835)
Twyford, Damian P 5:08:42 (27,929)
Tyas, David F 3:04:01 (1,449)
Tyce, Luke 4:42:31 (22,812)
Tyers, Jason P 4:19:36 (16,781)
Tyjas, Stephen J 6:38:16 (33,852)
Tyler, Anthony H 3:08:39 (1,846)
Tyler, John 2:57:31 (905)
Tyler, Mathew 4:35:00 (20,982)
Tyler, Richard C 4:11:44 (14,740)
Tyler, Stephen 5:11:37 (28,348)
Tyler, Stuart 3:54:52 (10,144)
Tyler Whittle, Jack T 4:47:21 (23,998)
Tymon, Shaun D 3:25:03 (3,939)
Tynan, David A 4:21:05 (17,204)
Tynan, Kieran 5:00:38 (26,725)
Tyndall, Jefrey A 3:47:27 (8,212)
Tyndall, Mark R 4:00:24 (11,948)
Tyne, Keith A 5:08:42 (27,929)
Tyreman, Glenn A 5:52:47 (32,329)
Tyrer, Nick 4:45:14 (23,473)
Tyrrell, Benjamin L 5:07:12 (27,719)
Tyrrell, Christopher W 4:30:20 (19,706)
Tyrrell, Jeffrey S 4:17:40 (16,268)
Tyrrell, Mark R 4:49:38 (24,514)
Tyrrell, Nigel P 3:16:19 (2,791)
Tysoe, Terry 4:19:31 (16,765)
Tyson, Graham 4:04:54 (13,021)
Tyszkiewicz, John Z 3:57:25 (10,935)
Udall, Neil S 5:54:52 (32,450)
Udell, Garreth C 5:16:57 (29,053)
Udell, Laurence C 5:16:57 (29,053)
Udell, Marcus A 5:16:56 (29,051)
Uffendell, James S 3:52:03 (9,318)
Ugwumadu, Austin H 4:10:44 (14,475)
Uhl, Kevin L 3:27:08 (4,301)
Ukrasin, Igor 3:59:37 (11,720)
Ullah, Sasta 4:54:06 (25,497)
Ulliott, Tom 5:13:27 (28,603)
Ullrich, Oliver 3:35:19 (5,757)
Ulrich, Kai-Uwe 3:37:41 (6,199)
Umpleby, Philip 5:52:07 (32,296)
Unai, Thomas E 5:18:28 (29,224)
Underhill, Richard 3:47:24 (8,197)
Underhill, Tom 3:27:47 (4,416)
Underwood, David L 3:55:27 (10,323)
Underwood, Justin K 4:10:44 (14,475)
Underwood, Mark J 3:46:32 (8,011)
Undy, Jonathan D 3:20:52 (3,337)
Unerman, Marti N 4:26:51 (18,773)
Unger, Simon C 3:57:31 (10,960)
Ungi, Thomas 4:56:52 (26,040)
Unitt, Andrew N 4:06:15 (13,346)
Unitt, Andrew V 3:17:35 (2,940)
Unwin, Barry 7:07:53 (34,292)
Unwin, Craig I 4:37:10 (21,518)
Unwin, Simon 4:07:27 (13,627)
Uppal, Amaritpal S 3:49:13 (8,632)
Upshon, Rupert L 4:52:11 (25,078)
Upson, Chris 2:54:55 (741)
Upton, Blaine D 3:49:37 (8,724)
Upton, Brian M 4:06:49 (13,476)
Upton, Martin 4:21:47 (17,402)
Ural, Can 4:37:52 (21,688)
Urban, Alex R 3:09:07 (1,897)
Urdaneta, Juan 4:21:30 (17,308)

Ure, Bruce C....3:53:46 (9,796)
U'Ren, Martyn P....4:07:48 (13,714)
Urquhart, Scott A....3:43:42 (7,387)
Urrutia, Ricardo A....6:03:14 (32,856)
Urwin, Anthony K....4:00:33 (11,987)
Urwin, Corey J....3:15:19 (2,678)
Urwin, Maison B....4:04:54 (13,021)
Usai, Pierpaolo....3:52:54 (9,536)
Usher, Will....3:22:33 (3,577)
Usui, Minoru....5:31:10 (30,579)
Utev, Alex....4:52:44 (25,207)
Uto, Futoru....4:22:04 (17,464)
Uto, Yuetsu....5:01:34 (26,883)
Utterson, Colin....3:43:52 (7,430)
Uttley, Jonathan....3:01:56 (1,308)
Vaccari, Stefano....4:49:20 (24,442)
Vaid, Manish....5:50:22 (32,160)
Vaidyanathan, Raju....5:32:13 (30,673)
Vais, Andrei....3:35:20 (5,760)
Valdenaire, Claude....4:25:21 (18,355)
Valdenaire, Yves....4:09:09 (14,073)
Vale, David J....5:00:13 (26,667)
Valente, Andrew M....3:56:04 (10,507)
Valente, Francesco....3:14:37 (2,573)
Valenti Gatto, Nico....4:01:15 (12,174)
Valentin, Antonio....3:30:43 (5,002)
Valentine, Chris J....4:31:52 (20,130)
Valentine, Keith R....4:57:36 (26,209)
Valentine-Penney, Daniel J....3:42:49 (7,198)
Valentino, Antony....5:50:50 (32,199)
Valenzuela Cruz, Ricardo....3:45:29 (7,790)
Valji, Vishram K....3:40:01 (6,641)
Vallance, Louis....3:42:25 (7,120)
Vallance, Roger W....3:06:52 (1,670)
Vallance, Stuart A....4:35:28 (21,104)
Vallis, Stuart L....4:56:43 (26,010)
Valverde, Javier....6:01:32 (32,798)
Vamben, Eric S....3:28:13 (4,508)
Van, Martin....3:34:37 (5,632)
Van Arkel, Fred....3:14:03 (2,474)
Van Aspert, Jack....3:21:00 (3,360)
Van Bilsen, Hendrikys P....3:32:34 (5,328)
Van Bladel, Rob....4:31:05 (19,906)
Van Bohemen, Trees....4:09:38 (14,209)
Van Buuren, Roger....3:46:27 (7,997)
Van Dam, Gerke G....4:25:37 (18,416)
Van Den Berg, Jan-Bery....3:39:22 (6,512)
Van Den Berghe, Philip M....4:28:16 (19,194)
Van Den Bossche, Patrick M....4:00:12 (11,897)
Van Den Broek, Leo....3:46:34 (8,018)
Van Den Houte, Walter....3:51:36 (9,196)
Van Der Hoek, Paul C....4:59:47 (26,608)
Van Der Kam, Erik....3:51:50 (9,254)
Van Der Merwe, John M....5:43:38 (31,621)
Van Der Pauw, Lex....3:52:25 (9,415)
Van Der Sloot, Bart J....3:58:38 (11,351)
Van Der Veen, Stado....4:05:38 (13,206)
Van Der Walt, Jurg....2:59:40 (1,138)
Van Doorn, Co M....4:21:39 (17,357)
Van Driel, Jan P....4:29:14 (19,459)
Van Geel, Arnoaldus R....4:45:13 (23,469)
Van Hamme, Danny....3:20:01 (3,229)
Van Houtte, Gabriel....5:54:55 (32,453)
Van Leeuwen, Michel....4:13:13 (15,091)
Van Lierde, Luc....3:41:00 (6,824)
Van Niekerk, Steven....5:23:02 (29,701)
Van Nieuwenhoven, Martinus L....3:46:01 (7,891)
Van Orsouw, Michael....3:59:39 (11,734)
Van Praag, Chris....4:08:37 (13,946)
Van Rij, Mark A....3:44:23 (7,530)
Van Staden, Gary....4:00:18 (11,926)
Van Stappershoef, Remco C....4:36:22 (21,339)
Van Tiggelen, Antonie J....3:50:14 (8,880)
Van Woerkom, Vincent S....2:48:28 (445)
Van Zyl, Heine....2:44:20 (305)
Vanden Nieuwenhof, Mark M....4:01:04 (12,128)
Vandepeer, Lee....4:04:47 (12,999)
Vandepol, John M....5:18:50 (29,265)
Vanderpump, Mark R....4:06:00 (13,291)
Vanni, Orlando....3:15:15 (2,664)
Vanotti, Antonio....2:53:09 (649)
Vanson, Richard J....3:28:28 (4,558)
Vanstone, Neale A....4:12:36 (14,950)
Vanvliet, Harm....5:05:03 (27,409)
Varah, Michael A....4:51:32 (24,944)
Varcin, Baris....4:18:26 (16,476)
Varden, Mark G....2:58:16 (977)
Vardy, Christopher P....3:48:49 (8,532)
Vardy, James E....4:14:10 (15,357)
Vargeson, Mark D....4:47:19 (23,989)
Vari, Claudio....2:45:25 (348)
Varley, Ashley D....3:29:29 (4,780)
Varley, Nicholas S....3:48:37 (8,493)
Varley, Paul....3:49:22 (8,668)
Varley, Robert A....4:21:38 (17,350)
Varndell, Andrew J....6:59:13 (34,202)
Varney, Steven R....3:20:18 (3,266)
Varsani, Kashyap D....5:02:23 (27,021)
Vasey, Matt M....3:46:44 (8,045)
Vasey, Stephen....5:55:26 (32,494)
Vashisht, Rahul....7:10:29 (34,325)
Vass, Simon O....3:10:21 (2,022)
Vatland, Magnus....5:33:17 (30,771)
Vaudin, David....3:39:13 (6,477)
Vaudin, John N....4:15:56 (15,819)
Vaughan, Allan....4:23:18 (17,816)
Vaughan, Andrew J....4:51:02 (24,852)
Vaughan, Antony R....5:58:13 (32,652)
Vaughan, Bryan J....4:02:16 (12,436)
Vaughan, David....3:29:28 (4,774)
Vaughan, Ian J....2:46:02 (363)
Vaughan, Mark W....4:35:59 (21,241)
Vaughan, Neville A....3:02:18 (1,329)
Vaughan, Patrick K....4:13:28 (15,153)
Vaughan, Rhodri....3:24:55 (3,914)
Vaughan, Richard T....3:46:07 (7,911)
Vaughan, Rod B....5:40:08 (31,347)
Vaughan, Steven R....3:59:54 (11,818)
Vavrovsky, Nikolaus....2:52:01 (596)
Vaz, Manuel....2:58:09 (961)
Veal, Richard S....5:14:52 (28,797)
Veale, David....3:41:15 (6,884)
Veale, Peter R....4:18:52 (16,589)
Veenhuis, Darren....4:55:56 (25,867)
Veiguela Nunez, Jesus....2:50:39 (541)
Veit, Nicolas....4:03:15 (12,670)
Veitch, Paul J....2:47:58 (421)
Veitlmeier, Hermann....3:32:46 (5,355)
Vekaria, Rupesh N....5:39:04 (31,268)
Velleley, Lucas....4:41:20 (22,522)
Velli, Aldo....4:43:30 (23,049)
Venet, Gilles....4:40:26 (22,294)
Venn, David....4:25:50 (18,491)
Venner, Ivor J....3:51:21 (9,141)
Venner, Michael P....5:04:28 (27,322)
Venning, Martin J....4:57:08 (26,115)
Venning, Stephen J....3:46:56 (8,093)
Ventham, Daniel J....4:06:07 (13,318)
Ventre, Phil W....3:37:23 (6,140)
Ventress, Michael O....4:58:30 (26,375)
Ventura, Gary J....4:18:36 (16,534)
Ventura, Jude R....5:41:23 (31,452)
Ventura, Stefano....2:59:43 (1,142)
Venturini, Mirko....3:30:50 (5,028)
Vera Bacallado, Juan M....4:20:33 (17,043)
Verboven, Vincent P....3:01:25 (1,275)
Vere, Derek....5:29:56 (30,472)
Vere, Richard W....4:41:39 (22,598)
Verita, Mario....4:12:17 (14,881)
Verity, Sean P....5:13:19 (28,580)
Verling, Ben F....3:36:22 (5,945)
Vermeesch, Pieter....2:24:23 (33)
Vernon, Christopher....4:17:40 (16,268)
Vernon, Mark L....3:58:06 (11,142)
Vernon, Mike....4:56:48 (26,025)
Vernon, Richard C....4:38:43 (21,890)
Vernon, Tony M....5:54:42 (32,439)
Vero, Richard....3:26:15 (4,145)
Verrall, Simon....3:54:58 (10,184)
Verwey, Frank N....5:26:26 (30,090)
Vescovi, Julian....3:43:03 (7,248)
Vesterlund, Jan-Ake....3:03:21 (1,407)
Vesty, Thomas D....5:59:04 (32,698)
Vesudevan, Ajit....4:31:57 (20,159)
Vial, Carlos A....4:46:08 (23,697)
Vialls, Ronald....3:09:09 (1,901)
Vianello, Nerino....4:27:57 (19,081)
Viborg, Jakob....3:59:06 (11,527)
Vicat, Andrew D....4:25:06 (18,288)
Vichion, Mark P....4:06:14 (13,341)
Vickerage, John A....4:27:27 (18,941)
Vickers, Donald F....4:47:06 (23,930)
Vickers, Douglas P....3:39:42 (6,576)
Vickers, Jamie J....3:49:41 (8,743)
Vickers, Simon G....3:26:05 (4,119)
Vickery, David C....3:10:21 (2,022)
Vickery, John P....3:26:46 (4,242)
Videfors, Bjorn....4:22:35 (17,611)
Viejo Belon, José L....3:41:13 (6,878)
Vieten, Holger R....3:18:09 (3,002)
Vigar, James....4:06:05 (13,309)
Vignogna, Angiolino....3:21:08 (3,377)
Vigors, Nick D....3:39:31 (6,540)
Vigurs, Robert J....3:27:02 (4,284)
Villa-Clarke, David V....5:03:48 (27,225)
Villars, Philip....4:23:04 (17,744)
Villiers, Christopher....4:49:46 (24,548)
Viltard, Bruno....3:07:16 (1,705)
Vinall, Erwin M....5:28:41 (30,342)
Vinas Bricall, Jordi....3:41:13 (6,878)
Vince, Ian F....5:59:40 (32,721)
Vince, Mark R....3:48:15 (8,414)
Vincent, Chris J....5:09:10 (27,991)
Vincent, Denis....3:51:06 (9,075)
Vincent, Marc....3:33:45 (5,515)
Vincent, Martin....4:22:09 (17,482)
Vincent, Ronald J....5:06:19 (27,605)
Vincent, Thierry....4:06:09 (13,326)
Vine, Desmond G....4:14:31 (15,453)
Vine, Terry....4:51:47 (25,001)
Vinken, Adrian C....4:02:08 (12,396)
Vint, David D....2:57:42 (921)
Vinten, Stephen....2:57:14 (890)
Vinyals, Victor....2:55:53 (802)
Vinyard, Nicholas L....3:29:39 (4,809)
Viollet, Paul-Anthony J....4:54:10 (25,515)
Vipond, Scott....4:56:59 (26,071)
Virton, Emeric P....3:02:06 (1,315)
Visram, Alexander S....4:15:01 (15,568)
Viswanathan, Narayanan....4:53:20 (25,337)
Vitale, Raffaele....4:09:20 (14,127)
Vitelli, Mario....4:43:26 (23,031)
Viveash, Ian....4:04:07 (12,848)
Vlasak, Martin....5:25:04 (29,926)
Vlcek, William B....4:49:34 (24,495)
Vlok, Deon I....3:38:01 (6,263)
Vlot, Adrianus....3:25:20 (3,984)
Voaden, Roger....3:17:56 (2,979)
Voegele, Juergen....3:54:35 (10,065)
Vogel, Christian....4:07:50 (13,725)
Vogwell, David....3:01:17 (1,259)
Voice, Simon....4:02:20 (12,454)
Voiculescu, Aurel....6:28:23 (33,631)
Voigt, Thomas....4:09:57 (14,287)
Voisey, Ian S....4:20:51 (17,138)
Von Arx, Hans-Peter....5:15:00 (28,820)
Von Ferscht-Fountain, Matt J....5:37:11 (31,131)
Von Hoff, Lucas M....3:18:44 (3,069)
Von Keitz, Alex....3:46:42 (8,039)
Von Kumberg, Wolf....4:24:39 (18,181)
Von Waldenfelsw, Hans-Albrecht....3:29:00 (4,669)
Vongo Neto, Miguel Sebastiao....3:20:49 (3,335)
Vonlanthen, Marc R....5:09:51 (28,125)
Vos, Ashley C....4:45:18 (23,495)
Vosper, Andy J....4:12:34 (14,944)
Vosper, Oliver....4:25:06 (18,288)
Vroom, Gerhardus M....3:48:57 (8,567)
Vu, Quoc-Dat....4:27:11 (18,868)
Vuillemez, Samuel....3:06:18 (1,626)
Vuillemez, Valentin....3:58:37 (11,341)
Vyas, Kiren....4:46:26 (23,765)
Vyse, Simon P....4:29:10 (19,444)
Vyvyan-Robinson, Mark W....3:29:15 (4,725)
Waby, Paul....2:41:00 (214)
Wackerhage, Henning....3:12:30 (2,266)
Waddell, Douglas R....3:30:36 (4,986)
Waddell, Ian....3:50:31 (8,931)
Waddell, James M....4:54:26 (25,569)
Waddington, Christopher D....4:41:03 (22,448)

Waddington, David	2:58:00 (948)	
Waddock, James W	4:23:45 (17,929)	
Wade, Calvin R	4:53:08 (25,303)	
Wade, Gary	3:37:51 (6,227)	
Wade, Ian J	4:17:18 (16,175)	
Wade, Ian M	4:40:34 (22,321)	
Wade, Jeff	4:16:46 (16,023)	
Wade, Matthew J	3:36:31 (5,972)	
Wade, Miles W	4:25:10 (18,310)	
Wade, Stephen	4:42:40 (22,846)	
Wade, Steven J	4:26:30 (18,667)	
Wade-Jones, Hugh	3:42:22 (7,111)	
Wadhams, Mark A	4:34:12 (20,758)	
Wadhwani, Suresh P	7:09:36 (34,315)	
Wadie, Abu	4:33:19 (20,516)	
Wadley, Steven L	5:17:31 (29,129)	
Wadmore, Mark	3:50:38 (8,968)	
Wadsworth, Des	4:53:01 (25,275)	
Wadsworth, John E	2:50:13 (518)	
Wadsworth, Simon	4:18:47 (16,567)	
Wadsworth, Simon	5:28:56 (30,371)	
Waggott, Martin R	4:03:08 (12,639)	
Waghorn, Gary J	5:06:12 (27,582)	
Wagland, Gareth W	4:06:26 (13,381)	
Wagner, Chris	4:38:26 (21,811)	
Wagner, John C	3:52:57 (9,553)	
Wagstaff, Simon	4:50:35 (24,743)	
Waheed, Khan	3:11:08 (2,108)	
Wahren, Karsten	3:11:58 (2,202)	
Waine, Michael T	3:30:01 (4,888)	
Wainewright, David	5:01:15 (26,834)	
Wainwright, Gordon L	6:45:01 (33,979)	
Wainwright, Richard J	4:24:09 (18,033)	
Wainwright, Rod G	4:19:53 (16,855)	
Waissman, Gary	4:03:34 (12,736)	
Wait, Ian	4:20:57 (17,164)	
Waite, Howard	3:12:11 (2,231)	
Waite, Iain D	5:16:40 (29,016)	
Waite, Mark	3:10:01 (1,989)	
Waite, Robert	4:49:52 (24,564)	
Waite, Stephen D	6:32:57 (33,724)	
Wakefield, Denis	5:21:39 (29,573)	
Wakefield, Ollie D	3:22:20 (3,538)	
Wakefield, Paul J	5:50:25 (32,166)	
Wakefield, Ryan D	3:35:04 (5,713)	
Wakeford, Malcolm J	5:24:13 (29,830)	
Wakeford, Stephen	3:23:17 (3,673)	
Wakeling, Mark A	6:38:05 (33,843)	
Wakeling, Mark O	3:32:12 (5,260)	
Wakely, Clive J	4:31:53 (20,135)	
Wakely, Robert A	4:28:30 (19,264)	
Wakem, Michael J	5:50:01 (32,123)	
Wakeman, Ashley	4:15:24 (15,670)	
Wakerley, Nick	4:31:18 (19,968)	
Walbrook, David R	3:39:55 (6,619)	
Walby, Chris	3:23:58 (3,774)	
Walch, Stephen P	3:43:39 (7,378)	
Walczak, Jonathan	4:52:30 (25,146)	
Walczak, Wojciech T	3:19:40 (3,186)	
Waldeier, Klaus	3:06:22 (1,632)	
Waldeland, Oddvar	3:43:46 (7,408)	
Walden, Adam J	4:59:28 (26,555)	
Walder, Graham T	5:38:57 (31,257)	
Walder, Nigel D	3:43:16 (7,300)	
Waldmann, Alex D	3:51:27 (9,164)	
Waldron, Paul A	5:05:24 (27,460)	
Waldron, Simeon P	3:34:01 (5,550)	
Waldron-Lynch, Tom	2:56:41 (854)	
Wales, Christopher	3:04:41 (1,494)	
Wales, Daniel J	4:03:16 (12,677)	
Wales, David J	5:43:55 (31,665)	
Wales, Peter	5:46:18 (31,861)	
Walford, Gary T	3:27:35 (4,376)	
Walford, Geoffrey	3:41:05 (6,841)	
Walford, Stuart	6:20:02 (33,397)	
Waliis, Patrick	3:00:56 (1,239)	
Walkden, Hugh P	5:15:27 (28,874)	
Walker, Alistair	4:59:43 (26,594)	
Walker, Andrew	4:26:27 (18,651)	
Walker, Andrew B	4:47:45 (24,088)	
Walker, Angus J	4:29:14 (19,459)	
Walker, Charlie	3:48:07 (8,380)	
Walker, Chris	3:43:45 (7,400)	

Walker, Colin A	4:35:22 (21,072)	
Walker, Damian	4:23:16 (17,804)	
Walker, Daniel C	4:24:49 (18,221)	
Walker, David	7:02:55 (34,239)	
Walker, David F	4:38:54 (21,941)	
Walker, Derek M	3:06:18 (1,626)	
Walker, Duncan	3:39:06 (6,452)	
Walker, Gary J	3:31:04 (5,060)	
Walker, Gary J	3:32:48 (5,363)	
Walker, Geof	3:53:52 (9,832)	
Walker, Graham	4:44:28 (23,294)	
Walker, Harry	3:37:40 (6,197)	
Walker, Henry M	4:27:49 (19,030)	
Walker, Ian	4:10:33 (14,423)	
Walker, James R	3:23:27 (3,701)	
Walker, John W	4:06:18 (13,355)	
Walker, Keith V	3:28:25 (4,538)	
Walker, Kelvin D	4:09:42 (14,228)	
Walker, Kenneth	5:08:27 (27,886)	
Walker, Kevin R	3:17:20 (2,905)	
Walker, Lewis A	3:53:49 (9,815)	
Walker, Mark G	3:10:29 (2,038)	
Walker, Martin	3:56:37 (10,669)	
Walker, Matthew J	4:28:06 (19,130)	
Walker, Mike	3:08:57 (1,872)	
Walker, Neal	2:58:24 (993)	
Walker, Neil	4:46:45 (23,838)	
Walker, Neil A	3:53:47 (9,800)	
Walker, Nigel J	5:21:58 (29,596)	
Walker, Oliver	4:44:58 (23,406)	
Walker, Paul	3:39:56 (6,623)	
Walker, Paul S	4:22:31 (17,591)	
Walker, Philip E	7:09:23 (34,311)	
Walker, Raymond	7:35:24 (34,471)	
Walker, Robert M	4:56:49 (26,029)	
Walker, Sam J	4:20:31 (17,032)	
Walker, Scott	5:02:05 (26,966)	
Walker, Scott A	3:48:28 (8,454)	
Walker, Stuart D	3:08:23 (1,827)	
Walker, Vincent	4:27:42 (18,997)	
Walker, Vincent J	6:20:27 (33,407)	
Walker, William	3:29:39 (4,809)	
Walker, William	5:39:36 (31,307)	
Walker-Reed, Roger G	4:02:34 (12,508)	
Walkey, Grant	3:44:10 (7,485)	
Walkingshaw, Grahame	4:57:45 (26,237)	
Wall, Ian	3:05:51 (1,585)	
Wall, Thomas C	4:39:21 (22,059)	
Wallace, David E	5:10:15 (28,183)	
Wallace, David F	3:20:19 (3,269)	
Wallace, David M	4:22:34 (17,601)	
Wallace, Ed	4:02:25 (12,479)	
Wallace, James J	3:51:15 (9,109)	
Wallace, John	6:22:25 (33,471)	
Wallace, John M	3:29:37 (4,803)	
Wallace, Martin C	3:25:35 (4,029)	
Wallace, Martyn E	3:57:55 (11,094)	
Wallace, Melvin	3:07:27 (1,729)	
Wallace, Paul	5:04:21 (27,303)	
Wallace, Richard A	3:13:44 (2,426)	
Wallace, Rob	3:50:54 (9,028)	
Wallace, Scott	4:18:27 (16,479)	
Wallace, Stephen C	4:10:51 (14,509)	
Walland, John	5:43:37 (31,618)	
Wallas, John R	4:38:46 (21,902)	
Wallbank, Robert A	3:29:42 (4,819)	
Waller, David	4:00:33 (11,987)	
Waller, Gary J	3:15:45 (2,722)	
Waller, Jason M	4:45:41 (23,577)	
Waller, Simon	3:29:44 (4,831)	
Waller, Tony	3:57:04 (10,816)	
Walling, Kevin D	3:52:05 (9,327)	
Wallis, Graham M	4:38:43 (21,890)	
Wallis, Ian M	3:59:15 (11,583)	
Wallis, Matthew S	5:53:18 (32,359)	
Wallis, Paul S	3:30:25 (4,955)	
Wallis, Peter	3:34:20 (5,594)	
Wallis, Thomas	5:29:34 (30,434)	
Wallsgrove, Jon S	4:41:01 (22,442)	
Wallwork, Roger I	4:14:24 (15,424)	
Walmesley, Daniel	3:45:56 (7,880)	
Walmsley, Alastair	3:53:08 (9,615)	
Walmsley, Chris	2:49:48 (500)	

Walmsley, David M	2:49:18 (477)	
Walmsley, Dennis G	2:35:28 (120)	
Walmsley, Steven M	3:56:59 (10,788)	
Walne, Steven	5:05:57 (27,543)	
Walsh, Allan J	4:16:02 (15,845)	
Walsh, Craig J	5:12:19 (28,435)	
Walsh, Daniel M	3:25:04 (3,941)	
Walsh, Danny S	4:30:31 (19,749)	
Walsh, David A	2:55:42 (787)	
Walsh, Frank J	4:50:52 (24,812)	
Walsh, John	4:08:19 (13,857)	
Walsh, Michael	2:42:38 (257)	
Walsh, Michael J	4:33:11 (20,475)	
Walsh, Paul M	3:13:23 (2,386)	
Walsh, Peter	4:34:58 (20,962)	
Walsh, Pierre	4:47:21 (23,998)	
Walsh, Raymond F	3:55:14 (10,273)	
Walsh, Robert M	4:00:10 (11,886)	
Walsh, Steve R	3:24:36 (3,857)	
Walsh, Stewart P	3:33:14 (5,426)	
Walsh, William T	3:59:18 (11,595)	
Walsham, Matthew J	3:47:51 (8,313)	
Walshaw, John	4:59:59 (26,631)	
Walshe, Donal P	4:43:22 (23,018)	
Walters, Ben J	6:06:31 (33,006)	
Walters, Humphrey J	5:02:58 (27,105)	
Walters, Iwan W	3:25:55 (4,091)	
Walters, John	4:00:38 (12,013)	
Walters, Mark	3:47:11 (8,149)	
Walters, Matthew J	4:25:18 (18,341)	
Walters, Morgan	3:14:26 (2,536)	
Walters, Paul	4:22:22 (17,542)	
Walters, Peter C	2:47:42 (411)	
Walters, Peter D	3:29:15 (4,725)	
Walters, Thomas J	4:43:53 (23,148)	
Walther, Jens	4:29:59 (19,631)	
Walton, Alan J	3:02:11 (1,320)	
Walton, Andrew E	4:18:37 (16,538)	
Walton, Anthony R	4:27:00 (18,812)	
Walton, Christopher P	4:27:49 (19,030)	
Walton, Colin J	4:33:37 (20,616)	
Walton, David S	4:38:53 (21,937)	
Walton, James M	5:40:48 (31,398)	
Walton, Michael J	4:57:34 (26,199)	
Walton, Patrick G	4:45:00 (23,412)	
Walton, Philip	4:54:55 (25,676)	
Walton, Tim J	3:32:27 (5,309)	
Walton, William	4:46:20 (23,750)	
Walton-Turner, Christopher R	4:17:47 (16,300)	
Wang, Yon Jon	5:01:15 (26,834)	
Wanjiru, Samuel	2:05:24 (2)	
Wanner, Peter	3:57:59 (11,109)	
Wantling, Andrew S	4:27:28 (18,946)	
Waples, Luke J	5:33:52 (30,823)	
Waraich, Fauzi	3:58:45 (11,389)	
Warburton, Kevin J	3:49:19 (8,653)	
Warburton, Terry	6:41:15 (33,903)	
Warchal, Christian	4:42:22 (22,766)	
Ward, Alexander J	4:24:27 (18,128)	
Ward, Anthony	4:26:15 (18,595)	
Ward, Charles E	4:15:35 (15,724)	
Ward, David	6:17:44 (33,346)	
Ward, David C	4:50:26 (24,694)	
Ward, David J	3:58:11 (11,182)	
Ward, Edward	3:35:47 (5,841)	
Ward, Gary N	4:24:53 (18,238)	
Ward, Grahame L	4:00:55 (12,086)	
Ward, Ian J	3:03:43 (1,432)	
Ward, Ian R	4:07:23 (13,608)	
Ward, James S	3:10:18 (2,018)	
Ward, Joe M	3:15:27 (2,694)	
Ward, John	5:28:11 (30,290)	
Ward, John	5:45:32 (31,804)	
Ward, John M	3:51:04 (9,068)	
Ward, Jonathan D	4:56:28 (25,963)	
Ward, Laurence	3:52:55 (9,544)	
Ward, Lea	4:59:56 (26,622)	
Ward, Lee	4:25:27 (18,382)	
Ward, Mark	3:35:12 (5,737)	
Ward, Matt	2:44:23 (308)	
Ward, Matthew J	3:21:57 (3,483)	
Ward, Neal	4:47:48 (24,100)	
Ward, Paul W	3:57:15 (10,877)	

Ward, Peter J 5:27:19 (30,183)
Ward, Peter M 3:38:15 (6,308)
Ward, Phil 3:25:29 (4,010)
Ward, Richard H 4:49:05 (24,392)
Ward, Robert D 4:13:47 (15,248)
Ward, Robin P 2:41:00 (214)
Ward, Simon J 4:29:50 (19,594)
Ward, Stephen M 4:15:11 (15,613)
Ward, Stephen R 3:49:51 (8,786)
Ward, Steve 4:54:06 (25,497)
Ward, Steven 5:04:09 (27,272)
Ward, Stuart J 4:07:51 (13,730)
Ward, Wayne 3:54:23 (9,987)
Warden, Martin J 5:49:27 (32,083)
Warden, Philip 5:12:11 (28,425)
Wardill, Edward 3:46:27 (7,997)
Wardle, David M 4:08:21 (13,869)
Wardle, Timothy J 4:12:15 (14,873)
Wardley, Robin 4:49:11 (24,410)
Wardman, Steve 4:17:30 (16,220)
Wardrope, David 3:57:20 (10,906)
Ware, Nicholas A 3:54:13 (9,932)
Ware, Richard 5:46:16 (31,859)
Ware, Richard J 3:39:52 (6,612)
Ware, Robert E 4:21:47 (17,402)
Ware, Simon J 4:23:54 (17,963)
Wareham, Andrew 4:28:20 (19,217)
Wareham, James 4:28:03 (19,116)
Wareham, Sean N 4:14:30 (15,451)
Warham, Ben J 4:19:13 (16,680)
Waring, Alfred J 3:40:03 (6,649)
Waring, Chris 5:11:31 (28,333)
Waring, Jonathan 4:28:06 (19,130)
Waring, Mark R 3:47:39 (8,270)
Waring, Miles A 4:00:58 (12,105)
Waring, Neill A 4:14:49 (15,518)
Waring, Seamus P 5:41:44 (31,482)
Warland, Gary M 5:14:47 (28,783)
Warland, John N 5:03:16 (27,143)
Warley, Roger G 5:00:13 (26,667)
Warman, Stephen 4:55:38 (25,810)
Warna, Raj 4:00:39 (12,017)
Warne, Barry A 3:19:35 (3,175)
Warne, Edward 3:56:24 (10,598)
Warner, Danny S 4:38:40 (21,871)
Warner, Edmond W 3:25:28 (4,007)
Warner, Graeme N 3:52:44 (9,490)
Warner, Graham K 4:45:44 (23,598)
Warner, Joe 3:29:47 (4,840)
Warner, Mark C 5:38:38 (31,234)
Warner, Michael 3:58:23 (11,256)
Warner, Michael B 3:36:54 (6,038)
Warner, Paul 5:13:33 (28,615)
Warner, Philip 4:35:56 (21,220)
Warner, Robert E 3:19:45 (3,200)
Warner, Robert M 3:43:16 (7,300)
Warner, Simon R 4:12:31 (14,931)
Warner, Stephen G 3:56:46 (10,714)
Warner, Stuart J 2:58:32 (1,013)
Warner, Tim J 3:50:27 (8,920)
Warner, Tony D 3:41:39 (6,959)
Warnes, Andrew 4:57:59 (26,278)
Warnes, Matthew D 4:24:52 (18,233)
Warnham, Stephen J 4:09:15 (14,104)
Warnock, John S 2:50:50 (545)
Warr, Andrew P 4:30:34 (19,766)
Warr, John E 5:26:05 (30,043)
Warr, Tim S 5:09:30 (28,048)
Warrack, Benedict J 3:55:50 (10,446)
Warran, Stephen J 4:15:00 (15,565)
Warren, Antony J 2:59:33 (1,119)
Warren, David J 4:53:34 (25,392)
Warren, Gary S 3:12:49 (2,308)
Warren, James L 4:26:39 (18,706)
Warren, Jamie D 3:38:21 (6,327)
Warren, John D 4:10:55 (14,527)
Warren, Kevin 5:53:36 (32,382)
Warren, Mark J 4:11:26 (14,656)
Warren, Nick J 4:16:45 (16,020)
Warren, Paul 4:28:35 (19,284)
Warren, Paul M 3:46:10 (7,922)
Warren, Paul N 4:27:41 (18,994)
Warren, Pete D 3:42:14 (7,076)
Warren, Peter 4:26:44 (18,738)
Warren, Philip A 5:40:08 (31,347)
Warren, Simon J 3:25:59 (4,103)
Warren, William S 4:29:07 (19,428)
Warrick, Michael J 2:59:21 (1,104)
Warrillow, James 3:58:11 (11,182)
Warrington, Nigel J 4:25:45 (18,463)
Warriss, Geoffrey R 5:18:57 (29,286)
Wartenberg, Joachim J 2:54:41 (728)
Warth, Benjamin D 6:42:30 (33,921)
Warwick, David 7:19:39 (34,392)
Warwick, Lee J 5:02:26 (27,031)
Warwick, Oliver W 3:58:50 (11,436)
Washer, Ben 4:16:18 (15,903)
Wasley, Gary B 5:19:00 (29,289)
Wassas, Sondre 5:06:20 (27,609)
Wasserman, Ian B 4:50:04 (24,617)
Waterfield, Jonathan L 3:02:30 (1,341)
Waterhouse, Andrew 3:52:06 (9,337)
Waterhouse, Christopher 3:14:41 (2,587)
Waterhouse, Ian D 4:51:52 (25,017)
Waterhouse, Simon 3:40:48 (6,780)
Waterhouse, Thomas E 4:56:57 (26,065)
Wateridge, Mark I 4:37:36 (21,619)
Waters, Christopher C 3:57:22 (10,913)
Waters, David J 4:25:50 (18,491)
Waters, Geoff 4:36:12 (21,296)
Waters, John 3:33:04 (5,394)
Waters, Richard J 4:10:18 (14,369)
Waters, Tony 5:40:39 (31,387)
Waterson, Steven J 3:37:50 (6,224)
Waterston, Paul 2:38:15 (173)
Wates, Neil E 4:52:28 (25,136)
Wates, Tim 5:47:23 (31,941)
Watkin, Andrew R 4:37:56 (21,699)
Watkin, Paul 4:44:38 (23,332)
Watkins, Andrew J 3:53:57 (9,854)
Watkins, Christopher R 4:33:11 (20,475)
Watkins, Michael C 4:03:45 (12,782)
Watkins, Rhys 3:24:52 (3,905)
Watkins, Richie K 4:54:19 (25,542)
Watkins, Stephen J 3:46:09 (7,919)
Watkins, Stephen R 4:39:04 (21,994)
Watkinson, Duncan C 4:07:30 (13,640)
Watkinson, George A 3:51:03 (9,064)
Watkinson, Peter G 3:12:42 (2,291)
Watmough, Stephen J 2:58:37 (1,020)
Watson, Alex F 5:05:59 (27,547)
Watson, Alex J 4:44:05 (23,200)
Watson, Alistair 3:14:01 (2,468)
Watson, Andrew 2:59:22 (1,106)
Watson, Andrew C 3:32:22 (5,293)
Watson, Andrew J 6:40:21 (33,890)
Watson, Andrew L 3:07:29 (1,731)
Watson, Andrew M 4:05:01 (13,053)
Watson, Anthony 4:56:06 (25,892)
Watson, Benjamin N 4:14:19 (15,401)
Watson, Darren D 5:58:34 (32,673)
Watson, David W 4:57:10 (26,119)
Watson, Duncan J 5:07:35 (27,778)
Watson, Frank R 3:59:44 (11,759)
Watson, Gerard M 3:46:26 (7,988)
Watson, Gregory N 3:18:04 (2,997)
Watson, James 4:20:55 (17,157)
Watson, James D 5:44:36 (31,728)
Watson, Julian A 4:33:14 (20,488)
Watson, Kenny 4:15:46 (15,774)
Watson, Kevin W 4:14:59 (15,553)
Watson, Lee D 4:36:32 (21,378)
Watson, Leonard A 5:05:09 (27,427)
Watson, Lloyd C 4:15:04 (15,584)
Watson, Malcolm D 3:44:43 (7,610)
Watson, Mark R 4:46:43 (23,833)
Watson, Michael J 5:39:03 (31,266)
Watson, Neil G 5:14:33 (28,752)
Watson, Paul 3:10:08 (2,002)
Watson, Paul M 2:56:35 (847)
Watson, Philip G 3:46:26 (7,988)
Watson, Richard 2:56:21 (835)
Watson, Richard 3:31:42 (5,169)
Watson, Richard G 4:38:33 (21,842)
Watson, Richard J 3:49:35 (8,715)
Watson, Robert J 5:07:42 (27,797)
Watson, Simon 3:23:22 (3,687)
Watson, Steven D 4:57:14 (26,132)
Watson, Timothy 4:33:04 (20,448)
Watson, Tom 2:56:15 (828)
Watson, Tom 3:15:16 (2,667)
Watson, William A 4:15:45 (15,768)
Watson, William I 3:32:29 (5,320)
Watt, Brian J 4:38:17 (21,775)
Watt, Chris 3:25:35 (4,029)
Watt, Frederick J 3:19:54 (3,215)
Watt, Michael 4:41:33 (22,565)
Wattenbach, Eddie J 3:21:46 (3,456)
Wattison, Dean E 5:57:58 (32,629)
Watts, Andrew J 3:12:49 (2,308)
Watts, Darren R 5:27:04 (30,149)
Watts, David 4:28:12 (19,171)
Watts, David 4:35:32 (21,113)
Watts, Duncan S 4:22:10 (17,486)
Watts, Graham Ian 4:16:20 (15,915)
Watts, Jonathan 5:12:05 (28,417)
Watts, Karl 3:44:21 (7,522)
Watts, Lee J 3:41:28 (6,932)
Watts, Matthew 5:28:06 (30,279)
Watts, Michael A 4:36:45 (21,429)
Watts, Michael B 3:56:55 (10,768)
Watts, Nicholas J 3:41:05 (6,841)
Watts, Paul A 5:13:24 (28,595)
Watts, Paul H 4:54:14 (25,531)
Watts, Peter A 3:48:42 (8,514)
Watts, Richard J 3:28:48 (4,624)
Watts, Richard J 5:37:29 (31,153)
Watts, Stephen H 4:16:26 (15,942)
Watts, Tim N 5:18:10 (29,194)
Waudby, Neil 4:30:06 (19,656)
Waugh, Andrew A 5:13:39 (28,630)
Waugh, Daniel 3:56:41 (10,684)
Waugh, Darren 3:11:43 (2,176)
Waugh, Glen 5:23:04 (29,706)
Waumsley, Peter J 2:42:16 (247)
Wax, Jonathan L 3:46:31 (8,009)
Way, Colin M 5:24:48 (29,887)
Way, Lawrence C 3:45:26 (7,780)
Way, Martin 3:29:56 (4,873)
Way, Steven 6:11:24 (33,152)
Way, Steven J 2:35:26 (118)
Wayland, James A 3:41:12 (6,873)
Wayne, David H 4:47:49 (24,101)
Wealthall, Nick 5:05:36 (27,498)
Weate, Geoff 6:05:48 (32,966)
Weatherall, John S 5:19:01 (29,291)
Weatherburn, James 3:27:03 (4,286)
Weatherhead, James 4:25:29 (18,388)
Weatherill, Alex L 3:06:10 (1,614)
Weatherley, Neil A 3:50:32 (8,937)
Weaver, Andrew S 3:54:43 (10,105)
Weaver, Cass 4:39:39 (22,108)
Weaver, John L 7:33:42 (34,467)
Weaver, Mark L 7:38:52 (34,479)
Weaver, Peter 4:43:55 (23,156)
Weaver, Stephen T 4:01:30 (12,241)
Weavers, David J 4:21:03 (17,197)
Weavers, Terry P 3:11:31 (2,151)
Weaving, Peter G 3:16:13 (2,778)
Webb, Adrian J 3:11:28 (2,146)
Webb, Alan 3:35:32 (5,798)
Webb, Alan 3:54:20 (9,968)
Webb, Alban J 5:26:19 (30,073)
Webb, Andrew C 3:59:52 (11,807)
Webb, Andrew R 4:08:40 (13,961)
Webb, Barnaby J 5:47:07 (31,917)
Webb, Craig 4:35:38 (21,148)
Webb, Daniel J 5:44:26 (31,715)
Webb, Danny 4:35:40 (21,157)
Webb, David J 3:49:00 (8,579)
Webb, David P 3:21:40 (3,441)
Webb, Edward W 4:44:10 (23,219)
Webb, Gregory J 4:35:30 (21,110)
Webb, Harvey J 3:36:51 (6,029)
Webb, Kevin N 5:08:19 (27,857)
Webb, Mark 3:47:33 (8,235)
Webb, Martin J 3:43:13 (7,290)
Webb, Mike 3:41:35 (6,952)
Webb, Nigel 4:04:53 (13,019)

White, Alexander J 4:29:34 (19,529)
White, Andrew J 3:07:41 (1,751)
White, Andrew J 3:55:15 (10,275)
White, Anthony J 4:07:51 (13,730)
White, Barry R 4:20:01 (16,890)
White, Barry S 4:18:23 (16,458)
White, Ben 3:59:58 (11,842)
White, Charles B 5:11:39 (28,354)
White, Charlie 4:24:02 (18,007)
White, Daniel J 5:14:50 (28,788)
White, Darren W 3:21:41 (3,443)
White, David J 4:42:51 (22,892)
White, David P 3:46:30 (8,007)
White, Douglas 5:47:20 (31,934)
White, Edwin 4:45:14 (23,473)
White, Eric G 4:00:51 (12,068)
White, Gary H 5:36:46 (31,100)
White, Graham A 4:31:34 (20,046)
White, Grahame K 4:05:38 (13,206)
White, Ian M 4:42:23 (22,770)
White, Ian P 5:17:16 (29,094)
White, Ian R 2:38:21 (174)
White, Ian R 3:15:47 (2,727)
White, James D 5:10:12 (28,175)
White, John F 4:42:42 (22,851)
White, Jonathan G 4:39:06 (22,005)
White, Keith R 3:25:15 (3,971)
White, Kevin M 5:39:25 (31,293)
White, Liam S 3:25:35 (4,029)
White, Louis F 5:17:24 (29,109)
White, Mark R 3:43:32 (7,350)
White, Mark S 3:43:23 (7,321)
White, Martin D 4:15:14 (15,626)
White, Michael G 4:28:22 (19,229)
White, Mike P 2:58:20 (982)
White, Myles B 3:20:05 (3,233)
White, Nick 3:04:53 (1,510)
White, Nick E 5:35:34 (30,983)
White, Nicky 4:20:14 (16,957)
White, Paul A 4:52:22 (25,118)
White, Paul J 4:51:42 (24,985)
White, Richard W 4:46:38 (23,807)
White, Rob J 4:21:01 (17,188)
White, Robert H 3:44:02 (7,461)
White, Robert J 3:30:23 (4,950)
White, Robert J 3:42:04 (7,042)
White, Robert P 4:37:34 (21,606)
White, Simon J 3:49:02 (8,587)
White, Stephen 3:20:23 (3,276)
White, Stephen A 4:52:16 (25,096)
White, Stephen J 3:20:33 (3,300)
White, Stephen J 6:00:16 (32,750)
White, Timothy G 5:25:14 (29,954)
White, Tom 5:41:40 (31,477)
White, Tomas E 4:33:16 (20,496)
White, Wayne 4:39:07 (22,008)
White, William 3:55:49 (10,440)
Whitechurch, Gavin A 4:59:56 (26,622)
Whitefield, Andrew W 4:07:21 (13,603)
Whitehead, Andrew S 3:56:55 (10,768)
Whitehead, Chris J 4:08:29 (13,905)
Whitehead, Daniel M 4:32:54 (20,401)
Whitehead, Glen 4:53:53 (25,456)
Whitehead, Ian D 3:24:50 (3,897)
Whitehead, John 3:22:45 (3,601)
Whitehead, Joshua C 3:04:13 (1,469)
Whitehead, Kevin M 4:20:36 (17,061)
Whitehead, Lee P 3:13:10 (2,355)
Whitehead, Matthew R 3:55:49 (10,440)
Whitehead, Paul A 4:18:17 (16,429)
Whitehead, Paul C 4:36:16 (21,315)
Whitehead, Stephen 2:44:34 (313)
Whitehouse, Andrew J 5:26:05 (30,043)
Whitehouse, David A 4:35:27 (21,098)
Whitehouse, Ian R 2:45:01 (333)
Whitehouse, James A 6:17:23 (33,331)
Whitehouse, Michael 5:03:56 (27,246)
Whitehouse, Mick 3:55:45 (10,422)
Whitehouse, Neil M 5:56:51 (32,572)
Whitehouse, Paul H 5:28:52 (30,360)
Whitehouse, Robert J 4:39:11 (22,022)
Whitehouse, Terry M 5:11:39 (28,354)
Whitelaw, David S 3:58:15 (11,198)
Whitelegg, Richard 2:44:02 (293)
Whiteley, Andrew J 5:09:57 (28,137)
Whiteley, David C 4:20:52 (17,144)
Whiteley, Dex 4:18:35 (16,526)
Whiteley, Martin H 3:41:58 (7,019)
Whiteley, Stephen P 3:08:27 (1,833)
Whitelock, Alan M 4:59:40 (26,588)
Whitelock, Ian T 3:49:26 (8,681)
Whiteman, Gary J 4:41:27 (22,546)
Whiteman, Paul J 4:07:36 (13,670)
Whitfield, Karl J 4:04:57 (13,038)
Whitfield, Mark 3:25:23 (3,992)
Whitfield, Matthew 3:11:47 (2,187)
Whitfield, Robert J 5:36:25 (31,073)
Whitford-Bartle, Jonathan 3:55:57 (10,477)
Whithead, Shane J 5:05:58 (27,544)
Whiting, Andrew C 4:58:35 (26,395)
Whiting, David C 5:29:57 (30,474)
Whiting, Richard 4:57:34 (26,199)
Whitley, Melvin 5:44:04 (31,670)
Whitlock, David R 4:14:38 (15,478)
Whitlock, Tony R 3:22:31 (3,570)
Whitlow, Todd W 5:07:46 (27,806)
Whitmore, Charles 4:56:40 (25,995)
Whitmore, Ivon E 3:17:55 (2,977)
Whitmore, Jason 4:55:46 (25,831)
Whitney, Michael R 4:15:13 (15,622)
Whitney, William L 6:49:13 (34,063)
Whittaker, Andrew H 3:09:42 (1,961)
Whittaker, Ben 3:07:01 (1,685)
Whittaker, David B 5:55:20 (32,487)
Whittaker, Dean 4:25:08 (18,302)
Whittaker, Keith 4:30:07 (19,660)
Whittaker, Michael 4:45:07 (23,438)
Whittem, Alex J 2:52:37 (619)
Whittingham, Andrew J 3:28:59 (4,665)
Whittingham, Dylan P 3:15:13 (2,656)
Whittington, Harvey 4:38:48 (21,912)
Whittington, Richard H 3:58:19 (11,226)
Whittington, Russell 2:50:20 (523)
Whittle, David 5:02:32 (27,044)
Whittle, Richard S 3:35:02 (5,708)
Whittle, Robert J 4:08:13 (13,833)
Whittle, Terry 4:51:57 (25,031)
Whittley, Shane 4:10:03 (14,305)
Whitton, Mark 4:24:19 (18,084)
Whitton, Peter R 5:05:31 (27,479)
Whitty, Iain A 3:47:55 (8,329)
Whitty, Maurice W 5:55:04 (32,465)
Whitwham, Simon C 4:07:34 (13,658)
Whitworth, Bill J 3:24:02 (3,783)
Whitworth, Brendan J 4:18:02 (16,352)
Whitworth, Martin J 3:38:27 (6,350)
Whitworth, Nicholas C 5:01:44 (26,921)
Whorwood, Thomas H 3:45:29 (7,790)
Whyatt, Paul D 5:11:03 (28,283)
Whymark, Paul 3:53:55 (9,839)
Whyte, Kyle D 4:52:16 (25,096)
Whyte, Michael 4:27:09 (18,858)
Whyte, Michael E 3:06:26 (1,638)
Wick, Darren 4:27:23 (18,928)
Wickenden, David 5:27:48 (30,236)
Wickenden, Lee C 4:14:14 (15,377)
Wickenden, Stephen 4:25:30 (18,397)
Wickens, James A 5:16:34 (29,003)
Wickens, Nigel M 4:19:49 (16,838)
Wickens, Robert 5:29:16 (30,405)
Wicker, William C 4:23:10 (17,770)
Wickett, Alexander J 3:26:45 (4,240)
Wickham, Wayne D 3:51:42 (9,229)
Wicks, Craig M 3:48:41 (8,507)
Wicks, Philip G 4:02:09 (12,404)
Wicks, Stephen J 3:19:13 (3,122)
Wictome, Matthew P 5:00:31 (26,710)
Widdowson, Nigel 4:01:50 (12,324)
Widdowson, Paul E 4:10:08 (14,320)
Widmer, David 4:27:54 (19,065)
Wiedel, Bengt 3:29:28 (4,774)
Wiegand, Paul A 4:03:43 (12,771)
Wieland, Herbert 3:23:11 (3,661)
Wield, Christopher 4:45:18 (23,495)
Wiggins, Michael 3:37:45 (6,210)
Wiggins, Robert S 4:12:04 (14,830)
Wigginton, Clive J 4:51:17 (24,898)
Wigglesworth, Christopher J 3:59:14 (11,574)
Wiggs, Richard I 4:58:05 (26,301)
Wigham, David 4:12:59 (15,027)
Wightman, Andrew C 5:37:43 (31,170)
Wightman, Paul M 4:33:22 (20,533)
Wigington, Denny S 4:02:19 (12,450)
Wigley, Andrew C 4:08:27 (13,895)
Wigley, Huw 5:02:39 (27,058)
Wignall, Ian 3:52:41 (9,476)
Wigniolle, Antoine 3:41:52 (7,008)
Wigniolle, Olivier 3:32:57 (5,380)
Wigzell, Clifford J 4:21:51 (17,412)
Wigzell, Edward 4:12:17 (14,881)
Wikeley, Adrian 4:32:57 (20,421)
Wilby, Darren J 5:03:08 (27,123)
Wilcke, Stephan 4:20:28 (17,015)
Wilcock, Martin 2:55:46 (792)
Wilcock, Martin 3:15:41 (2,716)
Wilcock, Pete J 5:59:37 (32,720)
Wilcock, Ross 4:44:25 (23,276)
Wilcox, Alan F 3:38:13 (6,303)
Wilcox, Andrew 4:17:10 (16,147)
Wilcox, Daniel T 4:54:37 (25,603)
Wilcox, Michael P 3:54:28 (10,013)
Wilcox, Peter J 5:21:58 (29,596)
Wild, Andrew D 5:19:13 (29,317)
Wild, Bob 4:01:10 (12,156)
Wild, James E 6:20:01 (33,395)
Wild, Mark S 3:59:08 (11,540)
Wild, Richard J 2:51:19 (565)
Wildblood, Andrew J 3:59:57 (11,836)
Wilde, Aaron R 5:23:48 (29,780)
Wilde, Andrew J 4:19:54 (16,861)
Wilde, John 4:41:01 (22,442)
Wilder, Andrew M 3:16:19 (2,791)
Wilder, Chris R 2:56:40 (852)
Wildgoose, Symon G 4:32:07 (20,204)
Wilding, Simon J 5:35:33 (30,981)
Wildman, Ben M 4:14:34 (15,464)
Wildman, Brian 3:33:42 (5,506)
Wildman, Philip J 5:39:32 (31,300)
Wilen, Allan J 3:39:30 (6,534)
Wiles, Gerald R 4:23:16 (17,804)
Wiles, Jonathon E 4:46:56 (23,895)
Wiles, William C 4:23:10 (17,770)
Wilford, Andrew R 3:50:14 (8,880)
Wilgoss, Andrew J 4:26:33 (18,679)
Wilhman, Carl C 3:42:04 (7,042)
Wili, Graham P 3:44:24 (7,534)
Wiliams, Gary 3:43:24 (7,323)
Wilkens, Nolan 3:10:21 (2,022)
Wilkes, Andrew 3:50:25 (8,913)
Wilkes, Bernard T 3:37:01 (6,067)
Wilkes, David J 4:01:31 (12,247)
Wilkes, Jeffrey W 5:07:36 (27,782)
Wilkes, Justin S 4:05:19 (13,125)
Wilkes, Paul 3:43:08 (7,273)
Wilkey, David H 4:05:16 (13,113)
Wilkins, Adrian 3:54:36 (10,071)
Wilkins, Andrew 4:38:12 (21,757)
Wilkins, Daran D 5:42:05 (31,507)
Wilkins, Derek V 4:23:07 (17,757)
Wilkins, Gareth J 4:15:28 (15,693)
Wilkins, James 5:50:03 (32,131)
Wilkins, Michael A 5:52:18 (32,307)
Wilkins, Peter J 4:01:04 (12,128)
Wilkinson, Dale M 2:55:21 (768)
Wilkinson, David R 3:38:44 (6,396)
Wilkinson, David R 3:45:50 (7,867)
Wilkinson, David R 5:09:32 (28,061)
Wilkinson, Geoffrey 5:09:49 (28,117)
Wilkinson, Ian J 2:52:59 (639)
Wilkinson, Ian M 4:28:06 (19,130)
Wilkinson, Ian S 3:31:28 (5,124)
Wilkinson, John 3:48:50 (8,534)
Wilkinson, John A 4:02:37 (12,520)
Wilkinson, Kevin 4:31:59 (20,169)
Wilkinson, Lawrence O 3:21:44 (3,451)
Wilkinson, Lee 4:38:34 (21,849)
Wilkinson, Martin J 3:09:22 (1,926)
Wilkinson, Matthew 4:44:29 (23,297)
Wilkinson, Michael 4:19:32 (16,768)

Wilkinson, Philip	3:52:19 (9,392)
Wilkinson, Ritchie	4:46:05 (23,685)
Wilkinson, Sam G	4:33:20 (20,523)
Wilkinson, Scott	4:14:10 (15,357)
Wilkinson, Stephen R	4:13:45 (15,240)
Wilkinson, Trevor	3:09:49 (1,972)
Wilks, Jon	4:32:00 (20,173)
Williams, Tom A	2:49:57 (510)
Willcocks, Charlie S	5:01:25 (26,864)
Willday, Trevor J	4:38:39 (21,868)
Willemsen, Hessel W	4:48:18 (24,208)
William, Trevor M	3:11:35 (2,161)
Williams, Aaron E	4:27:53 (19,058)
Williams, Adam A	4:38:26 (21,811)
Williams, Alex	3:15:11 (2,651)
Williams, Andrew	5:26:20 (30,077)
Williams, Andrew H	4:54:29 (25,577)
Williams, Andrew J	4:08:20 (13,864)
Williams, Andrew K	4:09:13 (14,095)
Williams, Andy	4:35:06 (21,011)
Williams, Andy T	5:40:49 (31,399)
Williams, Anthony D	4:28:27 (19,247)
Williams, Ashley	3:31:14 (5,087)
Williams, Barry	3:32:48 (5,363)
Williams, Barry J	4:30:35 (19,770)
Williams, Benjamin R	4:45:00 (23,412)
Williams, Brian G	4:56:45 (26,013)
Williams, Calum S	3:47:48 (8,296)
Williams, Chris D	4:45:42 (23,585)
Williams, Chris M	4:36:52 (21,454)
Williams, Chris M	4:56:57 (26,065)
Williams, Christopher J	4:51:42 (24,985)
Williams, Craig R	4:29:45 (19,578)
Williams, Damian	3:00:50 (1,229)
Williams, Dan	3:44:17 (7,512)
Williams, Daniel	4:25:39 (18,429)
Williams, Daniel H	3:14:32 (2,556)
Williams, Daniel R	3:46:18 (7,952)
Williams, Darren G	3:47:11 (8,149)
Williams, Darren M	4:11:05 (14,571)
Williams, David	4:12:50 (14,988)
Williams, David	5:47:25 (31,947)
Williams, David D	2:51:59 (593)
Williams, David John	4:28:17 (19,199)
Williams, David M	3:51:30 (9,175)
Williams, David M	5:26:46 (30,121)
Williams, David R	3:29:39 (4,809)
Williams, David S	4:08:14 (13,839)
Williams, Dennis S	4:34:10 (20,746)
Williams, Dominic J	5:08:50 (27,947)
Williams, Donald	3:25:20 (3,984)
Williams, Edward P	3:19:41 (3,188)
Williams, Gareth	6:59:10 (34,199)
Williams, Gareth I	4:16:23 (15,927)
Williams, Gareth J	2:48:47 (456)
Williams, Gareth T	4:19:36 (16,781)
Williams, Gary	3:56:03 (10,503)
Williams, Geraint	3:14:40 (2,583)
Williams, Glyn	4:38:59 (21,971)
Williams, Graham	3:57:30 (10,953)
Williams, Graham	5:41:24 (31,455)
Williams, Howard M	3:32:20 (5,286)
Williams, Huw L	4:13:17 (15,112)
Williams, Hywel	4:19:56 (16,868)
Williams, Ian	4:14:59 (15,553)
Williams, Ian J	4:14:21 (15,410)
Williams, Iwan W	3:32:49 (5,366)
Williams, Jack	4:15:42 (15,745)
Williams, James P	3:42:20 (7,100)
Williams, James R	3:30:46 (5,015)
Williams, James R	3:35:01 (5,706)
Williams, James R	4:12:14 (14,868)
Williams, Jamie R	5:27:49 (30,239)
Williams, Jared B	3:59:05 (11,521)
Williams, Jason	4:06:25 (13,375)
Williams, Jason M	2:43:07 (270)
Williams, Jason R	3:28:01 (4,462)
Williams, Jeremy G	3:52:25 (9,415)
Williams, Jerry L	5:17:56 (29,171)
Williams, Jesse J	2:25:43 (39)
Williams, John	3:14:12 (2,498)
Williams, John D	4:47:56 (24,132)
Williams, John E	3:58:26 (11,276)

Williams, John P	5:04:42 (27,359)
Williams, Jonathan D	3:16:55 (2,854)
Williams, Joseph M	4:33:14 (20,488)
Williams, Justin K	3:57:49 (11,066)
Williams, Keith E	3:20:09 (3,243)
Williams, Keith J	4:20:56 (17,159)
Williams, Ken	4:35:04 (20,998)
Williams, Kevin A	5:57:42 (32,614)
Williams, Kevin B	6:08:30 (33,067)
Williams, Leighton	3:21:18 (3,402)
Williams, Leslie	5:33:42 (30,798)
Williams, Lewis T	4:41:02 (22,445)
Williams, Lloyd	5:04:36 (27,342)
Williams, Mark	4:06:26 (13,381)
Williams, Mark A	4:29:11 (19,447)
Williams, Mark L	3:42:03 (7,038)
Williams, Martin	5:31:41 (30,632)
Williams, Martin D	3:47:50 (8,306)
Williams, Martin F	4:26:39 (18,706)
Williams, Martyn J	4:11:02 (14,551)
Williams, Matthew C	6:24:16 (33,524)
Williams, Matthew I	4:09:08 (14,069)
Williams, Michael	3:46:24 (7,979)
Williams, Michael J	3:51:43 (9,233)
Williams, Michael J	3:54:11 (9,928)
Williams, Nathaniel J	3:00:00 (1,169)
Williams, Neil	5:07:15 (27,732)
Williams, Neil A	3:28:06 (4,481)
Williams, Neil J	3:25:09 (3,956)
Williams, Neil M	4:11:32 (14,687)
Williams, Neville K	4:45:24 (23,510)
Williams, Nicholas J	3:45:23 (7,769)
Williams, Nik A	4:44:29 (23,297)
Williams, Oliver	4:36:00 (21,245)
Williams, Paul	4:25:17 (18,336)
Williams, Paul	5:01:57 (26,950)
Williams, Paul C	4:26:04 (18,558)
Williams, Paul D	3:56:17 (10,557)
Williams, Pete C	3:30:05 (4,904)
Williams, Peter H	3:32:13 (5,263)
Williams, Rhodri	4:03:51 (12,797)
Williams, Rhodri G	3:29:35 (4,795)
Williams, Rhys A	5:38:40 (31,238)
Williams, Rhys J	3:38:20 (6,321)
Williams, Richard	4:38:36 (21,858)
Williams, Richard	5:13:04 (28,552)
Williams, Richard S	3:40:01 (6,641)
Williams, Robbie H	4:27:12 (18,871)
Williams, Robert D	5:06:42 (27,652)
Williams, Robert E	4:27:48 (19,022)
Williams, Sam	4:42:22 (22,766)
Williams, Simon	3:55:37 (10,379)
Williams, Simon H	5:19:17 (29,330)
Williams, Simon J	3:16:11 (2,773)
Williams, Simon P	3:37:04 (6,074)
Williams, Stan	3:23:03 (3,645)
Williams, Stephen A	4:06:06 (13,313)
Williams, Stephen J	5:00:22 (26,688)
Williams, Stuart C	4:10:13 (14,340)
Williams, Tim	4:31:38 (20,063)
Williams, Timothy P	3:51:40 (9,220)
Williams, Tomos	5:47:22 (31,939)
Williams, Wesley D	6:22:49 (33,487)
Williams, William E	4:01:52 (12,329)
Williamson, Adam C	4:52:01 (25,048)
Williamson, Adrian E	6:09:33 (33,097)
Williamson, Andrew J	4:09:55 (14,283)
Williamson, Andrew L	3:58:47 (11,406)
Williamson, Dave J	4:22:53 (17,698)
Williamson, David	3:55:01 (10,201)
Williamson, Karl A	3:37:11 (6,098)
Williamson, Ken	3:11:45 (2,181)
Williamson, Mark	3:09:31 (1,942)
Williamson, Matt	2:36:48 (143)
Williamson, Matthew D	6:20:34 (33,410)
Williamson, Michael A	4:25:07 (18,296)
Williamson, Neil R	3:47:40 (8,273)
Williamson, Neil R	5:32:21 (30,686)
Williamson, Paul T	4:03:13 (12,658)
Williamson, Peter A	4:47:54 (24,123)
Willicott, Mark	3:40:31 (6,738)
Willis, Andrew D	6:27:45 (33,620)
Willis, Damien B	4:22:40 (17,639)

Willis, Darren	3:26:09 (4,130)
Willis, David	5:02:52 (27,091)
Willis, Howard A	4:34:02 (20,705)
Willis, James	5:41:32 (31,468)
Willis, John A	3:59:03 (11,507)
Willis, Matthew J	2:56:58 (869)
Willis, Norman S	3:36:35 (5,980)
Willis, Sean G	3:53:30 (9,711)
Willmes, Arie	5:23:22 (29,732)
Willmitt, Williams J	3:21:25 (3,415)
Willmore, Iain	5:51:32 (32,253)
Willmott, Andrew	3:55:27 (10,323)
Willmott, Dan	4:11:23 (14,640)
Willmott, Gary J	5:31:49 (30,641)
Willmott, Robin J	3:45:52 (7,873)
Willmott, Roy D	9:58:04 (34,588)
Willoughby, Gary K	3:44:33 (7,563)
Willow, Jack G	4:32:14 (20,238)
Wills, Andrew E	6:23:54 (33,514)
Wills, James	3:58:24 (11,261)
Wills, Robin J	5:43:52 (31,639)
Willsher, Anthony J	3:48:53 (8,549)
Willson, Anthony J	4:37:59 (21,711)
Wilmot, Andrew	3:45:27 (7,785)
Wilmot, Andrew H	3:37:47 (6,212)
Wilmot, Jack	5:41:47 (31,485)
Wilmot, Wayne D	4:58:26 (26,366)
Wilmshurst, Andrew P	2:45:49 (353)
Wilmshurst, Mark	4:18:22 (16,452)
Wilshaw, John T	5:26:57 (30,141)
Wilsher, Philip J	4:32:06 (20,197)
Wilsher, Tim A	3:44:11 (7,489)
Wilson, Adrian	4:42:14 (22,736)
Wilson, Andrew P	3:51:39 (9,211)
Wilson, Angus R	3:35:54 (5,859)
Wilson, Barry	2:50:26 (534)
Wilson, Benjamin J	4:07:10 (13,568)
Wilson, Brian	3:26:38 (4,213)
Wilson, Bruce	4:26:49 (18,761)
Wilson, Chris A	4:02:39 (12,533)
Wilson, Chris M	4:02:16 (12,436)
Wilson, Christopher B	5:35:56 (31,025)
Wilson, Christopher M	3:32:09 (5,253)
Wilson, Christopher M	4:37:11 (21,522)
Wilson, Colin	3:50:34 (8,944)
Wilson, Daren M	4:21:35 (17,332)
Wilson, David	6:05:14 (32,936)
Wilson, Dominic	3:53:55 (9,839)
Wilson, Eugene L	4:56:03 (25,885)
Wilson, Garry	4:04:36 (12,949)
Wilson, Geoffrey	3:03:00 (1,372)
Wilson, Glenn C	2:59:08 (1,077)
Wilson, Graham J	4:59:52 (26,613)
Wilson, Graham P	5:01:46 (26,925)
Wilson, Hamish G	5:07:07 (27,706)
Wilson, Iain A	2:58:11 (966)
Wilson, Ian	4:42:14 (22,736)
Wilson, James L	4:31:47 (20,097)
Wilson, James M	3:37:03 (6,071)
Wilson, Jason	4:43:33 (23,064)
Wilson, Jason L	3:31:36 (5,151)
Wilson, John P	3:30:54 (5,039)
Wilson, Jonathon B	4:20:51 (17,138)
Wilson, Kenneth J	4:04:19 (12,893)
Wilson, Kerry L	2:43:20 (278)
Wilson, Kevin A	5:02:19 (27,007)
Wilson, Lawrence M	6:36:37 (33,810)
Wilson, Leo J	3:58:59 (11,481)
Wilson, Leslie	4:12:19 (14,887)
Wilson, Mark	3:36:27 (5,956)
Wilson, Mark A	4:29:20 (19,481)
Wilson, Mark D	3:39:57 (6,628)
Wilson, Mark E	4:57:13 (26,127)
Wilson, Mark R	4:10:13 (14,340)
Wilson, Matthew T	3:57:53 (11,085)
Wilson, Matthew V	3:40:49 (6,784)
Wilson, Michael G	3:41:11 (6,866)
Wilson, Michael G	4:58:35 (26,395)
Wilson, Michael L	3:36:41 (5,995)
Wilson, Michael R	3:26:46 (4,242)
Wilson, Nicholas C	3:13:19 (2,376)
Wilson, Nicholas M	3:10:36 (2,054)
Wilson, Nicholas S	4:29:36 (19,542)

Wilson, Nick	3:41:00 (6,824)	
Wilson, Patrick J	3:09:43 (1,963)	
Wilson, Patrick N	5:09:31 (28,054)	
Wilson, Paul A	4:13:53 (15,273)	
Wilson, Paul S	3:38:39 (6,379)	
Wilson, Ralph A	4:33:36 (20,609)	
Wilson, Robert	2:56:10 (818)	
Wilson, Robert W	4:24:05 (18,017)	
Wilson, Robin H	4:57:01 (26,084)	
Wilson, Stephen V	4:22:27 (17,568)	
Wilson, Steve	4:44:46 (23,358)	
Wilson Hammond, Stuart	3:35:04 (5,713)	
Wilson Ramsay, Mark E	3:52:57 (9,553)	
Wilters, Hero	5:06:40 (27,647)	
Wilton, Graham G	2:49:44 (498)	
Wilton, Iain R	3:51:16 (9,113)	
Wilton, James M	4:20:16 (16,966)	
Wilton, Julian C	3:56:42 (10,690)	
Wilton, Matthew	3:41:09 (6,859)	
Wiltshire, Craig J	4:27:08 (18,851)	
Wiltshire, Glyn D	4:39:08 (22,011)	
Wiltshire, Simon L	4:27:35 (18,974)	
Wiman, Sebastian	3:22:37 (3,588)	
Wimmer, Anton E	5:25:01 (29,915)	
Wimpory, Howard P	3:26:59 (4,277)	
Windle, Paul J	3:04:12 (1,467)	
Windle, Rob A	4:26:02 (18,548)	
Windle, Scott	4:12:52 (14,996)	
Window, Chris D	4:24:37 (18,175)	
Windsor, Nicholas	4:14:59 (15,553)	
Winfield, David J	4:01:00 (12,112)	
Winfield, Mark L	5:27:58 (30,262)	
Winfield, Peter G	3:27:42 (4,396)	
Winfield, Russell A	4:18:25 (16,470)	
Winfield, Stephen J	3:47:38 (8,263)	
Winfieldale, John R	3:25:00 (3,930)	
Wing, Andrew T	3:27:04 (4,291)	
Wing, Gary	4:07:53 (13,745)	
Wing, Stephen	5:54:53 (32,451)	
Wingate, Eugene J	4:36:39 (21,402)	
Wingfield, Simon E	4:30:55 (19,870)	
Wingham, Mark	3:29:03 (4,681)	
Wingrove, Martin D	5:08:52 (27,952)	
Winkfield, David C	4:04:56 (13,035)	
Winkless, Neil S	4:57:06 (26,108)	
Winkworth, Toby	4:48:22 (24,218)	
Winn, Jonathan L	3:48:08 (8,385)	
Winn-Smith, Matt	2:49:02 (465)	
Winskill, Malcolm S	6:11:38 (33,157)	
Winsland, Derek	3:58:31 (11,306)	
Winsley, Nicholas P	4:43:40 (23,095)	
Winsley, Paul A	4:15:36 (15,730)	
Winslow, Michael P	4:02:53 (12,581)	
Winstanley, Martin T	4:31:32 (20,032)	
Winstanley, Sean G	6:47:52 (34,033)	
Winston, Deepak	5:24:29 (29,857)	
Winstone, Mark T	4:08:44 (13,978)	
Wint, Andrew	3:52:50 (9,514)	
Winter, Darren J	5:02:00 (26,958)	
Winter, Dean W	3:59:29 (11,668)	
Winter, Geoffrey P	3:58:22 (11,251)	
Winter, James	3:44:56 (7,665)	
Winter, John R	3:54:08 (9,915)	
Winter, Mark S	2:59:56 (1,163)	
Winter, Martin	3:55:27 (10,323)	
Winter, Tom	3:58:55 (11,460)	
Winterbourne, Daniel J	4:51:31 (24,941)	
Winterstein, Yaron	4:28:52 (19,367)	
Winterton, David J	4:15:15 (15,629)	
Wintle, David A	3:09:25 (1,930)	
Wintle, David M	3:30:03 (4,895)	
Wintle, George	4:55:18 (25,749)	
Winwood, Matthew R	5:22:21 (29,645)	
Wirsing, Uwe	3:06:11 (1,616)	
Wirth, Paul A	4:20:10 (16,936)	
Wisbey, Gavin L	4:26:13 (18,585)	
Wisdish, Robert J	4:59:07 (26,496)	
Wise, Chris A	3:19:57 (3,221)	
Wise, Daniel C	3:49:49 (8,774)	
Wise, David A	4:33:32 (20,586)	
Wise, David J	3:37:51 (6,227)	
Wise, John E	3:11:56 (2,200)	
Wise, Jonathan S	3:45:23 (7,769)	

Wise, Larry	4:18:30 (16,497)	
Wise, Raymond J	3:37:57 (6,252)	
Wise, Roger S	4:41:14 (22,496)	
Wise, Stephen	3:45:49 (7,863)	
Wisler, Michael A	3:36:04 (5,892)	
Wiswell, Paul	4:52:35 (25,166)	
Wiswell, Stephen J	4:32:30 (20,300)	
Witchell, John H	4:56:02 (25,881)	
Witherington, Clive R	4:17:07 (16,128)	
Witherington, Kieran D	4:22:10 (17,486)	
Withers, David G	3:58:47 (11,406)	
Withers, Gareth R	3:46:16 (7,946)	
Withers, Jim	3:44:51 (7,642)	
Withers, Peter F	4:37:35 (21,613)	
Withers, Scott D	3:57:42 (11,017)	
Withers, Scott P	4:37:00 (21,485)	
Witt, Jonathan J	4:33:32 (20,586)	
Witte, Rinus	2:58:06 (957)	
Witters, Barton J	4:13:09 (15,074)	
Wittred, Daniel	5:00:40 (26,730)	
Witts, James	3:35:25 (5,780)	
Wittusen, Thomas E	3:28:52 (4,641)	
Witty, Andrew P	4:26:13 (18,585)	
Wix, Jonathan R	4:09:25 (14,147)	
Wodarek-Black, Mark	5:53:59 (32,402)	
Woerner, Bernhard W	3:40:03 (6,649)	
Wohanka, Richard	3:57:23 (10,919)	
Wolfe, Andrew J	3:25:15 (3,971)	
Wolfe, Christopher M	4:32:24 (20,268)	
Wolfe, Henry L	6:43:39 (33,953)	
Wolfe, Shaun J	5:01:35 (26,887)	
Wolfendale, Stewart	3:54:49 (10,131)	
Wolfenden, Matthew	4:30:50 (19,843)	
Wolff, Andrew D	3:34:37 (5,632)	
Wolff, David A	4:48:35 (24,268)	
Wolff, Paul F	4:32:27 (20,282)	
Wollaston, Charles	4:38:23 (21,796)	
Wollaston, Lee	4:46:55 (23,888)	
Wolovitz, Lionel	3:18:48 (3,074)	
Wolstencroft, Shane M	3:14:43 (2,594)	
Wong, Alvin F	5:11:51 (28,391)	
Wood, Adam V	3:46:07 (7,911)	
Wood, Alasdair	3:54:10 (9,924)	
Wood, Andrew M	2:59:39 (1,135)	
Wood, Ben	4:22:31 (17,591)	
Wood, Brian E	4:05:55 (13,270)	
Wood, Christopher	6:04:12 (32,895)	
Wood, Colin G	3:20:55 (3,343)	
Wood, Darren J	3:11:25 (2,137)	
Wood, David C	4:13:53 (15,273)	
Wood, David J	5:34:10 (30,852)	
Wood, David L	3:13:06 (2,346)	
Wood, David M	3:16:48 (2,847)	
Wood, Derek J	5:54:44 (32,440)	
Wood, Derek L	5:08:23 (27,871)	
Wood, Duncan	5:05:59 (27,547)	
Wood, Fred J	4:26:26 (18,641)	
Wood, Freddie	3:50:07 (8,847)	
Wood, Gareth D	3:06:00 (1,596)	
Wood, Graham	4:11:54 (14,778)	
Wood, Hayden	4:12:17 (14,881)	
Wood, Ian D	3:03:12 (1,392)	
Wood, Ian S	5:25:49 (30,012)	
Wood, James	3:07:38 (1,745)	
Wood, Jody	3:59:04 (11,511)	
Wood, John M	3:52:14 (9,370)	
Wood, Jonathan	4:19:29 (16,750)	
Wood, Jonathan D	4:35:33 (21,116)	
Wood, Kevin	5:05:01 (27,405)	
Wood, Kevin G	4:47:35 (24,038)	
Wood, Kevin M	4:29:38 (19,547)	
Wood, Laurence A	5:04:13 (27,284)	
Wood, Mark	3:22:58 (3,631)	
Wood, Mark A	4:45:48 (23,624)	
Wood, Martin B	4:47:28 (24,015)	
Wood, Michael	3:55:40 (10,396)	
Wood, Michael A	4:26:42 (18,723)	
Wood, Nicholas A	5:04:42 (27,359)	
Wood, Nicholas F	6:01:17 (32,788)	
Wood, Paul J	2:49:22 (481)	
Wood, Paul L	4:53:00 (25,269)	
Wood, Peter C	3:45:16 (7,745)	
Wood, Peter J	3:37:14 (6,109)	

Wood, Phillip	4:22:12 (17,495)	
Wood, Reece	2:51:29 (570)	
Wood, Stephen M	3:16:20 (2,795)	
Wood, Steve W	3:30:43 (5,002)	
Wood, Steven D	3:44:01 (7,459)	
Wood, Tim J	4:14:42 (15,495)	
Wood, Tim K	5:04:51 (27,376)	
Wood, Tom D	4:51:04 (24,860)	
Wood, Vic	4:10:58 (14,537)	
Wood, William	3:47:11 (8,149)	
Wood, William M	3:43:00 (7,239)	
Woodard, Andrew P	4:19:09 (16,667)	
Woodcock, David	5:36:47 (31,101)	
Woodcock, John P	4:03:45 (12,782)	
Woodcock, Jonathan M	4:17:55 (16,329)	
Woodcock, Mark S	4:58:40 (26,410)	
Woodcock, Robert	4:48:24 (24,225)	
Woodcock, Shaun	3:33:03 (5,391)	
Woodcock, Stephen	3:54:09 (9,919)	
Wooderson, Andrew D	4:22:16 (17,514)	
Woodfield, Michael T	4:38:07 (21,743)	
Woodgate, Paul J	3:21:38 (3,438)	
Woodhams, Richard M	3:53:04 (9,596)	
Woodhead, Ian	3:43:11 (7,283)	
Woodhouse, Ben	3:11:39 (2,169)	
Woodhouse, David J	4:18:56 (16,610)	
Woodhouse, Jack	4:27:29 (18,950)	
Woodhouse, Keith E	5:30:06 (30,486)	
Woodhouse, Philip J	3:08:31 (1,840)	
Woodhouse, Richard A	4:40:05 (22,209)	
Woodier, Daniel R	3:39:01 (6,440)	
Wooding, Glen T	4:44:36 (23,321)	
Woodland, Clive R	4:31:47 (20,097)	
Woodland, Gregory W	5:27:57 (30,259)	
Woodley, Steve B	4:53:03 (25,286)	
Woodman, Adrian U	3:45:07 (7,711)	
Woodman, Grant C	3:35:57 (5,869)	
Woodman, Huw K	5:45:38 (31,808)	
Woodman, John M	3:20:03 (3,231)	
Woodman, Mark J	2:40:39 (207)	
Woodman, Philip C	3:32:37 (5,336)	
Woodman, William J	4:04:36 (12,949)	
Woodman-Smith, Oliver	3:56:04 (10,507)	
Woodroof, Neil	3:45:10 (7,719)	
Woodroofe, Paul	4:18:09 (16,386)	
Woodrow, Alan R	4:11:59 (14,806)	
Woodruff, Jeremy E	4:36:24 (21,344)	
Woodruff, Michael A	3:19:59 (3,224)	
Woods, Aaron K	5:47:45 (31,963)	
Woods, Andy T	3:10:40 (2,062)	
Woods, Brian P	3:53:39 (9,755)	
Woods, Christopher M	3:58:37 (11,341)	
Woods, Christopher N	4:08:30 (13,909)	
Woods, Garry	3:16:15 (2,781)	
Woods, Kevin	5:31:49 (30,641)	
Woods, Max J	3:21:13 (3,386)	
Woods, Nicholas M	3:15:27 (2,694)	
Woods, Philip R	3:15:10 (2,649)	
Woods, Richard M	4:34:51 (20,925)	
Woods, Robert A	4:06:31 (13,407)	
Woods, Scott C	3:50:37 (8,961)	
Woods, Shane D	3:51:58 (9,291)	
Woods, Tim	5:02:27 (27,036)	
Woods, Tim J	4:15:32 (15,715)	
Woodside, Dennis M	3:07:55 (1,780)	
Woodus, Stephen L	3:44:09 (7,482)	
Woodward, David J	3:59:19 (11,602)	
Woodward, Jeremy M	3:22:49 (3,612)	
Woodward, Keiron	4:14:37 (15,472)	
Woodward, Michael	4:54:30 (25,581)	
Woodward, Paul N	4:06:31 (13,407)	
Woodward, Peter G	2:53:40 (672)	
Woodward, Simon G	4:42:58 (22,924)	
Woodward, Tristan D	4:28:04 (19,118)	
Woodyard, Paul T	5:59:01 (32,694)	
Wooldridge, David P	3:40:19 (6,692)	
Wooldridge, John A	3:55:55 (5,862)	
Wooldridge, Symon A	5:59:55 (32,737)	
Woolerton, Philip J	4:25:18 (18,341)	
Woolfenden, Chris	5:05:55 (27,536)	
Woolford, Howard S	3:54:43 (10,105)	
Woolgar, Darren J	4:23:31 (17,872)	
Woolgard, Ed	5:44:56 (31,758)	

Woolham, Craig 4:45:15 (23,481)
Woollard, Tom L 4:11:59 (14,806)
Woollard, Wayne D 4:31:39 (20,067)
Woolley, Alan N 4:12:25 (14,910)
Woolley, Chris P 5:44:41 (31,736)
Woolley, Laurence M 4:14:44 (15,502)
Woolley, Philip R 5:31:10 (30,579)
Woolley, Simon M 3:29:10 (4,707)
Woolley, Stephen P 5:22:24 (29,650)
Woolmore, Scott T 5:08:20 (27,860)
Woolner, Paul V 3:50:36 (8,955)
Wooloff, Geoff P 5:43:52 (31,639)
Wooloughan, John C 6:08:08 (33,050)
Woolstenholmes, Peter L 4:42:33 (22,820)
Woolston, Mathew J 4:42:28 (22,793)
Woor, Stuart J 4:05:13 (13,105)
Woosey, Mark A 4:55:08 (25,723)
Wootley, Anthony B 4:12:58 (15,021)
Wootten, Keith R 4:25:57 (18,519)
Wootten, Ronald 4:04:13 (12,866)
Wootton, Kevin R 3:59:18 (11,595)
Wootton, Stephen R 4:41:56 (22,658)
Wootton, Terence E 4:40:34 (22,321)
Worboys, Tom H 3:53:38 (9,753)
Worcester, David J 2:59:03 (1,064)
Worden, Neil C 3:53:20 (9,673)
Workman, Malcolm J 4:40:02 (22,189)
Wormald, Carl E 3:06:53 (1,674)
Worner, Thomas 3:56:42 (10,690)
Worrall, Anthony G 4:33:34 (20,597)
Worrall, Elliot D 3:37:09 (6,088)
Worrall, Mark 4:39:02 (21,981)
Worrall, Stephen J 4:00:55 (12,086)
Worsfold, Mike J 3:49:06 (8,601)
Worsfold, Simon 4:04:05 (12,844)
Worswick, Neil D 3:17:13 (2,889)
Wort, Steven S 2:59:47 (1,150)
Worth, Daniel M 4:05:32 (13,185)
Worth, Darren J 4:19:40 (16,804)
Worthing-Smith, Jeremy B 3:15:35 (2,711)
Worthington, Brian 4:20:20 (16,983)
Worthington, John A 2:36:51 (144)
Worthley, Paul 4:20:47 (17,118)
Worthy, David S 4:25:52 (18,502)
Worthy, Laidlaw M 5:35:31 (30,979)
Wortley, Matthew 3:18:22 (3,029)
Worton, Chris 3:22:57 (3,628)
Wotton, Kevin M 2:59:04 (1,068)
Wotton, Mark A 4:02:29 (12,494)
Wouters, Wim 4:45:24 (23,510)
Wozencroft, Sean J 4:21:33 (17,319)
Wozniak, Michael J 4:27:24 (18,932)
Wozniak, Pawet 4:17:01 (16,100)
Wratten, Michael J 5:16:22 (28,977)
Wray, Alan A 3:27:44 (4,405)
Wray, Daniel 4:15:35 (15,724)
Wray, Scott J 4:20:57 (17,164)
Wreghitt, Guy 4:50:13 (24,644)
Wren, Graham F 5:04:51 (27,376)
Wren, James A 4:41:18 (22,513)
Wrench, James R 3:17:09 (2,880)
Wright, Alan 4:32:54 (20,401)
Wright, Alun D 4:22:54 (17,703)
Wright, Andrew 4:14:50 (15,520)
Wright, Andrew W 4:27:39 (18,986)
Wright, Annesley R 6:44:17 (33,963)
Wright, Anthony J 4:32:09 (20,212)
Wright, Anthony N 4:04:15 (12,876)
Wright, Ben S 4:27:17 (18,900)
Wright, Benjamin D 3:53:02 (9,586)
Wright, Benjamin N 3:53:35 (9,737)
Wright, Bernard A 4:01:56 (12,345)
Wright, Bill 5:00:29 (26,704)
Wright, Brian K 4:03:23 (12,695)
Wright, Daniel 3:50:49 (9,009)
Wright, Darren A 5:27:59 (30,264)
Wright, David 3:23:17 (3,673)
Wright, David 4:03:22 (12,689)
Wright, David A 3:37:19 (6,126)
Wright, David J 3:47:30 (8,223)
Wright, David J 4:26:19 (18,613)
Wright, David K 5:30:26 (30,520)
Wright, David P 3:42:41 (7,170)
Wright, Edward A 4:49:19 (24,436)
Wright, Gary 5:08:15 (27,849)
Wright, Gary P 3:30:25 (4,955)
Wright, Gavin C 4:50:53 (24,818)
Wright, Graham P 3:21:41 (3,443)
Wright, Ian 4:02:22 (12,469)
Wright, James C 4:44:53 (23,392)
Wright, John 4:18:06 (16,371)
Wright, John C 4:42:55 (22,912)
Wright, Justin J 4:09:32 (14,183)
Wright, Ken 5:52:59 (32,337)
Wright, Marcus 5:03:06 (27,118)
Wright, Mark F 4:43:01 (22,933)
Wright, Mark R 4:44:22 (23,271)
Wright, Matthew J 3:47:55 (8,329)
Wright, Michael G 6:12:39 (33,192)
Wright, Natanael 3:20:40 (3,315)
Wright, Neil 4:29:01 (19,402)
Wright, Neil H 5:14:08 (28,692)
Wright, Nicholas 4:15:59 (15,832)
Wright, Nick J 3:56:53 (10,756)
Wright, Nick J 4:11:09 (14,590)
Wright, Noel N 3:40:49 (6,784)
Wright, Paul D 7:27:04 (34,440)
Wright, Paul S 3:50:32 (8,937)
Wright, Peter 3:28:05 (4,477)
Wright, Peter 4:26:08 (18,571)
Wright, Peter A 3:27:17 (4,330)
Wright, Philip 5:25:30 (29,987)
Wright, Quintin E 3:11:04 (2,103)
Wright, Ralph E 3:32:20 (5,286)
Wright, Richard L 5:06:27 (27,623)
Wright, Shaun 4:09:53 (14,276)
Wright, Stephen 3:36:52 (6,033)
Wright, Stephen G 3:36:45 (6,003)
Wright, Stephen J 4:40:42 (22,353)
Wright, Stephen R 3:54:20 (9,968)
Wright, Stephen T 4:10:46 (14,485)
Wright, Steve M 3:58:06 (11,142)
Wright, Stuart L 3:38:28 (6,352)
Wright, Tim J 4:03:34 (12,736)
Wright, William F 4:40:21 (22,275)
Wrighton, Christopher J 3:14:26 (2,536)
Wrighton, James P 3:38:24 (6,339)
Wriglesworth, Nathan 3:10:31 (2,045)
Wroblewski, Steve J 4:02:55 (12,588)
Wroth, David W 4:52:47 (25,217)
Wroth, James J 4:52:26 (25,130)
Wu, William 3:26:31 (4,189)
Wu, Yeh Lap 4:05:25 (13,153)
Wyatt, Andrew 3:58:58 (11,478)
Wyatt, Andy 3:33:39 (5,495)
Wyatt, Cliff L 3:20:20 (3,270)
Wyatt, James A 3:55:10 (10,257)
Wyatt, James S 5:00:10 (26,663)
Wyatt, Paul 2:54:27 (718)
Wybouw, Erik W 4:29:41 (19,564)
Wybrow, Glyn 4:59:31 (26,564)
Wyeth, Chris 4:52:09 (25,076)
Wykes, David R 4:41:49 (22,641)
Wykes, Thomas H 4:27:50 (19,033)
Wylie, Andrew 4:41:00 (22,437)
Wylie, Ian G 3:51:48 (9,248)
Wylie, Mark C 5:03:44 (27,213)
Wylie, Robert J 3:43:06 (7,266)
Wylie, Robert S 5:35:34 (30,983)
Wylie, Samuel R 3:20:40 (3,315)
Wyllie, Stuart 3:55:42 (10,408)
Wynburne, John 5:15:41 (28,904)
Wynn, Darren A 6:16:32 (33,311)
Wynne, Steven P 4:17:28 (16,211)
Wynnes, Ian R 4:14:28 (15,443)
Wynn-Jones, William B 3:50:34 (8,944)
Wyse, Barry D 3:40:40 (6,751)
Xavier, Corey M 5:55:14 (32,484)
Yadave, Rush L 3:38:05 (6,281)
Yahiaoui, Mohammed 3:53:31 (9,715)
Yakubu, Funso 5:23:33 (29,751)
Yamada, Kent 4:07:31 (13,645)
Yandell, Duncan C 6:39:56 (33,877)
Yang, Clarence 4:59:45 (26,600)
Yano, Masaaki 3:45:50 (7,867)
Yardley, Stephen A 3:42:26 (7,124)
Yargici, Kaan 3:41:01 (6,829)
Yarnell, John 4:20:47 (17,118)
Yarrow, Andrew J 3:17:20 (2,905)
Yarwood, Robert A 4:39:32 (22,085)
Yasin, Nazar 3:21:55 (3,475)
Yates, Andrew F 2:55:28 (775)
Yates, Jason P 4:36:24 (21,344)
Yates, Kevin R 4:12:04 (14,830)
Yates, Peter E 5:40:08 (31,347)
Yates, Richard B 4:13:29 (15,154)
Yates, Robert J 5:40:07 (31,341)
Yates, Tim H 3:59:16 (11,585)
Yau, Robert C 4:42:31 (22,812)
Yazaki, Etsuro 3:14:19 (2,521)
Yeates, Andrew M 5:06:33 (27,630)
Yeats, Edwin 3:52:34 (9,448)
Yeldham, Ian J 5:01:22 (26,854)
Yelding, Steven R 4:47:17 (23,983)
Yell, William N 3:38:36 (6,369)
Yelland, David 4:28:03 (19,116)
Yelland, Jonathan D 4:16:19 (15,907)
Yelling, Christopher J 3:53:19 (9,667)
Yelling, Martin 2:48:24 (441)
Yendall, Keith A 2:59:05 (1,070)
Yeneralski, David N 3:40:17 (6,688)
Yeoman, Keith A 4:26:58 (18,806)
Yeomans, Richard J 4:35:43 (21,171)
Yeomans, Thomas S 3:22:37 (3,588)
Yerlikaya, Ziya 3:32:04 (5,237)
Yianni, Christopher 3:58:34 (11,326)
Ying, Leong 3:37:49 (6,219)
Yip, Gwan 4:43:15 (22,994)
Yoofoo, John R 5:08:15 (27,849)
York, Anthony G 4:05:57 (13,285)
York, Brian R 5:55:11 (32,476)
York, Paul A 4:29:19 (19,477)
Yorkston, Christopher A 4:35:35 (21,129)
Yoseflavi, Payam 4:24:50 (18,226)
Youds, Nigel J 4:21:22 (17,261)
Youell, James P 4:38:53 (21,937)
Younan, Paul I 4:25:59 (18,531)
Young, Aaron D 3:25:39 (4,044)
Young, Alex J 4:40:17 (22,254)
Young, Andrew F 4:03:39 (12,758)
Young, Andy 5:11:45 (28,376)
Young, Ben R 3:46:44 (8,045)
Young, Chris D 3:38:29 (6,356)
Young, Chris J 5:08:59 (27,967)
Young, Christopher J 3:29:52 (4,857)
Young, Christopher R 3:49:00 (8,579)
Young, Colin R 4:05:49 (13,249)
Young, Colin S 3:21:43 (3,447)
Young, Curtis 4:26:40 (18,712)
Young, David M 4:43:00 (22,926)
Young, Dominic M 3:11:40 (2,170)
Young, George 4:09:05 (14,060)
Young, Harvey 4:24:31 (18,147)
Young, Ian 4:40:29 (22,306)
Young, Kester R 3:28:40 (4,596)
Young, Mark 4:03:09 (12,641)
Young, Mark D 3:14:10 (2,494)
Young, Mark R 4:51:16 (24,897)
Young, Maurice W 5:09:41 (28,088)
Young, Michael 4:40:54 (22,402)
Young, Michael P 6:15:04 (33,270)
Young, Neil 5:35:47 (31,004)
Young, Patrick G 3:26:33 (4,192)
Young, Patrick J 3:12:53 (2,318)
Young, Peter H 3:56:46 (10,714)
Young, Philip A 4:34:44 (20,886)
Young, Richard S 4:55:25 (25,769)
Young, Robert J 4:27:35 (18,974)
Young, Rodney 3:35:04 (5,713)
Young, Sean M 4:28:24 (19,232)
Young, Simon 3:33:31 (5,476)
Young, Simon D 4:04:39 (12,968)
Young, Steve 4:16:12 (15,874)
Young, Thomas D 3:42:18 (7,094)
Young, Tim P 3:11:33 (2,156)
Youngman, Paul A 4:29:20 (19,481)
Yu, Nicholas 6:32:26 (33,713)
Yuan, Xiaolin 4:37:41 (21,641)
Yuill, Paul D 4:33:01 (20,434)

Zaagman, Richard E 5:04:25 (27,311)
Zachariades, Yiannis C.................3:50:52 (9,019)
Zaidi, Abbas..................................3:52:40 (9,472)
Zair, Chris G 3:56:31 (10,629)
Zajackowski, Jan 3:57:18 (10,890)
Zalewski, Robert G.......................4:31:20 (19,975)
Zandee, Matthijs...........................4:30:11 (19,675)
Zanich, Alex 5:31:57 (30,657)
Zanoni, Gilberto............................4:01:11 (12,159)
Zapata, Alfred I 4:00:19 (11,929)
Zaranko, Tadeusz 2:49:24 (484)
Zasadzki, Victor............................5:17:53 (29,165)
Zavatarelli, Maurizio 3:28:18 (4,518)
Zealand, Stephen J........................3:51:23 (9,149)
Zech, Manfred...............................4:15:42 (15,745)
Zeffert, Jonathan R 4:37:51 (21,683)
Zegers Reyes, Rodrigo E 2:54:28 (721)
Zephyr, Serge................................4:37:18 (21,550)
Zerafa, John...................................5:44:24 (31,712)
Zielinski, Jeremy...........................3:04:43 (1,496)
Zietek, John...................................4:16:09 (15,863)
Zietsman, Hendrik S....................2:30:30 (78)
Zikas, Nikolaos M.........................3:55:54 (10,465)
Zikri, Sherif 5:20:26 (29,459)
Zillig, Peter D 3:45:59 (7,888)
Zillikens, Stefan............................4:39:50 (22,157)
Zimmer, Michael............................3:46:26 (7,988)
Zinn, Mark......................................4:47:50 (24,102)
Zior, Franz 4:19:09 (16,667)
Zironi, Fausto 3:54:48 (10,125)
Zitnik, Juan A 3:47:24 (8,197)
Zlatic, Zlatko.................................4:42:59 (22,925)
Zoia, Mario 3:39:32 (6,545)
Zomerdijk, Herman........................3:19:04 (3,103)
Zubiria, Fernando...........................4:18:14 (16,409)
Zucconi, Devis................................2:31:51 (83)
Zucker, Jamie C.............................4:18:31 (16,503)
Zuddas, Marcello............................3:52:06 (9,337)
Zuercher, Roland 4:34:23 (20,794)
Zurawlin, Paul A............................3:40:40 (6,751)
Zurawski, Lui J...............................5:25:06 (29,936)
Zurwonne, Frank 3:54:53 (10,150)

FEMALE RUNNERS

Aagesen, Mariann 4:47:30 (24,021)
Abbott, Helen M 4:37:21 (21,560)
Abbott, Joanne 3:19:11 (3,116)
Abbott, Kathryn E 4:00:55 (12,086)
Abejide, Lola..................................6:27:02 (33,599)
Abercrombie, Lynne.......................4:19:44 (16,821)
Abraham, Beverley D 3:56:17 (10,557)
Abraham, Corinne S......................3:55:18 (10,289)
Abraham, Helena J 5:35:49 (31,011)
Abraham, Ingrid P 5:51:39 (32,264)
Abraham, Tracey............................5:25:57 (30,030)
Abrahamian, Paula..........................4:59:16 (26,527)
Abrams, Zoe 6:12:53 (33,205)
Abrey, Colene J..............................5:03:09 (27,126)
Achille, Karen.................................4:33:27 (20,562)
Ackers, Laura J 4:08:56 (14,026)
Ackers, Shelagh A 5:03:47 (27,222)
Ackroyd, Helen L...........................4:02:57 (12,598)
Ackroyd, Sue..................................4:55:21 (25,757)
Ackroyd, Zoe A..............................6:24:41 (33,538)
Acton, Carolyn C...........................5:31:57 (30,657)
Acton, Kate J.................................5:36:21 (31,071)
Adam, Candice J............................4:59:00 (26,477)
Adames, Elcie 5:27:23 (30,191)
Adams, Denise 5:09:29 (28,044)
Adams, Hazel P 4:44:13 (23,233)
Adams, Jean...................................3:41:12 (6,873)
Adams, Katy L...............................5:25:05 (29,933)
Adams, Linda 5:31:54 (30,647)
Adams, Louise W...........................3:15:31 (2,703)
Adams, Nina 4:35:23 (21,079)
Adams, Pam 4:17:06 (16,122)
Adams, Patricia C 7:04:50 (34,259)
Adams, Polly H 3:09:13 (1,912)
Adams, Sharon A...........................4:21:37 (17,341)
Adams, Susan P 4:51:05 (24,862)
Adams, Victoria J...........................4:43:46 (23,113)
Adams, Wendy S............................4:08:06 (13,789)
Adamson, Catherine......................4:35:26 (21,094)
Adamson, Yvette C 5:06:13 (27,585)
Adar, Sandra M..............................4:30:19 (19,702)
Addelsee, Helen M.........................5:00:56 (26,787)
Addison, Gemma M 4:55:14 (25,735)
Addison, Joanne C 4:42:28 (22,793)
Addleton, Lisa 4:41:07 (22,467)
Adere, Berhane 2:27:42 (46)
Adjei, Cynthia.................................5:42:58 (31,567)
Adkins, Deborah J..........................4:49:52 (24,564)
Adlam, Lisa C 5:28:11 (30,290)
Adlam, Rebecca..............................5:23:45 (29,775)
Adler, Alma J 4:07:54 (13,753)
Adlum, Jane...................................4:18:28 (16,486)
Aer, Tuula 4:06:12 (13,332)
Afrell, Maria I 4:00:27 (11,960)
Agar, Michelle 7:22:19 (34,411)
Aggett, Sian E 3:56:22 (10,582)
Aghera, Anita 5:30:16 (30,505)
Agnew, Geraldine R 4:08:59 (14,036)
Agrawal, Sheila E...........................4:36:13 (21,301)
Ahad, Lucy I 4:15:16 (15,632)
Ahern, Jane E 4:57:31 (26,190)
Ahmed, Nabeela.............................6:51:26 (34,103)
Ahmed, Zehra 6:39:59 (33,881)
Ahmet, Seniz 3:57:53 (11,085)
Ahned, Hattie..................................5:49:56 (32,117)
Ahnien, Marie-Claire 4:40:04 (22,198)
Aigner, Christine 3:28:35 (4,574)
Ainscough, Kirsty A.......................3:45:28 (7,786)
Ainsworth, Pat H 5:35:49 (31,011)
Airey-Rowlinson, Debbie 5:24:27 (29,853)
Ait Salem, Souad 2:27:41 (45)
Aitchison, Edda I............................4:20:14 (16,957)
Aitchison, Elise M 4:15:04 (15,584)
Aitken, Maryanne............................5:17:10 (29,086)
Ajadi, Bims......................................4:53:25 (25,354)
Akdeniz, Shereen...........................5:00:22 (26,688)
Akeroyd, Suzanne 3:29:05 (4,688)
Alabaster, Morag 5:37:07 (31,123)
Alberry, Sian H 4:03:25 (12,708)
Alcock, Brigitte...............................5:06:24 (27,614)
Alcock, Julie M 5:41:09 (31,426)
Alcock, Sarah..................................5:20:12 (29,430)
Alderman, Pauline M.....................4:06:19 (13,358)
Aldridge, Hilary E 5:06:38 (27,642)
Aldridge, Katherine S 3:21:15 (3,395)
Alers, Nicole L...............................4:00:24 (11,948)
Alessi, Adrianna 5:38:09 (31,203)
Alexander, Amanda 4:40:24 (22,289)
Alexander, Carol 5:05:03 (27,409)
Alexander, Chrstina 4:33:05 (20,452)
Alexander, Claire 3:59:35 (11,705)
Alexander, Elizabeth J...................4:15:31 (15,711)
Alexander, Genavieve 7:32:06 (34,464)
Alexander, Karen G 3:01:02 (1,245)
Alexander, Mary E.........................5:05:50 (27,521)
Alexander, Samantha.....................4:33:43 (20,639)
Alexanderou, Tracey A 3:22:21 (3,541)
Alfonzo, Nahir A 4:33:35 (20,601)
Alford, Rebecca J...........................3:43:42 (7,387)
Alfred, Sylvia..................................5:05:05 (27,414)
Aliane, Jane L 4:36:12 (21,296)
Aligon, Maria J 3:47:53 (8,321)
Alireza, Nirmeen............................4:25:04 (18,278)
Allan, Claire L 4:45:33 (23,549)
Allard, Véronique 5:08:31 (27,899)
Allcard, Catherine K......................5:40:54 (31,404)
Allen, Amanda................................3:56:15 (10,552)
Allen, Amy K..................................4:26:42 (18,723)
Allen, Becky A 6:48:26 (34,044)
Allen, Carla M 3:45:56 (7,880)
Allen, Christine A...........................5:25:50 (30,013)
Allen, Hayley 4:10:18 (14,369)
Allen, Heather.................................3:54:06 (9,903)
Allen, Janice L................................5:13:23 (28,592)
Allen, Jen L....................................4:46:06 (23,689)
Allen, Julie A 4:33:15 (20,493)
Allen, Katie.....................................6:01:01 (32,782)
Allen, Katie 6:25:57 (33,575)
Allen, Laura K 4:34:49 (20,908)
Allen, Laura M 3:35:25 (5,780)
Allen, Lucy M 3:34:01 (5,550)
Allen, Marion J...............................6:47:57 (34,036)
Allen, Nicola J 5:17:54 (29,168)
Allen, Sonya....................................4:14:56 (15,540)
Allen, Victoria M 5:33:12 (30,767)
Allenby, Jennifer K........................4:53:00 (25,269)
Allenby-Dilley, Nichola 6:08:29 (33,066)
Allerston, Catherine A..................6:00:54 (32,775)
Allford, Dan J 4:45:56 (23,660)
Allison, Clare A 5:00:50 (26,771)
Allison, Luzaan...............................5:37:47 (31,176)
Allistone, Sophie L........................3:32:19 (5,281)
Allman, Elizabeth H.......................4:29:17 (19,467)
Almeida, Dalva P 6:29:21 (33,644)
Alon, Sheila 4:54:40 (25,615)
Alonso, Marisa................................6:15:59 (33,294)
Alsford, Sheryl F.............................5:28:10 (30,285)
Alves de Sousa, Sarah J 4:08:59 (14,036)
Alwis, Rosemary V.........................6:17:37 (33,342)
Alzaga, Guadalupe 4:34:04 (20,712)
Ama, Tracey....................................7:03:58 (34,251)
Amato, Sophia.................................5:24:53 (29,903)
Ambrose, Jane S 4:51:10 (24,875)
Ames, Sally E 5:24:51 (29,900)
Amey, Karen M..............................5:01:07 (26,814)
Amiot, Clarisse 4:25:20 (18,352)
Amooty, Belle 4:11:11 (14,604)
Amor, Caron Lisa 5:08:36 (27,912)
Amos, Claire R...............................4:31:32 (20,032)
Amson-Orth, Karyn M 4:21:52 (17,415)
Amy, Chris 4:18:22 (16,452)
Andersen, Susanne J......................4:49:50 (24,556)
Anderson, Barbara A 4:40:23 (22,282)
Anderson, Britta..............................3:47:51 (8,313)
Anderson, Carolynn........................4:20:21 (16,985)
Anderson, Charlotte E...................4:56:10 (25,907)
Anderson, Clare 4:23:55 (17,968)
Anderson, Jacqueline E 5:07:30 (27,766)
Anderson, Jocelyn M.....................5:29:28 (30,420)
Anderson, Katherine L...................5:21:39 (29,573)
Anderson, Katy M...........................3:14:54 (2,617)
Anderson, Lucy 4:58:09 (26,315)
Anderson, Margaret........................5:50:01 (32,123)
Anderson, Margaret J.....................3:27:09 (4,304)
Anderson, Paula M.........................5:28:30 (30,323)
Anderson, Ruth...............................5:39:23 (31,290)
Anderson, Sarah J 6:44:47 (33,975)
Anderson, Shirley H 3:27:56 (4,449)
Anderson, Tracey 4:50:38 (24,752)
Anderson-Edward, Sarah E............3:56:38 (10,674)
Andreou, Chris................................6:04:15 (32,900)
Andreu, Maite 4:51:13 (24,884)
Andrew, Alison J............................4:22:34 (17,601)
Andrew, Lucy M 3:55:09 (10,251)
Andrew, Lynne R............................3:33:49 (5,523)
Andrew, Sharon..............................3:52:53 (9,532)
Andrews, Alexandra........................7:10:20 (34,324)
Andrews, Emma L..........................6:11:53 (33,162)
Andrews, Jacqueline.......................5:17:25 (29,111)
Andrews, Jo.....................................3:59:31 (11,680)
Andrews, Lisa 6:05:37 (32,960)
Andrews, Rachel.............................3:46:48 (8,059)
Andrews, Robin...............................4:38:48 (21,912)
Angel, Melanie R............................4:00:22 (11,941)
Angelides, Suzanne.........................4:27:38 (18,984)
Angell, Barbara 6:20:32 (33,409)
Angell, Harriet 5:37:16 (31,136)
Angus, Fiona M 3:30:41 (4,997)
Ankarett, Helen...............................4:05:25 (13,153)
Anki, Farida....................................4:32:31 (20,307)
Annabel, Angela H.........................6:29:36 (33,647)
Annan, Leonie C.............................6:56:43 (34,176)
Annequin, Nicole.............................4:28:29 (19,256)
Annesley, Sheila M 6:42:33 (33,925)
Annetts, Rachel M..........................4:35:08 (21,017)
Anning, Barbara J 6:21:37 (33,449)
Anscomb, Anne...............................4:14:16 (15,387)
Ansell, Christina M 5:07:25 (27,755)
Ansell, Sian.....................................6:51:11 (34,096)
Anslow, Ruth...................................5:08:11 (27,841)
Anstee, Jessica................................3:54:47 (10,121)
Anstey, Alyson J 5:00:55 (26,782)
Antell, Helen O 4:13:13 (15,091)
Anthias, Chloe................................3:35:15 (5,747)
Anthony, Christine M.....................3:33:24 (5,451)

Anthony, Helen M 3:34:06 (5,564)
Anthony, Natalie E 5:29:55 (30,470)
Anthony, Sally 6:31:13 (33,688)
Anthony, Sara L 4:57:21 (26,152)
Anthony, Shirley A 5:29:55 (30,470)
Antoniou, Angela 6:06:23 (32,999)
Aonso, Melanie J 5:51:31 (32,250)
Appanna, Madura G 5:34:18 (30,866)
Appel, Rona 5:24:45 (29,881)
Appleby, Gemma M 4:50:51 (24,805)
Appleby, Jenny 4:01:52 (12,329)
Appleby, Sally E 5:59:40 (32,721)
Appleton, Jane E 4:30:37 (19,780)
Appleton, Katharine E 6:05:01 (32,929)
Appleyard, Deborah A 5:22:17 (29,636)
Applin, Deborah 4:39:30 (22,080)
Applin, Susan I 4:49:18 (24,431)
Apps, Vanessa J 4:38:48 (21,912)
April, Merrill V 3:47:53 (8,321)
Aranda, Lucia 4:03:23 (12,695)
Archer, Julie M 4:37:12 (21,526)
Archer, Katie R 4:34:42 (20,876)
Archer, Skye J 4:27:02 (18,824)
Arellano, Olimpia 4:32:14 (20,238)
Ariss, Sarah 6:53:41 (34,134)
Armitage, Caroline 5:36:13 (31,054)
Armitage, Jacqueline A 3:57:47 (11,053)
Armitage, Rachel C 3:51:38 (9,206)
Armour, Rebecca 4:36:05 (21,263)
Armson, Jennifer M 3:07:08 (1,692)
Armstrong, Catherine 5:27:09 (30,163)
Armstrong, Christine 4:26:29 (18,662)
Armstrong, Denise 6:33:13 (33,727)
Armstrong, Jacqueline M 5:19:22 (29,335)
Armstrong, Julia H 3:20:52 (3,337)
Armstrong, Marlise C 4:36:30 (21,368)
Armstrong, Rosemary F 4:33:51 (20,671)
Armstrong, Vicky 4:42:34 (22,823)
Armstrong-Smith, Linsey K 4:15:36 (15,730)
Arnold, Christine 5:27:00 (30,144)
Arnold, Hannah 3:28:34 (4,573)
Arnold, Jana 4:08:02 (13,778)
Arnold, Katie A 4:21:16 (17,244)
Arnold, Louise E 5:12:27 (28,453)
Arnold, Tracy 4:15:17 (15,637)
Arnott, Barbara 5:26:03 (30,040)
Arpessella, Jessica 5:19:30 (29,354)
Arrowsmith, Hilary G 4:31:49 (20,112)
Arscott, Ann M 5:35:39 (30,992)
Arthan, Liz 4:07:38 (13,684)
Arthey, Kathryn L 5:11:00 (28,275)
Arthur, Zoe M 4:32:50 (20,383)
Artis, Susi E 4:49:16 (24,425)
Aryeetey, Camille 4:00:52 (12,074)
Aschan, Charlotte E 4:08:45 (13,980)
Aschmann, Debra A 3:52:54 (9,536)
Ascott, Claire L 5:28:34 (30,329)
Asghar, Anita 5:51:06 (32,215)
Ashbrook, Colette 5:50:19 (32,157)
Ashby, Jennifer D 3:35:23 (5,772)
Ashcroft, Cristine J 5:54:26 (32,428)
Ashdown, Jane 5:29:51 (30,462)
Ashdown, Kimberly M 6:48:19 (34,042)
Ashenden, Tracey 4:12:03 (14,824)
Asher, Carolyn 5:10:53 (28,263)
Ashford, Katherine H 3:55:46 (10,425)
Ashford-Smith, Paulette D 4:50:53 (24,818)
Ashley, Annette 4:22:08 (17,476)
Ashmead, Annie E 4:33:50 (20,667)
Ashpole, Lisa J 7:12:22 (34,346)
Ashton, Charlotte E 4:24:40 (18,186)
Ashton, Joanna C 5:04:57 (27,390)
Ashton, Karen M 4:49:27 (24,466)
Ashton, Wendy M 4:51:49 (25,010)
Ashton-Rigby, Lee C 4:38:40 (21,871)
Ashurst, Catherine M 4:09:54 (14,278)
Ashwell, Nicola D 4:50:57 (24,834)
Ashwood, Natalie R 4:52:20 (25,110)
Ashwood, Rachel A 4:17:08 (16,135)
Ashworth, Celia 5:52:23 (32,311)
Ashworth, Kerry A 4:28:56 (19,386)
Ashworth, Laura S 5:26:15 (30,064)
Ashworth, Nicola G 5:34:37 (30,897)
Asken, Sharon G 3:45:26 (7,780)
Askins, Louise 3:46:55 (8,088)
Aspinall, Rebecca C 4:40:29 (22,306)
Aspler, Annabel 4:29:47 (19,581)
Asplin, Lucy A 3:55:55 (10,470)
Astill, Mandy 6:19:17 (33,383)
Aston, Jen 3:55:53 (10,462)
Atkins, Beth M 4:31:37 (20,056)
Atkins, Katie 5:05:45 (27,516)
Atkins, Michelle L 4:57:53 (26,259)
Atkins, Wendy J 4:40:56 (22,418)
Atkinson, Alison G 5:15:38 (28,898)
Atkinson, Anna L 4:48:18 (24,208)
Atkinson, Deborah M 4:29:37 (19,544)
Atkinson, Fidelma M 3:58:55 (11,460)
Atkinson, Nicola C 5:58:33 (32,672)
Atkinson, Rachel L 4:50:32 (24,727)
Atkinson, Sue 4:57:51 (26,252)
Atkinson, Sue L 7:15:27 (34,367)
Attenboroough, Joanne M 4:41:11 (22,484)
Attenborough, Lisa A 3:59:52 (11,807)
Attree, Amanda J 4:12:43 (14,968)
Attrill, Patricia A 4:56:13 (25,919)
Attwell, Susannah K 3:37:56 (6,246)
Attwood, Angela J 4:28:01 (19,103)
Attwood, Kathy S 3:54:49 (10,131)
Atwell, Rachel L 6:27:19 (33,608)
Auckland, Julie 4:13:58 (15,292)
Audrain, Helen L 3:32:03 (5,234)
Auge, Benita L 5:05:12 (27,434)
Auger, Nathalie 3:36:54 (6,038)
Aujla, Jaskiran K 5:45:03 (31,773)
Auld, Deborarh A 6:34:32 (33,763)
Auld, Sally B 5:51:05 (32,213)
Aus der Fuenten, Karen 3:09:24 (1,927)
Aussenberg, Glenda J 7:53:16 (34,518)
Austick, Selina J 4:27:09 (18,858)
Austin, Sara K 4:47:18 (23,986)
Austin, Stephanie K 4:27:51 (19,040)
Austin, Theresa M 5:30:38 (30,539)
Austin, Tracey D 5:41:16 (31,441)
Austin-Harrison, Lisa J 4:46:41 (23,823)
Authers, Sandra D 4:02:45 (12,553)
Avenell, Dee 4:43:06 (22,962)
Avery, June 3:56:48 (10,727)
Aves, Susan M 3:59:00 (11,489)
Aydelott, Wanda Dee Ann 7:06:22 (34,276)
Ayers, Karen Q 4:16:33 (15,971)
Ayers, Samantha J 3:40:08 (6,662)
Ayliffe, Andrea 4:36:23 (21,342)
Ayling, Angela K 4:46:41 (23,823)
Ayling, Laura M 5:25:04 (29,926)
Aylward, Karen E 3:58:10 (11,174)
Babajide, Addy V 4:50:41 (24,762)
Bachra, Amandeep K 6:25:17 (33,552)
Backhouse, Bonita F 4:41:47 (22,628)
Bacon, Diane W 4:30:38 (19,783)
Badenhorst, Liesel 4:27:23 (18,928)
Badham, Tracey K 5:01:41 (26,912)
Badman, Helen 5:23:25 (29,736)
Badock, Lesley J 4:16:12 (15,874)
Baenziger, Detra 4:29:17 (19,467)
Baerselman, Tessa A 4:34:42 (20,876)
Baggaley, Elizabeth J 4:53:01 (25,275)
Baggaley, Sophie 5:54:32 (32,431)
Bagnall, Anne-Marie 5:05:30 (27,476)
Bagnall, Denise 5:49:18 (32,076)
Bagnall, Louise A 3:53:14 (9,644)
Bahrami, Elfrida R 4:09:01 (14,045)
Bailey, Catherine A 4:57:46 (26,241)
Bailey, Claire L 3:55:54 (10,465)
Bailey, Kath 4:22:42 (17,650)
Bailey, Madeline J 4:01:50 (12,324)
Bailey, Marianne 5:09:32 (28,061)
Bailey, Marie Clare 4:41:59 (22,667)
Bailey, Martine 5:05:31 (27,479)
Bailey, Nicola J 4:07:04 (13,534)
Bailey, Paula J 5:07:07 (27,706)
Bailey, Rosie C 4:00:16 (11,917)
Bailey, Sarah H 5:08:16 (27,853)
Bailey, Tina L 3:10:54 (2,089)
Bailey, Victoria G 6:38:09 (33,847)
Bailey, Wendy M 6:26:40 (33,589)
Bailie, Emma R 7:30:12 (34,456)
Baillie, Alexis J 5:33:02 (30,752)
Baillie, Louise E 4:17:09 (16,140)
Baily, Clare C 3:46:52 (8,074)
Bain, Judy A 4:34:09 (20,739)
Bain, Lindsey A 3:57:15 (10,877)
Bainbridge, Samantha R 4:36:45 (21,429)
Bainbridge, Wendy E 5:06:33 (27,630)
Baines, Joanne E 4:50:30 (24,715)
Bains, Rosemary M 4:23:15 (17,797)
Bajaj, Punam 4:27:55 (19,071)
Baker, Aimée V 3:21:51 (3,466)
Baker, Alison M 6:47:55 (34,034)
Baker, Bev 5:41:13 (31,437)
Baker, Bridget D 3:19:23 (3,147)
Baker, Carol 4:48:59 (24,370)
Baker, Ceri L 4:29:54 (19,606)
Baker, Christina 6:42:59 (33,940)
Baker, Debbie E 4:37:06 (21,506)
Baker, Denise S 3:56:07 (10,516)
Baker, Helen M 8:57:17 (34,580)
Baker, Judith 5:28:50 (30,353)
Baker, Juliette P 4:38:24 (21,800)
Baker, Louise C 5:03:40 (27,204)
Baker, Nadia 4:38:35 (21,855)
Baker, Nicola J 3:28:36 (4,580)
Baker, Sally H 2:57:28 (902)
Baker, Sally M 5:50:54 (32,204)
Baker, Stephanie A 4:34:46 (20,897)
Baker, Teresa 5:42:06 (31,511)
Baker, Trace A 3:30:53 (5,035)
Baker, Vivien L 5:06:45 (27,659)
Bakewell, Sally J 5:41:41 (31,478)
Balaam, Toni 4:29:59 (19,631)
Balbi, Maria C 5:29:05 (30,382)
Balchin, Amy E 4:07:52 (13,739)
Balchin, Jacqui J 4:55:23 (25,765)
Balcombe, Susan 4:18:43 (16,556)
Baldaro, Hannah C 5:51:31 (32,250)
Baldaro, Jan N 7:12:47 (34,347)
Baldazzi, Olivia 5:14:44 (28,778)
Balding, Kate M 5:18:10 (29,194)
Baldock, Dawn S 4:43:51 (23,141)
Baldwin, Katey A 5:27:12 (30,164)
Baldwin, Leona J 4:31:32 (20,032)
Baldwin, Nicola L 4:21:11 (17,220)
Baldwin, Sue R 4:07:24 (13,612)
Bale, Christine M 4:37:27 (21,585)
Bale, Rosamund C 4:53:42 (25,417)
Bale-Bovet, Anne 6:10:53 (33,137)
Bales, Rowena J 3:13:58 (2,462)
Ball, Ann 5:39:01 (31,263)
Ball, Becky J 5:01:56 (26,948)
Ball, Sarah E 4:59:41 (26,591)
Ball, Valarie G 4:03:48 (12,788)
Ball, Victoria E 5:28:51 (30,358)
Ballam, Lydia D 4:58:58 (26,468)
Ballantyne-Spiller, Elise J 4:49:02 (24,381)
Ballard, Natalie L 6:02:22 (32,828)
Ballinger, Cherie A 4:26:34 (18,685)
Balteskard, Angela M 3:58:30 (11,298)
Bamber, Kirsty E 3:58:19 (11,226)
Bancroft, Elizabeth K 4:43:01 (22,933)
Bancroft-Kent, Helen L 5:04:57 (27,390)
Banfield, Hazel J 3:37:36 (6,183)
Banfield, Linda 6:20:36 (33,413)
Bangs, Louise H 5:14:10 (28,697)
Banks, Angela L 3:35:51 (5,855)
Banks, Faye M 3:00:33 (1,207)
Bannerman, Helen R 6:20:43 (33,416)
Banning-Boddy, Nondus 4:30:48 (19,833)
Bannister, Helen A 5:42:00 (31,499)
Bannister, Laura 3:26:51 (4,253)
Bannister, Sharon P 4:38:40 (21,871)
Banville, Elaine M 3:46:25 (7,984)
Baran, Catherine T 6:08:45 (33,073)
Barber, Eli C 4:35:56 (21,220)
Barber, Ella J 4:33:10 (20,473)
Barber, Jo 4:13:53 (15,273)
Barber, Joanna M 6:21:34 (33,446)
Barber, Lynne E 4:45:44 (23,598)
Barber-Lane, Nicole 7:58:58 (34,530)
Barciauskas, Aimée R 4:10:10 (14,328)

Barden, Katie S 5:22:46 (29,683)
Bardswell, Sonya C 4:05:15 (13,110)
Bardwell, Sharon 4:48:08 (24,173)
Baretto, Barbara 3:57:04 (10,816)
Barford, Julie Ann 5:08:41 (27,928)
Barios, Nadine 5:55:19 (32,486)
Barker, Brenda M 4:49:31 (24,478)
Barker, Claire L 4:58:01 (26,284)
Barker, Emily 5:49:36 (32,092)
Barker, Gail J 4:35:18 (21,056)
Barker, Joanne L 5:25:26 (29,983)
Barker, Katherine 4:04:18 (12,891)
Barker, Kirsten L 4:28:54 (19,378)
Barker, Louise K 4:14:36 (15,470)
Barker, Marianne K 3:59:43 (11,756)
Barker, Nicola J 4:13:37 (15,191)
Barker, Pauline A 5:50:06 (32,135)
Barker, Penelope M 4:06:07 (13,318)
Barker, Rosamund A 3:00:31 (1,203)
Barker, Sue J 4:36:04 (21,258)
Barker, Tracey Anne 5:24:28 (29,856)
Barkes, Harriet 4:11:04 (14,563)
Barley, Julie A 3:19:47 (3,206)
Barlow, Angela M 4:39:08 (22,011)
Barlow, Deborah J 4:45:47 (23,617)
Barlow, Emma J 3:48:38 (8,496)
Barlow, Gemma L 4:47:36 (24,044)
Barlow, Sally 4:21:18 (17,254)
Barnard, Emma 5:47:36 (31,958)
Barnard, Heidi A 4:32:06 (20,197)
Barnard, Kate 4:12:31 (14,931)
Barnard, Katy V 4:50:34 (24,740)
Barnard, Mary E 4:39:06 (22,005)
Barnes, Carole S 3:56:59 (10,788)
Barnes, Claire A 6:49:13 (34,063)
Barnes, Ellie 3:20:24 (3,279)
Barnes, Jane V 3:55:49 (10,440)
Barnes, Julie A 5:10:11 (28,171)
Barnes, Lesley A 4:40:03 (22,193)
Barnes, Linda T 5:25:18 (29,965)
Barnes, Rosalind 4:08:06 (13,789)
Barnes, Tracy A 6:38:15 (33,851)
Barnes, Wendy A 3:50:49 (9,009)
Barnett, Alison C 6:06:01 (32,972)
Barnett, Karyn 4:03:57 (12,820)
Barnett, Kirsty G 3:28:58 (4,659)
Barnett, Lisa M 4:13:12 (15,081)
Barnett, Marion H 8:31:55 (34,567)
Barnett, Sarah L 5:41:37 (31,473)
Barnett, Sharon R 3:51:53 (9,271)
Barnett-Connolly, Angela C 5:44:58 (31,761)
Barney, Jane 5:19:14 (29,319)
Barney, Lucie 3:13:20 (2,377)
Barnfield, Catherine 4:25:26 (18,377)
Barnhouse, Laura F 5:36:00 (31,028)
Baron, Sarah J 4:22:17 (17,517)
Barr, Charlotte E 3:49:59 (8,821)
Barr, Iva D 5:50:45 (32,194)
Barr, Nicola 4:05:27 (13,161)
Barr, Valerie 4:17:00 (16,095)
Barraclough, Emma J 3:54:05 (9,899)
Barraclough, Tracey D 6:04:29 (32,908)
Barratt, Vicky C 3:33:53 (5,530)
Barrett, Angela N 4:17:55 (16,329)
Barrett, Angela S 4:00:11 (11,894)
Barrett, Julie A 5:13:34 (28,618)
Barrett, Lisa 4:25:10 (18,310)
Barrett, Louise R 4:27:01 (18,818)
Barrett, Sally 5:18:35 (29,239)
Barrett, Sherrill 4:05:12 (13,098)
Barrett, Victoria L 3:30:30 (4,971)
Barrow, Kathy M 5:39:59 (31,333)
Barrow, Michelle 5:36:06 (31,042)
Barrow-Green, June E 3:37:24 (6,149)
Barry, Helen F 4:44:21 (23,265)
Barry, Kirsty V 3:58:18 (11,219)
Barry, Natalie J 5:36:45 (31,099)
Barter, Amanda 5:36:57 (31,117)
Barter, Joanne 5:42:58 (31,567)
Barter, Lucy A 4:51:25 (24,925)
Barter Fitzgerald, Angela 4:16:08 (15,862)
Bartlett, Jacqueline A 4:22:39 (17,631)
Bartlett, Jessica A 5:09:47 (28,113)
Bartlett, Louise 3:19:16 (3,130)
Bartlett, Michelle J 3:28:08 (4,496)
Bartley, Aimée L 3:56:22 (10,582)
Bartley, Elaine S 5:08:35 (27,911)
Bartley, Heather D 4:56:52 (26,040)
Barulis, Caroline T 5:36:13 (31,054)
Basarab, Veronica 4:35:55 (21,217)
Basham, Caroline 4:12:56 (15,011)
Baska, Uma 4:32:12 (20,225)
Baskcomb, Sarah C 4:36:25 (21,352)
Bason, Caroline A 5:05:35 (27,495)
Basquill, Vikki 3:44:11 (7,489)
Bass, Josephine A 6:03:47 (32,880)
Bass, Rachel 5:11:49 (28,387)
Bass, Yvette 4:24:22 (18,098)
Bassett, Lisa 4:50:14 (24,650)
Bassett, Sarah J 4:38:02 (21,721)
Bastiaansen vd Staak, José G 4:13:03 (15,050)
Bastow, Kate N 5:50:35 (32,177)
Batchelor, Mary 3:39:23 (6,516)
Bateman, Chloe M 5:40:24 (31,366)
Bates, Brenda R 3:56:03 (10,503)
Bates, Helen S 5:02:46 (27,076)
Bates, Lesley A 4:46:32 (23,785)
Bates, Paula R 5:49:49 (32,107)
Bates, Sonya D 4:51:26 (24,928)
Bates, Tracy A 5:29:09 (30,392)
Bates, Wendy J 5:13:42 (28,635)
Batson, Chante C 4:14:14 (15,377)
Batt, Elaine A 5:01:52 (26,940)
Batten, Carina 5:13:21 (28,583)
Batten, Elizabeth F 5:04:04 (27,259)
Battersby, Alex C 5:09:21 (28,023)
Battisson, Alison M 4:34:57 (20,957)
Bauer, Bettina 4:36:10 (21,284)
Bauerreiss, Claudia 5:12:56 (28,537)
Bauldry, Georgina L 4:32:54 (20,401)
Baum, Clare 4:51:48 (25,003)
Baxter, Becky C 4:26:28 (18,654)
Baxter, Joanne 5:28:49 (30,351)
Baxter, Vicki 7:00:45 (34,212)
Baxter, Zoe L 6:47:03 (34,020)
Bayley, Sarah J 5:09:19 (28,014)
Bayley, Victoria L 4:09:40 (14,216)
Baylis, Susan M 4:03:39 (12,758)
Baylis, Vanessa R 4:03:41 (12,763)
Baynes, Natalie K 4:31:15 (19,950)
Bayuga, Marlene 6:04:04 (32,887)
Bazeley, Judith 4:37:23 (21,569)
Bazeley, Sarah 5:55:42 (32,507)
Bazely, Sarah J 5:32:25 (30,696)
Bazzy, Gail E 4:34:22 (20,790)
Beach, Claire J 3:47:26 (8,205)
Beacom, Hannah M 8:08:51 (34,545)
Beadle, Deborah J 4:38:59 (21,971)
Bean, Nicola L 4:46:07 (23,693)
Beaney, Catherine L 5:36:49 (31,105)
Beard, Karen L 4:20:18 (16,975)
Beare, Samantha 4:22:20 (17,527)
Bearley, Natalie 9:25:52 (34,584)
Beart, Caroline L 4:30:33 (19,764)
Beasant, Anna L 5:10:17 (28,186)
Beaton, Laura 5:18:29 (29,226)
Beaton, Pauline 5:18:30 (29,227)
Beattie, Joanne 4:47:13 (23,963)
Beattie, Michelle 5:02:43 (27,068)
Beaty, Sian E 4:06:15 (13,346)
Beauchamp, Barbara 4:22:37 (17,622)
Beaumont, Laura C 4:45:35 (23,555)
Beaumont, Maria L 4:36:30 (21,368)
Beaumont, Michelle 3:55:08 (10,246)
Beavan, Faye 4:26:32 (18,673)
Beavis, Joanne C 5:09:33 (28,064)
Beavis, Lynne M 4:00:01 (11,857)
Bebbington, Elizabeth C 4:04:08 (12,852)
Becconsall, Anna 5:08:07 (27,834)
Becko, Kimberley V 6:05:35 (32,955)
Beckwith, Clare 4:35:44 (21,175)
Beckwith, Moira A 3:59:14 (11,574)
Bedelian, Claire E 5:41:08 (31,425)
Bedells, Clare H 3:11:45 (2,181)
Bedford, Julie 3:46:08 (7,916)
Beech, Anna 4:37:56 (21,699)
Beecham, Fay A 4:04:47 (12,999)
Beecher, Sarah-Lee 4:05:19 (13,125)
Beechinor, Georgina A 4:45:17 (23,492)
Beecroft, Claire A 5:01:51 (26,936)
Beer, Désirée 3:56:12 (10,538)
Beere, Jane A 3:30:07 (4,909)
Beesley, Joanne 4:53:44 (25,422)
Beesley, Katherine 3:43:34 (7,357)
Beetles, Andrea C 5:30:15 (30,502)
Begbie, Joanne R 5:33:41 (30,795)
Begnor, Gill M 4:20:44 (17,101)
Beische Bechard, Clotilde 3:58:53 (11,451)
Bekker-Botha, Erna 4:20:38 (17,074)
Belallam, Soad 3:53:20 (9,673)
Belam, Wendy 4:03:59 (12,827)
Belaon, Sarah 4:07:00 (13,518)
Belcher, Clare L 4:58:13 (26,328)
Belcher, Joanne 3:24:35 (3,856)
Belcher, Rebecca A 4:11:04 (14,563)
Belem, Maria 5:10:23 (28,204)
Belfort, Alison J 6:27:50 (33,621)
Belham, Charlotte E 6:11:47 (33,159)
Bell, Annette 3:22:30 (3,564)
Bell, Caryn M 4:28:49 (19,351)
Bell, Corrie A 5:32:37 (30,712)
Bell, Josephine M 5:23:41 (29,767)
Bell, Joy 4:36:09 (21,280)
Bell, Linda J 4:18:55 (16,603)
Bell, Nina L 4:19:24 (16,723)
Bell, Tracy A 5:13:51 (28,655)
Bell, Wendy 5:30:33 (30,532)
Bellchambers, Emma L 4:58:58 (26,468)
Bellenger, Lesley K 4:57:03 (26,095)
Bellettini, Vincenza 4:14:59 (15,553)
Bellinger, Joanne E 5:59:59 (32,739)
Bellis, Lindsey 6:08:46 (33,075)
Bellis, Sue A 5:35:24 (30,968)
Bellwood, Natasha M 5:47:56 (31,976)
Bellworthy, Naomi R 7:09:17 (34,308)
Belsom, Ruth L 5:10:14 (28,180)
Belton, Alison 5:04:00 (27,252)
Belton, Emma J 4:35:27 (21,098)
Benbow, Jennifer L 5:00:43 (26,742)
Bench, Suzanne D 3:57:46 (11,049)
Bendeaux, Jill K 4:40:51 (22,393)
Bending, Michelle G 6:08:13 (33,053)
Benfield, Rebecca 6:14:48 (33,264)
Benjamin, Floella 5:53:29 (32,374)
Benjamin, Kelly 4:31:48 (20,103)
Benn, Sandra 4:35:22 (21,072)
Bennett, Amy K 5:23:44 (29,774)
Bennett, Anne-Marie 5:04:18 (27,293)
Bennett, Caroline A 5:29:27 (30,419)
Bennett, Cheryl 5:51:40 (32,265)
Bennett, Georgina E 3:33:27 (5,464)
Bennett, Hildy A 4:26:36 (18,695)
Bennett, Jemma J 4:37:23 (21,569)
Bennett, Julia J 5:10:56 (28,270)
Bennett, Karen L 4:15:51 (15,795)
Bennett, Kate A 5:38:57 (31,257)
Bennett, Katie L 6:34:32 (33,763)
Bennett, Layla 5:11:47 (28,383)
Bennett, Lisa J 4:32:29 (20,293)
Bennett, Lizzy C 4:32:16 (20,245)
Bennett, Louise 6:02:25 (32,831)
Bennett, Magda K 3:42:12 (7,071)
Bennett, Nichola M 4:01:12 (12,165)
Bennett, Sarah J 5:27:48 (30,236)
Bennett, Sophie J 3:27:50 (4,428)
Bennett, Victoria A 4:05:51 (13,257)
Bennett, Victoria E 4:18:31 (16,503)
Bennetts, Katherine A 4:24:40 (18,186)
Benneyworth, Anna K 5:05:28 (27,467)
Benson, Elizabeth J 4:19:21 (16,717)
Benson, Suzanne E 3:56:59 (10,788)
Bent, Caroline 4:53:42 (25,417)
Bentley, Alison 5:04:37 (27,348)
Bentley, Anna M 4:46:28 (23,769)
Bentley, Jennifer W 4:52:26 (25,130)
Bentley, Karen 4:44:46 (23,358)
Bentley, Karen L 4:20:56 (17,159)
Bentley, Sarah L 3:56:54 (10,762)
Bentley, Sharon J 4:17:27 (16,205)

Bouchet, Estelle	3:31:33 (5,141)	
Bouchou, Naoual	5:43:01 (31,573)	
Boud, Helen	5:20:29 (29,463)	
Bouley, Jennifer M	3:26:38 (4,213)	
Bourdier, Brigitte	4:44:25 (23,276)	
Bourdoux, Annie	4:31:43 (20,086)	
Bourgeay, Monique	4:13:26 (15,145)	
Bourne, Margaret Hannah H	6:14:17 (33,252)	
Bourne, Naomi A	3:29:24 (4,763)	
Bourton, Laura C	4:41:05 (22,452)	
Boustead, Jill	5:21:57 (29,595)	
Boutrolle, Dominique	5:21:34 (29,567)	
Bouvant, Annie M	3:39:49 (6,600)	
Bowdery, Paula	5:43:10 (31,583)	
Bowditch, Kathryn	3:39:50 (6,607)	
Bowe, Hannah E	3:21:16 (3,397)	
Bowen, Angela	4:23:39 (17,905)	
Bowen, Anna	5:37:53 (31,186)	
Bowen, Elizabeth A	3:53:50 (9,824)	
Bowen, Stacey	4:50:20 (24,673)	
Bowen Rees, Mary V	3:19:45 (3,200)	
Bower, Amanda J	4:37:34 (21,606)	
Bower, Rebecca	5:04:41 (27,354)	
Bowers, Gillian K	4:50:17 (24,663)	
Bowers, Heather A	4:44:30 (23,303)	
Bowers, Judith	4:24:38 (18,180)	
Bowers, Rachel A	6:27:43 (33,618)	
Bowers, Sandra	3:17:24 (2,919)	
Bowker, Rachel S	4:43:32 (23,059)	
Bowler, Jade R	4:42:28 (22,793)	
Bowles, Jacqueline F	3:58:27 (11,282)	
Bowles, Jane	4:35:40 (21,157)	
Bowles, Sarah L	3:59:38 (11,724)	
Bowley, Carmen L	4:52:15 (25,091)	
Bowman, Melanie J	5:15:27 (28,874)	
Bown, Helen E	4:20:41 (17,089)	
Bown, Sarah D	4:49:24 (24,457)	
Bowres, Pauline A	6:00:03 (32,741)	
Bowyer, Nicola J	4:10:30 (14,409)	
Bowyer-Jones, Pauline J	4:04:22 (12,909)	
Boyd, Caroline J	3:34:41 (5,641)	
Boyd, Judith	3:52:05 (9,327)	
Boyd, Laura E	4:38:27 (21,818)	
Boyd, Margaret R	4:46:44 (23,836)	
Boyd, Nicki J	4:55:21 (25,757)	
Boyd, Valerie	5:44:26 (31,715)	
Boydell, Sara	5:27:04 (30,149)	
Boyden, Julie	4:07:12 (13,578)	
Boyens, Victoria N	4:51:49 (25,010)	
Boyes, Elaine T	5:53:11 (32,352)	
Boyle, Catherine C	3:37:22 (6,137)	
Boyle, Ruth E	5:18:38 (29,246)	
Boys, Francesca R	4:52:46 (25,213)	
Braasch, Birgit	3:34:45 (5,654)	
Brace, Nicola J	5:35:04 (30,948)	
Bracher, Linda	4:00:44 (12,043)	
Brackstone, Annabel L	5:36:38 (31,091)	
Bradbury, Amanda M	3:56:45 (10,708)	
Bradbury, Nicola J	6:16:48 (33,321)	
Bradbury, Sarah	4:19:57 (16,874)	
Bradbury, Victoria E	4:19:35 (16,777)	
Braddon, Cathy A	5:30:17 (30,506)	
Bradford, Elizabeth A	4:35:02 (20,992)	
Bradford, Nikki M	3:13:02 (2,338)	
Bradley, Anna L	5:07:50 (27,809)	
Bradley, Dawn	4:48:29 (24,243)	
Bradley, Deanne	4:23:38 (17,900)	
Bradley, Jayne F	4:51:09 (24,870)	
Bradley, Lesley H	6:44:38 (33,971)	
Bradley, Mary	5:00:36 (26,718)	
Bradley, Melloney C	6:31:46 (33,698)	
Bradley, Sarah J	4:10:03 (14,305)	
Bradley, Susan	4:17:35 (16,244)	
Bradshaw, Caroline L	6:37:43 (33,836)	
Bradshaw, Julie K	3:25:27 (4,002)	
Bradshaw, Lizzie	3:36:18 (5,933)	
Brady, Denise	5:21:30 (29,555)	
Brady, Emma L	3:54:29 (10,022)	
Brady, Katherine L	4:14:42 (15,495)	
Brady, Kerry	5:04:27 (27,316)	
Brady, Lorna A	4:32:01 (20,177)	
Brady, Vanessa	4:20:13 (16,951)	
Braidwood, Jennifer E	4:38:27 (21,818)	

Brailsford, Julie V	4:11:55 (14,784)	
Brain, Nicky	4:38:27 (21,818)	
Brain, Sandra N	3:50:21 (8,900)	
Braine, Elizabeth	5:23:53 (29,787)	
Braithwaite, Joanne C	4:38:51 (21,929)	
Brakell, Sonja R	6:06:03 (32,978)	
Brambles, Sarah Eleanor	6:00:05 (32,743)	
Bramley, Nathalie L	5:18:12 (29,198)	
Bramley, Nicola J	3:37:16 (6,118)	
Brammer, Sian J	4:30:46 (19,823)	
Branca, Dionne D	5:34:21 (30,871)	
Brander, Fran A	4:43:53 (23,148)	
Brandt, Kaz R	4:00:45 (12,047)	
Brangan, Emer	3:20:15 (3,259)	
Branker, Patricia	7:23:05 (34,416)	
Branston, Stephanie J	5:37:39 (31,164)	
Braude, Hayley M	5:52:11 (32,299)	
Bray, Brydie	3:43:39 (7,378)	
Bray, Claire L	5:20:08 (29,419)	
Bray, Eleanor G	4:43:05 (22,954)	
Bray, Gill F	5:36:32 (31,084)	
Bray, Jody	5:16:26 (28,987)	
Bray, Laura L	3:47:35 (8,243)	
Bray, Sharyn M	5:12:56 (28,537)	
Brazewell, Gillian	4:34:55 (20,940)	
Brazil, Michelle M	4:55:23 (25,765)	
Breaden, Ann-Louise M	6:45:38 (33,995)	
Breaden, Donna	5:15:34 (28,887)	
Breagan, Heidi B	4:00:41 (12,029)	
Breaker, Jennifer H	5:08:36 (27,912)	
Breakwell, Alison	4:49:38 (24,514)	
Breakwell, Sophie L	4:35:14 (21,039)	
Brearley, Jo M	5:23:57 (29,799)	
Breeden, Laura S	5:26:17 (30,069)	
Bremner, Jane S	3:33:43 (5,509)	
Brench, Alison M	5:01:01 (26,798)	
Brennan, Lisa J	7:01:41 (34,226)	
Brennan, Melissa	3:46:53 (8,078)	
Brenton, Sarah J	4:14:08 (15,347)	
Breslin, Katie L	5:21:29 (29,551)	
Brett, Rosalind	4:34:04 (20,712)	
Breuil, Laetitia	4:16:03 (15,849)	
Brewer, Sally J	5:35:35 (30,986)	
Brewis, Hayley L	4:27:08 (18,851)	
Brewster, Joanne E	4:29:24 (19,500)	
Brewster, Vanessa	4:48:43 (24,298)	
Brewster, Victoria L	3:46:06 (7,905)	
Brian, Alison	5:44:11 (31,685)	
Brice, Michelle A	4:54:56 (25,683)	
Brichard, Marie-Thérèse	4:44:38 (23,332)	
Brickland, Patricia	4:11:30 (14,679)	
Brickley, Katherine E	3:56:22 (10,582)	
Bridge, Helen M	5:51:49 (32,276)	
Bridgman, Jackie	4:38:42 (21,888)	
Brierley, Michelle L	5:25:05 (29,933)	
Brierley, Susanne V	4:06:49 (13,476)	
Briggs, Clare	4:45:10 (23,456)	
Briggs, Katy V	4:24:55 (18,245)	
Briggs, Ruth G	2:50:20 (523)	
Brighouse, P. Maria	4:24:20 (18,091)	
Bright, Jennifer A	5:38:09 (31,203)	
Brightling, Jenny	5:30:41 (30,544)	
Brightman, Hanna	5:09:25 (28,031)	
Brightman, Pat A	5:49:25 (32,080)	
Brighton, Susan L	3:41:07 (6,851)	
Brincat, Brenda K	5:17:59 (29,178)	
Brincat, Sarah C	4:19:46 (16,829)	
Brindley, Heather J	3:50:23 (8,910)	
Brine, Helen K	5:33:14 (30,769)	
Briscoe, Jackie	7:21:49 (34,408)	
Bristow, Jo A	5:21:59 (29,599)	
Bristow, Mary	5:27:12 (30,164)	
Bristow Tyler, Linda	5:15:56 (28,929)	
Britnell, Claire L	3:53:09 (9,620)	
Brittain, Katie R	4:26:28 (18,654)	
Britten, Bryony J	3:36:39 (5,988)	
Britton, Christine A	5:46:35 (31,883)	
Britton, Eleanor S	6:24:14 (33,522)	
Britton, Toni	3:51:00 (9,046)	
Brittton, Caroline	4:47:59 (24,144)	
Broad, Lucinda C	4:07:47 (13,711)	
Broadway, Lynn D	4:51:18 (24,905)	
Broadwell, Nicola A	3:44:43 (7,610)	

Broady, Karin Y	4:46:35 (23,793)	
Brobin, Sarah	4:47:50 (24,102)	
Brocard, Pierrette	4:06:19 (13,358)	
Brockbank, Caroline S	4:22:27 (17,568)	
Brockman, Michelle J	3:53:10 (9,629)	
Broder, Marie T	4:54:26 (25,569)	
Broderick, Polly A	4:19:38 (16,790)	
Brody, Rachel H	4:50:59 (24,839)	
Broekhof, Mary K	4:03:02 (12,616)	
Brolin, Eva	4:03:12 (12,654)	
Brook, Diana L	4:25:44 (18,456)	
Brook, Karen H	4:37:11 (21,522)	
Brooke, Hannah L	4:27:27 (18,941)	
Brookes, Mandy J	4:34:11 (20,752)	
Brookes, Nicole M	5:43:05 (31,576)	
Brooks, Denise J	4:30:32 (19,758)	
Brooks, Emma-Louise V	7:28:52 (34,448)	
Brooks, Helen	4:41:31 (22,560)	
Brooks, Helen	5:00:23 (26,692)	
Brooks, Jade L	6:04:48 (32,916)	
Brooks, Julia E	4:02:56 (12,592)	
Brooks, Katharine E	3:38:12 (6,301)	
Brooks, Katherine E	4:28:53 (19,317)	
Brooks, Laurel P	4:16:58 (16,082)	
Brooks, Linda R	4:50:45 (24,782)	
Brooks, Melanie L	4:57:16 (26,137)	
Brook-Smith, Joanne	5:18:21 (29,212)	
Broome, Megan R	4:28:18 (19,207)	
Broome, Sara M	4:59:00 (26,477)	
Broomfield, Louise A	3:58:32 (11,310)	
Broomfield, Wendy E	5:58:03 (32,634)	
Broster, Linsey J	4:02:53 (12,581)	
Broughton, Angela	5:24:49 (29,891)	
Broughton, Jane E	6:03:42 (32,876)	
Brown, Abigail J	3:49:24 (8,674)	
Brown, Alison E	4:07:28 (13,633)	
Brown, Amanda	5:13:32 (28,610)	
Brown, Amanda M	3:20:59 (3,359)	
Brown, Amanda S	4:01:53 (12,338)	
Brown, Amy L	4:07:27 (13,627)	
Brown, Angela M	3:42:20 (7,100)	
Brown, Brenda	4:50:18 (24,667)	
Brown, Christine J	5:55:20 (32,487)	
Brown, Claudia	5:00:06 (26,654)	
Brown, Delia	4:15:13 (15,622)	
Brown, Esther J	6:08:23 (33,059)	
Brown, Fiona	4:47:07 (23,935)	
Brown, Fiona C	4:53:32 (25,382)	
Brown, Gillian	4:38:05 (21,736)	
Brown, Hayley	7:02:20 (34,234)	
Brown, Jacqueline	4:33:26 (20,556)	
Brown, Janet H	3:28:23 (4,534)	
Brown, Janine E	3:06:42 (1,656)	
Brown, Janis A	4:56:21 (25,940)	
Brown, Jennifer	5:03:43 (27,209)	
Brown, Jennifer L	6:04:46 (32,914)	
Brown, Jessica C	4:58:30 (26,375)	
Brown, Joanna S	4:44:57 (23,402)	
Brown, Judy	3:36:48 (6,021)	
Brown, Juli B	3:52:53 (9,532)	
Brown, Julie C	6:49:00 (34,051)	
Brown, Kate V	2:49:21 (480)	
Brown, Katherine L	3:48:51 (8,539)	
Brown, Lisa	4:31:12 (19,938)	
Brown, Loren M	4:42:39 (22,844)	
Brown, Louise J	4:30:07 (19,660)	
Brown, Lucienne	4:50:44 (24,774)	
Brown, Lucy V	4:22:22 (17,542)	
Brown, Madalaine S	4:31:51 (20,123)	
Brown, Marie	5:34:30 (30,885)	
Brown, Marie-Louise	5:44:22 (31,710)	
Brown, Maxine L	3:40:24 (6,718)	
Brown, Michelle A	5:17:50 (29,159)	
Brown, Nathalie M	6:17:08 (33,324)	
Brown, Rachael	4:58:05 (26,301)	
Brown, Rachael A	5:09:43 (28,097)	
Brown, Ruth E	6:11:10 (33,146)	
Brown, Sam	4:01:25 (12,220)	
Brown, Samantha A	4:08:55 (14,022)	
Brown, Sarah	3:59:14 (11,574)	
Brown, Sarah L	5:18:14 (29,201)	
Brown, Sheila L	3:49:34 (8,711)	
Brown, Sian C	3:43:00 (7,239)	

Campbell, Helen 4:17:54 (16,324)
Campbell, Ilidia M 3:57:36 (10,977)
Campbell, Isabelle E 4:40:14 (22,242)
Campbell, Joanna K 4:47:10 (23,949)
Campbell, Joanne 4:56:38 (25,990)
Campbell, Joyce 5:09:06 (27,981)
Campbell, Julia D 5:48:41 (32,025)
Campbell, Laura 4:58:33 (26,386)
Campbell, Lisa J 4:24:30 (18,143)
Campbell, Lori L 4:59:54 (26,617)
Campbell, Nicola 5:18:28 (29,224)
Campbell, Patricia 7:22:33 (34,413)
Campbell, Sarah 4:37:18 (21,550)
Campbell, Shirley P 4:57:27 (26,173)
Campbell, Sony 4:42:48 (22,877)
Campbell-Barr, Juliet A 4:28:27 (19,247)
Campion, Jane 3:14:19 (2,521)
Candland, Sonja K 4:19:48 (16,835)
Cane, Susan 4:38:20 (21,787)
Caney, Pauline J 4:29:44 (19,575)
Canfield, Caireen G 3:43:15 (7,296)
Cann, Jane 5:07:08 (27,711)
Cannell, Angela D 3:57:13 (10,868)
Cannell, Susan H 5:56:34 (32,561)
Cannock, Lucy J 3:51:18 (9,123)
Cannon, Catherine L 3:59:19 (11,602)
Cannon, Jessica L 4:48:11 (24,179)
Cannon, Patricia M 5:27:20 (30,184)
Cannon, Sarah R 3:44:41 (7,597)
Cant, Denise C 4:32:45 (20,363)
Cantley, Louise 4:30:40 (19,791)
Cantley, Louise M 4:27:01 (18,818)
Cantu, Ivonne 4:04:36 (12,949)
Capdevielle, Véronique 4:32:35 (20,318)
Capener, Rebecca A 3:32:57 (5,380)
Capes, Susan E 5:55:04 (32,465)
Capey, Sarah J 4:55:43 (25,821)
Caple, Anna 7:15:41 (34,369)
Capper, Suzan E 5:25:31 (29,988)
Carberry, Suzanne 5:04:08 (27,268)
Carboni, Roberta 4:39:54 (22,166)
Cardiff, Rebecca K 5:41:22 (31,447)
Cardwell, Deborah C 4:12:23 (14,904)
Cardwell, Jane 4:04:39 (12,968)
Cardy, Paula C 4:14:38 (15,478)
Carelsen, Brenda S 6:27:20 (33,609)
Carey, Elizabeth J 4:13:01 (15,037)
Carey, Shelley L 5:36:13 (31,054)
Carey-Jones, Mariclare D 4:59:40 (26,588)
Carini, Susie E 5:41:18 (31,442)
Carley, Wendy 4:08:28 (13,901)
Carlin, Annette K 3:36:34 (5,978)
Carlisle, Charlotte L 4:44:53 (23,392)
Carlson-Zyats, Anne G 3:39:41 (6,572)
Carlton, Maria L 6:29:49 (33,650)
Carmichael, Holly B 4:33:14 (20,488)
Carmichael, Isabella 4:09:30 (14,174)
Carmody, Kerry L 5:12:27 (28,453)
Carne, Julie 4:41:48 (22,637)
Carney, Rochelle 6:00:12 (32,748)
Carnwath, Gabriel J 3:12:04 (2,218)
Carpenter, Charlotte A 4:54:21 (25,549)
Carpenter, Eileen D 4:33:26 (20,556)
Carpenter, Gina T 4:41:37 (22,589)
Carpenter, Lisa 4:16:32 (15,969)
Carpenter, Shirley D 5:03:04 (27,113)
Carpenter, Sylvia P 4:44:18 (23,256)
Carr, Alison E 5:25:04 (29,926)
Carr, Caroline B 4:25:38 (18,422)
Carr, Karen E 5:14:29 (28,738)
Carr, Wendy M 5:12:20 (28,439)
Carradice, Joanne L 6:40:11 (33,886)
Carragher, Lindsey 4:48:12 (24,185)
Carre, Faye S 4:16:15 (15,892)
Carrick, Gillian R 4:14:26 (15,432)
Carrick, Marie J 4:04:52 (13,015)
Carrington, Annie M 3:38:41 (6,386)
Carrington, Samantha 6:49:52 (34,073)
Carrington, Sarah M 4:36:01 (21,246)
Carroll, Claire 4:32:07 (20,204)
Carroll, Michelle L 3:37:15 (6,114)
Carroll, Pamela 4:30:43 (19,806)
Carroll, Sarah L 4:39:49 (22,155)
Carrotte, Barbara 5:20:11 (29,425)
Carruth, Adrienne C 4:57:03 (26,095)
Carswell, Emma-Louise 4:20:11 (16,940)
Carter, Alexandra 5:01:21 (26,849)
Carter, Anna E 4:29:07 (19,428)
Carter, Bernadette 4:32:25 (20,273)
Carter, Clare L 3:53:08 (9,615)
Carter, Helen M 7:10:52 (34,328)
Carter, Jacqueline A 3:58:12 (11,190)
Carter, Jane 4:00:30 (11,975)
Carter, Janet 5:50:28 (32,170)
Carter, Joanne A 4:23:01 (17,733)
Carter, Julie E 3:04:52 (1,508)
Carter, Kerry 5:18:27 (29,220)
Carter, Louise E 5:37:16 (31,136)
Carter, Luce 5:34:34 (30,892)
Carter, Martine L 6:17:55 (33,355)
Carter, Rebecca 5:55:26 (32,494)
Carter, Sarah J 5:36:08 (31,046)
Carter, Shelley L 5:59:54 (32,736)
Carter, Suzanne 5:56:32 (32,558)
Carter, Suzanne L 4:18:45 (16,564)
Carter, Tina E 5:29:24 (30,411)
Carter, Zoe E 5:01:21 (26,849)
Cartlidge, Helen 3:34:00 (5,548)
Cartmell, Janine E 4:16:58 (16,082)
Carton, Anna C 5:00:55 (26,782)
Carton, Jo C 4:40:39 (22,337)
Cartwright, Katy 4:37:36 (21,619)
Cartwright, Kim L 5:18:51 (29,270)
Cascon Gonzalez, Teresa 3:51:55 (9,282)
Case, Bonita J 4:37:35 (21,613)
Casey, Angela M 4:26:32 (18,673)
Casey, Sinead M 5:54:09 (32,415)
Casey, Trudy 5:38:49 (31,251)
Cashell, Joanna L 5:28:50 (30,353)
Cason, Julie 4:20:38 (17,074)
Cass, Bridget M 5:55:51 (32,512)
Cassamally, Laura 4:50:52 (24,812)
Cassell, Karen A 4:39:40 (22,114)
Cassidy, Clare 4:56:46 (26,019)
Cast, Jacqueline L 4:54:22 (25,553)
Cast, Louse 6:22:43 (33,479)
Castan Salinas, Susana 3:41:17 (6,894)
Castelluccio, Lesleyann 5:08:55 (27,955)
Castle, Joanne 5:50:14 (32,147)
Castle, Rosemary A 4:22:21 (17,531)
Castleden, Kate 4:58:07 (26,310)
Castledine, Emma 6:30:46 (33,678)
Castronovo, Francesca A 5:35:06 (30,950)
Caswell, Sarah J 5:51:19 (32,238)
Caswell, Teresa 5:40:43 (31,393)
Cataldi, Grazia 4:03:35 (12,742)
Catchpole, Fiona F 6:38:41 (33,862)
Cathie, Helen 4:40:26 (22,294)
Catley, Alison 4:35:46 (21,184)
Caton, Carly J 4:41:38 (22,593)
Caton, Claire J 3:45:11 (7,724)
Catteau, Catherine 3:49:27 (8,686)
Cattell, Kate E 3:57:52 (11,079)
Caulfield, Vanda 3:20:33 (3,300)
Caulton, Jacqui 7:39:25 (34,481)
Caunter, Janice N 4:00:59 (12,110)
Caunter, Tina M 4:56:02 (25,881)
Causer, Linda S 5:32:13 (30,673)
Cavendish, Jodie 5:22:26 (29,656)
Cavendish, Lucinda 4:43:00 (22,926)
Cawkwell, Lucy C 4:34:58 (20,962)
Cawley, Linda A 7:21:51 (34,409)
Cawte, Lisa 3:59:07 (11,535)
Cawthorne, Helen M 3:16:42 (2,835)
Caylor, Chantal M 4:35:54 (21,211)
Cazot, Amita R 4:20:51 (17,138)
Cecil, Jayne A 4:19:38 (16,790)
Cecil, Juliet S 4:28:06 (19,130)
Cederstrom, Susan H 3:32:01 (5,228)
Cefferty, Margaret R 5:59:34 (32,719)
Cerrino, Flora M 7:11:49 (34,342)
Chadwell, Karen G 5:07:02 (27,700)
Chadwick, Clare E 7:30:12 (34,456)
Chadwick, Sophie 4:55:02 (25,706)
Chaffey, Heather C 4:29:06 (19,420)
Chaffey, Lorraine A 4:09:08 (14,069)
Challacombe, Sian F 5:09:03 (27,976)
Chamberlain, Anne 6:36:02 (33,793)
Chamberlain, Julie S 6:05:11 (32,934)
Chambers, Alison K 4:32:44 (20,355)
Chambers, Christine 4:25:32 (18,406)
Chambers, Hilary V 6:48:35 (34,047)
Chambers, Jennifer C 4:37:58 (21,708)
Chambers, Lisa 4:24:54 (18,241)
Chambers, Marcia C 4:24:05 (18,017)
Champs, Annamarie 5:03:14 (27,138)
Chan, Andrea 4:39:50 (22,157)
Chan, Ling K 3:57:04 (10,816)
Chan, Stacy S 4:56:16 (25,927)
Chance, Luanne 4:12:56 (15,011)
Chandler, Janine S 4:57:31 (26,190)
Chandler, Jemma A 6:22:09 (33,465)
Chandler, Lillian M 4:16:21 (15,922)
Chandler, Melanie J 6:40:11 (33,886)
Chandler, Natalie 4:32:29 (20,293)
Chandler, Sarah E 4:05:25 (13,153)
Chandola, Shalini 6:52:05 (34,113)
Chanell, Samantha M 4:38:24 (21,800)
Channer, Debbie 3:47:10 (8,142)
Channing, Tracy 4:40:44 (22,364)
Chant, Lottie 3:38:04 (6,277)
Chant, Michelle A 4:43:01 (22,933)
Chaplin, Stephanie L 6:08:04 (33,046)
Chaplin, Zara E 4:41:20 (22,522)
Chapman, Bee J 4:32:55 (20,411)
Chapman, Camilla 3:54:24 (9,994)
Chapman, Corinne W 4:45:29 (23,536)
Chapman, Cynthia M 4:13:20 (15,126)
Chapman, Denise A 3:15:17 (2,669)
Chapman, Jennifer K 3:56:52 (10,749)
Chapman, Kate 6:07:47 (33,037)
Chapman, Kate E 3:19:03 (3,102)
Chapman, Kathryn L 5:13:36 (28,622)
Chapman, Kathryn M 7:36:26 (34,474)
Chapman, Lesley 3:26:18 (4,154)
Chapman, Lisa 5:30:00 (30,479)
Chapman, Lucy J 4:43:43 (23,106)
Chapman, Marie P 4:05:29 (13,172)
Chapman, Marie-Clare 5:04:12 (27,280)
Chapman, Sally A 3:41:08 (6,856)
Chapman, Sarah 5:09:44 (28,103)
Chapman, Sarah A 4:47:13 (23,963)
Chapman, Sarah L 3:57:16 (10,883)
Chapman, Sonia 5:08:21 (27,865)
Chapman, Susan J 4:52:41 (25,196)
Chapman, Wendy 4:25:52 (18,502)
Chappell, Jane P 3:15:09 (2,647)
Chapple, Alice G 4:18:16 (16,421)
Chapple, Helen M 4:40:12 (22,240)
Chapple, Sarah J 4:31:56 (20,147)
Charalambous, Maria 4:46:57 (23,896)
Charalambous, Pat 4:11:48 (14,753)
Chard, Lucy C 3:54:25 (9,998)
Charles, Ellen L 6:30:38 (33,676)
Charles, Sarah E 4:52:51 (25,234)
Charles, Susan L 5:19:35 (29,369)
Charlton, Angela 4:45:02 (23,417)
Charlton, Carol 4:46:07 (23,693)
Charlton, Louise 4:26:17 (18,605)
Charlton, Mary P 4:29:06 (19,420)
Charlton, Nicola 4:42:40 (22,846)
Charman, Kathleen J 5:13:57 (28,668)
Charman, Louise A 4:30:44 (19,811)
Charman, Mary L 4:50:46 (24,787)
Charman, Rosemary 5:18:45 (29,260)
Charmley, Susan E 6:00:27 (32,755)
Charnley, Kim 4:25:21 (18,355)
Charter, Sue 4:05:35 (13,198)
Chastel de Boinville, Cornelia F 4:41:27 (22,546)
Chatburn, Denise 4:52:44 (25,207)
Chater, Ann-Marie 3:43:45 (7,400)
Chater, Christine A 5:35:51 (31,014)
Chatlani, Roma 5:05:22 (27,454)
Chauhan, Jyoti 5:43:38 (31,621)
Chavasse, Diane M 4:38:28 (21,825)
Cheaveau, Maria 4:50:50 (24,801)
Cheeseman, Carly A 4:33:55 (20,686)
Cheesworth, Helen T 5:45:15 (31,781)
Chessis, Carol R 5:00:34 (26,712)

Compton, Louise 5:53:26 (32,371)
Compton, Rachel L 4:47:37 (24,048)
Comrie, Louise S 6:08:57 (33,080)
Concannon, Donna R 5:05:59 (27,547)
Concheiro, Helen K 6:12:44 (33,197)
Condliffe, Rachel M 4:46:55 (23,888)
Conetta, Katherine F 5:09:30 (28,048)
Coney, Deborah C 3:23:58 (3,774)
Coney, Diane J 3:30:43 (5,002)
Confait, Rachel 5:52:21 (32,309)
Cong, Katherine 4:30:03 (19,646)
Conlon, Aimée L 5:15:04 (28,830)
Connaugton, Emma 4:33:24 (20,540)
Connell, Keeley W 3:50:52 (9,019)
Connell, Margaret A 5:33:24 (30,780)
Connell, Tracy 3:15:05 (2,641)
Connolly, Tara 8:37:50 (34,573)
Connor, Dannielle 5:19:16 (29,327)
Connor, Helena K 7:50:18 (34,511)
Connor, Lee-Ann 5:23:25 (29,736)
Connor, Linsey J 5:06:06 (27,568)
Connor, Lisa 4:40:01 (22,186)
Connor, Stacey 4:15:22 (15,655)
Constable, Jacqueline L 6:54:54 (34,152)
Constable, Rebecca J 3:43:16 (7,300)
Constant, Paula J 4:12:50 (14,988)
Constantin, Elisabeth 5:48:26 (32,006)
Conte, Helen A 4:48:23 (24,222)
Convert, Raffaelle J 4:21:15 (17,236)
Conway, Eloise 4:51:31 (24,941)
Conway, Julia 6:48:33 (34,045)
Conway, Tracy J 4:04:15 (12,876)
Conway, Victoria J 3:53:39 (9,755)
Conway, Yvonne A 4:28:01 (19,103)
Cooil, Jan M 3:43:57 (7,449)
Cook, Claire N 7:06:13 (34,273)
Cook, Donna 5:46:12 (31,853)
Cook, Emma L 6:33:55 (33,746)
Cook, Faith 4:50:55 (24,826)
Cook, Hayley A 4:17:45 (16,294)
Cook, Laura 6:51:55 (34,108)
Cook, Linda M 5:14:53 (28,801)
Cook, Lindsay C 4:43:46 (23,113)
Cook, Loretta 4:36:18 (21,324)
Cook, Lynda 6:24:47 (33,543)
Cook, Paula W 4:18:15 (16,413)
Cook, Phillippa S 4:00:32 (11,982)
Cook, Sarah 4:46:49 (23,863)
Cook, Sarah B 3:35:30 (5,791)
Cook, Sharon A 4:18:10 (16,393)
Cook, Sian 4:53:46 (25,432)
Cook, Sophie L 4:29:59 (19,631)
Cook, Stephanie M 3:20:16 (3,260)
Cook, Sylvia 3:46:29 (8,004)
Cook, Tonia M 4:09:11 (14,085)
Cook, Wendy J 4:35:10 (21,024)
Cooke, Anna K 4:46:39 (23,814)
Cooke, Anna L 3:21:50 (3,462)
Cooke, Beth M 4:32:06 (20,197)
Cooke, Elizabeth M 4:27:31 (18,953)
Cooke, Frances L 4:07:29 (13,636)
Cooke, Iona 5:56:10 (32,533)
Cooke, Joanne 4:13:02 (15,045)
Cooke, Lauren R 4:33:20 (20,523)
Cooke, Liz J 4:19:23 (16,720)
Cooke, Rachel 5:23:18 (29,725)
Cooke, Sonia N 7:54:08 (34,520)
Cooksey, Emma L 4:00:23 (11,944)
Cookson, Fiona 5:03:12 (27,131)
Cookson, Sarah A 5:45:25 (31,795)
Cookson, Serena L 5:51:13 (32,228)
Coombe, Emma V 4:36:27 (21,358)
Coombe, Pennie 4:57:40 (26,225)
Coombe, Penny F 5:43:52 (31,639)
Coomber, Isobel A 4:43:03 (22,944)
Coombs, Carla P 5:22:11 (29,623)
Coombs, Elinor 4:13:16 (15,105)
Coombs, Hannah K 3:32:16 (5,271)
Cooney, Margaret M 4:43:56 (23,162)
Cooper, Ann 4:45:41 (23,577)
Cooper, Anna 5:37:42 (31,168)
Cooper, Anna G 5:54:51 (32,448)
Cooper, Anne 4:02:05 (12,382)
Cooper, Cheryl L 8:06:13 (34,541)
Cooper, Helen 3:55:55 (10,470)
Cooper, Isabelle L 4:01:37 (12,273)
Cooper, Julie 3:49:29 (8,696)
Cooper, Julie 4:01:05 (12,132)
Cooper, Justine E 4:09:44 (14,239)
Cooper, Karen J 4:06:30 (13,400)
Cooper, Louise J 3:21:28 (3,421)
Cooper, Louise M 4:56:15 (25,926)
Cooper, Michelle 6:27:24 (33,610)
Cooper, Nichola 4:55:38 (25,810)
Cooper, Rachel M 5:00:44 (26,747)
Cooper, Sally A 4:52:34 (25,161)
Cooper, Sarah L 4:50:03 (24,613)
Cooper, Sonia O 5:29:03 (30,380)
Cooper, Sonya 4:29:01 (19,402)
Cooper, Susan M 4:15:49 (15,786)
Cooper, Yvonne L 4:59:19 (26,536)
Copas, Christine 4:40:23 (22,282)
Cope, Amy L 3:24:13 (3,806)
Cope, Lucy 3:32:35 (5,330)
Cope, Wendy A 4:06:14 (13,341)
Copeland, Kelly M 5:37:06 (31,122)
Copley, Rebecca 4:16:18 (15,903)
Copp, Rhona 3:21:53 (3,470)
Coppin, Sarah A 4:22:21 (17,531)
Copse, Georgina M 5:50:53 (32,201)
Copsey, Shirley A 4:08:29 (13,905)
Copson, Angela 3:16:54 (2,852)
Copson, Tracey K 4:01:09 (12,148)
Copus, Suzanne M 3:54:17 (9,954)
Corbett, Stephanie 4:04:00 (12,833)
Corbion, Virginie 4:38:51 (21,929)
Corbo, Amelia N 5:27:18 (30,180)
Corcut, Sarah M 3:44:55 (7,660)
Cordell, Hannah 5:29:15 (30,403)
Corden-Lloyd, Melanie R 4:03:29 (12,722)
Cordeux, Susan J 4:21:36 (17,334)
Cordon, Cheryl 4:40:08 (22,221)
Cordrey, Sue M 6:50:24 (34,080)
Cormack, Suzanne M 3:49:04 (8,593)
Cormie, Anna L 4:55:24 (25,767)
Cornic, Evelyne 4:22:40 (17,639)
Cornish, Deborah J 7:03:42 (34,249)
Cornthwaite, Carolyn 4:34:41 (20,870)
Cornwell, Emma J 5:05:52 (27,525)
Corrigan, Fiona L 6:23:50 (33,510)
Corry, Clare T 4:46:16 (23,733)
Corsi, Mary 4:31:24 (19,995)
Corsini, Alessandra 5:17:05 (29,075)
Coscione, Emily 8:27:30 (34,563)
Coslett, Deborah S 2:55:47 (793)
Coste, Aleth 5:10:44 (28,238)
Costello, Ananda M 5:12:10 (28,424)
Costello, Pamela M 4:15:00 (15,565)
Costello, Sinead M 5:19:28 (29,350)
Cottam, Jude 6:22:48 (33,483)
Cottam, Nicola J 4:23:53 (17,958)
Cottam, Ruth 4:14:01 (15,310)
Cotter, Gina A 6:15:07 (33,271)
Cotter, Melanie M 3:50:58 (9,040)
Cotter, Vicky 3:04:12 (1,467)
Cottereau, Thérèse 4:44:06 (23,202)
Cotterill, Brenda 6:16:09 (33,297)
Cotterrell, Lin A 4:48:34 (24,265)
Cotton, Emma J 3:30:05 (4,904)
Cotton, Helen V 4:20:17 (16,971)
Cotton, Katherine A 4:05:20 (13,133)
Cotton, Sarah T 3:45:02 (7,691)
Cotton, Tracy R 5:31:38 (30,626)
Cottrell, Sally 3:27:11 (4,310)
Couch, Carolyn P 4:53:06 (25,295)
Coucke, Catheline 4:14:51 (15,523)
Coulam, Amelia 4:13:01 (15,037)
Coulbert, Julie A 4:02:36 (12,513)
Coulter, Kylie J 3:53:59 (9,869)
Coulter, Rebecca M 4:15:04 (15,584)
Counihan, Gail 5:40:53 (31,402)
Coupland, Jennifer 5:04:15 (27,288)
Court, Ruth C 3:52:27 (9,423)
Court, Susan W 5:24:06 (29,817)
Courtemanche, Sophie 5:17:15 (29,090)
Courtier Dutton, Lucy K 5:07:57 (27,819)
Courtman, Karin A 6:24:45 (33,541)
Courtney, Hannah M 3:59:11 (11,554)
Courtney, Suzan A 5:41:52 (31,491)
Courtney, Sylvia 5:27:51 (30,246)
Cousins, Rosanna 3:45:48 (7,858)
Cousins, Sarah E 4:01:51 (12,327)
Cove, Hayley 4:56:13 (25,919)
Cover, Pamela J 4:40:41 (22,346)
Coverley, Lucy A 4:55:34 (25,792)
Cowan, Daniele J 5:01:35 (26,887)
Cowan, Heather 6:47:48 (34,032)
Coward, Nicola J 4:50:13 (24,644)
Cowburn, Louise H 4:41:50 (22,647)
Cowell, Sharon M 5:36:04 (31,039)
Cowen, Mary P 5:56:23 (32,552)
Cowley, Laura J 2:48:25 (443)
Cowling, Gert T 4:28:04 (19,118)
Cox, Donna E 6:34:40 (33,767)
Cox, Gillian 5:53:49 (32,394)
Cox, Hester C 4:08:31 (13,919)
Cox, Jacqueline L 7:10:44 (34,327)
Cox, Laura 3:58:24 (11,261)
Cox, Laura S 5:05:13 (27,437)
Cox, Lauren E 4:31:32 (20,032)
Cox, Lesley P 5:45:38 (31,808)
Cox, Lisa M 4:18:33 (16,513)
Cox, Louise A 4:45:24 (23,510)
Cox, Lucy J 4:43:59 (23,177)
Cox, Natasha 3:19:26 (3,151)
Cox, Nikki J 4:50:27 (24,697)
Cox, Sarah 7:42:56 (34,489)
Coxall, Kaylee 4:36:56 (21,474)
Coxhead, Dawn 3:58:23 (11,256)
Coxhead, Julie E 4:18:28 (16,486)
Coxhead, Patricia T 5:07:57 (27,819)
Coxshall, Fiona M 3:26:59 (4,277)
Coyle, Geraldine 4:22:05 (17,466)
Coyne, Linda 5:36:28 (31,080)
Crabtree, Linda C 3:27:43 (4,402)
Crabtree, Susan 3:30:13 (4,927)
Crack, Fiona M 5:03:19 (27,158)
Cragg, Sarah L 7:16:37 (34,374)
Craig, Lucy 4:30:48 (19,833)
Craig, Theresa K 4:38:48 (21,912)
Craigie, Louise 3:52:56 (9,549)
Craigie, Tamsin 4:50:51 (24,805)
Crain, Amy L 3:08:05 (1,798)
Cramp, Helen K 3:36:49 (6,024)
Crane, Joanne S 6:49:01 (34,052)
Crane, Meggie S 4:44:50 (23,380)
Crane, Moira V 6:44:47 (33,975)
Crane, Roberta J 5:09:49 (28,117)
Crane, Victoria L 5:09:48 (28,114)
Craney, Jean 4:37:51 (21,683)
Cranmer, Catherine E 4:05:04 (13,062)
Cranmer, Rosamund H 4:14:59 (15,553)
Crannage, Sarah 3:45:35 (7,808)
Cranston, Emma L 3:51:51 (9,261)
Cranton, Patti K 3:23:53 (3,758)
Craven, Margaret 5:58:24 (32,663)
Crawford, Arna J 5:04:15 (27,288)
Crawford, Elizabeth H 3:05:20 (1,540)
Crawford, Judith P 4:35:57 (21,228)
Crawford, Kylie M 4:43:27 (23,034)
Crawford, Mhairi 4:10:10 (14,328)
Cream, Tania J 3:28:03 (4,471)
Creaney, Kathryn 4:18:03 (16,354)
Creed, Gemma 3:59:47 (11,774)
Creegan, Gina M 4:05:02 (13,057)
Cregan, Nicola M 6:05:35 (32,955)
Cremen, Sandra 4:34:29 (20,820)
Cresswell, Caroline S 4:35:24 (21,082)
Cresswell, Gillian D 4:47:16 (23,976)
Cresswell, Jayne 5:47:50 (31,968)
Cresswell, Jenny A 4:03:40 (12,761)
Cresswell, Maria A 5:49:52 (32,109)
Crichton, Sophie 4:34:11 (20,752)
Crichton, Tracy 3:45:16 (7,745)
Crickmore, Sharon 4:26:00 (18,538)
Crideford, Freda 4:57:07 (26,110)
Crighton, Sally 4:47:52 (24,109)
Crilley, Kathy 5:45:02 (31,772)
Criminale, Suzanne J 4:48:16 (24,196)

Cripps, Suzanne 5:54:32 (32,431)
Crisford, Sarah 4:26:13 (18,585)
Crisp, Cheryl A 5:06:12 (27,582)
Crisp, Lorraine 5:04:58 (27,394)
Crisp, Lynda L 5:13:12 (28,571)
Crisp, Mary J 4:18:48 (16,572)
Critchley, Alix V 3:54:22 (9,978)
Critchlow, Anna E 3:05:56 (1,592)
Croad, Karen 5:02:51 (27,086)
Crocker, Christine 8:17:04 (34,556)
Crocker, Habe 3:43:38 (7,373)
Crocker, Marilyn J 5:03:47 (27,222)
Crocombe, Rebecca A 5:55:29 (32,501)
Crofton, Susan A 7:05:13 (34,264)
Crofts, Tanya E 3:26:44 (4,237)
Croker, Laura J 3:20:28 (3,289)
Crommie, Kirsty M 6:42:37 (33,930)
Crompton, Helen M 3:59:43 (11,756)
Cronin, Emma K 4:28:08 (19,142)
Cronk, Gina M 4:56:09 (25,903)
Crook, Amanda E 4:33:24 (20,540)
Crooke, Margaret E 5:15:03 (28,827)
Croot, Sarah E 4:06:25 (13,375)
Cropps, Natalie A 4:50:44 (24,774)
Crosbie, Virginia R 3:20:00 (3,227)
Crosland, Elaine 3:48:13 (8,403)
Cross, Amanda J 4:28:16 (19,194)
Cross, Charlotte L 4:14:40 (15,487)
Cross, Claire L 5:34:51 (30,923)
Cross, Linda M 5:12:58 (28,543)
Cross, Susan E 5:22:09 (29,621)
Cross, Suzanne J 5:47:11 (31,926)
Cross, Teresa 3:45:45 (7,845)
Crosskill, Grazia 4:24:16 (18,073)
Crossland, Sue 3:54:16 (9,950)
Crossley, Alexandra K 4:03:47 (12,785)
Crossley, Samantha 4:08:18 (13,853)
Crossman, Elisabeth M 3:38:50 (6,415)
Crouch, Debra L 4:37:12 (21,526)
Croucher, Cindy D 5:49:08 (32,063)
Croudass, Suzanne 3:35:08 (5,729)
Crow, Ceris A 5:02:12 (26,991)
Crowe, Gillian 4:03:22 (12,689)
Crowe, Susan M 5:58:06 (32,641)
Crowhurst, Paula 5:43:52 (31,639)
Crowley, Jacqueline C 4:53:39 (25,410)
Crowson, Jackie A 5:08:19 (27,857)
Crowther, Anastasia 4:33:53 (20,680)
Crowther, Dyan 5:16:35 (29,004)
Crowther, Lizanne 4:34:38 (20,855)
Croxford, Claire R 5:04:51 (27,376)
Cruddas, Claire 3:43:05 (7,263)
Cruickshank, Pauline K 5:00:19 (26,684)
Cruse, Julie 3:23:00 (3,636)
Crute, Catherine J 4:50:35 (24,743)
Cudmore, Angela 4:17:03 (16,108)
Cuff, Althea D 6:51:05 (34,092)
Cuffe, Elaine 5:10:50 (28,257)
Cuin, Susan A 4:25:37 (18,416)
Cullen, Emma J 3:55:43 (10,409)
Cullen, Wendy A 4:37:53 (21,693)
Culley, Carol A 4:44:10 (23,219)
Culling, Tina 4:12:21 (14,895)
Cullup, Catherine A 4:33:20 (20,523)
Culwin, Leah 5:50:15 (32,149)
Cumming, Erica J 4:42:29 (22,800)
Cumming, Fiona 4:54:16 (25,536)
Cummings, Joanna R 5:22:24 (29,650)
Cummings, Sandra 5:12:51 (28,525)
Cummins, Fiona S 3:32:04 (5,237)
Cummins, Michelle G 7:28:54 (34,450)
Cuningham, Suzanne L 5:01:54 (26,944)
Cunningham, Jenyth L 6:49:58 (34,074)
Cunningham, Julia M 5:33:17 (30,771)
Cunningham, Lynn 5:02:17 (27,003)
Cunningham, Michelle L 4:16:53 (16,054)
Cunningham, Natalie A 4:17:28 (16,211)
Curd, Chloe L 4:53:31 (25,379)
Curd, Natalie 4:53:30 (25,376)
Cure, Margaret R 7:12:12 (34,345)
Curkin, Tracey J 3:37:21 (6,130)
Curl, Tracey 3:16:29 (2,814)
Curnow, Denise C 5:35:52 (31,016)
Curnow, Emma J 3:48:05 (8,368)
Curnow, Gemma D 6:02:17 (32,827)
Currah, Yvonne 4:48:41 (24,285)
Curran, Brenda M 6:17:25 (33,332)
Curran, Lisa A 5:44:10 (31,682)
Currell, Justine A 3:51:32 (9,179)
Currie, Alexandra V 3:53:55 (9,839)
Currie, Emily A 3:57:25 (10,935)
Currie, Geraldine R 4:34:33 (20,834)
Curry, Cliona 4:31:39 (20,067)
Curry, Emma L 4:35:35 (21,129)
Curtin, Gwen P 5:18:05 (29,188)
Curtis, Brigid N 4:44:50 (23,380)
Curtis, Debbie 5:19:27 (29,346)
Curtis, Frances D 5:49:17 (32,073)
Curtis, Joanna H 3:45:23 (7,769)
Curtis, Katy V 4:10:26 (14,395)
Curtis, Pat M 3:33:11 (5,416)
Curtis, Sophie A 4:32:43 (20,351)
Curtis, Susan D 4:32:43 (20,351)
Cushnie, Lorraine S 4:56:55 (26,060)
Custance, Lucie J 3:12:07 (2,225)
Cuthbert, Janet M 4:45:42 (23,585)
Cuthbert, Jennifer A 6:46:35 (34,012)
Cuthbert, Julie C 5:03:31 (27,186)
Cutler, Joanne L 4:45:05 (23,432)
Cutler, Sarah 3:25:03 (3,939)
Cutmore, Sara L 4:14:06 (15,339)

Czajkowski, Maya J 4:26:48 (18,753)

It felt like a long, long way but the crowd and the atmosphere was fantastic. The best bit was coming round the corner by Buckingham Palace and running down The Mall to the finish line to that famous London Marathon music. I couldn't have done it without all the support from everyone who wished me luck and cheered me on and help me raise £1000.90p for the Oxford Transplant Foundation. How could I possibly have explained it if I had to drop out? My aim was to run the whole way. I did run it all except I stopped for a second to give Paul a big hug when I saw him spectating at mile 9. Then twice more to hug Anna at mile 18 then mile 24. The next day my legs were aching but I was still smiling!

Czifra, Aniko 4:29:39 (19,551)
D, Martha R 4:27:52 (19,051)
Da Costa, Adrienne V 4:49:20 (24,442)
Dace, Felicity 4:56:18 (25,931)
Dad, Naheed 7:46:53 (34,501)
Dada, Agnes O 6:50:34 (34,082)
Dadd, Charlotte 5:01:39 (26,901)
Daft, Hannah E 4:26:10 (18,579)
Daggers, Angela T 4:49:58 (24,594)
Dagnan, Victoria A 5:12:42 (28,494)
Dahlberg, Cecilia 5:43:39 (31,623)
Dahlberg, Johanna 4:57:39 (26,220)
Dainton, Rebecca T 5:12:21 (28,444)
Dainty, Deborah L 5:21:34 (29,567)
Dainty, Margery 4:27:21 (18,916)
Daldini, Antonella 5:03:18 (27,154)
Dale, Carolyn 5:51:57 (32,288)
Dale, Diane 6:11:44 (33,158)
Dale, Donna 4:43:04 (22,948)
Dale, Louise M 4:38:28 (21,825)
Dale, Nicola I 4:16:19 (15,907)
Dale, Victoria J 4:52:46 (25,213)
Dales, Jane M 5:46:40 (31,892)
Daley, Sally C 5:21:29 (29,551)
Daley, Stephanie J 3:38:11 (6,300)
Daley, Susan 7:26:34 (34,439)
Dalling, Toni 7:01:36 (34,223)
Dallison, Annick T 3:39:08 (6,456)
Dalrymple, Stella E 6:18:08 (33,358)
Dalton, Hannah R 5:34:22 (30,872)
Dalton, Laura 4:18:11 (16,399)
Dalton, Penny 3:54:09 (9,919)
Dalton, Sheryl 4:17:16 (16,166)
Daly, Elizabeth A 5:18:15 (29,203)
Daly, Gwen 4:01:26 (12,224)
Daly, Mary M 5:36:39 (31,092)
Daly, Patricia A 4:32:12 (20,225)
Dalzell, Julie 3:15:32 (2,705)
D'Amone, Marilena 4:17:34 (16,238)
Dancey, Sally C 3:49:42 (8,746)
Dando, Suzanne 4:38:54 (21,941)
Danes, Sarah 4:24:11 (18,045)
D'Angelosante, Onorina 4:59:35 (26,570)
Dangwa, Flora 6:28:44 (33,634)
Daniel, Beryl M 4:49:50 (24,556)
Daniels, Katherine C 7:42:25 (34,487)
Daniels, Susan F 4:54:55 (25,676)
Daniels, Tania 4:31:13 (19,942)
Danks, Emma J 4:09:31 (14,181)
Dann, Alexandra R 4:18:07 (16,374)
Dappiano, Sara M 5:32:34 (30,708)
Darby, Catherine M 3:27:13 (4,315)
Darby, Rachael M 4:32:08 (20,208)
Dare, Penelope R 4:32:01 (20,177)
Darke, Alice J 4:09:48 (14,251)
Darley, Joanna S 5:29:33 (30,429)
Darlington, Catherine E 5:08:00 (27,825)
Darlington-Smith, Jane 4:45:15 (23,481)
Darnell, Kim 4:54:02 (25,489)
Dartnall, Miki L 6:03:12 (32,852)
Darwood, Joanne 3:12:58 (2,330)
Dastous, Deirdre M 5:04:59 (27,397)
Dauer, Eva 4:18:11 (16,399)
Davanne, Francine 4:51:18 (24,905)
Davenport, Diane T 5:44:27 (31,718)
Davenport, Michelle M 5:12:50 (28,520)
Davenport, Pauline 6:38:08 (33,844)
Davenport, Victoria 4:31:35 (20,050)
Daverin, Claire 4:57:32 (26,194)
Davey, Alice 6:11:23 (33,151)
Davey, Antoinette 6:04:27 (32,906)
Davey, Joanne 5:31:26 (30,606)
Davey, Julie A 5:10:03 (28,153)
Davey, Lynwen J 4:39:48 (22,153)
Davey, Sue M 5:25:57 (30,030)
Davey, Susan C 3:56:44 (10,702)
Davidson, Anna V 5:37:14 (31,134)
Davidson, Anne 4:07:14 (13,586)
Davidson, Anne A 3:18:12 (3,008)
Davidson, Violet 4:22:20 (17,527)
Davies, Aimée E 5:35:01 (30,943)
Davies, Alison 4:08:56 (14,026)
Davies, Amanda J 3:31:33 (5,141)
Davies, Anne M 3:46:14 (7,936)
Davies, Bethan 6:16:40 (33,315)
Davies, Cate 5:39:51 (31,320)

Dinesen, Anne L	4:11:04 (14,563)
Dingley, Amanda I	4:57:57 (26,271)
Dingley, Jan A	5:16:59 (29,060)
Dinneen, Sarah J	4:01:59 (12,358)
Dinsdale, Stella	3:56:22 (10,582)
Diplock, Sarah J	4:33:09 (20,470)
Disney, Glennys	3:18:19 (3,022)
Diss, Joanna L	4:33:20 (20,523)
Diss, Rachel	5:30:32 (30,530)
Dita, Constantina	2:27:45 (47)
Ditchfield, Christine	4:00:42 (12,034)
Ditchfield, Penny	5:44:06 (31,674)
Dixon, Angela J	4:06:06 (13,291)
Dixon, Carol F	5:21:05 (29,506)
Dixon, Christine A	4:57:34 (26,199)
Dixon, Laura J	5:58:10 (32,647)
Dixon, Leonie	4:23:29 (17,864)
Dixon, Michelle A	4:14:53 (15,530)
Dixon, Patricia J	4:17:10 (16,147)
Dixon, Rachel	4:07:08 (13,553)
Dixon, Sally A	4:30:55 (19,870)
Dixon, Sally A	6:32:37 (33,718)
Dixon, Sharon	3:14:03 (2,474)
Dobbin, Caroline J	4:01:57 (12,348)
Dobbs, Helen A	6:31:13 (33,688)
Dobson, Claire	6:52:40 (34,121)
Dobson, Katie	5:12:02 (28,411)
Dobson, Lesley	3:43:38 (7,373)
Dobson, Lindsay	5:33:47 (30,813)
Docherty, Anne	4:26:14 (18,590)
Docherty, Anne H	4:18:47 (16,567)
Docherty, Wendy	6:10:22 (33,127)
Dockray, Beverley L	3:57:05 (10,829)
Dodd, Debbie E	4:23:44 (17,922)
Dodd, Frances	5:03:33 (27,191)
Dodd, Sharon L	5:51:10 (32,219)
Dodd, Susie M	4:02:48 (12,565)
Dodds, Chenoa	4:48:08 (24,173)
Dodds, Clare L	4:28:31 (19,268)
Dodds, Mandy	4:52:19 (25,107)
Dodds, Michelle	4:32:41 (20,345)
Dodgson, Jocelyn F	5:08:15 (27,849)
Dodgson, Stacey L	4:19:46 (16,829)
Dods, Melissa	4:01:11 (12,159)
Dodsworth, Elizabeth	5:01:25 (26,864)
Doebel, Katrin	4:20:48 (17,127)
Doheny, Laura	4:01:53 (12,338)
Doherty, Adele	5:06:37 (27,638)
Doherty, Emma D	4:58:01 (26,284)
Doherty, Tania	6:01:00 (32,781)
Doherty, Vicky J	4:27:40 (18,990)
Doig, Vanessa J	4:10:41 (14,457)
Dollar, Tessa S	3:20:07 (3,236)
Dollive, Leanne J	4:34:35 (20,839)
Domagala, Kamila	3:57:10 (10,856)
Doman, Theda F	4:56:52 (26,040)
Domina, Manuela	3:57:09 (10,852)
Dominey, Tanya J	4:31:22 (19,983)
Dominguez, Ana Paula	5:02:06 (26,967)
Donachie, Linda M	5:35:14 (30,955)
Donaghy, Katherine M	4:29:07 (19,428)
Donahue, Amy L	4:46:48 (23,854)
Donald, Cara	4:21:44 (17,387)
Donald, Jane	5:17:11 (29,087)
Donald, Joanna L	4:54:49 (25,653)
Donald, Julie	3:28:58 (4,659)
Donaldson, Anne C	4:19:11 (16,675)
Donaldson, Kim	4:56:13 (25,919)
Donaldson, Mandy S	4:33:15 (20,493)
Donato, Alice N	3:36:21 (5,938)
Donbavand, Nicky	5:02:11 (26,985)
Donelon, Laura	5:13:07 (28,558)
Doniselli, Michela	4:19:42 (16,814)
Donkersloot, Ann	6:32:28 (33,715)
Donkin, Anne	4:16:57 (16,074)
Donnelly, Nicola J	5:36:05 (31,041)
Donnelly, Susan A	4:15:23 (15,663)
Donnelly, Tracey	4:55:35 (25,797)
Donohoe, Alma L	5:28:34 (30,329)
Donohoe, Elizabeth J	5:08:14 (27,847)
Donohoe, Tara M	5:28:34 (30,329)
Donohoe, Tina L	4:29:14 (19,459)
Donovan, Andrea H	6:02:56 (32,846)

Donta, Helen	2:41:10 (221)
Dorman, Katie	4:24:57 (18,249)
Dorrington, Elizabeth A	4:59:53 (26,615)
Dorritt, Rayne	4:58:00 (26,281)
Dorrity, Miriam	4:16:03 (15,849)
Doshi, Mili	5:00:03 (26,643)
Dougall, Annie K	3:52:42 (9,479)
Dougan-Watt, Verity	4:48:10 (24,178)
Douglas, Adele L	5:50:08 (32,140)
Douglas, Claire E	5:25:23 (29,976)
Douglas, Claire J	4:18:22 (16,452)
Douglas, Emily L	5:53:25 (32,370)
Douglas, Joan E	5:41:37 (31,473)
Douthwaite, Vauneen	4:05:55 (13,270)
Dove, Claire L	4:22:18 (17,521)
Dover, Liz H	3:28:04 (4,473)
Dover, Margaret M	4:00:35 (11,998)
Dow, Ashley A	4:46:50 (23,867)
Dow, Katie L	4:45:35 (23,555)
Dowell, Melissa J	3:17:20 (2,905)
Dowling, Claire E	4:48:48 (24,320)
Dowling, Sarah H	3:23:16 (3,669)
Dowman, Sadie	4:50:56 (24,829)
Down, Alicia L	4:28:40 (19,303)
Down, Bernadette M	4:27:21 (18,916)
Down, Claire L	5:56:58 (32,581)
Downey, Christine C	5:49:20 (32,078)
Downham, Gemma L	4:42:03 (22,683)
Downie, Lauren	5:50:02 (32,128)
Downing, Paula J	3:47:38 (8,263)
Downs, Gabrielle A	3:36:08 (5,903)
Downton, Rachel H	5:11:58 (28,405)
Dowse, Marika E	3:56:26 (10,605)
Dowsett, Melissa K	5:21:09 (29,515)
Dowson, Jill C	3:56:49 (10,730)
Dowton, Christina S	4:54:13 (25,525)
Doy, Lindsay E	4:02:14 (12,423)
Doyle, Anna	3:58:51 (11,440)
Doyle, Camilla A	6:43:01 (33,941)
Doyle, Caroline J	3:30:10 (4,919)
Doyle, Elizabeth K	3:57:32 (10,964)
Doyle, Sheila	4:57:19 (26,145)
Drake, Deborah J	4:27:35 (18,974)
Drake, Sheila A	4:07:32 (13,650)
Drakes, Michelle N	4:19:52 (16,853)
Draper, Anne	4:43:50 (23,132)
Draper, Eleanor	4:18:25 (16,470)
Draper, Julie E	4:40:31 (22,313)
Draper, Katharine S	5:04:31 (27,329)
Draper, Kerry W	4:51:01 (24,847)
Draper, Pauline	5:10:17 (28,186)
Draper, Sarah V	5:26:09 (30,048)
Draycott, Lindsay	4:59:45 (26,600)
Dring, Jackie	4:48:58 (24,366)
Drinkall, Deborah A	4:16:10 (15,868)
Driscoll, Glenis K	3:25:00 (3,930)
Drozdowska, Dorota	4:34:37 (20,849)
Drumm, Karen A	4:10:43 (14,467)
Drury, Judith P	6:22:13 (33,466)
Dryhurst, Sarah E	4:44:33 (23,312)
Drysdale, Fiona	4:47:42 (24,068)
Du Plessis, Annelize	4:09:10 (14,077)
Du Plessis, Jenna V	4:53:54 (25,464)
Du Plessis, Sonja	5:04:50 (27,372)
Du Preez, Suzanne	6:08:33 (33,069)
Du Toit, Kate A	4:33:13 (20,485)
Dubber, Carrie A	4:19:01 (16,633)
Dubois, Catherine L	4:03:56 (12,812)
Duchaine, Muriel M	5:29:48 (30,457)
Duchar Clark, Marie V	5:03:49 (27,230)
Duck, Isabelle M	4:47:31 (24,025)
Ducker, Jackie A	3:36:36 (5,981)
Duckling, Louise A	5:09:39 (28,082)
Duckworth, Avril Mary M	3:31:15 (5,092)
Duckworth, Ruth E	4:10:32 (14,418)
Dudfield, Cathy J	3:42:14 (7,076)
Dudley, Emer B	3:22:52 (3,617)
Dudley, Katy	5:40:07 (31,341)
Dudley, Norma P	5:33:19 (30,775)
Duedale, Hannah L	4:00:48 (12,056)
Duerden, Kate F	4:12:52 (14,996)
Duffell, Linda J	3:48:01 (8,355)
Duffield, Clare	5:09:57 (28,137)

Duffy, Angela R	5:58:06 (32,641)
Duffy, Helen A	4:45:14 (23,473)
Duffy, Joanne M	4:51:06 (24,864)
Duffy, Miriam R	5:46:01 (31,835)
Duffy, Nicola	7:09:12 (34,307)
Duffy, Rachel	4:18:06 (16,371)
Duffy, Roisin M	6:38:30 (33,859)
Duffy, Therezia	3:34:58 (5,699)
Duggan, Andrea	4:37:00 (21,485)
Duggan, Gillian	4:24:42 (18,194)
Duggleby, Helen J	3:54:09 (9,919)
Dugourd, Catherine	5:17:35 (29,136)
Dulai, Navneet K	5:12:46 (28,508)
Dumbrell, Jeanette K	3:06:39 (1,651)
Dummer, Davina	5:49:16 (32,072)
Dummer, Samantha M	6:00:28 (32,757)
Dumontier, Martine	4:14:51 (15,523)
Dunbar, Sally L	5:24:49 (29,891)
Dunbar, Shelley S	6:33:25 (33,736)
Duncan, Aileen J	4:09:32 (14,183)
Duncan, Christina E	7:49:19 (34,508)
Duncan, Isobel	5:25:26 (29,983)
Duncan, Kathleen A	7:49:26 (34,510)
Duncan, Linsay J	4:25:31 (18,402)
Dunford, Jayne L	8:17:20 (34,557)
Dunham, Helen J	4:54:38 (25,606)
Dunham, Maria	4:01:56 (12,345)
Dunkley, Clare	5:08:25 (27,879)
Dunn, Barbara J	4:46:08 (23,697)
Dunn, Fiona	3:56:07 (10,516)
Dunn, Louise	3:51:03 (9,064)
Dunn, Louise F	5:12:03 (28,414)
Dunn, Marcia S	4:09:02 (14,050)
Dunn, Rebecca J	5:03:25 (27,167)
Dunne, Nichola J	4:22:36 (17,613)
Dunning, Hannah K	5:14:54 (28,806)
Dunning, Louise C	4:26:50 (18,765)
Dunstan, Coral	6:21:50 (33,454)
Dunstan, Karen J	4:25:23 (18,364)
Dupain, Emma L	4:13:15 (15,098)
Dupain, Hannah J	3:37:11 (6,098)
Dupre, Amanda D	4:41:19 (22,518)
Duquensnay, Celine F	4:25:42 (18,444)
Durbridge, Jacqueline A	4:52:02 (25,052)
Durney, Jane H	5:19:49 (29,390)
Durrans, Rebecca A	4:01:03 (12,121)
Durrant, Emma J	4:01:13 (12,169)
Durrant, Sue J	4:43:28 (23,035)
Duschl, Rita	3:30:04 (4,900)
Dusgate, Karen E	5:02:44 (27,072)
Dustan, Rowena C	3:30:08 (4,912)
Dutch, Liz	4:36:31 (21,372)
Dutka, Mel M	4:21:36 (17,334)
Dutton, Anna M	6:30:51 (33,683)
Duurloo, Miranda L	5:10:33 (28,221)
Dwan, Philippa J	7:00:16 (34,210)
Dyer, Amy M	5:01:28 (26,866)
Dyer, Danielle	5:26:10 (30,052)
Dyer, Louise	4:26:46 (18,745)
Dyer, Pamela J	3:59:27 (11,656)
Dyer, Susan E	4:58:54 (26,455)
Dyke, Caroline	4:55:51 (25,848)
Dykes, Erica	5:35:22 (30,966)
Dykes, Rita	4:20:00 (16,884)
Dymond, Penni C	3:57:05 (10,829)
Dyos, Megan R	6:37:23 (33,828)
Dyson, Joanna L	4:36:54 (21,464)
Dyu, Lily A	3:29:44 (4,831)
Dzialdow, Resi	4:24:03 (18,011)
Eade, Simone M	4:48:30 (24,252)
Eaden, Malgorzata	5:36:13 (31,054)
Eagle, Fiona	3:13:00 (2,334)
Eaglestone, Susan C	5:03:34 (27,194)
Eames, Louise A	6:33:53 (33,744)
Earl, Jacqueline A	6:55:01 (34,154)
Earnshaw, Angela J	4:07:08 (13,553)
Easden, Lisa-Anne	5:47:34 (31,955)
Eastbury, Justine A	3:40:20 (6,695)
Eastham, Jane E	4:27:21 (18,916)
Eastman, Adele	4:41:01 (22,442)
Eastmead, Tara E	3:59:53 (11,813)
Eastwood, Kathryn J	4:09:12 (14,088)
Eastwood, Kim	6:01:29 (32,796)

Eato, Lisa K	4:17:30	(16,220)
Eaton, Naomi A	3:51:39	(9,211)
Eaton, Penny	5:25:44	(30,005)
Ebel, Jane E	5:01:14	(26,832)
Eccles, Janice	6:56:44	(34,177)
Eccles, Kirstie A	6:56:44	(34,177)
Eccles, Tamsin J	6:56:44	(34,177)
Eckhoffcull, Amy C	4:21:24	(17,275)
Ecollan, Carole	4:08:51	(14,006)
Ecollan, Isabelle	4:26:03	(18,552)
Economu, Nicoleta M	4:33:51	(20,671)
Edgar, Rebekah	3:48:31	(8,469)
Edge, Lucy K	3:59:54	(11,818)
Edgson, Zoe L	3:54:11	(9,928)
Edmunds, Melanie G	5:24:26	(29,851)
Edom, Kathryn A	7:11:13	(34,331)
Edrich, Janet M	5:57:37	(32,610)
Edsell, Jane C	5:00:30	(26,707)
Edvardsdottir, Sigurbjorg	3:12:03	(2,217)
Edward, Anna L	3:55:44	(10,418)
Edwards, Bryony G	4:47:10	(23,949)
Edwards, Christine E	8:05:30	(34,538)
Edwards, Clare E	4:13:10	(15,076)
Edwards, Diane	4:18:07	(16,374)
Edwards, Eleanor H	5:27:44	(30,229)
Edwards, Emma	7:54:53	(34,523)
Edwards, Fiona M	4:13:25	(15,138)
Edwards, Fizzy G	4:59:24	(26,545)
Edwards, Helen	6:49:03	(34,053)
Edwards, Helen K	4:19:08	(16,663)
Edwards, Janet E	3:34:24	(5,605)
Edwards, Jo L	5:16:43	(29,020)
Edwards, Joanne K	4:09:02	(14,050)
Edwards, Kelly V	5:14:41	(28,772)
Edwards, Lauren L	3:41:51	(7,001)
Edwards, Linda K	3:46:44	(8,045)
Edwards, Lorna E	6:12:24	(33,184)
Edwards, Louisa-Jane	4:28:47	(19,343)
Edwards, Olivia G	3:45:00	(7,681)
Edwards, Paula	4:14:08	(15,347)
Edwards, Rebecca	4:14:18	(15,398)
Edwards, Victoria G	7:05:33	(34,270)
Edwardsl, Sharon L	4:49:02	(24,381)
Edwick, Lucy	4:15:28	(15,693)
Egan, Alison	4:34:41	(20,870)
Egan, Denise	5:02:27	(27,036)
Egan, Linda	5:09:16	(28,005)
Egan, Olivia M	4:22:33	(17,599)
Egan, Sharon M	4:42:29	(22,800)
Egerton, Ingrid	5:43:53	(31,660)
Eggington, Ann	3:44:24	(7,534)
Egglestone, Christine J	3:55:36	(10,371)
Egloff, Gwenaelle G	3:37:52	(6,230)
Ejaife, Efe M	6:22:57	(33,490)
Eke, Julie	6:25:55	(33,574)
Ekenbratt, Maria	3:57:45	(11,039)
Ekpe, Yetunde	5:50:07	(32,138)
Elachkar, Hala E	4:19:04	(16,647)
Elcome, Lynsey H	3:39:03	(6,445)
Elder, Caroline E	4:44:27	(23,286)
Eldridge, Anne E	5:11:32	(28,339)
Eldridge, Carla A	4:36:57	(21,477)
Eldridge, Charlotte	4:26:32	(18,673)
Elener, Claire L	3:54:30	(10,034)
Eley, Kerry A	3:51:23	(9,149)
Elford, Sophie	4:05:23	(13,140)
Elfver, Josefin	4:25:40	(18,434)
Elia, Amanda J	5:53:02	(32,339)
Elkington, Amanda T	3:43:44	(7,396)
Elks, Katy L	4:11:17	(14,622)
Elks, Teresa M	5:50:12	(32,144)
Ellen, Angela	5:44:59	(31,766)
Ellenburg, Rochelle	3:57:02	(10,805)
Ellerton, Joanne M	4:23:33	(17,883)
Ellett, Lesley A	4:26:59	(18,809)
Ellington, Cheryl	4:51:27	(24,930)
Elliot, Katherine R	4:21:34	(17,328)
Elliot, Tia D	4:11:39	(14,719)
Elliot, Victoria A	4:29:08	(19,434)
Elliot MBE, Virginia H	4:47:52	(24,109)
Elliott, Charlotte S	6:01:43	(32,807)
Elliott, Christine M	4:26:37	(18,700)
Elliott, Faith V	4:35:05	(21,005)
Elliott, Justine	5:25:46	(30,008)
Elliott, Kate	4:10:18	(14,369)
Elliott, Kate	4:20:24	(16,997)
Elliott, Shelley M	5:31:56	(30,651)
Elliott, Sue M	5:32:50	(30,730)
Elliott, Vanessa	4:14:08	(15,347)
Elliott, Vanessa J	4:31:04	(19,900)
Ellis, Alison J	5:58:10	(32,647)
Ellis, Debbie E	4:05:29	(13,172)
Ellis, Gill	4:37:51	(21,683)
Ellis, Louise	4:53:32	(25,382)
Ellis, Katherine A	3:56:08	(10,522)
Ellis, Rebecca H	5:40:56	(31,408)
Ellis, Rosie A	5:30:26	(30,520)
Ellis, Sarah J	4:29:20	(19,481)
Ellis Hoult, Dawn C	4:37:39	(21,630)
Ellison, Jane	3:58:41	(11,369)
Ellis-Williams, Gillian W	5:05:41	(27,508)
Ellman, Lucia	4:29:22	(19,494)
Ellwood, Sarah	3:25:20	(3,984)
Ellynn, Emma J	5:27:40	(30,220)
Elmes, Emma	4:19:37	(16,787)
Elmes, Simone M	4:07:25	(13,618)
Elmquist, Anne L	4:25:24	(18,367)
Elsdon, Helen A	3:58:16	(11,203)
Else, Claire A	3:58:27	(11,282)
Elsley, Sharon E	5:21:01	(29,497)
Elster, Frances J	4:36:17	(21,320)
Elugbadebo-Solomons, Adeola	4:48:32	(24,258)
Elvidge, Catherine E	5:28:59	(30,377)
Elwell, Jill	6:23:33	(33,506)
Elyeznassni, Karima	4:39:12	(22,027)
Emerton, Sally	4:21:11	(17,220)
Emmerson, Rebecca L	4:18:37	(16,538)
Emsley, Victoria L	3:36:51	(6,029)
Eneas, Tiffany	4:33:42	(20,635)
Engerer, Ramona	4:13:05	(15,063)
England, Lucy	5:01:06	(26,811)
England, Susannah	3:54:11	(9,928)
Englefield, Maureen P	6:57:53	(34,188)
English, Lesley H	4:09:47	(14,250)
English, Teresa J	3:17:02	(2,867)
Ennis, Claire E	5:16:32	(28,999)
Erangey, Emma L	5:50:24	(32,163)
Erasmus, Annemarie	4:54:21	(25,549)
Ercolani, Cesarina N	4:03:38	(12,755)
Erikson, Lene	4:31:23	(19,991)
Eriksson, Jessica M	4:04:20	(12,901)
Eriksson, Nell	5:15:25	(28,868)
Erskine, Lorraine A	4:57:20	(26,150)
Erskine, Stephanie M	5:36:14	(31,059)
Eschweiler, Trix	5:02:23	(27,021)
Espana, Yvonne	5:19:35	(29,369)
Espinosa, Sylvie	3:57:36	(10,977)
Estrada, Maria	4:56:54	(26,052)
Etchells, Barbara J	7:08:06	(34,294)
Etchells, Katy J	5:13:08	(28,562)
Etheridge, Josephine	4:31:01	(19,887)
Etherington, Laura E	4:02:56	(12,592)
Etienne, Charmaine E	3:54:20	(9,968)
Ettling, Penelope J	4:16:14	(15,888)
Evans, Alison	4:22:59	(17,722)
Evans, Amanda	4:25:38	(18,422)
Evans, Amanda J	3:28:33	(4,569)
Evans, Anne Marie	4:23:22	(17,835)
Evans, Caroline	4:56:51	(26,036)
Evans, Caroline J	4:35:14	(21,039)
Evans, Carolyn A	3:17:09	(2,880)
Evans, Christine M	5:31:11	(30,583)
Evans, Claire	4:00:49	(12,062)
Evans, Claire M	4:16:39	(15,997)
Evans, Dawn	4:41:37	(22,589)
Evans, Donna L	4:45:54	(23,651)
Evans, Emily J	5:46:23	(31,870)
Evans, Emma	4:48:11	(24,179)
Evans, Fiona L	4:19:51	(16,850)
Evans, Gill A	4:37:50	(21,679)
Evans, Helen C	4:26:36	(18,695)
Evans, Helen E	3:10:24	(2,030)
Evans, Hilary	4:32:26	(20,280)
Evans, Jane	4:12:44	(14,969)
Evans, Jennfier C	5:29:11	(30,400)
Evans, Kate	7:23:08	(34,417)
Evans, Kathryn L	5:23:06	(29,710)
Evans, Katrina J	3:53:15	(9,649)
Evans, Kerry L	5:29:38	(30,440)
Evans, Kim	6:27:31	(33,612)
Evans, Kim E	5:35:59	(31,027)
Evans, Klaire D	3:41:50	(6,996)
Evans, Linda S	5:52:57	(32,335)
Evans, Lorraine T	3:56:45	(10,708)
Evans, Louise S	5:52:08	(32,298)
Evans, Lucy	4:12:29	(14,928)
Evans, Marian	4:36:44	(21,423)
Evans, Marit	4:53:58	(25,474)
Evans, Mel E	5:29:05	(30,382)
Evans, Mieke	3:59:39	(11,734)
Evans, Natasha R	4:09:40	(14,216)
Evans, Nerys A	4:14:13	(15,373)
Evans, Rhian	4:21:05	(17,204)
Evans, Rhian	4:58:05	(26,301)
Evans, Sarah A	4:42:16	(22,746)
Evans, Susan	4:51:27	(24,930)
Evans, Taryn J	5:48:52	(32,038)
Evans, Tracey L	5:05:40	(27,507)
Evans, Valerie K	3:56:23	(10,594)
Eve, Henrietta F	5:28:46	(30,347)
Everett, Florence J	4:15:10	(15,610)
Everett, Julie A	4:58:00	(26,281)
Everett, Julie M	5:47:49	(31,966)
Everill, Elaine A	3:19:18	(3,135)
Everitt, Amanda	5:16:07	(28,948)
Everitt, Eileen G	4:49:44	(24,541)
Evers-Buckland, Elena	5:14:34	(28,754)
Eversden, Helen	4:45:58	(23,665)
Everton, Beverley	6:50:36	(34,084)
Eves, Honor	5:11:31	(28,333)
Ewart, Kathryn	4:14:07	(15,340)
Ewbank, Penelope J	5:31:37	(30,624)
Eyles, Julie	4:52:37	(25,174)
Eyre, Rachael E	5:09:12	(27,996)
Fackerell, Karon L	3:48:53	(8,549)
Fadli, Aisha	5:47:20	(31,934)
Fagan, Rachel E	3:14:28	(2,541)
Fahey, Rachael	3:45:05	(7,704)
Fahy, Anne-Marie	5:28:34	(30,329)
Faiola, Stacy L	4:51:34	(24,950)
Fairbard, Lorraine A	4:27:53	(19,058)
Fairbrother, Lisa M	4:54:33	(25,591)
Fairclough, Janet	5:08:43	(27,932)
Fairfax, Lydia A	3:58:23	(11,256)
Fairhurst, Debra	4:13:55	(15,283)
Fairley, Linda E	3:56:11	(10,533)
Faithfull, Sarah E	5:51:29	(32,248)
Fake, Anna E	5:04:26	(27,312)
Falcand, Nicole L	5:49:39	(32,096)
Falcus, Elaine C	3:51:05	(9,072)
Falkiner, Stephanie J	6:13:01	(33,211)
Falloon, Colleen N	4:38:42	(21,888)
Falsini, Helen	3:54:28	(10,013)
Famiglietti, Wendy F	5:03:55	(27,244)
Fane, Briony A	4:24:59	(18,259)
Fanning, Jane L	3:14:48	(2,607)
Faraone, Maria	4:38:46	(21,902)
Farbridge, Nicola L	3:58:48	(11,416)
Fardy, Catherine H	4:31:24	(19,995)
Farley, Angela J	4:34:06	(20,725)
Farley, Claire E	3:28:37	(4,583)
Farley, Joanne	4:52:29	(25,143)
Farmah, Neena	5:19:35	(29,369)
Farmbrough, Clare M	4:51:29	(24,935)
Farmer, Catherine A	4:54:53	(25,671)
Farmer, Libby J	4:36:11	(21,289)
Farmiloe, Elizabeth L	4:31:41	(20,074)
Farnham, Eleanor	6:15:36	(33,280)
Farnworth, Katherine	5:34:11	(30,854)
Farquhar, Katherine A	3:03:48	(1,438)
Farquharson, Jayne A	4:12:14	(14,868)
Farraday, Erica J	5:10:42	(28,236)
Farrall, Ali	3:22:44	(3,599)
Farrell, Ann	4:15:53	(15,804)
Farrell, Sara C	5:40:12	(31,353)
Farren, Natalie	5:26:23	(30,086)
Farrow, Alexandra	7:09:47	(34,318)
Farrow, Rozina E	7:10:02	(34,323)
Farrow, Sharon B	4:32:30	(20,300)

Fashoni, Kelly L....4:30:25 (19,724)
Faulkner, Susan T....4:02:30 (12,497)
Faulkner, Tracey S....5:38:18 (31,213)
Fauser, Birgit....3:19:48 (3,207)
Fawcett, Kelly A....4:52:50 (25,229)
Fawcett, Paula....4:41:18 (22,513)
Fawcett, Rebecca....6:45:02 (33,980)
Fawcett, Trudy J....2:55:00 (751)
Fawke, Kim....2:42:08 (244)
Fay, Josephine....4:23:53 (17,958)
Fay, Victoria J....5:05:52 (27,525)
Fear, Andi....7:01:37 (34,224)
Fearn, Margaret....4:30:41 (19,795)
Fearn, Sharon E....3:35:14 (5,745)
Fearnside, Maureen P....5:15:18 (28,850)
Fearon, Patricia M....4:26:51 (18,773)
Feary, Johanna R....4:22:14 (17,506)
Featherstone, Jenny....3:37:21 (6,130)
Febrer, Yvalia T....5:41:28 (31,462)
Fee, Deirdre....3:52:49 (9,506)
Fee, Monica....3:17:35 (2,940)
Feely, Christine....4:40:50 (22,389)
Feely, Joan....5:17:22 (29,104)
Feeney, Carol A....4:13:04 (15,054)
Feeney, Jaimie L....3:08:14 (1,815)
Feeney, Lisa....3:47:55 (8,329)
Fel, Armelle....4:32:28 (20,288)
Felice Pace, Claire....4:42:24 (22,780)
Fellows, Colette J....5:32:19 (30,684)
Fellows, Jacqueline A....6:00:17 (32,751)
Felmington, Helen E....5:53:27 (32,373)
Felstead, Julie....6:45:31 (33,992)
Felton, Lesley S....3:58:33 (11,317)
Feltwell, Anne L....4:35:17 (21,051)
Fenelon, Patsy E....3:58:10 (11,174)
Fenn, Catherine A....3:54:22 (9,978)
Fenn, Rhian M....4:31:23 (19,991)
Fenn, Sarah....7:01:47 (34,227)
Fennell, Kate....3:22:39 (3,593)
Fenner, Christine....5:56:50 (32,571)
Fennessy, Jacqueline....4:11:29 (14,674)
Fennings, Gloria A....7:45:32 (34,497)
Fensome, Tania J....7:01:21 (34,216)
Fentiman, Ella R....5:51:59 (32,290)
Fenton, Ann H....4:24:29 (18,137)
Fenwick, Caron....4:46:16 (23,733)
Ferguson, Christine....3:24:11 (3,802)
Ferguson, Julia....3:56:45 (10,708)
Ferguson, Lisa J....6:23:32 (33,505)
Ferguson, Paula A....7:10:52 (34,328)
Ferguson, Sarah V....4:22:24 (17,551)
Fergusson-Kelly, Helen....4:23:10 (17,770)
Fernandez, Emma L....5:19:56 (29,406)
Ferraby, Rachel....5:06:52 (27,677)
Ferreira, Sylvia....4:42:29 (22,800)
Ferrie, Clare M....5:03:32 (27,189)
Ferries, Hilary A....6:14:08 (33,244)
Ferris, Gillian L....4:18:35 (16,526)
Ferris, Kate....4:26:42 (18,723)
Ferry, Emma....4:14:37 (15,472)
Ferry, Lindsey J....4:19:42 (16,814)
Fewkes, Samantha J....5:31:12 (30,585)
Ffrench, Anja E....3:55:35 (10,367)
Field, Amanda....5:52:46 (32,326)
Field, Andrea F....6:42:31 (33,923)
Field, Carolyn J....4:49:19 (24,436)
Field, Janette A....4:39:14 (22,037)
Field, Jennifer E....6:54:17 (34,140)
Field, Laura....4:35:40 (21,157)
Field, Louise L....5:39:52 (31,322)
Field, Paula....4:12:44 (14,969)
Field, Sarah H....6:03:41 (32,874)
Fielden, Katherine M....4:43:20 (23,012)
Fielding, Claire L....3:55:52 (10,457)
Fields, Sarah....3:56:07 (10,516)
Fifield, Joanne....3:13:42 (2,422)
Figes, Wendy K....3:40:30 (6,737)
Figgis, Susan M....4:18:42 (16,552)
Filatotchev, Anne....4:19:28 (16,743)
Filby, Angela M....5:04:24 (27,310)
Fildes, Lisa R....5:32:39 (30,715)
Filesi, Anna....4:44:07 (23,206)
Filsell, Vikki C....3:22:24 (3,549)
Finch, Claire....7:14:32 (34,360)
Finch, Helen S....3:00:14 (1,181)
Finch, Laura S....6:39:21 (33,872)
Finch, Lydia L....6:35:49 (33,790)
Finch, Sophie A....4:38:21 (21,790)
Findlater, Lisa....4:38:18 (21,781)
Findlay, Caroline L....3:48:14 (8,407)
Findley, Pauline A....5:08:42 (27,929)
Finegan, Georgina....3:49:07 (8,606)
Finlay, Claire L....4:14:20 (15,406)
Finlay, Fiona A....4:50:57 (24,834)
Finn, Suzanne T....5:02:45 (27,074)
Finney, Helen L....3:56:26 (10,605)
Finniear, Kerry....4:19:25 (16,728)
Finning, Jessica L....3:52:49 (9,506)
Firkins, Kate A....5:49:35 (32,091)
Firn, Emily....4:48:31 (24,255)
Firpi, Claudia C....4:35:12 (21,032)
Firth, Margaret P....3:54:53 (10,150)
Firth, Melinda P....5:43:30 (31,607)
Firth, Samantha J....5:31:29 (30,613)
Firth, Susan A....5:08:10 (27,839)
Fischborn, Sylva....4:35:34 (21,122)
Fischer, Carmen....4:28:44 (19,321)
Fisher, Alison J....4:32:10 (20,215)
Fisher, Ann L....4:49:33 (24,491)
Fisher, Harriet....5:11:43 (28,369)
Fisher, Heather R....3:44:55 (7,660)
Fisher, Jackie K....7:23:08 (34,417)
Fisher, Sally....4:30:39 (19,785)
Fisher, Sonia E....5:13:55 (28,664)
Fisher, Sophie L....7:15:37 (34,368)
Fisher, Tina J....6:48:58 (34,050)
Fishwick, Rachael L....4:16:24 (15,932)
Fiss, Susanne....4:32:08 (20,208)
Fitch, Rebecca F....5:50:48 (32,196)
Fitt, Lisa J....6:23:53 (33,512)
Fitzgerald, Amy-Lucy....4:59:24 (26,545)
Fitzgerald, Kathrina P....4:56:32 (25,977)
Fitzgerald, Nicola C....5:17:22 (29,104)
Fitzgerald, Sara H....3:56:34 (10,650)
Fitzjohn, Monica....7:24:49 (34,426)
Fitzpatrick, Anna F....5:10:01 (28,147)
Fitzpatrick, Julie....4:18:03 (16,354)
Fitzpatrick, Kerry....5:08:37 (27,917)
Fitzpatrick, Leeana E....5:51:10 (32,219)
Fitzpatrick, Lorraine....5:19:50 (29,393)
Fitzpatrick, Siobhan C....5:02:52 (27,091)
Fitzroy, Julia R....3:58:33 (11,317)
Fitzsimmons, Emma K....5:09:06 (27,981)
Fitzsimons, Anthea....3:47:12 (8,154)
Flanagan, Jane M....4:36:38 (21,399)
Flannery, Julia L....3:48:25 (8,447)
Flavell, Margaret A....4:32:20 (20,260)
Flavell-Raybone, Jan....4:25:10 (18,310)
Flaxel, Christina....4:57:22 (26,159)
Flaxington, Frances V....5:46:06 (31,842)
Fleetwood, Angela A....5:00:09 (26,661)
Fleming, Clare L....3:37:52 (6,230)
Fleming, Dyan J....4:30:53 (19,863)
Fleming, Helen....3:24:48 (3,888)
Fleming, Morna R....4:02:59 (12,606)
Fleming, Susan A....6:27:02 (33,599)
Fletcher, Angela....4:35:45 (21,177)
Fletcher, Claire....4:57:05 (26,104)
Fletcher, Helen....4:39:42 (22,130)
Fletcher, Lonnie G....7:08:32 (34,297)
Fletcher, Sally....4:18:50 (16,582)
Fletcher, Vivienne A....6:51:12 (34,097)
Flitcroft, Tracey....6:30:08 (33,664)
Flood, Nicola A....4:29:17 (19,467)
Florendine-Roberts, Rebecca E....4:49:06 (24,397)
Flower, Clare L....5:11:02 (28,280)
Flower, Naomi J....5:32:24 (30,693)
Flowerdew, Laura A....3:57:15 (10,877)
Flury, Joanna C....3:26:27 (4,179)
Flury, Patricia M....7:04:13 (34,256)
Flynn, Deborah A....5:51:15 (32,235)
Flynn, Jessica J....5:52:54 (32,333)
Flynn, Louisa J....4:47:55 (24,126)
Foddering, Naomi L....5:13:19 (28,580)
Fogarty, Helen....3:54:58 (10,184)
Fogg, Emma C....4:29:56 (19,617)
Fogg, Erica J....3:04:44 (1,499)
Fogg, Jan....4:31:56 (20,147)
Fok, Rowena C....2:59:39 (1,135)
Foley, Claire E....5:28:43 (30,345)
Foley, Helen S....6:55:30 (34,161)
Foley, Jeanette....5:07:13 (27,722)
Foley, Katherine E....5:36:43 (31,096)
Foley, Lucy A....4:20:25 (17,003)
Folkes, Liz S....4:26:46 (18,745)
Follis, Lynda J....4:06:19 (13,358)
Follows, Stella E....5:01:38 (26,900)
Fooks, Katy....3:56:13 (10,540)
Foord, Liane....4:30:49 (19,838)
Foot, Susan....3:49:40 (8,736)
Foote, Barbara L....4:50:07 (24,625)
Foote, Sarah J....5:16:51 (29,036)
Foran, Gillian....4:09:43 (14,233)
Forbes, Abigail R....4:38:46 (21,902)
Forbes, Catriona M....3:40:04 (6,653)
Forbes, Kimberly J....5:56:15 (32,541)
Forbes, Ruth H....3:51:24 (9,152)
Ford, Alison....4:38:17 (21,775)
Ford, Claire L....4:21:33 (17,319)
Ford, Denise M....3:49:42 (8,746)
Ford, Heather C....4:41:16 (22,501)
Ford, Helen J....3:44:14 (7,496)
Ford, Liz....4:52:13 (25,084)
Ford, Lucy....5:30:45 (30,550)
Ford, Miranda....6:10:39 (33,133)
Ford, Morag H....4:55:14 (25,735)
Ford, Vanessa....3:50:00 (8,824)
Fordham, Jan M....4:25:24 (18,367)
Fordham, Sarah E....4:58:46 (26,436)
Foreman, Clare V....3:52:11 (9,356)
Forgione, Teresa M....4:47:33 (24,029)
Forrest, Ginny....5:21:16 (29,530)
Forrest, Jane....3:35:23 (5,772)
Forrester, Claire....5:50:01 (32,123)
Forrester, Karen....5:34:05 (30,843)
Forshaw, Sarah J....4:25:09 (18,306)
Forskitt, Mary....5:01:20 (26,847)
Forsner-Hansen, Anette....5:21:37 (29,571)
Forster, Denise....5:02:19 (27,007)
Forsyth, Gayle....4:35:28 (21,104)
Forsyth, Jennifer A....4:58:52 (26,446)
Forsyth, Mary M....5:34:32 (30,888)
Forsythe, Lynette....4:52:49 (25,227)
Fortenberry, Nancy Y....4:05:06 (13,069)
Fortunato, Franca....5:23:46 (29,778)
Fortune, Zoe M....5:08:36 (27,912)
Fosker, Denise J....4:09:51 (14,262)
Foster, Ann....5:26:50 (30,136)
Foster, Beverley K....5:06:55 (27,687)
Foster, Carol....6:43:06 (33,942)
Foster, Catherine S....5:03:19 (27,158)
Foster, Clare L....5:24:01 (29,808)
Foster, Clare V....4:19:57 (16,874)
Foster, Elizabeth A....5:41:18 (31,442)
Foster, Eve M....4:54:50 (25,657)
Foster, Joanna C....6:00:02 (32,740)
Foster, Julia K....5:49:58 (32,118)
Foster, Kerry L....5:43:46 (31,631)
Foster, Laura A....4:18:35 (16,526)
Foster, Lindsay C....4:39:55 (22,170)
Foster, Louise M....4:28:24 (19,232)
Foster, Sarah J....4:45:14 (23,473)
Foster, Sharon....4:51:58 (25,036)
Fothergill, Helen C....4:34:37 (20,849)
Foulds, Claire L....4:35:14 (21,039)
Foulser, Kelly J....4:08:30 (13,909)
Fourie, Erika....4:18:04 (16,361)
Fourie, Retha S....4:39:57 (22,174)
Fouweather, Michelle L....6:08:39 (33,070)
Fowler, Claire....3:23:31 (3,709)
Fowler, Kay....3:21:43 (3,447)
Fowler, Nicola....3:54:53 (10,150)
Fowles, Charlotte E....4:54:44 (25,632)
Fox, Anne M....4:23:02 (17,737)
Fox, Charlotte....4:18:39 (16,542)
Fox, Claire L....4:27:07 (18,847)
Fox, Joanna....6:09:13 (33,088)
Fox, Nicola....5:18:35 (29,239)
Fox, Sue....7:09:10 (34,306)

Fox, Wendy A 4:44:57 (23,402)
Foyle, Susan J............................5:41:20 (31,446)
Foyster, Mandy L.........................3:27:54 (4,439)
Frampton, Linda G.......................4:22:30 (17,582)
France, Hayley J..........................4:58:53 (26,450)
France, Jacqueline R...................3:05:40 (1,567)
Francis, Abby..............................4:09:17 (14,112)
Francis, Andrea K........................3:27:30 (4,363)
Francis, Anita C..........................6:21:18 (33,437)
Francis, Anna L...........................3:24:56 (3,916)
Francis, Gillian A........................6:41:49 (33,907)
Francis, Jill.................................6:08:04 (33,046)
Francis, Karen A..........................5:10:24 (28,208)
Francis, Sarah.............................5:13:02 (28,547)
Francis, Sarah.............................6:04:16 (32,902)
Francis, Sarah C..........................4:48:47 (24,315)
Francis, Selina.............................4:48:45 (24,307)
François, Marie-Ange...................4:09:28 (14,162)
Francombe, Faye.........................4:58:46 (26,436)
Frank, Flora.................................6:04:12 (32,895)
Frank, Lucinda M.........................4:22:37 (17,622)
Frankish, Helen E.........................5:07:07 (27,706)
Frankland, Sharon........................4:25:50 (18,491)
Franklin, Anna M..........................5:15:20 (28,858)
Franklin, Emma M.........................4:52:53 (25,247)
Franklin, Karen.............................5:27:27 (30,199)
Franklin, Kay E..............................5:04:51 (27,376)
Franklin, Lindsay A........................4:48:26 (24,233)
Franklin, Melanie A.......................6:20:11 (33,401)
Franklin, Mezzi E...........................4:57:19 (26,145)
Franks, Eleanor J...........................3:59:49 (11,789)
Franks, Helen L..............................6:21:24 (33,441)
Frankum, Alice..............................4:55:54 (25,859)
Frankum, Catherine E....................4:48:18 (24,208)
Franssen-Franken, Diana...............3:54:59 (10,191)
Fraser, Alice R...............................3:25:44 (4,058)
Fraser, Lauren...............................4:22:08 (17,476)
Fraser, Nadine M............................4:40:48 (22,379)
Fraser, Susan B..............................4:32:45 (20,363)
Frazier, Emma C.............................4:31:50 (20,120)
Frean, Sandy D...............................5:09:28 (28,042)
Freegard, Emilia.............................5:06:04 (27,564)
Freeman, Alexandra L.....................4:31:06 (19,910)
Freeman, Alison J...........................4:25:06 (18,288)
Freeman, Claire J............................4:42:50 (22,884)
Freeman, Genevieve.......................4:03:25 (12,708)
Freeman, Holly...............................4:10:55 (14,527)
Freeman, Karen M...........................4:39:08 (22,011)
Freeman-Attwood, Emmy M.............5:01:19 (26,842)
Freer, Lisa J....................................4:57:28 (26,177)
Freestone, Deborah........................4:18:14 (16,409)
French, Alison.................................4:42:02 (22,680)
French, Amanda A...........................5:56:09 (32,530)
French, Annette E...........................4:14:17 (15,392)
French, Georgina A.........................4:43:39 (23,088)
French, Margaret A.........................4:13:57 (15,286)
French, Michelle French L...............4:09:38 (14,209)
Frenken, Hildy.................................4:30:41 (19,795)
Fretwell, Stephanie E......................5:44:28 (31,721)
Freyd, Hana.....................................4:52:03 (25,056)
Fricker, Elizabeth J..........................6:21:49 (33,452)
Fricker, Faye....................................4:22:32 (17,594)
Fricker, Rosalind G..........................8:01:23 (34,532)
Friday, Abbie....................................4:25:03 (18,275)
Fritchley-Simpson, Jacqueline.........4:19:05 (16,651)
Frith, Lynne......................................4:27:25 (18,936)
Fritz, Danielle...................................4:44:55 (23,397)
Fritzel, Lucia.....................................4:40:25 (22,290)
Froeliger, Michelle............................4:51:17 (24,898)
Froes, Gabriella P.............................3:59:20 (11,610)
Froggatt, Carly L...............................4:24:44 (18,201)
Frogley, Helen E................................4:20:09 (16,928)
Froglia Simmonds, Sonia M...............7:16:57 (34,376)
Frost, Andrea E..................................3:24:51 (3,899)
Frost, Angelique N.............................5:40:40 (31,388)
Frost, Barbara M................................6:55:20 (34,158)
Frost, Debbie.....................................4:12:02 (14,816)
Frost, Helen A....................................4:06:40 (13,446)
Frost, Kerry..4:59:13 (26,520)
Frost, Michelle L................................8:36:32 (34,572)
Frost, Nicola.......................................4:22:00 (17,455)
Frost, Theresa E.................................3:27:01 (4,283)
Frost, Victoria....................................4:46:39 (23,814)
Froud, Nicola M.................................3:20:44 (3,322)
Fruin, Laura C....................................4:19:30 (16,757)
Fry, Natasha J.....................................5:24:50 (29,893)
Fry, Rachel L.......................................5:27:34 (30,206)
Fry, Samantha L.................................3:54:40 (10,089)
Fry, Sue..3:20:16 (3,260)
Frydman, Valerie................................4:29:34 (19,529)
Fryer, Natalie.....................................3:30:59 (5,053)
Fuentes, Teresa..................................4:30:54 (19,869)
Fullalove, Mary T.................................3:58:56 (11,468)
Fuller, Frances G.................................4:32:04 (20,190)
Fuller, Jacqueline J..............................4:52:02 (25,052)
Fuller, Janine L.....................................5:27:17 (30,176)
Fuller, Jessica C....................................6:21:11 (33,433)
Fullman, Caroline..................................8:02:45 (34,535)
Fullwood, Elizabeth A...........................4:48:09 (24,176)
Fullwood, Lesley J.................................4:50:32 (24,727)
Fulton, Andrea......................................4:38:53 (21,937)
Fulton, Vanessa K..................................5:24:17 (29,836)
Furbank, Valerie A.................................5:37:42 (31,168)
Furley, Kirsten F....................................3:28:17 (4,517)
Furmidge, Joy R....................................4:52:47 (25,217)
Furnell-Brennan, Zoe............................5:12:22 (28,446)
Furner, Sue M..5:49:04 (32,059)
Furnivall, Jane.......................................6:40:27 (33,894)
Furze, Elaine..5:55:51 (32,512)
Furzeland, Julie A..................................5:19:15 (29,323)
Fustos, Tunde..4:32:56 (20,415)
Futcher, Sarah.......................................4:49:56 (24,587)
Futter, Maria L.......................................5:01:40 (26,906)
Gabb, Nicola..6:04:52 (32,920)
Gadd, Sam J...4:14:53 (15,530)
Gadgil, Anjan R......................................3:28:28 (4,558)
Gahan, Lisa H...4:43:46 (23,113)
Gailhac, Colette.....................................4:40:41 (22,346)
Gaillard D Laubenque, Teresa J..3:10:30 (2,041)
Gaitskell, Linda......................................5:25:14 (29,954)
Gale, Sally-Anne.....................................4:58:55 (26,459)
Gallagher, Emily R..................................5:50:35 (32,177)
Gallagher, Jenna.....................................4:19:53 (16,855)
Gallagher, Joan.......................................6:40:56 (33,899)
Gallagher, Lynn.......................................6:05:31 (32,953)
Gallagher, Victoria E...............................4:30:40 (19,791)
Gallagher Brown, Victoria J.....................6:50:23 (34,079)
Gallardo, Maria De Lourdes.....................4:11:09 (14,590)
Gallimore, Alison C..................................4:16:34 (15,975)
Gallimore, Diane......................................3:35:34 (5,806)
Gallington, Piri L......................................5:14:52 (28,797)
Galliot, Valerie A......................................4:27:28 (18,946)
Gallivan, Angela K.....................................5:55:59 (32,519)
Galloway, Alison.......................................4:44:51 (23,385)
Galloway, Nicki H......................................4:38:27 (21,818)
Galpin, Karen M..3:43:51 (7,424)
Galvin, Alice K..4:45:46 (23,611)
Galvin, Joanna M......................................4:45:46 (23,611)
Gamble, Carole A......................................6:10:02 (33,117)
Gamble, Chris C..6:34:21 (33,756)
Gamble, Kimberley L..................................6:10:02 (33,117)
Gambrill, Jodie L.......................................4:22:01 (17,457)
Game, Emma..7:18:31 (34,386)
Gammoh, Sarah..5:03:44 (27,213)
Gamskjaer, Karin..4:11:09 (14,590)
Ganley, Joanne...4:45:36 (23,563)
Gannon, Elizabeth J....................................3:22:33 (3,577)
Gannon, Jean M..6:22:20 (33,468)
Gannon, Mary M..4:55:22 (25,761)
Gannon, Sharon K..3:13:53 (2,447)
Gapp, Kirsty V..4:54:36 (25,600)
Gappy, Tina L..3:41:58 (7,019)
Garbe, Marcia M...4:43:19 (23,007)
Garbett, Jill K...4:19:29 (16,750)
Garbould, Kathleen......................................4:42:40 (22,846)
Garcia, Amy L...4:47:04 (23,923)
Garcia, Ana...4:18:57 (16,616)
Garcia, Natalia..4:16:55 (16,065)
Garcia, Paula Maria.......................................4:04:40 (12,972)
Garcia Hernandez, Alejandra.........................4:06:35 (13,420)
Garciarguelles, Susana...................................4:19:23 (16,720)
Gardam, Deborah A..5:30:06 (30,486)
Gardener, Sue E..3:15:18 (2,674)
Garder-Hall, Sarah J..3:55:40 (10,396)
Gardiner, Ali..4:31:03 (19,896)
Gardiner, Julia..3:38:15 (6,308)
Gardner, Angela J...4:55:32 (25,786)
Gardner, Delaine A...5:43:25 (31,602)
Gardner, Helen S...4:39:24 (22,063)
Gardner, Jemma..5:17:51 (29,161)
Gardner, Julie R...6:20:57 (33,425)
Gardner, Louise...2:45:00 (331)
Gardner, Melissa D..3:50:41 (8,985)
Gardner, Nicola E..4:11:56 (14,788)
Gardner, Sarah E...5:06:27 (27,623)
Gardner, Susan..4:03:13 (12,658)
Garlick, Deborah...5:20:22 (29,446)
Garner, Kerry A..5:11:04 (28,284)
Garner, Susan L..4:07:04 (13,534)
Garnett, Justine...4:39:59 (22,181)
Garnett, Kathleen...4:42:08 (22,709)
Garnett, Suzanna M..5:16:27 (28,989)
Garnier, Brigitte..3:52:17 (9,384)
Garrard, Sharon D...5:11:13 (28,297)
Garratt, Anna M...3:51:03 (9,064)
Garratt, Emma..5:04:08 (27,268)
Garratt, Sandra H...5:44:45 (31,742)
Garrec, Cathy..5:06:11 (27,581)
Garrett, Barbara E...5:19:04 (29,298)
Garrett, Jo-Anne M..3:55:05 (10,225)
Garrod, Lorna E...3:23:05 (3,651)
Garrod, Susan A...4:01:19 (12,192)
Garside, Louise C...4:15:30 (15,704)
Garside, Theresa M..4:28:45 (19,327)
Garthwaite, Annie...4:23:45 (17,929)
Gartshore, Elizabeth S...5:30:40 (30,543)
Garwood, Samantha J...5:25:14 (29,954)
Gary, Christine E...5:11:51 (28,391)
Gaskell, Sophie..3:13:23 (2,386)
Gasnot, Françoise..4:17:25 (16,195)
Gaster, Sandra D...4:11:17 (14,622)
Gates, Kathie P...4:58:05 (26,301)
Gatfield, Jennifer S..4:28:53 (19,371)
Gault, Wendy M...4:44:42 (23,347)
Gaunt, Carole E...5:44:41 (31,736)
Gaunt, Catherine A..3:46:22 (7,971)
Gauvin, Sarah J..4:05:00 (13,050)
Gavin, Geraldine..6:20:09 (33,398)
Gawley, Susan J..3:35:42 (5,832)
Gay, Kate E...4:49:40 (24,525)
Gaye, Julia M..4:22:41 (17,645)
Gaylor, Barbara A...4:34:01 (20,699)
Gaynor, Carole A..4:56:12 (25,916)
Gaytten, Lorraine M..5:02:51 (27,086)
Gaywood, Shelley L...4:00:23 (11,944)
Geary, Franchesca A..4:46:12 (23,714)
Geary, Maggie E..6:13:17 (33,218)
Geaves, Geraldine...3:52:49 (9,506)
Gedge, Clare...5:22:55 (29,694)
Gee, Elaine...7:03:00 (34,241)
Gee, Sarah R...2:51:16 (560)
Gelder, Emily J..3:07:26 (1,727)
Gemmell, June..5:27:01 (30,147)
Gemmill, Joanna C..4:00:54 (12,080)
Gendle, Kathryn..4:43:59 (23,177)
Gendron, Kathleen B...3:49:35 (8,715)
Genney, Marie...4:48:29 (24,243)
George, Hannah...4:02:21 (12,460)
George, Imogen C...5:07:43 (27,802)
George, Jenny N..5:19:01 (29,291)
George, Johanna M..3:55:44 (10,418)
George, Rebecca M..4:58:25 (26,364)
Georghiou, Jane...3:29:52 (4,857)
Gerety, Nicola..4:36:03 (21,251)
Gerlach, Angelika...3:48:57 (8,567)
German, Gemma...4:36:52 (21,454)
German, Rachel L...4:00:25 (11,951)
Gerth, Sophia...4:15:22 (15,655)
Geschiere, Suzanne...3:49:55 (8,804)
Gettins, Lucy A...3:39:24 (6,519)
Gevrey, Valerie..3:04:31 (1,485)
Ghelani, Shailini..5:48:02 (31,980)
Giannotti, Monica...3:42:51 (7,205)
Gibb, Sandra M...3:54:45 (10,114)
Gibbard, Helen J...5:28:57 (30,374)
Gibbens, Nina M...3:57:51 (11,075)
Gibbins, Sara L..5:32:03 (30,667)
Gibbon, Laura A..5:22:05 (29,612)
Gibbons, Lynda R..4:57:00 (26,080)

Gibbs, Abi E	6:45:43 (33,998)	
Gibbs, Elaine R	4:15:16 (15,632)	
Gibbs, Helen J	3:33:25 (5,457)	
Gibbs, Jane A	4:54:12 (25,519)	
Gibbs, Jean	5:16:57 (29,053)	
Gibbs, Philippa L	4:35:54 (21,211)	
Gibbs, Samantha J	3:59:26 (11,646)	
Gibbs, Sonya L	4:38:16 (21,770)	
Gibbs, Yvonne D	5:58:05 (32,638)	
Gibson, Caroline M	4:32:17 (20,249)	
Gibson, Claire	2:50:30 (536)	
Gibson, Hazel C	5:57:03 (32,583)	
Gibson, Janet	4:24:04 (18,013)	
Gibson, Julie	3:58:55 (11,460)	
Gibson, Lorraine	4:55:43 (25,821)	
Gibson, Mary A	5:11:46 (28,379)	
Gibson, Shirley R	3:34:21 (5,598)	
Giddy, Claire L	4:43:39 (23,088)	
Gigg, Serena J	4:35:24 (21,082)	
Gilbert, Claire	5:36:54 (31,112)	
Gilbert, Emma L	5:04:45 (27,365)	
Gilbert, Rachel A	4:06:39 (13,441)	
Gilbert, Sally A	3:04:17 (1,473)	
Gilbert, Tina M	4:47:44 (24,080)	
Gilchrist, Samantha J	3:53:54 (9,836)	
Giles, Deborah-Anne	4:57:11 (26,122)	
Giles, Emma L	5:26:49 (30,132)	
Giles, Karie	5:26:49 (30,132)	
Giles, Susan B	5:48:08 (31,984)	
Gilham, Wendy A	4:42:23 (22,770)	
Gill, Ciara T	5:13:12 (28,571)	
Gill, Derrin P	4:13:51 (15,259)	
Gill, Helen L	5:00:04 (26,648)	
Gill, Laura J	4:40:36 (22,330)	
Gill, Lisa	5:03:36 (27,198)	
Gill, Ruth	5:47:01 (31,911)	
Gill, Siu-Anne M	6:01:29 (32,796)	
Gillam, Danielle	3:34:22 (5,601)	
Gillane, Olga B	3:47:20 (8,181)	
Gillespie, Denise R	5:54:47 (32,444)	
Gillet, Elisabeth	4:49:15 (24,424)	
Gillett, Nicola	5:53:23 (32,367)	
Gillham, Rebecca	4:34:58 (20,962)	
Gillie, Sheila	4:35:45 (21,177)	
Gillies, Jill	5:10:46 (28,243)	
Gillies, Stephanie R	3:38:29 (6,356)	
Gilmour, Stephanie F	3:53:19 (9,667)	
Gilpin, Anna K	4:01:45 (12,306)	
Ging, Sarah P	4:31:34 (20,046)	
Gingell, Clarissa Chloe	4:42:09 (22,713)	
Gingell, Lynne A	4:04:55 (13,031)	
Giordano, Luisa	4:32:57 (20,421)	
Giovanacci, Chiara M	4:54:51 (25,664)	
Giovanola, Stefania	4:34:10 (20,746)	
Gipp, Diana M	3:36:17 (5,929)	
Giraudet, Pascale	4:23:28 (17,862)	
Girdler, Karen M	5:34:27 (30,880)	
Girling, Jude	4:12:49 (14,986)	
Girling, Michaela J	3:56:52 (10,749)	
Gittens, Aimée L	6:06:45 (33,009)	
Gittins, Rosanne R	3:29:12 (4,714)	
Given, Joanne L	3:36:08 (5,903)	
Gladman, Karen	4:05:53 (13,262)	
Gladney, Hanne	3:46:11 (7,924)	
Gladwell, Kathryn J	4:49:02 (24,381)	
Glanville, Katie A	5:36:09 (31,048)	
Glas, Andrea	4:43:53 (23,148)	
Glass, Jackie A	4:08:49 (13,993)	
Glasse, Pamela E	6:01:42 (32,804)	
Glassup, Michele	4:55:20 (25,753)	
Glavan, Cornelia	4:32:35 (20,318)	
Gleadall, Victoria M	5:29:54 (30,466)	
Gleeson, Cassie	4:42:54 (22,907)	
Glencross, Julia L	5:01:10 (26,821)	
Glenday, Diana C	4:56:47 (26,023)	
Glenn, Jacquelyn M	5:17:46 (29,150)	
Glennon, Lynne	6:00:29 (32,759)	
Gliddon, Joanna C	5:25:48 (30,011)	
Glinwood, Yvonne B	5:44:07 (31,676)	
Glithro, Linda H	5:49:58 (32,118)	
Glock, Beverley	4:40:45 (22,367)	
Gloor, Barbara	4:23:00 (17,728)	
Glossy, Suzi M	5:53:20 (32,362)	

Glover, Elaine	5:25:01 (29,915)	
Glover, Faye	4:25:45 (18,463)	
Glover, Louise	6:09:25 (33,095)	
Glover, Susan C	5:42:49 (31,556)	
Glover, Susan E	4:57:00 (26,080)	
Glyn, Tessa C	3:59:11 (11,554)	
Goad, Jacqueline A	3:33:08 (5,407)	
Goater, Rachel	5:54:00 (32,404)	
Goatman, Clare	4:09:37 (14,204)	
Godage, Himali Y	4:07:05 (13,539)	
Godber, Emma J	4:07:12 (13,578)	
Godber, Kath A	5:01:40 (26,906)	
Goddard, Amanda J	3:54:38 (10,082)	
Goddard, Eleri W	4:26:37 (18,700)	
Goddard, Laura S	5:46:42 (31,894)	
Godden, Jacinta M	4:52:52 (25,241)	
Godfrey, Dawn M	5:34:31 (30,887)	
Godfrey, Emma L	5:56:00 (32,521)	
Godfrey, Jacqueline A	4:54:25 (25,564)	
Godfrey, Josephine F	5:25:24 (29,979)	
Godin, Diane F	5:49:13 (32,069)	
Goding, Dawn	4:06:59 (13,514)	
Godwin, Cynthia A	4:34:28 (20,816)	
Godwin, Lisa M	4:18:27 (16,479)	
Goergiou, Angela	5:02:10 (26,980)	
Gogarty, Rebekah	4:37:17 (21,547)	
Goh, Kim Hong	3:32:41 (5,344)	
Golach, Verena	3:53:36 (9,743)	
Goldburn, Janet	4:54:41 (25,618)	
Goldman, Elizabeth	4:11:57 (14,791)	
Goldsack, Elizabeth A	4:28:57 (19,390)	
Goldthorpe, Helen J	3:48:58 (8,572)	
Goldthorpe, Tegwnne E	4:26:20 (18,619)	
Goldwin, Eleanor K	4:21:23 (17,270)	
Gomersall, Deborah	5:44:09 (31,678)	
Gomes, Dawn	4:40:18 (22,257)	
Gomez Chumillas, Aurora	4:57:23 (26,161)	
Gonella, Jayne L	4:36:55 (21,471)	
Gonzalez, Adela	4:43:42 (23,102)	
Gonzalez, Monica	4:03:10 (12,644)	
Gonzalez, Roberta	4:24:02 (18,007)	
Gooch, Gemma L	4:21:21 (17,259)	
Gooch, Paula M	4:45:59 (23,671)	
Gooch-Smith, Shelley	4:44:13 (23,233)	
Good, Emma J	5:54:14 (32,420)	
Good, Libby	5:00:15 (26,676)	
Goodburn, Sandy F	5:39:41 (31,311)	
Goodchild, Lorna M	4:49:07 (24,399)	
Goodchild, Vickie	4:31:33 (20,039)	
Goode, Lisa C	3:49:45 (8,758)	
Goodearl, Kerry L	7:51:21 (34,514)	
Gooden, Rachel S	5:08:54 (27,954)	
Goodenough, Jenny	4:33:47 (20,658)	
Goodenough, Vicki E	4:35:59 (21,241)	
Goodenough, Vikki	4:43:39 (23,088)	
Gooderham, Emma L	2:54:51 (737)	
Goodey, Jane E	4:09:37 (14,204)	
Goodge, Sharon P	5:22:49 (29,688)	
Goodman, Hollie	5:48:00 (31,978)	
Goodman, Madeline	4:26:57 (18,798)	
Goodman, Tracey	4:06:03 (13,301)	
Goodwin, Dee	5:37:57 (31,190)	
Goodwin, Jacqueline A	6:07:00 (33,019)	
Goodwin, Jacqui	4:31:38 (20,063)	
Goodwin, Julie	4:40:49 (22,388)	
Goodwin, Lucie	6:15:26 (33,274)	
Goodwin, Nicola C	3:59:40 (11,741)	
Goodwin, Rebekah J	4:25:34 (18,408)	
Goodyear, Rachael B	7:02:59 (34,240)	
Gook, Andrea	4:46:55 (23,888)	
Goorney, Joanna M	3:28:26 (4,545)	
Goral, Louise C	4:31:16 (19,952)	
Gordon, Claire	4:18:49 (16,579)	
Gordon, Hila	4:30:45 (19,816)	
Gordon, Julie M	3:44:22 (7,527)	
Gordon, Karen	4:49:42 (24,534)	
Gordon, Katie	4:31:40 (20,071)	
Gordon, Kirsty J	5:05:06 (27,418)	
Gordon, Lucy J	4:08:22 (13,874)	
Gordon, Mary A	4:40:46 (22,372)	
Gordon Spence, Nicky	5:12:45 (28,502)	
Gore, Sophie J	4:44:46 (23,358)	
Gorga, Cheryl E	5:00:54 (26,779)	

Gorman, Barbara	5:27:37 (30,214)	
Gormley, Alison R	3:24:07 (3,792)	
Gormley, Teresa M	5:24:48 (29,887)	
Gosby, Karen L	4:21:45 (17,389)	
Goscomb, Glenda I	3:53:43 (9,775)	
Goscomb, Joanna C	4:00:43 (12,039)	
Gosling, Rosie C	4:13:53 (15,273)	
Gosling, Tracy A	5:22:47 (29,684)	
Gosmore, Sara J	4:59:11 (26,512)	
Goss, Breda M	4:06:01 (13,294)	
Gott, Angela M	4:23:50 (17,946)	
Gouge, Louise E	4:38:14 (21,762)	
Gough, Julie L	5:10:35 (28,228)	
Gough, Teresa	5:07:41 (27,796)	
Goulart, Sylvia	4:32:03 (20,184)	
Gould, Aimée E	5:53:43 (32,388)	
Gould, Ann L	5:02:26 (27,031)	
Gould, Karen	4:04:11 (12,859)	
Gould, Lara	4:03:10 (12,644)	
Goulding, Michelle L	4:54:56 (25,683)	
Gouldthorpe, Anne	5:07:37 (27,785)	
Goult, Catherine E	5:21:07 (29,513)	
Goumiri, Katja	7:04:11 (34,254)	
Gourlay, Gill L	4:18:18 (16,434)	
Gourlay, Susan J	4:40:08 (22,221)	
Gouverne, Françoise	5:18:43 (29,255)	
Govier, Elizabeth A	8:12:53 (34,548)	
Govindraj, Martina J	5:39:16 (31,282)	
Gow, Caroline F	4:15:30 (15,704)	
Gow, Elizabeth N	4:09:32 (14,183)	
Gower, Belinda	4:22:18 (17,521)	
Gower, Heidi	6:02:33 (32,837)	
Gowers, Natalie R	4:43:04 (22,948)	
Gowland, Deborah	4:44:11 (23,224)	
Graat, M	3:44:44 (7,617)	
Grabowski, Sarah J	3:58:33 (11,317)	
Grace, Adina E	6:26:47 (33,593)	
Grace, Amanda J	4:29:58 (19,625)	
Grace, Jennifer	6:39:57 (33,879)	
Gracey, Linda M	5:10:09 (28,168)	
Gradwell, Emma J	4:08:57 (14,032)	
Grady, Nidale A	4:35:41 (21,164)	
Grady, Sarah J	3:33:16 (5,434)	
Grafton, Amelia J	4:43:58 (23,172)	
Graham, Aileen	5:42:26 (31,529)	
Graham, Anna	4:42:43 (22,858)	
Graham, Beth	4:14:12 (15,367)	
Graham, Debbie A	5:11:31 (28,333)	
Graham, Julie E	4:09:48 (14,251)	
Graham, Louisa M	3:40:50 (6,789)	
Graham, Sarah F	6:01:20 (32,790)	
Graham, Sukuri K	4:45:20 (23,500)	
Graham, Tracey	4:08:46 (13,985)	
Graham, Zeata S	5:07:12 (27,719)	
Graham-Campbell, Hatty J	4:28:54 (19,378)	
Graham-Dobson, Fiona J	4:23:02 (17,737)	
Grahame, Samantha K	4:59:56 (26,622)	
Grainger, Miriam A	3:57:12 (10,862)	
Grainger, Morgan A	4:12:08 (14,843)	
Grainger, Rebecca E	4:23:17 (17,813)	
Grant, Evelyn M	3:55:07 (10,241)	
Grant, Fiona M	4:55:45 (25,830)	
Grant, Joanne S	3:40:25 (6,723)	
Grant, Kirsty	4:50:16 (24,661)	
Grant, Maria	4:13:23 (15,136)	
Grant, Pamela C	3:39:33 (6,551)	
Grant, Vicki M	3:55:06 (10,233)	
Granville, Gail	4:11:47 (14,745)	
Grassick, Katie L	4:31:26 (20,010)	
Grasso, Gina	5:42:08 (31,514)	
Gratton, Jacqui L	4:30:01 (19,639)	
Graudt, Svetlana	5:32:50 (30,730)	
Graveling, Anne K	4:47:56 (24,132)	
Graves, Lucinda J	3:10:01 (1,989)	
Graves, Susan A	4:32:09 (20,212)	
Gravis, Karen H	6:03:54 (32,884)	
Gray, Bethany	4:04:30 (12,931)	
Gray, Caroline	4:18:14 (16,409)	
Gray, Caroline A	4:19:25 (16,728)	
Gray, Delia C	4:08:34 (13,931)	
Gray, Elaine	5:04:56 (27,387)	
Gray, Emily J	4:14:12 (15,367)	
Gray, Emily M	5:34:48 (30,917)	

Gray, Harriet.................5:16:55 (29,047)
Gray, Heather L............5:40:22 (31,364)
Gray, Helen C...............4:42:54 (22,907)
Gray, Irene...................4:46:46 (23,845)
Gray, Jane....................4:47:19 (23,989)
Gray, Jennifer L............3:56:32 (10,639)
Gray, Jessica H.............4:47:11 (23,955)
Gray, Joanne................5:05:50 (27,521)
Gray, Margaret R..........5:47:01 (31,911)
Gray, Marian B.............4:38:33 (21,842)
Gray, Michelle L...........4:37:23 (21,569)
Gray, Natasha V...........5:16:52 (29,039)
Gray, Pamela A.............4:50:42 (24,766)
Gray, Rosaire P............3:46:59 (8,104)
Gray, Sally M................3:28:38 (4,587)
Gray, Sharon................4:45:11 (23,462)
Gray, Susan E...............5:45:38 (31,808)
Gray, Victoria...............5:58:07 (32,644)
Gray, Wendy M............4:31:11 (19,934)
Grayson, Elizabeth E.....3:52:57 (9,553)
Grazebrook, Sam..........6:22:02 (33,463)
Greatrix, Emma L.........3:26:19 (4,161)
Greaves, Tracey...........3:44:14 (7,496)
Greedus, Maria L..........4:24:26 (18,122)
Green, Aleksandra.........4:09:31 (14,181)
Green, Ana-Maria.........4:02:37 (12,520)
Green, Andrea..............5:00:25 (26,696)
Green, Beverley L..........5:43:46 (31,631)
Green, Catherine...........4:24:00 (17,994)
Green, Charlotte M........4:38:49 (21,919)
Green, Christine M........6:13:20 (33,222)
Green, Deborah L..........5:16:09 (28,954)
Green, Diana................5:58:47 (32,687)
Green, Emma E.............4:05:54 (13,266)
Green, Gail..................4:36:36 (21,393)
Green, Heather C..........4:22:54 (17,703)
Green, Jacqueline W.......3:55:03 (10,216)
Green, Joanne..............4:50:44 (24,774)
Green, Judith M............4:11:32 (14,687)
Green, Julie S...............4:28:43 (19,318)
Green, Kay..................4:24:04 (18,013)
Green, Lucy J...............7:05:21 (34,267)
Green, Lucy R...............5:05:52 (27,525)
Green, Mandy...............5:22:04 (29,606)
Green, Melanie.............3:47:46 (8,289)
Green, Pauline..............4:27:12 (18,871)
Green, Sara J................4:25:11 (18,318)
Green, Sharon J............3:37:09 (6,088)
Green, Shelley..............4:29:06 (19,420)
Green, Victoria R..........5:12:20 (28,439)
Greenall, Laura A..........5:07:11 (27,716)
Greenall, Vicki A...........3:21:14 (3,389)
Greenan, Kathleen A......5:08:17 (27,856)
Greenbank, Deb............5:05:00 (27,404)
Greene, Margaret A.......4:06:56 (13,501)
Greene-Fraser, Hayley M..5:43:52 (31,639)
Greener, Alison.............4:11:11 (14,604)
Greenfield, Jacqueline D...5:28:25 (30,312)
Greenhalgh, Christy A.....4:23:24 (17,838)
Greenhalgh, Tina J........5:21:17 (29,534)
Greenidge, Tara............4:56:08 (25,900)
Greenlay, Deborah L......6:04:43 (32,913)
Greenlees, Sarah...........5:04:19 (27,294)
Greenslade, Elizabeth E..3:46:09 (7,919)
Greenwalker, Jennie E....4:05:07 (13,074)
Greenwell, Davina L.......4:52:51 (25,234)
Greenwood, Amanda J....4:08:49 (13,993)
Greenwood, Charlotte V..6:09:38 (33,099)
Greenwood, Jane E........4:52:01 (25,048)
Greenwood, Rachael C....5:42:54 (31,561)
Greer, Cathryn L...........4:13:25 (15,138)
Greer, Sara A...............4:24:25 (18,114)
Greggains, Susan J........4:52:41 (25,196)
Greggor, Ruth W...........4:28:30 (19,264)
Gregorczyk, Claudia.......4:39:32 (22,085)
Gregory, Ebonee K........5:20:11 (29,425)
Gregory, Elizabeth D......3:42:07 (7,051)
Gregory, Jane...............5:24:29 (29,857)
Gregory, Joanna M........5:17:17 (29,095)
Gregory, Katharine A......4:57:54 (26,263)
Gregory, Lisa J..............4:19:15 (16,688)
Gregory, Nicola.............4:57:42 (26,230)
Gregory, Sally...............6:54:50 (34,150)

Gregory, Sarah L...........3:36:14 (5,919)
Gregory, Tamsin M........4:25:18 (18,341)
Gregson, Matthew.........6:37:15 (33,825)
Gregurec, Julia.............4:28:45 (19,327)
Greif, Jessica................7:16:21 (34,373)
Greig, Amanda L...........4:15:43 (15,752)
Greig, Lucy G...............6:54:17 (34,140)
Greig, Natasha C...........5:21:42 (29,578)
Greisman, Abbie............5:31:48 (30,640)
Grenmark, Sara............3:27:54 (4,439)
Gretton, Jessica S..........3:56:34 (10,650)
Greville-Heygate, Claire E..4:21:41 (17,368)
Grey, Alison J...............5:12:48 (28,514)
Grey, Gemma M............4:59:33 (26,565)
Grey, Lucy C................5:03:18 (27,154)
Greyling, Letitia............5:19:06 (29,303)
Grice, Eleanor A............4:48:29 (24,243)
Grice, Helen G..............5:35:41 (30,997)
Grievson, Hannah E.......4:38:46 (21,902)
Griffin, Alison...............3:56:26 (10,605)
Griffin, Ann M..............5:14:32 (28,745)
Griffin, Beverley J..........4:37:24 (21,574)
Griffin, Chanese............4:28:56 (19,386)
Griffin, Erin L...............5:56:33 (32,560)
Griffin, Leah.................3:52:34 (9,448)
Griffin, Liane................5:55:13 (32,480)
Griffin, Linda................3:34:46 (5,656)
Griffin, Patricia.............5:12:30 (28,464)
Griffin, Rachel L............4:30:16 (19,691)
Griffith, Hannah M........4:18:19 (16,440)
Griffiths, Helen C...........5:50:18 (32,155)
Griffiths, Helen S...........5:00:03 (26,643)
Griffiths, Jane...............4:49:04 (24,388)
Griffiths, Kathleen L.......4:06:22 (13,366)
Griffiths, Kim L.............7:11:45 (34,341)
Griffiths, Lisa M............5:07:42 (27,797)
Griffiths, Madeline.........3:13:49 (2,438)
Griffiths, Nicola.............5:03:31 (27,186)
Griffiths, Rachael A........7:11:33 (34,338)
Griffiths, Rhian E...........5:03:33 (27,191)
Griffiths, Sarah K...........7:11:33 (34,338)
Griffiths, Tamsin C........4:39:40 (22,114)
Griffiths Jeans, Pauline M..4:51:17 (24,898)
Griggs, Jill E................4:16:38 (15,989)
Grillet, Marie-France......4:45:06 (23,434)
Grima, Claire M............2:55:36 (781)
Grime, Maria M............3:31:30 (5,127)
Grimshaw, Hannah M.....4:54:22 (25,553)
Grimshaw, Julie V..........3:51:58 (9,291)
Grimwood, Nicola L.......6:30:36 (33,675)
Grindu, Christiane.........4:34:25 (20,804)
Grisdale, Charlotte J......4:22:36 (17,613)
Grizzell, Nicola.............4:39:32 (22,085)
Groat, Katherine H........4:47:47 (24,098)
Grogan, Clare..............4:26:44 (18,738)
Grogan, Joan A.............4:54:37 (25,603)
Gromett, Samantha J......3:49:43 (8,752)
Grondin, Terese M.........3:39:15 (6,483)
Groom, Victoria C.........4:41:25 (22,537)
Grosperrin, Elisabeth.....4:53:54 (25,464)
Grossick, Sarah............5:01:57 (26,950)
Grosvenor, Emma C.......3:15:32 (2,705)
Grounds, Rachel L.........4:18:34 (16,519)
Grout, Gwyneth B.........5:40:40 (31,388)
Grove, Anna-Marie........6:12:48 (33,200)
Grove, Fiona................5:13:37 (28,628)
Grove, Lorraine A..........4:59:18 (26,534)
Grover, Linda A.............6:11:17 (33,147)
Groves, Alison M...........6:06:13 (32,992)
Groves, Brigitte............4:29:06 (19,420)
Groves, Laura K............3:39:59 (6,636)
Groves, Vicki A.............4:40:42 (22,353)
Grubb, Kirsty...............5:08:29 (27,893)
Gruet, Julie E...............5:01:47 (26,927)
Gruffydd, Mari W..........5:14:40 (28,770)
Grundeken, Debbie........5:18:49 (29,264)
Grundy, Maria S...........4:09:51 (14,262)
Guarnieri, Patrizia.........3:31:01 (5,055)
Guderley, Madeleine R....4:49:01 (24,376)
Gudgeon, Thea K..........3:14:18 (2,519)
Guild, Wendy B.............4:16:04 (15,853)
Guilfoyle, Alison...........4:32:46 (20,367)
Guillemin, Alison...........4:16:39 (15,997)

Guillerme, Sylvie...........3:59:22 (11,622)
Guimah, Camilla...........5:08:22 (27,868)
Guldberg, Cathinka A.....4:50:04 (24,617)
Gulliver, Lynne.............7:29:22 (34,451)
Gundle, Joanna L..........3:41:30 (6,940)
Gunn, Carol.................5:20:55 (29,488)
Gunn, Carole...............4:33:19 (20,516)
Gunn, Elaine................4:58:54 (26,455)
Gunn, Kim...................4:52:13 (25,084)
Gunnell, Sarah A...........5:13:42 (28,635)
Guridge, Katryna G........6:12:36 (33,190)
Gurney, Lisa J..............5:14:31 (28,741)
Gurpinar, Sevda E.........4:42:24 (22,780)
Gurrin, Nicola J.............4:38:01 (21,720)
Guthrie, Anna L............3:53:33 (9,726)
Guttery, Heather D........5:13:10 (28,564)
Gutzan, Eva.................4:23:34 (17,888)
Guy, Annette S.............4:21:24 (17,275)
Guy, Helen M...............4:54:42 (25,623)
Guy, Julie...................4:35:45 (21,177)
Guyton, Teresa M..........5:32:24 (30,693)
Guyver, Deirdre F..........6:39:08 (33,868)
Guzy, Magdalena P........4:14:00 (15,302)
Gwaderi, Razia.............7:03:38 (34,248)
Gwenaelle, Jaouen........4:58:51 (26,443)
Gwilliam, Victoria L.......5:14:04 (28,683)
Gwilliams, Gillian K........4:38:25 (21,805)
Gwynne, Veronica M......4:48:23 (24,222)
Gyekye, Elizabeth..........5:09:50 (28,123)
Gyulafia, Erica.............5:32:21 (30,686)
Haagen, Inez-Anne........3:03:17 (1,400)
Habberley, Sarah J........4:43:02 (22,940)
Hack, Michelle L............5:54:15 (32,422)
Hackett, Leila C............3:43:25 (7,327)
Hacking, Tara..............4:06:18 (13,355)
Hacon, Gweneth L.........4:45:36 (23,563)
Haddon, Amanda J........4:42:16 (22,746)
Haddon, Imogen F.........4:24:00 (17,994)
Haddon, Perie H............4:31:22 (19,983)
Haddow, Carol A...........7:06:30 (34,279)
Haddow, Emma J..........4:11:38 (14,712)
Hadingham, Charlotte S...4:19:31 (16,765)
Hadley, Susan..............5:17:02 (29,066)
Hagan, Anne................4:37:30 (21,592)
Hageman, Caroline........5:31:42 (30,635)
Hagen, Gemma A..........5:44:19 (31,698)
Haggan, Nicoli A...........5:09:30 (28,048)
Haggar, Rachel M..........3:38:16 (6,312)
Haggarty, Elaine L.........5:08:55 (27,955)
Hagger, Emily...............4:37:14 (21,534)
Haggman, Ann-Christine M..3:55:06 (10,233)
Hague, Sara C..............4:43:08 (22,968)
Haigh, Alexandra L........4:02:07 (12,392)
Haigh, Emma R.............4:30:13 (19,683)
Haigh, Gayatri M...........3:59:04 (11,511)
Hailey, Dee.................4:39:02 (21,981)
Haines, Nicola C............4:22:51 (17,686)
Haines, Sally A..............4:31:47 (20,097)
Haining, Hayley.............2:29:18 (61)
Hairsine, Jane E............5:13:16 (28,579)
Hairsine, Jay E..............3:15:40 (2,715)
Haiselden, Sally R..........4:06:38 (13,436)
Haji, Aliya..................6:16:34 (33,313)
Halbert, Gail A.............5:38:37 (31,231)
Hale, Caroline J............3:09:07 (1,897)
Hale, Lynda R..............4:38:46 (21,902)
Hales, Diane C.............4:41:21 (22,524)
Hales, Sarah L..............3:55:51 (10,452)
Hales, Vanessa C..........7:24:15 (34,424)
Halewood, Bridget........3:57:23 (10,919)
Halford, Catherine D......4:31:48 (20,103)
Halksworth, Liz............5:52:25 (32,313)
Hall, Alice K................4:54:22 (25,553)
Hall, Amelia.................3:08:20 (1,824)
Hall, Anita C................4:15:30 (15,704)
Hall, Carol..................3:55:36 (10,371)
Hall, Caroline A............3:39:27 (6,526)
Hall, Cathy A...............3:31:08 (5,066)
Hall, Deborah A............3:53:24 (9,696)
Hall, Denise.................4:03:43 (12,771)
Hall, Elizabeth A...........4:25:28 (18,386)
Hall, Emma-Louise........3:58:25 (11,268)
Hall, Frances...............7:05:22 (34,268)

Hall, Jayne A 4:16:19 (15,907)
Hall, Julia A 4:21:16 (17,244)
Hall, Kate L 4:23:54 (17,963)
Hall, Linda 5:44:39 (31,733)
Hall, Margaret 7:08:56 (34,302)
Hall, Martha A 3:09:33 (1,948)
Hall, Moira 4:29:35 (19,537)
Hall, Monique 4:10:13 (14,340)
Hall, Natasha S 4:23:24 (17,838)
Hall, Rebecca A 4:09:41 (14,220)
Hall, Rebecca A 4:19:26 (16,735)
Hall, Samantha E 5:10:50 (28,257)
Hall, Samantha J 5:33:00 (30,749)
Hall, Sarah L 4:30:27 (19,735)
Hall, Suzanne 4:46:26 (23,765)
Hall, Teresa M 4:05:54 (13,266)
Hall, Toni 4:49:20 (24,442)
Hall, Tracy 5:09:35 (28,068)
Halliday, Freja A 3:55:51 (10,452)
Halliday, Sarah 3:54:57 (10,179)
Hallidie, Phyllida L 4:59:57 (26,627)
Halliwell, Katy R 5:36:33 (31,085)
Hallock, Kathryn L 4:35:50 (21,200)
Halpin, Jill R 4:17:41 (16,276)
Halsall, Christine E 4:36:34 (21,384)
Hambleton, Karen L 4:16:27 (15,949)
Hambley, Susan A 8:12:31 (34,547)
Hamborg, Chloe S 4:38:04 (21,729)
Hambsch, Annette 5:59:49 (32,730)
Hamel, Dominique 3:54:25 (9,998)
Hamer, Kate N 6:08:13 (33,053)
Hamer-Davies, Elizabeth A 4:40:12 (22,240)
Hames, Caroline S 4:22:18 (17,521)
Hamilton, Joyce 4:47:30 (24,021)
Hamilton, Kirsty E 4:22:39 (17,631)
Hamilton, Robyn T 4:30:35 (19,770)
Hamilton, Victoria J 3:53:00 (9,572)
Hamlett, Suzanne J 6:42:01 (33,911)
Hamlin, Victoria L 4:38:37 (21,861)
Hamlyn, Lucy 4:13:33 (15,172)
Hammick, Victoria L 4:42:05 (22,692)
Hammond, Chloe 3:32:21 (5,291)
Hammond, Kathryn O 4:37:32 (21,600)
Hammond, Katie L 5:52:51 (32,331)
Hammond, Lesley M 4:58:02 (26,289)
Hammond, Lucy 4:43:55 (23,156)
Hammond, Michelle 4:45:25 (23,517)
Hammond, Michelle L 7:38:53 (34,480)
Hammond, Nina E 5:22:11 (29,623)
Hammond, Samantha L 3:35:04 (5,713)
Hammond, Stacey T 5:48:48 (32,032)
Hammond, Susan I 4:35:34 (21,122)
Hammond, Vicki E 4:58:02 (26,289)
Hampsey, Catherine M 6:13:07 (33,215)
Hampshire, Shiralee J 6:50:10 (34,078)
Hampson, Lisa 5:09:51 (28,125)
Hampton, Lara M 3:49:00 (8,579)
Hampton-Jones, Linda M 3:59:07 (11,535)
Hamshere, Jane 5:37:03 (31,121)
Hancock, Claire 5:33:51 (30,820)
Hancock, Jane 4:58:53 (26,450)
Hancock, Natalie 4:09:40 (14,216)
Hancock, Nicola 5:06:36 (27,636)
Hancock, Sioned 4:24:17 (18,077)
Hancox, Rebecca J 5:48:49 (32,033)
Hands, Angela M 6:00:53 (32,773)
Handyside, Beth M 3:26:33 (4,192)
Haniver, Kelley T 2:58:51 (1,047)
Hankin, Lesley A 5:23:14 (29,722)
Hanmer, Frankie 4:40:54 (22,402)
Hanna, Laurine I 4:49:22 (24,455)
Hanna, Rosemary 4:23:55 (17,968)
Hannah, Xanthe 3:45:05 (7,704)
Hannam, Catherine L 5:03:16 (27,143)
Hannan, Amanda J 4:10:12 (14,338)
Hannan, Patricia J 4:45:31 (23,541)
Hannaway, Jasmine 4:57:59 (26,278)
Hannaway, Michelle C 7:07:51 (34,290)
Hanney, Lynne 5:36:01 (31,033)
Hanrahan, Niamh 3:44:43 (7,610)
Hanrahan, Sarah J 4:34:27 (20,811)
Hanratty, Krista 3:54:19 (9,963)
Hansen, Carla M 4:50:11 (24,640)
Hanson, Stephanie A 4:50:34 (24,740)
Happs, Gillian S 4:43:22 (23,018)
Haque, Francesca M 4:39:16 (22,040)
Harbage, Abigail 5:20:30 (29,465)
Harber, Sandra A 5:21:05 (29,506)
Hard, Bernadette M 4:30:51 (19,850)
Hardcastle, Karen 4:45:03 (23,423)
Hardie, Petra 4:08:35 (13,937)
Harding, Amber C 3:41:13 (6,878)
Harding, Belinda 4:11:21 (14,633)
Harding, Lisa 6:44:33 (33,968)
Harding, Ljiljana 3:54:27 (10,008)
Harding, Susan E 5:54:38 (32,435)
Hardman, Frances R 3:46:42 (8,039)
Hardman, Gina V 3:20:24 (3,279)
Hardman, Jackie S 4:20:31 (17,032)
Hardman, Julie A 7:34:09 (34,469)
Hards, Anna 5:27:05 (30,156)
Hardwick, Mary D 3:56:02 (10,501)
Hardy, Carol P 4:55:14 (25,735)
Hardy, Emma 5:13:32 (28,610)
Hardy, Gill 3:40:41 (6,756)
Hardy, Karolynn 4:51:22 (24,919)
Hardy, Lorraine A 3:37:59 (6,260)
Hardy, Rachel M 3:44:14 (7,496)
Hardy, Victoria L 4:21:00 (17,182)
Hare, Amanda J 6:39:11 (33,870)
Harfstrand, Kristina 4:53:16 (25,326)
Hargadon, Sue E 4:23:01 (17,733)
Hargie, Patricia G 5:54:45 (32,441)
Hargrave, Celia 3:47:31 (8,225)
Hargreaves, Ann P 5:07:31 (27,769)
Harirs, Sophie H 4:41:54 (22,652)
Harker, Danielle R 4:22:48 (17,668)
Harkin, Christina M 7:01:05 (34,213)
Harkin, Leona M 7:01:05 (34,213)
Harkness, Ruth M 3:25:58 (4,102)
Harland, Julie 6:09:17 (33,090)
Harlock, Beth V 4:39:55 (22,170)
Harman, Rachel 4:16:01 (15,842)
Harmer, Amanda M 5:33:30 (30,786)
Harne, Vicky R 5:07:29 (27,762)
Harold, Laura M 6:03:04 (32,849)
Harper, Gillian E 3:58:19 (11,226)
Harper, Isabel 4:59:58 (26,629)
Harper, Jenny C 4:58:20 (26,348)
Harper, Joy 5:07:25 (27,755)
Harper, Julie A 8:17:23 (34,558)
Harper, Lorraine 4:20:35 (17,055)
Harper, Louise A 4:09:46 (14,247)
Harper, Sarah L 4:42:51 (22,892)
Harper, Zena 4:41:46 (22,622)
Harrington, Fiona A 4:17:52 (16,318)
Harrington, Tracy L 3:47:43 (8,282)
Harrington-Frost, Emma S 5:00:16 (26,679)
Harris, Belinda T 5:04:09 (27,272)
Harris, Carli 4:09:02 (14,050)
Harris, Charlotte M 3:30:41 (4,997)
Harris, Clare E 4:21:47 (17,402)
Harris, Denise 3:34:51 (5,679)
Harris, Emma J 4:17:28 (16,211)
Harris, Gillian R 4:27:33 (18,964)
Harris, Heather A 3:47:51 (8,313)
Harris, Jane E 3:41:33 (6,949)
Harris, Julie P 4:47:15 (23,969)
Harris, Kathryn L 4:50:38 (24,752)
Harris, Kim A 4:06:27 (13,386)
Harris, Laura 4:27:54 (19,065)
Harris, Lynne 4:05:53 (13,262)
Harris, Michelle L 3:35:49 (5,850)
Harris, Nancy 4:45:43 (23,592)
Harris, Nicola A 7:07:11 (34,284)
Harris, Philippa 5:02:21 (27,014)
Harris, Samantha J 3:30:41 (4,997)
Harris, Samantha R 5:09:26 (28,032)
Harris, Sandra 5:49:46 (32,104)
Harris, Sharon A 7:19:54 (34,395)
Harris, Sharon C 4:20:42 (17,095)
Harris, Tammie A 5:39:31 (31,298)
Harris, Vikki 4:09:02 (14,050)
Harrison, Amy C 5:04:14 (27,285)
Harrison, Carmel F 3:58:03 (11,131)
Harrison, Gil M 3:29:05 (4,688)
Harrison, Helen 4:35:35 (21,129)
Harrison, Julie H 5:57:27 (32,604)
Harrison, Karen 3:28:06 (4,481)
Harrison, Lydia 6:29:14 (33,641)
Harrison, Lydia G 4:28:21 (19,223)
Harrison, Megan A 4:40:53 (22,398)
Harrison, Michelle A 5:34:27 (30,880)
Harrison, Michelle L 6:52:14 (34,116)
Harrison, Patricia S 3:49:26 (8,681)
Harrison, Rachel L 4:42:35 (22,827)
Harrison, Sarah 4:17:38 (16,258)
Harrison, Susan M 5:35:39 (30,992)
Harrison-Jeive, Bridget H 5:22:45 (29,681)
Harrison-Mirfield, Lucy J 5:06:52 (27,677)
Harriss, Celia M 3:57:30 (10,953)
Harrop, Elaine C 5:31:18 (30,596)
Harrop, Jennifer V 5:48:25 (32,004)
Harrop, Louise M 4:32:10 (20,215)
Hart, Catherine 4:29:35 (19,537)
Hart, Cherie-Anne C 3:51:10 (9,089)
Hart, Christine V 4:55:34 (25,792)
Hart, Harriet B 3:22:15 (3,524)
Hart, Joanne M 3:49:50 (8,778)
Hart, Julie 4:55:00 (25,700)
Hart, Louise A 3:55:48 (10,437)
Hart, Samantha J 4:38:57 (21,961)
Harte, Joanne M 5:33:45 (30,807)
Hartgill, Denby L 3:34:26 (5,610)
Hartland, Emily J 6:10:06 (33,120)
Hartle, Catherine 3:38:54 (6,427)
Hartley, Anna J 4:00:25 (11,951)
Hartley, Victoria H 4:08:07 (13,801)
Hartney, Liz E 2:49:24 (484)
Hartsilver, Emma L 3:56:00 (10,491)
Hartwell, Anna 4:34:15 (20,768)
Hartwright, Caryl E 4:22:30 (17,582)
Harvey, Caroline A 4:34:37 (20,849)
Harvey, Grace 5:12:52 (28,533)
Harvey, Rosemary C 4:33:48 (20,661)
Harvey, Toni 4:51:27 (24,930)
Harward, Nicola F 3:24:43 (3,872)
Harwood, Abigail E 5:11:49 (28,387)
Harwood, Lesley 5:22:29 (29,662)
Hasegawa, Mayuko 4:21:43 (17,380)
Hasell, Lucy 2:40:31 (205)
Haskin, Julia T 5:24:00 (29,806)
Haskins, Laura M 4:05:16 (13,113)
Haslam, Sally D 5:25:54 (30,021)
Hassler-De Vos, Silvia 4:15:04 (15,584)
Hastings, Kerry A 4:58:29 (26,373)
Hastings, Linda 5:26:51 (30,137)
Hastings, Sarah 5:00:36 (26,718)
Hatchard, Bryony E 5:18:00 (29,181)
Hathaway, Daphne L 4:44:30 (23,303)
Hatherley, Marilyn J 4:03:55 (12,807)
Hatton, Janet 3:14:13 (2,504)
Hatton, Karen L 4:21:55 (17,430)
Hauser, Anne C 3:43:28 (7,337)
Havers, Roberta I 4:33:07 (20,461)
Haverson, Gillian F 5:04:20 (27,298)
Haviland, Clare 4:27:22 (18,924)
Hawker, Sue D 4:56:27 (25,957)
Hawkes, Deborah J 4:02:39 (12,533)
Hawkes, Jennifer 4:46:15 (23,727)
Hawkes, Leigh S 4:07:26 (13,625)
Hawkins, Emma L 4:05:30 (13,178)
Hawkins, Fiona 3:10:30 (2,041)
Hawkins, Fiona E 4:00:32 (11,982)
Hawkins, Jennifer 4:34:22 (20,790)
Hawkins, Kelly L 5:14:34 (28,754)
Hawkins, Melissa 4:13:25 (15,138)
Hawkins, Naomi J 4:22:49 (17,676)
Hawkins, Sally 4:58:01 (26,284)
Hawkins, Sharon J 3:01:45 (1,292)
Hawkins, Simone E 4:39:17 (22,043)
Hawkins, Tilly J 5:14:06 (28,686)
Hawkins, Victoria M 4:35:53 (21,209)
Hawley, Charlotte E 6:36:53 (33,821)
Haworth, Emma C 3:44:38 (7,587)
Haworth, Madeline M 4:02:46 (12,556)
Hay, Jennifer P 4:36:03 (21,251)
Hayeems, Deborah 4:49:31 (24,478)
Hayes, Annabelle P 4:34:32 (20,829)

Hayes, Carla 4:28:05 (19,125)
Hayes, Carol A 4:24:13 (18,056)
Hayes, Dawn 5:50:13 (32,145)
Hayes, Donna 5:53:53 (32,399)
Hayes, Judy E 4:52:18 (25,104)
Hayes, Katherine A 4:40:08 (22,221)
Hayes, Sandie L 4:04:10 (12,856)
Hayes, Sandra C 6:01:43 (32,807)
Hayes-Gill, Claire S 3:24:40 (3,863)
Hayler, Hannah L 4:36:27 (21,358)
Hayler, Karen A 5:18:06 (29,190)
Hayley Bell, Catherine 4:09:41 (14,220)
Hayman, Lucy 4:54:48 (25,649)
Haynes, Clare 5:44:38 (31,732)
Haynes, Lisa A 4:35:51 (21,203)
Haynes, Lynne 3:22:50 (3,615)
Haynes, Susan J 4:43:28 (23,035)
Hayter, Jay C 5:07:40 (27,794)
Hayward, Joanne E 4:26:53 (18,784)
Hayward, Leanne 4:53:02 (25,280)
Hayward, Leanne 7:43:20 (34,491)
Hayward, Lizzie 4:57:25 (26,168)
Hayward, Samantha L 3:28:23 (4,534)
Haywood, Diane 3:22:30 (3,564)
Haywood, Elizabeth A 3:55:52 (10,457)
Haywood, Emma 4:57:26 (26,172)
Haywood, Gillian M 5:22:27 (29,657)
Haywood, Wendy M 5:07:13 (27,722)
Hazel, Sam J 7:01:57 (34,230)
Hazelden, Stephanie J 5:10:55 (28,268)
Hazeldine, Debra J 7:17:13 (34,377)
Hazell, Clair L 5:13:32 (28,610)
Hazell, Katharine E 4:13:27 (15,149)
Hazzard, Susan 3:37:11 (6,098)
Head, Andrea 5:05:10 (27,431)
Head, Joanna 5:46:18 (31,861)
Heading, Emily S 5:27:36 (30,209)
Headley, Fiona J 3:51:58 (9,291)
Headon, Leah R 3:32:52 (5,372)
Heal, Rebecca R 5:39:27 (31,294)
Heales, Carol J 3:50:54 (9,028)
Healey, Melanie J 4:51:41 (24,982)
Healey, Samantha 6:45:37 (33,994)
Healy, Fiona N 3:45:53 (7,877)
Healy, Sharon 5:06:46 (27,660)
Heapy, Karen A 4:45:20 (23,500)
Hearfield, Tessa 3:54:29 (10,022)
Hearn, Amy L 3:42:35 (7,150)
Hearn, Angela 6:05:29 (32,951)
Hearn, Claire A 5:17:56 (29,171)
Hearn, Jacqueline M 4:37:43 (21,644)
Hearn, Leona K 6:18:18 (33,366)
Hearn, Sarah J 5:35:29 (30,977)
Hearn, Trudy E 4:38:44 (21,893)
Heartford, Stacey L 5:35:36 (30,988)
Heasman, Jo M 5:57:20 (32,596)
Heath, Kirsty L 4:39:29 (22,076)
Heath, Nicola J 4:27:05 (18,834)
Heath, Rachel H 4:35:24 (21,082)
Heath, Theresa I 6:45:00 (33,978)
Heather, Lucy J 5:46:44 (31,897)
Heaton, Christine 3:23:13 (3,665)
Heaton, Mathilde M 3:16:55 (2,854)
Heavey, Laura K 4:24:26 (18,122)
Heavey, Sarah 3:56:51 (10,743)
Heaviside, Karen M 3:18:16 (3,012)
Hecher, Lisi 3:59:10 (11,548)
Heckman, Christine E 4:19:06 (16,659)
Hector, Kathy A 4:21:25 (17,284)
Hedberg, Maj N 5:24:04 (29,815)
Hedges, Angela M 3:57:33 (10,969)
Hedges, Georgina 5:19:15 (29,323)
Hedges, Julie A 3:40:34 (6,741)
Hedley Lewis, Penny A 4:10:17 (14,365)
Heenan, Rachael A 7:09:59 (34,320)
Heffer, Katharine L 4:16:03 (15,849)
Heffer, Lorna M 7:23:34 (34,420)
Hegerty, Gabrielle M 4:42:51 (22,892)
Hehn, Antje 3:11:28 (2,146)
Heighway, Jenny 5:17:36 (29,137)
Heimdal, Ann-Thérèse 4:39:29 (22,076)
Heine, Victoria A 5:09:49 (28,117)
Heite, Louise 4:17:39 (16,265)
Heller, Beatrice E 4:19:44 (16,821)
Hellings, Geraldine A 3:55:28 (10,331)
Helliwell, Annette 5:49:03 (32,057)
Helliwell, Rebecca A 4:16:58 (16,082)
Helme, Samantha J 7:26:20 (34,438)
Helsby, Genevieve E 3:35:46 (5,840)
Heminsley, Alexandra L 5:04:05 (27,261)
Heminsley, Caroline F 3:17:57 (2,981)
Hemmings, Kirston 5:51:18 (32,237)
Hemmings, Lisa 6:17:19 (33,330)
Hemmington, Caroline 4:54:07 (25,504)
Hempenius, Evelyn 5:23:18 (29,725)
Hempsall, Theresa K 3:16:58 (2,860)
Hemsley, Anne C 4:01:52 (12,329)
Hemsworth, Caroline 3:19:34 (3,172)
Hemsworth, Jane 4:14:16 (15,387)
Hemsworth, Marion V 4:01:03 (12,121)
Henderson, Gillian A 7:56:17 (34,527)
Henderson, Jacqueline 5:12:42 (28,494)
Henderson, Jennifer M 5:09:45 (28,107)
Henderson, Kate M 5:33:41 (30,795)
Henderson, Kerry L 4:29:45 (19,578)
Henderson, Krista P 3:58:59 (11,481)
Henderson, Noreen 3:55:59 (10,488)
Henderson, Tina J 4:18:36 (16,534)
Henderson, Winifred 7:09:59 (34,320)
Hendle, Joanna M 4:38:48 (21,912)
Hendrick, Louise 4:45:28 (23,534)
Hendry, Alexandra 7:54:55 (34,524)
Hendry, Ann M 6:15:29 (33,275)
Hendry, Jacquelyn M 5:58:05 (32,638)
Hendry, Susan C 4:56:31 (25,973)
Henkes, Renata 4:06:51 (13,484)
Hennigan, Kirsten E 3:42:46 (7,190)
Henrikson, Jacqueline T 5:22:41 (29,676)
Henry, Amanda 3:06:54 (1,675)
Henry, Carole A 4:45:54 (23,651)
Henry, Fredricka T 3:49:27 (8,686)
Henry, Katie 3:43:30 (7,345)
Henry, Kirsty A 4:00:44 (12,043)
Henry, Kirsty J 6:56:51 (34,181)
Henry, Nicola J 3:58:19 (11,226)
Henry, Victoria A 6:02:24 (32,830)
Henry-Brown, Rebecca L 4:41:30 (22,559)
Henshall, Angela C 5:35:55 (31,023)
Heracleous, Marie 5:33:55 (30,826)
Herath, Kirrily J 5:27:17 (30,176)
Herath, Suvendrini A 5:00:08 (26,659)
Herbert, Asha 4:26:43 (18,731)
Herbert-Evans, Hannah 4:02:11 (12,413)
Herbertson, Rebecca A 4:18:33 (16,513)
Herfert, Sandra 4:15:59 (15,832)
Herman, Elizabeth J 3:47:26 (8,205)
Hermer, Yasmina 4:35:17 (21,051)
Hermolle, Jennie L 4:32:36 (20,327)
Hernandez, Edith 4:06:49 (13,476)
Hernandez, Maria C 4:22:49 (17,676)
Hernon, Michelle K 4:55:16 (25,745)
Herold, Anne 3:06:36 (1,644)
Heron, Gill D 4:43:16 (22,998)
Heron, Joan E 4:15:13 (15,622)
Heron, Judith A 5:11:15 (28,301)
Herrington, Jane 5:09:01 (27,974)
Herterich, Kimberley 3:45:46 (7,849)
Heseltine, Emma L 6:21:52 (33,460)
Heseltine, Sarah 4:50:33 (24,733)
Hesketh, Jo Anne 3:13:57 (2,460)
Heslegrave, Amanda J 4:09:05 (14,060)
Heslip, Andrea L 4:20:41 (17,089)
Heslop, Karen R 3:55:55 (10,470)
Hester, Angela R 4:10:42 (14,462)
Hetherington, Alexandra M 3:38:46 (6,402)
Hetherington, Tracey 4:11:41 (14,729)
Hettich, Teresa N 3:54:03 (9,887)
Hewer, Sue J 5:10:21 (28,198)
Hewer, Susan E 5:55:03 (32,464)
Hewett, Lorraine F 4:28:25 (19,238)
Hewison, Frances M 5:48:56 (32,046)
Hewitson, Diane 4:38:11 (21,752)
Hewitt, Catherine E 3:16:48 (2,847)
Hewitt, Kirsty J 4:31:00 (19,882)
Hewlett, Zoe M 5:04:09 (27,272)
Hewson, Annabel R 4:46:02 (23,678)
Heycock, Carol 3:24:28 (3,840)
Heydecker, Deirdre A 3:41:58 (7,019)
Heyes, Fiona J 4:30:26 (19,728)
Heyland, Fiona H 5:32:02 (30,666)
Heywood, Victoria E 4:33:11 (20,475)
Hguhes, Elizabeth A 6:05:30 (32,952)
Hibberd, Briony 4:21:59 (17,449)
Hibbert, Babitah 4:05:07 (13,074)
Hibbert, Kate 5:14:46 (28,782)
Hickey, Alicia A 3:59:47 (11,774)
Hickey, Claire 5:27:30 (30,201)
Hickey, Sarah E 4:58:41 (26,417)
Hickey, Sarah H 5:09:55 (28,132)
Hickling, Francesca K 4:33:17 (20,504)
Hickling, Rizalina M 6:34:23 (33,758)
Hickling, Tina M 4:24:29 (18,137)
Hickman, Breeda M 3:39:00 (6,437)
Hickman, Helen E 4:27:32 (18,960)
Hickman, Julia M 4:30:45 (19,816)
Hickman, Susan 4:59:09 (26,500)
Hicks, Beverley A 5:07:17 (27,736)
Hicks, Caroline L 5:28:31 (30,326)
Hier, Diane R 3:09:47 (1,970)
Higgins, Sara N 4:11:28 (14,665)
Higgins, Tracey 4:32:43 (20,351)
Higgs, Alison J 6:16:03 (33,295)
Higgs, Laura A 4:15:44 (15,763)
Higgs, Lucinda S 4:38:44 (21,893)
Higham, Rosalie D 4:18:36 (16,534)
Highgate, Cath J 3:49:27 (8,686)
Higins, Angela 3:52:10 (9,351)
Higson, Susan M 5:05:07 (27,423)
Hildenbrandt, Birgit 4:46:46 (23,845)
Hilget, Ruth 4:16:27 (15,949)
Hili, Carmen 3:03:38 (1,426)
Hill, Anna 6:07:12 (33,027)
Hill, Caroline J 5:33:55 (30,826)
Hill, Catherine 4:45:47 (23,617)
Hill, Christine M 4:25:47 (18,473)
Hill, Deborah J 4:57:52 (26,255)
Hill, Hazel M 5:04:59 (27,397)
Hill, Janet M 3:55:21 (10,298)
Hill, Kate 6:07:43 (33,034)
Hill, Katherine J 3:42:04 (7,042)
Hill, Maxcine M 5:56:38 (32,564)
Hill, Naomi K 5:11:26 (28,323)
Hill, Nicola J 4:19:39 (16,797)
Hill, Paula 3:19:15 (3,128)
Hill, Rachael L 4:58:20 (26,348)
Hill, Rebecca L 3:38:46 (6,402)
Hill, Samantha L 4:10:45 (14,483)
Hill, Tracy J 4:23:46 (17,937)
Hill, Tracy M 5:04:50 (27,372)
Hill, Zoe C 6:24:43 (33,540)
Hillier, Ann B 3:33:19 (5,444)
Hillis, Kathryn M 5:52:24 (32,312)
Hillman, Donna S 3:03:01 (1,374)
Hillman, Joanna E 6:47:03 (34,020)
Hillman, Lucy A 4:31:53 (20,135)
Hills, Fiona 4:32:54 (20,401)
Hills, Frida A 5:33:18 (30,773)
Hills, Karen 4:23:58 (17,981)
Hills, Nicole L 4:39:52 (22,162)
Hills, Tanya A 6:35:32 (33,786)
Hilman, Paula K 4:24:26 (18,122)
Hilson, Lin 6:28:00 (33,624)
Hilton, Sarah C 4:37:43 (21,644)
Hiluk, Justine J 5:13:32 (28,610)
Hinchcliffe-Lancaste, Thea 6:02:29 (32,833)
Hinchelwood, Sarah L 8:36:04 (34,571)
Hind, Tia 3:27:45 (4,408)
Hinde, Helen S 4:29:18 (19,472)
Hindley, Jo C 3:54:22 (9,978)
Hinds, Georgina L 4:07:58 (13,767)
Hindson, Shelley 4:07:43 (13,702)
Hine, Sophie I 3:17:50 (2,965)
Hines, Emma L 4:05:13 (13,105)
Hines, Sarah E 5:55:13 (32,480)
Hinge, Caroline 4:49:14 (24,420)
Hinkley, Clare 4:41:35 (22,575)
Hinshelwood, Linda 4:17:49 (16,311)
Hinton, Frances 4:52:53 (25,247)
Hinton, Jessica L 3:52:05 (9,327)

Hinton, Sarah J 4:24:10 (18,039)
Hird, Linda D 3:44:52 (7,648)
Hirons, Sarah R 3:33:24 (5,451)
Hirotsuna, Shoko 5:48:31 (32,013)
Hirsch, Karin 7:24:12 (34,423)
Hirst, Marion P 5:59:44 (32,727)
Hirst, Susan E 4:06:16 (13,352)
Hiscox, Sarah M 3:34:36 (5,630)
Hiskett, Loretta 5:33:28 (30,783)
Hitch, Tracy D 5:00:37 (26,723)
Hitchcock, Joanne S 4:35:25 (21,088)
Hitchen, Abigail 5:21:58 (29,596)
Hitchman, Katy V 6:37:37 (33,832)
Hladun, Jana L 4:40:34 (22,321)
Ho, Renyung 5:32:53 (30,737)
Ho, Wendy 6:18:52 (33,376)
Hoare, Christina L 4:58:10 (26,320)
Hoare, Emma 4:14:43 (15,499)
Hoareay, Juliette R 4:07:01 (13,522)
Hobart, Kelly 4:14:59 (15,553)
Hobbs, Fiona A 3:54:32 (10,045)
Hobbs, Jenny 6:09:43 (33,109)
Hobbs, Samantha L 5:09:20 (28,019)
Hobbs, Sarah E 5:48:21 (31,998)
Hobden, Hannah F 3:56:17 (10,557)
Hobson, Amanda J 5:07:02 (27,700)
Hobson, Gemma K 4:31:13 (19,942)
Hobson, Jacqueline A 4:26:06 (18,566)
Hochfeld, Kim 3:48:40 (8,504)
Hodder, Rebecca J 3:28:18 (4,518)
Hodder, Tracey L 4:28:47 (19,343)
Hoddinott, Sarah R 4:47:22 (24,001)
Hoddle, Kirsten V 4:42:29 (22,800)
Hodge, Abbie L 5:52:12 (32,303)
Hodge, Nicola J 4:45:24 (23,510)
Hodges, Rachael L 4:46:23 (23,759)
Hodgson, Sharon A 4:45:24 (23,510)
Hodkinson, Julie 4:54:55 (25,676)
Hodkinson, Rachel A 6:24:37 (33,536)
Hodkinson, Susan 3:26:38 (4,213)
Hodson, Emma R 4:06:13 (13,333)
Hofbauer, Claudia 3:52:18 (9,386)
Hoffmann, Elisabeth 3:56:49 (10,730)
Hogarth, Sarah 4:35:40 (21,157)
Hogg, Janet E 4:33:18 (20,511)
Hoggins, Rachel D 5:03:44 (27,213)

Holden, Amanda 4:13:22 (15,132)

Holden, Amy R 3:46:45 (8,050)
Holden, Danielle C 5:02:47 (27,079)
Holden, Janet C 4:46:16 (23,733)
Holden, Sarah L 5:29:57 (30,474)
Holden, Vivienne A 4:51:44 (24,994)
Holder, Claire L 4:38:00 (21,716)
Holder, Kate S 3:58:53 (11,451)
Holding, Dawn 3:58:05 (11,137)
Holditch, Susan L 5:11:18 (28,308)
Holdridge, Lorraine 6:02:30 (32,835)
Holdstock, Anne E 5:05:54 (27,532)
Holdsworth, Catherine 4:22:59 (17,722)
Holdsworth, Sophia C 7:11:16 (34,332)
Hole, Gemma Louise 4:13:51 (15,259)
Hole, Sarah 4:07:07 (13,549)
Holl, Jennifer 4:44:06 (23,202)
Holland, Kay 5:14:50 (28,788)
Holland, Laura M 5:17:51 (29,161)
Holland, Marie 4:06:36 (13,428)
Holland, Michelle 4:27:53 (19,058)
Holland, Victoria M 5:21:16 (29,530)
Hollett, Georgie V 3:52:12 (9,360)
Holley, Kathryn G 6:05:49 (32,967)
Holley, Louise A 4:36:22 (21,339)
Hollgran, Sorcha 4:39:58 (22,175)
Holliday, Jill 4:32:52 (20,392)
Hollingsworth, Karen L 4:39:07 (22,008)
Hollington, Rachael 5:25:20 (29,970)
Hollington, Victoria 7:16:55 (34,375)
Hollins, Annick 4:24:11 (18,045)
Hollinshead, Elizabeth A 6:25:21 (33,557)
Hollinshead, Monique G 3:15:47 (2,727)
Hollis, Victoria A 4:08:06 (13,789)
Holloran, Kirsty L 5:05:17 (27,445)
Hollyer, Tracy-Jane 6:26:29 (33,584)
Holman, Aimée 4:06:48 (13,474)
Holmes, Caroline T 3:43:32 (7,350)
Holmes, Gill R 4:34:08 (20,733)
Holmes, Jasmine C 5:34:53 (30,927)
Holmes, Lorna G 6:04:27 (32,906)
Holmes, Lorna M 4:25:52 (18,502)
Holmes, Nicole 4:24:55 (18,245)
Holmes, Rachel M 4:16:48 (16,038)
Holohan, Caroline A 5:18:01 (29,183)
Holroyd, Annette B 4:54:11 (25,518)
Holsgrove, Anna 5:27:20 (30,184)
Holt, Carol 6:50:47 (34,087)
Holt, Jayne 4:24:11 (18,045)
Holt, Saba G 3:16:06 (2,766)
Holt, Tina 4:59:36 (26,574)
Home, Lynda A 4:03:00 (12,609)
Homer, Britta 3:42:42 (7,172)
Homer, Jo 6:12:51 (33,203)
Homewood, Ellen F 3:11:32 (2,153)
Hood, Anita J 5:19:56 (29,406)
Hood, Lindsey C 5:15:21 (28,860)
Hood, Sijbrigje A 6:22:08 (33,464)
Hook, Lyn 4:01:28 (12,232)
Hooke, Penelope E 4:20:52 (17,144)
Hooper, Emily J 4:38:45 (21,898)
Hooper, Helen A 5:19:04 (29,298)
Hooper, Rosie 6:04:05 (32,889)
Hooser, Daniele 4:59:35 (26,570)
Hooton, Jacqueline T 4:50:35 (24,743)
Hope, Geraldine 3:24:12 (3,804)
Hope, Helen J 3:55:04 (10,222)
Hope, Margaret 6:53:14 (34,127)
Hopgood, Jeannie 4:41:10 (22,478)
Hopkins, Alison C 3:03:15 (1,396)
Hopkins, Jill A 4:41:47 (22,628)
Hopkins, Jodie P 4:35:21 (21,068)
Hopkins, Sorrel 4:37:57 (21,704)
Hopkins, Victoria H 4:55:32 (25,786)
Hopkinson, Emma N 4:23:38 (17,900)
Hopwell, Sally A 4:41:06 (22,460)
Hopwood, Fiona J 3:31:13 (5,082)
Horabin, Bernadette A 4:20:01 (16,890)
Horder, Caroline M 3:32:38 (5,338)
Hordosva, Iveta 4:20:33 (17,043)
Hore, Angela 5:14:53 (28,801)
Horgan, Joanne L 4:33:25 (20,550)
Horler, Emma C 4:19:20 (16,711)
Horn, Shannon 5:29:25 (30,414)
Horne, Alexandra E 6:49:15 (34,066)
Horne, Emma M 4:35:10 (21,024)
Horne, Jennifer L 3:10:32 (2,048)
Horne, Jody 6:16:20 (33,302)
Horne, Pauline E 4:31:22 (19,983)
Horner, Nicola 5:38:47 (31,244)
Horner, Vanessa M 4:22:52 (17,691)
Hornett, Angela D 3:48:08 (8,385)
Hornsby, Suzanne 6:17:08 (33,324)
Horrell, Tara M 3:41:44 (6,974)
Horsburgh, Anne G 5:57:11 (32,588)
Horsman, Kathy 3:26:38 (4,213)
Horton, Carolyn A 4:21:32 (17,315)
Horton, Elaine R 4:51:49 (25,010)
Horton, Jacqueline 5:45:48 (31,820)
Horton, Lisa M 5:24:54 (29,905)
Horton, Lucy A 4:59:15 (26,523)
Horton, Rachel E 4:42:47 (22,874)
Hoskin, Fiona A 6:57:16 (34,183)
Hoskinson, Christie L 3:50:36 (8,955)
Hosono, Masae 4:49:55 (24,583)
Hosseini, Sophia 4:30:32 (19,758)
Hossick, Rhiannon M 5:06:15 (27,591)
Hostler, Emma L 3:58:13 (11,196)
Hostler, Rowan Tracey 3:51:36 (9,196)
Hothi, Rajinder 4:24:27 (18,128)
Hough, Stephanie L 5:32:15 (30,681)
Houghton, Carolyn 4:28:09 (19,151)
Houghton, Christina A 5:05:43 (27,512)
Houghton, Sharon D 4:27:50 (19,033)
Houghton, Teresa E 5:32:14 (30,677)
Houghton, Tracey 4:37:47 (21,663)
Houlden, Sarah J 4:19:36 (16,781)
Houlder, Melanie 4:35:56 (21,220)
Houlder, Sophie E 3:57:07 (10,842)
Houlihan-Burne, Caroline C 4:03:48 (12,788)
Houlston, Bridget J 4:04:21 (12,905)
House, Clare L 4:34:56 (20,949)
House, Kim M 5:46:53 (31,903)
House, Rachel L 5:32:33 (30,704)
House, Stephanie C 3:59:46 (11,770)
Housley, Kirsty D 4:48:54 (24,346)
Houston, Diane G 4:45:43 (23,592)
Houston, Lynette 4:43:05 (22,954)
Houtas, Lucy C 4:44:53 (23,392)
Hovden, Aase S 3:27:13 (4,315)
Hovell, Anne 4:49:40 (24,525)
Howard, Bobi M 6:42:46 (33,935)
Howard, Christine 3:41:32 (6,945)
Howard, Julie E 7:17:19 (34,378)
Howard, Katrina 4:56:54 (26,052)
Howard, Laura J 4:23:17 (17,813)
Howard, Lucy 6:22:48 (33,483)
Howard, Nicola J 3:59:35 (11,705)
Howard, Rebecca A 4:56:55 (26,060)
Howard, Samantha T 4:46:00 (23,674)
Howard, Sarah J 4:26:03 (18,552)
Howarth, Beverley H 4:31:19 (19,972)
Howarth, Camilla 4:28:05 (19,125)
Howarth, Cathrine 4:39:05 (21,999)
Howarth, Clare 4:00:26 (11,957)
Howarth, Elizabeth A 4:00:57 (12,102)
Howarth, Marie 4:41:47 (22,628)
Howarth, Sally E 3:52:04 (9,324)
Howden, Victoria K 4:45:44 (23,598)
Howe, Angela D 2:51:02 (556)
Howe, Angela L 6:15:07 (33,271)
Howe, Carolyn 4:42:07 (22,701)
Howe, Emma C 5:28:05 (30,276)
Howe, Tina 4:30:23 (19,719)
Howell, Anna P 4:44:25 (23,276)
Howell, Jacqueline S 5:25:55 (30,025)
Howell, Katrina E 6:05:36 (32,958)
Howell, Linda 3:15:17 (2,669)
Howell, Samantha J 4:32:52 (20,392)
Howes, Georgina 4:46:58 (23,900)
Howes, Helen A 5:36:30 (31,081)
Howes, Kim T 3:22:07 (3,503)
Howes, Pauline C 4:45:09 (23,452)
Howie, Margie L 3:15:51 (2,737)
Howkins, Linda J 3:58:10 (11,174)
Howles, Stephanie 4:04:27 (12,919)
Howlett, Midge E 4:20:28 (17,015)
Howlin, Michelle C 6:24:23 (33,529)
Howson, Christine 5:37:19 (31,144)
Hoyle, Antonia 4:02:58 (12,602)

Hoyle, Elizabeth A 4:33:52 (20,676)
Hoyle, Emily S 4:33:52 (20,676)
Hoyle, Helen E 3:17:47 (2,961)
Hoyle, Kathleen A 4:57:40 (26,225)
Hoyle, Stephanie J 4:10:38 (14,449)
Hoyte, Angela P 5:44:20 (31,701)
Hubbick, Joanne S 4:07:53 (13,745)
Hubert, Charlotte E 5:41:09 (31,426)
Huck, Alison J 5:26:13 (30,060)
Huckell, Melanie G 5:46:53 (31,903)
Huckle, Lita M 4:56:28 (25,963)
Huddy, Louisa C 4:54:25 (25,564)
Hudec-Plasencia, Monika 4:21:54 (17,422)
Hudson, Annabel J 5:25:09 (29,943)
Hudson, Catherine J 4:50:33 (24,733)
Hudson, Diane 4:02:49 (12,569)
Hudson, Jenny E 5:32:35 (30,710)
Hudson, Jude A 5:26:01 (30,038)
Hudson, Kathryn J 5:38:51 (31,253)
Hudson, Kerry 4:52:34 (25,161)
Hudson, Kym 3:55:19 (10,292)
Hudson, Lindsay 3:48:49 (8,532)
Hudson, Lisa J 4:00:42 (12,034)
Hudson, Lynn 3:47:58 (8,341)
Hudson, Naomi A 4:20:41 (17,089)
Hudson, Sarah J 3:49:04 (8,593)
Hudson, Sheila 5:29:42 (30,445)
Huestis, Gretchen 3:28:25 (4,538)
Huggett, Bridget M 5:06:34 (27,633)
Huggins, Celine 3:52:04 (9,324)
Hughes, Breda M 5:03:28 (27,177)
Hughes, Christina E 4:29:50 (19,594)
Hughes, Connie 4:05:42 (13,222)
Hughes, Helen C 6:52:46 (34,123)
Hughes, Jane 5:42:05 (31,507)
Hughes, Kate E 5:32:34 (30,708)
Hughes, Katharine S 3:54:40 (10,089)
Hughes, Leana R 6:13:31 (33,228)
Hughes, Liz 4:38:23 (21,796)
Hughes, Marina 6:45:23 (33,987)
Hughes, Megan 4:02:07 (12,392)
Hughes, Nicola R 4:47:51 (24,106)
Hughes, Penny J 6:33:52 (33,743)
Hughes, Rachael J 5:00:45 (26,751)
Hughes, Sally 4:50:15 (24,656)
Hughes, Shona 3:33:14 (5,426)
Hughes, Susan M 5:46:12 (31,853)
Hughes-Conway, Jacqueline K 4:30:05 (19,650)
Hugi, Christine 4:21:29 (17,300)
Huliat, Sharan 4:46:35 (23,793)
Hull, Elizabeth J 4:37:46 (21,659)
Hulland, Gaynor A 3:39:41 (6,572)
Hully, Anne 4:41:13 (22,493)
Humble, Susan J 5:05:34 (27,491)
Hume, Alison J 5:59:46 (32,729)
Hume, Michelle A 4:17:04 (16,112)
Humpage, Lorna 5:10:17 (28,186)
Humphreys, Alison 4:05:58 (13,289)
Humphreys, Jann 4:45:24 (23,510)
Humphreys, Linda F 6:19:45 (33,390)
Humphreys, Melitsa 4:17:25 (16,195)
Humphreys, Nicola J 6:15:30 (33,277)
Humphries, Frances P 4:06:37 (13,433)
Hung, Kitty S 4:49:21 (24,451)
Hunnable, Claire E 6:26:03 (33,578)
Hunninghake, Sara 3:41:30 (6,940)
Hunt, Helen D 4:47:56 (24,132)
Hunt, Jemma A 4:14:09 (15,354)
Hunt, Kim 8:30:28 (34,566)
Hunt, Lesley 4:39:44 (22,137)
Hunt, Lisa J 4:20:45 (17,103)
Hunt, Nicola J 3:28:42 (4,606)
Hunt, Rachel L 5:15:44 (28,910)
Hunt, Susanna J 5:03:21 (27,163)
Hunter, Annette T 4:11:08 (14,581)
Hunter, Charlotte E 5:45:21 (31,792)
Hunter, Dale 6:57:50 (34,186)
Hunter, Marianne J 5:52:16 (32,306)
Hunter, Marie C 4:55:36 (25,801)
Hunter, Marsha 5:55:30 (32,502)
Hunter, Nicola L 5:31:34 (30,617)
Hunter, Rachel S 3:33:44 (5,512)
Hurd, Tracey 5:16:16 (28,968)
Hurley, Cliona T 4:22:34 (17,601)
Hurley, Nicola 4:18:54 (16,599)
Hurran, Barbara 8:29:12 (34,565)
Hurst, Christine M 7:26:04 (34,436)
Hurst, Colette J 5:06:16 (27,598)
Hurst, Faye 4:31:42 (20,082)
Hurst, Jodie C 4:54:58 (25,694)
Hurst, Rana S 5:15:07 (28,834)
Hurtado Sanchez, Lorena 5:04:26 (27,312)
Hussey, Nicola J 5:51:17 (32,236)
Hussey, Nicola L 4:32:06 (20,197)
Hüsseyin, Çiğdem E 5:24:39 (29,873)
Hustler, Willa V 5:00:00 (26,633)
Hutchings, Joanna C 3:57:16 (10,883)
Hutchinson, Amy 4:30:25 (19,724)
Hutchinson, Elizabeth A 4:24:00 (17,994)
Hutchinson, Ellie F 4:50:56 (24,829)
Hutchinson, Judith 5:09:38 (28,079)
Hutchinson, Kira D 3:55:57 (10,477)
Hutchinson, Sally 5:38:49 (31,251)
Hutchinson, Samantha E 3:17:34 (2,937)
Hutchinson, Susan J 4:32:13 (20,233)
Hutchison, Kylie D 4:14:31 (15,453)
Hutley, Susannah L 5:13:43 (28,640)
Hutson, Tracey J 5:01:01 (26,798)
Hutton, Angela M 4:13:15 (15,098)
Hutton, Celina J 3:54:33 (10,052)
Hutton, Paraskevi 5:29:33 (30,429)
Huxham, Charlene J 4:22:46 (17,661)
Huxley, Tracey 5:34:11 (30,854)
Huxtable, Emily M 5:22:02 (29,602)
Huxtable, Fiona 4:37:38 (21,625)
Huxtable, Gail 4:02:18 (12,446)
Hyatt, Kate E 3:46:48 (8,059)
Hyatt-Williams, Sarah J 5:10:17 (28,186)
Hyde, Alison C 6:46:28 (34,008)
Hyland, Lorna J 4:39:58 (22,175)
Hynan, Kate 4:26:50 (18,765)
Hynd, Julie 4:04:11 (12,859)
Hyndman, Alexandra 5:53:10 (32,350)
Hyndman, Jody E 4:52:05 (25,062)
Hyne, Joanna 4:06:27 (13,386)
Hynes, Jane C 4:47:10 (23,949)
Hynes, Mary 6:51:24 (34,102)
Iannella, Pamela C 4:21:59 (17,449)
Ianson, Jennifer L 5:29:45 (30,453)
Ibell, Emma L 3:21:07 (3,376)
Igoe, Lorraine C 3:46:28 (8,001)
Igoe, Susan E 6:15:51 (33,290)
Iles, Amanda J 4:08:43 (13,973)
Iles, Kirsten 5:41:55 (31,493)
Illgner, Amalia 4:59:16 (26,527)
Illingworth, Barbara J 4:33:25 (20,550)
Illman, Sarah J 4:07:08 (13,553)
Iman, Safia 6:24:22 (33,528)
Imina, Grace 6:08:58 (33,081)
Imperato, Carmelina 5:17:14 (29,089)
Imrie, Claire E 3:06:35 (1,643)
Ince, Sarah L 5:12:27 (28,453)
Ind, Katherine C 4:20:36 (17,061)
Ingleden, Georgina J 3:43:13 (7,290)
Ingledew, Clare 4:25:52 (18,502)
Ingledew, Judith E 4:34:09 (20,739)
Ingledew, Sally 4:48:19 (24,212)
Ingleton, Beverley A 4:38:32 (21,831)
Inglis, Chloe 4:09:04 (14,058)
Ingram, Helen 3:47:10 (8,142)
Ingram, Judi E 5:01:08 (26,816)
Innes, Jennifer G 4:06:08 (13,322)
Innes, Jill M 5:44:09 (31,678)
Inzinger, Gabriele 3:59:29 (11,668)
Ireland, Esme M 4:18:40 (16,546)
Ireland, Nicola J 6:03:31 (32,868)
Ireland, Tracey 4:52:40 (25,190)
Irish, Victoria E 5:18:42 (29,253)
Irlam, Lisa J 4:02:10 (12,409)
Irons, Claire L 4:35:37 (21,145)
Irvine, Elizabeth M 4:58:03 (26,293)
Irwin, Ellen J 4:20:21 (16,985)
Isaac, Kristina 4:31:00 (19,882)
Isanzu, Maria 6:04:20 (32,904)
Isbill, Joanna F 3:50:08 (8,854)
Isherwood, Amanda P 4:50:09 (24,633)
Ishikawa, Marisa G 5:14:35 (28,757)
Island, Sheridan R 4:39:31 (22,082)
Ison, Lucy J 4:18:16 (16,421)
Israeli, Naama 5:31:50 (30,644)
Itani, Aysha A 5:44:47 (31,747)
Iturbide, Alejandra R 5:43:26 (31,604)
Iturbide, Maria 4:55:59 (25,875)
Ivantsoff, Mariana J 3:31:47 (5,186)
Ives, Alysia 5:29:42 (30,445)
Ives, Jane A 4:48:42 (24,290)
Ives, Tracy A 5:53:30 (32,377)
Iwanska, Anna K 4:33:50 (20,667)
Iwasaki, Yoko 4:44:49 (23,375)
Izelaar, Liesbeth 4:36:29 (21,364)
Jack, Nicola 4:14:10 (15,357)
Jack, Rhona W 3:58:46 (11,397)
Jack, Victoria A 5:02:24 (27,027)
Jackman, Kelly A 4:20:47 (17,118)
Jacks, Annette F 4:58:34 (26,390)
Jackson, Aimée D 3:47:51 (8,313)
Jackson, Amy E 4:58:25 (26,364)
Jackson, Amy E 5:42:32 (31,532)
Jackson, Anne 4:50:46 (24,787)
Jackson, Cat 5:19:01 (29,291)
Jackson, Connie 4:21:29 (17,300)
Jackson, Elaine 4:28:46 (19,335)
Jackson, Elizabeth L 4:49:20 (24,442)
Jackson, Gillian L 4:21:41 (17,368)
Jackson, Glen P 3:59:46 (11,770)
Jackson, Hannah L 6:06:09 (32,988)
Jackson, Hannah R 3:59:46 (11,770)
Jackson, Jayne E 4:44:55 (23,397)
Jackson, Jennifer A 4:15:58 (15,828)
Jackson, Kathy J 4:32:06 (20,197)
Jackson, Laura J 4:46:01 (23,677)
Jackson, Lisa J 4:29:38 (19,547)
Jackson, Lucy 4:12:11 (14,859)
Jackson, Maeve 5:04:00 (27,252)
Jackson, Rebecca L 5:11:41 (28,362)
Jackson, Ria 4:25:42 (18,444)
Jackson, Sarah L 4:01:30 (12,241)
Jackson, Sylvia C 5:44:29 (31,722)
Jackson, Tessa 6:34:49 (33,769)
Jackson, Zoe L 6:03:25 (32,862)
Jackson-Mayne, Susanne 5:53:12 (32,354)
Jackson-Smith, Hayley K 4:50:44 (24,774)
Jackson-Spillman, Janie D 4:25:39 (18,429)
Jacob, Mary R 4:49:07 (24,399)
Jacobs, Caroline S 4:31:21 (19,978)
Jacobs, Jennifer E 4:19:17 (16,701)
Jacobson, Glenys M 4:48:58 (24,366)
Jacques, Carly S 3:55:58 (10,483)
Jacques, Hayley L 4:29:08 (19,434)
Jaffe-Wilcockson, Roberta M 4:29:00 (19,399)
Jaggard, Caroline F 3:53:34 (9,732)
Jago, Angela S 4:42:29 (22,800)
Jamal, Rabia S 5:11:12 (28,295)
James, Ceinwen C 4:40:45 (22,367)
James, Christine J 4:54:45 (25,638)
James, Claire S 4:33:25 (20,550)
James, Dianne M 7:11:28 (34,336)
James, Emily J 4:22:06 (17,471)
James, Georgina A 5:21:54 (29,592)
James, Helen 4:19:00 (16,625)
James, Jane A 3:20:46 (3,327)
James, Joanna 4:15:52 (15,801)
James, Julia C 4:02:56 (12,592)
James, Katherine M 3:27:30 (4,363)
James, Kayrene 6:01:39 (32,799)
James, Kerry L 4:09:04 (14,058)
James, Laura 5:45:33 (31,805)
James, Laura J 5:16:37 (29,008)
James, Linda J 4:20:09 (16,928)
James, Louise E 5:15:06 (28,833)
James, Melanie D 6:16:21 (33,305)
James, Natasha J 5:39:06 (31,270)
James, Samantha L 6:09:41 (33,104)
James, Sarah 5:47:33 (31,954)
James, Sarah E 5:34:34 (30,892)
James, Sarah L 4:55:06 (25,718)
James, Susan M 4:32:16 (20,245)
James, Valerie M 5:09:23 (28,026)
James Duff, Nicola M 4:59:12 (26,516)

Jameson, Judy....4:44:10 (23,219)
Jamieson, Alexandra S....6:22:01 (33,462)
Jamieson, Bella M....4:40:22 (22,279)
Jamieson, Cathryn....5:50:15 (32,149)
Jamil, Saniya....4:24:57 (18,249)
Jane, Victoria....3:32:16 (5,271)
Janey, Corine....3:15:29 (2,700)
Janiaud, Muriel....5:38:59 (31,261)
Jannetta, Francesca A....4:21:54 (17,422)
Janse Van Rensburg, Alida M....5:12:29 (28,461)
Janse Van Rensburg, Deidre E....5:20:11 (29,425)
Jansen, Anna L....6:14:09 (33,245)
Jansen, Ellis....4:39:41 (22,122)
Jansen, Margaret....3:58:47 (11,406)
Jansen, Ruth J....4:23:13 (17,792)
Japheth, Alaw....4:31:57 (20,159)
Jaras, Francisca....4:34:38 (20,855)
Jardine, Lucy A....6:34:06 (33,752)
Jarman, Sarah L....4:33:15 (20,493)
Jarrett, Louise A....4:34:01 (20,699)
Jarrett, Rebecca....4:54:56 (25,683)
Jarvis, Anna R....6:03:31 (32,868)
Jarvis, Jacki L....3:15:00 (2,627)
Jarvis, Naomi L....4:48:08 (24,173)
Jarvis, Patricia J....4:28:49 (19,351)
Jaschke, Denise....4:42:31 (22,812)
Jasper, Rebecca A....3:56:48 (10,727)
Jay, Carinne M....3:42:18 (7,094)
Jayant, Tracy J....3:59:09 (11,544)
Jayawardena, Crishi....4:31:41 (20,074)
Jeacocke, Faye....4:09:30 (14,174)
Jeans, Polly E....4:09:52 (14,271)
Jedrej, Nicola S....4:10:39 (14,451)
Jefferies, Mary....5:08:03 (27,831)
Jefferson, Holly R....3:57:07 (10,842)
Jefferson, Nicola M....3:11:21 (2,132)
Jeffery, Debra J....4:47:21 (23,998)
Jeffery, Louise....5:17:40 (29,141)
Jeffery, Natalie D....5:42:06 (31,511)
Jeffery, Viviane J....4:56:11 (25,910)
Jeffries, Amber H....4:36:24 (21,344)
Jeffs, Laura D....6:33:20 (33,731)
Jellett, Victoria L....7:52:37 (34,517)
Jelley, Jodie L....4:09:29 (14,165)
Jemmett-Allen, Michelle....4:17:20 (16,181)
Jenkin, Sally C....4:17:26 (16,200)
Jenkins, Caroline C....4:10:15 (14,351)
Jenkins, Christina L....3:49:40 (8,736)
Jenkins, Francesca L....5:39:08 (31,272)
Jenkins, Greta....3:46:17 (7,948)
Jenkins, Jacqueline L....4:12:18 (14,885)
Jenkins, Katie R....4:52:08 (25,070)
Jenkins, Michelle....4:22:30 (17,582)
Jenkins, Rita....5:18:56 (29,282)
Jenkins, Susannah J....5:26:24 (30,088)
Jenkins, Teresa A....5:58:58 (32,693)
Jenkins, Wanda M....5:01:28 (26,866)
Jenkins-Bullmore, Cara....5:04:33 (27,336)
Jenks, Jennifer C....3:38:58 (6,436)
Jenner, Lizzie....4:20:24 (16,997)
Jenner, Lynsey C....5:40:26 (31,368)
Jennings, Amanda E....4:49:25 (24,462)
Jennings, Amy A....4:10:24 (14,388)
Jennings, Jennifer....5:11:37 (28,348)
Jennings, Samantha....4:51:36 (24,960)
Jennings, Sylvia M....5:14:36 (28,759)
Jennings, Yvonne S....5:13:24 (28,595)
Jennison, Cara A....4:30:50 (19,843)
Jensen, Alexandra F....5:25:23 (29,976)
Jensen, Margit....5:09:34 (28,066)
Jensen, Wendy....5:48:32 (32,014)
Jenssen, Linda....4:12:01 (14,814)
Jereissati, Heloisa M....6:49:05 (34,055)
Jerrom, Samantha L....4:43:54 (23,154)
Jesson, Maree....3:00:27 (1,199)
Jewell, Natalie A....3:57:58 (11,106)
Jewett, Melanie K....3:31:55 (5,203)
Jewitt, Yvette....4:05:27 (13,161)
Jewson, Rachel J....5:01:30 (26,871)
Jeynes, Anne J....3:46:38 (8,028)
Jhappan, Shauna....4:26:48 (18,753)
Job, Genevieve....5:17:25 (29,111)
Jobson, Diane....3:20:20 (3,270)
Jobsz, Nicole S....4:04:50 (13,007)
Johansen, Gerda....4:27:53 (19,058)
Johansson, Annette G....4:13:12 (15,081)
Johansson, Eva....3:36:31 (5,972)
John, Caroline V....3:33:39 (5,495)
John, Helen L....5:19:04 (29,298)
John, Helen M....3:54:54 (10,160)
John, Lorna....4:15:44 (15,763)
John, Lowri A....5:23:23 (29,733)
Johns, Catherine E....4:57:08 (26,115)
Johns, Imogen C....3:48:46 (8,525)
Johnson, Anita A....4:44:00 (23,180)
Johnson, Charlotte R....4:32:45 (20,363)
Johnson, Christine A....3:51:27 (9,164)
Johnson, Frances K....4:08:28 (13,901)
Johnson, Hayley....5:51:11 (32,223)
Johnson, Heather K....4:26:57 (18,798)
Johnson, Helen Y....4:53:25 (25,354)
Johnson, Jane M....4:54:29 (25,577)
Johnson, Jayne A....5:12:28 (28,458)
Johnson, Jeanette E....3:27:42 (4,396)
Johnson, Joann....5:35:42 (30,999)
Johnson, Katie M....5:30:41 (30,544)
Johnson, Kirstin F....4:00:38 (12,013)
Johnson, Kirsty M....4:57:04 (26,098)
Johnson, Lisa J....4:41:39 (22,598)
Johnson, Louise....3:53:18 (9,661)
Johnson, Michelle G....4:57:07 (26,110)
Johnson, Nicola S....5:32:00 (30,662)
Johnson, Riona....5:54:07 (32,413)
Johnson, Sara V....6:04:53 (32,921)
Johnson, Sarah....5:58:51 (32,689)
Johnson, Sarah J....5:32:31 (30,701)
Johnson, Sharon L....3:29:30 (4,782)
Johnson, Sophie A....4:49:00 (24,375)
Johnson, Susan R....4:50:22 (24,680)
Johnson, Treena....3:09:13 (1,912)
Johnson, Wendy S....5:02:15 (26,999)
Johnsson, Marion....4:04:23 (12,912)
Johnston, Carron....4:13:52 (15,266)
Johnston, Catherine....6:26:03 (33,578)
Johnston, Catherine E....3:58:10 (11,174)
Johnston, Clare M....4:10:43 (14,467)
Johnston, Emma....5:18:21 (29,212)
Johnston, Nicola D....5:37:57 (31,190)
Johnston, Sarah E....4:31:10 (19,928)
Johnston, Tracey....5:58:12 (32,651)
Johnston, Yvette....3:56:56 (10,774)
Johnstone, Jade E....3:39:23 (6,516)
Johnstone, Melanie....4:15:23 (15,663)
Johnstone, Ruth E....3:15:45 (2,722)
Jones, Amanda....3:49:06 (8,601)
Jones, Amanda E....5:15:27 (28,874)
Jones, Anna....4:35:24 (21,082)
Jones, Annbritt....5:09:18 (28,009)
Jones, Barbara A....4:14:42 (15,495)
Jones, Barbara E....4:33:41 (20,633)
Jones, Bethan....3:18:53 (3,084)
Jones, Caren P....6:16:40 (33,315)
Jones, Caroline A....3:13:07 (2,348)
Jones, Caroline S....4:19:18 (16,704)
Jones, Carys H....4:35:29 (21,108)
Jones, Catherine L....5:22:08 (29,619)
Jones, Catherine M....3:55:22 (10,304)
Jones, Ceri R....4:45:35 (23,555)
Jones, Christina....5:02:24 (27,027)
Jones, Claire A....3:50:46 (9,002)
Jones, Claire L....5:33:28 (30,783)
Jones, Clarissa L....4:42:28 (22,793)
Jones, Claudia E....4:41:11 (22,484)
Jones, Cynthia J....4:56:07 (25,898)
Jones, Donna E....5:16:49 (29,033)
Jones, Elisabeth....5:03:08 (27,123)
Jones, Elizabeth H....4:26:28 (18,654)
Jones, Elizabeth J....5:22:13 (29,629)
Jones, Eluned H....4:22:15 (17,509)
Jones, Emily J....4:33:01 (20,434)
Jones, Gillian E....4:31:12 (19,938)
Jones, Heather M....5:12:51 (28,525)
Jones, Heidi....7:28:53 (34,449)
Jones, Helen....4:53:48 (25,440)
Jones, Jacqueline....3:15:02 (2,635)
Jones, Jane....3:24:26 (3,835)
Jones, Jemma I....5:43:37 (31,618)
Jones, Jenni L....6:09:59 (33,116)
Jones, Jennifer A....5:12:40 (28,480)
Jones, Joanne S....4:47:56 (24,132)
Jones, Julie B....5:36:16 (31,060)
Jones, Karen....5:55:43 (32,508)
Jones, Karen....6:13:26 (33,225)
Jones, Kate E....3:41:27 (6,924)
Jones, Keston D....5:13:51 (28,655)
Jones, Kim S....4:59:03 (26,485)
Jones, Kimberley L....5:05:21 (27,450)
Jones, Kirsty D....4:15:46 (15,774)
Jones, Laura J....4:40:48 (22,379)
Jones, Lauren....4:12:25 (14,910)
Jones, Lauren J....4:30:30 (19,744)
Jones, Linda....6:46:39 (34,013)
Jones, Linda M....3:32:58 (5,383)
Jones, Liz....5:37:16 (31,136)
Jones, Lyndsey M....4:20:40 (17,084)
Jones, Mandy J....5:08:47 (27,943)
Jones, Marie E....4:29:50 (19,594)
Jones, Michelle....4:30:31 (19,749)
Jones, Michelle....5:50:25 (32,166)
Jones, Milly....4:20:42 (17,095)
Jones, Miss Vanessa....4:50:15 (24,656)
Jones, Nicola A....4:26:21 (18,621)
Jones, Patricia M....4:17:48 (16,305)
Jones, Rebecca....5:16:03 (28,943)
Jones, Rebecca....5:38:12 (31,207)
Jones, Rebecca L....3:56:02 (10,501)
Jones, Rebecca L....5:15:11 (28,843)
Jones, Ruth....5:04:51 (27,376)
Jones, Samantha K....5:27:53 (30,251)
Jones, Sarah....5:21:35 (29,570)
Jones, Sarah....5:58:19 (32,656)
Jones, Sarah J....5:43:12 (31,587)
Jones, Sarah L....3:51:20 (9,132)
Jones, Sharon L....4:21:30 (17,308)
Jones, Shirley A....5:21:53 (29,591)
Jones, Siana....3:52:36 (9,454)
Jones, Susan J....6:06:24 (33,000)
Jones, Teresa....6:10:50 (33,135)
Jones, Toni L....5:24:57 (29,908)
Jones, Tracey....3:51:40 (9,220)
Jones, Tracey....4:27:11 (18,868)
Jones, Tracy J....3:41:59 (7,022)
Jones, Vanessa D....4:28:45 (19,327)
Jones, Victoria R....4:32:29 (20,293)
Jones, Wendy....4:46:42 (23,829)
Jones, Wendy....5:01:46 (26,925)
Jones, Yvonne....4:14:29 (15,446)
Jones, Yvonne I....3:36:48 (6,021)
Jones, Yvonne J....4:32:57 (20,421)
Jones, Zoe....4:52:00 (25,042)
Jones, Zoe R....5:09:35 (28,068)
Jordaan, Antalene N....4:42:56 (22,915)
Jordan, Janet M....5:56:03 (32,525)
Jordan, Rebecca H....3:56:46 (10,714)
Jordanous, Anna K....5:11:54 (28,400)
Joseph, Christine....7:44:13 (34,493)
Joseph, Jacqueline H....5:21:47 (29,585)
Josette, Lange....5:48:55 (32,042)
Jowett, Nina S....4:01:24 (12,217)
Joyce, Carol B....4:13:02 (15,045)
Joyner, Lesley J....5:16:17 (28,969)
Joynson, Britt....4:42:57 (22,920)
Jpegrum, Louise....4:07:52 (13,739)
Jubb, Gail D....5:05:15 (27,442)
Juchau, Nathalie G....4:00:55 (12,086)
Juengling, Nina....5:00:43 (26,742)
Juillet, Laura H....4:49:33 (24,491)
Jukes, Victoria A....4:47:58 (24,139)
Julin, Barbro K....4:49:14 (24,420)
Juma, Fatma M....4:18:43 (16,556)
Jump, Alison J....4:10:13 (14,340)
Jump, Allison E....4:40:48 (22,379)
Juneja, Anita K....6:05:23 (32,941)
Junes, Louise A....5:35:36 (30,988)
Jupp, Tracy S....5:11:16 (28,305)
Jury, Pauline A....5:48:27 (32,008)
Just, Karin....3:39:53 (6,614)
Justin, Ellen E....4:50:13 (24,644)
Juszczyk, Agnieszka E....5:28:53 (30,364)

Jutte, Harvinder K 4:40:09 (22,226)
Kahl, Martine R 4:12:08 (14,843)
Kain Barrett, Emma L 3:59:46 (11,770)
Kajlich, Anya S 4:43:39 (23,088)
Kakitie, Patience I 4:31:45 (20,088)
Kakiuchi, Sahoko 4:37:37 (21,621)
Kakiuchi, Sawako 4:50:10 (24,637)
Kana, Pravina 5:25:09 (29,943)
Kane, Lesley G 4:34:46 (20,897)
Kane, Wendy L 4:58:52 (26,446)
Kapadia, Geeta M 6:00:49 (32,769)
Karanicola, Androulla 4:28:33 (19,279)
Karlsson, Helen 4:41:51 (22,651)
Karlsson, Lena 5:12:35 (28,472)
Karlsson, Mathilde 5:12:35 (28,472)
Kasak, Ella 5:06:09 (27,576)
Katory, Joanna E 4:08:06 (13,789)
Kaus, Kristen R 3:56:52 (10,749)
Kavanagh, Anne 3:37:02 (6,070)
Kavanagh, Janette S 4:28:01 (19,103)
Kavanagh, Pam A 4:36:06 (21,268)
Kavanagh-O'Brien, Susan J 5:51:42 (32,268)
Kawamura, Emiko 5:31:10 (30,579)
Kay, Angela 4:28:10 (19,159)
Kay, Catherine 5:31:12 (30,585)
Kay, Lucy A 4:42:54 (22,907)
Kay, Naomi 4:44:27 (23,286)
Kaye, Judith A 4:32:10 (20,215)
Kaye, Patricia 4:20:54 (17,152)
Keal, Irene 6:00:45 (32,766)
Keane, Francesca 5:18:09 (29,193)
Keane, Mandy I 4:50:51 (24,805)
Keane, Rowena M 4:50:56 (24,829)
Keaney, Jenny L 4:36:19 (21,328)
Keaney-Gahn, Sarah 6:01:42 (32,804)
Kear, Kim 5:34:12 (30,858)
Kear, Lisa M 4:03:57 (12,820)
Kearley, Emma 4:34:40 (20,865)
Kearley, Gwen A 5:13:52 (28,658)
Kearney, Lesley E 4:01:11 (12,159)
Kearney, Lucy V 6:12:17 (33,179)
Kearns, Lindsay E 4:01:27 (12,230)
Keast, Sarah A 3:27:18 (4,332)
Keating, Bernadette M 6:59:45 (34,206)
Keating, Janette C 6:42:41 (33,932)
Keeble, Jo 4:24:44 (18,201)
Keeble, Vivienne M 4:54:38 (25,606)
Keegans, Pauline 4:33:05 (20,452)
Keelan, Amanda E 4:24:28 (18,133)
Keeling, Woppy 3:54:45 (10,114)
Keenan, Mandy 4:42:38 (22,840)
Keenan, Nicola A 6:58:58 (34,196)
Keep, Myra 5:02:21 (27,014)
Kehoe, Megan 4:58:44 (26,432)
Keigher, Sally A 3:39:41 (6,572)
Keighley, Clare M 5:00:43 (26,742)
Keighley, Deborah J 5:16:09 (28,954)
Kejser, Lotte 3:35:04 (5,713)
Kelbie, Faye M 5:30:48 (30,553)
Kell, Lisa A 4:33:30 (20,577)
Keller, Françoise 4:39:12 (22,027)
Keller-Buchheit, Gudrun 5:25:33 (29,990)
Kellett, Deborah 4:47:58 (24,139)
Kelly, Angela J 6:17:51 (33,351)
Kelly, Beryl M 4:39:29 (22,076)
Kelly, Carolyn I 3:54:30 (10,034)
Kelly, Donna 4:55:27 (25,775)
Kelly, Doreen E 7:29:33 (34,454)
Kelly, Geraldine 4:30:20 (19,706)
Kelly, Jennifer 4:56:33 (25,980)
Kelly, Leigh S 5:08:19 (27,857)
Kelly, Margaret 3:45:06 (7,709)
Kelly, Maureen 5:06:42 (27,652)
Kelly, Melissa S 5:29:33 (30,429)
Kelly, Roni 5:56:19 (32,547)
Kelly, Sandra K 5:53:11 (32,352)
Kelly, Sarah L 4:43:19 (23,007)
Kelly, Sarah M 4:50:50 (24,801)
Kelly, Vanessa C 6:46:57 (34,018)
Kelly, Vicky M 3:12:45 (2,295)
Kelsey, Gita M 4:43:31 (23,054)
Kemp, Linda L 5:57:31 (32,606)
Kemp, Tracy A 4:58:28 (26,371)

Big numbers

300 litres of paint, marking the course, is steam-cleaned off as the last runner passes. It's put down on the eve of the race. There's 100 kilometres of barrier tape around the course. There are 1,100 marshals at the start, 2,500 at the finish and 3,500 on the route. You shouldn't get lost.

Kench, Tracey 5:48:22 (32,000)
Kendall, Anna R 5:21:21 (29,542)
Kendall, Charlie 4:44:37 (23,330)
Kendall, Jeanette F 3:30:32 (4,978)
Kendall, Jessica S 4:32:48 (20,374)
Kendall, Sarah 4:24:00 (17,994)
Kenden, Fran 3:46:18 (7,952)
Kenn, Amanda J 4:13:04 (15,054)
Kennard, Susan J 4:41:12 (22,488)
Kennedy, Caroline A 5:00:32 (26,711)
Kennedy, Catherine H 7:17:39 (34,381)
Kennedy, Helena 6:33:53 (33,744)
Kennedy, Iryna G 4:10:03 (14,305)
Kennedy, Linda 3:45:37 (7,817)
Kennedy, Maura T 4:05:24 (13,146)
Kennedy, Sandra F 5:05:36 (27,498)
Kennedy, Siobhan 4:50:17 (24,663)
Kennedy, Susan E 4:10:56 (14,531)
Kennedy, Wendy E 4:42:18 (22,755)
Kennelly, Michelle R 5:43:42 (31,627)
Kennerley, Elizabeth L 4:25:18 (18,341)
Kennet, Jane 3:55:15 (10,275)
Kennett, Elizabeth J 3:12:36 (2,276)
Kennett, Mandy E 4:43:04 (22,948)
Kent, Alison 4:44:27 (23,286)
Kent-Lemon, Belinda 6:45:58 (34,004)
Kenworthy, Adel 3:42:22 (7,111)
Kenyon, Caroline M 4:48:18 (24,208)
Kenyon, Sarah 3:32:13 (5,263)
Keogh, Deborah J 4:27:40 (18,990)
Keough, Julie 4:00:36 (12,004)
Keough, Lisa A 5:16:55 (29,047)
Ker, Christine E 5:36:27 (31,076)
Ker, Madeleine A 5:33:43 (30,801)
Kerai, Vasanti K 5:54:46 (32,443)
Kerby-Collins, Elizabeth A 3:36:26 (5,954)
Kerner, Caroll 3:40:51 (6,793)
Kerner, Lacie C 6:18:10 (33,360)
Kerr, Alison M 4:11:03 (14,559)
Kerr, Angela 3:53:09 (9,620)
Kerr, Carolyn J 5:48:56 (32,046)
Kerr, Katrina 4:08:23 (13,876)
Kerrison, Lois E 4:09:00 (14,041)
Kerry, Nicki 5:28:25 (30,312)
Kershaw, Caroline M 4:35:04 (20,998)
Kershaw, Cheryl A 3:53:09 (9,620)
Kershaw, Kay H 3:45:39 (7,827)
Kerven, Nicola 3:53:15 (9,649)
Keshwala, Nimisha 5:09:18 (28,009)
Kessell, Nicola L 4:32:40 (20,340)
Kessie, Emma 5:43:26 (31,604)
Kettle, Anthea J 4:26:57 (18,798)
Kettle, Gillian A 6:05:25 (32,944)
Kew, Joanne 5:11:25 (28,320)
Kew, Natalie 5:25:55 (30,025)
Key, Cherry 4:12:28 (14,920)
Key, Eva 4:22:32 (17,594)
Keylock, Louisa K 4:32:25 (20,273)
Keys, Morna A 4:21:23 (17,270)
Khakh, Joinder 5:03:07 (27,119)
Khan, Lucy C 3:48:39 (8,500)
Khan, Sabien 5:55:30 (32,502)
Khan, Tehmina 4:15:45 (15,768)
Khatri, Shaleen 5:36:21 (31,071)
Khoshnevis, Heather 3:25:49 (4,070)
Kibble, Sharron 4:37:37 (21,621)

Kidner, Karen J 3:56:28 (10,619)
Kiedaisch, Kandy 4:34:21 (20,785)
Kiell, Nicola K 5:22:37 (29,672)
Kiely, Jacqui L 4:30:11 (19,675)
Kienert, Paula 5:23:59 (29,803)
Kieran, Rosalind A 3:29:44 (4,831)
Kift, Joanne E 5:16:46 (29,026)
Kiggundu, Victoria Irene K 6:04:12 (32,895)
Kight, Kim 4:51:07 (24,867)
Kilbey, Gemma S 4:17:22 (16,184)
Kilbey, Sarah H 3:48:55 (8,559)
Kilbride, Kathleen B 3:24:43 (3,872)
Kilchmann, Ellen L 4:46:48 (23,854)
Kilduff, Emma L 5:35:02 (30,944)
Kilgour, Janette 3:47:53 (8,321)
Killeen, Emiliana H 4:19:56 (16,868)
Kilroy, Rachael V 3:54:54 (10,160)
Kilshaw, Meryl A 5:09:42 (28,094)
Kimmens, Nikki 6:17:30 (33,336)
Kimura, Sumie 4:00:37 (12,010)
Kindregan, Brenda 5:56:11 (32,536)
King, Alecto S 4:29:58 (19,625)
King, Ann M 5:40:25 (31,367)
King, Bryony J 3:49:51 (8,786)
King, Claire L 4:01:52 (12,329)
King, Clare 4:29:51 (19,600)
King, Elisabeth D 5:04:20 (27,298)
King, Emma M 4:52:43 (25,203)
King, Hannah J 5:09:20 (28,019)
King, Jacqueline 4:25:45 (18,463)
King, Jacqueline 4:39:53 (22,165)
King, Karen A 6:16:43 (33,318)
King, Katie A 4:50:33 (24,733)
King, Katie J 4:42:29 (22,800)
King, Lexie 5:46:11 (31,851)
King, Melanie 4:07:02 (13,527)
King, Nancy 4:05:21 (13,136)
King, Rachael A 4:21:09 (17,213)
King, Sally 4:14:44 (15,502)
King, Sarah A 4:50:23 (24,681)
King, Susan R 4:56:27 (25,957)
King, Tracey J 4:39:14 (22,037)
King, Tracey J 5:23:34 (29,753)
Kingdon, Elizabeth 6:01:49 (32,815)
Kingham, Marianne W 4:46:53 (23,880)
Kingham, Sarah 4:48:44 (24,303)
King-Lewis, Elaine C 4:35:57 (21,228)
Kingsford, Juliet A 4:31:39 (20,067)
Kingsley, Anna 4:50:07 (24,625)
Kingston, Alison L 3:20:27 (3,286)
Kingston, Marion R 4:23:35 (17,890)
Kinney, Gillian 3:55:29 (10,335)
Kirby, Alysia S 3:39:32 (6,545)
Kirby, Claire L 4:47:27 (24,011)
Kirby, Gemma R 5:02:48 (27,082)
Kirby, Jackie M 4:52:26 (25,130)
Kirby, Rebecca J 3:48:13 (8,403)
Kirkby, Carol 5:08:13 (27,845)
Kirkby, Jane C 3:56:16 (10,555)
Kirkham, Myshola 3:01:50 (1,300)
Kirkpatrick, Alison J 5:12:28 (28,458)
Kirkpatrick, Anna F 4:22:12 (17,495)
Kirschner, Elke 4:33:57 (20,691)
Kirsop, Susan M 5:22:48 (29,685)
Kirtsi, Soultana 6:56:05 (34,169)
Kirwan, Anne M 6:57:25 (34,184)
Kirwan, Elizabeth M 4:30:18 (19,698)
Kisbee, Laura J 6:43:35 (33,950)
Kisler, Jill E 3:48:21 (8,431)
Kita, Isabelle J 4:46:38 (23,807)
Kitchen, Diane B 3:40:24 (6,718)
Kitchen, Elizabeth 3:47:59 (8,345)
Kite, Wendy 5:10:46 (28,243)
Kitson, Joanna C 5:54:49 (32,447)
Kleijn, Catharina 3:57:04 (10,816)
Klein, Isabelle 3:46:56 (8,093)
Kletter, Alicia C 5:14:12 (28,704)
Klimczak, Anna E 3:35:33 (5,800)
Knappett, Charlotte 3:31:58 (5,217)
Knee, Susan E 5:16:47 (29,030)
Knee, Wendy 5:00:26 (26,700)
Knell, Sarah K 5:26:15 (30,064)
Knight, Audrey E 4:08:06 (13,789)

Leighton, Rebecca L.	4:46:06 (23,689)	
Leighton, Susan	5:33:10 (30,765)	
Leiper, Rosemary A.	4:12:04 (14,830)	
Le-Maguer, Nicole	5:35:40 (30,994)	
Lemanski, Charlotte L.	3:36:38 (5,984)	
Lenaghan, Chloe	5:09:36 (28,072)	
Lenaghan, Donna	3:23:25 (3,694)	
Lenaghan, Moira	4:11:54 (14,778)	
Leng, Jennifer M.	4:05:26 (13,158)	
Lennie, Christine R.	5:05:56 (27,539)	
Lennon, Carol L.	7:43:50 (34,492)	
Lennox, Carole A.	4:23:25 (17,842)	
Lenton, Barbara H.	4:13:37 (15,191)	
Leo, Asha	5:22:04 (29,606)	
Leon, Caroline D.	4:46:39 (23,814)	
Leon, Hannah F.	6:46:55 (34,015)	
Leonard, Bernadette	5:40:54 (31,404)	
Leonard, Sally A.	5:53:44 (32,390)	
Leonard, Sue S.	5:05:20 (27,446)	
Lepillier, Collette A.	4:43:32 (23,059)	
Leppard, Camilla A.	5:49:01 (32,054)	
Lerolland, Sophie	4:50:10 (24,637)	
Leslie, Ann M.	5:12:07 (28,421)	
Lester, Karen S.	5:04:10 (27,276)	
Lester, Michelle	7:18:39 (34,389)	
Letherby, Meg	2:55:50 (796)	
Letsch, Eliza C.	4:38:36 (21,858)	
Leven, Anna M.	3:51:33 (9,182)	
Lever, Caroline J.	6:34:40 (33,767)	
Levett, Theresa M.	3:57:07 (10,842)	
Levine, Clare	3:57:29 (10,948)	
Levinson, Jacqueline E.	5:23:55 (29,794)	
Levitton, Elaine K.	6:24:17 (33,525)	
Levy, Elizabeth M.	4:24:25 (18,114)	
Levy, Fiona	3:50:53 (9,023)	
Levy, Jennette	4:31:49 (20,112)	
Levy, Wendy	6:19:11 (33,379)	
Lewanowski, Melanie	3:56:59 (10,788)	
Lewellen, Tamsyn R.	4:41:59 (22,667)	
Lewington, Anne M.	4:15:25 (15,676)	
Lewis, Abena K.	4:34:59 (20,974)	
Lewis, Carol A.	6:16:32 (33,311)	
Lewis, Caroline A.	4:06:51 (13,484)	
Lewis, Caroline J.	4:13:33 (15,172)	
Lewis, Debbie J.	4:18:07 (16,374)	
Lewis, Diana R.	3:42:02 (7,035)	
Lewis, Hannah	4:10:04 (14,310)	
Lewis, Heidi B.	4:34:21 (20,785)	
Lewis, Jacqueline	5:08:34 (27,906)	
Lewis, Jennifer	5:02:44 (27,072)	
Lewis, Jenny C.	4:28:46 (19,335)	
Lewis, Julie	4:31:17 (19,961)	
Lewis, Justine F.	4:17:13 (16,159)	
Lewis, Kathleen A.	4:09:28 (14,162)	
Lewis, Laura R.	6:36:32 (33,806)	
Lewis, Lucie J.	8:48:28 (34,578)	
Lewis, Mia S.	4:45:34 (23,551)	
Lewis, Natalie	6:35:16 (33,777)	
Lewis, Natalie C.	5:30:22 (30,513)	
Lewis, Petra	4:50:44 (24,774)	
Lewis, Rebecca L.	5:23:59 (29,803)	
Lewis, Rose A.	4:39:38 (22,104)	
Lewis, Susan	4:45:41 (23,577)	
Lewis, Susan L.	4:38:49 (21,919)	
Lewis, Ursula R.	5:28:17 (30,303)	
Lewis, Valerie J.	4:54:32 (25,586)	
Lewis Wright, Angela I.	6:02:31 (32,836)	
Lewis-Meredith, Michelle M.	4:30:47 (19,828)	
Leworthy, Kathryn E.	6:32:56 (33,722)	
Lewry, Angela L.	6:01:01 (32,782)	
Leyshon, Deborah	4:51:33 (24,947)	
Lezard, Ashleigh	5:07:01 (27,698)	
Li, Mandy	3:56:17 (10,557)	
Li, May-Fay J.	3:49:50 (8,778)	
Liama, Evangelia L.	4:59:00 (26,477)	
Liberty, Darrelyn J.	4:31:46 (20,091)	
Licari, Stefania	5:16:57 (29,053)	
Lickfold, Kaye	4:38:56 (21,954)	
Liddle, Ailsa C.	5:31:19 (30,598)	
Liddle, Samantha L.	3:54:50 (10,139)	
Liesenfelt, Barbara A.	4:36:17 (21,320)	
Liet, Marielle	4:30:05 (19,650)	
Liggins, Lindsey D.	4:49:53 (24,569)	
Light, Fiona E.	3:35:31 (5,795)	
Light, Nicola	7:09:31 (34,313)	
Light, Sharon	4:03:07 (12,635)	
Lightfoot, Gill	4:28:13 (19,184)	
Liles, Charlotte A.	5:41:34 (31,471)	
Lilley, Daisy L.	4:28:45 (19,327)	
Lilley, Sarah K.	5:20:50 (29,484)	
Lilley-Bray, Clair	5:19:30 (29,354)	
Lim, Li Geok C.	5:38:25 (31,221)	
Lim, Lisa E.	4:46:30 (23,777)	
Limbert, Joanne	5:47:35 (31,957)	
Limbrick, Gudrun J.	4:54:06 (25,497)	
Lin, Sophia	3:35:34 (5,806)	
Lincoln, Abigail R.	5:47:34 (31,955)	
Lincoln, Anastasia	4:51:33 (24,947)	
Lincoln, Vicky	3:28:21 (4,528)	
Lindley, Denise	4:48:16 (24,196)	
Lindley, Sarah	4:39:43 (22,133)	
Lindop, Jane	4:08:51 (14,006)	
Lindsay, Gillian	4:16:39 (15,997)	
Lindsay, Olga M.	7:09:08 (34,305)	
Lindsell, Tracy	5:10:30 (28,217)	
Lindsey, Carolyn	5:09:37 (28,075)	
Lindsey, Sally	4:06:03 (13,301)	
Line, Julie A.	4:20:12 (16,942)	
Lines, Janet V.	4:08:04 (13,781)	
Ling, Lucy K.	5:33:44 (30,803)	
Ling, Melanie	3:30:03 (4,895)	
Linnell, Linda M.	4:55:00 (25,700)	
Linnell, Sarah M.	4:55:00 (25,700)	
Linnitt, Shirley	5:29:40 (30,443)	
Linsmeier, Petra	4:58:24 (26,361)	
Linton, Sara J.	4:15:55 (15,811)	
Linwood, Marjorie	4:31:51 (20,123)	
Lipparelli, Tania	4:35:33 (21,116)	
Lippett, Karen B.	4:21:37 (17,341)	
Lipton, Diana	4:52:19 (25,107)	
Lishman, Tracy L.	4:08:24 (13,882)	
Lisney, Lisa M.	5:03:54 (27,242)	
Liston, Fiona B.	4:35:06 (21,011)	
Listopad, Alina	5:16:30 (28,992)	
Litchfield, Anna	3:25:31 (4,017)	
Litchfield, Jenna D.	4:16:38 (15,989)	
Litterick, Emma C.	3:28:01 (4,462)	
Little, Clemency	5:16:07 (28,948)	
Little, Gina M.	4:11:15 (14,618)	
Little, Maureen	4:21:14 (17,233)	
Little, Rachael	4:13:12 (15,081)	
Little, Sue E.	6:21:01 (33,428)	
Little, Vicky C.	4:15:52 (15,801)	
Littlechild, Karen E.	3:51:51 (9,261)	
Littler, Katie	4:39:13 (22,034)	
Littler, Louise S.	4:29:47 (19,581)	
Littlewood, Hayley	4:40:09 (22,226)	
Liu, Michelle	3:40:44 (6,765)	
Liversedge, Samantha K.	4:46:57 (23,896)	
Livesey, Karen G.	4:53:07 (25,301)	
Livesey, Rachel	4:50:49 (24,799)	
Livingstone, Mandy J.	3:19:32 (3,169)	
Livingstone, Mandy P.	4:55:11 (25,730)	
Livingstone, Rachael	7:01:25 (34,221)	
Llewelyn-Jones, Belinda J.	5:03:25 (27,167)	
Lloyd, Jane B.	5:05:15 (27,442)	
Lloyd, Katie	5:01:59 (26,954)	
Lloyd, Philippa R.	6:24:26 (33,531)	
Lloyd, Sarah L.	5:01:12 (26,827)	
Lloyd, Susan M.	4:09:24 (14,141)	
Llwyd, Lowri M.	5:17:07 (29,077)	
Loach, Kate E.	3:26:35 (4,202)	
Loader, Carole A.	3:28:56 (4,650)	
Loat, Monica I.	4:47:13 (23,963)	
Lock, Dawn	7:06:23 (34,277)	
Lock, Debbie	7:54:42 (34,522)	
Lock, Jennifer L.	4:32:19 (20,255)	
Lock, Tracey	5:04:59 (27,397)	
Locke, Sarah J.	4:40:02 (22,189)	
Lockett, Rebecca J.	4:43:01 (22,933)	
Lockett, Rose A.	4:24:10 (18,039)	
Lockwood, Anne	4:19:11 (19,005)	
Lockwood, Linda A.	3:58:37 (11,341)	
Lockwood, Samantha J.	4:46:19 (23,745)	
Locock, Rosemary L.	5:39:14 (31,279)	
Lodge, Carol A.	5:39:23 (31,290)	
Lodge, Jackie L.	4:00:05 (11,873)	
Lodrick, Julie	3:57:58 (11,106)	
Loeffler, Claudia	3:42:46 (7,190)	
Logan, Julie A.	4:29:20 (19,481)	
Logue, Nicola	3:59:14 (11,574)	
Lomas, Emily S.	6:20:15 (33,402)	
Lomas, Helen	5:02:07 (26,974)	
Lomas, Jennifer	5:44:06 (31,674)	
Lomas, Sarah	3:08:14 (1,815)	
Lomax, Jayne D.	4:09:02 (14,050)	
Lomax, Lindsay	5:45:15 (31,781)	
Lombard, Celeste	4:57:32 (26,194)	
Lombard, Regina B.	3:54:50 (10,139)	
Loneden, Sian E.	6:34:22 (33,757)	
Long, Ann	6:22:43 (33,479)	
Long, Caroline A.	4:30:43 (19,806)	
Long, Caroline L.	4:33:37 (20,616)	
Long, Christine A.	6:13:00 (33,210)	
Long, Jane	5:36:04 (31,039)	
Long, Lavinia	4:31:31 (20,027)	
Long, Lorraine	4:06:38 (13,436)	
Long, Paula R.	6:00:51 (32,772)	
Long, Samantha J.	5:53:18 (32,359)	
Long, Sara E.	4:45:51 (23,633)	
Longden, Lorraine L.	3:53:56 (9,849)	
Longhurst, Nicola J.	5:03:10 (27,128)	
Longley, Zira K.	4:37:55 (21,698)	
Lonsdale, Rachel E.	4:36:57 (21,477)	
Loomes, Lynda A.	6:51:12 (34,097)	
Lopez, Anna L.	5:28:33 (30,327)	
Lopez Largo, Adabella	3:39:43 (6,580)	
Loprete, Fabiola	5:30:15 (30,502)	
Lord, Alexandra C.	4:16:25 (15,938)	
Lord, Catherine E.	4:41:50 (22,647)	
Lord, Sarah	5:34:12 (30,858)	
Lord, Susan	4:33:52 (20,676)	
Lord, Tamara	6:12:54 (33,206)	
Lothian, Adele	6:39:19 (33,871)	
Lotufo Alonso, Alessandra	4:25:41 (18,438)	
Louden, Caroline A.	3:58:16 (11,203)	
Lough, Claire L.	6:20:10 (33,399)	
Loughnane, Tilly A.	4:02:49 (12,569)	
Lourd, Mireille	3:52:05 (9,327)	
Louth, Candy J.	4:21:17 (17,249)	
Louth, Clare L.	4:30:29 (19,740)	
Lovatt, Ellen L.	4:18:53 (16,595)	
Love, Helen L.	6:24:20 (33,526)	
Love, Jo	4:33:12 (20,482)	
Love, Jonica A.	5:38:38 (31,234)	
Loveday, Andrea	5:47:00 (31,908)	
Loveless, Victoria L.	4:45:51 (23,633)	
Lovell, Nikki	3:39:43 (6,580)	
Lovell, Pam E.	4:14:39 (15,482)	
Lovell Anderson, Marilyn	5:57:48 (32,622)	
Lovell Knight, Jade	4:59:56 (26,622)	
Lovelock, Clare F.	4:51:44 (24,994)	
Lovelock, Rebecca P.	4:03:23 (12,695)	
Lovis, Claire P.	5:29:37 (30,437)	
Low, Alison	5:48:55 (32,042)	
Low, Susan J.	4:10:02 (14,303)	
Lowe, Davina N.	3:25:19 (3,982)	
Lowe, Janine L.	3:32:56 (5,378)	
Lowe, Katy	5:53:42 (32,386)	
Lowe, Wendy	4:31:14 (19,945)	
Lowin, Lucy J.	4:18:56 (16,610)	
Lowles, Nathalie	4:53:40 (25,413)	
Lowndes, Clare L.	4:52:21 (25,113)	
Lowson, Rebecca E.	5:13:44 (28,641)	
Lowther, Deborah	4:36:10 (21,284)	
Lowther, Sarah M.	4:56:48 (26,025)	
Lowthian, Lucy I.	6:54:34 (34,148)	
Loy, Francesca	4:49:29 (24,471)	
Loyd, Jane E.	5:35:36 (30,988)	
Lubbock, Sandra K.	4:31:55 (20,144)	
Luca, Cristina P.	3:50:36 (8,955)	
Lucas, Julie P.	4:04:37 (12,960)	
Lucas, Pauline A.	3:56:43 (10,699)	
Lucas, Theresa A.	5:23:31 (29,746)	
Lucking, Nicola S.	5:11:46 (28,379)	
Lucking, Samantha	6:34:36 (33,765)	
Lucocq, Carolyn M.	3:19:23 (3,147)	
Luebkeman, Laurel	4:39:33 (22,090)	
Luff, Machteld	4:17:42 (16,281)	

Lumber, Liz 3:25:40 (4,046)
Lund, Ceri 4:28:46 (19,335)
Lundy, Bronwen 3:58:39 (11,357)
Lundy, Caroline B 3:35:37 (5,815)
Lunt, Gillian 5:40:26 (31,368)
Lurring, Lisa J 4:40:01 (22,186)
Luscombe, Caroline R 5:02:39 (27,058)
Lush, Rachel E 6:31:30 (33,693)
Luth, Mariska 4:00:33 (11,987)
Luther, Aimée C 7:09:45 (34,317)
Luther Madsen, Anne K 4:41:09 (22,475)
Luthra, Archna 5:57:50 (32,624)
Lvey, Karen I 3:51:51 (9,261)
Lyddy, Sylvia 6:24:32 (33,534)
Lyle, Jenn C 5:31:13 (30,590)
Lyle, Susan V 3:55:38 (10,382)
Lynam, Glenys 5:19:11 (29,313)
Lynch, Emma 4:57:45 (26,237)
Lynch, Hayley J 6:21:11 (33,433)
Lynch, Janet M 6:35:16 (33,777)
Lynch, Susan E 4:42:45 (22,866)
Lyne, Debra S 5:49:27 (32,083)
Lyne, Jodie 4:37:25 (21,578)
Lynn, Michaela M 4:03:58 (12,826)
Lyon, Emily K 4:10:53 (14,516)
Lyon, Gemma C 4:47:54 (24,123)
Lyons, Alicia T 6:32:35 (33,716)
Lyons, Cheryl L 3:15:23 (2,690)
Lysne, Kristin S 3:34:30 (5,623)
Lytle, Lisa J 3:51:20 (9,132)
Lytle, Lynn 3:51:20 (9,132)
Mabbutt, Sheila M 6:27:53 (33,623)
Mabire, Maryse 4:08:33 (13,927)
Maby, Julie 7:51:43 (34,515)
MacAndrew, Karen D 4:58:30 (26,375)
Macartney, Catherine J 5:26:21 (30,082)
Macartney, Sarah C 4:59:37 (26,579)
MacAskill, Lesley F 3:59:24 (11,633)
Macaulay, Emily J 5:01:40 (26,906)
Macaulay, Janine 5:08:45 (27,937)
Macbeath, Irene 3:46:22 (7,971)
Maccariello, Bettina E 4:11:12 (14,607)
Macdonald, Alison 3:28:19 (4,522)
Macdonald, Gillian C 7:10:00 (34,322)
Macdonald, Kay V 4:47:16 (23,976)
Macdonald, Melissa J 5:19:58 (29,409)
Macdonald, Nakia 5:19:14 (29,319)
Macdonald, Patricia 5:45:38 (31,808)
Macdonald, Shauna 4:00:34 (11,994)
Macdonald Lockhart, Davina 4:35:45 (21,177)
MacDougall, Jane 4:36:04 (21,258)
Macduff, Anna-Jane 4:47:51 (24,106)
MacEwen, Elizabeth 4:41:24 (22,534)
Macey, Rebecca E 4:30:44 (19,811)
Macfarlane, Beth 4:44:08 (23,211)
Macfarlane, Roz 4:44:08 (23,211)
Macfarlane, Veronica I 5:36:59 (31,118)
MacGill, Edith M 4:27:19 (18,911)
MacGregor, Sue M 3:47:21 (8,187)
Machin, Amanda A 3:33:43 (5,509)
Machin, Frances H 4:29:06 (19,420)
Macintyre, Shona M 5:25:04 (29,926)
MacIver, Isabel 5:04:59 (27,397)
Mackay, Heather J 3:52:52 (9,526)
Mackay, Jennifer S 5:35:47 (31,004)
Mackay, Stacey A 6:21:17 (33,436)
Mackenny, Louise 4:36:36 (21,393)
Mackenzie, Davina L 4:28:42 (19,313)
Mackenzie, Kate E 3:53:02 (9,586)
Mackenzie, Lynn 4:50:46 (24,787)
Mackenzie-Wilson, Susan J 5:53:30 (32,377)
Mackerron, Sharee 4:46:09 (23,700)
Mackey, Jill L 6:44:44 (33,973)
Mackie, Caroline L 4:50:15 (24,656)
Mackie, Rebekah E 3:28:35 (4,574)
Mackinnon, Amy 5:45:27 (31,800)
Mackley, Veronica M 3:24:58 (3,921)
Mackrell, Louisa T 4:57:58 (26,277)
MacLaurin, Joanne C 5:50:41 (32,185)
MacLeary, Rebeckah 3:57:53 (11,085)
Macleay, Cariona M 5:16:54 (29,042)
Macleod, Catherine J 4:22:52 (17,691)
Macleod, Helen 3:38:44 (6,396)
Macleod, Rebecca 3:59:00 (11,489)
Macleod, Sadie L 4:42:23 (22,770)
Macmillan, Fiona V 4:34:50 (20,918)
Macmillan, Sonja A 5:42:59 (31,571)
MacNaughton, Beverley A 6:06:03 (32,978)
Macpherson, Alyson 3:28:33 (4,569)
Macpherson, Fiona L 4:22:25 (17,555)
Macpherson, Shona 3:52:36 (9,454)
MacQueen, Andrea L 4:15:41 (15,742)
Macrae, Sarah E 4:28:37 (19,296)
Mac Taggart, Dee 5:19:31 (29,362)
Madden, Anne K 5:09:07 (27,984)
Madders, Rachel C 3:58:05 (11,137)
Maddison, Laura 5:30:35 (30,538)
Maddocks, Carol 4:34:11 (20,752)
Madeley, Joanna 3:53:21 (9,677)
Maden, Deborah N 3:55:17 (10,286)
Madzoubia, Marie 5:17:44 (29,145)
Magee, Katherine P 3:10:25 (2,034)
Magee, Suzanna M 5:12:22 (28,446)
Mageean-Lee, Mary M 6:17:33 (33,341)
Magin, Stephanie 6:04:59 (32,924)
Magni, Monica 3:28:20 (4,523)
Magudia, Sangita 5:11:10 (28,289)
Maguire, Imelda M 5:51:10 (32,219)
Maguire, Jemma S 5:32:39 (30,715)
Maguire, Sarah 3:13:17 (2,369)
Maguire, Tess L 4:58:05 (26,301)
Mahadani, Netra 6:17:30 (33,336)
Maher, Heidi C 5:11:39 (28,354)
Mahiques, Philippa M 6:05:28 (32,950)
Mahmoud, Sonia E 4:16:26 (15,942)
Mahomed, Fathima 5:50:26 (32,168)
Mahon, Ruth 4:35:52 (21,205)
Mahon, Sarah E 5:36:35 (31,089)
Mahony, Helen M 6:48:49 (34,048)
Maingi, Deborah 3:39:04 (6,447)
Maisey, Louise 5:10:24 (28,208)
Maishman, Madeleine C 5:28:22 (30,309)
Maita, Hisayo 5:01:21 (26,849)
Majid, Kay E 4:58:35 (26,395)
Majithia, Roshni 4:13:44 (15,233)
Major, Emma 4:22:27 (17,568)
Major, Michelle 7:40:35 (34,482)
Major, Pippa J 3:15:51 (2,737)
Major, Sarah A 4:51:14 (24,887)
Makin, Cheryl L 4:41:41 (22,613)
Makinson-Friske, Anne L 3:52:56 (9,549)
Maksymiu, Debra M 5:45:21 (31,792)
Malcolm, Fiona J 3:59:57 (11,836)
Maldoni, Alessandra 4:33:38 (20,618)
Male, Ruth E 4:33:21 (20,530)
Male, Samantha J 4:52:33 (25,156)
Male, Teresa M 4:55:00 (25,700)
Malik, Simina K 7:54:40 (34,521)
Mallon, Emma L 4:41:36 (22,581)
Mallorie, Charlotte J 3:07:19 (1,713)
Mallows, Helen L 4:58:15 (26,335)
Malone, Erine E 4:30:52 (19,855)
Maltas, Angela 4:31:56 (20,147)
Malton, Elizabeth J 5:22:17 (29,636)
Manahan-Thomas, Elin 5:36:07 (31,045)
Manby, Jennifer C 5:46:37 (31,886)
Mancell, Sara K 4:19:16 (16,693)
Mandarelli, Anna Laura 3:21:44 (3,451)
Mandelman, Mariah J 3:01:30 (1,278)
Mangiamarchi, Paola E 4:45:43 (23,592)
Manifield, Catherine A 5:27:54 (30,254)
Mankowitz, Alexandra P 6:36:29 (33,804)
Manley, Angela J 5:11:04 (28,284)
Manlove, Lorraine 4:47:19 (23,989)
Mann, Isobel J 4:52:54 (25,256)
Mann, Josephine 5:19:17 (29,330)
Mann, Rosalind H 3:59:42 (11,750)
Manners, Janet 5:01:43 (26,916)
Manning, Alison 5:17:59 (29,178)
Manning, Kate 5:02:47 (27,079)
Manning, Lucy 5:24:17 (29,836)
Mannion, Deirbhle 4:13:25 (15,138)
Mansbridge, Kaye M 2:57:53 (934)
Mansbridge, Kelly M 5:36:12 (31,052)
Mansell, Claire J 6:43:06 (33,942)
Mansell, Kate G 4:32:55 (20,411)
Mansfield, Cally 4:21:22 (17,261)
Mansfield, Elizabeth J 6:00:08 (32,745)
Mansfield, Hazel P 3:48:58 (8,572)
Mansfield, Katherine A 5:59:22 (32,705)
Mansfield, Katie J 5:02:22 (27,018)
Mansfield, Kylie A 3:55:40 (10,396)
Mansfield, Laura A 5:30:29 (30,525)
Mansfield, Lauren H 4:58:34 (26,390)
Mansfield, Lynn S 3:46:35 (8,020)
Manso, Rita 3:54:23 (9,987)
Manton, Helen M 5:10:23 (28,204)
Maples, Marion J 4:26:29 (18,662)
Mapplebeck, Sarah 4:16:31 (15,965)
Mara, Deitra E 5:25:36 (29,996)
Marais, Sue-Ellen 4:17:34 (16,238)
Maraval, Collette D 4:53:59 (25,478)
March, Karla M 5:02:13 (26,994)
March, Liz 5:38:15 (31,210)
Marchant, Carmen L 3:19:19 (3,137)
Marchant, Judy C 3:45:43 (7,838)
Marchant-Jones, Alison 6:06:50 (33,013)
Marchesi, Kathryn 5:56:09 (32,530)
Marco Fabre, Maria E 4:31:02 (19,893)
Marcolini, Manuela 3:07:11 (1,697)
Marconato, Julie C 5:07:42 (27,797)
Marder, Swee L 4:10:53 (14,516)
Mardon, Sandrine C 4:15:43 (15,752)
Markham, Tamsyn C 5:12:15 (28,429)
Marks, Wendy E 4:06:51 (13,484)
Marlow, Amanda E 4:07:49 (13,720)
Marr, Niki 4:37:25 (21,578)
Marriner, Janet A 5:08:02 (27,828)
Marriott, Ivette 5:11:06 (28,286)
Marriott, Susan M 4:20:08 (16,920)
Marris, Jacqueline 5:08:31 (27,899)
Marsano, Tracy 6:08:03 (33,044)
Marsden, Claire L 4:19:16 (16,693)
Marsh, Carla J 3:58:17 (11,208)
Marsh, Clare L 4:52:48 (25,222)
Marsh, Jessica R 4:07:31 (13,645)
Marsh, Katy 3:52:05 (9,327)
Marsh, Kerry Anne 4:30:06 (19,656)
Marsh, Mary E 4:25:51 (18,496)
Marsh, Rachel 5:43:51 (31,638)
Marsh, Sara E 4:25:15 (18,328)
Marsh, Siobhan 6:33:18 (33,729)
Marsh, Veronica B 4:15:49 (15,786)
Marshall, Anne J 4:14:57 (15,544)
Marshall, Annita J 4:25:39 (18,429)
Marshall, Christine 4:22:53 (17,698)
Marshall, Emma V 4:13:03 (15,050)
Marshall, Julie C 5:07:17 (27,736)
Marshall, Kelly-Jay 4:55:14 (25,735)
Marshall, Linda A 3:53:41 (9,764)
Marshall, Paula R 6:30:27 (33,670)
Marshall, Sarah E 4:28:19 (19,213)
Marshall, Sharon L 6:10:56 (33,140)
Marshall, Zoe H 3:48:58 (8,572)
Marsham, Rebecca E 5:04:19 (27,294)
Mart, Jaymie 5:03:41 (27,206)
Martens, Ursula 4:49:39 (24,521)
Martin, Alice R 4:46:54 (23,885)
Martin, Amanda J 3:26:03 (4,113)
Martin, Antoinette S 5:27:56 (30,257)
Martin, Carol A 3:37:56 (6,246)
Martin, Clare E 2:51:08 (558)
Martin, Dawn R 3:44:17 (7,512)
Martin, Elizabeth A 4:15:28 (15,693)
Martin, Emma C 5:24:02 (29,812)
Martin, Erica L 3:13:36 (2,406)
Martin, Hayley 4:36:37 (21,396)
Martin, Heidi R 4:11:42 (14,733)
Martin, Joanne 6:38:08 (33,844)
Martin, Julie K 5:33:19 (30,775)

Martin, Katherine A....5:27:13 (30,167)
Martin, Kira-Lee A....4:21:26 (17,286)
Martin, Lindsay J....4:36:01 (21,246)
Martin, Lucie....4:48:50 (24,328)
Martin, Maxine J....5:47:49 (31,966)
Martin, Melissa R....5:28:14 (30,297)
Martin, Michele....4:57:05 (26,104)
Martin, Monica....4:49:20 (24,442)
Martin, Nicola....4:43:34 (23,070)
Martin, Patricia M....3:55:02 (10,210)
Martin, Rachel C....5:05:22 (27,454)
Martin, Rachel C....5:15:54 (28,921)
Martin, Rebecca C....4:34:54 (20,939)
Martin, Rebecca L....3:57:03 (10,811)
Martin, Rosemary E....7:07:21 (34,287)
Martin, Sarah E....3:57:04 (10,816)
Martin, Stephanie....4:10:51 (14,509)
Martin, Stephanie J....3:09:29 (1,940)
Martin, Teresa M....4:46:55 (23,888)
Martin-Consani, Debbie....3:31:00 (5,054)
Martindill, Louise E....4:59:49 (26,610)
Martino, Orsolina L....4:16:02 (15,845)
Martins, Marketa....4:43:29 (23,044)
Martyn-Smith, Patricia I....4:40:04 (22,198)
Marz, Alexis L....4:01:20 (12,196)
Mascall, Jacqueline A....5:29:37 (30,437)
Masden, Liz....5:20:18 (29,438)
Maskell, Rachel....4:25:59 (18,531)
Maskell, Susie....4:00:13 (11,901)
Maslin, Fiona K....4:37:49 (21,675)
Mason, Alice S....4:33:00 (20,431)
Mason, Angela....4:19:27 (16,739)
Mason, Angharad E....3:29:00 (4,669)
Mason, Emma....5:55:47 (32,509)
Mason, Hayley....4:26:44 (18,738)
Mason, Joanna K....4:59:19 (26,536)
Mason, Kim E....6:00:33 (32,762)
Mason, Lisa J....4:54:45 (25,638)
Mason, Rebecca H....4:00:10 (11,886)
Mason, Ruth E....4:20:07 (16,917)
Mason, Sarah J....5:51:21 (32,240)
Mason, Soraya....4:22:34 (17,601)
Mason, Terri L....4:01:45 (12,306)
Mason-Lodge, Louise....4:44:36 (23,321)
Massey, Beth F....3:16:02 (2,758)
Massey, Lara L....3:32:28 (5,318)
Massey, Theresa J....4:14:14 (15,377)
Masson, Kim C....3:09:26 (1,934)
Masson, Paula M....4:33:19 (20,516)
Massos, Jacky D....4:48:29 (24,243)
Masterman, Tanya J....7:23:09 (34,419)
Masters-Clark, Alison C....5:02:51 (27,086)
Mataria, Memuna....3:50:03 (8,834)
Mate, Suzanne J....4:27:46 (19,011)
Matharoo, Susan A....4:55:15 (25,742)
Mather, Angela....5:09:24 (28,028)
Mather, Nicola J....5:12:39 (28,477)
Mathers, Denise....3:41:59 (7,022)
Mathers, Julie B....3:58:59 (11,481)
Matheson, Michaela....4:28:16 (19,194)
Mathews, Carol J....4:41:23 (22,531)
Mathews, Ebony J....4:34:06 (20,725)
Mathias, Jennifer F....4:57:31 (26,190)
Mathias, Kate....5:14:36 (28,759)
Mathieson, Emma L....5:24:37 (29,870)
Mathison, Camilla T....3:23:48 (3,737)
Matijuk, Jill I....5:37:43 (31,170)
Matkin, Penelope A....3:59:23 (11,626)
Maton, Christine R....5:03:43 (27,209)
Matthams, Stacey L....5:18:33 (29,234)
Matthews, Christine....3:38:09 (6,296)
Matthews, Claire....4:43:19 (23,007)
Matthews, Clare E....3:59:25 (11,639)
Matthews, Deborah S....5:13:36 (28,622)
Matthews, Denise....3:59:38 (11,724)
Matthews, Georgina H....3:55:41 (10,399)
Matthews, Hannah....4:08:13 (13,833)
Matthews, Jane E....5:04:33 (27,336)
Matthews, Janice E....6:14:19 (33,254)
Matthews, Joanne L....8:08:27 (34,543)
Matthews, Karen L....8:08:24 (34,542)
Matthews, Linzi J....4:22:56 (17,710)
Matthews, Lucy A....5:18:24 (29,218)
Matthews, Nicola....4:28:36 (19,289)
Matthews, Ruth F....5:07:34 (27,776)
Matthews, Sally....4:24:23 (18,106)
Matthews, Sarah E....3:37:57 (6,252)
Matthews, Sarah M....4:39:20 (22,057)
Matthews, Sasha J....4:10:41 (14,457)
Matthews, Susan J....3:53:01 (9,582)
Matthews, Vanessa....4:51:00 (24,844)
Matthias, Fiona....5:06:39 (27,645)
Mattick, Suzanne L....4:07:06 (13,545)
Maudovit, Helene C....4:28:46 (19,335)
Maudsley, Joanne M....6:18:55 (33,378)
Mauger, Bev....3:55:27 (10,323)
Maund, Lesley....6:51:59 (34,110)
Maund, Louisa J....3:25:49 (4,070)
Maunder, Angela C....8:34:33 (34,570)
Mauri, Chiara....4:22:29 (17,575)
Maurice, Thérèse....4:08:28 (13,901)
Mavrogiorgis, Sophia A....4:18:35 (16,526)
Maw, Anne....5:09:39 (28,082)
Maw, Kirsten....5:02:01 (26,960)
Mawby, Claire K....5:26:31 (30,101)
Mawer, Helen K....4:49:04 (24,388)
Mawer, Lisa M....3:04:06 (1,454)
Maxwell, Gill M....4:16:47 (16,029)
Maxwell, Helen L....4:37:53 (21,693)
Maxwell, Kathy A....3:37:28 (6,167)
May, Gillian W....6:07:24 (33,030)
May, Hannah R....5:18:39 (29,247)
May, Helen....4:37:52 (21,688)
May, Jackie J....4:43:50 (23,132)
May, Jill M....3:28:55 (4,648)
May, Karen....4:54:23 (25,558)
May, Sian C....4:54:52 (25,669)
Maybury, Sarah L....5:24:53 (29,903)
Maycock, Fiona J....3:19:54 (3,215)
Maycock, Zoe E....4:17:14 (16,163)
Maydew, Provence A....5:31:17 (30,594)
Mayer, Lillian E....4:45:42 (23,585)
Mayer, Vicky A....5:11:34 (28,342)
Mayers, Sandra....4:43:18 (23,001)
Mayes, Amanda J....4:47:08 (23,940)
Mayhead, Benita A....4:35:11 (21,029)
Mayhew, Kate L....6:53:07 (34,125)
Maynard, Anna V....6:45:48 (34,001)
Maynard, Jayne E....4:40:25 (22,290)
Maynard, Kay P....6:12:42 (33,195)
Maynard, Susan L....6:21:28 (33,444)
Mayo, Caroline J....5:12:41 (28,489)
Maziere, Sandrine....4:56:40 (25,995)
Mazur, Jacqui A....5:48:34 (32,018)
Mazzeo, Katie....7:06:15 (34,274)
Mburu, Philomena W....3:54:06 (9,903)
Mc Alea, Phil-Marie K....4:43:09 (22,971)
McAleer, Paula....4:14:31 (15,453)
McAlister, Ariel F....3:52:53 (9,532)
McArdle, Emmeline....5:04:21 (27,303)
McArther, Lucy-Jane....3:55:54 (10,465)
McArthur, Claire V....3:33:24 (5,451)
McArthur, Erica....4:02:54 (12,585)
McAuley, Carol A....5:18:11 (29,196)
McAuliffe, Aileen....4:46:53 (23,880)
McBeth, Caroline A....3:30:12 (4,924)
McBride, Catherine M....4:02:10 (12,409)
McCabe, Brenda C....3:58:01 (11,122)
McCabe, Claire L....5:18:50 (29,265)
McCabe, Cynthia....4:14:23 (15,418)
McCabe, Jan....5:03:54 (27,242)
McCabe, Natalie C....3:53:28 (9,705)
McCabe, Tracie L....4:14:45 (15,508)
McCaffrey, Annmarie....3:22:13 (3,519)
McCaffrey, Beth....5:26:16 (30,067)
McCaffrey, Jessica C....5:26:16 (30,067)
McCall, Estralita L....4:14:17 (15,392)
McCann, Colleen A....4:46:23 (23,759)
McCardle, Rebecca....3:58:56 (11,468)
Mc Carron, Emer E....4:38:32 (21,831)
McCarron, Kellyann....6:36:19 (33,798)
McCarron, Sue E....5:46:30 (31,879)
McCarthy, Alison M....4:59:36 (26,574)
McCarthy, Christine....3:13:10 (2,355)
McCarthy, Gillian L....5:11:02 (28,280)
McCarthy, Helen....5:11:38 (28,351)
McCarthy, Jane M....4:49:46 (24,548)
McCarthy, Kerry A....3:38:50 (6,415)
McCartney, Gillian L....4:13:01 (15,037)
McCartney, Margaret A....4:40:19 (22,262)
McCaughan, Tracy J....3:48:17 (8,423)
McCauley, Treena....4:23:31 (17,872)
McCaw, Eileen E....4:21:14 (17,233)
McCleery, Sally J....5:48:41 (32,025)
McClellan, Renée M....5:23:50 (29,781)
McClellan, Sarah....7:11:28 (34,336)
McClellan, Su....5:25:25 (29,981)
McColl, Jacqueline A....5:50:51 (32,200)
McConkey, Alison....5:01:40 (26,906)
McConkey, Sarah....5:13:32 (28,610)
McConnell, Angela R....4:39:10 (22,020)
McConnell, Janey E....5:17:56 (29,171)
McCord, Kate....5:58:18 (32,655)
Mc Cormick, Fiona E....4:44:00 (23,180)
McCormick, Laura....4:12:35 (14,948)
McCorriston, Elaine M....4:43:04 (22,948)
McCourt, Maureen F....4:42:01 (22,676)
McCourtie, Sarah M....5:31:34 (30,617)
McCowan Hill, Harry....5:16:23 (28,979)
McCoy, Claire....5:29:25 (30,414)
McCracken, Dorothy C....3:33:31 (5,476)
McCreadie, Elspeth T....4:11:57 (14,791)
McCullagh, Melanie C....4:05:29 (13,172)
McCulloch, Frances A....5:24:27 (29,853)
McCullough, Sonya L....4:22:42 (17,650)
McDade, Geraldine....4:19:27 (16,739)
McDermott, Camilla F....4:11:50 (14,765)
McDermott, Jacqueline A....3:31:37 (5,156)
McDermott, Sarah....4:49:16 (24,425)
McDonagh, Tina A....3:58:06 (11,142)
McDonald, Dawn K....3:55:23 (10,309)
McDonald, Deborah A....6:30:15 (33,666)
McDonald, Julie....3:30:33 (4,981)
McDonald, Mandy H....5:27:16 (30,172)
McDonald, Sally M....6:54:28 (34,146)
McDonald-Hamilton, Heather....4:28:49 (19,351)
McDonnell, Caroline....4:22:42 (17,650)
McDonnell, Lyn M....4:19:38 (16,790)
McDonough, Annie....3:39:13 (6,477)
McDonough, Heather E....5:27:16 (30,172)
McDougall, Elizabeth....5:04:03 (27,258)
McDowall, Sarah J....3:46:11 (7,924)
McEachern, Victoria E....4:18:23 (16,458)
McEneaney, Paulette....5:28:25 (30,312)
McEwan, Flo....6:36:20 (33,801)
McEwan, Paula Jayne....6:22:40 (33,477)
McEwen, Donna....2:56:51 (862)
McFadyen, Angharad W....3:48:41 (8,507)
McFall, Josie....6:47:03 (34,020)
McFarland, Kim....4:21:40 (17,364)
McFerran, Nuala A....5:08:20 (27,860)
McGahey, Emily C....4:13:06 (15,066)
McGain, Sarah....5:10:18 (28,191)
McGarry, Yvonne C....3:15:20 (2,680)
McGeary, Christina C....3:41:02 (6,834)
McGee, Molly C....4:47:06 (23,930)
McGee, Nicola....6:32:11 (33,706)
McGeever, Siobhan M....3:56:53 (10,756)
McGeoch, Laura....3:47:26 (8,205)
McGibbon, Maryl S....3:55:27 (10,323)
McGill, Pamela....5:34:46 (30,909)
McGill, Susan I....4:23:50 (17,946)
McGinn, Anna M....4:38:12 (21,757)
McGinty, Roslyn A....3:34:29 (5,619)
McGirr, Clare M....4:08:44 (13,978)
McGlennon, Kirsten F....5:13:10 (28,564)
McGlynn, Joanna....4:38:41 (21,880)
McGoldrick, Carol....6:45:49 (34,003)
McGoldrick, Lesley....5:05:06 (27,418)
McGovern, Carole A....4:37:51 (21,683)
McGowan, Marianne....6:00:15 (32,749)
McGowan, Sarah....4:41:06 (22,460)
McGrane, Oonagh M....5:54:56 (32,454)
McGreevy, Adele M....3:50:28 (8,924)
McGregor, Kirsten....4:54:24 (25,560)
McGuinness, Cris....6:43:51 (33,956)
McGuire, Rebecca J....4:16:38 (15,989)
McHugh, Samina....4:47:52 (24,109)
McHugh, Zoe D....5:06:48 (27,666)

McIlhinney, Lucy P	3:23:59 (3,779)
McInally, Catherine J	3:25:54 (4,085)
McInman, Karen E	4:06:05 (13,309)
McInnes, Annette K	4:00:16 (11,917)
McIntosh, Caroline S	7:06:39 (34,280)
McIntosh, Shona	2:47:38 (406)
McIntyre, Elana M	5:25:35 (29,994)
McIntyre, Jill D	4:45:05 (23,432)
McIver, Jennie L	5:06:52 (27,677)
McKay, Anna L	4:23:04 (17,744)
McKay, Claire C	5:09:22 (28,025)
McKay, Leigh	4:23:21 (17,831)
McKee, Elaine	4:57:52 (26,255)
McKee, Hannah L	5:09:18 (28,009)
McKee, Jayne E	5:07:32 (27,771)
McKendrey, Bernie A	5:35:07 (30,951)
McKenna, Angela	5:09:31 (28,054)
McKenna, Christine M	5:03:30 (27,183)
McKenna, Gillian	4:30:22 (19,717)
McKenna, Sara L	5:22:54 (29,692)
McKenney, Emma-Louise M	5:43:50 (31,636)
McKenney, Kim A	5:35:54 (31,020)
McKenzie, Cheryl A	5:45:59 (31,831)
McKenzie, Louise J	4:50:31 (24,722)
McKeon-Clark, Rachel M	6:51:09 (34,093)
McKernan, Glynis	3:27:25 (4,354)
McKie, Elizabeth A	3:06:14 (1,622)
McKinlay, Sarah E	4:31:56 (20,147)
McLachlan, Antonia	5:34:47 (30,914)
McLachlan, Margaret E	3:14:17 (2,516)
McLaren, Donna	5:33:46 (30,812)
McLaren, Joanne	4:07:06 (13,545)
McLaughlin, Roshani	6:26:52 (33,595)
McLaughlin, Susan G	5:32:24 (30,693)
McLaurin, Helen	5:23:54 (29,792)
McLean, Alison	4:44:44 (23,352)
McLean, Lorraine	4:17:48 (16,305)
McLean, Lucie M	5:14:44 (28,778)
McLean, Theresa M	5:14:02 (28,677)
McLeary, Claire L	5:26:13 (30,060)
McLeish, Holly	5:01:17 (26,838)
McLellan, Kay	5:25:54 (30,021)
McLeod, Camille J	4:41:59 (22,667)
McLoughlin, Rebecca M	3:56:22 (10,582)
McMahon, Kathleen M	4:57:44 (26,234)
McMahon, Mella M	3:31:56 (5,208)
McMahon, Paula A	5:11:25 (28,320)
McManus, Claire M	5:32:59 (30,747)
McManus, Claire M	6:16:23 (33,306)
McManus, Laura	3:53:50 (9,824)
McMenamin, Catriona	5:16:58 (29,058)
McMillan, Isabel J	4:10:17 (14,365)
McMillan, Lyndal	5:08:45 (27,937)
McMullan, Clare	3:54:13 (9,932)
McMullen, Laura	3:59:11 (11,554)
McMullin, Lisa	4:51:38 (24,973)
McMurray, Louise J	4:42:25 (22,784)
McNally, Emily C	3:59:38 (11,724)
McNamee, Louise	4:14:41 (15,494)
McNeil, Iona	4:40:28 (22,304)
McNelis, Jan	5:15:16 (28,848)
McNelis, Nikki	3:48:14 (8,407)
McNicholas, Claire A	5:47:27 (31,948)
McNicholas, Kathryn S	5:34:20 (30,869)
McNidder, Carol D	6:09:13 (33,088)
McNulty, Barbara	4:29:27 (19,508)
McParlin, Catherine	4:25:27 (18,382)
McPartland, Bonnie	4:22:26 (17,560)
McPaul, Carol A	4:13:15 (15,098)
McPhail, Marian	4:15:24 (15,670)
McPhee, Lizzie	4:58:42 (26,420)
McPherson, Debbie	5:42:30 (31,531)
McPherson, Jennifer	5:46:25 (31,872)
McPherson, Trish	4:15:06 (15,600)
McQuade, Ciara C	5:43:32 (31,610)
McQuade, Claire	5:50:02 (32,128)
McQuade, Eileen	5:43:32 (31,610)
McQuade, Mandy M	5:05:44 (27,514)
McQueen, Avril M	4:40:20 (22,269)
McQueen, Rebecca J	5:31:41 (30,632)
McRae, Sandra M	3:58:41 (11,369)
McRobert, Philippa	4:45:48 (23,624)
McTaggart, Vicky L	3:39:40 (6,571)

McWilliams, Anne	5:48:55 (32,042)
Mead, Kim	5:36:00 (31,028)
Meade, Niamh M	4:50:33 (24,733)
Meadows, Angie	6:06:06 (32,985)
Meadows, Dawn E	4:08:46 (13,985)
Meads, Emma L	5:39:11 (31,273)
Meads, Rebecca F	5:37:52 (31,184)
Mealings, Lorraine A	4:48:07 (24,169)
Meaney, Katrina J	4:50:45 (24,782)
Mearing-Smith, Ellie E	4:51:06 (24,864)
Mears, Helen E	4:41:46 (22,622)
Medeiros, Ana C	4:56:45 (26,013)
Medes, Claire L	4:40:41 (22,346)
Medland, Louise C	5:28:02 (30,270)
Mee, Viki A	4:31:50 (20,120)
Meehan, Antoinette	3:45:13 (7,733)
Meese, Katie S	5:22:32 (29,667)
Megoran, Jane I	4:43:50 (23,132)
Meilmann, Daniela	6:50:35 (34,083)
Meilmann, Yphat	6:50:36 (34,084)
Mein, Michaela C	5:09:09 (27,990)
Meir, Rachel L	4:02:50 (12,574)
Meldrum, Tara J	4:55:04 (25,711)
Melhuish, Alyson K	4:04:21 (12,905)
Meller, Helen C	4:55:09 (25,725)
Mellish, Denise C	3:42:24 (7,116)
Mellor, Katie D	4:34:16 (20,771)
Mellors, Sharon	3:16:23 (2,801)
Melnyk, Chrysia M	4:48:46 (24,312)
Meloy, Jane G	5:39:45 (31,314)
Melrose, Donna	5:28:55 (30,369)
Melvin, Gemma E	4:38:32 (21,831)
Melvin, June R	5:27:14 (30,168)
Mendick, Nicola A	3:52:54 (9,536)
Menzies-Sacher, Rosie C	5:25:18 (29,965)
Meo, Catherine	4:21:31 (17,312)
Mercer, Claudine E	3:45:22 (7,767)
Mercer, Julie D	3:22:36 (3,584)
Mercer, Lesley J	4:36:12 (21,296)
Mercer, Rhainnon	4:53:45 (25,426)
Mercer-Leach, Lisa A	4:36:40 (21,409)
Mercer-Rees, Alixandra E	4:27:57 (19,081)
Meredith, Georgina	4:26:19 (18,613)
Meredith, Jean	5:43:49 (31,634)
Meredith, Katie A	3:17:16 (2,898)
Merley, Jean A	3:42:56 (7,218)
Merrett, Bridget M	4:47:42 (24,068)
Merrick, Eleanor	5:11:53 (28,395)
Merrick, Jane	4:49:05 (24,392)
Merritt, Diane P	4:46:57 (23,896)
Mertin, Marita	4:46:58 (23,900)
Messenger, Claire E	3:28:16 (4,515)
Messenger, Karen M	5:42:04 (31,503)
Meston, Nicky K	4:10:27 (14,404)
Meston, Niki	3:45:37 (7,817)
Metcalf, Julia	5:33:44 (30,803)
Metcalfe, Claire	5:11:42 (28,367)
Metcalfe, Gail M	4:29:22 (19,494)
Metcalfe, Margaret R	3:56:58 (10,781)
Metcalfe, Sally-Ann	4:59:43 (26,594)
Metcalfe, Teresa	4:28:53 (19,371)
Metham, Elaine	3:58:52 (11,444)
Metzger, Regina	5:07:04 (27,702)
Meuer, Christina	5:02:20 (27,009)
Meuer, Herma	5:36:00 (31,028)
Meugin, Fabienne	4:09:05 (14,060)
Meyers, Hilary	5:32:50 (30,730)
Mhina, Mary Ann W	5:37:10 (31,129)
Michael, Sheelagh	5:05:06 (27,418)
Michael-Ives, Adrienne A	5:14:48 (28,785)
Michalik, Izzy	6:09:19 (33,093)
Michalowski, Gwenola	4:03:36 (12,748)
Michel, Franziska E	3:47:50 (8,306)
Michon, Sylvie	4:11:03 (14,559)
Micklewright, Kelly A	5:01:23 (26,858)
Mico, Stephanie	4:57:47 (26,245)
Middle, Claire J	4:58:53 (26,450)
Middlemast, Lynda	8:47:51 (34,577)
Middleton, Bridget R	4:10:55 (14,527)
Middleton, Jennifer E	4:51:41 (24,982)
Middleton, Sarah	6:16:30 (33,308)
Middleweek, Lucy M	4:48:32 (24,258)
Midgley, Nicola	3:35:50 (5,852)

Miell-Ingram, Wendy K	3:17:45 (2,959)

Mikitenko, Irina 2:24:14 (32)

Irina Mikitenko is one of Germany's most successful long distance runners. She has set German national records for 3000m and 5000m, with lifetime bests of 8:30.39 and 14:42.03 respectively. Her 10,000m best is 31:29.55. But it was when she turned her attention to the marathon that she realised her full potential. She won the London Marathon in 2008 and 2009 and the 2008 Berlin Marathon, where she became the ninth runner to break the 2:20 marathon barrier. She was born Irena Volynskaya in Kazakhstan, in 1972 and represented that nation at the 5000m in the 1996 Olympics. She and her husband immigrated to Germany in 1996. She is married to her coach, Alexander Mikitenko, and they have a son Alexander and daughter Vanessa.

Milbank, Camilla	3:54:09 (9,919)
Milburn, Lauren	4:40:58 (22,425)
Miles, Bethan D	3:22:17 (3,530)
Miles, Elizabeth A	6:34:19 (33,755)
Miles, Jenny	5:17:08 (29,080)
Miles, Nicola J	5:34:49 (30,919)
Miles, Teresa M	6:58:17 (34,191)
Miles-Young, Sarah	4:36:57 (21,477)
Milford, Cindy	5:06:18 (27,603)
Milford, Gaby H	5:10:18 (28,191)
Milgrom, Tuesday	4:50:23 (24,681)
Milkins, Jo K	5:14:49 (28,786)
Millar, Gillian M	3:40:01 (6,641)
Millar, Helen A	4:50:20 (24,673)
Millard, Rosie	3:51:47 (9,245)
Mille, Sarah	4:04:36 (12,949)
Miller, Anglea	4:38:32 (21,831)
Miller, Carolann	3:51:58 (9,291)
Miller, Clare M	5:10:00 (28,145)
Miller, Erica	5:56:05 (32,527)
Miller, Hannah J	4:37:59 (21,711)
Miller, Helen P	4:16:22 (15,924)
Miller, Joanne	4:45:09 (23,452)
Miller, Leanne	4:36:39 (21,402)
Miller, Lucy	3:25:50 (4,075)
Miller, Maureen A	5:58:49 (32,688)
Miller, Rosemary	6:25:18 (33,554)
Miller, Samantha J	5:22:12 (29,626)
Miller, Susan J	4:51:56 (25,028)

Millidine, Karen J....5:02:41 (27,062)
Milligan, Jessica E....4:00:13 (11,901)
Millington, Clare....5:26:05 (30,043)
Millman, Katie J....4:42:50 (22,884)
Mills, Alison J....4:49:36 (24,503)
Mills, Amy....4:34:59 (20,974)
Mills, Charis S....4:20:35 (17,055)
Mills, Charlotte S....4:49:37 (24,507)
Mills, Debra J....4:46:33 (23,789)
Mills, Diana H....3:43:58 (7,452)
Mills, Francesca L....6:06:12 (32,991)
Mills, Helen C....5:14:12 (28,704)
Mills, Lee-Ann....4:28:12 (19,171)
Mills, Lorraine....4:44:13 (23,233)
Mills, Natasha....5:54:02 (32,409)
Mills, Pippa....5:09:43 (28,097)
Mills, Rachel....5:12:51 (28,525)
Mills, Victoria C....5:30:41 (30,544)
Millson, Carrie H....3:12:05 (2,221)
Millward, Harriet R....5:19:12 (29,315)
Millward, Jacky M....4:40:50 (22,389)
Millward, Katie....5:21:32 (29,560)
Milne, Ali Y....4:22:33 (17,599)
Milne, Carolyn E....3:32:27 (5,309)
Milne, Chrissy....5:03:21 (27,163)
Milne, Helen R....5:23:33 (29,751)
Milne, Kirsty J....4:25:40 (18,434)
Milne, Patricia....3:21:18 (3,402)
Milne, Sarah E....3:52:59 (9,566)
Milne, Seonaid C....5:43:45 (31,629)
Milner, Bernadette....3:37:09 (6,088)
Milner, Beth L....4:39:13 (22,034)
Milner, Victoria L....4:15:25 (15,676)
Milnes, Dianne....4:24:02 (18,007)
Milnor, Becky....4:22:50 (17,679)
Milsom, Georgina....5:25:38 (29,998)
Milsom, Jennifer M....4:31:05 (19,906)
Milton, Angela M....4:04:34 (12,942)
Milton, Caroline L....4:41:38 (22,593)
Milton, Gillian C....3:58:49 (11,426)
Milton, Jackie....5:27:55 (30,256)
Milton, Joanna....4:44:34 (23,313)
Minas, Argyro....4:11:42 (14,733)
Minas, Christalla....4:08:47 (13,990)
Mingay, Karen D....5:02:35 (27,048)
Mingo, Florencia....4:19:43 (16,818)
Minintt, Clare F....3:52:43 (9,484)
Minks, Sally A....5:23:45 (29,775)
Minter, Briony L....6:17:54 (33,354)
Minton, Jacqueline L....5:10:04 (28,158)
Miralles, Laurence....4:01:34 (12,259)
Mirfattahi, Mahya....4:20:35 (17,055)
Mischke, Susanne....3:50:32 (8,937)
Missen, Verity....3:48:16 (8,418)
Misth, Carolyn....6:49:05 (34,055)
Mistry, Jayshree....4:52:04 (25,059)
Mistry, Kumud....5:30:03 (30,481)
Mitchell, Alex M....4:48:49 (24,324)
Mitchell, Claire E....4:12:15 (14,873)
Mitchell, Elizabeth M....4:48:41 (24,285)
Mitchell, Heather M....4:01:21 (12,200)
Mitchell, Jackie A....4:36:19 (21,328)
Mitchell, Julie A....7:22:52 (34,414)
Mitchell, Kay....5:27:07 (30,159)
Mitchell, Lauren J....4:15:43 (15,752)
Mitchell, Michelle S....4:28:52 (19,367)
Mitchell, Pauline A....5:26:35 (30,109)
Mitchell, Rebecca....3:50:26 (8,916)
Mitchell, Tracy....3:14:16 (2,513)
Mitchell, Vanessa J....3:48:35 (8,483)
Mitchkovska, Ina....4:07:44 (13,704)
Miyahara, Yayoi....4:58:13 (26,328)
Miyashita, Miho....4:59:29 (26,561)
Mizukami, Ikuko....5:29:10 (30,394)
Moffat, Alex J....5:07:32 (27,771)
Moffat, Cheryl L....3:43:28 (7,337)
Moffat, Julia S....4:25:13 (18,323)
Moffatt, Fiona H....3:31:19 (5,102)
Moffett, Joanne F....5:21:01 (29,497)
Moffitt, Alison J....6:05:00 (32,926)
Moggan, Sarah J....4:35:10 (21,024)
Mohimani, Nooshin....7:27:54 (34,445)
Mold, Bridget E....5:11:51 (28,391)
Molland, Jennie E....5:02:11 (26,985)
Moloney, Jenny....3:39:55 (6,619)
Molyneaux, Alison J....4:24:47 (18,210)
Molyneaux, Heather V....5:25:44 (30,005)
Molyneaux, Jo....3:28:59 (4,665)
Molyneux, Julia....4:25:46 (18,468)
Monaghan, Siobhan M....4:52:30 (25,146)
Monahan, Rachel C....4:09:12 (14,088)
Moncrieff, Natasha E....4:22:44 (17,654)
Monday, Trudy....4:32:35 (20,318)
Mong, Lisa....4:12:52 (14,996)
Monk, Caroline A....3:59:38 (11,724)
Monk, Clare V....4:48:34 (24,265)
Monk, Gillian M....4:33:08 (20,468)
Monks, Taryn A....4:56:59 (26,071)
Montalbetti, Silvia....4:42:03 (22,683)
Montgomery, Britney A....4:20:47 (17,118)
Montgomery, Claire H....4:02:18 (12,446)
Montgomery, Mairi J....4:16:42 (16,010)
Moody, Denny P....4:47:28 (24,015)
Moody, Elaine....5:28:50 (30,353)
Moody, Margaret M....3:34:41 (5,641)
Moody, Pat....5:08:34 (27,906)
Moon, Clare J....3:52:00 (9,301)
Mooney, Alice M....4:10:51 (14,509)
Mooney, Catrina....3:58:38 (11,351)
Mooney, Gillian E....6:03:28 (32,863)
Moorcroft, Tiffany A....3:27:19 (4,336)
Moore, Caroline J....4:25:35 (18,411)
Moore, Catherine A....6:17:59 (33,356)
Moore, Jane L....5:28:52 (30,360)
Moore, Jenny....3:00:13 (1,180)
Moore, Jessica M....3:58:53 (11,451)
Moore, Katherine L....3:54:21 (9,974)
Moore, Katie L....4:37:04 (21,499)
Moore, Kerry L....4:48:44 (24,303)
Moore, Lucinda M....3:51:21 (9,141)
Moore, Nicola....3:21:23 (3,413)
Moore, Pamela....4:15:02 (15,574)
Moore, Patricia E....4:42:47 (22,874)
Moore, Sally....6:05:36 (32,958)
Moore, Sally A....4:30:45 (19,816)
Moore, Sarah E....4:14:01 (15,310)
Moore, Tracey K....4:52:22 (25,118)
Moore Fitzgerald, Lindsey J....4:19:00 (16,625)
Moors, Kate M....5:32:12 (30,672)
Morahan, Lonneke....5:05:14 (27,439)
Moran, Abigail E....4:25:31 (18,402)
Moran, Michele....3:26:06 (4,125)
Moran, Teresa L....6:26:25 (33,583)
Moreau, Denny A....6:01:11 (32,785)
Morecroft, Casey N....4:44:09 (23,214)
Morelli, Brenda....4:45:33 (23,549)
Moreton, Penny....4:06:56 (13,501)
Moreton, Sarah E....6:01:47 (32,814)
Moretti, Catherine R....5:40:32 (31,378)
Morgan, Amy H....5:00:13 (26,667)
Morgan, Angela....4:20:09 (16,928)
Morgan, Angela B....6:11:07 (33,144)
Morgan, Carol....3:33:15 (5,432)
Morgan, Carole A....3:49:59 (8,821)
Morgan, Catherine G....4:42:46 (22,868)
Morgan, Charissa....4:49:47 (24,552)
Morgan, Clarie L....4:30:30 (19,744)
Morgan, Debbie M....4:53:18 (25,332)
Morgan, Debra J....5:10:20 (28,196)
Morgan, Gemma....4:18:13 (16,405)
Morgan, Heather....7:14:25 (34,356)
Morgan, Helen C....4:49:39 (24,521)
Morgan, Karen....5:06:25 (27,617)
Morgan, Kay....5:47:21 (31,937)
Morgan, Kerry....4:54:46 (25,642)
Morgan, Linda A....3:59:12 (11,562)
Morgan, Louise....4:14:21 (15,410)
Morgan, Nicola J....5:04:20 (27,298)
Morgan, Pauline J....4:56:05 (25,889)
Morgan, Ruth....5:42:19 (31,523)
Morgan, Shan....2:57:57 (943)
Morgan, Sharon....5:10:11 (28,171)
Morgan, Sian....5:46:01 (31,835)
Morgan, Sian A....3:34:47 (5,659)
Morgan, Sian J....3:44:17 (7,512)
Morgan, Susan D....5:03:12 (27,131)
Morgan, Suzanne....4:53:46 (25,432)
Morgan, Trish A....4:20:18 (16,975)
Morgan Jones, Melanie M....6:47:55 (34,034)
Morgan-Barnes, Simoine C....6:41:23 (33,904)
Morgan-Bell, Julie D....4:01:44 (12,302)
Moriarty, Lucy E....4:43:31 (23,054)
Morley, Anna J....6:20:50 (33,420)
Morley, Diane N....4:04:48 (13,002)
Morley, Hannah E....4:34:22 (20,790)
Morley, Helen L....4:49:36 (24,503)
Morley, Jayne L....4:57:46 (26,241)
Morley, Joanne....4:37:24 (21,574)
Morley, Lindsay....4:33:07 (20,461)
Morley, Suzanne P....5:47:50 (31,968)
Morley, Syra....4:12:09 (14,852)
Mornement, Hannah L....5:19:48 (29,389)
Morosi Rizzi, Rezia....4:40:19 (22,262)
Morreale, Ivana....4:36:55 (21,471)
Morrey, Alison....4:29:47 (19,581)
Morris, Ann....4:20:12 (16,942)
Morris, Barbara J....7:35:48 (34,472)
Morris, Colette M....4:57:14 (26,132)
Morris, Eleanor J....5:48:58 (32,053)
Morris, Emma L....4:32:44 (20,355)
Morris, Gemma L....4:42:17 (22,752)
Morris, Grace H....4:37:57 (21,704)
Morris, Helen E....4:37:47 (21,663)
Morris, Helen J....4:28:13 (19,184)
Morris, Jayne L....5:10:28 (28,215)
Morris, Marcelle W....4:01:06 (12,136)
Morris, Margaret A....4:04:17 (12,882)
Morris, Mercy J....4:55:56 (25,867)
Morris, Michelle J....6:22:52 (33,488)
Morris, Neiline K....6:33:56 (33,748)
Morris, Patricia....7:01:40 (34,225)
Morris, Rachel J....3:32:23 (5,296)
Morris, Rosa....3:10:44 (2,067)
Morris, Rose L....4:25:44 (18,456)
Morris, Ruth N....6:31:06 (33,687)
Morris, Sara J....5:14:57 (28,813)
Morris, Sarah L....4:30:39 (19,785)
Morris, Sarah M....6:13:32 (33,229)
Morris, Sonya....5:04:04 (27,259)
Morris, Sophie L....4:02:05 (12,382)
Morris, Susan M....4:22:30 (17,582)
Morris, Tracey....4:58:10 (26,320)
Morris, Vanessa....4:05:06 (13,069)
Morrisey, Annabel R....3:47:23 (8,193)
Morrison, Diane L....3:49:22 (8,668)
Morrison, Hazel V....5:00:42 (26,737)
Morrison, Moira L....5:41:25 (31,459)
Morrison, Natalie G....5:00:25 (26,696)
Morrison, Sheila J....4:43:24 (23,026)
Morrison, Yvonne I....3:40:49 (6,784)
Morrissey, Martina....4:46:13 (23,717)
Morrow, Karen L....4:33:44 (20,647)
Morse, Hayley L....4:07:28 (13,633)
Mort, Helen R....3:10:08 (2,002)
Mortimer, Alison S....5:37:31 (31,154)
Mortimer, Diana J....3:20:58 (3,357)
Mortimer, Roz S....5:16:46 (29,026)
Mortimer, Verena N....4:26:43 (18,731)
Mortlock, Brenda D....5:16:22 (28,977)
Morton, Abi K....6:45:28 (33,989)
Morton, Caron M....4:30:40 (19,791)
Morton, Frances G....5:28:02 (30,270)
Morton, Lisa....4:37:59 (21,711)
Morton, Lisa C....4:39:02 (21,981)
Morton, Rebecca....4:56:41 (26,001)
Morton, Rebecca D....6:12:56 (33,208)
Morton, Sandra P....4:51:15 (24,893)
Morton, Shayne L....4:32:53 (20,397)
Morton, Tania B....4:45:31 (23,541)
Morton-Hunte, Ashley S....5:01:44 (26,921)
Mosbah, Dalila....6:50:47 (34,087)
Mosley, Dominique....4:48:22 (24,218)
Mosley, Polly C....3:45:39 (7,827)
Moss, Deirdre M....5:29:35 (30,435)
Moss, Gillian A....6:50:08 (34,077)
Moss, Harriet....5:17:57 (29,175)
Moss, Lorraine S....5:43:36 (31,614)
Moss, Patricia M....3:58:50 (11,436)
Mossop, Maureen....5:10:49 (28,256)

Mostacci, Odessa.............4:28:29 (19,256)	Naim, Angelina.............7:08:41 (34,300)	Newman, Rebecca L.............4:34:55 (20,940)
Mostert, Nadine.............5:27:06 (30,158)	Nairn, Fionn.............3:12:58 (2,330)	Newman, Sally A.............5:45:54 (31,828)
Mott, Jacqueline A.............4:50:02 (24,608)	Naish, Joanna M.............5:27:17 (30,176)	Newman, Sharon.............4:15:00 (15,565)
Mottley, Bev A.............4:05:04 (13,062)	Naismith, Julie.............4:49:21 (24,451)	Newnes, Hannah.............5:14:36 (28,759)
Moulton, Janice M.............4:58:08 (26,314)	Nakagawa, Yuriko.............4:16:24 (15,932)	Newport-Peace, Diana S.............4:17:50 (16,314)
Mountain, Denise S.............4:15:59 (15,832)	Nancolas, Hayley L.............3:28:09 (4,498)	Newson, Marian E.............5:22:22 (29,646)
Mountford, Sara.............4:33:42 (20,635)	Nandra, Kirat K.............4:34:06 (20,725)	Newstead, Deborah.............3:56:03 (10,503)
Mountfort, Toni.............5:38:06 (31,196)	Napier, Sara E.............5:52:44 (32,325)	Newton, Elie M.............4:16:25 (15,938)
Moussa, Sema.............5:13:22 (28,588)	Napper, Amanda.............4:30:48 (19,833)	Newton, Emma-Jane.............3:43:02 (7,246)
Moutarde, Margarita I.............5:10:22 (28,201)	Nash, Beverley J.............5:28:19 (30,305)	Newton, Helen A.............5:08:28 (27,848)
Mouzakitis, Helen.............4:10:46 (14,485)	Nash, Ellen R.............4:25:32 (18,406)	Newton, Jane.............4:06:47 (13,471)
Mouzer, Sandra A.............6:39:08 (33,868)	Nash, Helen.............5:18:14 (29,201)	Newton, Jane I.............6:40:47 (33,897)
Mowat, Nicky.............3:28:07 (4,491)	Nash, Jackie.............4:34:07 (20,731)	Newton, Kristina A.............4:10:53 (14,516)
Mowbray, Julie A.............5:38:28 (31,224)	Nash, Kaylie J.............5:56:38 (32,564)	Newton, Susan L.............5:19:06 (29,303)
Mower, Joy S.............5:06:15 (27,591)	Nash, Rachel E.............5:03:12 (27,131)	Newton-Fisher, Naomi K.............5:00:14 (26,672)
Mowle, Linda F.............5:12:42 (28,494)	Nash, Sarah.............3:55:31 (10,346)	Ng, Wai Foong.............4:39:03 (21,988)
Moxon, Kay.............3:53:04 (9,596)	Nassi, Nicola.............7:03:11 (34,244)	Ngalam, Kezia.............6:44:44 (33,973)
Moyer, Hallie M.............5:13:24 (28,595)	Nathan, Janine A.............4:35:47 (21,190)	Ngeow, Teresa P.............4:18:35 (16,526)
Moyse, Kerry.............6:35:02 (33,772)	Nathwani, Nisha.............4:41:42 (22,616)	Niarchos, Michelle L.............6:28:12 (33,646)
Mueller, Friederike.............4:15:09 (15,607)	Natrajan, Rachael C.............4:13:09 (15,074)	Nicholas, Brenda.............6:39:24 (33,873)
Muir, Clare H.............4:18:54 (16,599)	Naughton, Eileen C.............5:33:45 (30,807)	Nicholas, Linda.............6:08:04 (33,046)
Muir, Sarah.............4:34:27 (20,811)	Nauman, Zoe C.............5:21:10 (29,516)	Nicholas, Susie L.............4:48:38 (24,277)
Muirhead, Sarah J.............3:40:21 (6,704)	Nawrat, Jennifer C.............5:07:56 (27,817)	Nicholl, Emily M.............4:04:44 (12,992)
Mulcahy, Nora E.............3:45:04 (7,700)	Naylor, Ann J.............5:31:11 (30,583)	Nicholls, Alison.............3:47:07 (8,136)
Mulchay, Debbie.............5:06:03 (27,560)	Naylor, Anne.............3:46:26 (7,988)	Nicholls, Clair M.............4:54:54 (25,673)
Muldoon, Deborah H.............5:17:50 (29,159)	Naylor, Denise L.............5:14:04 (28,683)	Nicholls, Clare.............5:49:11 (32,066)
Muldoon, Nuala M.............4:24:19 (18,084)	Ncube, Zwe.............6:53:25 (34,130)	Nicholls, Emily R.............4:12:45 (14,974)
Mulinder, Theryn.............5:31:44 (30,637)	Neachell, Emma A.............5:42:35 (31,535)	Nicholls, Janice J.............6:12:23 (33,181)
Mullen, Helen.............6:00:59 (32,779)	Neal, Clare.............5:13:40 (28,631)	Nicholls, Kathryn.............3:57:57 (11,102)
Mullenger, Claire.............3:21:20 (3,408)	Neal, Helen L.............3:47:05 (8,130)	Nicholls, Susan A.............5:11:23 (28,315)
Muller, Severine.............3:41:47 (6,988)	Neal, Mary.............6:16:13 (33,300)	Nichols, Claire L.............4:18:50 (16,582)
Mulligan, Debra M.............5:33:48 (30,814)	Neal, Nikki H.............3:07:23 (1,722)	Nichols, Lisa M.............5:35:28 (30,973)
Mullin, Claire.............4:14:09 (15,354)	Neale, Mandy J.............4:31:47 (20,097)	Nichols, Tracy A.............4:36:11 (21,289)
Mullins, Anna L.............5:20:10 (29,422)	Nealon, Nicki J.............3:04:26 (1,480)	Nichols, Zara M.............4:57:37 (26,213)
Mullins, Karen.............3:44:16 (7,505)	Nealon, Sabina.............5:23:53 (29,787)	Nicholson, Alison J.............4:48:47 (24,315)
Mulvaney, Shona.............5:51:22 (32,241)	Neal-Smith, Kate C.............5:44:59 (31,766)	Nicholson, Camilla.............5:45:59 (31,831)
Mumby, Karen.............4:18:43 (16,556)	Neary, Patricia.............5:18:51 (29,270)	Nicholson, Dianne.............6:30:47 (33,679)
Mumford, Claire L.............6:12:13 (33,175)	Neate, Victoria L.............3:40:15 (6,684)	Nicholson, Emma D.............4:47:07 (23,935)
Mumford, Ruth M.............4:47:28 (24,015)	Neave, Marianne J.............4:55:14 (25,735)	Nicholson, Emma F.............5:33:30 (30,786)
Mummery, Lucy J.............4:41:07 (22,467)	Needham, Lindsay.............4:11:42 (14,733)	Nicholson, Joanne F.............5:00:48 (26,761)
Mundy, Suzanne J.............4:35:22 (21,072)	Needs, Jenny A.............4:55:50 (25,842)	Nicholson, Katie.............4:30:50 (19,843)
Munn, Fiona E.............5:17:03 (29,068)	Neenan, Trudi C.............4:23:41 (17,910)	Nicholson, Melissa.............4:31:52 (20,130)
Munn, Flavia.............3:43:11 (7,283)	Negus, Ruth E.............3:59:19 (11,602)	Nicholson, Nicolie J.............4:26:12 (18,584)
Munn, Suzanne.............4:18:51 (16,587)	Neill, Fiona S.............5:51:00 (32,208)	Nicholson, Rebecca C.............4:00:00 (11,853)
Munnion, Janette L.............4:34:04 (20,712)	Neill, Karen E.............4:00:15 (11,909)	Nicholson, Rebecca E.............4:50:27 (24,697)
Munro, Anna.............5:22:31 (29,664)	Neilson, Christine M.............3:43:34 (7,357)	Nicholson, Victoria A.............5:02:45 (27,074)
Munro, Diane.............3:20:39 (3,313)	Neligan, Fiona C.............4:11:54 (14,778)	Nickalls, Alice.............4:53:32 (25,382)
Munro, Lynsey.............3:34:54 (5,685)	Nelson, Catherine M.............3:52:47 (9,499)	Nicklin, Debbie E.............4:35:57 (21,228)
Munro, Patricia A.............3:17:25 (2,920)	Nelson, Clare E.............4:28:32 (19,274)	Nicks, Jessica A.............4:49:05 (24,392)
Murchie, Shonagh.............4:46:29 (23,774)	Nelson, Sarah.............3:57:39 (10,995)	Nicodemo, Luigia.............4:33:22 (20,533)
Murdoch, Felicity A.............4:07:06 (13,545)	Nelson, Sarah K.............4:53:53 (25,456)	Nicol, Barbara.............3:39:16 (6,490)
Murdoch, Gail E.............3:08:17 (1,819)	Neocleous, Julia E.............4:41:40 (22,608)	Nicol, Emma.............5:25:53 (30,019)
Murless, Catherine M.............4:24:57 (18,249)	Nestor, Frances M.............4:54:44 (25,632)	Nicol, Jackie A.............3:29:43 (4,824)
Murphy, Angela.............4:56:14 (25,924)	Nethercott, Kat H.............6:11:52 (33,161)	Nicol, Nicola J.............5:37:13 (31,133)
Murphy, Catherine.............3:45:37 (7,817)	Netherwood-Meek, Kirsteen A....3:57:45 (11,039)	Nicolaou, Clare N.............3:48:39 (8,500)
Murphy, Christine P.............4:41:36 (22,581)	Nettleton, Michele L.............4:34:49 (20,908)	Nicoll, Catherine R.............4:52:21 (25,115)
Murphy, Deborah J.............4:00:58 (12,105)	Netto, Lisa M.............4:32:02 (20,181)	Nicoll, Ruth S.............4:10:16 (14,356)
Murphy, Ellen.............4:03:13 (12,658)	Neuhaeuser, Hildegard.............4:30:30 (19,744)	Nicolle, Sue.............5:09:58 (28,139)
Murphy, Emma C.............5:09:46 (28,109)	Neuteboom-De Jong, Sonja.............4:48:22 (24,218)	Nield, Alison J.............5:03:29 (27,181)
Murphy, Helen L.............4:38:58 (21,967)	Neville, Denise.............4:55:04 (25,711)	Nielsen, Anja.............4:03:57 (12,820)
Murphy, Joanna L.............3:37:23 (6,140)	Neville, Elizabeth.............3:28:54 (4,644)	Nielsen, Karen C.............3:48:22 (8,436)
Murphy, Lucy J.............5:47:09 (31,922)	Neville, Lenka.............4:37:45 (21,652)	Nieuwenhuis, Victoria R.............5:02:38 (27,055)
Murphy, Pamela J.............6:45:09 (33,981)	Neville, Lindsay V.............5:31:57 (30,657)	Nightingale, Gail.............3:28:30 (4,562)
Murphy, Samantha A.............3:23:05 (3,651)	New, Abby R.............4:46:48 (23,854)	Nightingale, Teresa J.............4:22:48 (17,668)
Murphy, Susan M.............5:21:33 (29,563)	Newburn, Charlotte.............4:39:41 (22,122)	Nikbakht, Neda.............7:07:48 (34,289)
Murphy, Tracey M.............3:23:06 (3,654)	Newbury, Caroline C.............5:10:23 (28,204)	Nissim, Rachel.............3:57:40 (11,001)
Murphy, Zara J.............3:42:58 (7,227)	Newbury, Christine.............4:31:59 (20,169)	Niven, Stephanie.............3:58:16 (11,203)
Murray, Angela M.............7:09:57 (34,319)	Newby, Claire L.............4:31:37 (20,056)	Niven, Suzie.............4:10:27 (14,404)
Murray, Beverley A.............4:24:20 (18,091)	Newby, Nancy.............4:50:52 (24,812)	Nivoix, Bernadette.............4:53:45 (25,426)
Murray, Clare A.............3:54:27 (10,008)	Newcomb, Hannah D.............4:37:48 (21,671)	Nixon, Jackie.............4:24:29 (18,137)
Murray, Deborah.............4:46:42 (23,829)	Newcombe, Diana C.............5:06:49 (27,668)	Nixon, Jill.............4:28:18 (19,207)
Murray, Rebecca J.............4:02:08 (12,396)	Newcombe, Penny-Marie.............5:02:38 (27,055)	Nixon, Rosemary L.............4:05:50 (13,254)
Murray, Samantha J.............4:58:20 (26,348)	Newell, Angela C.............4:59:17 (26,529)	Nkonde, Natasha.............4:27:57 (19,081)
Musgrave, Rosie.............4:43:20 (23,012)	Newell, Claire F.............4:34:57 (20,957)	Noad, Joy.............3:25:24 (3,993)
Musk, Vicky.............4:36:29 (21,364)	Newens, Joanne C.............4:29:21 (19,489)	Nobbs, Tracy J.............4:06:47 (13,471)
Mustafa, Hatice.............6:15:40 (33,285)	Newman, Anita A.............4:03:30 (12,727)	Noble, Anne H.............3:51:25 (9,157)
Mustat, Lara.............2:54:35 (723)	Newman, Jacqueline D.............3:36:38 (5,984)	Noble, Cate M.............3:56:49 (10,730)
Musty, Maria J.............4:35:44 (21,175)	Newman, Jana A.............4:17:02 (16,104)	Noble, Emma.............4:16:14 (15,888)
Myatt, Debbie A.............4:46:40 (23,822)	Newman, Jo L.............4:03:27 (12,715)	Noble, Linda.............3:29:25 (4,766)
Myers, Amanda J.............4:09:58 (14,291)	Newman, Judith A.............4:55:47 (25,836)	Noble, Maria.............5:26:09 (30,048)
Myers, Cynthia.............5:54:48 (32,445)	Newman, Louise.............6:17:27 (33,333)	Noble, Victoria A.............4:34:18 (20,776)
Myers, Marie L.............5:53:32 (32,379)	Newman, Lucy H.............5:26:32 (30,106)	Nobles, Margaret.............4:22:15 (17,509)
Nagel, Lee J.............5:06:54 (27,682)		Noel, Lesley A.............5:11:43 (28,369)

Noel, Maureen 3:34:09 (5,571)
Nokes, Carol V 4:32:13 (20,233)
Nolan, Ann P.................................4:31:49 (20,112)
Nolan, Christina M 4:53:18 (25,332)
Noorian, Rebecca L 5:15:19 (28,855)
Norbury, Carol 5:21:40 (29,575)
Nordin, Breege J 3:13:59 (2,463)
Norman, Carmen 4:55:20 (25,753)
Norman, Chantel M 4:16:49 (16,041)
Norman, Diane 4:23:00 (17,728)
Norman, Eve 4:20:06 (16,913)
Norman, Jane A.............................5:02:23 (27,021)
Norman, Lindsay............................4:33:02 (20,439)
Norman, Louisa M 5:15:39 (28,899)
Norman, Melanie G 4:45:23 (23,506)
Norman, Samantha 4:43:47 (23,119)
Norman, Sarah A 5:19:00 (29,289)
Norman, Sarah J............................5:20:11 (29,425)
Normanton, Clare L 5:11:15 (28,301)
Norquay, Megan J..........................3:13:32 (2,401)
Norris, Bonita 4:51:57 (25,031)
Norrish, Donna M..........................3:26:03 (4,113)
North, Alison 6:08:24 (33,061)
North, Tracy S 4:16:47 (16,029)
Northey, Teresa J 3:45:50 (7,867)
Northwood, Emmilia C..................3:47:42 (8,280)
Northwood, Tina 4:37:11 (21,522)
Norton, Julie A...............................3:43:10 (7,281)
Noske, Juliette 5:07:16 (27,733)
Notley, Sandra J............................4:32:18 (20,254)
Nottage, Janine 4:46:22 (23,755)
Nowak, Maja 4:32:05 (20,192)
Nowell, Lucille M...........................6:05:58 (32,971)
Nozdar, Helen M 6:05:03 (32,930)
Nugent, Clare M.............................5:03:05 (27,115)
Nugent, Mandy...............................5:00:56 (26,787)
Nugent, Natasha M 4:52:15 (25,091)
Nulty, Josephine A..........................5:10:37 (28,233)
Nunn, Amy A..................................3:24:58 (3,921)
Nunn, Gill A 3:48:02 (8,358)
Nunn, Hazel L.................................4:27:21 (18,916)
Nunn, Melanie J..............................4:26:04 (18,558)
Nurcombe, Karen A........................3:58:28 (11,290)
Nurse, Linda J.................................4:07:09 (13,563)
Nurse, Sarah R................................4:26:42 (18,723)
Nutburn, Jennifer A.........................5:26:31 (30,101)
Nutland, Rebecca............................4:26:21 (18,621)
Nutt, Rebecca K 4:29:47 (19,581)
Nutt, Wendy J 4:18:27 (16,479)
Nuttall, Alison M.............................4:54:59 (25,698)
Nutting, Katie L..............................4:54:07 (25,504)
Nwaigwe, Otito 6:36:46 (33,815)
Nygren, Johanna.............................3:28:46 (4,618)
Nyguist, Janice E 5:00:48 (26,761)
Nys, Marie-Cecile...........................4:15:55 (15,811)
Oakes, Mhari E...............................3:59:33 (11,688)
Oakley, Karen I...............................4:38:40 (21,871)
Oakley, Lisa M 4:43:02 (22,940)
Oakley, Louise 4:02:28 (12,491)
Oakley, Ruth E................................4:01:18 (12,184)
Oates, Emma J................................4:21:26 (17,286)
O'Beney, Carol 5:00:44 (26,747)
O'Brien, Alex R...............................5:22:49 (29,688)
O'Brien, Christina J.........................6:51:36 (34,105)
O'Brien, Claudette F........................5:43:13 (31,590)
O'Brien, Hannah L..........................4:41:54 (22,652)
O'Brien, Kathryn H 4:54:44 (25,632)
O'Brien, Lesley J.............................5:27:54 (30,254)
O'Brien, Morag E............................4:45:25 (23,517)
O'Brien, Nina C 4:29:20 (19,481)
O'Brien, Tina Y 4:44:48 (23,367)
O'Brien, Victoria M 6:24:12 (33,521)
O'Brien, Yesmin.............................4:23:18 (17,816)
O'Callaghan, Ailish K 5:05:06 (27,418)
O'Callaghan, Ann 4:05:24 (13,146)
O'Callaghan, Lisa J.........................6:14:44 (33,260)
O'Callaghan, Sara J........................3:58:23 (11,256)
O'Connell, Alison 4:34:58 (20,962)
O'Connell, Susanne J 5:22:07 (29,616)
O'Connell, Tanya A.........................5:43:53 (31,660)
O'Connor, Carmel 4:44:49 (23,375)
O'Connor, Carol A..........................3:35:37 (5,815)
O'Connor, Cindy M 6:36:19 (33,798)

O'Connor, Kerrie A 3:13:56 (2,457)
O'Connor, Rachel E.........................3:50:04 (8,837)
Oddie, Elaine A...............................6:21:22 (33,439)
Odell, Julie 5:25:52 (30,016)
Odell, Maxine 4:40:29 (22,306)
O'Dell, Susie M 5:27:15 (30,170)
Odgers, Alix 5:30:17 (30,506)
O'Donnell, Anne Marie....................3:59:33 (11,688)
O'Donoghue, Shanleigh S 4:12:44 (14,969)
O'Donoghue, Terri A........................4:11:57 (14,791)
O'Duffy, Libby K 3:15:18 (2,674)
O'Dwyer, Sarah J 5:05:45 (27,516)
Oertwich, Marina 4:05:56 (13,275)
O'Farrell, Alison 4:50:29 (24,708)
Offer, Kirsten E...............................6:36:48 (33,817)
Offord, Catherine M........................5:15:07 (28,834)
O'Flaherty, Caroline F 5:10:33 (28,221)
Ogbemudia, Ann E 5:02:54 (27,098)
Ogilvie, Hannah 4:45:10 (23,456)
Ogne, Birgithe 4:20:29 (17,020)
O'Gorman, Elizabeth G....................4:11:47 (14,745)
O'Gorman, Katherine 4:19:00 (16,625)
O'Hagan, Collette M 4:47:07 (23,935)
O'Hagan, Rosie 4:16:04 (15,853)
O'Halloran, Madeline J 6:11:19 (33,148)
O'Hanlon, Denise S.........................4:12:05 (14,835)
O'Hanlon, Jenny A 4:03:16 (12,677)
O'Hara, Bryony F 3:43:45 (7,400)
O'Hara, Jane S 4:42:55 (22,912)
O'Hare, Rachel A............................5:57:09 (32,585)
O'Hare, Suzanne 4:48:29 (24,243)
Oie, Ingeborg D 4:25:58 (18,524)
Ojeaga, Jackie B 6:36:19 (33,798)
Okada, Megumi...............................4:49:45 (24,543)
O'Kane, Barbara J 6:12:44 (33,197)
O'Kane, Caroline E..........................6:36:07 (33,795)
Okello, Dolores 4:32:34 (20,315)
Okoye, Ginika S..............................4:53:03 (25,286)
Oldershaw, Tina J...........................3:03:56 (1,443)
Oldfield, Carla J 4:27:19 (18,911)
Oldfield, Nadine C...........................3:53:44 (9,783)
Oldham, Michelle 3:18:43 (3,066)
Oldham, Nicola S............................3:36:42 (5,999)
Oldham, Rebecca J 4:06:43 (13,455)
Olds, Denise 4:38:30 (21,829)
Oliver, Barbara 4:33:09 (20,470)
Oliver, Beverley R...........................5:10:46 (28,243)
Oliver, Cara 3:32:27 (5,309)
Oliver, Chantal E............................3:52:58 (9,560)
Oliver, Jo 5:41:59 (31,496)
Oliver, Kathleen 4:45:52 (23,637)
Oliver, Rosemary M 5:21:33 (29,563)
Oliver, Sue 4:54:41 (25,618)
Oliver-Hobley, Esme.......................4:44:54 (23,395)
Olliffe, Stephanie J..........................3:34:55 (5,688)
Ollis, Jan R.....................................4:25:25 (18,373)
Olney, Yvonne 3:57:48 (11,061)
Olsson, Kirsten B............................4:50:36 (24,746)
Olvier, Hannah...............................3:43:03 (7,248)
O'Mahony, Nora M 6:31:39 (33,696)
O'Malley, Susan A 4:31:37 (20,056)
O'Neil, Jane A 3:38:31 (6,361)
O'Neill, Alana I...............................5:04:37 (27,348)
O'Neill, Angela C............................4:48:40 (24,283)
O'Neill, Gail H 5:01:06 (26,811)
O'Neill, Katherine A........................4:05:08 (13,080)
O'Neill, Leigh 4:10:50 (14,503)
O'Neill-Berest, Suzanne P 4:22:29 (17,575)
Ong, Michelle.................................3:47:54 (8,326)
Onions, Kate 5:28:06 (30,279)
Onnie, Lisa 5:22:12 (29,626)
Onslow, Julie..................................4:51:21 (24,915)
Oomen, Fionnuala...........................4:51:44 (24,994)
Oosthuizen, Johannette..................4:42:13 (22,732)
Oosthuizen, Riette 3:47:13 (8,161)

Oosthuizen, Vicki-Ann H............3:53:02 (9,586)
Opara, Elaine M.............................4:33:29 (20,572)
Open, Sarah 6:30:35 (33,673)
Openshaw, Alexandra C 3:49:17 (8,649)
Opie, Catherine 4:49:50 (24,556)
Opie-Smith, Katherine.....................4:34:50 (20,918)
Orange, Helen 4:27:05 (18,834)
Orange, Liz M 4:57:54 (26,263)
Orban, Mary B.................................4:37:16 (21,539)
Orchard, Nicola 4:30:45 (19,816)
Orchard, Sara E..............................5:03:17 (27,149)
O'Regan, Catherine P......................4:18:32 (16,508)
O'Reilly, Beth M 3:53:00 (9,572)
O'Reilly, Tracey L 5:51:54 (32,284)
O'Riordan, Michelle H......................4:18:56 (16,610)
O'Riordan, Shelagh 4:40:43 (22,360)
Ormesher, Kelly L 3:55:10 (10,257)
Ormisher, Hannah J.........................5:50:13 (32,145)
Ormiston Smith, Kate H...................4:34:47 (20,904)
O'Rourke, Catherine M....................6:02:46 (32,844)
Orozco, Virginia..............................5:19:30 (29,354)
Orr, Christine M...............................3:52:43 (9,484)
Orr, Heather C................................4:55:22 (25,761)
Orrin, Zoe D 5:44:13 (31,688)
Orth, Barbara 3:31:54 (5,198)
Orton, Katie L.................................5:21:23 (29,545)
Orton, Rachel..................................4:18:56 (16,610)
Orvelind, Jacqueline A 5:56:02 (32,524)
Osborn, Lucie 3:54:14 (9,936)
Osborne, Julie 5:14:09 (28,694)
Osborne, Leela M 4:42:43 (22,858)
Osei-Gyamfi, Vera...........................5:03:45 (27,219)
Osei-Owusu, Genevieve L 5:40:35 (31,382)
Oseland, Anne M 4:38:03 (21,724)
Oseman, Rebecca 4:40:15 (22,245)
O'Shaughnessy, Catherine V............4:29:06 (19,420)
O'Shaughnessy, Linda A..................3:54:23 (9,987)
O'Shea, Louise O.............................6:36:46 (33,815)
O'Shea, Rebecca M.........................4:30:31 (19,749)
Oskarsdottir, Asta 5:00:39 (26,728)
Osman, Samantha J.........................5:08:57 (27,962)
Osorio, Ana H 4:02:21 (12,460)
Osorio, Jessica................................5:05:54 (27,532)
O'Sullivan, Deborah S 4:30:48 (19,833)
O'Sullivan, Elizabeth P 5:58:37 (32,678)
O'Sullivan, Jessica D 4:36:11 (21,289)
O'Sullivan, Kate M 3:59:34 (11,696)
O'Sullivan, Kerry.............................6:18:54 (33,377)
O'Sullivan, Kerry A 7:14:53 (34,364)
O'Sullivan, Maureen N.....................5:37:56 (31,188)
O'Sullivan, Nichola J........................4:54:41 (25,618)
Oswell, Rebecca C..........................5:52:12 (32,303)
Other, Helen V................................4:24:13 (18,056)
O'Toole, Claire L 4:56:11 (25,910)
O'Toole, Helen A.............................4:11:42 (14,733)
O'Toole, Karen P 4:09:18 (14,118)
Otte, Sabine...................................4:43:23 (23,023)
Otter, Sally H 4:40:15 (22,245)
Ott-Meyer, Kristy............................4:31:24 (19,995)
Outen, Samantha J..........................4:05:46 (13,235)
Outram, Jane..................................4:26:42 (18,723)
Overall, Heather M..........................4:49:36 (24,503)
Overy, Nicolette M..........................3:37:07 (6,084)
Ovstedal, Jenny L 4:00:54 (12,080)
Owen, Cecilia E...............................4:17:09 (16,140)
Owen, Christine C...........................5:16:33 (29,001)
Owen, Elisabeth J 4:42:21 (22,763)
Owen, Jennifer M............................4:23:09 (17,766)
Owen, Julie 4:45:46 (23,611)
Owen, Lyn 5:19:27 (29,346)
Owen, Mary B.................................3:12:40 (2,282)
Owen, Rebecca L 5:42:43 (31,551)
Owen, Rebecca S............................4:47:23 (24,004)
Owen, Samantha J...........................4:41:12 (22,488)
Owen, Sarah L................................4:12:23 (14,904)
Owen, Sian E..................................5:49:51 (32,108)
Owen, Wendy S 4:25:50 (18,491)
Owens, Angharad E 6:59:10 (34,199)
Owens, Caron S..............................5:09:20 (28,019)
Owens, Catherine...........................6:43:16 (33,946)
Owens, Emma C.............................4:01:32 (12,251)
Owens, Rhiannon 6:59:10 (34,199)
Owst, Jennie R................................3:56:40 (10,680)

LONDON MARATHON

Perrett, Shirley J 4:52:53 (25,247)
Perriman, Jacqui A 4:26:33 (18,679)
Perry, Christine M 4:34:27 (20,811)
Perry, Georgina 3:56:41 (10,684)
Perry, Jane M 4:35:46 (21,184)
Perry, Lisa A 4:31:14 (19,945)
Perry, Lucy M 4:33:32 (20,586)
Perry, Natasha 3:25:52 (4,081)
Perry, Philippa 6:10:38 (33,132)
Perry, Rachel 5:48:09 (31,986)
Perry, Victoria A 2:55:08 (759)
Perryman, Angela C 4:53:31 (25,379)
Persaud, Marcia C 5:36:18 (31,064)
Pertus, Lysianne 4:12:15 (14,873)
Perusko, Claire 4:03:02 (12,616)
Perveen, Rahat 4:33:22 (20,533)
Pescod, Mary E 5:59:12 (32,701)
Peters, Anna M 5:41:14 (31,439)
Peters, Laura J 4:50:05 (24,621)
Peters, Louise R 3:14:28 (2,541)
Peters, Rachel A 5:40:16 (31,358)
Peters, Tracey R 3:30:49 (5,024)
Petersen, Amy 4:48:06 (24,162)
Petersen, Helle R 4:06:02 (13,297)
Pethania, Yasmin B 7:19:08 (34,391)
Petken, Lorraine M 5:22:12 (29,626)
Petri, Katja 4:47:44 (24,080)
Petri, Maria 5:04:05 (27,261)
Petrova, Ludmila 2:26:45 (42)
Pettican, Kate M 3:52:14 (9,370)
Pettifer, Lorna E 4:10:43 (14,467)
Pettipiece, Jill 4:05:43 (13,226)
Pettit, Lorna J 5:17:29 (29,123)
Pettitt, Claire 4:50:17 (24,663)
Pettitt, Dianne E 4:28:02 (19,113)
Petzer, Alison C 4:52:17 (25,101)
Pezzani, Francesca R 5:11:38 (28,351)
Pfaender, Caroline 4:06:43 (13,455)
Pfeiffer, Gite 4:09:14 (14,097)
Phelan, Orpha 5:55:27 (32,497)
Philbrow, Rebecca 5:00:04 (26,648)
Philipps, Gemma E 5:50:32 (32,176)
Phillips, Abbie S 4:33:03 (20,442)
Phillips, Anna J 4:38:14 (21,762)
Phillips, Anna M 4:36:30 (21,368)
Phillips, Anna M 4:55:43 (25,821)
Phillips, Bethanie 4:24:36 (18,170)
Phillips, Carol A 4:50:14 (24,650)
Phillips, Carole 3:14:36 (2,567)
Phillips, Clare 3:01:47 (1,296)
Phillips, Cynthia M 4:25:05 (18,285)
Phillips, Emma 4:04:32 (12,937)
Phillips, Emma 5:16:44 (29,023)
Phillips, Gillian M 4:15:57 (15,823)
Phillips, Heather J 4:57:02 (26,094)
Phillips, Helen L 4:20:22 (16,988)
Phillips, Jacqueline 4:20:20 (16,983)
Phillips, Jane M 4:01:07 (12,141)
Phillips, Jean C 5:26:49 (30,132)
Phillips, Karen 4:19:00 (16,625)
Phillips, Kathryn M 3:26:21 (4,167)
Phillips, Laura E 4:24:52 (18,233)
Phillips, Lorraine V 4:30:52 (19,855)
Phillips, Lowri A 5:42:27 (31,530)
Phillips, Natalie L 6:49:05 (34,055)
Phillips, Nichola J 4:49:24 (24,457)
Phillips, Sarah J 5:09:44 (28,103)
Phillips, Susan 3:29:25 (4,766)
Phillips, Tracey B 5:16:45 (29,024)
Phillips, Tracey G 5:32:22 (30,689)
Philpot, Leonie 5:16:25 (28,985)
Phipps, Catriona 4:42:57 (22,920)
Phipson, Elizabeth R 4:23:23 (17,837)
Phiri, Niya M 5:39:03 (31,266)
Phoenix, Alexa J 4:04:50 (13,007)
Phythian Hawkes, Kelleyann 7:51:05 (34,512)
Piccinino, Cristina 3:58:44 (11,387)
Pichelski, Lorraine 4:06:39 (13,441)
Pickard, Anne 4:01:59 (12,358)
Pickard, Francesca 4:37:49 (21,675)
Pickering, Josephine 5:32:45 (30,723)
Pickering, Sharon M 5:14:37 (28,764)
Pickering, Tracy 4:38:17 (21,775)
Pickett, Jacqueline L 5:32:20 (30,685)
Pickford, Ali L 3:58:35 (11,331)
Pickford, Katy 4:21:07 (17,208)
Pickles, Grace M 5:08:55 (27,955)
Picksley, Mary L 3:41:07 (6,851)
Pickup, Ann T 5:21:33 (29,563)
Pickup, Karen T 5:21:31 (29,558)
Pidgeon, Moira E 4:44:28 (23,294)
Piears, Louise 3:56:28 (10,619)
Pieper, Lindsay P 4:03:42 (12,765)
Pierce, Clare M 5:40:40 (31,388)
Pierce, Laura A 4:08:21 (13,869)
Piercy, Sandra 4:00:56 (12,096)
Pieri, Melissa G 4:20:17 (16,971)
Pierzchalski, Emma M 6:47:58 (34,038)
Piggott, Catherine M 3:56:42 (10,690)
Piggott, Claire E 3:54:14 (9,936)
Pignatelli, Tizianan 3:15:51 (2,737)
Pike, Vivien 4:50:39 (24,757)
Pike, Yvonne C 5:48:14 (31,992)
Pike, Zoe M 2:56:26 (838)
Pikulski, Maria 5:50:28 (32,170)
Pilgrim, Mary J 4:26:14 (18,590)
Pilley, Laura 4:47:28 (24,015)
Pilling, Angela M 5:28:35 (30,333)
Pilling, Caroline A 4:33:48 (20,661)
Pimm, Maria E 6:18:26 (33,370)
Pimm, Melanie B 6:04:11 (32,894)
Pina, Jennie L 5:32:47 (30,727)
Pinder, Sarah 4:54:25 (25,564)
Pinkney, Charlotte 4:33:04 (20,448)
Pinkney, Olivia C 3:58:12 (11,190)
Pinnick, Abigail J 4:12:32 (14,936)
Piper, Beverley A 4:27:01 (18,818)
Piper, Julie 5:14:36 (28,759)
Pirtea, Adriana 2:28:52 (54)
Pita, Cecilia 4:23:59 (17,987)
Pitch, Amy 4:09:58 (14,291)
Pitcher, Paula J 4:08:27 (13,895)
Pite, Ayshea L 5:14:31 (28,741)
Piterkova, Miriam 4:45:10 (23,456)
Pitman, Natasha A 3:05:51 (1,585)
Pittard, Diane E 4:38:56 (21,954)
Pizzasegola, Federica 5:56:49 (32,570)
Plant, Caroline A 5:33:34 (30,792)
Plasencia-Ferrer, Ana I 4:21:55 (17,430)
Plaskitt, Lindsey 4:21:15 (17,236)
Platts, Cath 4:24:46 (18,208)
Plaxton, Alison C 4:57:21 (26,152)
Playell, Karen L 5:27:05 (30,156)
Player, Victoria M 5:10:04 (28,158)
Playle, Amanda J 5:31:49 (30,641)
Plowman, Nicki C 4:40:16 (22,249)
Plowman, Rosemary A 4:43:37 (23,078)
Pluck, Lynsey J 5:31:56 (30,651)
Pluck, Sally A 5:51:10 (32,219)
Plummer, Anna 4:34:20 (20,781)
Plumridge, Erika G 5:10:48 (28,250)
Pluves, Sarah H 4:30:05 (19,650)
Pogson, Angelica M 5:42:38 (31,541)
Pogson, Linda R 4:57:07 (26,110)
Pollard, Linda S 4:21:13 (17,231)
Pollard, Ruth S 5:05:50 (27,521)
Pomeroy-Kellinger, Melanie 4:40:00 (22,183)
Pomfret, Mary M 5:46:37 (31,886)
Pond, Sarra 7:13:52 (34,353)
Ponder, Rosamund A 3:14:58 (2,625)
Pons, Susan 4:49:31 (24,478)
Pontefract, Elaine C 4:23:00 (17,728)
Pontius, Sarah Y 3:54:01 (9,878)
Pook, Emma 4:18:25 (16,470)
Pool, Jenny R 5:24:20 (29,846)
Poole, Fiona L 3:54:13 (9,932)
Poole, Jennifer L 5:49:10 (32,065)
Poole, Joanna E 4:29:38 (19,547)
Poole, Olivia V 3:50:43 (8,994)
Pooles, Kerry 4:58:30 (26,375)
Pooley, Ellen 3:09:49 (1,972)
Pooloo, Fee 5:27:51 (30,246)
Pope, Kim 4:01:08 (12,145)
Pope, Margaret 4:42:52 (22,897)
Popham, Julia K 6:35:38 (33,789)
Poppleton, Amanda J 5:13:55 (28,664)
Pordardottir, Pordis E 4:18:03 (16,354)
Porritt, Bethan 5:18:47 (29,263)
Portaccio, Eleonora 4:48:57 (24,359)
Porter, Charlotte A 4:22:21 (17,531)
Porter, Charlotte E 4:41:36 (22,581)
Porter, Claire L 6:13:15 (33,217)
Porter, Gertrud F 3:45:09 (7,715)
Porter, Helen 5:30:14 (30,501)
Porter, Laura-Jayne 5:11:02 (28,280)
Porter, Rosalind C 4:45:34 (23,551)
Porter, Sinead L 3:38:43 (6,394)
Porter, Zoe G 3:30:47 (5,017)
Portsmore, Sophie R 4:02:36 (12,513)
Postings, Denise 6:34:23 (33,758)
Potgieter, Liesl 4:09:18 (14,118)
Potgieter, Riana 5:18:01 (29,183)
Potter, Alex J 3:30:02 (4,893)
Potter, Emma 4:22:41 (17,645)
Potter, Hannah L 5:55:01 (32,461)
Potter, Nicola F 5:12:20 (28,439)
Pottle, Alison 4:33:31 (20,579)
Potts, Janet M 6:20:47 (33,418)
Potts, Katherine L 4:28:04 (19,118)
Potts, Leeanne 4:15:43 (15,752)
Potts, Ruth C 5:18:56 (29,282)
Poulter, Jane 5:49:17 (32,073)
Poulter, Justine C 4:04:14 (12,871)
Poulton, Jane 5:15:36 (28,889)
Pountney, Helen J 4:24:43 (18,199)
Povall, Judit 4:57:39 (26,220)
Pover, Joanne E 5:44:50 (31,752)
Powell, Abigail K 4:35:12 (21,032)
Powell, Amanda 3:41:27 (6,924)
Powell, Catherine L 4:35:57 (21,228)
Powell, Emma J 7:04:09 (34,253)
Powell, Fiona L 3:28:47 (4,621)
Powell, Irene D 4:46:45 (23,838)
Powell, Lucy 4:30:47 (19,828)
Powell, Mariann 3:55:09 (10,251)
Powell, Pauline A 4:50:32 (24,727)
Powell, Rosemary J 5:19:15 (29,323)
Powell, Sasha 4:43:14 (22,990)
Powell, Terri R 5:00:45 (26,751)
Power, Avril P 4:42:46 (22,868)
Power, Kate 4:23:55 (17,968)
Power, Susan J 5:46:53 (31,903)
Powis, Andrea 6:31:24 (33,691)
Powis, Annie M 3:52:01 (9,305)
Powlitfch, Stephanie A 6:05:31 (32,953)
Powner, Harriet C 4:43:54 (23,154)
Powolozky, Carina 5:45:50 (31,824)
Powrie, Catherine 3:26:14 (4,142)
Pozsgai, Luca 3:51:57 (9,287)
Prain, Wanda 5:12:57 (28,540)
Prance, Carole 4:14:04 (15,326)
Prater, Holly M 4:24:49 (18,221)
Pratt, Aranka 4:46:11 (23,709)
Pratt, Erika J 4:42:07 (22,701)
Prazeres, Elizabeth M 4:43:39 (23,088)
Preece, Sophie A 4:35:57 (21,228)
Preen, Rebecca 6:15:33 (33,279)
Premoli, Daniela 4:11:13 (14,610)
Prentice, Carolanne 5:48:57 (32,049)
Pressey, Susan 6:10:42 (33,134)
Preston, Catherine L 4:50:07 (24,625)
Preston, Heather E 4:31:13 (19,942)
Preston, Kate F 5:02:53 (27,094)
Preston, Lisa 5:10:30 (28,217)
Preston, Sue L 4:07:08 (13,553)
Preston, Susan M 4:12:34 (14,944)
Prestridge, Julia 3:47:58 (8,341)
Pretlove, Gemma L 5:53:20 (32,362)
Pretorius, Cindy C 4:52:28 (25,136)
Prevett, Sarah 5:46:19 (31,865)
Price, Clare J 4:24:59 (18,259)
Price, Elizabeth J 5:13:12 (28,571)
Price, Elizabeth M 3:58:30 (11,298)
Price, Evette L 4:19:05 (16,651)
Price, Jane 6:17:51 (33,351)
Price, Joanne E 3:39:11 (6,469)
Price, Kiri E 3:52:49 (9,506)
Price, Robyn 6:47:13 (34,025)
Price, Samantha L 5:16:46 (29,026)

Price, Susan M 5:10:35 (28,228)
Price, Veronica M 5:28:19 (30,305)
Prichard, Georgina 6:08:28 (33,064)
Prickett, Andrea 4:37:10 (21,518)
Prideaux, Anna E 4:40:22 (22,279)
Prideaux, Rebecca A 4:39:18 (22,049)
Priestley, Carole I 4:24:16 (18,073)
Prince, Jane M 5:24:59 (29,910)
Prince, Louise 4:33:31 (20,579)
Prince, Rosemary 5:22:09 (29,621)
Prince, Susan 4:22:48 (17,668)
Prior, Elaine E 4:48:26 (24,233)
Prior, Elly 6:11:54 (33,164)
Prior, Jemma 5:39:29 (31,295)
Prior, Michelle J 3:39:08 (6,456)
Prior, Tracey 3:20:55 (3,343)
Pritchard, Cathryn 4:46:29 (23,774)
Pritchard, Kimberley 4:25:57 (18,519)
Pritchard, Sharon L 6:40:26 (33,892)
Pritchett, Jennifer A 4:09:16 (14,108)
Procter, Rebecca L 5:03:17 (27,149)
Proctor, Andrea 4:36:14 (21,308)
Proctor, Julia A 3:49:34 (8,711)
Proctor, Louise A 4:56:54 (26,052)
Profir, Diana 4:38:52 (21,934)
Prokopowicz, Liz A 4:37:06 (21,506)
Proto, Emma L 3:58:49 (11,426)
Proud, Lucy A 3:47:37 (8,257)
Proudhon, Christine 4:47:01 (23,915)
Prowse, Wendy 3:30:40 (4,993)
Pryce, Sandra 4:28:49 (19,351)
Pryke, Joanna M 3:57:03 (10,811)
Pryke, Martha 4:53:17 (25,329)
Pryse, Sian C 6:15:58 (33,293)
Pucan, Sanja 6:07:49 (33,039)
Puffett, Angela J 3:59:01 (11,496)
Pugh, Alis 5:33:49 (30,819)
Pugh, Jane M 3:58:28 (11,290)
Pugh, Janice M 5:03:48 (27,225)
Pugh, Jessica C 4:23:44 (17,922)
Pullen, Mandy 5:03:37 (27,200)
Purcell, Clare E 4:51:11 (24,878)
Purim, Dahlia 4:40:58 (22,425)
Purkiss, Sheila T 5:40:05 (31,337)
Purnell, Ann L 4:04:31 (12,934)
Pussard, Gail V 5:48:49 (32,033)
Pyane, Susan 3:55:41 (10,399)
Pyatt, Jane 3:59:34 (11,696)
Pyatt, Tracy 3:59:35 (11,705)
Pye, Hazel A 4:02:27 (12,488)
Pymont, Linda 4:05:41 (13,218)
Pyne, Janet L 5:23:26 (29,741)
Pyne, Katie J 5:23:26 (29,741)
Quaid, Olivia M 4:04:57 (13,038)
Quance, Betty 5:31:56 (30,651)
Quantrill, Sarah 3:18:03 (2,991)
Quartermaine, Paulette D 5:56:13 (32,539)
Quaye, Lynette K 4:40:25 (22,290)
Queally, Gemma L 3:45:48 (7,858)
Quelch, Katie 4:46:45 (23,838)
Quentin-Hicks, Kate E 4:46:11 (23,709)
Quesnel, Lise P 4:31:35 (20,050)
Quick, Kimberley 6:05:12 (32,935)
Quigley, Emma M 5:23:06 (29,710)
Quilter, Nicola H 6:54:19 (34,144)
Quin, Emily E 4:33:24 (20,540)
Quincey, Kerry A 5:48:57 (32,049)
Quincey, Nicole 4:59:38 (26,582)
Quine, Lynne 4:29:54 (19,606)
Quinlan, Rachel 3:53:03 (9,593)
Quinlivan, Claire M 4:34:58 (20,962)
Quinn, Colleen A 4:14:07 (15,340)
Quinn, Cora L 4:42:32 (22,816)
Quinn, Jacqueline M 5:46:42 (31,894)
Quinn, Nicky S 4:52:31 (25,151)
Quinn, Tara L 4:23:20 (17,825)
Quinn, Thirza J 4:55:21 (25,757)
Quinn-Ryan, Noreen 5:11:26 (28,323)
Quirke, Ruth 5:42:20 (31,524)
Quorning, Inger 3:47:59 (8,345)
Raaijmakers, Monique M 3:29:43 (4,824)
Rabin, Jenny 6:00:27 (32,755)
Rabitti, Delia 5:18:46 (29,261)
Raby, Beth A 4:50:19 (24,670)
Rachatathanatorn, Thanatorn 6:37:39 (33,833)
Radcliffe, Pauline 4:54:19 (25,542)
Radford, Caroline 5:27:35 (30,208)
Radford, Joy C 3:19:30 (3,166)
Radnedge, Elizabeth L 5:36:19 (31,067)
Rado, Alessandra 4:16:28 (15,954)
Radovich, Lisa A 4:18:50 (16,582)
Rafferty, Kylene 4:20:49 (17,130)
Rafferty, Lisa 6:30:48 (33,680)
Raidy, Davina J 3:19:21 (3,144)
Rainford-Batty, Sarah 7:25:36 (34,432)
Rainsden, Sara J 5:26:52 (30,138)
Rajani, Seeta 5:37:09 (31,127)
Rajiyah, Anushka L 4:46:50 (23,867)
Rajpar, Mariam H 6:25:31 (33,566)
Ralph, Barbara 3:19:56 (3,219)
Ralph, Lysa 3:43:52 (7,430)
Ramage, Anna M 4:15:41 (15,742)
Rampling, Patricia 3:55:12 (10,268)
Ramsay, Amanda G 3:43:04 (7,255)
Ramsay, Lucy 4:50:30 (24,715)
Ramsay, Paula J 4:27:06 (18,843)
Ramsay, Tana 4:33:33 (20,591)
Ramsbottom, Heather J 5:41:12 (31,435)
Ramsden, Tracy L 6:30:03 (33,661)
Ramsell, Judy 4:58:15 (26,335)
Ramsey, Paula 4:12:06 (14,838)
Ramsey Smith, Sarah M 3:33:07 (5,401)
Ramsundarsingh, Deniese 5:30:58 (30,563)
Rana, Gurjit K 4:53:34 (25,392)
Rance, Jaynie Y 5:31:08 (30,574)
Rand, Katherine P 4:45:07 (23,438)
Randall, Diane M 5:16:20 (28,973)
Randell, Carolyn 4:02:25 (12,479)
Randle, Joanne 5:15:25 (28,868)
Randle, Victoria L 4:22:25 (17,555)
Rankin, Helen C 7:45:16 (34,496)
Ransom, Kelly M 5:02:39 (27,058)
Ransome, Jennifer A 3:19:16 (3,130)
Ranson, Pauline F 4:37:50 (21,679)
Rapp, Sarah E 4:53:50 (25,449)
Rashid, Shamima 5:30:56 (30,558)
Ratcliffe, Alexa 3:54:31 (10,071)
Ratcliffe, Elizabeth M 4:57:20 (26,150)
Ratcliffe, Julia H 3:58:06 (11,142)
Ratcliffe, Megan E 3:44:21 (7,522)
Rath, Sally J 5:25:35 (29,994)
Rathborne, Vanessa L 3:31:53 (5,195)
Ratti, Claire R 4:49:01 (24,376)
Rattigan, Michelle 4:57:42 (26,230)
Rattu, Beneesha 5:51:54 (32,284)
Rattu, Lisa M 4:07:07 (13,549)
Raven, Daisy R 5:22:42 (29,679)
Ravenscroft, Corry A 3:31:56 (5,208)
Rawani, Kalpana 4:22:17 (17,517)
Rawden, Nicola C 4:59:09 (26,500)
Rawle, Michelle E 3:47:08 (8,138)
Rawlings, Donna M 4:43:28 (23,035)
Rawlings, Lynsey D 5:25:01 (29,915)
Rawlinson, Jody L 3:47:23 (8,193)
Rawson, Kimberley 4:41:47 (22,628)
Ray, Camilla A 4:11:32 (14,687)
Ray, Diane S 4:16:23 (15,927)
Raymond, Irma 5:08:26 (27,884)
Raymond, Madleine H 4:14:22 (15,415)
Rayner, Anne H 4:59:35 (26,570)
Rayner, Frances E 5:06:17 (27,599)
Rayner, Marion R 3:20:12 (3,249)
Rayner, Miranda J 4:53:41 (25,415)
Raynor, Claire G 4:11:58 (14,801)
Rayton, Allyson 6:59:46 (34,207)
Rea, Maureen 4:05:46 (13,235)
Read, Cheryl-Anne 4:44:29 (23,297)
Read, Michelle 4:23:32 (17,875)
Read, Paula A 4:16:13 (15,882)
Read, Sharon 4:26:41 (18,716)
Reader, Helen M 5:14:32 (28,745)
Reading, Avril 5:56:18 (32,545)
Reading, Gillian C 3:56:34 (10,650)
Reading, Kate S 4:01:14 (12,170)
Reading, Lisa M 4:42:27 (22,790)
Readings, Dianne G 4:19:30 (16,757)
Readman, Tamzin C 3:48:32 (8,473)
Reagh, Kate E 3:29:00 (4,669)
Reakes, Wendy G 5:00:10 (26,663)
Reardon, Sarah 4:15:04 (15,584)
Reay, Anna 3:43:36 (7,366)
Rebelo, Perpetua 6:49:24 (34,069)
Reber, Christine 6:00:56 (32,778)
Reckeweg, Susann 3:33:40 (5,501)
Reckova, Andrea 6:10:27 (33,129)
Redden, Kim D 3:20:36 (3,307)
Reddish, Diane Y 5:11:13 (28,297)
Reddish, Tonya R 4:31:56 (20,147)
Redfern, Diane 6:04:12 (32,895)
Redfern, Louise M 5:24:50 (29,893)
Redfern, Sally C 3:29:37 (4,803)
Redford, Julia M 4:24:23 (18,106)
Redgrove, Janine 5:52:54 (32,333)
Redhead, Amy 4:08:23 (13,876)
Redman, Annabelle L 4:22:59 (17,722)
Redmond, Amy E 3:36:40 (5,994)
Redmond, Anna 5:09:11 (27,992)
Redpath, Clare M 4:36:34 (21,384)
Redstone, Jenni E 3:51:38 (9,206)
Reece, Katherine V 5:07:36 (27,782)
Reece, Susan E 4:56:29 (25,967)
Reed, Annabelle J 5:16:06 (28,946)
Reed, Claire J 5:51:06 (32,215)
Reed, Emma A 5:11:31 (28,333)
Reed, Kirsten N 5:16:43 (29,020)
Reed, Melissa R 4:28:26 (19,243)
Reed, Nicola J 3:28:26 (4,545)
Reed, Rebecca 4:37:59 (21,711)
Reed, Sue 4:24:08 (18,029)
Reedy, Jane H 3:55:26 (10,316)
Rees, Angie C 5:01:51 (26,936)
Rees, Caroline S 4:17:27 (16,205)
Rees, Emma 4:21:00 (17,182)
Rees, Katherine 4:06:19 (13,358)
Rees, Katy 5:26:17 (30,069)
Rees, Nicola 4:10:43 (14,467)
Rees, Penelope A 3:48:25 (8,447)
Rees, Ruth 5:10:34 (28,225)
Rees, Sarah E 5:09:26 (28,032)
Rees, Wendy 4:35:33 (21,116)
Reeve, Rachel 4:18:09 (16,386)
Reeve, Sally A 6:12:49 (33,202)
Reeve, Sarah J 4:42:56 (22,915)
Reeves, Annabelle 6:12:04 (33,168)
Reeves, Gemma 4:38:18 (21,781)
Reeves, Julie A 3:46:23 (7,975)
Reeves, Justine 3:56:11 (10,533)
Reeves, Rachel M 5:43:08 (31,580)
Refson, Nicole 4:53:42 (25,417)
Regan, Julie A 6:17:45 (33,348)
Regan, Kathleen M 4:47:18 (23,986)
Regan, Lorraine 3:42:34 (7,147)
Regan, Suzanne E 3:55:47 (10,429)
Reid, Alexandra A 4:00:39 (12,017)
Reid, Carol A 3:35:42 (5,832)
Reid, Claire J 3:17:22 (2,916)
Reid, Jacqueline E 4:17:32 (16,232)
Reid, Rosemary J 4:34:30 (20,822)
Reid, Sarah L 4:22:38 (17,627)
Reid, Susan I 5:59:28 (32,715)
Reid, Zoe C 5:40:26 (31,368)
Reilly, Anna M 5:16:10 (28,956)
Remington, Joanne 3:38:39 (6,379)
Renfer, Fionuala T 3:40:51 (6,793)
Renfree, Hellen M 4:40:30 (22,310)
Renmant, Beverley J 3:21:32 (3,427)
Rennie, Felicity C 3:28:25 (4,538)
Renteria, Maria 3:56:05 (10,511)
Renwick, Pamela J 4:39:42 (22,130)
Renwick, Sally A 5:45:33 (31,805)
Reukers, Irene C 5:04:59 (27,397)
Reukers, Martine 5:04:59 (27,397)
Reviriaud, Julie 3:24:56 (3,916)
Rexe, Jessica 6:14:48 (33,264)
Reyes, Carolina 3:45:15 (7,741)
Reynders, Julia A 4:20:50 (17,133)
Reynish, Catherine A 4:34:21 (20,785)
Reynolds, Abigail M 4:03:03 (12,620)
Reynolds, Andrea 3:57:00 (10,796)

Reynolds, Catriona M 4:15:16 (15,632)
Reynolds, Jane L........................6:03:12 (32,852)
Reynolds, Julia...........................5:06:00 (27,552)
Reynolds, Julie M.......................3:17:12 (2,888)
Reynolds, Katherine...................4:53:44 (25,422)
Reynolds, Kathryn F...................3:41:07 (6,851)
Reynolds, Leigh..........................4:35:39 (21,152)
Reynolds, Lisa C.........................6:11:07 (33,144)
Reynolds, Rachel........................3:49:27 (8,686)
Reynolds, Sandra J.....................3:02:32 (1,343)
Rhodes, Catherine M..................4:50:28 (24,703)
Rhodes, Deborah A.....................3:21:44 (3,451)
Rhodes, Emma J.........................4:39:40 (22,114)
Rhodes, Gillian L........................5:02:35 (27,048)
Rhodes-Evans, Rebecca..............4:16:23 (15,927)
Rhys, Hannah.............................4:21:29 (17,300)
Ricco, Luisa...............................4:03:37 (12,751)
Rice, Anna E...............................4:24:04 (18,013)
Rice, Cheryl...............................4:48:20 (24,215)
Rice, Liz A.................................4:38:36 (21,858)
Richards, Alice L........................4:35:41 (21,164)
Richards, Cherilee J...................4:42:48 (22,877)
Richards, Dawn E.......................3:55:01 (10,201)
Richards, Diana E.......................4:36:52 (21,454)
Richards, Donna M.....................5:00:36 (26,718)
Richards, Elinor L.......................5:26:30 (30,098)
Richards, Elizabeth A..................5:30:38 (30,539)
Richards, Emma V.......................3:43:04 (7,255)
Richards, Erin.............................5:08:24 (27,876)
Richards, Faye L.........................4:02:47 (12,561)
Richards, Fiona..........................4:10:30 (14,409)
Richards, Hannah.......................4:49:07 (24,399)
Richards, Jacqueline K................4:37:40 (21,634)
Richards, Jane E.........................6:39:36 (33,875)
Richards, Katie...........................6:04:51 (32,918)
Richards, Maggie........................5:09:53 (28,128)
Richards, Maria S.......................4:10:54 (14,522)
Richards, Mary J.........................4:34:23 (20,794)
Richards, Nicola A......................4:57:13 (26,127)
Richards, Ruth G........................3:40:44 (6,765)
Richards, Sally...........................4:09:20 (14,127)
Richards, Susan J.......................5:12:50 (28,520)
Richards, Trudie.........................4:57:30 (26,188)
Richardson, Anna E....................4:56:08 (25,900)
Richardson, Chanel L..................4:53:30 (25,376)
Richardson, Helen E....................7:21:16 (34,404)
Richardson, Jill C.......................4:05:08 (13,080)
Richardson, Karen E....................4:04:42 (12,985)
Richardson, Kerry.......................4:07:52 (13,739)
Richardson, Lesley C...................3:54:41 (10,097)
Richardson, Shelley M.................4:53:17 (25,329)
Richardson, Sue L.......................4:49:41 (24,529)
Richardson, Susan......................5:07:46 (27,806)
Richardson, Val..........................4:40:14 (22,242)
Riches, Patricia O.......................4:56:42 (26,007)
Richmond, Petngam....................5:58:28 (32,668)
Richter, Carola...........................3:37:06 (6,081)
Rick, Gill...................................5:31:25 (30,604)
Rickaby, Emma J........................4:40:20 (22,269)
Rickard, Donna..........................4:15:32 (15,715)
Rickard, Lisa D...........................5:07:21 (27,743)
Rickerby, Sandra P.....................4:07:18 (13,597)
Rickett, Leanne..........................4:46:37 (23,801)
Ricketts, Rebecca J.....................4:11:28 (14,665)
Ricks, Sara J..............................5:26:40 (30,118)
Riddell, Amy..............................4:19:28 (16,743)
Riddell, Grainne.........................3:56:39 (10,677)
Riddock, Nicola..........................7:19:47 (34,394)
Ridehalgh, Emma L.....................4:23:37 (17,897)
Ridehalgh, Sarah E.....................3:13:04 (2,343)
Ridge, Julia D............................4:08:23 (13,876)
Ridge, Keeley J...........................4:31:02 (19,893)
Ridgley, Julie R..........................3:41:44 (6,974)
Ridgwell, Anne C........................4:58:58 (26,468)
Ridler, Mandy............................4:49:37 (24,507)
Ridley, Heather J........................4:23:15 (17,797)
Ridout, Frances V.......................4:27:46 (19,011)
Ridout, Heather Lb.....................4:04:36 (12,949)
Ridsdale, Esther J.......................5:01:02 (26,803)
Rigby, Katie J.............................3:54:58 (10,184)
Rigby, Rachel A..........................6:54:05 (34,137)
Rigby-Burr, Emma L....................4:01:57 (12,348)
Rigby-Jones, Ann E.....................6:12:40 (33,193)

Rijnsburger, Jolanda 4:38:57 (21,961)
Riley, Alexandra.........................5:04:36 (27,342)
Riley, Belinda J...........................4:08:56 (14,026)
Riley, Claire L.............................4:30:23 (19,719)
Riley, Donna R............................3:51:25 (9,157)
Riley, Ellie.................................3:45:26 (7,780)
Riley, Jennifer............................5:46:11 (31,851)
Riley, Karen R.............................5:15:47 (28,916)
Riley, Karen T.............................4:30:31 (19,749)
Riley, Sophie L............................4:48:11 (24,179)
Rindl, Deb C...............................5:15:17 (28,849)
Ringham, Liz J............................3:03:21 (1,407)
Ringwood, Zoe K.........................5:25:38 (29,998)
Risdale, Joanne S........................7:27:11 (34,441)
Riseley, Miriam 5:42:20 (31,524)
Risom, Ketti...............................4:59:33 (26,565)
Ritchie, Jessica E........................5:22:38 (29,674)
Ritchie, Kirsty-Jane.....................3:55:21 (10,298)
Ritchie, Louisa M........................4:39:43 (22,133)
Ritchie, Megan J.........................4:33:53 (20,680)
Ritson, Samantha.......................4:38:55 (21,948)
Rivers, Alison J...........................5:34:11 (30,854)
Rivers, Anna M...........................5:01:47 (26,927)
Rivers, Katherine M 4:19:11 (16,675)
Rivett, Alexandra........................4:41:05 (22,452)
Rix, Rowena...............................6:23:03 (33,493)
Rixon, Victoria...........................4:42:28 (22,793)
Riyat, Sheetal............................4:18:16 (16,421)
Rley, Harriet L............................4:27:54 (19,065)
Roach, Sandra............................6:08:22 (33,058)
Roback, Ylana.............................5:36:27 (31,076)
Robathano, Katharine L...............4:34:55 (20,940)
Robb, Pauline P..........................5:54:31 (32,430)
Robb, Victoria A..........................5:30:56 (30,558)
Robbie, Belinda..........................3:21:54 (3,473)
Robbins, Charlotte A...................4:40:47 (22,376)
Robbins, Joanna L.......................3:51:32 (9,179)
Roberts, Amanda M.....................5:35:16 (30,956)
Roberts, Beverley A.....................7:04:53 (34,261)
Roberts, Carole M.......................3:38:28 (6,352)
Roberts, Carolyne M....................5:06:07 (27,571)
Roberts, Dorothy J......................4:39:08 (22,011)
Roberts, Ellie J...........................4:10:53 (14,516)
Roberts, Fabienne.......................5:01:33 (26,880)
Roberts, Faye.............................4:05:32 (13,185)
Roberts, Glenda..........................3:51:14 (9,105)
Roberts, Gwendolyn....................5:34:19 (30,867)
Roberts, Helen 4:24:11 (18,045)
Roberts, Helen M........................6:05:51 (32,968)
Roberts, Jayne B.........................5:35:40 (30,994)
Roberts, Joan.............................6:28:27 (33,632)
Roberts, Josephine A 4:02:38 (12,530)
Roberts, Judith E........................4:43:55 (23,156)
Roberts, Karen J.........................4:58:14 (26,333)
Roberts, Kate.............................4:22:21 (17,531)
Roberts, Louse C.........................4:45:17 (23,492)
Roberts, Melanie N 5:53:03 (32,343)
Roberts, Nicola...........................5:56:51 (32,572)
Roberts, Penelope J.....................5:31:12 (30,585)
Roberts, Shan D..........................3:06:46 (1,663)
Roberts, Sophia K........................4:26:49 (18,761)
Roberts, Tanya G.........................5:08:43 (27,932)
Roberts, Victoria J.......................6:52:37 (34,120)
Robertshaw, Helen J....................4:46:31 (23,781)
Robertson, Elaine E.....................4:56:01 (25,879)
Robertson, Emma L......................5:19:49 (29,390)
Robertson, Kyra D.......................6:24:55 (33,547)
Robertson, Louise A 4:46:38 (23,807)
Robins, Leigh.............................5:06:34 (27,633)
Robins, Samantha.......................4:53:56 (25,468)
Robins, Suzanne M......................5:34:46 (30,909)
Robinson, Barbara.......................4:20:39 (17,080)
Robinson, Brenda C.....................4:48:01 (24,154)
Robinson, Davena A.....................6:05:23 (32,941)
Robinson, Deborah M 3:25:18 (3,978)
Robinson, Eleanor M....................4:00:41 (12,029)
Robinson, Emily H.......................4:27:39 (18,986)
Robinson, Emily S........................4:28:34 (19,280)
Robinson, Hannah M....................5:36:16 (31,060)
Robinson, Jackie.........................4:36:44 (21,423)
Robinson, Joanna H.....................4:48:06 (24,162)
Robinson, Joanne........................3:37:53 (6,235)
Robinson, Joy 4:30:42 (19,800)

Robinson, Julie A........................3:46:33 (8,013)
Robinson, Karen.........................5:56:51 (32,572)
Robinson, Karen A.......................3:28:48 (4,624)
Robinson, Karen P.......................4:48:41 (24,285)
Robinson, Katie E........................4:36:18 (21,324)
Robinson, Katy J.........................4:22:21 (17,531)
Robinson, Kylie L........................5:27:41 (30,224)
Robinson, Lisa C.........................4:32:41 (20,345)
Robinson, Liu.............................3:51:25 (9,157)
Robinson, Louise J......................4:18:18 (16,434)
Robinson, Louise S......................5:31:41 (30,632)
Robinson, Melinda D...................5:57:20 (32,596)
Robinson, Paula..........................4:13:01 (15,037)
Robinson, Pauline L.....................4:53:35 (25,398)
Robinson, Sara E.........................4:40:45 (22,367)
Robinson, Sarah..........................3:53:57 (9,854)
Robinson, Sharron.......................4:50:38 (24,752)
Robinson, Simone.......................4:14:31 (15,453)
Robinson, Simone.......................5:44:58 (31,761)
Robinson, Susan J.......................3:57:27 (10,942)
Robinson, Suzie..........................4:21:34 (17,328)
Robinson, Tracey J......................5:09:43 (28,097)
Robinson, Tracy L........................4:48:59 (24,370)
Robjohns, Karen S 5:07:34 (27,776)
Robson, Anne.............................5:05:32 (27,487)
Robson, Anne M..........................3:43:55 (7,445)
Robson, Dany L...........................3:24:49 (3,892)
Robson, Dawn E..........................3:44:07 (7,476)
Robson, Helen 3:31:48 (5,187)
Robson, Joanne P........................3:59:49 (11,789)
Robson, Kelly.............................4:37:17 (21,547)
Robson, Rebecca E......................4:08:30 (13,909)
Robson, Ruth.............................6:01:28 (32,795)
Robson, Trish.............................3:19:37 (3,178)
Robson-Gill, Samantha J.............5:01:37 (26,899)
Roch, Georgette..........................5:15:44 (28,910)
Rocha, Cecilia M.........................6:28:04 (33,625)
Roche, Clare A............................4:46:52 (23,876)
Roche, Elizabeth M......................6:26:52 (33,595)
Rochez, Hazel M.........................4:25:30 (18,397)
Rockefeller, Kathleen...................5:19:01 (29,291)
Rockett, Lisa M...........................5:24:42 (29,877)
Rockley, Jeanette........................5:18:20 (29,211)
Roddis, Suzanne C.......................3:13:39 (2,413)
Rodgers, Cathy M........................4:19:29 (16,750)
Rodgers, Jennifer A......................5:31:23 (30,601)
Rodgers, Sarah A.........................5:26:31 (30,101)
Roe, Lorna D..............................4:40:07 (22,215)
Roe, Nicola J..............................4:25:01 (18,266)
Roebuck, Elizabeth A...................7:03:58 (34,251)
Roevekamp, Marion.....................5:22:03 (29,604)
Roexssen, Sharon........................5:34:26 (30,877)
Rogan, Emma B...........................3:33:27 (5,464)
Roger, Collette............................5:09:37 (28,075)
Rogers, Alison L..........................4:46:28 (23,769)
Rogers, Beryl M..........................6:14:32 (33,258)
Rogers, Caron.............................4:17:11 (16,153)
Rogers, Charlie E........................5:01:42 (26,913)
Rogers, Charlotte L......................6:21:01 (33,428)
Rogers, Claire V..........................5:31:00 (30,568)
Rogers, Elizabeth A......................6:35:37 (33,788)
Rogers, Georgina L......................4:31:48 (20,103)
Rogers, Jennifer L........................4:41:03 (22,448)
Rogers, Karen A...........................4:53:57 (25,472)
Rogers, Kate...............................4:00:16 (11,917)
Rogers, Lisa C.............................4:57:07 (26,110)
Rogers, Louise V.........................4:53:10 (25,310)
Rogers, Margaret F......................5:19:40 (29,381)
Rogers, Melanie J........................5:34:46 (30,909)
Rogers, Patricia M.......................4:11:25 (14,650)
Rogers, Sarah M..........................3:33:20 (5,445)
Rogers, Tracey............................5:03:34 (27,194)
Rogers, Vanessa V.......................5:03:17 (27,149)
Rohloff, Nadine..........................3:57:03 (10,811)
Roine, Karen M...........................3:36:57 (6,050)
Roland, Lena A............................3:54:39 (10,086)
Rolfe, Jodie................................4:04:40 (12,972)
Rolfe, Marion F...........................6:30:02 (33,660)
Rolfe, Vanessa A.........................4:57:47 (26,245)
Rolfe, Virginia A..........................4:28:09 (19,151)
Rollin, Sophie A..........................5:12:41 (28,489)
Rollinson, Lorraine......................3:28:44 (4,609)
Rollitt, Jane A.............................3:55:38 (10,382)

Rollo, Linda 6:36:36 (33,809)
Rolls, Jacqueline F 5:47:47 (31,965)
Rolls-King, Jacqueline 4:46:52 (23,876)
Romaine, Kimberly K 3:43:17 (7,303)
Romecin, Lindsay H 3:36:19 (5,935)
Ronald, Natalie S 4:51:34 (24,950)
Rooke, Zoe S 3:10:42 (2,065)
Rooney, Michelle A 4:34:02 (20,705)
Rooney, Sharron D 4:46:18 (23,742)
Roope, Barbara M 6:03:06 (32,850)
Roose, Kathleen A 4:21:51 (17,412)
Rootes, Jane E 5:13:22 (28,588)
Roper, Helen 3:44:37 (7,582)
Roper, Janine R 3:09:18 (1,918)
Roques, Leonie P 3:52:46 (9,495)
Rosa, Jessica H 3:28:22 (4,531)
Rosa, Marie-Carol E 5:13:07 (28,558)
Rosborough, Diane M 7:36:00 (34,473)
Rose, Alison L 6:35:12 (33,776)
Rose, Angela E 5:16:19 (28,972)
Rose, Catherine J 4:08:35 (13,937)
Rose, Emily L 6:49:14 (34,065)
Rose, Heidi M 4:54:06 (25,497)
Rose, Heidi M 5:02:51 (27,086)
Rose, Joanne V 4:08:08 (13,810)
Rose, Julie M 4:08:01 (13,774)
Rose, Neva C 5:12:51 (28,525)
Rose, Phillippa 4:44:03 (23,194)
Rose, Yasmine 3:46:50 (8,068)
Rosenthal, Gaby O 2:54:42 (729)
Ross, Annabel 4:17:43 (16,284)
Ross, Clare L 5:50:36 (32,179)
Ross, Fiona 4:54:59 (25,698)
Ross, Jacqueline 6:14:27 (33,257)
Ross, Jillian M 5:02:47 (27,079)
Ross Gower, Angela D 4:44:51 (23,385)
Ross Russell, Fiona 3:11:22 (2,134)
Rosseboom, Dorry 3:16:32 (2,818)
Rosser, Maria H 4:51:44 (24,994)
Rossi, Criana 3:53:58 (9,863)
Rossi, Jane L 5:26:29 (30,095)
Rossi, Stefania 5:11:41 (28,362)
Rossi, Valeria 6:51:53 (34,107)
Rosso, Lula 4:24:57 (18,249)
Roth-Kahl, Elisabeth M 4:12:06 (14,838)
Rothwell, Kerry S 4:40:18 (22,257)
Rothwell, Tania 4:51:48 (25,003)
Roudette-Gregory, Lisa 4:49:21 (24,451)
Roughley, Victoria D 5:07:26 (27,758)
Roumania, Michele L 5:02:40 (27,061)
Rounce, Kate L 4:23:30 (17,867)
Round, Helen J 3:44:54 (7,656)
Round, Sarah 4:29:36 (19,542)
Roux, Helene C 4:43:09 (22,971)
Rowe, Carole A 4:06:04 (13,305)
Rowe, Catherine E 4:29:32 (19,524)
Rowe, Jessica 4:32:52 (20,392)
Rowe, Juliet 3:12:31 (2,272)
Rowe, Sue 5:59:24 (32,708)
Rowe, Trudi 4:54:01 (25,488)
Rowe, Zoe 4:11:18 (14,626)
Rowett, Ann 4:35:40 (21,157)
Rowe-Wakeling, Pippa A 4:22:15 (17,509)
Rowland, Gemma D 5:18:53 (29,274)
Rowland, Jude A 5:56:00 (32,521)
Rowland, Viv 4:19:00 (16,625)
Rowlands, Helen 5:11:19 (28,309)
Rowles, Claire M 5:19:01 (29,291)
Rowles, Nicola J 4:36:32 (21,378)
Rowley, Jenny E 4:18:39 (16,542)
Rowley, Michelle L 5:09:34 (28,066)
Rowlings, Amie D 4:40:48 (22,379)
Rowlinson, Helen E 5:09:33 (28,064)
Rowson, Kerrie A 4:48:44 (24,303)
Rowswell, Kathryn M 4:32:09 (20,212)
Roy, Diane 3:22:34 (3,579)
Roy, Fiona M 3:49:56 (8,808)
Roy, Jocelyne 4:04:15 (12,876)
Roy, Josiane 4:28:21 (19,223)
Royce, Siobhann 3:45:42 (7,836)
Royer, Rachel S 5:03:03 (27,111)
Roylance, Susan E 5:31:25 (30,604)
Roythorne, Denise C 4:13:34 (15,181)

Rozados, Patricia 4:04:45 (12,994)
Ruane, Helen 4:27:31 (18,953)
Ruano de Salado, Marta 4:53:06 (25,295)
Rudanec, Helen M 5:21:10 (29,516)
Rudd, Donna 4:47:32 (24,026)
Rudd, Louise N 3:39:20 (6,503)
Rudden, Victoria J 5:08:11 (27,841)
Ruddick, Sarah J 5:41:52 (31,491)
Ruddy, Elaine C 4:41:22 (22,526)
Ruderman, Louisa J 3:15:53 (2,746)
Rudge, Charlotte H 5:09:44 (28,103)
Rudge, Emma J 4:35:36 (21,137)
Rudge, Leanne S 5:18:27 (29,220)
Rudge, Megan J 5:06:31 (27,627)
Rudland, Deborah 5:21:14 (29,527)
Rudrum, Stefanie A 5:03:43 (27,209)
Ruff, Kerry L 4:46:00 (23,674)
Ruholl, Daniela 4:18:16 (16,421)
Rule, Helen 5:07:13 (27,722)
Rule, Nicola J 6:06:57 (33,016)
Rulka, Nicole M 5:06:54 (27,682)
Rulke, Diane L 4:29:23 (19,498)
Rullino, Vittoria 3:33:31 (5,476)
Rumble, Hannah E 4:26:03 (18,552)
Rundhaug Johansson, Helene 6:52:26 (34,118)
Runnacles, Julia R 4:55:26 (25,770)
Rushton, Michelle 3:20:34 (3,302)
Rushworth, Elaine 5:09:32 (28,061)
Ruskin, Elise G 4:22:03 (17,460)
Russell, Amanda C 4:32:56 (20,415)
Russell, Cathryn S 4:40:02 (22,189)
Russell, Chloe L 4:32:20 (20,260)
Russell, Frances J 4:21:19 (17,257)
Russell, Julie 4:55:26 (25,770)
Russell, Julie D 4:55:37 (25,803)
Russell, Lesley D 3:55:10 (10,257)
Russell, Marianne 6:38:49 (33,863)
Russell, Marlene 4:44:43 (23,349)
Russell, Rebecca 4:24:12 (18,050)
Russell, Valerie 6:36:52 (33,819)
Russell, Yvonne 3:59:07 (11,535)
Russell Grant, Helen 4:38:33 (21,842)
Russon, Tara L 4:03:37 (12,751)
Rusyn, Linda 4:28:58 (19,393)
Ruszkowski, Ania 4:17:00 (16,095)
Rutherford, Julia M 4:14:26 (15,432)
Rutherford, Kate 5:29:44 (30,452)
Rutherford, Pam 3:43:52 (7,430)
Rutherford, Susie 3:03:15 (1,396)
Rutland, Samantha 5:19:17 (29,330)
Rutter, Alison J 7:04:11 (34,254)
Rutter, Emma R 5:15:01 (28,821)
Ruttle, Margaret A 5:38:08 (31,199)
Ryan, Angela 7:26:02 (34,435)
Ryan, Caroline J 5:23:10 (29,714)
Ryan, Christine A 5:34:45 (30,908)
Ryan, Emma C 4:43:06 (22,962)
Ryan, Liesl J 5:26:39 (30,116)
Ryan, Lisbeth 5:43:42 (31,627)
Ryan, Mary C 4:42:45 (22,866)
Ryan, Maryanna 6:07:08 (33,025)
Ryan, Michele J 6:01:44 (32,809)
Ryan, Orla A 4:14:31 (15,453)
Ryan, Tamatha J 3:40:40 (6,751)
Ryder, Catherine A 4:04:29 (12,928)
Ryder, Helen S 3:29:52 (4,857)
Saberton, Allison J 5:48:55 (32,042)
Sachse, Laura 4:24:22 (18,098)
Sadd, Kim R 5:15:31 (28,882)
Sadler, Charlotte A 4:20:05 (16,908)
Saha, Rebecca 7:41:54 (34,486)
Saines, Caroline L 4:01:44 (12,302)
Saint, Debbie M 4:02:21 (12,460)
Saj, Maria A 5:12:50 (28,520)
Salanty, Cheryl 3:53:21 (9,677)
Sale, Elaine 5:55:59 (32,519)
Sale, Sally 5:56:24 (32,553)
Saleh, Rama A 5:08:28 (27,888)
Sales, Anne 4:19:13 (16,680)
Sales, Jayne E 6:23:53 (33,512)
Salih, Samira 3:52:21 (9,396)
Salisbury, Emma A 4:47:55 (24,126)
Salmon, Gillian P 4:36:06 (21,268)

Salmon, Victoria S 4:04:17 (12,882)
Salome-Bentley, Nicola 6:25:21 (33,557)
Salome-Keetley, Yvonne M 6:09:55 (33,113)
Salt, Adela M 2:48:23 (440)
Salt, Jennifer K 4:09:27 (14,156)
Salter, Arianne 4:31:07 (19,915)
Salter, Rebecca J 6:13:18 (33,221)
Saltigerald, Sharon 7:51:09 (34,513)
Saltrese, Maria 5:43:31 (31,609)
Salvage, Christine 3:54:05 (9,899)
Samara, Shereen M 7:20:44 (34,400)
Samblas-Deffekary, Cynthia 4:56:41 (26,001)
Sambles, Miranda E 4:32:28 (20,288)
Sam-Daliri, Nadia M 4:36:19 (21,328)
Sampson, Helen M 4:17:19 (16,179)
Sams, Lisa V 5:31:27 (30,610)
Samuel, Eirian 5:02:53 (27,094)
Samuel, Karen 3:59:29 (11,668)
Samuelson-Dean, Katie M 3:21:18 (3,402)
Samwell, Amanda 4:24:26 (18,122)
San, Abigail 6:58:04 (34,189)
Sanchez, Cecilia 4:39:05 (21,999)
Sanctuary, Joanne E 5:36:34 (31,087)
Sandall, Charlotte 6:49:12 (34,061)
Sandell, Liz 6:19:13 (33,381)
Sanderova, Olga 4:01:45 (12,306)
Sanders, Barbara E 4:49:35 (24,498)
Sanderson, Elizabeth A 3:30:16 (4,935)
Sanderson, Sandra D 5:03:26 (27,173)
Sanderson, Sheila 5:51:05 (32,213)
Sanderson, Zoe M 3:55:49 (10,440)
Sanders-Reece, Andrea 3:37:15 (6,114)
Sandfeld, Anne 4:06:46 (13,466)
Sandford, Wendy E 4:34:13 (20,760)
Sandilands, Helen 4:46:30 (23,777)
Sandilands, Marietta M 4:55:37 (25,803)
Sandom, Fiona 4:25:55 (18,513)
Sandover, Diane M 3:43:03 (7,248)
Sangster, Rachel S 4:34:35 (20,839)
Sanson, Kathryn A 5:50:31 (32,175)
Sargant, Sylvia R 4:38:54 (21,941)
Sargeant, Mary T 4:24:10 (18,039)
Sargeant, Pauline 5:47:54 (31,972)
Sargent, Beth F 3:53:28 (9,705)
Sarker-Bell, Sunanda 4:40:19 (22,262)
Sarup, Louise S 4:15:28 (15,693)
Saul, Jenny L 4:37:22 (21,565)
Sault, Deb 3:42:56 (7,218)
Saunders, Francesca E 6:35:16 (33,777)
Saunders, Juliet E 4:23:38 (17,900)
Saunders, Kathryn 6:14:11 (33,249)
Saunders, Paula M 5:16:54 (29,042)
Saunders, Rachel 4:09:17 (14,112)
Saunders, Rebecca J 7:22:52 (34,414)
Saunders, Rio 4:04:17 (12,882)
Saunders, Vicki G 4:00:21 (11,937)
Saunt, Tonia E 4:21:45 (17,389)
Savage, Juliet A 4:21:41 (17,368)
Savage, Maura K 4:25:42 (18,444)
Saville, Anna G 3:48:50 (8,534)
Saville, Nicky 4:54:45 (25,638)
Savoca, Katia 5:39:34 (31,304)
Sawford, Andrea 4:51:17 (24,898)
Sawyer, Evelyn B 7:18:31 (34,386)
Sawyer, Julia 3:25:30 (4,015)
Sawyer, Kate 6:47:13 (34,025)
Saye, Sheila 4:57:12 (26,124)
Sayers, Kim 5:49:30 (32,086)
Scanlan, Catherine 4:21:36 (17,334)
Scanlon, Sharon 6:41:49 (33,907)
Scantlebury, Kelly A 6:25:43 (33,569)
Scargill, Elizabeth M 4:42:54 (22,907)
Scarlett, Tracey M 4:22:14 (17,506)
Scarr-Hall, Rachael 5:15:14 (28,847)
Scarrott, Kate 5:52:43 (32,323)
Scarrott, Laura J 4:49:11 (24,410)
Scarrott, Yvonne C 3:14:24 (2,531)
Scarth, Anna M 4:25:01 (18,266)
Sceeny, Claire E 3:47:36 (8,251)
Schaerer, Patricia 3:52:01 (9,305)
Schall, Michelle G 4:37:48 (21,671)
Schalla, Monika 3:35:45 (5,838)
Schapira, Laura J 3:55:11 (10,261)

Schembri, Joslyn	4:39:41	(22,122)
Scherrer, Kanan Bala	6:20:28	(33,408)
Schmid, Erika R	3:13:51	(2,443)
Schmidt, Monika	4:35:35	(21,129)
Schmitt, Annette	4:35:34	(21,122)
Schmitt, Kathryn M	5:00:47	(26,756)
Schmitz, Gabi	4:35:35	(21,129)
Schneider, Andrea	3:32:40	(5,342)
Schneider, Joanne E	3:49:56	(8,808)
Schneider, Leah J	4:56:59	(26,071)
Schofield, Cheryl J	5:50:20	(32,159)
Schofield, Evie	3:54:18	(9,960)
Schofield, Lynn P	4:04:15	(12,876)
Schofield, Sarah J	4:41:47	(22,628)
Scholes, Rachel L	5:44:17	(31,695)
Scholtz, Ruth	5:17:00	(29,063)
Scholz, Bettina	4:45:25	(23,517)
Schonhofer, Robyn M	6:06:16	(32,995)
Schubert, Lindsey	3:48:06	(8,374)
Schuessler, Karin	4:35:36	(21,137)
Schuhle-Lewis, Jessica E	4:37:13	(21,531)
Schuller, Lynne	4:23:20	(17,825)
Schulz, Adele K	4:10:44	(14,475)
Schumann, Anne L	4:19:09	(16,667)
Schwarz, Marion	3:52:00	(9,301)
Scoble, Marie C	4:24:25	(18,114)
Scofield, Sharon L	6:38:16	(33,852)
Scorer, Beth	5:05:02	(27,406)
Scothern, Sally H	5:01:35	(26,887)
Scotland, Bev	4:49:30	(24,474)
Scott, Aileen	3:43:01	(7,243)
Scott, Amanda	7:28:48	(34,447)
Scott, Anne	3:39:07	(6,454)
Scott, Clare	3:48:37	(8,493)
Scott, Jacqueline M	4:55:37	(25,803)
Scott, Julia M	3:51:13	(9,101)
Scott, Karen J	5:30:48	(30,553)
Scott, Kate	4:48:12	(24,185)
Scott, Katie	4:49:45	(24,543)
Scott, May M	4:53:48	(25,440)
Scott, Miranda E	4:54:24	(25,560)
Scott, Rachel	4:28:08	(19,142)
Scott, Sallie J	5:01:58	(26,952)
Scott, Sandra M	4:43:47	(23,119)
Scott, Vicky L	4:39:31	(22,082)
Scott, Victoria L	6:16:20	(33,302)
Scott, Yvonne F	4:50:39	(24,757)
Scott-Wilson, Suzanne	5:15:46	(28,915)
Scrase, Emma L	4:15:35	(15,724)
Screen, Hazel R	3:56:32	(10,639)
Scrivener, Kelly L	3:53:33	(9,726)
Scrowther, Rosemary A	6:23:29	(33,503)
Scully, Teresa N	3:00:23	(1,194)
Scurfield, Marie L	5:03:59	(27,249)
Seabrook, Patricia H	5:09:36	(28,072)
Seagrove, Sandra A	4:45:35	(23,555)
Seal, Amy C	5:45:49	(31,823)
Seal, Laura A	6:05:24	(32,943)
Seaman, Francesca M	5:48:49	(32,033)
Searle, Amber	4:04:40	(12,972)
Searle, Liz	4:06:40	(13,446)
Searle, Lorna E	4:33:18	(20,511)
Searle, Olivia C	5:17:09	(29,084)
Sears, Tracey L	4:47:04	(23,923)
Seddon, Anna J	3:52:05	(9,327)
Sedgman, Katherine J	4:08:31	(13,919)
Sedgwick, Rebecca L	4:35:14	(21,039)
Sedman, Alison	3:03:26	(1,415)
See, Christina J	5:39:41	(31,311)
Seeley, Katie A	4:42:39	(22,844)
Sefton, Denise E	4:08:05	(13,784)
Segal, Jane C	3:51:41	(9,226)
Segal, Rachel E	6:37:00	(33,822)
Segawa, Kana	3:40:43	(6,761)
Sekkides-Lunn, Penny J	5:10:09	(28,168)
Selby, Julie E	4:54:20	(25,548)
Sell, Laura	3:23:49	(3,742)
Selman, Kay M	3:54:07	(9,909)
Selvon, Nathalie V	5:44:43	(31,740)
Selwood, Gemma A	6:41:12	(33,902)
Selwood, Katie M	4:12:03	(14,824)
Senatore, Anna	3:39:30	(6,534)
Senecal-Woolnough, Andrea	4:49:07	(24,399)
Senior, Gill V	3:37:42	(6,201)
Senior, Gina L	4:34:00	(20,697)
Sentenac, Ann-Marie	4:16:56	(16,070)
Sessions, Lucy	5:06:13	(27,585)
Severn, Eileen M	4:39:39	(22,108)
Seward, Tina M	4:32:38	(20,331)
Sewell, Rosalind G	4:24:37	(18,175)
Sexton, Claire E	5:49:12	(32,067)
Sexton, Dawn A	4:59:58	(26,629)
Sexton, Phillippa	4:49:08	(24,403)
Seymour, Angela L	4:25:07	(18,296)
Seymour, Ann C	3:51:27	(9,164)
Seymour, Laura A	4:24:23	(18,106)
Shackleton, Jane	5:22:33	(29,669)
Shackleton, Megan	3:03:35	(1,422)
Shacklock, Susan L	3:44:10	(7,485)
Shah, Kirti	4:58:42	(26,420)
Shah, Meera	4:09:36	(14,200)
Shah, Meera M	7:25:04	(34,427)
Shah, Nishma	3:53:36	(9,743)
Shah, Nita	5:21:55	(29,593)
Shah, Rajvi H	7:04:13	(34,256)
Shah, Shila	4:55:07	(25,721)
Shalloe, Julie A	4:28:49	(19,351)
Shambrook, Wendy M	5:36:33	(31,085)
Shams, Fari	3:08:48	(1,856)
Shang, Catherine A	4:50:30	(24,715)
Shannon, Marie M	4:42:01	(22,676)
Shannon-Jones, Sue D	5:21:30	(29,555)
Shapland, Julie	4:57:27	(26,173)
Sharland, Sharon L	3:43:06	(7,266)
Sharma, Poonam	6:35:16	(33,777)
Sharman, Charlotte A	4:01:07	(12,141)
Sharman, Rhiannon A	4:13:37	(15,191)
Sharp, Gemma	7:11:09	(34,330)
Sharp, Karen	4:41:23	(22,531)
Sharp, Lorna C	4:06:13	(13,333)
Sharp, Renata L	3:53:06	(9,607)
Sharp, Zoe A	4:46:13	(23,717)
Sharpe, Anthea L	3:46:03	(7,899)
Sharpe, Fiona M	4:10:07	(14,318)
Sharpe, Shelley	5:14:27	(28,735)
Sharrod, Sandra	4:54:21	(25,549)
Shaw, Amanda E	4:08:55	(14,022)
Shaw, Carol	4:46:14	(23,723)
Shaw, Deborah M	4:14:30	(15,451)
Shaw, Felicity	3:42:14	(7,076)
Shaw, Julie E	5:15:55	(28,926)
Shaw, Leah J	5:15:40	(28,902)
Shaw, Natasha J	5:00:42	(26,737)
Shaw, Nicola	5:31:28	(30,611)
Shaw, Rachel A	3:52:52	(9,526)
Shaw, Sacha	6:12:55	(33,207)
Shaw, Sarah	5:41:38	(31,476)
Shea, Margaret M	5:05:31	(27,479)
Shedden, Joanne	3:53:42	(9,771)
Sheffield, Gillian	3:23:55	(3,767)
Sheikh, Shaleena	6:08:09	(33,051)
Shelbourn, Nicola J	5:15:42	(28,905)
Shelbourn-Barrow, Jayne	5:18:27	(29,220)
Sheldon, Sheena F	4:52:38	(25,180)
Sheldon (née Chapman), Melanie	6:05:10	(32,933)
Shelley, Claire J	3:57:57	(11,102)
Shen, Aimée	3:27:07	(4,299)
Shen, Meng	5:18:03	(29,186)
Shenton, Fiona C	3:07:44	(1,757)
Shenton, Lucy J	4:27:24	(18,932)
Shephard, Sarah	3:51:16	(9,113)
Shepherd, Amanda L	4:13:48	(15,252)
Shepherd, Catherine M	5:23:19	(29,729)
Shepherd, Charlotte E	5:34:43	(30,906)
Shepherd, Jennifer A	4:23:26	(17,852)
Shepherd, Melissa	4:57:27	(26,173)
Shepherd, Rachel A	4:57:05	(26,104)
Shepherd, Sue L	3:33:26	(5,461)
Shepherd, Zoe	3:55:01	(10,201)
Sheppard, Kalli L	4:21:43	(17,380)
Sheppard, Vicky J	4:53:34	(25,392)
Shergill, Guzz	4:35:54	(21,211)
Sheridan, Alison J	4:30:49	(19,838)
Sheridan, Jeanette	4:45:14	(23,473)
Sheridan, Margaret M	4:16:40	(16,005)
Sheridan, Pauline B	5:24:10	(29,825)
Sherlock, Joanna	4:54:42	(25,623)
Sherriff, Virginia L	3:45:50	(7,867)
Sherwin, Christine Elizabeth C	5:42:40	(31,545)
Sherwin, Louise N	4:38:04	(21,729)
Shew, Julie F	4:47:59	(24,144)
Shields, Lynda C	5:29:40	(30,443)
Shiells, Patricia (George) J	5:10:03	(28,153)
Shiels, Donna	4:51:37	(24,969)
Shiels, Laura J	4:14:40	(15,487)
Shier, Karen L	4:26:27	(18,651)
Shilling, Vicky	5:34:07	(30,846)
Shillito, Annemarie	4:29:40	(19,557)
Shipman, Sue	7:42:25	(34,487)
Shipp, Rachel E	4:39:40	(22,114)
Shipperley, Elaine C	4:38:20	(21,787)
Shipton, Melissa C	5:46:46	(31,899)
Shire, Philippa J	5:51:12	(32,227)
Shirley, Marie L	3:50:54	(9,028)
Shore, Loren	7:11:23	(34,335)
Shori, Punam	4:57:34	(26,199)
Short, Lynette	5:10:22	(28,201)
Short, Sarah E	4:42:19	(22,758)
Short, Susan M	3:59:49	(11,789)
Shorten, Nicola E	5:42:24	(31,527)
Shotton, Bryanie S	4:34:46	(20,897)
Shotton, Kay L	5:40:59	(31,411)
Shrimpton, Karen B	3:57:45	(11,039)
Shrubsole, Clair	3:25:06	(3,947)
Shufflebottom, Tracy	4:17:31	(16,227)
Sidhu, Julie A	4:20:47	(17,118)
Sidoti, Eleonora	4:28:16	(19,194)
Sierwald, Samantha C	4:13:47	(15,248)
Sigward, Lorna J	4:18:54	(16,599)
Silberbauer, Victoria	5:17:58	(29,176)
Silke, Alison F	5:17:22	(29,104)
Silver, Sally A	4:38:21	(21,790)
Silverman, Ruth H	3:35:36	(5,813)
Silverside, Susan A	5:08:08	(27,836)
Sim, Helena	3:36:46	(6,005)
Simalova, Martina	4:28:12	(19,171)
Simcox, Rachael J	3:47:38	(8,263)
Simeon, Helga L	5:30:21	(30,511)
Simmonds, Jane	4:31:11	(19,934)
Simmonds, Sally-Jane	4:57:25	(26,168)
Simmonds, Tamsin M	3:17:32	(2,935)
Simmonds OBE, Brigid M	4:17:27	(16,205)
Simmons, Diane	4:24:50	(18,226)
Simmons, Eleanor	3:38:41	(6,386)
Simmons, Kathy	3:39:04	(6,447)
Simmons, Maxine P	5:27:20	(30,184)
Simon, Joann T	4:22:16	(17,514)
Simon, Pascale	4:20:40	(17,084)
Simon, Stacey	5:12:17	(28,432)
Simons, Emily-Claire C	4:31:14	(19,945)
Simons, Heather I	4:42:01	(22,676)
Simpson, Hannah	5:07:19	(27,741)
Simpson, Julia	4:43:48	(23,122)
Simpson, Linda	5:08:38	(27,921)
Simpson, Lynn A	4:40:20	(22,269)
Simpson, Michelle D	6:21:18	(33,437)
Simpson, Nicola J	5:46:23	(31,870)
Simpson, Patrice M	5:13:14	(28,578)
Simpson, Stephenie M	4:40:04	(22,198)
Sims, Amanda C	5:45:29	(31,803)
Sims, Denise	4:25:04	(18,278)
Sims, Natasha O	4:53:08	(25,303)
Sims, Rosemary D	5:40:22	(31,364)
Sims, Rosie G	3:43:38	(7,373)
Sims, Sarah L	5:08:22	(27,868)
Sinclair, Karen E	4:58:55	(26,459)
Sinclair, Kirsty	5:29:57	(30,474)
Sinclair, Kristel	5:41:41	(31,478)
Sinclair, Laura J	3:46:14	(7,936)
Singal, Ann M	5:44:15	(31,690)
Singer, Jo L	3:49:02	(8,587)

Singer, Sally 5:11:31 (28,333)
Sinkinson, Clare 3:54:47 (10,121)
Sinquin, Thérèse 4:43:25 (23,028)
Sipidias, Christine 4:21:53 (17,419)
Siret, Tracey L 4:24:49 (18,221)
Sirmen, Trish A 5:24:13 (29,830)
Sison, Kelly A 4:03:24 (12,700)
Sjoo, Solweig 4:59:45 (26,600)
Skapoullis, Debra 5:28:52 (30,360)
Skates, Lucie I 4:19:49 (16,838)
Skelton, Anna F 3:36:39 (5,988)
Skelton, Elizabeth 5:03:30 (27,183)
Skelton, Sophie 3:46:26 (7,988)
Skidmore, Flora 3:14:26 (2,536)
Skidmore, Gemma 5:08:45 (27,937)
Skingsley, Victoria L 5:28:00 (30,267)
Skinner, Belinda 5:10:51 (28,260)
Skinner, Catherine J 3:54:09 (9,919)
Skinner, Elizabeth A 6:12:42 (33,195)
Skinner, Joanna 3:31:33 (5,141)
Skinner, Lucy E 4:21:34 (17,328)
Skipper, Vikki 4:10:37 (14,440)
Skvortsova, Silvia 2:29:11 (58)
Slack, Clover E 4:36:01 (21,246)
Slack, Debbie A 5:29:26 (30,418)
Slack, Rebecca T 3:58:19 (11,226)
Slade, Louise 4:38:04 (21,729)
Slade, Nikki 4:48:00 (24,148)
Slade, Tracy M 4:36:06 (21,268)
Slamon, Lynne 4:51:02 (24,852)
Slane, Joanne V 3:47:10 (8,142)
Slanina, Theresa A 4:19:32 (16,768)
Slark-Hollis, Rebecca L 5:31:39 (30,627)
Slatcher, Deborah 4:28:34 (19,280)
Slater, Carolyn 5:20:32 (29,470)
Slater, Elizabeth A 4:50:00 (24,604)
Slater, Zoe D 6:21:51 (33,458)
Slattery, Margaret 4:29:39 (19,551)
Slattery Dillon, Franses E 5:34:39 (30,901)
Sleigh, Alice 4:09:13 (14,095)
Slinger, Tara L 4:50:40 (24,759)
Sliwerski, Claire L 4:56:40 (25,995)
Sloan, Paddy M 4:31:26 (20,010)
Smail, Amanda 3:12:09 (2,227)
Small, Christina 4:30:05 (19,650)
Small, Emma K 4:24:47 (18,210)
Small, Michele H 6:13:10 (33,216)
Smallamn, Judith R 4:19:01 (16,633)
Smallman, Sarah K 4:46:06 (23,689)
Smart, Bridgette A 4:06:08 (13,322)
Smart, Emma L 4:17:27 (16,205)
Smart, Louise A 4:35:08 (21,017)
Smeaton, Maxine T 5:10:46 (28,243)
Smedley, Dionne 5:27:04 (30,149)
Smedley, Parminder 5:15:08 (28,836)
Smee, Henrietta S 4:03:51 (12,797)
Smeeton, Samantha E 5:02:15 (26,999)
Smethurst, Anna K 4:01:48 (12,317)
Smith, Abby 4:01:33 (12,255)
Smith, Abigail 7:29:24 (34,452)
Smith, Aeron 4:26:35 (18,690)
Smith, Aileen 4:19:40 (16,804)
Smith, Ali C 7:11:22 (34,334)
Smith, Alison L 4:01:17 (12,178)
Smith, Andrea J 4:02:18 (12,446)
Smith, Angela K 4:08:08 (13,810)
Smith, Angela L 6:09:38 (33,099)
Smith, Angharad L 3:53:49 (9,815)
Smith, Ann-Marie 3:06:23 (1,634)
Smith, Barbara S 6:40:09 (33,885)
Smith, Bathsheba R 4:31:24 (19,995)
Smith, Becky 5:53:39 (32,384)
Smith, Caroline A 4:26:29 (18,662)
Smith, Carolyn 3:44:25 (7,539)
Smith, Cath 3:38:47 (6,405)
Smith, Catherine 4:48:00 (24,148)
Smith, Catherine H 4:32:15 (20,243)
Smith, Cathryn J 4:16:00 (15,837)
Smith, Celia 6:21:35 (33,447)
Smith, Charlotte N 4:57:29 (26,182)
Smith, Christina 3:37:48 (6,217)
Smith, Claire 3:54:29 (10,022)
Smith, Claire A 6:06:06 (32,985)
Smith, Claire L 5:36:10 (31,050)
Smith, Clare 4:52:33 (25,156)
Smith, Clare 5:27:00 (30,144)
Smith, Collette 5:08:59 (27,967)
Smith, Corin B 5:10:07 (28,164)
Smith, Cynthia A 5:22:13 (29,629)
Smith, Davina L 4:22:27 (17,568)
Smith, Deborah J 5:55:10 (32,473)
Smith, Debra 5:32:35 (30,710)
Smith, Dorothy A 4:39:02 (21,981)
Smith, Elaine G 4:03:20 (12,685)
Smith, Elizabeth A 4:11:02 (14,551)
Smith, Eloise A 4:32:35 (20,318)
Smith, Emily 5:10:09 (28,168)
Smith, Emma 5:09:58 (28,139)
Smith, Emma L 4:45:47 (23,617)
Smith, Emma L 6:05:42 (32,962)
Smith, Emma M 4:15:30 (15,704)
Smith, Fiona L 5:49:53 (32,112)
Smith, Frances C 4:44:22 (23,271)
Smith, Gemma A 4:33:54 (20,684)
Smith, Giselle R 5:10:12 (28,175)
Smith, Grace A 5:25:52 (30,016)
Smith, Hannah C 5:42:54 (31,561)
Smith, Hannah E 4:10:57 (14,535)
Smith, Heather A 4:35:46 (21,184)
Smith, Heidi J 4:37:02 (21,494)
Smith, Helen C 5:04:40 (27,352)
Smith, Helen M 7:07:16 (34,285)
Smith, Jackie 7:22:19 (34,411)
Smith, Jacqueline J 5:02:21 (27,014)
Smith, Jane 6:34:04 (33,749)
Smith, Joan 5:28:59 (30,377)
Smith, Joanne 3:41:01 (6,829)
Smith, Joanne L 5:52:32 (32,316)
Smith, Josephine 4:10:13 (14,340)
Smith, Kara L 6:49:22 (34,068)
Smith, Kathryn A 5:33:41 (30,795)
Smith, Kathryn L 5:14:20 (28,727)
Smith, Katy V 4:30:21 (19,712)
Smith, Kirsty D 4:24:30 (18,143)
Smith, Kirsty L 4:49:05 (24,392)
Smith, Kym M 4:51:23 (24,921)
Smith, Laura A 4:42:24 (22,780)
Smith, Lauren E 4:53:48 (25,440)
Smith, Lauren K 4:54:56 (25,683)
Smith, Libby H 5:29:15 (30,403)
Smith, Linda 3:38:08 (6,292)
Smith, Linda S 4:17:44 (16,291)
Smith, Louise C 4:09:41 (14,220)
Smith, Luzanne M 4:43:12 (22,982)
Smith, Melanie 3:54:40 (10,089)
Smith, Melanie A 5:20:50 (29,484)
Smith, Michelle L 5:49:58 (32,118)
Smith, Michelle L 6:09:17 (33,090)
Smith, Nichola E 6:33:55 (33,746)
Smith, Norma F 3:51:46 (9,241)
Smith, Pamela A 4:26:09 (18,574)
Smith, Pamela J 5:34:25 (30,875)
Smith, Patricia A 5:27:15 (30,170)
Smith, Paula 5:22:02 (29,602)
Smith, Paula J 4:09:46 (14,247)
Smith, Philippa K 4:33:21 (20,530)
Smith, Philomena 3:43:08 (7,273)
Smith, Rachael J 5:59:03 (32,697)
Smith, Rebecca L 4:01:48 (12,317)
Smith, Roisin K 3:48:13 (8,403)
Smith, Rosalind L 4:32:56 (20,415)
Smith, Sally 5:54:00 (32,404)
Smith, Samantha 5:21:33 (29,563)
Smith, Samantha J 3:44:34 (7,569)
Smith, Samantha J 4:46:52 (23,876)
Smith, Sandee J 5:34:28 (30,882)
Smith, Sheila D 4:50:52 (24,812)
Smith, Simone 4:24:17 (18,077)
Smith, Susan 4:32:05 (20,192)
Smith, Susan 4:38:44 (21,893)
Smith, Susan 4:57:01 (26,084)
Smith, Susan J 4:41:45 (22,620)
Smith, Susannah C 5:17:53 (29,165)
Smith, Tennille P 3:31:50 (5,190)
Smith, Tina L 4:56:50 (26,033)
Smith, Tracey J 4:20:40 (17,084)
Smith, Valerie 6:03:29 (32,865)
Smith, Vanessa E 4:24:20 (18,091)
Smith, Zoie 5:09:30 (28,048)
Smithard, Jacqueline 4:57:23 (26,161)
Smullen, Jean 4:09:12 (14,088)
Smy, Christa H 4:48:48 (24,320)
Smyth, Cara A 5:04:47 (27,370)
Smyth, Claire 4:49:46 (24,548)
Smyth, Nicola 3:36:38 (5,984)
Smyth, Nuala J 4:17:26 (16,200)
Smyth, Sarah 4:09:26 (14,151)
Sneddon, Stephanie 4:48:49 (24,324)
Sneezum, Beverley 5:01:31 (26,875)
Snelgrove, Elizabeth A 4:18:52 (16,589)
Snell, Marie E 6:20:34 (33,410)
Snellgrove, Kirste 4:59:40 (26,588)
Snippe, Marjolein 3:32:47 (5,360)
Snizek, Meredith H 4:49:01 (24,376)
Snoodyk, Kate 4:17:12 (16,157)
Snook, Tanya L 3:50:33 (8,941)
Snow, Alice F 3:54:31 (10,040)
Snow, Julia R 4:51:57 (25,031)
Snowden, Emma-Jane 4:35:37 (21,145)
Snowden, Marlena C 5:10:02 (28,150)
Snoxell, Joanna E 5:00:13 (26,667)
Snyder, Joanne 8:08:41 (34,544)
Soar, Susan R 4:17:41 (16,276)
Sofocleous, Paula 5:30:09 (30,491)
Sokal, Rachel 3:52:14 (9,370)
Sokhal, Emma J 5:19:28 (29,350)
Solaiman, Anna 6:22:29 (33,473)
Solbes, Isabelle 3:43:11 (7,283)
Soles, Harriet M 4:41:42 (22,616)
Solon, Adriana O 6:43:54 (33,959)
Soma, Champa 5:45:26 (31,797)
Somers, Laura 4:04:11 (12,859)
Somers-Edgar, Kirsty 3:03:31 (1,419)
Somerville, Jane Y 4:34:09 (20,739)
Somma, Anna 5:07:14 (27,728)
Sonnery-Cottet, Nathalie 3:43:29 (7,342)
Soper, Amanda K 3:40:46 (6,775)
Soper, Jennifer E 5:01:35 (26,887)
Sopp, Hazel M 4:43:58 (23,172)
Sorain, Françoise 3:47:00 (8,108)
Sordillo, Paola 4:30:49 (19,838)
Sorensen, Natascha H 4:22:55 (17,706)
Sotheby, Angela 4:34:32 (20,829)
Sott, Andrea H 3:56:18 (10,565)
South, Carole A 4:55:35 (25,797)
Southon, Emma 4:18:09 (16,386)
Southorn, Ingrid 3:47:38 (8,263)
Southwick, Kerry A 3:54:14 (9,936)
Southwood, Rhiannon J 4:52:39 (25,185)
Sowden-Taylor, Cari 4:08:21 (13,869)
Sowerby, Susan J 4:51:37 (24,969)
Spacey, Emma L 6:31:33 (33,694)
Sparkes, Ruth L 5:26:30 (30,098)
Sparks, Lara M 5:06:46 (27,660)
Sparling, Clare M 4:04:41 (12,979)
Sparrow, Julie M 5:13:46 (28,647)
Sparrow, Michelle A 6:27:51 (33,622)
Spatz, Angela F 3:51:33 (9,182)
Spaull, Sally A 6:29:16 (33,642)
Speak, Sue D 4:14:14 (15,377)
Speake, Celia 3:53:50 (9,824)
Speake, Rachel A 4:19:46 (16,829)
Speakman, Eva 4:52:47 (25,217)
Spears, Alison 6:04:49 (32,917)
Speas, Rachel L 4:27:32 (18,960)
Speck, Camilla 4:05:28 (13,168)
Speechley, Bernadette 3:54:02 (9,882)
Speirs, Rachael 4:19:50 (16,842)
Spence, Emma L 4:52:48 (25,222)
Spence, Irena J 5:25:02 (29,920)
Spence, Jannett C 7:45:32 (34,497)
Spence, Laura B 4:03:35 (12,742)
Spence, Laura E 3:18:28 (3,045)
Spence, Rebecca 7:49:18 (34,507)
Spencer, Emma J 4:33:39 (20,622)
Spencer, Gillian C 5:00:27 (26,702)
Spencer, Katherine W 4:30:01 (19,639)
Spencer, Rebecca H 5:46:13 (31,855)
Spicer, Julia M 7:56:18 (34,528)

Spicer, Katie......6:00:17 (32,751)
Spick, Claire 3:41:01 (6,829)
Spiers, Tracey C.......5:38:37 (31,231)
Spillane, Katie J.......4:43:20 (23,012)
Spittles, Kirsty A 4:25:21 (18,355)
Spong, Carole.......3:38:29 (6,356)
Spong, Sue 3:19:11 (3,116)
Spragg, Jane K.......4:03:02 (12,616)
Sprake, Alice A 4:18:15 (16,413)
Springall, Claire 4:05:31 (13,182)
Sproson, Criona A.......5:28:10 (30,285)
Sprules, Laura L 7:03:00 (34,241)
Spurr, Sarah J 4:51:13 (24,884)
Squire, Gemma L.......5:29:42 (30,445)
Stace, Katrina 4:41:25 (22,537)
Stacey, Ayshea D 7:07:54 (34,293)
Stacey, Elizabeth A 5:19:40 (29,381)
Stacey, Judith C 3:44:38 (7,587)
Stach-Keyitz, Adele 3:43:03 (7,248)
Staeck, Emma 5:42:49 (31,556)
Staelens, Aurelie.......4:04:20 (12,901)
Stafford, Ceri E.......4:14:59 (15,553)
Stafford, Julie 3:45:49 (7,863)
Stafford, Natalie R.......4:28:11 (19,164)
Stafford, Sally V 5:27:16 (30,172)
Staite, Jane C 3:23:10 (3,659)
Stalder, Martine L 6:27:32 (33,613)
Staley, Louise R 4:34:52 (20,931)
Stallard, Lizzy 3:45:14 (7,736)
Stamper, Linda.......4:22:27 (17,568)
Stanbridge, Amanda J.......6:45:30 (33,991)
Standing, Angie C.......4:36:37 (21,396)
Standley, Edna A 6:12:38 (33,191)
Standley, Gillian M.......4:48:17 (24,205)
Standring, Debbie 4:06:55 (13,496)
Stanfill, Sonnet.......4:22:40 (17,639)
Stanford, Paula J 4:34:04 (20,712)
Staniforth, Jane A.......4:26:25 (18,639)
Stanley, Isabella L.......4:31:37 (20,056)
Stanley, Ruth.......4:31:16 (19,952)
Stanley, Sarah 4:53:02 (25,280)
Stannett, Ann-Janet.......4:27:54 (19,065)
Stansfield, Judith C 6:36:28 (33,802)
Stanton, Claire M.......5:18:53 (29,274)
Stanton, Josephine 5:59:40 (32,721)
Stanton, Kate 3:42:21 (7,105)
Stanway, Rachel M.......5:49:08 (32,063)
Stapelberg, Michelle 5:28:48 (30,350)
Staples, Elizabeth A.......5:34:25 (30,875)
Staples, Phillippa L.......6:27:38 (33,616)
Stapley, Carolyn J 4:55:13 (25,732)
Stares, Diane B 4:06:35 (13,420)
Starr, Victoria J.......5:09:49 (28,117)
Statham, Pamela 4:25:13 (18,323)
Staton, Nicola 4:27:16 (18,896)
Stauffacher, Annette 4:03:13 (12,658)
Staveley, Shirley L.......3:42:47 (7,194)
Stavenuiter, Isobel.......4:35:41 (21,164)
Stavri, Georgina.......5:21:29 (29,551)
Stavri, Theodora.......5:26:36 (30,110)
Stead, Ann C.......4:22:39 (17,631)
Stead, Elaine J 4:57:55 (26,268)
Steadman, Victoria A 3:42:59 (7,233)
Steed, Maureen E.......4:53:58 (25,474)
Steeds, Lindsay L.......6:16:09 (33,297)
Steeds, Sandra I.......6:23:29 (33,503)
Steel, Emma V.......6:03:14 (32,856)
Steele, Adele L 5:06:12 (27,582)
Steer, Deborah A 2:58:38 (1,022)
Steggles, Ruth.......5:06:52 (27,677)
Stein, Lyndall 5:47:36 (31,958)
Stein du Pre, Debby 4:35:33 (21,116)
Steindorsdottir, Bjork 3:54:55 (10,170)
Steiner, Caroline A.......5:04:00 (27,252)
Steiner-Gnigler, Renate.......3:40:43 (6,761)
Stendall, Helen 5:18:22 (29,214)
Stenhouse, Michelle.......4:02:05 (12,382)
Stenner, Sue C.......5:24:18 (29,838)
Stephant, Patricia.......3:55:51 (10,452)
Stephen, Lynne 3:38:26 (6,347)
Stephens, Adele F 5:03:39 (27,202)
Stephens, Beth L.......4:11:17 (14,622)
Stephens, Jayne S 4:28:47 (19,343)

Stephens, Joanna C.......4:07:39 (13,689)
Stephens, Karen L.......4:54:14 (25,531)
Stephens, Nicola J.......4:08:34 (13,931)
Stephens, Phillippa G 3:12:45 (2,295)
Stephens, Sarah-Jane 4:09:49 (14,257)
Stephens, Vanessa A.......4:07:38 (13,684)
Stephenson, Carly L.......3:53:41 (9,764)
Stephenson, Christine M.......5:51:57 (32,288)
Stephenson, Helena E 4:20:31 (17,032)
Stephenson, Pamela L.......4:49:43 (24,537)
Stephenson, Rebecca H.......3:58:24 (11,261)
Stephenson, Susan V.......6:07:00 (33,019)
Stephenson, Tamsin 4:38:41 (21,880)
Stepler, Joan T.......3:39:19 (6,501)
Stepto, Michela M 4:03:34 (12,736)
Steptoe, Charlotte 3:12:46 (2,298)
Steptoe, Helen F 5:50:43 (32,190)
Stern, Lucy M 4:19:23 (16,720)
Steven, Jill K 4:50:29 (24,708)
Stevens, Alison 5:37:10 (31,129)
Stevens, Amanda 5:58:34 (32,673)
Stevens, Corrina 3:16:47 (2,843)
Stevens, Joanne 3:44:32 (7,558)
Stevens, Kerry L 5:37:11 (31,131)
Stevens, Lorna 5:09:16 (28,005)
Stevens, Rachel E 4:27:52 (19,051)
Stevens, Tanya 4:07:54 (13,753)
Stevenson, Gillian A.......3:41:41 (6,964)
Stevenson, Leanne M.......8:13:11 (34,549)
Stevenson, Lorraine J.......4:44:29 (23,297)
Stevenson, Louise.......3:57:36 (10,977)
Stevenson, Lucy 5:56:29 (32,556)
Stevenson, Nicola 4:33:46 (20,653)
Stevenson, Samantha 8:16:35 (34,554)
Stevenson, Victoria H 3:35:44 (5,837)
Stevenson-Baker, Sara L.......5:51:33 (32,256)
Steward, Adele M 4:55:10 (25,726)
Steward, Gemma J.......4:33:48 (20,661)
Steward, Ruth.......4:24:53 (18,238)
Stewart, Audrie 6:06:13 (32,992)
Stewart, Jennifer J 5:11:09 (28,287)
Stewart, Joanne 5:11:41 (28,362)
Stewart, Joanne M.......4:13:31 (15,164)
Stewart, Kelly 6:52:04 (34,112)
Stewart, Leith M 3:56:52 (10,749)
Stewart, Melanie J 4:27:28 (18,946)
Stewart, Monica 3:24:47 (3,885)
Stewart, Victoria 6:12:52 (33,204)
Stewart-Power, Anne M 3:15:32 (2,705)
Stibbs, Helen J 3:42:39 (7,164)
Stickland, Jessica A.......4:26:26 (18,641)
Stiff, Tracy L 5:49:01 (32,054)
Stiles, Laura J.......4:03:56 (12,812)
Still, Karen 4:49:53 (24,569)
Stimson, Juliet 4:28:29 (19,256)
Stirling, Laura J.......5:52:11 (32,299)
Stirrup, Johanna M 5:16:13 (28,961)
Stirrup, Sarah 6:53:06 (34,124)
Stirzaker, Amanda 7:03:45 (34,250)
Stoakes, Tina 4:55:02 (25,706)
Stock, Nadia 4:50:59 (24,839)
Stockdale, Katherine A 4:46:18 (23,742)
Stockill, Clare A.......5:32:28 (30,699)
Stocks, Alice E.......4:50:52 (24,812)
Stocks, Joanne 3:50:05 (8,843)
Stockton, Paula J 3:42:44 (7,181)
Stockton, Sarah T.......4:58:04 (26,297)
Stoddard, Amy S.......3:45:39 (7,827)
Stoddart, Elisabeth E 4:22:41 (17,645)
Stojkovic, Jelena 4:17:36 (16,250)
Stokes, Kimberley.......4:51:14 (24,887)
Stokes, Nikki 5:42:05 (31,507)
Stokes, Trudy S 3:47:38 (8,263)
Stonard, Sarah L 4:23:32 (17,875)
Stone, Alexandra.......5:14:37 (28,764)
Stone, Charlotte E.......4:20:49 (17,130)
Stone, Domini A.......5:46:56 (31,906)
Stone, Gillian 4:19:28 (16,743)
Stone, Jennifer M.......5:47:55 (31,975)
Stone, Rebecca L.......6:26:03 (33,578)
Stone, Sally A.......3:42:14 (7,076)
Stone, Sarah K.......4:31:40 (20,071)
Stoneman, April 4:56:45 (26,013)

Stoneman, Cara S.......5:00:02 (26,638)
Stoneman, Marion C.......4:03:59 (12,827)
Stones, Lorraine C.......5:12:57 (28,540)
Stones, Louisa P 4:21:15 (17,236)
Stooks, Melanie 5:24:01 (29,808)
Stopforth, Karen N 4:32:23 (20,267)
Stoppani, Julie M 3:39:09 (6,462)
Storck, Christiane.......3:41:27 (6,924)
Storey, Pamela J.......6:22:24 (33,470)
Storey, Simone 3:58:01 (11,122)
Storm, Lize-Marie.......3:37:24 (6,149)
Storr, Ann E.......4:31:48 (20,103)
Stott, Ami E.......5:24:11 (29,826)
Stott, Sarah 3:59:34 (11,696)
Stout, Christy L.......3:58:39 (11,357)
Stout, Katja 5:36:56 (31,116)
Stovell, Leonora M 4:46:51 (23,874)
Straccia, Carmen P.......5:45:22 (31,794)
Stracey, Amanda J.......4:24:24 (18,111)
Strachan, Iona 4:30:08 (19,663)
Stradling, Sarah.......2:51:48 (585)
Strang, Amanda C.......4:29:40 (19,557)
Strang, Camilla 5:01:35 (26,887)
Stratford, Karen 8:21:08 (34,560)
Strattan, Jenny E 4:40:48 (22,379)
Stratton, Julie M.......6:53:18 (34,128)
Strawbridge, Tracey M 5:12:47 (28,512)
Street, Stephanie A 3:49:11 (8,622)
Streeter, Anne 4:58:40 (26,410)
Stretton, Jackie M.......4:38:32 (21,831)
Stricker, Stephanie 5:03:15 (27,141)
Stringer, Judith F.......7:09:07 (34,304)
Stringer, Lynda K 4:18:56 (16,610)
Stringfellow, Sandra 5:17:08 (29,080)
Stronach, Joanna F.......6:09:08 (33,086)
Strong, Lucy F 4:49:41 (24,529)
Stronghill, Tracey J.......4:53:56 (25,468)
Stroud, Andrea T 4:31:33 (20,039)
Stroud, Kirsten L.......3:37:24 (6,149)
Stroud, Sue C 5:39:21 (31,288)
Strudwick, Jenny.......3:58:48 (11,416)
Strumm, Brianna L 5:00:28 (26,703)
Stuart, Jane 3:50:04 (8,837)
Stuart, Joanne L 5:48:43 (32,027)
Stubbings, Natasha E 5:03:37 (27,200)
Stubbs, Amanda P 4:32:12 (20,225)
Stubbs, Eleanor 5:59:26 (32,713)
Stubbs, Karen 4:57:32 (26,194)
Stuetzel, Heidi 4:27:52 (19,051)
Sturgeon, Julia M 5:33:52 (30,823)
Sturla, Alison M.......5:48:21 (31,998)
Sturtivant, Justine L 6:06:59 (33,018)
Sturzaker, Nicola A.......3:26:17 (4,150)
Styche, Jeanette 4:03:02 (12,616)
Styles, Joanna E 5:41:37 (31,473)
Stynes, Clare H 4:46:22 (23,755)
Suckling, Alison 4:21:52 (17,415)
Suckling, Marion 5:27:43 (30,228)
Suddaby, Tracey J 5:06:33 (27,630)
Sudra, Sheena 6:19:21 (33,384)
Sugden, Faye L 4:17:58 (16,338)
Sugden, Jean E 4:45:45 (23,605)
Sulaiman, Latiffawati 4:53:20 (25,337)
Sullivan, Carmel M.......3:19:52 (3,213)
Sullivan, Delilah 4:56:00 (25,877)
Sullivan, Marie S.......5:39:15 (31,281)
Sullivan, Nicole L.......3:24:49 (3,904)
Sully, Deborah L.......5:08:38 (27,921)
Sully, Jess L 5:15:50 (28,919)
Summerfield, Joanne K 5:47:44 (31,961)
Summerfield, Wendy A.......3:48:20 (8,429)
Summers, Elizabeth A.......3:52:51 (9,522)
Summers, Jo C.......4:28:06 (19,130)
Summers, Laura G 4:57:01 (26,084)
Summers, Linda 4:43:11 (22,978)
Summers, Melanie J 5:07:42 (27,797)
Summers, Rona 5:51:00 (32,208)
Sumner, Kate L 3:58:24 (11,261)
Sun, Weiwei 2:36:34 (139)
Surgay, Louise C.......4:03:01 (12,611)
Surplice, Holly.......5:19:31 (29,362)
Susans, Nicola D.......3:16:15 (2,781)
Sutcliffe, Helen M.......4:07:39 (13,689)

Thornton, Eirian 4:23:50 (17,946)
Thornton, Laura A. 4:10:19 (14,374)
Thornton-West, Vicky L 4:34:31 (20,824)
Thorp, Sallie Ann 4:42:46 (22,868)
Thorpe, Caroline E 4:19:54 (16,861)
Thoua, Nora M 3:51:34 (9,188)
Thriepland, Fiona 5:58:20 (32,657)
Thrippleton, Karen E 4:51:52 (25,017)
Throgmorton, Hannah 4:31:54 (20,141)
Thrower, Kristina 5:01:35 (26,887)
Thuillier, Sally F 4:41:16 (22,501)
Thurbin, Gaynor L 4:10:12 (14,338)
Thurlby, Rebecca J 5:26:38 (30,114)
Thurling, Kate E 5:32:58 (30,744)
Thursfield, Angela M 4:32:50 (20,383)
Thurston, Bridget M 4:09:52 (14,271)
Thwaites, Alexandra J 4:40:03 (22,193)
Thwaites, Anna-Louise 4:39:18 (22,049)
Thwaites, Victoria 4:40:03 (22,193)
Tibbott, Joanne 4:32:03 (20,184)
Tibby, Megan L 4:19:40 (16,804)
Tickner, Teri E 4:08:09 (13,817)
Tidder, Lucy 5:07:00 (27,694)
Tideswell, Fiona J 3:33:13 (5,425)
Tierney, Elaine M 4:24:03 (18,011)
Tift, Lindsay C 4:41:36 (22,581)
Tighe, Mary 5:00:42 (26,737)
Tilbury, Gay A 4:39:02 (21,981)
Tiller, Linni 4:05:09 (13,088)
Tilley, Sarah 4:11:23 (14,640)
Tillotson, Eleanor M 3:52:08 (9,348)
Tillson, Lisa 4:35:22 (21,072)
Timm, Kitty 5:28:54 (30,366)
Timmermann, Joanna P 4:40:55 (22,410)
Timms, Jacqueline M 4:33:06 (20,457)
Timms, Louise C 5:53:51 (32,395)
Timms, Victoria A 4:59:28 (26,555)
Timney, Anna 5:26:11 (30,056)
Tiney, Alison J 6:56:17 (34,173)
Tinker, Emma J 5:40:17 (31,359)
Tinsdale, Gemma J 4:22:28 (17,574)
Tinsley, Tylie S 4:56:13 (25,919)
Tinson, Gemma C 4:45:55 (23,657)
Tinton, Samantha M 4:34:51 (20,925)
Titley, Sandra B 6:12:25 (33,185)
Tizzard, Joanna 4:55:37 (25,803)
Tobey, Tina K 4:15:05 (15,594)
Tobin, Sarah B 4:02:46 (12,556)
Todd, Amy V 3:38:02 (6,268)
Todd, Suzanne P 5:02:01 (26,960)
Tolfree, Sophia 3:54:54 (10,160)
Tolley, Ceri Jane 7:09:30 (34,312)
Tolley, Samantha J 5:38:01 (31,194)
Tomic, Ana 4:06:59 (13,514)
Tomita, Yoshie 4:29:54 (19,606)
Tomkins, Gill 4:27:02 (18,824)
Tomlin, Jo F 4:24:07 (18,023)
Tomlins, Zoe D 4:29:01 (19,402)
Tomlinson, Christina J 3:13:33 (2,403)
Tomlinson, Helen 4:00:35 (11,998)
Tomlinson, Lisa A 4:44:16 (23,248)
Tomlinson, Natasha L 4:16:26 (15,942)
Tomlinson, Rebecca 3:45:11 (7,724)
Tompson, Juliette J 5:50:29 (32,174)
Toms, Faye 3:27:35 (4,376)
Toms, Sharron 4:05:45 (13,232)
Tonkin, Joanne 4:13:33 (15,172)
Tonner, Kimberley 5:47:07 (31,917)
Tonnessen, Amy L 3:58:27 (11,282)
Tooher, Bridie C 5:02:42 (27,064)
Tooke, Hayley E 4:14:12 (15,367)
Toole, Elizabeth S 4:23:11 (17,778)
Toothill, Diane M 4:01:35 (12,267)
Tooze, Louise A 4:25:08 (18,302)
Topping, Prudence A 6:17:31 (33,339)
Tori, Tiziana 6:26:45 (33,591)
Torii, Masami 4:31:52 (20,130)
Torrance, Sue H 4:53:47 (25,437)
Torrebiarte, Deborah 5:19:42 (29,384)
Torrecampo, Nicole 3:49:19 (8,653)
Totty, Harriet V 4:08:41 (13,965)
Tough, Caroline C 4:23:19 (17,820)
Toulson, Bonnie H 4:18:03 (16,354)
Tovey, Elizabeth G 3:49:26 (8,681)
Towers, Emily R 3:48:29 (8,460)
Towerton, Kate V 3:16:22 (2,798)
Towndrow, Susan 6:08:14 (33,055)
Towner, Susan K 5:43:22 (31,598)
Townley, Karen 5:48:04 (31,982)
Townley, Kerry A 4:58:22 (26,354)
Townley, Sharon 3:34:54 (5,685)
Townroe, Lynne 3:55:56 (10,473)
Towns, Jill M 4:38:39 (21,868)
Towns, Sharron 3:53:40 (9,758)
Townsend, Joanne 4:41:05 (22,452)
Townsend, Paula 4:41:05 (22,452)
Townsley, Meredith L 4:15:44 (15,763)
Townsley, Terri A 5:02:01 (26,960)
Trace, Ella E 4:02:04 (12,378)
Tracey, Charolotte 6:12:47 (33,199)
Traill, Elizabeth 5:25:03 (29,924)
Travis, Colaire E 5:39:30 (31,296)
Treacher, Natalie 3:54:15 (9,943)
Treadwell, Lorraine F 3:33:39 (5,495)
Tredant, Anna M 5:56:19 (32,547)
Tredwell, Gemma C 3:59:48 (11,782)
Tregellas, Carly J 7:09:44 (34,316)
Tregoning, Clare 5:55:09 (32,472)
Trembath, Katie M 4:52:46 (25,213)
Tremud, Olga 4:22:37 (17,622)
Trenas Hinojosa, Maria N 3:22:03 (3,497)
Trevena, Suzanne 5:35:30 (30,978)
Trezise, Marie G 4:24:32 (18,155)
Trigg, Joy N 4:33:14 (20,488)
Trigg, Michelle M 3:59:06 (11,527)
Triggs, Nicky J 4:04:41 (12,979)
Trimm, Caroline E 4:54:12 (25,519)
Tripp, Kate 4:54:56 (25,683)
Tripp, Lisa A 4:50:37 (24,749)
Troughton, Laura 5:34:53 (30,927)
Trowsdale, Katie V 3:33:28 (5,467)
Troy, Lisa J 4:04:34 (12,942)
Trubuhovich, Anna E 4:50:40 (24,759)
Trubuhovich, Michelle C 5:56:43 (32,567)
Trubuhovich, Rosemary M 6:55:07 (34,155)
True, Susan J 3:21:36 (3,434)
Trueman, Dawn A 4:13:42 (15,225)
Trueman, Ngaio 4:28:31 (19,268)
Truett, Alice 4:16:44 (16,013)
Truett, Dinah M 4:28:11 (19,164)
Trujillo, Julia 4:36:40 (21,409)
Tsang, Gigi 3:25:46 (4,065)
Tuazon, Gigi 6:11:03 (33,142)
Tubbs, Carol A 4:51:32 (24,944)
Tuck, Caroline M 3:32:03 (5,234)
Tuck, Jill 3:23:54 (3,764)
Tuck, Julia 3:18:59 (3,097)
Tuck, Philippa J 4:14:16 (15,387)
Tucker, Hayley D 4:15:04 (15,584)
Tucker, Julia 4:45:35 (23,555)
Tucker, Kirsten M 4:43:20 (23,012)
Tuddenham, Rachel E 4:06:32 (13,412)
Tudor, Ruth 5:57:59 (32,631)
Tudor, Sarah E 4:31:49 (20,112)
Tuer, Eva V 4:16:01 (15,842)
Tuff, Rebecca 4:58:03 (26,293)
Tulloch, Katerina M 6:20:42 (33,415)
Tulloch, Sandra M 3:47:26 (8,205)
Tumber, Clara E 4:11:58 (14,801)
Tunnard, Fleur 3:57:40 (11,001)
Tunstall, Helen C 4:05:08 (13,080)
Tunstall, Rebecca J 4:43:41 (23,098)
Turgoose, Susannah J 3:32:24 (5,300)
Turley, Fiona M 3:36:50 (6,026)
Turley, Heather 4:11:30 (14,679)
Turnbull, Heather 4:48:15 (24,190)
Turnbull, Jo 5:08:29 (27,893)
Turnbull, Marianne 4:45:57 (23,661)
Turnbull, Natalie 4:05:43 (13,226)
Turner, Adele L 4:59:10 (26,506)
Turner, Avril M 4:53:43 (25,421)
Turner, Donna L 3:55:23 (10,309)
Turner, Elinor 3:47:07 (8,136)
Turner, Elisabeth C 3:59:37 (11,720)
Turner, Janet C 5:07:51 (27,810)
Turner, Jessica L 4:39:43 (22,133)
Turner, Kathryn L 4:26:38 (18,704)
Turner, Katrina 5:08:53 (27,953)
Turner, Lorraine 5:01:55 (26,946)
Turner, Melanie E 4:58:41 (26,417)
Turner, Michele 4:26:21 (18,621)
Turner, Rebecca 4:37:43 (21,644)
Turner, Ruth M 4:17:18 (16,175)
Turner, Sabrina 6:15:37 (33,282)
Turner, Suzanne 5:46:19 (31,865)
Turner, Suzanne M 5:10:08 (28,167)
Turner, Verity S 3:56:54 (10,762)
Turpin, Caroline E 3:59:02 (11,499)
Turpin, Samantha V 6:04:09 (32,893)
Turrell, Jenna 4:44:21 (23,265)
Turton, Helen 3:20:26 (3,282)
Turvill, Julie 7:16:18 (34,372)
Tutin, Angela M 4:11:23 (14,640)
Twidle, Sarah L 4:44:12 (23,229)
Twigg, Kate 4:08:09 (13,817)
Twitchell, Sarah M 4:50:23 (24,681)
Twomey, Joy M 4:32:49 (20,377)
Twyman, Lucy M 4:49:11 (24,410)
Tydman, Kate 4:27:08 (18,851)
Tye, Sally A 4:48:43 (24,298)
Tyler, Deborah J 5:05:56 (27,539)
Tyler, Jacky A 3:43:09 (7,276)
Tyler, Kati 4:06:58 (13,508)
Tyler, Linda 3:56:31 (10,629)
Tyler, Sarah I 4:19:59 (16,882)
Tyler, Victoria L 3:57:18 (10,890)
Tyndale, Amelia L 5:37:17 (31,142)
Tyrrell, Jill P 4:40:21 (22,275)
Tyrrell, Nichola J 4:08:09 (13,817)
Tyson, Beverley 6:22:30 (33,474)
Tytler, Kathy 4:38:54 (21,941)
Uarciat, Monique D 5:15:59 (28,934)
U'Chong, Idy 5:29:08 (30,389)
Uden, Maggie E 4:40:53 (22,398)
Ukiah, Nicola J 4:56:10 (25,907)
Ulatowski, Kelly A 7:23:46 (34,421)
Ullen, Elisabeth 4:29:09 (19,439)
Ullger, Joanna 4:41:39 (22,598)
Underwood, Amy L 4:57:03 (26,095)
Underwood, Susan R 5:14:39 (28,768)
Unsworth, Tania 5:11:21 (28,313)
Unwin, Samantha L 5:17:52 (29,164)
Urbach, Penny J 4:56:11 (25,910)
Urban, Wendy H 3:02:23 (1,337)
Uren, Lisa C 3:25:01 (3,935)
Urquhart, Sarah L 3:52:00 (9,301)
Urquhart, Victoria-Jane 5:09:26 (28,032)
Urwin, Amanda L 4:50:32 (24,727)
Urwin-Mann, Sarah L 2:58:51 (1,047)
Usher, Karen D 5:13:03 (28,550)
Usher, Laura C 5:51:32 (32,253)
Vaatz, Stephanie 4:08:53 (14,014)
Vacher, Louise D 3:51:01 (9,052)
Valapinee, Anick M 3:40:24 (6,718)
Valdes, Ana M 4:34:56 (20,949)
Valentine, Catherine 4:37:06 (21,506)
Valentine, Lyne 4:11:33 (14,693)
Valentine-Anderson, Sally 4:25:39 (18,429)
Valentino, Raffaella 4:12:07 (14,840)
Vallance, Sandra A 4:09:56 (14,286)
Van De Pol, Loretta 4:29:20 (19,481)
Van Den Bergh, Stephanie L 5:32:38 (30,713)
Van Den Broek-Koster, Nelly 4:31:18 (19,968)
Van Den Dool, Nicole 4:54:09 (25,513)
Van Der Merwe, Caren L 4:44:27 (23,286)
Van Der Merwe, Maria 4:46:54 (23,885)
Van Der Putten, Rosemary A 3:55:00 (10,195)
Van Der Slootprumper, Corine J 4:32:13 (20,233)
Van Der Weyde, Carla Van Gyzel 4:37:22 (21,565)
Van Deventer-Taylor, Antonia 3:13:01 (2,336)
Van Genuchten Cain, Edith 4:49:14 (24,420)

Van Hotson, Victoria....5:21:16 (29,530)
Van Loen, Belinda C....4:16:46 (16,023)
Van Ostrand, Gigi....4:43:50 (23,132)
Van Rossum, Johanna....6:30:49 (33,682)
Van Wijk, Tarryn....4:19:50 (16,842)
Van Wittenberghe, Noelle....4:38:56 (21,954)
Vanderveldt, Helen....5:28:18 (30,304)
Vandevelde, Mell M....5:51:04 (32,212)
Vanegas, Clara E....5:17:30 (29,126)
Vanlint, Alisa....4:11:56 (14,788)
Vansant, Kaitlyn....4:11:05 (14,571)
Vargas, Patricia A....4:08:04 (13,781)
Varney, Sophie V....6:36:02 (33,793)
Varney, Suzanne G....4:47:45 (24,088)
Vaughan, Sarah L....4:08:38 (13,950)
Veasey, Hayley....3:55:05 (10,225)
Vega, Georgina....5:25:11 (29,947)
Vellacott, Jane K....5:05:21 (27,450)
Ven Den Berg, Karin....6:45:14 (33,983)
Venet, Bernadette....3:45:28 (7,786)
Vennik, Jane L....4:20:35 (17,055)
Venning, Ann....5:50:04 (32,132)
Ventress, Katia D....5:39:38 (31,309)
Ventura, Maria....5:54:17 (32,424)
Verduyn, Christine M....4:05:06 (13,069)
Vere, Louisa J....4:08:09 (13,817)
Vergara, Maria....4:23:41 (17,910)
Vermeersch, Heidi N....4:28:18 (19,207)
Vernazza, Patricia....4:29:02 (19,408)
Vernon, Elizabeth H....6:15:36 (33,280)
Vernon, Julie Ann....4:25:37 (18,416)
Verrill, Freda....3:52:06 (9,337)
Vezzu, Joanna....4:36:47 (21,437)
Vial, Kristine M....4:50:04 (24,617)
Vickers, Kelliney E....5:31:39 (30,627)
Vickers, Shona....8:21:10 (34,561)
Vickers, Suzy J....4:57:17 (26,139)
Vickery, Helen B....4:10:18 (14,369)
Victor, Christina....4:33:39 (20,622)
Vignudelli, Daniela....4:09:15 (14,104)
Vihl, Ana Regina....4:48:17 (24,205)
Vile, Margaret....6:40:38 (33,896)
Vinall, Lucy E....3:53:49 (9,815)
Vincent, Courtenay N....6:56:40 (34,175)
Vincent, Ellie....3:22:08 (3,505)
Vincent, Jackie J....5:50:17 (32,153)
Vincent, Jo....4:38:45 (21,898)
Vincent, Louise N....5:24:24 (29,847)
Vine, Susan....5:13:05 (28,554)
Viner, Jenni M....4:48:21 (24,216)
Viner, Kate R....3:39:17 (6,494)
Vinter, Julie L....3:49:41 (8,743)
Virani, Zahira....6:10:15 (33,124)
Virgin, Julie L....4:32:53 (20,397)
Virgo, Tamsin E....3:57:18 (10,890)
Visser, Elisabeth....3:35:24 (5,775)
Vitty, Caroline....4:25:34 (18,408)
Vivian, Christina....3:56:52 (10,749)
Vlaarkamp, Judith....3:37:47 (6,212)
Voas, Karen M....4:58:53 (26,450)
Vogel, Kirsty....3:47:45 (8,286)
Vogel, Miriam....4:07:51 (13,730)
Vogelsang, Kate J....4:47:37 (24,048)
Voisey, Lorraine B....5:09:17 (28,008)
Vollans, Francine A....4:40:34 (22,321)
Vollenbroker, Nina....4:09:33 (14,188)
Voller, Sophie L....3:21:33 (3,428)
Von Arx, Rosemarie....5:15:01 (28,821)
Von Knobloch, Ursula....3:35:19 (5,757)
Von Uthmann, Sabine....4:00:20 (11,933)
Voss, Patricia....6:38:29 (33,858)
Voss, Sharon....5:44:21 (31,706)
Voysey, Katherine....5:29:38 (30,440)
Vu, Tuyet T....5:00:45 (26,751)
Vyras, Elenie....5:07:43 (27,802)
Waddell, Arline K....5:09:43 (28,097)
Waddicor, Cathrine J....4:17:02 (16,104)
Wade, Anderley C....4:25:10 (18,310)
Wade, Angela....4:40:33 (22,319)
Wade, Hayley J....4:50:48 (24,795)
Wade, Susan....5:25:06 (29,936)
Wade, Tracey L....4:33:31 (20,579)
Wadeson, Carol E....4:33:26 (20,556)

Wadforth, Cath....3:55:13 (10,269)
Wadland, Pauline....5:59:24 (32,708)
Waghorn, Claire M....4:58:54 (26,455)
Wagland, Lisa J....4:57:04 (26,098)
Wagner-Schanz, Gisela....4:48:26 (24,233)
Wagstaff, Nina E....3:49:18 (8,650)
Wagstaffe, Claire E....4:00:10 (11,886)
Wahlers, Lucinda J....3:59:54 (11,818)
Wain, Amy L....6:17:44 (33,346)
Wain, Barbara....6:33:09 (33,726)
Wainwright, Angela....4:13:51 (15,259)
Waistell, Lisa....5:12:42 (28,494)
Wait, Lorraine....4:02:58 (12,602)
Waite, Gillian A....4:30:00 (19,636)
Waite, Lorna K....4:14:28 (15,443)
Waites, Adele R....4:55:46 (25,831)
Wakefield, Liz....4:57:15 (26,135)
Wakefield, Susan L....4:10:47 (14,488)
Wakeley, Suzanne C....6:26:34 (33,587)
Wakelin, Wendy R....5:02:23 (27,021)
Wakeling, Izzy A....3:23:37 (3,717)
Walden, Helen E....4:37:23 (21,569)
Waldron, Helen....5:44:10 (31,682)
Waldron, Jo....4:23:11 (17,778)
Wales, Alison A....4:41:46 (22,622)
Wales, Sandra....4:37:34 (21,606)
Walhout, Andra....4:23:32 (17,875)
Walker, Andrea....4:24:11 (18,045)
Walker, Beverley F....5:34:34 (30,892)
Walker, Brenda P....4:08:57 (14,032)
Walker, Bridget....4:42:02 (22,680)
Walker, Caroline....4:49:11 (24,410)
Walker, Caroline J....3:21:01 (3,362)
Walker, Christina M....4:07:34 (13,658)
Walker, Clare J....3:53:47 (9,800)
Walker, Dale B....6:32:03 (33,703)
Walker, Fiona A....6:20:45 (33,417)
Walker, Garthine....5:25:59 (30,034)
Walker, Helen M....4:08:15 (13,842)
Walker, Hilary....4:23:56 (17,975)
Walker, Holly A....5:48:10 (31,988)
Walker, Laura K....4:17:35 (16,244)
Walker, Loretta C....5:47:54 (31,972)
Walker, Louise A....4:43:57 (23,169)
Walker, Michelle J....7:20:43 (34,399)
Walker, Poppy H....4:34:31 (20,824)
Walker, Susan M....4:08:50 (14,001)
Walker, Tracey A....5:45:48 (31,820)
Walker, Tracy....3:19:59 (3,224)
Walker, Victoria H....4:09:10 (14,077)
Walkey, Kizzy A....5:30:29 (30,525)
Wall, Christine H....5:04:31 (27,329)
Wall, Denise....5:00:40 (26,730)
Wall, Jacqueline S....6:44:37 (33,969)
Wall, Mandy....4:28:13 (19,184)
Wall, Michala C....3:10:47 (2,075)
Wall, Rebecca J....3:21:41 (3,443)
Wall, Samantha....6:46:01 (34,006)
Wall, Sarah F....3:37:17 (6,122)
Wall, Tania....6:51:17 (34,100)
Wallace, Amelia....4:38:33 (21,842)
Wallace, Anna S....6:54:07 (34,138)
Wallace, Emma K....5:01:36 (26,896)
Wallace, Kathryn M....4:31:18 (19,968)
Wallace, Sarah C....5:48:50 (32,036)
Wallace, Sharon....4:00:14 (11,905)
Wallace, Stacey....4:36:31 (21,372)
Wallis, Caroline....5:20:01 (29,413)
Wallis, Nicky....5:27:36 (30,209)
Wallis, Nicola....6:04:14 (32,899)
Wallis, Samantha J....3:26:05 (4,119)
Wallis, Suzanne C....7:27:47 (34,444)
Walls, Jacqui C....4:09:51 (14,262)
Walmsley, Avril....3:42:21 (7,105)
Walpole, Tracy J....4:32:24 (20,268)
Walsgrove, Hilary J....4:46:22 (23,755)
Walsh, Clair F....4:54:10 (25,515)
Walsh, Edit....3:41:48 (6,991)
Walsh, Jane L....4:59:02 (26,482)
Walsh, Justina M....5:09:18 (28,009)
Walsh, Majella F....4:16:39 (15,997)
Walsh, Rosie M....4:29:43 (19,568)
Walsh, Susan....4:32:54 (20,401)

Walshe, Julianne K....4:57:36 (26,209)
Walter, Amanda J....4:59:09 (26,500)
Walter, Charlotte E....4:53:53 (25,456)
Walters, Gail R....3:24:28 (3,840)
Walters, Janet....5:26:48 (30,126)
Walters, Jessica R....4:57:54 (26,263)
Walters, Kathryn....4:16:52 (16,049)
Walters, Laura J....4:08:37 (13,946)
Walters, Nicole Y....3:53:41 (9,764)
Walther, Pernille....4:08:50 (14,001)
Walton, Jan D....4:39:52 (22,162)
Walton, Jenny....4:11:32 (14,687)
Walton, Laura....5:28:06 (30,279)
Walton, Laura M....4:45:15 (23,481)
Walton, Louise....4:47:09 (23,947)
Walton, Mari-Mar....3:45:43 (7,838)
Walton, Stacey C....5:19:52 (29,401)
Walton Gunn, Lesley C....6:25:20 (33,556)

Wami, Gete....2:25:37 (38)

Wane, Brenda....3:29:07 (4,697)
Wang, Mary....5:27:04 (30,149)
Wanner, Angela....4:23:46 (17,937)
Want, Victoria A....5:14:53 (28,801)
Waram, Hilary M....4:49:32 (24,484)
Warbrick, Laura A....6:23:18 (33,497)
Warburton, Claire....4:19:36 (16,781)
Warburton, Katy L....5:29:07 (30,388)
Ward, Alison S....4:18:26 (16,476)
Ward, Anna....4:59:49 (26,610)
Ward, Anna K....3:12:23 (2,258)
Ward, Ausrine....3:59:19 (11,602)
Ward, Carrie-Ann....3:26:40 (4,224)
Ward, Claire V....4:47:00 (23,910)
Ward, Cressida E....4:21:32 (17,315)
Ward, Deborah J....4:30:17 (19,694)
Ward, Deirdre....3:28:06 (4,481)
Ward, Elizabeth H....6:51:38 (34,106)
Ward, Emma C....3:57:46 (11,049)
Ward, Felicity J....3:37:05 (6,078)
Ward, Helen....5:22:15 (29,633)
Ward, Jessica....6:06:05 (32,983)
Ward, Joanna M....5:22:13 (29,629)
Ward, Joanne L....4:36:56 (21,474)
Ward, Jody....4:52:37 (25,174)
Ward, Julie....5:20:33 (29,471)
Ward, Karen L....4:51:51 (25,016)
Ward, Kathryn Y....3:54:49 (10,131)

Ward, Linda N 4:58:43 (26,427)
Ward, Lisa J 4:40:10 (22,229)
Ward, Melanie J 4:26:40 (18,712)
Ward, Michelle K 4:13:30 (15,159)
Ward, Rachel A 3:36:04 (5,892)
Ward, Rachel N 4:54:10 (25,515)
Ward, Ruth E 4:18:29 (16,491)
Ward, Susan 4:37:44 (21,651)
Ward, Suzanne M 5:06:23 (27,611)
Warden, Jacqueline L 5:49:26 (32,081)
Ward-Wyatt, Anne 6:45:46 (34,000)
Warlow, Karen M 4:54:34 (25,593)
Warne, Ruth C 5:41:55 (31,493)
Warner, Anne 4:42:00 (22,673)
Warner, Carley J 5:07:13 (27,722)
Warner, Claire L 3:36:27 (5,956)
Warner, Lindsay J 5:39:13 (31,278)
Warner, Marion 4:34:31 (20,824)
Warner, Sally L 5:33:02 (30,752)
Warnock, Danielle L 6:33:43 (33,741)
Warr, Naomi 3:17:15 (2,894)
Warren, Donna L 4:27:18 (18,906)
Warren, Julie 4:14:33 (15,462)
Warren, Karen 4:05:57 (13,285)
Warren, Kim I 5:29:05 (30,382)
Warren, Kimberley A 3:46:21 (7,965)
Warren, Lacey A 5:12:11 (28,425)
Warren, Lydia J 5:03:49 (27,230)
Warren, Suzanne J 4:46:39 (23,814)
Warren, Tracey A 6:26:49 (33,594)
Warrick, Stephanie M 4:13:25 (15,138)
Warrington, Frankie B 4:04:56 (13,035)
Warwick, Cathy 6:06:08 (32,987)
Warwick, Emma 3:57:38 (10,990)
Warwick, Karen 4:13:01 (15,037)
Warwick-Smith, Clare R 3:59:38 (11,724)
Washington, Paula J 4:24:47 (18,210)
Wasyliw, Antoinette 3:53:19 (9,667)
Watchorn-Rice, Ruth F 3:08:57 (1,872)
Waterer, Margaret 4:35:52 (21,205)
Waterfall, Emma E 4:01:05 (12,132)
Waterhouse, Shirley A 4:30:58 (19,875)
Waterman, Rose 3:16:43 (2,837)
Waters, Bel A 3:53:23 (9,693)
Waters, Felicity A 3:55:16 (10,279)
Waters, Lisa J 5:11:40 (28,359)
Wates, Joanna S 4:03:11 (12,649)
Watkin, Bridie 5:41:24 (31,455)
Watkins, Luisa I 5:16:45 (29,024)
Watkins, Sally 3:46:45 (8,050)
Watkins, Sharon 5:16:46 (29,026)
Watkins, Victoria J 4:31:38 (20,063)
Watkiss, Jo C 5:15:29 (28,880)
Wats, Nicola A 3:42:42 (7,172)
Watson, Carly 6:47:13 (34,025)
Watson, Cheryl J 4:10:19 (14,374)
Watson, Claire L 4:34:04 (20,712)
Watson, Debbie J 4:10:05 (14,313)
Watson, Fiona 7:07:21 (34,287)
Watson, Joanna 3:54:22 (9,978)
Watson, Kerry J 4:48:48 (24,320)
Watson, Lesley A 4:30:36 (19,775)
Watson, Libby 3:45:29 (7,790)
Watson, Lisa J 4:23:20 (17,825)
Watson, Lydia C 5:32:46 (30,725)
Watson, Nicola J 3:52:01 (9,305)
Watson, Stephanie 6:08:05 (33,049)
Watson, Susan J 3:05:07 (1,527)
Watson, Wendy 5:44:36 (31,728)
Watt, Glenys P 5:45:52 (31,826)
Watt, Jennifer R 3:39:48 (6,597)
Watt, Kathryn E 4:30:35 (19,770)
Watt, Tracy J 5:56:39 (32,566)
Watt, Vivien 4:37:27 (21,585)
Wattis, Lindsay J 6:29:50 (33,652)
Watts, Amy V 5:00:48 (26,761)
Watts, Angela M 5:05:31 (27,479)
Watts, Beverley A 6:02:36 (32,838)
Watts, Hannah 4:40:19 (22,262)
Watts, Hannah J 6:08:00 (33,042)
Watts, Heather E 4:29:56 (19,617)
Watts, Jane E 3:27:48 (4,421)
Watts, Laura M 6:05:35 (32,955)
Watts, Rosanne 7:12:51 (34,348)
Watts, Sally J 5:14:14 (28,710)
Watts, Sarah E 5:21:26 (29,550)
Wauchope, Kate 4:20:30 (17,028)
Waugh, Charlie M 4:14:48 (15,515)
Waugh, Melanie C 4:22:11 (17,492)
Wayman, Chantal L 4:13:40 (15,213)
Waymark, Leanne 4:18:17 (16,429)
Weale, Marsha R 4:45:49 (23,626)
Weall, Julia F 3:24:45 (3,878)
Weames, Joanne N 4:21:44 (17,387)
Weatherley, Anne P 4:30:36 (19,775)
Weaver, Jolanta U 4:15:25 (15,676)
Weaver, Norma 5:51:48 (32,275)
Weaver, Sophie A 4:33:01 (20,434)
Webb, Alison J 5:02:06 (26,967)
Webb, Camilla E 4:10:23 (14,384)
Webb, Carol A 3:36:33 (5,975)
Webb, Caroline 4:27:12 (18,871)
Webb, Helen 4:34:59 (20,974)
Webb, Judith 4:25:07 (18,296)
Webb, Julia A 4:58:52 (26,446)
Webb, Kirsty L 3:56:58 (10,781)
Webb, Lorna P 4:20:59 (17,177)
Webb, Mary L 3:45:38 (7,822)
Webb, Melanie J 4:42:11 (22,715)
Webb, Natalie L 5:05:23 (27,458)
Webb, Nicola C 3:26:44 (4,237)
Webb, Paula M 4:34:09 (20,739)
Webb, Rachel 4:23:25 (17,842)
Webb, Tanya E 5:47:07 (31,917)
Webb, Tracy J 6:14:09 (33,245)
Webber, Ann H 4:16:09 (15,863)
Webber, Heidi 5:48:32 (32,014)
Webber, Hilary A 3:54:33 (10,052)
Webber, Nicola E 4:23:20 (17,825)
Webber, Sarah 4:27:17 (18,900)
Webby, Jenny A 4:22:59 (17,722)
Weber, Martina 5:23:02 (29,701)
Websdale, Christina S 4:48:33 (24,262)
Webster, Andrea J 4:40:31 (22,313)
Webster, Charlotte A 4:04:40 (12,972)
Webster, Dorinda 7:24:26 (34,425)
Webster, Jayne A 5:05:09 (27,427)
Webster, Julie J 4:01:03 (12,121)
Webster, Katie A 5:16:00 (28,936)
Webster, Katy 2:53:39 (671)
Webster, Kirsten S 4:29:57 (19,621)
Webster, Morag 6:46:41 (34,014)
Webster, Nicola J 5:21:20 (29,540)
Webster, Rachel 4:07:29 (13,636)
Webster, Samantha C 3:56:19 (10,568)
Webster, Wendy 3:52:05 (9,327)
Webster-Newman, Emma 3:55:33 (10,354)
Weder, Ghislaine G 4:27:25 (18,936)
Weeden, Susan M 4:08:20 (13,864)
Weedon, Michelle R 4:39:12 (22,027)
Weekes, Bridget C 3:54:08 (9,915)
Weekes, Emma J 4:45:22 (23,503)
Weeks, Alison 4:02:02 (12,372)
Weeks, Rosa L 4:56:37 (25,989)
Wegener, Susan 6:42:33 (33,925)
Wehbe, Angeline 3:22:13 (3,519)
Weight, Catherine S 4:17:54 (16,324)
Weightman, Lisa 2:32:32 (91)
Weijand, Saskia 4:17:27 (16,205)
Weinberger, Amy J 5:44:20 (31,701)
Weir, Gail 4:40:35 (22,325)
Weir, Lorraine 4:45:47 (23,617)
Weisblatt, Emma J 4:28:21 (19,223)
Weiss, Sabine 3:21:35 (3,430)
Welbourne, Jacqueline 4:27:00 (18,812)
Welch, Diane 4:12:59 (15,027)
Welch, Hannah 4:35:04 (20,998)
Welch, Margaret A 5:10:03 (28,153)
Weldon, Katrina 4:32:48 (20,374)
Welham, Lisa J 3:47:47 (8,293)
Weller, Ruth E 4:22:25 (17,555)
Wellesley Wesley, Katherine A 4:33:11 (20,475)
Wellington, Claire H 5:14:53 (28,801)
Wells, Jane M 4:56:52 (26,040)
Wells, Lindsay E 4:41:29 (22,553)
Wellsmore, Ruth A 4:48:45 (24,307)
Welsh, Jaime 4:48:36 (24,271)
Welsh, Sarah G 5:33:04 (30,759)
Wemyss, Penny F 5:28:55 (30,369)
Wendel, Rebecca 5:16:08 (28,950)
Wenzel, Ilonna 4:52:11 (25,078)
Werner, Sarah J 5:03:25 (27,167)
West, Alison C 6:42:52 (33,937)
West, Charlotte E 5:15:27 (28,874)
West, Diane 5:55:13 (32,480)
West, Eleanor M 4:43:02 (22,940)
West, Elizabeth 4:45:41 (23,577)
West, Jennifer 3:54:03 (9,887)
West, Joanne M 4:43:02 (22,940)
West, Julie 4:44:14 (23,237)
West, Lydia B 5:47:54 (31,972)
West, Melissa 4:51:49 (25,010)
West, Olivia 3:30:55 (5,041)
West, Tracey-Anne 5:41:11 (31,434)
West, Zoe 3:22:19 (3,536)
Westbarn, Sarah 5:16:08 (28,950)
Westbrook, Karen 5:30:09 (30,491)
Westbrook, Susan M 5:54:27 (32,429)
Westcott, Liz F 4:07:49 (13,720)
Westen, Sian E 3:43:33 (7,355)
Westerlund, Elisabeth 4:45:07 (23,438)
Westerman, Elaine 4:16:47 (16,029)
Westlake, Claire 5:26:29 (30,095)
Westlake, Louise 5:05:56 (27,539)
Westlake, Mandy 3:32:36 (5,334)
Westley, Delia S 4:27:44 (19,005)
Weston, Alexandra C 4:57:22 (26,159)
Weston, Christine S 5:35:41 (30,997)
Weston, Denise 3:49:47 (8,769)
Weston, Ella J 3:57:45 (11,039)
Weston, Kathleen V 5:09:37 (28,075)
Weston, Susan M 4:54:07 (25,504)
Westrope, Jacqueline 4:48:41 (24,285)
Westwood, Caroline M 6:04:04 (32,887)
Westwood, Katie 3:45:24 (7,774)
Wetherall, Suzanne 4:28:05 (19,125)
Whalen, Tina M 4:56:46 (26,019)
Whang, Bonnie 4:20:57 (17,164)
Wharton, Emma L 3:20:32 (3,295)
Whately-Smith, Jess C 5:22:51 (29,690)
Wheatley, Andrée A 4:14:34 (15,464)
Wheatley, Angela 4:24:27 (18,128)
Wheaton, Anna 5:16:55 (29,047)
Wheaton, Mylena R 5:51:55 (32,287)
Wheeler, Amy 3:59:50 (11,797)
Wheeler, Dawn A 6:06:45 (33,009)
Wheeler, Jennifer M 5:04:58 (27,394)
Wheeler, Nicola 4:49:46 (24,548)
Wheeler, Suzanne E 4:56:05 (25,889)
Whetlor, Julia F 3:44:59 (7,676)
Whiddon, Kelly L 6:25:18 (33,554)
Whigham, Kirsty 2:58:40 (1,028)
Whiley, Lesley 3:03:07 (1,382)
Whitby, Sally J 5:31:03 (30,571)
White, Amanda J 5:21:00 (29,495)
White, Angela V 4:54:43 (25,627)
White, Clare M 4:17:47 (16,300)
White, Clare M 5:10:12 (28,175)
White, Deborah 3:46:12 (7,927)
White, Emily J 5:14:34 (28,754)
White, Emma 4:08:56 (14,026)
White, Hannah J 4:07:36 (13,670)
White, Iris 4:53:36 (25,400)
White, Jacqueline J 4:42:18 (22,755)
White, Jacqui H 3:42:00 (7,028)
White, Jae S 4:42:42 (22,851)
White, Jane L 3:51:31 (9,176)
White, Joanne 4:56:27 (25,957)
White, Julianne L 5:08:51 (27,950)
White, Julie A 3:47:34 (8,239)
White, Karen R 4:23:25 (17,842)
White, Katherine 4:51:20 (24,910)
White, Lesley M 4:40:39 (22,337)
White, Margaret E 4:38:28 (21,825)
White, Melanie J 4:00:40 (12,024)
White, Nicole 5:52:38 (32,321)
White, Patricia 4:30:32 (19,758)
White, Rebecca 4:41:18 (22,513)
White, Rebecca J 6:03:12 (32,852)

White, Sara E	5:51:29	(32,248)
White, Sarah L	5:55:20	(32,487)
White, Susan	4:28:55	(19,383)
White, Tina	5:54:40	(32,437)
White, Veronica C	4:26:22	(18,627)
Whitefield, Monica B	4:03:18	(12,681)
Whitehead, Amy	2:45:38	(352)
Whitehead, Helen L	5:12:39	(28,477)
Whitehead, Sarah	5:05:59	(27,547)
Whitehead, Sarah A	4:43:46	(23,113)
Whitehouse, Susan	5:48:28	(32,009)
Whitehurst, Michele A	4:40:47	(22,376)
Whitelaw, Alexandra	3:59:48	(11,782)
Whitelaw, Sally M	3:30:03	(4,895)
Whiteley, Alexandra E	5:38:07	(31,197)
Whiteley, Susan A	6:08:46	(33,075)
Whitelock, Vicky L	4:09:10	(14,077)
Whitemore, Nicola D	7:29:45	(34,455)
Whiter, Linda	4:31:25	(20,004)
Whitfield, Catherine T	5:49:20	(32,078)
Whitfield, Maz C	5:12:03	(28,414)
Whiting, Elizabeth	3:13:32	(2,401)
Whitlon, Tina M	5:53:35	(32,380)
Whitmore, Rachel L	4:59:10	(26,506)
Whitnall, Lynn K	4:37:43	(21,644)
Whitney, Danielle M	5:46:01	(31,835)
Whittaker, Lynsey S	5:55:20	(32,487)
Whittaker, Rachel L	3:20:42	(3,320)
Whittaker Axon, Emma	4:00:55	(12,086)
Whittam, Beverley A	4:55:14	(25,735)
Whittfield, Nicola J	4:29:13	(19,455)
Whittingham, Alison E	3:57:42	(11,017)
Whittingham, Susan C	4:15:35	(15,724)
Whitton, Kate S	5:05:31	(27,479)
Whitty, Marilyn A	4:16:19	(15,907)
Whitworth, Bethan W	4:30:10	(19,671)
Whitworth, Leigh S	5:17:18	(29,096)
Whitworth, Nicola	6:28:12	(33,626)
Whorwood, Amanda J	4:36:34	(21,384)
Why, Christina J	4:43:32	(23,059)
Whybrow, Jennifer A	3:36:30	(5,969)
Whyte, Katie J	4:20:10	(16,936)
Whytewood, Ann E	4:49:27	(24,466)
Wiblin, Julia S	3:59:38	(11,724)
Wicks, Marion C	3:51:48	(9,248)
Widdop, Anne	4:02:14	(12,423)
Widdowson, Elaine M	4:49:37	(24,507)
Widdowson, Victoria C	4:44:15	(23,241)
Wieland, Barbara	6:09:02	(33,082)
Wiener, Nikki C	3:29:12	(4,714)
Wiggett, Nina R	3:12:30	(2,266)
Wiggins, Natalie D	4:24:14	(18,063)
Wiggins, Rena	5:57:25	(32,602)
Wigglesworth, Rose	5:04:10	(27,276)
Wiggs, Helen C	4:56:54	(26,052)
Wightman, Helen F	4:25:42	(18,444)
Wigley, Lyn	6:42:52	(33,937)
Wigmore, Emma	4:43:56	(23,162)
Wigmore, Tina	5:34:49	(30,919)
Wignall, Julia E	4:41:49	(22,641)
Wilcke, Samantha J	4:05:38	(13,206)
Wilcox, Denise B	4:04:02	(12,841)
Wilcox, Mandy	4:50:45	(24,782)
Wild, Jane	3:33:05	(5,397)
Wild, Louise	3:35:37	(5,815)
Wilde, Nicola	3:47:57	(8,338)
Wilde, Sofia	4:15:04	(15,584)
Wildig, Kathryn A	5:18:50	(29,265)
Wilding, Anne	4:15:31	(15,711)
Wilding, Karen	5:16:17	(28,969)
Wilding, Linda J	4:56:49	(26,029)
Wilding, Polly	4:10:54	(14,522)
Wildman, Elizabeth	4:42:07	(22,701)
Wile, Alyson J	3:31:58	(5,217)
Wileman, Sarah	3:22:05	(3,501)
Wilen, Melissa Y	4:28:36	(19,289)
Wilford, Marie J	4:13:40	(15,213)
Wilkes, Anne-Marie A	3:55:36	(10,371)
Wilkes, Hayley J	4:00:32	(11,982)
Wilkes, Trudy D	5:02:37	(27,053)
Wilkes, Vivien A	5:10:18	(28,191)
Wilkie, Matgorzata L	3:55:05	(10,225)
Wilkin, Emma	4:24:31	(18,147)
Wilkins, Christine A	5:28:03	(30,273)
Wilkinson, Carolyn S	3:09:49	(1,972)
Wilkinson, Dorothy A	3:07:23	(1,722)
Wilkinson, Joanne	5:13:55	(28,664)
Wilkinson, Karen E	8:23:10	(34,562)
Wilkinson, Lisa	3:34:17	(5,587)
Wilkinson, Marilena Segnini	4:07:42	(13,698)
Wilkinson, Rebecca K	4:59:10	(26,506)
Wilks, Alexandra F	4:29:51	(19,600)
Wilks, Rachel A	4:51:53	(25,020)
Willbourne, Sian E	4:31:03	(19,896)
Willerton, Janet R	4:39:34	(22,095)
Willetts, Joanne E	4:09:20	(14,127)
Willetts, Marion J	5:41:10	(31,433)
Willgoose, Carol B	3:38:02	(6,268)
Willgoss, Amy	4:34:16	(20,771)
Williams, Bethan C	6:37:56	(33,840)
Williams, Carly L	4:26:32	(18,673)
Williams, Catherine A	5:33:42	(30,798)
Williams, Catherine J	6:46:34	(34,011)
Williams, Catherine M	4:21:01	(17,188)
Williams, Christine S	5:36:30	(31,081)
Williams, Claire L	4:06:05	(13,309)
Williams, Claire N	5:17:15	(29,090)
Williams, Delyth N	4:04:36	(12,949)
Williams, Diana M	5:06:03	(27,560)
Williams, Diane C	4:54:49	(25,653)
Williams, Dumisani S	3:10:14	(2,014)
Williams, Eifiona M	5:13:30	(28,608)
Williams, Eileen M	3:58:00	(11,116)
Williams, Emma	6:05:00	(32,926)
Williams, Emma L	3:25:37	(4,039)
Williams, Emma L	5:10:33	(28,221)
Williams, Fiona E	4:10:37	(14,440)
Williams, Gemma	5:18:16	(29,204)
Williams, Helen V	4:38:21	(21,790)
Williams, Jacqueline A	5:21:15	(29,529)
Williams, Jane M	5:07:53	(27,814)
Williams, Jayne A	4:50:51	(24,805)
Williams, Jayne M	3:23:25	(3,694)
Williams, Jennifer L	5:02:09	(26,978)
Williams, Joanne S	4:45:58	(23,665)
Williams, Julie A	5:42:44	(31,553)
Williams, Justine C	4:13:33	(15,172)
Williams, Karen L	4:02:21	(12,460)
Williams, Karly	5:05:41	(27,508)
Williams, Kathryn H	3:31:17	(5,098)
Williams, Katie L	6:36:37	(33,810)
Williams, Keely J	3:56:56	(10,774)
Williams, Kerry	5:27:44	(30,229)
Williams, Kerry S	4:01:31	(12,247)
Williams, Kim	4:53:53	(25,456)
Williams, Linda J	5:53:02	(32,339)
Williams, Lindsey	5:08:12	(27,844)
Williams, Madeleine M	4:21:47	(17,402)
Williams, Margaret	5:02:27	(27,036)
Williams, Maria J	4:52:41	(25,196)
Williams, Mary B	3:34:06	(5,564)
Williams, Maureen M	5:19:09	(29,309)
Williams, Maxine	5:50:41	(32,185)
Williams, Michelle H	7:05:45	(34,271)
Williams, Nancy H	3:58:25	(11,268)
Williams, Patricia M	4:53:53	(25,456)
Williams, Philippa C	4:40:05	(22,209)
Williams, Rosie	4:20:36	(17,061)
Williams, Samantha L	4:35:24	(21,082)
Williams, Sarah A	5:12:55	(28,534)
Williams, Sarah L	5:22:25	(29,654)
Williams, Shirley	5:10:34	(28,225)
Williams, Sian E	3:57:55	(11,094)
Williams, Silifa	4:59:59	(26,631)
Williams, Stephanie	5:39:37	(31,308)
Williams, Stephanie	6:07:40	(33,033)
Williams, Suzanne B	6:55:20	(34,158)
Williams, Tamsin	5:26:21	(30,082)
Williams, Tara A	5:34:29	(30,884)
Williams, Teresa	4:59:55	(26,619)
Williams, Teresa K	3:27:19	(4,336)
Williams, Teresa L	4:54:55	(25,676)
Williams, Tracy J	3:40:22	(6,708)
Williamson, Anne B	4:05:50	(13,254)
Williamson, Claire	4:04:37	(12,960)
Williamson, Eleanor M	5:48:19	(31,995)
Williamson, Elinor C	6:09:33	(33,097)
Williamson, Fiona	3:35:37	(5,815)
Williamson, Julia F	5:32:21	(30,686)
Williamson, Kate	3:32:59	(5,385)
Williamson, Kirsten	5:31:43	(30,636)
Willicott, Anne-Marie	3:57:09	(10,852)
Willis, Abigail E	4:46:07	(23,693)
Willis, Caroline A	4:39:24	(22,063)
Willis, Christine	4:44:36	(23,321)
Willis, Debbie J	4:13:04	(15,054)
Willis, Rachael	4:52:03	(25,056)
Willis, Rachel E	3:41:06	(6,846)
Wills, Amy K	6:58:16	(34,190)
Wilmer, Amanda J	4:07:51	(13,730)
Wilmington, Karen	5:03:53	(27,238)
Wilmot, Kathryn L	3:49:32	(8,706)
Wilshaw, Lynda J	5:26:57	(30,141)
Wilsher, Victoria L	4:06:14	(13,341)
Wilson, Aglen	3:54:54	(10,160)
Wilson, Antonia	4:34:13	(20,760)
Wilson, Barbara A	6:07:30	(33,031)
Wilson, Bernadette	5:48:13	(31,991)
Wilson, Beverley A	4:18:24	(16,464)
Wilson, Cara	3:58:48	(11,416)
Wilson, Charlotte J	3:33:18	(5,443)
Wilson, Claire L	4:00:04	(11,867)
Wilson, Dawn	5:34:48	(30,917)
Wilson, Donna M	5:19:51	(29,396)
Wilson, Emma L	4:05:37	(13,202)
Wilson, Helen C	5:24:25	(29,849)
Wilson, Jacqueline L	3:26:05	(4,119)
Wilson, Jade L	5:24:59	(29,910)
Wilson, Jenni	4:33:58	(20,693)
Wilson, Joanne C	3:22:39	(3,593)
Wilson, Karen J	4:36:52	(21,454)
Wilson, Katherine C	5:33:21	(30,778)
Wilson, Kayt	4:53:00	(25,269)
Wilson, Kim M	5:00:19	(26,684)
Wilson, Kimerley J	4:42:23	(22,770)
Wilson, Kristy J	4:14:39	(15,482)
Wilson, Lauren A	5:29:46	(30,454)
Wilson, Lisa	5:01:05	(26,807)
Wilson, Lucy	4:08:29	(13,905)
Wilson, Lynda	3:52:12	(9,360)
Wilson, Lynne	4:41:24	(22,534)
Wilson, Marlene F	4:40:23	(22,282)
Wilson, Patricia M	3:34:10	(5,573)
Wilson, Rosalie E	3:30:06	(4,906)
Wilson, Rosemary E	3:23:53	(3,758)
Wilson, Sally	4:17:07	(16,128)
Wilson, Sally A	4:54:39	(25,609)
Wilson, Sarah L	5:13:22	(28,588)
Wilson, Sharon E	4:45:54	(23,651)
Wilson, Simone C	3:22:57	(3,628)
Wilson, Thea R	4:18:23	(16,458)
Wilson, Trish	4:03:22	(12,689)
Wilson, Ursula R	3:24:07	(3,792)
Wilson, Vicky H	4:28:53	(19,371)
Wiltshire, Cheryl K	4:18:12	(16,403)
Wiltshire, Nicola J	4:01:01	(12,114)
Winder, Caroline L	4:47:43	(24,074)
Windsor, Louise	3:58:20	(11,236)
Winfield, Karen A	4:46:02	(23,678)
Wing, Julie A	5:10:27	(28,213)
Winn, Stephanie	6:24:06	(33,520)
Winstanley, Katherine J	5:27:16	(30,172)
Winstanley, Sommart	5:02:13	(26,994)
Winter, Lindsey	4:18:49	(16,579)
Winter, Lindsey	4:25:16	(18,330)
Winter, Rachel V	4:28:01	(19,103)
Winter, Sara C	2:49:56	(507)
Winters, Melissa H	3:10:16	(2,015)
Winterton, Sally M	6:33:20	(33,731)
Winterton, Sue M	4:55:50	(25,842)
Wintle, Sally A	3:48:53	(8,549)

LONDON MARATHON

Winton, Laura....4:51:48 (25,003)
Winward, Sarah J....4:08:43 (13,973)
Winwood, Nicola J....4:33:21 (20,530)
Wisbey, Gail F....4:52:00 (25,042)
Wiscombe, Rebecca....3:41:51 (7,001)
Wisdom, Jenny A....4:42:37 (22,836)
Wisdom, Linda A....5:40:31 (31,377)
Wise, Gaye S....6:04:53 (32,921)
Wiseman, Anne-Marie....4:27:01 (18,818)
Wiseman, Marianne....5:49:30 (32,086)
Wisniewska, Rowena....7:01:24 (34,220)
Wisniewska, Sarah....7:01:23 (34,219)
Wisson, Shirley A....4:07:13 (13,582)
Witherall, Rhian....6:19:46 (33,391)
Witheridge, April....5:53:29 (32,374)
Withers, Christina L....4:54:40 (25,615)
Withey, Jill....8:32:41 (34,569)
Withey, Sarah J....4:30:04 (19,649)
Witjes, Ella M....3:35:24 (5,775)
Witney, Kristin L....4:36:50 (21,449)
Witton, Wendi M....4:49:35 (24,498)
Wohanka, Oonagh....3:37:43 (6,203)
Woitke, Anne-Katrin....4:54:24 (25,560)
Wojcik, Estera....5:06:52 (27,677)
Wolanski, Sandra....3:20:08 (3,239)
Wolf, Christiane....5:16:37 (29,008)
Wolfe, Theresa C....6:43:38 (33,951)
Wolfsdorf, Amalaswintha V....3:57:22 (10,913)
Wollaston, Esther C....3:36:27 (5,956)
Wollaston, Jilly....5:29:46 (30,454)
Wolliter, Emma....5:08:40 (27,924)
Wolney, Janet....3:42:49 (7,198)
Wolstencroft, Kate....5:04:02 (27,256)
Wolstenholme, Jennifer M....3:48:42 (8,514)
Wong, Caroline S....4:05:39 (13,213)
Wood, Amanda E....4:44:25 (23,276)
Wood, Audrey B....5:28:47 (30,348)
Wood, Carla J....5:01:58 (26,952)
Wood, Caroline J....3:38:36 (6,369)
Wood, Denise....4:31:04 (19,900)
Wood, Fiona A....4:58:09 (26,315)
Wood, Jenni B....4:48:28 (24,240)
Wood, Joanna M....3:25:13 (3,962)
Wood, Joanna V....4:11:38 (14,712)
Wood, Julie M....5:02:23 (27,021)
Wood, Kerrie J....3:05:55 (1,589)
Wood, Laura....6:21:50 (33,454)
Wood, Lesley....4:44:04 (23,195)
Wood, Linda J....4:20:26 (17,008)
Wood, Lucy V....4:01:11 (12,159)
Wood, Patricia A....4:24:50 (18,226)
Wood, Pauline E....5:06:19 (27,605)
Wood, Rebecca J....4:30:46 (19,823)
Wood, Rebekah L....3:36:27 (5,956)
Wood, Roisin A....4:30:17 (19,694)
Wood, Stephanie L....3:58:17 (11,208)
Wood, Susanna M....4:46:14 (23,723)
Wood, Suzanne M....3:00:14 (1,181)
Woodard, Belinda J....4:41:05 (22,452)
Woodard, Louisa C....5:24:31 (29,860)
Woodcock, Anne L....4:01:41 (12,289)
Woodcock, Sarah A....4:36:41 (21,415)
Wooderson, Lisa....4:13:04 (15,054)
Woodford, Jodie N....4:16:38 (15,989)
Woodham, Sue D....6:03:40 (32,873)
Woodhead, Charlotte E....5:01:39 (26,901)
Woodhouse, Elaine....4:08:08 (13,810)
Woodhouse, Finola M....3:42:18 (7,094)
Woodhouse, Samantha J....6:22:30 (33,474)
Woodland, Beckie J....3:33:35 (5,486)
Woodley, Hannah....4:11:42 (14,733)
Woodley, Michelle F....3:17:39 (2,946)
Woodley, Sarah G....4:22:48 (17,668)
Woodman, Julie....4:20:24 (16,997)
Woodman, Robyn K....4:03:03 (12,620)
Woodrow, Victoria S....3:45:00 (7,681)
Woodruffe Peacock, Fiona C....4:58:49 (26,440)
Woods, Claire J....5:05:34 (27,491)
Woods, Donna M....4:28:25 (19,238)
Woods, Louise....5:17:28 (29,121)
Woods, Nicola J....4:23:40 (17,908)
Woodvine, Andrea....2:45:49 (353)
Woodward, Alison D....3:32:50 (5,367)
Woodward, Carol S....3:44:32 (7,558)
Woodward, Julie D....3:41:24 (6,916)
Woodward, Julie W....5:23:35 (29,756)
Woodyatt, Fiona M....4:02:16 (12,436)
Wooff, Louise D....4:46:47 (23,849)
Woolaway, Suzy E....4:27:26 (18,939)
Woolford, Nicola....3:25:04 (3,941)
Woolger, Joanna C....4:46:00 (23,674)
Woollcott, Katherine S....7:19:06 (34,390)
Wooller, Diane E....3:44:39 (7,593)
Woollett, Susan J....4:56:31 (25,973)
Woolley, Catherine A....4:47:55 (24,126)
Woolley, Helen....5:17:34 (29,135)
Woolley, Kelly....3:49:35 (8,715)
Woolley, Theresa....3:00:12 (1,179)
Woolmington, Elizabeth L....3:36:12 (5,915)
Woolven, Nicola T....4:12:28 (14,920)
Woon, Christine D....5:39:21 (31,288)
Wooster, Samantha J....4:41:15 (22,498)
Wootton, Liz M....5:58:46 (32,686)
Worden, Maxine C....3:11:28 (2,146)
Workman, Petula D....7:08:31 (34,296)
Worley, Joanne K....4:39:38 (22,104)
Worrall, Linda A....3:53:17 (9,657)
Worroll, Suzie....4:51:17 (24,898)
Worsfold, Anna L....5:34:52 (30,925)
Worth, Barbara R....6:54:18 (34,142)
Worth, Sara R....5:19:24 (29,337)
Worthington, Jennifer J....4:14:05 (15,331)
Worthington, Lindsey....4:29:27 (19,508)
Worthington, Ruth....6:13:46 (33,237)
Wosoba, Marca S....3:32:10 (5,257)
Wouters, Annelie M....4:57:37 (26,213)
Wray, Harriet A....4:20:01 (16,890)
Wray, Michelle C....4:25:07 (18,296)
Wray, Shelley A....4:09:42 (14,228)
Wreathall, Kate F....5:34:39 (30,901)
Wren, Aly K....4:04:20 (12,901)
Wren, Jessica L....4:03:47 (12,785)
Wren, Nicola J....5:24:19 (29,841)
Wrench, Claire....4:39:31 (22,082)
Wright, Beverley....4:20:13 (16,951)
Wright, Caroline....4:21:32 (17,315)
Wright, Claire L....4:24:04 (18,013)
Wright, Deborah J....4:10:36 (14,433)
Wright, Emma A....5:12:28 (28,458)
Wright, Fiona....3:54:29 (10,022)
Wright, Hollie G....4:39:45 (22,146)
Wright, Janet S....6:10:05 (33,119)
Wright, Joanna J....4:58:03 (26,293)
Wright, Joanne L....3:48:21 (8,431)
Wright, Julia L....5:40:07 (31,341)
Wright, Karen M....4:41:10 (22,478)
Wright, Kate....3:11:11 (2,113)
Wright, Laurel E....4:57:01 (26,084)
Wright, Linda....5:16:28 (28,991)
Wright, Maddy J....4:10:13 (14,340)
Wright, Megan F....2:52:44 (623)
Wright, Nadine A....4:40:59 (22,431)
Wright, Phyllis H....5:29:05 (30,382)
Wright, Rachel....4:37:54 (21,697)
Wright, Rebecca....4:13:44 (15,233)
Wright, Sarah J....5:06:01 (27,558)
Wright, Suzanne....4:30:31 (19,749)
Wright, Tracey....4:50:25 (24,688)
Wright, Yvonne....9:00:59 (34,581)
Wrobel, Carolyn N....3:27:08 (4,301)
Wu, Elizabeth....3:56:14 (10,545)
Wu, Tina....4:58:14 (26,333)
Wulkan, Nancy....4:39:58 (22,175)
Wyant, Julie J....4:10:10 (14,328)
Wyatt, Carole A....4:42:10 (22,714)
Wyatt, Dawn....6:17:08 (33,324)
Wyatt, Julie A....4:30:55 (19,870)
Wyatt, Natalie D....4:55:55 (25,864)
Wyatt, Nichola F....6:24:25 (33,530)
Wyatt, Sian T....4:21:01 (17,188)
Wyatt-Davies, Patricia L....5:57:17 (32,593)
Wyer, Karen....3:23:58 (3,774)
Wykeham, Antonia P....4:33:07 (20,461)
Wykes, Tracey....5:41:48 (31,487)
Wyldes, Emma A....5:15:43 (28,908)
Wylie, Anna E....4:05:30 (13,178)
Wylie, Candida A....4:40:04 (22,198)
Wyllie, Elizabeth M....3:43:09 (7,276)
Wynn, Hazel J....6:24:58 (33,549)
Wynn, Jenny A....4:48:36 (24,271)
Yacoub, Lisa....8:16:09 (34,553)
Yallop, Lauren E....4:48:06 (24,162)
Yamamoto, Kimiko....5:27:53 (30,251)
Yandle, Susan....5:14:47 (28,783)
Yarde, Alyson L....5:21:04 (29,503)
Yarham, Catherine A....4:37:38 (21,625)
Yarker, Anna....4:22:11 (17,492)
Yarnall, Katy L....3:09:18 (1,918)
Yarnley, Charlotte E....5:00:02 (26,638)
Yates, Catherine M....3:40:46 (6,775)
Yates, Clare....4:52:21 (25,113)
Yates, Jacquelyn....4:27:45 (19,009)
Yates, Jani L....4:50:18 (24,667)
Yates, Liz....5:48:57 (32,049)
Yates, Sarah....3:07:48 (1,765)
Yau, Ada K....5:06:51 (27,675)
Yau, Trudie G....5:42:48 (31,555)
Yaxley, Deborah J....6:22:42 (33,478)
Yazawa, Miyoko....4:09:24 (14,141)
Yearley, Lesley C....4:24:44 (18,201)
Yeld, Rophina O....4:15:51 (15,795)
Yelling, Liz....2:28:33 (51)
Yems, Sara T....4:17:30 (16,220)
Yendley, Susan E....3:58:27 (11,282)
Yeoman, Helen....4:36:45 (21,429)
Yeomans, Melanie D....5:06:55 (27,687)
Yerbury, Julia....3:56:32 (10,639)
Yesson, Carol....5:41:42 (31,480)
Yewdall, Louise....4:39:52 (22,162)
Yiasoumi, Fanny....5:31:24 (30,603)
Yim, Julie....4:22:30 (17,582)
Yoder, Joy B....5:55:36 (32,506)
Yong, Gladys F....3:46:51 (8,071)
York, Tamara C....5:43:45 (31,629)
Yorke, Joanne....3:54:19 (9,963)
Yorke, Mary P....8:40:13 (34,575)
Youel, Karen J....5:04:07 (27,265)
Young, Alison....3:56:22 (10,582)
Young, Alison J....3:20:44 (3,322)
Young, Catherine F....3:30:34 (4,983)
Young, Christine A....4:16:12 (15,874)
Young, Donna M....4:23:09 (17,766)
Young, Elizabeth H....5:35:48 (31,009)
Young, Joanna B....5:09:14 (28,002)
Young, Kristin....4:37:03 (21,498)
Young, Lesley A....5:38:48 (31,248)
Young, Lisa....6:23:43 (33,508)
Young, Lisa M....5:14:51 (28,794)
Youngman, Clare J....3:36:57 (6,050)
Zaccaria, Lia....3:54:25 (9,998)
Zachary, Breege....4:18:00 (16,345)
Zack, Linda R....6:06:05 (32,983)
Zakharova, Svetlana....2:24:39 (34)
Zaniewska, Katarzyna....4:04:18 (12,891)
Zapata Castellanos, Maria V....5:08:24 (27,876)
Zarpanely, Renée....5:55:22 (32,492)
Zass, Liz E....4:17:58 (16,338)
Zavareh, Sahar....7:13:15 (34,349)
Zeider, Naomi....4:59:39 (26,584)
Zeineidine, Ranya....4:45:02 (23,417)
Zenobi-Bird, Luisa....4:22:44 (17,654)
Zerdin, Dorothy....3:43:04 (7,255)
Zeytin, Simone....3:53:48 (9,808)
Zhang, Yuening....4:30:05 (19,650)
Zimmermann, Heike....4:46:05 (23,685)
Zitterkopf, Ann E....5:22:16 (29,635)
Ziyadeh, Nadia J....4:39:04 (21,994)
Zoeftig, Sara....3:54:32 (10,045)
Zucca, Marzia....4:49:17 (24,429)
Zuckerman, Rachel....3:03:56 (1,443)

WHEELCHAIR ENTRANTS

Alldis, Brian....1:37:23 (8)
Bottello Jimenez, Rafael....1:37:26 (9)
Cheek, Andrew....2:09:55 (18)
Downing, Peter....3:11:36 (32)
Fearnley, Kurt....1:34:00 (2)
Frei, Heinz....1:34:03 (5)
George, Joshua....1:34:46 (7)

Golightly, Andy...........................2:35:04 (25)

Graf, Sandra 1:48:04 (11)

Sandra Graf from Switzerland (born 9 December 1969) won the London and Padova marathons in 2008. She set a 5000m world record in 2004, competed in athletics at the Summer Paralympics three times from 2000 to 2008, and took the bronze medal in the marathon at the 2008 Beijing Paralympic Games. She has twice interrupted her sporting career to have children. Shortly before the European championships in 2003 she suffered a lung embolism and was unable to participate in the marathon and the 5000m. As a compromise she took part in the 800m and 1500m. In 2008, during her first London Marathon wheelchair race, she beat American Amanda McGrory and Briton Shelly Woods and set a new course record of 1:48:04.

Grazier, Edward...........................2:15:51 (20)
Holiday, Robert 2:25:27 (22)
Hunt, Paul 2:56:42 (30)
Hussain, Ifhakhar........................2:25:21 (21)
Lemeunier, Denis........................1:34:01 (3)
McGrory, Amanda.......................1:51:58 (14)
Patel, Tushar...............................1:48:17 (12)
Phipps, Aaron.............................2:30:32 (23)
Piercy, Sarah 2:35:54 (27)
Porcellato, Francesca 2:04:48 (17)
Powell, Richard 2:01:23 (15)
Rea, Paul....................................2:14:59 (19)
Riggs, Stuart 2:33:58 (24)
Schabort, Krige 1:34:02 (4)
Smith, Robert 2:35:27 (26)
Telford, Mark 1:51:33 (13)
Turner, James 2:38:48 (29)
Turner, Jonathan.........................2:38:47 (28)

Van Dyk, Ernst............................1:34:25 (6)
Ward, Kevin 2:56:43 (31)

Weir, David 1:33:56 (1)

Woods, Shelly 2:01:59 (16)
Yasuoka, Choke 1:39:50 (10)

The 2009 London Marathon

Marathon day, 26 April 2009, dawned sunny and still and looked like an ideal day for records. Kenya's Sammy Wanjiru completed the fastest marathon ever run on the streets of London. His time, 2:05:10, beat the course record by five seconds.

Sadly, London's favourite British runner Paula Radcliffe did not take part because of a broken toe and reigning champion Irina Mikitenko of Germany was the women's winner. Mikitenko, 36, wearing long white socks, dominated the race as she broke away from the women's field after 20 miles and crossed the line in 2:22:11, improving on her 2008 time by more than two minutes. Mara Yamauchi of Britain crossed the finish line to huge cheers to finish second, just 61 seconds behind in a career-best performance.

Kenyan Martin Lel, the defending champion from 2008, dropped out on the eve of the men's race with a hip injury. His countryman, Sammy Wanjiru, had predicted he would break Haile Gebrselassie's world record of 2:03:59. When he lined up in near-perfect conditions, with light winds, hardly a cloud in the sky, and temperatures expected to rise no higher than 15 degrees, Wanjiru must have believed it was on. But, as is so often in marathons, over-enthusiastic pace-making wrote off hopes of a world record as the leaders raced through half way in 61:35. The three Kenyan pacemakers took the lead through the third mile in 4:22 and through the 5km point in 14:06.

Shortly after mile 20, Wanjiru made his break and opened a lead on Ethiopia's Tsegaye Kebede. Just as he had in the Beijing Olympic Marathon in 2008, the young Kenyan seemed immune to the early, suicidal pace. He ran 4:40 and 4:46 for miles 20 and 21, winning the race with Kebede just 10 seconds behind.

This was the sixth victory in a row for Kenya in the men's race, making Kenya the most successful country in London Marathon history, with one more men's winner than Great Britain whose last victory came in 1993. The first Briton home this year was Andi Jones, who was thirteenth in 2:15:20.

The men's wheelchair race was won in a new course record by Australian Kurt Fearnley, age 28. The Paralympic gold medallist grabbed Briton David Weir's 2008 title as well as his 2006 course record. Fearnley crossed the line in a new course record of 1:28:56, with Weir just one second behind.

The women's wheelchair race was won by Amanda McGrory, 22, in what many considered to be the most exciting marathon race since the Beijing Paralympics. The American held off last year's winner Sandra Graf of Switzerland to win by one second in 1:50:39, while only seven seconds separated the six top women.

Celebrities who ran the 2009 London Marathon, the last of the series sponsored by Flora, included Katie Price and then-husband Peter Andre. Among the competitors was Major Phil Packer, a paraplegic who was injured in Iraq and who hoped to complete the course in two weeks.

Major Packer, of the Royal Military Police, was injured in a rocket attack in Basra in February 2008 and was originally told he would never walk again. The 36-year-old from Warminster raised money for Help for Heroes. After two painstaking weeks on crutches at a speed of just less than two miles every day, he was presented with his

marathon medal by Olympic legend Sir Steve Redgrave. He raised over £762,000.

There were unfounded fears on the eve of the Marathon that part of the route would have to change because of an ongoing protest by Sri Lankan Tamils at Parliament Square. But even that couldn't put off the couple who veered briefly off course to marry 24 miles into the race

Rachel Pitt, 37, and Garry Keates, 44, demonstrated their stamina by taking a detour to jog down the aisle of St Bride's Church on Fleet Street to exchange vows. It was the first time in the event's history that a couple have married mid-race in a Christian ceremony in a church.

The couple ran in a top hat and tails for the groom, and a short dress and floral headpiece for the bride. As they knelt breathlessly at the altar, only their trainers would have given them away.

ELITE ATHLETES

Explanation of placing system

Each London Marathon year in this register is divided up into four categories: first, a summary of the **Elite Athletes**, containing names (last, first) and times (hours : minutes : seconds) of the top 50 male runners, top 50 female runners, top 3 male and top 2 female wheelchair entrants; then **Male Runners**, **Female Runners** and **Wheelchair Entrants**. These last three sections display the individual names and times of *every* entrant, including elite athletes, alphabetically and with their overall finishing position in that year's Marathon displayed in brackets alongside.

Some entrants have chosen to enhance past London Marathon entries with photos and recollections online at **www.aubreybooks.com**. Please visit the website to find out more about appearing in future editions.

Top 50 male runners

Wanjiru, Samuel	2:05:10
Kebede, Tsegaye	2:05:20
Gharib, Jaouad	2:05:27
Mutai, Emmanuel	2:06:53
Ramaala, Hendrick	2:07:44
Goumri, Abderrahim	2:08:25
Kifle, Yonas	2:08:28
Sato, Atsushi	2:09:16
Keflezighi, Meb	2:09:21
Limo, Felix	2:09:47
Ritzenhein, Dathan	2:10:00
Abshiro, Tessema	2:11:18
Jones, Andi	2:15:20
Dent, Marty	2:15:24
Wojcik, Rafal	2:16:41
Whitby, Benedict	2:18:14
Sibanda, Nkosiyazi	2:19:02
Gardiner, Richard	2:19:48
Abyu, Tomas	2:20:09
Renault, Neil	2:20:30
McFarlane, John	2:20:44
Cooray, Anuradha I	2:21:02
Pierson, Matthew	2:22:15
Williams, Martin	2:23:02
Bilton, Darran E	2:23:32
Williams, Nathaniel J	2:23:48
Lennox, Jethro D	2:24:11
Way, Steven J	2:25:00
Frost, Jonathan	2:25:03
Simpson, Eddie	2:25:04
Greene, Owen J	2:26:06
Martelletti, Paul V	2:26:16
Sumpter, James P	2:26:21
Robertson, Kevin	2:26:43
Molyneux, Paul M	2:26:58
Thake, Andrew	2:27:37

(continued)

Wilson, Christopher	2:27:40
Ryde, Carl L	2:27:45
Stirk, Nigel A	2:27:55
North, Steffan J	2:28:25
Littler, Steve	2:28:36
Marchant, Paul A	2:28:40
Martyn, Nicholas A	2:28:41
Baker, Julian D	2:28:43
Harroufi, Ridouane	2:28:52
Brooks, Cameron M	2:28:53
Hope, Ben T	2:29:08
Moran, Stuart I	2:29:11
Weir, Andrew P	2:29:13
Matthews, Martin	2:29:14

Top 50 female runners

Mikitenko, Irina	2:22:11
Yamauchi, Mara	2:23:12
Shobukova, Liliya	2:24:24
Zakharova, Svetlana	2:25:06
Adere, Berhane	2:25:30
Abitova, Inga	2:25:55
Ndereba, Catherine	2:26:22
Morimoto, Tomo	2:26:29
Wami, Gete	2:26:54
Petrova, Lyudmila	2:27:42
Kano, Yuri	2:28:44
Chunxiu, Zhou	2:29:02
O'Neill, Kate	2:34:48
Okunaga, Mika	2:35:36
Lobacevske, Diana	2:38:26
Centeno, Yesenia	2:40:13
Decker, Helen J	2:42:08
Gee, Sarah R	2:45:35
Cowley, Laura J	2:46:45
Ganiel-O'Neill, Gladys	2:47:53
Dyke, Helen A	2:49:52

(continued)

Stradling, Sarah L	2:49:54
Amend, Samantha	2:49:55
Gooderham, Emma L	2:52:12
Grima, Claire M	2:52:56
Loubser, Rona C	2:53:11
Perry, Victoria A	2:53:15
Kieran, Rosalind A	2:53:30
Patrick, Eileen	2:53:49
Steer, Deborah A	2:54:08
Gill, Victoria L	2:54:44
Penty, Rebecca H	2:55:12
Clark, Tamsin L	2:55:32
Pike, Zoe M	2:56:25
Dickens, Jayne	2:56:26
McIntosh, Shona L	2:56:35
Hazlitt, Karen N	2:56:54
Barney, Lucie	2:57:31
Fletcher, Johanna	2:57:52
Lomas, Sarah	2:57:52
Ransome, Jennifer A	2:57:56
Hutchison, Anne-Marie	2:58:18
Von Opel, Sonja	2:58:36
Rea, Isobel	2:58:40
Taranowski, Helen L	2:58:44
Oakes, Fiona L	2:58:48
Kimberley, Simone	2:59:07
Phillips, Clare	2:59:14
Briggs, Julie L	2:59:19
Gordon, Claire	2:59:38

Top 3 male and top 2 female wheelchair entrants

Fearnley, Kurt	1:28:56
Weir, David	1:28:57
Van Dyk, Ernst	1:28:58
McGrory, Amanda M	1:50:39
Graf, Sandra	1:50:40

MALE RUNNERS

Aarden, Aart ... 4:09:30 (12,719)
Aarons, Philip D ... 4:39:20 (20,526)
Aartse-Tuyn, Guy ... 3:14:10 (2,143)
Abate, Michael B ... 4:25:50 (16,945)
Abbasi, Nasser A ... 5:04:53 (26,521)
Abbasi, Naveed S ... 6:25:38 (34,262)
Abbey, Ben ... 4:27:44 (17,459)
Abbey, Graeme J ... 5:48:01 (32,171)
Abbey, Nick J ... 4:12:26 (13,499)
Abbot, Richard L ... 3:36:35 (5,250)
Abbotson, James P ... 5:34:30 (30,915)
Abbott, Clif ... 4:52:58 (23,970)
Abbott, Donald Foster ... 4:35:42 (19,599)
Abbott, Gordon D ... 3:49:23 (7,704)
Abbott, Graham P ... 4:22:17 (16,020)
Abbott, Jason P ... 4:41:02 (20,969)
Abbott, Keith J ... 4:22:10 (15,995)
Abbott, Kerrigan J ... 4:28:57 (17,818)
Abbott, Matthew J ... 3:49:43 (7,783)
Abbott, Nicky C ... 4:09:53 (12,827)
Abbott, Paul M ... 4:09:43 (12,779)
Abbotts, Patrick ... 3:52:25 (8,386)
Abbs, Richard R ... 4:49:30 (23,116)
Abdala, Ramon ... 4:03:44 (11,368)
Abedeen, Bobby Z ... 4:11:14 (13,168)
Abel, Clive Edward ... 4:09:36 (12,753)
Abene, Gabe ... 6:01:54 (33,162)
Abercrombie, Ian R ... 4:07:21 (12,199)
Abercrombie, Paul A ... 4:25:40 (16,899)
Abeykoon, Anil ... 5:29:20 (30,312)
Abhyankar, Amit ... 4:13:37 (13,829)
Abood, Ahid ... 4:21:13 (15,744)
Abraham, Adam M ... 4:38:27 (20,288)
Abraham, Alexander M ... 6:02:58 (33,228)
Abraham, John ... 5:35:15 (30,993)
Abraham, Martin J ... 4:05:57 (11,870)
Abraham, Philip I ... 3:35:31 (5,049)
Abraham, Scott ... 3:23:39 (3,211)
Abrahams, Daniel ... 4:30:05 (18,121)
Abrahim, Harry S ... 3:22:23 (3,054)
Abramovich, Ruben ... 5:17:45 (28,757)
Abratt, David ... 4:59:30 (25,497)
Absalom, Wesley ... 3:50:45 (8,007)
Abshiro, Tessema ... 2:11:18 (12)
Abyu, Tomas ... 2:20:09 (19)
Acheson, Graeme ... 4:17:03 (14,658)
Acid, Rab ... 4:02:30 (11,126)
Ackerman, Steve ... 5:00:31 (25,703)
Ackland-Snow, Mark ... 4:34:34 (19,282)
Ackroyd, Andrew M ... 4:43:18 (21,543)
Ackroyd, John S ... 4:11:34 (13,273)
Ackroyd, Mark E ... 4:46:45 (22,420)
Ackroyd, Patrick ... 4:41:02 (20,969)
Acton, Christy ... 3:52:16 (8,353)
Acton, Keith S ... 3:57:48 (9,873)
Acton, Robert P ... 3:36:30 (5,236)
Adair, Henry ... 4:11:15 (13,176)
Adam, James A ... 5:36:05 (31,085)
Adami, Franco ... 2:48:50 (419)
Adams, Christopher A ... 2:57:38 (816)
Adams, Daniel R ... 3:50:06 (7,855)
Adams, Darryl ... 3:49:25 (7,708)
Adams, David ... 4:52:30 (23,863)
Adams, Dennis ... 4:26:48 (17,205)
Adams, Douglas V ... 5:39:55 (31,485)
Adams, Gareth M ... 6:53:24 (34,867)
Adams, Ian G ... 4:11:44 (13,320)
Adams, James E ... 3:36:03 (5,166)
Adams, James R ... 3:18:46 (2,595)
Adams, James R ... 3:55:45 (9,243)
Adams, Jeffrey P ... 3:11:49 (1,864)
Adams, John D ... 3:44:05 (6,648)
Adams, Kevin J ... 3:17:58 (2,523)
Adams, Lee S ... 3:30:54 (4,314)
Adams, Mark A ... 4:57:59 (25,135)
Adams, Max R ... 5:17:05 (28,655)
Adams, Nick J ... 5:12:50 (27,954)
Adams, Paul Anthony ... 5:15:40 (28,450)
Adams, Paul D ... 5:28:17 (30,187)
Adams, Paul R ... 2:36:45 (135)
Adams, Phil ... 3:43:24 (6,510)
Adams, Sean R ... 4:30:42 (18,279)
Adams, Steve ... 3:13:38 (2,080)
Adams, Steve ... 6:10:51 (33,595)
Adams, Steven M ... 5:01:50 (25,976)
Adams, Steven P ... 4:12:19 (13,473)
Adams, Tom ... 4:06:56 (12,090)
Adams, Tom M ... 5:14:35 (28,252)
Adams, Tony ... 4:05:48 (11,843)
Adams, William ... 3:59:57 (10,537)
Adams-Cairns, Hamish I ... 3:33:14 (4,639)
Adamson, Jim ... 3:48:27 (7,504)
Adamson, Stuart A ... 4:36:45 (19,848)
Adan, Andrew N ... 5:09:09 (27,298)
Adan, Iain A ... 5:04:59 (26,542)
Addati, Ferdinando ... 4:30:02 (18,106)
Addison, Joe M ... 5:00:04 (25,608)
Addison, Owen A ... 4:28:44 (17,754)
Addison, Tony G ... 5:07:24 (26,987)
Addison-Evans, Nigel ... 5:53:10 (32,563)
Addley, Michael ... 5:18:35 (28,891)
Addrison, Martin K ... 3:38:37 (5,609)
Addy, Tim ... 4:12:07 (13,418)
Addyman, Nick ... 5:27:26 (30,086)
Adekoya, Anthony D ... 3:56:35 (9,483)
Adhikari, Bhupal ... 4:31:53 (18,602)
Adkins, Daniel ... 3:29:10 (4,033)
Adkins, Peter J ... 3:37:24 (5,385)
Adlam, Michael J ... 4:08:53 (12,594)
Adler, Thomas J ... 4:00:28 (10,656)
Adlington, Ben ... 3:32:17 (4,514)
Adlington, Paul J ... 4:05:56 (11,866)
Adnitt, Robert I ... 3:15:59 (2,334)
Adriano, Laudato ... 3:45:38 (6,918)
Adu, Alex O ... 6:25:28 (34,254)
Affleck, Clive M ... 5:16:44 (28,607)
Affleck, Michael V ... 3:39:55 (5,838)
Affleck, Robert J ... 3:04:29 (1,261)
Afforselles, Ben J ... 2:58:49 (897)
Afinowi, Rasheed A ... 4:40:14 (20,781)
Afonso Guerra, Juan Eduardo ... 3:54:33 (8,904)
Afshar, Dan ... 3:02:07 (1,127)
Agar, Simon ... 3:44:39 (6,740)
Agbayani, Rafael ... 5:11:36 (27,749)
Agbo, Celestine O ... 4:13:39 (13,837)
Ager, Stephen ... 3:12:55 (1,993)
Agestam, Lennart ... 4:13:20 (13,760)
Aggerholm, Jan ... 3:31:56 (4,458)
Aggleton, Hugh S ... 2:47:40 (382)
Agnew, Rodney ... 3:41:26 (6,108)
Agostara, Filippo ... 4:42:49 (21,412)
Agran, Alex M ... 4:18:09 (14,934)
Agrawal, Sanjay ... 4:05:56 (11,866)
Aguilar, Fitz ... 4:31:42 (18,552)
Aguizy, Tarek ... 5:37:42 (31,246)
Agus, Fabrizio ... 4:05:03 (11,665)
Aherne, Lee L ... 2:34:08 (101)
Ahmad, Mohsin A ... 5:02:48 (26,182)
Ahmed, Belal ... 3:02:47 (1,166)
Ahmed, Hussein A ... 2:34:19 (102)
Ahmed, Saleem ... 4:38:10 (20,221)
Ahmed, Syed ... 4:30:50 (18,312)
Ahrens, Mark Michael ... 4:14:15 (13,974)
Ahrens, Tobias ... 3:46:37 (7,116)
Ahroon, Per ... 3:33:33 (4,683)
Aigner, Leopold ... 3:26:32 (3,603)
Aijieenthan, Sampasivamoorthy ... 5:28:14 (30,180)
Aiken, Gordon D ... 4:58:46 (25,330)
Aiken, Scott M ... 2:58:32 (871)
Ainscow, Robert B ... 4:38:46 (20,369)
Ainsley, David C ... 3:28:18 (3,899)
Ainslie, Paul ... 3:12:42 (1,958)
Ainsworth, Richard ... 4:53:30 (24,071)
Aird, Alastair G ... 4:34:43 (19,321)
Airey, Richard P ... 4:09:38 (12,762)
Airlie, Brian S ... 3:50:03 (7,848)
Aitchison, Darren ... 4:11:45 (13,323)
Aitchison, Rob J ... 3:24:27 (3,335)
Aitken, Angus J ... 4:31:55 (18,611)
Aitken, Clive ... 3:53:58 (8,745)
Aitken, Gordon A ... 4:30:48 (18,303)
Aitken, John ... 3:09:44 (1,683)
Aitken, Mark W ... 4:41:05 (20,984)
Aitkenhead, Ian P ... 4:04:40 (11,578)
Ajmar, Andrea ... 3:49:00 (7,619)
Akehurst, Brian ... 3:38:58 (5,675)
Akehurst, Paul A ... 4:45:14 (22,022)
Akeroyd, Alan ... 5:39:03 (31,402)
Akinluyi, Ayo O ... 5:14:58 (28,308)
Akinrinmade, Ronald Adedayo ... 5:59:22 (33,011)
Akio, Kamosawa ... 6:22:16 (34,120)
Akister, Lee ... 4:12:45 (13,593)
Akpojaro, Princeton E ... 3:58:50 (10,205)
Al Chalabi, Richard ... 6:01:22 (33,133)
Al Mehairi, Ali Mohd Ali Juma ... 5:37:25 (31,218)
Alaganandasundaram, S ... 5:25:29 (29,856)
Alain, Boquet ... 4:41:26 (21,065)
Alain, Lediouron ... 2:31:57 (82)
Alain, Schirrer ... 3:31:45 (4,430)
Alam, Mahfooz ... 6:41:50 (34,660)
Alamouti, Maziar ... 5:03:20 (26,261)
Alban, Jayne ... 4:23:25 (16,281)
Albinson, Mike N ... 4:18:52 (15,124)
Albon, Gary P ... 5:08:03 (27,094)
Albrecht, Steven ... 3:55:46 (9,253)
Albrizio, Salvatore ... 3:25:58 (3,527)
Albuquerque, Carlos ... 5:03:34 (26,294)
Albur, Mahableshwar S ... 4:55:20 (24,535)
Albury, Adrian T ... 4:12:29 (13,518)
Albutt, Chris ... 4:24:48 (16,654)
Alcock, Ben ... 3:43:16 (6,481)
Alcock, David ... 2:31:16 (75)
Alcock, Ian Richard ... 4:13:30 (13,796)
Alder, Chris C ... 5:00:54 (25,787)
Alder, Christopher A ... 3:13:48 (2,100)
Alderson, Ian D ... 4:45:51 (22,177)
Alderson, Richard J ... 4:10:47 (13,060)
Aldiss, Richard B ... 3:55:04 (9,050)
Aldred, Lee R ... 3:58:00 (9,931)
Aldred, Mark ... 4:13:12 (13,712)
Aldred, Tom C ... 3:06:41 (1,419)
Aldrich, Michael J ... 4:17:50 (14,846)
Aldrich, Stuart ... 3:56:40 (9,523)
Aldridge, Ian ... 4:46:53 (22,444)
Aldridge, Peter M ... 6:24:14 (34,200)
Aldus, Daniel R ... 3:39:34 (5,772)
Alessandrini, Pietro ... 3:26:15 (3,566)
Alexander, Adam B ... 5:22:53 (29,494)
Alexander, Alan ... 4:38:25 (20,280)
Alexander, Brian ... 3:27:14 (3,722)
Alexander, David W ... 5:49:52 (32,327)
Alexander, James W ... 3:20:08 (2,773)
Alexander, Jeffrey R ... 3:56:07 (9,344)
Alexander, Marcus D ... 4:09:45 (12,788)
Alexander, Matthew J ... 3:04:46 (1,290)
Alexander, Paul ... 3:32:41 (4,569)
Alexander, Paul J ... 3:28:16 (3,894)
Alexander, Philip D ... 3:29:45 (4,146)
Alexander, Robert ... 4:28:17 (17,644)
Alexander, Robert ... 5:18:22 (28,848)
Alexander, Rohan G ... 4:02:02 (11,024)
Alexander, Ross C ... 5:29:26 (30,323)
Alexander, Steven ... 5:18:22 (28,848)
Alford, Bryce ... 3:10:20 (1,725)
Algie, Robert S ... 4:15:31 (14,287)
Ali, Abul B ... 4:32:33 (18,769)
Ali, Ashraf ... 5:41:09 (31,597)
Ali, Erol ... 3:31:03 (4,335)
Ali, Ghassan ... 4:35:21 (19,506)
Ali, Huseyin ... 5:19:21 (29,016)
Ali, Mohsin A ... 4:37:40 (20,081)
Ali, Shahib M ... 4:39:49 (20,670)
Ali, Shahjahan S ... 4:43:36 (21,625)
Ali, Urfan ... 4:24:44 (16,636)
Ali, Wais Mahdi ... 4:28:08 (17,587)
Ali, Yassar ... 5:12:35 (27,909)
Alias Garcia, Juan ... 3:30:11 (4,205)
Alison, Daniel D ... 4:43:56 (21,700)
Alister, Gallichan ... 4:03:56 (11,428)
Alizai, Naved K ... 4:59:23 (25,468)
Alker, Paul ... 4:39:32 (20,591)
Allaker, Julian ... 3:44:03 (6,639)
Allan, Alistair G ... 3:22:47 (3,106)
Allan, Christopher T ... 4:30:19 (18,185)
Allan, David G ... 4:51:24 (23,595)
Allan, Greg M ... 4:20:28 (15,548)
Allan, James R ... 4:59:42 (25,535)
Allan, Jamie ... 3:29:40 (4,127)

Allan, Marcus 5:23:13 (29,553)
Allard, Charles J Jnr 3:28:50 (3,981)
Allberry, Michael 4:10:56 (13,089)
Allchin, Martin Geoffrey 4:34:58 (19,400)
Allcock, Henry 5:42:29 (31,722)
Alldis, Michael A 3:20:04 (2,762)
Allen, Andrew Patrick 3:29:05 (4,022)
Allen, Brian M 3:54:09 (8,796)
Allen, Charles F 4:10:38 (13,016)
Allen, Chris 4:31:36 (18,528)
Allen, Christian 3:58:08 (9,982)
Allen, Christopher G 5:03:04 (26,219)
Allen, Darryl J 3:57:04 (9,638)
Allen, David H 5:35:46 (31,047)
Allen, David J 4:32:16 (18,701)
Allen, David P 4:51:36 (23,649)
Allen, Dean 4:00:15 (10,611)
Allen, Derek C 4:22:22 (16,040)
Allen, Ed J 4:52:10 (23,791)
Allen, Gavin P 3:54:35 (8,914)
Allen, Graham 5:22:21 (29,414)
Allen, Grant G 5:11:30 (27,730)
Allen, Greg J 3:34:44 (4,913)
Allen, Gregory 2:49:18 (434)
Allen, Gregory R 4:45:36 (22,105)
Allen, James A 3:45:44 (6,933)
Allen, James A 4:58:40 (25,312)
Allen, James N 3:07:09 (1,451)
Allen, Jimmy 5:04:00 (26,387)
Allen, Jonathan 4:13:48 (13,869)
Allen, Keith W 5:11:53 (27,789)
Allen, Ken R 3:21:33 (2,953)
Allen, Kevin M 4:02:10 (11,057)
Allen, Lee J 6:13:55 (33,742)
Allen, Lee M 6:14:56 (33,789)
Allen, Lee P 5:01:59 (26,014)
Allen, Martin 3:43:45 (6,574)
Allen, Michael 3:41:39 (6,138)
Allen, Michael 4:55:04 (24,468)
Allen, Mike J 3:10:46 (1,760)
Allen, Nick 5:30:28 (30,457)
Allen, Paul M 3:05:45 (1,352)
Allen, Peter R 5:01:19 (25,879)
Allen, Philip S 4:33:01 (18,901)
Allen, Richard 4:13:11 (13,707)
Allen, Richard 5:18:57 (28,967)
Allen, Richard G 3:56:27 (9,446)
Allen, Richard O 4:16:00 (14,395)
Allen, Robert C 4:46:46 (22,426)
Allen, Robert E 5:48:00 (32,170)
Allen, Roger 4:56:50 (24,890)
Allen, Russell G 3:34:59 (4,955)
Allen, Simon G 4:43:01 (21,473)
Allen, Simon P 3:36:46 (5,273)
Allen, Stephen A 5:02:33 (26,129)
Allen, Stephen R 5:36:08 (31,089)
Allen, Steven 4:56:07 (24,710)
Allen, Terence C 6:47:26 (34,755)
Allen, Tim 4:22:24 (16,050)
Allen, Tim H 3:44:31 (6,724)
Allen, Tristan M 4:32:26 (18,743)
Allen, William 4:11:09 (13,153)
Allford, Simon John 3:23:56 (3,252)
Allingham, Richard 5:24:31 (29,736)
Allinson, Chris A 3:21:03 (2,892)
Allison, Clive J 3:12:13 (1,904)
Allison, David 4:14:20 (13,994)
Allison, Edward 4:39:40 (20,634)
Allison, Gordon A 3:29:16 (4,057)
Allison, Jason C 2:51:48 (518)
Allison, Philip 3:52:16 (8,353)
Allon, Clive 4:06:28 (11,984)
Allon, Greg 4:39:31 (20,587)
Allport, Trevor Anthony 4:35:00 (19,406)
Allpress, Thomas 4:39:05 (20,461)
Allsop, Timothy K 3:00:33 (1,024)
Allsopp, Brian 6:18:42 (33,984)
Alltimes, Alec 4:02:26 (11,115)
Allum, Conrad 5:33:13 (30,777)
Allum, Philip W 4:52:28 (23,859)
Allwork, Phillip R 5:39:28 (31,444)
Almeida, Bruno B 4:06:36 (12,016)
Alonso, Javier 4:06:55 (12,084)
Alonso Alonso, Eudosio Jesus 3:58:00 (9,931)
Alonzo Castillo, Auber Manuel 4:28:45 (17,760)
Alquraishi, Assaf A 3:47:45 (7,336)
Al-Rawni, Zaid A 3:51:42 (8,208)
Al-Salihi, Nawzad 6:10:58 (33,599)
Alsey, Simon J 3:59:01 (10,254)
Alsford, Julian 4:25:34 (16,861)
Alsop, Daniel 2:49:22 (438)
Alston, Richard A 3:28:41 (3,954)
Alsworth, Michael D 4:03:50 (11,403)
Alting, Jan 4:16:46 (14,596)
Alvarez, Jorge Ivan 4:27:34 (17,404)
Alvarez, Teodoro 6:40:01 (34,628)
Alwell, John 3:00:59 (1,050)
Aly Hamed, Abd Allah 4:50:27 (23,358)
Amankwah, Nyuito 4:34:32 (19,267)
Amar, James H 4:29:04 (17,850)
Ambery, William D 4:16:27 (14,509)
Ambite, Tony 5:48:19 (32,201)
Ambrose, John E 4:37:32 (20,045)
Ambrose, Ronine 4:02:33 (11,141)
Ambrosi, Simon O 3:43:06 (6,441)
Amelia, Reynolds S 4:10:06 (12,879)
Amelung, Holger 3:35:43 (5,099)
Amery, Nathan G 3:48:01 (7,405)
Amery, Richard 3:57:47 (9,870)
Ames, Steve 4:26:45 (17,195)
Amico, Giuseppe 4:01:28 (10,905)
Amico, Pietro 3:36:43 (5,265)
Amiga, Robin J 5:00:38 (25,736)
Amin, James A 4:13:02 (13,664)
Amin, Saj 5:13:21 (28,046)
Amla, Ismail 3:48:49 (7,574)
Amohia, Sohan S 3:51:13 (8,103)
Amoils, Peter I 3:49:48 (7,799)
Amoo, Paul J 3:50:33 (7,959)
Amooquaye, Eno 4:28:20 (17,658)
Amoroso, Peter 5:57:29 (32,875)
Amos, Chris 3:41:37 (6,132)
Amos, Kelvin J 2:50:58 (494)
Amos, Mark D 3:09:12 (1,639)
Amos, Shane 5:15:17 (28,381)
Amos, Steve 5:21:49 (29,346)
Amphoux, Didier 5:20:04 (29,104)
Amyes, Nigel M 3:55:32 (9,162)
Anahory, David 4:24:14 (16,508)
Anam, James 4:58:42 (25,319)
Anand, Sanjay K 3:36:09 (5,182)
Ancock, George 6:01:40 (33,152)
Anders, Mark C 5:48:20 (32,204)
Andersen, Finn 4:01:20 (10,868)
Andersen, Howard J 3:06:05 (1,377)
Andersen, Jens Rud 4:21:36 (15,844)
Andersen, Mark J 3:57:19 (9,712)
Anderson, Adrian E 5:02:32 (26,124)
Anderson, Alan T 5:29:30 (30,335)
Anderson, Andrew J 5:36:01 (31,080)
Anderson, Andy J 5:33:19 (30,790)
Anderson, Craig 4:46:08 (22,232)
Anderson, Daniel J 2:40:24 (202)
Anderson, Daniel J 6:11:16 (33,611)
Anderson, David 4:01:35 (10,939)
Anderson, David A 3:09:49 (1,691)
Anderson, Dean Clayton 4:38:38 (20,336)
Anderson, Duncan M 3:08:54 (1,608)
Anderson, Duncan W 3:49:44 (7,787)
Anderson, Greig 4:17:39 (14,806)
Anderson, Harry S 4:14:05 (13,925)
Anderson, James 4:06:09 (11,915)
Anderson, James 4:47:21 (22,565)
Anderson, James 5:23:23 (29,582)
Anderson, James H 4:35:03 (19,425)
Anderson, Jamie 4:31:52 (18,597)
Anderson, Jamie R 2:45:48 (326)
Anderson, John 3:38:03 (5,501)
Anderson, John M 4:40:54 (20,941)
Anderson, Lee J 4:07:34 (12,248)
Anderson, Mark R 3:19:45 (2,717)
Anderson, Matthew D 4:05:33 (11,785)
Anderson, Patrick 3:46:37 (7,116)
Anderson, Peter M 3:50:18 (7,903)
Anderson, Philip 3:45:48 (6,948)
Anderson, Philip 5:04:57 (26,535)
Anderson, Philip J 3:49:21 (7,696)
Anderson, Richard J 3:52:20 (8,369)
Anderson, Robbie E 4:04:00 (11,450)
Anderson, Roy 4:51:48 (23,701)
Anderson, Simon 3:57:37 (9,806)
Anderson, Stephen L 4:25:32 (16,847)
Anderson, Steven R 4:38:39 (20,339)
Anderson, Tony 4:22:32 (16,084)
Anderson, Warwick A 3:07:32 (1,484)
Anderssen, Knut 4:36:51 (19,883)
Andersson, Joakim 5:11:43 (27,761)
Andersson, Krister 5:39:26 (31,440)
Andersson, Lars-Eric 4:17:36 (14,795)
Anderton, Dave 3:49:18 (7,686)
Anderton, James P 4:54:57 (24,437)
Andrade, Arthur 4:01:01 (10,800)
Andrade, Peter J 4:11:44 (13,320)
Andrade-Claros, Ivar 4:19:59 (15,425)
Andre, Peter J 7:11:02 (35,064)
Andrew, Christopher 3:12:54 (1,989)
Andrew, Jamie D 3:59:03 (10,268)
Andrew, Kevin J 3:35:52 (5,125)
Andrew, Paul 4:52:38 (23,887)
Andrew, Paul 5:34:46 (30,949)
Andrew, Stuart C 3:17:54 (2,519)
Andrews, Ben 5:11:03 (27,652)
Andrews, Brian M 4:33:18 (18,977)
Andrews, Christopher S 4:13:43 (13,854)
Andrews, David 3:52:37 (8,435)
Andrews, Frederick R 4:23:20 (16,260)
Andrews, Gary F 3:53:29 (8,621)
Andrews, Ian A 5:17:27 (28,710)
Andrews, Jason M 3:20:14 (2,789)
Andrews, Joe J 3:50:03 (7,848)
Andrews, Marcus 5:16:30 (28,562)
Andrews, Mark 4:24:08 (16,483)
Andrews, Mark 4:37:53 (20,138)
Andrews, Mark V 3:26:17 (3,571)
Andrews, Martin N 5:16:28 (28,555)
Andrews, Nick 5:01:39 (25,943)
Andrews, Paul J 3:23:54 (3,248)
Andrews, Paul J 4:12:52 (13,617)
Andrews, Roger D 5:20:41 (29,173)
Andrews, Stuart N 3:38:54 (5,654)
Andrews, Thomas 5:09:47 (27,428)
Andrews, Tim J 4:16:31 (14,525)
Andrla, Eric C 3:53:14 (8,568)
Andronikos, Alexandros 5:38:45 (31,363)
Angell, Dean J 5:48:16 (32,192)
Angell, John 3:54:09 (8,796)
Angell, Richard S 5:24:46 (29,760)
Angier, John B 4:22:56 (16,172)
Angiolin, Marco 4:29:06 (17,858)
Angiolini, Dominic 5:03:00 (26,210)
Angus, Nigel L 4:23:20 (16,260)
Angus, Terry 5:47:07 (32,106)
Anholm, Matthew C 3:32:45 (4,582)
Anjoyeb, Adam 5:32:37 (30,706)
Annable, Andrew D 4:02:25 (11,108)
Annable, David A 4:05:24 (11,752)
Annear, David 5:27:33 (30,097)
Anner, Martin 3:56:43 (9,541)
Annetts, Sean 4:12:29 (13,518)
Annis, Chris D 3:54:05 (8,776)
Annison, Mike 4:36:52 (19,885)
Anscomb, Lee F 4:29:01 (17,834)
Anscombe, Kevin 5:49:10 (32,265)
Anscombe, Nicholas 4:34:32 (19,267)
Ansell, John P 5:19:52 (29,081)
Ansell, Thomas P 5:12:00 (27,800)
Anslow, Gary A 5:24:31 (29,736)
Anslow, Mike 3:11:43 (1,851)
Anstead, Stuart M 3:40:19 (5,916)
Antcliffe, Mark J 3:26:29 (3,596)
Antell, Alastair J 4:50:02 (23,244)
Anthony, Alasdair 2:39:52 (190)
Anthony, Andrew 4:08:07 (12,395)
Anthony, Darren E 6:18:33 (33,950)
Anthony, Greg 3:42:08 (6,238)
Anton, John 3:55:41 (9,211)
Antonelli, Ugo 4:17:52 (14,851)
Antonio, Ernesto 4:17:30 (14,769)
Antoniou, Alexandros 4:48:41 (22,897)

Austin, Henry D 4:18:02 (14,900)
Austin, Matt 3:29:26 (4,093)
Austin, Melvyn R 4:21:25 (15,791)
Austin, Patrick B 4:23:01 (16,189)
Austin, Paul 4:50:20 (23,323)
Austin, Richard 4:32:14 (18,689)
Austin, Rick D 4:12:36 (13,547)
Austin, Simon J 3:50:07 (7,859)
Austing, John W 5:27:03 (30,055)
Autie, Sam J 4:50:18 (23,318)
Autton, Steven M 4:47:48 (22,671)
Avalos, Hiram 4:48:51 (22,932)
Avara, Oner 3:56:00 (9,309)
Avenell, Jamie P 3:39:52 (5,821)
Avenell, Keith A 4:00:03 (10,557)
Avenell, Matthew C 5:31:16 (30,555)
Avent, Martin 3:27:01 (3,684)
Avery, Graham N 4:49:25 (23,085)
Avery, Joe A 5:21:05 (29,234)
Avery, Mark N 5:13:11 (28,025)
Avery, Philip M 2:43:59 (285)
Avery, Thomas 3:01:29 (1,080)
Avey, Darren 5:07:06 (26,926)
Avigliano, Raffaele 3:53:00 (8,506)
Avis, Charles E 5:43:34 (31,822)
Avis, Patrick W 4:26:48 (17,205)
Avis, Sean 4:01:05 (10,812)
Awofolaju, Tunde 6:10:17 (33,575)
Axelsson, Patrik 5:08:50 (27,234)
Axon, Terry 3:46:16 (7,032)
Ayliffe, Mark C 5:20:35 (29,158)
Ayling, Colin J 5:20:54 (29,206)
Ayling, John V 5:35:14 (30,989)
Ayling, Nathanael J 3:34:18 (4,830)
Aylmer, Kerry W 4:38:04 (20,189)
Aylott, Dan 4:41:53 (21,178)
Aylward, Francis 5:15:18 (28,387)
Ayres, Bob J 5:03:53 (26,360)
Ayres, David 5:01:36 (25,933)
Ayres, John G 3:54:08 (8,790)
Ayres, Keith Anthony 4:01:16 (10,852)
Azdad, Abel 3:26:57 (3,676)
Azevedo, Miguel J 3:56:29 (9,454)
Aziz, Aresmouk 3:19:48 (2,725)
Baalham, John 4:21:01 (15,697)
Babb, Andrew 5:11:06 (27,659)
Babb, Chris C 3:27:03 (3,691)
Babb, Steven M 2:48:21 (408)
Babbage, Matthew P 4:38:12 (20,230)
Babbage, Stuart 4:24:16 (16,517)
Babbington, Richard 4:44:34 (21,848)
Baber, Cavin T 4:05:57 (11,870)
Babington, Duncan J 3:38:46 (5,638)
Bacchini, Rocco 3:33:37 (4,695)
Baccouche, Mohamed Ali 3:47:48 (7,351)
Bach, Alisdair E 5:39:30 (31,449)
Bach, Paul Patrick Anthony 4:58:23 (25,233)
Bacher, Antoine 3:39:54 (5,834)
Baci, Perparin 4:12:47 (13,602)
Back, Adam R 5:08:39 (27,205)
Back, George H 4:55:09 (24,491)
Backhouse, Tim J 4:35:24 (19,522)
Bacon, Gary 3:51:51 (8,240)
Bacon, Guy T 3:46:23 (7,062)
Bacon, Matthew J 3:54:00 (8,757)
Bacon, Matthew T 3:41:30 (6,118)
Bacon, Roger P 4:04:19 (11,511)
Bacon, Russell 5:02:59 (26,207)
Badcock, David 5:18:31 (28,874)
Badcock, Matthew 5:18:31 (28,874)
Bader, Brett S 6:27:48 (34,351)
Bader, Ronald 3:38:37 (5,609)
Badger, Len 3:38:51 (5,648)
Badham, Neil A 3:58:53 (10,221)
Badillo, José 4:19:09 (15,197)
Badouraly-Rajan, Malik 3:44:37 (6,733)
Badreddine, Nouhad 3:32:46 (4,584)
Badrock, Bruce 3:37:08 (5,348)
Badyal, Jaspal 5:51:48 (32,467)
Baenziger, Walter 4:47:08 (22,525)
Baffard, Jean Michel 4:41:41 (21,139)
Bagdady, Lee D 4:53:27 (24,061)
Bage, Steven 3:29:56 (4,173)
Baggaley, Lee G 3:38:57 (5,667)
Baggott, Paul M 6:01:40 (33,152)
Baggs, Darren 4:47:04 (22,501)
Baggs, Len 4:40:43 (20,890)
Bagley, Stephen P 4:56:38 (24,836)
Baglione, Nino 4:35:49 (19,630)
Bagnall, Mark 6:19:13 (34,008)
Bagnall, Robert C 4:37:40 (20,081)
Bagnall, Stephen J 4:51:32 (23,631)
Bagnall, Wayne 4:28:19 (17,651)
Bagnold, Richard A 4:41:25 (21,058)
Bagshaw, Allan K 4:46:16 (22,267)
Bagshaw, Andrew G 5:12:18 (27,853)
Bagshaw, Daniel James 3:55:22 (9,126)
Bagster, Nigel 4:36:58 (19,909)
Bahar, Adil 6:06:51 (33,425)
Baigorri, Alejandro 4:15:05 (14,185)
Bailes, Jonathan 5:35:23 (31,011)
Bailey, Adrian J 4:09:56 (12,840)
Bailey, Andrew J 6:23:09 (34,156)
Bailey, Andy N 4:01:01 (10,800)
Bailey, Bart John 4:07:00 (12,106)
Bailey, Chris 4:47:45 (22,664)
Bailey, David M 3:48:15 (7,456)
Bailey, David M 4:03:11 (11,269)
Bailey, David P 5:05:31 (26,642)
Bailey, Frank 4:25:59 (16,983)
Bailey, Frank J 4:24:28 (16,564)
Bailey, Geoffrey K 4:26:15 (17,051)
Bailey, Guy C 3:57:05 (9,644)
Bailey, Guy M 4:20:38 (15,584)
Bailey, Hugh M 4:00:05 (10,571)
Bailey, Ian 3:21:43 (2,973)
Bailey, Ian M 4:59:00 (25,386)
Bailey, Jason 4:24:58 (16,700)
Bailey, John G 3:55:29 (9,154)
Bailey, Jon J 4:11:03 (13,124)
Bailey, Jonathon 4:52:48 (23,927)
Bailey, Les E 4:37:12 (19,963)
Bailey, Mark 3:12:47 (1,974)
Bailey, Mark S 4:43:34 (21,617)
Bailey, Matthew W 4:02:31 (11,135)
Bailey, Nick G 4:54:47 (24,404)
Bailey, Paul R 4:54:14 (24,268)
Bailey, Peter L 3:27:26 (3,759)
Bailey, Richard J 4:15:05 (14,185)
Bailey, Robert J 5:23:05 (29,531)
Bailey, Steven R 6:12:36 (33,665)
Bailey, Stuart 5:23:05 (29,531)
Bailey, Stuart Henry 4:44:36 (21,856)
Bailey, Thomas 6:10:08 (33,571)
Bailey, Tony 4:33:59 (19,151)
Bailey-House, James J 3:39:31 (5,761)
Bailie, Mark M 4:07:50 (12,322)
Baillie, Douglas A 5:24:13 (29,684)
Baillie, Murray A 5:24:13 (29,684)
Baillie, Stuart J 5:24:13 (29,684)
Bailly, Jean Philippe 3:33:09 (4,631)
Bain, Andrew M 4:56:57 (24,924)
Bain, Darren 4:22:23 (16,044)
Bain, David V 4:32:19 (18,710)
Bainbridge, Matthew 4:19:48 (15,371)
Baines, Carl C 7:51:55 (35,294)
Baines, Dean P 4:09:53 (12,827)
Baines, Ian 3:37:41 (5,436)
Baines, Mark A 4:59:47 (25,552)
Baines, Mark J 5:33:00 (30,754)
Baird, Colin 4:14:34 (14,047)
Baird, Phil 4:25:04 (16,732)
Bairstow, Karl 4:49:00 (22,974)
Bajaj, Robert 4:13:42 (13,848)
Bajwa, Jasdeep 4:20:26 (15,542)
Baker, (An)tony R 4:33:44 (19,080)
Baker, Alex James 4:08:57 (12,606)
Baker, Alex P 4:44:44 (21,896)
Baker, Brett 5:54:22 (32,646)
Baker, Carl 3:11:40 (1,847)
Baker, Charlie C 5:13:58 (28,154)
Baker, Colin 4:26:03 (16,999)
Baker, Daniel C 4:49:24 (23,080)
Baker, Darren R 5:00:29 (25,697)
Baker, Dave J 4:12:27 (13,507)
Baker, David 4:46:47 (22,430)
Baker, David W 4:13:31 (13,802)
Baker, Gary 4:58:54 (25,362)
Baker, Graeme C 4:27:06 (17,282)
Baker, Greig 5:04:59 (26,542)
Baker, Ian D 3:44:19 (6,685)
Baker, James C 4:38:35 (20,319)
Baker, John 4:19:20 (15,238)
Baker, John 4:55:34 (24,584)
Baker, Joost 5:13:43 (28,104)
Baker, Joseph 4:37:00 (19,920)
Baker, Julian D 2:28:43 (54)
Baker, Karl 4:41:07 (20,989)
Baker, Laurence 3:44:03 (6,639)
Baker, Lee W 6:01:50 (33,158)
Baker, Mark A 3:39:30 (5,758)
Baker, Mark E 3:16:32 (2,385)
Baker, Mark S 3:16:39 (2,400)
Baker, Martin 4:16:09 (14,438)
Baker, Martyn J 3:28:41 (3,954)
Baker, Neil 4:37:06 (19,942)
Baker, Nicholas A 7:10:59 (35,060)
Baker, Nick M 2:40:11 (196)
Baker, Patrick 3:51:03 (8,066)
Baker, Paul 4:35:34 (19,564)
Baker, Paul J 5:03:57 (26,374)
Baker, Philip A 3:58:34 (10,119)
Baker, Robert 4:30:50 (18,312)
Baker, Robert B 5:25:59 (29,933)
Baker, Robert J 2:30:17 (67)
Baker, Ross D 3:43:50 (6,601)
Baker, Scott 4:42:02 (21,206)
Baker, Simon 3:14:01 (2,124)
Baker, Steven A 4:31:47 (18,578)
Baker, Steven G 4:40:29 (20,829)
Baker, Stuart W 4:27:12 (17,309)
Bakewell, Rob A 3:58:17 (10,031)
Bakhshi, Omar 3:54:07 (8,786)
Baki, Adam 5:54:05 (32,624)
Baki, Nada 5:11:14 (27,680)
Bakken, Harald 3:51:22 (8,133)
Balaam, Robert 4:52:23 (23,838)
Balach, Julian A 4:53:23 (24,056)
Balbierer, Chris 4:34:56 (19,393)
Balchin, Stephen D 4:31:42 (18,552)
Balcombe, Mike 4:27:48 (17,487)
Baldisserri, Enrico 4:00:31 (10,677)
Baldock, Anthony J 3:17:49 (2,513)
Baldock, Graham 5:06:49 (26,871)
Baldwin, David M 3:29:50 (4,157)
Baldwin, Elwyn 3:37:00 (5,320)
Baldwin, Gareth R 4:52:48 (23,927)
Baldwin, Graham 5:21:20 (29,275)
Baldwin, Huw J 6:18:41 (33,977)
Baldwin, Michael J 4:23:23 (16,274)
Baldwin, Neil 5:00:32 (25,713)
Baldwin, Nick C 4:57:27 (25,021)
Baldwin, Richard 4:34:04 (19,164)
Baldwin, Richard 5:24:10 (29,677)
Baldwin, Russell A 4:12:09 (13,426)
Baldwin, Simon 3:38:58 (5,675)
Bale, Benjamin 4:01:31 (10,919)
Bale, Mark A 3:04:08 (1,243)
Bale, Mons 2:50:05 (473)
Bale, Simon M 3:23:34 (3,199)
Bales, Robert G 5:12:03 (27,810)
Balfour, Alastair 4:25:42 (16,910)
Balfour, Kevin 4:45:07 (22,003)
Balfour, Neil 4:53:14 (24,027)
Balfourth, Winston R 3:16:36 (2,394)
Ball, Alan 5:56:42 (32,806)
Ball, Andrew 3:17:31 (2,484)
Ball, Andrew M 4:07:53 (12,336)
Ball, Christopher J 4:45:26 (22,062)
Ball, Daniel 4:46:10 (22,237)
Ball, David J 3:52:14 (8,341)
Ball, Elliott G 4:17:59 (14,886)
Ball, Ian 5:18:22 (28,848)
Ball, Jim R 4:32:55 (18,876)
Ball, Michael D 3:34:12 (4,811)
Ball, Peter J 4:35:03 (19,425)
Ball, Richard L 6:07:47 (33,472)
Ball, Robert 4:23:18 (16,253)
Ball, Tim J 4:20:02 (15,437)

Ball, Tony M 5:01:47 (25,967)
Ballagan, Dalvir S 5:32:06 (30,652)
Ballard, Jonathan J 6:52:23 (34,854)
Ballard, Marc A 4:26:08 (17,020)
Ballard, Martin D 5:06:40 (26,837)
Ballard, Neil 3:40:01 (5,863)
Ballard, Stuart 4:25:14 (16,773)
Ballard, Stuart 5:26:59 (30,050)
Ballast, Ronald 4:26:37 (17,158)
Ballesteros Jeronimo, José Luis 3:33:14 (4,639)
Ballinger, Ian P 4:49:04 (22,989)
Ballisai, Antonello 4:56:32 (24,809)
Ballivian, Rodrigo 5:03:18 (26,252)
Ballorin, Christophe 4:03:05 (11,246)
Balls, Eddie W 5:22:08 (29,376)
Balmer, Jon R 3:28:29 (3,927)
Balmer, Martin R 5:31:29 (30,581)
Balmer, William R 4:39:29 (20,576)
Balshaw, Richard J 3:03:20 (1,189)
Bamford, David 4:48:28 (22,843)
Bamford, David R 5:10:20 (27,517)
Bamford, Dean S 5:45:41 (31,993)
Bamford, Justin R 3:15:58 (2,332)
Bamford, Mark 4:30:02 (18,106)
Bamford, Mark C 4:29:18 (17,927)
Bamford, Mike 4:48:27 (22,841)
Bampton, Richard J 3:49:36 (7,747)
Bance, Elliott J 5:00:31 (25,703)
Bancroft, Andrew 4:43:21 (21,567)
Bancroft, Daniel P 4:04:22 (11,518)
Bancroft, Ian R 3:42:53 (6,395)
Bancroft, Tom 4:22:49 (16,145)
Banfield, Alistair 3:56:46 (9,554)
Bang, Goo Man 4:13:46 (13,863)
Bangay, Stephen S 3:40:44 (5,978)
Bangura, Mohamed A 3:34:25 (4,856)
Banham, David 4:52:46 (23,919)
Banham, Mark R 4:14:13 (13,964)
Banim, Ivor M 4:05:54 (11,861)
Banks, Alan E 4:35:20 (19,501)
Banks, Chris 5:04:51 (26,511)
Banks, Colin J 5:01:56 (26,001)
Banks, Doug 4:56:29 (24,795)
Banks, Ed 2:51:53 (520)
Banks, Edward J 3:42:21 (6,276)
Banks, John 3:52:35 (8,420)
Banks, John W 4:24:04 (16,459)
Banks, Martin P 4:32:21 (18,715)
Banks, Stephen 3:59:31 (10,395)
Bannatyne, Tom 4:00:25 (10,640)
Banner, Charles E 3:08:18 (1,552)
Bannister, Duncan 3:45:52 (6,957)
Bannister, Paul 4:47:35 (22,624)
Bannon, Damian 4:59:04 (25,406)
Bansal, Ravi S 4:53:08 (24,007)
Bansal, Vikrant 3:17:25 (2,478)
Bant, Philip J 4:38:50 (20,384)
Baraldi, Carlo 4:29:39 (18,003)
Barber, Andrew D 4:36:09 (19,712)
Barber, Charles J 4:46:44 (22,416)
Barber, Ian B 3:39:21 (5,736)
Barber, Jeffrey 7:11:24 (35,070)
Barber, John D 4:02:03 (11,030)
Barber, Jon 5:10:01 (27,462)
Barber, Kevin P 3:49:21 (7,696)
Barber, Malcolm P 4:29:53 (18,068)
Barber, Martin P 4:39:16 (20,511)
Barber, Matthew 5:50:32 (32,382)
Barber, Nigel C 3:58:11 (10,002)
Barber, Paul G 3:36:08 (5,180)
Barber, Phil Andrew 3:41:51 (6,175)
Barber, Thomas L 4:57:24 (25,012)
Barber, Timothy P 3:48:31 (7,513)
Barbini, Nicola 3:31:30 (4,399)
Barbosa, Martin 4:03:07 (11,253)
Barbour, Malcolm B 4:10:13 (12,913)
Barclay, David 4:41:37 (21,122)
Barclay, Greig I 4:46:27 (22,331)
Barclay, Ian S 5:38:43 (31,357)
Barclay, Nicholas A 4:01:06 (10,819)
Bardell, Graham P 4:38:07 (20,204)
Barden, Stefan 4:24:09 (16,490)
Bardsley, Adam 2:58:49 (897)
Bardsley, Craig H 3:43:51 (6,604)
Bardsley, David W 3:47:00 (7,201)
Barfoot, Steve 4:42:35 (21,357)
Bargh, Robbie J 4:16:57 (14,634)
Barham, Andrew 5:08:42 (27,212)
Barke, Paul J 4:01:34 (10,934)
Barker, Adam J 4:38:40 (20,342)
Barker, Andrew 3:47:05 (7,210)
Barker, Anthony A 5:50:55 (32,410)
Barker, Anthony C 4:31:24 (18,471)
Barker, Clive 4:42:49 (21,412)
Barker, Clive A 4:20:02 (15,437)
Barker, Darron 3:58:58 (10,243)
Barker, David 2:58:19 (862)
Barker, Douglas M 4:12:28 (13,512)
Barker, Ellery 4:45:24 (22,057)
Barker, Graham R 4:00:33 (10,687)
Barker, Jeremy 4:56:58 (24,925)
Barker, Jeremy C 4:39:45 (20,657)
Barker, Kevin 4:47:58 (22,728)
Barker, Lee 5:07:22 (26,976)
Barker, Mark S 5:09:58 (27,453)
Barker, Matthew J 5:10:38 (27,571)
Barker, Michael A 5:54:56 (32,686)
Barker, Michael M 4:49:54 (23,217)
Barker, Neil M 5:01:31 (25,917)
Barker, Nick 4:25:23 (16,814)
Barker, Steven 4:54:17 (24,284)
Barker, Tom A 3:40:47 (5,994)
Barley, David P 4:27:19 (17,348)
Barley, Paul 3:44:22 (6,695)
Barlow, Antony J 5:11:12 (27,672)
Barlow, Charles 4:56:39 (24,843)
Barlow, Chris 4:31:44 (18,560)
Barlow, Graham S 3:12:27 (1,926)
Barlow, James 3:37:39 (5,432)
Barlow, Jeremy A 4:01:31 (10,919)
Barlow, Lee 2:58:18 (858)
Barlow, Peter A 3:54:42 (8,945)
Barlow, Simon R 3:34:06 (4,789)
Barltrop, Verne 3:31:05 (4,341)
Barnaby, Harold M 6:08:58 (33,511)
Barnacle, Adrian M 3:56:56 (9,603)
Barnacle, Gary J 5:55:44 (32,742)
Barnard, Carl 4:50:08 (23,267)
Barnard, Christopher D 6:25:08 (34,234)
Barnard, Craig 4:46:04 (22,218)
Barnard, Jacobus 4:30:15 (18,166)
Barnard, James 4:45:51 (22,177)
Barnard, Matt J 3:59:17 (10,331)
Barnard, Sebastiaan 4:30:15 (18,166)
Barnbrook, Gregory J 4:47:49 (22,675)
Barnes, Al E 3:58:27 (10,083)
Barnes, Bruce 5:14:26 (28,232)
Barnes, Daniel R 5:23:10 (29,542)
Barnes, Daniel S 4:48:39 (22,890)
Barnes, David 3:54:14 (8,821)
Barnes, David 4:10:34 (13,000)
Barnes, David G 3:04:30 (1,263)
Barnes, David M 6:19:18 (34,011)
Barnes, Jack B 4:52:18 (23,827)
Barnes, James R 4:27:41 (17,441)
Barnes, James R 5:06:51 (26,877)
Barnes, Jason 4:18:28 (15,021)
Barnes, Julian A 4:55:08 (24,485)
Barnes, Mick 3:19:23 (2,665)
Barnes, Nick A 3:52:03 (8,287)
Barnes, Nigel Anthony 4:51:09 (23,521)
Barnes, Peter 3:19:54 (2,741)
Barnes, Richard W 3:58:05 (9,963)
Barnes, Robert E 4:11:40 (13,303)
Barnes, Ross 4:36:43 (19,843)
Barnes, Russell P 4:03:57 (11,436)
Barnes, Simon A 4:28:58 (17,823)
Barnes, Simon P 2:54:14 (612)
Barnes, Stuart M 5:08:36 (27,193)
Barnes, Stuart R 3:25:57 (3,523)
Barnes, Tim M 4:37:55 (20,143)
Barnes-Smith, Martin J 3:43:26 (6,515)
Barnett, Christopher M 5:41:34 (31,636)
Barnett, Dave 4:36:57 (19,900)
Barnett, David W 5:45:26 (31,967)
Barnett, Hardey 3:52:31 (8,406)
Barnett, Ian J 3:37:34 (5,417)
Barnett, Matthew J 4:41:04 (20,976)
Barnett, Oliver J 3:12:59 (2,005)
Barnett, Phillip 4:44:30 (21,837)
Barnett, Sam L 3:44:57 (6,794)
Barnett, Stephen J 3:26:17 (3,571)
Barnett, Stewart H 3:41:52 (6,180)
Barnhoorn, Rob 4:23:39 (16,349)
Barningham, Richard A 5:58:46 (32,977)
Barns, Brendan A 5:44:39 (31,901)
Barnshaw, Daniel T 3:46:52 (7,171)
Barnwal, Pravin 4:38:45 (20,365)
Baron, Jonathan J 3:51:30 (8,170)
Baron, Michael R 4:01:27 (10,899)
Baroth, Emmanuel 4:30:44 (18,292)
Barr, Adam W 3:39:03 (5,697)
Barr, Dave A 3:24:16 (3,306)
Barr, Richard 3:54:39 (8,934)
Barr, Robert D 3:38:31 (5,594)
Barr, Simon J 5:37:04 (31,180)
Barraclough, Adam A 4:07:20 (12,191)
Barraclough, Clive A 3:44:56 (6,791)
Barraclough, Stephen P 5:02:02 (26,028)
Barradell, Adrian 4:12:46 (13,596)
Barran, Nick E 4:45:41 (22,130)
Barrance, Tony R 5:17:01 (28,639)
Barrass, Daniel James 4:09:50 (12,816)
Barrass, Richard T 4:45:05 (21,993)
Barratt, Clinton D 3:57:34 (9,796)
Barratt, David C 4:56:18 (24,751)
Barratt, Gareth 3:44:33 (6,726)
Barratt, James 3:46:01 (6,990)
Barratt, Nick 5:20:09 (29,115)
Barratt, Stephen 5:00:36 (25,727)
Barrell, Julian P 4:39:53 (20,688)
Barrera, Pedro 3:19:04 (2,624)
Barrera, Ruben 2:42:15 (242)
Barrera Portillo, Javier Maria 3:10:45 (1,758)
Barrett, Adrian 3:46:55 (7,182)
Barrett, Brian M 4:33:53 (19,124)
Barrett, Darren 3:52:32 (8,409)
Barrett, Darren 4:11:19 (13,194)
Barrett, David S 3:46:22 (7,056)
Barrett, Duane P 4:08:56 (12,600)
Barrett, Gordon D 3:13:58 (2,115)
Barrett, John P 4:16:09 (14,438)
Barrett, Kevin 4:04:45 (11,594)
Barrett, Mark D 4:46:32 (22,355)
Barrett, Michael A 4:06:19 (11,953)
Barrett, Michael J 5:03:35 (26,300)
Barrett, Oliver J 3:15:02 (2,239)
Barrett, Patrick A 3:28:40 (3,948)
Barrett, Philip A 3:38:49 (5,643)
Barrett, Thomas 4:18:56 (15,146)
Barrett, Tim W 3:26:14 (3,564)
Barrett, Tom 4:08:15 (12,430)
Barrett, Wayne 4:36:35 (19,813)
Barretto Ko, Percival 4:23:06 (16,207)
Barrie, Allan G 2:54:03 (604)
Barrington, Samuel 4:14:21 (14,000)
Barriskell, Simon 4:03:29 (11,327)
Barron, Giles 4:52:31 (23,869)
Barron, Jeremy Daniel 4:36:11 (19,716)
Barron, Jonathan 4:54:54 (24,429)
Barrow, Frederick N 3:54:17 (8,835)
Barrow, Richard J 4:46:14 (22,255)
Barrow, Stefan Magnus 3:53:48 (8,703)
Barrows, Darren J 3:49:08 (7,651)
Barry, Andrew J 3:09:39 (1,677)
Barry, Matthew J 4:17:32 (14,776)
Barry, Philip P 4:57:46 (25,081)
Barry, Stephen G 5:34:28 (30,912)
Barry, Stuart 5:48:01 (32,171)
Barson, Carl Joseph 4:49:10 (23,009)
Barstow, Michael J 3:30:30 (4,256)
Bartels, Andreas H 3:18:54 (2,610)
Barter, Paul M 4:31:00 (18,347)
Barth, Florent 3:57:10 (9,664)
Bartholome, Burkhard 5:13:31 (28,068)
Bartholome, Frank 5:36:04 (31,083)
Bartholome, Nico 6:35:51 (34,539)
Bartholomew, Adam T 5:13:25 (28,051)
Bartholomew, Jon 5:06:28 (26,800)

Barthorpe, Scott	4:30:00 (18,095)	
Bartle, Darryl	6:02:14 (33,185)	
Bartlett, Charles K	4:32:05 (18,660)	
Bartlett, Daniel	6:03:53 (33,282)	
Bartlett, Graham	4:03:17 (11,288)	
Bartlett, James S	3:41:00 (6,028)	
Bartlett, John H	5:14:31 (28,247)	
Bartlett, Martin	4:37:38 (20,078)	
Bartlett, Martin I	5:46:01 (32,015)	
Bartlett, Nigel P	4:23:18 (16,253)	
Bartlett, Oliver J	4:21:45 (15,892)	
Bartlett, Scott	5:48:58 (32,248)	
Bartlett, Scott J	4:56:33 (24,814)	
Bartlett, Simon E	4:09:41 (12,769)	
Bartlett, Stephen J	4:20:57 (15,674)	
Bartley, Mark G	5:11:28 (27,721)	
Bartloff, Sascha	4:45:50 (22,171)	
Bartman, Nick M	3:54:49 (8,973)	
Barton, Anthony	4:39:33 (20,595)	
Barton, Desmond P	4:24:38 (16,601)	
Barton, James	4:39:34 (20,602)	
Barton, Neil J	4:55:39 (24,605)	
Barton, Nick	3:53:52 (8,718)	
Barton, Paul	4:28:34 (17,716)	
Barton, Paul E	3:55:47 (9,258)	
Barton, Robert	3:22:58 (3,125)	
Barton, Rollin P	5:29:12 (30,299)	
Barton, Russell C	4:51:31 (23,625)	
Barton, Scott	4:39:33 (20,595)	
Barton, Stanley R	5:32:58 (30,749)	
Barton, Stephen	5:55:42 (32,739)	
Bartram, Ian J	4:06:03 (11,893)	
Bartram, Lee	4:14:24 (14,013)	
Bartram, Sam	3:49:37 (7,753)	
Bartrip, Lee	4:21:00 (15,692)	
Barua, Anjohn P	3:55:14 (9,092)	
Barus, Stephane	4:04:29 (11,541)	
Barwick, Jamie R	3:44:45 (6,758)	
Barwick, Paul	5:38:52 (31,379)	
Basa, Mauro	4:32:35 (18,783)	
Bascombe, Tom	5:32:38 (30,709)	
Basford, Pete J	3:54:14 (8,821)	
Basham, Craig	5:51:51 (32,473)	
Basham, Ross	5:51:51 (32,473)	
Bashford, Gary R	3:54:02 (8,763)	
Bashford, Julian I	4:48:46 (22,915)	
Bashford, Simon R	3:50:41 (7,989)	
Basmaa, Yousef	5:26:25 (29,982)	
Bason, David J	4:22:31 (16,078)	
Bason, Graham A	4:23:25 (16,281)	
Bason, Peter J	3:56:37 (9,500)	
Basra, Melvinder S	3:52:56 (8,491)	
Bass, Andrew P	2:46:59 (368)	
Bass, David	3:38:44 (5,630)	
Bass, Neil	4:06:16 (11,945)	
Bassam, Kevin J	3:48:40 (7,543)	
Bassett, David J	4:01:30 (10,915)	
Bassett, Paul	4:53:28 (24,066)	
Bassett, Paul	6:06:13 (33,396)	
Bassett, Stephen	4:08:23 (12,481)	
Bassett-Myers, Ted	6:00:09 (33,059)	
Bassford, Dan	3:55:13 (9,089)	
Bassi, Sanraj Bobby Singh	5:38:14 (31,300)	
Bassindale, Craig R	4:29:53 (18,068)	
Bassinder, John	3:41:40 (6,142)	
Bassiri, Maurice	4:50:32 (23,381)	
Bastock, Luke S	4:02:05 (11,037)	
Bastow, David A	4:02:26 (11,115)	
Bastow-Coultiss, James D	3:59:03 (10,268)	
Batchelor, Robert J	5:20:03 (29,100)	
Batchelor, William J	5:24:22 (29,715)	
Batcup, Marc B	4:54:53 (24,426)	
Bate, Geoff M	6:28:13 (34,364)	
Bate, Lawrence	3:16:30 (2,378)	
Bateman, Adrian	4:10:59 (13,104)	
Bateman, Alasatair N	3:44:45 (6,758)	
Bateman, Anthony P	3:17:59 (2,527)	
Bateman, David	4:24:37 (16,595)	
Bateman, Edward D	5:27:36 (30,102)	
Bateman, Jonathan S	2:55:37 (703)	
Bateman, Nicholas	3:09:57 (1,703)	
Bateman, Paul	4:16:59 (14,642)	
Bateman, Peter	4:23:45 (16,374)	

Bateman, Richard J	3:52:06 (8,301)	
Bateman, Rory	3:56:00 (9,309)	
Bater, Bernie	3:42:57 (6,409)	
Bates, Christopher W	5:06:21 (26,781)	
Bates, Daniel S	3:34:29 (4,873)	
Bates, Dean	3:43:17 (6,487)	
Bates, Giles D	4:29:37 (17,988)	
Bates, Ian W	4:11:45 (13,323)	
Bates, Joe	4:19:03 (15,173)	
Bates, John	4:08:51 (12,585)	
Bates, John C	3:50:32 (7,958)	
Bates, Lukas J	3:29:21 (4,079)	
Bates, Neville A	3:34:18 (4,830)	
Bates, Rick	5:50:33 (32,384)	
Bates, Rob	4:12:28 (13,512)	
Bates, Robin	5:38:21 (31,310)	
Bateson, Colin	5:30:15 (30,434)	
Bateson, Graham A	3:29:28 (4,097)	
Bateson, Steven	2:30:35 (70)	
Batey, Trevor J	3:14:53 (2,218)	
Bathgate, Andy S	4:46:52 (22,441)	
Batista, Mark A	4:18:41 (15,077)	
Batley, Lloyd E	5:06:52 (26,879)	
Batrick, Lee	5:09:02 (27,280)	
Batsford, Mark	4:31:56 (18,618)	
Batstone, Andrew	7:13:36 (35,089)	
Batt, James C	4:21:48 (15,900)	
Batterbee, Gareth	5:32:14 (30,662)	
Batterbee, Robert F	4:32:27 (18,748)	
Batterbury, Clive E	4:23:34 (16,331)	
Battersby, Ian W	5:05:26 (26,629)	
Battersby, Nick P	3:16:39 (2,400)	
Battye, Adam M	5:22:49 (29,482)	
Battye, Michael	5:22:49 (29,482)	
Baty, Edward S	4:03:44 (11,368)	
Baty, John	4:50:59 (23,483)	
Baudry, Denis	3:39:52 (5,821)	
Bauer, Joerg	3:54:14 (8,821)	
Baulch, James	2:41:52 (234)	
Baumgaertel, Dirk	4:15:03 (14,176)	
Baumgart, William	3:28:11 (3,878)	
Baur, Nicolas	3:19:19 (2,657)	
Baur, Tobias	4:12:49 (13,609)	
Bausor, Neil T	4:12:19 (13,473)	
Bavetta, Tom	6:03:10 (33,240)	
Bavetta, Vince	5:52:45 (32,536)	
Bavey-Neal, Darren J	6:01:11 (33,119)	
Bavin, Trevor	5:57:00 (32,836)	
Bawden, Tom	5:11:26 (27,715)	
Bax, Trevor J	3:45:16 (6,848)	
Baxendale, Sam	4:09:50 (12,816)	
Baxter, Anthony J	4:17:19 (14,725)	
Baxter, Eric G	3:33:02 (4,615)	
Baxter, Greg	2:44:44 (308)	
Baxter, John M	5:24:03 (29,660)	
Baxter, Mark	4:40:29 (20,829)	
Baxter, Paul David	4:40:30 (20,833)	
Baxter, Robert J	4:37:37 (20,070)	
Baxter, Simon S	4:10:05 (12,874)	
Baxter, Tamsin L	5:40:22 (31,531)	
Bayes, Jonathan	4:30:56 (18,331)	
Bayes, Mark	4:45:06 (22,000)	
Bayfield, Simon	5:10:09 (27,489)	
Bayfield-Hill, Kevin	5:57:39 (32,889)	
Bayliss, Alastair J	2:49:43 (456)	
Bayliss, Gerald	4:57:51 (25,097)	
Bayliss, James A	4:01:32 (10,926)	
Bayliss, Mark	3:37:05 (5,339)	
Bayliss, Mark J	3:58:02 (9,950)	
Bayliss, Michael C	5:18:39 (28,904)	
Bayliss, Simon M	3:46:49 (7,159)	
Bayne, Les	4:46:17 (22,274)	
Bayne, Stuart B	4:00:51 (10,755)	
Baynes, Neil S	4:00:33 (10,687)	
Bayon, Bernard	3:20:19 (2,801)	
Bayramoglu, Alperhan	5:04:36 (26,481)	
Bazeley, Geoffrey Mark	5:04:28 (26,450)	
Bazeley, Matthew	4:10:28 (12,973)	
Bazell, Steven C	2:48:19 (406)	
Bazley, Graham	4:01:23 (10,881)	
Bazley, John Charles	3:47:43 (7,331)	
Bazley, Peter G	3:53:29 (8,621)	
Bazzocchi, Domenico	3:48:24 (7,487)	

Beach, Tom	6:02:56 (33,226)	
Beach, William J	3:42:35 (6,325)	
Beadle, David	2:56:52 (765)	
Beadle, Michael	4:13:36 (13,824)	
Beadle, Mike S	3:53:15 (8,572)	
Beagley, Andrew	6:00:56 (33,109)	
Beagley, Mark H	4:38:43 (20,354)	
Beal, Kevin P	5:09:04 (27,283)	
Beale, John	4:36:49 (19,870)	
Beale, Nikki	4:05:05 (11,675)	
Beales, Chris	4:57:19 (24,989)	
Beales, Edward F	4:33:50 (19,108)	
Beall, Jonathan L	4:10:20 (12,943)	
Beamish, Eoghan	5:27:52 (30,134)	
Beamond, Jeffery	5:07:31 (27,011)	
Bean, Andrew J	3:55:12 (9,085)	
Bean, John	3:44:55 (6,787)	
Beaney, John	4:39:56 (20,701)	
Beard, David P	5:25:04 (29,806)	
Beard, Mark	4:49:02 (22,981)	
Beard, Matthew	3:54:40 (8,936)	
Beard, Mike K	3:24:12 (3,299)	
Beard, Richard	4:56:22 (24,764)	
Beard, Steve	4:20:16 (15,502)	
Beardmore, Roger C	3:11:48 (1,860)	
Beardsmore, Keith J	3:13:00 (2,006)	
Beare, Martin A	3:34:12 (4,453)	
Bearman, Jordan M	5:27:35 (30,100)	
Bearwish, Andy	3:49:40 (7,761)	
Bearwish, Darren R	4:21:04 (15,706)	
Bearwish, Neil S	3:04:21 (1,253)	
Bearyman, Rob P	3:31:54 (4,453)	
Beathe, Carl J	3:10:32 (1,740)	
Beaton, Andrew	4:13:38 (13,834)	
Beaton, Kevin C	4:00:55 (10,778)	
Beattie, Alan W	4:55:48 (24,640)	
Beattie, Brian W	3:46:44 (7,140)	
Beattie, David I	3:14:57 (2,225)	
Beattie, Ian J	3:06:12 (1,390)	
Beattie, Kenneth P	3:31:15 (4,366)	
Beaudry, Raymond	4:22:13 (16,006)	
Beaumont, Charlie H	4:31:34 (18,518)	
Beaumont, Craig S	4:06:26 (11,978)	
Beaumont, Paul J	4:30:39 (18,269)	
Beauvallet, Francis	4:29:20 (17,932)	
Beauvallet, Julien	4:29:19 (17,931)	
Beavan, Robert	5:23:11 (29,543)	
Beavis, Andrew	4:59:02 (25,394)	
Beavis, Joey	3:32:15 (4,510)	
Beazeley, Christopher D	3:22:39 (3,032)	
Beazer, Derek G	5:41:40 (31,645)	
Bebbington, Colin	3:48:13 (7,449)	
Becher, Anthony J	4:15:25 (14,262)	
Becher, Harry R	4:31:21 (18,455)	
Bechoo, Santosh	4:53:49 (24,177)	
Bechtle, Joachim	3:22:56 (3,123)	
Beck, Andrew S	5:03:57 (26,374)	
Beck, Gerald	4:26:29 (17,111)	
Becker, Mark J	3:33:04 (4,620)	
Beckett, Christopher H	4:41:18 (21,037)	
Beckett, Kelvin W	4:11:36 (13,284)	
Beckett, Matthew	3:58:16 (10,027)	
Beckett, Peter G	3:46:46 (7,148)	
Beckingham, Ian J	3:04:26 (1,259)	
Beckingham, Nicholas J	4:27:49 (17,495)	
Beckley, Daniel	4:43:54 (21,691)	
Beckmann, Timothy J	4:40:03 (20,739)	
Beckmann, Wolfgang	4:30:19 (18,185)	
Beckmans, Marcus	3:24:57 (3,395)	
Beckwith, Ben J	4:46:21 (22,294)	
Beddard, Roger S	4:06:13 (11,931)	
Beddow, Jay	3:08:38 (1,583)	
Bedford, Andrew J	6:49:28 (34,804)	
Bedford, Geoffrey	4:57:00 (24,930)	
Bedford, Matt	4:06:24 (11,969)	
Bednall, Claire L	4:35:42 (19,599)	
Bednarek, Krzysztof	3:40:11 (5,899)	
Bedson, Peter A	5:20:13 (29,119)	
Bedwell, Peter J	4:16:50 (14,615)	
Bee, Giles S	3:58:53 (10,221)	
Beecher, Colin	3:35:58 (5,147)	
Beechey, Paul D	3:03:51 (1,229)	
Beecroft, David	3:08:34 (1,571)	

Beeden, Paul 4:13:37 (13,829)
Beenham, Ian E....4:13:29 (13,791)
Beer, James A....5:27:50 (30,130)
Beer, Robert J 4:35:19 (19,496)
Beer, Roger E 5:35:01 (30,972)
Beerkens, Bart....5:45:28 (31,969)
Beerling, Mark M....5:01:51 (25,980)
Beese-Raybould, Jamie R 4:31:27 (18,487)
Beeslee, Paul....4:20:42 (15,604)
Beesley, Carl B....4:31:00 (18,347)
Beesley, Ian S....4:04:20 (11,515)
Beesley, Jeremy....4:26:41 (17,176)
Beesley, Luke I....4:32:34 (18,777)
Beeton, Andrew John 3:32:12 (4,504)
Beffort, Marc 3:27:12 (3,716)
Beggs, Gary J....5:39:06 (31,410)
Beggs, William Kenneth 4:05:21 (11,742)
Begley, Andrew....4:20:53 (15,657)
Begley, Charles A....5:17:55 (28,780)
Begsteinn, Gunnarsson....3:35:36 (5,071)
Behagg, David J 3:43:24 (6,510)
Behling, Alessandro A 3:39:16 (5,723)
Behrendt, Matthias 4:36:49 (19,870)
Behrman, Grant....3:57:49 (9,880)
Beider, Rufus H....4:07:34 (12,248)
Beighton, Nick T....5:39:47 (31,474)
Bekerman, Marek....4:27:11 (17,305)
Bekker, Olav 3:51:07 (8,076)
Belcher, Martin 3:42:55 (6,402)
Belcher, Ryan M 5:11:35 (27,746)
Bell, Andrew....4:36:55 (19,894)
Bell, Andrew....5:24:04 (29,663)
Bell, Austin 3:59:12 (10,310)
Bell, Craig L....4:58:13 (25,193)
Bell, Daniel S....2:52:18 (536)
Bell, Duncan C....2:43:20 (264)
Bell, Geoffrey David....4:55:33 (24,581)
Bell, Gordon....4:52:40 (23,895)
Bell, Graham 2:48:09 (403)
Bell, Graham P....5:14:56 (28,303)
Bell, Jimmy S 4:14:21 (14,000)
Bell, John D 3:20:24 (2,811)
Bell, Jon D 6:25:33 (34,259)
Bell, Jonathan....4:59:34 (25,512)
Bell, Keith....4:13:25 (13,780)
Bell, Martin A....3:42:01 (6,212)
Bell, Matthew....4:41:09 (20,995)
Bell, Michael D....3:56:14 (9,372)
Bell, Nicholas G....3:46:56 (7,187)
Bell, Nick 3:58:38 (10,137)
Bell, Paul....3:00:17 (1,013)
Bell, Robert 3:54:15 (8,828)
Bell, Robert 3:58:13 (10,018)
Bell, Robert S 4:32:19 (18,710)
Bell, Robert W....3:59:32 (10,398)
Bell, Rupert T....4:47:08 (22,525)
Bell, Simon 4:29:25 (17,952)
Bell, Simon J....2:49:18 (434)
Bell, Steven J....4:45:36 (22,105)
Bell, Stuart....5:23:04 (29,526)
Bell, Wayne P....2:54:56 (658)
Bellamy, Darren W....4:47:11 (22,542)
Bellamy, Hugh G....3:58:42 (10,162)
Bellamy, Richard K....4:36:34 (19,808)
Bellinger, Nicholas J....4:48:51 (22,932)
Bellingham, Geoff....4:39:35 (20,606)
Bellingham, Neil J....4:25:27 (16,829)
Bellingham, Steve J 3:43:16 (6,481)
Bellis, Deryn S 3:39:59 (5,856)
Bell-Nevin, Shane....4:57:01 (24,933)
Bello, Aurelio M....4:49:04 (22,989)
Bello, Diego....3:51:04 (8,072)
Bellver Aullana, Alfonso 3:00:36 (1,027)
Bellwood, David D....5:57:27 (32,873)
Bellwood, Paul....4:07:28 (12,228)
Belotti, Claudio 3:34:35 (4,889)
Belpedio, Cristian 3:25:24 (3,444)
Belson, Damain 4:32:15 (18,698)
Belson, Joseph 3:42:44 (6,363)
Belton, Robert Bryan 4:03:49 (11,398)
Bemment, Glenn....3:45:39 (6,920)
Ben Ayed, Nizou....4:30:39 (18,269)
Benak, Martin....4:28:43 (17,751)
Benamara, Samir....3:44:59 (6,800)
Benamy - Hackel, Klaus 4:18:23 (14,990)
Benatre, Christian....3:35:05 (4,975)
Benavides, Javier 5:38:41 (31,353)
Bence, Christopher R 4:33:14 (18,954)
Bendall, Mark....2:33:53 (96)
Bendel, Colin P....4:08:26 (12,493)
Bender, Michael G 4:10:26 (12,962)
Bendikas, Peter J 4:50:28 (23,362)
Bendle, Gavin S....5:01:51 (25,980)
Bendle, Jeremy Philip....3:43:45 (6,574)
Benfield, Bradley....4:31:28 (18,494)
Benger, Nick....3:55:46 (9,253)
Bengisu, Mete....5:11:15 (27,684)
Beniston, Paul 4:07:05 (12,129)
Benjamin, Daniel 4:04:50 (11,616)
Benkwitz, Adam P 5:16:07 (28,521)
Bennet, George C 3:47:57 (7,384)
Bennet, Tom D....3:55:14 (9,092)
Bennett, Adrian Charles....4:06:06 (11,903)
Bennett, Adrian P 4:15:20 (14,240)
Bennett, Bill 3:19:04 (2,624)
Bennett, Brian 5:04:22 (26,438)
Bennett, Christopher....3:44:35 (6,729)
Bennett, Christopher....5:04:10 (26,409)
Bennett, Christopher G....5:15:42 (28,456)
Bennett, Christopher J....3:57:51 (9,896)
Bennett, Christopher M 3:39:39 (5,784)
Bennett, Dan 4:14:33 (14,042)
Bennett, Daniel J....5:04:29 (26,452)
Bennett, Dave A 5:15:23 (28,398)
Bennett, David H 3:24:55 (3,392)
Bennett, George B 6:05:02 (33,341)
Bennett, Grant T....4:12:42 (13,575)
Bennett, James 4:37:02 (19,928)
Bennett, John J....3:53:25 (8,609)
Bennett, John M....4:23:45 (16,374)
Bennett, Jonathan D....4:58:03 (25,148)
Bennett, Jonathan M 4:06:00 (11,880)
Bennett, Kevin J 4:57:17 (24,980)
Bennett, Marc D....5:47:47 (32,155)
Bennett, Mike T 4:39:24 (20,552)
Bennett, Neil 4:34:06 (19,172)
Bennett, Oliver....4:16:35 (14,550)
Bennett, Paul....3:55:12 (9,085)
Bennett, Raymond 3:59:58 (10,540)
Bennett, Richard A 4:56:10 (24,720)
Bennett, Richard J....6:50:17 (34,821)
Bennett, Robert C....5:22:20 (29,408)
Bennett, Simeon A....2:56:55 (768)
Bennett, Stephen 4:13:46 (13,863)
Bennett, Stephen 5:27:30 (30,093)
Bennett, Steven A....3:08:58 (1,618)
Bennett, Steven M....6:54:38 (34,890)
Bennett, Tony C 4:42:26 (21,309)
Benneworth, Clive M 5:20:52 (29,204)
Bennion, Chris....4:18:14 (14,949)
Bennison, John....4:54:33 (24,345)
Bennison, Matthew S 4:42:02 (21,206)
Benoit, Austruit....2:42:37 (247)
Benoit, Dubots 3:45:11 (6,832)
Benoit, Pierre-Alain 5:02:46 (26,170)
Benskin, Ian D....3:11:50 (1,866)
Benson, Bob F 3:24:22 (3,323)
Benson, David 4:41:27 (21,072)
Benson, David J 4:05:32 (11,780)
Benson, Ian C....3:29:50 (4,157)
Benson, James 2:38:48 (172)
Benson, James 4:15:24 (14,256)
Benson, Kevin G....4:23:31 (16,319)
Benson, Philip....4:31:24 (18,471)
Benson, Tristan J 3:29:00 (4,006)
Benstead, Anthony J 3:54:09 (8,796)
Benstead, Mark 4:45:02 (21,973)
Bent, Alan....3:40:00 (5,859)
Bentley, Christopher W....4:30:31 (18,235)
Bentley, Daryl C....3:43:52 (6,607)
Bentley, Gary....4:56:35 (24,825)
Bentley, Justin D....3:15:37 (2,295)
Bentley, Mark....3:14:24 (2,163)
Bentley, Mike....3:38:38 (5,615)
Bentley, Paul D 4:44:39 (21,871)
Bentley, Philip J 4:12:55 (13,635)
Bentley, Robert W 4:17:58 (14,882)
Bentley, Roy....3:15:43 (2,307)
Bentley, Simon 3:46:22 (7,056)
Benton, Brian A 4:43:44 (21,655)
Benton, Jonathan....3:50:47 (8,019)
Benton, Lewis....6:38:52 (34,603)
Benton, Mark 3:42:55 (6,402)
Benton, Mark P 3:46:12 (7,017)
Benton, Peter C....4:07:08 (12,138)
Benton, Wesley J....2:55:39 (706)
Benz, Reinhold....4:12:29 (13,518)
Beque, Jozef....3:11:32 (1,832)
Berendsen, René J....4:19:04 (15,177)
Beresford, Simon C....6:15:08 (33,796)
Berg, Andrew P 4:52:46 (23,919)
Bergin, Ian R....3:40:29 (5,941)
Bergman, Bengt 3:52:04 (8,291)
Bergmann, Elmar....4:08:25 (12,485)
Berkeley, Neil J....6:23:04 (34,153)
Berks, Graham I 3:18:10 (2,544)
Berks, Michael A 3:19:02 (2,621)
Berlenz, Elmar....4:00:12 (10,599)
Berlyn, Paul P 4:17:23 (14,740)
Berman, Steven 4:11:07 (13,145)
Bernabei, Bruno....3:07:30 (1,481)
Bernard, Blanc 4:07:02 (12,114)
Bernard, Duncan 4:19:18 (15,232)
Bernard, Peter....6:00:34 (33,084)
Bernard, Ralph M 5:28:55 (30,264)
Bernardi, Graziano 3:43:00 (6,418)
Bernardi, Mark O....3:35:54 (5,136)
Bernas, François....3:59:55 (10,523)
Berney, Nicholas E 4:37:34 (20,060)
Bernstein, David....4:48:29 (22,846)
Bernstein, Jon....6:08:03 (33,484)
Bernstein, Peter S....3:44:12 (6,663)
Berrett, Andy S 4:49:17 (23,046)
Berridge, Adrian 3:56:18 (9,394)
Berrill, Lee....3:51:27 (8,156)
Berriman, Paul G 4:37:40 (20,081)
Berrizbeita, Luis Enrique 3:50:02 (7,845)
Berry, Adrian 4:08:54 (12,596)
Berry, Andrew R....3:22:36 (3,085)
Berry, Clifford....3:03:15 (1,185)
Berry, Craig P 5:04:40 (26,489)
Berry, David H....5:11:49 (27,780)
Berry, Ian J....2:39:36 (187)
Berry, James D 4:08:48 (12,573)
Berry, Jason....3:14:22 (2,160)
Berry, Jason....4:33:18 (18,977)
Berry, Karl....4:08:23 (12,481)
Berry, Kevin M....5:38:49 (31,374)
Berry, Mark A 4:10:44 (13,049)
Berry, Martin G 5:29:14 (30,303)
Berry, Michael P 4:39:04 (20,456)
Berry, Mike A....3:54:52 (8,988)
Berry, Richard T....5:07:12 (26,944)
Berry, Scott S 4:15:24 (14,256)
Berthold, Grant I 4:53:42 (24,138)
Bertol, Roald 4:15:50 (14,357)
Bertorelli, Joseph F 3:48:11 (7,442)
Bertram, Jeff....4:41:56 (21,188)
Bertrand, Christophe....3:50:44 (8,001)
Berwick, Adam 3:53:37 (8,653)
Besford, Sarah M....4:30:21 (18,194)
Besly, Adrian....5:03:17 (26,248)
Bessant, Philip M....5:15:08 (28,341)
Best, Andrew J 4:09:14 (12,668)
Best, Anthony....5:46:37 (32,056)
Best, Chris....5:34:58 (30,963)
Best, Luke....4:05:30 (11,768)
Best, Martin B....3:56:05 (9,335)
Best, Roy 4:47:41 (22,647)
Best, Scott 4:39:35 (20,606)
Best, Simon D....4:48:38 (22,887)
Best, Steven....5:39:15 (31,423)
Bestwick, Paul F....2:58:57 (914)
Beswick, Tim C....4:26:11 (17,034)
Betambeau, Alexander 5:36:35 (31,129)
Betteridge, Gareth 4:48:04 (22,756)
Betton, Andrew D 3:03:42 (1,215)
Betts, Kevin J....3:30:57 (4,320)
Betts, Mark P 2:47:50 (388)

Bettsworth, Richard G 3:00:00 (997)
Beullard, Eddy 3:32:08 (4,492)
Bevan, Alexander J 3:21:42 (2,971)
Bevan, Charles E 6:15:09 (33,798)
Bevan, David J 4:59:47 (25,552)
Bevan, Gareth 4:24:48 (16,654)
Bevan, Jason 6:18:41 (33,977)
Bevan, John A 4:45:58 (22,208)
Bevan, Nick 4:47:43 (22,657)
Bevan, Richard F 4:00:07 (10,575)
Bevan, Robin J 4:49:43 (23,182)
Bevan, Steve 3:56:26 (9,437)
Bevan, Steven P 3:31:44 (4,426)
Bevans, Joel T 4:57:41 (25,066)
Bevan-Smith, Sean B 3:58:00 (9,931)
Bevan-Thomas, Tim G 4:38:35 (20,319)
Beverley, David H 3:56:09 (9,351)
Beverley, Thor P 4:20:29 (15,554)
Bew, Tom 5:18:49 (28,938)
Bewsher, Peter A 4:05:36 (11,798)
Bey, Jide 4:45:33 (22,090)
Beynon, Peter N 4:40:10 (20,768)
Bhadressa, Nisshan 4:49:29 (23,110)
Bhala, Neeraj 5:19:44 (29,065)
Bhamidipati, Joshi 6:11:04 (33,603)
Bhatti, Mandeep 4:38:18 (20,251)
Bhogal, Hardial S 4:17:06 (14,664)
Bhupal, Kulvinder S 4:13:57 (13,895)
Bianchi, Nick P 4:44:02 (21,729)
Bibby, Gary 4:03:08 (11,257)
Bibby, Gary 5:55:44 (32,742)
Bickers, Christopher J 5:32:56 (30,744)
Bickers, Richard A 4:21:33 (15,832)
Bickerstaff, Neil D 4:46:21 (22,294)
Bickerstaffe, Philip K 4:58:30 (25,268)
Bickerton, David J 3:35:02 (4,965)
Bicknell, Jonathan 3:51:38 (8,196)
Bicknell, Tony J 5:58:33 (32,961)
Biddick, Dominic S 2:40:47 (211)
Biddle, Timothy J 6:03:51 (33,280)
Biddulph, Daniel E 4:16:18 (14,473)
Bidmead, James D 4:09:42 (12,774)
Bidston, Mark J 4:01:47 (10,980)
Bidwell, Matthew J 2:41:21 (223)
Bienkowski, Stephen 5:19:59 (29,090)
Bierbaumer, Ulrich 3:36:25 (5,219)
Bieris, Stan 4:08:25 (12,485)
Biggane, Nicholas J 3:56:04 (9,329)
Biggar, Andrew J 4:22:03 (15,954)
Biggin, Chris S 3:21:49 (2,985)
Biggin, Matthew James 3:29:47 (4,150)
Biggs, Andy J 3:46:59 (7,198)
Biggs, Duncan L 5:17:27 (28,710)
Biggs, Geoff D 4:24:41 (16,621)
Biggs, Liam 3:45:54 (6,960)
Biggs, Rachel L 8:41:36 (35,346)
Biggs, Roger 3:42:08 (6,238)
Bigley, Alastair J 3:42:47 (6,374)
Bigley, Matt 5:34:43 (30,940)
Bigmore, Paul T 3:53:16 (8,575)
Bill, David R 3:56:44 (9,544)
Bill, Nick D 3:54:25 (8,867)
Billingham, Matthew A 3:54:59 (9,018)
Billinghurst, Antony 3:51:51 (8,240)
Billings, Jon 4:58:49 (25,341)
Billington, Ian R 4:41:32 (21,098)
Billington, Keith S 4:09:34 (12,741)
Bills, Stephen A 4:41:40 (21,136)
Billson, Simon N 5:36:35 (31,129)
Billups, Russ John 5:43:11 (31,792)
Bilsbury, Allan D 5:46:23 (32,040)
Biltcliffe, Steve J 4:18:50 (15,113)
Bilton, Darran E 2:23:32 (27)
Binding, Patrick D 5:05:49 (26,700)
Bingham, Luke Jonathan 4:43:33 (21,613)
Bingham, Stephen M 4:12:06 (13,414)
Bingham, Stuart J 4:12:06 (13,414)
Bingham, William E 4:27:55 (17,520)
Bingley, Kenneth 4:38:26 (20,283)
Binks, Dominic F 4:50:14 (23,292)
Binnie, Brian 5:38:02 (31,283)
Binnington, Tim J 3:36:54 (5,295)
Binns, David 4:58:03 (25,148)
Binns, David A 3:07:40 (1,498)
Binstock, Yisroel 5:22:40 (29,464)
Birch, Alex 4:41:01 (20,965)
Birch, Christopher B 3:54:10 (8,804)
Birch, Christopher J 4:03:34 (11,351)
Birch, Francis A 4:12:04 (13,405)
Birch, Michael 5:03:50 (26,348)
Birch, Simon 4:56:58 (24,925)
Birchall, James 3:28:11 (3,878)
Birchall, Matthew J 2:53:21 (576)
Bird, Andrew A 5:53:03 (32,550)
Bird, Anthony 4:01:10 (10,827)
Bird, David J 3:03:43 (1,217)
Bird, David J 5:45:35 (31,982)
Bird, David W 4:37:57 (20,155)
Bird, Gavin D 2:41:06 (217)
Bird, James A 7:07:49 (35,038)
Bird, Jamie E 3:51:23 (8,136)
Bird, Jason A 3:57:46 (9,863)
Bird, Jeffrey 3:43:08 (6,448)
Bird, Jonathan A 3:42:27 (6,288)
Bird, Jonathan C 4:21:23 (15,778)
Bird, Mark W 4:24:43 (16,627)
Bird, Matthew 3:54:59 (9,018)
Bird, Nicholas 5:18:35 (28,891)
Bird, Nick J 3:26:01 (3,535)
Bird, Patrick R 3:47:36 (7,309)
Bird, Paul S 4:51:16 (23,558)
Bird, Phillip 4:15:41 (14,317)
Bird, Robert J 4:25:08 (16,746)
Bird, Simon 4:04:17 (11,506)
Bird, Thomas R 3:56:19 (9,399)
Bird, Tim G 3:54:16 (8,833)
Bird, Wayne 4:34:54 (19,382)
Birdi, Gurpreet 5:39:25 (31,438)
Biriny, Kevin P 4:23:25 (16,281)
Birkby, David B 4:34:31 (19,264)
Birkby, Nicholas 4:32:35 (18,783)
Birke-Gagel, Anton 4:30:34 (18,245)
Birkeland, Johan E 3:51:29 (8,164)
Birkeland, Mads E 5:33:38 (30,827)
Birkett, Daniel J 4:42:12 (21,249)
Birkinshaw, David Mark Poynton 4:28:53 (17,806)
Birks, David L 3:21:45 (2,979)
Birks, Ian D 4:53:51 (24,189)
Birrane, Paul Anthony 3:46:56 (7,187)
Birru, Samuel A 5:17:03 (28,647)
Birt, Ashley S 3:27:05 (3,695)
Birt, Christopher H 4:36:27 (19,787)
Birtles, Alex D 3:19:53 (2,736)
Birtwhistle, Andy J 4:02:06 (11,043)
Bisby, David G 3:38:32 (5,598)
Bish, David M 4:12:54 (13,628)
Bishop, Andrew R 5:16:47 (28,617)
Bishop, Daniel T 2:54:22 (622)
Bishop, Gary 5:33:02 (30,758)
Bishop, Ian M 3:01:08 (1,063)
Bishop, James J 4:47:16 (22,556)
Bishop, Jim M 3:49:28 (7,723)
Bishop, Mark J 4:26:05 (17,006)
Bishop, Nick 5:25:38 (29,883)
Bishop, Peter I 4:33:58 (19,145)
Bishop, Philip J 4:43:01 (21,473)
Bishop, Philip M 4:19:18 (15,232)
Bishop, Robert 4:50:12 (23,282)
Bishop, Scott 3:36:41 (5,261)
Bishop, Sebastien B 5:59:56 (33,045)
Bishop, Simon 3:49:40 (7,761)
Bishop, Simon 5:01:29 (25,910)
Bishop, Stephen C 3:51:01 (8,058)
Bishop, Steven R 5:05:58 (26,722)
Bishop, Tim 3:46:18 (7,045)
Bishopp, Stephen Richard 4:39:09 (20,482)
Bisiker, Richard 5:54:42 (32,660)
Bisoni, David 4:13:25 (13,780)
Biss, Wayne S 4:56:51 (24,898)
Bisschop, Murray 4:27:33 (17,402)
Bisset, Ian 4:19:42 (15,340)
Bisset, James A 5:38:00 (31,274)
Bisson, Antoine 3:49:01 (7,622)
Bistrong, Richard T 4:11:35 (13,279)
Bittighofer, Hubert 4:06:36 (12,016)
Bitting, John H 4:11:18 (13,189)
Bittner, Jiri 3:20:05 (2,766)
Biwersi, Guenter 3:55:01 (9,030)
Bjerrum, Mads 3:04:49 (1,294)
Bjoerkoey, Magne Vik 3:19:46 (2,722)
Black, Alistair 2:59:37 (965)
Black, Daniel Charles 4:18:04 (14,909)
Black, Eamonn C 5:03:52 (26,353)
Black, Grant 3:31:06 (4,346)
Black, James H 3:03:38 (1,211)
Black, Kenneth J 4:00:07 (10,575)
Black, Paul D 5:12:35 (27,909)
Black, Roger 5:06:43 (26,846)
Black, Simon J 2:57:30 (805)
Black, Stephen E 3:16:44 (2,408)
Black, Steven 4:18:01 (14,891)
Blackburn, Chris 5:25:36 (29,878)
Blackburn, Will E 4:26:48 (17,205)
Blacketer, Paul 6:13:29 (33,721)
Blackford, Derek W 5:20:40 (29,171)
Blackham, Stuart 4:18:15 (14,951)
Blackledge, Mark 6:13:45 (33,737)
Blackledge, Robert W 6:03:59 (33,289)
Blackmore, Andrew 3:38:56 (5,661)
Blackmore, Darren T 3:33:10 (4,633)
Blackmore, Ivor 6:48:14 (34,777)
Blackwell, Daniel 4:00:04 (10,564)
Blackwell, Kevin M 4:15:05 (14,185)
Blackwell, Mark S 6:26:59 (34,320)
Blackwell, Nicholas A 3:25:10 (3,416)
Blackwell, Oliver 4:22:19 (16,025)
Blackwell, Tom D 3:29:41 (4,132)
Blackwood, Des L 3:59:48 (10,495)
Blades, Andrew 3:51:12 (8,098)
Bladon, Charles C 4:31:45 (18,567)
Bladon, Dave 3:36:05 (5,171)
Bladon, Mark 4:27:01 (17,260)
Blagg, John R 4:12:11 (13,437)
Blain, Chris J 4:50:56 (23,467)
Blaine, John S 3:07:07 (1,448)
Blair, Andrew D 3:35:21 (5,022)
Blair, John 4:19:46 (15,363)
Blaize, Andy J 3:04:55 (1,301)
Blaize-Smith, Matthew S 4:04:38 (11,569)
Blake, Ben M 4:32:33 (18,769)
Blake, Cian 3:56:00 (9,309)
Blake, Edward M 2:40:11 (196)
Blake, James 4:44:12 (21,766)
Blake, James W 4:21:35 (15,837)
Blake, Jamie 5:26:00 (29,939)
Blake, Jermaine 4:44:55 (21,933)
Blake, John 3:41:30 (6,118)
Blake, John D 3:22:12 (3,036)
Blake, Neil A 4:21:35 (15,837)
Blake, Nigel 4:51:09 (23,521)
Blake, Peter 3:53:43 (8,682)
Blake, Stephen J 3:07:43 (1,503)
Blake, Steve J 4:17:49 (14,842)
Blakeley, Andrew J 5:13:57 (28,151)
Blakemore, Ian 3:16:44 (2,408)
Blakemore, Ian 4:42:52 (21,431)
Blake-Smith, Mark J 4:35:46 (19,620)
Blake-Turner, Joe 5:41:29 (31,634)
Blakey, Edward J 4:38:03 (20,179)
Blakey, Simon C 4:47:49 (22,675)
Blampied, Peter 5:09:10 (27,303)
Blanc, Cyril 4:14:41 (14,074)
Blanc, Daniel 3:29:13 (4,044)
Blanchard, Colin 6:13:23 (33,715)
Blanchard, Luke J 3:59:04 (10,274)
Blanco Castro, Xoan Xesus 3:19:25 (2,672)
Blanco Ortiz, Fabian 3:21:30 (2,946)
Bland, Dan 4:40:20 (20,802)
Bland, Dave J 3:43:43 (6,570)
Blandin, Marc 4:16:48 (14,605)
Blaney, Geoffrey 3:58:08 (9,982)
Blantz, Andrew 5:14:38 (28,257)
Blantz, Steven D 5:37:15 (31,198)
Blatcher, James R 4:50:49 (23,449)
Blaylock, Mark R 4:46:44 (22,416)
Blazye, Robert 4:49:55 (23,221)
Blease, Simon T 4:35:13 (19,472)
Bleay, Michael A 5:06:33 (26,812)
Bleazard, Sam J 3:54:47 (8,964)

Blencowe, Rupert D 5:02:32 (26,124)
Blenkharn, John M 6:26:10 (34,288)
Blessley, Christopher 6:07:04 (33,438)
Blewett, Steve G 3:40:04 (5,871)
Blewitt, Richard D 3:04:11 (1,247)
Blewitt, Tim A 4:27:15 (17,325)
Bligh, Peter 3:56:05 (9,335)
Blin, Michel 4:28:37 (17,730)
Blinman, Leigh 4:33:35 (19,046)
Bliss, Edward R 5:21:05 (29,234)
Blissitt, Stuart 4:36:34 (19,808)
Blizzard, Andrew 5:09:43 (27,405)
Block, Robert John 3:28:27 (3,922)
Blockus, Willy 4:37:41 (20,088)
Blofeld, Roger J 4:32:30 (18,758)
Blofeld, Stuart 3:42:16 (6,262)
Blogg, Kieran M 3:04:32 (1,267)
Blogg, Nick J 4:05:11 (11,703)
Blois, James 4:43:19 (21,554)
Blok, Gezinus 4:29:31 (17,969)
Bloomfield, Crispian J 2:34:41 (108)
Bloomfield, David C 4:04:33 (11,556)
Bloomfield, Paul M 3:26:58 (3,678)
Bloor, Charles 4:27:47 (17,479)
Blott, Stephen A 4:40:34 (20,851)
Blount, Tony K 6:18:18 (33,941)
Blower, Kev M 5:16:28 (28,555)
Blower, Michael D 4:44:02 (21,729)
Blowers, Simon C 4:04:12 (11,489)
Blowes, Benjamin D 2:50:41 (487)
Bloxham, Clive 4:55:05 (24,476)
Bluefield, Paul 5:08:50 (27,234)
Bluett, Nicholas 4:15:09 (14,203)
Blunden, Matthew 2:34:40 (107)
Blyth, Christopher A 4:32:25 (18,735)
Blythe, Roy 4:04:03 (11,459)
Boakye, Christopher L 4:24:12 (16,497)
Boakye, Rob 4:50:46 (23,437)
Board, Matthew J 4:54:13 (24,264)
Boarder, Stephen 4:56:09 (24,716)
Boardley, Ian D 2:51:58 (521)
Boardman, Allan Neville 5:09:32 (27,370)
Boardman, Andrew D 3:10:09 (1,711)
Boardman, Chris 3:19:27 (2,676)
Boardman, Liam John 3:41:17 (6,086)
Boardman, Wayne 4:38:24 (20,279)
Boase, Duncan K 4:33:35 (19,046)
Boatman, Ben 5:58:48 (32,979)
Bobeldijk, Volkert 4:20:05 (15,453)
Bobo, Richard 4:12:15 (13,453)
Bocking, Andrew Warren 3:57:08 (9,658)
Boddington, Richard 4:00:03 (10,557)
Boddy, Tim D 4:20:26 (15,542)
Bodfish, Stephen 4:35:08 (19,446)
Bodie, Alex 5:01:27 (25,904)
Bodman, Daniel J 3:48:13 (7,449)
Bodnar, Paul 4:02:08 (11,048)
Bodrozic, Valdimir 4:05:08 (11,690)
Bodson, Bertrand 3:10:37 (1,747)
Body, Paul 3:11:07 (1,796)
Boelter, Dirk 3:30:21 (4,228)
Boettcher, René 3:41:22 (6,099)
Boggan, Matt A 4:02:15 (11,077)
Boggi, Daniel 4:17:24 (14,742)
Boggis, Mark A 4:03:53 (11,420)
Bogoevski, Sasho 5:11:55 (27,792)
Bogue, James Y 3:30:07 (4,192)
Bogush, Jeremy H 4:00:29 (10,664)
Bohan, Eamonn J 5:36:17 (31,100)
Bohn, Joerg 3:56:24 (9,429)
Bohr, Werner 3:07:06 (1,445)
Bohssein, Eric 3:55:36 (9,191)
Boi, Alberto 3:13:35 (2,071)
Bojesen, Soeren B 4:46:22 (22,302)
Boland, Colum 4:29:23 (17,945)
Bold, Matt 3:56:58 (9,610)
Bolden, David K 3:44:27 (6,710)
Bolding, Shaun D 4:33:40 (19,066)
Boler, Richard 4:51:21 (23,578)
Boler, Timothy J 5:28:38 (30,226)
Bolger, Liam M 4:08:04 (12,376)
Bollack, Olivier P 4:38:30 (20,296)
Bollen, Charles H 5:39:56 (31,487)
Bollington, Simon J 4:41:43 (21,144)
Bolsher, Scott 4:39:53 (20,688)
Bolt, Philip J 3:05:14 (1,319)
Bolt, Thomas 3:52:28 (8,396)
Bolton, Ashley J 4:04:03 (11,459)
Bolton, Ben 4:58:52 (25,355)
Bolton, Carl P 3:02:07 (1,127)
Bolton, Clive 4:35:57 (19,664)
Bolton, David J 5:30:21 (30,443)
Bolton, Matthew 4:10:26 (12,962)
Bolton, Neil M 4:20:19 (15,515)
Bolton, Nick D 4:29:34 (17,976)
Bolton, Robert T 3:53:52 (8,718)
Bolton, Steve 2:58:28 (865)
Boltwood, Dave J 4:31:30 (18,505)
Bolwell, Jeremy 4:18:42 (15,081)
Bom, Michiel J 5:01:28 (25,907)
Bommarco, Giorgio 3:17:00 (2,429)
Bonaccolta, Carmelo 4:08:07 (12,395)
Bonarius, John Derek 4:35:23 (19,518)
Bond, Andrew W 4:54:04 (24,235)
Bond, David 4:24:53 (16,679)
Bond, David J 5:01:58 (26,010)
Bond, Francis D 3:24:19 (3,314)
Bond, Greg J 4:11:35 (13,279)
Bond, Ian D 3:12:45 (1,965)
Bond, Jonathan 3:46:06 (7,003)
Bond, Joseph 3:48:43 (7,548)
Bond, Mark G 4:35:43 (19,607)
Bond, Martin 4:21:53 (15,917)
Bond, Michael J 2:53:24 (578)
Bond, Richard 4:52:11 (23,793)
Bond, Stewart Allan 3:37:05 (5,339)
Bone, Andy G 3:02:14 (1,134)
Bone, Christian 6:44:50 (34,705)
Bone, David B 5:18:18 (28,833)
Bonell, Simon J 3:42:42 (6,356)
Bonelli, Paolo 3:37:01 (5,321)
Bones, Jonathan A 3:53:42 (8,677)
Bones, Richard M 3:05:11 (1,316)
Bonfatti, Luca 4:03:48 (11,393)
Bonham, Keith A 4:31:40 (18,542)
Bonhommet, Christophe 4:16:03 (14,407)
Boniface, Andrew 4:36:11 (19,716)
Boniface, Phillip 3:59:06 (10,278)
Boninsegna, Alessandro 3:45:40 (6,924)
Bonner, Mark 4:57:51 (25,097)
Bonning, Mark 3:52:24 (8,381)
Bonnyman, Ewen 5:50:54 (32,407)
Bono, Vincent 5:32:10 (30,659)
Bonomo, John 3:46:40 (7,131)
Bonthrone, Steven A 3:33:16 (4,648)
Bontoft, Alan 3:35:41 (5,096)
Boocock, James C 3:37:21 (5,379)
Boocock, Scott 4:14:02 (13,913)
Book, Avigdor Z 3:15:18 (2,259)
Booker, Alex D 3:49:39 (7,758)
Booker, John D 4:23:56 (16,423)
Booker, Nicholas E 3:42:36 (6,330)
Booker, Paul 3:58:39 (10,144)
Bookless, John 5:38:32 (31,336)
Boom, Gary 4:22:40 (16,119)
Boon, Clive A 4:21:05 (15,710)
Boon, Jamie 4:35:11 (19,458)
Boon, Malcolm D 4:10:35 (13,003)
Boon, Martin R 4:51:43 (23,679)
Boon, Richard 4:33:39 (19,060)
Boon, Robert 3:06:04 (1,375)
Boot, David 4:07:20 (12,191)
Boote, Jonathan I 4:46:53 (22,444)
Booth, Andrew A 4:17:57 (14,872)
Booth, Brian M 5:08:46 (27,225)
Booth, Gavin C 5:24:06 (29,669)
Booth, John 3:18:30 (2,577)
Booth, Martin L 3:22:18 (3,050)
Booth, Peter J 3:41:30 (6,118)
Booth, Roger 2:59:58 (995)
Booth, Stephen 4:06:33 (12,005)
Booth, Stephen J 4:25:26 (16,823)
Booth, Thomas D 3:21:27 (2,939)
Booth, Vincent A 2:54:20 (621)
Boothroyd, Bobby 3:30:25 (4,243)
Bopp, James 3:59:46 (10,481)
Boram, John 4:44:16 (21,783)
Bord, Thomas 3:23:15 (3,154)
Borda, Alan Lawrence 4:34:48 (19,355)
Boreel, Jacob 4:02:25 (11,108)
Borel, Philip 4:19:52 (15,395)
Borghoff, Michael 3:21:35 (2,957)
Borgman, Paul 3:43:03 (6,429)
Borgmann, Janek 4:47:22 (22,571)
Borgund, Ole Jan 4:01:28 (10,905)
Borkin, Simon N 4:28:53 (17,806)
Borland, Cameron J 5:14:10 (28,190)
Borley, Harry 4:38:20 (20,264)
Borondy, Steve 3:32:24 (4,530)
Borschmann, Rohan D 4:16:24 (14,499)
Bosak, Bryan 3:56:00 (9,309)
Bosch, Jan K 4:13:16 (13,736)
Bosch, Ulf 3:10:57 (1,777)
Boscherel, Fabrice 3:50:56 (8,047)
Bosley, Stuart N 4:01:43 (10,969)
Boss, Michael 3:52:03 (8,287)
Bossi, Paolo 3:01:28 (1,079)
Bossier, Eddy 2:32:25 (84)
Bostock, David P 5:14:54 (28,294)
Bostock, Giles 4:28:26 (17,678)
Bostock, Nigel B 3:00:31 (1,022)
Bostock, Teddy 5:02:57 (26,200)
Bostock, Will 4:41:11 (21,008)
Boston, Stewart J 3:40:33 (5,948)
Boswell, Guy M 3:14:42 (2,197)
Boswell, Matthew H 4:36:59 (19,914)
Boswell, Robert J 6:11:29 (33,621)
Boswell, Stuart N 3:28:42 (3,957)
Botha, Harry 5:24:01 (29,652)
Botha, Nico 4:19:02 (15,167)
Bott, Jeremy 4:56:54 (24,913)
Bottley, Jeremy R 5:01:09 (25,849)
Bottom, Tristan 6:03:10 (33,240)
Bottomley, David J 5:54:02 (32,621)
Botwright, Robert 4:17:08 (14,677)
Bouchard, Bruno 5:08:34 (27,187)
Boucher, Ian T 4:28:14 (17,628)
Boucher, Joseph F 3:22:32 (3,072)
Boucher, Michael B 2:31:13 (74)
Boucher, William J 3:27:32 (3,783)
Boucherrab, Akli 2:51:46 (515)
Bouchet, Jean-Claude 5:04:14 (26,416)
Boud, Jonny 4:23:52 (16,405)
Bouda, Christopher M 4:55:16 (24,522)
Boughen, Brian T 4:52:49 (23,934)
Boughen, Simon 5:09:37 (27,386)
Boughton, James R 4:02:58 (11,221)
Bougourd, Steve W 4:07:34 (12,248)
Boukelia, Boukhemis 2:37:40 (150)
Boulter, David 3:50:40 (7,983)
Boulter, Robert W 6:23:33 (34,175)
Boulton, Chris G 5:16:42 (28,600)
Boulton, Norman A 5:48:30 (32,217)
Boulton, Robert R 5:53:42 (32,597)
Bourdalle, Daniel 3:24:52 (3,387)
Bourke, Tony L 5:03:44 (26,330)
Bourne, Andrew R 5:01:18 (25,877)
Bourne, Christopher 4:46:42 (22,400)
Bourne, Kevin G 5:24:02 (29,655)
Bourne, Mark 5:13:41 (28,095)
Bourne, Richie 5:26:43 (30,015)
Bourne, Simon 6:15:56 (33,842)
Bourne, William J 2:47:56 (392)
Bourner, Graham A 6:07:16 (33,448)
Bournes, Mike 4:27:23 (17,362)
Boussen, Hamouda 4:19:29 (15,277)
Boutcher, Jon 4:01:46 (10,976)
Bouteyre, Jean-Yves 3:17:25 (2,478)
Bouvet, Dominic 4:17:48 (14,839)
Boux, Jonny 4:29:57 (18,082)
Bowcott, Chris 4:11:37 (13,292)
Bowden, Andrew 5:16:16 (28,536)
Bowden, David A 3:15:18 (2,259)
Bowden, Jonathan P 5:13:35 (28,078)
Bowden, Nigel C 4:23:40 (16,355)
Bowden, Stuart 4:07:35 (12,252)
Bowen, Brett 4:02:06 (11,043)
Bowen, David A 3:25:14 (3,424)
Bowen, Gary B 4:35:43 (19,607)

Bowen, Jon V.......5:05:11 (26,589)
Bowen, Keith J.......3:22:38 (3,089)
Bowen, Michael C.......4:48:46 (22,915)
Bowen, Richard A.......5:22:58 (29,513)
Bowen, Rob A.......4:16:20 (14,482)
Bowen, Robert M.......3:59:09 (10,297)
Bowen, Thaddeus J.......4:41:10 (20,998)
Bowen-Jones, Craig A.......3:46:31 (7,091)
Bower, Andrew.......4:42:49 (21,412)
Bower, David P.......3:55:35 (9,183)
Bower, Michael L.......4:16:31 (14,525)
Bower, Robert W.......4:37:42 (20,090)
Bower, William.......3:59:35 (10,413)
Bowers, Andrew P.......3:43:55 (6,617)
Bowers, Clifford.......5:06:08 (26,752)
Bowes, Oliver.......5:47:14 (32,113)
Bowker, David.......3:52:43 (8,450)
Bowker, Richard H.......2:51:15 (500)
Bowkett, Andrew.......5:26:41 (30,013)
Bowkett, James W.......5:15:20 (28,390)
Bowkley, Michael.......4:20:06 (15,459)
Bowles, Matthew.......4:04:57 (11,645)
Bowles, Peter L.......3:25:54 (3,518)
Bowling, Gosia.......6:22:33 (34,128)
Bowman, Ian.......4:15:55 (14,369)
Bowman, John.......4:54:23 (24,307)
Bowman, Kevin S.......4:18:44 (15,088)
Bowman, Sam.......3:21:06 (2,900)
Bowman, Stephen J.......4:16:15 (14,458)
Bowring, Simon John.......3:43:00 (6,418)
Bowser, Richard J.......4:51:46 (23,692)
Bowyer, Barry W.......5:31:23 (30,563)
Bowyer, Gary A.......3:59:54 (10,515)
Bowyer, Malcolm J.......3:03:04 (1,175)
Bowyer, Paul R.......5:55:51 (32,752)
Bowyer, Simon W.......3:58:10 (9,996)
Box, Ashley P.......3:35:59 (5,152)
Box, Christopher J.......3:57:25 (9,746)
Box, Dan James.......3:41:26 (6,108)
Box, Nathan.......3:57:29 (9,762)
Box, Richard H.......4:36:22 (19,757)
Box, Timothy J.......4:52:27 (23,856)
Boxall, Colin.......3:38:41 (5,621)
Boxall, Daniel J.......5:17:19 (28,686)
Boxall, Mark.......4:38:14 (20,238)
Boxell, Neil A.......3:47:29 (7,285)
Boxhall, Richard J.......3:58:46 (10,179)
Boxley, Daniel J.......5:29:35 (30,347)
Boxley, Keith.......3:59:21 (10,351)
Boyall, Tim J.......3:36:54 (5,295)
Boyce, Benjamin.......5:07:26 (26,993)
Boyce, Christopher J.......5:12:49 (27,952)
Boyce, David.......4:38:09 (20,215)
Boyce, Ian.......4:13:18 (13,745)
Boyce, James.......3:56:42 (9,535)
Boyce, James A.......5:01:37 (25,936)
Boyce, James R.......4:04:51 (11,618)
Boyce, Matthew.......4:09:03 (12,631)
Boyd, Gareth John.......4:23:14 (16,238)
Boyd, Gareth W.......3:29:39 (4,124)
Boyd, Ian O.......6:34:51 (34,520)
Boyd, Len.......7:56:34 (35,306)
Boyd, Philip M.......4:53:43 (24,148)
Boyd, Scott.......5:00:57 (25,799)
Boyd, Stephen.......5:00:52 (25,779)
Boyd, Stephen P.......5:09:29 (27,360)
Boyd, Timothy.......3:51:23 (8,136)
Boyde, Martin R.......4:28:25 (17,676)
Boyde, Steven W.......4:02:59 (11,226)
Boyden, Mark P.......4:54:27 (24,326)
Boyer, Edward J.......4:30:40 (18,272)
Boyer, Guilhem.......3:48:59 (7,616)
Boyer, Jean-Louis.......3:26:52 (3,659)
Boyers, Andrew J.......4:04:38 (11,569)
Boyes, Ian.......3:53:53 (8,721)
Boyinapalli, Prithvi.......5:07:18 (26,960)
Boylan, James.......3:40:05 (5,875)
Boyle, Alan.......4:31:34 (18,518)
Boyle, David.......4:04:31 (11,550)
Boyle, David R.......4:06:49 (12,065)
Boyle, Graeme.......3:53:32 (8,630)
Boyle, James.......5:37:55 (31,263)
Boyle, James R.......3:12:45 (1,965)
Boyle, Jonathan.......5:30:24 (30,447)
Boyle, Matt J.......4:54:36 (24,360)
Boyle, Raymond.......3:56:26 (9,437)
Boyling, Samuel J.......3:17:03 (2,436)
Boyne, Chris S.......3:58:04 (9,958)
Bozman, Neale A.......6:27:08 (34,329)
Brabham, Paul C.......4:40:32 (20,843)
Bracey, Jonathan E.......3:42:04 (6,226)
Bracken, Carl J.......3:42:53 (6,395)
Bracken, Cathal.......3:55:03 (9,040)
Brackenbury, Steve.......4:55:55 (24,667)
Brackin, Philip.......3:49:08 (7,651)
Brackley, Mark.......5:02:26 (26,100)
Bradbrook, Johnny A.......5:36:12 (31,094)
Bradbrook, Simon C.......4:08:08 (12,403)
Bradbury, Alan K.......3:43:37 (6,548)
Bradbury, Alexis James.......3:26:01 (3,535)
Bradbury, Guy W.......4:00:37 (10,700)
Bradbury, Ian J.......3:51:39 (8,199)
Bradbury, Mark.......5:14:21 (28,214)
Bradbury, Michael.......4:25:30 (16,836)
Bradbury, Mike M.......4:21:25 (15,791)
Bradbury, Shaun P.......3:51:37 (8,191)
Bradbury, Tom E.......4:20:31 (15,563)
Braddon, Nicholas C.......4:08:54 (12,596)
Brades, Keith J.......5:07:39 (27,035)
Bradford, David.......2:43:26 (267)
Bradford, Paul S.......4:03:54 (11,423)
Bradley, Andrew.......5:46:58 (32,087)
Bradley, Barry.......3:50:54 (8,038)
Bradley, Ciaran P.......4:07:51 (12,326)
Bradley, Darren M.......4:58:12 (25,189)
Bradley, David.......4:06:52 (12,076)
Bradley, Eamon.......3:50:00 (7,833)
Bradley, Harvey.......4:05:42 (11,822)
Bradley, Ian.......4:40:19 (20,799)
Bradley, Ian.......5:04:32 (26,468)
Bradley, Jack.......4:38:17 (20,250)
Bradley, John.......3:51:24 (8,142)
Bradley, John T.......4:07:12 (12,152)
Bradley, Julian C.......3:49:26 (7,712)
Bradley, Mark D.......4:31:01 (18,352)
Bradley, Matthew.......5:26:52 (30,033)
Bradley, Matthew G.......4:58:42 (25,319)
Bradley, Michael.......5:51:05 (32,419)
Bradley, Neil J.......3:37:48 (5,459)
Bradley, Nigel T.......4:07:40 (12,274)
Bradley, Peter I.......4:09:26 (12,712)
Bradley, Philip P.......3:02:33 (1,152)
Bradley, Roger D.......5:07:12 (26,944)
Bradley, Thomas.......4:22:35 (16,096)
Bradley, William J.......4:14:15 (13,974)
Bradnam, Stephen E.......3:10:54 (1,771)
Bradney, Stuart J.......4:14:51 (14,128)
Bradshaw, Allan.......5:24:32 (29,739)
Bradshaw, Austin.......5:40:01 (31,498)
Bradshaw, Brian S.......5:29:47 (30,370)
Bradshaw, Eric G.......4:53:11 (24,020)
Bradshaw, Gary.......3:57:29 (9,762)
Bradshaw, Gary J.......4:30:49 (18,309)
Bradshaw, John.......4:13:53 (13,880)
Brady, Anthony.......4:25:22 (16,806)
Brady, John J.......4:37:26 (20,018)
Brady, Matthew P.......5:12:09 (27,834)
Brady, Michael J.......3:37:53 (5,469)
Brady, Shaun.......4:38:04 (20,189)
Braganza, Ricardo.......4:15:14 (14,220)
Bragg, Anthony.......4:35:01 (19,411)
Bragg, Matthew S.......3:00:23 (1,018)
Brahams, Nigel R.......4:10:48 (13,064)
Braharnyk, Rostyslav.......3:43:46 (6,580)
Braid, Richard.......3:27:09 (3,707)
Braidwood, Billy G.......3:29:38 (4,122)
Brain, Douglas H.......3:52:13 (8,335)
Brain, Robert A.......5:18:11 (28,815)
Brainch, Michael.......4:44:01 (21,725)
Braithwaite, Alex.......5:02:53 (26,195)
Braithwaite, Carl S.......3:38:00 (5,489)
Braithwaite, Mark.......4:19:04 (15,177)
Braley, Dave.......5:39:31 (31,450)
Braley, Mark P.......2:52:17 (534)
Brambles, Neil.......3:13:43 (2,091)
Brame, Paul F.......4:11:05 (13,133)
Brameld, Andrew J.......4:58:31 (25,274)
Bramwell, Donald J.......6:19:33 (34,017)
Bramwell, Nicholas C.......3:33:44 (4,710)
Brancato, Marco.......4:47:04 (22,501)
Brand, Douglas E.......4:39:29 (20,576)
Brand, Jon.......4:43:57 (21,703)
Brand, Matthew J.......3:29:04 (4,013)
Brand, Philip.......4:18:26 (15,009)
Brand, Roger J.......3:41:38 (6,134)
Brand, Tom.......3:41:39 (6,138)
Brandish, Stephen E.......4:40:24 (20,814)
Brangan, Adam.......4:11:40 (13,303)
Brangwin, Richard.......3:24:53 (3,388)
Brankin, Paul Nicholas.......4:37:49 (20,125)
Brannam, Glen D.......4:55:48 (24,640)
Brannigan, Malachy.......3:53:29 (8,621)
Brannigan, Niall S.......5:37:52 (31,258)
Branson, Damon.......5:02:11 (26,061)
Branston, Rob J.......3:47:43 (7,331)
Brant, John R.......4:43:09 (21,503)
Brant, Mark S.......4:55:08 (24,485)
Brant, Raymond P.......4:35:03 (19,425)
Branthwaite, Ian C.......3:43:56 (6,621)
Brar, Satwant Singh.......5:58:37 (32,967)
Brasch, Simon.......4:43:24 (21,575)
Brash, Adam N.......3:48:55 (7,599)
Brashier, Gary H.......4:26:36 (17,148)
Brasse, Frederic.......3:26:59 (3,680)
Brassington, Wayne.......3:29:04 (4,013)
Bratberg, Nils.......3:56:53 (9,592)
Braude, Jonathan H.......5:43:03 (31,777)
Braun, Scott.......4:41:10 (20,998)
Brauns, Simon R.......5:05:40 (26,671)
Brawn, Nick C.......3:59:38 (10,428)
Bray, Alan.......4:18:26 (15,009)
Bray, Jonathan.......4:13:45 (13,859)
Bray, Luke.......4:42:21 (21,283)
Bray, Ruth.......6:15:56 (33,842)
Bray, Simon T.......5:15:12 (28,353)
Bray, Steven L.......3:20:26 (2,817)
Bray, Wayne.......4:31:19 (18,445)
Bray, William R.......4:50:46 (23,437)
Braybrook, Colin A.......3:05:04 (1,307)
Brayshaw, Tony.......3:35:17 (5,008)
Brazier, Matthew R.......4:43:55 (21,694)
Brazier, Paul N.......4:18:47 (15,101)
Brazil, Simon A.......3:05:17 (1,322)
Breach, Darren P.......4:20:00 (15,428)
Breach, Hamish.......3:55:15 (9,099)
Breaker, Ben.......3:29:44 (4,143)
Breakspear, Kevin N.......4:05:53 (11,858)
Breakspear, Nick.......5:07:36 (27,024)
Brear, Stephen E.......4:50:02 (23,244)
Brearey, Vincent I.......5:09:16 (27,321)
Brearley, Kenneth R.......4:31:49 (18,588)
Brearley, Mark.......5:30:53 (30,506)
Brearley, Michael.......2:54:16 (614)
Brecht, Philip T.......4:14:49 (14,116)
Brede, Riley.......6:21:07 (34,079)
Bredenschey, Gert.......4:52:00 (23,750)
Breen, Derek.......2:59:56 (993)
Breen, Graham J.......2:32:56 (91)
Breen, John.......5:03:04 (26,219)
Breese, Ian C.......4:32:23 (18,723)
Brehmer, Reiner.......4:43:37 (21,628)
Bremnar, Jonathan M.......4:45:14 (22,022)
Bremner, Thomas.......4:26:24 (17,088)
Bremnes, Jonfinn.......3:47:13 (7,236)
Brennan, Aaron.......5:41:41 (31,646)
Brennan, Christopher M.......4:52:47 (23,923)
Brennan, Daire J.......2:53:25 (581)
Brennan, David.......5:48:34 (32,225)
Brennan, Ian H.......5:48:35 (32,226)
Brennan, Lee J.......3:57:21 (9,729)
Brennan, Mark.......5:30:07 (30,417)
Brennan, Michael O.......3:38:23 (5,560)
Brennan, Mike.......3:59:00 (10,250)
Brennan, Peter G.......7:32:02 (35,234)
Brennan, Richard D.......3:36:19 (5,208)
Brennand, Steven K.......4:07:04 (12,124)
Brent, Michael J.......5:42:06 (31,680)
Brequeville, David.......4:05:38 (11,812)
Bresland, Noel P.......4:03:31 (11,340)

Breslin, David T....4:27:36 (17,412)
Breslin, Peter G....4:40:36 (20,860)
Bresnahan, Mark....4:28:47 (17,769)
Bresnan, Steve....4:10:28 (12,973)
Brett, Alison....4:48:42 (22,902)
Brett, Andrew J....3:52:58 (8,498)
Brett, Mark R....4:45:31 (22,085)
Brett, Michael P....4:56:52 (24,902)
Brett, Stephen....3:04:41 (1,277)
Brettell, Neil D....4:32:43 (18,819)
Breure, Gerardus....4:55:02 (24,455)
Brew, Patrick....3:33:53 (4,736)
Brewer, Andy....3:58:18 (10,033)
Brewer, John....4:32:25 (18,735)
Brewer, John....4:45:48 (22,155)
Brewer, Lyndon D....4:06:47 (12,056)
Brewer, Timothy R....3:55:43 (9,232)
Breydin, Patrick J....5:25:32 (29,866)
Breyne, Dimitri N....5:39:03 (31,402)
Briant, Russell S....4:31:26 (18,484)
Briars, Paul....3:56:36 (9,489)
Brice, Nicholas....7:16:35 (35,116)
Bridge, John D....3:17:17 (2,463)
Bridge, Nigel....5:40:02 (31,500)
Bridge, Paul....5:29:57 (30,395)
Bridge, Tom S....4:13:14 (13,724)
Bridgeland, Michael J....2:46:10 (335)
Bridgens, John M....4:54:11 (24,255)
Bridger, Andrew L....4:01:57 (11,011)
Bridger, Gary S....4:14:13 (13,964)
Bridger, Robert W....5:16:39 (28,587)
Bridges, Alex....3:49:01 (7,622)
Bridges, Donald J....4:36:05 (19,698)
Bridges, Edward Bridges W....3:57:33 (9,789)
Bridges, Gareth M....4:01:54 (11,003)
Bridges, James....6:33:37 (34,487)
Bridges, Mark....3:06:22 (1,400)
Bridges, Paul T....4:24:57 (16,698)
Bridgman, Lewis....3:51:28 (8,159)
Bridgman, William T....3:05:30 (1,336)
Bridgwater, Chris....6:03:20 (33,250)
Brien, Patrick H....4:20:52 (15,653)
Brierley, Andrew S....2:43:30 (270)
Briggs, Andrew R....4:05:35 (11,794)
Briggs, Daniel P....4:12:08 (13,421)
Briggs, David R....5:33:55 (30,855)
Briggs, Dennis J....5:06:44 (26,853)
Briggs, Gareth....2:40:27 (204)
Briggs, Guy A....4:05:07 (11,685)
Briggs, James L....4:53:57 (24,211)
Briggs, Jonathan K....4:22:48 (16,140)
Briggs, Martin P....4:49:55 (23,221)
Briggs, Michael....3:22:02 (3,017)
Briggs, Thomas M....4:09:07 (12,644)
Brigham, Josh....4:01:26 (10,893)
Brigham, Michael J....3:55:57 (9,297)
Bright, Andy....4:23:00 (16,184)
Bright, Jason....3:47:48 (7,351)
Bright, Jonty....3:11:52 (1,871)
Bright, Neil A....5:22:45 (29,474)
Bright, Simon....4:59:43 (25,538)
Brightling, Michael J....5:38:11 (31,296)
Brighton, David C....4:43:59 (21,715)
Brighton, James....5:44:43 (31,908)
Brighton, Mark....3:09:37 (1,669)
Bril, Martinus....4:23:22 (16,268)
Brimicombe, Leigh D....4:20:12 (15,484)
Brims, Edward T....4:17:12 (14,693)
Brinded, Tom J....3:59:12 (10,310)
Brindle, David John....3:47:06 (7,213)
Brindley, Martin J....4:42:52 (21,431)
Brindley, Paul W....3:38:13 (5,537)
Brindley, Robert P....4:40:21 (20,806)
Brindley, Roger....5:19:23 (29,022)
Brine, Martin R....3:19:44 (2,716)
Brine, Tony A....7:10:28 (35,055)
Bringloe, James B....2:57:00 (773)
Brinin, Mark A....4:33:45 (19,086)
Brinkley, Paul A....5:08:54 (27,253)
Brinkley, Robert M....4:05:57 (11,870)
Brinklow, James M....4:25:54 (16,961)
Briozzo, Mirko G....5:05:34 (26,653)
Brisbane, Mark D....4:57:30 (25,029)
Brisco, Douglas A....2:59:21 (947)
Briscoe, Matthew J....6:07:49 (33,476)
Briscombe, Stephen P....4:22:51 (16,156)
Brislen, Christopher....4:38:45 (20,365)
Brisley, Christopher N....3:50:19 (7,907)
Bristow, Andrew T....5:08:11 (27,123)
Bristow, John P....5:26:17 (29,964)
Bristow, Jonathan P....4:37:47 (20,115)
Bristow, Martin J....4:35:40 (19,587)
Bristow, Nick....4:47:53 (22,701)
Bristowe, Graham R....4:34:10 (19,187)
Britnell, Adrian R....3:43:09 (6,457)
Brito Pereira, Jorge....3:42:57 (6,409)
Britschgi, Daniel....4:04:43 (11,590)
Britt, Anthony....5:17:15 (28,681)
Brittain, Paul....3:38:24 (5,566)
Brittain, Richard D....3:29:36 (4,116)
Britten, Daniel....3:38:45 (5,637)
Britten, Jake C....3:38:44 (5,630)
Britten, Kit John....4:53:01 (23,979)
Britton, Gary....3:53:42 (8,677)
Britton, Philip L....4:57:39 (25,060)
Britton, Shaun A....4:11:39 (13,300)
Britton, Stephen....4:01:39 (10,956)
Britton-Hall, Stephen J....3:34:08 (4,796)
Broad, Chris....5:39:01 (31,398)
Broad, John....4:45:12 (22,014)
Broadbent, Alexander B....3:45:48 (6,948)
Broadbent, Allan....4:01:58 (11,014)
Broadbent, Chris J....3:47:39 (7,318)
Broadbent, David....3:57:22 (9,736)
Broadbent, David J....4:36:32 (19,801)
Broadbent, Richard J....5:17:25 (28,700)
Broadbent, Steven Scott....3:42:29 (6,295)
Broadhead, Ian....4:48:17 (22,804)
Broadhurst, Colin....6:02:40 (33,207)
Broadhurst, Daniel J....4:43:51 (21,678)
Broadhurst, Henry S....4:39:22 (20,536)
Broadhurst, Thomas....2:58:57 (914)
Broadley, David C....3:02:44 (1,162)
Broadley, Duncan K....3:47:21 (7,257)
Broadley, Kenneth....5:00:26 (25,688)
Broadley, Thomas W....4:36:12 (19,726)
Broadribb, William....4:13:56 (13,891)
Broccoli, Marco....3:14:20 (2,157)
Brockett, Martin A....4:23:30 (16,314)
Brockington, Martin J....5:37:38 (31,241)
Brocklebank, Adam J....4:52:38 (23,887)
Brocklebank, Ian P....3:03:14 (1,183)
Brocklebank, Scott M....5:04:20 (26,430)
Brocklehurst, Aaron....4:14:08 (13,941)
Brocklehurst, Robert....3:58:01 (9,941)
Brocklesby, Keith A....4:21:05 (15,710)
Brocklesby, Mathew....4:13:17 (13,742)
Brocklesby, Robert....4:31:28 (18,494)
Brockley, Mark W....4:27:57 (17,528)
Broder, James N....6:26:59 (34,320)
Broderick, Derek....5:39:10 (31,417)
Brodie, Andrew D....5:12:42 (27,926)
Brodrick, Michael John....4:15:17 (14,231)
Broekhof, Joop....4:09:30 (12,719)
Broendum Lund Jensen, Thomas.3:31:51 (4,448)
Broer, Wout....4:14:49 (14,116)
Brogan, Michael....3:39:28 (5,752)
Brolly, Martin D....4:12:12 (13,439)
Bromige, Robert M....3:20:05 (2,766)
Bromiley, Neil M....4:14:40 (14,067)
Bromley, Karl L....6:28:56 (34,381)
Bromley, Nigel....4:24:59 (16,706)
Bromley, Paul A....5:54:01 (32,615)
Brook, Andy....4:27:24 (17,368)
Brook, Ashley....3:18:11 (2,546)
Brook, Martin....3:22:47 (3,106)
Brook, Matthew J....4:54:16 (24,279)
Brook, Michael A....4:06:55 (12,084)
Brook, Roland S....4:08:18 (12,454)
Brook, Thomas....4:42:03 (21,212)
Brooke, Anthony C....3:52:00 (8,277)
Brooke, David....4:29:51 (18,056)
Brooker, James D....4:27:37 (17,417)
Brooker, Kevin....5:13:03 (27,995)
Brooker, Matthew J....4:11:34 (13,273)
Brookes, Jamie W....4:21:41 (15,876)
Brookes, Paul....3:34:27 (4,867)
Brookes, Steven....4:38:36 (20,330)
Brookman, Chris J....3:51:01 (8,058)
Brookmyre, John M....4:54:57 (24,437)
Brooks, Adam....3:52:49 (8,471)
Brooks, Alex....2:34:22 (103)
Brooks, Andrew J....4:07:13 (12,155)
Brooks, Andrew P....4:06:49 (12,065)
Brooks, Anthony....5:41:58 (31,667)
Brooks, Cameron M....2:28:53 (57)
Brooks, Charles V....5:41:26 (31,628)
Brooks, Charlie G....3:46:57 (7,191)
Brooks, Christopher....4:19:41 (15,333)
Brooks, Christopher A....4:41:21 (21,048)
Brooks, Danny L....4:28:00 (17,542)
Brooks, David....5:39:11 (31,418)
Brooks, David....6:13:39 (33,728)
Brooks, Duncan G....5:19:17 (29,004)
Brooks, John W....4:34:40 (19,307)
Brooks, Julian G....5:37:34 (31,237)
Brooks, Lee....3:59:45 (10,477)
Brooks, Michael J....4:21:32 (15,824)
Brooks, Neil R....4:35:21 (19,506)
Brooks, Nigel....3:57:20 (9,721)
Brooks, Paul....3:57:51 (9,896)
Brooks, Peter J....5:16:42 (28,600)
Brooks, Richard A....4:24:13 (16,504)
Brooks, Richard D....4:17:22 (14,736)
Brooks, Ryan G....4:07:45 (12,302)
Brooks, Sabin....3:11:16 (1,805)
Brooks, Sam....4:23:35 (16,333)
Brooks, Simon....4:10:39 (13,019)
Brooks, Tim C....3:16:10 (2,348)
Brooks, Tom J....3:43:23 (6,505)
Brooks, Tommy....5:19:18 (29,006)
Brooks, Victor K....3:51:23 (8,136)
Brookshaw, Ben I....3:25:53 (3,515)
Broom, Peter....3:58:05 (9,963)
Broom, Richard....4:38:07 (20,204)
Broom, Shaun T....5:01:59 (26,014)
Broom, Tim J....5:03:39 (26,315)
Broome, Clive....5:49:12 (32,267)
Broomfield, Mark T....4:22:42 (16,127)
Brosnan, Patrick W....3:21:44 (2,976)
Brostroem, Leif....4:01:20 (10,868)
Brough, John J....5:33:19 (30,790)
Brough, Jon R....3:15:54 (2,326)
Brough, Steven R....5:29:29 (30,328)
Broughton, Stephen P....4:00:47 (10,741)
Brouillard, Raymond....3:58:23 (10,065)
Brown, Adrian P....3:55:42 (9,221)
Brown, Alan....4:02:21 (11,091)
Brown, Alan G....4:41:39 (21,132)
Brown, Alastair M....4:07:30 (12,236)
Brown, Andrew....3:34:50 (4,934)
Brown, Andrew....4:03:10 (11,266)
Brown, Andrew....5:49:34 (32,295)
Brown, Andrew B....4:34:52 (19,371)
Brown, Andrew J....4:20:39 (15,587)
Brown, Andrew M....3:13:20 (2,039)
Brown, Andrew N....5:26:39 (30,010)
Brown, Andy....3:44:29 (6,717)
Brown, Anthony....3:36:56 (5,307)
Brown, Antony W....4:50:26 (23,350)
Brown, Benjamin J....4:22:02 (15,950)
Brown, Buster....5:27:00 (30,052)
Brown, Charles Duncan D....3:31:22 (4,378)
Brown, Charles E....6:13:32 (33,724)
Brown, Charlie....5:33:17 (30,785)
Brown, Chris B....4:36:00 (19,683)
Brown, Christopher I....4:13:14 (13,724)
Brown, Christopher S....3:59:29 (10,384)
Brown, Daniel R....6:18:40 (33,952)
Brown, Dave....4:29:58 (18,088)
Brown, David....5:17:39 (28,738)
Brown, David....5:25:31 (29,860)
Brown, David....7:30:19 (35,220)
Brown, David J....4:19:54 (15,400)
Brown, David J....4:27:31 (17,395)
Brown, Derek....2:36:25 (131)
Brown, Derek....4:34:38 (19,296)
Brown, Dominic Z....3:48:08 (7,425)
Brown, Duncan J....4:19:17 (15,231)

Brown, Edward B 5:04:22 (26,438)
Brown, Edward O............4:12:30 (13,526)
Brown, Elliot C............4:03:33 (11,348)
Brown, Francis H 4:37:46 (20,111)
Brown, Gavin............3:23:03 (3,131)
Brown, Graham P............5:30:40 (30,484)
Brown, Greg A............4:15:16 (14,226)
Brown, Iain 4:26:28 (17,104)
Brown, Iain P............5:09:00 (27,274)
Brown, Ian 4:32:14 (18,689)
Brown, James A 5:36:19 (31,103)
Brown, James D 4:28:48 (17,776)
Brown, James D 5:17:03 (28,647)
Brown, James H............3:17:39 (2,496)
Brown, James L 5:25:48 (29,905)
Brown, James M 3:07:28 (1,477)
Brown, James R 3:46:14 (7,025)
Brown, James R 5:25:41 (29,887)
Brown, Jason............5:44:28 (31,889)
Brown, John A............6:25:04 (34,232)
Brown, John J 3:34:53 (4,939)
Brown, John W 5:22:15 (29,397)
Brown, Justin L............5:22:16 (29,402)
Brown, Justin S 4:32:42 (18,817)
Brown, Keith Alan............3:24:05 (3,277)
Brown, Kelvin David 3:57:39 (9,826)
Brown, Kevin............3:28:20 (3,907)
Brown, Kevin A............5:19:29 (29,035)
Brown, Kevin G 3:02:08 (1,129)
Brown, Kevin Paul............3:51:42 (8,208)
Brown, Lee 4:17:08 (14,677)
Brown, Lee D............6:04:47 (33,324)
Brown, Mark............3:56:26 (9,437)
Brown, Mark A 4:06:35 (12,014)
Brown, Mark D 4:47:38 (22,639)
Brown, Martin T............3:47:51 (7,361)
Brown, Matthew 4:22:02 (15,950)
Brown, Matthew G 4:37:57 (20,155)
Brown, Matthew P............4:05:01 (11,655)
Brown, Michael J 3:03:09 (1,180)
Brown, Mike Richard............3:45:57 (6,977)
Brown, Miles E 4:17:19 (14,725)
Brown, Neil A............4:52:44 (23,912)
Brown, Nicholas L............3:31:50 (4,445)
Brown, Nicholas P............4:41:06 (20,988)
Brown, Patrick V 5:18:27 (28,863)
Brown, Patrick W 5:09:08 (27,295)
Brown, Paul 5:18:40 (28,910)
Brown, Paul A............5:48:29 (32,214)
Brown, Paul J............3:43:24 (6,510)
Brown, Paul John 5:42:20 (31,705)
Brown, Paul M............5:04:48 (26,506)
Brown, Paul N 3:47:39 (7,318)
Brown, Paul N 4:13:34 (13,813)
Brown, Peter............5:11:09 (27,663)
Brown, Peter A 3:50:16 (7,898)
Brown, Peter J 4:54:17 (24,284)
Brown, Peter M 5:10:23 (27,528)
Brown, Peter M 5:12:27 (27,881)
Brown, Phil D............4:44:41 (21,885)
Brown, Philip............5:34:16 (30,886)
Brown, Philip G............5:12:10 (27,838)
Brown, Ray............4:11:57 (13,374)
Brown, Raymond P 4:17:02 (14,654)
Brown, Richard E............5:10:57 (27,633)
Brown, Richard J 3:29:52 (4,162)
Brown, Richard M............4:26:10 (17,031)
Brown, Robert............3:22:26 (3,058)
Brown, Robert............4:27:35 (17,409)
Brown, Robert............4:51:38 (23,655)
Brown, Robert H 4:35:21 (19,506)
Brown, Robert N 3:22:28 (3,063)
Brown, Roger J 4:56:05 (24,700)
Brown, Russell............4:17:42 (14,819)
Brown, Sean M 4:03:10 (11,266)
Brown, Simon............5:27:28 (30,089)
Brown, Stephen............6:57:49 (34,928)
Brown, Stuart............4:01:33 (10,931)
Brown, Stuart Charles............3:25:49 (3,504)
Brown, Stuart J 4:30:51 (18,318)
Brown, Thomas William 3:14:43 (2,201)
Brown, Tim M 4:39:22 (20,536)
Brown, Tim P 3:23:49 (3,239)
Browne, Anthony J............3:51:21 (8,128)
Browne, Arthur 5:07:29 (27,005)
Browne, Brendan C 4:06:57 (12,094)
Browne, Chris A 4:05:05 (11,675)
Browne, Edward............4:11:57 (13,374)
Browne, Jason............4:51:59 (23,748)
Browne, Liam C 3:28:40 (3,948)
Browne, Martin L............6:18:40 (33,952)
Browne, Mathew J 3:11:26 (1,817)
Browne, Nathan J............4:43:06 (21,493)
Browne, Patrick J............3:57:23 (9,742)
Browne, Robert J............3:57:57 (9,917)
Browne, Robert Timothy............4:48:49 (22,922)
Brownhill, Alison............3:10:49 (1,761)
Browning, Andrew 4:57:37 (25,056)
Browning, David W 4:33:04 (18,915)
Brownlee, Daniel P 4:19:29 (15,277)
Brownlee, Simon J............2:38:43 (169)
Brownless, Stephen A 6:09:14 (33,523)
Brownlie, Francis............4:04:51 (11,618)
Brownlie, John A............4:10:21 (12,944)
Brownlow-Smith, Lucy A............6:18:00 (33,925)
Bruce, Adrian L............6:13:09 (33,703)
Bruce, Andrew K............3:54:53 (8,992)
Bruce, Charles D 2:46:54 (365)
Bruce, Chris............3:47:07 (7,217)
Bruce, Richard J 3:44:35 (6,729)
Bruce, Sam A............2:56:29 (746)
Bruce, Sandy............4:49:09 (23,004)
Bruce, Simon J 5:00:31 (25,703)
Bruce, Stephen............4:33:10 (18,932)
Bruce-Smith, Adam R 4:12:45 (13,593)
Brudenell, Ryan J 3:29:27 (4,095)
Bruessow, Gerfried............5:16:34 (28,573)
Bruinsma, Rob............3:48:09 (7,433)
Brumby, Ged............4:55:12 (24,506)
Brumby, Ian R 4:48:05 (22,759)
Brummitt-Brown, Angus............4:44:57 (21,945)
Brumpton, Martyn 3:43:53 (6,611)
Bruneau, Dominic E 3:33:43 (4,706)
Brunjes, Andrew John McCormack 3:46:06 (7,003)
Brunner, Thomas M............3:32:15 (4,510)
Brunning, Peter E 4:15:32 (14,291)
Bruno, Alan C 3:52:43 (8,450)
Bruno, Carlo J 5:27:49 (30,127)
Brunt, James............5:48:28 (32,213)
Brunt, Jamie 5:33:18 (30,788)
Brunton, Ian A 5:56:32 (32,793)
Brunton, Terry 4:50:19 (23,321)
Brunyee, Jonathan S 3:51:15 (8,108)
Bruun, Kim Bye............3:48:10 (7,438)
Bruun, Yngve Bye............3:56:49 (9,573)
Bruun-Jensen, Jacob 3:56:19 (9,399)
Bryan, Adrian 3:19:19 (2,657)
Bryan, Dave 4:19:36 (15,313)
Bryan, Luke 4:26:29 (17,111)
Bryan, Philip E 4:44:37 (21,861)
Bryan, Richard T............5:05:08 (26,575)
Bryans, Christopher E............5:20:46 (29,187)
Bryant, Adam L 3:50:26 (7,929)
Bryant, Ben L 4:35:02 (19,419)
Bryant, Chris............3:50:09 (7,872)
Bryant, Daniel 4:35:45 (19,617)
Bryant, Edmund B 3:35:27 (5,040)
Bryant, James M 3:35:10 (4,990)
Bryant, Jason 5:05:37 (26,662)
Bryant, John W............5:22:04 (29,371)
Bryant, Kevin I............7:33:41 (35,243)
Bryant, Mark............3:53:01 (8,510)
Bryant, Peter R............3:43:51 (6,604)
Bryant, Simon D............3:47:31 (7,292)
Bryars, Richard............3:33:10 (4,633)
Bryce, David A 3:34:52 (4,936)
Bryce, Ian............5:11:19 (27,695)
Brydon, Derrick W............3:15:09 (2,249)
Bryning, John P............3:27:44 (3,816)
Bryson, Kenneth M 3:14:03 (2,130)
Bryson, Thomas E 5:33:09 (30,768)
Bubb, Nick J 5:00:33 (25,717)
Buchan, Andrew............3:03:51 (1,229)
Buchan, Helen L............5:02:14 (26,068)
Buchanan, Andrew 3:25:29 (3,456)
Buchanan, Andrew G............5:34:07 (30,869)
Buchanan, Geoff M............3:43:11 (6,469)
Buchanan, Jason C............4:17:57 (14,872)
Buchanan-Dunne, Michael J 4:29:57 (18,082)
Buchbauer, Michael 3:21:21 (2,927)
Bucheli, Michael 3:10:49 (1,761)
Buck, Jethro............3:29:01 (4,010)
Buck, Martin D............3:23:50 (3,242)
Buck, Oliver............5:06:03 (26,734)
Buckby, Mark............4:38:01 (20,170)
Buckee, John 5:30:39 (30,480)
Buckell, Adam J............5:04:29 (26,452)
Buckett, Andrew............3:52:54 (8,487)
Buckett, Chris J 4:44:20 (21,801)
Buckett, Daniel C............5:42:21 (31,708)
Buckey, Michael W............4:19:30 (15,287)
Buckingham, Peter J 3:20:44 (2,859)
Buckingham, Richard............3:10:00 (1,706)
Buckle, Dan J............3:58:00 (9,931)
Buckle, Darren H............4:56:55 (24,917)
Buckle, Jim 3:34:20 (4,839)
Buckler, Dean R 4:45:21 (22,045)
Buckley, Anthony R............3:13:43 (2,091)
Buckley, Colin............5:28:18 (30,189)
Buckley, Matthew 5:29:06 (30,284)
Buckley, Paul D............3:33:05 (4,622)
Buckley, Sean P 4:36:08 (19,707)
Buckley, Timothy A............3:39:20 (5,734)
Buckley, Timothy A............5:09:44 (27,412)
Buckley, William T 4:47:51 (22,689)
Bucknell, Ian R............4:34:10 (19,187)
Buckton, Stephen 4:30:04 (18,116)
Buckwell, Jonathan M............4:35:06 (19,439)
Budd, Matt J 4:42:04 (21,215)
Budd, Robert A 3:59:09 (10,297)
Budd, Tim T............3:46:16 (7,032)
Buddenhagen, Volker............4:02:45 (11,178)
Budge, Grant............4:54:48 (24,408)
Budge, Jonathan L............3:21:33 (2,953)
Budworth, Martin............3:58:31 (10,107)
Buehn, Klaus 3:34:58 (4,954)
Buenger, Jens-Uwe 3:36:33 (5,245)
Bugajny, Pawel............4:28:51 (17,795)
Bugby, Antony R............5:41:42 (31,648)
Buglass, Tom............6:59:23 (34,941)
Buick, Jim 2:59:38 (969)
Buick, Tim M............3:57:15 (9,690)
Buisson, Phlippe 4:18:03 (14,905)
Bulbarella, Elio Victor 4:34:47 (19,348)
Bulbulia-McLean, Shawn P............4:47:58 (22,728)
Bull, Andrew............3:54:15 (8,828)
Bull, Andrew C 5:06:07 (26,749)
Bull, David I............4:12:46 (13,596)
Bull, Geoffrey S 4:49:58 (23,234)
Bull, John R............3:50:54 (8,038)
Bull, Martyn G............7:25:11 (35,180)
Bull, Peter B 4:04:29 (11,541)
Bull, Ross 8:26:17 (35,337)
Bullamore, Andrew............4:59:33 (25,508)
Bullen, Colin R............3:58:10 (9,996)
Bullen, Nigel C............3:49:56 (7,818)
Bullen, Paul A............4:27:22 (17,358)
Bulley, David A 3:14:42 (2,197)
Bullivant, Paul A............4:06:32 (11,997)
Bullo, Daniele............3:53:34 (8,640)
Bulloch, Jason R............4:31:57 (18,623)
Bullock, Alastair R............4:07:52 (12,331)
Bullock, Darren J 4:56:01 (24,682)
Bullock, David J 4:01:56 (11,006)
Bullock, Guy S............4:58:02 (25,147)
Bullock, Iain M............5:00:19 (25,658)
Bullock, Mike 3:24:03 (3,270)
Bullock, Paul D............5:17:26 (28,708)
Bullock, Peter K 5:37:29 (31,222)
Bullock, Steve 5:59:54 (33,044)
Bulmer, Craig A............3:46:28 (7,081)
Bulmer, Peter Grant............4:13:10 (13,700)
Bulmer, Richard 4:12:08 (13,421)
Bulmer, Tim 3:54:06 (8,781)
Bumpstead, Leon 4:43:14 (21,524)
Bunce, Craig............3:59:17 (10,331)
Bunce, Gerald 3:41:58 (6,197)
Bunce, Nicholas H 4:03:15 (11,282)
Bunce, Stephen A 6:14:28 (33,765)

Bunch, Trevor I	3:12:38 (1,948)	
Bundey, Paul	3:42:43 (6,359)	
Bundy, Terry J	4:56:14 (24,737)	
Bungay, Alan	5:32:04 (30,648)	
Bunn, Daniel	4:49:41 (23,176)	
Bunn, Westley	4:59:45 (25,544)	
Bunner, Colin	3:39:03 (5,697)	
Bunney, Allen	3:58:59 (10,248)	
Bunning, Dean	5:10:52 (27,616)	
Bunten, Andrew	4:08:03 (12,374)	
Bunting, Colin	3:27:34 (3,796)	
Bunting, Naz J	3:49:10 (7,660)	
Bunting, Simon J	4:44:58 (21,948)	
Bunton, Neil	4:22:39 (16,111)	
Bunyard, Simon	4:31:17 (18,429)	
Buono, Richard	3:46:51 (7,167)	
Burbidge, Edward	4:11:50 (13,343)	
Burbridge, Paul	7:19:44 (35,147)	
Burchett, Gary P	3:37:50 (5,462)	
Burchett, James E	4:18:24 (14,995)	
Burchett, Rainer H	4:06:40 (12,037)	
Burchnall, Adam D	4:24:03 (16,453)	
Burden, Glenn	3:44:17 (6,680)	
Burden, Phil G	4:12:39 (13,560)	
Burdett, Dan	4:14:45 (14,096)	
Burdett, Simon L	4:52:37 (23,883)	
Burdin, Ian	3:33:23 (4,663)	
Burdon, David J	3:40:28 (5,937)	
Burdsey, Tim	4:30:50 (18,312)	
Burfoot, Mark J	4:28:03 (17,557)	
Burford, Bruce Warren	4:06:44 (12,048)	
Burford, Lawrence C	5:32:08 (30,654)	
Burford, Peter D	3:29:42 (4,135)	
Burge, Raymond L	5:07:25 (26,988)	
Burge, Robert C	4:24:30 (16,569)	
Burger, Primarius	3:49:02 (7,627)	
Burgess, Andrew R	4:29:07 (17,865)	
Burgess, David	2:49:12 (430)	
Burgess, Henry H	5:13:42 (28,099)	
Burgess, John	3:57:02 (9,628)	
Burgess, John	3:58:28 (10,090)	
Burgess, John Alun	3:27:05 (3,695)	
Burgess, John F	4:04:38 (11,569)	
Burgess, Keith J	3:35:30 (5,047)	
Burgess, Michael J	4:37:35 (20,065)	
Burgess, Richard Michael	3:52:35 (8,420)	
Burgess, Stuart L	4:19:38 (15,323)	
Burgin, Neil D	4:12:56 (13,643)	
Burgos Lopez, Luis	4:12:25 (13,494)	
Burgoyne, Chris	2:54:53 (655)	
Burgoyne, Robert S	4:15:23 (14,251)	
Burin, Christopher A	4:45:21 (22,045)	
Burke, Adam J	3:31:42 (4,422)	
Burke, Aiden L	3:40:59 (6,026)	
Burke, Alastair	4:30:19 (18,185)	
Burke, Andrew S	5:03:00 (26,210)	
Burke, Anthony P	4:03:48 (11,393)	
Burke, David	4:40:57 (20,953)	
Burke, David A	3:48:04 (7,419)	
Burke, Desmond A	4:57:16 (24,978)	
Burke, Iain A	3:41:11 (6,067)	
Burke, James M	5:35:56 (31,066)	
Burke, Neil	3:32:06 (4,484)	
Burke, Nicholas S	4:12:28 (13,512)	
Burke, Paul M	3:29:54 (4,167)	
Burke, Peter D	3:00:04 (1,002)	
Burke, Robert	3:55:35 (9,183)	
Burke, Robert	5:24:50 (29,772)	
Burke, Terry	4:15:23 (14,251)	
Burkhalter, Beat	3:38:54 (5,654)	
Burkhill, Graeme	5:32:27 (30,680)	
Burkitt, Henry W	4:00:54 (10,776)	
Burleigh, Philip J	4:02:47 (11,186)	
Burleton, Ian S	6:01:22 (33,133)	
Burlingham, Dave L	4:39:30 (20,584)	
Burlingham, Richard	5:01:29 (25,910)	
Burman, Darren M	5:49:05 (32,257)	
Burne, David M	3:42:38 (6,341)	
Burne, Rick	4:35:22 (19,514)	
Burnett, Christopher	4:30:44 (18,292)	
Burnett, Michael A	4:43:31 (21,665)	
Burnett, Richard H	4:40:20 (20,802)	
Burnham, Darrell R	4:38:54 (20,409)	
Burningham, Leo J	3:21:59 (3,012)	
Burns, Andrew M	4:37:16 (19,978)	
Burns, Ben G	4:25:03 (16,726)	
Burns, Craig D	3:54:51 (8,986)	
Burns, Daniel	3:42:52 (6,391)	
Burns, Francis	5:40:49 (31,571)	
Burns, Graham S	5:55:08 (32,697)	
Burns, Iain J	4:17:34 (14,787)	
Burns, James	4:12:55 (13,635)	
Burns, John	5:33:18 (30,788)	
Burns, John P	4:45:16 (22,031)	
Burns, John S	3:29:33 (4,108)	
Burns, Matthew R	4:08:20 (12,464)	
Burns, Michael L	3:39:26 (5,749)	
Burns, Paul R	4:59:57 (25,587)	
Burns, Peter F	3:34:26 (4,862)	
Burns, Rawson N	4:43:42 (21,649)	
Burns, Thomas L	4:13:41 (13,842)	
Burnside, William A	3:47:29 (7,285)	
Burow, Stephan	4:38:02 (20,174)	
Burr, Martin	3:23:23 (3,174)	
Burr, Matthew J	4:59:55 (25,581)	
Burr, Paul D	4:06:34 (12,010)	
Burrage, Peter	5:25:03 (29,804)	
Burrell, Chris L	4:30:10 (18,142)	
Burrell, Jason	5:42:30 (31,728)	
Burrell, Mark	5:08:10 (27,119)	
Burrill, Ben	4:14:05 (13,925)	
Burrill, Ed W	3:35:44 (5,104)	
Burrow, Craig P	3:19:52 (2,733)	
Burrowes, Robin	3:59:47 (10,488)	
Burrows, Anthony C	3:12:12 (1,901)	
Burrows, Craig M	4:01:38 (10,951)	
Burrows, Geoff C	5:09:23 (27,345)	
Burrows, Karen J	4:40:37 (20,865)	
Burrows, Nicholas K	5:09:15 (27,316)	
Burrows, Paul S	3:55:26 (9,139)	
Burt, Alan M	4:06:31 (11,994)	
Burt, Jon G	4:58:06 (25,162)	
Burt, Matt	6:00:45 (33,095)	
Burt, Nick	3:16:40 (2,403)	
Burt, Peter E	4:24:46 (16,646)	
Burtenshaw, Martin	4:03:50 (11,403)	
Burtness, Peter	5:05:10 (26,585)	
Burton, Alexander	3:30:24 (4,237)	
Burton, Alistair J	3:55:45 (9,243)	
Burton, Andrew	4:22:09 (15,989)	
Burton, Chris J	3:11:33 (1,834)	
Burton, Chris R	6:15:33 (33,816)	
Burton, Craig B	5:55:20 (32,711)	
Burton, David	4:42:10 (21,239)	
Burton, David J	5:00:33 (25,717)	
Burton, George	4:28:24 (17,670)	
Burton, Joseph J	4:48:22 (22,819)	
Burton, Kenny	5:00:34 (25,721)	
Burton, Mike	4:51:01 (23,494)	
Burton, Ollie P	4:59:21 (25,464)	
Burton, Phil	4:53:07 (24,004)	
Burton, Robert J	2:43:33 (274)	
Burton, Roland	4:12:33 (13,538)	
Burton, Terence C	6:25:30 (34,255)	
Burton, Tony L	4:42:37 (21,366)	
Burtonshaw, David	5:28:22 (30,197)	
Burtt, William R	5:41:19 (31,611)	
Burtwell, Mark C	3:10:54 (1,771)	
Burville, Ryan M	5:21:47 (29,339)	
Bury, Robert D	4:32:44 (18,826)	
Busby, Khan	4:50:35 (23,392)	
Busby, Steve Rowland	3:57:19 (9,712)	
Buscall Terrones, Pilar	7:07:17 (35,030)	
Busch, Graham	3:34:23 (4,850)	
Buscke, Graeme C	2:57:00 (773)	
Busetto, Sergio	4:11:06 (13,139)	
Bush, David W	4:15:06 (14,190)	
Bush, John L	4:02:31 (11,135)	
Bush, Nigel G	4:14:58 (14,158)	
Bush, Stephen	4:38:15 (20,241)	
Bush, Timothy J	4:36:58 (19,909)	
Bushell, David	4:00:22 (10,628)	
Bushell, Julian A	5:31:09 (30,549)	
Bushell, Stuart C	4:53:03 (23,986)	
Bussey, James R	3:48:18 (7,465)	
Bussola, Gennaro	3:43:07 (6,446)	
Bussolari, Alberto	3:37:06 (5,341)	
Buswell, Andy M	3:51:10 (8,088)	
Buswell, Peter J	6:15:49 (33,836)	
Butcher, Darryl	4:44:29 (21,833)	
Butcher, Giles	4:25:58 (16,978)	
Butcher, James	5:23:01 (29,520)	
Butcher, Martin E	4:26:57 (17,246)	
Butcher, Richard	4:22:30 (16,075)	
Butfield, Colin P	3:23:05 (3,133)	
Butland, Andrew R	3:24:28 (3,336)	
Butland, Richard	3:35:16 (5,002)	
Butler, Adrian Woodman	3:37:24 (5,385)	
Butler, Andrew J	2:50:47 (490)	
Butler, Bruce C	4:15:56 (14,374)	
Butler, Carl A	4:11:06 (13,139)	
Butler, Christopher P	6:12:49 (33,682)	
Butler, Dave I	3:22:13 (3,040)	
Butler, David A	2:52:11 (530)	
Butler, David P	5:38:38 (31,347)	
Butler, Eoin	3:46:43 (7,138)	
Butler, Glen	3:56:18 (9,394)	
Butler, Grant J	3:12:09 (1,896)	
Butler, Iain J	4:28:53 (17,806)	
Butler, Jamie	3:35:02 (4,965)	
Butler, Jason P	3:55:26 (9,139)	
Butler, Jeffrey	3:04:28 (1,260)	
Butler, Matthew	4:03:47 (11,386)	
Butler, Nigel J	4:03:13 (11,275)	
Butler, Norman D	5:27:51 (30,133)	
Butler, Oliver M	4:26:52 (17,229)	
Butler, Paul W	4:27:31 (17,395)	
Butler, Robert A	3:37:16 (5,365)	
Butler, Robin J	3:53:40 (8,667)	
Butler, Ross S	4:29:25 (17,952)	
Butler, Sam	3:37:46 (5,450)	
Butler, Simon	3:33:07 (4,627)	
Butler, Simon	4:55:55 (24,667)	
Butler, Stephen	3:56:10 (9,357)	
Butler, Stephen D	3:08:34 (1,571)	
Butt, Jawaad K	4:34:47 (19,348)	
Butterfield, Karl M	5:47:46 (32,151)	
Butterfield, Sam	4:05:44 (11,828)	
Butterworth, Christopher	5:00:23 (25,675)	
Butterworth, Francis	3:55:44 (9,240)	
Buttery, Andrew J	2:37:29 (147)	
Buttleman, James H	3:29:39 (4,124)	
Buttler, Brian	5:10:48 (27,602)	
Button, John	4:12:55 (13,635)	
Button, Kevin	4:55:10 (24,494)	
Button, Tim	3:59:40 (10,445)	
Buxton, Frank N	3:33:46 (4,719)	
Buzza, David	2:31:35 (78)	
Buzzard, David James	4:01:53 (10,999)	
Byansi, Malachi	2:39:23 (183)	
Byard, Christopher	3:57:20 (9,721)	
Byatt, Vinny J	3:47:58 (7,391)	
Bye, Alan F	3:32:41 (4,569)	
Byerley, Andrew L	3:14:58 (2,228)	
Byers, Richard J	3:03:45 (1,221)	
Byfield, David	5:29:46 (30,367)	
Byford, Steve C	3:36:39 (5,259)	
Bygrave, Garry	5:23:13 (29,553)	
Bygrave, Kelvin R	4:19:49 (15,379)	
Byne, Edward John	3:25:31 (3,461)	
Byram, Andrew	3:28:20 (3,907)	
Byram, Stephen G	3:19:31 (2,684)	
Byres, Kelvin J	4:13:59 (13,905)	
Byrne, Adrian J	3:50:42 (7,994)	
Byrne, Barrie	4:53:21 (24,046)	
Byrne, Damian	4:06:36 (12,016)	
Byrne, David A	2:48:25 (410)	
Byrne, John J	4:21:40 (15,872)	
Byrne, Justin D	3:51:33 (8,174)	
Byrne, Kevin	4:09:53 (12,827)	
Byrne, Laurence	3:45:48 (6,948)	
Byrne, Neil S	4:03:50 (11,403)	
Byrne, Nick	4:25:50 (16,945)	
Byrne, Nick D	5:38:32 (31,336)	
Byrne, Patrick	5:00:16 (25,646)	
Byrne, Paul	5:10:01 (27,462)	
Byrne, Stephen K	4:12:36 (13,547)	
Byrne, Tom	4:47:55 (22,712)	
Byrom, Chris E	5:10:39 (27,575)	

Byrom, Matthew W........................3:30:10 (4,202)
Byron, Robert W..........................4:09:35 (12,747)
Byron-Davies, Justin M.................3:52:08 (8,304)
Bysouth, Richard..........................4:34:34 (19,282)
Bytheway, David J.........................4:21:41 (15,876)
Byworth, Giles..............................3:02:19 (1,138)
Cabeza, David...............................2:49:16 (433)
Cabezutto, Peter...........................4:17:53 (14,858)
Cable, Andrew J............................3:56:28 (9,449)
Cable, Matthew S..........................3:33:41 (4,700)
Cable, Oliver B.............................6:27:36 (34,347)
Cable, Paul A................................3:50:17 (7,900)
Cable, Paul J.................................4:17:43 (14,826)
Caborn, Neil..................................3:43:35 (6,541)
Cabrera, Edwin V..........................5:13:27 (28,056)
Cackett, Richard Alan...................4:53:48 (24,175)
Caddy, Derek.................................5:12:48 (27,947)
Caddy, James W.............................3:52:53 (8,483)
Cade, Jason J.................................5:29:00 (30,274)
Cadman, Karl.................................4:21:36 (15,844)
Cadogan, Tom................................3:59:49 (10,500)
Cady, Ben R...................................4:13:05 (13,680)
Cahill, Edward N...........................4:25:26 (16,823)
Cahill, Graham..............................4:32:34 (18,777)
Cahill, Niel M................................4:50:28 (23,362)
Cahill, Tim....................................3:27:48 (3,825)
Cahling, Thomas............................4:17:30 (14,769)
Cahusac, George R.........................4:11:12 (13,162)
Caillaud, Jean Philippe..................3:30:03 (4,186)
Cain, Christopher Edward..............3:38:28 (5,581)
Cain, Justin A................................4:33:03 (18,911)
Cain, Paul D..................................3:24:01 (3,262)
Caines, Jonathan R........................5:59:50 (33,037)
Caird, Andrew...............................4:12:23 (13,488)
Cairns, Duncan J...........................3:26:32 (3,603)
Cairns, Ian W................................4:17:43 (14,826)
Cairns, Josh...................................3:55:32 (9,162)
Cairns, Mark K..............................4:01:37 (10,947)
Cairns, Steven M...........................2:42:58 (255)
Cajigas, Juan P..............................4:48:12 (22,783)
Cake, Phil J...................................2:43:43 (280)
Cakebread, George H.....................8:58:34 (35,355)
Cakebread, John............................3:18:20 (2,560)
Calame, Andrew B.........................4:11:05 (13,133)
Calder, Gavin E..............................5:08:09 (27,112)
Calder, Murray J............................3:42:34 (6,321)
Caldwell, Mark..............................3:56:31 (9,465)
Caley, Jeffrey T.............................6:15:49 (33,836)
Caliendo, Chris T...........................3:27:27 (3,768)
Calladine, Paul A...........................5:37:39 (31,243)
Callaghan, David...........................4:17:42 (14,819)
Callaghan, Michael D....................4:33:13 (18,948)
Callaghan, Peter J..........................3:50:44 (8,001)
Callanan, Gerry P..........................5:01:58 (26,010)
Callanan, Mike M..........................5:37:06 (31,187)
Callanan, Richard..........................4:41:08 (20,991)
Callear, Robert I............................4:45:38 (22,113)
Callender, Stephen........................4:19:43 (15,344)
Caller, John D...............................4:24:25 (16,555)
Caller, Mark J...............................5:32:41 (30,721)
Calles, Luis....................................4:12:56 (13,643)
Callingham, Paul A........................4:04:54 (11,630)
Callow, James...............................3:46:24 (7,067)
Callow, Terry W............................4:38:13 (20,234)
Calo, Armando...............................3:35:40 (5,090)
Calthrop, Ben................................3:31:44 (4,426)
Calvert, Philip...............................4:38:11 (20,227)
Calvert, Stuart...............................3:59:47 (10,488)
Calvey, Alexander..........................3:55:45 (9,243)
Calway, Paul Andrew......................4:17:39 (14,806)
Camara, Nick M.............................5:34:00 (30,861)
Cambier, Philippe..........................3:30:02 (4,181)
Cameron, James.............................4:17:06 (14,664)
Cameron, James A..........................4:08:47 (12,566)
Cameron, Michael W......................4:23:01 (16,189)
Cameron, Paul J.............................5:46:33 (32,050)
Cameron, Rob I..............................5:14:16 (28,202)
Cameron, Ronald A........................5:26:32 (29,995)
Cameron, Scott..............................4:49:45 (23,192)
Camfield, Bryan.............................2:45:32 (323)
Camilleri, Vincent J........................5:20:03 (29,100)
Cammidge, Peter Y........................5:48:04 (32,177)
Camorali, Pier Luigi.......................4:15:22 (14,246)
Camp, Duncan P............................4:25:41 (16,904)
Camp, Paul J.................................3:56:57 (9,606)
Campany, Timothy W.....................5:09:17 (27,329)
Campbell, Andrew.........................4:39:57 (20,707)
Campbell, Andrew A......................5:23:13 (29,553)
Campbell, Andrew Stuart...............4:55:58 (24,676)
Campbell, Brian J..........................3:19:18 (2,650)
Campbell, Geoff............................2:52:19 (538)
Campbell, Graham.........................4:16:43 (14,587)
Campbell, Iain M...........................3:30:13 (4,209)
Campbell, Iain R............................5:54:15 (32,633)
Campbell, James P.........................4:40:55 (20,943)
Campbell, John..............................3:27:05 (3,695)
Campbell, Jonathan.......................3:26:35 (3,617)
Campbell, Kenneth M....................3:45:45 (6,937)
Campbell, Kenny...........................4:01:36 (10,945)
Campbell, Martin...........................4:03:51 (11,412)
Campbell, Matthew D....................3:33:02 (4,615)
Campbell, Nathan D......................4:31:27 (18,487)
Campbell, Nicholas M....................3:25:13 (3,420)
Campbell, Paul..............................3:59:46 (10,481)
Campbell, Paul A...........................4:32:15 (18,698)
Campbell, Peter S..........................3:26:32 (3,603)
Campbell, Pierre............................4:45:29 (22,075)
Campbell, Raymond.......................4:44:21 (21,805)
Campbell, Richard.........................4:04:12 (11,489)
Campbell, Robert S........................4:21:54 (15,924)
Campbell, Rory G...........................4:04:11 (11,484)
Campbell, Ryan..............................3:37:42 (5,440)
Campbell, Scott R..........................5:41:53 (31,661)
Campbell, Simon............................3:31:13 (4,363)
Campbell, Stuart P.........................4:27:28 (17,382)
Campbell, Thomas Duncan.............3:55:34 (9,176)
Campbell, Tim...............................5:29:36 (30,349)
Campbelton, Ben M........................5:01:42 (25,951)
Campey, Jon..................................5:03:36 (26,307)
Campion, James P..........................3:36:12 (5,190)
Campion, John..............................4:31:54 (18,607)
Campion, Mark A...........................2:47:49 (386)
Campion, Stephen W.....................3:08:03 (1,527)
Campion, Timothy C......................4:19:00 (15,160)
Camplin, James..............................4:39:05 (20,461)
Campling, Peter.............................4:55:49 (24,646)
Campolungo, Giovanni...................4:04:45 (11,594)
Canavan, Ciaran Michael................3:03:54 (1,233)
Canca Hurtado, José Francisco.......3:46:34 (7,100)
Candy, Martyn James......................5:07:10 (26,935)
Cane, Peter S.................................4:18:42 (15,081)
Canenti, Roberto...........................4:46:53 (22,444)
Cann, Simon..................................4:55:12 (24,506)
Cann, Stephen...............................5:38:56 (31,386)
Cannell, David P............................4:36:36 (19,821)
Cannell, Neal A.............................4:55:48 (24,640)
Canning, Andrew J.........................4:34:15 (19,209)
Canning, Mark A...........................3:32:23 (4,529)
Cannon, Damian B.........................3:16:32 (2,385)
Cannon, Jocelyn C..........................5:00:36 (25,727)
Cannon, John................................4:56:36 (24,829)
Cannon, Paul A.............................4:06:56 (12,090)
Cannon, Thomas............................4:40:01 (20,730)
Cannon, Tony................................5:41:01 (31,586)
Canosa Barandalla, David..............3:42:02 (6,218)
Cantalamessa, Cesare.....................3:22:14 (3,043)
Cantarelli, Davide..........................4:06:15 (11,941)
Cantell, Darren..............................3:45:43 (6,930)
Cantwell, Peter B...........................5:22:19 (29,406)
Capamagian, Gareth R...................3:38:11 (5,532)
Caparini, Davide Carlo..................3:25:20 (3,433)
Capel, Alan S................................5:37:16 (31,201)
Capel, Dom....................................3:58:52 (10,218)
Capeling, Michael..........................5:25:43 (29,894)
Capes, Adrian N.............................3:29:24 (4,089)
Capewell, Nicholas R.....................4:42:45 (21,397)
Caplan, Elliot A.............................5:34:34 (30,922)
Caple, Kevin J...............................3:25:37 (3,476)
Capon, Daniel J..............................4:10:58 (13,102)
Capon, Ian....................................4:49:09 (23,004)
Capon, John O...............................3:43:45 (6,574)
Caponi, Daniele.............................3:42:43 (6,359)
Capper, Simon...............................4:39:59 (20,719)
Capperauld, Kris............................3:41:25 (6,104)
Capps, Christopher S.....................4:31:30 (18,505)
Cappuccio, Peter............................4:00:24 (10,635)
Capriglione, Bernardino L..............4:31:55 (18,611)
Capriles, Andrés.............................3:36:10 (5,185)
Carabba, Dario...............................5:29:16 (30,308)
Carassus, Jean-Marc.......................3:24:25 (3,330)
Carbone, Nick................................6:20:57 (34,067)
Carbonnier, Frederic......................5:18:12 (28,817)
Carby, Joe M.................................5:50:15 (32,360)
Card, David W...............................5:06:57 (26,894)
Card, John A.................................4:07:24 (12,216)
Carding, Neil M.............................3:48:47 (7,562)
Cardwell, James S..........................4:11:48 (13,337)
Cardy, Alex...................................5:24:07 (29,670)
Carey, Andrew J.............................5:53:06 (32,555)
Carey, Denis John..........................4:50:28 (23,362)
Carey, Ian J...................................4:57:07 (24,948)
Carey, Moray W.............................4:52:59 (23,973)
Carey, Paul....................................4:27:55 (17,520)
Carissimi, Daniele..........................4:12:03 (13,398)
Carley, Lee....................................6:44:15 (34,698)
Carley, Martin T............................4:37:50 (20,128)
Carli, Silvio...................................2:56:34 (750)
Carlin, Brian E...............................3:11:09 (1,797)
Carlin, Paul...................................4:33:50 (19,108)
Carlisle, Colin................................4:56:03 (24,694)
Carløn, Jan....................................5:35:14 (30,989)
Carlsen, Trond Inge........................3:01:44 (1,099)
Carlson, Floyd...............................4:18:51 (15,118)
Carlsson, Dick................................3:44:51 (6,779)
Carlsson, Neil P.............................6:07:40 (33,470)
Carlsson, Olle................................5:09:07 (27,292)
Carlyle, Colin J..............................5:15:04 (28,335)
Carlyle, Mark.................................3:26:29 (3,596)
Carmichael, Andrew.......................4:28:14 (17,628)
Carmichael, Ian..............................4:17:18 (14,717)
Carmichael, Jeremy Robert.............3:40:20 (5,919)
Carmichael, Rob H.........................5:05:21 (26,613)
Carmichael, Stephen.......................3:16:14 (2,353)
Carmody, Kieran............................3:21:17 (2,919)
Carmona, Diego.............................4:04:11 (11,484)
Carnall, Simon J.............................3:40:42 (5,971)
Carnegie, John...............................3:11:02 (1,780)
Carnevali, Giorgio..........................3:02:43 (1,161)
Carney, Michael..............................4:59:15 (25,443)
Carnochan, Graeme I......................4:44:53 (21,924)
Carnwell, Simon A..........................4:14:49 (14,116)
Carol, Riel.....................................2:59:52 (987)
Carolan, Hugh................................5:42:00 (31,675)
Carolan, Malcolm V........................6:51:31 (34,837)
Carolan, Thomas.............................4:22:19 (16,025)
Caron, Marc...................................4:09:13 (12,663)
Carpenter, Colin B..........................5:15:13 (28,357)
Carpenter, David............................3:57:03 (9,634)
Carpenter, Edward.........................3:50:07 (7,859)
Carpenter, Joseph H.......................5:12:34 (27,903)
Carpenter, Richard.........................4:53:53 (24,197)
Carpenter, Tim P............................4:56:46 (24,867)
Carr, Adrian N...............................3:59:08 (10,290)
Carr, David....................................4:45:42 (22,133)
Carr, Dean H.................................3:20:00 (2,755)
Carr, Frazer....................................3:30:56 (4,317)
Carr, Gerard...................................3:31:32 (4,403)
Carr, John......................................2:43:25 (266)
Carr, Leigh Glenn...........................3:38:06 (5,514)
Carr, Malcolm.................................4:33:46 (19,090)
Carr, Malcolm A.............................3:24:24 (3,328)
Carr, Mark.....................................3:49:45 (7,791)
Carr, Martin G...............................3:58:52 (10,218)
Carr, Oliver M................................4:05:29 (11,766)
Carr, Phillip...................................3:07:22 (1,463)
Carr, Robert..................................3:31:06 (4,346)
Carragher, Andrew O.....................4:32:55 (18,876)
Carrapiett, Myles............................3:41:13 (6,075)
Carrea, Michael..............................3:29:51 (4,160)
Carretero, Julio..............................4:16:16 (14,464)
Carrick, Hugh.................................4:51:44 (23,685)
Carrier, Nicholas A.........................3:33:57 (4,750)
Carrington-Wilde, Robin B.............5:54:08 (32,627)
Carroll, Adam J..............................4:43:17 (21,541)
Carroll, Gideon..............................5:49:30 (32,294)
Carroll, John..................................4:02:23 (11,102)
Carroll, Joseph...............................4:24:38 (16,601)
Carroll, Mark M.............................6:13:16 (33,709)
Carroll, Pat....................................6:04:13 (33,300)

Carroll, Stuart P 2:58:57 (914)
Carroll, Tony J 3:58:06 (9,971)
Carson, Alan 5:24:45 (29,758)
Carson, Alex 3:36:25 (5,219)
Carson, Kevin M 4:06:16 (11,945)
Cartailler, Mathias 2:49:22 (438)
Carter, Alun J 3:15:18 (2,259)
Carter, Andrew D 3:26:17 (3,571)
Carter, Andrew M 5:55:13 (32,706)
Carter, Andrew S 2:58:10 (850)
Carter, Barry C 3:44:54 (6,784)
Carter, Charles G 4:12:26 (13,499)
Carter, Colin 4:44:31 (21,840)
Carter, Darryl 2:54:50 (653)
Carter, Dave 3:51:44 (8,215)
Carter, Dave A 2:34:35 (106)
Carter, Dave C 3:37:01 (5,321)
Carter, Dave J 5:18:10 (28,812)
Carter, David Charles 6:27:51 (34,352)
Carter, David F 5:31:15 (30,554)
Carter, David John 4:22:20 (16,031)
Carter, David R 5:48:56 (32,244)
Carter, Dennis J 4:16:38 (14,567)
Carter, Graham J 3:31:37 (4,409)
Carter, Jake 4:50:37 (23,400)
Carter, Jeffrey J 4:49:26 (23,088)
Carter, John A 3:49:02 (7,627)
Carter, Jonathan A 4:19:24 (15,255)
Carter, Keith G 4:40:36 (20,860)
Carter, Mark C 3:53:20 (8,587)
Carter, Matt 5:09:46 (27,420)
Carter, Neil A 3:28:25 (3,915)
Carter, Nigel G 4:14:24 (14,013)
Carter, Richard J 4:14:11 (13,955)
Carter, Rory C 3:53:45 (8,692)
Carter, Simon 4:25:35 (16,868)
Carter, Stephen F 6:04:25 (33,308)
Carter, Tim R 3:57:13 (9,678)
Carter, Tom 4:34:32 (19,267)
Carter Shaw, Nicholas P 3:48:39 (7,541)
Cartwirght, Adrian P 5:07:03 (26,915)
Cartwright, Anton P 3:50:57 (8,049)
Cartwright, Daniel 5:24:59 (29,797)
Cartwright, Dominic 4:33:10 (18,932)
Cartwright, Gary C 5:00:28 (25,694)
Cartwright, Jamie 3:35:19 (5,012)
Cartwright, Jason L 6:07:15 (33,447)
Cartwright, Joe R 5:13:01 (27,990)
Cartwright, Kevin A 4:50:22 (23,335)
Cartwright, Nicky 4:35:08 (19,446)
Cartwright, Paul Nigel 3:32:42 (4,573)
Cartwright, Phil J 6:00:03 (33,056)
Cartwright, Robert G 6:39:49 (34,625)
Cartwright, Spencer F 4:21:06 (15,714)
Cartwright, Stephen 3:21:06 (2,900)
Cartwright, Thomas Allen 3:45:19 (6,860)
Carty, Nick J 5:39:38 (31,459)
Caruana, Paul 3:35:55 (5,138)
Carvalho, Maritz T 3:42:01 (6,212)
Carvill, Charley 5:27:12 (30,066)
Carwardine, Mark Richard 3:19:08 (2,630)
Casady, Tim 3:33:24 (4,666)
Cascapera, Fabrizio 3:35:16 (5,002)
Case, Adam P 5:39:03 (31,402)
Case, Barry John 4:43:16 (21,534)
Case, Daniel 4:16:43 (14,587)
Case, Robert 4:36:55 (19,894)
Casement, William R 4:21:39 (15,863)
Casey, James R 4:43:17 (21,541)
Casey, John 4:38:26 (20,283)
Casey, Mark F 4:39:49 (20,670)
Casey, Michael P 3:29:35 (4,114)
Casey, Sean 4:38:26 (20,283)
Cash, Jamie L 4:16:11 (14,443)
Cashen, Thomas 5:33:44 (30,834)
Cass, Marc 4:56:12 (24,728)
Casserley, Dominic J 4:32:04 (18,656)
Cassidy, Anthony J 4:44:19 (21,800)
Cassidy, Gary 3:02:36 (1,156)
Cassidy, Robin P 4:12:57 (13,651)
Cassidy, Seain B 5:27:03 (30,055)
Cassidy, Stuart J 5:28:11 (30,175)
Castagnola, Barry 3:56:41 (9,529)
Castaldo, Paul 3:30:37 (4,272)
Castelo Branco, Fernando 3:16:08 (2,344)
Castilho, José 3:46:34 (7,100)
Castle, David 4:56:33 (24,814)
Castle, David M 2:53:47 (597)
Castle, Robert B 4:03:17 (11,288)
Castle, Toby A 3:33:29 (4,675)
Castle, Will L 6:36:24 (34,551)
Castrey, Simon 3:44:26 (6,705)
Castro Estevez, Benito 3:50:35 (7,966)
Castrodeza Via, Javier 3:32:51 (4,592)
Casula, Maria 6:19:12 (34,007)
Catantan, Fidel 5:26:17 (29,964)
Catchpole, Charles F 3:52:24 (8,381)
Catchpole, Chris R 3:58:56 (10,233)
Catchpole, Gary J 3:26:28 (3,595)
Catchpole, Tony 4:24:28 (16,564)
Catchpole, William A 5:11:46 (27,770)
Cates, Sam E 4:55:07 (24,479)
Catleugh, Peter 3:50:53 (8,034)
Catlin, Henry G 5:12:38 (27,913)
Catlow, Ian J 4:19:07 (15,188)
Catt, Daniel John 3:21:54 (2,998)
Catt, Mark R 4:55:07 (24,479)
Catterall, Christopher 5:08:57 (27,261)
Catto, Stephen K 3:36:07 (5,175)
Catton, Giles 4:53:05 (23,994)
Cauchi, Anthony 4:04:11 (11,484)
Caulder, Graham A 4:13:18 (13,745)
Caulfield, Andrew J 3:52:51 (8,476)
Caulfield, James H 4:11:55 (13,362)
Caulfield, Russell E 5:38:40 (31,351)
Cautley, Steven N 4:12:04 (13,405)
Cavalcante, Amadeu 3:55:41 (9,211)
Cavaliere, Angelo 4:10:16 (12,930)
Cavalla, Albert D 5:55:48 (32,749)
Cavalla, Paul 3:43:23 (6,505)
Cavanagh, Kristian 5:25:27 (29,853)
Cavanagh, Michael J 3:38:02 (5,497)
Cavanagh, Scott J 5:12:51 (27,958)
Cave, Adrian J 3:21:35 (2,957)
Cave, Rhodri S 4:42:07 (21,235)
Caveney, Terence J 3:18:47 (2,601)
Cavey, Ben W 3:55:07 (9,072)
Cawkwell, Andrew A 4:45:27 (22,068)
Cawley, John W 3:55:03 (9,040)
Cawte, Martin I 3:35:10 (4,990)
Cawte, Stephen J 5:15:14 (28,366)
Cawthorne, Timothy James 4:13:08 (13,691)
Caygill, Paul 4:23:28 (16,299)
Cazala, Didier 4:38:30 (20,296)
Cazalet, James A 4:34:53 (19,376)
Cecchetto, Domenico 2:49:11 (428)
Cecil, Rupert L 3:43:16 (6,481)
Celandroni, Lorenzo 4:25:02 (16,719)
Celinski, Robert 3:06:20 (1,397)
Cenni, Massimiliano 3:48:08 (7,425)
Cerely, Francis P 4:42:52 (21,431)
Cerretani, Paolo 3:52:19 (8,362)
Cerveny, Frank 3:13:05 (2,013)
Cesarz, Dom A 4:08:00 (12,359)
Ceustermans, Franswa 4:53:53 (24,197)
Chadaway, Andrew K 4:23:05 (16,205)
Chadfield, Jonathan N 4:18:26 (15,009)
Chadwick, Jonathan M 4:14:54 (14,140)
Chafer, Anthony R 4:45:47 (22,152)
Chaffart, Kim 4:21:03 (15,704)
Chahal, Kuljeet S 3:59:37 (10,423)
Chahal, Palwinder 3:37:18 (5,372)
Chainey, Christopher 3:48:18 (7,465)
Chainey, Ross A 3:33:01 (4,612)
Chakraborty, Suhash 5:18:47 (28,931)
Chalamet, Adrien 3:51:34 (8,178)
Chalk, Chris J 3:52:05 (8,295)
Chalk, David R 4:50:18 (23,318)
Chalk, Jason A 3:52:11 (8,323)
Chalk, Lewis S 3:15:43 (2,307)
Chalkley, John W 4:03:59 (11,445)
Chalkley, Nick S 3:59:02 (10,261)
Chalkley, Stephen 4:04:19 (11,511)
Chalkley, Steve R 3:31:18 (4,371)
Challenor, Mark O 3:55:02 (9,032)
Challis, Kevin D 3:30:09 (4,197)
Challis, Leigh J 3:48:35 (7,529)
Challiss, Jason S 4:53:30 (24,071)
Chalmers, Hugh A 3:51:02 (8,065)
Chalmers, Julian 3:45:13 (6,839)
Chalmers, William 5:19:04 (28,980)
Chaloner, Mark 5:04:51 (26,511)
Chaloner, Steve 4:51:10 (23,528)
Chamberlain, Brian 4:32:49 (18,850)
Chamberlain, Kevin C 4:03:52 (11,414)
Chamberlain, Robert Edward 4:44:13 (21,772)
Chamberlain, Robert S 5:12:59 (27,981)
Chambers, Alistair 3:20:46 (2,865)
Chambers, Ben D 4:25:49 (16,940)
Chambers, Craig 3:52:10 (8,317)
Chambers, Dean K 3:53:38 (8,658)
Chambers, Howard 3:21:49 (2,985)
Chambers, Joseph 4:12:21 (13,483)
Chambers, Mark 3:43:30 (6,525)
Chambers, Michael 3:57:28 (9,756)
Chambers, Peter J 5:05:29 (26,637)
Chambers, Stephen 4:27:44 (17,459)
Chambers, Tony 4:56:11 (24,723)
Chambon, Patrick 6:14:45 (33,781)
Champion, Richard J 3:37:47 (5,452)
Champneys, Simon 3:27:29 (3,771)
Chan, Alfie 5:28:04 (30,155)
Chan, Dennis 5:14:58 (28,308)
Chan, Merit S 4:45:30 (22,079)
Chan, Paul 5:31:07 (30,541)
Chan, Peter G 2:46:49 (363)
Chan, Royce 5:32:44 (30,730)
Chan, Tony 5:05:39 (26,666)
Chan, Wai Wah D 5:31:26 (30,569)
Chana, Jaswant 4:49:50 (23,205)
Chandak, Akhil 4:35:18 (19,488)
Chandioux, Stephane 3:54:13 (8,815)
Chandler, Gary W 2:34:56 (114)
Chandler, James 3:59:06 (10,278)
Chandler, James J 3:52:16 (8,353)
Chandler, Jason R 5:00:20 (25,663)
Chandler, Michael J 4:22:15 (16,011)
Chandler, Nigel 5:22:45 (29,474)
Chandler, Peter J 3:25:53 (3,515)
Chandler, Richard J 4:55:35 (24,591)
Chandler, Simon D 3:04:47 (1,291)
Chandler, Stephen J 5:42:17 (31,702)
Chang, David C 3:47:59 (7,396)
Chang, Joseph E 3:00:01 (998)
Channell, Thomas 7:02:17 (34,974)
Channer, Aeon R 3:50:59 (8,054)
Channon, Stuart 4:47:56 (22,721)
Chant, Ian R 2:57:05 (781)
Chant, Nicholas J 4:52:12 (23,795)
Chantry, Peter T 4:08:56 (12,600)
Chaplin, Colin F 4:07:04 (12,124)
Chaplin, Gordon J 5:35:19 (31,000)
Chapman, Alan E 5:39:41 (31,465)
Chapman, Andrew J 6:18:13 (33,937)
Chapman, Anthony C 5:13:56 (28,148)
Chapman, Anthony S 5:05:41 (26,678)
Chapman, Ashley J 5:13:55 (28,144)
Chapman, Chris J 4:55:24 (24,553)
Chapman, Chris S 4:44:06 (21,748)
Chapman, Christopher P 4:25:30 (16,836)
Chapman, Darren 4:43:10 (21,508)
Chapman, David A 5:58:08 (32,928)
Chapman, Desmond M 3:45:42 (6,927)
Chapman, Gary 5:52:13 (32,495)
Chapman, Gary I 3:11:10 (1,799)
Chapman, Graham J 3:02:04 (1,123)
Chapman, Ian P 5:12:51 (27,958)
Chapman, James 3:26:20 (3,579)
Chapman, James 4:16:08 (14,434)
Chapman, Jim W 4:48:31 (22,856)
Chapman, Jody C 3:15:43 (2,307)
Chapman, Karl 3:49:04 (7,635)
Chapman, Kenneth W 5:50:01 (32,335)
Chapman, Nathan T 3:56:41 (9,529)
Chapman, Neville 3:36:19 (5,208)
Chapman, Nik 4:22:29 (16,073)
Chapman, Oliver V 3:25:22 (3,438)
Chapman, Paul 5:13:50 (28,123)
Chapman, Paul A 4:24:00 (16,440)

Chapman, Paul D....4:33:06 (18,921)
Chapman, Philip D....4:38:02 (20,174)
Chapman, Reg M....3:41:13 (6,075)
Chapman, Richard....3:54:23 (8,858)
Chapman, Richard M....3:13:18 (2,034)
Chapman, Robert I....3:58:21 (10,057)
Chapman, Ross....7:19:29 (35,146)
Chapman, Roy....5:22:12 (29,391)
Chapman, Simon L....3:47:26 (7,271)
Chapman, Stephen Michael....4:05:33 (11,785)
Chapman, Tim....4:03:40 (11,362)
Chapman, Torquil I....3:57:36 (9,802)
Chapman-Sheath, Philip J....4:57:56 (25,127)
Chappatte, Sam....3:45:25 (6,873)
Chappell, Adam....4:27:49 (17,495)
Chappell, Anthony D....4:51:19 (23,571)
Chappell, Danny....4:22:23 (16,044)
Chappell, Ian S....4:34:18 (19,222)
Chappell, Michael J....4:26:26 (17,093)
Chappell, Richard I....4:50:02 (23,244)
Chappelle, Gavin S....4:06:05 (11,897)
Chard, Adam N....4:20:53 (15,657)
Chard, Ken R....3:06:05 (1,377)
Chard, Matthew J....3:16:26 (2,373)
Charles, Jason....6:37:44 (34,586)
Charles, Mark A....4:46:12 (22,248)
Charles, Nathan....5:05:06 (26,566)
Charles, Simon P....4:06:10 (11,919)
Charles, William S....4:28:00 (17,542)
Charles-Jones, Richard J....4:03:29 (11,327)
Charleston, Andrew S....4:00:00 (10,544)
Charleston, Dan....3:07:27 (1,473)
Charles-Williams, Ben....4:41:48 (21,166)
Charlesworth, James W....4:14:25 (14,017)
Charlesworth, Luke P....4:02:46 (11,182)
Charlesworth, Simon....3:53:42 (8,677)
Charley, Richard M....3:45:30 (6,897)
Charlick, Alan R....4:00:39 (10,707)
Charlsworth, Ben....3:16:11 (2,350)
Charlton, Adrian J....6:14:54 (33,787)
Charlton, Alan....4:10:51 (13,078)
Charlton, David G....4:11:47 (13,334)
Charlton, James....5:30:56 (30,515)
Charman, Nigel R....3:12:45 (1,965)
Charman, Philip G....4:33:54 (19,129)
Charnley, Edward J....3:40:12 (5,902)
Charnley, James R....3:29:14 (4,046)
Charry, Jean-Paul....4:56:31 (24,807)
Chart, Robert J....3:36:30 (5,236)
Charter, Nick V....4:46:27 (22,331)
Charters, Matthew....3:47:55 (7,377)
Charters, Paul W....4:02:10 (11,057)
Charters, Simon....3:40:10 (5,892)
Chase, Andrew....6:17:18 (33,890)
Chase, James W....5:10:01 (27,462)
Chatee, Martin G....5:51:11 (32,428)
Chater, Andrew N....4:00:01 (10,550)
Chater, Paul....4:47:00 (22,484)
Chater, Richard J....4:26:37 (17,158)
Chatfield, David I....4:17:39 (14,806)
Chati, Ahmad-Zukai....3:35:08 (4,985)
Chatt, Mike J....4:37:09 (19,954)
Chattenton, Michael S....4:07:18 (12,176)
Chaudhari, Sohail....4:13:42 (13,848)
Chaudhury, Sajad....4:11:40 (13,303)
Chauhan, Anandkumar....6:19:39 (34,022)
Chauhan, Shashi....6:14:39 (33,774)
Chaumet, Laurent....3:23:11 (3,146)
Chaves Costa, Antonio....3:32:22 (4,526)
Chaytor, Trevor....4:34:05 (19,170)
Chaytow, Ben K....3:47:04 (7,207)
Cheal, David J....4:51:14 (23,547)
Cheal, Jonathan I....3:48:48 (7,569)
Checkley, Christian....3:58:11 (10,002)
Checkley, Edward....4:47:27 (22,589)
Chedraui Lopez, Alfredo....4:14:49 (14,116)
Cheeseman, Dean W....3:54:33 (8,904)
Cheeseman, James....4:45:30 (22,079)
Cheeseman, Kevin J....4:51:53 (23,723)
Cheeseman, Matthew....5:23:46 (29,622)
Cheesman, Alex....4:49:38 (23,159)
Cheesman, Charles R....6:26:52 (34,314)
Cheetham, Stephen G....3:49:02 (7,627)
Cheetham, Thomas R....3:32:55 (4,600)
Cheffins, Patrick....3:58:46 (10,179)
Chellingworth, Peter D....5:06:50 (26,874)
Chelule, Kenneth....4:48:12 (22,783)
Chenery, Alexander M....4:28:05 (17,570)
Chenery, Colin A....5:42:46 (31,743)
Cheney, Andrew....3:55:47 (9,258)
Cheney, Mark J....4:54:52 (24,420)
Chenhall, Richard J....4:22:26 (16,060)
Chequer, James R....3:57:29 (9,762)
Cherry, Dan....3:52:36 (8,426)
Cherry, Graeme J....4:22:19 (16,025)
Cherry, Nick W....4:15:57 (14,381)
Cherry, Shaun A....4:11:12 (13,162)
Cherry, Steven T....4:43:05 (21,488)
Cheseldine, James G....3:56:31 (9,465)
Chesher, Thomas A....3:29:05 (4,022)
Chesney, Jon....6:20:50 (34,062)
Chessell, Bruce....4:26:34 (17,139)
Chessell, Guy....4:22:38 (16,105)
Chester, Cal....4:03:58 (11,443)
Chesterman, John....5:13:55 (28,144)
Chettaoui, Rafik....3:20:39 (2,847)
Chettle, James....2:55:32 (699)
Cheung, Jamie....4:40:01 (20,730)
Chevin, Robert W....4:39:47 (20,666)
Chi Yin, Ho....5:25:12 (29,825)
Chiaramonte, Ivan Antonio....3:44:50 (6,774)
Chiarelli, Nicola....4:34:49 (19,358)
Chick, Gareth....7:02:02 (34,972)
Chick, Hayden J....3:26:53 (3,663)
Chick, Joseph E....4:22:20 (16,031)
Chicken, Michael J....4:42:06 (21,226)
Chidell, Anthony R....5:41:54 (31,663)
Chignell, Will....5:01:04 (25,834)
Chilcott, Darren....4:17:05 (14,662)
Chilcott, Duncan....4:11:12 (13,162)
Child, David A....2:43:48 (281)
Child, Dean E....4:39:25 (20,558)
Child, Robert....3:36:16 (5,201)
Childe, Michael....4:05:31 (11,773)
Childe-Freeman, Paul R....4:36:45 (19,848)
Childerhouse, Paul....4:44:16 (21,783)
Childerley, Neil A....3:50:07 (7,859)
Childs, Paul....4:25:20 (16,796)
Childs, Paul A....2:54:40 (639)
Childs, Phillip....3:42:18 (6,268)
Childs, Stephen John....4:43:57 (21,703)
Childs, Tim M....6:55:09 (34,896)
Chiles, Matthew....3:52:35 (8,420)
Chilman, Michael J....5:32:16 (30,667)
Chilvers, Simon R....5:31:32 (30,585)
Chin, Raymond....4:58:29 (25,263)
Chinnock, Ian....4:31:41 (18,546)
Chino, John....4:54:56 (24,433)
Chipeur, Gerald....5:18:43 (28,921)
Chisholm, Alastair....4:49:15 (23,036)
Chisholm, David....5:01:56 (26,001)
Chiswell, Ian....4:56:32 (24,809)
Chittock, Robert....3:50:39 (7,978)
Chitty, Bryan Adam....3:51:12 (8,098)
Chitty, James A....5:17:55 (28,780)
Chivers, Luke R....3:24:09 (3,289)
Choi, James....4:26:04 (17,002)
Choi, Trevor....3:49:27 (7,718)
Chojnacki, Grzegorz....4:32:25 (18,735)
Cholmondeley, Kristian....3:54:43 (8,952)
Chorley, Martin....2:57:02 (776)
Choudhary, Sharjeel S....4:16:18 (14,473)
Choudhury, Junayeed....6:14:05 (33,749)
Chouraqui, Laurent....3:12:21 (1,918)
Chowdhury, Arshad Ahmed....5:42:58 (31,767)
Chowdhury, Shafait Momen....6:26:29 (34,298)
Chrispo, Biyiha....3:10:39 (1,752)
Christensen, Simon....4:33:52 (19,118)
Christian, Blanc....4:36:36 (19,821)
Christian, Giral....4:35:01 (19,411)
Christian, Gourland....4:34:39 (19,300)
Christian, Iacono....5:40:27 (31,539)
Christian, Jenny....3:08:44 (1,593)
Christian, Nick....4:39:49 (20,670)
Christian, Peter....3:15:37 (2,295)
Christian, Reynaud....3:33:53 (4,736)
Christian, Seiler....3:26:41 (3,633)
Christian, Seyfritz....4:04:40 (11,578)
Christian, William....3:58:55 (10,230)
Christie, David....4:20:28 (15,548)
Christie, Paul....4:43:30 (21,598)
Christie, Sandy....3:12:27 (1,926)
Christley, Andy....4:00:11 (10,593)
Christophe, Gosset....3:22:08 (3,028)
Christophe, Toulouse....4:22:11 (16,000)
Christopher, Derek....3:42:33 (6,317)
Christopher, John M....3:12:58 (2,002)
Christopher, Rob J....4:42:39 (21,373)
Christy, John R....2:59:33 (962)
Chrysostomou, Tom....5:34:33 (30,921)
Chu, Alan C....5:07:40 (27,039)
Chu, Brian....3:19:27 (2,676)
Chubb, Daniel P....4:21:19 (15,767)
Chubb, Richard A....4:17:53 (14,858)
Chuck, Gavin....5:21:47 (29,339)
Chui, Wai....4:23:24 (16,280)
Chum, Peter W....4:16:15 (14,458)
Chumber, Vinod K....5:27:34 (30,099)
Chung, Kawai....2:59:55 (991)
Chung, Ying....4:13:20 (13,760)
Church, Ed....3:55:43 (9,232)
Church, John W....4:31:45 (18,567)
Church, Leigh D....3:42:27 (6,288)
Church, Trevor E....4:01:38 (10,951)
Churchill, Keith....5:15:17 (28,381)
Churchill, Kim J....5:21:29 (29,296)
Churchill, Nigel....4:26:15 (17,051)
Churton, Mark A....3:54:58 (9,010)
Ciancimino, Filippo....4:05:36 (11,798)
Ciano, Phillip....3:47:14 (7,239)
Ciarrapico, Tullio....4:15:44 (14,329)
Cilia, Charles....2:34:04 (100)
Cilira, Milton....2:53:04 (562)
Cilli, Fabio....4:16:32 (14,531)
Cima, Keith M....4:00:41 (10,716)
Cinesi, Mirco....4:52:53 (23,945)
Cinesi, Pietro....3:08:37 (1,579)
Cinieri, Ciro....3:15:08 (2,246)
Cinnamon, Paul T....3:25:48 (3,501)
Cinque, Giulio A....3:07:12 (1,453)
Ciociola, Matteo....2:45:52 (328)
Cirio, Alberto....3:03:42 (1,215)
Cisternino, Angelo....3:20:30 (2,826)
Clack, Graham M....5:20:00 (29,093)
Clague, Andrew J....4:17:29 (14,764)
Clancey, Steve M....4:00:45 (10,731)
Clancy, Paul....4:00:24 (10,635)
Clapham, Mark J....4:01:19 (10,862)
Clapp, Mark C....5:10:23 (27,528)
Clapp, Matthew N....2:48:00 (397)
Clapton, Roland A....4:26:02 (16,994)
Clarabut, Ray....4:10:57 (13,094)
Clare, Benjamin....3:46:23 (7,062)
Clare, Jonathan R....3:01:35 (1,088)
Clare, Paul....5:21:17 (29,266)
Clare, Peter....6:04:21 (33,307)
Clare, Tony J....4:39:03 (20,452)
Clarey, Simon K....4:21:51 (15,911)
Clargo, Adrian John....4:25:46 (16,928)
Claridge, Benjamin D....4:24:53 (16,679)
Clark, Adam A....4:32:55 (18,876)
Clark, Andrew....4:39:26 (20,562)
Clark, Andrew N....3:45:20 (6,862)
Clark, Andrew N....6:24:09 (34,194)
Clark, Antony S....3:56:53 (9,592)
Clark, David....5:25:25 (29,844)
Clark, David I....4:41:04 (20,976)
Clark, Derek J....3:18:44 (2,590)
Clark, Edward D....3:55:04 (9,050)
Clark, Francis....3:29:14 (4,046)
Clark, Gareth....5:34:45 (30,947)
Clark, Gavin....4:46:15 (22,262)
Clark, Iain L....4:02:14 (11,074)
Clark, Ian A....3:57:48 (9,873)
Clark, Ian R....3:30:58 (4,325)
Clark, Jason....4:24:08 (16,483)
Clark, Jason....4:24:45 (16,638)
Clark, Jason D....4:25:38 (16,885)
Clark, Joel S....4:02:29 (11,125)

Clark, John	4:03:01 (11,234)
Clark, John	4:29:04 (17,850)
Clark, Jonathan E.	3:34:52 (4,936)
Clark, Jonathan L.	6:08:17 (33,488)
Clark, Joseph T.	3:30:19 (4,222)
Clark, Kelvin A	4:50:13 (23,285)
Clark, Lorenzo	3:59:12 (10,310)
Clark, Luke D	4:10:44 (13,049)
Clark, Mark A	3:47:06 (7,213)
Clark, Martin J.	3:57:33 (9,789)
Clark, Matthew J.	3:54:08 (8,790)
Clark, Michael	3:34:25 (4,856)
Clark, Michael A.	4:31:08 (18,391)
Clark, Nicholas	3:58:47 (10,189)
Clark, Nicholas E.	4:16:57 (14,634)
Clark, Oliver G	3:27:24 (3,749)
Clark, Paul	3:43:33 (6,532)
Clark, Paul	3:59:21 (10,351)
Clark, Paul Christopher	5:59:27 (33,016)
Clark, Paul D	3:07:19 (1,459)
Clark, Peter L	4:48:23 (22,825)
Clark, Phil	4:50:57 (23,474)
Clark, Philip	5:36:25 (31,113)
Clark, Richard Ashton	5:28:41 (30,234)
Clark, Rick	3:28:11 (3,878)
Clark, Robert	3:03:00 (1,173)
Clark, Robert	4:21:15 (15,755)
Clark, Robert M	4:33:15 (18,959)
Clark, Robert N	5:28:41 (30,234)
Clark, Robert P	3:31:09 (4,352)
Clark, Roy D	4:31:17 (18,429)
Clark, Sam Reece	5:14:55 (28,296)
Clark, Samuel T	4:09:04 (12,635)
Clark, Scott C	4:58:10 (25,184)
Clark, Simon	4:01:17 (10,853)
Clark, Simon A	4:03:04 (11,244)
Clark, Simon G	5:07:13 (26,949)
Clark, Steve	5:03:43 (26,327)
Clark, Tim M	3:46:07 (7,008)
Clark, Trevor G.	4:30:23 (18,202)
Clark, Trevor J	4:42:56 (21,456)
Clark, Trevor J	5:41:58 (31,667)
Clark, William A	4:05:32 (11,780)
Clark, William J	4:34:01 (19,155)
Clarke, Aidan M	4:11:25 (13,228)
Clarke, Alan L	6:30:06 (34,414)
Clarke, Alex R	5:02:41 (26,150)
Clarke, Alistair D	3:21:31 (2,949)
Clarke, Andrew T	3:14:28 (2,170)
Clarke, Andrew T	4:25:19 (16,791)
Clarke, Andy	3:35:40 (5,090)
Clarke, Barry	4:14:05 (13,925)
Clarke, Billy	4:44:04 (21,740)
Clarke, Craig C.	3:31:17 (4,368)
Clarke, Dale R	4:31:40 (18,542)
Clarke, Daniel J	3:31:43 (4,424)
Clarke, Dave Alan	3:58:35 (10,124)
Clarke, David B	5:34:45 (30,947)
Clarke, David P.	4:31:55 (18,611)
Clarke, David R	3:30:08 (4,194)
Clarke, Dennis G.	5:58:11 (32,937)
Clarke, Graham P.	5:42:00 (31,675)
Clarke, Ian J	3:24:19 (3,314)
Clarke, Ian J	4:14:42 (14,079)
Clarke, James	5:19:09 (28,989)
Clarke, James E	4:37:16 (19,978)
Clarke, James J	4:37:07 (19,945)
Clarke, Joe W	4:12:56 (13,643)
Clarke, John B	5:44:01 (31,852)
Clarke, John E	3:39:49 (5,812)
Clarke, John F	5:52:24 (32,508)
Clarke, John R	3:57:28 (9,756)
Clarke, Jonathan P	3:48:44 (7,550)
Clarke, Lee	5:16:34 (28,573)
Clarke, Mark J	4:31:41 (18,546)
Clarke, Matthew A.	4:06:18 (12,032)
Clarke, Mick F	4:05:37 (11,807)
Clarke, Neil B	5:09:20 (27,337)
Clarke, Neil S.	4:49:36 (23,147)
Clarke, Neville P.	3:34:11 (4,808)
Clarke, Nic	3:16:32 (2,385)
Clarke, Patrick C	4:43:43 (21,654)
Clarke, Paul D	3:23:24 (3,178)
Clarke, Paul S	4:21:12 (15,741)
Clarke, Peter J	7:01:52 (34,971)
Clarke, Peter Michael	4:16:59 (14,642)
Clarke, Phil	4:43:18 (21,543)
Clarke, Phillip T	5:02:42 (26,155)
Clarke, Renaud L	4:33:18 (18,977)
Clarke, Richard	4:56:01 (24,682)
Clarke, Richard	5:43:13 (31,797)
Clarke, Robert	3:46:08 (7,010)
Clarke, Robert	3:58:25 (10,071)
Clarke, Robert A	4:23:22 (16,268)
Clarke, Robert P	4:57:23 (25,010)
Clarke, Robert W	5:43:12 (31,795)
Clarke, Russell W	5:01:32 (25,918)
Clarke, Sean T	5:28:07 (30,164)
Clarke, Simon D	3:51:57 (8,269)
Clarke, Simon P	4:09:01 (12,624)
Clarke, Steve R	4:27:55 (17,520)
Clarke, Steven F	4:46:24 (22,315)
Clarke, Stuart	4:22:57 (16,177)
Clarke, Thomas G	4:34:15 (19,209)
Clarke, Tom	4:33:51 (19,113)
Clarke, Wayne	6:54:25 (34,887)
Clarke, William	3:56:51 (9,583)
Clarkson, Chris J	4:32:18 (18,706)
Clarkson, Greegan P	2:43:04 (257)
Clarkson, Gustav	5:50:17 (32,362)
Clarkson, Nigel	4:30:36 (18,255)
Clarkson, Rick J	4:19:28 (15,269)
Claro, Carlos F	3:56:26 (9,437)
Clasby, Andrew W	4:53:55 (24,204)
Claude, Meyer	3:47:45 (7,336)
Claude, Simonian	4:42:17 (21,272)
Claveau, Mathias A	3:35:58 (5,147)
Clawson, Mark	3:46:41 (7,134)
Clawson, Matt R	5:14:34 (28,250)
Clay, David	4:28:59 (17,826)
Clay, David P.	4:14:53 (14,136)
Clay, Nick J.	3:24:02 (3,265)
Claydon, Andrew	3:30:50 (4,302)
Claydon, Lewis	4:11:00 (13,110)
Claydon, Nicholas A	3:42:58 (6,412)
Claydon, Paul	4:21:35 (15,837)
Clayman, John	3:49:16 (7,682)
Clays, Jonathan M	4:30:50 (18,312)
Clayton, Alex	4:56:21 (24,761)
Clayton, Dean	4:31:15 (18,416)
Clayton, Harry C	4:27:02 (17,264)
Clayton, James V	4:22:01 (15,944)
Clayton, Jonathan B	4:00:32 (10,680)
Clayton, Liam	4:35:13 (19,472)
Clayton, Mark R	3:24:26 (3,332)
Clayton, Michael	5:37:19 (31,207)
Clayton, Peter P	3:06:51 (1,425)
Clayton, Robert	3:33:31 (4,678)
Clayton, Steven Anthony	4:47:53 (22,701)
Cleal, Simon J	4:54:01 (24,225)
Cleall, Leonard	6:13:06 (33,699)
Clear, Nigel T	4:28:05 (17,570)
Cleary, Christopher F	3:05:35 (1,340)
Cleasby, Neil M	3:36:53 (5,291)
Cleaver, Andrew D	4:43:25 (21,583)
Clegg, David E	5:02:27 (26,102)
Cleland, James R	3:15:23 (2,271)
Clelland, Alastair W	5:02:43 (26,159)
Clemens, John B	3:46:00 (6,986)
Clemens, Stewart R	4:21:53 (15,917)
Clemens, Tim	3:58:22 (10,059)
Clement, Roger	4:23:12 (16,231)
Clements, Andrew C	2:44:46 (310)
Clements, Andrew P	5:02:38 (26,142)
Clements, Gavin	4:09:42 (12,774)
Clements, Graham R	4:05:50 (11,849)
Clements, Jon A	4:29:55 (18,072)
Clements, Mark J	6:59:04 (34,935)
Clements, Martin R	4:37:07 (19,945)
Clements, Paul	3:52:14 (8,341)
Clements, Phil	4:29:22 (17,940)
Clements, Ross	3:31:17 (4,368)
Clements, Trevor W	3:08:05 (1,532)
Clemmet, Lyle G	4:55:10 (24,494)
Clenaghan, Stuart J	4:41:39 (21,132)
Clench, Gary	3:11:57 (1,877)
Cleveland, Richard R	5:07:29 (27,005)
Cleverdon, Andy M	4:16:49 (14,609)
Cleverley, Martin R.	3:40:44 (5,978)
Cleverley, Paul H	4:16:15 (14,458)
Cleverly, William	3:45:08 (6,824)
Clewley, Thomas	3:42:48 (6,377)
Clews, William M	3:09:54 (1,698)
Cliff, Stuart	4:20:28 (15,548)
Cliff, Tom	3:41:30 (6,118)
Cliffe, Shane	3:59:07 (10,285)
Clifford, Bill J	4:46:07 (22,230)
Clifford, Paul S	3:43:21 (6,499)
Clifford, Stephen W	3:31:59 (4,467)
Clifford, Stewart	6:02:24 (33,196)
Clift, Simon	4:03:30 (11,334)
Clifton, Ian J	5:38:15 (31,305)
Clifton, Matt J	4:00:56 (10,782)
Clifton, Richard J	3:12:02 (1,884)
Clinch, Michael J	4:44:43 (21,890)
Clinton, Joe M	4:58:07 (25,170)
Clinton, Peter	3:54:27 (8,876)
Clinton-Tarestad, Gregory	6:09:18 (33,524)
Clive, Gary B	5:10:54 (27,620)
Clogger, Liam T	4:36:02 (19,689)
Close, Ashley J	4:58:25 (25,247)
Close, Dan J	3:13:43 (2,091)
Close, James D	2:58:36 (875)
Close, Matt	3:59:53 (10,512)
Closey, Mike	4:37:37 (20,070)
Clough, Jack	5:12:52 (27,962)
Clough, Jonathan N	5:34:13 (30,880)
Clough, Trevor	2:55:36 (702)
Clover, Quintin	4:34:39 (19,300)
Clues, Mark A	3:13:18 (2,034)
Clulow, James A	4:06:15 (11,941)
Clutterbuck, Jason S	4:19:07 (15,188)
Clutterbuck, Paul A	4:06:37 (12,026)
Clyne, Mike	4:50:56 (23,467)
Coard, Dave	3:33:42 (4,703)
Coate, Clive A	4:30:50 (18,312)
Coates, Brian W	3:05:27 (1,334)
Coates, John	4:00:29 (10,664)
Coates, Mark A	3:46:26 (7,071)
Coates, Matthew S	5:35:10 (30,985)
Coates, Michael	5:04:04 (26,394)
Coates, Nigel J	2:59:29 (956)
Coates, Oliver	4:37:21 (19,994)
Coates, Paul	5:08:41 (27,209)
Coates, Paul R	4:26:39 (17,168)
Coates, Robert	3:53:51 (8,714)
Coats, Richard P	4:44:04 (21,740)
Cobb, Jon P	5:14:08 (28,185)
Cobb, Robert J	3:53:57 (8,738)
Cobbin, Terry	4:56:29 (24,795)
Cobbold, Chris P	4:48:01 (22,745)
Cobbold, Paul	4:40:56 (20,948)
Cobby, Peter G	5:17:38 (28,736)
Cocco, Giulio	4:12:03 (13,398)
Cochet, Michel	3:38:23 (5,560)
Cochran, Chris A.	6:06:13 (33,396)
Cochran, Nicholas	4:18:53 (15,128)
Cochrane, Ian	4:46:42 (22,400)
Cochrane, Niall P	5:37:38 (31,241)
Cockayne, James P	3:53:57 (8,738)
Cockburn, Jim	5:24:48 (29,767)
Cockburn, Lee	4:10:32 (12,989)
Cockburn, Simon	5:32:23 (30,674)
Cockcroft, Martin A	5:50:06 (32,351)
Cockell, Terry J	4:51:52 (23,717)
Cocker, David J	3:43:16 (6,481)
Cocker, Robert	3:37:37 (5,427)
Cockerell, William V	2:31:25 (77)
Cockerill, Michael L	5:58:42 (32,971)
Cockhill, Andy J	4:30:09 (18,139)
Cockill, Simon	4:49:21 (23,071)
Cocking, Samuel	5:15:30 (28,416)
Cockram, Stuart A.	4:29:35 (17,980)
Cockrell, Steven N	2:53:37 (591)
Cockroft, Guy H	3:38:29 (5,585)
Cockshoot, David	4:09:22 (12,699)
Codling, Geoffrey J	4:21:16 (15,759)
Codner, Dave	4:32:45 (18,832)
Codrington, Toby S	4:15:07 (14,195)

Cody, Eddie	5:06:34 (26,815)	
Cody, Mike	4:53:46 (24,163)	
Coe, Steven M	4:16:46 (14,596)	
Coene, Lieven	3:56:11 (9,364)	
Coffey, Colm	4:05:33 (11,785)	
Coffey, Thomas	5:07:58 (27,082)	
Cogan, Chris	5:07:35 (27,019)	
Coggan, Ben D	4:43:20 (21,559)	
Coggan, Thomas M	4:43:20 (21,559)	
Coggins, Joe	4:08:06 (12,390)	
Coghill, Chris	3:37:03 (5,330)	
Coghlan, Duncan	4:12:25 (13,494)	
Coglan, Julian J	4:02:27 (11,118)	
Cohen, Darren	4:45:55 (22,192)	
Cohen, Darren	5:14:55 (28,296)	
Cohen, David P	4:27:10 (17,301)	
Cohen, Gavriel	4:56:24 (24,774)	
Cohen, Joel	3:50:53 (8,034)	
Cohen, Lewis	4:40:36 (20,860)	
Cohen-Price, Daniel L	5:47:57 (32,166)	
Coianiz, Alessandro	2:45:07 (319)	
Cok, Nigel A	3:13:59 (2,117)	
Coke, Gus	4:07:33 (12,244)	
Coker, David	4:06:19 (11,953)	
Coker, Jeremy	4:16:00 (14,395)	
Colahan, Chris	3:42:30 (6,303)	
Colangelo, Carmelo	3:15:20 (2,265)	
Colberg, Daniel S	5:10:59 (27,638)	
Colborne, Peter A	3:32:10 (4,497)	
Colborne, Peter J	4:09:19 (12,689)	
Colburn, Tom J	4:30:25 (18,211)	
Colby, James	4:37:25 (20,014)	
Colby, Vincent	3:41:38 (6,134)	
Colcombe, Andrew	4:12:27 (13,507)	
Coldham, Mark L	3:16:31 (2,383)	
Cole, Alan	3:44:03 (6,639)	
Cole, Alex M	3:40:09 (5,888)	
Cole, Andrew	3:37:54 (5,473)	
Cole, Ben C	4:49:49 (23,203)	
Cole, Craig	4:25:12 (16,766)	
Cole, David	5:17:31 (28,719)	
Cole, Ernie H	4:22:07 (15,970)	
Cole, Geoff R	3:46:00 (6,986)	
Cole, Graham	3:33:15 (4,647)	
Cole, Gregory A	4:03:35 (11,352)	
Cole, Ian M	4:14:40 (14,067)	
Cole, Jack E	4:08:20 (12,464)	
Cole, John D	3:31:20 (4,375)	
Cole, Kevin D	3:57:55 (9,909)	
Cole, Leon J	3:57:54 (9,903)	
Cole, Mark	4:17:57 (14,872)	
Cole, Mark D	3:17:32 (2,485)	
Cole, Matt G	4:25:00 (16,712)	
Cole, Nicholas	4:19:01 (15,164)	
Cole, Paul S	4:55:08 (24,485)	
Cole, Richard P	4:53:57 (24,211)	
Cole, Robert	3:44:10 (6,659)	
Cole, Samuel G	4:52:01 (23,753)	
Cole, Stephen Harwood	4:11:17 (13,185)	
Cole, Thomas Martin	3:53:13 (8,566)	
Cole, Tom	5:47:30 (32,131)	
Cole, Warren M	5:04:16 (26,425)	
Colebatch, Brenton	7:14:52 (35,102)	
Colebourn, Mark R	4:21:39 (15,863)	
Coleby, James W	5:10:55 (27,627)	
Cole-Edwardes, Jon G	5:14:38 (28,257)	
Cole-Fletcher, Nigel	6:19:38 (34,020)	
Coleman, Andrew	4:42:02 (21,206)	
Coleman, Anthony J	4:07:18 (12,176)	
Coleman, Anthony J	4:47:21 (22,565)	
Coleman, Gareth	6:15:22 (33,808)	
Coleman, Glen	3:04:31 (1,265)	
Coleman, Ian	5:35:51 (31,057)	
Coleman, James C	4:02:32 (11,138)	
Coleman, James N	4:15:08 (14,200)	
Coleman, John A	4:09:16 (12,673)	
Coleman, John P	7:10:15 (35,053)	
Coleman, John W	4:59:32 (25,506)	
Coleman, Paul J	6:31:59 (34,451)	
Coleman, Paul R	4:27:04 (17,274)	
Coleman, Peter	4:18:55 (15,139)	
Coleman, Rory J	4:00:04 (10,564)	
Coleman, Russell B	3:29:20 (4,074)	

Coleman, Steve J	3:07:59 (1,524)	
Coles, Anthony J	4:49:13 (23,024)	
Coles, Clive A	4:27:51 (17,502)	
Coles, Owen D	4:10:15 (12,921)	
Coles, Paul	3:50:23 (7,918)	
Coles, Robert J	4:43:35 (21,621)	
Coles, Stuart	4:52:32 (23,870)	
Coles, Terence G	3:53:02 (8,514)	
Colfer, James J	3:55:30 (9,158)	
Colitti, Umberto	3:47:22 (7,261)	
Collard, Stephen M	4:15:39 (14,312)	
Colledge, James M	5:09:58 (27,453)	
Collett, Steven	3:14:17 (2,151)	
Colley, Ian R	4:48:34 (22,866)	
Collie, Phil M	5:04:33 (26,472)	
Collier, Andrew	5:14:05 (28,177)	
Collier, Arthur	3:58:47 (10,189)	
Collier, Christopher	3:55:45 (9,243)	
Collier, David	4:33:34 (19,041)	
Collier, David S	3:02:45 (1,163)	
Collier, John R	3:54:38 (8,928)	
Collier, Lee P	4:52:44 (23,912)	
Collier, Paul D	3:37:45 (5,448)	
Collier, Paul E	3:17:04 (2,439)	
Collier, Paul J	4:14:10 (13,949)	
Collier, Simon T	4:58:54 (25,362)	
Collin, Mark R	4:57:45 (25,078)	
Colling, Kevan	4:26:02 (16,994)	
Collings, Antony	3:49:23 (7,704)	
Collings, Gary	3:48:01 (7,405)	
Collings, Stuart	4:17:52 (14,851)	
Collingwood, Mark S	4:14:43 (14,088)	
Collingwood, Matthew R	4:15:19 (14,233)	
Collingwood, Paul S	2:49:41 (454)	
Collini, Stefan	3:49:12 (7,670)	
Collins, Adam J	4:55:03 (24,460)	
Collins, Adam N	3:53:56 (8,734)	
Collins, Barry J	4:42:25 (21,305)	
Collins, Ben D	3:45:00 (6,804)	
Collins, Bradley E	3:18:06 (2,539)	
Collins, Bradley J	5:38:57 (31,389)	
Collins, Craig	3:58:25 (10,071)	
Collins, David M	3:55:31 (9,160)	
Collins, Duncan	2:46:38 (350)	
Collins, Gary	4:55:01 (24,452)	
Collins, Gary	5:11:05 (27,657)	
Collins, Gary	6:35:08 (34,525)	
Collins, James A	4:21:01 (15,697)	
Collins, Jamie M	5:02:31 (26,120)	
Collins, John	5:56:14 (32,773)	
Collins, Joseph	5:19:19 (29,009)	
Collins, Lee Paul	4:45:13 (22,016)	
Collins, Mark	3:46:35 (7,104)	
Collins, Mark	4:03:21 (11,303)	
Collins, Mark	4:38:19 (20,257)	
Collins, Martin A	3:05:46 (1,354)	
Collins, Matthew	4:44:06 (21,748)	
Collins, Maurice S	3:00:13 (1,010)	
Collins, Michael	4:31:44 (18,560)	
Collins, Michael P	5:51:51 (32,473)	
Collins, Niall	5:06:00 (26,726)	
Collins, Paul J	3:40:19 (5,916)	
Collins, Paul M	3:16:34 (2,392)	
Collins, Peter D	5:29:49 (30,377)	
Collins, Phil	4:38:48 (20,378)	
Collins, Phil	5:10:09 (27,489)	
Collins, Richard A	3:43:06 (6,441)	
Collins, Rob F	5:18:01 (28,797)	
Collins, Robert P	4:26:44 (17,187)	
Collins, Robin	3:45:14 (6,842)	
Collins, Rodney J	6:06:25 (33,408)	
Collins, Shaun S	3:27:20 (3,739)	
Collins, Simon L	3:10:35 (1,742)	
Collins, Stephen G	4:13:30 (13,796)	
Collins, Tolan S	4:05:23 (11,749)	
Collinson, Anthony	3:14:38 (2,186)	
Collinson, Jason	5:12:06 (27,819)	
Collinson, Mark C	3:25:44 (3,492)	
Collinson, Rich	2:56:06 (727)	
Collis, Guy W	3:02:25 (1,143)	
Collis, James G	3:50:14 (7,892)	
Collis, Paul A	5:50:54 (32,407)	
Collister, Christopher	4:12:42 (13,575)	

Colman, Brian D	5:15:34 (28,432)	
Colman, Graham P	3:35:26 (5,037)	
Colquhoun, John	5:00:15 (25,643)	
Colver, Phillip M	3:44:14 (6,671)	
Colverd, Christien J	3:15:00 (2,232)	
Colvill, Steve	6:39:07 (34,611)	
Colwell, Andy J	5:02:12 (26,065)	
Colyer, Robin A	5:04:52 (26,518)	
Combarro, Yrineo	3:38:57 (5,667)	
Combeau, Bernard	5:15:12 (28,353)	
Comber, Duncan P	5:41:27 (31,630)	
Combos, Michael	5:05:01 (26,549)	
Combstock, Emerson	2:46:10 (335)	
Common, Ian R	4:02:05 (11,037)	
Compaan, Donovan A	4:37:08 (19,950)	
Comport, David J	3:40:27 (5,934)	
Compton, Andy	4:46:57 (22,469)	
Compton, Derek K	6:01:25 (33,137)	
Compton, John P	3:19:21 (2,661)	
Compton, Ollie S	3:20:40 (2,850)	
Condotti, Matthew A	5:09:32 (27,370)	
Conduit, Tim	3:13:30 (2,061)	
Conejero Roos, Cristian A	4:17:24 (14,742)	
Congdon, Andrew J	3:29:04 (4,013)	
Coniam, Simon J	4:08:11 (12,415)	
Coniglio, Tony	5:42:07 (31,682)	
Conley, Neil M	3:58:51 (10,211)	
Conlin, Jonathan G	4:44:52 (21,921)	
Conlon, Michael G	4:56:52 (24,902)	
Conlon, Toby J	4:45:31 (22,085)	
Conn, Adam	4:33:02 (18,906)	
Connan, Neil P	4:00:09 (10,583)	
Connaughton, Michael B	4:27:17 (17,338)	
Connell, James P	7:35:00 (35,246)	
Connell, Paul	4:22:49 (16,145)	
Connell, Richard	3:48:21 (7,480)	
Connell, Richard J	4:27:39 (17,430)	
Connell, Robert M	4:15:34 (14,300)	
Connell, Thomas C	4:03:31 (11,340)	
Connelly, Martin G	3:09:42 (1,680)	
Conner, Brenden	6:04:51 (33,330)	
Connery, Matthew B	5:18:25 (28,857)	
Connick, Roger M	4:25:48 (16,937)	
Connolly, Brendan M	4:49:24 (23,080)	
Connolly, Dan S	4:08:31 (12,508)	
Connolly, David	4:27:55 (17,520)	
Connolly, David A	4:15:27 (14,271)	
Connolly, Laurence C	3:44:59 (6,800)	
Connolly, Steve R	3:49:32 (7,736)	
Connon, James M	3:16:22 (2,365)	
Connor, Alec W	4:16:49 (14,609)	
Connor, Calvin M	7:56:04 (35,304)	
Connor, Christopher G	3:45:25 (6,873)	
Connor, David	2:36:22 (130)	
Connor, Gavin	5:40:34 (31,551)	
Connor, Ian G	3:49:19 (7,688)	
Connor, Paul	4:23:11 (16,228)	
Connor, Paul	5:12:20 (27,857)	
Connor, Richard	2:55:48 (714)	
Connor, Robert A	4:20:57 (15,674)	
Connor, Shaun S	3:19:58 (2,752)	
Connors, Andrew A	3:20:46 (2,865)	
Connors, Edmund P	4:44:12 (21,766)	
Conoley, Michael P	5:40:24 (31,536)	
Conqueror, Martin R	3:57:08 (9,658)	
Conrad, David J	5:51:48 (32,467)	
Conron, Nick	3:41:01 (6,033)	
Conroy, Christopher C	5:05:27 (26,631)	
Conroy, Gary	5:26:53 (30,038)	
Conroy, Ian M	4:54:43 (24,390)	
Conroy, Lee H	4:41:12 (21,014)	
Consani, Paul C	3:54:38 (8,928)	
Consden, Michael A	5:59:16 (33,003)	
Constant, David A	5:28:31 (30,213)	
Constantinedes, Antoine	6:27:00 (34,324)	
Contino, Domenico	5:56:20 (32,779)	
Convents, André	5:16:38 (28,586)	
Conway, Guy M	3:41:23 (6,101)	
Conway, James A	4:15:58 (14,387)	
Conway, Jim C	5:19:08 (28,987)	
Conway, Neil J	5:04:07 (26,405)	
Conway, Richard M	3:50:28 (7,938)	
Conway, Sam H	4:18:24 (14,995)	

Conway, Steve P................4:43:05 (21,488)
Conyers, Daniel................4:53:43 (24,148)
Conyers-Silverthorn, Rex............4:26:36 (17,148)
Cook, Adam D................3:49:05 (7,642)
Cook, Adam M................3:28:28 (3,924)
Cook, Alan R................4:37:01 (19,922)
Cook, Alex................4:25:40 (16,899)
Cook, Alex J................3:39:52 (5,821)
Cook, Brian N................5:24:57 (29,790)
Cook, Cameron J................4:01:49 (10,987)
Cook, Chris M................3:50:51 (8,027)
Cook, Christopher J................5:04:53 (26,521)
Cook, Darren A................4:24:08 (16,483)
Cook, David................4:19:41 (15,333)
Cook, Dewitt................4:39:48 (20,668)
Cook, Gary J................3:01:27 (1,078)
Cook, Gary P................5:11:49 (27,780)
Cook, Glen Alan................4:05:17 (11,728)
Cook, Glenn W................4:30:30 (18,228)
Cook, Gregg................5:49:15 (32,272)
Cook, James G................4:45:20 (22,040)
Cook, James R................3:57:32 (9,781)
Cook, Jason M................5:02:32 (26,124)
Cook, Jonathan D................3:52:34 (8,415)
Cook, Keith Alexander................4:17:58 (14,882)
Cook, Leonard J................5:07:22 (26,976)
Cook, Malcolm K................4:38:00 (20,165)
Cook, Martin................4:32:30 (18,758)
Cook, Michael J................3:34:15 (4,819)
Cook, Nathan................4:34:10 (19,187)
Cook, Neil................3:57:28 (9,756)
Cook, Neil J................4:49:17 (23,046)
Cook, Paul................3:17:38 (2,493)
Cook, Peter W................3:11:04 (1,786)
Cook, Phil J................2:42:58 (255)
Cook, Philip Michael................5:30:57 (30,519)
Cook, Simon................3:30:52 (4,305)
Cook, Simon G................4:57:58 (25,132)
Cook, Stephen................4:13:42 (13,848)
Cook, Steve P................5:02:04 (26,038)
Cook, Steven C................5:28:07 (30,164)
Cook, Tim M................5:55:10 (32,701)
Cooke, Alistair D................4:21:04 (15,706)
Cooke, Christopher................4:21:59 (15,940)
Cooke, Craig G................4:06:57 (12,094)
Cooke, Darryl J................4:40:27 (20,822)
Cooke, Edward W................4:21:33 (15,832)
Cooke, Gareth................4:24:59 (16,706)
Cooke, Gareth................4:31:21 (18,455)
Cooke, James P................4:00:45 (10,731)
Cooke, Jason L................3:08:46 (1,598)
Cooke, Jon A................4:05:04 (11,670)
Cooke, Kevin J................5:52:31 (32,515)
Cooke, Peter J................5:03:14 (26,243)
Cooke, Richard D................4:00:07 (10,575)
Cooke, Samuel P................3:57:18 (9,706)
Cooke, Stephen P................4:51:31 (23,625)
Cookham, Marcus R................3:21:16 (2,915)
Cookman, Graham R................3:46:24 (7,067)
Cooknell, Andrew J................4:15:03 (14,176)
Cooksey, Andrew P................3:56:46 (9,554)
Cooksley, Sean................4:21:06 (15,714)
Cookson, William D................4:34:30 (19,263)
Coolahan, Fred................6:56:23 (34,911)
Cooling, Stuart M................5:29:37 (30,350)
Coomber, Rob W................4:19:36 (15,313)
Coombes, Martin................4:04:39 (11,572)
Coombes, Matt................4:14:04 (13,922)
Coombes, Timothy G................4:14:39 (14,065)
Coombs, Callum David................4:32:07 (18,666)
Coombs, Richard C................3:11:33 (1,834)
Cooner, Jagdeep S................5:14:02 (28,170)
Cooney, Andrew G................4:06:00 (11,880)
Cooney, Andrew S................3:09:06 (1,626)
Cooney, Brett S................4:13:54 (13,884)
Cooney, Stephen J................3:23:23 (3,174)
Cooper, Aaron C................4:17:45 (14,833)
Cooper, Andrew K................2:52:33 (545)
Cooper, Andy D................4:55:16 (24,522)
Cooper, Bomi................5:08:15 (27,135)
Cooper, Charles E................3:19:32 (2,686)
Cooper, Clive................4:27:38 (17,426)
Cooper, Craig................4:07:49 (12,319)

Preparation Bedford-style

David Bedford these days is the Race Director of the London Marathon. But in 1981, at around 11pm the night before the first London race, a friend bet Bedford he could not run the marathon. At that time he had not run a step for 12 months. He was at work in his nightclub, the *Mad Hatter* in Luton. But, having accepted the £250 wager, he began his preparations by switching from beer to pina coladas followed by a late-night curry. By the time he stumbled over Tower Bridge he hit a wall of his own and he was caught on television, being violently sick, his head hanging sadly over a drain with Brendan Foster providing the commentary. Incidentally, the wager was never paid.

Cooper, Dale R................3:58:12 (10,007)
Cooper, Daniel S................5:35:27 (31,013)
Cooper, David................3:38:26 (5,574)
Cooper, David A................2:59:16 (940)
Cooper, Dean................5:35:32 (31,022)
Cooper, Gary................4:26:43 (17,185)
Cooper, Gerard M................4:55:49 (24,646)
Cooper, Ian J................4:24:19 (16,532)
Cooper, Ian R................4:50:14 (23,292)
Cooper, James D................3:01:39 (1,093)
Cooper, Jamie H................5:13:30 (28,063)
Cooper, Jeremy J................4:18:25 (15,001)
Cooper, John A................5:29:50 (30,379)
Cooper, John P................3:02:37 (1,157)
Cooper, Jon................3:47:48 (7,351)
Cooper, Jonathan E................3:15:23 (2,271)
Cooper, Kelvin E................4:50:08 (23,267)
Cooper, Lee N................4:08:41 (12,544)
Cooper, Leonard P................3:31:16 (4,367)
Cooper, Mark................6:35:53 (34,541)
Cooper, Martin A................5:24:07 (29,670)
Cooper, Martin D................4:57:53 (25,104)
Cooper, Martin S................3:45:26 (6,878)
Cooper, Michael F................5:10:32 (27,554)
Cooper, Neil A................4:10:15 (12,921)
Cooper, Niall................3:45:31 (6,899)
Cooper, Nicholas G................3:07:18 (1,458)
Cooper, Nicholas P................3:44:37 (6,733)
Cooper, Nick J................3:29:36 (4,116)
Cooper, Paul C................4:30:15 (18,166)
Cooper, Peter................4:45:20 (22,040)
Cooper, Peter J................4:40:00 (20,726)
Cooper, Philip John................3:00:39 (1,028)
Cooper, Ricky................4:44:47 (21,906)
Cooper, Rob J................5:47:55 (32,162)
Cooper, Robert C................4:09:59 (12,851)
Cooper, Sean F................3:59:48 (10,495)
Cooper, Stephen J................3:44:01 (6,632)
Cooper, Stephen J................5:47:56 (32,164)
Cooper, Stephen R................4:16:05 (14,420)
Cooper, Steve W................3:42:53 (6,395)
Cooper, Terence B................4:36:05 (19,698)
Cooper, Terry................5:58:31 (32,960)
Cooper, Tim E................4:09:43 (12,779)
Cooper, William G................5:01:23 (25,893)
Cooper-Mitchell, William................4:32:37 (18,794)
Coopey, Simon J................4:36:06 (19,703)
Cooray, Anuradha I................2:21:02 (22)
Coote, Mark R................4:35:57 (19,664)
Cope, David................3:36:01 (5,158)
Cope, Gareth R................5:08:53 (27,250)
Cope, Grahame M................3:26:10 (3,551)

Cope, Jared................4:15:33 (14,294)
Copeland, Maurice H................6:40:11 (34,632)
Copeland, Peter J................3:32:04 (4,479)
Copeland, Tom J................5:47:07 (32,106)
Copestick, Robin J................2:56:07 (728)
Copley, Neil................5:26:08 (29,954)
Copnall, Daniel M................4:18:09 (14,934)
Copnall, Mark................4:39:24 (20,552)
Copp, Daniel................4:58:18 (25,213)
Coppack, Simon W................5:33:15 (30,781)
Coppard, Kenneth P................3:50:30 (7,944)
Coppens, Filip................3:45:10 (6,830)
Coppin, Andrew R................4:48:54 (22,945)
Coppin, Scott J................4:27:40 (17,436)
Coppinger, Eugene................3:12:30 (1,932)
Coppock, Benjamin................4:11:25 (13,228)
Coppock, John D................6:02:04 (33,174)
Coppola, Laurent................4:04:43 (11,590)
Copsey, Mark J................5:04:56 (26,530)
Copus, Christopher D................3:40:43 (5,974)
Copus, Martin R................3:36:58 (5,314)
Copus, Toby W................5:35:51 (31,057)
Corallo, Paul................3:24:15 (3,304)
Coram, Julian................5:01:18 (25,877)
Corben, Alan................5:18:46 (28,925)
Corbet Burcher, James................4:05:22 (11,744)
Corbett, David T................3:45:54 (6,960)
Corbett, Jason................3:24:22 (3,323)
Corbett, Peter M................4:30:22 (18,197)
Corbett, Phillip J................3:27:25 (3,752)
Corbett, Richard C................3:34:01 (4,761)
Corbin, Bryan T................4:11:46 (13,328)
Corbo, Mike A................5:15:30 (28,416)
Corby, Andy P................5:25:43 (29,894)
Corby, Richard John................3:41:24 (6,102)
Corcoran, Chris................3:28:50 (3,981)
Corcoran, Philip Anthony................4:56:01 (24,682)
Corden, Luke................6:21:05 (34,075)
Corderoy, Dave................4:22:18 (16,023)
Cordier, Paul................4:20:34 (15,574)
Cordiner-Barton, Mark J................5:37:32 (31,231)
Cording, James................4:28:05 (17,570)
Cording, Stephen J................4:28:05 (17,570)
Cordingley, Frank J................3:26:11 (3,555)
Cordingley, Jason W................5:32:40 (30,716)
Cordingley, Simon N................4:22:20 (16,031)
Corfield, Mike H................3:30:42 (4,283)
Corkrey, Larry................6:04:49 (33,328)
Corlett, Brian................4:18:22 (14,980)
Corley, Steven M................3:24:56 (3,394)
Cormano, Tony................3:40:32 (5,943)
Cormell, Matthew S................4:30:51 (18,318)
Cornelius, Paul................4:25:37 (16,877)
Cornell, Andrew................4:24:47 (16,651)
Corner, Ian G................4:37:55 (20,143)
Corner, James................5:23:24 (29,583)
Cornes, Christopher J................5:06:34 (26,815)
Corney, Nick................3:27:35 (3,799)
Cornick, Terry J................4:25:11 (16,762)
Cornish, James E................4:28:16 (17,638)
Cornish, Neil A................5:06:14 (26,768)
Cornock, David E................3:12:08 (1,892)
Corns, Ian E................5:01:55 (25,996)
Cornwell, Clive E................5:00:56 (25,795)
Cornwell, Simon A................6:55:09 (34,896)
Corp, John C................5:10:29 (27,545)
Corr, John P................4:05:14 (11,717)
Corrall, Ken T................4:33:48 (19,097)
Corrick, Ian................4:00:27 (10,650)
Corrie, Justin J................2:59:16 (940)
Corrigan, John J................4:54:26 (24,322)
Corry-Reid, Edward B................3:58:03 (9,954)
Corsini, Russell................2:52:59 (557)
Cortes Vallarin, José Hernan................4:01:21 (10,873)
Cortese, Guiseppe................4:27:41 (17,441)
Cosco, Antonio................5:37:53 (31,262)
Costa, Bob................4:56:48 (24,879)
Costa, Gaspar................4:32:57 (18,885)
Costa, Marc................3:39:57 (5,849)
Costain, Michael G................4:04:01 (11,455)
Costanzo, Filippo................3:50:02 (7,845)
Costanzo, Marco................3:40:04 (5,871)
Costas, Paul................3:16:58 (2,424)

Coste, Claude 4:30:35 (18,250)
Costello, Anthony G.........3:53:37 (8,653)
Costello, Steven...............4:11:25 (13,228)
Costello, Tony...................5:30:27 (30,456)
Coster, Ian C....................5:06:05 (26,741)
Coster, Michael................7:09:01 (35,042)
Costiff, Nigel L.................3:57:32 (9,781)
Cota, Brian S....................5:01:22 (25,890)
Cotsen, Jonathan.............4:15:24 (14,256)
Cottee, Simon C...............4:29:11 (17,884)
Cotter, Ian J....................2:58:50 (903)
Cotter, James E................4:37:28 (20,027)
Cotter, Nick J...................5:30:08 (30,423)
Cotter, Steven M..............5:03:35 (26,300)
Cotterell, Steven J...........5:24:28 (29,728)
Cotterill, Matthew D 3:58:03 (9,954)
Cottin, Jean-Benoit 3:40:17 (5,913)
Cotton, Anthony E............7:00:22 (34,950)
Cotton, Keith...................4:22:34 (16,091)
Cotton, Stuart R..............4:11:51 (13,350)
Cottrell, Brendan M..........3:31:31 (4,400)
Cottrell, Richard.............4:09:13 (12,663)
Couch, Adam H.................3:48:28 (7,506)
Couchman, Kevin A...........3:02:02 (1,121)
Couchman, Neil R 4:29:16 (17,913)
Coudret, Jean-Luc...........4:24:34 (16,585)
Coughlan, Alan P.............4:16:42 (14,584)
Coughlan, Mark A............4:15:07 (14,195)
Coughlan, Simon..............3:42:52 (6,391)
Couldridge, David C 5:02:04 (26,038)
Couldridge, Paul J............2:41:35 (226)
Coulon, Laurence.............6:14:45 (33,781)
Coulson, Alex...................4:11:23 (13,222)
Coulson, Chris..................4:23:00 (16,184)
Coulson, Ian.....................4:11:34 (13,273)
Coulson, Joshua S 3:58:01 (9,941)
Coulson, Paul A................5:17:32 (28,723)
Coulson, Stephen Hugh 4:13:44 (13,857)
Coulson, Wayne A.............3:21:03 (2,892)
Coulthurst, Benjamin 4:18:43 (15,085)
Counihan, Shaun..............4:50:58 (23,478)
Coupe, Joseph S 5:26:52 (30,033)
Coupe, Matthew R 3:36:00 (5,154)
Coupe, Michael.................4:25:57 (16,974)
Coupes, Chris...................5:14:19 (28,211)
Coupes, Dominic John 4:05:46 (11,837)
Coupland, Lee...................5:37:06 (31,187)
Courage, Toby B...............2:49:14 (431)
Court, Alan R 3:17:51 (2,515)
Court, Andrew P...............4:18:30 (15,029)
Court, Andy G...................5:55:15 (32,708)
Court, David L...................4:32:43 (18,819)
Court, Jon P.....................3:23:00 (3,126)
Court, Steven R.................4:36:13 (19,729)
Courtenay-Clack, Charlie E 4:21:27 (15,797)
Courtney, Daniel C............4:50:05 (23,261)
Courtney, John.................5:35:48 (31,051)
Courtney, Paul D..............4:37:49 (20,125)
Courtney, Robert..............4:38:32 (20,307)
Courtney, Trevor A............4:57:10 (24,957)
Cousens, Charles L............4:58:51 (25,349)
Cousin, Simon J................5:11:10 (27,667)
Cousins, Lee.....................4:00:43 (10,724)
Cousins, Roger Norman 4:27:34 (17,404)
Coutant, Eric....................3:35:38 (5,082)
Coutinho, Jo.....................4:04:12 (11,489)
Coutts, David....................4:38:21 (20,266)
Couvreur, Pierre................3:34:03 (4,770)
Covell, Andrew..................4:41:01 (20,965)
Covey, Wayne...................5:50:19 (32,365)
Covus, Steven D...............5:41:14 (31,600)
Cowan, Angus..................5:43:22 (31,811)
Cowan, Callum..................3:51:49 (8,231)
Cowan, William M.............4:49:42 (23,179)
Coward, David A................4:50:09 (23,274)
Coward, Jonathan M..........4:21:56 (15,931)
Coward, Richard 4:48:40 (22,891)
Cowdrill, Andrew..............4:24:57 (16,698)
Cowdroy, David Robert.......3:59:53 (10,512)
Cowell, Antony J...............3:16:50 (2,416)
Cowen, Chris....................4:42:50 (21,422)
Cowhig, Jeff.....................4:22:51 (16,156)
Cowie, James...................6:00:34 (33,084)

Cowling, Mark A...............4:37:08 (19,950)
Cowling, Michael L.............4:42:01 (21,202)
Cowlishaw, Steven G..........3:03:24 (1,196)
Cowper-Smith, Adam.........3:13:37 (2,075)
Cox, Alan D......................5:52:24 (32,508)
Cox, Alan M......................3:07:52 (1,516)
Cox, Allan........................5:06:49 (26,871)
Cox, Barry S.....................4:37:34 (20,060)
Cox, Brett M.....................3:45:53 (6,958)
Cox, Brian Antony.............6:02:18 (33,190)
Cox, Christopher 4:01:44 (10,970)
Cox, Christopher S 4:27:43 (17,451)
Cox, Colin.........................5:18:18 (28,833)
Cox, Darren 3:49:36 (7,747)
Cox, David L......................3:40:55 (6,017)
Cox, David M.....................5:12:38 (27,913)
Cox, David R......................4:05:30 (11,768)
Cox, David R......................4:13:33 (13,811)
Cox, Elliot H.....................4:48:16 (22,801)
Cox, Gareth B....................6:20:03 (34,035)
Cox, Gary.........................6:00:44 (33,094)
Cox, Ian G........................3:43:49 (6,592)
Cox, Ian M........................4:39:04 (20,456)
Cox, James........................3:26:35 (3,617)
Cox, James E.....................4:54:37 (24,365)
Cox, Jason........................3:50:51 (8,027)
Cox, Jason B.....................5:08:58 (27,265)
Cox, Jonathan R................3:23:40 (3,214)
Cox, Liam R......................5:46:53 (32,077)
Cox, Mark A 3:42:34 (6,321)
Cox, Mark S......................4:43:53 (21,688)
Cox, Martin L....................5:52:07 (32,487)
Cox, Matthew J.................5:02:09 (26,051)
Cox, Matthew R................4:49:28 (23,102)
Cox, Michael 3:24:39 (3,362)
Cox, Michael A..................4:10:00 (12,853)
Cox, Michael P..................5:08:02 (27,090)
Cox, Nicholas G................3:32:45 (4,582)
Cox, Paul A.......................3:49:40 (7,761)
Cox, Peter G.....................5:01:32 (25,918)
Cox, Robert C....................5:29:48 (30,374)
Cox, S..............................4:37:03 (19,932)
Cox, Simon.......................4:12:44 (13,587)
Cox, Simon P....................4:31:50 (18,590)
Cox, Stephen M................3:48:13 (7,449)
Cox, Tim...........................3:41:01 (6,033)
Cox, Trevor D....................4:45:13 (22,016)
Coyle, David M..................4:55:13 (24,512)
Coyle, James R.................3:54:50 (8,985)
Coyle, Michael..................5:22:26 (29,428)
Coyle, Paul S....................3:59:38 (10,428)
Coyle, Roger.....................3:27:32 (3,783)
Coyle, Terry P...................2:54:18 (617)
Cozens, David M...............4:58:51 (25,349)
Crabb, Kieron N................5:01:13 (25,865)
Crabtree, Mark..................2:59:13 (934)
Crabtree, Nik....................4:42:45 (21,397)
Cracknell, Andrew P 3:20:31 (2,827)
Cracknell, Rob...................5:00:36 (25,727)
Cracknell, Sam C...............4:47:55 (22,712)
Cradden, Brendan 3:55:27 (9,148)
Craddock, Christopher J.............4:30:50 (18,312)
Craddock, Dean A..............4:52:26 (23,851)
Craddock, Peter M.............4:17:26 (14,753)
Crader, Michael.................5:25:59 (29,933)
Craen, Peter R..................4:58:50 (25,346)
Craft, Alan W....................3:38:09 (5,527)
Cragg, Paul J....................4:56:16 (24,742)
Craggs, Tom L...................2:54:55 (657)
Craig, Chris......................3:46:36 (7,110)
Craig, Gerard E.................2:54:57 (659)
Craig, John L....................5:37:24 (31,214)
Craig, Michael...................2:53:35 (589)
Craig, Phillip M.................5:23:24 (29,583)
Craig, Richard J.................5:28:51 (30,254)
Craig, Robert J..................4:46:33 (22,360)
Craig, Scott......................3:22:31 (3,071)
Cramphorn, Jon B 4:29:51 (18,056)
Crampsey, James M 2:43:29 (268)
Crampton, Ian..................2:30:23 (68)
Crampton, Simon 4:52:41 (23,903)
Cran, Alex N.....................2:58:37 (879)
Crane, Andrew J................4:14:17 (13,986)

Crane, Barry M..................3:30:59 (4,330)
Crane, Carl Laurence 3:27:00 (3,683)
Crane, Christopher 5:34:39 (30,927)
Crane, David.....................4:35:40 (19,587)
Crane, Gregory L................4:34:40 (19,307)
Crane, Lee........................4:18:22 (14,980)
Crane, Mark......................3:22:47 (3,106)
Crane, Mark John 3:57:44 (9,856)
Crane, Martin A.................3:33:25 (4,669)
Crane, Michael A...............4:50:02 (23,244)
Crane, Oliver P..................4:55:56 (24,672)
Crang, Paul A....................5:18:19 (28,837)
Crannage, Jonathan 3:03:50 (1,227)
Cranston, Jonathan M 4:21:35 (15,837)
Cranwell, Mark A 3:06:51 (1,425)
Crashley, Sue M................4:27:11 (17,305)
Craske, Neil B...................4:00:47 (10,741)
Craven, James N...............4:22:31 (16,078)
Craven, John C..................3:12:17 (1,911)
Craven, Martin 4:30:30 (18,228)
Craven, Philip...................6:26:15 (34,291)
Crawford, Ben...................3:54:01 (8,760)
Crawford, Daniel...............3:35:03 (4,968)
Crawford, Daniel T 3:37:42 (5,440)
Crawford, David J..............4:26:49 (17,211)
Crawford, David J..............4:57:59 (25,135)
Crawford, John..................4:27:48 (17,487)
Crawford, Kamau...............6:30:49 (34,430)
Crawford, Lee A.................5:30:06 (30,411)
Crawford, Paul..................5:04:35 (26,479)
Crawford, Samuel..............2:43:29 (268)
Crawford, Steve A..............4:37:59 (20,161)
Crawley, William 4:58:58 (25,380)
Crayford, Dean A...............5:09:09 (27,298)
Crayston, David 3:07:01 (1,436)
Craze, Lee D.....................5:52:59 (32,542)
Creal, Joe........................5:08:07 (27,106)
Creamer, Jonathan M 4:10:07 (12,884)
Crease, Greg B..................6:03:31 (33,259)
Creasy, Ian A....................3:30:13 (4,209)
Creaven, Dylan L...............4:15:46 (14,340)
Creech, Stuart D...............2:59:10 (930)
Creed, Andrew 4:08:48 (12,573)
Creed, Gareth...................3:20:04 (2,762)
Creed, Phil.......................4:55:33 (24,581)
Creed, Steve.....................5:56:09 (32,766)
Creegan, Dermot F 4:42:25 (21,305)
Crees, Stuart E..................2:39:16 (180)
Cregan, David E 4:17:55 (14,866)
Creighton, Mark G.............4:54:04 (24,235)
Cremins, David..................4:12:36 (13,547)
Crenol, Kevin N.................2:40:10 (195)
Crestani, James E 3:42:35 (6,325)
Crichton, Jamie.................3:29:56 (4,173)
Crichton, Thomas G 4:00:32 (10,680)
Crick, Steve......................4:07:19 (12,183)
Crighton, Timothy P 4:29:37 (17,988)
Crimmins, John D 3:52:38 (8,440)
Cripps, David L..................4:34:23 (19,235)
Cripps, Peter G.................4:24:08 (16,483)
Crisp, David E...................5:08:25 (27,167)
Crisp, Derek J...................4:54:02 (24,229)
Crisp, John C....................5:23:04 (29,526)
Crisp, Mark.......................4:44:31 (21,840)
Crisp, Matthew D 3:14:59 (2,230)
Crisp, Philip......................4:19:36 (15,313)
Crisp-Harrison, Daniel M 3:58:37 (10,132)
Crispie, Gerard..................2:56:20 (736)
Critchfield, John R 4:21:27 (15,797)
Critchley, David J..............4:39:29 (20,576)
Critchlow, Martin 3:06:00 (1,372)
Critchlow, Nigel................3:34:34 (4,886)
Critoph, Jason 4:57:40 (25,064)
Croal, Jeremy P 4:35:24 (19,522)
Croasdale, Mark J..............2:33:59 (99)
Crocker, Matthew M...........3:23:08 (3,141)
Crocker, Neil J..................4:26:32 (17,126)
Crocker, Russell P 5:11:15 (27,684)
Crocker, Shaun..................4:59:11 (25,430)
Crocket, Graham................3:12:40 (1,952)
Croft, Stephen P................5:14:58 (28,308)
Croft, Stuart K..................4:44:27 (21,828)
Crofts, Stephen 4:55:57 (24,674)

Crol, Ludo 3:13:37 (2,075)
Crole-Rees, Matthew J 3:30:16 (4,217)
Crombie, Hugo D 5:18:20 (28,844)
Crompton, Howard R 4:12:33 (13,538)
Crompton, Neil W 2:52:55 (554)
Cronin, Aindriu J 4:44:39 (21,871)
Cronin, Alexander 4:42:41 (21,381)
Cronin, David A 5:02:46 (26,170)
Cronin, Iain D 4:53:47 (24,169)
Cronin, Matthew C 4:36:23 (19,766)
Cronin, Neil J 4:27:17 (17,338)
Cronin, Stephen M 4:42:42 (21,388)
Cronin, Tony J 5:02:47 (26,179)
Cronk, Anthony J 3:59:56 (10,530)
Crook, Andrew 4:03:24 (11,315)
Crook, Andrew P 4:10:23 (12,952)
Crook, Christopher 4:12:24 (13,493)
Crook, David F 3:31:09 (4,352)
Crook, Graham 5:50:21 (32,367)
Crook, Jonathan F 4:29:50 (18,048)
Crook, Warren S 3:57:48 (9,873)
Crooks, Lee 3:59:48 (10,495)
Crooks, Martin 3:40:40 (5,965)
Croook, Ian T 5:09:20 (27,337)
Crosbie, David A 4:25:58 (16,978)
Crosbie, Neil J 3:57:31 (9,775)
Crosby, Ian 4:39:08 (20,473)
Cross, Adrian 4:47:08 (22,525)
Cross, Andrew 5:58:33 (32,961)
Cross, Andrew D 5:23:19 (29,573)
Cross, David M 4:44:59 (21,957)
Cross, Giles M 5:02:41 (26,150)
Cross, Jonathan M 4:17:29 (14,764)
Cross, Kevin J 3:57:15 (9,690)
Cross, Peter 3:41:20 (6,093)
Cross, Peter H 5:47:17 (32,120)
Cross, Philip J 2:48:04 (400)
Cross, Ryan 3:51:34 (8,178)
Cross, Stephen A 3:18:14 (2,548)
Cross, Stephen D 4:09:53 (12,827)
Cross, Stephen V 5:21:22 (29,281)
Cross, Tim 4:41:24 (21,055)
Cross, Toby A 4:45:35 (22,101)
Crossan, Bill 4:58:11 (25,187)
Crossan, James Vincent 4:22:26 (16,060)
Crossley, Anthony 3:27:32 (3,783)
Crossley, Mark R 4:58:38 (25,304)
Crossman, John M 4:35:59 (19,675)
Crossman, John S 4:27:15 (17,325)
Crosthwaite, Calum G 4:45:46 (22,147)
Crosthwaite, Tom W 4:26:33 (17,130)
Croston, Yanik 4:54:52 (24,420)
Crotte Alvarado, Amado 5:20:56 (29,213)
Crotty, Andrew D 3:38:40 (5,619)
Crotty, Damian 4:21:01 (15,697)
Crotty, Michael 5:38:22 (31,313)
Crouch, Lewis C 5:02:11 (26,061)
Crouch, Matthew J 5:10:29 (27,545)
Crouch, Michael 3:25:07 (3,410)
Crouch, Robert J 3:46:38 (7,120)
Crouch, Steven J 4:39:56 (20,701)
Crouch, Stuart J 5:08:18 (27,140)
Croud, Andrew T 4:18:38 (15,064)
Crow, Allan 5:23:55 (29,638)
Crow, Barry W 4:02:22 (11,100)
Crow, Graham 3:31:25 (4,386)
Crowder, Greville 5:14:57 (28,306)
Crowder, Robert 3:46:05 (6,998)
Crowe, Graham 5:32:58 (30,749)
Crowhurst, Paul M 3:53:49 (8,705)
Crowie, Rowan 4:59:41 (25,529)
Crowle, Ian K 3:24:32 (3,346)
Crowley, David M 4:05:57 (11,870)
Crowley, Gregory S 3:06:14 (1,394)
Crowley, Jonnie R 4:09:48 (12,803)
Crowley, Vincent P 3:46:23 (7,062)
Crowther, Adam J 3:49:54 (7,814)
Crowther, David 3:38:07 (5,518)
Croydon, Stuart Anthony 3:05:47 (1,356)
Crozier, Peter 3:35:53 (5,131)
Cruddas, Peter H 4:59:11 (25,430)
Crudge, Simon S 4:18:09 (14,934)
Crudgington, David J 4:37:17 (19,982)
Cruickshank, Brian 3:02:34 (1,154)
Cruickshank, George A 4:31:31 (18,510)
Crump, Steve 5:17:29 (28,716)
Crumpton, Anthony Loris 4:19:41 (15,333)
Crundwell, Gary 4:04:48 (11,609)
Cruse, Alastair J 4:16:41 (14,580)
Cruse, Peter 3:00:19 (1,015)
Crussell, Nicholas 5:47:45 (32,146)
Crutcher, Wesley D 5:54:55 (32,683)
Crutchley, Andrew 3:48:25 (7,490)
Crutchley, Wayne 4:30:23 (18,202)
Cruz, Pedro 4:57:18 (24,985)
Cryan, Bernard T 4:44:55 (21,933)
Cryer, Mark 4:04:32 (11,552)
Crysell, Adam T 5:05:34 (26,653)
Crysell, Trevor 4:22:08 (15,978)
Crystal, Roger 4:48:45 (22,912)
Cubbison, John M 5:16:08 (28,523)
Cubbon, Paul R 3:13:50 (2,102)
Cudmore, Jonathan L 5:19:53 (29,082)
Cue Pandal, Eduardo 4:13:49 (13,873)
Cuff, Pete 4:01:49 (10,987)
Culclough, David 6:24:07 (34,192)
Cull, Matthew J 3:58:49 (10,198)
Cull, Mick 3:36:11 (5,188)
Cull, Steven R 3:37:18 (5,372)
Cullen, Andrew 3:04:51 (1,297)
Cullen, Anne F 4:50:20 (23,323)
Cullen, Benjamin J 3:59:11 (10,306)
Cullen, Bryan 3:19:56 (2,745)
Cullen, Declan A 4:50:30 (23,371)
Cullen, Gary J 3:43:34 (6,536)
Cullern, Doug A 4:48:30 (22,851)
Cullinane, John 3:57:18 (9,706)
Cullingworth, Ian 3:23:14 (3,153)
Cullum, Gordon G 4:08:51 (12,585)
Cully, Patrick 4:27:26 (17,377)
Cully, Rob J 4:50:56 (23,467)
Culpan, Charlie J 4:13:15 (13,729)
Culshaw, Jamie 3:55:29 (9,154)
Culver, David 5:18:12 (28,817)
Culwin, Fintan 4:53:38 (24,109)
Cumber, Geoffrey 3:04:48 (1,293)
Cumberworth, Paul 4:05:02 (11,659)
Cumming, Alastair J 4:29:31 (17,969)
Cumming, Iain 3:02:11 (1,132)
Cumming, John 3:56:17 (9,383)
Cumming, Mick 5:11:48 (27,775)
Cumming, Robert G 5:11:32 (27,733)
Cummings, Alan T 3:59:32 (10,398)
Cummings, Allan 5:58:12 (32,938)
Cummings, Simon J 3:51:29 (8,164)
Cummins, Mark Craig 3:47:45 (7,336)
Cummins, Timothy D 3:49:21 (7,696)
Cundall, Ian 3:57:20 (9,721)
Cundy, David E 5:03:55 (26,366)
Cundy, Kevin J 3:58:30 (10,097)
Cunliffe, Rory 3:53:09 (8,548)
Cunnah, Liam 4:14:09 (13,945)
Cunniffe, Matthew P 5:27:11 (30,064)
Cunningham, Colin M 4:27:10 (17,301)
Cunningham, Dan 4:03:45 (11,375)
Cunningham, Daniel J 4:33:30 (19,022)
Cunningham, Fraser K 5:37:08 (31,190)
Cunningham, Gary 5:57:49 (32,896)
Cunningham, George A 5:40:21 (31,528)
Cunningham, Ian A 3:59:56 (10,530)
Cunningham, James J 4:30:42 (18,279)
Cunningham, James M 3:43:49 (6,592)
Cunningham, Kevin 5:03:18 (26,252)
Cunningham, Mark 4:49:16 (23,042)
Cunningham, Philip P 3:01:30 (1,083)
Cunningham, Steve 2:48:19 (406)
Cunningham, Steve 4:09:57 (12,843)
Cunningham, Stuart J 2:42:32 (246)
Cunnison, Martin P 4:57:18 (24,985)
Cuppello, Perry D 4:59:18 (25,453)
Curant, Mark A 4:27:27 (17,380)
Curd, Christopher D 4:59:03 (25,399)
Curnier, Bruno D 4:38:03 (20,179)
Curnow, Steve 5:51:30 (32,448)
Curphey, Paul T 3:20:58 (2,887)
Curran, Jeremy 3:15:31 (2,285)
Curran, Mathew E 5:23:15 (29,563)
Curran, Quentin S 3:26:37 (3,621)
Curran, Steven W 4:01:39 (10,956)
Curran, Tony 4:26:17 (17,064)
Curran, William R 3:13:36 (2,073)
Curreli, Francesco 3:55:19 (9,112)
Currell, Geoffrey 4:18:18 (14,962)
Currie, Andrew I 4:49:36 (23,147)
Currie, Glenn 4:00:12 (10,599)
Currie, Matthew J 4:03:15 (11,282)
Currie, Michael A 4:08:06 (12,390)
Currie, Tom 4:02:27 (11,118)
Currier, Simon 5:33:01 (30,756)
Currin, Robert A 5:29:51 (30,384)
Currington, Darren L 3:40:08 (5,885)
Curry, Andrew J 4:55:19 (24,531)
Curson, Ashley D 4:28:15 (17,633)
Curtin, Samuel 4:23:06 (16,207)
Curtis, Adam 4:16:33 (14,536)
Curtis, Adam 4:41:10 (20,998)
Curtis, Alan M 4:17:10 (14,687)
Curtis, Andy B 3:53:41 (8,673)
Curtis, Barry J 5:24:13 (29,684)
Curtis, Ben W 5:02:41 (26,150)
Curtis, Gary L 6:04:18 (33,305)
Curtis, Ian S 5:08:41 (27,209)
Curtis, James R 4:47:49 (22,675)
Curtis, Jason 5:13:46 (28,115)
Curtis, Jeremy 3:22:13 (3,040)
Curtis, Jonathon 4:53:09 (24,012)
Curtis, Keith 3:57:14 (9,682)
Curtis, Len P 3:33:11 (4,635)
Curtis, Marc S 3:21:26 (2,936)
Curtis, Martin John 4:58:46 (25,330)
Curtis, Michael 4:52:40 (23,895)
Curtis, Michael 6:18:40 (33,952)
Curtis, Nicky L 3:52:19 (8,362)
Curtis, Richard 3:39:39 (5,784)
Curtis, Simon 5:02:39 (26,146)
Curtis, Steven A 3:47:54 (7,374)
Curwen, Philip T 4:53:51 (24,189)
Curzon, Jason B 4:59:59 (25,594)
Cushing, George S 4:24:47 (16,651)
Cushway, Darren T 3:46:39 (7,122)
Custance, Stephen 4:12:14 (13,447)
Custodio, Ricardo 5:40:35 (31,554)
Cusworth, Stuart M 4:42:32 (21,339)
Cuthbert, Paul Jeremy 3:44:38 (6,738)
Cuthbert, Philip D 3:33:41 (4,700)
Cuthbertson, Graham 4:16:33 (14,536)
Cutler, Colin J 4:33:33 (19,036)
Cutler, Dereck D 4:33:25 (19,006)
Cutler, Paul F 4:03:27 (11,320)
Cutting, Andy J 4:11:25 (13,228)
Cutting, Stuart 5:37:46 (31,251)
Cutts, Nigel Philip 3:44:02 (6,636)
Cuzzol, Davide 5:31:46 (30,614)
Czaja, Mark 4:57:26 (25,016)
Czerwinski, David A 4:39:00 (20,435)
Da Gama, Paul S 4:55:17 (24,527)
Da Silva, Panta 4:23:55 (16,419)
Da Silva Pereira, David E 3:14:49 (2,210)
Dable, Julian P 4:35:18 (19,488)
Dable, Neil A 3:40:26 (5,931)
D'Acampo, Gino 5:13:19 (28,041)
Dachtler, Christopher 3:42:01 (6,212)
Dackow, Sven 3:24:34 (3,351)
Dacosta, Marva 5:49:06 (32,259)
Dadd, Tony W 2:54:45 (646)
Dade, John P 3:45:38 (6,918)
Dade, Richard C 4:12:46 (13,596)
Dade, Stuart J 5:18:33 (28,880)
Dadgostar, Simon 4:48:28 (22,843)
Dadi, Rav S 5:13:56 (28,148)
Dadson, James S 4:53:04 (23,990)
Daffern, Andrew S 6:15:05 (33,794)
Daffit, Herve 3:12:56 (1,995)
Dagger, Richard 4:03:14 (11,279)
Dagless, John W 3:27:49 (3,827)
Dagonas, James 5:48:37 (32,230)
Dagul, Robert 4:15:14 (14,220)
Dahanayake, Kit 4:32:30 (18,758)
Daines, Paul J 4:38:29 (20,292)

Dajda, Nick......4:06:47 (12,056)	Darby, Iain M......2:52:07 (525)	Davies, Carwyn......4:16:46 (14,596)
Dakin, Jon A......4:41:08 (20,991)	Darby, Paul......4:42:12 (21,249)	Davies, Ceri Rhys......4:07:10 (12,144)
Dakin, Simon J......2:57:31 (806)	Darby, Richard J......4:50:15 (23,301)	Davies, Chris......5:03:21 (26,265)
Dala, Anil......4:29:01 (17,834)	Darch, Gary C......5:49:46 (32,315)	Davies, Chris N......3:52:46 (8,460)
Daldry, Simon J......5:23:16 (29,566)	Darcy, Lee G......4:54:07 (24,247)	Davies, Christopher A......4:25:18 (16,786)
Dale, Alex J......5:09:55 (27,442)	D'Arcy, Adrian......3:44:07 (6,653)	Davies, Christopher J......3:41:06 (6,048)
Dale, Dave M......4:27:38 (17,426)	D'Arcy, Ross......4:41:24 (21,055)	Davies, Clive T......3:21:14 (2,912)
Dale, Graham Thomas......4:37:15 (19,974)	Dare, Steve J......5:25:25 (29,844)	Davies, Craig A......4:46:17 (22,274)
Dale, Jonathan......5:11:02 (27,645)	Dario, Luciano......4:46:14 (22,255)	Davies, Daniel A......3:35:08 (4,985)
Dale, Matt J......3:41:44 (6,156)	Dark, Kevin P......5:53:21 (32,574)	Davies, Darren M......5:42:49 (31,751)
Dale, Simon L......4:38:21 (20,266)	Darkins, Alan......5:29:31 (30,339)	Davies, David W......3:20:44 (2,859)
Dale, Steve G......5:20:08 (29,111)	Darkins, Peter S......4:08:31 (12,508)	Davies, Gareth......4:09:06 (12,642)
Daley, John R......5:44:21 (31,882)	Darley, Glenn......3:51:50 (8,234)	Davies, Gareth Richard......3:58:08 (9,982)
Dalgleish, Michael......5:25:23 (29,841)	Darley, Vince M......3:19:24 (2,668)	Davies, Gary Paul......4:08:48 (12,573)
Dalies, Guillaume J......5:13:38 (28,085)	Darling, Richard J......2:45:52 (328)	Davies, Gavin R......2:38:01 (158)
Dallimore, Aaron J......4:28:12 (17,613)	Darnbrook, Bob N......5:20:22 (29,135)	Davies, Geraint......4:36:41 (19,835)
D'Alton, Charles H......3:28:06 (3,868)	Darnell, Peter......4:25:43 (16,915)	Davies, Gethin C......7:30:18 (35,219)
Dalton, Jonathan C......4:24:53 (16,679)	Darnell, Peter F......5:09:07 (27,292)	Davies, Glenn......3:37:34 (5,417)
Dalton, Julian......5:34:27 (30,907)	Darnell, Scott......5:08:10 (27,119)	Davies, Goronwy H......6:18:40 (33,952)
Dalton, Mark S......3:01:05 (1,056)	Darragh, Matthew......5:18:36 (28,898)	Davies, Graham M......4:24:31 (16,573)
Dalton, Patrick M......5:15:20 (28,390)	Darrock, Bernard T......4:29:04 (17,850)	Davies, Hadleigh James......3:30:23 (4,232)
Dalton, Stephen A......5:09:59 (27,458)	Darrock, Robert L......6:18:40 (33,952)	Davies, Henry......4:31:46 (18,574)
Dalton, Thomas J......4:35:01 (19,411)	Darroze, Marc......4:02:44 (11,173)	Davies, Howard......3:41:51 (6,175)
Dalton, Tony J......4:40:40 (20,878)	Darton, David F......3:28:51 (3,985)	Davies, Hywel J......3:45:24 (6,871)
Daly, Anthony L......3:54:49 (8,973)	Darton-Smith, Alan......6:49:04 (34,796)	Davies, Iaan G......3:46:12 (7,017)
Daly, Chris......3:55:27 (9,148)	Darvill, Ian......5:19:05 (28,981)	Davies, Ivor J......4:51:51 (23,709)
Daly, Christian......5:57:36 (32,882)	Das, Saroj......7:12:43 (35,079)	Davies, James T......4:13:15 (13,729)
Daly, Edward V......3:57:56 (9,912)	Das, Shailendra......6:48:58 (34,795)	Davies, Jamie A......3:06:37 (1,413)
Daly, George......3:51:53 (8,249)	Dasgupta, Prokar......5:57:29 (32,875)	Davies, Jeffrey......3:43:49 (6,592)
Daly, Gerard M......4:09:29 (12,717)	Dashper, Wayne R......2:38:50 (173)	Davies, Jerome......5:31:36 (30,594)
Daly, Hugh D......4:20:07 (15,464)	Date, Malcolm......4:00:11 (10,593)	Davies, Jerry M......4:56:51 (24,898)
Daly, Ian J......4:16:57 (14,634)	Datson, Richard J......6:08:00 (33,480)	Davies, John......4:16:18 (14,473)
Daly, John A......4:51:04 (23,505)	Datson, Sean R......5:00:19 (25,658)	Davies, Johnny H......4:40:55 (20,943)
Daly, Joseph......3:59:43 (10,467)	Datta, Julian......4:43:12 (21,517)	Davies, Jonathan......5:22:25 (29,425)
Daly, Kieran D......3:48:54 (7,595)	Datta, Milton......4:33:16 (18,965)	Davies, Jonathan Charles......3:36:06 (5,173)
Daly, Michael P......7:19:46 (35,149)	Datta, Roger N......5:31:36 (30,594)	Davies, Jonathan H......4:09:22 (12,699)
Daly, Stephen J......4:08:09 (12,407)	Daugherty, Duane W......3:36:53 (5,291)	Davies, Keith J......3:03:07 (1,178)
Dalziel, Stephen M......5:04:57 (26,535)	Daughtrey, James......4:20:27 (15,545)	Davies, Kevin......5:18:18 (28,833)
Damant, Clive......4:39:59 (20,719)	Daum, Peter R......4:05:28 (11,762)	Davies, Kevin M......4:19:44 (15,348)
Danaher, Kieran J......4:18:26 (15,009)	Daumen, Vincent......3:32:43 (4,575)	Davies, Lee......3:20:02 (2,758)
Danby, Christopher J......7:01:38 (34,969)	Davenport, Robert R......4:29:51 (18,056)	Davies, Lee......3:33:08 (4,630)
Dance, James Frederick......4:45:17 (22,033)	Davenport, Roy......5:01:35 (25,929)	Davies, Lee Davies......4:58:37 (25,302)
Dancer, Andrew......2:57:41 (820)	Daveridge, Jamie I......4:55:51 (24,653)	Davies, Lee J......4:03:04 (11,244)
Dando, Dan......5:07:14 (26,951)	Davesne, Laurent Tony......3:45:31 (6,899)	Davies, Lee M......4:09:41 (12,769)
D'Andrea, Alex......4:49:52 (23,212)	Davey, Adrian R......2:59:43 (977)	Davies, Lian......3:17:58 (2,523)
Dane, Lindsay J......4:38:01 (20,170)	Davey, Andrew J......4:57:32 (25,040)	Davies, Lyndon H......4:07:50 (12,322)
Danel, Philippe......3:52:53 (8,483)	Davey, David P......4:27:16 (17,333)	Davies, Mark A......4:31:11 (18,400)
Danelli, Fabio......2:53:31 (585)	Davey, Ian P......3:56:23 (9,423)	Davies, Mark Marcello......3:48:51 (7,585)
Danelli, Manlio......3:19:55 (2,743)	Davey, Kelly......3:05:33 (1,338)	Davies, Martin V......3:11:26 (1,817)
Daniel, Anthony W......4:20:46 (15,627)	Davey, Michael J......4:29:41 (18,011)	Davies, Matt......5:57:10 (32,842)
Daniel, Guilleminet......4:08:25 (12,485)	Davey, Peter R......4:55:22 (24,542)	Davies, Matthew E......3:45:43 (6,930)
Daniel, Jasper......6:02:21 (33,194)	Davey, Steve J......4:26:55 (17,241)	Davies, Matty......5:09:53 (27,439)
Daniel, Lehr......3:40:32 (5,943)	David, Alastair C......4:03:28 (11,323)	Davies, Michael......4:48:58 (22,962)
Daniel, Neil......7:31:15 (35,228)	David, Arab......4:00:56 (10,782)	Davies, Michael H......3:45:53 (6,958)
Daniel, Richard W......4:16:03 (14,407)	David, George......5:06:02 (26,731)	Davies, Michael H......5:14:31 (28,247)
Daniel, Stephen......3:59:57 (10,537)	David, Neville G......5:12:25 (27,873)	Davies, Mike J......3:53:54 (8,723)
Daniele, Gennaro......4:10:05 (12,874)	Davidson, Colin I......3:05:08 (1,312)	Davies, Morgan......4:59:48 (25,555)
Danieli, Stefano......3:30:52 (4,305)	Davidson, Eric R......4:37:16 (19,978)	Davies, Nathan......5:04:18 (26,427)
Daniels, David J......3:01:43 (1,097)	Davidson, Ewan J......3:16:09 (2,346)	Davies, Nicholas......4:54:38 (24,374)
Daniels, Gary......5:31:54 (30,626)	Davidson, George Fraser......3:42:32 (6,310)	Davies, Paul......3:52:01 (8,280)
Daniels, Guy......5:01:51 (25,980)	Davidson, Graham J......5:51:09 (32,426)	Davies, Paul......4:02:45 (11,178)
Daniels, Hywel J......4:11:36 (13,284)	Davidson, Iain......4:37:20 (19,990)	Davies, Paul David......3:31:26 (4,391)
Daniels, Michael......3:01:32 (1,085)	Davidson, Ian C......3:23:38 (3,206)	Davies, Paul R......4:18:25 (15,001)
Daniels, Michael......5:15:48 (28,474)	Davidson, Julian......3:49:14 (7,672)	Davies, Paul W......3:17:08 (2,404)
Daniels, Neil......3:21:00 (2,890)	Davidson, Malcolm K......5:23:04 (29,526)	Davies, Peter B......3:42:14 (6,255)
Daniels, Paul......3:52:53 (8,483)	Davidson, Michael......5:15:10 (28,347)	Davies, Philip B......4:59:35 (25,513)
Daniels, Paul......4:20:06 (15,459)	Davidson, Mick......3:47:18 (7,248)	Davies, Philip C......4:47:34 (22,617)
Daniels, Terence......6:25:32 (34,257)	Davidson, Neil M......4:19:05 (15,181)	Davies, Philip R......4:23:40 (16,355)
Danielsson, Mathias......4:32:05 (18,660)	Davidson, Sean......5:12:59 (27,981)	Davies, Raymond......4:19:09 (15,197)
Danilla Herrera, Mohamed......5:14:58 (28,308)	Davidson, Simon......4:12:30 (13,526)	Davies, Richard......5:02:13 (26,066)
Danks, Richard......5:06:41 (26,839)	Davie, Keith......4:01:22 (10,879)	Davies, Richard A......4:12:53 (13,623)
Danks, Simon R......5:56:43 (32,810)	Davie, Tim D......3:25:44 (3,492)	Davies, Richard J......5:40:04 (31,504)
Dann, Graham S......4:29:08 (17,872)	Davies, Ade......5:34:54 (30,957)	Davies, Robert......4:29:05 (17,856)
Dann, Stephen J......4:44:26 (21,827)	Davies, Andrew......5:12:44 (27,932)	Davies, Robert J......6:03:13 (33,243)
Dann, Steven A......4:00:40 (10,713)	Davies, Andrew J......3:26:18 (3,575)	Davies, Rohan B......4:29:22 (17,940)
D'Anna, Vincenzo......4:45:17 (22,033)	Davies, Andrew M......3:55:25 (9,135)	Davies, Russell G......3:55:45 (9,243)
Dannatt, Adam Christopher......3:28:32 (3,930)	Davies, Anthony P......4:39:39 (20,627)	Davies, Sam G......6:00:10 (33,060)
Dannatt, Edward R......4:14:32 (14,037)	Davies, Anthony M......4:27:28 (17,382)	Davies, Simon B......5:05:30 (26,639)
Danskin, Ian A......4:23:28 (16,299)	Davies, Antony......4:11:43 (13,317)	Davies, Stephen P......4:22:04 (15,960)
Danter, Mark......5:37:30 (31,224)	Davies, Ben......4:26:44 (17,187)	Davies, Steven......6:18:40 (33,952)
D'Aquino, Antonio......3:37:04 (5,333)	Davies, Benedikt C......3:32:34 (4,558)	Davies, Stuart M......5:12:01 (27,803)
D'Aquino, Francesco......2:56:10 (729)	Davies, Brian......4:20:09 (15,471)	Davies, Thomas E......3:30:12 (4,208)
Darby, Christopher B......3:30:58 (4,325)	Davies, Bryn......4:08:25 (12,485)	Davies, Thomas R......3:58:19 (10,039)

Davies, Tony M	5:16:50 (28,623)	
Davies, Vivian H	6:08:56 (33,510)	
Davies, Wayne A	3:34:44 (4,913)	
Davies, William Martin	4:42:04 (21,215)	
Davila, Rodrigo	4:39:58 (20,710)	
Davis, Aaron	4:24:06 (16,471)	
Davis, Alex J	4:43:41 (21,644)	
Davis, Anthony	3:15:33 (2,289)	
Davis, Anthony L	3:05:42 (1,349)	
Davis, Anthony P	3:43:52 (6,607)	
Davis, Cem J	6:14:28 (33,765)	
Davis, Colin L	4:04:23 (11,520)	
Davis, Evan	4:43:30 (21,598)	
Davis, Ewen	3:45:27 (6,885)	
Davis, Francis	4:50:32 (23,381)	
Davis, Jeffrey	3:41:20 (6,093)	
Davis, Joe A	4:00:47 (10,741)	
Davis, John R	3:43:46 (6,580)	
Davis, Lee A	6:47:24 (34,753)	
Davis, Marcus W	3:29:48 (4,155)	
Davis, Mark A	4:22:58 (16,178)	
Davis, Mark J	3:27:32 (3,783)	
Davis, Mark J	4:03:44 (11,368)	
Davis, Mark J	4:23:06 (16,207)	
Davis, Martin J	3:48:16 (7,459)	
Davis, Martin N	3:53:11 (8,561)	
Davis, Matthew	3:50:16 (7,898)	
Davis, Matthew S	5:28:15 (30,183)	
Davis, Michael Philip	5:06:37 (26,824)	
Davis, Paul T	4:20:16 (15,502)	
Davis, Peter	4:25:52 (16,951)	
Davis, Phillip F	6:26:06 (34,283)	
Davis, Richard J	5:10:30 (27,550)	
Davis, Richard M	3:15:44 (2,310)	
Davis, Robert	3:32:35 (4,562)	
Davis, Roger M	4:58:20 (25,222)	
Davis, Sean L	5:27:17 (30,077)	
Davis, Sean P	4:05:05 (11,675)	
Davis, Simon J	3:43:42 (6,565)	
Davis, Simon W	4:14:16 (13,982)	
Davis, Spencer	4:55:58 (24,676)	
Davis, Stephen	5:21:05 (29,234)	
Davis, Steve	5:01:55 (25,996)	
Davis, Todd	3:22:28 (3,063)	
Davis, Trevor D	7:36:13 (35,252)	
Davis, Trevor J	3:55:41 (9,211)	
Davis, Vaughan	4:13:23 (13,774)	
Davison, Scott H	4:51:04 (23,505)	
Davison, Stephen J	5:57:18 (32,855)	
Davison, Tim J	5:16:44 (28,607)	
Davison-Poltock, Lee	3:31:45 (4,430)	
Davitt, Paul	4:01:26 (10,893)	
Davy, Paul	5:30:37 (30,478)	
Daw, Thomas	4:26:27 (17,097)	
Dawe, Andrew M	3:19:32 (2,686)	
Dawe, Andrew P	3:14:54 (2,220)	
Dawe, Nicholas C	4:15:01 (14,168)	
Dawes, Andrew John	5:25:08 (29,816)	
Dawes, Chris	3:27:55 (3,842)	
Dawes, Mike G	5:14:00 (28,161)	
Dawkins, Terence P	5:26:38 (30,009)	
Dawnay, Giles	3:25:43 (3,491)	
Dawood, Adam	5:18:00 (28,794)	
Daws, Peter M	3:14:04 (2,131)	
Dawson, Alan R	3:07:14 (1,455)	
Dawson, Allen J	4:47:54 (22,707)	
Dawson, Carl	4:41:50 (21,171)	
Dawson, Daniel D	4:12:29 (13,518)	
Dawson, Douglas	5:25:35 (29,875)	
Dawson, Gary J	3:59:25 (10,374)	
Dawson, Guy C	4:38:23 (20,272)	
Dawson, John	6:15:08 (33,796)	
Dawson, Jon G	4:45:14 (22,022)	
Dawson, Jonathan	5:10:22 (27,526)	
Dawson, Matthew I	4:44:52 (21,921)	
Dawson, Oli J	3:35:41 (5,096)	
Dawson, Stephen	3:26:48 (3,651)	
Dawson, Tim M	4:45:38 (22,113)	
Dawson, Will	5:00:00 (25,601)	
Day, Adrian M	4:57:44 (25,073)	
Day, Andy P	5:06:11 (26,759)	
Day, Daniel	5:17:03 (28,647)	
Day, David	3:38:59 (5,683)	

Day, Gary	4:26:35 (17,144)	
Day, Graham	4:52:19 (23,829)	
Day, Ian	3:44:26 (6,705)	
Day, Julian E	4:12:19 (13,473)	
Day, Kevin G	3:34:40 (4,906)	
Day, Lee D	3:58:07 (9,978)	
Day, Michael T	5:07:03 (26,915)	
Day, Paul	3:30:10 (4,202)	
Day, Paul G	4:28:32 (17,706)	
Day, Richard J	4:22:23 (16,044)	
Day, Richard N	4:53:52 (24,193)	
Day, Robert N	3:44:46 (6,763)	
Day, Simon G	5:12:02 (27,807)	
Day, Thomas F	4:19:37 (15,320)	
Day, Thomas J	3:52:24 (8,381)	
Daye, Paul M	5:25:33 (29,868)	
Daykin, Adam	3:37:30 (5,400)	
De Berry, Simon	3:38:33 (5,600)	
De Biasio, Enrico	4:52:16 (23,814)	
De Boer, Anne	3:59:54 (10,515)	
De Boltz, David	4:45:04 (21,986)	
De Castro, John	3:12:39 (1,950)	
De Cruz, Benjamin	4:43:11 (21,511)	
De Diago Pacheco, Gerardo	4:10:03 (12,864)	
De Feo, Vincenzo	3:07:30 (1,481)	
De Freyne, Stuart P	3:57:38 (9,818)	
De Glanville, Jack E	3:30:16 (4,217)	
De Groot, Bernadus Johannes G.	3:45:57 (6,977)	
De Groot, Sebastian M	4:26:19 (17,071)	
De Jong, Henno	3:43:29 (6,520)	
De Jong, Ludo	4:09:48 (12,803)	
De La Cruz, David	3:00:56 (1,048)	
De La Motte, JP	4:31:01 (18,352)	
De La Pena, David R	4:31:43 (18,558)	
De La Pena, José	3:57:02 (9,628)	
De Lacy, Jean-Paul	4:21:12 (15,741)	
De Livio, David	4:24:49 (16,661)	
De Luca, Andrea	3:27:56 (3,846)	
De Luca, Luca	3:27:57 (3,850)	
De Luca, Nicola	2:57:53 (828)	
De Luca, Paolo	4:40:42 (20,886)	
De Luca, Paolo A	3:31:49 (4,443)	
De Montfort, Oliver Edward	3:18:19 (2,556)	
De Mooi, Connagh J	4:13:02 (13,664)	
De Nill, Chris J	4:27:08 (17,290)	
De Pater, Henri	4:40:56 (20,948)	
De Pear Brown, Matthew B	3:50:22 (7,915)	
De Roeck, Diederik	3:28:54 (3,993)	
De Smedt, Laurent	3:56:47 (9,561)	
De Souza, Douglas R	4:04:56 (11,639)	
De Souza, Geoffrey P	3:58:09 (9,990)	
De Vos, Johan	4:09:47 (12,800)	
De Wolf, Nick A	4:47:03 (22,498)	
Deacon, Clifford	5:43:08 (31,785)	
Deacon, Gary A	3:55:58 (9,300)	
Deacon, Kenneth R	6:44:20 (34,699)	
Deacon, Peter T	4:47:52 (22,693)	
Deal, Andrew P	4:18:15 (14,951)	
Deal, Harry	4:04:40 (11,578)	
Deaman, Peter E	3:16:29 (2,376)	
Deamer, Russell M	4:33:18 (18,977)	
Dean, Alexander D	5:03:31 (26,287)	
Dean, Andrew	3:39:45 (5,799)	
Dean, Ben	4:09:51 (12,822)	
Dean, Ben	4:44:03 (21,736)	
Dean, Craig William	4:43:49 (21,671)	
Dean, David	5:52:03 (32,484)	
Dean, David E	4:00:46 (10,733)	
Dean, Gary	2:57:17 (796)	
Dean, Ian G	4:39:17 (20,513)	
Dean, Jason A	4:49:15 (23,036)	
Dean, Kevin G	3:48:03 (7,413)	
Dean, Mark R	3:13:12 (2,028)	
Dean, Matthew F	6:46:31 (34,728)	
Dean, Michael S	5:52:09 (32,490)	
Dean, Mike	3:26:01 (3,535)	
Dean, Philip G	4:59:28 (25,488)	
Dean, Simon J	4:32:22 (18,721)	
Dean, Will	5:34:05 (30,866)	
Deane, Leo J	4:24:56 (16,691)	
Deans, Mark	4:33:41 (19,073)	
Dear, Jay	5:41:04 (31,590)	
Dear, Rhys Jonathan	4:05:55 (11,862)	

Dear, Richard A	4:42:13 (21,255)	
Dear, Stephen G	3:40:54 (6,014)	
Dearing, Jon S	6:36:32 (34,553)	
Dearing, Mark G	5:45:36 (31,985)	
Dearman, Craig W	6:15:21 (33,806)	
Deaville, Stephen P	5:06:19 (26,778)	
Debney, Graham A	3:56:42 (9,535)	
Debono, Jason	4:16:16 (14,464)	
Debruyne, Gerard	4:02:15 (11,077)	
Decair, Thomas	6:56:21 (34,910)	
Decanniere, Olivier	3:19:36 (2,697)	
Declerck, Didier	3:48:36 (7,534)	
Deddis, Jonathan	4:12:41 (13,573)	
Dee, Peter F	3:29:21 (4,079)	
Deed, Michael E	4:31:35 (18,524)	
Deed, Nigel R	3:39:17 (5,726)	
Deegan, Justin Wayne	4:47:25 (22,582)	
Deegan, Stephen J	3:38:56 (5,661)	
Deeljur, Dilan	5:13:55 (28,144)	
Deeprose, Jon	4:45:36 (22,105)	
Deer, Tony S	4:28:54 (17,811)	
Defillet, Erik	3:39:58 (5,854)	
Defillet, Hugo	4:23:13 (16,235)	
Defillet, Jokke	4:15:57 (14,381)	
Defillet, Joris	3:43:06 (6,441)	
Defillet, Wilfried	5:13:50 (28,123)	
Defillet, Wim	4:39:19 (20,523)	
Defty, Ian M	5:42:13 (31,696)	
Degnan, Gregory D	5:03:11 (26,233)	
Deighan, Andrew J	4:50:57 (23,474)	
Deighan, Hugh A	3:48:01 (7,405)	
Deighton, Justin L	4:29:11 (17,884)	
Deighton, Kevin E	4:21:56 (15,931)	
Dekas, Ioannis	5:22:38 (29,458)	
Del Castillo, José	2:50:16 (475)	
Del Giudice, Guido	3:32:22 (4,526)	
Del Vecchio, Antonello	3:51:53 (8,249)	
Delahaye, Nick J	4:37:07 (19,945)	
Delahoy, Trevor R	4:07:41 (12,281)	
Delamare, Paul E	4:52:57 (23,965)	
Delander, John K	4:14:21 (14,000)	
Delaney, Lee D	4:41:28 (21,077)	
Delbast, Pierre	3:45:31 (6,899)	
Delderfield, Kris	4:22:08 (15,978)	
Deledda, Francesco	4:01:45 (10,972)	
Delew, Russell P	4:03:21 (11,303)	
De-Liege, René	5:24:14 (29,690)	
Dell, Graeme J	5:13:34 (28,075)	
Dell, Stephen Jeffrey Raymond	4:09:46 (12,794)	
Dell'Accio, Vito	4:18:30 (15,029)	
Dell'Aringa, Stefano	3:36:14 (5,195)	
Delling, Thomas	3:02:01 (1,118)	
Dell'Orletta, Domenico	3:11:53 (1,874)	
Dell'Oste, Giancarlo	4:27:01 (17,260)	
Delogne, Jean Claude	3:04:42 (1,280)	
Delogu, Sebastiano	4:53:38 (24,109)	
Deluca, Tony	5:43:58 (31,847)	
Demarigny, Sebastien	3:30:40 (4,280)	
Demetriou, Chris	6:48:47 (34,791)	
Demetriou, David R	4:08:04 (12,376)	
Demetropoulos, John	2:49:50 (466)	
Demick, Alastair L	5:23:11 (29,543)	
Deminier, Loic	3:41:57 (6,195)	
Demmetran, Victor J	6:13:37 (33,727)	
Dempsey, Dee	5:01:41 (25,949)	
Dempsey, Shane	5:28:44 (30,242)	
Dempsey, Simon R	3:55:58 (9,300)	
Dempsey, Tim	4:33:52 (19,118)	
Dempster, Clive G	5:02:35 (26,134)	
Demur, Daniel	4:39:10 (20,487)	
Den Hoed, Arie	4:22:59 (16,181)	
Den Hoed, Lennaert	3:43:09 (6,457)	
Dendy, Will P	4:54:00 (24,219)	
Denham, Nick	5:13:49 (28,121)	
Denison, Colin J	5:01:52 (25,988)	
Denman, Phil M	3:56:05 (9,335)	
Denman, Tom	4:43:24 (21,575)	
Denney, Graham	4:48:59 (22,971)	
Dennis, Christopher J	4:08:19 (12,459)	
Dennis, Julian	5:17:47 (28,760)	
Dennis, Matt J	4:19:57 (15,408)	
Dennis, Neil	4:53:42 (24,138)	
Dennis, Paul A	3:12:21 (1,918)	

Dennis, Paul J	2:59:40 (973)
Dennison, Nicholas J	4:33:14 (18,954)
Denny, Jason	4:35:30 (19,546)
Denny, Lynden K	4:56:51 (24,898)
Denny, Mark A	4:52:50 (23,935)
Denny, Reginald F	4:51:05 (23,511)
Denny, Simon J	3:58:19 (10,039)
Denny, Steve D	4:44:12 (21,766)
Denstone, Gary J	5:08:46 (27,225)
Dent, Andrew	4:53:04 (23,990)
Dent, James P	3:49:42 (7,774)
Dent, Marty	2:15:24 (14)
Denton, Chris	4:35:08 (19,446)
Denton, Jon W	3:03:32 (1,205)
Denwood, Thomas J	2:56:35 (751)
Denyer, William	4:34:22 (19,232)
Derbyshire, David	4:11:41 (13,310)
Derbyshire, Jamie	4:06:02 (11,889)
Derbyshire, Michael J	3:49:32 (7,736)
Derbyshire, Scott R	4:04:13 (11,495)
Derham, Chris Alan	3:52:10 (8,317)
Derham, Richard O	5:23:12 (29,550)
Deria, Fuad	6:48:38 (34,789)
Dermit, Jean-Paul	5:12:05 (27,814)
Deroide, Antoine	4:39:24 (20,552)
Derrett, Robin	4:29:01 (17,834)
Derrick, Terry	6:30:16 (34,418)
Derstroff, Thomas	5:05:49 (26,700)
Derveaux, Pierre	4:21:32 (15,824)
Derzypilskyj, Christopher J	3:58:46 (10,179)
Desai, Kalpesh	5:04:49 (26,509)
Desborough, Dudley M	3:14:52 (2,214)
Desborough, Steve	4:28:49 (17,780)
Desenlis, Bruno	4:09:31 (12,728)
Desgoutte, Pierre Yves	4:42:48 (21,409)
Desmond, Paul	4:10:09 (12,898)
Despic, Tim	3:43:47 (6,586)
Dettwiler, Andy	3:35:41 (5,096)
Devalia, Arvind	7:25:37 (35,182)
Devennie, David J	3:49:41 (7,772)
Devereux, Ross I	4:45:30 (22,079)
Devereux, Steven G	4:08:17 (12,447)
Deverick, George M	4:27:32 (17,400)
Deverill, Stephen	4:07:07 (12,135)
Devey, Dennis	6:05:20 (33,355)
Deville, Gerard	4:14:09 (13,945)
Devine, Ciaran	4:03:11 (11,269)
Devine, George	3:59:06 (10,278)
Devine, Martin E	5:10:16 (27,508)
Devine, Ronan	4:46:20 (22,290)
Devitt, Russell	3:53:52 (8,718)
Devlin, Giles	4:11:24 (13,226)
Devlin, Joseph W	3:42:40 (6,350)
Devlin, Mark	4:33:14 (18,954)
Dew, Kelvin R	4:52:57 (23,965)
Dewar, Gordon	4:18:21 (14,975)
Dewhirst, Greg	4:17:06 (14,664)
Dewick, Mark C	4:08:34 (12,517)
Dexter, Shaun K	6:09:34 (33,538)
Dey, Andrew J	4:53:06 (23,998)
Dey, James M	5:07:14 (26,951)
Dey, Joseph	5:49:46 (32,315)
Dhers, Jean-Philippe	4:41:18 (21,037)
Dhinsa, Makinder S	4:18:47 (15,101)
D'Hoker, Dirk	4:30:13 (18,154)
Di Benedetto, Davide Massimo	3:37:25 (5,388)
Di Bonito, Vincenzo	4:56:23 (24,769)
Di Geronimo, Michele	4:15:00 (14,164)
Di Girolamo, Alessio	3:41:09 (6,057)
Di Nella, Donato	3:22:52 (3,115)
Di Nonno, Costanzo	3:29:00 (4,006)
Di Pace, Giuseppe	4:50:03 (23,253)
Di Rubba, Domenico	4:23:58 (16,432)
Di Somma, Antonio	2:49:47 (461)
Diaper, Jonathan P	4:08:37 (12,528)
Dias, Adam L	4:26:07 (17,014)
Dias, Henrique	4:21:59 (15,940)
Dibb-Fuller, Jason	3:26:14 (3,564)
Dicio, Domenico	3:54:18 (8,839)
Dick, Alistair	3:04:38 (1,272)
Dick, Barry G	5:47:03 (32,099)
Dick, Christopher J	3:51:43 (8,212)
Dick, Michael J	3:37:29 (5,395)

Dick, Robert T	3:15:17 (2,257)
Dick, Stewart M	4:46:11 (22,244)
Dickens, Andrew S	4:32:34 (18,777)
Dickens, Ivan A	4:29:51 (18,056)
Dickens, Mark I	4:44:48 (21,907)
Dickens, Matthew	3:50:36 (7,972)
Dickens, Peter	4:45:25 (22,059)
Dickens, Stephen J	3:22:35 (3,082)
Dicker, Adam	6:03:39 (33,265)
Dickerson, Andrew M	5:12:39 (27,918)
Dickins, Ben R	3:52:04 (8,291)
Dickinson, Anthony M	5:25:31 (29,860)
Dickinson, Duncan F	4:32:50 (18,855)
Dickinson, Kelvin B	3:09:36 (1,667)
Dickinson, Mark	2:35:22 (121)
Dickinson, Ralph W	4:38:54 (20,409)
Dickinson, Stephen J	4:25:41 (16,904)
Dickman, Stewart J	4:25:10 (16,757)
Dickson, Christopher M	3:16:14 (2,353)
Dickson, Colin L	3:39:47 (5,807)
Dickson, Hugh	4:24:01 (16,444)
Didd, Jamie	4:31:37 (18,531)
Dieppe, James	3:29:43 (4,139)
Dierckxsens, Joris	3:57:50 (9,890)
Dietz, Hans-Joachim	4:31:05 (18,382)
Difrancesco, Stefano	5:20:00 (29,093)
Digby-Baker, Hugh J	5:27:47 (30,120)
Diggens, Timothy M	4:50:49 (23,449)
Diggines, Graham A	3:51:06 (8,074)
Dignan, Kieran	3:28:36 (3,938)
Digwa, Gurmukh S	3:41:00 (6,028)
Di-Lieto, Sergio D	5:10:03 (27,473)
Dilks, Justin M	3:30:31 (4,260)
Dilks, Mark R	5:25:34 (29,873)
Dill, John W	4:02:41 (11,165)
Dill, Simon C	4:21:30 (15,812)
Dill, Torsten	3:32:39 (4,567)
Dillabaugh, Joe	3:08:57 (1,615)
Dilley, Brian J	4:11:00 (13,110)
Dilley, Thomas J	3:48:58 (7,610)
Dilliway, Nathan	4:33:37 (19,054)
Dillon, Jeff	4:10:31 (12,984)
Dillon, Nick B	3:57:58 (9,873)
Dilworth, Jason P	3:30:43 (4,284)
Dilworth, Joseph R	4:58:07 (25,170)
Dilworth, Mark T	3:56:17 (9,383)
Dimbleby, Peter J	2:45:50 (327)
Dimelow, Geoffrey	4:00:26 (10,646)
Dimelow, Glenn C	3:38:05 (5,510)
Diment, Daniel	3:54:43 (8,952)
Diment, Joe M	3:51:53 (8,249)
Dimmock, Lee J	5:30:59 (30,526)
Din, Kashif	5:19:35 (29,046)
Dina, Sergio	2:48:03 (398)
Dineen, John	6:01:17 (33,127)
Dineen, Paul	3:43:09 (6,457)
Dingley, Kane D	4:53:55 (24,204)
Dingwall, Alex	4:19:58 (15,419)
Dinsdale, Danny T	3:58:09 (9,990)
Dinsmore, Barry	3:46:30 (7,087)
Dinwoodie, Stuart J	3:13:17 (2,033)
Diogo, Joao P	3:41:30 (6,118)
Dionisio, Tiago	3:41:47 (6,166)
Dippenaar, Rory Dereck	5:25:41 (29,887)
Dipple, Paul A	5:37:20 (31,209)
Direnzo, Robert	3:45:14 (6,842)
Dirkes, Charles E	4:14:59 (14,162)
Disley, Andrew G	3:35:22 (5,026)
Ditcham, Robert J	3:41:02 (6,038)
Dix, Lemuel L	4:29:24 (17,951)
Dix, Richard H	3:26:30 (3,600)
Dixon, Alex M	3:46:05 (6,998)
Dixon, Andrew	4:10:31 (12,984)
Dixon, Andrew	4:33:22 (18,998)
Dixon, Andrew J	3:13:29 (2,059)
Dixon, Andy	5:17:25 (28,700)
Dixon, Bob	3:55:58 (9,300)
Dixon, Clem N	2:47:29 (380)
Dixon, Craig L	3:17:18 (2,465)
Dixon, Daniel T	4:27:15 (17,325)
Dixon, Davey A	4:25:38 (16,885)
Dixon, David	3:31:56 (4,458)
Dixon, Edward J	3:42:16 (6,262)

Dixon, Garry J	2:29:40 (65)
Dixon, Gary	6:43:08 (34,683)
Dixon, Gordon M	2:43:35 (276)
Dixon, Grant	3:52:28 (8,396)
Dixon, Joe	5:05:31 (26,642)
Dixon, Mark J	3:19:56 (2,745)
Dixon, Nicholas J	4:14:16 (13,982)
Dixon, Russ M	3:52:14 (8,341)
Dixon, Russell J	4:48:07 (22,766)
Dixon, Tony	3:43:04 (6,434)
Dixon, Trevor J	3:04:13 (1,249)
Dixon-Box, Russell Beaumont	4:16:49 (14,609)
D'Netto, Matthew J	4:38:21 (20,266)
Doak, Ian D	4:46:45 (22,420)
Doak, Robert J	4:40:01 (20,730)
Dobbie, Adam Stephen	3:28:21 (3,910)
Dobbie, David R	4:10:25 (12,958)
Dobbie, Peter	4:39:34 (20,602)
Dobbin, Wallace	4:54:12 (24,259)
Dobbins, Gregg	6:24:44 (34,223)
Dobbs, Patrick A	3:31:03 (4,335)
Dobbs, Simon C	2:42:41 (249)
Dobby, Andrew M	2:49:01 (424)
Dobson, Adrian P	4:28:27 (17,683)
Dobson, Andy	4:08:47 (12,566)
Dobson, Mark C	7:44:38 (35,277)
Dobson, Neal R	3:34:26 (4,862)
Dobson, Neil J	4:04:46 (11,599)
Dobson, Oliver H	4:12:54 (13,628)
Dobson, Robin	3:39:23 (5,741)
Dobson, Stephen M	5:22:54 (29,500)
Dobson, Tim	3:34:03 (4,770)
Docherty, Alex J	3:41:20 (6,093)
Docherty, Nick J	3:39:08 (5,706)
Docherty, Steven	4:35:02 (19,419)
Dockerill, Steve C	3:47:02 (7,205)
Dodd, Andrew C	4:36:33 (19,804)
Dodd, Andrew K	3:25:26 (3,452)
Dodd, Matthew B	4:34:10 (19,187)
Dodd, Michael	4:48:07 (22,766)
Dodd, Richard S	5:25:20 (29,836)
Dodds, Ian	4:01:29 (10,909)
Dodds, Jeffrey	4:28:05 (17,570)
Dodds, Richard M	4:41:05 (20,984)
Dodgson, Darryl K	4:05:22 (11,744)
Dodkin, Mike J	4:04:51 (11,618)
Dodman, James	5:31:42 (30,606)
Dodsley, Andrew	3:57:12 (9,673)
Dodsworth, Neville	3:39:55 (5,838)
Dodwell, Chris W	4:58:29 (25,263)
Dodwell, Declan J	4:53:00 (23,977)
Doe, Don G	3:17:53 (2,518)
Doel, Robert	4:46:41 (22,391)
Doerr, Alan J	4:38:46 (20,369)
Doerr, Dean S	4:54:57 (24,437)
Doerr, Norbert	4:00:46 (10,733)
Doherty, Daniel J	3:35:37 (5,074)
Doherty, Martin	4:46:19 (22,284)
Doherty, Martin J	5:12:08 (27,828)
Doherty, Oliver	5:02:19 (26,085)
Doherty, Patrick	2:54:16 (614)
Doherty, Paul	3:34:23 (4,850)
Doherty, Thomas A	3:23:12 (3,151)
Doidge, William	3:44:54 (6,784)
Doig, Henry R	4:50:32 (23,381)
Dokus, Klaus	3:51:59 (8,273)
Dolan, Chris J	4:31:54 (18,607)
Dolan, Mark	4:01:05 (10,812)
Dolan, Peter	3:23:46 (3,228)
Dolan, Robert	3:13:38 (2,080)
Dolan, Robert	3:34:08 (4,796)
Doleman, Stephen R	3:58:01 (9,941)
Dolinar, Robert J	3:25:49 (3,504)
Dolle, Gaston A	5:16:05 (28,514)
Dollet, André	5:02:57 (26,200)
Domanski, Michal	3:11:51 (1,869)
Dombrandt, Stephen W	5:24:30 (29,734)
Dominique, Bordet	4:21:40 (15,872)
Dominique, Boussat	3:17:16 (2,460)
Dommersnes, Sam R	6:03:36 (33,263)
Dommett, Robert A	6:46:50 (34,735)
Don, Christopher R	4:52:28 (23,859)
Donaghy, Nigel	6:40:01 (34,628)

Donaghy, Tim J	4:42:10	(21,239)
Donahue, Charles	3:42:29	(6,295)
Donald, Ewan W	6:07:36	(33,464)
Donald, James W	2:59:41	(974)
Donald, John	3:52:59	(8,502)
Donaldson, Graham M	2:52:07	(525)
Donaldson, Kenneth	3:20:22	(2,806)
Donaldson, Nick E	4:57:40	(25,064)
Donat, Martin	3:38:19	(5,553)
Donegan, Barry J	4:40:37	(20,865)
Doni, Lorenzo	4:50:25	(23,347)
Donnachie, Jason P	6:19:25	(34,013)
Donnan, Adam J	3:40:44	(5,978)
Donnelly, Adam Samuel	3:48:32	(7,520)
Donnelly, David	4:51:40	(23,667)
Donnelly, Jeffrey	5:35:00	(30,970)
Donnelly, John	4:18:38	(15,064)
Donnelly, John A	3:06:34	(1,409)
Donnelly, Shane R	5:48:18	(32,199)
Donnelly, Shaun	4:53:52	(24,193)
Donnelly, Stephen M	3:20:26	(2,817)
Donnelly, Stephen P	4:22:12	(16,002)
Donnelly, Turlough M	2:38:31	(165)
Donoghue, Adam J	3:16:07	(2,341)
Donoghue, Anthony	8:07:42	(35,323)
Donoghue, Barry	4:45:04	(21,986)
Donoghue, Christopher	3:17:45	(2,509)
Donoghue, Gary John	3:36:48	(5,276)
Donoghue, Kevin M	3:08:41	(1,588)
Donoghue, Oliver	4:21:13	(15,744)
Donoghue, Paul	3:43:27	(6,516)
Donovan, Joe M	7:05:10	(35,006)
Donovan, Paul	4:13:16	(13,736)
Donovan, Robert J	4:29:34	(17,976)
Doodson, Gary J	3:55:33	(9,171)
Doolan, Matthew M	3:29:21	(4,079)
Dooley, Andrew J	3:55:05	(9,059)
Dooley, Anthony B	4:33:53	(19,124)
Dooley, John Patrick	4:14:49	(14,116)
Dooley, Michael S	2:47:16	(375)
Dooley, Robert E	4:44:27	(21,828)
Dooley, William M	3:38:57	(5,667)
Dooling, Graham C	4:29:10	(17,876)
Doolittle, Anthony I	3:03:32	(1,205)
Doran, Andrew T	3:30:29	(4,249)
Doran, Colin C	4:20:15	(15,498)
Doran, David J	3:54:56	(9,004)
Doran, Matt	5:06:57	(26,894)
Doran, Phil J	5:08:11	(27,123)
Doran, Stephen	4:56:21	(24,761)
Dorenbos, Sander	5:37:03	(31,177)
Dorgan, Sean	3:47:27	(7,278)
Dorin, Christian P	3:31:26	(4,391)
Dorin, Paul	6:11:24	(33,619)
Dorman, Laurence	3:00:46	(1,035)
Dormer, Adam C	4:17:27	(14,757)
Dorrell, Ian	4:58:21	(25,225)
Dorrian, Brendan	4:39:23	(20,542)
Dorward, Neil L	3:01:53	(1,107)
Dos Santos Neves, Jorge	3:39:00	(5,686)
Doshi, Rajen Anil	3:59:54	(10,515)
Dott, Charles	3:23:57	(3,254)
Dou, Carl C	4:47:18	(22,560)
Double, Michael	4:47:04	(22,501)
Doubleday, Jamie C	4:02:59	(11,226)
Dougall, Alan C	3:38:03	(5,501)
Dougherty, John P	4:37:28	(20,027)
Doughty, John J	5:17:48	(28,765)
Doughty, Tim	3:19:49	(2,729)
Douglas, Andrew	3:17:12	(2,454)
Douglas, Gary R	4:42:29	(21,329)
Douglas, Ian	3:34:05	(4,783)
Douglas, Keith	3:50:07	(7,859)
Douglas, Neil A	3:01:32	(1,085)
Douglas, Philip	3:39:56	(5,843)
Douglas, Robert N	3:05:04	(1,307)
Douglas, Stuart D	3:54:20	(8,847)
Douglas, Stuart J	2:59:28	(953)
Douglass, Guy	4:35:43	(19,607)
Douglass, Paul E	5:39:07	(31,413)
Douse, James	5:21:05	(29,234)
Doust, David R	4:46:55	(22,454)
Douthwaite, Neil	3:46:44	(7,140)

Dovadola, Krishna	2:49:51	(467)
Dovedi, Stephen S	4:31:22	(18,462)
Dover, Gary William	3:19:42	(2,710)
Dovey, Andrew G	4:53:38	(24,109)
Dovey, Tom	4:44:44	(21,896)
Dow, Adrian	3:09:52	(1,694)
Dow, Peter J	3:12:27	(1,926)
Dowd, Liam S	3:37:55	(5,476)
Dowdall, Tim C	4:29:53	(18,068)
Dowding, Andy E	5:03:43	(26,327)
Dowding, Chris	4:49:09	(23,004)
Dowds, Liam	3:48:19	(7,470)
Dowds, Niall	5:35:02	(30,975)
Dowdy, Nicholas H	4:25:56	(16,968)
Dowell, Dom	4:24:44	(16,636)
Dowen, Chris E	6:38:57	(34,607)
Dowie, Paul R	3:41:31	(6,125)
Dowie, Sean J	4:17:27	(14,757)
Dowle, Simon J	5:35:56	(31,066)
Dowler, Robert	5:24:11	(29,680)
Dowling, Adam	5:02:27	(26,102)
Dowling, James M	5:46:28	(32,047)
Dowling, Michael W	4:47:32	(22,605)
Dowling, Patrick Dermot	4:03:41	(11,363)
Dowling, Rohan	5:12:08	(27,828)
Dowling, Shaun	4:06:27	(11,982)
Down, Nick	4:44:10	(21,763)
Downer, Michael J	3:46:03	(6,996)
Downes, Benjamin T	5:54:01	(32,615)
Downes, David R	4:36:48	(19,864)
Downes, Graeme M	4:50:34	(23,389)
Downes, Paul A	5:24:05	(29,666)
Downes, Philip A	3:56:40	(9,523)
Downes, Ryk	5:27:44	(30,114)
Downes, Tony	3:57:49	(9,880)
Downey, Des D	4:50:08	(23,267)
Downey, James	4:20:58	(15,681)
Downey, Kevin	5:20:43	(29,178)
Downham, Antony S	4:02:09	(11,054)
Downing, Oliver J	3:23:28	(3,183)
Downs, David J	3:25:38	(3,479)
Downs, Rob H	2:33:23	(95)
Dowse, Matthew J	3:32:12	(4,504)
Dowsell, Graham J	4:55:20	(24,535)
Dowsett, Mike J	4:14:15	(13,974)
Dowsett, Owen	3:25:37	(3,476)
Dowsett, Robert Elliot	4:29:26	(17,956)
Doxford, Paul	2:58:01	(837)
Doyle, Alastair K	3:11:15	(1,801)
Doyle, Andrew James	3:31:44	(4,426)
Doyle, Geoffrey E	3:22:35	(3,082)
Doyle, Gerard	4:12:05	(13,410)
Doyle, Ian	3:24:33	(3,349)
Doyle, James	5:23:59	(29,645)
Doyle, John C	3:40:44	(5,978)
Doyle, Kevin	2:59:04	(925)
Doyle, Nigel M	3:15:28	(2,280)
Doyle, Pete	3:28:13	(3,888)
Doyle, Richard B	4:02:06	(11,043)
Doyle, Stuart	4:38:47	(20,372)
Drabble, Dean	3:45:22	(6,866)
Drabwell, Lee S	4:12:46	(13,596)
Drake, Jeffrey T	4:06:33	(12,005)
Drake, Nathan	4:36:34	(19,808)
Drake, Peter L	3:50:34	(7,962)
Drake, Tim	3:05:10	(1,314)
Drake-Norris, Andrew G	2:58:05	(842)
Draper, Dennis	4:36:34	(19,808)
Draper, Edward	3:24:02	(3,265)
Draper, Hedde	3:47:46	(7,341)
Draper, Jason L	6:18:40	(33,952)
Draper, Sidney P	5:41:46	(31,653)
Drasdo, Duncan N	3:20:11	(2,778)
Drax, Richard G	4:49:30	(23,116)
Dray, Nick J	3:19:45	(2,717)
Dray, Philip A	6:19:34	(34,018)
Dray, Rudi A	3:18:27	(2,571)
Draycott, Mark	5:08:17	(27,139)
Draycott, Paul M	3:29:46	(4,148)
Draysey, Matt	4:24:19	(16,532)
Drayton, Paul A	4:15:46	(14,340)
Dreau, Lionel	6:00:59	(33,112)
Drew, John R	4:08:59	(12,616)

Drew, Michael P	4:31:15	(18,416)
Drew, Paul	3:48:46	(7,557)
Drew, Paul	4:33:12	(18,944)
Drew, Peter	3:22:44	(3,100)
Drew, Robert Stefan S	6:14:42	(33,779)
Drew, Simon Jefferey	3:27:53	(3,838)
Drewe, Julian A	4:19:57	(15,408)
Drewitt, Christopher A	4:46:17	(22,274)
Drewitt, Christopher J	3:46:26	(7,071)
Driscoll, Daron N	4:10:50	(13,071)
Driscoll, Patrick A	5:03:31	(26,287)
Driscoll, Richard W	4:28:21	(17,660)
Driscoll, Steve	4:44:35	(21,853)
Driver, Michael J	4:08:07	(12,395)
Driver, Samuel	4:32:23	(18,723)
Drogan, Christian M	4:56:25	(24,777)
Droznika, Simon	4:47:09	(22,532)
Druce, Phillip	5:19:34	(29,044)
Drummond, Alastair C	3:59:01	(10,254)
Drummond, James A	4:40:30	(20,833)
Drummond, John R	4:25:36	(16,874)
Drummond, Samuel	2:52:11	(530)
Drury, David	3:34:25	(4,856)
Drury, James S	3:49:08	(7,651)
Drury, Neil W	4:22:32	(16,048)
Dry, Peter F	4:29:00	(17,829)
Dryden, Alex	5:22:49	(29,482)
Dryden, Gordon P	3:43:08	(6,448)
Dryden, Kenny T	5:56:12	(32,770)
Drysdale, Luke S	4:33:31	(19,026)
D'Silva, Graham	5:33:36	(30,821)
D'Souza, Franz	4:24:04	(16,459)
D'Souza, John	5:06:23	(26,787)
D'Souza, Nigel	4:26:35	(17,144)
Du Plessis, Murray T	5:41:47	(31,655)
Dubery, Robert P	6:18:02	(33,928)
Dubin, Drake L	3:18:50	(2,606)
Dublish, Shashank	4:12:18	(13,468)
Ducasse, Michel	4:37:33	(20,054)
Duce, Greg	4:08:56	(12,600)
Duck, Ian L	3:51:58	(8,272)
Duckett, Oliver C	5:39:41	(31,465)
Duckworth, David	5:15:53	(28,490)
Duckworth, Iain A	3:25:47	(3,500)
Duckworth, Kevin	2:51:06	(497)
Duckworth, Mark D	4:46:32	(22,355)
Duddy, Gerry M	2:46:25	(342)
Dude, Viesturs	2:41:39	(227)
Dudfield, Stuart K	4:25:34	(16,861)
Dudley, Paul	5:37:10	(31,192)
Dudley, Peter	5:26:52	(30,033)
Dudney, Alan G	4:34:13	(19,199)
Duell, Kevin	4:00:00	(10,544)
Duez, Philippe	4:26:05	(17,006)
Dufauret, Paul	3:53:26	(8,612)
Duff, Andrew	5:24:39	(29,749)
Duff, Christopher E	3:55:05	(9,059)
Duff, Craig	3:40:47	(5,994)
Duff, Harry S	4:38:35	(20,319)
Duff, Scott J	4:23:23	(16,274)
Duff, Simon	3:56:40	(9,523)
Duffaure, François	3:54:29	(8,885)
Duffell, Craig S	3:43:39	(6,556)
Duffey, Sean J	3:40:57	(6,021)
Duffield, Richard J	3:31:37	(4,409)
Duffy, Andrew D	3:19:41	(2,708)
Duffy, Darren	4:35:07	(19,442)
Duffy, Dean	4:19:54	(15,400)
Duffy, Jonathan	4:30:23	(18,202)
Duffy, Jonathan P	4:58:31	(25,274)
Duffy, Keith D	3:52:33	(8,410)
Duffy, Laurence B	3:19:21	(2,661)
Duffy, Liam James	3:23:44	(3,222)
Duffy, Patrick J	4:01:12	(10,835)
Duffy, Simon M	3:59:16	(10,327)
Duffy, William	4:39:14	(20,502)
Duffy, William B	3:41:22	(6,099)
Duffy-Penny, Keith	4:48:46	(22,915)
Dufour, Yves	3:59:01	(10,254)
Dufton, Neil	4:24:15	(16,511)
Dugdale, Andrew	3:37:58	(5,481)
Duggan, Mike	3:22:33	(3,074)
Duggan, Neil	4:58:16	(25,206)

Duggan, Patrick	4:06:10 (11,919)
Duggan, Patrick M	4:07:26 (12,221)
Dugmore, Paul	4:02:12 (11,068)
Duguid, William R	4:20:12 (15,484)
Duhan, Michael K	5:54:01 (32,615)
Duivenvoorden, Kees	3:58:46 (10,179)
Dujardin, Jean-Jacques	4:06:55 (12,084)
Dukes, Alan C	4:19:23 (15,254)
Dukes, Nicholas J	2:45:04 (317)
Dumbell, Alex C	5:11:59 (27,799)
Dumbell, James C	4:08:46 (12,562)
Dumonteil, Armand	4:59:20 (25,459)
Dumout, Fabrice	3:14:02 (2,126)
Dun, Craig	4:39:58 (20,710)
Duncan, Alasdair W	3:23:29 (3,186)
Duncan, Alex J	4:11:22 (13,214)
Duncan, Benjamin J	4:46:35 (22,370)
Duncan, Benjamin T	3:14:24 (2,163)
Duncan, Craig	5:05:59 (26,723)
Duncan, Mark	3:34:29 (4,873)
Duncan, Mark R	3:26:50 (3,654)
Duncan, Matthew C	4:39:51 (20,682)
Duncanson, Malcolm	4:10:42 (13,040)
Duncton, Ross	4:44:48 (21,907)
Duncumb, Lee	4:45:47 (22,152)
Dundee, Roger	4:02:06 (11,043)
Dunford, Anthony J	4:19:43 (15,344)
Dunford, Nick R	4:12:57 (13,651)
Dunham, Ralph J	3:55:03 (9,040)
Dunkin, Chris J	5:13:00 (27,988)
Dunkley, Christopher J	4:47:34 (22,617)
Dunkley, Dominic	3:26:41 (3,633)
Dunkley, Simon G	3:41:45 (6,159)
Dunlea, Brian C	4:48:13 (22,791)
Dunleavy, Martin	3:23:11 (3,146)
Dunmall, Peter J	3:55:04 (9,050)
Dunn, Aaron P	6:15:38 (33,822)
Dunn, Barrie	3:20:22 (2,806)
Dunn, Chris	4:40:57 (20,953)
Dunn, Christopher H	3:06:39 (1,417)
Dunn, Gary D	3:48:09 (7,433)
Dunn, James S	4:18:26 (15,009)
Dunn, John F	4:31:18 (18,438)
Dunn, Julian	5:05:33 (26,652)
Dunn, Karl S	4:49:22 (23,075)
Dunn, Kenneth T	4:08:05 (12,382)
Dunn, Martin	3:50:29 (7,941)
Dunn, Matthew	4:19:12 (15,211)
Dunn, Peter M	3:51:52 (8,246)
Dunn, Phil J	3:57:27 (9,752)
Dunn, Simon	4:16:56 (14,632)
Dunn, Simon J	4:49:36 (23,147)
Dunne, Aaron	4:09:41 (12,769)
Dunne, Gerry A	3:27:50 (3,829)
Dunne, John	5:08:07 (27,106)
Dunn-Parrant, Glenn D	3:37:34 (5,417)
Dunsby, Andrew J	5:31:56 (30,631)
Dunscombe, Mark	3:06:00 (1,372)
Dunstall, Dave	3:07:26 (1,471)
Dunstan, Andrew G	4:28:04 (17,564)
Dunstan, Philip A	4:31:31 (18,510)
Dunstan, Richard E	5:07:05 (26,921)
Dunwoody, Andrew S	2:40:58 (215)
Dupain, Christopher N	4:34:04 (19,164)
Dupire, Philippe	3:28:12 (3,886)
Du-Prat, Dominic	4:22:54 (16,167)
Dupree, Steven	5:03:29 (26,282)
Dupriez, Pierre	4:48:40 (22,891)
Durance, Richard	4:46:56 (22,461)
Durand, Benoit	3:05:41 (1,348)
Durand, Wilfried	3:30:23 (4,232)
Durant, Andrew C	4:47:10 (22,536)
Durant, Samuel W	4:36:08 (19,707)
Durantini, Cristiano	3:13:24 (2,052)
Durantini, Pierstefano	3:53:41 (8,673)
Durband, Ian	4:10:50 (13,071)
Durden, William	4:11:40 (13,303)
Durham, Andrew G	3:42:32 (6,310)
Durham, Jamie A	3:51:53 (8,249)
Durham, Neil Jonathan	4:54:20 (24,299)
Durham, Richard	4:52:30 (23,863)
Durick, Gary J	4:08:14 (12,425)
Durie, Steven J	4:08:39 (12,533)
Duron, Gerald	5:08:59 (27,270)
Durrani, Amer J	5:57:49 (32,896)
Durrant, George	6:04:11 (33,297)
Durrant, Kevin J	4:16:53 (14,624)
Durrant, Peter J	4:26:49 (17,211)
Durrant, Philip	4:53:44 (24,152)
Durrant, Thomas A	4:44:39 (21,871)
Dursley, Paul	3:39:39 (5,784)
D'Urso, Paul	3:58:33 (10,114)
Durston, Mark E	3:31:36 (4,407)
Dury, Baxter	4:39:09 (20,482)
Dury, Michael J	2:56:24 (739)
Dury, Simon M	3:47:06 (7,213)
Dusek, Tomas	4:16:33 (14,536)
Dusi, Carlo	3:37:53 (5,469)
Dutch, James	5:15:52 (28,488)
Dutch, Peter	5:10:33 (27,556)
Dutnall, Nick J	5:09:44 (27,412)
Duton, Patrick	2:53:26 (582)
Dutton, Giles E	5:08:05 (27,100)
Dutton, John A	6:03:49 (33,277)
Dutton, Matthew	4:53:40 (24,123)
Dutton, Peter G	4:54:19 (24,292)
Duval, Dominique	4:01:56 (11,006)
Duxbury, Robert	3:48:25 (7,490)
Duzgunoglu, Ozgur O	3:58:24 (10,070)
Dwan, Jason J	6:01:05 (33,117)
Dwyer, Kevin J	3:56:50 (9,579)
Dyckes, John J	3:11:25 (1,815)
Dyde, Alasdair L	4:20:20 (15,519)
Dye, Mark J	5:12:02 (27,807)
Dye, Richard J	3:50:52 (8,031)
Dyer, Andrew J	5:16:40 (28,590)
Dyer, Ian	5:58:29 (32,956)
Dyer, Ioan N	10:20:47 (35,365)
Dyer, Louise	5:02:05 (26,041)
Dyer, Nick	3:20:26 (2,817)
Dyer, Paul D	4:06:44 (12,048)
Dyer, William J	5:01:14 (25,869)
Dyke, Adrian Vivian	4:04:42 (11,586)
Dykes, Edward	4:56:31 (24,807)
Dymond, Stephen J	4:24:23 (16,545)
Dyson, Darren J	4:17:20 (14,732)
Dyson, Graham	3:51:51 (8,240)
Dyson, Michael	5:32:47 (30,736)
Dyson, Paul J	3:18:00 (2,530)
Dyson, Tom A	3:44:10 (6,659)
Eaborn, Gary N	3:19:27 (2,676)
Eade, Isaac W	4:02:55 (11,213)
Eade, Jacob W	4:44:12 (21,766)
Eade, Robert J	4:06:09 (11,915)
Eades, Lee R	3:45:57 (6,977)
Eades, Paul D	4:50:21 (23,327)
Eadie, Christopher J	3:47:05 (7,210)
Eadie, Gordon M	4:08:18 (12,454)
Eadie, James	3:38:34 (5,602)
Eadon, Roger A	3:52:09 (8,311)
Eady, Timothy	5:05:04 (26,563)
Ealand, Nigel W	3:35:12 (4,995)
Eales, Darryl C	5:27:48 (30,124)
Eales, James R	5:12:47 (27,944)
Eales, Robert	4:19:43 (15,344)
Eames, James P	4:44:16 (21,783)
Eames, John S	6:12:07 (33,645)
Earl, David W	4:47:06 (22,515)
Earl, Dennis	3:22:34 (3,079)
Earl, Derek W	4:07:43 (12,290)
Earl, Geoff C	3:31:23 (4,383)
Earl, Jonathan R	4:18:24 (14,995)
Earl, Stephen James	3:20:16 (2,795)
Earley, Nick S	5:00:00 (25,601)
Earley, Simon	3:25:15 (3,427)
Eason, Ben J	4:04:30 (11,547)
Eason, Paul	7:17:54 (35,126)
East, Brian A	4:36:31 (19,797)
East, Jason	3:33:56 (4,745)
East, Michael D	4:44:27 (21,828)
Eastaff, John M	5:03:38 (26,313)
Easter, Greg	4:06:50 (12,068)
Eastham, Fred	6:00:01 (33,053)
Easton, David J	4:10:28 (12,973)
Easton, Richard J	3:28:43 (3,959)
Easton, Thomas H	3:56:00 (9,309)
Eastwood, Andrew W	4:16:55 (14,626)
Eastwood, Stephen G	4:16:42 (14,584)
Eaton, Colin M	4:47:25 (22,582)
Eaton, Daniel	4:34:25 (19,243)
Eaton, James M	3:13:38 (2,080)
Eaton, James R	4:43:31 (21,605)
Eaton, Nick	4:07:23 (12,209)
Eaton, Paul D	3:47:26 (7,271)
Eaton, Richard A	4:16:13 (14,452)
Eaton, Simon A	3:26:24 (3,587)
Eaton, Stephen Douglas	4:16:12 (14,448)
Eatough, Chris	4:34:57 (19,395)
Eatwell, David J	4:53:36 (24,100)
Eatwell, James R	4:01:13 (10,839)
Eaves, Phil	2:55:16 (684)
Eaves, Thomas E	4:23:04 (16,200)
Eburah, Fred	4:30:18 (18,176)
Eburah, Nicholas	4:14:08 (13,941)
Eccles, Gary J	5:11:45 (27,767)
Eccles, Jonny	3:21:34 (2,955)
Eccleston, Gary J	5:28:39 (30,230)
Eckersall, Matthew J	4:28:23 (17,665)
Eckersley, Jonathan M	5:18:44 (28,922)
Eckert, Bjoern M	5:35:44 (31,044)
Eckley, Adam J	5:20:47 (29,194)
Eckley, Mark J	6:18:40 (33,952)
Eddleston, Mike J	3:24:03 (3,270)
Eddolls, Graham	6:17:18 (33,890)
Ede, David John	5:06:32 (26,810)
Eden, Christopher G	5:03:39 (26,315)
Edgar, Bryan	2:53:04 (562)
Edgar, Ross R	4:14:46 (14,102)
Edgecliffe-Johnson, Robin R	3:26:38 (3,625)
Edgecombe, Russell	6:04:29 (33,312)
Edgell, Lawrence Arthur	4:12:39 (13,560)
Edgell, Steve J	4:46:33 (22,360)
Edgerton, Richard P	5:04:31 (26,459)
Edgington, Stephen F	4:09:05 (12,640)
Edington, Christopher	4:21:01 (15,697)
Edmond, Barry J	5:57:58 (32,913)
Edmond, Peter J	5:55:53 (32,754)
Edmonds, Andrew	3:35:19 (5,012)
Edmonds, Ian	4:32:41 (18,812)
Edmonds, Matthew	4:34:57 (19,395)
Edmonds, Paul S	3:49:14 (7,672)
Edmonds, Richard C	3:15:36 (2,293)
Edmondson, Robert	4:57:03 (24,938)
Edmondson Jones, Andrew M	2:59:25 (950)
Edmunds, Marlon A	5:19:35 (29,046)
Edmunds, Tom W	3:59:41 (10,451)
Edmundson, Joe	4:12:56 (13,643)
Edmundson, Martin I	5:25:46 (29,901)
Edmundson, Paul J	3:54:38 (8,928)
Edridge, Norman F	4:27:56 (17,524)
Edser, Matthew James	5:15:16 (28,378)
Edward, John D	3:59:29 (10,384)
Edwards, Adrian W	4:08:20 (12,464)
Edwards, Alex C	5:06:53 (26,884)
Edwards, Alistair	5:07:27 (26,996)
Edwards, Anthony C	6:03:39 (33,265)
Edwards, Anthony Raymond	4:04:24 (11,525)
Edwards, Barry L	4:37:23 (20,004)
Edwards, Carl	4:05:51 (11,850)
Edwards, Charles T	4:03:21 (11,303)
Edwards, Chris	5:32:02 (30,643)
Edwards, Darren J	3:54:42 (8,945)
Edwards, Darren M	4:15:45 (14,335)
Edwards, David	5:16:46 (28,614)
Edwards, David	5:46:00 (32,012)
Edwards, David Arwel	3:58:30 (10,097)
Edwards, David B	5:06:34 (26,815)
Edwards, David C	4:10:07 (12,884)
Edwards, Duncan	5:14:56 (28,303)
Edwards, Dylan L	4:46:43 (22,413)
Edwards, Edward E	4:19:42 (15,340)
Edwards, Elise M	4:18:44 (15,088)
Edwards, Gareth K	4:28:31 (17,701)
Edwards, Glyn P	3:34:55 (4,943)
Edwards, Graeme S	4:26:12 (17,038)
Edwards, Harry	3:48:58 (7,610)
Edwards, Jamie M	5:35:42 (31,042)
Edwards, Jason B	4:17:26 (14,753)
Edwards, Jeremy	3:06:11 (1,387)

Edwards, John 4:37:40 (20,081)
Edwards, Jonathan M 5:00:11 (25,630)
Edwards, Jonathan M 5:31:08 (30,548)
Edwards, Jonathan P 4:43:58 (21,711)
Edwards, Julian W 5:25:07 (29,813)
Edwards, Justin Paul 6:20:16 (34,043)
Edwards, Keith J 3:34:04 (4,778)
Edwards, Kenneth D 4:12:00 (13,387)
Edwards, Kirk 3:56:53 (9,592)
Edwards, Lloyd P 3:50:18 (7,903)
Edwards, Marc 4:18:27 (15,017)
Edwards, Marc David 4:06:33 (12,005)
Edwards, Mark 3:15:39 (2,300)
Edwards, Mark 4:05:20 (11,739)
Edwards, Mark A 4:23:58 (16,432)
Edwards, Martin G 4:18:15 (14,951)
Edwards, Michael D 3:12:24 (1,920)
Edwards, Neil A 3:29:12 (4,039)
Edwards, Neil C 4:26:58 (17,251)
Edwards, Neil John 4:07:55 (12,344)
Edwards, Nigel J 3:08:08 (1,536)
Edwards, Paul D 3:47:09 (7,228)
Edwards, Paul K 3:53:56 (8,734)
Edwards, Philip 4:27:39 (17,430)
Edwards, Rhidian W 5:44:44 (31,909)
Edwards, Rick 3:27:32 (3,783)
Edwards, Robert J 3:07:48 (1,513)
Edwards, Robert T 4:59:45 (25,544)
Edwards, Rory 3:53:43 (8,682)
Edwards, Rory P 3:54:42 (8,945)
Edwards, Sam I 4:20:24 (15,537)
Edwards, Steve 2:57:54 (829)
Edwards, Tim J 3:43:35 (6,541)
Edwards, William N 3:02:23 (1,141)
Edwards-Morgan, Richard 4:40:50 (20,920)
Edwardson, Mark J 4:46:57 (22,469)
Eeles, Alex M 3:35:39 (5,086)
Eeles, Matthew 3:36:44 (5,269)
Effer, Jonathan 4:17:45 (14,833)
Efstratiou, Stratos 4:51:40 (23,667)
Efthimiou, Panikos 3:50:13 (7,889)
Egan, Arthur 3:46:35 (7,104)
Egan, Michael A 3:31:48 (4,438)
Egan, Paul 3:27:30 (3,778)
Egan, Peter C 4:24:50 (16,663)
Egbor, Michael A 6:17:54 (33,923)
Egbujie, Chidi 4:38:23 (20,272)
Egelie, Eduard C 3:08:04 (1,530)
Eggeman, Alexander S 2:46:04 (332)
Eggett, Christopher J 3:48:03 (7,413)
Eggington, Simon 5:08:05 (27,100)
Eggle, Gareth P 4:18:41 (15,077)
Eggleton, Bernard J 3:52:33 (8,410)
Eggleton, Steven F 3:55:42 (9,221)
Eglinton, Nick 5:09:30 (27,363)
Ehlen, Jon B 3:22:06 (3,025)
Ehren, Gary R 5:44:24 (31,885)
Ehrhart, Andy P 4:17:33 (14,781)
Ehrich, Desmond 5:19:00 (28,974)
Eigelaar, Floors 3:34:19 (4,837)
Eijo, Ferderico 4:26:29 (17,111)
Einarsson, Ingolfur 3:22:34 (3,079)
Einarsson, Petur 4:14:50 (14,122)
Eisenbach, Andreas 4:17:00 (14,649)
Ekanger, Frank 3:54:37 (8,922)
Eke, Shane E 4:17:15 (14,702)
Ekstrom, Anders 4:40:03 (20,739)
El Filali, Youssef 2:59:37 (965)
Elazab, Sammy A 4:47:09 (22,532)
Elbrow, John E 6:03:06 (33,236)
Elcome, Robert 5:01:24 (25,896)
Elderfield, Adam J 3:30:14 (4,214)
Elderton, Dan R 4:01:53 (10,999)
Elding, Joe A 4:03:52 (11,414)
Eldred, Ben J 4:30:26 (18,214)
Eldred, Nigel 3:58:23 (10,065)
Eldred, Steffen 4:08:22 (12,475)
Eldridge, David J 3:55:35 (9,183)
Eldridge, Reg W 4:50:23 (23,340)
Eley, Allan J 3:56:47 (9,561)
Eley, David C 5:25:06 (29,810)
Elgar, Greg S 4:01:39 (10,956)
Elgey, Jason J 4:24:20 (16,537)
Elhag, Omar Muhammad 4:41:39 (21,132)
Elia, Charlie 5:37:35 (31,240)
Elia, Nick 5:17:54 (28,778)
Elis, Mike B 3:34:47 (4,925)
Elkan, Stephen J 4:29:21 (17,936)
El-Khoueiry, Marwan 3:35:34 (5,061)
Elkington, Simon 4:20:37 (15,580)
Elkins, Chris 4:58:38 (25,304)
Elkins, John Barry 4:29:01 (17,834)
Elkins, Peter J 5:57:38 (32,888)
Elkins, Stephen 3:27:28 (3,769)
Ellacott, Tom M 2:42:17 (243)
Ellam, Darren J 3:57:54 (9,903)
Ellaway, Nick J 5:00:18 (25,655)
Elleman, Peter 6:11:21 (33,615)
Ellender, Murray 4:31:52 (18,597)
Ellens, Nigel A 3:59:43 (10,467)
Ellerbeck, James A 6:06:47 (33,423)
Ellerby, Kevin G 4:06:00 (11,880)
Ellerby, Roger K 3:39:53 (5,830)
Ellerby, Stuart E 3:09:33 (1,660)
Ellerington, Anthony J 3:38:15 (5,543)
Ellershaw, Robert 3:55:21 (9,119)
Ellett, Ryan 3:29:50 (4,157)
Elliff, Steve R 4:56:11 (24,723)
Elliman, Max 6:34:29 (34,510)
Ellingham, Keith 6:03:41 (33,271)
Ellingham, Keith R 4:01:18 (10,858)
Ellingham, Reece C 4:54:45 (24,395)
Elliot, Ben 5:35:20 (31,002)
Elliot, Richard K 5:03:35 (26,300)
Elliott, Andrew J 3:53:22 (8,599)
Elliott, Andy C 4:36:22 (19,757)
Elliott, Carl R 5:10:18 (27,513)
Elliott, Daren P 3:56:28 (9,449)
Elliott, David A 4:09:35 (12,747)
Elliott, David W 4:39:39 (20,627)
Elliott, Garry J 4:05:10 (11,701)
Elliott, Graham M 6:43:32 (34,688)
Elliott, Joe V 3:00:47 (1,037)
Elliott, Keith 3:30:24 (4,237)
Elliott, Kevin M 4:51:11 (23,535)
Elliott, Mark A 4:01:56 (11,006)
Elliott, Mark C 6:20:24 (34,048)
Elliott, Matthew James 3:53:03 (8,519)
Elliott, Mike D 4:12:30 (13,526)
Elliott, Oliver J 4:17:53 (14,858)
Elliott, Peter 4:17:07 (14,671)
Elliott, Richard J 3:20:09 (2,774)
Elliott, Russ 4:54:17 (24,284)
Elliott, Samuel K 4:38:57 (20,421)
Elliott, Scott J 5:05:40 (26,671)
Elliott, Simon G 3:24:46 (3,378)
Elliott, Steve O 3:54:04 (8,772)
Elliott, Stuart G 6:21:14 (34,085)
Elliott-Smith, Lewis M 5:11:12 (27,672)
Ellis, Andrew 5:21:18 (29,272)
Ellis, Andrew Jeremy Dalrymple . 3:43:57 (6,625)
Ellis, Brent L 4:42:50 (21,422)
Ellis, Chris 5:46:26 (32,044)
Ellis, Chris B 6:46:36 (34,731)
Ellis, Chris P 3:24:08 (3,286)
Ellis, Christopher R 3:43:08 (6,448)
Ellis, David A 3:26:08 (3,546)
Ellis, David A 4:43:14 (21,524)
Ellis, David W 4:40:30 (20,833)
Ellis, Gareth S 3:17:38 (2,493)
Ellis, Ian 5:36:32 (31,126)
Ellis, James A 2:44:42 (306)
Ellis, John R 5:10:34 (27,561)
Ellis, Keith 6:25:26 (34,252)
Ellis, Lawren I 3:32:41 (4,569)
Ellis, Matthew P 4:16:05 (14,420)
Ellis, Michael P 3:35:16 (5,002)
Ellis, Orlando 3:09:22 (1,652)
Ellis, Ralph 4:18:35 (15,049)
Ellis, Richard J 4:36:26 (19,777)
Ellis, Ricky J 4:35:40 (19,587)
Ellis, Rob W 5:54:43 (32,662)
Ellis, Robert H 4:47:09 (22,532)
Ellis, Samuel J 4:04:44 (11,593)
Ellis, Samuel R 4:07:44 (12,295)
Ellis, Steve D 4:17:18 (14,717)
Ellis, Steven J 3:51:29 (8,164)
Ellis, Timothy C 3:39:34 (5,772)
Ellis, Timothy H 3:11:16 (1,805)
Ellis, Tony 3:23:47 (3,229)
Ellis, Vincent J 3:22:35 (3,082)
Ellison, Andrew J 2:46:43 (356)
Ellison, Chris 3:44:38 (6,738)
Ellison, Chris 3:56:47 (9,561)
Ellison, Matthew 4:38:18 (20,251)
Ellison, Wayne A 4:50:13 (23,285)
Ellman, Jeremy 3:39:00 (5,686)
Ellsbury, Stuart J 4:49:50 (23,205)
Ellson, Matthew 3:53:05 (8,528)
Ellwood, Mike 4:28:34 (17,716)
Ellwood, Robert C 5:44:51 (31,919)
Elmes, Andrew 4:46:42 (22,400)
Elmes, Mike C 3:41:38 (6,134)
Elms, Mike R 4:44:53 (21,924)
Elmy, Glen 4:20:41 (15,596)
Elsby, Dominic A 2:38:58 (177)
Elsey, Thomas C 4:24:59 (16,706)
Elsmere, Alan 3:10:14 (1,716)
Elsmoortel, Jean Claude 4:01:51 (10,991)
Elsom, Dave 4:15:55 (14,369)
Elsom, Simon Gregory 5:10:35 (27,565)
Elson, Ian 7:56:34 (35,306)
Elson, Nigel C 3:09:25 (1,656)
Elson, Richard M 3:59:22 (10,359)
Elston, Adam D 3:26:05 (3,543)
Elston, Tony M 3:46:41 (7,134)
Elswood, Dan E 3:55:34 (9,176)
Elsworth, Damon E 3:24:17 (3,309)
Elton, Colin R 4:50:56 (23,467)
Elverd, Stephen C 3:27:15 (3,726)
Elvidge, Dean 4:23:06 (16,207)
Elvidge, Douglas M 4:13:41 (13,842)
Elvidge, Nicholas 3:35:47 (5,112)
Elvin, Peter 4:20:21 (15,524)
Elvin, Roger E 4:25:05 (16,734)
Elward, Mike J 3:59:12 (10,310)
Elwell, Thomas W 5:53:17 (32,571)
Elwick, Kevin 3:48:19 (7,470)
Ely, Martin P 4:32:15 (18,698)
Emberson, Paul 4:23:10 (16,223)
Embleton, Dennis 4:41:10 (20,998)
Embry, John W 5:23:00 (29,517)
Emeny, Mark 3:59:34 (10,411)
Emerson, Bruce 3:15:17 (2,257)
Emerson, Jamie R 4:24:02 (16,448)
Emerson, John E 5:33:27 (30,799)
Emery, Daryl 4:01:51 (10,991)
Emery, Dominic V 4:25:31 (16,842)
Emery, Paul 4:42:11 (21,244)
Emery, Paul R 4:29:07 (17,865)
Emery, Peter K 3:26:55 (3,669)
Emes, Robert 3:56:52 (9,588)
Emmerson, Bob 4:44:34 (21,848)
Empsall, Craig 3:20:16 (2,795)
Emson, Darren R 4:24:58 (16,700)
Endersby, James 4:22:38 (16,105)
Engelmann, Paul Manson 4:19:51 (15,390)
England, John R 5:14:48 (28,283)
England, Paul A 4:59:53 (25,573)
Engledow, Maria A 4:57:20 (24,992)
Englefield, Bruce 4:43:15 (21,529)
Engley, Robin 5:41:51 (31,659)
English, Allan 4:19:21 (15,246)
English, Jeremy G 4:58:28 (25,258)
English, Mark 4:20:11 (15,482)
English, Michael J 4:33:43 (19,077)
Enjuanes, Andrew M 4:44:40 (21,879)
Ennis, Gary 7:05:21 (35,007)
Enock, Adam C 5:31:57 (30,634)
Enock, Eric B 5:31:58 (30,635)
Enskat, Damian A 4:28:11 (17,608)
Ensor, Simon 4:10:06 (12,879)
Enstone, Robin W 3:51:18 (8,120)
Enstone, Simon P 4:44:09 (21,757)
Entwistle, Colin 4:07:10 (12,144)
Enville, Thomas P 6:15:41 (33,825)
Eric, Goguet 4:12:09 (13,426)
Eric, Maggi 3:47:39 (7,318)
Eric, Radicchi 4:28:14 (17,628)

Eric, Serot 3:57:14 (9,682)
Eric, Zonca 4:01:14 (10,844)
Erichsen, Bjorn 3:57:21 (9,729)
Eriksen, Asger S 4:36:24 (19,773)
Eriksson, Johan 4:05:53 (11,858)
Erkan, Yucel 5:42:20 (31,705)
Errichiello, Domenico 3:25:08 (3,412)
Errington, Jonathon T 3:48:31 (7,513)
Erskine, Alex 4:08:17 (12,447)
Erskine, Kevin A 2:51:25 (505)
Eschle, Luke D 4:20:57 (15,674)
Esclapon, Cristiano 3:59:36 (10,419)
Eskelund, Vidar 4:11:29 (13,248)
Espinasa, Jorge 4:13:39 (13,837)
Esplin, Stephen F 3:47:46 (7,341)
Essex, John 4:37:21 (19,994)
Essex-Crosby, Chris E 3:34:00 (4,758)
Essig, Alexander 3:54:37 (8,922)
Esson, Andy B 4:13:48 (13,869)
Estela, Roger 3:55:39 (9,207)
Estevez Nuñez, Pedro 3:19:18 (2,650)
Estick, Ian 5:17:41 (28,745)
Estick, Peter V 5:24:29 (29,730)
Estienne, Mark P 4:20:00 (15,428)
Etches, Adam 3:50:59 (8,054)
Etherden, Cliff R 4:24:48 (16,654)
Etheridge, Brian R 3:39:41 (5,791)
Etherington, Dave 4:18:03 (14,905)
Etherington, John T 4:50:16 (23,308)
Etienne, Kolly 3:20:33 (2,832)
Etty, Peter G 4:37:00 (19,920)
Eufrate, Alfredo 4:18:37 (15,058)
Eugeni, Ray 4:28:30 (17,697)
Eustace, Bryan R 4:31:47 (18,578)
Eva, Paul D 4:36:47 (19,859)
Evans, Alan W 4:43:16 (21,534)
Evans, Alexander P 4:56:49 (24,883)
Evans, Andrew N 4:01:22 (10,879)
Evans, Andrew W 3:26:58 (3,678)
Evans, Anthony 4:33:07 (18,924)
Evans, Ashley M 4:17:46 (14,836)
Evans, Barrie J 4:58:29 (25,263)
Evans, Ben Lawrence Gordon 3:32:44 (4,578)
Evans, Benjamin R 4:13:53 (13,880)
Evans, Brandon J 6:05:56 (33,383)
Evans, Carl S 5:57:36 (32,882)
Evans, Chris David 4:35:25 (19,525)
Evans, Chris J 4:03:19 (11,298)
Evans, Chris P 4:31:17 (18,429)
Evans, Christopher H 4:35:06 (19,439)
Evans, Colin 3:16:36 (2,394)
Evans, Conrad R 4:38:00 (20,165)
Evans, Daniel 3:00:06 (1,005)
Evans, Daniel 4:05:13 (11,715)
Evans, Darin 4:04:51 (11,618)
Evans, Dylan R 4:53:51 (24,189)
Evans, Evan R 4:34:00 (19,153)
Evans, Gareth A 5:32:08 (30,654)
Evans, Gareth P 6:11:44 (33,626)
Evans, Gary 4:45:59 (22,210)
Evans, Geraint 5:00:05 (25,610)
Evans, Geraint R 3:35:52 (5,125)
Evans, Graham 3:41:18 (6,088)
Evans, Graham A 4:21:13 (15,744)
Evans, Gwyn William 4:40:40 (20,878)
Evans, Ian 4:54:35 (24,352)
Evans, Jason 4:51:47 (23,695)
Evans, Jason 4:51:54 (23,729)
Evans, Jason S 6:35:48 (34,538)
Evans, Jerome 3:13:52 (2,105)
Evans, Jim 3:08:12 (1,545)
Evans, John A 4:32:13 (18,686)
Evans, John E 3:36:28 (5,229)
Evans, John E 4:10:12 (12,911)
Evans, John Lloyd 4:19:51 (15,390)
Evans, John M 4:11:59 (13,383)
Evans, Jonathan D 5:41:43 (31,650)
Evans, Kevin 4:35:33 (19,558)
Evans, Lee A 5:09:38 (27,392)
Evans, Marc T 2:53:59 (603)
Evans, Mark A 3:53:21 (8,592)
Evans, Mark A 5:03:52 (26,353)
Evans, Mark Anthony 4:25:48 (16,937)
Evans, Mark D 5:00:33 (25,717)
Evans, Mark H 3:42:32 (6,310)
Evans, Mark Stephen 4:54:41 (24,382)
Evans, Mark W 4:18:17 (14,959)
Evans, Martin 3:50:08 (7,867)
Evans, Michael A 5:00:22 (25,669)
Evans, Nicholas C 3:36:45 (5,272)
Evans, Nicholas J 4:56:25 (24,777)
Evans, Nicholas O 4:23:26 (16,290)
Evans, Nicholas P 4:05:32 (11,780)
Evans, Pascal 2:58:46 (890)
Evans, Paul 4:17:58 (14,882)
Evans, Paul R 3:49:00 (7,619)
Evans, Paul S 4:50:21 (23,327)
Evans, Philip B 4:15:26 (14,268)
Evans, Philip G 3:26:26 (3,593)
Evans, Philippe M 4:54:55 (24,432)
Evans, Phillip 3:27:24 (3,749)
Evans, Phillip 3:39:38 (5,782)
Evans, Phillip T 4:18:38 (15,064)
Evans, Richard A 4:44:01 (21,725)
Evans, Richard D 5:03:37 (26,308)
Evans, Richard L 4:42:21 (21,283)
Evans, Richard P 4:13:27 (13,785)
Evans, Robert 3:54:33 (8,904)
Evans, Ross L 5:20:04 (29,104)
Evans, Russell James 4:23:10 (16,223)
Evans, Sam 4:51:19 (23,571)
Evans, Sam J 4:29:10 (17,876)
Evans, Sam J 6:05:41 (33,375)
Evans, Scott 3:11:30 (1,829)
Evans, Simon L 3:25:13 (3,420)
Evans, Stephen 2:55:37 (703)
Evans, Stephen J 5:12:48 (27,947)
Evans, Stephen P 5:53:07 (32,556)
Evans, Stephen R 5:42:53 (31,756)
Evans, Stuart C 4:01:04 (10,807)
Evans, Timothy 4:27:16 (17,333)
Evans, Tommy H 4:50:48 (23,448)
Eve, Patrick 3:55:42 (9,221)
Everett, Barry 4:57:39 (25,060)
Everett, Grahame J 3:16:47 (2,413)
Everett, Herbert J 4:46:55 (22,454)
Everett, Richard 3:59:47 (10,488)
Everington, Nick K 4:18:22 (14,980)
Everitt, Matt P 4:02:26 (11,115)
Everitt, Matthew R 5:53:27 (32,581)
Everitt, Michael J 3:59:09 (10,297)
Evers, André 3:32:57 (4,604)
Everson, Ben E 4:00:28 (10,656)
Everson, David 3:29:30 (4,102)
Eves, Robert 6:06:13 (33,396)
Eves, Terance C 4:09:21 (12,698)
Evett, Jon P 4:10:36 (13,006)
Evins, Stephen John 3:34:09 (4,802)
Evi-Parker, Christopher C 4:51:54 (23,729)
Evison, Gareth 5:20:17 (29,129)
Ewart, Michael David 3:40:21 (5,923)
Ewart, Tim 5:03:53 (26,360)
Ewart-Perks, George G 3:06:50 (1,423)
Ewbank, Tim D 4:24:40 (16,614)
Ewen, Colin 3:54:03 (8,769)
Ewen, James 4:33:49 (19,101)
Ewing, Andy J 3:58:56 (10,233)
Ewing, Tom J 4:07:22 (12,205)
Ewington, Simon J 3:58:46 (10,179)
Exell, Gary P 3:49:21 (7,696)
Exley, Andrew R 3:11:57 (1,877)
Exley, Martin J 2:50:29 (481)
Exton, Gareth J 4:49:02 (22,981)
Exton, Graham 4:10:52 (13,081)
Eyers, Jonathan A 3:51:03 (8,066)
Eyole, Mbou 6:11:44 (33,626)
Eyre, Matt 4:39:11 (20,495)
Eyre, Torbjorn K 4:49:17 (23,046)
Eyre-Brook, David G 3:57:09 (9,662)
Ezen, Alan J 4:08:49 (12,577)
Ezingeard, Jean-Noel 4:39:19 (20,523)
Fabley, Michel 5:02:18 (26,081)
Fabrice, Bidault 2:40:30 (207)
Facciponte, Cataldo 3:29:47 (4,150)
Facey, Nigel A 4:22:37 (16,103)
Fadiora, George E 3:22:21 (3,053)
Faerestrand, Ben 5:08:50 (27,234)
Fagan, Alan B 4:20:31 (15,563)
Fagioli, Raffaele 4:39:33 (20,595)
Faherty, Aidan 4:19:45 (15,357)
Fahey, Christian 3:57:35 (9,798)
Fahy, Peter M 3:05:08 (1,312)
Fairbairn, Scott H 3:57:37 (9,806)
Fairbrass, Keith 4:37:56 (20,149)
Fairbrother, Nick 4:57:50 (25,094)
Fairbrother, Paul 3:10:49 (1,761)
Fairburn, David L 5:28:34 (30,215)
Fairclough, Lee J 5:01:02 (25,825)
Fairclough, Stuart J 4:47:49 (22,675)
Fairclough, Thomas 3:47:51 (7,361)
Fairfield, James 3:59:07 (10,285)
Fairhall, Jack H 4:22:16 (16,017)
Fairhead, Darryl J 3:59:06 (10,278)
Fairhurst, Charlie B 4:58:53 (25,357)
Fairhurst, Paul 4:18:41 (15,077)
Fairhurst, Russell L 3:47:54 (7,374)
Fairhurst, Wayne 3:04:29 (1,261)
Fairlamb, Ian 3:34:08 (4,796)
Fairley, Lee M 3:51:22 (8,133)
Fairlie, Kenneth W 3:49:30 (7,730)
Fairman, Paul 5:00:06 (25,616)
Fairs, Jon P 2:37:47 (153)
Fairs, Steve 4:30:14 (18,160)
Fairs, Steven 4:19:04 (15,177)
Fairweather, Hamish K 4:31:37 (18,531)
Fajardo, Marcos R 6:09:18 (33,524)
Falgate, Steve 3:41:59 (6,200)
Falk, Johan 4:31:44 (18,560)
Falk, Roland 4:31:45 (18,567)
Falkingham, John M 4:55:02 (24,455)
Fallman (Naylor), Tomas 3:33:04 (4,620)
Fallon, Darren 4:46:40 (22,386)
Fallon, Declan J 5:19:19 (29,009)
Fallows, David 3:48:24 (7,487)
Fallows, Martin 5:21:20 (29,275)
Fallows, Michael L 5:43:13 (31,797)
Fancy, Peter R 3:53:50 (8,710)
Fanner, Sarah J 4:03:36 (11,356)
Fanning, Patrick 4:05:09 (11,695)
Fanning, Scott M 3:59:53 (10,512)
Fantham, Wayne 4:30:01 (18,103)
Fanthome, Phillip J 5:52:07 (32,487)
Fantoni, Luigi G 4:18:21 (14,975)
Faotto, Giovanni 5:18:15 (28,830)
Farago, Gaetano 3:35:15 (5,000)
Fararoni, Rafael 4:17:57 (14,872)
Farazmand, Tim B 6:12:16 (33,654)
Fardy, David R 5:22:51 (29,490)
Faria, Joaquim 4:01:56 (11,006)
Farias, Carlos Frederico 4:38:47 (20,372)
Farias, Rodrigo 4:03:08 (11,257)
Farid, Aidoud 3:30:44 (4,288)
Faries, Ryan 4:53:01 (23,979)
Fariña Fraga, José Manuel 3:48:18 (7,465)
Farioli, Maurizio 4:08:57 (12,606)
Farley, Adam 5:03:02 (26,214)
Farley-Thompson, Mark J 4:20:50 (15,644)
Farmer, Andrew M 5:09:24 (27,347)
Farmer, David A 4:10:58 (13,102)
Farmer, Joe F 4:10:40 (13,025)
Farmer, Nigel K 3:54:03 (8,769)
Farmer, Phil A 4:12:16 (13,459)
Farmer, Ricky 5:48:55 (32,243)
Farmer, Stephen 3:49:11 (7,665)
Farmer, Stuart Michael 3:55:55 (9,292)
Farmery, David J 5:20:23 (29,138)
Farnan, Stuart 4:19:40 (15,331)
Farndell, Terry J 3:54:08 (8,790)
Farnell, Mark A 2:58:18 (858)
Farnetani, Riccardo 3:37:02 (5,325)
Farnham, Lyndon 4:41:37 (21,122)
Farnsworth, Benjamin L 5:14:30 (28,242)
Farnsworth, Graham 3:07:49 (1,514)
Farrah, Abdul 4:56:23 (24,769)
Farrar, John 4:00:28 (10,656)
Farrell, Andrew J 3:47:21 (7,257)
Farrell, Andrew James 4:44:49 (21,913)
Farrell, Bernard 3:57:17 (9,702)
Farrell, Donal J 4:12:50 (13,613)

Finnis, Steven M 4:28:34 (17,716)
Finotto, Alessandro 3:21:49 (2,985)
Finsveen, Bernt Ove 3:34:41 (4,909)
Fiordi, Luca 3:59:47 (10,488)
Firetto, Andrew J 3:56:09 (9,351)
Firman, Andrew J 7:36:03 (35,251)
Firouzi, Mazeyar 2:47:57 (395)
Firth, David A 4:57:07 (24,948)
Firth, Martin J 2:49:46 (460)
Firth, Michael 4:31:55 (18,611)
Firth, Peter M 3:39:48 (5,809)
Firth, Wayne 5:17:42 (28,747)
Fischer, Alfons 3:36:36 (5,255)
Fischer, Stephan 4:47:05 (22,511)
Fish, Bradley David 5:48:17 (32,195)
Fish, Jonathan P 3:09:58 (1,704)
Fish, Richard M 4:15:15 (14,222)
Fishburn, Andrew 4:29:43 (18,019)
Fishel, Matthew 4:08:50 (12,580)
Fisher, Anthony P 7:31:21 (35,229)
Fisher, Chris R 4:04:18 (11,509)
Fisher, Edward 4:29:30 (17,967)
Fisher, Jerry 3:46:39 (7,122)
Fisher, John D 5:26:00 (29,939)
Fisher, Mark 4:09:58 (12,846)
Fisher, Martin L 3:29:35 (4,114)
Fisher, Matthew C 3:59:33 (10,404)
Fisher, Matthew R 5:57:16 (32,848)
Fisher, Neil L 4:27:46 (17,474)
Fisher, Nicholas 4:32:58 (18,888)
Fisher, Paul 6:48:01 (34,770)
Fisher, Scott E 4:40:42 (20,886)
Fisher, Simon 5:05:59 (26,723)
Fisher, Stephen 5:02:16 (26,074)
Fisher, Stuart J 4:45:25 (22,059)
Fisher, Tom 4:35:16 (19,483)
Fisher, Wayne G 4:29:49 (18,041)
Fishman, Oliver J 3:54:02 (8,763)
Fishwick, Ian R 3:52:16 (8,353)
Fishwick, Mark 4:00:00 (10,544)
Fishwick, Mary C 6:02:36 (33,203)
Fiske, Neal 5:24:13 (29,684)
Fissneider, Werner 3:45:39 (6,920)
Fitch, Ian R 4:27:00 (17,257)
Fitch, Jamie Frederick 4:16:37 (14,560)
Fitchett, Simon 5:04:06 (26,403)
Fitsakis, Yiannis 2:56:29 (746)
Fitter, Carl 3:40:32 (5,943)
Fitter, Gary A 3:23:00 (3,126)
Fittock, Ian J 4:35:03 (19,425)
Fittock, Paul J 2:57:21 (799)
Fitton, Brian 4:26:41 (17,176)
Fitton, Simon 3:49:33 (7,742)
Fitzgerald, Craig 3:50:46 (8,016)
Fitzgerald, David P 4:33:55 (19,133)
Fitzgerald, Dean R 4:04:12 (11,489)
Fitzgerald, Jon-Paul H 4:21:53 (15,917)
Fitzgerald, Joshua 5:03:34 (26,294)
Fitzgerald, Justin 3:18:18 (2,553)
Fitzgerald, Karl W 3:44:17 (6,680)
Fitzgerald, Mark J 4:36:40 (19,830)
Fitzgerald, Martyn 4:48:52 (22,936)
Fitzgerald, Michael T 5:10:08 (27,485)
Fitzgerald, Paddy M 3:55:16 (9,102)
Fitzgerald, Patrick J 3:04:39 (1,275)
Fitzgerald, Tom 5:25:12 (29,825)
Fitz-Gerald, Philip 4:53:53 (24,197)
Fitzgibbon, Francis 4:05:04 (11,670)
Fitzgibbon, Mike R 4:54:38 (24,374)
Fitzjohn, Daniel 3:23:17 (3,157)
Fitzjohn, Malcolm G 5:01:03 (25,829)
Fitzpatrick, David 2:47:04 (370)
Fitzpatrick, Dean M 4:24:23 (16,545)
Fitzpatrick, Michael M 4:04:14 (11,499)
Fitzpatrick, Niall 5:06:58 (26,901)
Fitzpatrick, Tomas 4:21:07 (15,721)
Fitzsimmons, Joseph A 3:54:53 (8,992)
Fitzsimmons, Thomas 6:54:03 (34,882)
Fitzsimon, James P 3:26:08 (3,546)
Fixter, Adam 6:26:04 (34,282)
Flack, Chris J 3:53:21 (8,592)
Flade, Peter 4:19:41 (15,333)
Flaherty, John L 3:56:17 (9,383)
Flaherty, Michael A 3:27:33 (3,790)
Flanagan, Brian 4:00:51 (10,755)
Flanagan, David C 4:20:54 (15,662)
Flanagan, Mark 3:18:46 (2,595)
Flanagan, Tony 3:07:06 (1,445)
Flanaghan, David J 5:08:27 (27,171)
Flannery, James O 4:07:25 (12,218)
Flashman, Keith 5:06:22 (26,784)
Flatt, Christopher J 3:15:08 (2,246)
Flawn, Guy O 3:57:34 (9,796)
Flaxman, John W 4:53:47 (24,169)
Fleet, Paul J 5:32:18 (30,669)
Fleming, Christopher N 4:01:04 (10,807)
Fleming, James S 5:52:06 (32,485)
Fleming, John A 3:46:45 (7,145)
Fleming, Michael D 5:45:49 (32,003)
Fleming, Neil D 4:03:12 (11,273)
Fleming, Nicholas J 4:07:11 (12,148)
Fleming, Roger W 4:15:31 (14,287)
Fleming, Scott 4:05:41 (11,821)
Fleming, Simon C 4:59:20 (25,459)
Fleming, Tim J 3:35:27 (5,040)
Flemmings, Richard 3:27:41 (3,811)
Flesher, Roy 3:39:32 (5,764)
Fletcher, Alan J 4:34:06 (19,172)
Fletcher, Anthony B 4:29:47 (18,031)
Fletcher, Brendan S 7:15:14 (35,107)
Fletcher, Cedric J 3:00:44 (1,033)
Fletcher, Danny 4:01:51 (10,991)
Fletcher, David P 4:18:52 (15,124)
Fletcher, Gordon 4:02:30 (11,126)
Fletcher, Graham A 3:41:49 (6,171)
Fletcher, Harvey W 4:54:05 (24,241)
Fletcher, James 4:21:08 (15,727)
Fletcher, Jonathan C 4:38:03 (20,179)
Fletcher, Neil S 5:37:12 (31,193)
Fletcher, Paul David 3:41:39 (6,138)
Fletcher, Richard 4:28:41 (17,744)
Fletcher, Robert W 4:29:50 (18,048)
Fletcher, Sean K 3:14:19 (2,155)
Fletcher, Stuart 4:50:46 (23,437)
Fletcher, Thomas N 5:45:31 (31,975)
Fletcher, Wayne G 4:39:41 (20,639)
Flett, Douglas G 3:57:30 (9,772)
Flint, Daniel 2:46:20 (341)
Flint, Jonathan 4:19:35 (15,308)
Flint, Kevin R 4:28:00 (17,542)
Flint, Thomas 3:16:21 (2,362)
Flitcroft, Graeme 4:47:25 (22,582)
Flitcroft, Robert A 4:07:45 (12,302)
Flitney, Paul 2:58:09 (849)
Flockhart, Kevin Robert 5:34:32 (30,920)
Flood, Colin J 4:04:09 (11,478)
Flood, Gavin D 4:56:39 (24,843)
Flood, Tim 5:42:06 (31,680)
Floris, Francesco 4:02:10 (11,057)
Flower, Roger 5:50:49 (32,400)
Flowerday, Crispin E 4:09:36 (12,753)
Floyd, Darren L 3:53:24 (8,604)
Floyd, Mark R 5:02:36 (26,137)
Floyd, Michael 3:58:18 (10,033)
Floyd, Peter 3:23:31 (3,191)
Floyd, Robert J 3:48:26 (7,496)
Floyd, Warren S 4:19:44 (15,348)
Flygare, Klas 3:41:46 (6,161)
Flynn, Christopher 5:05:06 (26,566)
Flynn, Daniel 7:26:16 (35,191)
Flynn, John 5:26:00 (29,939)
Flynn, John P 4:47:06 (22,515)
Flynn, Jonathan P 4:40:14 (20,781)
Flynn, Paul G 3:46:25 (7,069)
Flynn, Paul T 5:23:01 (29,520)
Flynn, Russell 5:05:47 (26,694)
Flynn, Timothy B 4:36:11 (19,716)
Foad, Martin C 5:30:31 (30,463)
Foale, Trevor R 4:16:28 (14,514)
Foddering, Ian 4:10:01 (12,858)
Foden, Dean 3:46:43 (7,138)
Fog, Torben 4:30:31 (18,235)
Fogarty, James P 4:11:31 (13,258)
Fogden, Kieran G 4:06:50 (12,068)
Fogelman, Clive S 3:58:01 (9,941)
Fogelman, David J 4:30:49 (18,309)
Fogelman, Richard 5:31:22 (30,562)
Fogerty, David 5:52:41 (32,528)
Fogg, Brian 4:44:18 (21,794)
Fogwill, Alex 4:02:13 (11,072)
Folan, Paul 5:30:19 (30,442)
Foley, Benjamin J 4:05:36 (11,798)
Foley, Colm P 4:57:17 (24,980)
Foley, David J 4:03:21 (11,303)
Foley, David M 4:35:12 (19,465)
Foley, David O 5:14:48 (28,283)
Foley, Dean W 3:29:47 (4,150)
Foley, Ian 4:21:53 (15,917)
Foley, Keith 3:19:12 (2,637)
Foley, William P 4:16:48 (14,605)
Folkard, Jeremy R 4:51:28 (23,612)
Folkes, Peter JT 5:08:58 (27,265)
Folkesson, Erik A 3:35:53 (5,131)
Follan, Michael G 3:35:21 (5,022)
Follett, Jeremy C 3:47:24 (7,265)
Follis, Tim M 4:52:53 (23,945)
Follows, Dominic R 4:06:32 (11,997)
Follows, Gordon 4:43:04 (21,484)
Foo, Kim A 3:02:32 (1,148)
Foord, Michael R 6:53:29 (34,871)
Foord, Tim J 5:05:03 (26,558)
Foot, Peter G 6:17:15 (33,889)
Foote, Andy 6:11:49 (33,632)
Foote, Colin J 4:44:49 (21,913)
Foote, Jamie 4:45:04 (21,986)
Foote, Simon J 3:59:09 (10,297)
Foppele, Tim 4:38:31 (20,303)
Foran, Clark 4:33:06 (18,921)
Foran, Ian S 5:38:14 (31,300)
Forbes, Christopher J 3:57:43 (9,850)
Forbes, David G 4:08:00 (12,359)
Forbes, David W 4:29:11 (17,884)
Forbes, Dominic 3:57:28 (9,756)
Forbes, Jerry J 5:14:24 (28,224)
Ford, Ben 3:27:07 (3,698)
Ford, Chris 4:46:04 (22,218)
Ford, Christopher J 3:32:33 (4,553)
Ford, Darran 3:48:56 (7,603)
Ford, David 3:37:19 (5,375)
Ford, David A 3:58:12 (10,007)
Ford, David J 5:23:39 (29,607)
Ford, David J 6:20:44 (34,060)
Ford, David R 6:22:11 (34,116)
Ford, Gary J 3:30:40 (4,280)
Ford, Graham 4:03:08 (11,257)
Ford, Greg C 3:50:25 (7,925)
Ford, Ian J 6:34:33 (34,512)
Ford, John A 3:19:18 (2,650)
Ford, Julian 4:12:51 (13,616)
Ford, Mark S 2:56:36 (753)
Ford, Martin C 3:10:35 (1,742)
Ford, Martin L 3:34:35 (4,889)
Ford, Matt 5:30:25 (30,449)
Ford, Nicholas L 3:45:47 (6,945)
Ford, Peter J 4:15:23 (14,251)
Ford, Timothy A 4:25:09 (16,751)
Forde, David M 4:14:50 (14,122)
Forde, James 3:55:46 (9,253)
Fordyce, Alex 3:50:34 (7,962)
Fordyce, Bruce N 3:59:19 (10,340)
Foreman, Dan 4:51:40 (23,667)
Foreman, Edward 4:00:56 (10,782)
Foreman, Keith D 4:19:14 (15,218)
Foreman, Tim 3:35:46 (5,109)
Foreman, Timothy James 3:30:09 (4,197)
Fores, Shaun 3:18:37 (2,585)
Forest, Daniel 4:10:07 (12,884)
Forester, Simon 3:29:05 (4,022)
Forgione, Giuseppe 4:54:34 (24,351)
Forman, Mark E 4:07:59 (12,355)
Forman, Oliver P 4:22:09 (15,989)
Forman, Thomas W 4:34:41 (19,314)
Formisano, Fabio 3:10:53 (1,769)
Formstone, Martin D 2:31:05 (72)
Forrat, Olivier 3:51:11 (8,093)
Forrest, Alex W 4:28:05 (17,570)
Forrester, George W 4:44:29 (21,833)
Forrester, Tom D 3:49:14 (7,672)
Forsdyke, Dale M 3:48:33 (7,523)

Forshaw, Antony A	6:40:00 (34,627)
Forster, David M	4:42:36 (21,361)
Forsyth, Dirk J	4:10:24 (12,955)
Forsythe, Alex	5:23:24 (29,583)
Forte, Philip	3:23:17 (3,157)
Fortune, Damien	4:12:15 (13,453)
Fortune, David J	4:20:10 (15,478)
Fortune, Gary J	4:11:20 (13,202)
Fosker, Steven P	4:11:01 (13,112)
Fossey, James	4:42:51 (21,425)
Foster, Adam R	4:56:42 (24,856)
Foster, Andrew J	4:10:43 (13,044)
Foster, Charlie G	6:44:30 (34,701)
Foster, David	4:48:12 (22,783)
Foster, David	4:49:20 (23,064)
Foster, David I	4:37:49 (20,125)
Foster, David John	3:43:49 (6,592)
Foster, David R	4:54:24 (24,310)
Foster, James W	3:11:09 (1,797)
Foster, Mark	5:54:19 (32,641)
Foster, Mark G	5:56:04 (32,761)
Foster, Mark John	4:52:53 (23,945)
Foster, Martin S	4:11:30 (13,255)
Foster, Matthew S	4:08:51 (12,585)
Foster, Nigel I	3:34:09 (4,802)
Foster, Oliver C	4:49:48 (23,199)
Foster, Paul	4:48:12 (22,783)
Foster, Robert P	3:20:28 (2,823)
Foster, Simon	3:35:03 (4,968)
Foster, Simon E	4:15:54 (14,368)
Foster, Stephen John	4:05:11 (11,703)
Foster, Stephen P	4:55:35 (24,591)
Foster, Steven M	3:58:38 (10,137)
Foster, Stuart	3:26:29 (3,596)
Foster, Timothy J	6:08:32 (33,494)
Fotheringham, Duncan W	4:52:46 (23,919)
Fotheringham, Ian A	5:45:10 (31,941)
Foulerton, Mark	3:13:21 (2,041)
Foulkes, Andy D	4:08:44 (12,558)
Foulkes, Chris A	4:28:00 (17,542)
Fountain, Johnathan W	4:56:39 (24,843)
Fourie, Johan	5:27:47 (30,120)
Fournier, Bob	4:23:56 (16,423)
Fourny, Eric	4:51:37 (23,650)
Fowell, Mark A	3:02:31 (1,147)
Fowler, Alun J	4:21:24 (15,785)
Fowler, Andy J	3:20:33 (2,832)
Fowler, Carwyn I	5:46:56 (32,083)
Fowler, Charlie	4:45:35 (22,101)
Fowler, Craig A	3:20:48 (2,868)
Fowler, David J	5:22:39 (29,461)
Fowler, Dean Martin	4:21:52 (15,913)
Fowler, Justin P	3:12:16 (1,909)
Fowler, Marc H	4:27:39 (17,430)
Fowler, Matthew N	3:53:22 (8,599)
Fowler, Nick T	3:59:30 (10,393)
Fowler, Simon	4:39:58 (20,710)
Fowler, Terry	2:49:22 (438)
Fowler, Timothy E	4:18:18 (14,962)
Fowler, Vincent C	2:55:10 (676)
Fowles, Chris	5:25:49 (29,906)
Fowles, Stephen W	3:24:29 (3,339)
Fox, Barrie	3:26:22 (3,584)
Fox, Barry P	5:43:00 (31,770)
Fox, Gary	5:31:38 (30,599)
Fox, Malcolm F	6:13:03 (33,696)
Fox, Martin	4:41:25 (21,058)
Fox, Martin R	4:20:21 (15,524)
Fox, Nick	5:31:38 (30,599)
Fox, Nick J	4:11:07 (13,145)
Fox, Noel	4:11:51 (13,350)
Fox, Shaun T	3:41:10 (6,061)
Fox, Stevan	4:57:24 (25,012)
Fox, Steve W	5:13:05 (28,001)
Fox, Thomas W	3:37:07 (5,344)
Foxall, Martin P	4:26:06 (17,010)
Foyle, Christopher N	3:59:32 (10,398)
Fozzard, Jamie	5:27:41 (30,111)
Frain, Diarmaid	3:41:42 (6,151)
Fraiz, Wayne	5:49:28 (32,287)
Frampton, Craig R	3:55:32 (9,162)
Frampton, Duncan R	3:15:41 (2,302)
Frampton, Robin A	5:25:11 (29,824)

Frampton, Scott	4:56:03 (24,694)
France, Colin	3:14:36 (2,182)
France, Paul C	5:08:51 (27,242)
France, Peter	4:35:13 (19,472)
France, Peter K	4:33:34 (19,041)
Franceschini, Pietro D	3:34:47 (4,925)
Franchi, Juri	3:17:21 (2,472)
Francis, Brian P	4:50:16 (23,308)
Francis, Christopher	3:28:18 (3,899)
Francis, Christopher T	3:52:23 (8,378)
Francis, Colin B	5:34:13 (30,880)
Francis, Daniel	4:25:35 (16,868)
Francis, David Charles	5:01:52 (25,988)
Francis, David Terence	5:32:11 (30,660)
Francis, Hugh R	6:14:19 (33,757)
Francis, Ian D	4:07:46 (12,310)
Francis, James S	4:54:42 (24,386)
Francis, Marcus D	7:44:32 (35,276)
Francis, Mark A	3:07:55 (1,519)
Francis, Mark D	4:45:19 (22,037)
Francis, Michael J	3:56:00 (9,309)
Francis, Richard C	3:01:29 (1,080)
Francis, Seb	5:59:45 (33,029)
Francis, Steven	4:01:21 (10,873)
Francis, Vale	5:55:07 (32,696)
Franck, Chalumeau	3:15:01 (2,234)
Franck, Schmitz	3:37:01 (5,321)
Franco, Daniel	3:43:42 (6,565)
Franco, Rocco	4:04:08 (11,474)
François, Denis	4:33:11 (18,939)
François, René J	4:45:03 (21,981)
Frank, Glen D	4:25:34 (16,861)
Franke, Hans	4:45:22 (22,050)
Frankiewicz, Maciej	4:11:12 (13,162)
Frankis, Richard	5:10:21 (27,522)
Franklin, Kelvin	4:35:22 (19,514)
Franklin, Leslie	4:37:19 (19,989)
Franklin, Mark V	3:50:06 (7,855)
Franklin, Martin A	3:58:49 (10,198)
Franklin, Nicholas	3:44:47 (6,765)
Franklin, Peter	4:22:21 (16,036)
Franklin, Richard J	3:49:19 (7,688)
Franklin, Robert C	4:02:50 (11,195)
Franklin, Stephen M	3:48:23 (7,482)
Franks, David A	3:27:57 (3,850)
Frankum, Stuart	4:26:23 (17,083)
Fransham, James M	3:31:02 (4,334)
Franz, Karl P	3:56:10 (9,357)
Franz, Xaver F	4:00:29 (10,664)
Fraquelli, Andrea	2:55:20 (687)
Fraser, Anthony	3:42:02 (6,218)
Fraser, Barry J	3:16:47 (2,413)
Fraser, David E	5:21:46 (29,336)
Fraser, David F	4:41:43 (21,144)
Fraser, David M	3:22:11 (3,035)
Fraser, Derek	3:31:59 (4,467)
Fraser, Edward	4:51:40 (23,667)
Fraser, Fred	5:01:11 (25,858)
Fraser, Jeremy	5:58:51 (32,983)
Fraser, Matthew J	4:09:19 (12,689)
Fraser, Paul G	4:02:51 (11,198)
Fraser, Ricky B	3:42:00 (6,206)
Fraser, Ryan	4:26:28 (17,104)
Fraser, Simon N	2:49:28 (442)
Fraser, Stuart J	2:54:19 (619)
Fraser-Looen, Oliver	3:48:01 (7,405)
Fratangelo, Claudio	4:20:06 (15,459)
Frater, Bruce M	4:15:32 (14,291)
Frati, Francesco	4:01:25 (10,887)
Frattaroli, David	4:19:33 (15,299)
Frattini, Tommaso	3:20:32 (2,829)
Fray, Martin D	3:03:36 (1,208)
Frazer, Anthony	3:13:44 (2,094)
Frazer, Kevin D	3:33:03 (4,617)
Frederic, Gibert	5:10:54 (27,620)
Frederic, Lacombe	3:27:36 (3,801)
Frederic, Melnyk	3:38:07 (5,518)
Frederic, Paschal	3:05:53 (1,363)
Free, Robert	6:15:39 (33,823)
Freeborn, David R	4:27:44 (17,459)
Freebury, Ross	5:01:55 (25,996)
Freedman, Ben M	4:34:33 (19,276)
Freedman, Paul	6:19:52 (34,028)

Freeland, John A	4:51:15 (23,553)
Freeland, Tim	4:19:11 (15,209)
Freeley, Mark J	5:05:35 (26,658)
Freeman, Anthony W	4:56:12 (24,728)
Freeman, Danny	4:49:18 (23,053)
Freeman, Darren W	4:17:23 (14,740)
Freeman, David J	2:35:21 (120)
Freeman, Derek P	3:28:04 (3,864)
Freeman, Jason W	5:12:01 (27,803)
Freeman, John F	4:52:30 (23,863)
Freeman, Mark D	4:20:33 (15,571)
Freeman, Martin	4:33:40 (19,066)
Freeman, Michael	4:54:47 (24,404)
Freeman, Nathanael W	3:41:28 (6,114)
Freeman, Paul	3:24:44 (3,373)
Freeman, Peter M	4:01:32 (10,926)
Freeman, Philip M	4:57:52 (25,102)
Freeman, Simon B	2:49:44 (458)
Freemantle, William H	4:47:01 (22,487)
Freer, Richard B	4:42:44 (21,394)
Freestone, Oliver	3:51:08 (8,081)
Frehner, Ruedi	3:03:56 (1,235)
Freire, José Carlos	5:00:35 (25,723)
Freitas, José	3:50:35 (7,966)
French, Adam J	4:29:06 (17,858)
French, Anthony Thomas	5:05:55 (26,715)
French, Frederick	5:07:13 (26,949)
French, Graham T	3:11:46 (1,855)
French, Joel	4:47:15 (22,553)
French, Luke J	5:10:07 (27,481)
French, Malcolm J	4:14:57 (14,154)
French, Richard	3:51:50 (8,234)
French, Stephen E	4:08:41 (12,544)
Fresco, Patrick	5:18:39 (28,904)
Fresson, William R	4:31:16 (18,419)
Frewer, Martyn F	5:32:28 (30,683)
Freymann, Daniel	3:13:37 (2,075)
Freyne, Tom G	4:24:56 (16,691)
Fribbens, Mark I	4:17:26 (14,753)
Fricker, Simon D	4:38:59 (20,429)
Friedman, Jonathan	4:51:10 (23,528)
Friedman, Jonathan	5:18:11 (28,815)
Friedman, Lawrence	5:30:35 (30,472)
Friel, Liam J	3:14:27 (2,168)
Friel, Peter	3:59:56 (10,530)
Friel, Philip C	4:28:59 (17,826)
Friel, Robert H	4:49:37 (23,155)
Friend, Brian S	3:41:46 (6,161)
Friend, Bryan J	3:12:00 (1,882)
Friend, Darren C	5:20:48 (29,197)
Friend, David	4:45:18 (22,036)
Friend, Matthew J	4:42:01 (21,202)
Frietman, Juan Carlos	4:43:05 (21,488)
Frisby, Carl S	3:51:50 (8,234)
Frischmuth, Carsten	3:35:43 (5,099)
Frith, Andy	3:29:52 (4,162)
Frith, Glynn S	4:52:17 (23,823)
Fritz, Stephan	4:25:31 (16,842)
Frodsham, Carl	4:12:13 (13,443)
Froestad, Kaare	3:45:02 (6,812)
Froggatt, Richard	4:13:56 (13,891)
Frohlich, Shaun	5:49:01 (32,251)
Fromme, Paul	3:12:45 (1,965)
Frost, Ashley	4:51:22 (23,581)
Frost, Benjamin	5:40:12 (31,518)
Frost, Daryl	3:55:49 (9,267)
Frost, Dean	4:46:26 (22,326)
Frost, Duncan	4:31:16 (18,419)
Frost, John K	6:39:35 (34,620)
Frost, Jonathan	2:25:03 (32)
Frost, Kevin Dean	3:35:27 (5,040)
Frost, Malcolm J	5:52:15 (32,498)
Frost, Michael	5:43:27 (31,815)
Froud, Nigel P	4:16:55 (14,626)
Frugoni, Enrico	3:53:02 (8,514)
Fry, John W	3:38:33 (5,600)
Fry, Kenneth J	4:45:49 (22,161)
Fry, Les	4:51:17 (23,562)
Fry, Malcolm M	4:27:14 (17,317)
Fry, Mark A	4:33:56 (19,136)
Fry, Nigel J	3:35:46 (5,109)
Fry, Robert A	5:28:10 (30,173)
Fry, Tim V	5:39:24 (31,434)

Fryer, Mark V 5:16:20 (28,542)
Fryer, Matthew 3:54:17 (8,835)
Fryer, Stephen J 3:20:13 (2,784)
Fubini, Renzo 4:21:18 (15,764)
Fudulu, Liviu 3:16:56 (2,422)
Fuggle, Tony J 5:19:55 (29,086)
Fulcher, Chris J 3:02:47 (1,166)
Fulcher, David J 3:56:19 (9,399)
Fulco, Daniel N 4:26:36 (17,148)
Fullalove, Guy 5:39:41 (31,465)
Fullalove, Paul Andrew 3:44:36 (6,732)
Fullbrook, Richard 4:08:13 (12,419)
Fuller, Adrian H 2:59:48 (983)
Fuller, Christopher 3:57:32 (9,781)
Fuller, David J 4:25:04 (16,732)
Fuller, Dean 4:48:12 (22,783)
Fuller, Mark A 5:15:26 (28,408)
Fuller, Martin G 2:55:10 (676)
Fuller, Martin N 3:34:23 (4,850)
Fuller, Nick L 4:11:20 (13,202)
Fuller, Richard N 3:12:12 (1,901)
Fuller, Robert P 5:37:27 (31,221)
Fuller, Samuel R 4:48:55 (22,949)
Fuller, William R 3:15:19 (2,263)
Fullick, Paul 4:34:52 (19,371)
Fullilove, Michael J 3:37:47 (5,452)
Fulton, Harold 5:47:56 (32,164)
Fulton, Paul W 4:55:45 (24,624)
Fulton, Peter 4:20:03 (15,442)
Fumich, Frank 3:25:03 (3,404)
Fumio, Yoda 5:47:06 (32,105)
Funnell, Ian David 4:58:00 (25,140)
Funnell, Keith A 3:58:28 (10,090)
Furey, Dara E 3:19:42 (2,710)
Furlong, Antony 3:56:15 (9,377)
Furlong, Brian A 4:39:44 (20,652)
Furlong, James C 5:10:51 (27,610)
Furlong, Michael 4:18:18 (14,962)
Furlong, Paul G 4:54:04 (24,235)
Furlong, Rob 3:27:49 (3,827)
Furlong, Terence M 3:54:23 (8,858)
Furman, Max 5:54:23 (32,648)
Furmidge, Sean A 3:27:26 (3,759)
Furness, Jason A 4:18:26 (15,009)
Furness, Tom 4:46:37 (22,375)
Furzer, Paul M 4:00:40 (10,713)
Furzer, William 4:39:39 (20,627)
Fusco, Jeremy 4:48:56 (22,955)
Fusi, Riccardo 3:20:18 (2,800)
Futter, Paul 4:44:04 (21,740)
Futtit, Mike 3:55:03 (9,040)
Fyall, Drummond 4:59:35 (25,513)
Fyfield, David J 4:14:11 (13,955)
Fyles, Wayne 5:06:45 (26,859)
Fysh, Robert J 4:23:22 (16,268)
Gabriel, Arron J 6:09:34 (33,538)
Gabriel, Brian J 5:32:51 (30,739)
Gabriel, Steven D 3:45:18 (6,854)
Gadd, Adam 4:45:26 (22,062)
Gadd, Andrew 5:41:21 (31,615)
Gadd, Chris H 6:21:08 (34,081)
Gadd, Jonathan 3:13:22 (2,046)
Gadd, Kev 2:45:04 (317)
Gadd, Louis 3:14:32 (2,174)
Gadd, Stephen M 5:42:10 (31,686)
Gadsden, Marc J 2:59:59 (996)
Gaffey, Dominic James 4:12:42 (13,575)
Gaffney, Marcus J 4:24:51 (16,670)
Gaffney, Nigel S 4:58:15 (25,202)
Gager, Terry C 3:52:08 (8,304)
Gahagan, James 5:28:51 (30,254)
Gahagan, Patrick A 3:30:34 (4,267)
Gaile, Thomas P 2:53:15 (569)
Gair, Scott 3:57:49 (9,880)
Gaisburgh-Watkyn, Graham 6:52:08 (34,847)
Gait, Simon R 3:58:45 (10,174)
Gaizley, Gavin 4:37:21 (19,994)
Gaizley, Jason 4:19:10 (15,203)
Gajbutowicz, Andrzej 4:09:24 (12,706)
Gajree, Ritesh 6:17:19 (33,894)
Gal, Danny A 3:26:10 (3,551)
Galang, Nathaniel 3:56:26 (9,437)
Galati, Antonio 3:31:26 (4,391)
Galbraith, Scott 3:14:48 (2,208)
Gale, Ben J 4:16:37 (14,560)
Gale, Oliver L 5:17:24 (28,697)
Galie, Filippo 3:44:01 (6,632)
Galkowski, Richard A 4:24:46 (16,646)
Gall, Stuart 4:38:51 (20,388)
Gallacher, Adam J 3:14:37 (2,184)
Gallacher, Russell S 3:37:58 (5,481)
Gallacher, Steven 3:38:07 (5,518)
Gallagher, Andrew 5:02:03 (26,033)
Gallagher, Brian G 3:17:38 (2,493)
Gallagher, David 5:23:33 (29,599)
Gallagher, Kevin 5:19:11 (28,995)
Gallagher, Leslie J 5:11:26 (27,715)
Gallagher, Mark A 4:17:39 (14,806)
Gallagher, Martin D 2:46:34 (348)
Gallagher, Michael 4:57:51 (25,097)
Gallagher, Michael H 5:47:33 (32,137)
Gallagher, Niall Patrick 5:10:17 (27,511)
Gallagher, Nick 3:25:49 (3,504)
Gallagher, Paul 3:33:45 (4,713)
Gallagher, Peter Anthony 4:20:30 (15,557)
Gallanagh, Peter 2:57:03 (777)
Galley, André G 3:32:08 (4,492)
Gallien, Cedrik 4:34:54 (19,382)
Galliford, Gary G 4:14:32 (14,037)
Gallimore, Mark 3:08:46 (1,598)
Gallimore, William 4:24:41 (16,621)
Gallinaro, Andrea 4:20:03 (15,442)
Gallivan, John F 7:07:12 (35,028)
Gallo, Eddy 3:22:46 (3,103)
Gallo, Simon 6:22:33 (34,128)
Gallon, Derek 4:30:18 (18,176)
Galloway, Michael D 3:34:11 (4,808)
Galloway, Neil J 3:58:49 (10,198)
Galloway, Paul 4:22:38 (16,105)
Galpin, Peter C 2:46:53 (364)
Galsinh, Suraj S 6:56:54 (34,919)
Galvani, Tony A 5:45:00 (31,928)
Galvin, Barry 4:38:02 (20,174)
Galvin, Michael 3:26:53 (3,663)
Gamadia, Russell 4:43:59 (21,715)
Gambaro, Gianmassimo 3:11:15 (1,801)
Gamble, Julian 7:14:06 (35,097)
Gamble, Lukas 4:19:00 (15,160)
Gambs, Christopher D 3:13:10 (2,023)
Game, Kevin J 3:32:04 (4,479)
Gammage, Brian H 3:58:06 (9,971)
Gammell, Alastair D 4:30:26 (18,214)
Gammon, Carl 5:11:35 (27,746)
Gammon, Robert J 4:04:32 (11,552)
Gammon, Rodney H 4:14:07 (13,937)
Gammon, Steve J 5:44:50 (31,916)
Gammon, Vincent John 4:18:48 (15,105)
Ganderton, Maximus G 4:52:52 (23,940)
Gandhi, Eric 4:58:16 (25,206)
Gandy, Stuart 4:22:50 (16,149)
Gandy, Ray D Jnr 4:31:12 (18,405)
Gange, Tom 3:24:28 (3,336)
Gannon, Ciaran 4:37:29 (20,035)
Garbett, Adrian 5:00:07 (25,617)
Garbett, Carl A 5:04:05 (26,398)
Garbow, Geoff J 4:26:43 (17,185)
Garbutt, Kevin 3:09:37 (1,669)
Garcha, Parvinder 6:19:29 (34,015)
Garcha, Sukhdip S 4:57:34 (25,048)
Garcia, Andy 5:14:16 (28,202)
García Briseno, José 5:49:19 (32,277)
Garcia Oliver, Carlos 4:21:00 (15,692)
Garcia Ramirez, José Manuel 4:12:11 (13,437)
Garcia Rangel, Luis 3:48:26 (7,496)
Garcia Teruel, Adolfo 2:57:13 (795)
Garcia Teruel, David 2:57:06 (782)
Garcia-Delgado, José C 4:58:25 (25,247)
Gard, Merlin 6:27:14 (34,332)
Gardam, Matthew R 5:27:14 (30,071)
Gardarsson, Karl 4:28:08 (17,587)
Gardham, Lee J 4:21:43 (15,884)
Gardham, Russell B 3:56:36 (9,489)
Gardiner, Andrew 5:12:55 (27,970)
Gardiner, Gary 4:12:35 (13,544)
Gardiner, Neil M 3:49:26 (7,712)
Gardiner, Richard 2:19:48 (18)
Gardner, Andrew J 3:52:19 (8,362)
Gardner, Carl W 3:29:12 (4,039)
Gardner, Clive D 3:25:15 (3,427)
Gardner, Giles 4:30:45 (18,295)
Gardner, Glen 4:54:30 (24,334)
Gardner, John A 5:14:06 (28,180)
Gardner, Leighton J 3:17:00 (2,429)
Gardner, Mark S 3:56:55 (9,598)
Gardner, Neal T 6:18:41 (33,977)
Gardner, Paul Antony 4:17:01 (14,651)
Gardner, Pete 4:19:24 (15,255)
Gardner, Roger S 5:11:52 (27,786)
Gardner, Wayne 3:50:27 (7,933)
Gardner, William R 3:10:09 (1,711)
Gare, Peter 4:58:22 (25,228)
Gargan, Nicholas J 4:54:01 (24,225)
Gargaro, Steven 4:57:34 (25,048)
Garland, Andrew 4:17:20 (14,732)
Garland, Andrew S 5:02:28 (26,109)
Garland, Christopher J 3:58:48 (10,194)
Garland, David P 5:39:47 (31,474)
Garland, Jon A 5:52:37 (32,519)
Garland, Peter J 4:01:02 (10,803)
Garland, Stephen D 4:50:35 (23,392)
Garlichs, Wilfried 5:21:21 (29,279)
Garlick, Chris J 4:10:41 (13,033)
Garner, Adam F 5:48:17 (32,195)
Garner, Alan 4:31:28 (18,494)
Garner, David 2:53:24 (578)
Garner, David 3:23:50 (3,242)
Garner, Geoff 5:44:18 (31,878)
Garner, George R 4:41:11 (21,008)
Garner, Ian 5:20:02 (29,099)
Garner, Victor Douglas 3:34:05 (4,783)
Garner, William 3:03:50 (1,227)
Garnham, Darran F 5:04:09 (26,407)
Garnham, Gary G 4:49:43 (23,182)
Garnham, Russell J 3:57:16 (9,695)
Garnish, Mark R 5:16:53 (28,628)
Garratt, Christopher J 3:38:52 (5,651)
Garratt, Matt 5:52:40 (32,522)
Garratt, Thomas 4:27:12 (17,309)
Garrett, Adam J 5:40:49 (31,571)
Garrett, Andrew 4:57:43 (25,072)
Garrett, Ben J 3:44:01 (6,632)
Garrett, Jeremy P 4:06:06 (11,903)
Garrett, Michael A 3:08:39 (1,585)
Garrett, Paul S 4:44:34 (21,848)
Garrett, Philip A 4:58:05 (25,158)
Garrett, Rob O 3:23:06 (3,136)
Garrett, Thomas O 3:55:06 (9,065)
Garrett, Will 5:02:46 (26,170)
Garrido, Reginald L 3:42:29 (6,295)
Garrigos Mascarell, José Vicente 2:49:39 (449)
Garrity, Troy C 2:46:47 (361)
Garrod, Neil 4:16:50 (14,615)
Garrood, Steve 3:48:32 (7,520)
Garry, Paul F 5:10:56 (27,629)
Garry, Tony J 6:16:15 (33,853)
Garside, Duncan 5:14:07 (28,182)
Garside, Paul M 6:28:05 (34,358)
Garside, Roger 4:44:01 (21,725)
Garth, Michael J 4:25:45 (16,923)
Gartland, John 5:12:54 (27,966)
Gartside, James H 5:07:57 (27,078)
Garuti, Enrico 4:18:32 (15,038)
Garvey, David J 4:45:50 (22,171)
Garvey, Hugh E 6:21:07 (34,079)
Garvey, Stephen 3:25:56 (3,522)
Garwood, Barry I 4:58:14 (25,197)
Gascoyn-Day, Tim 4:35:38 (19,574)
Gaskell, Alex P 3:04:55 (1,301)
Gaskell, Jack W 4:10:57 (13,094)
Gaskell, Paul 3:34:10 (4,805)
Gaskin, Neil D 4:08:21 (12,469)
Gasparotto, Manlio 5:15:56 (28,494)
Gasson, James 4:34:42 (19,317)
Gasson, Paul J 4:35:53 (19,648)
Gatehouse, Andrew 5:27:17 (30,077)
Gates, Andrew S 4:09:00 (12,620)
Gatrell, Christopher A 4:37:37 (20,070)
Gaudion, Shane G 4:26:58 (17,251)
Gauld, Stephen Gordon 4:33:35 (19,046)

Gault, Peter J	4:45:56 (22,198)
Gault, Steve A	4:34:53 (19,376)
Gaunt, Craig J	3:32:09 (4,495)
Gaunt, Martin	2:46:27 (344)
Gaunt-Edwards, Stephen M	4:32:46 (18,835)
Gaut, Matthew	4:01:07 (10,821)
Gautier, Benoit	5:12:17 (27,852)
Gavin, David M	5:25:54 (29,917)
Gavin, Oliver B	3:00:10 (1,009)
Gavriel, Andrew	4:43:47 (21,663)
Gawne, Richard A	4:37:42 (20,090)
Gay, Christopher D	3:44:43 (6,751)
Gay, Daniel R	2:42:10 (239)
Gay, Paul E	3:55:25 (9,135)
Gay, Trevor E	5:31:55 (30,629)
Gayle, Terry	3:30:53 (4,311)
Gayner, Ronald G	3:53:24 (8,604)
Gaze, Christopher Gaze D	5:09:25 (27,351)
Gaze, Nick C	6:19:04 (33,999)
Gazeley, Neil A	4:39:33 (20,595)
Gazi, Laurence B	4:13:08 (13,691)
Gazzillo, Mario	4:16:58 (14,638)
Geaix, Christophe	3:07:20 (1,461)
Gear, Adam T	3:35:40 (5,090)
Gear, Allan R	3:59:25 (10,374)
Gear, Ian	4:23:39 (16,349)
Gear, Neil H	3:42:14 (6,255)
Gearing, John	5:02:49 (26,185)
Geddes, Fraser H	4:29:35 (17,980)
Geddes, Ian J	4:11:57 (13,374)
Geddes, Stuart	3:33:55 (4,743)
Gedge, Duncan James	4:04:20 (11,515)
Gedin, Mats R	2:43:55 (283)
Gedling, Luke W	5:25:14 (29,828)
Gee, Alexander P	3:59:22 (10,359)
Gee, Fenton	6:10:33 (33,588)
Gee, Patrick R	5:21:30 (29,298)
Geen, Peter R	4:58:21 (25,225)
Geenrits, Alain	5:37:01 (31,170)
Geering, Janos	5:43:55 (31,842)
Geikie, Jamie D	3:33:53 (4,736)
Geitner, Joseph J	3:02:28 (1,145)
Gelin, Benoit	4:05:39 (11,815)
Gelis, Mathieu	3:51:41 (8,206)
Gell, Colin	2:49:11 (428)
Gelley, Abraham	5:28:18 (30,189)
Gemmell, Keith	5:09:30 (27,363)
Gemmell, Scott M	4:14:42 (14,079)
Gendron, Eric	5:28:18 (30,189)
Gengembre, Jean-Marc	3:38:26 (5,574)
Genn-Bromley, James R	4:26:23 (17,083)
Gentle, Christopher R	3:34:02 (4,763)
Gentry, Mark E	5:21:28 (29,295)
Genz, Markus	3:36:33 (5,245)
George, Christopher	4:16:22 (14,486)
George, David M	5:57:10 (32,842)
George, Iain	5:03:13 (26,241)
George, Ian L	7:09:10 (35,044)
George, Martin J	2:58:01 (837)
George, Martin P	3:49:04 (7,635)
George, Neil	3:58:47 (10,189)
George, Phillip M	2:44:38 (300)
George, Rayner C	3:56:57 (9,606)
George, Ronald	4:08:21 (12,469)
Georges, Grolleau	3:31:27 (4,396)
Georgiadis, Nikos	5:59:45 (33,029)
Gerard, Naud	5:05:21 (26,613)
Gerber, Steve W	5:35:40 (31,038)
Gerlack, Danny	4:06:44 (12,048)
Germain, Lucas	4:57:15 (24,975)
German, Peter M	4:09:22 (12,699)
Gerrard, Daniel M	5:38:09 (31,292)
Gerrard, Simon C	3:58:11 (10,002)
Gerundini, Anthony R	3:13:59 (2,117)
Gerver, Richard M	5:39:40 (31,462)
Gethin, David	5:59:21 (33,009)
Ghadiri-Zare, Reza M	4:35:29 (19,634)
Ghafoor, Farhan	5:01:43 (25,956)
Gharib, Jaouad	2:05:27 (3)
Ghazi-Nouri, Seyed M	5:42:54 (31,759)
Ghent, Miles S	3:31:52 (4,451)
Ghezzi, Mario	4:50:26 (23,350)
Ghomshei, Amir	5:19:35 (29,046)

Giacomin, Mark	5:08:44 (27,219)
Giami, Davis	3:39:49 (5,812)
Gibb, Martin	5:56:38 (32,802)
Gibb, Robin J	4:28:13 (17,622)
Gibb, Tim M	3:46:31 (7,091)
Gibbard, Jon R	4:08:50 (12,580)
Gibbins, Alex N	2:36:54 (139)
Gibbins, Brian	3:41:52 (6,180)
Gibbins, Simon M	3:22:47 (3,106)
Gibbon, Adrian Christopher	3:47:18 (7,248)
Gibbon, Brian R	4:38:33 (20,311)
Gibbon, Dominic	4:08:16 (12,439)
Gibbons, Alastair R	3:13:27 (2,055)
Gibbons, Carl	4:19:35 (15,308)
Gibbons, Gary Michael	4:40:16 (20,790)
Gibbons, Jeremy	4:45:38 (22,113)
Gibbons, John T	4:42:27 (21,313)
Gibbons, Mark	4:03:17 (11,288)
Gibbons, Martin J	4:24:23 (16,545)
Gibbons, Martin S	5:22:45 (29,474)
Gibbons, Matthew H	6:09:33 (33,535)
Gibbons, Paul A	4:47:22 (22,571)
Gibbons, Robbie	5:07:35 (27,019)
Gibbons, Stephen	2:58:52 (907)
Gibbs, Christopher J	5:48:57 (32,246)
Gibbs, David W	3:56:20 (9,406)
Gibbs, Donald O	5:03:14 (26,243)
Gibbs, Edward B	3:09:01 (1,620)
Gibbs, Gibbs	3:17:18 (2,465)
Gibbs, Graham	4:44:22 (21,809)
Gibbs, Ian	4:58:23 (25,233)
Gibbs, Leslie	6:54:11 (34,885)
Gibbs, Matthew A	3:50:07 (7,859)
Gibbs, Michael R	4:23:40 (16,355)
Gibbs, Paul	4:16:31 (14,525)
Gibbs, Phillip	3:36:33 (5,245)
Gibbs, Richard W	4:30:16 (18,171)
Gibbs, Stephen P	2:59:36 (963)
Gibling, Mark	5:15:30 (28,416)
Gibson, Adam Lewis	3:55:25 (9,135)
Gibson, Alex J	3:15:54 (2,326)
Gibson, Andrew	3:49:19 (7,688)
Gibson, Brian	6:21:27 (34,092)
Gibson, Darren	4:12:18 (13,468)
Gibson, Ian	5:17:43 (28,749)
Gibson, Ian G	4:41:11 (21,008)
Gibson, Jeremy J	4:12:14 (13,447)
Gibson, John D	4:39:18 (20,521)
Gibson, Patrick	3:47:56 (7,381)
Gibson, Paul	4:53:44 (24,152)
Gibson, Robert	3:46:15 (7,028)
Gibson, Ryan S	4:36:32 (19,801)
Gibson, Thomas D	4:42:15 (21,265)
Gibson, William J	3:25:34 (3,469)
Gidley, Michael A	4:37:31 (20,042)
Giger, Hans	4:36:26 (19,777)
Gilbert, Andrew	3:39:43 (5,795)
Gilbert, Anthony William	5:09:57 (27,446)
Gilbert, David G	3:57:19 (9,712)
Gilbert, Geoff R	3:36:19 (5,208)
Gilbert, Graeme	4:30:06 (18,126)
Gilbert, Ian J	5:25:34 (29,873)
Gilbert, Jonathan P	4:25:10 (16,757)
Gilbert, Justin H	4:26:48 (17,205)
Gilbert, Kevin A	3:43:23 (6,505)
Gilbert, Lee	4:41:18 (21,037)
Gilbert, Mark	4:31:11 (18,400)
Gilbert, Mark	4:32:21 (18,715)
Gilbert, Matt	4:20:44 (15,615)
Gilbert, Nick D	5:13:36 (28,082)
Gilbert, Paul	5:23:59 (29,645)
Gilbert, Peter F	5:57:59 (32,914)
Gilbert, Richard	5:05:06 (26,566)
Gilbert, Sean W	5:02:29 (26,115)
Gilbert, Simon M	3:16:00 (2,335)
Gilbert, Tim P	4:45:12 (22,014)
Gilbert, Wayne	5:33:09 (30,768)
Gilbertson, John P	3:59:35 (10,413)
Gilbertson, Jonathan	4:15:33 (14,294)
Gilbertson, Michael Q	5:13:08 (28,012)
Gilbertson, Paul E	4:48:36 (22,877)
Gilbey, Kenneth	4:35:44 (19,616)
Gilbey, Stephen G	5:43:11 (31,792)

Gilbride, Darren T	4:08:41 (12,544)
Gilbride, Michael F	3:33:36 (4,692)
Gilby, Daniel S	4:02:32 (11,138)
Gilby, Simon P	4:55:27 (24,563)
Gilchrist, Alastair J	5:04:18 (26,427)
Gilchrist, Brian W	4:11:48 (13,337)
Gilchrist, Ewen J	4:07:11 (12,148)
Gilchrist, Robin A	4:51:15 (23,553)
Gilchrist, Tyrone	5:52:26 (32,510)
Gildove, Neil	4:24:40 (16,614)
Giles, Antony C	3:06:30 (1,404)
Giles, Geraint J	4:30:52 (18,321)
Giles, Ian R	2:59:53 (989)
Giles, Nicholas J	4:34:03 (19,163)
Giles, Paul R	4:18:47 (15,101)
Gilfillan, Dean A	3:20:02 (2,758)
Gilkes, Alex	5:17:56 (28,783)
Gilkes, Benedict	5:17:56 (28,783)
Gilkes, Edward L	5:17:57 (28,786)
Gilkes, Oliver	5:17:56 (28,783)
Gill, Adam C	4:49:40 (23,171)
Gill, Amarjit	6:16:08 (33,847)
Gill, Andrew D	5:08:44 (27,219)
Gill, Andrew M	4:33:48 (19,097)
Gill, Benjamin Angus	4:56:38 (24,836)
Gill, Christopher	5:22:22 (29,416)
Gill, Daljit S	4:25:37 (16,877)
Gill, Daniel T	3:57:32 (9,781)
Gill, Dave	4:47:01 (22,487)
Gill, Duane T	5:20:59 (29,216)
Gill, Graeme J	4:27:09 (17,297)
Gill, Greg	3:53:08 (8,541)
Gill, James R	3:12:33 (1,937)
Gill, John	7:26:24 (35,193)
Gill, Kenneth J	4:15:52 (14,362)
Gill, Matt	6:02:07 (33,180)
Gill, Oliver W	3:32:43 (4,575)
Gill, Paul	4:40:01 (20,730)
Gill, Robert N	3:15:01 (2,234)
Gill, Shaminder S	3:42:15 (6,258)
Gill, Steve	4:22:30 (16,075)
Gillam, Ross	3:39:18 (5,729)
Gillan, Alistair	3:56:36 (9,489)
Gillanders, James A	3:04:03 (1,240)
Gillard, Barry W	4:42:54 (21,445)
Gillard, James	4:30:55 (18,328)
Gillard, Mathew	4:14:36 (14,058)
Gillespie, Andrew	4:11:11 (13,158)
Gillespie, Andrew J	3:51:21 (8,128)
Gillespie, Frank G	3:58:04 (9,958)
Gillespie, Mark	4:28:28 (17,688)
Gillett, Stephen M	4:16:13 (14,452)
Gilliard, Ken J	4:03:32 (11,344)
Gillibrand, Christian Steven	3:27:09 (3,707)
Gillibrand, Colin	4:16:40 (14,575)
Gillibrand, Jonny	3:31:48 (4,438)
Gillibrand, Kit	3:43:05 (6,439)
Gillies, Adam J	3:57:44 (9,856)
Gillies, Stuart	4:37:50 (20,128)
Gillingham, Craig	3:23:48 (3,236)
Gillis, John W	4:00:50 (10,752)
Gillman, Darren	3:46:33 (7,097)
Gillman, Roy	4:51:33 (23,637)
Gill-Martin, Rupert P	3:41:56 (6,191)
Gillmore, Ben	4:39:28 (20,571)
Gillmore, Ricky	4:16:23 (14,495)
Gillon, Charlie A	3:20:45 (2,862)
Gillot, Leslie	4:50:00 (23,239)
Gillott, Stuart J	4:58:35 (25,290)
Gilmartin, Noel Patrick	4:02:36 (11,151)
Gilmore, Eddie	3:23:30 (3,189)
Gilmore, Nigel A	6:04:38 (33,320)
Gilmour, Duncan N	3:34:05 (4,783)
Gilpin, Jonathan	3:34:40 (4,906)
Gilroy, Francis J	3:06:51 (1,425)
Gilroy, Robert	3:00:27 (1,020)
Gilson, Ben W	3:51:27 (8,156)
Gimson, Simon G	4:13:05 (13,694)
Ginet, François	4:46:37 (22,375)
Ginger, Paul J	4:32:14 (18,689)
Ginn, Alan P	3:15:35 (2,292)
Ginn, Richard C	3:04:21 (1,253)
Ginnaw, Colin	6:00:30 (33,075)

Ginnaw, Gary R.	4:36:21 (19,750)
Giorgione, Federico	3:37:35 (5,420)
Giovannoni, Alberto	5:03:35 (26,300)
Gipp, Peter	3:10:15 (1,717)
Girard, Patrice	2:53:27 (583)
Girardot, Paul M	4:08:02 (12,369)
Girbane, Prashant	5:20:12 (29,117)
Girdlestone, Richard M	4:19:20 (15,238)
Girdwood, Callum G	5:38:41 (31,353)
Girling, Thomas	4:05:49 (11,847)
Girmay, Aregai	3:09:18 (1,649)
Girolami, Alberto	3:52:11 (8,323)
Gissendanner, Daniel	3:51:42 (8,208)
Gíthe, Johan	4:06:21 (11,962)
Githui, Davidson M	5:37:01 (31,170)
Gittens, Jonathan	4:39:41 (20,639)
Gittins, Andrew J	4:25:21 (16,800)
Gittins, James R	3:53:04 (8,523)
Gittins, Martin F	3:42:24 (6,282)
Gittins, Tim J	5:02:14 (26,068)
Giuliani, Michele	3:24:01 (3,262)
Giuntoli, Lorenzo	3:56:35 (9,483)
Giusti, Luciano	4:14:17 (13,986)
Given, Vernon	4:07:23 (12,209)
Gjytetza, Adrian	5:24:29 (29,730)
Glackin, Stephen P	3:10:03 (1,709)
Glading, Mark A	3:42:32 (6,310)
Gladman, Andrew	5:38:30 (31,333)
Gladstone, James A	5:10:25 (27,535)
Gladstone, Paul S	5:33:46 (30,839)
Gladwin, Pete A	5:03:54 (26,364)
Glaister, Jonathan	4:38:57 (20,421)
Glaister, Keith	4:38:57 (20,421)
Glanfield, Martin	5:22:44 (29,470)
Glass, Andy	3:14:21 (2,159)
Glass, Raphael	4:44:33 (21,844)
Glass, Samuel T	5:05:22 (26,617)
Glass, Steve J	5:09:52 (27,436)
Glasscock, David	4:02:50 (11,195)
Glasscok, Christopher P	5:44:35 (31,897)
Glassock, Stephen	5:39:20 (31,428)
Glassup, Ben S	6:18:18 (33,941)
Glavin, Danny William Alfie	3:44:27 (6,710)
Glaysher, Stefan N	2:54:57 (659)
Gleave, Harold	4:18:04 (14,909)
Gledhill, Andrew	4:15:45 (14,335)
Gledson, Jonathan B	3:43:14 (6,476)
Gleeson, Jonathan	4:59:29 (25,494)
Glen, Andrew	3:22:17 (3,047)
Glen, David Philip	4:54:40 (24,380)
Glendenning, John W	3:58:12 (10,007)
Glendinning, Tom B	3:29:21 (4,079)
Glendon, Leo	3:41:49 (6,171)
Glenn, Andrew	3:49:16 (7,682)
Glenn, Felix	3:40:16 (5,910)
Glennon, Martin	4:24:39 (16,605)
Glennon, Steve J	5:46:33 (32,050)
Glisson, Matthew J	5:02:45 (26,169)
Glonek, Alexander J	5:20:47 (29,194)
Glover, Brian K	4:55:04 (24,468)
Glover, Ian George	4:06:55 (12,084)
Glover, Jeremy	4:27:51 (17,502)
Glover, Jerry R	4:00:20 (10,623)
Glover, John	4:17:55 (14,866)
Glover, Mark	4:11:20 (13,202)
Glover, Richard	6:56:37 (34,915)
Gloyens, Mark	3:30:37 (4,272)
Gluckman, Michael	4:23:37 (16,341)
Gluschke, Michael	3:46:15 (7,028)
Glynn, John	4:11:05 (13,133)
Glynn, Michael	3:21:44 (2,976)
Glynn, Michael P	5:34:14 (30,882)
Gnanadesikan, Ram	6:05:04 (33,342)
Goadsby, Charles W	5:24:38 (29,747)
Goakes, Andrew	3:30:38 (4,274)
Goater, Douglas G	8:28:32 (35,340)
Goatly, Robert	5:35:17 (30,997)
Gobbo, Fabiano	3:45:37 (6,915)
Gobin, Patrice	3:11:39 (1,844)
Godbold, Alan Roger	4:00:34 (10,690)
Godbold, Tom	5:45:32 (31,977)
Goddard, Chris A	4:25:35 (16,868)
Goddard, Chris M	3:50:12 (7,881)

Goddard, George	4:45:39 (22,121)
Goddard, Graham John	4:58:42 (25,319)
Goddard, Matthew	4:33:47 (19,094)
Goddard, Paul E	3:41:26 (6,108)
Goddard, Roger	3:00:35 (1,026)
Goddard, Simon L	4:50:55 (23,464)
Goddard, Trevor E	2:59:43 (977)
Godden, James P	3:04:44 (1,285)
Godel, Hans-Joachim	5:29:32 (30,341)
Godel, Tim	5:29:33 (30,342)
Goden, David	4:37:48 (20,120)
Godfrey, Alan S	5:13:10 (28,021)
Godfrey, Andrew	3:48:30 (7,508)
Godfrey, Chidinma Charles	4:19:16 (15,226)
Godfrey, Chris	5:04:00 (26,387)
Godfrey, Christopher A	4:48:25 (22,831)
Godfrey, Clint D	3:59:54 (10,515)
Godfrey, Matt	5:02:00 (26,018)
Godfrey-Faussett, Thomas	4:00:22 (10,628)
Godsall, Matt	5:02:24 (26,094)
Goerens, Leonard	5:15:51 (28,484)
Goetsch, Otto	3:53:27 (8,615)
Goff, Christopher R	3:45:54 (6,960)
Goff, Matthew P	4:00:51 (10,755)
Goffin, Jez N	5:12:02 (27,807)
Gogarty, Ben	4:56:34 (24,820)
Gohil, Himesh	4:50:36 (23,396)
Gold, David A	3:54:31 (8,894)
Gold, Jeremy A	2:44:35 (298)
Gold, Joel A	4:43:10 (21,508)
Gold, Mark J	3:20:04 (2,762)
Gold, Paul A	4:51:15 (23,553)
Gold, Peter	3:59:54 (10,515)
Gold, Peter C	4:09:01 (12,624)
Golden, Michael	3:58:13 (10,018)
Golding, Andrew	3:39:34 (5,772)
Golding, David A	3:40:52 (6,009)
Golding, Matthew Scott	4:23:23 (16,274)
Golding, Neville A	4:31:17 (18,429)
Golding, Tom P	3:51:36 (8,187)
Goldsack, Stuart	6:09:53 (33,555)
Goldsmith, Andrew W	4:16:22 (14,486)
Goldsmith, Christopher R	4:15:47 (14,344)
Goldsmith, David L	3:49:26 (7,712)
Goldsmith, Jeremy M	5:29:20 (30,312)
Goldsmith, Robert	4:51:32 (23,631)
Goldsmith, Stuart G	3:34:38 (4,902)
Goldstein, Jacob	4:31:17 (18,429)
Goldstein, Mark A	2:58:55 (910)
Goldthorpe, Jonathan M	4:51:18 (23,566)
Goligher, Nick William	4:21:44 (15,889)
Goligher, Scott	3:30:57 (4,320)
Golland, Scott	4:40:47 (20,906)
Golledge, Nick J	3:53:17 (8,580)
Gomersall, Tim	4:29:40 (18,008)
Gomez, Hugo	4:32:07 (18,666)
Gomez, Julio	3:57:44 (9,856)
Gomez, Luis F	2:52:18 (536)
Gomez Delgado, Javier	3:31:25 (4,386)
Gomez Garcia, Ulpiano	3:40:16 (5,910)
Gomm, Philip M	4:42:15 (21,265)
Gompertz, Henry	4:28:49 (17,780)
Goncalves, Joel	3:30:22 (4,230)
Goniszewski, Jan	6:26:47 (34,311)
Gonsalves, Victor	4:28:15 (17,633)
Gonzalez, Alejandro	4:32:03 (18,648)
Gonzalez, Cyril	5:02:46 (26,170)
Gonzalez, Fernando	4:32:03 (18,648)
Gonzalez, Jorge E	3:23:28 (3,183)
Gonzalez, Paul J	4:08:17 (12,447)
Gonzalez, Richard	5:42:53 (31,756)
Gonzalez, Simon	4:35:50 (19,638)
Gonzalez-George, Victor	3:37:23 (5,381)
Gooch, Clive Andrew	4:06:59 (12,100)
Gooch, Daniel A	3:30:56 (4,317)
Gooch, Warwick	3:08:55 (1,610)
Gooch-Smith, Nigel A	3:47:11 (7,233)
Good, Christopher R	3:23:31 (3,191)
Good, Michael Edward	3:43:45 (6,574)
Goodacre, Robert J	4:14:51 (14,128)
Goodall, David	3:59:39 (10,437)
Goodall, James A	5:24:20 (29,708)
Goodall, Malcolm	3:59:38 (10,428)

Goodall, Robert	4:58:31 (25,274)
Goodbun, Mark	4:29:01 (17,834)
Goodchild, Julian P	4:21:23 (15,778)
Goodchild, Paul D	4:09:51 (12,822)
Goodchild, Robert C	4:35:22 (19,514)
Goode, Jonny M	3:33:45 (4,713)
Goode, Justine	4:59:27 (25,484)
Goode, Nigel C	4:05:09 (11,695)
Goode, Paul J	4:27:07 (17,285)
Goode, Tom	6:39:47 (34,624)
Goodenough, Ian E	3:59:14 (10,320)
Gooder, Stephen A	4:43:54 (21,691)
Gooderham, Ian R	4:18:48 (15,105)
Goodey, David M	5:01:59 (26,014)
Goodfellow, Stephen C	4:34:28 (19,254)
Goodfield, Paul	4:08:21 (12,469)
Goodge, Stephen A	5:22:27 (29,430)
Goodger, James L	4:43:24 (21,575)
Goodhall, Pete A	3:57:03 (9,634)
Goodhew, Robert C	6:27:24 (34,342)
Goodin, Matthew	4:24:41 (16,621)
Gooding, Alex	4:53:42 (24,138)
Gooding, David O	4:25:56 (16,968)
Gooding, Paul	4:58:08 (25,174)
Goodley, Simon	4:49:46 (23,194)
Goodman, Chris	3:47:27 (7,278)
Goodman, James E	4:14:38 (14,063)
Goodman, John E	4:19:35 (15,308)
Goodman, Kevin M	4:58:35 (25,155)
Goodridge, Ian D	5:33:07 (30,765)
Goodrum, Paul J	3:59:27 (10,379)
Goodsell, Mark R	4:51:12 (23,541)
Goodson, Edward	4:42:14 (21,260)
Goodwin, Alan D	5:27:46 (30,119)
Goodwin, Andrew	5:17:40 (28,741)
Goodwin, Bartholomew J	4:53:42 (24,138)
Goodwin, David	5:40:14 (31,520)
Goodwin, Dominic	5:50:19 (32,365)
Goodwin, Edward C	5:32:54 (30,742)
Goodwin, Graham S	6:03:20 (33,250)
Goodwin, Ian S	5:12:42 (27,926)
Goodwin, Jack	5:08:50 (27,234)
Goodwin, Julian	3:02:32 (1,148)
Goodwin, Kevin	4:11:27 (13,242)
Goodwin, Kevin D	3:58:31 (10,107)
Goodwin, Leon	2:59:31 (959)
Goodwin, Mark I	3:05:10 (1,314)
Goodwin, Michael J	5:30:46 (30,497)
Goodwin, Nick R	4:11:43 (13,317)
Goodwin, Peter	5:14:49 (28,285)
Goodwin, Peter E	5:09:58 (27,453)
Goodwin, Peter J	4:29:56 (18,077)
Goodwin, Richard	4:11:30 (13,255)
Goodwin, Richard	5:26:30 (29,989)
Goodwin, Ryan T	3:31:31 (4,400)
Goodwin, Stephen H	5:15:35 (28,435)
Goodwin, Tony D	4:11:55 (13,362)
Goodwyn, Edward	3:54:06 (8,781)
Goody, James C	4:11:28 (13,246)
Goold, Tom	3:53:25 (8,609)
Gordon, Adrian	3:49:53 (7,813)
Gordon, Andrew J	4:43:49 (21,671)
Gordon, Brian	4:31:34 (18,518)
Gordon, Chris I	4:22:07 (15,910)
Gordon, Christopher R	6:09:50 (33,554)
Gordon, Ian P	4:52:25 (23,849)
Gordon, Jeffrey	5:07:21 (26,971)
Gordon, Joseph E	4:42:34 (21,348)
Gordon, Norman C	6:23:01 (34,151)
Gordon, Rob	3:27:53 (3,838)
Gordon, Stephen	2:57:17 (796)
Gordon, Tim B	4:45:04 (21,986)
Gordon-Dean, Rufus	3:47:27 (7,278)
Gore, Matt	4:28:09 (17,593)
Gorham, Michael	6:09:33 (33,535)
Gorin, Edward A	4:27:10 (17,301)
Gorman, Cathal	4:08:04 (12,376)
Gorman, Martin J	2:55:45 (712)
Gorman, Tom D	4:18:50 (15,113)
Gornall, Robert J	2:49:04 (425)
Gorozarri Del Valle, Carlos	4:05:09 (11,695)
Gorrigan, John H	4:49:12 (23,017)
Gorringe, Dez	5:05:02 (26,555)

Gorrod, Mark	4:58:55	(25,368)
Gorton, Peter R	4:39:59	(20,719)
Gosbee, Norman	4:38:33	(20,311)
Gosling, Chris P	5:14:59	(28,314)
Gosney, Jason	4:54:24	(24,310)
Gosrani, Visesh	4:47:21	(22,565)
Goss, Benjamin B	4:29:08	(17,872)
Goss, Clive M	4:26:52	(17,229)
Goss, David	4:37:18	(19,984)
Goss, Paul D	4:20:12	(15,484)
Goubel, Clement	4:34:29	(19,257)
Gough, Adrian J	7:17:50	(35,124)
Gough, Brian E	5:24:31	(29,736)
Gough, David R	3:09:11	(1,637)
Gough, James	5:14:47	(28,282)
Gough, Neil M	4:28:02	(17,551)
Gough, Sam M	4:33:17	(18,968)
Gough, Tim M	4:49:39	(23,165)
Goulbourn, Stuart R	4:53:42	(24,138)
Gould, Don	5:05:32	(26,649)
Gould, Jeremy	5:02:52	(26,189)
Gould, Leo A	4:14:19	(13,992)
Gould, Norman	7:56:57	(35,311)
Gould, Robert A	3:56:26	(9,437)
Gould, Simon A	3:50:47	(8,019)
Gouldbourn, Simon S	4:02:21	(11,091)
Goulden, Mike C	6:51:18	(34,834)
Gouldin, Michael P	3:56:42	(9,535)
Goulding, Jonathan	3:54:46	(8,960)
Goulds, Nicholas	5:33:55	(30,855)
Goumri, Abderrahim	2:08:25	(6)
Goundry, Andrew C	3:25:28	(3,455)
Gournay, Kevin J	4:35:39	(19,581)
Gout, Robert D	4:04:24	(11,525)
Gouteux, Gilles	3:52:26	(8,388)
Govier, Huw	4:04:40	(11,578)
Gow, Chris	3:59:29	(10,384)
Gow, Matthew	5:29:31	(30,339)
Goward, Mark T	4:39:22	(20,536)
Gower, Alistair J	3:54:31	(8,894)
Gower, Andy M	4:14:13	(13,964)
Gowers, John Robert	5:10:01	(27,462)
Gowers, Tobias	3:30:43	(4,284)
Goy, Nick	4:19:31	(15,292)
Grabham, Mark M	4:46:10	(22,237)
Grace, Andrew	3:47:34	(7,303)
Grace, Kevin	4:55:47	(24,632)
Grace, Mark	3:21:52	(2,996)
Grace, Matthew R	4:42:36	(21,361)
Grace, Ray W	5:09:31	(27,367)
Gradden, Michael D	4:34:08	(19,179)
Gradwell, Andrew	4:19:45	(15,357)
Graf, Gerrard S	3:27:17	(3,729)
Graffi, John	3:48:12	(7,446)
Grafton-Reed, Clive	4:10:48	(13,064)
Graham, Alan	4:30:06	(18,126)
Graham, David C	3:13:27	(2,055)
Graham, Dominic E	4:59:10	(25,428)
Graham, Douglas J	3:44:10	(6,659)
Graham, James	4:37:52	(20,135)
Graham, Mark A	5:29:40	(30,355)
Graham, Martin W	2:43:10	(260)
Graham, Michael J	4:03:35	(11,352)
Graham, Neil D	4:06:00	(11,880)
Graham, Neil W	4:50:19	(23,321)
Graham, Ray K	4:20:15	(15,498)
Graham, Richard J	4:09:34	(12,741)
Graham, Roderick	3:17:56	(2,521)
Graham, Rodney D	4:59:30	(25,497)
Graham, Stewart	5:40:19	(31,524)
Graham, Stuart J	4:11:14	(13,168)
Graham, Warren V	4:54:28	(24,329)
Graham-Clare, Philip J	4:45:11	(22,012)
Grahamj, Martin	4:53:32	(24,083)
Grahn, Richard	5:18:47	(28,931)
Grainge, Matthew J	2:53:36	(590)
Grainger, Darren James	4:06:38	(12,032)
Grainger, Neal S	4:45:13	(22,016)
Grainger, Richard J	4:21:38	(15,858)
Grainger, Robert P	3:23:09	(3,142)
Gramann, Jens	3:51:24	(8,142)
Grandfils, Eric	4:11:40	(13,303)
Graney, Barry M	2:57:54	(829)

Grange, Brett	5:56:16	(32,774)
Grange, Ian V	3:56:10	(9,357)
Grange, Robert P	4:44:05	(21,745)
Granger, Paul A	4:06:05	(11,897)
Granholm, John H	3:11:02	(1,780)
Grant, Andy	5:17:36	(28,730)
Grant, David R	3:54:30	(8,890)
Grant, Elliot	4:20:23	(15,534)
Grant, Frank	5:13:29	(28,062)
Grant, James	3:55:19	(9,112)
Grant, Mark L	5:56:21	(32,783)
Grant, Matthew	3:45:29	(6,891)
Grant, Michael J	3:41:52	(6,180)
Grant, Neil	3:46:45	(7,145)
Grant, Neil W	4:00:28	(10,656)
Grant, Nicholas	5:26:33	(29,998)
Grant, Shane D	4:19:49	(15,379)
Grant, Stephen	6:59:16	(34,939)
Grant, Stuart T	4:49:54	(23,217)
Grant, Wayne A	5:12:06	(27,819)
Grantham, Richard	4:55:01	(24,452)
Gras, Vincent	5:00:58	(25,802)
Grasso, Luigi P	5:41:25	(31,621)
Gratrix, Ian D	5:14:49	(28,285)
Grattan-Kane, Duncan R	4:28:03	(17,557)
Gratton, Craig	4:58:34	(25,288)
Gratton, Ralph V	4:14:39	(14,065)
Gratz, Detlet	3:34:59	(4,955)
Graves, Simon S	4:33:06	(18,921)
Graves, Stuart R	4:14:24	(14,013)
Gray, Adam	4:36:07	(19,705)
Gray, Andrew	5:00:20	(25,663)
Gray, Andrew C	3:32:57	(4,604)
Gray, Andrew R	4:52:32	(23,870)
Gray, Anthony D	3:32:49	(4,587)
Gray, Ben	4:50:39	(23,412)
Gray, Ben J	4:19:02	(15,167)
Gray, Christopher	4:56:02	(24,691)
Gray, Christopher W	3:54:54	(8,999)
Gray, Daniel J	3:26:04	(3,542)
Gray, David A	4:02:45	(11,178)
Gray, David Russell	4:57:49	(25,089)
Gray, Dean	5:03:10	(26,232)
Gray, Geoffrey I	2:49:47	(461)
Gray, Ian	3:31:25	(4,386)
Gray, Ian James	4:35:19	(19,496)
Gray, James Christopher	4:43:57	(21,703)
Gray, Jamie	6:14:04	(33,748)
Gray, John	4:24:13	(16,504)
Gray, John A	4:42:08	(21,237)
Gray, Neil R	3:54:45	(8,956)
Gray, Neil W	3:01:16	(1,071)
Gray, Oliver S	4:28:46	(17,766)
Gray, Patrick J	4:45:27	(22,068)
Gray, Paul	3:57:50	(9,619)
Gray, Paul W	5:06:27	(26,799)
Gray, Simon	3:20:17	(2,799)
Gray, Simon	4:19:43	(15,344)
Gray, Stephen R	4:18:04	(14,909)
Gray, Steven C	4:22:09	(15,989)
Gray, Stuart E	4:42:08	(21,237)
Grayson, Matthew M	4:22:36	(16,100)
Graziano, Gennaro	3:24:11	(3,296)
Grealy, Michael J	3:39:13	(5,718)
Greaney, Paul R	4:26:19	(17,071)
Greatorex, Gary	4:30:21	(18,194)
Greatrex, Warren	4:19:58	(15,419)
Greaves, Anthony	3:53:55	(8,726)
Greaves, Jonathan M	4:58:07	(25,170)
Greaves, Peter	3:57:25	(9,746)
Greco, Carlo	5:30:03	(30,403)
Greed, Tom J	3:56:46	(9,554)
Green, Adam M	4:47:41	(22,647)
Green, Alan R	3:50:28	(7,938)
Green, Alex	4:23:46	(16,379)
Green, Alex M	3:54:09	(8,796)
Green, Allan	4:15:05	(14,185)
Green, Andrew D	5:29:43	(30,363)
Green, Andrew J	2:44:45	(309)
Green, Andrew J	5:12:56	(27,971)
Green, Anthony	4:04:42	(11,586)
Green, Bradley	5:05:07	(26,573)
Green, Charles D	4:05:45	(11,834)

Green, Charles E	3:34:35	(4,889)
Green, Chris	5:41:45	(31,652)
Green, Colin	4:13:31	(13,802)
Green, Danny J	4:07:30	(12,236)
Green, David C	2:42:50	(252)
Green, David E	4:27:10	(17,301)
Green, David Paul	4:05:08	(11,690)
Green, David R	3:11:22	(1,812)
Green, Eric	2:59:57	(994)
Green, Francis A	6:12:03	(33,644)
Green, James	7:13:31	(35,087)
Green, James A	5:07:19	(26,963)
Green, James Alexander	4:11:42	(13,312)
Green, James J	3:32:32	(4,549)
Green, James R	4:04:36	(11,563)
Green, Jason D	4:27:57	(17,528)
Green, John J	4:27:40	(17,436)
Green, John K	2:58:30	(868)
Green, Jonathon	4:24:39	(16,605)
Green, Karl J	5:45:10	(31,941)
Green, Keith A	4:56:49	(24,883)
Green, Lawrence C	4:45:13	(22,016)
Green, Mark A	5:08:19	(27,144)
Green, Matt A	4:01:24	(10,885)
Green, Matthew	4:48:20	(22,814)
Green, Michael D	5:27:35	(30,100)
Green, Nicholas	4:22:26	(16,060)
Green, Nigel	3:56:11	(9,364)
Green, Nigel	4:12:52	(13,617)
Green, Nigel G	4:33:24	(19,004)
Green, Nigel M	4:40:55	(20,943)
Green, Paul A	3:18:36	(2,583)
Green, Peter K	3:45:18	(6,854)
Green, Philip S	3:55:14	(9,092)
Green, Richard	3:58:15	(10,025)
Green, Richard	4:18:35	(15,049)
Green, Richard A	3:40:16	(5,910)
Green, Rosemary	5:08:13	(27,127)
Green, Russell	4:28:39	(17,736)
Green, Shaun F	4:22:30	(16,075)
Green, Simon E	5:05:01	(26,549)
Green, Simon M	4:45:50	(22,171)
Green, Steven L	3:19:17	(2,647)
Green, Steven M	4:13:10	(13,700)
Green, Thomas	4:35:49	(19,630)
Green, Tony	3:51:36	(8,187)
Green, Will	2:46:37	(349)
Greenan, Alastair J	6:10:07	(33,567)
Greenaway, Justin P	3:49:32	(7,736)
Greenaway, Ryan	6:15:37	(33,819)
Greenblatt, Michael	3:50:12	(7,881)
Greene, Brian	5:10:39	(27,575)
Greene, Owen J	2:26:06	(37)
Greenep, Paul	4:33:29	(19,020)
Greener, John P	3:18:19	(2,556)
Greener, Michael A	2:58:16	(854)
Greengrass, Ian S	4:20:18	(15,512)
Greenhalgh, Bruce A	4:14:54	(14,140)
Greenhalgh, Clifford	5:00:46	(25,763)
Greenhalgh, Gordon A	4:48:32	(22,861)
Greenham, Peter A	4:51:15	(23,553)
Greenham, Peter A	5:41:28	(31,632)
Greening, Stephen G	5:12:51	(27,958)
Greenland, Edward C	3:37:47	(5,452)
Greenleaf, Andrew H	2:33:13	(94)
Greenleaf, Paul H	3:42:04	(6,226)
Greenley, Neil F	4:40:26	(20,821)
Greenop, Paul C	3:54:36	(8,919)
Greenshields, Ross	4:08:19	(12,459)
Greenslade, Christopher W	4:36:31	(19,797)
Greenslade, Daevid	5:08:46	(27,225)
Greenslade, Daniel	4:05:27	(11,760)
Greenslade, Heath	4:15:11	(14,211)
Greenslade, John	3:55:32	(9,162)
Greenway, Andrew	4:58:35	(25,290)
Greenwell, Andrew P	4:10:26	(12,962)
Greenwell, Jeremy	4:19:21	(15,246)
Greenwell, Robert N	6:06:21	(33,403)
Greenwood, Alan	5:21:33	(29,310)
Greenwood, Jonathan	4:27:58	(17,532)
Greenwood, Mark A	2:40:57	(214)
Greenwood, Matthew A	3:40:26	(5,931)
Greenwood, Michael J	3:14:00	(2,122)

Greenwood, Peter M	7:03:16	(34,984)
Greenwood, Richard J	4:49:29	(23,110)
Gregg, Martin	4:55:46	(24,628)
Gregg, Paul	2:40:11	(196)
Gregg, William S	3:51:59	(8,273)
Gregory, Darren	5:30:32	(30,464)
Gregory, David	4:07:46	(12,310)
Gregory, Ian	5:34:27	(30,907)
Gregory, Ian J	3:22:19	(3,052)
Gregory, James	3:39:52	(5,821)
Gregory, James	4:59:31	(25,505)
Gregory, Jeffrey S	5:24:18	(29,700)
Gregory, John A	3:37:40	(5,435)
Gregory, John A	4:55:31	(24,578)
Gregory, Marcus	5:55:25	(32,718)
Gregory, Mark	3:52:36	(8,426)
Gregory, Mark	4:41:31	(21,093)
Gregory, Mark	4:41:46	(21,158)
Gregory, Mark J	3:57:10	(9,664)
Gregory, Matthew	4:33:40	(19,066)
Gregory, Neil K	4:41:00	(20,962)
Gregory, Neil R	3:57:09	(9,662)
Gregory, Nick A	3:09:47	(1,688)
Gregory, Paul F	2:38:52	(175)
Gregory, Paul R	4:20:46	(15,627)
Gregory, Sonia L	4:15:34	(14,300)
Gregory, Stephen	3:59:29	(10,384)
Gregory, Stuart	3:52:56	(8,491)
Gregory, Wilhelm F	4:39:37	(20,618)
Gregory-Peake, Brett A	4:07:14	(12,162)
Gregson, Andrew	4:31:52	(18,597)
Greig, Alan R	3:30:55	(4,315)
Greig, Andrew T	4:02:06	(11,043)
Greig, Jon M	2:54:04	(606)
Greig, Lionel	4:09:15	(12,671)
Greiner, Matthias	5:05:13	(26,595)
Greiner, Zang	4:00:58	(10,792)
Grek, Jonny	4:12:30	(13,526)
Grek, Mike	4:12:29	(13,518)
Gresham, Paul R	5:23:25	(29,587)
Gresham, Steven A	4:12:09	(13,426)
Gresse, Gavin S	3:50:00	(7,833)
Gresty, Paul J	3:15:37	(2,295)
Greville, Richard	5:07:45	(27,052)
Grewal, Jeff	4:31:51	(18,592)
Grewal, Randeep S	4:11:08	(13,149)
Grey, Chris R	4:42:55	(21,450)
Gribben, Iain M	5:12:28	(27,889)
Gribble, Tom	3:54:25	(8,867)
Grice, Andy D	6:09:00	(33,512)
Grice, Neil	5:39:59	(31,495)
Grice, Zippy	2:54:07	(608)
Gridley, Marc	3:22:51	(3,113)
Grier, Alex A	4:49:20	(23,064)
Grieve, Steven	4:26:59	(17,256)
Grieves, Mark C	4:13:47	(13,868)
Grieveson, Peter	3:46:50	(7,162)
Grifa, Michele	3:09:03	(1,623)
Griffin, Alan W	4:53:35	(24,093)
Griffin, Ian C	4:26:26	(17,093)
Griffin, John J	5:55:11	(32,704)
Griffin, Jonathan L	3:43:08	(6,448)
Griffin, Kristian T	4:59:58	(25,591)
Griffin, Mark	4:37:04	(19,934)
Griffin, Patrick S	4:47:29	(22,594)
Griffin, Roger F	3:49:04	(7,635)
Griffin, Simon C	3:09:55	(1,700)
Griffith, John O	5:26:24	(29,978)
Griffith, Mark	4:40:20	(20,802)
Griffith, Owen Evan	4:50:00	(23,239)
Griffiths, Alan P	3:38:24	(5,566)
Griffiths, Alan T	4:36:02	(19,689)
Griffiths, Andrew	4:00:47	(10,741)
Griffiths, Andrew	5:03:33	(26,292)
Griffiths, Ashley P	4:13:36	(13,824)
Griffiths, Bryn	4:15:20	(14,240)
Griffiths, Charlie	4:33:58	(19,145)
Griffiths, Chris	6:18:14	(33,938)
Griffiths, Craig P	4:13:07	(13,687)
Griffiths, David J	5:09:16	(27,321)
Griffiths, David J	5:21:23	(29,282)
Griffiths, Dewi E	5:11:14	(27,680)
Griffiths, Gywnn	5:03:18	(26,252)
Griffiths, Ian	4:36:21	(19,750)
Griffiths, James M	3:53:33	(8,634)
Griffiths, Lewis	4:22:55	(16,168)
Griffiths, Mark C	3:20:54	(2,879)
Griffiths, Martin S	3:18:32	(2,579)
Griffiths, Nicholas D	3:58:37	(10,132)
Griffiths, Owain P	3:54:41	(8,940)
Griffiths, Paul W	3:17:35	(2,490)
Griffiths, Phil	4:52:48	(23,927)
Griffiths, Rhidian G	5:12:01	(27,803)
Griffiths, Simon G	5:10:41	(27,583)
Griffiths, Steve M	5:33:34	(30,813)
Griffiths, Thomas P	3:44:34	(6,727)
Griffiths, Thomas W	4:21:11	(15,739)
Griggs, Justin H	4:56:49	(24,883)
Griggs, Karl A	4:10:43	(13,044)
Griggs, Tim	4:54:30	(24,334)
Grigoleit, Peter M	3:31:58	(4,464)
Grim, Robert J	4:00:52	(10,766)
Grima, David V	3:10:56	(1,774)
Grimbley, David	3:34:13	(4,815)
Grime, Chris J	4:21:29	(15,804)
Grimes, David	5:15:37	(28,441)
Grimes, Dylan	3:29:52	(4,162)
Grimes, Shane M	4:26:49	(17,211)
Grimm, Heinz	4:29:59	(18,092)
Grimm, Joerg	3:29:12	(4,039)
Grimshaw, Chris	5:36:31	(31,125)
Grimshaw, Graham	3:46:46	(7,148)
Grimwood, Andrew	3:35:37	(5,074)
Grindell, Philip	3:24:50	(3,384)
Grindu, Louis	4:35:34	(19,564)
Grinsted, Rob T	4:55:48	(24,640)
Grint, Lee S	6:12:09	(33,648)
Grismond, Matt	4:16:16	(14,464)
Grist, Andrew	3:19:12	(2,637)
Grist, Matthew R	5:40:52	(31,577)
Grist, Paul J	3:59:44	(10,472)
Grist, Reginald D	4:46:18	(22,281)
Grist, Roger W	3:26:56	(3,674)
Gristwood, Clive C	3:58:11	(10,002)
Grobe, Carsten	4:02:28	(11,121)
Grobler, Daniel F	5:22:38	(29,458)
Grobler, Gerrie P	4:03:59	(11,445)
Grodard, Philippe	4:13:30	(13,796)
Groen, Gerrit	3:38:01	(5,495)
Groen, Johannes	4:15:45	(14,335)
Groenewald, Siewert	4:10:27	(12,970)
Grogan, Adam M	3:57:02	(9,628)
Grogan, Geoff	4:37:02	(19,928)
Grogan, Robert	5:22:55	(29,503)
Groom, Aidan	4:45:22	(22,050)
Groom, Benjamin	4:19:48	(15,371)
Groom, Lloyd	4:50:23	(23,340)
Groom, Stephen H	3:20:49	(2,871)
Grosbois, Gilles	4:00:35	(10,694)
Gross, Christian	3:38:25	(5,570)
Grossmann, Joseph	4:20:09	(15,471)
Grosvenor, David Michael	4:29:40	(18,008)
Grosvenor, Justin	5:08:34	(27,187)
Groth, Andreas	2:34:44	(109)
Grotto, Antonio	4:05:52	(11,854)
Ground, Paul W	3:50:13	(7,889)
Grout, Alan C	5:42:56	(31,763)
Grout, Steven R	3:26:17	(3,571)
Grove, Jonathan P	4:32:00	(18,640)
Grover, Jonathan P	6:25:57	(34,279)
Grover, Rhett	4:47:12	(22,546)
Groves, Paul	5:37:39	(31,243)
Groves, Peter J	4:06:02	(11,889)
Groves, Robert	4:26:57	(17,246)
Grubb, Timothy J	5:35:18	(30,999)
Gruber, Thomas E	5:00:25	(25,680)
Grundy, Andrew Stephen	4:00:13	(10,603)
Grundy, Christopher J	4:36:26	(19,777)
Grundy, Kieran J	3:21:32	(2,951)
Grundy, Stephen	4:43:30	(21,598)
Gruzinski, Ryan J	4:45:44	(22,139)
Guanter, Xavier	4:01:23	(10,881)
Guatelli, Francesco	3:01:13	(1,068)
Gubbins, Matthw J	6:51:03	(34,830)
Gudgeirsson, Steinar Thor	5:53:03	(32,550)
Gudjonsson, Arnar	3:45:48	(6,948)
Gudjonsson, Heidar	3:40:48	(6,000)
Gudjonsson, Thorarinn	5:15:31	(28,423)
Gudka, Ganesh H	5:16:39	(28,587)
Gudka, Piyush	3:49:19	(7,688)
Guerin, Geoff	4:23:03	(16,197)
Guerlot, Guillaume	3:33:51	(4,731)
Guerreiro, Francisco	5:12:20	(27,857)
Guerrero, Francisco José	3:54:03	(8,769)
Guerrier, Jean François	3:32:32	(4,549)
Guest, Andrew	3:54:39	(8,934)
Guest, Karl D	5:13:15	(28,029)
Guest, Lee Dylan	4:01:29	(10,909)
Guest, Thomas	4:12:28	(13,512)
Guest, William R	4:54:52	(24,420)
Gugelmann, Christoph	4:27:51	(17,502)
Guibourg, Phlippe	4:16:31	(14,525)
Guildford, Jonathan	4:01:53	(10,999)
Guilhermino Rodrigues, Antënio	4:31:59	(18,629)
Guillemain, Philippe	4:12:25	(13,494)
Guillot, Jean François	4:08:44	(12,558)
Guimaraes, Manoel	3:57:43	(9,850)
Guinan, Paul E	2:41:14	(219)
Guinchard, Marcel A	3:52:08	(8,304)
Guinness, Dominic	4:27:48	(17,487)
Guinness, Gary	6:15:11	(33,800)
Guinsberg, Myer	3:29:43	(4,139)
Guiseley, Andrew	2:48:08	(402)
Guitton, Alain	3:22:46	(3,103)
Guiver, Richard J	2:58:00	(835)
Gulc, Peter	2:58:59	(920)
Gull, William E	4:05:36	(11,798)
Gulland, Phil James	4:31:28	(18,494)
Gullis, Michael A	3:41:24	(6,102)
Gulliver, John	5:05:23	(26,622)
Gumbrell, Nick C	4:28:04	(17,564)
Gummer, Andrew J	3:59:33	(10,404)
Gundogdu, Volkan	5:37:25	(31,218)
Gundry, Martin	3:33:43	(4,706)
Gunn, Eleanor C	6:10:01	(33,563)
Gunn, Graham	5:08:49	(27,232)
Gunn, John F	4:06:32	(11,997)
Gunn, Mark L	5:03:47	(26,338)
Gunnarsson, Haukur	4:14:55	(14,147)
Gunning, Brinsley	3:50:55	(8,042)
Gunningham, Ian R	4:50:16	(23,308)
Gunstone, Douglas W	3:54:42	(8,945)
Gunther, Steven Peter	4:19:50	(15,385)
Gurd, Marc J	4:47:04	(22,501)
Gurd, Richard	3:45:41	(6,926)
Gurney, Henry	3:21:54	(2,998)
Gurney, Paul	3:47:39	(7,318)
Gurria, Angel	3:59:23	(10,365)
Gurry, Harvey D	3:15:46	(2,316)
Gush, Mike H	4:14:40	(14,067)
Gushlow, Alan	5:25:58	(29,929)
Gustafson, Michael J	4:05:04	(11,670)
Gustard, Paul	4:09:16	(12,673)
Gustavsson, Christer	2:53:43	(594)
Gutcher, Lee	4:44:58	(21,948)
Guth, Karl-Josef	4:48:45	(22,912)
Guthrie, Neil L	3:52:41	(8,446)
Guthrie-Brown, Thurstan S	3:19:43	(2,713)
Gutman, Nimrod	4:03:16	(11,287)
Guttenplan, Don D	4:34:33	(19,276)
Guveya, John	2:55:08	(673)
Guy, David J	4:22:13	(16,006)
Guy, Ian V	4:27:19	(17,348)
Guy, Luke S	4:42:27	(21,313)
Guy, Thomas R	3:28:19	(3,903)
Guyver, Chris	4:57:07	(24,948)
Gwatkin, Paul F	5:35:04	(30,979)
Gwenter, Matthew J	4:04:15	(11,502)
Gwilliam, Dave	3:42:41	(6,352)
Gwilliam, Steve	4:50:22	(23,335)
Gwilliam, Steven J	4:29:25	(17,952)
Gwillim, John A	4:38:05	(20,195)
Gye, Emmanuel	4:47:06	(22,515)
Haak, Willem	3:26:33	(3,609)
Haarhuis, Ben	4:12:30	(13,526)
Haas, Laurent	3:40:05	(5,875)
Haber, Brett A	4:27:48	(17,487)
Haberstroh, Friedrich	4:21:23	(15,778)
Haberstroh, Theophil	4:21:23	(15,778)

Hancock, Richard 4:42:46 (21,402)
Hancock, Wayne A 4:19:40 (15,331)
Hancox, Duncan J 4:50:03 (23,253)
Hancox, Grenville 4:53:50 (24,183)
Hancox, Karl A 3:20:12 (2,780)
Hancox, Matthew J 3:37:35 (5,420)
Hancox, Michael J 4:36:09 (19,712)
Hancox, Robert G 4:07:03 (12,119)
Hancox, Robert N 3:37:33 (5,412)
Hand, Colin T 5:45:23 (31,960)
Hand, Edward 4:56:20 (24,758)
Handasyde Dick, Oliver 4:47:37 (22,634)
Handley, Graham 4:32:24 (18,728)
Handley, James 4:16:15 (14,458)
Handley, Mark 4:42:57 (21,459)
Handley, Mark D 5:03:57 (26,374)
Handley, William K 5:08:23 (27,157)
Haneef, Mohammed 3:59:37 (10,423)
Hankin, Antony P 4:59:01 (25,391)
Hanks, Lee 5:16:31 (28,564)
Hanks, Steve 4:17:03 (14,658)
Hanks, Tom G 3:54:49 (8,973)
Hanley, Jonathan G 2:40:32 (208)
Hanlon, John 3:55:42 (9,221)
Hann, Kevin P 4:50:40 (23,414)
Hanna, Colin M 4:42:42 (21,388)
Hannaford, Chris P 4:48:31 (22,856)
Hannah, Errick 3:30:32 (4,262)
Hannan, Jon M 3:32:19 (4,518)
Hannibal, Alan Ronald 5:00:14 (25,639)
Hannon, Patrick J 4:34:11 (19,193)
Hannula, Todd K 4:23:30 (16,314)
Hanrahan, John T 4:06:55 (12,084)
Hanrahan, Paul T 3:44:02 (6,636)
Hansen, Bart 4:20:02 (15,437)
Hansen, David L 4:04:36 (11,563)
Hansen, Jason 3:43:35 (6,541)
Hansen, Olov H 4:28:06 (17,580)
Hansen, Paul 3:11:48 (1,860)
Hansen, Volker 3:49:04 (7,635)
Hanson, Carl 5:45:35 (31,982)
Hanson, David A 3:53:05 (8,528)
Hanson, Joel T 4:06:21 (11,962)
Hanson, Kevin A 3:57:18 (9,706)
Hanson, Paul 3:36:18 (5,207)
Hanvey, Richard 4:30:31 (18,235)
Happe, Joseph 3:20:49 (2,871)
Haque, Eyeedul 4:52:39 (23,892)
Haran, Brian V 5:11:12 (27,672)
Harasek, Thomas 4:22:05 (15,961)
Harbert, Barrie John 3:44:05 (6,648)
Harborow, Adam J 2:59:01 (922)
Harbour, Ryan 3:08:20 (1,554)
Harbron, Christopher G 3:21:17 (2,919)
Harchowal, Binu 4:01:13 (10,839)
Harcinovic, Adi 4:53:15 (24,033)
Hardcastle, David R 6:45:25 (34,715)
Hardcastle, Richard 3:31:55 (4,457)
Harden, Samuel T 4:29:26 (17,956)
Harden, Tim R 5:12:40 (27,920)
Hardie, Stuart W 5:48:06 (32,179)
Hardiman, Mark 4:55:30 (24,572)
Harding, Dan D 3:22:27 (3,061)
Harding, Derek J 5:28:07 (30,164)
Harding, James A 4:48:40 (22,891)
Harding, Jason A 3:33:36 (4,692)
Harding, Jason P 2:57:33 (813)
Harding, Jason P 4:31:04 (18,376)
Harding, John M 5:29:21 (30,315)
Harding, Michael J 4:25:36 (16,874)
Harding, Nick 5:31:04 (30,537)
Harding, Paul 5:22:31 (29,442)
Harding, Peter M 3:38:58 (5,675)
Harding, Roger J 5:08:30 (27,178)
Harding, Trevor T 7:02:31 (34,975)
Hardman, Matthew 4:13:53 (13,880)
Hardman, Nigel 4:56:50 (24,890)
Hards, Stephen John 3:55:20 (9,117)
Hardstone, Roger G 4:09:20 (12,695)
Hardwell, Keith J 3:34:02 (4,763)
Hardwick, Chris 4:58:45 (25,327)
Hardwick, David W 4:57:15 (24,975)
Hardy, Frank S 3:49:10 (7,660)
Hardy, James E 5:23:11 (29,543)
Hardy, Mark 6:08:28 (33,491)
Hardy, Michael S 4:19:51 (15,390)
Hardy, Robert 4:43:14 (21,524)
Hardy, Roy William 4:47:59 (22,736)
Hare, Ian M 3:47:57 (7,384)
Hare, Michael R 3:58:35 (10,124)
Hare, Sam 5:29:52 (30,387)
Haresign, Martin R 4:59:03 (25,399)
Haresnape, Alan J 3:57:15 (9,690)
Harfield, Patrick D 6:51:09 (34,832)
Harfoot, Michael 3:47:56 (7,381)
Hargreaves, Ben R 4:13:11 (13,707)
Hargreaves, David 3:54:27 (8,876)
Hargreaves, Mark 3:26:44 (3,640)
Hargreaves, Michael S 4:55:28 (24,566)
Hargreaves, Phillip 5:06:22 (26,784)
Hargreaves, William A 4:50:46 (23,437)
Hariram, Lloyd A 4:46:54 (22,451)
Harker, Andrew J 3:20:51 (2,877)
Harkin, Derek 3:45:54 (6,960)
Harkin, James L 5:07:19 (26,963)
Harkin, Max 4:05:07 (11,685)
Harkness, Ian M 4:24:37 (16,595)
Harkness, Lee R 4:24:38 (16,601)
Harkness, Roger 3:49:26 (7,712)
Harkus, Gavin M 2:54:54 (656)
Harland, Alan 3:17:16 (2,460)
Harland, Jason 3:35:10 (4,990)
Harley, Andrew K 4:42:10 (21,239)
Harloff, Michael 5:00:42 (25,748)
Harlow, Andrew 5:07:04 (26,920)
Harlow, Gary 3:59:41 (10,451)
Harlow, Steven 4:36:59 (19,914)
Harman, Craig 3:59:54 (10,515)
Harmer, Mark 4:41:38 (21,129)
Harmes, Paul 3:46:34 (7,100)
Harmsworth, Mark 4:58:27 (25,253)
Harness, Ian 5:24:46 (29,760)
Harness, Robert 4:20:23 (15,534)
Harney, Brian 3:47:58 (7,391)
Harney, Mark 3:16:12 (2,351)
Harper, Andrew 4:29:49 (18,041)
Harper, Ed 4:43:07 (21,497)
Harper, Greg 5:30:55 (30,510)
Harper, Kevin A 3:31:03 (4,335)
Harper, Richard D 5:11:43 (27,761)
Harper, Robert 3:55:41 (9,211)
Harper, Robert J 4:25:17 (16,780)
Harper, Simon P 3:27:40 (3,809)
Harper, Terence 6:29:54 (34,407)
Harper, Theo 2:59:12 (933)
Harpham, John 5:43:46 (31,831)
Harpur, Gavin P 4:11:54 (13,358)
Harridge, Jonathan D 5:02:30 (26,117)
Harries, Hugo 5:09:11 (27,306)
Harries, Iwan 3:48:09 (7,433)
Harries, Mark W 3:21:09 (2,907)
Harries, Owen D 2:54:33 (635)
Harrington, Patrick 3:20:40 (2,850)
Harrington, Richard 3:33:05 (4,622)
Harrington, Roland M 3:42:09 (6,242)
Harris, Alastair J 4:14:42 (14,079)
Harris, Chris 3:59:25 (10,374)
Harris, Chris J 4:25:07 (16,739)
Harris, Chris P 4:04:32 (11,552)
Harris, Chris R 4:28:34 (17,716)
Harris, Clive 5:54:09 (32,628)
Harris, Daniel A 3:39:51 (5,817)
Harris, Dave 3:46:57 (7,191)
Harris, Ed J 4:52:34 (23,876)
Harris, Giles M 2:55:18 (686)
Harris, Ian 4:10:40 (13,025)
Harris, Jackson H 5:00:37 (25,733)
Harris, Jason 2:53:17 (572)
Harris, John 4:18:46 (15,094)
Harris, Jonathan C 5:44:53 (31,922)
Harris, Joseph Luther 3:37:36 (5,424)
Harris, Keith 6:18:02 (33,928)
Harris, Keith N 4:53:44 (24,152)
Harris, Keith R 3:38:00 (5,489)
Harris, Luke D 4:59:07 (25,415)
Harris, Mark Robert 4:40:29 (20,829)
Harris, Matt 4:49:55 (23,221)
Harris, Matthew D 4:53:02 (23,985)
Harris, Michael 6:16:51 (33,878)
Harris, Michael D 3:34:38 (4,902)
Harris, Michael J 2:59:31 (959)
Harris, Micheal Terry 4:09:19 (12,689)
Harris, Patrick B 5:00:47 (25,767)
Harris, Paul 3:40:37 (5,961)
Harris, Paul H 4:35:59 (19,675)
Harris, Paul J 7:15:58 (35,113)
Harris, Paul M 4:33:56 (19,136)
Harris, Pete J 6:05:11 (33,349)
Harris, Peter 5:47:28 (32,129)
Harris, Phillip J 4:04:29 (11,541)
Harris, Richard Lewis 3:30:13 (4,209)
Harris, Robert B 2:55:26 (693)
Harris, Simon P 4:21:20 (15,768)
Harris, Steven M 4:56:14 (24,737)
Harris, Tim J 3:57:40 (9,836)
Harrison, Adam M 4:50:38 (23,409)
Harrison, Andrew 4:23:28 (16,299)
Harrison, Andrew J 2:37:15 (144)
Harrison, Ben John 4:02:55 (11,213)
Harrison, Chad A 5:55:46 (32,748)
Harrison, David A 3:25:18 (3,431)
Harrison, David R 3:15:45 (2,313)
Harrison, Derek J 3:31:48 (4,438)
Harrison, Glenn J 3:50:31 (7,951)
Harrison, Jeremy PP 3:59:00 (10,250)
Harrison, Jody 3:57:58 (9,924)
Harrison, John 5:10:46 (27,598)
Harrison, John R 3:40:52 (6,009)
Harrison, John T 3:56:42 (9,535)
Harrison, Jonathan 3:27:03 (3,691)
Harrison, Matt 2:51:39 (512)
Harrison, Matthew 3:31:48 (4,438)
Harrison, Matthew 4:21:27 (15,797)
Harrison, Matthew 4:23:44 (16,370)
Harrison, Matthew D 4:10:26 (12,962)
Harrison, Matthew E 3:59:37 (10,423)
Harrison, Max 3:34:03 (4,770)
Harrison, Patrick 5:25:50 (29,910)
Harrison, Paul C 3:06:11 (1,387)
Harrison, Paul D 4:34:39 (19,300)
Harrison, Paul J 4:39:55 (20,696)
Harrison, Paul L 4:50:25 (23,347)
Harrison, Peter 5:27:48 (30,124)
Harrison, Philip D 4:26:01 (16,991)
Harrison, Piers W 3:32:53 (4,596)
Harrison, Richard D 5:17:06 (28,658)
Harrison, Richard J 4:46:15 (22,262)
Harrison, Robert E 4:00:09 (10,583)
Harrison, Simon A 3:38:43 (5,629)
Harrison, Simon E 7:07:13 (35,029)
Harrison, Stephen 3:47:52 (7,367)
Harrison, Stephen D 4:27:03 (17,269)
Harrison, Tim 3:22:41 (3,096)
Harrison, Tim J 5:12:32 (27,897)
Harrison, Tom 4:24:45 (16,638)
Harrison, Tom C 7:16:54 (35,118)
Harrison-Church, John N 3:11:15 (1,801)
Harrod, Craig Bergen 3:59:14 (10,320)
Harrold, Bruce 2:44:48 (311)
Harrold, Jonathan 4:49:17 (23,046)
Harrop, Philip 3:53:19 (8,585)
Harrop, Simon 3:50:35 (7,966)
Harroufi, Ridouane 2:28:52 (56)
Harrow, Simon J 4:09:37 (12,757)
Harrowing, Keith D 5:04:12 (26,413)
Harry, Richard 2:53:01 (559)
Harstedt, Goran 3:29:12 (4,039)
Hart, Al 2:37:45 (152)
Hart, Andrew D 4:56:16 (24,742)
Hart, Damian 5:16:11 (28,525)
Hart, David 4:31:03 (18,370)
Hart, David J 3:26:00 (3,533)
Hart, David W 2:56:38 (754)
Hart, Michael J 4:17:17 (14,712)
Hart, Patrick 4:50:13 (23,285)
Hart, Peter J 3:20:50 (2,874)
Hart, Peter J 4:12:58 (13,654)
Hart, Robert W 5:52:16 (32,501)
Hart, Simon 2:47:10 (371)

Hart, Stuart M 4:34:20 (19,226)
Hart, Stuart P 4:56:32 (24,809)
Hart, Tim P 4:21:06 (15,714)
Harte, Michael V 3:26:50 (3,654)
Harte, Serge 5:09:00 (27,274)
Harte, Tony 3:30:52 (4,305)
Hartin, Alan D 4:42:37 (21,366)
Hartley, Adam 3:59:54 (10,515)
Hartley, Allan 3:32:11 (4,500)
Hartley, Chris D 3:20:14 (2,789)
Hartley, Matthew B 3:58:48 (10,194)
Hartley, Richard A 3:57:31 (9,775)
Hartley, Simon G 4:24:12 (16,497)
Hartley, Steve 4:05:36 (11,798)
Hartley, Stuart 4:54:25 (24,317)
Hartmann, Oliver 3:59:22 (10,359)
Hartmann, Peter 3:57:25 (9,746)
Hartnell, Haydn 2:59:10 (930)
Hartopp, Ben J 4:56:22 (24,764)
Hartridge, James H 3:32:16 (4,513)
Hartropp, Jon S 3:37:32 (5,409)
Hartshorn, Andy 3:51:48 (8,227)
Hartshorn, George B 3:26:40 (3,629)
Hartt, Leslie R 3:35:07 (4,981)
Harvey, Adam 4:49:36 (23,147)
Harvey, Alexander 3:59:13 (10,317)
Harvey, Bob 5:02:55 (26,197)
Harvey, Christopher J 4:27:27 (17,380)
Harvey, Clive S 3:28:42 (3,957)
Harvey, Colin N 4:39:43 (20,648)
Harvey, David 4:08:07 (12,395)
Harvey, David 4:57:14 (24,971)
Harvey, Ian E 5:04:39 (26,485)
Harvey, Ian H 3:11:37 (1,842)
Harvey, James M 3:48:50 (7,580)
Harvey, Jonathan 4:25:54 (16,961)
Harvey, Matthew J 2:41:57 (235)
Harvey, Nicholas 3:16:08 (2,344)
Harvey, Stephen 3:57:39 (9,826)
Harvey, Tim J 5:15:26 (28,408)
Harwood, Andrew J 3:53:15 (8,572)
Harwood, Christopher C 5:48:19 (32,201)
Harwood, Ian M 4:39:53 (20,688)
Harwood, Jim 4:38:15 (20,241)
Harwood, Neil J 5:21:45 (29,334)
Harwood, Paul 4:55:36 (24,597)
Harwood, Paul M 4:39:23 (20,542)
Harwood, Simon J 5:09:59 (27,458)
Haselden, Adrian 5:24:24 (29,720)
Hasell, Adam D 3:13:29 (2,059)
Haskell, James D 4:25:22 (16,806)
Haslam, Andy J 3:46:05 (6,998)
Haslam, John P 5:15:29 (28,414)
Haslam, Tom Sebastian 5:02:41 (26,150)
Haslehurst, Tim 5:55:45 (32,745)
Haslett, Francis P 7:10:58 (35,059)
Haslett, Jeremy R 3:57:29 (9,762)
Hassal, Graham N 4:49:11 (23,012)
Hassall, Andrew C 4:19:55 (15,404)
Hassall, Glyn R 4:51:26 (23,605)
Hassall, Mark M 5:05:06 (26,566)
Hassall, Robert R 4:50:53 (23,458)
Hassan, Carl A 4:05:03 (11,665)
Hassan, Hasan M 4:52:04 (23,769)
Hassan, Medhat 6:11:16 (33,611)
Hassell, Jim 5:09:43 (27,405)
Hassett, Simon R 4:08:44 (12,558)
Hasslacher, James M 4:32:59 (18,895)
Haste, Carl T 3:44:21 (6,689)
Hastie, David I 3:26:18 (3,575)
Hastings, Mark 6:20:12 (34,042)
Hastings, Paul S 4:22:34 (16,091)
Hatch, Steven 5:32:03 (30,646)
Hatfield, Alexander J 4:04:17 (11,506)
Hatfield, Dan E 3:58:41 (10,155)
Hatfield, Jonathon 5:15:03 (28,328)
Hatfield, Richard 4:35:02 (19,419)
Hatfield, Robert J 3:17:58 (2,523)
Hatfield, Stephen 4:44:09 (21,757)
Hathaway, David John 7:07:25 (35,032)
Hathaway, Marc Daniel 4:45:45 (22,144)
Hathaway, Paul J 4:12:48 (13,605)
Hather, Keith H 3:46:35 (7,104)
Hatheway, Larry 4:55:14 (24,514)
Hatt, Jack 4:17:53 (14,858)
Hatto, David 4:10:18 (12,935)
Hatvany, Alan P 3:20:37 (2,842)
Hauenstein, Johannes 3:54:29 (8,885)
Haugh, David 4:49:29 (23,110)
Haughey, Duncan J 3:01:07 (1,060)
Haughey, John F 4:05:19 (11,737)
Haurum, Steffen 4:12:55 (13,635)
Hausken, Oddvar 3:25:58 (3,527)
Havard, Allan 5:20:27 (29,148)
Havard, Michael 3:12:53 (1,985)
Havenhand, David C 3:16:30 (2,378)
Havers, James M 4:23:15 (16,241)
Havill, Neil Stanley 3:47:48 (7,351)
Havis, Stuart 4:12:21 (13,483)
Havlock, Pedro 3:42:58 (6,412)
Hawcutt, Michael J 4:22:50 (16,149)
Hawes, Andrew K 4:07:01 (12,111)
Hawes, Crispin 6:30:21 (34,424)
Hawes, Dougie 4:29:49 (18,041)
Hawes, Micheal L 6:16:21 (33,861)
Hawgood, Peter W 4:51:34 (23,640)
Hawker, Ian F 4:10:36 (13,006)
Hawker, Kyle P 4:09:43 (12,779)
Hawker, Nick J 4:14:46 (14,102)
Hawker, Steve 4:47:52 (22,693)
Hawkes, Andrew 3:59:17 (10,331)
Hawkes, Andrew 4:25:37 (16,877)
Hawkes, Andrew P 4:10:08 (12,892)
Hawkes, David 4:25:37 (16,877)
Hawkes, Dexter N 6:04:11 (33,297)
Hawkes, Ian P 5:31:25 (30,567)
Hawkes, Keith S 3:11:29 (1,826)
Hawkes, Mark L 5:21:30 (29,298)
Hawkes, Martyn J 2:55:20 (687)
Hawkes, Michael 5:08:52 (27,245)
Hawkes, Tony J 4:03:07 (11,253)
Hawkins, Andrew P 3:45:17 (6,852)
Hawkins, Andrew R 3:09:13 (1,644)
Hawkins, Ben 3:29:21 (4,079)
Hawkins, Christopher F 4:09:50 (12,816)
Hawkins, Daniel 4:46:15 (22,262)
Hawkins, David J 4:16:30 (14,522)
Hawkins, Dominic A 3:28:37 (3,942)
Hawkins, Graeme 3:24:36 (3,356)
Hawkins, Joe D 3:18:54 (2,610)
Hawkins, Keith R 5:25:57 (29,927)
Hawkins, Marc L 4:27:46 (17,474)
Hawkins, Mark J 3:54:24 (8,864)
Hawkins, Martin S 3:24:25 (3,330)
Hawkins, Sam E 4:31:20 (18,451)
Hawkins, Stephen 2:53:03 (560)
Hawkins, Thomas 4:06:20 (11,957)
Hawkins, William A 4:32:41 (18,812)
Hawksley, Gary Julian 3:20:13 (2,784)
Hawkswood, Jamie I 5:49:04 (32,256)
Hawksworth, John 4:46:27 (22,331)
Hawley, Graham 3:43:39 (6,556)
Hawliczek, Edward J 4:12:39 (13,560)
Haworth, Adrian 4:21:49 (15,905)
Haworth, Dominic P 3:33:45 (4,713)
Haworth, Richard C 4:21:50 (15,909)
Hawse, Robert J 4:18:34 (15,044)
Hawthorn, Chris A 3:39:52 (5,821)
Hay, James 4:27:32 (17,400)
Hay, Roy 5:24:43 (29,753)
Hay, Stephen 7:33:21 (35,241)
Hayakawa, Dominic P 4:43:34 (21,617)
Haycock, Christopher A 4:54:04 (24,235)
Haycock, Nick R 4:34:12 (19,197)
Hayday, Rob J 4:02:03 (11,030)
Hayden, Alan C 4:32:05 (18,660)
Hayden, Darrin P 4:50:14 (23,292)
Hayden, John M 4:00:58 (10,792)
Hayden, Paul 4:01:46 (10,976)
Hayden, Stuart R 4:25:27 (16,829)
Hayer, Gurpal S 4:13:20 (13,760)
Hayes, Daniel F 3:44:06 (6,651)
Hayes, Daniel P 5:32:42 (30,722)
Hayes, Guy 4:45:23 (22,054)
Hayes, James 3:08:50 (1,603)
Hayes, Kevin 4:03:32 (11,344)
Hayes, Kim J 5:56:20 (32,779)
Hayes, Matt G 4:33:13 (18,948)
Hayes, Michael A 3:17:01 (2,434)
Hayes, Mike 5:13:20 (28,042)
Hayes, Philip 4:03:56 (11,428)
Hayes, Simon 4:07:57 (12,348)
Hayes, William A 4:52:23 (23,838)
Hayhurst, Chris M 3:55:41 (9,211)
Hayler, Douglas W 4:18:59 (15,156)
Hayler, Ronald S 4:18:58 (15,152)
Haylock, Adam C 5:34:10 (30,873)
Haylock, Colin A 4:52:06 (23,775)
Haylock, Garry 5:21:50 (29,352)
Haylock, Keith J 4:59:53 (25,573)
Haylock, Michael John 4:00:44 (10,726)
Haylor, Simon 5:05:40 (26,671)
Hayman, Nick P 5:29:29 (30,328)
Hayman, Tom 4:39:36 (20,613)
Haynes, Jason L 3:28:17 (3,896)
Haynes, John R 3:12:54 (1,989)
Haynes, Kevin C 3:28:47 (3,971)
Haynes, Kevin J 3:13:31 (2,063)
Haynes, Rupert J 4:11:19 (13,194)
Haynes, Stephen C 4:37:05 (19,937)
Haynes, Stewart P 3:23:59 (3,257)
Haysom, Robert James 3:42:36 (6,330)
Hayter, Nick P 4:04:52 (11,623)
Hayward, Alexander D 4:20:28 (15,548)
Hayward, Byron 4:31:00 (18,347)
Hayward, Dean L 4:04:49 (11,612)
Hayward, Gavin P 3:50:52 (8,031)
Hayward, Jason D 4:29:35 (17,980)
Hayward, Joshua J 4:22:31 (16,078)
Hayward, Justin 3:53:51 (8,714)
Hayward, Michael 4:46:26 (22,326)
Hayward, Michael J 4:19:48 (15,371)
Hayward, Nick E 4:32:52 (18,864)
Hayward, Steve M 4:42:32 (21,339)
Haywood, Kevin 3:33:59 (4,754)
Haywood, Phil 4:03:56 (11,428)
Hayworth, Scott 4:05:30 (11,768)
Hazeldene, Richard 3:38:06 (5,514)
Hazell, Graham 4:58:23 (25,233)
Hazell, Justin L 4:10:17 (12,931)
Hazell, Peter 4:12:52 (13,617)
Hazell, Tim 3:31:22 (4,378)
Head, Alastaire J 3:50:58 (8,052)
Head, Douglas J 3:58:46 (10,179)
Head, Marcus 3:50:58 (8,052)
Head, Michael D 4:22:44 (16,131)
Head, Peter J 5:50:54 (32,407)
Heade, Stuart L 3:45:42 (6,927)
Heading, Richard 3:39:31 (5,761)
Headly, Nicholas I 5:03:35 (26,300)
Headly, William A 4:18:54 (15,133)
Heads, Stephen D 4:18:38 (15,064)
Heafey, Daniel B 5:20:23 (29,138)
Heaford, Matthew R 4:37:27 (20,024)
Heal, Gareth A 4:13:26 (13,783)
Heal, James E 6:18:47 (33,986)
Heal, Matthew W 3:12:16 (1,909)
Heal, Nicholas 4:04:55 (11,634)
Heal, Sam W 4:06:36 (12,016)
Heald, David S 4:42:17 (21,272)
Heale, Stanley K 4:54:07 (24,247)
Healey, Brynley 6:18:53 (33,991)
Healey, James R 6:03:19 (33,248)
Healing, Matthew J 4:05:59 (11,878)
Healy, Christopher M 3:23:11 (3,146)
Healy, Dan 4:03:27 (11,320)
Healy, Niall 5:10:18 (27,513)
Healy, Patrick 4:41:14 (21,024)
Healy, Sean 3:53:43 (8,682)
Healy, Tom 5:16:06 (28,518)
Heaney, Colm P 5:27:02 (30,053)
Heaney, Jon 5:14:24 (28,224)
Heap, Clive R 4:28:09 (17,593)
Heap, Jonathan 3:38:04 (5,505)
Heard, Andrew J 5:11:33 (27,737)
Heard, Peter A 4:18:26 (15,009)
Heargreaves, Stephen 4:16:37 (14,560)
Hearn, Andy D 3:59:09 (10,297)
Hearn, Clive D 3:22:51 (3,113)

Hearn, Tom 3:14:44 (2,205)
Hearne, David 3:59:33 (10,404)
Hearne, Matthew F 3:42:41 (6,352)
Heaselgrave, Daryl R 4:37:48 (20,120)
Heath, Adam S 4:34:09 (19,183)
Heath, Alan J 8:36:26 (35,344)
Heath, Andrew 4:31:59 (18,629)
Heath, Brenhan 4:22:40 (16,119)
Heath, Chris P 4:12:19 (13,473)
Heath, Frederick C 3:45:29 (6,891)
Heath, Russell 4:38:19 (20,257)
Heath, Tony H 4:49:59 (23,236)
Heath, Tristan 3:36:54 (5,295)
Heathcoat Amory, Simon 4:49:33 (23,133)
Heathcock, Laurence P 3:01:55 (1,111)
Heathcote, Adam 4:51:24 (23,595)
Heathcote, Alastair R 2:58:36 (875)
Heathcote, Daniel J 4:05:33 (11,785)
Heathcote, John 4:39:42 (20,645)
Heather, Alistair 4:20:00 (15,428)
Heather, Darren L 5:16:51 (28,624)
Heather, Richard 4:35:57 (19,664)
Heather, Simon P 4:56:27 (24,785)
Heaton, Andrew 4:02:43 (11,171)
Heaton, David C 5:00:49 (25,769)
Heaton, Jeremy P 4:38:34 (20,315)
Heaton, Michael 4:48:01 (22,745)
Heaven, Matthew P 3:51:16 (8,112)
Heaver, Mick J 4:32:58 (18,888)
Heaver, Simon 4:24:40 (16,614)
Heaviside, Richard J 3:42:55 (6,402)
Hebbron, Ross 5:29:48 (30,374)
Hebden, Mark A 4:18:09 (14,934)
Hebden, Paul 4:24:59 (16,706)
Hebreard, Jean Marc 4:59:30 (25,497)
Heck, Jochen 5:00:15 (25,643)
Heck, Matthew J 3:14:12 (2,146)
Heddon, Tony P 5:09:52 (27,436)
Hedger, Graham 2:56:05 (726)
Hedges, James J 4:44:18 (21,794)
Hedley, Nick J 3:58:19 (10,039)
Hedley, Richard J 4:07:54 (12,340)
Heeks, Paul J 4:37:42 (20,090)
Heeley, David G 3:24:24 (3,328)
Heeley, John 4:34:52 (19,371)
Heelis, James C 4:55:55 (24,667)
Heeramun, Kris 4:53:48 (24,175)
Hefesse, Ronnie 4:35:43 (19,607)
Heffell, Joseph 4:45:30 (22,079)
Heffer, Tim A 5:00:59 (25,805)
Hefferman, Terry 4:55:48 (24,640)
Hefford, Philip 5:33:39 (30,829)
Hefni, Mohamed 5:33:15 (30,781)
Hefni, Sherif 5:24:48 (29,767)
Hegarty, Anthony J 5:00:37 (25,733)
Hegarty, Hugo 4:00:54 (10,776)
Hegarty, Thomas A 4:19:20 (15,238)
Hegemann, Karsten 3:48:36 (7,534)
Heggarty, Colum 5:17:25 (28,700)
Heggie, Steven J 4:08:11 (12,415)
Hegley, Marc Richard 6:17:27 (33,902)
Hegvold, Knut 2:39:18 (181)
Hehir, Gerry 3:42:09 (6,242)
Heinrich, Fred 3:41:40 (6,142)
Helliwell, Alasdair W 3:29:40 (4,127)
Helliwell, Paul 2:46:39 (352)
Hellmers, Christopher L 3:31:08 (4,349)
Hellum, Frode 3:55:12 (9,085)
Hellyer, Patrick 3:28:36 (3,938)
Helne, Mark R 3:38:57 (5,667)
Helps, Michael W 4:57:55 (25,119)
Heltne, Svein Robert 3:45:47 (6,945)
Heming, Tim K 3:05:26 (1,330)
Heming Johnson, Alex E 4:11:08 (13,149)
Hemingway, Wayne 3:32:20 (4,520)
Hemmila, Jari A 2:58:48 (893)
Hemming, Gary 3:38:46 (5,638)
Hemming, Neil 4:43:48 (21,670)
Hemmings, James 4:53:37 (24,106)
Hemmings, Joseph P 4:49:01 (22,978)
Hemmings, Lance R 3:23:57 (3,254)
Henaughan, Andrew D 4:46:59 (22,478)
Hencher, Steve 6:01:59 (33,170)
Henchie, Richard W 5:03:18 (26,252)
Henderson, Andrew N 2:51:22 (504)
Henderson, Bernard J 3:13:58 (2,115)
Henderson, Brian S 4:23:58 (16,432)
Henderson, David 4:55:36 (24,597)
Henderson, David G 2:46:19 (340)
Henderson, Duncan L 5:14:01 (28,165)
Henderson, Gareth J 3:36:23 (5,212)
Henderson, Graham R 4:43:16 (21,534)
Henderson, Iain 4:50:22 (23,335)
Henderson, Jason 3:15:38 (2,298)
Henderson, Mark 4:35:55 (19,656)
Henderson, Matthew J 3:54:19 (8,844)
Henderson, Richard 4:40:37 (20,865)
Henderson, Rob 4:47:47 (22,669)
Henderson, Tom 5:26:19 (29,969)
Henderson, William John C 4:21:44 (15,889)
Henderson Russell, Charlie G 4:18:49 (15,108)
Hendrie, Clifford J 4:55:29 (24,569)
Hendry, Paul 3:54:26 (8,872)
Hendy, Manya 7:10:00 (35,050)
Heneghan, Jarlath T 3:20:10 (2,777)
Heneghan, Peter 3:39:52 (5,821)
Henesy, Ewan H 3:34:40 (4,906)
Heney, Kenneth J 3:05:01 (1,305)
Henley, Simon J 4:30:03 (18,113)
Henley, Stephen 6:00:39 (33,091)
Hennessey, Andrew R 5:45:10 (31,941)
Hennessey, Jamie 4:02:04 (11,033)
Hennessy, Paul 4:36:12 (19,726)
Henning, Stephen J 4:17:30 (14,769)
Hennis, Richard 3:57:42 (9,846)
Henry, Adam 4:03:52 (11,414)
Henry, Derek 4:13:09 (13,695)
Henry, Jean Maurice 3:00:06 (1,005)
Henry, Stephen 4:10:22 (12,947)
Henry, Steve 3:39:08 (5,706)
Hensby, Paul A 2:52:28 (542)
Henshaw, John 4:15:57 (14,381)
Henshaw, John A 3:44:04 (6,643)
Henshaw, Paul A 3:44:26 (6,705)
Henson, Jason 3:26:37 (3,621)
Henson, Karl A 4:22:55 (16,168)
Henson, Steven 4:05:24 (11,752)
Henville, Andrew 4:54:51 (24,418)
Henwood, Phillip W 4:13:22 (13,772)
Hepburn, Gerard S 4:10:46 (13,056)
Hepburn, Paul A 3:55:06 (9,065)
Hepditch, William 3:33:43 (4,706)
Hepworth, George W 3:52:59 (8,502)
Hepworth, Ian D 4:05:11 (11,703)
Herbert, Andrew J 5:33:11 (30,773)
Herbert, David R 4:06:46 (12,053)
Herbert, Edward B 3:38:32 (5,598)
Herbert, Graham A 5:23:07 (29,537)
Herbert, Neil M 4:42:30 (21,334)
Herbert, Raymond L 7:20:14 (35,152)
Herbert, Richard C 5:43:02 (31,774)
Hercules, Tyrone A 4:14:23 (14,012)
Herd, Marc 4:25:57 (16,974)
Herd, Martin W 3:12:53 (1,985)
Herd, Michael K 4:46:06 (22,227)
Herden, Ulrich 5:47:00 (32,094)
Herdman, Allan 3:14:16 (2,148)
Herenguel, Jean-Marie 3:58:50 (10,205)
Herentrey, Klaus 4:22:39 (16,111)
Heritage, Mick 4:10:29 (12,978)
Hernandez Garcia, Alberto 3:35:20 (5,018)
Hernon, Philip M 4:07:51 (12,326)
Heron, Derek 4:14:33 (14,042)
Heron, James R 3:08:36 (1,578)
Herrero Morales, Ivan 3:55:26 (9,139)
Herridge, Shaun A 4:34:33 (19,276)
Herridge, Steve 4:19:09 (15,197)
Herring, Dean 4:39:50 (20,676)
Herring, Matthew J 6:18:40 (33,952)
Herring, Michael 4:58:03 (25,148)
Herring, Stephen P 2:46:31 (346)
Herrington, Ian E 4:07:21 (12,199)
Herrington, Richard C 3:08:37 (1,579)
Herriott, Bryan P 4:18:06 (14,920)
Herron, Neil 3:45:02 (6,812)
Herve, Alliot 3:53:58 (8,745)
Herzmark, Thomas 4:29:23 (17,945)
Hesketh, Ben H 3:59:41 (10,451)
Hesketh, Will J 5:07:21 (26,971)
Heslop, Robert 4:25:17 (16,780)
Hession, Darren 4:51:44 (23,685)
Hester, Mark 4:36:18 (19,739)
Hetherington, Chris 5:56:42 (32,806)
Hetherington, Christopher 4:46:12 (22,248)
Hetherington, David 4:49:39 (23,165)
Hetherington, Graham D 3:31:21 (4,376)
Hetherington, Jeff 3:53:09 (8,548)
Hetherington, Jeff 4:52:40 (23,895)
Hetherington, Julian M 5:06:06 (26,745)
Hettinga, Dries 4:34:38 (19,296)
Heuer, Ingmar 4:08:29 (12,504)
Hevingham, Richard 4:55:47 (24,632)
Heward, James D 4:17:06 (14,664)
Hewer, David 5:05:03 (26,558)
Hewett, David 4:54:16 (24,279)
Hewett, Richard J 3:48:31 (7,513)
Hewison, Matthew R 5:15:02 (28,324)
Hewitson, Geoff F 3:14:41 (2,194)
Hewitt, Cameron L 5:55:29 (32,725)
Hewitt, Colin 4:28:50 (17,789)
Hewitt, Damien F 4:22:13 (16,006)
Hewitt, Kevan 3:54:38 (8,928)
Hewitt, Kevin 4:31:22 (18,462)
Hewitt, Kevin 5:46:06 (32,026)
Hewitt, Martyn G 3:46:37 (7,116)
Hewitt, Stefan 5:01:46 (25,965)
Hewitt, Stephen C 3:45:57 (6,977)
Hewitt, Stephen D 4:06:37 (12,026)
Hewitt, Thomas 4:43:33 (21,613)
Hewitt, Timothy C 3:21:40 (2,967)
Hewitt, Will 5:10:51 (27,610)
Hewlett, Benjamin A 5:37:18 (31,205)
Hewlett, David J 5:12:45 (27,934)
Hewlett, Ian M 4:05:00 (11,652)
Hewlett, Martin 3:11:35 (1,839)
Hewson, James 5:15:06 (28,337)
Hewson, Ross 4:53:01 (23,979)
Hext, Andrew 4:31:55 (18,611)
Hey, Andy 4:15:02 (14,172)
Hey, Peter 4:46:12 (22,248)
Heymann, Daniel 4:01:04 (10,807)
Heys, Andrew 3:53:17 (8,580)
Heys, Gary 4:38:05 (20,195)
Heys, Simon R 3:38:30 (5,588)
Heywood, Brian J 4:48:36 (22,877)
Heywood, Dave R 5:01:29 (25,910)
Heywood, Simon V 4:08:22 (12,475)
Hiatt, David 3:36:24 (5,215)
Hibberd, Daniel P 3:30:22 (4,230)
Hibberd, David 4:58:37 (25,302)
Hibberd, John 5:30:24 (30,447)
Hibberd, Roy George Frederick 4:52:06 (23,775)
Hibbert, Christopher S 3:26:21 (3,582)
Hibbert, Michael J 3:28:25 (3,915)
Hibbert, William J 4:23:18 (16,253)
Hibbott, Simon P 4:21:34 (15,834)
Hickey, Colm F 5:28:01 (30,148)
Hickey, James P 5:06:11 (26,759)
Hickey, Mark A 5:51:05 (32,419)
Hickey, Paul T 5:11:33 (27,737)
Hickey, Thomas 4:59:36 (25,518)
Hickling, Jeffrey P 4:38:35 (20,319)
Hickling, Phill 4:57:42 (25,069)
Hickman, Michael J 3:39:54 (5,834)
Hickman, Paul 4:17:38 (14,800)
Hickman, Simon C 3:38:28 (5,581)
Hickman, Stephen P 4:02:05 (11,037)
Hicks, Adrian T 4:45:58 (22,208)
Hicks, Brian W 5:07:31 (27,011)
Hicks, Chris J 4:24:45 (16,638)
Hicks, Dominic B 5:18:50 (28,947)
Hicks, Geoff I 4:32:51 (18,860)
Hicks, Harry 4:24:15 (16,511)
Hicks, Lee D 4:12:59 (13,656)
Hicks, Michael 5:35:30 (31,018)
Hicks, Peter J 5:25:07 (29,813)
Hicks, Robert C 4:01:40 (10,963)
Hicks, Russell D 4:49:23 (23,078)
Hicks, Stephen D 3:56:36 (9,489)

Hicks, Stuart M....3:08:45 (1,596)
Hicks, Thomas....3:45:29 (6,891)
Hickson, Spencer....4:25:38 (16,885)
Hidekazu, Chayama....4:00:16 (10,614)
Hieber, Ben G....3:07:58 (1,522)
Hiely, Philippe....4:57:59 (25,135)
Higgins, Brian D....5:24:17 (29,697)
Higgins, Christopher....5:42:45 (31,741)
Higgins, Daniel J....2:40:03 (193)
Higgins, Daniel M....4:19:48 (15,371)
Higgins, Ian M....3:51:03 (8,066)
Higgins, Rob W....4:29:17 (17,919)
Higgins, Robert A....3:40:42 (5,971)
Higgins, Sean....4:32:14 (18,689)
Higgins, Stuart....5:14:13 (28,195)
Higginson, Liam T....3:45:42 (6,927)
Higginson, Martin J....3:56:27 (9,446)
Higginson, Paul....4:40:54 (20,941)
Higginson, Sam J....4:10:19 (12,938)
Higglesden, Matt W....3:17:59 (2,527)
Higgs, Adam C....3:08:02 (1,526)
Higgs, Robert G....3:58:38 (10,137)
Higgs, Rowley T....4:02:20 (11,090)
Highfield, Colin Robert....3:33:40 (4,697)
Highfield, Terry D....4:05:16 (11,724)
Highfield-Robert, Guy....5:09:23 (27,345)
Highlands, Angus M....4:05:31 (11,773)
Hight, Chris M....5:20:26 (29,146)
Hilbery, Graham J....4:23:29 (16,308)
Hilbrands, Chris R....4:24:35 (16,590)
Hildebrandt, Rüdiger....4:46:21 (22,294)
Hildesley, Charlie....4:08:56 (12,600)
Hildrew, Ross George....4:23:47 (16,382)
Hiley, Andrew....5:45:34 (31,981)
Hill, Alex....5:23:58 (29,642)
Hill, Andrew G....3:51:00 (8,056)
Hill, Andrew J....4:38:02 (20,174)
Hill, Andrew M....4:32:26 (18,743)
Hill, Andy P....5:58:00 (32,916)
Hill, Bernie....4:32:14 (18,689)
Hill, Brett....4:27:40 (17,436)
Hill, Christian L....4:16:26 (14,506)
Hill, David R....4:13:12 (13,712)
Hill, Jonathan E....4:12:56 (13,643)
Hill, Jonathan M....3:21:03 (2,892)
Hill, Justin....4:46:59 (22,478)
Hill, Kenneth....3:12:06 (1,891)
Hill, Laurie B....3:57:39 (9,826)
Hill, Mark....4:23:00 (16,184)
Hill, Martin S....3:33:46 (4,719)
Hill, Matt G....4:23:53 (16,409)
Hill, Matthew T....4:28:26 (17,678)
Hill, Michael T....7:03:41 (34,987)
Hill, Michael V....3:39:28 (5,752)
Hill, Nick E....3:57:39 (9,826)
Hill, Nigel S....3:54:53 (8,992)
Hill, Patrick A....3:35:45 (5,107)
Hill, Peter D....3:01:36 (1,090)
Hill, Raymond....3:21:54 (2,998)
Hill, Richard D....3:30:20 (4,225)
Hill, Richard Hugh....4:38:57 (20,421)
Hill, Robert....4:44:43 (21,890)
Hill, Robert....6:14:34 (33,769)
Hill, Rodger P....4:45:59 (22,210)
Hill, Roy....4:15:41 (14,317)
Hill, Ryan M....4:22:36 (16,100)
Hill, Samuel L....4:25:55 (16,965)
Hill, Simon J....3:06:59 (1,432)
Hill, Simon R....4:31:19 (18,445)
Hill, Stephen D....7:17:45 (35,123)
Hill, Steve....3:26:32 (3,603)
Hill, Stuart K....3:38:04 (5,505)
Hill, Stuart P....3:16:33 (2,389)
Hill, Terry....4:25:28 (16,832)
Hill, Walter J....3:11:28 (1,823)
Hillas, Stephen E....3:43:32 (6,528)
Hiller, Christopher B....5:22:44 (29,470)
Hillery, Timothy B....5:00:52 (25,779)
Hilliard, Steve W....3:43:08 (6,448)
Hillier, Guy R....4:14:22 (14,007)
Hillier, Paul....3:52:13 (8,335)
Hillis, Tom P....4:40:56 (20,948)
Hillman, Mark W....4:05:23 (11,749)
Hillman, Matthew John....3:30:02 (4,181)
Hillman, Thomas....4:22:10 (15,995)
Hills, Adam S....3:21:43 (2,973)
Hills, Ben J....4:25:06 (16,736)
Hills, David I....4:50:28 (23,362)
Hills, Jamie P....4:26:14 (17,048)
Hills, Malcolm....5:09:43 (27,405)
Hills, Paul D....3:31:03 (4,335)
Hills, Richard D....6:05:38 (33,370)
Hills, Robert D....5:39:58 (31,493)
Hills, Stuart....4:05:22 (11,744)
Hillson, Martin D....4:26:06 (17,010)
Hillwood, Carl G....4:19:57 (15,408)
Hilmi, Aykut S....4:36:23 (19,766)
Hilpert, Dirk....4:18:25 (15,001)
Hilson, David....4:03:14 (11,279)
Hilton, Alan Gary....4:39:49 (20,670)
Hilton, Guy....5:09:08 (27,295)
Hilton, John....5:19:06 (28,985)
Hilton, Matthew....3:24:35 (3,355)
Hilton, Mick....4:06:32 (11,997)
Hinchliffe, Robert J....4:00:42 (10,720)
Hind, Lee Matthew....3:24:32 (3,346)
Hind, Robert D....3:31:35 (4,406)
Hindle, Shaun....5:59:14 (33,002)
Hindle Fisher, Robin C....5:06:43 (26,846)
Hinds, Andrew P....4:17:09 (14,683)
Hinds, David B....3:49:25 (7,708)
Hindson, Liam....4:35:46 (19,620)
Hine, Edward....4:16:05 (14,420)
Hine, William....4:11:16 (13,179)
Hines, Adam....3:25:01 (3,399)
Hines, Christopher W....3:47:15 (7,242)
Hines, Ian M....4:15:50 (14,357)
Hines, James....4:47:43 (22,657)
Hines, Mark F....5:11:16 (27,688)
Hines, Stuart C....3:44:08 (6,655)
Hingston, Robert....3:51:56 (8,263)
Hinojosa, Edelmiro....4:22:53 (16,164)
Hinson, Michael C....3:51:43 (8,212)
Hinson, Robert John....4:42:52 (21,431)
Hinton, Lee....5:00:44 (25,755)
Hinton, Lee Stiles....3:36:54 (5,295)
Hinton, Martin P....5:01:37 (25,936)
Hipshon, Mark....4:00:52 (10,766)
Hipworth, Antony E....4:46:24 (22,315)
Hird, Nick....3:29:12 (4,039)
Hirons, Trevor M....4:09:39 (12,764)
Hirotaka, Nunomiya....4:36:27 (19,787)
Hirsch, Michael....4:48:57 (22,960)
Hirschi, Markus....3:25:46 (3,497)
Hirst, Alastair R....3:15:31 (2,285)
Hirst, John....5:38:39 (31,348)
Hirst, Kelvin P....4:24:07 (16,477)
Hirst, Martyn J....3:34:54 (4,941)
Hirst, Simon C....4:42:12 (21,249)
Hiscock, Gareth David Lewis....4:23:04 (16,200)
Hiscocks, Eddie....3:58:06 (9,971)
Hiscox, Darren....2:36:51 (137)
Hiscutt, Benjamin S....4:05:15 (11,721)
Hisee, Robert....5:26:25 (29,982)
Hita Hita, Luis....3:07:02 (1,437)
Hitchcock, Mark....4:12:37 (13,555)
Hitchcock, Stephen J....3:54:23 (8,858)
Hitchcroft, Nicholas J....3:48:43 (7,548)
Hitchen, Mike....4:28:51 (17,795)
Hitchens, Richard J....4:03:31 (11,340)
Hitching, Ian....4:18:33 (15,042)
Hitchings, Stephen James....4:05:31 (11,773)
Hitner, Phillip R....5:37:04 (31,180)
Hitner, Simon R....4:20:10 (15,478)
Hitoshi, Takenoshita....3:59:40 (10,445)
Hitt, Dave....4:08:09 (12,407)
Hjorth, Kasper....3:46:37 (7,116)
Ho, Chiu Ling....3:43:34 (6,536)
Ho, Simon....5:44:34 (31,893)
Ho, Wai Tung....5:22:35 (29,450)
Hoang, David....4:14:10 (13,949)
Hoang, Man V....5:22:11 (29,388)
Hoare, Andrew S....5:23:05 (29,531)
Hoare, Dan J....4:01:48 (10,984)
Hoare, Ian P....2:58:55 (910)
Hoare, Lee....3:22:33 (3,074)
Hoare, Philip M....4:41:46 (21,158)
Hobbis, Stuart....4:39:15 (20,508)
Hobbs, Adam D....3:50:31 (7,951)
Hobbs, Charles....3:27:45 (3,819)
Hobbs, Daniel J....5:54:21 (32,642)
Hobbs, David....4:27:06 (17,282)
Hobbs, David P....5:23:37 (29,603)
Hobbs, Jonathan M....2:58:31 (869)
Hobbs, Mark S....2:49:15 (432)
Hobbs, Matthew D....5:17:43 (28,749)
Hobbs, Mike J....3:09:22 (1,652)
Hobbs, Nicholas D....5:20:18 (29,130)
Hobbs, Richard....3:28:11 (3,878)
Hobbs, Robert....4:16:46 (14,596)
Hobbs, Roger M....4:24:53 (16,679)
Hobbs, Stephen....5:25:59 (29,933)
Hobbs, Steve....2:57:27 (804)
Hobbs, Steve....3:33:05 (4,622)
Hobbs-Shoulder, Mark....6:05:46 (33,378)
Hobday, Alastari G....3:12:15 (1,908)
Hobday, Barry V....3:55:29 (9,154)
Hobden, David B....5:36:19 (31,103)
Hobe, Marc....4:24:15 (16,511)
Hobin, Kevin J....5:56:35 (32,798)
Hobins, Tom D....3:03:13 (1,182)
Hobson, Christopher W....4:47:58 (22,728)
Hobson, John D....3:39:53 (5,830)
Hobson, Kevin M....6:45:09 (34,712)
Hobson, Morne....3:12:45 (1,965)
Hobson, Robert G....3:41:44 (6,156)
Hockenhull, Robert J....3:31:10 (4,357)
Hockin, David I....5:35:27 (31,013)
Hocking, Peter L....4:00:34 (10,690)
Hocking, Thomas A....5:22:20 (29,408)
Hockley, Ryan P....3:57:32 (9,781)
Hoddell, David L....3:08:49 (1,601)
Hoddy, Liam S....4:20:58 (15,681)
Hodge, Brian M....5:22:07 (29,375)
Hodge, Justin....5:15:12 (28,353)
Hodge, Paul M....4:50:54 (23,459)
Hodge, Richard F....3:19:14 (2,642)
Hodge, Tony G....3:48:26 (7,496)
Hodges, Frederick P....4:21:35 (15,837)
Hodges, Nick....4:55:14 (24,514)
Hodges, Nick B....2:40:20 (201)
Hodges, Peter....5:48:56 (32,244)
Hodgetts, Andrew....3:51:03 (8,066)
Hodgetts, Benjamin....3:56:02 (9,322)
Hodgetts, Nathan J....6:24:38 (34,219)
Hodgins, David C....2:48:42 (415)
Hodgkin, Christopher J....3:27:26 (3,759)
Hodgkins, David A....4:51:25 (23,601)
Hodgkinson, Andy J....4:40:07 (20,757)
Hodgkiss, Guy J....4:33:52 (19,118)
Hodgkiss, Ian J....5:30:56 (30,515)
Hodgson, Chris L....2:51:42 (513)
Hodgson, David S....4:20:46 (15,627)
Hodgson, Duncan....3:05:42 (1,349)
Hodgson, Ian C....3:29:34 (4,110)
Hodgson, Keith A....6:26:13 (34,290)
Hodgson, Lee....3:42:58 (6,412)
Hodgson, Thomas E....5:23:25 (29,587)
Hodgson, Wayne....3:46:17 (7,037)
Hodson, Dominic....4:11:54 (13,358)
Hodson, Gregory A....4:14:11 (13,955)
Hodson, James A....5:12:22 (27,864)
Hodson, Philip....4:02:56 (11,217)
Hoeblyn, Oliver....5:01:34 (25,927)
Hoefling, Juergen....2:54:46 (649)
Hoejbjerg, Peter....4:26:28 (17,104)
Hoejbjerg, Torben....3:44:58 (6,796)
Hoejgaard, Steen....4:16:12 (14,448)
Hoepken, Wolfgang....3:16:33 (2,389)
Hoey, Jonathan R....4:18:37 (15,058)
Hoez, Jean Luc....4:33:21 (18,991)
Hoff, Kevin M....3:56:29 (9,454)
Hoffman, Andrew....4:33:10 (18,932)
Hoffmann, Reinhard....4:47:06 (22,515)
Hoffmann, Stefan....4:57:34 (25,048)
Hoffmeister, Marc....3:08:59 (1,619)
Hofmann, Raymond....3:26:51 (3,656)
Hogan, Adrian....6:01:30 (33,142)
Hogan, Dan....4:27:02 (17,264)

Hogan, James 3:48:28 (7,506)
Hogan, Michael 3:16:37 (2,396)
Hogan, Pat M 5:10:43 (27,588)
Hogan, Paul 3:40:00 (5,859)
Hogan, Sean 2:58:54 (909)
Hogarth, William T 5:12:03 (27,810)
Hogben, Richard L 4:38:54 (20,409)
Hogeman, Jozefus 4:15:45 (14,335)
Hogeveen, Marco 4:12:39 (13,560)
Hogg, Alastair 5:06:47 (26,865)
Hogg, Darren Thomas 3:58:25 (10,071)
Hogg, David 3:16:46 (2,411)
Hogg, Gerry F 2:38:51 (174)
Hogg, Graham T 3:56:19 (9,399)
Hogg, Iain W 3:31:09 (4,352)
Hogg, Simon 4:57:44 (25,073)
Hogger, Harry B 3:28:45 (3,964)
Hoglund, Greger 5:59:08 (32,995)
Hoglund, Mats 4:25:41 (16,904)
Hogsflesh, Philip Andrew 3:52:08 (8,304)
Holah, Daniel J 3:32:02 (4,472)
Holborn, Adrian 3:56:41 (9,529)
Holbourn, Mark W 5:16:45 (28,610)
Holbrook, Adam J 3:57:08 (9,658)
Holbrook, Michael B 4:01:32 (10,926)
Holbrook, Stuart J 5:34:38 (30,924)
Hold, Ian 5:07:35 (27,019)
Holda, Bartlomiej H 3:09:12 (1,639)
Holdcroft, Leslie D 2:50:35 (484)
Holden, Chris 4:52:50 (23,935)
Holden, Clive J 4:37:46 (20,111)
Holden, David F 3:50:40 (7,983)
Holden, Frank 5:04:35 (26,479)
Holden, Lee Stuart 3:05:30 (1,336)
Holden, Peter J 4:38:04 (20,189)
Holden, Stephen 3:48:25 (7,490)
Holden, Trevor I 3:24:08 (3,286)
Holding, Martin 3:43:47 (6,586)
Holding, Neil H 3:08:55 (1,610)
Holding, Phil 4:35:45 (19,617)
Holdsworth, Mark 5:17:25 (28,700)
Hole, Gareth M 4:37:25 (20,014)
Hole, Knut Eraker 2:43:13 (261)
Hole, Mark R 3:51:23 (8,136)
Hole, Richard J 4:08:51 (12,585)
Holehouse, Benjamin W 4:34:14 (19,204)
Holey, Graham B 5:13:34 (28,075)
Holford, Mark 5:58:36 (32,964)
Holford, Simon 3:48:24 (7,487)
Holgate, Craig 2:39:38 (189)
Holgate, Paul 4:34:53 (19,376)
Holinski, Paul A 5:12:27 (27,881)
Holladay, Michael R 3:26:10 (3,551)
Holland, Adam J 2:51:48 (518)
Holland, Brian N 3:56:01 (9,319)
Holland, Christian 4:54:28 (24,329)
Holland, John D 3:09:02 (1,621)
Holland, Kevin David 4:25:56 (16,968)
Holland, Mike 5:07:17 (26,957)
Holland, Paul 3:50:35 (7,966)
Holland, Paul M 4:17:39 (14,806)
Holland, Richard E 4:54:59 (24,444)
Holland, Stephen J 3:54:17 (8,835)
Hollands, Graham John 4:23:28 (16,299)
Hollands, John R 4:34:07 (19,176)
Holleran, Clive N 2:57:12 (794)
Hollick, Kevin 5:36:21 (31,108)
Hollick, Warren 5:48:50 (32,241)
Holliday, Alex 4:07:20 (12,191)
Holliday, Andrew P 4:59:11 (25,430)
Holliday, Asa 5:13:08 (28,012)
Holliday, Joel J 4:12:14 (13,447)
Holliday, John R 4:34:57 (19,395)
Holliday, Stuart 3:51:30 (8,170)
Holliday, Vincent J 4:33:34 (19,041)
Hollidge, David R 3:15:48 (2,318)
Hollidge, Paul 3:25:59 (3,529)
Hollinger, Graeme S 3:35:24 (5,033)
Hollings, Kevin Paul 3:56:57 (9,606)
Hollingsworth, Mark S 5:35:32 (31,022)
Hollingsworth, Noel S 4:19:24 (15,255)
Hollington, Michael D 5:24:20 (29,708)
Hollingworth, Ian 4:27:21 (17,356)
Hollingworth, Paul J 4:15:25 (14,262)
Hollinshead, Christopher D 2:49:57 (471)
Hollis, Anthony 4:00:27 (10,650)
Hollis, Keith L 3:32:31 (4,547)
Hollis, Paul H 3:19:55 (2,743)
Hollis, Stephen 6:21:25 (34,090)
Holliwell, Mark 6:19:09 (34,005)
Holloran, Alex 4:11:41 (13,310)
Holloway, Byron 4:25:31 (16,842)
Holloway, Chris R 3:58:18 (10,033)
Holloway, Darren P 3:58:42 (10,162)
Holloway, Martin J 3:46:54 (7,177)
Holloway, Nick 4:18:25 (15,001)
Holloway, Paul C 3:55:42 (9,221)
Holloway, Steve 5:25:01 (29,801)
Hollyoak, David 3:19:56 (2,745)
Hollywood, Adam 4:04:39 (11,572)
Holman, Andrew J 4:53:44 (24,152)
Holman, Mark C 4:13:58 (13,900)
Holmes, Aaron R 3:41:08 (6,055)
Holmes, Andrew P 4:19:57 (15,408)
Holmes, Chris J 5:53:26 (32,579)
Holmes, Clint Marcel 4:25:47 (16,933)
Holmes, Colin 3:24:43 (3,370)
Holmes, Damian 3:50:33 (7,959)
Holmes, Damian J 4:50:13 (23,285)
Holmes, Daniel J 4:30:08 (18,135)
Holmes, Daniel S 3:22:16 (3,046)
Holmes, Darrell 4:50:04 (23,257)
Holmes, Derrick W 3:54:58 (9,010)
Holmes, Dominic 3:54:09 (8,796)
Holmes, Dominic S 4:31:17 (18,429)
Holmes, Frank E 5:28:01 (30,148)
Holmes, Fraser 4:23:09 (16,220)
Holmes, Ian H 3:14:09 (2,141)
Holmes, Jamie A 3:38:12 (5,536)
Holmes, Karl 5:39:14 (31,420)
Holmes, Matthew M 4:10:08 (12,892)
Holmes, Michael A 4:45:49 (22,161)
Holmes, Mike 4:30:47 (18,299)
Holmes, Nick 5:21:37 (29,318)
Holmes, Paul K 3:39:13 (5,718)
Holmes, Robert W 5:24:23 (29,716)
Holmes, Robin 3:15:20 (2,265)
Holmes, Rory D 3:54:23 (8,858)
Holmes, Stephen P 4:08:36 (12,524)
Holmes, Stuart 6:26:58 (34,319)
Holmes, Thomas R 4:21:32 (15,824)
Holness, Gary 5:24:00 (29,648)
Holohan, Tom J 3:51:47 (8,225)
Holroyd, Christopher J 4:50:59 (23,483)
Holt, Alan W 5:23:34 (29,600)
Holt, Bob J 4:05:08 (11,690)
Holt, Chris P 3:54:31 (8,894)
Holt, Colin Alan 4:42:41 (21,381)
Holt, Jonathan D 4:00:32 (10,680)
Holt, Jonathan P 3:50:37 (7,974)
Holt, Malcom R 6:38:14 (34,595)
Holt, Mark 5:37:31 (31,228)
Holt, Martyn 5:22:27 (29,430)
Holt, Oliver 4:53:01 (23,979)
Holt, Roy S 4:29:13 (17,899)
Holt, Stewart G 4:40:23 (20,813)
Holt, Tim 4:43:52 (21,681)
Holterman, Jan 3:33:48 (4,724)
Holtmann, Klaus 4:39:29 (20,576)
Holtom, Geoffrey 4:36:22 (19,757)
Holton, Adam 3:35:16 (5,002)
Holubjowsky, John 4:34:54 (19,382)
Holyoak, Ian D 5:29:39 (30,353)
Holyoak, Tim S 3:55:04 (9,050)
Holyoake, Jamie 5:20:29 (29,150)
Homann, Heinz 3:52:15 (8,347)
Hombaiah, Umapathy (Umesh) 4:38:09 (20,215)
Home, Paul F 4:24:04 (16,459)
Homer, Mark 3:33:31 (4,678)
Homer, Nathan P 3:53:29 (8,621)
Homer, Richard D 7:15:36 (35,109)
Homersham, Jayce C 5:04:41 (26,490)
Homes, Simon P 3:36:49 (5,279)
Homewood, Gordon A 5:17:05 (28,655)
Homeyard, Lee J 4:01:34 (10,934)
Hommel, Sven 3:27:58 (3,852)
Hone, Dennis V 4:35:04 (19,434)
Hone, Eddie 3:59:40 (10,445)
Hones, Stephen R 2:57:35 (815)
Honeyball, Willie 4:24:33 (16,581)
Honeyman, Adam 4:42:40 (21,376)
Honeyman, Nicky 5:11:02 (27,645)
Honeyman, Richard N 4:04:53 (11,626)
Honeywood, Ian A 5:05:43 (26,685)
Honnor, Ian 3:21:31 (2,949)
Honour, Andrew M 3:34:16 (4,824)
Honour, Chris 4:03:22 (11,310)
Hontas, Patrick 3:57:20 (9,721)
Hooban, Matt S 4:16:25 (14,503)
Hood, Andrew 4:13:14 (13,724)
Hood, Graeme 4:06:52 (12,076)
Hood, Paul 2:56:44 (758)
Hood, Peregrine A 3:45:13 (6,839)
Hoods, Karl J 5:14:55 (28,296)
Hook, John C 3:06:21 (1,399)
Hook, Jonathon H 4:15:21 (14,243)
Hook, Joseph 3:20:45 (2,862)
Hook, Mathew 3:07:43 (1,503)
Hook, Maxwell J 3:08:14 (1,550)
Hook, Myles 5:07:38 (27,031)
Hook, Simon 4:16:34 (14,542)
Hooke, Andrew P 5:52:40 (32,522)
Hookway, Billy A 3:39:07 (5,703)
Hooper, Graham 6:04:04 (33,291)
Hooper, Gregg P 3:01:58 (1,114)
Hooper, Jason R 4:08:50 (12,580)
Hooper, Martin 3:26:29 (3,596)
Hooper, Martin J 4:02:59 (11,226)
Hooper, Michael G 4:11:59 (13,383)
Hooper, Nicholas J 3:01:23 (1,075)
Hooper, Patrick David 5:11:27 (27,719)
Hooper, Shaun I 3:58:11 (10,002)
Hooper, Steven C 2:58:46 (890)
Hooper, Tony 3:20:59 (2,888)
Hooton, Nick 4:14:37 (14,060)
Hope, Ben T 2:29:08 (59)
Hope, Geoff C 5:26:05 (29,948)
Hope, Jason N 3:59:36 (10,419)
Hope, Lee C 6:36:17 (34,548)
Hope, Martin A 4:29:38 (17,994)
Hope, Richard N 5:01:38 (25,940)
Hopgood, Tom J 4:20:30 (15,557)
Hopkin, William R 5:23:05 (29,531)
Hopkins, Andy P 3:57:25 (9,746)
Hopkins, Anthony P 4:29:14 (17,908)
Hopkins, Greg 3:55:03 (9,040)
Hopkins, James A 3:52:26 (8,388)
Hopkins, James D 5:00:55 (25,790)
Hopkins, Mark S 4:40:05 (20,752)
Hopkins, Martin J 3:55:57 (9,297)
Hopkins, Martin P 4:59:53 (25,573)
Hopkins, Michael D 3:42:37 (6,336)
Hopkins, Neil A 4:42:17 (21,272)
Hopkins, Neil W 4:31:02 (18,361)
Hopkins, Robert D 3:24:50 (3,384)
Hopkins, Scott D 3:05:39 (1,347)
Hopkins, Stephen D 3:34:01 (4,761)
Hopkins, Steven 5:55:10 (32,701)
Hopkins, Stuart D 2:58:34 (873)
Hopkins, Tony R 4:37:47 (20,115)
Hopkinson, Chris P 5:55:02 (32,690)
Hopkinson, David 4:21:24 (15,785)
Hopkinson, Giles H 5:36:26 (31,117)
Hopkinson, Tom 3:52:38 (8,440)
Hopper, Robert B 4:39:26 (20,562)
Hopping, Martyn J 5:21:35 (29,315)
Hopton, Steve 4:28:16 (17,638)
Horan, Gerald A 4:31:03 (18,370)
Horan, Glenn 4:30:56 (18,331)
Horch, Klaus 4:31:13 (18,409)
Hordern, Chris P 4:00:29 (10,664)
Hordley, Jeff 3:48:56 (7,603)
Horgan, James 3:17:39 (2,496)
Horler, Mark 5:07:25 (26,988)
Horman, James 2:47:53 (389)
Horn, Chris J 4:21:32 (15,824)
Horn, Colin M 5:17:34 (28,727)
Horn, Rolf 4:44:14 (21,775)
Horn, Steve 3:57:43 (9,850)

Horn, Steven Mark....4:29:43 (18,019)
Hornby, Colin J....3:59:03 (10,268)
Horne, Oliver R....4:17:36 (14,795)
Hornett, Andrew M....4:53:44 (24,152)
Hornsby, Graham R....3:39:07 (5,703)
Hornsby, Terry P....5:40:33 (31,548)
Horrell, Charlie....4:46:30 (22,345)
Horridge, Chris R....4:47:37 (22,634)
Horritt, Ian....3:21:28 (2,941)
Horrocks, Craig A....4:42:32 (21,339)
Horrocks, Rodney J....4:19:19 (15,235)
Horsenail, Rob J....4:13:18 (13,745)
Horsewell, Lewis....5:02:44 (26,162)
Horsfall, Donald Isaac....3:49:40 (7,761)
Horsfield, Craig....3:49:34 (7,743)
Horslen, Rob....4:51:33 (23,637)
Horsley, Andrew J....3:20:16 (2,795)
Horsley, Ben....3:27:48 (3,825)
Horsley, James....4:31:34 (18,518)
Horst, Latif....3:30:28 (4,248)
Horstead, Matt....4:56:40 (24,852)
Hort, Patrick R....3:53:29 (8,621)
Horth, Jody J....4:23:30 (16,314)
Horton, Andrew R....4:34:00 (19,153)
Horton, Anthony D....4:26:08 (17,020)
Horton, Clive....3:30:24 (4,237)
Horton, Colin....3:48:49 (7,574)
Horton, David....3:36:48 (5,276)
Horton, David Leslie....5:11:40 (27,757)
Horton, James A....6:22:46 (34,144)
Horton, John....3:33:53 (4,736)
Horton, Michael Eric....3:40:18 (5,915)
Horton, Peter H....3:12:02 (1,884)
Horton, Steven....5:30:06 (30,411)
Horwood, Alan....4:45:57 (22,206)
Hose, Sam J....4:37:24 (20,009)
Hoshi, Augusto....5:50:05 (32,345)
Hosie, Nick M....3:46:26 (7,071)
Hoskin, Jeremy D....4:13:52 (13,877)
Hoskin, Niall P....4:15:47 (14,344)
Hosking, David....6:07:30 (33,458)
Hosking, Paul J....4:09:02 (12,629)
Hoskins, Richard....3:11:22 (1,812)
Hoskyn, John....5:36:14 (31,095)
Hossain, Syed Z....4:55:13 (24,512)
Hostler, Keir M....4:42:36 (21,361)
Hothi, Gurdeep....5:25:52 (29,913)
Houchin, Anthony M....4:43:11 (21,511)
Hough, Julian....2:42:17 (243)
Hough, Tim M....4:02:49 (11,191)
Houghton, Dave....3:34:12 (4,811)
Houghton, Jamie N....5:11:52 (27,786)
Houghton, Mark E....4:39:40 (20,634)
Houghton, Michael J....3:18:46 (2,595)
Houghton, Phil D....4:38:47 (20,372)
Houghton, Steve D....3:57:08 (9,658)
Houghton, Toby J....3:40:11 (5,899)
Houghton, Tony D....5:30:18 (30,440)
Houlgrave, Paul....5:18:19 (28,837)
Houlihan, Colin....5:55:27 (32,723)
Hoult, Nigel S....3:07:57 (1,521)
Hoult, Spencer G....4:24:51 (16,670)
Houlton, Nicholas J....2:35:17 (118)
Hourican, Brendan Louis....5:29:20 (30,312)
Hourigan, Patrick....4:26:51 (17,222)
House, Daniel R....3:49:21 (7,696)
House, Dean....3:14:35 (2,180)
House, Paul G....3:12:38 (1,948)
House, Rich....3:57:40 (9,836)
House, Stephen W....3:23:26 (3,181)
Houston, Duncan....5:51:58 (32,481)
Houston, Michael....3:33:50 (4,729)
Houston, Michael A....6:35:05 (34,523)
Houston, Robert....4:59:08 (25,418)
Houston, Ross D....2:31:48 (80)
Hovden, Jon....3:38:57 (5,667)
Hovell, Andrew N....4:28:19 (17,651)
Hovell, David I....4:39:28 (20,571)
Howard, Andrew....5:10:08 (27,485)
Howard, Andrew S....3:27:58 (3,852)
Howard, Andrew T....4:06:28 (11,984)
Howard, Ben R....3:15:01 (2,234)
Howard, Charles D....3:24:07 (3,282)
Howard, Christian....5:09:26 (27,353)
Howard, Gareth S....3:27:58 (3,852)
Howard, Gary....5:39:34 (31,453)
Howard, Graham I....5:09:06 (27,289)
Howard, Jonathan....4:06:10 (11,919)
Howard, Mark C....5:14:56 (28,303)
Howard, Mark W....4:28:41 (17,744)
Howard, Milton E....5:19:32 (29,039)
Howard, Paul J....3:36:39 (5,259)
Howard, Roger John Dymoke....4:51:45 (23,689)
Howard, Stephen....4:56:53 (24,906)
Howard, Tom....3:07:04 (1,439)
Howarth, Alastair G....4:44:42 (21,889)
Howarth, Mark W....4:09:45 (12,788)
Howarth, Neil....4:00:57 (10,786)
Howarth, Peter D....4:10:06 (12,879)
Howarth, Raymond....4:23:33 (16,327)
Howarth, Raymond P....3:29:16 (4,057)
Howarth, Richard J....2:45:01 (316)
Howarth, Simon J....4:48:13 (22,791)
Howat, Gordon J....4:35:30 (19,546)
Howden, Stephen D....4:05:02 (11,659)
Howden-Windell, Nicholas J....4:15:12 (14,214)
Howe, Andrew M....5:13:09 (28,015)
Howe, Bradley E....4:05:29 (11,766)
Howe, Christopher....3:25:45 (3,494)
Howe, Clayton....5:02:32 (26,124)
Howe, David A....3:52:12 (8,328)
Howe, David J....4:40:07 (20,757)
Howe, Gary....5:42:25 (31,711)
Howe, Kevin J....4:34:55 (19,391)
Howe, Martin....4:01:14 (10,844)
Howe, Sean T....5:07:18 (26,960)
Howe, Thomas....4:47:11 (22,542)
Howell, Christopher E....7:22:36 (35,162)
Howell, David R....3:54:49 (8,973)
Howell, Gareth....3:58:32 (10,110)
Howell, John....4:10:24 (12,955)
Howell, Mark....4:33:10 (18,932)
Howell, Matthew....4:23:55 (16,419)
Howell, Scott....2:55:44 (710)
Howell, Scott L....4:55:54 (24,665)
Howell, Simon....3:58:03 (9,954)
Howells, David C....4:53:37 (24,106)
Howells, Mark R....4:39:13 (20,499)
Howells, Robert D....3:37:39 (5,432)
Howers, Simon....4:40:31 (20,840)
Howes, Alan D....5:38:14 (31,300)
Howes, Chris....4:45:50 (22,171)
Howes, Jeremy P....4:30:39 (18,269)
Howes, José A....4:27:29 (17,387)
Howes, Neil R....4:47:08 (22,525)
Howes, Paul R....3:56:26 (9,437)
Howes, Paul R....4:13:36 (13,824)
Howes, William J....3:21:36 (2,960)
Howie, Jonathan R....4:24:32 (16,577)
Howkins, Josh J....3:43:59 (6,627)
Howlett, James E....6:32:53 (34,470)
Howlett, Kevin C....3:26:13 (3,560)
Howlett, Richard J....5:33:08 (30,767)
Howley, Vincent I....3:14:19 (2,155)
Howton, Rupert....5:14:13 (28,195)
Hoye, Alex....5:12:10 (27,838)
Hoyle, Andrew J....4:04:36 (11,563)
Hoyle, Christopher J....6:10:07 (33,567)
Hoyle, Jon R....4:28:45 (17,760)
Huang, Eugene J....3:36:26 (5,222)
Hubbard, John R....4:19:29 (15,277)
Hubble, Peter L....5:15:44 (28,462)
Huber, Manfred....4:01:35 (10,939)
Hubert, Werner....4:15:21 (14,243)
Huck, Ernest F....3:39:11 (5,715)
Hucker, Mark....3:01:02 (1,053)
Huckett, James....5:21:26 (29,288)
Hucks, David....3:29:14 (4,046)
Hudd, David....3:19:52 (2,733)
Huddleston, Chris J....5:57:39 (32,889)
Hudi-Dinnage, David....3:54:58 (9,010)
Hudson, Damian R....4:05:56 (11,866)
Hudson, Daniel....4:13:11 (13,707)
Hudson, David....3:38:29 (5,585)
Hudson, Frank....3:31:13 (4,363)
Hudson, John M....4:23:10 (16,223)
Hudson, John W....4:49:51 (23,209)
Hudson, Mark....3:01:43 (1,097)
Hudson, Mark....5:24:23 (29,716)
Hudson, Nicholas P....5:21:59 (29,363)
Hudson, Pat....3:11:19 (1,811)
Hudson, Paul R....3:54:02 (8,763)
Hudson, Paul R....7:18:53 (35,138)
Hudson, Philip....4:29:11 (17,884)
Hudspith, John E....3:04:44 (1,285)
Hufton, Daniel....3:38:30 (5,588)
Huggett, Nick J....3:52:21 (8,372)
Huggett, Ross....5:14:27 (28,234)
Huggins, Peter C....4:30:41 (18,276)
Huggins, Richard....4:55:03 (24,460)
Hughes, Aidan P....4:49:03 (22,985)
Hughes, Andrew....4:41:25 (21,058)
Hughes, Andrew B....4:20:38 (15,584)
Hughes, Andy....4:41:20 (21,045)
Hughes, Aneirin Mason....5:09:47 (27,428)
Hughes, Ceri D....4:44:16 (21,783)
Hughes, Chris J....4:33:22 (18,998)
Hughes, Craig W....5:08:14 (27,132)
Hughes, Dafydd A....3:55:00 (9,025)
Hughes, Darren....3:52:58 (8,498)
Hughes, Darren....6:07:32 (33,462)
Hughes, Dave....3:06:27 (1,403)
Hughes, David J....3:32:56 (4,603)
Hughes, David P....4:33:43 (19,077)
Hughes, David R....3:11:14 (1,800)
Hughes, Dean....2:52:49 (553)
Hughes, Duncan R....3:47:15 (7,242)
Hughes, Frank D....3:34:36 (4,896)
Hughes, Gareth D....4:38:21 (20,266)
Hughes, Gareth J....3:59:56 (10,530)
Hughes, Gary J....3:28:35 (3,936)
Hughes, Giles....4:37:57 (20,155)
Hughes, Ian....5:09:43 (27,405)
Hughes, Ian M....5:46:03 (32,021)
Hughes, James....5:35:47 (31,049)
Hughes, James....5:48:35 (32,226)
Hughes, Jeff....6:19:09 (34,005)
Hughes, Jeremy George....4:16:59 (14,642)
Hughes, Jerome....6:43:55 (34,694)
Hughes, John....4:08:33 (12,513)
Hughes, John....4:40:37 (20,865)
Hughes, John F....6:42:12 (34,668)
Hughes, Jonathan D....3:12:24 (1,920)
Hughes, Jonathan R....3:56:28 (9,449)
Hughes, Justin....6:07:31 (33,461)
Hughes, Keith M....6:55:14 (34,898)
Hughes, Kevin Anthony....4:50:05 (23,261)
Hughes, Marc A....4:57:03 (24,938)
Hughes, Mark A....4:02:23 (11,102)
Hughes, Mark A....4:38:32 (20,307)
Hughes, Martin....5:04:31 (26,459)
Hughes, Michael W....3:58:30 (10,097)
Hughes, Nicholas J....4:27:17 (17,338)
Hughes, Nigel P....4:44:35 (21,853)
Hughes, Paul....4:30:00 (18,095)
Hughes, Peter G....3:46:53 (7,174)
Hughes, Richard G....5:05:17 (26,603)
Hughes, Richard G....5:48:35 (32,226)
Hughes, Richard J....4:17:06 (14,664)
Hughes, Robert....4:54:36 (24,360)
Hughes, Samuel D....3:25:46 (3,497)
Hughes, Simon David....4:21:21 (15,774)
Hughes, Simon G....4:21:57 (15,933)
Hughes, Steve A....4:03:06 (11,249)
Hughes, Tom J....3:39:18 (5,729)
Hughes, Wayne A....4:41:11 (21,008)
Hughes, William R....3:23:11 (3,146)
Hughes-Morris, Trefor....4:31:18 (18,438)
Hugill, Tim....4:03:09 (11,260)
Huguet, Christian....4:42:34 (21,348)
Huisken, Wilhelmus....4:23:23 (16,274)
Huitson, Tom....4:39:08 (20,473)
Huizer, Pieter....3:49:14 (7,672)
Hulbert, Graham....4:43:42 (21,649)
Hulbert, Martin....3:14:34 (2,176)
Hulcoop, Stephen V....4:51:35 (23,644)
Hulett, Carl S....3:31:22 (4,378)
Hull, Andrew....4:11:33 (13,266)
Hull, Ben....4:22:19 (16,025)

Hull, Dean	5:13:20	(28,042)
Hull, Geoffrey R	5:54:17	(32,637)
Hull, Jonathan A	3:58:12	(10,007)
Hull, Keith	3:21:40	(2,967)
Hull, Patrick C	4:30:01	(18,103)
Hull, Richard	5:29:52	(30,387)
Hull, Stephen J	3:55:38	(9,203)
Hullett, Dave C	4:50:56	(23,467)
Hully, Andrew S	3:22:40	(3,094)
Hulme, Alex M	3:46:05	(6,998)
Hulme, Jeremy	9:11:45	(35,360)
Hulme, Mark S	4:27:20	(17,352)
Hulme, Simon J	4:13:18	(13,745)
Hulme, Steve J	4:21:08	(15,727)
Hulme, Tony	4:34:49	(19,358)
Hulse, Christopher T	3:04:43	(1,284)
Humble, Jonathan R	4:08:27	(12,496)
Hume, David	3:51:37	(8,191)
Hume, Marc S	5:22:06	(29,374)
Humfrey, David	6:17:30	(33,906)
Humm, Andrew M	3:46:53	(7,174)
Hummerson, Jonathan J	4:47:22	(22,571)
Humpherson, Roy	3:22:38	(3,089)
Humphrey, Chris	4:28:02	(17,551)
Humphrey, David A	4:22:35	(16,096)
Humphrey, John G	5:05:54	(26,713)
Humphrey, Richard A	4:02:42	(11,168)
Humphreys, Andy	3:26:46	(3,645)
Humphreys, Ian S	3:19:40	(2,704)
Humphreys, Jake G	4:29:47	(18,031)
Humphreys, Kent	4:28:52	(17,801)
Humphreys, Matthew	6:00:47	(33,100)
Humphreys, Nick	4:48:24	(22,830)
Humphreys, Paul	4:38:40	(20,342)
Humphreys, Peter I	2:53:10	(565)
Humphreys, Tony	3:50:56	(8,047)
Humphreys, Troy D	4:09:50	(12,816)
Humphreys-Evans, Giles W	3:08:11	(1,544)
Humphries, Darren Nicholas	5:30:11	(30,428)
Humphries, Del A	6:16:21	(33,861)
Humphries, Stephen D	5:25:27	(29,853)
Humpreies, Graham A	6:02:19	(33,191)
Hundley, Rob J	3:50:00	(7,833)
Hunjan, Sanjay	4:58:00	(25,140)
Hunsdale, Jamie P	5:07:36	(27,024)
Hunstone, David P	4:48:34	(22,866)
Hunt, Andrew C	4:34:15	(19,209)
Hunt, Andy J	5:26:37	(30,007)
Hunt, Anthony	4:33:58	(19,145)
Hunt, Anthony C	3:58:42	(10,162)
Hunt, Christopher P	3:12:41	(1,955)
Hunt, Christopher W	3:43:32	(6,528)
Hunt, Dan	4:45:14	(22,022)
Hunt, Daniel J	4:54:31	(24,341)
Hunt, Daniel M	5:30:58	(30,522)
Hunt, David M	4:58:54	(25,362)
Hunt, Jeffrey P	4:36:46	(19,856)
Hunt, Jonathan P	3:37:24	(5,385)
Hunt, Lee J	6:48:13	(34,774)
Hunt, Mark P	5:06:24	(26,793)
Hunt, Matt	3:24:40	(3,364)
Hunt, Matt G	3:01:50	(1,104)
Hunt, Matthew J	4:26:15	(17,051)
Hunt, Matthew J	5:34:59	(30,965)
Hunt, Michael I	6:46:18	(34,727)
Hunt, Paul A	5:23:15	(29,563)
Hunt, Richard S	4:29:06	(17,858)
Hunt, Simon A	3:09:08	(1,633)
Hunt, Stephen J	4:11:09	(13,153)
Hunt, Steve B	6:48:13	(34,774)
Hunt, Steven	3:39:01	(5,689)
Hunt, Terry	4:26:14	(17,048)
Hunt, Thomas	6:39:53	(34,626)
Hunt, Thomas C	3:38:16	(5,546)
Hunt, Tim	5:31:35	(30,590)
Hunt, Wayne	4:52:12	(23,795)
Hunt, William J	4:37:50	(20,128)
Hunter, Alistair N	4:20:55	(15,668)
Hunter, Allistair	4:53:15	(24,033)
Hunter, Andrew	5:35:54	(31,061)
Hunter, Bruce W	4:09:07	(12,644)
Hunter, Chris	6:56:45	(34,916)
Hunter, Craig R	3:33:56	(4,745)
Hunter, David	4:47:12	(22,546)
Hunter, Gareth	3:28:28	(3,924)
Hunter, Harry W	3:53:55	(8,726)
Hunter, Ian	4:47:57	(22,724)
Hunter, Ian Francis	3:25:26	(3,452)
Hunter, Ian W	3:24:00	(3,259)
Hunter, Joel E	4:10:40	(13,025)
Hunter, John W	4:03:42	(11,366)
Hunter, Jon M	3:48:57	(7,605)
Hunter, Kevin T	4:49:15	(23,036)
Hunter, Luke	5:39:24	(31,434)
Hunter, Mark Iain	3:45:26	(6,878)
Hunter, Mark R	4:29:07	(17,865)
Hunter, Paul	4:04:09	(11,478)
Hunter, Richard J	5:21:24	(29,283)
Hunter, Richard S	3:56:20	(9,406)
Hunter, Simon	3:37:14	(5,359)
Hunter, Tony	3:02:46	(1,165)
Hunter, Winston A	3:54:53	(8,992)
Huntley, David	4:43:20	(21,559)
Huntley, George E	5:27:45	(30,116)
Huntley, Simon T	3:50:44	(8,001)
Hunton, James	4:12:03	(13,398)
Hunziker, Urs	4:57:01	(24,933)
Hurd, Andrew J	3:31:40	(4,418)
Hurd, Chris F	5:03:18	(26,252)
Hurdley, Paul	3:26:53	(3,663)
Hurdman, Peter J	4:03:17	(11,288)
Hurley, Bevan	3:53:14	(8,568)
Hurley, Joe	3:22:30	(3,068)
Hurley, Michael T	5:15:44	(28,462)
Hurley, Patrick	6:49:25	(34,801)
Hurley, Russell	6:26:01	(34,281)
Hurrell, Darren	6:01:02	(33,114)
Hurrell, Geoff	3:35:08	(4,985)
Hurrell, Mark J	3:12:45	(1,965)
Hurren, Mark A	4:27:44	(17,459)
Hurry, Graeme J	3:30:08	(4,194)
Hursey, Martin I	4:42:26	(21,309)
Hurst, Alan	5:16:32	(28,567)
Hurst, David	7:31:47	(35,233)
Hurst, Mike	4:16:08	(14,434)
Hurst, Paul	3:29:53	(4,166)
Hursthouse, Carl D	4:01:17	(10,853)
Hurtado, Gustavo	4:29:37	(17,988)
Hurworth, Mark L	4:33:13	(18,948)
Husband, Ian S	3:13:45	(2,095)
Hush, Graham W	4:18:15	(14,951)
Huskinson, Nick B	3:33:18	(4,651)
Hussain, Jamil	5:32:36	(30,703)
Hussein, Abid	7:06:04	(35,016)
Hussein, Liaquat	3:56:37	(9,500)
Hussey, Alexander D	2:58:58	(918)
Hussey, Gareth	4:27:45	(17,470)
Hussey, John	3:41:12	(6,071)
Hussey, John Paul	5:07:42	(27,043)
Hussey, Paul	4:09:32	(12,732)
Hussey, Richard D	3:59:02	(10,261)
Hutchence, Tim	3:55:37	(9,199)
Hutcheson, Adam	4:26:17	(17,064)
Hutcheson, Chris	4:48:36	(22,877)
Hutcheson, Luke	4:09:06	(12,642)
Hutchin, Anthony D	3:18:46	(2,595)
Hutchings, David	4:34:33	(19,276)
Hutchings, Lian R	4:13:03	(13,667)
Hutchings, Mark	4:02:17	(11,084)
Hutchings, Mark Andrew	4:15:44	(14,329)
Hutchins, Cheryl W	4:51:37	(23,650)
Hutchins, Tim R	4:09:06	(13,163)
Hutchinson, Barry	5:25:19	(29,833)
Hutchinson, James	3:33:59	(4,754)
Hutchinson, James Robert	3:11:46	(1,855)
Hutchinson, Keith C	4:53:45	(24,159)
Hutchinson, Neil	3:34:15	(4,819)
Hutchinson, Paul A	3:46:50	(7,162)
Hutchinson, Peter G	3:01:58	(1,114)
Hutchinson, Peter R	4:49:30	(23,116)
Hutchison, Stuart	3:35:48	(5,117)
Hutchon, Grant	4:57:11	(24,962)
Huthwaite, Philip	4:43:47	(21,663)
Hutson, Daniel J	4:23:59	(16,437)
Hutten Czapski, Stanislas	4:15:01	(14,168)
Hutton, Ben	5:57:59	(32,914)
Hutton, Charles D	3:18:07	(2,541)
Hutton, Kenneth M	4:02:25	(11,108)
Hutton, Kieran J	4:03:21	(11,303)
Hutton, Martin	5:04:51	(26,511)
Hutton, Paul M	4:08:39	(12,533)
Hutton, Stephen G	4:13:41	(13,842)
Hutton-Squire, Doug J	3:23:47	(3,229)
Huxford, Jonathan	4:45:55	(22,192)
Huxley, Philip J	4:20:32	(15,568)
Huynh, Phuc Minh	4:28:09	(17,593)
Huyser, Riaan	4:35:11	(19,458)
Huysse-Smith, Jon R	6:11:10	(33,607)
Hviid, Morten	4:17:38	(14,800)
Hyam, David G	3:22:25	(3,056)
Hyam, Richard E	3:55:03	(9,040)
Hyams, James	3:54:06	(8,781)
Hyatt, Gary Francis	4:21:53	(15,917)
Hyde, Carl	4:07:54	(12,340)
Hyde, Chris	4:41:55	(21,184)
Hyde, David B	4:43:37	(21,628)
Hyde, Ian	6:15:11	(33,800)
Hyde, Jonathan M	3:41:40	(6,142)
Hyde, Matthew E	3:14:34	(2,176)
Hyde, Richard	4:08:08	(12,403)
Hyde, Simon Robert	4:40:53	(20,936)
Hydes, Gareth M	4:27:03	(17,269)
Hyland, Andrew	3:08:37	(1,579)
Hyland, Glynn M	5:18:04	(28,801)
Hyland, Gordon	5:28:36	(30,222)
Hylton, Neville	4:06:34	(12,010)
Hyman, Michael	5:42:44	(31,738)
Hynd, Michael	5:23:39	(29,607)
Hynes, Richard	3:44:44	(6,754)
Hynes, Stephen	4:48:25	(22,831)
Hynes, Stuart M	4:21:31	(15,820)
Hyun, Seong Chan	4:59:03	(25,399)
Iaboni, Sandro	5:02:47	(26,179)
Iafrate, Marcus B	3:57:29	(9,762)
Ianich, Aido	3:25:24	(3,444)
I'Anson, Anthony	5:13:39	(28,088)
Iball, John K	3:59:55	(10,523)
Ibbotson, Ian R	3:14:25	(2,166)
Ibeson, David C	5:18:14	(28,826)
Ibiza, José M	3:31:49	(4,443)
Ibrahim, Nader	5:34:39	(30,927)
Icardi, Sebastien	3:23:12	(3,151)
Iceton, Ben	4:29:48	(18,036)
Iceton, Glenn P	4:00:22	(10,628)
Iddenden, Andrew S	6:25:55	(34,276)
Ide, Philip J	3:24:36	(3,356)
Ide, Steve W	4:08:40	(12,539)
Ideus, Ken	4:20:42	(15,604)
Idle, Matthew R	3:57:33	(9,789)
Iglesias, Luis	4:55:20	(24,535)
Ignoto Gil, Manu	2:43:30	(270)
Iles, Stephen B	3:50:54	(8,038)
Ilie, Ciprian S	4:33:49	(19,101)
Illien, Dominique	4:42:36	(21,361)
Illingworth, Colin J	5:28:08	(30,168)
Illman, Christopher H	2:32:51	(89)
Illsley, Robert J	6:44:46	(34,703)
Imam, Hisham	4:44:58	(21,948)
Imeson, Benjamin G	3:26:34	(3,615)
Imeson, Michael D	4:05:06	(11,679)
Immos, Reto	3:58:20	(10,046)
Impey, Grant H	4:56:29	(24,795)
Imray, Daniel	3:28:19	(3,903)
Imrie, Gavin A	4:13:28	(13,787)
Imrie, Graeme	4:34:12	(19,197)
Imschoot, Jurgen	4:03:35	(11,352)
Inbar, Tomer J	4:13:19	(13,752)
Ince, Carl S	4:06:26	(11,978)
Ince, Mark Goodman	3:15:48	(2,318)
Ind, Andrew J	3:07:05	(1,442)
Ineson, Andrew	4:39:02	(20,444)
Ineson, James	4:29:38	(17,994)
Ineson, Philip	4:56:41	(24,854)
Ing, Martin S	5:39:18	(31,426)
Ingham, Lee R	4:18:42	(15,081)
Ingham, Richard F	4:13:16	(13,736)
Ingle, Neil	3:37:02	(5,325)
Ingle, Phil	4:55:15	(24,520)
Ingle, Steve	3:27:29	(3,771)

Ingledew, Neil	3:28:46 (3,967)	
Ingles, James H	4:18:08 (14,929)	
Ingles, Philip	4:38:53 (20,407)	
Inglis, Aaron S	4:50:02 (23,244)	
Inglis, Alan J	3:34:44 (4,913)	
Inglis, Glenn	5:11:48 (27,775)	
Inglis, Jon J	5:25:24 (29,843)	
Ingold, Andrew James	3:55:59 (9,307)	
Ingram, Anthony	5:06:47 (26,865)	
Ingram, Guy	4:17:17 (14,712)	
Ingram, Mark A	5:29:29 (30,328)	
Ingram, Michael	3:40:46 (5,990)	
Ingram, Michael ;	4:05:11 (11,703)	
Ingram, Steven J	3:36:10 (5,185)	
Ingram-Tedd, Paul	5:38:59 (31,394)	
Ingrey, Vince W	7:27:57 (35,206)	
Ings, Ross A	3:12:58 (2,002)	
Inman, Mathew J	3:42:31 (6,305)	
Inman, Paul	3:36:07 (5,175)	
Innes, Adrian	5:21:41 (29,329)	
Innes, Andrew P	4:22:59 (16,181)	
Innes, Richard G	3:59:08 (10,290)	
Inwood, David P	3:48:07 (7,424)	
Inwood, Laurence	4:13:10 (13,700)	
Ioannou, Ioannis	5:06:40 (26,837)	
Ioannou, John M	5:19:37 (29,052)	
Ions, Philip John	3:20:35 (2,835)	
Ioseliani, George	5:20:44 (29,182)	
Iqbal, Mohammad M	3:59:43 (10,467)	
Iqbal, Omar	3:34:34 (4,886)	
Iratzoquy, Jean-Christophe	3:28:28 (3,924)	
Irby, Jonathan	5:21:17 (29,266)	
Irens, Duncan R	3:40:41 (5,968)	
Irlam, Michael J	4:42:05 (21,220)	
Irlam, Stewart	4:42:05 (21,220)	
Irons, Alan G	5:45:25 (31,965)	
Irons, Matthew	4:14:28 (14,023)	
Irvine, Andrew	3:41:58 (6,197)	
Irvine, Angus D	4:52:43 (23,910)	
Irvine, Duncan Stuart	3:23:26 (3,181)	
Irvine, James	2:55:05 (668)	
Irvine, Justin S	4:08:47 (12,566)	
Irvine, Kevin	4:27:25 (17,374)	
Irvine, Robert D	3:49:08 (7,651)	
Irvine, Scott	4:57:51 (25,097)	
Irvine-Smith, Paul	3:57:41 (9,842)	
Irving, John	4:21:55 (15,927)	
Irving, Michael	4:23:38 (16,346)	
Irving, Stephen C	6:03:03 (33,233)	
Irwin, Mark	5:02:44 (26,162)	
Irwin, Steven R	4:20:04 (15,446)	
Isaac, Robert	5:45:13 (31,947)	
Isaacs, Richard Michael	4:29:50 (18,048)	
Isaacs, William	3:53:07 (8,536)	
Isbitsky, Reuben	4:23:42 (16,364)	
Iseke, Hans	3:49:11 (7,665)	
Isenberg, Steve F	3:43:59 (6,627)	
Ishmael, Michael F	3:53:30 (8,628)	
Isip, Darryl	5:20:45 (29,186)	
Islam, Rejaul	5:06:36 (26,823)	
Islam, Sayeed Z	3:50:45 (8,007)	
Islas, José	4:04:45 (11,594)	
Isley, Simon	4:22:38 (16,105)	
Islip, Alastair M	4:51:35 (23,644)	
Isman, Renaud	3:46:57 (7,191)	
Isnardi, Tino	3:50:26 (7,929)	
Isola, Nicholas	4:18:01 (14,891)	
Ison, Daniel	4:58:09 (25,179)	
Ispahani, Adil	5:25:55 (29,922)	
Issa, Salim	3:58:50 (10,205)	
Isted, Andrew J	4:56:56 (24,921)	
Isted, Ian Barry	4:03:46 (11,379)	
Ito, Yo	3:09:55 (1,700)	
Iuliano, Domenico	4:07:45 (12,302)	
Ivanic, Vladimir	4:56:36 (24,829)	
Ive, Martin J	3:08:43 (1,591)	
Ivens, Derek M	3:02:39 (1,159)	
Ivens, Gareth R	3:59:46 (10,481)	
Ivers, David P	3:53:40 (8,667)	
Iveson, William J	4:26:05 (17,006)	
Ivie, Jody	4:55:17 (24,527)	
Ivins, Scott	3:56:02 (9,322)	
Ivory, Adrian	4:15:19 (14,233)	

Ivory, Graham J	3:08:01 (1,525)	
Ivory, Julian	4:08:26 (12,493)	
Ivory, Kenneth	3:00:34 (1,025)	
Ivory, Stephen	5:39:07 (31,413)	
Izard, Daivd	5:11:11 (27,670)	
Izza, Michael D	5:29:54 (30,390)	
Izzard, Matthew J	5:46:01 (32,015)	
Izzidien, Ali	3:49:09 (7,658)	
Jaaskelainen, Kari	4:16:59 (14,642)	
Jabour, Stephen J	4:05:18 (11,734)	
Jabri, Oussama	3:15:44 (2,310)	
Jack, Graeme	4:33:10 (18,932)	
Jack, Grisoni	4:59:10 (25,428)	
Jack, Hugo	4:14:41 (14,074)	
Jack, Lee	4:37:01 (19,922)	
Jack, Peter	4:14:43 (14,088)	
Jacklin, Mark	3:52:29 (8,403)	
Jackman, Mark	5:39:52 (31,482)	
Jacks, Chistopher A	4:45:17 (22,033)	
Jacks, Jeff C	5:14:23 (28,219)	
Jackson, Allan G	3:30:53 (4,311)	
Jackson, Andrew	2:43:15 (262)	
Jackson, Andrew	3:47:27 (7,278)	
Jackson, Andrew	5:13:32 (28,071)	
Jackson, Anthony C	2:51:34 (509)	
Jackson, Anthony R	2:37:37 (149)	
Jackson, Barry	4:26:34 (17,139)	
Jackson, Chris A	4:33:35 (19,046)	
Jackson, Christopher A	3:36:51 (5,287)	
Jackson, David	3:48:06 (7,422)	
Jackson, Derek	3:30:58 (4,325)	
Jackson, Duncan M	4:10:41 (13,033)	
Jackson, Edward P	4:41:51 (21,174)	
Jackson, Gareth	4:26:06 (17,010)	
Jackson, George D	3:00:55 (1,046)	
Jackson, Gregor M	4:57:49 (25,089)	
Jackson, Guy R	5:25:08 (29,816)	
Jackson, James	3:51:55 (8,262)	
Jackson, Jonathan P	5:26:41 (30,013)	
Jackson, Joshua K	4:37:45 (20,104)	
Jackson, Kevin J	3:15:01 (2,234)	
Jackson, Lewis J	5:04:45 (26,500)	
Jackson, Malcolm C	3:53:08 (8,541)	
Jackson, Mark	5:17:24 (28,697)	
Jackson, Mark B	4:10:06 (12,879)	
Jackson, Martyn R	4:22:53 (16,164)	
Jackson, Mathew I	4:16:49 (14,609)	
Jackson, Mick E	6:47:24 (34,753)	
Jackson, Neil	2:56:16 (731)	
Jackson, Nick M	3:58:57 (10,237)	
Jackson, Nick W	5:47:39 (32,140)	
Jackson, Nigel	7:56:34 (35,306)	
Jackson, Nigel G	3:34:08 (4,796)	
Jackson, Paul B	3:14:54 (2,220)	
Jackson, Paul Terence	4:26:25 (17,090)	
Jackson, Paul Timothy	3:19:02 (2,621)	
Jackson, Phil D	4:12:26 (13,499)	
Jackson, Philip	4:03:46 (11,379)	
Jackson, Richard A	5:00:55 (25,790)	
Jackson, Robert	2:49:34 (446)	
Jackson, Robert P	5:49:22 (32,283)	
Jackson, Sam J	4:16:26 (14,506)	
Jackson, Simon	3:20:36 (2,838)	
Jackson, Simon A	3:09:12 (1,639)	
Jackson, Simon D	2:58:45 (889)	
Jackson, Simon W	3:57:37 (9,806)	
Jackson, Stephen P	3:02:24 (1,142)	
Jackson, Stephen R	4:57:28 (25,026)	
Jackson, Stephen R	5:53:09 (32,561)	
Jackson, Stuart	4:37:56 (20,149)	
Jackson, Stuart R	3:01:29 (1,080)	
Jackson, Tim S	4:49:40 (23,171)	
Jacky, Leenaert	4:52:36 (23,880)	
Jacob, Mark R	4:34:15 (19,209)	
Jacobs, David	4:15:58 (14,387)	
Jacobs, Gavin	3:58:12 (10,007)	
Jacobs, Jon	5:36:29 (31,122)	
Jacobs, Michael F	7:54:07 (35,301)	
Jacobs, Paul	3:43:09 (6,457)	
Jacobs, Raymond	4:33:37 (19,054)	
Jacobs, Robert E	5:35:19 (31,000)	
Jacobs, Simon	4:44:21 (21,805)	
Jacobs, Thomas	4:51:31 (23,625)	

Jacobs, Wayne	4:00:18 (10,618)	
Jacobson, Brett A	3:18:29 (2,573)	
Jacobson, Paul A	3:50:29 (7,941)	
Jacobson, Scott M	4:02:33 (11,141)	
Jaconelli, Matthew	4:07:02 (12,114)	
Jacquenin, Laurent	3:58:19 (10,039)	
Jacques, Daniel	3:14:47 (2,207)	
Jacques, Gros	3:48:46 (7,557)	
Jacques, Juchs	4:23:51 (16,399)	
Jacques, Lepreux	3:54:53 (8,992)	
Jacques, Norbert	5:05:53 (26,711)	
Jacques, Piccoli	4:46:22 (22,302)	
Jacques, Reverberri	3:53:14 (8,568)	
Jadwat, Junaid	5:15:25 (28,404)	
Jafarov, Fuad	4:50:42 (23,424)	
Jaffe, Felix W	3:10:45 (1,758)	
Jago, Daniel S	5:02:08 (26,049)	
Jago, Stephen J	4:28:39 (17,736)	
Jagpal, Sukhijit Singh S	7:31:36 (35,231)	
Jahans, Stephen Desmond	5:10:15 (27,505)	
Jahn, Uwe	3:04:45 (1,289)	
Jakeway, Paul	4:06:05 (11,897)	
Jakob, Andreas	5:19:20 (29,014)	
Jal, Conan R	5:00:51 (25,773)	
Jales, John A	4:50:37 (23,400)	
Jalloh, Abraham A	2:59:26 (951)	
James, Adrian	5:54:21 (32,642)	
James, Alan	5:38:43 (31,357)	
James, Andrew	3:58:49 (10,198)	
James, Anthony Mark	5:35:05 (30,981)	
James, Arthur J	5:43:10 (31,789)	
James, Ashley	3:50:45 (8,007)	
James, Ben	4:25:01 (16,716)	
James, Benjamin A	4:20:49 (15,641)	
James, Brad	3:05:47 (1,356)	
James, Brian R	5:01:10 (25,853)	
James, Bruce E	6:20:20 (34,046)	
James, Colin	2:49:07 (426)	
James, David C	4:29:04 (17,850)	
James, David R	4:10:43 (13,044)	
James, Edward	4:04:00 (11,450)	
James, Edward	4:46:29 (22,341)	
James, Gary	5:07:45 (27,052)	
James, Huw	3:40:44 (5,978)	
James, Ian F	2:42:06 (236)	
James, Kevan J	2:43:21 (265)	
James, Martyn	3:20:06 (2,769)	
James, Matthew R	4:27:41 (17,441)	
James, Michael B	5:30:03 (30,403)	
James, Michael J	4:19:55 (15,404)	
James, Michael P	5:36:36 (31,133)	
James, Mick	4:14:50 (14,122)	
James, Mike	4:33:30 (19,022)	
James, Oliver	4:03:53 (11,420)	
James, Paul D	4:20:45 (15,619)	
James, Philip L	4:00:10 (10,587)	
James, Richard G	2:54:19 (619)	
James, Robert S	2:42:37 (247)	
James, Roy L	3:45:27 (6,885)	
James, Ryan P	3:35:28 (5,043)	
James, Simon A	2:38:26 (163)	
James, Simon W	4:37:45 (20,104)	
James, Steve	4:53:57 (24,211)	
James, Steve	5:18:31 (28,874)	
James, Thomas	4:09:01 (12,624)	
James, Vernon	5:00:46 (25,763)	
James-Bowen, Rod M	5:02:11 (26,061)	
James-Cuthbert, Declan C	5:58:25 (32,952)	
Jameson, William	4:30:11 (18,146)	
Jamieson, Alex	3:17:08 (2,449)	
Jamieson, David I	4:31:20 (18,451)	
Jamieson, Fraser W	3:09:37 (1,669)	
Jamieson, Neil	4:28:32 (17,706)	
Jamieson, Stuart	4:41:37 (21,122)	
Jammes, Thierry	3:59:21 (10,351)	
Jandl, Helmut	4:42:14 (21,260)	
Janes, Edward M	4:09:34 (12,741)	
Janes, Steve R	4:40:29 (20,829)	
Janes, Trevor B	4:34:54 (19,382)	
Janker, Andreas	2:41:46 (228)	
Jankowski, Mark	5:06:43 (26,846)	
Jannerling, Jon-Hakan	5:35:32 (31,022)	
Janowski, Peter	3:49:08 (7,651)	

Jansen, Adrianus	4:12:05 (13,410)	
Janvrin, Benoit	3:57:00 (9,619)	
Jaques, Martin C	5:42:14 (31,698)	
Jarach, Stefano	5:46:59 (32,089)	
Jardot, Daniel	3:39:12 (5,716)	
Jarman, Daniel C	4:24:39 (16,605)	
Jarman, Lucy M	5:32:59 (30,752)	
Jarman, Matt	4:05:32 (11,780)	
Jarman, Michael	4:50:30 (23,371)	
Jarman, Nick	3:24:13 (3,302)	
Jarman, Nick D	3:55:42 (9,221)	
Jarman, Paul	3:53:27 (8,615)	
Jarratt, Matthew J	3:35:14 (4,997)	
Jarrett, Andy	3:49:42 (7,774)	
Jarrett, Dean	5:37:29 (31,222)	
Jarrett, Michael T	3:46:45 (7,145)	
Jarrett, Neale A	3:42:35 (6,325)	
Jarrett, Nicholas S	4:09:54 (12,833)	
Jarrett, Robert N	3:17:25 (2,478)	
Jarrett, Thomas L	2:56:10 (729)	
Jarrey, Christopher D	6:11:22 (33,617)	
Jarrold, Robert S	5:01:04 (25,834)	
Jarry, Florent	3:18:10 (2,544)	
Jarvest, Christian J	3:51:07 (8,076)	
Jarvis, Andrew	3:58:09 (9,990)	
Jarvis, Daniel	5:39:14 (31,420)	
Jarvis, Daniel M	5:04:58 (26,539)	
Jarvis, Ian	4:52:30 (23,863)	
Jarvis, Keith P	4:54:00 (24,219)	
Jarvis, Lee David	4:43:59 (21,715)	
Jarvis, Paul	5:45:49 (32,003)	
Jarvis, Sam D	4:26:33 (17,130)	
Jarvis, Steve	4:31:56 (18,618)	
Jarvis, William R	3:59:45 (10,477)	
Jashapara, Dipak	7:50:08 (35,289)	
Jason, Stephen	4:56:37 (24,832)	
Jasper, Andrew	5:40:16 (31,521)	
Jaubert, Fabrice	4:20:40 (15,591)	
Jauffres, Jerome	2:50:23 (478)	
Javadi, Mustafa	4:18:18 (14,962)	
Javangwe, Spencer Dzimbanhete	5:58:37 (32,967)	
Javicoli, Gerard	4:28:52 (17,801)	
Javkin, Daniel	4:21:53 (15,917)	
Jaworski, Markus	3:13:23 (2,050)	
Jay, Christopher	4:01:18 (10,858)	
Jay, Edward	4:52:44 (23,912)	
Jay, Nick	3:57:57 (9,917)	
Jay, Paul	4:35:17 (19,487)	
Jay, Stephen	4:35:42 (19,599)	
Jayasekaran, Julius K	5:41:25 (31,621)	
Jeacock, Simon	4:20:54 (15,662)	
Jeal, Damian T	5:31:28 (30,577)	
Jeal, Stephen A	4:11:23 (13,222)	
Jean Aime, Boutelier	3:18:46 (2,595)	
Jean Christophe, Alessandra	3:07:07 (1,448)	
Jean Louis, Estrata	5:22:59 (29,515)	
Jean Luc, Cherriere	3:48:06 (7,422)	
Jean Luc, Quelo	4:43:15 (21,529)	
Jean Marc, Hebert	3:36:01 (5,158)	
Jean Michel, Gsell	4:03:02 (11,237)	
Jean Michel, Lecointe	3:07:37 (1,493)	
Jean Noel, Ober	3:37:31 (5,405)	
Jean Paul, Hubert	4:37:41 (20,088)	
Jean Pierre, Dorval	5:28:19 (30,193)	
Jean-Baptiste, Emeka	3:30:20 (4,225)	
Jeanes, Robert	5:17:38 (28,736)	
Jeanes, Sean R	5:17:39 (28,738)	
Jean-Paul, Desmond	4:46:24 (22,315)	
Jeevan, Joshua	6:27:02 (34,327)	
Jefferies, Chris	4:59:21 (25,464)	
Jefferies, Daniel	4:49:36 (23,147)	
Jefferies, David	5:06:43 (26,846)	
Jefferies, David L	4:54:08 (24,250)	
Jefferies, Tom	3:17:07 (2,444)	
Jefferies, William Edward	3:25:02 (3,400)	
Jefferson, Neil S	3:48:32 (7,520)	
Jeffery, Anthony	3:41:54 (6,186)	
Jeffery, Graham	6:27:53 (34,354)	
Jeffery, John R	4:18:37 (15,058)	
Jeffery, Martin J	3:51:57 (8,269)	
Jeffery, Michael	4:53:09 (24,012)	
Jeffery, Robert J	4:48:03 (22,754)	
Jeffery, Stephen P	2:38:13 (162)	
Jefford, Mark	3:27:40 (3,809)	
Jeffrey, David	5:48:51 (32,242)	
Jeffrey, Mark Andrew	4:27:14 (17,317)	
Jeffrey, Ricky J	4:20:13 (15,490)	
Jeffrey, Steven	3:44:04 (6,643)	
Jeffrey, Tom	3:44:04 (6,643)	
Jeffreys, Aled R	3:04:37 (1,271)	
Jeffreys, John	3:54:49 (8,973)	
Jeffries, Alan	5:54:51 (32,673)	
Jeffries, John L	3:59:40 (10,445)	
Jeffries, Kevin J	3:05:53 (1,363)	
Jeffries, Stacey	3:20:15 (2,792)	
Jeffries, Tom	3:44:55 (6,787)	
Jeffs, Neal	3:12:20 (1,917)	
Jeggo, Stuart	5:47:45 (32,146)	
Jehu, Gareth E	3:34:22 (4,846)	
Jelbert, Mark J	3:17:07 (2,444)	
Jelfs, Luke E	3:35:01 (4,962)	
Jelley, David G	3:02:20 (1,139)	
Jelley, Derek A	4:32:33 (18,769)	
Jelley, Nick Duncan	3:50:18 (7,903)	
Jelley, Paul J	3:34:06 (4,789)	
Jellicoe, Will B	5:45:00 (31,928)	
Jenkin, Daniel L	2:55:42 (709)	
Jenkin, Philip T	4:15:28 (14,275)	
Jenkins, Adam M	4:46:14 (22,255)	
Jenkins, Alun Rhys	4:14:13 (13,964)	
Jenkins, Andrew	4:04:28 (11,538)	
Jenkins, Antony	4:53:31 (24,074)	
Jenkins, Ben C	3:55:25 (9,135)	
Jenkins, Christopher	4:21:29 (15,804)	
Jenkins, David William	4:14:46 (14,102)	
Jenkins, Jody K	3:57:49 (9,880)	
Jenkins, John H	5:08:02 (27,090)	
Jenkins, Jonathan M	4:18:51 (15,118)	
Jenkins, Keith N	4:28:43 (17,751)	
Jenkins, Michael Anthony	4:14:01 (13,910)	
Jenkins, Michael D	4:19:16 (15,226)	
Jenkins, Paul	3:55:36 (9,191)	
Jenkins, Paul J	3:37:27 (5,391)	
Jenkins, Peter H	5:58:05 (32,925)	
Jenkins, Rhodri	4:17:34 (14,787)	
Jenkins, Robert Alun Stephen	4:28:28 (17,688)	
Jenkins, Robert E	4:46:25 (22,324)	
Jenkins, Steve J	4:58:22 (25,228)	
Jenkins, Tim	6:23:12 (34,160)	
Jenkins, Tim D	3:18:18 (2,553)	
Jenkinson, Damian	4:20:52 (15,653)	
Jenkinson, Douglas M	5:15:03 (28,328)	
Jenkinson, John J	6:00:00 (33,051)	
Jenkinson, Timothy	3:46:44 (7,140)	
Jenks, Andrew	5:38:12 (31,298)	
Jenner, Christopher	4:48:50 (22,928)	
Jenner, Damien B	4:29:13 (17,899)	
Jenner, Marc	5:45:41 (31,993)	
Jenner, Martin W	3:42:58 (6,412)	
Jenner, Nigel	5:14:22 (28,218)	
Jenner, Rick	3:09:09 (1,634)	
Jennings, Adrian E	4:58:41 (25,316)	
Jennings, Andrew	3:19:15 (2,645)	
Jennings, Colin S	3:21:27 (2,939)	
Jennings, Edward	7:03:37 (34,986)	
Jennings, George C	4:29:36 (17,986)	
Jennings, John F	4:11:33 (13,266)	
Jennings, Mark	4:25:34 (16,861)	
Jennings, Odran J	4:24:06 (16,471)	
Jennings, Paul J	4:57:55 (25,119)	
Jennings, Robert	3:06:32 (1,405)	
Jennings, Stuart P	4:17:44 (14,830)	
Jensen, Herluf	3:54:23 (8,858)	
Jensen, Peter Munk	5:07:00 (26,908)	
Jensson, Eirikur Magnus	3:21:07 (2,903)	
Jephcott, Mat	4:43:34 (21,617)	
Jerrit, Giles Z	3:56:02 (9,322)	
Jess, Michael	4:30:18 (18,176)	
Jesson, Allen	6:38:58 (34,609)	
Jessop, Martin T	4:07:21 (12,199)	
Jessop, Simon J	3:58:05 (9,963)	
Jessop, Steve	4:17:25 (14,749)	
Jewell, Daniel	3:18:51 (2,607)	
Jewell, Ian E	4:35:36 (19,571)	
Jewell, Kevin J	4:32:59 (18,895)	
Jewell, Michael J	4:15:19 (14,233)	
Jewell, Neville	4:04:00 (11,450)	
Jewell, Steven	3:54:55 (9,000)	
Jewitt, Anthony J	3:07:25 (1,468)	
Jewitt, Darren C	3:42:31 (6,305)	
Jewkes, Simon	4:52:19 (23,829)	
Jeyes, Eric	4:37:45 (20,104)	
Jhina, Pritesh	5:46:41 (32,064)	
Jimenez Garcia, Jesus Manuel	3:52:29 (8,403)	
Jimenez Garcia, José Juan	3:49:46 (7,792)	
Jimeno Enrique, Miguel Angel	3:50:26 (7,929)	
Jina, Amit	4:15:22 (14,246)	
Jinabhai, Rajesh	5:20:24 (29,142)	
Joannou, Victor	3:59:31 (10,395)	
Joannou, Xenephos	4:37:21 (19,994)	
Jobe, Nick	5:43:50 (31,834)	
Jobson, Simon	4:05:34 (11,792)	
Jobson, Stephen	3:56:46 (9,554)	
Joddrell, Peter	4:26:48 (17,205)	
Joel, Deharte	3:21:19 (2,923)	
Joel, Fievet	3:15:36 (2,293)	
Joel, Grant	4:35:49 (19,630)	
Joenson, Lars	4:13:05 (13,680)	
Johal, Gurvir	5:52:28 (32,513)	
Johal, Manpreet S	5:08:23 (27,157)	
Johal, Rana S	7:11:47 (35,075)	
Johannesen, Stein H.	3:39:17 (5,726)	
Johansen, Anders Gunnar	2:58:15 (852)	
Johansen, Torbjoern-Einar	4:01:18 (10,984)	
Johansson, Patrik	3:12:57 (1,998)	
Johansson, Roger	4:09:32 (12,732)	
John, Andrew R	3:49:28 (7,723)	
John, Ben	5:11:01 (27,642)	
John, Chris	4:05:13 (11,715)	
John, Nicholas W	4:35:21 (19,506)	
John, Oliver C	3:30:39 (4,278)	
Johns, Alwyn M	4:27:31 (17,395)	
Johns, Colin A	4:38:44 (20,360)	
Johns, Matthew P	4:06:19 (11,953)	
Johns, Nicholas	4:49:50 (23,205)	
Johnsen, Trond-Rolf	5:45:10 (31,941)	
Johnson, Andrew D	4:37:47 (20,115)	
Johnson, Andrew R	4:51:01 (23,494)	
Johnson, Andrew William	4:39:02 (20,444)	
Johnson, Andy	5:23:11 (29,543)	
Johnson, Andy J	5:19:28 (29,032)	
Johnson, Anthony J	5:01:01 (25,815)	
Johnson, Ben	4:11:33 (13,266)	
Johnson, Ben R	4:32:34 (18,777)	
Johnson, Ben Sambourne Romann	4:23:15 (16,241)	
Johnson, Billy	5:06:55 (26,887)	
Johnson, Brian	5:42:09 (31,685)	
Johnson, Chris J	4:44:56 (21,936)	
Johnson, Chris S	4:43:57 (21,703)	
Johnson, Christopher A	4:38:00 (20,165)	
Johnson, Colm M	3:59:38 (10,428)	
Johnson, David	4:50:28 (23,362)	
Johnson, David	5:01:48 (25,970)	
Johnson, David C	4:33:17 (18,968)	
Johnson, David J	4:58:51 (25,349)	
Johnson, David P	5:24:28 (29,728)	
Johnson, David T	3:25:49 (3,504)	
Johnson, David William W	3:41:40 (6,142)	
Johnson, Eustace	4:58:27 (25,253)	
Johnson, Gary	4:16:05 (14,420)	
Johnson, Gerald C	4:11:26 (13,238)	
Johnson, Iain A	4:10:01 (12,858)	
Johnson, Ian	3:50:36 (7,972)	
Johnson, James	5:15:56 (28,494)	
Johnson, Jeremy J	4:45:14 (22,022)	
Johnson, John S	5:24:15 (29,693)	
Johnson, Karl	3:37:16 (5,365)	
Johnson, Kenny	4:04:55 (11,634)	
Johnson, Kirk	4:57:38 (25,057)	
Johnson, Lee	3:33:53 (4,736)	
Johnson, Malcolm R	3:59:39 (10,437)	
Johnson, Mark C	3:53:04 (8,523)	
Johnson, Mark S	3:48:11 (7,442)	
Johnson, Mark S	4:07:57 (12,348)	
Johnson, Matthew	4:59:45 (25,544)	
Johnson, Michael	5:13:45 (28,113)	
Johnson, Michael	6:37:30 (34,581)	
Johnson, Michael B	5:06:00 (26,726)	
Johnson, Michael D	5:00:38 (25,736)	

Johnson, Michael John	4:08:17 (12,447)
Johnson, Miles David	4:29:10 (17,876)
Johnson, Neil	3:52:34 (8,415)
Johnson, Nicholas	4:16:38 (14,567)
Johnson, Nicholas A	4:40:11 (20,774)
Johnson, Nicky M	5:18:28 (28,864)
Johnson, Olafur	6:06:32 (33,412)
Johnson, Patrick	5:22:22 (29,416)
Johnson, Paul T	4:30:34 (18,245)
Johnson, Paul W	3:15:08 (2,246)
Johnson, Pete G	3:35:47 (5,112)
Johnson, Peter G	5:12:19 (27,856)
Johnson, Phillip R	5:28:11 (30,175)
Johnson, Ray D	4:01:26 (10,893)
Johnson, Richard A	5:15:19 (28,389)
Johnson, Robert	4:16:20 (14,482)
Johnson, Robin	5:06:54 (26,886)
Johnson, Robert P	3:10:09 (1,711)
Johnson, Steve C	5:24:14 (29,690)
Johnson, Tim	4:28:23 (17,665)
Johnson, Tony	3:01:30 (1,083)
Johnson, William David	4:06:25 (11,975)
Johnston, Gordon A	3:37:41 (5,436)
Johnston, Graham	2:59:50 (985)
Johnston, Greg	4:55:42 (24,614)
Johnston, Guy	4:06:59 (12,100)
Johnston, Kim Hawley	4:38:52 (20,396)
Johnston, Magnus D	4:07:00 (12,106)
Johnston, Peter M	3:58:57 (10,237)
Johnston, Scott	4:31:05 (18,382)
Johnston, Tom	3:51:25 (8,147)
Johnston Stewart, Edward	4:14:43 (14,088)
Johnstone, Allan D	4:13:32 (13,807)
Johnstone, Iain R	4:02:08 (11,048)
Johnstone, Paul S	3:58:22 (10,059)
Johnstone, Robert M	3:57:28 (9,756)
Johnstone-Scott, Giles	4:51:54 (23,729)
Johnstone-Scott, Ian	4:51:54 (23,729)
Joliffe, George W	4:22:41 (16,124)
Jolliffe, David T	4:40:00 (20,726)
Jolly, Neil M	4:39:50 (20,676)
Jolly, Simon J	4:39:59 (20,719)
Jolly, Steve D	3:54:36 (8,919)
Jolly, Tom	4:50:14 (23,292)
Jones, Adrian	3:44:58 (6,796)
Jones, Alex N	2:59:38 (969)
Jones, Allan	4:38:08 (20,211)
Jones, Allan S	2:55:39 (706)
Jones, Andi	2:15:20 (13)
Jones, Andrew D	3:53:08 (8,541)
Jones, Andrew L	4:55:55 (24,667)
Jones, Andrew M	4:43:34 (21,617)
Jones, Andy D	3:09:07 (1,629)
Jones, Andy S	4:38:52 (20,396)
Jones, Anthony	4:03:29 (11,327)
Jones, Anthony A	5:14:16 (28,202)
Jones, Anthony Mark	4:32:24 (18,728)
Jones, Ashley	4:08:59 (12,616)
Jones, Ben	3:14:24 (2,163)
Jones, Bernard	4:18:17 (14,959)
Jones, Bevis	4:29:02 (17,843)
Jones, Brian	5:21:17 (29,266)
Jones, Brian J	4:07:52 (12,331)
Jones, Bryan	4:06:05 (11,897)
Jones, Bryan A	5:08:22 (27,155)
Jones, Carl	5:02:30 (26,117)
Jones, Carl G	4:26:39 (17,168)
Jones, Chris	4:24:50 (16,663)
Jones, Chris	4:42:10 (21,239)
Jones, Chris	4:44:11 (21,765)
Jones, Chris Edward Francis	4:25:50 (16,945)
Jones, Christopher	4:32:25 (18,735)
Jones, Christopher	4:33:09 (18,931)
Jones, Christopher E	5:32:18 (30,669)
Jones, Christopher J	6:18:40 (33,952)
Jones, Christopher W	3:30:05 (4,189)
Jones, Christopher W	4:26:44 (17,187)
Jones, Clive G	4:55:14 (24,514)
Jones, Craig J	4:38:52 (20,396)
Jones, Craig W	4:57:10 (24,957)
Jones, Damien	5:00:00 (25,601)
Jones, Dan	3:59:20 (10,345)
Jones, Daniel	3:48:51 (7,585)

Jones, Daniel G	5:31:52 (30,624)
Jones, Daniel T	4:29:35 (17,980)
Jones, Danny J	3:21:42 (2,971)
Jones, Danny W	5:38:32 (31,336)
Jones, Darren	4:33:14 (18,954)
Jones, Darren	4:37:03 (19,932)
Jones, Darren	2:55:09 (675)
Jones, Darren F	4:03:00 (11,232)
Jones, Darren S	4:58:01 (25,146)
Jones, Darrin R	4:26:13 (17,044)
Jones, Dave	4:13:37 (13,829)
Jones, David	3:15:44 (2,310)
Jones, David	5:09:24 (27,347)
Jones, David A	4:45:01 (21,967)
Jones, David A	5:06:09 (26,753)
Jones, David F	4:30:15 (18,166)
Jones, David H	3:59:22 (10,359)
Jones, David J	4:39:40 (20,634)
Jones, David L	4:44:07 (21,754)
Jones, David M	3:59:04 (10,274)
Jones, David O	4:29:23 (17,945)
Jones, David P	4:16:39 (14,571)
Jones, David R	4:20:30 (15,557)
Jones, Dennis	5:39:24 (31,434)
Jones, Emlyn V	5:00:31 (25,703)
Jones, Francis D	5:15:15 (28,370)
Jones, Fraser L	5:34:26 (30,903)
Jones, Gareth	3:39:56 (5,843)
Jones, Gareth D	4:06:58 (12,097)
Jones, Gareth P	3:14:08 (2,137)
Jones, Gareth P	6:18:41 (33,977)
Jones, Gareth Richard	5:25:12 (29,825)
Jones, Gareth V	3:57:01 (9,625)
Jones, Gareth W	4:56:53 (24,906)
Jones, Garry	3:24:09 (3,289)
Jones, Gary	2:41:50 (230)
Jones, Gary A	4:02:33 (11,141)
Jones, Gavin C	4:12:43 (13,584)
Jones, Gavin M	4:46:48 (22,434)
Jones, Geoff J	5:09:46 (27,420)
Jones, Geoffrey C	3:38:07 (5,518)
Jones, Giles W	4:04:57 (11,645)
Jones, Glyn	4:54:09 (24,253)
Jones, Glyn R	3:19:28 (2,680)
Jones, Graham G	4:56:17 (24,747)
Jones, Graham P	5:06:19 (26,778)
Jones, Grahame	3:43:56 (6,621)
Jones, Greg	6:05:57 (33,385)
Jones, Guy R	4:15:29 (14,279)
Jones, Huw	4:20:32 (15,568)
Jones, Hywel S	3:24:41 (3,366)
Jones, Hywel W	3:13:14 (2,032)
Jones, Ian R	4:20:12 (15,484)
Jones, James H	3:39:53 (5,830)
Jones, John	3:40:33 (5,948)
Jones, John A	4:47:01 (22,487)
Jones, John D	2:56:59 (772)
Jones, John E. M	5:39:31 (31,450)
Jones, Jonathan	4:57:11 (24,962)
Jones, Karl J	5:09:34 (27,379)
Jones, Keith	3:54:27 (8,876)
Jones, Kelvin	3:19:32 (2,686)
Jones, Kenneth I	5:06:06 (26,745)
Jones, Kevin	4:32:03 (18,648)
Jones, Kristian	5:02:05 (26,041)
Jones, Lee	3:58:10 (9,996)
Jones, Lee D	4:03:06 (11,249)
Jones, Llewelyn	3:49:54 (7,814)
Jones, Marc	6:41:08 (34,649)
Jones, Marcus F	3:34:28 (4,869)
Jones, Mark A	4:03:03 (11,239)
Jones, Mark N	2:59:13 (934)
Jones, Mark P	3:44:28 (6,713)
Jones, Mark S	3:33:18 (4,651)
Jones, Martin	3:47:08 (7,222)
Jones, Martin	6:04:26 (33,310)
Jones, Martyn H	5:05:02 (26,555)
Jones, Mathew	4:49:56 (23,225)
Jones, Mathew W	4:11:43 (13,317)
Jones, Matthew	3:45:00 (6,804)
Jones, Matthew J	3:18:54 (2,610)
Jones, Matthew S	4:14:33 (14,042)
Jones, Meirion	5:51:42 (32,461)

Jones, Melvin	6:57:01 (34,921)
Jones, Michael	4:29:39 (18,003)
Jones, Michael A	4:57:10 (24,957)
Jones, Michael D	2:57:23 (801)
Jones, Michael D	4:44:02 (21,729)
Jones, Michael G	4:46:31 (22,347)
Jones, Michael R	4:58:54 (25,362)
Jones, Michael W	4:21:10 (15,733)
Jones, Mike	3:59:44 (10,472)
Jones, Neil	4:08:06 (12,390)
Jones, Neil	4:26:08 (17,020)
Jones, Neil R	4:17:50 (14,846)
Jones, Nick	3:42:34 (6,321)
Jones, Nick	5:02:05 (26,041)
Jones, Nick H	4:48:58 (22,962)
Jones, Nick J	5:41:06 (31,594)
Jones, Nick W	3:58:27 (10,083)
Jones, Nigel L	4:01:27 (10,899)
Jones, Nigel L	4:55:49 (24,646)
Jones, Norman V	7:06:40 (35,023)
Jones, Oliver	2:58:05 (842)
Jones, Owain C	2:53:00 (558)
Jones, Paul	4:31:01 (18,352)
Jones, Paul	4:34:27 (19,249)
Jones, Paul	4:42:37 (21,366)
Jones, Paul D	3:35:34 (5,061)
Jones, Paul Hedley	3:53:24 (8,604)
Jones, Peter D	6:29:59 (34,410)
Jones, Quentin N	3:34:19 (4,837)
Jones, Richard	4:11:48 (13,337)
Jones, Richard A	4:29:51 (18,056)
Jones, Richard E	5:40:39 (31,560)
Jones, Richard L	2:58:07 (845)
Jones, Richard L	3:20:44 (2,859)
Jones, Richard M	3:37:41 (5,436)
Jones, Robert A	3:59:35 (10,413)
Jones, Robert A	4:41:33 (21,103)
Jones, Robert D	4:44:06 (21,748)
Jones, Robert M	4:04:48 (11,609)
Jones, Robert S	3:48:20 (7,475)
Jones, Roderic	4:45:22 (22,050)
Jones, Rodri	2:37:50 (154)
Jones, Rolant R	4:25:26 (16,823)
Jones, Rory	4:08:17 (12,447)
Jones, Rue	3:46:39 (7,122)
Jones, Russell A	3:45:34 (6,909)
Jones, Ryan	4:25:07 (16,793)
Jones, Scott	3:48:08 (7,425)
Jones, Simon	3:20:37 (2,842)
Jones, Simon	3:58:54 (10,224)
Jones, Simon	4:12:43 (13,584)
Jones, Simon	4:28:45 (17,760)
Jones, Simon	5:12:33 (27,900)
Jones, Simon P	3:12:14 (1,906)
Jones, Simon P	4:20:09 (15,471)
Jones, Spencer	4:43:04 (21,484)
Jones, Steffan	4:22:25 (16,057)
Jones, Stephen	2:52:33 (545)
Jones, Stephen	4:22:09 (15,989)
Jones, Stephen	4:38:39 (20,339)
Jones, Stephen A	4:56:13 (24,733)
Jones, Stephen M	6:02:49 (33,216)
Jones, Steve A	4:19:42 (15,340)
Jones, Steve P	4:33:54 (19,129)
Jones, Steven	4:22:26 (16,060)
Jones, Steven	4:49:24 (23,080)
Jones, Stewart M	2:59:24 (949)
Jones, Stuart	4:09:29 (12,717)
Jones, Stuart A	6:18:40 (33,952)
Jones, Stuart David	3:28:46 (3,967)
Jones, Stuart L	6:22:28 (34,125)
Jones, Thomas	5:31:59 (30,638)
Jones, Thomas A	3:12:42 (1,958)
Jones, Thomas Patrick	4:01:12 (10,885)
Jones, Tim S	4:09:22 (12,699)
Jones, Toby William	4:48:01 (22,745)
Jones, Tony	6:17:02 (33,885)
Jones, Tony P	5:30:18 (30,440)
Jones, Trevor	4:00:48 (10,749)
Jones, Trevor	4:58:08 (25,174)
Jones, Trevor Bryant	3:54:55 (9,000)
Jones, Trevor W	5:10:05 (27,475)
Jones, Vince	4:52:08 (23,781)

Jones, Vincent E.................5:44:04 (31,858)
Jones, Vincent M.................4:12:00 (13,387)
Jones, Walter.................6:45:02 (34,708)
Jones, William D.................4:38:29 (20,292)
Jones, William J.................4:58:26 (25,251)
Jones, William K.................4:12:04 (13,405)
Jones, William W.................4:06:25 (11,975)
Jonker, William.................3:48:54 (7,595)
Jootna, Vijay.................4:54:24 (24,310)
Jopling, Raymond.................4:24:18 (16,527)
Jordan, Andy.................3:22:36 (3,085)
Jordan, Chris R.................2:39:13 (178)
Jordan, Ian R.................6:15:00 (33,791)
Jordan, Mark.................4:06:24 (11,969)
Jordan, Michael.................4:58:45 (25,327)
Jordan, Michael J.................4:49:12 (23,017)
Jordan, Miles J.................4:28:06 (17,580)
Jordan, Nick.................6:43:52 (34,692)
Jordan, Peter E.................4:56:12 (24,728)
Jordan, Robert H.................4:41:20 (21,045)
Jordan, Ross.................4:57:20 (24,992)
Jordan, Simon.................5:06:02 (26,731)
Jordan, Tom N.................4:46:49 (22,435)
Jordan Oncins, Francisco.................3:59:39 (10,437)
Jorlett, Joe.................4:55:04 (24,468)
José Domingo, Gonzalez Rios.....4:26:50 (17,216)
Josefsson, Patrik.................3:50:04 (7,850)
Joseph, Andrew J.................6:18:40 (33,955)
Joseph, Cinneri.................3:35:40 (5,090)
Joseph, Foggetta.................3:48:45 (7,552)
Joseph, Podmilsak.................2:57:08 (787)
Joseph, Revanie.................4:09:38 (12,762)
Josephine, Didier.................4:03:29 (11,327)
Josephs, David S.................3:55:15 (9,099)
Josephs, Merrick L.................4:33:39 (19,060)
Joslin, Paul J.................6:24:58 (34,228)
Joslin, Tom J.................4:23:50 (16,395)
Joubert, Jan.................4:35:20 (19,501)
Joubert, Salomon W.................4:18:57 (15,150)
Joule, Tom S.................3:52:14 (8,341)
Joules, Keith.................2:58:55 (910)
Jowett, Rob P.................2:55:35 (701)
Joyce, Austin P.................5:19:28 (29,032)
Joyce, Ben.................4:45:40 (22,126)
Joyce, Dominic.................5:14:59 (28,314)
Joyce, Ian P.................4:24:02 (16,448)
Joyce, Lewis M.................5:54:57 (32,688)
Joyce, Michael.................3:24:29 (3,339)
Joyce, Michael E.................6:03:05 (33,235)
Joyce, Noel.................4:07:02 (12,114)
Joyce, Paul.................4:43:41 (21,644)
Joyce, Simon R.................5:49:49 (32,321)
Joyce, Thomas.................4:22:44 (16,131)
Joyner, Matt.................5:30:58 (30,522)
Joyner, Timothy D.................4:33:42 (19,075)
Jubb, Stephen A.................5:57:27 (32,873)
Jud, Christian.................4:25:26 (16,823)
Judd, Andrew.................4:11:11 (13,158)
Judd, Mike.................3:14:45 (2,206)
Judd, Nathan P.................3:45:01 (6,808)
Jude, Neil.................4:17:08 (14,677)
Judge, Declan.................3:46:15 (7,028)
Juett, Michael.................6:37:43 (34,584)
Jugnarain, Pravin J.................4:28:10 (17,604)
Jukes, Daniel P.................4:57:11 (24,962)
Jukes, David.................5:42:11 (31,690)
Jukes, Matthew J.................3:45:26 (6,878)
Jukes, Paul.................4:54:37 (24,365)
Julian, Danny.................5:04:58 (26,539)
Julien, Dervillers.................4:40:58 (20,958)
Juliff, Mike.................4:32:23 (18,723)
Julyan, Martin K.................5:07:00 (26,908)
Jung, Ki Chul.................4:32:12 (18,685)
Juniper, Adam.................3:01:06 (1,058)
Junkin, Mark W.................5:33:00 (30,754)
Jupp, Malcolm.................4:47:34 (22,617)
Jupp, Peter R.................4:37:44 (20,101)
Jury, Alistair H.................4:31:08 (18,391)
Kaal, Giles S.................4:53:13 (24,024)
Kachhala, Pradeep.................5:37:55 (31,263)
Kaczmarski, Jeffrey.................3:49:44 (7,787)
Kadambari, Swaroop.................4:26:37 (17,158)
Kading, Jan P.................4:08:28 (12,500)

Kaelin, Remo.................3:38:44 (5,630)
Kafton, Lloyd D.................5:07:43 (27,045)
Kahl, Christoph.................4:39:29 (20,576)
Kahlow, Edward J.................3:40:06 (5,879)
Kainth, Ranjiet.................3:21:28 (2,941)
Kaker, Nazir A.................5:36:20 (31,106)
Kaland, Tom Ove.................3:12:43 (1,961)
Kalek, Dean M.................4:42:27 (21,313)
Kallstrom, Rolf.................4:45:26 (22,062)
Kalsi, Nirmal Singh.................4:59:02 (25,394)
Kaluzny, Marcin P.................4:35:53 (19,648)
Kamal, Mohammed J.................6:07:13 (33,445)
Kamara, Mykay I.................5:58:07 (32,927)
Kaminski, Marek.................4:00:34 (10,690)
Kämpfer, Matthias.................6:07:36 (33,464)
Kane, Graham.................3:42:29 (6,295)
Kane, Jonathan J.................4:12:58 (13,654)
Kane, Kevan R.................3:51:46 (8,220)
Kane, Ross A.................4:40:46 (20,902)
Kane, Stephen.................4:58:40 (25,312)
Kang, Ajmer.................5:38:11 (31,296)
Kang, Roger.................4:36:22 (19,757)
Kanji, Abid.................4:36:33 (19,804)
Kanji, Mohamed.................4:48:08 (22,770)
Kanngiesser, Gerd.................3:16:30 (2,378)
Kanumilli, Naresh.................3:58:07 (9,978)
Kanzaria, Kanti.................4:40:37 (20,865)
Kapadia, Hatim.................4:22:23 (16,044)
Kapoor, Neil.................2:44:09 (287)
Kapor, Humberto.................3:23:21 (3,169)
Karachalios, Theofilos.................5:36:48 (31,155)
Karagozian, Dino.................4:40:24 (20,814)
Karavias, Michael G.................4:34:58 (19,400)
Karger, Oliver R.................3:21:16 (2,915)
Karibu, Paul Gibson.................4:19:29 (15,277)
Karim, Lee.................4:21:26 (15,793)
Karl, Menard.................2:52:40 (548)
Karley, Christopher J.................4:36:57 (19,900)
Karlsson, Einar Gunnar.................4:34:18 (19,222)
Karlsson, Karl-Eric.................6:26:36 (34,302)
Karlstrom, Hakan.................3:51:29 (8,164)
Karrim, Mahomed Z.................6:12:58 (33,691)
Karunaratne, Rosh.................3:44:27 (6,710)
Kasander, Cornelis.................4:19:02 (15,167)
Kashmiri, Bashir.................5:15:10 (28,347)
Kasprzyk, Jakub.................4:11:54 (13,358)
Kassell, Tom.................3:12:43 (1,961)
Kasthuri, Madhavan.................5:16:47 (28,617)
Kästner, Wolfgang.................4:37:37 (20,070)
Kat, Gregory H.................3:36:32 (5,241)
Katechia, Bhagesh C.................3:38:08 (5,524)
Katon, Steven J.................4:24:04 (16,459)
Kaul, Arun.................5:14:19 (28,211)
Kavanagh, Kevin S.................3:26:23 (3,585)
Kavanagh, Terry F.................5:13:02 (27,991)
Kay, Ben R.................3:45:12 (6,835)
Kay, Jonathan.................4:52:29 (23,862)
Kay, Jonathan D.................4:53:45 (24,159)
Kay, Martin J.................3:27:19 (3,736)
Kay, Nick P.................3:40:51 (6,008)
Kay, Robert.................3:55:16 (9,102)
Kay, Tim.................3:58:43 (10,168)
Kaye, Samuel B.................3:55:02 (9,032)
Kaye, Simon A.................5:10:51 (27,610)
Kaye, Stuart C.................5:32:13 (30,661)
Kaynes, Paul.................4:06:34 (12,010)
Kayser, Karl-Wilhelm.................4:13:42 (13,848)
Keady, John Kaz.................6:58:53 (34,934)
Kean, Jon.................3:01:21 (1,073)
Kean, Raymond.................4:30:05 (18,121)
Keane, Ged C.................2:56:04 (725)
Kear, Alexander J.................5:21:25 (29,285)
Kear, Neil.................4:32:29 (18,755)
Kear, Tony.................4:58:49 (25,341)
Kearney, Andrew Joseph.................3:48:19 (7,470)
Kearney, Martin F.................3:28:40 (3,948)
Kearney, Stuart.................4:13:09 (13,695)
Kearney, Thomas C.................3:57:20 (9,721)
Kearns, Adrian.................3:07:43 (1,503)
Kearon, Thomas P.................5:13:34 (28,075)
Kearsey, Martin H.................4:56:01 (24,682)
Kearsley, Peter.................3:30:08 (4,194)
Keary, Andrew J.................3:45:43 (6,930)

Keasey, Damion J.................4:51:48 (23,701)
Keast, Tim.................3:14:02 (2,126)
Keates, Garry C.................7:03:46 (34,990)
Keates, Robin.................4:42:48 (21,409)
Keating, Jared R.................3:35:52 (5,125)
Keating, Nicholas M.................3:54:58 (9,010)

Keating, Ronan.................4:15:33 (14,294)

Kebede, Tsegaye.................2:05:20 (2)
Keeble, Daniel T.................4:12:53 (13,623)
Keeble, Ford A.................5:18:08 (28,809)
Keeble, Ian R.................2:54:25 (628)
Keeble, Sam.................3:17:22 (2,474)
Keeble, Thomas.................4:50:36 (23,396)
Keech, Edward J.................5:49:13 (32,269)
Keech, Paul Alan.................3:50:19 (7,907)
Keech, Tony.................3:30:27 (4,245)
Keegan, Joseph.................5:40:45 (31,567)
Keegan, Mark.................5:54:51 (32,673)
Keegan, Martin E.................4:11:47 (13,334)
Keehn, David.................4:40:27 (20,822)
Keelan, Peter S.................6:37:18 (34,575)
Keeler, Nicholas.................3:52:52 (8,482)
Keeley, Anthony Joseph.................3:45:20 (6,862)
Keeley, James W.................4:29:57 (18,082)
Keeling, David H.................5:43:58 (31,847)
Keeling, Tim.................4:30:32 (18,240)
Keen, Chris.................4:28:03 (17,557)
Keen, Philip J.................3:39:33 (5,766)
Keen, Warren H.................5:24:21 (29,711)
Keenan, Barry J.................3:45:02 (6,812)
Keenan, Brian.................4:44:49 (21,913)
Keenan, Garry.................3:24:17 (3,309)
Keenan, Noel F.................3:35:18 (5,009)
Keenan, Steven.................3:02:16 (1,137)
Keenan, Thomas S.................4:23:59 (16,437)
Keene, Ben G.................3:25:42 (3,487)
Keene, Hamish A.................3:57:06 (9,648)
Keene, Oliver N.................4:14:07 (13,937)
Keenleyside, Piers B.................4:39:02 (20,444)
Keep, Mark.................4:01:05 (10,812)
Keep, Matthew.................4:34:44 (19,326)
Keevil, Christopher J.................6:03:14 (33,244)
Keflezighi, Meb.................2:09:21 (9)
Keher, Aidan.................4:47:04 (22,501)
Kehoe, Gerard.................4:49:51 (23,209)
Kehoe, Robert F.................4:43:36 (21,625)
Kehoe, Vincent P.................4:42:34 (21,348)
Keighley, Paul C.................3:56:37 (9,500)
Keitch, Arthur.................6:06:24 (33,406)
Keith, Kevin.................4:35:18 (19,488)
Kellal, Madjid.................3:54:28 (8,880)
Kelley, David C.................3:55:45 (9,243)
Kelley, Luke.................5:31:42 (30,606)
Kelly, Alan T.................5:26:46 (30,022)
Kelly, Andrew P.................3:39:07 (5,703)

La Cour, Poul 3:54:44 (8,954)
La Franca, Massimiliano 5:06:57 (26,894)
La Mola, Angelo 3:41:32 (6,128)
La Noce, Emanuele 4:09:37 (12,757)
La Rocca, Stefano 4:34:53 (19,376)
La Roche, Lee 6:14:13 (33,753)
La Vecchia, Raffaello 3:57:46 (9,863)
Labropoulos, Alexander 5:47:30 (32,131)
Labuschagne, Timothy 4:38:44 (20,360)
Lacey, Kenneth 4:58:13 (25,193)
Lacey, Matthew 6:33:21 (34,479)
Lacey, Neville J 5:34:15 (30,885)
Lacy, Neil 4:46:37 (22,375)
Lacy, Terry W 3:58:30 (10,097)
Lad, Mahesh 6:26:35 (34,301)
Ladanowski, John Daniel 3:48:03 (7,413)
Ladd, Julian A 4:24:02 (16,448)
Ladhams, Steve Richard 3:41:13 (6,075)
Lafferty, David A 4:10:34 (13,000)
Lafferty, Ron R 4:10:08 (12,892)
Lafferty, Stephen P 3:51:25 (8,147)
Lafleche, Trevor 4:09:16 (12,673)
Lagerwall, Kenneth R 5:34:12 (30,876)
Lagerweij, Egbert 5:06:04 (26,739)
Laggar, Rob W 4:58:17 (25,209)
Lagnado, Max 3:08:22 (1,556)
Lague, David 3:37:04 (5,333)
Lai, Lai 5:57:54 (32,905)
Laidlaw, Jack R 4:04:40 (11,578)
Laidlaw, Michael 4:15:57 (14,381)
Laidler, David J 3:40:38 (5,963)
Lain, Frank 3:39:27 (5,750)
Laing, Warwick Karl Bruce Roy ...4:29:51 (18,056)
Laingui, Yves 4:36:45 (19,848)
Laird, James A 3:51:50 (8,234)
Laister, Nicholas D 4:00:44 (10,726)
Lake, Christopher J 4:50:11 (23,280)
Lake, David M 4:13:17 (13,742)
Lake, James T 5:30:58 (30,522)
Lake, John R 5:39:39 (31,461)
Lake, Oliver J 3:59:38 (10,428)
Lake, Simon S 3:47:09 (7,228)
Lakeman, Thomas A 5:01:42 (25,951)
Laken, Oli W 4:21:27 (15,797)
Lakomy, Lukasz 4:13:29 (13,791)
Lalley, Chris J 3:27:58 (3,852)
Lally, Kevin W 2:58:39 (881)
Lally, Mark C 4:34:28 (19,254)
Lally, Michael J 4:45:10 (22,010)
Lam, Ken K 4:37:26 (20,018)
Lam, Tung 4:16:15 (14,458)
Lamb, Bryan 3:11:49 (1,864)
Lamb, David A 4:53:44 (24,152)
Lamb, Haydn E 5:24:18 (29,700)
Lamb, James M 4:24:40 (16,614)
Lamb, Jonathan D 4:46:26 (22,326)
Lamb, Keith 3:41:11 (6,067)
Lamb, Ken D 3:53:23 (8,603)
Lamb, Martin James 4:39:42 (20,645)
Lamb, Paul J 4:59:08 (25,418)
Lamb, Spencer C 4:47:01 (22,487)
Lamb, William 3:54:38 (8,928)
Lamba, Justin H 4:03:32 (11,344)
Lambarth, Brian David 3:57:30 (9,772)
Lambden, Murray M 2:45:59 (331)
Lambe, Andrew J 5:05:00 (26,544)
Lambe, Anthony 4:26:08 (17,020)
Lambert, Geoff 6:12:52 (33,687)
Lambert, James 4:45:10 (22,010)
Lambert, John S 5:08:45 (27,223)
Lambert, Mark 3:56:24 (9,429)
Lambert, Matthew J 4:20:22 (15,527)
Lambert, Peter 3:38:25 (5,570)
Lambert, Philip W 3:11:15 (1,801)
Lambert, Richard C 4:32:37 (18,794)
Lambert, Russell F 6:08:54 (33,509)
Lambkin, Gary P 3:19:54 (2,741)
Lambourne, Chris J 4:36:47 (19,859)
Lambrick, Geoff J 4:30:13 (18,154)
Lambrou, Geoff 3:44:16 (6,677)
Lambrou, Tony 5:01:08 (25,848)
Lamige, Alain 3:59:30 (10,393)
Lammas, Edward 3:17:33 (2,487)
Lamont, Andrew K 2:51:08 (498)
Lamont, Fraser M 4:05:02 (11,659)
Lampard, Clive 4:32:14 (18,689)
Lampard, James M 4:54:59 (24,444)
Lamri, Belarbi 2:58:32 (871)
Lamy, Thomas 4:44:25 (21,824)
Lan, Kevin 3:57:40 (9,836)
Lancashire, Michael 4:45:27 (22,068)
Lancaster, Elliot K 5:30:26 (30,450)
Lancaster, James A 4:28:49 (17,780)
Lancaster, James E 4:19:06 (15,185)
Lancaster, John 4:01:37 (10,947)
Lancaster, Julie B 5:24:39 (29,749)
Lancaster, Richard P 3:56:20 (9,406)
Land, Christopher J 4:25:11 (16,762)
Land, Christopher R 4:03:49 (11,398)
Land, Graham D 4:55:47 (24,632)
Lande, Jon Helge 4:14:46 (14,102)
Lande, Kjell Roger 5:15:15 (28,370)
Landells, Martin R 2:58:31 (869)
Lander, Mark N 4:20:06 (15,459)
Landers, Gary E 3:58:12 (10,007)
Landers, Steven 5:10:07 (27,481)
Landles, Simon J 4:17:56 (14,869)
Landstad, Finn Kristian 3:58:20 (10,046)
Landy, Michael T 5:28:55 (30,264)
Lane, Andrew J 3:52:09 (8,311)
Lane, Anton D 5:27:02 (30,053)
Lane, Brian 4:16:19 (14,479)
Lane, Damien J 3:10:33 (1,741)
Lane, Daniel J 5:34:55 (30,959)
Lane, Dave 5:04:56 (26,530)
Lane, David J 3:07:05 (1,442)
Lane, Gary R 3:47:27 (7,278)
Lane, Ian R 4:52:41 (23,903)
Lane, Jerome D 5:21:21 (29,279)
Lane, Johnathan C 4:40:45 (20,898)
Lane, Jon 3:55:23 (9,127)
Lane, Michael 5:07:54 (27,075)
Lane, Michael P 4:20:46 (15,627)
Lane, Richard 4:35:47 (19,625)
Lane, Robert John 3:40:17 (5,913)
Lane, Ronald 3:51:37 (8,191)
Lane, Spenser 3:40:01 (5,863)
Lang, Chris P 5:12:58 (27,979)
Lang, David P 5:03:53 (26,360)
Lang, John 4:18:19 (14,969)
Langdon, Jeremy 3:14:43 (2,201)
Langdon, Tom 3:55:06 (9,065)
Langdown, Louis 3:42:33 (6,317)
Langford, David 4:42:57 (21,459)
Langford, Phil A 4:17:54 (14,862)
Langham, Simon 5:50:02 (32,337)
Langler, Ian J 3:12:42 (1,958)
Langley, Dan 3:41:14 (6,081)
Langley, Tom J 4:23:33 (16,327)
Langlois, Tim 5:28:59 (30,272)
Langly-Smith, Pete 4:55:45 (24,624)
Langman, Jack 4:53:05 (23,994)
Langrish, Ray J 5:43:17 (31,802)
Langthorne, Simon 4:19:57 (15,408)
Langton, Harry C 3:16:29 (2,376)
Langton, John S 3:47:24 (7,265)
Langton, Jonathan C 5:18:32 (28,878)
Langton, Michael S 5:07:25 (26,988)
Langton, Richard J 3:35:50 (5,121)
Langton, Simon 4:11:25 (13,228)
Lanham, James P 4:10:00 (12,853)
Lanik, Robert 4:51:25 (23,601)
Lannon, Adam 4:32:11 (18,683)
Lannon, Richie 5:15:20 (28,390)
Lanoe, JB 4:35:59 (19,675)
Lansberry, Richard C 4:55:47 (24,632)
Lansdown, Chris 5:26:16 (29,963)
Lapish, John Andrew 5:16:01 (28,503)
Lappin, Zek A 5:04:55 (26,529)
Larder, Darren M 3:09:05 (1,625)
Larderet, François 5:00:59 (25,805)
Large, Barney R 5:04:33 (26,472)
Large, David E 4:25:21 (16,800)
Large, Phillip 3:06:40 (1,418)
Largey, James J 4:43:24 (21,575)
Largey, James Michael L 3:42:20 (6,275)
Lark, Shaun A 3:06:13 (1,392)
Lark, Stephen J 4:12:05 (13,410)
Larkin, Brian J 4:51:23 (23,585)
Larkin, James A 5:54:12 (32,631)
Larkin, Jonathan 5:09:22 (27,340)
Larmour, Chris L 6:42:51 (34,677)
Larmour, James D 4:04:26 (11,530)
Larner, Emmett 4:28:28 (17,688)
Larsen, Bjarke 3:47:46 (7,341)
Larsen, Jan Magne 4:14:09 (13,945)
Larsen, Morten T 4:18:10 (14,940)
Larsen, Peter 3:38:05 (5,510)
Lashley, Wayne 3:06:45 (1,421)
Lashmar, Anthony 3:00:20 (1,016)
Lasmi, Azzez 3:58:19 (10,039)
Lass, Charlie 5:02:41 (26,150)
Lassnig, Cliff 3:32:07 (4,486)
Last, Kevin F 3:22:17 (3,047)
Last, Shane W 3:43:17 (6,487)
Latham, Andrew S 6:02:34 (33,202)
Latham, David P 3:53:47 (8,701)
Latham, Jarrod D 4:13:03 (13,667)
Latham, Tim J 5:48:11 (32,187)
Lathwell, Gary 4:30:10 (18,142)
Lathwell, Simon G 3:10:38 (1,748)
Latif, Iqbal 3:33:11 (4,635)
Latorre, Antonio B 3:51:03 (8,066)
Latter, Darren J 3:36:43 (5,265)
Lattuada, Giorgio 3:58:36 (10,126)
Lattuada, Riccardo 3:02:47 (1,166)
Lau, Alfred 5:10:09 (27,489)
Lau, Chris K 4:07:33 (12,244)
Laud, Jon D 4:13:12 (13,712)
Lauder, Neil D 5:52:15 (32,498)
Lauder, Oliver N 4:44:29 (21,833)
Lauder, Trevor R 4:24:55 (16,688)
Laughlin, Dale 2:42:45 (250)
Laughton, Douglas E 4:50:52 (23,455)
Laughton, Nicholas E 3:22:41 (3,096)
Laundon, Ben 3:49:04 (7,635)
Laurent, Michellier 3:16:18 (2,358)
Laurent, Pierre François 3:17:19 (2,468)
Laurent, Tarroux 3:03:57 (1,236)
Laurenti, Tim 4:46:34 (22,367)
Laurie, Brian 4:01:35 (10,939)
Laurie, Steven J 3:25:42 (3,487)
Lautizi, Claudio 3:10:59 (1,778)
Lauwers, Erik 4:11:50 (13,343)
Lauwers, Stefaan 3:38:29 (5,585)
Laval, Sean 4:39:28 (20,571)
Lavan, Nicholas T 3:20:35 (2,835)
Lavender, Andrew M 3:42:52 (6,391)
Laverick, Adam 5:18:59 (28,973)
Laverty, Sean A 2:47:49 (386)
Lavesen, Martin 4:08:05 (12,382)
Lavidalle, Laurent 3:31:23 (4,383)
Lavin, Christopher M 5:00:16 (25,646)
Lavington, Jamie S 4:08:41 (12,544)
Law, Adam 4:32:36 (18,789)
Law, Alan G 4:44:52 (21,921)
Law, Andrew J 4:46:45 (22,420)
Law, Andrew Puryer 3:54:57 (9,007)
Law, Christopher N 3:19:46 (2,722)
Law, Dominic 3:45:27 (6,885)
Law, Simon N 2:58:03 (839)
Lawes, Leslie J 6:22:48 (34,146)
Lawler, Ben 5:17:43 (28,749)
Lawler, Rob W 4:22:08 (15,978)
Lawless, Anthony J 3:51:44 (8,215)
Lawless, Matt S 4:13:31 (13,802)
Lawlor, Colin R 4:00:29 (10,664)
Lawlor, James M 5:58:42 (32,971)
Lawlor, Sean 4:08:06 (12,390)
Lawman, Darren J 4:38:53 (20,407)
Lawn, Simon 5:25:19 (29,833)
Lawrance, Lee James 4:24:30 (16,569)
Lawrence, Adam P 4:18:36 (15,054)
Lawrence, Andrew J 4:11:04 (13,130)
Lawrence, Andrew S 5:08:59 (27,270)
Lawrence, Anthony C 5:13:43 (28,104)
Lawrence, Chris D 4:19:31 (15,292)
Lawrence, David 4:43:36 (21,625)
Lawrence, Graham 4:10:39 (13,019)

Lawrence, James Keith................4:45:09 (22,009)
Lawrence, Jeffrey..........................4:35:19 (19,496)
Lawrence, Joe...............................4:53:53 (24,197)
Lawrence, Mark.............................4:37:05 (19,937)
Lawrence, Martin...........................4:49:52 (23,212)
Lawrence, Martin David.................4:43:22 (21,573)
Lawrence, Matthew J......................4:21:38 (15,858)
Lawrence, Nicholas.........................4:28:45 (17,760)
Lawrence, Rupert J.........................3:53:36 (8,650)
Lawrence, Stephen D......................5:18:34 (28,886)
Lawrie, Jonathan............................4:37:52 (20,135)
Laws, Richard................................5:01:58 (26,010)
Lawson, Andy James.......................3:58:12 (10,007)
Lawson, Ian J..................................3:14:57 (2,225)
Lawson, Mark A..............................3:30:48 (4,298)
Lawson, Nick..................................4:31:14 (18,414)
Lawson, Philip H.............................3:26:24 (3,587)
Lawson, Ron E.................................3:50:55 (8,042)
Lawson, Simon................................5:38:04 (31,286)
Lawson, Stephen.............................5:15:35 (28,435)
Lawson, Steve.................................3:55:45 (9,243)
Lawson-Smith, Stev.........................5:21:06 (29,243)
Lawton, Bryan W.............................3:18:32 (2,579)
Lawton, Jim....................................3:44:21 (6,689)
Lawton, Peter J................................4:27:48 (17,487)
Lawton, Steven J..............................3:41:06 (6,048)
Lax, James P....................................3:57:54 (9,903)
Lay, Kevin J.....................................4:00:29 (10,664)
Lay, Peter A.....................................3:25:02 (3,400)
Lay, Peter A.....................................6:00:54 (33,108)
Laycock, Graeme..............................3:25:23 (3,441)
Laycock, John W..............................4:01:27 (10,899)
Laycock, Michael E..........................5:11:48 (27,775)
Layland, Paul...................................4:07:28 (12,228)
Layne, William Leonard...................4:03:47 (11,386)
Layton, Jonathan A..........................4:20:59 (15,687)
Layton, Neil.....................................4:52:58 (23,970)
Lazarus, Alex...................................4:22:03 (15,954)
Lazell, Luke A..................................3:08:45 (1,596)
Lazell, Richard J..............................2:44:41 (305)
Le Bertre, Thomas R.........................4:26:19 (17,071)
Le Blevennec, Philippe.....................3:55:58 (9,300)
Le Bosquet, Charles..........................3:52:28 (8,396)
Le Bris, Pascal..................................4:28:25 (17,676)
Le Compte, Ben.................................3:50:31 (7,951)
Le Duc, Andrew P.............................6:06:53 (33,431)
Le Geyt, Shaun G.............................3:54:34 (8,911)
Le Good, Andrew K..........................3:28:01 (3,860)
Le Good, Daniel Saul.......................3:27:11 (3,712)
Le Hir, Patrice..................................4:10:44 (13,049)
Le Lorrain, Guido.............................3:49:51 (7,809)
Le Miere, Gerard...............................3:35:33 (5,056)
Le Miere, Julian................................3:35:36 (5,071)
Le Moigne, Olivier............................2:58:41 (885)
Le Normand, Jean Philippe...............4:17:49 (14,842)
Le Roux, Carl F.................................5:14:17 (28,209)
Le Roux, Tienie.................................5:18:13 (28,820)
Lea, Christopher E............................4:57:20 (24,992)
Lea, Colin..3:36:57 (5,309)
Leach, Brian J....................................4:17:05 (14,662)
Leach, Dave A....................................5:21:18 (29,272)
Leach, David A...................................5:14:30 (28,242)
Leach, Eric C.....................................6:28:28 (34,370)
Leach, Mark A....................................4:36:41 (19,835)
Leach, Nigel G...................................4:36:17 (19,736)
Leach, Robert J..................................3:07:46 (1,508)
Leadbetter, David M.........................3:53:46 (8,697)
Leader, David A.................................3:40:20 (5,919)
Leal, Alberto......................................4:58:05 (25,158)
Leal, Juan...4:28:44 (17,754)
Leaney, Stuart.....................................2:51:27 (506)
Lear, Rob E..3:44:21 (6,689)
Learman, Simon J...............................4:11:50 (13,343)
Learoyd, Craig A................................3:37:49 (5,460)
Leary, Andrew C................................3:08:25 (1,559)
Leary, Ben...4:25:06 (16,736)
Leary-Joyce, John S...........................6:06:33 (33,414)
Leat, Martin..4:14:42 (14,079)
Leatham, Matthew..............................4:21:07 (15,721)
Leatham, Michael R...........................5:06:01 (26,729)
Leather, David A.................................4:18:25 (15,001)
Leather, Martin B...............................3:55:01 (9,030)
Leather, Richard.................................4:11:36 (13,284)
Leathers, John.....................................4:56:38 (24,836)
Lebel, Louis...3:47:57 (7,384)
Leblanc, Anthony.................................4:36:55 (19,894)
Lebus, Willie O....................................4:45:55 (22,192)
Lécand-Harwood, Chris......................4:21:16 (15,759)
Leckie, Marc..5:17:22 (28,691)
Leclerc, Denis......................................4:42:40 (21,376)
Lecomte, Etienne.................................4:03:36 (11,356)
Lecount, Paul.......................................5:02:01 (26,025)
Leddy, Brendan....................................4:22:49 (16,145)
Leddy, Matthew D................................4:32:09 (18,677)
Lederer, Mark F...................................4:12:36 (13,547)
Ledgard, Simon O.................................4:03:22 (11,310)
Ledger, William P.................................4:56:13 (24,733)
Ledsam, Charles E................................4:41:32 (21,098)
Ledwidge, Alan S.................................4:14:05 (13,925)
Lee, Alan D..5:35:54 (31,061)
Lee, Alan K..3:53:10 (8,556)
Lee, Andrew J.......................................3:07:56 (1,520)
Lee, Andrew S......................................4:08:19 (12,459)
Lee, Brenan..5:27:28 (30,089)
Lee, Byung Ryong................................3:59:33 (10,404)
Lee, Charles...4:00:52 (10,766)
Lee, Chris...5:59:24 (33,013)
Lee, Chris D...5:46:38 (32,057)
Lee, Colin A...4:59:26 (25,480)
Lee, Conrad..3:57:27 (9,752)
Lee, David..5:18:32 (28,878)
Lee, Dennis K.......................................4:23:59 (16,437)
Lee, Derek D..6:03:39 (33,265)
Lee, Gareth...4:11:56 (13,368)
Lee, Gary..3:37:11 (5,353)
Lee, James M..5:20:39 (29,169)
Lee, John C..4:07:50 (12,322)
Lee, Jonathan W...................................4:22:08 (15,978)
Lee, Laurie C..3:35:33 (5,056)
Lee, Martyn A......................................4:43:13 (21,521)
Lee, Matthew H....................................5:51:32 (32,451)
Lee, Michael...4:06:33 (12,005)
Lee, Michael I.......................................4:07:45 (12,302)
Lee, Michael J.......................................4:39:30 (20,584)
Lee, Nicolas R.......................................3:22:55 (3,119)
Lee, Nigel..3:51:51 (8,240)
Lee, Peter R..4:00:00 (10,544)
Lee, Richard C.......................................3:56:22 (9,418)
Lee, Richard J..4:28:02 (17,551)
Lee, Robert S...4:53:14 (24,027)
Lee, Roger D...4:17:52 (14,851)
Lee, Sang Kwan.....................................4:30:34 (18,245)
Lee, Simon A...4:43:16 (21,534)
Lee, Steven...6:49:49 (34,809)
Lee, Studley..5:17:31 (28,719)
Lee, Thomas..5:34:53 (30,956)
Lee, Victor..4:59:19 (25,455)
Lee, William T.......................................5:15:03 (28,328)
Lee, Yuk-On..4:11:19 (13,194)
Lee, Yun Woo..4:35:30 (19,546)
Leech, Christopher................................7:51:27 (35,290)
Leech, Matthew D.................................4:26:25 (17,090)
Leedham, Gavin A.................................3:48:00 (7,401)
Leedham, Richard J...............................3:54:57 (9,007)
Leek, Alistair C......................................5:20:36 (29,165)
Leek, Robert I...5:03:45 (26,334)
Leek, Shawn J...4:27:29 (17,387)
Leek, Steve...4:08:23 (12,481)
Leeke, Chris L..3:54:14 (8,821)
Leeke, Matthew W..................................4:08:13 (12,419)
Leeming, Chris.......................................4:36:35 (19,813)
Leeming, John D.....................................4:32:27 (18,748)
Leeming, Nicholas..................................3:27:09 (3,707)
Lees, Fraser J..3:48:20 (7,475)
Lees, Keith A...6:07:05 (33,440)
Lees, Michael...5:26:34 (30,003)
Lees, Phil...5:48:04 (32,177)
Lees, Richard R......................................4:23:02 (16,195)
Lees, Steven D.......................................5:02:56 (26,199)
Lees, Tim...4:36:23 (19,766)
Leet-Cook, Charlie E..............................3:53:04 (8,523)
Lefebvre, Stephane D.............................4:48:46 (22,915)
Legard, Paul C..4:26:28 (17,104)
Legassick, David T..................................3:08:25 (1,559)
Legendre, Stephane.................................3:04:03 (1,240)
Legg, Benjamin.......................................4:25:36 (16,874)
Legg, Daniel H..3:37:09 (5,351)
Legg, Mark C..6:11:55 (33,637)
Leggat, Robert A.....................................4:53:39 (24,114)
Leggat, William......................................4:51:26 (23,605)
Legge, Edwin..5:33:21 (30,794)
Legge, Neale S..3:27:45 (3,819)
Legrand, Stephane...................................5:22:49 (29,482)
Lehnhardt, Marcus..................................4:08:25 (12,485)
Leigh, Alex J...4:50:26 (23,350)
Leigh, Andrew J......................................3:38:09 (5,527)
Leigh, Andrew R.....................................3:58:41 (10,155)
Leigh, Christopher J................................3:55:19 (9,112)
Leigh, Christopher W.............................3:46:30 (7,087)
Leigh, David...6:06:07 (33,390)
Leigh, Graham B.....................................4:00:26 (10,646)
Leigh, Jon...3:23:40 (3,214)
Leigh, Michel E.......................................5:23:20 (29,574)
Leigh, Peter C...4:09:30 (12,719)
Leigh, Philip...4:29:38 (17,994)
Leighton, Adrian W.................................4:24:23 (16,545)
Leighton, Nigel.......................................2:41:16 (221)
Leinweber, Matthias................................3:58:18 (10,033)
Leiria Pinto, Tomas.................................4:13:11 (13,707)
Leitch, James O..4:18:28 (15,021)
Leite, Paulo A..3:45:00 (6,804)
Leith, Clifford W.....................................2:56:25 (740)
Lejeune, Nicolas......................................3:40:59 (6,026)
Lejoly, Franck..3:03:26 (1,198)
Lelliott, Stephen......................................3:15:32 (2,288)
Leloup, Vincent..3:42:39 (6,346)
Lelu, Bernard...4:13:21 (13,768)
Lemaire, Georges......................................4:27:43 (17,451)
Lemass, Frank...4:15:07 (14,195)
Lemery, Christophe..................................2:51:00 (495)
Lemery, Jean-Charles................................4:57:39 (25,060)
Lemming, Mark...3:47:48 (7,351)
Lemon, Scott J...3:38:31 (5,594)
Lemos, Filippos...3:34:04 (4,778)
Lemstom, Kjell M.....................................3:05:52 (1,360)
Lenaghan, John..4:19:22 (15,249)
Lenaghan, Maximillian.............................4:55:14 (24,514)
Lench, Joseph P...3:45:56 (6,972)
Lendvai-Lintner, Geza...............................4:42:35 (21,357)
Lenehan, Raymond.....................................3:31:26 (4,391)
Leney, Paul A..4:23:56 (16,423)
Lenihan, Kevin G.......................................3:38:39 (5,618)
Lennon, James...4:14:50 (14,122)
Lennox, Adam Paul...................................3:41:15 (6,083)
Lennox, Andrew...5:00:07 (25,617)
Lennox, Jethro D..2:24:11 (29)
Lenon, Mark...4:47:13 (22,550)
Lenski, Matt...3:56:55 (9,598)
Lensley, Rudi..3:56:26 (9,437)
Lenthall, Alex W..3:43:44 (6,571)
Lenton-Cliffe, Chris...................................5:54:55 (32,683)
Leonard, Andrew P.....................................3:56:45 (9,549)
Leonard, Mark J..4:37:24 (20,009)
Leonard, Michael A....................................5:00:51 (25,773)
Leonard, Terry M.......................................4:46:29 (22,341)
Leontiou, Marios M...................................5:13:30 (28,063)
Leonzio, Generoso.......................................3:20:50 (2,874)
Lepine, Brent...5:28:55 (30,264)
Leppard, Robert A......................................4:06:13 (11,931)
Lepper, Leslie A..3:33:16 (4,648)
Lequenne, Bruno..4:28:56 (17,814)
Lernout, Patrick..3:26:38 (3,625)
Leroy, Bart...4:28:16 (17,638)
Lerpiniere, Ernie C.....................................4:20:06 (15,459)
Leslau, Ori M..4:16:38 (14,567)
Lesley, Richard J..4:08:55 (12,598)
Leslie, Ben..4:21:01 (15,697)
Leslie, Bill...4:26:12 (17,038)
Leslie, Hugh A...4:16:14 (14,455)
Lessell, James S...4:12:14 (13,447)
Lester, Ian H..4:11:20 (13,202)
Lester, Richard...4:22:22 (16,040)
Lester, Roy E...4:58:41 (25,316)
Lester, Simon...4:10:37 (13,010)
Lethaby, Raymond J.....................................5:32:56 (30,744)
Lethbridge, Paul J..4:33:49 (19,101)
Letley, Matthew R..4:50:26 (23,350)
Letts, Antony W...3:21:44 (2,976)
Letts, Sam...3:45:36 (6,913)

Leung, Wai Leung 3:31:32 (4,403)
Leusink, Job J 4:24:43 (16,627)
Leutert, Christoph 4:12:15 (13,453)
Leuw, Peter Jonathan Dudley 4:03:50 (11,403)
Leuzzi, Gianluca 2:58:00 (835)
Levene, Ben 6:03:09 (33,238)
Levene, Russell 4:42:19 (21,277)
Leveque, Nicolas 3:46:47 (7,153)
Leverett, Craig 3:52:09 (8,311)
Levett, Jonathon Mark 4:02:30 (11,126)
Levett, Peter D 5:29:28 (30,326)
Levick, Andrew P 4:15:43 (14,323)
Levin, Jules 4:30:40 (18,272)
Levine, Hugh A 4:49:42 (23,179)
Levison, Andrew V 4:59:44 (25,541)
Levy, Adam C 3:57:55 (9,909)
Levy, David P 6:05:00 (33,338)
Levy, Frederic 3:48:19 (7,470)
Levy, Jason E 5:01:26 (25,900)
Levy, Mark 4:48:09 (22,772)
Levy, Will 4:33:37 (19,054)
Lewington, Simon D 4:49:19 (23,058)
Lewis, Alan G 3:41:05 (6,045)
Lewis, Andy 3:12:26 (1,924)
Lewis, Brett R 4:27:22 (17,358)
Lewis, Cormac C 3:32:08 (4,492)
Lewis, Dafydd 5:14:58 (28,308)
Lewis, Daniel R 4:04:06 (11,468)
Lewis, David John 3:56:39 (9,518)
Lewis, Gary J 6:14:36 (33,770)
Lewis, Giles C 5:05:51 (26,705)
Lewis, Giles R 3:58:40 (10,151)
Lewis, Graham 4:17:38 (14,800)
Lewis, Greg 5:15:21 (28,394)
Lewis, Ian C 4:34:02 (19,158)
Lewis, Jack M 4:48:05 (22,759)
Lewis, James C 4:00:55 (10,778)
Lewis, James H 4:07:36 (12,255)
Lewis, Jason 5:13:20 (28,042)
Lewis, Jeremy 4:06:01 (11,888)
Lewis, Jeremy M 4:12:50 (13,613)
Lewis, Joe 4:05:01 (11,655)
Lewis, Joe 5:34:25 (30,902)
Lewis, John Daniel 4:02:44 (11,173)
Lewis, Jonathan 4:39:04 (20,456)
Lewis, Julian D 4:02:58 (11,221)
Lewis, Kevin W 4:55:07 (24,479)
Lewis, Kieron D 2:56:55 (768)
Lewis, Lee 4:50:54 (23,459)
Lewis, Leonard J 4:44:02 (21,729)
Lewis, Mark 5:36:19 (31,103)
Lewis, Mark J 2:54:49 (652)
Lewis, Martin G 2:35:11 (117)
Lewis, Michael P 5:18:30 (28,869)
Lewis, Neil B 3:13:07 (2,017)
Lewis, Nicholas J 5:13:02 (27,991)
Lewis, Paul 5:03:18 (26,252)
Lewis, Paul A 2:34:27 (105)
Lewis, Peter 3:16:42 (2,406)
Lewis, Roy 5:00:14 (25,639)
Lewis, Russell G 4:08:29 (12,504)
Lewis, Sebastian C 4:54:06 (24,245)
Lewis, Seth 3:38:17 (5,548)
Lewis, Simon D 4:14:06 (13,931)
Lewis, Simon W 5:07:30 (27,008)
Lewis, Sion 3:15:20 (2,265)
Lewis, Stanley 5:59:51 (33,038)
Lewis, Stephen 5:33:42 (30,832)
Lewis, Terence J 4:12:37 (13,555)
Lewis, Thomas M 3:51:17 (8,117)
Lewis, Tim 4:59:16 (25,445)
Lewis, Trevor A 5:01:38 (25,940)
Lewis Russell, Mark A 5:23:39 (29,607)
Lewis-Jones, Bleddyn 4:12:40 (13,566)
Lewis-Jones, Jules W 4:48:53 (22,938)
Lewys-Lloyd, Tegid William 4:29:12 (17,896)
Ley, Richard D 4:40:14 (20,781)
Leyenda, Manuel 3:59:18 (10,335)
Leygues, Roger 4:59:25 (25,475)
Leys, Calum P 4:16:02 (14,405)
Leyton, Richard I 3:56:35 (9,483)
Leyval, Olivier 4:00:28 (10,656)
Libby, Jason R 4:09:19 (12,689)
Liberson, Max J 4:58:24 (25,243)
Liburd, Garfield N 5:17:31 (28,719)
License, Darren P 4:24:20 (16,537)
Lickman, Paul R 5:08:54 (27,253)
Liddle, Alan 4:13:46 (13,863)
Liddle, John P 4:17:29 (14,764)
Lidgate-Taylor, Steven P 2:59:36 (963)
Liebers, Jonathan 3:55:51 (9,274)
Liebhauser, Daniel 3:31:03 (4,335)
Liebhold, Hartmut 5:12:15 (27,847)
Liebing, Lars 4:26:51 (17,222)
Liebling, Simon F 3:21:58 (3,009)
Lien, Knut 4:31:55 (18,611)
Liew, Michael 5:30:41 (30,489)
Liffen, Scott 4:21:37 (15,849)
Liggins, Anthony N 4:50:21 (23,327)
Light, Barry J 3:59:24 (10,369)
Light, Richard D 3:56:07 (9,344)
Lightning, David W 4:13:34 (13,813)
Lightwood, Barry 5:48:09 (32,181)
Liley, Phillip 4:15:48 (14,349)
Lilja, Peter 4:48:12 (22,783)
Lilla, Kerstin 5:14:25 (28,229)
Lilla, Olaf 5:14:25 (28,229)
Lilley, Craig D 4:30:08 (18,135)
Lilley, Richard J 4:56:46 (24,867)
Lilley, Sam E 3:49:58 (7,828)
Lilley, Simon 4:05:02 (11,659)
Lillie, Gary D 5:57:25 (32,867)
Lim, Eng B 6:12:19 (33,655)
Lim, Jerome C 4:11:01 (13,112)
Lim, Marc T 3:48:09 (7,433)
Lim, Mark C 6:00:51 (33,105)
Lim, Young Jae 5:07:43 (27,045)
Lima, Marcus 3:59:35 (10,413)
Limbirons, Steve J 4:40:46 (20,902)
Limo, Felix 2:09:47 (10)
Lincoln, David W 5:11:52 (27,786)
Lindebotten, John 3:32:37 (4,563)
Lindgren, Bengt 3:54:59 (9,018)
Lindley, Chris 4:08:16 (12,439)
Lindley, Paul 3:47:38 (7,313)
Lindon, James D 4:36:43 (19,843)
Lindon, Matthew A 4:47:12 (22,546)
Lindop, Nigel K 4:25:41 (16,904)
Lindop, Peter M 4:34:20 (19,226)
Lindsay, David 2:42:14 (241)
Lindsay, Iain S 4:07:37 (12,259)
Lindsay, Simon D 3:59:23 (10,365)
Lindsell, Scott 4:28:11 (17,608)
Lindsey, Anthony L 4:10:50 (13,071)
Lindsey, Paul D 4:21:16 (15,759)
Lindsey-Clark, Matthew P 4:14:15 (13,974)
Line, Chris J 5:27:58 (30,142)
Line, Stephen 3:38:03 (5,501)
Lines, Keith J 4:12:26 (13,499)
Lines, Mike R 4:42:21 (21,283)
Lines, Nicholas 4:06:08 (11,910)
Lines, Peter T 4:07:08 (12,138)
Lines, Stuart M 5:30:06 (30,411)
Linford, Matthew J 5:02:09 (26,051)
Ling, James S 3:44:32 (6,725)
Lingard, Brett 3:45:18 (6,854)
Lingard, John 3:26:34 (3,615)
Linger, Paul Hayden 4:28:11 (17,608)
Linley-Adams, William 4:32:10 (18,679)
Linn, Mark 4:42:06 (21,226)
Linnane, Declan J 7:09:04 (35,043)
Linnemann, Heinz-Georg 4:38:04 (20,189)
Linney, Scott 6:05:24 (33,358)
Linton, Mark 3:45:54 (6,960)
Linton, Perry I 4:53:35 (24,093)
Liondaris, Panicos A 5:30:11 (30,428)
Lipczynski, Nicholas J 4:42:47 (21,408)
Lippert, Marcus 4:33:34 (19,041)
Lippert, Max P 3:03:15 (1,185)
Lippiett, Thomas 3:57:20 (9,721)
Lips, Markus 4:59:26 (25,480)
Lips, Roland 4:32:33 (18,769)
Lipscomb, Simon 5:01:16 (25,872)
Lipscombe, Sam 4:31:46 (18,574)
Lira, Alejandro 3:54:33 (8,904)
Lisle, Richard A 3:24:44 (3,373)
Lister, Allan D 6:48:22 (34,782)
Lister, Darron 5:10:23 (27,528)
Lister, Ewart G 3:31:05 (4,341)
Lister, James D 5:50:27 (32,375)
Lister, Neil S 3:59:21 (10,351)
Lister, Robert C 4:38:10 (20,221)
Lister, Tom 4:48:19 (22,811)
Litchfield, Andrew J 3:38:35 (5,604)
Litchfield, Derek R 3:37:35 (5,420)
Little, Christopher Mark 4:28:48 (17,776)
Little, Ciaran 3:37:19 (5,375)
Little, Craig B 3:27:42 (3,812)
Little, Daniel J 3:56:33 (9,475)
Little, Eddy Bayor 3:49:10 (7,660)
Little, Ian J 4:54:13 (24,264)
Little, Mark D 4:11:29 (13,248)
Little, Mark R 3:47:57 (7,384)
Little, Martin R 4:12:26 (13,499)
Little, Paul J 3:18:02 (2,532)
Littlebury, Gary 5:18:18 (28,833)
Littlecott, Stephen R 3:55:32 (9,162)
Littlefield, Aaron Jon 4:10:40 (13,025)
Littlejohns, Marcus 4:21:10 (15,733)
Littleproud, Jim 4:01:35 (10,939)
Littler, Francis Henry 3:55:27 (9,148)
Littler, Steve 2:28:36 (51)
Littlewood, Mike 4:45:21 (22,045)
Littlewood, Richard Kevin 4:59:06 (25,410)
Littlewood, Richard S 3:15:24 (2,274)
Litton, Thomas G 3:59:08 (10,290)
Litwin, Kevin 4:33:58 (19,145)
Lively, Joshua P 3:52:08 (8,304)
Livermore, Robert F 4:19:46 (15,363)
Livesey, James E 5:17:01 (28,639)
Livesey, Mark 4:41:43 (21,144)
Livesey, Shaun 3:05:16 (1,320)
Livett, Edward 5:01:12 (25,861)
Living, Neil C 5:17:08 (28,664)
Livings, Gareth K 5:13:54 (28,142)
Livingston, Campbell 3:44:47 (6,765)
Livingstone, Adrian J 4:29:01 (17,834)
Livingstone-Learmonth, Max 3:03:32 (1,205)
Lizart, Nicolas 3:11:04 (1,786)
Llewellyn, Adam J 4:25:28 (16,832)
Llewellyn, Derran L 4:57:24 (25,012)
Llewellyn, Mark 5:31:54 (30,626)
Llewellyn, Robert 4:32:45 (18,832)
Llewellyn, Tony 4:13:39 (13,837)
Llewelyn, Clement H 3:48:04 (7,419)
Llewlyn, Marc L 6:25:17 (34,242)
Lloyd, Adam 3:35:07 (4,981)
Lloyd, Adrian 3:39:46 (5,803)
Lloyd, Christopher 4:08:22 (12,475)
Lloyd, David S 4:35:49 (19,630)
Lloyd, Derek 4:01:12 (10,835)
Lloyd, George 4:08:43 (12,556)
Lloyd, Ian 3:33:42 (4,703)
Lloyd, James 7:31:04 (35,224)
Lloyd, Joanne 4:37:25 (20,014)
Lloyd, John Paul 3:38:55 (5,658)
Lloyd, Kevin 4:36:53 (19,890)
Lloyd, Martin P 3:26:55 (3,669)
Lloyd, Matthew B 4:48:48 (22,921)
Lloyd, Michael C 4:23:10 (16,223)
Lloyd, Nigel 5:36:27 (31,120)
Lloyd, Paul 4:50:23 (23,340)
Lloyd, Peter David 3:56:58 (9,610)
Lloyd, Ralph J 3:54:37 (8,922)
Lloyd, Ryan 4:29:41 (18,011)
Lloyd, Thomas M 3:55:05 (9,059)
Lloyd, Thomas W 4:26:08 (17,020)
Lloyd, Tim 5:36:08 (31,089)
Lloyd, Timothy D 3:32:59 (4,609)
Lo, Wallace F 3:57:57 (9,917)
Loach, Mark A 4:42:34 (21,348)
Loach, Simon J 3:00:09 (1,008)
Lobb, Matt 6:26:47 (34,311)
Lobo, Jeremy P 3:01:50 (1,104)
Lochead, Malcolm 4:01:36 (10,945)
Lochray, Ian 3:31:51 (4,448)
Lock, Alan 3:28:33 (3,932)
Lock, Andrew J 3:54:02 (8,763)
Lock, Dave S 6:13:05 (33,697)

Lock, Jonathan D 5:08:50 (27,234)
Lock, Michael 5:25:26 (29,849)
Lock, Neil W 4:34:47 (19,348)
Lock, Peter R 4:49:43 (23,182)
Locke, Andrew 4:03:21 (11,303)
Locke, Ashley 4:27:25 (17,374)
Locke, David 4:32:39 (18,806)
Locke, Eric V 5:20:44 (29,182)
Locke, Malcolm 4:12:21 (13,483)
Locke, Matthew 4:07:37 (12,259)
Locke, Simon 4:07:24 (12,216)
Locke, William J 4:08:15 (12,430)
Locker, Gary J 3:46:14 (7,025)
Lockett, Mark J 5:26:33 (29,998)
Lockett, Patrick 3:27:47 (3,823)
Lockey, Kevin M 4:57:36 (25,052)
Lockhart, Allan D 4:09:26 (12,712)
Lockhart, Anthony J 4:26:11 (17,034)
Lockley, Paul M 3:54:37 (8,922)
Lockstone, Steven G 4:20:39 (15,587)
Lockwood, Paul R 4:50:30 (23,371)
Lockwood, Richard D 4:44:24 (21,821)
Lockwood, Simon R 4:19:54 (15,400)
Lockwood, Victoria T 6:20:26 (34,050)
Lockwood-Cowell, Stuart 4:54:19 (24,292)
Lockyer, Chris D 4:14:35 (14,053)
Lockyer, Paul Anthony 3:39:28 (5,752)
Locmelis, Andriy A 4:23:32 (16,323)
Loddo, Arthur J 4:42:38 (21,371)
Loden, James M 3:02:54 (1,171)
Loder, Adam R 3:21:57 (3,007)
Lodge, Darren M 3:57:14 (9,682)
Lodge, Stuart 3:38:19 (5,553)
Logan, Michael B 4:32:35 (18,783)
Logenthiran, Baheerathan 4:57:55 (25,119)
Logie, Peter W 5:36:39 (31,140)
Logie, Steven J 3:55:32 (9,162)
Logue, Toby 4:25:39 (16,893)
Loi, Rossano 3:19:59 (2,754)
Loi, Su Han 4:53:47 (24,169)
Loizou, Christopher 5:34:58 (30,963)
Lok, Joseph 4:51:11 (23,535)
Lole, Matthew J 2:39:30 (184)
Lomas, Chris M 3:38:52 (5,651)
Lomas, Terry A 4:27:47 (17,479)
Lomax, Norman J 3:30:11 (4,205)
Lomb, Ruediger B 3:21:18 (2,921)
Lombardo, Domenico 5:12:08 (27,828)
Lonergan, John W 2:57:11 (791)
Loney, Ben 3:44:50 (6,774)
Long, Andrew R 3:50:02 (7,845)
Long, Andy 4:21:23 (15,778)
Long, Brian 5:18:31 (28,874)
Long, Darren M 3:51:33 (8,174)
Long, David W 2:58:17 (856)
Long, Edward W 3:34:56 (4,951)
Long, Gary 4:57:56 (25,127)
Long, Gavin 5:17:06 (28,658)
Long, Joseph Daniel 4:38:48 (20,378)
Long, Martin K 4:41:44 (21,149)
Long, Matthew 3:47:44 (7,334)
Long, Matthew 5:02:05 (26,041)
Long, Nick A 3:46:33 (7,097)
Long, Oliver J 5:06:58 (26,901)
Long, Sam 3:56:56 (9,603)
Long, Stuart D 5:03:57 (26,374)
Long, Wayne C 5:06:58 (26,901)
Longefaye, Jean André 3:18:16 (2,552)
Longfield, Paul T 4:07:21 (12,199)
Longhurst, Adam 5:39:06 (31,410)
Longland, Craig R 4:48:54 (22,945)
Longland, Peter C 5:02:32 (26,124)
Longland, Steven J 4:30:11 (18,146)
Longley, Dean T 2:59:23 (948)
Longley, Gavin D 3:26:53 (3,663)
Longley, Greg M 5:31:50 (30,620)
Longman, Dominic 3:34:11 (4,808)
Longmead, Andrew 3:46:23 (7,062)
Longo, Alfredo 3:21:49 (2,985)
Longstaff, Andrew 4:53:13 (24,024)
Longstaff, Chris D 3:42:00 (6,206)
Longstaff, Christopher E 5:45:27 (31,968)
Longstaff, Martyn W 4:06:28 (11,984)
Longthorpe, Simon 2:43:09 (259)
Lonnroth, Johnny-Stefan 2:47:48 (385)
Lonsdale, Adrian J 3:53:55 (8,726)
Lonsdale, David T 4:25:24 (16,819)
Looby, Michael J 5:53:04 (32,552)
Lopapa, Carmelo 3:55:47 (9,258)
Lopes, Antonio T 4:52:17 (23,823)
Lopez, Gabriel 4:30:25 (18,211)
Lopez Peña, Pedro 4:02:51 (11,198)
Lopez Portela, Antonio 3:57:06 (9,648)
Lopez Rodriguez, Oscar 3:34:24 (4,853)
Loran, Jeremy N 4:16:45 (14,594)
Lord, Chris J 5:55:08 (32,697)
Lord, David A 3:29:11 (4,035)
Lord, Gordon J 5:21:40 (29,327)
Lord, James M 4:26:50 (17,216)
Lord, Mike 5:22:37 (29,455)
Lord, Stephen D 5:46:53 (32,077)
Lordan, Shaun M 4:09:33 (12,737)
Lorenzato, Neil 5:06:05 (26,741)
Lorimer, Stephen J 6:12:52 (33,687)
Lorusso, Angelo 3:21:21 (2,927)
Lorusso, Peter 5:13:35 (28,078)
Loseby, Stephen J 3:23:45 (3,226)
Losio, Renato 4:52:41 (23,903)
Lotinga, Nicholas 4:20:03 (15,442)
Loton, Jon J 3:56:14 (9,372)
Lott, David 3:10:40 (1,754)
Loubser, Jonathan L 4:57:53 (25,104)
Louden, Adrian R 4:35:41 (19,592)
Loughlin, Tim G 5:02:42 (26,155)
Loughrey, Patrick T 5:07:03 (26,915)
Louis, Patrick 4:12:55 (13,635)
Lound, Charles A 2:41:47 (229)
Lourenco, Manuel 6:12:58 (33,691)
Lourenco, Pascal 4:41:02 (20,969)
Louw, Bertus J 3:43:53 (6,611)
Lovatt, John 4:01:09 (10,825)
Love, Adrian O 3:30:29 (4,249)
Love, Andrew J 4:28:47 (17,769)
Love, Christopher C 5:36:35 (31,129)
Love, Ian 4:53:15 (24,033)
Love, Jay D 4:09:03 (12,631)
Love, Martin R 3:26:35 (3,617)
Love, Nick J 5:51:42 (32,461)
Love, Robert A 5:39:24 (31,434)
Loveday, Richard M 4:56:47 (24,871)
Loveday, Scott C 3:50:20 (7,911)
Lovelace, Craig Barry 3:47:42 (7,328)
Loveless, Byron J 3:59:03 (10,268)
Loveless, Martin G 3:20:14 (2,789)
Lovell, Bruce M 2:55:15 (683)
Lovell, James 3:57:50 (9,890)
Lovell, John C 3:46:44 (7,140)
Lovell, Joseph Frank 3:55:21 (9,119)
Lovell, Paul N 3:49:07 (7,649)
Lovell, Richard J 4:17:08 (14,677)
Lovell, Robert D 4:41:35 (21,115)
Lovelock, Robert 7:47:54 (35,286)
Lovett, Andrew V 4:15:58 (14,387)
Lovett, Jamie 4:45:44 (22,139)
Lovewell, David B 5:52:19 (32,503)
Lovitt, Jason 6:17:21 (33,895)
Low, Ashley H 4:16:50 (14,615)
Low, Grace 3:38:23 (5,560)
Low, Roger L 3:44:22 (6,695)
Low, Stephen A 2:57:32 (809)
Low, Stewart W 4:51:31 (23,625)
Lowe, Alistair J 5:47:16 (32,118)
Lowe, Andrew 4:04:09 (11,478)
Lowe, Andrew J 4:45:06 (22,000)
Lowe, Andrew Martin 4:15:46 (14,340)
Lowe, Antony V 4:01:15 (10,847)
Lowe, Benjamin 5:30:33 (30,469)
Lowe, Christian 4:45:20 (22,040)
Lowe, Christopher 5:23:04 (29,526)
Lowe, Dean 2:55:31 (698)
Lowe, Gary M 4:20:13 (15,490)
Lowe, Graham 6:24:05 (34,189)
Lowe, Jake 3:13:09 (2,021)
Lowe, Matt J 4:41:15 (21,026)
Lowe, Michael J 5:47:17 (32,120)
Lowe, Neal M 5:06:38 (26,830)
Lowe, Rick 4:50:09 (23,274)
Lowe, Simon J 3:42:01 (6,212)
Lower, Robert 3:32:13 (4,507)
Lowes, Kelvin 5:23:11 (29,543)
Lowis, Kevin J 3:33:53 (4,736)
Lowis, Michael D 5:16:24 (28,548)
Lownds, Melvyn T 7:00:38 (34,956)
Lowrie, Andrew D 4:32:27 (18,748)
Lowrie, James 3:21:32 (2,951)
Lowry, Ian J 5:28:36 (30,222)
Lowry, Patrick L 4:22:39 (16,111)
Lowther, Adrian 2:34:24 (104)
Lowther, Mark D 5:04:26 (26,445)
Lowthian, Drew L 3:14:35 (2,180)
Loxam, Jamie L 2:33:53 (96)
Loy, Dicon J 3:28:27 (3,922)
Loy, Martin 3:23:09 (3,142)
Loynes, Chris J 4:32:47 (18,842)
Loynes, Greg 5:04:20 (26,430)
Lozano, Alfredo 4:23:50 (16,395)
Lozano, Fernando 3:56:16 (9,382)
Luca, Antongiulio 3:29:42 (4,135)
Lucas, Alan 3:42:18 (6,268)
Lucas, Jay 6:09:02 (33,513)
Lucas, Stuart R 5:10:46 (27,598)
Lucas, Timothy 3:20:39 (2,847)
Lucas Ponce, Jorge 3:34:36 (4,896)
Lucas-Lucas, Adam W 3:25:21 (3,434)
Lucass, David M 4:18:03 (14,905)
Luce, Philip A 4:24:08 (16,483)
Lucitt, Stewart A 4:42:32 (21,339)
Lucitt-Rees, Sam D 4:29:29 (17,966)
Luckhurst, Anthony P 6:09:43 (33,547)
Lucskai, Valentin 4:08:28 (12,500)
Ludlow, Chris A 5:18:20 (28,844)
Ludlow, Craig D 3:27:53 (3,838)
Ludlow, Jamie 3:23:47 (3,229)
Ludman, Andrew 3:45:54 (6,960)
Ludwig, Juergen 4:31:44 (18,560)
Lue, Anthony 4:39:41 (20,639)
Luengo-Fernandez, Ramon 3:50:55 (8,042)
Luetz, Hans-Gernot 3:50:08 (7,867)
Luff, Adrian F 3:52:25 (8,386)
Luff, Darrell 6:25:27 (34,253)
Lugauer, Dietmar 4:41:45 (21,154)
Luiters, Keegan J 3:15:06 (2,244)
Luka, David E 3:36:26 (5,222)
Luke, Charles 4:47:21 (22,565)
Lulham, Gary 5:38:53 (31,382)
Lum Young, John 3:35:39 (5,086)
Lumb, Christopher J 4:20:04 (15,446)
Lumby, Alex D 5:04:44 (26,499)
Lumby, Paul Leonard 3:58:20 (10,046)
Lumley, Ian L 4:01:27 (10,899)
Lumley, Matthew Armstrong 3:57:42 (9,846)
Lund, Robert 6:25:10 (34,235)
Lund, Simon N 2:57:48 (823)
Lundgren, Andreas 3:47:45 (7,336)
Lundgren, Olov 4:08:15 (12,430)
Lundy, Leo 4:14:34 (14,047)
Lunn, Alex J 4:49:27 (23,092)
Lunn, Gary J 3:06:56 (1,430)
Lunt, Keith R 3:28:44 (3,961)
Lupo, Patrick A 4:57:31 (25,037)
Lupp, Leif 4:20:51 (15,647)
Lupton, Chris 4:52:12 (23,795)
Luscombe, Adrian R 5:50:02 (32,337)
Luscombe, Barrie J 5:30:13 (30,430)
Luscombe, Nick C 4:21:28 (15,801)
Lush, Dale M 3:28:35 (3,936)
Lush, Michael F 5:46:01 (32,015)
Luson, David 4:06:56 (12,090)
Luson, Mark 4:56:28 (24,791)
Luther, Bjoern 5:43:06 (31,781)
Luther, David 4:06:40 (12,037)
Luther, Ralf A 3:19:24 (2,668)
Luther, Ulrich 3:38:44 (5,630)
Luxton, Martin J 3:47:45 (7,336)
Luxton, Neville 4:03:56 (11,428)
Luyt, David 4:13:07 (13,687)
Ly, Tuan 4:36:19 (19,742)
Lyall, David I 3:44:34 (6,727)
Lycett, Redvers A 4:12:03 (13,398)

Lyddon, Martin G 6:14:13 (33,753)
Lyddon, Simon D 3:56:36 (9,489)
Lydon, Chris W 4:40:10 (20,768)
Lydon, Martin Wayne 4:43:52 (21,681)
Lye, Albert 4:14:02 (13,913)
Lygo, Mark 4:20:15 (15,498)
Lyle, David 4:23:16 (16,248)
Lynagh, Jonathan 4:04:25 (11,527)
Lynan, David 3:58:13 (10,018)
Lynch, Andrew 5:07:05 (26,921)
Lynch, Chris 4:21:37 (15,849)
Lynch, Jim 5:29:26 (30,323)
Lynch, Joe 4:55:47 (24,632)
Lynch, Martin 4:33:11 (18,939)
Lynch, Paul R 4:44:09 (21,757)
Lynch, Robert J 3:32:52 (4,594)
Lynch, Rory J 4:23:55 (16,419)
Lynch, Simon D 3:56:34 (9,478)
Lynch, Simon N 4:21:22 (15,776)
Lynd, Nick 3:49:16 (7,682)
Lyndon, Ogbourne 4:33:32 (19,029)
Lyne, Andrew 4:24:17 (16,522)
Lyne, Geoffrey S 3:30:24 (4,237)
Lyne-Pirkis, Matthew 6:49:29 (34,806)
Lyner, Matthew Grahame 4:58:10 (25,184)
Lynes, Matthew I 4:45:16 (22,031)
Lynes, Samuel B 4:20:27 (15,545)
Lyngholm, Jonas 2:58:04 (840)
Lyngnes, Baard 3:32:00 (4,469)
Lynott, Mark M 5:38:57 (31,389)
Lyon, Andy M 4:29:39 (18,003)
Lyon, David J 3:12:58 (2,002)
Lyon, Michael William 4:30:14 (18,160)
Lyon, Roger J 5:18:07 (28,807)
Lyons, Dale R 6:40:53 (34,643)
Lyons, Edward H 4:55:27 (24,563)
Lyons, Gary 4:20:26 (15,542)
Lyons, Graham G 3:02:47 (1,166)
Lyons, Jack M 4:22:08 (15,978)
Lyons, Jonathan P 3:24:39 (3,362)
Lyons, Joseph 4:25:24 (16,819)
Lyons, Liam Stuart 4:59:26 (25,480)
Lyons, Stephen E 4:34:40 (19,307)
Lyons, Stephen L 3:48:30 (7,508)
Lyons, Tony J 4:01:30 (10,915)
Lythgoe, Lynton J 3:31:54 (4,453)
Lyttle, John 4:17:16 (14,706)
Lyttle, Jonathan A 5:45:40 (31,992)
Mabbutt, Bradley J 4:33:16 (18,965)
Maber, Giles 4:33:44 (19,080)
Mabey, Peter F 3:17:04 (2,439)
Mabon, Philip J 5:58:18 (32,945)
MacAdam-Slater, Paul 7:35:53 (35,249)
MacAlister, Gary S 5:06:46 (26,862)
MacAllan, Ray 4:27:46 (17,474)
MacAllister, Andrew J 4:39:09 (20,482)
MacAndrew, Keith M 5:49:52 (32,327)
MacAninch, Cal 3:16:19 (2,360)
Macarthur, Robert James 4:49:13 (23,024)
MacAskill, Andy 2:48:38 (412)
Macaulay, Adam 3:56:43 (9,541)
MacBay, Paul H 4:09:37 (12,757)
Macbeath, Niall A 3:10:52 (1,768)
Macbeth, Kenneth D 2:49:39 (449)
Macchia, Alberto 4:02:01 (11,020)
MacConnell, Ross 3:59:42 (10,460)
MacCormac, Oscar J 4:13:23 (13,774)
MacCuish, Donald 5:42:27 (31,717)
Macdonald, Alexander J 3:47:46 (7,341)
Macdonald, Alistair Andrew 4:47:51 (22,689)
Macdonald, Andrew P 3:54:49 (8,973)
Macdonald, David C 4:02:33 (11,141)
Macdonald, David M 2:58:48 (893)
Macdonald, George A 3:48:01 (7,405)
Macdonald, Graham M 5:14:08 (28,185)
Macdonald, Jay 5:10:42 (27,584)
Macdonald, Julian 2:35:47 (125)
Macdonald, Robert J 5:50:55 (32,410)
Macdonald, Stephen G 5:09:09 (27,298)
Macdonald, Steve S 4:17:52 (14,851)
Macdonald, Thomas 3:44:52 (6,783)
Macdonough, Paul J 4:08:05 (12,382)
MacDougall, Robert M 3:42:01 (6,212)

Mace, Simon J 2:52:06 (524)
MacEnhill, Justin J 3:10:31 (1,738)
Macey, Terence J 4:10:49 (13,068)
MacFadyen, Matthew 4:54:44 (24,392)
Macfarlane, Angus 4:09:59 (12,851)
MacGibbon, Sam 3:14:16 (2,148)
MacGillivray, Andrew S 3:43:50 (6,601)
MacGregor, Alain 3:39:41 (5,791)
MacGregor, Philip R 3:25:37 (3,476)
MacGregor, Stuart 3:41:10 (6,061)
MacHale, Martin 3:56:37 (9,500)
Machin, Bryn D 3:43:12 (6,473)
Mächler, Daniel 4:38:16 (20,246)
Macintosh, Andrew G 3:53:46 (8,697)
Mack, Antony 4:10:15 (12,921)
Mack, Daniel 5:12:27 (27,881)
Mack, Harry 5:12:27 (27,881)
Mackay, Alexander D 3:37:45 (5,448)
Mackay, Alexander P 6:17:49 (33,921)
Mackay, Blake M 3:53:32 (8,630)
Mackay, Frazer David 3:57:04 (9,638)
Mackay, Graeme G 3:11:31 (1,830)
Mackay, Jonathan H 5:13:24 (28,050)
Mackay, Ross 5:19:09 (28,989)
Mackel, Jeannot 3:22:00 (3,014)
Macken, Graham M 5:00:25 (25,680)
Macken, Kevin D 5:00:25 (25,680)
Mackenzie, Colin A 5:10:42 (27,584)
Mackenzie, John 4:15:58 (14,387)
Mackenzie, Neil R 3:40:46 (5,990)
Mackenzie, Nigel James 3:51:40 (8,203)
Mackenzie, Robert E 3:32:24 (4,530)
Mackertich, David S 3:10:26 (1,731)
Mackey, James E 4:10:26 (12,962)
Mackie, Colin 4:36:39 (19,829)
Mackie, Scott A 2:51:46 (515)
Mackie, Steve 4:31:21 (18,455)
Mackintosh, Al 4:29:38 (17,994)
Mackintosh, Jamie S 3:58:27 (10,083)
Mackley, Jonathan N 3:55:24 (9,132)
Mackley, Stuart 4:36:06 (19,703)
Macklin, Julian H 3:50:07 (7,859)
Mackness, John N 5:18:33 (28,880)
Mackrell, Peter 3:12:54 (1,989)
MacLachlan, Alastair J 2:54:58 (661)
Maclaren, Donald B 2:59:27 (952)
Maclean, Richard Alan 5:03:26 (26,270)
MacLennan, Michael 4:24:34 (16,585)
Macleod, Alaistair 4:11:05 (13,133)
Macleod, Andrew J 3:37:37 (5,427)
Macleod, Darren 4:02:57 (11,219)
Macleod, Iain 5:06:55 (26,887)
Macleod, James Roderick 3:44:28 (6,713)
Macleod-Miller, Leslie 3:44:28 (6,713)
MacLure, Matthew J 4:51:10 (23,528)
MacManus, Paul A 3:42:00 (6,206)
Macmillan, Robert 4:29:11 (17,884)
MacNab, Robbie J 4:15:58 (14,387)
MacPhail, Scott H 3:59:42 (10,460)
Macpherson, Donald 4:30:13 (18,154)
MacQueen, Anthony 3:04:32 (1,267)
MacQueen, Ian M 5:01:13 (25,865)
MacQueen, Peter J 6:20:43 (34,059)
Macrae, Laurence M 4:56:35 (24,825)
Maddage, Vinny 4:04:27 (11,532)
Madden, Joseph D 4:26:06 (17,010)
Madden, Mike T 5:38:53 (31,382)
Maddison, David A 3:52:21 (8,372)
Maddison-Roberts, Ian J 4:02:23 (11,102)
Maddock, Andrew T 4:18:24 (14,995)
Maddock, Craig W 4:59:16 (25,445)
Maddock, Michael P 4:20:40 (15,591)
Maddock, Richard T 4:27:41 (17,441)
Maddocks, Terry 6:36:57 (34,561)
Maddox, Steven J 4:11:50 (13,343)
Maddy, John D 3:57:14 (9,682)
Madelin, Gary 4:02:05 (11,037)
Madell, Christopher 4:01:10 (10,827)
Madges, Karl A 6:28:53 (34,379)
Madges, Mark 6:28:54 (34,380)
Madigan, Sean Edward 5:21:32 (29,307)
Maeda, Malcolm T 4:20:08 (15,468)
Maess, Jens 4:24:45 (16,638)

Maestranzi, Matthew A 3:29:15 (4,053)
Mafaraud, Stephane 4:02:24 (11,106)
Magalhaes, José 4:59:40 (25,525)
Maged, Jack 4:03:13 (11,275)
Magee, Paul D 6:24:51 (34,225)
Magee, Peter 4:57:30 (25,029)
Maggs, Steve J 3:49:52 (7,811)
Magi, Antonio 3:25:15 (3,427)
Magill, Daniel J 4:40:34 (20,851)
Magill, John R 5:13:40 (28,091)
Magni, Fabio 4:46:08 (22,232)
Magnussen, Oeivind O. 4:36:26 (19,777)
Magnusson, Tord 5:14:05 (28,177)
Maguire, Alex C 4:02:49 (11,191)
Maguire, Mark 3:26:25 (3,591)
Maguire, Michael J 4:27:34 (17,404)
Maguire, Neil J 4:13:04 (13,672)
Magwood, David 6:29:08 (34,385)
Mahal, Tulbinder 6:25:41 (34,266)
Maher, Andrew D 3:54:20 (8,847)
Maher, Brian P 3:56:28 (9,449)
Maher, Derek P 4:39:09 (20,482)
Maher, Terry J 5:58:10 (32,932)
Mahmood, Kamran 5:41:41 (31,646)
Mahmood, Talat M 5:00:40 (25,743)
Mahnut, Ahmet 5:25:10 (29,822)
Mahon, Keith 4:00:42 (10,720)
Mahon, Oliver J 4:03:10 (11,266)
Mahon, Peter 4:23:49 (16,391)
Mahon, Scott B 4:19:02 (15,167)
Mahon, Tony J 4:55:42 (24,614)
Mahoney, Danny Thomas 3:01:44 (1,099)
Mahoney, Jim 3:20:12 (2,780)
Mahoney, Nicholas G 4:09:46 (12,794)
Mahood, George M 3:55:26 (9,139)
Maida Junior, José 3:42:46 (6,370)
Maiden, Alastair J 4:33:33 (19,036)
Maiden, Kyle R 4:23:58 (16,432)
Maiden, Richard P 5:22:41 (29,467)
Maidment, John A 4:29:12 (17,896)
Maidment, Nicholas M 4:08:13 (12,419)
Maile, James 4:06:26 (11,978)
Mailie, Michael 4:20:55 (15,668)
Maillard, Gerard 5:02:14 (26,068)
Mainwaring, Gareth S 4:26:20 (17,078)
Mainwaring, Robert 4:39:57 (20,707)
Mainwaring, Rupert C 3:42:34 (6,321)
Mairs, Graham 2:55:37 (703)
Maisey, Jonathan G 5:07:16 (26,955)
Maitland, Lewis 3:57:29 (9,762)
Majekodunmi, Seni 4:30:29 (18,222)
Majer, Peter Edward 3:52:58 (8,498)
Maji, Bhaskar S 5:30:23 (30,446)
Major, Andy 4:06:36 (12,016)
Major, Daniel E 3:17:52 (2,516)
Major, Dave J 4:06:18 (11,948)
Major, Louis 4:46:06 (22,227)
Major, Paul A 5:22:09 (29,381)
Major, Philip J 5:08:21 (27,151)
Major, Sean 5:06:23 (26,787)
Major, Steven John 3:54:24 (8,864)
Makin, Frank H 4:12:38 (13,558)
Makin, Stuart 4:08:10 (12,410)
Makins, David A 4:45:02 (21,973)
Makoto, Mishima 3:59:51 (10,508)
Makuwa, Bill M 2:48:55 (420)
Mal, Firouz 3:41:51 (6,175)
Malacrida, Richard G 3:42:57 (6,409)
Malagoli, Glauco 3:42:12 (6,250)
Malaspina, Michael 4:37:32 (20,045)
Malavolta, Marco 3:04:51 (1,297)
Malcolm, Thomas E 3:50:40 (7,983)
Male, Nick 4:19:11 (15,209)
Male, Stuart L 3:07:22 (1,463)
Maleedy, Christian Andrew 4:14:21 (14,000)
Maleh, Lewis 3:56:11 (9,364)
Malekos, George 6:52:43 (34,858)
Males, Shane 4:53:36 (24,100)
Malherbe, Martin J 3:25:30 (3,457)
Malhotra, Aneil 5:24:56 (29,788)
Malhotra, Deepak 3:51:42 (8,208)
Malik, Khawar 3:52:48 (8,465)
Malin, Richard A 2:46:47 (361)

Malk, Johan 3:18:01 (2,531)
Mall, Sadik 4:30:34 (18,245)
Mallaber, Richard J 3:59:42 (10,460)
Mallalieu, Karl 4:43:52 (21,681)
Mallen, Garry C 4:04:39 (11,572)
Mallet, Karl A 5:01:12 (25,861)
Mallett, Anthony S 3:57:07 (9,655)
Mallett, Christopher 5:51:15 (32,432)
Mallett, Tim J 5:51:55 (32,479)
Malley, Michael A 4:21:42 (15,880)
Mallick, James L 4:02:53 (11,206)
Mallinson, Chris 3:10:13 (1,714)
Mallmann, Peter 4:47:33 (22,612)
Mallon, Anthony M 4:28:21 (17,660)
Mallon, Ben Alan 4:49:32 (23,127)
Mallon, Guy R 4:55:16 (24,522)
Malmqvist, Tony 3:18:07 (2,541)
Malone, Derek F 4:36:43 (19,843)
Malone, John 4:24:07 (16,477)
Malone, Kevin 4:28:49 (17,780)
Malone, Lawerence J 3:40:58 (6,024)
Maloney, Philip J 3:59:36 (10,419)
Malsom, Dominic J 3:16:59 (2,428)
Malton, Russell J 5:02:09 (26,051)
Mameli, Sergio 4:00:36 (10,698)
Maña Ribo, Enric 5:13:48 (28,120)
Manasco, Tyrone J 4:26:32 (17,126)
Manby, Christopher P 3:50:30 (7,944)
Mancer, Jez 2:46:45 (357)
Manchester, Neil D 3:42:08 (6,238)
Mancini, Clarke S 4:42:55 (21,450)
Mancini, John Alan 5:32:18 (30,669)
Mancoo, Jay 5:21:27 (29,291)
Mandelli, Marco 4:00:28 (10,656)
Mandeman, Daniel 4:58:32 (25,282)
Manden, Hendrik 4:38:45 (20,365)
Mandizvidza, Tinashe M 6:01:18 (33,129)
Manenti, Andrea 3:48:14 (7,454)
Manero Font, Jaume 5:17:04 (28,654)
Mangalum, Alvin M 4:52:21 (23,832)
Mangion, Stuart J 4:09:31 (12,728)
Mangold, Ryan D 4:02:02 (11,024)
Mangwiro, Denver I 4:06:41 (12,041)
Mani, Rahul 4:05:36 (11,798)
Mankee, Grant 3:22:54 (3,117)
Manktelow, Stuart J 3:14:07 (2,136)
Manley, Adam R 4:10:56 (13,089)
Manley, Stuart T 4:46:19 (22,284)
Manlow, Christopher J 4:41:53 (21,178)
Manlow, John D 2:55:54 (720)
Mann, Craig 2:58:39 (881)
Mann, Dave K 3:53:31 (8,629)
Mann, James R 3:53:34 (8,640)
Mann, John William 3:59:36 (10,419)
Mann, Joseph 6:08:38 (33,500)
Mann, Peter C 3:02:01 (1,118)
Mann, Raj 6:20:17 (34,044)
Mann, Stuart H 3:19:45 (2,717)
Mann, Stuart I 5:13:17 (28,033)
Manners, Warren 4:39:17 (20,513)
Manning, Andrew J 3:49:26 (7,712)
Manning, Carl R 3:42:46 (6,370)
Manning, Charles B 4:39:13 (20,499)
Manning, Chris 4:05:23 (11,749)
Manning, Jason I 3:16:58 (2,424)
Manning, Joseph A 4:34:06 (19,172)
Manning, Julian H 2:50:36 (485)
Manning, Richard J 4:14:59 (14,162)
Manning, Robert J 4:18:11 (14,942)
Manning, Sean M 4:51:01 (23,494)
Manning, Steve D 5:10:28 (27,544)
Mannion, Mike 4:15:48 (14,349)
Mannion, Paul 3:17:36 (2,491)
Mannion, Peter J 3:17:57 (2,522)
Manns, Shaun D 5:01:01 (25,815)
Manoj, Padeepa 3:13:00 (2,006)
Mansbridge, Paul M 4:14:20 (13,994)
Mansfield, Ben R 4:11:18 (13,189)
Mansfield, Christopher C 4:42:40 (21,376)
Mansfield, David N 5:38:48 (31,372)
Mansfield, Luke N 4:22:25 (16,057)
Mansfield, Michael S 2:51:45 (514)
Mansfield, Stephen P 4:34:31 (19,264)
Mansfield, William A 4:24:53 (16,679)
Manship, Alan 4:46:44 (22,416)
Mansi, Andrew J 3:32:03 (4,477)
Manson, Neil 3:10:28 (1,733)
Manson, Stuart D 5:16:42 (28,600)
Mansour, Marc R 4:11:53 (13,355)
Mantell, Stephen D 4:23:53 (16,409)
Manthorpe, Richard 5:34:35 (30,923)
Mantle, Damien 3:50:10 (7,876)
Manton, Christopher J 4:09:35 (12,747)
Manuel, Gareth 4:20:48 (15,636)
Manuel, Tim K 5:10:02 (27,467)
Manville, Paul R 4:23:55 (16,419)
Manwaring, Mark T 4:50:32 (23,381)
Mapes, Simon 4:27:37 (17,417)
Maple, Kevin 4:26:44 (17,187)
Maple, Simon 4:49:27 (23,092)
Mapp, Stuart 3:06:32 (1,405)
Mapperson, Ian M 2:57:48 (823)
Marais, Paul R 3:42:06 (6,235)
Marantz, Jason M 4:38:52 (20,396)
Maranzano, Michael A 3:12:33 (1,937)
Marc-Alain, Schaer 3:41:44 (6,156)
Marcar, Rik M 4:10:48 (13,064)
Marcelle, Nick P 3:32:27 (4,536)
March, Chris 7:06:03 (35,014)
March, Justin 3:39:51 (5,817)
March, Neil E 5:12:28 (27,889)
March, Simon 3:59:27 (10,379)
Marchant, Jon 3:58:16 (10,027)
Marchant, Paul A 2:28:40 (52)
Marchant, Peter M 6:43:27 (34,687)
Marchetti, Maurizio 5:10:25 (27,535)
Marco, Marcello 3:52:26 (8,388)
Marco, Peter 4:40:03 (20,739)
Marcondes, Pedro 4:46:58 (22,474)
Marconi, Massimo 3:27:17 (3,729)
Marcoz, Rinaldo 4:40:25 (20,819)
Marcus, Harvey 3:57:50 (9,890)
Mardell, Kevin 3:57:48 (9,873)
Mardlin, Ricky J 3:40:24 (5,927)
Maree, Christiaan 3:45:54 (6,960)
Marenghi, Marcel 5:09:43 (27,405)
Maresta, Paolo 4:00:38 (10,705)
Maret Mercier, Sidoine Robert 3:18:49 (2,604)
Mareta, Petr 4:11:20 (13,202)
Margetts, Daryll C 6:56:57 (34,920)
Mariani, Jean 4:45:04 (21,986)
Mariano Da Costa, Jeferson 4:01:52 (10,996)
Mariette, Louis 4:48:56 (22,955)
Marin, José 3:34:30 (4,879)
Marin, Mario Eduardo 3:48:53 (7,591)
Marinelli, Massimiliano 3:46:56 (7,187)
Marinko, John 3:04:21 (1,253)
Maripuri, Naidu 4:37:23 (20,004)
Maris, Graham C 3:36:38 (5,257)
Mark, Jonathan D 3:46:15 (7,028)
Mark, Mullin J 4:33:17 (18,968)
Mark, Roland M 4:23:28 (16,299)
Mark, Scott 5:19:09 (28,989)
Mark, Tyler 4:32:10 (18,679)
Markham, John C 3:31:42 (4,422)
Markham, Matthew L 4:07:31 (12,240)
Markhoff, Burkhard E 4:12:48 (13,605)
Marklew, Paul F 5:32:06 (30,652)
Marklew, Steve 2:36:58 (141)
Markley, Simon A 3:07:29 (1,478)
Marks, Craig N 6:21:29 (34,093)
Marks, Dan 4:49:56 (23,225)
Marks, Elliot 4:03:28 (11,323)
Marks, Henry 5:52:51 (32,537)
Marks, Richard 3:57:10 (9,664)
Marks, Stephen R 5:28:34 (30,215)
Markslag, Jan 3:48:45 (7,552)
Markwell, Kevin M 6:15:14 (33,802)
Markwick, David C 4:20:22 (15,527)
Marlais, Matko 5:22:59 (29,515)
Marland, John 4:33:13 (18,948)
Marler, David R 5:03:45 (26,334)
Marletta, Giuseppe 4:16:27 (14,509)
Marley, Nigel R 2:31:08 (73)
Marlow, Richard J 5:09:52 (27,436)
Marlowe, Andrew Daniel 4:54:14 (24,268)
Marmolejo, Julian E 6:46:01 (34,721)
Marnoch, Adam 3:39:55 (5,838)
Marquenet, Lawrence 3:08:31 (1,568)
Marques, Miguel 3:45:18 (6,854)
Marques Da Silva, Eloi 3:47:14 (7,239)
Marquez, Miguel 4:57:18 (24,985)
Marquis-Jones, Peter H 2:56:56 (770)
Marr, Irvine 3:43:49 (6,592)
Marr, Peter 3:46:16 (7,032)
Marrai, Sandro R 2:57:07 (785)
Marriott, Jeff R 3:51:56 (8,263)
Marriott, John D 3:11:38 (1,843)
Marriott, Paul 3:32:27 (4,536)
Marriott, Sean J 4:33:22 (18,998)
Marsch, Paul A 4:09:20 (12,695)
Marsden, Andrew F 4:46:42 (22,400)
Marsden, Angus A 4:04:03 (11,459)
Marsden, Gary 4:11:02 (13,121)
Marsden, Hugh 2:59:53 (989)
Marsden, Ian N 3:27:55 (3,842)
Marsden, John 5:45:32 (31,977)
Marsden, Lee E 4:32:23 (18,723)
Marsden, William 3:25:46 (3,497)
Marseglia, Pasquale 2:56:42 (757)
Marsh, Clive F 4:50:46 (23,437)
Marsh, Colin 5:33:35 (30,819)
Marsh, Daniel D 3:57:20 (9,721)
Marsh, David J 4:28:02 (17,551)
Marsh, Gary 5:01:01 (25,815)
Marsh, Jim 3:54:26 (8,872)
Marsh, John E 3:50:42 (7,994)
Marsh, Nicholas P 4:18:34 (15,044)
Marsh, Patrick C 4:14:32 (14,037)
Marsh, Pete 3:06:13 (1,392)
Marsh, Philip J 3:57:11 (9,670)
Marsh, Richard 3:35:57 (5,145)
Marsh, Richard P 3:53:21 (8,592)
Marsh, Samuel 4:29:02 (17,843)
Marsh, Stephen R 5:40:04 (31,504)
Marshall, Andrew 4:36:23 (19,766)
Marshall, Andrew 5:20:19 (29,131)
Marshall, Andrew J 3:08:55 (1,610)
Marshall, Andrew J 3:45:14 (6,842)
Marshall, Christopher W 6:23:09 (34,156)
Marshall, Craig P 4:10:36 (13,006)
Marshall, Craig S 5:12:43 (27,929)
Marshall, Damon L 3:54:31 (8,894)
Marshall, Darren A 5:14:38 (28,257)
Marshall, Dave 4:56:29 (24,795)
Marshall, Dean G 5:34:24 (30,899)
Marshall, Ian 4:11:11 (13,158)
Marshall, James 3:36:49 (5,279)
Marshall, James J 4:27:15 (17,325)
Marshall, Jason 4:58:03 (25,148)
Marshall, John A 3:58:33 (10,114)
Marshall, Kevin J 3:05:35 (1,340)
Marshall, Michael V 5:16:12 (28,528)
Marshall, Neil S 4:04:49 (11,612)
Marshall, Norman H 4:14:10 (13,949)
Marshall, Paul M 4:48:21 (22,817)
Marshall, Peter M 4:22:00 (15,943)
Marshall, Raymond 3:15:01 (2,234)
Marshall, Rob 3:13:42 (2,089)
Marshall, Sam 5:14:59 (28,314)
Marshall, Simon Paul 4:00:41 (10,716)
Marshall, Stephen 3:00:45 (1,034)
Marshall, Timothy 4:18:36 (15,054)
Marshall, Timothy J 6:00:33 (33,080)
Marshall, Tom J 2:50:28 (480)
Marsland, Steve 3:56:02 (9,322)
Marsters, Michael 3:05:49 (1,358)
Marston, Andrew 5:08:26 (27,170)
Marston, Duncan A 5:22:16 (29,402)
Marston, Geoffrey M 3:51:06 (8,074)
Marston, Jeremy 3:23:33 (3,196)
Marston, Lee 3:42:35 (6,325)
Martell, Richard L 4:18:37 (15,058)
Martelletti, Paul V 2:26:16 (38)
Martial, Aranaz 4:54:30 (24,334)
Martin, Alan J 6:41:16 (34,650)
Martin, Alastair D 3:42:27 (6,288)
Martin, Alejandro 4:30:34 (18,245)
Martin, Alex L 4:38:03 (20,179)

Martin, Andrew C.	4:59:44 (25,541)	
Martin, Andrew E.	5:49:47 (32,319)	
Martin, Andrew J.	3:37:28 (5,392)	
Martin, Anthony J.	3:27:11 (3,712)	
Martin, Bruce A.	3:48:13 (7,449)	
Martin, Carleton E.	3:52:51 (8,476)	
Martin, Colin S.	4:02:24 (11,106)	
Martin, Craig R.	4:05:52 (11,854)	
Martin, David T.	4:27:12 (17,309)	
Martin, Denzil	3:59:20 (10,345)	
Martin, George	3:55:43 (9,232)	
Martin, Gerard P.	5:33:24 (30,796)	
Martin, Glenn S.	4:20:09 (15,471)	
Martin, Graeme J.	5:07:15 (26,953)	
Martin, Graham R.	5:40:23 (31,533)	
Martin, James T.	3:53:50 (8,710)	
Martin, Jeffrey M.	4:47:55 (22,712)	
Martin, Jim	4:47:32 (22,605)	
Martin, John	4:48:18 (22,809)	
Martin, John S.	4:48:11 (22,779)	
Martin, Jonathan S.	4:35:52 (19,644)	
Martin, Karl J.	4:35:53 (19,648)	
Martin, Matthew	5:30:30 (30,462)	
Martin, Matthew D.	5:14:16 (28,202)	
Martin, Neil P.	3:13:25 (2,053)	
Martin, Nick J.	4:40:36 (20,860)	
Martin, Pablo	3:29:06 (4,028)	
Martin, Paul	3:59:41 (10,451)	
Martin, Paul	5:11:10 (27,667)	
Martin, Paul A.	5:01:07 (25,844)	
Martin, Paul J.	4:27:50 (17,501)	
Martin, Paul R.	6:37:16 (34,574)	
Martin, Philip A.	3:19:37 (2,699)	
Martin, Richard A.	5:39:59 (31,495)	
Martin, Richard H.	5:01:37 (25,936)	
Martin, Rick J.	3:50:17 (7,900)	
Martin, Robert	4:03:29 (11,327)	
Martin, Robert	5:38:04 (31,286)	
Martin, Sean	3:07:38 (1,495)	
Martin, Sean	5:28:34 (30,215)	
Martin, Shaun S	3:58:57 (10,237)	
Martin, Steve	4:00:07 (10,575)	
Martin, Steve P	3:53:43 (8,682)	
Martin, Steven J	3:58:47 (10,189)	
Martin, Stewart W	4:38:36 (20,330)	
Martin, Stuart A.	5:28:28 (30,207)	
Martin Gonzalez, Angel L.	3:26:11 (3,555)	
Martina, Reynaldo V	4:43:18 (21,543)	
Martinez, Isidro	4:12:53 (13,623)	
Martinez, Martin	5:04:48 (26,506)	
Martinez Diez, Miguel Angel M.	3:59:10 (10,303)	
Martinez Fuster, Alejandro	3:48:59 (7,616)	
Martinez Hermida, Manuel I	3:24:34 (3,351)	
Martinez Pumares, Jorge	6:25:14 (34,239)	
Martinez Saavedra, Raimundo	3:39:45 (5,799)	
Martin-Kitchen, Ryan J	4:19:47 (15,368)	
Martins, Antonio M.	3:14:39 (2,188)	
Martins, Gabriel R.	4:34:47 (19,348)	
Martyn, Nicholas A.	2:28:41 (53)	
Maru, Tony C.	3:14:23 (2,162)	
Marval, Jonathan	3:49:27 (7,718)	
Marval, Paul D.	3:08:52 (1,606)	
Marven, Roger A.	4:51:34 (23,640)	
Marwood, Keiren	4:12:29 (13,518)	
Marzullo, Clemente	4:29:17 (17,919)	
Maskell, Chris	4:40:12 (20,775)	
Maskell, Robert E	4:51:54 (23,729)	
Maskell, Scott	5:40:59 (31,585)	
Maskens, David	3:57:31 (9,775)	
Maskill, Simon L	3:23:37 (3,204)	
Maslin, Mark	4:42:23 (21,297)	
Maslin, Paul J.	4:35:52 (19,644)	
Mason, Alex	6:15:10 (33,799)	
Mason, Andrew J	4:39:38 (20,621)	
Mason, Anthony J.	4:53:29 (24,069)	
Mason, Brian	4:29:13 (17,899)	
Mason, Charles	3:12:50 (1,978)	
Mason, Chris J	6:02:57 (33,227)	
Mason, Chris L.	2:58:04 (840)	
Mason, Christopher J.	3:08:34 (1,571)	
Mason, Dale	5:26:30 (29,989)	
Mason, Daniel	5:34:52 (30,955)	
Mason, David	4:17:09 (14,683)	
Mason, Eamon	3:38:55 (5,658)	
Mason, Glenn	4:37:43 (20,099)	
Mason, Ian	5:18:13 (28,820)	
Mason, James H.	2:46:32 (347)	
Mason, Jamie P.	4:14:05 (13,925)	
Mason, Joe	4:49:06 (22,998)	
Mason, John B.	5:10:23 (27,528)	
Mason, John S.	4:43:57 (21,703)	
Mason, Mark L	5:39:45 (31,471)	
Mason, Neil	4:07:13 (12,155)	
Mason, Neil	5:06:20 (26,780)	
Mason, Paul	4:17:50 (14,846)	
Mason, Paul A.	3:07:27 (1,473)	
Mason, Pete N	3:50:41 (7,989)	
Mason, Peter J	3:45:47 (6,945)	
Mason, Rich	3:39:33 (5,766)	
Mason, Richard	3:29:14 (4,046)	
Mason, Richard K.	5:43:50 (31,834)	
Mason, Ross M	4:04:19 (11,511)	
Mason, Simon J	4:18:31 (15,035)	
Mason, Simon J	4:31:16 (18,419)	
Mason, Spencer S	4:03:26 (11,317)	
Mason, Thomas E.	4:38:36 (20,330)	
Mason, Toby	4:18:31 (15,035)	
Mason, Tom	4:02:00 (11,017)	
Massa, Andrea	4:10:15 (12,921)	
Massam, Stephen	4:38:19 (20,257)	
Massbery, David J.	3:39:00 (5,686)	
Massey, Adrian P.	3:23:22 (3,171)	
Massey, Edward	5:19:32 (29,039)	
Massey, Paul A	5:13:15 (28,029)	
Massey, Raymond C.	4:22:40 (16,119)	
Massey, Richard J.	4:43:46 (21,659)	
Massey, Simon J	6:05:18 (33,353)	
Massey, Stephen	3:25:21 (3,434)	
Massey, William M	3:40:28 (5,937)	
Massingham, Jonathan P	2:57:06 (782)	
Masson, Richie	3:34:35 (4,889)	
Massy, Robert L	4:00:35 (10,694)	
Masters, Andrew	3:24:06 (3,279)	
Masters, Gary	3:39:52 (5,821)	
Masters, Lee G.	3:49:13 (7,671)	
Masters, Nolan	3:59:22 (10,359)	
Masters, Stephen P.	4:20:09 (15,471)	
Masters, Stuart J	4:48:22 (22,819)	
Masterson, Andrew J	4:19:10 (15,203)	
Masterson, Jonathan D	4:16:03 (14,407)	
Masterson, Paul	4:56:47 (24,871)	
Masterton, Simon H.	3:32:30 (4,543)	
Mastroianni, Giuseppe A	4:47:50 (22,684)	
Mastrovita, Matteo	4:11:22 (13,214)	
Masullo, Mauro	3:57:14 (9,682)	
Matamala Roa, Hardy A.	3:01:17 (1,072)	
Materazzi, Francesco	4:12:55 (13,635)	
Matev, Dimitar S.	3:56:07 (9,344)	
Mathai, Oliver K	4:32:50 (18,855)	
Mathe, Philip P.	4:25:53 (16,958)	
Mather, Alan	4:17:39 (14,806)	
Mather, Anthony M.	4:37:08 (19,950)	
Mathes, Fernand	3:59:31 (10,395)	
Matheson, Peter Donald	5:01:23 (25,893)	
Matheson, Shaun	4:28:18 (17,647)	
Matheson, Stuart Thomas	3:55:34 (9,176)	
Mathew Collins, Duanne M	5:16:36 (28,581)	
Mathews, Peter	4:45:55 (22,192)	
Mathias, David C	4:23:06 (16,207)	
Mathie, Richard P	3:05:51 (1,359)	
Mathie, Rod A	3:38:15 (5,543)	
Mathieson, David	5:41:25 (31,621)	
Mathieu, Remy	3:52:12 (8,328)	
Matisonn, Mark	4:48:09 (22,772)	
Matisonn, Shaun	3:38:51 (5,648)	
Matley, Will	5:42:14 (31,698)	
Matloob, Samir A	5:16:32 (28,567)	
Matonti, Vincenzo	3:50:49 (8,024)	
Mattessi, Peter	3:42:30 (6,303)	
Matthai, Clarence C.	4:33:12 (18,944)	
Matthams, David J	4:38:27 (20,288)	
Matthew, David L	5:28:48 (30,251)	
Matthews, Adrian S	4:25:33 (16,856)	
Matthews, Alan	4:36:49 (19,870)	
Matthews, Anthony R	4:42:45 (21,397)	
Matthews, Ben D	2:44:38 (300)	
Matthews, Bertie J	4:49:18 (23,053)	
Matthews, Elis A	5:14:46 (28,277)	
Matthews, Gair Richard	3:13:23 (2,050)	
Matthews, Graham D	4:37:38 (20,078)	
Matthews, Guy W.	3:57:19 (9,712)	
Matthews, Hayden	3:53:33 (8,634)	
Matthews, Ian R.	3:18:14 (2,548)	
Matthews, James H.	3:34:13 (4,815)	
Matthews, John	5:05:01 (26,549)	
Matthews, Jon	4:55:28 (24,566)	
Matthews, Jon James	4:50:15 (23,301)	
Matthews, Jonathan	4:19:05 (15,181)	
Matthews, Jonathan	4:54:24 (24,310)	
Matthews, Karl A	4:59:06 (25,410)	
Matthews, Kevin R.	5:25:14 (29,828)	
Matthews, Luke J	3:13:33 (2,066)	
Matthews, Martin	2:29:14 (62)	
Matthews, Neal A	3:52:12 (8,328)	
Matthews, Nicholas	4:07:44 (12,295)	
Matthews, Paul	4:23:57 (16,430)	
Matthews, Peter I.	4:04:03 (11,459)	
Matthews, Ray E	3:28:00 (3,858)	
Matthews, Roy T	4:53:53 (24,197)	
Matthews, Sean I	3:29:18 (4,068)	
Matthews, Stuart J	3:11:06 (1,794)	
Matthews, Thomas	3:11:29 (1,826)	
Matthews, Tim I	5:37:52 (31,258)	
Matthews, Vernon G	5:08:09 (27,112)	
Mattinson, Neil	4:47:03 (22,498)	
Mattioli, Sandro	3:34:28 (4,869)	
Mattison, Michael J	3:42:11 (6,248)	
Mattock, Jonathan R	3:34:18 (4,830)	
Mattocks, Craig J	2:44:12 (291)	
Mattocks, Ian	4:50:29 (23,368)	
Maughan, Nigel	4:58:33 (25,284)	
Mauloni, Fabio	4:42:27 (21,313)	
Maunder, Adam T	5:08:03 (27,094)	
Maunder, Jamie R	4:37:37 (20,070)	
Maurel, Olivier	4:05:35 (11,794)	
Maurello, Domenico	4:25:42 (16,910)	
Maurer, Mike	4:08:00 (12,359)	
Mauro, Lorenzo	5:17:22 (28,691)	
Maury, Neil	3:20:55 (2,881)	
Mauschitz, Christian	6:00:32 (33,077)	
Mavian, Alex	4:29:17 (17,919)	
Mavor, Alastair J	4:18:39 (15,072)	
Maw, Philip	3:45:07 (6,819)	
Maw, Phillip	4:00:04 (10,564)	
Mawby, Michael R	3:40:47 (5,994)	
Mawdsley, Joel E	4:33:48 (19,097)	
Mawdsley, Keith John	4:47:37 (22,634)	
Mawer, Roger	5:20:41 (29,173)	
Mawer, Simon T	5:46:40 (32,062)	
Mawson, Matt G	4:06:23 (11,967)	
Maxmin, Peter T	4:33:49 (19,101)	
Maxwell, Anthony T	5:05:34 (26,653)	
Maxwell, Antony S	3:42:40 (6,350)	
Maxwell, Mark	3:50:12 (7,881)	
Maxwell, Ross	4:16:18 (14,473)	
May, Adrian A	3:50:25 (7,925)	
May, Brian	5:03:37 (26,308)	
May, Dan J	5:43:36 (31,823)	
May, Darren	3:47:16 (7,245)	
May, Darren J	4:30:56 (18,331)	
May, Fredrick A	3:45:19 (6,860)	
May, Kev	3:13:25 (2,053)	
May, Lee Charles	3:34:04 (4,778)	
May, Mike	4:02:08 (11,048)	
May, Peter S	4:45:37 (22,109)	
May, Rob W	5:55:49 (32,750)	
May, Stuart	4:47:32 (22,605)	
Mayall, Adrian J	5:51:04 (32,416)	
Mayall, Philip	3:46:27 (7,077)	
Mayall, Shawn	5:51:05 (32,419)	
Maycock, Jeremy F	4:31:27 (18,487)	
Maycock, Stuart T	2:34:49 (113)	
Maydon, Will	4:48:44 (22,910)	
Maye, Brian	3:53:55 (8,726)	
Mayers, Louis	3:04:13 (1,249)	
Mayes, Jon	3:54:22 (8,855)	
Mayes, Nigel C.	4:39:31 (20,587)	
Mayes, Paul	3:48:23 (7,482)	
Mayes, Robert	4:23:40 (16,355)	

Mayhew, Allen M	4:32:43 (18,819)	
Mayhew, Dave M	3:40:46 (5,990)	
Mayhew, Jon E	4:11:18 (13,189)	
Mayhew, Steve	6:00:24 (33,068)	
Mayles, Gregg	3:52:50 (8,474)	
Maynard, Graham L	3:13:19 (2,037)	
Maynard, Kristian	3:42:33 (6,317)	
Maynard, Steven	4:06:44 (12,048)	
Maynard, Trevor B	6:07:37 (33,467)	
Maynard-Connor, Giles	3:53:55 (8,726)	
Mayne, Christopher S	3:57:11 (9,670)	
Mayo, Matt G	4:52:17 (23,823)	
Mayo, Philip I	3:19:18 (2,650)	
Mayoh, Leigh R	3:55:02 (9,032)	
Mayson, Howard J	3:58:40 (10,151)	
Maytham, Gary D	4:30:48 (18,303)	
Maytum, Jez D	4:05:06 (11,679)	
Maywood, Paul C	7:33:31 (35,242)	
Mazza, Alfio	4:18:58 (15,152)	
Mazzaferro, Matthew A	3:36:04 (5,169)	
Mazzantini, Maurizio	3:21:25 (2,934)	
Mazzei, Giovanni	3:06:20 (1,397)	
Mbuyi, Joseph	3:45:18 (6,854)	
McAllen, Jonathan	3:36:03 (5,166)	
McAllister, Andrew P	4:37:26 (20,018)	
McAllister, Darren	3:00:04 (1,002)	
McAllister, Francis J	5:40:24 (31,536)	
McAllister, William A	4:17:02 (14,654)	
McAndie, Stewart	3:14:52 (2,214)	
McAndrew, Tom M	4:09:48 (12,803)	
McAnea, Thomas C	4:32:06 (18,664)	
McAneny, Robert	4:30:58 (18,340)	
McArthur, Andrew	5:05:55 (26,715)	
McAuley, Chris J	4:12:10 (13,433)	
McAuley, Michael	5:03:34 (26,294)	
McBean, Benjamin E	6:20:24 (34,048)	
McBean, Craig James	4:41:57 (21,191)	
McBean, Matthew R	5:34:12 (30,876)	
McBride, Alistair	4:50:41 (23,418)	
McBride, Martin J	3:17:24 (2,476)	
McBrown, Philip A	3:50:40 (7,983)	
McCabe, Ciaran	3:20:25 (2,815)	
McCabe, Gerry	4:21:18 (15,764)	
McCabe, Liam F	3:11:53 (1,874)	
McCabe, Peadar	4:49:27 (23,092)	
McCabe, Scott	5:07:48 (27,059)	
McCabe, Sean P	4:21:30 (15,812)	
McCaffrey, Robert J	3:56:56 (9,603)	
McCaig, James	3:40:01 (5,863)	
McCain, Neil J	5:33:46 (30,839)	
McCairn, Dice	3:58:49 (10,198)	
McCall, Robert B	6:00:47 (33,100)	
McCall, Steven D	4:05:48 (11,843)	
McCallum, Iain	4:36:07 (19,705)	
McCallum, Kenneth	5:37:31 (31,228)	
McCandless, Huw	4:18:01 (14,891)	
McCann, Gerard	3:05:35 (1,340)	
McCann, John	3:50:49 (8,024)	
McCarrick, Anthony	4:26:22 (17,080)	
McCarrick MBE, Derek	5:48:09 (32,181)	
McCarroll, Anthony R	3:40:49 (6,003)	
McCarron, Darragh	4:15:45 (14,335)	
McCarron, Richard	3:41:46 (6,161)	
McCarry, Patrick	3:51:56 (8,263)	
McCartan, Patrick J	3:21:56 (3,003)	
McCarter, Dominic	2:44:58 (315)	
McCarthy, Adam J	4:33:16 (18,965)	
McCarthy, Conor	5:07:51 (27,069)	
McCarthy, Donal	4:09:36 (12,753)	
McCarthy, Francis	4:31:22 (18,462)	
McCarthy, Gregory	7:00:47 (34,959)	
McCarthy, Ian	3:54:11 (8,808)	
McCarthy, James D	3:52:15 (8,347)	
McCarthy, Jason	4:53:10 (24,017)	
McCarthy, Keith Douglas	6:12:50 (33,685)	
McCarthy, Kevin C	3:43:29 (6,520)	
McCarthy, Martin R	4:15:21 (14,243)	
McCarthy, Michael G	9:03:06 (35,357)	
McCarthy, Michael J	6:12:30 (33,661)	
McCarthy, Michael R	5:04:46 (26,501)	
McCarthy, Paul F	5:25:59 (29,933)	
McCarthy, Pete J	5:48:37 (32,230)	
McCarthy, Scott	3:11:41 (1,849)	
McCarthy, Shane	3:13:22 (2,046)	
McCartney, David F	3:52:16 (8,353)	
McCatty, Alex G	5:36:38 (31,136)	
McCaughey, Tim	4:35:29 (19,536)	
McCleave, Damian P	3:50:42 (7,994)	
McClelland, Glenn B	4:51:43 (23,679)	
McClelland, Michael B	3:31:48 (4,438)	
McClelland, Peter N	3:32:24 (4,530)	
McClintock, Stephen C	5:01:40 (25,945)	
McCloskey, Gavin	5:10:05 (27,475)	
McClunan, Eric	4:21:40 (15,872)	
McClure, Greg M	3:03:31 (1,203)	
McCluskie, Kristen	4:21:49 (15,905)	
McClutchie, Mike	3:54:06 (8,781)	
McClymont, Ian W	3:58:09 (9,990)	
McColgan, Martin	4:11:19 (13,194)	
McColl, Ewen M	3:05:52 (1,360)	
McComb, Phil	5:10:34 (27,561)	
McConnell, Andrew J	3:43:00 (6,418)	
McConnell, David	4:49:20 (23,064)	
McConnell, David	5:40:07 (31,510)	
McConville, Cahal M	3:30:48 (4,298)	
McConville, John P	3:09:44 (1,683)	
McConville, Kevin	3:55:55 (9,292)	
McConville, Paul R	4:10:14 (12,916)	
McCormack, Ade G	4:22:40 (16,119)	
McCormack, Gavin M	4:48:01 (22,745)	
McCormick, Andrew D	4:37:32 (20,045)	
McCormick, Chris	4:37:14 (19,969)	
McCormick, John E	5:26:32 (29,995)	
McCormick, Peter	3:56:58 (9,610)	
McCormick-Houston, Johnnie	5:01:12 (25,861)	
McCouaig, Jason A	4:40:09 (20,763)	
McCourt, George	2:44:34 (297)	
McCourt, Kevin	5:54:51 (32,673)	
McCourt, Kevin B	4:17:35 (14,790)	
McCoy, Edward J	5:36:27 (31,120)	
McCoy, Gerard M	3:56:06 (9,341)	
McCoy, Phil J	2:44:37 (299)	
McCoy, Robin E	3:10:44 (1,757)	
McCreesh, Patrick	5:13:43 (28,104)	
McCrimmon, Neil K	3:35:29 (5,045)	
McCrory, Patrick	3:37:53 (5,469)	
McCrudden, Ian Joseph	4:18:25 (15,001)	
McCubbin, David A	6:59:06 (34,936)	
McCullagh, Philip E	4:48:15 (22,799)	
McCullie, John	4:58:20 (25,222)	
McCulloch, Philip F	3:54:40 (8,936)	
McCulloch, Stephen J	3:47:51 (7,361)	
McCulloch, Thomas A	3:17:04 (2,439)	
McCulloch, Willie	5:04:27 (26,449)	
McCullough, Stephen	3:33:17 (4,650)	
McCullough, Stephen	6:14:28 (33,765)	
McCully, John	5:07:36 (27,024)	
McCusker, John	3:47:34 (7,303)	
McDade, Norman	5:21:30 (29,298)	
McDavid, Nigel A	5:26:50 (30,028)	
McDermott, Christopher B	6:19:01 (33,997)	
McDermott, Darren Leslie	3:23:47 (3,229)	
McDermott, Garry	4:48:29 (22,846)	
McDermott, Gary	4:58:51 (25,349)	
McDermott, Greg	3:13:39 (2,084)	
McDermott, Nigel	3:42:55 (6,402)	
McDermott, Sean P	3:11:44 (1,852)	
McDonagh, Luke	3:33:39 (4,696)	
McDonagh, Michael A	3:05:24 (1,329)	
McDonald, Alan	3:02:05 (1,125)	
McDonald, Andrew	5:01:43 (25,956)	
McDonald, Corey S	4:27:43 (17,451)	
McDonald, Daniel C	4:02:25 (11,108)	
McDonald, Darren	4:07:38 (12,265)	
McDonald, David John	4:50:14 (23,292)	
McDonald, Glynn W	3:26:41 (3,633)	
McDonald, Gordon A	3:59:21 (10,351)	
McDonald, Ian G	3:27:13 (3,719)	
McDonald, Jamie	3:15:51 (2,323)	
McDonald, Mark M	4:35:16 (19,483)	
McDonald, Maurice G	6:40:41 (34,636)	
McDonald, Neil	3:13:01 (2,009)	
McDonald, Neil	3:28:18 (3,899)	
McDonald, Peter	3:28:56 (4,000)	
McDonald, Robert	3:37:42 (5,440)	
McDonald, Scott	4:08:15 (12,430)	
McDonald, Scott K	4:13:04 (13,672)	
McDonald, Shaun H	4:13:00 (13,659)	
McDonald, Stephen P	4:07:26 (12,221)	
McDonald, Terry J	4:09:22 (12,699)	
McDonnell, John J	7:03:35 (34,985)	
McDonnell, John R	4:36:33 (19,804)	
McDonnell, Mark P	3:32:34 (4,558)	
McDonnell, Martin	4:42:53 (21,440)	
McDonough, Alister	4:05:44 (11,828)	
McDonough, Kevin	4:41:18 (21,037)	
McDonough, Trevor J	4:39:55 (20,696)	
McDougall, Grant Robert	4:48:31 (22,856)	
McDowell, Jody W	4:41:08 (20,991)	
McDowell, William M	4:47:48 (22,671)	
McElhatton, Nic S	5:10:42 (27,584)	
McElroy, Brain	3:33:47 (4,722)	
McElroy, Craig J	3:35:39 (5,086)	
McEntaggart, Eamonn A	6:02:16 (33,187)	
McEntaggart, Tim	4:44:39 (21,871)	
McEntee, Aidan	3:51:27 (8,156)	
McEntee, John	3:21:20 (2,924)	
McEntee, Scott	4:11:54 (13,358)	
McEntee, Stephen	3:34:26 (4,862)	
McEvoy, Andrew John	4:49:38 (23,159)	
McEvoy, Jonathan	4:42:27 (21,313)	
McEwan, Alastair D	3:38:21 (5,557)	
McEwan, David L	5:01:12 (25,861)	
McEwan, Fraser	4:27:52 (17,509)	
McEwan, Graham	3:41:45 (6,159)	
McEwan, Stephen	4:59:29 (25,494)	
McEwen, Craig J	5:15:16 (28,378)	
McEwen, Malcolm J	5:42:44 (31,738)	
McFadden, Roger S	3:36:29 (5,232)	
McFadyen, Michael	5:11:22 (27,705)	
McFall, Andrew R	3:29:32 (4,104)	
McFall, Kevin J	4:31:05 (18,382)	
McFarland, Andrew	4:51:46 (23,692)	
McFarland, Luke Francis	3:01:53 (1,107)	
McFarlane, Graham W	3:58:18 (10,033)	
McFarlane, James W	3:21:09 (2,907)	
McFarlane, John	2:20:44 (21)	
McFarlane, Paul	3:53:08 (8,541)	
McFarlane, Sean L	4:26:15 (17,051)	
McFaul, Richard W	4:10:11 (12,907)	
McFerran, Robert	4:05:18 (11,734)	
McGarr, Anthony R	4:03:52 (11,414)	
McGarrie, Callum H	3:42:58 (6,412)	
McGarry, Richard D	4:17:01 (14,651)	
McGarvie, Alan G	3:48:57 (7,605)	
McGeachan, Garry	5:03:56 (26,370)	
McGeary, Simon	4:17:13 (14,697)	
McGee, John	4:09:33 (12,737)	
McGeever, Patrick D	2:48:06 (401)	
McGeoch, Mick	2:53:20 (574)	
McGeorge, Alistair K	4:44:00 (21,723)	
McGhee, James Arthur	3:36:33 (5,245)	
McGibbon, Jason S	3:48:30 (7,508)	
McGill, Colin N	2:36:30 (133)	
McGillan, David P	4:35:26 (19,527)	
McGillicuddy, Christopher J	3:32:31 (4,547)	
McGilligan, Charles G	3:03:49 (1,226)	
McGilligan, Joe M	4:25:09 (16,751)	
McGinley, Stephen P	6:19:05 (34,002)	
McGinty, John Peter	4:22:24 (16,050)	
McGinty, Sean	4:19:01 (15,164)	
McGlade, John	6:01:53 (33,160)	
McGlennon, David L	4:06:46 (12,053)	
McGlyn, Andrew	4:47:49 (22,675)	
McGlynn, Stephen	3:30:47 (4,296)	
McGough, James	4:17:40 (14,814)	
McGouran, Jonathan G	3:48:35 (7,529)	
McGovern, Terence Christopher	4:34:33 (4,983)	
McGowan, Andrew J	4:30:11 (18,146)	
McGowan, Grant J	4:35:52 (19,644)	
McGowan, Kevin	4:41:17 (21,034)	
McGowan, Peter J	7:03:59 (34,994)	
McGowan, Scott G	4:31:01 (18,352)	
McGowan, Tim J	4:06:24 (11,969)	
McGrane, Larry R	4:58:07 (25,170)	
McGrann, Ian	4:14:25 (14,017)	
McGrath, Andrew	3:56:00 (9,309)	
McGrath, Benjamin L	3:45:29 (6,891)	

McGrath, David 3:16:48 (2,415)
McGrath, Michael J 3:35:48 (5,117)
McGraw, Sean 5:00:08 (25,620)
McGregor, Andrew K 4:17:07 (14,671)
McGregor, Ian D 3:51:46 (8,220)
McGregor, Ian D 5:29:50 (30,379)
McGregor, Roddy 2:43:05 (258)
McGrory, Raymond 5:32:14 (30,662)
McGuckin, Michael 4:32:21 (18,715)
McGuigan, Duncan 5:57:19 (32,856)
McGuigan, James 4:05:38 (11,812)
McGuill, Mike D 4:47:41 (22,647)
McGuiness, Jonathan O 4:25:32 (16,847)
McGuinness, Harold 4:15:01 (14,168)
McGuinness, Liam 4:37:48 (20,120)
McGuire, Andrew J 5:01:47 (25,967)
McGuire, Craig 4:05:20 (11,739)
McGuire, David M 3:02:22 (1,140)
McGuire, Dominic 3:02:32 (1,148)
McGuire, Stewart P 3:41:11 (6,067)
McGurk, Paul 3:38:05 (5,510)
McHale, Barry D 6:20:07 (34,036)
McHenry, Gareth D 5:22:14 (29,394)
McHugh, Derek F 4:38:12 (20,230)
McHugh, Edward 3:19:09 (2,632)
McHugh, Gerard B 4:23:33 (16,327)
McHugh, Michael P 4:55:30 (24,572)
McHugh, Noel 3:40:43 (5,974)
McHugh, Sean 4:44:16 (21,783)
McIlroy, James S 2:47:24 (379)
McIlwee, Ian 2:44:54 (312)
McIlwee, Laurie 4:44:16 (21,783)
McInally, Michael 4:14:08 (13,941)
McInerney, Michael C 4:32:40 (18,808)
McInnes, John 3:58:36 (10,126)
McIntosh, Andrew G 4:07:47 (12,315)
McIntosh, Dennis A 6:26:39 (34,305)
McIntosh, Edward 4:28:06 (17,580)
McIntosh, Graeme 4:26:44 (17,187)
McIntyre, Adam J 6:48:53 (34,793)
McIntyre, Alan J 3:41:38 (6,134)
McIntyre, John P 4:05:31 (11,773)
McIntyre, Russell 4:25:02 (16,719)
McIver, Gary P 5:51:54 (32,478)
McKane, Robert C 6:06:35 (33,417)
McKay, Alan 4:38:56 (20,416)
McKay, Ben V 3:42:32 (6,310)
McKay, Craig J 5:29:48 (30,374)
McKay, Ewan W 2:55:02 (665)
McKay, George C 5:15:49 (28,476)
McKay, Stuart D 4:38:19 (20,257)
McKean, Gary 4:59:27 (25,484)
McKean, Matthew 4:11:21 (13,210)
McKechnie, Anthony 4:21:38 (15,858)
McKechnie, James D 4:46:16 (22,267)
McKee, Gavin M 4:02:51 (11,198)
McKeeman, Alan H 3:59:10 (10,303)
McKeen, Kenneth R 4:07:28 (12,228)
McKeeney, Paul 4:10:25 (12,958)
McKeever, Andrew L 3:35:40 (5,090)
McKeith, Stuart G 4:42:33 (21,345)
McKellar, James R 4:45:49 (22,161)
McKendrick, Hugh R 4:07:19 (12,183)
McKendrick, Rob J 5:10:06 (27,478)
McKenna, Michael P 3:16:55 (2,421)
McKensey, Andrew B 3:51:01 (8,058)
McKenzie, Grant W 3:29:52 (4,162)
McKenzie, James M 3:03:59 (1,238)
McKenzie, John 4:51:09 (23,521)
McKenzie, Phil 4:46:31 (22,347)
McKenzie, Sam 5:32:55 (30,743)
McKenzie-Cook, Scott 3:58:01 (9,941)
McKeown, Des Michael 3:27:21 (3,742)
McKeown, James P 4:21:29 (15,804)
McKeown, Phillip 3:19:40 (2,704)
McKeown, Donal 4:57:44 (25,073)
McKernan, Bernard V 5:15:09 (28,344)
McKevitt, David 3:55:44 (9,240)
McKibbin, Peter 3:59:19 (10,340)
McKie, Nick 5:11:06 (27,659)
McKiernan, Adrian 3:50:54 (8,038)
McKillop Paley, Stuart J 3:46:20 (7,048)
McKinney, James 4:10:22 (12,947)
McKinniss, Pete 6:10:33 (33,588)
McKinnon, Neil 4:54:16 (24,279)
McKinstrie, Jim H 3:57:29 (9,762)
McKinstry, Danny 4:10:42 (13,040)
McKirdy, Gordon James 6:48:15 (34,780)
McKnight, Anthony 2:56:19 (734)
McKrill, Daniel 5:19:51 (29,079)
McLachlan, Fergus R 6:33:39 (34,491)
McLachlan, Robert L 4:15:24 (14,256)
McLane, Andy J 4:57:01 (24,933)
McLardie, Geoffrey D 3:56:29 (9,454)
McLardy, Gordon 5:06:55 (26,887)
McLaren, Bruce 3:34:35 (4,889)
McLaren, Guy N 2:52:09 (528)
McLaren, James A 6:27:35 (34,345)
McLaren, James C 3:27:37 (3,804)
McLaughlan, Sam P 5:01:05 (25,837)
McLaughlin, Brian J 4:35:04 (19,434)
McLaughlin, Christopher D 4:14:52 (14,132)
McLaughlin, Christopher W 4:31:16 (18,419)
McLaughlin, Danny 4:10:09 (12,898)
McLaughlin, Danny R 4:53:21 (24,046)
McLaughlin, David A 4:46:26 (22,326)
McLaughlin, Ian M 3:43:23 (6,505)
McLaughlin, John L 3:13:31 (2,063)
McLaughlin, Martin 5:05:08 (26,575)
McLaughlin, Peter 3:28:59 (4,005)
McLaughlin, Simon 6:18:30 (33,947)
McLaughlin, Stephen J 4:50:34 (23,389)
McLean, Andrew J 3:26:18 (3,575)
McLean, Brian D 4:21:37 (15,849)
McLean, Charles F 4:59:36 (25,518)
McLean, Henry 4:39:02 (20,444)
McLean, Ian A 4:06:11 (11,926)
McLean, Jeff B 3:30:51 (4,303)
McLean, Kyle 3:13:21 (2,041)
McLean, Paul A 4:29:08 (17,872)
McLeavery, Mark P 3:36:02 (5,164)
McLelland, Steve 3:58:01 (9,941)
McLemont, Stephen 3:22:29 (3,066)
McLening, Marc S 5:05:16 (26,601)
McLennan, Andrew 4:19:28 (15,269)
McLennan, Steven R 4:20:15 (15,498)
McLeod, Ben C 3:47:32 (7,296)
McLeod, Gordon G 3:58:51 (10,211)
McLeod, Gregg S 3:32:11 (4,500)
McLeod, Kirk 4:20:30 (15,557)
McLoughlin, David C 4:30:31 (18,235)
McLoughlin, Mark T 3:35:36 (5,071)
McLucas, Tom R 3:48:49 (7,574)
McLuckie, Garwen 4:19:39 (15,328)
McMahon, Aidan K 3:44:59 (6,800)
McMahon, Brian K 4:59:25 (25,475)
McMahon, Lee 5:15:46 (28,469)
McMahon, Nicholas J 3:49:59 (7,830)
McMahon, Paul 4:39:11 (20,495)
McMahon, Stephen B 4:02:37 (11,156)
McManamey, Kip 3:45:07 (6,819)
McManus, Sean 5:26:43 (30,015)
McMaster, Philip J 3:38:14 (5,540)
McMaster, Steven 4:45:45 (22,144)
McMeehan-Roberts, Jim 4:55:23 (24,549)
McMillan, Craig L 3:54:18 (8,839)
McMillan, Graeme 4:16:16 (14,464)
McMillan, Jeff T 4:28:06 (17,580)
McMillan, Kenny T 3:49:58 (7,828)
McMillan, Matthew J 3:56:04 (9,329)
McMillan, Rory J 5:17:18 (28,683)
McMillan, Ross A 4:12:52 (13,617)
McMonagle, Noel 3:54:48 (8,970)
McMullan, Dominic 4:25:07 (16,739)
McMullan, Kevin J 3:22:43 (3,099)
McMullan, Luke 3:38:56 (5,661)
McMullan, Stephen J 4:19:38 (15,323)
McMullen, Mark B 4:26:16 (17,060)
McMullen, Simon 4:34:04 (19,164)
McNab, Robert D 4:09:54 (12,833)
McNabb, Cormac 4:06:36 (12,016)
McNabb, John C 4:13:30 (13,796)
McNabb, Phil 5:30:16 (30,438)
McNally, James W 3:18:32 (2,579)
McNally, Mark J 4:30:02 (18,106)
McNally, Thomas M 3:14:37 (2,184)
McNamara, David 3:58:04 (9,958)
McNamara, Gerard C 5:10:20 (27,517)
McNamara, Kerry 4:16:47 (14,602)
McNamara, Peter J 5:31:25 (30,567)
McNamara, Stuart J 6:29:13 (34,387)
McNamee, Simon D 3:57:18 (9,706)
McNeice, Patrick G 4:07:17 (12,170)
McNeila, Joseph 4:33:21 (18,991)
McNeilage, Ben 4:27:44 (17,459)
McNeill, Andrew S 2:36:01 (127)
McNeill, Eric J 4:23:54 (16,416)
McNeill, Ian 3:34:02 (4,763)
McNelis, Robin N 2:51:01 (496)
McNerney, John 4:22:24 (16,050)
McNicol, Alex 3:34:28 (4,869)
McNiff, John W 5:01:01 (25,815)
McNulty, John 4:22:33 (16,089)
McPhail, Rob 3:56:37 (9,500)
McPherson, Wayne K 4:10:59 (13,104)
McPherson, William A 5:36:53 (31,164)
McPhilemy, Anthony P 4:28:01 (17,549)
McPhillips, Russ R 5:49:39 (32,301)
McQuade, James H 2:48:15 (405)
McQueen, Daniel 4:19:13 (15,213)
McQueen, Lee 4:22:49 (16,145)
McQueen, Matt J 4:48:57 (22,960)
McQuillan, Darryl R 4:19:09 (15,197)
McQuillen, Jason P 3:42:09 (6,242)
McRoberts, Dermot J 4:23:44 (16,370)
McShane, Dessie C 3:09:35 (1,665)
McShane, John M 4:06:00 (11,880)
McShea, Brian 4:18:11 (14,942)
McShea, Dean 4:23:53 (16,409)
McSweeny, James 4:22:10 (15,995)
McTague, Matthew J 5:06:57 (26,894)
McTavish, Douglas A 4:25:52 (16,951)
McTeare, Andy C 4:37:51 (20,132)
McVeigh, Kieron P 4:09:14 (12,668)
McVeigh, Stephen J 4:47:08 (22,525)
McVinish, Andrew B 5:01:33 (25,923)
McWilliam, Rob G 3:06:54 (1,429)
McWilliams, Brendan F 5:15:59 (28,498)
McWilliams, Robert 5:02:27 (26,102)
Meacock, Miles A 3:43:21 (6,499)
Mead, Adrian M 3:09:12 (1,639)
Mead, Ben 4:13:48 (13,869)
Mead, Christopher J 3:13:53 (2,109)
Mead, Harry F 4:37:22 (20,000)
Mead, Scott 4:34:36 (19,288)
Mead, Stuart E 2:48:36 (411)
Meaden, Paul 3:47:30 (7,291)
Meadowcroft, Ian C 3:00:17 (1,013)
Meadowcroft, Mike 3:17:01 (2,434)
Meadows, Christopher S 4:43:38 (21,633)
Meadows, Samuel W 3:27:01 (3,684)
Meadows, Terry 4:09:05 (12,640)
Meager, Graham S 3:52:43 (8,450)
Meagher, Mark Thomas 4:59:00 (25,386)
Meagor, Lucas R 4:00:03 (10,557)
Meakes, Tim G 4:11:01 (13,112)
Meakin, Gary 5:18:25 (28,857)
Meakin, Ian R 4:20:05 (15,453)
Meakin, James 4:49:31 (23,124)
Mears, Bradley 3:55:14 (9,092)
Mears, Garrett 3:53:22 (8,599)
Mears, Michael P 3:12:43 (1,961)
Mears, Phillip R 4:20:34 (15,574)
Measor, Daniel 4:10:25 (12,958)
Medcalf, John 3:43:10 (6,463)
Medcraft, Jonathan P 6:37:02 (34,565)
Meddings, Andy J 4:12:47 (13,602)
Medhurst, Steve 4:33:15 (18,959)
Medley, Dave J 4:35:59 (19,675)
Medley, Ray S 4:28:26 (17,678)
Medlock, Scott 4:39:23 (20,542)
Medrano, Pablo 4:21:58 (15,935)
Medsker, Mike 3:46:36 (7,110)
Medway, Jim 3:49:40 (7,761)
Mee, Gary J 4:56:33 (24,814)
Mee, Jim 5:46:16 (32,034)
Mee, Paul 3:19:56 (2,745)
Mee, Rory 4:29:59 (18,092)
Meech, Ellis 5:06:28 (26,800)

Meehan, Alex 3:03:29 (1,202)
Meehan, Anthony J 3:27:26 (3,759)
Meehan, David J 3:49:28 (7,723)
Meehan, Tony 4:49:30 (23,116)
Meek, Stephen J 4:36:46 (19,856)
Meekcoms, Dean 5:26:13 (29,957)
Meen, David J 4:07:53 (12,336)
Meenan, Declyn Anthony 4:55:34 (24,584)
Meenan, Kieran 4:02:01 (11,020)
Meering, Richard J 4:54:26 (24,322)
Megali, Aldo 4:36:50 (19,881)
Megarrell, Hugh J 5:52:54 (32,540)
Meghjee, Ashif 3:14:30 (2,173)
Mehew, Bruce 5:10:43 (27,588)
Mehmet, Mehmet K 4:30:38 (18,265)
Mehmet, Nick 4:30:18 (18,176)
Mehmi, Michael 5:18:44 (28,922)
Mehta, Ajay 5:08:42 (27,212)
Mehta, Paresh 4:22:38 (16,105)
Meier, Stefan 5:11:13 (27,676)
Meiklejohn, Graham K 3:53:54 (8,723)
Meir, Thomas J 3:28:55 (3,997)
Meiring, Carl E 5:07:59 (27,086)
Melbourne, David 5:24:09 (29,674)
Melchert, Alex 4:16:33 (14,536)
Meldrum, James D 2:36:42 (134)
Melhem, Marcel 4:29:37 (17,988)
Melhuish-Thomas, Ceri C 4:19:37 (15,320)
Melia, Denis M 4:24:28 (16,564)
Meller, David 2:49:41 (454)
Mellinger, Simon 5:21:05 (29,234)
Mellings, Lachlan 3:49:43 (7,783)
Mellish, Phil C 4:31:08 (18,391)
Mellon, Jimmy 7:10:00 (35,050)
Mellon, Mark L 3:00:32 (1,023)
Mellor, Alex J 4:49:18 (23,053)
Mellor, James W 5:18:09 (28,811)
Mellor, Samuel R 3:43:19 (6,493)
Mellor, Tom 2:51:35 (510)
Melloy, Scott 3:39:02 (5,692)
Melly, Joe P 3:38:41 (5,621)
Melmoe, Alexander J 5:33:39 (30,829)
Melvin, Lindsay V 4:46:47 (22,430)
Melvin, Simon W 4:27:11 (17,305)
Menchise, Franco 6:13:10 (33,706)
Mende, Jens 3:07:25 (1,468)
Mendelsohn, Rafi 4:46:33 (22,360)
Mendelssohn, James 5:40:04 (31,504)
Mendes, Alberto 4:00:51 (10,755)
Mendes, Manuel 2:50:16 (475)
Mendes Da Costa, Niall 5:03:27 (26,275)
Meneely, Paul J 3:46:32 (7,096)
Menegale, Germano 4:52:15 (23,809)
Menhinnitt, Dan 5:18:12 (28,817)
Menzefricke-Koitz, Magnus 4:20:46 (15,627)
Mepham, Derek 3:48:00 (7,401)
Mercati, Guido 4:22:24 (16,050)
Mercer, Andrew P 4:14:20 (13,994)
Mercer, Edward 4:45:52 (22,183)
Mercer, Jason R 4:30:43 (18,286)
Mercer, Simon N 3:00:51 (1,041)
Merchant, Adam E 4:07:46 (12,310)
Meredith, Adrian R 5:18:40 (28,910)
Meredith, Brian 6:02:49 (33,216)
Meredith, Jeremy J 3:55:06 (9,065)
Meredith, Martin 3:24:02 (3,265)
Meredith, Roy 4:26:11 (17,034)
Meredith, Stephen J 4:25:26 (16,823)
Meredith, Timothy D 4:41:55 (21,184)
Meredith, Tom 3:58:58 (10,243)
Meredith, Tom O 5:09:44 (27,412)
Meredith-Hardy, Charlie A 4:19:31 (15,292)
Merki, Juerg 4:58:34 (25,288)
Merlin, David J 6:12:13 (33,651)
Merrell, Christopher 4:33:56 (19,136)
Merrett, Richard G 5:10:11 (27,493)
Merrey, James 3:31:56 (4,458)
Merrick, Paul 3:27:37 (3,804)
Merrick, Peter D 5:22:10 (29,384)
Merris, Andy H 3:28:45 (3,964)
Merritt, Anthony E 5:00:15 (25,643)
Merritt, David 6:26:37 (34,304)
Merritt, David R 4:36:22 (19,757)
Merritt, Glyn I 4:07:01 (12,111)
Merritt, Jason M 4:09:16 (12,673)
Merron, Bernard J 3:29:18 (4,068)
Merrylees, Chris R 3:23:01 (3,129)
Merryweather, James G 4:15:11 (14,211)
Merrywest, Mark Andrew 3:49:32 (7,736)
Mersmann, Hans 4:48:11 (22,779)
Merwood, Simon D 3:05:00 (1,304)
Mesnil, Patrick 4:43:42 (21,649)
Messa, José I 4:20:59 (15,687)
Messenger, Andrew M 4:43:26 (21,587)
Messenger, Mark 3:45:48 (6,948)
Messer, Robin P 3:49:56 (7,818)
Mestres Domenech, Josep 3:36:31 (5,238)
Mestrom, Jack 3:24:00 (3,259)
Metcalf, Craig 3:03:48 (1,223)
Metcalf, Graham 6:12:44 (33,677)
Metcalfe, Alastair F 4:43:02 (21,476)
Metcalfe, Alistair 3:42:58 (6,412)
Metcalfe, Andrew L 5:24:58 (29,796)
Metcalfe, Carlo 3:27:08 (3,702)
Metcalfe, James S 2:57:18 (798)
Metcalfe, John 8:12:52 (35,329)
Metcalfe, Leon D 4:00:51 (10,755)
Metcalfe, Tom 5:14:07 (28,182)
Metelski, Ludwik 4:49:56 (23,225)
Metsanvirta, Miikka 4:34:54 (19,382)
Metters, Paul J 3:57:48 (9,873)
Metzgen, Fred 5:43:41 (31,826)
Metzl, Ulrich 3:26:15 (3,566)
Mewes, Jon 3:26:01 (3,535)
Mewse, Dale L 4:49:47 (23,195)
Mewse, Nicholas 5:30:40 (30,484)
Mexter, Anthony 4:41:04 (20,976)
Meyer, Gilbert 4:29:45 (18,025)
Meyer, Nick F 4:10:45 (13,054)
Meylan, Roland Terence 3:39:24 (5,743)
Meyler, Philip J 3:02:35 (1,155)
Miah, Saiful 3:52:50 (8,474)
Miccio, Claudio 5:32:51 (30,739)
Micelli, Giuseppe 3:45:09 (6,827)
Michael, Andrew 4:37:29 (20,035)
Michael, Roger 5:53:56 (32,612)
Michael, Steven 4:30:42 (18,279)
Michaels, Simon 4:48:45 (22,912)
Michallef, Charles 3:33:21 (4,658)
Michau, Mikael 4:16:32 (14,531)
Michel, Burguet 5:11:11 (27,670)
Michel, Erich 4:36:38 (19,826)
Michel, Hollenstein 3:49:05 (7,642)
Michel, Passe 4:03:45 (11,375)
Michel, Roussel 4:43:38 (21,633)
Michel, Soler 5:23:59 (29,645)
Michel, Vilault 4:56:27 (24,785)
Micheli, Carlo 3:18:33 (2,582)
Michell, Sam 3:33:26 (4,670)
Michelsen, Tore 3:20:29 (2,824)
Michi, Stefano 4:04:45 (11,594)
Mickael, Rault 3:09:06 (1,626)
Micklewright, Colin 5:00:55 (25,790)
Micklewright, Ian 5:42:59 (31,769)
Mickovski, Goran 3:19:27 (2,676)
Middle, David G 4:28:26 (17,678)
Middlebrook, Alan 3:25:19 (3,432)
Middlebrook, Ian 3:21:51 (2,994)
Middleditch, Henry S 3:51:33 (8,174)
Middlemiss, Peter J 3:21:14 (2,912)
Middleton, Andrew 5:30:57 (30,519)
Middleton, Chris N 5:38:46 (31,370)
Middleton, Daniel J 3:10:13 (1,714)
Middleton, Guy C 3:27:34 (3,796)
Middleton, Hugo R 3:55:06 (9,065)
Middleton, Philip D 4:25:44 (16,920)
Middleton, Philip H 4:12:32 (13,535)
Middleton, Simon 3:56:35 (9,483)
Middleton, Stephen J 3:56:45 (9,549)
Middleton, William Stanley 3:58:26 (10,079)
Midgley, Martin N 3:17:33 (2,487)
Midung'a, Mark E 5:03:23 (26,266)
Mikellides, Andy 3:59:11 (10,306)
Mikkelsen, Vidar 3:29:51 (4,160)
Milano, Walter 4:44:46 (21,903)
Milbourn, Gervase M 4:27:11 (17,305)
Milburn, Alastair 4:50:24 (23,343)
Milburn, Mark W 5:39:03 (31,402)
Milburn, Neil 4:21:11 (15,739)
Mileham, Richard P 4:40:10 (20,768)
Miles, Adrian J 5:38:00 (31,274)
Miles, Albert J 4:49:01 (22,978)
Miles, Andrew B 5:12:56 (27,971)
Miles, Andrew W 3:34:20 (4,839)
Miles, Andy 3:43:18 (6,491)
Miles, Christopher M 4:12:56 (13,643)
Miles, Christopher T 4:50:16 (23,308)
Miles, Dominic J 3:09:54 (1,698)
Miles, James J 2:55:39 (706)
Miles, Jason M 6:09:59 (33,561)
Miles, Martin 4:26:46 (17,199)
Miles, Matt 5:15:33 (28,427)
Miles, Nicholas 5:48:47 (32,239)
Miles, Oliver A 3:29:44 (4,143)
Miles, Paul J 4:08:42 (12,553)
Miles, Philip J 5:24:54 (29,780)
Mileson, Alison J 4:19:48 (15,371)
Milford, Shaun 2:39:57 (191)
Millar, Ben 4:27:35 (17,409)
Millar, Clive 4:21:55 (15,927)
Millar, Daniel 4:11:25 (13,228)
Millar, James M 4:38:07 (20,204)
Millar, Robert D 4:52:01 (23,753)
Millar, William H 5:09:32 (27,370)
Millard, Alex W 3:41:52 (6,180)
Millard, Ben 4:49:22 (23,075)
Millard, Iain V 5:28:52 (30,256)
Millard, Leigh A 3:27:33 (3,790)
Millard-Beer, Matthew W 4:09:25 (12,710)
Millbank, Paul Andrew 3:49:43 (7,783)
Miller, Alexander C 3:25:59 (3,529)
Miller, Alexander J 4:20:19 (15,515)
Miller, Alexander M 3:37:29 (5,395)
Miller, Allan R 6:12:45 (33,678)
Miller, Andrew D 4:24:39 (16,605)
Miller, Chris J 3:20:39 (2,847)
Miller, Christopher J 4:13:55 (13,887)
Miller, Daniel 4:09:04 (12,635)
Miller, Daniel 6:25:12 (34,238)
Miller, Darren 4:03:17 (11,288)
Miller, Dave 3:07:35 (1,491)
Miller, David M 3:43:49 (6,592)
Miller, David Phillip 4:41:10 (20,998)
Miller, Gareth D 3:38:07 (5,518)
Miller, Glenn A 4:07:42 (12,286)
Miller, Graham F 3:16:13 (2,352)
Miller, Greg 3:55:05 (9,059)
Miller, James 4:18:05 (14,912)
Miller, John 5:14:34 (28,250)
Miller, Karl 3:58:54 (10,224)
Miller, Lee 4:14:43 (14,088)
Miller, Les 5:56:25 (32,786)
Miller, Neil 5:14:58 (28,308)
Miller, Nick W 4:39:35 (20,606)
Miller, Nigel 5:00:52 (25,779)
Miller, Paul 2:36:11 (128)
Miller, Paul D 4:52:16 (23,814)
Miller, Paul H 5:58:19 (32,948)
Miller, Paul J 5:04:50 (26,510)
Miller, Philip A 5:22:10 (29,384)
Miller, Robert J 5:12:01 (27,803)
Miller, Robin N 7:43:22 (35,274)
Miller, Samuel N 3:32:30 (4,543)
Miller, Simon 4:33:21 (18,991)
Miller, Simon C 4:45:48 (22,155)
Miller, Steve 5:24:56 (29,788)
Miller, Steve A 4:28:29 (17,693)
Miller, William H 4:35:01 (19,411)
Millership, Anthony J 3:54:48 (8,970)
Millertson, Fredrik 4:11:21 (13,210)
Milles, Humphrey H 5:21:34 (29,312)
Millett, Paul 5:06:38 (26,830)
Millett, Tony N 3:59:23 (10,365)
Millican, Keith M 3:11:16 (1,805)
Milligan, Gordon 3:27:50 (3,829)
Milligan, Jonny 4:27:30 (17,393)
Milliken-Smith, Mark G 5:45:44 (31,998)
Millington, James Stuart 4:08:37 (12,528)
Millington, Max R 4:36:23 (19,766)

Millinship, James G......5:18:51 (28,954)
Millman, Dom......4:10:59 (13,104)
Millross, Nigel D......4:16:22 (14,486)
Mills, Aaron P......5:07:20 (26,969)
Mills, David John......3:26:46 (3,645)
Mills, David T......3:28:25 (3,915)
Mills, Ian W......4:44:35 (21,853)
Mills, Ian W......5:25:31 (29,860)
Mills, Jeremy V......4:00:08 (10,580)
Mills, Jonathan R......5:04:09 (26,407)
Mills, Lee E......4:16:07 (14,429)
Mills, Lee J......4:20:49 (15,641)
Mills, Mark......4:37:05 (19,937)
Mills, Mark H......4:44:12 (21,766)
Mills, Martin D......4:34:42 (19,317)
Mills, Martin G......5:05:39 (26,666)
Mills, Nathan E......2:57:51 (825)
Mills, Nicholas J......3:19:23 (2,665)
Mills, Peter J......4:32:47 (18,842)
Mills, Philip......4:14:47 (14,108)
Mills, Robert A......3:16:51 (2,417)
Mills, Robert S......3:19:32 (2,686)
Mills, Robert S......5:00:35 (25,723)
Mills, Ron S......4:23:14 (16,238)
Mills, Simon......4:51:13 (23,545)
Mills, Simon G......3:54:05 (8,776)
Mills, Stephen B......5:03:05 (26,221)
Mills, Stephen J......4:20:48 (15,636)
Mills, Tom C......4:21:26 (15,793)
Millsom, Barry P......5:05:21 (26,613)
Millward, Gary B......4:35:05 (19,438)
Millwood, Nigel......4:12:27 (13,507)
Millyard, Brian A......6:06:53 (33,431)
Milmoe, Michael......4:08:40 (12,539)
Milne, Alex......3:50:43 (7,999)
Milne, Alex J......3:22:13 (3,040)
Milne, Andrew......4:20:16 (15,502)
Milne, David M......4:10:41 (13,033)
Milne, James......4:58:28 (25,258)
Milne, Nicholas J......4:43:05 (21,488)
Milne, Ross......2:29:20 (64)
Milne, Stephen......3:20:45 (2,862)
Milner, David M......3:47:58 (7,391)
Milner, Peter L......5:58:01 (32,919)
Milsom, Michael P......3:02:40 (1,160)
Milson, Paul J......3:29:33 (4,108)
Milton, Paul......4:40:32 (20,843)
Milton, Paul......6:00:25 (33,069)
Milton, Trevor......4:24:40 (16,614)
Milwain, Kevin I......4:44:59 (21,957)
Minakov, Alexander......6:14:58 (33,790)
Minas, Charilaos P......8:43:57 (35,350)
Minchin, Andrew E......3:47:32 (7,296)
Minervini, Mauro......4:27:51 (17,502)
Mingay, Simon......3:16:16 (2,357)
Minhas, Pardip......4:45:28 (22,071)
Minney, Hugo......4:33:12 (18,944)
Minns, Nicholas E......3:27:20 (3,739)
Minns, Phillip I......3:43:16 (6,481)
Minogue, Eugene P......4:58:53 (25,357)
Minogue, James A......6:15:19 (33,804)
Minondo Toruno, Roberto José......4:04:30 (11,547)
Minor, Gary I......4:27:46 (17,474)
Minoru, Ueda......4:36:22 (19,757)
Minshull, Ian S......4:49:55 (23,221)
Minter, Andrew J......4:24:08 (16,483)
Minter, Daniel J......4:52:16 (23,814)
Minter, Kevin P......3:06:05 (1,377)
Minto, Robert......4:51:44 (23,685)
Minton, Kevin......4:40:28 (20,827)
Minty, Kevin J......2:55:44 (710)
Miquel Planas, Ramon......5:47:32 (32,136)
Mir, Zlatan......4:57:13 (24,968)
Mirams, Jeremy E......3:25:31 (3,461)
Miranda, Giuseppe......4:16:55 (14,626)
Mirjan, Razzak......3:28:40 (3,948)
Miskelly, Fergus P......4:53:59 (24,217)
Misra, Rajnish......6:16:38 (33,872)
Missing, Neil D......5:30:26 (30,450)
Missions, David W......5:15:34 (28,432)
Misson, Trevor......3:34:29 (4,873)
Mistry, Bharat......5:49:08 (32,262)
Mistry, Chetan......4:29:11 (17,884)
Mistry, Chetan N......3:26:37 (3,621)
Mistry, Dharmesh V......4:55:10 (24,494)
Mistry, Hiran......4:20:04 (15,446)
Mistry, Jayanti......5:41:48 (31,657)
Mistry, Prashant......6:23:45 (34,181)
Mistry, Shashi M......6:24:23 (34,209)
Mistry, Vinod P......6:10:21 (33,582)
Mitcham, David J......3:53:41 (8,673)
Mitchel, Paul......4:47:52 (22,693)
Mitchell, Andrew Charles John......3:51:10 (8,088)
Mitchell, Andrew D......4:10:40 (13,025)
Mitchell, Andrew M......3:44:37 (6,733)
Mitchell, Andy M......3:37:07 (5,344)
Mitchell, Anthony L......4:45:56 (22,198)
Mitchell, Brian John......5:09:51 (27,434)
Mitchell, Christopher A......4:00:18 (10,618)
Mitchell, Christopher J......4:21:23 (15,778)
Mitchell, David......3:28:57 (4,002)
Mitchell, Edward P......3:16:00 (2,335)
Mitchell, Gary......3:41:41 (6,149)
Mitchell, George......3:04:38 (1,272)
Mitchell, Ian B......4:57:30 (25,029)
Mitchell, James Thomas......5:29:30 (30,335)
Mitchell, Jason M......4:47:07 (22,522)
Mitchell, Jim K......3:29:38 (4,122)
Mitchell, Jon R......7:18:41 (35,135)
Mitchell, Julian......3:49:39 (7,758)
Mitchell, Justin A......2:35:35 (122)
Mitchell, Kevin......3:34:37 (4,899)
Mitchell, Kieron J......3:08:24 (1,558)
Mitchell, Mark......3:43:44 (6,571)
Mitchell, Matthew J......4:22:21 (16,036)
Mitchell, Matthew Joseph......3:48:50 (7,580)
Mitchell, Nigel M......3:01:11 (1,067)
Mitchell, Paul......4:59:41 (25,529)
Mitchell, Paul D......4:34:16 (19,215)
Mitchell, Paul K......4:05:03 (11,665)
Mitchell, Paul R......3:08:48 (1,600)
Mitchell, Paul S......4:18:29 (15,027)
Mitchell, Peter......3:59:38 (10,428)
Mitchell, Peter J......5:37:00 (31,169)
Mitchell, Robert......3:50:25 (7,925)
Mitchell, Robert C......3:41:13 (6,075)
Mitchell, Robert J......3:33:14 (4,639)
Mitchell, Sam P......4:45:40 (22,126)
Mitchell, Scott N......3:48:47 (7,562)
Mitchell, Simon E......3:45:46 (6,941)
Mitchell, Steve G......4:34:45 (19,329)
Mitchell, Stuart G......3:46:21 (7,052)
Mitchell, Timothy J......3:22:25 (3,056)
Mitchell, Wayne G......4:21:39 (15,863)
Mitchell-Brown, Daniel......5:23:21 (29,577)
Mitchelmore, Andrew......4:19:44 (15,348)
Mitchener, Paul J......3:43:48 (6,589)
Mitson, David......5:11:14 (27,680)
Miyazaki, Hideichi......5:58:58 (32,990)
Mizzi, Peter V......5:42:13 (31,696)
Moate, Simon......3:49:11 (7,665)
Moate, Toby J......4:37:29 (20,035)
Moberg, Lars......4:58:19 (25,218)
Moberly, Tom......3:47:33 (7,300)
Mocatta, Simon......3:54:05 (8,776)
Modaher, Jasvir S......5:23:34 (29,600)
Modaher, Tejinder S......6:25:15 (34,241)
Modoni, Abdur......4:10:51 (13,078)
Moelchand, Parmanan......5:50:23 (32,368)
Moffa, John J......5:01:36 (25,933)
Moffat, David J......3:48:53 (7,591)
Moffatt, Alastair J......2:55:49 (716)
Moffatt, Ben......5:12:38 (27,913)
Moffatt, Graham D......2:57:22 (800)
Moffett, Alasdair S......3:38:07 (5,518)
Moffett, David J......4:23:56 (16,423)
Moffitt, Gavin J......3:56:08 (9,348)
Mogensen, Bjorn Reinhardt......3:53:20 (8,587)
Moger, Richard J......4:53:04 (23,990)
Mogford, David J......5:44:20 (31,881)
Mogford, Philip B......5:36:34 (31,127)
Moggan, Frank Martin......4:03:50 (11,403)
Moggs, David......3:51:28 (8,159)
Mohamed, Bekkari......3:35:21 (5,022)
Mohamed, Jamal......2:58:55 (910)
Mohan, Kevin P......5:13:04 (27,998)
Moir, Nick C......4:44:17 (21,793)
Mol, Michal G......5:05:04 (26,563)
Mole, Andrew A......4:44:41 (21,885)
Mole, Robert A......3:36:44 (5,269)
Mole, Samuel......5:07:03 (26,915)
Moles, Chris M......4:28:50 (17,789)
Molesworth, Tony......4:06:06 (11,903)
Molho, Nick......3:26:43 (3,637)
Molina, Ricardo......5:03:55 (26,366)
Mollart, Jamie A......5:43:44 (31,828)
Moller, Hanan Z......4:05:21 (11,742)
Mollett, Nathan......4:21:08 (15,727)
Mollison, John A......4:39:02 (20,444)
Molloy, Bernard M......5:01:01 (25,815)
Moloele, Sekgwane E......3:48:13 (7,449)
Moloney, Kevin P......5:17:07 (28,662)
Moloney, Simon......4:28:38 (17,734)
Molyneux, Paul M......2:26:58 (44)
Molyneux, Sidney A......4:50:09 (23,274)
Momoniat, Faizal......4:43:25 (21,583)
Mompalao, Ricky......4:44:53 (21,924)
Monaghan, Keith D......4:51:28 (23,612)
Monaghan, Paul E......4:47:47 (22,669)
Monahan, Andrew G......5:36:52 (31,163)
Monahan, Charles......6:00:29 (33,072)
Monclus Fraga, Santiago......3:55:10 (9,079)
Mondelli, Michele......2:54:07 (608)
Monfreda, Francesco......3:30:20 (4,225)
Monger-Godfrey, Timothy J......3:38:24 (5,566)
Moniatis, Jonathan F......4:42:25 (21,305)
Moniz, Steve......4:24:46 (16,646)
Monks, Colin J......4:37:11 (19,961)
Monks, James......4:17:49 (14,842)
Monksfield, Darren L......4:00:47 (10,741)
Monkton, Andrew D......3:45:45 (6,937)
Monroy, Juan Manuel......3:39:38 (5,782)
Monson, Andrew......4:28:31 (17,701)
Montagnino, Michael......6:34:33 (34,512)
Montagnon, Eric......3:42:05 (6,230)
Montague, Justin M......2:43:17 (263)
Montagu-Williams, Robert Peter......3:14:49 (2,210)
Montalvo Hernandez, Francisco......5:04:05 (26,398)
Montanari, Giorgio......3:56:50 (9,579)
Montanari, Riccardo......3:23:06 (3,136)
Montaut, Ricki J......5:35:33 (31,025)
Monte, Steven......2:39:35 (186)
Montero, Mario......3:23:32 (3,195)
Montgomery, Craig......5:48:33 (32,221)
Montgomery, Gary......4:03:17 (11,288)
Montgomery, Gerard......3:04:09 (1,245)
Montgomery, Harvie E......4:40:14 (20,781)
Montgomery, John......3:49:36 (7,747)
Montgomery, Peter F......4:31:08 (18,391)
Montgomery, Richard R......4:16:48 (14,605)
Montgomery, Stephen D......5:44:11 (31,869)
Montgomery, William I......7:16:51 (35,117)
Mon-Williams, Mark......3:13:52 (2,105)
Moody, Colin A......3:07:10 (1,452)
Moody, James......4:01:52 (10,996)
Moody, Mark......6:00:36 (33,089)
Moody, Oliver N......3:11:52 (1,871)
Moody, Robert J......5:04:03 (26,393)
Moody, Steve......3:25:02 (3,400)
Moolla, Ahmad......3:31:28 (4,397)
Moon, Antony......3:51:53 (8,249)
Moon, Benjamin D......3:33:07 (4,627)
Moon, Chris......3:58:51 (10,211)
Moon, Daniel S......3:56:49 (9,573)
Moon, James K......2:56:49 (762)
Mooney, Bertie......3:57:28 (9,756)
Moor, Gary......4:28:13 (17,622)
Moore, Aaron J......4:10:47 (13,060)
Moore, Alan......4:44:30 (21,837)
Moore, Andrew......3:00:53 (1,043)
Moore, Andrew P......3:49:57 (7,823)
Moore, Anthony......4:43:42 (21,649)
Moore, Bruce......4:09:54 (12,833)
Moore, Charles J......3:53:38 (8,658)
Moore, Christopher......4:55:29 (24,569)
Moore, Christopher J......4:19:36 (15,313)
Moore, Christopher J......4:51:55 (23,737)
Moore, Craig J......3:17:43 (2,505)
Moore, David......3:22:12 (3,036)

Moore, Derek 5:01:44 (25,960)
Moore, Dominic.........................4:18:16 (14,956)
Moore, Duncan J........................4:18:01 (14,891)
Moore, Gordon 4:52:13 (23,801)
Moore, Graham S.......................2:50:11 (474)
Moore, Jason 4:50:52 (23,455)
Moore, Jim I 3:36:32 (5,241)
Moore, Julian N.........................3:22:32 (3,072)
Moore, Justin H.........................4:50:13 (23,285)
Moore, Justin M.........................2:56:19 (734)
Moore, Lee 4:45:37 (22,109)
Moore, Matt D............................4:45:41 (22,130)
Moore, Melwyn J 4:19:22 (15,249)
Moore, Michael K 3:42:04 (6,226)
Moore, Mick 3:56:29 (9,454)
Moore, Mick J.............................4:51:24 (23,595)
Moore, Nick J..............................4:29:07 (17,865)
Moore, Peter...............................5:22:25 (29,425)
Moore, Phil 5:03:06 (26,224)
Moore, Philip 3:32:52 (4,594)
Moore, Philip J............................3:46:49 (7,159)
Moore, Rich J..............................3:46:35 (7,104)
Moore, Richard 5:23:11 (29,543)
Moore, Richard J.........................5:12:34 (27,903)
Moore, Richard J.........................5:14:15 (28,200)
Moore, Robert G 3:19:53 (2,736)
Moore, Robert J...........................5:40:34 (31,551)
Moore, Shaun P 7:07:19 (35,031)
Moore, Stephen A........................5:09:36 (27,384)
Moore, Timothy J........................4:35:41 (19,592)
Moores, David J 5:15:33 (28,427)
Moorhouse, Adam S...................4:52:51 (23,938)
Moorhouse, Mark J 4:52:24 (23,842)
Moorhouse, Simon......................3:39:10 (5,713)
Moosbauer, Jean-Marie 3:42:42 (6,356)
Moppett, Samuel A 4:32:34 (18,777)
Mora, Martin 4:54:17 (24,284)
Morais Leitão, Pedro 5:00:44 (25,755)
Moralee, Alastair 3:53:51 (8,714)
Morales, Alexandre José F 3:23:00 (3,126)
Morales, Edgar 3:41:54 (6,186)
Morales de Leon, Roberto E 3:35:43 (5,099)
Moran, Craig A............................4:42:34 (21,348)
Moran, David..............................3:09:22 (1,652)
Moran, James M 4:02:02 (11,024)
Moran, John 5:10:18 (27,513)
Moran, Kev 5:18:25 (28,857)
Moran, Nick M 5:45:09 (31,938)
Moran, Paschal P.........................3:36:12 (5,190)
Moran, Stuart I 2:29:11 (60)
Moran Cubero, Javier 4:13:22 (13,772)
Morcom, Jonathon......................5:15:03 (28,328)
Mordi, Ebolum O........................4:29:48 (18,036)
Morel, Philippe 3:13:59 (2,117)
Moreland, Nicholas.....................3:54:09 (8,796)
More-Molyneux, Michael G.........5:50:49 (32,400)
Moreno-Galindo, Francisco.........4:36:52 (19,885)
Moreton, Ian 5:19:09 (28,989)
Moreton, Lloyd 5:53:07 (32,556)
Morfey, Michael J 7:00:42 (34,957)
Morfitt, David J...........................4:08:27 (12,496)
Morgan, Andrew 4:17:52 (14,851)
Morgan, Andrew C......................5:26:31 (29,992)
Morgan, Ben...............................4:32:55 (18,876)
Morgan, Benedict E 4:24:46 (16,646)
Morgan, Casey P.........................2:54:27 (632)
Morgan, Charles J 3:08:43 (1,591)
Morgan, Chris 4:40:14 (20,781)
Morgan, Darren 6:00:58 (33,111)
Morgan, Gareth...........................4:08:27 (12,496)
Morgan, Gareth David 3:38:00 (5,489)
Morgan, Iain J.............................5:14:37 (28,255)
Morgan, Ian J 6:18:40 (33,952)
Morgan, James D.........................5:05:01 (26,549)
Morgan, James Stuart 3:58:12 (10,007)
Morgan, Jason 5:10:43 (27,588)
Morgan, Jonathan G 3:24:20 (3,321)
Morgan, Michael P......................4:25:46 (16,928)
Morgan, Neil 3:48:54 (7,595)
Morgan, Neil T............................5:44:50 (31,916)
Morgan, Nicholas........................3:29:22 (4,085)
Morgan, Nicholas G.....................3:29:04 (4,013)
Morgan, Paul G 3:32:27 (4,536)

Morgan, Richard P.......................3:45:44 (6,933)
Morgan, Richie J 4:49:28 (23,102)
Morgan, Roger Lee 3:17:00 (2,429)
Morgan, Russell J 3:16:03 (2,338)
Morgan, Sean R...........................5:34:50 (30,952)
Morgan, Simon D........................3:33:59 (4,754)
Morgan, Stephen 5:32:58 (30,749)
Morgan, Wesley J........................3:38:54 (5,654)
Morgan, William 3:50:18 (7,903)
Morgan-Jones, Gethin................4:33:25 (19,006)
Morgan-Smith, Oliver 5:59:18 (33,007)
Morganti, Francesco 3:46:47 (7,153)
Morgenstern, Ron 4:47:18 (22,560)
Moriarty, Brendan 3:20:41 (2,854)
Moriarty, Francis M 3:48:23 (7,482)
Moriarty, Neil M 3:03:54 (1,233)
Moriarty, Paul C 5:42:31 (31,729)
Moriarty, Richard 4:23:44 (16,370)
Moriarty, Sean B 5:05:53 (26,711)
Morineau, Philippe......................3:48:26 (7,496)
Morjaria, Shamil.........................5:05:09 (26,581)
Morley, Alex J 3:51:14 (8,107)
Morley, Bryan 3:21:51 (2,994)
Morley, Chris M...........................3:59:17 (10,331)
Morley, Colin J 4:08:01 (12,366)
Morley, Dean 3:11:02 (1,780)
Morley, Duncan 5:15:50 (28,481)
Morley, James E 3:45:23 (6,869)
Morley, Kevin 4:55:07 (24,479)
Morley, Paul Anthony 3:40:09 (5,888)
Morley, Phil A.............................3:04:47 (1,291)
Morley-Smith, James 4:32:54 (18,871)
Moroney, Mark 4:18:18 (14,962)
Morphett, Keith S 4:46:14 (22,255)
Morreale, Adrian.........................5:09:16 (27,321)
Morrell, Thomas F 4:39:29 (20,576)
Morrin, Cyril J 4:55:38 (24,602)
Morris, Aaron 4:00:57 (10,786)
Morris, Alexander L.....................4:16:28 (14,514)
Morris, Andy P............................3:42:06 (6,235)
Morris, Anthony 4:16:11 (14,443)
Morris, Barrie D 4:07:04 (12,124)
Morris, Ben 4:36:29 (19,791)
Morris, Chris...............................3:55:54 (9,289)
Morris, Chris J 3:43:02 (6,423)
Morris, Chris R............................5:13:28 (28,060)
Morris, Clive Russell....................4:24:48 (16,654)
Morris, Colin 5:38:28 (31,328)
Morris, Colin A............................6:18:41 (33,977)
Morris, Craig C............................4:54:04 (24,235)
Morris, Darren J 3:48:39 (7,541)
Morris, David C 5:37:14 (31,196)
Morris, David T 3:48:47 (7,562)
Morris, Dean R............................3:50:14 (7,892)
Morris, Duncan G 4:19:08 (15,194)
Morris, Gareth 6:19:04 (33,999)
Morris, Gareth W 5:31:51 (30,622)
Morris, Gary................................5:22:44 (29,470)
Morris, Glyn Evan 3:25:08 (3,412)
Morris, Greg 3:35:55 (5,138)
Morris, Houston 4:45:57 (22,206)
Morris, Iestyn.............................5:08:28 (27,175)
Morris, Jason J 3:20:24 (2,811)
Morris, John F 4:35:43 (19,607)
Morris, Julian 5:03:26 (26,270)
Morris, Kevin D 3:49:19 (7,688)
Morris, Kieron 4:40:45 (20,898)
Morris, Luke 5:47:02 (32,098)
Morris, Mark 3:28:11 (3,878)
Morris, Mark 7:19:07 (35,139)
Morris, Neil 4:15:29 (14,279)
Morris, Nigel 4:06:54 (12,079)
Morris, Oliver J...........................3:29:17 (4,060)
Morris, Paul 3:35:06 (4,978)
Morris, Peter E 4:39:59 (20,719)
Morris, Peter F............................5:42:05 (31,679)
Morris, Richard 5:07:02 (26,912)
Morris, Richard David 4:14:40 (14,067)
Morris, Richard G 3:24:36 (3,356)
Morris, Rob P 4:47:58 (22,728)
Morris, Ryan M............................3:50:10 (7,876)
Morris, Simeon J 3:46:46 (7,148)
Morris, Simon A 3:00:58 (1,049)

Morrisey, Lee C 5:01:53 (25,991)
Morrish, Luke 4:04:27 (11,532)
Morrish, Stuart Raymond 3:18:21 (2,562)
Morris-Jones, Stephen................4:49:11 (23,012)
Morrison, Alex R 4:40:00 (20,726)
Morrison, Andy 4:21:54 (15,924)
Morrison, Cairn C........................3:53:47 (8,701)
Morrison, Christopher 2:58:15 (852)
Morrison, David 4:31:04 (18,376)
Morrison, David A........................4:34:32 (19,267)
Morrison, Gordon 4:56:40 (24,852)
Morrison, Gregg 6:10:32 (33,587)
Morrison, Rafael L 5:14:40 (28,261)
Morrison, Sidney.........................3:40:10 (5,892)
Morrison, Stephen 4:49:32 (23,127)
Morrison, Steven.........................3:35:35 (5,069)
Morrissey, Ian 4:06:12 (11,927)
Morrow, Andrew J 3:26:11 (3,555)
Morrow, Charlie 4:47:59 (22,736)
Morrow, Dave G 3:34:16 (4,824)
Morrow, Doug 4:21:52 (15,913)
Morrow, Martin 3:19:52 (2,733)
Morse, Andy C.............................6:50:23 (34,823)
Morse, Oliver 3:36:42 (5,264)
Mortensen, Thomas F 4:01:19 (10,862)
Mortimer, Andrew.......................4:37:40 (20,081)
Mortimer, Andrew D 6:40:10 (34,630)
Mortimer, Carl C 6:38:11 (34,593)
Mortimer, Christopher J 4:40:13 (20,779)
Mortimer, Karl 4:09:54 (12,833)
Mortimore, Robert O...................3:27:08 (3,702)
Morton, Colin J 4:25:08 (16,746)
Morton, Derek 5:32:38 (30,709)
Morton, Jonathan M 3:57:04 (9,638)
Morton, Paul O 6:08:32 (33,494)
Morton, Scott 3:36:15 (5,198)
Morton-Kemp, Paul L 5:26:50 (30,028)
Moruzzi, Paul..............................5:09:18 (27,334)
Moscrop, Jonathan S...................3:30:02 (4,181)
Mosedale, Simon A 4:10:32 (12,989)
Moseley, Alan J 3:20:55 (2,881)
Moseley, Stuart J.........................4:14:06 (13,931)
Moses, Nick.................................4:26:57 (17,246)
Moses, Richard 4:45:03 (21,981)
Mosley, Paul 4:15:43 (14,323)
Mosley, Philip 2:52:48 (552)
Mosney, Ryan P 5:57:49 (32,896)
Mosquera, Nestor 5:27:58 (30,142)
Moss, Anthony W 3:52:34 (8,415)
Moss, Barney J 4:31:35 (18,524)
Moss, Benjamin R 5:10:15 (27,505)
Moss, Colin A 5:21:37 (29,318)
Moss, David P 4:20:51 (15,647)
Moss, Gary D 4:57:58 (25,132)
Moss, Gavin P 3:52:27 (8,392)
Moss, Gerrard A 3:29:07 (4,030)
Moss, Graham R 4:03:09 (11,260)
Moss, James I 3:15:02 (2,239)
Moss, Keith 3:48:26 (7,496)
Moss, Matthew 4:53:35 (24,093)
Moss, Moddy J 4:08:46 (12,562)
Moss, Paul 5:09:13 (27,311)
Moss, Simon C.............................3:27:23 (3,746)
Mostari, Lee 4:41:01 (20,965)
Mothersole, Richard G 6:30:16 (34,418)
Motherway, Thomas.....................3:44:16 (6,677)
Motsi, Tawanda 5:53:13 (32,567)
Mott, Robert 4:14:46 (14,102)
Mott, Timothy 4:39:17 (20,513)
Mott, Warren J............................4:19:28 (15,269)
Mottershead, Alan.......................3:54:12 (8,812)
Motyka, Didier............................3:40:36 (5,958)
Motz, Markus..............................5:22:14 (29,394)
Moughan, Eamonn M..................3:52:18 (8,359)
Mougin, Eric...............................3:39:57 (5,849)
Moulding, Lee 4:52:00 (23,750)
Moule, Gavin S............................3:37:30 (5,400)
Moulovasilis, Anthansios.............4:23:11 (16,228)
Moulson, Stuart C 3:56:38 (9,511)
Mouncey, Dave J 3:20:11 (2,778)
Mound, David G...........................5:21:01 (29,223)
Mounter, Garry...........................4:51:19 (23,571)
Mourant, Anthony F 5:02:16 (26,074)

Mouritsen, Lars M....4:03:41 (11,363)
Mousdale, Anthony....3:14:17 (2,151)
Moverley, Ian....5:27:06 (30,060)
Mowbury, Roy D....5:36:55 (31,167)
Mowitz, Mikael....3:50:00 (7,833)
Mowle, Lee C....3:10:19 (1,722)
Moxham, Bruce R....3:39:56 (5,843)
Moxon, David S....3:50:08 (7,867)
Moxon, Howard....5:07:30 (27,008)
Moylan, Will G....4:40:50 (20,920)
Moyle, Fraser....3:59:56 (10,530)
Moyle, Richard J....4:07:02 (12,114)
Moynihan, Humphrey....5:59:45 (33,029)
Moyse, Gary P....4:00:51 (10,755)
Moyse, Warren....4:08:07 (12,395)
Mozaffar, Hasnain....4:48:34 (22,866)
Mozziconacci, Laurent....3:47:27 (7,278)
Muboro, Edward K....3:09:51 (1,693)
Muchall, Gordon J....4:36:45 (19,848)
Mudge, Ian D....3:16:44 (2,408)
Mudge, Jason R....5:09:34 (27,379)
Mudie, Douglas....3:47:52 (7,367)
Mueller, Andreas....5:11:13 (27,676)
Mueller, Philippe....4:30:29 (18,222)
Muffett, Paul J....2:54:45 (646)
Muffett, Peter G....7:53:07 (35,296)
Muggleton, Jonathan J....4:34:09 (19,183)
Mughal, Muntzer....4:51:42 (23,676)
Mugliston, David P....4:02:52 (11,203)
Muhammad, Faruq....4:57:44 (25,073)
Mühlbauer, Winfried....4:17:12 (14,693)
Muid, Leo T....3:52:20 (8,369)
Muir, Cameron J....5:22:27 (29,430)
Muir, Graham M....3:54:32 (8,900)
Muir, Jamie....4:42:37 (21,366)
Muir, Malcolm J....3:58:58 (10,243)
Muirhead, Linus....4:50:20 (23,323)
Mujica Mota, Ruben E....4:57:17 (24,980)
Mukerjea, Sunil....5:36:15 (31,096)
Mukherjee, Benjamin....2:59:06 (927)
Mulchrone, Jonathan E....3:46:22 (7,056)
Mulder, Johannes....3:55:16 (9,102)
Mulea, Richard L....6:15:06 (33,795)
Mulgrew, Gerry Ciaran....5:06:56 (26,892)
Mulholland, Brian J....4:44:58 (21,948)
Mulholland, Harry....3:27:08 (3,702)
Mullan, Ryan....3:34:59 (4,955)
Mullan, Steve....4:25:05 (16,734)
Mullane, Grant....4:12:15 (13,453)
Mullany, Richard....5:56:04 (32,761)
Mullarkey, James M....5:39:29 (31,445)
Mullen, Michael J....4:51:07 (23,513)
Muller, Arnaud....4:18:28 (15,021)
Muller, Claude....4:55:12 (24,506)
Muller, Marius A....5:54:28 (32,650)
Muller, René....4:07:00 (12,106)
Müller, Uwe B....3:33:49 (4,726)
Mullery, Peter J....3:15:27 (2,277)
Mullett, Alex S....4:08:00 (12,359)
Mulligan, Brian H....4:11:36 (13,284)
Mulligan, Martin....4:06:42 (12,042)
Mulligan, Michael....3:37:33 (5,412)
Mulligan, Paul E....3:45:10 (6,830)
Mulligan, Peter A....3:10:49 (1,761)
Mulligan, Stephen E....4:22:43 (16,129)
Mullin, Daniel....5:22:54 (29,500)
Mullin, Daniel J....4:41:52 (21,177)
Mullin, Henry....3:28:54 (3,993)
Mullin, William R....3:02:59 (1,172)
Mullins, Andrew P....4:40:03 (20,739)
Mullins, Gerard....3:32:40 (4,568)
Mullis, Justin....4:20:04 (15,446)
Mullish, Elliot....3:27:20 (3,739)
Mulock, Michael L....5:51:39 (32,460)
Mulroy, Brad J....5:41:25 (31,621)
Multani, Gurvinder....4:59:14 (25,438)
Mulvenna, Mark A....4:17:32 (14,776)
Mumford, Kieron M....3:24:17 (3,309)
Munce, James....4:40:02 (20,735)
Munday, Christopher....4:52:11 (23,793)
Munday, John R....5:12:05 (27,814)
Munday, Russell J....4:14:31 (14,032)
Munday, Simon E....4:25:54 (16,961)
Mundy, Andrew S....3:42:11 (6,248)
Mundy, Robert....5:00:59 (25,805)
Munford, Andrew....4:44:06 (21,748)
Mungavin, Michael....3:25:57 (3,523)
Munkley, Carl....3:57:38 (9,818)
Munn, Geoffrey....6:24:32 (34,212)
Munn, Richard G....2:48:48 (418)
Munro, Jonathan C....4:00:19 (10,622)
Munroe, Andy J....3:43:42 (6,565)
Munroe, Lee....4:53:47 (24,169)
Munson, William B....6:37:02 (34,565)
Murani, Ali....4:38:44 (20,360)
Muraro, Maurizio....2:59:19 (943)
Murch, David B....3:49:48 (7,799)
Murdoch, Andrew P....3:46:01 (6,990)
Murdoch, Christopher A....3:56:53 (9,592)
Murdoch, Graeme A....3:31:36 (4,407)
Murdoch, Michael....3:17:18 (2,465)
Murdoch, Michael J....5:11:44 (27,765)
Murdoch, Steven J....2:50:36 (485)
Mureithi, David M....4:38:20 (20,264)
Murgatroyd, Steven....5:00:26 (25,688)
Murgia, Giovanni....3:25:23 (3,441)
Murney, Ian H....4:58:19 (25,218)
Murnieks, Andrew P....3:05:36 (1,345)
Murphy, Brendan....4:58:33 (25,284)
Murphy, Chris P....3:57:38 (9,818)
Murphy, Christian M....3:26:33 (3,609)
Murphy, Christopher D....4:57:20 (24,992)
Murphy, Colin D....3:40:02 (5,869)
Murphy, David....5:00:12 (25,633)
Murphy, Declan D....4:18:36 (15,054)
Murphy, Gary....5:38:08 (31,290)
Murphy, Gerard....3:50:39 (7,978)
Murphy, Glen J....4:27:44 (17,459)
Murphy, John A....4:36:00 (19,683)
Murphy, John G....3:51:34 (8,178)
Murphy, John P....3:09:11 (1,637)
Murphy, Kelvin J....5:24:10 (29,677)
Murphy, Kevin C....3:35:38 (5,082)
Murphy, Kieron T....4:28:31 (17,701)
Murphy, Lee K....3:19:56 (2,745)
Murphy, Luke A....5:07:44 (27,050)
Murphy, Mark D....4:45:39 (22,121)
Murphy, Martin....4:29:18 (17,927)
Murphy, Martin F....4:31:57 (18,623)
Murphy, Matthew....5:03:44 (26,330)
Murphy, Michael G....4:09:12 (12,661)
Murphy, Nick James....4:26:36 (17,148)
Murphy, Peter A....3:44:46 (6,763)
Murphy, Peter G....4:08:21 (12,469)
Murphy, Peter John....3:42:50 (6,385)
Murphy, Peter K....4:53:18 (24,042)
Murphy, Richard....4:55:38 (24,602)
Murphy, Robert....4:19:27 (15,266)
Murphy, Sam A....4:08:00 (12,359)
Murphy, Sean A....4:43:38 (21,633)
Murphy, Stephen....4:37:06 (19,942)
Murphy, William J....4:07:39 (12,270)
Murray, Alasdair J....3:27:33 (3,790)
Murray, Alex....4:35:57 (19,664)
Murray, Alexander D....3:50:07 (7,859)
Murray, Andrew Charles....3:54:59 (9,018)
Murray, Anthony....4:22:55 (16,168)
Murray, Benjamin R....6:28:07 (34,361)
Murray, Dan N....3:05:36 (1,345)
Murray, Daniel C....4:08:39 (12,533)
Murray, Garry N....4:05:34 (11,792)
Murray, Hugh D....3:52:40 (8,444)
Murray, Ian....4:18:55 (15,139)
Murray, James....5:34:22 (30,891)
Murray, James I....3:11:28 (1,823)
Murray, Jamie....3:48:08 (7,425)
Murray, John A....4:46:17 (22,274)
Murray, Jonathan J....3:38:27 (5,578)
Murray, Mark....5:15:49 (28,476)
Murray, Matt S....4:31:16 (18,419)
Murray, Paul....4:23:45 (16,374)
Murray, Paul F....4:06:51 (12,075)
Murray, Rob....3:55:26 (9,139)
Murray, Robert J....2:59:41 (974)
Murray, Stephen M....4:39:26 (20,562)
Murray, Thomas D....3:11:02 (1,780)
Murray, Tom P....4:20:41 (15,596)
Murrills, Christopher D....5:01:16 (25,872)
Murrin, Thomas W....5:39:22 (31,433)
Mursell, John W....3:24:02 (3,265)
Mursell, Phillip I....4:14:42 (14,079)
Murtagh, Mark....4:08:02 (12,369)
Murtagh, Matthew J....4:42:36 (21,361)
Murtagh, Stephen J....2:49:29 (443)
Murteira, Nicholas....4:46:52 (22,441)
Murugananthavel, Senthoran K..4:42:26 (21,309)
Murwill, John....5:01:45 (25,963)
Murwill, Phil....4:00:52 (10,766)
Musa, Gbadebo Olawole....5:23:11 (29,543)
Muscroft, Marco....4:56:32 (24,809)
Mushtaq, Wasim....6:01:35 (33,145)
Musselwhite, James D....4:11:09 (13,153)
Musselwhite, Paul T....5:40:20 (31,526)
Musson, Anthony R....4:49:21 (23,071)
Musson, Harry J....4:44:39 (21,871)
Mustafa, Mustafa....4:40:56 (20,948)
Mustill, Oliver....5:30:05 (30,408)
Mutai, Emmanuel....2:06:53 (4)
Mutch, George M....4:46:46 (22,426)
Mutch, Jonathan M....5:25:57 (29,927)
Mutimer, Daniel....5:16:22 (28,545)
Mutini, Lorenzo....3:23:07 (3,139)
Mutsaers, Adrian R....3:47:38 (7,313)
Mutter, Dave W....4:39:07 (20,467)
Muttett, David Colin....4:35:57 (19,664)
Mutton, Andrew Martin....3:23:20 (3,163)
Mycock, Gareth J....5:31:07 (30,541)
Myers, Aron....3:41:59 (6,200)
Myers, Jon R....5:26:44 (30,018)
Myers, Martin A....4:34:24 (19,241)
Myers, Matt J....4:10:26 (12,962)
Myers, Nathan....5:03:34 (26,294)
Myers, Nick....4:59:49 (25,556)
Myers, Peter....4:56:19 (24,755)
Myers, Tony....4:07:52 (12,331)
Myerscough, Steve V....3:06:32 (1,405)
Myles, Patrick....4:48:41 (22,897)
Mynett, Michael....4:02:21 (11,091)
Nachbaur, Kurt....3:39:12 (5,716)
Nafzger, Gerard....3:59:24 (10,369)
Nagashige, Sakaguchi....4:36:57 (19,900)
Nagel, Horst....4:18:53 (15,128)
Nagorski, John J....4:31:01 (18,352)
Nahar, Naveen....4:12:08 (13,421)
Nairn, Charlie....3:41:06 (6,048)
Naisby, Eddie....5:15:02 (28,324)
Naish, Keith D....5:24:02 (29,655)
Nakan, Lee V....5:15:33 (28,427)
Nakanishi, Kohei....5:25:28 (29,855)
Nakrani, Mitul....5:23:14 (29,561)
Naldrett, Andrew J....4:38:00 (20,165)
Nall, Simon....4:11:34 (13,273)
Nallen, Noel....4:33:02 (18,906)
Naman, Colin....4:20:57 (15,674)
Namian, Christophe....4:07:38 (12,265)
Nancarrow, James....3:55:57 (9,297)
Nandha, Bhavesh P....4:40:15 (20,788)
Nandi, Sanjay....3:51:18 (8,120)
Nanton, Kingsley P....2:49:40 (452)
Napleton, Matthew....4:57:26 (25,016)
Napthen, Richard D....4:54:37 (24,365)
Nascimento, Jo....3:41:58 (6,197)
Naseem, Muhammad S....4:42:32 (21,339)
Nash, Charles P....4:02:52 (11,203)
Nash, David C....4:33:51 (19,113)
Nash, Gary J....5:52:41 (32,528)
Nash, Nick J....4:39:56 (20,701)
Nash, Paul A....4:33:55 (19,133)
Nash, Pete S....3:44:42 (6,749)
Nash, Stephen....3:56:25 (9,434)
Nash, Steven J....3:33:21 (4,658)
Nash, Steven P....6:00:02 (33,055)
Nash, Tim C....5:44:10 (31,867)
Nash, William A....5:25:59 (29,933)
Natali, Giulio....3:48:03 (7,413)
Natali, Ivan....3:58:20 (10,046)
Natali, Paul E....3:36:03 (5,166)
Nathan, Aaron B....4:59:11 (25,430)
Nathan, Clive....3:32:27 (4,536)

Nathan, Joseph A 3:44:28 (6,713)
Nathan, Paul J 3:25:36 (3,473)
Nathwani, Aashish 4:37:09 (19,954)
Nation, Richard 3:49:31 (7,733)
Nattino, Arturo 3:09:37 (1,669)
Naudi, Matthew A 3:59:54 (10,515)
Naughton, Aidan A 4:34:59 (19,404)
Naughton, Liam R 4:16:01 (14,401)
Nauroy, Luc 3:22:18 (3,050)
Navarre, Paul 3:53:50 (8,710)
Navrady, Jeremy 4:15:44 (14,329)
Nayager, Preven 4:27:03 (17,269)
Nayler, Darren 5:21:02 (29,227)
Nayler, Robert J 5:21:02 (29,227)
Naylor, Andy W 2:32:39 (87)
Naylor, Antony J 3:31:19 (4,374)
Naylor, Charles E 4:17:43 (14,826)
Naylor, David H 4:22:16 (16,017)
Naylor, David M 3:16:10 (2,348)
Naylor, Robert 4:33:25 (19,006)
Naylor, Timothy R 4:59:49 (25,556)
Nayyar, Micky B 6:16:33 (33,868)
Nazzi, Francesco 3:25:25 (3,449)
Ndirangu, Solomon 3:29:43 (4,139)
Ndlovu, Nkosiyabo N 4:51:50 (23,707)
Neal, Martin J 4:26:52 (17,229)
Neal, Steven J 4:00:04 (10,564)
Neal, Trevor J 6:05:35 (33,367)
Neale, David M 5:12:20 (27,857)
Neale, Nickolas 3:34:51 (4,935)
Neale, Ulen 4:30:58 (18,340)
Neale-May, Simon M 5:10:03 (27,473)
Neary, David 5:00:12 (25,633)
Nee, Michael 4:49:45 (23,192)
Needham, David W 3:34:49 (4,933)
Needham, Gary J 4:37:04 (19,934)
Needham, Michael J 4:12:10 (13,433)
Needham, Stephen 4:45:31 (22,085)
Needham, Stephen D 3:54:30 (8,890)
Needham, Wayne F 3:48:51 (7,585)
Neel, George A 3:56:18 (9,394)
Neep, Andrew B 3:49:34 (7,743)
Neeson, Andrew 5:09:44 (27,412)
Neeson, Patrick J 4:08:31 (12,508)
Negri, Lorenzo 3:29:55 (4,169)
Neicho, Scott M 4:16:24 (14,499)
Neighbour, Chris J 4:37:21 (19,994)
Neighbour, Matthew R 4:28:08 (17,587)
Neighbour, William J 4:01:18 (10,858)
Neil, James R 3:44:22 (6,695)
Neil, Martin Loudon 3:36:23 (5,212)
Neill, Gary D 3:52:59 (8,502)
Neill, Jamie S 5:23:22 (29,579)
Neill, Jonathan 4:27:49 (17,495)
Neill, Peter T 6:57:18 (34,924)
Neill, Steven M 2:29:51 (66)
Neill, Tom J 4:02:40 (11,163)
Neilly, Gordon J 4:36:19 (19,742)
Neish, Richard 4:58:38 (25,304)
Neller, Joe A 4:36:30 (19,793)
Nellins, Christopher T 3:30:23 (4,232)
Nelmes, Paul A 4:42:07 (21,235)
Nelson, Adam J 4:08:17 (12,447)
Nelson, Colin R 4:51:57 (23,741)
Nelson, Frik 6:36:45 (34,555)
Nelson, James M 5:15:29 (28,414)
Nelson, Janusz J 3:55:33 (9,171)
Nelson, John 4:54:42 (24,386)
Nelson, John E 3:08:35 (1,575)
Nelson, Jonathan James 4:32:53 (18,868)
Nelson, Matt 4:25:30 (16,836)
Nelson, Nicholas 4:22:46 (16,136)
Nelson, Paul S 3:24:06 (3,279)
Nelson, Rick 5:24:01 (29,652)
Nelson, Ricky D 4:25:57 (16,974)
Nelson, Russell J 4:18:57 (15,150)
Nenning, Siegfried 4:35:01 (19,411)
Neocleous, Richard R 5:29:47 (30,370)
Nero, Josef T 4:51:40 (23,667)
Nesden, Patrick 4:52:39 (23,892)
Ness, Patrick 4:26:35 (17,144)
Nester, Christopher J 3:59:01 (10,254)
Neter, Nicholas J 5:59:51 (33,038)
Nethercott, Steve J 3:10:41 (1,755)
Neto, Pedro 3:57:16 (9,695)
Nettleton, Philip D 4:13:03 (13,667)
Netto, Tim D 4:55:41 (24,610)
Netzel, Thomas 4:12:12 (13,439)
Neubauer, Christian 3:15:45 (2,313)
Neuberger, Oliver 4:47:35 (22,624)
Neugebauer, James 3:49:48 (7,799)
Nevard, Stephen P 4:03:17 (11,288)
Nevill, Mark G 5:12:18 (27,853)
Nevill, Timothy J 4:29:28 (17,963)
Neville, Philip E 4:00:13 (10,603)
Nevin, Austin F 3:56:48 (9,569)
Nevison, David S 5:51:48 (32,467)
New, Keith S 4:24:56 (16,691)
New, Simon D 4:19:30 (15,287)
Newall, Brian J 4:53:40 (24,123)
Newall, Mark R 4:12:35 (13,544)
Newbould, Andrew J 3:07:03 (1,438)
Newbould, Lee R 3:47:53 (7,372)
Newbury, William 3:54:14 (8,821)
Newby, Dave S 5:33:35 (30,819)
Newby, Gavin 3:58:51 (10,211)
Newcombe, George F 4:42:31 (21,336)
Newcombe, Tom J 4:19:58 (15,419)
Newell, Guy R 4:54:24 (24,310)
Newell, Jonathan E 3:59:44 (10,472)
Newell, Mark 5:14:40 (28,261)
Newell, Mark S 4:23:29 (16,308)
Newington-Bridges, Charlie 3:40:34 (5,951)
Newins, Mathew 3:34:18 (4,830)
Newitt, Steve 4:43:33 (21,613)
Newman, Alun G 3:22:09 (3,029)
Newman, Antony 4:43:58 (21,711)
Newman, Clive W 4:13:27 (13,785)
Newman, David 5:05:43 (26,685)
Newman, David A 3:22:49 (3,111)
Newman, Guy 4:15:49 (14,354)
Newman, Jason J 5:27:13 (30,068)
Newman, Mark E 4:19:07 (15,188)
Newman, Maurice Thomas 4:06:24 (11,969)
Newman, Neil 4:44:45 (21,899)
Newman, Neville 4:00:32 (10,680)
Newman, Nick 3:54:05 (8,776)
Newman, Nick 4:50:20 (23,323)
Newman, Richard D 3:37:33 (5,412)
Newman, Roberto 4:37:13 (19,964)
Newman, Steven 2:57:31 (806)
Newman, Stuart R 3:55:18 (9,110)
Newns, Luke J 4:39:18 (20,521)
Newport, Alan B 4:52:40 (23,895)
Newsome, Peter 3:07:49 (1,514)
Newsum-Smith, Jon P 3:20:21 (2,803)
Newton, David 3:50:19 (7,907)
Newton, Graham 3:55:54 (9,289)
Newton, James A 3:53:17 (8,580)
Newton, James E 4:17:33 (14,781)
Newton, Mark B 4:42:15 (21,265)
Newton, Martin J 3:59:24 (10,369)
Newton, Matthew R 2:52:24 (541)
Newton, Matthew T 4:18:10 (14,940)
Newton, Oli P 4:25:53 (16,958)
Newton, Peter 3:54:46 (8,960)
Newton, Peter J 3:08:09 (1,538)
Newton, Philip C 5:06:01 (26,729)
Newton, Robert 4:06:32 (11,997)
Newton, Ronald A 4:31:44 (18,560)
Newton, Samuel D 3:15:57 (2,330)
Newton, Simon 2:38:35 (168)
Newton, Wayne D 3:30:05 (4,189)
Newton-Lee, Andy 4:06:26 (11,978)
Nex, Andrew P 4:08:59 (12,616)
Neylon, William 6:28:32 (34,371)
Ng, Pak Ho 4:13:13 (13,717)
Ng, Thomas 4:45:26 (22,062)
Nibbelke, Peter 3:51:16 (8,112)
Niblett, Richard M 4:00:02 (10,552)
Niblock, Craig 5:09:11 (27,306)
Nice, Matthew A 4:11:05 (13,133)
Nice, Richard D 5:29:51 (30,384)
Nicel, John M 4:51:50 (23,707)
Nicholas, Daryl P 3:17:41 (2,500)
Nicholas, Gary 4:47:42 (22,653)
Nicholas, Peter C 4:33:44 (19,080)
Nicholl, Ali C 5:46:27 (32,045)
Nicholl, Gary A 5:01:21 (25,885)
Nicholls, Andrew S 3:22:28 (3,063)
Nicholls, Craig 4:10:01 (12,858)
Nicholls, Darren J 4:42:38 (21,371)
Nicholls, Guy 4:25:11 (16,762)
Nicholls, Jeremy J 4:39:44 (20,652)
Nicholls, John W 3:57:38 (9,818)
Nicholls, Jonathon 5:45:12 (31,946)
Nicholls, Luke William 4:17:22 (14,736)
Nicholls, Martin Clive 3:43:20 (6,497)
Nicholls, Matthew 4:05:58 (11,875)
Nicholls, Matthew T 4:15:43 (14,323)
Nicholls, Paul Keith 5:36:00 (31,078)
Nicholls, Peter 5:00:43 (25,751)
Nicholls, Robert 3:58:45 (10,174)
Nicholls, Seb 3:37:38 (5,429)
Nicholls, Tom 4:36:18 (19,739)
Nichols, Charles E 4:18:46 (15,094)
Nichols, Dave 3:54:15 (8,828)
Nichols, Edward 4:14:34 (14,047)
Nichols, Grant 5:58:01 (32,919)
Nichols, John D 3:53:45 (8,692)
Nichols, Kenneth B 4:59:21 (25,464)
Nichols, Michael 2:50:24 (479)
Nichols, Paul 3:44:11 (6,662)
Nichols, Richard W 5:08:32 (27,180)
Nichols, Tom A 4:26:27 (17,097)
Nicholson, Angus 5:05:00 (26,544)
Nicholson, Ben 3:11:47 (1,859)
Nicholson, Ben S 5:09:42 (27,403)
Nicholson, Chris D 3:33:12 (4,637)
Nicholson, Christopher J 5:53:22 (32,576)
Nicholson, Daniel 3:19:12 (2,637)
Nicholson, David 4:02:28 (11,121)
Nicholson, Ian P 5:37:01 (31,170)
Nicholson, Jonathan P 3:56:49 (9,573)
Nicholson, Joseph 3:51:26 (8,150)
Nicholson, Keith 4:00:08 (10,580)
Nicholson, Nick E 5:53:09 (32,561)
Nicholson, Nigel 3:58:13 (10,018)
Nicholson, Paul M 4:32:29 (18,755)
Nicholson, Richard David 3:06:50 (1,423)
Nicholson, Stuart H 3:27:15 (3,726)
Nicholson, Tom E 3:36:28 (5,229)
Nickalls, James 3:32:34 (4,558)
Nicklin, Edward R 5:06:38 (26,830)
Nickolds, Stephen V 4:53:07 (24,004)
Nicol, Alan 3:46:59 (7,198)
Nicol, Alister 3:43:19 (6,493)
Nicol, Chris 4:29:26 (17,956)
Nicol, David Grant 4:36:08 (19,707)
Nicolaci, Giovanni 2:48:43 (416)
Nicolas, Besnard 5:55:08 (32,697)
Nicolas, Charrier 5:13:42 (28,099)
Nicolas, Darren 4:57:26 (25,016)
Nicolas, Mentha 3:50:53 (8,034)
Nicolas, Suard 4:02:46 (11,182)
Nicole, Steven 4:53:06 (23,998)
Nicoll, David R 5:22:08 (29,376)
Nida, James 4:52:22 (23,835)
Nieder, Thomas 6:04:34 (33,317)
Nield, Duncan W 3:19:57 (2,750)
Nield, Peter J 3:43:29 (6,520)
Nielsen, Bjorn D 5:15:39 (28,447)
Nielsen, Christian B 3:35:34 (5,061)
Nielsen, Henning 3:39:56 (5,843)
Nielsen, Leif Broechner 4:21:36 (15,844)
Niemann, Willem A 5:03:32 (26,290)
Nieuwpoort, Rudolf 4:46:49 (22,435)
Nightingale, Benjamin P 4:38:51 (20,388)
Nightingale, Mark J 3:20:36 (2,838)
Nightingale, Paul 5:12:23 (27,865)
Nihill, Robbie 4:38:35 (20,319)
Nilsson, Gíran 2:54:43 (643)
Nimmo, Steven G 2:56:33 (748)
Nisbet, Andrew I 3:42:09 (6,242)
Niven, Chris 4:32:04 (18,656)
Nix, Edward J 4:20:33 (15,571)
Nix, Kevin J 5:56:51 (32,821)
Nixson, Michael 5:06:03 (26,734)
Nizar, Jamal 3:52:00 (8,277)

Noades, Ryan T 5:22:08 (29,376)
Nobbs, David J 4:29:21 (17,936)
Nobes, Lee A 3:47:12 (7,234)
Noble, Brian J 4:27:24 (17,368)
Noble, David 4:49:10 (23,009)
Noble, Gerrard G 4:12:27 (13,507)
Noble, Graham 4:10:21 (12,944)
Noble, Jamie 4:51:00 (23,488)
Noble, Jason R 3:47:08 (7,222)
Noble, Matthew D 3:12:56 (1,995)
Noble, Paul M 3:37:51 (5,465)
Nobuyuki, Yawata 5:46:16 (32,034)
Nock, Graham S 3:20:26 (2,817)
Nock, Simon 4:46:19 (22,284)
Nodder, George 4:03:30 (11,334)
Noel, Lesley 4:42:21 (21,283)
Noe-Nordberg, Markus 3:15:28 (2,280)
Nogami, Yoshiyuki 4:31:35 (18,524)
Nokes, Andrew 4:59:07 (25,415)
Nolan, Adrian 5:34:23 (30,894)
Nolan, Andrew 3:57:02 (9,628)
Nolan, David M 3:57:41 (9,842)
Nolan, Jim 4:54:48 (24,408)
Nolan, Joe 3:53:42 (8,677)
Nolan, Keiran 4:46:57 (22,469)
Nolan, Martin J 4:23:29 (16,308)
Nolan, Richard 3:53:07 (8,536)
Nolan, Steven 4:06:13 (11,931)
Nolan, Timothy C 4:35:01 (19,411)
Nombreuse, Georges 5:20:22 (29,135)
Noorbaccus, Mike 5:22:55 (29,503)
Norbury, Antony 4:08:02 (12,369)
Norbury, David 3:53:07 (8,536)
Norbury, Stephen F 3:33:30 (4,677)
Norcott, Lee 4:33:28 (19,016)
Nordin, Abdurauf Bin 5:15:15 (28,370)
Norgrove, Gary 2:52:17 (534)
Norgrove, Michael 3:01:38 (1,091)
Noriega, Jorge 4:34:45 (19,329)
Norley, Lyndon E 3:55:14 (9,092)
Norman, Daniel G 2:41:06 (217)
Norman, Eddie 4:29:02 (17,843)
Norman, Greg 4:26:56 (17,245)
Norman, John D 5:57:13 (32,845)
Norman, Martin J 4:42:22 (21,293)
Norman, Matthew B 2:56:52 (765)
Norman, Nick C 3:59:39 (10,437)
Norman, Paul 4:04:16 (11,504)
Norman, Phil 4:24:48 (16,654)
Norman, Richard T 3:46:57 (7,191)
Norman, Robert I 3:38:26 (5,574)
Norman, Ross 4:32:40 (18,808)
Norman, Tim R 3:53:55 (8,726)
Normoyle, Trevor F 4:06:59 (12,100)
Norridge, Christopher 4:02:36 (11,151)
Norris, Andrew 3:59:43 (10,467)
Norris, Barry M 4:08:36 (12,524)
Norris, Ben J 5:48:01 (32,171)
Norris, Christopher 5:04:31 (26,459)
Norris, Gary 4:50:28 (23,362)
Norris, Gerard A 3:35:08 (4,985)
Norris, Graham L 4:05:30 (11,768)
Norris, John F 4:21:48 (15,900)
Norris, Patrick A 5:40:03 (31,503)
Norris, Paul A 5:44:09 (31,866)
Norris, Steve R 4:48:17 (22,804)
Norris, Stuart B 4:04:13 (11,495)
North, Ian K 4:34:39 (19,300)
North, Steffan J 2:28:25 (50)
Northcote, Robert 4:15:39 (14,312)
Northcott, Adrian Peter 3:24:55 (3,392)
Northeast, Graham P 3:35:52 (5,125)
Northey, Kevin 3:51:50 (8,234)
Northmore, Andrew B 3:42:31 (6,305)
Northmore, David J 6:10:53 (33,598)
Northway, Oliver J 4:54:43 (24,390)
Northway, Simon A 4:58:25 (25,247)
Norton, Andrew R 4:08:33 (12,513)
Norton, Barry P 4:54:53 (24,426)
Norton, Gary 5:02:50 (26,187)
Norton, Jerry P 4:10:04 (12,869)
Norton, Jonathan 3:56:09 (9,351)
Norton, Jonathan F 3:58:42 (10,162)
Norton, Paul R 4:43:14 (21,524)
Norton, Simon 4:16:11 (14,443)
Norton, Simon N 4:42:20 (21,280)
Nottidge, Vincent 4:17:08 (14,677)
Nottingham, Ross 3:51:21 (8,128)
Notton, Christopher J 3:54:28 (8,880)
Nouillan, Bill 5:36:10 (31,092)
Noungu, Stephen N 3:59:46 (10,481)
Nourse, Robert A 6:19:57 (34,031)
Novak, Ondrej 5:18:50 (28,947)
Novelli, Pio Eugenio 3:35:01 (4,962)
Novello, Andrea Gianluigi 4:13:35 (13,821)
Nowak, Jean-Marc 5:12:15 (27,847)
Nowakowski, David 4:59:44 (25,541)
Nugari, Paolo 3:50:08 (7,867)
Nugari, Paolo Filippo 3:18:15 (2,550)
Nugent, Ashley J 5:39:04 (31,406)
Nugent, Daniel Christian 3:40:56 (6,019)
Nugent, Jenny J 6:46:34 (34,730)
Nunn, Ashley 3:38:36 (5,608)
Nunn, David 6:23:07 (34,155)
Nunn, Luke 3:55:35 (9,183)
Nunn, Matthew 5:24:55 (29,782)
Nutbean, James 5:00:24 (25,677)
Nutkin, Kevin S 4:59:49 (25,556)
Nutt, Matthew R 2:52:55 (554)
Nuttall, Philip R 3:30:49 (4,300)
Nutton, David E 3:25:52 (3,514)
Nuyts, Wim D 3:50:27 (7,933)
Nydahl, Stig 5:47:48 (32,157)
Nye, Alan D 4:21:55 (15,927)
Nye, Graham 4:12:01 (13,392)
Nye, John 5:55:11 (32,704)
Nye, Simon W 5:02:25 (26,098)
Nyeki, Jan 3:44:48 (6,770)
Nyland, Sean 4:59:49 (25,556)
Nylon, Nils 3:07:22 (1,463)
Oakes, Mark A 3:43:49 (6,592)
Oakland, Simon N 3:48:47 (7,562)
Oakley, Andrew J 3:27:58 (3,852)
Oakley, Kevin C 5:01:25 (25,898)
Oakley, Mark I 4:43:20 (21,559)
Oakley, Philip S 3:36:11 (5,188)
Oakley MBE, Les 5:47:45 (32,146)
Oates, David A 4:29:32 (17,974)
Oatham, Philip W 3:04:08 (1,243)
Oatts, Christopher M 4:33:15 (18,959)
Obank, Simon 4:39:56 (20,701)
O'Beirne, Edward 4:35:28 (19,534)
O'Beirne, Gerry B 3:48:33 (7,523)
Oberwinkler, Manfred 3:42:37 (6,336)
Obie, Gareth 5:50:35 (32,388)
Obie, Nicholas M 6:14:21 (33,761)
O'Boyle, Jeff M 5:21:02 (29,227)
O'Brien, Andrew A 4:21:49 (15,905)
O'Brien, Chris 4:12:34 (13,542)
O'Brien, Cornelius P 5:53:36 (32,592)
O'Brien, Darragh 3:44:51 (6,779)
O'Brien, Darron J 4:21:07 (15,721)
O'Brien, David J 4:50:31 (23,376)
O'Brien, David J 5:05:12 (26,592)
O'Brien, Frank 5:19:07 (28,986)
O'Brien, Gerard F 3:16:32 (2,385)
O'Brien, Ian 3:51:22 (8,133)
O'Brien, James 4:59:40 (25,525)
O'Brien, Lee 4:39:52 (20,685)
O'Brien, Lee R 5:21:01 (29,223)
O'Brien, Michael 7:19:15 (35,144)
O'Brien, Mike 5:44:08 (31,864)
O'Brien, Neil 5:35:30 (31,018)
O'Brien, Nigel D 4:43:18 (21,543)
O'Brien, Richard M 3:41:10 (6,061)
O'Brien, Tony 4:15:53 (14,364)
O'Callaghan, Eugene P 3:27:22 (3,744)
O'Callaghan, Gavin 4:52:04 (23,769)
O'Callaghan, James R 3:10:51 (1,765)
O'Callaghan, John 4:34:45 (19,329)
O'Callaghan, Mark 4:57:54 (25,111)
O'Connell, Andrew 3:49:02 (7,627)
O'Connell, Geoffrey 4:41:13 (21,017)
O'Connell, Iain A 4:25:08 (16,746)
O'Connor, Denis J 3:35:06 (4,978)
O'Connor, James T 5:52:36 (32,518)
O'Connor, John 3:06:25 (1,401)
O'Connor, Kevin 3:40:05 (5,875)
O'Connor, Mark 4:33:08 (18,928)
O'Connor, Patrick P 5:24:34 (29,743)
O'Connor, Paul 5:20:47 (29,194)
O'Connor, Ray 3:32:05 (4,483)
O'Connor, Richard I 2:58:50 (903)
O'Connor, Richard R 4:12:23 (13,488)
O'Connor, Rory 4:27:56 (17,524)
O'Connor, Shane 3:04:52 (1,299)
O'Connor, Thomas J 5:58:12 (32,938)
O'Connor, Tom P 4:02:48 (11,187)
O'Connor, William J 4:50:43 (23,428)
Odell, Dustin 3:19:23 (2,665)
Odell, Graham 4:18:35 (15,049)
O'Dell, Mark J 3:18:15 (2,550)
Odling, Richard J 4:27:15 (17,325)
Odonnell, John 3:30:29 (4,249)
O'Donnell, Anthony M 4:19:41 (15,333)
O'Donnell, Ben J 3:52:12 (8,328)
O'Donnell, Gary P 4:13:59 (13,905)
O'Donnell, Jonathan 4:10:37 (13,010)
O'Donnell, Martin J 4:03:35 (11,352)
O'Donnell, Mike 3:42:50 (6,385)
O'Donnell, Paul 3:44:14 (6,671)
O'Donnell, Paul V 3:09:02 (1,621)
O'Donoghue, Brett 4:10:40 (13,025)
O'Donoghue, Thomas 3:28:05 (3,866)
O'Donohoe, David M 4:44:14 (21,775)
O'Driscoll, Barry 3:52:02 (8,282)
Odurny, Allan 4:06:47 (12,056)
O'Dwyer, David 3:09:20 (1,650)
O'Dwyer, Eamonn Gerrard 3:32:50 (4,590)
O'Dwyer, Michael C 5:20:46 (29,187)
Oeen, Erlend 4:55:50 (24,649)
Oelze, Joerg 4:20:49 (15,641)
O'Farrell, Edmund 4:02:37 (11,156)
O'Farrell-Ross, Graeme A 4:39:16 (20,511)
Offinger, Johannes 5:58:02 (32,921)
Offord, Richard 4:06:15 (11,941)
Offord, Simon P 4:12:47 (13,602)
Ogden, David M 2:55:11 (678)
Ogden, Dean 3:52:55 (8,489)
Ogden, Kevin P 2:47:37 (381)
Ogden, Nick D 3:06:59 (1,432)
Ogden, Simon M 3:41:39 (6,138)
Ogeron, Stephane 3:49:03 (7,633)
Ogierman, Andrew 5:02:01 (26,025)
Ogilvie, Ian 4:26:52 (17,229)
Ogilvie, Paul N 4:41:04 (20,976)
Ognedal, Tormod 4:20:09 (15,471)
O'Gorman, Eddie P 2:53:16 (571)
O'Gorman, Keith Patrick 4:32:25 (18,735)
O'Gorman, Tim J 4:17:19 (14,725)
O'Grady, Jim 4:25:58 (16,978)
O'Grady, Vinny C 3:08:32 (1,570)
Ogunsanlu, Ayo O 4:37:27 (20,024)
Ogunyemi, Jackson 5:36:24 (31,111)
O'Hagan, Michael 4:10:41 (13,033)
O'Halloran, Conor P 7:02:46 (34,980)
O'Hanlon, Thomas 5:27:44 (30,114)
O'Hara, Andy W 4:42:21 (21,283)
O'Hara, Michael John 4:24:16 (16,517)
O'Hara, Raymond J 4:10:49 (13,068)
O'Hare, Brian J 4:47:10 (22,536)
O'Hare, James P 4:16:34 (14,542)
O'Hare, John 4:57:32 (25,040)
O'Hare, Mark 3:57:20 (9,721)
O'Herlihy, Donal 3:50:11 (7,878)
O'Kane, Sean 4:43:32 (21,609)
Okazaki, Jay 4:45:44 (22,139)
O'Keefe, Christopher S 4:19:24 (15,255)
O'Keefe, Steven L 5:09:02 (27,280)
O'Keeffe, Jeremiah J 4:08:26 (12,493)
O'Keeffe, William F 4:46:51 (22,438)
Okolo, Patrick 5:21:31 (29,305)
Okura, Masamitsu 3:17:42 (2,502)
Olausson, Karl Anders 3:44:48 (6,770)
Old, George 3:40:10 (5,892)
Old, Jack 5:10:33 (27,556)
Oldcorn, Mike 4:33:39 (19,060)
Oldfield, David 4:42:01 (21,202)
Oldfield, James 5:27:40 (30,106)

Oldfield, Mark A.........5:09:45 (27,417)
Oldfield, Richard.........5:27:40 (30,106)
Oldfield-Hodge, Trefor.........5:00:18 (25,655)
Olding, Andrew.........4:10:43 (13,044)
Oldmeadow, Keith R.........5:22:08 (29,376)
Oldreive, Mike A.........3:22:02 (3,017)
O'Leary, Grant.........3:25:14 (3,424)
O'Leary, Jim A.........4:51:51 (23,709)
O'Leary, John.........5:43:07 (31,784)
O'Leary, Steven J.........5:20:46 (29,187)
Oleen, Brian.........7:17:08 (35,119)
Oletzky, Torsten.........3:58:22 (10,059)
Oliphant, Andy.........5:51:28 (32,444)
Oliphant, Robert.........5:14:04 (28,175)
Olival, Joe.........6:02:52 (33,219)
Oliveira, Joao.........3:35:00 (4,960)
Oliveira, Paul.........4:23:37 (16,341)
Oliver, Andrew R.........3:16:09 (2,346)
Oliver, David J.........2:59:28 (953)
Oliver, David M.........5:45:13 (31,947)
Oliver, Geoffrey J.........3:34:48 (4,930)
Oliver, Mark R.........4:04:54 (11,630)
Oliver, Paul J.........3:47:26 (7,271)
Oliver, Paul R.........3:17:13 (2,455)
Oliver, Phillip J.........4:28:45 (17,760)
Oliver, Richard.........3:42:02 (6,218)
Oliver, Richard T.........4:30:31 (18,235)
Oliver, Robert J.........3:39:53 (5,830)
Oliver, Stephen R.........3:18:11 (2,546)
Olivier, Bertrand M.........4:15:44 (14,329)
Olivier, Darrel L.........3:19:37 (2,699)
Ollington, Jon.........5:09:48 (27,431)
Olney, Lee Steven.........5:58:47 (32,978)
Olney, Paul John.........4:03:13 (11,275)
O'Loughlin, Julian.........3:33:56 (4,745)
O'Loughlin, Shaun P.........3:51:08 (8,081)
Olozulu, Marcus N.........5:52:53 (32,539)
Olsen, Jeremy.........4:53:49 (24,177)
Olsen, Mark J.........5:03:57 (26,374)
Olsen, Nathan J.........4:10:26 (12,962)
Olszowski, Rupert T.........4:39:48 (20,668)
Olver, George.........3:35:30 (5,047)
Olvier, Mark R.........4:57:46 (25,081)
O'Mahoney, Bernard.........6:28:43 (34,375)
O'Mahoney, Gerard.........4:12:42 (13,575)
O'Malley, Michael J.........4:38:52 (20,396)
Ombler, Simon.........4:37:07 (19,945)
O'Meara, Philip.........3:59:07 (10,285)
Omiyale, Wale.........4:40:38 (20,875)
Omonkhua, Daniel.........5:05:08 (26,575)
Omori, Mark.........3:17:40 (2,499)
Omran, Ramzy.........4:16:28 (14,514)
Onclin, Hendrik Martinus.........3:39:01 (5,689)
O'Neill, Adam.........4:06:09 (11,915)
O'Neill, Christopher.........4:12:53 (13,623)
O'Neill, Eamonn C.........2:58:08 (846)
O'Neill, James A.........6:47:55 (34,769)
O'Neill, Kevin F.........3:50:45 (8,007)
O'Neill, Patrick G.........3:07:32 (1,484)
O'Neill, Patrick N.........5:00:54 (25,787)
O'Neill, Patrick R.........4:39:08 (20,473)
O'Neill, Rory H.........3:12:27 (1,926)
O'Neill, Vincent.........3:41:20 (6,093)
Ong, Dennis.........5:20:26 (29,146)
Onions, Darren.........5:21:45 (29,334)
Onkelbach, Michael.........3:49:25 (7,708)
Openshaw, Lee C.........4:36:21 (19,750)
Opperman, Richard E.........3:30:29 (4,249)
Oprych, Joe.........4:49:02 (22,981)
Oram, Hugh.........3:57:01 (9,625)
O'Rathaille, Conn O.........5:55:23 (32,715)
Orchard, Allen M.........5:20:35 (29,158)
Orchard, Mark Anthony.........4:40:33 (20,848)
Orchard, Stephen R.........4:32:47 (18,842)
Ordish, Ian A.........4:25:37 (16,877)
O'Regan, John.........3:29:30 (4,102)
O'Reilley, Brian J.........3:19:37 (2,699)
O'Reilly, Bob.........4:43:20 (21,559)
O'Reilly, Christopher J.........6:27:35 (34,345)
O'Reilly, Kevin.........4:13:21 (13,768)
O'Reilly, Patrick.........4:33:26 (19,013)
O'Reilly, Peter J.........6:03:33 (33,262)
O'Reilly, Sean.........4:40:53 (20,936)
O'Reilly, Stephen P.........5:36:25 (31,113)
O'Reilly, Tom.........4:51:14 (23,547)
Orford, Martin I.........4:19:53 (15,396)
Organ, Adrian C.........3:31:21 (4,376)
Oricci, Giuseppe.........3:35:58 (5,147)
Orishaguna, George B.........5:36:23 (31,110)
Orlando, Camillo.........3:42:22 (6,277)
Orme, Michael T.........4:10:04 (12,869)
Orme, Paul Matthew.........4:23:12 (16,231)
Orme, Steven.........4:49:41 (23,176)
Ormerod, Clive R.........3:18:57 (2,614)
Ormiston, Chris J.........4:25:08 (16,746)
Ormond, Ian.........5:11:04 (27,655)
Ormond, John M.........4:39:08 (20,473)
Ormond, Paul A.........3:53:35 (8,644)
Ormston, Jeff R.........5:07:25 (26,988)
Ornolfsson, Magnus Palmi.........4:52:08 (23,781)
Orpin, Michael John.........4:07:55 (12,344)
Orr, Andrew.........3:08:03 (1,527)
Orr, Billy.........3:09:53 (1,696)
Orr, Stuart.........4:55:36 (24,597)
Orrin, Stuart W.........3:51:39 (8,199)
Orsanigo, Pierluigi.........5:10:24 (27,532)
Orsman, Christopher J.........5:27:23 (30,084)
Orton, Ryan.........4:13:13 (13,717)
Orton, Steven D.........4:05:00 (11,652)
Osafo-Asare, Rex.........5:26:26 (29,988)
Osawa, Manabu.........4:05:25 (11,756)
Osbiston, Alan G.........4:18:12 (14,945)
Osborn, Andrew S.........5:17:39 (28,738)
Osborn, Ben J.........2:41:51 (231)
Osborn, Kevan.........5:05:15 (26,600)
Osborn, Mark E.........4:34:14 (19,204)
Osborn, Matthew N.........4:08:39 (12,533)
Osborn, Roger J.........3:42:43 (6,359)
Osborne, Adrian J.........4:24:14 (16,508)
Osborne, Andrew.........3:29:37 (4,120)
Osborne, Andrew J.........3:41:05 (6,045)
Osborne, David G.........5:00:36 (25,727)
Osborne, Douglas.........4:22:12 (16,002)
Osborne, Ed.........3:43:04 (6,434)
Osborne, Godfrey W.........4:21:43 (15,884)
Osborne, Ian W.........4:32:57 (18,885)
Osborne, James R.........4:28:43 (17,751)
Osborne, Jeremy J.........4:19:29 (15,277)
Osborne, John.........6:18:48 (33,987)
Osborne, John K.........3:20:22 (2,806)
Osborne, Lyndon J.........4:49:33 (23,133)
Osborne, Matthew W.........3:45:22 (6,866)
Osborne, Michael A.........2:47:17 (376)
Osborne, Nicolas C.........3:30:00 (4,178)
Osborne, Paul W.........4:18:02 (14,900)
Osborne, Peter M.........3:55:50 (9,272)
Osborne, Richard R.........4:18:56 (15,146)
Osborne, Steve.........4:52:26 (23,851)
Osborne Hill, Matt.........6:03:43 (33,273)
Osgerby, Jay.........4:57:09 (24,955)
Osgood, Neil R.........3:53:01 (8,510)
O'Shaughnessy, John B.........4:07:21 (12,199)
O'Shea, David.........3:58:41 (10,155)
O'Shea, James P.........4:49:04 (22,989)
O'Shea, Johnny.........4:49:22 (23,075)
O'Shea, Kevin.........6:27:24 (34,342)
O'Shea, Stephen W.........3:33:23 (4,663)
Osinowo, Remi A.........3:37:55 (5,476)
Osis, Gunar.........4:40:04 (20,746)
Osman, Rick.........4:58:13 (25,193)
Osmond, Paul.........5:10:51 (27,610)
Osmond, Tom.........4:42:52 (21,431)
Ostrehan, Neil J.........5:11:19 (27,695)
O'Sullivan, Andrew J.........5:13:49 (28,121)
O'Sullivan, Chris J.........4:36:17 (19,736)
O'Sullivan, Ciaran J.........3:21:59 (3,012)
O'Sullivan, Conal.........4:14:38 (14,063)
O'Sullivan, Dominic.........5:21:49 (29,346)
O'Sullivan, Gary M.........4:18:17 (14,959)
O'Sullivan, John.........3:36:12 (5,190)
O'Sullivan, John D.........3:59:38 (10,428)
O'Sullivan, Mark.........3:57:32 (9,781)
O'Sullivan, Michael P.........3:24:30 (3,342)
O'Sullivan, Nick J.........4:28:06 (17,580)
O'Sullivan, Peter D.........5:14:41 (28,266)
O'Sullivan, Richard J.........3:53:49 (8,705)
Oswald, James R.........4:07:39 (12,270)
Otero-Perez, Allen J.........5:30:35 (30,472)
Otis, Bill.........5:28:38 (30,226)
Otkay, Emir.........5:04:00 (26,387)
O'Toole, Fintan.........5:12:14 (27,843)
O'Toole, Peter R.........4:14:12 (13,961)
Ottarsson, Hakon Bergmann.........3:36:16 (5,201)
Ottaviani, Fabien.........3:53:36 (8,650)
Otten, Frank T.........4:49:10 (23,009)
Ottosson, Leif.........3:53:32 (8,630)
Otwal, Mukhtiar S.........3:47:07 (7,217)
Oudin, Herve.........3:18:18 (2,553)
Oughton, Charlie.........3:23:04 (3,132)
Oughton, Nic.........4:52:07 (23,779)
Oughton, Simon A.........3:54:24 (8,864)
Ouilleres, Jean Paul.........3:44:16 (6,677)
Ousby, Daniel.........4:19:46 (15,363)
Outten, Jonathan C.........4:42:21 (21,283)
Overall, Mark.........4:41:45 (21,154)
Overbeeke, Marinus.........5:11:45 (27,767)
Overland, Michael F.........3:35:37 (5,074)
Overman, David W.........4:24:22 (16,541)
Overton, Darren.........3:26:00 (3,533)
Overton, Dave J.........4:37:58 (20,159)
Overton, Frederick H.........5:37:15 (31,198)
Overton, Richard W.........5:02:27 (26,102)
Overton, Stewart.........4:03:30 (11,334)
Overy, Mike.........4:47:53 (22,701)
Owdud, Abdul.........5:38:27 (31,326)
Owen, Alan.........4:54:48 (24,408)
Owen, Alan W.........4:36:59 (19,914)
Owen, Andrew J.........5:23:26 (29,589)
Owen, Benjamin T.........3:28:04 (3,864)
Owen, Chris.........4:29:38 (17,994)
Owen, Christopher S.........4:56:12 (24,728)
Owen, David A.........5:08:05 (27,100)
Owen, Dewi W.........6:57:16 (34,923)
Owen, James E.........5:28:43 (30,241)
Owen, Jonathan A.........4:10:21 (12,944)
Owen, Kai.........5:15:53 (28,490)
Owen, Mark.........4:31:05 (18,382)
Owen, Mark.........5:05:08 (26,575)
Owen, Martin J.........3:54:21 (8,853)
Owen, Mei.........4:02:12 (11,068)
Owen, Patrick B.........3:41:19 (6,090)
Owen, Shaun W.........3:53:54 (8,723)
Owen, Tom.........4:11:49 (13,341)
Owens, Dean D.........5:18:53 (28,960)
Owens, Elliot.........5:43:19 (31,807)
Owens, Graham J.........5:33:37 (30,823)
Owens, John P.........3:09:44 (1,683)
Owens, Michael D.........4:13:34 (13,813)
Owens, Simon C.........4:35:03 (19,425)
Owens, Stacy J.........7:06:27 (35,022)
Owens, Susan M.........8:01:30 (35,315)
Owers, David J.........4:15:05 (14,185)
Owles, Adrian Huge Beaumont.........5:26:53 (30,038)
Oxby, Andrew D.........3:56:47 (9,561)
Oxlade, Chris.........6:33:24 (34,482)
Oxlade, Ray G.........4:19:22 (15,249)
Oxley, Jonathon P.........3:39:30 (5,758)
Oxley, Martyn.........5:39:57 (31,490)
Oxley, Philip M.........4:26:37 (17,158)
Oxley, Scott A.........3:24:29 (3,339)
Oyston, Jared R.........4:55:26 (24,559)
Oza, Amit.........5:44:53 (31,922)
Ozanne, David L.........3:26:18 (3,575)
Ozdemir, Jacob.........5:04:33 (26,472)
Oziem, Christopher.........3:50:06 (7,855)
Ozols, Nathan A.........3:19:41 (2,708)
Ozsakin, Sal.........4:00:51 (10,755)
Pabla, Gursharnjit S.........4:23:42 (16,364)
Pacchetti, Davide.........3:18:22 (2,563)
Pace, John W.........3:43:17 (6,487)
Pace, Michael J.........3:47:36 (7,309)
Pace, Neil D.........5:18:58 (28,969)
Pace, Nick J.........6:23:44 (34,178)
Pace, Roy E.........3:45:07 (6,819)
Pacey, Nick J.........3:03:53 (1,232)
Pacini, Damian B.........3:29:20 (4,074)
Paciotti, Enrico.........3:35:37 (5,074)
Pack, Mark A.........3:36:32 (5,241)
Pack, Michael.........4:51:14 (23,547)

Partridge, James A....6:22:32 (34,127)
Partridge, Jeff L....4:24:00 (16,440)
Partridge, Robert D....5:23:32 (29,598)
Partridge, Simon....3:34:25 (4,856)
Partridge, Simon D....3:59:29 (10,384)
Paruta, Massimiliano....5:11:02 (27,645)
Pascal, Batime....4:04:16 (11,504)
Pascal, Buttet....4:27:38 (17,426)
Pascal, Emery....4:28:16 (17,638)
Pascal, Gousse....5:06:56 (26,892)
Pascal, Schubnel....3:23:05 (3,133)
Päschel, Marc-Raimon....4:41:35 (21,115)
Pascoe, Barry....4:48:09 (22,772)
Pascoe, Daniel J....4:28:24 (17,670)
Pascoe, Jason R....4:44:28 (21,831)
Pascoe, Kevin F....5:19:26 (29,027)
Pashen, Martin....4:37:45 (20,104)
Pask, Jonathan M....4:26:02 (16,994)
Paskin, Daniel....4:51:08 (23,516)
Paskin, Gavin S....3:26:45 (3,642)
Pass, Ian John....3:08:09 (1,538)
Passingham, Leonard J....2:38:45 (170)
Passmore, Kevin J....3:28:41 (3,954)
Passmore, Lee....4:36:33 (19,804)
Pasturel, Jean-Marie....5:05:31 (26,642)
Patchett, Rob N....6:48:14 (34,777)
Pate, Chris R....5:05:21 (26,613)
Patel, Amit....4:20:56 (15,671)
Patel, Anshul H....5:31:07 (30,541)
Patel, Bhupendrabhai....4:03:06 (11,249)
Patel, Chirag....5:43:30 (31,820)
Patel, Deepesh Rasikbhai....3:43:13 (6,475)
Patel, Dharmesh P....4:43:00 (21,468)
Patel, Ghansham....5:29:33 (30,342)
Patel, Jeetesh V....5:10:38 (27,571)
Patel, Ketan....3:56:20 (9,406)
Patel, Keyur....4:16:07 (14,429)
Patel, Kiran D....4:50:29 (23,368)
Patel, Mishal....5:42:25 (31,711)
Patel, Mitesh....5:13:59 (28,157)
Patel, Mitesh T....4:02:44 (11,173)
Patel, Narendra M....5:29:04 (30,280)
Patel, Nehal....3:46:25 (7,069)
Patel, Rajesh....5:21:08 (29,246)
Patel, Shamir....4:01:32 (10,926)
Patel, Shian....4:33:44 (19,080)
Patel, Shivlal H....4:59:41 (25,529)
Patel, Vijay....5:29:35 (30,347)
Patel, Vinod....4:44:59 (21,957)
Patel, Vinod M....4:40:44 (20,892)
Paterson, David....3:58:30 (10,097)
Paterson, Ewan S....3:28:51 (3,985)
Paterson, James....5:09:15 (27,316)
Paterson, James M....3:54:00 (8,757)
Paterson, Jamie M....4:23:01 (16,189)
Paterson, Mark....4:32:46 (18,835)
Paterson, Mark H....6:22:56 (34,150)
Paterson, Peter L....4:47:55 (22,712)
Paterson, Stephen J....2:38:12 (161)
Paterson, Stewart....4:13:54 (13,884)
Patey, Daniel F....5:56:22 (32,784)
Patey, Ian W....3:58:12 (10,007)
Patience, Kevin S....4:56:50 (24,890)
Patil, Advait Krishna....4:47:48 (22,671)
Paton, Colin....2:40:27 (204)
Paton, Daren....3:58:18 (10,033)
Paton, Gary L....4:54:47 (24,404)
Paton, Ian R....5:38:45 (31,363)
Paton, Luke K....3:53:02 (8,514)
Paton, Malcolm....4:28:27 (17,683)
Paton, Martin J....3:42:10 (6,246)
Paton, Philip S....3:50:41 (7,989)
Patrice, Baudoin....4:24:14 (16,508)
Patrice, Nanniot....4:57:14 (24,971)
Patrice, Pfeuty....3:53:49 (8,705)
Patrick, Adam J....5:41:27 (31,630)
Patrick, Alfred....4:26:22 (17,080)
Patrick, Alleaume....3:47:41 (7,324)
Patrick, Andy D....4:07:39 (12,270)
Patrick, Andy J....5:21:34 (29,312)
Patrick, Ceintre....3:24:22 (3,323)
Patrick, Lehmann....3:39:03 (5,697)
Patrick, Lutzelschwab....4:03:42 (11,366)
Patrick, Melzer....4:28:49 (17,780)
Patrick, Puchades....5:04:12 (26,413)
Patrick, Stanley....4:35:55 (19,656)
Patrick, Weil....4:15:56 (14,374)
Patten, Kevin Anthony William....4:53:05 (23,994)
Patterson, Colin....5:50:13 (32,356)
Patterson, Dean K....4:12:07 (13,418)
Patterson, Hylton....4:27:42 (17,448)
Patterson, Jacob....6:14:52 (33,785)
Patterson, John....3:18:38 (2,586)
Patterson, Jonathan M....3:08:30 (1,565)
Patterson, Lametha....5:44:14 (31,874)
Patterson, Norman J....6:41:54 (34,663)
Patterson, Paul D....5:13:46 (28,115)
Patterson, Richard E....4:35:38 (19,574)
Patterson, Stephen J....4:46:27 (22,331)
Patti, Pasquale....5:00:39 (25,740)
Pattison, Dan....4:54:38 (24,374)
Pattison, David G....5:24:02 (29,655)
Pattison, Mark A....4:56:44 (24,860)
Pattison, Nicholas J....3:43:08 (6,448)
Pattni, Sharad B....6:14:15 (33,755)

Patton, Shaun C....7:07:35 (35,036)

This was my very first time running a marathon. I was raising money for The Stroke Association Charity. I was running in memory of my grandad who died from a massive stroke. The Marathon didn't really go to plan as I had a nasty fall, so needed to walk most of the way. I still had an amazing day, as the crowd keep you going. The atmosphere around London on Marathon day is amazing. The crowds are so big, all shouting your name and supporting. I can't put into words what it feels like to cross the finish line after 26.2 miles. I do remember saying at the finish line 'never again'. I can't explain the pain I was in. The pain is soon forgotten as I am now planning my next London Marathon.

Paugh, Richard....3:58:13 (10,018)
Paul, Alastair J....4:10:31 (12,984)
Paul, Alex R....4:01:19 (10,862)
Paul, Buret....4:24:58 (16,700)
Paul, Carlo D....2:52:31 (543)
Paul, David....3:43:10 (6,463)
Paul, David W....4:56:38 (24,836)
Paul, Emerson....4:03:07 (11,253)
Paul, Jesus....3:10:53 (1,769)
Paul, Jonathan B....5:12:39 (27,918)
Paul, Martin....4:16:11 (14,443)
Paul, Robert....6:15:15 (33,803)
Paul, Stuart S....3:39:28 (5,752)
Paul, Tim F....4:07:20 (12,191)
Paul, Tim J....3:36:12 (5,190)
Pauley, George D....3:05:19 (1,323)
Paulides, Jordie....4:09:30 (12,719)
Paul-Marshall, Phillip D....5:51:37 (32,458)
Paulsen, Rune....3:20:49 (2,871)
Paulson, Alex....5:00:43 (25,751)
Pausch, Helmut....3:52:23 (8,378)
Pavesi, Giovanni....4:12:54 (13,628)
Pavey, Giles H....3:56:45 (9,549)
Pavey, Richard M....3:39:58 (5,854)
Pavia Fernandez, José Carlos....3:26:51 (3,656)
Paviour, Benjamin A....2:29:17 (63)
Pavitt, David....3:06:09 (1,384)
Pawlowski, Christopher P....3:55:36 (9,191)
Pawluk, Ivan M....2:53:37 (591)
Pay, Alan J....4:07:19 (12,183)
Payette, Adrian Richard....4:14:41 (14,074)
Payne, Adam R....5:36:54 (31,165)
Payne, Alastair W....2:45:58 (330)
Payne, Andrew M....4:09:31 (12,728)
Payne, Anthony....3:24:46 (3,378)
Payne, Barry J....5:16:37 (28,582)
Payne, Bradley....5:24:55 (29,782)
Payne, Christopher James....4:54:26 (24,322)
Payne, David....4:32:53 (18,868)
Payne, David S....5:00:20 (25,663)
Payne, Dean A....3:15:30 (2,283)
Payne, Edward C....4:53:32 (24,083)
Payne, Gareth....3:51:45 (8,218)
Payne, Garry P....2:38:34 (167)
Payne, Gary F....4:59:03 (25,399)
Payne, Ian F....4:51:10 (23,528)
Payne, James A....4:31:04 (18,376)
Payne, Joel M....3:43:55 (6,617)
Payne, John L....2:55:26 (693)
Payne, Julian....4:21:13 (15,744)
Payne, Mark....5:38:54 (31,384)
Payne, Martin C....4:07:04 (12,124)
Payne, Matthew R....3:52:13 (8,335)
Payne, Neil....4:57:07 (24,948)
Payne, Neil J....4:05:07 (11,685)
Payne, Rod M....4:34:20 (19,226)
Payne, Trevor A....4:32:27 (18,748)
Peace, Daniel E....3:12:25 (1,923)
Peace, Michael S....3:32:07 (4,486)
Peach, Matthew P....5:07:51 (27,069)
Peachey, Michael....3:30:33 (4,264)
Peacock, Kieron J....4:16:33 (14,536)
Peacock, Mark A....3:33:14 (4,639)
Peacock, Robert....3:43:40 (6,559)
Peacock, William R....3:41:33 (6,130)
Peak, Michael J....3:37:04 (5,333)
Peake, Charlie....4:22:19 (16,025)
Peake, Paul M....4:01:47 (10,980)
Peake, Stan E....4:26:16 (17,060)
Peaks, Garry....7:00:30 (34,952)
Pealling, Ian D....4:28:12 (17,613)
Pearce, Adrian J....4:46:10 (22,237)
Pearce, Andrew M....4:01:11 (10,831)
Pearce, Andrew Philip....3:26:52 (3,659)
Pearce, David....5:49:39 (32,301)
Pearce, David A....3:34:33 (4,883)
Pearce, David A....4:52:37 (23,883)
Pearce, David M....4:23:25 (16,281)
Pearce, David M....4:37:32 (20,045)
Pearce, David R....6:19:45 (34,024)
Pearce, Jeremy R....4:55:39 (24,605)
Pearce, Jon....4:07:41 (12,281)
Pearce, Jonathan M....6:26:36 (34,302)
Pearce, Mark A....3:32:34 (4,558)
Pearce, Michael W....4:34:42 (19,317)
Pearce, Neal D....5:20:46 (29,187)
Pearce, Rob D....4:22:41 (16,124)
Pearce, Robert E....3:21:16 (2,915)
Pearce, Steve J....3:50:01 (7,840)
Pearce, Steve J....4:19:34 (15,303)
Pearce, Tim....5:53:11 (32,565)
Pearce, William S....6:40:45 (34,639)
Pearce Gould, Edward....4:52:09 (23,786)
Pearcey, Wessley J....4:53:08 (24,007)
Pearl, Andrew H....3:09:03 (1,623)
Pearman, Brad....4:22:09 (15,989)
Pearman, Robert....4:11:21 (13,210)
Pears, Richard....3:48:54 (7,595)
Pearsall, Steven....4:43:47 (21,663)
Pearse, Mark S....4:16:22 (14,486)
Pearse, William J....4:03:26 (11,317)
Pearson, Andrew E....4:10:04 (12,869)
Pearson, Anthony....3:53:11 (8,561)
Pearson, Anthony....4:27:41 (17,441)
Pearson, Antony S....3:06:58 (1,431)
Pearson, Charles J....4:58:18 (25,213)
Pearson, Charlie L....2:41:51 (231)
Pearson, Darren....5:30:07 (30,417)
Pearson, David R....4:10:05 (12,874)
Pearson, Donald K....4:16:58 (14,638)
Pearson, Graham A....4:51:26 (23,605)
Pearson, Hugh A....3:23:33 (3,196)
Pearson, James C....4:04:56 (11,639)
Pearson, Jamie....6:46:55 (34,736)
Pearson, John H....4:05:16 (11,724)
Pearson, Kris....4:56:29 (24,795)
Pearson, Paul....5:12:47 (27,944)
Pearson, Robert E....3:28:51 (3,985)
Pearson, Simon Carl....4:39:55 (20,696)
Pearson, Stephen....4:06:13 (11,931)
Pearson, Stephen S....3:57:01 (9,625)
Pearson, Toby S....2:41:00 (216)
Peart, David Brodie....4:56:44 (24,860)

Peart, Gary C	3:44:44 (6,754)	
Pease, Alastair K	3:49:01 (7,622)	
Pease, Alex	4:41:54 (21,181)	
Pease, Alex M	4:21:57 (15,933)	
Peasland, Garry	5:25:06 (29,810)	
Peat, Dan	5:22:24 (29,423)	
Peat, James G	4:11:36 (13,284)	
Peate, Aaron	4:25:43 (16,915)	
Peate, Gareth J	4:25:43 (16,915)	
Peatfield, Toby G	4:02:46 (11,182)	
Pecha, Richard	4:40:40 (20,878)	
Peck, Andrew R	4:11:39 (13,300)	
Peck, David R	3:34:10 (4,805)	
Pedder, Mark J	3:55:23 (9,127)	
Peddie, Neil A	4:39:26 (20,562)	
Peddie, Peter	4:14:57 (14,154)	
Pedersen, Anders	3:13:42 (2,089)	
Pedersen, Poul-Erik	3:27:55 (3,842)	
Pedgrift, Alex A	4:13:41 (13,842)	
Pediconi, Francesco Maria	4:30:49 (18,309)	
Peel, David	3:11:16 (1,805)	
Peel, David	4:37:20 (19,990)	
Peel, Kevin P	3:56:09 (9,351)	
Peel, Mike	4:45:08 (22,007)	
Peel, Steve J	4:15:06 (14,190)	
Peel Cross, Andy G	4:44:37 (21,861)	
Pegg, Jonathan Charles William	4:18:27 (15,017)	
Pegg, Martyn	5:03:11 (26,233)	
Pegler, David B	4:06:37 (12,026)	
Pegler, Timothy	4:01:10 (10,827)	
Pegram, Dominick	4:34:38 (19,296)	
Peischl, Joseph J	3:55:21 (9,119)	
Pelaez, Jean-Paul	3:59:32 (10,398)	
Pelan, John H	4:35:18 (19,488)	
Peled, Asaf	4:28:33 (17,711)	
Peled, Nadav	6:24:36 (34,218)	
Pell, Gary Matthew	3:58:54 (10,224)	
Peltzer, Dirk	4:46:31 (22,347)	
Pemberton, Stephen N	4:41:42 (21,143)	
Pemberton, Tom	3:50:53 (8,034)	
Pembroke, John P	3:03:36 (1,208)	
Pembrooke, Robin E	4:53:08 (24,007)	
Penagos Goldberg, Carlos	3:47:41 (7,324)	
Penaluna, Karl S	4:37:17 (19,982)	
Penberthy, Mike	3:48:50 (7,580)	
Pendarves, George W	4:17:40 (14,814)	
Pender, Jon R	3:40:47 (5,994)	
Pendlebury, Christopher John	3:45:11 (6,832)	
Pendlebury, Mark L	4:00:15 (10,611)	
Penfold, Jon	4:00:59 (10,797)	
Penfold, Keith J	5:00:11 (25,630)	
Pengelly, Eifion A	6:18:40 (33,952)	
Pengelly, Gary P	4:55:08 (24,485)	
Pengelly, Steven	5:02:09 (26,051)	
Penn, Kevin A	3:58:49 (10,198)	
Penn, Thomas	4:10:11 (12,907)	
Pennell, Iain	3:55:13 (9,089)	
Penney, Nigel C	4:45:23 (22,054)	
Pennicott, James	3:01:48 (1,103)	
Pennington, Christopher	4:15:12 (14,214)	
Pennington, Jason	4:23:13 (16,235)	
Pennington, John	3:47:57 (7,384)	
Pennock, Richard L	3:44:06 (6,651)	
Penny, Anthony	4:58:56 (25,371)	
Penny, Brian	2:55:16 (684)	
Penny, Chris C	4:50:02 (23,244)	
Penny, Jonathan L	3:57:46 (9,863)	
Penny, Martin C	3:09:34 (1,663)	
Penny, William J	4:00:32 (10,680)	
Penrose, Ronald K	3:28:08 (3,873)	
Penswick, Stuart Paul	5:52:19 (32,503)	
Pentecost, Rick A	5:27:58 (30,142)	
Pentin, Richard P	3:56:44 (9,544)	
Pentland, Bob	3:15:49 (2,320)	
Penverne, Max	4:20:34 (15,574)	
Penza, Andrew J	4:42:20 (21,280)	
Pepe, Raymond J	4:08:29 (12,504)	
Pepes, Peter	3:25:42 (3,487)	
Pepper, David	4:25:56 (16,968)	
Pepper, David G	3:52:21 (8,372)	
Pepper, Matt	4:40:44 (20,892)	
Peppercorn, Michael J	5:44:49 (31,915)	
Peppercorn, Nathan	5:59:26 (33,014)	

Perarnau Grau, Juan	3:54:11 (8,808)	
Perceval, Arnaud	3:23:53 (3,246)	
Percey, Steven John	4:13:13 (13,717)	
Percival, Alan Howard	4:34:54 (19,382)	
Percival, Steve	3:57:36 (9,802)	
Percival, Thomas D	3:18:23 (2,565)	
Percy, Alex	4:05:44 (11,828)	
Percy, Ian D	4:26:14 (17,048)	
Perdichizzi, Mario Salvatore	4:23:20 (16,260)	
Perego, Stefano	3:52:36 (8,426)	
Pereira, Luis	4:53:25 (24,058)	
Pereira, Oliver J	5:10:52 (27,616)	
Pereira, Simao	3:57:50 (9,890)	
Perey, Patrick	3:32:25 (4,534)	
Perez, Maria Del Carmen	3:40:43 (5,974)	
Perez, Sion Daniel	3:56:01 (9,319)	
Perez Cruz, Eduardo	3:17:46 (2,511)	
Perez Reyes, Enrique	3:35:56 (5,142)	
Perez Sanchez, José	3:43:45 (6,574)	
Perfect, Richard S	3:29:24 (4,089)	
Perine, Kelly	5:15:42 (28,456)	
Perkins, Alex T	4:51:47 (23,695)	
Perkins, Chris A	4:46:10 (22,237)	
Perkins, Christian E	5:12:27 (27,881)	
Perkins, Jake W	4:33:25 (19,006)	
Perkins, John P	4:20:17 (15,508)	
Perkins, John S	4:08:56 (12,600)	
Perkins, Martyn	3:25:13 (3,420)	
Perkins, Matthew J	5:07:23 (26,982)	
Perkins, Matthew N	4:17:24 (14,742)	
Perkins, Michael P	4:41:57 (21,191)	
Perkins, Phil J	4:31:23 (18,469)	
Perkins, Robert K	3:29:29 (4,100)	
Perkins, Simon D	5:35:40 (31,038)	
Perkins, Tom J	5:24:05 (29,666)	
Perkins, Tony J	4:49:11 (23,012)	
Perks, Ben A	4:38:32 (20,307)	
Perks, Matthew Raymond	3:41:48 (6,167)	
Perks, Wesley J	4:23:28 (16,299)	
Perl, Jeremy R	3:38:08 (5,524)	
Perle, Gary	5:33:33 (30,810)	
Perotto, Bruno	3:59:10 (10,303)	
Perret, Christophe	4:01:03 (10,804)	
Perrett, John E	4:13:56 (13,891)	
Perri, Craig	3:48:58 (7,610)	
Perrin, Andrew F	5:24:53 (29,778)	
Perrin, Laurent	4:39:25 (20,558)	
Perrin, Marc E	4:22:50 (16,149)	
Perrin, Sebastian T	6:24:10 (34,196)	
Perring, Alex	5:00:32 (25,713)	
Perring, David A	3:45:58 (6,982)	
Perrone, Alessandro	4:06:43 (12,044)	
Perrott, Anthony M	3:19:29 (2,683)	
Perry, Adam	2:51:33 (507)	
Perry, Andrew L	4:41:57 (21,191)	
Perry, Ben	3:47:51 (7,361)	
Perry, Darren L	3:39:21 (5,736)	
Perry, David G	4:44:02 (21,729)	
Perry, Dean R	3:36:50 (5,283)	
Perry, Greg N	3:58:15 (10,025)	
Perry, Justin N	5:08:28 (27,175)	
Perry, Kevin M	4:32:58 (18,888)	
Perry, Lee	4:11:22 (13,214)	
Perry, Luke B	5:06:22 (26,784)	
Perry, Martin J	3:44:56 (6,791)	
Perry, Nick	4:05:26 (11,757)	
Perry, Nick	4:52:40 (23,895)	
Perry, Richard I	4:33:56 (19,136)	
Perry, Stephen	3:20:26 (2,817)	
Perry, Stephen	4:54:16 (24,279)	
Perry, Stephen J	3:46:18 (7,045)	
Perry, Thomas E	4:25:33 (16,856)	
Pertile, Paolo	4:13:52 (13,877)	
Peryer, Keith G	4:14:35 (14,053)	
Pesce, Claudio	3:37:17 (5,369)	
Peschiera, Luis	3:55:41 (9,211)	
Peskett, Chris	4:45:03 (21,981)	
Pesquero, Gary D	3:28:49 (3,977)	
Pestat, Christian	4:33:17 (18,968)	
Pestridge, Simon J	3:33:09 (4,631)	
Peters, Christopher M	4:52:35 (23,877)	
Peters, Colin W	3:44:41 (6,743)	
Peters, David	2:48:40 (413)	

Peters, Gary R	3:38:58 (5,675)	
Peters, Ian M	4:00:57 (10,786)	
Peters, James A	5:56:18 (32,776)	
Peters, Jeff A	5:23:01 (29,520)	
Peters, John R	4:10:47 (13,060)	
Peters, Matthew E	4:52:35 (23,877)	
Peters, Michael J	3:53:44 (8,688)	
Peters, Philip J	4:16:14 (14,455)	
Peters, René	4:03:45 (11,375)	
Pethe, Sameer M	5:02:44 (26,162)	
Pethers, Rick W	5:18:36 (28,898)	
Petit, Emmanuel	3:24:11 (3,296)	
Petitcolas, Didier	4:02:43 (11,171)	
Petker, Hassan	5:05:12 (26,592)	
Peto, Alexander	4:39:10 (20,487)	
Petracci, Vincenzo	4:04:47 (11,603)	
Petreni, Enzo Giuseppe	6:23:09 (34,156)	
Petrie, Andrew J	5:23:22 (29,579)	
Petrie, David	5:20:55 (29,211)	
Petrie, Simon	4:08:03 (12,374)	
Petrou, Arron	5:06:38 (26,830)	
Petruso, Tony	3:54:35 (8,914)	
Pettersson, Conny	5:15:48 (28,474)	
Pettet, David A	5:24:29 (29,730)	
Pettifer, John	4:33:17 (18,968)	
Pettit, Stephen M	2:44:10 (288)	
Pettitt, Neil M	5:38:45 (31,363)	
Pettitt, Nick	3:53:59 (8,751)	
Petty, Bruce	5:19:15 (29,002)	
Petty, Chris P	3:54:32 (8,900)	
Petty, Nathan	5:57:19 (32,856)	
Pewter, Ben	4:02:09 (11,054)	
Pewter, Graham	4:33:50 (19,108)	
Pewtner, Joe P	3:34:21 (4,843)	
Peyton, Tom C	5:30:05 (30,408)	
Pez, Jacques	4:39:01 (20,438)	
Pfaff, Marcus	3:46:55 (7,182)	
Pfeiffer, Marcel	3:48:40 (7,543)	
Pfeuffer, Ulrich	3:47:49 (7,357)	
Phair, Liam G	3:58:42 (10,162)	
Pheasant, Colin R	4:17:48 (14,839)	
Phelan, Patrick J	3:33:27 (4,674)	
Phelps, Brian	5:25:37 (29,880)	
Phethean, Tom S	6:11:40 (33,625)	
Philbin, Tony R	3:58:49 (10,198)	
Philcox, James A	5:16:41 (28,597)	
Philip, David	3:19:14 (2,642)	
Philip, Douglas	2:59:52 (987)	
Philip, Iain M	3:27:02 (3,689)	
Philip, Jamie	2:56:20 (736)	
Philip, John D	4:32:20 (18,713)	
Philip, Patrick	4:06:09 (11,915)	
Philippe, Josso	3:27:56 (3,846)	
Philippe, Jule	3:34:15 (4,819)	
Philippe, Simon	4:30:05 (18,121)	
Philippe, Urwyler	5:30:41 (30,489)	
Philippou, Pedro	5:15:47 (28,471)	
Philipps, Andrew E	4:55:35 (24,591)	
Phillips, Adam	3:53:06 (8,532)	
Phillips, Alan P	3:44:37 (6,733)	
Phillips, Andrew	3:21:29 (2,944)	
Phillips, Anthony R	5:01:07 (25,844)	
Phillips, Ashley A	6:34:19 (34,509)	
Phillips, Benedict C	4:05:07 (11,685)	
Phillips, Brian	4:28:36 (17,724)	
Phillips, Brian	5:38:51 (31,376)	
Phillips, Dale	3:55:03 (9,040)	
Phillips, Daniel	3:46:11 (7,014)	
Phillips, Dave	3:42:49 (6,380)	
Phillips, Eric S	2:46:42 (354)	
Phillips, Gary C	4:17:16 (14,706)	
Phillips, Glenn Stephen	4:09:18 (12,682)	
Phillips, Greg C	5:42:19 (31,704)	
Phillips, Iain J	4:15:32 (14,291)	
Phillips, Ian D	4:32:33 (18,769)	
Phillips, Ian R	4:24:43 (16,627)	
Phillips, James P	4:02:36 (11,151)	
Phillips, John	6:00:45 (33,095)	
Phillips, Johnny D	3:31:54 (4,453)	
Phillips, Justin A	4:38:52 (20,306)	
Phillips, Kevin	3:46:01 (6,990)	
Phillips, Kevin J	3:40:32 (5,943)	
Phillips, Lee M	3:31:03 (4,335)	

Phillips, Leonard J 3:59:44 (10,472)
Phillips, Mark G 5:05:49 (26,700)
Phillips, Matthew 3:58:33 (10,114)
Phillips, Matthew A 5:31:35 (30,590)
Phillips, Michael 5:52:10 (32,492)
Phillips, Michael P 5:51:02 (32,415)
Phillips, Mitch W 3:19:43 (2,713)
Phillips, Neil M 3:58:36 (10,126)
Phillips, Owen J 6:18:22 (33,944)
Phillips, Paul 3:23:44 (3,222)
Phillips, Paul D 6:04:57 (33,337)
Phillips, Paul S 4:39:46 (20,662)
Phillips, Richard 6:18:40 (33,952)
Phillips, Robert A 4:20:02 (15,437)
Phillips, Robin J 4:28:10 (17,604)
Phillips, Stephen Rupert 4:42:11 (21,244)
Phillips, Steve 5:45:24 (31,962)
Phillips, Steven 3:23:45 (3,226)
Phillips, Tomas E 5:59:59 (33,049)
Phillips, Trevor 5:13:39 (28,088)
Phillips, Wade P 5:51:28 (32,444)
Phillips, Zack 5:45:24 (31,962)
Phillipson, David 4:35:42 (19,599)
Phillipson, Mark 4:47:00 (22,484)
Phillipson, Stuart J 4:10:41 (13,033)
Phillis, Marc Weston 4:07:19 (12,183)
Phillpot, Neil James 4:09:18 (12,682)
Phillpott, Luke W 4:52:25 (23,849)
Philp, Andrew 3:51:13 (8,103)
Philp, Paul 5:15:25 (28,404)
Philp, Richard L 4:32:46 (18,835)
Philpot, Saul T 4:39:10 (20,487)
Philpott, Andy J 4:31:57 (18,623)
Philpott, David R 5:15:58 (28,496)
Philpott, Garry C 5:28:28 (30,207)
Philpott, Ryan 4:05:04 (11,670)
Philpott, Timothy R 3:43:22 (6,503)
Phipps, David J 5:07:21 (26,971)
Phipps, Ian M 4:14:49 (14,116)
Phipps, Kevin M 4:10:57 (13,094)
Phipps, Patrick 3:50:34 (7,962)
Phipps, Stephen R 4:59:14 (25,438)
Phoenix, Andrew 4:28:44 (17,754)
Phoenix, Ian 4:15:51 (14,361)
Phull, Gurvinder 5:28:38 (30,226)
Phypers, Jason 4:11:52 (13,354)
Piana, Michel 5:05:31 (26,642)
Pichetta, Stefan 3:20:15 (2,792)
Pick, David A 5:20:08 (29,111)
Pickard, Iain 4:31:42 (18,552)
Pickard, John 5:11:19 (27,695)
Pickard, Oliver G 3:36:57 (5,309)
Picken, Thomas J 3:40:45 (5,985)
Pickering, David T 5:08:37 (27,196)
Pickering, Derrick J 5:55:23 (32,715)
Pickering, Mike 7:17:37 (35,122)
Pickering, Scott 4:37:33 (20,054)
Pickering, Steven D 3:08:28 (1,563)
Pickering, Warren M 4:42:56 (21,456)
Pickering, William M 5:13:06 (28,006)
Pickers, Jerry R 4:43:26 (21,587)
Pickett, Benjamin J 3:59:12 (10,310)
Pickett, Lewis K 3:42:03 (6,225)
Pickett, Paul D 6:49:40 (34,808)
Pickford, Chris 4:17:22 (14,736)
Pickford, Samuel G 4:29:52 (18,066)
Picking, Thomas M 3:34:26 (4,862)
Pickles, Tim 4:09:45 (12,788)
Pickthall, Chris 3:58:47 (10,189)
Pickup, Andrew 2:59:47 (981)
Pickup, John A 5:02:38 (26,142)
Picton, Ian 3:25:05 (3,407)
Piddington, Martin 4:47:52 (22,693)
Piddock, Michael 5:59:10 (32,999)
Pidduck, Mark J 3:10:54 (1,771)
Pidgeon, Paul 4:47:34 (22,617)
Piedade, Tony 5:08:51 (27,242)
Pienaar, Stephen 5:28:03 (30,152)
Pierce, Charles 6:02:43 (33,210)
Pierce, David 4:16:28 (14,514)
Pierce, Mark 5:23:06 (29,535)
Pierce, Robert E 4:13:14 (13,724)
Pierce, Simon D 3:55:49 (9,267)
Pierce, Tom 3:54:41 (8,940)
Pierides, Mike 4:50:40 (23,414)
Pierpoint, David J 4:16:18 (14,473)
Pierre, Jacques 4:09:41 (12,769)
Pierre-Alain, Wenger 3:29:14 (4,046)
Piers, Chris 3:52:44 (8,456)
Pierson, Matthew 2:22:15 (24)
Pieterse, Justin J 3:04:42 (1,280)
Pietersen, Bryan 4:57:31 (25,037)
Pietersen, Gregg D 4:13:30 (13,796)
Pietersen, Jannie F 4:20:42 (15,604)
Pietersen, Tony 4:34:04 (19,164)
Pietrak, Robert 5:39:06 (31,410)
Pigford, Mark 2:55:26 (693)
Piggott, Christopher H 4:46:03 (22,216)
Piggott, James M 4:56:39 (24,843)
Piggott, Jonathan D 6:08:08 (33,487)
Piggott, Nick 3:53:59 (8,751)
Pigorini, Luigi 4:25:17 (16,780)
Pigott, Timothy M 3:40:28 (5,937)
Pigram, Matt D 5:11:24 (27,711)
Pike, Alan 7:07:28 (35,034)
Pike, Christopher A 3:37:30 (5,400)
Pike, Daniel R 3:35:19 (5,012)
Pike, David J 3:50:38 (7,975)
Pike, David J 5:21:26 (29,288)
Pike, Derek J 4:38:35 (20,319)
Pike, Ed 6:13:49 (33,740)
Pike, Graham 5:28:22 (30,197)
Pike, Karl 5:35:03 (30,978)
Pilcher, Martin K 3:45:46 (6,941)
Pilcher, Simon M 3:29:26 (4,093)
Pile, Jon 4:31:54 (18,607)
Pill, Tony 3:50:39 (7,978)
Pillar, Alan R 4:47:58 (22,728)
Pilling, Kristian J 4:17:38 (14,800)
Pilling, Paul M 3:00:28 (1,021)
Pincher, Ian 3:19:40 (2,704)
Pinder, David K 3:54:29 (8,885)
Pinder, Ian J 4:26:12 (17,038)
Pinder, John 5:20:29 (29,150)
Pinder, Nick G 3:45:39 (6,920)
Ping, Darren J 3:12:40 (1,952)
Pinha, Pedro 3:12:05 (1,888)
Pinhey, Richard 3:31:39 (4,413)
Pink, Colin M 4:40:04 (20,746)
Pink, John D 4:05:36 (11,798)
Pink, Mitchell 5:00:39 (25,740)
Pinkham, Thomas A 4:00:11 (10,593)
Pinkney, Andy P 4:01:37 (10,947)
Pinney, James E 4:38:45 (20,365)
Pinnick, Mark A 5:15:41 (28,452)
Pinnock, Thomas P 5:31:28 (30,577)
Pino, Alberto 3:46:17 (7,037)
Pioche, Patrick 4:03:05 (11,246)
Piotrowski, Tad 5:58:23 (32,950)
Piozin, Daniel 4:36:26 (19,777)
Piper, Daniel W 5:19:23 (29,022)
Piper, David J 4:14:21 (14,000)
Piper, Duncan J 6:50:53 (34,829)
Piper, Kevin G 5:18:37 (28,903)
Piper, Paul J 3:59:06 (10,278)
Piper, Simon Mark 3:09:13 (1,644)
Piper, Stephen D 6:21:26 (34,091)
Pippenger, Alan 4:34:27 (19,249)
Pirie, Leslie 5:06:28 (26,800)
Pirozzolo, Mario 5:23:08 (29,539)
Pisu, Silvestro 3:24:57 (3,395)
Pitchell, Ian 3:36:51 (5,287)
Pitcher, Julian N 3:52:04 (8,291)
Pitchford, Steven 4:08:51 (12,585)
Piterzak, John 4:46:24 (22,315)
Pitkethley, Ryan J 4:24:23 (16,545)
Pitkethly, Rob J 3:20:05 (2,766)
Pitman, Gary 4:22:51 (16,156)
Pitman, Mike 5:06:33 (26,812)
Pitt, Richard M 4:05:12 (11,711)
Pittaway, Mark 2:49:40 (452)
Pittaway, Simon 4:10:39 (13,019)
Pitter, Frederik T 3:40:25 (5,929)
Pittman, Andrew R 3:01:01 (1,052)
Pitts, Jonathan 3:23:58 (3,256)
Piva, Nicola 4:33:53 (19,124)
Piwecki, Paul S 4:57:21 (25,001)
Pizzey, Alex R 6:09:56 (33,557)
Placer, Dieter 3:47:26 (7,271)
Plaister, Luke 3:39:09 (5,710)
Plane, Stuart J 3:36:55 (5,301)
Plant, Benjamin G 3:55:58 (9,300)
Plant, Gary A 4:05:06 (11,679)
Plant, Paul K 5:31:07 (30,541)
Plantinga, Douwe 4:22:34 (16,091)
Plasett, Malcolm 5:42:28 (31,718)
Plaskowski, Bron 3:50:22 (7,915)
Platt, Andrew C 5:06:47 (26,865)
Platt, Gary 3:14:02 (2,126)
Platt, James S 4:14:04 (13,922)
Platt, Richard J 5:06:47 (26,865)
Platt, Richard L 4:05:43 (11,826)
Platt, Rob M 4:29:11 (17,884)
Platt, Ryan P 4:06:29 (11,988)
Platten, Paul 3:27:37 (3,804)
Platts, Tom N 4:27:05 (17,278)
Plaw, Adrian 4:42:46 (21,402)
Playdon, James R 4:31:59 (18,629)
Playford, Luke J 3:52:56 (8,491)
Pleasance, Guy 6:34:32 (34,511)
Pledger, Carl P 4:03:12 (11,273)
Plenderleith, Scott 4:05:26 (11,757)
Plested, Stuart 4:50:35 (23,392)
Plets, Lieven 3:16:14 (2,353)
Plowman, Ian E 3:47:51 (7,361)
Plowman, Jamie F 5:18:05 (28,804)
Plume, Andrew 4:44:04 (21,740)
Plummer, Anthony P 4:11:56 (13,368)
Plummer, Bradley C 3:44:15 (6,673)
Plummer, Daniel J 5:25:58 (29,929)
Plummer, Matt R 5:02:02 (26,028)
Plumridge, Neil J 3:14:08 (2,137)
Plumstead, Pat 3:22:10 (3,031)
Plunkett, Mark 3:34:45 (4,916)
Plunkett, Matt 6:26:07 (34,285)
Plunkett, Richard 3:28:07 (3,871)
Pochat, Amedee 3:34:09 (4,802)
Pochin, Seph 3:46:09 (7,011)
Pocklington, Paul D 3:59:02 (10,261)
Pocock, Andrew John Cullum 4:12:54 (13,628)
Pocock, Martin J 5:28:29 (30,209)
Pocock, Michael J 3:26:43 (3,637)
Poggio, Roberto 3:27:33 (3,790)
Pogose, Peter D 5:40:37 (31,556)
Pointer, Daniel M 4:25:23 (16,814)
Pointet, David A 5:11:22 (27,705)
Pointon, Matt C 3:03:47 (1,222)
Poland, Michael J 4:46:46 (22,426)
Pole, Terry 4:27:18 (17,343)
Polehonski, David L 6:03:39 (33,265)
Poletyllo, James W 5:15:37 (28,441)
Poli, Danilo 3:50:41 (7,989)
Pollard, Anthony G 3:05:55 (1,367)
Pollard, Brian D 6:35:26 (34,534)
Pollard, Gary J 3:44:56 (6,791)
Pollard, Jonathan D 3:20:25 (2,815)
Pollard, Michael I 5:16:05 (28,514)
Pollard, Neil R 4:08:40 (12,539)
Pollard, Nicholas B 4:46:19 (22,284)
Pollard, Simon 4:24:39 (16,605)
Pollard, Simon R 4:20:11 (15,482)
Polledro, Patrizio 3:29:05 (4,022)
Pollen, Samuel 3:50:06 (7,855)
Polley, Keith A 5:13:33 (28,074)
Polley, Richard 4:23:17 (16,250)
Pollitt, Alastair 3:42:49 (6,380)
Pollock, Martin 4:59:51 (25,565)
Pollock, Neil A 3:05:26 (1,330)
Pollock, Steve J 3:47:37 (7,312)
Polman, Alphons 4:24:51 (16,670)
Polman, Darren M 6:04:33 (33,315)
Polman, Paul 4:12:15 (13,453)
Polyblank, Darron R 4:25:12 (16,766)
Polycarpou, Louis 3:53:08 (8,541)
Polydorou, Stephen 4:20:34 (15,574)
Pomeroy, Andrew J 4:58:10 (25,184)
Pomfret, Robert M 4:18:59 (15,156)
Pompei, Marino 4:45:41 (22,130)
Poncelet, Loic 3:27:31 (3,781)

Record Breakers

LONDON MARATHON

Breaking a record in the London Marathon is a sure way of hitting the headlines. The London Marathon was awarded the Guinness World Record for the Largest Annual Fundraising Event – generating the most money to date of some £47.2 million. The amount raised for charity by runners in the London Marathon since 1981 topped half a billion pounds when it celebrated its 30th anniversary in 2010.

In 2009 ten new Guinness World Records were set:

- Paul Simons, 45, broke the record for the **Fastest marathon dressed as Santa Claus** – 2:55:50

- Ian Benskin, 35, as Virgil Tracey from Thunderbirds; **Fastest marathon in a film character costume** – 3:11:50

- Robert Prothero, in full carrot costume; **Fastest marathon dressed as a vegetable** – 3:34:55

- Darren Stone, 22, in Banana Man costume; **Fastest marathon dressed as a cartoon character** – 3:36:07

- Alastair Martin, 41, ran as an ostrich; **Fastest marathon in an animal costume** – 3:42:27

- Thomas Day, 32; **Fastest marathon dressed in full suit, complete with bowler hat** – 4:19:37

- Irishman Jack Lyons; **Fastest marathon dressed as a leprechaun** – 4:22:08

- Sally Orange, dressed as an orange; **Fastest marathon dressed as a fruit** – 4:32:28

- Gordon Chaplin, running for 'Help for Heroes'; **Fastest marathon carrying a 40lb pack** – 5:35:19

- Neal Gardner and 29 friends from Wales linked together; **Fastest marathon for the most runners linked** – 6:18:41

Prime, Dave D	4:42:02 (21,206)	
Prince, Kevin J	5:19:46 (29,068)	
Prince, Luke	3:33:06 (4,626)	
Pring, Nick	3:51:47 (8,225)	
Pring, Richard A	4:40:50 (20,920)	
Pringle, Chris	4:41:04 (20,976)	
Pringle, Iain	3:47:46 (7,341)	
Pringle, Neil	3:18:29 (2,573)	
Print, Robert	5:01:07 (25,844)	
Prior, Dave J	4:40:48 (20,911)	
Prior, David J	4:39:23 (20,542)	
Prior, Oli	5:03:09 (26,227)	
Prior, Toby C	5:16:19 (28,540)	
Pritchard, Andrew J	7:38:03 (35,261)	
Pritchard, David J	5:01:13 (25,865)	
Pritchard, Edward W	3:37:36 (5,424)	
Pritchard, Gary R	4:16:40 (14,575)	
Pritchard, George	4:41:48 (21,166)	
Pritchard, James	3:36:41 (5,261)	
Pritchard, Michael	4:07:23 (12,209)	
Pritchett, Andrew N	4:25:03 (16,726)	
Pritchett, Simon M	4:10:09 (12,898)	
Probert, Damon	4:29:57 (18,082)	
Probert, David C	6:29:44 (34,405)	
Prochazka, Ivo	3:08:38 (1,583)	
Procter, Daniel Francis	4:40:40 (20,878)	
Procter, Jonathan G	4:24:15 (16,511)	
Procter, Ryan	3:07:29 (1,478)	
Proctor, Adam	3:49:44 (7,787)	
Proctor, Benjamin	4:34:46 (19,337)	
Proctor, Chris	6:29:19 (34,393)	
Proctor, David A	3:19:35 (2,694)	
Proctor, Robert	4:34:20 (19,226)	
Proctor, Stewart S	5:08:37 (27,196)	
Profaska, Detlef	3:33:47 (4,722)	
Prosperi, Luciano	3:37:53 (5,469)	
Prothero, Robert A	3:34:55 (4,943)	
Proud, Hector H	4:51:39 (23,661)	
Proudley, Gavin J	3:29:42 (4,135)	
Proudlove, Andrew	4:25:09 (16,751)	
Proust, Jerome	3:34:41 (4,909)	
Prout, Ryan	2:34:44 (109)	
Provan, Andrew D	3:56:42 (9,535)	
Provito, Antonino	4:24:56 (16,691)	
Prowse, Peter	4:53:57 (24,211)	
Prowse, William G	3:21:37 (2,964)	
Prudham, Joseph P	4:35:27 (19,532)	
Pryce, Andrew J	3:56:17 (9,383)	
Pryce, Simon P	3:29:13 (4,044)	
Pryce, Steve E	4:58:09 (25,179)	
Pryke, Andy H	3:01:10 (1,064)	
Pryor, Adam J	4:06:29 (11,988)	
Pryor, Jonathan	3:56:08 (9,348)	
Pryor, Jonathan P	4:28:49 (17,780)	
Psaila, Marc	2:57:54 (829)	
Psink, Eric	4:03:29 (11,327)	
Puckett, Graham J	3:55:35 (9,183)	
Puckey, Steve J	4:06:18 (11,948)	
Puddick, Julian U	3:38:22 (5,559)	
Puddicombe, Vince J	4:51:00 (23,488)	
Puddifant, Jon D	4:33:05 (18,919)	
Puddle, Mark R	5:12:47 (27,944)	
Pudney, Christopher D	3:06:15 (1,396)	
Pudney, Noel B	4:58:35 (25,290)	
Puente, Hector	4:02:33 (11,141)	
Pugh, Adrian E	3:35:43 (5,099)	
Pugh, Neil	4:07:26 (12,221)	
Pugh, Patrick	3:28:00 (3,858)	
Pugh, Roderick M	3:39:59 (5,856)	
Pugh, Wayne J	4:07:15 (12,165)	
Pugliese, Domenico	5:07:58 (27,082)	
Pugliese, Francesco	2:58:08 (846)	
Pugnetti, Maurizio	3:09:06 (1,626)	
Pugsley, Chris A	4:23:56 (16,423)	
Pukacz, Peter	5:27:16 (30,075)	
Pulford, Mark C	4:21:59 (15,940)	
Pulford, Tom G	5:15:30 (28,416)	
Pulis, Anthony R	4:31:57 (18,623)	
Pullan, Nick D	4:43:09 (21,503)	
Pullen, Matthew G	4:32:31 (18,761)	
Pullen, Matthew T	4:23:04 (16,200)	
Pullen, Miles	4:01:26 (10,893)	
Pullen, Timothy J	3:38:13 (5,537)	
Pullinger, Jerry A	3:20:29 (2,824)	
Puls, Richard	4:10:50 (13,071)	
Pumfleet, Jon P	4:38:47 (20,372)	
Pummell, Mike A	4:21:32 (15,824)	
Punch, Julian E	4:17:14 (14,700)	
Punchard, Gavin M	2:58:22 (863)	
Purcell, Owen	4:39:56 (20,701)	
Purches, John R	5:03:34 (26,294)	
Purdon, Nick T	3:44:09 (6,657)	
Purdy, Mark A	2:59:38 (969)	
Puri, Amit S	4:25:39 (16,893)	
Purkiss, Christopher R	3:50:04 (7,850)	
Purkiss, Michael	3:36:09 (5,182)	
Purkiss, Michael T	4:53:12 (24,021)	
Purr, Andrew W	5:54:49 (32,671)	
Purslow, David J	5:00:10 (25,629)	
Purslow, Philip	4:08:35 (12,519)	
Purves, James A	3:40:55 (6,017)	
Purvey, Alan	4:45:29 (22,075)	
Purvis, Darrell A	4:49:42 (23,179)	
Purvis, Darren M	2:38:47 (171)	
Purvis, Ian	4:36:19 (19,742)	
Purvis, John F	3:37:12 (5,354)	
Purvor, Mark B	5:09:36 (27,384)	
Pusch, Juergen	4:31:02 (18,361)	
Pusey, Andrew	3:47:05 (7,210)	
Puxty, James M	4:55:34 (24,584)	
Pyatt, Chris D	4:13:45 (13,859)	
Pye, Alan E	3:24:02 (3,265)	
Pye, David L	4:13:05 (13,680)	
Pye, Thomas D	6:07:06 (33,441)	
Pygall, Anthony	5:14:16 (28,202)	
Pyle, Chris J	2:58:46 (890)	
Pyle, Tim	5:22:35 (29,450)	
Pyne, Daniel T	2:55:53 (718)	
Pyper, Darryl J	3:47:40 (7,323)	
Qi Chao, Foo	4:34:32 (19,267)	
Quadt, Andreas	4:10:56 (13,089)	
Quaile, James P	4:39:44 (20,652)	
Quaile, Rob E	4:39:44 (20,652)	
Quant, Tony	5:32:04 (30,648)	
Quantrill, Philip	2:55:48 (714)	
Quantrill, Richard J	2:50:51 (492)	
Quarrell, Andrew P	6:18:40 (33,952)	
Quartel, Adrian W	5:08:57 (27,261)	
Quartermaine, Richard A	3:44:15 (6,673)	
Quarterman, Paul	4:50:09 (23,274)	
Quarton, Henry J	4:54:36 (24,360)	
Quattromini, Gianriccardo	4:15:16 (14,226)	
Quayle, Jonathan C	4:46:58 (22,474)	
Quayle, Scott John	4:10:46 (13,056)	
Quehen, Gilles	4:25:39 (16,893)	
Quelch, Danny	6:23:32 (34,173)	
Quick, James H	3:19:01 (2,620)	
Quicke, Michael C	4:37:22 (20,000)	
Quijo, Thierry	5:29:03 (30,278)	
Quilligan, James	4:56:05 (24,700)	
Quilter, Nicholas J	3:10:17 (1,721)	
Quilter, Stuart J	4:15:53 (14,364)	
Quin, Paul A	5:12:45 (27,934)	
Quincey, Scott	3:57:50 (9,890)	
Quinlan, Lee S	4:21:01 (15,697)	
Quinn, Aaron	3:32:20 (4,520)	
Quinn, Anthony	4:48:46 (22,915)	
Quinn, Carl P	2:57:03 (777)	
Quinn, Danny M	5:25:53 (29,914)	
Quinn, David	5:37:55 (31,263)	
Quinn, Don	6:43:10 (34,684)	
Quinn, Eamonn	5:56:41 (32,805)	
Quinn, James	4:09:09 (12,650)	
Quinn, James J	4:51:16 (23,558)	
Quinn, Jamie C	4:32:17 (18,705)	
Quinn, John P	4:03:36 (11,356)	
Quinn, Marc	4:47:49 (22,675)	
Quinn, Martin A	4:32:03 (18,648)	
Quinn, Peter	3:44:04 (6,643)	
Quinn, Thomas S	3:09:33 (1,660)	
Quinn, Timothy F	4:55:11 (24,499)	
Quinsee, Paul	3:41:26 (6,108)	
Quinton, Matthew J	3:21:53 (2,997)	
Quirk, Jeremy	4:30:48 (18,303)	
Quirk, Tom M	4:46:27 (22,331)	
Quirke, Stephen J	4:51:18 (23,566)	
Quistgaard, Jacob	5:07:47 (27,056)	
Ra, Seung Hwan	4:03:09 (11,260)	
Raaijmakers, Tuur	3:51:12 (8,098)	
Rabaey, Maarten	3:56:50 (9,579)	
Rabanal, Lisa	4:39:54 (20,693)	
Rabicano, Thomas C	4:23:07 (16,215)	
Rabin, Jeremy J	4:19:34 (15,303)	
Rabinowitz, Gideon P	4:43:59 (21,715)	
Rabjohns, Peter	3:02:33 (1,152)	
Raboldt, Marco	4:31:25 (18,480)	
Rabone, Martin J	4:28:56 (17,814)	
Race, Andrew A	4:08:13 (12,419)	
Race, Regis	4:46:19 (22,284)	
Rackham, Nigel D	2:37:30 (148)	
Rackind, Kevin N	5:13:30 (28,063)	
Rackley, Trevor	3:56:36 (9,489)	
Racktoo, Andrew J	6:05:08 (33,345)	
Rad Carrera, Juan Antonio	3:34:06 (4,789)	
Radcliffe, James J	3:24:07 (3,282)	
Radcliffe, Richard	3:19:33 (2,690)	
Radford, Andrew J	4:31:12 (18,405)	
Radford, Ian	3:54:01 (8,760)	
Radford, Martin F	4:17:03 (14,658)	
Radford, Max A	3:40:34 (5,951)	
Radford, Paul J	3:23:47 (3,229)	
Radford, Sean R	3:30:49 (4,300)	
Radjen, Steve	3:52:51 (8,476)	
Radley, Lee	3:40:36 (5,958)	
Radley, Simon K	3:29:42 (4,135)	
Radway, Jon	4:14:50 (14,122)	
Rae, Colin G	4:12:08 (13,421)	
Rae, Jonathan M	2:54:36 (637)	
Rae, Neil	3:32:02 (4,472)	
Raffaelli, Sergio	5:54:36 (32,655)	
Raffegeau, Christophe	4:52:55 (23,956)	
Rafferty, Brendan P	3:48:57 (7,605)	
Rafferty, Paul	4:44:54 (21,931)	
Raffo, Paul	4:52:40 (23,895)	
Raftery, Patrick	5:55:25 (32,718)	
Raftery, Simon P	5:02:46 (26,170)	
Ragatzu, Pierpaolo	3:38:52 (5,651)	
Raggett, Brian	2:54:18 (617)	
Raggett, Ian S	3:55:45 (9,243)	
Raggett, Phil J	4:14:25 (14,017)	
Ragnarsson, Birgir Mar	4:04:52 (11,623)	
Rahim, Mohammed	2:43:40 (279)	
Rai, Hiradhan	7:38:33 (35,264)	
Raimondi, Renzo	3:04:50 (1,296)	
Rain, Stuart M	4:24:23 (16,545)	
Rainbow, Christopher M	2:53:03 (560)	
Rainbow, Matthew S	3:40:21 (5,923)	
Raincock, Adam	3:57:40 (9,836)	
Raine, Andrew	4:16:33 (14,536)	
Rainer, James R	3:31:47 (4,434)	
Raineteau, Herve	3:30:38 (4,274)	
Rainey, Timothy	3:14:43 (2,201)	
Rainier, Paul J	3:52:59 (8,502)	
Rainsford, Mark A	5:34:08 (30,870)	
Rajadeva, Haran	5:13:07 (28,009)	
Rajkumar, Thiagarajah	5:12:28 (27,889)	
Rajwani, Hanif	4:41:23 (21,051)	
Rake, Toby	4:03:30 (11,334)	
Rakusen, Lloyd	4:34:11 (19,193)	
Ralph, Daniel	4:42:34 (21,348)	
Ralph, John Peter	3:20:59 (2,888)	
Ralph, Philip	5:01:00 (25,811)	
Ralton, Paul J	3:04:23 (1,257)	
Rama, Jayesh	4:23:52 (16,405)	
Rama, Perparim	5:06:07 (26,749)	
Ramaala, Hendrick	2:07:44 (5)	
Ramada Pereira, Luis	3:46:55 (7,182)	
Ramage, Alan	2:39:22 (182)	
Rambo, Troy	5:20:46 (29,187)	
Rambourg, Guillaume	3:11:04 (1,786)	
Ramchandani, Neil	5:05:22 (26,617)	
Ramdhian, David K	4:31:58 (18,627)	
Rament, Dave J	3:20:24 (2,811)	
Ramini, Stefano	3:41:04 (6,039)	
Ramonas, Andrius	2:32:54 (90)	
Ramsay, Allan	3:57:36 (9,802)	
Ramsay, Gordon	4:05:02 (11,659)	
Ramsay, Grant M	2:37:25 (146)	

Reilly, Christopher S	5:09:13 (27,311)
Reilly, David G	3:07:27 (1,473)
Reilly, John	5:05:16 (26,601)
Reilly, Leon	5:14:43 (28,268)
Reilly, Michael W	4:21:06 (15,714)
Reilly, Peter A	4:34:07 (19,176)
Reilly, Stuart C	3:14:34 (2,176)
Reimer, Max	4:41:38 (21,129)
Reimers, Kevin C	4:52:41 (23,903)
Reinhardt, Benjamin A	5:52:22 (32,506)
Reis, Goncalo A	4:24:59 (16,706)
Reisman, Paul S	4:30:22 (18,197)
Reisser, Peter	2:44:03 (286)
Rejdal, Djemal	4:20:32 (15,568)
Rejza, Henryk	3:51:18 (8,120)
Remnant, Aaron S	4:50:44 (23,431)
Renaltner, Markus	3:58:34 (10,119)
Renard, Philippe	3:41:51 (6,175)
Renault, Neil	2:20:30 (20)
Rendall, Brendan O	3:13:12 (2,028)
Rendall, Julian I	2:31:54 (81)
Rendell, Graham	3:58:39 (10,144)
Render, Moz	5:21:36 (29,317)
Rennard, Alan	5:01:53 (25,991)
Rennie, David	3:57:43 (9,850)
Rennie, Gordon	3:55:34 (9,176)
Rennox, Daniel J	4:39:17 (20,513)
Renshaw, Arthur W	4:11:07 (13,145)
Renton, Nick J	5:47:46 (32,151)
Renwick, Chris P	4:19:09 (15,197)
Renwick, Iain R	4:07:51 (12,326)
Reque, Juan	2:54:40 (639)
Resnick, Brian	5:38:23 (31,317)
Retallack, Jack A	4:08:02 (12,369)
Rethoret, Christophe	3:47:41 (7,324)
Retkoceri, Ben	4:20:48 (15,636)
Revell, Edward C	3:56:15 (9,377)
Revell, Justin P	3:00:51 (1,041)
Revell, Kevin	2:58:49 (897)
Revell, Pete	5:22:50 (29,487)
Revell, Sean P	4:59:17 (25,450)
Revill, Adam	3:54:09 (8,796)
Revill, Craig I	5:09:18 (27,334)
Revill, Keith J	6:02:33 (33,200)
Revill, Sean	5:02:23 (26,092)
Rew, Ben Paul	3:26:49 (3,652)
Rexilius, Hartmut	6:47:11 (34,747)
Rexilius, Sebastian	5:54:52 (32,677)
Reyes Arroyo, Juan Antonio	3:22:37 (3,087)
Reyes-Montes, Juan M	4:36:49 (19,870)
Reyna, Luis	4:48:23 (22,825)
Reynolds, Andrew	5:30:49 (30,501)
Reynolds, Ben	4:05:17 (11,728)
Reynolds, Benjamin B	2:33:06 (93)
Reynolds, Bryan Mark	3:38:34 (5,602)
Reynolds, Carl	5:08:52 (27,245)
Reynolds, Chris	5:21:42 (29,332)
Reynolds, David J	4:06:59 (12,100)
Reynolds, JL	4:12:40 (13,566)
Reynolds, James N	4:14:10 (13,949)
Reynolds, Jamie	5:23:04 (29,526)
Reynolds, John	4:43:37 (21,628)
Reynolds, Leigh E	5:14:43 (28,268)
Reynolds, Mark A	3:53:09 (8,548)
Reynolds, Mark G	2:54:22 (622)
Reynolds, Mark P	4:00:53 (10,770)
Reynolds, Martin	3:51:52 (8,246)
Reynolds, Matthew W	3:35:56 (5,142)
Reynolds, Nicholas J	5:36:42 (31,143)
Reynolds, Paul	2:58:53 (908)
Reynolds, Paul P	5:30:33 (30,469)
Reynolds, Peter	4:45:15 (22,028)
Reynolds, Philip J	3:37:58 (5,481)
Reynolds, Richard W	5:30:54 (30,507)
Reynolds, Rob	5:23:21 (29,577)
Reynolds, Thomas W	3:29:29 (4,100)
Rezannah, Jason	3:29:34 (4,110)
Rhead, Robert J	4:58:55 (25,368)
Rhimes, Godfrey H	2:58:48 (893)
Rhoda, Matthew W	4:28:09 (17,593)
Rhodes, Chris	3:14:02 (2,126)
Rhodes, Chris	6:14:41 (33,777)
Rhodes, Hamish	4:11:35 (13,279)
Rhodes, Sam	3:48:48 (7,569)
Rhodes, Steven	4:20:18 (15,512)
Rhodes, Trevor	5:00:31 (25,703)
Rhodes-Baxter, James	4:51:27 (23,611)
Rhys-Davies, Russell B	3:58:00 (9,931)
Rianey, Jackson	4:01:04 (10,807)
Ribalet, André	4:39:20 (20,526)
Ribas, José	3:58:01 (9,941)
Ribbens, Chris	3:56:10 (9,357)
Ribeiro, Joaquim	3:00:59 (1,050)
Ricard, Pascal	5:25:26 (29,849)
Ricci, Lorenzo	3:25:24 (3,444)
Riccio, Paolo	4:32:05 (18,660)
Rice, Dennis B	4:28:41 (17,744)
Rice, James B	5:47:11 (32,110)
Rice, Jonathan	3:43:46 (6,580)
Rice, Mark A	3:22:04 (3,022)
Rice, Martin J	3:29:05 (4,022)
Rice, Matt E	4:54:14 (24,268)
Rice, Michael J	5:16:18 (28,538)
Rice, Mike F	4:17:29 (14,764)
Rice, Robert J	6:04:48 (33,326)
Rice, Tim S	6:08:36 (33,498)
Rice, Tom	3:56:46 (9,554)
Rice-Jones, Malcolm R	3:44:02 (6,636)
Rich, Andrew John	5:00:31 (25,703)
Rich, Joe	4:47:15 (22,553)
Rich, Mark C	4:31:11 (18,400)
Rich, Simon S	3:53:08 (8,541)
Rich, Steve J	3:58:07 (9,978)
Richard, Valentini	3:37:03 (5,330)
Richards, Ben	3:41:04 (6,039)
Richards, Craig	3:56:13 (9,370)
Richards, Daniel	4:45:28 (22,071)
Richards, Daniel	4:53:31 (24,074)
Richards, Daniel	5:38:34 (31,340)
Richards, David	3:47:32 (7,296)
Richards, David Brian	4:17:19 (14,725)
Richards, Dean	4:39:50 (20,676)
Richards, Drummond W	3:40:57 (6,021)
Richards, Gavin H	3:34:53 (4,939)
Richards, Glyn	3:33:56 (4,745)
Richards, Glyn	4:16:29 (14,519)
Richards, James I	4:35:15 (19,477)
Richards, Jason T	2:53:32 (587)
Richards, John	3:54:49 (8,973)
Richards, John J	6:04:09 (33,296)
Richards, Jonathan	4:17:28 (14,761)
Richards, Kevin	5:37:01 (31,170)
Richards, Mark	3:07:47 (1,511)
Richards, Mark	4:27:01 (17,260)
Richards, Mark J	3:48:37 (7,537)
Richards, Neil A	3:08:25 (1,559)
Richards, Neil A	5:07:21 (26,971)
Richards, Neil T	5:39:13 (31,419)
Richards, Paul	4:09:49 (12,813)
Richards, Paul A	3:24:06 (3,279)
Richards, Paul I	3:42:49 (6,380)
Richards, Simon L	5:41:47 (31,655)
Richards, Timothy R	2:49:49 (463)
Richards, Timothy R	5:12:40 (27,920)
Richards, Tom	3:48:55 (7,599)
Richardson, Andrew T	4:10:11 (12,907)
Richardson, Brian	3:54:38 (8,928)
Richardson, Danny J	3:06:07 (1,382)
Richardson, James E	3:30:43 (4,284)
Richardson, Jeremy P	4:44:44 (21,896)
Richardson, John A	4:40:15 (20,788)
Richardson, Jordan	3:43:04 (6,434)
Richardson, Julian	2:44:14 (293)
Richardson, Kevin A	5:09:33 (27,374)
Richardson, Lee	4:16:42 (14,584)
Richardson, Mark	4:00:47 (10,741)
Richardson, Martin	4:58:39 (25,310)
Richardson, Martin P	3:50:57 (8,049)
Richardson, Matthew G	4:20:10 (15,478)
Richardson, Neil	4:02:54 (11,211)
Richardson, Oliver J	4:40:37 (20,865)
Richardson, Paul	4:43:02 (21,476)
Richardson, Paul W	5:09:33 (27,374)
Richardson, Peter	4:06:53 (12,078)
Richardson, Peter G	4:37:46 (20,111)
Richardson, Scott	4:35:02 (19,419)
Richardson, Scott A	4:35:49 (19,630)
Richardson, Simon C	2:57:56 (833)
Richardson, Stephen	3:38:13 (5,537)
Richardson, Stephen J	4:56:49 (24,883)
Richardson, Steve	4:03:57 (11,436)
Richardson, Stuart I	3:57:35 (9,798)
Richardson, Tim C	4:55:12 (24,506)
Richardson, Tom	4:27:05 (17,278)
Richardson-Perks, Tim R	3:24:04 (3,276)
Riches, Andrew	6:24:32 (34,212)
Riches, Edward	5:45:53 (32,007)
Riches, Mark C	2:58:44 (887)
Riches, Philip G	3:19:38 (2,702)
Richford, Ben P	3:00:02 (1,000)
Richford, Duncan A	4:22:29 (16,073)
Richman, Dave	4:35:31 (19,552)
Richman, Simon	4:43:41 (21,644)
Richmond, Aaron L	3:42:15 (6,258)
Richmond, Ben T	4:13:04 (13,672)
Richmond, Colin	3:59:39 (10,437)
Richmond, David F	3:12:55 (1,993)
Richmond, Graham K	4:14:11 (13,955)
Richmond, Steve	6:04:27 (33,311)
Richter, Klaus-Peter	3:58:19 (10,039)
Richter, Ralf	3:47:34 (7,303)
Richter, Simon A	4:25:22 (16,806)
Rickaby, Richard	3:55:24 (9,132)
Rickard, Stuart J	4:25:47 (16,933)
Rickards, Jason	4:51:11 (23,535)
Rickards, Simon	3:56:38 (9,511)
Rickett, Jacob O	4:41:18 (21,037)
Ricketts, Bart L	5:16:15 (28,534)
Ricketts, Damien J	4:53:40 (24,123)
Ricketts, Michael J	4:17:20 (14,732)
Ricketts, Toby J	4:28:47 (17,769)
Rickey, Charles H	4:12:17 (13,464)
Rickman, Nigel J	4:36:35 (19,813)
Rickus, Michael S	3:46:14 (7,025)
Rickwood, Tony	3:36:00 (5,154)
Rico, Willi	3:28:30 (3,929)
Ricoux, Jean-Luc	5:03:37 (26,308)
Riddell, Gareth	2:37:11 (143)
Riddick, Matt	4:12:08 (13,421)
Riddle, Martin	5:03:12 (26,235)
Riddleston, Ross G	3:49:40 (7,761)
Rider, Jess C	4:20:40 (15,591)
Ridge, Terry	3:51:12 (8,098)
Ridgeon, Jon D	5:40:52 (31,577)
Ridgeway, Paul B	3:47:13 (7,236)
Ridgewell, Keith A	5:56:49 (32,817)
Ridgewell, Stan Leonard	3:41:17 (6,086)
Ridler, Adam	5:23:29 (29,594)
Ridley, Cheryl L	5:43:10 (31,789)
Ridley, David J	4:12:55 (13,635)
Ridley, Jason	4:06:31 (11,994)
Ridley, Jonathan	3:52:27 (8,392)
Ridout, Simon J	4:46:12 (22,248)
Ridsdale, John C	3:50:38 (7,975)
Ridsdale, Neil	4:07:40 (12,274)
Ridsdale, Tom N	4:07:40 (12,274)
Rieder, Hubert	3:19:34 (2,691)
Riedi, Christian	3:30:56 (4,317)
Riedl, Martin	4:19:21 (15,246)
Riedweg, Franz	3:44:13 (6,667)
Rieley, Hugh	3:18:29 (2,573)
Riemke, Thomas	4:46:17 (22,274)
Rigabert, Juan	3:12:35 (1,943)
Rigarlsford, Giles A	3:30:51 (4,303)
Rigby, Alan D	5:42:47 (31,745)
Rigby, Chris	6:36:54 (34,559)
Rigby, Gareth A	4:11:49 (13,341)
Rigby, Neil A	4:19:39 (15,328)
Rigby, Reginald K	5:37:52 (31,258)
Rigby, Simon M	4:02:18 (11,088)
Rigg, Nigel K	3:25:22 (3,438)
Riggens, Stephen G	4:51:53 (23,723)
Riggs, David G	5:45:09 (31,938)
Rigler, David S	3:33:26 (4,670)
Rigoni, Angelo	4:07:07 (12,135)
Rikken, Sjors	3:11:56 (1,876)
Riley, Adam	4:25:49 (16,940)
Riley, Brett D	5:06:37 (26,824)
Riley, Bryan A	3:42:04 (6,226)

Riley, Christopher J 2:33:03 (92)
Riley, Damian J 4:19:28 (15,269)
Riley, Daniel A 3:48:34 (7,525)
Riley, Duncan S 4:46:53 (22,444)
Riley, Jason M 5:45:28 (31,969)
Riley, John L 4:57:05 (24,947)
Riley, John L 5:46:30 (32,049)
Riley, Joseph L 3:51:01 (8,058)
Riley, Malcolm T 3:36:29 (5,232)
Riley, Mark F 5:00:43 (25,751)
Riley, Michael P 4:06:49 (12,065)
Riley, Patrick 3:14:29 (2,171)
Riley, Peter J 4:45:51 (22,177)
Riley, Robert M 5:08:40 (27,207)
Riley, William 4:28:39 (17,736)
Rímer, Florian 3:37:29 (5,395)
Rimmer, Colin 3:36:17 (5,203)
Rimmer, John R 3:29:57 (4,175)
Rimmer, Michael 3:06:04 (1,375)
Rimmer, Paul 5:30:52 (30,504)
Rimmington, Glen 4:45:06 (22,000)
Ring, Chris 3:13:54 (2,111)
Ring, Gerard C 3:59:39 (10,437)
Ring, Mark R 4:20:13 (15,490)
Ringham, Simon P 3:20:56 (2,884)
Ringshaw, Daniel 4:29:32 (17,974)
Rinsler, Alex 3:54:25 (8,867)
Rintari, Lawrence K 4:46:50 (22,437)
Rio, Jonathan P 6:53:57 (34,878)
Riou, Yann 3:46:06 (7,003)
Ripamonti, Paolo 3:11:46 (1,855)
Ripley, Michael S 4:48:37 (22,885)
Ripol Malet, Javier 3:28:44 (3,961)
Ripolles, Robert 4:02:48 (11,187)
Risa, Arne 3:29:44 (4,143)
Risbridger, Paul J 5:16:55 (28,633)
Risby, Floyd T 4:11:36 (13,284)
Rising, Chris J 4:30:04 (18,116)
Rissik, Angus 3:21:46 (2,980)
Ritchie, Alan 3:43:59 (6,627)
Ritson, Martin 5:12:46 (27,939)
Ritter, Gordon 3:48:41 (7,545)
Ritter, Nicholas 4:42:04 (21,215)
Ritzenhein, Dathan 2:10:00 (11)
Rivellini, Andrea 3:48:47 (7,562)
Rivers, Brian 3:33:19 (4,654)
Rivers, Terry 3:52:27 (8,392)
Rivett, Colin K 4:31:25 (18,480)
Rivett, Tim J 3:54:10 (8,804)
Rivolta, Jason 4:21:48 (15,900)
Rixon, Andy 6:22:33 (34,128)
Rizzo Gomez, Alexandro M 3:55:14 (9,092)
Roach, Dave J 4:12:38 (13,558)
Roach, David 5:22:30 (29,438)
Roach, Marcus 3:48:34 (7,525)
Roach, Robert 5:51:47 (32,465)
Roach, Shane 3:35:04 (4,972)
Roach, Stephen W 5:26:19 (29,969)
Roadnight, James H 5:01:35 (25,929)
Robb, Andy J 4:53:54 (24,202)
Robb, Anthony F 4:52:32 (23,870)
Robb, Lee 3:48:18 (7,465)
Robb, Tim W 4:37:23 (20,004)
Robbie, Neil 3:42:53 (6,395)
Robbins, Andrew 2:57:32 (809)
Robbins, Gordon A 5:08:23 (27,157)
Robbins, Keith G 6:04:33 (33,315)
Robbins, Martin 5:52:26 (32,510)
Robbins, Stephen John 3:49:41 (7,772)
Robello, Mauro 4:48:42 (22,902)
Roberson, Paul 3:37:10 (5,352)
Robert, Iain A 2:48:59 (422)
Robert, Patrick 2:59:13 (934)
Roberton, John A 4:27:43 (17,451)
Roberts, Alan F 3:12:05 (1,888)
Roberts, Alick J 3:57:53 (9,901)
Roberts, Andrew D 4:01:39 (10,956)
Roberts, Chris 3:12:12 (1,901)
Roberts, Christopher J 4:17:30 (14,769)
Roberts, Clive B 3:53:01 (8,510)
Roberts, Colin D 4:53:35 (24,093)
Roberts, Darren 4:21:12 (15,741)
Roberts, David A 3:59:24 (10,369)
Roberts, David E 3:22:26 (3,058)
Roberts, David W 4:52:07 (23,779)
Roberts, Dean C 3:19:53 (2,736)
Roberts, Gareth A 4:50:38 (23,409)
Roberts, Gareth H 5:58:10 (32,932)
Roberts, George 4:34:47 (19,348)
Roberts, Glyn 4:34:23 (19,235)
Roberts, Guy J 2:47:21 (378)
Roberts, Ian 4:42:16 (21,269)
Roberts, Ian D 4:54:46 (24,397)
Roberts, James 6:08:34 (33,497)
Roberts, James D 4:20:57 (15,674)
Roberts, James R 5:05:43 (26,685)
Roberts, James S 3:04:30 (1,263)
Roberts, Justin D 4:30:25 (18,211)
Roberts, Kerry J 2:45:35 (324)
Roberts, Malcolm 3:28:48 (3,973)
Roberts, Mark D 3:45:01 (6,808)
Roberts, Mark J 5:29:26 (30,323)
Roberts, Mark W 5:55:51 (32,752)
Roberts, Martyn 4:39:00 (20,435)
Roberts, Neil M 4:11:22 (13,214)
Roberts, Owain 4:01:34 (10,934)
Roberts, Paul 4:09:58 (12,846)
Roberts, Paul G 4:33:53 (19,124)
Roberts, Paul M 5:43:51 (31,837)
Roberts, Philip J 4:40:19 (20,799)
Roberts, Richard A 3:54:41 (8,940)
Roberts, Richard H 4:22:52 (16,161)
Roberts, Russell W 5:10:32 (27,554)
Roberts, Simon G 3:13:46 (2,099)
Roberts, Simon W 4:33:17 (18,968)
Roberts, Stephen W 4:50:22 (23,335)
Roberts, Stewart M 4:59:03 (25,399)
Roberts, Thomas Alwyn 3:56:11 (9,364)
Roberts, Thomas D 4:05:09 (11,695)
Roberts, Tim 4:10:59 (13,104)
Roberts, Vince 3:46:50 (7,162)
Roberts, William 4:12:06 (13,414)
Roberts, William 5:48:29 (32,214)
Robertshaw, Keith 2:41:51 (231)
Robertshaw, Tom 3:08:49 (1,601)
Robertson, Alexander D 4:07:41 (12,281)
Robertson, Alexander S 4:30:27 (18,217)
Robertson, Anthony M 4:01:21 (10,873)
Robertson, Craig T 5:05:18 (26,607)
Robertson, Frazer 4:16:07 (14,429)
Robertson, George 5:05:18 (26,607)
Robertson, Iain D 3:03:16 (1,187)
Robertson, Iain T 4:51:39 (23,661)
Robertson, Ian 3:17:29 (2,483)
Robertson, Ian M 4:54:25 (24,317)
Robertson, Jamie T 3:43:04 (6,434)
Robertson, John R 2:44:57 (314)
Robertson, Kevin 2:26:43 (42)
Robertson, Michael P 4:19:15 (15,221)
Robertson, Paul 2:59:31 (959)
Robertson, Paul 4:07:20 (12,191)
Robertson, Paul J 3:54:49 (8,973)
Robertson, Peter C 4:10:33 (12,994)
Robertson, Richard 4:56:26 (24,782)
Roberts-Thomson, Harold J 4:11:26 (13,238)
Robey, Nick 4:58:31 (25,274)
Robin, Sias 4:28:14 (17,628)
Robineau, Fabien 4:11:01 (13,112)
Robins, Alan N 4:42:33 (21,345)
Robins, Andrew 3:51:23 (8,136)
Robins, Andrew C 3:49:31 (7,733)
Robins, Ian M 5:22:23 (29,419)
Robins, Paul 4:49:59 (23,236)
Robins, Stephen David 3:37:25 (5,388)
Robinson, Alan 5:22:05 (29,373)
Robinson, Andy 4:04:39 (11,572)
Robinson, Angus William B 3:29:34 (4,110)
Robinson, Antony 5:07:29 (27,005)
Robinson, Antony W 4:14:41 (14,074)
Robinson, Barry J 3:35:19 (5,012)
Robinson, Brian J 4:27:20 (17,352)
Robinson, Charles J 3:41:10 (6,061)
Robinson, Clive R 3:27:55 (3,842)
Robinson, Craig 4:20:22 (15,527)
Robinson, Craig A 4:55:09 (24,491)
Robinson, Daniel 3:51:26 (8,150)
Robinson, Daniel 4:56:29 (24,795)
Robinson, Daniel P 5:38:09 (31,292)
Robinson, David 5:23:43 (29,615)
Robinson, David A 3:03:28 (1,199)
Robinson, David J 3:45:01 (6,808)
Robinson, David J 5:25:31 (29,860)
Robinson, David K 2:58:14 (851)
Robinson, David W 4:42:25 (21,305)
Robinson, Edward G 3:53:11 (8,561)
Robinson, Gary A 5:41:16 (31,603)
Robinson, Gary M 5:48:42 (32,237)
Robinson, Howard J 6:10:21 (33,582)
Robinson, Ian 4:34:15 (19,209)
Robinson, Ian B 5:29:49 (30,377)
Robinson, James 4:48:22 (22,819)
Robinson, James 5:33:34 (30,813)
Robinson, James E 5:01:21 (25,885)
Robinson, James N 2:58:06 (844)
Robinson, John L 4:53:46 (24,163)
Robinson, Jonathan C 4:55:57 (24,674)
Robinson, Juan De Dios 6:05:49 (33,381)
Robinson, Julian J 4:56:45 (24,865)
Robinson, Keith Richard 5:04:29 (26,452)
Robinson, Mark D 4:07:01 (12,111)
Robinson, Neil A 3:57:00 (9,619)
Robinson, Neil J 4:46:47 (22,430)
Robinson, Neil Stuart 6:00:33 (33,080)
Robinson, Neville H 4:00:18 (10,618)
Robinson, Nick 3:17:43 (2,505)
Robinson, Patrick 4:10:15 (12,921)
Robinson, Patrick 4:27:59 (17,540)
Robinson, Paul 4:30:56 (18,331)
Robinson, Paul 5:11:02 (27,645)
Robinson, Peter 3:30:33 (4,264)
Robinson, Peter R 3:45:20 (6,862)
Robinson, Rupert G 4:25:59 (16,983)
Robinson, Shaun E 3:43:09 (6,457)
Robinson, Simon 4:00:13 (10,603)
Robinson, Simon A 4:32:08 (18,671)
Robinson, Simon C 4:01:19 (10,862)
Robinson, Simon J 4:30:33 (18,242)
Robinson, Stephen R 5:31:16 (30,555)
Robinson, Steve 4:57:22 (25,005)
Robinson, Steve J 4:41:34 (21,109)
Robinson, Tom 3:01:06 (1,058)
Robinson, Tony V 4:51:18 (23,566)
Robinson, William R 7:26:04 (35,187)
Roblin, David G 4:02:30 (11,126)
Roborgh, Dominic L 4:07:40 (12,274)
Robson, Dale 5:19:25 (29,026)
Robson, David A 4:47:16 (22,556)
Robson, David J 4:55:41 (24,610)
Robson, David N 3:49:05 (7,642)
Robson, Derek 4:52:06 (23,775)
Robson, Ian 4:14:20 (13,994)
Robson, James E 3:49:34 (7,743)
Robson, John N 4:11:16 (13,179)
Robson, John P 3:56:01 (9,319)
Robson, Mark 4:29:28 (17,963)
Robson, Mark A 4:12:44 (13,587)
Robson, Stephen M 3:13:38 (2,080)
Roca Biosca, David 3:16:34 (2,392)
Rocchi, Maurice 4:38:23 (20,272)
Roche, Mark 4:51:47 (23,695)
Roche, Paul M 4:05:42 (11,822)
Roche Soler, Manuel 3:07:39 (1,497)
Rochester, Steve R 5:26:50 (30,028)
Rockett, Chris D 5:13:50 (28,123)
Rodaway, Steven J 3:39:46 (5,803)
Rodger, Edward 4:51:51 (23,709)
Rodger, Mr P 4:39:53 (20,688)
Rodgers, Alun 3:35:23 (5,030)
Rodgers, Ian Gordon 3:23:34 (3,199)
Rodgers, Josh 4:11:31 (13,258)
Rodgers, Stephen Anthony 3:45:17 (6,852)
Rodi, Christopher M 3:49:09 (7,658)
Rodriguez, Carlos 3:29:43 (4,139)
Rodriguez, Renato 3:53:58 (8,745)
Rodway, Marty 4:50:00 (23,239)
Roe, Matthew James 3:04:14 (1,251)
Roe, Richard R 4:35:16 (19,483)
Roebuck, Mark J 5:13:53 (28,139)
Roeed, Bernt Erik 3:47:09 (7,228)

Roelofsz, Ian	4:01:28 (10,905)	
Roennow, Tor	4:48:35 (22,873)	
Roer, Adam A	4:08:41 (12,544)	
Roesgaard, Henrik	3:29:14 (4,046)	
Roessler, Silvio	3:42:22 (6,277)	
Roff, Anthony D	4:21:34 (15,834)	
Roff, Tom M	3:18:02 (2,532)	
Roffe, Jamie	5:46:33 (32,050)	
Roffey, Robert I	4:42:52 (21,431)	
Rogan, Ian	3:38:56 (5,661)	
Roger, Alan M	5:29:11 (30,296)	
Rogers, Adam	5:31:36 (30,594)	
Rogers, Andrew	4:21:15 (15,755)	
Rogers, Benjamin	4:20:00 (15,428)	
Rogers, Christopher James	5:02:05 (26,041)	
Rogers, David	4:56:01 (24,682)	
Rogers, David W	6:18:40 (33,952)	
Rogers, Dennis	3:42:22 (6,277)	
Rogers, Geoff	4:22:03 (15,954)	
Rogers, Ian	4:19:44 (15,348)	
Rogers, Ian J	3:40:35 (5,953)	
Rogers, James	5:01:35 (25,929)	
Rogers, James O	4:22:03 (15,954)	
Rogers, Jim	2:49:44 (458)	
Rogers, John	3:55:51 (9,274)	
Rogers, John B	4:48:12 (22,783)	
Rogers, Kevin C	4:38:23 (20,272)	
Rogers, Lee A	3:59:27 (10,379)	
Rogers, Lee E	5:07:23 (26,982)	
Rogers, Luke	4:20:42 (15,604)	
Rogers, Malcolm	3:46:26 (7,071)	
Rogers, Mark	3:35:50 (5,121)	
Rogers, Mathew	4:51:51 (23,709)	
Rogers, Matthew J	3:56:40 (9,523)	
Rogers, Matthew S	3:59:46 (10,481)	
Rogers, Neil	4:36:55 (19,894)	
Rogers, Peter	2:55:28 (696)	
Rogers, Peter J	4:04:13 (11,495)	
Rogers, Philip A	3:09:09 (1,634)	
Rogers, Phillip	4:05:57 (11,870)	
Rogers, S	3:22:38 (3,089)	
Rogers, Shaun A	5:12:57 (27,974)	
Rogers, Stuart J	5:35:10 (30,985)	
Rogers, Stuart M	4:36:11 (19,716)	
Rogers, Tom	3:52:18 (8,359)	
Rogers, Wayne N	5:40:29 (31,540)	
Rogiers, Luc	3:47:47 (7,346)	
Rogiers, Walter	4:14:13 (13,964)	
Rohde, Ben	4:04:32 (11,552)	
Rohder, Arno	5:00:01 (25,605)	
Rohland, Martin	5:13:06 (28,006)	
Rojas, Jacobo	3:36:51 (5,287)	
Rojas, Stephen R	2:41:21 (223)	
Rojas Castillo, Fernando	6:13:59 (33,743)	
Roland, Lionel	3:13:05 (2,013)	
Roland, Wyss M	3:14:55 (2,222)	
Roles, James	4:18:30 (15,029)	
Rolf, Kevin J	4:57:08 (24,953)	
Rolfe, Clive J	3:09:13 (1,644)	
Rolfe, Kevin John	4:45:32 (22,089)	
Rolfe, Les J	4:47:29 (22,594)	
Rolison, Aaron R	5:02:24 (26,094)	
Rolley, James W	3:55:33 (9,171)	
Rollings, Andrew P	5:23:43 (29,615)	
Rollings, Jamie L	3:46:11 (7,014)	
Rollings, Simon	5:14:43 (28,268)	
Rollinson, Jason	5:00:22 (25,669)	
Rolls, Chris J	5:15:24 (28,402)	
Rolls, David	5:15:24 (28,402)	
Rolls, Shaun F	4:58:14 (25,197)	
Rolls, Spencer C	5:54:48 (32,667)	
Rolt, Patrick A	3:48:53 (7,591)	
Romagnolo, Alan	4:59:08 (25,418)	
Romain, Gary	3:51:38 (8,196)	
Romano, David	4:29:07 (17,865)	
Rombaut, Eric	3:17:22 (2,474)	
Rombaut, Walter	3:32:03 (4,477)	
Romecin, Tom J	3:28:01 (3,860)	
Romero, Joanne	5:27:28 (30,089)	
Romero, José	4:00:10 (10,587)	
Romero Arguello, Cuauhtemoc	3:40:01 (5,863)	
Romine, Stephen	4:42:51 (21,425)	
Ronaki, Kramer Rawharetua KK	6:36:22 (34,550)	
Ronald, James C	4:02:00 (11,017)	
Ronan, Gareth J	5:38:29 (31,331)	
Ronnan, Andrew	5:33:45 (30,837)	
Rook, Spencer J	3:01:35 (1,088)	
Roome, Peter	3:04:42 (1,280)	
Rooney, David J	5:18:19 (28,837)	
Rooney, Frank S	3:07:23 (1,466)	
Roos, Paul	7:22:37 (35,163)	
Root, Mark B	5:16:14 (28,532)	
Ropars, Olivier	3:37:14 (5,359)	
Roper, Bill	4:26:28 (17,104)	
Roper, Daniel	5:23:24 (29,583)	
Roper, Edward B	6:06:57 (33,434)	
Roper, Graham R	4:43:08 (21,500)	
Roper, Miles	4:14:01 (13,910)	
Roper, Stephen	4:20:24 (15,537)	
Roper, Tom	5:01:05 (25,837)	
Rosa, Andrew M	3:39:18 (5,729)	
Rosa, Robin C	5:03:49 (26,344)	
Rosato, Domenico A	6:13:19 (33,712)	
Rosborg, Gorm B	4:29:42 (18,016)	
Rosbrook, Simon J	4:22:35 (16,096)	
Roscoe, Andy	4:51:10 (23,528)	
Roscoe, Clive A	5:01:51 (25,980)	
Rose, Alan	5:06:37 (26,824)	
Rose, Alun M	2:56:26 (742)	
Rose, Andrew	4:27:29 (17,387)	
Rose, Andrew M	4:18:27 (15,017)	
Rose, Chris	4:55:17 (24,527)	
Rose, Christian	3:56:15 (9,377)	
Rose, Daniel	4:28:53 (17,806)	
Rose, Daniel	5:11:32 (27,733)	
Rose, David A	3:10:36 (1,745)	
Rose, David P	4:22:07 (15,970)	
Rose, Gary	4:53:49 (24,177)	
Rose, Ian P	4:46:03 (22,216)	
Rose, James	4:38:25 (20,280)	
Rose, John	3:29:48 (4,155)	
Rose, John P	3:30:29 (4,249)	
Rose, Mark	4:06:50 (12,068)	
Rose, Mark R	4:26:31 (17,121)	
Rose, Martin	4:33:38 (19,058)	
Rose, Martin D	5:35:49 (31,052)	
Rose, Michael	4:03:03 (11,239)	
Rose, Nigel A	4:17:51 (14,850)	
Rose, Paul	5:30:28 (30,457)	
Rose, Paul A	3:30:00 (4,178)	
Rose, Paul J	2:43:30 (270)	
Rose, Paul J	6:10:22 (33,585)	
Rose, Philip J	3:51:36 (8,187)	
Rose, Sean A	2:46:04 (332)	
Rose, Stuart	4:31:59 (18,629)	
Rose, Stuart T	3:45:26 (6,878)	
Roseborne, Nicholas	4:22:26 (16,060)	
Rosell, Martin J	4:18:06 (14,920)	
Rosenbach, Jonathan T	3:18:24 (2,567)	
Rosenberg, Stuart D	5:00:04 (25,608)	
Rosenblatt, Ollie	4:36:13 (19,729)	
Rosenfeld, David J	4:27:13 (17,314)	
Rosenstein, Andrew P	4:14:12 (13,961)	
Rosien, Sebastian	3:16:28 (2,374)	
Rosland, Nils Svein	5:32:17 (30,668)	
Ross, Alex	3:57:00 (9,619)	
Ross, Allan	3:50:39 (7,978)	
Ross, David E	3:03:14 (1,183)	
Ross, Ewan A	4:09:33 (12,737)	
Ross, George J	4:34:37 (19,294)	
Ross, George S	3:54:13 (8,815)	
Ross, John	4:27:22 (17,358)	
Ross, Jonathan D	4:39:35 (20,606)	
Ross, Mark D	4:07:51 (12,326)	
Ross, Matthew G	3:56:36 (9,489)	
Ross, Matthew J	4:01:45 (10,972)	
Ross, Nicholas J	4:54:25 (24,317)	
Rosser, David R	4:39:50 (20,676)	
Rosser, Keith G	3:30:09 (4,197)	
Rosser, Kevin	5:50:43 (32,395)	
Rosser, Nick J	5:02:52 (26,189)	
Rosser, Simon James	3:44:55 (6,787)	
Rosser, Stephen J	3:52:16 (8,353)	
Ross-Gower, Sam	4:03:28 (11,323)	
Rossini, Andrea	3:24:16 (3,306)	
Rossiter, Martin R	3:24:16 (3,306)	
Rossiter, Miki	3:41:59 (6,200)	
Rossiter, Paul	5:36:36 (31,133)	
Rossiter, Philippe R	4:11:34 (13,273)	
Rostern, Paul	3:10:28 (1,733)	
Roth, Anselm	4:08:20 (12,464)	
Roth, Benjamin	4:48:14 (22,797)	
Rothe, Carsten	4:13:06 (13,685)	
Rothwell, Alan	4:47:42 (22,653)	
Rothwell, Colin	2:54:22 (622)	
Rothwell, Ian	4:49:47 (23,195)	
Rothwell, Neil R	4:55:21 (24,539)	
Rouby, Bruno	3:43:37 (6,548)	
Rough, Mark C	4:58:19 (25,218)	
Roughley, Jon	4:20:59 (15,687)	
Rought-Rought, Craig D	3:54:27 (8,876)	
Round, Derek	4:38:18 (20,251)	
Round, Matt D	5:16:25 (28,551)	
Rounsley, Jim S	3:56:45 (9,549)	
Rouquier, Raphael	3:24:44 (3,373)	
Roure, Patrick	3:28:09 (3,876)	
Rourke, Ciaran	5:07:49 (27,066)	
Rourke, Steven J	4:29:57 (18,082)	
Rous, James A	3:44:09 (6,657)	
Rouse, David	3:52:13 (8,335)	
Rouse, David G	4:19:20 (15,238)	
Rouse, James	4:16:59 (14,642)	
Rousseau, Frederic	4:59:14 (25,438)	
Routledge, George	5:34:05 (30,866)	
Rowan, Darren J	4:41:51 (21,174)	
Rowan, Gordon	3:54:18 (8,839)	
Rowbotham, Neil	4:13:15 (13,729)	
Rowbury, James L	4:04:56 (11,639)	
Rowbury, Matthew D	3:28:26 (3,921)	
Rowden, David J	3:11:03 (1,785)	
Rowe, Brandon	4:42:53 (21,440)	
Rowe, Chris	5:03:02 (26,214)	
Rowe, David	3:30:18 (4,221)	
Rowe, David M	3:19:46 (2,722)	
Rowe, Davied L	6:22:41 (34,140)	
Rowe, George	4:09:08 (12,647)	
Rowe, Gerard	4:28:29 (17,693)	
Rowe, Martin	3:27:14 (3,722)	
Rowe, Mike S	5:28:10 (30,173)	
Rowe, Phil	8:21:22 (35,335)	
Rowe, Simon A	5:05:17 (26,603)	
Rowe, Tim N	3:29:21 (4,079)	
Rowe, Timothy	4:54:27 (24,326)	
Rowell, Ben	4:07:05 (12,129)	
Rowell, Jason	4:56:46 (24,867)	
Rowell, Paul Robert	3:24:42 (3,368)	
Rowell, Tony	4:27:41 (17,441)	
Rowland, Adam J	4:46:41 (22,391)	
Rowland, Andrew	4:03:49 (11,398)	
Rowland, Andrew J	2:53:31 (585)	
Rowland, Darius	4:42:53 (21,440)	
Rowland, David A	4:25:12 (16,766)	
Rowland, Kevin P	3:29:32 (4,104)	
Rowland, Mike J	6:05:18 (33,353)	
Rowland, Reginald	5:37:02 (31,174)	
Rowland, Shaun Richard	5:39:29 (31,445)	
Rowlands, Alun L	5:09:40 (27,399)	
Rowlands, Gary	3:59:59 (10,541)	
Rowlands, Kevin	3:30:31 (4,260)	
Rowlands, Marc N	3:52:35 (8,420)	
Rowlands, Peter	5:03:02 (26,214)	
Rowlands, Trefor	4:46:11 (22,244)	
Rowlatt, Gary	4:22:33 (16,089)	
Rowles, Alex	4:51:30 (23,620)	
Rowley, Benjamin P	3:57:31 (9,775)	
Rowley, Chris R	4:21:13 (15,744)	
Rowley, Kevin David	4:27:49 (17,495)	
Rowley, Matthew	4:37:44 (20,101)	
Rowley, Paul	3:11:04 (1,786)	
Rowlinson, Paul D	4:18:05 (14,912)	
Rowntree, Ben	6:25:38 (34,262)	
Rowntree, Paul D	4:35:20 (19,501)	
Rowswell, Huw R	4:00:39 (10,707)	
Royall, Mike S	5:17:50 (28,770)	
Royer, Gerd H	4:05:06 (11,679)	
Royer, Michael	4:05:08 (11,690)	
Royle, Tim J	4:49:00 (22,974)	
Rozanski, Rafal K	5:01:20 (25,882)	
Rthwell, Nigel T	3:12:57 (1,998)	

Ruane, Jack	4:30:43 (18,286)	
Ruane, James C	3:01:22 (1,074)	
Ruault, James E	3:35:43 (5,099)	
Ruban, Franck	3:54:49 (8,973)	
Ruban, Jerome	3:54:49 (8,973)	
Rubenstein, Ezra	4:13:12 (13,712)	
Rubio Eguiluz, Juan	3:22:05 (3,024)	
Ruck, Ian	3:26:49 (3,652)	
Rucker, Michael	4:45:24 (22,057)	
Rucklidge, Paul K	4:53:22 (24,054)	
Ruczynski, Zeniek	4:28:13 (17,622)	
Rudall, Ben	5:10:17 (27,511)	
Rudd, Adrian	4:01:13 (10,839)	
Rudd, John	4:17:15 (14,702)	
Rudd-Clarke, Peter J	3:22:54 (3,117)	
Rudderham, Lee	4:32:09 (18,677)	
Ruddock, James I	4:13:04 (13,672)	
Ruddy, Barry J	4:16:05 (14,420)	
Ruddy, Paul	6:17:27 (33,902)	
Rudge, Anthony Edward	5:28:30 (30,210)	
Rudge, Antony D	5:43:08 (31,785)	
Rudge, Lee A	5:34:41 (30,935)	
Rudman, Jason M	2:53:14 (567)	
Rudnick, Errol	3:50:45 (8,007)	
Rud-Petersen, Kim	3:35:23 (5,030)	
Ruf, Nico	3:46:47 (7,153)	
Ruff, Elliot M	4:01:13 (10,839)	
Ruff, Neil M	5:55:31 (32,727)	
Ruffe, Frederick W	4:18:55 (15,139)	
Ruffle, Ged	3:16:30 (2,378)	
Rufus, Renato	5:43:12 (31,795)	
Ruggles, Nikita	4:17:22 (14,736)	
Ruggles-Brice, Edward	4:18:33 (15,042)	
Ruhnke, Andreas	4:17:35 (14,790)	
Ruia, Alok	4:30:35 (18,250)	
Ruinoff, Andrew M	4:11:26 (13,238)	
Ruiz, Lorenzo	4:15:56 (14,374)	
Ruiz Oliver, Laura M	4:18:38 (15,064)	
Rule, Ally D	4:04:23 (11,520)	
Rule, Richard J	4:37:01 (19,922)	
Rumbelow, Nick A	3:12:45 (1,965)	
Rumble, Daniel F	3:15:28 (2,280)	
Rumley, Simon	5:47:34 (32,138)	
Rumohr, Marco	3:15:13 (2,255)	
Rundle, Alan	5:00:25 (25,680)	
Rundle, Christopher R	4:11:46 (13,328)	
Ruppersbery, Daniel J	3:43:02 (6,423)	
Ruprai, John	5:33:37 (30,823)	
Rusbridge, Rob	4:20:58 (15,681)	
Rusby, Philip D	3:38:58 (5,675)	
Rush, Andrew J	4:49:29 (23,110)	
Rush, Kristopher A	3:14:36 (2,182)	
Rush, Martin C	4:39:14 (20,502)	
Rush, Tom G	4:52:09 (23,786)	
Rushby, Dean	4:31:47 (18,578)	
Rushmer, Gary	3:25:51 (3,512)	
Rushovich, Athos	5:15:31 (28,423)	
Russell, Alan J	4:54:46 (24,397)	
Russell, Alex	3:54:40 (8,936)	
Russell, Andrew P	3:27:31 (3,781)	
Russell, Andrew W	4:29:49 (18,041)	
Russell, Ben R	3:27:04 (3,693)	
Russell, Brian	4:35:36 (19,571)	
Russell, Colin D	4:56:25 (24,777)	
Russell, Daniel	3:45:35 (6,911)	
Russell, Daniel J	3:50:38 (7,975)	
Russell, David L	5:31:24 (30,564)	
Russell, Dean	3:28:49 (3,977)	
Russell, Derek J	3:07:29 (1,478)	
Russell, Geoff L	4:34:40 (19,307)	
Russell, George	3:30:35 (4,269)	
Russell, Gordon	4:15:10 (14,208)	
Russell, James	3:46:30 (7,087)	
Russell, John A	4:11:50 (13,343)	
Russell, John George	2:57:11 (791)	
Russell, Joseph G	6:47:04 (34,740)	
Russell, Julian L	4:39:17 (20,513)	
Russell, Keith E	3:48:00 (7,401)	
Russell, Keith S	5:04:26 (26,445)	
Russell, Mark A	4:11:12 (13,162)	
Russell, Martyn	4:45:39 (22,121)	
Russell, Matt P	5:11:50 (27,782)	
Russell, Michael	3:20:56 (2,884)	
Russell, Mike	5:15:38 (28,445)	
Russell, Oscar	4:42:21 (21,283)	
Russell, Philip	4:33:51 (19,113)	
Russell, Phillip	3:05:46 (1,354)	
Russell, Phillip	5:10:13 (27,501)	
Russell, Robert	5:09:29 (27,360)	
Russell, Roy A	4:07:48 (12,316)	
Russell, Shaun	4:44:13 (21,772)	
Russell, Stephen F	3:30:30 (4,256)	
Russell, Steven	4:28:26 (17,678)	
Russell, Zane	5:58:10 (32,932)	
Rustler, Tobias	3:56:34 (9,478)	
Rutherford, Andrew P	4:46:39 (22,383)	
Rutherford, Dominic	3:56:47 (9,561)	
Rutherford, Simon J	3:10:16 (1,718)	
Rutland, Ashley C	5:18:54 (28,961)	
Rutland, Neil Andrew	4:21:58 (15,935)	
Rutland-Mantle, Gary	5:54:16 (32,636)	
Rutstein, Dan N	6:16:40 (33,874)	
Rutt, Dave	5:08:38 (27,203)	
Rutter, Andy G	3:36:26 (5,222)	
Rutter, Arnaud	4:28:13 (17,622)	
Rutter, Jonathan C	3:54:41 (8,940)	
Rutter, Mark	5:09:41 (27,401)	
Rutter, Matthew J	4:19:51 (15,390)	
Rutter, Neil E	4:23:15 (16,241)	
Ryan, Anthony G	3:13:39 (2,084)	
Ryan, Chris J	4:49:13 (23,024)	
Ryan, Christopher	3:38:18 (5,551)	
Ryan, Clayton M	4:52:22 (23,835)	
Ryan, Declan	4:48:06 (22,763)	
Ryan, Enda O	5:16:56 (28,634)	
Ryan, Gary	4:55:14 (24,514)	
Ryan, James T	5:33:03 (30,760)	
Ryan, John	4:16:28 (14,514)	
Ryan, Keith M	3:38:57 (5,667)	
Ryan, Lee M	3:27:58 (3,852)	
Ryan, Neil S	4:28:40 (17,740)	
Ryan, Peter James	3:21:50 (2,992)	
Ryan, Peter K	4:54:44 (24,392)	
Ryan, Sean	5:03:57 (26,374)	
Ryan, Shaun	5:05:31 (26,642)	
Ryan, Simon C	5:15:15 (28,370)	
Ryan, Tim	3:35:14 (4,997)	
Ryazantsev, Sasha A	4:59:24 (25,472)	
Ryazantsev, Vladimir V	3:15:27 (2,277)	
Rybarczuk, Douglas G	4:37:18 (19,984)	
Ryde, Carl L	2:27:45 (48)	
Ryder, Gary O	5:06:46 (26,862)	
Ryder, Mark J	3:51:17 (8,117)	
Rye, Andrew E	2:58:49 (897)	
Rye, Joseph M	2:40:14 (200)	
Ryecart, Fred W	4:07:49 (12,319)	
Rye-Florentz, Frederik	3:13:55 (2,113)	
Ryerson, Jim	5:24:48 (29,767)	
Rylah, Fred	4:28:08 (17,587)	
Ryles, Nicholas D	3:21:07 (2,903)	
Ryman, Paul	5:51:25 (32,440)	
Saadie, Gary	4:59:00 (25,386)	
Sabater, Alvaro	4:14:32 (14,037)	
Sablayrolles, Jean-François	4:08:40 (12,539)	
Sacks, Jonathan	3:03:22 (1,192)	
Sacre, Andrew	4:43:21 (21,567)	
Sacristan Sanz, Fernando	3:56:18 (9,394)	
Sadler, Adrian G	4:44:57 (21,945)	
Sadler, David	5:00:09 (25,624)	
Sadler, Derek J	4:24:12 (16,497)	
Sadler, Duncan T	3:12:53 (1,985)	
Sadler, Neil	6:16:27 (33,864)	
Sadler, Paul E	3:13:39 (2,084)	
Sadler, Paul J	5:09:04 (27,283)	
Sadler, Peter J	6:09:38 (33,543)	
Sadler, Phil L	4:40:30 (20,833)	
Sage, Neil K	5:14:00 (28,161)	
Sagebiel, Klaus	3:52:24 (8,381)	
Saggars, Peter	4:38:37 (20,333)	
Saggs, Mark A	5:09:37 (27,386)	
Sahin, Alan	3:42:37 (6,336)	
Sainsbury, Noel W	5:49:40 (32,303)	
Sainter, Andrew	5:22:41 (29,467)	
Sait, Nick R	4:12:31 (13,533)	
Saiyed, Moinuddin	6:08:26 (33,490)	
Saiz, Gabriel	2:43:35 (276)	
Saker, Andrew Mark	3:26:46 (3,645)	
Saker, Graeme A	2:52:04 (522)	
Saklow, Alex J	3:39:36 (5,776)	
Saksida, Robert	3:18:36 (2,583)	
Sala, Alberto	3:29:10 (4,033)	
Salacinski, Christopher M	4:56:18 (24,751)	
Saladin, Vincent P	4:38:44 (20,360)	
Salam, Lakhmiri	5:13:41 (28,095)	
Salamanca, Orlando	4:49:11 (23,012)	
Salas, Samuel	4:39:06 (20,465)	
Salas Ortiz, Arturo	3:39:59 (5,856)	
Salawu, Adebambo	5:47:15 (32,114)	
Sale, Nicholas J	2:57:08 (787)	
Saleem, Stefan A	5:06:34 (26,815)	
Salem, Husein	4:59:39 (25,523)	
Salem, Murtaza K	4:07:06 (12,131)	
Salerno, Gaetano	4:04:48 (11,609)	
Sales, Alexander J	3:32:02 (4,472)	
Sales, Mike Robert	5:17:57 (28,786)	
Sales, Roger J	4:56:03 (24,694)	
Salinas, Roberto	4:00:53 (10,770)	
Salisbury, Robert L	4:27:54 (17,518)	
Salkeld, Jason C	5:48:25 (32,209)	
Sallaba, Milan	3:34:06 (4,789)	
Sallows, Alan	3:21:25 (2,934)	
Salmen, Mark P	4:01:57 (11,011)	
Salmon, Alec	4:29:00 (17,829)	
Salmon, Arran B	4:45:08 (22,007)	
Salmon, Mirek	4:11:29 (13,248)	
Salmon, Nicolas	3:21:38 (2,966)	
Salmons, Malcolm D	4:27:28 (17,382)	
Salmons, Mark A	3:49:40 (7,761)	
Salmons, Neil	3:24:10 (3,292)	
Salt, Paul R	3:53:21 (8,592)	
Salt, Stephen A	4:58:38 (25,304)	
Salter, Dan P	2:55:06 (669)	
Salter, Luke	4:36:21 (19,750)	
Saltmarsh, Douglas J	6:21:48 (34,107)	
Saltmer, Matthew	3:50:17 (7,900)	
Salton, Matthew	3:26:33 (3,609)	
Salvador, Jean-Michel	3:37:29 (5,395)	
Salvador, Stephane	4:21:00 (15,692)	
Salvini, Richard M	5:09:10 (27,303)	
Salzer, Joerg	4:24:04 (16,459)	
Salzgeber, Guenter	3:23:29 (3,186)	
Samarasinghe, James	4:07:29 (12,233)	
Sambridge, Kevin John	3:19:11 (2,635)	
Sambrook, Dominic C	5:09:38 (27,392)	
Sames, Paul	4:54:45 (24,395)	
Saminipour, Kourosh	6:00:38 (33,090)	
Samkin, James P	4:40:39 (20,876)	
Sammons, Christopher M	4:35:26 (19,527)	
Sammons, Paul	4:58:18 (25,213)	
Sampathkumar, Kandasamy	4:53:41 (24,133)	
Sampson, Barry P	2:50:53 (493)	
Sampson, George A	4:59:09 (25,424)	
Sampson, Matthew P	4:00:25 (10,640)	
Sampson, Ross	3:51:01 (8,058)	
Sampson, Stuart	4:29:20 (17,932)	
Sampson, Tom	4:49:56 (23,225)	
Samra, Harjap S	3:43:16 (6,481)	
Sams, Christopher R	4:37:31 (20,042)	
Samson, Douglas W	3:54:08 (8,790)	
Samson, Mark	3:30:44 (4,288)	
Samson, Nathaniel	3:51:40 (8,203)	
Samuel, Harry J	5:09:15 (27,316)	
Samuels, Adam	4:25:56 (16,968)	
Samuels, Stephen	5:12:46 (27,939)	
Samways, Paul	3:15:19 (2,263)	
Samways, Shane A	4:24:18 (16,527)	
Samwell, Mathew	3:41:00 (6,028)	
Samyn, Dries	4:12:44 (13,587)	
San Juan, Juan Carlos	3:20:48 (2,868)	
San Martin, Orlando	3:59:18 (10,335)	
Sanchez, Ernesto	4:47:05 (22,511)	
Sanchez, Gonzalo	4:14:31 (14,032)	
Sanchez, Joe A	3:34:39 (4,905)	
Sanchez Carnerero, Blas	4:22:16 (16,017)	
Sanchez-Roselly, Juan De Dios	4:31:51 (18,592)	
Sandall, Ed	4:46:42 (22,400)	
Sandell, Bruce	3:51:13 (8,103)	
Sandeman, Edward G	4:34:32 (19,267)	
Sander, Peter	4:29:16 (17,913)	

Sandercork, Graham M 4:28:02 (17,551)
Sanders, Clive 4:18:56 (15,146)
Sanders, Gary D 4:38:18 (20,251)
Sanders, Gerald Kevin 4:20:40 (15,591)
Sanders, Keith 3:09:10 (1,636)
Sanders, Kevin D 4:48:59 (22,971)
Sanders, Mark 5:36:26 (31,117)
Sanders, Noel C 4:53:03 (23,986)
Sanders, Pete 4:37:42 (20,090)
Sanders, Phil H 4:42:03 (21,212)
Sanderson, Andy M 3:16:06 (2,339)
Sanderson, Brian J 4:14:27 (14,022)
Sanderson, Marc C 6:07:23 (33,454)
Sanderson, Nick 4:46:12 (22,248)
Sanderson, Nigel Paul 3:20:52 (2,878)
Sanderson, Robert E 4:19:36 (15,313)
Sanderson, Simon B 3:51:23 (8,136)
Sandford, Darrel 5:36:40 (31,141)
Sandford, Lee R 4:29:30 (17,967)
Sandford, Richard Paul 4:03:56 (11,428)
Sandham, David A 3:14:39 (2,188)
Sandhu, Harpreet 5:59:09 (32,997)
Sandhu, John S 3:13:33 (2,066)
Sandhu, Kelvin S 3:36:15 (5,198)
Sandroni, Gabriele 4:26:34 (17,139)
Sands, Lee 4:41:30 (21,087)
Sands, Mark 4:29:51 (18,056)
Sands, Nick 4:07:53 (12,336)
Sandy, Nick 4:26:30 (17,118)
Sangalli, Giorgio 3:23:39 (3,211)
Sangenis Salvo, Jordi 3:29:39 (4,124)
Sanger, Philip B 2:43:38 (278)
Sangha, Charanjit 4:49:39 (23,165)
Sangha, Larkhbir 4:41:51 (21,174)
Sanghera, Jas 3:25:38 (3,479)
Sanghera, Kirn K 4:56:49 (24,883)
Sangiorgio, Enrico 4:57:26 (25,016)
Sangster, Andrew P 4:43:28 (21,593)
Sanjoaquin, Pascal 4:28:27 (17,683)
Sankey, Paul W 2:39:32 (185)
Sankey, Stuart C 6:01:28 (33,140)
Sankoff, Neil 4:39:59 (20,719)
Sannino, Marino 6:14:10 (33,752)
Sanotra, Sumeet 6:01:02 (33,114)
Sanseverino, Julio César 4:26:07 (17,014)
Santarelli, Felice 3:07:05 (1,442)
Sant-Cassia, Sean F 4:00:10 (10,587)
Santiago, Joseph 3:20:41 (2,854)
Santos, José S 4:29:23 (17,945)
Santos, Luis 4:08:21 (12,469)
Santosh, Jamie 6:48:11 (34,772)
Sapsford, James 3:15:54 (2,326)
Saqui, Glenn A 2:36:51 (137)
Sara, Charlie 5:14:11 (28,192)
Saracino, Massimo 4:47:36 (22,629)
Saraga, Mauro 4:26:57 (17,246)
Sarai, Jass Singh 3:51:11 (8,093)
Saraiva, Artur 4:26:26 (17,093)
Sardu, Pier Paolo 5:09:46 (27,420)
Sarfati, Jean-Charles 3:20:27 (2,822)
Sargeant, Ben P 4:43:52 (21,681)
Sargeant, Christopher N 5:23:39 (29,607)
Sargeant, Jonathan D 3:21:14 (2,912)
Sargeant, Jonathan D 4:48:50 (22,928)
Sargeant, Robert J 3:37:42 (5,440)
Sargeant, Rodney 4:34:44 (19,326)
Sargeant, Steve G 4:09:10 (12,652)
Sargent, Kevin 5:39:00 (31,395)
Sargent, Lee 5:31:27 (30,574)
Sargent, Neil 4:23:41 (16,362)
Sargent, Rob 3:30:01 (4,180)
Sargood, John P 3:47:20 (7,254)
Sarjant, Alan J 4:20:48 (15,636)
Sarkar, Bidesh 3:47:29 (7,285)
Sarling, Andrew J 4:30:29 (18,222)
Sarr, Omar 3:31:00 (4,331)
Sarson, Peter 3:34:24 (4,853)
Sartori, Mark 4:46:25 (22,324)
Sartoris, Stephen 4:35:38 (19,574)
Satchell, Peter James 3:57:39 (9,826)
Sato, Atsushi 2:09:16 (8)
Satya, Prabhu 3:49:40 (7,761)
Sauer, Hans 3:50:20 (7,911)
Sauer, Uli 3:35:31 (5,049)
Sauerbier, Hans-Josef 4:39:07 (20,467)
Saunders, Andrew 3:20:37 (2,842)
Saunders, Chris J 4:48:26 (22,836)
Saunders, Darren 4:18:56 (15,146)
Saunders, David A 3:06:53 (1,428)
Saunders, Joss 4:11:22 (13,214)
Saunders, Justin G 4:44:08 (21,756)
Saunders, Ken 6:47:14 (34,748)
Saunders, Kevin J 4:42:12 (21,249)
Saunders, Malcolm J 4:01:31 (10,919)
Saunders, Mark 4:12:44 (13,587)
Saunders, Mark A 2:54:14 (612)
Saunders, Mark D 3:58:33 (10,114)
Saunders, Mark J 4:35:28 (19,534)
Saunders, Peter J 3:47:59 (7,396)
Saunders, Richard P 3:55:04 (9,050)
Saunders, Robert J 4:43:18 (21,543)
Saunders, Stefan P 4:26:08 (17,020)
Saunders, Tim R 5:06:06 (26,745)
Saunderson, Eric M 5:18:29 (28,867)
Saunderson, Lee 3:45:31 (6,899)
Saurin, Zak 3:25:38 (3,479)
Saut, Dominique 3:53:33 (8,634)
Savage, Anthony K 4:34:06 (19,172)
Savage, Brian 3:31:57 (4,462)
Savage, Colin 4:52:56 (23,960)
Savage, Gerard 3:38:28 (5,581)
Savage, James S 2:36:48 (136)
Savage, Mark T 3:24:54 (3,391)
Savage, Martin 3:30:04 (4,187)
Savage, Paul 4:04:33 (11,556)
Savage, Peter C 4:31:28 (18,494)
Savage, Ross D 4:31:56 (18,618)
Savage, Thomas J 3:03:22 (1,192)
Savani, Jitu 6:01:47 (33,156)
Savery, Andrew 2:35:00 (115)
Savill, Keith 3:54:19 (8,844)
Savill, Neil 3:15:23 (2,271)
Savill, Shayne J 5:17:18 (28,683)
Saville, Graham 4:51:57 (23,741)
Saville, Robert D 4:27:47 (17,479)
Savory, Harry J 4:11:08 (13,149)
Savoya, Remy 3:46:11 (7,014)
Sawa, Peter F 4:59:33 (25,508)
Sawbridge, Mark 4:52:27 (23,856)
Sawicki, Mike H 5:51:37 (32,458)
Sawko, Peter W 4:32:38 (18,801)
Sawyer, Duncan 3:36:57 (5,309)
Sawyer, Greg 5:09:16 (27,321)
Sawyer, James R 4:15:58 (14,387)
Sawyer, Keith J 4:10:33 (12,994)
Sawyer, Nicholas C 4:58:35 (25,290)
Sawyer, Rob J 5:24:35 (29,745)
Saxby, Graham 5:48:39 (32,233)
Saxby, Roy 5:32:32 (30,696)
Sayer, Andrew 3:24:53 (3,388)
Sayer, Darren R 4:03:26 (11,317)
Sayer, Timothy M 4:58:09 (25,179)
Sayers, Alan M 5:49:01 (32,251)
Scaife, Ian 5:24:44 (29,756)
Scalelli, Serge 5:02:58 (26,204)
Scales, Ben 4:26:48 (17,205)
Scales, Mark 5:57:25 (32,867)
Scales, Robin 4:27:28 (17,382)
Scally, John R 4:19:34 (15,303)
Scally, Sean J 6:47:21 (34,751)
Scamans, Oliver M 4:05:16 (11,724)
Scambler, Peter J 3:36:24 (5,215)
Scammell, Steve J 3:42:36 (6,330)
Scanlan, Tim E 5:05:13 (26,595)
Scanlon, Andy 4:19:44 (15,348)
Scannell, Andrew J 5:12:21 (27,861)
Scannell, Nicholas 4:25:02 (16,719)
Scaramanga, Peter R 4:52:58 (23,970)
Scarborough, Glenn 5:23:46 (29,622)
Scarborough, Linton J 2:54:45 (646)
Scarff, Matthew D 5:36:07 (31,088)
Scarle, Andrew 4:24:29 (16,567)
Scarlett, Laurence S 3:07:37 (1,493)
Scarpati, Pasquale 3:15:24 (2,274)
Scarr, Richard C 4:10:14 (12,916)
Scarrott, Ian J 3:43:46 (6,580)
Scarrow, Paul C 4:56:43 (24,858)
Scerensen, Jens Peter H 4:14:06 (13,931)
Schade, Marko 4:02:10 (11,057)
Schaefer, Alexander 3:57:26 (9,750)
Schafer, Chris 3:49:57 (7,823)
Schandl, Werner 3:43:11 (6,469)
Scharf, Karl-Heinz 3:46:18 (7,045)
Scharmacher, Stephen 5:28:25 (30,204)
Schauenburg, Cristoph 3:28:48 (3,973)
Scheepers, Dawie 4:11:30 (13,255)
Scheer, Andrew D 3:30:43 (4,284)
Scheidig, Thomas 4:19:19 (15,235)
Scheinert, Stefan 4:20:58 (15,681)
Schenker, Stefan 5:18:50 (28,947)
Schepens, Dirk 3:28:13 (3,888)
Schepisi, Oliver 3:24:10 (3,292)
Scherer, Charlie G 4:04:26 (11,530)
Scherg, Andreas 3:36:01 (5,158)
Schiebler, Daniel 3:14:01 (2,124)
Schiffer-Harte, Benjamin G 4:33:08 (18,928)
Schilling, Frederic 4:00:43 (10,724)
Schilling, William F 3:55:04 (9,050)
Schiltz, Stephen L 7:13:00 (35,082)
Schimatschek, Josef 4:14:14 (13,971)
Schinaia, Cosimo 4:37:56 (20,149)
Schindler, David 6:53:19 (34,864)
Schínheit-Kenn, Ursula 4:07:36 (12,255)
Schippel, John 6:52:59 (34,861)
Schlagman, Aron 5:13:04 (27,998)
Schloder, Kurt 3:12:27 (1,926)
Schmaedt, Knut 4:20:41 (15,596)
Schmidt, Christian 3:37:33 (5,412)
Schmidt, Lars 4:41:13 (21,017)
Schmidt, Wolfgang 3:47:55 (7,377)
Schmitz, Michael 5:18:42 (28,916)
Schmitz, Nicolas 4:15:50 (14,357)
Schneider, David Neil 4:01:11 (10,831)
Schneider, Josef 3:41:54 (6,186)
Schneider, Michael 4:11:55 (13,362)
Schneider, Thomas 3:55:20 (9,117)
Schnell, Ryan A 5:08:56 (27,258)
Schofield, James 3:16:18 (2,358)
Schofield, Paul 5:17:25 (28,700)
Schofield, Paul P 4:17:18 (14,717)
Schofield, Robert A 4:11:14 (13,168)
Scholer, Dieter 5:01:01 (25,815)
Scholes, Michael A 3:07:54 (1,517)
Scholes, Roderick 4:33:02 (18,906)
Schollhammer, Jeffrey 6:23:19 (34,164)
Scholte, Paul 4:01:41 (10,965)
Scholz, Lothar 3:27:30 (3,778)
Scholz, Sebastian 4:52:01 (23,753)
Schooling, Robert J 5:00:59 (25,805)
Schouest, Clay M 3:23:21 (3,169)
Schrell, Torsten 3:21:46 (2,980)
Schreuder, Fred B 3:51:26 (8,150)
Schroeter-Janssen, Helge 3:52:15 (8,347)
Schropsdorff, Gerno 3:47:49 (7,357)
Schubert, Dave 3:04:49 (1,294)
Schultheis, Markus 3:33:19 (4,654)
Schulz, Hans-Juergen 5:41:34 (31,636)
Schumann, Paul 2:59:04 (925)
Schwartz, Jeremy 3:46:27 (7,077)
Schwarz, Andreas 3:02:14 (1,134)
Schwarz, Gerardo 4:58:03 (25,148)
Schwegmann, David 3:57:32 (9,781)
Schweinberger, Bernhard 5:38:56 (31,386)
Schwendinger, Hans-Joerg 3:42:15 (6,258)
Schwenzer, Michael 4:18:01 (14,891)
Sciver, Richard J 4:06:38 (12,032)
Scobie, Duncan H 2:50:32 (482)
Scoble, Neil 4:41:26 (21,065)
Scollard, Donncha J 4:03:50 (11,403)
Scollin, Nigel R 4:20:28 (15,548)
Scope, Philip 4:05:12 (11,711)
Scopelliti, Massimo 3:42:18 (6,268)
Scopes, John A 4:10:53 (13,084)
Scotland, Jason 8:04:07 (35,320)
Scotney, Michael R 3:36:55 (5,301)
Scott, Aaron 5:31:33 (30,587)
Scott, Adam C 4:43:35 (21,621)
Scott, Alan L 5:04:36 (26,481)
Scott, Alasdair 4:39:28 (20,571)

Scott, Alex J 5:01:55 (25,996)
Scott, Andrew J 5:29:24 (30,319)
Scott, Andrew James Thomas 3:45:45 (6,937)
Scott, Anthony C 4:12:50 (13,613)
Scott, Brian C 5:13:15 (28,029)
Scott, Christopher E 3:29:07 (4,030)
Scott, Clive R 4:34:13 (19,199)
Scott, Darren M 5:35:49 (31,052)
Scott, David 3:27:26 (3,759)
Scott, David 4:53:55 (24,204)
Scott, David R 3:53:56 (8,734)
Scott, Gareth 4:31:28 (18,494)
Scott, Gary 3:53:15 (8,572)
Scott, Gary L 3:40:49 (6,003)
Scott, Hamish A 4:28:44 (17,754)
Scott, Ian 3:13:11 (2,026)
Scott, Ian S 3:45:26 (6,878)
Scott, Ian T 3:54:23 (8,858)
Scott, James A 3:49:35 (7,746)
Scott, Jim Anthony 3:35:07 (4,981)
Scott, John W 5:56:34 (32,796)
Scott, Jonathan A 2:44:10 (288)
Scott, Keith 6:09:10 (33,520)
Scott, Kevin 3:50:31 (7,951)
Scott, Lee C 3:33:24 (4,666)
Scott, Lloyd E 7:56:33 (35,305)
Scott, Mark Anthony 4:47:29 (22,594)
Scott, Matthew 4:20:16 (15,502)
Scott, Michael J 6:52:28 (34,856)
Scott, Michael K 4:05:58 (11,875)
Scott, Nathan P 3:21:49 (2,985)
Scott, Neil S 3:12:57 (1,998)
Scott, Oliver J 4:32:32 (18,762)
Scott, Peter 4:41:37 (21,122)
Scott, Robin 3:14:06 (2,135)
Scott, Roy G 2:39:36 (187)
Scott, Samuel F 4:47:55 (22,712)
Scott, Simon 5:56:29 (32,791)
Scott, Stephen M 3:33:20 (4,657)
Scott-Buccleuch, James 3:03:31 (1,203)
Scott-Harden, Oliver C 4:26:57 (17,246)
Scott-Mullen, Caine 3:57:19 (9,712)
Scott-Smith, Jason 5:49:10 (32,265)
Scourfield, Keith R 4:09:10 (12,652)
Scourfield, Tom D 3:54:47 (8,964)
Scovell, Keith 3:10:36 (1,745)
Scragg, Peter J 4:10:08 (12,892)
Scrase, Paul 4:08:00 (12,359)
Scrase, Russell J 4:20:54 (15,662)
Scrivener, Chris 3:00:39 (1,028)
Scrivener, Russell J 4:07:37 (12,259)
Scrutton, Claire B 3:42:50 (6,385)
Seaberg, Alan 3:55:41 (9,211)
Seabourne, Ben 4:38:08 (20,211)
Seabrook, Jonathan D 3:56:58 (9,610)
Seager, John K 4:28:30 (17,697)
Seager, Richard J 5:50:51 (32,406)
Seal, Adrian P 4:09:34 (12,741)
Sealey, Jonathan R 4:43:46 (21,659)
Sealey, Robert M 6:10:05 (33,565)
Sealey, Stefan 5:30:56 (30,515)
Seaman, Martyn J 4:51:05 (23,511)
Seaman, Oliver R 5:25:19 (29,833)
Sear, Michael C 5:18:02 (28,799)
Sear, Paul A 4:55:43 (24,620)
Searcy, Angus 4:00:08 (10,580)
Searil, David 4:31:47 (18,578)
Searle, Daniel M 4:26:10 (17,031)
Searle, David A 3:54:28 (8,880)
Searle, John Richard 3:43:02 (6,423)
Searle, Lachlan 5:26:00 (29,939)
Searle, Michael 4:09:13 (12,663)
Searle, Michael A 4:36:09 (19,712)
Searle, Ronald E 3:07:19 (1,459)
Searle, Yann N 5:04:39 (26,485)
Sears, Richard J 3:58:25 (10,071)
Sears, Tony 5:44:51 (31,919)
Seaton, Richard M 4:04:42 (11,586)
Seatter, Anton M 3:31:05 (4,341)
Sebastiani, Jacopo 3:57:41 (9,842)
Sebastien, Labisse 3:48:17 (7,460)
Seberry, Mark K 4:13:12 (13,712)
Sebire, Pascal 3:36:55 (5,301)
Secci, Giorgio 4:11:16 (13,179)
Secker, Christopher R 4:47:04 (22,501)
Secker, Theo 3:43:01 (6,422)
Seddon, David A 4:16:36 (14,553)
Seddon, Jonathan F 3:53:06 (8,532)
Seddon, Paul 3:09:50 (1,692)
Sedge, Martyn J 3:05:02 (1,306)
Sedgwick, Glenn C 4:34:08 (19,179)
Sedgwick, John 3:46:40 (7,131)
Sedgwick, Robert 4:51:57 (23,741)
Sedman, Michael W 5:23:09 (29,540)
Sedman, Nigel H 3:25:57 (3,523)
See, Jason 5:29:29 (30,328)
Seeck, Stephan 4:14:47 (14,108)
Seed, Daniel Anthony 4:39:58 (20,710)
Seehawer, Michael 3:09:37 (1,669)
Seelandt, Frank 3:53:16 (8,575)
Seelochan, David 3:34:04 (4,778)
Sefton, Kevin 4:55:04 (24,468)
Sefton, Robert J 4:56:34 (24,820)
Segrott, Alan J 3:27:38 (3,807)
Seidel, Uwe 3:38:17 (5,548)
Seivewright, Andrew 4:10:50 (13,071)
Sek, Matt 5:29:50 (30,379)
Selby, Adam 5:10:25 (27,535)
Selby, Mark G 4:21:18 (15,764)
Selby, Paul 5:42:57 (31,765)
Selby, Robin C 3:52:47 (8,461)
Seldon, Keith 4:59:22 (25,467)
Selemba, Andy S 5:00:22 (25,669)
Self, Richard J 2:59:08 (929)
Selfe, Christopher 3:42:49 (6,380)
Sell, Charlie 4:27:37 (17,417)
Sell, Matthew J 4:31:59 (18,629)
Sell, Richard L 3:33:45 (4,713)
Sellars, Ashley I 4:57:56 (25,127)
Sellay, Abdul 4:23:22 (16,268)
Seller, Mark J 5:25:42 (29,891)
Sellers, Calvin 4:24:27 (16,560)
Sellers, Ian R 4:10:48 (13,064)
Sellers, Mark 3:34:45 (4,916)
Sellers, Mark J 4:49:20 (23,064)
Sellers, Michael N 3:33:23 (4,663)
Sellers, Peter 5:26:33 (29,998)
Sellers, Steven R 5:55:31 (32,727)
Sellick, Jo 5:09:09 (27,298)
Sellick, Phil 4:30:23 (18,202)
Sellwood, Michael J 4:26:42 (17,182)
Selman, Andrew 4:19:10 (15,203)
Selman, Andrew J 3:50:55 (8,042)
Selves, Stephen J 4:31:44 (18,560)
Selway, Richard P 3:15:42 (2,305)
Semple, Graeme W 4:34:35 (19,285)
Senaldi, Giorgio 3:51:40 (8,203)
Seneviratna, Dineth A 3:58:56 (10,233)
Senker, Jonathan 3:34:47 (4,925)
Senkiw, Walter 4:29:58 (18,088)
Senni, Pierpaolo 3:36:59 (5,318)
Sensicle, Luke J 4:55:50 (24,649)
Sensier, James J 3:52:33 (8,410)
Sepio, Jean Marc 5:02:25 (26,098)
Serdet, Stuart P 4:50:43 (23,428)
Serrano Ceballos, Angel 3:32:30 (4,543)
Serrant, Frederic O 3:41:31 (6,125)
Sese Poisat, Rafael 4:30:45 (18,295)
Setchell, Alex 4:43:08 (21,500)
Setford, John A 4:39:36 (20,613)
Seth, Mohit 3:46:17 (7,037)
Sethard Wright, Matt G 4:52:50 (23,935)
Severa, Tonino 3:38:54 (5,654)
Severs, Jonathan R 4:11:14 (13,168)
Seward, Len 4:49:44 (23,187)
Sewell, Andrew P 3:32:53 (4,596)
Sewell, Mark L 5:28:08 (30,168)
Sewter, Lance 5:15:15 (28,370)
Sexon, Nathan 4:51:23 (23,585)
Sexton, Jonathan N 3:54:58 (9,010)
Sexton, Stephen T 7:44:39 (35,278)
Seymour, Adam J 4:38:32 (20,307)
Seymour, Ashley 5:42:41 (31,737)
Seymour, Ben 4:45:21 (22,045)
Seymour, Craig D 5:57:24 (32,866)
Seymour, Matthew A 4:47:58 (22,728)
Sforza, Michele 5:29:25 (30,321)
Shackleford, Mark J 4:58:09 (25,179)
Shackleton, Andrew I 3:17:25 (2,478)
Shackleton, Martin 3:23:20 (3,163)
Shackleton, Paul R 3:30:32 (4,262)
Shackman, Alistair J 6:12:45 (33,678)
Shadick, James J 4:20:54 (15,662)
Shadrack, Mark A 5:33:29 (30,802)
Shadwell, Michael T 3:13:06 (2,016)
Shadwell, Scott 4:42:04 (21,215)
Shafier, Alex 4:45:52 (22,183)
Shafier, Lawrence E 3:07:44 (1,506)
Shafto, Ainslee C 3:05:55 (1,367)
Shah, Akhil 5:38:48 (31,372)
Shah, Amit 4:19:42 (15,340)
Shah, Binoi 3:40:07 (5,881)
Shah, Dhaval 3:33:32 (4,682)
Shah, Dilan P 4:29:17 (17,919)
Shah, Harshad 6:24:23 (34,209)
Shah, Kavit 4:08:49 (12,577)
Shah, Kirti R 4:24:50 (16,663)
Shah, Neil Niraj 5:45:36 (31,985)
Shah, Nishal 4:44:43 (21,890)
Shah, Rajen 5:14:45 (28,272)
Shah, Ritesh 7:17:51 (35,125)
Shah, Romal 3:42:41 (6,352)
Shah, Vivek S 5:13:03 (27,995)
Shaid, Wasim 7:12:45 (35,080)
Shaikh, Haroon 3:37:43 (5,445)
Shailes, Joseph J 4:48:50 (22,928)
Shalders, Michael 3:43:52 (6,607)
Shand, Alan J 4:07:23 (12,209)
Shandley, Adrian P 4:04:04 (11,463)
Shanks, Scott 4:15:35 (14,303)
Shanley, John 5:49:44 (32,308)
Shannon, Jack 4:12:45 (13,593)
Shannon, James A 4:58:28 (25,258)
Shannon, Kevin J 4:34:14 (19,204)
Shapland, Tim 4:40:43 (20,890)
Shapleski, Oliver Richard 3:56:23 (9,423)
Shardlow, Richard A 2:55:22 (692)
Sharland, Richard J 3:19:21 (2,661)
Sharland, Roger J 3:36:36 (5,255)
Sharma, Neil 6:16:51 (33,878)
Sharma, Pankaj 4:46:32 (22,355)
Sharma, Rishi 4:45:03 (21,981)
Sharma, Sanjai 2:56:48 (761)
Sharman, Ben 3:22:56 (3,123)
Sharman, Glen W 3:06:06 (1,381)
Sharman, Ian M 2:43:33 (274)
Sharp, Andrew 4:25:54 (16,961)
Sharp, Andrew 4:38:18 (20,251)
Sharp, Christopher 5:45:36 (31,985)
Sharp, David 4:52:52 (23,940)
Sharp, David E 5:09:24 (27,347)
Sharp, Ian 4:46:12 (22,248)
Sharp, Langley C 3:33:50 (4,729)
Sharp, Matt A 3:53:45 (8,692)
Sharp, Michael J 5:28:40 (30,232)
Sharp, Nicholas 4:00:53 (10,770)
Sharp, Timothy 4:06:08 (11,910)
Sharp, Tony 7:33:01 (35,239)
Sharpe, Chris 3:51:21 (8,128)
Sharpe, Christopher 3:33:29 (4,675)
Sharpe, Darren 3:03:28 (1,199)
Sharpe, David W 5:35:01 (30,972)
Sharpe, Ian 4:56:39 (24,843)
Sharpe, Keith 3:33:49 (4,726)
Sharpe, Paul J 2:49:35 (447)
Sharpe, Richard W 4:13:13 (13,717)
Sharpe, Sam P 2:54:24 (626)
Sharples, Matthew Edward James 4:21:37 (15,849)
Sharples, Richard W 3:28:25 (3,915)
Sharran, Nasser 5:12:51 (27,958)
Sharrock, John K 4:36:13 (19,729)
Sharrod, Martin 5:31:16 (30,555)
Shaswar, Mashkhall 3:39:32 (5,764)
Shatford, John Donald 4:18:59 (15,156)
Shave, Adam R 4:26:34 (17,139)
Shave, Martin 5:08:34 (27,187)
Shaw, Alan 7:27:13 (35,199)
Shaw, Alistair P 3:19:15 (2,645)
Shaw, Andrew J 5:45:25 (31,965)

Shaw, Andrew M	4:13:09 (13,695)	Sheppard, David	4:15:56 (14,374)	Short, Michael D	3:52:48 (8,465)
Shaw, Anthony J	3:53:57 (8,738)	Sheppard, Edward H	4:52:23 (23,838)	Short, Richard G	4:32:49 (18,850)
Shaw, Anthony T	3:42:38 (6,341)	Sheppard, Edward Y	4:29:54 (18,071)	Short, Simon J	5:19:41 (29,061)
Shaw, Barry	3:59:19 (10,340)	Sheppard, Jonathan N	7:36:28 (35,255)	Shortall, James N	4:43:25 (21,583)
Shaw, Chris J	3:36:50 (5,283)	Sheppard, Justin D	4:51:34 (23,640)	Shortall, Martin P	3:50:12 (7,881)
Shaw, Craig I	4:57:38 (25,057)	Sheppard, Leon G	4:19:58 (15,419)	Shorter, Lee	6:32:41 (34,467)
Shaw, Darren A	4:36:26 (19,777)	Sheppard, Michael D	4:37:35 (20,065)	Shotbolt, Adrian W	3:42:05 (6,230)
Shaw, David A	3:23:49 (3,239)	Sheppard, Philip J	4:36:19 (19,742)	Shoults, Will C	3:53:29 (8,621)
Shaw, David K	4:33:39 (19,060)	Sheppard, Raymond G	5:03:31 (26,287)	Showell, David	3:41:59 (6,200)
Shaw, Gareth	4:46:54 (22,451)	Sheppard, Richard	4:38:10 (20,221)	Showell, Steven D	4:46:39 (22,383)
Shaw, Geoff	3:34:03 (4,770)	Sheppard, Stephen	4:52:16 (23,814)	Shrimpton, Benjamin J	2:56:27 (744)
Shaw, Gerry A	3:17:07 (2,444)	Sheppard, Thomas	4:07:43 (12,290)	Shrimpton, Daniel J	2:55:01 (663)
Shaw, Ian	6:07:36 (33,464)	Sheppard, Timothy N	5:11:07 (27,662)	Shrubsole, Andy G	4:54:12 (24,259)
Shaw, James	4:36:20 (19,748)	Sheraton, Matt D	5:45:00 (31,928)	Shrubsole, Ben	5:42:53 (31,756)
Shaw, Jody M	4:23:36 (16,334)	Shergill, Darren	5:17:27 (28,710)	Shuck, Steve P	3:14:05 (2,132)
Shaw, Jon D	5:21:11 (29,254)	Sheridan, Chris	3:47:29 (7,285)	Shulman, Robert I	3:03:52 (1,231)
Shaw, Lee A	5:03:40 (26,321)	Sheridan, Gerard	5:22:20 (29,408)	Shulver, Edward J	3:56:27 (9,446)
Shaw, Luke Joshua James	4:09:56 (12,840)	Sheridan, Mark	5:24:51 (29,775)	Shulver, Roderick L	5:33:51 (30,851)
Shaw, Michael	5:31:31 (30,584)	Sheridan, Pat	5:07:58 (27,082)	Shurlock, Matthew P	3:21:56 (3,003)
Shaw, Mike	3:41:48 (6,167)	Sheridan, Philip O	3:05:21 (1,326)	Shute, Rupert N	2:38:33 (166)
Shaw, Neil M	3:38:00 (5,489)	Sheriffs, Iain N	3:47:29 (7,285)	Shutt, Alistair	4:13:19 (13,752)
Shaw, Paul	5:12:30 (27,895)	Sherman, Adam	4:42:55 (21,450)	Shutt, James R	4:33:11 (18,939)
Shaw, Paul A	4:49:56 (23,225)	Sherman, Howard	4:36:23 (19,766)	Shuttle, Jamie	3:42:15 (6,258)
Shaw, Robert	5:53:18 (32,572)	Sherpa, Jangbu	3:32:19 (4,518)	Shuttlewood, Andrew	4:25:16 (16,778)
Shaw, Robert D	4:18:54 (15,133)	Sherratt, Adam	3:35:46 (5,109)	Shuttleworth, Colin	3:25:07 (3,410)
Shaw, Steven	3:59:08 (10,290)	Sherratt, Andrew J	4:46:09 (22,236)	Shuttleworth, Craig C	4:23:25 (16,281)
Shaw, Steven P	3:59:20 (10,345)	Sherratt, Craig D	4:09:47 (12,800)	Shuttleworth, Ian D	4:38:03 (20,179)
Shaw, Stuart A	2:50:42 (488)	Sherrell, Paul	5:26:00 (29,939)	Shuttleworth, Kris	4:00:02 (10,552)
Shaw, Tim	4:13:55 (13,887)	Sherriff, Mark D	2:49:19 (436)	Sibanda, Nkosiyazi	2:19:02 (17)
Shaw, Timothy J	4:31:18 (18,438)	Sherring, Justin E	4:22:56 (16,172)	Sibbald, Andrew	4:24:16 (16,517)
Shawe, David J	4:11:36 (13,284)	Sherry, Dominic	4:41:21 (21,048)	Sibbald, Terry	6:09:06 (33,518)
Shayler, David C	3:46:13 (7,023)	Sherwin, Mark G	4:08:33 (12,513)	Sibbons, Paul D	4:34:20 (19,226)
Shea, Nicholas J	3:14:58 (2,228)	Sherwood, Adrian T	3:23:53 (3,246)	Sibley, Kevin	3:45:46 (6,941)
Sheahan, Alan E	4:41:30 (21,087)	Sherwood, Malcolm S	5:28:34 (30,215)	Sibley, Neil	3:19:13 (2,640)
Sheard, Bryan A	4:28:37 (17,730)	Shewan, John	3:38:37 (5,609)	Sibley, Paul W	3:16:02 (2,337)
Sheard, Steven P	3:29:47 (4,150)	Shewry, Christopher J	5:16:04 (28,508)	Sidat, Mohammed	4:10:37 (13,010)
Shearer, Paul	5:50:41 (32,393)	Shickell, Matt J	3:30:52 (4,305)	Siddall, Mark I	4:47:44 (22,663)
Sheath, Peter N	4:00:51 (10,755)	Shiel, Paul E	3:14:29 (2,171)	Siddall, Paul D	5:01:21 (25,885)
Sheehan, Adrian	4:25:10 (16,757)	Shield, Andrew T	5:20:31 (29,155)	Siddell, Steven	3:33:03 (4,617)
Sheehan, Andrew	4:33:21 (18,991)	Shield, Jerry M	2:55:12 (680)	Siddens, John	2:41:33 (225)
Sheehan, Paul Kelley	3:10:06 (1,710)	Shields, Dominic J	3:44:15 (6,673)	Sidders, Andrew J	3:41:16 (6,084)
Sheehan, Philip W	4:06:57 (12,094)	Shields, James	6:21:32 (34,094)	Siddiqi, Abdul Q	4:12:42 (13,575)
Sheehan, Tim G	3:35:16 (5,002)	Shields, Keith T	4:11:26 (13,238)	Siddique, Abubakor	4:36:49 (19,870)
Sheen, Richard	3:28:36 (3,938)	Shields, Spencer R	5:29:47 (30,370)	Siddon, Tony J	3:54:41 (8,940)
Sheen, Rory	5:06:10 (26,756)	Shields, Timothy J	3:25:21 (3,434)	Siderfin, Justin Frank	3:22:04 (3,022)
Sheen, William G	4:16:22 (14,486)	Shields, Vincent N	4:56:49 (24,883)	Sidgwick, David	3:25:45 (3,494)
Sheera, Navdeep S	4:49:16 (23,042)	Shigeki, Yamauchi	3:20:38 (2,845)	Sidhu, Rajdeep	6:25:00 (34,229)
Sheerin, John	3:50:00 (7,833)	Shihab, Zane	4:40:45 (20,898)	Sidhu, Satvinder	5:38:26 (31,320)
Sheils, Thomas J	4:28:19 (17,651)	Shimmin, Robert Joseph	3:31:47 (4,434)	Sidley, David Mark	4:44:57 (21,945)
Sheldon, Paul	5:27:54 (30,138)	Shin, Kyung Woo	4:47:41 (22,647)	Siebler, Andreas	4:12:04 (13,405)
Sheldon, Toby H	6:25:02 (34,231)	Shingadia, Deepak	4:52:54 (23,951)	Siegel, Matt	3:13:33 (2,066)
Shelford, Mark J	4:55:40 (24,608)	Shingler, Marcus R	5:47:01 (32,095)	Siegfried, John S	5:05:37 (26,662)
Shell, David	4:25:52 (16,951)	Shingler, Matthew	5:18:21 (28,846)	Sienkiewicz, Marek	3:42:10 (6,246)
Shelley, Alan W	6:05:13 (33,350)	Shinn, Andrew D	3:27:52 (3,834)	Siesenop, Frank	3:23:18 (3,160)
Shelley, Neil D	3:39:16 (5,723)	Shinn, Ian A	4:40:27 (20,822)	Sievers, Stephan	3:51:59 (8,273)
Shelley, Peter M	3:57:12 (9,673)	Ship, Gareth P	4:42:39 (21,373)	Siffre, Christian	2:58:51 (906)
Shelley, Richard N	3:07:46 (1,508)	Shipley, Adrian J	4:10:53 (13,084)	Siguenza Hernandez, Pedro A	3:58:42 (10,162)
Shelton, Ben	4:53:44 (24,152)	Shipley, David H	5:05:24 (26,625)	Sigurdsson, Benedikt	3:32:44 (4,578)
Shelton, Chris A	5:20:24 (29,142)	Shipley, Peter D	3:52:49 (8,471)	Sigurgeirsson, Petur	4:05:47 (11,838)
Shelton, Richard J	4:29:42 (18,016)	Shipman, Alan	3:42:02 (6,218)	Sikka, Charanpal S	6:27:00 (34,324)
Shelton, Stuart M	4:48:17 (22,804)	Shipman, Ryan A	3:08:20 (1,554)	Silcock, Ross	4:05:03 (11,665)
Shemming, Mark A	5:02:55 (26,197)	Shipp, Anthony	5:19:26 (29,027)	Silcock, Stephen M	4:11:44 (13,320)
Shemoon, David L	4:05:49 (11,847)	Shipton, Edward J	4:36:50 (19,881)	Silk, Elliott J	4:41:25 (21,058)
Shephard, Steve	6:34:18 (34,507)	Shipton, Stewart J	4:31:27 (18,487)	Silk, James	3:34:15 (4,819)
Shepheard, Paul J	4:08:51 (12,585)	Shipway, Kris S	5:06:51 (26,877)	Sillett, Garry J	4:10:37 (13,010)
Shepherd, Alan G	5:23:51 (29,630)	Shipway, Richard M	3:19:26 (2,674)	Sillett, Ian M	3:26:45 (3,642)
Shepherd, Andrew	4:39:52 (20,685)	Shirazi, Seyed	6:08:33 (33,496)	Sillitoe, Michael	4:48:30 (22,851)
Shepherd, Christopher R	3:54:05 (8,776)	Shires, Paul M	5:07:41 (27,042)	Silsbury-Basey, Russell D	6:00:00 (33,051)
Shepherd, Darren	4:35:55 (19,656)	Shirley, Dean A	3:56:17 (9,383)	Silva, César M	4:36:59 (19,914)
Shepherd, Douglas	4:55:51 (24,653)	Shirley, Glen R	4:56:03 (24,694)	Silva, James A	5:17:45 (28,757)
Shepherd, Gary J	5:04:54 (26,526)	Shoebridge, Christopher J	3:48:58 (7,610)	Silva, Joao	4:10:32 (12,989)
Shepherd, Gavin	5:11:05 (27,657)	Shoefield, Ross M	3:55:41 (9,211)	Silva, Mario Augusto	3:26:37 (3,621)
Shepherd, Jacob	3:57:56 (9,912)	Shone, Peter R	4:44:23 (21,817)	Silva, Ruy	4:47:52 (22,693)
Shepherd, John D	4:32:32 (18,762)	Shoobert, James	4:27:47 (17,479)	Silvani, Christian P	3:36:10 (5,185)
Shepherd, Mark D	3:08:09 (1,538)	Shore, Daniel J	3:54:20 (8,847)	Silvennoinen, Janne	4:34:29 (19,257)
Shepherd, Roger K	5:08:42 (27,212)	Shore, Karl	4:50:29 (23,368)	Silverthorn, Kevin R	3:24:47 (3,380)
Shepherd, Trevor	3:53:35 (8,644)	Shorrock, Lee T	5:31:45 (30,611)	Silvester, Adam J	3:18:49 (2,604)
Shepherd, Trevor J	5:26:40 (30,011)	Short, Andrew P	4:32:24 (18,728)	Silvester, Carl L	5:08:52 (27,245)
Shepley, Chris A	4:46:42 (22,400)	Short, Arthur V	3:14:22 (2,160)	Silvester, Neil	5:42:10 (31,646)
Shepley, Tim C	3:55:38 (9,203)	Short, Chris T	3:40:56 (6,019)	Silvey, Melvin	3:12:51 (1,981)
Sheppard, Andrew	3:46:02 (6,994)	Short, Graeme	3:39:25 (5,747)	Silvey, Michael A	5:26:13 (29,957)
Sheppard, Andrew	5:26:56 (30,045)	Short, Kevin	3:16:40 (2,403)	Sim, Andrew	3:34:05 (4,783)
Sheppard, Bill H	4:05:11 (11,703)	Short, Mark A	5:36:38 (31,136)	Sim, Paul	4:32:18 (18,706)

Sim, Richard A	4:19:31	(15,292)
Simajchl, Erich	4:02:08	(11,048)
Simart, Jacques	3:33:05	(4,622)
Simcock, Andy	3:47:24	(7,265)
Sime, Andrew J	4:30:30	(18,228)
Simkins, Mark	4:42:23	(21,297)
Simkins, Paul J	4:31:59	(18,629)
Simlett, John	4:12:29	(13,518)
Simmonds, Jon D	4:34:40	(19,307)
Simmonds, Kevin	6:01:28	(33,140)
Simmonds, Paul	5:05:51	(26,705)
Simmonds, Rob F	3:56:38	(9,511)
Simmonds, Rob J	7:49:01	(35,288)
Simmons, Chris	5:16:05	(28,514)
Simmons, David S	4:58:53	(25,357)
Simmons, Edward A	3:36:53	(5,291)
Simmons, Gary C	4:38:11	(20,227)
Simmons, Matthew	4:24:01	(16,444)
Simmons, Paul	3:51:12	(8,098)
Simmons, Tony D	4:02:14	(11,074)
Simms, Christopher J	4:32:13	(18,686)
Simo, Jordi	4:09:45	(12,788)
Simon, David A	5:32:29	(30,686)
Simon, Lloyd	4:42:51	(21,425)
Simon, Paul F	3:48:46	(7,557)
Simoneit, Frank	3:59:42	(10,460)
Simons, Craig	5:55:38	(32,735)
Simons, Justin	5:54:50	(32,672)
Simons, Paul R	2:55:50	(717)
Simons, Stefan	6:01:18	(33,129)
Simons, Tim	4:23:40	(16,355)
Simons, Trevor J	5:15:58	(28,496)
Simpkins, David C	3:59:41	(10,451)
Simpson, Alan	3:56:36	(9,489)
Simpson, Alexander J	6:06:52	(33,429)
Simpson, Alun	3:17:06	(2,443)
Simpson, Bradley J	4:38:33	(20,311)
Simpson, Brian A	4:19:50	(15,385)
Simpson, Charles A	4:23:06	(16,207)
Simpson, Colin	3:14:39	(2,188)
Simpson, Duncan	4:14:56	(14,149)
Simpson, Eddie	2:25:04	(33)
Simpson, Hugh	3:57:57	(9,917)
Simpson, Joe	4:40:08	(20,760)
Simpson, John C	6:31:06	(34,436)
Simpson, Keith A	3:58:54	(10,224)
Simpson, Kevin A	4:44:25	(21,824)
Simpson, Leo J	5:20:35	(29,158)
Simpson, Malcolm J	5:16:33	(28,570)
Simpson, Michael A	5:24:24	(29,720)
Simpson, Paul	4:51:40	(23,667)
Simpson, Peter	4:23:02	(16,195)
Simpson, Peter	4:35:11	(19,458)
Simpson, Peter J	3:23:31	(3,191)
Simpson, Robert J	3:37:18	(5,372)
Simpson, Robert R	4:05:33	(11,785)
Simpson, Thomas	5:51:59	(32,482)
Simpson, Thomas A	3:58:41	(10,155)
Simpson, William	3:37:31	(5,405)
Simpson, William G	3:53:46	(8,697)
Sims, Andrew V	4:39:23	(20,542)
Sims, Andy J	3:19:00	(2,617)
Sims, Darren	5:49:44	(32,308)
Sims, James	4:13:34	(13,813)
Sims, Jonathan R	4:22:53	(16,164)
Sims, Matthew D	3:22:10	(3,031)
Sims, Nicholas J	4:03:56	(11,428)
Sims, Paul R	4:31:16	(18,419)
Sinclair, Callum	3:53:41	(8,673)
Sinclair, Daniel	5:20:25	(29,144)
Sinclair, David	5:52:20	(32,505)
Sinclair, Donald	3:57:23	(9,742)
Sinclair, Graham D	4:33:32	(19,029)
Sinclair, Hamish W	5:49:07	(32,261)
Sinclair, Joe M	3:29:04	(4,013)
Sinclair, Malcolm	3:01:10	(1,064)
Sinclair, Mark	6:26:07	(34,285)
Sinclair, Nicholas	5:40:55	(31,580)
Sinclair-Day, Aaron C	6:29:37	(34,400)
Sincock, Andrew M	4:02:30	(11,126)
Sinfield, Colin	4:40:34	(20,851)
Sinfield, Matthew S	3:22:10	(3,031)
Sinfield, Paul D	4:17:02	(14,654)
Singer, Jamie J	4:57:50	(25,094)
Singh, Baldev	4:25:17	(16,780)
Singh, Baljinder	4:35:38	(19,574)
Singh, Ciaran	4:33:32	(19,029)
Singh, Harmander	6:14:19	(33,757)
Singh, Harminderjit	5:59:59	(33,049)
Singh, Jagjit	4:26:41	(17,176)
Singh, Makhan	4:49:40	(23,171)
Singh, Malkiat	8:19:12	(35,332)
Singh, Manjit	3:39:22	(5,739)
Singh, Manjit	3:52:09	(8,311)
Singh, Manminder	5:37:57	(31,269)
Singh, Raghbir A	4:51:18	(23,566)
Singh, Rajdave	3:01:40	(1,094)
Singh, Resham	3:33:46	(4,719)
Singh, Vijay	5:32:40	(30,716)
Singh Samra, Pavinder	4:39:03	(20,452)
Singleton, Simon	4:58:48	(25,338)
Singleton, Wayne	6:12:12	(33,650)
Sinnott, Colin E	3:53:03	(8,519)
Sinnott, Matt A	3:23:10	(3,145)
Sinton, Mark A	3:44:45	(6,758)
Siou, Vincent	2:44:31	(296)
Sipe, Stephen	5:23:13	(29,553)
Siriett, Stephen C	6:10:52	(33,596)
Sirs, Nicholas J	3:12:50	(1,978)
Sisson, Mark J	5:06:23	(26,787)
Siu, Alan	3:40:45	(5,985)
Sivertsen, Atle	4:33:45	(19,086)
Siveyer, Adam A	3:50:24	(7,920)
Siviter, Michael J	4:28:31	(17,701)
Sjíí, Hákan	5:08:22	(27,155)
Sjoberg, Leif	4:01:47	(10,980)
Skaraas, Steinar	4:03:54	(11,423)
Skehan, Niall	3:47:57	(7,384)
Skellorn, Raymond	4:15:19	(14,233)
Skelly, Mark A	3:14:40	(2,193)
Skelton, Chris	3:13:53	(2,109)
Skelton, Chris R	4:20:42	(15,604)
Skelton, John	3:12:11	(1,899)
Skelton, Martin	4:56:47	(24,871)
Skelton, Terry James	3:48:48	(7,569)
Skerratt, Clark I	3:08:57	(1,615)
Skerrow, Richard	5:32:19	(30,672)
Skevington, Timothy M	3:15:20	(2,265)
Skiba, Georg	4:35:49	(19,630)
Skidmore, Andrew	4:40:48	(20,911)
Skidmore, Mark A	3:47:57	(7,384)
Skillington, Joseph	3:17:19	(2,468)
Skinner, Benjamin W	3:58:22	(10,059)
Skinner, Bob J	5:20:49	(29,198)
Skinner, Chris	4:49:28	(23,102)
Skinner, Christopher Hugh	4:00:12	(10,599)
Skinner, Christopher J	4:58:22	(25,228)
Skinner, David	4:29:16	(17,913)
Skinner, Gregory	5:45:19	(31,958)
Skinner, Jeremy	4:01:05	(10,812)
Skinner, Mark D	5:45:53	(32,007)
Skinner, Mark E	4:01:26	(10,893)
Skipper, David L	4:21:01	(15,697)
Skirrow, Dave	4:02:56	(11,217)
Skjoerestad, Kurt	4:09:17	(12,679)
Skott, Jakob	3:19:35	(2,694)
Skovgaard, Jakob	3:58:41	(10,155)
Skriker, Dustin	4:36:53	(19,890)
Skyner, Leo	4:25:12	(16,766)
Slack, Andrew J	4:16:03	(14,407)
Slack, Mark Andrew	4:35:26	(19,527)
Slack, William A	3:44:23	(6,698)
Slade, Colin W	4:41:09	(20,995)
Slade, Glen	3:11:46	(1,855)
Slade, Richard	5:21:09	(29,248)
Slade, Rob	5:37:03	(31,177)
Slade, Sharon	5:37:04	(31,180)
Sladeczek, Franz Josef	5:05:24	(26,625)
Slaney, Mark A	3:22:48	(3,110)
Slaski, Mark	5:12:57	(27,974)
Slater, Benjamin D	5:05:09	(26,581)
Slater, Colin J	4:43:15	(21,529)
Slater, Darren Michael	5:53:21	(32,574)
Slater, Leslie G	4:49:12	(23,017)
Slater, Malcolm	5:22:53	(29,494)
Slater, Michael	4:33:49	(19,101)
Slater, Philip H	4:19:08	(15,194)
Slater, Stephen	5:33:17	(30,785)
Slater, Stephen William	6:21:40	(34,101)
Slator, Clive C	3:43:22	(6,503)
Slatter, Barry	5:28:54	(30,263)
Slavin, John	4:09:52	(12,825)
Slavin, Shan	4:16:15	(14,458)
Sleath, Andrew	4:58:53	(25,357)
Slender, Jason	4:28:50	(17,789)
Slessor, Tony	3:26:55	(3,669)
Sleurs, Willem P	4:46:32	(22,355)
Sleuyter, Steven	3:05:42	(1,349)
Slevin, David J	5:09:59	(27,458)
Sliman, Steven A	4:25:21	(16,800)
Slingo, Paul	6:00:42	(33,093)
Slinn, Greg J	5:27:26	(30,086)
Slinn, Simon J	4:14:52	(14,132)
Sloan, Geoff A	3:08:12	(1,545)
Sloan, Martin T	5:23:18	(29,571)
Sloan, Patrick A	4:08:35	(12,519)
Slocombe, Christopher D	3:56:31	(9,465)
Sloman, Alan P	4:28:03	(17,557)
Slootweg, James K	4:55:36	(24,597)
Slowly, Daniel J	4:01:07	(10,821)
Sluman, Philip S	3:57:05	(9,644)
Sly, Andy	2:49:43	(456)
Smailes, Nicky	4:18:00	(14,889)
Smailes, Paul	4:12:26	(13,499)
Smailes, Robert D	4:54:32	(24,343)
Smails, Ian B	2:58:16	(854)
Smale, Barry	5:04:20	(26,430)
Smale, Dan	5:57:44	(32,893)
Smale, Ian N	3:56:42	(9,535)
Smale, Nick J	3:36:21	(5,211)
Small, Alexander	5:03:16	(26,246)
Small, Andrew	5:51:34	(32,454)
Small, Edward W	5:26:24	(29,978)
Small, James	4:00:09	(10,583)
Small, Michael F	3:56:17	(9,383)
Small, Michael L	5:15:20	(28,390)
Small, Steve G	5:09:01	(27,277)
Smallcombe, Stuart J	5:12:33	(27,900)
Smallman, Darryl	4:43:38	(21,633)
Smallman, Neil J	4:35:41	(19,592)
Smallpage, Matthew	3:57:22	(9,736)
Smallwood, Daryl A	4:32:35	(18,783)
Smart, Andrew D	4:03:44	(11,368)
Smart, Benjamin Toby Edward	4:07:46	(12,310)
Smart, Darren	3:21:09	(2,907)
Smart, Jeremy N	4:26:17	(17,064)
Smart, John C	4:51:00	(23,488)
Smart, Julian D	4:26:19	(17,071)
Smart, Kev S	3:24:58	(3,397)
Smart, Michael	3:17:59	(2,527)
Smart, Paul	3:48:21	(7,480)
Smart, Tomas	4:01:54	(11,003)
Smee, first name unknown	3:23:41	(3,217)
Smee, Graham	3:26:13	(3,560)
Smillie, Martin A	4:06:36	(12,016)
Smink, Luc J	4:12:55	(13,635)
Smit, Morgan	3:37:06	(5,341)
Smith, Adam A	3:31:39	(4,413)
Smith, Adam L	4:44:15	(21,778)
Smith, Adam R	3:48:27	(7,504)
Smith, Adrian J	5:59:35	(33,022)
Smith, Alan	5:30:03	(30,403)
Smith, Alan H	4:28:13	(17,622)
Smith, Alan N	4:50:05	(23,261)
Smith, Alan P	4:55:51	(24,653)
Smith, Alan R	4:07:32	(12,243)
Smith, Alan W	4:22:15	(16,011)
Smith, Alastair J	4:35:46	(19,620)
Smith, Alex G	4:34:05	(19,170)
Smith, Allan H	5:01:57	(26,008)
Smith, Andrew	4:11:31	(13,258)
Smith, Andrew Charles	4:57:04	(24,942)
Smith, Andrew E	4:25:19	(16,791)
Smith, Andrew J	3:26:06	(3,544)
Smith, Andrew J	4:09:43	(12,779)
Smith, Andrew J	4:28:05	(17,570)
Smith, Andrew J	7:40:12	(35,269)
Smith, Andrew K	3:49:46	(7,792)
Smith, Andrew P	6:00:33	(33,080)

Smith, Andrew R 4:07:12 (12,152)
Smith, Andrew S 5:11:18 (27,693)
Smith, Andy 3:44:20 (6,687)
Smith, Andy J 3:23:34 (3,199)
Smith, Andy J 4:06:14 (11,938)
Smith, Anthony J 4:39:01 (20,438)
Smith, Anthony N 4:15:52 (14,362)
Smith, Anthony P 3:00:48 (1,039)
Smith, Anthony R 4:40:47 (20,906)
Smith, Anthony R 4:46:57 (22,469)
Smith, Antony J 3:24:10 (3,292)
Smith, Ashley B 4:12:16 (13,459)
Smith, Ashley M 3:37:43 (5,445)
Smith, Athole J 3:06:11 (1,387)
Smith, Barrie 5:53:33 (32,586)
Smith, Barry 5:39:17 (31,425)
Smith, Barry Sean 3:13:36 (2,073)
Smith, Ben James 4:09:58 (12,846)
Smith, Bradley S 4:50:24 (23,343)
Smith, Brett L 3:56:04 (9,329)
Smith, Brian 4:49:23 (23,078)
Smith, Brian 4:53:46 (24,163)
Smith, Brian R 4:32:03 (18,648)
Smith, Carl 3:14:20 (2,157)
Smith, Carl 4:22:17 (16,020)
Smith, Carl L 3:44:20 (6,687)
Smith, Carl P 3:34:14 (4,818)
Smith, Charles E 4:14:53 (14,136)
Smith, Chris 3:05:59 (1,371)
Smith, Chris 4:57:53 (25,104)
Smith, Chris E 4:11:46 (13,328)
Smith, Chris J 4:38:30 (20,296)
Smith, Christopher E 3:47:56 (7,381)
Smith, Christopher P 4:32:26 (18,743)
Smith, Christopher R 5:46:23 (32,040)
Smith, Clive 5:04:00 (26,387)
Smith, Craig 5:19:13 (28,999)
Smith, Craig A 3:39:09 (5,710)
Smith, Craig Paul 3:23:20 (3,163)
Smith, Craig S 3:58:50 (10,205)
Smith, Damion J 4:37:33 (20,054)
Smith, Daniel 4:00:00 (10,544)
Smith, Daniel 4:36:42 (19,838)
Smith, Daniel J 3:16:33 (2,389)
Smith, Daniel R 4:48:00 (22,744)
Smith, Darren M 4:28:41 (17,744)
Smith, Darren M 5:14:26 (28,232)
Smith, Daryl L 4:44:40 (21,879)
Smith, David 4:54:36 (24,360)
Smith, David A 3:39:51 (5,817)
Smith, David G 4:00:29 (10,664)
Smith, David M 2:47:44 (384)
Smith, Dean 4:07:22 (12,205)
Smith, Dean 4:13:02 (13,664)
Smith, Dean Michael 4:04:40 (11,578)
Smith, Derek A 5:20:54 (29,206)
Smith, Derek N 4:04:57 (11,645)
Smith, Dermot A 3:51:48 (8,227)
Smith, Donald 4:25:21 (16,800)
Smith, Duncan H 3:54:49 (8,973)
Smith, Dylan 4:31:37 (18,531)
Smith, Edd 5:22:55 (29,503)
Smith, Edward G 5:39:40 (31,462)
Smith, Edward W 3:59:47 (10,488)
Smith, Edwin 4:49:44 (23,187)
Smith, Edwin J 3:46:46 (7,148)
Smith, Gary 3:13:09 (2,021)
Smith, Gary 3:41:19 (6,090)
Smith, Gary 4:26:27 (17,097)
Smith, Gary 5:24:14 (29,690)
Smith, Gary J 3:44:12 (6,663)
Smith, Gary J 5:33:15 (30,781)
Smith, Gary N 5:03:30 (26,284)
Smith, Gary P 4:42:12 (21,249)
Smith, Geoff Robert William 4:44:48 (21,907)
Smith, Geoffrey B 3:37:17 (5,369)
Smith, George A 5:08:06 (27,104)
Smith, Gilbert H 6:22:16 (34,120)
Smith, Glen 4:59:12 (25,435)
Smith, Glyn E 4:41:45 (21,154)
Smith, Graham 5:11:38 (27,751)
Smith, Graham A 4:39:44 (20,652)
Smith, Graham P 3:42:05 (6,230)
Smith, Graham T 4:01:21 (10,873)
Smith, Greg 5:34:08 (30,870)
Smith, Greg J 4:28:12 (17,613)
Smith, Greg J 4:32:24 (18,728)
Smith, Gregory J 4:31:27 (18,487)
Smith, Harvey J 5:07:53 (27,074)
Smith, Henry O 4:34:09 (19,183)
Smith, Howard J 3:31:38 (4,411)
Smith, Iain M 4:08:38 (12,532)
Smith, Ian D 4:08:10 (12,410)
Smith, Ian H 3:38:59 (5,683)
Smith, Ian M 3:03:23 (1,195)
Smith, James C 4:27:37 (17,417)
Smith, James Robert Lincoln 3:35:56 (5,142)
Smith, Jamie 3:41:34 (6,131)
Smith, Jamie C 4:20:31 (15,563)
Smith, Jared H 4:07:06 (12,131)
Smith, Jason M 4:24:43 (16,627)
Smith, Jason M 4:38:01 (20,170)
Smith, Jeffrey D 4:30:14 (18,160)
Smith, Jeremy 3:54:55 (9,000)
Smith, John 4:14:45 (14,096)
Smith, John A 5:35:33 (31,025)
Smith, John M 4:16:37 (14,560)
Smith, Jonathan 4:02:08 (11,048)
Smith, Jonathan D 3:58:40 (10,151)
Smith, Jonathan S 5:22:00 (29,365)
Smith, Jonathan T 6:18:40 (33,952)
Smith, Julian A 4:03:53 (11,420)
Smith, Kenneth 6:48:31 (34,788)
Smith, Kenny 4:55:21 (24,539)
Smith, Kevin 6:39:23 (34,614)
Smith, Kevin J 4:22:46 (16,136)
Smith, Kevin W 2:51:46 (515)
Smith, Lawrence Graham 4:53:46 (24,163)
Smith, Lee G 3:01:46 (1,101)
Smith, Leigh A 5:13:08 (28,012)
Smith, Leigh Raymond 5:07:51 (27,069)
Smith, Les 5:25:55 (29,922)
Smith, Lindsay R 4:47:10 (22,536)
Smith, Malcolm 4:31:52 (18,597)
Smith, Mark 6:00:46 (33,099)
Smith, Mark A 4:00:53 (10,770)
Smith, Mark A 4:20:46 (15,627)
Smith, Mark A 4:48:27 (22,841)
Smith, Mark A 5:23:17 (29,569)
Smith, Mark C 5:01:44 (25,960)
Smith, Mark D 4:15:02 (14,172)
Smith, Mark J 6:12:49 (33,682)
Smith, Mark N 5:06:44 (26,853)
Smith, Martin 3:58:51 (10,211)
Smith, Martin 4:08:22 (12,475)
Smith, Martin 5:02:18 (26,081)
Smith, Martin B 4:08:05 (12,382)
Smith, Martin D 3:51:09 (8,085)
Smith, Martin G 4:00:25 (10,640)
Smith, Martin J 3:14:08 (2,137)
Smith, Mary 4:40:59 (20,959)
Smith, Matt J 5:34:44 (30,945)
Smith, Matthew 3:11:27 (1,819)
Smith, Matthew 4:26:20 (17,078)
Smith, Matthew 4:34:59 (19,404)
Smith, Matthew D 4:38:19 (20,257)
Smith, Matthew J 4:53:12 (24,021)
Smith, Matthw 4:12:34 (13,542)
Smith, Michael 4:18:08 (14,929)
Smith, Michael J 4:44:15 (21,778)
Smith, Michael John 5:47:04 (32,100)
Smith, Michael P 5:38:58 (31,392)
Smith, Mike P 4:31:18 (18,438)
Smith, Mike W 5:56:11 (32,768)
Smith, Nathan Daniel 5:51:23 (32,437)
Smith, Nathan R 3:19:13 (2,640)
Smith, Neil 4:17:57 (14,872)
Smith, Neil Andrew 4:42:44 (21,394)
Smith, Neil B 4:11:36 (13,284)
Smith, Neil K 4:50:14 (23,292)
Smith, Neil M 5:33:13 (30,777)
Smith, Niall F 4:22:39 (16,111)
Smith, Nicholas J 4:22:34 (16,091)
Smith, Nick 3:41:13 (6,075)
Smith, Nick 3:45:29 (6,891)
Smith, Nick D 5:24:47 (29,766)
Smith, Nigel C 4:11:38 (13,297)
Smith, Patrick J 3:52:47 (8,461)
Smith, Paul 3:53:56 (8,734)
Smith, Paul 4:03:24 (11,315)
Smith, Paul 4:34:26 (19,244)
Smith, Paul A 3:48:15 (7,456)
Smith, Paul D 6:22:34 (34,133)
Smith, Paul E 4:57:50 (25,094)
Smith, Paul J 4:35:08 (19,446)
Smith, Paul N 4:15:25 (14,262)
Smith, Paul P 4:34:31 (19,264)
Smith, Paul R 3:53:34 (8,640)
Smith, Pete J 5:07:49 (27,066)
Smith, Peter 5:11:57 (27,797)
Smith, Peter C 4:12:22 (13,486)
Smith, Peter E 3:35:31 (5,049)
Smith, Peter M 4:55:51 (24,653)
Smith, Phil P 4:49:32 (23,127)
Smith, Phil R 5:51:34 (32,454)
Smith, Philip 4:44:18 (21,794)
Smith, Philip A 3:04:21 (1,253)
Smith, Rhys R 3:43:53 (6,611)
Smith, Richard 3:22:29 (3,066)
Smith, Richard 3:45:56 (6,972)
Smith, Richard 3:53:12 (8,564)
Smith, Richard 4:24:39 (16,605)
Smith, Richard 4:29:43 (18,019)
Smith, Richard N 2:58:34 (873)
Smith, Ricky 3:51:54 (8,257)
Smith, Robert 4:40:47 (20,906)
Smith, Robert J 3:56:38 (9,511)
Smith, Robert J 5:15:14 (28,366)
Smith, Robert L 5:28:12 (30,178)
Smith, Robert M 5:47:25 (32,127)
Smith, Robert W 4:54:35 (24,352)
Smith, Roderick W 5:02:17 (26,076)
Smith, Ronald 5:36:42 (31,143)
Smith, Ronald J 4:01:55 (11,005)
Smith, Ross W 5:42:47 (31,745)
Smith, Roy 4:40:59 (20,959)
Smith, Royston P 6:20:29 (34,054)
Smith, Russell 4:18:03 (14,905)
Smith, Russell I 4:33:12 (18,944)
Smith, Ruth B 4:41:55 (21,184)
Smith, Sandy H 3:32:07 (4,486)
Smith, Scott A 3:56:21 (9,415)
Smith, Scott P 3:52:28 (8,396)
Smith, Sean 3:12:36 (1,945)
Smith, Sebastian 4:14:21 (14,000)
Smith, Shaun 4:46:11 (22,244)
Smith, Simon 3:32:04 (4,479)
Smith, Simon A 4:33:30 (19,022)
Smith, Simon C 4:22:08 (15,978)
Smith, Simon E 3:40:53 (6,012)
Smith, Simon J 3:53:37 (8,653)
Smith, Simon L 4:29:46 (18,029)
Smith, Stephen A 4:42:49 (21,412)
Smith, Stephen J 4:23:18 (16,253)
Smith, Stephen J 4:39:07 (20,467)
Smith, Stephen L 6:18:40 (33,952)
Smith, Stephen M 4:54:15 (24,273)
Smith, Stephen R 3:51:36 (8,187)
Smith, Stephen T 3:55:16 (9,102)
Smith, Steve 3:34:46 (4,921)
Smith, Steve 5:01:40 (25,945)
Smith, Steve J 3:15:51 (2,323)
Smith, Steven A 3:54:04 (8,772)
Smith, Steven B 3:56:28 (9,449)
Smith, Steven G 5:32:35 (30,701)
Smith, Stewart 5:31:24 (30,564)
Smith, Stuart 6:43:17 (34,685)
Smith, Stuart James 3:48:31 (7,513)
Smith, Stuart L 4:07:40 (12,274)
Smith, Terry A 4:16:17 (14,469)
Smith, Thomas 4:10:07 (12,884)
Smith, Thomas 6:30:01 (34,413)
Smith, Tim 4:47:26 (22,587)
Smith, Timohty M 4:00:25 (10,640)
Smith, Timothy A 3:28:34 (3,935)
Smith, Toby P 5:01:52 (25,988)
Smith, Tom 3:48:26 (7,496)
Smith, Tom G 4:23:01 (16,189)
Smith, Tony J 6:25:55 (34,276)

Smith, Tony P 4:47:40 (22,644)
Smith, Trevor J 5:31:56 (30,631)
Smith, William 4:18:49 (15,108)
Smith, William E 3:24:32 (3,346)
Smitham, David L 4:04:14 (11,499)
Smith-Calvert, John 3:04:54 (1,300)
Smithers, Roger K 4:06:08 (11,910)
Smithey, John 5:14:55 (28,296)
Smith-Pryor, Justin E 5:30:33 (30,469)
Smithson, Ben 4:36:48 (19,864)
Smojver, Stephane 5:11:19 (27,695)
Smout, Grahame D 6:25:00 (34,229)
Smulouic, Steve 3:58:58 (10,243)
Smyth, David 5:05:06 (26,566)
Smyth, Edward 3:46:36 (7,110)
Smyth, Joe N 4:38:57 (20,421)
Smyth, John Paul 5:53:46 (32,603)
Smyth, Kieron P 5:14:55 (28,296)
Smyth, Liam T 3:57:52 (9,900)
Smyth, Louis 5:10:12 (27,499)
Smyth, Michael D 4:39:32 (20,591)
Smyth, Rory 3:39:02 (5,692)
Smyth, William H 5:06:53 (26,884)
Smythe, Stephen 2:47:55 (391)
Snape, Carl 4:40:52 (20,929)
Snart, David J 4:07:00 (12,106)
Snazel, David 4:39:14 (20,502)
Snazell, Chris W 5:52:10 (32,492)
Snead, Martin P 4:20:04 (15,446)
Snell, Alex J 4:26:12 (17,038)
Snelson, Dewi L 4:17:07 (14,671)
Snoad, Alex A 4:29:37 (17,988)
Snodgrass, Ryan 3:13:33 (2,066)
Snook, Christopher 5:03:17 (26,248)
Snook, Michael T 5:51:07 (32,423)
Snow, Andrew Lawrence 3:55:54 (9,289)
Snow, Simon S 4:30:00 (18,095)
Snow, Stewart D 6:09:18 (33,524)
Snowden, John A 4:38:19 (20,257)
Snowden, Laurence B 4:31:22 (18,462)
Snowdon, David R 3:44:17 (6,680)
Sockett, Sam 4:05:37 (11,807)
Soderberg, Phil D 3:28:38 (3,944)
Sodje, Stephen O 5:24:07 (29,670)
Soendergaard, Knud 3:48:23 (7,482)
Soerensen, Steen 3:09:59 (1,705)
Sofia, Mauro 4:32:10 (18,679)
Sohal, Manjit 7:34:54 (35,245)
Sohal, Sundip 6:07:47 (33,472)
Sokoya, Babatunde O 5:13:50 (28,123)
Soler Rodriguez, Francisco 4:09:18 (12,682)
Soliman, Mohamed T 5:24:11 (29,680)
Solkow, Paul 4:12:00 (13,387)
Sollitt, Paul 6:23:44 (34,178)
Solly, Robert A 4:39:58 (20,710)
Solomon, Daniel H 3:49:56 (7,818)
Solti, Nicholas L 4:28:36 (17,724)
Soltys, Daniel J 3:52:15 (8,347)
Soltysik, Andrew 3:12:35 (1,943)
Somarakis, Philip J 3:38:27 (5,578)
Somers, John 4:28:19 (17,651)
Somersall, David A 3:29:57 (4,175)
Somerset, Quentin 4:30:03 (18,113)
Somerville-Cotton, Justin C 4:52:27 (23,856)
Sonante, Alfredo Ciro 4:10:04 (12,869)
Sondergaard, Michael 4:56:06 (24,707)
Soor, Apar 5:43:56 (31,845)
Soper, Keith 4:21:20 (15,768)
Soper, Olly M 3:52:11 (8,323)
Sorce, Giuseppe 3:17:32 (2,485)
Sorel, Michel 3:53:53 (8,721)
Sorensen, Per L 4:16:44 (14,593)
Soria, Francisco 5:13:38 (28,085)
Sorrentino, Lawrence D 3:28:14 (3,890)
Sotillo Acero, José Antonio 4:05:18 (11,734)
Sotoca, Christian 5:11:43 (27,761)
Sotomi, Matt 3:45:51 (6,955)
Soucier, Jean-Pierre 4:11:42 (13,312)
Soula, Philippe 5:14:01 (28,165)
Soulier, Dominique 4:01:06 (10,819)
Soulsby, Paul D 3:34:24 (4,853)
South, Clifford R 4:12:40 (13,566)
South, Dominic A 4:36:48 (19,864)
Southall, Paul C 3:42:39 (6,346)
Southam, Christopher 2:32:45 (88)
Southby, David P 3:13:07 (2,017)
Southern, Anthony 4:44:33 (21,844)
Southern, Michael 3:59:23 (10,365)
Southgate, Charlie D 5:28:46 (30,245)
Southgate, David J 5:36:50 (31,159)
Southwell, Niall James 4:15:06 (14,190)
Southwick, Wayne 4:28:24 (17,670)
Sovegjarto, Pete 3:56:32 (9,469)
Sowells, David E 4:22:26 (16,060)
Sowerby, Dave M 5:02:37 (26,139)
Sowry, Gerrard 5:29:05 (30,283)
Spackman, Steve J 5:58:18 (32,945)
Spadotto, Massimo 4:48:10 (22,776)
Spaetling, Robin 4:24:53 (16,679)
Spain, Joe M 5:08:09 (27,112)
Spalding, Kevin G 5:18:13 (28,820)
Spanos, Stephanos 3:23:41 (3,217)
Sparkes, Stuart 3:48:25 (7,490)
Sparks, Glyn D 3:56:40 (9,523)
Sparks, Ian 3:57:22 (9,736)
Sparks, Martin J 4:55:28 (24,566)
Spayne, John 4:39:01 (20,438)
Spayne, Nicholas J 4:54:25 (24,317)
Speake, Malcolm D 4:20:38 (15,584)
Speake, Peter G 2:53:57 (602)
Speake, William J 2:38:02 (160)
Speakman, Christian 4:19:07 (15,188)
Speakman, Peter R 4:22:01 (15,944)
Spear, Jon R 3:28:06 (3,868)
Spear, Timothy 6:48:11 (34,772)
Speare, Adam C 4:27:46 (17,474)
Spearman, Rod 5:04:54 (26,526)
Speck, Adam 3:22:30 (3,068)
Speck, Andrew D 5:09:11 (27,306)
Speck, David P 7:51:41 (35,293)
Speck, Dennis R 2:44:40 (304)
Speed, Ian 4:40:42 (20,886)
Speedy, Philip P 4:25:42 (16,910)
Speight, Chris 4:03:11 (11,269)
Speirs, Ivie A 5:50:26 (32,371)
Speke, Jeffrey 4:38:16 (20,246)
Spelling, Paul 3:19:10 (2,634)
Spelman, Peter J 3:56:36 (9,489)
Spence, Geoffrey M 3:29:17 (4,060)
Spence, James M 5:56:46 (32,814)
Spenceley, Vincent J 3:51:53 (8,249)
Spencer, Andrew M 3:10:56 (1,774)
Spencer, Bert 5:35:56 (31,066)
Spencer, Christopher J 3:59:41 (10,451)
Spencer, Damian Paul 5:47:39 (32,140)
Spencer, David E 3:50:08 (7,867)
Spencer, David P 4:33:54 (19,129)
Spencer, David R 6:18:21 (33,943)
Spencer, Ian H 4:18:55 (15,139)
Spencer, Jordan P 4:35:37 (19,573)
Spencer, Lee James 3:42:23 (6,281)
Spencer, Richard D 4:20:17 (15,508)
Spencer-Perkins, Michael D 5:14:28 (28,237)
Spencer-Smith, Jason 4:52:39 (23,892)
Spencer-Wood, Julian E 3:38:30 (5,588)
Spender, Alex 3:59:55 (10,523)
Spendlove, Lee Paul 4:26:36 (17,148)
Spensley, Robert A 5:32:37 (30,706)
Sper, Andreas 4:36:08 (19,707)
Spicer, Simon 5:06:04 (26,739)
Spiers, Ben 3:52:41 (8,446)
Spiers, Gareth A 6:24:14 (34,200)
Spillard, Terry K 4:24:21 (16,540)
Spink, Adam J 3:27:50 (3,829)
Spinks, Philip D 5:21:32 (29,307)
Spinner, Remy 3:50:04 (7,850)
Spires, Tim 3:46:20 (7,048)
Spiteri, George P 3:27:30 (3,778)
Spittle, Andrew Michael 3:51:10 (8,088)
Spitzer, Soeren 4:27:45 (17,470)
Spitzer, Wolfgang 4:15:49 (14,354)
Spivey, Caroline 5:18:49 (28,938)
Spokes, Edward J 5:46:03 (32,021)
Spong, Albert 5:56:56 (32,829)
Spooner, Cliff D 5:36:15 (31,096)
Spotswood, Eric R 5:15:13 (28,357)
Spratt, Andy 4:47:04 (22,501)
Spreafico, Ambrogio 3:57:53 (9,901)
Spreafico, Roberto 4:02:32 (11,138)
Spriggs, Andrew W 4:58:03 (25,148)
Spriggs, Benjamin W 4:27:20 (17,352)
Spring, Jonathan 4:55:34 (24,584)
Springer, Gideon 3:37:30 (5,400)
Springett, Mark I 5:18:46 (28,925)
Springthorpe, Robert N 4:45:02 (21,973)
Sproston, David 4:25:20 (16,796)
Sprot, Michael 2:44:28 (294)
Sprowson, Andrew 4:43:31 (21,605)
Spruntulis, Ben 3:39:57 (5,849)
Spurling, Ian G 4:06:18 (11,948)
Spurling, Laurence S 5:35:59 (31,076)
Spurr, James C 4:52:48 (23,927)
Spurr, Tim 3:25:50 (3,509)
Squibb, Jason A 3:39:36 (5,776)
Squibb, Rick 4:59:59 (25,594)
Squire, David F 4:47:01 (22,487)
Squire, Jason 5:21:14 (29,262)
Squire, Richard J 4:08:57 (12,606)
Squires, Kim M 4:23:27 (16,296)
Squires, Paul 5:56:56 (32,829)
Sri-Ganeshan, Muhuntha 4:46:55 (22,454)
St Clair, Richard 3:07:42 (1,501)
St Croix, Denis 4:57:48 (25,085)
St George, Dominic 3:39:28 (5,752)
St J Reynolds, Robin 5:19:13 (28,999)
St John, Anthony 3:06:38 (1,414)
St John, Ian L 3:34:10 (4,805)
St Pierre, James E 3:52:08 (8,304)
Stacchini, Alexis O 4:24:32 (16,577)
Stacey, Andrew 3:43:48 (6,589)
Stacey, Lee 4:59:24 (25,472)
Stacey, Mark J 4:47:59 (22,736)
Stacey, Paul A 4:09:46 (12,794)
Stacey, Sam 4:00:56 (10,782)
Stacey, Steve John 3:50:12 (7,881)
Stacey, Tony 3:52:28 (8,396)
Stacey, Tony 4:00:04 (10,564)
Stachowiak, Lukasz M 3:51:34 (8,178)
Stack, Paul W 4:23:38 (16,346)
Stack, Peter 4:38:30 (20,296)
Staddon, Michael 5:57:25 (32,867)
Staehr, Martin 3:35:37 (5,074)
Staff, Colin Robert 3:41:30 (6,118)
Stafford, Richard J 4:50:16 (23,308)
Stafford, Tom 5:20:39 (29,169)
Stagg, Antony R 3:55:10 (9,079)
Stagg, Matthew 5:15:23 (28,398)
Staggs, Jason C 4:38:08 (20,211)
Staggs, Robert P 4:29:41 (18,011)
Stainer, Peter 2:38:55 (176)
Staines, Toby N 3:09:52 (1,694)
Stainthorpe, David 4:51:24 (23,595)
Stainton, Paul 5:55:05 (32,693)
Stallard, Michael J 5:10:06 (27,478)
Stalley, Andrew C 3:18:56 (2,613)
Stambrook, Paul S 4:53:38 (24,109)
Stammers, Andy 4:09:07 (12,644)
Stamos, Steve 3:27:10 (3,711)
Stamp, Duncan 5:20:37 (29,166)
Stamp, Jack 4:31:40 (18,542)
Stamp, Paul M 3:23:50 (3,242)
Stanbridge, Mark 4:42:41 (21,381)
Standing, Alexander W 4:06:12 (11,927)
Standing, Robert D 5:03:42 (26,325)
Stanford, John R 3:54:29 (8,885)
Stanger, Mike J 3:51:16 (8,112)
Stangroom, Richard 5:22:23 (29,419)
Stanhope, Ian C 4:03:30 (11,334)
Staniforth, Andrew M 3:10:27 (1,732)
Stanley, Dennis 5:46:46 (32,071)
Stanley, Douglas A 5:02:37 (26,139)
Stanley, Ian 4:02:02 (11,024)
Stanley, Jack 5:16:20 (28,542)
Stanley, Sean 6:12:14 (33,653)
Stannard, Richard 4:09:42 (12,774)
Stannett, Charlie 4:56:16 (24,742)
Stansfield, Rob 3:40:27 (5,934)
Stanski, Franz 3:23:54 (3,248)
Stanton, Mark W 4:43:57 (21,703)

Stanton, Peter 3:35:50 (5,121)
Stanton, Ross P 2:59:28 (953)
Staples, Anthony E 4:21:10 (15,733)
Staples, James F 4:59:39 (25,523)
Stapley, Colin M 6:06:08 (33,392)
Stapley, Paul J 5:24:26 (29,724)
Starbrook, Samuel J 5:28:44 (30,242)
Starkey, Chris 3:33:03 (4,617)
Starkey, Jason P 6:26:00 (34,280)
Starkings, Martin 5:52:40 (32,522)
Starr, Ben 5:19:58 (29,088)
Startup, Paul 3:40:45 (5,985)
Statham, Jez 3:27:13 (3,719)
Statham, Kerry 4:21:00 (15,692)
Staton, Derek L 4:37:37 (20,070)
Statter, Ian G 4:19:36 (15,313)
Staudt, Bernd 3:26:25 (3,591)
Staunton, John 4:33:45 (19,086)
Staunton, John 5:50:03 (32,341)
Staunton, Michael 4:16:47 (14,602)
Staveley, James K 3:41:04 (6,039)
Stavenuiter, Kees 3:39:35 (5,775)
Stavrou, Dinos 5:43:27 (31,815)
Stavrou, George 5:43:27 (31,815)
Stawman, Colin 4:16:08 (14,434)
Stawowski, Peter 3:38:56 (5,661)
Stclair, Henry 5:06:23 (26,787)
Stead, Colin 3:20:03 (2,761)
Stead, Kent R 3:05:20 (1,324)
Steadman, Jon P 4:20:05 (15,453)
Steadman, Terence R 3:58:34 (10,119)
Stearn, Martyn K 4:07:17 (12,170)
Stearn, Nicholas 3:33:35 (4,691)
Stearn, Tom F 3:28:11 (3,878)
Stearne, Chris 5:46:39 (32,060)
Steatfield, Fred W 4:53:22 (24,054)
Steatham, Royston J 4:38:10 (20,221)
Stebbing, David A 4:27:47 (17,479)
Stecher, Thomas 2:42:52 (253)
Steckelberg, Edgar 5:40:20 (31,526)
Steckelberg, Ulf 3:53:45 (8,692)
Stedmann, Kevin 4:41:40 (21,136)
Steed, Mark S 4:28:46 (17,766)
Steede, Calvin 3:38:08 (5,524)
Steel, Alistair W 4:22:56 (16,172)
Steel, Arron J 3:57:33 (9,789)
Steel, John 4:51:07 (23,513)
Steel, Jonathon A 5:39:00 (31,395)
Steel, Martin A 3:22:55 (3,119)
Steel, Mike 5:10:57 (27,633)
Steel, Paul R 4:23:17 (16,250)
Steele, Chris 5:19:27 (29,030)
Steele, Colin G 5:00:53 (25,785)
Steele, Colin M 4:05:22 (11,744)
Steele, David P 4:46:17 (22,274)
Steele, Matthew J 4:43:18 (21,543)
Steele, Paul T 6:17:33 (33,908)
Steer, Nicholas 4:18:36 (15,054)
Steer, Simon M 4:48:58 (22,962)
Steevens, Nick P 4:08:49 (12,577)
Stefanowicz, Andrew 6:17:06 (33,887)
Steffan, Odino 5:02:57 (26,200)
Stege-Dietl, Oliver 3:26:55 (3,669)
Steiger, Ian 4:26:04 (17,002)
Stein, Samuel M 7:04:23 (34,998)
Steiner, Manfred 2:56:16 (731)
Steinhauer, Thomas 3:19:28 (2,680)
Steinle, Jon 7:53:53 (35,299)
Steitz, Jonathan 4:57:41 (25,066)
Stelfox, Mark C 4:23:36 (16,334)
Stenhouse, Douglas A 5:11:29 (27,726)
Stent, Bradley S 5:05:01 (26,549)
Stentaford, Mark P 3:57:31 (9,775)
Stenton, Raymond 5:00:53 (25,785)
Stephane, Pierre François 3:55:45 (9,243)
Stephen, Christopher S 4:51:16 (23,558)
Stephen, Graeme R 3:53:19 (8,585)
Stephen, Ian 4:44:05 (21,745)
Stephens, Adam 5:56:01 (32,759)
Stephens, Gareth 6:18:40 (33,952)
Stephens, George A 4:55:02 (24,455)
Stephens, Graham C 2:47:57 (395)
Stephens, Jeff 4:49:20 (23,064)
Stephens, Joshua J 5:27:49 (30,127)
Stephens, Marc R 4:36:42 (19,838)
Stephenson, Andrew J 4:12:19 (13,473)
Stephenson, Arran L 3:55:43 (9,232)
Stephenson, Mark 5:50:36 (32,390)
Stephenson, Mark Richard 3:37:59 (5,487)
Stephenson, Mathew 2:46:38 (350)
Stephenson, Matthew J 4:36:53 (19,890)
Stephenson, Phil 3:58:45 (10,174)
Stepney, Tony 5:42:32 (31,730)
Steptoe, Colin G 2:49:49 (463)
Sterlini, Peter J 5:16:13 (28,529)
Stern, Elliott A 3:38:57 (5,667)
Sternkopf, Stefan 2:53:20 (574)
Stersi Filho, Roberto 3:28:38 (3,944)
Steurer, Paul 3:42:37 (6,336)
Stevanovic, Alexander P 6:09:49 (33,553)
Stevens, Andrew K 3:54:56 (9,004)
Stevens, Andrew P 3:25:32 (3,467)
Stevens, Anthony 5:26:34 (30,003)
Stevens, Chris 5:02:52 (26,189)
Stevens, Christian J 4:15:50 (14,357)
Stevens, Darren 3:28:57 (4,002)
Stevens, David A 2:46:46 (360)
Stevens, Edward 3:35:31 (5,049)
Stevens, Gavin R 2:32:06 (83)
Stevens, Giles 4:07:20 (12,191)
Stevens, Graham J 3:35:50 (5,121)
Stevens, Greg P 2:54:48 (650)
Stevens, John P 3:53:01 (8,510)
Stevens, Kevin A 4:18:23 (14,990)
Stevens, Mark 4:45:45 (22,144)
Stevens, Martin J 2:44:43 (307)
Stevens, Matt T 3:56:15 (9,377)
Stevens, Mike B 6:33:51 (34,495)
Stevens, Neil T 5:10:24 (27,532)
Stevens, Robert 3:39:20 (5,734)
Stevens, Robert G 6:47:15 (34,749)
Stevens, Scott B 4:36:57 (19,900)
Stevens, Simon P 4:52:53 (23,945)
Stevens, Thomas L 4:44:04 (21,740)
Stevens, Todd 2:53:48 (598)
Stevens, Tony 4:45:01 (21,967)
Stevens, Wayne 5:17:35 (28,728)
Stevens-Olsen, Andy 3:39:30 (5,758)
Stevenson, Alastair S 3:22:27 (3,061)
Stevenson, Antony M 5:10:45 (27,592)
Stevenson, Iain 3:56:02 (9,322)
Stevenson, James P 3:57:14 (9,682)
Stevenson, John 7:03:59 (34,994)
Stevenson, John R 4:36:26 (19,777)
Stevenson, Matthew 3:05:16 (1,320)
Stevenson, Michael H 4:46:33 (22,360)
Stevenson, Michael J 3:30:09 (4,197)
Stevenson, Neil 4:53:03 (23,986)
Stevenson, Nigel J 3:17:03 (2,436)
Stevenson, Stuart J 4:51:32 (23,631)
Stevenson, William C 4:17:35 (14,790)
Steventon, Alan G 4:30:43 (18,286)
Stevick, Joseph W 3:01:55 (1,111)
Steward, Gary D 5:16:02 (28,506)
Stewart, Alan 4:23:39 (16,349)
Stewart, Alex J 3:52:43 (8,450)
Stewart, Alex M 3:51:07 (8,076)
Stewart, Brian 3:42:25 (6,285)
Stewart, Colin G 4:57:55 (25,119)
Stewart, Craig 5:12:26 (27,877)
Stewart, Gavin 4:49:28 (23,102)
Stewart, George 2:32:28 (85)
Stewart, Graeme S 4:19:05 (15,181)
Stewart, Iain 4:34:29 (19,257)
Stewart, Iain S 3:41:28 (6,114)
Stewart, Ian 4:16:07 (14,429)
Stewart, Jack 4:51:19 (23,571)
Stewart, Kevin 4:21:42 (15,880)
Stewart, Mark R 4:51:00 (23,488)
Stewart, Neville A 4:59:28 (25,488)
Stewart, Nick M 4:11:06 (13,139)
Stewart, Philip D 4:07:16 (12,167)
Stewart, Philip J 3:50:51 (8,027)
Stewart, Rob A 3:35:33 (5,056)
Stewart, Ryan 3:16:24 (2,371)
Stewart, Tim D 3:26:40 (3,629)
Stewart, Toby V 5:45:36 (31,985)
Stewart, William Paul 4:13:16 (13,736)
Stezaker, Matthew 4:02:57 (11,219)
Stickland, Paul A 4:28:17 (17,644)
Stiff, Simon D 5:09:37 (27,386)
Stiglich, Roberto 3:53:40 (8,667)
Stiles, Andrew D 3:08:03 (1,527)
Stilgoe, James L 4:13:58 (13,900)
Still, Colin J 3:56:05 (9,335)
Still, James W 3:23:25 (3,179)
Still, Nathan 3:54:02 (8,763)
Still, Peter R 4:28:12 (17,613)
Still, Stuart N 2:56:46 (759)
Stillwell, Paul A 5:10:27 (27,541)
Stinton, Daren R 3:35:05 (4,975)
Stirk, Adam D 3:35:53 (5,131)
Stirk, Nigel A 2:27:55 (49)
Stirland, Barry R 4:07:14 (12,162)
Stirling, Rory J 5:24:59 (29,797)
Stirling, Ross M 4:10:08 (12,892)
Stirling, Samuel 4:50:46 (23,437)
Stirna, Martin A 4:06:36 (12,016)
Stjernfeldt, Tobias 4:15:01 (14,168)
Stoakley, Robin E 4:05:19 (11,737)
Stoate, Howard G 4:10:07 (12,884)
Stock, Andy 5:41:08 (31,596)
Stock, David 3:07:26 (1,471)
Stock, James D 4:17:43 (14,826)
Stock, Nigel J 3:32:06 (4,484)
Stock, Richard 7:12:49 (35,081)
Stockdale, Peter C 2:57:40 (818)
Stocker, Gerhard 4:59:58 (25,591)
Stocker, John L 3:24:45 (3,377)
Stocker, Paul 3:50:45 (8,007)
Stocker, Paul 5:38:01 (31,279)
Stocking, David J 5:10:18 (27,513)
Stockley, Simon N 5:55:44 (32,742)
Stockman, David 5:45:42 (31,997)
Stocks, Chris I 5:00:09 (25,624)
Stocks, Chris T 5:43:51 (31,837)
Stocks, Robert 3:53:28 (8,619)
Stockton, Ian 3:53:21 (8,592)
Stockwell, Jonathan P 3:40:41 (5,968)
Stoddard, Mark 3:45:26 (6,878)
Stoddard, Mark S 3:19:26 (2,674)
Stoddart, Keith W 5:29:56 (30,393)
Stoeckel, Daniel L 3:19:14 (2,642)
Stokes, Andrew 5:45:15 (31,955)
Stokes, Clifford R 4:45:46 (22,147)
Stokes, Colin 5:08:36 (27,193)
Stokes, Derek H 5:09:17 (27,329)
Stokes, John 5:04:32 (26,468)
Stokes, John 6:49:25 (34,801)
Stokes, Jonathan J 4:47:12 (22,546)
Stokes, Mark H 4:58:04 (25,155)
Stokes, Michael 4:39:34 (20,602)
Stokey, Paul 4:39:23 (20,542)
Stolarek, Tomasz 4:28:04 (17,564)
Stolerman, Alexander C 4:12:57 (13,651)
Stolker, Jacobus Cornelis 3:23:22 (3,171)
Stone, Chris 4:04:54 (11,630)
Stone, Christopher 4:39:10 (20,487)
Stone, Darren L 3:36:07 (5,175)
Stone, David M 2:46:18 (338)
Stone, Desmond G 5:03:56 (26,370)
Stone, Fabian A 6:24:13 (34,197)
Stone, Gab 4:24:37 (16,595)
Stone, Garry 5:04:20 (26,430)
Stone, Gavin N 5:46:29 (32,048)
Stone, John 4:05:17 (11,728)
Stone, Kevin J 3:02:03 (1,122)
Stone, Kieran P 3:57:16 (9,695)
Stone, Martin 4:58:23 (25,233)
Stone, Matthew 4:10:03 (12,864)
Stone, Nicholas W 3:53:24 (8,604)
Stone, Paul 4:00:47 (10,741)
Stone, Paul 4:14:15 (13,974)
Stone, Philip A 5:14:10 (28,190)
Stone, Steven D 5:00:57 (25,799)
Stone, Tim J 5:56:54 (32,825)
Stone, Tim R 5:43:38 (31,825)
Stoneley, Norman W 4:40:18 (20,795)
Stones, Christopher 6:23:06 (34,154)

Stones, Daniel P	3:38:02 (5,497)	
Stones, Kevin J	4:00:50 (10,752)	
Stones, Nicholas	3:58:09 (9,990)	
Stonier, Chris D	3:06:59 (1,432)	
Stoop, Ben M	4:05:24 (11,752)	
Stopher, Andy	2:48:12 (404)	
Stopher, Brian	2:55:54 (720)	
Stopher, Jed	5:52:40 (32,522)	
Storer, Dan F	4:43:20 (21,559)	
Storer, Graham N	4:10:33 (12,994)	
Storer, Sam	3:34:03 (4,770)	
Storer, Thomas	4:04:56 (11,639)	
Storey, Ben P	4:29:50 (18,048)	
Storey, Iain E	3:07:32 (1,484)	
Storey, James A	4:50:56 (23,467)	
Storey, Matthew H	3:32:33 (4,553)	
Storey, Nigel H	3:44:41 (6,743)	
Storie, Ian P	3:47:19 (7,251)	
Stormont, Edward	3:47:08 (7,222)	
Storr, Geoffrey M	4:00:22 (10,628)	
Storrie, Martin James	4:14:02 (13,913)	
Storrs, Martin	6:12:07 (33,645)	
Story, Tom	4:26:25 (17,090)	
Stothard, Peter	4:13:58 (13,900)	
Stothert, Jonathan	7:23:39 (35,167)	
Stott, Peter J	4:52:56 (23,960)	
Stottor, Chris B	4:20:24 (15,537)	
Stout, Brian R	2:54:36 (637)	
Stout, Paul A	4:33:01 (18,901)	
Strachan, Alan	3:05:52 (1,360)	
Strachan, Ali R	4:50:13 (23,285)	
Strachan, David	4:16:09 (14,438)	
Strachan, Michael S	3:55:23 (9,127)	
Strachan, Oliver J	5:07:10 (26,935)	
Strain, Michael S	5:13:39 (28,088)	
Stramer, Brian	2:55:30 (697)	
Strang, Gus	4:06:42 (12,042)	
Strange, Kit	5:34:20 (30,888)	
Strange, Peter F	4:37:15 (19,974)	
Stratford, Barry	3:00:55 (1,046)	
Stratford, Gary C	3:07:06 (1,445)	
Stratton, Garry D	3:29:08 (4,032)	
Stratton, Martin	4:04:33 (11,556)	
Strawbridge, James	5:10:38 (27,571)	
Street, Alan B	3:39:51 (5,817)	
Street, Chris G	5:02:18 (26,081)	
Street, Christopher	3:56:13 (9,370)	
Street, Christopher J	4:20:52 (15,653)	
Street, Graeme P	3:52:44 (8,456)	
Street, Paul A	2:58:58 (918)	
Street, René	3:54:33 (8,904)	
Street, Richard	4:28:00 (17,542)	
Street, William M	3:28:40 (3,948)	
Streeter, Dominic	4:00:28 (10,656)	
Streets, Craig	5:04:14 (26,416)	
Strickland, Richard	4:25:27 (16,829)	
Stride, Richard	4:41:41 (21,139)	
Stringer, Gary J	3:46:13 (7,023)	
Stringer, Justin E	3:52:19 (8,362)	
Stronach, Chris	5:17:06 (28,658)	
Strong, Alex H	4:37:32 (20,045)	
Strong, Nigel G	4:45:33 (22,090)	
Strong, Stuart A	4:39:32 (20,591)	
Stroud, Tom M	4:37:33 (20,054)	
Strowger, Alan L	4:51:30 (23,620)	
Strudwick, Daniel	4:28:12 (17,613)	
Struthers, Mike J	4:38:38 (20,336)	
Struthers, Thomas W	5:02:17 (26,076)	
Strutt, Barry J	5:41:38 (31,643)	
Struyf, Antoine	3:29:18 (4,068)	
Struyf, Bruno	3:39:57 (5,849)	
Struzak, Bernd	5:05:34 (26,653)	
Strydom, Nico	5:25:42 (29,891)	
Stuart, Dyer	4:31:24 (18,471)	
Stuart, Graham	3:42:44 (6,363)	
Stuart, Michael J	3:50:45 (8,007)	
Stuart, Nick	4:01:23 (10,881)	
Stuart, Peter	3:43:38 (6,551)	
Stubba, Werner	4:26:18 (17,069)	
Stubberfield, James R	4:46:16 (22,267)	
Stubberfield, John A	4:34:04 (19,164)	
Stubbings, Andy	4:52:33 (23,875)	
Stubbings, Darren J	5:47:05 (32,103)	

Stubbings, Matt	4:24:22 (16,541)	
Stubbins, Graham J	3:17:45 (2,509)	
Stubbs, Russell	5:01:20 (25,882)	
Stuckey, Richard J	3:09:38 (1,676)	
Stupples, Philip J	4:48:30 (22,851)	
Sturdgess, Ian C	6:00:32 (33,077)	
Sturgess, Benjamin J	3:20:54 (2,879)	
Sturgess, Gary F	4:13:29 (13,791)	
Sturgess, Gavin O	4:18:14 (14,949)	
Sturgess, James	4:18:52 (15,124)	
Sturgess, Philip	6:26:34 (34,300)	
Sturgess, Phillip J	3:53:37 (8,653)	
Sturla, Tim	3:46:26 (7,071)	
Sturley, John	5:09:27 (27,356)	
Stutznaecker, Peter	3:33:26 (4,670)	
Stylianou, Mark	4:51:07 (23,513)	
Stylski, Gregory	5:37:34 (31,237)	
Stynes, Michael J	3:53:43 (8,682)	
Subia, Marcos	4:12:56 (13,643)	
Subia, Marcos Fernando	4:23:22 (16,268)	
Sudbury, Nick D	4:14:34 (14,047)	
Suddes, David	5:10:40 (27,579)	
Sudell, Greg J	3:52:55 (8,489)	
Sudupe Iturbe, Felipe	3:50:30 (7,944)	
Suehiro, Eto.	4:59:45 (25,544)	
Suenaga, Manoel	4:35:15 (19,477)	
Suff, Maxwell P	3:10:01 (1,708)	
Sugarman, Daniel	3:52:06 (8,301)	
Sugden, George	4:54:30 (24,334)	
Sugden, Peter H	3:24:11 (3,296)	
Sughayer, Najeeb	4:37:29 (20,035)	
Sullivan, Chris J	4:23:47 (16,382)	
Sullivan, Christopher J	4:20:47 (15,634)	
Sullivan, Daniel J	6:03:57 (33,287)	
Sullivan, David J	6:04:56 (33,336)	
Sullivan, Dieter L	6:04:38 (33,320)	
Sullivan, Francis G	4:08:57 (12,606)	
Sullivan, Ian M	4:15:35 (14,303)	
Sullivan, John	5:21:09 (29,248)	
Sullivan, Joseph W	4:41:31 (21,093)	
Sullivan, Luke	3:37:35 (5,420)	
Sullivan, Mark	5:11:22 (27,705)	
Sullivan, Matthew J	6:11:04 (33,603)	
Sullivan, Michael	5:33:44 (30,834)	
Sullivan, Nigel J	3:55:37 (9,199)	
Sullivan, Paul D	3:01:05 (1,056)	
Sullivan, Paul G	4:00:03 (10,557)	
Sullivan, Peter	5:11:23 (27,709)	
Sullivan, Peter J	4:33:57 (19,143)	
Sullivan, Steve	4:55:14 (24,514)	
Sullivan, Stuart	4:04:54 (11,630)	
Sullivan, Thomas F	4:26:18 (17,069)	
Sullivan, Tim	3:15:41 (2,302)	
Summerfield, Nicholas	4:43:16 (21,534)	
Summerley, Michael J	5:49:46 (32,315)	
Summers, Clark R	4:25:44 (16,920)	
Summers, Darren	5:13:10 (28,021)	
Summers, David	6:15:55 (33,841)	
Summers, David L	4:59:35 (25,513)	
Summers, Derek G	4:46:15 (22,262)	
Summers, John W	5:18:39 (28,904)	
Summers, Jonathon J	4:51:51 (23,709)	
Summers, Mike	3:54:31 (8,894)	
Summers, Pete	2:51:20 (503)	
Summerscales, Damian J	4:31:53 (18,602)	
Summersgill, David	3:19:51 (2,731)	
Summerton, John M	7:28:07 (35,207)	
Sumner, Alan	4:00:39 (10,707)	
Sumner, Andrew A	4:43:07 (21,497)	
Sumner, Marc	4:21:03 (15,704)	
Sumner, Michael J	4:37:20 (19,990)	
Sumner, Rob	4:57:55 (25,119)	
Sumpter, James P	2:26:21 (39)	
Sumpter, Lee	4:47:59 (22,736)	
Sumpton, Christopher A	4:40:56 (20,948)	
Sumpton, Martin C	5:07:48 (27,059)	
Sunger, Darshan S	5:04:10 (26,409)	
Sunley, Michael C	4:49:32 (23,127)	
Sunner, Pavitar S	5:35:49 (31,052)	
Surgey, Dave A	3:53:48 (8,703)	
Suri, Keitel	4:33:51 (19,113)	
Surman, Andrew J	5:35:05 (30,981)	
Surrel, Nicolas	4:42:48 (21,409)	

Surrey, Sam	3:08:44 (1,593)	
Surry, Michael	5:27:40 (30,106)	
Suryajaya, Billy	6:33:51 (34,495)	
Sussams, Brendon J	4:00:35 (10,694)	
Susumu, Ueno	4:30:37 (18,260)	
Sutch, David	5:19:22 (29,020)	
Sutch, Kevin	4:56:09 (24,716)	
Sutcliffe, Christopher D	6:24:15 (34,205)	
Sutcliffe, Ian	3:42:36 (6,330)	
Sutcliffe, John M	5:41:43 (31,650)	
Sutcliffe, Peter R	3:08:16 (1,551)	
Suter, David E	5:42:55 (31,762)	
Suter, Frank T	4:38:05 (20,195)	
Suter, Joachim	3:51:56 (8,263)	
Suter, Paul	4:43:30 (21,598)	
Sutherland, Alex J	3:54:04 (8,772)	
Sutherland, Azad T	4:55:03 (24,460)	
Sutherland, David J	4:08:52 (12,591)	
Sutherland, Dougal W	3:51:03 (8,066)	
Sutherland, Eric	7:12:32 (35,077)	
Sutherland, Graham T	3:39:54 (5,834)	
Sutherland, Leslie	5:24:57 (29,790)	
Sutherland, Neil	5:56:28 (32,790)	
Suttle, Stephen D	3:38:21 (5,557)	
Sutton, Andy J	4:11:06 (13,139)	
Sutton, Ian C	4:51:16 (23,558)	
Sutton, Jonathan L	3:19:45 (2,717)	
Sutton, Julian D	7:00:34 (34,953)	
Sutton, Kevin	5:20:07 (29,108)	
Sutton, Malcolm J	4:22:50 (16,149)	
Sutton, Roger J	6:03:44 (33,274)	
Sutton, Russell	4:22:44 (16,131)	
Sutton, Timothy J	3:28:45 (3,964)	
Svahn, Peter	4:25:49 (16,940)	
Svanekjaer, Morten	4:18:29 (15,027)	
Svedlund, Ove	4:57:13 (24,968)	
Svedman, Kjell	3:20:13 (2,784)	
Svennson, Gary M	4:44:18 (21,794)	
Svensson, Síren	4:47:29 (22,594)	
Sverrisson, Vignir Thor	3:42:31 (6,305)	
Swaby, Steven M	4:08:59 (12,616)	
Swain, James	5:51:07 (32,423)	
Swaisland, Kevin W	3:52:02 (8,282)	
Swales, Keith	4:05:09 (11,695)	
Swallow, Phil	4:28:12 (17,613)	
Swallow, Richard J	3:52:20 (8,369)	
Swan, Alan	3:23:55 (3,250)	
Swan, David P	4:18:31 (15,035)	
Swan, Kim R	3:33:14 (4,639)	
Swan, Paul	3:06:09 (1,384)	
Swan, Paul	7:19:52 (35,150)	
Swann, Andrew D	3:29:36 (4,116)	
Swannell, Jonathan R	5:01:07 (25,844)	
Swanton, Neil D	4:59:08 (25,418)	
Swanton, Paul N	3:04:38 (1,272)	
Swarbrick, David.	4:05:58 (11,875)	
Swart, André	5:37:59 (31,273)	
Swart, Clayton	5:10:25 (27,535)	
Swash, Chris T	3:41:48 (6,167)	
Sweeney, Andrew	4:45:54 (22,188)	
Sweeney, Derek F	3:57:17 (9,702)	
Sweeney, Gary W	3:53:00 (8,506)	
Sweeney, John M	3:49:42 (7,774)	
Sweeney, Jonathan	3:27:50 (3,829)	
Sweeney, Tommy E	3:34:00 (4,758)	
Sweeney, William F	4:51:17 (23,562)	
Sweeney, William R	2:50:49 (491)	
Sweet, Andrew	7:56:34 (35,306)	
Sweet, David	5:17:58 (28,788)	
Sweet, Tony J	3:18:06 (2,539)	
Sweet, William H	3:04:44 (1,285)	
Sweetlove, Bob	3:34:29 (4,873)	
Sweetlove, Mark	4:55:42 (24,614)	
Swift, Derrick J	3:08:51 (1,604)	
Swift, Lee J	4:41:26 (21,065)	
Swift, Nicholas J	4:37:01 (19,922)	
Swimer, Greg	3:56:24 (9,429)	
Swinbank, Peter D	5:27:36 (30,102)	
Swinburne, Andrew	3:12:19 (1,916)	
Swindin, Robin T	3:23:38 (3,206)	
Swingler, David G	3:52:49 (8,471)	
Swingler, Richard J	4:28:47 (17,769)	
Switzer, Matthew K	3:58:10 (9,996)	

Sworn, Adrian....4:30:44 (18,292)
Sycamore, Paul C....5:40:56 (31,582)
Syers, Graham E....3:04:17 (1,252)
Sykes, Chris P....4:12:09 (13,426)
Sykes, Christopher A....4:29:45 (18,025)
Sykes, Duncan....3:57:49 (9,880)
Sykes, Edward....4:07:44 (12,295)
Sykes, Jason....4:03:59 (11,445)
Sykes, John....5:12:24 (27,867)
Sykes, Jonathan D....3:55:46 (9,253)
Sykes, Paul....4:42:03 (21,212)
Sylvester, Raphael....3:55:53 (9,282)
Sylvestre, Philippe....4:15:44 (14,329)
Syme, Bob....4:24:24 (16,553)
Syme, James....5:26:17 (29,964)
Syme, Neil....3:57:49 (9,880)
Symeou, Nicos....4:42:06 (21,226)
Symes, Tony....4:18:19 (14,969)
Symmonds, Mark D....3:56:06 (9,341)
Symns, Paul D....3:26:27 (3,594)
Symon, Witney D....4:14:22 (14,007)
Symonds, Andrew....3:00:21 (1,017)
Symonds, Dean....4:12:09 (13,426)
Symonds, Tom....5:00:39 (25,740)
Symonds, Warren....5:28:17 (30,187)
Symons, Mike....4:47:43 (22,657)
Symons, Paul R....4:31:41 (18,546)
Synan, Paul Edward....4:52:09 (23,786)
Synnott, Colin....5:29:41 (30,357)
Syrett, Jason K....3:18:46 (2,595)
Syrett, Stephen....4:02:25 (11,108)
Syvret, Mark R....3:53:12 (8,564)
Szafnauer, Otmar M....4:50:26 (23,350)
Szczepura, Matthew J....3:31:10 (4,357)
Szkwarok, Stefan....4:26:40 (17,175)
Sztarkman, Herve....3:12:08 (1,892)
Szukalski, Darren A....4:05:55 (11,862)
Szulc, Ryszard D....4:53:09 (24,012)
Szwajkowski, Adam S....4:24:43 (16,627)
Szwardcbord, Nimrod....4:24:50 (16,663)
Szynaka, Stefan....4:36:40 (19,830)
Taam, Chafik....3:28:25 (3,915)
Tabor, James E....6:03:15 (33,245)
Tabor, Marc....4:21:22 (15,776)
Tabor, Paul A....4:48:26 (22,836)
Tadie, Laexis J....3:19:07 (2,629)
Tadman, Miles....4:52:51 (23,938)
Taffs, Miles J....3:42:27 (6,288)
Taft, David A....4:42:22 (21,293)
Tagg, Chris J....4:27:04 (17,274)
Taggart, James....4:41:11 (21,008)
Taggart, Mark J....5:13:28 (28,060)
Tague, Harrison....5:18:35 (28,891)
Taha, Omar....4:17:13 (14,697)
Tai, Frank....2:55:54 (720)
Tailor, Dennis....6:30:19 (34,422)
Tait, John....6:39:09 (34,612)
Tait, Richard A....3:12:36 (1,945)
Takamatsu, Naoto....3:18:45 (2,592)
Takano, Hideo....4:05:55 (11,862)
Takeshi, Furuichi....4:44:58 (21,948)
Talbot, Alastair G....5:05:50 (26,704)
Talbot, Andrew....4:13:28 (13,787)
Talbot, Bruce J....4:37:02 (19,928)
Talbot, Christopher....2:59:03 (924)
Talbot, Colin....3:27:11 (3,712)
Talbot, Cy....4:29:39 (18,003)
Talbot, Hugo P....2:58:37 (879)
Talbot, Jonathan....3:52:37 (8,435)
Talbot, Lee R....5:03:49 (26,344)
Talbot, Simon J....5:00:18 (25,655)
Talijancich, Milan....3:33:55 (4,743)
Tallentire, Mark A....4:17:07 (14,671)
Talwatte, Gehan....3:51:54 (8,257)
Tamblyn, Matthew....4:34:43 (19,321)
Tamlyn, Gregory J....4:22:48 (16,140)
Tan, Wallace K....4:38:25 (20,280)
Tan, Ying Hsien....4:16:39 (14,571)
Tandy, Simon....5:41:55 (31,664)
Tang, Keith....3:40:10 (5,892)
Tang, Matthew J....4:04:11 (11,484)
Tangri, Abhineet....4:19:15 (15,221)
Tanikawa, Hideo....4:59:20 (25,459)
Tank, Shai....4:52:23 (23,838)
Tankard, Kerry W....4:26:36 (17,148)
Tann, Michael B....5:21:47 (29,339)
Tann, Simon....3:55:17 (9,107)
Tannahill, Brad R....4:12:35 (13,544)
Tanner, Colin R....4:11:11 (13,158)
Tanner, Joseph E....4:22:52 (16,161)
Tanner, Kirk....3:35:04 (4,972)
Tanner, Lea G....5:15:03 (28,328)
Tannian, Mark E....3:49:31 (7,733)
Tansey, Andrew R....5:11:31 (27,731)
Tansley, Kim....4:44:48 (21,907)
Tant, Mark D....4:07:11 (12,148)
Tanzi, Massimo....3:53:33 (8,634)
Taoussi, Mohammed....4:11:32 (13,263)
Tapley, Matthew....4:21:21 (15,774)
Taplin, Derek R....5:13:38 (28,085)
Tapparo, Peter....6:14:25 (33,762)
Tappin, Mark D....3:09:48 (1,690)
Tapscott, Paul J....5:13:31 (28,068)
Tarantino, William....2:30:25 (69)
Tarawik, Dan L....8:50:41 (35,354)
Tarleton, James W....3:52:05 (8,295)
Tarn, Peter....4:51:51 (23,709)
Tarpey, Patrick G....4:00:53 (10,770)
Tarplee, Simon R....3:03:22 (1,192)
Tarr, John N....5:15:05 (28,336)
Tarrant, Derek....4:46:59 (22,478)
Tarrant, Kieran J....4:29:13 (17,899)
Tarrant, Stuart P....3:46:22 (7,056)
Tarver, Andrew J....4:26:52 (17,229)
Tasker, Ian D....4:19:49 (15,379)
Tate, Alexander J....2:54:22 (622)
Tate, Simon A....4:33:13 (18,948)
Tate, Steve J....3:28:06 (3,868)
Tateossian, Gilles....3:34:20 (4,839)
Tatham, Alasdair G....2:40:07 (194)
Tatler, David M....4:33:43 (19,077)
Tatsuo, Ikeda....5:29:18 (30,310)
Tattam, Karl J....4:46:23 (22,310)
Tattan, David....4:20:30 (15,557)
Tattersall, Matthew F....4:56:29 (24,795)
Tattersall, Robert S....4:13:18 (13,745)
Tattersdill, Paul J....5:10:40 (27,579)
Tatum, Nicholas B....4:15:11 (14,211)
Taupin, Vincent R....4:35:39 (19,581)
Tavener, Ben....6:02:31 (33,198)
Tavener, Chris....4:13:04 (13,672)
Taverner, Ron....3:51:26 (8,150)
Tavner, Adam C....3:41:43 (6,152)
Tawell, Adam J....4:35:30 (19,546)
Tawell, Ben R....4:31:32 (18,513)
Tawfik, Alex W....5:27:38 (30,104)
Tawn, Paul R....3:57:19 (9,712)
Tay, Michael....4:42:49 (21,412)
Taylor, Adam....3:57:39 (9,826)
Taylor, Adam A....3:21:08 (2,905)
Taylor, Adam C....3:40:35 (5,953)
Taylor, Adrian M....4:46:08 (22,232)
Taylor, Alan J....6:06:56 (33,433)
Taylor, Alan L....3:55:21 (9,119)
Taylor, Alexander J....4:36:12 (19,726)
Taylor, Andrew....4:51:32 (23,631)
Taylor, Andrew W....3:50:14 (7,892)
Taylor, Andy....5:46:00 (32,012)
Taylor, Andy J....4:50:46 (23,437)
Taylor, Arron E....3:58:39 (10,144)
Taylor, Ben....4:37:42 (20,090)
Taylor, Billy....4:03:57 (11,436)
Taylor, Birger....3:43:30 (6,525)
Taylor, Bryon A....5:43:53 (31,840)
Taylor, Chris A....4:40:57 (20,953)
Taylor, Christopher....4:13:36 (13,824)
Taylor, Christopher....4:42:31 (21,336)
Taylor, Christopher S....4:52:42 (23,908)
Taylor, Colin....3:40:45 (5,985)
Taylor, Daniel J....2:58:26 (864)
Taylor, Daniel J....3:29:01 (4,010)
Taylor, Darren L....6:08:41 (33,502)
Taylor, David....4:33:51 (19,113)
Taylor, David....5:35:30 (31,018)
Taylor, David A....3:55:32 (9,162)
Taylor, David Ernest....3:36:49 (5,279)
Taylor, David J....3:46:05 (6,998)
Taylor, David J....3:47:35 (7,307)
Taylor, David J....5:38:45 (31,363)
Taylor, David Ronald....4:29:31 (17,969)
Taylor, Dean M....4:39:43 (20,648)
Taylor, Dominic C....3:39:37 (5,780)
Taylor, Donald G....3:56:39 (9,518)
Taylor, Edward....4:36:58 (19,909)
Taylor, Eric....3:13:27 (2,055)
Taylor, Gary....3:37:50 (5,462)
Taylor, Geoffrey....4:34:54 (19,382)
Taylor, George K....2:40:53 (212)
Taylor, Glen....3:50:09 (7,872)
Taylor, Graham C....3:11:31 (1,830)
Taylor, Graham P....4:05:32 (11,780)
Taylor, Howard G....3:46:21 (7,052)
Taylor, Ian D....5:42:38 (31,734)
Taylor, Ian J....3:13:45 (2,095)
Taylor, Ian K....3:13:03 (2,012)
Taylor, James....3:19:18 (2,650)
Taylor, James A....3:53:40 (8,667)
Taylor, James D....7:11:31 (35,072)
Taylor, James P....4:13:33 (13,811)
Taylor, Jeremy N....4:23:01 (16,189)
Taylor, Joe....6:21:45 (34,105)
Taylor, Joe C....6:25:33 (34,259)
Taylor, John....5:04:31 (26,459)
Taylor, John V....5:17:14 (28,680)
Taylor, Justin....4:29:02 (17,843)
Taylor, Keith....4:06:08 (11,910)
Taylor, Keith R....3:56:53 (9,592)
Taylor, Kevin....3:29:17 (4,060)
Taylor, Kevin A....4:19:27 (15,266)
Taylor, Kevin C....3:54:58 (9,010)
Taylor, Leon....3:52:58 (8,498)
Taylor, Les Robert....3:58:04 (9,958)
Taylor, Luke D....5:12:57 (27,974)
Taylor, Mark B....3:32:21 (4,523)
Taylor, Mark M....3:26:32 (3,603)
Taylor, Mark T....4:00:01 (10,550)
Taylor, Mark W....4:24:06 (16,471)
Taylor, Martin J....3:57:37 (9,806)
Taylor, Matthew....3:21:22 (2,932)
Taylor, Matthew....3:39:16 (5,723)
Taylor, Matthew....4:24:40 (16,614)
Taylor, Matthew D....5:47:15 (32,114)
Taylor, Matthew J....4:23:49 (16,391)
Taylor, Maximilian....3:26:31 (3,601)
Taylor, Michael....4:48:36 (22,877)
Taylor, Michael A....4:20:45 (15,619)
Taylor, Michael A....5:18:40 (28,910)
Taylor, Michael Fred....3:49:59 (7,830)
Taylor, Michael J....3:59:15 (10,324)
Taylor, Neil....6:06:16 (33,401)
Taylor, Neil A....3:11:58 (1,879)
Taylor, Neil C....4:28:31 (17,701)
Taylor, Neil D....4:30:20 (18,192)
Taylor, Nigel G....5:56:38 (32,802)
Taylor, Paul....4:12:27 (13,507)
Taylor, Paul....5:05:03 (26,558)
Taylor, Paul....5:16:40 (28,590)
Taylor, Paul Anthony....4:31:46 (18,574)
Taylor, Paul R....4:05:17 (11,728)
Taylor, Paul R....5:15:30 (28,416)
Taylor, Paul S....6:38:54 (34,606)
Taylor, Peter G....4:44:53 (21,924)
Taylor, Peter M....5:30:46 (30,497)
Taylor, Philip A....4:59:30 (25,497)
Taylor, Phillip G....2:46:18 (338)
Taylor, Ralph G....3:51:38 (8,196)
Taylor, Richard....4:44:56 (21,936)
Taylor, Richard J....4:53:27 (24,061)
Taylor, Richard K....4:35:50 (19,638)
Taylor, Richard N....3:52:48 (8,465)
Taylor, Richard S....3:02:45 (1,163)
Taylor, Richard T....4:29:26 (17,956)
Taylor, Rob....3:59:41 (10,451)
Taylor, Robert....3:41:16 (6,084)
Taylor, Robert M....4:33:04 (18,915)
Taylor, Roland J....4:40:10 (20,768)
Taylor, Russell J....4:21:24 (15,785)
Taylor, Russell J....4:42:06 (21,226)
Taylor, Russell J....6:51:38 (34,838)

Taylor, Ryan D 4:40:10 (20,768)
Taylor, Ryan P 4:01:23 (10,881)
Taylor, Sam 5:26:35 (30,005)
Taylor, Simon 4:06:54 (12,079)
Taylor, Simon C 5:21:39 (29,326)
Taylor, Steve 4:58:38 (25,304)
Taylor, Stuart J 5:19:30 (29,036)
Taylor, Zac S 2:56:00 (724)
Taylorson, Simon 3:18:45 (2,592)
Teague, Alan R 4:31:22 (18,462)
Teague, Paul Wayne 5:11:17 (27,692)
Teague, Steven R 4:00:57 (10,786)
Teale, Chris J 4:45:05 (21,993)
Teale, Richard 4:13:10 (13,700)
Teale, Simon P 4:13:30 (13,796)
Tear, Steven 3:01:13 (1,068)
Teare, Adrian 4:24:51 (16,670)
Tebbit, Christopher M 4:56:26 (24,782)
Tedford, Barry R 3:39:04 (5,700)
Tedstone, Geoff A 4:00:10 (10,587)
Tedstone, Nicholas M 5:09:29 (27,360)
Tee, Paul 3:55:09 (9,075)
Teece, Paul A 4:25:18 (16,786)
Teece, Philip R 2:55:07 (671)
Teed, Paul L 5:18:13 (28,820)
Teer, Ryan C 4:15:09 (14,203)
Teers, Nigel P 3:45:12 (6,835)
Tees, Andrew P 3:43:50 (6,601)
Teesdale, Michael 4:57:14 (24,971)
Teeton, Andrew 4:02:00 (11,017)
Teeuwen, Jurrie 5:15:08 (28,341)
Teji, Shalinder 3:21:08 (2,905)
Telfer, George M 4:37:20 (19,990)
Telford, David J 3:58:38 (10,137)
Telford, Gary Robert 4:49:57 (23,231)
Telford-Reed, Nicholas J 4:17:13 (14,697)
Telson, Andrew M 6:32:01 (34,452)
Temerlies, Simon 3:53:26 (8,612)
Temple, Alex J 4:42:40 (21,376)
Temple, Paul 6:49:33 (34,807)
Temple, Stephen 3:59:14 (10,320)
Templer, Mark 3:07:58 (1,522)
Templer, Peter 4:27:23 (17,362)
Templeton, Calum P 3:50:30 (7,944)
Tennant, David M 5:44:50 (31,916)
Tennant, James 3:07:25 (1,468)
Tennant, Mark 4:43:50 (21,676)
Tennant, Mark J 3:29:41 (4,132)
Teodori, Luigi 3:14:41 (2,194)
Ter Horst, Timothy J 3:53:24 (8,604)
Teranne, Pascal 3:44:45 (6,758)
Terrace, David J 4:56:47 (24,871)
Terrell, Andrew M 3:38:19 (5,553)
Terrill, Paul K 5:28:22 (30,197)
Terry, Andrew L 5:08:33 (27,185)
Terry, Andrew R 5:20:43 (29,178)
Terry, Dean 4:18:08 (14,929)
Terry, James T 3:47:27 (7,278)
Terry, Jeffrey C 4:58:21 (25,225)
Terry, Mark P 3:35:20 (5,018)
Terry, Michael B 4:40:55 (20,943)
Terry, Nick J 5:24:00 (29,648)
Terry, Paul S 4:42:52 (21,431)
Teruhisa, Natsume 6:07:20 (33,452)
Teruo, Shimoda 2:52:45 (550)
Tesfay, Habtom 4:09:15 (12,671)
Tesolin, Tiziano 4:11:53 (13,355)
Tessels, Dick 4:40:41 (20,884)
Tester, Andrew F 4:33:54 (19,129)
Tetsuo, Kojima 6:32:28 (34,462)
Teuscher, Mathias 4:26:19 (17,071)
Tevenan, John F 4:56:39 (24,843)
Tew, Gavin 4:50:55 (23,464)
Tewater, Sam 3:52:06 (8,301)
Thacker, Simon 3:04:41 (1,277)
Thackeray, Richard P 3:13:52 (2,105)
Thackeray, Ryan Steven 4:06:50 (12,068)
Thackray, James A 4:04:58 (11,650)
Thackwell, James A 4:54:50 (24,415)
Thake, Andrew 2:27:37 (45)
Thakrar, Sanjay 5:10:57 (27,633)
Thandi, Mandip S 4:12:25 (13,494)
Thapa, Ben V 4:59:49 (25,556)

Tharakan, Tharu T 4:18:16 (14,956)
Tharp, Andy 5:13:26 (28,052)
Tharratt, James 4:01:20 (10,868)
Thatcher, Andrew 5:42:28 (31,718)
Thatcher, Matthew J 3:40:39 (5,964)
Thayaparan, Piranaven T 3:54:18 (8,839)
Themans-Hales, Simon J 4:48:07 (22,766)
Theobald, Edward 3:52:56 (8,491)
Theobald, John D 5:04:21 (26,437)
Theobald, Paul 4:15:42 (14,319)
Theokli, Tony 4:20:21 (15,524)
Theron, Willem J 3:37:07 (5,344)
Theuri, George 6:22:41 (34,140)
Thewlis, AR 5:20:51 (29,201)
Thibault, PJ 3:23:39 (3,211)
Thibierge, Christophe 3:54:46 (8,960)
Thierry, Buil 3:29:23 (4,088)
Thierry, Pittavino 3:12:53 (1,985)
Thill, Christophe 3:02:08 (1,129)
Thind, Kulbir S 5:32:40 (30,716)
Thírner, Klaus 3:57:35 (9,798)
Thirsk, Michael 4:56:01 (24,682)
Thistlethwaite, Anthony E 3:27:35 (3,799)
Thogersen, Martin 3:34:15 (4,819)
Thom, David J 5:56:36 (32,800)
Thomas, Alex 4:54:49 (24,414)
Thomas, Allun E 3:36:12 (5,190)
Thomas, Andrew 3:40:54 (6,014)
Thomas, Andrew J 3:34:00 (4,758)
Thomas, Andrew J 4:13:37 (13,829)
Thomas, Andrew R 4:52:12 (23,795)
Thomas, Andrew Roger 4:18:11 (14,942)
Thomas, Barry D 3:39:24 (5,743)
Thomas, Benjamin G 5:33:46 (30,839)
Thomas, Brett R 6:23:53 (34,185)
Thomas, Brian 3:25:51 (3,512)
Thomas, Carwyn 3:18:02 (2,532)
Thomas, Charles R 4:00:29 (10,664)
Thomas, Chris 3:49:28 (7,723)
Thomas, Christophe 4:01:33 (10,931)
Thomas, Christopher C 4:46:16 (22,267)
Thomas, Christopher P 5:36:17 (31,100)
Thomas, Daniel Richard 4:24:06 (16,471)
Thomas, Dave H 4:05:51 (11,850)
Thomas, David 4:07:03 (12,119)
Thomas, David A 4:58:46 (25,330)
Thomas, David G 4:29:43 (18,019)
Thomas, David I 4:09:10 (12,652)
Thomas, David I 4:16:13 (14,452)
Thomas, David M 4:49:44 (23,187)
Thomas, David M 5:28:38 (30,226)
Thomas, David Simon 4:47:39 (22,641)
Thomas, David W 3:37:47 (5,452)
Thomas, Dean A 3:00:46 (1,035)
Thomas, Derek W 5:17:25 (28,700)
Thomas, Didier A 3:19:43 (2,713)
Thomas, Edward 5:08:43 (27,216)
Thomas, Eric J 3:32:38 (4,566)
Thomas, Frank W 4:06:48 (12,060)
Thomas, Gareth 3:34:03 (4,770)
Thomas, Gavin 4:20:37 (15,580)
Thomas, George A 5:10:09 (27,489)
Thomas, Geraint A 6:13:59 (33,743)
Thomas, Gethin 5:32:46 (30,735)
Thomas, Glynn L 3:06:34 (1,409)
Thomas, Graeme 4:37:35 (20,065)
Thomas, Graham D 3:48:49 (7,574)
Thomas, Graham Kenneth 3:57:22 (9,736)
Thomas, Grahame G 4:09:13 (12,663)
Thomas, Harry C 4:05:01 (11,655)
Thomas, Harvey 3:30:19 (4,222)
Thomas, Henry J 3:13:51 (2,103)
Thomas, Ian 4:11:06 (13,139)
Thomas, Iwan 3:58:45 (10,174)
Thomas, James 3:34:46 (4,921)
Thomas, James A 4:03:37 (11,359)
Thomas, James J 3:23:56 (3,252)
Thomas, James M 3:19:51 (2,731)
Thomas, James R 3:47:15 (7,242)
Thomas, Jason 4:16:45 (14,594)
Thomas, Jeff L 4:38:03 (20,179)
Thomas, Jeffrey C 3:28:17 (3,896)
Thomas, John 3:55:55 (9,292)

Thomas, Justin L 2:59:29 (956)
Thomas, Keith 2:49:49 (463)
Thomas, Kevin P 5:21:30 (29,298)
Thomas, Laurence J 5:32:56 (30,744)
Thomas, Lee Jarad 3:41:19 (6,090)
Thomas, Leighton N 4:30:15 (18,166)
Thomas, Mark S 4:26:54 (17,239)
Thomas, Martin 5:39:58 (31,493)
Thomas, Matt 4:22:48 (16,140)
Thomas, Max W 4:16:08 (14,434)
Thomas, Mike 4:47:01 (22,487)
Thomas, Nicholas R 3:50:12 (7,881)
Thomas, Nick D 2:54:35 (636)
Thomas, Nigel G 4:39:04 (20,456)
Thomas, Nigel V 7:04:50 (35,001)
Thomas, Oliver R 4:10:34 (13,000)
Thomas, Paul Bruno 4:46:51 (22,438)
Thomas, Perrin R 5:57:42 (32,892)
Thomas, Peter L 4:24:38 (16,601)
Thomas, Philip 5:14:21 (28,214)
Thomas, Richard 3:29:17 (4,060)
Thomas, Richard L 4:22:48 (16,140)
Thomas, Richard M 2:57:03 (777)
Thomas, Simon H 5:13:26 (28,052)
Thomas, Simon M 3:42:26 (6,287)
Thomas, Stephen 3:41:59 (6,200)
Thomas, Stephen James 4:20:43 (15,612)
Thomas, Steve 6:12:34 (33,662)
Thomas, Trevor J 5:05:10 (26,585)
Thomas, Warren D 3:50:11 (7,878)
Thomas, Wayne 5:05:02 (26,555)
Thomas, Will O 4:36:45 (19,848)
Thomason, Francis L 4:51:00 (23,488)
Thomason, Gary 4:07:03 (12,119)
Thomason, Paul J 5:57:21 (32,861)
Thomason, Sam 3:36:05 (5,171)
Thompson, Adam 4:17:17 (14,712)
Thompson, Andrew J 3:35:23 (5,030)
Thompson, Andrew Neil 4:38:43 (20,354)
Thompson, Andrew R 4:45:01 (21,967)
Thompson, Andrew W 4:30:38 (18,265)
Thompson, Andy 4:23:10 (16,223)
Thompson, Anthony J 3:34:54 (4,941)
Thompson, Barry S 2:53:37 (591)
Thompson, Ben 4:14:30 (14,026)
Thompson, Campbell 4:51:02 (23,498)
Thompson, Chris 3:21:50 (2,992)
Thompson, Chris J 5:04:05 (26,398)
Thompson, Colin W 3:20:42 (2,858)
Thompson, Craig D 4:54:08 (24,250)
Thompson, Daniel J 3:57:02 (9,628)
Thompson, Darren 3:58:36 (10,126)
Thompson, David 3:32:15 (4,510)
Thompson, David J 3:11:04 (1,786)
Thompson, David J 3:48:03 (7,413)
Thompson, Francis 3:36:35 (5,250)
Thompson, Gary J 3:11:28 (1,823)
Thompson, Gary P 5:09:33 (27,374)
Thompson, Gladstone 4:26:41 (17,176)
Thompson, Guy Ashley 3:49:20 (7,694)
Thompson, Ian J 3:03:41 (1,213)
Thompson, Ian J 5:46:02 (32,018)
Thompson, James Leonard 4:33:49 (19,101)
Thompson, John V 4:51:08 (23,516)
Thompson, Keith N 3:11:48 (1,860)
Thompson, Kevin 4:10:00 (12,853)
Thompson, Kevin E 4:33:39 (19,060)
Thompson, Kit 5:12:53 (27,964)
Thompson, Lee David 4:03:23 (11,313)
Thompson, Leo A 3:18:28 (2,572)
Thompson, Luke D 4:25:22 (16,806)
Thompson, Mark 4:32:03 (18,648)
Thompson, Mark A 5:12:08 (27,828)
Thompson, Mark P 3:44:12 (6,663)
Thompson, Matt E 4:08:15 (12,430)
Thompson, Michael J 4:36:37 (19,825)
Thompson, Neil C 3:07:31 (1,483)
Thompson, Nicholas P 3:38:14 (5,540)
Thompson, Nigel P 2:40:29 (206)
Thompson, Paul L 4:46:41 (22,391)
Thompson, Paul R 3:48:49 (7,574)
Thompson, Pete J 4:11:56 (13,368)
Thompson, Peter C 5:20:15 (29,121)

Thompson, Peter D	3:46:34	(7,100)
Thompson, Peter F	4:09:00	(12,620)
Thompson, Phil	4:39:56	(20,701)
Thompson, Phil	4:48:43	(22,908)
Thompson, Ralph	4:50:57	(23,474)
Thompson, Richard A	3:01:07	(1,060)
Thompson, Richard C	5:52:59	(32,542)
Thompson, Richard W	4:37:45	(20,104)
Thompson, Robert	6:55:52	(34,904)
Thompson, Ryan	5:49:46	(32,315)
Thompson, Shaun	4:26:55	(17,241)
Thompson, Simon	4:11:59	(13,383)
Thompson, Stephen G	2:58:49	(897)
Thompson, Steven W	6:01:36	(33,147)
Thompson, Stuart	5:11:45	(27,767)
Thompson, Stuart S	5:00:45	(25,759)
Thompson, Tony	3:05:54	(1,366)
Thompson, William R	5:18:24	(28,856)
Thompson, Winston C	5:41:57	(31,665)
Thomsen, Henning	3:21:23	(2,933)
Thomson, Alex	6:54:00	(34,880)
Thomson, Alistair J	3:37:23	(5,381)
Thomson, Allan D	3:38:37	(5,609)
Thomson, Arthur G	4:43:24	(21,575)
Thomson, Bertie	4:25:42	(16,910)
Thomson, Dave	3:22:23	(3,054)
Thomson, Doug C	4:25:32	(16,847)
Thomson, Gary	4:17:11	(14,689)
Thomson, George R	3:57:10	(9,664)
Thomson, Harvey	4:52:13	(23,801)
Thomson, Ian	5:15:27	(28,410)
Thomson, Ian J	5:23:39	(29,607)
Thomson, Neil	5:23:00	(29,517)
Thomson, Nicholas J	5:50:58	(32,413)
Thomson, Peter R	4:01:11	(10,831)
Thomson, Shaine	5:21:27	(29,291)
Thomson, Stephen	3:05:26	(1,330)
Thorburn, Jason A	3:47:23	(7,264)
Thorley, Matt Simon	3:44:44	(6,754)
Thorman-Jones, Dilwyn	5:40:44	(31,565)
Thorn, Barry J	3:36:01	(5,158)
Thorn, Michael A	4:14:31	(14,032)
Thornber, David	3:38:41	(5,621)
Thornby, David G	4:01:57	(11,011)
Thorne, Adrian	4:24:43	(16,627)
Thorne, Andrew	4:52:24	(23,842)
Thorne, Colin T	5:08:23	(27,157)
Thorne, John	3:58:48	(10,194)
Thorne, Scott	4:55:55	(24,667)
Thorne, William A	4:43:52	(21,681)
Thornely, Nigel S	4:30:02	(18,106)
Thorner, Roderick B	4:31:24	(18,471)
Thorneywork, David J	4:59:53	(25,573)
Thorns, Andrew	4:12:42	(13,575)
Thornton, Alisdair M	3:34:06	(4,789)
Thornton, Craig C	4:08:25	(12,485)
Thornton, James	3:09:45	(1,687)
Thornton, James	4:29:23	(17,945)
Thornton, James	4:49:21	(23,071)
Thornton, John	4:26:33	(17,130)
Thornton, Keith J	2:57:40	(818)
Thornton, Simon A	4:29:23	(17,945)
Thornton, Simon R	2:58:50	(903)
Thornton, Stanley	5:04:20	(26,430)
Thorogood, Roy D	5:49:00	(32,250)
Thorp, Andy J	3:19:28	(2,680)
Thorp, Caspar	3:35:24	(5,033)
Thorp, Nick J	4:08:13	(12,419)
Thorpe, Adam J	4:00:11	(10,593)
Thorpe, David A	4:38:42	(20,350)
Thorpe, John A	3:25:23	(3,441)
Thorpe, Jon	4:30:36	(18,255)
Thorpe, Martin A	3:48:31	(7,513)
Thorpe, Matt	4:18:01	(14,891)
Thorpe, Ric C	4:25:49	(16,940)
Thorpe, Richard	4:17:35	(14,790)
Thorpe, Richard	4:19:44	(15,348)
Thorpe, Robert J	4:27:18	(17,343)
Thorpe, Scott	4:43:59	(21,715)
Thrasher, Danny	3:08:37	(1,579)
Thraves, Jon M	2:57:39	(817)
Threadgold, Kavan	4:18:23	(14,990)
Threadgold, Mark	5:04:48	(26,506)

Thresher, Terrence H	4:46:34	(22,367)
Thrift, Jonathan M	3:43:32	(6,528)
Throssell, Stephen	3:01:23	(1,075)
Thrower, David N	4:51:38	(23,655)
Thunecke, Rolf	5:55:22	(32,714)
Thurgood, Hugh A	3:59:20	(10,345)
Thurgood, Joe Vince	3:59:21	(10,351)
Thurgood, Lyndon	4:05:33	(11,785)
Thurgood, Marc	3:31:09	(4,352)
Thurgood, Peter S	6:22:51	(34,148)
Thurkettle, David J	6:10:36	(33,591)
Thurley, Mathew R	3:47:08	(7,222)
Thurnham, Jason	5:21:27	(29,291)
Thwaite, Paul	3:39:50	(5,815)
Thyne, Oliver	4:47:57	(22,724)
Tibbals, Adam	4:10:10	(12,904)
Tibbles, Matt	3:44:50	(6,774)
Ticehurst, Martyn D	3:57:45	(9,860)
Tickel, James L	4:54:21	(24,302)
Tickle, Matthew	4:11:28	(13,246)
Tickner, Paul	4:40:27	(20,822)
Tidder, Anthony R	4:18:21	(14,975)
Tidder, Robert G	5:28:14	(30,180)
Tidy, Gary D	3:52:36	(8,426)
Tierney, Liam A	4:05:53	(11,858)
Tiersen, Jean	5:30:04	(30,406)
Tigg, David P	3:54:51	(8,986)
Tighe, Anthony R	4:42:15	(21,265)
Tighe, Steve J	3:32:21	(4,523)
Tigwell, Ralph	5:16:28	(28,555)
Tihcq, Daniel	4:45:00	(21,962)
Tijdhof, Benno	4:40:31	(20,840)
Tijdhof, Johan	4:24:52	(16,677)
Tilbrook, Christopher J	2:52:34	(547)
Tilbury, Adam J	6:03:36	(33,263)
Tilbury, Jonathan E	4:38:21	(20,266)
Tildesley, Kevan G	5:06:57	(26,894)
Tildesley, Lewis R	7:29:04	(35,213)
Tilke, Warren	4:10:01	(12,858)
Till, Dennis B	4:26:49	(17,211)
Tillbrooke, Ton Y	4:53:50	(24,183)
Tiller, Nicholas B	3:50:39	(7,978)
Tiller, Trevor J	5:12:43	(27,929)
Tillery, Andrewe J	2:52:08	(527)
Tilley, David	3:37:38	(5,429)
Tilley, Ian R	5:32:28	(30,683)
Tilley, Jason A	3:05:35	(1,340)
Tilley, Rob A	5:04:00	(26,387)
Tillman, Wayne R	5:07:17	(26,957)
Tillotson, John	3:27:26	(3,759)
Tilly, Ross	4:33:10	(18,932)
Tillyard, Robert F	4:50:26	(23,350)
Tillyer, Dave W	5:35:20	(31,002)
Tilstone, Phil	4:44:22	(21,809)
Tilt, Ralph	3:19:35	(2,694)
Timbrell, Greg	4:44:09	(21,757)
Timeneys, Ricky	3:56:31	(9,465)
Timmins, Andrew	3:41:06	(6,048)
Timmins, Chris	3:42:12	(6,250)
Timms, Giles M	3:24:47	(3,380)
Timms, Jason	5:23:18	(29,571)
Timms, Mark	4:06:27	(11,982)
Timms, Mitchell J	4:11:29	(13,248)
Timney, David	3:08:57	(1,615)
Timossi, Luca	4:28:10	(17,604)
Timpson, Edward	3:58:36	(10,126)
Tindall, Dave W	4:59:00	(25,386)
Tindall, Iain	5:11:14	(27,680)
Tindall, James	4:23:36	(16,334)
Tindall, Mark	4:26:47	(17,203)
Tindle, Robert J	3:32:18	(4,516)
Tinegate, Paul W	4:07:38	(12,265)
Tinena, Alfons	3:47:59	(7,396)
Tiney, Nick K	4:15:57	(14,381)
Tingle, Andrew J	4:36:11	(19,716)
Tink, Andy Edward	3:49:50	(7,807)
Tinker, Antony A	3:47:03	(7,206)
Tinkler, Mark	3:28:49	(3,977)
Tinling, Simon M	3:19:40	(2,704)
Tinoco, Gerardo	4:35:07	(19,442)
Tinsley, Miles L	4:22:05	(15,961)
Tinsley, Peter Alan	3:51:16	(8,112)
Tinti, Marco	4:49:37	(23,155)

Tinton, Glen	4:30:59	(18,346)
Tipacti, Marcos	5:31:45	(30,611)
Tippet, Simon J	4:54:41	(24,382)
Tironi, Stefano	3:38:58	(5,675)
Tisdall, David C	5:10:55	(27,627)
Titcombe, Graham N	4:35:04	(19,434)
Titley, Howard William	4:51:53	(23,723)
Titshall, Colin A	4:37:47	(20,115)
Titshall, Jamie C	4:37:47	(20,115)
Tittle, Dave J	4:21:32	(15,824)
To, Ken	3:41:56	(6,191)
Tobias, Read	3:00:05	(1,004)
Tobin, Anthony	4:00:03	(10,557)
Tobin, Michael J	5:07:26	(26,993)
Tobin, Simon	3:29:04	(4,013)
Tobin, Tony	5:00:50	(25,771)
Todd, Andy	3:12:34	(1,940)
Todd, Colin J	4:48:05	(22,759)
Todd, David J	5:35:29	(31,017)
Todd, Edward M	3:47:38	(7,313)
Todd, James J	3:52:04	(8,291)
Todd, James K	4:07:23	(12,209)
Todd, Kevin	3:47:49	(7,357)
Todd, Matthew R	5:44:42	(31,907)
Todd, Paul	4:52:43	(23,910)
Todd, Richard J	3:29:37	(4,120)
Todman, David	4:35:12	(19,465)
Tognarelli, Adrian	3:38:27	(5,578)
Toher, John-Paul	4:32:57	(18,885)
Tokarczyk, Karol	3:09:35	(1,665)
Tolan, Colm	4:31:03	(18,370)
Toland, Ben	3:56:59	(9,616)
Tolhurst, Patrick J	4:22:42	(16,127)
Toller, Mark S	5:12:45	(27,934)
Tolley, Nicky J	5:18:26	(28,861)
Tolliday, Clive W	4:40:19	(20,799)
Tollington, Peter G	4:27:37	(17,417)
Tombling, Anthony R	5:18:34	(28,886)
Tombs, Jonathan M	3:31:50	(4,445)
Tomkins, Matthew P	3:48:30	(7,508)
Tomkinson, Mark D	5:20:29	(29,150)
Tomlin, Ben S	3:39:27	(5,750)
Tomlin, Charles A	4:58:59	(25,383)
Tomlin, Darren	4:43:09	(21,503)
Tomlin, James R	3:57:21	(9,729)
Tomlinson, Dean L	4:51:29	(23,617)
Tomlinson, Fred G	6:50:30	(34,824)
Tomlinson, Ian M	4:19:38	(15,323)
Tomlinson, Oliver C	5:36:41	(31,142)
Tompsett, Gary	4:40:07	(20,757)
Toms, Malcolm	5:55:31	(32,727)
Toms, Simon J	3:43:54	(6,616)
Tomsett, Peter L	4:23:23	(16,274)
Toner, David	4:49:27	(23,092)
Toner, Gary M	4:52:53	(23,945)
Toner, Neil	3:16:53	(2,419)
Tonge, Steven	4:24:55	(16,688)
Tongue, Gareth	4:22:24	(16,050)
Tonkin, Ben T	4:19:03	(15,173)
Tonkinson, Robert M	4:15:04	(14,180)
Toole, Daniel	3:27:51	(3,833)
Tooley, Frank A	3:48:57	(7,605)
Toolin, Iain H	4:10:27	(12,970)
Toomey, Gary	4:48:58	(22,962)
Toone, Michael G	4:56:50	(24,890)
Tootell, Andrew R	3:31:45	(4,430)
Tootell, Simon P	3:18:42	(2,587)
Topper, Steve	3:37:20	(5,377)
Topping, Simon	3:48:10	(7,438)
Tordoff, Phil	3:33:45	(4,713)
Torkington, Mark	4:34:36	(19,288)
Torley, Bob	4:12:23	(13,488)
Tormi, Mikko	3:02:06	(1,126)
Tornusciolo, Giovanni	5:14:39	(28,260)
Torquati, Francesco	4:24:07	(16,477)
Torres, Gerardo	4:00:13	(10,603)
Torrington, Bruce E	5:46:47	(32,073)
Torry, Hugh J	2:44:13	(292)
Tosh, Philip P	5:35:04	(30,979)
Toshinobu, Katashiba	3:36:52	(5,290)
Toshitake, Ono	4:51:22	(23,581)
Tosney, Jonah J	5:08:55	(27,255)
Totterdell, Graham W	4:04:29	(11,541)

Twizell, David W 5:17:09 (28,667)
Twomey, Andrew J 3:57:59 (9,927)
Twomey, Eamon G 3:03:57 (1,236)
Twose, Paul 4:06:39 (12,035)
Twydell, Will 4:58:58 (25,380)
Twyford, Damian P 4:59:33 (25,508)
Twyman, Luke G 3:25:48 (3,501)
Tyburski, Marcin 4:20:45 (15,619)
Tye, Christian H 4:44:10 (21,763)
Tye, Christopher 5:59:13 (33,001)
Tyers, Brian W 6:31:21 (34,441)
Tyers, Simon J 5:08:20 (27,146)
Tyler, Adam J 6:09:39 (33,544)
Tyler, Anthony H 3:09:14 (1,647)
Tyler, Bill 4:34:40 (19,307)
Tyler, David A 4:54:29 (24,331)
Tyler, David J 5:29:28 (30,326)
Tyler, Jamie 3:54:31 (8,894)
Tyler, John 3:08:42 (1,589)
Tyler, Richard C 3:53:59 (8,751)
Tyley, Gwynfor 3:27:47 (3,823)
Tylianakis, Matt M 4:24:12 (16,497)
Tymon, Shaun David 3:37:58 (5,481)
Tyrrell, Clive A 6:37:02 (34,565)
Tyrrell, Mark 4:07:23 (12,209)
Tyrrell, Nigel P 3:38:28 (5,581)
Tyrrell, Tommy 5:17:37 (28,734)
Tyrwhitt-Drake, Tom W 5:21:17 (29,266)
Tysoe, Terry 4:37:59 (20,161)
Tyszkiewicz, John Z 3:55:31 (9,160)
Tzannes-Kastritis, Andreas 4:32:20 (18,713)
Uberto, Giovanni 4:00:46 (10,733)
Ubhi, Amit S 6:06:15 (33,400)
Ubsdell, Simon 2:59:16 (940)
Uddin, Jomir 5:07:08 (26,929)
Uden, Matthew 4:47:26 (22,587)
Udvardi, Mario 4:08:35 (12,519)
Uebelgunne, Detlef-Ruidiger 6:18:58 (33,995)
Uff, Chris E 2:54:17 (616)
Ugarte Garagalza, Carlos 4:00:27 (10,650)
Uggerhoj, Jesper 4:13:37 (13,829)
Uglow, Pete M 4:59:51 (25,565)
Uittermark, Paul 5:54:01 (32,615)
Ulatowski, Peter 5:09:49 (27,432)
Ullrich, Frank 3:18:42 (2,587)
Ulrich, Kai Uwe 3:25:36 (3,473)
Umfreville, Paul 5:02:44 (26,162)
Umlauf, Peter 3:58:03 (9,954)
Underdown, Kevin C 3:36:28 (5,229)
Underhill, Richard 3:47:08 (7,222)
Underwood, Mark 3:46:12 (7,017)
Underwood, Mark 5:12:42 (27,926)
Underwood, Paul K 3:38:17 (5,548)
Unerman, Martin H 4:29:20 (17,932)
Ung, Hy C 4:29:11 (17,884)
Unger, Andreas 4:18:53 (15,128)
Ungi, Tom 5:22:27 (29,430)
Unitt, Dennis J 5:12:31 (27,896)
Unitt, Keith 4:08:14 (12,425)
Unsted, Paul S 3:49:39 (7,758)
Unsworth, Ben D 3:56:38 (9,511)
Unti, Marco 4:58:19 (25,218)
Unwin, Peter 4:59:57 (25,587)
Unwin, Richard J 4:59:09 (25,424)
Unwin, Shane D 4:28:48 (17,776)
Upellini, Alexandre 4:31:02 (18,361)
Upham, Mark A 4:20:24 (15,537)
Upjohn, Dave 4:09:08 (12,647)
Upson, Chris 2:54:09 (611)
Upson, Tom G 4:51:09 (23,521)
Upton, Brian M 3:44:23 (6,698)
Ural, Can 4:47:25 (22,582)
Ure, Bruce 4:41:44 (21,149)
Urquiza, José Augusto J 2:51:19 (501)
Urrunaga, Roberto 3:08:35 (1,575)
Urry, Martyn J 4:41:07 (20,989)
Urwin, Robert James 3:28:46 (3,967)
Urwin, Stephen P 5:35:57 (31,071)
Usher, Wayne J 2:49:00 (423)
Utley, David 3:49:36 (7,747)
Utteridge, Glenn R 3:43:33 (6,532)
Utz, Hans-Juergen 5:58:59 (32,992)
Uzzell, Kevin 3:31:12 (4,361)

Vacher, Rupert P 4:18:27 (15,017)
Vadehra, Aseem 3:45:16 (6,848)
Vadera, Rupin 6:35:51 (34,539)
Vadgama, Damien 3:04:09 (1,245)
Vaezinejad, Mehrad 6:12:48 (33,681)
Vagi, Andrew C 2:57:54 (829)
Vaidyanathan, Raju 5:45:48 (32,002)
Vaillant, Edmond 3:48:49 (7,574)
Valdes, Pablo 3:13:32 (2,065)
Vale, John R 6:01:31 (33,143)
Valentin, Eric 3:50:09 (7,872)
Valentin, Patrick 4:37:50 (20,128)
Valentine, David 4:46:56 (22,461)
Valentine, Tony J 4:45:22 (22,050)
Valentini, Mick J 3:03:43 (1,217)
Valentino, Antony 6:05:01 (33,340)
Valji, Vishram K 4:07:17 (12,170)
Vallance, Andrew J 2:47:00 (369)
Vallance, Simon P 5:16:13 (28,529)
Vallance, Stephen J 3:48:55 (7,599)
Vallee, Laurent 3:49:01 (7,622)
Vamben, Eric S 2:37:15 (144)
Van Agteren, Sebastian 4:12:18 (13,468)
Van Alderwegen, Francis S 4:46:21 (22,294)
Van Alderweggen, Damian 3:56:30 (9,461)
Van Ansem, Jan 3:39:40 (5,789)
Van Arendonk, Jan 3:56:37 (9,500)
Van Arkel, Gerardus 3:11:44 (1,852)
Van Breda, Marc 3:21:13 (2,911)
Van Damme, Frank 3:26:12 (3,559)
Van Den Berg, André 4:54:16 (24,279)
Van Den Berg, Dannis 5:27:31 (30,095)
Van Den Bossche, Patrick 3:49:38 (7,755)
Van Den Broek, Adam J 4:25:30 (16,836)
Van Den Broek, Ton 4:29:28 (17,963)
Van Der Bijl, Wouter 3:48:35 (7,529)
Van Der Graaf, Harry 4:09:18 (12,682)
Van Der Heim, Bradley 5:39:27 (31,441)
Van Der Linden, Johannis 3:13:21 (2,041)
Van Der Meer, Wietze 4:23:39 (16,349)
Van Der Merwe, Brett A 4:25:46 (16,928)
Van Der Merwe, Willem B 3:14:52 (2,214)
Van Der Ven, Hans 4:01:49 (10,987)
Van Der Walt, Jurg 2:58:28 (865)
Van Der Wilt, Ben 4:36:51 (19,883)
Van Deventer, Paul M 5:12:06 (27,819)
Van Dijen, Rob 4:38:51 (20,388)
Van Hal, Erik 3:29:57 (4,175)
Van Heerden, Jaco 6:37:05 (34,569)
Van Helmond, Gerrie 3:04:06 (1,242)
Van Leeuwen, Michel 4:18:02 (14,900)
Van Mersbergen, Howard 3:28:14 (3,890)
Van Minden, Nils 3:56:41 (9,529)
Van Niekerk, Johan Gysbert 3:11:34 (1,836)
Van Olmen, Erik 4:56:50 (24,890)
Van Oranje, Pieter-Christiaan 3:42:45 (6,367)
Van Overmeeren, Bram 4:36:42 (19,838)
Van Rij, Jaap J 3:29:05 (4,022)
Van Trommel, Hielke 3:16:30 (2,378)
Van Velsen, Koen 3:34:38 (4,902)
Van Waardenberg, Rens 4:15:08 (14,200)
Van Weert, Jean-Paul 3:42:53 (6,395)
Van West, Alain 5:00:13 (25,637)
Van Wijk, Danny 3:09:47 (1,688)
Van Wissen, Wout G 3:58:10 (9,996)
Van Woerkom, Vincent S 2:53:21 (576)
Van Zyl, Heine 2:58:18 (858)
Vandenlindenloof, Erwin 3:58:44 (10,170)
Vanderpump, Mark R 3:58:30 (10,097)
Vanderschueren, Mattias 4:02:21 (11,091)
Vanetzian, Greg 4:09:18 (12,682)
Vanhooijdonk, Jan P 5:17:28 (28,715)
Vannen, David J 3:35:37 (5,074)
Vanrenen, Daniel 4:22:03 (15,954)
Vanson, Neil A 4:47:10 (22,536)
Vanstone, Justin 4:14:30 (14,026)
Vantreen, Tom 5:00:16 (25,646)
Vara, Sanjay 4:04:46 (11,599)
Varathadasan, Nadarajah 4:03:55 (11,427)
Varela, Rodolfo 3:16:22 (2,365)
Vargeson, Mark D 4:59:01 (25,391)
Vargeson, Simon J 4:36:18 (19,739)
Vari, Claudio 2:48:24 (409)

Varley, Andrew M 4:01:13 (10,839)
Varley, Ashley D 3:28:40 (3,948)
Varley, Christian 2:54:31 (634)
Varley, Mark 3:40:48 (6,000)
Varley, Peter C 4:46:04 (22,218)
Varney, Oli H 4:14:56 (14,149)
Varney, Steven R 3:01:13 (1,068)
Varney, Terry 5:09:27 (27,356)
Varu, Kunal 3:58:08 (9,982)
Vas, David A 3:38:38 (5,615)
Vasir, Shindy S 5:48:22 (32,206)
Vassallo, Peter C 5:54:44 (32,663)
Vassie, Christopher J 4:08:57 (12,606)
Vassiliou, Vasso 4:32:51 (18,860)
Vaudin, David 3:35:18 (5,009)
Vaudin, John N 5:07:21 (26,971)
Vaudin, Mark 5:01:11 (25,858)
Vaudrecourt, Eduardo 3:49:05 (7,642)
Vaughan, Allan 4:37:22 (20,000)
Vaughan, Bryan J 3:43:47 (6,586)
Vaughan, Duncan A 4:01:39 (10,956)
Vaughan, Huw John 4:18:38 (15,064)
Vaughan, Mark 3:51:39 (8,199)
Vaughan, Michael Anthony 3:37:33 (5,412)
Vaughan, Neville Adrian 3:15:09 (2,249)
Vaughan, Oliver R 4:50:15 (23,301)
Vaughan, Rhodri J 4:00:06 (10,572)
Vaughnley, Craig 5:58:12 (32,938)
Vaughnley, Jason K 5:58:12 (32,938)
Vauth, Hermann 3:49:57 (7,823)
Vauth, Jürgen 3:58:40 (10,151)
Vaz, Manuel 2:55:13 (682)
Veal, Clive 4:11:56 (13,368)
Veale, David 3:23:20 (3,163)
Veale, James A 4:37:42 (20,090)
Veale, Peter R 4:17:27 (14,757)
Veck, Sean 5:16:37 (28,582)
Veerman, Gerrard 5:09:08 (27,295)
Veevers, James J 6:53:26 (34,870)
Vega, Manolo 3:57:46 (9,863)
Vegro, Symon 4:08:16 (12,439)
Veiguela Nuñez, Jesus 2:57:32 (809)
Veihl, Dagmar 4:33:17 (18,968)
Vekaria, Dinal 5:29:23 (30,317)
Vekaria, Navin V 4:33:46 (19,090)
Velagapudi, Vamsi K 3:52:48 (8,465)
Velebit, Dragoljub 3:37:46 (5,450)
Velez, Pablo 4:06:13 (11,931)
Vellante, Franco 5:01:14 (25,869)
Velthuis, Jeroen 3:29:24 (4,089)
Velut, Jean-Gabriel 4:05:39 (11,815)
Venables, Martin 4:45:29 (22,075)
Venn, Wesley J 4:47:18 (22,560)
Venta, Carlos 4:09:30 (12,719)
Venter, Peter M 4:00:57 (10,786)
Ventham, Graham M 4:52:09 (23,786)
Ventrice, Rocco 3:09:07 (1,629)
Ventura, Peter 4:53:56 (24,208)
Venturi, Stefano 4:24:45 (16,638)
Verblis, Daniel P 5:18:49 (28,938)
Verde, Nick 4:18:18 (14,962)
Vere, Derek 6:21:42 (34,103)
Vere, Graham 4:27:26 (17,377)
Vergnes, Nicolas 3:32:28 (4,540)
Verhoef, Ronald 3:31:40 (4,418)
Verity, Lee R 3:52:14 (8,341)
Verity, Martin J 5:28:36 (30,222)
Verling, Ben F 4:19:50 (15,385)
Vermeesch, Pieter 2:30:37 (71)
Vernaci, Francesco 3:08:55 (1,610)
Vernersson, Lars 3:45:18 (6,854)
Vernon, Christopher Russell 4:52:57 (23,965)
Vernon, Darren L 3:00:03 (1,001)
Vernon, Gary H 2:58:08 (846)
Vernon, Mike 5:21:49 (29,346)
Vernon, Nigel S 4:45:04 (21,986)
Vernon, Phil 4:35:29 (19,536)
Verrept, Marc 4:55:08 (24,485)
Verth, Alistair 4:35:13 (19,472)
Very, Jean-Pierre 4:25:07 (16,739)
Vesperini, Luigi 4:26:07 (17,014)
Vessichelli, Maurizio 4:05:02 (11,659)
Vetter, Georg 4:54:05 (24,241)

Vey, Frederic 4:59:28 (25,488)
Vezzi, Fulvio 3:37:50 (5,462)
Vials, Russell D 5:17:01 (28,639)
Vianello, Nerino 4:51:52 (23,717)
Vicente, Victor 3:33:48 (4,724)
Vicente Do Souto, Carlos 3:31:18 (4,371)
Vichion, Mark 3:55:29 (9,154)
Vickers, Benjamin H 3:11:35 (1,839)
Vickers, Graham M 3:24:36 (3,356)
Vickers, John A 4:27:25 (17,374)
Vickers, Mark 5:37:24 (31,214)
Vickers, Paul G 3:51:56 (8,263)
Vickers, Stacy 7:10:44 (35,057)
Vickers, Thomas G 4:08:42 (12,553)
Vickers, Tony 3:29:28 (4,097)
Vickery, David C 3:28:39 (3,947)
Vickery, Robert 3:37:44 (5,447)
Victor, David 3:57:49 (9,880)
Vidal, Marco Arturo 4:13:18 (13,745)
Vidor, Luca 4:46:55 (22,454)
Vieira, Erik R 5:03:50 (26,348)
Vieira, Sam C 4:59:16 (25,445)
Vigar, Robert J 5:38:30 (31,333)
Vignati, Stefano 5:12:54 (27,966)
Viletta, Rudolf 4:14:11 (13,955)
Villarreal, Eduardo Maximo 3:49:49 (7,803)
Villars, Philip 4:52:26 (23,851)
Villiers, Christopher 4:48:20 (22,814)
Villiers, Freddie 3:58:25 (10,071)
Vincent, Alun 3:49:08 (7,651)
Vincent, Andrew 3:50:01 (7,840)
Vincent, David 4:39:08 (20,473)
Vincent, Edward 4:21:06 (15,714)
Vincent, Edward M 3:41:12 (6,071)
Vincent, Kenny A 6:06:27 (33,410)
Vincent, Kevin M 3:55:04 (9,050)
Vincent, Paul 4:14:56 (14,149)
Vine, Adrian P 4:47:30 (22,601)
Vine, Desmond G 4:04:08 (11,474)
Vines, Daniel J 5:01:27 (25,904)
Virdee, Inderpal S 4:58:31 (25,274)
Virgona, Angelo J 2:59:01 (922)
Visi, Vincenzo 3:38:25 (5,570)
Vithlani, Diven 7:13:17 (35,086)
Vittorini, Piergiorgio 5:00:44 (25,755)
Vivian, John E 5:33:12 (30,774)
Vizard, Trevor J 5:11:03 (27,652)
Vlaar, Henry J 3:09:30 (1,658)
Voaden, Roger 2:54:24 (626)
Voase, Stephen 3:36:43 (5,265)
Voce, Ananda 3:41:55 (6,189)
Vodden, Ed D 4:55:50 (24,649)
Voegele, Jens 5:39:02 (31,399)
Voelzer, Robert 4:43:06 (21,493)
Vogt, Michael 3:31:22 (4,378)
Vogwell, David J 3:15:04 (2,241)
Vohra, Arun 6:06:12 (33,395)
Voix, Fabien 3:25:25 (3,449)
Vojtek, Hartmut 4:55:35 (24,591)
Vojtek, René 3:10:16 (1,718)
Volans, Ian J 3:46:36 (7,110)
Volante, Neil J 4:57:27 (25,021)
Volke, John 4:19:35 (15,308)
Vollar, Simon D 5:45:06 (31,933)
Vollentine, Brian 4:10:33 (12,994)
Vollstedt, Klaus 4:38:06 (20,201)
Von Kumberg, Wolf 5:16:00 (28,499)
Von Othegraven, Thomas 5:05:30 (26,639)
Vonasek, Stefan 4:28:35 (17,722)
Vongo Neto, Miguel Sebastiao 3:06:09 (1,384)
Vooght, Stephen J 4:19:22 (15,249)
Vora, Bhimji 4:34:36 (19,288)
Vorres, Dimitri 2:57:06 (782)
Vos, Chris A 4:35:06 (19,439)
Vosper, Matthew P 4:11:19 (13,194)
Voss, Neil 5:09:51 (27,434)
Vowles, Nicholas W 3:49:51 (7,809)
Vreken, Jan 4:55:48 (24,640)
Vreken, Jan H 4:55:47 (24,632)
Vrhunc, Matjaz 2:53:45 (595)
Vrignaud, Dominiqu 4:23:53 (16,409)
Vurnum, Mark 5:50:49 (32,400)
Vyas, Kiren 5:02:52 (26,189)
Vye Taylor, Edward H 4:33:39 (19,060)
Waby, Paul 2:37:52 (156)
Waddams, Peter L 4:55:25 (24,556)
Waddell, Douglas R 3:43:24 (6,510)
Waddell, Josh 4:29:22 (17,940)
Waddingham, Andrew 3:51:41 (8,206)
Waddingham, Keith 3:36:54 (5,295)
Waddington, Neil 4:27:16 (17,333)
Wade, Christopher P 5:20:54 (29,206)
Wade, Gary 3:53:33 (8,634)
Wade, Ian M 4:55:03 (24,460)
Wade, Mark A 5:20:54 (29,206)
Wade, Neil S 3:49:22 (7,703)
Wade, Richard M 3:42:50 (6,385)
Wade, Tom E 3:12:56 (1,995)
Wade-Jones, Hugh P 3:28:46 (3,967)
Wadeson, Craig D 5:14:23 (28,219)
Wadeson, Ivan 4:07:19 (12,183)
Wadey, Christopher C 3:43:53 (6,611)
Wadey, Ross 4:23:44 (16,370)
Wadey, Roy B 2:56:38 (754)
Wadhams, Mark Anthony 4:23:16 (16,248)
Wadher, Bhavesh V 5:17:36 (28,730)
Wadlow, Phil J 3:57:37 (9,806)
Wadmore, Mark 4:02:41 (11,165)
Wadsworth, Adrian M 3:34:04 (4,778)
Wadsworth, Lee 3:05:45 (1,352)
Wadsworth, Patrick John 3:33:54 (4,742)
Wadsworth, Philip 5:33:05 (30,764)
Waelde, Martin 3:26:46 (3,645)
Wagener, Daniel F 3:57:32 (9,781)
Wagener, Markus 3:43:52 (6,607)
Waghorn, Philip R 4:59:45 (25,544)
Waghorn, Robert 6:47:47 (34,766)
Wagland, Roger 4:05:31 (11,773)
Wagner, Bernd 4:05:56 (11,866)
Wagner, Charles 4:25:59 (16,983)
Wagner, Christoph 3:49:14 (7,672)
Wagner, Markus 5:37:52 (31,258)
Wagner, Rolf 5:47:15 (32,114)
Wagner, Sam M 5:54:42 (32,660)
Wagner, Steve 3:35:40 (5,090)
Wagstaff, Matthew J 4:19:07 (15,188)
Waiman, Alex 5:12:59 (27,981)
Wainhouse, Owen 3:39:48 (5,809)
Wainman, Phil 5:04:53 (26,521)
Wainwright, Ben 4:18:34 (15,044)
Wainwright, Christopher J 7:31:42 (35,232)
Wainwright, Mark 4:47:58 (22,728)
Wainwright, Tim D 5:26:44 (30,018)
Wainwright, Tom 5:02:40 (26,147)
Wait, Andrew 3:33:19 (4,654)
Wait, Christopher M 3:36:26 (5,222)
Waite, Colin R 5:23:20 (29,574)
Waite, Gareth T 4:15:37 (14,308)
Waite, Gary 4:02:45 (11,178)
Waite, Howard 3:05:11 (1,316)
Waite, James D 2:47:18 (377)
Waite, Luke A 3:48:30 (7,508)
Waite, Mark 3:20:36 (2,838)
Waites, Malcolm J 4:49:15 (23,036)
Waites, Tim 5:35:42 (31,042)
Wakefield, Antony 3:48:51 (7,585)
Wakefield, David W 4:54:12 (24,259)
Wakefield, Gary F 4:29:13 (17,899)
Wakefield, Robin M 4:51:58 (23,746)
Wakeford, Paul 4:13:20 (13,760)
Wakeford, Stephen 3:54:00 (8,757)
Wakeham, David R 4:10:29 (12,978)
Wakelam, Paul C 4:01:15 (10,847)
Wakeling, Geoffrey I 4:30:36 (18,255)
Wakerley, Nick 4:30:10 (18,142)
Walbank, Philip C 5:02:17 (26,076)
Walberton, Michael A 3:23:15 (3,154)
Walburn, Stephen R 5:09:22 (27,340)
Walby, Chris 3:21:20 (2,924)
Walby, Ollie J 3:25:34 (3,469)
Walden, Barry L 5:18:23 (28,854)
Walden, Phillip 5:32:45 (30,732)
Walder, Chris 5:16:04 (28,508)
Walder, Stevyn C 4:18:55 (15,139)
Waldie, Doug 3:27:33 (3,790)
Walding, Aaron J 4:58:24 (25,243)
Waldron, Bernard 4:29:20 (17,932)
Waldron, David T 5:58:49 (32,980)
Waldron, Nicholas P 6:11:03 (33,602)
Waldron, Russell J 4:25:03 (16,726)
Waldron, Simeon P 3:12:52 (1,984)
Waldron-Lych, Tom 3:13:05 (2,013)
Waldschütz, Alois 3:17:11 (2,452)
Waldwyn, Graham B 6:17:28 (33,904)
Wales, Chris J 3:08:30 (1,565)
Wales, Lee A 4:55:19 (24,531)
Walford, Stuart A 5:37:19 (31,207)
Walia, Viren 5:08:40 (27,207)
Walkden, Simon E 3:53:20 (8,587)
Walker, Aaron R 6:40:34 (34,635)
Walker, Allan P 4:45:50 (22,171)
Walker, Andrew D 4:27:12 (17,309)
Walker, Andrew M 4:29:14 (17,908)
Walker, Anthony P 4:26:15 (17,051)
Walker, Brian 6:02:05 (33,176)
Walker, Chris J 4:10:13 (12,913)
Walker, Christopher J 4:27:48 (17,487)
Walker, Clive 4:55:50 (24,649)
Walker, Craig 4:50:06 (23,264)
Walker, Craig J 3:43:38 (6,551)
Walker, Daimon J 4:36:40 (19,830)
Walker, Dave M 5:34:57 (30,962)
Walker, David F 4:38:46 (20,369)
Walker, David W 4:50:14 (23,292)
Walker, Frank 5:18:23 (28,854)
Walker, Garry J 4:33:19 (18,982)
Walker, Garth E 4:39:41 (20,639)
Walker, Grant William Thomas 6:46:08 (34,722)
Walker, Ian 4:49:35 (23,141)
Walker, James R 2:42:06 (236)
Walker, James R 3:58:00 (9,931)
Walker, Jason 3:38:56 (5,661)
Walker, John 4:35:42 (19,599)
Walker, John 4:39:40 (20,634)
Walker, John W 4:33:42 (19,075)
Walker, Jon 5:30:13 (30,430)
Walker, Joseph A 4:01:56 (11,006)
Walker, Julian A 4:00:42 (10,720)
Walker, Keith E 6:26:22 (34,295)
Walker, Kelvin Darren Charles 4:16:04 (14,416)
Walker, Kenny 4:52:16 (23,814)
Walker, Kieith V 3:44:13 (6,667)
Walker, Lee M 5:36:22 (31,109)
Walker, Liam D 4:17:33 (14,781)
Walker, Mark 4:24:27 (16,560)
Walker, Mark D 3:21:48 (2,984)
Walker, Mark G 3:36:54 (5,295)
Walker, Martin 4:09:35 (12,747)
Walker, Martin D 4:26:38 (17,164)
Walker, Martin J 5:24:21 (29,711)
Walker, Michael J 5:51:20 (32,434)
Walker, Neil 4:19:24 (15,255)
Walker, Neil A 4:08:39 (12,533)
Walker, Nigel M 4:44:18 (21,794)
Walker, Paul 3:38:02 (5,497)
Walker, Paul 6:46:55 (34,736)
Walker, Paul A 3:46:20 (7,048)
Walker, Peter J 3:57:03 (9,634)
Walker, Peter R 3:48:26 (7,496)
Walker, Robert J 4:28:56 (17,814)
Walker, Robert L 4:34:57 (19,395)
Walker, Russell J 4:39:38 (20,621)
Walker, Ryan M 4:31:34 (18,518)
Walker, Scott M 5:10:29 (27,545)
Walker, Simon 5:54:10 (32,629)
Walker, Simon A 3:33:52 (4,734)
Walker, Stephen A 3:30:35 (4,269)
Walker, Stephen D 3:27:25 (3,752)
Walker, Stephen J 4:43:04 (21,484)
Walker, Steven W 3:17:52 (2,516)
Walker, Stuart D 3:11:52 (1,871)
Walker, Stuart L 5:25:31 (29,860)
Walker, Tim M 3:07:40 (1,498)
Walker, Timothy-John 4:17:57 (14,872)
Walker, Tony 7:06:51 (35,026)
Walker, Warren R 4:06:02 (11,889)
Walkley, Darrell T 4:30:18 (18,176)
Walklin, Steven A 4:48:42 (22,902)
Wall, Brendan 4:06:30 (11,991)

Wall, David C.......4:55:19 (24,531)
Wall, Ian.......2:59:50 (985)
Wall, James H.......4:29:10 (17,876)
Wall, Jason M.......3:55:53 (9,282)
Wallace, Colin R.......3:59:29 (10,384)
Wallace, David A.......4:39:32 (20,591)
Wallace, David F.......3:27:18 (3,733)
Wallace, Edmund J.......4:14:30 (14,026)
Wallace, James.......3:22:09 (3,029)
Wallace, John.......6:51:46 (34,841)
Wallace, Justin.......5:41:25 (31,621)
Wallace, Keven P.......4:44:16 (21,783)
Wallace, Leonard D.......4:28:00 (17,542)
Wallace, Martin C.......3:30:44 (4,288)
Wallace, Martyn Edward.......3:38:06 (5,514)
Wallace, Nathan A.......5:21:49 (29,346)
Wallace, Richard A.......3:16:14 (2,353)
Wallace, Stuart J.......5:43:51 (31,837)
Wallace, Tony.......3:49:27 (7,718)
Wallace-Mason, Nigel J.......4:12:44 (13,587)
Wallbank, Daren.......5:08:59 (27,270)
Wallenberg, Marc J.......4:34:14 (19,204)
Waller, Anthony E.......5:09:15 (27,316)
Waller, David M.......3:59:21 (10,351)
Waller, Douglas W.......4:00:23 (10,632)
Waller, Gary B.......5:09:16 (27,321)
Waller, Ian.......4:06:14 (11,938)
Wallington, Darren J.......4:04:01 (11,455)
Wallis, Alan.......4:51:47 (23,695)
Wallis, Patrick.......3:11:04 (1,786)
Wallis, Paul J.......4:46:53 (22,444)
Wallis, Peter John.......3:14:09 (2,141)
Wallis, Philip J.......3:46:58 (7,196)
Walls, Fabio.......4:54:22 (24,305)
Walls, Jonathan.......5:31:07 (30,541)
Walls, Rob M.......4:29:18 (17,927)
Wallsgrove, Jon S.......5:06:37 (26,824)
Wallwork, Roger I.......3:52:28 (8,396)
Walsgrove, John D.......2:55:08 (673)
Walsh, Alistair J.......4:45:15 (22,028)
Walsh, Allan J.......4:48:30 (22,851)
Walsh, Andrew.......4:28:34 (17,716)
Walsh, Anthony.......7:24:16 (35,172)
Walsh, Bernie.......3:51:35 (8,183)
Walsh, Carl M.......5:16:04 (28,508)
Walsh, David.......4:14:40 (14,067)
Walsh, Dylan L.......5:01:29 (25,910)
Walsh, Francis E.......3:12:45 (1,965)
Walsh, Frank J.......4:55:58 (24,676)
Walsh, Guy.......4:07:45 (12,302)
Walsh, James.......4:25:17 (16,780)
Walsh, Mark.......6:04:47 (33,324)
Walsh, Michael I.......2:44:10 (288)
Walsh, Nathan J.......4:08:25 (12,485)
Walsh, Patrick J.......4:07:31 (12,240)
Walsh, Paul M.......3:14:42 (2,197)
Walsh, Pete.......4:33:40 (19,066)
Walsh, Phillip I.......3:26:59 (3,680)
Walsh, Richard J.......3:57:46 (9,863)
Walsh, Robin.......4:11:32 (13,263)
Walsh, Sean S.......5:31:32 (30,585)
Walsh, Shane P.......4:36:49 (19,870)
Walsh, Stephen C.......4:25:09 (16,751)
Walsh, Steve R.......3:23:40 (3,214)
Walsh, Timothy P.......4:05:47 (11,838)
Walsh, William T.......3:45:27 (6,885)
Waltenspul, Christoph.......3:53:10 (8,556)
Walter, Andrew.......4:41:04 (20,976)
Walters, Adrian.......4:01:35 (10,939)
Walters, Andrew.......5:37:20 (31,209)
Walters, Cyril.......3:46:52 (7,171)
Walters, David.......4:28:09 (17,593)
Walters, Edwyn J.......3:53:57 (8,738)
Walters, Humphrey J.......5:02:34 (26,132)
Walters, John.......4:11:02 (13,121)
Walters, John F.......3:35:31 (5,049)
Walters, Paul.......3:41:08 (6,055)
Walters, Paul.......3:59:13 (10,317)
Walters, Simon D.......5:25:14 (29,828)
Walton, Christopher D.......4:16:59 (14,642)
Walton, Jack.......3:30:57 (4,320)
Walton, James.......4:18:42 (15,081)
Walton, James M.......5:01:51 (25,980)
Walton, Neil S.......4:56:27 (24,785)
Walton, Oliver E.......4:08:37 (12,528)
Walton, Paul R.......5:21:48 (29,343)
Walton, Robert.......4:10:31 (12,984)

Wanjiru, Samuel.......2:05:10 (1)

Sammy Wanjiru is one of the greatest Kenyan marathoners of all time. Born in 1986, his greatest achievement was winning the 2008 Olympic marathon in Beijing in 2:06:32, but he also set the world record in the half-marathon three times and a world junior record for 10,000m. Wanjiru started running at the age of 15. In 2002 he moved to Japan where he achieved great success on the Japanese cross-country circuit. He was subsequently coached by 1992 Olympic marathon silver medallist Koichi Morishita. His stated goal is to better Haile Gebrselassie's world record in the marathon and says he feels capable of clocking a sub 2 hours time for the distance. In the 2008 London Marathon he came second, breaking 2:06 for the first time. Wanjiru forgot his racing shoes in Beijing, so he had to run the Olympic marathon in his warm-up shoes. He wanted to defend his title at the 2010 London Marathon, but he encountered knee trouble at the midway point of the race and decided to drop out to avoid further injury.

Wanlin, Greg.......3:41:01 (6,033)
Wannell, Ray.......4:28:12 (17,613)
Waplington, Mark.......3:17:17 (2,463)
Warburton, Bradley.......3:51:29 (8,164)
Warburton, Gavin S.......6:42:46 (34,675)
Warburton, John.......4:31:41 (18,546)
Ward, Adam D.......4:27:05 (17,278)
Ward, Andrew.......4:32:51 (18,860)
Ward, Andrew D.......3:16:46 (2,411)
Ward, Andrew J.......3:49:48 (7,799)
Ward, Andrew M.......4:34:58 (19,400)
Ward, Anthony Keith.......4:23:37 (16,341)
Ward, Barry.......4:07:13 (12,155)
Ward, Christopher A.......3:15:41 (2,302)
Ward, Colin.......3:59:42 (10,460)
Ward, DR.......5:25:26 (29,849)
Ward, Daniel.......3:56:32 (9,469)
Ward, David.......5:58:56 (32,988)
Ward, David C.......4:37:46 (20,111)
Ward, David G.......6:14:41 (33,777)
Ward, David J.......3:49:47 (7,796)
Ward, David J.......4:15:40 (14,315)
Ward, David J.......5:51:29 (32,447)
Ward, Duncan L.......4:10:29 (12,978)
Ward, Frazer R.......5:39:18 (31,426)
Ward, Gary N.......3:56:20 (9,406)
Ward, Ian J.......3:07:17 (1,457)
Ward, Ian R.......4:42:57 (21,459)
Ward, James D.......3:57:04 (9,638)
Ward, James R.......2:55:57 (723)
Ward, John.......3:33:44 (4,710)
Ward, John.......5:35:23 (31,011)
Ward, John R.......3:36:34 (5,249)
Ward, Jon.......3:56:52 (9,588)
Ward, Jonathan.......3:25:02 (3,400)
Ward, Lee.......3:48:04 (7,419)
Ward, Mark.......4:14:05 (13,925)
Ward, Mark.......4:34:49 (19,358)
Ward, Mark W.......5:07:10 (26,935)
Ward, Matt.......3:22:50 (3,112)
Ward, Matt.......3:47:26 (7,271)
Ward, Matthew.......4:34:09 (19,183)
Ward, Matthew.......4:55:11 (24,499)
Ward, Mike J.......4:08:14 (12,425)
Ward, Paul.......3:24:53 (3,388)
Ward, Philip R.......4:36:49 (19,870)
Ward, Richard G.......4:49:00 (22,974)
Ward, Robert.......5:08:18 (27,140)
Ward, Robert.......5:16:04 (28,508)
Ward, Robert A.......3:39:02 (5,692)
Ward, Roly.......3:42:19 (6,272)
Ward, Simon.......3:45:44 (6,933)
Ward, Stephen P.......2:48:43 (416)
Ward, Steven C.......4:24:27 (16,560)
Ward, Steven P.......4:05:45 (11,834)
Ward, Thomas.......3:38:11 (5,532)
Wardell, Francis.......3:54:53 (8,992)
Warden, Philip.......4:33:57 (19,143)
Ward-Horner, Jason.......3:45:55 (6,969)
Wardlaw, Robert G.......3:13:01 (2,009)
Wardle, David E.......5:18:36 (28,898)
Wardle, Tim J.......4:27:04 (17,274)
Wardley, Keith P.......4:15:36 (14,306)
Wardman, Andy E.......5:28:57 (30,269)
Wardrope, Adam Boyd.......3:57:05 (9,644)
Ware, Callan.......4:47:36 (22,629)
Ware, Ian M.......4:08:07 (12,395)
Ware, Jonathan G.......5:22:30 (29,438)
Ware, Nicholas A.......4:05:15 (11,721)
Ware, Steven E.......4:54:29 (24,331)
Wareham, Andrew J.......4:52:54 (23,951)
Wareham, David J.......4:47:52 (22,693)
Warham, Ben J.......3:39:55 (5,838)
Warhurst, Matthew R.......3:51:15 (8,108)
Waring, Chris.......5:36:48 (31,155)
Waring, Don.......4:11:42 (13,312)
Waring, John.......5:36:47 (31,153)
Waring, Martin H.......4:36:48 (19,864)
Warlow, David J.......3:00:16 (1,012)
Warman, Adrian.......4:30:00 (18,095)
Warmerdam, Arthur.......3:56:05 (9,335)
Warnar, Henk.......3:55:53 (9,282)
Warne, Mark.......4:31:24 (18,471)
Warner, Andrew R.......3:39:14 (5,720)
Warner, Bradley J.......4:35:02 (19,419)
Warner, Carl.......4:09:02 (12,629)
Warner, David A.......2:59:11 (932)
Warner, David C.......5:08:24 (27,164)
Warner, Graeme N.......3:54:37 (8,922)
Warner, Joe.......4:09:03 (12,631)
Warner, Jonathan S.......5:42:26 (31,716)
Warner, Matthew.......4:08:10 (12,410)
Warner, Michael.......5:46:58 (32,087)
Warner, Paul.......4:59:54 (25,578)
Warner, Tony D.......3:13:18 (2,034)
Warner Smith, James.......4:06:37 (12,026)
Warnes, Andrew.......4:42:26 (21,309)
Warnes, Gavin J.......4:47:22 (22,571)
Warnett, John A.......4:51:28 (23,612)
Warnett, Steven.......3:55:04 (9,050)
Warnock, Dennis J.......5:51:57 (32,480)
Warnock, John S.......2:44:28 (294)
Warr, Christopher N.......4:35:10 (19,456)
Warr, John E.......6:07:02 (33,437)
Warran, Stephen John.......4:08:19 (12,459)
Warren, Alex M.......4:20:07 (15,464)
Warren, Andrew D.......5:16:42 (28,600)
Warren, Ben.......6:01:11 (33,119)
Warren, Chris.......3:40:14 (5,907)
Warren, John.......4:38:07 (20,204)
Warren, John D.......3:56:51 (9,583)

Weldin, Jonathan Michael 3:33:40 (4,697)
Weldon, Paul 4:01:17 (10,853)
Welfare, Simon 4:39:14 (20,502)
Welford, Mark J 3:51:56 (8,263)
Welham, Robert A 4:21:28 (15,801)
Wellborn, Sacha P 6:10:07 (33,567)
Weller, Allan 4:54:42 (24,386)
Wellesley, Christopher 5:09:27 (27,356)
Wellesley, Gerald V 4:58:30 (25,268)
Wellfair, Peter J 6:23:19 (34,164)
Wellings, Gareth M 4:13:05 (13,680)
Wellman, Timothy S 3:56:10 (9,357)
Wells, Anthony 5:02:22 (26,090)
Wells, Ben J 3:44:21 (6,689)
Wells, Brian 6:33:55 (34,498)
Wells, Colin 4:56:34 (24,820)
Wells, Colin J 5:50:00 (32,333)
Wells, David M 4:00:24 (10,635)
Wells, Edward 4:43:53 (21,688)
Wells, Gary B 5:49:14 (32,270)
Wells, Martin J 5:19:41 (29,061)
Wells, Matthew L 3:32:32 (4,549)
Wells, Michael L 5:38:36 (31,343)
Wells, Mike J 5:01:33 (25,923)
Wells, Neal 5:06:45 (26,859)
Wells, Paul 4:48:26 (22,836)
Wells, Paul D 4:20:41 (15,596)
Wells, Simon J 4:06:50 (12,068)
Wells, Steven T 4:08:43 (12,556)
Wells, Trevor G 3:35:37 (5,074)
Welsh, Christopher 5:30:59 (30,526)
Welsh, Martin 3:45:13 (6,839)
Welton, William H 3:33:58 (4,752)
Wemyss, Robin A 4:10:51 (13,078)
Wendleken, Dylan W 4:10:42 (13,040)
Wenlock, Tony 4:02:04 (11,033)
Wenman, David R 4:24:51 (16,670)
Wenman, Mark 3:11:25 (1,815)
Wennberg, Benny 4:05:14 (11,717)
Wentzell, David J 4:53:27 (24,061)
Wenzel, Peter F 4:26:33 (17,130)
Wesley, Lee A 4:50:36 (23,396)
Wessinghage, Thomas 3:11:17 (1,809)
West, Alex J 4:37:56 (20,149)
West, Andrew J 3:26:55 (3,669)
West, Ashton 4:21:47 (15,898)
West, Brian P 3:47:34 (7,303)
West, Chris P 4:14:47 (14,108)
West, Darren 5:50:02 (32,337)
West, David 3:22:37 (3,087)
West, David P 5:18:34 (28,886)
West, Dean 5:19:21 (29,016)
West, Frank 3:46:29 (7,084)
West, Greg F 4:49:25 (23,085)
West, Jamie Robert 3:18:03 (2,537)
West, John J 4:49:53 (23,215)
West, Justin P 2:45:10 (320)
West, Kevin M 2:54:04 (606)
West, Mark A 3:53:13 (8,566)
West, Nolan L 4:49:25 (23,085)
West, Paul D 4:18:50 (15,113)
West, Phil C 3:00:54 (1,044)
West, Rupert 4:22:39 (16,111)
West, Sam 3:09:42 (1,680)
West, Stephen V 5:11:47 (27,772)
West, Steve 5:08:09 (27,112)
West, Tony W 3:29:55 (4,169)
Westacott, David 4:12:59 (13,656)
Westall, Mark 4:26:26 (17,093)
Westbrook, James 5:07:01 (26,910)
Westbrook, Jon L 4:05:37 (11,807)
Westbury, Damon 4:05:44 (11,828)
Westbury, Lewis G 4:33:36 (19,052)
Westbury, Philip 4:04:19 (11,511)
Westby, Andrew 4:10:15 (12,921)
Westcott, Chris 4:43:56 (21,700)
Westcott, Mike 3:56:22 (9,418)
Westerby, David P 5:13:17 (28,033)
Western, John 5:27:20 (30,082)
Westhead, Karl S 2:53:53 (600)
Westhead, Terence A 3:21:12 (2,910)
Weston, Asher J 4:05:16 (11,724)
Weston, Daniel J 2:37:51 (155)
Weston, Edward 3:39:48 (5,809)
Weston, Grant 4:59:32 (25,506)
Weston, Paul C 4:18:01 (14,891)
Weston, Shane P 3:26:39 (3,628)
Weston, Steven J 3:14:17 (2,151)
Westvig, Karl H 3:12:41 (1,955)
Westwood, Dave B 4:11:56 (13,368)
Westwood, Guy N 3:16:07 (2,341)
Westwood, Jamie I 2:59:47 (981)
Westwood, Mark D 4:44:51 (21,918)
Westwood, Steven 4:13:50 (13,875)
Wetherell, Jon 4:29:41 (18,011)
Wethers, Nigel 3:38:10 (5,529)
Weyler, Javier 4:57:04 (24,942)
Weyler, Pablo 4:57:04 (24,942)
Whale, Matt 3:33:14 (4,639)
Whale, Richard C 5:06:21 (26,781)
Whall, Anthony J 5:21:38 (29,322)
Wharton-Malcolm, Cory A 5:59:47 (33,032)
Whateley, John 3:22:06 (3,025)
Whatford, Howard Martin 4:39:23 (20,542)
Whatley, David K 5:05:38 (26,664)
Whatley, Gavin J 3:16:58 (2,424)
Whatling, Anthony N 4:09:11 (12,658)
Wheal, Adrian 3:40:08 (5,885)
Wheatley, Iain E 3:58:57 (10,237)
Wheatley, Joshua J 5:24:30 (29,734)
Wheatley, Richard M 4:22:06 (15,966)
Wheatley, Robert 6:37:44 (34,586)
Wheatley, Stephen A 4:38:10 (20,221)
Wheeldon, Paul 4:11:21 (13,210)
Wheele, Matthew S 5:21:10 (29,251)
Wheeler, Adam M 4:20:13 (15,490)
Wheeler, Adam P 3:37:47 (5,452)
Wheeler, Alan J 3:52:14 (8,341)
Wheeler, Andrew G 3:03:36 (1,208)
Wheeler, Ben 4:22:52 (16,161)
Wheeler, Chris F 4:32:34 (18,777)
Wheeler, Christian D 4:51:12 (23,541)
Wheeler, David 4:18:12 (14,945)
Wheeler, Graham 4:00:37 (10,700)
Wheeler, Ian 4:45:56 (22,198)
Wheeler, Ian 6:23:20 (34,168)
Wheeler, Jonathan C 4:49:03 (22,985)
Wheeler, Keiron J 5:32:37 (30,706)
Wheeler, Kevin T 4:28:06 (17,580)
Wheeler, Malcolm L 4:32:37 (18,794)
Wheeler, Michael J 4:51:29 (23,617)
Wheeler, Patrick W 3:05:22 (1,328)
Wheeler, Philip J 4:51:18 (23,566)
Wheeler, Philip L 4:32:21 (18,715)
Wheeler, Richard 4:41:31 (21,093)
Wheeler, Steve 6:21:42 (34,103)
Wheeler, Sydney J 5:08:27 (27,171)
Whelan, Andrew M 4:28:49 (17,780)
Whelan, Chris 3:23:47 (3,229)
Whelan, Liam 4:01:38 (10,951)
Whelan, Paul A 4:56:21 (24,761)
Wheldon, Alexander J 4:26:12 (17,038)
Wherry, Steven M 2:55:20 (687)
Whetton, Michael 3:17:05 (2,442)
Whibley, Drew D 4:35:35 (19,568)
Whiffin, Toby 4:58:47 (25,335)
Whiles, Stephen J 4:15:28 (14,275)
Whiley, Matt 4:13:19 (13,752)
Whipman, Timothy 4:12:42 (13,575)
Whishaw, Bernard W 4:16:52 (14,621)
Whiston, Arthur 3:20:01 (2,756)
Whitaker, Alistair M 5:44:46 (31,913)
Whitaker, David S 4:02:01 (11,020)
Whitaker, Gary 5:13:13 (28,027)
Whitby, Benedict 2:18:14 (16)
Whitby, Chris 4:18:00 (14,889)
Whitby, Colin 4:16:38 (14,567)
Whitby, Mark 4:01:00 (10,798)
Whitby, Richard J 4:00:31 (10,677)
Whitby, Stuart M 4:19:39 (15,328)
Whitcombe, Jonathan 3:35:33 (5,056)
White, Adrian J 3:55:50 (9,272)
White, Adrian J 5:03:05 (26,221)
White, Alan 4:36:03 (19,692)
White, Andrew R 3:34:02 (4,763)
White, Andy R 3:49:14 (7,672)
White, Andy S 5:36:00 (31,078)
White, Antony 3:37:51 (5,465)
White, Benjamin A 4:14:03 (13,919)
White, Bijan V 4:23:47 (16,382)
White, Brendan F 4:19:45 (15,357)
White, Charles Leslie 4:30:57 (18,338)
White, Chris J 4:43:01 (21,473)
White, Colin G 3:47:09 (7,228)
White, David C 4:07:40 (12,274)
White, David J 6:15:39 (33,823)
White, Desmond G 3:46:54 (7,177)
White, Douglas J 2:56:16 (731)
White, Douglas M 5:44:27 (31,888)
White, Edward J 4:00:25 (10,640)
White, Gary A 5:06:46 (26,862)
White, Gavin R 5:18:36 (28,898)
White, Geoffrey B 3:07:35 (1,491)
White, Graham K 4:43:42 (21,649)
White, Ian P 3:53:18 (8,583)
White, Jack A 4:35:39 (19,581)
White, James 3:21:36 (2,960)
White, Jamie 4:06:46 (12,053)
White, Jason H 4:25:01 (16,716)
White, Jerry M 4:08:28 (12,500)
White, John A 4:11:55 (13,362)
White, John D 3:55:43 (9,232)
White, Jonathan M 4:55:37 (24,601)
White, Jonathan P 4:21:30 (15,812)
White, Kevin A 2:59:45 (979)
White, Lee F 5:21:17 (29,266)
White, Malcolm D 4:48:56 (22,955)
White, Mark 4:09:42 (12,774)
White, Mark J 5:13:50 (28,123)
White, Martin 3:56:44 (9,544)
White, Martin J 5:35:37 (31,031)
White, Matthew 4:51:39 (23,661)
White, Matthew B 4:02:52 (11,203)
White, Michael A 3:38:44 (5,630)
White, Michael J 4:08:22 (12,475)
White, Myles 3:15:38 (2,298)
White, Neil B 2:54:27 (632)
White, Nicholas A 3:55:03 (9,040)
White, Nick 3:12:50 (1,978)
White, Nick I 5:18:50 (28,947)
White, Paul A 3:17:26 (2,482)
White, Paul M 3:32:02 (4,472)
White, Phil 3:31:28 (4,397)
White, Philip 4:48:28 (22,843)
White, Philip D 4:42:18 (21,275)
White, Rhys 3:45:25 (6,873)
White, Ricky 4:27:12 (17,309)
White, Robert 4:46:14 (22,255)
White, Robert H 3:45:57 (6,977)
White, Ronny P 4:56:53 (24,906)
White, Simon M 3:55:59 (9,307)
White, Stephen 4:55:16 (24,522)
White, Steven 3:35:11 (4,993)
White, Thomas R 4:25:00 (16,712)
White, Vincent J 4:47:01 (22,487)
White, Wayne George 4:47:56 (22,721)
Whiteford, Stuart R 4:13:23 (13,774)
Whitehead, Ben J 4:47:38 (22,639)
Whitehead, Ian David 3:27:19 (3,736)
Whitehead, Justin R 4:34:33 (19,276)
Whitehead, Lee P 3:35:55 (5,138)
Whitehead, Mike 4:47:27 (22,589)
Whitehead, Rob 4:55:51 (24,653)
Whitehead, Stephen 2:45:21 (321)
Whitehill, Craig J 4:47:34 (22,617)
Whitehouse, Andrew 5:39:49 (31,479)
Whitehouse, Andrew G 3:40:00 (5,859)
Whitehouse, Ben 5:01:43 (25,956)
Whitehouse, Michael 5:00:16 (25,646)
Whitehouse, Nick T 4:33:47 (19,094)
Whitelaw, Patrick J 4:14:22 (14,007)
Whitelegg, Richard M 2:36:18 (129)
Whiteley, David C 4:10:02 (12,863)
Whiteley, Leo 4:30:27 (18,217)
Whiteley, Martin H 3:28:20 (3,907)
Whiteley, Nigel P 3:29:47 (4,150)
Whiteley, Philip 4:54:33 (24,345)
Whiteley, Stephen P 3:13:45 (2,095)
Whiteman, Greg P 4:16:01 (14,401)

Whitemore, David J 7:38:34 (35,265)
Whitemore, Kevin A 4:59:37 (25,522)
Whiteside, Gareth John 5:08:02 (27,090)
Whitestone, Dean 3:28:58 (4,004)
Whitfield, Adam 3:57:36 (9,802)
Whitfield, Gary 3:45:07 (6,819)
Whitfield, Kenneth J 5:36:38 (31,136)
Whitfield, Mark 3:30:46 (4,293)
Whitfield, Matthew 3:42:02 (6,218)
Whitfield, Peter D 4:34:17 (19,218)
Whitfield, Scott A 5:24:13 (29,684)
Whitfield, Timothy E 4:17:16 (14,706)
Whitford, Adrian 4:54:46 (24,397)
Whiting, Daniel 4:32:24 (18,728)
Whiting, Darren J 3:47:00 (7,201)
Whiting, John M 6:48:25 (34,785)
Whiting, Richard 4:53:55 (24,204)
Whiting, Stephen A 5:38:43 (31,357)
Whiting, Stephen J 2:41:17 (222)
Whitley, Richard B 4:37:56 (20,149)
Whitlock, Kevin R 5:02:02 (26,028)
Whitlock, Tony Robert 3:21:55 (3,001)
Whitmarsh, Jim 3:53:59 (8,751)
Whitmarsh, Michael 4:47:23 (22,577)
Whitmore, Ivon E 3:19:20 (2,659)
Whittaker, David N 4:06:10 (11,919)
Whittaker, Paul S 3:49:30 (7,730)
Whittaker, Robert J 5:18:42 (28,916)
Whittall, Phil R 4:47:04 (22,501)
Whittell, Simon K 3:54:35 (8,914)
Whittell, Stuart K 4:15:56 (14,374)
Whittingham, Adrian J 6:16:11 (33,849)
Whittingham, Dylan P 3:03:03 (1,174)
Whittingham, Kevin 4:29:06 (17,858)
Whittingham, Paul 4:31:02 (18,361)
Whittington, Russell 3:03:08 (1,179)
Whittington, William R 4:11:47 (13,334)
Whittle, Christopher D 4:08:41 (12,544)
Whittle, Stephen J 4:16:03 (14,407)
Whittock, Mark D 4:57:36 (25,052)
Whitton, Peter R 5:06:11 (26,759)
Whitty, Michael 5:05:10 (26,585)
Whitworth, Richard 5:47:15 (32,114)
Whoriskey, Teague 3:51:10 (8,088)
Whyment, Andrew D 4:48:23 (22,825)
Whyte, Bruce W 4:55:44 (24,623)
Whyte, Michael E 3:25:40 (3,485)
Whyte, Steven 3:38:47 (5,640)
Wiblin, David J 4:26:53 (17,236)
Wickenden, Stephen 4:34:49 (19,358)
Wickens, Geoff 6:02:17 (33,188)
Wickens, Ian K 4:30:36 (18,255)
Wickens, Stuart J 4:10:07 (12,884)
Wickham, Ian 2:57:24 (802)
Wickham, Wayne D 3:32:50 (4,590)
Wickins, Richard 4:40:02 (20,735)
Wickramasinghe, Eranda P 4:28:57 (17,818)
Wicks, Martyn J 5:04:12 (26,413)
Wicks, Peter Leslie 3:59:02 (10,261)
Wicks, Thomas A 5:06:31 (26,809)
Widdows, Michael D 5:26:08 (29,954)
Widdowson, Tim 5:04:33 (26,472)
Widegger, David 5:39:50 (31,480)
Widegren, Stefan 5:20:50 (29,199)
Widelski, Gregg P 4:15:42 (14,319)
Wiehahn, Adrian Charl 3:59:11 (10,306)
Wienk, Hans 4:01:42 (10,967)
Wigan, Thomas 3:49:05 (7,642)
Wigens, John 3:46:09 (7,011)
Wiggins, Andrew S 2:55:04 (667)
Wiggins, Derek A 4:41:17 (21,034)
Wiggins, Ian D 4:56:01 (24,682)
Wiggins, Michael 3:08:04 (1,530)
Wiggins, Simon P 4:27:47 (17,479)
Wigglesworth, James R 4:10:41 (13,033)
Wightman, John 5:14:59 (28,314)
Wikeley, Adrian 4:48:51 (22,932)
Wilbraham, Stephen J 3:20:50 (2,874)
Wilby, Michael A 5:18:41 (28,914)
Wilby, Rob J 2:58:17 (856)
Wilcock, Martin 2:50:44 (489)
Wilcock, Stephen J 4:42:41 (21,381)
Wilcox, Ashley 4:34:57 (19,395)
Wilcox, David J 4:27:30 (17,393)
Wilcox, Mark A 6:58:23 (34,932)
Wilcox, Michael P 3:34:16 (4,824)
Wilcox, Paul 3:54:22 (8,855)
Wilcox, Steven James 3:49:04 (7,635)
Wilczkiewicz, Nenryk W 4:58:38 (25,304)
Wild, Bob C 4:13:38 (13,834)
Wild, Dave 5:05:39 (26,666)
Wild, Ian M 5:01:11 (25,858)
Wild, James 3:33:33 (4,683)
Wild, James A 4:24:07 (16,477)
Wild, Richard 4:01:05 (10,812)
Wild, Richard J 2:56:33 (748)
Wilde, Anthony 5:44:45 (31,912)
Wilde, John S 4:32:46 (18,835)
Wilde, Michael 4:54:54 (24,429)
Wilden, Jonathan J 4:40:50 (20,920)
Wilder, Paul 4:39:17 (20,513)
Wildey, Richard 5:07:34 (27,016)
Wilding, Mark 5:28:42 (30,237)
Wilding, Michael I 4:05:37 (11,807)
Wildman, Brian 3:44:29 (6,717)
Wildman, Christopher P 3:43:24 (6,510)
Wildy, Neil J 4:09:11 (12,658)
Wileman, Michael T 4:03:46 (11,379)
Wiles, Craig 4:54:39 (24,377)
Wiles, Jonathan C 4:59:16 (25,445)
Wiley, Keith 3:10:39 (1,752)
Wilford, Andrew R 3:50:34 (7,962)
Wililams, Graham D 4:55:10 (24,494)
Wilke, Robert 3:53:09 (8,548)
Wilke, Sascha 4:30:19 (18,185)
Wilken, Olaf 4:15:59 (14,394)
Wilkens, Nolan 2:57:26 (803)
Wilkes, Bernard Terry 3:56:51 (9,583)
Wilkes, Colin 4:13:20 (13,760)
Wilkes, Jerry P 3:50:42 (7,994)
Wilkes, Neil H 3:51:35 (8,183)
Wilkes, Stephen G 3:16:37 (2,396)
Wilkie, Ross 4:37:10 (19,959)
Wilkie, Stuart H 3:14:05 (2,132)
Wilkins, Adrian 4:31:45 (18,567)
Wilkins, Ben 3:56:17 (9,383)
Wilkins, Daran D 5:00:37 (25,733)
Wilkins, Geoffrey D 6:58:04 (34,931)
Wilkins, Huw Richard 3:47:36 (7,309)
Wilkins, Jonathan 5:18:33 (28,880)
Wilkins, Mark J 2:46:15 (337)
Wilkins, Michael 4:15:19 (14,233)
Wilkins, Robert Michael 4:52:12 (23,795)
Wilkins, Shaun M 5:24:33 (29,740)
Wilkinson, Andrew 3:38:06 (5,514)
Wilkinson, Andy 3:33:36 (4,692)
Wilkinson, Andy 5:56:13 (32,771)
Wilkinson, Ben L 3:04:31 (1,265)
Wilkinson, Dominic 4:28:49 (17,780)
Wilkinson, Geoff 4:04:10 (11,481)
Wilkinson, Geoffrey 4:56:02 (24,691)
Wilkinson, Gerald 4:57:11 (24,962)
Wilkinson, Graeme 3:15:11 (2,251)
Wilkinson, Ian M 4:15:27 (14,271)
Wilkinson, James A 4:25:12 (16,766)
Wilkinson, James M 3:11:51 (1,869)
Wilkinson, Jeffrey K 4:50:54 (23,459)
Wilkinson, John 3:50:46 (8,016)
Wilkinson, Jon 4:05:38 (11,812)
Wilkinson, Lee W 2:43:49 (282)
Wilkinson, Mark 4:39:10 (20,487)
Wilkinson, Mark A 4:12:28 (13,512)
Wilkinson, Martin 4:34:51 (19,370)
Wilkinson, Martin 4:56:34 (24,820)
Wilkinson, Martin M 3:15:39 (2,300)
Wilkinson, Michael B 4:28:47 (17,769)
Wilkinson, Nick L 4:49:27 (23,092)
Wilkinson, Peter W 3:30:15 (4,215)
Wilkinson, Philip C 4:39:39 (20,627)
Wilkinson, Richard E 4:07:13 (12,155)
Wilkinson, Roger 3:57:39 (9,826)
Wilkinson, Sean 7:14:25 (35,100)
Wilkinson, Sean V 4:14:13 (13,964)
Wilkinson, Steven M 3:55:04 (9,050)
Wilkinson, Trevor 2:59:19 (943)
Wilks, Stephen J 4:34:53 (19,376)
Willatgamuwa, Don S 5:21:46 (29,336)
Willatt, Iain G 4:08:35 (12,519)
Willcock, Craig A 6:20:56 (34,066)
Willcock, Gary A 3:20:41 (2,854)
Willcox, John R 3:47:59 (7,396)
Willcox, Richard W 4:25:31 (16,842)
Willdridge, William D 3:52:19 (8,362)
Willems, Bart 3:59:24 (10,369)
Willgrass, Elvin C 5:52:52 (32,538)
William, Celea 4:37:15 (19,974)
Williams, Adam 4:24:55 (16,688)
Williams, Alastair P 3:18:02 (2,532)
Williams, Aled M 4:50:37 (23,400)
Williams, Alex T 3:12:26 (1,924)
Williams, Andrew D 4:03:02 (11,237)
Williams, Andrew P 4:19:16 (15,226)
Williams, Andrew P 4:24:24 (16,553)
Williams, Andy 4:49:47 (23,195)
Williams, Andy J 3:51:46 (8,220)
Williams, Anthony 4:22:27 (16,068)
Williams, Anthony Aaron 3:41:00 (6,028)
Williams, Anton F 4:18:50 (15,113)
Williams, Barrie A 3:42:29 (6,295)
Williams, Barry 5:25:25 (29,844)
Williams, Barry J 5:13:02 (27,991)
Williams, Ben L 4:39:15 (20,508)
Williams, Ben S 4:56:56 (24,921)
Williams, Charles A 4:58:14 (25,197)
Williams, Chris 3:52:43 (8,450)
Williams, Chris 3:59:55 (10,523)
Williams, Chris 4:57:21 (25,001)
Williams, Chris J 4:53:03 (23,986)
Williams, Chris Leigh 3:51:49 (8,231)
Williams, Christopher James 5:29:11 (30,296)
Williams, Christopher Neil 5:11:51 (27,785)
Williams, Colin W 3:58:46 (10,179)
Williams, Dan 3:35:34 (5,061)
Williams, Daniel T 4:39:12 (20,498)
Williams, Darren 3:38:04 (5,505)
Williams, Darren 4:14:36 (14,058)
Williams, Daryl 4:15:09 (14,203)
Williams, Dave W 3:11:27 (1,819)
Williams, David 4:42:43 (21,393)
Williams, David 4:42:46 (21,402)
Williams, David 4:52:56 (23,960)
Williams, David J 5:13:27 (28,056)
Williams, David M 3:56:00 (9,309)
Williams, David P 5:17:42 (28,747)
Williams, Dean J 4:51:26 (23,605)
Williams, Dennis Selby 5:27:53 (30,136)
Williams, Dewi G 4:01:04 (10,807)
Williams, Dominic H 4:04:18 (11,509)
Williams, Dwight 4:23:54 (16,416)
Williams, Edward B 4:21:39 (15,863)
Williams, Edward H 3:20:48 (2,868)
Williams, Edward James 4:14:20 (13,994)
Williams, Gareth 3:28:50 (3,981)
Williams, Gareth 3:58:37 (10,132)
Williams, Gareth E 3:55:43 (9,232)
Williams, Gareth J 2:52:09 (528)
Williams, Gary 5:55:14 (32,707)
Williams, Gary J 3:21:58 (3,009)
Williams, Gavin 4:01:45 (10,972)
Williams, Iain 2:55:06 (669)
Williams, Ian 4:13:54 (13,884)
Williams, Ian 5:03:59 (26,385)
Williams, Ian G 2:31:41 (79)
Williams, Jack M 4:51:30 (23,620)
Williams, James 4:50:21 (23,327)
Williams, James 5:07:57 (27,078)
Williams, James H 3:20:02 (2,758)
Williams, James M 5:43:43 (31,827)
Williams, Jason M 2:40:39 (210)
Williams, Joel 5:42:29 (31,722)
Williams, John A 5:00:32 (25,713)
Williams, John E 4:18:07 (14,926)
Williams, John E 4:48:13 (22,791)
Williams, John R 4:30:33 (18,242)
Williams, John R 6:18:40 (33,954)
Williams, John W 6:07:57 (33,479)
Williams, Jonathan 4:56:55 (24,917)
Williams, Jonathan D 4:43:53 (21,688)
Williams, Jordan M 4:23:03 (16,197)

Williams, Keith 3:13:52 (2,105)
Williams, Keith M 5:14:11 (28,192)
Williams, Kenneth 5:31:58 (30,635)
Williams, Kevin 3:49:15 (7,679)
Williams, Kevin 4:38:28 (20,290)
Williams, Kim T 3:50:44 (8,001)
Williams, Kory 3:23:17 (3,157)
Williams, Kristian Michael 3:28:43 (3,959)
Williams, Leslie E 3:08:34 (1,571)
Williams, Lewis D 4:28:36 (17,724)
Williams, Lloyd 4:12:03 (13,398)
Williams, Mark 3:44:42 (6,749)
Williams, Mark 4:15:39 (14,312)
Williams, Mark A 4:24:07 (16,477)
Williams, Mark Andrew 4:44:22 (21,809)
Williams, Mark P 5:14:46 (28,277)
Williams, Mark R 4:25:34 (16,861)
Williams, Martin 2:23:02 (25)
Williams, Martin J 3:49:57 (7,823)
Williams, Matt 4:25:55 (16,965)
Williams, Matthew 3:37:07 (5,344)
Williams, Matthew 4:39:02 (20,444)
Williams, Michael 3:56:22 (9,418)
Williams, Michael 4:46:53 (22,444)
Williams, Michael A 4:32:08 (18,671)
Williams, Michael H 4:55:26 (24,559)
Williams, Michael K 4:24:22 (16,541)
Williams, Nathaniel J 2:23:48 (28)
Williams, Neil J 3:10:25 (1,730)
Williams, Neil R 4:20:09 (15,471)
Williams, Neil R 5:58:44 (32,975)
Williams, Nicholas 4:40:48 (20,911)
Williams, Nick 4:02:05 (11,037)
Williams, Nick F 3:39:36 (5,776)
Williams, Nigel 3:18:45 (2,592)
Williams, Owen J 4:02:59 (11,226)
Williams, Owen J 5:25:25 (29,844)
Williams, Paul 4:58:00 (25,140)
Williams, Paul C 4:42:11 (21,244)
Williams, Paul D 3:07:47 (1,511)
Williams, Paul D 4:55:42 (24,614)
Williams, Paul M 3:53:38 (8,658)
Williams, Peter H 3:52:45 (8,459)
Williams, Ray 6:34:18 (34,507)
Williams, Richard T 3:08:05 (1,532)
Williams, Sam 4:48:09 (22,772)
Williams, Simon 4:34:48 (19,355)
Williams, Simon J 3:42:12 (6,250)
Williams, Simon M 3:29:45 (4,146)
Williams, Steph 4:57:01 (24,933)
Williams, Steve J 6:06:59 (33,436)
Williams, Steve R 4:10:47 (13,060)
Williams, Steven D 5:01:01 (25,815)
Williams, Steven P 5:05:40 (26,671)
Williams, Steven R 5:00:11 (25,630)
Williams, Sullivan 3:44:40 (6,741)
Williams, Timothy 5:39:05 (31,409)
Williams, Timothy M 4:19:05 (15,181)
Williams, Tony R 4:41:36 (21,119)
Williams-Gunn, Andrew 3:51:18 (8,120)
Williamson, Adam D 4:07:57 (12,348)
Williamson, Anthony P 4:18:35 (15,049)
Williamson, Blair C 3:28:52 (3,988)
Williamson, Christopher J 4:33:58 (19,145)
Williamson, David 3:23:06 (3,136)
Williamson, Duncan 3:49:40 (7,761)
Williamson, James A 4:39:21 (20,532)
Williamson, Josh D 3:54:34 (8,911)
Williamson, Karl Andrew 3:31:40 (4,418)
Williamson, Ken 3:51:10 (8,088)
Williamson, Matthew C 5:36:25 (31,113)
Williamson, Michael H 5:25:49 (29,906)
Williamson, Neil R 5:28:14 (30,180)
Williamson, Paul 4:38:07 (20,204)
Williamson, Paul T 3:41:01 (6,033)
Williamson, Peter A 4:05:55 (11,862)
Williamson, Robin D 3:50:31 (7,951)
Williamson, Stephen W 2:46:58 (367)
Williamson, Steve 3:18:24 (2,567)
Williamson, Thomas Robert 3:59:50 (10,505)
Willicott, Mark 3:36:26 (5,222)
Willingham, Mark 4:46:07 (22,230)
Willis, Andrew 3:25:31 (3,461)
Willis, Andrew 4:10:42 (13,040)
Willis, Andrew P 4:12:46 (13,596)
Willis, Barry P 5:05:24 (26,625)
Willis, Brian A 4:32:38 (18,801)
Willis, Daniel S 3:58:55 (10,230)
Willis, David J 4:52:19 (23,829)
Willis, Fred 3:55:35 (9,183)
Willis, Gary S 3:15:06 (2,244)
Willis, Gavin 4:22:22 (16,040)
Willis, Ivan W 4:48:10 (22,776)
Willis, James 4:10:05 (12,874)
Willis, Jonathan T 6:52:22 (34,850)
Willis, Matthew 4:46:20 (22,290)
Willis, Roger T 5:01:59 (26,014)
Willis, Simon 4:43:51 (21,678)
Willis, Simon B 3:23:25 (3,179)
Willis, Tim 3:48:42 (7,546)
Willis, William J 4:35:15 (19,477)
Willis-Owen, Charles A 2:46:45 (357)
Willmitt, William J 3:28:01 (3,860)
Willmore, Rob D 4:33:07 (18,924)
Willmott, Martin G 3:44:05 (6,648)
Willmott, Victor 4:32:33 (18,769)
Willoughby, Stefan J 3:55:47 (9,258)
Wills, Andrew E 5:27:15 (30,073)
Wills, Colin 6:31:47 (34,448)
Wills, Dennis A 3:36:29 (5,232)
Wills, John R 5:35:27 (31,013)
Wills, Stuart 4:22:02 (15,950)
Willsher, Neil D 3:27:29 (3,771)
Willson, Jamie S 4:25:34 (16,861)
Willson, Keith J 3:59:19 (10,340)
Willson, Nick 3:52:05 (8,295)
Willson, Simon 4:34:23 (19,235)
Wilmes, Martin 4:25:38 (16,885)
Wilmont, Andrew 4:27:44 (17,459)
Wilmot, Ben 6:31:28 (34,443)
Wilmot, Tom 4:24:27 (16,560)
Wilsher, Reginald 4:43:46 (21,659)
Wilson, Alan 3:41:10 (6,061)
Wilson, Alan 4:24:41 (16,621)
Wilson, Alastair F 4:59:51 (25,565)
Wilson, Andrew 3:08:56 (1,614)
Wilson, Andrew 3:43:14 (6,476)
Wilson, Andrew 4:32:41 (18,812)
Wilson, Andrew R 5:04:22 (26,438)
Wilson, Andy 4:35:32 (19,555)
Wilson, Ben G 5:15:15 (28,370)
Wilson, Benjamin 4:39:31 (20,587)
Wilson, Benjamin J 5:00:43 (25,751)
Wilson, Brendan J 4:34:54 (19,382)
Wilson, Bruce M 3:13:45 (2,095)
Wilson, Chris J 4:07:10 (12,144)
Wilson, Chris J 4:09:58 (12,846)
Wilson, Christopher 2:27:40 (46)
Wilson, Colin 4:03:50 (11,403)
Wilson, Colin P 4:22:56 (16,172)
Wilson, Colin S 3:51:37 (8,191)
Wilson, Daniel 3:35:07 (4,981)
Wilson, Daryl L 3:27:33 (3,790)
Wilson, Dave 4:04:04 (11,463)
Wilson, David 3:37:14 (5,359)
Wilson, David 3:50:49 (8,024)
Wilson, David A 4:40:51 (20,927)
Wilson, David C 3:52:15 (8,347)
Wilson, David P 6:13:06 (33,699)
Wilson, David T 3:30:05 (4,189)
Wilson, Eugene L 4:51:03 (23,500)
Wilson, Gareth E 2:46:42 (354)
Wilson, Gary 4:31:02 (18,361)
Wilson, Gary 6:00:26 (33,070)
Wilson, Gary A 3:48:48 (7,569)
Wilson, Geoffrey 3:37:16 (5,365)
Wilson, Iain 5:51:20 (32,434)
Wilson, James 4:39:06 (20,465)
Wilson, James R 5:09:42 (27,403)
Wilson, James S 5:31:02 (30,533)
Wilson, John 3:53:05 (8,528)
Wilson, John G 5:04:38 (26,484)
Wilson, John R 4:16:14 (14,455)
Wilson, John S 3:40:47 (5,994)
Wilson, Jon 4:03:46 (11,379)
Wilson, Kenneth J 4:43:39 (21,639)
Wilson, Larry 3:13:11 (2,026)
Wilson, Lee J 4:29:17 (17,919)
Wilson, Les 4:08:41 (12,544)
Wilson, Mark 6:01:48 (33,157)
Wilson, Mark A 3:13:20 (2,039)
Wilson, Mark A 3:57:37 (9,806)
Wilson, Mark A 5:03:14 (26,243)
Wilson, Mark D 3:43:38 (6,551)
Wilson, Mark R 4:27:02 (17,264)
Wilson, Martin 3:34:55 (4,943)
Wilson, Matthew T 3:24:05 (3,277)
Wilson, Michael G 3:47:29 (7,285)
Wilson, Nicholas M 3:29:22 (4,085)
Wilson, Nicholas T 3:57:43 (9,850)
Wilson, Nick 3:22:17 (3,047)
Wilson, Nick C 3:21:05 (2,898)
Wilson, Paul P 3:57:05 (9,644)
Wilson, Peter 3:50:30 (7,944)
Wilson, Richard 4:07:35 (12,252)
Wilson, Richard 4:49:54 (23,217)
Wilson, Richard A 7:18:28 (35,132)
Wilson, Richard J 3:50:07 (7,859)
Wilson, Rick 3:43:48 (6,589)
Wilson, Robert J 3:20:06 (2,769)
Wilson, Robin H 5:04:20 (26,430)
Wilson, Ross 3:18:26 (2,570)
Wilson, Russell Christopher 5:11:37 (27,750)
Wilson, Shane 3:27:43 (3,814)
Wilson, Simon H 3:15:14 (2,256)
Wilson, Simon M 4:42:39 (21,373)
Wilson, Simon S 4:08:40 (12,539)
Wilson, Stephen S 4:31:21 (18,455)
Wilson, Stephen W 4:11:16 (13,179)
Wilson, Stevan J 4:10:59 (13,104)
Wilson, Steven D 4:56:11 (24,723)
Wilson, Stuart A 3:58:36 (10,126)
Wilson, Tim 5:23:26 (29,589)
Wilson, Toby J 6:24:33 (34,215)
Wilson, Tom 3:57:46 (9,863)
Wilson-Beales, Steven L 4:38:35 (20,319)
Wilton, David 4:38:35 (20,319)
Wilton, Graham G 2:54:42 (642)
Wilton, Herman 4:50:59 (23,483)
Wilton, Matthew 3:35:34 (5,061)
Wilton, Nicholas M 4:22:48 (16,140)
Wiltshire, Chris 4:16:07 (14,429)
Wiltshire, Craig J 4:45:50 (22,171)
Wiltshire, Paul A 4:19:56 (15,407)
Wimborne, Alex J 4:26:13 (17,044)
Wimmer, Richard J 4:00:51 (10,755)
Wimpory, Howard P 3:14:59 (2,230)
Wimshurst, Thomas H 3:07:21 (1,462)
Winbanks, Gavin J 5:15:17 (28,381)
Winch, Jamie 5:29:41 (30,357)
Winch, Kevin 3:55:46 (9,253)
Winch, Martin James 4:05:22 (11,744)
Windle, Christopher D 5:36:46 (31,149)
Windle, Jason M 4:07:42 (12,286)
Windle, Patrick 5:15:41 (28,452)
Windle, Paul J 2:59:14 (937)
Windle, Robin 3:49:23 (7,704)
Windows, Max O 4:17:59 (14,886)
Winfield, Brian N 4:22:06 (15,966)
Winfield, Simon 4:15:28 (14,275)
Wing, Andrew T 3:47:47 (7,346)
Wing, Stephen 6:33:53 (34,497)
Wingate, Matthew B 3:29:19 (4,073)
Wingate, Simon 4:54:14 (24,268)
Wingate-Pearse, Jared 5:11:12 (27,672)
Wingfield, Simon E 3:53:29 (8,621)
Wingham, Mark 3:50:24 (7,920)
Winkfield, Len 4:58:23 (25,233)
Winn, Andy 4:26:09 (17,030)
Winn, Mike J 3:28:32 (3,930)
Winnery, Keith A 4:46:41 (22,391)
Winsley, Paul A 4:31:16 (18,419)
Winstanley, Sam J 3:42:24 (6,282)
Winston, Deepak 5:28:45 (30,244)
Winstone, Mark T 4:36:30 (19,793)
Winter, Andrew J 6:43:17 (34,685)
Winter, Anthony M 3:09:33 (1,660)
Winter, James 3:40:10 (5,892)
Winter, James 4:20:30 (15,557)

Winter, Mark S 3:19:08 (2,630)
Winter, Martin 3:55:52 (9,279)
Winter, Martin D 7:35:22 (35,247)
Winter, Mike 3:27:01 (3,684)
Winter, Neil 4:38:41 (20,347)
Winter, Paul L 5:17:22 (28,691)
Winter, Reuben 3:55:36 (9,191)
Winter, Wayne 4:13:19 (13,752)
Winterton, Matt J 4:47:50 (22,684)
Wintle, David A 3:07:38 (1,495)
Wintle, David M 3:21:34 (2,955)
Winward, Charles S 4:54:52 (24,420)
Winyard, Joe 4:02:46 (11,182)
Winyard, Mark 4:11:45 (13,323)
Wisbey, Carl 4:35:15 (19,477)
Wisbey, Matt J 4:49:57 (23,231)
Wisdom, Martin J 3:41:52 (6,180)
Wisdom, Richard J 5:22:53 (29,494)
Wise, Alan 3:08:35 (1,575)
Wise, Andrew S 4:35:38 (19,574)
Wise, Ben J 4:12:01 (13,392)
Wise, Daniel C 3:56:50 (9,579)
Wise, John 3:32:46 (4,584)
Wise, Jonathan 3:49:57 (7,823)
Wiseman, Mark 4:09:35 (12,747)
With, Christoffer 3:36:01 (5,158)
Withalm, Johann 4:43:21 (21,567)
Withecombe, Mark W 3:09:32 (1,659)
Withers, Alex 4:57:09 (24,955)
Withey, Guy 5:13:59 (28,157)
Withey, Jonathan M 2:42:49 (251)
Withington, Justin 4:18:55 (15,139)
Withrington, Paul 4:05:03 (11,665)
Witt, Jonathan J 4:31:59 (18,629)
Wittet, Mark J 4:06:50 (12,068)
Witton, Ross A 4:58:03 (25,148)
Witts, Stephen H 4:25:33 (16,856)
Witty, Andrew P 4:32:04 (18,656)
Wixey, John D 4:58:42 (25,319)
Wizard, Danny N 3:35:02 (4,965)
Wodzianski, Juliusz V 5:10:39 (27,575)
Woensdregt, Joseph W 3:53:42 (8,677)
Woerle, Roland 3:35:37 (5,074)
Wohanka, Richard 4:11:17 (13,185)
Wojcik, Rafal 2:16:41 (15)
Wolf, Torsten 4:13:03 (13,667)
Wolfendale, Stewart 3:38:35 (5,604)
Wolfenden, Matthew 5:13:40 (28,091)
Wolfensberger, Christian 4:25:58 (16,978)
Wolfmayr, Norbert 4:05:33 (11,785)
Wolkov, Benjamin 3:56:03 (9,328)
Wollaston, Lee 4:46:08 (22,232)
Wollon, Andy C 3:58:43 (10,168)
Wolovitz, Lionel 3:32:28 (4,540)
Wolowczuk, Richard 4:18:37 (15,058)
Wolschow, Mathias 4:03:46 (11,379)
Wolsey, Peter 3:44:26 (6,705)
Wolstencroft, John A 4:51:38 (23,655)
Wolstencroft, Michael P 5:17:26 (28,708)
Wolstencroft, Shane M 3:18:19 (2,556)
Wolters, Alexander 3:00:14 (1,011)
Womack, Darren 5:32:43 (30,727)
Wong, Andrew 3:55:40 (9,210)
Wong, Baldwin 3:38:37 (5,609)
Wong, Christopher X 4:55:24 (24,553)
Wong, Ing H 4:39:30 (20,584)
Wong, Michael 4:52:02 (23,760)
Wong, Terence 4:42:05 (21,220)
Wong, Voi Shim 6:41:48 (34,659)
Woo, Ian S 5:41:59 (31,671)
Wood, Adrian 6:44:47 (34,704)
Wood, Alan D 3:40:36 (5,958)
Wood, Alan D 6:12:45 (33,678)
Wood, Andrew R 4:14:58 (14,158)
Wood, Anthony J 4:54:19 (24,292)
Wood, Bernard J 4:05:05 (11,675)
Wood, Bradley J 4:10:09 (12,898)
Wood, Dan 4:18:06 (14,920)
Wood, Dave 3:49:54 (7,814)
Wood, David A 3:49:49 (7,803)
Wood, David M 3:37:14 (5,359)
Wood, Duncan 4:36:57 (19,900)
Wood, Gary 4:28:04 (17,564)
Wood, Graham J 4:40:42 (20,886)
Wood, Ian D 3:13:10 (2,023)
Wood, James 2:55:20 (687)
Wood, James M 3:58:58 (10,243)
Wood, John D 4:09:14 (12,668)
Wood, Joseph D 3:20:41 (2,854)
Wood, Kevin 6:53:46 (34,876)
Wood, Lee 5:40:18 (31,522)
Wood, Louis 3:41:57 (6,195)
Wood, Mark 4:35:55 (19,656)
Wood, Mark A 4:03:27 (11,320)
Wood, Mark J 3:16:22 (2,365)
Wood, Martin 4:00:44 (10,726)
Wood, Matthew P 4:41:34 (21,109)
Wood, Matthew S 4:16:29 (14,519)
Wood, Oliver J 4:18:30 (15,029)
Wood, Olly J 3:52:02 (8,282)
Wood, Owen M 5:18:52 (28,958)
Wood, Peter A 5:18:50 (28,947)
Wood, Peter C 4:15:43 (14,323)
Wood, Phillip A 4:18:15 (14,951)
Wood, Reece 2:49:39 (449)
Wood, Rob J 3:32:11 (4,500)
Wood, Robert M 3:52:57 (8,496)
Wood, Sam D 3:56:17 (9,383)
Wood, Simon 4:35:55 (19,656)
Wood, Simon J 3:52:15 (8,347)
Wood, Stephen 4:36:05 (19,698)
Wood, Victor W 4:30:37 (18,260)
Wood, William M 3:50:40 (7,983)
Woodall, David A 4:54:58 (24,441)
Woodall, Marc 3:22:15 (3,045)
Woodbridge, Andrew M 4:22:26 (16,060)
Woodbridge, Jamie A 5:36:51 (31,162)
Woodburn, Peter J 3:04:42 (1,280)
Woodcock, John P 3:30:13 (4,209)
Woodcock, Mark S 4:39:49 (20,670)
Woodcock, Paul 4:36:26 (19,777)
Woodcock, Shaun 3:10:29 (1,736)
Woodfield, Craig J 4:56:10 (24,720)
Woodford, Stephen W 4:25:43 (16,915)
Woodgate, Daniel M 3:42:08 (6,238)
Woodhams, Rich M 3:43:56 (6,621)
Woodhead, Mark 4:01:39 (10,956)
Woodhead, Stephen R 4:34:52 (19,371)
Woodhouse, Nigel 3:56:19 (9,399)
Woodhouse, Paul J 3:51:11 (8,093)
Woodhouse, Philip J 3:19:53 (2,736)
Woodhouse, Richard A 4:38:59 (20,429)
Woodhouse, Stephen 4:15:37 (14,308)
Wooding, Glen T 4:24:03 (16,453)
Wooding, Ross 5:14:46 (28,277)
Woodley, Steven M 3:36:50 (5,283)
Woodman, Ian H 4:28:44 (17,754)
Woodman, Mark J 2:40:55 (213)
Woodman, Tim J 5:35:56 (31,066)
Woodmore, Chris M 4:17:59 (14,886)
Woodrow, Graham 3:58:41 (10,155)
Woodrow, Michael 4:00:28 (10,656)
Woodrow, Nick T 3:29:20 (4,074)
Woodrow, Thomas 3:36:31 (5,238)
Woodruff, Glenn A 6:09:23 (33,531)
Woodruff, Raymond 3:38:38 (5,615)
Woodruff, Thomas G 3:25:38 (3,479)
Woods, Benjamin 4:01:03 (10,804)
Woods, Christopher F 3:48:58 (7,610)
Woods, Christopher J 6:01:02 (33,114)
Woods, Garry 4:03:51 (11,412)
Woods, Ian J 4:20:16 (15,502)
Woods, James M 4:34:55 (19,391)
Woods, Jonathan 4:26:19 (17,071)
Woods, Lee M 3:01:03 (1,054)
Woods, Neil 4:47:37 (22,634)
Woods, Neil J 5:12:29 (27,893)
Woods, Paul 5:06:09 (26,753)
Woods, Paul A 3:54:25 (8,867)
Woods, Phil R 3:18:22 (2,563)
Woods, Roger K 4:43:21 (21,567)
Woods, Ross D 4:04:42 (11,586)
Woods, Shane 4:50:14 (23,292)
Woods, Shane W 4:46:33 (22,360)
Woods, Shaun 4:44:32 (21,843)
Woods, Sheldon 5:38:34 (31,340)
Woods, Simon G 4:01:45 (10,972)
Woods, Tristan M 4:07:25 (12,218)
Woodward, Aaron R 4:52:01 (23,753)
Woodward, Lee J 6:00:32 (33,077)
Woodward, Peter G 3:04:11 (1,247)
Woodward, Robert A 4:55:04 (24,468)
Woodward, Simon P 2:56:22 (738)
Woodward, Teifion J 6:15:24 (33,809)
Woodworth, James P 4:38:42 (20,350)
Woodyard, Jamie 3:51:37 (8,191)
Woodyard, Paul T 5:33:12 (30,774)
Woolard, Clive 4:35:21 (19,506)
Woolard, Leigh 3:55:15 (9,099)
Woolcock, Anthony 4:24:50 (16,663)
Woolcock, Graham John 4:50:34 (23,389)
Woolcock, Mark 4:47:46 (22,667)
Woolcott, Karl 3:24:28 (3,336)
Wooldridge, Claire 4:43:45 (21,656)
Wooldridge, David 4:53:32 (24,083)
Wooldridge, David P 3:46:54 (7,177)
Woolf, Michael S 4:17:55 (14,866)
Woolf, Robert 6:54:26 (34,888)
Woolf, Ryan J 3:43:23 (6,505)
Woolf, Stephen 4:16:17 (14,469)
Woolford, Colin 4:32:43 (18,819)
Woolgar, Adam D 3:33:13 (4,638)
Woolger, Philip A 4:39:51 (20,682)
Woolhouse, David 4:23:47 (16,382)
Woollard, Tom 3:52:51 (8,476)
Woollett, Stephen R 3:31:12 (4,361)
Woolley, Andrew 3:12:47 (1,974)
Woolley, Devon 4:25:00 (16,712)
Woolley, Michael 5:04:32 (26,468)
Woolley, Philip R 5:19:09 (28,989)
Woolley, Simon M 3:20:09 (2,774)
Woollons, Martin J 5:23:12 (29,550)
Woolman, Paul L 4:23:58 (16,432)
Wooloughan, John J 4:46:32 (22,355)
Woolsey, Jack 5:12:21 (27,861)
Woolston, David A 4:23:15 (16,241)
Woolston, Mathew J 4:20:29 (15,554)
Wootten, Scott G 3:43:03 (6,429)
Wootton, Richard O 3:51:54 (8,257)
Wootton, Shaun 3:31:14 (4,365)
Wootton, Stephen R 4:54:18 (24,290)
Wootton, Terence E 4:39:05 (20,461)
Worboys, Tom 3:39:24 (5,743)
Worfolk-Smith, Barney J 4:01:31 (10,919)
Worgan, Steven 4:41:13 (21,017)
World, Paul L 3:51:43 (8,212)
Worley, Richard J 4:46:21 (22,294)
Worlidge, Ali J 4:43:32 (21,609)
Wormald, Carl 4:57:45 (25,078)
Worrall, Colin 4:24:58 (16,700)
Worrall, Kevin 4:02:10 (11,057)
Worrall, Mark 3:25:30 (3,457)
Worrell, Jeffrey W 4:51:02 (23,498)
Worrow, Jeff 4:26:39 (17,168)
Worsley, Nick 4:30:22 (18,197)
Worsley, Philip James 3:59:07 (10,285)
Worssell, Mark A 3:50:13 (7,889)
Wort, Gary 5:28:05 (30,158)
Wort, Steven S 2:58:57 (914)
Worth, Dan A 4:22:01 (15,944)
Worth, James B 3:28:53 (3,989)
Worthington, Andrew M 5:05:08 (26,575)
Worthington, Barrie V 4:22:06 (15,966)
Worthington, Luke 3:55:00 (9,025)
Worthy, David S 4:19:46 (15,363)
Worthy, Ian 4:26:30 (17,118)
Worton, Chris 4:39:37 (20,618)
Wotton, David A 3:55:42 (9,221)
Wotton, Gary D 3:52:05 (8,295)
Wotton, Kevin M 2:59:00 (921)
Wotton, Mark A 4:23:51 (16,399)
Wozencroft, Richard G 4:25:00 (16,712)
Wragg, Matthew 3:55:11 (9,081)
Wragg, Philip 4:06:12 (11,927)
Wraight, Oliver R 3:28:12 (3,886)
Wraith, Jonathan 3:53:39 (8,663)
Wratten, David J 3:52:35 (8,420)
Wray, Alan 2:42:12 (240)
Wray, Andy 4:00:30 (10,675)

Wray, Mike G 5:25:44 (29,897)
Wray, Paul G 4:38:43 (20,354)
Wray, Peter P 6:03:30 (33,258)
Wreford, David G 4:41:12 (21,014)
Wreford, Joe H 5:16:53 (28,628)
Wren, Anthony P 5:58:14 (32,943)
Wren, James 4:37:31 (20,042)
Wren, James R 4:21:40 (15,872)
Wrenn, Ceri T 4:00:18 (10,618)
Wright, Andrew J 4:39:03 (20,452)
Wright, Andrew M 4:41:27 (21,072)
Wright, Andrew T 3:38:41 (5,621)
Wright, Andrew William 4:18:46 (15,094)
Wright, Barry J 6:01:55 (33,164)
Wright, Carl 2:47:42 (383)
Wright, Chris 5:44:05 (31,859)
Wright, Chris J 3:56:57 (9,606)
Wright, Christopher 6:05:58 (33,386)
Wright, Darryl L 5:06:12 (26,763)
Wright, David 3:22:33 (3,074)
Wright, David G 3:01:41 (1,095)
Wright, David J 4:51:22 (23,581)
Wright, David P 3:52:40 (8,444)
Wright, David P 5:22:54 (29,500)
Wright, David W 5:22:29 (29,436)
Wright, Dominic 4:31:53 (18,602)
Wright, Edward D 4:57:54 (25,111)
Wright, Edward J 4:29:31 (17,969)
Wright, Gary 4:02:12 (11,068)
Wright, Gary A 4:14:47 (14,108)
Wright, Helen L 4:39:05 (20,461)
Wright, Ian S 4:22:21 (16,036)
Wright, James 4:24:40 (16,614)
Wright, James W 6:33:58 (34,500)
Wright, Jason 4:57:20 (24,992)
Wright, Jason W 4:03:13 (11,275)
Wright, John 3:21:56 (3,003)
Wright, John G 3:59:38 (10,428)
Wright, John J 4:24:18 (16,527)
Wright, Jonathan 4:44:28 (21,831)
Wright, Jonathon B 4:22:05 (15,961)
Wright, Justin 3:56:23 (9,423)
Wright, Keith 3:53:45 (8,692)
Wright, Ken C 5:26:43 (30,015)
Wright, Kristian 4:00:58 (10,792)
Wright, Mark 4:39:00 (20,435)
Wright, Mark A 2:58:36 (875)
Wright, Mark D 4:48:22 (22,819)
Wright, Matt J 3:25:11 (3,417)
Wright, Matthew 4:51:08 (23,516)
Wright, Matthew A 4:40:01 (20,730)
Wright, Matthew W 5:19:59 (29,090)
Wright, Michael 4:14:42 (14,079)
Wright, Michael 5:06:44 (26,853)
Wright, Michael R 3:37:01 (5,321)
Wright, Neil 4:42:45 (21,397)
Wright, Neil J 3:57:57 (9,917)
Wright, Nick 4:43:55 (21,694)
Wright, Peter A 4:30:57 (18,338)
Wright, Peter J 4:14:06 (13,931)
Wright, Philip J 4:51:28 (23,612)
Wright, Simon B 5:03:12 (26,235)
Wright, Simon R 4:23:31 (16,319)
Wright, Stuart 4:07:25 (12,218)
Wright, Thomas W 4:52:30 (23,863)
Wright, Tom A 4:40:36 (20,860)
Wright, Tony 4:43:32 (21,609)
Wrighton, Chris J 2:49:33 (445)
Wrighton, David T 3:57:06 (9,648)
Wrigley, Russell D 4:07:41 (12,281)
Wring, Matthew G 3:56:47 (9,561)
Wu, Jean-Michel S 6:03:02 (33,231)
Wuestenenk, Garrit Jan Willem 3:32:37 (4,563)
Wunderlich, Marcel 4:41:39 (21,132)
Wurmbock, Arrigo 3:46:51 (7,167)
Wyatt, Ben 4:08:00 (12,359)
Wyatt, Ben 4:14:20 (13,994)
Wyatt, Colin A 5:17:40 (28,741)
Wyatt, Danny 3:27:12 (3,716)
Wyatt, Darren 4:16:05 (14,420)
Wyatt, David R 4:31:08 (18,391)
Wyatt, Steven J 3:20:22 (2,806)
Wyatt, Terry A 6:14:20 (33,760)
Wyatt, William J 6:01:35 (33,145)
Wybrow, Andrew 4:14:42 (14,079)
Wydell, Ben D 5:17:51 (28,771)
Wye, Mark A 4:16:40 (14,575)
Wyldes, Mark E 4:02:53 (11,206)
Wylie, Stephen 2:34:47 (111)
Wyllie, Stuart D 4:23:28 (16,299)
Wynn, Gareth J 4:10:11 (12,907)
Wynn, Richard D 4:37:51 (20,132)
Wynne, Richard 8:20:45 (35,333)
Wynne, Rob H 3:09:37 (1,669)
Wynne Morgan, Jamie 4:26:10 (17,031)
Wyse, Barry David 3:47:51 (7,361)
Wysocki, Richard 4:11:58 (13,382)
Xanders, Nick 4:27:34 (17,404)
Xavier, Prats 4:03:57 (11,436)
Xenophontos, Chris 4:24:39 (16,605)
Yabluchanskiy, Andriy 5:18:28 (28,864)
Yadave, Rush L 3:28:19 (3,903)
Yakubu, Funso 5:30:54 (30,507)
Yam, Perry 3:56:44 (9,544)
Yanover, Darren 7:28:31 (35,211)
Yao, N'guessan Alain Maxime 7:18:42 (35,136)
Yap, Wooi Huen 3:47:22 (7,261)
Yardley-Rees, Guy P 3:19:53 (2,736)
Yarham, Ian M 4:33:00 (18,899)
Yarker, Andrew J 2:42:57 (254)
Yarker, Kit 3:36:15 (5,198)
Yarnall, Matt J 3:26:41 (3,633)
Yarnall, Terry L 4:08:31 (12,508)
Yasin, Abdur Razzak Md 6:26:30 (34,299)
Yates, Andrew J 2:53:33 (588)
Yates, Andy 5:12:28 (27,889)
Yates, Chris 5:25:05 (29,809)
Yates, Chris 5:54:38 (32,656)
Yates, Christopher E 4:10:52 (13,081)
Yates, David A 3:40:50 (6,007)
Yates, Fredi J 4:48:58 (22,962)
Yates, Graham R 3:50:25 (7,925)
Yates, Ian R 3:34:30 (4,879)
Yates, Mark A 3:19:05 (2,626)
Yates, Matthew 5:23:55 (29,638)
Yates, Nick D 4:15:03 (14,176)
Yates, Peter 3:35:32 (5,054)
Yates, Peter J 3:56:09 (9,351)
Yates, Philip 4:07:29 (12,233)
Yates, Simon R 5:27:47 (30,120)
Yates, Steven 4:40:34 (20,851)
Yates, Stewart 3:29:00 (4,006)
Yates, Tim 4:24:01 (16,444)
Yau, Jason 3:55:23 (9,127)
Yazaki, Etsuro 3:19:00 (2,617)
Yeates, Andrew 5:03:52 (26,353)
Yeates, Anthony 3:15:42 (2,305)
Yeates, Daniel R 4:42:02 (21,206)
Yeats, Gavin R 3:46:51 (7,167)
Yeldham, Ian J 4:59:59 (25,594)
Yelland, David J 4:16:16 (14,464)
Yelland, Peter 4:53:34 (24,089)
Yemez, Zeki 4:07:43 (12,290)
Yeo, Steve N 4:29:50 (18,048)
Yeoman, Allan J 4:09:08 (12,647)
Yeomans, Martin 4:08:39 (12,533)
Yeomans, Stuart J 4:58:08 (25,174)
Yerby, Ben E 4:43:16 (21,534)
Yiasoumi, Antonakis 5:08:47 (27,229)
Yip, Gwan 4:48:51 (22,932)
Yoong, Lee 4:45:51 (22,177)
York, Oliver T 4:14:30 (14,026)
Yorke, Christopher J 3:15:49 (2,320)
You, Jean François 3:26:47 (3,650)
Youlten, Robert M 3:57:10 (9,664)
Youmans, Christopher 3:56:37 (9,500)
Younan, Paul I 4:15:37 (14,308)
Young, Adam 4:32:46 (18,835)
Young, Alan 3:35:52 (5,125)
Young, Alan A 5:14:35 (28,252)
Young, Alastair 4:26:28 (17,104)
Young, Alex D 3:20:40 (2,850)
Young, Andrew 3:26:45 (3,642)
Young, Andrew W 5:15:12 (28,353)
Young, Andy 5:17:01 (28,639)
Young, Chris D 3:21:05 (2,898)
Young, Christopher J 4:25:03 (16,726)
Young, Darren B 4:25:47 (16,933)
Young, David J 4:56:43 (24,858)
Young, Gary J 3:40:13 (5,904)
Young, Harry R 4:42:35 (21,357)
Young, Harvey 4:45:34 (22,097)
Young, Hedley 4:34:19 (19,225)
Young, Ian A 5:24:03 (29,660)
Young, James P 4:23:51 (16,399)
Young, John P 5:50:59 (32,414)
Young, Justin M 2:59:41 (974)
Young, Keith L 4:58:57 (25,377)
Young, Mark 4:18:20 (14,973)
Young, Mark A 5:05:06 (26,566)
Young, Mark D 3:12:32 (1,934)
Young, Michael 4:28:23 (17,665)
Young, Mickey 5:24:55 (29,782)
Young, Nick 4:17:33 (14,781)
Young, Richard E 4:49:44 (23,187)
Young, Scott A 3:58:51 (10,211)
Young, Scott J 4:17:50 (14,846)
Young, Simon D 4:47:18 (22,560)
Young, Stephen 5:20:12 (29,117)
Young, Stephen J 5:14:29 (28,239)
Young, Thomas A 3:45:56 (6,972)
Young, Willie 3:34:02 (4,763)
Younger, Michael 5:37:49 (31,255)
Youngson, Robert G 3:23:19 (3,161)
Youssef, Mourou 4:09:48 (12,803)
Yousuf, Ali 3:01:32 (1,085)
Yout, Tony R 3:04:41 (1,277)
Yoxall, Anthony J 4:02:58 (11,221)
Yu, Nicholas 6:18:32 (33,948)
Yuill, Charles L 5:21:24 (29,283)
Yuill, Paul D 5:47:46 (32,151)
Yuill, Peter 3:46:50 (7,162)
Yule, Craig 3:58:08 (9,982)
Yule, Michael A 3:40:42 (5,971)
Yule, Scott 3:28:29 (3,927)
Yusuf, Sherif O 4:33:17 (18,968)
Yves, Duval 4:53:07 (24,004)
Zaagman, Richard E 5:21:41 (29,329)
Zaccariello, Benito 5:30:09 (30,426)
Zaffran, Laurent 5:33:30 (30,803)
Zagarella, Giuseppe 3:56:47 (9,561)
Zaher, Yousef 4:21:48 (15,900)
Zakay, Uri 4:39:41 (20,639)
Zaldua, Iñaki 3:50:30 (7,944)
Zallot, Lucio 4:09:23 (12,705)
Zallot, Tiziano 4:11:03 (13,124)
Zamir, Nasar 4:56:50 (24,890)
Zamparelli, Ugo 2:49:59 (472)
Zanardi, Nicola 5:03:35 (26,300)
Zandonella, Laurent 2:57:44 (822)
Zangari, Alain 4:27:02 (17,264)
Zanon, Fabio 5:05:05 (26,565)
Zapata, Jairo 4:15:22 (14,246)
Zaranko, Tadeusz 2:55:46 (713)
Zardini, Max 3:39:50 (5,815)
Zastresek, Ladislav 3:42:43 (6,359)
Zazzetta, Vittorio 3:17:10 (2,451)
Zeffert, Jonathan R 4:44:21 (21,805)
Zeifman, Clifford 5:13:59 (28,157)
Zeima, Mohamed 2:40:02 (192)
Zelinger, Simon 5:36:42 (31,143)
Zembashis, Antony A 5:03:39 (26,315)
Zemori, Jacques 4:25:46 (16,928)
Zhor, Radim 4:58:46 (25,330)
Zia, Shahzad 4:05:31 (11,773)
Zielinski, Jeremy V 3:11:00 (1,779)
Zietsman, Hendrik S 2:35:02 (116)
Ziff, Alex 3:34:03 (4,770)
Zimmer, Martin 3:43:08 (6,448)
Zimmer, Michael 4:05:08 (11,690)
Zimmermann, Christophe 5:21:53 (29,357)
Zimmermann, Mark R 5:22:36 (29,453)
Zingor, Peter 4:05:01 (11,655)
Zinn, Mark 3:59:55 (10,523)
Zorn, Georg 4:40:50 (20,920)
Zouras, Arthur 4:17:14 (14,700)
Zsitvai, Peter P 5:05:28 (26,632)
Zuber, Pascal 3:11:58 (1,879)
Zuber, Stefan 2:59:29 (956)

Zucconi, Anthony 4:27:07 (17,285)
Zuliani, Walter 4:31:18 (18,438)
Zurawski, Lui 4:15:53 (14,364)
Zurlo, Lorenzo 4:41:27 (21,072)
Zverev, Vasily 2:47:12 (373)
Zwirner, Jens 4:36:00 (19,683)

FEMALE RUNNERS

Aaron, Elin 5:11:43 (27,761)
Abate, Sian G 3:25:59 (3,529)
Abbey, Claire 5:48:01 (32,171)
Abbott, Elizabeth M 3:04:23 (1,257)
Abbott, Joanne 3:30:46 (4,293)
Abbott, Sue Linda 6:21:59 (34,112)
Abela, Cheryl 4:14:17 (13,986)
Abernethy, Paula 3:46:07 (7,008)
Abhyankar, Tay 4:07:08 (12,138)
Abitova, Inga 2:25:55 (36)
Abraham, Claire M 5:32:25 (30,676)
Abraham, Rebecca C 4:46:20 (22,290)
Abrams, Julie 4:01:58 (11,014)
Ackland, Sian 5:45:30 (31,974)
Ackroyd, Jayne 3:59:40 (10,445)
Ackroyd, Sarah 4:33:21 (18,991)
Acors, Carrie R 5:18:47 (28,931)
Acott, Susan M 4:43:23 (21,574)
Acton, Nikki A 3:56:55 (9,598)
Adair, Anne T 4:18:46 (15,094)
Adames, Alexandra 4:54:02 (24,229)
Adams, Annie 4:56:58 (24,925)
Adams, Carrie-Anne 5:39:35 (31,456)
Adams, Christina M 4:31:17 (18,429)
Adams, Claire M 4:12:30 (13,526)
Adams, Clare L 3:42:29 (6,295)
Adams, Emma L 5:09:13 (27,311)
Adams, Erika B 4:42:54 (21,445)
Adams, Helen A 4:05:47 (11,838)
Adams, Jean 3:39:21 (5,736)
Adams, Jennifer 6:06:42 (33,420)
Adams, Kimberley 6:52:22 (34,850)
Adams, Nicola P 4:35:19 (19,496)
Adams, Rowena 5:51:11 (32,428)
Adams, Shani A 4:15:07 (14,195)
Adams, Susan P 5:05:59 (26,723)
Adamson, Jolene C 4:45:28 (22,071)
Adamson, Sarah H 3:37:38 (5,429)
Adcock, Miranda J 3:27:34 (3,796)
Adcock, Rosemary A 4:57:30 (25,029)
Adcock, Sarah J 5:13:35 (28,078)
Addison, Gemma M 5:07:47 (27,056)
Adelmann, Doris 4:41:55 (21,184)
Adere, Berhane 2:25:30 (35)
Adigun, Abiola 5:00:02 (25,606)
Adlam, Charlotte E 5:09:57 (27,446)
Adlam, Melissa 4:01:34 (10,934)
Adlard, Victoria L 4:24:49 (16,661)
Adler, Kat 6:03:22 (33,253)
Adnams, Jacqueline D 3:54:08 (8,790)
Affleck, Patricia M 3:21:58 (3,009)
Agbulos, Jasmine 5:22:52 (29,491)
Agestam, Maria 4:31:41 (18,546)
Aghanti, Julie I 6:09:45 (33,549)
Agostara, Cinzia 4:11:40 (13,303)
Ahl, Jo 6:01:15 (33,125)
Ahl, Lucie A 3:24:15 (3,304)
Ahlqwist, Anna 3:53:58 (8,745)
Ahmed, Shahana A 4:25:16 (16,778)
Ahnien, Marie-Claire A 4:42:19 (21,277)
Aigner, Christine 3:27:01 (3,684)
Aikman, Jane 4:08:58 (12,614)
Ailey, Jacqueline K 6:19:48 (34,027)
Ainsley, Susan H 3:56:47 (9,561)
Ainsworth, Pat H 6:15:00 (33,791)
Aitchison, Edda I 4:03:59 (11,445)
Aitchison, Pauline A 3:32:07 (4,486)
Aitken, Jayne A 4:28:38 (17,734)
Aitken, Marianne L 5:01:28 (25,907)
Akeroyd, Suzanne 3:40:08 (5,885)
Aki, Ishii 5:17:30 (28,717)
Akin, Aylin 7:15:06 (35,105)
Akin, Tracy 4:43:18 (21,543)
Aknai, Mandy 4:34:16 (19,215)
Alabede, Abimbola I 5:59:08 (32,995)
Al-Ali, Nesem 7:40:24 (35,271)
Alami-Merrouni, Sue 5:48:09 (32,181)
Albayrak, Aylin 4:57:51 (25,097)
Alberry, Sian H 3:39:43 (5,795)
Albin-Jones, Chris 5:08:13 (27,127)
Albon, Lorraine M 4:29:49 (18,041)
Albrecht, Annika 3:46:55 (7,182)
Albutt, Nancy E 5:49:20 (32,280)
Alcock, Helen L 5:20:10 (29,116)
Alcock, Sarah L 5:56:50 (32,819)
Alder, Helen 5:00:35 (25,723)
Alder, Louise 6:09:46 (33,550)
Alderman, Henrietta 4:25:52 (16,951)
Alderman, Pauline 4:11:20 (13,202)
Aldous-Critchley, Amy-Jo 4:21:58 (15,935)
Aldred, Deborah L 4:30:20 (18,192)
Aldred, Victoria C 5:10:33 (27,556)
Aldridge, Katherine S 3:26:33 (3,609)
Aldridge, Lucy V 4:22:31 (16,078)
Alekna, Amie E 4:11:42 (13,312)
Aleknavicius, Carol 4:09:50 (12,816)
Alexander, Alison 4:12:02 (13,397)
Alexander, Eleanor M 6:25:25 (34,249)
Alexander, Michelle 5:17:13 (28,676)
Alexander-Cahill, Gail 5:15:07 (28,338)
Alexandrou, Tracey A 3:18:43 (2,589)
Aley, Rachel 4:25:47 (16,933)
Alford, Sara 4:44:45 (21,899)
Alice, Tillin 6:07:48 (33,474)
Alim, Navene 4:26:19 (17,071)
Allan, Allison 4:56:06 (24,707)
Allan, Dotty 4:00:51 (10,755)
Allan, Kirsty E 6:03:58 (33,288)
Allan, Nicola 4:36:08 (19,707)
Allen, Amanda 4:09:25 (12,710)
Allen, Angela M 4:45:51 (22,177)
Allen, Annabel J 4:22:05 (15,961)
Allen, Della 4:07:27 (12,226)
Allen, Della A 5:15:00 (28,320)
Allen, Emma L 4:27:08 (17,290)
Allen, Erica M 4:13:28 (13,787)
Allen, Heather 4:01:21 (10,873)
Allen, Helen E 4:51:55 (23,737)
Allen, Jennifer L 5:32:53 (30,741)
Allen, Joanna 4:48:53 (22,938)
Allen, Joanna 5:18:56 (28,966)
Allen, Karen M 6:30:51 (34,431)
Allen, Katherine 5:14:02 (28,170)
Allen, Katie 6:06:51 (33,425)
Allen, Katy 4:20:12 (15,484)
Allen, Lucy 6:32:19 (34,459)
Allen, Melanie G 5:05:03 (26,558)
Allen, Naomi 5:24:52 (29,776)
Allen, Nicola J 4:59:01 (25,391)
Allen, Nikki 4:28:00 (17,542)
Allen, Sara Ann 5:56:35 (32,798)
Allen, Sarah J 4:21:20 (15,768)
Allen, Stephanie J 3:46:29 (7,084)
Allen, Susan M 5:17:43 (28,749)
Allen, Tanya 6:01:11 (33,119)
Allenby, Zoe D 4:50:40 (23,414)
Alley, Janet L 5:50:26 (32,371)
Allison, Joanne L 4:16:57 (14,634)
Allison, Lois C 4:03:47 (11,386)
Alliston, Kelly 4:19:27 (15,266)
Allman, Katherine E 5:32:38 (30,709)
Allocco, Andrea 3:34:37 (4,899)
Allport, Jan M 4:35:00 (19,406)
Allsopp, Lucy V 6:18:43 (33,985)
Allum, Theresa 5:23:48 (29,625)
Allwright, Fran A 5:46:23 (32,040)
Almond, Katherine M 4:57:42 (25,069)
Almond, Sally 5:07:50 (27,068)
Alphonso, Annabel 4:16:34 (14,542)
Alston, Heather M 3:39:23 (5,741)
Altayeb, Dina A 4:28:23 (17,665)
Altini, Giovanna M 4:07:34 (12,248)
Alvarez Sieiro, Rosa Maria 5:08:24 (27,164)
Alves, Renata 3:50:57 (8,049)
Amarteifio, Peggy 5:23:55 (29,638)
Ambrose, Helen 6:29:28 (34,395)
Amend, Samantha 2:49:55 (470)
Amer, Lisa J 4:04:23 (11,520)
Ames, Sally E 5:10:38 (27,571)
Amies, Wendy T 5:16:11 (28,525)
Amin, Mohaia M 6:20:08 (34,039)
Amorese, Stefania L 6:13:45 (33,737)
Amos, Emma L 5:16:32 (28,567)
Amos, Libby 4:42:35 (21,357)
Amroussi, Aza 5:40:11 (31,515)
An, Jung Ja 4:45:25 (22,059)
Andersen, Katie 4:36:00 (19,683)
Andersen, Thora 5:06:34 (26,815)
Anderson, Alicia 6:04:16 (33,301)
Anderson, Alison M 5:38:51 (31,376)
Anderson, Amanda 3:56:55 (9,598)
Anderson, Carolynn 5:11:28 (27,721)
Anderson, Charlotte K 4:09:30 (12,719)
Anderson, Claire E 4:55:27 (24,563)
Anderson, Elaine 4:33:18 (18,977)
Anderson, Isabel C 4:52:30 (23,863)
Anderson, Jenni L 4:39:19 (20,523)
Anderson, Jennie A 6:06:22 (33,405)
Anderson, Johanne G 4:28:09 (17,593)
Anderson, Martina 4:32:22 (18,721)
Anderson, Nicole 4:29:39 (18,003)
Anderson, Shirley H 3:32:14 (4,508)
Anderson, Susan J 3:46:48 (7,157)
Anderson, Victoria J 5:34:42 (30,938)
Anderson-Bain, Jules 7:02:31 (34,975)
Andrade, Silvia 4:58:52 (25,355)
Andrade-Brown, Fiona J 4:46:21 (22,294)
Andreae, Emma L 4:15:43 (14,323)
Andrés Abdo, Carolina 4:56:50 (24,890)
Andrew, Catherine 3:31:25 (4,386)
Andrew, Claire L 3:05:33 (1,338)
Andrew, Jane A 4:42:34 (21,348)
Andrew, Sharon 3:43:35 (6,541)
Andrews, Amanda J 4:36:03 (19,692)
Andrews, Angela 4:14:45 (14,096)
Andrews, Angela I 3:47:31 (7,292)
Andrews, Denise C 4:17:41 (14,818)
Andrews, Emma J 3:37:28 (5,392)
Andrews, Heather J 5:22:12 (29,391)
Andrews, Julie D 3:34:02 (4,763)
Andrews, Katie H 3:56:04 (9,329)
Andrews, Michelle L 4:21:24 (15,785)
Andrews, Robin 4:12:59 (13,656)
Andrews, Sarah L 4:22:21 (16,036)
Andrews, Sharon A 3:40:07 (5,881)
Andrews, Sheridan 5:25:35 (29,875)
Andrews, Ulele H 4:28:48 (17,776)
Andrews King, Angela T 4:31:47 (18,578)
Andrieux, Martine 4:31:37 (18,531)
Aneck-Hahn, Claire Elizabeth 4:00:04 (10,564)
Angel, Melanie R 3:57:48 (9,873)
Angell, Anila 5:45:14 (31,952)
Angell, Sarah J 4:53:43 (24,148)
Ankrah, Stephanie V 5:26:46 (30,022)
Ankrett, Helen 4:07:15 (12,165)
Anlander, Denise U 4:28:27 (17,683)
Anne, Landry 5:51:04 (32,416)
Annear, Diane M 5:10:02 (27,467)
Annear, Parveen Z 4:15:27 (14,271)
Annetts, Elizabeth A 3:46:17 (7,037)
Ansbro, Cassandra Dawn 5:19:09 (28,989)
Anscomb, Anne 4:28:37 (17,730)
Antell, Helen O 4:46:33 (22,360)
Anthony, Christine M 3:37:59 (5,487)
Anthony, Karen M 3:35:21 (5,022)
Anton, Susan 3:49:11 (7,665)
Antony Roberts, Rachel H 5:13:17 (28,033)
Aplin, Helen M 6:02:39 (33,206)
Appelhans, Sarah L 4:31:42 (18,552)
Appleton, Carly J 6:12:40 (33,675)
Appleton, Emma 3:42:02 (6,218)
Appleyard, Deborah A 5:19:12 (28,997)
Apps, Vanessa J 3:49:04 (7,635)
Arbaret, Dominique 4:27:49 (17,495)
Arbuthnot, Diana 5:01:01 (25,815)
Arbuthnot, Suzanne K 3:29:17 (4,060)
Archbold, Karen 3:41:04 (6,039)
Archer, Catriona M 3:43:03 (6,429)
Archer, Louise 6:40:57 (34,644)
Archer, Maritha 5:06:42 (26,842)
Archer, Skye J 4:01:19 (10,862)

Archer, Sue K.	5:07:18 (26,960)
Archibald, Helen R.	5:40:04 (31,504)
Archibald, Samantha J.	4:19:25 (15,263)
Arens, Katrina I.	4:34:46 (19,337)
Argyle, Jennifer E.	6:01:37 (33,149)
Arias, Ana Laura	5:49:08 (32,262)
Arkinstall, Melissa J.	3:26:16 (3,569)
Armes, Robyn Z.	6:06:07 (33,390)
Armitage, Jacqueline A.	3:57:37 (9,806)
Armitage, Jane E.	4:36:56 (19,898)
Armour, Victoria L.	4:53:50 (24,183)
Armstrong, Clare A.	4:18:35 (15,049)
Armstrong, Elizabeth J.	5:03:27 (26,275)
Armstrong, Hazel M.	5:11:46 (27,770)
Armstrong, Helen E.	4:43:55 (21,694)
Armstrong, Jane	4:54:37 (24,365)
Armstrong, Victoria	5:45:23 (31,960)
Arnold, Fiona M.	3:45:23 (6,869)
Arnold, Joanne	6:03:20 (33,250)
Arnold, Kate A.	5:02:59 (26,207)
Arnold, Katie	5:32:59 (30,752)
Arnott, Leah	4:33:35 (19,046)
Arrowsmith, Elizabeth L.	5:02:27 (26,102)
Arrowsmith, Jacqueline R.	4:30:09 (18,139)
Arscott, Ann	4:34:37 (19,294)
Arthan, Liz	4:17:58 (14,882)
Arthur, Janet R.	5:56:57 (32,832)
Arthur, Rachel	5:09:22 (27,340)
Artus, Ingrid J.	4:50:54 (23,459)
Aryeetey, Camille	3:40:02 (5,869)
Ash, Hayley E.	5:09:41 (27,401)
Ash, Rebecca	3:37:04 (5,333)
Ashbolt, Alison J.	5:33:56 (30,857)
Ashbridge, Louise S.	5:04:42 (26,494)
Ashby, Jennifer D.	3:44:00 (6,630)
Ashcroft, Cynthia	4:34:23 (19,235)
Ashdown, Jane M.	5:55:45 (32,745)
Ashdown, Rebecca L.	3:53:25 (8,609)
Ashford, Sally L.	5:40:11 (31,515)
Ashley, Anna J.	5:30:32 (30,464)
Ashley, Elizabeth M.	4:29:55 (18,072)
Ashley, Linda	3:55:11 (9,081)
Ashman, Katie E.	4:05:44 (11,828)
Ashman, Laura Suzanne	4:53:32 (24,083)
Ashraff, Victoria L.	6:35:05 (34,523)
Ashton, Leila J.	5:08:01 (27,089)
Ashton, Lindsay	4:27:37 (17,417)
Ashton, Lisa	4:12:00 (13,387)
Ashwell, Emily Jane	4:48:34 (22,866)
Ashworth, Andrea	5:17:02 (28,645)
Ashworth, Kerry A.	4:31:16 (18,419)
Ashworth, Tanya J.	3:41:12 (6,071)
Asken, Dannii M.	5:36:05 (31,085)
Askew, Jennifer	4:34:11 (19,193)
Askew, Sophie I.	5:31:03 (30,535)
Askey, Dawn	5:16:54 (28,631)
Aspinall, Mary B.	4:42:52 (21,431)
Aspinwall, Pennie J.	5:23:54 (29,634)
Asplin, Nicola L.	4:49:03 (22,985)
Aston, Gemma L.	6:06:29 (33,411)
Aston, Sarah F.	4:38:28 (20,290)
Atherton, Anne E.	4:22:27 (16,068)
Atherton, Clair L.	3:52:26 (8,388)
Atkin, Anne Mary	4:39:31 (20,587)
Atkins, Alison S.	6:03:42 (33,272)
Atkins, Gillian C.	5:08:56 (27,258)
Atkins, Lindsay V.	6:18:09 (33,936)
Atkins, Lisa	5:33:32 (30,807)
Atkins, Michelle L.	5:26:57 (30,047)
Atkins, Rebecca J.	3:16:20 (2,361)
Atkinson, Alice	5:25:37 (29,880)
Atkinson, Claire L.	5:21:52 (29,355)
Atkinson, Janette L.	4:54:40 (24,380)
Atkinson, Katharine J.	3:55:13 (9,089)
Atkinson, Keely	3:34:45 (4,916)
Atkinson, Lindsey M.	4:08:04 (12,376)
Atkinson, Michelle L.	4:55:34 (24,584)
Atkinson, Sue	4:26:27 (17,097)
Atkinson, Sue E.	5:18:39 (28,904)
Attard, Anna	4:55:32 (24,579)
Attenborough, Joanne M.	5:52:38 (32,520)
Attenborough, Lisa A.	3:57:13 (9,678)
Atthowe, Helen	4:25:29 (16,834)
Attwell, Susannah K.	3:43:21 (6,499)
Attwood, Gill	5:26:21 (29,973)
Attwood, Laura A.	5:18:54 (28,961)
Attwood, Susan M.	4:13:32 (13,807)
Aubin, Melanie J.	5:42:47 (31,745)
Auckland, Julie M.	4:22:07 (15,970)
Auld, Sarah	5:25:29 (29,856)
Aussenber, Glenda J.	7:47:30 (35,284)
Aussenberg, Rochelle	6:50:13 (34,818)
Austin, Angela	4:49:13 (23,024)
Austin, Debbie L.	5:28:46 (30,245)
Austin, Hayley	7:32:53 (35,235)
Austin, Kathryn E.	4:38:34 (20,315)
Austin, Sarah Helen	3:45:14 (6,842)
Austin, Sue	5:00:45 (25,759)
Austin, Zandra M.	5:52:14 (32,496)
Auzanneau, Isabelle	4:27:14 (17,317)
Avermaete, Marleen	3:39:09 (5,710)
Avery, Kathryn L.	5:26:25 (29,982)
Avery, Lisa A.	6:56:49 (34,917)
Avidic, Aida	5:51:49 (32,470)
Aviet, Anne-Marie	4:22:56 (16,172)
Avril, Jo	3:41:56 (6,191)
Ayako, Nakamura	5:20:44 (29,182)
Ayling, Caroline J.	5:17:32 (28,723)
Aylmer-Pearse, Christina M.	4:52:40 (23,895)
Aylott, Caroline V.	5:40:19 (31,524)
Ayre, Ally	3:28:18 (3,899)
Ayre, Sarah E.	5:40:49 (31,571)
Ayres, Jane C.	3:08:31 (1,568)
Azkornik, Lucy	4:47:59 (22,736)
Babalola, Anne	7:25:57 (35,186)
Babb, Kim	4:49:38 (23,159)
Babor De Abramovich, Patricia	4:38:13 (20,234)
Bache, Susanne E.	4:38:10 (20,221)
Back, Martha M.	4:40:18 (20,795)
Backer, Karin	4:53:39 (24,114)
Backhouse, Alison	5:10:56 (27,629)
Backshell, Kerry M.	3:27:25 (3,752)
Bacon, Pat M.	4:22:51 (16,156)
Badger, Angela	5:26:18 (29,967)
Badham, Rachel	3:27:52 (3,834)
Baenziger, Petra	4:47:08 (22,525)
Baerlocher-Leitch, Jenny	3:56:49 (9,573)
Baeyens, Lise	4:00:46 (10,733)
Baeza, Paloma	4:12:18 (13,468)
Baggott, Pat A.	7:27:50 (35,203)
Bagley, Laura A.	5:45:04 (31,932)
Bagnall, Jessica J.	4:19:10 (15,203)
Bagster, Kathy	4:21:45 (15,892)
Baguena, Marie	4:04:49 (11,612)
Bahadori, Sara	3:51:48 (8,227)
Bailey, Corinne	5:46:56 (32,083)
Bailey, Davina M.	5:30:01 (30,398)
Bailey, Donna M.	5:31:48 (30,617)
Bailey, Eleanor B.	4:49:54 (23,217)
Bailey, Eliana M.	4:46:42 (22,400)
Bailey, Gill R.	5:18:13 (28,820)
Bailey, Heather	5:14:52 (28,290)
Bailey, Julia	6:05:40 (33,374)
Bailey, Laura E.	4:19:29 (15,277)
Bailey, Maureen	4:34:26 (19,244)
Bailey, Nicola	4:47:28 (22,592)
Bailey, Nicola C.	4:47:33 (22,612)
Bailey, Rachel L.	4:54:27 (24,326)
Bailey, Sarah	3:52:39 (8,443)
Bailey, Sarah L.	3:17:39 (2,496)
Bailey, Susan M.	5:30:13 (30,430)
Bailey, Tamsin	4:34:08 (19,179)
Bailey, Tina L.	3:25:17 (3,430)
Baillie, Louise E.	4:19:41 (15,333)
Baillie, Samantha E.	4:03:50 (11,403)
Bain, Lisa	4:18:28 (15,021)
Bainbridge, Jill	3:35:38 (5,082)
Baines, Lydia J.	6:14:52 (33,785)
Bains, Devinder K.	4:33:35 (19,046)
Bains, Rosemary M.	4:08:36 (12,524)
Bajaj, Punam Z.	4:51:42 (23,676)
Baker, Alexis A.	4:55:34 (24,584)
Baker, Amanda M.	3:50:55 (8,042)
Baker, Andrea	4:00:44 (10,726)
Baker, Annabelle	4:44:01 (21,725)
Baker, Annette F.	4:55:21 (24,539)
Baker, Christina A.	6:22:13 (34,117)
Baker, Clare A.	5:13:41 (28,095)
Baker, Deborah C.	4:42:44 (21,394)
Baker, Denise S.	4:22:20 (16,031)
Baker, Emma J.	4:26:15 (17,051)
Baker, Hannah E.	4:23:17 (16,250)
Baker, Hayley L.	5:54:55 (32,683)
Baker, Joanna E.	6:03:32 (33,260)
Baker, Joanne M.	4:46:22 (22,302)
Baker, Joss	7:24:14 (35,171)
Baker, Juliet	4:26:01 (16,991)
Baker, Kate E.	6:12:13 (33,651)
Baker, Lucy M.	5:11:04 (27,655)
Baker, Rachel J.	4:21:13 (15,744)
Baker, Sally G.	4:02:17 (11,084)
Baker, Sarah E.	4:23:34 (16,331)
Baker, Sarah J.	5:05:22 (26,617)
Baker, Sheila A.	5:43:06 (31,781)
Baker, Tara L.	6:34:38 (34,514)
Baker, Theresa M.	6:05:24 (33,358)
Bakewell, Sharon L.	5:32:28 (30,683)
Bakunina, Yana	3:59:22 (10,359)
Balch, Wendy	5:31:58 (30,635)
Baldry, Tracey D.	5:28:47 (30,249)
Baldwin, Jayne L.	3:19:45 (2,717)
Bales, Rowena J.	3:08:09 (1,538)
Baliol-Key, Eleanor	5:38:17 (31,307)
Balkham, Jade L.	4:57:19 (24,989)
Ball, Ann Sandra	4:15:22 (14,246)
Ball, Carly A.	5:23:37 (29,603)
Ball, Carole	4:36:52 (19,885)
Ball, Charlotte	4:06:54 (12,079)
Ball, Gill	5:52:27 (32,512)
Ball, Juliet S.	4:11:33 (13,266)
Ball, Kate G.	4:21:05 (15,710)
Ball, Michelle A.	4:49:44 (23,187)
Ball, Rosie	4:47:40 (22,644)
Ball, Samantha	6:34:45 (34,518)
Ball, Shirley Gail	4:40:04 (20,746)
Ball, Victoria G.	5:44:01 (31,852)
Ballard, Jane S.	4:45:00 (21,962)
Ballard, Sue L.	5:15:14 (28,366)
Balsillie, Kirsty L.	5:52:58 (32,541)
Bamber, Emma J.	5:43:17 (31,802)
Bamber, Keeley A.	5:08:41 (27,209)
Bamber, Laura	4:44:03 (21,736)
Bamford, Alicia J.	4:00:51 (10,755)
Bamford, Anna M.	5:17:21 (28,690)
Bampton, Pauline J.	4:11:56 (13,368)
Bancroft, Karen M.	6:49:26 (34,803)
Bancroft-Kent, Helen Louise	5:05:38 (26,664)
Banfield, Katie J.	4:31:12 (18,405)
Banfield, Zoe L.	8:17:52 (35,331)
Bangle-Jones, Fiona L.	5:26:35 (30,005)
Banks, Angela L.	3:27:29 (3,771)
Banks, Claire J.	3:53:00 (8,506)
Banks, Faye M.	3:10:43 (1,756)
Banks, Gillian S.	4:18:40 (15,075)
Banks, Louise E.	5:20:46 (29,187)
Banks, Wendy	5:39:20 (31,428)
Banner, Paula J.	4:14:45 (14,096)
Banning, Ruth H.	6:29:30 (34,396)
Banning-Boddy, Nondus	4:45:42 (22,133)
Bannister, Laura	3:27:08 (3,702)
Bannister, Linda	5:46:33 (32,050)
Bannister, Pamela J.	6:06:49 (33,424)
Bannister, Sharon P.	4:51:59 (23,748)
Banwell, Kirsty A.	4:49:27 (23,092)
Baran, Catherine T.	5:36:03 (31,081)
Barber, Cecily A.	3:40:11 (5,899)
Barber, Charlotte	5:21:01 (29,223)
Barber, Jeanette E.	4:16:01 (14,401)
Barber, Jennifer L.	3:51:51 (8,240)
Barber, Kenwynne E.	5:49:44 (32,308)
Barber, Rachel D.	4:07:41 (12,281)
Barber Lane, Nicole	6:29:37 (34,400)
Barbour, Laura C.	4:18:22 (14,980)
Barbuti, Sandra A.	4:51:03 (23,500)
Barclay, Jessica A.	3:57:33 (9,593)
Barden, Sandra L.	4:50:04 (23,257)
Bardin, Alicia	6:23:12 (34,160)
Bardrick, Karen M.	4:54:50 (24,415)
Bardswell, Sonya C.	3:55:48 (9,263)

Bardwell, Sharon 3:58:26 (10,079)
Barge, Lisa 4:47:04 (22,501)
Barham, Claire 7:01:35 (34,968)
Bark, Caroline S 4:37:42 (20,090)
Barker, Celia H 5:21:51 (29,354)
Barker, Emma E 5:12:41 (27,923)
Barker, Faye R 4:40:44 (20,892)
Barker, Gail Josephine 4:51:14 (23,547)
Barker, Jackie S 4:20:27 (15,545)
Barker, Jessica 3:57:11 (9,670)
Barker, Joan C 5:37:16 (31,201)
Barker, Katie J 5:37:16 (31,201)
Barker, Liz 5:48:33 (32,221)
Barker, Ned M 5:57:52 (32,901)
Barker, Pamela J 5:24:16 (29,695)
Barker, Paula M 4:11:05 (13,133)
Barker, Rosamund A 3:04:44 (1,285)
Barker, Rosamund J 3:25:57 (3,523)
Barker, Sarah J 5:46:05 (32,025)
Barker, Susan J 5:01:39 (25,943)
Barlow, Amanda M 4:16:59 (14,642)
Barlow, Janice M 4:30:22 (18,197)
Barlow, Katrina M 5:15:37 (28,441)
Barlow-Graham, Mish 4:22:32 (16,084)
Barltrop, Philippa 6:23:49 (34,182)
Barnard, Alice 5:54:03 (32,623)
Barnes, Bethany 5:35:02 (30,975)
Barnes, Beverley A 4:11:01 (13,112)
Barnes, Carol E 5:45:10 (31,941)
Barnes, Carole S 4:13:10 (13,700)
Barnes, Ellie 3:19:06 (2,628)
Barnes, Judy 7:19:27 (35,145)
Barnes, Katherine V 5:16:01 (28,503)
Barnes, Laura J 4:53:31 (24,074)
Barnes, Marina R 4:25:48 (16,937)
Barnes, Rosalind 4:46:11 (22,244)
Barnes, Victoria Michelle 4:14:53 (14,136)
Barnes, Yvonne W 4:48:13 (22,791)
Barnes, Zoe L 4:35:53 (19,648)
Barnett, Corinne 4:17:44 (14,830)
Barnett, Gemma L 3:18:57 (2,614)
Barnett, Helen R 5:34:23 (30,894)
Barnett, Lisa S 5:51:52 (32,477)
Barnett, Pamela M 5:34:24 (30,899)
Barnett, Tracy D 5:22:08 (29,376)
Barnett-Roberts, Helen S 5:33:58 (30,858)
Barnett-Roberts, Jane E 4:53:35 (24,093)
Barney, Lucie 2:57:31 (806)
Barr, Charlotte E 3:51:31 (8,172)
Barr, Evelyn M 4:19:26 (15,265)
Barr, Helen M 3:40:00 (5,859)
Barratt, Vicky C 3:27:02 (3,689)
Barret, Pippa 5:07:12 (26,944)
Barrett, Alex F 7:39:46 (35,268)
Barrett, Andrea 3:39:52 (5,821)
Barrett, Annette 5:04:30 (26,456)
Barrett, Caroline 5:03:09 (26,227)
Barrett, Dharam 7:26:19 (35,192)
Barrett, Esther R 4:00:50 (10,752)
Barrett, Lorraine C 6:37:49 (34,588)
Barrett, Sam J 5:33:46 (30,839)
Barrett, Samantha J 3:32:37 (4,563)
Barrett, Sarah S 6:26:12 (34,289)
Barrett, Vanessa Anne 4:11:32 (13,263)
Barrett-Seward, Kellie A 4:41:28 (21,077)
Barrick, Zoe A 5:33:54 (30,853)
Barron, Claire 4:28:57 (17,818)
Barron, Emma M 5:30:07 (30,417)
Barrow, Jennifer C 4:50:47 (23,445)
Barrow, Kathryn R 5:24:25 (29,723)
Barrow, Lisa J 5:05:43 (26,685)
Barrow-Green, June E 3:35:35 (5,069)
Barry, Alison 3:56:51 (9,583)
Barry, Charlotte 4:19:28 (15,269)
Barry, Deborah A 4:23:36 (16,334)
Barry, Elizabeth R 3:16:57 (2,423)
Barry, Lorraine K 5:24:55 (29,782)
Barter, Emma E 4:50:24 (23,343)
Barter, Laura M 3:57:57 (9,917)
Bartishel, Kate R 4:20:08 (15,468)
Bartlett, Carolyn L 5:15:30 (28,416)
Bartlett, Johanna S 4:07:53 (12,336)
Bartlett, Susan P 5:10:42 (27,584)
Bartlett, Zoe Alexandra 5:23:00 (29,517)
Bartley, Heather 4:52:13 (23,801)
Bartley, Lisa 5:44:10 (31,867)
Bartley, Maureen A 4:57:15 (24,975)
Barton, Alfreda C 7:08:10 (35,041)
Barton, Brieanne 5:24:48 (29,767)
Barton, Elizabeth Mary R 6:14:18 (33,756)
Barton, Fionnuala R 4:09:44 (12,787)
Barton, Julie A 4:06:32 (11,997)
Barton, Liz 6:37:03 (34,568)
Barton, Nadia 4:44:53 (21,924)
Barwell, Lorraine 4:53:29 (24,069)
Barwick, Kathryn A 6:50:02 (34,814)
Basden, Claire 5:43:06 (31,781)
Baskcomb, Sarah 4:32:37 (18,794)
Bassett, Sam J 4:42:16 (21,269)
Bassett, Samantha J 5:20:15 (29,121)
Bassiri, Sedi 5:27:45 (30,116)
Bassitt, Catherina A 5:10:45 (27,592)
Batchelor, Emma R 5:14:02 (28,170)
Batchelor, Lynette 4:35:15 (19,477)
Batchelor, Mary 3:45:31 (6,899)
Bates, Claire L 3:35:03 (4,968)
Bates, Elaine 4:44:02 (21,729)
Bates, Gillian M 4:27:36 (17,412)
Bates, Gina 5:28:55 (30,264)
Bates, Katherine J 3:39:45 (5,799)
Bates, Nicky J 5:23:50 (29,629)
Bates, Pauline 4:44:33 (21,844)
Bateson, Natalie J 4:24:04 (16,459)
Bath, Ann C 3:49:21 (7,696)
Batheja, Maya 3:45:09 (6,827)
Bathmaker, Gillian H 3:17:46 (2,511)
Batley, Louie 5:38:04 (31,286)
Batson, Cat V 3:55:33 (9,171)
Battell, Rebecca 4:38:05 (20,195)
Batten, Carina 5:02:46 (26,170)
Batten, Jacqueline M 3:50:51 (8,027)
Battersby, Alexandra C 5:05:57 (26,720)
Battersby, Lucy K 4:50:15 (23,301)
Battistuzzi, Laura 4:48:42 (22,902)
Batts, Sara 5:32:29 (30,686)
Batup, Sophie M 5:41:02 (31,587)
Baty, Catherine A 5:11:10 (27,667)
Baucher, Danielle 4:56:29 (24,795)
Baugh, Betsy 4:49:17 (23,046)
Baughman, Tracey 3:58:30 (10,097)
Baumber, Paula 6:57:28 (34,925)
Baxter, Anna C 4:30:56 (18,331)
Baxter, Annabel C 4:37:43 (20,099)
Baxter, Catherine M 4:52:18 (23,827)
Baxter, Emma L 4:57:44 (25,073)
Baxter, Heather 4:21:43 (15,884)
Baxter, Helen M 6:30:09 (34,416)
Baxter, Joanne 5:33:12 (30,774)
Baxter, Laura 5:43:04 (31,778)
Baxter, Madeleine Carmel 4:42:02 (21,206)
Baxter, Marie 5:55:16 (32,709)
Baxter, Ruth 4:40:12 (20,775)
Baxter, Sarah L 3:26:13 (3,560)
Baxter, Zoe 5:07:08 (26,929)
Baxter-Warman, Fleur N 6:32:10 (34,455)
Baybut, Joanne M 5:48:57 (32,246)
Bayford, Michelle 6:47:53 (34,767)
Bayley, Georgina C 3:54:32 (8,900)
Baylis, Isobel 4:06:13 (11,931)
Bayliss, Lesley A 5:19:27 (29,030)
Bazeley, Judith M 4:47:35 (22,624)
Bazeley, Sarah 4:38:23 (20,272)
Bazely, Sarah J 5:24:12 (29,683)
Bazzardi, Bartolomea 4:00:26 (10,646)
Beale, Donna 5:47:04 (32,100)
Beale, Sharon A 4:36:36 (19,821)
Beals, Kristen 4:32:18 (18,706)
Beames, Joanne C 5:02:10 (26,056)
Beamont, Maria 4:54:13 (24,264)
Bear, Angie 4:20:22 (15,527)
Beard, Gill M 7:05:34 (35,010)
Beardall, Katie 6:00:01 (33,053)
Beardsmore, Kerry J 5:44:34 (31,893)
Beardsmore, Suzanne L 5:17:12 (28,673)
Bearman, Ruth C 6:53:05 (34,862)
Beasant, Lynne 4:25:38 (16,885)
Beasley, Thirzah R 5:30:41 (30,489)
Beaton, Eve 5:13:46 (28,115)
Beatrice, Watin 5:51:04 (32,416)
Beattie, Rachel 6:30:59 (34,435)
Beattie, Victoria S 5:38:23 (31,317)
Beausire, Anna 3:59:05 (10,277)
Beavis, Gemma L 5:02:52 (26,189)
Beazeley, Deborah J 5:02:40 (26,147)
Bebbington, Lisa 5:07:08 (26,929)
Beccaara, Kaleigh 6:22:37 (34,134)
Becerra, Katie 4:59:46 (25,549)
Bechelli, Kaye 4:59:08 (25,418)
Beck, Wendy A 4:35:20 (19,501)
Becker, Joanna N 4:46:10 (22,237)
Becker, Maria 4:53:40 (24,123)
Becker, Robyn A 5:35:11 (30,988)
Beckett, Julie L 5:19:51 (29,079)
Beckett, Kirsten 5:10:11 (27,493)
Beckford, Rosie C 4:38:03 (20,179)
Beckley, Cynthia 4:54:02 (24,229)
Beckoff, Emma 4:06:40 (12,037)
Beckwith, Clare 4:59:05 (25,407)
Becvar, Nicola 5:07:39 (27,035)
Beddoes, Allison 5:06:55 (26,887)
Bedi, Sapna 5:27:40 (30,106)
Bediako, Melissa 7:05:00 (35,004)
Bedier, Olivia G 4:20:20 (15,519)
Bedry, Kim P 5:06:28 (26,800)
Bee, Zoe C 4:57:54 (25,111)
Beeby, Sally J 4:52:21 (23,832)
Beecham, Fay A 3:56:39 (9,518)
Beecham, Helen C 4:25:31 (16,842)
Beel, Megan E 4:56:16 (24,742)
Beerling, Julie 5:15:03 (28,328)
Beer-Robson, Kerensa K 4:58:00 (25,140)
Beesley, Katherine 3:42:55 (6,402)
Beeson, Semirah 3:42:36 (6,330)
Beever, Margaret M 3:14:18 (2,154)
Beggs, Abbi J 5:39:08 (31,415)
Begley, Tracey M 5:43:00 (31,770)
Begum, Nhaid 4:55:26 (24,559)
Behan, Jane O 4:21:30 (15,812)
Behnam, Soraya 6:34:11 (34,505)
Beidas, Elspeth N 5:35:09 (30,984)
Belam, Wendy 4:16:48 (14,605)
Belaon, Sarah 3:42:32 (6,310)
Belcher, Angela H 4:56:09 (24,716)
Belcher, Louise E 5:11:35 (27,746)
Beldova, Barbora 6:47:40 (34,761)
Bell, Abigail Dorothy 4:51:19 (23,571)
Bell, Caroline 4:56:11 (24,723)
Bell, Deborah 4:13:03 (13,667)
Bell, Denise 5:40:41 (31,563)
Bell, Fiona 5:50:04 (32,342)
Bell, Jacqueline 4:59:47 (25,552)
Bell, Jill 6:23:32 (34,173)
Bell, June 4:23:29 (16,308)
Bell, Katherine A 5:07:57 (27,078)
Bell, Linda J 3:55:26 (9,139)
Bell, Lynn 4:49:51 (23,209)
Bell, Lynsey 4:57:54 (25,111)
Bell, Marsha J 4:57:26 (25,016)
Bell, Michelle 5:14:23 (28,219)
Bell, Nicola K 4:51:55 (23,737)
Bell, Rachael S 4:31:13 (18,409)
Bell, Samantha 4:11:50 (13,343)
Bell, Sharon 4:58:05 (25,158)
Bellamy, Deborah 4:45:46 (22,147)
Bellamy, Jill 4:06:32 (11,997)
Bellamy, Joanne C 4:24:34 (16,585)
Bellamy, Melanie L 4:47:55 (22,712)
Bellamy, Susan J 3:40:48 (6,000)
Bellis, Lindsey 5:02:59 (26,207)
Bellis, Sue A 5:14:25 (28,229)
Bellsham-Revell, Catherine J 4:27:09 (17,297)
Belson, Mary 8:48:58 (35,353)
Belton, Sharon A 5:10:08 (27,485)
Belyavin, Julia R 3:10:51 (1,765)
Benee, Shelley L 5:17:02 (28,645)
Benfield, Becky 6:15:26 (33,813)
Benham, Sarah L 5:39:50 (31,480)
Benjamin-Taylor, Alvina 5:07:48 (27,059)
Bennellick, Charlotte A 5:38:27 (31,326)

Bennett, Amy R 5:07:36 (27,024)
Bennett, Andrea M 3:59:15 (10,324)
Bennett, Caroline T 5:56:25 (32,786)
Bennett, Carolyn T 4:43:24 (21,575)
Bennett, Elettra T 5:08:25 (27,167)
Bennett, Helen A 5:30:39 (30,480)
Bennett, Jane Y 5:25:53 (29,914)
Bennett, Jo L 5:11:55 (27,792)
Bennett, Kim M 8:15:38 (35,330)
Bennett, Lisa J 3:22:10 (3,031)
Bennett, Lisa Jayne 4:28:32 (17,706)
Bennett, Magda K 3:34:56 (4,951)
Bennett, Michelle J 3:55:02 (9,032)
Bennett, Naomi A 4:08:46 (12,562)
Bennett, Nichola 4:49:34 (23,139)
Bennett, Roberta J 7:47:52 (35,285)
Bennett, Sarah 4:13:43 (13,854)
Bennett, Sarah 4:34:35 (19,285)
Bennett, Sarah B 4:35:41 (19,592)
Bennett, Sarah L 5:50:34 (32,386)
Bennett, Susan Margaret 4:08:46 (12,562)
Bennett-Jones, Hayley L 4:43:28 (21,593)
Bennetts, Jessica J 5:05:13 (26,595)
Benney, Margaret A 6:07:08 (33,444)
Benning, Jenna H 4:52:36 (23,880)
Benning, Lorna Jane 5:28:30 (30,210)
Benning, Sarah J 7:14:30 (35,101)
Benson, Elizabeth J 4:17:18 (14,717)
Benson, Gaynor A 3:53:38 (8,658)
Bensted, Amy J 5:36:04 (31,083)
Bentley, Angela N 4:28:58 (17,823)
Bentley, Elizabeth A 4:38:42 (20,350)
Bentley, Karen 5:03:12 (26,235)
Bentley, Louise 5:29:30 (30,335)
Bentley, Zoe 4:25:59 (16,983)
Benton, Nathalie J 5:25:08 (29,816)
Benton, Sally 3:36:58 (5,314)
Benzimra, Ruth E 4:27:29 (17,387)
Bephune, Deirdre 4:17:44 (14,830)
Beresford-Wood, Melanie 4:58:39 (25,310)
Berger, Eva 4:01:31 (10,919)
Bergin Goncalves, Samantha 4:17:28 (14,761)
Bergkvist, Britt 5:08:35 (27,190)
Bergman, Eva 4:46:14 (22,255)
Bergman, Rachael 5:30:00 (30,396)
Bergonzi, Emily-Louise 5:23:48 (29,625)
Berkeley, Ailsa 4:00:26 (10,646)
Berkeley, Anita N 6:23:03 (34,152)
Bernard, Elizabeth J 4:49:12 (23,017)
Bernard, Lisa A 7:10:22 (35,054)
Bernas, Anne 4:04:39 (11,572)
Berner, Juliet C 3:41:04 (6,039)
Bernhard, Marion 3:32:51 (4,592)
Berry, Carol A 5:42:03 (31,678)
Berry, Charlotte C 5:35:56 (31,066)
Berry, Charmain 6:22:31 (34,126)
Berry, Cheryle J 6:21:13 (34,084)
Berry, Jakki A 4:21:45 (15,892)
Berry, Karen 5:18:13 (28,820)
Berry, Louise C 4:13:07 (13,687)
Berry, Stephanie P 5:36:36 (31,133)
Berry, Sue M 3:43:49 (6,592)
Berry, Vicky 4:43:59 (21,715)
Besser, Sarah Jane 5:42:15 (31,700)
Besson, Lesley F 4:35:09 (19,453)
Best, Alexandra 5:46:54 (32,080)
Best, Nicola 4:20:50 (15,644)
Best-Shaw, Charlotte L 4:42:57 (21,459)
Bestwick, Rachel E 4:30:19 (18,185)
Bethell, Susanne S 4:13:55 (13,887)
Betmead, Caroline J 3:03:05 (1,176)
Betteridge, Helen 5:22:45 (29,474)
Betteridge, Jennifer L 5:04:24 (26,442)
Bettey, Deborah A 5:42:25 (31,711)
Bettinson, Louise N 4:55:26 (24,559)
Bettle, Abi R 6:02:12 (33,183)
Betts, Carol A 4:00:14 (10,610)
Betts, Caroline C 6:44:04 (34,696)
Betts, Fiona H 3:33:41 (4,700)
Bevan, Dannielle 3:41:59 (6,200)
Bevan, Marion C 4:26:33 (17,130)
Bevan, Tracy D 6:05:39 (33,371)
Bevan-Jones, Katie B 4:25:41 (16,904)
Beveridge, Lisa 6:27:17 (34,337)
Beveridge, Louise A 3:11:48 (1,860)
Beveridge, Sarah L 5:26:03 (29,946)
Beverley-Jones, Tina S 5:26:06 (29,951)
Bewlex, Jennifer 5:47:01 (32,095)
Bewley, Rikki 8:10:20 (35,327)
Bexson, Emma J 3:35:06 (4,978)
Beyer, Kristin L 4:01:05 (10,812)
Bezzant, Charlotte 4:47:43 (22,657)
Bi, Yesret 4:59:33 (25,508)
Biant, Rupa M 4:42:10 (21,239)
Bickerton, Ruth 4:38:38 (20,336)
Bicknell, Elizabeth 3:22:30 (3,068)
Biddle, Solvej C 5:29:15 (30,305)
Bidgood, Susan 3:51:05 (8,073)
Bidston, Joanna H 3:46:35 (7,104)
Bielawski, Ellen J 7:14:54 (35,103)
Biggas, Marie 4:06:07 (11,908)
Billig, Alexandra 4:47:05 (22,511)
Billingham, Amanda L 4:36:16 (19,735)
Billingham, Anna 4:34:42 (19,317)
Billingham, Carole J 4:29:05 (17,856)
Billingham, Lauren 6:08:37 (33,499)
Billington, Aimée 3:53:46 (8,697)
Billington, Felicity C 4:40:32 (20,843)
Billington, Tracey 6:32:03 (34,453)
Bills, Alison 5:13:14 (28,028)
Billsberry-Grass, Rachel J 5:20:22 (29,135)
Billson, Diana 6:43:01 (34,680)
Billson, Sarah G 4:27:43 (17,451)
Bingham, Ruth J 4:38:40 (20,342)
Binks, Susan E 3:52:36 (8,426)
Binks, Yvonne A 5:41:24 (31,620)
Binns, Angela 5:00:36 (25,727)
Binns, Janet V 3:36:55 (5,301)
Birch, Clare E 4:34:47 (19,348)
Birch, Olivia R 4:29:45 (18,025)
Bircher, Kerry 3:36:23 (5,212)
Birch-Machin, Juliet M 4:11:16 (13,179)
Bird, Angela 5:03:26 (26,270)
Bird, Clare M 4:01:41 (10,965)
Bird, Karen 4:13:08 (13,691)
Bird, Katy 6:08:38 (33,500)
Bird, Marion 5:16:45 (28,610)
Bird, Sara 4:03:39 (11,360)
Bird, Valerie J 6:17:34 (33,912)
Birdwood, Alice S 5:08:28 (27,175)
Birley, Susanne J 5:06:39 (26,835)
Birnie, Helen S 4:12:19 (13,473)
Birru, Sara J 5:17:03 (28,647)
Birt, Louise H 3:58:38 (10,137)
Bischof, Monique 4:06:19 (11,953)
Bish, Lynda M 5:13:53 (28,139)
Bishop, Laura J 5:14:24 (28,224)
Bishop, Lisa B 4:35:12 (19,465)
Bishop, Sophie A 3:23:43 (3,220)
Bisset-Smith, Jo C 4:03:01 (11,234)
Bissett, Tina M 4:50:42 (23,424)
Bisson, Sharon A 5:34:44 (30,945)
Bithell, Samantha T 5:01:21 (25,885)
Bitmead, Valerie S 4:25:03 (16,726)
Bizouarn, Keri-Anne 5:57:19 (32,856)
Bjelland, Ingunn Hoeiby 5:09:11 (27,306)
Bjírk, Jenny 4:33:46 (19,090)
Blace, Joan 4:43:02 (21,476)
Black, Charlotte 3:35:13 (4,996)
Black, Gillian 4:40:49 (20,917)
Black, Julia M 3:14:42 (2,197)
Black, Kathryn 4:26:16 (17,060)
Black, Linda M 5:15:45 (28,466)
Black, Veronica 4:45:39 (22,121)
Blackburn, Deborah E 5:04:53 (26,521)
Blackburn, Patricia A 4:41:23 (21,051)
Blackburn, Tracey 7:19:11 (35,142)
Blackburne, Annie 5:53:42 (32,597)
Blackburne, Helen C 5:45:51 (32,005)
Blackford, Hilary 4:56:52 (24,902)
Blackford, Lindsey J 5:13:50 (28,123)
Blackford, Robyne A 3:57:21 (9,729)
Blackhurst, Melanie W 3:36:02 (5,164)
Blackmore, Dianne Helen 3:58:01 (9,941)
Blackmore, Louise A 5:07:27 (26,996)
Blackwell, Amy J 5:13:05 (28,001)
Blackwell, Lesley A 4:55:47 (24,632)
Blackwell, Natasha V 6:26:59 (34,320)
Blackwell, Samantha J 5:43:58 (31,847)
Blackwood, Cheryl 3:35:47 (5,112)
Blackwood, Deborah 4:36:49 (19,870)
Blagg, Tiffany 4:12:10 (13,433)
Blain, Soraya 4:13:19 (13,752)
Blair, Janet 5:12:57 (27,974)
Blais, Celine 5:02:47 (26,179)
Blake, Jane I 4:19:16 (15,226)
Blake, Jayne P 4:18:13 (14,947)
Blake, Rebecca 6:53:08 (34,863)
Blake, Sarah 5:04:18 (26,427)
Blake, Sarah 5:56:34 (32,796)
Blake, Tracy Lorraine 4:41:04 (20,976)
Blake-James, Molly R 5:49:44 (32,308)
Blakeman, Lucy 4:38:15 (20,241)
Blakemore, Caoire 5:19:43 (29,063)
Blakey, Maria A 5:22:26 (29,428)
Blamire, Rebecca 4:47:34 (22,617)
Bland, Debbie L 3:59:44 (10,472)
Bland, Gillian 5:39:04 (31,406)
Blandford, Wendy W 4:09:17 (12,679)
Blane, Jennifer A 4:50:27 (23,358)
Blanks, Joanne 5:44:39 (31,901)
Blewitt, Cheryl L 4:27:15 (17,325)
Blick, Philippa J 7:30:27 (35,221)
Bliss, Sarah A 5:21:04 (29,233)
Blisson, Christine 3:42:45 (6,367)
Bloom, Chloe 4:10:22 (12,947)
Bloomfield, Jenny S 5:29:22 (30,316)
Bloor, Vanessa N 5:19:15 (29,002)
Blott, Camilla S 3:47:24 (7,265)
Blount, Sukeallia 6:18:08 (33,935)
Blowers, Sandra 4:55:20 (24,535)
Blows, Jo 6:26:07 (34,285)
Bloxham, Charmaine C 6:08:44 (33,505)
Bloxidge, Emily J 4:32:49 (18,850)
Bluck, Donna Caroline 5:20:00 (29,093)
Bluett, Kerry-Lee 4:15:33 (14,294)
Blunden, Katrina 4:30:52 (18,321)
Blunt, Michelle I 4:45:56 (22,198)
Bluston, Katy 5:14:45 (28,272)
Blyde, Natalie 4:22:01 (15,944)
Blyth, Helen E 4:11:14 (13,168)
Boardman, Leanne 5:10:56 (27,629)
Boardman, Madeline J 3:03:05 (1,176)
Boast, Nicola L 4:29:43 (18,019)
Boby, Giulia 3:43:56 (6,621)
Bodie, Alison R 5:46:44 (32,067)
Bodie, Hilary J 5:46:44 (32,067)
Bogaerts, Nathalie Fabienne 4:17:12 (14,693)
Boggis, Emma L 3:59:46 (10,481)
Bogle, Johanna 3:31:26 (4,391)
Bohrer, Juliane 4:11:46 (13,328)
Bohssein, Marianne 5:16:25 (28,551)
Bolanos Romero, Cristina 4:18:06 (14,920)
Bolden, Michelle L 4:36:21 (19,750)
Bolden, Victoria 7:32:55 (35,237)
Boleor, Rose Aimée 4:08:16 (12,439)
Boller, Jenny E 4:54:03 (24,233)
Bolorinos, Alyette 5:05:30 (26,639)
Bolsher, Kirsten 4:51:08 (23,516)
Bolt, Lucy 3:59:49 (10,500)
Bolton, Alison F 5:33:59 (30,859)
Boltwood, Kathy 4:34:13 (19,199)
Bonar, Kirsty J 5:03:26 (26,270)
Bond, Frances E 3:24:34 (3,351)
Bond, Helen 4:09:30 (12,719)
Bond, Jane J 5:13:23 (28,049)
Bond, Mary J 4:43:10 (21,508)
Bond, Nicola 3:49:40 (7,761)
Bone, Carrie A 5:07:22 (26,976)
Bone, Jackie W 4:50:12 (23,282)
Bone, Jennifer 5:58:45 (32,976)
Boneham, Sarah J 4:08:04 (12,376)
Bonell, Elizabeth 3:48:08 (7,425)
Boniface, Mishelle A 4:51:09 (23,521)
Bonnel, Laura J 4:41:31 (21,093)
Bonnick, Clare J 3:34:55 (4,943)
Bonnor, Linda D 5:27:27 (30,088)
Booker, Helen B 5:31:49 (30,619)
Bool, Lorraine M 4:58:28 (25,258)

Boomer, Sandra	4:58:50 (25,346)
Boon, Jennifer A	4:40:09 (20,763)
Boora, Julie J	3:52:10 (8,317)
Boorman, Nicola J	4:25:32 (16,847)
Boot, Claire	4:58:27 (25,253)
Booth, Alexandra	6:24:18 (34,207)
Booth, Alison	4:35:31 (19,552)
Booth, Christine M	5:33:03 (30,760)
Booth, Frances M	5:24:55 (29,782)
Booth, Karen	4:58:15 (25,202)
Booth, Rachel L	5:01:29 (25,910)
Booth, Sandra	5:16:06 (28,518)
Booth, Sarah L	5:04:51 (26,511)
Booth, Trinity A	3:37:04 (5,333)
Boothby, Julieann	4:59:51 (25,565)
Boreham-Bevan, Clare E	5:19:19 (29,009)
Borg, Lesley Jane	4:00:24 (10,635)
Borgmann, Malene	4:47:22 (22,571)
Borland, Julie A	4:06:36 (12,016)
Borland, Philippa D	4:02:27 (11,118)
Borowiak, Wendy	4:46:44 (22,416)
Borst-Tyroll, Eva	7:31:05 (35,225)
Bosch, Lynn	5:22:55 (29,503)
Bosher, Fiona E	3:49:42 (7,774)
Bosio, Teresa J	5:16:29 (28,559)
Boskovic, Jelena C	4:27:18 (17,343)
Bosomworth, Bethany A	5:16:05 (28,514)
Bosomworth, Kate	4:48:07 (22,766)
Bostick, Sharon	6:18:40 (33,952)
Bostock, Rebecca	5:23:42 (29,614)
Bostwick-Beevers, Sarah E	3:15:58 (2,332)
Bosustow, Suzy J	3:01:59 (1,117)
Botha, Esme	4:19:03 (15,173)
Botha, Petronella B	5:13:05 (28,001)
Botsis, Roxane	5:03:39 (26,315)
Botterill, Zoe A	4:17:11 (14,689)
Bottomley, Elizabeth	4:24:01 (16,444)
Bottomley, Sue M	4:43:58 (21,711)
Bottomley, Victoria L	4:38:07 (20,204)
Botwright, Claire Elizabeth	5:05:47 (26,694)
Boucher, Jackie	4:49:58 (23,234)
Boud, Helen	4:48:31 (22,856)
Boulter, Gill M	5:28:06 (30,161)
Boulton, Amanda J	6:27:15 (34,333)
Bourne, Jacqueline	4:29:37 (17,988)
Bourne, Katy	5:58:52 (32,986)
Bourne, Sarah	5:24:02 (29,655)
Bouttell, Janet	4:34:46 (19,337)
Bovill, Gillian M	4:27:34 (17,404)
Bowden, Tracy A	7:37:50 (35,260)
Bowdery, Paula	5:39:27 (31,441)
Bowditch, Kathryn	4:05:00 (11,652)
Bowen, Anjie R	5:27:05 (30,058)
Bowen, Laura	5:30:02 (30,400)
Bowen, Stacey	4:53:21 (24,046)
Bower, Angela L	5:17:24 (28,697)
Bower, Charlotte	6:51:56 (34,844)
Bowerman, Rosie Anne	4:02:58 (11,221)
Bowers, Amanda V	4:55:52 (24,659)
Bowers, Judith	4:31:26 (18,484)
Bowers, Sandra	3:21:30 (2,946)
Bowes, Leia C	4:03:48 (11,393)
Bowie, Christine A	3:40:40 (5,965)
Bowlas, Rachel L	4:27:24 (17,368)
Bowles, Jane	4:43:47 (21,663)
Bowles, Sarah L	4:07:57 (12,348)
Bowles, Theresa M	5:16:34 (28,573)
Bowman, Claire	3:43:06 (6,441)
Bowman, Elizabeth A	5:55:36 (32,732)
Bowman, Katie	6:07:55 (33,477)
Bown, Rachel H	3:38:00 (5,489)
Bowness, Lisa J	7:45:08 (35,280)
Bowring, Joanna	5:17:30 (28,717)
Bowyer, Laura E	4:31:09 (18,396)
Boyd, Julie A	3:44:50 (6,774)
Boyde, Nikola	3:31:44 (4,426)
Boyer, Helen N	5:09:38 (27,392)
Boyer, Nadine	4:26:05 (17,006)
Boyer-Besant, Catherine J	5:42:32 (31,730)
Boylan, Alexandra	5:21:49 (29,346)
Boyle, Brenda M	4:46:34 (22,367)
Boyle, Catherine A	5:30:26 (30,450)
Boyle, Kate	5:05:55 (26,715)

Boyle, Vicki J	3:06:36 (1,412)
Boyne, Coral J	4:33:03 (18,911)
Boynton, Katherine S	4:37:23 (20,004)
Braat, Lisa	5:24:54 (29,780)
Bracey, Jade	6:21:08 (34,081)
Brackenbury, Victoria J	4:45:49 (22,161)
Brackley, Sharon L	4:34:36 (19,288)
Bradbrook, Jo L	4:06:29 (11,988)
Bradburn, Karen M	4:51:51 (23,709)
Bradbury, Amanda	4:32:11 (18,683)
Bradbury, Cheryl E	4:09:50 (12,816)
Bradbury, Helen M	4:44:59 (21,957)
Bradbury, Sue	4:45:56 (22,198)
Brades, Kathleen A	5:25:29 (29,856)
Bradfield, Katy H	5:18:48 (28,934)
Bradford, Nicola M	3:31:39 (4,413)
Bradgate, Maggi A	4:41:29 (21,083)
Bradley, Alison	5:46:50 (32,075)
Bradley, Angela	6:54:09 (34,884)
Bradley, Claire	4:44:20 (21,801)
Bradley, Dawn L	4:43:33 (21,613)
Bradley, Gail C	4:23:53 (16,409)
Bradley, Julie	7:10:14 (35,052)
Bradley, Patsy A	5:21:38 (29,322)
Bradley, Una P	4:46:21 (22,294)
Bradley, Victoria	5:46:51 (32,076)
Bradshaw, Claire E	5:10:51 (27,610)
Bradshaw, Helen M	5:24:39 (29,749)
Bradshaw, Karen E	5:08:32 (27,180)
Bradshaw, Lizzie	3:31:39 (4,413)
Brady, Bethany C	5:20:30 (29,153)
Brady, Caroline	5:03:37 (26,308)
Brady, Emma L	3:58:28 (10,090)
Brady, Kathy L	3:34:18 (4,830)
Brady, Lesley Anne T	6:04:40 (33,323)
Brady, Pamela J	4:38:03 (20,179)
Braeger, Louise	4:33:26 (19,013)
Bragg, Lisa	6:33:38 (34,489)
Braham, Jane M	4:26:03 (16,999)
Braithwaite, Suzanna M	4:12:52 (13,617)
Bramley, Nicola J	3:43:03 (6,429)
Bramley, Sarah R	6:11:48 (33,631)
Bramwell, Ruth E	5:30:07 (30,417)
Brand, Cassandra L	6:03:08 (33,237)
Brandenburg, Helga	4:49:17 (23,046)
Brandie, Pamela M	4:16:24 (14,499)
Brandon, Alice M	4:50:41 (23,418)
Brandon, Orla	4:25:10 (16,757)
Branfoot, Sarah J	5:02:44 (26,162)
Brannan, Cathryn	5:41:02 (31,587)
Brannigan, Charlotte E	4:20:45 (15,619)
Brannigan, Christina M	6:03:45 (33,275)
Brant, Kate E	6:09:20 (33,529)
Brass, Louise E	3:24:19 (3,314)
Braude, Hayley	5:43:02 (31,774)
Braun, Claudia	4:44:33 (21,844)
Braun, Katherine W	4:47:11 (22,542)
Bray, Alice Louise	4:13:44 (13,857)
Bray, Caroline O	5:57:25 (32,867)
Bray, Lorraine	4:01:29 (10,909)
Bray, Rosie	4:50:21 (23,327)
Brazener, Sally C	6:01:23 (33,136)
Brazier, Jacqueline V	3:51:00 (8,056)
Brazier, Michelle L	4:43:55 (21,694)
Brazil, Michelle M	4:42:27 (21,313)
Breaker, Jennifer H	5:07:22 (26,976)
Breaker, Linda F	5:48:16 (32,192)
Breathet, Kristy-Jo	6:55:59 (34,906)
Bredenschey, Ilona	4:52:00 (23,750)
Breed, Anna	5:15:31 (28,423)
Breen, Julia J	4:20:37 (15,580)
Breeze, Jill	4:21:39 (15,863)
Breeze, Lynsey V	5:40:34 (31,551)
Breitmeyer, Sophie	4:42:13 (21,255)
Brennan, Anne-Marie B	9:03:05 (35,356)
Brennan, Julia F	3:43:40 (6,559)
Brennan, Sara H	4:46:00 (22,213)
Brennan, Terri M	6:25:05 (34,233)
Brentnall, Lucy E	4:45:42 (22,133)
Brenton, Sarah J	4:13:24 (13,779)
Bresch, Louise E	6:16:17 (33,856)
Breslan, Kirstie	5:09:44 (27,412)
Breslin, Kathryn L	4:05:48 (11,843)

Bresnahan, Cassie	4:03:01 (11,234)
Bresnahan, Una	5:46:00 (32,012)
Bresnik, Sylvia	5:26:19 (29,969)
Bretherick, Katie	3:54:30 (8,890)
Brett, Katy	4:27:39 (17,430)
Brett, Sandra Y	3:12:13 (1,904)
Brett, Vanessa A	5:14:45 (28,272)
Brett, Zoe	5:42:56 (31,763)
Brew, Sarah J	3:23:28 (3,183)
Brewer, Cherry L	5:29:42 (30,359)
Brewer, Linda M	5:14:21 (28,214)
Brewin, Hazel A	5:06:41 (26,839)
Brewin, Jennifer J	4:25:18 (16,786)
Brewster, Vanessa M	4:19:28 (15,269)
Brian, Joanne L	4:21:04 (15,706)
Bridge, Helen M	6:02:40 (33,207)
Bridgen, Melanie J	4:24:53 (16,679)
Bridges, Denise	3:43:15 (6,479)
Bridges, Teresa J	5:19:53 (29,082)
Bridges, Valerie P	4:57:22 (25,005)
Brien, Laura	5:11:28 (27,721)
Brient, Mairead	5:13:57 (28,151)
Brierley, Anne J	4:55:22 (24,542)
Briffett, Jane	5:54:56 (32,686)
Brigati, Carolina	4:16:06 (14,426)
Briggs, Clare	6:22:41 (34,140)
Briggs, Julie L	2:59:19 (943)
Briggs, Kathryn J	5:07:43 (27,045)
Briggs, Katy V	4:23:06 (16,207)
Briggs, Kristyn	6:13:43 (33,735)
Briggs, Michelle E	5:16:15 (28,534)
Briggs, Sarah	4:38:56 (20,416)

Briggs, Susannah B 6:37:15 (34,573)

After being rejected for five years, or should I say not being successful in the public ballot, the morning of the 2009 London Marathon dawned – this was my opportunity to fulfil my dream. I am 67, have three grown up children and seven grandchildren all wondering, 'Should she be doing this?' I had taken part in the Beachy Head Marathon twice, Great North and Great South, plus shorter races so why not? It was a lovely morning and the excitement was unbelievable and very emotional. As I made my way around the course the cheering and calling out of my name will always be remembered. I finished having had a wonderful time, not even feeling tired. 6 hours 37 minutes never to be forgotten.

Bright, Kellie	4:19:35 (15,308)
Brightman, Patricia A	6:09:13 (33,522)
Brighton, Susan L	3:50:20 (7,911)
Brightwell, Maria G	3:53:36 (8,650)
Brightwell, Natalie Anne	3:55:42 (9,221)
Brigstocke, Hannah	3:44:13 (6,667)
Brigstocke, Laura M	5:11:34 (27,743)
Brimson, Emily R	5:33:59 (30,859)
Brind, Bridget D	4:35:08 (19,446)
Brindle, Dawn	4:43:07 (21,497)
Bringlow, Véronique M	3:14:52 (2,214)
Brink, Liz	4:32:16 (18,701)
Brinkley, Joanna P	6:52:09 (34,848)
Brint, Emma M	5:01:46 (25,965)
Brisbane, Julia	4:57:30 (25,029)
Briscoe, Jackie M	6:51:07 (34,831)
Brissenden, Abbi J	5:06:33 (26,812)
Bristow Tyler, Linda	5:12:34 (27,903)
Brittain, Lindsey	5:06:44 (26,853)
Britteon, Carol	5:37:58 (31,270)
Britton, Kate	5:14:46 (28,277)
Broadbent, Susan	4:12:37 (13,555)
Broadley, Patricia M	5:14:45 (28,272)
Brock, Helen	3:58:56 (10,233)
Brock, Helen C	4:45:23 (22,054)
Brock, Natasha E	4:05:14 (11,717)
Brockbank, Nicola J	3:41:10 (6,061)
Brockett, Samone E	3:13:59 (2,117)
Brockie, Rachel C	3:34:48 (4,930)
Brocklehurst, Jaine J	3:38:04 (5,505)
Brocklesby, Claire	4:10:04 (12,869)
Brocklesby, Lorna	4:30:06 (18,126)
Brockmann, Andrea	4:30:19 (18,185)
Broda, Krysia B	4:28:17 (17,644)
Broder, Marie T	6:26:59 (34,320)
Broers, Jacqueline D	4:11:38 (13,297)
Broesche, Kelly	5:18:35 (28,891)
Bromley, Sally A	5:00:41 (25,745)
Brook, Christine E	4:00:02 (10,552)
Brook, Frances A	5:36:42 (31,143)
Brook, Katharine	4:21:30 (15,812)
Brook, Robyn C	4:47:43 (22,657)
Brooke, Diana A	5:42:21 (31,708)
Brooker, Esther M	4:50:13 (23,285)
Brookes, Caroline M	4:54:03 (24,233)
Brookes, Maria	5:35:10 (30,985)
Brookes, Natasha A	5:18:58 (28,969)
Brookes-Duncan, Katy	4:57:17 (24,980)
Brooklin Smith, Fleur	4:42:49 (21,412)
Brookman, Helen N	4:59:51 (25,565)
Brooks, Claire H	3:49:29 (7,727)
Brooks, Nicola-Jane	4:23:51 (16,399)
Brooks, Sarah J	4:57:54 (25,111)
Brooks, Susan	5:59:26 (33,014)
Brooks, Tracy C	4:09:55 (12,837)
Brook-Smith, Joanne	5:09:30 (27,363)
Brooks-Sheppard, Tess C	6:40:22 (34,634)
Broom, Dawn A	3:10:19 (1,722)
Broom, Felicity A	6:19:42 (34,023)
Broom, Karen L	4:56:33 (24,814)
Broom, Linda J	4:04:37 (11,567)
Broomfield, Wendy E	5:51:12 (32,430)
Brosnan, Tina L	4:16:27 (14,509)
Brotherhood, Clare E	5:47:54 (32,161)
Broughton, Julie	4:12:54 (13,628)
Brown, Alison F	3:56:34 (9,478)
Brown, Ana L	4:45:07 (22,003)
Brown, Anna Lucy	5:15:02 (28,324)
Brown, April S	4:54:11 (24,255)
Brown, Bernie M	5:47:55 (32,162)
Brown, Carolyn	3:59:38 (10,428)
Brown, Catherine M	6:33:34 (34,486)
Brown, Cecilia M	3:20:09 (2,774)
Brown, Debbie	5:22:47 (29,479)
Brown, Debra J	4:51:23 (23,585)
Brown, Donna A	3:34:22 (4,846)
Brown, Elizabeth W	4:53:40 (24,123)
Brown, Ellie D	4:01:52 (10,996)
Brown, Emma	6:24:43 (34,222)
Brown, Emma L	3:28:09 (3,876)
Brown, Emma T	5:43:25 (31,813)
Brown, Frances C	4:50:50 (23,452)
Brown, Gillian	4:28:19 (17,651)

Brown, Gillian	4:36:58 (19,909)
Brown, Hannah C	5:29:12 (30,299)
Brown, Hannah R	4:56:04 (24,698)
Brown, Helen E	4:05:35 (11,794)
Brown, Helen L	3:48:26 (7,496)
Brown, Helen P	5:09:06 (27,289)
Brown, Janice B	4:20:07 (15,464)
Brown, Janis A	4:31:18 (18,438)
Brown, Jennifer D	4:50:07 (23,266)
Brown, Jo	6:41:20 (34,652)
Brown, Johanna E	4:59:09 (25,424)
Brown, Josephine	4:03:48 (11,393)
Brown, Judy	3:48:25 (7,490)
Brown, Julie	4:38:40 (20,342)
Brown, Karen L	4:41:20 (21,045)
Brown, Kerry A	5:06:18 (26,776)
Brown, Laura A	6:00:40 (33,092)
Brown, Lizzie	4:01:20 (10,868)
Brown, Lizzie	5:03:47 (26,338)
Brown, Lorraine	3:25:21 (3,434)
Brown, Lynda J	4:09:04 (12,635)
Brown, Mairead C	3:40:57 (6,021)
Brown, Mandy	5:02:14 (26,068)
Brown, Melanie A	4:56:41 (24,854)
Brown, Natalie C	5:33:16 (30,784)
Brown, Rachael A	6:18:38 (33,951)
Brown, Rachel C	5:12:46 (27,939)
Brown, Rebecca O	5:05:11 (26,589)
Brown, Rosie E	4:09:36 (12,753)
Brown, Samantha	5:40:18 (31,522)
Brown, Samantha J	3:56:10 (9,357)
Brown, Samantha J	3:58:39 (10,144)
Brown, Sheena	4:11:38 (13,297)
Brown, Sophie	5:55:37 (32,734)
Brown, Sue A	8:03:38 (35,319)
Brown, Susan	3:53:09 (8,548)
Brown, Valerie	4:24:19 (16,532)
Brown, Vicky	5:18:35 (28,891)
Brown, Victoria E	3:36:25 (5,219)
Browne, Kelly A	5:56:04 (32,761)
Browne, Lauren	5:55:50 (32,751)
Browne, Rachael C	5:19:40 (29,057)
Browne, Sue E	4:27:08 (17,290)
Browning, Attracta	4:04:23 (11,520)
Browning, Barbara	3:37:08 (5,348)
Bruce, Christina L	6:01:54 (33,162)
Bruce, Elizabeth G	4:34:28 (19,254)
Bruce, Gillian S	4:39:49 (20,670)
Bruce, Lindsay M	4:23:48 (16,389)
Bruce, Mieghan M	3:40:09 (5,888)
Bruce, Roselyn R	4:58:15 (25,202)
Bruce, Sarah J	4:33:04 (18,915)
Bruce-Green, Sarah J	4:01:51 (10,991)
Brudenell, Kate	4:49:08 (23,002)
Bruen, Rachel L	5:12:59 (27,981)
Bruinsma-Stibbe, Gerda	4:30:04 (18,116)
Brummell, Zoe	3:53:44 (8,688)
Brunaccini, Teresa	4:43:19 (21,554)
Brundle, Katherine M	4:29:56 (18,077)
Brunn, Beate H	5:24:55 (29,782)
Bruton, Jane	3:49:46 (7,792)
Bryan, Jeanette	5:26:23 (29,976)
Bryan, Victoria	5:20:07 (29,108)
Bryant, Jennifer A	3:50:12 (7,881)
Bryant, Nia J	3:59:41 (10,451)
Bryant, Rebecca M	4:02:34 (11,148)
Bryant, Zoe	6:06:51 (33,425)
Bryden, Susan M	4:56:27 (24,785)
Brydon, Kathryn J	4:15:29 (14,279)
Buchan, Jane C	4:45:05 (21,993)
Buchan, Laura A	3:39:37 (5,780)
Buchan, Nicola L	6:10:17 (33,575)
Buchanan, Dawn A	7:36:00 (35,250)
Buchanan, Francesca D	4:46:31 (22,347)
Buchanan, Jennifer	5:21:13 (29,260)
Buchanan, Katie J	4:37:37 (20,070)
Buchanan, Lindsay J	4:42:28 (21,324)
Buck, Nicola J	7:02:38 (34,979)
Buck, Rachel A	4:23:08 (16,218)
Buckby, Gillian M	5:20:35 (29,158)
Buckee, Angela	5:30:39 (30,480)
Buckingham, Catherine	4:43:45 (21,656)
Buckingham, Kathleen C	3:55:02 (9,032)

Buckingham, Laura C	5:08:36 (27,193)
Buckle, Michelle L	6:35:18 (34,531)
Buckley, Beatrice D	7:07:49 (35,038)
Buckley, Emily J	6:53:57 (34,878)
Buckley, Judy A	5:00:19 (25,658)
Buckley, Julia J	5:05:36 (26,660)
Buckley, Julie	5:49:14 (32,270)
Buckley, Natasha K	3:32:33 (4,553)
Buckley, Nicola Jayne	5:13:09 (28,015)
Buckley, Susan	5:04:51 (26,511)
Bucknall, Sarah	3:53:09 (8,548)
Buckwell, Lorna Anne	4:14:15 (13,974)
Budge, Rose E	5:41:17 (31,604)
Budge, Theresa	3:40:26 (5,931)
Buesser, Odette	3:58:22 (10,059)
Buff, Teresa M	4:25:12 (16,766)
Buffini, Lauren	3:52:47 (8,461)
Bufton, Clare A	5:59:39 (33,026)
Builder, Rachel	4:34:47 (19,348)
Bujakowski, Susan T	4:30:18 (18,176)
Buker, Sue	4:22:24 (16,050)
Bulbeck, Lynn J	4:27:35 (17,409)
Buldum, Sarah Rose	4:49:39 (23,165)
Bulgin, Amanda J	5:33:51 (30,851)
Bull, Catherine	6:20:29 (34,054)
Bull, Helen C	5:15:36 (28,438)
Bull, Jenny	4:34:35 (19,285)
Bull, Sarah K	5:54:02 (32,621)
Buller, Fiona	6:30:44 (34,429)
Bulley, Tina	6:04:07 (33,293)
Bullock, Emma L	3:51:13 (8,103)
Bullock, Emma N	5:57:52 (32,901)
Bullock, Karri S	5:14:23 (28,219)
Bullock, Katie Anne	5:17:25 (28,700)
Bullock, Sara L	5:10:43 (27,588)
Bumfrey, Deborah	5:28:18 (30,189)
Bumpus-Bosch, Sarah J	3:57:29 (9,762)
Bunce, Gemma	3:32:20 (4,520)
Bunce, Janet F	5:38:36 (31,343)
Bunce, Michelle C	5:01:41 (25,949)
Bunch, Susana	6:13:01 (33,695)
Bundy, Deborah J	4:54:46 (24,397)
Bundy, Jennifer Louise	5:09:02 (27,280)
Bunston, Clare A	3:35:34 (5,061)
Bunten, Susan E	3:56:06 (9,341)
Bunting, Jennie C	3:32:12 (4,504)
Burch, Cally M	4:56:05 (24,700)
Burch, Heather	4:00:39 (10,707)
Burchett, Judith S	4:26:36 (17,148)
Burd, Serane L	3:13:35 (2,071)
Burden, Hannah L	5:49:09 (32,264)
Burge, Jill P	4:50:24 (23,343)
Burge, Tracy	5:03:12 (26,235)
Burgess, Catherine T	3:54:45 (8,956)
Burgess, Christina	6:31:34 (34,445)
Burgess, Heather B	5:53:12 (32,566)
Burgess, Joanne	5:51:44 (32,463)
Burgess, Tracy A	4:42:46 (21,402)
Burgess, Tracy A	6:05:25 (33,361)
Burgess, Vernie	6:27:09 (34,330)
Burgham, Moira	4:51:48 (23,701)
Burgoyne, Michele	5:50:26 (32,371)
Burke, Christina	6:42:25 (34,671)
Burke, Elaine	5:25:49 (29,906)
Burke, Paula C	4:41:30 (21,087)
Burke, Sarah I	4:49:35 (23,141)
Burkhill, Helen	5:35:44 (31,044)
Burley, Caroline L	3:54:47 (8,964)
Burmeister, Anne	5:00:35 (25,723)
Burn, Tracey Deborah Marie	5:13:41 (28,095)
Burnett, Angela	5:08:42 (27,212)
Burnett, Barbara	4:10:19 (12,938)
Burnett, Caroline M	5:45:31 (31,975)
Burnett, Jackie	4:35:14 (19,476)
Burnett, Karen	4:38:09 (20,215)
Burnett, Nicola M	5:00:29 (25,697)
Burniston, Ann M	5:48:27 (32,212)
Burns, Amanda J	4:45:46 (22,147)
Burns, Donna L	5:21:01 (29,223)
Burns, Elisabeth A	4:23:41 (16,362)
Burns, Jennifer	4:49:24 (23,080)
Burns, Pru L	4:43:15 (21,529)
Burns, Stephanie	4:33:50 (19,108)

Burnside, Kirstie A 6:12:58 (33,691)
Burr, Laura 4:51:39 (23,661)
Burr, Susan J 5:45:08 (31,936)
Burrough, Alexandra E 6:41:55 (34,664)
Burrows, Angela M 6:44:08 (34,697)
Burrows, Catherine 4:35:09 (19,453)
Burrows, Jacqui Carol 4:18:01 (14,891)
Burrows, Janet F 4:26:53 (17,236)
Burrows, Johanna 5:44:17 (31,876)
Bursack, Jennifer 4:58:36 (25,294)
Burston, Nicola 5:05:40 (26,671)
Burt, Charlie 5:38:14 (31,300)
Burton, Amy L 5:39:29 (31,445)
Burton, Elizabeth 6:22:49 (34,147)
Burton, Jane L 3:47:24 (7,265)
Burton, Joanne M 6:11:52 (33,635)
Burton, Kim A 5:22:01 (29,366)
Burton, Linda J 4:46:30 (22,345)
Burton, Michelle M 5:10:51 (27,610)
Burton, Teresa 4:12:36 (13,547)
Burwood, Kerry Louise 5:05:43 (26,685)
Bury, Corinne 4:12:40 (13,566)
Busby, Louise 5:05:25 (26,628)
Bush, Lucy A 5:22:33 (29,446)
Bushnell, Julie-Ann 4:23:25 (16,281)
Bushnell, Margaret C 4:55:32 (24,579)
Bussell, Jennifer C 5:55:36 (32,732)
Bussell, Rickki J 6:40:44 (34,638)
Bussey-Jones, Elisabeth B 4:41:25 (21,058)
Bussy, Gemma 5:56:32 (32,793)
Butcher, Bryony R 3:42:13 (6,254)
Butcher, Caroline 5:37:04 (31,180)
Butcher, Leane 4:27:09 (17,297)
Butcher, Nicola D 5:37:04 (31,180)
Butland, Orlanda C 4:48:35 (22,873)
Butler, Audrey L 6:49:49 (34,809)
Butler, Claire L 4:37:28 (20,027)
Butler, Gail Ceridwen 4:23:04 (16,200)
Butler, Jane C 4:20:18 (15,512)
Butler, Kristina F 4:51:26 (23,605)
Butler, Naomi Helen 3:57:06 (9,648)
Butler, Noel 8:46:46 (35,352)
Butler, Rowena T 3:13:59 (2,117)
Butler, Sarah 3:45:16 (6,848)
Butler, Vanessa L 3:47:58 (7,391)
Butt, Carmel D 5:18:52 (28,958)
Butterfield, Shannon E 5:44:39 (31,901)
Butterworth, Sarah F 6:24:34 (34,217)
Buttle, Samantha 5:52:14 (32,496)
Buxton, Carol 6:27:51 (34,352)
Buxton, Gemma G 4:50:02 (23,244)
Bvaughan, Sarah L 4:30:30 (18,228)
Bygrave, Angela 5:23:13 (29,553)
Byrne, Anne Marie 3:42:33 (6,317)
Byrne, Katie B 4:22:01 (15,944)
Byrnes, Doreen A 4:58:13 (25,193)
Byrom, Lynda G 6:29:24 (34,394)
Byron, Katy A 6:12:49 (33,682)
Byron, Laura 4:51:23 (23,585)
Cacace, Helene 5:20:51 (29,201)
Caddy, Anita E 5:49:12 (32,267)
Cadei, Marina A 6:42:30 (34,672)
Cadenas Fernandez, Natalia 4:31:04 (18,376)
Cadenas Saez, Maria Eugenia 4:21:00 (15,692)
Cadman, Stacey 4:04:10 (11,481)
Cadogan, Nicola 5:54:52 (32,677)
Cafferky, Emma 5:23:52 (29,631)
Caines, Jodie Lousie 4:41:37 (21,122)
Cairney, Shirley 4:23:51 (16,399)
Cairns, Hayley Dawn 6:00:45 (33,095)
Cakebread, Louise V 4:16:56 (14,632)
Calcutt, Michelle 4:43:45 (21,656)
Calderbank, Tara A 3:49:21 (7,696)
Caldicott, Lucy W 4:56:15 (24,740)
Calesky, Vicky A 4:41:48 (21,166)
Caley, Elizabeth M 6:15:47 (33,834)
Caley, Kathy 4:43:47 (21,663)
Callaghan, Nicole L 5:15:02 (28,324)
Callaghan, Sarah 5:19:45 (29,066)
Callanan, Collette 4:19:44 (15,348)
Callaway, Amanda 4:59:25 (25,475)
Callingham, Debbie 5:17:10 (28,669)
Calliste, Gillian L 5:12:41 (27,923)
Callus, Gillian A 5:39:16 (31,424)
Calver, Sarah J 3:39:14 (5,720)
Calvert, Christine 4:54:00 (24,219)
Camassa, Alessandra 3:44:59 (6,800)
Camenzuli, Ellena J 5:26:14 (29,961)
Cameron, Aileen M 7:09:58 (35,049)
Cameron, Alison 5:31:28 (30,577)
Cameron, Fiona 3:41:28 (6,114)
Cameron, Jacqueline 4:19:24 (15,255)
Cameron, Lorraine A 6:49:13 (34,798)
Camilleri, Elizabeth 4:58:31 (25,274)
Cammell, Rhona 7:07:25 (35,032)
Cammidge, Kathryn 4:34:56 (19,393)
Camp, Debbie 3:41:18 (6,088)
Campbell, Alex E 5:13:09 (28,015)
Campbell, Alice Wright 3:52:05 (8,295)
Campbell, Amanda 5:23:13 (29,553)
Campbell, Andrea 4:39:21 (20,532)
Campbell, Angela J 4:53:16 (24,038)
Campbell, Brenda 4:35:40 (19,587)
Campbell, Claire L 3:40:01 (5,863)
Campbell, Deborah 4:32:14 (18,689)
Campbell, Emily Kate 4:32:32 (18,762)
Campbell, Emma 5:30:40 (30,484)
Campbell, Gail F 4:05:31 (11,773)
Campbell, Ilidia M 3:53:58 (8,745)
Campbell, Jennifer E 5:52:07 (32,487)
Campbell, Joyce 4:52:01 (23,753)
Campbell, Kathryn E 4:05:07 (11,685)
Campbell, Kathy 6:51:56 (34,844)
Campbell, Laura 5:01:10 (25,853)
Campbell, Lucy A 4:37:13 (19,964)
Campbell, Marina 3:29:15 (4,053)
Campbell, Mary 3:30:09 (4,197)
Campbell, Mehrnaz 4:49:13 (23,024)
Campbell, Melissa 4:29:51 (18,056)
Campbell, Nicola 4:19:57 (15,408)
Campbell, Olivia 4:44:39 (21,871)
Campbell, Paula R 6:16:59 (33,883)
Campbell, Sarah E 3:19:36 (2,697)
Campbell, Stephanie B 3:55:02 (9,032)
Campbell-Stanway, Camilla L 4:12:56 (13,643)
Campese, Anna 4:15:40 (14,315)
Campion, Anne-Marie 4:31:54 (18,607)
Camps, Cherylene T 5:14:45 (28,272)
Cane, Susan 5:10:29 (27,545)
Caney, Pauline J 4:16:40 (14,575)
Cann, Sally E 3:51:34 (8,178)
Cannell, Lucy A 6:12:21 (33,656)
Cannell, Lucy C 3:42:22 (6,277)
Cannell, Susan H 6:08:00 (33,480)
Canning, Clare A 4:55:22 (24,542)
Cannings, Deena L 5:41:23 (31,619)
Cantley, Louise 5:25:45 (29,898)
Cantrill, Lisa 3:50:01 (7,840)
Cantu, Ivonne 3:41:11 (6,067)
Capdeville, Corinne 3:54:13 (8,815)
Capel, Claire E 4:43:40 (21,642)
Capel, Lara L 5:09:46 (27,420)
Capeling, Nicola L 4:30:00 (18,095)
Capobianco, Lucia 4:47:59 (22,736)
Capper, Hayley P 6:42:59 (34,678)
Capper, Rachel E 4:31:37 (18,531)
Capper, Suzan E 5:29:42 (30,359)
Capstick, Christine A 4:28:58 (17,823)
Capstick, Dorothy M 3:56:29 (9,454)
Capstick, Nina 4:23:28 (16,299)
Carassus, Nathalie 4:05:06 (11,679)
Carberry, Nicola 5:06:13 (26,766)
Cardno-Strachan, Gillian 3:43:07 (6,446)
Cardy, Kyria E 5:24:46 (29,760)
Cardy, Sarah L 4:45:19 (22,037)
Careddu, Giuseppina 4:36:27 (19,787)
Carelsen, Brenda 7:13:50 (35,093)
Carey, Frances H 4:59:26 (25,480)
Carey, Samantha 5:18:26 (28,861)
Cargan, Sonia G 4:37:28 (20,027)
Carless, Anjie J 6:47:06 (34,744)
Carley, Helen R 5:08:11 (27,123)
Carli, Mariafrancesca 4:16:31 (14,525)
Carlile, Jacqui M 5:27:58 (30,142)
Carlson, Katherine 4:48:11 (22,779)
Carman, SJ 3:37:54 (5,473)
Carmen, Delarue 3:33:07 (4,627)
Carmichael, Lauren 3:56:51 (9,583)
Carney, Renée T 4:06:34 (12,010)
Carnwath, Gabriel 3:06:59 (1,432)
Carole, Lauk 4:46:37 (22,375)
Caroline, Butterfield 6:47:28 (34,756)
Carpenter, Hannah 4:26:30 (17,118)
Carpenter, Jennifer 6:15:43 (33,828)
Carpenter, Sue 5:53:52 (32,609)
Carr, Aimée 4:44:16 (21,783)
Carr, Caroline B 5:04:33 (26,472)
Carr, Dannie 5:23:27 (29,591)
Carr, Gillian 3:16:42 (2,406)
Carr, Helen A 4:28:47 (17,769)
Carr, Iris 4:50:32 (23,381)
Carr, Joanne L 6:25:14 (34,239)
Carr, Olivia S 5:06:52 (26,879)
Carr, Roxy 4:39:09 (20,482)
Carr, Susie 4:39:02 (20,444)
Carrick, Gill 5:54:11 (32,630)
Carritt, Charlotte 3:52:42 (8,449)
Carritt, Joanna 3:01:38 (1,091)
Carroll, Amy V 5:14:21 (28,214)
Carroll, Brenna S 4:16:47 (14,602)
Carroll, Claire L 4:31:05 (18,382)
Carroll, Emma J 5:26:02 (29,945)
Carroll, Laura 4:34:27 (19,249)
Carroll, Nicky 4:34:27 (19,249)
Carroll, Pamela 4:53:56 (24,208)
Carruthers, Alex 6:23:30 (34,171)
Carruthers, Kathryn M 3:53:03 (8,519)
Carruthers, Sheila 3:58:20 (10,046)
Carsberg, Jillian D 5:26:44 (30,018)
Carsley, Lauren 5:21:37 (29,318)
Carson, Christine A 5:43:55 (31,842)
Carter, Angela J 6:17:21 (33,895)
Carter, Camilla E 5:12:09 (27,834)
Carter, Denise 5:36:11 (31,093)
Carter, Elizabeth M 4:02:40 (11,163)
Carter, Gemma M 5:23:54 (29,634)
Carter, Gill 3:40:35 (5,953)
Carter, Helen R 4:02:15 (11,077)
Carter, Helen S 4:03:59 (11,445)
Carter, Jacqueline A 4:27:52 (17,509)
Carter, Kim 5:12:24 (27,867)
Carter, Krystina 6:03:50 (33,278)
Carter, Nicola 3:24:33 (3,349)
Carter, Penny C 5:00:19 (25,658)
Carter, Rebecca J 5:45:16 (31,956)
Carter, Samantha 5:41:25 (31,621)
Carter, Sue J 5:02:26 (26,100)
Carter, Susan 4:11:35 (13,279)
Carter, Victoria E 3:37:28 (5,392)
Cartlidge, Delia A 6:42:12 (34,668)
Cartwright, Lucy B 3:03:10 (1,181)
Cartwright-Clamp, Claire E 5:23:55 (29,638)
Carvalho Dias, Maria de Lurdes (Lutzy) 4:59:05 (25,407)
Carver, Alison J 4:53:05 (23,994)
Carver, Jacqueline A 4:49:26 (23,088)
Carver, Karen E 5:15:10 (28,347)
Carver, Sheridan J 4:48:04 (22,756)
Cary, Catherine J 4:53:40 (24,123)
Cary, Helena J 4:51:49 (23,705)
Casali, Patrizia Maria Luisa 5:24:24 (29,720)
Casault, Ashley R 4:28:13 (17,622)
Case, Melissa K 4:32:59 (18,895)
Caseley, Kathryn M 3:57:47 (9,870)
Caseley, Samantha Kimberley 4:46:58 (22,474)
Casey, Lauren 4:41:36 (21,119)
Casey Evans, Diane 4:23:25 (16,281)
Casey Evans, Kathryn 4:23:25 (16,281)
Cash, Diana 4:09:33 (12,737)
Cashen, Rebekah L 4:29:18 (17,927)
Cashmore, Ashling 3:58:29 (10,096)
Cason, Julie 5:23:58 (29,642)
Cass, Bridget M 6:05:47 (33,379)
Cassidy, Louise M 4:45:49 (22,161)
Cassidy, Vivienne Louise 4:45:49 (22,161)
Cassie, Kathleen G 5:54:06 (32,625)
Castelo Branco, Luciana 4:44:22 (21,809)
Castillo, Hilda 4:19:02 (15,167)
Castle, Jennifer 4:36:14 (19,732)

Castle, Rosemary A....4:27:23 (17,362)
Castles, Dawn M....4:37:59 (20,161)
Catchpole, Zoe J....4:11:20 (13,202)
Catherine, Cinneri....4:00:10 (10,587)
Catherine, Guillaume....4:22:37 (16,103)
Catherine, Lemahieu....3:28:54 (3,993)
Catley, Katie....5:40:05 (31,508)
Cattell, Louise....5:29:50 (30,379)
Cattell, Sarah J....3:59:55 (10,523)
Catterall, Victoria....5:38:12 (31,298)
Caulfield, Sarah L....5:28:21 (30,195)
Caulton, Jacqui....7:46:15 (35,281)
Caunter, Janice N....4:15:33 (14,294)
Causon, Jacky....5:45:28 (31,969)
Cavalot, Jennifer M....7:00:35 (34,954)
Cavanagh, Kathleen....5:45:24 (31,962)
Cavanagh, Nicola J....5:27:12 (30,066)
Cave, Elizabeth....4:36:42 (19,838)
Cave, Elizabeth....4:58:43 (25,324)
Cave, Lucy J....4:31:56 (18,618)
Cavedaschi, Rosemarie S....5:00:28 (25,694)
Caven, Alexandra J....3:33:33 (4,683)
Cavendish, Lucinda....4:40:52 (20,929)
Cawley, Danielle B....4:29:03 (17,849)
Caws, Tara L....4:48:40 (22,891)
Cechova, Viktoria....4:49:36 (23,147)
Cecil, Gemma E....5:43:22 (31,811)
Cederberg, Maria....4:05:06 (11,679)
Centeno, Yesenia....2:40:13 (199)
Ceranowska, Aleksandra....5:05:28 (26,632)
Cerveny, Gretchen B....3:58:06 (9,971)
Cessford, Alison M....5:00:45 (25,759)
Chadha, Angela....6:21:03 (34,071)
Chadwell, Karen G....4:39:33 (20,595)
Chadwick, Lindsey J....4:45:01 (21,967)
Chadwick, Lindsey N....4:19:41 (15,333)
Chaffey, Heather C....5:01:42 (25,951)
Chaffey, Lerryn T....3:48:12 (7,446)
Chaggar, Inder....5:31:59 (30,638)
Chahed, Georgina K....5:37:50 (31,257)
Chakraborti, Angeli....5:59:51 (33,038)
Chalice, Leighann....5:33:49 (30,848)
Chalk, Natalie L....5:13:56 (28,148)
Chalkley, Kelly....7:02:34 (34,977)
Chalkley, Naomi....4:42:18 (21,275)
Chalmers, Katie....4:32:36 (18,789)
Chalmers, Lana....3:54:28 (8,880)
Chalmers, Tracy Teresa....4:41:59 (21,198)
Chaloner, Elizabeth V....4:48:29 (22,846)
Chamberlain, Anne....6:41:57 (34,665)
Chamberlain, Bethany....5:17:35 (28,728)
Chamberlain, Claire E....5:12:59 (27,981)
Chambers, Hayley L....4:56:25 (24,777)
Chambers, Jennifer C....4:03:41 (11,363)
Chambers, Joanne L....4:35:15 (19,477)
Chambers, Lisa....4:18:50 (15,113)
Chambers, Liz....4:11:24 (13,226)
Chambers, Nicola....5:13:27 (28,056)
Chambers, Pam D....5:38:50 (31,375)
Chambers, Sally B....6:06:24 (33,406)
Chambers, Sarah L....5:15:14 (28,366)
Champion, Laura H....3:53:59 (8,751)
Champion, Louise....5:21:58 (29,361)
Champney, Christine M....5:41:05 (31,592)
Chan, Ling K....3:47:47 (7,346)
Chan, Michelle....5:13:21 (28,046)
Chan, Shun-Kai....4:47:09 (22,532)
Chance, Katie L....4:16:32 (14,531)
Chandler, Jane....4:50:50 (23,452)
Chandler, Jemma A....6:00:29 (33,072)
Chandler, Lillian M....3:57:22 (9,736)
Chandler, Selina....6:00:29 (33,072)
Channon, Heather A....4:19:30 (15,287)
Chant, Lottie....3:58:05 (9,963)
Chantal, Le Luduec....5:37:24 (31,214)
Chantal, Renaudeau....4:13:56 (13,891)
Chaparro-Rincon, Maria Paula....5:02:00 (26,018)
Chaplin, Nicola J....4:47:36 (22,629)
Chapman, Adele....6:17:50 (33,922)
Chapman, Bee J....4:26:29 (17,111)
Chapman, Caroline J....5:12:56 (27,971)
Chapman, Cheryl E....4:32:33 (18,769)
Chapman, Claire L....4:27:36 (17,412)

Chapman, Cynthia M....4:27:53 (17,513)
Chapman, Janie....3:24:19 (3,314)
Chapman, Lesley....3:36:57 (5,309)
Chapman, Lisa....5:13:07 (28,009)
Chapman, Lucy J....4:57:20 (24,992)
Chapman, Mary....6:04:04 (33,291)
Chapman, Natalie E....5:41:21 (31,615)
Chapman, Sally A....3:48:35 (7,529)
Chappell, Alissa H....5:33:30 (30,803)
Chappell, Jayne....4:19:03 (15,173)
Chappelle, Jane K....4:47:56 (22,721)
Charalambous, Pat....4:14:22 (14,007)
Charkiewicz, Angela G....5:22:28 (29,434)
Charles, Joanne....5:00:31 (25,703)
Charles, Marvelyn....5:27:23 (30,084)
Charles, Sara C....4:03:39 (11,360)
Charlesworth, Susan....4:07:26 (12,221)
Charlton, Catherine M....3:28:38 (3,944)
Charnock, Hannah M....3:47:59 (7,396)
Charters, Gemma G....5:44:39 (31,901)
Chase, Sarah A....4:44:58 (21,948)
Chase Pevsner, Elaine....5:11:21 (27,702)
Chaston, Natalie M....6:10:06 (33,566)
Chater, Ann-Marie....3:57:57 (9,917)
Chater, Frances....5:23:17 (29,569)
Chater, Rosemary....5:08:43 (27,216)
Chaudhri, Sarah E....3:56:22 (9,418)
Chaudhri, Shaista....5:38:37 (31,345)
Cheeseman, Sarah....5:57:31 (32,877)
Chen, Jacqueline....3:59:08 (10,290)
Chenet, Stefania....4:10:36 (13,006)
Cheng, Susan....5:52:34 (32,516)
Cherry, Rosie J....5:00:52 (25,779)
Chessis, Carol R....5:11:38 (27,751)
Chessum, Deborah Susanne....4:26:15 (17,051)

Chesworth, Sharon B....8:08:09 (35,324)

I ran the last ever Flora London Marathon for Macmillan Cancer Support in memory of my beloved cousin Michelle. She was only 38 years old. She suffered so much. It was heartbreaking watching her pass away. My cousin sadly lost her battle with cancer shortly before 3pm Sunday 22nd March 2009. I completed the London Marathon in 8 hours 8 minutes and 9 seconds. It may seem a long time but I was determined to finish. I started off well but just after half way I had to slow down and walk the remaining 13 miles. I had blisters and my feet hurt but the crowd was amazing, they kept cheering me on. I was so emotional I burst into tears when I crossed the finish line. I will never forget you Michelle x

---

Cheung, Paula....5:25:59 (29,933)
Chhabra, Sumita....4:46:56 (22,461)
Chick, Amanda K....4:16:00 (14,395)
Chick, May L....5:15:13 (28,357)
Chicken, Rachel L....3:56:37 (9,500)
Chikako, Kurazumi....4:38:15 (20,241)
Childs, Chris P....4:56:37 (24,832)
Childs, Daisy C....4:33:24 (19,004)
Childs, Stacy A....4:12:40 (13,566)
Chillingworth, Jacqueline K....5:04:25 (26,443)
Chilton, Katie L....4:24:10 (16,493)
Chilvers, Alyson E....5:50:11 (32,355)
Chima, Rajpreet....4:38:11 (20,227)

Chimes, Jane....4:51:35 (23,644)
Ching, Anna....3:53:49 (8,705)
Ching, Susanna J....4:37:42 (20,090)
Chinwala, Yasmine....5:14:03 (28,174)
Chipperfield, Caroline L....5:18:46 (28,925)
Chivers, Ella....4:52:44 (23,912)
Chivers, Lizzie A....5:28:37 (30,225)
Chna, Rupinder K....4:51:53 (23,723)
Chohan, Bhavna....6:05:27 (33,362)
Chohan, Nayla....5:50:01 (32,335)
Chokore, Lizih....3:34:13 (4,815)
Chong Yoke Kwi, Evelyn....5:38:26 (31,320)
Choudhry, Louise A....5:06:16 (26,772)
Chow, Ally....6:13:40 (33,730)
Christie, Jill....3:24:00 (3,259)
Christie, Nathalie....3:02:29 (1,146)
Christie, Sarah E....4:13:31 (13,802)
Christie, Sharon E....4:46:56 (22,461)
Christmas, Leanne J....4:20:31 (15,563)
Christy, Carol A....5:03:52 (26,353)
Chrstie, Erica....3:08:29 (1,564)
Chung, Angela....4:18:08 (14,929)
Chung, Wendy....6:40:46 (34,640)
Chunxiu, Zhou....2:29:02 (58)
Church, Moya A....4:48:02 (22,751)
Churchill, Joanne M....3:56:39 (9,518)
Churchill, Natalie K....4:30:00 (18,095)
Churchill, Simone J....6:41:16 (34,650)
Chuttha, Kiren....6:34:44 (34,517)
Cilliers, Desiré....5:59:09 (32,997)
Cinotto, Ilaria....5:46:13 (32,029)
Clack, Liz E....5:20:00 (29,093)
Clack, Tracey L....3:48:14 (7,454)
Clair, Bridie....6:38:53 (34,605)
Claisse, Annette....4:16:32 (14,531)
Clampett, Linda S....4:12:05 (13,410)
Clampin, Shelley J....7:02:11 (34,973)
Clancy, Rebecca....4:53:42 (24,138)
Clanza, Gretel....6:21:05 (34,075)
Clapham, Penelope E....5:04:15 (26,422)
Clare, Sarbjit....5:43:27 (31,815)
Clarey, Clare M....4:13:34 (13,813)
Claridge, Emma....4:49:28 (23,102)
Clark, Alison C....4:57:32 (25,040)
Clark, Alison M....5:28:06 (30,161)
Clark, Barbara S....4:51:03 (23,500)
Clark, Carol A....6:43:05 (34,681)
Clark, Dawn....3:39:46 (5,803)
Clark, Emma L....5:00:16 (25,646)
Clark, Helen....4:58:56 (25,371)
Clark, Jo....4:16:04 (14,416)
Clark, Joanna E....3:36:46 (5,273)
Clark, Karen D....4:14:02 (13,913)
Clark, Karen L....3:43:34 (6,536)
Clark, Kate E....5:53:47 (32,604)
Clark, Kelly....5:55:10 (32,701)
Clark, Lauren A....3:33:22 (4,661)
Clark, Liz....4:28:42 (17,749)
Clark, Lynn J....5:48:17 (32,195)
Clark, Marie D....3:42:44 (6,363)
Clark, Melanie....4:56:50 (24,890)
Clark, Michelle....6:30:25 (34,425)
Clark, Nicci S....4:39:02 (20,444)
Clark, Rachael....6:11:15 (33,608)
Clark, Sarah L....4:56:38 (24,836)
Clark, Sheryl L....3:40:13 (5,904)
Clark, Sue....6:08:17 (33,488)
Clark, Tamsin L....2:55:32 (699)
Clark, Tessa L....6:36:41 (34,554)
Clark, Wendy M....3:38:50 (5,644)
Clarke, Alison E....5:32:42 (30,722)
Clarke, Christina M....4:54:35 (24,352)
Clarke, Elle M....5:16:00 (28,499)
Clarke, Francesca A....3:30:21 (4,228)
Clarke, Jenny L....5:55:09 (32,700)
Clarke, June Ann....5:02:28 (26,109)
Clarke, Lauren J....3:46:12 (7,017)
Clarke, Lesley C....3:18:52 (2,608)
Clarke, Lorraine....6:40:47 (34,641)
Clarke, Maxine D....3:55:32 (9,162)
Clarke, Michelle M....3:05:20 (1,324)
Clarke, Miranda M....3:57:14 (9,682)
Clarke, Nina....5:25:41 (29,887)

Clarke, Penelope A	4:55:42 (24,614)	
Clarke, Rachel J	5:16:01 (28,503)	
Clarke, Una	8:26:37 (35,338)	
Clarke, Wendy A	5:28:30 (30,210)	
Clarke, Zoe L	4:14:51 (14,128)	
Clarkson, Emilie	3:58:30 (10,097)	
Clarkson, Lydia J	4:49:31 (23,124)	
Claudianos, Pagona	4:10:40 (13,025)	
Claudine, Juchs	4:26:02 (16,994)	
Claxton, Lea M	4:55:35 (24,591)	
Claxton, Rachael	4:37:32 (20,045)	
Claxton, Rosalyn Y	3:47:08 (7,222)	
Claydon, Cheryll A	5:33:25 (30,797)	
Clayton, Bernadette A	3:57:03 (9,634)	
Clayton, Frances L	4:12:03 (13,398)	
Clayton, Lucy	3:35:44 (5,104)	
Clayton, Michelle L	5:58:02 (32,921)	
Clayton, Rachel	4:21:24 (15,785)	
Clayton, Sallyanne	4:15:29 (14,279)	
Clear, Anne F	4:11:33 (13,266)	
Cleary, Rachel	4:05:28 (11,762)	
Cleave, Claire	4:13:57 (13,895)	
Cleaver, Irene	4:30:14 (18,160)	
Cleere, Genevieve	4:16:10 (14,441)	
Cleland-James, Alexandra	5:14:16 (28,202)	
Clements, Angela T	4:28:41 (17,744)	
Clements, Diane J	5:38:28 (31,328)	
Clements, Jo M	4:49:34 (23,139)	
Clements, Michelle C	3:50:35 (7,966)	
Clemmensen, Tina E	3:10:35 (1,742)	
Cleverly, Karen	4:47:49 (22,675)	
Clibbon, Lara	5:31:24 (30,564)	
Cliff, Jill M	3:22:33 (3,074)	
Clifford, Catherine A	3:45:58 (6,982)	
Clifford, Marcia	5:06:49 (26,871)	
Clifton, Tania E	3:49:10 (7,660)	
Clinch, Agnes M	3:58:00 (9,931)	
Clinch, Georgina	3:58:37 (10,132)	
Clinck, Annick	3:50:09 (7,872)	
Cloke, Kerrie	4:51:10 (23,528)	
Close, Claire L	3:53:10 (8,556)	
Close, Kate	4:14:35 (14,053)	
Close, Martha K	6:23:36 (34,176)	
Clough, Lucy M	3:32:24 (4,530)	
Clough, Sally	4:53:32 (24,083)	
Clout, Charlotte L	4:10:46 (13,056)	
Clowes, Lauren	4:30:41 (18,276)	
Cluitt, Sonia	4:39:45 (20,657)	
Clune, Tina	5:03:49 (26,344)	
Clunie, Libby	6:16:39 (33,873)	
Coaker, Louise A	5:05:52 (26,708)	
Coates, Bev	4:20:39 (15,587)	
Coates, Emily A	4:39:21 (20,532)	
Coates, Samantha E	3:51:29 (8,164)	
Coates, Zoe H	3:22:02 (3,017)	
Coats, Maria V	5:30:36 (30,474)	
Cobaine, Faith A	3:52:05 (8,295)	
Cobban, Claire-Joanna	6:11:55 (33,637)	
Cobby, Janet A	4:08:15 (12,430)	
Cobby, Ruth M	5:02:00 (26,018)	
Cochrane, Barbara K	4:30:13 (18,154)	
Cochrane, Isabel C	6:08:00 (33,480)	
Cockburn, Sally J	5:28:50 (30,253)	
Cockle, Hannah V	4:44:55 (21,933)	
Codner, Barbara L	4:32:46 (18,835)	
Codou, Marie	3:35:48 (5,117)	
Coelho, Rosa R	3:45:09 (6,827)	
Coggins, Kate M	5:16:35 (28,577)	
Cohen, Abi L	5:18:35 (28,891)	
Cohen, Tamara J	4:56:22 (24,764)	
Coignard, Nadege	4:22:44 (16,131)	
Coker, Amanda A	4:14:07 (13,937)	
Colahan, Claire	4:18:45 (15,092)	
Colchester, Joanne	5:13:52 (28,134)	
Cole, Felicity J	3:58:59 (10,248)	
Cole, Julie D	7:27:50 (35,203)	
Cole, Michelle	3:25:03 (3,404)	
Cole, Nicola A	4:10:39 (13,019)	
Cole, Patricia N	5:26:24 (29,978)	
Cole, Sacena L	5:56:53 (32,824)	
Cole, Sarah J	4:43:12 (21,517)	
Cole, Vicky	5:20:15 (29,121)	
Colebrook, Hollie L	6:00:49 (33,102)	
Coleman, Amanda M	4:28:51 (17,795)	
Coleman, Elizabeth J	4:03:07 (11,253)	
Coleman, Hayley C	6:14:39 (33,774)	
Coleman, Joanne S	4:05:59 (11,878)	
Coleman, Kathryn J	5:34:59 (30,965)	
Coleman, Kim	4:52:56 (23,960)	
Coleman, Linda	8:03:29 (35,318)	
Coleman, Patricia J	5:34:59 (30,965)	
Coleman, Susie E	3:57:46 (9,863)	
Coleman, Tamara J	4:50:21 (23,327)	
Coleridge, Joanna	5:46:22 (32,039)	
Coles, Anne	4:35:32 (19,555)	
Coll, Rachel L	4:02:35 (11,149)	
Collard, Caroline F	4:14:10 (13,949)	
Collard-Woolmer, Odette L	5:06:55 (26,887)	
Collen, Gillian A	4:26:49 (17,211)	
Colley, Rachael S	4:32:08 (18,671)	
Collier, Barbara A	6:15:46 (33,833)	
Collier, Celeste	4:20:12 (15,484)	
Collier, Gemma L	3:51:11 (8,093)	
Collier, Jane	6:36:15 (34,545)	
Colligan, Sian A	3:55:14 (9,092)	
Collings, Gemma L	3:28:50 (3,981)	
Collingwood, Jane E	5:26:05 (29,948)	
Collins, Amy E	4:59:05 (25,407)	
Collins, Carol	5:48:06 (32,179)	
Collins, Claire M	6:06:25 (33,408)	
Collins, Clare E	4:43:52 (21,681)	
Collins, Ellie R	5:04:26 (26,445)	
Collins, Gemma	7:13:44 (35,090)	
Collins, Georgina	4:53:41 (24,133)	
Collins, Jacqui	5:21:32 (29,307)	
Collins, Kelly J	4:16:43 (14,587)	
Collins, Lisa	4:49:43 (23,182)	
Collins, Louise	3:14:48 (2,208)	
Collins, Louise	4:43:52 (21,681)	
Collins, Lucy	4:53:42 (24,138)	
Collins, Natalie J	5:26:59 (30,050)	
Collins, Rebecca	3:56:58 (9,610)	
Collins, Rosie A	7:06:15 (35,019)	
Collins, Sheelagh M	4:16:34 (14,542)	
Collins, Susan M	5:25:40 (29,885)	
Collins, Tracy A	4:32:54 (18,871)	
Collins, Virginia D	4:13:29 (13,791)	
Collinson, Libby (Helen) E	3:51:01 (8,058)	
Collinson, Rachel A	5:02:23 (26,092)	
Collip, Helen E	5:43:01 (31,773)	
Collis, Rebecca C	4:08:14 (12,425)	
Collisson, Fiona E	3:11:34 (1,836)	
Collyer, Lucy E	4:09:11 (12,658)	
Colman, Lindsey J	3:50:28 (7,938)	
Colquhoun, Laura E	5:57:14 (32,846)	
Colquhoun, Shirley J	3:35:45 (5,107)	
Coltman, Elizabeth	5:29:15 (30,305)	
Colville-Foley, Tatiana M	4:37:13 (19,964)	
Colvin, Hati A	4:37:18 (19,984)	
Colwell, Cathy	4:38:23 (20,272)	
Colwell, Christine N	4:36:03 (19,692)	
Colwell, Katy L	6:13:29 (33,721)	
Colwell, Michaela R	3:24:38 (3,361)	
Colwill, Samantha K	4:54:02 (24,229)	
Combrink, Marisca	5:08:48 (27,230)	
Concannon, Gina	3:57:17 (9,702)	
Coney, Deborah	3:24:43 (3,370)	
Coney, Diane J	3:30:58 (4,325)	
Coney, Sarah J	4:32:54 (18,871)	
Confalone, Antonia M	5:00:25 (25,680)	
Congdon, Gillian M	3:44:45 (6,758)	
Conlon, Ruth D	5:56:40 (32,804)	
Conn, Gemma	5:20:35 (29,158)	
Conneely, Janet	4:04:47 (11,603)	
Connell, Keeley J	4:52:53 (23,945)	
Conner, Karen	6:04:51 (33,330)	
Conniffe-Jones, Sarah L	4:50:25 (23,347)	
Connolly, Bernadette	5:33:22 (30,795)	
Connolly, Fieona	6:20:26 (34,050)	
Connolly, Lynne	4:40:27 (20,822)	
Connor, Donna P	6:38:08 (34,592)	
Connor, Karen Mary	5:26:50 (30,028)	
Connor, Shirley A	4:58:36 (25,294)	
Conrad, Lucy R	6:17:37 (33,913)	
Conroy, Julie	4:08:12 (12,418)	
Convery, Sue C	4:59:54 (25,578)	
Conway, Jackie	5:43:05 (31,780)	
Conway, Jennifer	4:49:49 (23,203)	
Conway, Tracy J	4:20:42 (15,604)	
Conway, Wendy A	4:57:20 (24,992)	
Conybeer, Sarah	4:17:57 (14,872)	
Cooil, Jan M	3:54:15 (8,828)	
Cook, Allison	4:40:37 (20,865)	
Cook, Barbara	3:43:35 (6,541)	
Cook, Emily J	3:56:14 (9,372)	
Cook, Jane	4:17:19 (14,725)	
Cook, Janet L	5:11:09 (27,663)	
Cook, Joanna M	4:27:17 (17,338)	
Cook, Katherine A	5:36:46 (31,149)	
Cook, Kirstie R	5:24:00 (29,648)	
Cook, Lesley A	5:49:40 (32,303)	
Cook, Lorna J	5:06:06 (26,745)	
Cook, Michelle D	5:59:17 (33,005)	
Cook, Paula E	5:02:31 (26,120)	
Cook, Ruth	5:13:50 (28,123)	
Cook, Sian R	4:49:19 (23,058)	
Cook, Susan A	4:44:56 (21,936)	
Cook, Susanna J	5:26:52 (30,033)	
Cook, Terena M	5:47:27 (32,128)	
Cook, Tonia M	4:20:56 (15,671)	
Cook, Vanessa	4:37:11 (19,961)	
Cooke, Hannah C	3:42:00 (6,206)	
Cooke, Jennifer J	5:07:33 (27,013)	
Cooke, Susan	3:55:06 (9,065)	
Cooke-Priest, Charlotte J	4:29:58 (18,088)	
Cooke-Simmons, Julia K	4:46:31 (22,347)	
Cookson, Anna L	4:02:39 (11,161)	
Cooley, Gemma Lesley Sylvia	5:39:55 (31,485)	
Coombe, Pennie	4:48:49 (22,922)	
Coonan, Caren	3:16:23 (2,369)	
Cooney, Lauren N	5:57:49 (32,896)	
Coop, Andrea T	4:55:05 (24,476)	
Cooper, Alison	3:13:19 (2,037)	
Cooper, Amy	5:04:41 (26,490)	
Cooper, Anna L	5:15:25 (28,404)	
Cooper, Anne	4:39:35 (20,606)	
Cooper, Chloe J	6:18:05 (33,933)	
Cooper, Claire	4:28:04 (17,564)	
Cooper, Elena Sophie	4:40:08 (20,760)	
Cooper, Elizabeth	4:41:15 (21,026)	
Cooper, Helen R	4:55:25 (24,556)	
Cooper, Helene L	5:58:51 (32,983)	
Cooper, Jacqueline P	3:42:45 (6,367)	
Cooper, Jennifer	7:21:27 (35,158)	
Cooper, Jennifer Anne	4:10:57 (13,094)	
Cooper, Judith	4:14:21 (14,000)	
Cooper, Katherine	6:34:08 (34,502)	
Cooper, Linda M	5:16:33 (28,570)	
Cooper, Lindsey J	4:07:37 (12,259)	
Cooper, Lisa	5:41:21 (31,615)	
Cooper, Louise J	3:26:11 (3,555)	
Cooper, Louise M	4:46:51 (22,438)	
Cooper, Lucy C	5:53:47 (32,604)	
Cooper, Patience A	4:12:19 (13,473)	
Cooper, Pauline A	5:21:14 (29,262)	
Cooper, Sarah	5:44:34 (31,893)	
Cooper, Sian A	4:04:04 (11,463)	
Cooper, Sonya	4:20:46 (15,627)	
Cooper, Stephanie C	5:58:10 (32,932)	
Cooper, Stephanie J	5:01:45 (25,963)	
Cooper, Susan M	3:37:32 (5,409)	
Cooper, Susan M	3:55:17 (9,107)	
Cooper, Tanja	4:52:08 (23,781)	
Cooper, Theresa M	5:09:27 (27,356)	
Cooper, Tracey J	4:39:55 (20,696)	
Cooper, Valerie J	5:07:02 (26,912)	
Cooper, Wendy A	4:50:08 (23,267)	
Cooper, Zoe J	4:23:50 (16,395)	
Coopey, Victoria L	4:01:27 (10,890)	
Coote, Tracey L	5:01:53 (25,991)	
Cootes, Hilary F	4:28:29 (17,693)	
Cope, Amy L	3:20:32 (2,829)	
Cope, Lucy	3:30:02 (4,181)	
Cope, Lucy A	5:39:00 (31,395)	
Cope, Wendy A	4:07:02 (12,114)	
Copeman, Clare	4:13:19 (13,752)	
Copley, Helen M	5:01:48 (25,970)	
Copp, Janet H	4:38:59 (20,429)	
Coppin, Kylie L	7:16:31 (35,115)	

Coppola, Alison J	4:29:31 (17,969)	Cowie, Natalie S	4:51:52 (23,717)	Cross, Sophia G	4:45:38 (22,113)
Copsey, Shirley	4:18:48 (15,105)	Cowley, Carol	3:46:53 (7,174)	Cross, Suzie P	4:38:51 (20,388)
Copson, Angela	3:14:51 (2,213)	Cowley, Laura J	2:46:45 (357)	Crossman, Elisabeth M	3:42:16 (6,262)
Corben, Louisa	5:45:13 (31,947)	Cowley Antelo, Maria A	5:12:50 (27,954)	Croucher, Sinead	5:17:44 (28,755)
Corben, Sarah	4:59:43 (25,538)	Cowmeadow, Nicola	4:32:37 (18,794)	Crouchman, Nina	6:09:10 (33,520)
Corbet Burcher, Georgina	4:03:47 (11,386)	Cowsill, Elaine M	4:42:28 (21,324)	Crouse, Anna	6:37:20 (34,576)
Corbett, Georgina S	3:46:31 (7,091)	Cox, Chantal	5:04:54 (26,526)	Crowdy, Victoria L	5:30:32 (30,464)
Corcoran, Kate	4:25:59 (16,983)	Cox, Gemma	5:33:07 (30,765)	Crowe, Emily	4:42:51 (21,425)
Cordingley, Jacqueline A	3:33:26 (4,670)	Cox, Hailey A	4:42:53 (21,440)	Crowe, Samantha J	4:31:35 (18,524)
Corfe, Ashlee S	6:14:03 (33,747)	Cox, Heather	6:01:05 (33,117)	Crowhurst, Flossie E	4:02:16 (11,082)
Cork, Caroline L	4:40:06 (20,755)	Cox, Jacqueline L	6:35:09 (34,526)	Crowhurst, Paula	5:44:02 (31,855)
Corke, Hilary R	6:08:53 (33,508)	Cox, Jo B	5:23:01 (29,520)	Crowley, Amy	5:05:28 (26,632)
Corless, Hilary N	5:59:34 (33,020)	Cox, Mary	5:50:32 (32,382)	Crowley, Louise	4:45:35 (22,101)
Corley, Sarah A	4:27:07 (17,285)	Cox, Rachel Elizabeth	4:13:58 (13,900)	Crowson, Jackie L	5:06:52 (26,879)
Cormack, Claire H	5:16:59 (28,636)	Cox, Sally A	4:24:04 (16,459)	Crowther, Anastasia	5:07:20 (26,969)
Cormack, Fiona A	4:36:42 (19,838)	Cox, Sarah A	4:16:36 (14,553)	Crowther, Jacqueline F	4:39:38 (20,621)
Cormack, Lisa	4:35:30 (19,546)	Cox, Sarah E	6:57:44 (34,927)	Crowther, Jacqueline L	4:23:05 (16,205)
Cormack, Sarah J	3:33:57 (4,750)	Coxhead, Julie E	4:18:54 (15,133)	Crowther, Jane E	4:34:29 (19,257)
Cormie, Anna L	4:56:12 (24,728)	Coy, Mary	5:19:21 (29,016)	Crowther, Libby	3:43:04 (6,434)
Cornell, Tracy A	3:40:31 (5,942)	Coyne, Glenis V	4:48:36 (22,877)	Croxford, Claire R	5:22:14 (29,394)
Cornfield, Tamsin C	4:28:52 (17,801)	Coyte, Amy	4:35:39 (19,581)	Cruddas, Claire	3:39:24 (5,743)
Cornish, Jennifer L	3:35:34 (5,061)	Coyte, Rachel	4:37:27 (20,024)	Crummay, Fiona Mary	4:21:41 (15,876)
Cornwell, Helen E	3:50:00 (7,833)	Cozzi, Anna L	5:49:49 (32,321)	Crundall, Amanda	3:02:49 (1,170)
Cornwell, Laura L	4:14:47 (14,108)	Crabb, Tracy A	4:12:19 (13,473)	Cruse, Sharon	4:42:29 (21,329)
Cornwell, Victoria L	5:46:59 (32,089)	Crabtree, Kim	5:15:13 (28,357)	Cuckney, Kate J	4:23:38 (16,346)
Corra, Loredana	4:48:41 (22,897)	Crabtree, Linda C	3:32:17 (4,514)	Cuddy, Michaela L	4:41:34 (21,109)
Corriette, Lianne	5:23:45 (29,618)	Crabtree, Sue	3:36:00 (5,154)	Cudlip, Helen E	6:24:03 (34,187)
Corsini, Susan	3:27:52 (3,834)	Craig, Carrie L	4:37:14 (19,969)	Cudmore, Angela	4:05:45 (11,834)
Corvill, Lorna E	5:21:00 (29,220)	Craig, Katie L	6:25:42 (34,267)	Cue Pandal, Coral	3:54:45 (8,956)
Cory, Sarah A	3:41:12 (6,071)	Craigie, Tamsin	4:20:45 (15,619)	Cuff, Ashley	4:57:33 (25,047)
Cosh, Charlotte F	5:00:14 (25,639)	Crain, Amy L	3:15:27 (2,277)	Cull, Wendy J	4:32:21 (18,715)
Costa, Emily	6:40:10 (34,630)	Craine, Rachael B	5:02:33 (26,129)	Culley, Laura E	4:32:42 (18,817)
Costa, Olivia J	5:31:02 (30,533)	Cramp, Belinda	4:37:34 (20,060)	Cullimore, Rosemary J	4:13:26 (13,783)
Coste, Catherine	4:13:11 (13,707)	Cramsie, Camilla	3:41:13 (6,075)	Culling, Tina	5:12:50 (27,954)
Costello, Lisa A	6:46:13 (34,726)	Cran, Kelly-Anne	4:35:18 (19,488)	Cullin-Moir, Linda	4:53:36 (24,100)
Costello, Tiarnagh N	4:47:06 (22,515)	Crandon, Shirley A	5:48:13 (32,189)	Cully, Katy	5:53:35 (32,590)
Coster, Niki J	5:23:15 (29,563)	Crane, Claire L	5:38:00 (31,274)	Cummine, Alexandra	4:21:38 (15,858)
Costiff, Christine	3:27:32 (3,783)	Crane, Jane L	4:32:00 (18,640)	Cumming, Erica J	4:46:52 (22,441)
Costley, Tracey	5:43:27 (31,815)	Cranidge, Ruth	4:23:53 (16,409)	Cummings, Rebecca	4:51:54 (23,729)
Cottafava, Annita	4:31:28 (18,494)	Craven, Hazel L	3:44:13 (6,667)	Cummins, Christine	4:51:23 (23,585)
Cotter, Colleen	5:59:58 (33,047)	Craven, Margaret	6:13:20 (33,714)	Cummins, Karen Teresa	4:29:11 (17,884)
Cotter, Victoria	3:04:01 (1,239)	Crawford, Barbara M	4:51:47 (23,695)	Cummins, Kathryn A	4:07:38 (12,265)
Cotterell, Caroline	3:43:33 (6,532)	Crawford, Grace	5:43:46 (31,831)	Cunningham, Janet M	4:05:44 (11,828)
Cotterell, Liz C	5:11:19 (27,695)	Crawford, Joanna	4:44:18 (21,794)	Cunningham, Julie E	3:57:26 (9,750)
Cotterell-East, Max L	5:59:47 (33,032)	Crawford, Julie A	4:28:18 (17,647)	Cunningham, Linda M	4:31:38 (18,537)
Cottey, Laura J	4:44:20 (21,801)	Crawford, Kerry	5:41:18 (31,608)	Cunningham, Lisa J	4:24:47 (16,651)
Cottini, Georgina	4:25:37 (16,877)	Crawford, Oona	4:52:17 (23,823)	Cunningham, Lynn	4:51:04 (23,505)
Cottiss, Michele	5:42:54 (31,759)	Crawford, Sarah E	4:37:34 (20,060)	Cunningham-Reid, Amy	3:40:01 (5,863)
Cottle, Agnes	6:10:58 (33,599)	Crawford, Sophie H	5:03:30 (26,284)	Cunningham-White, Wendy A	5:42:29 (31,722)
Cotton, Emma J	3:29:46 (4,148)	Crawley, Julie A	4:56:48 (24,879)	Cupman, Katie M	4:03:58 (11,443)
Cotton, Jody E	4:48:19 (22,811)	Creaney, Kathryn A	4:11:37 (13,292)	Curant, Kelly A	6:34:13 (34,506)
Cotton, Nicola J	4:19:20 (15,238)	Creech, Heidi J	3:26:24 (3,587)	Curd, Chloe L	4:47:55 (22,712)
Cottrell, Diana	5:32:03 (30,646)	Creedon, Sheila O	3:48:50 (7,580)	Curd, Janine N	5:20:44 (29,182)
Cottrell, Jeannette	5:08:03 (27,094)	Creek, Emily V	5:11:33 (27,737)	Curley, Donna R	5:31:48 (30,617)
Cottrell, Rebecca E	5:31:19 (30,559)	Creighton, Denise M	5:15:21 (28,394)	Curnow, Lucy J	3:44:01 (6,632)
Couch, Georgina I	5:29:02 (30,275)	Creighton, Paula	5:00:24 (25,677)	Currall, Tatiana A	4:34:17 (19,218)
Coulson, Alison P	4:02:16 (11,082)	Creuza, Marie-Claude	4:31:29 (18,502)	Curran, Brenda M	5:53:10 (32,563)
Coulson, Gina	4:46:45 (22,420)	Crick, Anette	3:57:40 (9,836)	Curran, Hyral S	6:13:41 (33,733)
Coulson, Samantha	6:12:39 (33,670)	Cringle, Tara L	3:39:36 (5,776)	Curran, Jane A	4:02:14 (11,074)
Coulson, Sarah E	5:53:26 (32,579)	Crisp, Clare J	4:40:05 (20,752)	Curran, Julie A	6:07:26 (33,456)
Coupe, Helen L	3:58:54 (10,224)	Crisp, Lynda L	5:00:29 (25,697)	Currid, Angela Caroline	4:15:16 (14,226)
Couper, Susan	4:30:14 (18,160)	Crispin, Jason D	3:44:37 (6,733)	Currie, Clare E	4:40:06 (20,755)
Couper, Tracie K	5:46:46 (32,071)	Croall, Kate	5:09:46 (27,420)	Currie, Laura	3:28:22 (3,913)
Court, Emily	6:54:59 (34,895)	Crocker, Andrea	5:10:07 (27,481)	Currie, Melissa J	5:12:00 (27,800)
Courtenay, Christine M	6:41:21 (34,654)	Crocker, Linda C	5:18:33 (28,880)	Currie, Nicola D	5:28:53 (30,259)
Courtney, Sylvia	5:35:47 (31,049)	Croft, Bev S	4:16:39 (14,571)	Currie-Godbolt, Denise	4:07:04 (12,124)
Cousen, Sharon L	4:14:33 (14,042)	Croft, Rowan P	4:12:15 (13,453)	Currington, Debra J	4:35:03 (19,425)
Cousens, Barbara A	5:39:45 (31,471)	Croker, Laura J	3:15:45 (2,313)	Curry, Georgina E	4:38:52 (20,396)
Cousins, Jenny	5:10:45 (27,592)	Crompton, Barbara A	5:08:20 (27,146)	Curtin, Orlaith	4:40:03 (20,739)
Cousins, Katie A	3:39:56 (5,843)	Crompton, Susan J	4:04:05 (11,467)	Curtis, Cheryl K	4:01:25 (10,887)
Cousins, Wendy A	6:35:31 (34,535)	Cronin, Breda M	4:29:00 (17,829)	Curtis, Hannah L	3:36:35 (5,250)
Coutts, Marla	4:01:25 (10,887)	Cronin, Emma Kate	4:30:58 (18,340)	Curtis, Joanna H	3:30:30 (4,256)
Cove, Hayley J	4:33:20 (18,985)	Crook, Christine	7:13:14 (35,084)	Curtis, Lisa	4:59:06 (25,410)
Coveney, Susan T	5:37:30 (31,224)	Crook, Fern	5:14:15 (28,200)	Curtis, Lucill J	5:02:38 (26,142)
Coverdale, Heather F	4:25:06 (16,736)	Crook, Nicola	4:47:14 (22,552)	Curtis, Margaret T	4:34:32 (19,267)
Cowan, Eleanor F	4:57:18 (24,985)	Crosbie, Laura E	3:44:41 (6,743)	Curtis, Nadine	5:13:52 (28,134)
Cowan, Heather	5:41:18 (31,608)	Crosbie, Margot J	3:48:35 (7,529)	Cusack, Rosemary	5:22:39 (29,461)
Cowan, Judy	6:23:22 (34,169)	Crosby, Jennifer C	6:06:51 (33,425)	Cushnaghan, Fiona C	3:47:01 (7,203)
Cowan, Margaret M	4:41:23 (21,051)	Crosby, Kirsty	7:26:07 (35,188)	Cusick, Karin Elisabeth Odegaard	4:39:46 (20,662)
Cowdrey, Melanie J	5:44:44 (31,909)	Cross, Carole E	5:11:20 (27,700)	Custance, Jane E	4:12:14 (13,447)
Cowen, Sarah C	5:53:20 (32,573)	Cross, Janette M	4:58:36 (25,294)	Cutliffe, Caroline	5:21:40 (29,327)
Cowen, Selina M	4:12:39 (13,560)	Cross, Lindsay	4:06:40 (12,037)	Cutmore, Michaela	5:30:36 (30,474)
Cowie, Katrina C	7:27:49 (35,202)	Cross, Sally L	5:15:13 (28,357)	Cutner, Christine J	4:37:04 (19,934)

Cutting, Dawn A....4:59:56 (25,584)
Cutuk-Short, Andjelka....5:13:30 (28,063)
Czarnowska, Ros A....6:25:54 (34,275)
Czifra, Aniko....4:33:15 (18,959)
Dacey, Claire L....4:22:28 (16,072)
Dachtler, Deborah A....7:05:42 (35,012)
Dadlani, Emma....3:28:54 (3,993)
Dados, Julie....4:56:47 (24,871)
D'Agostino, Paola....5:09:49 (27,432)
Dahle, Astrid....3:24:13 (3,302)
Dahlkvist, Irina....4:32:19 (18,710)
Dailly, Kirsty A....4:42:13 (21,255)
Dalby, Mary....4:26:37 (17,158)
Dale, Charlotte....3:16:39 (2,400)
Dale, Emma K....4:44:00 (21,723)
Dale, Julie....3:38:50 (5,644)
Dale, Louise M....4:58:33 (25,284)
Dale, Nicola I....4:08:41 (12,544)
Dale, Oenone....4:37:07 (19,945)
Dale, Samantha....4:01:18 (10,858)
Dale, Sue I....3:37:12 (5,354)
Dalessandro, Jalanie....3:23:43 (3,220)
Daley, Susan....7:29:24 (35,215)
Dalgleish, Hannah S....4:31:12 (18,405)
Daloise, Brenna L....4:10:29 (12,978)
Dalton, Jo....4:48:38 (22,887)
Dalton, Karen S....5:01:03 (25,829)
Dalton, Pauline....3:27:26 (3,759)
Dalton, Sheryl C....4:48:34 (22,866)
Daly, Andrea L....6:12:10 (33,649)
Daly, Deborah Alicia....3:56:22 (9,418)
Daly, Louise....4:21:39 (15,863)
Daly, Maria F....5:18:46 (28,925)
Daly, Sinead....5:36:46 (31,149)
Daly, Teresa....3:50:27 (7,933)
Daly, Vanessa....4:48:49 (22,922)
Dalzell, Julie....3:32:49 (4,587)
Dalzell, Rebecca L....4:55:11 (24,499)
Dalziel, Joanne....4:02:48 (11,187)
Damant, Sandy....3:51:28 (8,159)
D'Amone, Marilena....4:33:14 (18,954)
Danaher, Eleanor....4:18:25 (15,001)
Dance, Helen....4:25:22 (16,806)
Dando, Louise M....5:56:04 (32,761)
Daniel, Beryl M....4:28:23 (17,665)
Daniels, Corinne....5:48:01 (32,171)
Daniels, Sally A....4:30:17 (18,175)
Daniels, Tanya M....4:21:37 (15,849)
Danks, Caroline J....4:44:40 (21,879)
Danks, Emma J....3:49:23 (7,704)
Dannatt, Emma M....4:14:32 (14,037)
Danson, Claire F....3:34:22 (4,846)
Darby, Elizabeth R....5:25:55 (29,922)
Darby, Rachael M....4:30:35 (18,250)
Dargan, Lesley E....4:41:44 (21,149)
Dargan, Susan E....5:07:48 (27,059)
Dargie, Kate E....4:27:47 (17,479)
Darley, Vanessa M....6:23:50 (34,184)
Darling, Mary....3:15:18 (2,259)
Darmody, Michelle....6:23:19 (34,164)
Darne, Elizabeth R....4:40:09 (20,763)
Darroch, Liza Q....4:35:33 (19,558)
Datson, Lynne F....6:08:01 (33,483)
Dav Ies-Raimbault, Angela M....5:13:35 (28,078)
Davenport, Clare....4:02:33 (11,141)
Davenport, Victoria....4:44:39 (21,871)
Daveport, Beth....5:10:53 (27,618)
Davey, Angela....4:25:32 (16,847)
Davey, Antoinette....5:54:59 (32,689)
Davey, Judy M....3:38:35 (5,604)
Davey, Kelly L....4:48:52 (22,936)
Davey, Lesley J....5:25:04 (29,806)
Davey, Rebecca J....3:56:24 (9,429)
David, Anna....4:04:46 (11,599)
David, Donna....5:17:59 (28,792)
David, Elizabeth J....4:22:58 (16,178)
David, Jamie A....5:39:25 (31,438)
David, Kelly A....4:49:40 (23,171)
Davidson, Anne A....3:24:09 (3,289)
Davidson, Anne D....3:45:34 (6,909)
Davidson, Charlotte....5:32:29 (30,686)
Davidson, Claire....4:33:49 (19,101)
Davidson, Hannah K....5:13:07 (28,009)

Iron lady motivation

Journalist and former conservative politician Matthew Parris holds the record for the fastest MP to complete the London Marathon. He nailed the 26 miles in 2 hours and 32 minutes in 1985. He says that he used Margaret Thatcher as an inspiration for his training: 'I was terrified of her'. Since 1981, over 40 MPs have run in the London Marathon. The slowest was Conservative Bill Wiggin who ran 6:32:43 in 2002. 'I'm not a very good runner,' he said, 'but I never give up.' Apparently none of the MPs charged their entry fee to expenses.

Davidson, Leanne R....5:30:44 (30,493)
Davidson, Lesley A....4:18:22 (14,980)
Davidson, Violet....5:11:34 (27,743)
Davie, Sue M....5:30:06 (30,411)
Davies, Alex P....4:04:07 (11,470)
Davies, Alexandra....4:15:35 (14,303)
Davies, Amanda J....3:37:57 (5,479)
Davies, Angharad S....4:29:00 (17,829)
Davies, Anna C....5:19:03 (28,978)
Davies, Anne....3:28:53 (3,989)
Davies, Beverley F....6:18:40 (33,952)
Davies, Cara C....5:55:40 (32,738)
Davies, Caroline....5:38:47 (31,371)
Davies, Caryl....3:59:02 (10,261)
Davies, Cate....6:06:52 (33,429)
Davies, Christine A....5:42:57 (31,765)
Davies, Delyth C....3:51:24 (8,142)
Davies, Elaine....3:12:30 (1,932)
Davies, Ellen M....4:52:38 (23,887)
Davies, Emma E....6:18:41 (33,977)
Davies, Emma L....3:49:10 (7,660)
Davies, Fay E....5:21:48 (29,343)
Davies, Helen....4:26:44 (17,187)
Davies, Helen A....5:07:15 (26,953)
Davies, Helen L....5:54:48 (32,667)
Davies, Jane A....3:17:37 (2,492)
Davies, Joanna K....5:15:50 (28,481)
Davies, Josie M....5:38:22 (31,313)
Davies, Kerra M....5:00:57 (25,799)
Davies, Kerry A....6:59:47 (34,944)
Davies, Kim L....5:41:59 (31,671)
Davies, Laura....4:59:56 (25,584)
Davies, Laura A....6:21:47 (34,106)
Davies, Lisa....6:09:57 (33,558)
Davies, Louise....6:41:28 (34,655)
Davies, Louise M....4:27:59 (17,540)
Davies, Lyn....4:12:28 (13,512)
Davies, Michelle L....4:12:03 (13,398)
Davies, Nicola M....5:38:22 (31,313)
Davies, Rachel....6:30:57 (34,434)
Davies, Rachel S....4:49:39 (23,165)
Davies, Rita....4:25:56 (16,968)
Davies, Rose A....5:32:45 (30,732)
Davies, Sarah H....5:25:47 (29,903)
Davies, Sarah L....5:06:14 (26,768)
Davies, Sarah V....4:10:56 (13,089)
Davies, Siobhan....5:54:48 (32,667)
Davies, Susan J....5:06:41 (26,839)
Davies, Susan M....5:31:30 (30,582)
Davies, Tryphena L....4:32:52 (18,864)
Davies, Valerie....4:24:25 (16,555)
Davies, Vicki A....3:52:44 (8,456)
Davies, Victoria....4:28:27 (17,683)
Davies, Zoe M....5:31:09 (30,549)
Davies Jones, Caroline R....4:43:09 (21,503)
Davila, Justine R....4:36:31 (19,797)
Davis, Alex C....5:47:12 (32,111)
Davis, Bonnie J....6:26:18 (34,292)
Davis, Carol Ann A....6:06:34 (33,416)
Davis, Cathy....5:34:54 (30,957)
Davis, Cheryl L....5:11:48 (27,775)
Davis, Christine L....5:08:21 (27,151)
Davis, Claire E....4:02:53 (11,206)
Davis, Connie E....5:09:06 (27,289)
Davis, Dawn Y....5:38:52 (31,379)
Davis, Jacqueline A....5:44:26 (31,887)
Davis, Jayne L....4:24:09 (16,490)
Davis, Jo J....6:22:37 (34,134)
Davis, Joanna....5:02:40 (26,147)
Davis, Karen E....4:06:48 (12,060)
Davis, Kelly....3:46:02 (6,994)
Davis, Lydia....3:23:23 (3,174)
Davis, Lyn A....4:31:05 (18,382)
Davis, Margaret C....5:29:46 (30,367)
Davis, Maria....6:11:05 (33,605)
Davis, Merilyn J....3:57:12 (9,673)
Davis, Nicola K....4:32:00 (18,640)
Davis, Rachel....5:14:20 (28,213)
Davis, Samantha J....4:23:20 (16,260)
Davis, Tina A....5:58:21 (32,949)
Davis, Ulla B....7:10:55 (35,058)
Davison, Ruth M....5:20:53 (29,205)
Davison, Sue....4:20:08 (15,468)
Davoren, Sinead M....4:55:47 (24,632)
Daw, Eve....4:50:08 (23,267)
Daw, Sharon L....3:12:48 (1,976)
Dawe, Emma L....4:35:34 (19,564)
Dawid-Ernst, Doris....4:55:16 (24,522)
Dawkins, Margaret E....4:41:41 (21,139)
Dawnay, Sophia P....5:02:08 (26,049)
Dawson, Andrea M....4:28:34 (17,716)
Dawson, Christine E....5:56:56 (32,829)
Dawson, Elizabeth....4:56:47 (24,871)
Dawson, Gemma C....4:45:38 (22,113)
Dawson, Hayley....4:30:35 (18,250)
Dawson, Natalie K....5:48:17 (32,195)
Dawson, Rebecca....4:59:06 (25,410)
Day, Amanda J....4:16:51 (14,619)
Day, Gillian....5:25:58 (29,929)
Day, Jenny....5:58:33 (32,961)
Day, Julia M....3:46:39 (7,122)
Day, Natalie....5:22:33 (29,446)
Day, Sarah E....4:53:47 (24,169)
Dayawala, Geeta....5:37:22 (31,213)
De Albuquerque, Katie E....4:10:39 (13,019)
De Bohun, Andrea C....4:32:49 (18,850)
De Castro, Victoria....4:31:07 (18,389)
De Giovanni, Silvana....3:39:02 (5,692)
De Graaf, Marjan....5:02:46 (26,170)
De Graaff, Natascha C....4:36:19 (19,742)
De Juniac, Alexandra K....4:16:55 (14,626)
De Klerk, Ismari....4:33:44 (19,080)
De La Guerre, Annelize....5:18:48 (28,934)
De Ridder, Amanda....4:45:34 (22,097)
De Smedt, Beryl....4:03:50 (11,403)
De Smedt, Marina....4:46:41 (22,391)
De Sousa, Claire J....4:48:33 (22,864)
De Verdiere, Morgane....4:28:03 (17,557)
De Villiers, Natalie K....3:16:23 (2,369)
De Wal, Christa....5:00:23 (25,675)
De Winter, Genevieve M....4:18:07 (14,926)
De Wit, Melanie....6:21:03 (34,071)
Deadman, Alison Catherine....4:46:23 (22,310)
Dean, Dixie H....4:54:20 (24,299)
Dean, Donna M....7:00:52 (34,961)
Dean, Elizabeth....4:47:41 (22,647)
Dean, Erin E....4:28:11 (17,608)
Dean, Hazel....3:27:36 (3,801)
Dean, Julia M....4:44:53 (21,924)
Dean, Suzanne E....4:44:37 (21,861)
Deane, Linda A....4:47:53 (22,701)
Deane, Sophie....5:22:37 (29,455)
Dearlove, Hannah L....5:11:40 (27,757)
Deary, Jane....5:17:53 (28,775)
Deathe, Kirsty....4:52:52 (23,940)
Debling, Kim Anne....5:26:05 (29,948)
Decker, Helen J....2:42:08 (238)
Decosta, Karyn P....5:26:06 (29,951)
Deed, Katherine E....3:39:17 (5,726)
Deeley, Rebecca H....5:16:04 (28,508)

Deere, Gabrielle L....3:47:50 (7,360)
Deering, Sarah....4:54:21 (24,302)
Degeir-Mawdsley, Lisa....5:02:01 (26,025)
Degg, Karen E....6:18:02 (33,928)
Deighton, Avelline M....4:26:51 (17,222)
Dejonckeere, Els....3:56:40 (9,523)
Delagneau, Jocelyne....4:07:51 (12,326)
Delahaye-Slater, Julie E....5:00:27 (25,692)
Delapenwa Grant, Inger....7:23:54 (35,168)
Delderfield, Diane L....4:40:13 (20,779)
Delderfield, Sophie L....3:20:13 (2,784)
Delf, Jacqueline A....5:09:40 (27,399)
Della, Meyers....5:35:16 (30,996)
Dellar, Natalie E....4:35:42 (19,599)
Deller, Kim Y....5:57:23 (32,864)
Deloubes, Lynne M....5:53:30 (32,585)
Delves, Frances M....3:49:42 (7,774)
Demand, Noelle....4:25:02 (16,719)
Dempster, Tina M....4:58:30 (25,268)
Dench, Rachel Elizabeth....4:01:44 (10,970)
Denham, Jo N....4:33:02 (18,906)
Denham, Vicky E....4:22:08 (15,978)
Denison, Laura J....3:21:47 (2,982)
Denman, Kate L....4:38:14 (20,238)
Dennis, Julie A....4:15:30 (14,285)
Dennis, Sarah E....4:27:08 (17,290)
Dennison, Andrea M....3:10:38 (1,748)
Dennison, Jennifer M....5:54:46 (32,665)
Dennison, Kelly L....3:18:30 (2,577)
Denniss, Rachel....5:55:21 (32,713)
Denniston, Iona....5:34:00 (30,861)
Denny, Sarai....4:51:38 (23,655)
Denyer, Judith J....5:00:05 (25,610)
Denzey, Clare M....5:16:23 (28,546)
Depangher, Cristina....5:37:21 (31,212)
Depear, Sharron....4:50:58 (23,478)
Dermit, Mirentxu....5:12:06 (27,819)
Derry, Mary....5:05:43 (26,685)
Dervish, Sheree....6:16:56 (33,881)
Desai, Priya....5:04:31 (26,459)
Desmond, Pauline E....4:38:13 (20,234)
Devaney, Catryn A....4:53:35 (24,093)
Devaney, Claire E....6:15:35 (33,817)
Devereux, Christine V....3:51:17 (8,117)
Devine, Laura M....3:29:41 (4,132)
Devine, Sandra M....4:08:04 (12,376)
Devlin, Hannah L....4:11:37 (13,292)
Devlin, Kate....5:42:20 (31,705)
Devonshire, Sarah....7:11:16 (35,068)
Dew, Sheryl A....4:52:57 (23,965)
Dewar, Jane....4:44:36 (21,856)
Dewberry, Michelle....4:26:23 (17,083)
Dewey, Alison Jill....6:29:57 (34,409)
Dewhirst, Lesley....4:18:22 (14,980)
Dewhurst, Alice C....4:49:38 (23,159)
Dewhurst, Andrea J....4:51:21 (23,578)
Dewis, Karen L....4:39:33 (20,595)
Dews, Jacqui H....3:23:48 (3,236)
Dews, Tracey....4:16:51 (14,619)
Dhadwal, Arbind....5:16:52 (28,626)
Dhaliwal, Manjiv....5:01:30 (25,916)
Di Padova, Daniela A....4:55:42 (24,614)
Diaz, Selfi....4:46:22 (22,302)
Dibbs, Emma L....5:36:49 (31,157)
Dibbs, Juliet C....3:57:22 (9,736)
Dick, Eleanor M....3:09:39 (1,677)
Dick, Julia A....4:02:33 (11,141)
Dick, Patricia A....3:35:53 (5,131)
Dickens, Abby F....4:52:48 (23,927)
Dickens, Jayne....2:56:26 (742)
Dickens, Maggie....6:20:53 (34,065)
Dickinson, Emma T....4:41:46 (21,158)
Dickinson, Pamela J....3:35:20 (5,018)
Dicks, Michaela L....5:49:36 (32,298)
Dickson, Georgina M....4:43:37 (21,628)
Diggens, Laura K....4:43:13 (21,521)
Diggines, Linda J....6:10:21 (33,582)
Diggins, Lexi J....7:07:45 (35,037)
Dihal- Rikkelman, Joyce A....4:16:00 (14,395)
Dillon, Caroline L....5:38:44 (31,361)
Dillon, Elizabeth....4:56:22 (24,764)
Dimmer, Alexandra....6:05:36 (33,368)
Dimmock, Natalie C....4:37:05 (19,937)
Dimond, Nicola J....5:30:05 (30,408)
Dina, Debs....6:31:49 (34,450)
Ding, Nicola....5:58:00 (32,916)
Dingemans, Jayne M....4:21:08 (15,727)
Dingle, Tracey H....5:18:46 (28,925)
Dinwoodie, Maddie....5:34:27 (30,907)
Disbury, Rebecca H....4:36:35 (19,813)
Ditton, Carolyn P....5:04:47 (26,503)
Dixon, Angela J....3:59:46 (10,481)
Dixon, Elisabeth C....4:14:54 (14,140)
Dixon, Joanna C....4:21:37 (15,849)
Dixon, Lucy....4:23:33 (16,327)
Dixon, Sally A....4:48:06 (22,763)
Dixon, Sara J....6:25:18 (34,243)
Dixon, Sharon....3:30:30 (4,256)
Dobbin, Claire....4:47:23 (22,577)
Dobson, Jane L....4:46:40 (22,386)
Dobson, Joanne M....4:40:52 (20,929)

Dobson, Judith E....3:24:03 (3,270)

I ran London Marathon in 2001, 2002, 2008 and 2009. In 2009 I raised funds (£500) for the British Heart Foundation as heart disease can affect people of all ages and fitness. I finished the 2009 race in exactly the same time as I ran in 2008 i.e. 3:24:03. I was amazed by this coincidence and wonder if it has ever happened to anybody else?

Docherty, Alison A....3:05:56 (1,369)
Docherty, Anne H....4:29:10 (17,876)
Docherty, Sarah....5:03:51 (26,350)
Doctor, Gillian....5:06:28 (26,800)
Dodd, Caroline M....5:37:05 (31,185)
Dodd, Gianna....6:43:35 (34,689)
Dodd, Louise....4:35:29 (19,536)
Dodd, Mikyla....5:55:05 (32,693)
Dodd, Sarah....4:17:32 (14,776)
Dodd, Susan....5:50:04 (32,342)
Dodd, Tracey....5:29:46 (30,367)
Dodds, Clare L....4:47:42 (22,653)
Dodds, Elaine....6:05:39 (33,371)
Dodds, Pam J....4:25:50 (16,945)
Dodds, Sarah L....5:54:18 (32,639)
Dodds, Victoria A....4:54:19 (24,292)
Dodson, Rosemary....6:40:15 (34,633)
Dodsworth, Catherine M....4:31:01 (18,352)
Dodwell, Hannah....4:46:24 (22,315)
Doe, Sarah K....3:39:01 (5,689)
Doggett, Janine E....4:00:30 (10,675)
Doherty, Alli....7:01:10 (34,963)
Doherty, Christina A....4:51:39 (23,661)
Doherty, Claire M....5:48:59 (32,249)
Dolan, Amy F....3:47:39 (7,318)
Dolan, Carla J....5:53:58 (32,613)
Dolan, Rose....5:53:58 (32,613)
Dolis, Isabelle....5:02:27 (26,102)
Dominique, Hofman....4:44:15 (21,778)
Dominy, Kathy M....4:52:16 (23,814)
Donald, Gina P....4:02:17 (11,084)
Donald, Julie D....3:38:14 (5,540)
Donald, Pauline....4:45:01 (21,967)
Donaldson, Claire....4:35:00 (19,406)
Done, Sarah R....5:18:29 (28,867)
Donelan, Joanna L....5:24:00 (29,648)
Donne, Danielle....5:16:46 (28,614)
Donnelly, Dolores M....4:47:32 (22,605)
Donnelly, Michelle A....4:20:44 (15,615)
Donnelly, Nicola J....3:42:35 (6,325)
Donnelly, Rachael....4:31:46 (18,574)
Donnelly, Rebecca A....4:32:38 (18,801)
Donnelly, Ursula....5:27:19 (30,081)
Donoho, Kelly J....4:53:06 (23,998)
Donoyou, Heather M....4:15:24 (14,256)
Doody, Eleanor....4:15:22 (14,246)
Dooley, Sharon M....4:56:15 (24,740)
Doorgachurn, Frances....6:44:56 (34,707)
Dopson, Sarah L....4:06:54 (12,079)
Dorey, Sarah J....6:04:53 (33,334)
Dorling, Julie....5:02:10 (26,056)
Dorman, Vicki....4:31:51 (18,592)
Dorrity, Miriam....4:13:52 (13,877)
Dos Santos, Marie Isabel....4:16:34 (14,542)
Dosanjh, Bindar K....5:17:49 (28,767)
Dosanjh, Herdeep....5:12:21 (27,861)
Dossa, Cressida....4:07:45 (12,302)
Dougall, Annie K....3:53:49 (8,705)
Dougall, Rebecca J....5:46:45 (32,069)
Dougherty, Kirsty L....4:07:54 (12,340)
Doughton, Jane S....4:46:10 (22,237)
Doughty, Kay M....5:17:48 (28,765)
Douglas, Cheryl....5:38:26 (31,320)
Douglas, Fiona I....5:01:56 (26,001)
Douglas, Nighean M....5:16:54 (28,631)
Douglas, Ronnie....5:27:38 (30,104)
Douglas-Pennant, Caroline M....6:12:22 (33,657)
Doulton, Lindsay M....3:49:08 (7,651)
Douthwaite, Donna M....4:32:28 (18,752)
Dove, Emma L....5:50:30 (32,381)
Dove, Peter W....6:09:47 (33,551)
Doven, Emma J....4:49:43 (23,182)
Dow, Deborah Suzanne....3:56:20 (9,406)
Dowe Davies, Carol D....6:02:53 (33,221)
Dowen, Meg....4:48:53 (22,938)
Dowie, Claire L....5:47:19 (32,122)
Dowman, Sadie....4:31:55 (18,611)
Downer, Aimée S....4:02:11 (11,064)
Downey, Irene M....4:21:13 (15,744)
Downey, Mary E....7:13:31 (35,087)
Downie, Anne....3:53:55 (8,726)
Downie, Lauren....5:14:05 (28,177)
Downs, Gabrielle A....3:44:47 (6,765)
Downton, Kate R....4:38:56 (20,416)
Dowsett, Laura L....4:24:42 (16,626)
Doyce, Caroline J....3:38:00 (5,489)
Doyle, Aileen P....4:28:24 (17,670)
Doyle, Carly H....3:46:27 (7,077)
Doyle, Carly V....7:26:37 (35,195)
Doyle, Helen J....5:22:04 (29,371)
Doyle, Katina....7:21:06 (35,156)
Doyle, Kiersten L....4:13:28 (13,787)
Doyle, Mary T....4:25:22 (16,806)
Doyle, Michelle A....6:21:17 (34,087)
Doyle, Siobhan....4:44:38 (21,867)
Drake, Cheryl D....4:57:38 (25,057)
Drake, Deborah J....4:49:12 (23,017)
Drake, Elizabeth J....7:02:48 (34,981)
Drake, Janet F....5:13:59 (28,157)
Drake, Sheila....4:17:00 (14,649)
Drake-Norris, Zoe G....4:05:11 (11,703)
Draper, Claire....4:35:11 (19,458)
Draper, Clare L....4:56:10 (24,720)
Draper, Jacqueline....6:05:16 (33,351)
Drasdo, Alison D....3:10:21 (1,728)
Draycott, Ella....6:24:03 (34,187)
Draycott, Michelle....4:00:15 (10,611)
Draysey, Zelda A....4:06:43 (12,044)
Dredge, Sally L....4:58:05 (25,158)
Drew, Catherine....4:10:12 (12,911)
Drewett, Sandi....5:12:24 (27,867)
Drewitt, Julia Denise....4:44:56 (21,936)
Dreyer, Sigrid....4:55:41 (24,610)
Driscoll, Kathryn L....5:21:00 (29,220)
Driver, Katrin....3:07:24 (1,467)
Drohan, Janice G....4:33:13 (18,948)
Drouet, Annick....4:11:48 (13,337)
Druce, Sarah J....5:15:23 (28,398)
Drury, Chris M....4:33:19 (18,982)
Druvaskalns, Lina E....6:02:13 (33,184)
Drysdale, Fiona D....7:25:43 (35,183)
D'Santos, Karen L....5:09:57 (27,446)
Dsouza, Jennifer....5:51:32 (32,451)
Du Plessis, Sonja A....5:26:22 (29,974)
Dubbink, Sophie E....5:22:50 (29,487)
Duboise, Patricia....5:16:40 (28,590)
Duce, Abigail....5:34:23 (30,894)
Duck, Deborah M....5:03:49 (26,344)
Ducker, Angela....6:49:52 (34,811)
Ducker, Jackie A....4:13:00 (13,659)
Duckett, Catherine....4:47:07 (22,522)
Duckworth, Avril M....3:25:25 (3,449)
Duckworth, Ruth E....5:09:56 (27,444)
Duddy, Sarah....4:46:04 (22,218)
Dudfield, Cathy J....4:00:06 (10,572)

Dudgeon, Sarah P	3:09:12 (1,639)	
Dudin, Elizabeth M	3:45:31 (6,899)	
Dudley, Emer B	3:32:49 (4,587)	
Duez, Pascale	4:02:04 (11,033)	
Duff, Jenny A	5:12:11 (27,840)	
Duff, Joanne L	4:32:43 (18,819)	
Duff, Kirsty	4:03:03 (11,239)	
Duff, Louisa I	5:48:13 (32,189)	
Duffell, Linda Jane	3:51:35 (8,183)	
Duffell, Lynsey	4:12:39 (13,560)	
Duffett, Juanita	4:53:51 (24,189)	
Duffin, Bronagh A	5:47:22 (32,123)	
Duffin, Janet K	5:01:09 (25,849)	
Duffin, Roberta P	7:28:45 (35,212)	
Duffy, Fiona M	3:55:00 (9,025)	
Duffy, Kim	6:16:47 (33,877)	
Duffy, Louise M	6:17:41 (33,916)	
Duffy, Nicola Jane	4:50:37 (23,400)	
Duffy, Paula	6:59:18 (34,940)	
Duffy, Sinead	4:06:08 (11,910)	
Duffy, Una	4:21:15 (15,755)	
Dufour, Mireille	4:08:47 (12,566)	
Dugdale, Catherine	3:15:54 (2,326)	
Dugdale, Julie C	5:17:19 (28,686)	
Duggan, Andrea	4:56:27 (24,785)	
Duggan, Becky	3:46:39 (7,122)	
Duguid, Petra	3:47:17 (7,247)	
Duke, Jennifer A	4:34:14 (19,204)	
Dulla, Catherine N	3:12:10 (1,897)	
Dumergue, Simone L	4:38:58 (20,426)	
Dunbar, Amanda K	4:31:13 (18,409)	
Dunbar, Susan M	6:51:16 (34,833)	
Duncan, Christina	3:56:49 (9,573)	
Duncan, Lucy J	4:38:43 (20,354)	
Dunder, Katarina	4:22:31 (16,078)	
Dunford, Ashley E	4:00:37 (10,700)	
Dunford, Bethan C	6:01:45 (33,154)	
Dunkel-Benz, Friederike	4:30:42 (18,279)	
Dunkeld, Katrina M	5:04:04 (26,394)	
Dunkley, Nicola	9:11:41 (35,359)	
Dunmore, Clare M	4:33:33 (19,036)	
Dunn, Caroline A	3:27:42 (3,812)	
Dunn, Julie A	4:37:13 (19,964)	
Dunn, Nadia	4:54:48 (24,408)	
Dunn, Olivia	5:08:08 (27,110)	
Dunn, Tracey	6:03:01 (33,229)	
Dunne, Clare E	4:16:23 (14,495)	
Dunne, Lyn P	4:00:53 (10,770)	
Dunne, Tracy	5:05:54 (26,713)	
Dunnett, Brenda M	5:02:11 (26,061)	
Dunning, Alison M	5:46:18 (32,037)	
Dunning, Nicky M	4:53:46 (24,163)	
Dunsire, Zoe M	4:41:31 (21,093)	
Dunster, Carol A	5:33:44 (30,834)	
Dupain, Emma L	3:52:03 (8,287)	
Dupay, Teresa	4:59:27 (25,484)	
Dupont, Laura	6:28:10 (34,362)	
Durance, Helen A	4:46:55 (22,454)	
Durance, Penny L	4:46:56 (22,461)	
Durber, Kathryn Louise	4:46:05 (22,224)	
Durham, Lee C	6:05:39 (33,371)	
Durham, Lisa M	5:41:36 (31,639)	
Durn, Carol	4:55:03 (24,460)	
Durnin, Angela E	5:17:09 (28,667)	
Durow, Sandra	4:28:49 (17,780)	
Durrand, Marie	5:08:50 (27,234)	
Durrant, Pam M	5:21:20 (29,275)	
Durston, Beverly A	4:41:46 (21,158)	
Durston, Lisa	4:25:35 (16,868)	
Dutnall, Jude S	5:01:03 (25,829)	
Dutoit, Susie	4:41:33 (21,103)	
Dutton, Clare E	7:00:01 (34,949)	
Duxbury, Alex	4:32:24 (18,728)	
Dwight, Helen J	4:14:29 (14,024)	
Dyer, Amy M	4:38:05 (20,195)	
Dyer, Holly M	4:46:16 (22,267)	
Dyer, Liza M	5:48:29 (32,214)	
Dyke, Helen A	2:49:52 (468)	
Dyke, Tia J	4:04:39 (11,572)	
Dyker, Rachel S	3:36:46 (5,273)	
Dykes, Karen	5:13:17 (28,033)	
Dykes, Rita A	4:31:04 (18,376)	
Dyson, Joanna	4:30:28 (18,220)	
Dzialdow, Resi	4:18:23 (14,990)	
Eade, Barbara L	4:40:04 (20,746)	
Eade, Charlotte L	5:07:38 (27,031)	
Eades, Antonia	5:07:54 (27,075)	
Eagling, Becky	3:59:56 (10,530)	
Earis, Harriet L	5:17:51 (28,771)	
Earl, Deborah S	4:20:31 (15,563)	
Earl, Diana L	5:19:38 (29,054)	
Earl, Jayne E	5:43:18 (31,806)	
Earl, Judi A	4:21:39 (15,863)	
Earle, Jayne K	4:53:09 (24,012)	
Earle, Joanna Earle L	4:17:16 (14,706)	
Early, Gemma D	4:32:33 (18,769)	
Early, Ruth E	4:34:27 (19,249)	
Earnshaw, Charlotte D	5:25:33 (29,868)	
Easom, Anette J	5:03:43 (26,327)	
East, Gill S	4:36:22 (19,757)	
East, Gillian	4:57:52 (25,102)	
Eastbury, Justine A	4:16:04 (14,416)	
Easter, Aimée L	5:29:29 (30,328)	
Easton, Julie A	4:37:51 (20,132)	
Eastwood, Kim	6:23:30 (34,171)	
Eaton, Elise H	4:49:40 (23,171)	
Ebden, Caroline	6:22:15 (34,119)	
Ebrahimoff, Mindy S	3:46:09 (7,011)	
Ecclestone, Bethan S	5:30:21 (30,443)	
Eckersley, Jeni	4:53:06 (23,998)	
Economu, Nicoleta M	3:52:51 (8,476)	
Edeam, Catherine	4:09:48 (12,803)	
Edgar, Hazel T	7:11:43 (35,074)	
Edgar, Sarah G	5:04:57 (26,535)	
Edge, Joanne	4:13:58 (13,900)	
Edge, Kerry	4:58:18 (25,213)	
Edghill, Sharon L	4:27:45 (17,470)	
Edith, Didier	4:26:36 (17,148)	
Edmead, Tammy A	3:56:43 (9,541)	
Edmeades, Nerieda K	4:17:56 (14,869)	
Edmond, Anna	5:06:14 (26,768)	
Edmonds, Julia	5:47:47 (32,155)	
Edmondson, Rowena M	3:30:24 (4,237)	
Edmondson, Tanya E	4:19:30 (15,287)	
Edmunds, Anthea	6:18:51 (33,990)	
Edwards, Adele	4:03:56 (11,428)	
Edwards, Angela S	6:15:24 (33,809)	
Edwards, Celia	4:26:38 (17,164)	
Edwards, Christine E	7:27:54 (35,205)	
Edwards, Claire M	6:50:14 (34,819)	
Edwards, Diane L	5:13:32 (28,071)	
Edwards, Elizabeth M	5:57:07 (32,839)	
Edwards, Fizzy (Felicity) G	5:16:18 (28,538)	
Edwards, Georgina L	4:26:50 (17,216)	
Edwards, Halina S	4:41:27 (21,072)	
Edwards, Helen	4:58:36 (25,294)	
Edwards, Helen	6:36:58 (34,564)	
Edwards, Jane A	4:37:42 (20,090)	
Edwards, Janet L	5:12:13 (27,842)	
Edwards, Joanne	4:39:38 (20,621)	
Edwards, Karen L	4:26:42 (17,182)	
Edwards, Linda K	4:14:53 (14,136)	
Edwards, Melissa J	5:31:37 (30,598)	
Edwards, Natalie R	3:49:15 (7,679)	
Edwards, Nicola R	3:28:55 (3,997)	
Edwards, Sally-Anne	3:59:25 (10,374)	
Edwards, Sian H	3:52:19 (8,362)	
Edwards, Siobhan E	5:10:14 (27,503)	
Edwards, Stephanie Anne	5:22:03 (29,369)	
Edwards, Tracy E	4:13:34 (13,813)	
Edwards, Vivienne A	5:21:34 (29,312)	
Edwards, Wendy E	5:47:04 (32,100)	
Edwards, Yvonne	3:52:19 (8,362)	
Edwardson, Jane A	3:52:37 (8,435)	
Edwards-Smith, Valerie	5:33:13 (30,777)	
Egan, Sharon M	6:34:49 (34,519)	
Egbulefu, Susan H	5:11:22 (27,705)	
Egeberg, Aina	5:08:08 (27,110)	
Egglestone, Christine J	3:49:29 (7,727)	
Eghbal, Media	6:52:54 (34,860)	
Egloff, Sandra J	4:46:40 (22,386)	
Egon, Annick	5:55:39 (32,737)	
Ehren, Karen L	5:44:24 (31,885)	
Ehrenreich, Carmen	5:36:17 (31,100)	
Eilerts De Haan, Carin	4:41:01 (20,965)	
Ejalu, Sheila	5:18:50 (28,947)	
Eklof, Carin	4:33:11 (18,939)	
Elbro, Kate	4:35:24 (19,522)	
Eldridge, Marianne	5:19:47 (29,069)	
Elener, Claire L	3:23:38 (3,205)	
Elisabeth, Marion-Camille	5:28:15 (30,183)	
El-Khazen, Soraya	5:33:10 (30,771)	
Elkington, Margaret H	8:27:03 (35,339)	
Ellender, Michelle A	7:05:29 (35,009)	
Ellerker, Katie K	5:05:41 (26,678)	
Ellerton, Joanne M	3:42:14 (6,255)	
Ellicott, Barbara	8:35:23 (35,343)	
Ellingford, Nicky C	5:34:39 (30,927)	
Elliott, Anouschka	5:32:29 (30,686)	
Elliott, John	3:49:56 (7,818)	
Elliott, Katrina J	6:21:14 (34,085)	
Elliott, Pauline	4:55:11 (24,499)	
Elliott, Sharon	6:20:00 (34,032)	
Elliott, Teresa	5:47:30 (32,131)	
Elliott, Vicki J	4:51:52 (23,717)	
Ellis, Alison J	5:56:59 (32,834)	
Ellis, Debbie	4:27:23 (17,362)	
Ellis, Francis	6:50:36 (34,827)	
Ellis, Irene R	6:04:29 (33,312)	
Ellis, Janine	3:40:20 (5,919)	
Ellis, Julia	4:09:39 (12,764)	
Ellis, Lucy A	5:24:10 (29,677)	
Ellis, Mary E	5:03:27 (26,275)	
Ellis, Tracy M	6:05:59 (33,387)	
Ellis-Brown, Nia M	6:05:56 (33,383)	
Ellison, Bryony	5:00:26 (25,688)	
Ellison, Corinne Elizabeth	4:41:00 (20,962)	
Ellison, Joann	4:04:00 (11,450)	
Ellison, Julia	3:36:53 (5,291)	
Ellison, Katy M	5:25:17 (29,832)	
Ellsmore, Rebecca	6:28:32 (34,371)	
Ellwood, Paula	4:43:46 (21,659)	
Elmore, Lynda A	6:15:48 (33,835)	
Elms, Liz	4:29:56 (18,077)	
Elmy, Sophie	4:55:08 (24,485)	
Elsadek, Soraya	5:52:59 (32,542)	
Elsawey, Jihanne P	4:59:30 (25,497)	
Elsdon, Katryna	7:00:46 (34,958)	
Else, Claire A	4:02:55 (11,213)	
Elson, Naomi R	4:09:37 (12,757)	
Elswood, Enya	4:37:28 (20,027)	
Eltham, Heather R	5:18:22 (28,848)	
Elvin, Jacqueline	6:10:20 (33,579)	
Elwen, Caroline	5:44:17 (31,876)	
Emblem, Lorien C	4:46:27 (22,331)	
Emerson, Deana J	3:51:50 (8,234)	
Emery, Roxanne	5:38:25 (31,319)	
Emmerson, Jane E	8:06:12 (35,321)	
Emmerson, Rachel A	4:44:16 (21,783)	
Emmert-Sealey, Rosita	5:25:01 (29,801)	
Emms, Gail E	3:47:14 (7,239)	
Emsley, Victoria L	3:28:49 (3,977)	
Emslie, Linda M	4:20:17 (15,508)	
Emson, Katy M	3:41:26 (6,108)	
Emson, Lorna	3:41:26 (6,108)	
Engin, Carmel M	6:01:11 (33,119)	
England, Daisy	5:37:33 (31,234)	
England, Maureen	5:34:31 (30,918)	
Engle, Alison	4:30:41 (18,276)	
Englefield, Maureen P	4:02:28 (11,121)	
English, Sharon	4:47:32 (22,605)	
Ennals, Philippa	5:33:48 (30,844)	
Entwistle, Jane	4:41:57 (21,191)	
Entwistle, Jean J	4:35:53 (19,648)	
Entwistle-Barstow, Leanne	4:26:34 (17,139)	
Epps, Anna	4:19:30 (15,287)	
Epsom, Joe	5:24:34 (29,743)	
Erikson, Lene	4:54:56 (24,433)	
Eriksson, Christina	5:54:17 (32,637)	
Ernest, Andrea J	4:38:15 (20,241)	
Erwood, Becky S	4:21:51 (15,911)	
Escudero, Rocio Amparo	6:08:49 (33,506)	
Eshmade, Rebecca J	5:11:55 (27,792)	
Esward, Gemma	5:59:58 (33,007)	
Etheridge, Alison I	6:15:44 (33,830)	
Etheridge, Helen C	6:15:44 (33,830)	
Etheridge, Jo L	5:38:30 (31,333)	
Etheridge, Lucinda	5:23:40 (29,613)	
Etheridge, Nicola J	4:45:13 (22,016)	

Etherington, Denise M 5:50:24 (32,369)
Euridge, Katryna G 5:00:28 (25,694)
Eusebi, Marisa 4:40:37 (20,865)
Euwe, Jacqueline 5:12:12 (27,841)
Evans, Alison J 5:07:08 (26,929)
Evans, Amanda 3:25:08 (3,412)
Evans, Amanda J 6:25:45 (34,270)
Evans, Angela M 5:49:34 (32,295)
Evans, Angharad E 6:33:58 (34,500)
Evans, Ann 5:30:17 (30,439)
Evans, Annabel 5:26:25 (29,982)
Evans, Annette 4:46:42 (22,400)
Evans, Becky V 5:17:16 (28,682)
Evans, Brenda J 5:00:41 (25,745)
Evans, Bryony A 7:17:55 (35,127)
Evans, Claire 3:57:40 (9,836)
Evans, Desmond 4:37:44 (20,101)
Evans, Eiri 4:14:58 (14,158)
Evans, Emma 5:14:29 (28,239)
Evans, Fleur L 4:35:30 (19,546)
Evans, Hannah 4:54:41 (24,382)
Evans, Harriet F 4:46:46 (22,426)
Evans, Jane C 6:31:18 (34,440)
Evans, Jenny S 4:01:25 (10,887)
Evans, Karen 4:10:19 (12,938)
Evans, Karon 7:19:12 (35,143)
Evans, Kate J 7:00:27 (34,951)
Evans, Kelly M 5:47:24 (32,126)
Evans, Kelly S 5:31:03 (30,535)
Evans, Lesley V 4:04:59 (11,651)
Evans, Lisa J 3:57:39 (9,826)
Evans, Lorraine T 3:58:08 (9,982)
Evans, Lowri A 5:35:20 (31,002)
Evans, Lucy G 6:33:08 (34,474)
Evans, Maggie E 4:50:17 (23,316)
Evans, Mandy J 3:46:57 (7,191)
Evans, Marie 3:31:47 (4,434)
Evans, Marit 4:55:53 (24,662)
Evans, Penny 6:31:06 (34,436)
Evans, Rebecca L 4:49:37 (23,155)
Evans, Rhea 4:26:17 (17,064)
Evans, Sally A 4:38:56 (20,416)
Evans, Samantha J 10:17:12 (35,364)
Evans, Sandra 5:10:16 (27,508)
Evans, Sarah Kathrine 5:11:50 (27,782)
Evans, Sarah L 5:02:20 (26,088)
Evans, Sharon M 5:23:28 (29,592)
Evans, Sioned W 4:29:48 (18,036)
Evans, Victoria A 4:58:30 (25,268)
Evans, Victoria A 5:27:33 (30,097)
Evans-Olsen, Maureen 5:39:57 (31,490)
Evelyne, Carbonne 4:43:31 (21,605)
Everall, Sarah J 4:27:54 (17,518)
Everest, Isobel A 3:42:16 (6,262)
Everitt, Melanie J 3:45:56 (6,972)
Everitt, Patricia A 5:23:31 (29,595)
Eversden, Helen M 4:36:57 (19,900)
Evershed, Sarah B 4:03:03 (11,239)
Ewens, Estelle J 4:27:22 (17,358)
Ewing, June 4:43:19 (21,554)
Exall, Annina T 4:59:55 (25,581)
Exelby, Emma J 5:30:55 (30,510)
Eynon, Marcia 5:20:20 (29,133)
Eyre, Rosalind H 4:26:23 (17,083)
Fabb, Debbie 4:55:54 (24,665)
Fabb, Lisa S 5:09:46 (27,420)
Fabianova, Marty 6:07:38 (33,469)
Fabiny, Sarah 3:48:46 (7,557)
Facer, Sarah Jane 4:53:31 (24,074)
Facey, Caroline J 5:21:30 (29,298)
Fackerell, Karon L 4:02:25 (11,108)
Fagan, Rachel E 3:10:20 (1,725)
Fagg, Kirsten S 6:03:03 (33,233)
Fair, Laila 5:58:05 (32,925)
Fairclough, Julie 5:01:01 (25,815)
Fairclough, Lisa M 3:46:36 (7,110)
Fairclough, Susan A 4:47:49 (22,675)
Fairfax, Susan G 3:32:00 (4,469)
Fairhall, Victoria 3:01:54 (1,109)
Fairhurst, Claire 7:24:40 (35,174)
Fairhurst, Helen R 7:24:40 (35,174)
Fairhurst, Victoria J 3:57:58 (9,924)
Fairlamb, Patricia A 3:33:59 (4,754)
Fairweather, Sonia 5:34:18 (30,887)
Falconer, Jenni S 3:53:16 (8,575)
Falcus, Elaine C 3:38:01 (5,495)
Falcus, Karen 4:45:43 (22,136)
Falkingham, Elizabeth 5:10:00 (27,461)
Falla, Hannah 6:25:25 (34,249)
Fallace, Lauren N 5:12:15 (27,847)
Fallon, Janine L 3:53:34 (8,640)
Fallon, Patricia A 4:40:30 (20,833)
Falloon, Nancy Clare H 4:44:48 (21,907)
Fanchie, Claire 6:33:38 (34,489)
Fani, Valeria 4:22:12 (16,002)
Fanning, Caroline A 5:08:37 (27,196)
Faraone, Maria 4:36:38 (19,826)
Farias, Georgiana 4:57:41 (25,066)
Farley, Amanda J 7:31:26 (35,230)
Farman, Michelle C 3:21:57 (3,007)
Farmer, Susanna E 6:20:26 (34,050)
Farnell, Sophie J 4:06:03 (11,893)
Farnsworth, Christine A 4:58:29 (25,263)
Farnworth, Catherine M 6:16:18 (33,858)
Farr, Kathryn A 6:04:16 (33,301)
Farrall, Ali 3:27:32 (3,783)
Farrand, Clare E 5:24:53 (29,778)
Farrand, Laura 5:26:13 (29,957)
Farrant, Ellen M 6:21:52 (34,110)
Farrell, Anne 4:17:25 (14,749)
Farrell, Emma 5:01:40 (25,945)
Farrell, Stephanie 3:22:44 (3,100)
Farrer, Allison 4:32:02 (18,646)
Farrington, Kathryn L 4:00:06 (10,572)
Farrington, Michelle 5:56:51 (32,821)
Farrow, Louise 3:52:09 (8,311)
Farthing, Jenny A 4:20:05 (15,453)
Fasolato, Donatella 5:03:20 (26,261)
Fatima, Debbaghi 4:54:35 (24,352)
Fatt, Hannah 3:47:19 (7,251)
Faulkner, Lauren 5:34:21 (30,889)
Faulkner, Lynda J 3:23:44 (3,222)
Faure, Tessa 3:44:41 (6,743)
Faure Walker, Julia F 3:52:36 (8,426)
Faust, Nicola E 3:59:56 (10,530)
Fawaz, Hana 5:24:46 (29,760)
Fawcett, Elizabeth A 4:25:21 (16,800)
Fawcett, Helen 4:15:08 (14,200)
Fawell, Andrea J 5:20:51 (29,201)
Fawke, Delphine R 5:04:31 (26,459)
Fawthorp, Angela M 4:45:56 (22,198)
Fay, Victoria J 5:25:09 (29,821)
Faye, Suzanne C 5:29:30 (30,335)
Fayolle, Chantal 4:54:14 (24,268)
Fazzino, Joanna 4:55:41 (24,610)
Fearnhead, Debbie J 6:36:15 (34,545)
Fearnley, Henrietta C 4:35:29 (19,536)
Fearnley, Louisa 4:24:33 (16,581)
Fearon, Anne 6:18:06 (33,934)
Featherstone, Catherine E 3:59:32 (10,398)
Feazey, Angela J 3:57:19 (9,712)
Fecci, Katie E 4:25:52 (16,951)
Feculak, Helen 4:30:08 (18,135)
Fee, Deirdre 4:17:07 (14,671)
Fekri, Reem F 5:03:55 (26,366)
Feldberg, Emily J 4:56:07 (24,710)
Feldman, Sandra P 7:04:23 (34,998)
Fell, Christine M 4:06:32 (11,997)
Fell, Sue 4:44:58 (21,948)
Fellows, Samantha 4:35:23 (19,518)
Felton, Jo-Ann 4:24:31 (16,573)
Felton, Judith E 4:46:37 (22,375)
Felton, Lesley S 3:56:33 (9,475)
Feminier, Chloe M 4:41:27 (21,072)
Fend, Martina 3:54:15 (8,828)
Fenelon, Patsy E 3:47:38 (7,313)
Fenn, Charlotte R 5:33:42 (30,832)
Fenn, Holly 4:41:05 (20,984)
Fennell, Alison 4:33:58 (19,145)
Fennell, Caroline L 5:53:08 (32,558)
Fenner, Christine 6:02:00 (33,171)
Fenton, Ceri 5:30:02 (30,400)
Fenton, Claire 5:40:32 (31,546)
Fenton, Lynne 5:40:55 (31,580)
Fenwick, Alison L 5:42:28 (31,718)
Fenwick, Caron L 4:39:29 (20,576)
Ferenczi, Emily A 3:03:41 (1,213)
Ferguson, Christine 3:30:04 (4,187)
Ferguson, Claire 4:37:55 (20,143)
Ferguson, Helen M 5:06:02 (26,731)
Ferguson, Sarah J 4:43:13 (21,521)
Fergusson, Karen 5:13:05 (28,001)
Fergusson, Leanne 3:29:28 (4,097)
Fern, Alison M 4:42:42 (21,388)
Fern, Lucy S 4:23:46 (16,379)
Fernandes, Ninette 4:56:05 (24,700)
Fernandez, Teresa 5:10:31 (27,552)
Ferrari, Kandy J 4:51:23 (23,585)
Ferraz, Celeste 5:14:06 (28,180)
Ferreira, Natalina D 5:51:24 (32,438)
Ferris, Anne 5:25:32 (29,866)
Ferris, Nancy 3:48:03 (7,413)
Ferry, Emma 3:55:53 (9,282)
Fertil, Gaelle 4:57:36 (25,052)
Fetterroll, Wendy C 5:33:30 (30,803)
Fewkes, Helen 5:11:27 (27,719)
Field, Catherine N 5:12:46 (27,939)
Field, Jane M 3:41:04 (6,039)
Field, Julie A 3:36:32 (5,241)
Field, Julie A 5:37:05 (31,185)
Field, Vanessa K 4:51:55 (23,737)
Fields, Anthanette 3:48:10 (7,438)
Figes, Wendy K 4:01:29 (10,909)
Figg, Debra A 5:05:32 (26,649)
Filby, Melissa P 5:53:50 (32,607)
Fildes, Poppy J 4:44:40 (21,879)
Filer, Sara-Marie 4:52:52 (23,940)
Finch, Katy A 3:24:44 (3,373)
Fincham, Sally J 4:16:36 (14,553)
Fincken, Kelly M 6:56:49 (34,917)
Findlay, Celia A 3:31:08 (4,349)
Findlay, Claire 5:24:50 (29,772)
Findon, Elaine J 4:37:01 (19,922)
Finill, Joanna M 5:08:21 (27,151)
Finlay, Claire L 4:19:59 (15,425)
Finlay, Helen A 5:32:19 (30,672)
Finn, Samantha 3:45:45 (6,937)
Finnegan, Michelle 6:41:42 (34,657)
Finney, Amanda L 3:19:17 (2,647)
Fioretti, Mariaassunta 4:08:56 (12,600)
Firmager, Carolyn 3:37:54 (5,473)
Firman, Sarah-Jane 4:26:51 (17,222)
Firmin, Anna 5:47:46 (32,151)
Firth, Chris 5:01:16 (25,872)
Firth, Mel 5:29:39 (30,353)
Fischer, Carmen 4:23:47 (16,382)
Fish, Emma J 4:59:59 (25,594)
Fisher, Alison J 4:31:27 (18,487)
Fisher, Anika J 3:58:41 (10,155)
Fisher, Ann Louise 4:56:35 (24,825)
Fisher, Chloe L 4:03:49 (11,398)
Fisher, Denise C 7:14:17 (35,099)
Fisher, Heather R 3:51:09 (8,085)
Fisher, Justine S 6:02:20 (33,193)
Fisher, Laura J 4:32:58 (18,888)
Fisher, Lisa S 5:32:39 (30,714)
Fisher, Nancy 3:48:58 (7,610)
Fisher, Rachel J 3:32:10 (4,497)
Fisher, Rebecca C 5:31:01 (30,530)
Fisher, Victoria J 3:58:25 (10,071)
Fishwick, Rachael L 4:12:16 (13,459)
Fisk, Selena M 6:25:10 (34,235)
Fitchie, Catherine 6:59:07 (34,937)
Fitzgerald, Amanda H 6:37:27 (34,580)
Fitzgerald, Amy-Lucy 4:48:23 (22,825)
Fitzgerald, Denise 3:37:51 (5,465)
Fitzgerald, Evelynn M 4:35:12 (19,465)
Fitzgerald, Lindsay A 3:38:31 (5,594)
Fitzgerald, Lucy A 5:54:32 (32,651)
Fitzgerald, Sarah A 4:39:17 (20,513)
Fitzgerald Devine, Karen 4:38:41 (20,347)
Fitzhugh, Laura J 4:56:24 (24,774)
Fitzpatrick, Alexandra J 5:17:58 (28,788)
Flanagan, Catherine M 5:32:35 (30,701)
Flanagan, Helen M 5:21:11 (29,254)
Flannery, Clare 3:23:35 (3,202)
Flavell, Margaret A 5:02:18 (26,081)
Flavell, Sophie G 5:15:07 (28,338)
Flavell-Raybone, Jan 4:30:32 (18,240)

Fleck, Polly A 5:29:14 (30,303)
Fleckney, Rebecca G 4:38:14 (20,238)
Fleet, Catherine J 4:13:40 (13,840)
Fleischman, Charmaine 3:37:03 (5,330)
Fleming, Alison 6:16:51 (33,878)
Fleming, Clare L 3:22:01 (3,015)
Fleming, Dyan 4:18:08 (14,929)
Fleming, Kathryn E 6:04:36 (33,318)
Fleming, Louise E 4:02:30 (11,126)
Fleming, Natalie J 3:55:35 (9,183)
Fletcher, Dawn 3:58:14 (10,023)
Fletcher, Elizabeth 5:24:41 (29,752)
Fletcher, Jacqueline S 4:11:46 (13,328)
Fletcher, Jill 4:16:12 (14,448)
Fletcher, Johanna 2:57:52 (826)
Fletcher, Natalie J 5:44:23 (31,883)
Fletcher, Rachael 4:40:39 (20,876)
Fletcher, Samantha J 3:42:44 (6,363)
Fletcher, Timothy G 4:08:06 (12,390)
Flew, Elizabeth J 4:50:37 (23,400)
Flexer, Susannah 4:01:15 (10,847)
Flint, Joanna 5:08:52 (27,245)
Flockhart, Kelly 5:29:44 (30,365)
Flood, Jane L 7:21:10 (35,157)
Flood, Kelly T 4:25:07 (16,739)
Florence, Anne 4:31:44 (18,560)
Flower, Rachel L 4:52:41 (23,903)
Floyd, Helena M 6:00:53 (33,106)
Flury, Joanna C 3:32:43 (4,575)
Flynn, Kirsty L 5:09:57 (27,446)
Flynn, Una M 3:57:39 (9,826)
Flynn, Victoria A 5:32:49 (30,738)
Foad, Deborah J 6:27:17 (34,337)
Foden, Jo M 4:25:02 (16,719)
Fogarty, Helen M 3:54:04 (8,772)
Foiera, Patrizia 5:07:52 (27,072)
Foley, Felicity 4:11:25 (13,228)
Foley, Isabel M 4:33:08 (18,928)
Follis, Sarah E 4:49:19 (23,058)
Fong, Jeanne 4:00:10 (10,587)
Fong, Lorraine S 4:58:47 (25,335)
Fong, Sophia S 4:23:40 (16,355)
Fonnereau, Julia V 3:49:36 (7,747)
Fontaine, Marie 3:59:18 (10,335)
Fooks, Helen L 5:30:29 (30,460)
Foot, Kerryn 4:08:19 (12,459)
Foote, Judy 6:03:01 (33,229)
Forbes, Catrin 4:49:06 (22,998)
Forbes, Daniela J 4:26:58 (17,251)
Forbes, Stephanie Joanne 5:45:37 (31,990)
Forbes, Véronique 4:21:14 (15,753)
Ford, Denise Michelle 3:52:29 (8,403)
Ford, Jan 6:47:37 (34,760)
Ford, Jodie L 6:16:15 (33,853)
Ford, Kim M 4:42:30 (21,334)
Ford, Shelly A 6:10:13 (33,573)
Fordham, Julia Z 3:49:32 (7,736)
Fordham, Lindsey J 4:26:29 (17,111)
Fordyce, Paula A 7:24:09 (35,170)
Foreman, Sarah 4:50:30 (23,371)
Forman, Julia R 4:34:36 (19,288)
Formosa, Sarah C 4:47:53 (22,701)
Forrest, Maureen I 6:25:53 (34,272)
Forrest, Sarah M 5:33:03 (30,760)
Forrester, Claire 5:31:41 (30,603)
Forrest-Jones, Emillie 4:47:25 (22,582)
Forrow, Sarah E 4:53:58 (24,216)
Forsell, Lena 5:59:17 (33,005)
Forster, Kim 4:17:28 (14,761)
Forster, Lisa M 3:58:48 (10,194)
Forte, Liz A 5:25:45 (29,898)
Fortescue, Melanie L 4:35:23 (19,518)
Fortunova, Miroslava 4:07:22 (12,205)
Fosbury, Clare F 4:22:39 (16,111)
Foscoe, Ceri F 4:44:40 (21,879)
Fosker, Denise J 4:18:05 (14,912)
Foskett, Laura 6:16:36 (33,869)
Fossey, Janine E 6:00:07 (33,057)
Foster, Emily A 4:45:33 (22,090)
Foster, Hannah Elisabeth 5:12:08 (27,828)
Foster, Jackie 5:38:34 (31,340)
Foster, Joanne 5:19:56 (29,087)
Foster, Joanne L 4:37:28 (20,027)
Foster, Lindsay Catrina 4:15:34 (14,300)
Foster, Louise J 3:59:09 (10,297)
Foster, Robert A 5:04:11 (26,411)
Foster, Stephanie 5:04:52 (26,518)
Foster, Victoria R 4:45:34 (22,097)
Foulds, Annie 4:00:03 (10,557)
Fountain, Wendy A 5:35:14 (30,989)
Fourie, Susan 3:24:03 (3,270)
Fournier, Dawn 5:21:17 (29,266)
Fouweather, Marilyn G 6:31:33 (34,444)
Fovargue, Fiona A 7:27:18 (35,200)
Fowler, Anna E 4:41:35 (21,115)
Fowler, Claire 3:29:36 (4,116)
Fowler, Kathryn A 4:53:21 (24,046)
Fowler, Lucy E 6:08:04 (33,485)
Fowler, Natasha 6:25:42 (34,267)
Fowler, Penelope R 5:09:16 (27,321)
Fowler, Sarah L 5:20:59 (29,216)
Fowler, Surinder K 5:06:21 (26,781)
Fox, Alison M 6:20:19 (34,045)
Fox, Amanda C 5:21:12 (29,257)
Fox, Elle A 4:54:33 (24,345)
Fox, Jane E 4:41:24 (21,055)
Fox, Stephanie F 5:11:21 (27,702)
Fox, Sue 4:43:19 (21,554)
Fox-Perry, Jane M 6:19:36 (34,019)
Foy, Emily C 4:19:47 (15,368)
Foyster, Mandy L 3:55:16 (9,102)
Fraley, Polly K 4:31:22 (18,462)
Frampton, Kimberley J 3:56:19 (9,399)
Frampton, Lenni A 5:50:33 (32,384)
Francine, Blanc 4:03:47 (11,386)
Francis, Ann M 5:20:14 (29,120)
Francis, Anna 3:25:45 (3,494)
Francis, Carly J 4:17:32 (14,776)
Francis, Donna M 5:51:27 (32,443)
Francis, Jade Candice 4:37:58 (20,159)
Francis, Laura E 4:59:23 (25,468)
Francis, Laura L 4:24:37 (16,595)
Francis, Sandra C 6:46:00 (34,720)
Francis, Sarah L 5:32:25 (30,676)
Francis, Victoria A 3:59:57 (10,537)
François, Kat 5:23:37 (29,603)
Françoise, Daney De Marcillac 3:30:52 (4,305)
Françoise, Pfeuty 4:42:24 (21,302)
Frank, Christine J 3:57:21 (9,729)
Frank, Flora 6:01:39 (33,150)
Franklin, Sarah L 4:45:37 (22,109)
Franks, Catherine 4:35:42 (19,599)
Franks, Helen C 4:28:21 (17,660)
Franqueira, Bianca 5:58:49 (32,980)
Franz, Johanna 4:31:26 (18,484)
Fraser, Claire 5:16:00 (28,499)
Fraser, Katie E 4:33:01 (18,901)
Fraser, Liz 4:14:30 (14,026)
Fraser, Nadine M 4:21:37 (15,849)
Fraser, Paula L 5:28:53 (30,259)
Fraser, Rose 4:44:46 (21,903)
Fraser, Tom 5:32:43 (30,727)
Fraser-Armstrong, Annie 5:55:25 (32,718)
Fravigar-Roots, Dawn 4:44:23 (21,817)
Frazer, Donna Michelle 3:45:59 (6,984)
Freak, Jane 6:20:02 (34,034)
Freeland, Julie Rosemarie 4:32:36 (18,789)
Freeman, Alison J 5:51:51 (32,473)
Freeman, Anne-Marie 5:39:56 (31,487)
Freeman, Elaine T 6:27:21 (34,340)
Freeman, Laura J 5:59:52 (33,042)
Freeman, Sylvia C 5:34:42 (30,938)
Freeman-Phillips, Janice 5:11:25 (27,713)
Freemantle, Lucy A 4:25:15 (16,775)
Freer, Lisa J 5:51:12 (32,430)
Freeston, Deborah M 4:15:15 (14,222)
French, Amy F 6:53:44 (34,875)
French, Annette 4:23:00 (16,184)
French, Emma J 6:20:21 (34,047)
French, Georgina B 4:24:12 (16,497)
French, Margaret A 4:26:46 (17,199)
French, Michelle 3:53:14 (8,568)
French, Michelle L 6:28:16 (34,365)
French, Sheila C 5:17:53 (28,775)
French, Stephanie J 3:36:07 (5,175)
Fresco, Chantal 5:18:39 (28,904)
Freshwater, Dawn S 5:00:29 (25,697)
Friars, Claire 6:25:21 (34,246)
Friberg, Helle 4:45:53 (22,186)
Fricker, Elizabeth J 6:55:17 (34,899)
Fricker, Joanne L 4:29:17 (17,919)
Friedman, Laura 4:54:56 (24,433)
Friesen, Trina L 4:22:15 (16,011)
Frietman, Clare L 5:30:57 (30,519)
Friggnes, Jennifer A 5:40:21 (31,528)
Frith, Emma 5:01:06 (25,842)
Frith, Lynne 4:32:44 (18,826)
Fritz, Sara 7:44:39 (35,278)
Froggatt, Cindy 5:25:23 (29,841)
Frost, Amy 4:41:16 (21,030)
Frost, Charlotte 3:58:54 (10,224)
Frost, Michelle L 6:35:15 (34,527)
Frost, Shelley A 6:23:15 (34,162)
Frost, Sophie C 5:12:04 (27,813)
Frost, Tamara 5:19:39 (29,056)
Frost, Tara L 5:43:30 (31,820)
Frost, Tracey 4:55:12 (24,506)
Froud, Melina 6:31:11 (34,439)
Fry, Gillian 4:22:25 (16,057)
Fry, Jacqui 3:29:04 (4,013)
Fry, Samantha Louise 3:54:44 (8,954)
Fryer, Natalie L 3:27:25 (3,752)
Fryer, Paula 5:25:08 (29,816)
Fuller, Frances 5:34:14 (30,882)
Fuller, Karen A 5:03:01 (26,213)
Fuller, Stacey Emma 4:53:16 (24,038)
Fuller, Sue 4:44:24 (21,821)
Fullwood, Lesley J 5:04:56 (26,530)
Fullylove, Roz J 4:56:14 (24,737)
Fulton, Alexandra A 4:40:53 (20,936)
Furbank, Valerie A 5:46:15 (32,032)
Furlong, Julie E 4:19:57 (15,408)
Furlong, Paula M 5:56:50 (32,819)
Furness, Sara J 5:54:21 (32,642)
Furzer, Penny 4:17:24 (14,742)
Fyfe, Michelle 4:53:26 (24,060)
Fynney, Catherine M 4:17:17 (14,712)
Gabb, Ania M 4:14:03 (13,919)
Gabbarelli, Jennifer R 4:11:14 (13,168)
Gadd, Patricia S 5:29:06 (30,284)
Gaddes, Deborah M 5:35:01 (30,972)
Gaiger, Zoe A 4:54:48 (24,408)
Galbraith, Helen L 3:42:05 (6,230)
Galda, April 4:14:06 (13,931)
Gale, Nicola 5:42:49 (31,751)
Galea, Lauren 4:50:16 (23,308)
Gallagher, Elaine 5:05:13 (26,595)
Gallagher, Lyndsey 5:18:10 (28,812)
Gallagher, Sarah E 6:30:54 (34,432)
Gallagher, Tess M 4:06:05 (11,897)
Gallanagh, Anne M 5:02:03 (26,033)
Gallantry, Karen 4:44:25 (21,824)
Galleway, Julia 5:06:00 (26,726)
Galley, Louise T 3:54:01 (8,760)
Gallichan, Sharon 4:09:32 (12,732)
Gallimore, Diane 3:39:45 (5,799)
Gallo, Sally L 4:41:32 (21,098)
Galloway, Alison 4:33:15 (18,959)
Galloway, Clare S 4:21:10 (15,733)
Galloway, Joanne C 4:35:59 (19,675)
Galloway, Louise J 5:30:55 (30,510)
Galloway, Sheila 4:37:48 (20,120)
Galloway-Hale, Kate J 6:02:41 (33,209)
Galpin, Karen M 3:57:49 (9,880)
Galster, Cordula 3:27:29 (3,771)
Galvin, Sophia E 4:16:23 (14,495)
Gambold, Susie J 4:27:15 (17,325)
Gambrill, Julie 4:42:05 (21,220)
Gambrill, Karen 4:43:58 (21,711)
Gamez, Kate S 5:07:23 (26,982)
Gammage, Becky 5:05:56 (26,718)
Ganczakowski, Helena L 3:47:09 (7,228)
Gandiya, Tariro N 5:24:17 (29,697)
Ganiel-O'Neill, Gladys 2:47:53 (389)
Gannon, Elizabeth J 3:18:59 (2,616)
Ganose, Beverley A 3:29:20 (4,074)
Gappy, Tina L 3:30:11 (4,205)
Garby, Mette 4:16:22 (14,486)
García Gonzales, Pamela 5:49:20 (32,280)

Garden, Jennifer A....4:29:48 (18,036)
Gardener, Tracy....5:11:55 (27,792)
Gardiner, Di....5:03:55 (26,366)
Gardiner, Tina....5:48:37 (32,230)
Gardner, Angela J....5:28:33 (30,214)
Gardner, Hannah J....5:05:52 (26,708)
Gardner, Jo E....7:40:55 (35,273)
Gardner, Julie A....4:34:58 (19,400)
Gardner, Kate E....4:31:16 (18,419)
Gardner, Michelle....4:46:06 (22,227)
Gardner-Hall, Sarah J....5:14:16 (28,202)
Garey, Lynne V....4:45:14 (22,022)
Garge, Nicola R....4:06:25 (11,975)
Garland, Sarah....6:34:42 (34,516)
Garner, Angela....7:04:06 (34,996)
Garner, Jane S....6:08:42 (33,504)
Garner, Julie A....4:31:15 (18,416)
Garner, Kerry A....4:58:54 (25,362)
Garner, Susan L....4:23:50 (16,395)
Garnett, Donna....5:21:35 (29,315)
Garnett, Kathleen....5:15:00 (28,320)
Garnham, Sally....5:35:58 (31,075)
Garrard, Katharyn A....5:10:35 (27,565)
Garrett, Barbara E....4:49:01 (22,978)
Garrett, Sarah A....4:36:19 (19,742)
Garrett, Sarah L....4:17:31 (14,774)
Garrigan, Keira B....3:58:23 (10,065)
Garrod, Rachel E....4:25:38 (16,885)
Garside, Catherine E....6:15:49 (33,836)
Garside, Heather....5:23:54 (29,634)
Garside, Theresa M....4:35:31 (19,552)
Garsleitner, Carmen-Ina....4:29:27 (17,960)
Garth, Jennifer....4:14:56 (14,149)
Garth, Louise E....4:10:03 (12,864)
Garth, Susanne Marie Rose....4:36:09 (19,712)
Garwood, Debbie M....4:57:03 (24,938)
Garwood, Samantha J....4:48:55 (22,949)
Gash, Michelle....4:40:30 (20,833)
Gashe, Victoria J....3:55:48 (9,263)
Gaskell, Sophie....3:21:49 (2,985)
Gaskill, Claire L....3:32:44 (4,578)
Gasking, Mireille F....5:03:09 (26,227)
Gasper, Amy V....4:22:39 (16,111)
Gates, Caroline E....5:28:24 (30,202)
Gates, Catherine....5:49:01 (32,251)
Gates, Nicol L....5:25:29 (29,856)
Gatesman, Deborah....4:24:15 (16,511)
Gatzweiler, Iris....5:03:09 (26,227)
Gaudie, Jane M....5:51:35 (32,456)
Gault, Sarah J....3:59:51 (10,508)
Gault, Stephanie L....4:00:33 (10,687)
Gaunt, Alison V....5:08:14 (27,132)
Gaunt, Catherine Anne....3:48:20 (7,475)
Gavin, Eleanor Z....6:45:40 (34,717)
Gavrilloff, Suzie....4:23:32 (16,323)
Gay, Annie C....5:31:55 (30,629)
Gaze, Wendy....6:19:03 (33,998)
Gazzard, Deborah L....5:10:29 (27,545)
Gebbett, Colette....4:32:32 (18,762)
Gebbett, Emily S....5:57:34 (32,881)
Gee, Samantha H....5:08:23 (27,157)
Gee, Sarah R....2:45:35 (324)
Geer, Betty....7:25:56 (35,184)
Geering, Sarah L....6:26:53 (34,315)
Geeson-Orsgood, Sarah E....4:27:31 (17,395)
Gehlhausen, Savanna D....4:37:59 (20,161)
Geier, Marlies....5:45:28 (31,969)
Geisler, Katrin....4:55:23 (24,549)
Gelder, Emily J....3:04:34 (1,270)
Gemmell, Claire M....3:11:27 (1,819)
Gemmill, Joanna C....4:09:10 (12,652)
Gent, Jennifer A....7:24:40 (35,174)
George, Tracey D....5:31:54 (30,626)
Georgeson, Christina....4:28:09 (17,593)
Georghiou, Jane....3:28:53 (3,989)
Gerber, Roz H....5:35:40 (31,038)
German, Sarah L....7:11:30 (35,071)
Gerono, Jane Stewart....4:49:03 (22,985)
Gerrard, Nicola J....5:09:43 (27,405)
Gerreli, Juliet A....5:33:48 (30,844)
Gershon, Anneka L....4:12:17 (13,464)
Gething, Nichola....3:36:14 (5,195)
Gettins, Lucy A....3:17:13 (2,455)
Ghadiri, Nousheh....4:01:32 (10,926)
Gibbins, Caroline E....4:29:40 (18,008)
Gibbon, Lisa....4:38:33 (20,311)
Gibbons, Adelle L....7:04:53 (35,003)
Gibbons, Carla....3:42:24 (6,282)
Gibbons, Helen M....4:42:41 (21,381)
Gibbs, Elaine R....4:39:39 (20,627)
Gibbs, Jennifer EE....4:44:21 (21,805)
Gibbs, Victoria L....4:38:31 (20,303)
Gibson, Caroline J....4:36:23 (19,766)
Gibson, Deborah C....4:20:41 (15,596)
Gibson, Heather M....5:14:49 (28,285)
Gibson, Kate L....5:20:15 (29,121)
Gibson, Katy L....5:02:35 (26,134)
Gibson, Louise....4:41:09 (20,995)
Gibson, Lucia E....3:43:10 (6,463)
Gibson, Ruth C....4:31:51 (18,592)
Gibson, Vix....6:22:00 (34,113)
Giddings, Helen J....4:22:18 (16,023)
Gidney, Michelle A....5:28:05 (30,158)
Gilbert, Christina C....5:51:06 (32,422)
Gilbert, Kathryn....4:21:07 (15,721)
Gilbert, Sally A....3:05:26 (1,330)
Gilbride, Caroline....4:36:34 (19,808)
Gilchrist, Helen L....3:55:02 (9,032)
Gilchrist, Joanna....3:30:57 (4,320)
Gilchrist, Sam....3:54:35 (8,914)
Gilderdale, Jeanette A....6:35:17 (34,529)
Giles, Alexandra C....6:32:52 (34,469)
Giles, Della....3:34:45 (4,916)
Giles, Emilie....3:19:09 (2,632)
Giles, Judy N....8:34:38 (35,342)
Giles, Melanie R....4:57:20 (24,992)
Giles, Vikki....6:37:05 (34,569)
Gilham, Wendy A....4:26:04 (17,002)
Gilkes, Polly D....4:00:29 (10,664)
Gill, Anna....4:32:43 (18,819)
Gill, Ellie....5:36:43 (31,148)
Gill, Jennifer....5:16:42 (28,600)
Gill, Jo C....4:18:41 (15,077)
Gill, Lisa....5:01:34 (25,927)
Gill, Marie E....4:37:18 (19,984)
Gill, Nicola....5:57:52 (32,901)
Gill, Susannah Cordelia....3:34:47 (4,925)
Gill, Victoria L....2:54:44 (644)
Gillam, Sally E....4:10:43 (13,044)
Gillan, Pauline P....5:47:05 (32,103)
Gillen, Linda M....3:56:20 (9,406)
Gillespie, Kate Louisa....4:51:11 (23,535)
Gillie, Shaunna....6:50:01 (34,813)
Gillies, Alison....4:11:27 (13,242)
Gillies, Ruth F....3:20:23 (2,810)
Gillmore, Kirsty E....3:38:37 (5,609)
Gillon, Louisa....5:19:20 (29,014)
Gillow, Marie A....5:55:32 (32,730)
Gilly, Virginie....4:11:37 (13,292)
Gilman, Natalie....5:07:16 (26,955)
Gilmour, Lydnsey....4:02:53 (11,206)
Gilson, Helen R....4:56:53 (24,906)
Gina, Gouaux....5:02:00 (26,018)
Gingell, Clarissa C....4:26:08 (17,020)
Ginger, Tracey M....4:34:41 (19,314)
Girvan, Anita C....4:07:44 (12,295)
Gisby, Amanda V....7:06:20 (35,021)
Gittos, Hannah....5:30:06 (30,411)
Gladwell, Katharyn....4:54:21 (24,302)
Gladwin, Karen....4:51:32 (23,631)
Glassup, Michele....5:33:32 (30,807)
Gledhill, Emma K....4:36:35 (19,813)
Gledhill, Rachael C....5:46:27 (32,045)
Gleeson, Cassie....4:20:04 (15,446)
Gleeson, Julia M....3:41:21 (6,098)
Glockler, Sarah....4:41:43 (21,144)
Glover, Elaine....4:29:50 (18,048)
Glover, Margaret A....4:22:01 (15,944)
Glover, Nicola J....4:19:16 (15,226)
Glover, Rachel S....3:46:20 (7,048)
Glover, Rikki Marie....4:36:49 (19,870)
Glyde, Sarah....4:26:00 (16,990)
Godber, Amanda L....4:49:48 (23,199)
Godber, Charlotte J....4:21:24 (15,785)
Godber, Emma J....4:12:00 (13,387)
Goddard, Joanne L....6:30:08 (34,415)
Godden, Emily R....4:19:37 (15,320)
Godel, Linda....5:29:33 (30,342)
Godfrey, Joanne E....4:54:15 (24,273)
Godfrey, Rebecca....4:25:21 (16,800)
Godfrey, Vicky....4:48:47 (22,920)
Godfrey, Victoria R....4:13:20 (13,760)
Godoliffe, Katie....5:21:52 (29,355)
Godwin, Claire....5:24:21 (29,711)
Godwin, Lisa M....3:54:10 (8,804)
Godwin, Lucy C....4:36:49 (19,870)
Godwin-Brown, Alex B....5:16:51 (28,624)
Goel, Kerry....4:26:33 (17,130)
Golach, Verena....3:56:38 (9,511)
Golder, Vicky....5:17:01 (28,639)
Goldfinch, Michelle....5:00:25 (25,680)
Goldie, Clare M....5:40:33 (31,548)
Golding, Carol L....4:03:30 (11,334)
Golding, Nicola....4:49:14 (23,031)
Goldring, Shelly....4:23:47 (16,382)
Goldsack, Elizabeth A....4:19:12 (15,211)
Goldsmith, Joanne....3:59:51 (10,508)
Goldsmith, Stephanie....4:57:47 (25,083)
Goldthorpe, Helen J....4:25:55 (16,965)
Golland, Kayti....4:00:32 (10,680)
Gomes, Dawn R....4:18:22 (14,980)
Gomme, Sarah V....5:06:52 (26,879)
Gompertz, Valerie....6:05:00 (33,338)
Goncalves, Anna....5:01:42 (25,951)
Gonzales, Norma....4:37:09 (19,954)
Gonzales, Rita V....5:21:05 (29,234)
Gonzales, Vanessa L....5:06:03 (26,734)
Gooch, Zoe M....5:07:43 (27,045)
Good, Esther Paula....3:48:50 (7,580)
Good, Libby....5:17:12 (28,673)
Goodacre, Christine E....6:39:38 (34,622)
Goodall, Greta....5:50:40 (32,392)
Goodall, Kelly A....4:40:14 (20,781)
Goodall, Rachael J....4:29:55 (18,072)
Goode, Sally R....5:37:32 (31,231)
Goode, Sarah-Jane....6:34:59 (34,522)
Gooderham, Emma L....2:52:12 (532)
Goodfellow, Andrea....5:08:57 (27,261)
Goodliffe, May B....4:38:00 (20,165)
Goodliffe, Penny R....6:56:33 (34,914)
Goodman, Emily L....5:59:16 (33,003)
Goodman, Emma S....5:40:56 (31,582)
Goodman, Madeline....4:36:05 (19,698)
Goodman, Naomi L....5:13:26 (28,052)
Goodman, Victoria E....5:54:33 (32,654)
Goodram, Claire R....4:53:32 (24,083)
Goodridge, Nicola J....4:24:06 (16,471)
Goodridge, Shirley....4:37:24 (20,009)
Goodsell, Clare L....4:22:13 (16,006)
Goodsell, Jackie A....5:06:47 (26,865)
Goodwin, Denise E....5:34:31 (30,918)
Goodwin, Gillian F....5:15:35 (28,435)
Goodwin, Julie....4:39:34 (20,602)
Goodwin, Katherine Frances....5:26:18 (29,967)
Goodwin, Margaret J....3:46:06 (7,003)
Goodwin, Nicola C....4:08:18 (12,454)
Goodwin, Sandra M....3:50:12 (7,881)
Goodwin, Vicki H....3:27:22 (3,744)
Goodwin, Vivien C....4:37:18 (19,984)
Goorney, Hilary R....5:06:52 (26,879)
Goorney, Joanna M....3:23:59 (3,257)
Goosey, Caitlin S....4:47:03 (22,498)
Gopalakrishnan, Gayatri....5:16:47 (28,617)
Gordon, Alexandra J....4:29:01 (17,834)
Gordon, Anna C....4:37:54 (20,141)
Gordon, Claire....2:59:38 (969)
Gordon, Elizabeth J....5:37:44 (31,250)
Gordon, Genevieve....6:10:02 (33,564)
Gordon, Helen E....5:08:33 (27,185)
Gordon, Julie M....3:46:00 (6,986)
Gordon, Lisa J....4:28:08 (17,587)
Gore, Cristi....4:31:03 (18,370)
Gore, Fiona....5:50:47 (32,397)
Gore, Kate....4:57:53 (25,104)
Gorga, Cheryl E....4:51:04 (23,505)
Gorman, Barbara....6:09:33 (33,535)
Gorman, Clare D....4:59:28 (25,488)
Gormley, Katie A....4:22:59 (16,181)
Gornall, Helen....4:59:11 (25,430)

Gornall, Lisa 4:09:30 (12,719)
Gornall, Marie J 4:39:25 (20,558)
Gorst, Tammy M 6:25:20 (34,245)
Goscomb, Glenda 3:51:19 (8,125)
Goslett, Harriet J 4:26:38 (17,164)
Gosling, Fiona A 4:37:28 (20,027)
Gosling, Rachel E 5:16:45 (28,610)
Gosney, Laura 5:18:50 (28,947)
Goss, Hayley 3:55:19 (9,112)
Goss, Jill 3:43:02 (6,423)
Gotink, Esther H 5:47:10 (32,109)
Gough, Pip 4:29:00 (17,829)
Gough, Sharon 5:45:09 (31,938)
Gough, Teresa 5:16:34 (28,573)
Gould, Chloe A 3:52:02 (8,282)
Gould, Kathryn J 5:53:36 (32,592)
Gould, Sarah H 4:28:37 (17,730)
Gouldthorpe, Anne 5:24:09 (29,674)
Gourlay, Gill L 4:38:48 (20,378)
Gourves, Raphaelle 4:50:59 (23,483)
Gove, Sarah J 4:15:28 (14,275)
Gow, Jane E 5:18:21 (28,846)
Gow, Kim 5:25:20 (29,836)
Gow, Neil 3:46:16 (7,032)
Gower, Katy E 3:49:14 (7,672)
Gowing, Anne M 4:23:26 (16,290)
Graber, Carolyne 7:51:57 (35,295)
Gracey, Sarah M 4:54:33 (24,345)
Grady, Kerry 4:30:12 (18,151)
Grady, Sarah J 3:27:44 (3,816)
Grafton-Green, Charlotte 5:12:53 (27,964)
Graham, Alison M 4:42:27 (21,313)
Graham, Caroline A 4:44:31 (21,840)
Graham, Christine 5:06:14 (26,768)
Graham, Hannah 5:04:30 (26,456)
Graham, Julie E 4:09:48 (12,803)
Graham, Kerry L 4:39:47 (20,666)
Graham, Maria 5:17:53 (28,775)
Graham, Martine E 3:55:33 (9,171)
Graham, Michelle 6:14:38 (33,772)
Graham, Michelle A 4:38:50 (20,384)
Graham, Nicky J 5:00:50 (25,771)
Graham, Polly 5:42:17 (31,702)
Graham, S 4:15:23 (14,251)
Graham, Susan W 5:58:39 (32,970)
Graham-Dobson, Fiona 4:51:43 (23,679)
Graham-Enock, Camilla A 4:33:36 (19,052)
Grahamslaw, Margaret 5:09:26 (27,353)
Grainger, Catherine T 4:47:42 (22,653)
Grainger, Diana 5:58:09 (32,930)
Grainger, Joanne M 5:01:02 (25,825)
Grainger, Suzanne E 5:17:03 (28,647)
Grainger (née Williams),
Carolyn N 3:31:05 (4,341)
Granger, Dawn E 6:14:19 (33,757)
Grannell, Lena 4:41:10 (20,998)
Grant, Anita M 5:04:39 (26,485)
Grant, Jane P 4:20:53 (15,657)
Grant, Lorraine D 4:30:30 (18,228)
Grant, Lorraine M 5:25:43 (29,894)
Grant, Pamela C 4:03:31 (11,340)
Grant, Samantha E 4:44:37 (21,861)
Grant, Sarah 3:59:08 (10,290)
Grant, Sophie A 3:23:47 (3,229)
Grant, Virginia 3:41:25 (6,104)
Gration, Judith 3:18:02 (2,532)
Gratrick, Emma R 4:19:45 (15,357)
Grattage, Louise M 5:18:49 (28,938)
Grattidge, Charlotte 4:46:59 (22,478)
Gratz, Katharina 3:34:59 (4,955)
Gravell, Rhiannon M 4:17:35 (14,790)
Graves, Alison C 4:58:16 (25,206)
Graves, Karen J 4:13:09 (13,695)
Graviles, Alanah L 5:48:25 (32,209)
Grawehr, Cezanne M 5:56:51 (32,821)
Gray, Abigail J 5:30:10 (30,427)
Gray, Anna S 4:53:42 (24,138)
Gray, Deborah I 3:07:42 (1,501)
Gray, Jenny F 3:22:52 (3,115)
Gray, Karen 4:34:29 (19,257)
Gray, Karen A 5:29:29 (30,328)
Gray, Katherine E 4:19:48 (15,371)
Gray, Lauren 5:38:08 (31,290)
Gray, Lorraine S 5:05:42 (26,682)
Gray, Louise B 5:04:26 (26,445)
Gray, Margaret L 6:20:50 (34,062)
Gray, Marian B 4:55:46 (24,628)
Gray, Natalie 4:24:17 (16,522)
Gray, Pamela V 5:10:49 (27,604)
Gray, Sally M 3:20:15 (2,792)
Gray, Sam L 5:10:11 (27,493)
Gray, Sam L 6:47:06 (34,744)
Gray, Sara-Jane E 6:54:52 (34,892)
Gray, Vivienne R 6:37:20 (34,576)
Grayson, Gillian M 5:43:04 (31,778)
Greaney, Lisa 3:56:48 (9,569)
Greatorex-Day, Suzanne L 3:42:07 (6,237)
Greatrix, Emma L 3:30:47 (4,296)
Greaves, Kate 5:10:49 (27,604)
Greeley-Ward, Loretta 4:29:17 (17,919)
Green, Aleksandra 5:09:05 (27,287)
Green, Alison 5:34:38 (30,924)
Green, Amy Alexandra 5:08:52 (27,245)
Green, Amy K 3:12:51 (1,981)
Green, Anna 5:08:13 (27,127)
Green, Barbara 5:38:45 (31,363)
Green, Beth 4:56:39 (24,843)
Green, Carol M 4:51:58 (23,746)
Green, Carole M 5:08:37 (27,196)
Green, Charlotte E 4:57:58 (25,132)
Green, Chloe E 6:06:57 (33,434)
Green, Diana M 6:38:20 (34,597)
Green, Emma Louise 5:55:55 (32,757)
Green, Fiona J 4:20:54 (15,662)
Green, Francesca H 3:41:40 (6,142)
Green, Gail 4:32:14 (18,689)
Green, Hannah 4:43:24 (21,575)
Green, Helena M 5:16:40 (28,590)
Green, Janet E 4:06:37 (12,026)
Green, Jemma L 5:15:33 (28,427)
Green, Kylie 4:06:18 (11,948)
Green, Linda 6:28:26 (34,368)
Green, Nicola G 3:08:07 (1,534)
Green, Pauline M 4:14:54 (14,140)
Green, Philippa A 4:29:45 (18,025)
Green, Ruth E 4:19:24 (15,255)
Green, Sandra J 4:51:31 (23,625)
Green, Sarah J 3:43:35 (6,541)
Green, Sheila L 6:49:15 (34,799)
Green, Sophie A 5:21:10 (29,251)
Green, Stephanie J 5:07:52 (27,072)
Green, Susan L 7:51:37 (35,291)
Greenan, Ellie J 6:10:07 (33,567)
Greenaway, Beth J 5:11:26 (27,715)
Greenaway, Tracy 5:15:47 (28,471)
Greenblatt, Elaine 3:24:03 (3,270)
Greene, Helen P 5:19:48 (29,072)
Greene, Jenny K 3:58:23 (10,065)
Greene, Mary P 6:19:54 (34,029)
Greenfield, Lisa C 3:13:08 (2,019)
Greenhalgh, Christy A 4:13:23 (13,774)
Greenhalgh, Rose 5:36:06 (31,087)
Greenhead, Sian 4:40:52 (20,929)
Greenidge, Tara 5:00:42 (25,748)
Greenway, Pamela 6:15:37 (33,819)
Greenwood, Becky 4:53:04 (23,990)
Greenwood, Deborah M 4:28:50 (17,789)
Greenwood, Gemma 3:48:47 (7,562)
Greenwood, Jade 5:03:42 (26,325)
Greenwood, Judy A 4:42:50 (21,422)
Greenwood, Laura M 4:50:04 (23,257)
Greenwood, Susan M 6:55:30 (34,901)
Gregory, Abigail 5:28:07 (30,164)
Gregory, Holly 5:17:33 (28,725)
Gregory, Jo 4:17:03 (14,658)
Gregory, Lisa J 4:18:32 (15,038)
Gregory, Marie 5:40:08 (31,511)
Gregory, Melanie T 4:39:26 (20,562)
Gregory, Samantha Jane 4:50:49 (23,449)
Gregory, Tamsin M 4:30:45 (18,295)
Grehan, Monica M 4:56:56 (24,921)
Greig, Natasha C 5:12:48 (27,947)
Grewal, Hapal K 5:28:19 (30,193)
Grey, Debra C 5:10:15 (27,505)
Grey, Pippa R 3:57:56 (9,912)
Grice, Annie E 4:14:22 (14,007)
Grice, Leanne J 5:25:33 (29,868)
Griffin, Chanese 3:20:16 (2,795)
Griffin, Hayley B 6:02:52 (33,219)
Griffin, Liane 5:56:20 (32,779)
Griffin, Louise 3:59:29 (10,384)
Griffin, Sarah J 5:37:42 (31,246)
Griffin, Zoe H 3:54:56 (9,004)
Griffith, Becky L 3:21:03 (2,892)
Griffiths, Alison J 4:00:58 (10,792)
Griffiths, Evelyn 4:37:05 (19,937)
Griffiths, Joanna 3:43:39 (6,556)
Griffiths, Laura J 4:38:35 (20,319)
Griffiths, Lillias M 4:32:44 (18,826)
Griffiths, Linda J 4:48:13 (22,791)
Griffiths, Louisa B 6:25:19 (34,244)
Griffiths, Mari 6:11:55 (33,637)
Griffiths, Nicola 5:35:50 (31,056)
Griffiths, Pamela J 5:33:34 (30,813)
Griffiths, Samantha R 6:26:20 (34,294)
Griffiths, Serena Lennox 4:58:32 (25,282)
Griffiths, Siobhan D 3:34:46 (4,921)
Griffiths, Thalia R 4:51:24 (23,595)
Griffiths, Zoe C 4:27:13 (17,314)
Grigorian, Violetta 4:49:13 (23,024)
Grima, Claire M 2:52:56 (556)
Grimes, Nicola J 4:00:35 (10,694)
Grimshaw, Emma 4:57:54 (25,111)
Grimshaw, Sarah M 3:43:20 (6,497)
Grindle, Keeley J 4:28:50 (17,789)
Grindu, Christiane 4:48:35 (22,873)
Grist, Fiona 5:06:17 (26,775)
Grobbelaar, Leigh 4:19:31 (15,292)
Grobler, Babette C 3:52:28 (8,396)
Grobler, Gina E 4:55:43 (24,620)
Grogan, Sarah 5:33:02 (30,758)
Gronow, Karen E 4:15:00 (14,164)
Groom, Jacqueline A 5:04:07 (26,405)
Grossgebauer, Kathrin 4:20:20 (15,519)
Grosvenor, Susan A 5:51:32 (32,451)
Grout, Madeleine J 6:36:29 (34,552)
Grove, Judith L 5:25:50 (29,910)
Grove, Victoria 3:54:08 (8,790)
Grover, Neha 4:07:28 (12,228)
Grummitt, Jo 3:27:08 (3,702)
Grundy, Amy J 4:28:04 (17,564)
Grundy, Karen L 5:11:02 (27,645)
Grunow, Heike 5:16:35 (28,577)
Gu, Jia-Yan 4:16:01 (14,401)
Guard, Maureen P 5:34:01 (30,863)
Gubbay, Shani 5:17:13 (28,676)
Gue, Stephanie S 4:26:27 (17,097)
Guerrier, Helen Claire 4:14:08 (13,941)
Guerrina, Roberta 4:55:53 (24,662)
Guest, Lisa C 5:26:32 (29,995)
Guha, Parul 5:10:30 (27,550)
Guilfoyle, Claire 4:12:16 (13,459)
Gulick, Lisa 5:01:33 (25,923)
Gulson, Christabel 4:53:12 (24,021)
Gulvin, Teleri 4:43:35 (21,621)
Gumbel, Lizanne 4:47:21 (22,565)
Gundersen, Ariane M 6:33:06 (34,472)
Gundle, Joanna L 3:40:46 (5,990)
Gunn, Catherine J 4:15:04 (14,180)
Gunner, Frances 4:59:51 (25,565)
Guram, Sandi K 5:15:15 (28,370)
Gush, Laura 4:44:09 (21,757)
Gutherless, Kim 4:52:38 (23,887)
Guthrie-Brown, Juliet K 5:03:02 (26,214)
Guy, Chana D 4:44:13 (21,772)
Guy, Frances J 4:55:22 (24,542)
Guy, Sylvia J 4:44:15 (21,778)
Guyver, Helen 4:54:35 (24,352)
Gwaderi, Razia 6:53:25 (34,869)
Gwilliams, Bernadette Kathryn 4:41:40 (21,136)
Gwilliams, Gillian K 4:58:00 (25,140)
Gyamtso, Cassandra 4:59:14 (25,438)
Haag, Angela 3:46:17 (7,037)
Haagensen, May Britt 5:21:55 (29,359)
Haaland, Elin Rasdal 3:13:12 (2,028)
Haaland, Kristin Rasdal 3:13:22 (2,046)
Haase, Jutta 3:35:24 (5,033)
Habgood, Samantha 5:01:44 (25,960)
Habib-Shaheed, Claire 4:46:27 (22,331)

Hart, Portia I 4:10:46 (13,056)
Harte, Jo M 5:32:48 (30,737)
Hartfield, Sally L 4:31:59 (18,629)
Hartiss, Rachael...........................4:30:55 (18,328)
Hartlebury, Catherine...................5:38:45 (31,363)
Hartley, Catherine L 5:15:44 (28,462)
Hartley, Emma L..........................4:16:46 (14,596)
Hartley Miller, Emma....................4:28:32 (17,706)
Hartshorne, Deborah A..............4:56:39 (24,843)
Hartshorne, Kylie M....................3:56:46 (9,554)
Hartsilver, Jessica H....................3:44:19 (6,685)
Hartwright, Caryl E......................4:17:31 (14,774)
Harvey, Angie J 3:45:25 (6,873)
Harvey, Cate 6:38:40 (34,602)
Harvey, Charlotte 4:56:28 (24,791)
Harvey, Gillian E 4:19:53 (15,396)
Harvey, Jacqui A..........................4:56:47 (24,871)
Harvey, Kathy L...........................3:20:57 (2,886)
Harvey, Katie J 5:34:21 (30,889)
Harvey, Laura E...........................4:50:58 (23,478)
Harvey, Liz 4:53:21 (24,046)
Harvey, Lucy 4:34:02 (19,158)
Harvey, Margaret J 4:38:51 (20,388)
Harvey, Penny J...........................4:17:11 (14,689)
Harvey, Rachel.............................4:33:25 (19,006)
Harvey, Rosemary C 4:57:00 (24,930)
Harvey-Jones, Kelly......................4:56:05 (24,700)
Harward, Nicola F........................3:39:43 (5,795)
Harwood, Lyndsey A....................3:48:36 (7,534)
Haskell, Charlotte A.....................6:10:47 (33,594)
Haslam, Joanne 3:42:53 (6,395)
Hasler, Emma C 3:56:34 (9,478)
Hasler, Natasha M 5:19:12 (28,997)
Hassan, Sara 4:37:55 (20,143)
Hassell, Alison B..........................5:04:43 (26,496)
Hassell, Paula S 3:30:23 (4,232)
Hassett, Valerie 5:39:48 (31,477)
Hassler-De Vos, Silvia 4:42:06 (21,226)
Hastings, Emma 5:23:54 (29,634)
Hatch, Melinda K.........................6:40:42 (34,637)
Hatcher, Rachel L 4:36:45 (19,848)
Hatchett, Tina L...........................5:07:33 (27,013)
Hatton, Anna 4:45:44 (22,139)
Hatton, Janet 3:10:51 (1,765)
Hatton, Jeanette 4:52:48 (23,927)
Hatton, Karen L 4:24:22 (16,541)
Haughton, Louise M 4:27:42 (17,448)
Havey, Allison B...........................4:38:09 (20,215)
Hawes, Louise E 5:08:32 (27,180)
Hawes, Nicola J............................4:14:24 (14,013)
Hawken, Amy K............................4:09:48 (12,803)
Hawken, Valerie E........................5:50:28 (32,377)
Hawkes, Michelle A......................4:26:29 (17,111)
Hawkins, Anne C..........................5:53:54 (32,611)
Hawkins, Deirdre A......................5:10:06 (27,478)
Hawkins, Diana S 3:45:33 (6,906)
Hawkins, Fiona 3:17:43 (2,505)
Hawkins, Laura 4:36:26 (19,777)
Hawkins, Melissa 4:09:00 (12,620)
Hawkins, Sarah L 6:01:22 (33,133)
Hawkins, Sharon J........................3:06:34 (1,409)
Hawkins, Theresa A 5:20:55 (29,211)
Hawley, Rosie E 6:48:21 (34,781)
Haworth, Emma C 3:40:10 (5,892)
Haworth, Emma L.........................4:06:48 (12,060)
Hawse, Sheryl M 4:01:39 (10,956)
Hawthorn, Jacqui R......................4:08:53 (12,594)
Hawthorne, Kerry L......................4:36:14 (19,732)
Hay, Philippa L.............................6:18:53 (33,991)
Haycocks, Kate A 4:53:45 (24,159)
Haydon, Ronnie R 4:13:35 (13,821)
Hayes, Beverley S.........................4:03:52 (11,414)
Hayes, Carol A.............................4:39:41 (20,639)
Hayes, Claire 4:46:29 (22,341)
Hayes, Elly M 4:26:07 (17,014)
Hayes, Fiona A..............................6:08:31 (33,492)
Hayes, Joanne 4:44:45 (21,899)
Hayes, Natasha M 3:37:42 (5,440)
Hayes, Sandie L............................4:05:47 (11,838)
Hayes, Sophie E 4:21:20 (15,768)
Hayes, Susan E 4:07:48 (12,316)
Hayford, Helen 6:41:50 (34,660)
Haygarth, Sally.............................4:50:02 (23,244)

Hayhow, Prunella V.....................3:28:16 (3,894)
Hayhurst, Charlotte 4:50:12 (23,282)
Hayles, Laura 5:15:31 (28,423)
Haylett, Ainslie J..........................3:56:10 (9,357)
Hayley Bell, Catherine 4:22:23 (16,044)
Haylock, Laura 4:55:24 (24,553)
Haylock, Tricia 5:21:10 (29,251)
Hayman, Victoria K......................4:11:09 (13,153)
Haynes, Elizabeth A 3:57:33 (9,789)
Haynes, Lynne 3:21:40 (2,967)
Haynes, Rebecca 5:30:13 (30,430)
Hays, Mandy 4:36:40 (19,830)
Hayter, Suzanne 5:10:49 (27,604)
Hayward, Josephine M 5:28:41 (30,234)
Hayward, Samantha L...................3:19:48 (2,725)
Hayward, Sarah 5:22:19 (29,406)
Hayward, Zoe A 6:35:55 (34,543)
Hazell, Cathryn J..........................5:31:50 (30,620)
Hazell, Lisa M 6:13:27 (33,718)
Hazell, Tracy 7:20:38 (35,154)
Hazlehurst, Caroline....................4:46:16 (22,267)
Hazlewood, Debbie J....................4:07:16 (12,167)
Hazlitt, Karen N...........................2:56:54 (767)
Hazzard, Susan 3:35:08 (4,985)
Head, Katrina H 3:44:49 (6,773)
Heade, Josie C 3:46:21 (7,052)
Headland, Kelly...........................5:03:58 (26,381)
Headley, Meg J 4:21:39 (15,863)
Heafield, Nicola J.........................5:44:35 (31,897)
Healey, Jill C 3:57:54 (9,903)
Healey, Rebecca 4:17:54 (14,862)
Healy, Joanne 3:55:19 (9,112)
Healy, Marie M 5:00:25 (25,680)
Heaney, Bronagh 5:17:22 (28,691)
Hearfield, Tessa J.........................4:11:57 (13,374)
Hearn, Amy L 3:36:17 (5,203)
Hearn, Karen A 5:19:40 (29,057)
Heasman, Helen E 4:31:30 (18,505)
Heath, Gilliam Y...........................5:35:28 (31,016)
Heath, Heather 4:19:06 (15,185)
Heath, Kate A 6:01:20 (33,132)
Heathfield, Kathryn L...................7:07:52 (35,040)
Heathwood, Hannah M 4:10:53 (13,084)
Heaton, Mathilde M 3:08:54 (1,608)
Heaver, Melanie J.........................4:32:58 (18,888)
Heavey, Judith D..........................4:56:44 (24,860)
Heaviside, Karen M......................3:08:30 (1,565)
Heck, Miranda 3:49:25 (7,708)
Hedges, Anita E............................3:52:38 (8,440)
Hedges, Julie A.............................3:43:14 (6,476)
Hedges, June 3:33:18 (4,651)
Hedley, Lesley J............................6:47:22 (34,752)
Hedley, Sarah A 4:06:48 (12,060)
Hedley Lewis, Amanda J 4:07:33 (12,244)
Hedley Lewis, Melissa S...............4:07:33 (12,244)
Hedley Lewis, Penny A 4:11:04 (13,130)
Hedley-Goddard, Francine...........5:23:09 (29,540)
Heduan, Phyllis 4:18:26 (15,009)
Heenan, Rachael..........................7:00:36 (34,955)
Hegerty, Gabby 4:12:40 (13,566)
Hehir, Natalie L............................5:56:03 (32,760)
Heidemann, Martine D 6:33:23 (34,481)
Hellier, Sheree A..........................4:29:06 (17,858)
Helliwell, Christine 4:30:45 (18,295)
Helliwell, Claire L 3:50:46 (8,016)
Helm, Emilie 4:16:36 (14,553)
Helm, Nikki 6:12:38 (33,668)
Helme, Naomi 3:51:24 (8,142)
Helmn, Karen 5:15:36 (28,438)
Helmsley, Julia C 5:25:10 (29,822)
Helps, Liza B 5:36:08 (31,089)
Heminsley, Caroline F 3:21:20 (2,924)
Hemley, Maureen G 4:37:25 (20,014)
Hemphill, Clare 5:28:13 (30,179)
Hemsworth, Jane.........................4:27:18 (17,343)

Hemsworth, Marion V 3:44:04 (6,643)
Henderson, Alice B.......................4:44:22 (21,809)
Henderson, Claudia C 5:34:50 (30,952)
Henderson, Doreen I....................4:33:23 (19,003)
Henderson, Jane A 4:45:28 (22,071)
Henderson, Katie R 4:34:45 (19,329)
Henderson, Kirsteen M 3:43:17 (6,487)
Henderson, Louise E 4:45:55 (22,192)
Henderson, Melanie 5:25:06 (29,810)
Henderson, Teresa N 5:56:55 (32,827)
Hendry, Jennifer 3:47:38 (7,313)
Hendry, Joanna Z.........................4:36:43 (19,843)
Hendry, Tracy 4:49:35 (23,141)
Heneage, Alice R..........................4:30:55 (18,328)
Heney, Sonya 3:58:39 (10,144)
Henley, Joanne S 6:03:28 (33,257)
Henley, Rebecca A 6:17:33 (33,908)
Henley, Rebecca E 4:05:43 (11,826)
Hennelly, Paula 5:30:15 (30,434)
Henners, Debbra M 4:47:45 (22,664)
Hennessy, Tatiana M 6:04:36 (33,318)
Hennighan, Emma L 5:23:07 (29,537)
Henniker-Major, Anna M 4:11:35 (13,279)
Henry, Amanda 3:14:10 (2,143)
Henry, Bridgette J 4:31:07 (18,389)
Henry, Roberta J..........................5:18:51 (28,954)
Henshaw, Sandy A........................4:13:23 (13,774)
Henshaw, Susan L 6:46:09 (34,724)
Henwood, Scarlett A 3:46:46 (7,148)
Hepburn, Tracy L..........................3:55:47 (9,258)
Hepworth, Angela C.....................5:34:26 (30,903)
Heras Perez, Maria Del Mar 4:32:40 (18,808)
Herbert, Zoe 7:02:34 (34,977)
Herd, Samantha J 7:25:04 (35,179)
Hermon, Carolyn 4:39:28 (20,571)
Heron, Barbara 4:22:08 (15,978)
Heron, Fiona E 3:55:44 (9,240)
Heron, Nicola R 3:55:41 (9,211)
Herring, Penny D 5:42:15 (31,700)
Herrington, Kate 4:07:21 (12,199)
Herriott, Thanyalak 5:05:45 (26,693)
Hersh, Julie K 4:18:39 (15,072)
Hertzberg, Golda 6:39:06 (34,610)
Herz, Janice 5:14:07 (28,182)
Heseltine, Emma L 5:35:15 (30,993)
Hesketh, Jo Anne 3:09:44 (1,683)
Hesp, Charlotte L.........................4:42:21 (21,283)
Hesp, Sara 5:49:28 (32,287)
Hess, Josephine B.........................6:02:03 (33,173)
Hetherington, Jackie A.................4:36:11 (19,716)
Hetrick, Cyndy J 3:28:48 (3,973)
Hettle, Elizabeth C.......................4:33:31 (19,026)
Heuff, Pauline 4:06:06 (11,903)
Heum, Marina B 4:21:20 (15,768)
Hewer, Natalie 4:57:22 (25,005)
Hewett, Ally H 4:28:18 (17,647)
Hewings, Irene E 4:49:12 (23,017)
Hewison, Deborah S 4:19:58 (15,419)
Hewitt, Adrienne 4:43:00 (21,468)
Hewitt, Catherine E 3:24:26 (3,332)
Hewitt, Clare S 4:46:42 (22,400)
Hewitt, Paula 4:40:09 (20,763)
Hewitt-Gray, Jill S 3:57:38 (9,818)
Hewlett, Hannah..........................4:39:50 (20,676)
Hewson, Julie 3:32:58 (4,607)
Hext, Catherine 5:36:46 (31,149)
Heyburn, Amanda........................5:26:31 (29,992)
Heycock, Carol R 3:15:52 (2,325)
Heydecker, Deidre A....................3:38:10 (5,529)
Heywood, Elizabeth K..................4:35:58 (19,672)
Hibberd, Sally-Ann 6:38:38 (34,600)
Hibbert, Haylee P.........................4:55:11 (24,499)
Hibbert, Louise E 5:50:05 (32,345)
Hibbs, Angela E............................4:24:17 (16,522)
Hibbs, Samantha 6:42:37 (34,674)
Hickey, Lynn J 4:42:41 (21,381)
Hickey, Mairead P 7:01:29 (34,967)
Hickey, Sarah H............................4:06:58 (12,097)
Hickford, Stephanie.....................5:04:05 (26,398)
Hickman, Breeda M......................3:39:15 (5,722)
Hickman, Carol Annw 6:16:37 (33,870)
Hickman, Kate..............................4:23:08 (16,218)
Hickman, Sarah............................5:53:50 (32,607)

Hicks, Beverley A.	4:29:56 (18,077)	
Hicks, Emma L.	5:40:52 (31,577)	
Hicks, Helen L.	3:35:26 (5,037)	
Hicks, Rosamond F.	4:11:15 (13,176)	
Hicks, Sally A.	4:45:00 (21,962)	
Hider-Bayford, Nicola	7:26:40 (35,197)	
Hier, Diane	3:21:26 (2,936)	
Higenbottam, Adele D.	4:01:19 (10,862)	
Higginbottom, Wendy E.	3:24:22 (3,323)	
Higgins, Anne	4:53:57 (24,211)	
Higgins, Bernie	4:22:15 (16,011)	
Higgins, Jane	5:06:39 (26,835)	
Higgins, Jane R.	5:10:50 (27,607)	
Higgins, Sara N	3:51:21 (8,128)	
Higgins, Susie C	4:50:50 (23,452)	
Higgins, Tracey M	4:39:43 (20,648)	
Higginson, Ruth A	4:49:04 (22,989)	
Higginson, Sally K	4:46:24 (22,315)	
Higgs, Collette	6:23:49 (34,182)	
Higgs, Laura J	5:40:31 (31,544)	
Higgs, Lucinda S	5:17:40 (28,741)	
Higgs, Portia E	6:21:12 (34,083)	
Higgs, Shelagh L	3:27:17 (3,729)	
Hilaire, Margaret J	5:25:08 (29,816)	
Hill, Adele	4:35:02 (19,419)	
Hill, Annabelle J	4:33:53 (19,124)	
Hill, Beth	6:50:02 (34,814)	
Hill, Beth J	4:45:05 (21,993)	
Hill, Carmen	6:03:09 (33,238)	
Hill, Charlotte A	6:27:20 (34,339)	
Hill, Collette H	7:18:10 (35,129)	
Hill, Deborah	3:51:59 (8,273)	
Hill, Della P	4:45:49 (22,161)	
Hill, Denise M	6:52:22 (34,850)	
Hill, Denya	5:04:30 (26,456)	
Hill, Elaine C	5:49:52 (32,327)	
Hill, Heather R	4:08:17 (12,447)	
Hill, Isabel A	4:41:29 (21,083)	
Hill, Jessica R	4:35:51 (19,641)	
Hill, Joanna M	4:49:38 (23,159)	
Hill, Kathryn E	4:18:43 (15,085)	
Hill, Katie R	3:56:37 (9,500)	
Hill, Kim	5:19:19 (29,009)	
Hill, Melanie L	4:49:48 (23,199)	
Hill, Nicola E	5:13:20 (28,042)	
Hill, Paula	3:16:07 (2,341)	
Hill, Rebecca	4:25:33 (16,856)	
Hill, Sarah	4:12:40 (13,566)	
Hiller, Sandra L	5:52:09 (32,490)	
Hilliard, Sarah J	4:46:26 (22,326)	
Hillier, Janet R	4:19:01 (15,164)	
Hillman, Lisa	4:47:02 (22,497)	
Hills, Alexandra J	5:15:38 (28,445)	
Hills, Charlotte E	4:59:02 (25,394)	
Hills, Nicole	4:00:49 (10,751)	
Hill-Trevor, Caroline A	4:29:16 (17,913)	
Hilton, Janet M.	5:26:24 (29,978)	
Hilton, Sarah C	5:11:29 (27,726)	
Hilton, Wendy E	4:14:04 (13,922)	
Hinch, Alex	5:32:43 (30,727)	
Hindle, Anna E	3:49:43 (7,783)	
Hindle, Rebecca A	5:41:20 (31,612)	
Hindlet, Lesley Susan	5:22:34 (29,449)	
Hinds, Olivia L	6:15:53 (33,839)	
Hine, Clare	5:15:08 (28,341)	
Hines, Emma L	5:13:40 (28,091)	
Hines, Tonya S.	5:46:36 (32,055)	
Hinks, Gillian M	4:58:14 (25,197)	
Hinshelwood, Linda	4:29:55 (18,072)	
Hipkins, Danielle E	4:24:31 (16,573)	
Hipwell, Adele	5:09:16 (27,321)	
Hird, Elizabeth	5:00:51 (25,773)	
Hird, Linda D	4:11:51 (13,350)	
Hirons, Catherine M	6:20:01 (34,033)	
Hirons, Claire Marie	5:10:45 (27,592)	
Hirons, Hita	4:57:10 (24,957)	
Hirotsuna, Shoko	6:15:41 (33,825)	
Hirsch, Karin	6:13:06 (33,699)	
Hirst, Nicola J	6:42:31 (34,673)	
Hirst, Tricia A	4:13:41 (13,842)	
Hiscock, Karli M	5:50:35 (32,388)	
Hiscock, Sophie	4:14:57 (14,154)	
Hita, Natasha L	4:47:32 (22,605)	
Hitchcock, Frances K	8:20:48 (35,334)	
Hitchcock, Joanna M	4:05:35 (11,794)	
Hitchen, Louisa A	6:26:44 (34,308)	
Hitchens, Wietske	3:54:42 (8,945)	
Hitchings, Josie S	5:22:32 (29,444)	
Hitner, Claudia E	4:55:53 (24,662)	
Hlela, Carol	5:11:23 (27,709)	
Hlusovicka, Dana Bernatova	3:52:12 (8,328)	
Ho, Mai-Ling S	3:58:19 (10,039)	
Hoadley, Annabel C	4:10:17 (12,931)	
Hoare, Emma	3:59:01 (10,254)	
Hoare, Sarah	4:42:14 (21,260)	
Hoare, Susan	4:32:08 (18,671)	
Hobbs, Heather	4:14:00 (13,907)	
Hobbs, Jane L	5:50:49 (32,400)	
Hobbs, Jane M	3:39:18 (5,729)	
Hobbs, Rachel A	4:48:16 (22,801)	
Hobbs, Wendy	5:23:45 (29,618)	
Hobbs, Zita K.	4:53:35 (24,093)	
Hobday, Katharine	4:07:48 (12,316)	
Hobden, Adele M	5:06:05 (26,741)	
Hobin, Carolyne M	4:43:06 (21,493)	
Hobson, Emma M	4:00:29 (10,664)	
Hobson, Laura J	7:11:41 (35,073)	
Hobson, Nina V.	4:34:49 (19,358)	
Hoche, Daniela	4:27:48 (17,487)	
Hockey, Nina C	5:45:47 (32,001)	
Hocking, Debs E	5:57:19 (32,856)	
Hocking, Hannah R	5:57:19 (32,856)	
Hocking, Rosie	5:22:20 (29,408)	
Hocking, Sarah J	5:34:30 (30,915)	
Hockley, Aimée L	4:35:07 (19,442)	
Hockley, Anna M	3:35:48 (5,117)	
Hockney, Karen A	4:30:22 (18,197)	
Hodges, Alexandra	4:42:45 (21,397)	
Hodges, Rachael L	4:27:08 (17,290)	
Hodges, Tracy A	6:05:06 (33,343)	
Hodgetts, Lynne	5:17:52 (28,774)	
Hodgkins, Lesley A	4:51:25 (23,601)	
Hodgkinson, Lucy C	3:57:43 (9,850)	
Hodgkinson, Tara	5:27:53 (30,136)	
Hodgson, Caroline	4:27:49 (17,495)	
Hodgson, Hayley	3:48:37 (7,537)	
Hodgson, Joanne	5:00:31 (25,703)	
Hodgson, Kate L	3:11:29 (1,826)	
Hodgson, Kelly S	5:30:39 (30,480)	
Hodgson, Rebecca L	4:39:26 (20,562)	
Hodgson, Sarah L	4:30:28 (18,220)	
Hodnett, Maria	5:26:53 (30,038)	
Hodnett, Nicola A	5:50:08 (32,353)	
Hoebem, Sonja	6:10:38 (33,592)	
Hoefling, Susan Elizabeth	5:02:04 (26,038)	
Hoff, Claire J	4:50:45 (23,434)	
Hogan, Katherine A	4:56:02 (24,691)	
Hogan, Renée	5:38:37 (31,345)	
Hogarth, Sharon	5:12:03 (27,810)	
Hogarty, Louisa C	5:52:41 (32,528)	
Hogg, Alison L	4:50:09 (23,274)	
Hogg, Jillian E	4:13:04 (13,672)	
Hogg, Lisa F	4:42:23 (21,297)	
Hoggarth, Jess F	4:41:05 (20,984)	
Hogsflesh, Roma J	4:56:13 (24,733)	
Holcroft, Victoria	4:02:54 (11,211)	
Holden, Abigail J	4:17:42 (14,819)	
Holden, Janet Cecily	4:49:13 (23,024)	
Holden, Katherine L	4:14:35 (14,053)	
Holden, Nikki P	4:38:26 (20,283)	
Holden, Sarah	4:10:38 (13,016)	
Holden, Sharon	3:16:51 (2,417)	
Holden-Peters, Ana E	4:48:26 (22,836)	
Holding, Casey-Louise	4:32:54 (18,871)	
Holdsworth, Gilly	3:59:43 (10,467)	
Holford, Rachael E	3:53:27 (8,615)	
Holland, Aileen L	4:32:26 (18,743)	
Holland, Bethany M	4:21:47 (15,898)	
Holland, Chantelle	4:27:38 (17,426)	
Holland, Christine Clare C	3:59:14 (10,320)	
Holland, Davina E	4:19:47 (15,368)	
Holland, Deborah	6:18:50 (33,989)	
Holland, Jennifer R	3:51:54 (8,257)	
Holland, Rebecca	5:01:20 (25,882)	
Holland, Sian	3:55:58 (9,300)	
Hollands, Emma L	3:58:14 (10,023)	
Holle, Hayley J	3:09:36 (1,667)	
Hollick, Joanne L	4:07:40 (12,274)	
Holliday, Susan M	4:15:02 (14,172)	
Hollingsworth, Jayne E	6:29:31 (34,397)	
Hollington, Lee H	6:08:06 (33,486)	
Hollins, Teresa A	4:01:40 (10,963)	
Hollinshead, Monique G	3:15:00 (2,232)	
Hollis, Bianca I	4:01:42 (10,967)	
Holliss, Tara L	5:41:37 (31,642)	
Hollocks, Karen E	4:52:55 (23,956)	
Holloway, Natalie	4:35:47 (19,625)	
Holly, Jennifer	5:20:32 (29,156)	
Holman, Tracy L	4:33:30 (19,022)	
Holmes, Corina T	3:37:36 (5,424)	
Holmes, Jane	4:29:47 (18,031)	
Holmes, Kate	4:21:36 (15,844)	
Holmes, Laura A	4:26:46 (17,199)	
Holmes, Liz	4:39:23 (20,542)	
Holmes, Lucia M	4:21:32 (15,824)	
Holmes, Lyndsey J	4:26:37 (17,158)	
Holmes, Sarah H	5:26:37 (30,007)	
Holmes, Teresa	4:53:47 (24,169)	
Holroyd, Annette B	5:19:28 (29,032)	
Holroyd, Julie	4:39:08 (20,473)	
Holt, Debbie	4:09:01 (12,624)	
Holt, Elizabeth A	4:48:58 (22,962)	
Holt, Joanne	4:59:30 (25,497)	
Holt, Sarah J	3:43:00 (6,418)	
Holt, Tina	6:34:55 (34,521)	
Holt, Toni	3:42:28 (6,294)	
Holyfield, Rachel S	4:11:46 (13,328)	
Homent, Angie	6:05:10 (33,347)	
Homer, Britta	3:32:55 (4,600)	
Homer, Chantal K	5:01:03 (25,829)	
Homer, Laura	4:36:57 (19,900)	
Homer, Samantha L	4:35:12 (19,465)	
Homersham, Nicola D	5:21:00 (29,220)	
Hommel, Carry	5:02:43 (26,159)	
Hone, Nyree L	4:59:19 (25,455)	
Honey, Kim F	5:15:49 (28,476)	
Honey, Vivienne P	5:14:30 (28,242)	
Honeybourne, Julie R	6:42:11 (34,666)	
Honeysett, Nicola J	4:40:47 (20,906)	
Hontas, Joelle	4:19:09 (15,197)	
Hood, Flora	3:56:14 (9,372)	
Hood, Sian	4:27:00 (17,257)	
Hood, Zoe T	6:18:40 (33,953)	
Hook, Vanessa M	5:41:39 (31,644)	
Hooke, Penny	5:35:38 (31,037)	
Hookham, Samantha	6:24:14 (34,200)	
Hool, Sue E	3:28:02 (3,863)	
Hooper, Ayisha M	4:31:29 (18,502)	
Hooper, Melanie T	5:41:58 (31,667)	
Hooper, Tina Jane	4:40:17 (20,792)	
Hoornaert, Emma J	4:45:30 (22,079)	
Hoos, Debra M	4:02:15 (11,077)	
Hope, Geraldine	4:11:18 (13,189)	
Hopegood, Karen J	4:38:55 (20,414)	
Hopgood, Jeannie	4:42:16 (21,269)	
Hopkin, Amanda	3:47:44 (7,334)	
Hopkins, Alison C	3:02:04 (1,123)	
Hopkins, Claire L	4:31:02 (18,361)	
Hopkins, Gillian E	4:54:35 (24,352)	
Hopkins, Katheryn E	7:19:09 (35,141)	
Hopkins, Mary M	4:12:20 (13,481)	
Hopkins, Rhian S	4:11:57 (13,374)	
Hopkins, Sandra A	3:27:56 (3,846)	
Hopkins, Sorrel	4:28:19 (17,651)	
Hopkinson, Emma N	4:27:36 (17,412)	
Hopp, Caroline	4:33:33 (19,036)	
Hoppe, Gisela	3:25:12 (3,418)	
Hopper, Julie P	7:18:52 (35,137)	
Hopper, Louisa D	4:16:30 (14,522)	
Horbury, Kate	4:47:32 (22,605)	
Horder, Caroline M	4:41:10 (20,998)	
Hore, Angela T	5:00:55 (25,790)	
Horgan, Clare V	7:20:44 (35,155)	
Horn, Janette	5:19:47 (29,069)	
Horn, Kerry F	6:29:33 (34,398)	
Horne, Jennifer L	3:10:38 (1,748)	
Horne, Joanne C	5:01:29 (25,910)	
Horne, Kate H	3:59:34 (10,411)	
Horne, Pauline E	5:02:42 (26,155)	

Horrell, Tara ... 4:14:34 (14,047)
Horrigan, Debbie M ... 6:41:53 (34,662)
Horsfall, Charlotte ... 5:11:33 (27,737)
Horsfall, Samantha ... 3:35:32 (5,054)
Horswood, Karen ... 3:59:47 (10,488)
Horta-Osorio, Ana ... 3:57:16 (9,695)
Horton, Claire V ... 6:07:13 (33,445)
Horton, Jessica L ... 6:22:46 (34,144)
Hosburn, Cassie H ... 3:51:08 (8,081)
Hosker, Joanne R ... 5:18:58 (28,969)
Hoskin, Fiona A ... 9:13:35 (35,361)
Hough, Cara L ... 6:10:20 (33,579)
Hough, Charlotte ... 5:00:00 (25,601)
Hough, Kathryn M ... 3:30:29 (4,249)
Houghton, Joanne M ... 3:47:21 (7,257)
Houghton, Tracy A ... 5:15:42 (28,456)
Houlston, Bridget J ... 3:59:33 (10,404)
Houseman, Rachel H ... 3:47:20 (7,254)
Housley, Kirsty D ... 4:32:56 (18,882)
Houston, Nicola ... 4:59:08 (25,418)
Houston, Rebecca J ... 5:08:07 (27,106)
Houston, Samantha E ... 4:11:12 (13,162)
Hovden., Aase S. ... 3:32:07 (4,486)
Howard, Annabel ... 3:32:47 (4,586)
Howard, Catherine S ... 3:55:21 (9,119)
Howard, Emily J ... 5:37:13 (31,195)
Howard, Jo S ... 6:05:09 (33,346)
Howard, Joanne C ... 4:40:37 (20,865)
Howard, Kate ... 5:24:38 (29,747)
Howard, Michelle ... 5:57:07 (32,839)
Howard, Rachael A ... 3:57:16 (9,695)
Howard, Samantha T ... 5:16:11 (28,525)
Howard, Zoe R ... 5:19:32 (29,039)
Howarth, Jill A ... 5:24:18 (29,700)
Howarth, Marie ... 4:43:59 (21,715)
Howarth, Sally E ... 4:16:29 (14,519)
Howarth, Tracey ... 5:28:34 (30,215)
Howat, Jenny ... 5:03:57 (26,374)
Howden, Tammie C ... 5:05:10 (26,585)
Howe, Annabel ... 4:38:55 (20,414)
Howe, Kirsty R ... 4:32:41 (18,812)
Howe, Nicola ... 4:14:17 (13,986)
Howe, Simone D ... 6:37:49 (34,588)
Howell, Anna P ... 4:52:48 (23,927)
Howell, Katrina E ... 7:22:35 (35,161)
Howell, Toni K ... 4:17:40 (14,814)
Howells, Hannah M ... 5:20:00 (29,093)
Howells, Lesley A ... 4:59:16 (25,445)
Howells, Sue M ... 5:22:52 (29,491)
Howes, Kim T ... 3:31:25 (4,386)
Howes, Lorna S ... 6:27:06 (34,328)
Howes, Pauline C ... 4:37:32 (20,045)
Howlett, Angie ... 6:00:18 (33,063)
Howlett, Emma ... 4:58:23 (25,233)
Howlett, Victoria A ... 5:31:01 (30,530)
Howson, Elizabeth ... 5:28:53 (30,259)
Howson, Tracey M ... 7:09:37 (35,047)
Hoy, Anna C ... 4:05:48 (11,843)
Hoyle, Helen E ... 3:24:03 (3,270)
Hoyle, Helen M ... 5:03:17 (26,248)
Hoyle, Laura ... 4:28:29 (17,693)
Hoyle, Tina ... 5:02:19 (26,085)
Hoyles, Wyn ... 7:24:01 (35,169)
Hoyne, Sarah-Jane M ... 4:30:01 (18,103)
Huband, Bronwyn M ... 4:42:49 (21,412)
Hubbard, Caroline T ... 3:45:30 (6,897)
Hubbard, Claire B ... 5:18:49 (28,938)
Hucker, Jackie M ... 5:29:15 (30,305)
Huckle, Julian T ... 4:04:08 (11,474)
Huckle, Lita M ... 5:03:44 (26,330)
Hudgell, Jolene ... 6:55:57 (34,905)
Hudson, Janet N ... 5:01:49 (25,974)
Hudson, Karen E ... 5:42:47 (31,745)
Hudson, Kathleen P ... 4:27:23 (17,362)
Hudson, Kerrie E ... 4:29:10 (17,876)
Hudson, Kerry ... 5:02:10 (26,056)
Hudson, Kym ... 4:03:15 (11,282)
Hudson, Laura E ... 4:18:05 (14,912)
Hudson, Maria T ... 5:14:49 (28,285)
Hudson, Marie G ... 6:00:23 (33,065)
Hudson, Nadia M ... 5:44:11 (31,869)
Hudson, Sarah J ... 5:08:18 (27,140)
Hudson, Vanessa H ... 4:38:02 (20,174)
Hudson, Zoe J ... 3:45:37 (6,915)
Huffman, Holly ... 3:50:15 (7,895)
Hufton, Elizabeth J ... 5:14:43 (28,268)
Huggett, Bridget M ... 5:55:54 (32,755)
Huggett, Lucy K ... 4:55:29 (24,569)
Huggins, Celine ... 4:01:58 (11,014)
Huggins, Laura ... 6:16:43 (33,875)
Hughes, Alison ... 4:15:19 (14,233)
Hughes, Ann-Marie ... 4:57:48 (25,085)
Hughes, Briony F ... 5:11:16 (27,688)
Hughes, Carly M ... 5:02:13 (26,066)
Hughes, Caroline ... 4:11:57 (13,374)
Hughes, Catherine Ellen ... 4:49:28 (23,102)
Hughes, Clare M ... 4:26:55 (17,241)
Hughes, Deborah D ... 5:06:03 (26,734)
Hughes, Deborah M ... 4:16:58 (14,638)
Hughes, Eirwen ... 5:18:42 (28,916)
Hughes, Emma J ... 4:26:46 (17,199)
Hughes, Gail ... 6:17:32 (33,907)
Hughes, Heather ... 6:27:15 (34,333)
Hughes, Jane ... 5:18:04 (28,801)
Hughes, Jane M ... 4:41:12 (21,014)
Hughes, Jo M ... 4:44:05 (21,745)
Hughes, Karen E ... 5:18:39 (28,904)
Hughes, Linda A ... 5:13:42 (28,099)
Hughes, Lisa Anne ... 4:13:01 (13,663)
Hughes, Maureen ... 6:35:22 (34,532)
Hughes, Rachel C ... 5:15:23 (28,398)
Hughes, Sarah L ... 3:31:31 (4,400)
Hughes, Shirley M ... 4:35:43 (19,607)
Hughes, Shona ... 3:25:50 (3,509)
Hughes, Sonja Karen ... 4:48:26 (22,836)
Hughes, Susanne K ... 6:09:54 (33,556)
Hughes, Tanya K ... 4:00:47 (10,741)
Hughes, Tanya R ... 4:43:02 (21,476)
Hughes, Victoria ... 5:44:11 (31,869)
Hughes-Morris, Carol ... 4:46:10 (22,237)
Huguet, Anne ... 4:07:20 (12,191)
Hull, Helen S ... 4:15:18 (14,232)
Hull, Tina ... 3:26:10 (3,551)
Hullock, Sharron ... 4:56:52 (24,902)
Hume, Alison C ... 4:31:45 (18,567)
Hume, Helen R ... 5:10:31 (27,552)
Hume, Melissa ... 5:42:44 (31,738)
Hume, Shirley H ... 3:51:01 (8,058)
Hume-Almeida, Bernadette T ... 4:58:23 (25,233)
Humphrey, Joanne L ... 4:07:31 (12,240)
Humphrey, Karen C ... 5:30:58 (30,522)
Humphreys, Jann ... 4:28:30 (17,697)
Humphreys, Kate ... 5:46:40 (32,062)
Humphreys-Elvis, Becky ... 4:41:56 (21,188)
Humphries, Nazila ... 4:53:36 (24,100)
Humpidge, Kath ... 4:43:08 (21,500)
Hundley, Dale J ... 3:49:50 (7,807)
Hung, Kitty S ... 4:40:55 (20,943)
Hunt, Amanda O ... 6:55:37 (34,902)
Hunt, Erin F ... 3:34:29 (4,873)
Hunt, Glynis ... 6:24:42 (34,221)
Hunt, Holly ... 5:30:50 (30,502)
Hunt, Jayne ... 4:42:27 (21,313)
Hunt, Joanne ... 3:57:50 (9,890)
Hunt, Kate E ... 4:04:55 (11,634)
Hunt, Nicola J ... 3:24:12 (3,299)
Hunt, Sarah ... 3:46:00 (6,986)
Hunt, Suzanne ... 6:09:58 (33,559)
Hunter, Alison K ... 5:48:09 (32,181)
Hunter, Ann R ... 4:11:51 (13,350)
Hunter, Collette T ... 4:11:22 (13,214)
Hunter, Jaimie L ... 3:41:41 (6,149)
Hunter, Jen ... 5:42:52 (31,755)
Hunter, Joy ... 5:02:28 (26,109)
Hunter, Kate V ... 5:58:08 (32,928)
Hunter, Marianne J ... 7:30:50 (35,222)
Hunter Blair, Pol ... 5:03:56 (26,370)
Huntriss, Emmaclare P ... 4:49:14 (23,031)
Hunziker, Agnes ... 3:53:37 (8,653)
Hunziker, Eng Hiang ... 5:00:12 (25,633)
Hurcum, Charlie E ... 4:26:33 (17,130)
Hurd, Katherine ... 5:05:41 (26,678)
Hurdle, Brittany C ... 4:05:12 (11,711)
Hurley, Joanne M ... 4:23:29 (16,308)
Hurley, Nicola ... 4:24:03 (16,453)
Hurley, Patricia ... 4:23:49 (16,391)
Hurrell, Katie A ... 5:49:25 (32,284)
Hurwitz Bremner, Marjorie F ... 5:23:13 (29,553)
Hussell, Elizabeth ... 4:48:05 (22,759)
Hussey, Alexandra ... 4:48:01 (22,745)
Hussey, Deborah ... 4:17:46 (14,836)
Hussey, Linsey ... 5:00:49 (25,769)

Hüsseyin, Çiğdem E ... 5:27:56 (30,140)

Wow, this is my 5th London Marathon. I always say 'never again' but the emotions that pass through me at the finish line are overwhelming and I know that I will run again. My children, Sema, Eren and Sevgi have been my inspiration since they were born and throughout every race I carry them in my heart and soul. Not only do they attend every race but they cheer and support me through every event. Seeing their smiles and hearing their cheers makes me so proud that I keep going on no matter what!

Hutchins, Sarah M ... 4:24:32 (16,577)
Hutchinson, Ann Patricia ... 4:53:14 (24,027)
Hutchinson, Claire L ... 3:17:34 (2,489)
Hutchinson, Jaqui ... 7:36:13 (35,252)
Hutchison, Anne-Marie ... 2:58:18 (858)
Hutter, Louise H ... 6:35:17 (34,529)
Hutton, Hannah ... 5:04:51 (26,511)
Hutton, Lorna ... 6:10:58 (33,599)
Hutton, Ruth F ... 3:17:07 (2,444)
Hutton, Toni L ... 5:12:05 (27,814)
Huxtable, Emily M ... 5:50:29 (32,379)
Huxtable, Gail ... 3:51:53 (8,249)
Hyatt, Kate E ... 3:40:32 (5,943)
Hyde, Helen S ... 4:52:59 (23,973)
Hyde, Jodie ... 4:41:10 (20,998)
Hyde, Katrina M ... 5:15:28 (28,413)
Hyland, Laura H ... 4:54:37 (24,365)
Hyland, Ruth ... 4:17:32 (14,776)
Hyland, Sara L ... 4:54:37 (24,365)
Hynd, Julie ... 5:23:39 (29,607)
Hynes, Kate V ... 4:59:54 (25,578)
Hyslop, Andrea ... 4:25:39 (16,893)
Iannella, Pamela C ... 3:59:50 (10,505)
Iannelli, Elisabetta ... 4:37:22 (20,000)
I'Anson, Helen E ... 4:12:44 (13,587)
Ibbotson, Rachel ... 3:47:52 (7,367)
Ibell, Emma L ... 3:55:26 (9,139)
Iborra, Joanne R ... 3:20:32 (2,829)
Ibrahim, Zoe S ... 4:40:53 (20,936)
Iddon, Keri ... 5:38:56 (31,386)
Illien, Martine ... 4:07:20 (12,191)
Imanaka, Arlene ... 6:51:52 (34,843)
Imeson, Hazel ... 3:48:34 (7,525)
Imrie, Claire E ... 3:04:32 (1,267)
Ince, Ayse S ... 4:50:58 (23,478)
Inch, Christine A ... 3:27:17 (3,729)
Ingham, Hayley M ... 5:34:43 (30,940)
Ingham, Yvonne A ... 5:30:36 (30,474)
Ingle, Kristy M ... 5:53:42 (32,597)
Inglis, Jean ... 3:55:42 (9,221)
Ingram, Nicola K ... 5:22:56 (29,508)
Ingram, Rachael ... 5:24:43 (29,753)
Inkster, Clare ... 4:30:02 (18,106)
Inness, Vicky L ... 3:19:31 (2,684)
Inns, Heidi L ... 4:56:32 (24,809)
Ioannou, Sarah ... 5:19:37 (29,052)
Ip, Dot ... 4:34:54 (19,382)
Ip, Jacey ... 5:41:17 (31,604)
Iratzoqui, Valerie ... 4:01:38 (10,951)
Iredale, Vicky ... 6:25:22 (34,247)
Ireladn, Tracy ... 3:44:08 (6,655)
Ireland, Michelle L ... 5:00:31 (25,703)
Ireland, Rachel M ... 5:05:28 (26,632)
Irvine, Lesley A ... 4:48:21 (22,817)
Irving, Elly ... 5:09:22 (27,340)
Irving, Sarah J ... 4:24:30 (16,569)
Irwin, Katie ... 4:45:04 (21,986)
Irwin, Kellie ... 4:10:01 (12,858)
Isaac, Sandra ... 5:45:13 (31,947)
Isaacs, Zoe A ... 5:18:00 (28,794)

Isabelle, Defendini 5:02:00 (26,018)
Isbitsky, Abi 4:23:31 (16,319)
Israeli, Naama 5:15:51 (28,484)
Isted, Emily E 4:51:33 (23,637)
Ithier-Aimée, Jane E 5:34:28 (30,912)
Ivanov, Jennifer 5:14:52 (28,290)
Ivantsoff, Mariana 3:34:46 (4,921)
Iversen, Rachael J 4:02:51 (11,198)
Ives, Caroline J 4:31:24 (18,471)
Ives, Hayley E 5:53:38 (32,594)
Ives, Jacqueline 5:11:34 (27,743)
Jack, Melissa J 4:59:55 (25,581)
Jackaman, Edwina 5:26:55 (30,044)
Jackets, Nicola 5:18:33 (28,880)
Jackman, Lara 5:15:40 (28,450)
Jackman, Sarah J 4:11:09 (13,153)
Jackman, Stephanie L 4:14:14 (13,971)
Jackson, Amy E 5:21:50 (29,352)
Jackson, Amy J 5:43:00 (31,770)
Jackson, Belinda A 5:34:46 (30,949)
Jackson, Charlotte R 5:49:21 (32,282)
Jackson, Chris 4:13:42 (13,848)
Jackson, Deborah R 3:29:40 (4,127)
Jackson, Diane L 5:28:34 (30,215)
Jackson, Elizabeth J 4:35:43 (19,607)
Jackson, Elizabeth J 4:54:30 (24,334)
Jackson, Emily J 6:01:31 (33,143)
Jackson, Gemma 5:05:22 (26,617)
Jackson, Georgina M 5:11:47 (27,772)
Jackson, Geraldine A 5:15:37 (28,441)
Jackson, Glen P 3:57:37 (9,806)
Jackson, Jayne 5:27:15 (30,073)
Jackson, Katie L 4:49:30 (23,116)
Jackson, Kerrie L 4:59:00 (25,386)
Jackson, Lisa J 4:32:16 (18,701)
Jackson, Louise 4:47:08 (22,525)
Jackson, Nikki 4:28:24 (17,670)
Jackson, Philippa D 4:10:54 (13,088)
Jackson, Rachel 5:12:33 (27,900)
Jackson, Sandre D 3:51:25 (8,147)
Jackson, Valerie A 5:46:17 (32,036)
Jackson, Victoria A 4:13:57 (13,895)
Jackson (née Shedden), Joanne 3:50:42 (7,994)
Jackson-Leach, Rachel 5:14:30 (28,242)
Jacobs, Louise A 4:22:32 (16,084)
Jacobs, Polly V 3:50:35 (7,966)
Jacobsen, Jenny F 3:59:12 (10,310)
Jacques, Marie 4:06:02 (11,889)
Jacques, Sarah J 5:43:08 (31,785)
Jagger, Joanne 4:21:20 (15,768)
Jainu-Deen, Nikki M 4:29:02 (17,843)
Jakeman, Marion J 5:04:58 (26,539)
Jakeway, Michelle J 4:31:25 (18,480)
Jalaly, Aisha 5:40:02 (31,500)
James, Caroline A 4:16:24 (14,499)
James, Cherry I 4:42:19 (21,277)
James, Elaine L 3:57:58 (9,924)
James, Emma L 5:15:11 (28,351)
James, Frances M 5:46:13 (32,029)
James, Georgina F 5:56:26 (32,788)
James, Jennifer E 4:00:44 (10,726)
James, Lowri A 4:17:19 (14,725)
James, Lysbeth 5:21:20 (29,275)
James, Melanie 5:21:38 (29,322)
James, Miems 5:00:46 (25,763)
James, Olivia K 6:47:42 (34,764)
James, Paula Jane 3:54:11 (8,808)
James, Rebecca T 3:56:20 (9,406)
James, Sandra 4:56:35 (24,825)
James, Sarah Louise 4:31:43 (18,558)
James, Stephanie J 3:12:51 (1,981)
James, Susan M 3:33:14 (4,639)
Jameson, Judy 5:32:42 (30,722)
Jamieson, Aileen A 4:31:29 (18,502)
Jamieson, Amanda S 3:24:18 (3,313)
Jamieson, Emily 5:23:03 (29,525)
Jamieson, Faith L 4:19:29 (15,277)
Jamieson, Georgina K 3:17:11 (2,452)
Jamieson, Hilary 4:53:15 (24,033)
Jamieson, Sandra L 5:00:40 (25,743)
Jammes, Isabelle 4:11:23 (13,222)
Jandl, Silvia 4:42:14 (21,260)
Janes, Caroline 3:33:42 (4,703)
Jansen, Ruth J 4:33:29 (19,020)
Japheth, Alaw 4:19:29 (15,277)
Jaques, Hilary A 4:01:25 (10,887)
Jaques, Naomi W 4:38:30 (20,296)
Jarosilova, Petra 3:38:31 (5,594)
Jarrett, Karen 6:14:00 (33,745)
Jarrold, Claire M 5:41:42 (31,648)
Jarrold, Tracy 5:32:27 (30,680)
Jarvis, Jacki L 3:19:18 (2,650)
Jarvis, Katie 4:28:57 (17,818)
Javkin, Melina 5:26:40 (30,011)
Jay, Carinne M 3:29:55 (4,169)
Jayasekera, Menaka S 5:12:49 (27,952)
Jayawardena, Crishi 4:53:14 (24,027)
Jaycock, Louise C 5:22:15 (29,397)
Jeacocke, Faye 3:58:27 (10,083)
Jean-Baptiste, Gisele 5:04:41 (26,490)
Jean-Elie, Liliane 3:34:08 (4,796)
Jeanes, Dawn 7:03:49 (34,992)
Jeanmart, Stephane 3:29:15 (4,053)
Jeanne, Lisa 4:47:31 (22,603)
Jearrad, Victoria C 4:38:37 (20,333)
Jefferies, Linda C 4:27:36 (17,412)
Jefferies, Sarah R 4:33:04 (18,915)
Jefferson, Holly R 3:58:06 (9,971)
Jeffery, Beverley T 4:55:22 (24,542)
Jeffery, Louise 7:18:36 (35,133)
Jeffery, Tamsin C 4:21:29 (15,804)
Jeffrey, Jayne L 4:04:23 (11,520)
Jeffrey, Kerry J 4:37:36 (20,068)
Jeffrey, Laura 5:53:52 (32,609)
Jeffrey, Laura R 4:50:03 (23,253)
Jeffrey, Maxine M 4:27:15 (17,325)
Jeffries, Alex J 3:45:25 (6,873)
Jeffries, Dawn 5:19:21 (29,016)
Jeffs, Clare W 3:32:59 (4,609)
Jeffs, Laura 5:34:30 (30,915)
Jehu, Melanie R 5:16:41 (28,597)
Jelbert, Ruth 5:17:51 (28,771)
Jelley, Diana M 4:42:11 (21,244)
Jenkin, Linda D 6:22:00 (34,113)
Jenkins, Amy 4:52:15 (23,809)
Jenkins, Beverley J 7:11:00 (35,061)
Jenkins, Claire L 4:46:53 (22,444)
Jenkins, Elizabeth M 5:31:26 (30,569)
Jenkins, Helen 3:56:30 (9,461)
Jenkins, Jackie L 4:07:17 (12,170)
Jenkins, Kate 3:19:48 (2,725)
Jenkins, Laura 4:52:15 (23,809)
Jenkins, Lindsay 5:20:19 (29,131)
Jenkins, Rachel 4:48:44 (22,910)
Jenkins, Sarah L 6:31:48 (34,449)
Jenkins, Tracy I 3:48:08 (7,425)
Jenkinson, Anne M 4:17:18 (14,717)
Jenkinson, Cheryl L 4:23:57 (16,430)
Jenkinson, Clare E 4:08:25 (12,485)
Jenkinson, Kathleen 6:51:21 (34,835)
Jenkinson, Kirsty F 5:13:02 (27,991)
Jenkinson, Lauren M 4:35:19 (19,496)
Jenks, Jane 4:25:45 (16,923)
Jenks, Jennifer C 3:50:31 (7,951)
Jenner, Karen D 4:48:55 (22,949)
Jenner, Kate E 5:10:12 (27,499)
Jenner, Lynsey C 5:45:41 (31,993)
Jennings, Azra E 5:42:45 (31,741)
Jennings, Karen R 6:07:33 (33,463)
Jennings, Louise R 4:22:08 (15,978)
Jennings, Sylvia M 5:20:00 (29,093)
Jensen, Helle E 3:55:52 (9,279)
Jensen, Janni Mosberg Sund 3:46:41 (7,134)
Jensen, Pernille 4:26:17 (17,064)
Jersild, Helle 3:36:35 (5,250)
Jess, Samantha J 4:14:40 (14,067)
Jesson, Samantha 5:34:23 (30,894)
Jewels, Judith 6:07:30 (33,458)
Jewett, Melanie K 3:32:04 (4,479)
Jeyes, Joy M 4:29:22 (17,940)
Jinks, Marion 4:49:41 (23,176)
Jobsz, Nicole S 4:17:42 (14,819)
Joelle, Leymonie 3:48:00 (7,401)
Joenson, Helle Broechner 4:33:21 (18,991)
Johanson, Suzanne L 5:16:28 (28,555)
Johansson, Ann 3:27:14 (3,722)
Johansson, Susanne 5:31:35 (30,590)
John, Amanda L 3:38:42 (5,626)
John, Angharad R 4:20:01 (15,435)
John, Caroline V 3:21:35 (2,957)
Johns, Hannah M 3:55:35 (9,183)
Johns, Rhiannon M 3:49:30 (7,730)
Johnson, Amanda 4:19:38 (15,323)
Johnson, Anita A 5:22:56 (29,508)
Johnson, Annette 5:55:30 (32,726)
Johnson, Bebe M 5:35:33 (31,025)
Johnson, Carolyn T 3:39:33 (5,766)
Johnson, Clare E 5:21:14 (29,262)
Johnson, Elizabeth S 4:53:13 (24,024)
Johnson, Faye N 5:54:53 (32,681)
Johnson, Frances K 3:44:40 (6,741)
Johnson, Gladys I 6:26:53 (34,315)
Johnson, Heather C 4:09:10 (12,652)
Johnson, Helen M 5:00:38 (25,736)
Johnson, Hilary C 3:51:28 (8,159)
Johnson, Jacqueline A 3:59:55 (10,523)
Johnson, Joanne 3:26:03 (3,539)
Johnson, Joanne 5:53:34 (32,589)
Johnson, Julia 4:25:01 (16,716)
Johnson, Laura 4:58:12 (25,189)
Johnson, Laura 5:00:17 (25,652)
Johnson, Leanne L 4:50:47 (23,445)
Johnson, Naomi G 6:55:48 (34,903)
Johnson, Rebecca A 3:02:37 (1,157)
Johnson, Riona 6:04:49 (33,328)
Johnson, Rosealeen 4:56:28 (24,791)
Johnson, Ruth E 5:45:32 (31,977)
Johnson, Samantha E 5:44:32 (31,890)
Johnson, Sharon L 3:27:25 (3,752)
Johnson, Sheona E 4:56:29 (24,795)
Johnson, Tracy J 5:47:45 (32,146)
Johnson, Trudi J 4:39:58 (20,710)
Johnston, Donna L 5:49:57 (32,331)
Johnston, Emma L 5:12:50 (27,954)
Johnston, Patricia 5:21:12 (29,257)
Johnston, Samantha E 4:09:27 (12,715)
Johnston, Sandra E 4:30:13 (18,154)
Johnstone, Caroline A 5:47:49 (32,158)
Johnstone, Julie A 4:48:16 (22,801)
Johnstone, Melanie 4:09:48 (12,803)
Johnstone, Ruth E 5:31:26 (30,569)
Jolley, Janet 4:56:08 (24,714)
Jolleys, Dawn L 5:22:30 (29,438)
Jolly, Joanne M 4:41:44 (21,149)
Jolly, Liz 4:40:24 (20,814)
Jonas, Anji D 5:13:09 (28,015)
Jones, Abigail S 4:30:18 (18,176)
Jones, Albane 4:00:38 (10,705)
Jones, Amparo P 4:50:41 (23,418)
Jones, Amy E 5:09:46 (27,420)
Jones, Anita D 3:30:44 (4,288)
Jones, Anita J 3:58:04 (9,958)
Jones, Anna 4:24:33 (16,581)
Jones, Anne Marie 4:25:18 (16,786)
Jones, Barbara A 6:19:31 (34,016)
Jones, Barbara E 4:19:33 (15,299)
Jones, Bethan L 4:51:23 (23,585)
Jones, Bridget E 5:31:27 (30,574)
Jones, Carla S 5:00:20 (25,663)
Jones, Carole 4:09:35 (12,747)
Jones, Caroline J 3:12:46 (1,973)
Jones, Caroline J 5:34:29 (30,914)
Jones, Catherine F 4:12:54 (13,628)
Jones, Ceri Ann 4:52:22 (23,835)
Jones, Charmain S 4:41:32 (21,098)
Jones, Christine 3:48:42 (7,546)
Jones, Claire E 4:31:01 (18,352)
Jones, Debbie S 5:12:15 (27,847)
Jones, Eleanor K 4:18:18 (14,962)
Jones, Eleri 5:30:04 (30,406)
Jones, Elizabeth P 4:25:23 (16,814)
Jones, Emma E 5:25:15 (29,831)
Jones, Emma J 5:34:38 (30,924)
Jones, Emma L 6:11:27 (33,620)
Jones, Emma M 5:29:50 (30,379)
Jones, Emma R 4:49:05 (22,994)
Jones, Enfys A 3:09:07 (1,629)
Jones, Gemma H 3:47:55 (7,377)
Jones, Gwenan 4:04:10 (11,481)

Jones, Hazel L 5:07:28 (27,001)
Jones, Heather R 5:23:16 (29,566)
Jones, Helen C 5:10:53 (27,618)
Jones, Helen L 5:10:54 (27,620)
Jones, Hilary A 4:24:58 (16,700)
Jones, Janice A 3:22:33 (3,074)
Jones, Jennifer 7:38:28 (35,262)
Jones, Jennifer B 6:14:42 (33,779)
Jones, Joanne 3:40:20 (5,919)
Jones, Joanne 4:45:02 (21,973)
Jones, Judith Clare 3:58:55 (10,230)
Jones, Julie 5:41:18 (31,608)
Jones, June E 4:45:43 (22,136)
Jones, Kali 4:49:27 (23,092)
Jones, Karen L 5:18:51 (28,954)
Jones, Kate E 3:51:15 (8,108)
Jones, Katherine M 5:18:02 (28,799)
Jones, Katie E 6:45:03 (34,709)
Jones, Kimberley L 5:15:34 (28,432)
Jones, Kyle 3:47:04 (7,207)
Jones, Laraine 5:49:18 (32,275)
Jones, Laura A 6:35:16 (34,528)
Jones, Laura J 4:47:28 (22,592)
Jones, Laura S 5:13:00 (27,988)
Jones, Lauren 3:56:09 (9,351)
Jones, Lisa S 6:11:45 (33,628)
Jones, Lorraine K 4:15:30 (14,285)
Jones, Louise 7:46:18 (35,282)
Jones, Lucy-Ann R 4:01:15 (10,847)
Jones, Lynn 4:27:37 (17,417)
Jones, Lynne Lloyd 5:29:34 (30,346)
Jones, Marie C 4:54:09 (24,253)
Jones, Marie C 5:40:45 (31,567)
Jones, Marie E 4:37:24 (20,009)
Jones, Nicola 6:10:20 (33,579)
Jones, Nikki A 3:43:12 (6,473)
Jones, Penny A 3:34:18 (4,830)
Jones, Philippa 4:31:14 (18,414)
Jones, Rachel 4:24:12 (16,497)
Jones, Rebecca Margaret 4:47:17 (22,558)
Jones, Sarah A 4:55:07 (24,479)
Jones, Sarah J 3:38:47 (5,640)
Jones, Serena 4:56:54 (24,913)
Jones, Sharon L 5:22:53 (29,494)
Jones, Shirley A 4:47:23 (22,577)
Jones, Shirley A 5:00:51 (25,773)
Jones, Sophie A 5:34:59 (30,965)
Jones, Susan L 4:23:32 (16,323)
Jones, Taru K 5:32:38 (30,709)
Jones, Tessa E 3:58:06 (9,971)
Jones, Tina 3:51:54 (8,257)
Jones, Tracey 4:20:54 (15,662)
Jones, Victoria A 4:40:33 (20,848)
Jones, Wendy 5:00:17 (25,652)
Jones, Wendy A 3:44:29 (6,717)
Jones, Yvonne J 3:59:52 (10,511)
Jones, Yvonne T 5:19:18 (29,006)
Jones, Zoe 5:24:19 (29,704)
Jones-Baldock, Carolyna L 3:39:52 (5,821)
Jones-Crofts, Helen L 4:21:10 (15,733)
Jones-Reading, Rebecca F 4:23:20 (16,260)
Jonsson, Eva M 4:47:54 (22,707)
Jordaan, Antalene N 4:44:43 (21,890)
Jordan, Alexandra C 7:18:24 (35,131)
Jordan, Angela C 3:28:05 (3,866)
Jordan, Helen-Louisa 6:21:36 (34,098)
Jordan, Julie A 5:42:48 (31,749)
Jordan, Nicola A 4:09:13 (12,663)
Jordan, Sarah L 5:48:33 (32,221)
Jordan-Owers, Lorna H 4:33:21 (18,991)
Joseph, Christine 6:47:53 (34,767)
Joseph, Laura 4:12:43 (13,584)
Joseph, Marie A 4:29:47 (18,031)
Joshi, Neema 6:24:52 (34,226)
Joubert, Jolandie 5:07:35 (27,019)
Jowett, Nina 3:58:38 (10,137)
Joy, Samantha J 4:42:31 (21,336)
Joyce, Ann E 6:12:54 (33,689)
Joyce, Carol B 4:30:58 (18,340)
Joyce, Jackie S 5:02:52 (26,189)
Joyce, Lisa 4:20:47 (15,634)
Joyce, Shelley 3:49:19 (7,688)
Joyner, Kate 4:54:30 (24,334)

Jubane, Nellie 6:25:38 (34,262)
Jubb, Gail Dornice 5:01:50 (25,976)
Jubb, Gillian 3:37:02 (5,325)
Juby, Louise 3:47:42 (7,328)
Judd, Lorna 4:53:37 (24,106)
Judd, Mandy 4:09:22 (12,699)
Judd, Vikkie 4:58:06 (25,162)
Jude, Suzanne C 5:50:06 (32,351)
Juggins, Lucy C 4:25:15 (16,775)
Jukes, Victoria 5:25:53 (29,914)
Junglas, Tracey 4:59:02 (25,394)
Jupp, Sacha M 5:49:40 (32,303)
Justice, Claire Rozalia 4:34:33 (19,276)
Kaas, Ena 3:56:21 (9,415)
Kakar, Neera 4:45:20 (22,040)
Kalek, Claire 4:42:27 (21,313)
Kana, Homma 4:43:11 (21,511)
Kanda, Synthia 5:12:00 (27,800)
Kane, Eleanor A 3:42:29 (6,295)
Kane, Kerry 4:19:44 (15,348)
Kane, Kerry A 5:07:27 (26,996)
Kane, Wendy L 4:13:15 (13,729)
Kanesalingam, Kavitha 5:26:04 (29,947)
Kangeson, Hema 5:44:36 (31,899)
Kano, Yuri 2:28:44 (55)
Kaphan, Alice 4:58:24 (25,243)
Kapoor, Lesley 4:06:35 (12,014)
Kaposi, Anna 4:18:58 (15,152)
Kapur, Annette 5:12:45 (27,934)
Karbowiak, Anna L 5:13:43 (28,104)
Karia, Bindi 5:20:59 (29,216)
Karpitskaya, Yekaterina 3:54:13 (8,815)
Kast, Jennifer A 4:36:26 (19,777)
Kataria, Ravita 6:20:07 (34,036)
Kater, Candice 3:45:33 (6,906)
Kater, Lorien 5:48:24 (32,208)
Katkin, Yildiz 6:33:22 (34,480)
Katzman, Gili 4:12:49 (13,609)
Kaur, Baljinder 6:00:49 (33,102)
Kaur, Carol 4:59:57 (25,587)
Kaur, Harpal K 4:00:41 (10,716)
Kaushal, Anita B 3:58:25 (10,071)
Kavanagh, Ann C 5:23:14 (29,561)
Kavanagh, Breda 5:20:15 (29,121)
Kavanagh, Elizabeth 6:33:31 (34,483)
Kavanagh, Sheila E 4:02:49 (11,191)
Kay, Annabel J 4:19:08 (15,194)
Kay, Teresa M 4:29:17 (17,919)
Kaye, Lesley C 4:43:32 (21,609)
Kayr Jones, Priya 7:56:34 (35,306)
Kayser, Fenella K 5:07:36 (27,024)
Kayum, Elene E 3:53:43 (8,682)
Kazandag, Gulden 4:11:42 (13,312)
Keable, Lyn A 5:08:20 (27,146)
Keable, Shelley A 5:05:39 (26,666)
Keane, Jacinta 3:52:00 (8,277)
Keane, Kathy 5:27:52 (30,134)
Keane, Sarah J 5:33:17 (30,785)
Keane, Susie M 5:05:56 (26,718)
Keaney, Katie 4:57:30 (25,029)
Kearney, Clare 5:01:25 (25,898)
Kearney, Deborah 5:33:10 (30,771)
Kearns, Julia 5:11:32 (27,733)
Kearsley, Christine 5:13:58 (28,154)
Keavney, Jacqueline S 3:14:10 (2,143)
Keay, Eleanor 5:21:55 (29,359)
Keddy, Ann M 6:22:22 (34,122)
Keech, Julie 5:24:46 (29,760)
Keegan, Sarah 4:24:13 (16,504)
Keen, Angela 4:43:57 (21,703)
Keen, Heather G 6:26:57 (34,318)
Keen, Pauline Elaine 4:59:18 (25,453)
Keenan, Janet 4:40:20 (20,802)
Keenan, Joanna C 5:51:44 (32,463)
Keenan, Marie A 5:54:51 (32,673)
Keer, Angela 4:02:31 (11,135)
Kehoe, Donna M 5:23:06 (29,535)
Kehyaian, Emma F 5:00:51 (25,773)
Keiller, Susan J 4:33:56 (19,136)
Keith, Catherine 4:42:06 (21,226)
Keller, Gertrud-Maria 4:59:57 (25,587)
Kelly, Caroline 6:14:27 (33,764)
Kelly, Catherine E 4:57:39 (25,060)

Kelly, Julie A 5:31:35 (30,590)
Kelly, Karen 5:45:35 (31,982)
Kelly, Kerry A 4:40:33 (20,848)
Kelly, Krista L 5:53:45 (32,601)
Kelly, Lorna C 3:49:38 (7,755)
Kelly, Lucy 4:30:43 (18,286)
Kelly, Lucy 4:47:00 (22,484)
Kelly, Penny L 5:44:56 (31,924)
Kelly, Sandra K 5:26:06 (29,951)
Kelly, Victoria C 4:31:52 (18,597)
Kelly-White, Rhonda A 3:53:26 (8,612)
Kelsall, Sarah Louise L 6:05:54 (33,382)
Kelsey, Vicky J 6:19:45 (34,024)
Kelty, Emma Tamsin 4:56:23 (24,769)
Kemp, Ashleigh 5:00:09 (25,624)
Kemp, Daisy M 4:25:22 (16,806)
Kemp, Hilary D 3:59:37 (10,423)
Kemp, Louise J 4:18:06 (14,920)
Kemp, Rebecca L 4:15:24 (14,256)
Kemp, Sarah L 3:54:33 (8,904)
Kempton, Jane 4:41:34 (21,109)
Kendall, Clare E 4:12:36 (13,547)
Kendall, Wendy 3:53:04 (8,523)
Kenden, Fran 3:52:53 (8,483)
Kendon, Elizabeth J 3:03:20 (1,189)
Kendrew, Emma L 4:45:55 (22,192)
Kenley, Natalie N 5:42:35 (31,732)
Kennard, Lisa J 4:24:02 (16,448)
Kennard, Nikki 4:10:22 (12,947)
Kennedy, Adele 4:45:31 (22,085)
Kennedy, Aletta 4:05:26 (11,757)
Kennedy, Andrea L 4:04:25 (11,527)
Kennedy, Diane 5:12:34 (27,903)
Kennedy, Jayne M 5:10:54 (27,620)
Kennedy, Joanne 6:16:19 (33,859)
Kennedy, Linda 3:40:33 (5,948)
Kennedy, Liz L 5:01:50 (25,976)
Kennedy, Rachel J 6:01:01 (33,113)
Kennedy, Siobhan 4:57:25 (25,015)
Kennelly, Julia 4:22:31 (16,078)
Kennett, Mia R 4:14:15 (13,974)
Kenney, Kathleen R 5:01:27 (25,904)
Kenny, Anna V 4:54:23 (24,307)
Kent, Charlotte 5:10:34 (27,561)
Kent, Karen 5:49:49 (32,321)
Kent, Linda A 5:11:57 (27,797)
Kent, Margaret 4:54:35 (24,352)
Kent, Sarah 6:46:56 (34,738)
Keogh, Joanna M 4:41:53 (21,178)
Keogh, Joanne 4:44:38 (21,867)
Ker, Grace M 4:48:53 (22,938)
Kerley, Ruth 5:58:36 (32,964)
Kerly, Joanne 5:19:11 (28,995)
Kern, Sharon 5:52:10 (32,492)
Kerr, Clare 3:23:05 (3,133)
Kerr, Emily V 5:56:46 (32,814)
Kerr, Maria 4:43:49 (21,671)
Kerr, Ruth H 4:23:15 (16,241)
Kerr, Selina M 5:43:21 (31,810)
Kerrigan, Colette M 4:10:26 (12,962)
Kerrigan, Emma L 5:19:50 (29,076)
Kerrison, Lois E 5:18:55 (28,965)
Kerry, Claire 5:46:39 (32,060)
Kersting, Elke 4:50:57 (23,474)
Kesavan, Shenaz 4:54:22 (24,305)
Ketley, Angela L 4:30:14 (18,160)
Ketley, Fern E 3:55:26 (9,139)
Ketteridg, Tracy A 3:47:06 (7,213)
Kettle, Sally J 5:20:38 (29,168)
Key, Cherry 4:49:16 (23,042)
Keys, Tammy J 4:30:24 (18,210)
Keywood, Laura J 4:18:58 (15,152)
Khan, Alisha 6:19:56 (34,030)
Khan, Ameana 6:14:25 (33,762)
Khan, Imrana 7:29:05 (35,214)
Khan, Noreen 5:12:26 (27,877)
Khatib, Sarah 4:58:14 (25,197)
Khetani, Heidi J 5:39:14 (31,420)
Khoshnevis, Heather M 3:21:37 (2,964)
Khosla, Aimée 5:49:06 (32,259)
Kidd, Janet L 4:23:00 (16,184)
Kidd, Judith A 6:56:13 (34,908)
Kiddell, Lianna 4:24:17 (16,522)

Kiely, Heidi 7:15:14 (35,107)
Kiemel, Annmarie 4:14:37 (14,060)
Kieran, Rosalind A 2:53:30 (584)
Kiernan, Lorraine L 4:44:24 (21,821)
Kign, Berengaria M 4:15:00 (14,164)
Kilbey, Karen 4:43:39 (21,639)
Kilbey, Sarah 3:37:47 (5,452)
Kilburn, Carole A 5:20:15 (29,121)
Kilgour, Janette 4:08:41 (12,544)
Kilgour, Vivien 4:00:37 (10,700)
Kilic, Sultan 5:07:48 (27,059)
Killgren, Alexia L 5:36:54 (31,165)
Killick, Katie L 5:45:59 (32,010)
Killip, Liz 3:34:36 (4,896)
Kim, Sung Yeul 5:41:59 (31,671)
Kimberley, Simone 2:59:07 (928)
Kimura, Maki 3:40:27 (5,934)
Kinch, Brenda E 4:06:39 (12,035)
Kinder, Mary A 5:22:22 (29,416)
Kinder, Monica H 4:14:02 (13,913)
King, Anita M 6:17:56 (33,924)
King, Carolyn P 4:22:24 (16,050)
King, Chris 3:15:33 (2,289)
King, Christine L 5:14:14 (28,199)
King, Claire L 3:53:44 (8,688)
King, Denise 6:04:18 (33,305)
King, Elaine F 7:15:54 (35,110)
King, Elizabeth A 5:46:33 (32,050)
King, Emma M 4:39:55 (20,696)
King, Emma R 5:10:16 (27,508)
King, Hannah J 6:04:12 (33,299)
King, Helen E 4:35:23 (19,518)
King, Julia 3:39:10 (5,713)
King, Karen A 6:16:31 (33,866)
King, Katie A 4:44:36 (21,856)
King, Maria S 3:56:41 (9,529)
King, Michelle 4:34:20 (19,226)
King, Michelle 6:02:14 (33,185)
King, Nadine M 3:56:32 (9,469)
King, Nicola A 5:07:48 (27,059)
King, Rachael A 4:35:26 (19,527)
King, Sara E 6:15:37 (33,819)
King, Sarah L 6:02:53 (33,221)
King, Sarah R 4:00:55 (10,778)
King, Shirley C 6:21:39 (34,100)
King, Stephanie L 4:40:52 (20,929)
King, Terry E 4:20:05 (15,453)
King, Thila 5:49:34 (32,295)
King, Tracey M 4:08:27 (12,496)
King, Veronica M 4:58:48 (25,338)
King, Wendy 3:07:32 (1,484)
Kingdon, Nina J 4:46:42 (22,400)
Kingdon, Paula 4:12:23 (13,488)
Kingscott, Sally G 4:25:03 (16,726)
Kingsland, Sheila 6:20:52 (34,064)
Kingsnorth, Mary B 4:34:36 (19,288)
Kingston, Ali M 3:53:27 (8,615)
Kingston, Belinda 4:30:00 (18,095)
Kinney, Gillian 4:10:14 (12,916)
Kinniburgh-Dickie, Julie M 5:10:50 (27,607)
Kinsella, Julie E 7:13:05 (35,083)
Kinsella, Michele M 4:46:15 (22,262)
Kinsey, Michelle 4:09:19 (12,689)
Kinzett, Laura 4:01:49 (10,987)
Kírber, Jana 5:02:02 (26,028)
Kirby, Cressida L 4:35:39 (19,581)
Kirby, Jeni J 4:27:57 (17,528)
Kirby, Maureen 4:29:58 (18,088)
Kirby, Sandie D 5:09:39 (27,396)
Kirby, Trina L 5:03:47 (26,338)
Kirby, Val 5:10:34 (27,561)
Kirk, Elizabeth A 5:38:26 (31,320)
Kirk, Emma 4:25:32 (16,847)
Kirk, Natasha 4:32:07 (18,666)
Kirk, Rachel 5:18:51 (28,954)
Kirk, Rebecca C 3:46:21 (7,052)
Kirk, Tricia A 4:28:46 (17,766)
Kirka, Danica J 4:35:09 (19,453)
Kirkbride, Jessica M 5:33:27 (30,799)
Kirkbride, Maria A 5:16:04 (28,508)
Kirkby, Hayley J 4:52:45 (23,918)
Kirke, Linda M 6:02:08 (33,181)
Kirkham, Jane 4:06:00 (11,880)
Kirkham, Mary 4:53:08 (24,007)
Kirkwood, Anne 4:31:00 (18,347)
Kirkwood, Christine 5:40:38 (31,559)
Kirwan, Karen 5:15:46 (28,469)
Kisbee, Amanda 5:44:11 (31,869)
Kisseleva, Victoria 5:03:07 (26,226)
Kitchen, Diane B 3:43:09 (6,457)
Kitchen, Kathryn J 5:27:14 (30,071)
Kitchener, Tracey Sharon 4:45:33 (22,090)
Kitchin, Lorraine 4:57:03 (24,938)
Kite, Helen 4:47:51 (22,689)
Kivelainen, Pirjo H 3:34:33 (4,883)
Kjaergaard, Lone S 5:10:27 (27,541)
Kleanthous, Natasha 4:40:31 (20,840)
Kleinhans, Adele 4:05:14 (11,717)
Klimczak, Anna E 3:36:56 (5,307)
Klimowicz, Emma E 4:14:45 (14,096)
Klingel, Andrea 4:18:51 (15,118)
Klintworth, Gail A 4:38:12 (20,230)
Kloosterman, José 4:04:43 (11,590)
Knai, Cecile 5:57:01 (32,837)
Knapman, Louise A 4:48:37 (22,885)
Knee, Wendy 4:45:01 (21,967)
Knight, Amanda J 4:48:17 (22,804)
Knight, Carin J 3:55:49 (9,267)
Knight, Dawn R 5:08:21 (27,151)
Knight, Emily K 4:29:38 (17,994)
Knight, Fran 4:31:19 (18,445)
Knight, Gemma 6:26:18 (34,292)
Knight, Helen S 4:36:17 (19,736)
Knight, Jane E 5:17:10 (28,669)
Knight, Janet E 5:10:57 (27,633)
Knight, Jill A 3:46:27 (7,077)
Knight, Judith L 6:19:04 (33,999)
Knight, Julie 4:23:30 (16,314)
Knight, Julie 6:01:56 (33,166)
Knight, Kate 6:26:45 (34,310)
Knight, Laura 5:42:11 (31,690)
Knight, Lisa N 4:42:52 (21,431)
Knight, Louise 6:14:38 (33,772)
Knight, Lucie C 5:44:34 (31,893)
Knighton, Joanne P 4:42:14 (21,260)
Knights, Victoria M 4:53:39 (24,114)
Knill, Collette L 4:19:49 (15,379)
Knott, Jennifer C 6:09:25 (33,533)
Knott, Sue 3:56:21 (9,415)
Knowles, Sarah D 4:50:41 (23,418)
Knowlton, Jillian M 4:50:01 (23,242)
Knox, Fiona M 5:31:39 (30,601)
Knox, Jessica M 5:19:38 (29,054)
Knudson, Ashley A 5:28:03 (30,152)
Kober, Lesley R 4:39:26 (20,562)
Kobylinski, Marta 5:35:49 (31,052)
Kohlmann, Parwin Sarah 4:46:12 (22,248)
Koklschka, Hannah L 6:38:52 (34,603)
Komolafe, Bukola B 4:44:06 (21,748)
Konieczna, Joanna 5:17:19 (28,686)
Konrad, Birgit 4:36:00 (19,683)
Konstanty, Kelly 4:02:36 (11,151)
Koppang, Dee A 4:54:57 (24,437)
Kordel, Louise F 4:44:41 (21,885)
Korolova, Zarina 6:06:32 (33,412)
Kotas, Jo A 4:19:19 (15,235)
Koth, Melanie 3:26:57 (3,676)
Kovash, Carolyn 4:27:19 (17,348)
Kowollik, Sabrina M 4:29:14 (17,908)
Kraetschmer, Nancy 3:43:08 (6,448)
Krafft, Alison E 3:53:07 (8,536)
Kramer, Fabri J 5:01:37 (25,936)
Krawczyk, Donna 4:46:22 (22,302)
Kremer, Moira E 4:40:12 (20,775)
Krempff, Margaret A 4:24:05 (16,466)
Kristiansen, Lara 3:28:48 (3,973)
Kruger, Jeanette H 5:36:49 (31,157)
Krugmann, Tilda 4:02:36 (11,151)
Kuijk, Eleonora 5:24:02 (29,655)
Kulik, Annette M 7:40:36 (35,272)
Kulkarni, Valerie C 4:36:30 (19,793)
Kullova, Lucie K 4:25:09 (16,751)
Kumar, Rosemary 4:54:01 (24,225)
Kunze, Birgit 6:13:28 (33,720)
Kurdyla, Helen C 5:01:36 (25,933)
Kury, Anita 4:10:57 (13,094)
Kyari, Ayesha 4:52:16 (23,814)
Kyle, Sally E 3:52:11 (8,323)
Labram, Clare Louise 4:43:18 (21,543)
Labram, Sandra A 6:48:05 (34,771)
Lacey, Emma 5:05:49 (26,700)
Lacey, Liz 5:28:02 (30,151)
Lacey, Sarah J 5:10:57 (27,633)
Lachman, Wendy C 6:23:42 (34,177)
Lacroix, Gwendolyn 4:43:02 (21,476)
Ladd, Judith C 3:49:42 (7,774)
Ladkin, Angela 3:35:34 (5,061)
Lafferty, Anna K 3:59:28 (10,382)
Laforet, Kate 3:25:31 (3,461)
Lafosse, Geves C 5:08:11 (27,123)
Lagden, Natasha F 3:49:15 (7,679)
Lai, Nai One 4:08:01 (12,366)
Laidlar, Philippa K 5:03:09 (26,227)
Laidlaw, Dawn 6:09:04 (33,514)
Laing, Jo M 3:25:48 (3,501)
Laird, Doreen 6:13:09 (33,703)
Lake, Claire L 5:21:08 (29,246)
Lake, Gillian M 4:55:25 (24,556)
Laker, Ciara M 4:54:37 (24,365)
Lakhlef, Farida 5:07:11 (26,941)
Lakin, Maria J 6:38:22 (34,598)
Laliberte, Sophie 4:51:26 (23,605)
Lalor, Sinead E 4:54:19 (24,292)
Lam, Sai-Yee 4:22:06 (15,966)
Lamb, Cherie 4:30:05 (18,121)
Lamb, Louise 4:26:04 (17,002)
Lambe, Annette J 5:36:24 (31,111)
Lambert, Debra L 6:52:22 (34,850)
Lambert, Jennie L 4:47:11 (22,542)
Lambert, Lorna F 5:31:45 (30,611)
Lambert, Vicky 3:51:57 (8,269)
Lammas, Sara F 7:32:56 (35,238)
Lammiman, Jane L 6:12:42 (33,676)
Lamond, Anna C 5:19:54 (29,084)
Lamont, Jackie 5:27:13 (30,068)
Lamont, Mary A 5:35:37 (31,031)
Lampe, Sabrina 3:53:04 (8,523)
Lampen-Smith, Rosalie A 4:09:43 (12,779)
Lampkin, Sarah H 5:11:09 (27,663)
Lancaster, Emma G 5:37:58 (31,270)
Lancaster, Tracey L 3:36:55 (5,301)
Lanceley, Catherine A 4:54:11 (24,255)
Lande, Hilde S. 3:41:46 (6,161)
Landi, Karen 6:32:32 (34,465)
Landragin, Alice J 4:07:38 (12,265)
Landsman, Candice 5:35:54 (31,061)
Landy, Helen 3:45:46 (6,941)
Lane, Alison J 3:21:18 (2,921)
Lane, Anita 5:27:56 (30,140)
Lane, Leah 5:01:56 (26,001)
Lane, Sallyann 5:25:58 (29,929)
Lang, Carol 5:36:30 (31,124)
Lang, Geraldine M 4:04:57 (11,645)
Lang, Isobel 4:27:07 (17,285)
Lang, Stefanie 4:42:04 (21,215)
Langaro, Daniela 3:45:32 (6,905)
Langdon, Helena J 5:19:14 (29,001)
Langdon, Jennifer A 5:04:39 (26,485)
Langdon, Rachel M 3:38:55 (5,658)
Langdon, Sally 4:31:20 (18,451)
Langford, Sarah L 5:26:09 (29,956)
Langham, Katy 4:32:18 (18,706)
Langham, Michelle 5:50:02 (32,337)
Langley, Catherine J 4:54:17 (24,284)
Langley, Georgina K 4:11:53 (13,355)
Langley, Irene A 5:45:36 (31,985)
Langley, Katherine E 5:50:05 (32,345)
Langstaff, Emma M 4:23:49 (16,391)
Langton, Clementine D 5:34:05 (30,866)
Langton, Francesca K 6:45:15 (34,714)
Langton, Georgie 5:24:03 (29,660)
Langton, India R 5:27:21 (30,083)
Langton, Michelle R 4:47:51 (22,689)
Lankester, Melanie 7:07:28 (35,034)
Lannon, Laura J 4:04:02 (11,457)
Lansdown, Caroline A 4:56:53 (24,906)
Lantz, Meredith 6:06:16 (33,401)
Lapper, Alison M 4:23:47 (16,382)
Lapper, Sandi 7:27:48 (35,201)

Larbalestier, Jane M 4:04:29 (11,541)
Larderet, Edith 5:00:59 (25,805)
Large, Hayley J 5:22:44 (29,470)
Large, Krista F 5:33:54 (30,853)
Larke, Wendy 6:00:50 (33,104)
Larkin, Jacqui L 5:20:37 (29,166)
Larkin, Rachel C 3:54:06 (8,781)
Larkin, Valerie J 4:29:36 (17,986)
Larkman, Alice 4:05:42 (11,822)
Larnach, Kim N 5:38:54 (31,384)
Larnder, Sarah 4:11:01 (13,112)
Larsson, Charlotta 4:03:05 (11,246)
Larsson, Karin 4:29:10 (17,876)
Larvin, Jo Emma B 4:11:14 (13,168)
Laryea, Edmee 5:42:54 (31,759)
Lashwood, Alison 4:09:31 (12,728)
Laslo, Shikira A 5:28:42 (30,237)
Lau, Che-Man 5:57:56 (32,911)
Lauder, Sarah N 3:50:22 (7,915)
Laurence, Patricia A 5:50:00 (32,333)
Laurens, Kristin R 4:40:46 (20,902)
Laurie, Coffin 4:28:45 (17,760)
Laverty, Clare E 5:33:33 (30,810)
Lavia, Lisa 5:02:24 (26,094)
Lavis, Janet E 4:14:34 (14,047)
Lawler, Bethan 4:54:39 (24,377)
Lawler, Caroline 5:52:44 (32,535)
Lawler, Kate 4:40:35 (20,858)
Lawrence, Chris L 3:25:33 (3,468)
Lawrence, Helen J 4:13:46 (13,863)
Lawrence, Helen M 4:05:17 (11,728)
Lawrence, Julia F 4:40:49 (20,917)
Lawrence, Natalie R 5:18:48 (28,934)
Lawrence, Nichola E 5:44:19 (31,879)
Laws, Amy 4:38:04 (20,189)
Laws, Bridget M 4:07:22 (12,205)
Laws, Faye E 5:15:33 (28,427)
Laws, Linda J 4:54:13 (24,264)
Lawson, Elspeth C 4:18:45 (15,092)
Lawson, Jocelyn 4:30:47 (18,299)
Lawson, Sarah 3:55:12 (9,085)
Lawson-Smith, Maxine 5:13:22 (28,048)
Lawton, Barbara 5:12:40 (27,920)
Lawton, Faith Janet 4:39:38 (20,621)
Lawton, Jayne 4:00:36 (10,698)
Lawton, Kate L 4:28:36 (17,724)
Lawton, Victoria J 4:27:48 (17,487)
Lawton-Archer, Paula 4:38:35 (20,319)
Lax, Nicolette T 5:29:19 (30,311)
Laxton, Lois N 4:24:33 (16,581)
Laxton-Kane, Martha 4:00:46 (10,733)
Laycock, Helen J 5:53:33 (32,586)
Lazard, Penny J 4:42:29 (21,329)
Le Fanu, Celia R 3:58:02 (9,950)
Le Vay, Lulu D 5:09:32 (27,370)
Lea, Joanna R 5:21:03 (29,231)
Lea, Pauline E 4:47:06 (22,515)
Leach, Helen 5:02:17 (26,076)
Leach, Patricia C 6:57:05 (34,922)
Leadbetter, Tracey A 6:43:00 (34,679)
Leader, Gillian M 5:24:17 (29,697)
Leader, Zoe M 4:18:01 (14,891)
Leahy, Caoimhe B 3:19:20 (2,659)
Leahy, Kate P 4:43:54 (21,691)
Learoyd, Jo 4:41:29 (21,083)
Learoyd, Rowen 4:41:29 (21,083)
Leary-Joyce, Miriam E 6:06:33 (33,414)
Leask, Mary 4:37:01 (19,922)
Leatham, Naomi A 7:26:08 (35,190)
Leavy, Julie 7:18:07 (35,128)
Leavy, Yvette E 4:41:15 (21,026)
Leberl, Marie Jane A 3:47:31 (7,292)
Leckey, Louise A 6:03:39 (33,265)
Lecky, Martina A 4:57:27 (25,021)
Lederer, Tracy 5:03:24 (26,267)
Ledger, Alison J 4:54:01 (24,225)
Ledgister, Christine E 5:22:57 (29,511)
Lee, Anne 3:34:55 (4,943)
Lee, Carol A 6:00:34 (33,084)
Lee, Christine M 6:40:50 (34,642)
Lee, Chun Duk 6:09:22 (33,530)
Lee, Denise Y 4:30:21 (18,194)
Lee, Elaine Y 4:23:27 (16,296)
Lee, Gayle M 3:55:39 (9,207)
Lee, Hannah 6:45:10 (34,713)
Lee, Jackie 6:12:35 (33,664)
Lee, Jane 3:57:00 (9,619)
Lee, Jay Elizabeth 4:30:43 (18,286)
Lee, Jo M 7:07:04 (35,027)
Lee, Joanna F 5:17:44 (28,755)
Lee, Justine 5:56:36 (32,800)
Lee, Lorraine 6:25:53 (34,272)
Lee, Louise A 5:54:01 (32,615)
Lee, Nicola J 3:46:44 (7,140)
Lee, Rebecca E 3:50:24 (7,920)
Lee, Rebecca J 4:51:43 (23,679)
Lee, Sang Sook 4:18:54 (15,133)
Lee, Sarah 4:55:51 (24,653)
Lee, Susannah 3:59:33 (10,404)
Lee, Tracey D 4:59:41 (25,529)
Lee, Tracy 4:54:25 (24,317)
Lee, Victoria 4:32:25 (18,735)
Lee, Zhongwen 5:32:08 (30,654)
Leech, Maxine R 4:58:15 (25,202)
Leed, Karen E 4:37:33 (20,054)
Leeds, Anna D 5:58:03 (32,923)
Lee-Goodall, Jessica 5:31:41 (30,603)
Leeson, Catherine M 3:54:13 (8,815)
Leeson, Sharon 5:21:30 (29,298)
Leeson, Yvonne 3:45:55 (6,969)
Leeves, Nicola 4:24:36 (16,592)
Lefevre, Chantal J 3:58:20 (10,046)
Leftley, Becky 5:25:54 (29,917)
Leftley, Sarah C 4:43:49 (21,671)
Legat, Jennie K 4:30:06 (18,126)
Legesse, Beth 6:58:46 (34,933)
Legg, Alison J 4:51:01 (23,494)
Legg, Angie M 4:09:46 (12,794)
Legg, Caroline E 5:51:22 (32,436)
Leggate, Jane 4:34:08 (19,179)
Legge, Victoria L 6:04:08 (33,294)
Leggett, Anne 4:05:51 (11,850)
Leggett, Leanne J 6:46:41 (34,733)
Leishman, Maria 5:28:24 (30,202)
Lejeune, Valerie 3:41:00 (6,028)
Lemanski, Charlotte L 4:03:28 (11,323)
Lemay, Nita Kay 6:13:00 (33,694)
Lemon, Michelle G 4:20:55 (15,668)
Lemon, Tessa A 4:23:26 (16,290)
Lenaghan, Alison L 3:26:43 (3,637)
Lenaghan, Chloe 5:51:50 (32,472)
Lench, Abbie 4:43:03 (21,481)
Lench, Angie 4:36:35 (19,813)
Lennard, Lucinda 5:25:22 (29,840)
Lennon, Kathryn A 7:26:07 (35,188)
Lens, Charlotte 6:18:41 (33,977)
Lenton, Barbara H 4:41:34 (21,109)
Lenton-Cliffe, Clare 5:42:12 (31,694)
Leonard, Annette M 5:37:34 (31,237)
Leonard, Eileen A 4:36:24 (19,773)
Leonard, Jennifer 4:48:20 (22,814)
Leonard, Sue S 5:05:13 (26,595)
Leslie, Alex 4:48:25 (22,831)
Leslie, Anna S 6:07:22 (33,453)
Leslie, Jane 4:27:58 (17,532)
Leslie, Jenny L 6:02:02 (33,172)
Leslie, Wilma 5:19:31 (29,038)
Lesorgen, Yona 4:50:03 (23,253)
Lester, Samantha 4:39:23 (20,542)
Letts, Debbie A 5:27:13 (30,068)
Letts, Rachel Jane 4:12:31 (13,533)
Leung, Tina K 4:56:55 (24,917)
Levett, Kim Marie 4:02:30 (11,126)
Levins, Sharon M 4:44:34 (21,848)
Levitt, Shelley 5:27:30 (30,093)
Levy, Fiona 3:56:02 (9,322)
Levy, Laura A 6:10:19 (33,578)
Levy, Michelle J 4:53:09 (24,012)
Levy, Wendy 6:03:48 (33,276)
Lewin, Claire L 3:55:34 (9,176)
Lewis, Amanda J 5:14:52 (28,290)
Lewis, Beverley A 4:53:19 (24,044)
Lewis, Caroline J 4:13:38 (13,834)
Lewis, Christine 5:03:17 (26,248)
Lewis, Debbie A 4:02:15 (11,077)
Lewis, Eileen 3:54:45 (8,956)
Lewis, Evelyn Isobel C 5:18:00 (28,794)
Lewis, Hannah O 4:43:11 (21,511)
Lewis, Heidi E 3:56:36 (9,489)
Lewis, Jayne L 5:04:29 (26,452)
Lewis, Jodie A 4:32:39 (18,806)
Lewis, Julie I 5:20:32 (29,156)
Lewis, Karen 6:57:35 (34,926)
Lewis, Karen L 4:54:37 (24,365)
Lewis, Kate 5:11:26 (27,715)
Lewis, Kate D 4:42:49 (21,412)
Lewis, Katharine 6:25:32 (34,257)
Lewis, Kathryn A 6:16:04 (33,845)
Lewis, Laura C 5:20:23 (29,138)
Lewis, Melanie 4:54:59 (24,444)
Lewis, Menna I 4:13:15 (13,729)
Lewis, Non 5:43:11 (31,792)
Lewis, Siobhan A 5:00:44 (25,755)
Lewis, Susan L 4:57:16 (24,978)
Lewis, Vanessa D 4:55:04 (24,468)
Lewry, Angela Louise 4:34:39 (19,300)
Lewry, Siobhan M 4:34:32 (19,267)
Ley, Marianne 5:26:50 (30,028)
Li, Jayne 5:03:29 (26,282)
Li, Sarah 4:10:10 (12,904)
Liberman, Amanda C 5:49:51 (32,325)
License, Kerry 4:49:30 (23,116)
Lichman, Zoe E 5:18:07 (28,807)
Liddiard, Heather 5:08:10 (27,119)
Liddle, Helen J 4:46:29 (22,341)
Lieber, Margot M 5:54:40 (32,657)
Lightfoot, Cathryn L 4:11:27 (13,242)
Lightfoot, Claire E 4:41:37 (21,122)
Lightfoot, Joyce 6:45:43 (34,718)
Lightman, Sarah J 5:25:46 (29,901)
Lillie, Julie B 5:57:25 (32,867)
Lilwall, Deborah A 4:41:47 (21,162)
Lim, Nicola 4:51:57 (23,741)
Limpenny, Charlotte 4:12:25 (13,494)
Lincoln, Anastasia 4:47:52 (22,693)
Lincoln, Michelle L 4:32:41 (18,812)
Lincoln, Victoria M 3:14:57 (2,225)
Linderoth, Ann-Christine 4:09:52 (12,825)
Lindley, Holly 4:04:57 (11,645)
Lindley, Rachel E 4:26:27 (17,097)
Lindley, Sarah 4:21:35 (15,837)
Lindon, Jacqueline 6:20:09 (34,041)
Lindsay, Claire L 4:27:56 (17,524)
Lindsay, Jenny 5:04:31 (26,459)
Lindsay, Judy 4:36:02 (19,689)
Lindsay, Rachael L 4:54:11 (24,255)
Lindsay, Tiffany M 6:00:16 (33,061)
Lines, Julia 4:39:22 (20,536)
Ling, Ann E 6:16:31 (33,866)
Ling, Catherine 6:00:30 (33,075)
Ling, Melanie J 3:43:55 (6,617)
Ling, Melanie J 4:38:58 (20,426)
Ling, Victoria H 4:55:45 (24,624)
Lingley, Ruth 4:50:47 (23,445)
Link, Britta 4:00:13 (10,603)
Linsell, Ellie K 4:34:16 (19,215)
Linton, Emma L 5:01:00 (25,811)
Linton, Sara Jayne 3:59:42 (10,460)
Linwood, Joanna K 5:07:34 (27,016)
Lipparelli, Tania M 4:43:18 (21,543)
Lisney, Lisa M 5:09:35 (27,382)
Lister, Gillian F 3:50:05 (7,853)
Lister, Jill F 4:26:28 (17,104)
Lister, June 4:20:53 (15,657)
Lister, Karen G 6:48:22 (34,782)
Lister, Sandra A 7:14:55 (35,104)
Litadier, Irene Marie Claire 4:30:02 (18,106)
Littell, Sarah A 3:43:34 (6,536)
Litterick, Emma C 3:24:41 (3,366)
Little, Adrienne 4:26:31 (17,121)
Little, Catherine J 4:43:37 (21,628)
Little, Deborah 5:17:00 (28,638)
Little, Gina M 3:57:06 (9,648)
Little, Liesl 4:47:49 (22,675)
Little, Louise M 3:30:52 (4,305)
Littlechild, Karen E 3:49:49 (7,803)
Littlecott, Amanda C 5:26:56 (30,045)
Littlefield, Angelina E 3:57:56 (9,912)
Littler, Mary T 5:24:57 (29,790)

Littlewood, Janet E......3:29:11 (4,035)
Litton, Tara Jayne......4:26:08 (17,020)
Liu, Michelle......3:59:45 (10,477)
Liu, Susan......4:49:39 (23,165)
Livesey, Jennifer L......5:00:12 (25,633)
Livesey, Laura......5:50:14 (32,357)
Livesey, Rachel......5:19:30 (29,036)
Livesey, Tracy......4:32:55 (18,876)
Livingstone, Mandy J......3:19:58 (2,752)
Lizart, Florence......3:56:32 (9,469)
Lloyd, Androulla......5:01:23 (25,893)
Lloyd, Christine E......4:50:31 (23,376)
Lloyd, Joanne M......7:31:05 (35,225)
Lloyd, Katie M......4:24:12 (16,497)
Lloyd, Rhiannon Eleanor Iris......4:12:33 (13,538)
Lloyd, Sally C......5:22:40 (29,464)
Lloyd, Susan D......4:15:47 (14,344)
Loach, Deborah......4:11:25 (13,228)
Loach, Kate E......3:39:49 (5,812)
Loader, Carole A......3:26:52 (3,659)
Lobacevske, Diana......2:38:26 (163)
Lobb, Michele I......6:15:53 (33,839)
Lock, Anne P......4:35:21 (19,506)
Lock, Claire P......6:54:55 (34,893)
Lock, Maria E......4:11:02 (13,121)
Locke, Helen R......4:45:44 (22,139)
Locket, Sophie J......5:25:49 (29,906)
Lockett, Ellen R......3:44:51 (6,779)
Lockett, Hannah......4:30:47 (18,299)
Lockett, Rebecca J......4:53:54 (24,202)
Lockey, Anne C......4:43:28 (21,593)
Lockhart, Emily......4:19:15 (15,221)
Lockhart-Gregg, Jennifer......4:45:21 (22,045)
Lockley, Dawn M......5:35:22 (31,009)
Lockley, Joanne......7:22:04 (35,160)
Lockton, Nathalie......4:07:18 (12,176)
Lockwood, Linda A......4:52:47 (23,923)
Locock, Rosemary L......5:35:55 (31,064)
Lodge, Kerry A......6:03:32 (33,260)
Lodwig, Clare E......3:41:53 (6,185)
Loffhagen, Judith......5:09:58 (27,453)
Lofts, Fiona J......5:33:45 (30,837)
Logan, Alaina Louise......4:39:45 (20,657)
Lohmus, Gerli......4:30:06 (18,126)
Lomas, Hayley......3:40:37 (5,961)
Lomas, Jennifer M......7:05:49 (35,013)
Lomas, Sarah......2:57:52 (826)
London, Carol......5:06:26 (26,797)
Lonergan, Kate E......4:06:24 (11,969)
Lonergan, Rachel L......5:19:49 (29,074)
Long, Cheryl A......4:24:41 (16,621)
Long, Christine A......5:14:28 (28,237)
Long, Jackie C......6:36:46 (34,557)
Long, Jennifer E......5:00:05 (25,610)
Long, Lorraine......3:58:52 (10,218)
Long, Michelle R......5:35:37 (31,031)
Long, Sandra J......4:28:22 (17,663)
Longford, Anouska......3:53:33 (8,634)
Longhurst, Claire J......4:49:11 (23,012)
Longley, Zira K......4:38:16 (20,246)
Lonsdale, Caroline L......4:08:28 (12,500)
Looker, Lisa K......4:23:37 (16,341)
Loosemore, Georgina C......3:43:37 (6,548)
Loosemore, Kathryn......4:53:10 (24,017)
Lopez, Shelley A......3:27:07 (3,698)
Lopez De La Puente, Carmen......5:08:24 (27,164)
Lopez Graña, Maria Del Pilar......3:50:26 (7,929)
Loraine, Sally J......5:52:22 (32,506)
Lord, Anna......4:46:41 (22,391)
Lord, Octavia N......5:53:24 (32,577)
Lorgeray, Jocelyne......4:18:02 (14,900)
Lorimer, Bryony F......3:41:25 (6,104)
Lorimer, Erica E......3:54:22 (8,855)
Lorraine, Veronica......4:29:01 (17,834)
Lort-Phillips, Rachel......5:49:16 (32,274)
Lota-Zunino, Isabelle......4:35:57 (19,664)
Lott, Gabrielle S......4:56:13 (24,733)
Lotz, Anne Lise......6:26:24 (34,296)
Loubser, Rona C......2:53:11 (566)
Lough, Rosie......4:08:14 (12,425)
Loughlin, Sarah J......5:20:03 (29,100)
Lour, Sylvia......4:20:03 (15,442)
Lovatt, Ellen L......4:47:41 (22,647)
Love, Sarah L......5:00:05 (25,610)
Lovell, Helen M......4:06:20 (11,957)
Lovell, Nicola......3:43:33 (6,532)
Lovell, Sally......3:29:32 (4,104)
Lovell-Knight, Jade A......4:17:42 (14,819)
Lovelock, Victoria E......4:32:51 (18,860)
Lovesy, Jennifer......3:56:24 (9,429)
Lovett, Sally......4:34:22 (19,232)
Lovett, Tamsin V......4:21:16 (15,759)
Lovett, Zoe......6:54:51 (34,891)
Loveys, Lara F......4:55:46 (24,628)
Low, Alexandra Diane......5:21:05 (29,234)
Low, Claire L......4:55:12 (24,506)
Low, Rebecca J......6:28:27 (34,369)
Lowe, Alison C......3:57:06 (9,648)
Lowe, Angela......5:47:16 (32,118)
Lowe, Jaki......4:30:37 (18,260)
Lowe, Sanchia......5:33:48 (30,844)
Lowe, Stephanie......4:32:55 (18,876)
Lowe, Vanessa S......3:35:29 (5,045)
Lowe, Vicki A......3:39:55 (5,838)
Lowes, Kim L......3:57:37 (9,806)
Lowing, Bethan......5:41:15 (31,602)
Lowman, Sarah L......4:20:13 (15,490)
Lowndes, Jane L......4:48:34 (22,866)
Lowndes, Sally A......4:15:03 (14,176)
Lowndes, Valerie......6:12:39 (33,670)
Lowry, Brenda E......5:09:33 (27,374)
Lowry, Noelle J......4:36:57 (19,900)
Lowther, Deborah......4:42:41 (21,381)
Lowther, Emma A......4:44:56 (21,936)
Lubbock, Sandra K......4:41:33 (21,103)
Lucas, Jillian C......6:38:01 (34,591)
Lucas, Jody K......4:52:37 (23,883)
Lucas, Sarah......4:45:33 (22,090)
Lucas, Stephanie K......4:53:01 (23,979)
Lucas Munce, Joanna C......4:54:15 (24,273)
Luce, Nicola A......4:53:49 (24,177)
Lucena, Gemma......6:22:33 (34,128)
Lucien, Eldica M......4:29:51 (18,056)
Luck, Lorraine E......4:28:28 (17,688)
Luck, Nicky J......5:48:12 (32,188)
Lucken, Andrea M......4:32:16 (18,701)
Lucy, Clair E......5:29:53 (30,389)
Lucy, Samantha......4:55:01 (24,452)
Ludlam, Melissa Kate......4:27:16 (17,333)
Ludlow, Samantha R......4:04:07 (11,470)
Luis, Mary M......4:02:23 (11,102)
Luji-Ross, Latifah......4:11:55 (13,362)
Luke, Emily......4:11:22 (13,214)
Lumby, Philly S......6:07:17 (33,450)
Lumley, Joan I......6:50:41 (34,828)
Lundemose, Anker......4:28:20 (17,658)
Lunn, Chris J......3:38:59 (5,683)
Luong, Ling......4:24:56 (16,691)
Lurani, Carola......4:20:22 (15,527)
Luscombe, Clare L......4:32:44 (18,826)
Luscombe, Jennifer A......4:32:44 (18,826)
Lusty, Elizabeth R......3:48:17 (7,460)
Luthman, Elizabeth C......6:16:17 (33,856)
Luton, Nicola J......5:11:48 (27,775)
Luxford, Louise R......6:29:18 (34,391)
Lyddy, Sylvia......7:04:22 (34,997)
Lydon, Carole......4:12:26 (13,499)
Lyle, Rachel......5:16:35 (28,577)
Lyman Smith, Helen......4:58:17 (25,209)
Lynch, Anna S......5:09:37 (27,386)
Lynch, Catherine L......4:47:04 (22,501)
Lynch, Donna J......5:13:46 (28,115)
Lynch, Helen......5:42:40 (31,736)
Lynch, Jo L......6:37:36 (34,582)
Lynch, Madeline F......4:39:50 (20,676)
Lynch, Nicola......4:09:45 (12,788)
Lyness, Catherine......6:11:50 (33,633)
Lyon, Anita K......4:51:31 (23,625)
Lyon, Nicola C......4:34:26 (19,244)
Lyons, Alice R......4:24:19 (16,532)
Lyons, Alison......4:42:06 (21,226)
Lyons, Zoe E......3:55:42 (9,221)
Lysne, Kristin S......3:32:18 (4,516)
Lysons, Alison Julie......4:42:57 (21,459)
Lyubova, Julia......5:31:12 (30,553)
MacAndrew, Karen D......4:58:09 (25,179)
MacArthur, Georgina......4:14:03 (13,919)
Macatonia, Eve C......5:22:39 (29,461)
Macaulay, Sheila M......4:25:50 (16,945)
Macbeth, Jo L......4:44:34 (21,848)
Macdonald, Abigail......5:03:37 (26,308)
Macdonald, Alison......3:34:02 (4,763)
Macdonald, Kym......5:37:58 (31,270)
Macdonald, Linda......4:09:48 (12,803)
Macdonald, Roberta N......5:50:56 (32,412)
Macdonald, Wanda......3:50:29 (7,941)
MacDougall, Jane......4:31:36 (18,528)
Mace, Joanne......5:49:47 (32,319)
MacEnhill, Tina......4:03:44 (11,368)
Macfarlane, Fiona M......5:06:57 (26,894)
Macfarlane, Lisa L......5:24:08 (29,673)
Macfarlane, Nicola L......4:39:40 (20,634)
MacGregor, Helen......3:48:31 (7,513)
MacGregor, Sue M......4:15:20 (14,240)
MacGregor, Victoria R......3:30:44 (4,288)
Macham, Ann......5:15:45 (28,466)
Machen, Sarah E......3:42:46 (6,370)
Machin, Carolyn A......4:57:55 (25,119)
Machin, Juliet A......6:31:46 (34,447)
Machin, Victoria S......4:24:45 (16,638)
MacIver, Isabel......5:07:57 (27,078)
Mack, Anne......5:07:30 (27,008)
Mackaill, Linda......5:38:44 (31,361)
Mackay, Heather J......4:19:38 (15,323)
Mackay, Jenny......4:30:40 (18,272)
Mackay, Julia D......4:32:24 (18,728)
Mackay, Lucy S......3:42:56 (6,408)
Mackay, Penny......5:05:44 (26,691)
Mackenzie, Emily R......4:36:29 (19,791)
Mackenzie, Kaeti A......3:08:44 (1,593)
Mackie, Jill......3:33:52 (4,734)
Mackin, Mary......3:40:05 (5,875)
Mackinney, Beccy J......6:09:47 (33,551)
Mackintosh, Sarah L......4:50:32 (23,381)
Macklin, Becky......3:57:39 (9,826)
Macklin, Yolande E......4:06:12 (11,927)
Mackness, Sarah......4:49:27 (23,092)
Mackrell, Allison......4:54:37 (24,365)
Maclaren, Lesley A......5:08:44 (27,219)
Maclaren, Sarah Jane......4:32:38 (18,801)
MacLennan, Joanna M......5:58:38 (32,969)
MacLennan, Katherine L......4:25:20 (16,796)
Macleod, Helen......3:43:46 (6,580)
Macleod, Kirsty......4:39:53 (20,688)
MacNab, Sheila M......4:14:45 (14,096)
MacNeall, Lisa H......4:53:34 (24,089)
Macrae, Chris D......5:47:58 (32,167)
Macrae, Vivien M......5:11:01 (27,642)
MacRitchie, Fiona......3:30:10 (4,202)
MacWilliams, Fallon......5:11:13 (27,676)
Madden, Anna L......3:29:40 (4,127)
Madden, Christina......5:02:46 (26,170)
Madden, Kate A......5:50:15 (32,360)
Madden, Vicky A......5:59:21 (33,009)
Maddison, Gemma......5:31:46 (30,614)
Maddock, Sheila E......4:02:21 (11,091)
Maddock, Suzanne E......4:29:38 (17,994)
Maddocks, Hazel......6:36:57 (34,561)
Madelaine, Lemoine......5:05:17 (26,603)
Maden, Deborah N......4:25:53 (16,958)
Madigan, Leonie V......5:12:25 (27,873)
Madsen, Line......4:34:26 (19,244)
Magali, Rouard......4:23:07 (16,215)
Magee, Jo......4:24:45 (16,638)
Magee, Julia......4:11:16 (13,179)
Magee, Katherine......3:30:57 (4,320)
Maggs, Nicola K......4:25:43 (16,915)
Maggs, Yasmine S......3:49:52 (7,811)
Magness, Teresa......5:32:15 (30,665)
Magnusson, Margaret......4:37:09 (19,954)
Magny, Angela......3:56:17 (9,383)
Maguire, Anna L......5:10:40 (27,579)
Maguire, Helen E......3:36:58 (5,314)
Maguire, Joanna D......3:58:20 (10,046)
Maguire, Rosemarie......5:14:57 (28,306)
Maguire, Sarah C......5:19:48 (29,072)
Maguire, Tina L......5:23:53 (29,633)
Maguire, Veronica J......5:24:15 (29,693)
Mahany, Sara-Jayne L......4:30:36 (18,255)

Maher, Bernadette M....3:43:15 (6,479)
Maher, Fiona L....4:26:54 (17,239)
Maher, Kim....5:57:33 (32,880)
Mah-Ford, Linda....4:15:31 (14,287)
Mahon, Sarah....4:14:10 (13,949)
Mahoney, Patricia A....5:30:15 (30,434)
Maidment, Marilyn F....3:35:16 (5,002)
Maidment, Terry....4:47:24 (22,581)
Maile, Joanne....5:02:28 (26,109)
Maillard, Amelie....4:06:56 (12,090)
Maillard, Josette....3:57:35 (9,798)
Main, Katy S....4:07:59 (12,355)
Maindment, Jacqui....5:37:33 (31,234)
Mainwaring, Xanthe A....6:02:22 (33,195)
Maiolino, Lucia....3:55:11 (9,081)
Mair, Anne....6:19:38 (34,020)
Maison, Margaret Cyrilene....5:42:10 (31,686)
Major, Emma....5:14:52 (28,290)
Majteles, Lisa J....4:24:54 (16,686)
Majury, Anna....6:03:27 (33,256)
Makepeace, Joe L....4:30:23 (18,202)
Makin, Cheryl Lesley....4:34:11 (19,193)
Mal, Lynis G....4:07:46 (12,310)
Malcolm, Sarah....3:59:01 (10,254)
Male, Anthony K....5:44:57 (31,925)
Male, Emma L....5:33:39 (30,829)
Maley, Hannah....4:08:05 (12,382)
Malhan, Puneeta D....7:00:49 (34,960)
Malik, Ashi M....5:35:57 (31,071)
Malin, Frances C....3:24:19 (3,314)
Malin, Victoria....5:10:45 (27,592)
Malir, Sarah A....3:06:48 (1,422)
Mallery, Lynne....5:35:53 (31,060)
Mallorie-Williams, Jennifer L....5:06:24 (26,793)
Malloy, Ann....4:47:58 (22,728)
Malloy, Marie....5:36:38 (31,136)
Malmberg, Lena....5:09:17 (27,329)
Malmsten, Ann....3:38:11 (5,532)
Maloney, Louise A....4:40:24 (20,814)
Maltby, Luci J....5:28:34 (30,215)
Maltby, Vicki M....5:14:01 (28,165)
Maltseva, Valentina....4:36:21 (19,750)
Mamouri, Jihane....5:26:13 (29,957)
Mancuso, Lucia....4:08:05 (12,382)
Mandel, Lindsey....5:00:20 (25,663)
Mandelman, Mariah J....3:14:08 (2,137)
Maneely, Dany....4:18:23 (14,990)
Mangel, Astrid....5:53:28 (32,582)
Mangione, Rita....4:48:49 (22,922)
Manhood, Sue J....5:05:34 (26,653)
Manifold, Andreana C....3:58:05 (9,963)
Mankelow, Kate-Emily....4:29:52 (18,066)
Manktelow, Holly J....4:16:03 (14,407)
Manley, Donna D....4:30:42 (18,279)
Mann, Carmel A....5:22:09 (29,381)
Mann, Eleanor J....4:44:38 (21,867)
Mann, Melanie....3:55:56 (9,296)
Mann, Nikola....4:31:28 (18,494)
Mannering, Laura M....5:09:56 (27,444)
Manning, Anna K....4:47:55 (22,712)
Manning, Katie E....5:56:45 (32,813)
Manning, Pamela J....5:57:14 (32,846)
Manning, Susan A....4:24:05 (16,466)
Manning, Tracy....5:31:09 (30,549)
Manning-Brown, Melissa C....4:27:14 (17,317)
Mannion, Deirbhle....4:22:27 (16,068)
Mansbridge, Holly J....5:03:47 (26,338)
Mansbridge, Rebecca M....6:03:39 (33,265)
Mansell, Anita....4:24:17 (16,522)
Mansell, Carol....4:21:43 (15,884)
Mansfield, Sarah....4:21:04 (15,706)
Mansfield, Victoria....4:52:04 (23,769)
Manso, Rita....3:41:48 (6,167)
Mant, Anita L....5:11:20 (27,700)
Manthorpe, Karen....4:59:59 (25,594)
Mantin, Becky....4:46:18 (22,281)
Mantle, Ruth J....5:51:24 (32,438)
Manton, Helen Mary....4:45:52 (22,183)
Manvell, Gabrielle J....4:47:54 (22,707)
Manzolini, Katy E....5:30:07 (30,417)
Mapp, Emma....6:09:06 (33,518)
Mapp, Jane E....4:20:40 (15,591)
Maranzano, Nadia....6:55:21 (34,900)
March, Abi....6:25:11 (34,237)
March, Joanna B....7:06:03 (35,014)
March, Victoria M....5:13:37 (28,083)
Marchant, Carmen L....3:25:36 (3,473)
Marchant, Judy C....4:05:04 (11,670)
Marchant, Michelle E....5:35:37 (31,031)
Marden, Amanda J....4:33:15 (18,959)
Mardon, Helen R....3:40:09 (5,888)
Marfitt, Linda M....4:26:39 (17,168)
Margetts, Lynne....6:42:18 (34,670)
Margolis, Laura....5:54:23 (32,648)
Margree, Anna-Kathryn....5:21:42 (29,332)
Marie Claude, Tournadre....3:53:59 (8,751)
Marie Jeanne, Charrier....5:13:42 (28,099)
Mariko, Miura....5:57:32 (32,879)
Markey, Shelagh A....5:48:23 (32,207)
Markham, Andrea H....4:45:30 (22,079)
Markham, Hannah M....4:42:42 (21,388)
Marks, Anna....5:08:49 (27,232)
Marks, Leander G....3:55:05 (9,059)
Marnoch, Victoria....4:35:18 (19,488)
Marples, Joanne S....5:10:46 (27,598)
Marques, Storme....5:08:50 (27,234)
Marquis, Emily....4:32:47 (18,842)
Marr, Kathy....4:08:05 (12,382)
Marr, Leanne V....4:48:25 (22,831)
Marras, Tiziana....3:55:34 (9,176)
Marrett, Roisin....5:51:35 (32,456)
Marriott, Catherine T....4:32:56 (18,882)
Marriott, Kirsty D....5:46:57 (32,086)
Marriott, Lee....7:57:07 (35,312)
Marriott, Rosemary S....3:35:53 (5,131)
Marsden, Debbie C....5:17:58 (28,788)
Marsden, Helen C....4:38:06 (20,201)
Marsden, Lauren....3:37:58 (5,481)
Marsh, Angela H....6:03:17 (33,247)
Marsh, Kerry Anne....4:38:37 (20,333)
Marsh, Rachel M....5:01:43 (25,956)
Marshall, Anne L....5:59:47 (33,032)
Marshall, Carol E....4:50:39 (23,412)
Marshall, Emma J....3:42:17 (6,267)
Marshall, Fiona Rachel....4:37:56 (20,149)
Marshall, Gwenda L....6:03:15 (33,245)
Marshall, Heather A....3:48:18 (7,465)
Marshall, Kate J....4:46:59 (22,478)
Marshall, Katrina E....4:34:07 (19,176)
Marshall, Kelly-Jay....4:48:53 (22,938)
Marshall, Laura E....5:27:47 (30,120)
Marshall, Lavinia G....6:43:06 (34,682)
Marshall, Leigh A....6:47:36 (34,759)
Marshall, Lisa M....4:21:28 (15,801)
Marshall, Lorraine....3:58:05 (9,963)
Marshall, Louise A....4:35:59 (19,675)
Marshall, Marlee B....6:00:33 (33,080)
Marshall, Maxine....5:17:41 (28,745)
Marshall, Zoe....3:51:39 (8,199)
Martelle Climas, Sher....6:36:56 (34,560)
Martin, Abigail M....5:04:06 (26,403)
Martin, Alison J....5:57:46 (32,894)
Martin, Amy J....4:26:52 (17,229)
Martin, Cheryl T....5:02:33 (26,129)
Martin, Emma K....6:44:54 (34,706)
Martin, Erica L....3:05:07 (1,311)
Martin, Hayley A....5:19:36 (29,050)
Martin, Jackie R....5:14:24 (28,224)
Martin, Joanna....4:13:43 (13,854)
Martin, Joanna....5:41:33 (31,635)
Martin, Katie G....5:21:09 (29,248)
Martin, Lorna J....4:42:22 (21,293)
Martin, Nina Isabella....3:41:50 (6,173)
Martin, Samantha....5:08:03 (27,094)
Martin, Sara E....4:56:17 (24,747)
Martin, Sarah....4:32:07 (18,666)
Martin, Serena....4:16:32 (14,531)
Martin, Stephanie A....4:13:21 (13,768)
Martin, Tessa....5:49:19 (32,277)
Martin, Tisha A....4:29:49 (18,041)
Martin, Tracey A....4:24:19 (16,532)
Martin, Victoria J....5:54:40 (32,657)
Martindale, Fiona....4:00:46 (10,733)
Martino, Orsolina Irma....4:20:23 (15,534)
Martins, Marketa....3:57:30 (9,772)
Martin-Sierra, Véronique....4:32:38 (18,801)
Marvel, Alison J....4:23:56 (16,423)
Marwa, Jude....4:15:43 (14,323)
Marwick, Denise....5:50:25 (32,370)
Marzaioli, Sarah L....3:51:46 (8,220)
Marzullo, Jennifer M....4:51:43 (23,679)
Mascarenhas, Emily....4:46:35 (22,370)
Mascitti, Rita....3:18:24 (2,567)
Masding, Deborah J....4:38:52 (20,396)
Maskell, Shelly A....5:39:44 (31,469)
Maslen, Charlotte J....4:59:15 (25,443)
Mason, Dawn....4:18:49 (15,108)
Mason, Helen L....4:51:35 (23,644)
Mason, Lucy....5:57:37 (32,886)
Mason, Nichola J....5:34:41 (30,935)
Mason, Rachel A....4:57:08 (24,953)
Mason, Saroya....4:08:15 (12,430)
Mason, Wendy A....4:52:10 (23,791)
Masquere, Catherine....4:48:58 (22,962)
Mass, Pippa L....5:15:45 (28,466)
Massey, Helen R....5:02:34 (26,132)
Massey, Joanne....5:16:40 (28,590)
Massey, Louise A....3:38:23 (5,560)
Massie, Jennifer C....5:31:10 (30,552)
Masterman, Julie....3:33:45 (4,713)
Masters, Anne....5:03:13 (26,241)
Masterton, Hollie E....5:30:08 (30,423)
Masuda, Yuko....4:53:50 (24,183)
Matchan, Angela....4:16:40 (14,575)
Mather, Fiona L....5:44:08 (31,864)
Mather, Karen....6:26:44 (34,308)
Mather, Lynda C....4:11:03 (13,124)
Mathers, Jo-Anne....3:52:12 (8,328)
Mathias, Michi....4:52:06 (23,775)
Mathie, Louise....4:35:49 (19,630)
Mathieson, Emma L....5:15:41 (28,452)
Mathieson, Rachel....4:29:35 (17,980)
Mathison, Camilla T....3:15:22 (2,270)
Matson, Mel J....4:19:57 (15,408)
Mattey, Celeste L....5:27:03 (30,055)
Matthams, Karys L....5:08:09 (27,112)
Matthews, Claire M....5:08:10 (27,119)
Matthews, Denise....3:57:19 (9,712)
Matthews, Eileen....6:14:02 (33,746)
Matthews, Jackie I....5:33:34 (30,813)
Matthews, Karen....5:16:14 (28,532)
Matthews, Karen L....4:17:10 (14,687)
Matthews, Louise....4:45:49 (22,161)
Matthews, Lucy C....4:57:56 (25,127)
Matthews, Nic T....6:48:25 (34,785)
Matthews, Nina J....4:38:09 (20,215)
Matthews, Samantha J....4:03:46 (11,379)
Matthews, Sarah L....4:09:34 (12,741)
Matveeva, Sophia....4:42:37 (21,366)
Mauchaza, Farai....5:16:00 (28,499)
Maude, Karen M....4:20:19 (15,515)
Mauger, Beverley C....4:04:13 (11,495)
Maulkerson, Rosalind I....4:29:13 (17,899)
Maurice, Alexandra L....6:15:56 (33,842)
Maury, Nancy....4:42:54 (21,445)
Maxwell, Jill Elizabeth....4:15:27 (14,271)
Maxwell, Louise M....6:03:50 (33,278)
Maxwell, Michelle J....3:03:43 (1,217)
May, Jill M....3:34:31 (4,881)
Maya, Irazu....3:42:00 (6,206)
Mayall, Sarah-Jane....5:28:04 (30,155)
Maycock, Carol....4:23:43 (16,367)
Maycock, Fiona J....3:14:14 (2,147)
Maycock, Jacqueline....4:31:32 (18,513)
Mayfield, Elaine S....3:32:21 (4,523)
Mayfield, Lucy E....4:22:23 (16,044)
Mayles, Rebecca A....3:48:44 (7,550)
Maynard, Lisa M....6:05:27 (33,362)
Mayne, Sarah J....3:59:02 (10,261)
Mayo, Victoria....4:34:17 (19,218)
Mazey, Katherine....4:09:16 (12,673)
Mazuir, Karine....4:30:18 (18,176)
Mburu, Philomena W....3:46:39 (7,122)
McAdams, Alison....5:59:48 (33,035)
McAlister, Andrea M....4:29:16 (17,913)
McAllister, Donna L....3:51:49 (8,231)
McAllister, Tracy J....4:38:30 (20,296)
McAndrew, Claire M....4:45:46 (22,147)
McAndrew, Nell....3:10:20 (1,725)

McAneny, Laura E	4:30:58 (18,340)
McArdle, Emmeline	4:31:59 (18,629)
McArdle, Sarah	6:37:43 (34,584)
McArthur, Claire V	3:01:07 (1,060)
McAulay, Marie	6:50:07 (34,816)
McAvoy, Clare	3:39:29 (5,757)
McAvoy, Liza	5:37:49 (31,255)
McBeth, Caroline A	4:25:23 (16,814)
McCabe, Julia A	5:49:45 (32,313)
McCabe, Laura	4:40:16 (20,790)
McCabe, Maureen A	5:32:30 (30,692)
McCaffrey, Annmarie	3:26:23 (3,585)
McCaffrey, Heather A	4:15:04 (14,180)
McCaffrey, Joanne R	3:56:17 (9,383)
McCann, Elaine A	5:19:22 (29,020)
McCann, Nicola C	4:57:11 (24,962)
McCappin, Lucy K	5:01:53 (25,991)
McCardle, Claire	5:10:07 (27,481)
McCarthy, Christine	3:09:37 (1,669)
McCarthy, Clair	4:43:38 (21,633)
McCarthy, Jane	4:37:30 (20,041)
McCarthy, Michelle K	4:50:56 (23,467)
McCarthy, Patricia	4:54:53 (24,426)
McCarthy, Gail B	4:31:39 (18,538)
McCartney, Christine A	5:53:28 (32,582)
McCaul, Ashley H	6:16:07 (33,846)
McCloskey, Carol	4:50:17 (23,316)
McCloud, Karen E	4:54:15 (24,273)
McClure, Mel E	4:18:38 (15,064)
McCluskey, Gareth S	3:34:41 (4,909)
McConkey, Susan K	4:11:07 (13,145)
McConnell, Lucy	6:52:24 (34,855)
McCook, Patsy	5:08:20 (27,146)
McCormick, Sheree A	3:48:17 (7,460)
McCowen-Smith, Linda	5:49:19 (32,277)
McCracken, Morag	3:28:07 (3,871)
McCrae, Lori	3:21:04 (2,897)
McCrea, Sarah L	4:40:37 (20,865)
McCreath, Natalie S	3:43:35 (6,541)
McCredie, Holly	5:39:38 (31,459)
McCreery, Claire E	3:28:14 (3,890)
McCreeth, Joanna	5:57:36 (32,882)
McCulloch, Amy A	5:19:34 (29,044)
McCune, Samantha M	5:46:55 (32,082)
McCurdie, Fiona K	6:01:26 (33,138)
McCurdie, Susan M	6:01:26 (33,138)
McCusker, Colleen M	6:20:08 (34,039)
McDade, Irene E	4:29:01 (17,834)
McDermott, Claire M	4:26:50 (17,216)
McDermott, Elisabeth S	4:47:46 (22,667)
McDermott, Helen	6:30:16 (34,418)
McDermott, Katie R	5:09:16 (27,321)
McDermott, Shirley M	5:27:50 (30,130)
McDevitt, Hannah L	5:27:08 (30,061)
McDonagh, Lynn	3:52:27 (8,392)
McDonagh, Margaret M	4:35:03 (19,425)
McDonald, Claire	4:54:06 (24,245)
McDonald, Eleanor L	5:05:23 (26,622)
McDonald, Joanne M	5:31:52 (30,624)
McDonald, Linda E	4:04:07 (11,470)
McDonald, Sophia	4:46:55 (22,454)
McDonald, Sophie E	4:50:04 (23,257)
McDonald-Hamilton, Heather	4:39:21 (20,532)
McDonnell, Claire F	3:43:53 (6,611)
McDonnell, Elizabeth L	5:03:40 (26,321)
McDonnell, Rebecca	5:48:32 (32,218)
McDonnell, Tracy	4:26:51 (17,222)
McDougal, Lisa	5:09:09 (27,298)
McEniery, Carmel M	3:48:37 (7,537)
McEvoy, Louise	6:26:43 (34,307)
McEvoy, Sinead H	4:31:30 (18,505)
McEwan, Paula Jayne	6:00:18 (33,063)
McFadyen, Claire C	5:40:56 (31,582)
McFadyen, Georgina E	4:02:41 (11,165)
McFadyen, Jacomina F	4:56:07 (24,710)
McFall, Josie	6:18:54 (33,993)
McFarlane, Kirsty A	4:51:47 (23,695)
McGarry, Gill M	4:13:16 (13,736)
McGarvey, Yvonne C	3:13:21 (2,041)
McGarvey, Agnes	3:35:05 (4,975)
McGhee, Angela	5:49:51 (32,325)
McGibbon, Lisa M	7:13:47 (35,091)
McGill, Andrea	6:25:37 (34,261)

McGill, Jo	5:13:50 (28,123)
McGill, Karen A	4:45:35 (22,101)
McGinn, Carole	5:29:55 (30,392)
McGinn, Ellen	5:31:26 (30,569)
McGinty, Roslyn A	3:20:55 (2,881)
McGlashan, Kerry	4:43:55 (21,694)
McGowan, Joanne M	5:09:13 (27,311)
McGowan, Laura C	4:49:19 (23,058)
McGrath, Allison J	4:37:26 (20,018)
McGrath, Emma	4:13:15 (13,729)
McGrath, Julie	4:44:36 (21,856)
McGrath, Laura	4:09:00 (12,620)
McGrath, Maria T	4:35:10 (19,456)
McGrath, Mary R	5:07:05 (26,921)
McGrath, Susan E	6:39:29 (34,618)
McGrattan, Andrea J	5:45:41 (31,993)
McGregor, Jane K	5:42:46 (31,743)
McGregor, Katie M	6:22:53 (34,149)
McGregor, Kirsten	4:57:00 (24,930)
McGregor, Susan	5:53:08 (32,558)
McGrory, Keelin	3:50:01 (7,840)
McGuinness, Joan T	4:41:02 (20,969)
McHale, Victoria	4:05:20 (11,739)
McHugh, Bridie C	4:17:37 (14,799)
McHugh, Sue J	5:41:17 (31,604)
McHugh, Zoe D	5:44:46 (31,913)
McIlwham, Harriet N	5:22:36 (29,453)
McInally, Catherine J	3:38:23 (5,560)
McInnes, Shona	4:19:49 (15,379)
McInnes, Suzanne	5:01:17 (25,876)
McIntosh, Anne	4:54:05 (24,241)
McIntosh, Joyce	6:54:15 (34,886)
McIntosh, Julia K	3:38:02 (5,497)
McIntosh, Shona L	2:56:35 (751)
McIntosh, Val M	4:14:57 (14,154)
McIntyre, Rossalyn	4:48:18 (22,809)
McIvor, Jenny E	4:14:26 (14,021)
McKail, Shelagh	5:18:48 (28,934)
McKay, Fiona	4:03:18 (11,296)
McKeand, Sadie A	4:09:41 (12,769)
McKee, Alexandra	5:10:20 (27,517)
McKendrick, Fiona M	4:07:18 (12,176)
McKendry, Marlene	7:36:14 (35,254)
McKenna, Angie	5:57:54 (32,905)
McKenna, Diane	4:40:53 (20,936)
McKenna, Sara L	5:05:52 (26,708)
McKenny, Michelle E	5:41:51 (31,659)
McKenzie, Calum P	4:42:27 (21,313)
McKenzie, Katie	6:18:01 (33,926)
McKeown, Carolyn A	4:18:51 (15,118)
McKerrell, FA	5:13:57 (28,151)
McKerrow, Kate C	3:58:57 (10,237)
McKevitt, Una F	5:02:44 (26,162)
McKiernan, Elizabeth	4:28:16 (17,638)
McKillop, Jaqueline	4:04:21 (11,517)
McKinlay, Kirsty	4:47:01 (22,487)
McKinley-Hutchinson, Oonagh S	5:19:05 (28,981)
McKinney, Janice	4:24:31 (16,573)
McKinnon, Victoria	3:17:16 (2,460)
McKittrick, Julie A	5:27:10 (30,063)
McLachlan, Margaret E	3:17:00 (2,429)
McLachlan, Marisa A	5:38:26 (31,320)
McLaren, Leah K	4:41:22 (21,050)
McLaughlin, Barbara	6:59:59 (34,948)
McLaughlin, Frances	3:56:00 (9,309)
McLaughlin, Hazel C	4:37:32 (20,045)
McLean, Evelyn E	4:20:44 (15,615)
McLean, Kate J	4:05:27 (11,760)
McLean, Samantha	5:05:23 (26,622)
McLean, Sarah E	5:42:50 (31,753)
McLean, Sharon J	5:44:07 (31,862)
McLean, Tracey J	4:29:21 (17,936)
McLean, Tracy L	5:59:58 (33,047)
McLean, Vicky	4:59:40 (25,525)
McLees, Beverley	4:36:11 (19,716)
McLellan, Wendy A	5:32:38 (30,709)
McLeod, Alexandra	4:41:10 (20,998)
McLeod, Angela	5:37:06 (31,187)
McLeod, Jacqui	4:55:05 (24,476)
McLeod, Joan M	5:07:38 (27,031)
McLoughlin, Helen J	3:48:59 (7,616)
McLuckie, Kerrin	5:26:33 (29,998)
McMahon, Emily A	4:15:09 (14,203)

McMahon, Yvonne C	4:21:58 (15,935)
McMaster, Jill	4:27:14 (17,317)
McMath, Melanie C	4:07:08 (12,138)
McMillan, Caroline	4:50:45 (23,434)
McMillan, Denise	6:30:27 (34,426)
McMillan, Kelly	4:09:17 (12,679)
McMullan, Danielle	6:20:38 (34,058)
McMullen, Juliet	5:18:41 (28,914)
McMurtrie, Valerie M	4:58:51 (25,349)
McNabb, Gwyneth	5:22:25 (29,425)
McNamara, Joanne	5:26:53 (30,038)
McNamara, Lucy	5:26:53 (30,038)
McNeice, Sonia C	5:09:37 (27,386)
McNeil, Kirstin	5:28:09 (30,172)
McNeill, Hannah	5:20:57 (29,215)
McNeill-Rogers, Bronwyn L	3:13:49 (2,101)
McNerney, Jayne	4:45:48 (22,155)
McParlin, Catherine L	7:57:21 (35,314)
McQuaid, Linda D	5:56:27 (32,789)
McQueen, Elise	4:30:27 (18,217)
McQueen, Toni C	4:06:33 (12,005)
McRoberts, Janet	3:49:02 (7,627)
McRuvie, Jill E	4:47:48 (22,671)
McShane, Paula J	6:02:55 (33,225)
McShannon, Emma	5:32:24 (30,675)
McSharry, Sinead M	5:20:15 (29,121)
McShea, Lisa M	4:49:37 (23,155)
McShea, Thérèse	7:05:21 (35,007)
McSkeane, Patricia	5:14:02 (28,170)
McTaggart, Jackie A	6:02:04 (33,174)
McVann, Lisa	5:31:04 (30,537)
McWhinnie, Laura J	5:13:46 (28,115)
McWilliams, Jo K	4:49:26 (23,088)
Mead, Anna V	5:15:41 (28,452)
Meade, Ashley	5:36:50 (31,159)
Meade, Denise E	6:18:16 (33,940)
Meads, Roberta R	5:28:42 (30,237)
Meakin, Kathryn A	4:19:55 (15,404)
Meaney, Julie A	5:22:53 (29,494)
Meanwell, Katie E	4:35:59 (19,675)
Measures, Julie D	4:31:37 (18,531)
Medawar, Laya	4:52:01 (23,753)
Medcalf, Pippa	5:04:52 (26,518)
Medeiros, Ana C	4:54:51 (24,418)
Medland, Joan V	3:55:06 (9,065)
Medley, Elizabeth L	4:16:31 (14,525)
Meek, Hayley	3:55:53 (9,282)
Meek, Rebecca E	5:30:55 (30,510)
Meek, Tessa	5:10:54 (27,620)
Meek-Welsh, Beverley	4:39:58 (20,710)
Megarrell, Susan G	5:57:55 (32,908)
Megaw, Hannah	5:06:43 (26,846)
Melbourne, Rowena	3:54:49 (8,973)
Meldrum, Helen C	6:14:51 (33,783)
Melhuish, Alyson K	4:08:20 (12,464)
Meline, Lindsay	4:26:31 (17,121)
Mella, Lucy A	5:32:04 (30,648)
Mellor, Anne E	5:06:58 (26,901)
Mellor, Georgina R	5:52:17 (32,502)
Mellor, Sally	4:25:32 (16,847)
Melmoe, Victoria A	5:43:45 (31,830)
Melville, Sarah E	4:58:42 (25,319)
Melvin, Gillian R	5:29:42 (30,359)
Melvin, Helen M	4:56:33 (24,814)
Menadue, Felicity J	3:37:15 (5,364)
Mendez, Dalia	5:56:13 (32,771)
Mendis, Dinesha	7:15:55 (35,112)
Mendoza, Lisa Caroline	3:58:07 (9,978)
Mendus-Edwards, Nicola L	4:28:42 (17,749)
Menzies, Issy	3:05:12 (1,318)
Mepsted, Kim M	4:23:22 (16,268)
Mercer, Abigail S	4:22:05 (15,961)
Mercer, Kimberley G	5:13:26 (28,052)
Mercer, Lesley J	4:20:58 (15,681)
Mercer, Susan E	6:22:27 (34,124)
Mercer-Leach, Lisa A	5:08:53 (27,250)
Meredith, Deborah	4:19:10 (15,203)
Meredith, Jayne	5:57:03 (32,838)
Meredith, Jean	6:27:23 (34,341)
Meredith, Katie A	3:20:21 (2,803)
Meredith, Katie L	5:06:35 (26,821)
Meredith, Louise	4:44:37 (21,861)
Meredith, Stephanie E	4:55:52 (24,659)

Merredy, Lucy J 4:16:10 (14,441)
Merredy, Victoria A....................4:13:29 (13,791)
Merrett, Rosina B....................4:04:27 (11,532)
Merrick, Deborah....................5:34:26 (30,903)
Merryweather, Marilyn....................4:48:29 (22,846)
Merryweather, Ruth 3:22:42 (3,098)
Merton, Jules....................5:59:29 (33,017)
Messanger, Prue 4:44:51 (21,918)
Messervy-Evans, Anna 4:42:51 (21,425)
Meta, Natalia 4:39:36 (20,613)
Metcalf, Heidi L 6:39:11 (34,613)
Metcalf, Julia....................5:08:07 (27,106)
Metcalf, Victoria J....................6:28:06 (34,359)
Metson, Louise S....................4:51:40 (23,667)
Meurice, Penelope A 5:25:54 (29,917)
Meuwissen, Jeanne....................4:48:49 (22,922)
Meyer, Marie-Josee 4:09:55 (12,837)
Meyer, Sophie Victoria....................4:24:29 (16,567)
Meyer-Schall, Ingrid....................4:41:19 (21,043)
Micallef, Ricarda 5:23:36 (29,602)
Michael, Julie-Ann 4:45:34 (22,097)
Michael, Mary....................6:20:26 (34,050)
Michel, Marie Odile....................4:30:09 (18,139)
Michele, Deharte 4:00:11 (10,593)
Micklewright, Kelly A....................5:00:55 (25,790)
Middleburgh, Lorraine....................5:54:52 (32,677)
Middleton, Helen....................5:59:38 (33,024)
Middleton, Sally A....................4:19:57 (15,408)
Middleton, Sarah 6:23:56 (34,186)
Middleton, Sophie M....................4:25:51 (16,950)
Middleton, Victoria L 5:04:25 (26,443)
Midgley, Heather E 5:54:44 (32,663)
Midlane, Toni J....................4:20:42 (15,604)
Mihangel, Mari H....................5:15:10 (28,347)
Miho, Taoka....................4:51:39 (23,661)

Mikitenko, Irina 2:22:11 (23)

TIMEX
FLORA LONDON MARATHON 2009
FLORA

Mikkonen, Ira K....................5:08:48 (27,230)
Mikulski, Maureen 4:31:39 (18,538)
Miles, Annette P....................5:32:02 (30,643)
Miles, Bethan D....................3:02:32 (1,148)
Miles, Charlotte R 5:52:28 (32,513)
Miles, Fiona A....................5:32:14 (30,662)
Miles, Jenny 5:15:44 (28,462)
Miles, Joanna....................4:51:40 (23,667)
Miles, Lucy J 5:13:52 (28,134)
Miles, Nannette H....................5:32:32 (30,696)
Miles, Rebecca....................6:37:39 (34,583)
Miles, Rebecca L 4:39:37 (20,618)
Milewski, Julie....................4:41:18 (21,037)
Mill, Lesley M 4:13:10 (13,700)
Millan, Lesley 4:53:36 (24,100)
Millar, Alicia S 5:37:48 (31,253)
Millar, Andrea 4:29:04 (17,850)
Millar, Helen 5:34:22 (30,891)
Millar, Penelope C 4:20:13 (15,490)
Millen, Angela D 4:41:58 (21,195)
Miller, Claire E 4:46:35 (22,370)
Miller, Debbie J 4:41:25 (21,058)
Miller, Eleanor....................4:40:00 (20,726)
Miller, Hannah E....................5:37:33 (31,234)
Miller, Jane E....................6:17:26 (33,901)
Miller, Joanne....................4:58:44 (25,325)
Miller, Julia A....................4:40:04 (20,746)
Miller, Kate 4:40:24 (20,814)
Miller, Kathleen M 4:45:48 (22,155)
Miller, Louise....................4:30:52 (18,321)
Miller, Marie J....................5:13:09 (28,015)
Miller, Mary J....................4:12:13 (13,443)
Miller, Mhairi E....................4:51:20 (23,576)
Miller, Michelle J....................4:32:52 (18,864)
Miller, Sadie M 5:07:10 (26,935)
Miller, Tracey....................4:41:28 (21,077)
Millest, Alice F....................4:30:23 (18,202)
Millett, Anne E 4:02:08 (11,048)
Millington, Hayley....................4:19:13 (15,213)
Millman, Natalie L 4:22:51 (16,156)
Mills, Cathryn L....................6:01:17 (33,127)
Mills, Claire L 4:59:43 (25,538)
Mills, Jacqueline....................5:03:25 (26,268)
Mills, Karen E....................6:01:16 (33,126)
Mills, Kate S....................4:59:50 (25,563)
Mills, Samantha L 4:47:59 (22,736)
Mills, Simon 3:40:14 (5,907)
Mills, Tracy Diane....................5:13:44 (28,110)
Mills Cooper, Sadie 5:01:19 (25,879)
Millward, Laura J....................4:36:03 (19,692)
Milne, Caroline M....................4:21:39 (15,863)
Milne, Juliet N....................4:40:10 (20,768)
Milne, Patricia 3:30:13 (4,209)
Milner, Gillian 4:32:06 (18,664)
Milton, Amanda E....................4:27:24 (17,368)
Milton, Angela....................3:47:25 (7,270)
Minas, Argyro 4:01:31 (10,919)
Minchella, Christine A....................4:55:11 (24,499)
Minchella, Marie....................5:40:49 (31,571)
Minhas, Reena....................5:54:18 (32,639)
Mirande, Marie Josee....................4:28:30 (17,697)
Miras, Rena E 4:50:40 (23,414)
Mishra, Nini....................6:27:00 (34,324)
Miskell, Louise 3:54:58 (9,010)
Miskiw, Lida....................4:08:57 (12,606)
Misselyn, Marie....................5:38:00 (31,274)
Mitchell, Alison C....................4:49:56 (23,225)
Mitchell, Chloe F....................3:39:05 (5,702)
Mitchell, Clare K....................4:07:03 (12,119)
Mitchell, Elizabeth C 4:47:34 (22,617)
Mitchell, Heather....................4:22:09 (15,989)
Mitchell, Heather M 4:05:42 (11,822)
Mitchell, Holly E 4:57:29 (25,028)
Mitchell, Joanna E....................5:02:58 (26,204)
Mitchell, Judith A....................4:35:18 (19,488)
Mitchell, Kelly 5:48:49 (32,240)
Mitchell, Kirsten....................5:14:01 (28,165)
Mitchell, Moira A 4:38:18 (20,251)
Mitchell, Paola T....................4:29:38 (17,994)
Mitchell, Pauline M....................5:14:01 (28,165)
Mitchell, Sally L....................5:22:41 (29,467)
Mitchell, Sarah K....................5:24:59 (29,797)
Mitchell, Sarah L....................3:26:32 (3,603)
Mitchell, Susanna E 6:32:57 (34,471)
Mitchell, Theresa A....................5:03:18 (26,252)
Mitchell, Tracy M 3:08:25 (1,559)
Mitchell-Rose, Poppy 4:30:56 (18,331)
Mitchelmore, Alison 4:38:31 (20,303)
Mitra, Ritu 6:16:11 (33,849)
Mittoo, Denise....................6:03:10 (33,240)
Mize, Rachel 5:42:11 (31,690)
Mockford, Fay L....................5:50:08 (32,353)
Modelska, Zofia Maria 4:09:55 (12,837)
Modern, Helen....................5:37:12 (31,193)
Moehring-Bengisu, Caroline....................5:31:42 (30,606)
Moffat, Cheryl L....................3:48:55 (7,599)
Moffat, Dawn L....................6:09:37 (33,541)
Moffat, Julie M 4:43:55 (21,694)
Moffatt, Fiona H....................3:40:07 (5,881)
Moffatt, Samantha E 5:01:51 (25,980)
Moffatt, Sarah....................5:20:25 (29,144)
Mohamed Shafi, Aziza 6:30:00 (34,411)
Molan, Sara E 4:58:30 (25,268)
Mole, Jennifer M....................5:21:47 (29,339)
Molloy, Gillian 4:24:46 (16,646)
Molloy, Stephanie....................4:31:02 (18,361)
Molony, Debra A 5:04:15 (26,422)
Molyneaux, Jo....................3:27:25 (3,752)
Molyneux, Julia 4:37:16 (19,978)
Monaghan, Michelle....................3:55:34 (9,176)
Monaghan, Siobhan M 4:24:15 (16,511)
Monk, Delia J....................4:44:43 (21,890)
Monk, Michelle 5:42:25 (31,711)
Monks, Catherine L 7:17:16 (35,120)
Monks, Margaret H....................7:17:16 (35,120)
Monnington, Rebecca L....................5:28:42 (30,237)
Montague, Olivia M 4:34:02 (19,158)
Montague, Peter....................7:37:29 (35,258)
Montague-Williams, Rebecca 3:57:49 (9,880)
Montano, Marie A....................6:22:39 (34,138)
Montgomery, Amy....................3:48:57 (7,605)
Monti, Kim E 5:23:13 (29,553)
Moodie, Clemmie 3:55:27 (9,148)
Moody, Anna C....................5:42:51 (31,754)
Moody, Elaine 6:00:35 (33,087)
Moody, Mary....................5:18:35 (28,891)
Moody, Pat....................5:09:17 (27,329)
Moody, Patricia M 4:19:44 (15,348)
Moonlight, Pamela....................3:55:07 (9,072)
Moor, Victoria C....................6:50:34 (34,826)
Moore, Amanda T....................4:36:35 (19,813)
Moore, Emily....................4:51:35 (23,644)
Moore, Emma C....................7:20:08 (35,151)
Moore, Fiona....................4:51:38 (23,655)
Moore, Helen J....................5:07:05 (26,921)
Moore, Jacey....................5:31:43 (30,609)
Moore, Jane N....................4:33:28 (19,016)
Moore, Kirsty....................4:51:24 (23,595)
Moore, Kirsty D 5:10:46 (27,598)
Moore, Liz....................3:52:47 (8,461)
Moore, Lucinda M 4:39:14 (20,502)
Moore, Lyndsey L....................4:12:12 (13,439)
Moore, Nicola....................3:28:11 (3,878)
Moore, Rachel L....................5:23:28 (29,592)
Moore, Rebecca S 4:59:25 (25,475)
Moore, Sarah....................4:08:22 (12,475)
Moore, Sarah....................4:51:21 (23,578)
Moore, Tarryn L....................4:03:57 (11,436)
Moore, Terri M....................6:02:33 (33,200)
Moore, Tracy 5:32:42 (30,722)
Moore, Vanessa 5:30:40 (30,484)
Moores, Alexandra M 4:40:48 (20,911)
Moorhouse, Jane 5:39:48 (31,477)
Morales Morales, Anunciacion....................3:55:26 (9,139)
Morel, Frederique....................3:28:36 (3,938)
More-Molyneux, Sarah 6:28:43 (34,375)
Moreton, Christina 4:08:15 (12,430)
Moreton, Penny 4:34:49 (19,358)
Morford, Anna....................4:26:51 (17,222)
Morgan, Alison E 3:24:30 (3,342)
Morgan, Amanda J....................4:03:20 (11,300)
Morgan, Carole A....................4:07:19 (12,183)
Morgan, Claire 4:03:32 (11,344)
Morgan, Debra J....................5:38:01 (31,279)
Morgan, Harriet R 3:30:02 (4,181)
Morgan, Helen C 6:05:07 (33,344)
Morgan, Jennie 5:32:57 (30,748)
Morgan, Jessica R....................4:30:12 (18,151)
Morgan, Jo....................6:20:58 (34,069)
Morgan, Kate....................4:23:36 (16,334)
Morgan, Kathryn L 4:54:19 (24,292)
Morgan, Kelly....................3:11:34 (1,836)
Morgan, Lesley P....................5:11:56 (27,796)
Morgan, Lon 4:27:37 (17,417)
Morgan, Louise 3:57:59 (9,927)
Morgan, Lucy....................5:56:24 (32,785)
Morgan, Michelle D....................5:08:37 (27,196)
Morgan, Michelle P....................7:25:28 (35,181)
Morgan, Ruth C 4:35:25 (19,525)
Morgan, Sharon 4:46:35 (22,370)
Morgan, Sheila....................5:28:39 (30,230)
Morgan, Sian 3:38:25 (5,570)
Moriarty, Joanna E 5:30:59 (30,526)
Morimoto, Tomo....................2:26:29 (41)

Morineau, Evelyne 4:07:11 (12,148)
Morley, Anne M....................5:09:04 (27,283)
Morley, Camilla 4:12:18 (13,468)
Morley, Emma 3:47:54 (7,374)
Morley, Pattie A....................4:21:26 (15,793)
Morley, Syra 4:10:32 (12,989)
Mornemont, Hannah 5:24:57 (29,790)
Morosi Rizzi, Rezia....................4:15:48 (14,349)
Morris, Becky J 5:40:39 (31,560)
Morris, Bianca 5:08:38 (27,203)
Morris, Brenda M....................4:34:48 (19,355)
Morris, Carole 4:00:27 (10,650)
Morris, Cassandra 5:49:29 (32,289)
Morris, Colette M....................5:02:30 (26,117)
Morris, Diane K....................5:44:58 (31,927)
Morris, Jan E....................3:48:45 (7,552)
Morris, Jane 4:32:23 (18,723)
Morris, Janet L 7:19:08 (35,140)
Morris, Jennifer A 6:46:39 (34,732)
Morris, Jennifer G....................3:35:18 (5,009)
Morris, Kate M....................3:29:40 (4,127)
Morris, Lauren C....................5:57:17 (32,851)
Morris, Madeleine....................3:54:13 (8,815)
Morris, Mandy J....................5:22:09 (29,381)
Morris, Marion J....................5:12:32 (27,897)
Morris, Natalie F 6:24:13 (34,197)
Morris, Phillippa L....................3:11:35 (1,839)
Morris, Rachel J....................3:31:17 (4,368)
Morris, Sara M....................6:24:47 (34,224)
Morris, Sarah L....................3:49:02 (7,627)
Morris, Sarah L....................5:04:42 (26,494)
Morris, Sonya....................4:25:02 (16,719)
Morris, Susan K....................7:36:48 (35,256)
Morris, Susan M 3:43:40 (6,559)
Morris, Tamarisk 5:17:58 (28,788)
Morris, Zoe....................5:04:56 (26,530)
Morris-Mullins, Elen 5:16:21 (28,544)
Morrison, Angelica 5:40:48 (31,569)
Morrison, Ellen M....................4:22:20 (16,031)
Morrison, Moira....................6:03:19 (33,248)
Morrissey, Elizabeth L....................4:31:19 (18,445)
Morse, Hayley L....................4:10:52 (13,081)
Mortimer, Alison S 5:37:32 (31,231)
Mortimer, Marie-Helene R....................5:06:13 (26,766)
Morton, Christine M....................5:01:32 (25,918)
Morton, Collette A....................5:32:31 (30,695)
Morton, Jacqueline A....................3:48:11 (7,442)
Morton, Lisa C 5:45:53 (32,007)
Morton, Lucy J 4:04:53 (11,626)
Morton, Mandy 5:34:39 (30,927)
Morton-Turner, Emma J 5:37:42 (31,246)
Mosca, Francesco 4:33:45 (19,086)
Mosedale, Emily A....................3:37:32 (5,409)
Moseley, Alison E 5:41:13 (31,599)
Moseley, Carol L....................3:36:29 (5,232)
Mosheshe, Oreke D 5:49:03 (32,254)
Moss, Annika....................4:14:13 (13,964)
Moss, Gwen....................5:17:31 (28,719)
Moss, Linda 4:56:30 (24,805)
Moss, Patricia M 6:11:50 (33,633)
Moss, Racheal....................4:04:28 (11,538)
Moss, Stephanie A....................3:45:54 (6,960)
Mossman, Bernadette 3:49:01 (7,622)
Motion, Caroline M 5:32:02 (30,643)
Motley, Anne P 6:00:53 (33,106)
Mott, Geraldine M 6:41:02 (34,647)
Mottershaw, Elizabeth....................4:32:48 (18,847)
Mottram, Charlotte A 5:15:21 (28,394)
Mould, Gaye L....................4:14:44 (14,093)
Mould, Gillian S 3:37:04 (5,333)
Moult, Penelope J 5:38:09 (31,292)
Mountjoy, Rebecca S....................7:23:17 (35,166)
Moutrie, Madeleine P P....................4:30:48 (18,303)
Mouzer, Sandra A....................6:05:47 (33,379)
Mowat, Isobel C....................4:36:38 (19,826)
Mowatt, Lucy C....................6:13:12 (33,707)
Moxham, Victoria 5:43:17 (31,802)
Moye, Jennifer E 4:35:54 (19,654)
Moyle, Janet....................4:59:27 (25,484)
Moynier, Daphne C....................6:14:28 (33,765)
Mtya, Unathi....................5:12:07 (27,826)
Muckley, Dawn 5:50:26 (32,371)
Muir, Jan 4:11:57 (13,374)
Muir, Sharon J 4:38:30 (20,296)
Mulcrone, Natalie 4:25:40 (16,899)
Mulholland, Bronagh 3:54:10 (8,804)
Mulholland, Jenny A....................5:38:43 (31,357)
Mulholland, Justine M....................6:18:02 (33,928)
Mulholland, Ros A 6:59:50 (34,945)
Mullan, Lucy....................4:12:36 (13,547)
Mullan, Nivette K....................4:14:46 (14,102)
Mullany, Lisa A....................5:08:46 (27,225)
Mullenger, Clare 3:13:00 (2,006)
Muller, Nicole....................5:12:14 (27,843)
Mulley, Rebecca J 3:49:11 (7,665)
Mullin, Annabel J....................5:00:17 (25,652)
Mullinger, Louise 4:25:52 (16,951)
Mullins, Brid....................6:01:11 (33,119)
Mullins, Sophie A....................3:40:49 (6,003)
Mullins, Tina 7:32:53 (35,235)
Mulvenna, Claire L 4:45:07 (22,003)
Mumford, Jane A....................4:39:01 (20,438)
Mumford, Jo N 4:56:28 (24,791)
Mumford, Joanne L 3:25:06 (3,409)
Muncey, Felicity....................5:11:33 (27,737)
Munday, Susanna M....................4:33:33 (19,036)
Mundim, Ana Paula....................4:39:15 (20,508)
Mundle, Claire A....................5:40:00 (31,497)
Mundy, Dawn E 5:41:20 (31,612)
Munn, Flavia....................3:47:20 (7,254)
Munn, Jane L....................5:28:15 (30,183)
Munnoch, Andrea M 4:44:58 (21,948)
Munro, Anna R 5:34:03 (30,865)
Munro, Anna L....................6:16:56 (33,881)
Munro, Patricia A....................3:12:41 (1,955)
Munroe, Jean....................4:59:41 (25,529)
Munthali, Waleke T 5:22:15 (29,397)
Murdoch, Gail E....................3:21:36 (2,960)
Murdoch, Katie R....................5:15:11 (28,351)
Murdoch, Wendy....................4:02:42 (11,168)
Murphy, Alisa....................4:43:18 (21,543)
Murphy, Andrea L....................3:30:17 (4,219)
Murphy, Angela....................5:15:09 (28,344)
Murphy, Angela....................5:41:07 (31,595)
Murphy, Carol 4:53:31 (24,074)
Murphy, Ciara....................5:04:33 (26,472)
Murphy, Denise 7:01:26 (34,966)
Murphy, Eleanor C....................4:02:58 (11,221)
Murphy, Helen 5:46:45 (32,069)
Murphy, Janice 7:18:37 (35,134)
Murphy, Julie A 5:33:36 (30,821)
Murphy, Kelley 4:16:04 (14,416)
Murphy, Kerrie A 5:47:49 (32,158)
Murphy, Louise M....................4:39:52 (20,685)
Murphy, Rebecca F....................6:49:28 (34,804)
Murphy, Samantha L 5:34:08 (30,870)
Murphy, Sarah J....................3:11:50 (1,866)
Murphy, Sarah Louise....................5:27:18 (30,079)
Murphy, Tracey M 3:25:31 (3,461)
Murray, Amy A....................6:39:28 (34,617)
Murray, Anna K....................4:41:36 (21,119)
Murray, Carol M 5:41:36 (31,639)
Murray, Carol S 3:48:25 (7,490)
Murray, Charlotte J 4:00:12 (10,599)
Murray, Claire L....................6:04:52 (33,333)
Murray, Helen F 4:10:57 (13,094)
Murray, Jacqueline M....................4:41:58 (21,195)
Murray, Jane E....................5:06:23 (26,787)
Murray, Jennifer 4:49:16 (23,042)
Murray, Karen A....................5:37:55 (31,263)
Murray, Morag....................5:22:55 (29,503)
Murray, Nicola....................4:49:27 (23,092)
Murray-Brown, Joanne....................4:38:16 (20,246)
Musandu, Bwalya N....................9:03:11 (35,358)
Musson, Sally M....................3:11:39 (1,844)
Muston, Jennifer C....................3:08:22 (1,556)
Mutch, Esther M 5:50:29 (32,379)
Muttitt, Christine J 4:22:07 (15,970)
Muxworthy, Anja J....................3:53:39 (8,663)
Muxworthy, Katy....................4:34:24 (19,241)
Mycock, Gemma L 4:15:13 (14,218)
Myers, Amanda J 3:56:45 (9,549)
Myers, Helen 4:49:35 (23,141)
Myles, Selina....................5:14:40 (28,261)
Mylvaganam, Faye A....................3:41:37 (6,132)
Naden, Debra E....................4:07:42 (12,286)
Nagni, Roberta....................3:00:23 (1,018)
Naidu, Shantell J 4:58:36 (25,294)
Nairn, Fionn M....................3:09:53 (1,696)
Naismith, Amanda 4:36:11 (19,716)
Najim, Rana....................4:46:33 (22,360)
Namagiri, Srinivas....................5:36:34 (31,127)
Nandra, Kirat K....................4:32:32 (18,762)
Napleton, Bridgit F 3:33:44 (4,710)
Narang, Satwant K....................5:09:58 (27,453)
Narey, Susan E....................4:41:13 (21,017)
Nash, Rachel E 4:41:17 (21,034)
Nash, Sarah A 4:39:27 (20,569)
Nash, Sharlene J....................5:12:52 (27,962)
Nash, Valerie 5:21:05 (29,234)
Nash-King, Tara R 4:31:04 (18,376)
Nathalie, Meniel....................4:14:35 (14,053)
Nathan, Laura S 4:48:38 (22,887)
Nathan, Vinotha....................4:44:22 (21,809)
Natoli, Courtney B 5:46:10 (32,028)
Naughton, Eileen....................4:52:05 (23,773)
Navyte, Ruta....................5:13:03 (27,995)
Naylor, Poppy S 5:08:59 (27,270)
Nazer, Zeina....................6:11:20 (33,614)
Ndereba, Catherine 2:26:22 (40)
Neal, Anne....................5:21:03 (29,231)
Neale, Mandy J 4:23:18 (16,253)
Neale, Rachel 4:44:09 (21,757)
Nealon, Sabina 4:48:59 (22,971)
Neary, Helen P 4:02:09 (11,054)
Neate, Victoria L 3:50:44 (8,001)
Neath, Tracy 4:33:01 (18,901)
Needham, Lou E....................5:04:14 (26,416)
Needs, Karen P....................4:40:21 (20,806)
Negri, Annita....................3:12:17 (1,911)
Negus, Ruth E 3:52:37 (8,435)
Neill, Fiona....................3:53:16 (8,575)
Neilson, Christine M....................3:42:38 (6,341)
Nel, Désirée....................6:15:25 (33,811)
Nel, Lesia S....................4:40:57 (20,953)
Nelhams, Sally....................4:29:06 (17,858)
Nelmes, Nadina....................4:37:36 (20,068)
Nelsey, Thomas S 4:03:22 (11,310)
Nelson, Abigail....................5:27:40 (30,106)
Nelson, Caroline E....................6:07:06 (33,441)
Nelson, Deborah L....................8:44:17 (35,351)
Nelson, Hantie 6:36:45 (34,555)
Nelson, Melany L 4:28:33 (17,711)
Nelson, Sandra J....................4:26:41 (17,176)
Neocleous, Julia E 4:46:05 (22,224)
Nery, Charlotte....................5:34:39 (30,927)
Neseyif, Helen M....................4:56:47 (24,871)
Ness, Rina D 4:59:14 (25,438)
Nester, Rachel 4:12:06 (13,414)
Nethisinghe, Chandima....................3:57:59 (9,927)
Nettle, Anna V....................3:37:20 (5,377)
Neve, Janice....................4:23:42 (16,364)
Neville, Claire L 5:43:44 (31,828)
Neville, Helen....................6:18:28 (33,946)
Neville, Liz....................4:04:25 (11,527)
New, Sam 5:39:44 (31,469)
Newall, Shelly K....................5:16:19 (28,540)
Newberry, Dorothy....................5:15:51 (28,484)
Newbery, Gemma....................4:35:08 (19,446)
Newbery, Helen A 4:16:37 (14,560)
Newbould, Catherine J 5:00:24 (25,677)
Newbury, Joanne 4:12:53 (13,623)
Newby, Nancy 5:11:25 (27,713)
Newell, Louise E....................4:48:13 (22,791)
Newington, Deborah A....................7:06:14 (35,018)
Newington, Ella....................4:50:15 (23,301)
Newington, Lynette E 4:50:15 (23,301)
Newlands, Claire M....................4:10:24 (12,955)
Newlands, Maxine....................6:10:08 (33,571)
Newman, Carly....................6:36:15 (34,545)
Newman, Claire J 3:58:50 (10,205)
Newman, Eileen J....................4:16:55 (14,626)
Newman, Elaine D 4:15:10 (14,208)
Newman, Linda C 5:53:33 (32,586)
Newman, Tracey....................4:44:15 (21,778)
Newson, Marian E....................5:51:47 (32,465)
Newstead, Deborah....................4:14:29 (14,024)
Newstead, Johanne 4:17:54 (14,862)
Newstead, Julie....................3:48:45 (7,552)

Newton, Charlotte 4:39:43 (20,648)
Newton, Christina M 5:16:46 (28,614)
Newton, Elizabeth A 5:49:18 (32,275)
Newton, Helen A 4:46:24 (22,315)
Newton, Lisa J 5:10:02 (27,467)
Newvell, Kelly 5:08:44 (27,219)
Ng, Chin Chin 5:33:26 (30,798)
Ngo, Hoa V 5:22:12 (29,391)
Nguyen-Quan, Kim L 6:11:05 (33,605)
Nhende, Ketiwe E 4:17:11 (14,689)
Nic Fhogartaigh, Caoimhe 3:32:22 (4,526)
Nicholas, Alexandra F 4:18:51 (15,118)
Nicholas, Becky 4:17:19 (14,725)
Nicholas, Clare J 4:21:26 (15,793)
Nicholas, Jane K 3:55:39 (9,207)
Nicholas, Rebecca S 4:31:36 (18,528)
Nicholls, Clair M 4:28:33 (17,711)
Nicholls, Jackie A 4:29:50 (18,048)
Nicholls, Sally A 5:26:01 (29,944)
Nicholls, Sarah C 5:32:44 (30,730)
Nicholls, Shelley 6:17:02 (33,885)
Nicholls, Tracey 5:34:10 (30,873)
Nichols, Lisa M 5:44:02 (31,855)
Nicholson, Anne 5:22:49 (29,482)
Nicholson, Clare M 3:35:11 (4,993)
Nicholson, Frances S 5:47:42 (32,145)
Nicholson, Natacha M 6:48:55 (34,794)
Nicholson, Natalie 5:51:17 (32,433)
Nicholson, Nichola G 4:16:43 (14,587)
Nicholson, Olivia J 5:10:21 (27,522)
Nicholson, Wendy 3:51:11 (8,093)
Nicklin, Jacqueline K 4:51:44 (23,685)
Nickson, Ruth 3:35:58 (5,147)
Nicol, Barbara 3:48:20 (7,475)
Nicol, Donna M 5:11:42 (27,760)
Nicol, Eileen N 4:09:39 (12,764)
Nicolai, Susan T 4:26:15 (17,051)
Nicole, Rege Colet 4:47:57 (22,724)
Nicoll, Helen Anne 5:30:44 (30,493)
Nicolson, Krissie B 4:33:11 (18,939)
Niederländer, Susanne 5:59:34 (33,020)
Niedzwiedzka, Malgorzata 4:56:36 (24,829)
Nield, Martine Zena 3:52:18 (8,359)
Nielsen, Claire L 6:47:15 (34,749)
Nielsen, Wendy 4:24:45 (16,638)
Nightingale, Sharon J 4:46:42 (22,400)
Nightingale, Teresa A 5:12:24 (27,867)
Nilsen, Jessica F 4:59:24 (25,472)
Nippard, Kaye M 4:24:35 (16,590)
Nixon, Jackie 4:36:21 (19,750)
Njaka, Chinelo L 5:29:06 (30,284)
Njoroge, Rahab 5:55:45 (32,745)
Noake, Alyson J 3:23:15 (3,154)
Noakes, Beth 5:18:05 (28,804)
Noakes, Jan C 5:14:08 (28,185)
Noakes, Kimberley M 5:34:39 (30,927)
Noble, Beverley M 3:42:47 (6,374)
Noble, Eileen R 5:26:22 (29,974)
Noble, Hannah P 5:02:53 (26,195)
Noble, Heather L 4:40:09 (20,763)
Noble, Linda 3:23:38 (3,206)
Nobles, Margaret 4:40:57 (20,953)
Nodder, Jane C 3:37:23 (5,381)
Noden, Susan K 5:39:34 (31,453)
Nojd, Margareta 4:55:07 (24,479)
Nolan, Christina Mary 4:27:52 (17,509)
Nolan, Jeanette K 4:56:46 (24,867)
Noone, Zita M 5:50:28 (32,377)
Noordhuis-Kooijman, Joke 4:58:40 (25,312)
Nordhagen, Stella 4:07:28 (12,228)
Nordin, Breege J 3:30:38 (4,274)
Norman, Alice 4:51:12 (23,541)
Norman, Amy 4:10:57 (13,094)
Norman, Carmen A 5:05:48 (26,697)
Norman, Gary J 5:30:00 (30,396)
Norman, Laura E 4:21:10 (15,733)
Norman, Lindsay 4:19:29 (15,277)
Norman, Lucy A 3:27:43 (3,814)
Norman, Sarah 4:38:09 (20,215)
Norris, Caroline E 5:21:07 (29,245)
Norris, Ellen V 4:27:53 (17,513)
Norris, Jo 5:47:01 (32,095)
Norris, Kate E 5:18:42 (28,916)
Norris, Louise 5:20:43 (29,178)
Norris, Morag 5:29:07 (30,288)
Norris, Patricia 5:06:34 (26,815)
Norris, Shelley 4:17:27 (14,757)
Norris, Stacey 5:54:52 (32,677)
Norris, Susan E 3:59:16 (10,327)
Norrish, Donna M 3:38:30 (5,588)
North, Hannah K 5:59:22 (33,011)
North, Tracy S 3:57:17 (9,702)
Northeast, Caireen 4:36:22 (19,757)
Northern, Susan E 4:16:27 (14,509)
Northey, Teresa J 3:47:52 (7,367)
Northover, Sarah N 5:46:59 (32,089)
Norton, Charlotte A 5:08:58 (27,265)
Norton, Helen A 5:35:46 (31,047)
Norton, Julie A 4:06:15 (11,941)
Norton, Samantha J 3:57:12 (9,673)
Norwood, Hopewell 4:42:53 (21,440)
Norwood, Jennifer E 4:01:24 (10,885)
Noschese, Jenny 5:51:31 (32,450)
Novak, Laura 5:49:38 (32,300)
Noyce, Jemima L 6:54:04 (34,883)
Noyce, Stephanie J 3:44:29 (6,717)
N'Sola, Baby 6:13:40 (33,730)
Nuding, Ann 4:58:56 (25,371)
Nugent, Kelly A 3:59:03 (10,268)
Nugent, Natasha Margaret 4:29:34 (17,976)
Nunes, Sonia P 4:23:04 (16,200)
Nunn, Alison N 5:34:12 (30,876)
Nunn, Charlotte E 4:45:19 (22,037)
Nunn, Gill A 3:54:02 (8,763)
Nunn, Lisa E 4:13:48 (13,869)
Nutter, Christine A 5:05:09 (26,581)
Nydahl, Eivor 7:44:18 (35,275)
Nydegger, Thérèse 5:12:32 (27,897)
Nyman, Nina 4:19:15 (15,221)
Nystad, Vera V 3:27:28 (3,769)
Oakes, Catherine A 4:22:26 (16,060)
Oakes, Fiona L 2:58:48 (893)
Oakins, Mandy 6:49:57 (34,812)
Oakley, Louise S 4:15:44 (14,329)
Oakshott, Cheryl E 3:12:54 (1,989)
Oates, Claire 4:02:25 (11,108)
Oates, Elizabeth A 4:34:13 (19,199)
Oates, Kate E 4:08:52 (12,591)
Oates, Kyra M 5:53:48 (32,606)
Oates, Verity R 4:37:23 (20,004)
Obank, Natasha G 4:39:54 (20,693)
Obiago, Didi 5:33:28 (30,801)
Oborne, Laura J 5:13:50 (28,123)
O'Borne, Kathryn S 4:36:47 (19,859)
O'Boyle, Barbara J 4:12:52 (13,617)
O'Brien, Alexandra 5:16:49 (28,621)
O'Brien, Bernadette E 3:44:24 (6,703)
O'Brien, Carla 5:28:04 (30,155)
O'Brien, Catherine P 6:56:30 (34,913)
O'Brien, Claudette F 5:32:45 (30,732)
O'Brien, Fiona A 5:08:55 (27,255)
O'Brien, Josephine A 5:49:42 (32,307)
O'Brien, Maire M 4:18:05 (14,912)
O'Brien, Maureen E 6:26:47 (34,311)
O'Brien, Sheila 5:10:40 (27,579)
O'Brien, Susan 4:21:49 (15,905)
O'Brien, Tara 5:47:40 (32,143)
O'Brien, Tina Yvette 4:39:38 (20,621)
O'Byrne, Emer S 6:12:54 (33,689)
O'Callaghan, Ailish K 5:07:06 (26,926)
O'Callaghan, Jennifer A 6:24:32 (34,212)
O'Callaghan, Sara J 3:45:49 (6,953)
Ockendon, Ana M 3:51:19 (8,125)
O'Connell, Annmarie 5:05:31 (26,642)
O'Connell, Fiona 5:05:42 (26,682)
O'Connell, Pam J 5:15:00 (28,320)
O'Connell, Sally A 4:52:54 (23,951)
O'Connell, Susan E 4:07:49 (12,319)
O'Connor, Claire 4:28:57 (17,818)
O'Connor, Hayley 4:54:23 (24,307)
O'Connor, Kerry A 5:08:57 (27,261)
Oddie, Elaine A 6:51:58 (34,846)
O'Dea-Hughes, Catherine 4:27:24 (17,368)
O'Dell, Charlotte 5:34:27 (30,907)
O'Dell, Emma L 5:39:57 (31,490)
O'Dell, Sarah R 3:56:18 (9,394)
O'Dowd, Claire 4:21:06 (15,714)
O'Dowd, Joanne M 3:39:31 (5,761)
O'Driscoll, Maria 4:14:02 (13,913)
O'Duffy, Libby K 3:12:49 (1,977)
O'Dwyer, Rachel 4:30:10 (18,142)
O'Farrell, Alison 4:52:08 (23,781)
O'Farrell, Genevieve 4:03:49 (11,398)
Offer, Caroline V 4:28:51 (17,795)
Offley, Vicky A 5:24:18 (29,700)
Offord, Amelia 6:15:26 (33,813)
Offord, Jennifer 6:05:27 (33,362)
Offredi, Doreen 7:34:10 (35,244)
Ogan, Leyla 4:34:50 (19,365)
Ogan, Rhoda 4:53:15 (24,033)
Ogden, Rosanne D 6:21:24 (34,089)
Ogg, Susan C 4:33:22 (18,998)
Ogilvie, Hannah J 5:10:11 (27,493)
Ogilvie, Michelle L 4:25:19 (16,791)
O'Grady, Claire E 4:45:02 (21,973)
O'Halloran, Laura C 4:20:37 (15,580)
O'Hara, Jane S 4:26:22 (17,080)
O'Hara, Michelle 4:17:47 (14,838)
O'Hara, Rebecca A 4:17:57 (14,872)
O'Hare, Joanne 4:33:38 (19,058)
Ohtani, Marika 3:54:18 (8,839)
O'Kane, Karen D 3:56:58 (9,610)
O'Keefe, Jayne L 4:43:47 (21,663)
O'Keeffe, Clare E 4:07:30 (12,236)
O'Keeffe, Patricia A 3:47:47 (7,346)
Okine, Okailey 5:03:38 (26,313)
Okunaga, Mika 2:35:36 (123)
Okwiri, Caroline 4:38:41 (20,347)
Okwu, Antonia S 3:54:32 (8,900)
Old, Kim Theresa Mary 6:20:29 (34,054)
Old, Melody B 5:03:05 (26,221)
Old, Neeley 5:58:50 (32,982)
Oldershaw, Tina 3:04:39 (1,275)
Oldham, Nicola S 3:30:55 (4,315)
Oldland, Gretchen Lynn 4:24:43 (16,627)
O'Leary, Vickie Hazel 4:48:32 (22,861)
Oliver, Christine 4:35:00 (19,406)
Oliver, Cleo 3:17:15 (2,459)
Oliver, Deborah K 3:57:54 (9,903)
Oliver, Hannah J 3:34:25 (4,856)
Oliver, Katherine A 5:15:52 (28,488)
Oliver, Lauren A 4:57:21 (25,001)
Oliver, Philippa 5:34:01 (30,863)
Oliver, Susan M 3:12:18 (1,913)
Oliver, Susannah L 4:30:04 (18,116)
Ollerton, Linda J 6:22:23 (34,123)
Ollis, Jan R 4:13:49 (13,873)
O'Loghlen, Kate 4:19:13 (15,213)
O'Loghlen, Laura C 4:54:58 (24,441)
Olsson, Marie 3:21:49 (2,985)
O'Malley, Sandra M 4:53:42 (24,138)
Ombler, Sharon L 3:57:06 (9,648)
O'Neil, Stacey J 6:22:13 (34,117)
O'Neill, Kate 2:34:48 (112)
O'Neill, Lindsay 4:51:46 (23,692)
O'Neill, Melanie J 6:28:06 (34,359)
Ong, Denise 3:54:28 (8,880)
Ool, Sandra 5:50:14 (32,357)
Orange, Sally Jane 4:32:28 (18,752)
Orban, Marybrdget 4:46:31 (22,347)
Orchard, Julia 5:06:26 (26,797)
Orchard, Sara E 4:56:38 (24,836)
O'Regan, Donna 5:38:39 (31,348)
O'Regan, Sheryl M 4:22:55 (16,168)
Oreglia, Federica 3:13:54 (2,111)
O'Reilly, Elma 5:13:04 (27,998)
O'Reilly, Jean 4:50:26 (23,350)
O'Reilly, Natalie 4:03:20 (11,300)
Orfanos, Thekla 6:11:23 (33,618)
Ormsby, Heidi J 4:07:56 (12,347)
Orr, Christine E 4:45:56 (22,198)
Orr, Deborah J 5:24:05 (29,666)
Orr, Nicola J 4:07:13 (12,155)
Orrin, Zoe D 5:41:20 (31,612)
Orth, Barbara 4:07:52 (12,331)
Ortiquet Climent, Maria 4:08:23 (12,481)
Orwin, Lynn M 4:56:17 (24,747)
Osborn, Gemma V 4:27:44 (17,459)
Osborn, Kathryn M 4:25:25 (16,822)

Name	Time (Position)
Osborne, Clare A	4:26:13 (17,044)
Osborne, Janine	4:36:48 (19,864)
Osborne, Katherine A	5:30:51 (30,503)
Osborne, Lucy A	5:59:52 (33,042)
Oscroft, Jennifer V	3:58:01 (9,941)
O'Shea, Jacinta K	4:37:33 (20,054)
O'Shea, Niamh M	5:19:50 (29,076)
Osmond, Amy G	4:58:20 (25,222)
Osmond, Melissa	5:17:03 (28,647)
Osonowo, Oyinda	7:29:35 (35,216)
Ostrehan, Bridget L	3:25:12 (3,418)
O'Sullivan, Elaine J	3:47:07 (7,217)
O'Sullivan, Elizabeth	5:48:16 (32,192)
O'Sullivan, Maureen N	5:38:21 (31,310)
O'Sullivan, Michele	4:08:31 (12,508)
O'Sullivan, Ros	3:58:32 (10,110)
O'Sullivan, Tina	4:42:24 (21,302)
Otache, Joy	4:22:47 (16,139)
Ougier, Severine K	3:53:03 (8,519)
Outram, Susan D	7:24:40 (35,174)
Overall, Julie	4:31:03 (18,370)
Overall, Sarah J	6:09:04 (33,514)
Owen, Eleanor	5:16:53 (28,628)
Owen, Kerrie	4:26:45 (17,195)
Owen, Laura E	3:42:39 (6,346)
Owen, Linda P	5:31:17 (30,558)
Owen, Mary Bridget	4:59:23 (25,468)
Owen, Tegwen	8:11:45 (35,328)
Owens, Danielle L	4:35:03 (19,425)
Owens, Karen J	4:35:38 (19,574)
Owens, Kate	7:06:17 (35,020)
Owens, Kate L	6:06:46 (33,422)
Owens, Susan A	4:20:36 (15,579)
Owston, Jennifer A	4:13:55 (13,887)
Ozier, Patricia Maria	4:17:15 (14,702)
Pace, Mone	6:02:06 (33,179)
Pace, Rebecca A	4:30:38 (18,265)
Pacey, Angela J	5:24:33 (29,740)
Pacey, Victoria	6:29:37 (34,400)
Paddock, Laura J	4:12:29 (13,518)
Padget, Beverley J	4:54:26 (24,322)
Padgett, Jan	5:08:03 (27,094)
Padgham, Samantha	5:32:30 (30,692)
Padley, Kerry L	5:05:18 (26,607)
Page, Amanda J	5:48:18 (32,199)
Page, Annie B	6:02:45 (33,211)
Page, Geraldine L	4:19:06 (15,185)
Page, Hayley	4:20:20 (15,519)
Page, Janice	4:15:29 (14,279)
Page, Kelley	5:52:06 (32,485)
Page, Louise M	5:33:37 (30,823)
Page, Nicola A	4:49:19 (23,058)
Page, Sarah E	3:56:07 (9,344)
Paggetta, Katia	4:41:26 (21,065)
Pain, Lucy C	4:58:06 (25,162)
Paling, Sarah	5:13:32 (28,071)
Palladino, Camilla A	4:38:43 (20,354)
Palles, Katherine	4:49:14 (23,031)
Pallot, Nerina N	5:02:28 (26,109)
Palmadori, Valentina	4:39:22 (20,536)
Palmer, Clare D	4:21:42 (15,880)
Palmer, Elaine	4:13:00 (13,659)
Palmer, Ella L	3:25:42 (3,487)
Palmer, Janet	5:05:01 (26,549)
Palmer, Jenni	4:57:47 (25,083)
Palmer, Julia	3:12:57 (1,998)
Palmer, Louise E	4:52:54 (23,951)
Palmer, Melissa N	5:39:40 (31,462)
Palmer, Susannah Frances	4:24:16 (16,517)
Paloniemi, Tuula	4:41:03 (20,974)
Palser, Jenny A	4:41:37 (21,122)
Pamplin, Diane R	3:51:07 (8,076)
Panay, Claire A	4:36:49 (19,848)
Panayis, Eleni	5:03:58 (26,381)
Panayis, Tania	5:03:58 (26,381)
Panday, Kamala	5:56:17 (32,775)
Panetta, Thérèse	3:49:44 (7,787)
Panther, Vicky	3:40:14 (5,907)
Pape, Alexandra L	4:48:54 (22,945)
Papworth, Rachel T	4:40:25 (20,819)
Pardoe, Karmen M	3:10:00 (1,706)
Paredes, Jenny E	3:54:34 (8,911)
Paremain, Gillian A	5:00:33 (25,717)
Parfitt, Lisa	4:01:28 (10,905)
Parfitt, Sarah L	3:59:08 (10,290)
Parfoot, Katie D	3:30:36 (4,271)
Park, Chung Cha	5:01:13 (25,865)
Park, Karen	4:09:56 (12,840)
Parke, Hannah	4:29:21 (17,936)
Parker, Annabel	4:25:33 (16,856)
Parker, Caroline M	5:33:37 (30,823)
Parker, Cheryl L	5:40:25 (31,538)
Parker, Helen J	5:18:57 (28,967)
Parker, Jo L	5:38:57 (31,389)
Parker, Josephine D	5:43:20 (31,809)
Parker, Justine D	5:19:43 (29,063)
Parker, Karen	4:13:35 (13,821)
Parker, Karen L	4:39:17 (20,513)
Parker, Kelly A	4:03:09 (11,260)
Parker, Laura	3:58:12 (10,007)
Parker, Linda	5:08:19 (27,144)
Parker, Liz M	5:14:12 (28,194)
Parker, Michaela J	5:50:48 (32,399)
Parker, Pamela Anne	4:19:33 (15,299)
Parker, Rache J	4:14:14 (13,971)
Parker, Tarnya	3:46:35 (7,104)
Parker, Yvonne E	5:58:25 (32,952)
Parker-Smith, Kelly-Anne	5:17:10 (28,669)
Parkes, Isabelle M	4:33:22 (18,998)
Parkes, Sally M	4:20:24 (15,537)
Parkes, Samantha	5:19:45 (29,066)
Parkes, Sarah J	4:11:29 (13,248)
Parkin, Claire Louise	5:09:46 (27,420)
Parkin, Kate E	4:46:31 (22,347)
Parkin, Lara A	4:09:04 (12,635)
Parkin, Laura A	4:31:59 (18,629)
Parkins, Sally Jane	4:10:38 (13,016)
Parkinson, Barbara	4:04:30 (11,547)
Parkinson, Katharine R	4:16:34 (14,542)
Parkinson, Sara N	4:34:50 (19,365)
Parkinson, Shelley	4:16:17 (14,469)
Parmar, Manisha V	4:24:56 (16,691)
Parncutt, Sarah J	5:50:49 (32,400)
Parnell, Vicki	6:21:36 (34,098)
Parr, Kathryn E	4:00:02 (10,552)
Parr, Sarah J	5:25:03 (29,804)
Parratt, Louise S	5:42:01 (31,677)
Parri, Catrin L	5:10:24 (27,532)
Parrick, Sarah M	7:03:44 (34,988)
Parrish, Pauline	5:31:07 (30,541)
Parrott, Madeleine	4:33:31 (19,026)
Parrott, Margaret A	4:42:54 (21,445)
Parry, Anne M	4:21:45 (15,892)
Parry, Camilla R	5:07:08 (26,929)
Parry, Leanne	3:57:27 (9,752)
Parry, Liz	5:35:00 (30,970)
Parry, Victoria	3:43:40 (6,559)
Parry-Williams, Jessica	3:02:01 (1,118)
Parsonage, Kate A	5:01:26 (25,900)
Parsons, Alexandra G	5:46:59 (32,089)
Parsons, Beth L	5:55:23 (32,715)
Parsons, Catherine H	4:10:03 (12,864)
Parsons, Connie	6:17:21 (33,895)
Parsons, Elizabeth J	5:03:52 (26,353)
Parsons, Jackie A	4:07:07 (12,135)
Parsons, Louise	5:04:56 (26,530)
Parsons, Polly C	4:21:05 (15,710)
Parsons, Sarah J	4:24:16 (16,517)
Parsons, Tamarin	4:16:50 (14,615)
Partington, Elizabeth A	5:01:01 (25,815)
Partridge, Charlotte	4:39:24 (20,552)
Partridge, Kathryn B	6:10:52 (33,596)
Partridge, Mandie M	6:53:24 (34,867)
Partridge, Rachael F	4:50:21 (23,327)
Pascall, Nina	3:38:58 (5,675)
Pascoe, Angela	5:30:01 (30,398)
Pass, Donna L	3:43:40 (6,559)
Passfield, Diane J	5:04:14 (26,416)
Pastor, Jennie A	4:35:01 (19,411)
Patanchon, Marie-Laure	4:14:54 (14,140)
Patandin, Jane	4:57:54 (25,111)
Patching, Katrina J	5:45:07 (31,934)
Patel, Anita T	5:15:54 (28,492)
Patel, Anjana	4:52:59 (23,973)
Patel, Chaya P	6:27:12 (34,331)
Patel, Gargi S	3:53:35 (8,644)
Patel, Heena	6:29:05 (34,382)
Patel, Jeegna	4:04:35 (11,561)
Patel, Komal	6:11:56 (33,640)
Patel, Krupa	5:43:02 (31,774)
Patel, Leena	5:21:59 (29,363)
Patel, Meena M	6:24:25 (34,211)
Patel, Meera P	5:18:19 (28,837)
Patel, Mukta Ranjit	5:29:42 (30,359)
Patel, Prabha	4:58:26 (25,251)
Patel, Purvi	5:14:54 (28,294)
Patel, Resh	7:09:18 (35,046)
Patel, Sangeeta	6:21:33 (34,096)
Paterson, Ailsa	5:39:09 (31,416)
Paterson, Becky	4:49:14 (23,031)
Paterson, Fiona M	5:18:05 (28,804)
Paterson, Rachel M	4:06:59 (12,100)
Paterson, Sarah	3:33:51 (4,731)
Paterson, Susan	4:28:09 (17,593)
Patmore, Tracey M	3:05:04 (1,307)
Paton, Janet A	5:38:45 (31,363)
Paton, Kim A	4:27:58 (17,532)
Patricia, Brunetto	4:58:56 (25,371)
Patricia, Lepreux	3:44:41 (6,743)
Patrick, Eileen	2:53:49 (599)
Patrick, Kayleigh	5:13:51 (28,133)
Patten, Penelope A	3:52:31 (8,406)
Patterson, Amanda M	5:38:21 (31,310)
Patterson, Julia E	4:06:03 (11,893)
Patterson, Julie E	4:51:04 (23,505)
Patterson, Laurie Beth	4:07:12 (12,152)
Patterson, Tanya L	5:25:33 (29,868)
Pattinson, Angela J	3:41:50 (6,173)
Pattinson, Helen M	6:27:37 (34,348)
Pattis, Rosa Lucia	4:24:11 (16,494)
Pattison, Michelle J	3:56:04 (9,329)
Paul, Carol	4:38:34 (20,315)
Paul, Georgina Frances	5:21:31 (29,305)
Paul, Helen C	4:52:42 (23,908)
Paul, Hina	5:19:02 (28,976)
Paul, Miranda J	4:16:43 (14,587)
Paull, Irene H	5:01:02 (25,825)
Paulsson, Tara E	5:20:20 (29,133)
Paveley, Tracey	5:07:11 (26,941)
Pavey, Patricia J	5:22:58 (29,513)
Pawson, Katherine	3:35:19 (5,012)
Paxton, Emma L	5:23:52 (29,631)
Paxton, Lindsay C	4:48:41 (22,897)
Payne, Anna L	5:51:25 (32,440)
Payne, Belinda L	4:54:48 (24,408)
Payne, Karen M	4:16:43 (14,587)
Payne, Linda J	5:35:59 (31,076)
Payne, Louise A	5:41:57 (31,665)
Payne, Sarah	3:36:55 (5,301)
Payne, Sarah L	4:45:53 (22,186)
Peacock, Alison	4:53:52 (24,193)
Peacock, Jill	4:59:28 (25,488)
Peacock, Laura	3:41:56 (6,191)
Peacock, Suzy D	5:01:35 (25,929)
Pearce, Caroline E	6:12:01 (33,642)
Pearce, Donna M	3:59:15 (10,324)
Pearce, Flora E	4:43:20 (21,559)
Pearce, Jo	4:51:13 (23,545)
Pearce, Katharine E	5:10:33 (27,556)
Pearce, Miranda	6:52:13 (34,849)
Pearce, Sue	4:10:25 (12,958)
Pearce, Wanda L	4:51:51 (23,709)
Pearce, Zoe	3:56:48 (9,569)
Pearcey, Jo-Anne	5:33:32 (30,807)
Pearcy, Karen M	5:04:32 (26,468)
Pearson, Alison K	5:12:25 (27,873)
Pearson, Allison J	6:46:56 (34,738)
Pearson, Andrea	4:09:57 (12,843)
Pearson, Elizabeth H	5:00:05 (25,610)
Pearson, Gwen	5:36:20 (31,106)
Pearson, Lynne M	4:21:15 (15,755)
Pearson, Melanie L	7:06:43 (35,024)
Pearson, Rebecca	4:43:03 (21,481)
Pearson, Sue	4:58:57 (25,377)
Peart, Julie-Ann M	4:26:58 (17,251)
Peasgood, Teresa J	3:36:31 (5,238)
Peat, Gemma A	6:24:09 (34,194)
Peck, Gemma M	3:46:28 (7,081)
Peck, Gillian	3:43:05 (6,439)

Peck, Rita	4:05:37 (11,807)
Peck, Sarah G	3:43:10 (6,463)
Pedder, Amy-Leigh	4:40:32 (20,843)
Pedder-Smith, Hannah L.	3:54:58 (9,010)
Pedersen, Kjersti Tunheim	4:25:09 (16,751)
Pedersen, Signe	3:34:16 (4,824)
Pedleham, Tracey	6:49:18 (34,800)
Pedlow, Rachel V.	5:28:26 (30,206)
Peebles, Adrienne K.	4:15:38 (14,311)
Pegg, Kate A	5:20:43 (29,178)
Pell, Anna L.	5:39:56 (31,487)
Pell, Valerie M	4:14:17 (13,986)
Pellicciari, Maria Luisa	4:53:52 (24,193)
Penalver, Ruth A.	6:31:21 (34,441)
Pender, Claire S.	4:04:12 (11,489)
Penfold, Helen	4:51:38 (23,655)
Pennell, Charlotte	4:38:39 (20,339)
Penney, Carol A.	4:29:50 (18,048)
Penney, Samantha A	5:22:56 (29,508)
Penny, Nicola J	4:41:30 (21,087)
Penny, Sarah	5:15:22 (28,397)
Penrose, Katherine M	4:23:26 (16,290)
Pentland, Debbie	6:01:56 (33,166)
Pentland, Emma L	5:24:46 (29,760)
Penton, Emma	4:21:07 (15,721)
Penty, Rebecca H	2:55:12 (680)
Pereira, Teresa	4:06:54 (12,079)
Pereira-Lopes, Indira	5:22:35 (29,450)
Perera, Helen A.	3:32:30 (4,543)
Perez Bravo, Gema	3:35:20 (5,018)
Perez Espinoza, Rosalia	4:17:57 (14,872)
Perfect, Nicola	5:01:48 (25,970)
Perkins, Georgina	6:12:36 (33,665)
Perkins, Janine D	5:58:09 (32,930)
Perkins, Joanne	5:50:17 (32,362)
Perkins, Tracey M	4:07:43 (12,290)
Perriand, Monique	4:07:00 (12,106)
Perrin, Clare E.	5:33:33 (30,810)
Perrin, Tara	5:27:49 (30,127)
Perry, Anne-Marie	4:27:29 (17,387)
Perry, Fiona A	5:40:09 (31,512)
Perry, Jayne	3:47:52 (7,367)
Perry, Jayne L	4:17:24 (14,742)
Perry, Jennifer	4:29:11 (17,884)
Perry, Juliet Ruth	4:43:56 (21,700)
Perry, Kate	4:50:06 (23,264)
Perry, Louise	7:01:25 (34,965)
Perry, Lucy M.	4:23:21 (16,266)
Perry, Mandy J	4:26:55 (17,241)
Perry, Melissa E	4:28:44 (17,754)
Perry, Rachel A.	5:28:40 (30,232)
Perry, Rebecca J	5:11:54 (27,790)
Perry, Susan M	4:26:12 (17,038)
Perry, Victoria A	2:53:15 (569)
Perryman, Sarah A	4:37:15 (19,974)
Perugini, Nicola F	5:17:46 (28,759)
Perusko, Claire	3:30:19 (4,222)
Perveen, Rahat P.	5:02:09 (26,051)
Pescod, Debbie	5:10:21 (27,522)
Peskett, Amy A.	5:20:23 (29,138)
Pete, Jacqueline	4:06:05 (11,897)
Peters, Becky L	6:14:08 (33,750)
Peters, Lorraine	6:00:23 (33,065)
Peters, Louise R.	3:21:40 (2,967)
Peters, Sharon L	3:38:50 (5,644)
Peters, Tracey R.	3:26:21 (3,582)
Petit, Nathalie	4:04:27 (11,532)
Petkovic, Charlotte J	5:30:29 (30,460)
Petrie, Mona	5:12:06 (27,819)
Petrova, Lyudmila	2:27:42 (47)
Pettifer, Tracy E	4:32:25 (18,735)
Phelan, Sarah M	4:10:35 (13,003)
Phelps, Jane Alison	5:25:36 (29,878)
Phibbs, Laura K.	3:48:09 (7,433)
Philipps, Laura A.	5:31:05 (30,539)
Philips, Jenny C	3:30:34 (4,267)
Phillip, Sarah	3:29:22 (4,085)
Phillips, Amanda D	4:08:18 (12,454)
Phillips, Carole	3:37:12 (5,354)
Phillips, Carolyn E.	5:58:42 (32,971)
Phillips, Clare	2:59:14 (937)
Phillips, Clare A.	4:12:42 (13,575)
Phillips, Cynthia M.	4:30:47 (18,299)

Phillips, Debbie L	5:31:26 (30,569)
Phillips, Debra A	4:54:12 (24,259)
Phillips, Emma L	3:56:15 (9,377)
Phillips, Jill	3:43:45 (6,574)
Phillips, Joanne	6:39:45 (34,623)
Phillips, Juliet	5:41:26 (31,628)
Phillips, Kirsty A	5:00:22 (25,669)
Phillips, Louise A	5:04:14 (26,416)
Phillips, Maria S	4:14:42 (14,079)
Phillips, Natasha	5:21:25 (29,285)
Phillips, Patricia A	4:56:27 (24,785)
Phillips, Rebecca	4:20:13 (15,490)
Phillips, Sarah J	8:43:47 (35,349)
Phillips, Sarah L	5:17:25 (28,700)
Phillips, Sonia E	3:59:29 (10,384)
Phillips, Sue	3:23:38 (3,206)
Phillips, Tasha	6:01:53 (33,160)
Phillips, Vicky	5:56:43 (32,810)
Phillips, Victoria	5:12:34 (27,903)
Philp, Catherine R	3:25:22 (3,438)
Philp, Linda K	3:31:09 (4,352)
Philpot, Lucy D	4:26:31 (17,121)
Philpot, Pam S	4:24:51 (16,670)
Philpott, Emma J	5:46:23 (32,040)
Philpott, Helen E	4:18:49 (15,108)
Philpott, Tracy	5:06:42 (26,842)
Phoenix, Alexa J	3:59:16 (10,327)
Piana, Martine	4:55:23 (24,549)
Pickard, Francesca A	4:42:27 (21,313)
Pickard, Linda A	4:45:38 (22,113)
Pickard, Lynsay	4:34:10 (19,187)
Pickering, Karen S	5:04:04 (26,394)
Pickering, Sharon	5:01:40 (25,945)
Pickford, Delaine W	6:02:05 (33,176)
Picksley, Mary L	3:43:29 (6,520)
Pickup, Karen T	4:36:04 (19,697)
Picton, Alison	4:42:21 (21,283)
Picton, Sioned L	5:25:54 (29,917)
Pidgen, Briony	4:34:15 (19,209)
Piech, Aggy	4:29:51 (18,056)
Piekos, Laura	6:53:31 (34,872)
Pienaar, Eleanor	7:14:13 (35,098)
Pierce, Nicole	6:34:09 (34,503)
Pierrot, Lucy	4:50:18 (23,318)
Piggott, Stephanie K	5:55:20 (32,711)
Pike, Alison J	4:32:25 (18,735)
Pike, Hazel	4:25:08 (16,746)
Pike, Julie M	6:25:56 (34,278)
Pike, Karen J	4:57:13 (24,968)
Pike, Nichola M.	5:40:23 (31,533)
Pike, Zoe M.	2:56:25 (740)
Pilati, Lydia J.	5:24:09 (29,674)
Pilgrim, Jan	4:20:39 (15,587)
Pilgrim, Lorraine	4:53:28 (24,066)
Pilling, Angela M	5:16:40 (28,590)
Pilling, Samantha L	4:44:56 (21,936)
Pinas, Emmy E.	5:43:15 (31,799)
Pinder, Melanie M.	4:58:50 (25,346)
Pineda-Langford, Clare A	4:20:04 (15,446)
Pini, Daniela	5:24:19 (29,704)
Pinkerton, Sarah	4:46:22 (22,302)
Pinkney, Susan	5:14:33 (28,249)
Pinkus, Molly C	3:49:27 (7,718)
Pinner, Sharon N	4:51:29 (23,617)
Pinnes, Katie	6:02:46 (33,212)
Pinnington, Deborah A	6:10:00 (33,562)
Pinto, Wanda	4:53:46 (24,163)
Pipe, Clare M.	5:04:17 (26,426)
Pipe, Katie L	4:54:17 (24,284)
Piper, Catherine A.	5:01:42 (25,951)
Piper, Lucy	4:57:55 (25,119)
Piper, Stella A	4:35:03 (19,425)
Pirie, Beth F	4:24:36 (16,592)
Pirie, Claire	5:07:22 (26,976)
Pitchford, Heather D	5:24:04 (29,663)
Pither, Louise	4:53:50 (24,183)
Pitt, Rachel F	7:03:46 (34,990)
Pittam, Laura	4:51:04 (23,505)
Pitts, Simon M	3:57:23 (9,742)
Pittson, Susan G	5:05:39 (26,666)
Plaat, Felicity	5:06:10 (26,756)
Plaatjies, Gail	4:17:20 (14,732)
Plant, Gillian	6:13:09 (33,703)

Plant, Natalie A	5:07:19 (26,963)
Plantiga Nieuwland, Rinskje	4:27:21 (17,356)
Plas, Marlene	3:35:39 (5,086)
Plaskett, Ting	6:28:48 (34,377)
Plaskowski, Carol M	4:47:39 (22,641)
Plassen, Hilde	3:12:34 (1,940)
Platt, Emma C	6:53:33 (34,874)
Platts, Cath F	4:32:01 (18,645)
Playford-Wall, Lizzie	5:57:56 (32,911)
Playle, Nicola A	5:23:16 (29,566)
Plebias, Claire A	6:18:03 (33,932)
Pletinckx, Martine	5:10:05 (27,475)
Plumb, Anna	4:35:42 (19,599)
Plumbley, Joanne C.	3:49:07 (7,649)
Plumbridge, Sarah Jane	4:54:07 (24,247)
Plume, Jennifer L	5:45:29 (31,973)
Plummer, Kate E	3:53:32 (8,630)
Plumstead, Karen	5:03:20 (26,261)
Plunkett, Claire J	5:04:57 (26,535)
Pobereskin, Lisa	4:53:40 (24,123)
Pockert, Aneta J	6:21:06 (34,078)
Podbury, Anna C.	3:27:19 (3,736)
Poirault, Marie-Agnes	3:58:17 (10,031)
Polcerova, Denisa	3:31:43 (4,424)
Pollard, Joanne P	3:52:43 (8,450)
Pollard, Kelly J	4:21:55 (15,927)
Pollard, Kirsty	4:27:17 (17,338)
Pollecutt, Alison L	4:46:40 (22,386)
Polley, Rosemary G.	4:15:06 (14,190)
Pomfret, Katherine	5:26:25 (29,982)
Ponsford, Claire	4:33:20 (18,985)
Pontefract, Elaine Carrina	4:58:06 (25,162)
Ponti, Hilary G	3:59:01 (10,254)
Pontin, Emma T	5:30:22 (30,445)
Poole, Amy R	3:55:05 (9,059)
Poole, Beryl E	8:23:27 (35,336)
Poole, Louise A	4:11:25 (13,228)
Poole, Nardia D	3:12:39 (1,950)
Poole, Sarah J	5:03:56 (26,370)
Pooley, Ellen	3:07:12 (1,453)
Poore, Karen	4:45:38 (22,113)
Poortman-Gerritsma, Marjolein	5:24:19 (29,704)
Pope, Amy L	3:42:29 (6,295)
Pope, Emma L	4:44:16 (21,783)
Pope, Jenny	5:01:32 (25,918)
Popplewell, Anna K	6:15:43 (33,828)
Porritt, Catherine	3:48:17 (7,460)
Porteous, Nel	6:47:40 (34,761)
Porter, Anna R	4:25:34 (16,861)
Porter, Christine M	5:20:50 (29,199)
Porter, Gertrud F	3:49:37 (7,753)
Porter, Karen	4:57:12 (24,967)
Porter, Keiko	4:50:41 (23,418)
Porter, Laura Anne	4:28:03 (17,557)
Porter, Pauline J	5:37:30 (31,224)
Porter, Zoe G	3:43:42 (6,565)
Portus, Joanna I.	5:16:25 (28,551)
Posnett, Catherine	4:04:12 (11,489)
Postance, Samantha	6:25:22 (34,247)
Potter, Catherine	6:41:02 (34,647)
Potter, Dawn	5:00:26 (25,688)
Potter, Lauren Y	3:49:49 (7,803)
Potter, Lucy C	4:17:36 (14,795)
Potts, Christian E.	4:40:51 (20,927)
Potts, Jacqueline I	6:41:00 (34,645)
Potts, Karen E	4:32:08 (18,671)
Potts, Katie J	6:59:45 (34,943)
Potts, Leeanne	4:01:33 (10,931)
Potts, Peggy A	6:59:44 (34,942)
Pouchain, Marie-Pierre	4:19:25 (15,263)
Poulain, Nicky J	4:33:32 (19,029)
Poulton, Patricia A	4:01:47 (10,980)
Povey, Samantha M	5:07:19 (26,963)
Powell, Carly	4:32:37 (18,794)
Powell, Catrin M.	4:37:29 (20,035)
Powell, Catriona	7:01:45 (34,970)
Powell, Fiona L	3:33:34 (4,688)
Powell, Karen A.	3:55:49 (9,267)
Powell, Leona	3:39:18 (5,729)
Powell, Michelle	4:04:52 (11,623)
Powell, Sarah E.	4:03:57 (11,436)
Powell, Sarah L.	3:55:23 (9,127)
Power, Anna V	4:26:38 (17,164)

Power, Cassandra....3:41:51 (6,175)
Power, Elizabeth M....5:13:44 (28,110)
Power, Nina M....4:05:10 (11,701)
Power, Rebecca....4:52:36 (23,880)
Powers-Moore, Kathy A....5:28:59 (30,272)
Powles, Jacqueline....5:20:35 (29,158)
Powlett, Abby J....4:32:03 (18,648)
Powter, Ann....4:13:00 (13,659)
Powys, Sian C....4:33:32 (19,029)
Poxon, Nicola....4:31:33 (18,515)
Poynton, Claire M....4:51:57 (23,741)
Poyo, Linda W....2:52:31 (543)
Pozzani, Esther....4:34:01 (19,155)
Pozzi Gurung, Helen O....4:14:48 (14,115)
Prats, Esther....4:36:20 (19,748)
Pratt, Gillian....5:31:07 (30,541)
Pratt, Jenny M....5:14:27 (28,234)
Prcychodny, Susan....6:36:53 (34,558)
Prebble, Katherine....4:57:53 (25,104)
Precey, Gretchen....5:18:01 (28,797)
Precious, Sally....4:55:15 (24,520)
Preece, Nina....4:18:53 (15,128)
Preedy, Clare A....3:57:42 (9,846)
Prendergast, Maureen V....5:32:40 (30,716)
Prentis, Clare L....6:11:15 (33,608)
Prescott, Vashti....4:49:28 (23,102)
Pressly, Laura M....5:45:14 (31,952)
Prest, Jennie....6:24:13 (34,197)
Preston, Christine....3:43:11 (6,469)
Preston, Emily....3:29:34 (4,110)
Preston, Rachel C....5:14:40 (28,261)
Preston, Sharon....5:22:47 (29,479)
Preston, Susan L....4:52:24 (23,842)
Pretlove, Gemma Louise....4:46:59 (22,478)
Price, Bernadette....5:07:36 (27,024)
Price, Jackie H....4:37:32 (20,045)
Price, Jane....6:01:36 (33,147)
Price, Jennifer....5:08:50 (27,234)
Price, Joanne E....3:55:18 (9,110)
Price, Julie C....4:48:31 (22,856)
Price, Kathryn H....4:07:18 (12,176)

Price, Katie....7:11:00 (35,061)

Price, Klara....5:38:33 (31,339)
Price, Leigh M....5:01:19 (25,879)
Price, Lucy A....5:28:05 (30,158)
Price, Maggie....5:45:07 (31,934)
Price, Marie....6:39:23 (34,614)
Price, Rebecca J....4:34:46 (19,337)
Price, Sheila....4:22:10 (15,995)
Price, Sophie....6:12:08 (33,647)
Price, Stephanie J....4:41:48 (21,166)
Price, Tracey A....5:52:43 (32,532)
Priddle-Higson, Fiona A....5:28:25 (30,204)
Prideaux, Lena E....5:53:08 (32,558)
Priest, Luciana....4:15:55 (14,369)
Priestland, Liz M....5:03:12 (26,235)
Prietzel, Helen L....6:07:46 (33,471)
Prime, Laura J....4:35:27 (19,532)
Prince, Adele....5:19:50 (29,076)
Prince, Jenny D....5:34:49 (30,951)
Pring, Fiona E....4:41:54 (21,181)
Printon, Alexandra T....5:19:36 (29,050)
Prior, Michelle J....3:32:11 (4,500)
Prior, Susan C....4:18:22 (14,980)
Priseman, Clare....3:19:22 (2,664)
Pritchard, Christine L....4:31:40 (18,542)
Pritchard, Lisa....4:26:47 (17,203)
Pritchett, Jennifer A....4:11:01 (13,112)
Procter, Stephanie H....5:19:19 (29,009)
Proctor, Julia A....4:01:30 (10,915)
Proctor, Lesley A....4:57:04 (24,942)
Proctor, Nicola A....6:41:44 (34,658)
Proctor, Susan K....4:54:46 (24,397)
Profaska, Martina....3:45:28 (6,889)
Proitsi, Petroula....5:13:52 (28,134)
Protasiuk, Nicola K....5:35:21 (31,007)
Protheroe, Sallyann....5:05:44 (26,691)
Proudlock, Liz P....6:38:37 (34,599)
Proudlove, Joanne D....3:12:36 (1,945)
Proudlove, Sally E....4:19:28 (15,269)
Prowse, Wendy....3:26:54 (3,667)
Pryce, Joanna S....4:16:52 (14,621)
Pryke, Gail....3:51:33 (8,174)
Pugh, Andrea....5:19:00 (28,974)
Pugh, Daphne W....5:53:28 (32,582)
Pugh, Denise G....4:57:34 (25,048)
Pugh, Jane....4:06:18 (11,948)
Pugh, Rachel....7:11:20 (35,069)
Pugh, Tracy....5:24:27 (29,726)
Pulcini, Anna Maria....4:40:05 (20,752)
Pulford, Helen C....4:47:06 (22,515)
Pull, Juliet C....5:12:06 (27,819)
Pullen, Helen A....4:44:23 (21,817)
Pullen, Linda....6:20:57 (34,067)
Pullen, Michelle....3:50:48 (8,023)
Pullinger, Amanda J....5:22:52 (29,491)
Pullman, Dorothy M....4:30:30 (18,228)
Pumphrey, Amelia J....5:08:58 (27,265)
Purdie Scott, Helen....4:56:23 (24,769)
Purkiss, Jane S....4:27:43 (17,451)
Purton, Diane C....3:54:16 (8,833)
Pussard, Gail V....6:23:23 (34,170)
Puttock, Lucy J....5:01:16 (25,872)
Pye, Katherine D....3:37:06 (5,341)
Pyke, Catharine G....4:02:21 (11,091)
Pykett, Rebecca....4:22:08 (15,978)
Pyne, Janet Lynne....5:17:43 (28,749)
Quaife, Julie L....6:16:13 (33,851)
Quantrill, Natalie J....6:47:04 (34,740)
Quarrell, Julie P....5:03:58 (26,381)
Quarterman, Hannah L....4:17:36 (14,795)
Quatresols, Alison....5:43:59 (31,851)
Quayle, Allie....4:24:26 (16,558)
Queyroy, Martine....4:11:31 (13,258)
Quick, Juliet A....6:08:51 (33,507)
Quick, Louise....5:59:05 (32,994)
Quigg, Deirdre....4:00:55 (10,778)
Quincey, Kerry....5:42:21 (31,708)
Quine, Ninette L....5:29:45 (30,366)
Quinn, Aileen....5:28:46 (30,245)
Quinn, Clare P....5:28:46 (30,245)
Quinn, Dolores A....4:14:09 (13,945)
Quinn, Laura....5:17:47 (28,760)
Quinn, Lisa J....3:45:54 (6,960)
Quinn, Lucy J....4:33:25 (19,006)
Quirico, Clare E....5:05:00 (26,544)
Quirke, Laura A....5:28:21 (30,195)
Rabbetts, Lisa J....5:09:57 (27,446)
Race, Odile....4:24:03 (16,453)
Radcliffe, Gemma....4:10:39 (13,019)
Radcliffe, Helen E....5:14:41 (28,266)
Radcliffe, Johanna....5:58:54 (32,987)
Radcliffe, Sarah V....5:27:18 (30,079)
Radley, Brooke....4:18:19 (14,969)
Rae, Allyson M....4:47:30 (22,601)
Rae, Jane E....4:05:40 (11,818)
Rae, Sheila C....3:36:41 (5,261)
Rafferty, Helen L....4:23:51 (16,399)
Raharisoa, Annick....4:10:41 (13,033)
Rahma, Letexier....3:58:46 (10,179)
Rainbird, Claire L....4:50:42 (23,424)
Rainbird, Nicholas....5:07:23 (26,982)
Rainbow, Elizabeth M....5:08:27 (27,171)
Rainey, Janette....3:37:17 (5,369)
Raitt, Sarah....4:41:47 (21,162)
Rajah, Osma....4:40:30 (20,833)
Rajah, Ruby A....5:55:06 (32,695)
Rajput, Jagruti....6:43:54 (34,693)
Ralph, Barbara....3:18:53 (2,609)
Ralston, Valerie R....4:58:27 (25,253)
Rampley, Ann-Marie....3:57:59 (9,927)
Ramsay, Amanda G....3:39:47 (5,807)
Ramsay, Catriona A....4:17:52 (14,851)
Ramsay, Sam J....4:20:50 (15,644)
Ramsay, Tana....4:34:44 (19,326)
Ramsden, Anna-Marika A....4:26:31 (17,121)
Ramsden, Victoria L....7:51:37 (35,291)
Ramsell, Judy....5:08:09 (27,112)
Ramsey, Alison J....4:05:11 (11,703)
Ramsey, Gillian R....5:49:55 (32,330)
Ramsey, Jennifer S....4:42:06 (21,226)
Ramsey, Nicola J....3:22:01 (3,015)
Ramsey Smith, Sarah....3:34:16 (4,824)
Rana, Naheed....4:35:57 (19,664)
Rand, Anne-Marie L....5:51:49 (32,470)
Randall, Bernice....3:32:54 (4,599)
Randall, Emma J....5:31:34 (30,589)
Randall, Laura M....5:57:21 (32,861)
Randall, Pat A....6:02:54 (33,223)
Randall, Rebecca....4:26:11 (17,034)
Randall, Wendy Lynn....4:39:27 (20,569)
Randall, Zoe....3:49:47 (7,796)
Rang, Vicki....4:16:41 (14,580)
Ransom, Carol M....4:07:36 (12,255)
Ransome, Jennifer A....2:57:56 (833)
Ransome, Susan....3:39:54 (5,834)
Rantell, Kerry L....5:20:28 (29,149)
Ratcliffe, Martine A....4:51:40 (23,667)
Ratcliffe, Shelley....6:34:38 (34,514)
Rauscher, Erika....4:17:02 (14,654)
Raven, Daisy R....4:31:21 (18,455)
Raven, Lisa D....6:15:44 (33,830)
Ravenscroft, Sophie L....4:10:32 (12,989)
Rawal, Anjla....5:31:00 (30,529)
Rawle, Michelle E....3:45:14 (6,842)
Rawling, Eleanor M....4:20:07 (15,464)
Rawlings, Rebecca A....4:11:03 (13,124)
Rawlings-Brown, Nicole....4:20:43 (15,612)
Rawlins, Emma J....6:45:06 (34,711)
Rawlins, Katherine A....5:05:42 (26,682)
Rawlinson, Aine....5:06:29 (26,805)
Rawlinson, Susan....5:52:15 (32,498)
Rawson, Kate J....4:11:57 (13,374)
Ray, Diane S....5:26:33 (29,998)
Ray, Helen J....3:58:34 (10,119)
Ray, Lisa S....7:53:47 (35,298)
Raybould, Sara L....4:48:11 (22,779)
Raycraft, Gaynor L....4:55:30 (24,572)
Rayment, Heather A....4:48:42 (22,902)
Raymond, Helen....4:04:56 (11,639)
Raymond, Muriel M....5:12:48 (27,947)
Rayner, Adele L....5:24:45 (29,758)
Rayner, Marion R....3:24:31 (3,344)
Rayner, Michaela....5:00:22 (25,669)
Rayner, Miranda J....5:29:17 (30,309)
Raynor, Sophie A....6:43:46 (34,691)
Rea, Isobel....2:58:40 (884)
Rea, Maureen....4:25:59 (16,983)
Rea, Pamela K....4:59:23 (25,468)
Reach, Lucy E....3:26:08 (3,546)
Read, Caroline A....5:28:08 (30,168)
Read, Cathy....4:50:31 (23,376)
Read, Christine M....5:33:19 (30,790)
Read, Kate J....6:48:40 (34,790)
Read, Kellee....5:15:13 (28,357)
Read, Natalie C....5:01:56 (26,001)
Read, Nicky....6:53:22 (34,866)
Read, Sheila A....6:54:29 (34,889)
Read, Tina E....4:23:39 (16,349)
Reade, Kirsty E....3:35:33 (5,056)
Reader, Amanda E....4:30:43 (18,286)
Reader, Susan J....4:31:42 (18,552)
Readman, Emily H....4:33:17 (18,968)
Readman, Tamzin C....3:46:33 (7,097)
Ready, Deborah J....4:04:35 (11,561)
Reagan, Helen....3:36:14 (5,195)
Reaney, Anne....4:33:02 (18,906)
Reason, Janette S....4:53:16 (24,038)

Rebane, Glenys M 4:07:10 (12,144)
Rebbeck, Zoe 4:21:30 (15,812)
Redbart, Simone T 5:34:43 (30,940)
Redburn, Denise 4:41:03 (20,974)
Redden, Peter J 4:56:39 (24,843)
Reddy, Samantha J 5:13:17 (28,033)
Reddy, Shilpa 6:37:06 (34,572)
Reddy, Siobhan A 3:46:39 (7,122)
Redfearn, Debbie L 4:44:56 (21,936)
Redman, Lisa Joanne 4:25:11 (16,762)
Redman, Lorna 4:54:58 (24,441)
Redmond, Amy E 3:44:00 (6,630)
Redpath, Janet M 5:06:37 (26,824)
Redshaw, Helena C 5:37:24 (31,214)
Reece, Katherine V 3:58:38 (10,137)
Reed, Catherine E 3:59:07 (10,285)
Reed, Kim E 4:27:03 (17,269)
Reed, Larraine M 7:02:54 (34,982)
Reed, Louise M 6:12:39 (33,670)
Reed, Rachel L 4:34:02 (19,158)
Reed, Rebecca J 4:55:34 (24,584)
Reed, Sarah P 5:21:58 (29,361)
Rees, Carolyn A 4:44:07 (21,754)
Rees, Kate 4:02:53 (11,206)
Rees, Katherine A 4:15:33 (14,294)
Rees, Katherine L 3:40:12 (5,902)
Rees, Lexi 5:19:05 (28,981)
Rees, Linda P 4:42:05 (21,220)
Rees, Sandra P 5:13:27 (28,056)
Rees, Sarah A 4:43:00 (21,468)
Rees, Wendy M 4:52:03 (23,765)
Reeve, Lucy V 4:06:22 (11,966)
Reevell, Helen 5:01:21 (25,885)
Reeves, Nathalie 5:45:52 (32,006)
Regan, Jenni 5:19:54 (29,084)
Regan, Maria L 4:52:44 (23,912)
Regan, Sharon 6:28:36 (34,374)
Rehwald, Megan 3:56:36 (9,489)
Reiber, Michelle 5:00:42 (25,748)
Reid, Claire J 3:21:28 (2,941)
Reid, Debbie D 7:10:32 (35,056)
Reid, Donna J 3:57:51 (9,896)
Reid, Jacqueline A 6:32:35 (34,466)
Reid, Jacqueline E 3:59:33 (10,404)
Reid, Michelle L 5:32:05 (30,651)
Reid, Riona A 6:04:39 (33,322)
Reid, Sarah 3:27:44 (3,816)
Reid, Sharon V 5:30:08 (30,423)
Reid, Victoria A 4:09:51 (12,822)
Reidy, Anne-Marie 4:54:39 (24,377)
Reilly, Caroline M 4:29:47 (18,031)
Reilly, Darinka 4:13:32 (13,807)
Reilly, Sheila 5:02:31 (26,120)
Reilly, Tracey 4:23:26 (16,290)
Reincke, Jolyn H 4:49:07 (23,000)
Reinke-Wiese, Birgit 4:12:20 (13,481)
Relph, Sarah 4:57:27 (25,021)
Remzi, Allison L 6:25:50 (34,271)
Renfrew, Hollie 4:58:28 (25,258)
Renham, Penny A 4:19:24 (15,255)
Rennie, Deborah 6:37:05 (34,569)
Renny, Joanne E 5:38:41 (31,353)
Renton, Judith 4:25:07 (16,739)
Renwick-Bradford, Sharon 5:09:39 (27,396)
Revell, Fiona M 5:32:08 (30,654)
Revell, Kristy L 5:29:10 (30,291)
Rex, Jayne 4:59:20 (25,459)
Reyal, Yasmin 3:48:08 (7,425)
Reynolds, Angela 5:30:32 (30,464)
Reynolds, Claire 6:05:28 (33,365)
Reynolds, Deborah 5:06:44 (26,853)
Reynolds, Dianne 5:45:13 (31,947)
Reynolds, Emma 4:27:07 (17,285)
Reynolds, Frances M 4:07:19 (12,183)
Reynolds, Frances M 4:42:01 (21,202)
Reynolds, Heather C 5:46:02 (32,018)
Reynolds, Jessica 5:57:17 (32,851)
Reynolds, Linsey 4:35:59 (19,675)
Reynolds, Lisa 4:03:45 (11,375)
Reynolds, Tracy Carol 5:09:17 (27,329)
Rhodes, Debbie A 3:38:26 (5,574)
Rhodes, Elizabeth G 4:24:32 (16,577)
Rhodes, Louisa 4:16:41 (14,580)
Rhodes, Tracey H 3:53:57 (8,738)
Rhule, Justine L 4:31:09 (18,396)
Rhule, Suzanne 5:09:33 (27,374)
Rhys, Elin 5:54:15 (32,633)
Riccio, Gina M 5:06:03 (26,734)
Ricco, Ylenia 3:54:20 (8,847)
Rice, Cheryl 5:02:17 (26,076)
Rice, Francesca E 4:35:47 (19,625)
Rice, Jennifer S 3:53:09 (8,548)
Rice, Lisa J 6:45:04 (34,710)
Rice, Rachel E 5:44:33 (31,892)
Richards, Alison J 4:19:49 (15,379)
Richards, Anna L 5:34:40 (30,933)
Richards, Bethan 5:13:43 (28,104)
Richards, Caryl 4:29:48 (18,036)
Richards, Cherilee J 4:23:01 (16,189)
Richards, Deborah L 3:01:58 (1,114)
Richards, Emma 5:09:47 (27,428)
Richards, Emma V 3:35:57 (5,145)
Richards, Jan N 3:59:06 (10,278)
Richards, Jeannette S 5:35:30 (31,018)
Richards, Karen 5:50:27 (32,375)
Richards, Katie J 5:37:02 (31,174)
Richards, Lynne 4:24:48 (16,654)
Richards, Marie Clare 4:25:32 (16,847)
Richards, Mary E 4:16:00 (14,395)
Richards, Maxine L 6:17:18 (33,890)
Richards, Megan L 4:59:51 (25,565)
Richards, Pamela A 3:50:33 (7,959)
Richards, Ruth G 3:44:44 (6,754)
Richards, Wendy L 5:20:41 (29,173)
Richardson, Alice 5:11:29 (27,726)
Richardson, Angela 4:56:33 (24,814)
Richardson, Angela Louise 4:20:57 (15,674)
Richardson, Belinda S 5:11:29 (27,726)
Richardson, Helen E 4:58:08 (25,174)
Richardson, Helen J 4:51:15 (23,553)
Richardson, Jen G 5:56:31 (32,792)
Richardson, Jenny 4:24:23 (16,545)
Richardson, Karen 5:00:16 (25,646)
Richardson, Kerry 3:51:51 (8,240)
Richardson, Lisa 5:48:19 (32,201)
Richardson, Mandie J 4:56:49 (24,883)
Richardson, Nicola L 7:28:10 (35,208)
Richardson, Pamela 4:59:19 (25,455)
Richardson, Pamela 7:05:02 (35,005)
Richardson, Patricia 3:26:31 (3,601)
Richardson, Pauline H 5:03:27 (26,275)
Richardson, Susan G 6:26:28 (34,297)
Richardson, Tamara C 4:36:58 (19,909)
Richardson, Tracy 4:46:27 (22,331)
Riches, Patricia D 5:12:48 (27,947)
Richmond, Petngam 5:46:06 (32,026)
Richmond, Rachel 5:32:39 (30,714)
Richter, Carola 4:22:32 (16,084)
Rickard, Anna T 5:25:39 (29,884)
Rickerby, Christina 5:29:10 (30,291)
Ricoux, Katherine 5:03:35 (26,300)
Riddell, Grainne 3:41:07 (6,052)
Riddle, Kayley M 4:35:45 (19,617)
Riddy, Myrianthe 5:24:43 (29,753)
Ridehalgh, Sarah E 3:00:47 (1,037)
Ridgeon, Christine 6:13:43 (33,735)
Ridger, Joan M 5:30:43 (30,492)
Ridgley, Edith J 5:20:15 (29,121)
Ridgley, Julie R 3:59:40 (10,445)
Ridgway, Debra Anne 4:23:52 (16,405)
Ridgway, Sandy L 4:00:46 (10,733)
Ridley, Elysia 3:32:25 (4,534)
Ridley, Paul R 3:49:42 (7,774)
Rigby, Brenda E 7:25:56 (35,184)
Rigden, Kate 4:48:03 (22,754)
Rigg, Rachel J 5:25:20 (29,836)
Riley, Alexandra 4:39:45 (20,657)
Riley, Carolyn J 4:32:47 (18,842)
Riley, Elizabeth O 4:53:40 (24,123)
Riley, Ellie J 5:29:24 (30,319)
Riley, Joanna L 4:26:24 (17,088)
Rimmer, Lucy B 4:41:38 (21,129)
Ringham, Gypsy Rose 3:45:05 (6,816)
Rinn, Joanne 4:39:14 (20,502)
Ripley, Christine 5:40:29 (31,540)
Risa, Mette 4:09:18 (12,682)
Risby, Kay Elizabeth 3:50:23 (7,918)
Riseley, Miriam E 4:54:59 (24,444)
Rissbrook, Sally 4:27:57 (17,528)
Ritchie, Amy K 4:42:28 (21,324)
Ritchie, Eva M 4:56:53 (24,906)
Ritchie, Lucy 4:23:09 (16,220)
Rivers, Alison C 3:48:19 (7,470)
Rivers, Valerie A 5:15:16 (28,378)
Rix, Jemma 6:46:10 (34,725)
Rixon, Angela M 3:40:28 (5,937)
Rixon, Diana 4:07:59 (12,355)
Roach, Karen M 5:17:55 (28,780)
Roake, Karen N 3:44:23 (6,698)
Robb, Allyson 4:48:19 (22,811)
Robb, Tracy A 3:40:49 (6,003)
Robbins, Ashley L 3:32:58 (4,607)
Robbins, Linda M 5:56:46 (32,814)
Robert, Rebecca 4:48:04 (22,756)
Robert, Vanessa L 4:48:32 (22,861)
Roberts, Ann C 4:30:11 (18,146)
Roberts, Anna L 4:45:33 (22,090)
Roberts, Annika L 4:35:22 (19,514)
Roberts, Bethan 4:10:05 (12,874)
Roberts, Cali M 5:22:20 (29,408)
Roberts, Carly 4:56:19 (24,755)
Roberts, Carole M 3:55:53 (9,282)
Roberts, Charlotte P 6:21:05 (34,075)
Roberts, Danielle C 4:58:45 (25,327)
Roberts, Deborah 4:39:20 (20,526)
Roberts, Eve 4:26:23 (17,083)
Roberts, Georgina 4:59:25 (25,475)
Roberts, Gill 4:33:03 (18,911)
Roberts, Hannah 5:19:49 (29,074)
Roberts, Hayley A 6:02:54 (33,223)
Roberts, Jayne E 4:58:56 (25,371)
Roberts, Jeanette 4:35:33 (19,558)
Roberts, Jennifer C 4:19:22 (15,249)
Roberts, Jenny 5:13:40 (28,091)
Roberts, Julia 4:08:16 (12,439)
Roberts, Kanina K 5:18:49 (28,938)
Roberts, Kate L 5:09:13 (27,311)
Roberts, Katherine S 3:42:25 (6,285)
Roberts, Laura J 5:37:39 (31,243)
Roberts, Lynn C 5:36:42 (31,143)
Roberts, Pauline 4:30:23 (18,202)
Roberts, Rachael K 6:06:36 (33,419)
Roberts, Rebekah L 4:39:46 (20,662)
Roberts, Samantha J 5:24:20 (29,708)
Roberts, Shan D 3:00:54 (1,044)
Roberts, Victoria M 4:47:27 (22,589)
Robertson, Abby K 4:48:58 (22,962)
Robertson, Annette V 6:32:25 (34,461)
Robertson, Charlotte 5:10:48 (27,602)
Robertson, Elizabeth A 7:11:02 (35,064)
Robertson, Flora 5:15:42 (28,456)
Robertson, Gillian 4:28:54 (17,811)
Robertson, Ila R 4:17:38 (14,800)
Robertson, Jo 5:18:15 (28,830)
Robertson, Katia 4:49:05 (22,994)
Robertson, Sarah C 4:40:17 (20,792)
Robertson, Vanessa E 6:37:22 (34,579)
Robertson, Zoe C 5:00:31 (25,703)
Robertson-Cowley, Fran E 5:53:38 (32,594)
Robertson-Ross, Catherine 4:48:55 (22,949)
Robinson, Abigail 4:56:23 (24,769)
Robinson, Anesa S 3:27:25 (3,752)
Robinson, Ann M 5:30:44 (30,493)
Robinson, Anne Christine 4:13:45 (13,859)
Robinson, Deborah M 3:23:48 (3,236)
Robinson, Debra A 5:10:45 (27,592)
Robinson, Deena S 4:22:35 (16,096)
Robinson, Emily H 4:56:37 (24,832)
Robinson, Fiona C 3:34:22 (4,846)
Robinson, Gill E 5:07:22 (26,976)
Robinson, Helen E 4:38:21 (20,266)
Robinson, Janet K 6:23:16 (34,163)
Robinson, Jayne 5:13:58 (28,154)
Robinson, Jemma L 5:34:59 (30,965)
Robinson, Joanne 4:01:03 (10,804)
Robinson, Julia A 4:53:40 (24,123)
Robinson, Julie A 3:36:48 (5,276)
Robinson, Karen A 3:36:57 (5,309)
Robinson, Kay H 7:09:16 (35,045)

Robinson, Laura....4:14:54 (14,140)
Robinson, Lizzie....4:01:09 (10,825)
Robinson, Mandy....5:02:38 (26,142)
Robinson, Margaret A....6:04:55 (33,335)
Robinson, Michael J....4:34:41 (19,314)
Robinson, Nicky....5:58:00 (32,916)
Robinson, Pauline A....6:17:18 (33,890)
Robinson, Rosella J....3:50:01 (7,840)
Robinson, Sarah L....4:14:11 (13,955)
Robinson, Sarah L....4:52:32 (23,870)
Robinson, Sarah V....4:31:41 (18,546)
Robinson, Tracey J....5:29:47 (30,370)
Robinson, Urszula E....5:54:22 (32,646)
Robjohns, Karen Susan....4:46:36 (22,374)
Robson, Anastasia H....4:32:07 (18,666)
Robson, Dawn E....4:10:59 (13,104)
Robson, Jane S....4:25:39 (16,893)
Robson, Jaqueline....6:21:03 (34,071)
Robson, Linda R....4:41:58 (21,195)
Robson, Louise C....4:45:54 (22,188)
Roche, Anna....4:53:25 (24,058)
Roche, Claudine....4:38:04 (20,189)
Roche-Kelly, Clodagh F....4:02:55 (11,213)
Rochford, Nikki A....3:54:26 (8,872)
Rock, Sarah J....3:42:36 (6,330)
Rockett, Jackie....5:41:14 (31,600)
Rockey, Katrina....4:12:32 (13,535)
Rodarte, Sharon....4:15:15 (14,222)
Roddis, Suzanne C....3:22:55 (3,119)
Rodger, Donna....4:15:04 (14,180)
Rodger, Gillian....4:44:41 (21,885)
Rodgers, Cathy M....4:12:07 (13,418)
Rodgers, Mandy Jane....4:13:08 (13,691)
Roe, Angela J....5:10:54 (27,620)
Roe, Joanne E....3:27:54 (3,841)
Roe, Stephanie C....4:54:19 (24,292)
Roebuck, Emily....4:46:22 (22,302)
Roebuck, Liz....6:47:41 (34,763)
Rogan, Emma B....3:32:07 (4,486)
Rogan, Marion G....4:32:48 (18,847)
Rogers, Adam J....4:19:54 (15,400)
Rogers, Amanda....4:11:01 (13,112)
Rogers, Carina A....3:54:46 (8,960)
Rogers, Caroline M....4:20:33 (15,571)
Rogers, Denise....5:39:21 (31,431)
Rogers, Gemma A....4:27:43 (17,451)
Rogers, Janet E....6:22:37 (34,134)
Rogers, Karla L....4:38:42 (20,350)
Rogers, Kate....5:13:15 (28,029)
Rogers, Linda A....3:40:35 (5,953)
Rogers, Sarah M....3:31:23 (4,383)
Rogers, Suzanne....4:25:30 (16,836)
Rogers, Tracey A....4:54:04 (24,235)
Rogerson, Naomi....5:18:34 (28,886)
Roissetter, Lucy E....4:34:26 (19,244)
Rolande, Peiffer....3:58:44 (10,170)
Rolfe, Jodie....4:05:12 (11,711)
Rollings, Isabel S....4:52:26 (23,851)
Rollinson, Michelle A....4:50:02 (23,244)
Rolston, Lisa J....6:01:58 (33,169)
Romecin, Lindsay H....3:25:14 (3,424)
Romijn, Werenfrieda....5:21:33 (29,310)
Ronald, Lorna A....6:21:49 (34,108)
Ronan, Sue....5:34:41 (30,935)
Roni, Nat....5:40:40 (31,562)
Rooke, Jan....5:49:41 (32,306)
Rooke, Laura Louise....4:43:25 (21,583)
Rooke, Zoe S....3:41:40 (6,142)
Rookes, Debra M....4:18:55 (15,139)
Rooney, Alison J....4:39:08 (20,473)
Rooney, Sharron....4:25:41 (16,904)
Roos, Annette....5:26:54 (30,043)
Roper, Helen....4:25:17 (16,780)
Roper, Ling M....4:47:01 (22,487)
Rosales, Marisol....3:56:23 (9,423)
Roscoe, Elizabeth W....4:58:46 (25,330)
Rose, Bronwyn D....6:57:52 (34,929)
Rose, Debbie....6:32:30 (34,464)
Rose, Emily L....6:15:19 (33,804)
Rose, Faye Rebecca....4:22:13 (16,006)
Rose, Katharine....4:24:00 (16,440)
Rose, Lisa....4:04:29 (11,541)
Rose, Nickie L....5:12:18 (27,853)
Roseblade, Eleanor....4:35:07 (19,442)
Rose-Cunningham, Emma....4:53:49 (24,177)
Roshier, Lizzie S....4:55:03 (24,460)
Ross, Alexandra....5:15:09 (28,344)
Ross, Alison....3:54:14 (8,821)
Ross, Andrea....4:35:46 (19,620)
Ross, Denise....3:54:20 (8,847)
Ross, Emma Z....3:38:44 (5,630)
Ross, Joanne....3:31:54 (4,453)
Ross, Lisa....6:39:30 (34,619)
Ross, Michele....4:06:00 (11,880)
Ross, Penny J....4:56:29 (24,795)
Ross, Sue A....4:05:40 (11,818)
Ross Gower, Angela D....4:40:50 (20,920)
Rosser, Margaret T....5:25:04 (29,806)
Rossi, Delia....4:28:32 (17,706)
Rossi, Valeria....6:19:14 (34,010)
Roth, Laura J....6:02:46 (33,212)
Rothwell, Kerry S....4:29:02 (17,843)
Rothwell, Valerie....4:49:47 (23,195)
Roughley, Suzanne E....5:59:03 (32,993)
Roughley, Victoria D....5:07:27 (26,996)
Rougier., Siv B....3:07:04 (1,439)
Rouse, Janice J....5:30:46 (30,497)
Rouse, Victoria L....6:19:45 (34,024)
Routledge, Tracy....5:58:58 (32,990)
Rowan, Joanna Frances....5:11:18 (27,693)
Rowan, Kathryn E....4:30:13 (18,154)
Rowan, Louise....8:08:23 (35,326)
Rowe, Catherine D....3:56:14 (9,372)
Rowe, Claire....8:08:21 (35,325)
Rowe, Jennifer L....4:27:13 (17,314)
Rowe, Jessica....4:16:37 (14,560)
Rowe, Rachael....5:24:11 (29,680)
Rowland, Pamela Mary....5:19:26 (29,027)
Rowlands, Fleur E....6:12:02 (33,643)
Rowlands, Gillian D....3:56:38 (9,511)
Rowlands, Kate L....4:33:01 (18,901)
Rowlands-Wong, Christina P....5:23:45 (29,618)
Rowley, Gemma K....4:24:43 (16,627)
Rowley, Jennie L....5:43:37 (31,824)
Rowley, Joanne M....4:52:59 (23,973)
Rowlings, Amie D....5:11:39 (27,755)
Rowntree, Olivia J....6:25:39 (34,265)
Rowswell, Kathryn M....4:49:18 (23,053)
Roxburgh, Katherine L....3:28:25 (3,915)
Roy, Diane M....3:14:38 (2,186)
Roy, Morag....5:11:50 (27,782)
Ruakere, Bianca....4:51:37 (23,650)
Rubicini, Elisabetta....5:29:23 (30,317)
Rubino, Giuseppina....5:24:33 (29,740)
Rubino, Natalia....3:45:03 (6,815)
Rubis, Anita Victoria....4:09:03 (12,631)
Ruch, Alexandra....4:58:24 (25,243)
Ruckwied, Kim....4:23:15 (16,241)
Rudd, Philippa G....4:19:32 (15,298)
Ruddick, Sarah....4:41:32 (21,098)
Rudman, Amanda....4:18:07 (14,926)
Rumens, Nicky J....5:16:31 (28,564)
Rumgay, Clare....4:15:31 (14,287)
Rummell, Lyn M....6:54:00 (34,880)
Rump, Franchine H....3:50:27 (7,933)
Rusby, Linda A....4:51:14 (23,547)
Rush, Lorraine J....5:35:02 (30,975)
Rushton, Nicola H....4:57:42 (25,069)
Rusling, Barbara....3:40:04 (5,871)
Russ, Sarah A....4:49:18 (23,053)
Russell, Angela C....5:22:32 (29,444)
Russell, Catherine....4:25:58 (16,978)
Russell, Chloe L....4:30:53 (18,325)
Russell, Delma R....5:01:48 (25,970)
Russell, Judith E....4:08:36 (12,524)
Russell, Julie....5:10:13 (27,501)
Russell, Lucy E....4:44:06 (21,748)
Russell, Marilyn....5:14:40 (28,261)
Russell, Sarah....6:02:10 (33,182)
Russell, Vanessa....4:19:29 (15,277)
Russo, Deborah E....3:58:27 (10,083)
Russon, Tara L....3:42:48 (6,377)
Rust, Fiona A....3:54:29 (8,885)
Rutherfoord, Paula M....3:00:40 (1,030)
Rutherford, Nicola M....4:07:58 (12,354)
Rutherford, Pamela L....3:35:28 (5,043)
Rutherford, Sandra....5:02:43 (26,159)
Ruthven, Stephanie....3:55:11 (9,081)
Rutledge, Leigh....5:49:36 (32,298)
Rutt, Rebecca L....3:56:11 (9,364)
Rutter, Alison J....6:21:32 (34,094)
Rutter, Emma Rachel Florence....5:31:06 (30,540)
Ruxton, Ashleigh....4:51:30 (23,620)
Ryall, Karen A....5:56:58 (32,833)
Ryan, Carmel....4:31:48 (18,584)
Ryan, Catherine A....4:04:53 (11,626)
Ryan, Fiona....4:20:16 (15,502)
Ryan, Tamatha J....3:37:39 (5,432)
Ryan, Wendy P....4:58:55 (25,368)
Ryder, Helen S....3:32:44 (4,578)
Rymer, Jane....5:25:02 (29,803)
Sabatini, Heather....4:50:27 (23,358)
Sabin, Anna L....4:46:43 (22,413)
Sachdev, Nimisha....6:14:51 (33,783)
Sackfield, Consuela P....5:21:25 (29,285)
Sadler, Angela S....3:10:29 (1,736)
Sadler, Dawn....5:36:26 (31,117)
Sadler, Janet C....5:22:11 (29,388)
Sadler, Joanne....6:09:39 (33,544)
Sadler, Maria L....4:56:20 (24,758)
Sadler, Rachel....3:59:26 (10,378)
Sadler, Sally A....5:01:10 (25,853)
Saeed, Zina....4:29:59 (18,092)
Safa, Zerin T....6:13:29 (33,721)
Saffron, Janet L....6:30:43 (34,428)
Saffuri, Kelly C....7:09:40 (35,048)
Saffuri, Nina E....5:08:30 (27,178)
Sage, Elaine....4:51:52 (23,717)
Sage, Jane E....5:59:11 (33,000)
Sage, Rosie....6:38:38 (34,600)
Said, Rowina A....5:04:14 (26,416)
Saint, Debbie M....3:58:32 (10,110)
Saint, Elizabeth J....3:49:20 (7,694)
Saker, Laura....5:06:25 (26,796)
Salcedo, Veronica....4:10:44 (13,049)
Saldanha, Emily A....5:31:30 (30,582)
Saleem, Irm....5:58:10 (32,932)
Sales, Catherine A....4:26:58 (17,251)
Sales, Katie L....4:56:04 (24,698)
Saliba, Adeline....5:50:43 (32,395)
Saliba, Carla....6:25:25 (34,249)
Saliba, Gaylee....4:40:02 (20,735)
Salisbury, Dee....3:57:18 (9,706)
Sallis, Jodie....5:02:10 (26,056)
Sally, Friend....4:31:02 (18,361)
Salmon, Jenny E....3:57:37 (9,806)
Salomons, Pauline....4:52:04 (23,769)
Salt, Melanie P....4:27:31 (17,395)
Samara, Samir....3:47:16 (7,245)
Sampson, Laura....5:01:57 (26,008)
Sams, Nicola L....4:47:50 (22,684)
Samuel, Adele....4:32:32 (18,762)
Samuel, Lyndsay J....4:46:21 (22,294)
Samuelson-Dean, Katie M....3:25:41 (3,486)
Samuelsson, Eva-Britt....4:26:08 (17,020)
Samways, Carol A....4:55:43 (24,620)
Samways, Pauline....6:29:18 (34,391)
Sanchez, Karen E....4:43:00 (21,468)
Sanchez, Maria de la Nieves....4:02:17 (11,084)
Sandbach, Carly....3:53:00 (8,506)
Sandell, Nikki J....3:47:33 (7,300)
Sanders, Beverley A....6:29:17 (34,388)
Sanders, Emily A....3:43:38 (6,551)
Sanders, Lyn K....5:26:23 (29,976)
Sanders, Natalie....5:36:35 (31,129)
Sanderson, Georgina M....5:32:15 (30,665)
Sanderson, Jayne....4:47:35 (22,624)
Sanderson, Karen....6:02:05 (33,176)
Sanderson, Sarah L....6:38:19 (34,596)
Sandford, Eleanor K....3:56:35 (9,483)
Sandford, Elizabeth J....3:46:28 (7,081)
Sandover, Diane M....3:59:32 (10,398)
Sandrine, Hayo....4:26:39 (17,168)
Sandrine, Messager....4:04:31 (11,550)
Sands, Charlotte J....6:03:54 (33,284)
Sands, Fiona....5:22:02 (29,368)
Sangha, Rameet....4:33:28 (19,016)
Sankey, Rebecca....4:14:17 (13,986)
Sant-Cassia, Rebecca P....4:08:57 (12,606)

Santos, Maria Lucia....6:10:16 (33,574)
Santos Taylor, Waleria....5:39:36 (31,458)
Sapsford, Jean Y....5:09:25 (27,351)
Sapwell, Eleanor J....6:33:50 (34,494)
Saqui, Sonja L....3:34:55 (4,943)
Sarah, Stone J....5:40:11 (31,515)
Saravia, Carol....3:37:14 (5,359)
Sarce Ballorin, Karine....3:51:44 (8,215)
Sardone, Janice A....5:27:16 (30,075)
Sargeant, Caroline....6:41:00 (34,645)
Sargent, Rebecca C....5:18:28 (28,864)
Sargent, Tania Marie....6:04:25 (33,308)
Sargent Wong, Suzanne....4:58:53 (25,357)
Sargood, Joanne C....5:29:02 (30,275)
Sarner, Helen Petra Sarah....5:12:38 (27,913)
Sarsfield, Kaye L....4:45:47 (22,152)
Saul, Nikki A....6:32:43 (34,468)
Saunders, Alexandra....4:11:03 (13,124)
Saunders, Alison J....3:56:32 (9,469)
Saunders, Charlotte L....3:47:26 (7,271)
Saunders, Clare M....4:21:50 (15,909)
Saunders, Gerry....6:04:16 (33,301)
Saunders, Jane A....4:33:20 (18,985)
Saunders, Jennie L....5:05:40 (26,671)
Saunders, Judy C....4:24:18 (16,527)
Saunders, Lucy E....6:15:00 (33,791)
Saunt, Tonia E....4:20:13 (15,490)
Savage, Catherine L....6:26:41 (34,306)
Savage, Jane....4:53:40 (24,123)
Savage, Melissa M....4:39:07 (20,467)
Savage, Tamara....4:30:05 (18,121)
Savage Eames, Nicola E....4:55:22 (24,542)
Savic, Donna....4:46:24 (22,315)
Savill, Anna K....3:35:04 (4,972)
Savill, Bridget C....4:24:39 (16,605)
Savoca, Katia....5:29:03 (30,278)
Sawdon, Alison Jane....4:57:19 (24,989)
Sawyer, Helen....4:18:51 (15,118)
Sawyer, Jennifer M....6:12:24 (33,658)
Sawyer, Philippa....4:35:41 (19,592)
Sayer, Nicholette....5:03:39 (26,315)
Sayers, Pamela J....4:49:33 (23,133)
Scadding, Jeanette....5:35:21 (31,007)
Scales, Carmen....5:00:25 (25,680)
Scanlan, Catherine....5:05:12 (26,592)
Scannell, Linda....5:43:16 (31,801)
Scarisbrick, Jane....4:17:25 (14,749)
Scarle, Eve R....3:54:17 (8,835)
Scarratt, Rebecca J....5:42:12 (31,694)
Scarrott, Yvonne C....3:17:19 (2,468)
Schaad, Carline....3:47:48 (7,351)
Schandl, Roswitha....4:11:19 (13,194)
Scherg, Anja....3:36:01 (5,158)
Scheuber, Mathilda F....4:27:14 (17,317)
Schiess, Fabienne....4:47:54 (22,707)
Schilling, Valerie....4:00:42 (10,720)
Schipporeit, Klaudia S....4:28:09 (17,593)
Schlaeppi, Louise P....3:39:57 (5,849)
Schloder, Monika....4:12:13 (13,443)
Schmid, Erika R....3:20:40 (2,850)
Schmitz, Jutta....4:21:29 (15,804)
Schneider, Inga....4:41:19 (21,043)
Schnell, Lauren....5:08:55 (27,255)
Schofield, Helen....4:16:35 (14,550)
Schofield, Susan....5:18:49 (28,938)
Scholes, Kate B....4:57:31 (25,037)
Scholes, Rachel I....5:25:25 (29,844)
Scholey, Georgina L....5:30:52 (30,504)
Schooling, Tracey C....4:12:04 (13,405)
Schorr, Barbara....6:11:39 (33,624)
Schulz, Kirstin....4:17:49 (14,842)
Schulz, Ursula G....3:08:13 (1,547)
Schumacher, Christina....4:32:58 (18,888)
Schuster, Penelope....4:39:39 (20,627)
Schwartz, Nicola....5:05:32 (26,649)
Schwarz, Marion....4:02:12 (11,068)
Sciarrino, Barbara A....6:37:58 (34,590)
Scobie, Erin T....5:42:58 (31,767)
Scoby, Ailsa J....6:13:33 (33,725)
Scofield, Dianne E....4:30:02 (18,106)
Scoot, Tanya E....4:24:07 (16,477)
Scorah, Kelly S....5:17:40 (28,741)
Scott, Amy....3:27:36 (3,801)
Scott, Angela Gail....4:37:55 (20,143)
Scott, Caroline A....4:29:41 (18,011)
Scott, Carolyn....5:22:37 (29,455)
Scott, Catherine M....6:22:02 (34,115)
Scott, Cathryn....5:15:15 (28,370)
Scott, Clare L....4:50:38 (23,409)
Scott, Donna C....3:47:55 (7,377)
Scott, Edy L....4:51:53 (23,723)
Scott, Isobel A....5:09:35 (27,382)
Scott, Janet M....4:58:23 (25,233)
Scott, Julia L....3:42:39 (6,346)
Scott, Karen A....5:04:37 (26,483)
Scott, Kelly....5:15:13 (28,357)
Scott, Lauren M....5:54:47 (32,666)
Scott, Lorraine....4:54:00 (24,219)
Scott, Louise....5:04:28 (26,450)
Scott, Louise N....5:46:47 (32,073)
Scott, Myrna L....4:53:27 (24,061)
Scott, Rachel....3:38:30 (5,588)
Scott, Sandy....6:07:16 (33,448)
Scott-Collis, Susan....5:08:51 (27,242)
Scott-Tabron, Amanda....5:22:24 (29,423)
Scovell, Gillian....4:59:29 (25,494)
Screech, Rebecca M....3:16:53 (2,419)
Screen, Hazel....4:06:13 (11,931)
Scrivens, Alex....5:40:21 (31,528)
Scrivens, Debbie....4:32:56 (18,882)
Scruton, Kathy M....5:52:40 (32,522)
Scudellaro, Kate....6:53:31 (34,872)
Seaberg, Stacy A....4:31:21 (18,455)
Seabrook, Patricia H....5:33:34 (30,813)
Sealey, Carys....6:17:33 (33,908)
Seals, Mandy....5:40:36 (31,555)
Seaman, Claire L....5:16:37 (28,582)
Seaman, Lucy A....5:16:37 (28,582)
Searle, Belinda J....5:09:34 (27,379)
Searle, Olivia C....5:32:00 (30,640)
Searle, Tina E....4:58:51 (25,349)
Seaton, Allys J....4:46:23 (22,310)
Seaton, Jane M....4:18:59 (15,156)
Sedgwick, Rebecca L....4:57:30 (25,029)
Sedman, Alison....3:01:10 (1,064)
Sedman, Kerry J....4:40:44 (20,892)
Seedat, Sarah B....5:57:36 (32,882)
Seedhouse, Donna L....5:07:58 (27,082)
Seeling, Sabine....4:29:07 (17,865)
Seelinger, Lisa E....5:09:00 (27,274)
Seem, Tracy R....4:16:22 (14,486)
Sejersen, Gitte....4:50:01 (23,242)
Sekkides-Lunn, Penny J....5:28:22 (30,197)
Selby, Elizabeth A....4:40:45 (20,898)
Selby, Linda....4:24:37 (16,595)
Selby, Rachel A....4:37:53 (20,138)
Sellers, Suneeta....4:23:20 (16,260)
Sellwood, Chloe....4:48:36 (22,877)
Selway-Swift, Lydia....4:04:04 (11,463)
Selwood, Gemma A....5:46:04 (32,023)
Semikin, Allison K....4:49:30 (23,116)
Semmelink, Marilise....3:47:26 (7,271)
Semper, Kelly-Ann....5:11:47 (27,772)
Senatore, Anna....3:11:32 (1,832)
Senior, Gina L....4:25:23 (16,814)
Senior, Katherine A....3:58:33 (10,114)
Sephton, Karen L....4:30:30 (18,228)
Serfontein, Ilse....4:16:34 (14,542)
Serobe, Queen....4:59:56 (25,584)
Serop, Dorte....5:27:11 (30,064)
Service, Catherine A....5:13:37 (28,083)
Sesto, Valeria A....3:02:15 (1,136)
Setch, Ann....6:48:14 (34,777)
Setz, Cathryn....5:57:52 (32,901)
Seward, Tina M....5:11:15 (27,684)
Sewell, Carina Lynn....4:00:21 (10,626)
Sexton-Wainwright, Francesca P....4:35:58 (19,672)
Seymour, Angela Lucy....4:34:52 (19,371)
Seymour-Willcox, Rebecca....4:27:14 (17,317)
Shackleton, Katy L....3:53:10 (8,556)
Shacklock, Susan L....3:21:21 (2,927)
Shadbolt, Tammy....4:34:43 (19,321)
Shadforth, Jane E....4:42:23 (21,297)
Shadick, Janet L....4:49:32 (23,127)
Shah, Bella R....5:01:49 (25,974)
Shah, Kavita....4:58:06 (25,162)
Shah, Neeta....5:57:41 (32,891)
Shaikh, Zohra....6:29:34 (34,399)
Shalders, Donna....5:52:59 (32,542)
Shannon, Catriona M....3:50:24 (7,920)
Shannon, Margaret Anna....4:38:03 (20,179)
Shapland, Tracy L....5:07:10 (26,935)
Sharam, Trudy J....5:55:17 (32,710)
Sharman, Charlotte A....3:57:07 (9,655)
Sharman, Jemma R....4:27:58 (17,532)
Sharman, Lucinda E....5:12:05 (27,814)
Sharp, Caroline L....4:09:46 (12,794)
Sharp, Claire....7:33:01 (35,239)
Sharp, Heather J....3:52:24 (8,381)
Sharp, Lisa....4:03:09 (11,260)
Sharp, Yvonne....4:58:48 (25,338)
Sharpe, Anthea L....3:41:31 (6,125)
Sharpe, Fiona M....4:19:45 (15,357)
Sharpe, Sarah M....4:12:32 (13,535)
Sharpe, Shelley....5:09:26 (27,353)
Sharpe, Toni J....5:56:00 (32,758)
Sharpe, Zoe....3:59:20 (10,345)
Sharpner, Natalie J....4:25:35 (16,868)
Sharrod, Sandra....4:49:35 (23,141)
Shattock, Chloe....3:37:16 (5,365)
Shave, Donna E....5:18:19 (28,837)
Shave, Sarah J....4:52:12 (23,795)
Shaw, Alexie....3:09:55 (1,700)
Shaw, Anna C....5:17:23 (28,696)
Shaw, Carol A....4:58:54 (25,362)
Shaw, Caroline M....4:03:29 (11,327)
Shaw, Deborah A....3:41:20 (6,093)
Shaw, Emma L....4:09:24 (12,706)
Shaw, Felicity....3:35:14 (4,997)
Shaw, Gemma L....4:18:34 (15,044)
Shaw, Hannah E....4:31:39 (18,538)
Shaw, Holly D....4:19:13 (15,213)
Shaw, Jennie....5:24:29 (29,730)
Shaw, Jennifer A....5:56:43 (32,810)
Shaw, Linda....5:22:53 (29,494)
Shaw, Lisa M....6:07:48 (33,474)
Shaw, Olivia J....4:53:41 (24,133)
Shaw, Ruth M....4:03:47 (11,386)
Shaw, Samantha....6:13:13 (33,708)
Shaw, Susan....4:47:37 (22,634)
Shaw, Suzanne....3:44:41 (6,743)
Shaw, Tanya....3:13:39 (2,084)
Shaw, Wendy L....4:18:38 (15,064)
Shea, Samantha L....4:55:46 (24,628)
Sheaf, Mary E....5:54:01 (32,615)
Shearer, Joanna M....4:16:54 (14,625)
Sheehan, Sheila....6:27:53 (34,354)
Sheldrake, Rebekah....7:37:23 (35,257)
Shelton, Joanne M....4:32:14 (18,689)
Shephard, Debbie....4:55:02 (24,455)
Shepherd, Antonia G....6:01:46 (33,155)
Shepherd, Barbara J....4:35:40 (19,587)
Shepherd, Carrie D....5:16:06 (28,518)
Shepherd, Catherine H....5:33:30 (30,803)
Shepherd, Gemma....4:21:36 (15,844)
Shepherd, Karen L....5:02:07 (26,046)
Shepherd, Samantha J....4:28:03 (17,557)
Shepherd, Sarah A....4:36:27 (19,787)
Shepherd, Suzie E....4:45:00 (21,962)
Shepherd, Wendy A....5:32:09 (30,658)
Sheppard, Gail S....6:04:17 (33,304)
Sheppard, Jayne....4:38:59 (20,429)
Sheppard, Joanna L....4:45:02 (21,973)
Sheppard, Kate E....4:51:37 (23,650)
Shergill, Guzz....4:17:06 (14,664)
Sheridan, Alison J....4:49:28 (23,102)
Sheridan, Sonia....4:12:48 (13,605)
Sherman, Gemma R....4:59:19 (25,455)
Sherman, Shelia A....4:48:30 (22,851)
Sherriff, Virginia L....3:44:17 (6,680)
Shevlin, Claire H....6:31:08 (34,438)
Shian, Angela....4:34:49 (19,358)
Shields, Debra....3:52:31 (8,406)
Shields, Julie C....4:41:04 (20,976)
Shields-Peach, Tracey-Anne....6:10:43 (33,593)
Shier, Katherine L....5:44:19 (31,879)
Shilland, Kate E....4:00:02 (10,552)
Shilling, Claire E....5:04:46 (26,501)
Shilling, Rebecca E....5:53:24 (32,577)

Shindler, Miriam F 4:28:12 (17,613)
Shing, Lindsey 3:33:31 (4,678)
Shipley, Adele Victoria................3:57:31 (9,775)
Shipley, Nicola 5:34:22 (30,891)
Shipp, Elizabeth A.......................4:15:26 (14,268)
Shippey, Sue M 5:18:08 (28,809)
Shipton, Alison M 5:13:50 (28,123)
Shirley, Laura A...........................4:26:32 (17,126)
Shirley, Lorraine C 4:34:04 (19,164)
Shirley, Marie L 3:17:41 (2,500)
Shirt, Andrea Mary 4:52:14 (23,806)
Shobukova, Liliya 2:24:24 (30)
Shoebridge, Polly A......................4:03:54 (11,423)
Shore, Danielle M 4:50:26 (23,350)
Shorrock, Dorothy M....................5:06:11 (26,759)
Short, Susan M 4:13:18 (13,745)
Shorter, Tracey C..........................5:17:07 (28,662)
Shorunkeh-Sawyerr, Brenda R 5:01:26 (25,900)
Shotton, Faye 4:38:50 (20,384)
Shrimpton, Annette C 3:52:13 (8,335)
Shrimpton, Charlotte E 5:48:32 (32,218)
Shrosbree, Tracy A 6:07:06 (33,441)
Shudell, Emma-Jayne 6:56:28 (34,912)
Shynn, Sarah J 3:56:37 (9,500)
Siblon, Feria V 4:41:33 (21,103)
Sidaway, Renée 5:01:04 (25,834)
Siddons, Kate 4:27:44 (17,459)
Siddons, Melanie Sarah S 4:43:51 (21,678)
Siderfin, Catherine L 4:53:01 (23,979)
Sidhu, Rupinder...........................5:14:50 (28,289)
Siepiela, Lauren 4:14:07 (13,937)
Sieracki, Helen J 4:30:12 (18,151)
Sierwald, Samantha C 3:50:47 (8,019)
Sigismondi, Clio 4:41:50 (21,171)
Signorelli, Helen 5:00:56 (25,795)
Sikka, Seema 6:02:31 (33,198)
Silbernagl, Martha 3:32:01 (4,471)
Silcock, Tracey D 8:07:18 (35,322)
Silk, Rebecca 5:06:16 (26,772)
Sillars, Anne 3:34:21 (4,843)
Sillitoe, Amy C 4:37:26 (20,018)
Sills, Hannah R 4:34:46 (19,337)
Silvani, Anja 4:37:14 (19,969)
Silver, Rachel A 5:04:20 (26,430)
Silver, Sally A 4:23:48 (16,389)
Silverman, Claudene E 4:17:07 (14,671)
Silverman, Ruth H 3:33:01 (4,612)
Silverthorn, Gillian 5:07:01 (26,910)
Silverwood, Emma 3:45:29 (6,891)
Silverwood, Janet C 4:18:05 (14,912)
Silvey, Emma J 6:28:51 (34,378)
Silvey, Victoria J 5:34:24 (30,899)
Sim, Helena 3:33:56 (4,745)
Simber, Jane 4:27:51 (17,502)
Sime, Sarah L 6:11:45 (33,628)
Simington, Naomi 4:11:08 (13,149)
Simmonds, Leanne R....................4:14:50 (14,122)
Simmonds, Sian 4:59:59 (25,594)
Simmonds, Stephanie M...............4:48:49 (22,922)
Simmons, Kathy 3:34:20 (4,839)
Simmons, Meinou 3:29:25 (4,092)
Simms, Jennifer E 3:46:49 (7,159)
Simon, Joann T 4:37:14 (19,969)
Simon, Mary-Anne J 4:36:41 (19,835)
Simonetti, Fabiola 4:35:43 (19,607)
Simons, Emily S 4:04:53 (11,626)
Simons, Jodie 5:55:54 (32,755)
Simphal, Josephine J....................4:48:55 (22,949)
Simpkin, Lorna S 4:30:53 (18,325)
Simpkins, Emma M 3:56:33 (9,475)
Simpkins, Rachel M 5:08:20 (27,146)
Simpson, Abigail 4:18:37 (15,058)
Simpson, Becky J 5:39:04 (31,406)
Simpson, Deidre A 4:31:18 (18,438)
Simpson, Diana R 5:28:00 (30,147)
Simpson, Jennifer 6:09:18 (33,524)
Simpson, Joanna B 6:06:10 (33,393)
Simpson, Kaye S 5:02:03 (26,033)
Simpson, Margaret.......................4:58:12 (25,189)
Simpson, Patricia (Trish) M 4:15:48 (14,349)
Simpson, Penny A 5:59:57 (33,046)
Simpson, Sarah A 5:24:59 (29,797)
Simpson, Susan B 6:09:24 (33,532)

Sims, Belinda G 4:01:29 (10,909)
Sims, Karen 6:35:53 (34,541)
Sims, Rosie G 3:32:42 (4,573)
Sims, Sharon M 5:52:40 (32,522)
Sinclair, Hayley M 4:49:29 (23,110)
Sinclair, Karen 4:22:03 (15,954)
Sinclair, Kristel 6:24:05 (34,189)

Sinclair-Day, Jennifer 6:02:51 (33,218)

This was one of the best days of my life, from the
training to the actual day. The training was hard
but great fun (sometimes). I have always wanted to
run the London Marathon. It was my nephew who
gave me the inspiration to do it and I'm so glad
that he did. This was my first Marathon, which I
ran with my nephew Aaron who has MS. It will
not be my last. The weather was great for me as
I love to run in the sun. What can I say about the
atmosphere? It was fantastic. Friends, family and
the crowd cheering you on, pubs playing music,
live bands and even the bagpipes at the Cutty Sark.
I would recommend anyone to run the London
Marathon. Derek Smiley (a great friend) took up
the challenge in 2010. XX

Singer, Jo L 3:13:30 (2,061)
Singer, Shani 7:26:39 (35,196)
Singleton, Veronica C..................3:30:17 (4,219)
Sinnett, Ann F..............................3:10:38 (1,748)
Sinnott, Giselle H 4:24:43 (16,627)
Sinnott, June 5:39:02 (31,399)
Sipos, Adriana 6:13:17 (33,710)
Sisk, Aoife 4:08:07 (12,395)
Sittmann, Liezl 4:52:14 (23,806)
Sivamberam, Karen 5:35:17 (30,997)
Sivertsen, Vikki J 4:03:17 (11,288)
Sixsmith, Gemma Francesca 4:53:14 (24,027)
Skaalen, Jennifer C 5:43:50 (31,834)
Skates, Tracey D 5:59:40 (33,028)
Skea, Katie 3:45:55 (6,969)
Skegg, Nicola A 5:58:57 (32,989)
Skelton, Helen E 4:43:30 (21,598)
Skene, Caryl 4:55:04 (24,468)
Skidmore, Flora 3:18:29 (2,573)
Skilton, Sarah 4:41:35 (21,115)
Skinner, Catherine 3:46:17 (7,037)
Skinner, Deidre J 7:24:29 (35,173)
Skinner, Katrina N 5:38:17 (31,307)
Skinner, Sarah J 5:15:25 (28,404)
Skinner, Vicky A 6:05:59 (33,387)
Skinns, Jessica 3:48:02 (7,411)
Skinns, Layla 3:50:30 (7,944)
Skipper, Sally E 4:31:45 (18,567)
Skirving, Chloe J 4:59:30 (25,497)
Skudal, Linda 4:12:12 (13,439)
Slachmuylders, Saskia 4:21:13 (15,744)
Slade, Gemma M 6:47:04 (34,740)
Slade, Louise H 4:56:06 (24,707)
Slade, Lydia 4:36:57 (19,900)
Slade, Maxine M...........................5:58:26 (32,955)
Slamon, Emma L...........................5:01:53 (25,991)
Slamon, Lynne 5:08:05 (27,100)
Slapp, Janette 4:18:49 (15,108)
Slater, Abigail 5:00:09 (25,624)
Slater, Carolyn 5:45:45 (31,999)
Slater, Catherine L 4:09:42 (12,774)
Slater, Debbie A............................6:37:21 (34,578)
Slater, Morag M 4:38:51 (20,388)
Slater, Ruth 4:48:50 (22,928)
Slattery, Franses E 5:26:46 (30,022)
Slaughter, Hollie S 5:25:42 (29,891)
Slevin, Sara 6:17:01 (33,884)
Slide, Catherine E 6:02:24 (33,196)
Slinn, Clare H 5:12:27 (27,881)
Slipp, Hannah 4:59:06 (25,410)
Sliwerski, Lynn 6:11:30 (33,622)
Slow, Amber K 7:06:05 (35,017)
Smail, Amanda 3:25:35 (3,472)
Smale, Philippa A.........................5:56:55 (32,827)
Small, Elizabeth A 5:07:48 (27,059)

Smalley, Wendy............................5:00:52 (25,779)
Smart, Sandra A 4:39:57 (20,707)
Smart, Tamsin C 4:44:22 (21,809)
Smart, Terry J 6:11:30 (33,622)
Smedley, Dionne 5:21:29 (29,296)
Smiles, Hilary 4:12:33 (13,538)
Smillie, Lesley H 4:46:42 (22,400)
Smillie, Madeline C 4:09:43 (12,779)
Smillie, Odette M 5:00:08 (25,620)
Smit, Bridget G.............................3:59:48 (10,495)
Smit, Lize 4:23:43 (16,367)
Smith, Abigail 6:26:55 (34,317)
Smith, Abigail C 5:56:54 (32,825)
Smith, Aileen 4:09:46 (12,794)
Smith, Alexandra F 4:38:43 (20,354)
Smith, Alexandra G 3:55:27 (9,148)
Smith, Amanda J 5:31:56 (30,631)
Smith, Amanda S 6:17:46 (33,917)
Smith, Amy L 3:28:44 (3,961)
Smith, Amy L 4:50:08 (23,267)
Smith, Angela M 4:43:12 (21,517)
Smith, Ann 6:11:15 (33,608)
Smith, April L 5:03:39 (26,315)
Smith, Barbara 6:07:17 (33,450)
Smith, Barbara A 5:05:08 (26,575)
Smith, Barbara S 6:34:10 (34,504)
Smith, Becky R 4:25:18 (16,786)
Smith, Bryony H 5:21:11 (29,254)
Smith, Cara L 4:39:46 (20,662)
Smith, Catherine M 3:27:18 (3,733)
Smith, Cathryn J 4:01:30 (10,915)
Smith, Chantal 4:35:11 (19,458)
Smith, Christina 3:39:33 (5,766)
Smith, Claire 3:30:53 (4,311)
Smith, Claire A 5:47:31 (32,135)
Smith, Corrina L 4:10:56 (13,089)
Smith, Corrine L 5:00:19 (25,658)
Smith, Debbie 4:42:13 (21,255)
Smith, Deborah A 4:43:19 (21,554)
Smith, Deborah E 4:33:28 (19,016)
Smith, Diana 5:16:29 (28,559)
Smith, Donna L 4:53:56 (24,208)
Smith, Elaine G 4:18:09 (14,934)
Smith, Elizabeth 4:26:39 (17,168)
Smith, Emily D 5:30:06 (30,411)
Smith, Emily K 3:11:17 (1,809)
Smith, Emily L 3:38:48 (5,642)
Smith, Emma E 5:07:38 (27,031)
Smith, Emma L 4:41:08 (20,991)
Smith, Emma V 5:06:44 (26,853)
Smith, Faye M 4:10:17 (12,931)
Smith, Frances 5:07:40 (27,039)
Smith, Gemma A 4:55:30 (24,572)
Smith, Ginette 4:07:35 (12,252)
Smith, Harriett 7:12:29 (35,076)
Smith, Hilary J 4:35:12 (19,465)
Smith, Hillary 4:59:36 (25,518)
Smith, Hollie 4:45:54 (22,188)
Smith, Jacqueline 6:33:42 (34,492)
Smith, Jane E 6:05:41 (33,375)
Smith, Jane Elizabeth...................4:21:32 (15,824)
Smith, Jayne 5:00:54 (25,787)
Smith, Jayne Y 6:22:38 (34,137)
Smith, Jeanette M 4:37:48 (20,120)
Smith, Jemma L 4:50:08 (23,267)
Smith, Jennifer L 5:26:48 (30,027)
Smith, Jessica S 4:58:57 (25,377)
Smith, Jo J 4:35:29 (19,536)
Smith, Josephine 4:04:27 (11,532)
Smith, Julie 4:08:09 (12,407)
Smith, Julie B 4:55:39 (24,605)
Smith, Kara L 6:36:02 (34,544)
Smith, Karen L 5:17:37 (28,734)
Smith, Karen M 4:27:16 (17,333)
Smith, Kathryn A 5:08:18 (27,140)
Smith, Kathryn A 6:32:28 (34,462)
Smith, Katie F 5:02:15 (26,072)
Smith, Kerry L 5:02:37 (26,139)
Smith, Kim M 3:54:42 (8,945)
Smith, Kirsten N 5:03:46 (26,337)
Smith, Lara R 4:35:33 (19,558)
Smith, Linda 3:20:04 (2,762)
Smith, Linda E 3:45:16 (6,848)

Smith, Lorraine R 4:06:28 (11,984)
Smith, Louise 3:55:38 (9,203)
Smith, Louise 4:53:42 (24,138)
Smith, Louise E 4:51:30 (23,620)
Smith, Louise S 6:13:39 (33,728)
Smith, Lucy 5:38:28 (31,328)
Smith, Mary 5:37:55 (31,263)
Smith, Mary E 5:13:18 (28,040)
Smith, Melanie 5:47:22 (32,123)
Smith, Naomi 5:38:39 (31,348)
Smith, Norma F 4:15:04 (14,180)
Smith, Patricia E 4:35:35 (19,568)
Smith, Philippa K 4:23:36 (16,334)
Smith, Polly A 6:54:56 (34,894)
Smith, Rachel C 4:01:07 (10,821)
Smith, Rachel J 4:33:07 (18,924)
Smith, Rebecca 5:13:43 (28,104)
Smith, Rebecca 6:17:25 (33,900)
Smith, Rebecca J 4:49:17 (23,046)
Smith, Rebecca L 5:36:47 (31,153)
Smith, Rozalind K 4:12:01 (13,392)
Smith, Sally A 5:26:31 (29,992)
Smith, Sallyanne 4:38:54 (20,409)
Smith, Samantha D 5:25:33 (29,868)
Smith, Sandee J 5:08:27 (27,171)
Smith, Sarah 4:35:34 (19,564)
Smith, Sarah J 5:33:49 (30,848)
Smith, Sarah-Jane 5:02:03 (26,033)
Smith, Shella 4:14:43 (14,088)
Smith, Sheree 6:47:34 (34,757)
Smith, Sian 7:04:52 (35,002)
Smith, Souad 6:39:23 (34,614)
Smith, Susan 4:38:54 (20,409)
Smith, Susan K 4:28:09 (17,593)
Smith, Tanya A 5:40:05 (31,508)
Smith, Teresa 4:13:20 (13,760)
Smith, Tina M 4:48:55 (22,949)
Smith, Tracey J 5:24:57 (29,790)
Smith, Una J 5:03:45 (26,334)
Smith, Vanessa E 4:19:53 (15,396)
Smith, Vanessa H 3:54:59 (9,018)
Smith, Vanessa K 4:06:47 (12,056)
Smith, Wendy J 5:42:25 (31,711)
Smith, Zoe P 5:40:02 (31,500)
Smith-Calvert, Elizabeth H 4:02:04 (11,033)
Smither, Deborah J 5:01:02 (25,825)
Smullen, Jean 3:57:29 (9,762)
Smyth, Anne E 4:40:44 (20,892)
Smyth, Katie L 4:40:44 (20,892)
Smyth, Kelly A 5:47:09 (32,108)
Smyth, Nuala J 3:57:55 (9,909)
Smyth, Penny J 3:46:42 (7,137)
Smyth, Sarah 3:53:38 (8,658)
Smythe, Elizabeth J 5:51:07 (32,423)
Smyton, Amanda J 4:34:22 (19,232)
Snape, Sandra E 3:51:45 (8,218)
Sneade, Rhian 5:06:50 (26,874)
Sneddon, Linda 5:12:15 (27,847)
Snellgrove, Kirste L 6:05:36 (33,368)
Snelling, Jean E 5:31:27 (30,574)
Snodgrass, Tatiana P 4:10:49 (13,068)
Snook, Louisa A 4:24:54 (16,686)
Snook, Rachel 5:05:41 (26,678)
Snook, Tanya 4:04:28 (11,538)
Soar, Susan R 4:44:45 (21,899)
Soden-Roberts, Lisa J 5:09:43 (27,405)
Soffe, Angela S 4:29:44 (18,024)
Sohl, Inderjit 5:40:13 (31,519)
Sohl, Justina 5:22:30 (29,438)
Soldal, Elisabeth 4:44:03 (21,736)
Solomon Williams, Rachel 3:49:42 (7,774)
Somers, Grainne H 5:25:40 (29,885)
Soobul, Natasha 6:08:41 (33,502)
Soremski, Claudia 4:15:47 (14,344)
Sorensen, Lotte H 3:24:59 (3,398)
Sosimi, Atiti 6:47:45 (34,765)
Soula, Fta 5:01:22 (25,890)
Soumya, Bendada 5:40:22 (31,531)
South, Elaine 5:09:10 (27,303)
South, Jayne E 4:39:42 (20,645)
Southern, Joanne H 4:58:23 (25,233)
Sowerbutts, Julia R 5:29:10 (30,291)
Sowerby, Joanne H 4:35:32 (19,555)
Sowerby, Kay 5:39:29 (31,445)
Sowter, Lee 5:07:05 (26,921)
Spain, Helen M 4:07:55 (12,344)
Spalluto, Cosma 4:16:03 (14,407)
Spanswick, Emma J 5:14:04 (28,175)
Sparkes, Lizzie M 5:41:28 (31,632)
Sparrow, Sam 4:26:03 (16,999)
Sparshatt, Anna C 5:56:32 (32,793)
Spearing, Luretta L 3:46:58 (7,196)
Spearman, Susan J 4:19:00 (15,160)
Speed, Lucy 5:55:03 (32,691)
Speight, Gail 5:13:44 (28,110)
Speirs, Christine 5:38:26 (31,320)
Speirs, Fiona 4:00:40 (10,713)
Speirs, Rachael F 4:33:34 (19,041)
Spelzini, Charlotte 4:22:07 (15,970)
Spence, Sarah 4:55:56 (24,672)
Spence, Shelagh F 6:46:43 (34,734)
Spence, Tina M 4:38:52 (20,396)
Spencer, Claire 4:36:56 (19,898)
Spencer, Claire L 3:12:24 (1,920)
Spencer, Deborah 5:12:59 (27,981)
Spencer, Deborah A 4:33:32 (19,029)
Spencer, Freeston-Smith 4:02:30 (11,126)
Spencer, Gillian M 4:12:10 (13,433)
Spencer, Imogen K 5:14:13 (28,195)
Spencer, Jasmine 4:33:59 (19,151)
Spencer, Sally A 3:26:56 (3,674)
Spencer, Shelley A 4:07:14 (12,162)
Spencer, Sue 4:35:56 (19,662)
Spencer, Yvonne E 5:09:31 (27,367)
Sperl, Andrea 4:08:48 (12,573)
Spice, Joanna E 5:01:05 (25,837)
Spiers, Anna B 6:24:14 (34,200)
Spiers, Sally 6:27:16 (34,336)
Spight, Carolyn 5:17:47 (28,760)
Spiller, Elizabeth C 3:52:10 (8,317)
Spiller, Karen F 5:19:40 (29,057)
Spink, Charlotte V 5:22:29 (29,436)
Spink, Hannah E 5:07:47 (27,056)
Spinks, Danielle 5:07:28 (27,001)
Spinks, Rebecca E 5:24:04 (29,663)
Spittal, Tanja 4:27:47 (17,479)
Spong, Carole 4:02:11 (11,064)
Spowart, Bethan 5:25:41 (29,887)
Spreckelsen, Katharina 4:28:12 (17,613)
Sprenkel, Angela 5:07:28 (27,001)
Sprich, Sabine 4:29:22 (17,940)
Sprigings, Paula H 5:57:25 (32,867)
Spring, Georgie 4:44:51 (21,918)
Sprintall, Sarah 5:35:14 (30,989)
Sproson, Nicola E 4:34:45 (19,329)
Spruntulis, Madeline N 4:11:29 (13,248)
Squibbs, Emma 6:18:32 (33,948)
Squire, Susan M 4:50:37 (23,400)
Sranding, Angie C 5:02:35 (26,134)
Stacey, Marie 5:28:16 (30,186)
Stacey, Susan J 4:19:51 (15,390)
Stacey, Tracy 4:42:58 (21,466)
Stafferton, Lois 4:51:14 (23,547)
Stafford, Clare 4:55:23 (24,549)
Stafford, Fleur M 4:53:18 (24,042)
Stagg, Sophie A 4:39:59 (20,719)
Stallard, Emma L 3:00:40 (1,030)
Stanborough, Lindsey A 6:21:01 (34,070)
Stancliffe, Josephine Carmidy 5:12:45 (27,934)
Standing, Helen S 3:44:17 (6,680)
Standish, Rebecca J 5:46:02 (32,018)
Standley, Gillian M 5:05:19 (26,610)
Stanescu, Silvia 4:10:09 (12,898)
Stanfield, Christine 4:43:40 (21,642)
Stanford, Paula 4:35:46 (19,620)
Stanley, Andrea N 4:04:00 (11,450)
Stanley, Caryn N 4:26:50 (17,216)
Stanley, Jillian J 4:22:50 (16,149)
Stanley, Nicola S 5:13:53 (28,139)
Stansell, Amandeep 4:28:05 (17,570)
Stansfield, Jane E 5:16:13 (28,529)
Stansfield, Sarah M 6:15:25 (33,811)
Stanton, Amanda 3:56:34 (9,478)
Stanton, Tracy A 4:32:48 (18,847)
Stanyard, Philippa J 3:27:24 (3,749)
Staplehurst, Diane 5:18:30 (28,869)
Stapleton, Clare L 5:09:57 (27,446)
Stapleton, Joanne 4:24:50 (16,663)
Starbuck, Juliet C 3:48:46 (7,557)
Stark, Michelle Heather 3:54:07 (8,786)
Stark, Sophie A 4:21:58 (15,935)
Starkey, Debbie 4:59:42 (25,535)
Starkey, Karla H 4:31:53 (18,602)
Starling, Marion D 4:31:13 (18,409)
Starmer, Clare 4:56:42 (24,856)
Starr, Victoria Joanna 4:48:29 (22,846)
Starrs, Debbie M 5:40:29 (31,540)
Starvis, Samantha 4:49:05 (22,994)
Staton, Lorrel D 5:08:16 (27,137)
Staunton, Louise J 3:34:55 (4,943)
Staunton, Marie 4:59:46 (25,549)
Staunton, Rebecca L 4:17:54 (14,862)
Stead, Clare E 6:03:56 (33,285)
Stearn, Becca H 3:41:01 (6,033)
Stearn, Michelle L 4:55:22 (24,542)
Stearns, Annabelle V 2:59:46 (980)
Steavenson, Laura 4:28:40 (17,740)
Steckelberg-Mevert, Silke 5:48:21 (32,205)
Steed, Rebecca C 5:49:44 (32,308)
Steel, Emma 4:54:24 (24,310)
Steel, Janice A 4:07:45 (12,302)
Steer, Daniella Marie 4:21:31 (15,820)
Steer, Deborah A 2:54:08 (610)
Steer, Gail 4:31:48 (18,584)
Steer, Jodie 4:03:52 (11,414)
Stefanowicz, Courtney 6:17:06 (33,887)
Stegmeyer, Kelly S 4:55:30 (24,572)
Stein, Chantal S 3:53:02 (8,514)
Steinman, Linda 4:28:36 (17,724)
Stenner, Sue C 4:55:38 (24,602)
Stenning, Gemma E 4:34:13 (19,199)
Stenning, Nicola 5:06:23 (26,787)
Stephen, Vivienne J 3:37:08 (5,348)
Stephens, Karen S 6:21:55 (34,111)
Stephens, Miranda J 4:06:24 (11,969)
Stephenson, Jane Susan 5:40:37 (31,556)
Stephenson, Jo 4:08:34 (12,517)
Stephenson, Joanne 4:24:25 (16,555)
Stephenson, Kim 3:14:33 (2,175)
Stephenson, Pamela 5:52:34 (32,516)
Steptoe, Charlotte 3:13:02 (2,011)
Sterba, Gemma L 5:35:44 (31,044)
Sterling, Amanda 3:35:59 (5,152)
Stevens, Clare 3:27:09 (3,707)
Stevens, Gillian 4:13:19 (13,752)
Stevens, Helen E 4:28:53 (17,806)
Stevens, Laura J 4:34:46 (19,337)
Stevens, Rachel E 4:21:52 (15,913)
Stevens, Sandra 4:54:08 (24,250)
Stevens, Sarah L 5:29:56 (30,393)
Stevens, Tina J 5:24:44 (29,756)
Stevens, Tracy A 4:03:00 (11,232)
Stevens, Wendy 5:17:49 (28,767)
Stevens, Yvonne J 6:26:06 (34,283)
Stevenson, Belinda M 4:13:06 (13,685)
Stevenson, Danielle M 4:21:14 (15,753)
Stevenson, Debbie A 7:54:14 (35,302)
Stevenson, Elizabeth C 5:15:47 (28,471)
Stevenson, Fiona C 6:13:27 (33,718)
Stevenson, Gemma 3:57:07 (9,655)
Stevenson, Kate L 5:30:07 (30,417)
Stevenson, Liz 5:37:30 (31,224)
Stevenson, Philippa 4:42:49 (21,412)
Stevenson, Rebecca A 5:59:32 (33,019)
Stevenson, Sonya 6:28:16 (34,365)
Stevenson, Tracy 4:29:11 (17,884)
Steward, Claire E 3:23:11 (3,146)
Stewart, Alex Y 5:09:15 (27,316)
Stewart, Ann M 3:48:01 (7,405)
Stewart, Breanne E 5:12:20 (27,857)
Stewart, Carol 4:20:17 (15,508)
Stewart, Helen 4:42:57 (21,459)
Stewart, Julie 3:40:04 (5,871)
Stewart, Lucinda Jane 4:12:09 (13,426)
Stewart, Monica 3:24:01 (3,262)
Stewart, Rachel L 5:14:59 (28,314)
Stewart, Rachel L 5:44:51 (31,919)
Stewart, Sarah 4:19:59 (15,425)
Stewart, Verka 4:12:48 (13,605)

Stibbs, Cath J	3:42:32 (6,310)	
Stibbs, Helen J	3:49:47 (7,796)	
Stickler, Carol L	3:50:31 (7,951)	
Stiles, Carol A	6:27:41 (34,349)	
Stimson, Juliet	4:36:32 (19,801)	
Stirling, Debbie L	4:49:36 (23,147)	
Stirling, Lisa	3:35:03 (4,968)	
Stoakes, Tina	4:29:14 (17,908)	
Stoate, Amy C	6:00:27 (33,071)	
Stobbard, Sarah J	4:21:38 (15,858)	
Stock, Kerry A	6:24:19 (34,208)	
Stockdale, Samantha M	3:53:21 (8,592)	
Stocker, Aimée D	5:27:54 (30,138)	
Stocker, Audrey	5:12:58 (27,979)	
Stocker, Cara E	5:39:35 (31,456)	
Stockham, Elizabeth A	4:24:06 (16,471)	
Stockley, Naomi	5:00:46 (25,763)	
Stockman, Hanny E	3:20:12 (2,780)	
Stockton, Elizabeth S	3:58:53 (10,221)	
Stockton, Hannah A	6:13:19 (33,712)	
Stockton, Paula J	3:42:37 (6,336)	
Stoddart, Sian E	4:47:55 (22,712)	
Stoffell, Caroline L	6:30:00 (34,411)	
Stokes, Anna L	5:04:11 (26,411)	
Stokes, Cheri	5:04:00 (26,387)	
Stokes, Claire	4:24:34 (16,585)	
Stokes, Laura J	4:41:13 (21,017)	
Stokes, Marie A	3:23:55 (3,250)	
Stokes, Samantha J	7:14:02 (35,095)	
Stokes, Sarah L	4:01:10 (10,827)	
Stokes, Sharon A	5:16:44 (28,607)	
Stokes, Trudy S	3:41:09 (6,057)	
Stone, Emma J	5:11:28 (27,721)	
Stone, Natasha	4:57:32 (25,040)	
Stone, Penelope	3:45:50 (6,954)	
Stone, Sally A	3:58:09 (9,990)	
Stone, Sarah K	4:22:11 (16,000)	
Stone, Susan C	4:54:32 (24,343)	
Stone, Veronica A	4:50:59 (23,483)	
Stone, Zoe M	3:51:16 (8,112)	
Stoneman, Camilla	6:19:06 (34,003)	
Stones, Joanne P	4:19:36 (15,313)	
Stopforth, Karen N	5:04:31 (26,459)	
Stoppani, Julie M	3:45:24 (6,871)	
Storer, Dawn Lesley	3:57:13 (9,678)	
Storer, Helen	6:24:14 (34,200)	
Storey, Elaine	3:12:14 (1,906)	
Storey, Pamela J	6:51:45 (34,840)	
Storey, Susan M	6:25:30 (34,255)	
Storm, Ruth	5:40:42 (31,564)	
Storr, Ann E	5:19:24 (29,024)	
Storr, Helen E	4:15:56 (14,374)	
Storr, Sophie J	5:03:54 (26,364)	
Storrie, Marie	3:48:10 (7,438)	
Story, Sue P	5:01:28 (25,907)	
Stott, Kay A	5:41:35 (31,638)	
Stott, Nicola Clare	4:47:36 (22,629)	
Stout, Caroline P	4:06:10 (11,919)	
Stpehen, Lisa	3:34:59 (4,955)	
Stracey, Victoria J	4:10:15 (12,921)	
Stradling, Claire P	4:07:17 (12,170)	
Stradling, Sarah L	2:49:54 (469)	
Strain, Paula	5:22:17 (29,404)	
Stratford, Christine K	4:59:35 (25,513)	
Stratton, Karen K	4:29:10 (17,876)	
Streatfeild, Rachel Anne	4:41:43 (21,144)	
Stredwick, Marian	5:32:32 (30,696)	
Street, Hannah L	4:19:48 (15,371)	
Street, Joanne	5:44:32 (31,890)	
Street, Stephanie A	3:43:51 (6,604)	
Street, Virginia B	5:02:15 (26,072)	
Streeter, June A	5:17:59 (28,792)	
Stretch, Samantha	4:17:39 (14,806)	
Strickland, Caroline J	5:51:26 (32,442)	
Stringer, Jennifer J	6:16:44 (33,876)	
Stringfellow, Hayley	4:17:24 (14,742)	
Strom, Sue	7:13:16 (35,085)	
Stromer, Lindsay S	5:40:31 (31,544)	
Strong, Claire J	4:01:35 (10,939)	
Strong, Sarah E	4:28:50 (17,789)	
Stroud, Andrea T	3:52:33 (8,410)	
Stuart, Laura	5:00:13 (25,637)	
Stubbs, Eleanor S	5:03:30 (26,284)	
Stubbs, Jill A	4:36:48 (19,864)	
Stubbs, Sally J	3:35:54 (5,136)	
Studer, Leah	4:41:50 (21,171)	
Stueber, Alexandra	4:11:27 (13,242)	
Stuetzel, Heidi	4:27:40 (17,436)	
Sturges, Elizabeth C	5:27:29 (30,092)	
Sturgess, Penny J	5:08:53 (27,250)	
Sturgess, Rachael	6:27:15 (34,333)	
Sturman, Darren L	4:56:08 (24,714)	
Sturzaker, Nicola A	3:23:37 (3,204)	
Subramanian, Suchitra	5:04:47 (26,503)	
Such, Louise C	4:18:09 (14,934)	
Suckling, Vicky A	5:21:26 (29,288)	
Sudlow, Alexis	4:11:22 (13,214)	
Sugar, Natasha J	4:31:58 (18,627)	
Sugden, Ingrid	5:28:58 (30,271)	
Sullivan, Carmel M	3:13:37 (2,075)	
Sullivan, Cindy A	4:50:14 (23,292)	
Sullivan, Fiona E	4:41:45 (21,154)	
Sullivan, Joanne	4:23:28 (16,299)	
Sullivan, Kate E	5:54:32 (32,651)	
Sullivan, Megan	6:18:48 (33,987)	
Sullivan, Michelle	4:35:11 (19,458)	
Sullivan, Rachel	5:47:58 (32,167)	
Sullivan, Sheila	4:05:47 (11,838)	
Summers, Karen	5:24:27 (29,726)	
Summers, Michelle M	5:13:52 (28,134)	
Summers, Rona	4:54:36 (24,360)	
Summerskill, Chloe J	4:04:27 (11,532)	
Summerson, Una	4:53:31 (24,074)	
Summerville, Karen	4:08:30 (12,507)	
Sund, Berit	4:07:13 (12,155)	
Sunderland, Caroline	4:32:43 (18,819)	
Suppas, Barbara	5:42:29 (31,722)	
Surrey, Anouska	4:34:45 (19,329)	
Sutcliffe, Laura E	4:20:01 (15,435)	
Sutcliffe, Rachel L	6:24:15 (34,205)	
Suter, Emma L	4:27:26 (17,377)	
Sutherland, Fiona M	4:04:14 (11,499)	
Sutherland, Helen C	3:52:08 (8,304)	
Sutherland, Judith A	4:56:45 (24,865)	
Sutherland, Stephanie C	4:52:55 (23,956)	
Sutton, Andrea	4:12:13 (13,443)	
Sutton, Jill	4:24:05 (16,466)	
Sutton, Kira	6:53:19 (34,864)	
Sutton, Louise	5:41:05 (31,592)	
Sutton, Nicola	5:40:37 (31,556)	
Swain, Charlotte E	4:22:43 (16,129)	
Swaine, Hayley	4:08:35 (12,519)	
Swaine, Suzanne Lucy	3:58:20 (10,046)	
Swale Pope, Rosie	6:07:37 (33,467)	
Swallow, Alison J	4:44:12 (21,766)	
Swan, Eileen M	4:46:39 (22,383)	
Swan, Emily C	4:54:56 (24,433)	
Swan, Hayley J	4:51:03 (23,500)	
Swannell, Lisa J	4:48:42 (22,902)	
Swanson, Katherine M	3:24:40 (3,364)	
Swart, Sunette	5:38:00 (31,274)	
Sweeney, Emily C	4:28:36 (17,724)	
Sweeney, Orla J	5:41:53 (31,661)	
Sweet, Jennifer	3:57:00 (9,619)	
Sweeting, Alison	5:45:37 (31,990)	
Swift, Alannah G	4:19:58 (15,419)	
Swift, Annabel	4:46:45 (22,420)	
Swift, Anne M	3:47:13 (7,236)	
Swift, Claire M	4:41:25 (21,058)	
Swift, Claudine N	6:41:39 (34,656)	
Swift, Kerry M	5:37:03 (31,177)	
Swigciski, Amy	6:50:15 (34,820)	
Swinburne, Linsey J	4:31:24 (18,471)	
Swindell, DA	4:32:00 (18,640)	
Swindin, Caroline	4:42:11 (21,244)	
Swingler, Val M	3:25:30 (3,457)	
Swinnerton, Grace E	6:24:56 (34,227)	
Syed, Rachel	3:41:43 (6,152)	
Sykes, Melanie	4:09:26 (12,712)	
Sykes, Rachel C	6:41:20 (34,652)	
Symes, Sylvia M	6:29:12 (34,386)	
Symonds, Sheila M	6:45:26 (34,716)	
Symons-Jones, Georgina T	4:02:35 (11,149)	
Synnott, Kim	5:21:37 (29,318)	
Synnott-Wells, Marie	3:10:56 (1,774)	
Syrett, Kerry D	5:19:35 (29,046)	
Syson, Catherine E	4:31:20 (18,451)	
Syvret, Claire L	4:18:46 (15,094)	
Szerman Ostergaard, Lorena A	4:40:34 (20,851)	
Szulc, Linda	4:53:08 (24,007)	
Tabony, Natalie J	5:08:37 (27,196)	
Tabor, Rosalind M	3:55:30 (9,158)	
Taccuso, Simonetta	3:52:48 (8,465)	
Tadd, Cheryl	5:07:12 (26,944)	
Tae, Young Hee	4:34:43 (19,321)	
Tage, Tina J	4:10:13 (12,913)	
Tagg, Susan G	4:02:59 (11,226)	
Tait, Gayle M	3:58:39 (10,144)	
Tait, Joanne L	6:33:16 (34,477)	
Tait, Kimberley D	4:06:03 (11,893)	
Tait, Nicola	5:34:50 (30,952)	
Tait, Stephanie J	4:53:34 (24,089)	
Takako, Katayama	4:46:56 (22,461)	
Talbot, Camilla Helen	4:04:07 (11,470)	
Talbot, Catherine	4:15:58 (14,387)	
Talbot, Joyce A	4:31:51 (18,592)	
Talbot, Julie	5:08:35 (27,190)	
Talbot, Julie A	4:33:07 (18,924)	
Talbot, Julie D	4:43:26 (21,587)	
Talbot, Michele A	5:31:01 (30,530)	
Talby, Donna L	4:31:09 (18,396)	
Taliadoros, Helen	5:02:28 (26,109)	
Tamburella, Claire	4:24:26 (16,558)	
Tamm, Angela	4:41:33 (21,103)	
Tan, Chew Kwee	4:21:23 (15,778)	
Tandon, Anjali	5:13:10 (28,021)	
Tang, Luveon Y	5:57:31 (32,877)	
Tanner, Christine	3:44:47 (6,765)	
Tanner, Diane	3:47:12 (7,234)	
Tanner, Pauline F	4:06:43 (12,044)	
Taphouse, Karin	5:22:10 (29,384)	
Tapley, Julie	3:56:30 (9,461)	
Taranowski, Helen L	2:58:44 (887)	
Tardrew, Helen	4:27:01 (17,260)	
Tarpey, Kim	3:32:32 (4,549)	
Tarr, Belinda A	5:07:01 (26,968)	
Tarrach, Chevaun	3:27:23 (3,746)	
Tarrach, Zoe C	3:21:03 (2,892)	
Tartoosie, Lee-Anne	6:14:40 (33,776)	
Tasker, Vicki E	5:15:49 (28,476)	
Tatchley, Maria	4:14:58 (14,158)	
Tate, Dominique L	3:58:28 (10,090)	
Tattersall, Philippa J	3:42:51 (6,389)	
Tatton, Kate L	5:08:32 (27,180)	
Tauber, Gillian	5:02:58 (26,204)	
Tavener, Mary G	3:31:50 (4,445)	
Taverner, Zoe	5:19:17 (29,004)	
Tavner, Gill	3:41:43 (6,152)	
Tay, Alison P	4:18:21 (14,975)	
Taylor, Alice	4:58:11 (25,209)	
Taylor, Alison E	4:36:53 (19,890)	
Taylor, Angie R	4:54:47 (24,404)	
Taylor, Anna L	3:24:49 (3,383)	
Taylor, Anne	6:30:37 (34,427)	
Taylor, Beverley M	4:57:23 (25,010)	
Taylor, Camilla R	3:50:45 (8,007)	
Taylor, Caroline T	5:01:56 (26,001)	
Taylor, Catherine R	3:43:10 (6,463)	
Taylor, Christina B	5:47:13 (32,112)	
Taylor, Christine	5:55:28 (32,724)	
Taylor, Claire M	5:44:36 (31,899)	
Taylor, Clare E	4:05:51 (11,850)	
Taylor, Debbie	5:17:43 (28,749)	
Taylor, Eleanor	4:01:51 (10,991)	
Taylor, Emma L	4:37:09 (19,954)	
Taylor, Eve	4:36:05 (19,698)	
Taylor, Frances R	6:48:22 (34,782)	
Taylor, Helen	6:00:45 (33,095)	
Taylor, Helen M	4:04:49 (11,612)	
Taylor, Isla K	4:48:12 (22,783)	
Taylor, Jane M	4:15:02 (14,172)	
Taylor, Jayne M	3:11:45 (1,854)	
Taylor, Julie K	4:48:54 (22,945)	
Taylor, Kate	4:40:14 (20,781)	
Taylor, Leila	4:39:35 (20,606)	
Taylor, Lindsay J	5:46:53 (32,077)	
Taylor, Louise A	6:18:01 (33,926)	
Taylor, Lynne	7:05:38 (35,011)	
Taylor, Margaret	4:52:16 (23,814)	

Traylen, Jane M	4:40:32 (20,843)
Traynor, Lucy M	4:56:54 (24,913)
Traynor, Mary P	3:31:00 (4,331)
Tredant, Anna	6:12:34 (33,662)
Tregear, Jacqueline	5:17:22 (28,691)
Tregunno, Stacey M	6:42:11 (34,666)
Treharne, Ruth Louise	4:31:33 (18,515)
Trembath, Emily A	5:49:29 (32,289)
Trenowden, Hannah	4:58:40 (25,312)
Tresler, Gabrielle M	4:56:01 (24,682)
Triana-Abbott, Carmen Sofia	4:58:22 (25,228)
Tribe, Sarah	5:08:43 (27,216)
Tribe, Stefanie A	4:36:36 (19,821)
Trim, Teresa	7:16:23 (35,114)
Trimbee, Olivia R	5:43:15 (31,799)
Tristham, Lisa M	4:41:15 (21,026)
Troni, Pamela	5:03:27 (26,275)
Trotter, Kirsty V	5:21:12 (29,257)
Trotter, Suzanne C	4:54:20 (24,299)
Trowsdale, Katie V	3:36:06 (5,173)
Trudgeon, Helen D	5:05:36 (26,660)
True, Susan J	3:17:42 (2,502)
Trust, Helen M	5:10:37 (27,569)
Tsai, Jany	3:43:19 (6,493)
Tubb, Claire Rosemary	4:55:03 (24,460)
Tubb, Samantha F	5:47:45 (32,146)
Tubbs, Carol A	4:36:52 (19,885)
Tuck, Caroline M	3:35:55 (5,138)
Tucker, Caroline A	5:31:47 (30,616)
Tucker, Hannah J	5:23:49 (29,627)
Tucker, Jo	3:47:33 (7,300)
Tucker, Rachel H	4:18:54 (15,133)
Tucker, Sally L	3:55:28 (9,153)
Tucker, Samantha R	4:51:45 (23,689)
Tucker, Sarra L	4:58:36 (25,294)
Tudor-Jones, Catherine	3:47:04 (7,207)
Tugman, Gill E	3:58:30 (10,097)
Tulett, Catherine A	4:20:57 (15,674)
Tull, Emily S	6:27:44 (34,350)
Tulley, Mary E	6:33:20 (34,478)
Tulloch, Lotte E	6:01:11 (33,119)
Tunsley, Victoria J	4:10:45 (13,054)
Tuohy, Christa	6:17:22 (33,898)
Tuoyo, Tosan	5:06:37 (26,824)
Turello, Daniela	3:34:03 (4,770)
Turk, Elizabeth J	4:23:56 (16,423)
Turketo, Clair M	5:35:15 (30,993)
Turkington, Frances	5:07:23 (26,982)
Turl, Kelly J	4:37:29 (20,035)
Turley, Frances M	5:53:13 (32,567)
Turley, Susan	4:50:31 (23,376)
Turnbull, Fiona C	4:23:45 (16,374)
Turnbull, Lone	4:44:02 (21,729)
Turnbull, Margo	4:33:40 (19,066)
Turner, Alison J	4:54:59 (24,444)
Turner, Antonia	4:32:28 (18,752)
Turner, Beverley	5:05:20 (26,611)
Turner, Caroline M	3:26:24 (3,587)
Turner, Emma L	4:14:16 (13,982)
Turner, Helen K	4:30:07 (18,131)
Turner, Helene C	4:37:57 (20,155)
Turner, Hollie J	4:49:12 (23,017)
Turner, Jenny A	3:35:26 (5,037)
Turner, Justine	4:32:45 (18,832)
Turner, Justine	5:49:29 (32,289)
Turner, Kate	3:58:02 (9,950)
Turner, Katie Louise	5:28:11 (30,175)
Turner, Lorna J	4:21:52 (15,913)
Turner, Michele	4:39:24 (20,552)
Turner, Rebekah K	4:19:18 (15,232)
Turner, Sarah J	3:43:42 (6,565)
Turner, Stephanie L	4:04:41 (11,585)
Turner, Tracy A	4:45:37 (22,109)
Turner, Vanessa K	4:59:53 (25,573)
Turner, Victoria	4:53:31 (24,074)
Turner, Victoria M	4:35:55 (19,656)
Turner Traill, Frances C	4:12:01 (13,392)
Turner-Smith, Anna C	5:39:31 (31,450)
Turton, Fiona M	5:20:08 (29,111)
Turton, Judy	4:52:02 (23,760)
Tuson, Caroline L	4:56:51 (24,898)
Tutin, Helen Rebecca	5:26:45 (30,021)
Tweed, Beverly	3:47:07 (7,217)

Tweed, Claire	4:10:50 (13,071)
Tweed, Jo L	3:12:32 (1,934)
Twelvetree, Sarah J	5:57:17 (32,851)
Twelvetree, Yvonne	3:50:27 (7,933)
Twiss, Katina N	5:06:43 (26,846)
Twynham, Georgia L	5:58:51 (32,983)
Tyce, Harriet L	6:08:31 (33,492)
Tyczynska, Anna	6:32:04 (34,454)
Tydeman, Natalie	3:45:36 (6,913)
Tyers, Natasha M	4:39:51 (20,682)
Tyler, Catrin V	4:26:07 (17,014)
Tyler, Kerry	4:52:24 (23,842)
Tyler, Linda A	4:11:17 (13,185)
Tyrrell, Lucinda J	6:52:43 (34,858)
Tyrrell, Lynn	5:54:21 (32,642)
Tyte, Nicola	5:40:10 (31,514)
Uglow, Lyndsey S	4:10:07 (12,884)
Ulivi, Gemma	5:42:48 (31,749)
Uminski, Nicola J	4:37:08 (19,950)
Underwood, Amy E	5:42:38 (31,734)
Underwood, Amy L	4:50:15 (23,301)
Underwood, Jane E	4:32:50 (18,855)
Underwood, Lorraine H	4:27:56 (17,524)
Ungi, Sheleen	5:12:44 (27,932)
Unterhalter, Gina N	5:09:24 (27,347)
Upson, Sarah A	4:35:04 (19,434)
Upstone, Trudy A	4:28:51 (17,795)
Upton, Lynn	5:10:50 (27,607)
Urbaine, Ginette	4:11:40 (13,303)
Uren, Lisa C	4:02:42 (11,168)
Urie, Alex	5:06:45 (26,859)
Urquhart, Sarah L	3:55:52 (9,279)
Usborne, Helen P	3:22:03 (3,020)
Usher, Karen L	4:45:40 (22,126)
Usher, Marie	4:25:38 (16,885)
Usher, Tanya I	3:43:18 (6,491)
Usiskin, Louise R	5:01:03 (25,829)
Utako, Suzuki	4:01:15 (10,847)
Uthamakunan, Vani	5:22:31 (29,442)
Uva, Rebecca	5:29:38 (30,352)
Vaccaro, Amie S	4:57:22 (25,005)
Vadher, Monica	5:28:03 (30,152)
Vaghi, Teresa	4:59:20 (25,459)
Vaile, Karla	5:30:55 (30,510)
Valdes, Frances E	7:04:48 (35,000)
Vale, Cathy H	5:18:19 (28,837)
Valentine, Catherine	4:33:10 (18,932)
Valentine, Kim J	5:17:03 (28,647)
Valentine, Sally L	3:57:49 (9,880)
Vallier, Louise A	3:01:41 (1,095)
Van Assche, Christiane	4:10:23 (12,952)
Van Deelen, Jennifer M	3:18:05 (2,538)
Van Den Aardweg, Stacey	3:47:31 (7,292)
Van Den Berg, Jacqueline A	5:09:55 (27,442)
Van Den Herik, Yvonne	4:15:13 (14,218)
Van Der Graaf, Johanna Elisabeth	6:09:37 (33,541)
Van Der Meer, Maria A	5:07:54 (27,075)
Van Der Merwe, Maria P	4:38:23 (20,272)
Van Der Merwe, Pamela	6:01:57 (33,168)
Van Der Putten, Rosemary A	3:43:40 (6,559)
Van Der Watt, Elzanne R	5:42:29 (31,722)
Van Dijk, Suzan M	4:53:39 (24,114)
Van Dongen, Kim	5:12:35 (27,909)
Van Graan, Stephanie	3:44:03 (6,639)
Van Hees-Anhalt, Gunda	5:03:27 (26,275)
Van Helden, Elles	3:51:46 (8,220)
Van Huyssteen, Jane	5:15:13 (28,357)
Van Huyssteen, Sue A	3:29:17 (4,060)
Van Lelyveld, Sherryl L	5:16:42 (28,600)
Van Oers, Kim	3:46:29 (7,084)
Van Oudtshoorn, Ingrid L	4:33:40 (19,066)
Van Rensburg, Erika	5:29:37 (30,350)
Van Staeyen, Nicole F	5:39:53 (31,484)
Van Tiel, Cara L	4:10:19 (12,938)
Van Tilburg, Lilian	4:28:16 (17,638)
Van Weelden-Klop, Heiltje	4:15:09 (14,203)
Van West, Virginia C	4:51:54 (23,729)
Vane, Hannah M	5:03:00 (26,210)
Vango, Jeannette K	4:23:31 (16,319)
Vanhinsbergh, Carol	4:05:52 (11,854)
Vanslambrouck, Veerle	3:43:27 (6,516)
Vant, Sarah L	5:15:42 (28,456)
Vantol, Vanessa E	5:29:10 (30,291)

Varcoe, Sarah	3:58:05 (9,963)
Vargas, Jackeline	4:27:00 (17,257)
Varley, Joanne	6:06:11 (33,394)
Varley, Karen	4:20:43 (15,612)
Varley, Laura C	5:43:58 (31,847)
Varley, Niki J	4:50:36 (23,396)
Varney, Sam J	5:10:02 (27,467)
Vartz, Stephanie	4:14:42 (14,079)
Vaslavsky, Natalie	4:39:07 (20,467)
Vatin, Laure	3:26:33 (3,609)
Vaudin, Annie	3:54:25 (8,867)
Vaughan, Amanda L	4:25:19 (16,791)
Vaughan, Diane Elizabeth	3:54:33 (8,904)
Vaughan, Gillian R	6:17:39 (33,914)
Vaughan, Jo M	4:33:03 (18,911)
Vaughan, Penelope A	3:56:32 (9,469)
Vaughan, Rachel M	4:36:03 (19,692)
Vaughan, Rebecca L	4:05:24 (11,752)
Vawer, Deborah H	5:53:01 (32,547)
Vazquez, Nadine Anne	4:58:56 (25,371)
Veasey, Hayley A	3:34:52 (4,936)
Veith, Camilla L	6:06:42 (33,420)
Veldkamp- Nab, Yvonne	4:47:05 (22,511)
Venables, Lucy M	4:58:49 (25,341)
Vendette, Nathalie	3:56:08 (9,348)
Ventura, Marisa	4:46:28 (22,340)
Verdon, Heike	4:48:43 (22,908)
Verga, Gillian	4:00:24 (10,635)
Verma, Kalpana	5:38:22 (31,313)
Vernon, Nadine M	7:21:40 (35,159)
Vernum, Abbie J	4:38:35 (20,319)
Véronique, Gardet	6:13:41 (33,733)
Véronique, Haselwander	4:01:17 (10,853)
Véronique, Valette	4:50:32 (23,381)
Verrall, Sandra M	7:15:54 (35,110)
Very, Annie	4:55:00 (24,450)
Vesey, Alison	3:15:04 (2,241)
Vetter, Sylvia	4:54:05 (24,241)
Vick, Sarah	3:46:56 (7,187)
Vickers, Kelliney	5:49:49 (32,321)
Victor, Christina	4:31:34 (18,518)
Vidler, Anthea	5:18:14 (28,826)
Vigo Saunders, Julie	5:35:57 (31,071)
Villiers, Carlie	3:58:27 (10,083)
Vince, Nikki J	6:24:33 (34,215)
Vincent, Angela D	5:11:33 (27,737)
Vincent, Laura N	3:55:03 (9,040)
Vine, Susan E	4:40:52 (20,929)
Viner, Kate E	3:40:52 (6,009)
Viner, Kerry	3:59:59 (10,541)
Viner, Nicola	5:52:43 (32,532)
Vinton, Linda A	4:18:46 (15,094)
Violette, Bonny	6:18:15 (33,939)
Virdi, Tina	4:52:24 (23,842)
Vitoulova, Jana Vitoulova	4:38:29 (20,292)
Vivash, Laura	5:05:20 (26,611)
Vivian, Christina	3:55:41 (9,211)
Vivian, Holly E	4:10:03 (12,864)
Vogel, Kirsty L	4:07:57 (12,348)
Vohmann, Angela	5:36:55 (31,167)
Voigt, Natalie F	4:51:34 (23,640)
Voller, Karin	3:44:30 (6,722)
Voller, Sophie L	3:09:26 (1,657)
Vollstedt, Regine	5:19:05 (28,981)
Von Opel, Sonja	2:58:36 (875)
Voong, Cam	5:26:52 (30,033)
Voong, Va	5:06:50 (26,874)
Voss, Tara	4:43:50 (21,676)
Vowles, Deborah L	4:44:22 (21,809)
Voykin, Deirdre J	4:53:30 (24,071)
Vye, Charlotte L	4:10:09 (12,898)
Wackett, Caireen E	4:32:08 (18,671)
Waddell, Debra C	4:20:10 (15,478)
Wade-Jones, Charlotte H	4:17:39 (14,806)
Wadeley, Kerstin B	4:22:15 (16,011)
Wadey, Lara R	4:17:42 (14,819)
Wadey, Maria J	3:45:00 (6,804)
Wadforth, Cath	4:03:33 (11,348)
Wadsley, Donna M	7:27:10 (35,198)
Wadsworth, Caroline M	5:08:25 (27,167)
Wagner, Laura E	3:54:12 (8,812)
Wahlen, Kerstin	5:07:36 (27,024)
Wain, Chloe L	6:12:39 (33,670)

Wain, Jess	4:49:20 (23,064)	
Waine, Alison J	6:17:46 (33,917)	
Wainwright, Janice	4:49:09 (23,004)	
Wainwright, Jean	5:22:48 (29,481)	
Waite, Gill	4:56:38 (24,836)	
Waite, Sarah	3:48:08 (7,425)	
Waith, Liz	4:13:19 (13,752)	
Wajid, Sara	5:06:43 (26,846)	
Wakefield, Dorothy L	6:52:41 (34,857)	
Wakefield, Natasha Maria M	4:36:46 (19,856)	
Wakeley, Camilla	4:35:47 (19,625)	
Wakeling, Helen C	4:17:01 (14,651)	
Wake-Smith, Sarah M	5:08:39 (27,205)	
Wakley, Julie G	5:49:29 (32,289)	
Walbridge, Fiona K	4:49:08 (23,002)	
Walden, Susan E	5:25:35 (29,875)	
Walden, Wendy J	5:13:09 (28,015)	
Waldron, Helen E	5:19:02 (28,976)	
Waldrup, Frances	4:25:40 (16,899)	
Walford, Julie	4:53:00 (23,977)	
Walker, Alice Victoria	5:48:40 (32,236)	
Walker, Anneka L	4:29:09 (17,875)	
Walker, Charlotte Aimée	4:49:24 (23,080)	
Walker, Christina M	4:11:15 (13,176)	
Walker, Debbie	9:19:30 (35,362)	
Walker, Helen M	3:57:04 (9,638)	
Walker, Hilary C	4:11:06 (13,139)	
Walker, Julia J	6:46:08 (34,722)	
Walker, Lisa	6:29:39 (34,404)	
Walker, Lucia J	5:12:08 (27,828)	
Walker, Maria T	4:20:51 (15,647)	
Walker, Martha A	5:39:27 (31,441)	
Walker, Mary	5:56:04 (32,761)	
Walker, Rebecca	6:30:55 (34,433)	
Walkey, Kizzy A	4:41:59 (21,198)	
Walklate, Anna R	3:54:52 (8,988)	
Walklate, Rachel J	3:54:52 (8,988)	
Walkley, Claire S	3:54:21 (8,853)	
Wall, Dianne	4:42:32 (21,339)	
Wall, Emma L	4:42:20 (21,280)	
Wall, Joanna D	5:42:11 (31,690)	
Wall, Joanne L	4:35:41 (19,592)	
Wall, Karen L	4:01:34 (10,934)	
Wall, Michala C	3:25:39 (3,483)	
Wall, Rebecca J	3:24:26 (3,332)	
Wall, Sara L	5:00:03 (25,607)	
Wall, Sarah F	3:42:00 (6,206)	
Wall, Theresa M	3:42:46 (6,370)	
Wallace, Amie K	4:38:56 (20,416)	
Wallace, Anna W	3:27:15 (3,726)	
Wallace, Jenny J	5:16:49 (28,621)	
Wallace, Louisa	4:17:25 (14,749)	
Wallace, Shar L	5:13:06 (28,006)	
Wallace, Sue M	5:15:30 (28,416)	
Wallder, Carrie	4:26:50 (17,216)	
Waller, Jade	4:53:45 (24,159)	
Waller, Lee	6:57:55 (34,930)	
Waller, Lisa A	5:36:15 (31,096)	
Walley, Nicole	4:28:11 (17,608)	
Wallington, Dawn	5:56:18 (32,776)	
Wallis, Ann	5:10:56 (27,629)	
Wallis, Diana P	5:22:23 (29,419)	
Wallis, Emma	4:34:10 (19,187)	
Wallis, Joanna	4:14:47 (14,108)	
Wallis, Lucy	4:43:39 (21,639)	
Walmsley, Mary E	5:10:11 (27,493)	
Walsh, Edit	3:25:08 (3,412)	
Walsh, Fiona M	7:38:30 (35,263)	
Walsh, Frances C	5:38:16 (31,306)	
Walsh, Kate E	5:33:50 (30,850)	
Walsh, Katie M	4:17:34 (14,787)	
Walsh, Nicole	4:51:25 (23,601)	
Walsh, Rebecca A	4:07:44 (12,295)	
Walsh, Samantha L	4:43:28 (21,593)	
Walter, Angela J	4:16:30 (14,522)	
Walter, Lisa	4:44:29 (21,833)	
Walters, Emma K	5:12:43 (27,929)	
Walters, Kim L	5:34:14 (30,882)	
Walthall, Kate E	5:28:56 (30,268)	
Walton, Caroline L	4:58:06 (25,162)	
Walton, Faye R	4:14:40 (14,067)	
Walton, Gaye C	7:12:32 (35,077)	
Walton, Jennifer R	4:54:41 (24,382)	

Walton, Laura J	3:57:42 (9,846)	
Walton, Louise	4:35:18 (19,488)	
Walton-Grant, Carol	4:34:50 (19,365)	
Wami, Gete	2:26:54 (43)	
Wang'Ombe, Hannah	6:20:30 (34,057)	
Wanklyn, Ann	6:56:17 (34,909)	
Want, Victoria A	4:49:15 (23,036)	
Warburton, Claire L	4:29:15 (17,912)	
Warburton, Helena M	4:32:26 (18,743)	
Warcup, Clare M	4:11:03 (13,124)	
Ward, Alison Sarah	4:26:13 (17,044)	
Ward, Ausrine	3:56:26 (9,437)	
Ward, Claire Victoria	4:44:54 (21,931)	
Ward, Deirdre	3:29:27 (4,095)	
Ward, Diane	6:02:19 (33,191)	
Ward, Emma	5:50:05 (32,345)	
Ward, Jody	4:39:13 (20,499)	
Ward, Kerstin J	4:25:39 (16,893)	
Ward, Leanne M	4:45:49 (22,161)	
Ward, Liz	4:34:50 (19,365)	
Ward, Nicola Rachel	4:32:50 (18,855)	
Ward, Rachel	3:33:14 (4,639)	
Ward, Stella	4:24:39 (16,605)	
Ward, Tracey	5:34:40 (30,933)	
Ward, Vicky E	5:07:10 (26,935)	
Ward, Zoe	5:03:52 (26,353)	
Warder, Fiona	6:45:58 (34,719)	
Wardill, Katie-Emma	4:46:24 (22,315)	
Wardle, Elizabeth L	4:38:08 (20,211)	
Wardle, Rachel L	3:50:00 (7,833)	
Ward-Rotherham, Julie	4:15:42 (14,319)	
Ware, Ann Marie	3:20:24 (2,811)	
Wareing, Tracey A	5:31:19 (30,559)	
Waring, Mary	4:50:58 (23,478)	
Waring, Stephanie	3:55:48 (9,263)	
Warmer, Paula J	4:39:36 (20,613)	
Warne, Catherine P	4:00:57 (10,786)	
Warner, Lorena	5:01:47 (25,967)	
Warner-Smith, Alex B	4:14:01 (13,910)	
Warran, Patricia	5:14:00 (28,161)	
Warren, Alison J	4:45:33 (22,090)	
Warren, Berenice	4:14:44 (14,093)	
Warren, Gail E	5:01:10 (25,853)	
Warren, Kathryn	5:08:56 (27,258)	
Warren, Katy E	3:56:05 (9,335)	
Warren, Sara D	4:26:16 (17,060)	
Warrick, Stephanie M	4:13:51 (13,876)	
Warshaw, Emma L	4:23:13 (16,235)	
Warwick, Beki A	4:46:16 (22,267)	
Warwick, Cathy	7:35:46 (35,248)	
Warwick, Frances M	6:04:08 (33,294)	
Washington, Diane	4:33:32 (19,029)	
Washington, Victoria	4:53:21 (24,046)	
Wason, Wendy	5:09:11 (27,306)	
Wastell, Sarah L	4:39:24 (20,552)	
Waterfall, Emma	4:01:11 (10,831)	
Waterhouse, Caroline M	3:52:10 (8,317)	
Waterhouse, Dawn	5:43:17 (31,802)	
Waterhouse, Joanne	5:47:30 (32,131)	
Wateridge, Sharon	5:14:29 (28,239)	
Waterlow, Lucy M	3:19:17 (2,647)	
Waters, Anne-Marie	3:54:07 (8,786)	
Waters, Cara M	3:29:04 (4,013)	
Waters, Helen	5:29:10 (30,291)	
Waters, Louise H	5:00:14 (25,639)	
Watkin, Bridie	8:43:04 (35,347)	
Watkin, Susan	8:43:08 (35,348)	
Watkins, Georgina L	4:06:14 (11,938)	
Watkins, Pip	5:26:46 (30,022)	
Watkins, Zoe T	3:52:41 (8,446)	
Watkinson, Susan Patricia	4:30:00 (18,095)	
Watson, Alison T	4:34:38 (19,296)	
Watson, Ann M	6:29:44 (34,405)	
Watson, Caroline A	5:34:12 (30,876)	
Watson, Catherine J	5:45:46 (32,000)	
Watson, Claire	3:28:23 (3,914)	
Watson, Hannah L	4:16:34 (14,542)	
Watson, Hilary J	5:32:36 (30,703)	
Watson, Jacqui	3:25:24 (3,444)	
Watson, Joanna L	6:17:39 (33,914)	
Watson, Karen	3:46:31 (7,091)	
Watson, Melanie J	6:03:23 (33,254)	
Watson, Nanette G	5:40:23 (31,533)	

Watson, Pamela	7:53:58 (35,300)	
Watson Jones, Lucy	4:25:30 (16,836)	
Watt, Jean	5:22:01 (29,366)	
Watt, Kathryn E	4:23:40 (16,355)	
Watt, Neva M	4:35:49 (19,630)	
Watt, Vivien	4:18:32 (15,038)	
Watters, Clare L	3:54:19 (8,844)	
Watters, Elizabeth A	4:39:36 (20,613)	
Watts, Amanda J	4:13:34 (13,813)	
Watts, Ann L	4:10:35 (13,003)	
Watts, Beverley A	5:29:11 (30,296)	
Watts, Charlotte H	5:04:53 (26,521)	
Watts, Kalin	6:02:47 (33,214)	
Watts, Kerry Ann	5:42:29 (31,722)	
Watts, Lucy K	5:10:39 (27,575)	
Watts, Lynn C	4:45:20 (22,040)	
Watts, Maggie	5:35:37 (31,031)	
Watts, Penny A	6:02:47 (33,214)	
Watts, Rebecca M	4:38:29 (20,292)	
Watts, Samantha J	5:20:56 (29,213)	
Watts, Suzanne	7:03:50 (34,993)	
Waud, Vicki M	5:41:02 (31,587)	
Waymark, Leanne S	4:37:10 (19,959)	
Weall, Julia F	4:04:47 (11,603)	
Weare, Tracy	3:25:30 (3,457)	
Weatherhogg, Keri J	3:06:25 (1,401)	
Weatherley, Lisa	4:22:44 (16,131)	
Weaver, Caroline M	3:53:51 (8,714)	
Weaver, Kerry	5:46:38 (32,057)	
Weaver, Lyndsey C	4:43:09 (21,503)	
Weaver, Sophie A	4:55:40 (24,608)	
Weaver, Victoria A	4:02:44 (11,173)	
Webb, Alison J	4:39:23 (20,542)	
Webb, Celia	5:10:35 (27,565)	
Webb, Elizabeth G	5:06:29 (26,805)	
Webb, Helen Elizabeth	4:31:02 (18,361)	
Webb, Jo	5:32:01 (30,642)	
Webb, Kathryn	5:36:25 (31,113)	
Webb, Natasha W	4:28:33 (17,711)	
Webb, Tia	5:17:08 (28,664)	
Webb-Carter, Rose	4:11:29 (13,248)	
Webber, Louise M	4:22:50 (16,149)	
Webber, Sarah J	4:49:15 (23,036)	
Webster, Amy S	4:48:34 (22,866)	
Webster, Charlotte A	4:18:30 (15,029)	
Webster, Katherine	4:46:37 (22,375)	
Webster, Louise	5:14:35 (28,252)	
Webster, Lucy	4:24:23 (16,545)	
Webster, Morag E	7:15:10 (35,106)	
Webster, Samantha	4:27:44 (17,459)	
Webster, Sian	3:57:51 (9,896)	
Wedlock, Kiri J	3:46:48 (7,157)	
Weekes, Bridgit C	4:37:24 (20,009)	
Weeks, Debra L	3:48:34 (7,525)	
Wegner, Natalia	4:51:45 (23,689)	
Wehofer, Margarethe	5:29:04 (30,280)	
Weight, Catherine S	4:24:34 (16,585)	
Weightman, Claire L	5:15:07 (28,338)	
Weisfeld, Emily C	5:26:57 (30,047)	
Welch, Claire L	4:58:11 (25,187)	
Welch, Diana	4:19:48 (15,371)	
Welch, Maree	4:00:13 (10,603)	
Welch, Pat	4:31:11 (18,400)	
Welfare, Amy	4:40:18 (20,795)	
Welham, Lauren	5:20:41 (29,173)	
Weller, Susan J	5:30:26 (30,450)	
Weller, Victoria	4:41:26 (21,065)	
Wellington, Catherine	6:04:29 (33,312)	
Wells, Amanda	4:37:28 (20,027)	
Wells, Bridget M	5:09:45 (27,417)	
Wells, Donna L	3:51:09 (8,085)	
Wells, Jane M	4:52:13 (23,801)	
Wells, Jennifer A	5:11:21 (27,702)	
Wells, Kay H	5:42:08 (31,683)	
Wells, Sophie J	4:08:16 (12,439)	
Wellstead, Rita S	6:33:11 (34,475)	
Welsby, Pauline A	3:34:27 (4,867)	
Wendy, Lowe	4:27:24 (17,368)	
Wenman, Barbara H	3:21:01 (2,891)	
Wenman, Sarah L	4:07:23 (12,209)	
Wepplo, Katie	4:14:52 (14,132)	
Weskamp, Bettina	4:40:40 (20,878)	
Wesson, Heather L	4:51:17 (23,562)	

West, Carolyn E 4:58:31 (25,274)
West, Debbie A 4:06:00 (11,880)
West, Diane 5:56:20 (32,779)
West, Helen 4:44:43 (21,890)
West, Janet M 5:49:15 (32,272)
West, Katherine E 3:18:23 (2,565)
West, Lindsay J 5:24:21 (29,711)
West, Michelle K 4:46:57 (22,469)
West, Nicola 4:31:22 (18,462)
West, Salena A 5:15:36 (28,438)
West, Samantha 5:18:22 (28,848)
West, Samantha J 4:38:47 (20,372)
West, Tracy J 3:11:41 (1,849)
West, Victoria L 5:20:06 (29,107)
Westcott, Clare L 5:38:14 (31,300)
Westcott, Joanne L 5:01:58 (26,010)
Western, Dawn 4:31:45 (18,567)
Westlake, Sonia 4:11:14 (13,168)
Westle, Sue J 4:58:36 (25,294)
Westley, Fay 5:17:10 (28,669)
Weston, Helen E 6:43:36 (34,690)
Weston, Phyl A 4:18:02 (14,900)
Weston, Rebecca 3:38:42 (5,626)
Weston, Sharon 4:46:27 (22,331)
Westrope, Joanna 5:14:09 (28,189)
Wetheridge, Mandy L 4:08:47 (12,566)
Wetz, Amanda J 5:19:58 (29,088)
Whaites, Joanne 4:01:46 (10,976)
Wharam, Hilary 5:29:40 (30,355)
Wharton, Michelle 5:03:52 (26,353)
Whatley, Sarah J 3:55:43 (9,232)
Wheatman, Mia 5:28:47 (30,249)
Wheeler, Clare H 4:50:16 (23,308)
Wheeler, Helen 3:06:05 (1,377)
Wheeler, Nicola 5:13:42 (28,099)
Wheeler, Sarah 5:22:15 (29,397)
Wheelwright, Amelia 3:55:32 (9,162)
Whelan, Carol A 4:53:39 (24,114)
Whelan, Francina 4:58:25 (25,247)
Whicheloe, Claire A 5:09:45 (27,417)
While, Jenny E 5:29:02 (30,275)
Whiley, Lesley 3:02:12 (1,133)
Whipman, Melanie 4:08:10 (12,410)
Whitaker, Lynn T 4:56:11 (24,723)
Whitby, Brenda V 5:22:23 (29,419)
Whitby, Carly H 4:00:23 (10,632)
Whitby, Nicola H 3:54:57 (9,007)
Whitby, Sally J 5:02:50 (26,187)
Whitchurch, Annette 4:34:50 (19,365)
Whitcroft, Kay 4:51:09 (23,521)
White, Alexandra K 4:02:11 (11,064)
White, Alison 4:57:54 (25,111)
White, Angela J 5:16:16 (28,536)
White, Berry F 5:18:10 (28,812)
White, Bonny J 5:22:15 (29,397)
White, Cheryl L 5:03:03 (26,218)
White, Gillian 6:35:22 (34,532)
White, Heidi L 5:09:53 (27,439)
White, Helene 3:53:35 (8,644)
White, Jacqueline J 4:58:33 (25,284)
White, Jane L 3:29:11 (4,035)
White, Jane L 4:40:08 (20,760)
White, Jenny S 4:20:44 (15,615)
White, Jo-Anne 4:53:06 (23,998)
White, Julia Anne 5:07:45 (27,052)
White, Kate 4:09:30 (12,719)
White, Katherine J 5:08:35 (27,190)
White, Kirsty 5:39:20 (31,428)
White, Kris A 6:50:30 (34,824)
White, Laura J 4:39:22 (20,536)
White, Melanie J 3:55:51 (9,274)
White, Nicola J 4:18:47 (15,101)
White, Nicola S 4:01:48 (10,984)
White, Pamela L 3:13:33 (2,066)
White, Philippa C 5:36:03 (31,081)
White, Rebecca 4:43:21 (21,567)
White, Rebecca J 6:00:56 (33,109)
White, Rebecca L 6:09:43 (33,547)
White, Sarah V 5:32:56 (30,744)
White, Sharon A 5:26:15 (29,962)
White, Sian A 4:17:08 (14,677)
White, Teresa A 4:15:49 (14,354)
White, Veronica 4:21:16 (15,759)

Whitefield, Monica Bridget 4:03:20 (11,300)
Whitehead, Alice C 5:04:34 (26,478)
Whitehead, Louise A 5:07:25 (26,988)
Whitehead, Sarah L 5:34:26 (30,903)
Whitehead, Susannah J 4:42:21 (21,283)
Whitehead, Vivienne J 6:24:08 (34,193)
Whitehouse, Susan 5:16:41 (28,597)
Whitehouse, Susan 6:28:16 (34,365)
Whitehurst, Louise M 4:29:46 (18,029)
Whiteley, Charlotte L 5:31:21 (30,561)
Whiteley, Melanie J 3:46:04 (6,997)
Whitelock, Joanne M 4:59:40 (25,525)
Whitemore, Nicola D 6:44:20 (34,699)
Whiteson, Denisa 4:16:36 (14,553)
Whitfield, Annelie M 4:43:15 (21,529)
Whitfield, Beverley E 3:25:53 (3,515)
Whitfield, Lorna J 5:43:46 (31,831)
Whitman, Maureen P 5:04:47 (26,503)
Whitmarsh, Lorraine E 3:51:53 (8,249)
Whitmarsh, Shani M 5:50:05 (32,345)
Whitnall, Lynn K 4:51:11 (23,535)
Whitney, Claire N 4:58:23 (25,233)
Whittaker, Claire R 4:51:10 (23,528)
Whittaker, Jenny 4:35:50 (19,638)
Whittaker, Joanna L 6:32:19 (34,459)
Whittaker, Naomi J 4:23:23 (16,274)
Whittington, Lisa 5:35:52 (31,059)
Whittle, Carrie J 4:56:44 (24,860)
Whittle, Debbie D 5:06:18 (26,776)
Whittle, Deborah A 4:57:17 (24,980)
Whittle, Ersuline 3:59:39 (10,437)
Whittle, Sally Anne 3:58:37 (10,132)
Whittle, Terry 4:50:16 (23,308)
Whitton, Kate S 5:06:12 (26,763)
Whitty, Emma L 5:53:04 (32,552)
Whitty, Janet E 6:19:00 (33,996)
Whitty, Marilyn A 3:59:41 (10,451)
Whitworth, Bethan W 4:44:50 (21,917)
Whitworth, Natalie C 6:33:32 (34,485)
Whjitlock, Pat 4:43:04 (21,484)
Whybrow, Jennifer A 3:30:33 (4,264)
Whyman, Louise A 5:33:20 (30,793)
Whyte, Louise M 4:24:50 (16,663)
Whyte, Mary J 6:05:32 (33,366)
Wickham, Jill 6:05:22 (33,357)
Wicks, Joanne Emma E 5:10:02 (27,467)
Wicks, Kay A 3:58:00 (9,931)
Wicks, Marion C 4:14:51 (14,128)
Wickson, Maureen 5:00:05 (25,610)
Wiener, Nikki C 3:57:56 (9,912)
Wierzgacz, Magdalena J 5:27:48 (30,124)
Wigg, Amy 4:23:30 (16,314)
Wiggett, Nina R 3:19:05 (2,626)
Wiggins, Debbie 4:51:11 (23,535)
Wiggins, Rena 6:12:51 (33,686)
Wiggins, Samantha G 4:47:31 (22,603)
Wightman, Claire K 3:45:44 (6,933)
Wiglesworth, Alison L 4:21:29 (15,804)
Wiiliamson, Evelyn J 4:40:49 (20,917)
Wijkens, Linda 5:11:02 (27,645)
Wilbraham, Elizabeth M 7:13:55 (35,094)
Wilcock, Helen 4:32:03 (18,648)
Wild, Caroline 4:59:59 (25,594)
Wild, Laura 4:47:13 (22,550)
Wild, Tilly 5:37:15 (31,198)
Wilderink, Vanessa 5:07:19 (26,963)
Wilding, Olivia 4:46:23 (22,310)
Wilding, Samantha M 5:01:10 (25,853)
Wildman, Elizabeth 4:43:47 (21,663)
Wildon, Dale T 4:06:45 (12,052)
Wildridge, Josephine R 4:30:16 (18,171)
Wileman, Sarah 3:15:11 (2,251)
Wileman, Sue 5:46:43 (32,066)
Wilford, Marie J 4:02:13 (11,072)
Wiliams, Frances A 5:12:38 (27,913)
Wilkes, Carol 5:16:40 (28,590)
Wilkes, Deborah J 4:00:03 (10,557)
Wilkes, Elizabeth S 5:59:31 (33,018)
Wilkes, Sally E 4:15:16 (14,226)
Wilkie, Malgorzata L 4:23:18 (16,253)
Wilkins, Amanda J 7:01:01 (34,962)
Wilkins, Jo 4:15:15 (14,222)
Wilkins, Joanna 5:11:32 (27,733)

Wilkins, Joanne K 5:22:57 (29,511)
Wilkins, Julie Y 4:13:13 (13,717)
Wilkins, Maureen E 4:39:58 (20,710)
Wilkins, Rachel 5:56:59 (32,834)
Wilkins, Richard D 3:19:02 (2,621)
Wilkins, Sarah 4:17:18 (14,717)
Wilkinson, Alexandra E 6:49:10 (34,797)
Wilkinson, Carole L 5:31:40 (30,602)
Wilkinson, Carolyn S 3:00:01 (998)
Wilkinson, Davina A 4:12:41 (13,573)
Wilkinson, Emilie M 4:35:11 (19,458)
Wilkinson, Frances 4:17:16 (14,706)
Wilkinson, Gemma 5:59:51 (33,038)
Wilkinson, Julie E 5:24:49 (29,771)
Wilkinson, Kate S 4:16:26 (14,506)
Wilkinson, Lisa 3:47:21 (7,257)
Wilkinson, Lisa J 4:35:01 (19,411)
Wilkinson, Melanie 5:05:06 (26,566)
Wilkinson, Sonia 4:48:23 (22,825)
Willbond, Andrea F 4:23:54 (16,416)
Willday, Julie A 4:49:35 (23,141)
Willetts, Stephanie 7:31:12 (35,227)
Williams, Angela J 3:41:07 (6,052)
Williams, Anita 4:53:28 (24,066)
Williams, Annick M 4:32:54 (18,871)
Williams, Beverley A 5:53:02 (32,548)
Williams, Carol A 4:50:52 (23,455)
Williams, Caroline 4:32:49 (18,850)
Williams, Caroline 5:30:28 (30,457)
Williams, Carys 4:36:11 (19,716)
Williams, Chris M 4:45:39 (22,121)
Williams, Claire 5:54:54 (32,682)
Williams, Claire R 5:44:06 (31,860)
Williams, Deborah 4:16:22 (14,486)
Williams, Deborah A 4:23:27 (16,296)
Williams, Delyth N 4:16:06 (14,426)
Williams, Emily 7:13:48 (35,092)
Williams, Erin 5:44:44 (31,909)
Williams, Gaynor A 4:37:40 (20,081)
Williams, Jenny F 4:59:51 (25,565)
Williams, Jenny Louise 4:41:44 (21,149)
Williams, Julie 4:41:13 (21,017)
Williams, Karen 4:42:24 (21,302)
Williams, Katherine L 4:06:07 (11,908)
Williams, Katie M 4:42:49 (21,412)
Williams, Kelly 4:47:33 (22,612)
Williams, Khema D 4:16:02 (14,405)
Williams, Laura M 4:04:47 (11,603)
Williams, Layla 5:45:32 (31,977)
Williams, Lesley K 4:20:22 (15,527)
Williams, Linda J 5:31:36 (30,594)
Williams, Lizzie S 4:37:38 (20,078)
Williams, Louise 4:05:11 (11,703)
Williams, Louise J 5:15:00 (28,320)
Williams, Lynwen 5:06:59 (26,907)
Williams, Margaret O 5:37:56 (31,268)
Williams, Mechelle D 4:25:32 (16,847)
Williams, Melanie C 4:07:09 (12,143)
Williams, Nancy H 3:58:16 (10,027)
Williams, Natalie A 5:43:10 (31,789)
Williams, Nicola I 5:11:15 (27,684)
Williams, Nicola L 4:48:22 (22,819)
Williams, Nina E 4:27:14 (17,317)
Williams, Paula H 4:17:48 (14,839)
Williams, Rachel 5:41:50 (31,658)
Williams, Rebecca C 4:20:45 (15,619)
Williams, Rebecca J 4:39:03 (20,452)
Williams, Rhian E 5:54:12 (32,631)
Williams, Sara 4:33:48 (19,097)
Williams, Sarah A 3:15:57 (2,330)
Williams, Sarah A 5:19:33 (29,043)
Williams, Shirley A 6:23:44 (34,178)
Williams, Sioned 4:34:23 (19,235)
Williams, Susan A 5:25:55 (29,922)
Williams, Susan E 3:53:02 (8,514)
Williams, Teresa K 3:38:40 (5,619)
Williams, Vicky E 3:45:35 (6,911)
Williams, Victoria Catherine 3:55:51 (9,274)
Williams, Wendy 3:58:26 (10,079)
Williamson, Amy 6:20:07 (34,036)
Williamson, Andrea J 5:32:29 (30,686)
Williamson, Anne B 4:04:55 (11,634)
Williamson, Carol A 4:56:48 (24,879)

Williamson, Guy F	3:38:16 (5,546)
Williamson, Julia F	4:23:39 (16,349)
Willis, Gemma	6:30:15 (34,417)
Willis, Georgina L	4:07:27 (12,226)
Willis, Karen P	5:46:15 (32,032)
Willis, Laura H	4:18:28 (15,021)
Willis, Rachael	5:22:11 (29,388)
Willis, Tracey J	5:17:36 (28,730)
Willmott, Jane	5:00:32 (25,713)
Willows, Mary	4:52:35 (23,877)
Wills, Anna	4:10:00 (12,853)
Wills, Donna	5:39:34 (31,453)
Wills, Nicola	4:01:05 (10,812)
Wills, Sara	5:20:40 (29,171)
Willsher, Natalie	4:57:04 (24,942)
Willson, Emma	5:25:07 (29,813)
Willson, Francesca	5:55:43 (32,741)
Wilmer, Amanda J	3:44:23 (6,698)
Wilsher, Andrea	3:58:08 (9,982)
Wilson, Abigail H	4:13:10 (13,700)
Wilson, Alison F	3:45:14 (6,842)
Wilson, Amanda	3:20:06 (2,769)
Wilson, Annette	3:43:10 (6,463)
Wilson, Beverley J	4:10:22 (12,947)
Wilson, Catherine J	4:27:08 (17,290)
Wilson, Claire	5:41:36 (31,639)
Wilson, Claire L	3:58:34 (10,119)
Wilson, Claire L	4:10:18 (12,935)
Wilson, Denise K	4:24:05 (16,466)
Wilson, Emma R	5:10:20 (27,517)
Wilson, Fiona	4:29:49 (18,041)
Wilson, Flora L	4:41:00 (20,962)
Wilson, Gillian H	4:43:14 (21,524)
Wilson, Heather	6:15:36 (33,818)
Wilson, Heidi J	3:14:39 (2,188)
Wilson, Helen	4:52:01 (23,753)
Wilson, Isobel R	5:12:09 (27,834)
Wilson, Jade L	6:05:42 (33,377)
Wilson, Jennifer H	4:20:41 (15,596)
Wilson, Jennifer H	4:55:17 (24,527)
Wilson, Joanne C	3:23:29 (3,186)
Wilson, Judith C	5:51:30 (32,448)
Wilson, Kate	3:57:45 (9,860)
Wilson, Mags C	5:40:48 (31,569)
Wilson, Melanie	5:00:59 (25,805)
Wilson, Michelle A	3:45:26 (6,878)
Wilson, Michelle M	7:29:42 (35,217)
Wilson, Natalie F	3:42:48 (6,377)
Wilson, Nicola	5:01:50 (25,976)
Wilson, Patricia M	4:14:00 (13,907)
Wilson, Penny	4:54:30 (24,334)
Wilson, Rebecca A	4:57:32 (25,040)
Wilson, Sandra	3:47:01 (7,203)
Wilson, Sara J	7:53:22 (35,297)
Wilson, Sarah C	4:14:31 (14,032)
Wilson, Sarah E	4:24:08 (16,483)
Wilson, Sarah V	5:54:07 (32,626)
Wilson, Sharon E	5:18:34 (28,886)
Wilson, Teresa H	6:19:13 (34,008)
Wilson, Theresa M	4:53:14 (24,027)
Wilson, Veronica G	6:04:48 (33,326)
Wiltshire, Cheryl K	4:28:10 (17,604)
Winchester, Clare J	4:45:05 (21,993)
Winfield, Laura A	4:49:00 (22,974)
Winfield, Jane E	4:49:14 (23,031)
Wing, Julia A	4:46:58 (22,474)
Wing, Sarah M	5:43:19 (31,807)
Wingrove, Cher M	4:57:28 (25,026)
Wingrove, Rebecca L	5:16:23 (28,546)
Winn-Smith, Joanna E	4:03:23 (11,313)
Winter, Becca	6:06:21 (33,403)
Winter, Einat	4:33:52 (19,118)
Winter, Julia H	4:52:52 (23,940)
Winter, Michaela E	4:43:49 (21,671)
Winter, Sarah L	3:24:50 (3,384)
Winter, Verity	6:05:20 (33,355)
Winterbottom, Anne C	4:17:29 (14,764)
Winters, Clare	4:38:49 (20,383)
Winters, Melissa H	3:06:38 (1,414)
Winterson, Victoria	4:20:00 (15,428)
Wintgens, Tess	4:52:28 (23,859)
Wintle, Sarah	3:41:14 (6,081)
Winton, Caroline S	4:48:35 (22,873)
Winwood, Marion	5:32:26 (30,679)
Winwood, Nicola J	4:57:45 (25,078)
Wisbey, Gail	4:36:47 (19,859)
Wischhusen, Elaine	5:34:10 (30,873)
Wisdom, Carole J	4:21:48 (15,900)
Wise, Charlotte R	4:25:02 (16,719)
Wise, Hannah L	4:58:36 (25,294)
Wise, Vicki C	5:30:26 (30,450)
Wiseman, Angela M	4:50:55 (23,464)
Wiseman, Louise M	5:24:52 (29,776)
Wisson, Joanne Y	5:09:37 (27,386)
Wisson, Shirley A	4:46:19 (22,284)
Witham, Nondyebo G	6:16:23 (33,863)
Witherley, Janet E	4:33:05 (18,919)
Withers, Pamela R	3:53:18 (8,583)
Withington, Sarah	5:00:48 (25,768)
Withycombe, Angela A	3:50:15 (7,895)
Witt, Joanna M	5:21:49 (29,346)
Wogel, Catherine L	5:59:39 (33,026)
Wohanka, Oonagh	3:48:53 (7,591)
Wojna, Joanna M	4:51:42 (23,676)
Wokes, Rebecca	4:40:21 (20,806)
Wolanski, Sandra	3:25:39 (3,483)
Wold., Ellen	4:13:13 (13,717)
Wolf, Janice	4:51:53 (23,723)
Wolfenden, Claire M	5:15:50 (28,481)
Wolff, Gillian M	5:09:39 (27,396)
Wollaston, Esther C	3:28:08 (3,873)
Wolstenholme, Alison E	5:57:46 (32,894)
Wolujewicz, Adele	4:24:52 (16,677)
Wolvaardt, Renette	3:58:50 (10,205)
Wong, Allison Z	4:27:03 (17,269)
Wong, Grace	3:58:28 (10,090)
Wong, Kathy	6:03:26 (33,255)
Wong, Patsy	4:10:53 (13,084)
Woo, Lai Ping	3:44:55 (6,787)
Wood, Alison L	3:52:22 (8,376)
Wood, Alison M	4:15:06 (14,190)
Wood, Anna E	5:00:45 (25,759)
Wood, Caroline L	4:45:13 (22,016)
Wood, Celia J	6:33:06 (34,472)
Wood, Charlotte A	6:17:33 (33,908)
Wood, Christina	6:09:35 (33,540)
Wood, Emily L	5:50:39 (32,391)
Wood, Emma L	4:07:57 (12,348)
Wood, Felicity	4:42:34 (21,348)
Wood, Hannah C	5:27:45 (30,116)
Wood, Harriet R	4:57:55 (25,119)
Wood, Janice	4:08:16 (12,439)
Wood, Joanna M	4:30:26 (18,214)
Wood, Joanne L	6:56:01 (34,907)
Wood, Karen L	3:27:12 (3,716)
Wood, Katie M	5:57:17 (32,851)
Wood, Laura J	5:08:13 (27,127)
Wood, Lindsey C	4:38:44 (20,360)
Wood, Lisa F	3:56:55 (9,598)
Wood, Lorna C	5:39:46 (31,473)
Wood, Lucy A	4:08:42 (12,553)
Wood, Marion E	3:11:02 (1,780)
Wood, Nicola M	4:32:44 (18,826)
Wood, Rachel A	4:10:29 (12,978)
Wood, Rachel J	5:07:34 (27,016)
Wood, Rebecca J	5:56:49 (32,817)
Wood, Rebekah L	3:43:21 (6,499)
Wood, Ruth D	5:02:48 (26,182)
Wood, Seona E	5:30:36 (30,474)
Wood, Sue H	4:54:42 (24,386)
Wood, Susanna M	4:39:04 (20,456)
Wood, Suzanne M	3:01:03 (1,054)
Wood, Victoria E	5:45:01 (31,931)
Wood, Victoria J	5:00:36 (25,727)
Wood, Vivien J	5:03:25 (26,268)
Woodburn, Louise	4:33:41 (19,073)
Woodcock, Amy	6:50:20 (34,822)
Woodcock, Angela	5:48:39 (32,233)
Woodcock, Kate A	4:15:57 (14,381)
Woodgate, Elizabeth S	4:40:17 (20,792)
Woodham, Helene E	4:27:41 (17,441)
Woodham, Kerre	5:10:35 (27,565)
Woodham, Sue	5:44:40 (31,906)
Woodhams, Lucy A	3:20:38 (2,845)
Woodhead, Chloe L	5:39:52 (31,482)
Woodhead, Marie	5:29:04 (30,280)
Woodhouse, Emma J	6:18:27 (33,945)
Woodland, Naomi A	4:49:21 (23,071)
Woodman, Gill	7:11:15 (35,067)
Woodman, Jill M	5:03:26 (26,270)
Woods, Abigail L	3:31:08 (4,349)
Woods, Aimée D	3:52:36 (8,426)
Woods, Anne	7:20:25 (35,153)
Woods, Caroline L	3:57:54 (9,903)
Woods, Geraldine R	4:41:54 (21,181)
Woods, Helen J	4:48:36 (22,877)
Woods, Jacqui	3:53:44 (8,688)
Woods, Joanne	5:01:26 (25,900)
Woods, Katie S	5:46:04 (32,023)
Woods, Nicole	4:41:34 (21,109)
Woods, Sandra D	6:28:12 (34,363)
Woods, Susan M	4:00:48 (10,749)
Woodvine, Amanda	4:24:48 (16,654)
Woodward, Amanda C	4:24:36 (16,592)
Woodward, Charlotte	4:52:05 (23,773)
Woodward, Clare	4:47:20 (22,564)
Woodward, Kathryn E	4:09:32 (12,732)
Woodward, Polly	5:41:21 (31,615)
Woodward, Samantha K	5:06:30 (26,807)
Woodward, Stacy	4:21:31 (15,820)
Woodyard, Tracey S	3:20:34 (2,834)
Wooff, Louise D	4:35:29 (19,536)
Wookey, Francesca	4:43:11 (21,511)
Woolcock, Larraine Katrina M	4:50:09 (23,274)
Wooldridge, Kate R	3:39:39 (5,784)
Woolford, Nicola	3:12:18 (1,913)
Woolgar, Allyson G	5:35:40 (31,038)
Woollard, Claire L	3:53:09 (8,548)
Woollard, Faye M	4:48:08 (22,770)
Woollard, Pauline	4:38:40 (20,342)
Wooler, Diane E	3:44:21 (6,689)
Woolley, Erin L	4:04:22 (11,518)
Woolley, Kelly A	3:44:29 (6,717)
Woolley, Laura C	5:48:35 (32,226)
Woolley, Sarah H	3:57:15 (9,690)
Woolley, Theresa	3:08:09 (1,538)
Woolnough, Jennifer L	4:14:25 (14,017)
Woolnough, Leigh	6:19:06 (34,003)
Wootton, Helen E	3:41:46 (6,161)
Worboys, Caroline	5:29:08 (30,289)
Worboys-Hodgson, Joanne	4:50:44 (23,431)
Worley, Charlotte E	4:15:36 (14,306)
Wormald, Katy	3:58:05 (9,963)
Worraker, Sara	4:33:40 (19,066)
Worrall, Marie L	4:09:10 (12,652)
Worsley, Lucy K	4:57:21 (25,001)
Worswick, Catherine B	4:18:25 (15,001)
Worth, Stephanie	4:26:33 (17,130)
Worthington, Hannah Kate	4:43:38 (21,633)
Worthington, Lindsey	4:49:33 (23,133)
Woshalo, Helen	6:09:05 (33,516)
Wouters, Annelie M	5:15:51 (28,484)
Wozniczka, Katarzyna	4:20:00 (15,428)
Wrabel, Kasia A	5:06:16 (26,772)
Wraith, Emeline	5:19:32 (29,039)
Wray, Lisa M	3:16:28 (2,374)
Wreford, Anita B	4:03:56 (11,428)
Wrigglesworth, Julia	3:46:36 (7,110)
Wright, Annette	6:07:24 (33,455)
Wright, Beveley A	3:12:34 (1,940)
Wright, Caroline	4:01:12 (10,835)
Wright, Caroline	4:19:14 (15,218)
Wright, Catherine	3:26:08 (3,546)
Wright, Christine J	7:24:53 (35,178)
Wright, Eileen A	5:03:16 (26,246)
Wright, Elaine A	4:59:41 (25,529)
Wright, Fiona	3:56:19 (9,399)
Wright, Hannah E	4:11:59 (13,383)
Wright, Helen L	6:21:18 (34,088)
Wright, Hilary S	4:33:56 (19,136)
Wright, Jane A	4:45:56 (22,198)
Wright, Jayne A	5:03:59 (26,385)
Wright, Jeannie	5:00:08 (25,620)
Wright, Jessica C	5:18:54 (28,961)
Wright, Joanne L	4:14:47 (14,108)
Wright, Julia	4:06:30 (11,991)
Wright, Katherine E	4:00:20 (10,623)
Wright, Kathryn	4:24:03 (16,453)
Wright, Kerry	5:08:09 (27,112)

Wright, Kirsty J 4:06:20 (11,957)
Wright, Linda A........................6:53:53 (34,877)
Wright, Lisa 4:54:12 (24,259)
Wright, Lucy A.........................5:08:37 (27,196)
Wright, Melanie 4:51:09 (23,521)
Wright, Natasha P 6:14:55 (33,788)
Wright, Paula J.........................4:59:30 (25,497)
Wright, Rebecca J.....................3:53:50 (8,710)
Wright, Rosalind A 4:46:05 (22,224)
Wright, Sally L.........................5:17:08 (28,664)
Wright, Sarah 6:32:16 (34,458)
Wright, Sheila E 4:20:45 (15,619)
Wright, Stephanie 5:51:28 (32,444)
Wright, Tracey L.......................5:44:06 (31,860)
Wright, Vicky 4:19:33 (15,299)
Wrighton, Sophie E...................4:25:45 (16,923)
Wrigley, Nicola Claire 4:54:52 (24,420)
Wroe, Elizabeth A 5:38:03 (31,285)
Wuyts, Wanda 4:49:53 (23,215)
Wyatt, Abbe L 5:35:35 (31,030)
Wyatt, Helen P..........................5:11:41 (27,759)
Wyatt, Margaret A 5:21:02 (29,227)
Wyatt, Rebeca J........................4:53:36 (24,100)
Wyatt, Sharon E........................4:27:51 (17,502)
Wyatt, Shelley 5:13:31 (28,068)
Wyatt, Vickry...........................4:31:30 (18,505)
Wye, Helen C............................4:41:16 (21,030)
Wye, Vicki E.............................4:41:16 (21,030)
Wykes, Kate 4:34:46 (19,337)
Wyllie, Elizabeth M 3:55:38 (9,203)
Wynes, Susan S 5:32:30 (30,692)
Wynn, Hannah 4:08:11 (12,415)
Wynne, Amanda J......................6:59:58 (34,947)
Wynne, Nicky A 5:59:48 (33,035)
Wynne-Eyton, Kate 4:27:29 (17,387)
Yale, Julie 3:34:45 (4,916)
Yam, Deborah 4:43:18 (21,543)
Yamada, Hideto.........................3:56:48 (9,569)

Yamauchi, Mara.........................2:23:12 (26)

Yarbrough, Susan 7:55:36 (35,303)
Yarnall, Katy L 3:29:20 (4,074)
Yates, Emily..............................5:13:45 (28,113)
Yates, Joanna L 5:35:34 (31,028)
Yates, Michelle L 5:12:34 (27,903)
Yates, Sarah E 3:27:46 (3,822)
Yates, Suzanne 3:30:58 (4,325)
Yearley, Lesley C 4:50:35 (23,392)
Yellowley, Heather.....................4:59:09 (25,424)
Yems, Sara Thérèse 3:48:45 (7,552)
Yendell, Anne E.........................4:13:32 (13,807)
Yendley, Sue E 3:56:25 (9,434)
Yeo, Sarah N 4:09:24 (12,706)
Yeoman, Vivienne J 4:41:30 (21,087)
Yeomans, Zoe G.........................4:48:25 (22,831)
Yerbury, Christine J 5:06:58 (26,901)
Yerbury, Julia 5:06:58 (26,901)
Yerbury, Katrina 4:44:39 (21,871)
Yi, Eunok 6:06:00 (33,389)
Yli-Ojanpera, Heidi C................5:45:08 (31,936)
Yoon, Diana D 6:13:05 (33,697)
York, Marie L............................3:55:36 (9,191)
Youings, Helen 5:45:59 (32,010)

Youle, Orla A 5:02:49 (26,185)
Young, Aisha............................4:27:39 (17,430)
Young, Alison J 3:20:31 (2,827)
Young, Andrea...........................4:40:47 (20,906)
Young, Angela B 5:01:55 (25,996)
Young, Cath 3:40:19 (5,916)
Young, Claire J..........................4:45:54 (22,188)
Young, Hilary 3:21:47 (2,982)
Young, Holly A 5:15:18 (28,387)
Young, Ishbel S..........................6:29:54 (34,407)
Young, Jane 4:30:08 (18,135)
Young, Lesley A 5:57:37 (32,886)
Young, Linzi 5:58:43 (32,974)
Young, Melanie 3:26:54 (3,667)
Young, Nicola J 4:50:27 (23,358)
Young, Pam I 5:21:05 (29,234)
Young, Sally A 4:58:18 (25,213)
Young, Zoe B 4:55:59 (24,680)
Younge, Amanda J......................5:36:50 (31,159)
Younger, Clare Susan 4:07:43 (12,290)
Younghusband, Louisa J 4:26:01 (16,991)
Yoxall, Karen A 4:28:40 (17,740)
Yu, Bing 5:16:39 (28,587)
Yukiko, Teruyama 6:07:30 (33,458)
Yule, Michelle 5:58:04 (32,924)
Zachariou, Diane 4:38:31 (20,303)
Zäger, Karin 3:08:53 (1,607)
Zago, Letizia 3:44:51 (6,779)
Zak, Minoda J 6:13:40 (33,730)
Zakharova, Svetlana 2:25:06 (34)
Zakrzewski, Nicola.....................4:42:12 (21,249)
Zani, Miriam 5:40:29 (31,540)
Zass, Liz E 4:43:03 (21,481)
Zellbi, Helene 4:26:08 (17,020)
Zhu, Yinan 4:39:58 (20,710)
Ziaian, Caroline M 4:20:41 (15,596)
Ziegert, Josephine A 5:00:38 (25,736)
Ziem, Kerstin 4:29:25 (17,952)
Zillig, Rebecca T 4:15:25 (14,262)
Zirngast, Julie M........................5:16:52 (28,626)
Zlattinger, Ruth L......................4:16:41 (14,580)
Zorn, Ursula 4:40:52 (20,929)
Zotti, Ana M 4:49:07 (23,000)
Zu Putlitz, Dagmar.....................4:53:31 (24,074)
Zubizarreta, Maria.....................3:28:11 (3,878)
Zwahr, Amber 5:02:22 (26,090)

WHEELCHAIR ENTRANTS

Alldis, Brian G 1:40:15 (10)
Botello Jimenez, Rafael................1:37:38 (8)
Cheek, Andrew J 2:05:10 (21)
Clarke, Matthew L......................2:17:01 (25)
Dawes, Christie A 1:50:43 (18)
Derwin, Steve............................3:09:04 (37)
Downing, Peter L 2:53:22 (34)
Emerson, Nikki 3:17:37 (38)

Fearnley, Kurt.............................1:28:56 (1)

Born without the lower portion of his spine, Kurt Fearnley (born 23 May 1981) from New South Wales, Australia, will tackle any challenge. The youngest of five children, Fearnley took up wheelchair racing at 14 and went from pushing his wheelchair on grass tracks at school to man-handling his chair the last three miles of the marathon at the 2004 Athens Olympic Games on a flat tyre to win gold. He trains up to four hours each

day. His hands are raw from pushing the chair; his arms are scarred from rubbing against the rims; he has battle scars on his face and back and he's suffered broken bones and cracked teeth from race crashes. In Beijing 2008, Kurt won two silver medals (800m and 5000m) and bronze in the 1500m. On the last day of competition he won gold when he defended his Athens title in the marathon. Fearnley finished second in the 2007 and 2008 London Marathons behind Britain's David Weir.

Frei, Heinz................................1:30:15 (5)
Golightly, Andy...........................2:26:10 (28)
Graf, Sandra 1:50:40 (15)
Holliday, Rob D 2:47:15 (33)
Hunkeler, Edith 1:50:42 (17)
Iniguez, José Antonio 1:39:17 (9)
Kapinowski, Jacqui 2:57:49 (36)
Kent, Geoff A.............................2:10:34 (23)
Lemeunier, Denis........................1:32:40 (6)
Lopez, Bayron G 2:10:27 (22)
Ludovic, Gapenne.......................1:47:27 (11)

McGrory, Amanda M 1:50:39 (14)

Amanda McGrory (born 9 June 1986) is an American wheelchair athlete who held off the 2008 winner Sandra Graf of Switzerland to win by one second in 1:50:39. McGrory earned four medals during the 2008 Summer Paralympics in Beijing: she won gold in the 5000m, silver in the marathon, and bronze in both the 800m and the 4 × 100m relay. She won the 2006 New York Marathon wheelchair race. McGrory also competes in wheelchair basketball. Her interest in wheelchair sports began at a summer camp in Pennsylvania. She started out playing basketball, and then moved on to track and field. While she continues to compete in both sports at the University of Illinois, where she is studying psychology, she says track and field is definitely her favourite.

Mendoza, Saul............................1:37:12 (7)
Molina Sibaja, Laurens 2:27:31 (29)
Phipps, Aaron D.........................1:59:09 (20)
Price, James A............................2:54:29 (35)
Qadir, Shaho 2:26:09 (27)
Rayment, Alan E.........................2:33:42 (31)
Rea, Paul M 2:13:09 (24)
Riggs, Stuart J 2:31:04 (30)
Robin, Crevel............................1:48:52 (12)
Roy, Diane................................1:50:41 (16)
Smith, Rob P.............................2:20:23 (26)
Soejima, Masazumi......................1:30:13 (4)
Telford, Mark 1:49:49 (13)
Van Dyk, Ernst 1:28:58 (3)
Weir, David 1:28:57 (2)
Whiteford, Margo L....................2:46:10 (32)
Woods, Shelly 1:50:46 (19)

The 2010 London Marathon

In 2010, Princess Beatrice, 21, running for Children in Crisis became the first royal to complete the London Marathon. She and her American boyfriend David Clark set off in pouring rain as part of a 'human caterpillar' of 34 people who ran the course tied together with bungee cords.

The princess, wearing a lime green tutu, was congratulated at the finishing line by her parents the Duke and Duchess of York. The charity team – which also included entrepreneur Sir Richard Branson's two children Sam and Holly – completed the course in 5:13:03, setting a new world record for the most people to finish a marathon while tied together. Sir Richard Branson, wearing a colourful pair of butterfly wings, ran alongside the human caterpillar. The company that he founded, Virgin, has taken over sponsorship of the event from Flora for the first time.

It was the year that the cloud of ash from the Icelandic volcano grounded many aircraft, and threatened the majority of elite entries from overseas athletes. These included the runner-up in the women's race, Briton Mara Yamauchi, who was apparently wearied by a catalogue of travels and came home in tenth place. Yamauchi's 6,500-mile journey from her training base in Albuquerque, New Mexico took six days. Her odyssey of planes, trains and cars was really a journey too far and must have left her jaded and unprepared, and although she declined to make excuses, she finished four minutes behind the leader, Russian Liliya Shobukhova.

After leading for much of the second half of the race, Shobukhova, the 32-year-old European 5000m record holder, used her finishing speed to outpace Inga Abitova. In a time of 2:22:00, Ethiopia's Aselefech Mergia was third.

In the men's race, Ethiopia's Tsegaye Kebede, the world and Olympic bronze medallist and runner-up in London the previous year, dominated, finishing in 2:05:19. Kenyan runner-up Emmanuel Mutai was more than a minute behind him, while veteran Moroccan Jaouad Gharib was third.

The decisive moment came with five miles remaining when Kebede, 23, produced a blistering 4:33 mile that left his rivals stretched out behind him. It was too much for Kenyan world champion Abel Kirui, who, having looked the man most likely to challenge Kebede, fell apart and eventually finished fifth.

Andrew Lemoncello was the first Briton home in his debut over the marathon distance, crossing the line in eighth place. But the 27-year-old Scot will need to improve on his time of 2:13:40 if he has any hope of being among the leaders at the 2012 Olympics.

Two first-timers secured London Wheelchair Marathon titles in the men's and women's sections: Canadian Josh Cassidy (1:35:21) and Japan's Wakako Tsuchida (1:52:33) respectively. But there were problems for the leading two British Paralympic racers. David Weir was denied a fifth London title, in spite of being four minutes ahead at one point, after two flat tyres enabled Cassidy to overhaul him on the Embankment.

In the women's race, Wakako – the first wheelchair athlete to win the Boston and London marathons within a week – and Switzerland's Sandra Graf edged out defending champion Amanda McGrory in a sprint finish. But Britain's Shelly Woods, who, like Weir, had lead earlier in the race, suffered a puncture at 21 miles.

Wounded war veteran Major Phil Packer finished the London Marathon in 26 hours on the following Monday, smashing his personal best by

13 days. The ex-officer, who suffered serious spinal injuries in 2008, crossed the line after 25 hours 55 minutes, completing the marathon in aid of 26 charities.

Finally, a runner who was thought to have recorded the fastest time for the London Marathon for someone aged over 65 took a ten-mile short cut. Anthony Gaskell, 69, crossed the finishing line in just three hours and five minutes. He was due to receive a plaque to mark his record time but plans were abandoned after an analysis of the second half of his race, checking on the chip findings fitted to each entrant's shoes, revealed that he would have had to have run the second half in under an hour.

Gaskell, a grandfather from the Wirral, Merseyside, was stripped of his unofficial 'fastest OAP' title after admitting that he took a short cut, but claims he did so because he was injured and never intended to finish the race. Anthony Gaskell's disqualification meant that Colin Rathbone, 66, who finished 38 seconds behind Mr Gaskell after completing the full 26 miles and 385 yards, received the plaque.

Explanation of placing system

Each London Marathon year in this register is divided up into four categories: first, a summary of the **Elite Athletes**, containing names (last, first) and times (hours : minutes : seconds) of the top 50 male runners, top 50 female runners, top 3 male and top 2 female wheelchair entrants; then **Male Runners**, **Female Runners** and **Wheelchair Entrants**. These last three sections display the individual names and times of *every* entrant, including elite athletes, alphabetically and with their overall finishing position in that year's Marathon displayed in brackets alongside.

Some entrants have chosen to enhance past London Marathon entries with photos and recollections online at **www.aubreybooks.com**. Please visit the website to find out more about appearing in future editions.

ELITE ATHLETES

Top 50 male runners

Kebede, Tsegaye	2:05:19
Mutai, Emmanuel	2:06:23
Gharib, Jaouad	2:06:55
Bouramdane, Abderrahime	2:07:33
Kirui, Abel	2:08:04
Gomes Dos Santos, Marilson	2:08:46
Tadese, Zersenay	2:12:03
Lemoncello, Andrew	2:13:40
Kifle, Yonas	2:14:39
Jones, Andi	2:16:38
Moreau, Ben	2:16:46
Merrien, Lee	2:16:48
Perrett, Clint	2:18:15
Renault, Neil	2:18:29
Norman, Dave	2:19:05
Irifune, Satoshi	2:19:25
Way, Steven	2:19:38
Raven, Gareth	2:19:55
Osterlund, Kristoffer	2:20:06
Vermeesch, Pieter	2:20:16
Martelletti, Paul	2:21:02
Connor, James	2:21:04
Matsumiya, Takayuki	2:21:34
Houston, Ross D	2:22:49
Carroll, Michael J	2:22:52
Green, Michael	2:23:48
Desplanques, Frederic	2:23:49
Wilder, Brian J	2:24:18
Wardle, David	2:24:21
Bilton, Darran E	2:25:08
Edwards, Orlando	2:25:15
Gamble, Ben P	2:25:17
Lennox, Jethro	2:25:51
Kjaell-Ohlsson, Martin	2:26:00
Cope, Nicholas	2:26:18
Stirk, Nigel A	2:26:46

Baker, Robert J	2:26:58
Nowill, Peter	2:27:16
Marchant, Paul A	2:27:20
Gilbert, John J	2:27:27
Williams, Ian G	2:27:37
Vautier, Stephane	2:27:53
Killingley, Phil S	2:28:06
Kay, Richard A	2:28:34
McFarlane, John	2:28:38
Bell, Matthew J	2:28:39
Dickinson, Mark	2:28:46
Greenleaf, Andrew H	2:28:51
Keal, Robert J	2:28:58
Tucker, Peter R	2:29:27

Top 50 female runners

Shobukhova, Liliya	2:22:00
Abitova, Inga	2:22:19
Mergia, Aselefech	2:22:38
Bekele, Bezunesh	2:23:17
Tafa, Askale	2:24:39
Akaba, Yukiko	2:24:55
Bai, Xue	2:25:18
Smith, Kim	2:25:21
Ozaki, Mari	2:25:43
Yamauchi, Mara	2:26:16
Zakharova, Svetlana	2:31:00
Habtamu, Atsede	2:31:41
Ozaki, Yoshimi	2:32:26
Adere, Berhane	2:33:46
Maxwell, Tanith	2:34:24
Konovalova, Maria	2:35:21
Partridge, Sue	2:35:57
Kastor, Deena	2:36:20
Decker, Helen	2:36:56
Robinson, Rebecca	2:37:14
Wilkinson, Jo	2:37:44

Docherty, Fiona	2:37:55
Rush, Holly	2:37:56
Harrison, Sue	2:38:53
Gee, Sarah R	2:40:06
Dita, Constantina	2:41:12
Ganiel O'Neill, Gladys	2:41:45
Penty, Becky	2:42:07
Archer, Nicky	2:42:22
Dixon, Alyson	2:43:48
Gardner, Claire L	2:44:29
Gibbs, Rachel C	2:46:19
Amend, Samantha	2:47:01
Cowley, Laura J	2:47:30
McIntosh, Shona	2:48:46
Humphrey, Sam H	2:49:01
Blizard, Jenny	2:49:10
Firth, Charlotte	2:50:56
Bird, Sharon	2:51:44
Stewart, Lauren L	2:51:58
Palmer, Lisa A	2:53:16
Wood, Georgia E	2:53:35
Powell, Fiona L	2:53:42
Perry, Victoria A	2:53:46
Hutchison, Anne-Marie	2:54:13
Knass, Jenny E	2:54:47
Guiney, Megan	2:55:11
Kirk, Laura	2:55:29
Christie, Nathalie	2:55:52
Bosman, Jenny Mairi	2:55:59

Top 3 male and top 2 female wheelchair entrants

Cassidy, Josh	1:35:21
Hug, Marcel	1:36:07
Weir, David	1:37:01
Tsuchida, Wakako	1:52:33
Graf, Sandra	1:52:34

MALE RUNNERS

Aarons, Anthony 5:38:17 (32,235)
Aartse-Tuyn, Guy 3:13:29 (2,252)
Aattal, Joseph 4:27:10 (18,137)
Abad, Jesus 3:23:17 (3,339)
Abare, John 4:27:06 (18,120)
Abati, Mauro 4:25:47 (17,745)
Abato, Robert 4:08:09 (12,994)
Abbey, Graeme James 5:01:42 (26,792)
Abbey, Nick 4:28:09 (18,397)
Abbey, Paul Edward 4:32:28 (19,553)
Abbinett, Ian 3:27:41 (3,995)
Abbott, Aaron 4:05:09 (12,241)
Abbott, Barry Wayne 4:55:34 (25,424)
Abbott, Donald Foster 4:03:18 (11,801)
Abbott, Douglas C 3:55:26 (9,602)
Abbott, John 4:58:54 (26,189)
Abbott, Julian Richard 4:59:36 (26,366)
Abbott, Laurence 3:51:42 (8,587)
Abbott, Michael David 4:41:37 (21,927)
Abbott, Nicky C 3:56:50 (10,041)
Abbott, Phil 3:11:40 (2,066)
Abbott, Ryan J 3:58:07 (10,423)
Abbott, Stuart I 4:37:35 (20,904)
Abdulkadir, Nurdin Shariff 3:04:11 (1,407)
Abdullah, Ali 7:13:42 (36,346)
Abel, James 4:28:45 (18,591)
Abel, Kevin 4:38:11 (21,026)
Abel, Lawrence J 3:13:57 (2,309)
Ab-Elwyn, Rhys 3:40:59 (6,320)
Abercrombie, Ian Ross 4:54:59 (25,302)
Aberra, Ben 3:44:30 (6,987)
Abid, Khaled 4:53:34 (24,934)
Abou El Fadel, Mohamed 3:17:23 (2,695)
Abouzeid, Andrew R 3:09:54 (1,899)
Abraham, Xavier 3:41:00 (6,329)
Abrahams, Michael S 4:50:18 (24,116)
Abrahart, Jon Michael 3:44:49 (7,058)
Abrahart, Stephen Roger 3:45:45 (7,259)
Abrahim, Harry S 3:14:31 (2,385)
Abram, Barry E 3:03:11 (1,336)
Abram, Oliver 3:27:05 (3,882)
Abrams, Alexander N 2:52:02 (567)
Abrams, Gary Paul 4:52:17 (24,633)
Abrams-Humphries, Stuart 5:38:46 (32,287)
Abrons, Andrew 4:38:14 (21,037)
Abundis, Fancisco 3:48:01 (7,741)
Abusin, Wadah 4:55:41 (25,458)
Acheson, Gary John 3:50:20 (8,275)
Acheson, Graeme 3:46:12 (7,353)
Acheson, Marc 4:38:22 (21,078)
Acid, Rab 3:32:07 (4,761)
Ackland-Snow, James 4:59:07 (26,242)
Ackroyd, Paul Stephen 4:25:52 (17,779)
Acland, David 4:53:28 (24,905)
Acton, John 5:24:31 (30,558)
Acton, Simon 5:05:06 (27,386)
Acton, Steve Brian 4:48:42 (23,719)
Adamally, Irfaan 5:40:36 (32,443)
Adamczuk, James Stefan 4:39:19 (21,334)
Adamczyk, Eric 3:26:14 (3,775)
Adamis, Antonio 4:03:31 (11,849)
Adamjee, Juzar 5:10:40 (28,359)
Adams, Alexander 2:55:53 (796)
Adams, Andrew 4:46:00 (23,024)
Adams, Andrew C 3:44:51 (7,066)
Adams, Andrew J 4:19:45 (16,030)
Adams, Anthony Kenneth 4:03:26 (11,828)
Adams, David Eugene 4:05:27 (12,325)
Adams, Ian Geoffrey 3:45:12 (7,139)
Adams, Jason 4:22:36 (16,875)
Adams, Jeffrey P 3:04:51 (1,452)
Adams, John A 5:15:36 (29,163)
Adams, John R 3:39:09 (5,973)
Adams, Keith J 4:32:08 (19,468)
Adams, Kevin J 3:11:17 (2,025)
Adams, Laurence Eliot 4:29:36 (18,842)
Adams, Lee S 3:07:45 (1,680)
Adams, Lee Thomas 5:19:39 (29,800)
Adams, Leslie 4:25:02 (17,531)
Adams, Michael Ian 5:47:58 (33,134)
Adams, Nathan H 5:24:12 (30,510)
Adams, Neil 4:48:04 (23,561)
Adams, Neil Richard 4:08:58 (13,201)
Adams, Paul 5:03:27 (27,093)
Adams, Paul 5:27:16 (30,939)
Adams, Paul Anthony 5:41:40 (32,545)
Adams, Paul N 3:27:22 (3,934)
Adams, Paul R 5:28:45 (31,120)
Adams, Paul Simon 3:54:34 (9,344)
Adams, Richard 4:53:07 (24,826)
Adams, Richard L 4:52:52 (24,771)
Adams, Robert 4:59:05 (26,236)
Adams, Robert 6:29:41 (35,483)
Adams, Robin 3:31:44 (4,701)
Adams, Simon Christopher 5:07:41 (27,846)
Adams, Steven P 4:40:54 (21,743)
Adams, Thomas F 4:07:32 (12,843)
Adams, Tomos C 3:53:55 (9,186)
Adamson, Harry 4:40:50 (21,733)
Adamson, Michael 3:52:32 (8,804)
Adamson, Simon David 3:56:59 (10,084)
Adaway, Christopher J 3:58:44 (10,637)
Adby, Geoff Craig 5:00:43 (26,590)
Adcock, George Graham 3:54:00 (9,211)
Addati, Ferdinando 4:24:52 (17,481)
Adderley, Mark 5:30:57 (31,412)
Addicott, Phil Wallace 5:02:06 (26,867)
Addis, Ken James 3:41:51 (6,491)
Addis, Simon 4:46:45 (23,237)
Addison, Chris 3:26:56 (3,865)
Addison, Iain 4:22:52 (16,954)
Addison, Jason Peter 4:25:36 (17,690)
Addison, Jim M 2:44:25 (319)
Addison, Joe M 5:17:06 (29,403)
Addison, Simon Jack 4:54:08 (25,075)
Addison-Evans, Nigel 5:32:55 (31,654)
Addley, Michael 5:07:24 (27,790)
Addrison, Martin Kenneth 3:30:13 (4,456)
Addyman, Nick 5:33:20 (31,697)
Adelaido, Artemio 3:48:12 (7,782)
Adelsberg, Dennis O 7:18:47 (36,391)
Adissa, Jalal 3:54:45 (9,402)
Adkin, Matthew 3:38:43 (5,890)
Adkins, Daniel 3:34:33 (5,163)
Adkins, John S 3:39:02 (5,946)
Adlard, Simon C 3:14:22 (2,363)
Adlington, Ben J 3:44:25 (6,975)
Adnitt, Robert I 3:07:58 (1,696)
Adu-Bonsra, Hywel 4:09:28 (13,330)
Affleck, Michael V 3:31:03 (4,587)
Affleck, Robert J 2:52:37 (600)
Afforselles, Ben J 3:09:40 (1,876)
Afshar, Dan 3:18:54 (2,861)
Agar, Simon 4:12:51 (14,194)
Agard, Jean Pascal 4:21:19 (16,494)
Agbamu, Alex 4:16:22 (15,130)
Agbohlah, Senyo 5:06:02 (27,539)
Ager, Iain N 4:05:57 (12,445)
Ager, Stephen 2:56:42 (843)
Aggarwal, Vinod 5:07:16 (27,761)
Aggleton, Hugh S 2:41:18 (234)
Agius, Russell Alexander 3:38:29 (5,841)
Agliocchi, Luigi 4:53:54 (25,022)
Agmon, Gil 4:51:32 (24,426)
Agossou, Jean François 5:49:08 (33,250)
Agostini, Aldo 3:58:23 (10,517)
Agrawal, Dave 3:35:01 (5,253)
Aguerre, François 3:00:59 (1,205)
Ahlers, Michael 4:50:08 (24,078)
Ahmad, Mohammad Haroon 5:29:58 (31,289)
Ahmad, Omer 6:18:46 (35,069)
Ahmad, Rafat 4:07:00 (12,711)
Ahmed, Amjad Khan 4:38:42 (21,171)
Ahmed, Rashed 5:46:55 (33,043)
Ahmed, Shahzad 5:32:25 (31,588)
Ahmed, Sheeraz 4:25:10 (17,566)
Ahmed, Syed 4:43:33 (22,382)
Ahrend, Norbert 4:37:47 (20,944)
Aidoo, Colin Rohan 4:35:21 (20,309)
Aidroos, Fred 3:28:55 (4,214)
Aiken, Scott M 2:57:08 (864)
Aikens, Tom 3:53:35 (9,084)
Aikman, Neil Robert 3:43:46 (6,821)
Ailes, Derek Anthony 7:32:33 (36,481)
Ailes, Warwick 4:56:56 (25,753)
Aime, Michel 4:56:41 (25,689)
Ainger, Matthew R 4:10:35 (13,614)
Ainslie, Paul 3:13:56 (2,307)
Ainsworth, Robert W 6:44:33 (35,897)
Ainsworth, Roland William 4:35:38 (20,375)
Ainsworth, Tom 4:40:43 (21,700)
Aird, William Rowley 3:15:22 (2,481)
Airey, John 5:29:07 (31,165)
Aisthorpe-Buckley, Peter George 8:56:10 (36,612)
Aitken, John 3:28:12 (4,094)
Aitken, John 3:59:45 (10,932)
Aitken, Nigel James 3:45:22 (7,175)
Aked, Terry B 5:41:45 (32,556)

Akenhead, David 6:51:33 (36,027)

Ideal running conditions, but not for me, alas! Everything fine until Surrey Quays – then left ankle (broken last year when I did not run) went on strike – rest of run (17.2 miles) reduced to march and hobble! Completed my 10th London Marathon eventually in 6:51.33 having started in 2000 for St Jo's.

Akeret, Eric 3:30:51 (4,558)
Akerman, Hugo 4:13:20 (14,324)
Akinluyi, Ayo 5:43:47 (32,755)
Akinrinmade, Ronald Adedayo 6:09:10 (34,623)
Alabaster, Andrew 4:38:23 (21,088)
Alain, Rouillon 3:45:36 (7,228)
Alan, Meredith 6:00:44 (34,105)
Alba, Urbano F 3:59:16 (10,799)
Albagly, Serge 3:30:48 (4,548)
Albaz, Gilles 4:53:36 (24,941)
Albers, Simon James 5:40:14 (32,415)
Albert, Daniel Philip 4:31:07 (19,245)
Albert, Simon Mark 3:39:41 (6,073)
Alberto, Castello 3:30:44 (4,534)
Albes, Jean Luc 3:05:13 (1,474)
Albiges, James M 3:56:37 (9,964)
Albon, Gary Peter 5:30:35 (31,369)
Albuquerque, Carlos 5:40:43 (32,453)
Alcantara, André 3:26:59 (3,874)
Alciati, Maurizio 3:16:32 (2,618)
Alcock, Andrew 4:27:49 (18,316)
Alcock, Ian Richard 4:04:27 (12,066)
Alcock, Mark Benjamin 5:25:15 (30,655)
Alcock, Stephen Roy 4:26:04 (17,830)
Alden, Chris 5:53:56 (33,637)
Alder, Alex Mark 3:53:22 (9,018)
Alder, Chris A 3:13:35 (2,269)
Alder, Christopher 5:05:11 (27,401)
Alderman, Neil 3:37:49 (5,726)
Alders, Steve 5:08:55 (28,032)
Alderson, David M 4:10:46 (13,658)
Alderson, John Richard 5:47:46 (33,122)
Alderson, Paul 4:01:13 (11,300)
Aldred, Timothy Norman 3:50:09 (8,237)
Aldrich, Stuart 8:06:08 (36,590)
Aldridge, Jason 6:54:10 (36,089)
Aldridge, Matthew 4:04:03 (11,973)
Aldwinckle, Mark Thomas 5:15:42 (29,177)
A'Lee, Che J 5:01:20 (26,721)
Alen, Nicholas Robert 5:43:20 (32,704)
Alexander, Adam Benjamin 4:43:33 (22,382)
Alexander, Ian Joseph 5:21:26 (30,065)
Alexander, John 4:46:33 (23,180)
Alexander, Niall 4:10:44 (13,649)
Alexander, Paul 3:14:25 (2,372)
Alexander, Paul 3:26:34 (3,808)
Alexander, Peter David 4:35:24 (20,325)
Alexander, Ratan 3:30:13 (4,456)
Alexander, Robin 6:05:28 (34,419)
Alexander, Rohan 3:46:04 (7,330)
Alexander, Steve 3:48:21 (7,816)
Alexander, Steven D 3:59:10 (10,764)
Alexander, Tom 3:30:11 (4,447)
Alexander Lee, Kieran 4:40:49 (21,728)
Alexander-Bown, Scott 4:33:51 (19,953)
Alexandre, Denis 3:40:34 (6,252)
Alfermann, Georg 4:04:39 (12,114)

Alford, Jonathan Mark...............4:15:18 (14,861)
Alford, Kieran...............4:14:43 (14,719)
Algar, Neil James...............4:59:11 (26,260)
Al-Hakim, Ali...............4:43:44 (22,432)
Ali, Altan...............3:38:49 (5,908)
Ali, Ashraf...............5:42:33 (32,643)
Ali, Erol...............3:47:55 (7,723)
Ali, Gulam Mostafa...............6:11:04 (34,703)
Ali, Ibrar...............3:53:41 (9,117)
Ali, Iqbal...............3:21:10 (3,107)
Ali, Jahid...............5:33:06 (31,677)
Ali, Kausar...............4:21:22 (16,513)
Ali, Malik...............4:54:32 (25,188)
Ali, Somsuddin...............5:16:28 (29,304)
Aliane, Djelloul...............4:07:12 (12,749)
Alibert, Pascal...............4:29:29 (18,800)
Alison, Duncan J...............4:17:13 (15,354)
Alison, Philip...............4:06:03 (12,463)
Alizai, Naved Kamal...............5:04:55 (27,351)
Al-Kaabi, Ali Khalaf...............4:52:46 (24,742)
Alker, Paul Martin...............4:19:04 (15,866)
Alladyce, Tim...............4:20:02 (16,115)
Allafranchino, Cosimo...............4:54:45 (25,245)
Allain, Jonathan...............5:07:19 (27,772)
Allan, Bruce David...............5:35:45 (31,961)
Allan, David John...............4:00:14 (11,041)
Allan, John J...............4:20:35 (16,287)
Allan, Peter M...............3:55:15 (9,544)
Allan, Simon R...............3:25:12 (3,607)
Allan, Thomas...............4:30:08 (19,010)
Allard, François...............4:18:54 (15,828)
Allard, Lee...............4:38:36 (21,143)
Allard, Patrice...............3:29:42 (4,360)
Allard, Rod K...............4:11:08 (13,753)
Allard, Charles J Jnr...............3:12:23 (2,124)
Allardyce, Richard C...............5:55:08 (33,730)
Allaway, Dean A...............3:21:57 (3,191)
Allaway, Grant Kennth...............3:55:48 (9,719)
Allchin, Martin Geoffrey...............5:02:06 (26,867)
Allder, Colin Roy...............4:31:55 (19,411)
Alldis, Daniel Thomas...............4:48:42 (23,719)
Allen, Andrew Patrick...............3:27:46 (4,008)
Allen, Andrew William...............3:54:04 (9,225)
Allen, Brian M...............4:05:23 (12,303)
Allen, Chris...............4:12:05 (14,003)
Allen, Chris M...............3:10:31 (1,949)
Allen, Chris M...............3:52:46 (8,857)
Allen, David...............5:00:24 (26,535)
Allen, Dean Arthur...............4:38:11 (21,026)
Allen, Frederick Tristan Beresford...4:20:14 (16,173)
Allen, Gareth...............5:13:49 (28,896)
Allen, Gavin P...............3:56:10 (9,832)
Allen, Grant Gavin...............5:25:04 (30,634)
Allen, James...............3:55:56 (9,760)
Allen, James A...............3:26:46 (3,842)
Allen, James Edward...............4:48:31 (23,671)
Allen, Jamie...............3:27:11 (3,905)
Allen, Jimmy...............5:31:25 (31,466)
Allen, John F...............7:21:35 (36,413)
Allen, Jon...............3:31:19 (4,632)
Allen, Jonathan David...............3:34:42 (5,190)
Allen, Keith William...............4:27:30 (18,236)
Allen, Ken R...............3:18:54 (2,861)
Allen, Kevin...............4:04:08 (11,993)
Allen, Lee...............3:40:21 (6,206)
Allen, Lee Michael...............5:54:08 (33,653)
Allen, Mark William...............5:22:20 (30,197)
Allen, Martin J...............3:59:10 (10,764)
Allen, Michael E...............6:21:15 (35,171)
Allen, Michael Robert...............4:19:33 (15,985)
Allen, Paul M...............3:08:30 (1,754)
Allen, Paul Ronald...............3:55:35 (9,632)
Allen, Peter Edward...............4:53:10 (24,839)
Allen, Richard Tony...............5:18:55 (29,688)
Allen, Robert...............4:37:16 (20,806)
Allen, Roger Hugh...............5:21:08 (30,024)
Allen, Roy...............4:53:11 (24,845)
Allen, Steve P...............3:49:33 (8,102)
Allen, Stuart...............3:59:47 (10,942)
Allen, Tim...............4:41:21 (21,851)
Allen, Tim...............4:46:11 (23,085)
Allenby, Stephen J...............3:51:18 (8,492)
Allewell, Michael James...............3:51:08 (8,456)

Alley, Clive S...............2:52:35 (596)
Allinson, Steven Paul...............4:52:57 (24,785)
Allison, Gary Mark...............4:34:50 (20,202)
Allison, Jamie...............6:01:13 (34,140)
Allison, Jim Melville...............4:41:45 (21,952)
Allison, Sean William...............5:22:28 (30,215)
Allory, Patrick...............3:22:52 (3,273)
Allport, Trevor Anthony...............3:25:40 (3,681)
Allsey, Steve Edward...............4:58:48 (26,165)
Allsopp, Lewis Danie...............6:10:07 (34,673)
Allton, Christopher R...............3:09:52 (1,898)
Allton, Paul G...............4:02:35 (11,624)
Allum, Robin...............4:41:04 (21,784)
Ally, Geert...............3:16:12 (2,574)
Almgren, Marius...............4:05:12 (12,255)
Almond, James...............4:21:53 (16,664)
Almond, Martin P...............4:36:19 (20,551)
Almond, Stephen...............4:05:11 (12,251)
Alnaimi, Nasser Mohd SA...............6:00:59 (34,131)
Alogaga, Sol...............3:43:51 (6,845)
Alovisi, Julian...............3:23:49 (3,410)
Alsop, Daniel...............2:45:04 (343)
Alsop, Doug A...............3:12:11 (2,107)
Alston, Richard...............4:37:12 (20,795)
Alston, Sean W...............4:17:20 (15,386)
Alterauge, Bernd...............4:35:43 (20,392)
Althey, Charles...............3:01:24 (1,224)
Alvarado, Alexis...............3:58:06 (10,414)
Alvarado, David...............4:20:35 (16,287)
Alviarez Alonso, José Manuel......4:37:56 (20,974)
Alvidrez, Octavio...............3:43:46 (6,821)
Alwell, John A...............3:37:39 (5,699)
Alwen, Jon...............4:50:51 (24,254)
Amadio, Giorgio...............3:20:28 (3,017)
Amador, Daniel M...............5:58:51 (33,981)
Amatt, Robert...............4:51:24 (24,398)
Ambrose, Gary John Alfred.........4:00:15 (11,044)
Ambrose, Mickey B...............6:10:41 (34,689)
Ambuhl, Vincent...............4:42:15 (22,079)
Amer, Tarik...............4:02:51 (11,688)
Amerat, Imraan Hashim...............5:51:32 (33,464)
Amery, Richard...............3:26:19 (3,784)
Ames, Daniel...............5:26:49 (30,874)
Amesbury, Chris John...............3:53:53 (9,177)
Amic, Etienne A...............3:28:23 (4,121)
Amin, Agni...............4:44:23 (22,609)
Amin, Bhavesh...............3:34:57 (5,240)
Amin, Saj...............5:22:50 (30,278)
Amin, Tohkeel...............6:06:24 (34,470)
Amlot, Dylan...............3:58:12 (10,459)
Amner, James...............4:23:19 (17,049)
Amoo, Paul J...............3:39:42 (6,078)
Amoo-Bediako, Michael...............3:53:19 (9,004)
Amoros, Fabien...............6:38:09 (35,730)
Amos, Chris...............3:32:15 (4,780)
Amos, Graham...............6:26:28 (35,363)
Amos, Jordan Alexander...............6:26:29 (35,365)
Amos, Kelvin J...............3:09:05 (1,815)
Amos, Mark D...............3:09:33 (1,864)
Amos, Nigel T...............4:27:16 (18,171)
Amouroux, Valery Florent...............3:12:51 (2,171)
Amroussi, Amir...............5:34:36 (31,835)
Amy, Thomas...............3:43:47 (6,828)
Anand, Sanjay...............3:13:24 (2,236)
Anandakumar, Naveen...............5:27:20 (30,944)
Anders, Peter...............4:15:24 (14,886)
Andersen, Gert...............4:29:59 (18,976)
Anderson, Allan...............3:47:54 (7,717)
Anderson, Andy...............4:58:18 (26,040)
Anderson, Andy David...............4:11:06 (13,744)
Anderson, Chris H...............3:38:56 (5,926)
Anderson, Christopher...............4:40:50 (21,733)
Anderson, Christopher M...........4:01:09 (11,287)
Anderson, Craig...............3:33:32 (4,978)
Anderson, Damien...............7:01:34 (36,210)
Anderson, Daniel...............5:07:19 (27,772)
Anderson, David R...............4:35:42 (20,390)
Anderson, Dean Clayton...............4:51:13 (24,358)
Anderson, Gavin Alistair John......4:00:23 (11,085)
Anderson, Ian Clive...............3:46:33 (7,433)
Anderson, Ian S...............2:50:44 (515)
Anderson, James...............5:25:39 (30,728)
Anderson, Jamie R...............2:50:46 (518)

Anderson, Jeff...............5:42:12 (32,609)
Anderson, John...............3:40:13 (6,184)
Anderson, Mark...............5:26:51 (30,880)
Anderson, Mark William...............6:06:07 (34,457)
Anderson, Michael...............5:27:57 (31,017)
Anderson, Peter...............4:51:28 (24,411)
Anderson, Peter...............5:00:50 (26,617)
Anderson, Philip...............3:48:41 (7,896)
Anderson, Philip...............3:57:51 (10,345)
Anderson, Philip J...............4:23:02 (16,988)
Anderson, Richard...............4:32:56 (19,680)
Anderson, Robert James...............3:59:57 (10,976)
Anderson, Simon...............3:08:24 (1,739)
Anderson, Simon Francis...............3:19:20 (2,902)
Anderson, Stephen...............4:42:01 (22,017)
Anderson, Tony...............3:46:37 (7,444)
Anderson, Trevor...............4:31:03 (19,230)
Anderson, Warwick A...............3:21:54 (3,182)
Anderson, Wayne...............4:31:03 (19,230)
Anderson, Will James Benedict...4:35:33 (20,354)
Andersson, Björn...............3:54:00 (9,211)
Andersson, Jan...............4:35:58 (20,468)
Andersson, Joakim...............4:51:24 (24,398)
Anderton, Alan...............5:23:47 (30,440)
Anderton, Rupert J...............4:55:35 (25,429)
Ando, Toyohiko...............5:13:41 (28,868)
André, Jean-Christophe...............2:51:11 (528)
Andreck, Gerard...............4:05:10 (12,245)
Andrei, Pascal...............4:14:32 (14,659)
Andrew, Christopher P...............4:25:33 (17,677)
Andrew, John Richard...............4:58:04 (25,980)
Andrew, Murray...............4:53:06 (24,822)
Andrew, Nicholas Paul...............3:57:19 (10,186)
Andrew, Peter James...............4:55:17 (25,378)
Andrewes, Freddie...............5:13:04 (28,763)
Andrews, Ben...............4:22:35 (16,868)
Andrews, Ben,...............4:26:58 (18,069)
Andrews, Benjamin D...............4:47:18 (23,366)
Andrews, Brent...............4:41:50 (21,980)
Andrews, Damian...............4:11:25 (13,824)
Andrews, David John...............3:52:55 (8,904)
Andrews, David L...............3:20:15 (2,984)
Andrews, Glen Hoddle...............3:53:10 (8,963)
Andrews, Ian...............5:52:56 (33,576)
Andrews, John William...............5:00:02 (26,463)
Andrews, Jonathan...............3:24:40 (3,533)
Andrews, Marc...............4:28:00 (18,365)
Andrews, Marcus Lloyd...............4:46:00 (23,024)
Andrews, Michael Jeffrey...............4:56:04 (25,551)
Andrews, Paul Dennis...............5:01:24 (26,733)
Andrews, Paul J...............3:17:34 (2,722)
Andrews, Robert...............7:40:44 (36,525)
Andrews, Steve...............4:14:56 (14,768)
Andrews, Tim...............3:41:14 (6,378)
Andrews, Tim...............4:31:33 (19,342)
Andrews, Toby Joseph William...3:28:57 (4,223)
Andrews, Walter C...............3:09:00 (1,809)
Andrews, Wayne Allen...............4:27:07 (18,127)
Andrews, Wayne George...............4:42:39 (22,168)
Angel, Jimeel T...............4:49:31 (23,911)
Angel, Robert...............3:34:40 (5,185)
Angell, Phil...............4:54:53 (25,279)
Angelopoulos, Panos...............3:51:04 (8,440)
Angless, John Murray...............3:15:04 (2,446)
Anglin, Morris Anthony...............5:53:50 (33,631)
Angus, Steve...............2:47:13 (393)
Anker, Guy...............4:50:10 (24,088)
Ankers, Stephen Allan...............4:18:14 (15,641)
Ankrah, Michael...............4:14:46 (14,732)
Anley, Brian John...............5:05:21 (27,424)
Annable, Jon...............4:40:14 (21,553)
Annand, Nathan...............4:58:09 (26,004)
Annis, Chris David...............4:07:54 (12,930)
Anrig, Marco...............3:44:16 (6,928)
Anscombe, Robert...............6:10:23 (34,679)
Ansell, Jake...............4:43:35 (22,391)
Ansell, Martin...............4:05:07 (12,230)
Anson, Steven Patrick...............5:33:29 (31,715)
Anstee, Nick J...............4:36:52 (20,704)
Anstiss, Lee...............4:51:44 (24,168)
Anstruther-Gough-Calthorpe, JR 5:13:03 (28,747)
Antell, Ally...............4:02:21 (11,565)
Anthony, Alasdair...............2:33:06 (91)

Anthony, Carl J 3:35:02 (5,254)
Anthony, Ian J 3:00:37 (1,182)
Anthony, James K 3:49:39 (8,134)
Anthony, Mark Noel 5:48:14 (33,166)
Anthony, Michael 4:16:06 (15,052)
Anthony, Michael John 3:17:29 (2,708)
Anthonypillai, Jonathan 5:25:45 (30,741)
Antoine, Kerjean 4:14:39 (14,700)
Antonin, Olivier 4:21:22 (16,513)
Antonio, Andrew 6:18:54 (35,077)
Anwar, Twana 5:34:50 (31,862)
Anwyl, Mathew 2:58:33 (1,010)
Anyiam, Seun 4:05:17 (12,281)
Anzalichi, Steve 4:53:12 (24,847)
Apiou-Goussau, Stephane 3:45:19 (7,167)
Apolloni, Renzo 3:15:38 (2,511)
Apostolakis, Andy 4:58:27 (26,078)
Appah, Andrew W 5:10:04 (28,251)
Apperley, Hugh C 3:42:08 (6,535)
Applebee, Matthew E 4:36:42 (20,659)
Appleby, Luke Phillip 4:30:38 (19,129)
Appleton, Michael A 2:48:18 (424)
Applewhite, Robert 3:36:49 (5,525)
Appleyard, Timothy R 3:54:33 (9,340)
Apps, Paul 3:58:00 (10,376)
Apps, Peter David 4:46:23 (23,146)
Aqeel, Uzair 5:36:14 (32,021)
Arai, Yoshihiro 4:06:14 (12,506)
Aram, Jim W 4:57:39 (25,896)
Aramayo, Michael 3:57:15 (10,172)
Aranburu, Jon 2:50:08 (490)
Aranda, Jaime 5:22:19 (30,194)
Araujo, Miguel 3:07:02 (1,612)
Arbouine, Leroy Anthony 5:35:32 (31,931)
Arbourne, Mark 5:47:34 (33,105)
Arbury, John 3:56:12 (9,841)
Arcasenza, Claudio 3:10:12 (1,923)
Archer, Andrew N 3:18:56 (2,864)
Archer, Christopher Andrew 5:10:13 (28,279)
Archer, Nick 3:54:09 (9,245)
Archer, Paul J 2:54:04 (675)
Archer, Simon 4:05:04 (12,223)
Archibald, Fraser 3:32:37 (4,831)
Archibald, Greig 5:26:21 (30,829)
Archibald, Matthew W 3:34:05 (5,074)
Arckless, Richard Ian 4:18:36 (15,744)
Arden, Peter 4:26:18 (17,900)
Arden-Brown, Clive 3:55:32 (9,621)
Ardin, James C 2:50:45 (517)
Arding, Matt 5:24:12 (30,510)
Arding, Paul 5:58:12 (33,945)
Ardissone, Davide 3:58:35 (10,590)
Ardron, David 4:38:26 (21,099)
Arena, Bartolo 3:37:32 (5,673)
Argent, Stephen 6:11:35 (34,728)
Argyle, Edward W 3:46:25 (7,402)
Argyle, Neil Anthony 4:13:25 (14,345)
Ariyo, Femi 4:12:04 (14,000)
Arkell, Robin Jeffrey 3:49:53 (8,184)
Arkinstall, Ivan Paul 4:03:20 (11,809)
Arkley, Kevin 5:46:38 (33,019)
Arliguie, Francis 3:42:59 (6,695)
Armand, Gabriel 5:25:06 (30,640)
Armenia, Fabrizio 4:18:41 (15,769)
Armitage, Andrew Richard 4:44:08 (22,541)
Armitage, Chris 6:52:16 (36,054)
Armitage, James 4:34:10 (20,030)
Armitage, Mark E 3:30:52 (4,560)
Armitage, Mark Marius 5:07:32 (27,819)
Armour, Robert James 4:48:49 (23,754)
Armour, William 4:48:23 (23,634)
Armson, Mick 4:07:35 (12,853)
Armstrong, Alex 2:58:13 (980)
Armstrong, Benjamin Joshua 4:51:06 (24,333)
Armstrong, David 4:01:53 (11,466)
Armstrong, Gary 4:44:45 (22,712)
Armstrong, James Ralph Fenwick 4:05:57 (12,445)
Armstrong, John Paul 4:38:52 (21,223)
Armstrong, Mark 3:04:31 (1,435)
Armstrong, Nigel J 3:03:42 (1,363)
Armstrong, Robert J 3:16:15 (2,581)
Armstrong, Thomas 4:49:56 (24,037)
Arnaiz, Gustavo 4:29:50 (18,920)
Arnel, Richard 4:40:44 (21,708)
Arnesen, Sven Gjermund 4:15:19 (14,865)
Arnold, Andy 3:55:39 (9,661)
Arnold, Carl John 4:39:18 (21,329)
Arnold, David 3:29:34 (4,334)
Arnold, Edward 3:54:05 (9,231)
Arnold, James 4:48:20 (23,616)
Arnold, John J 3:49:57 (8,199)
Arnold, Mark J 3:26:44 (3,836)
Arnold, Martin Robert 4:45:12 (22,820)
Arnold, Nick 4:35:47 (20,417)
Arnold, Olie 3:58:25 (10,532)
Arnold, Paul A 5:40:36 (32,443)
Arnold, Paul R 3:54:42 (9,387)
Arnold, Phil Joseph 5:09:43 (28,184)
Arnold, Robert Lewis 6:10:31 (34,683)
Arnott, David Masterton 3:43:49 (6,835)
Arnott, Rob 6:23:15 (35,247)
Arnott, Ross 3:55:11 (9,523)
Arnott, Stuart 6:23:15 (35,247)
Arnst, Jonathon 3:51:03 (8,435)
Aronld, Bill 3:26:34 (3,808)
Arrand, Gary John 4:09:55 (13,448)
Arrol, Mark 3:47:14 (7,583)
Arrowsmith, Jonathan 3:53:44 (9,132)
Arslan, Tanju 5:31:02 (31,420)
Art, Az 4:16:13 (15,079)
Arthur, Kevin John 4:17:22 (15,396)
Arthurton, Roy 4:41:42 (21,941)
Artist, Steven 3:13:41 (2,281)
Artus, Tim 2:44:55 (338)
Arundale, Jonathan 4:42:38 (22,163)
Arundel, Stuart Thomas 3:35:23 (5,300)
Arvidsson, Martin 5:19:24 (29,761)
Asboe Christensen, Anders 2:36:26 (136)
Asbury, Shane A 3:42:36 (6,609)
Ascough, James Michael 5:35:58 (31,989)
Ash, Benjamin Robert 4:20:36 (16,297)
Ash, Chris 4:17:35 (15,464)
Ash, Scott Lee 5:15:37 (29,166)
Ashburner, David A 3:50:58 (8,414)
Ashby, Gareth J 5:36:41 (32,072)
Ashby, Gerald 5:30:36 (31,372)
Ashby, Jonathan 4:56:32 (25,658)
Ashby, Mark 2:54:30 (701)
Ashby, Mike J 2:51:59 (565)
Ashby, Neil 4:32:54 (19,673)
Ashby, Sean Russell 5:22:30 (30,220)
Ashby, Tom 3:15:35 (2,510)
Ashdown, Jeremy Charles 5:47:43 (33,117)
Ashdown, Roger William 5:48:26 (33,187)
Ashe, Gary J 3:14:32 (2,387)
Asher, Christopher 4:26:35 (17,977)
Asher, Darren 4:03:21 (11,813)
Asher, Mark P 3:37:31 (5,666)
Ashford, Christopher Andrew 2:55:57 (798)
Ashford, Paul 4:14:11 (14,566)
Ashforth, Richard 3:51:58 (8,649)
Ashington, Jamie 6:47:05 (35,951)
Ashley, Gregory Robert 3:20:23 (3,002)
Ashley, Philip John 4:50:13 (24,096)
Ashley, Scott 6:16:42 (34,961)
Ashley, Stuart Robin 4:48:22 (23,627)
Ashman, Rod James 5:47:19 (33,079)
Ashmead, Matthew 3:53:14 (8,979)
Ashmore, Mark A 3:53:53 (9,177)
Ashmore, Matthew Alan 6:47:46 (35,960)
Ashmore, Michael Alan 3:42:27 (6,587)
Ashover, John R 4:00:33 (11,126)
Ashton, Carl 3:47:15 (7,586)
Ashton, Edward 4:25:34 (17,681)
Ashton, Paul 3:20:53 (3,068)
Ashton, Richard Michael 3:52:02 (8,667)
Ashton-Rigby, Mark 3:51:43 (8,592)
Ashurst, Clive 3:01:35 (1,234)
Ashworth, Anthony N 2:59:06 (1,064)
Ashworth, David Martin 3:19:26 (2,910)
Ashworth, Jonathan D 3:29:06 (4,250)
Ashworth, Mike I 4:14:38 (14,696)
Ashworth, Robert J 5:17:40 (29,492)
Ashworth, Tim 4:25:53 (17,783)
Asiedu, Eric K 4:05:24 (12,313)
Askari, Kareem Charles 4:16:12 (15,071)
Asker, James 4:42:38 (22,163)
Askew, Jamie 3:17:28 (2,705)
Askew, Jeffrey Michael 5:24:00 (30,481)
Askew, Peter Nicholas 5:10:55 (28,395)

Askew, Ryan 5:06:32 (27,635)

My dad has completed eight London Marathons since 1995. Through his running he has raised over £30,000 for charity. Seeing him run over Tower Bridge and down Birdcage Walk made me really proud! My dad is my inspiration and in 2010 I took over the family tradition and completed my first London Marathon!

Askham, James Robert 4:21:00 (16,412)
Aspel, Ed 5:10:54 (28,393)
Aspinall, David 5:20:24 (29,905)
Aspinall, Dean Phillip 5:04:09 (27,221)
Aspinall, Nathan E 2:40:41 (218)
Aspinall, Nicholas 5:22:13 (30,177)
Aspinall, Steve 4:21:32 (16,556)
Aspinall, Steven William 6:01:54 (34,181)
Asquier, Thierry 4:40:08 (21,518)
Asseo, David 3:40:29 (6,235)
Asser, Jeffrey D 3:02:32 (1,303)
Asten, Mark 4:12:46 (14,176)
Astill, Bryan 2:54:38 (711)
Astin, Gavin R 2:50:44 (515)
Astin, Stephen 2:57:26 (894)
Astley, Oliver Paul 4:30:27 (19,075)
Astley, Steven David 5:34:38 (31,841)
Aston, Andrew 3:07:25 (1,644)
Aston, Ben 4:21:49 (16,643)
Aston, Darran 3:14:44 (2,412)
Aston, David 4:51:31 (24,423)
Aston, Edgar 3:34:27 (5,144)
Aston, Jeffrey R 4:18:34 (15,732)
Aston, Matthew Daniel 6:16:55 (34,971)
Astruc, Michel 4:16:41 (15,215)
Astruc, Olivier 4:16:42 (15,222)
Asua, Juan 4:07:29 (12,826)
Atfield, Peter J 5:26:31 (30,843)
Atherton, James 6:51:56 (36,039)
Atherton, Joe James 3:35:39 (5,353)
Atherton, Mark R 4:24:48 (17,468)
Athorn, Daniel 4:33:37 (19,897)
Athreya, Kannan 3:53:23 (9,024)
Atkin, Kevin Charles 5:32:22 (31,583)
Atkins, Colin James 4:09:21 (13,296)
Atkins, Craig George 4:36:35 (20,625)
Atkins, David John 4:02:08 (11,518)
Atkins, Ed A.J 4:33:12 (19,767)
Atkins, Gary J 4:47:46 (23,483)
Atkins, Jason 5:05:24 (27,431)
Atkins, Jeff 5:43:33 (32,724)
Atkins, Richard D 3:42:39 (6,624)
Atkinson, Adam E 5:06:41 (27,667)
Atkinson, Charles 4:57:40 (25,901)
Atkinson, David 4:05:29 (12,331)
Atkinson, James 4:45:20 (22,849)
Atkinson, Jason 3:12:02 (2,094)
Atkinson, John 3:04:06 (1,401)
Atkinson, Jonathan David 4:16:39 (15,204)
Atkinson, Lewis 5:00:48 (26,613)
Atkinson, Nathan John 3:28:03 (4,063)
Atkinson, Peter R 3:24:50 (3,554)
Atkinson, Stephen M 3:45:10 (7,132)
Atkinson, Stephen 3:51:06 (8,450)
Atkinson, Tim 4:52:34 (24,701)
Attalia, Hardip 5:18:23 (29,605)
Attar, Joel 4:37:59 (20,985)
Attard, Martin 5:31:58 (31,532)
Attelsey, Philip John 4:35:29 (20,343)
Attoe, Gerry 4:40:11 (21,533)
Attree, Mark Christopher 5:29:33 (31,228)
Attryde, Nik 5:08:00 (27,895)
Attwell, Timothy L 3:46:43 (7,464)
Attwood, Anthony Norman 6:10:49 (34,692)
Attwood, Howard Martin 4:28:20 (18,465)
Attwood, Mark John 4:16:18 (15,106)

Atwell, Steven 5:37:52 (32,195)
Audas, Allen 3:33:42 (5,006)
Audenshaw, Tony 3:13:30 (2,255)
Audis, Gilles 4:38:15 (21,041)
Audu, Joshua 5:59:50 (34,049)
Audu, Serge 2:57:11 (868)
Auer, Andreas 4:50:08 (24,078)
Augeri, John-Paul 4:02:24 (11,580)
Auld, William 4:46:35 (23,193)
Ault, Colin 4:27:06 (18,120)
Auray, Marcel 5:37:19 (32,146)
Aust, Nicholas Charles Vincent 4:47:20 (23,374)
Austerberry, Gareth G 4:02:06 (11,513)
Austin, Andrew Christopher 4:30:39 (19,135)
Austin, Andrew N 4:00:44 (11,179)
Austin, Anthony 5:09:12 (28,086)
Austin, Ben 5:09:22 (28,120)
Austin, Craig 5:24:11 (30,508)
Austin, Elliot 4:38:56 (21,241)
Austin, Frederick Henry 3:52:30 (8,796)
Austin, Gerald Patrick 3:18:48 (2,851)
Austin, James 4:11:30 (13,848)
Austin, Jonathan L 5:03:19 (27,076)
Austin, Melvyn Rodney 4:10:17 (13,545)
Austin, Peter R 4:16:17 (15,099)
Autie, Sam 4:48:34 (23,686)
Auty, Simon 4:26:32 (17,967)
Auville, Jean-François 3:30:53 (4,563)
Avau, Benoit 4:23:21 (17,060)
Avenell, Keith Antony 5:03:32 (27,108)
Avener, Daniel 5:32:10 (31,559)
Avery, David Stephen 4:05:18 (12,283)
Avery, Gary Andrew 4:51:12 (24,351)
Avery, Joe A 6:50:07 (35,998)
Avery, Philip Nicholas 4:32:53 (19,669)
Aves, Clayton A 3:19:17 (2,893)
Avis, Peter 5:21:51 (30,122)
Avison, Matthew Francis 4:16:23 (15,135)
Avondoglio, Dan 3:38:36 (5,869)
Awal, Danyal 4:26:23 (17,923)
Awan, Barry 3:12:40 (2,151)
Awbery, Nicholas M 2:43:58 (305)
Awofolaju, Tunde 5:41:46 (32,561)
Axon, Craig Paul 4:31:12 (19,272)
Axon, Kristopher R 2:54:46 (720)
Axon, Terry 4:04:59 (12,200)
Axson, Peter 5:07:05 (27,739)
Axtell, Graham C 5:19:01 (29,703)
Ayers, Jamie 3:55:00 (9,479)
Aylett, Nick 5:30:23 (31,333)
Ayliffe, James 4:06:12 (12,496)
Ayliffe, Neil 3:31:18 (4,626)
Ayling, Alex 4:07:07 (12,735)
Ayling, David J 4:49:13 (23,852)
Aylmore, James R 3:14:01 (2,322)
Aylott, Paul J 5:21:28 (30,072)
Aymard, Stephane 4:42:06 (22,037)
Aymon, Jean Claude 2:48:49 (437)
Ayres, James 3:45:17 (7,159)
Ayres, Jon H 3:24:45 (3,545)
Ayres, Keith Anthony 3:57:59 (10,373)
Ayres, Richard 4:14:28 (14,637)
Ayshford-Sanford, Crispin 4:11:29 (13,844)
Azzam, Mahmoud 3:58:37 (10,598)
Azzano, Bruno 3:04:21 (1,418)
Azzopardi, Malcolm John 3:29:55 (4,403)
Baba, Michael 3:06:10 (1,545)
Babb, Stephen 4:11:55 (13,966)
Babb, Steven M 2:51:29 (544)
Babbage, Matthew 4:01:33 (11,383)
Babcock-Lumish, Brian 3:45:39 (7,241)
Babeau, Jean Luc 4:24:18 (17,319)
Baber, Barnaby Edward Geoffrey 5:20:28 (29,919)
Babinet, Luke 4:09:04 (13,224)
Babington, Duncan Johm 3:34:16 (5,106)
Babynec, Wayne A 4:23:58 (17,229)
Bacchoo, Damian 4:20:27 (16,248)
Bacci, Antonio 2:58:01 (958)
Baccolini, Massimo 3:51:14 (8,482)
Bach, Alisdair E 5:20:12 (29,877)
Bachler, Steve 4:09:58 (13,463)
Bachmann, Ralf 4:20:18 (16,200)
Bachmann, Winfried 4:16:36 (15,192)
Bachu, Abdalla 3:07:07 (1,620)
Baci, Perparim 4:32:33 (19,572)
Backhouse, Ian 5:04:41 (27,315)
Backhouse, Oliver 5:59:40 (34,030)
Backhouse, Roger Charles Francis 5:59:40 (34,030)
Bacon, Christopher J 2:47:14 (396)
Bacon, Ellis James 3:52:22 (8,761)
Bacon, Guy 3:35:58 (5,407)
Bacon, John 5:01:45 (26,808)
Bacon, Lawrence Francis 4:48:43 (23,728)
Bacon, Richard Jim 3:59:47 (10,942)
Bacon, Roger Philip 3:38:28 (5,839)
Badcock, David 3:58:23 (10,517)
Badcock, Mark 3:51:08 (8,456)
Badcock, Matthew James 3:49:55 (8,191)
Badcott, Mike 4:38:21 (21,071)
Badcott, Nicholas 3:54:58 (9,468)
Baddiley, Stuart 5:12:18 (28,620)
Badero, Paolo 3:18:56 (2,864)
Badger, Jonathan 3:06:52 (1,598)
Badr, Ishmail 3:11:50 (2,079)
Badrock, Bruce 3:29:56 (4,406)
Badyal, Jaspal 5:19:24 (29,761)
Bagdady, Lee Daniel 5:54:20 (33,667)
Bage, Simon Lloyd 4:28:46 (18,598)
Bage, Steven 3:13:49 (2,297)
Baggaley, Clive R 3:43:04 (6,712)
Baggott, Michael Lee 3:26:37 (3,820)
Baggs, Stewart 5:32:57 (31,657)
Bagheri, Siamack 4:05:14 (12,263)
Baginsky, Chris Robert 4:42:47 (22,208)
Bagley, David 5:14:39 (29,011)
Bagley, James 4:08:20 (13,036)
Bagnall, Graeme 4:11:13 (13,771)
Bagshaw, Andrew Geoffrey 5:20:33 (29,937)
Bagshaw, Martin 4:37:37 (20,910)
Bagust, Jonathan Scott 3:56:39 (9,978)
Bagwell, David John 4:36:37 (20,637)
Baigent, Tim George 5:01:25 (26,738)
Bailey, Adrian J 4:08:36 (13,117)
Bailey, Andrew 4:25:21 (17,619)
Bailey, Andrew Nicholas 4:38:57 (21,244)
Bailey, Chris Richard 4:03:24 (11,820)
Bailey, Conan 4:59:07 (26,242)
Bailey, Daniel R 5:56:46 (33,848)
Bailey, Devan 6:41:46 (35,828)
Bailey, Edmund 3:10:59 (1,992)
Bailey, Henry 3:55:56 (9,760)
Bailey, Ian 2:53:16 (627)
Bailey, Ian M 5:04:49 (27,334)
Bailey, Jason 3:30:30 (4,499)
Bailey, Jonathan Andrew 4:31:00 (19,216)
Bailey, Kevin J 5:09:31 (28,153)
Bailey, Lee 3:47:18 (7,600)
Bailey, Lee 6:51:56 (36,039)
Bailey, Mark James 4:33:13 (19,772)
Bailey, Michael Edward 4:47:57 (23,535)
Bailey, Mike 3:56:37 (9,964)
Bailey, Nicholas 5:23:16 (30,349)
Bailey, Oliver 3:39:52 (6,119)
Bailey, Peter John 4:41:27 (21,878)
Bailey, Ross 3:31:07 (4,598)
Bailey, Russell 3:44:39 (7,024)
Bailey, Scott Edward Joseph 4:04:38 (12,111)
Bailey, Simon 5:58:46 (33,976)
Bailey, Simon R 3:44:19 (6,942)
Bailey, Steve 4:00:28 (11,111)
Baileyt, David A 3:47:26 (7,628)
Bailey-Wood, Colin M 3:13:41 (2,281)
Baillie, Jason Douglas 5:21:37 (30,098)
Baillie, Scott 4:36:54 (20,715)
Baillie, Steve 3:45:55 (7,290)
Baillie,, Ben, 3:44:46 (7,047)
Bailliere, Dirk 4:08:35 (13,111)
Bainbridge, Barry Alun 4:16:46 (15,239)
Bainbridge, James L 3:36:36 (5,496)
Bainbridge, Lee 5:49:37 (33,294)
Baines, Declan 5:35:05 (31,887)
Baines, Ian 3:45:38 (7,235)
Baines, Ian 6:14:05 (34,840)
Baines, Lee Adam 4:36:04 (20,495)
Baines, Michael Stephen 5:04:57 (27,355)
Baines, Thomas 6:39:50 (35,779)
Bainger, Graham E 4:14:22 (14,607)
Bains, Binderpal Singh 5:09:47 (28,193)
Bains, Chris 4:28:25 (18,494)
Bains, Jagdeep Singh 4:03:59 (11,956)
Bains, Shamsher 4:32:10 (19,476)
Baird, Gordon J 3:33:10 (4,921)
Baird, Stuart 3:57:46 (10,318)
Bairstow, Dale C 5:04:03 (27,197)
Baker, Adam 4:41:59 (22,012)
Baker, Alex George 4:12:27 (14,083)
Baker, Andrew J 4:59:25 (26,318)
Baker, Andy 6:12:16 (34,772)
Baker, Christopher David 4:16:51 (15,257)
Baker, Craig 4:09:12 (13,260)
Baker, Darren P 5:14:47 (29,032)
Baker, David John 7:14:27 (36,358)
Baker, David William 3:56:40 (9,984)
Baker, Gareth D 5:04:59 (27,363)
Baker, Geoff 4:14:32 (14,659)
Baker, Geoff 4:29:43 (18,888)
Baker, Ian 4:03:52 (11,940)
Baker, Ian Mark 3:00:55 (1,202)
Baker, Jamie 4:46:49 (23,259)
Baker, Jimmy P 4:52:03 (24,558)
Baker, Joel 4:39:02 (21,266)
Baker, Jonathan Paul 4:24:13 (17,291)
Baker, Karl 4:26:31 (17,961)
Baker, Les Michael 4:52:37 (24,710)
Baker, Marcus James 5:24:05 (30,490)
Baker, Mark 3:36:50 (5,532)
Baker, Martin 4:05:24 (12,313)
Baker, Matt John 4:49:46 (24,001)
Baker, Matthew 5:03:39 (27,127)
Baker, Matthew Duncan 4:00:37 (11,145)
Baker, Nicholas 4:03:13 (11,781)
Baker, Nicholas 4:37:25 (20,850)
Baker, Nick M 2:37:38 (154)
Baker, Paul William 5:55:43 (33,770)
Baker, Richard P 5:08:46 (28,011)
Baker, Robert J 2:26:58 (47)
Baker, Sam Stephen 4:32:55 (19,677)
Baker, Simon D 4:13:35 (14,398)
Baker, Steve D 3:27:51 (4,025)
Baker, Terry 4:09:16 (13,274)
Baker, Terry R 5:01:11 (26,678)
Baker, Tom 3:02:19 (1,282)
Baker-Heyes, Philip 4:02:10 (11,529)
Bakes, Wayne 5:32:52 (31,649)
Bakovic, Srdjan 3:51:37 (8,571)
Bakrania, Mehul 4:02:33 (11,616)
Balback, Stephen 4:16:52 (15,261)
Balcombe, Michael J 4:19:16 (15,920)
Baldan, Mauro 3:04:21 (1,418)
Balding, Kevin 4:01:11 (11,294)
Baldini, Alessandro 4:16:56 (15,282)
Baldock, Andrew James 4:11:36 (13,883)
Baldock, Andrew N 3:50:17 (8,268)
Baldock, Graham 5:45:17 (32,892)
Baldock, John 4:27:03 (18,097)
Baldry, Vic 4:16:51 (15,257)
Baldwin, Andrew David 6:34:19 (35,632)
Baldwin, David Paul 6:22:57 (35,235)
Baldwin, Gary Philip 5:32:16 (31,570)
Baldwin, James Antony 3:38:07 (5,785)
Baldwin, Kelvin James 3:56:49 (10,036)
Baldwin, Mark E 4:45:40 (22,940)
Baldwin, Matthew Robert 5:11:02 (28,410)
Baldwin, Nick Robert 3:52:52 (8,890)
Baldwin, Phil Andrew 5:29:22 (31,207)
Baldwin, Richard 5:35:15 (31,898)
Baldwin, Roy 5:17:13 (29,421)
Baldwin, William 4:49:33 (23,922)
Bale, Mons 3:09:21 (1,840)
Bale, Simon M 3:15:23 (2,484)
Bales, Bob 5:13:17 (28,815)
Balfour, Kevin 3:43:55 (6,861)
Ball, Andrew J 4:15:51 (14,987)
Ball, Anthony 4:33:00 (19,698)
Ball, Brian David 5:14:48 (29,036)
Ball, Chris 4:42:10 (22,053)
Ball, Graham 3:16:51 (2,656)
Ball, Jason Kenneth 3:20:22 (2,999)
Ball, John R 4:27:19 (18,187)

Ball, Lance I 4:07:56 (12,940)
Ball, Leon (Bobby) 4:46:35 (23,193)
Ball, Martin..................3:52:07 (8,682)
Ball, Matt 4:12:38 (14,132)
Ball, Michael William 5:08:29 (27,972)
Ball, Neil Thomas.............4:55:39 (25,447)
Ball, Nicholas A 3:17:17 (2,692)
Ball, Nick A 3:58:21 (10,512)
Ball, Oliver James 4:31:30 (19,334)
Ball, Pete 4:24:10 (17,279)
Ball, Robin Gordon............4:25:49 (17,760)
Ball, Steven J 4:11:02 (13,726)
Ball, Tim 3:58:31 (10,560)
Ballantine, Robert Keith......5:36:58 (32,098)
Ballard, Andrew Lloyd.........4:30:23 (19,061)
Ballard, George 3:35:47 (5,374)
Ballard, Martin David 4:55:36 (25,437)
Ballard, Michael 4:55:01 (25,310)
Ballard, Nigel William........5:26:55 (30,894)
Ballard, William 3:52:58 (8,911)
Ballard, William F 5:16:52 (29,367)
Baller, Steve 4:14:36 (14,680)
Balls, David 4:11:27 (13,835)
Balmer, Martin Howard.........4:50:37 (24,187)
Balmer, Martin Roger..........5:27:47 (31,000)
Balmforth, John Philip 5:26:51 (30,880)
Balsar, David 5:15:45 (29,188)
Balshaw, Richard J............2:56:47 (845)
Balsiger, Olivier 3:57:37 (10,268)
Balto, Jan Helge 3:12:39 (2,150)
Bamber, Ian J.................2:58:52 (1,032)
Bambury, Bernard..............5:58:46 (33,976)
Bamford, Ian 3:51:53 (8,632)
Bamford, James Edward 4:07:05 (12,730)
Bamford, Mark 4:01:46 (11,439)
Bamford, Paul Andrew 3:42:33 (6,605)
Bamford, Steven Paul 5:43:49 (32,756)
Bamforth, Gary Luke 4:39:00 (21,258)
Bamforth, John Richard........3:57:51 (10,345)
Bamforth, Peter...............4:03:05 (11,748)
Bamsey, Robert W 3:37:40 (5,703)
Ban, Andrew 4:28:28 (18,512)
Banbury, Kelvin Peter 3:07:34 (1,660)
Banbury, Neil A 3:29:03 (4,238)
Bancroft, Andrew J............4:05:58 (12,453)
Bancroft, Tom 4:46:42 (23,232)
Banfi, Michael J..............3:28:42 (4,173)
Banfield, Alistair 3:49:43 (8,150)
Bangani, Pumlani..............2:36:57 (142)
Bangert, Alexander J..........3:47:54 (7,717)
Bangert, Lee 5:17:20 (29,445)
Banim, Ivor M 3:52:26 (8,772)
Banin, Daniel 4:16:09 (15,060)
Bankier, Alistair 4:38:28 (21,110)
Banks, Charles 4:49:49 (24,013)
Banks, Chris Geoffrey 4:53:06 (24,822)
Banks, Edward 2:44:54 (337)
Banks, Glen 4:28:30 (18,521)
Banks, Martin 4:56:03 (25,548)
Banks, Neale Thomas 4:43:12 (22,302)
Banks, Neil...................5:47:22 (33,086)
Banks, Nick Woodgate 4:47:16 (23,355)
Banks, Paul Daniel 3:59:45 (10,932)
Banks, Simon 4:23:34 (17,125)
Banks, Wayne P 4:16:05 (15,047)
Banner, Charles...............3:07:40 (1,674)
Bannister, Adam 6:40:02 (35,787)
Bannister, Clive 4:19:43 (16,019)
Bannister, Daniel 3:48:57 (7,962)
Bannister, Nick 4:21:53 (16,664)
Bannister, Peter D 3:25:19 (3,618)
Bannister, Ross 4:45:48 (22,979)
Bansback, Michael J...........4:45:15 (22,828)
Banwell, Mark David 5:36:57 (32,094)
Banyard, Ashley 4:18:59 (15,847)
Baptista-Goncalves, Rui M 3:51:27 (8,531)
Baranda Molina, Alvaro........4:24:41 (17,440)
Baransky, Patrick 3:28:24 (4,126)
Baratte Du Vignaud, Gabriel...4:48:55 (23,776)
Barazzuol, Andrea.............3:32:38 (4,835)
Barbato, Dario................4:25:55 (17,790)
Barbato, Tom..................4:42:39 (22,168)
Barbay, Olivier...............4:11:14 (13,776)

Barber, Ashley Thomas..........4:09:44 (13,401)
Barber, Blythe Allan Douglas ...4:28:10 (18,406)
Barber, Daniel JP..............3:12:38 (2,149)
Barber, Harry..................3:06:22 (1,560)
Barber, Nick J.................4:15:46 (14,973)
Barber, Phil Alan 3:56:16 (9,861)
Barber, Phil Andrew............3:38:54 (5,920)
Barber, Robert David 3:32:24 (4,801)
Barber, Thomas.................5:34:35 (31,833)
Barber, Thomas Ian James.......4:21:37 (16,583)
Barber, Tim....................4:04:14 (12,016)
Barber, Timothy T..............5:12:44 (28,689)
Barberis Negra, Nicola.........2:59:24 (1,095)
Barbet, Guillaume..............4:37:10 (20,786)
Barbet, Matt...................4:12:06 (14,008)
Barboteau, Laurent.............5:08:43 (28,007)
Barbour, Iain 5:39:20 (32,336)
Barcaioni, Marco...............3:37:17 (5,614)
Barclay, David 4:04:25 (12,058)
Barclay, Simon 3:34:03 (5,068)
Barclay, Steven James..........3:50:46 (8,375)
Barden, Daniel 5:21:33 (30,083)
Bardey, Joe....................4:53:37 (24,947)
Bardsley, Adam 2:39:39 (187)
Bardsley, Malcolm T............3:20:24 (3,007)
Bardsley, Richard L............6:59:00 (36,176)
Bareham, Iain 3:29:23 (4,299)
Bareham, Ian...................4:28:42 (18,581)
Barette, Paul 3:52:31 (8,801)
Barff, Rob Alan 4:04:18 (12,029)
Barfield, James Anthony........4:49:26 (23,903)
Barham, Andrew 4:53:40 (24,961)
Barham, Darren 3:46:19 (7,378)
Baric, Nicolas.................2:54:34 (705)
Bark, Nick.....................3:49:36 (8,115)
Barke, Christopher 5:37:07 (32,118)
Barker, Carl Andrew 3:33:47 (5,020)
Barker, Dave Sharky............6:43:42 (35,877)
Barker, David S 5:01:42 (26,792)
Barker, Ed.....................4:56:13 (25,589)
Barker, Edward P...............2:59:15 (1,078)
Barker, Ernest.................5:40:41 (32,451)
Barker, Gavin John 4:51:52 (24,511)
Barker, Jeff...................3:56:49 (10,036)
Barker, Julian 4:54:19 (25,137)
Barker, Martin Richard.........6:01:54 (34,181)
Barker, Michael David 4:05:23 (12,303)
Barker, Nicholas Robert Lueders 5:16:48 (29,352)
Barker, Paul Sydney 4:23:21 (17,060)
Barker, Ralph..................3:17:25 (2,699)
Barker, Robert Ivor 3:45:44 (7,255)
Barker, Sean J.................3:11:09 (2,012)
Barker, Stuart Charles.........4:28:19 (18,458)
Barker, Tom A P................3:35:00 (5,249)
Barker, William J..............5:21:04 (30,012)
Barker Platt, Daniel...........5:26:43 (30,865)
Barkes, Benjamin Rogerson 3:01:21 (1,221)
Barkes, Jonathan Stuart........3:41:21 (6,395)
Barkman, Mårten................2:55:31 (772)
Barkway, Symon P 4:39:48 (21,462)
Barley, Alasdair 4:37:27 (20,866)
Barley, Clive 5:14:34 (28,998)
Barlow, Ben....................5:21:20 (30,049)
Barlow, Chris 4:23:50 (17,196)
Barlow, Dave John 4:07:52 (12,924)
Barlow, Gerald A 4:16:25 (15,147)
Barlow, Graham S...............3:27:35 (3,976)
Barlow, Lee....................2:57:35 (913)
Barlow, Mike...................4:12:06 (14,008)
Barlow, Nicholas...............4:15:26 (14,893)
Barlow, Paul...................3:41:41 (6,455)
Barlow, Roger 3:58:59 (10,718)
Barlow, Simon R................3:26:34 (3,808)
Barlow, Stephen T..............4:03:30 (11,844)
Barnard, Adam A 3:35:58 (5,407)
Barnard, Gawain 4:17:37 (15,473)
Barnard, Gordon................6:19:15 (35,093)
Barnard, James 4:21:37 (16,506)
Barnard, Luke 5:32:48 (31,639)
Barnard, Nigel Anthony 4:19:05 (15,869)
Barnatt, Stephane 4:50:13 (24,096)
Barnert, Paul 3:52:48 (8,870)
Barnes, Adrian Mark............4:14:22 (14,607)

Barnes, Alastair Clive 5:06:26 (27,612)
Barnes, Aron...................3:52:31 (8,801)
Barnes, Brian M 4:43:01 (22,263)
Barnes, Chris J H..............3:47:30 (7,647)
Barnes, Christopher 3:31:17 (4,624)
Barnes, Christopher Michael ...3:29:28 (4,315)
Barnes, Clinton Carl 3:42:21 (6,570)
Barnes, Daniel Leslie 5:16:31 (29,312)
Barnes, Darren 3:52:56 (8,908)
Barnes, David 3:56:43 (10,003)
Barnes, David John 3:48:44 (7,909)
Barnes, David John 5:09:11 (28,083)
Barnes, Delroy Alfred 3:59:26 (10,848)
Barnes, Garry..................4:41:40 (21,937)
Barnes, Graeme Richard 3:26:45 (3,838)
Barnes, James 3:29:24 (4,302)
Barnes, Jim 4:59:13 (26,267)
Barnes, Jody 5:24:41 (30,579)
Barnes, Kevin Jonathan 5:33:24 (31,706)
Barnes, Lee 3:58:48 (10,661)
Barnes, Michael David 4:44:26 (22,626)
Barnes, Mick B 3:28:52 (4,200)
Barnes, Nigel 4:50:20 (24,123)
Barnes, Nigel Anthony 4:31:07 (19,245)
Barnes, Oliver Jason...........4:10:58 (13,703)
Barnes, Peter D 4:20:31 (16,265)
Barnes, Richard A 5:01:43 (26,800)
Barnes, Roy J 4:04:14 (12,016)
Barnes, Simon Andrew 4:46:02 (23,037)
Barnes, Simon Paul 3:05:35 (1,505)
Barnes, Stephen Stannard 4:42:21 (22,105)
Barnett, Ed Guy................4:49:35 (23,937)
Barnett, Ian Charles 4:29:41 (18,875)
Barnett, Jonathan R 3:34:21 (5,129)
Barnett, Matthew A 5:53:10 (33,588)
Barnett, Nicholas J 3:51:36 (8,567)
Barney, Steve 4:44:18 (22,591)
Barnfather, Simon 3:01:56 (1,252)
Barnfield, David Graham........4:43:55 (22,481)
Barns, Steven 4:52:37 (24,710)
Baron, Gary 7:02:38 (36,222)
Baron, Gerald James 3:55:44 (9,688)
Baron, Jonathan Joseph 3:54:30 (9,328)
Baroni, Adolfo 3:35:54 (5,399)
Barquero, José Manuel 3:07:28 (1,650)
Barr, David 4:52:50 (24,764)
Barr, David A 3:10:36 (1,954)
Barr, Graham 3:45:43 (7,249)
Barr, James Douglas 3:57:34 (10,253)
Barr, Jonathan 5:01:18 (26,709)
Barr, Robert David 3:46:13 (7,357)
Barr, Roger M 2:47:04 (389)
Barr, Samuel 5:01:17 (26,703)
Barr, Tom 3:48:09 (7,778)
Barraclough, Paul 4:37:12 (20,795)
Barradell, Adrian Paul 4:09:30 (13,341)
Barran, Nick 4:23:21 (17,060)
Barrance, Tony Robert..........5:14:03 (28,930)
Barrand, Drew 4:08:06 (12,989)
Barratt, Colin Stuart..........3:40:25 (6,217)
Barratt, Damian Luke 4:34:16 (20,062)
Barratt, Stephen Ellis 4:44:36 (22,670)
Barratt, Trevor J..............5:24:07 (30,498)
Barre, Armand 3:55:48 (9,719)
Barre, Thierry.................3:59:17 (10,808)
Barrell, Andrew P 4:48:03 (23,557)
Barrett, Alan 3:50:55 (8,404)
Barrett, Chris 4:09:19 (13,288)
Barrett, Craig Andrew 4:25:01 (17,524)
Barrett, Giles Peter...........3:41:05 (6,337)
Barrett, Gregg S 3:55:20 (9,571)
Barrett, Ian 3:44:10 (6,909)
Barrett, Jason 4:03:25 (11,823)
Barrett, John Douglas 4:56:16 (25,601)
Barrett, Jonathan Paul 4:25:39 (17,701)
Barrett, Michael 3:34:17 (5,111)
Barrett, Michael 3:38:07 (5,785)
Barrett, Michael J 4:16:39 (15,204)
Barrett, Nick 4:43:54 (22,479)
Barrett, Patrick A 3:32:18 (4,788)
Barrett, Peter 3:20:27 (3,012)
Barrett, Richard Younger.......3:32:35 (4,823)
Barrett, Sean 4:34:19 (20,074)

Barrett, Stephen 3:57:55 (10,359)
Barrett, Thomas 3:29:29 (4,317)
Barretto-Ko, Percival 4:27:44 (18,295)
Barrie, Allan G 2:47:30 (402)
Barrie, John 4:36:21 (20,562)
Barrie, Martin J 5:07:26 (27,793)
Barrington, Harvey John Duke 4:45:37 (22,919)
Barrington, Steve 4:21:22 (16,513)
Barron, Daniel 4:03:35 (11,868)
Barron, Duncan S 4:52:37 (24,710)
Barron, Jeremy Daniel 4:26:15 (17,893)
Barron, Paul J 4:36:20 (20,554)
Barron, Phil 4:37:52 (20,959)
Barrow, Edmond Oneal 3:09:09 (1,820)
Barrowcliffe, Craig James 4:33:56 (19,977)
Barrows, Darren J 3:34:57 (5,240)
Barr-Sim, Andrew 4:10:10 (13,517)
Barry, Jamie Vincent Joseph 5:24:33 (30,562)
Barry, Richard A 4:40:32 (21,655)
Barry, Roy 5:48:39 (33,209)
Barry, Tobie Michael 5:17:20 (29,445)
Barsley, Will 4:32:21 (19,529)
Barstow, David R 4:44:19 (22,595)
Bartel, Franz-Josef 4:27:10 (18,137)
Bartholomew, Ash 5:50:31 (33,389)
Bartholomew, James 4:01:22 (11,325)
Bartholomew, Neil 4:25:39 (17,701)
Barthorp, Edward Michael 4:47:40 (23,459)
Bartle, Andrew 5:23:03 (30,315)
Bartle, Chris 4:18:22 (15,678)
Bartle, John Paul 4:15:33 (14,916)
Bartlett, Ben 3:52:29 (8,792)
Bartlett, Christopher Peter Yves 3:57:01 (10,102)
Bartlett, John 4:33:40 (19,910)
Bartlett, Scott 5:25:20 (30,667)
Bartlett, Stephen William 5:45:45 (32,929)
Bartley, Philip Alexander 4:22:35 (16,868)
Bartley, Scott 3:48:28 (7,837)
Barton, Andrew Philip 4:45:43 (22,955)
Barton, Anthony Barton 4:04:09 (11,996)
Barton, Chris 4:42:02 (22,024)
Barton, Ian Jon 4:08:38 (13,125)
Barton, Marc Andrew 3:55:22 (9,587)
Barton, Patrick 4:36:25 (20,580)
Barton, Simon 3:48:43 (7,905)
Bartram, Colin Ronald 3:55:57 (9,766)
Bartram, David Charles 4:55:32 (25,414)
Bartram, Matt 3:48:18 (7,805)
Bartup, Ross Jonathan 3:29:10 (4,263)
Barwick, Gary R 3:20:29 (3,022)
Basak, Saikat 4:17:42 (15,497)
Baseggio, John T 4:06:50 (12,670)
Basey, James 4:48:54 (23,773)
Basger, Oliver 5:25:21 (30,669)
Basham, Lee Antony 5:34:16 (31,792)
Basher, Jonathan 3:32:42 (4,843)
Bashford-Squires, Andrew 5:08:04 (27,908)
Bashforth, Jonathan 4:09:48 (13,421)
Bashir, Zaheir 3:27:21 (3,930)
Basit, Abdul 3:57:03 (10,118)
Baskaran, Jason 4:16:23 (15,135)
Baskaran, Paratharajan 5:22:24 (30,207)
Baskerville, James B 5:10:59 (28,403)
Bason, David, 4:01:49 (11,450)
Bass, Andrew P 2:59:52 (1,145)
Bass, Bernard N 3:30:55 (4,568)
Bass, Christopher G 5:41:07 (32,497)
Bass, Paul Alan 4:15:06 (14,808)
Bassett, Chris James 4:37:49 (20,948)
Bassett, Christopher Simon 4:20:45 (16,356)
Bassett, David J 4:08:05 (12,983)
Bassett, Duncan 5:15:39 (29,172)
Bassett, Paul J 4:23:02 (16,988)
Bassett, Sean 3:57:34 (10,253)
Bassett, Thomas Robert 4:25:18 (17,599)
Bassil, Alan 5:23:36 (30,404)
Basso, Vincenzo 3:10:39 (1,958)
Bastianelli, Federico 3:50:27 (8,297)
Bastick, Damian 3:37:24 (5,637)
Bastick, Mark Paul 4:42:53 (22,238)
Baston, Tim Dean 3:34:10 (5,090)
Baston-Pitt, Jon David 4:17:16 (15,368)
Bastow, Paul Graham 4:52:06 (24,573)
Basu, Subhashis 3:18:58 (2,870)
Batchelor, Daniel M 4:21:54 (16,674)
Batchelor, John Michael 3:32:42 (4,843)
Batchelor, Paul 4:58:31 (26,092)
Batchelor, Robert James 5:37:03 (32,106)
Bate, Lawrence 3:14:42 (2,406)
Bateman, David Alan 4:17:12 (15,351)
Bateman, Jack 4:49:42 (23,978)
Bateman, Jeremy D 3:20:29 (3,022)
Bateman, Jonathan S 3:07:28 (1,650)
Bateman, Kelly John 3:58:42 (10,625)
Bateman, Nicholas 2:58:59 (1,045)
Bateman, Rob 4:37:30 (20,881)
Bates, Chris 4:37:46 (20,938)
Bates, Daniel James 3:43:10 (6,727)
Bates, James (Grant) Edward 4:34:31 (20,124)
Bates, Kevin T 3:54:10 (9,248)
Bates, Mark 4:10:22 (13,562)
Bates, Matt Simon 4:49:51 (24,019)
Bates, Neville A 4:45:16 (22,833)
Bates, Peter 4:38:03 (20,997)
Bates, Richard Peter 4:52:19 (24,643)
Bateson, Graham A 3:25:55 (3,721)
Bateson, Marcus 4:54:20 (25,140)
Bateson, Nathaniel A 5:04:13 (27,237)
Batey, Trevor 3:02:50 (1,318)
Bather, Grant 3:56:19 (9,877)
Bathers, Steve David 4:18:02 (15,589)
Batley, Lloyd E 4:47:56 (23,528)
Batman, Gavin 5:29:59 (31,295)
Batterbury, Mark 4:31:38 (19,362)
Battersby, John A 3:46:26 (7,407)
Batterton, Daniel Thomas 3:50:51 (8,390)
Battison, Ian 4:28:08 (18,395)
Batts, Andrew J 4:03:41 (11,896)
Batty, Alex 5:51:46 (33,488)
Batty, Anthony James 3:24:44 (3,543)
Batty, Grant Michael 5:00:04 (26,471)
Baty, Andrew 3:26:45 (3,838)
Baty, John 4:55:42 (25,463)
Bauschulte, Klaus 4:33:39 (19,906)
Bavari, Giordano 3:55:47 (9,711)
Baverstock, Neil 5:16:40 (29,333)
Bavia, Silvano 5:54:55 (33,709)
Bawden, Phillip U 4:57:35 (25,875)
Bawden, Simon Northley 4:09:18 (13,283)
Baxendale, Richard 4:46:03 (23,043)
Baxter, Charlie Joseph 3:29:53 (4,393)
Baxter, Clifford John 4:59:12 (26,264)
Baxter, Colin 3:22:10 (3,206)
Baxter, Colin Richard 4:58:26 (26,071)
Baxter, Harry B 3:56:09 (9,822)
Baxter, John 5:20:39 (29,953)
Baxter, Mike 5:28:45 (31,120)
Baxter, Neil 4:54:58 (25,296)
Baxter, Nicholas W 4:21:50 (16,651)
Baxter, Paul David 4:23:24 (17,080)
Baxter, Robert Jeremy 4:44:23 (22,609)
Baxter, Steve D 5:07:14 (27,755)
Baxter, Steven D 4:42:13 (22,069)
Baxter, Tyler-John Marc David 3:59:54 (10,967)
Bayes, Graham P 4:39:38 (21,424)
Bayfield, Simon 5:08:06 (27,911)
Bayfield-Hill, Kevin 5:18:18 (29,591)
Bayles, Chris 3:29:37 (4,345)
Bayles, Neil 4:01:58 (11,482)
Bayley-Dainton, Stuart J 4:24:05 (17,259)
Baylis, Charles 3:45:23 (7,184)
Bayliss, Danyel 3:44:30 (6,987)
Bayliss, Graham 5:23:02 (30,312)
Bayliss, John C 5:20:35 (29,941)
Baynes, Chris P 2:51:26 (540)
Bayon, Tony P 4:21:17 (16,487)
Bazant, Jakub 3:10:42 (1,962)
Bazeley, Geoffrey Mark 4:32:54 (19,673)
Bazley, Andrew Robert 3:55:37 (9,647)
Beacham, Nigel John 4:05:43 (12,384)
Beacher, Neil D 2:56:30 (830)
Beacon, Miles 3:51:42 (8,587)
Beadle, Craig Adam 4:45:52 (22,992)
Beadle, David 2:59:35 (1,120)
Beadle, John Stewart 3:10:15 (1,928)
Beaken, David Joseph 4:54:20 (25,140)
Beal, Cliff 4:46:38 (23,217)
Beale, Andrew William 5:50:57 (33,427)
Beale, Darren 4:24:57 (17,504)
Beale, Fraser Benedict 5:22:15 (30,181)
Beale, Nicholas C 4:24:01 (17,242)
Beales, Chris 5:17:28 (29,465)
Bealing, Adrian James 5:16:57 (29,379)
Beament, Jeremy 3:50:10 (8,242)
Beamish, Liam 4:36:06 (20,506)
Beamiss, Graham A 3:27:24 (3,942)
Beamonte Cordoba, Eduardo 4:13:47 (14,452)
Bean, David Robert 4:10:52 (13,686)
Beaney, Jason William 4:22:54 (16,962)
Beaney, John Alexander 4:20:16 (16,185)
Beaney, Stuart J 3:19:32 (2,919)
Beanland, Alexander David 3:58:51 (10,670)
Beanland, Christopher 5:20:23 (29,897)
Beanland, Michael David 4:34:31 (20,124)
Beard, Christopher Adam N 4:26:21 (17,916)
Beard, Graham David 3:36:47 (5,520)
Beard, Matthew W 4:01:52 (11,462)
Beardall, Charles 4:52:24 (24,665)
Beardmore, Anthony John 3:50:38 (8,343)
Beardshall, Martin J 4:16:13 (15,079)
Beardsley, Andrew 3:11:11 (2,015)
Beare, Gerard 4:31:30 (19,334)
Beare, Martin A 3:37:04 (5,578)
Bearwish, Neil S 3:07:31 (1,653)
Beasley, Benjamin 4:55:09 (25,347)
Beasley, Chris 3:56:40 (9,984)
Beasley, Paul 3:48:46 (7,914)
Beasley, Richard Mark 5:12:31 (28,658)
Beathe, Carl J 3:13:01 (2,192)
Beaton, Andrew 4:05:36 (12,353)
Beattie, André 4:00:14 (11,041)
Beattie, Brian W 3:54:11 (9,254)
Beattie, Ian J 3:16:00 (2,556)
Beattie, Roger Charles 4:41:21 (21,851)
Beattie, Sean 4:46:48 (23,255)
Beattie, William Ryan 2:56:59 (859)
Beatty, Philip 3:39:51 (6,114)
Beaumont, Alec John 4:10:33 (13,608)
Beaumont, Craig 3:57:56 (10,362)
Beaumont, Gino Burnett 4:20:35 (16,287)
Beaumont, Kelvin Darrel 4:47:16 (23,355)
Beaumont, Mark J 3:28:01 (4,051)
Beaumont, Mark Thomas 5:44:32 (32,818)
Beaumont, Richard Garrett 3:58:06 (10,414)
Beaumont, Steve 4:24:54 (17,490)
Beauvais, Peter 3:11:16 (2,024)
Beaver, Mark G 3:52:51 (8,883)
Beaver, Michael Leonard 3:10:01 (1,907)
Beazeley, Chris 3:23:15 (3,332)
Bebbington, Richard 3:46:26 (7,407)
Beck, Alexander Charles 3:35:51 (5,385)
Beck, Andrew Scott 4:45:32 (22,897)
Beck, Eric 4:15:23 (14,883)
Beck, Gary Robert 4:21:46 (16,631)
Beck, Graham N 4:57:18 (25,820)
Beck, John W 3:28:44 (4,179)
Beck, Michael John 5:33:33 (31,721)
Beck, Nicolas 3:54:05 (9,231)
Beck, Robert 5:10:33 (28,340)
Becker, Ryan Anton 4:55:11 (25,352)
Beckett, Daniel J 3:20:23 (3,002)
Beckett, Huw 4:48:22 (23,627)
Beckett, Nick George 4:16:55 (15,275)
Beckett, Steve 4:20:43 (16,341)
Beckingham, Roy John 3:53:16 (8,988)
Beckwith, Alan 4:09:19 (13,288)
Beckwith, Anthony James 4:45:40 (22,940)
Bedding, Nick 4:21:38 (16,591)
Beddis, Graham R 5:16:35 (29,319)
Beddoe, Gareth David 4:18:22 (15,678)
Beddows, Rob Anthony 4:06:49 (12,660)
Bedford, Gary J 3:20:14 (2,982)
Bedford, Graham James 4:21:01 (16,420)
Bedford, Patrick 6:19:35 (35,109)
Bedford, Paul S 3:44:43 (7,038)
Bedford, Peter J 4:35:49 (20,426)
Bedford, Russell 4:18:18 (15,661)
Bedington, Terence J 3:55:51 (9,733)
Bedu, Jean-Philippe 3:44:41 (7,034)

Bedwell, Alexander Philip	4:02:51 (11,688)	
Bee, Anthony J	4:53:42 (24,973)	
Bee, Carwyn	5:07:17 (27,766)	
Beeby, Chris	3:54:23 (9,298)	
Beech, Carl	5:13:42 (28,871)	
Beech, James	3:20:49 (3,060)	
Beech, Samuel	4:23:52 (17,205)	
Beechey, Mike G.	3:43:29 (6,774)	
Beecroft, David John	4:56:34 (25,662)	
Beeden, Paul	3:36:13 (5,450)	
Beedie, Mark Anthony James S	5:37:31 (32,168)	
Beedie, Neil	3:38:44 (5,897)	
Beedle, Jonathan	4:13:26 (14,348)	
Beedle, Paul	4:10:18 (13,547)	
Beeley, Simon	4:30:00 (18,977)	
Beelitz, Ralf	4:59:22 (26,301)	
Beeney, Robert	4:07:26 (12,810)	
Beeney, Robert	4:38:41 (21,165)	
Beer, Nigel E.	3:51:10 (8,464)	
Beer, Rob James	3:25:29 (3,645)	
Beers, Darren Malcom	3:44:14 (6,921)	
Beers, Graham E	4:25:54 (17,786)	
Beeslee, Paul	4:15:17 (14,853)	
Beesley, Alan	5:40:55 (32,473)	
Beesley, Lee R	4:17:28 (15,431)	
Beesley, Paul	5:32:31 (31,605)	
Beeson, Nigel Adrian Laurence	4:32:20 (19,525)	
Beeston, Matthew	4:59:05 (26,236)	
Beet, Simon Trevor	5:14:49 (29,039)	
Beetham, Stephen	3:26:17 (3,782)	
Beeton, Andrew John	3:35:51 (5,385)	
Beffort, Marc	3:24:19 (3,488)	
Beggs, William Kenneth	4:56:13 (25,589)	
Behan, Gary	4:37:33 (20,896)	
Behan, Kenneth J	3:12:20 (2,114)	
Beharrell, Matthew Jared	3:32:12 (4,770)	
Behrens, Dietmar	3:53:15 (8,983)	
Bejarano Ejarque, Antonio M	4:18:22 (15,678)	
Belbin, Simon J	4:42:50 (22,225)	
Belet, Daniele	5:02:26 (26,935)	
Belk, Chris	4:54:17 (25,126)	
Belker, Peter	3:54:41 (9,381)	
Bell, Andrew	6:02:28 (34,215)	
Bell, Andrew K	5:09:19 (28,111)	
Bell, Chris	3:41:05 (6,337)	
Bell, Chris	4:18:50 (15,803)	
Bell, Colin	5:21:29 (30,075)	
Bell, Colin Alistair	3:54:30 (9,328)	
Bell, Daniel James	3:51:20 (8,500)	
Bell, Duncan Edward	6:05:54 (34,444)	
Bell, Graham	2:59:17 (1,082)	
Bell, Graham	3:49:49 (8,168)	
Bell, Graham	5:10:39 (28,357)	
Bell, Jeremy	3:36:16 (5,453)	
Bell, John Philip Richard	5:09:24 (28,126)	
Bell, Mark	3:17:28 (2,705)	
Bell, Martin	3:43:09 (6,723)	
Bell, Martin	5:03:31 (27,104)	
Bell, Martin Geoffrey	4:06:04 (12,468)	
Bell, Martyn	4:32:29 (19,556)	
Bell, Matthew J	2:28:39 (56)	
Bell, Michael Kenneth	6:49:11 (35,981)	
Bell, Nick Graham	3:56:08 (9,818)	
Bell, Paul Michael	6:01:59 (34,188)	
Bell, Roger I	4:05:21 (12,296)	
Bell, Tom James	5:50:18 (33,362)	
Bellamy, Darren	4:55:10 (25,350)	
Bellamy, Edward James	3:08:56 (1,804)	
Bellenbaum, Uwe	3:59:24 (10,839)	
Bellers, Lance Mark	3:27:35 (3,976)	
Belletti, Fabio	3:32:45 (4,852)	
Bellinfantie, Paul D	6:39:07 (35,755)	
Belling, Ernst	3:57:07 (10,131)	
Bellingham, Geoff	4:58:32 (26,097)	
Bellingham, Stuart J	3:49:51 (8,176)	
Bellis, Stephen	3:35:17 (5,286)	
Bello, Aurelio M	4:29:52 (18,935)	
Belloir, Gwenael	4:14:23 (14,610)	
Bellows, Guy	3:49:52 (8,180)	
Belmore, Jason Karl	4:41:38 (21,930)	
Beloulou, Jean-Marc	5:27:34 (30,972)	
Belsham, Simon	4:25:28 (17,650)	
Belshaw, Ryan	3:48:40 (7,890)	
Belshaw, Victor	3:32:44 (4,849)	
Belson, Simon	4:42:48 (22,213)	
Belton, Robert Bryan	3:55:21 (9,582)	
Bembridge, Simon	4:06:30 (12,575)	
Benato, Paolo	5:04:46 (27,330)	
Benavente, Pablo	3:39:15 (5,991)	
Benbow, Edward	3:34:43 (5,194)	
Benbow, Philip	4:34:15 (20,061)	
Benbrook, Dean	6:02:05 (34,192)	
Bendix, Rodney Malcolm	4:39:13 (21,317)	
Bendle, Stephen	3:47:28 (7,638)	
Benee, Ryan	4:25:29 (17,657)	
Benett, Marcus James Phillip	5:03:11 (27,056)	
Benetti, Arnaldo	4:59:04 (26,230)	
Benetz, Roland	4:19:58 (16,096)	
Beneventi, Michel	4:12:05 (14,003)	
Benfredj, Sacha Marc	4:19:08 (15,886)	
Benfredj, Stefan	4:19:08 (15,886)	
Beninger, Richard	4:45:27 (22,874)	
Benison, Dave	4:18:16 (15,648)	
Benitz, Alexander	3:26:30 (3,801)	
Benjamin, Daniel	3:50:24 (8,289)	
Benjamin, Isaac	4:13:08 (14,272)	
Benjie, Goss	3:55:03 (9,491)	
Benmore, Harry Edward	4:51:29 (24,419)	
Benn, Melvin	5:26:33 (30,845)	
Ben-Nathan, Marc I	4:55:01 (25,310)	
Bennet, Julian	4:16:22 (15,130)	
Bennet, Neil J	4:31:36 (19,352)	
Bennett, Adrian Charles	3:52:00 (8,659)	
Bennett, Alan John	4:00:31 (11,118)	
Bennett, Andrew John	4:46:10 (23,078)	
Bennett, Benjamin	4:15:40 (14,944)	
Bennett, Carl	4:32:49 (19,635)	
Bennett, Chris	3:49:09 (8,010)	
Bennett, David G.	4:13:18 (14,312)	
Bennett, David H	3:26:08 (3,757)	
Bennett, Graham	4:50:37 (24,187)	
Bennett, James	5:30:56 (31,406)	
Bennett, John	6:28:28 (35,445)	
Bennett, Kevin M	3:36:57 (5,554)	
Bennett, Marc	3:43:25 (6,764)	
Bennett, Marc	5:10:59 (28,403)	
Bennett, Mark	5:07:03 (27,733)	
Bennett, Mark D.	4:15:10 (14,826)	
Bennett, Mark H	3:42:18 (6,562)	
Bennett, Mark S	4:06:28 (12,562)	
Bennett, Michael	4:29:15 (18,743)	
Bennett, Michael J	3:52:22 (8,761)	
Bennett, Neil Andrew	3:54:46 (9,407)	
Bennett, Nigel David	4:26:25 (17,930)	
Bennett, Patrick	4:50:37 (24,187)	
Bennett, Paul	5:36:18 (32,033)	
Bennett, Robert	3:48:14 (7,789)	
Bennett, Stephen	4:31:04 (19,235)	
Bennett, Steven Edward	5:07:43 (27,849)	
Bennett, Stuart Paul	4:17:36 (15,469)	
Bennett, Tony	4:46:50 (23,270)	
Bennetta, Christoper William	5:01:12 (26,680)	
Bennington, Mark	5:36:25 (32,045)	
Bennison, Craig	3:50:38 (8,343)	
Bennison, Mark Brian	4:20:15 (16,181)	
Bennison, Richard	3:55:02 (9,485)	
Benskin, Anthony John	4:44:58 (22,759)	
Benskin, Benjamin Alexander	4:34:02 (20,000)	
Benson, Andrew Telford	5:22:07 (30,167)	
Benson, Colin	3:47:09 (7,556)	
Benson, Ian C.	3:10:44 (1,965)	
Benson, Ian Edward	3:56:25 (9,903)	
Benson, James	2:40:03 (200)	
Benson, James	4:52:44 (24,735)	
Benson, Mark Mckinley	4:33:34 (19,877)	
Benson, Russell	4:47:24 (23,389)	
Benson, Steven	4:46:03 (23,043)	
Benstead, Chris	4:18:41 (15,769)	
Bensted, Duncan I	4:45:25 (22,865)	
Bent, Alan	3:42:02 (6,517)	
Bent, Tim	3:42:03 (6,521)	
Bentall, George	4:16:04 (15,042)	
Bentemam, Boualem	3:17:05 (2,671)	
Bentham, Harry	4:47:10 (23,337)	
Bentley, Alan H	3:27:18 (3,922)	
Bentley, Chris William	4:22:38 (16,890)	
Bentley, James Martin	4:59:19 (26,292)	
Bentley, Jamin	7:15:53 (36,368)	
Bentley, John	3:57:56 (10,362)	
Bentley, Mark	3:23:53 (3,416)	
Bentley, Mike	3:38:04 (5,776)	
Bentley, Nick George	3:40:56 (6,316)	
Bentley, Robin J	2:43:12 (286)	
Bentley, Stephen	4:47:57 (23,535)	
Benton, Andy	4:56:11 (25,579)	
Benton, Craig Stuart	3:26:47 (3,845)	
Benton, David Christopher	5:46:45 (33,030)	
Benton, David John	3:07:46 (1,683)	
Benton, Mark R	3:48:38 (7,878)	
Benton, Nick James	4:58:44 (26,152)	
Benton, Tom	4:20:05 (16,131)	
Benzikie, Stephen	4:18:30 (15,715)	
Benzoni, Fabrizio	4:56:22 (25,624)	
Beraldo, Maurizio	3:27:42 (3,997)	
Beresford, John Paul	3:35:36 (5,342)	
Beresford, Lee M.	3:18:57 (2,866)	
Beresford, Mark	5:13:59 (28,921)	
Beresford, Martin	4:23:56 (17,221)	
Beresford, Steve	4:00:20 (11,068)	
Berg, Jens-Kristian	2:34:35 (105)	
Berg, Joerg	4:48:57 (23,788)	
Berger, David R	4:02:12 (11,540)	
Berggren, Roy	4:48:45 (23,734)	
Bergin, Mark	3:48:48 (7,927)	
Bergland, Lars	4:52:39 (24,722)	
Berlie, Adrian J	3:29:52 (4,391)	
Berlyn, Paul Philip	3:54:22 (9,296)	
Berman, Gavin B	5:46:43 (33,019)	
Bermond, Michel	3:37:49 (5,726)	
Bermond, Sebastien	4:21:41 (16,600)	
Bernadeau, François	4:08:33 (13,103)	
Bernard, Frederic	3:43:09 (6,723)	
Bernard, Jason	4:19:18 (15,929)	
Bernard, Ralph	5:41:12 (32,510)	
Berndt, Karsten	3:35:09 (5,265)	
Berndtson, Daniel John	6:54:17 (36,093)	
Bernier, Martin Richard	5:47:11 (33,069)	
Bernier, Victor	3:16:49 (2,654)	
Bernstein, Simon	4:04:00 (11,959)	
Berntsen, Guus	4:11:54 (13,959)	
Berogna, Richard	3:13:52 (2,301)	
Berresford, James	3:24:55 (3,568)	
Berry, Andrew	3:54:44 (9,397)	
Berry, Clifford	2:58:19 (988)	
Berry, Craig	5:21:50 (30,121)	
Berry, Daniel	4:12:57 (14,216)	
Berry, Grant Rostron	5:02:33 (26,950)	
Berry, Harry George	5:03:27 (27,093)	
Berry, Ian	4:33:25 (19,829)	
Berry, Ian J	2:54:52 (728)	
Berry, Jacade	3:33:53 (5,042)	
Berry, Karl	4:22:36 (16,875)	
Berry, Karl Wayne	5:36:22 (32,042)	
Berry, Kevin James	4:59:22 (26,301)	
Berry, Lee	2:46:07 (362)	
Berry, Mark Stephen	4:50:41 (24,203)	
Berry, Mike	6:20:29 (35,146)	
Berry, Paul Francis	4:55:56 (25,520)	
Berry, Paul Gerakd	3:20:29 (3,022)	
Berry, Stephen David	3:48:33 (7,861)	
Berry, Steve James	4:18:28 (15,704)	
Berry, Stuart	4:41:49 (21,977)	
Berry, Terry	6:10:51 (34,693)	
Berry, Tom Andrew Boyd	3:53:46 (9,147)	
Berryman, Nick	3:19:58 (2,960)	
Bertin, Moreno	4:43:23 (22,342)	
Bertolani, Piero	3:49:10 (8,016)	
Bertram, Michael	5:52:37 (33,540)	
Beskeen, Lee	4:02:52 (11,694)	
Besley, Daniel	4:15:56 (15,011)	
Besnard, Bernard Glyn Alfred	7:29:28 (36,469)	
Bessant, Philip Michael	5:10:25 (28,313)	
Best, Ben David	5:37:12 (32,125)	
Best, Chris	4:50:34 (24,179)	
Best, Craig Gordon	4:57:16 (25,817)	
Best, Daniel Stephen	5:37:12 (32,125)	
Best, Ian John	3:37:53 (5,739)	
Best, Lloyd S	3:08:57 (1,805)	
Beszterczey, Andras	3:59:00 (10,722)	

Betegon, José Maria	2:55:51 (791)
Bethell, Jared Charles Robert	2:52:42 (604)
Bethell, Richard	5:07:58 (27,889)
Bethoule, Mickael	3:22:00 (3,195)
Bethume, Bernard	3:20:46 (3,054)
Bettany, Sam Russell	3:34:31 (5,159)
Betteridge, St John	4:25:48 (17,749)
Bettles, Ian John	4:37:10 (20,786)
Bettridge, Mark	4:59:58 (26,442)
Betts, Benjamin C	4:27:28 (18,228)
Betts, Christopher	5:16:44 (29,341)
Betts, Jack	3:02:10 (1,269)
Betts, Jim	4:45:30 (22,884)
Betts, Mark	3:55:20 (9,571)
Betts, Mark P	2:53:01 (619)
Beuselinck, Peter	5:11:30 (28,480)
Bevan, Daniel Hugh	6:20:39 (35,150)
Bevan, David A	4:47:40 (23,459)
Bevan, Ross Michael	4:53:54 (25,022)
Bevan, Stephen John	3:42:25 (6,580)
Bevan, Steve	3:53:31 (9,061)
Bevans, Toby	4:09:06 (13,229)
Bever, Patrick J	3:44:22 (6,955)
Bewick, Jeremy Brett	4:19:04 (15,866)
Bewley, James Timothy	3:10:57 (1,988)
Beyer-Kay, Mark	4:08:23 (13,054)
Bezzant, Martin	6:00:49 (34,117)
Bhadressa, Nisshan	4:33:01 (19,703)
Bhagalia, Yogesh	4:38:50 (21,212)
Bhandarkar, Sandeep	4:45:04 (22,788)
Bhardwaj, Rajiv	5:00:17 (26,515)
Bhargava, Vijay	4:45:00 (22,770)
Bhogal, Sunjay	4:11:00 (13,715)
Bhojani, Yogesh Arvind	5:37:39 (32,177)
Bhugon, Daniel	3:19:33 (2,921)
Bhundia, Vinod	6:05:18 (34,410)
Biagini, Andrea	7:30:02 (36,471)
Bialaszewski, Charlie William	4:17:43 (15,501)
Bianchini, Alberto	3:49:22 (8,055)
Biasutti, Emanuele	4:10:50 (13,676)
Bibani, Alex	3:28:22 (4,118)
Bibring, Lee	3:41:05 (6,337)
Bickers, Michael Adrian	3:18:45 (2,846)
Bickhan, Zakir	6:05:05 (34,389)
Bickley, Anthony	3:24:47 (3,549)
Bickmore, Roger	4:28:54 (18,642)
Bicknell, Martin	5:07:54 (27,880)
Bicknell, Richard J	3:41:19 (6,389)
Biddle, Nick	3:55:08 (9,513)
Biddle, Steve	4:10:11 (13,524)
Bidgood, Kenneth A	4:27:26 (18,213)
Bidwell, Alex	3:46:02 (7,314)
Bidwell, Peter Mervin	5:10:52 (28,389)
Bidwell, Stephen H	5:05:46 (27,487)
Bielby, Luke	3:53:47 (9,154)
Bigaignon, François Louis Gilbert	4:46:53 (23,279)
Biggane, Nick	3:48:31 (7,852)
Biggin, James Richard	3:01:12 (1,213)
Biggin, Matthew James	3:35:22 (5,297)
Biggin, Rupert L	3:03:25 (1,341)
Biggs, Andrew J	3:55:24 (9,594)
Biggs, Jamie	4:09:36 (13,370)
Biggs, Matthew James	3:10:10 (1,920)
Biggs, Paul David	4:36:20 (20,554)
Biggs, Robert	3:39:39 (6,068)
Biggs, Roger	3:51:48 (8,608)
Biggs, Steven R	3:54:45 (9,402)
Biggs, Timothy	4:11:00 (13,715)
Biggs-Hayes, Tom	5:20:43 (29,965)
Bignell, Philip J	4:41:02 (21,777)
Bilboe, Ian H	4:03:58 (11,954)
Bilbrough, Mark	5:19:51 (29,829)
Bilgorri, Guy	3:25:02 (3,584)
Bilham, Lee	3:53:10 (8,963)
Bill, Stuart John	4:55:12 (25,359)
Billa, Bernard	4:23:55 (17,220)
Billinger, Christian	4:22:25 (16,826)
Billingham, Andy	4:49:38 (23,953)
Billingham, David P	3:05:40 (1,511)
Billingham, Huw Warwick	4:04:12 (12,010)
Billingham, Joe	6:09:50 (34,653)
Billinghay, Peter Mark	6:14:24 (34,856)
Billington, Keith	3:37:52 (5,734)

Billington, Richard J	3:12:57 (2,184)
Billsborough, Graham Mark	5:26:16 (30,813)
Billups, Russ John	5:20:19 (29,891)
Bilsby, Roger	3:53:22 (9,018)
Bilsland, Roger	5:12:53 (28,717)
Bilton, Darran E	2:25:08 (36)
Binder, Jan Kristiansen	5:48:49 (33,223)
Bines, Adrian	5:25:30 (30,691)
Bingham, George Frederick	7:36:57 (36,505)
Bingham, Grant	4:10:05 (13,491)
Bingham, Hugh	2:54:37 (708)
Bingham, Luke Jonathan	4:53:25 (24,895)
Bingham, Paul	4:55:45 (25,480)
Bingham, Raymond Stuart	4:22:44 (16,913)
Bingham, Roger Charles	4:50:18 (24,116)
Bingham, Stephen M	4:09:34 (13,358)
Bingham, Stuart J	4:09:34 (13,358)
Bingle, Michael Alan	3:53:13 (8,978)
Binnie, Brian	5:40:37 (32,446)
Binns, David	4:38:35 (21,137)
Binns, Leslie	5:23:06 (30,320)
Birch, Craig John	5:07:32 (27,819)
Birch, David	3:17:46 (2,739)
Birch, Mark	3:55:47 (9,711)
Birch, Matthew	3:58:19 (10,499)
Birch, Michael	4:48:41 (23,715)
Birch, Nick	3:41:53 (6,496)
Birch, Peter	4:53:28 (24,905)
Birch, Sean Robert	4:38:39 (21,154)
Birch, Warren Peter	3:30:54 (4,566)
Birchall, James C	3:20:15 (2,984)
Bircher, Martin	5:24:30 (30,556)
Bird, Alan Douglas Harvey	4:45:26 (22,870)
Bird, Andy	4:58:21 (26,054)
Bird, Benjamin	5:11:00 (28,405)
Bird, Damian	5:35:36 (31,936)
Bird, Dave J	3:08:30 (1,754)
Bird, David Kenneth	5:11:38 (28,491)
Bird, Derek	4:18:28 (15,704)
Bird, Graham John	4:04:25 (12,058)
Bird, James A	7:43:28 (36,540)
Bird, Jamie E	3:31:20 (4,636)
Bird, Jonathan	4:19:17 (15,922)
Bird, Martin G	4:07:37 (12,860)
Bird, Peter David	4:10:01 (13,479)
Bird, Phil	3:55:33 (9,626)
Bird, Terence	5:33:49 (31,749)
Birkby, Lance J	3:24:59 (3,577)
Birkby, Nicholas	3:33:04 (4,904)
Birkedale, Christopher	4:10:52 (13,686)
Birkenhead, Adam	5:51:01 (33,430)
Birkerdike, Iana	5:23:51 (30,448)
Birkinshaw, David Mark Poynton	4:45:35 (22,909)
Birnbaum, Maurice S	5:25:39 (30,728)
Birse, Scott	4:02:42 (11,650)
Birt, Andrew Jeaffreson	3:28:22 (4,118)
Birtles, Linus	5:12:59 (28,738)
Birtwhistle, John Charles	5:07:59 (27,891)
Birtwistle, Robin Wynne	3:56:12 (9,841)
Bisdee, Trevor	4:40:18 (21,574)
Bishop, Edward Thornhill	3:30:46 (4,541)
Bishop, Gareth L	5:07:21 (27,783)
Bishop, Ian M	2:52:44 (606)
Bishop, James Denise	5:32:13 (31,564)
Bishop, James Iain	3:15:33 (2,504)
Bishop, Jason Paul	4:10:21 (13,556)
Bishop, John	4:35:12 (20,270)
Bishop, Jonathan Paul	5:08:05 (27,910)
Bishop, Nick	5:10:27 (28,319)
Bishop, Paul	4:57:12 (25,804)
Bishop, Phil	4:16:19 (15,112)
Bishop, Philip James	4:54:45 (25,245)
Bishop, Roger Douglas	3:53:54 (9,183)
Bishop, Simon	4:05:09 (12,241)
Bispham, Adam	4:59:14 (26,272)
Bispo, Reinaldo A	3:46:07 (7,342)
Biss, Colin John	6:00:56 (34,126)
Biss, Mark	4:44:37 (22,676)
Biss, Neil	3:04:30 (1,434)
Bisset, Gordon	6:56:29 (36,137)
Bissett, Nigel Anthony	5:27:14 (30,937)
Bissett, Stuart	4:22:36 (16,875)
Bisson, Michael J	3:29:38 (4,348)

Bitcheno, Matt	4:38:25 (21,092)
Bitici, Albert	5:25:40 (30,730)
Bitting, John Hal	3:40:26 (6,221)
Bittner, Tomas	4:24:09 (17,272)
Bitton, Simon	7:08:55 (36,301)
Bixley, Aaron	4:48:55 (23,776)
Bjaaland Andersen, Morten	2:37:26 (149)
Bjoerge, Eirik	4:41:57 (22,002)
Bjornsson, Bjorn Asgeir	5:03:04 (27,034)
Black, Alistair	3:00:33 (1,178)
Black, Billy	5:32:59 (31,661)
Black, Clive Darren	5:29:36 (31,237)
Black, David	5:34:22 (31,808)
Black, Kenny John	3:49:11 (8,021)
Black, Marc Harrison	4:14:01 (14,508)
Black, Peter	4:27:18 (18,181)
Black, Roger	4:28:26 (18,499)
Black, Simon J	2:57:26 (894)
Black, Steven	4:36:44 (20,665)
Black, Stuart	4:08:16 (13,020)
Blackall, Graham	6:26:26 (35,362)
Blackburn, Ben David Harold	4:59:43 (26,388)
Blackburn, David	4:02:33 (11,616)
Blackburn, Graham M	3:24:28 (3,506)
Blackburn, Ian Mark	3:25:50 (3,709)
Blackburn, Luke	4:19:06 (15,872)
Blackburn, Paul	5:12:49 (28,703)
Blackburn, Stephen	4:38:40 (21,158)
Blackburn, Stuart	5:17:10 (29,413)
Blacker, Marcus Andrew	3:08:52 (1,799)
Blackett, Lee	3:56:55 (10,063)
Blackford, Robert G	6:21:16 (35,174)
Blackledge, Mark	6:30:04 (35,502)
Blackman, Gary	4:27:23 (18,205)
Blackman, Peter	3:42:20 (6,568)
Blackman, Robert	3:34:26 (5,142)
Blackmore, Andrew	3:25:35 (3,665)
Blackmore, Cory	3:52:10 (8,699)
Blackmore, Michael T	2:36:50 (139)
Blackmore, Robert J	3:41:23 (6,403)
Blackmore, Simon M	4:07:32 (12,843)
Blackmore, Stephen	5:17:45 (29,508)
Blackshaw, Simon Lee	4:29:50 (18,920)
Blackwell, Christian M	3:28:03 (4,063)
Blackwell, Paul A	4:38:52 (21,223)
Blad, Edward Jonathan	4:11:13 (13,771)
Bladen, Alan J	5:21:07 (30,021)
Blades, Kenneth	4:31:22 (19,304)
Bladier, Marc	3:51:49 (8,612)
Bladon, Glenn Andrew	4:33:14 (19,778)
Blagrove, Owen P	6:47:13 (35,954)
Blaine, John S	3:05:37 (1,506)
Blair, Alan J	3:46:14 (7,362)
Blair, Michael	4:21:31 (16,552)
Blake, Adam	5:08:08 (27,918)
Blake, David	5:40:31 (32,432)
Blake, James	3:55:29 (9,611)
Blake, John R	4:11:17 (13,786)
Blake, Jonathan Douglas	4:08:36 (13,117)
Blake, Kevin C	4:27:22 (18,200)
Blake, Kevin M	4:47:15 (23,353)
Blake, Mark Russell	4:49:13 (23,852)
Blake, Stephen J	2:57:39 (927)
Blake, Stephen J	4:17:24 (15,405)
Blake, Steve J	3:22:03 (3,197)
Blake, Stuart Robert	5:51:29 (33,462)
Blakeley, Paul Raymond	5:22:38 (30,245)
Blakeman, Kerry	4:19:57 (16,086)
Blakey, James	4:57:30 (25,858)
Blakey, Kelvin	7:00:49 (36,203)
Blamey, René Peter	4:34:03 (20,005)
Blamire, Christopher I	4:03:46 (11,914)
Blanch, Christian Marshall Hall	4:03:48 (11,924)
Blanco, José A	2:34:17 (101)
Bland, Nathan	4:31:09 (19,254)
Bland, Nicholas Mathew	5:16:15 (29,258)
Bland, Paul John	5:23:32 (30,390)
Bland, Philip Anthony	3:53:58 (9,201)
Blanford, William	4:19:44 (16,027)
Blaquiere, Ronnie Patrick	5:31:39 (31,493)
Blasi, Francesco	3:27:53 (4,033)
Blaxell, Tony David	4:41:10 (21,815)
Blayne, Simon Lee	4:49:38 (23,953)

Blazey, Nigel James 5:08:12 (27,929)
Blazquez, Carlos Alberto 3:55:19 (9,567)
Bleckwehl, Joachim 3:49:02 (7,983)
Blee, Adam Matthew 6:14:59 (34,886)
Bleeck, Peter J 4:33:13 (19,772)
Bleker, Robert Nicolas 3:59:23 (10,834)
Blewett, Simon 6:02:49 (34,236)
Bligh, Lee Alan 5:24:06 (30,494)
Bligh, Peter Tommy 3:36:06 (5,429)
Blight, Andrew Roy 4:20:25 (16,239)
Blight, James 3:57:51 (10,345)
Blinman, Gareth 3:42:28 (6,590)
Bliss, Kevin 3:34:02 (5,063)
Bliss, Paul 3:58:01 (10,384)
Blissett, Andrew 9:34:24 (36,625)
Blissett, Norman 4:20:30 (16,260)
Bloch, Paul W 4:35:43 (20,392)
Block, Robert John 3:16:53 (2,658)
Blofeld, Stuart 3:30:06 (4,432)
Blom, Leonard John 3:30:09 (4,439)
Blom Pettersen, John Inge 3:23:58 (3,427)
Bloom, Andrew 4:15:01 (14,790)
Bloom, Matthew John 4:49:55 (24,031)
Bloomfield, Colin F 4:45:07 (22,803)
Bloomfield, Crispian J 2:33:24 (96)
Bloomfield, Philip A 5:12:39 (28,671)
Bloomfield, Stephen L 3:59:00 (10,722)
Bloomfield, Toby 6:36:34 (35,689)
Bloor, Michael 3:52:01 (8,663)
Bloore, Alastair David 4:09:38 (13,380)
Blora, Gianluca 6:00:08 (34,076)
Blowes, Benjamin D 2:59:16 (1,079)
Blowing, Michael 4:42:43 (22,193)
Bloxam, Andrew 2:53:31 (640)
Bloxham, Clive 4:38:18 (21,054)
Bloy, Kevin 3:08:22 (1,735)
Bluett, Robert Andrew 6:40:28 (35,803)
Blum, Bernhard 3:41:20 (6,392)
Blundell, Neil 4:19:15 (15,913)
Blundell, Simon 3:47:35 (7,666)
Blunden, Keith 4:15:09 (14,821)
Blunden, Matthew J 2:29:38 (64)
Blunden, Nathan Anthony James 3:16:26 (2,601)
Blyth, Paul M 4:05:45 (12,395)
Blyth, Robert 3:39:14 (5,988)
Boarder, Timothy 5:03:08 (27,043)
Boardley, Ian D 2:53:23 (636)
Boardman, Andrew D 3:01:47 (1,241)
Boardman, David 4:57:22 (25,834)
Boardman, Keith 2:49:39 (471)
Boardman, Mark Russell 4:30:52 (19,182)
Boase, Duncan K 4:26:54 (18,049)
Boast, Andrew J 3:09:48 (1,895)
Bobbett, Michael Jonathan 4:29:53 (18,943)
Bobbin, Andy Thomas 3:54:59 (9,474)
Bobo, Richard 4:21:53 (16,664)
Bock, Manfred 4:10:08 (13,506)
Bockenheim, Zygmunt C 3:40:06 (6,165)
Bockenstette, Gregory 3:52:38 (8,832)
Boddeke, Rob 4:09:59 (13,471)
Boddington, Ralf 4:45:41 (22,945)
Boddington, Roy 4:32:08 (19,468)
Boden, Ed 2:58:20 (989)
Boden, Kevin 3:59:53 (10,961)
Boden, Lazloe 2:40:44 (220)
Bodman, Daniel J 2:58:58 (1,042)
Bodson, Bertrand 3:43:20 (6,746)
Bodsworth, James Edward 4:36:12 (20,528)
Boettger, Klauspeter 4:26:30 (17,952)
Boggan, Matthew Andrew 4:11:59 (13,984)
Boggi, Daniel 4:23:57 (17,225)
Boggia, Graham 5:07:10 (27,746)
Bogush, Jeremy 4:11:31 (13,852)
Bohbot, Alain 4:05:05 (12,225)
Bohbot, Charles 4:03:50 (11,933)
Boisseau, Thierry 4:05:00 (12,210)
Bokelmann, Michael 4:41:34 (21,912)
Bokobza, Idan 3:37:22 (5,631)
Bola, Narindar Singh 5:38:15 (32,231)
Bolderson, Mark 4:27:11 (18,143)
Bolding, Keith Roy 4:53:04 (24,806)
Bole, Robert D 3:21:38 (3,153)
Boles, Robin 4:25:11 (17,572)
Bolger, Liam 3:54:05 (9,231)
Bolger, Robert M 4:38:38 (21,149)
Bolland, Stephen 4:01:56 (11,478)
Boloorsaz-Allen, Thomas Robert 5:03:34 (27,116)
Bolster, Eric 4:37:37 (20,910)
Bolt, Philip J 3:09:16 (1,830)
Bolt, Ricky 4:40:23 (21,607)
Bolton, Andrew John 3:44:36 (7,014)
Bolton, Clive Daniel 4:34:49 (20,198)
Bolton, David 5:19:24 (29,761)
Bolton, Delme John 4:22:41 (16,897)
Bolton, Gavin 5:05:25 (27,434)
Bolton, James 3:52:53 (8,895)
Bolton, Jamie 4:07:37 (12,860)
Bolton, Mike 4:24:44 (17,450)
Bolton, Phil 4:40:09 (21,524)
Bolton, Reuben Solomon Joab 3:51:50 (8,614)
Bolton, Steve J 3:00:54 (1,201)
Bolton,, Alexander, Thomas 4:15:09 (14,821)
Bolwell, Jeremy 4:23:40 (17,147)
Bombelka, Andreas 4:36:24 (20,576)
Bona, Henrik 4:51:21 (24,387)
Bonaccolta, Carmelo 4:15:55 (15,007)
Bonacina, Angelo 4:58:25 (26,068)
Bond, Chris 4:55:06 (25,335)
Bond, Edward 4:01:05 (11,276)
Bond, Edward R 3:29:15 (4,280)
Bond, Mark 6:31:26 (35,553)
Bond, Michael J 2:54:02 (672)
Bond, Paul A 2:49:02 (444)
Bond, Richard M 5:46:37 (33,015)
Bond, Samuel Luke 4:45:38 (22,927)
Bond, Steven N 4:12:44 (14,165)
Bond, Stewart Allan 4:02:39 (11,638)
Bone, Andy G 2:54:58 (745)
Bone, Christopher 4:18:58 (15,843)
Bone, Krister 2:59:32 (1,116)
Bonelli, Paolo 4:00:02 (10,992)
Bonham, Jonathan James 4:22:15 (16,786)
Bonham, Mark James 4:31:36 (19,352)
Boniface, Kevin 4:31:29 (19,331)
Bonne, Yves 4:29:05 (18,709)
Bonner, Christopher Thomas 4:45:39 (22,935)
Bonner, John Anthony 5:56:06 (33,795)
Bonner, Jon L 3:54:49 (9,427)
Bonner, Mark 5:48:13 (33,162)
Bonner, Richard E 3:44:28 (6,984)
Bonnet, Olivier 3:44:34 (7,005)
Bonnett, David E 3:58:20 (10,505)
Bonnett, Glenn Steven 3:58:20 (10,505)
Bonnett, Terry 4:59:20 (26,298)
Bonney, Sam 3:54:28 (9,317)
Bonnick, Mitchell Lloyd 4:36:03 (20,490)
Bonning, Arron K 4:14:09 (14,547)
Bonning, Paul Kevin 4:31:43 (19,377)
Bonser, Steve 4:05:28 (12,329)
Bonsignore, Mario J 3:44:22 (6,955)
Bontoft, Alan 3:16:41 (2,642)
Bonuccelli, Silvano 4:49:11 (23,844)
Book, Avigdor 3:05:34 (1,501)
Booker, Julian 6:12:36 (34,787)
Booker, Ronald Frederick 4:31:11 (19,266)
Booker, Simon Karl 5:29:43 (31,255)
Boon, Andrew 4:45:26 (22,870)
Boon, David R 5:57:44 (33,914)
Boon, Jason 4:50:39 (24,195)
Boon, Julian Michael 3:50:44 (8,367)
Boon, Robert 3:08:42 (1,783)
Boorer, Gavin Neil 3:57:32 (10,238)
Boorman, Andy R 4:22:05 (16,730)
Boorman, Martin 4:26:09 (17,858)
Boorman, Nicholas 4:50:58 (24,292)
Boosey, Christopher 4:57:51 (25,936)
Boote, Peter Henry George 6:52:08 (36,047)
Booth, Adam Michael 3:44:04 (6,891)
Booth, Andrew 5:27:42 (30,988)
Booth, Christopher 3:44:03 (6,889)
Booth, Jason Kenneth 5:08:17 (27,948)
Booth, John 4:37:57 (20,977)
Booth, Marcus 4:55:43 (25,472)
Booth, Mark James 5:10:12 (28,277)
Booth, Martin P 4:46:05 (23,055)
Booth, Robert Alexander 3:48:37 (7,876)
Booth, Roger 2:58:56 (1,039)
Booth, Simon 3:34:16 (5,106)
Booth, Tristan 4:02:52 (11,694)
Booth, Vincent A 3:15:02 (2,441)
Booth, William 3:27:24 (3,942)
Booth, William Louis 3:44:51 (7,066)
Boothroyd, Bobby 3:12:07 (2,103)
Booty, Graham H 2:45:52 (354)
Booyens, Greg 3:33:03 (4,901)
Boozer, Andrew 4:18:01 (15,582)
Borda, Alan Lawrence 4:19:19 (15,935)
Boreham, Paul 4:30:11 (19,022)
Borg, Yaroslaff 4:47:11 (23,339)
Borge, Gerald 5:05:36 (27,468)
Borgman, Paul S 4:05:44 (12,386)
Borgman, Stuart A 4:25:17 (17,595)
Borgogni, Gianni 3:45:43 (7,249)
Borgoo, Bertrand 4:14:52 (14,753)
Borgund, Ole Jan 3:50:56 (8,409)
Borley, Harry William 4:24:20 (17,333)
Borlin, Enrico 4:35:54 (20,446)
Borner, Colin S 4:12:28 (14,089)
Bornet, Yvan 3:49:53 (8,184)
Borondy, Steve 3:34:28 (5,147)
Borrett, James N 3:41:49 (6,480)
Borrett, Keith 5:10:46 (28,372)
Borthwick, Moray 3:28:47 (4,185)
Borthwick, Robert 3:27:35 (3,976)
Borthwick, Stuart 3:56:05 (9,807)
Bortoft, Arron 3:35:38 (5,349)
Borwell, Kevin John 3:53:16 (8,988)
Bory, Marc 3:18:02 (2,771)
Boscarini, Andrea 3:28:50 (4,194)
Bosch, Ulf 3:17:57 (2,759)
Bose, Rajiv 5:28:17 (31,061)
Bosenberg, Geoff Donovan 4:26:03 (17,825)
Bosher, John Paul 6:04:53 (34,377)
Bosley, David 4:59:05 (26,236)
Bosshard, Markus 4:18:16 (15,648)
Bossi, Paolo 3:04:07 (1,402)
Bossuyt, Ivan 6:40:18 (35,797)
Bostock, Colin R 4:03:07 (11,762)
Bostock, David Heath 4:04:01 (11,962)
Bostock, Malcolm S 3:29:57 (4,408)
Boston, Stewart John 3:53:42 (9,122)
Boswell, Bob John 6:34:52 (35,651)
Boswell, Graham 5:22:05 (30,159)
Boswell, Stuart N 3:07:24 (1,642)
Boswell, Thomas D 2:58:10 (971)
Boswell, Tim 4:22:51 (16,949)
Bosworth, Andrew 3:44:13 (6,919)
Botha, Sean P 3:09:29 (1,855)
Botha, Theunis L 3:54:45 (9,402)
Botha, Wiltus 4:42:40 (22,176)
Bott, Adam James 6:49:24 (35,987)
Bottacco, Enrico 3:58:59 (10,718)
Bottani, Leopoldo 6:31:29 (35,555)
Botterill, Samuel 5:44:33 (32,821)
Botterill, Shaun 4:36:55 (20,719)
Bottomley, Mark Sebastian 4:51:59 (24,549)
Bottomley, Simon J 4:13:24 (14,335)
Bottomley, Steven Jes 5:44:10 (32,783)
Bouadjar, Bakar 4:28:22 (18,472)
Bouaziz, Fessal 4:41:11 (21,820)
Bouchat, Albert 4:10:32 (13,600)
Boucher, Charles 3:51:44 (8,596)
Boucher, Jonathan Allan 4:37:18 (20,818)
Boucher, Llewellyn Peter Scott 4:27:27 (18,220)
Boucher, Michael B 2:35:25 (121)
Boucher, Stuart Charles 4:13:13 (14,290)
Boudevin, Bertrand 4:04:59 (12,200)
Boudou, Jerome 4:33:03 (19,715)
Boughen, Simon 4:34:19 (20,074)
Boughton, Oliver 4:14:07 (14,542)
Bougourd, Mark Peter 4:02:03 (11,502)
Bouhana, Armand 4:12:59 (14,229)
Bouillon, François 3:27:55 (4,038)
Boukeba, Mourad 4:01:22 (11,325)
Boulter, Daniel James 5:00:12 (26,499)
Boulter, Matt S 5:12:04 (28,577)
Boulter, Simon Andrew 4:10:14 (13,536)
Boumelha, Ahmed 3:16:48 (2,652)
Bouramdane, Abderrahime 2:07:33 (4)

Bourdin, François 3:19:26 (2,910)
Bourg, Eric 4:53:37 (24,947)
Bourne, Charles 3:21:07 (3,101)
Bourne, Richard 4:09:07 (13,234)
Bourne, Rowland Mead 5:22:06 (30,163)
Bourne, Wayne 3:10:26 (1,941)
Bourne, Will John 5:37:36 (32,174)
Bourton, Tom 4:48:58 (23,795)
Boutcher, Jon 3:54:04 (9,225)
Bouten, Pieter-Jan 4:17:30 (15,439)
Bouttell, Wayne A 3:15:25 (2,488)
Bovaird, Chris 4:15:02 (14,798)
Bovington, Tom 4:00:34 (11,131)
Bowden, Bob 4:46:23 (23,146)
Bowden, Gary John 6:01:03 (34,134)
Bowden, Ian Phillip 5:43:41 (32,739)
Bowden, Phillip 5:08:12 (27,929)
Bowden, Roman 4:41:47 (21,964)
Bowden, Stephen 5:11:49 (28,525)
Bowdery, Kim Anthony 5:48:27 (33,189)
Bowen, Andy 3:24:56 (3,570)
Bowen, Anthony M 4:43:18 (22,320)
Bowen, David J 3:20:14 (2,982)
Bowen, Jack 5:01:42 (26,792)
Bowen, James K 2:53:05 (620)
Bowen, Mark 3:32:23 (4,796)
Bowen, Matthew 4:26:05 (17,837)
Bowen, Paul 5:59:47 (34,047)
Bowen, Sean 2:52:11 (577)
Bowen, Simon J 3:26:34 (3,808)
Bowen-Jones, Craig Anthony 3:28:33 (4,152)
Bowen-Morris, Ian David 4:25:30 (17,661)
Bower, John Simon 3:40:19 (6,202)
Bower, Julian C 3:31:55 (4,725)
Bowers, David 4:21:57 (16,688)
Bowers, Jason M 2:58:04 (962)
Bowes, Jeffrey 5:18:24 (29,608)
Bowes, Phil 5:25:53 (30,762)
Bowie, David 4:33:08 (19,740)
Bowie, Gregor G 4:44:39 (22,688)
Bowie, Luke 3:43:53 (6,854)
Bowie, Richard M 4:04:27 (12,066)
Bowker, Richard H 2:47:34 (404)
Bowker, Robert 4:33:50 (19,948)
Bowkett, William 4:27:05 (18,114)
Bowkley, Michael 4:00:10 (11,022)
Bowler, Robert S 3:58:32 (10,570)
Bowler, Ryan David 4:33:40 (19,910)
Bowles, Peter 3:13:42 (2,283)
Bowley, Matthew J 3:31:27 (4,659)
Bowling, John F 5:51:28 (33,460)
Bowlzer, Nicholas M 4:19:40 (16,002)
Bowmaker, David 4:11:23 (13,812)
Bowman, Alexander Phillip 3:51:37 (8,571)
Bowman, Ian 4:08:45 (13,149)
Bowman, John 6:04:26 (34,347)
Bowman, Neil Stuart 4:03:15 (11,792)
Bowman, Nick 4:14:03 (14,520)
Bowman, Paul 3:48:35 (7,871)
Bown, Jonathan 3:59:51 (10,952)
Bowness, Paul 4:11:04 (13,738)
Bowring, Simon John 3:17:14 (2,687)
Bowser, Phillip Raymond 4:44:18 (22,591)
Bowtell, Glen Michael 6:03:40 (34,301)
Bowyer, Ian Richard 5:19:23 (29,759)
Box, Dan James 3:23:29 (3,364)
Box, Ian 3:20:48 (3,056)
Box, Julian 4:56:46 (25,707)
Box, Mark 4:15:02 (14,798)
Boxall, David Edward 5:05:28 (27,443)
Boxshall, David 4:50:03 (24,059)
Boy, Peter 5:18:15 (29,582)
Boyce, Darren John 4:27:12 (18,149)
Boyce, Jason Cameron 5:11:56 (28,547)
Boyce, Sean Peter 5:22:41 (30,253)
Boyd, Adrian 4:20:17 (16,194)
Boyd, Bradley 4:39:32 (21,397)
Boyd, Chris 5:23:33 (30,393)
Boyd, Gareth John 4:07:52 (12,924)
Boyd, Keith Hamilton 5:23:59 (30,477)
Boyd, Leonard 3:11:59 (2,090)
Boyd, Stuart 4:08:35 (13,111)
Boyd-Carpenter, Harry 4:30:11 (19,022)

Boyes, Ian R 4:03:24 (11,820)
Boylan, Robert Francis 4:57:21 (25,830)
Boyland, Alexander J 5:11:13 (28,439)
Boyle, Alan 4:29:50 (18,920)
Boyle, Andrew Ian 5:11:07 (28,423)
Boyle, Brian 4:22:41 (16,897)
Boyle, Christopher Alan 3:24:38 (3,528)
Boyle, James 5:44:00 (32,767)
Boyle, Kevin 4:38:31 (21,118)
Boyle, Mark 3:47:08 (7,551)
Boylett, Martin 5:01:02 (26,656)
Boyling, Edward A 4:44:30 (22,638)
Bozzoli, Andrea 5:06:17 (27,581)
Brabazon, Ben Stewart 3:59:58 (10,980)
Braben, Owen G 5:50:11 (33,349)
Brace, Martin John 3:10:10 (1,920)
Bracegirdle, Jon 4:26:05 (17,837)
Bracegirdle, Matthew 3:37:29 (5,658)
Bracher, Joe R 3:29:23 (4,299)
Bracken, Alan 4:23:03 (16,994)
Bracken, Chris 6:19:11 (35,090)
Bracken, James Mark 4:35:23 (20,321)
Brackett, Paul J 3:36:37 (5,499)
Brackin, Philip 3:35:48 (5,379)
Brackley, Adam 4:42:03 (22,028)
Brackley, Mark Adrian 5:09:37 (28,170)
Brackpool, Tim 4:54:58 (25,296)
Brackstone, Robert L 4:32:05 (19,453)
Bradbeer-Dubery, Dominic 4:16:46 (15,239)
Bradbury, Alex 4:46:11 (23,085)
Bradbury, Alexis James 3:16:59 (2,667)
Bradbury, Andy 4:13:24 (14,335)
Bradbury, Jacob 4:06:31 (12,578)
Bradbury, James 5:12:13 (28,606)
Bradbury, Timothy Mark 6:19:21 (35,098)
Bradford, Darren V 3:42:58 (6,689)
Bradford, David 2:38:24 (170)
Bradford, Matt S 3:06:44 (1,589)
Bradford, Nathan J 2:54:49 (725)
Bradford, Paul 4:29:54 (18,953)
Bradie, Stuart 4:33:09 (19,748)
Bradley, Adam 3:47:16 (7,591)
Bradley, Alan Mark 3:44:58 (7,089)
Bradley, Barry 3:45:14 (7,147)
Bradley, Ben Michael 3:56:12 (9,841)
Bradley, Ciaran 3:51:50 (8,614)
Bradley, Darren Mark 4:19:57 (16,086)
Bradley, David 3:44:43 (7,038)
Bradley, Eamon 3:19:33 (2,921)
Bradley, Gavin 3:37:49 (5,726)
Bradley, Ian 4:40:47 (21,719)
Bradley, Ian 4:44:30 (22,638)
Bradley, Ian Brenden Peter 5:06:07 (27,552)
Bradley, Jack 4:23:29 (17,099)
Bradley, John T 4:02:09 (11,522)
Bradley, Kyran George 4:26:30 (17,952)
Bradley, Lawrence 3:39:32 (6,050)
Bradley, Mark 3:58:13 (10,463)
Bradley, Mark S 3:58:31 (10,560)
Bradley, Martin 4:16:12 (15,071)
Bradley, Nick 4:04:18 (12,029)
Bradley, Paul 4:59:18 (26,286)
Bradley, Scott 2:35:16 (117)
Bradley, Scott 6:01:05 (34,136)
Bradley-Barnard, Harry 4:09:07 (13,234)
Bradshaw, Chris 5:48:30 (33,197)
Bradshaw, Chris W 4:06:55 (12,689)
Bradshaw, David 4:15:19 (14,865)
Bradshaw, Eric G 4:48:06 (23,567)
Bradshaw, Lee Thomas 3:48:17 (7,800)
Bradshaw, Stephen L 4:44:38 (22,682)
Brady, Anthony 4:56:00 (25,535)
Brady, Edward W 3:16:40 (2,638)
Brady, Gerald J 6:06:54 (34,501)
Brady, Grant N 2:52:20 (585)
Brady, Hugh Joseph Martin 5:30:29 (31,352)
Brady, Martin George 3:41:20 (6,392)
Brady, Owen 5:17:35 (29,485)
Braehler, Rainer 4:07:37 (12,860)
Braeuer, Ingo 4:47:26 (23,396)
Braganza, Ricardo 4:09:54 (13,443)
Bragg, Marcus Chester 4:50:44 (24,219)
Bragg, Russell Philip 4:27:31 (18,241)

Brahin, Brice 4:24:44 (17,450)
Brahmawar, Sanjay 4:38:41 (21,165)
Braid, Colin 5:47:07 (33,061)
Braid, Gordon 4:27:20 (18,190)
Braidwood, Billy G 4:04:13 (12,012)
Brailsford, Craig Stephen 3:38:33 (5,854)
Braim, Mark Edward 4:07:30 (12,834)
Brainch, Michael 3:52:27 (8,777)
Braithwaite, Iain 4:19:56 (16,082)
Braithwaite, Nicholas 4:00:16 (11,048)
Brake, Martin 5:01:01 (26,652)
Brameld, Andrew 4:40:16 (21,565)
Bramham, Richard M 3:34:29 (5,149)
Bramley, Matthew 3:50:51 (8,390)
Bramley,, Peter, John 4:23:34 (17,125)
Brammer, Paul 5:14:52 (29,048)
Bramston, Nick 4:54:09 (25,079)
Branch, David 3:58:42 (10,625)
Brand, Gerson Luiz 3:55:19 (9,567)
Brand, Philip 4:59:17 (26,283)
Brand, Roger J 3:42:14 (6,553)
Brandås, Sven-Åke 5:11:52 (28,538)
Brandon, Toby 3:29:18 (4,289)
Braniff, Ian John 3:39:44 (6,084)
Brannan, Andrew 5:38:19 (32,244)
Brannigan, Peter 5:02:17 (26,904)

Branson, Richard 5:02:24 (26,927)

Branson, Sam 5:13:03 (28,747)
Branston, Michael Richard Philip 3:17:30 (2,712)
Brant, Andrew 4:04:41 (12,122)
Brant, Mark Simon 4:26:04 (17,830)
Brant, Raymond Peter 5:20:49 (29,979)
Brar, Diljit 5:37:12 (32,125)
Brasse, Jonathan David 4:24:11 (17,281)
Brassington, Alexander 6:09:55 (34,657)
Brasted, Dominic John 4:10:10 (13,517)
Brathwaite, Leon 5:43:52 (32,760)
Braude, Jonathan H 5:51:23 (33,454)
Braund, Roland 4:47:16 (23,355)
Brawley, Brendan 3:45:18 (7,162)
Brawn, Chris Stuart 3:40:13 (6,184)
Brawn, Christopher 5:19:16 (29,742)
Brawn, James Alexander 5:33:48 (31,748)
Bray, Jamie 5:55:28 (33,752)
Bray, Justin 3:56:36 (9,958)
Bray, Michael S 3:46:31 (7,423)
Bray, Paul Steven 4:14:02 (14,514)
Bray, Richard 5:25:57 (30,774)
Braybrook, Colin A 3:02:41 (1,311)
Braybrooke, Jason Roy 3:49:23 (8,059)
Brazendale, Owen 4:07:51 (12,918)
Brazil, Raphael Sean 4:45:46 (22,973)
Breaker, Ben 4:22:10 (16,747)
Brearley, Mick 4:16:57 (15,285)
Brede, Jan 4:27:53 (18,335)
Breen, Christopher Martin 3:10:47 (1,970)
Breen, Eric William 5:38:19 (32,244)
Breen, Gary S 4:16:30 (15,170)

Breen, Graham J	2:29:28 (61)
Breen, Rowan A.	2:40:01 (199)
Breen, Stephen	4:16:16 (15,092)
Breingan, David S	3:41:12 (6,367)
Breker, Markus	4:41:37 (21,927)
Bremner, Stuart	5:03:12 (27,060)
Brend, Colin Antony	4:44:01 (22,509)
Brendell, Stephen	5:05:51 (27,504)
Brendryen, Staale	4:23:54 (17,213)
Brennan, Alex	3:26:49 (3,851)
Brennan, David	5:07:42 (27,847)
Brennan, Greg	3:40:36 (6,260)
Brennan, Joe	3:51:32 (8,544)
Brennan, John Joseph	4:47:23 (23,386)
Brennan, Lee James	3:47:09 (7,556)
Brennan, Mike	3:53:38 (9,101)
Brennan, Norbert	3:44:19 (6,942)
Brennan, Shaun Francis	4:42:52 (22,234)
Brennan, Stewart	4:27:06 (18,120)
Brennand, Michael S	4:16:19 (15,112)
Brennand, Simon	3:33:58 (5,052)
Brennand, Steven K	3:40:59 (6,320)
Brent, Dan	6:02:34 (34,222)
Bresciani, Fabio	3:28:02 (4,058)
Bresciani, Stefano	3:34:35 (5,171)
Bresland, Noel	4:32:52 (19,661)
Bretaudeau, Alain	4:31:27 (19,321)
Brethous, Jacques	3:55:12 (9,528)
Breton, Geoffrey Thomas	4:10:23 (13,564)
Brett, Alex	3:36:38 (5,501)
Brett, Charlie	4:38:33 (21,131)
Brett, Colin M	3:29:50 (4,385)
Brett, Edward	3:57:39 (10,280)
Brett, Gavin Peter	3:25:24 (3,631)
Brett, Justin	3:36:05 (5,424)
Brett, Stephen	3:05:40 (1,511)
Brett, Tim	4:29:33 (18,820)
Brettell, Neil	4:10:19 (13,548)
Breugel, Wim Van	4:11:32 (13,860)
Brewer, Adam	4:01:50 (11,455)
Brewer, Craig Matthew	3:36:47 (5,520)
Brewer, John	4:25:42 (17,715)
Brewer, John Edward	4:40:19 (21,579)
Brewster, Ben David	3:33:50 (5,031)
Brewster, Jorden	3:55:39 (9,661)
Brewster, Matthew J	3:58:57 (10,704)
Brewster, Paul A	3:51:53 (8,632)
Breydin, Patrick	5:46:39 (33,022)
Brial, Marc	3:40:00 (6,147)
Brian, Nick	3:44:43 (7,038)
Briano, José Ignacio	4:32:11 (19,483)
Bridge, Andrew John	3:15:45 (2,524)
Bridge, John D	3:18:42 (2,841)
Bridge, Paul	4:54:18 (25,134)
Bridge, Peter Ernest	5:44:45 (32,847)
Bridgeland, Michael J	2:48:54 (441)
Bridgeman, Shane	4:05:51 (12,421)
Bridgen, Jason	4:19:27 (15,961)
Bridges, Anthony M	3:03:54 (1,381)
Bridges, David L	3:49:50 (8,169)
Bridges, Keith A	6:25:17 (35,326)
Bridges, Paul Thomas	4:18:01 (15,582)
Bridges, Russell T	4:39:25 (21,363)
Bridgman, Andy	4:29:38 (18,860)
Bridle, Steven	4:14:37 (14,687)
Bridon, David John	4:52:29 (24,681)
Bridson, Mark A	3:54:07 (9,236)
Brien, Ashley	4:12:46 (14,176)
Brierley, Andrew S	2:46:50 (380)
Brierley, John Paul	5:10:42 (28,363)
Briffitt, Nicholas John	2:59:00 (1,049)
Brigden, Lewis Daniel	5:05:53 (27,512)
Brigginshaw, Alex Paul	4:36:05 (20,500)
Briggs, Andrew J	3:25:55 (3,721)
Briggs, Ben Edward	5:37:53 (32,198)
Briggs, Brian Thomas	3:21:36 (3,148)
Briggs, Daniel	6:12:31 (34,783)
Briggs, Marcus	5:06:14 (27,573)
Briggs, Mark Alan	3:52:37 (8,826)
Briggs, Martin	6:00:34 (34,097)
Briggs, Matthew	4:58:32 (26,097)
Briggs, Paul	4:42:08 (22,045)
Briggs, Shaun	5:01:18 (26,709)
Briggs, Shaun Alan	4:53:49 (24,998)
Briggs, Simon	4:58:04 (25,980)
Brigham, Josh	3:16:53 (2,658)
Brighouse, Mark	4:01:09 (11,287)
Bright, Andrew	3:58:07 (10,423)
Bright, Chris	4:41:38 (21,930)
Bright, David	4:31:19 (19,295)
Brightling, David	3:52:21 (8,755)
Brightmore, Daniel Walsham	5:30:45 (31,385)
Brighton, Michael J	4:42:13 (22,069)
Brightwell, Ian R	4:51:33 (24,431)
Brightwell, Simon L	3:08:42 (1,783)
Brighty, Keith G	3:39:59 (6,139)
Briley, Stephen Andrew	5:29:36 (31,237)
Brimacombe, Steven John	4:13:31 (14,369)
Brimley, Dave	4:55:44 (25,476)
Brimson, Jason Howard	4:52:58 (24,788)
Brind, Gary Clive	3:56:39 (9,978)
Brindle, Liam Mark	4:51:35 (24,438)
Brink, Daniel Brink Adrian	4:56:56 (25,753)
Brinkley, Ian	3:48:33 (7,861)
Brinkley, Lee G	3:33:16 (4,930)
Briozzo, Cesare	4:10:27 (13,579)
Briozzo, Mirko Gianluca	4:26:02 (17,822)
Brisco, Douglas A	3:00:57 (1,204)
Briscoe, Noel A	4:13:15 (14,297)
Briseno, Jesus	4:10:16 (13,542)
Brisola, Leandro P	3:53:23 (9,024)
Bristow, Nicholas James	6:08:49 (34,603)
Bristow, Robert A	4:22:12 (16,761)
Britschgi, Daniel D B	3:20:23 (3,002)
Britt, Brendan Michael	4:25:22 (17,625)
Britt, Paul Andrew	3:21:13 (3,111)
Brittain, Richard D	3:09:57 (1,903)
Brittain, Tony Ian	5:29:20 (31,199)
Britten, Kit John	4:23:00 (16,984)
Britten, Nicholas	4:19:32 (15,978)
Britten, Tony R	3:49:30 (8,093)
Britton, Alan R	4:06:58 (12,705)
Britton, Lee S	4:17:29 (15,433)
Broad, Chris	5:37:46 (32,191)
Broad, Glenn	5:57:57 (33,928)
Broad, Mathew	2:59:30 (1,110)
Broadbent, Rick M	4:25:49 (17,760)
Broadbent, Sam	4:55:49 (25,492)
Broadbent, Steven Scott	3:35:59 (5,411)
Broadfoot, Peter	3:58:24 (10,523)
Broadhead, Andrew Richard	4:49:42 (23,978)
Broadhead, Richard	4:00:53 (11,211)
Broadhurst, Carl	3:55:52 (9,740)
Broadhurst, Jeff	4:42:30 (22,141)
Broadley, Paul	3:49:25 (8,070)
Broadley, Rob	4:55:21 (25,392)
Broadley, Robert	5:17:07 (29,408)
Broadman, James B	4:06:03 (12,463)
Broadribb, Will	3:19:42 (2,937)
Brobin, James M	5:08:16 (27,946)
Brock, Greg	3:12:56 (2,179)
Brockington, Martin J	4:49:47 (24,005)
Brocklehurst, Robert	3:54:49 (9,427)
Brocklesby, Adam	4:22:28 (16,839)
Brockley, Anthony Joseph	4:32:08 (19,468)
Brockley, Stephen John	4:13:53 (14,478)
Brockwell, Roberto	3:41:37 (6,442)
Brodie, Andrew G	4:29:35 (18,833)
Brodie, David	4:46:49 (23,259)
Brodie, Mark James	4:28:24 (18,487)
Brodnicki, Ralf	3:22:46 (3,267)
Brodrick, Ian	3:34:04 (5,070)
Brodrick, Michael John	3:55:00 (9,479)
Brodziak, Andy	3:45:23 (7,184)
Brohan, Stephen	5:06:01 (27,533)
Brolly, Martin	4:00:40 (11,159)
Bromige, Robert Michael	3:28:55 (4,214)
Bromley, Alec	4:57:27 (25,849)
Bromley, Callum Peter	3:18:10 (2,791)
Brons, Dave	5:32:31 (31,605)
Brook, Andrew	4:03:15 (11,792)
Brook, Daniel Christopher	3:43:54 (6,859)
Brook, Julian	4:28:52 (18,632)
Brook, Matthew James	4:05:05 (12,225)
Brook, Peter	4:38:31 (21,118)
Brook, Sean	3:56:38 (9,973)
Brooke, Anthony D	3:16:54 (2,661)
Brooke, James	3:08:24 (1,739)
Brooke, James Allan	4:33:10 (19,752)
Brooke, Louis	3:33:51 (5,036)
Brooke, William John	4:26:51 (18,039)
Brooker, Darren	3:52:02 (8,667)
Brooker, John	3:51:18 (8,492)
Brooker, Michael George Peter	5:14:57 (29,059)
Brooker, Terry	4:16:16 (15,092)
Brooker, Vincent R	4:35:48 (20,420)
Brookes, Adrian P	3:14:16 (2,355)
Brookes, Anton	4:46:11 (23,085)
Brookes, Ian W	3:55:22 (9,587)
Brookes, Malcolm	5:03:01 (27,029)
Brookes, Mark	4:43:57 (22,492)
Brookes, Paul Damian	3:39:56 (6,135)
Brookes, Richard A	4:03:37 (11,878)
Brookes, Robert J	4:02:14 (11,545)
Brookes, Stephen John	4:22:28 (16,839)
Brookes, Stephen John	5:16:48 (29,352)
Brookhouse, Paul Jonathan	4:26:23 (17,923)
Brookman, Chris	3:27:30 (3,961)
Brooks, Alex	4:43:31 (22,372)
Brooks, Alex D	2:38:52 (174)
Brooks, Anthony David	5:45:03 (32,875)
Brooks, Carl	4:26:10 (17,865)
Brooks, Charles	5:22:23 (30,204)
Brooks, Darryl John	3:38:36 (5,869)
Brooks, David	4:26:11 (17,868)
Brooks, David	6:28:57 (35,461)
Brooks, David C	3:33:22 (4,945)
Brooks, Edmond David	5:22:23 (30,204)
Brooks, Edward	3:06:01 (1,535)
Brooks, Matt	4:37:34 (20,900)
Brooks, Matthew	5:42:50 (32,657)
Brooks, Michael	4:17:39 (15,483)
Brooks, Michael G	4:24:31 (17,395)
Brooks, Neil	4:01:43 (11,415)
Brooks, Paul John	3:55:44 (9,688)
Brooks, Paul S	3:55:44 (9,688)
Brooks, Paul Tinothy	4:12:15 (14,045)
Brooks, Peter	4:49:27 (23,906)
Brooks, Richard D	3:45:48 (7,265)
Brooks, Roger	3:41:45 (6,469)
Brooks, Roger Michael	4:13:21 (14,328)
Brooks, Sam	4:19:51 (16,056)
Brooks, Sean Kevin	3:21:21 (3,124)
Brooks, Steve J	3:51:00 (8,423)
Broom, Anthony	4:15:10 (14,826)
Broom, David Christopher	3:43:44 (6,811)
Broom, Shaun S	4:56:04 (25,551)
Broome, David	4:24:18 (17,319)
Broome, Gareth Andrew	3:46:31 (7,423)
Broome, Marcus Robin	3:40:51 (6,301)
Broomfield, James Geoffrey	3:59:37 (10,896)
Brosnan, Michael F	6:27:05 (35,398)
Broude, Daniel Oliver	4:11:34 (13,867)
Brough, Dickon M	3:11:27 (2,045)
Brough, Paul A	3:21:09 (3,105)
Broughton, David	3:32:52 (4,875)
Broughton, Dean	4:52:33 (24,699)
Broughton, Stuart C	4:51:15 (24,366)
Brousseau, Christophe	4:04:24 (12,050)
Brower, Derek	5:01:42 (26,792)
Brown, Alan Steven	4:23:33 (17,119)
Brown, Allan G	5:31:40 (31,497)
Brown, Andrew	3:50:12 (8,247)
Brown, Andrew	4:06:46 (12,645)
Brown, Andrew	4:14:57 (14,771)
Brown, Andrew	4:28:38 (18,564)
Brown, Andrew Christopher	4:41:45 (21,952)
Brown, Andrew Neil	6:23:26 (35,258)
Brown, Andy	4:43:27 (22,359)
Brown, Andy C	4:39:17 (21,326)
Brown, Anthony	4:10:37 (13,620)
Brown, Anthony Christopher	5:54:40 (33,683)
Brown, Barnaby David	5:01:56 (26,835)
Brown, Chris	4:53:32 (24,928)
Brown, Chris	5:55:47 (33,714)
Brown, Christopher	3:52:23 (8,764)
Brown, Christopher Shenton	4:22:04 (16,723)
Brown, Christopher Stiles	4:34:23 (20,091)
Brown, Daniel	5:56:09 (33,806)

Brown, Dave	5:18:04 (29,556)	
Brown, David	3:54:47 (9,416)	
Brown, David	4:31:53 (19,404)	
Brown, David G	4:56:40 (25,686)	
Brown, David Peter	4:36:45 (20,670)	
Brown, David R	3:56:29 (9,926)	
Brown, David Rodney	6:23:15 (35,247)	
Brown, Dean Carl	4:40:15 (21,560)	
Brown, Edward	3:56:15 (9,857)	
Brown, Edward	4:00:44 (11,179)	
Brown, Garry Edward	4:17:16 (15,368)	
Brown, Gary	4:40:16 (21,565)	
Brown, Gavin Daniel	6:19:33 (35,106)	
Brown, Gavin Raymond	5:29:49 (31,270)	
Brown, Graeme	3:58:25 (10,532)	
Brown, Graeme J	4:11:53 (13,950)	
Brown, Howard	5:30:12 (31,316)	
Brown, Hugh James	3:23:45 (3,401)	
Brown, Ian M	2:57:55 (950)	
Brown, Ian Samuel	4:50:54 (24,269)	
Brown, Ian Stephen	4:36:33 (20,618)	
Brown, Jake	4:58:03 (25,979)	
Brown, James	5:20:40 (29,958)	
Brown, James A	3:25:28 (3,642)	
Brown, James F	6:06:04 (34,455)	
Brown, Jamie	4:59:22 (26,301)	
Brown, Jason	4:26:34 (17,972)	
Brown, Jim H	3:30:26 (4,489)	
Brown, John Alan	6:19:53 (35,120)	
Brown, John J	3:37:44 (5,715)	
Brown, John P	4:24:34 (17,411)	
Brown, Jon	4:25:07 (17,552)	
Brown, Jonathan	3:14:35 (2,396)	
Brown, Jonathan Charles	3:02:02 (1,261)	
Brown, Jonathan Francis	3:32:25 (4,804)	
Brown, Jonathan Mark	3:56:22 (9,887)	
Brown, Jonathan Paul	4:20:18 (16,200)	
Brown, Keith Alan	3:20:58 (3,082)	
Brown, Luke A	5:09:06 (28,067)	
Brown, Luke Bradley Thomas	3:55:31 (9,617)	
Brown, Mark	3:27:25 (3,947)	
Brown, Mark	4:59:18 (26,286)	
Brown, Matthew	5:22:23 (30,204)	
Brown, Michael E	4:09:42 (13,396)	
Brown, Nathan	3:58:19 (10,499)	
Brown, Nicholas	3:46:46 (7,478)	
Brown, Nicholas Hugh	3:47:04 (7,538)	
Brown, Nicholas R	3:40:23 (6,208)	
Brown, Nick	4:17:13 (15,354)	
Brown, Nigel	3:01:00 (1,207)	
Brown, Oliver	3:33:15 (4,929)	
Brown, Oly	4:49:03 (23,813)	
Brown, Paul	3:53:18 (8,997)	
Brown, Paul	4:03:43 (11,901)	
Brown, Paul D	4:04:55 (12,178)	
Brown, Paul Michael	4:02:25 (11,587)	
Brown, Peter	4:37:00 (20,742)	
Brown, Peter	5:00:52 (26,623)	
Brown, Peter Alan	5:23:21 (30,365)	
Brown, Philip G	4:46:34 (23,185)	
Brown, Phillip	4:28:38 (18,564)	
Brown, Ray	3:54:01 (9,215)	
Brown, Richard	4:11:10 (13,762)	
Brown, Richard J	4:00:13 (11,036)	
Brown, Richard Marc	6:20:09 (35,132)	
Brown, Robert	5:03:43 (27,140)	
Brown, Robert	6:14:44 (34,873)	
Brown, Robert James	4:44:16 (22,583)	
Brown, Russell	3:57:50 (10,337)	
Brown, Ryan	3:47:21 (7,609)	
Brown, Sean Daniel	3:57:02 (10,109)	
Brown, Sebastian	4:35:52 (20,437)	
Brown, Simon	5:40:36 (32,443)	
Brown, Stephane	4:47:14 (23,349)	
Brown, Stephen D	3:21:43 (3,163)	
Brown, Stephen Irwin	4:35:22 (20,318)	
Brown, Steven A	3:27:05 (3,882)	
Brown, Stuart Charles	3:29:30 (4,320)	
Brown, Stuart R	3:44:39 (7,024)	
Brown, Thomas	6:27:30 (35,402)	
Brown, Thomas William	3:12:09 (2,105)	
Brown, Trevor Graham	4:27:12 (18,149)	
Brown, Wesley	4:43:40 (22,410)	
Brown, William Robin	4:15:06 (14,808)	
Browne, Alex	4:19:23 (15,950)	
Browne, Charlie	5:32:02 (31,536)	
Browne, Chris	4:10:38 (13,625)	
Browne, Gavin	2:55:31 (772)	
Browne, Kevin S	5:44:52 (32,857)	
Browne, Liam P	3:31:42 (4,697)	
Browne, Matthew Vincent K	4:29:48 (18,913)	
Browne, Nicholas J	2:44:42 (328)	
Browne, Robert J	4:06:34 (12,591)	
Browne, Robert Timothy	4:32:05 (19,453)	
Browne, Simon Mark Francis	4:50:42 (24,208)	
Browning, Keith Michael	6:00:40 (34,101)	
Browning, Warwick E	3:36:56 (5,551)	
Brownlee, Simon J	2:34:41 (106)	
Brownlie, John Alan	5:03:53 (27,171)	
Brownlie, Ryan James	4:57:41 (25,905)	
Brownsdon, Michael	4:50:57 (24,289)	
Broyden, Chris Charles	5:34:08 (31,771)	
Bruand, Martin	3:53:33 (9,073)	
Bruce, Adrian	6:04:10 (34,330)	
Bruce, Alan C	4:17:21 (15,391)	
Bruce, Andrew Keith	3:56:54 (10,056)	
Bruce, Chris Joseph	3:59:39 (10,903)	
Bruce, Clive John	4:39:06 (21,280)	
Bruce, David	4:20:52 (16,381)	
Bruce, David	5:19:26 (29,769)	
Bruce, Edward	4:32:49 (19,635)	
Bruce, Gary	4:04:54 (12,174)	
Bruce, Graeme R	4:13:12 (14,286)	
Bruce, Kevin	6:02:34 (34,222)	
Bruce, Mark	4:17:31 (15,449)	
Bruce, Martin	4:34:59 (20,228)	
Bruce, Matt	3:33:48 (5,025)	
Bruce, Robert	4:09:13 (13,266)	
Bruce, Robert D	4:03:32 (11,854)	
Bruen, Andy	4:15:32 (14,911)	
Bruggenthijs, Johannes	4:18:26 (15,694)	
Brugman, Arie	3:58:44 (10,637)	
Bruguier, Patrice	3:21:02 (3,090)	
Brumby, Paul	3:07:32 (1,654)	
Bruni, Roberto	3:19:06 (2,882)	
Brunjes, Andrew John McCormack	3:39:23 (6,021)	
Bruno, Boucher	3:37:55 (5,746)	
Bruno, Michel	3:59:09 (10,760)	
Bruns, Jon	3:38:09 (5,795)	
Brunsden, Gareth Robert	4:01:29 (11,362)	
Brunswick, Andrew Neil	5:18:21 (29,597)	
Brunt, Craig	5:41:00 (32,483)	
Brunt, James	5:10:08 (28,262)	
Brunton, Christopher Michael	4:26:31 (17,961)	
Brunton, David Antoni	3:42:58 (6,689)	
Brunton, Keith Andrew	4:27:27 (18,220)	
Brunton, Mark	5:26:07 (30,792)	
Brunyee, Jonathan Stephen	3:54:54 (9,450)	
Brushett, Matthew Joseph	3:46:24 (7,397)	
Bruton, James	4:59:05 (26,236)	
Bruwer, François	4:37:35 (20,904)	
Bryan, Andrew Paul	5:33:49 (31,749)	
Bryan, Jason David	4:59:02 (26,223)	
Bryan, Jerry S	3:17:45 (2,738)	
Bryan, Patrick W	3:42:52 (6,671)	
Bryan, Robert Louis	4:16:34 (15,185)	
Bryant, Chris	5:30:29 (31,352)	
Bryant, Danny J	4:14:09 (14,547)	
Bryant, Gareth J	4:25:48 (17,749)	
Bryant, Graham Paul	5:33:01 (31,668)	
Bryant, James	3:44:02 (6,888)	
Bryant, John W	4:57:14 (25,810)	
Bryant, Jonathan	3:36:38 (5,501)	
Bryant, Jonathan	3:54:57 (9,460)	
Bryant, Matthew A	3:53:36 (9,092)	
Bryant, Nick	2:55:47 (787)	
Bryant, Rodney S	3:50:57 (8,411)	
Bryant, Wayne	5:09:08 (28,075)	
Bryant, William G	4:57:58 (25,963)	
Brydon, Richard	5:31:52 (31,519)	
Bryenton, Paul Christopher	5:18:41 (29,653)	
Brysgel, Ethan	4:35:48 (20,420)	
Bryson, Adam	4:20:24 (16,232)	
Bryson, Kenneth M	3:09:08 (1,819)	
Bubb, Ashley	4:18:15 (15,644)	
Bubb, Ian James	3:42:51 (6,669)	
Buchan, Andrew Mark	2:59:58 (1,150)	
Buchan, Stuart	3:00:28 (1,171)	
Buchanan, Anthony	4:41:01 (21,774)	
Buchanan, Barry	5:33:35 (31,724)	
Buchanan, Christopher	2:59:50 (1,140)	
Buchanan, John	4:14:14 (14,579)	
Buchanan-Smith, Beppo	3:56:50 (10,041)	
Bucher, William	4:48:53 (23,768)	
Buck, Alex	5:00:55 (26,638)	
Buck, William L	3:48:38 (7,878)	
Bucket, Andrew Peter	3:47:08 (7,551)	
Buckfield, Nick	3:44:48 (7,056)	
Buckham, Paul	3:00:42 (1,189)	
Buckingham, Gary	3:25:32 (3,652)	
Buckingham, Graham	5:07:31 (27,816)	
Buckland, Erik	4:51:57 (24,538)	
Buckle, Matthew	3:51:04 (8,440)	
Buckle, Michael John	4:43:48 (22,441)	
Buckle, Nick	4:48:06 (23,567)	
Buckle, Robert	5:51:26 (33,458)	
Buckle, Stephen	4:40:05 (21,514)	
Buckle, Stephen	4:40:41 (21,687)	
Buckles, Nick Peter	3:57:17 (10,178)	
Buckley, Alan	2:46:05 (360)	
Buckley, Brian W	3:17:51 (2,749)	
Buckley, Mark	3:55:46 (9,706)	
Buckley, Neil	5:02:53 (27,007)	
Buckley, Stephen	5:51:34 (33,468)	
Bucknall, Martyn David	3:38:33 (5,854)	
Bucknell, Andrew	4:26:48 (18,024)	
Buckwell, Lee W	2:44:01 (310)	
Budalles, Santiago	4:05:53 (12,428)	
Budd, Michael	4:27:50 (18,319)	
Buddin, Paul	5:11:07 (28,423)	
Buder, Karl-Heinz	4:01:30 (11,368)	
Budwig, Asher	4:33:37 (19,897)	
Buecker, Karsten	2:59:25 (1,100)	
Buehler, Helmut	3:51:06 (8,450)	
Bueldt, Stefan	4:02:25 (11,587)	
Bueso, Francisco	3:24:26 (3,504)	
Buffery, Farhad	3:54:19 (9,282)	
Bugby, Antony R	5:50:23 (33,373)	
Bugden, Robin	3:09:03 (1,812)	
Bugg, Barry Martin	4:15:39 (14,937)	
Buglass, Tom	7:13:40 (36,345)	
Buick, Jim	3:25:50 (3,709)	
Buick, Tim	3:46:13 (7,357)	
Bukavs, Neil James	3:39:42 (6,078)	
Bulaitis, Peter A	3:47:06 (7,544)	
Buley, Derek	3:49:40 (8,139)	
Bulezuik, Chris Charles	4:28:01 (18,371)	
Bull, Andrew Richard	5:37:56 (32,205)	
Bull, Christopher John	3:49:35 (8,112)	
Bull, Derek S	7:46:06 (36,550)	
Bull, Henry	4:05:16 (12,276)	
Bull, John	3:27:51 (4,025)	
Bull, John David	3:54:46 (9,407)	
Bull, Mark Darren	5:03:22 (27,083)	
Bull, Martyn G	7:39:38 (36,518)	
Bull, Michael James	3:55:12 (9,528)	
Bull, Peter B	4:19:19 (15,935)	
Bull, Richard Edward	3:52:49 (8,877)	
Bull, Richard Owen	4:01:58 (11,482)	
Bull, Simon	4:01:50 (11,455)	
Bull, Steve R	3:17:46 (2,739)	
Bullard, Michael A	4:28:33 (18,539)	
Bullard, Nick M	3:16:07 (2,564)	
Bullen, Andrew G	7:16:48 (36,377)	
Bullen, Joe P	3:51:33 (8,549)	
Bullock, Craig	4:50:33 (24,173)	
Bullock, Matthew	3:37:56 (5,751)	
Bullock, Mike Lee	3:19:02 (2,873)	
Bullock, Peter K	5:55:16 (33,740)	
Bullock, Rob	4:00:31 (11,118)	
Bullock, Terry	2:52:46 (608)	
Bullows, Ryan Thomas	3:18:01 (2,768)	
Bulman, Aled	4:23:44 (17,175)	
Bulmer, Marvin	4:35:09 (20,264)	
Bultz, Peter Mark	4:45:48 (22,979)	
Bumstead, Stephen Stuart	3:10:22 (1,935)	
Bunbury, Anthony G	4:51:20 (24,381)	
Bunce, Anthony Graham	4:07:29 (12,826)	
Bunce, Jamie Stuart	5:13:44 (28,879)	

Bunclark, Nick James Grant........3:56:19 (9,877)
Bunday, Simon P.........4:13:56 (14,486)
Bungay, Alan M.........5:52:44 (33,556)
Buniting, Darren J.........4:56:16 (25,601)
Bunn, Richard.........4:55:03 (25,321)
Bunn, Richard William James.....3:35:31 (5,327)
Bunnage, Russell J.........4:14:24 (14,613)
Bunney, Allen.........3:42:28 (6,590)
Bunney, David Robert.........4:19:07 (15,879)
Bunston, Michael John.........3:48:57 (7,962)
Bunting, Andrew James.........3:35:53 (5,395)
Bunting, Daniel.........4:39:29 (21,381)
Bunting, David.........4:50:15 (24,107)
Bunting, Naz.........3:38:33 (5,854)
Bunting, Simon J.........5:17:30 (29,471)
Buono, Richard.........5:45:08 (32,879)
Buonopane, Carlo.........3:23:16 (3,337)
Buquet, Olivier.........4:47:39 (23,455)
Burbage, Frank.........4:08:58 (13,201)
Burbidge, Thomas.........3:48:02 (7,747)
Burborough, Nick.........4:23:34 (17,125)
Burborough, Peter F.........4:14:30 (14,647)
Burbury, Simon.........3:48:17 (7,800)
Burch, Matthew I.........4:34:35 (20,145)
Burchell, Mark Thomas.........4:30:54 (19,190)
Burchell, Neil.........4:38:03 (20,997)
Burchett, Rainer H.........4:09:54 (13,443)
Burchnall, Nicholas.........3:25:49 (3,705)
Burden, John P.........3:48:58 (7,966)
Burden, Keith Michael.........3:04:35 (1,436)
Burden, Stuart Myles.........4:36:23 (20,573)
Burdett, Jim L.........2:46:43 (378)
Burdett, John William.........6:11:41 (34,731)
Burdett, Simon Lee.........5:04:50 (27,339)
Burdett, William A.........4:08:01 (12,966)
Burdon, Brian.........4:45:44 (22,962)
Burdsey, Timothy David.........4:55:45 (25,480)
Burdzik, Julian.........3:06:33 (1,574)
Burfoot, Peter D.........3:44:15 (6,923)
Burford, Nicholas Lawrence.......3:59:36 (10,893)
Burford, Peter G.........4:00:15 (11,044)
Burford, Phillip B.........3:42:11 (6,546)
Burford, Piers Raymond.........3:55:29 (9,611)
Burge, Daniel Peter.........6:05:43 (34,435)
Burge, Nigel J.........4:41:33 (21,910)
Burge, Ray Lee.........4:45:46 (22,973)
Burge, Steve O.........3:49:58 (8,204)
Burger, Primarius.........4:21:55 (16,680)
Burger, Richard.........4:42:49 (22,220)
Burgess, David.........2:54:53 (731)
Burgess, David.........4:29:39 (18,866)
Burgess, David Christopher.........4:40:14 (21,553)
Burgess, John.........5:25:21 (30,669)
Burgess, John Alun.........3:29:08 (4,259)
Burgess, John Leonard.........9:02:35 (36,615)
Burgess, Mike John.........3:25:28 (3,642)
Burgess, Neil John.........5:11:16 (28,447)
Burgess, Paul Greyson.........3:54:35 (9,347)
Burgess, Shaun C.........5:40:49 (32,457)
Burgess, Stephen James.........5:21:33 (30,083)
Burgess, Trevor.........4:41:56 (22,001)
Burggraaff, Hans.........4:54:30 (25,179)
Burghardt, Peter.........3:55:23 (9,591)
Burghes, Christopher Robert......3:18:23 (2,815)
Burgin, Jarod Simon.........4:55:48 (25,490)
Burgin, Neil Dougall.........3:44:32 (6,997)
Burgman, David.........4:13:19 (14,318)
Burke, Chris James.........5:12:26 (28,640)
Burke, Christopher Mark.........4:37:25 (20,850)
Burke, Christopher Matthew.......2:58:00 (956)
Burke, Desmond Anthony.........5:07:21 (27,783)
Burke, Geoffrey Patrick.........3:51:28 (8,533)
Burke, Iain Anthony.........3:50:16 (8,264)
Burke, James.........4:43:22 (22,339)
Burke, James.........5:27:33 (30,971)
Burke, Jonjo.........4:02:51 (11,688)
Burke, Joseph.........3:30:11 (4,447)
Burke, Martin J.........5:53:10 (33,588)
Burke, Martin S.........4:24:53 (17,485)
Burke, Michael Robert.........3:28:44 (4,179)
Burke, Nicholas.........4:26:16 (17,895)
Burke, Paul Dominic.........5:18:55 (29,688)
Burke, Steve.........4:20:14 (16,173)
Burke, Tim.........4:53:59 (25,045)
Burkett, Mark.........3:22:26 (3,233)
Burkhart, Kevin.........3:51:05 (8,445)
Burland, David.........3:49:57 (8,199)
Burleigh, Philip J.........3:24:13 (3,471)
Burleton, Paul.........3:41:50 (6,486)
Burley, George.........4:33:03 (19,715)
Burley, Matthew.........3:36:24 (5,468)
Burley, Nick.........4:45:43 (22,955)
Burlinson, Peter.........3:41:50 (6,486)
Burman, Dan.........4:14:58 (14,773)
Burn, Richard William.........3:46:51 (7,500)
Burnard, Alex.........4:07:09 (12,744)
Burness, John.........5:04:10 (27,222)
Burnett, Christopher.........4:47:13 (23,344)
Burnett, Daniel Christian.........4:03:38 (11,884)
Burnett, Kevin J.........3:39:48 (6,104)
Burnham, Andrew.........3:24:28 (3,506)
Burnham, Russell F.........4:21:55 (16,680)
Burnham-Jones, Gary Andrew.....5:03:01 (27,029)
Burnip, Glenn K.........5:03:50 (27,162)
Burnley, Paul D.........3:24:59 (3,577)
Burns, Alastair.........4:40:12 (21,538)
Burns, Benjamin Matthew.........4:33:22 (19,815)
Burns, Carl Peter.........3:19:29 (2,915)
Burns, Christopher R.........4:11:20 (13,800)
Burns, Craig.........4:30:00 (18,977)
Burns, Danny.........5:24:44 (30,587)
Burns, David.........5:03:11 (27,056)
Burns, Garry.........4:02:30 (11,601)
Burns, Jack.........4:25:55 (17,790)
Burns, James.........4:29:53 (18,943)
Burns, James.........5:58:26 (33,961)
Burns, John P.........3:39:31 (6,046)
Burns, Kevin Christopher.........5:50:12 (33,355)
Burns, Lee Rodney.........5:10:10 (28,270)
Burns, Mark Joseph.........4:05:52 (12,424)
Burns, Neil Leslie.........3:21:59 (3,194)
Burns, Paul.........4:53:00 (24,792)
Burns, Paul Laurence.........5:48:06 (33,150)
Burns, Paul Raymond.........5:03:04 (27,034)
Burns, Richard Paul.........3:56:57 (10,071)
Burns, Robert.........5:48:52 (33,227)
Burns, Simon J.........4:25:22 (17,625)
Burr, Mike.........4:03:14 (11,785)
Burrage, Adam.........4:46:44 (23,236)
Burrage, Andrew Neal.........4:36:30 (20,605)
Burrage, Chris.........4:55:21 (25,392)
Burrell, Alan.........5:06:36 (27,643)
Burrell, Anthony.........3:13:39 (2,274)
Burrell, John Frederick.........4:15:42 (14,952)
Burrett, Michael D.........2:31:11 (77)
Burridge, Cody.........4:12:16 (14,048)
Burridge, Ian Martin.........4:51:58 (24,545)
Burrow, Geoff Mark.........4:32:18 (19,514)
Burrows, Alan.........4:43:36 (22,394)
Burrows, Anthony C.........3:11:26 (2,042)
Burrows, Chris.........6:01:15 (34,143)
Burrows, David.........5:33:55 (31,755)
Burrows, James.........5:00:14 (26,505)
Burrows, Lee.........3:25:22 (3,624)
Burrows, Mark.........4:07:41 (12,883)
Burslem, Paul.........2:59:50 (1,140)
Bursztyn, Danny.........4:02:55 (11,710)
Burt, John G.........3:25:09 (3,600)
Burt, Jonathan Brenton.........3:28:08 (4,079)
Burt, Stephen W.........3:29:53 (4,393)
Burton, Andrew James.........3:41:06 (6,345)
Burton, Chris J.........2:59:29 (1,107)
Burton, Cliff.........3:51:34 (8,554)
Burton, Hugh R.........3:33:45 (5,013)
Burton, James Edward.........4:19:13 (15,903)
Burton, Kenny.........5:06:56 (27,710)
Burton, Matthew Charles.........3:44:01 (6,886)
Burton, Nathan James.........4:33:22 (19,815)
Burton, Oliver P.........4:38:25 (21,092)
Burton, Paul.........3:26:06 (3,749)
Burton, Paul.........4:32:48 (19,630)
Burton, Philip.........5:08:35 (27,985)
Burton, Robert.........2:48:04 (417)
Burton, Robert Graham.........5:47:09 (33,066)
Burton, Ross Alexnder.........5:21:42 (30,108)
Burton, Shaun.........3:54:24 (9,300)
Burton, Tim.........5:00:32 (26,557)
Burtwell, Mark C.........3:15:02 (2,441)
Burvill, Ray.........6:51:13 (36,017)
Burwell, Oliver David.........3:44:14 (6,921)
Burwood, Chris Malcolm.........3:52:58 (8,911)
Busbridge, Hugo.........4:14:30 (14,647)
Busch, Graham.........3:41:11 (6,362)
Busch, Wolfgang.........4:54:52 (25,272)
Buscke, Graeme C.........2:49:12 (454)
Bush, Andrew P.........4:44:09 (22,550)
Bush, Andrew Stuart.........3:24:29 (3,510)
Bush, John L.........5:25:19 (30,665)
Bush, Mark A.........3:55:53 (9,745)
Bush, Matthew J.........4:00:24 (11,090)
Bush, Nick.........3:39:50 (6,110)
Bush, Paul William.........4:26:11 (17,868)
Bush, Steve.........6:05:14 (34,407)
Bush, Steven John.........5:19:51 (29,829)
Bushby, Ray.........3:58:35 (10,590)
Bushell, David.........4:11:20 (13,800)
Bushell, Jeremy.........3:39:59 (6,139)
Bushell, Les George.........5:29:47 (31,266)
Buskin, Aaron Robert Jones.........5:37:33 (32,170)
Buss, Jonathan.........3:59:23 (10,834)
Buss, Mike.........4:58:55 (26,192)
Bussell, Terry.........7:38:52 (36,513)
Bussey, Steven Charles.........3:45:46 (7,261)
Bussolati, Antonio.........3:27:14 (3,912)
Bussy, Richard James.........3:56:31 (9,938)
Bustin, Mark.........4:10:02 (13,483)
Bustin, Paul Graham.........4:22:14 (16,776)
Buswell, Andy Martin.........3:14:22 (2,363)
Butcher, Alexander George.........6:52:43 (36,065)
Butcher, Andrew Steven.........4:37:25 (20,850)
Butcher, Antony.........5:38:55 (32,299)
Butcher, Gary.........2:56:09 (811)
Butcher, Mark.........4:15:18 (14,861)
Butcher, Philip J.........3:53:35 (9,084)
Butcher, Sam.........3:24:43 (3,541)
Butfield, Colin.........3:14:15 (2,349)
Butini, Alberto.........4:16:21 (15,125)
Butko, Paul John.........3:43:11 (6,729)
Butler, Andrew James.........4:30:31 (19,091)
Butler, Andrew P.........4:29:52 (18,935)
Butler, Anthony.........3:27:46 (4,008)
Butler, Brian David.........5:35:39 (31,947)
Butler, Carl R.........5:04:12 (27,230)
Butler, Chris.........6:20:53 (35,160)
Butler, Colin.........4:23:42 (17,156)
Butler, Craig.........3:58:45 (10,644)
Butler, Daniel.........6:33:22 (35,607)
Butler, Danny Aidan Phllip.........3:54:57 (9,460)
Butler, David.........5:21:10 (30,031)
Butler, David A.........2:54:53 (731)
Butler, Denis.........5:00:05 (26,474)
Butler, Gary.........3:58:57 (10,704)
Butler, Gethin J.........2:47:35 (405)
Butler, Glen.........4:37:19 (20,824)
Butler, Jason.........3:55:29 (9,611)
Butler, Jeffrey.........3:13:57 (2,309)
Butler, Kenneth John.........5:01:09 (26,674)
Butler, Lee David James.........3:29:26 (4,312)
Butler, Lyle William.........3:26:35 (3,814)
Butler, Mark David.........5:05:35 (27,464)
Butler, Matthew Stephen.........3:09:55 (1,900)
Butler, Raymond K.........3:09:33 (1,864)
Butler, Robert A.........3:37:55 (5,746)
Butler, Ryan William.........6:21:17 (35,177)
Butler, Simon.........5:02:35 (26,956)
Butler, Simon Gordon.........4:50:42 (24,208)
Butler, Stephen.........3:39:45 (6,090)
Butler, Stephen D.........5:26:53 (30,887)
Butler, Stephen P.........4:00:55 (11,225)
Butler, Terence John.........6:04:04 (34,327)
Butler, Timothy J.........5:09:48 (28,196)
Buttell, George L.........4:44:34 (22,658)
Butterfield, John Alexander.........4:30:46 (19,164)
Butterfill, Ross.........5:11:59 (28,558)
Butters, Michael John.........4:47:21 (23,379)
Butterworth, James Kent.........4:48:57 (23,788)
Buttery, Andrew J.........2:42:49 (269)
Butti, Marco.........3:47:36 (7,669)
Buttler, James Edward.........4:13:39 (14,417)

Button, Martin Andrew Colin	3:18:19 (2,806)	
Button, Paul	4:34:31 (20,124)	
Buttress, Mark Anthony	4:29:35 (18,833)	
Buxton, Graham	6:02:39 (34,228)	
Buxton, Joe	4:02:41 (11,646)	
Buxton, Kevin	2:59:42 (1,129)	
Buxton, Michael	5:16:07 (29,244)	
Buxton, Nigel	3:11:04 (2,007)	
Buzzard, David James	3:53:10 (8,963)	
Buzzoni, Daniele	3:41:12 (6,367)	
Byansi, Malachi	2:37:31 (150)	
Bye, Alan F	3:35:25 (5,306)	
Bye, Graham	4:51:23 (24,394)	
Byers, Richard J	4:44:12 (22,563)	
Byfleet, Jeremy A	3:45:44 (7,255)	
Byford, Adam	5:15:40 (29,174)	
Byford, Marc Adrian	4:44:33 (22,654)	
Byford, Richard Daniel	4:00:45 (11,183)	
Bygott, Adrian Stephen	5:12:57 (28,730)	
Bygrave, Gary	3:53:33 (9,073)	
Byles, Rohan Thomas	3:57:00 (10,089)	
Byran, Johan Nagulendran	5:36:12 (32,018)	
Byrne, Andy	4:44:01 (22,509)	
Byrne, Anthony James	4:42:06 (22,037)	
Byrne, Carl P	5:34:37 (31,837)	
Byrne, David Andrew	2:47:23 (400)	
Byrne, Duncan	5:28:06 (31,043)	
Byrne, Gary M	4:19:36 (15,994)	
Byrne, John	4:22:58 (16,977)	
Byrne, Laurence	4:02:49 (11,677)	
Byrne, Nicholas	5:09:51 (28,209)	
Byrne, Stephen	4:38:54 (21,231)	
Byrnes, Edward Mark	4:20:55 (16,390)	
Byrom, Christopher E	5:08:23 (27,961)	
Byrom, David	3:55:36 (9,636)	
Byron, Joel Christopher	4:17:25 (15,410)	
Bywater, Nigel	4:38:45 (21,185)	
Byworth, Giles	2:56:07 (809)	
Cabban, Paul Cathcart	5:00:22 (26,529)	
Cable, Adam	5:31:08 (31,427)	
Cable, Alexander	4:16:48 (15,247)	
Cable, Jamie	3:57:18 (10,182)	
Cable, Paul	5:59:54 (34,052)	
Cable, Paul A	3:57:39 (10,280)	
Cable, Simon A	4:34:44 (20,179)	
Cable, Stephen D	3:54:50 (9,431)	
Cabrera, Chris	4:52:46 (24,742)	
Cabrera, Francisco	3:57:43 (10,308)	
Cabrini, Franco	4:29:47 (18,909)	
Cacciati, Aldo	5:17:49 (29,514)	
Cacia, Daniel James	5:18:34 (29,632)	
Cader, Marcin	4:32:10 (19,476)	
Cadman, Mike C	4:50:51 (24,254)	
Cadogan, Tom	3:37:36 (5,690)	
Cafferty, Paul Patrick	3:28:35 (4,160)	
Caffyn, Tim	4:11:45 (13,922)	
Cahill, Brian	3:12:25 (2,127)	
Cahill, Chris J	4:24:42 (17,445)	
Cahill, Jason Dean	4:36:50 (20,695)	
Cahill, Rhys James	3:42:01 (6,511)	
Cahu, Jean-François	3:56:43 (10,003)	
Cain, Christopher Edward	3:39:09 (5,973)	
Cain, Isidoro	4:24:57 (17,504)	
Cain, Jonathan	4:02:09 (11,522)	
Cain, Paul D	3:30:47 (4,544)	
Cain, Scott Javon	3:42:55 (6,678)	
Cain, Steven Edward	5:19:01 (29,703)	
Caine, Steven R	4:52:06 (24,573)	
Cainey, Robert	4:35:45 (20,406)	
Cairnes, Simon	4:37:29 (20,873)	
Cairns, David Howard	4:00:03 (10,994)	
Cairns, George W	2:51:26 (540)	
Cairns, Graeme P	4:39:03 (21,269)	
Cairns, Jarrod A	4:57:50 (25,931)	
Cairns, John M	3:03:58 (1,387)	
Cairns, Paul Michael	4:37:41 (20,921)	
Cajet, Alain	3:25:55 (3,721)	
Cake, Phil J	2:39:52 (194)	
Cakebread, David	5:19:48 (29,823)	
Cakebread, John	3:13:59 (2,319)	
Cakebread, Peter	4:45:43 (22,955)	
Calabrese, Paul E	3:25:22 (3,624)	
Calame, Andrew B	3:54:40 (9,375)	
Calcraft, Robert	3:34:11 (5,093)	
Calder, Stuart	3:29:43 (4,366)	
Caldicott, Joel	4:02:15 (11,547)	
Caldiroli, Gianluigi	3:12:30 (2,133)	
Caldon, Kevin T	4:45:11 (22,815)	
Caldwell, Alex	5:35:47 (31,968)	
Caldwell, Damian	3:50:09 (8,237)	
Caldwell, Mark Anthony	3:41:47 (6,473)	
Caldwell, Ryan	4:11:00 (13,715)	
Caldwell Smith, Craig	3:41:10 (6,354)	
Caley, Jeffrey T	5:43:20 (32,704)	
Calfe, Andrew Peter	4:24:59 (17,515)	
Callachan, David	7:10:33 (36,315)	
Callaghan, Christopher	4:09:58 (13,463)	
Callaghan, James Robert	4:30:16 (19,040)	
Callaghan, Julian Robert	6:46:34 (35,938)	
Callaghan, Paul	3:19:05 (2,879)	
Callaghan, Paul John	3:33:48 (5,025)	
Callaghan-Wetton, James A	4:40:06 (21,515)	
Callanan, William C	4:02:22 (11,572)	
Callander, Ian S	3:08:15 (1,722)	
Callard, James Richard	3:29:51 (4,388)	
Callard, Jonathan William	5:24:05 (30,490)	
Callender, Paul David	5:23:41 (30,422)	
Callens, Joris	4:08:20 (13,036)	
Callinan, Stephen Thomas	4:13:16 (14,304)	
Callow, James S	4:09:40 (13,388)	
Calo, Armando	3:24:51 (3,556)	
Calow, Andy John	4:08:39 (13,126)	
Caltagirone, Fabrizio	3:07:23 (1,641)	
Calthrop, Ben Christian	3:34:02 (5,063)	
Calverley, Anthony R	3:55:50 (9,730)	
Calvey, John C	4:41:53 (21,989)	
Calvia, Luca	3:38:05 (5,779)	
Camanzi, Maurizio	4:54:23 (25,154)	
Camara, Nick	6:01:32 (34,160)	
Cambers, Gary	5:13:48 (28,894)	
Cameriere, Roberto	5:04:13 (27,237)	
Cameron, Angus James	5:43:10 (32,683)	
Cameron, Dougal	5:43:09 (32,681)	
Cameron, Duncan Alexander G	5:43:10 (32,683)	
Cameron, Edward	4:36:31 (20,611)	
Cameron, Gavin	4:23:07 (17,007)	
Cameron, Hamish Charles A	5:43:10 (32,683)	
Cameron, Iain	5:32:48 (31,639)	
Cameron, John L	6:32:27 (35,575)	
Cameron, Neil	3:45:57 (7,299)	
Cameron, Paul	4:59:58 (26,442)	
Cameron, Philip	3:58:29 (10,551)	
Cameron, Scott	2:58:36 (1,013)	
Cameron, Scott	3:34:03 (5,068)	
Camfield, Bryan	2:44:43 (330)	
Camillo, Marco	5:27:15 (30,938)	
Campbell, Adrian J	3:27:57 (4,047)	
Campbell, Alasdair	2:58:58 (1,042)	
Campbell, Alex Glenn	3:57:01 (10,102)	
Campbell, Andrew A	4:36:21 (20,562)	
Campbell, Andrew Stuart	5:32:14 (31,568)	
Campbell, Cameron James	3:05:17 (1,482)	
Campbell, David	4:09:59 (13,471)	
Campbell, David	4:14:27 (14,632)	
Campbell, David G	3:53:27 (9,039)	
Campbell, Donald Ross	4:02:27 (11,595)	
Campbell, Doug John Lister	4:50:35 (24,183)	
Campbell, Douglas John	5:15:01 (29,069)	
Campbell, Graeme	2:48:25 (428)	
Campbell, Graeme	3:57:12 (10,156)	
Campbell, Ian P	3:24:20 (3,491)	
Campbell, Julian	3:45:32 (7,216)	
Campbell, Neil	4:59:22 (26,301)	
Campbell, Peter Adrian	3:55:57 (9,766)	
Campbell, Robert K	3:26:06 (3,749)	
Campbell, Rory	4:41:35 (21,918)	
Campbell, Sam	3:48:38 (7,878)	
Campbell, Simon Alan Grant	4:28:26 (18,499)	
Campbell, Stuart	4:34:53 (20,212)	
Campbell, Thomas Duncan	4:00:39 (11,155)	
Campbell, Tim	4:28:56 (18,660)	
Campbell, Will Marcus C	4:09:51 (13,431)	
Campbell-Gray, Robert	4:59:35 (26,362)	
Campher, Frans	4:37:37 (20,910)	
Campion, Andrew	5:05:22 (27,427)	
Campion, Craig W	5:13:14 (28,808)	
Campion, Daniel J	3:12:52 (2,173)	
Campion, James P	3:31:03 (4,587)	
Campion, John	4:40:25 (21,617)	
Campion, Mark A	2:53:48 (656)	
Campion, Peter	4:56:06 (25,561)	
Campion, Stephen W	3:10:17 (1,930)	
Campos, Joao	4:37:44 (20,931)	
Camps, Christopher	4:59:40 (26,373)	
Campsie, Nick James	3:12:34 (2,143)	
Canavan, Ciaran Michael	3:05:38 (1,509)	
Canavera, Luca	4:08:16 (13,020)	
Candille, Xavier	3:35:28 (5,316)	
Candy, Martyn James	5:18:08 (29,564)	
Candy, Stephen Charles	5:09:58 (28,225)	
Candy, Steve	5:16:18 (29,269)	
Caney, Mark William	4:20:44 (16,347)	
Canham, Colin Raymond	4:17:54 (15,546)	
Canham, Raymond D	3:53:30 (9,054)	
Cann, Andrew	4:32:01 (19,441)	
Cann, Gary James	3:53:47 (9,154)	
Cann, Simon	4:50:43 (24,211)	
Cannaerts, Ronny	3:09:51 (1,896)	
Cannavacciuolo, Carmine	3:21:08 (3,104)	
Cannell, Neal	5:09:29 (28,141)	
Canning, James John	4:37:31 (20,888)	
Canning, Stephen Nigel John	3:10:03 (1,910)	
Cannon, Doug S	3:32:05 (4,754)	
Cannon, Jason	5:21:42 (30,108)	
Cannon, Stephen	4:13:43 (14,436)	
Cannon, William	4:43:09 (22,288)	
Cannon Brookes, Charlie	3:59:04 (10,737)	
Cano, Angel	3:06:59 (1,606)	
Cano-Lopez, Jonathan Peter	3:47:02 (7,531)	
Canovi, Giuliano	4:13:19 (14,318)	
Cantacessi, Nicola	4:16:50 (15,254)	
Cantell, Darren Lee	3:46:15 (7,367)	
Cantes, Alan	4:40:23 (21,607)	
Canty, Patrick	3:21:20 (3,122)	
Canueto, Steven	4:11:44 (13,917)	
Capasso, Marco	3:08:43 (1,787)	
Capel, Daren P	3:26:13 (3,773)	
Caperan, Nicolas Bruno	4:52:39 (24,722)	
Capetti, Giacomo	3:05:34 (1,501)	
Caplen, Stephen Gerard	3:51:13 (8,474)	
Caplin, Dean	4:53:38 (24,952)	
Capon, Daniel J	3:59:56 (10,970)	
Caporali, Rodolfo	3:24:13 (3,471)	
Cappello, Andrea	3:29:57 (4,408)	
Capper, Paul A	5:18:37 (29,645)	
Cappi, Stephen George	4:46:03 (23,043)	
Capponi, Simone	3:16:13 (2,577)	
Caprara, Giacomo	3:48:40 (7,890)	
Capriotti, Matteo	3:33:29 (4,967)	
Captan, Safi	4:31:52 (19,402)	
Caputi, Gaetano	3:15:00 (2,439)	
Carberry, Billy Sean	6:28:03 (35,424)	
Carbonnier, Anders E	3:15:55 (2,542)	
Carbonnier, Frederic	7:52:40 (36,568)	
Card, Andrew William	5:58:23 (33,957)	
Card, Simon James	3:58:31 (10,560)	
Cardnell, Simon Robert	3:31:52 (4,720)	
Cardow, Scott Stephen	5:05:52 (27,511)	
Cardy, Mark Paul	5:13:03 (28,747)	
Care, Andrew Michael	4:44:07 (22,537)	
Carey, Aidan G	4:34:38 (20,154)	

Carey, Chris 4:34:03 (20,005)

Aged 64, I ran my second marathon in 4hrs 34mins in aid of Juvenile Diabetes (JDRF) as my grandson, aged 5 yrs, was diagnosed with type 1 diabetes earlier in the year. My time was 26 minutes quicker than I ran four years earlier and I raised approximately £3,000 for the charity.

Carey, Dominic Patrick	5:12:06 (28,584)	
Carey, Ian	4:46:13 (23,096)	
Carey, Martin Ian	5:22:26 (30,212)	
Carey, Paul	4:09:11 (13,253)	
Carey, Stephen J	4:41:31 (21,899)	
Cargill, Ross Christopher	3:24:30 (3,511)	

Cariven, Philippe 4:10:41 (13,635)
Carlegrim, Magnus 4:17:41 (15,493)
Carles, Eric 4:11:59 (13,984)
Carley, Ian P 2:52:11 (577)
Carley, Lee Michael 4:49:20 (23,879)
Carlin, Ian 4:17:51 (15,533)
Carlin, Patrick Joseph 4:26:01 (17,817)
Carlin, Paul 4:28:40 (18,573)
Carlisle, Stephen 3:39:47 (6,099)
Carlos, Vera 4:04:34 (12,087)
Carlsson, Philip 4:40:23 (21,607)
Carlton, Jeff 4:25:42 (17,715)
Carlton, Tom 3:51:18 (8,492)
Carlyle, John W 4:24:18 (17,319)
Carman, Paul 4:45:03 (22,782)
Carmassi, Massimo 3:12:32 (2,136)
Carmel, Ed 3:37:16 (5,612)
Carmichael, Jeremy Robert 3:44:45 (7,043)
Carmichael, Luke 3:18:34 (2,827)
Carmichael, Nick 3:42:29 (6,593)
Carmon, Eyal 3:45:37 (7,230)
Carnazza, Antonio 3:31:09 (4,605)
Carnegie, John 3:42:37 (6,613)
Carnell, Richard James 4:53:38 (24,952)
Carnelley, Lee Sean 3:55:39 (9,661)
Carney, Michael 5:00:52 (26,623)
Carnochan, Graeme Ian 4:46:31 (23,174)
Caro, Manuel 3:58:16 (10,478)
Carol, Riel 2:59:50 (1,140)
Carotti, Jean-Marie 4:34:03 (20,005)
Carpanini, Sebastian Paul Victor 3:45:30 (7,207)
Carpenter, Daniel Robert 4:32:27 (19,550)
Carpenter, Ian 5:27:59 (31,026)
Carpenter, Philip 4:42:52 (22,234)
Carpenter, Richard J 4:55:41 (25,458)
Carpenter, Robert J 3:16:31 (2,610)
Carpi, Maurizio 3:37:22 (5,631)
Carr, Adrian 3:14:13 (2,345)
Carr, Adrian 4:00:56 (11,231)
Carr, Barry John 5:39:53 (32,375)
Carr, Bruce Roy 3:23:38 (3,383)
Carr, David Gavin 4:56:39 (25,681)
Carr, Graham E 4:32:24 (19,538)
Carr, Ian 4:15:01 (14,790)
Carr, John 2:45:07 (347)
Carr, Leigh Glenn 4:00:59 (11,245)
Carr, Malcolm Robert 4:53:38 (24,952)
Carr, Martin G 3:42:46 (6,651)
Carr, Patrick 5:38:18 (32,241)
Carr, Paul 4:25:18 (17,599)
Carr, Paul Joseph 3:59:11 (10,771)
Carr, Phillip R 3:13:47 (2,295)
Carr, Robert 3:22:18 (3,218)
Carr, Simon 5:03:09 (27,048)
Carr, Simon 6:01:48 (34,174)
Carr, Steve 4:04:15 (12,020)
Carr, Tom William David 5:13:04 (28,763)
Carragher, Andrew O 4:15:10 (14,826)
Carrigan, Ben 4:50:59 (24,300)
Carrillo, José Maria 4:45:03 (22,782)
Carrington, Gavin Lee Anthony 5:44:44 (32,844)
Carrington, Guy Matthew 3:20:27 (3,012)
Carrington, Stuart 4:41:09 (21,807)
Carritt, David 5:13:36 (28,857)
Carritt, Sean 3:50:43 (8,362)
Carroll, Adrian José 4:02:20 (11,564)
Carroll, Michael J 2:22:52 (28)
Carroll, Nathan J 4:35:41 (20,387)
Carroll, Paul A 3:03:31 (1,348)
Carroll, Raymond L 5:14:30 (28,989)
Carroll, Sean J 4:21:51 (16,655)
Carroll, Stephen Patrick 4:04:53 (12,172)
Carroll, Stuart P 2:54:41 (715)
Carroll, Tom 3:54:35 (9,347)
Carrott, Daniel 5:30:41 (31,382)
Carsley, Keith 4:04:06 (11,985)
Carson, Connor 3:22:41 (3,258)
Carson, Jeremy 4:23:23 (17,076)
Carson, Robert Martin 3:52:07 (8,682)
Carswell, Jeremy 4:22:01 (16,711)
Carter, Adam L 4:14:02 (14,514)
Carter, Alan John 4:33:35 (19,884)
Carter, Andrew 4:25:01 (17,524)
Carter, Andrew Keith 6:08:37 (34,590)
Carter, Andrew S 2:52:29 (591)
Carter, Anthony 3:21:03 (3,091)
Carter, Barry 4:36:30 (20,605)
Carter, Billy 4:18:55 (15,832)
Carter, Daren D 4:35:05 (20,245)
Carter, Dave 4:21:42 (16,606)
Carter, Dave J 5:26:12 (30,804)
Carter, David 5:12:27 (28,643)
Carter, David Charles 6:08:52 (34,609)
Carter, Dean 3:25:55 (3,721)
Carter, Gary 4:14:06 (14,533)
Carter, Graham S 3:46:18 (7,377)
Carter, Jamie Richard 4:22:10 (16,747)
Carter, Jason Lee 5:20:46 (29,972)
Carter, John Anthony 3:37:56 (5,751)
Carter, John D 3:32:47 (4,855)
Carter, Luke 3:40:28 (6,228)
Carter, Luke D 4:19:46 (16,033)
Carter, Matt James 5:25:58 (30,782)
Carter, Nick Peter 3:47:29 (7,644)
Carter, Oliver 4:11:23 (13,812)
Carter, Oliver 4:21:09 (16,452)
Carter, Paul J 3:06:51 (1,596)
Carter, Paul L 3:20:49 (3,060)
Carter, Richard 4:05:19 (12,288)
Carter, Rob James 4:02:43 (11,657)
Carter, Ross 6:20:00 (35,125)
Carter, Simon 3:03:40 (1,361)
Carter, Stephen G 4:33:51 (19,953)
Carter, Steve 4:40:20 (21,587)
Carter, Tim 4:27:36 (18,257)
Carter, Timothy N 2:50:49 (519)
Carter-Lee, Andy Robert 4:09:49 (13,424)
Cartin, John Joseph 2:57:25 (892)
Cartledge, Robert 3:53:37 (9,098)
Cartwright, Carl William 5:57:50 (33,921)
Cartwright, James 3:11:57 (2,088)
Cartwright, Joe 4:25:54 (17,786)
Cartwright, Jonathan Paul 3:47:41 (7,682)
Cartwright, Mark C 4:20:40 (16,324)
Cartwright, Paul Nigel 3:21:56 (3,187)
Cartwright, Simon Richard 4:28:09 (18,397)
Carvell, Paul Andrew 4:19:57 (16,086)
Carvell, Robin 3:33:05 (4,906)
Carver, Tom Alan 3:41:51 (6,491)
Carville, James Kevin 4:28:20 (18,465)
Carvin, Adam 4:20:18 (16,200)
Carwardine, Mark Richard 2:58:45 (1,026)
Cary, Nicholas George C 3:46:57 (7,518)
Cary, Sam Michael 3:17:53 (2,751)
Casali, Ernesto 3:59:09 (10,760)
Case, Michael David 4:02:10 (11,529)
Casey, Craig 5:47:40 (33,109)
Cash, Chris 4:33:42 (19,918)
Cash, James 4:02:24 (11,580)
Cash, Nick 6:18:06 (35,034)
Cash, Simon J 5:17:07 (29,408)
Casielles, Rafael 3:30:50 (4,554)
Casini, Enrico 4:08:36 (13,117)
Cassaro, Joel 4:27:37 (18,264)
Casse, Mark Robert 3:59:35 (10,891)
Cassels, John James 4:16:54 (15,271)
Cassere, Peter John 5:22:08 (30,168)
Casserley, Robert William 2:59:28 (1,101)
Cassidy, Ian 4:22:00 (16,705)
Cassidy, John 4:28:58 (18,670)
Cassidy, Patrick 4:27:56 (18,352)
Cassimon, Stefan 4:15:50 (14,986)
Casson, William 3:20:03 (2,967)
Cast, Robert 5:05:57 (27,523)
Castaldo, Paul 3:32:51 (4,871)
Castellon, Patrick 4:22:59 (16,983)
Castellon, Sylvain 3:51:01 (8,429)
Castillo, Christian 3:07:34 (1,660)
Castillo, Richard 5:43:25 (32,715)
Castle, Daniel 4:40:44 (21,708)
Castle, Kevin Arthur 3:59:06 (10,747)
Castle, Nick 6:08:56 (34,612)
Castle, Tim William 6:02:21 (34,208)
Castle-Doughty, Joshua Frederick 3:55:59 (9,779)
Castleton, John K 3:02:53 (1,320)
Castrey, Gary 3:57:46 (10,318)
Castrique, Ivon 3:35:39 (5,353)
Castro, David 4:08:16 (13,020)
Castro Huergo, Luis 3:50:27 (8,297)
Caswell, Jamie 4:32:50 (19,649)
Catalan Bernia, Vicente Luis 3:28:08 (4,079)
Catarino, Paulo 4:28:17 (18,448)
Catchpole, Andrew Peter 4:49:18 (23,872)
Catchpole, Chris 3:31:18 (4,626)
Catchpole, Philip 4:26:35 (17,977)
Catchpole, William A 4:37:14 (20,803)
Cater, Geoffrey David 3:41:50 (6,486)
Cater, James S 3:00:00 (1,151)
Cates, Liam 3:53:34 (9,080)
Catley, Matthew Stephen 4:50:29 (24,158)
Catling, James F 4:31:00 (19,216)
Catlow, Ian J 4:05:03 (12,220)
Catlow, Michael Jonathan 4:17:10 (15,339)
Catmull, Julian A 3:08:17 (1,728)
Catt, Daniel J 3:38:43 (5,890)
Catt, Simon 3:30:57 (4,572)
Cattaneo, Bruno 3:37:01 (5,564)
Cattaruzzi, Daniele 3:14:15 (2,349)
Catterall, David M 3:42:45 (6,646)
Cattini, Alessandro 3:38:45 (5,899)
Caudwell, Stephen J 6:54:52 (36,107)
Caulfield, Marc Jason 4:29:52 (18,935)
Caunce, Peter 4:03:46 (11,914)
Causey, Mark 3:32:51 (4,871)
Causton, Barry 6:07:39 (34,541)
Cavanagh, Sean Alan 4:08:51 (13,173)
Cave, Michael James 3:56:24 (9,899)
Cave, Richard 3:40:59 (6,320)
Caveney, Craig 3:36:18 (5,458)
Cavey, Benjamin William 3:47:27 (7,634)
Cawley, Mark Colin 4:05:01 (12,212)
Cawley, Nick 5:02:07 (26,871)
Caws, Graham 3:59:49 (10,947)
Cawthorne, Timothy James 4:01:24 (11,339)
Cawthray, Sam 4:09:07 (13,234)
Cayford, Robb 4:56:30 (25,646)
Cecarini, Roberto 5:28:04 (31,038)
Cederstrom, Jan B 3:40:59 (6,320)
Celine, Lopez 5:12:40 (28,677)
Celoni, Gilberto 5:05:07 (27,389)
Cenni, Max 3:24:20 (3,491)
Cepok, Theodor 4:14:14 (14,579)
Cernik, Philip Anthony Edmund 4:54:35 (25,199)
Cesaris, Filippo 3:52:24 (8,767)
Chaban, Taras 4:34:57 (20,222)
Chabani, Sid-Ali 4:04:32 (12,080)
Chacksfield, Charles P 5:04:03 (27,197)
Chadbourne, Martin 4:46:20 (23,133)
Chadburn, Michael 3:21:16 (3,115)
Chadd, Hugo 3:17:25 (2,699)
Chaddaer, Gurjit 6:16:25 (34,944)
Chadwick, Ben 3:50:49 (8,383)
Chadwick, David 4:33:55 (19,972)
Chadwick, Nicholas 3:49:12 (8,026)
Chadwick, Nicholas James 4:19:47 (16,038)
Chadwick, Nick 3:53:55 (9,186)
Chadwick, Nick Paul 3:54:37 (9,359)
Chadwick, Paul 5:48:35 (33,202)
Chadwick, Peter J 5:33:52 (31,753)
Chadwick, Simon 6:28:41 (35,452)
Chadwick, Tom 3:30:38 (4,517)
Chaffart, Kim 4:12:03 (13,997)
Chaffer, Peter 2:57:45 (936)
Chaffey, Jamie 3:35:52 (5,392)
Chahal, Gopinder Singh 4:51:36 (24,440)
Chahal, Palwinder Singh 3:34:26 (5,142)
Chahal, Rajinder Singh 5:06:36 (27,643)
Chahal, Runthir Singh 5:28:38 (31,100)
Chait, Albert Sebastian 6:54:34 (36,095)
Chaldecott, Mike 3:37:05 (5,582)
Chalk, Jason 3:54:03 (9,224)
Chalke, Daniel John 4:25:34 (17,681)
Chalkley, Andrew Lee 3:10:40 (1,959)
Chalkley, Steve R 3:42:42 (6,634)
Challice, Lee 5:12:11 (28,599)
Challis, Adrian Ronald C 4:13:34 (14,390)
Challis, Leigh J 7:40:10 (36,523)
Challis, Mark Richard 6:14:11 (34,843)
Challis, Paul David 6:42:16 (35,845)

Challis, Simon Mark......5:52:31 (33,534)
Chalmers, Charlie Scott......5:10:50 (28,381)
Chalmers, Julian......3:38:49 (5,908)
Chalmers, William......5:39:52 (32,374)
Chaloner, Andrew......6:00:59 (34,131)
Chamberlain, Brian......4:14:28 (14,637)
Chamberlain, Mark J......2:57:39 (927)
Chamberlain, Michael D......3:44:32 (6,997)
Chamberlain, Roger Brian......5:52:01 (33,506)
Chamberlain, Ross......5:07:34 (27,826)
Chamberlain, Steven A......3:56:40 (9,984)
Chambers, Alan......4:05:23 (12,303)
Chambers, Alistair......2:56:13 (815)
Chambers, Christopher George..5:23:02 (30,312)
Chambers, Craig......3:58:23 (10,517)
Chambers, Damon A......3:04:19 (1,416)
Chambers, Dean Kristen......3:52:55 (8,904)
Chambers, Duncan......3:51:01 (8,429)
Chambers, John......6:03:49 (34,309)
Chambers, Joseph......4:24:42 (17,445)
Chambers, Lloyd......4:20:11 (16,157)
Chambers, Matthew......3:31:05 (4,592)
Chambers, Robert I......3:35:45 (5,367)
Chambers, Sam......3:50:55 (8,404)
Chambers, Scott......5:00:34 (26,564)
Chambers, Timothy David......4:00:07 (11,011)
Chambers, Victor Stephen......5:50:30 (33,383)
Chamley, Paul......5:19:41 (29,805)
Champion, Dan......4:12:25 (14,075)
Champion, Mark S......3:06:08 (1,542)
Champion, Russell Stephen......4:12:08 (14,021)
Chan, Alan......4:51:06 (24,333)
Chan, David......5:09:19 (28,111)
Chan, Dillon......5:21:22 (30,055)
Chan, Ka Wai......3:53:52 (9,174)
Chan, Merit......4:18:57 (15,840)
Chan, Nicholas......3:53:30 (9,054)
Chan, Peter G......3:00:31 (1,173)
Chander, Deepak......4:49:00 (23,800)
Chandler, Chris David......4:03:48 (11,924)
Chandler, Darrell Grant......4:29:21 (18,763)
Chandler, David......3:21:09 (3,105)
Chandler, Gary James......3:54:29 (9,322)
Chandler, Gary W......2:40:39 (217)
Chandler, Mark......3:41:11 (6,362)
Chandler, Mark......3:52:00 (8,659)
Chandler, Michael......3:45:10 (7,132)
Chandler, Paul Holmes......3:30:52 (4,560)
Chandler, Paul James......4:30:51 (19,180)
Chandler, Paul Thomas......4:35:54 (20,446)
Chandler, Simon......5:06:26 (27,612)
Chandler, Simon D......3:21:38 (3,153)
Chandler, Timothy James......3:27:51 (4,025)
Chandley, Paul J......4:25:46 (17,742)
Chang, Michael J......2:52:26 (590)
Chang, Se Yong......4:58:29 (26,082)
Channon, Mark......4:34:21 (20,080)
Channon, Scott......5:25:36 (30,709)
Chant, Ian R......2:59:28 (1,101)
Chant, William David Oliver......4:14:15 (14,583)
Chanter, Will......4:18:45 (15,786)
Chantry, Rob......4:53:00 (24,792)
Chaplin, David I......3:10:27 (1,944)
Chaplin, Paul......4:54:14 (25,109)
Chapman, Alan Eward......5:15:27 (29,135)
Chapman, Alan G......3:09:37 (1,872)
Chapman, Alistair J......3:33:21 (4,942)
Chapman, Anthony......5:09:58 (28,225)
Chapman, Ben......4:44:22 (22,605)
Chapman, Craig G......2:56:22 (823)
Chapman, Darren H......4:06:44 (12,635)
Chapman, David......4:17:09 (15,337)
Chapman, Fraser......4:42:15 (22,079)
Chapman, Gary I......3:11:47 (2,073)
Chapman, Glenn......4:09:42 (13,396)
Chapman, Graham J......3:02:43 (1,313)
Chapman, Grant......4:16:24 (15,145)
Chapman, Jamie Richard......5:18:59 (29,699)
Chapman, Jason......5:26:07 (30,792)
Chapman, John......3:20:45 (3,051)
Chapman, Karl......3:52:15 (8,719)
Chapman, Kenny......3:31:38 (4,688)
Chapman, Kevin......4:45:33 (22,901)
Chapman, Luke......4:22:02 (16,716)
Chapman, Mark......5:06:28 (27,618)
Chapman, Mark E......3:32:44 (4,849)
Chapman, Matthew J......3:20:48 (3,056)
Chapman, Matthew James......3:53:30 (9,054)
Chapman, Matthew John......4:21:26 (16,531)
Chapman, Neil A......3:20:11 (2,976)
Chapman, Nicholas Kenneth......3:58:13 (10,463)
Chapman, Nick......6:41:20 (35,816)
Chapman, Nick......6:50:58 (36,012)
Chapman, Nick Paul......4:00:48 (11,194)
Chapman, Olly......3:48:49 (7,935)
Chapman, Paul......4:30:34 (19,113)
Chapman, Paul......4:57:40 (25,901)
Chapman, Paul Matthew......3:08:38 (1,773)
Chapman, Richard......4:26:55 (18,054)
Chapman, Robert......5:23:55 (30,464)
Chapman, Simon......4:22:54 (16,962)
Chapman, Simon L......3:42:09 (6,540)
Chapman, Steven......4:39:12 (21,313)
Chapman, Thomas......2:54:20 (689)
Chapman, Trevor......4:16:36 (15,192)
Chapman,, Bob......5:10:45 (28,366)
Chapman-Edwards, Stuart......5:25:30 (30,691)
Chappell, James Edward......4:14:06 (14,533)
Chappell, Simon J......5:14:33 (28,994)
Chappelle, Gavin Stewart......3:48:47 (7,922)
Chapuis, Bernard......3:27:48 (4,013)
Charalambous, Nick......4:08:35 (13,111)
Chard, Ken R......3:28:38 (4,168)
Chard, Paul R......4:29:09 (18,721)
Chard, Terence Edwin......4:30:10 (19,017)
Charity, Dan......4:39:49 (21,465)
Charlebois, Patrick......2:42:43 (265)
Charlery, Sebastian......4:57:02 (25,768)
Charles, Andrew......4:49:09 (23,840)
Charles, Greg......3:29:02 (4,234)
Charles, Hare Thomas......4:12:20 (14,062)
Charles, John......2:52:16 (582)
Charles, Jonathan R......3:59:10 (10,764)
Charles, Peter Alan......5:51:27 (33,459)
Charles-Barks, Paul......5:07:57 (27,887)
Charles-Brady, Jonathan......4:45:50 (22,985)
Charley, Mark Anthony......4:29:03 (18,704)
Charloteaux, Stephane......3:57:41 (10,293)
Charlton, Alan......4:27:27 (18,220)
Charlton, Christopher James......4:16:40 (15,209)
Charlton, Paul Thomas......5:20:05 (29,861)
Charlton, Ray......5:29:58 (31,289)
Charlton, Raymond......4:27:31 (18,241)
Charlton, Robert Jamie......5:24:34 (30,565)
Charman, Benjamin Thomas......4:05:30 (12,334)
Charman, Dan......3:20:20 (2,995)
Charman, Glen Ian......4:00:05 (11,002)
Charman, Michael John......4:12:37 (14,129)
Charman, Nigel R......3:00:18 (1,162)
Charnley, Andrew Graham......5:01:25 (26,738)
Charnley, Joe......4:06:32 (12,583)
Charnock, Ian James......3:45:38 (7,235)
Charoy Castellani, Franck......4:38:16 (21,047)
Chart, Robert J......3:26:30 (3,801)
Charters, Jonathan Daniel......3:24:02 (3,435)
Charters, Matthew......4:23:12 (17,024)
Charters, Paul William......3:53:29 (9,051)
Chase, Steven......4:52:36 (24,706)
Chase, Tim Alexander......4:30:20 (19,054)
Chatfield, Gary......4:20:43 (16,341)
Chattaway, David......3:39:29 (6,038)
Chattaway, Robert......3:42:09 (6,540)
Chatterton, Andy......3:12:50 (2,169)
Chatterton, Thomas......4:28:59 (18,679)
Chattey, Peter......4:34:23 (20,091)
Chauhan, Abhishek......4:10:26 (13,574)
Chauhan, Chatenya......6:30:24 (35,514)
Chauhan, Narinder......4:02:08 (11,518)
Chauhan, Niteen......6:42:07 (35,838)
Chauhan, Rishi......4:50:43 (24,211)
Chavasse, Steven John......5:23:54 (30,458)
Chavda, Jai......6:01:28 (34,154)
Chavida, Jesus......4:52:23 (24,657)
Cheah, Winston......4:31:07 (19,245)
Cheale, Andrew Michael......4:26:51 (18,039)
Chedzey, Paul......4:45:21 (22,852)
Cheek, Neil......4:11:23 (13,812)
Cheema, Amanpreet S......5:00:10 (26,493)
Cheesbrough, Paul......4:51:43 (24,466)
Cheeseman, Jack Anthony......3:45:51 (7,278)
Cheesman, Alex......5:03:36 (27,120)
Cheesmur, Stephen D......4:23:49 (17,193)
Cheetham, Thomas Richard......3:30:37 (4,514)
Chell, Ian M......3:28:14 (4,097)
Chelule, Kenneth......4:33:45 (19,933)
Cheng, Jason......5:34:55 (31,871)
Cherot, Jason Anthony......5:12:06 (28,584)
Cherrington, Jason......5:39:03 (32,307)
Cherry, Adrian Mark......4:19:43 (16,019)
Cherry, Felix......4:27:29 (18,229)
Cherry, James George......4:16:52 (15,261)
Cherry, Paul......4:51:58 (24,545)
Cherry, Steven T......5:02:51 (26,998)
Chesa, Christophe......4:19:54 (16,075)
Cheseldine, Noel......4:18:21 (15,672)
Cheshire, Paul J......4:09:58 (13,463)
Chester, Richard Paul......5:08:00 (27,895)
Chesterman, Paul......4:21:59 (16,700)
Chesters, Graham M......3:15:13 (2,463)
Chesterton, Neil Douglas......3:49:23 (8,059)
Chesterton, Nigel John......4:37:01 (20,749)
Chettle, James......2:44:19 (317)
Cheung, Kwok Kee......4:52:27 (24,669)
Cheung, Leslie Paul......4:14:36 (14,680)
Chidley, David A......4:34:31 (20,124)
Chilcott, Darren......5:20:01 (29,853)
Chilcott, Peter......6:17:46 (35,022)
Child, Karl Bryan......5:48:21 (33,178)
Child, Russell......4:31:37 (19,358)
Childe, Michael......4:39:12 (21,313)
Childs, Alexis J......4:45:32 (22,897)
Childs, Darren......4:35:32 (20,352)
Childs, David Joseph......4:56:31 (25,653)
Childs, Paul A......2:54:31 (702)
Childs, Peter Richard......4:43:37 (22,400)
Chilkoti, Budhi B......4:42:02 (22,024)
Chilton, Paul J......4:29:42 (18,878)
Chilton, William T......4:19:32 (15,978)
Chilvers, George......4:36:29 (20,598)
Chinnery, Clive Richard......6:02:36 (34,225)
Chipchase, David Alan......3:38:09 (5,795)
Chipchase, Peter John......4:22:03 (16,717)
Chipperfield, Richard Paul......4:53:12 (24,847)
Chisholm, Neil......2:39:41 (188)
Chiteculo, Abilio Antonio F......3:39:02 (5,946)
Chivers, Benjamin Rhodri......3:35:31 (5,327)
Chivers, Craig......4:36:03 (20,490)
Chivers, Simon James......3:34:07 (5,083)
Chivers, Steve A......3:29:07 (4,254)
Chleffer, Frederic......4:27:16 (18,171)
Chlopas, Paul......4:14:13 (14,573)
Choi, Jung Sup......4:52:40 (24,725)
Choi, Victor C......3:39:01 (5,942)
Chorlton, Gordon C......4:27:30 (18,236)
Chorlton, Michael David......4:46:22 (23,141)
Chothia, Andrew Paul......4:54:39 (25,219)
Choudhury, Reza Hussain......6:30:55 (35,532)
Choules, David......2:54:38 (711)
Chow, Kun Fai......4:55:35 (25,429)
Chow, Ritchie H......3:23:29 (3,364)
Chowdhury, Mahbubur......4:39:25 (21,363)
Chowles, Dennis Edward......6:10:23 (34,679)
Chrestia Blanchine, Bernard......4:02:01 (11,494)
Chrisanthou, Daniel......3:41:17 (6,386)
Christen, Daniel......4:08:18 (13,028)
Christensen, Soeren......3:56:26 (9,908)
Christensen, Toby James......4:47:51 (23,510)
Christer, Jason......4:59:51 (26,414)
Christian, Steven John......3:41:35 (6,437)
Christie, David......3:16:30 (2,609)
Christie, David AM......4:10:23 (13,564)
Christie, Emlyn D......2:49:46 (477)
Christie, Neil A......3:53:16 (8,988)
Christie, Sandy......3:10:45 (1,968)
Christie, Simon......4:24:17 (17,311)
Christie, Stuart......6:12:08 (34,762)
Christley, Andy......3:37:16 (5,612)
Christophe, Racine......5:02:46 (26,988)
Christopher, James......4:28:55 (18,650)

Christopherson, Michael 3:53:44 (9,132)
Christou, Panayiotis 5:16:50 (29,359)
Christy, Mark 4:49:31 (23,911)
Chritchlow, Philip 2:38:19 (167)
Chronis, Iason 3:46:14 (7,362)
Chrystie, Ian 6:07:14 (34,521)
Chu, Vi 3:31:05 (4,592)
Chuck, Gavin 5:11:01 (28,408)
Chudher, Bilal Younis 4:56:15 (25,595)
Chudy, Bernard 5:47:42 (33,114)
Chudy, David 4:56:52 (25,737)
Chugh, Rohit 6:05:36 (34,425)
Chung, Tony 4:40:10 (21,530)
Church, Chris 5:10:46 (28,372)
Church, Colin James 5:30:30 (31,357)
Church, Colin W 4:07:31 (12,837)
Church, Martin 6:00:01 (34,065)
Church, Martin Mark 4:47:48 (23,494)
Church, Simon Alec 4:57:37 (25,884)
Church, Trevor Edward 3:53:00 (8,925)
Churchill, David James 4:15:19 (14,865)
Churchill, Duncan Robert 3:40:40 (6,273)
Churchill, Matthew D 3:52:03 (8,672)
Churchill, Paul Michael 5:26:22 (30,830)
Churton, Mark A 3:33:03 (4,901)
Ciampoli, Tommaso 3:37:24 (5,637)
Ciano, Phillip 3:40:00 (6,147)
Ciarla, Giuseppe Antonio 4:06:44 (12,635)
Cichowlas, Marcin 5:29:10 (31,173)
Cigolotti, Marco 3:33:10 (4,921)
Cima, Keith H 4:08:35 (13,111)
Cineri, Ciro 3:26:34 (3,808)
Cinque, Giulio A 3:06:58 (1,604)
Cinque, Giuseppe 3:55:06 (9,505)
Cipolli, Roberto 3:13:02 (2,198)
Ciritella, Tommaso 4:04:32 (12,080)
Cirota, Vincenzo 3:35:20 (5,291)
Ciruzi, Roger Monga Basedeke 5:15:00 (29,065)
Cite, Jacques 2:53:54 (663)
Citterbard, John 5:53:13 (33,592)
Ciucci, Giuseppe 5:06:24 (27,601)
Ciulli, Gianni 4:20:07 (16,140)
Clack, Paul Charles 4:52:21 (24,649)
Claereboudt, Jan 3:41:44 (6,464)
Clafferty, Robert 4:36:24 (20,576)
Clague, Mark W 2:57:12 (871)
Clair, Jonathan 4:38:36 (21,143)
Clamp, David 3:59:38 (10,900)
Clapham, Fred R 3:52:40 (8,839)
Clapham, Mike Alan 3:28:51 (4,198)
Clapp, Matthew 2:42:56 (274)
Clapson, Barrie 4:22:47 (16,934)
Clapton, Bruce Vincent 4:47:26 (23,396)
Clapton, Roland Anthony 4:23:36 (17,136)
Clare, Andrew J 3:24:52 (3,558)
Clare, Ben 4:00:11 (11,025)
Clare, Danny 4:20:37 (16,302)
Clare, Matt 3:58:28 (10,544)
Claridge, Lewis J 4:52:28 (24,673)
Claridge, Matthew A 5:18:42 (29,656)
Clark, Adam James 4:37:32 (20,891)
Clark, Adam P 5:34:40 (31,845)
Clark, Adam Stephen 4:39:44 (21,445)
Clark, Alan 3:51:40 (8,581)
Clark, Andrew David 4:40:54 (21,743)
Clark, Andrew Mark 4:53:39 (24,957)
Clark, Andrew Paul 5:19:02 (29,705)
Clark, Anthony 3:01:01 (1,208)
Clark, Colin P 4:14:27 (14,632)
Clark, Daniel Martin 4:33:42 (19,918)
Clark, Darren 3:50:05 (8,226)
Clark, Darren 4:05:09 (12,241)
Clark, David 4:59:30 (26,340)
Clark, David 5:13:03 (28,747)
Clark, David 5:18:49 (29,669)
Clark, Derek 3:15:02 (2,441)
Clark, Ed 4:41:54 (21,995)
Clark, Gavin 3:48:48 (7,927)
Clark, Geoffrey M 4:49:48 (24,007)
Clark, Graham R 5:05:59 (27,527)
Clark, Graham S 3:09:39 (1,875)
Clark, Greg Thomas 4:17:15 (15,364)
Clark, Gregg Peter 6:34:16 (35,631)
Clark, Howard 2:58:12 (977)
Clark, Iain Murray 4:52:01 (24,555)
Clark, James Stephen 3:18:09 (2,787)
Clark, John 3:24:32 (3,514)
Clark, John 5:32:24 (31,585)
Clark, Jonathan S 4:28:44 (18,587)
Clark, Jonathan Wyndham 5:21:16 (30,038)
Clark, Joseph Thomas 3:08:34 (1,764)
Clark, Justin Leon 3:59:42 (10,920)
Clark, Lewis James 6:05:04 (34,386)
Clark, Mark 3:53:32 (9,067)
Clark, Mark Anthony 3:13:23 (2,235)
Clark, Martin Andrew 4:40:28 (21,633)
Clark, Matthew 4:45:29 (22,880)
Clark, Matthew A 3:18:09 (2,787)
Clark, Michael 3:11:18 (2,028)
Clark, Michael Andrew 4:56:19 (25,616)
Clark, Mike 4:41:21 (21,851)
Clark, Nick 3:11:39 (2,065)
Clark, Oliver Grant 3:37:29 (5,658)
Clark, Paul D 4:01:53 (11,466)
Clark, Philip Andrew 4:43:21 (22,333)
Clark, Richard 4:36:45 (20,670)
Clark, Richard James Joseph 4:09:32 (13,349)
Clark, Robert 4:16:44 (15,228)
Clark, Ross 4:08:45 (13,149)
Clark, Sam 4:25:43 (17,725)
Clark, Stephen 4:32:14 (19,494)
Clark, Stephen 7:32:54 (36,483)
Clark, Steven J 3:50:15 (8,259)
Clark, Steven Thornton 3:18:11 (2,793)
Clark, Stu 3:58:00 (10,376)
Clark, Thomas 4:36:02 (20,485)
Clark, Toby 4:43:55 (22,481)
Clark, Trevor Graham 4:13:18 (14,312)
Clark, Walter 4:49:46 (24,001)
Clark, William Arthur 3:59:45 (10,932)
Clark, William C 2:53:38 (647)
Clarke, Alan 5:42:20 (32,621)
Clarke, Allan Peter 4:40:22 (21,601)
Clarke, Andrew T 3:58:43 (10,631)
Clarke, Antony 3:55:49 (9,725)
Clarke, Barry 4:24:01 (17,242)
Clarke, Barry James 3:30:26 (4,489)
Clarke, Chris 5:14:20 (28,966)
Clarke, Christian Michael 4:32:18 (19,514)
Clarke, Dave Alan 4:07:45 (12,897)
Clarke, David 4:48:33 (23,679)
Clarke, David R 2:45:45 (353)
Clarke, David T 4:29:23 (18,773)
Clarke, Dominic 5:34:22 (31,808)
Clarke, Duncan 5:00:40 (26,581)
Clarke, Gary Douglas 3:31:37 (4,686)
Clarke, Gervase 4:38:19 (21,061)
Clarke, James Lewis George 4:50:27 (24,150)
Clarke, John Matthew 4:26:14 (17,882)
Clarke, Martin H 3:10:46 (1,969)
Clarke, Matthew 4:07:25 (12,804)
Clarke, Matthew J 3:36:55 (5,547)
Clarke, Michael 5:14:16 (28,959)
Clarke, Michael T 4:00:46 (11,185)
Clarke, Mick F 3:57:10 (10,146)
Clarke, Mike 3:28:53 (4,207)
Clarke, Mike David Alexander 6:48:19 (35,965)
Clarke, Neil 4:29:36 (18,842)
Clarke, Nicholas Paul 3:31:21 (4,642)
Clarke, Paul 3:13:33 (2,264)
Clarke, Paul 3:52:21 (8,755)
Clarke, Paul J 4:38:46 (21,193)
Clarke, Peter C 4:31:39 (19,366)
Clarke, Peter Michael 3:54:55 (9,455)
Clarke, Philip B 4:28:53 (18,636)
Clarke, Richard James Robert 5:18:09 (29,567)
Clarke, Richard John 3:37:21 (5,629)
Clarke, Richard Paul 5:05:23 (27,428)
Clarke, Robert 5:42:27 (32,633)
Clarke, Robert Ian 5:09:50 (28,205)
Clarke, Robert William 5:18:10 (29,568)
Clarke, Ronan M 4:14:27 (14,632)
Clarke, Russell J 3:33:36 (4,986)
Clarke, Ryan Henry 5:32:37 (31,619)
Clarke, Simon P 3:35:25 (5,306)
Clarke, Simon R 3:34:23 (5,135)
Clarke, Stephen B 4:26:08 (17,852)
Clarke, Steven Kenneth 3:58:44 (10,637)
Clarke, Stuart Matthew 3:56:36 (9,958)
Clarke, Ted 3:37:41 (5,706)
Clarke, Tom 4:31:43 (19,377)
Clarke, Tom George 4:02:52 (11,694)
Clarkson, Alan 4:10:32 (13,600)
Clarkson, Chris 4:56:10 (25,572)
Clarkson, Craig William 3:58:13 (10,463)
Clarkson, Gregan P 2:58:35 (1,012)
Clarkson, Matt P 4:05:40 (12,371)
Clarkson, Paul 5:25:49 (30,757)
Clarkson, Rick 3:59:40 (10,913)
Classen, Carl A 3:38:00 (5,761)
Clatworthy, Graham Paul 4:24:17 (17,311)
Clauzel, Sebastien 4:29:55 (18,957)
Clavel, Manuel 3:30:31 (4,500)
Claverie, Serge 3:57:25 (10,206)
Clavilla, Claus 5:07:37 (27,836)
Clawson, Mark 3:58:29 (10,551)
Claxton, Marc 3:56:56 (10,070)
Claxton, Michael David 4:41:32 (21,905)
Clay, Terry George 6:11:11 (34,708)
Clayden, Stephen 3:34:28 (5,147)
Claydon, Paul 3:55:44 (9,688)
Clayson, Thomas James 3:48:07 (7,769)
Clayton, Andrew John 3:56:46 (10,021)
Clayton, Andrew R 3:53:45 (9,140)
Clayton, Carl 6:29:14 (35,473)
Clayton, Iain 4:57:35 (25,875)
Clayton, Jonathan B 3:46:25 (7,402)
Clayton, Marc S 2:43:58 (305)
Clayton, Richard M 4:05:55 (12,435)
Clayton, Stephen Francis Robert 3:43:14 (6,733)
Cleary, Richard 3:53:39 (9,105)
Cleary, Stephen 3:31:21 (4,642)
Cleasby, Neil Martin 3:40:57 (6,319)
Cleator, Brian 4:52:16 (24,619)
Cleave, Christopher Alan 3:22:12 (3,209)
Cleaver, Stephen P 5:23:25 (30,375)
Cleaves, David John 5:43:08 (32,679)
Cleeton, Philip 5:23:54 (30,458)
Clegg, Dave 4:33:50 (19,948)
Clegg, Dean James 4:28:39 (18,567)
Cleife, Daniel Jon 3:48:59 (7,969)
Clemens, Leonard 3:21:05 (3,096)
Clement, Christian 4:45:53 (22,997)
Clement, Jean Christophe 3:47:10 (7,566)
Clement, Roger 4:24:51 (17,479)
Clements, Andrew C 2:33:14 (93)
Clements, Andrew P 6:17:27 (35,006)
Clements, Anthony G 4:54:38 (25,214)
Clements, Carl John 4:35:20 (20,301)
Clements, Clint 3:56:14 (9,853)
Clements, Ed George 3:07:08 (1,622)
Clements, Edward 4:52:06 (24,573)
Clements, Jon Alan 4:32:49 (19,635)
Clements, Marc Stewart 4:09:37 (13,375)
Clements, Mark J 4:51:11 (24,346)
Clements, Nikki 3:27:22 (3,934)
Clements, Stephen John 4:30:59 (19,212)
Clements, Stephen Mark 3:26:10 (3,765)
Clements, Steven B 3:50:22 (8,281)
Clements, Trevor W 3:10:51 (1,978)
Clemerson, Cedric 3:04:27 (1,425)
Clempson, Andrew 3:55:20 (9,571)
Clemson, Jonathan B 3:53:49 (9,166)
Clemson, Simon Charles 4:12:09 (14,022)
Clerkin, Duncan 3:48:49 (7,935)
Clerkin, Emmett Paul 4:02:11 (11,536)
Clerkin, Stephen Joseph 3:33:06 (4,907)
Cleveland, David 4:24:18 (17,319)
Cleveley, Mike John 4:43:56 (22,486)
Cleverly, Martin John 4:10:49 (13,670)
Clews, Malcolm D 4:49:02 (23,809)
Clews, Paul 4:44:38 (22,682)
Cliff, Simon 4:25:45 (17,738)
Cliffe, Shane 3:38:23 (5,827)
Clifford, Michael 3:44:45 (7,043)
Clifford, Robin P 2:47:06 (391)
Clifford, Stephen J 3:00:49 (1,199)
Clifford, Stephen William 3:32:23 (4,796)
Clift, Kevin 4:09:20 (13,293)

Clifton, Andrew 4:36:49 (20,689)
Clifton, Michael William 3:28:40 (4,169)
Clifton, Paul Raymond 3:52:11 (8,705)
Clifton, Richard J 3:02:11 (1,271)
Clifton, Scott 5:05:24 (27,431)
Clifton-Welker, Matthew Anton 4:01:53 (11,466)
Clinton, Peter 4:04:57 (12,191)
Clinton-Tarestad, Gregory 4:57:05 (25,777)
Clinton-Tarestad, Piers 3:49:17 (8,043)
Clipsham, Andrew James 4:49:24 (23,893)
Clist, Richard 4:28:10 (18,406)
Cloak, David Paul 4:09:25 (13,320)
Close, Sam 4:07:27 (12,817)
Close, Steven A 5:09:55 (28,214)
Close-Smith, James 4:53:05 (24,814)
Clough, Paul Robert Bernard 3:49:34 (8,109)
Clough, Robin D 3:44:09 (6,905)
Clough, Tom Harold 3:41:02 (6,331)
Clover, Quintin 4:07:26 (12,810)
Clowes, Robert 4:40:01 (21,506)
Clues, Mark A 3:16:27 (2,604)
Cluett, Stephen Paul 3:39:14 (5,988)
Clune, Dave 5:27:03 (30,913)
Clutten, Paul 4:14:10 (14,560)
Clutterbuck, Paul A 4:20:03 (16,117)
Clyburn, Nicholas Peter 4:59:22 (26,301)
Clyne, Andrew 4:44:35 (22,666)
Clyne, James Rutley 4:48:55 (23,776)
Clyne, Mike 4:42:25 (22,115)
Coad, Michael 4:09:58 (13,463)
Coade, David 3:27:43 (3,999)
Coakley, Shaun 4:15:17 (14,853)
Coales, David J 2:42:50 (270)
Coales, Matt 4:13:41 (14,429)
Coard, Dave 3:17:27 (2,702)
Coates, Andrew Richard 4:02:35 (11,624)
Coates, Brian W 6:14:14 (34,848)
Coates, Bryan Frederick 5:56:07 (33,797)
Coates, Craig John 3:44:34 (7,005)
Coates, Demian 4:52:37 (24,710)
Coates, Mark Lee 3:57:13 (10,161)
Coates, Martin R 3:53:37 (9,098)
Coates, Nigel J 3:02:40 (1,309)
Coates, Oliver 4:30:35 (19,120)
Coates, Richard John 4:32:32 (19,568)
Coates, Stephen T 2:54:19 (687)
Coats, Ed 3:42:39 (6,624)
Coats, Jack 5:31:37 (31,490)
Cobain, Robert Thomas 4:17:58 (15,569)
Cobb, Craig Andrew 4:09:45 (13,407)
Cobb, Ray Walker 4:58:21 (26,054)
Cobbett, Peter L 4:14:42 (14,715)
Cobbin, Toby 4:31:41 (19,373)
Cobbold, Chris 4:49:45 (23,994)
Cobbold, Jason 4:43:34 (22,386)
Coberman, Richard Ian Lionel 3:38:03 (5,774)
Cobley, Nick 5:27:24 (30,955)
Coburn, Christopher John 3:45:11 (7,135)
Coburn, Terry Joseph 5:10:58 (28,398)
Cocco, Danilo 4:18:28 (15,704)
Cochrane, Garry T 4:50:33 (24,173)
Cochrane, Graham 5:23:33 (30,393)
Cochrane, Sean S 4:06:55 (12,689)
Cochrane, Thomas James 3:55:37 (9,647)
Cock, Darren 3:54:41 (9,381)
Cock, Malcolm 4:00:40 (11,159)
Cockayne, John 5:39:21 (32,339)
Cockbain, Richard I 3:18:09 (2,787)
Cockbill, Simon 6:24:09 (35,286)
Cockburn, Richard Antony 3:31:57 (4,729)
Cocker, Tom 4:28:45 (18,591)
Cockerill, Andrew 3:13:39 (2,274)
Cockerill, Christopher Ruston 5:39:08 (32,312)
Cockerill, Tony 4:31:14 (19,279)
Cockerton, John 5:04:12 (27,230)
Cockram, Benjamin George A 4:09:53 (13,437)
Cockram, Kevin James 3:44:37 (7,020)
Cocks, David 3:52:02 (8,667)
Cockwell, Stephen John 3:56:06 (9,811)
Cocquyt, Michael 2:50:11 (491)
Codd, Angus Edridge 3:54:57 (9,460)
Codina, Antonio 4:38:24 (21,090)
Codling, Andrew David 4:59:55 (26,432)
Codling, Stuart 3:57:37 (10,268)
Coe, Derek 5:11:54 (28,543)
Coe, Gavin James 6:16:19 (34,935)
Coe, Jonathan 3:56:06 (9,811)
Coe, Michael John 5:07:43 (27,849)
Coen, Nick 4:43:14 (22,307)
Coffey, Damian N 3:05:17 (1,482)
Coffey, David L 4:06:59 (12,707)
Coffey, Richard James 3:58:09 (10,435)
Cogan, Allan David 5:36:28 (32,054)
Cogan, Ray 3:33:49 (5,028)
Coggan, Ben David 4:33:59 (19,987)
Coggins, Neil 4:09:28 (13,330)
Cogman, David 4:43:39 (22,405)
Cohen, Adam P 3:41:57 (6,504)
Cohen, Anthony P 3:44:19 (6,942)
Cohen, Paul 3:58:49 (10,666)
Cohen, Steffan K 3:16:08 (2,565)
Cohen, Toby 4:25:51 (17,768)
Cohen Romano, Alberto 3:57:07 (10,131)
Cohen-Price, Daniel L 6:04:49 (34,372)
Coianiz, Alessandro 2:55:07 (754)
Coiffait, Louis 5:39:58 (32,385)
Coker, Ben M 4:58:15 (26,028)
Coker, Geoff 4:44:29 (22,632)
Colairo, Paul 5:32:21 (31,581)
Colbourne, Steve J 3:19:19 (2,899)
Cole, Alexander M 3:57:27 (10,214)
Cole, Andrew George 3:28:03 (4,063)
Cole, Bill 4:11:40 (13,898)
Cole, Brian J 2:40:19 (205)
Cole, Daniel 3:30:53 (4,563)
Cole, Daniel Graham 3:22:21 (3,222)
Cole, Jamie J 3:09:20 (1,838)
Cole, Joe 3:29:46 (4,372)
Cole, Joseph W 4:34:05 (20,016)
Cole, Josh 5:08:00 (27,895)
Cole, Kraig A 3:48:59 (7,969)
Cole, Kye L 5:28:00 (31,029)
Cole, Leon Julian 4:03:56 (11,948)
Cole, Marc 3:30:09 (4,439)
Cole, Martin 4:34:05 (20,016)
Cole, Martin R 4:42:20 (22,101)
Cole, Nicholas 4:35:20 (20,301)
Cole, Nick A 3:08:20 (1,734)
Cole, Paul 4:44:00 (22,504)
Cole, Ray 2:55:04 (750)
Cole, Richard Edward 5:07:55 (27,883)
Cole, Simon Mark 4:52:16 (24,619)
Cole, Stephen Harwood 4:14:37 (14,687)
Colegate, Andrew 3:18:45 (2,846)
Colegrave, Colin 3:18:16 (2,804)
Coleman, Andrew 4:38:05 (21,005)
Coleman, Andrew M 3:53:09 (8,955)
Coleman, Ben Thomas John 5:12:33 (28,663)
Coleman, Daniel 5:28:17 (31,061)
Coleman, Hamish Andrew 3:29:41 (4,357)
Coleman, Jamie C 4:13:16 (14,304)
Coleman, John Patrick 6:59:14 (36,180)
Coleman, Neil M 3:25:45 (3,699)
Coleman, Phillip M 5:56:20 (33,818)
Coleman, Rhodri 4:48:18 (23,607)
Coleman, Rory J 4:02:04 (11,507)
Coleman, Russell G 2:44:58 (341)
Coleman, Steve 4:17:40 (15,487)
Coles, Bradley John 3:33:37 (4,989)
Coles, Clive Andrew 4:30:20 (19,054)
Coles, David 4:54:15 (25,114)
Coles, David Lesley 4:49:53 (24,026)
Coles, Jonathan D 2:57:35 (913)
Coles, Martin S 4:30:56 (19,203)
Coles, Matthew H 3:55:04 (9,495)
Coles, Nicholas I 3:39:49 (6,106)
Coles, Owen 3:55:41 (9,672)
Coles, Simon D 5:16:25 (29,295)
Coles, Stuart 5:05:15 (27,414)
Coletti, Francesco 3:46:33 (7,433)
Coley, Giles A 4:04:24 (12,050)
Coley, Mark D 4:37:26 (20,861)
Collaco, Kevin 6:33:03 (35,598)
Collado, Francisco 4:34:11 (20,037)
Collenette, John 4:33:13 (19,772)
Collet, Jean-Paul 5:31:39 (31,493)
Collett, Matthew Richard 3:48:33 (7,861)
Collett, Ryan 4:53:56 (25,031)
Collett, Steven G 3:34:17 (5,111)
Colletti, John Sebastian 3:52:21 (8,755)
Colley, Christopher 3:52:26 (8,772)
Colley, Mark 3:57:07 (10,131)
Colley, Sion 4:25:36 (17,690)
Collicutt, Gary J 5:28:23 (31,073)
Collier, Andrew Paul 4:36:55 (20,719)
Collier, Andy 4:05:30 (12,334)
Collier, Darren 4:22:22 (16,811)
Collier, David S 3:00:12 (1,158)
Collier, Geoff 3:50:47 (8,378)
Collier, Jeffrey E 4:19:36 (15,994)
Collier, John R 2:52:04 (570)
Collier, Lee Patrick 6:03:02 (34,255)
Collier, Mark Garry 5:34:21 (31,803)
Collier, Stuart 3:26:02 (3,741)
Colligan, Thomas 5:00:53 (26,629)
Collin, Michael P 3:06:00 (1,534)
Collin, Robert Keith 4:51:14 (24,361)
Collings, John 3:57:10 (10,146)
Collingwood, Edwin Jonathan 4:04:24 (12,050)
Collingwood, Max 5:07:40 (27,843)
Collingwood, Paul S 3:01:51 (1,248)
Collins, Allan 4:35:30 (20,344)
Collins, Andrew 4:48:14 (23,593)
Collins, Ben 3:39:08 (5,970)
Collins, Ben 5:33:02 (31,670)
Collins, Ben Stewart 3:41:22 (6,399)
Collins, Clive 5:26:36 (30,854)
Collins, Dan 3:55:12 (9,528)
Collins, Daniel 5:14:42 (29,018)
Collins, Danny Robert 3:52:45 (8,854)
Collins, David 2:58:24 (996)
Collins, Duncan 2:49:52 (479)
Collins, Eric 6:18:13 (35,043)
Collins, Gary 3:41:49 (6,480)
Collins, Gary F 4:50:32 (24,170)
Collins, Glen James 4:31:48 (19,393)
Collins, Iain Paul 4:50:20 (24,123)
Collins, John 5:32:26 (31,592)
Collins, John 5:36:05 (32,005)
Collins, Jon 3:37:45 (5,718)
Collins, Jonathan David 4:21:49 (16,643)
Collins, Kevin 4:31:56 (19,418)
Collins, Lee Marc 5:24:16 (30,520)
Collins, Lee Paul 4:58:26 (26,071)
Collins, Malcolm 3:17:35 (2,724)
Collins, Mark A 4:31:30 (19,334)
Collins, Mark D 5:15:43 (29,183)
Collins, Michael John 5:36:27 (32,050)
Collins, Michael William 4:44:09 (22,550)
Collins, Mike 5:46:57 (33,047)
Collins, Patrick John 5:34:07 (31,769)
Collins, Paul 4:25:16 (17,593)
Collins, Paul Michael 4:05:19 (12,288)
Collins, Paul Robin 4:30:54 (19,190)
Collins, Peter James 3:39:12 (5,981)
Collins, Phil 4:08:53 (13,181)
Collins, Phil 4:36:50 (20,695)
Collins, Richard 5:07:34 (27,826)
Collins, Rob 5:14:11 (28,948)
Collins, Robbie 4:43:29 (22,367)
Collins, Stephen Lee 3:31:48 (4,708)
Collins, Steven 4:45:25 (22,865)
Collinson, Andrew 4:39:46 (21,452)
Collinson, Nathan 3:33:47 (5,020)
Collinson, Sean D 5:39:19 (32,332)
Collis, Ben Charles 5:12:32 (28,659)
Collischon, Adrian Robert 4:20:03 (16,117)
Collis-Smith, David F 4:45:32 (22,897)
Collister, Mark 3:46:31 (7,423)
Collom, Robert I 4:25:42 (17,715)
Colls, Stewart Charles 3:37:19 (5,626)
Collum, Joseph 3:14:05 (2,331)
Collyer, Daniel Robert 3:29:39 (4,352)
Collyer, Nicholas Michael 5:51:36 (33,473)
Colman, Ivan Nigel 3:42:24 (6,579)
Colney, Neil M 4:00:19 (11,062)
Colon, William T 5:30:53 (31,401)
Colonelli, Alfredo 3:35:26 (5,311)
Colson, Andrew David 6:45:49 (35,926)

Colson, George William Grant....4:08:58 (13,201)
Colton, Jason Paul....5:20:28 (29,919)
Colton, Matthew....4:21:31 (16,552)
Colvill, Richard....4:01:04 (11,271)
Colvill, Steve....6:19:19 (35,095)
Colville, Robert J....4:01:49 (11,450)
Colvin, Rich....4:01:54 (11,472)
Colwill, Martin W....2:54:12 (680)
Colwill, Stuart....4:52:50 (24,764)
Colyer, Mark Colin....5:12:46 (28,694)
Comacle, Gerard....3:44:00 (6,883)
Coman, Brian David....6:34:08 (35,627)
Combarro, Yrineo....3:53:48 (9,162)
Combellack, Ian F....3:13:14 (2,215)
Combrink, Shawn....5:12:01 (28,568)
Combstock, Emerson....2:44:19 (317)
Comerford, Gary Michael....4:40:16 (21,565)
Comin, Rudi....3:14:51 (2,424)
Commander, Richard A....3:27:10 (3,900)
Common, Ian....4:22:07 (16,738)
Commons, Anthony J....4:30:31 (19,091)
Comport, David....3:37:43 (5,713)
Compton, Jonathan Charles A....4:21:06 (16,439)
Compton, Peter....5:36:10 (32,012)
Conaghan, Daniel Noel....4:59:40 (26,373)
Conaghan, Tom Joseph....4:21:28 (16,539)
Concannon, Philip....4:53:42 (24,973)
Conder, Jonathan....5:14:11 (28,948)
Condron, Brian....3:48:48 (7,927)
Condron, Chris John....4:14:54 (14,763)
Condron, Jack....3:26:36 (3,818)
Conlan, Joseph James....4:24:21 (17,344)
Conley, Sean....4:04:22 (12,044)
Conlin, Steve....4:22:32 (16,857)
Conlon, Gary....3:59:03 (10,733)
Conlon, Neal Stuart....4:47:37 (23,444)
Conlon, Tim C....5:02:35 (26,956)
Conn, Peter....3:13:39 (2,274)
Connell, David Benedict....2:52:54 (615)
Connell, James Brian....5:16:14 (29,257)
Connell, Jonathan Paul....4:59:51 (26,414)
Connell, Robert M....4:24:31 (17,395)
Connelly, James....4:15:57 (15,013)
Connery, Neil E....3:59:16 (10,799)
Connick, Paul....5:11:51 (28,534)
Conniffe, Matthew John....6:03:04 (34,258)
Connolly, Damian Jordan....4:39:43 (21,440)
Connolly, Daniel Thomas....6:29:50 (35,490)
Connolly, Gregory....5:33:15 (31,689)
Connolly, James....3:51:21 (8,503)
Connolly, James W....3:36:51 (5,537)
Connolly, Jonathan Graham....4:01:43 (11,415)
Connolly, Neil Donald....4:32:00 (19,436)
Connolly, Sean F....4:09:10 (13,250)
Connolly, Terry....4:40:04 (21,510)
Connor, Alec....3:44:24 (6,968)
Connor, Craig....5:30:26 (31,341)
Connor, David P....2:39:58 (198)
Connor, James....2:21:04 (22)
Connor, Karl J....3:51:59 (8,654)
Connor, Louis....3:35:46 (5,372)
Connor, Michael Joseph....3:56:29 (9,926)
Connor, Paul A....3:44:18 (6,938)
Connor, Rik....6:25:39 (35,334)
Connor, Simon P....5:17:12 (29,415)
Conquest, Johnny....4:44:07 (22,537)
Conroy, Grayson Richard....4:22:45 (16,918)
Constandinou, Costas....4:11:34 (13,867)
Constantine, Wayne....4:54:55 (25,287)
Constantinou, Cos....5:10:00 (28,235)
Contat, Damien....3:01:05 (1,210)
Contoret, Adam....5:27:17 (30,940)
Convertini, Donato....5:44:27 (32,810)
Convery, Matt....2:49:40 (473)
Convey, Michael John....6:38:43 (35,749)
Conway, Darren John....4:25:58 (17,803)
Conway, Jim....6:43:42 (35,877)
Conway, Matthew Benjamin....5:35:03 (31,880)
Conway, Phil....4:00:20 (11,068)
Conway, Robert Stephen....6:25:26 (35,328)
Conway, Shaun Philip....3:52:36 (8,822)
Conyers, Daniel....4:52:45 (24,739)
Cook, Adam....4:05:21 (12,296)
Cook, Alan Richard....5:05:26 (27,439)
Cook, Alex John....4:02:04 (11,507)
Cook, Arthur William....5:21:16 (30,038)
Cook, Barnaby....4:26:09 (17,858)
Cook, Christopher....5:29:46 (31,264)
Cook, Christopher Michael....3:56:43 (10,003)
Cook, David....5:09:17 (28,102)
Cook, David G....4:26:01 (17,817)
Cook, David James....4:13:34 (14,390)
Cook, David Lee....4:29:32 (18,817)
Cook, Edward....4:35:25 (20,332)
Cook, Gareth....3:07:35 (1,665)
Cook, Graham Philip....4:07:40 (12,878)
Cook, James....4:58:41 (26,134)
Cook, James Gerard....4:27:12 (18,149)
Cook, John....5:26:33 (30,845)
Cook, Julian K....4:07:22 (12,791)
Cook, Mark....4:46:37 (23,209)
Cook, Martin....3:40:21 (6,206)
Cook, Martin....4:16:10 (15,062)
Cook, Martin....4:34:32 (20,132)
Cook, Matthew....4:16:58 (15,287)
Cook, Nigel Vincent....3:42:29 (6,593)
Cook, Nigel W....3:34:29 (5,149)
Cook, Peter W....3:28:33 (4,152)
Cook, Phil J....2:48:29 (431)
Cook, Richard Andrew....3:13:44 (2,288)
Cook, Robert James....4:36:49 (20,689)
Cook, Robert Samuel....4:37:16 (20,806)
Cook, Sam....5:34:45 (31,854)
Cook, Terry....3:57:13 (10,161)
Cook, Tony Alan....4:55:13 (25,361)
Cooke, Gary....4:06:45 (12,642)
Cooke, James....4:17:43 (15,501)
Cooke, John Frederick....5:13:40 (28,866)
Cooke, Jon Alaistair....4:02:49 (11,677)
Cooke, Jonathan....4:39:08 (21,291)
Cooke, Jonathan R....4:35:17 (20,292)
Cooke, Nicolas Robert....4:51:23 (24,394)
Cooke, Stephen Robert James....7:13:54 (36,352)
Cooke, Timothy L....2:54:54 (734)
Cookman, Ben....4:22:35 (16,868)
Cooksey, Andrew....3:43:59 (6,879)
Cookson, Noel....4:20:09 (16,150)
Cooling, Mark David....5:18:20 (29,596)
Cooling, Philip....3:57:46 (10,318)
Coombe, Andy P....4:38:58 (21,252)
Coombes, David....4:54:10 (25,083)
Coombes, Mark....4:06:32 (12,583)
Coombes, Mark W....3:54:25 (9,304)
Coomer, Bradley....4:42:40 (22,176)
Cooney, Andrew S....3:03:34 (1,357)
Cooper, Alastair....4:02:58 (11,721)
Cooper, Alex....4:17:06 (15,321)
Cooper, Alex....4:25:20 (17,612)
Cooper, Andrew....5:01:32 (26,764)
Cooper, Andrew Christopher....5:16:20 (29,281)
Cooper, Andrew K....4:33:57 (19,980)
Cooper, Barry....5:12:09 (28,591)
Cooper, Ben....7:19:05 (36,396)
Cooper, Ben Michael....3:32:02 (4,745)
Cooper, Bob....3:58:40 (10,613)
Cooper, Christopher....3:47:25 (7,625)
Cooper, Darren....3:51:57 (8,647)
Cooper, Darren....5:15:38 (29,169)
Cooper, Daryn Lawrence....4:55:32 (25,414)
Cooper, David....4:00:39 (11,155)
Cooper, David....4:32:43 (19,610)
Cooper, David P....3:47:28 (7,638)
Cooper, Dean....4:26:55 (18,054)
Cooper, Douglas N....2:59:40 (1,125)
Cooper, Gary....3:56:26 (9,908)
Cooper, Gary....4:44:40 (22,692)
Cooper, Gordon F....4:28:13 (18,424)
Cooper, Graeme....5:24:03 (30,487)
Cooper, Ian L....5:26:34 (30,848)
Cooper, Ian T....5:21:43 (30,112)
Cooper, James....4:08:00 (12,963)
Cooper, James D....2:55:51 (791)
Cooper, James Robert....4:00:01 (10,989)
Cooper, John....4:06:08 (12,484)
Cooper, John F....3:43:59 (6,879)
Cooper, John M....3:53:19 (9,004)
Cooper, Jon....4:07:10 (12,747)
Cooper, Julian Peter....4:19:12 (15,898)
Cooper, Kelvin....4:02:31 (11,608)
Cooper, Luke....5:23:45 (30,434)
Cooper, Mark Alan....5:16:35 (29,319)
Cooper, Martin Stephen....3:29:01 (4,230)
Cooper, Matthew....4:33:04 (19,720)
Cooper, Matthew J....3:40:47 (6,288)
Cooper, Michael....3:24:49 (3,553)
Cooper, Michael Paul....5:10:45 (28,366)
Cooper, Mitchell Aaron....5:31:36 (31,488)
Cooper, Paul David....5:01:18 (26,709)
Cooper, Paul Steven....5:26:02 (30,785)
Cooper, Philip....4:26:38 (17,984)
Cooper, Raphael....3:28:33 (4,152)
Cooper, Richard Neil....4:09:09 (13,240)
Cooper, Rob....4:19:15 (15,913)
Cooper, Robert....4:08:40 (13,131)
Cooper, Roy Stephen....3:51:22 (8,507)
Cooper, Sam John....3:58:09 (10,435)
Cooper, Simon....3:42:06 (6,530)
Cooper, Stephen James....4:47:27 (23,400)
Cooper, Stephen Robert....4:22:09 (16,741)
Cooper, Steven William....4:08:40 (13,131)
Cooper, William....4:42:29 (22,136)
Cooper-Haime, Mark Anthony....5:03:09 (27,048)
Copas, Nicholas....2:59:05 (1,062)
Copas, Wayne....3:57:40 (10,286)
Cope, Ben....3:08:45 (1,788)
Cope, Grahame Michael....3:19:37 (2,929)
Cope, James Patrick....5:19:54 (29,836)
Cope, Nicholas....2:26:18 (45)
Cope, Robert....4:36:50 (20,695)
Cope, Trevor A....5:34:17 (31,794)
Cope, Vince L....4:13:29 (14,358)
Copeland, Richard....4:25:21 (17,619)
Copley, Dale B....4:41:40 (21,937)
Copley, David Alan....4:10:05 (13,491)
Copner, Guy....3:32:03 (4,749)
Copp, Daniel....4:15:36 (14,927)
Coppard, Chas....4:12:38 (14,132)
Coppen, Matthew....5:40:42 (32,452)
Coppin, Robert....4:35:24 (20,325)
Copping, Bradley....4:10:14 (13,536)
Copping, Christopher PS....5:13:43 (28,876)
Coppins, Benjamin David....3:42:14 (6,553)
Coppola, Giovanni....5:09:53 (28,212)
Cops, Simon Russell....5:02:04 (26,856)
Copson, Paul Justin....4:04:34 (12,087)
Copus, Christopher D....3:40:43 (6,277)
Copus, Peter....6:22:54 (35,231)
Cora Decunto, Adrian....3:29:24 (4,302)
Corallo, Paul....3:23:40 (3,390)
Corbersmith, Steven L....5:45:48 (32,932)
Corbet Burcher, James....5:07:14 (27,755)
Corbett, Andrew D....3:15:52 (2,538)
Corbett, David J....4:05:31 (12,338)
Corbett, David Thomas....3:52:17 (8,734)
Corbett, Glen....4:50:16 (24,110)
Corbett, Lance....4:21:34 (16,567)
Corbett, Paul....4:19:19 (15,935)
Corbett, Peter....4:30:28 (19,081)
Corbett, Philip J....3:21:35 (3,145)
Corbin, James....4:00:23 (11,085)
Corbishley, Wayne Harold....5:09:24 (28,126)
Corbishley-Forbes, Wayne....5:23:55 (30,464)
Corbould, Clive....5:57:13 (33,881)
Corcoran, Alex John....3:53:59 (9,205)
Corcoran, Chris....3:21:05 (3,096)
Corcoran, Stephen J....3:55:53 (9,745)
Cordell, Daniel....5:40:33 (32,439)
Corden, James M....2:42:21 (259)
Corden-Lloyd, Warwick Ron....3:46:57 (7,518)
Corderoy, David W....3:48:32 (7,853)
Cordes, Andrew....4:27:58 (18,357)
Cording, James....4:59:03 (26,227)
Cording, Stephen J....4:59:04 (26,230)
Cordner, Ross Stuart....4:33:07 (19,734)
Cordova, Edison Omar....4:25:59 (17,807)
Core, Kevin....4:01:02 (11,258)
Corfield, James....5:16:21 (29,286)
Corigliano, Antonio....4:02:42 (11,650)
Corke, Martin Andrew....4:13:12 (14,286)

Corke, Stephen A..................3:52:39 (8,836)
Corless, Ian J.....................2:58:01 (958)
Corlett, Brian.....................4:16:23 (15,135)
Corlett, James William.........3:59:08 (10,758)
Cormack, Ian Francis............4:25:49 (17,760)
Cormano, Tony....................3:23:01 (3,294)
Corn, David J.....................5:37:03 (32,106)
Cornelio, Thomas J...............5:17:14 (29,425)
Cornelio, Thomas William.......4:06:16 (12,516)
Cornelius, Matthew Philip.......4:41:45 (21,952)
Cornelius, Robert Ian...........5:15:46 (29,190)
Cornell, Andrew R................3:43:24 (6,757)
Corneloues, Roy..................5:44:00 (32,767)
Corney, Sam.......................4:35:54 (20,446)
Cornfield, Ed.....................3:37:49 (5,726)
Cornford, Adam....................4:32:44 (19,617)
Cornford, Adrian..................3:19:56 (2,954)
Cornhill, Lee Edward.............4:24:26 (17,370)
Cornhill, Phil....................3:37:52 (5,734)
Cornish, Dean Antony.............5:04:19 (27,246)
Cornock, Ian John................4:24:29 (17,384)
Cornock, Paul Stanley............4:58:14 (26,019)
Cornwall, Matt James.............4:39:47 (21,457)
Cornwall, Michael D..............4:41:29 (21,887)
Cornwell, David...................4:49:22 (23,886)
Cornwell, James Keith............5:00:23 (26,533)
Cornwell, Richard................4:39:00 (21,258)
Corp, John.........................4:39:53 (21,483)
Corr, David John..................4:29:54 (18,953)
Corr, Patrick.....................4:04:33 (12,084)
Corr, Tom Peter....................3:47:56 (7,726)
Corria, Anthony Paul..............3:47:52 (7,711)
Corrie, Justin J..................2:53:31 (640)
Corrigall, Douglas...............4:41:26 (21,873)
Corrigan, Howard.................4:07:58 (12,953)
Corrigan, John J..................5:20:15 (29,882)
Corrigan, Michael John...........4:08:20 (13,036)
Corry, James M....................6:16:34 (34,957)
Corry, Matthew James.............4:29:37 (18,852)
Corse, Chris......................3:48:53 (7,947)
Corse, Tom........................4:00:26 (11,100)
Corsini, Russell G...............2:56:20 (821)
Cort, Matthew John...............4:06:00 (12,456)
Cortese, Guiseppe.................4:24:26 (17,370)
Corti, Dominic Francis...........4:58:59 (26,210)
Cory, Timothy.....................3:15:23 (2,484)
Cosgrove, Christopher.............4:23:07 (17,007)
Cosker, Michael...................5:29:02 (31,154)
Cosker, Thomas Anthony...........3:30:01 (4,421)
Cossell, Paul.....................4:39:24 (21,353)
Cossey, Paul Graham...............4:15:09 (14,821)
Cosstick, Anthony J..............4:21:46 (16,631)
Costa, Michael....................3:49:16 (8,039)
Costanzo, Filippo.................3:42:50 (6,661)
Costarella, Luciano..............3:53:44 (9,132)
Costas, Paul......................3:27:51 (4,025)
Costello, Andrew..................4:08:21 (13,043)
Coster, Luke David...............4:16:40 (15,209)
Coster, Michael...................6:11:32 (34,724)
Coster, Paul J....................4:35:51 (20,433)
Costil, Pierre....................6:03:56 (34,319)
Costin, Mark William.............5:16:16 (29,261)
Costin, Richard David............5:29:19 (31,194)
Cote, Daniel......................4:55:04 (25,326)
Cotgrave, Andrew Peter...........5:00:14 (26,505)
Cottage, Darren Richard..........4:59:01 (26,219)
Cotter, Keith Fergus.............3:35:27 (5,313)
Cotterell, Alan James............4:01:34 (11,385)
Cotterill, Mark Andrew...........3:33:29 (4,967)
Cotterill, Phil James............4:22:06 (16,735)
Cotterill, Richard...............6:12:08 (34,762)
Cottier, Andrew C................2:52:47 (609)
Cottis, John D....................3:54:47 (9,416)
Cottis, Roy Anthony..............4:09:40 (13,388)
Cotton, Chris J...................2:59:31 (1,113)
Cotton, Keith.....................4:16:51 (15,257)
Cotton, Nicholas..................6:17:14 (34,992)
Cottrell, Dale....................3:21:00 (3,083)
Cottrell, Michael John...........4:54:42 (25,230)
Cottrell, Simon D.................4:09:00 (13,213)
Cottrill, Gary P..................3:54:20 (9,289)
Couch, Kevin......................3:56:15 (9,857)
Couch, Vince Kenneth.............4:13:36 (14,404)

Couchman, Kevin A.................3:02:54 (1,321)
Coudriet, Jacques.................4:05:14 (12,263)
Coughlan, Noel Thomas............5:03:00 (27,026)
Couldwell, Alan J.................3:58:17 (10,484)
Coull, Douglas....................5:25:09 (30,646)
Coulson, Charles Anthony Albert .4:35:39 (20,378)
Coulson, Jack.....................3:24:09 (3,460)
Coulson, Joseph...................4:06:49 (12,660)
Coulson, Myles Robert.............4:10:00 (13,475)

Coulson, Paul.....................5:56:42 (33,843)

My first London Marathon was in 1991 when it hosted the World Marathon Cup. That was my best time. This year I decided to dress up, and how glad I am that I did. Race day people kept asking to be photographed with me. As we set off it began. 'Come on fairy', they shouted. I waved my wand in acknowledgement. As I came along the embankment a line of girls chanted 'Paul, Paul' – a real boost when it's hurting. I met my daughter Rebecca a mile from the finish. A hug brought tears to my eyes. Megan, my other daughter, had rung me every 30 mins to encourage me and check how I was doing. As I crossed the finish I did a twirl and thought 'the sugar plum fairy has nothing on me'. I had made it, job done.

Coulson, Phil.....................2:40:31 (213)
Coulson, Robert...................5:08:55 (28,032)
Coulson, Stephen Hugh............4:25:37 (17,694)
Coulson, Wayne A..................3:18:40 (2,838)
Coultart, Gary T..................4:50:16 (24,110)
Coultas, Stephen Robert..........4:45:41 (22,945)
Coulter, Kenny....................3:34:49 (5,216)
Coulter, Michael John............4:05:10 (12,245)
Coulthard, Garry..................3:53:42 (9,122)
Coulthard, Neil...................4:32:28 (19,553)
Coulton, Robert...................4:08:31 (13,090)
Coupe, Michael F..................3:43:42 (6,805)
Coupe, Mike.......................4:25:03 (17,537)
Coupes, Dominic John.............4:09:38 (13,380)
Courau, Bertrand..................3:10:26 (1,941)
Courouble, Philippe..............5:21:32 (30,077)
Court, Steve......................3:36:51 (5,537)
Courtenay-Bishop, Harry Edward .3:38:58 (5,934)
Courtney, Christopher James......5:20:35 (29,941)
Courtney, John....................4:58:35 (26,112)
Courtney, John....................5:47:05 (33,059)
Courtney, Paul D..................4:17:45 (15,512)
Courtney, Rhys....................5:51:56 (33,500)
Courtney, Trevor Anthony.........4:58:19 (26,045)
Cousens, Andrew...................5:27:59 (31,026)
Cousens, Charles L...............4:51:45 (24,475)
Cousin, Simon James..............4:49:14 (23,861)
Cousins, Brian Jeffrey...........5:08:49 (28,017)
Cousins, Geoffrey.................4:36:56 (20,723)
Cousins, James....................3:46:44 (7,468)
Cousins, Kevin....................4:09:04 (13,224)
Cousins, Martyn Anthony..........4:43:13 (22,303)
Cousins, Roger Norman............4:43:11 (22,290)
Cousseau, Raphaël.................4:33:00 (19,698)
Coutts, Philip....................3:44:08 (6,901)
Cove, David J.....................4:44:11 (22,557)

Coventry, Christian Nevinson......5:24:22 (30,535)
Coverdale, John E................3:10:06 (1,915)
Coverley, Richard................4:52:34 (24,701)
Covey, David John.................4:38:51 (21,218)
Covill, Martin....................5:08:50 (28,019)
Covre, Fabio......................3:30:28 (4,495)
Cowan, Ben Vernon.................4:59:43 (26,388)
Cowan, Jonty......................3:05:37 (1,506)
Cowan, Nick.......................4:30:35 (19,120)
Cowan, Nigel......................4:34:33 (20,134)
Cowan, Toby.......................4:17:07 (15,329)
Cowap, Donald.....................4:39:59 (21,499)
Coward, John......................3:52:46 (8,857)
Coward, Richard...................4:51:52 (24,511)
Cowcher, Billy....................5:18:02 (29,552)
Cowdray, Andrew...................3:53:15 (8,983)
Cowdroy, Jim......................3:50:59 (8,416)
Cowell, David E...................4:17:32 (15,452)
Cowell, Ian Michael..............5:30:10 (31,312)
Cowell, Jon M.....................2:59:00 (1,049)
Cowell, Justin Kimborough........4:30:27 (19,075)
Cowell, Kevin S...................3:51:09 (8,461)
Cowell, Stephen J.................5:14:05 (28,936)
Cowen, Andy.......................4:29:21 (18,763)
Cowham, Michael...................6:27:33 (35,403)
Cowie, James......................5:47:56 (33,132)
Cowley, Ian.......................4:09:40 (13,388)
Cowley, John......................4:36:02 (20,485)
Cowlin, Jonny.....................4:11:40 (13,898)
Cowling, Johnny Paul.............4:58:36 (26,116)
Cowling, Peter C..................5:49:37 (33,294)
Cowling, Richard Martin..........4:18:38 (15,753)
Cowlishaw, Steven G..............3:12:43 (2,157)
Cowls, Stephen J..................4:08:12 (13,009)
Cowpertwait, Colin James.........4:49:04 (23,820)
Cox, Alistair Nicholas James.....4:18:50 (15,803)
Cox, Allan........................5:24:41 (30,579)
Cox, Andrew David.................4:35:49 (20,426)
Cox, Andrew Michael..............5:42:01 (32,588)
Cox, Brian L......................4:38:43 (21,175)
Cox, Chris........................3:35:12 (5,272)
Cox, Chris........................3:57:21 (10,194)
Cox, Christopher Stephen.........3:59:32 (10,870)
Cox, Dan James....................4:04:48 (12,153)
Cox, Darren James.................5:01:19 (26,718)
Cox, David........................4:11:23 (13,812)
Cox, David........................4:24:30 (17,388)
Cox, David Alan...................5:48:28 (33,193)
Cox, David Anthony................4:25:13 (17,578)
Cox, David Michael...............3:10:54 (1,982)
Cox, Dean.........................4:23:25 (17,084)
Cox, Ed...........................3:51:41 (8,584)
Cox, Gerald.......................5:33:05 (31,675)
Cox, Iain.........................3:42:39 (6,624)
Cox, James........................5:17:19 (29,442)
Cox, Kevin I......................3:26:04 (3,744)
Cox, Lee M........................4:44:50 (22,728)
Cox, Matthew......................4:24:12 (17,287)
Cox, Paul.........................5:26:17 (30,818)
Cox, Paul.........................6:57:58 (36,157)
Cox, Paul J.......................4:33:08 (19,740)
Cox, Peter........................4:20:05 (16,131)
Cox, Simon........................4:38:49 (21,207)
Cox, Simon John...................4:08:48 (13,161)
Cox, Simon Peter..................5:39:58 (32,385)
Cox, Steve Jon....................6:25:46 (35,339)
Cox, Steven Paul..................4:05:02 (12,217)
Cox, Vincent......................5:37:08 (32,120)
Coxhead, Ian......................3:42:12 (6,549)
Coxhead, Mark A...................4:33:28 (19,843)
Coxon, Peter Jeffrey.............4:05:57 (12,445)
Coxon, Robert David..............4:26:05 (17,837)
Coyle, Daniel Brendan............6:17:58 (35,029)
Coyle, Danny......................4:16:38 (15,197)
Coyle, Gareth.....................4:08:31 (13,090)
Coyle, Jade.......................4:33:38 (19,902)
Coyle, James......................3:46:02 (7,314)
Coyle, James Barry...............7:07:18 (36,282)
Coyle, James Richard.............3:43:45 (6,813)
Coyle, Terence P..................2:52:19 (584)
Coyne, Craig Matthew.............4:59:42 (26,386)
Coyne, Mark.......................4:38:40 (21,158)
Coyne, Paul.......................4:39:25 (21,363)

Coyne, Stephen 5:01:44 (26,803)
Crabb, Adam 5:18:26 (29,617)
Crabb, Bobby 4:53:50 (25,002)
Crabb, Kieron Niall 4:50:04 (24,064)
Crabbe, Rudi 4:44:42 (22,698)
Crabtree, Jason Karl 4:54:06 (25,072)
Crabtree, Joseph Ryan 4:23:25 (17,084)
Crabtree, Mark 3:34:45 (5,202)
Cracknell, Andrew P 2:51:35 (548)
Cracknell, Keith 4:22:56 (16,972)
Cracknell, Robert 5:52:21 (33,525)
Cradden, Brendan P 4:10:24 (13,568)
Craddock, Charles Thomas John 4:34:23 (20,091)
Craddock, Dean J 4:55:14 (25,367)
Craddock, Peter Martin 4:29:46 (18,905)
Cradock, Tommy 3:47:18 (7,600)
Craft, David C 4:54:19 (25,137)
Cragg, Richard Nicholas 4:21:02 (16,425)
Craggs, Michael R 5:46:41 (33,028)
Craig, Christopher 3:28:56 (4,219)
Craig, David Alexander 3:58:47 (10,652)
Craig, David Edwin 4:23:54 (17,213)
Craig, Gerard E 2:53:31 (640)
Craig, Graeme 6:13:03 (34,808)
Craig, Jamie 4:40:25 (21,617)
Craig, Michael 2:52:51 (613)
Craig, Robbie 3:58:14 (10,471)
Craig, Stevie 5:31:49 (31,516)
Craig, Thomas P 4:35:06 (20,251)
Craig-Corbett, Lewin 3:33:40 (5,001)
Craig-McFeely, Richard 3:18:08 (2,783)
Craik, Alexander David 4:55:23 (25,399)
Cram, James 4:28:36 (18,548)
Cramer, Lawrence Edward 7:08:23 (36,294)
Cramp, Graham M 3:39:46 (6,092)
Cramphorn, Jon Ben 4:17:01 (15,302)
Cramphorn, Russell 4:35:16 (20,287)
Crampton, Ian 2:30:02 (70)
Cran, Alexander N 2:54:29 (700)
Cran, Mike 4:17:14 (15,359)
Crandley, Royston 5:11:44 (28,509)
Crane, Andrew John 4:57:58 (25,963)
Crane, Barry Mackenzie 3:30:24 (4,485)
Crane, Carl Laurence 3:33:26 (4,958)
Crane, Mark A 4:32:33 (19,572)
Crane, Melvin Ian 5:14:41 (29,016)
Crane, Ric 3:54:15 (9,272)
Cranfield, Richard James 4:11:08 (13,753)
Crangle, Robert 3:42:07 (6,533)
Cranmer, Kevin 4:17:57 (15,563)
Cranshaw, Joel 3:59:05 (10,740)
Cranwell, Mark Andrew 3:11:37 (2,061)
Crashaw, Justin Raymond 4:06:34 (12,591)
Crate, Malcolm John 5:39:14 (32,324)
Craven, Jonathan 4:08:19 (13,033)
Craven, Mark J 3:42:58 (6,689)
Craven, Terry 3:55:15 (9,544)
Craw, Gavin 4:54:33 (25,190)
Crawford, Colin 3:47:49 (7,703)
Crawford, Duncan 4:18:39 (15,758)
Crawford, Mark 4:28:12 (18,417)
Crawford, Mark B 4:17:56 (15,557)
Crawford, Mark David 4:35:36 (20,367)
Crawford, Paul 4:03:04 (11,743)
Crawford, Steven 6:43:10 (35,868)
Crawley, Craig Graham 4:54:27 (25,168)
Craxton, Nick J 5:36:05 (32,005)
Cray, Adam Thomas 4:49:05 (23,828)
Creamer, Richard Andrew 3:52:27 (8,777)
Creasey, Daniel Paul 5:01:18 (26,709)
Creech, Andrew Martin C 4:44:13 (22,568)
Creech, Stuart D 2:50:18 (497)
Creed, Gary 4:10:09 (13,512)
Creed, Hugh 3:45:13 (7,145)
Creed, Paul D 4:24:06 (17,260)
Creed, Phil 5:24:21 (30,531)
Cregor, Paul D 4:30:46 (19,164)
Creighton, Luke 3:03:31 (1,348)
Cremer, Arne 4:23:30 (17,104)
Cremin, James 6:08:34 (34,587)
Cremosnik, Martin 3:20:41 (3,046)
Crerie, Marc K 4:32:13 (19,491)
Cresey, Michael 5:39:55 (32,381)
Crespin, Jocelyn 4:58:06 (25,986)
Crespo, Pablo 4:02:25 (11,587)
Cresser, Henry S 3:32:12 (4,770)
Cresswell, Dean 3:57:04 (10,122)
Cresswell, Peter Edward 4:35:57 (20,466)
Crews, Jon E 3:15:31 (2,499)
Cribb, Stephen T 6:06:57 (34,504)
Cribbin, David 5:38:29 (32,262)
Cribbin, Thomas 5:38:27 (32,255)
Cribier, Guillaume J 2:42:53 (272)
Crichton, Andrew Trevor Mark 4:04:06 (11,985)
Crick, Jonathan 3:31:13 (4,612)
Crick, Terence R 5:29:23 (31,210)
Crighton, Colin 4:29:55 (18,957)
Crighton, Matthew Daniel 3:21:05 (3,096)
Crijns, Jos 4:39:19 (21,334)
Crilly, Richard 4:18:03 (15,597)
Cripps, James Alexander 3:29:46 (4,372)
Cripps, Leonard Samuel Anthony 3:28:53 (4,207)
Crisp, Charles Philip 5:06:55 (27,708)
Crisp, Derek J 4:54:44 (25,238)
Crisp, John Cunningham 5:15:04 (29,078)
Crisp, John F 2:56:30 (830)
Crisp, Martin Timothy Palmer 5:55:18 (33,745)
Crisp, Philip 3:54:50 (9,431)
Crispie, Gerard T 3:10:23 (1,937)
Crispin, Stuart J 4:37:50 (20,951)
Cristal, James 4:58:23 (26,061)
Cristalli, Giuseppe 3:27:47 (4,011)
Critchlow, Guy 4:01:09 (11,287)
Critchlow, Martin 3:01:54 (1,250)
Critchlow, Nigel 3:37:59 (5,758)
Croasdale, Mark J 2:40:21 (207)
Croasdell, Leigh 5:32:43 (31,635)
Crocker, James Benjamin 4:30:24 (19,064)
Crocker, Matthew 3:51:57 (8,647)
Crocker, Matthew M 3:21:52 (3,178)
Crocker, Paul David 4:14:13 (14,573)
Crocker, Russell Paul 3:39:27 (6,033)
Crocket, Graham 3:06:18 (1,553)
Crockett, Steve 4:53:39 (24,957)
Crockwell, David J 4:08:05 (12,983)
Croft, Alex J 5:17:12 (29,415)
Croft, James Douglas 4:15:22 (14,881)
Croft, Simon 4:03:07 (11,762)
Crofts, Mark D 3:40:13 (6,184)
Crofts, Matt 4:12:38 (14,132)
Croll, Darren L 4:25:47 (17,745)
Crompton, Matthew 3:29:11 (4,266)
Crompton, Sam 4:09:05 (13,228)
Cronimus, Charles 6:07:10 (34,517)
Cronin, Iain 5:23:24 (30,372)
Cronin, Kieron Joseph 5:43:50 (32,758)
Cronin, Stephen Michael 5:15:46 (29,190)
Cronin,, Mark, Paul 6:39:32 (35,772)
Crook, David F 3:39:36 (6,061)
Crook, Ed 6:45:57 (35,930)
Crook, Gavin A 4:47:38 (23,449)
Crook, Mark 5:12:24 (28,629)
Crook, Paul Anthony 4:36:59 (20,738)
Crook, Philip 4:28:30 (18,521)
Crook, Richard David 5:07:25 (27,792)
Crookall, Jonathan 3:35:47 (5,374)
Crooke, Reece Michael 3:15:56 (2,546)
Cropper-Joyce, Ian Thomas 6:16:20 (34,938)
Cropton, Jason Graham 3:21:56 (3,187)
Crosby, Garry Robert 4:15:48 (14,979)
Crosby, Ian 4:48:37 (23,699)
Crosby, Jon W 4:01:07 (11,280)
Crosby, Luke Owen 3:47:10 (7,566)
Cross, Anthony W 3:49:11 (8,021)
Cross, Daniel 5:01:11 (26,678)
Cross, David Michael 4:44:08 (22,541)
Cross, Jeremy S 3:43:31 (6,778)
Cross, John 4:00:54 (11,218)
Cross, Julian 4:52:47 (24,751)
Cross, Peter 5:45:44 (32,926)
Cross, Peter R 3:46:44 (7,468)
Cross, Richard 3:30:20 (4,475)
Cross, Richard 4:51:59 (24,549)
Cross, Roger J 3:47:00 (7,524)
Cross, Stephen David 5:07:14 (27,755)
Cross, Tim 4:05:23 (12,303)
Crosse, David 4:45:11 (22,815)
Crosse, Matthew P 3:02:30 (1,301)
Crossen, David 5:21:26 (30,065)
Crossett, Gary R 5:17:58 (29,542)
Crossland, Charles 4:28:27 (18,508)
Crossland, Jamie 4:05:23 (12,303)
Crossland, Matthew 4:59:40 (26,373)
Crossley, Mark Raymond 4:32:49 (19,635)
Crossman, Philip 3:50:59 (8,416)
Crouch, Alan 3:41:43 (6,460)
Crouch, Oliver 3:59:01 (10,725)
Crouchman, Simon 5:03:39 (27,127)
Croud, Bryan 4:20:43 (16,341)
Crowder, Dave John 4:17:40 (15,487)
Crowe, Andrew John 4:58:48 (26,165)
Crowe, Douglas J 4:57:20 (25,827)
Crowe, Stuart 4:02:26 (11,592)
Crowe, Thomas 4:56:20 (25,619)
Crowhurst, Barry James 6:11:49 (34,742)
Crowhurst, Jake 3:55:52 (9,740)
Crowley, Gary Stephen 4:54:31 (25,184)
Crowley, Gregory S 3:13:27 (2,241)
Crowley, Jim 4:39:19 (21,334)
Crowley, Phillip J 4:17:20 (15,386)
Crowley, Vincent Patrick 4:07:54 (12,930)
Crowther, Jonathan 5:05:12 (27,408)
Crowther, Neil M 4:41:21 (21,851)
Crowther, Steven Brian 5:46:25 (32,998)
Croxall, Mark 4:54:10 (25,083)
Croxen-John, Dan 4:40:42 (21,693)
Croxford, David Robert 4:09:26 (13,325)
Croydon, Stuart Anthony 3:06:29 (1,569)
Crozier, Alan David 3:16:31 (2,610)
Cruden, Graham 4:33:07 (19,734)
Cruickshank, Brian 2:52:33 (594)
Cruickshank, George A 5:13:12 (28,800)
Cruickshank, Gus 4:22:30 (16,847)
Cruickshank, Ian 3:56:47 (10,027)
Cruise, Paul Stephen 4:51:22 (24,390)
Crumpler, Dan 5:00:53 (26,629)
Crumpton, Anthony Loris 4:07:26 (12,810)
Crumpton, Matthew 4:38:57 (21,244)
Crundwell, Alastair 5:12:09 (28,591)
Cruse, Peter 2:53:44 (652)
Crutcher, James G 3:29:31 (4,325)
Crute, George S 5:11:26 (28,471)
Cruttenden, Joe 3:29:44 (4,368)
Cruz, Ignacio 3:53:30 (9,054)
Cuañado, Antonio 4:08:17 (13,024)
Cubbage, Kevin J 4:51:06 (24,333)
Cubbin, Derek 4:36:39 (20,648)
Cubbon, Paul 3:08:25 (1,743)
Cubin, Michael Clarke 3:43:49 (6,835)
Cucchiara, Vincenzo 4:40:41 (21,687)
Cudd, James 5:12:49 (28,703)
Cudd, Simon 4:38:49 (21,207)
Cuddihy, Paul 2:34:49 (108)
Cudmore, Johnathan Luke 4:54:59 (25,302)
Cuell, Wesley Paul 4:56:09 (25,567)
Cuff, Paul E 3:08:16 (1,725)
Culbert, Philip J 3:33:26 (4,958)
Culkin, Giles 4:38:36 (21,143)
Cull, Alexander John 3:58:03 (10,397)
Cull, Mick 3:47:55 (7,723)
Cull, Stewart 6:03:20 (34,273)
Cullen, Christopher J 4:24:33 (17,407)
Cullen, James 4:00:16 (11,048)
Cullen, Martin J 4:01:49 (11,450)
Cullen, Robert 5:43:40 (32,734)
Cullen, Robert G 4:22:10 (16,747)
Cullen, Robert John 3:52:36 (8,822)
Cullern, Doug A 4:20:39 (16,320)
Culligan, Ciaran 3:18:40 (2,838)
Cullinane, John 4:10:12 (13,531)
Culling, Kevin 5:31:22 (31,456)
Culling, Ryland B 5:31:22 (31,456)
Cully, Matt 4:22:22 (16,811)
Cully, Robert J 5:20:58 (30,000)
Culmer, Anthony 4:49:44 (23,991)
Culpan, Charlie 4:33:00 (19,698)
Culshaw, Edmund 4:08:10 (12,998)
Culwin, Fintan 4:15:41 (14,948)
Cumber, Gary 5:06:54 (27,702)

Cumber, Geoffrey	3:06:44 (1,589)
Cumberland, Joseph R	3:16:52 (2,657)
Cuming, Nicholas P	4:52:07 (24,578)
Cumley, Stephen	3:11:32 (2,052)
Cumming, Iain	3:18:51 (2,859)
Cummings, Graham P	5:30:05 (31,306)
Cummings, Jonathan	4:19:57 (16,086)
Cummings, Neil	4:45:43 (22,955)
Cummings, Oliver	3:33:35 (4,983)
Cummins, Gerry	4:24:35 (17,414)
Cummins, Kevin P	4:20:41 (16,328)
Cummins, Simon C	4:08:52 (13,177)
Cummins, Timothy D	4:01:55 (11,474)
Cundall, André M	5:06:59 (27,720)
Cunliffe, Michael P	3:57:00 (10,089)
Cunliffe, Scott	4:07:40 (12,878)
Cunnah, Richard Joseph	5:54:53 (33,706)
Cunningham, Aidan	4:21:28 (16,539)
Cunningham, Andrew John	4:08:40 (13,131)
Cunningham, Anthony	4:12:31 (14,103)
Cunningham, Dan	3:41:25 (6,408)
Cunningham, David	4:11:48 (13,932)
Cunningham, Frazer	4:24:47 (17,462)
Cunningham, Gordon John	5:48:36 (33,203)
Cunningham, James	3:34:16 (5,106)
Cunningham, James	4:20:02 (16,115)
Cunningham, James Joseph	4:16:33 (15,181)
Cunningham, John A	4:28:59 (18,679)
Cunningham, Kevin	5:04:16 (27,243)
Cunningham, Mark	5:11:22 (28,460)
Cunningham, Neil John	4:46:47 (23,250)
Cunningham, Paul	5:45:32 (32,913)
Cunningham, Robert J	3:19:58 (2,960)
Cunningham, Sean P	3:21:34 (3,143)
Cunningham, Stuart J	2:46:12 (367)
Cuoq, Christophe	3:29:53 (4,393)
Curabet, Dominique	4:26:41 (17,994)
Curd, Richard James	6:05:47 (34,440)
Curia, Nicolas	4:29:38 (18,860)
Curley, Dermot	2:58:18 (987)
Curley, Garry A	4:51:26 (24,406)
Curley, John A	4:51:26 (24,406)
Curling, Andrew Peter	4:41:28 (21,884)
Curnier, Benjamin	4:16:12 (15,071)
Curphey, Paul T	3:21:39 (3,155)
Curran, Chris	4:25:54 (17,786)
Curran, James	4:04:35 (12,096)
Curran, John	3:44:30 (6,987)
Curran, John James	3:54:50 (9,431)
Curran, Len	4:40:46 (21,714)
Curran, Mark	5:08:40 (27,999)
Currell, Mark William	5:44:25 (32,806)
Currie, Alaster Paul	4:41:44 (21,948)
Currie, Alistair	4:17:47 (15,522)
Currie, Antony	4:45:32 (22,897)
Currie, Glenn Robert	3:52:51 (8,883)
Currie, Ian	4:12:53 (14,204)
Currie, John Stewart	3:58:13 (10,463)
Currie, Luke M	5:45:36 (32,917)
Currie, Tom Andrew	4:08:58 (13,201)
Curry, Ian David	3:46:44 (7,468)
Curry, Jeff	4:23:21 (17,060)
Curry, Sean	4:16:26 (15,151)
Cursons, Charles	6:49:19 (35,984)
Curtain, Andrew	6:21:13 (35,169)
Curtin, Matthew J	4:22:47 (16,934)
Curtin, Shane JJ	4:46:28 (23,159)
Curtis, Chris	5:05:17 (27,421)
Curtis, Daniel	4:02:09 (11,522)
Curtis, Daniel	4:38:57 (21,244)
Curtis, Francis J	4:14:30 (14,647)
Curtis, James R	2:57:36 (919)
Curtis, Joe	3:22:56 (3,282)
Curtis, John R	3:10:23 (1,937)
Curtis, Len	3:30:04 (4,429)
Curtis, Mark Christopher	4:40:35 (21,664)
Curtis, Martin John	4:58:02 (25,974)
Curtis, Matthew J	3:18:38 (2,834)
Curtis, Paul F	2:50:43 (512)
Curtis, Paul M	5:25:06 (30,640)
Curtis, Richard	4:03:31 (11,849)
Curtis, Robert B	3:20:31 (3,027)
Curtis, Ryan Anthony	4:38:16 (21,047)

LONDON MARATHON

Curtis, Simon D	4:19:21 (15,942)
Curtis, Tony Ian	4:34:43 (20,176)
Curzon, Matt J	5:24:56 (30,609)
Cusden, Fergus Andrew	5:03:43 (27,140)
Cushing, Spencer	4:13:34 (14,390)
Cushley, David	5:49:42 (33,308)
Cushway, William	3:56:55 (10,063)
Cussins, Timothy	3:38:06 (5,783)
Cutchey, Matthew	3:19:01 (2,872)
Cuthbert, Kevin Richard	4:24:34 (17,411)
Cuthbert, Simon	3:27:31 (3,966)
Cuthbertson, Graham	4:35:04 (20,242)
Cuthbertson, Richard Michael	3:55:29 (9,611)
Cutler, Chris	4:05:30 (12,334)
Cutler, Matt	3:41:34 (6,433)
Cutts, Mathew	5:05:15 (27,414)
Cutts, Nigel Philip	3:42:50 (6,661)
Da Bank, Rob	4:46:49 (23,259)
Dable, Julian	4:41:58 (22,005)
Dacey, Patrick W	4:25:19 (17,605)
D'Achille, Max	5:23:16 (30,349)
Dachtler, Christopher	3:30:41 (4,527)
Dack, Gary M	3:30:50 (4,554)
Dack, James	4:52:05 (24,568)
Dack, Jeremy Edward	3:15:54 (2,540)
Dade, Richard	4:14:26 (14,626)
Daft, Ben James	3:58:53 (10,682)
Dagless, John William	3:16:09 (2,566)
Daglish, Henry	4:48:56 (23,782)
Dahdouh, Fadi	4:29:09 (18,721)
Dahlke, Fryderyk	3:47:26 (7,628)
Dahlkvist, Göran	5:56:13 (33,812)
Dailey, Tom	4:20:18 (16,200)
Daines, Michael	5:47:59 (33,136)
Daines, Nick	4:25:28 (17,650)
Dainty, Grant	4:08:04 (12,978)
Dainty, Joe Andrew	4:52:50 (24,764)
Daisley, Kyle	4:03:59 (11,956)
Dajlid, James Mark	4:17:29 (15,433)
Dakin, Keith Alan	4:00:33 (11,126)
Dakin, Richard J	4:56:50 (25,728)
Dale, Graham Thomas	4:17:46 (15,519)
Dale, Kris Paul	4:49:41 (23,974)
Dale, Lee John	3:59:16 (10,799)
Dale, Stephen G	3:43:05 (6,715)
Dale, Steve	5:27:55 (31,013)
D'Alessandro, Robert Francis	3:38:53 (5,918)
Daley, Chris	3:50:31 (8,317)
Daley, Justin Michael	5:20:44 (29,970)
Dallard, Steve	5:00:44 (26,595)
Dallimore, Mark	7:07:00 (36,280)
Dallyn, Paul Simon	4:47:13 (23,344)
Dalrymple, David John	3:35:15 (5,278)
Dalton, Jason Christopher	4:32:12 (19,488)
Dalton, Jody Alan	5:03:33 (27,110)
Dalton, Julian	5:20:36 (29,946)
Dalton, Paul William	4:21:23 (16,521)
Dalton, Pedro	4:10:17 (13,545)
Dalton, Robert	3:40:19 (6,202)
Dalton, Stephen W	4:53:41 (24,965)
Dalton-Morris, Robert	4:19:17 (15,922)
Daly, Edward Vincent	3:29:13 (4,273)
Daly, George Samuel	3:43:42 (6,805)
Daly, Ian Joseph	3:42:08 (6,535)
Daly, Paul	2:51:28 (543)
Daly, William J	5:29:40 (31,247)
Dalziel, Julian Andrew	3:35:54 (5,399)
Damato, Nikolas	4:20:16 (16,185)
D'Amelio, Gian Piero	4:00:16 (11,048)
Dammermann, Nikolaus J	3:41:16 (6,383)
Damon, Dan	5:18:35 (29,634)
Danagher-Smith, Kevin Mark	4:18:45 (15,786)
Danbury, Robert	4:02:52 (11,694)
Danby, Tom J	2:38:16 (165)
Dance, Anthony	5:39:10 (32,318)
Dance, Gerry	3:55:59 (9,779)
Dance, James Frederick	4:56:57 (25,757)
Dancer, Simon	4:32:49 (19,635)
Danciger, Simon L	3:11:03 (2,003)
Dando, Richard Lee	2:59:43 (1,130)
Dane, Nicolai	4:22:23 (16,818)
D'Angelo, Claudio	3:36:36 (5,496)
Daniel, Christopher	4:26:40 (17,991)
Daniel, David P	6:42:09 (35,841)
Daniel, Neil	5:06:14 (27,573)
Daniel, Paul	4:19:17 (15,922)
Daniel, Paul Jeremy	6:34:42 (35,647)
Daniel, Ron B	3:32:40 (4,838)
Daniell, Stephen Alan Gary	4:32:29 (19,556)
Daniels, Adrian P	5:12:05 (28,582)
Daniels, David M	4:56:29 (25,643)
Daniels, Ian M	3:42:13 (6,551)
Daniels, Mark	5:15:55 (29,213)
Daniels, Michael	3:05:29 (1,495)
Daniels, Nat	4:54:33 (25,190)
Daniels, Paul A	4:05:19 (12,288)
Daniels, Paul K	3:29:35 (4,339)
Daniels, Paul W	4:34:34 (20,140)
Daniels, Richard Jeffrey	3:27:53 (4,033)
Daniels, Thomas	4:00:09 (11,019)
Danielsen, Staale	3:59:33 (10,882)
Danits, John	4:25:19 (17,605)
Dankl, Christian	5:14:51 (29,044)
Danks, Simon John	3:05:49 (1,522)
Dann, Graham	4:53:28 (24,905)
Dann, Mitchell	3:04:25 (1,421)
Dann, Neil Robert	3:01:57 (1,254)
Dannatt, Adam Christopher	3:17:27 (2,702)
Danobrega, James John	3:46:42 (7,460)
Dansey, Matt	7:22:30 (36,421)
Danter, Scott Francis William	3:58:01 (10,384)
Danzey, Mark Simon	3:33:02 (4,899)
Dar, Nir	4:01:11 (11,294)
Darbha, Sriram	5:36:27 (32,050)
Darby, Howard John	4:06:48 (12,657)
Darby, Jason C	4:08:15 (13,017)
Darby, Paul	4:20:08 (16,145)
Darbyshire, Stephen	4:11:57 (13,977)
Dardis, Mike John	3:34:59 (5,245)
Dare, James	4:13:26 (14,348)
Dargan, Lee Jack	5:32:03 (31,538)
Darge, Stewart K	3:28:01 (4,051)
Dargue, Kevin R	4:43:50 (22,456)
Dariani, Ramin	4:35:53 (20,439)
Darias, Ricardo	3:12:16 (2,111)
Dark, Lewis	3:31:31 (4,670)
Darke, Christopher John	3:37:22 (5,631)
Darkins, Alan	5:04:58 (27,360)
Darling, Richard J	2:40:32 (214)
Darling, Rob	4:59:18 (26,286)
Darlington, Nik	3:34:04 (5,070)
Darnell, Neil	3:29:20 (4,292)
Darnell, Peter	4:29:51 (18,927)
Darque, Jean-Pierre	4:04:36 (12,101)
Darrington, Robert	4:13:57 (14,492)
Darroch, Brian James	4:40:20 (21,587)
Dartois, David	3:46:30 (7,415)
Dartois, Yannis	4:09:34 (13,358)
Darvell, Gavin J	5:23:44 (30,432)
Darvill,, Simon,	4:21:23 (16,521)
Darvill-Evans, Mark	3:36:49 (5,525)
Darvishi, Kevin	3:46:02 (7,314)
Darwin, Chris John	3:24:45 (3,545)
Darwin, Nigel	4:40:26 (21,623)
Dary, Philippe	3:30:39 (4,518)
Das, Anupam	2:37:42 (155)
Das, Rajiv	4:41:44 (21,948)
D'Ascoli, Federico	4:21:09 (16,452)
Dasey, Andrew Gavin	4:12:16 (14,048)
Dashper, Wayne R	3:35:21 (5,295)
Dattani, Dilip	3:13:48 (2,296)
Daugherty, Duane W	3:28:19 (4,107)
Daughtry, Mark C	4:33:30 (19,852)
Daumer, Michel	3:57:33 (10,246)
Daun, Fraser William	3:43:09 (6,723)
Daunter, Mark C	4:20:42 (16,333)
Davanzo, Andrew	4:04:56 (12,186)
Davenport, Carl Neil	4:17:07 (15,329)

Davenport, Jay 4:35:53 (20,439)
Davenport, Simon James 3:48:23 (7,820)
Davesne, Laurent Tony 3:37:36 (5,690)
Davey, Carl Stewart 3:49:36 (8,115)
Davey, Craig 3:20:22 (2,999)
Davey, Daniel 5:18:13 (29,576)
Davey, Henry William 3:34:40 (5,185)
Davey, Keiron 4:18:16 (15,648)
Davey, Mat 4:25:15 (17,586)
Davey, Michael Jonn 4:15:48 (14,979)
Davey, Paul 4:17:17 (15,374)
Davey, Ralph 4:25:48 (17,749)
Davey, Stephen 4:27:25 (18,210)
Davey, Trevor 6:18:48 (35,073)
David, Cedric M 3:46:51 (7,500)
David, Leiglat 3:27:33 (3,971)
David, Pascal 4:04:08 (11,993)
David, Richard 5:10:46 (28,372)
David, William T 4:05:46 (12,402)
Davidson, Alistair 3:33:16 (4,930)
Davidson, Andrew 4:03:35 (11,868)
Davidson, Andrew Stuart 4:03:47 (11,920)
Davidson, Chris Steven 4:11:45 (13,922)
Davidson, Christian John 2:57:19 (881)
Davidson, Darren 4:25:42 (17,715)
Davidson, Ewan I 3:33:55 (5,043)
Davidson, Grant 4:58:46 (26,159)
Davidson, Ian 3:17:03 (2,669)
Davidson, Len 3:51:13 (8,474)
Davidson, Peter 4:06:24 (12,549)
Davies, Andrew G 3:52:38 (8,832)
Davies, Anthony N 4:48:24 (23,638)
Davies, Carl R 3:02:27 (1,293)
Davies, Ceri Rhys 3:52:10 (8,699)
Davies, Chris 4:23:33 (17,119)
Davies, Christopher Morgan 3:06:35 (1,579)
Davies, Clive T 3:33:26 (4,958)
Davies, Dai 3:26:13 (3,773)
Davies, Darhyl N 3:43:56 (6,865)
Davies, Darren 5:14:08 (28,942)
Davies, David B 4:13:14 (14,295)
Davies, Delfryn Arfon 3:54:47 (9,416)
Davies, Edward J 3:08:49 (1,795)
Davies, Eiros Wyn 4:50:46 (24,231)
Davies, Eric 3:51:22 (8,507)
Davies, Eurwyn 4:07:50 (12,912)
Davies, Gareth 4:12:05 (14,003)
Davies, Gareth 5:14:20 (28,966)
Davies, Gareth Fenton 5:53:41 (33,622)
Davies, Gareth James 4:12:35 (14,120)
Davies, Gareth Richard 4:17:55 (15,550)
Davies, Gary Paul 3:55:37 (9,647)
Davies, Gavin Joseph 4:18:42 (15,774)
Davies, Geoffrey Mark 5:08:45 (28,010)
Davies, Gethin Cai 7:10:02 (36,307)
Davies, Glen 3:49:10 (8,016)
Davies, Grahame 4:26:25 (17,930)
Davies, Hadleigh James 3:32:14 (4,778)
Davies, Haydn 5:49:40 (33,304)
Davies, Huw Meredydd 4:01:32 (11,376)
Davies, Hywel John 3:19:13 (2,892)
Davies, Ian I 4:04:57 (12,191)
Davies, Ian M 3:27:48 (4,013)
Davies, Ioan Rhys 4:06:37 (12,604)
Davies, James 3:51:02 (8,432)
Davies, James 7:06:34 (36,273)
Davies, James Lee 4:49:42 (23,978)
Davies, Jamie A 2:57:23 (886)
Davies, Jason 5:09:45 (28,189)
Davies, Jason L 4:10:06 (13,498)
Davies, John D 4:00:25 (11,094)
Davies, Jon 5:21:52 (30,124)
Davies, Jonathan 4:13:56 (14,486)
Davies, Jonathan Charles 3:38:13 (5,805)
Davies, Joss 4:21:06 (16,439)
Davies, Julian 3:49:55 (8,191)
Davies, Kelvin P 3:47:59 (7,736)
Davies, Kevin Maurice 4:58:41 (26,134)
Davies, Laurie David 4:03:48 (11,924)
Davies, Lian 2:58:39 (1,015)
Davies, Malcolm John 4:39:07 (21,286)
Davies, Mark 4:22:29 (16,841)
Davies, Mark 7:03:48 (36,238)
Davies, Mark Anthony 4:27:59 (18,361)
Davies, Mark John 4:23:13 (17,027)
Davies, Mark Marcello 3:39:19 (6,010)
Davies, Mark W 4:59:34 (26,356)
Davies, Martin Howard 4:31:44 (19,381)
Davies, Martin L 3:21:21 (3,124)
Davies, Martin V 3:08:47 (1,791)
Davies, Martyn Paul 4:48:48 (23,747)
Davies, Martyn Rhys 4:20:44 (16,347)
Davies, Michael 3:25:44 (3,692)
Davies, Michael H 3:25:23 (3,627)
Davies, Michael J 2:53:53 (661)
Davies, Mike 3:29:46 (4,372)
Davies, Neil 4:24:58 (17,509)
Davies, Neil Martin 5:14:55 (29,054)
Davies, Neil R 4:17:32 (15,452)
Davies, Nicholas 4:00:42 (11,170)
Davies, Nick Paul 4:10:53 (13,690)
Davies, Noel 3:45:33 (7,220)
Davies, Paul 3:35:38 (5,349)
Davies, Paul 4:59:16 (26,278)
Davies, Paul A 3:47:52 (7,711)
Davies, Paul David 3:28:10 (4,086)
Davies, Paul S 4:48:25 (23,647)
Davies, Peter 3:44:54 (7,080)
Davies, Peter 4:24:06 (17,260)
Davies, Peter 4:57:35 (25,875)
Davies, Peter Jonathan 3:39:19 (6,010)
Davies, Peter R 3:44:19 (6,942)
Davies, Raymond 4:05:42 (12,378)
Davies, Richard 4:06:42 (12,625)
Davies, Richard 5:24:44 (30,587)
Davies, Richard Llewellyn 3:29:29 (4,317)
Davies, Robert 4:10:58 (13,703)
Davies, Robert John 4:13:02 (14,249)
Davies, Robert Matthew 4:37:13 (20,798)
Davies, Robert Michael 3:45:13 (7,145)
Davies, Robert N 4:53:50 (25,002)
Davies, Robin 3:54:54 (9,450)
Davies, Roger Peter 4:46:37 (23,209)
Davies, Ronald 7:16:55 (36,378)
Davies, Sam 3:13:15 (2,217)
Davies, Shane 4:03:21 (11,813)
Davies, Simon 3:58:20 (10,505)
Davies, Spencer 4:22:39 (16,892)
Davies, Stephen C 2:50:31 (505)
Davies, Stuart Michael 4:45:44 (22,962)
Davies, Terry 4:39:56 (21,488)
Davies, Tony Michael 5:00:01 (26,457)
Davies, Will 4:35:41 (20,387)
Davies, William Martin 4:35:55 (20,453)
Davis, Aaron 4:09:16 (13,274)
Davis, Andy R 3:10:59 (1,992)
Davis, Anthony D 3:33:38 (4,994)
Davis, Barry 4:26:51 (18,039)
Davis, Benjamin H 3:10:57 (1,988)
Davis, Chris 5:26:56 (30,895)
Davis, Colin Llewellyn 4:16:01 (15,034)
Davis, Daniel 4:50:30 (24,161)
Davis, Frank 4:01:02 (11,258)
Davis, Greg Alexander 3:22:28 (3,235)
Davis, John 4:53:39 (24,957)
Davis, John Richard 3:48:47 (7,922)
Davis, Jon 4:27:31 (18,241)
Davis, Jonathan 4:54:35 (25,199)
Davis, Mark A 2:55:07 (754)
Davis, Martin J 2:55:13 (758)
Davis, Michael 3:05:16 (1,480)
Davis, Nick 5:03:15 (27,066)
Davis, Paul 4:59:18 (26,286)
Davis, Paul 5:23:36 (30,404)
Davis, Paul Kenneth 4:19:33 (15,985)
Davis, Paul W 2:46:58 (387)
Davis, Peter Bryan 5:03:33 (27,110)
Davis, Richard M 3:12:45 (2,161)
Davis, Richard Mark 4:29:24 (18,777)
Davis, Simon Allan 4:55:13 (25,361)
Davis, Spencer Michael 5:28:52 (31,133)
Davis, Stefan None 4:55:41 (25,458)
Davis, Timothy 3:32:14 (4,778)
Davis, Trevor John 4:04:28 (12,070)
Davis, Warren Keith 5:33:56 (31,756)
Davison, Andrew 3:37:41 (5,706)
Davison, Gary S 3:02:19 (1,282)
Davison, Mark 3:51:20 (8,500)
Davison, Neil A 2:39:01 (177)
Davison, Scott Harvey 4:04:11 (12,006)
Davison, Stephen James 5:20:15 (29,882)
Davitt, Andrew 3:52:08 (8,689)
Davy, Noel 4:53:23 (24,889)
Davy, Simon 4:54:57 (25,293)
Daw, Alasdair S 4:29:53 (18,943)
Daw, Jack Michael 4:45:24 (22,862)
Dawber, Craig Stephen 4:29:57 (18,971)
Dawe, Andrew M 3:13:17 (2,221)
Dawe, Andrew P 3:07:57 (1,693)
Dawe, Jamie 4:12:51 (14,194)
Dawe, Quentin 5:13:41 (28,868)
Dawes, Stacey William 4:59:35 (26,362)
Dawes, Tom Benjamin 3:38:55 (5,924)
Dawkins, Neil Keith 4:23:06 (17,003)
Dawkins, Stephen 5:45:14 (32,886)
Dawkins, Steven G 3:57:25 (10,206)
Dawney, Kevin Richard 5:27:38 (30,981)
Daws, Peter M 3:22:43 (3,261)
Dawson, Alan PS 4:15:32 (14,911)
Dawson, Andrew Charles 5:19:34 (29,785)
Dawson, Ben William 7:35:46 (36,493)
Dawson, Carl 4:49:02 (23,809)
Dawson, Christopher R 3:30:49 (4,552)
Dawson, Corey William 3:13:01 (2,192)
Dawson, David 4:21:14 (16,469)
Dawson, Elliott Fraser 5:51:05 (33,436)
Dawson, Fraser 2:57:36 (919)
Dawson, Graham 4:18:28 (15,704)
Dawson, Grant M 3:14:04 (2,329)
Dawson, Howard 4:15:13 (14,838)
Dawson, John 5:09:59 (28,230)
Dawson, Mark Anthony Richard 4:24:12 (17,287)
Dawson, Matt 5:07:18 (27,770)
Dawson, Matthew Thomas 3:51:56 (8,645)
Dawson, Richard 4:42:16 (22,084)
Dawson, Richard Leslie 4:06:39 (12,617)
Dawson, Simon 4:29:24 (18,777)
Dawson, Stephen Kenneth 4:09:21 (13,296)
Dawson, Steve 4:56:45 (25,704)
Dawson, Steven M 4:58:15 (26,028)
Dawson, Vince Michael 4:55:04 (25,326)
Day, Anthony Alan 6:14:56 (34,883)
Day, Anthony Stephen 6:03:46 (34,307)
Day, Arron John 4:13:48 (14,457)
Day, Christopher L 2:58:57 (1,041)
Day, Colin Leon Neal 4:33:26 (19,836)
Day, David Christopher 3:34:46 (5,206)
Day, Graham 4:28:47 (18,600)
Day, Grant 3:55:29 (9,611)
Day, Ian 2:46:29 (372)
Day, Jason 4:50:59 (24,300)
Day, Kevin G 3:29:06 (4,250)
Day, Marcus Francis 5:07:28 (27,804)
Day, Mark Anthony 4:28:50 (18,621)
Day, Martin 5:34:28 (31,819)
Day, Oliver John 3:55:23 (9,591)
Day, Paul Gary 4:15:40 (14,944)
Day, Richard James 4:31:55 (19,411)
Day, Rob 3:51:13 (8,474)
Day, Robert 3:50:23 (8,284)
De Azevedo, Rodrigo 4:46:16 (23,118)
De Boer, Nero Kamal 4:07:41 (12,883)
De Boer Lloyd, Mark 3:58:53 (10,682)
De Boise, Matthew 4:35:44 (20,397)
De Bruyn, Paul 3:42:32 (6,602)
De Courcey, Charles 4:06:38 (12,611)
De Ferry Foster, Harry 3:37:04 (5,578)
De Giorgio, Alex 3:42:02 (6,517)
De Guichen, Erwan 4:16:16 (15,092)
De Jager, Petrus 4:28:38 (18,564)
De Lacy, Jean-Paul 5:55:11 (33,732)
De Lathauwer, Michael 4:08:21 (13,043)
De Luca, Adrian 4:49:36 (23,943)
De Mooi, CJ 3:25:44 (3,692)
De Mulder, Freddy 4:06:16 (12,516)
De Penning, Johannes 4:35:35 (20,362)
De Santi, Manrico 3:30:40 (4,521)
De Schuyter, Nicolas 3:56:03 (9,800)
De Simone, Giuseppe 3:21:36 (3,148)

De Sousa, Carlos 5:17:58 (29,542)
De Sousa, George 4:55:36 (25,437)
De Souza, Adrian Michael 4:17:19 (15,380)
De Tarnowsky, Clinton Craig 3:37:32 (5,673)
De Vooght-Johnson, Ryan Luc 3:20:21 (2,996)
De Voogt, Freddy 4:37:18 (20,818)
De Vry, Jaco 3:54:45 (9,402)
De Waal, Gerard Mathew 4:08:00 (12,963)
De Waldner, Christian 4:16:15 (15,091)
De Wolf, Nicholas 5:07:52 (27,872)
Deacon, Craig M 2:54:37 (708)
Deag, James Michael 4:42:46 (22,206)
Deahl, Simon J 3:59:02 (10,729)
Deakin, Kevin 4:26:01 (17,817)
Deal, Sam George 6:45:50 (35,927)
Dean, Andrew C 3:30:42 (4,529)
Dean, Andrew Gerald 5:22:34 (30,232)
Dean, Christopher 3:48:06 (7,761)
Dean, Eaton 4:25:29 (17,657)
Dean, Edward Thomas 4:16:26 (15,151)
Dean, Gary 3:00:36 (1,181)
Dean, Gary James 5:09:07 (28,073)
Dean, Glyn 5:38:29 (32,262)
Dean, James Andrew David 2:55:43 (782)
Dean, Mark R 3:47:38 (7,674)
Dean, Mike 3:23:47 (3,405)
Dean, Richard David Allen 6:04:52 (34,375)
Dean, Richard Thomas 4:33:02 (19,708)
Dean, Stuart Richard 5:07:39 (27,841)
Dean, Tim J 3:56:53 (10,051)
Deane, James 2:56:37 (841)
Deane, Michael 4:29:35 (18,833)
Deane, Robert Stephen 4:37:32 (20,891)
Dear, Martin John 4:14:04 (14,526)
Dear, Matthew 5:22:56 (30,298)
Dear, Richard 4:32:51 (19,654)
Dearden, John A 5:18:15 (29,582)
Dearden, Tim 7:49:28 (36,562)
Dearing, Rob 4:29:55 (18,957)
Dearlove, Paul 3:44:12 (6,916)
Deas, Jon 4:24:24 (17,360)
Deatrick, Chris 4:01:23 (11,332)
Deaville, Andrew Peter 6:52:15 (36,053)
Debbah, Redha 4:25:31 (17,668)
Debray, Joel 4:20:16 (16,185)
Debusscher, Gilles 4:38:06 (21,008)
Deddis, Jonathan Suthee Phlek 4:15:39 (14,937)
Dedynski, Adam 4:36:29 (20,598)
Deed, Daniel 4:37:30 (20,881)
Deegan, Justin Wayne 4:46:10 (23,078)
Deegan, Stephen J 3:19:04 (2,875)
Deeks, Andrew William 4:32:37 (19,585)
Deen, Paul J 3:26:07 (3,752)
Deen, Simon 5:02:42 (26,979)
Deeney, Michael 3:45:04 (7,108)
Deeprose, Tim 4:08:22 (13,049)
Deering, Georgie 5:57:32 (33,905)
Deering, Robert 3:25:44 (3,692)
Deery, Ian P 4:37:22 (20,836)
Defaux, Olivier Benoit 4:17:26 (15,416)
Defaye, Alex 4:24:20 (17,333)
Defina, Ferdinando 3:33:58 (5,052)
Defries, Richard Mark 3:39:48 (6,104)
Degan, Gianluigi 3:07:13 (1,628)
Degand, Jean Charles 4:13:21 (14,328)
Degge, Austin Maxwell 4:35:18 (20,295)
Deidda, Giuseppe 4:06:48 (12,657)
Deighan, Eamon Eugene Paul 3:16:09 (2,566)
Del Carlo, Leri 3:46:43 (7,464)
Del Dotto, Stefano 2:57:11 (868)
Del Monte, Fernando 4:19:05 (15,869)
Del Moral Ramos, Carlos 3:07:00 (1,608)
Del Negro, Giorgio 4:33:28 (19,843)
Del Rosso, Alessandro 3:37:29 (5,658)
Delander, John 4:09:12 (13,260)
Delaney, Christopher P 4:21:02 (16,425)
Delaney, Dominic 4:46:50 (23,270)
Delaney, Joe Michael 4:40:53 (21,740)
Delaney, Mark 4:26:20 (17,910)
Delany, Paul John 4:30:58 (19,209)
Delany, Simon 4:09:55 (13,448)
Delatouche, David P 4:42:29 (22,136)
Delay, Jean-Luc 4:18:16 (15,648)
Delcamp, Jean Paul 4:09:24 (13,313)
Delderfield, Barry P 4:43:30 (22,369)
Delderfield, James Michael 4:18:53 (15,822)
Delderfield, Luke F 2:39:43 (191)
Deleersnyder, Chris 3:30:14 (4,461)
Delew, Russell 4:15:55 (15,007)
Delignieres, Lionel 3:36:45 (5,517)
Dell, Graeme 3:44:35 (7,008)
Dell, Stephen Jeffrey Raymond 4:11:34 (13,867)
Dell'Orletta, Domenico 3:03:59 (1,388)
Dellow, Chris 3:34:20 (5,126)
Dellow, Michael 4:20:04 (16,126)
Delmas, Olivier 4:35:26 (20,337)
Delmas, Stephane 3:08:13 (1,720)
Delvaux, Joe 4:09:50 (13,428)
Delve, James 4:40:06 (21,515)
Delves, Timothy 3:28:59 (4,226)
Demaine, Cedric 3:25:55 (3,721)
Demarais, Romain G 6:26:04 (35,353)
Demartis, Angelo Gesuino 4:44:22 (22,605)
Demay, Cyril 3:33:51 (5,036)
Dempsey, Ian Mathew 4:13:25 (14,345)
Demuth, Juergen 3:02:01 (1,260)
Demuynck, Bruno 3:12:27 (2,131)
Den Hartog, Jan A 3:49:50 (8,169)
Denbow, Richard James 5:02:48 (26,993)
Denby, Chris 4:34:04 (20,013)
Denby, Karl N 5:42:27 (32,633)
Dendy, Kevin 5:45:04 (32,876)
Dendy, Mark 4:59:24 (26,313)
Dendy, Sim 4:59:24 (26,313)
De-Neef, Gerald 4:16:28 (15,157)
Denford, Anthony B 4:59:15 (26,277)
Denham, Alan 4:47:56 (23,528)
Denham, Lee William 4:50:55 (24,279)
Denham, Matthew 4:18:33 (15,725)
Denholm, Mark Geoffrey 5:24:08 (30,501)
Dening, Joe 4:22:12 (16,761)
Denisov, Alexander 4:04:54 (12,174)
Denman, Chris 5:27:12 (30,935)
Dennett, Andrew 4:10:56 (13,695)
Denney, Matthew John 3:55:51 (9,733)
Denning, Joel 4:24:55 (17,494)
Denning, Michael 4:45:50 (22,985)
Dennis, Darren John 5:12:59 (28,738)
Dennis, David Robert 4:00:40 (11,159)
Dennis, George William 3:59:03 (10,733)
Dennis, Mark 4:55:36 (25,437)
Dennis, Paul 3:11:51 (2,081)
Dennis, Paul A 3:09:13 (1,827)
Dennis, Richard J 3:09:12 (1,824)
Dennis, Rob 5:47:07 (33,061)
Dennison, Jeremy Morgan C 3:50:52 (8,396)
Dennison, Kevin Terence Michael 4:41:30 (21,893)
Denny, Simon 3:50:49 (8,383)
Denny, Stephen D 4:27:11 (18,143)
Denselow, James 3:57:05 (10,126)
Dent, Adrian 5:51:05 (33,436)
Dent, David Renner 5:29:04 (31,160)
Dent, Ernest 6:05:13 (34,403)
Dent, James 3:04:52 (1,453)
Dent, Michael 4:04:28 (12,070)
Dent, Robert 4:48:26 (23,655)
Dent, Robert James 5:51:04 (33,434)
Dent, Trevor Ian 5:51:04 (33,434)
Dentith, Guy 3:55:28 (9,606)
Denton, James Charles 5:31:35 (31,483)
Denton, John 3:06:49 (1,594)
Denton, Mark 4:30:57 (19,205)
Denton, Paul Matthew 4:26:00 (17,812)
Denzer, Christian 5:49:08 (33,250)
Depala, Hardik 4:37:07 (20,776)
Derbyshire, Christopher Alan 3:51:13 (8,474)
Derbyshire, David 4:01:03 (11,264)
Derbyshire, Jonathan Robert 3:54:58 (9,468)
Derbyshire, Russell J 4:41:05 (21,790)
Derbyshire, Stephen J 5:35:51 (31,975)
Derham, Chris Alan 4:09:09 (13,240)
Dering, David 3:37:14 (5,605)
Derissy, Zakaria 6:14:12 (34,844)
Dermody, John Patrick 5:15:35 (29,161)
Dernis, David 3:49:43 (8,150)
Deroubaix, Raphael 4:01:56 (11,478)
Derow, Paul 4:17:14 (15,359)
Derrick, Mark Stephen 4:20:44 (16,347)
Derrington, Richard Paul 4:26:32 (17,967)
Derzypilskyj, John 4:09:13 (13,266)
Desai, Rahul 5:41:54 (32,579)
Deseneen, Vittorio 4:13:19 (14,318)
Desmond, Colin 3:25:31 (3,649)
Desmond, Paul 4:08:57 (13,193)
Desmond, Robert 4:42:48 (22,213)
Desnoues, Philippe 4:54:45 (25,245)
Desplanques, Frederic 2:23:49 (31)
Desvaux, Frederic 3:16:57 (2,663)
Devaney, Gareth Thomas 5:22:47 (30,267)
Deverill, James Ian 4:41:43 (21,944)
Devile, Simon 3:33:59 (5,056)
Devin, Paul 4:40:08 (21,518)
Devine, Ciaran 3:47:50 (7,704)
Devine, Jonathan 4:53:37 (24,947)
Devine, Martin 3:16:24 (2,598)
Devine, Martin P 4:48:20 (23,616)
Devitt, Russell 3:50:34 (8,328)
Devlin, Brendan John 3:45:03 (7,106)
Devlin, Mark 4:35:36 (20,367)
Devon, Stephen 5:01:31 (26,758)
Devonshire, Peter Gordon 4:57:20 (25,827)
Dew, Christopher 5:32:20 (31,577)
Dew, Simon J 2:44:03 (312)
Dewar, Gordon 4:49:00 (23,800)
Dewar, Lochie 5:13:04 (28,763)
Dewey, Christopher J 3:12:20 (2,114)
Dewey, Stephen Arthur 3:41:20 (6,392)
Dewhurst, Joseph 4:38:26 (21,099)
Dewinkel, Peter 4:22:45 (16,918)
Dewland, Paul Michael 5:11:45 (28,511)
Dexter, Matt John 4:08:42 (13,143)
Dexter, Ray 6:12:08 (34,762)
Dhadra, Onkar 4:19:49 (16,045)
Dhaliwal, Kawaljit 4:20:18 (16,200)
Dhanapala, Raj Manishin 5:41:31 (32,535)
Dhariwal, Navraj S 5:02:41 (26,974)
Dhaussy, Pierre 3:11:08 (2,011)
Dhillon, Amandeep 4:16:11 (15,068)
Dhillon, Amandeep S 4:40:41 (21,687)
Dhillon, John 4:18:22 (15,678)
Dhimar, Dipesh 3:53:58 (9,201)
Di Francesco, Stefano 5:29:52 (31,274)
Di Lenardo, Luciano 5:12:46 (28,694)
Di Mario, Bruno 5:39:47 (32,367)
Di Monaco, Vincenzo 2:53:40 (649)
Di Rubba, Enrico 3:26:46 (3,842)
Di Somma, Antonio 2:52:07 (573)
Diallo, Oumar 3:46:00 (7,311)
Diamond, James 5:15:37 (29,166)
Diamond, Philip 3:51:51 (8,622)
Dias, Charles J 4:04:16 (12,023)
Dias Bueno, Rodrigo 5:16:04 (29,238)
Diaz, Valentin 3:30:50 (4,554)
Dibb, David 5:09:18 (28,107)
Dibdin, Craig 4:00:25 (11,094)
Dick, Alistair 3:18:07 (2,781)
Dick, Stuart 4:39:12 (21,313)
Dickens, Andrew 5:18:38 (29,649)
Dickens, James 4:54:36 (25,204)
Dickens, Phil M 2:36:11 (132)
Dickens, Steven 4:54:27 (25,168)
Dicker, Clive Anthony 4:27:42 (18,288)
Dicker, Daniel 5:27:04 (30,916)
Dickerson, Andy 5:14:14 (28,955)
Dickerson, Tom 4:22:46 (16,928)
Dickins, Ben 4:11:26 (13,827)
Dickinson, Carl F 3:14:42 (2,406)
Dickinson, David 5:50:07 (33,344)
Dickinson, Gavin Leslie 5:16:19 (29,277)
Dickinson, Jeremy Roy 5:58:02 (33,936)
Dickinson, Kelvin B 2:57:18 (880)
Dickinson, Mark 2:28:46 (57)
Dickinson, Martin 3:37:12 (5,599)
Dickinson, Paul J 3:08:33 (1,761)
Dickinson, Peter Simon 4:40:36 (21,670)
Dickinson, Robert James 5:24:58 (30,616)
Dickinson, Sam 6:34:47 (35,649)
Dickinson, Simon Craig 4:03:41 (11,896)
Dickinson, Steve 4:55:42 (25,463)

Dickinson, Tim.........................2:59:21 (1,091)
Dickson, Alan 3:47:10 (7,566)
Dickson, Andrew.......................4:16:40 (15,209)
Dickson, Neil Andrew 4:14:12 (14,569)
Dickson, Paul Darren................4:11:50 (13,940)
Dickson, Robert W 4:37:13 (20,798)
Dickson, William 3:24:59 (3,577)
Didailler, Gael 5:03:10 (27,051)
Didier, Jean-Philippe................3:29:34 (4,334)
Didsbury, Christopher James.......3:38:46 (5,902)
Diers, William 3:11:34 (2,057)
Diesveld, Alistair John..............3:35:24 (5,301)
Dietsch, Peter 4:23:44 (17,175)
Digby, Craig.............................5:27:43 (30,991)
Digby, Peter 5:49:49 (33,319)
Digby-Baker, Hugh 4:44:57 (22,755)
Diggens, Timothy M 4:04:59 (12,200)
Diggins, Dominic 5:18:05 (29,559)
Dignan, Graeme 4:14:51 (14,750)
Dignum, Matthew Giles 5:24:25 (30,544)
Digweed, Andrew 4:40:34 (21,660)
Dillnutt, Sean 4:48:48 (23,747)
Dillon, Chris 5:16:00 (29,229)
Dillon, Matthew Robert 4:34:39 (20,156)
Dillon, Thomas 3:44:10 (6,909)
Dilworth, Joseph R 4:12:07 (14,018)
Dima, Mariano 4:24:31 (17,395)
Dimarellis, Serge 3:49:26 (8,075)
Dimbleby, Paul James................4:01:34 (11,385)
Dimbleby, Peter J......................2:43:17 (289)
Dimbylow, Matthew 3:43:49 (6,835)
Dimelow, Geoffrey....................4:00:41 (11,166)
Dimmick, Steve 3:54:40 (9,375)
Dimmock, Graeme D.................6:54:46 (36,105)
Dimmock, Neil 3:29:51 (4,388)
Dimond, Stephen John...............3:23:42 (3,394)
Dine, Nicholas A 4:13:33 (14,385)
Dineen, John 4:46:48 (23,255)
Dineen, Paul 4:03:29 (11,838)
Dinley, Luke 6:20:03 (35,126)
Dinning, Antony Michael 3:53:09 (8,955)
Dinsdale, Danny 3:57:33 (10,246)
Dinsmore, Barry 3:21:01 (3,087)
Dinwoodie, Stuart J 3:14:32 (2,387)
Dippenaar, Arend Allewyn 4:27:10 (18,137)
Dippenaar, Rory Dereck 4:58:51 (26,177)
Dipper, Robert 5:27:44 (30,992)
Dippie, Andrew 3:13:49 (2,297)
Dipple, Peter 4:08:22 (13,049)
Dipre, Stephen Thomas 3:00:40 (1,184)
Diprose, Rob Ian 4:15:52 (14,994)
Dirocco, Jerry Anthony..............5:01:31 (26,758)
Dirrane, Daniel Anthony............4:36:14 (20,532)
Disberry, Alan John 5:02:11 (26,886)
Ditcham, Robert James..............3:51:11 (8,469)
Diver, Philip Alan 3:40:18 (6,197)
Dix, Chris D..............................4:24:04 (17,252)
Dix, Daniel Richard 4:03:05 (11,748)
Dix, Edward J............................4:22:11 (16,757)
Dix, Rupert 3:29:21 (4,295)
Dixon, Alex 4:46:00 (23,024)
Dixon, Andrew 3:19:06 (2,882)
Dixon, Andrew 3:47:58 (7,731)
Dixon, Basil 3:58:08 (10,426)
Dixon, Brian James 5:19:18 (29,745)
Dixon, Charles 4:31:27 (19,321)
Dixon, Christopher Ian 4:01:45 (11,435)
Dixon, Clem N 5:14:10 (28,945)
Dixon, Dave 5:16:22 (29,289)
Dixon, David.............................3:48:11 (7,780)
Dixon, David John 3:38:46 (5,902)
Dixon, Garry J 2:34:56 (111)
Dixon, Gary 4:46:07 (23,065)
Dixon, Jim 4:53:45 (24,985)
Dixon, Jonathan James..............5:10:11 (28,275)
Dixon, Mark 3:49:21 (8,052)
Dixon, Mark John 4:55:58 (25,530)
Dixon, Paul Antony 3:49:00 (7,974)
Dixon, Peter D 3:56:43 (10,003)
Dixon, Richard F.......................3:46:02 (7,314)
Dixon, Robert John....................5:17:31 (29,476)
Dixon, Thomas Matthew 3:10:49 (1,973)
Dixon, Wayne 4:48:36 (23,694)

Dixon , Stephen Marc.................4:46:08 (23,071)
Dizier, Michel 5:22:19 (30,194)
Dobai, Lajos 3:10:07 (1,917)
Dobbert, Michael 4:30:32 (19,098)
Dobbie, Adam Stephen 3:41:39 (6,447)
Dobbie, Peter 4:15:31 (14,909)

Dobbin, Henry 4:18:06 (15,608)

I was nervous, I had trained, but my lifestyle is not athletic. It was my first marathon. I knew family and friends were rooting for me back home in Ireland, in the Braid and Carnlough. I was running for Health, Poverty, Action. But news my wife was pregnant again, four years after the birth of our son Malachy, was my driving force. I was elated. When the race started the rain stopped and London shone in many ways. People cheered, bands played and I felt like a hero. At 17 miles my wife and son Malachy, his cousins Charlie, Frankie, and Anna and their parents where there to greet me. It was a great moment I'll never forget the experience and thinking about the little one kicking inside.

Dobbs, Matthew 3:58:55 (10,691)
Dobbs, Patrick A.......................4:07:48 (12,906)
Dobbs, Simon C 2:43:58 (305)
Dobby, Andrew M......................2:47:15 (397)
Dobson, Christopher James 4:01:44 (11,429)
Dobson, David A 4:34:25 (20,099)
Dobson, Karl Samuel 5:06:22 (27,598)
Dobson, Lee A...........................3:48:16 (7,796)
Dobson, Mark Christopher 8:11:20 (36,594)
Dobson, Mike 5:28:28 (31,085)
Dobson, Neil.............................4:07:37 (12,860)
Dobson, Robin 3:51:22 (8,507)
Docherty, James Robert 3:33:10 (4,921)
Docherty, Nick..........................3:36:55 (5,547)
Doctor, Mark D..........................4:13:35 (14,398)
Docwra, Chris 5:27:57 (31,017)
Dodd, Adam Mark 5:27:20 (30,944)
Dodd, Alex John 5:18:32 (29,631)
Dodd, David 5:00:07 (26,483)
Dodd, Jon 4:54:44 (25,238)
Dodd, Martin 3:38:05 (5,779)
Dodd, Robert Edward James 5:39:27 (32,342)
Dodds, Andrew 4:32:29 (19,556)
Dodi, Simon 5:10:20 (28,297)
Dods, Richard William 4:51:48 (24,492)
Dodsley, Andrew 3:34:19 (5,118)
Dodsworth, Ian.........................6:00:50 (34,118)

Dodwell, Stephen......................5:05:03 (27,377)
Dodwell, Tristram 3:49:33 (8,102)
Doe, Don G...............................3:13:10 (2,206)
Doe, Mark 4:41:25 (21,870)
Doel, Adam James.....................5:14:36 (29,003)
Doggett, Chris 5:02:52 (27,000)
Doherty, Brian Coleman.............7:41:10 (36,529)
Doherty, Damian Pascal 3:48:52 (7,944)
Doherty, Dan J..........................3:28:01 (4,051)
Doherty, Des 4:07:21 (12,787)
Doherty, Frank 7:11:07 (36,323)
Doherty, Gerard P 3:20:45 (3,051)
Doherty, James David.................3:52:02 (8,667)
Doherty, Matthew J....................3:32:00 (4,738)
Doherty, Shane 3:02:28 (1,295)
Doherty, Thomas A 3:25:03 (3,587)
Dol, Eric 5:04:36 (27,297)
Dolah, Mohd Puzi 3:22:17 (3,217)
Dolan, Eric 4:43:42 (22,417)
Dolan, Michael 3:42:49 (6,659)
Dolan, Robert 3:25:25 (3,636)
Dolan, Stuart G 4:24:58 (17,509)
Dolby, Ryan Matthew 5:22:31 (30,222)
Dole, Tim P 4:44:26 (22,626)
Dolecki, Ronald.........................4:38:25 (21,092)
Dolinar, Robert 3:13:32 (2,259)
Dolle, Ulrich 3:46:49 (7,494)
Doll-Steinberg, Daniel 4:24:19 (17,329)
Dolman, Adam 4:35:53 (20,439)
Dolman, Ben Michael 4:05:12 (12,255)
Dolman, Mark 4:25:26 (17,642)
Dolphin, James H.......................3:07:58 (1,696)
Dolphin, Mark 4:04:42 (12,129)
Dolz Muedra, Vicente José 3:34:37 (5,175)
Domantay, Joe Glenn.................5:36:03 (32,003)
Dombrovskis, Andrejs.................4:16:32 (15,177)
Dominic, Roger 4:51:40 (24,455)
Dominy, Guy Robert 5:49:23 (33,271)
Dominy, Shawn.........................4:50:56 (24,286)
Dommisse, William 6:05:42 (34,432)
Donaghy, Gavin Leo 4:41:25 (21,870)
Donaghy, Nigel..........................6:12:44 (34,795)
Donaghy, Simon Paul.................3:45:09 (7,127)
Donald, James W.......................2:53:55 (664)
Donald, Kelvin 4:11:55 (13,966)
Donaldson, Alastair Philip...........5:00:41 (26,584)
Donaldson, Andrew 4:03:10 (11,769)
Donaldson, Graham M 2:50:43 (512)
Donaldson, James Arthur 4:30:39 (19,135)
Donaldson, James Peter..............3:37:51 (5,731)
Donaldson, Sean Anthony...........3:52:03 (8,672)
Donaldson, Tony 5:12:02 (28,570)
Donati, Alessandro....................4:39:20 (21,338)
Donegan, Christopher.................4:37:30 (20,881)
Donkin, Keith L 3:06:37 (1,581)
Donlon, Anthony James 3:41:22 (6,399)
Donnan, Karl 4:57:21 (25,830)
Donnarumma, Antimo 3:52:14 (8,716)
Donne, Michael.........................3:36:29 (5,478)
Donnelly, Adam Samuel 4:45:33 (22,901)
Donnelly, Bernard......................5:12:37 (28,670)
Donnelly, John A 3:29:10 (4,263)
Donnelly, Michael 3:39:06 (5,963)
Donnelly, Philip.........................3:46:38 (7,449)
Donoghue, Anthony 3:34:37 (5,175)
Donoghue, Chris........................3:03:38 (1,359)
Donoghue, Damien 4:57:27 (25,849)
Donoghue, Gary John.................3:26:49 (3,851)
Donohoe, Bernie 4:51:19 (24,378)
Donohoe, Paul 3:42:18 (6,562)
Donohue, Jack...........................4:41:36 (21,923)
Donovan, Chris 4:53:15 (24,862)
Donovan, Dick 4:32:26 (19,545)
Donovan, Edward J 2:41:40 (242)
Donovan, John Terence...............3:47:27 (7,634)
Donovan, Neil Philip 5:02:04 (26,856)
Donovan, Paul 4:55:37 (25,443)
Donovan, Peter 5:42:01 (32,588)
Donoyou, Timothy Liam 3:52:15 (8,719)
Dooley, John 4:40:09 (21,524)
Dooley, Michael S......................2:49:10 (449)
Doolittle, Anthony I...................2:58:11 (974)
Doradoux, François 4:03:26 (11,828)

Doran, Brian....4:17:33 (15,458)
Doran, Carl Eric....4:02:11 (11,536)
Doran, Carl G....4:31:17 (19,289)
Doran, Colin C....4:26:42 (17,998)
Doran, Matt....4:43:48 (22,441)
Doran, Tim....2:33:42 (97)
Doran, Trevor....4:27:57 (18,353)
Dordel, Sebastian....3:59:31 (10,866)
Dore, Stefon Terence....3:42:53 (6,674)
Dorey, Adam....3:28:02 (4,058)
Dorey, Nick Graham....5:02:35 (26,956)
Dorgan, Philip John....5:25:53 (30,762)
Dorin, Dominic J....4:06:33 (12,588)
Dorling, Eamonn E....3:09:25 (1,846)
Dorn, Mat Peter....5:09:19 (28,111)
Dorward, Neil Lawrence....3:14:34 (2,391)
Dosanjh, Jatinder....4:48:38 (23,705)
Doshi, Rajen Anil....4:08:33 (13,103)
Dost, Bill....5:56:52 (33,856)
Dott, Charles....3:11:42 (2,070)
Dotti, Giacomo....4:15:17 (14,853)
Double, James....3:23:39 (3,387)
Doughty, Paul....4:20:42 (16,333)
Douglas, George John....4:25:59 (17,807)
Douglas, Neil A....2:58:27 (1,003)
Douglas, Paul....3:07:32 (1,654)
Douglas, Stuart J....2:57:42 (932)
Doull, Paul George....5:59:05 (33,998)
Doulton, Grant Edward....5:02:15 (26,898)
Doutch, Ian James....4:38:27 (21,105)
Douthart, Dominic....4:12:06 (14,008)
Douthwaite, Neil....3:43:02 (6,703)
Doutney, Chris....3:45:43 (7,249)
Dove, Christopher D....3:44:58 (7,089)
Dove, Gavin....4:01:53 (11,466)
Dove, Iain....4:44:08 (22,541)
Dove, Paul Johnathon....4:56:45 (25,704)
Dover, Gary William....3:01:47 (1,241)
Dover, Mark....3:53:31 (9,061)
Dovey, Ivan....3:27:22 (3,934)
Dow, Adrian....3:20:21 (2,996)
Doward, Will....5:30:08 (31,311)
Dowd, John....4:09:28 (13,330)
Dowd, John Joseph....4:49:13 (23,852)
Dowden, Michael Thomas....4:14:37 (14,687)
Dowden, Tony M....6:14:04 (34,839)
Dowding, James....4:11:19 (13,796)
Dowding, Mark A....4:25:23 (17,629)
Dowding, Philip Richard....5:52:36 (33,538)
Dowds, Liam....3:51:26 (8,524)
Dowdy, Will....3:54:50 (9,431)
Dowe, Cornell A....7:36:24 (36,496)
Dowell, Allan J....4:27:15 (18,167)
Dower, Liam Gerald....3:40:51 (6,301)
Dowle, Chris....4:13:39 (14,417)
Dowler, Andrew James....4:45:40 (22,940)
Dowler, John....4:47:47 (23,489)
Dowling, James....4:07:13 (12,755)
Down, Gary Michael....3:59:12 (10,779)
Down, Joel....4:20:38 (16,314)
Down, Martyn C....6:02:11 (34,195)
Down, Nigel Stuart....4:11:26 (13,827)
Down, Terry D....3:36:03 (5,419)
Downer, Greg Owen....5:07:43 (27,849)
Downer, Neil A....3:31:33 (4,674)
Downes, Craig John....5:22:02 (30,151)
Downes, Mark....4:43:51 (22,464)
Downey, Chris....4:37:26 (20,861)
Downey, Desmond D....4:38:37 (21,148)
Downey, James....3:25:17 (3,617)
Downey, Kevin....4:55:52 (25,504)
Downey, Peter....4:07:15 (12,764)
Downey, Sean Thomas....4:38:21 (21,071)
Downey, William S....2:43:28 (295)
Downham, Danny William....4:55:07 (25,341)
Downing, Nicholas....4:45:04 (22,788)
Downing, Oliver J....3:29:06 (4,250)
Downing, Stephen D....3:52:42 (8,848)
Downs, Alan....5:10:15 (28,282)
Downs, Ricky....3:32:25 (4,804)
Downs, Rob H....2:37:33 (151)
Dowrick, Michael J....3:31:42 (4,697)
Dowse, Ray....4:16:00 (15,026)
Dowsett, Frederick J....3:59:53 (10,961)
Dowsett, Kevin R....4:17:29 (15,433)
Dowson, John Russell....4:27:33 (18,250)
Dowson, Richard M....3:40:59 (6,320)
Doxford, Paul....2:58:28 (1,006)
Doyle, Alan....4:00:25 (11,094)
Doyle, Alastair K....3:18:28 (2,818)
Doyle, Bernie....5:27:13 (30,936)
Doyle, Frank P....3:56:30 (9,933)
Doyle, Geoffrey E....2:58:12 (977)
Doyle, Jason Noel....4:58:46 (26,159)
Doyle, Karl....3:35:29 (5,321)
Doyle, Kevin....2:57:27 (896)
Doyle, Kirk....4:28:40 (18,573)
Doyle, Liam J....5:22:52 (30,286)
Doyle, Peter J....3:31:23 (4,647)
Doyle, Philip....3:58:20 (10,505)
Doyle, Rob Brendan....5:36:31 (32,059)
Doyle, Sean J....3:37:56 (5,751)
Doyle, Simon J....3:32:40 (4,838)
Doyle, Simon Paul....5:20:46 (29,972)
Doyle, Tim....5:04:04 (27,202)
Doyle, Tommy....6:01:28 (34,154)
Drabwell, Alan L....5:03:59 (27,186)
Drabwell, Lee Stanley....4:11:38 (13,889)
Draijer, Erik....3:53:46 (9,147)
Draine, Stephen Thomas....3:40:18 (6,197)
Drake, Andrew....3:48:44 (7,909)
Drake, Geoff J....4:58:20 (26,050)
Drake, James....5:13:49 (28,896)
Drake, Nick T....3:36:21 (5,463)
Drake, Steve....3:30:32 (4,501)
Drakes, Gordon....3:40:47 (6,288)
Drakes, Malcolm....3:40:36 (6,260)
Draper, Arthur....3:41:13 (6,374)
Draper, Dennis....4:47:11 (23,339)
Draper, Edward James....3:55:36 (9,636)
Draper, Martyn John....4:25:09 (17,560)
Drasdo, Duncan....2:58:55 (1,035)
Drayton, Mark Kenneth....4:22:51 (16,949)
Drew, Darren....4:17:02 (15,306)
Drew, Jonathan....4:51:24 (24,398)
Drew, Jonathan David....5:25:52 (30,761)
Drew, Simon Jefferey....3:16:40 (2,638)
Drew, Steve....4:27:19 (18,187)
Drewe, Julian A....3:45:20 (7,169)
Drewe, Martin....4:18:09 (15,620)
Drewery, David....5:30:11 (31,314)
Drewitt, Mark C....2:57:48 (940)
Drewitz, Piet....4:04:29 (12,074)
Dring, Daniel....3:38:42 (5,888)
Dring, Steven Barry....4:52:29 (24,681)
Drinkwater, Sam John....4:54:08 (25,075)
Driscoll, Daron Nigel....4:19:59 (16,103)
Driscoll, Jon....3:59:02 (10,729)
Driscoll, Sean Patrick....3:11:23 (2,036)
Driscoll, Steve....4:47:01 (23,315)
Driskell, Michael....5:29:44 (31,261)
Driver, Andrew P....3:54:46 (9,407)
Driver, Graham S....4:05:56 (12,440)
Driver, Neil James....4:35:53 (20,439)
Drobek, Robert Stuart....3:47:02 (7,531)
Drolon, Christophe....5:00:14 (26,505)
Drozak, Jacek....3:45:18 (7,162)
Druce, Edward....3:35:36 (5,342)
Drucker, Warwick....4:03:56 (11,948)
Druett, Nick....4:43:16 (22,317)
Drugan, Frances Anne....6:20:18 (35,138)
Drummond, Alan....3:22:27 (3,234)
Drummond, Christopher James....4:51:20 (24,381)
Drummond, Colin....4:48:27 (23,659)
Drummond, James Andrew....3:49:43 (8,150)
Drummond, Neil James....4:15:19 (14,865)
Drury, Craig....5:14:22 (28,976)
Drury, Warren J....3:36:32 (5,484)
Dry, Peter F....3:41:07 (6,348)
Dryden, Steven....4:59:34 (26,356)
Dryer, Darren....3:53:45 (9,140)
Dryland, Keith....4:19:17 (15,922)
Drymalski, Thomas George....4:52:55 (24,779)
Du Preez, Deon....4:15:14 (14,845)
Duarte, José Joaquin....3:36:51 (5,537)
Dube, Melusi....4:58:26 (26,071)
Dublish, Shashank....4:17:51 (15,533)
Dubois, Anthony H....3:47:18 (7,600)
Dubro, Christian....4:56:16 (25,601)
Ducept, Michel....3:28:52 (4,200)
Duchateau, Didier....5:46:57 (33,047)
Duchen, Theo....4:23:39 (17,143)
Duck, Christopher Colin....5:52:14 (33,519)
Duckers, Andrew....4:42:03 (22,028)
Duckham, Tom A....3:40:43 (6,277)
Duckworth, Kevin P....2:50:59 (524)
Duckworth, Robert Peter....4:28:06 (18,390)
Duddell, Michael Alan....5:23:04 (30,319)
Duddell, Steve J....2:57:53 (945)
Duddridge, Chris James....5:00:11 (26,497)
Duddridge, Joe....5:00:10 (26,493)
Duddy, Ian....3:51:08 (8,456)
Dudgeon, James....3:19:04 (2,875)
Dudley, Andy....4:16:44 (15,228)
Dudley, Dale Anthony....4:47:46 (23,483)
Dudley, Kris Jason....4:41:34 (21,912)
Dudley, Martyn....3:37:32 (5,673)
Dudley, Ross....4:44:31 (22,645)
Dudley, Roy....5:21:17 (30,041)
Dudman, Neil Andrew....5:37:22 (32,156)
Dufeal, Chris....4:01:43 (11,415)
Duff, Craig H....4:14:29 (14,643)
Duff, Graham....4:29:31 (18,812)
Duff, Michael Peter....5:24:00 (30,481)
Duff, Nigel Richard....4:34:19 (20,074)
Duff, Stephen Ronald....5:45:10 (32,883)
Duffaud, Olivier....4:30:52 (19,182)
Duffell, Craig Steven....3:33:22 (4,945)
Duffett, Chris....5:46:23 (32,995)
Duffield, Gary Geddes....3:52:22 (8,761)
Duffield, Richard James....3:25:54 (3,720)
Duffill, Steve....5:29:04 (31,160)
Duffin, Mark Stephen....3:46:45 (7,472)
Duffy, Andy....4:13:23 (14,333)
Duffy, Arthur Joseph....4:22:52 (16,954)
Duffy, Brian J....2:57:31 (903)
Duffy, Dean....4:44:13 (22,568)
Duffy, Jonathan Patrick....5:50:54 (33,419)
Duffy, Laurence B....3:03:31 (1,348)
Duffy, Liam James....3:51:48 (8,608)
Duffy, Michael....3:16:49 (2,654)
Duffy, Michael....3:49:03 (7,987)
Duffy, Steven....4:33:23 (19,820)
Duffy, William B....3:12:42 (2,154)
Dugard, Kirk....4:30:33 (19,106)
Dugdale, Oliver....3:25:20 (3,621)
Duggal, Rishi....5:28:01 (31,033)
Duggal, Sunil....4:44:04 (22,523)
Duggan, Mike....3:24:25 (3,499)
Duggan, Patrick....3:33:40 (5,001)
Duggan, Robin J....3:26:38 (3,822)
Duhamel, Jean-Paul....3:48:13 (7,784)
Duke, Gavin....3:48:55 (7,953)
Duke, Geoff....4:56:37 (25,671)
Dukes, Nicholas J....2:43:16 (288)
Duley, Russell....5:25:14 (30,654)
Dulieu, Paul....5:29:12 (31,175)
Dullemond, Kees....3:46:42 (7,460)
Dulson, Nick....4:58:50 (26,173)
Duly, Patrick W....3:42:39 (6,624)
Dumas, Fabien....3:56:05 (9,807)
Dumbell, James....4:03:39 (11,890)
Dumbreck, Peter James....3:56:20 (9,883)
Dumelow, Matthew William....3:56:53 (10,051)
Dummer, Richard....3:54:34 (9,344)
Dunbar, Daniel....4:52:23 (24,657)
Dunbar, Jeff....2:54:15 (684)
Dunbar, Jonathan Grant....3:58:24 (10,523)
Dunbar, Robert....4:33:30 (19,852)
Duncan, Bill A....3:36:21 (5,463)
Duncan, Mark....5:40:13 (32,414)
Duncan, Mark G....3:46:47 (7,484)
Duncan, Paul....3:48:56 (7,955)
Duncan, Rob....4:01:35 (11,392)
Duncan, Rory....5:13:04 (28,763)
Duncan, Steven....3:37:17 (5,614)
Duncan, Steven....5:20:17 (29,888)
Duncum, Daniel....7:02:59 (36,224)
Dunford, Johnathan....5:46:56 (33,046)

Dunford, Robert 3:36:09 (5,437)
Dunford, Steve C 3:11:24 (2,041)
Dungate, Keith S 3:37:51 (5,731)
Dunham, Christopher 4:46:01 (23,030)
Dunk, Nicholas 4:28:09 (18,397)
Dunlea, Brian 4:57:23 (25,839)
Dunlop, Daniel Mark 3:52:17 (8,734)
Dunlop, Stuart 4:45:44 (22,962)
Dunmall, Andy 4:14:26 (14,626)
Dunn, Adam 4:47:56 (23,528)
Dunn, Andrew 4:11:34 (13,867)
Dunn, Chris 4:39:03 (21,269)
Dunn, Gareth 4:39:28 (21,377)
Dunn, Gareth 5:22:46 (30,262)
Dunn, George 5:13:00 (28,743)
Dunn, Karl 4:49:22 (23,886)
Dunn, Martin 5:05:31 (27,452)
Dunn, Mike Robert 3:39:04 (5,956)
Dunn, Peter M 4:09:44 (13,401)
Dunn, Simon John 4:46:42 (23,232)
Dunn, Stuart W 2:54:38 (711)
Dunnachie, Mark 3:37:33 (5,678)
Dunne, Christopher J 3:44:31 (6,995)
Dunne, Derek J 2:55:01 (747)
Dunne, Gerry Anthony 3:38:56 (5,926)
Dunne, Jason Michael 3:56:43 (10,003)
Dunne, Jerome 2:52:17 (583)
Dunne, Jonathan R 6:11:55 (34,750)
Dunne, Kevin 3:27:29 (3,958)
Dunne, Martin Patrick 3:16:24 (2,598)
Dunne, Michael Jonathon 4:43:42 (22,417)
Dunne, Richard T 3:23:55 (3,423)
Dunnett, Keith 4:51:41 (24,457)
Dunnico, Clive R 7:19:40 (36,402)
Dunning, Guy 4:54:21 (25,144)
Dunnington, Gary 4:48:44 (23,733)
Dunn-Parrant, Glenn D 3:12:14 (2,109)
Dunscombe, Guy Christopher 3:01:56 (1,252)
Dunscombe, Mark 3:07:20 (1,638)
Dunsire, Magnus Fraser 3:43:12 (6,730)
Dunstall, David 2:59:03 (1,057)
Dunster, Jaime 5:22:27 (30,214)
Dunwoody, Keith Mervyn 4:05:46 (12,402)
Dupont, Sebastien 3:33:56 (5,048)
Dupre, Eric 3:48:13 (7,784)
Durance, Richard 4:15:20 (14,872)
Durand, Jean Dominique 4:13:43 (14,436)
Durant, Adam John 3:13:34 (2,266)
Durham, Lewis Chea 4:48:17 (23,605)
Durham, Neil Jonathan 4:30:33 (19,106)
Durkan, Kevin Joseph 3:37:39 (5,699)
Durose, Stuart William 4:33:39 (19,906)
Durrant, David W 3:58:23 (10,517)
Durst, Janos 4:15:39 (14,937)
Durston-Smith, Simon 3:51:59 (8,654)
Dury, Michael J 2:53:17 (629)
Dussault, Didier 4:11:03 (13,736)
Dustan, Andrew John 3:53:37 (9,098)
Duthoit, Anthony M 4:40:25 (21,617)
Duthoit, Jacques 4:40:40 (21,683)
Dutnall, Barry 4:54:44 (25,238)
Dutoit, Thomas 3:18:44 (2,845)
Dutton, David 3:32:36 (4,827)
Dutton, David Allan 3:52:32 (8,804)
Dutton, Gavin Mark 5:13:14 (28,808)
Dutton, Ian 4:21:46 (16,631)
Dutton, Ian 4:59:19 (26,292)
Duval, Bruno 4:09:26 (13,325)
Duval, Oliver 4:59:51 (26,414)
Duxbury, Richard Henry 3:46:02 (7,314)
Duxbury, Robert A 3:27:31 (3,966)
Dwyer, Ben 5:49:01 (33,242)
Dwyer, Maurice 4:53:07 (24,826)
Dwyer, Ross 3:36:19 (5,459)
Dyble, Dean Michael 4:21:15 (16,477)
Dyckes, John J 3:15:06 (2,449)
Dyckhoff, Matthew 3:33:25 (4,954)
Dyde, Robert 2:54:28 (696)
Dye, Mark 4:47:46 (23,483)
Dye, Richard J 3:40:25 (6,217)
Dye, Tom 3:24:50 (3,554)
Dyer, Chris 4:17:37 (15,473)
Dyer, Dominic 3:55:01 (9,482)
Dyer, Graham J 3:37:39 (5,699)
Dyer, Kevin 4:39:11 (21,308)
Dyer, Kevin John 4:29:51 (18,927)
Dyer, Robert Charles William 4:21:16 (16,484)
Dyet, William T 3:08:11 (1,717)
Dyke, Adrian Vivian 4:19:19 (15,935)
Dyke, Clive 3:29:20 (4,292)
Dymond, Garry 3:19:51 (2,947)
Dymond, Stephen James 4:32:20 (19,525)
Dymott, Steven 5:21:39 (30,103)
Dyne, Jeff 3:27:19 (3,924)
Dyson, Andy 4:45:17 (22,835)
Dyson, Graham 3:55:17 (9,556)
Dyson, Matthew 4:51:00 (24,306)
Dyson, Ron 6:01:20 (34,147)
Dyson, Steve William 5:14:28 (28,985)
Dytor, Nathan 5:27:10 (30,930)
Dzenkowski, Daniel Jacob 4:29:40 (18,870)
Eachus, Peter 5:46:40 (33,025)
Eacott, Mark 4:56:41 (25,689)
Eaden, Ken 4:45:13 (22,823)
Eady, John 5:31:18 (31,449)
Eakin, William 5:40:34 (32,442)
Ealand, Nigel W 3:54:09 (9,245)
Eales, Darryl Charles 4:44:03 (22,516)
Eames, John 3:23:40 (3,390)
Eames, Nick William 5:14:20 (28,966)
Eames, Rob 4:09:28 (13,330)
Earl, David W 4:49:13 (23,852)
Earl, Derek W 3:56:58 (10,077)
Earl, Martin James 3:52:47 (8,863)
Earl, Martyn 3:36:56 (5,551)
Earl, Richard John 4:20:05 (16,131)
Earl, Stuart 4:15:51 (14,987)
Earles, Jono 3:23:23 (3,349)
Earley, Simon 3:03:09 (1,334)
Earley, Stephen 2:44:32 (322)
Earls-Davis, James Gratwicke 4:22:04 (16,723)
Earney, Derek W 6:04:52 (34,375)
Earp, Andrew 4:57:37 (25,884)
Earp, Anthony 4:08:30 (13,085)
Eary, Nick 5:22:10 (30,173)
Eason, Adam Dennis 4:28:49 (18,617)
Eason, Benjamin J 4:10:52 (13,686)
East, Adrian John 5:28:55 (31,141)
East, Ian Robert 4:04:41 (12,122)
East, John Howard 3:51:19 (8,496)
East, Matthew J 2:51:26 (540)
East, Tony Geoffrey 6:32:30 (35,582)
Eastbury, Steven D 4:11:22 (13,805)
Easter, Peter 6:03:18 (34,272)
Easterbrook, Karim Colin 6:17:14 (34,992)
Easterby, William Andrew 4:56:47 (25,711)
Easterling, Tom 3:46:19 (7,378)
Easters, Matthew J 4:01:20 (11,319)
Eastham, Fred 5:43:40 (32,734)
Eastham, John Michael 4:59:47 (26,403)
Eastment, Andy 2:58:06 (965)
Eastment, Lee 6:05:32 (34,422)
Eastment, Neil G 3:13:27 (2,241)
Easton, Jonathan Mark 5:02:16 (26,900)
Eastwell, Judah Benjamin 4:09:11 (13,253)
Eastwood, Philip 5:06:17 (27,581)
Eastwood, Robert 3:28:48 (4,189)
Eaton, Simon A 3:56:22 (9,887)
Eaton, Stephen Douglas 4:53:19 (24,880)
Eatwell, James 4:08:27 (13,067)
Eavis, Ben 5:34:13 (31,782)
Ebbing, W 3:23:29 (3,364)
Ebdy, Richard 4:34:56 (20,220)
Ebedes, Neil Colin 4:52:58 (24,788)
Ebison, Howard James Northcote 4:59:39 (26,370)
Ebrey, Simon Dominic 4:36:22 (20,568)
Ebsworth, David Michael 4:13:19 (14,318)
Eburne, Rich 3:54:29 (9,322)
Eccleston, Gary James 5:10:22 (28,304)
Ecclestone, James Paul 5:09:30 (28,148)
Ecclestone, Leigh 3:08:25 (1,743)
Echegaray, José 5:03:30 (27,100)
Echeverria, José Antonio 3:49:28 (8,080)
Eckman, Harry 5:14:09 (28,943)
Ecrement, Richard 5:32:24 (31,585)
Edbrooke, Peter John 5:11:20 (28,455)
Eddleston, Mike J 3:35:35 (5,339)
Ede, David John 4:49:34 (23,929)
Ede, Philip Andrew 4:12:52 (14,199)
Ede, Stuart James Paterson 4:15:57 (15,013)
Eden, Anthony Richard 4:26:20 (17,910)
Eden, Neil 3:43:15 (6,735)
Edenborough, Iain Stuart 3:56:41 (9,992)
Edensor, Ray J 4:36:15 (20,536)
Edey, William Paul 4:08:06 (12,989)
Edgar, James W 3:05:27 (1,491)
Edge, Michael 3:22:28 (3,235)
Edgell, Damien John 5:01:29 (26,750)
Edgell, Matthew Paul 6:26:48 (35,376)
Edginton, James 5:44:32 (32,818)
Edginton, Nigel David 2:52:10 (575)
Edlin, David A 4:03:05 (11,748)
Edmond, Graham Mc Neil 4:14:00 (14,504)
Edmonds, Matthew 4:21:22 (16,513)
Edmonds, Ross 3:54:12 (9,256)
Edmondson, Andrew 3:07:57 (1,693)
Edmondson, Henry John Ronald 5:41:33 (32,538)
Edmondson, Richard 3:59:57 (10,976)
Edmondson, Sam Peter 3:21:04 (3,094)
Edmondson-Jones, Andrew M 2:55:20 (763)
Edmunds, Thomas William Arthur 3:47:00 (7,524)
Edmunds, Tim 6:18:46 (35,069)
Edney, Seamus Jude 5:17:06 (29,403)
Edward, Eurwyn 4:00:11 (11,025)
Edwards, Alan 4:44:51 (22,730)
Edwards, Alan Robert Thomas 5:22:49 (30,274)
Edwards, Alex W 3:45:51 (7,278)
Edwards, Anthony Raymond 4:11:56 (13,972)
Edwards, Benjamin John 4:12:42 (14,158)
Edwards, Carl 3:51:39 (8,577)
Edwards, Chris 5:37:02 (32,105)
Edwards, Christopher John W 4:46:54 (23,283)
Edwards, Craig Thomas 3:56:44 (10,009)
Edwards, Dave Bernard 5:02:19 (26,908)
Edwards, David A 3:37:11 (5,594)
Edwards, David Arwel 4:12:50 (14,187)
Edwards, David F 3:16:21 (2,592)
Edwards, David Peter 3:57:37 (10,268)
Edwards, Geraint Vaughan 4:34:14 (20,054)
Edwards, Gethin R 4:13:42 (14,432)
Edwards, Glenn 4:13:08 (14,272)
Edwards, Glyn Frank 4:38:19 (21,061)
Edwards, Harry John 3:51:52 (8,629)
Edwards, Huw 4:16:19 (15,112)
Edwards, Ian 4:53:41 (24,965)
Edwards, Ieuan 4:40:02 (21,507)
Edwards, Jerome M 2:44:50 (335)
Edwards, John 3:53:25 (9,033)
Edwards, John 5:37:16 (32,138)
Edwards, Jonathan Mark 4:40:57 (21,759)
Edwards, Justin Paul 3:38:25 (5,834)
Edwards, Kenneth Leonard 5:30:40 (31,380)
Edwards, Kevin D 3:09:26 (1,849)
Edwards, Kevin J 3:39:13 (5,985)
Edwards, Lloyd 3:41:32 (6,427)
Edwards, Marc David 4:03:20 (11,809)
Edwards, Marc Emerson 4:26:39 (17,986)
Edwards, Marcus 6:20:59 (35,161)
Edwards, Mark 3:15:07 (2,452)
Edwards, Mark 4:38:27 (21,105)
Edwards, Mark Ashley 4:39:34 (21,406)
Edwards, Matthew 5:11:03 (28,413)
Edwards, Matthew Anthony 3:39:00 (5,937)
Edwards, Matthew John 3:53:57 (9,196)
Edwards, Matthew S 4:53:51 (25,006)
Edwards, Matthew Stewart 3:05:58 (1,531)
Edwards, Merrick 5:37:54 (32,201)
Edwards, Mike Craig 4:31:41 (19,373)
Edwards, Nathan 3:23:02 (3,298)
Edwards, Niall K 6:38:39 (35,744)
Edwards, Nicholas A 6:02:02 (34,191)
Edwards, Nick 5:02:45 (26,987)
Edwards, Nigel J 3:09:33 (1,864)
Edwards, Orlando 2:25:15 (37)
Edwards, Patrick Darren 4:05:56 (12,440)
Edwards, Paul 3:38:00 (5,761)
Edwards, Paul Anthony Keep 3:37:53 (5,739)
Edwards, Peter 3:28:10 (4,086)
Edwards, Peter William 5:46:10 (32,968)

Edwards, Philip Michael 3:19:56 (2,954)
Edwards, Philip Stephen 4:02:47 (11,671)
Edwards, Phillip Mark 6:07:01 (34,507)
Edwards, Richard 3:14:56 (2,430)
Edwards, Richard 4:03:25 (11,823)
Edwards, Richard Darren 4:33:13 (19,772)
Edwards, Richard G 3:49:28 (8,080)
Edwards, Roy Anthony 5:31:03 (31,422)
Edwards, Scott 3:53:36 (9,092)
Edwards, Steve 3:09:44 (1,884)
Edwards, Terry 5:42:26 (32,630)
Edwards, Thomas Stuart 5:30:28 (31,351)
Edwards, Timothy Alan 5:17:35 (29,485)
Edwards, Toby James 3:28:26 (4,136)
Edwards, William Nicholas 4:01:59 (11,486)
Edwards-Broome, Joe 4:39:11 (21,308)
Eeles, Philip Anthony 4:20:35 (16,287)
Eels, Stuart William 4:53:44 (24,982)
Efrat, Eyal 4:17:56 (15,557)
Efstathiou, Michael 4:00:16 (11,048)
Eg, Ole 4:47:28 (23,404)
Egan, Declan J 3:58:11 (10,449)
Egan, Hugh 4:28:41 (18,579)
Egan, John 3:52:26 (8,772)
Egan, Michael Anthony 4:14:20 (14,603)
Egan, Paul 3:28:29 (4,138)
Egan, Sean P 4:21:36 (16,580)
Egan, Simon Andrew 2:58:25 (998)
Egdell, Carl A 2:49:16 (458)
Egeland, Frode 3:05:55 (1,528)
Egelie, Eduard C 2:59:16 (1,079)
Eggbeer, Peter Kevan 3:09:04 (1,814)
Eggelton, Matthew 3:20:41 (3,046)
Eggenschwiler, Peter 3:37:05 (5,582)
Eggers, Peter 4:10:20 (13,554)
Eggerton, Matt 5:07:50 (27,866)
Eggesvik, Tor 4:14:17 (14,592)
Eggleston, Pete 3:12:32 (2,136)
Eggleton, Bernard 4:06:07 (12,478)
Eggleton, Lawrence 3:47:32 (7,655)
Egley, James A 4:39:49 (21,465)
Egry, François 4:22:27 (16,834)
Ehmann, Jurg 3:58:31 (10,560)
Ehren, Gary 5:06:04 (27,543)
Ehrlich, Alexander David John 4:24:23 (17,350)
Eijsink, Geert 3:46:53 (7,505)
Eisenbach, Andreas 4:21:55 (16,680)
Eisenhut, Paul 3:24:01 (3,433)
Eismann, Thomas 3:24:08 (3,455)
Ejdelbaum, Henry 6:18:41 (35,064)
Ejdelbaum, Joshua 6:18:41 (35,064)
Ekberg, Carl 4:47:51 (23,510)
Eksteen, Bertus 3:56:23 (9,892)
El-Atribi, Omar Ibrahim 3:22:04 (3,199)
Elazab, Sammy 4:11:53 (13,950)
Elcome, Robert 4:34:44 (20,179)
Eld, Daniel 4:06:10 (12,490)
Elder, Andrew 4:10:14 (13,536)
Eldred, Nick R 4:03:32 (11,854)
Eldring, Hans-Olav 4:52:37 (24,710)
Eley, Allan John 3:51:34 (8,554)
Eley, Dean Edward 5:25:19 (30,665)
Eley, Matthew 4:27:21 (18,195)
Elferine, Alex 3:13:33 (2,264)
Elflett, Mark 4:49:43 (23,987)
Elgey, Jason Jay 3:47:32 (7,655)
Elia, Nick 4:28:47 (18,600)
Elias, Glyn 4:54:33 (25,190)
Eliasson, Kennerth 4:22:31 (16,854)
Eliott, Jon A 4:04:09 (11,996)
El-Kadey, Mohamed Ali 3:54:14 (9,269)
Elkerton, William James Stuart 5:26:18 (30,821)
Elkington, Simon 3:53:18 (8,997)
Elkins, John Barry 4:54:09 (25,079)
El-Kour, Ala 3:47:07 (7,545)
Ellerby, Mark 3:16:31 (2,610)
Ellerington, James M 4:41:15 (21,832)
Ellerington, Ross 6:38:44 (35,750)
Ellerton, Steve 3:29:37 (4,345)
Elles, Mark John 5:21:48 (30,116)
Ellett, Michael J 3:28:44 (4,179)
Ellice, Simon J 4:37:43 (20,928)
Ellice, William 3:45:05 (7,111)

Ellingford, David Anthony 5:27:45 (30,994)
Elliot, Charlie 4:22:27 (16,834)
Elliot, Robin Christopher 3:47:02 (7,531)
Elliott, Chris 4:53:15 (24,862)
Elliott, Christopher 3:40:55 (6,313)
Elliott, Craig Darren 4:12:02 (13,994)
Elliott, Dale Jonathan 5:13:03 (28,747)
Elliott, Daniel James 4:43:00 (22,259)
Elliott, Daren D 3:19:04 (2,875)
Elliott, David 5:07:27 (27,799)
Elliott, David 5:08:13 (27,936)
Elliott, David W 5:18:08 (29,564)
Elliott, Graeme Robert 4:21:53 (16,664)
Elliott, Howard C 3:09:45 (1,888)
Elliott, Joe Victor 3:00:07 (1,156)
Elliott, Justin 4:18:12 (15,629)
Elliott, Mark C 6:16:32 (34,954)
Elliott, Matthew James 4:04:07 (11,989)
Elliott, Nick 3:47:12 (7,576)
Elliott, Oliver James 4:26:20 (17,910)
Elliott, Peter J 3:40:00 (6,147)
Elliott, Phillip Paul 4:49:36 (23,943)
Elliott, Rob 4:38:45 (21,185)
Elliott, Robert Alan 3:43:07 (6,718)
Elliott, Thomas R 2:54:54 (734)
Ellis, Adam 4:36:29 (20,598)
Ellis, Andrew 5:14:13 (28,952)
Ellis, Andrew Jeremy Dalrymple 3:56:17 (9,866)
Ellis, Barrie 6:07:05 (34,511)
Ellis, Dave 4:02:39 (11,638)
Ellis, David W 4:32:13 (19,491)
Ellis, Dominic C 5:49:36 (33,293)
Ellis, Don 4:52:16 (24,619)
Ellis, Gregory Anthony 4:51:41 (24,457)
Ellis, James A 2:40:45 (221)
Ellis, John 5:10:10 (28,270)
Ellis, Matt J 2:51:25 (539)
Ellis, Matthew Lee 3:41:25 (6,408)
Ellis, Michael P 3:23:26 (3,357)
Ellis, Mike 3:50:19 (8,272)
Ellis, Nicholas 5:34:36 (31,835)
Ellis, Peter David Eric 3:28:00 (4,049)
Ellis, Peter V 3:28:29 (4,138)
Ellis, Philip 5:14:35 (29,000)
Ellis, Ralph 4:16:51 (15,257)
Ellis, Ray 5:59:45 (34,042)
Ellis, Richard F 4:44:24 (22,617)
Ellis, Ricky James 4:39:50 (21,473)
Ellis, Samuel John 3:58:45 (10,644)
Ellis, Samuel Ruskin 3:56:08 (9,818)
Ellis, Sean 4:08:18 (13,028)
Ellis, Stephen 4:06:52 (12,680)
Ellis, Steven D 4:02:12 (11,540)
Ellis, Stuart James 5:03:55 (27,175)
Ellis, Vince 3:31:27 (4,659)
Ellis, Wayne Mark 2:53:40 (649)
Ellison, Robert Grant 3:32:26 (4,809)
Ellison, William 3:20:33 (3,032)
Ellison-Burns, Simon J 4:04:39 (12,114)
Ellis-Smith, Jon Phillip 3:57:58 (10,370)
Ellson, Mark Andrew 5:27:11 (30,932)
Ellwood, Mike 4:03:19 (11,804)
Ellwood, Thomas Edward 4:44:55 (22,745)
Ellwood, Tim 3:29:22 (4,297)
Elmer, Gregory George 5:10:30 (28,327)
Elms, David 4:05:46 (12,402)
Elms, Nicholas Reginald 4:06:28 (12,562)
Elmy, Glen Charles 3:36:11 (5,444)
Elo, Moises 4:27:32 (18,246)
Elsby, Dominic A 3:09:16 (1,830)
Elsden, Keith A 5:48:00 (33,139)
Elsey, Matthew 4:45:44 (22,962)
Elsmere, Alan 3:16:14 (2,580)
Elsmore, Nigel Raymond 3:28:10 (4,086)
Elson, Ian 4:44:14 (22,575)
Elson, Stephen 3:39:54 (6,132)
Elson, Stephen 3:58:08 (10,426)
Elson, Steven Paul 3:58:25 (10,532)
Elston, Adam 3:30:26 (4,489)
Elustondo, Aitor 3:00:39 (1,183)
Elvin, Peter 3:56:45 (10,014)
Embiricos, Nick Stamati George 3:33:25 (4,954)
Emden, Bryan Jeremy 4:55:35 (25,429)

Emden, Samuel 4:55:35 (25,429)
Emeny, Mark 4:10:10 (13,517)
Emerson, Derek 4:29:01 (18,691)
Emerson, Jack Oliver 4:41:58 (22,005)
Emerton, James 4:01:50 (11,455)

Emery, Graham P 6:09:38 (34,641)

What a day April 26, 2010 was. It was my third London Marathon, but by far my most important and meaningful. Running for Cancer Research and running as a 7ft tall Gingerbread man! In the late 1980s when I was at school, my best mate Antony Waghorn was diagnosed with cancer. After many years of treatment he was given the all clear, and from him (and his wife!) I have two fantastic godsons, Elliott and Frazer. Late last year my brother's partner Jacqui Arnott was also diagnosed with cancer. She too has had treatment and is recovering well. I loved every mile of those 26 miles, the crowd support was fantastic. I made the TV with an interview at Cutty Sark. Best of all it was for Ants & Jacq.

Emery, Peter K 3:35:59 (5,411)
Emery, Philippe 4:15:27 (14,897)
Emery, Simon 4:58:06 (25,986)
Emery, Stephen James 5:23:10 (30,333)
Eminson, Richard 7:04:18 (36,248)
Emirali, Orbray 4:48:10 (23,582)
Emmett, Darren Thomas 4:32:39 (19,594)
Emmett, Simon Edward George 4:58:41 (26,134)
Empl, Georg 5:25:56 (30,771)
Emsden, Hugh A 4:16:32 (15,177)
Emtage, James 4:34:37 (20,150)
Emuss, Andrew Victor 4:26:51 (18,039)
Endean, David 4:31:37 (19,358)
Endean, Edward 3:35:31 (5,327)
Endemano, Mark 3:17:05 (2,671)
Enders, Scott 4:23:33 (17,119)
Endersby, James William Rowse 3:37:51 (5,731)
Engelbert, Ric 5:08:02 (27,903)
Engelhardt, Andreas 4:04:36 (12,101)
England, Chris John 3:43:58 (6,871)
England, Christopher 3:58:13 (10,463)
England, Daryn J 4:19:32 (15,978)
England, James 3:44:23 (6,964)
England, Russell 4:19:32 (15,978)
Englander, David 3:41:39 (6,447)
English, Aaron Michael 5:10:29 (28,325)
English, David James 4:30:32 (19,098)
English, Paul Jonathan 4:00:31 (11,118)
English, Stephen D 3:57:57 (10,366)
Engwell, Paul 5:27:44 (30,992)
Enkov, Artiom Olegovich 6:28:01 (35,421)
Enoch, Nigel Paul 4:39:39 (21,427)
Enrieu, Roberto 6:03:05 (34,259)
Enright, Mick 5:24:09 (30,505)
Entwistle, Dan James 4:17:57 (15,563)
Entwistle, Iain 4:46:10 (23,078)
Entwistle, Peter R 3:15:12 (2,462)
Ephgrave, Paul 4:20:47 (16,363)
Epifani, Antonio 4:27:54 (18,339)
Eplett, Liam C 4:34:24 (20,097)
Epsom, Joe 5:31:40 (31,497)
Epton, Jeremy 4:23:48 (17,191)

Erdilek, Richard 4:35:35 (20,362)
Ereku, Morgan 5:31:41 (31,501)
Erftemeijer, Jan 4:24:58 (17,509)
Eric, Aubay 3:46:37 (7,444)
Eric, Hamon 3:13:10 (2,206)
Eric, Herbin 3:55:45 (9,699)
Erleigh, Julian 5:13:04 (28,763)
Ernest Russell, Michael 4:37:25 (20,850)
Erpetto, Mario 3:50:31 (8,317)
Errington, Jonathan T 3:25:14 (3,613)
Errington, Mark Richard 4:06:46 (12,645)
Erskine, Stuart 4:44:35 (22,666)
Erwood, James 5:54:11 (33,659)
Escamilla, Victor Fidel 3:23:31 (3,370)
Escott, Justin Thomas 5:06:31 (27,628)
Escott, Mark 3:45:05 (7,111)
Espig, Mirko 4:50:58 (24,292)
Espinal, Rafael 3:21:42 (3,161)
Espinasa, Jorge 4:56:47 (25,711)
Espley, Daniel James 4:56:42 (25,695)
Esposito, Antonio 3:23:02 (3,298)
Essex, Trevor 4:36:16 (20,540)
Esslemont, Keith 5:32:29 (31,600)
Essom, Andrew 5:22:21 (30,200)
Esson, Andrew Balfour 4:13:29 (14,358)
Estall, Jim H 3:48:23 (7,820)
Estermann, Christophe 3:02:06 (1,265)
Estreich, Steven 5:01:48 (26,812)
Etherden, Clifford R 4:10:38 (13,625)
Etheridge, Royston Charles 4:48:19 (23,609)
Etherington, Roger 4:28:26 (18,499)
Etminan, Jonny 4:53:42 (24,973)
Ettinger, Lance 5:08:36 (27,991)
Etty, Peter Gordon 4:07:39 (12,871)
Etuazim, Andrew C. 5:59:31 (34,017)
Euden, Martin J 3:32:59 (4,891)
Euskirchen, Norbert 5:18:31 (29,627)
Evan-Hughes, Jonathan D 3:53:51 (9,172)
Evans, Adam Armytage 4:21:59 (16,700)
Evans, Aled 3:23:25 (3,354)
Evans, Alun T 3:10:10 (1,920)
Evans, Andrew 4:28:02 (18,375)
Evans, Andrew Richard 3:46:09 (7,345)
Evans, Andrew Richard 4:48:09 (23,579)
Evans, Anthony Mark 3:55:34 (9,628)
Evans, Barry J 4:09:58 (13,463)
Evans, Brian 4:33:08 (19,740)
Evans, Ceri 4:50:54 (24,269)
Evans, Chris 3:39:53 (6,122)
Evans, Chris David 4:48:26 (23,655)
Evans, Christian William 4:16:53 (15,266)
Evans, Colin Glyn 4:48:31 (23,671)
Evans, Dan Martin 9:12:20 (36,620)
Evans, Daniel 2:32:43 (89)
Evans, Daniel 3:23:13 (3,326)
Evans, Daniel 4:17:55 (15,550)
Evans, Daniel S 4:28:33 (18,539)
Evans, David 3:23:04 (3,303)
Evans, David 4:49:38 (23,953)
Evans, David 5:18:24 (29,608)
Evans, David John 6:21:19 (35,179)
Evans, David M 3:57:11 (10,154)
Evans, Edwin 3:59:11 (10,771)
Evans, Emlyn E 4:23:57 (17,225)
Evans, Frank C 5:00:00 (26,454)
Evans, Gareth 3:55:57 (9,766)
Evans, Gareth 4:52:16 (24,619)
Evans, Gareth J 3:20:56 (3,076)
Evans, Gareth Linton 3:53:14 (8,979)
Evans, Gavin M 2:49:25 (466)
Evans, Gerry R 4:29:53 (18,943)
Evans, Glyn R 3:39:19 (6,010)
Evans, Glynn 3:38:08 (5,791)
Evans, Graham 3:37:46 (5,720)
Evans, Gwyn William 3:35:42 (5,359)
Evans, Iain 4:06:18 (12,524)
Evans, Ian K 4:36:52 (20,704)
Evans, Ivor Robert 4:36:44 (20,665)
Evans, Jamie 3:39:29 (6,038)
Evans, Jamie John 5:50:41 (33,403)
Evans, Jason 4:37:17 (20,813)
Evans, Jeffrey 3:02:51 (1,319)
Evans, John E 3:45:07 (7,119)
Evans, John V 4:29:27 (18,790)
Evans, Jonathan 3:57:33 (10,246)
Evans, Jonathan 4:27:03 (18,097)
Evans, Joshua 5:18:01 (29,550)
Evans, Justin Curtis Robert 5:56:37 (33,837)
Evans, Kevan 3:35:20 (5,291)
Evans, Lee 4:55:10 (25,350)
Evans, Lee L 4:39:00 (21,258)
Evans, Leigh 4:50:30 (24,161)
Evans, Lloyd 3:46:35 (7,440)
Evans, Mark Anthony 4:23:17 (17,041)
Evans, Martyn 5:40:50 (32,460)
Evans, Michael 3:57:38 (10,275)
Evans, Mike 4:18:23 (15,686)
Evans, Neil Raymond 4:12:56 (14,214)
Evans, Nicholas William 4:48:23 (23,634)
Evans, Pascal J 2:55:33 (775)
Evans, Paul 3:50:28 (8,305)
Evans, Paul 6:58:53 (36,171)
Evans, Paul D 3:20:32 (3,030)
Evans, Paul Desmond 5:04:37 (27,300)
Evans, Paul Kenneth 4:01:59 (11,486)
Evans, Paul Thomas 3:40:53 (6,306)
Evans, Peter Gwyn 6:33:09 (35,603)
Evans, Richard 5:00:08 (26,488)
Evans, Richard Edward 4:53:05 (24,814)
Evans, Richard M 3:57:32 (10,238)
Evans, Rob David 5:08:03 (27,907)
Evans, Robert 4:14:27 (14,632)
Evans, Robert 4:22:47 (16,934)
Evans, Robert L 3:55:00 (9,479)
Evans, Robin 3:59:43 (10,925)
Evans, Ryan James 4:53:57 (25,034)
Evans, Scott 2:57:40 (929)
Evans, Steven 5:24:02 (30,486)
Evans, Stuart 3:25:32 (3,652)
Evans, Terry 5:11:46 (28,515)
Evans, Terry Alan 6:18:12 (35,042)
Evans, Thomas 3:54:04 (9,225)
Evans, Thomas Richard 3:59:12 (10,779)
Evans, Tim 4:46:37 (23,209)
Evans, Tony 4:16:49 (15,252)
Evelegh, Jon 3:57:38 (10,275)
Everest, Lawrence 3:46:03 (7,322)
Everett, Andrew 4:36:07 (20,510)
Everett, Barry 4:48:22 (23,627)
Everitt, Lee Michael 4:31:13 (19,274)
Everitt, Robert M 3:36:54 (5,545)
Everton, Lee David 6:44:57 (35,906)
Everton, Ray 4:32:16 (19,505)
Every, Alan J 2:58:44 (1,023)
Every, Duane 4:29:49 (18,918)
Eves, Dean J 4:20:42 (16,333)
Eves, Kyle 4:32:21 (19,529)
Eves, Martin Leonard 4:43:10 (22,292)
Eves, Ralph R 5:36:47 (32,080)
Evins, Stephen John 3:32:16 (4,783)
Evison, Gary John 4:05:22 (12,300)
Evlogimenos, Costa 4:31:06 (19,243)
Ewart, Michael David 3:52:27 (8,777)
Ewart, Tim 4:49:45 (23,994)
Ewbank, Tim David 4:08:03 (12,975)
Ewe, Patrik Bengt 3:31:38 (4,688)
Ewen, Colin 4:02:21 (11,565)
Ewen, Robert C 5:02:04 (26,856)
Ewens, Mark S 4:39:10 (21,304)
Ewing, Tom 4:27:20 (18,190)
Ewles, Stuart 3:59:22 (10,827)
Exley, Richard 6:27:02 (35,386)
Exley, Stephen David 3:52:07 (8,682)
Eybalin, Stephane 3:52:12 (8,706)
Eykyn, Alastair 3:45:19 (7,167)
Eyles, Ray 5:05:01 (27,371)
Eyley, Robert 3:58:51 (10,670)
Eymard, Julien 3:29:50 (4,385)
Eyre, Dave J 3:36:38 (5,501)
Eyre, Douglas 4:16:38 (15,197)
Eyre, Marcus Jamieson 4:11:04 (13,738)
Eyre, Torbjorn 5:20:49 (29,979)
Eznasni, Mohamed 3:27:10 (3,900)
Ezro, Daniel 4:29:01 (18,691)
Fabbri, Filippo 4:36:51 (20,702)
Fabian, Shaun B 5:11:47 (28,518)
Fabrizi, Mauro 4:04:59 (12,200)
Facer, Brian 4:14:37 (14,687)
Facey, Trevor 5:15:51 (29,205)
Facey, William 4:51:39 (24,450)
Fache, Olivier 4:01:23 (11,332)
Faenzi, Marco 3:30:19 (4,473)
Faerber, Steve Brian 6:38:24 (35,736)
Fagan, Chris A 5:39:23 (32,341)
Fagbohunka, Funso 4:36:36 (20,631)
Fagelson, Alon 4:44:45 (22,712)
Fahey, Michael 3:06:39 (1,583)
Fahey, Paul 5:39:45 (32,362)
Fairall, Matt Thomas 5:30:33 (31,364)
Fairbrother, George 3:58:42 (10,625)
Fairbrother, Justin 3:33:36 (4,986)
Fairbrother, Nick 4:46:59 (23,304)
Fairburn, Andrew 3:52:15 (8,719)
Fairclough, David 4:17:05 (15,317)
Fairclough, David 6:05:55 (34,445)
Fairclough, John 3:50:12 (8,247)
Fairclough, Thomas 3:52:20 (8,750)
Fairfax, Chris 4:21:31 (16,552)
Fairfield, James C 4:30:55 (19,201)
Fairhead, Paul Jeremy 5:00:10 (26,493)
Fairhurst, Jack Nathaniel 4:53:30 (24,917)
Fairhurst, Robin A 4:32:46 (19,622)
Fairhurst, Shaun 4:09:23 (13,304)
Fairhurst, Wayne 3:29:49 (4,382)
Fairs, Jon P 3:13:57 (2,309)
Fairs, Michael John 4:38:07 (21,011)
Fairs, Steve 4:46:01 (23,030)
Fairweather, Henry Nicholas 5:43:46 (32,751)
Faisal, Julian 4:20:49 (16,369)
Faithfull, Joe T 4:58:58 (26,207)
Falaschy, Georgio 4:25:44 (17,732)
Falconer, Jamie 3:28:18 (4,103)
Falconer, Owen G 3:51:26 (8,524)
Falconer, Robert 3:08:47 (1,791)
Falkiner, Max 5:12:55 (28,726)
Falla, Adam 4:18:03 (15,597)
Fallan, Tyran 5:45:27 (32,904)
Fallbrink, Krister 4:06:46 (12,645)
Fallon, Gary M 3:20:45 (3,051)
Fallon, Gerald James 3:52:27 (8,777)
Fallowfield-Smith, Mark 3:08:29 (1,752)
Falzon, Simon J 5:37:35 (32,172)
Fancourt, Andy 4:53:09 (24,835)
Fanfarillo, Stefano 5:41:10 (32,504)
Fantini, Rino 4:42:01 (22,017)
Fantoni, Luigi Gino 4:12:55 (14,210)
Farag, Ben M 3:05:27 (1,491)
Faries, David 4:34:44 (20,179)
Farland, Joel 3:58:42 (10,625)
Farley, Andrew 5:03:52 (27,167)
Farley, Anthony McKenzie 3:43:52 (6,848)
Farley, Darron P 3:29:11 (4,266)
Farley, Jon 4:50:05 (24,070)
Farmer, Darren O 4:43:27 (22,359)
Farmer, Dennis Karl, Eric 5:00:46 (26,606)
Farmer, Paul 3:07:53 (1,688)
Farmer, Stuart Michael 2:59:09 (1,071)
Farmery, Ian 3:21:20 (3,122)
Farnan, Stuart Andrew 4:08:31 (13,090)
Farnell, Lee Edward 3:26:10 (3,765)
Farnell, Norman 4:13:49 (14,460)
Farnham, Lyndon John 4:25:57 (17,798)
Farnsworth, Gary Alan 4:26:53 (18,048)
Farnworth, Richard 5:03:18 (27,073)
Farr, Charlie Nicholas 4:29:02 (18,697)
Farr, Rick 4:20:51 (16,375)
Farrant, Andrew J 4:08:47 (13,156)
Farrant, Nick 5:46:09 (32,965)
Farrant, Stuart Anthony 3:40:10 (6,179)
Farrants, George 3:58:37 (10,598)
Farrar, John 3:41:51 (6,491)
Farrar, Matthew 5:37:16 (32,138)
Farrell, Andrew James 4:13:24 (14,335)
Farrell, Bernard 4:14:58 (14,773)
Farrell, Conor Edward 4:25:55 (17,790)
Farrell, David Edward 4:42:39 (22,168)
Farrell, Dom 4:30:56 (19,203)
Farrell, Ed 3:50:03 (8,221)
Farrell, Joe 3:44:09 (6,905)

Farrell, John 5:21:55 (30,132)
Farrell, John Mark 4:15:13 (14,838)
Farrell, Ken 3:44:46 (7,047)
Farrell, Matthew 5:00:50 (26,617)
Farrell, Robert Joseph 5:45:17 (32,892)
Farrell, Sean 4:12:24 (14,068)
Farrell, Tyron L 3:39:26 (6,029)
Farren, Patrick Joseph 3:52:46 (8,857)
Farren-Handford, Matt 5:00:32 (26,557)
Farrer, Jonathan 3:38:34 (5,863)
Farres, Richard 4:04:46 (12,148)
Farrington, Phillip 4:08:52 (13,177)
Farrington, Stephen Joseph 4:04:37 (12,106)
Farris, Rob 3:58:10 (10,445)
Farrow, Gavin 4:23:23 (17,076)
Farrow, Martin Keith 4:48:03 (23,557)
Farrow, Nicky Ross 4:24:31 (17,395)
Farrow, Nigel A 4:48:55 (23,776)
Farrow, Simon 4:05:55 (12,435)
Farsides, Tom 2:57:23 (886)
Fassnidge, Andrew 4:02:04 (11,507)
Fassnidge, John 4:00:39 (11,155)
Fassnidge, Paul 4:37:03 (20,758)
Fast, Spencer 3:17:59 (2,763)
Faulkner, Jonh William 5:55:30 (33,756)
Faulkner, Kevin Michael 3:54:12 (9,256)
Faulkner, Mark 4:23:07 (17,007)
Faulkner, Simon 3:45:16 (7,156)
Faulkner, Simon 7:00:46 (36,200)
Faulkner, Simon P 4:34:53 (20,212)
Faurisson, Olivier R 3:34:08 (5,086)
Fauvel, Fabrice 3:42:36 (6,609)
Faveau, Fabien 4:53:08 (24,832)
Fawcett, Chris 4:50:12 (24,094)
Fawcett, Craig Andrew 4:28:02 (18,375)
Fawcett, Nick 4:48:43 (23,728)
Fawke, Mark 4:22:12 (16,761)
Fawkes, Paul Ian 5:24:18 (30,526)
Fawzy, Moustafa 4:13:56 (14,486)
Fay, James Andrew 5:53:41 (33,622)
Fear, Alan 4:32:49 (19,635)
Fear, Bob 5:08:46 (28,011)
Fearn, David J 3:48:44 (7,909)
Fearnhead, Gary John 3:31:47 (4,706)
Fearns, Mark Alan 3:49:37 (8,122)
Fearon, Marcus 4:55:13 (25,361)
Fearon, Sean Patrick 5:34:01 (31,765)
Feary, Brendon 4:27:52 (18,330)
Featherstone, James Andrew 5:51:28 (33,460)
Featherstone, James Mark 3:14:51 (2,424)
Feehan, Mark 6:03:44 (34,303)
Fegan, Paul 4:37:25 (20,850)
Feherty, Brian J 4:00:55 (11,225)
Feild, Jonathan Gordon 4:26:30 (17,952)
Feist, Richard 4:06:35 (12,596)
Felce, James 3:02:29 (1,297)
Felce, Jonathan 4:58:32 (26,097)
Feleus, Laurens 5:32:21 (31,581)
Fell, Simon James 3:19:53 (2,950)
Felley, Jean Yves 2:42:29 (262)
Fellows, Kevin Michael 5:46:26 (33,002)
Felstead, James Martin 3:44:52 (7,071)
Feltham, Andrew Robert 7:38:24 (36,510)
Feltham, Richard Kevin 4:49:22 (23,886)
Felton, Alistair N 4:35:25 (20,332)
Felton, David J 3:27:49 (4,019)
Felton, Richard 4:44:55 (22,745)
Fender, David Coutts 3:46:29 (7,413)
Fendley, Peter Anthony 3:44:57 (7,088)
Fenemore, James Steven 4:32:33 (19,572)
Fenn, Geoff 3:38:40 (5,886)
Fennell, David Andrew 3:39:50 (6,110)
Fennell, Michael 3:09:26 (1,849)
Fennell, Robert James Michael 4:10:01 (13,479)
Fennell, Russell John 4:06:55 (12,689)
Fennell, Sean P 3:49:01 (7,978)
Fennell, Stephen David 4:30:54 (19,190)
Fenton, Clark 4:28:47 (18,600)
Fenton, Dave 3:37:35 (5,684)
Fenton, Miguel 5:16:52 (29,367)
Fenton, Paul 3:41:34 (6,433)
Fenton, Robert Leslie 4:08:05 (12,983)
Fenwick, Bob 5:11:59 (28,558)
Fenwick, Ian S 3:28:43 (4,178)
Fenwick, John W 3:54:02 (9,223)
Fenwick, Sean P 2:34:53 (110)
Fenwick, Warren 6:51:18 (36,018)
Feo, Giorgio 3:12:06 (2,101)
Fereday, David H 5:27:46 (30,997)
Ferguson, Andrew 3:52:41 (8,843)
Ferguson, Andrew James 4:45:57 (23,012)
Ferguson, Carl Alexander 4:06:56 (12,697)
Ferguson, Gary 3:26:07 (3,752)
Ferguson, Iain 4:26:24 (17,927)
Ferguson, Ian 6:04:45 (34,366)
Ferguson, Jock Y 3:43:30 (6,776)
Ferguson, John W 2:52:11 (577)
Ferguson, Mark Nicholas 5:14:52 (29,048)
Ferguson, Michael T 3:09:42 (1,878)
Ferguson, Raymond G 3:36:39 (5,505)
Fergusson, Ian Ross 4:12:29 (14,097)
Fermor-Dunman, Alex 4:23:22 (17,071)
Fernandes, Clifford 4:28:01 (18,371)
Fernandes, Jason 4:33:55 (19,972)
Fernandes, Leo Joseph 4:29:51 (18,927)
Fernandez, Julio Francisco 4:50:59 (24,300)
Fernandez, Matthew J 5:56:34 (33,833)
Fernandez, Paul M 2:38:44 (172)
Fernandez Marin, José André 3:56:32 (9,944)
Fernando, Milan Angelo 5:35:19 (31,906)
Fernando, Ras 3:43:52 (6,848)
Fernando, Rohan Sextus 4:12:40 (14,143)
Fernyhough, Philip D 4:28:20 (18,465)
Fernyhough, Richard 3:21:07 (3,101)
Ferrante, Pietro 3:28:44 (4,179)
Ferrari, Paul 4:53:14 (24,858)
Ferrari, Roberto 4:32:23 (19,535)
Ferreira, José P 3:14:03 (2,327)
Ferreira, Mario 4:26:42 (17,998)
Ferreira, William 3:34:05 (5,074)
Ferrell, Mark James 5:00:48 (26,613)
Ferrer, Michel 3:50:56 (8,409)
Ferretti, Vincenzo 3:23:06 (3,305)
Ferri, Patrick 3:44:32 (6,997)
Ferriday, Ernest 4:55:40 (25,452)
Ferrier, Colin John 5:25:25 (30,682)
Ferris, Glenn 4:03:05 (11,748)
Ferris, Ryan Paul 4:44:00 (22,504)
Fettah, Allan M 3:07:16 (1,629)
Fetti, Sertan 4:37:10 (20,786)
Fettroll, Zak 3:55:36 (9,636)
Few, Andrew D 4:36:04 (20,495)
Few, Gregory Mark 4:41:25 (21,870)
Few, Richard 4:36:31 (20,611)
Fewings, Tom Bernard 3:40:27 (6,225)
Fewster, Thomas G 2:43:59 (309)
Fewtrell, Nicholas John 5:28:46 (31,123)
Fiddis, Richard William 3:58:31 (10,560)
Fidler, Nick 3:07:37 (1,669)
Fiel, Goncalo 4:17:55 (15,550)
Field, Andrew 4:07:38 (12,867)
Field, David A 5:09:08 (28,075)
Field, Lee Gary 6:25:11 (35,319)
Field, Peter 4:53:54 (25,022)
Field, Robert M 3:29:53 (4,393)
Field, Robert Owen 7:59:23 (36,587)
Field, Simon J 3:31:36 (4,683)
Field, William Philip 4:38:01 (20,990)
Fielden, Simon 3:30:07 (4,434)
Fielder, David James 5:25:26 (30,686)
Fielder, Justin 3:56:32 (9,944)
Fields, Daniel 4:20:33 (16,275)
Fieldson, Peter C 3:52:37 (8,826)
Fiennes, Michael 5:58:54 (33,985)
Fiford, Carl 3:00:33 (1,178)
Figgins, William Alan 4:44:04 (22,523)
Filby, Raymond 3:58:45 (10,644)
Filby, Stefan Peter 4:53:06 (24,822)
Filet, Vincent 3:38:00 (5,761)
Filkin, Matthew 4:26:25 (17,930)
Fillingham, Martin John 4:01:58 (11,482)
Fillion, Jean-Luc 3:39:16 (5,996)
Fillon, Nicolas 3:04:55 (1,455)
Filmer, Glenn Richard 4:34:16 (20,062)
Filmer, Graham 4:16:47 (15,244)
Finan, Richard Christopher 4:25:34 (17,681)
Finch, Brian Ashley 4:00:30 (11,116)
Finch, David 4:49:03 (23,813)
Finch, Howard John 4:56:43 (25,697)
Finch, John William 4:54:10 (25,083)
Finch, Matt 4:15:12 (14,834)
Finch, Oliver 4:35:56 (20,461)
Finch, Stephen Paul 3:41:39 (6,447)
Finden, John 3:50:50 (8,386)
Findlay, Alexander D 5:18:55 (29,688)
Findlay, Gordon 2:54:08 (677)
Findlay, Gordon Cameron 5:56:05 (33,794)
Findlay, Russell 5:50:26 (33,377)
Findley, Michael Anthony 4:24:22 (17,346)
Fine, Jon 4:06:30 (12,575)
Finill, Chris T 2:52:05 (571)
Finlay, Matthew 3:59:32 (10,870)
Finlay, Michael James 3:43:50 (6,842)
Finlay, Richard John 4:33:33 (19,867)
Finn, Allan G 4:42:59 (22,255)
Finn, Andrew M 2:58:25 (998)
Finn, Conor 5:06:52 (27,698)
Finn, Craig 3:25:39 (3,673)
Finn, James Alexander 3:56:33 (9,948)
Finn, Mark David 4:11:49 (13,936)
Finn, Peter James 3:51:17 (8,490)
Finn, Sean 3:10:42 (1,962)
Finnegan, Angus John 4:51:12 (24,351)
Finnerty, Andrew Thomas David 4:34:03 (20,005)
Finney, Colin J 3:21:47 (3,170)
Finney, John R 4:20:26 (16,244)
Fiore, Dominic P 3:58:25 (10,532)
Firetto, Andrew John 3:51:16 (8,488)
Firkins, Jonathan Graham 5:29:30 (31,222)
Firmstone, Michael J 3:31:08 (4,600)
Firn, Stephen 4:35:46 (20,410)
Firouzi, Mazeyar 2:38:20 (169)
Firth, Adrian 4:49:15 (23,865)
Firth, Andy 5:50:22 (33,371)
Firth, David Allan 5:20:04 (29,858)
Firth, David J 3:16:32 (2,618)
Firth, Edward 4:21:57 (16,688)
Firth, Mike 4:15:48 (14,979)
Fischer, Jez 4:48:15 (23,599)
Fischer, Stephan 3:54:52 (9,441)
Fischer, Tristan 3:27:08 (3,892)
Fish, Ben 2:33:06 (91)
Fish, Bradley David 5:13:35 (28,853)
Fish, Jonathan P 3:14:19 (2,360)
Fishburn, James 3:07:18 (1,634)
Fisher, Adrian Stuart 4:19:58 (16,096)
Fisher, Antony Gordon 5:00:52 (26,623)
Fisher, Ben 4:04:11 (12,006)
Fisher, Ben 4:46:32 (23,175)
Fisher, David 4:16:28 (15,157)
Fisher, David Peter 4:14:13 (14,573)
Fisher, David Ronald 4:35:15 (20,283)
Fisher, Edward John 4:02:51 (11,688)
Fisher, Jerry 3:39:27 (6,033)
Fisher, John Dennis 4:05:50 (12,418)
Fisher, Keith 6:21:49 (35,192)
Fisher, Lee 3:56:00 (9,787)
Fisher, Mark 4:10:23 (13,564)
Fisher, Mark 5:17:17 (29,435)
Fisher, Martyn 3:29:36 (4,342)
Fisher, Matt 4:04:42 (12,129)
Fisher, Paul 4:06:55 (12,689)
Fisher, Paul 5:06:12 (27,567)
Fisher, Peter 4:07:38 (12,867)
Fisher, Robert Peter 3:57:04 (10,122)
Fisher, Scott E 3:53:54 (9,183)
Fisher, Steve Peter 4:06:30 (12,575)
Fisher, Stuart 4:16:17 (15,099)
Fisher, Tom 4:50:12 (24,094)
Fisher, Wayne 4:44:03 (22,516)
Fisher,, Anthony, 4:08:40 (13,131)
Fishwick, Ian Robert 3:34:01 (5,061)
Fishwick, Matthew Paul 5:26:16 (30,813)
Fisk, Luke Daniel 4:55:32 (25,414)
Fisk, Nicholas 5:41:12 (32,510)
Fissenden, John 4:20:56 (16,394)
Fitch, Andrew 3:26:12 (3,771)
Fitch, Ian Robert 4:29:42 (18,878)
Fitchett, Ian 3:29:07 (4,254)

Fitchett, Simon 5:44:30 (32,814)
Fitsakis, Yiannis 2:52:06 (572)
Fitter, Carl 3:19:57 (2,959)
Fitzell, John 4:16:46 (15,239)
Fitzgerald, Aaron 3:31:35 (4,679)
Fitzgerald, Darren Paul 5:56:54 (33,859)
Fitzgerald, Dean Robert 4:50:50 (24,250)
Fitzgerald, Desmond 4:28:44 (18,587)
Fitzgerald, Jack Jerome Louis 3:58:05 (10,407)
Fitzgerald, John 4:05:57 (12,445)
Fitzgerald, Kieren 5:17:23 (29,457)
Fitzgerald, Liam 4:37:22 (20,836)
Fitzgerald, Mark 4:57:56 (25,953)
Fitzgerald, Patrick J 2:57:56 (951)
Fitzjohn, Tom 3:51:26 (8,524)
Fitzmaurice, James Patrick 4:27:21 (18,195)
Fitzmaurice, Jon-Paul 4:41:10 (21,815)
Fitzpatrick, Adam Sebastian 4:18:01 (15,582)
Fitzpatrick, Brendon Anthony 3:19:41 (2,935)
Fitzpatrick, David 4:53:32 (24,928)
Fitzpatrick, Dean 3:55:22 (9,587)
Fitzpatrick, Gary Eugene 5:04:41 (27,315)
Fitzpatrick, Peter G 4:27:17 (18,174)
Fitzsimmons, Luke 3:32:35 (4,823)
Fitzwalter, Keith Graham 5:17:44 (29,504)
Fiveash, Dean 4:54:39 (25,219)
Fjeld-Olsen, Per 5:59:35 (34,023)
Flack, Kevin Richard 4:20:44 (16,347)
Flade, Peter 4:21:13 (16,465)
Flaherty, Michael A 3:18:33 (2,825)
Flamarique, Ignacio 3:10:08 (1,918)
Flanagan, Desmond 4:15:25 (14,889)
Flanagan, Tony 2:49:23 (464)
Flashman, Martin 4:40:54 (21,743)
Flatt, Darren John 3:50:27 (8,297)
Flatt, Mark Alexander 4:32:05 (19,453)
Flavell, Mike 3:35:53 (5,395)
Fleckney, Mark Andrew 4:18:42 (15,774)
Fleet, Matthew J 4:03:49 (11,928)
Fleming, Andrew R 3:41:51 (6,491)
Fleming, Christopher J 4:45:54 (22,999)
Fleming, Malcolm 4:12:36 (14,127)
Fleming, Nathan Robert 5:36:00 (31,997)
Fleming, Peter J 3:48:03 (7,750)
Flemmings, Richard 3:40:18 (6,197)
Fletcher, Brett Michael 4:34:58 (20,226)
Fletcher, Chris D 2:59:04 (1,060)
Fletcher, Dan 4:17:06 (15,321)
Fletcher, Eddie 3:23:37 (3,379)
Fletcher, Gary John 3:52:16 (8,729)
Fletcher, Gavin Peter 4:07:16 (12,769)
Fletcher, Graham W 5:23:03 (30,315)
Fletcher, James William 3:35:50 (5,380)
Fletcher, John Stephen 3:36:47 (5,520)
Fletcher, Jonathan Peter 3:29:08 (4,259)
Fletcher, Kevin 4:44:52 (22,734)
Fletcher, Matthew John 3:44:55 (7,082)
Fletcher, Michael James 3:28:07 (4,077)
Fletcher, Paul David 3:35:00 (5,249)
Fletcher, Richard 4:04:13 (12,012)
Fletcher, Robert William 4:37:32 (20,891)
Fletcher, Robin 3:35:03 (5,259)
Flick, Anthony 3:34:25 (5,140)
Flick, Darren James 4:06:29 (12,569)
Flight, Paul 3:30:48 (4,548)
Flint, Harry 7:16:00 (36,371)
Flint, Paul Andrew 4:55:55 (25,518)
Flint, Steve Peter 4:21:22 (16,513)
Flint, Thomas David 4:15:24 (14,886)
Flitcroft, Robert Andrew 4:58:46 (26,159)
Flitney, Neil 4:40:26 (21,623)
Flitton, Alan G 3:50:47 (8,378)
Flockhart, Kevin Robert 5:34:44 (31,853)
Flood, Brian 4:01:42 (11,409)
Flood, James C 2:35:15 (116)
Flood, John 3:15:40 (2,519)
Flood, Seamus Slowlydoesit 4:03:12 (11,777)
Florent, Ajas 4:10:24 (13,568)
Floureux, Alain 4:44:48 (22,721)
Flower, Ed 5:31:34 (31,482)
Flower, Kevin 3:19:42 (2,937)
Flowers, Mike 3:28:13 (4,096)
Flowers, Neil 4:50:44 (24,219)
Fluege, Michael 3:23:42 (3,394)
Flynn, David 5:01:30 (26,754)
Flynn, John 5:28:25 (31,077)
Flynn, John R 4:23:47 (17,187)
Flynn, Kevin 4:54:59 (25,302)
Flynn, Liam J 4:43:06 (22,282)
Flynn, Patrick John 4:39:24 (21,353)
Flynn, Sean Thomas 3:50:37 (8,338)
Flynn, Stuart 5:42:40 (32,647)
Flynn, Stuart David 6:15:19 (34,901)
Foat, John Robert, Frederick 4:47:37 (23,444)
Foat, Michael 5:52:44 (33,556)
Foden, Adam Nicholas Baron 3:51:05 (8,445)
Fodor, Carl 4:35:30 (20,344)
Fogarty, Martino E 4:23:24 (17,080)
Fogg, Brian 5:51:16 (33,446)
Fohetaha, David 5:20:51 (29,985)
Folaranmi, Eniola 5:14:52 (29,048)
Foley, Danny 4:36:40 (20,651)
Foley, David James 4:03:26 (11,828)
Foley, David Owen 5:13:46 (28,884)
Foley, Gary Martin 4:54:36 (25,204)
Foley, Jack 5:19:25 (29,766)
Foley, William 3:59:39 (10,903)
Folger, Sam 4:18:03 (15,597)
Folkman, David 3:25:29 (3,645)
Folliard, Robin James 4:33:26 (19,836)
Fontaine, Christophe 4:05:44 (12,386)
Fontaine, Olivier 4:07:55 (12,933)
Fontana, Biagio 4:12:39 (14,139)
Fontana, Sergio 3:30:39 (4,518)
Foo, Qi Chao 4:18:07 (15,614)
Fooks-Bale, James 2:56:44 (844)
Foord, Matthew 3:24:32 (3,514)
Foote, Andy L 7:04:03 (36,246)
Foote, Simon John 4:12:35 (14,120)
Forber, Gareth Robert 7:14:07 (36,354)
Forbes, Jerry 5:23:10 (30,333)
Forbes, Jonathan 3:44:56 (7,085)
Forbes, Steve W 3:02:02 (1,261)
Forbes, Will 3:09:09 (1,820)
Ford, Benjamin Thomas 4:19:35 (15,990)
Ford, Brian C 3:27:26 (3,950)
Ford, Chris 3:24:40 (3,533)
Ford, Chris Justin 3:55:40 (9,668)
Ford, David 5:57:41 (33,913)
Ford, David John 5:40:03 (32,394)
Ford, Gary 5:12:27 (28,643)
Ford, Gavin 4:26:13 (17,877)
Ford, John 4:44:43 (22,701)
Ford, Kirk J 3:56:35 (9,955)
Ford, Leigh Stephen 6:08:43 (34,598)
Ford, Martin C 3:10:50 (1,975)
Ford, Neal 6:03:54 (34,315)
Ford, Peter 7:21:51 (36,417)
Ford, Simon 3:54:26 (9,312)
Ford, Tony 4:38:09 (21,016)
Ford, William John Allen 3:37:26 (5,642)
Forde, Douglas Stuart 5:01:35 (26,772)
Forde, Ian 5:39:55 (32,381)
Forde, James 3:51:23 (8,512)
Forde, Matt 6:06:33 (34,483)
Fordham, David I 4:16:55 (15,275)
Fordham, Michael Roy 5:19:18 (29,745)
Fordyce, Bruce 3:20:23 (3,002)
Foreman, Ian 3:12:27 (2,131)
Foreman, Peter S 3:49:42 (8,145)
Foreman, Timothy F 4:14:26 (14,626)
Foreman, Timothy James 3:12:20 (2,114)
Fores, Shaun 3:18:13 (2,797)
Forest, Philippe 3:43:09 (6,723)
Forey, Gerald 3:26:35 (3,814)
Forey, Martin C 6:05:58 (34,450)
Forey, Simon 5:09:42 (28,180)
Forgan, Jamie 5:10:24 (28,309)
Formisano, Fabio 3:15:50 (2,530)
Formosa, Alan 4:39:41 (21,432)
Forni, Raffaele 3:52:44 (8,851)
Forni, Ruggero 2:53:09 (621)
Forrer, Benjamin David 5:13:42 (28,871)
Forrest, Duncan James 4:25:44 (17,732)
Forrest, Stephen A 4:15:43 (14,958)
Forrester, Bob 4:15:35 (14,924)
Forrester, Ken 5:22:06 (30,163)
Forrester, Paul 5:56:07 (33,797)
Forrester, Peter J 4:31:19 (19,295)
Forrester, Thomas 3:17:33 (2,720)
Forristall, James 5:23:42 (30,426)
Forry, Sean William 3:58:09 (10,435)
Forsbrook, Russell M 3:03:55 (1,383)
Forsgren, Ivan 4:49:31 (23,911)
Forster, Ged 4:02:39 (11,638)
Forsyth, Mark 3:51:58 (8,649)
Forsyth, Shaun Robert 4:44:02 (22,511)
Forsythe, Alex 3:55:21 (9,582)
Forsythe, Michael 4:21:01 (16,420)
Forte, Philip 3:33:26 (4,958)
Foskett, Graham P 4:08:28 (13,069)
Foskett, Jamie 4:23:41 (17,151)
Foskett, Robert 4:52:07 (24,578)
Foskett, Samuel 4:21:21 (16,506)
Foss, John 3:10:57 (1,988)
Foss, Neil 3:59:20 (10,818)
Fossett, James J 3:55:51 (9,733)
Foster, Andrew 3:51:32 (8,544)
Foster, Andrew 3:53:42 (9,122)
Foster, Chris 5:25:02 (30,630)
Foster, David 5:11:22 (28,460)
Foster, David Ian 3:50:57 (8,411)
Foster, Harry Richard 4:30:22 (19,058)
Foster, James 4:29:32 (18,817)
Foster, James William 3:13:46 (2,292)
Foster, John 3:29:46 (4,372)
Foster, John Martin 4:08:20 (13,036)
Foster, Lee Stephen 4:48:14 (23,593)
Foster, Len J 3:53:23 (9,024)
Foster, Leon 2:54:28 (696)
Foster, Mark John 4:20:34 (16,281)
Foster, Michael Francis 3:58:18 (10,491)
Foster, Nick J D 3:28:50 (4,194)
Foster, Paul 3:58:16 (10,478)
Foster, Paul C 3:40:11 (6,181)
Foster, Paul R 6:16:15 (34,930)
Foster, Philip A 2:39:42 (190)
Foster, Robert 4:47:01 (23,315)
Foster, Stephen John 4:11:31 (13,852)
Foster, Steven 4:14:10 (14,560)
Foster, Steven James 3:35:47 (5,374)
Foster, Steven Leonard 5:40:00 (32,389)
Foster, Tim 4:25:15 (17,586)
Foster, Vernon 4:02:27 (11,595)
Foucher, Alain 3:44:23 (6,964)
Fouga, Alexandre 2:57:33 (908)
Foulkes, John S 4:29:17 (18,752)
Foulsham, Mark Damian Stuart 3:58:21 (10,512)
Fountain, Andy 4:33:34 (19,877)
Fouquet, Denis 4:26:54 (18,049)
Fouracres, Andrew Mark 3:50:16 (8,264)
Fourie, Clifford Louis 5:35:27 (31,921)
Fourie, Jon-Pierre Frederick 4:57:09 (25,791)
Fourie, Louis 3:50:51 (8,390)
Fournil, Gilles 4:37:16 (20,806)
Fourny, Eric 4:27:45 (18,299)
Foustok, Mohamed Naji 3:47:24 (7,620)
Fowell, Mark A 2:57:24 (889)
Fowle, Gary 4:14:28 (14,637)
Fowler, Andy James 3:08:29 (1,752)
Fowler, Anthony J 3:47:50 (7,704)
Fowler, Ben Andrew 4:16:53 (15,266)
Fowler, Dean Martin 5:25:48 (30,754)
Fowler, Greg 4:21:07 (16,443)
Fowler, Ian J 3:05:29 (1,495)
Fowler, James R 3:18:09 (2,787)
Fowler, Keith 3:56:49 (10,036)
Fowler, Kelvin E 3:08:32 (1,760)
Fowler, Martin G 3:41:24 (6,405)
Fowler, Matthew C 3:24:57 (3,572)
Fowler, Matthew D 2:44:38 (324)
Fowler, Nicholas Paul David 3:35:33 (5,336)
Fowler, Richard John 3:46:28 (7,412)
Fowler, Stephen P 4:18:22 (15,678)
Fowler, Tom 3:14:30 (2,383)
Fox, Andrew David 4:58:33 (26,104)
Fox, Andrew R 4:10:05 (13,491)
Fox, Barrie Reginald 3:35:16 (5,282)
Fox, Brian T 3:35:08 (5,263)

Gallagher, Charles Michael 4:54:15 (25,114)
Gallagher, Gareth 3:47:44 (7,688)
Gallagher, Gary 3:48:28 (7,837)
Gallagher, John 4:52:54 (24,777)
Gallagher, John Michael 5:46:27 (33,006)
Gallagher, Martin 4:43:43 (22,423)
Gallagher, Michael A 2:49:02 (444)
Gallagher, Neil Alan William 4:57:37 (25,884)
Gallagher, Nicholas T 3:26:47 (3,845)
Gallagher, Patrick J 2:59:20 (1,087)
Gallagher, Peter Anthony 4:32:49 (19,635)
Gallagher, Richard G 3:44:50 (7,062)
Gallagher, Ryan C 3:14:43 (2,409)
Gallagher, Sean Francis 4:17:51 (15,533)
Gallen, Gerry 6:53:33 (36,077)
Galley, André G 3:38:26 (5,835)
Galley, Andrew J 4:37:52 (20,959)
Galley, David 3:59:03 (10,733)
Galliano, Gianfranco 4:53:18 (24,876)
Gallimore, Stuart 4:44:45 (22,712)
Gallivan, John Francis 7:16:55 (36,378)
Gallo, Simon James 6:36:37 (35,690)
Galloway, Alan Paul 4:54:46 (25,252)
Galloway, Allan 4:30:00 (18,977)
Galloway, Paul R 4:19:30 (15,973)
Gallyer-Barnett, Michael 3:58:47 (10,652)
Galpin, John T. 4:16:00 (15,026)
Galpin, Robert J 3:56:55 (10,063)
Galsworthy, David P. 3:46:12 (7,353)
Galvin, Barry 4:33:13 (19,772)
Galvin, Brian Thomas 5:28:19 (31,066)
Galvin, Justin 4:46:22 (23,141)
Gamble, Ben P 2:25:17 (38)
Gamble, Christopher 4:33:40 (19,910)
Gamble, Philip 4:07:38 (12,867)
Gambs, Christopher D 3:30:07 (4,434)
Game, Barry 4:33:16 (19,791)
Game, Kevin J 2:49:56 (483)
Game, Paul J 3:47:54 (7,717)
Gami, Manji 4:40:51 (21,737)
Gammage, Brian 3:56:18 (9,871)
Gammon, Robert J 3:39:11 (5,979)
Gammon, Rod 4:24:08 (17,268)
Gammon, Trevor 5:58:37 (33,970)
Gammon, Vincent John 6:35:17 (35,658)
Gamper, Roger 4:54:03 (25,061)
Gander, Ashley Russell 4:54:25 (25,164)
Gander, Stuart James 4:59:22 (26,301)
Gandhi, Achal 5:04:08 (27,216)
Gandon, Peter 4:28:02 (18,375)
Gangar, Sunil 5:30:50 (31,397)
Ganguly, Stephen 4:52:03 (24,558)
Gann, John C. 4:46:15 (23,109)
Gant, Matthew J 3:34:29 (5,149)
Ganthi, Kiran Kumar R 4:56:41 (25,689)
Garaway, Danny Clive 4:22:32 (16,857)
Garbett, Adrian 5:08:52 (28,025)
Garbharran, Dinesh 3:39:58 (6,137)
Garbutt, Chris 6:36:57 (35,698)
Garbutt, Rob 3:42:08 (6,535)
Garcha, Jas 4:08:20 (13,036)
Garcha, Parvinder 6:12:30 (34,781)
Garcha, Sukhdip Singh 5:11:05 (28,418)
Garcia, Andy 5:04:12 (27,230)
Garcia, Benjamin 4:28:16 (18,443)
Garcia, Higinio 2:58:37 (1,014)
Garcia, José Luis 3:58:11 (10,449)
Garcia, Julian 3:37:28 (5,652)
Garcia, Marc 4:21:27 (16,535)
Garcia, Rolan 4:45:06 (22,799)
Garcia Juanino, Jorge 2:57:44 (935)
Garcia Teruel, David 2:49:28 (467)
Garcia-Amero, Hector 3:55:17 (9,556)
Garcka, David Eric Stephen 4:23:41 (17,151)
Garden, Greg 3:46:53 (7,505)
Gardener, Lee 4:01:26 (11,353)
Gardiner, Graham 4:57:12 (25,804)
Gardiner, John P 4:48:14 (23,593)
Gardiner, Mark 5:57:39 (33,912)
Gardiner, Rob 4:35:58 (20,468)
Gardiner, Simon 4:22:05 (16,730)
Gardiner, Tim James 4:12:24 (14,068)
Gardner, Barry 3:38:46 (5,902)
Gardner, Bruce Christopher 4:20:24 (16,232)
Gardner, Craig Andrew 3:29:27 (4,313)
Gardner, Damian Christopher 6:23:42 (35,267)
Gardner, David 4:07:50 (12,912)
Gardner, David Taylor 4:28:55 (18,650)
Gardner, Des 4:48:15 (23,599)
Gardner, Giles 4:24:15 (17,302)
Gardner, Jamie D 5:35:55 (31,984)
Gardner, Jason 3:52:12 (8,706)
Gardner, Jeremy 4:00:43 (11,176)
Gardner, Joe S 3:25:40 (3,681)
Gardner, John A 5:20:32 (29,933)
Gardner, Joshua C. 4:49:36 (23,943)
Gardner, Keith D 4:29:02 (18,697)
Gardner, Kevin 4:16:17 (15,099)
Gardner, Leighton J 3:26:27 (3,798)
Gardner, Mark 5:49:38 (33,301)
Gardner, Mark Andrew 5:10:40 (28,359)
Gardner, Patrick, ... 3:35:58 (5,407)
Gardner, Paul 4:54:30 (25,179)
Gardner, Paul Antony 3:45:30 (7,207)
Gardner, Tony 3:37:46 (5,720)
Gardner, Wayne Andrew 3:12:26 (2,129)
Garfield, Paul 3:36:32 (5,484)
Gargaro, Steven 4:34:23 (20,091)
Gargaro, Vincent 6:16:42 (34,961)
Gargett, Matthew Thomas 4:30:40 (19,139)
Garland, George W 5:09:04 (28,058)
Garland, Michael Christopher 3:31:01 (4,579)
Garland, Nick 3:40:05 (6,163)
Garlick, Paul 4:03:34 (11,864)
Garlick, Steven G. 4:47:09 (23,334)
Garlington, Ian James 4:59:37 (26,367)
Garman, John 4:09:07 (13,234)
Garmeson, Paul 3:39:49 (6,106)
Garner, Alex 3:42:58 (6,689)
Garner, Andrew C 5:00:01 (26,457)
Garner, Daren 4:07:14 (12,759)
Garner, James Adam 5:20:23 (29,897)
Garner, John Anthony 4:39:37 (21,418)
Garner, Mark John 6:03:35 (34,294)
Garner, Neil Edward 5:36:29 (32,055)
Garner, Oliver David Sebastian 4:44:13 (22,568)
Garner, Paul David 3:28:18 (4,103)
Garner, Steven 4:20:10 (16,154)
Garner, Victor Douglas 3:24:13 (3,471)
Garoppo, Gilles 4:14:06 (14,533)
Garran, Tim 5:02:11 (26,886)
Garrard, Boyd Stuart 4:09:09 (13,240)
Garrard, Phil 4:48:48 (23,747)
Garratt, Paul Anthony 5:35:46 (31,964)
Garratt, Paul Thomas 4:25:30 (17,661)
Garratty, Lee James 4:57:03 (25,770)
Garrelts, Gerald 4:12:32 (14,109)
Garrett, Christopher John 5:45:33 (32,915)
Garrett, Darren 6:25:40 (35,338)
Garrett, David R 4:21:20 (16,500)
Garrett, Lloyd 3:45:24 (7,188)
Garrett, Mark 3:23:15 (3,332)
Garrett, Philip Raymond 7:06:33 (36,271)
Garrett, Rupert 4:41:36 (21,923)
Garrido, Jean-François 3:14:35 (2,396)
Garrigan, Liam 4:13:49 (14,460)
Garrity, Dan 6:17:16 (34,998)
Garrod, James 4:34:14 (20,054)
Garrod, Leslie 4:00:15 (11,044)
Garrod, Wayne 5:36:46 (32,078)
Garrood, Steve 4:23:28 (17,095)
Garry, Dean M 4:05:18 (12,283)
Garry, Tony James 5:32:04 (31,543)
Garston, Chris 4:55:14 (25,367)
Garteiz-Gogeascoa, Asis 4:17:35 (15,464)
Garth, Crispian 4:18:12 (15,629)
Garthwaite, Jonathan 4:48:08 (23,577)
Gartland, Pat Francis 4:43:51 (22,464)
Gartshore, Andrew 3:39:53 (6,122)
Garvey, Daniel 4:07:01 (12,714)
Garvey, Eoin Thomas 3:40:18 (6,197)
Garvey, Stephen 3:10:50 (1,975)
Garzarolli, Christian Philip 4:59:47 (26,403)
Gaschler, Fredy 3:55:07 (9,508)
Gascoigne, Ian Vaughan 4:39:02 (21,266)
Gascoigne, Mike 4:46:26 (23,155)
Gascoigne-Pees, Edward Max 5:12:55 (28,726)
Gash, Simon William 4:17:51 (15,533)
Gaskell, David 5:55:34 (33,759)
Gaskell, Harry 4:13:27 (14,355)
Gaskell, Paul 3:46:23 (7,394)
Gaskell, Tim 3:54:36 (9,354)
Gasson, Daniel Scott 5:17:00 (29,389)
Gatenby, Mark 4:24:00 (17,236)
Gater, Andy Arthur 4:22:58 (16,977)
Gates, Daniel 5:09:15 (28,092)
Gates, Justin R 4:34:29 (20,119)
Gates, Tim James 3:43:22 (6,751)
Gatfield, Simon 6:00:01 (34,065)
Gath, Daniel 4:28:03 (18,379)
Gath, Matthew James 4:29:42 (18,878)
Gatrell, Adam 4:47:52 (23,514)
Gattepaille, Jacques 4:40:48 (21,721)
Gatward, Steve 5:28:23 (31,073)
Gauci, Oliver 4:34:11 (20,037)
Gaudinat, Jean Paul 3:27:19 (3,924)
Gaudry, Christophe 3:12:22 (2,119)
Gaukroger, Craig 5:12:40 (28,677)
Gauld, Stephen Gordon 4:03:29 (11,838)
Gaulder, Nicholas Ralph 3:40:07 (6,171)
Gaulon, Philippe 3:59:51 (10,952)
Gaunt, Martin 2:47:13 (393)
Gaunt, Stephen J 4:48:45 (23,734)
Gaut, Matthew James 3:50:55 (8,404)
Gautelier, Laurent 3:18:50 (2,857)
Gautier, Bruno 3:45:04 (7,108)
Gautier, Jacques 4:10:32 (13,600)
Gautier, Oudine 3:30:03 (4,428)
Gavin, Oliver 2:54:19 (687)
Gavriani, Paul 3:53:19 (9,004)
Gawler, Patrick A 5:21:57 (30,136)
Gay, Daniel R 2:41:53 (249)
Gay, Richard 3:29:31 (4,325)
Gay, Russel 4:06:20 (12,534)
Gayle, Richard 5:09:49 (28,201)
Gaze, Anthony Robert 5:04:55 (27,351)
Gazeley, Neil A 4:40:16 (21,565)
Gazzard, Michael 5:07:27 (27,799)
Gazzini, Graziano 4:05:57 (12,445)
Gazzotti, Corrado 4:42:59 (22,255)
Geake, Andrew James 3:29:18 (4,289)
Gear, Allan R 4:47:39 (23,455)
Gear, Iain Michael 4:39:13 (21,317)
Gear, Jason Alan Sumner 5:03:26 (27,090)
Gear, Martin James 3:50:20 (8,275)
Gearing, Daniel L 3:34:19 (5,118)
Geary, Robert David 4:55:04 (25,326)
Gebhard-Clark, Carl 5:24:37 (30,570)
Gebler, Marc 4:53:52 (25,009)
Geckler, Soeren 4:12:06 (14,008)
Gedaly, Roberto 4:53:26 (24,901)
Geddes, Euan G 2:54:08 (677)
Geddes, Ian James 4:20:11 (16,157)
Geddes, Readford R 5:41:16 (32,515)
Gedge, Duncan James 3:57:24 (10,202)
Gee, Harry 3:09:55 (1,900)
Gee, Kevin William 3:34:55 (5,234)
Gee, Matthew 3:51:45 (8,597)
Gee, Patrick 5:31:14 (31,436)
Gee, Paul 4:22:46 (16,928)
Gee, Raymond L 4:53:01 (24,800)
Gee, Ross 4:39:37 (21,418)
Gee, Stuart 4:30:47 (19,170)
Geen, Wayne 4:11:11 (13,764)
Geere, Stephen 4:09:49 (13,424)
Geldenhuys, Mattheus Lourens 5:02:52 (27,000)
Geldsetzer, Klaus 3:24:19 (3,488)
Geleit, Ryan James 4:41:38 (21,930)
Gelister, Benjamin 5:47:10 (33,068)
Gelson, William 4:31:02 (19,226)
Geneletti, Francesco 3:53:45 (9,140)
Genevet, Bruno 3:18:10 (2,791)
Genge, Bernard J 3:17:31 (2,714)
Genovesi, Athos 3:55:58 (9,772)
Gent, Chris 4:54:54 (25,286)
Gentle, Christopher R 3:13:51 (2,300)
Gentric, Didier 3:30:04 (4,429)
Gentry, Ian 7:15:20 (36,360)
George, Andrew R 5:23:16 (30,349)

George, Christopher 4:00:14 (11,041)
George, James 5:40:50 (32,460)
George, Jason 3:41:29 (6,419)
George, Mark 3:25:10 (3,604)
George, Martin J 3:10:40 (1,959)
George, Michael 4:58:41 (26,134)
George, Phillip M 2:41:46 (248)
George, Richard 3:33:38 (4,994)
George, Richard 3:50:31 (8,317)
George, Simon 3:48:05 (7,754)
George, Steven Scott 4:39:31 (21,391)
Georgeson, Thomas 3:45:52 (7,285)
Georgiou, Marios A 3:34:59 (5,245)
Georgiou, Matthew Joseph Albert. 4:48:52 (23,765)
Gerald, Rupert 3:20:57 (3,079)
Germain, Denis 3:59:24 (10,839)
Germain, Matthew Paul 3:44:30 (6,987)
Gerrard, Timothy 3:40:08 (6,175)
Gerrish, Willoughby John 3:47:44 (7,688)
Gersdorff, Charles 3:40:03 (6,157)
Gersdorff, Frederic 3:34:15 (5,104)
Gershfield, Oliver 4:06:00 (12,456)
Gertler, Christoph 3:12:45 (2,161)
Gethin, Martin Peter 4:10:37 (13,620)
Gethin, Steven John 4:10:38 (13,625)
Gething Lewis, Neale R 4:09:35 (13,365)
Getty, Christopher 4:05:54 (12,434)
Getty, Simon P 3:55:10 (9,520)
Gharib, Jaouad 2:06:55 (3)
Ghauri, Carlos 5:10:10 (28,270)
Ghebreindiras, Samson T 4:09:00 (13,213)
Ghelfi, André N 3:56:09 (9,822)
Ghezzi, Giampiero 3:57:00 (10,089)
Ghomshei, Amir 5:36:57 (32,094)
Ghysel, Walter 4:07:01 (12,714)
Giachetti, Roberto 4:14:26 (14,626)
Giacomini, Claudio 5:48:27 (33,189)
Giancristofano, Dario Jorge 3:49:59 (8,210)
Gibb, Scott Forbes 4:11:19 (13,796)
Gibb, Stephen 3:46:09 (7,345)
Gibben, John G 6:23:58 (35,276)
Gibbens, Richard 3:46:22 (7,387)
Gibbins, Alex N 2:36:00 (127)
Gibbon, Adam C 2:59:29 (1,107)
Gibbon, Adrian Christopher 3:58:07 (10,423)
Gibbons, Andrew 4:15:51 (14,987)
Gibbons, Gary Michael 4:58:23 (26,061)
Gibbons, Pat G 4:23:42 (17,156)
Gibbons, Robert Anthony 4:37:28 (20,870)
Gibbons, Stephen 2:57:35 (913)
Gibbons, Thomas E 3:36:54 (5,545)
Gibbons, Tom W 3:08:42 (1,783)
Gibbs, Aran Edward 3:45:42 (7,245)
Gibbs, Colin M 6:58:14 (36,158)
Gibbs, Graham 4:24:00 (17,236)
Gibbs, Jonathan 4:17:04 (15,311)
Gibbs, Mark A 5:31:27 (31,472)
Gibbs, Matthew James 5:20:36 (29,946)
Gibbs, Richard 5:41:26 (32,526)
Gibbs, Stephen P 2:53:00 (618)
Gibbs, Tony S 4:29:15 (18,743)
Gibert, Guillaume 5:38:06 (32,218)
Gibier, Julien 2:44:45 (332)
Giblin, John F 4:50:43 (24,211)
Gibson, Brian 6:02:15 (34,202)
Gibson, Christopher J 4:39:08 (21,291)
Gibson, David 3:18:21 (2,810)
Gibson, David 3:59:11 (10,771)
Gibson, Ewan D 4:01:51 (11,461)
Gibson, Giles 4:11:54 (13,959)
Gibson, James Alexander 4:14:19 (14,597)
Gibson, Jeremy John 4:19:28 (15,963)
Gibson, Joe Derek 3:53:25 (9,033)
Gibson, John Derek 4:28:10 (18,406)
Gibson, Jonathan Michael 4:02:23 (11,575)
Gibson, Kevin D 4:25:22 (17,625)
Gibson, Peter R 4:49:08 (23,835)
Gibson, Richard 3:47:20 (7,605)
Gibson, Richard J 3:12:58 (2,186)
Gibson, Stuart W 5:06:31 (27,628)
Gibson, William J 3:29:15 (4,280)
Giddens, Wayne 3:37:10 (5,592)
Giddings, Steven Martin 6:07:13 (34,520)
Gidman, Alan 4:28:55 (18,650)
Gierjatowicz, Patryk D 2:40:20 (206)
Giffen, Darren 5:04:42 (27,321)
Gifford, Alan P 4:04:49 (12,157)
Gigg, Terry John 5:44:42 (32,839)
Giggs, Ian 3:25:03 (3,587)
Giglietti, Simone 2:47:08 (392)
Gilbank, Mark 4:56:38 (25,673)
Gilbank, Paul 4:18:23 (15,686)
Gilbert, David 4:15:37 (14,929)
Gilbert, John J 2:27:27 (50)
Gilbert, Jon 4:57:34 (25,872)
Gilbert, Jonathan PW 4:14:45 (14,726)
Gilbert, Justin Hamilton 4:33:00 (19,698)
Gilbert, Kevin Martin 3:28:21 (4,116)
Gilbert, Matt 4:50:25 (24,146)
Gilbert, Michael A 5:30:12 (31,316)
Gilbert, Richard 4:07:37 (12,860)
Gilbert, Richard Thomas 4:31:35 (19,347)
Gilbert, Robert John 4:17:24 (15,405)
Gilbert, Simon M 3:04:04 (1,399)
Gilbert, Tony 3:18:17 (2,805)
Gilberthorpe, Tom George 3:53:27 (9,039)
Gilbery, Matthew 5:54:47 (33,694)
Gilbody, Daniel 5:04:02 (27,196)
Gilchrist, Rob Kennedy 3:34:29 (5,149)
Gilchrist, Tyrone 5:49:21 (33,264)
Gilder, Colin 4:44:23 (22,609)
Gilderdale, Philip H 6:14:50 (34,879)
Giles, Alan 5:27:02 (30,910)
Giles, Austin Anthony 5:19:18 (29,745)
Giles, Danny J 4:33:47 (19,942)
Giles, Ian 3:55:28 (9,606)
Giles, Ian R 2:57:46 (938)
Giles, Martin R 2:48:13 (422)
Gilfillan, Dean Anthony 3:08:07 (1,711)
Gilham, Daniel James 5:55:13 (33,736)
Gill, Amarjit Singh 6:31:09 (35,542)
Gill, Chris 3:26:12 (3,771)
Gill, David 3:26:19 (3,784)
Gill, Dominic 5:31:29 (31,473)
Gill, James 2:59:48 (1,136)
Gill, James S 3:59:06 (10,747)
Gill, Jason 5:00:05 (26,474)
Gill, John 3:42:22 (6,574)
Gill, Ken John 3:59:29 (10,861)
Gill, Mark D 4:04:15 (12,020)
Gill, Matthew 3:55:05 (9,501)
Gill, Matthew Robert 5:42:18 (32,617)
Gill, Nicholas J 3:27:46 (4,008)
Gill, Paul David 3:54:40 (9,375)
Gill, Robert John 4:19:49 (16,045)
Gill, Sikander 4:20:15 (16,181)
Gill, Steve 3:36:33 (5,490)
Gill, Tim 3:55:14 (9,538)
Gillam, David Lloyd 5:18:11 (29,570)
Gillard, Mathew K 3:56:42 (10,000)
Gillard, Tom 5:06:24 (27,601)
Gillard, Vernon Mark 4:05:55 (12,435)
Gillard-Moss, Peter 3:47:36 (7,669)
Gillatt, Dean 6:08:58 (34,615)
Gillert, Daniel J 4:03:37 (11,878)
Gilles, Dominique 4:37:39 (20,917)
Gillespie, Andrew J 4:03:38 (11,884)
Gillespie, Frank Gerard 4:20:23 (16,228)
Gillespie, John Richard 6:23:54 (35,272)
Gillespie, Keith 4:44:24 (22,617)
Gillett, Daniel J 2:50:29 (502)
Gillham, Paul J 2:49:52 (479)
Gillies, Frazer David Watt 3:53:33 (9,073)
Gillies, Robert 4:30:44 (19,156)
Gilling, Jonathan C 2:55:20 (763)
Gilling, Nigel David 4:26:27 (17,939)
Gillingham, Neil J 4:42:11 (22,058)
Gillings, Tom 5:44:04 (32,777)
Gillman, Mike Barry 4:30:08 (19,010)
Gillman, Thomas Andrew G 4:11:43 (13,908)
Gillmore, Ricky Lee 4:46:47 (23,250)
Gillon, Barry John 4:44:58 (22,759)
Gillon, Charles A 3:27:26 (3,950)
Gillott, Peter 6:16:06 (34,926)
Gillott, Stuart John 4:29:22 (18,768)
Gillott, Timothy Alan 4:18:46 (15,793)
Gilmartin, Noel Patrick 4:05:49 (12,417)
Gilmore, Christopher Bewick 5:20:47 (29,974)
Gilmore, Jonathan 3:58:00 (10,376)
Gilpin, John R 4:31:32 (19,340)
Gilroy, Francis J 3:11:07 (2,010)
Gilroy, Nick 5:47:14 (33,072)
Gilroy-Scott, Michael 3:43:16 (6,737)
Gimblett, Richard Jeremy 4:25:48 (17,749)
Gimblett, Wayne J 3:11:00 (1,995)
Gimenes, Miguel 3:56:25 (9,903)
Gimeno, Francisco 4:50:20 (24,123)
Gingell, Graham W 5:54:54 (33,707)
Gingell, Matthew Owen 4:31:13 (19,274)
Ginn, Andrew P 5:55:55 (33,786)
Ginn, Marcus William 5:59:24 (34,013)
Ginn, Mick Joesph 5:21:04 (30,012)
Ginn, Richard C 3:03:49 (1,374)
Ginnaw, Colin 5:27:06 (30,923)
Ginty, Paul 4:37:16 (20,806)
Giraudo, Loris 3:31:28 (4,662)
Girelli, Diego 3:26:11 (3,768)
Girling, Adam C 2:57:11 (868)
Girling, James 3:54:22 (9,296)
Girones, Jordi 4:38:17 (21,050)
Gisborne, Stephen P 3:28:17 (4,102)
Gisby, Tomas 4:04:00 (11,959)
Gischen, Hilton 4:43:50 (22,456)
Gittins, Andrew J 4:46:54 (23,283)
Gittins, Andrew John 5:29:43 (31,255)
Given, Vernon 3:55:35 (9,632)
Gladman, Alan 4:59:30 (26,340)
Gladstone, Michael 4:11:12 (13,766)
Gladwell, Mark 3:40:28 (6,228)
Glander, Kaz 3:52:12 (8,706)
Glasscock, David 3:55:06 (9,505)
Glasse-Davies, Wayne 5:30:15 (31,321)
Glatman, Daniel Benjamin 5:10:18 (28,288)
Glaysher, Michael 4:26:11 (17,868)
Glazebrook, Roger L 6:28:20 (35,437)
Gleadall, Sam Richard 3:56:04 (9,802)
Gleadall, Stephen 3:59:38 (10,900)
Gleave, Oliver 3:33:09 (4,915)
Gledhill, Andrew 4:19:08 (15,886)
Gleeson, Kieran John 5:10:26 (28,317)
Glen, Andrew 3:53:39 (9,105)
Glen, Christopher 3:45:10 (7,132)
Glen, David Philip 4:05:56 (12,440)
Glencross, Iain M 5:36:32 (32,061)
Glenn , Felix 4:26:29 (17,945)
Glew, Steve C 3:57:00 (10,089)
Glibbery, Robert J 4:48:20 (23,616)
Glithro, Alex 3:53:39 (9,105)
Gloch, Philipp 3:57:21 (10,194)
Gloch, Volkhard 4:19:34 (15,989)
Glover, Brian R 5:06:39 (27,662)
Glover, Ian George 4:35:20 (20,301)
Glover, Jamie George 4:38:57 (21,244)
Glover, Lindsey Richard 4:13:22 (14,330)
Glover, Michael 4:38:46 (21,193)
Glover, Sam 5:30:47 (31,391)
Glover, Simon 4:42:58 (22,250)
Gluning, Mark 3:46:21 (7,386)
Glynn, Kevin 3:51:25 (8,518)
Glynn, Mark J 3:09:36 (1,870)
Glynn, Michael P 4:46:05 (23,055)
Glynn, Paul M 5:32:40 (31,624)
Glynn, Terry Alan 4:57:32 (25,868)
Gnoyke, Bjoern 3:30:19 (4,473)
Goater, John 5:13:08 (28,795)
Goc, Milan 2:54:25 (695)
Godber, Duncan E 4:07:48 (12,906)
Godbold, Alan Roger 3:53:34 (9,080)
Godbold, Brian 4:02:55 (11,710)
Godby, Simon Mark 4:58:40 (26,130)
Goddard, Barry 4:32:26 (19,545)
Goddard, David Simon 3:32:01 (4,740)
Goddard, Jeremy 4:43:45 (22,435)
Goddard, Matthew J 5:17:12 (29,415)
Goddard, Neil D 4:27:16 (18,171)
Goddard, Paul Eric 3:39:06 (5,963)
Goddard, Tom 4:38:27 (21,105)
Goddard, Trevor E 3:32:49 (4,864)
Godden, Ian D 3:10:06 (1,915)

Godding, Justin	3:46:08 (7,344)	Goodbourn, Trevor	3:22:28 (3,235)	Gormley, Terry	5:32:08 (31,555)
Godfrey, Chidinma Charles	4:42:16 (22,084)	Goodburn, Mark	3:54:43 (9,392)	Gornall, Robert	2:45:31 (351)
Godfrey, David J	7:05:55 (36,265)	Goodchild, Keith A	3:59:01 (10,725)	Gorospe, Unai	4:03:14 (11,785)
Godfrey, James	5:13:25 (28,829)	Goodchild, Ralph	4:38:30 (21,117)	Gorringe, Tom Howard	5:08:43 (28,007)
Godfrey, John	4:09:36 (13,370)	Goode, Mark Richard	5:08:15 (27,939)	Gorton, John C	3:56:26 (9,908)
Godfrey, Paul Christopher	4:24:08 (17,268)	Goode, Philip	3:13:58 (2,315)	Gosling, Christopher Paul	5:20:27 (29,912)
Godfrey, Paul Milton	5:35:23 (31,914)	Goodenough, Nigel	5:13:30 (28,843)	Gosling, Darren John	3:47:34 (7,662)
Godhania, Vinesh	5:02:39 (26,967)	Goodey, Andrew M	4:20:11 (16,157)	Gosling, Hywel James	4:10:51 (13,680)
Godwin, Peter Charles William	3:18:34 (2,827)	Goodfellow, Dave Alan	4:07:55 (12,933)	Goss, Sam	4:32:12 (19,488)
Goessweiner, Herwig Christian	3:33:09 (4,915)	Goodfellow, Mark	4:07:29 (12,826)	Gossop, Stephen B	4:59:55 (26,432)
Goffe, James Robert	3:31:29 (4,664)	Goodfellow, Richard Michael	5:01:15 (26,694)	Gotfryd, Przemyslaw Pawel	3:53:46 (9,147)
Goffin, Julian	5:20:24 (29,905)	Goodhew, Kevin Peter	5:37:12 (32,125)	Gothard, John	4:04:21 (12,043)
Gogay, Craig John	4:01:52 (11,462)	Goodier, Mark	3:45:49 (7,267)	Gotobed, Ben	5:07:29 (27,808)
Goggin, Ben	5:08:15 (27,939)	Goodin, Eugene M	3:47:45 (7,694)	Gottlieb, Kim	5:10:02 (28,244)
Gohel, Sagar	4:11:53 (13,950)	Gooding, James Francis	5:03:19 (27,076)	Gouache, Antoine	3:37:04 (5,578)
Gohil, Arun Dayalal	5:23:19 (30,361)	Gooding, Paul	3:07:58 (1,696)	Gouache, Benoit	4:11:58 (13,983)
Goiri, Iñaki	3:48:32 (7,853)	Gooding, Peter J	4:07:56 (12,940)	Gouas, Alain	3:57:50 (10,337)
Gois, Manuel	3:05:22 (1,489)	Goodings, Kevin Richard	5:49:16 (33,259)	Goubet, Sylvain	3:32:07 (4,761)
Golby, Dan	4:49:49 (24,013)	Goodlad, Robin	4:52:15 (24,614)	Goudal, Jean-Louis	3:23:30 (3,368)
Golby, Kevin John	4:53:10 (24,839)	Goodlake, Wayne	4:06:56 (12,697)	Goude, Christian	4:15:53 (14,998)
Golcher, Tom	5:08:55 (28,032)	Goodliffe, Andrew R	4:01:59 (11,486)	Gouge, Ian	4:47:06 (23,328)
Gold, Adam Jon	3:36:51 (5,537)	Goodman, Allan	3:38:56 (5,926)	Gough, Darren Paul	4:10:01 (13,479)
Gold, Charlie Michael	4:33:21 (19,812)	Goodman, David	4:31:12 (19,272)	Gough, David R	3:10:03 (1,910)
Gold, Darren	7:02:24 (36,219)	Goodman, Dean	5:25:11 (30,648)	Gough, Frank	4:31:23 (19,306)
Gold, Jeremy A	3:00:35 (1,180)	Goodman, Ian J	3:53:12 (8,971)	Gough, James	5:09:56 (28,217)
Gold, Nick	3:02:27 (1,293)	Goodman, James N	3:55:20 (9,571)	Gough, Jamie Jonathan	5:32:37 (31,619)
Gold, Paul	4:58:45 (26,155)	Goodman, Martin	4:49:04 (23,820)	Gough, Peter George	4:38:22 (21,078)
Gold, Steven Paul	5:42:41 (32,648)	Goodreid, Ian C	3:03:48 (1,373)	Gough, Stephen Josheph	6:37:17 (35,706)
Goldau, Andreas	3:46:14 (7,362)	Goodrich, Paul Anthony	4:35:56 (20,461)	Gough, William J	4:37:48 (20,946)
Goldfinch, Doug	5:02:33 (26,950)	Goodrich, Thomas	3:54:48 (9,424)	Goulbourn, Stuart Roger	4:05:11 (12,251)
Golding, James Matthew	4:34:44 (20,179)	Goodrick, Paul Jonathan	5:04:38 (27,305)	Gould, Andrew	3:37:47 (5,724)
Golding, Neville	4:55:40 (25,452)	Goodsell, Terry James	4:01:36 (11,393)	Gould, Andrew	4:43:48 (22,441)
Golding, Reginald	5:22:40 (30,249)	Goodson, Mark A	4:02:38 (11,636)	Gould, Andrew	5:23:37 (30,410)
Golding, Stuart	4:12:26 (14,078)	Goodway, Samuel Lewis	4:39:24 (21,353)	Gould, Anthony	6:32:28 (35,577)
Goldring, Simon	4:05:52 (12,424)	Goodwin, Christopher	4:09:34 (13,358)	Gould, Daniel	6:38:27 (35,739)
Goldschmidt, David Charles	4:10:25 (13,573)	Goodwin, Colin David	5:08:32 (27,978)	Gould, Edward	3:15:38 (2,511)
Goldsmith, David Lee	3:27:39 (3,991)	Goodwin, Craig Alan	4:24:15 (17,302)	Gould, Matthew	3:50:52 (8,396)
Goldsmith, Paul	5:11:23 (28,465)	Goodwin, David Andrew	6:08:41 (34,594)	Gould, Richard Paul	2:51:57 (561)
Goldsmith, Simon	4:01:21 (11,322)	Goodwin, Julian	2:55:34 (777)	Goulding, Allister J	3:17:53 (2,751)
Goldsmith, Stuart Glenn	5:29:37 (31,240)	Goodwin, Kevin Michael	4:13:45 (14,448)	Goulding, Stephen J	3:04:26 (1,423)
Goldstein, Jonathan Simon	4:00:55 (11,225)	Goodwin, Mark	3:59:13 (10,786)	Goupil, François	3:27:22 (3,934)
Goldstein, Paul	5:59:40 (34,030)	Goodwin, Mark Ian	3:11:40 (2,066)	Gourlay, Douglas John	4:07:56 (12,940)
Goldstone, Barry G	4:55:59 (25,534)	Goodwin, Neil	4:06:29 (12,569)	Gourley, Peter	4:46:39 (23,224)
Goldsworthy-Ellson, Donald	5:04:41 (27,315)	Goodwin, Paul	3:30:59 (4,575)	Gouveris, John Nicolas	3:41:11 (6,362)
Goldup, Nicholas C	4:33:11 (19,757)	Goodwin, Paul	4:45:31 (22,891)	Gover, Kevin	3:43:59 (6,876)
Golledge, Brett St John	4:15:59 (15,019)	Goodwin, Rod	4:27:36 (18,257)	Govier, Adam Christian	4:24:27 (17,376)
Gomersall, Andrew	4:19:33 (15,985)	Goodwin, Ryan Thomas	3:59:51 (10,952)	Govindji, Rizwan	4:27:18 (18,181)
Gomes, Carlos	4:56:14 (25,593)	Goodwin, Scott	3:26:14 (3,775)	Govus, Simon Peter	3:52:53 (8,895)
Gomes Dos Santos, Marilson	2:08:46 (6)	Goody, Craig Phillip	5:13:19 (28,820)	Gow, Andrew	3:54:47 (9,416)
Gomez, James Sam	5:02:13 (26,893)	Goodyear, Nicholas Lewis	5:44:11 (32,785)	Gow, Chris	4:12:02 (13,994)
Gomez, Luis F.	2:53:52 (660)	Gora, Simon	4:00:55 (11,225)	Gowar, Jack David	3:53:27 (9,039)
Gomez Millan, Juan Gabriel	3:31:33 (4,674)	Goraparthi, Raja Mahendra	4:57:45 (25,920)	Gower, Kelvin Andrew	4:00:08 (11,015)
Gomez-Ragio Carrera, José Agustin	4:59:29 (26,333)	Gordon, Adam Raphael	5:43:13 (32,692)	Gower, Kevin Andrew	4:43:57 (22,492)
Gomm, Philip M	4:33:37 (19,897)	Gordon, Adrian Thomas	3:54:29 (9,322)	Gower, Mark	3:28:49 (4,193)
Gomme, Daniel	3:37:02 (5,570)	Gordon, Brian	4:23:27 (17,090)	Gower, Neil Jonathan	3:02:31 (1,302)
Gong, Sul Hee	4:28:19 (18,458)	Gordon, Chris John	4:20:10 (16,154)	Gowers, Ian J	3:47:44 (7,688)
Goniszewski, Jan	5:49:08 (33,250)	Gordon, Frank	3:36:28 (5,476)	Gowers, John Robert	5:25:48 (30,754)
Gonsalves, Victor	4:17:45 (15,512)	Gordon, Gary	4:45:35 (22,909)	Gozi, Sandro	4:01:47 (11,443)
Gonzalez, David	2:47:42 (409)	Gordon, Iain	5:06:10 (27,558)	Graca, Nuno A.	2:43:03 (280)
Gonzalez, José Roman	3:27:30 (3,961)	Gordon, James	4:25:52 (17,779)	Grace, Mark	3:10:35 (1,953)
Gonzalez, Juan Carlos	4:50:36 (24,185)	Gordon, James Robert	4:58:49 (26,169)	Gracey, Peter	4:05:55 (12,435)
Gonzalez, Richard Donald	5:20:13 (29,879)	Gordon, Jeffrey	5:06:26 (27,612)	Gracie, Nick J	2:58:32 (1,008)
Gonzalez, Victor	4:50:37 (24,187)	Gordon, Luke	5:12:52 (28,714)	Grady, Paul Alexander	4:36:35 (20,625)
Gonzalez Pacheco, José Manuel	3:03:50 (1,375)	Gordon, Mel	4:39:07 (21,286)	Graftiaux, Franck	3:46:12 (7,353)
Gonzalez-George, Victor	3:15:51 (2,536)	Gordon, Paul A	4:40:30 (21,640)	Graham, Alan	4:16:10 (15,062)
Gooch, Alexander	4:45:37 (22,919)	Gordon, Robert Innes	4:54:15 (25,114)	Graham, Alex	3:57:43 (10,308)
Gooch, Clive Andrew	4:27:38 (18,270)	Gordon, Steven J	3:24:42 (3,540)	Graham, Andrew	4:34:12 (20,044)
Gooch, Darren	6:12:43 (34,794)	Gordon-Martin, Alex	3:48:32 (7,853)	Graham, David I	4:07:45 (12,897)
Gooch, Karl Anthony	4:37:55 (20,970)	Gore, Andy K	2:41:38 (241)	Graham, Howard	4:24:33 (17,407)
Gooch, Lars James	4:47:47 (23,489)	Gore, Jeremy	3:56:58 (10,077)	Graham, Ian Christopher	4:12:07 (14,018)
Good, Craig Anthony	3:32:12 (4,770)	Gore, Lawrence	4:07:23 (12,796)	Graham, Jamie	4:38:19 (21,061)
Good, Michael Edward	3:27:40 (3,993)	Gore, Martin John	4:20:37 (16,302)	Graham, Jonathan	3:35:22 (5,297)
Good, Paul Antony	4:51:49 (24,497)	Gorgerat, Jean-Philippe	3:05:00 (1,457)	Graham, Keith R	5:20:11 (29,875)
Goodacre, Adam	5:25:25 (30,682)	Gorham, John	3:52:15 (8,719)	Graham, Martin John	4:42:55 (22,241)
Goodale, Gavin S	3:50:27 (8,297)	Gorham, Scott	5:09:18 (28,107)	Graham, Martin P	5:03:58 (27,179)
Goodale, Paul	5:29:16 (31,184)	Gorman, Brian Richard	4:43:09 (22,288)	Graham, Michael J	4:07:22 (12,791)
Goodall, Dave James	4:20:17 (16,194)	Gorman, Cathal	3:58:47 (10,652)	Graham, Neil Dominic	4:04:16 (12,023)
Goodall, David	3:37:09 (5,590)	Gorman, Ciaran	3:43:02 (6,703)	Graham, Patrick	4:05:50 (12,418)
Goodall, Gareth	4:37:34 (20,900)	Gorman, Justin Sacha	4:18:46 (15,793)	Graham, Paul	3:12:07 (2,103)
Goodall, Mark F	4:33:10 (19,752)	Gorman, Stephen J	4:21:45 (16,628)	Graham, Paul A	3:33:07 (4,910)
Goodall, Tim Michael Charles	5:56:25 (33,824)	Gormanns, Franz	3:33:17 (4,933)	Graham, Richard John Giles	4:20:20 (16,215)
Goodall, William K	5:24:06 (30,494)	Gormley, Matthew	4:51:54 (24,521)	Graham, Robert	5:22:40 (30,249)
Goodbody, Simon Christopher	3:24:02 (3,435)	Gormley, Stephen P	2:56:04 (804)	Graham, Stuart	3:52:30 (8,796)

Graham, Vanaka 3:13:32 (2,259)
Grain, Thomas T 4:20:23 (16,228)
Grainger, Eric 4:41:12 (21,824)
Grainger, Simon 4:51:25 (24,403)
Grajer, Peter 5:36:58 (32,098)
Granato, Salvatore 3:26:08 (3,757)
Grancea, Adrian 3:15:11 (2,458)
Grandy, Mark 3:23:55 (3,423)
Grange, Ian 3:53:22 (9,018)
Grant, Alan 4:40:17 (21,570)
Grant, Andrew 4:00:18 (11,059)
Grant, Brian W 4:44:38 (22,682)
Grant, Daniel 5:35:38 (31,945)
Grant, David 3:36:27 (5,474)
Grant, Iain Alexander 3:30:41 (4,527)
Grant, Ian L 4:19:26 (15,957)
Grant, James R 4:54:11 (25,093)
Grant, Jeffrey 4:08:58 (13,201)
Grant, Mark 5:56:44 (33,845)
Grant, Mark S 3:45:22 (7,175)
Grant, Martin 5:35:21 (31,912)
Grant, Mike 4:14:02 (14,514)
Grant, Neil Oliver 4:27:36 (18,257)
Grant, Ross 5:16:15 (29,258)
Grant, Stefan C 5:32:20 (31,577)
Grant, Steven John 4:25:56 (17,795)
Grant, Warren 4:35:02 (20,237)
Grantham, Simon 3:24:28 (3,506)
Grapes, Tom Jack 5:16:16 (29,261)
Grassick, Mark Richard 5:09:30 (28,148)
Grassick, Richard K 5:09:30 (28,148)
Graveling, Stephen John 4:35:55 (20,453)
Gravell, Thomas 4:45:08 (22,805)
Graves, Derek R 3:58:04 (10,401)
Graves, Ian C 4:28:45 (18,591)
Graves, Lee Edwin Fisher 3:12:52 (2,173)
Graves, Mal John 5:04:56 (27,354)
Graves, Paul Michael 2:58:47 (1,029)
Graves, Richard M 3:51:06 (8,450)
Graves-Morris, Rob William 4:10:44 (13,649)
Gray, Aaron 4:18:29 (15,711)
Gray, Alan 4:57:43 (25,912)
Gray, Andrew N 4:20:29 (16,256)
Gray, Andy 4:18:30 (15,715)
Gray, Anthony D 3:22:24 (3,227)
Gray, Antony Mark 4:19:06 (15,872)
Gray, Barry 4:28:36 (18,548)
Gray, Barry David 3:33:39 (4,998)
Gray, Bryan Gilbert 3:42:36 (6,609)
Gray, David 3:21:00 (3,083)
Gray, Glen 4:32:29 (19,556)
Gray, Ian James 3:55:09 (9,516)
Gray, Jack 4:53:04 (24,806)
Gray, Jay K. C. 4:10:40 (13,629)
Gray, Mark Lindley 5:19:42 (29,808)
Gray, Martin 4:59:52 (26,422)
Gray, Michael 5:24:59 (30,622)
Gray, Michael D 5:27:47 (31,000)
Gray, Myles Robert 4:08:19 (13,033)
Gray, Neil 5:37:59 (32,211)
Gray, Neil R 3:46:35 (7,440)
Gray, Nigel W 4:30:33 (19,106)
Gray, Patrick John 4:53:04 (24,806)
Gray, Paul 5:01:15 (26,694)
Gray, Paul William 4:42:48 (22,213)
Gray, Peter 4:13:13 (14,290)
Gray, Richard 3:11:22 (2,034)
Gray, Rob 5:24:41 (30,579)
Gray, Steve P 3:38:43 (5,890)
Gray, Stuart Robert 3:45:15 (7,151)
Gray, Thomas Benjamin 4:24:24 (17,360)
Gray, Todd Craig 3:34:19 (5,118)
Grealish, Ciaran 3:53:50 (9,169)
Greany, Liam James 3:49:28 (8,080)
Greasby, Dennis 3:44:19 (6,942)
Greasby, Oliver William 4:27:54 (18,339)
Greasby, Peter William 5:17:08 (29,412)
Greasley, Robert 4:42:11 (22,058)
Greatbatch, Nick 3:58:00 (10,376)
Greatholder, Jacko 5:11:08 (28,427)
Greatorex, Ian Robin 6:17:50 (35,025)
Greatwood, Glen 4:23:41 (17,151)
Greaves, James 4:01:08 (11,282)
Grecco, Chris 2:48:19 (425)
Grechi, Alberto 3:19:32 (2,919)
Gredley, Tim 3:39:17 (6,000)
Greedy, Stephen 3:05:01 (1,459)
Greeff, Neil 4:15:21 (14,879)
Green, Adrian John 5:47:59 (33,136)
Green, Alan 3:52:27 (8,777)
Green, Andrew 4:12:19 (14,059)
Green, Andrew J 2:42:03 (253)
Green, Andrew J 3:37:35 (5,684)
Green, Andrew J 4:10:59 (13,710)
Green, Andrew John 3:20:49 (3,060)
Green, Benjamin 4:08:18 (13,028)
Green, Chris 6:14:54 (34,881)
Green, Christopher John 3:17:44 (2,734)
Green, Colin Martin 3:10:54 (1,982)
Green, Daniel James 5:08:37 (27,995)
Green, Darryl 4:27:55 (18,347)
Green, David 5:16:28 (29,304)
Green, David Henry 4:48:51 (23,760)
Green, David Paul 5:01:16 (26,699)
Green, David R 2:54:50 (726)
Green, Dominic J 5:36:51 (32,087)
Green, Edward Simon 4:59:41 (26,380)
Green, Eric 3:08:17 (1,728)
Green, Gavin A 3:44:53 (7,075)
Green, Harry 3:56:44 (10,009)
Green, James Alexander 3:50:08 (8,232)
Green, Jez 4:36:37 (20,637)
Green, John Joseph 4:32:38 (19,589)
Green, John K 3:13:19 (2,226)
Green, Joseph 4:24:58 (17,509)
Green, Kevin Alan 5:50:41 (33,403)
Green, Kevin John 4:47:04 (23,322)
Green, Kristian 5:16:46 (29,347)
Green, Malcolm 5:02:08 (26,877)
Green, Marcus Paul Douglas 3:18:21 (2,810)
Green, Mark Stephen 4:38:33 (21,131)
Green, Martin 3:35:36 (5,342)
Green, Martin H 3:10:54 (1,982)
Green, Matthew 4:10:00 (13,475)
Green, Michael 2:23:48 (30)
Green, Michael D 4:39:51 (21,477)
Green, Michael Robert 4:19:37 (15,997)
Green, Micky Steven 4:10:40 (13,629)
Green, Miles 4:37:48 (20,946)
Green, Norman G 3:07:40 (1,674)
Green, Paul A 3:13:19 (2,226)
Green, Phil John 5:17:52 (29,520)
Green, Richard 5:20:29 (29,925)
Green, Richard Dennis 4:44:00 (22,504)
Green, Rob 4:17:24 (15,405)
Green, Robert 3:59:27 (10,853)
Green, Samuel 5:03:43 (27,140)
Green, Shane A 4:02:23 (11,575)
Green, Simon Edward 5:18:08 (29,564)
Green, Steven Andrew 4:08:55 (13,188)
Green, Steven James 5:18:25 (29,610)
Green, Tim 4:26:48 (18,024)
Green, Tony John 5:41:01 (32,486)
Greenaway, Alexander Rufus 4:14:42 (14,715)
Greene, Alan 5:56:46 (33,848)
Greene, Matthew James 5:26:59 (30,902)
Greene, Robert 4:15:51 (14,987)
Greener, John Philip 3:14:49 (2,420)
Greener, Michael A 2:54:31 (702)
Greenfield, Mark 4:25:24 (17,636)
Greenhalgh, Andy 4:53:44 (24,982)
Greenhalgh, Clifford 5:20:28 (29,919)
Greenhalgh, Eric 4:48:35 (23,690)
Greenhalgh, Gamel 4:40:21 (21,596)
Greenhalgh, Lee 3:33:20 (4,939)
Greenhalgh, Philip 4:29:53 (18,943)
Greenhalgh, Stephen Christopher 4:42:19 (22,098)
Greenhalgh, Tony 7:19:24 (36,400)
Greenhill, Ewan F 3:25:44 (3,692)
Greenhill, Simon Derek 4:13:26 (14,348)
Greenhough, Karl 5:05:23 (27,428)
Greenland, Richard 4:37:53 (20,962)
Greenleaf, Andrew H 2:28:51 (58)
Greenshields, Fraser 4:00:46 (11,185)
Greenshields, Gregor 4:10:14 (13,536)
Greensill, Matthew 4:25:29 (17,657)
Greenslade, Daevid Victor 5:21:01 (30,008)
Greenslade, Nicholas 3:13:16 (2,219)
Greensmith, Geoff 4:16:10 (15,062)
Greenstein, David 3:37:52 (5,734)
Greenway, Mark Alexander 3:55:50 (9,730)
Greenwood, Alan 4:49:35 (23,937)
Greenwood, Brett 3:52:33 (8,809)
Greenwood, Mark A 2:37:06 (143)
Greenwood, Matt 4:54:24 (25,160)
Greenwood, Richard 3:44:04 (6,891)
Greer, Alan 5:19:06 (29,719)
Greer, Mervyn Robert 5:45:02 (32,873)
Greer, Neale 4:57:51 (25,936)
Greer, Neil 5:06:37 (27,649)
Greer, Richard Paul 4:01:23 (11,332)
Greet, Mark A 2:47:40 (408)
Grefsheim, Matthew Franklin 4:48:02 (23,554)
Greg, Levine David 4:58:56 (26,196)
Gregg, John Alexander 7:54:24 (36,577)
Gregg, Matthew J 6:17:37 (35,011)
Gregg, Paul 2:44:44 (331)
Gregg, William 4:07:59 (12,957)
Gregor, Zdenek 4:08:29 (13,074)
Gregory, David Hayden 4:36:58 (20,734)
Gregory, Guy 4:19:22 (15,944)
Gregory, Ian 4:39:15 (21,321)
Gregory, Jackson Martin 4:32:42 (19,607)
Gregory, James A 4:15:01 (14,790)
Gregory, Jeff 4:51:14 (24,361)
Gregory, John A 3:38:04 (5,776)
Gregory, John Anthony 4:41:06 (21,798)
Gregory, Justin 4:37:13 (20,798)
Gregory, Keith 4:33:31 (19,857)
Gregory, Kevin C 3:53:35 (9,084)
Gregory, Mark 5:27:55 (31,013)
Gregory, Mark Thomas 4:36:16 (20,540)
Gregory, Nicholas John 4:50:06 (24,073)
Gregory, Nick A 3:12:32 (2,136)
Gregory, Paul Dennis 4:06:34 (12,591)
Gregory, Richard Mark 4:46:33 (23,180)
Greig, Alan R 3:24:02 (3,435)
Greig, Alan R 6:33:14 (35,605)
Greig, Peter 5:07:27 (27,799)
Greig, Stuart 4:17:11 (15,345)
Gresham, Matt 3:48:26 (7,832)
Gressin, Philippe 3:39:11 (5,979)
Grethe, Robert Charles 6:24:08 (35,285)
Grew, Fergus 4:52:54 (24,777)
Grew, Gareth 2:47:13 (393)
Grey, William Mark Falconer 3:00:40 (1,184)
Gribben, Adam Lawrence 3:58:24 (10,523)
Gribben, Iain 5:14:06 (28,938)
Gribben, Lawrence David 6:10:55 (34,696)
Gribble, Andy 5:17:06 (29,403)
Grice, Peter 6:09:39 (34,642)
Grier, Alistair Robert 4:47:27 (23,400)
Grierson, Marc 2:57:27 (896)
Grieve, Richard William 2:54:52 (728)
Grieves, Mark Christopher 3:45:20 (7,169)
Grieveson, Peter 3:25:37 (3,670)
Griffey, Jack 3:46:16 (7,373)
Griffin, Andrew A 5:02:06 (26,867)
Griffin, Andrew Paul 5:36:49 (32,085)
Griffin, Chris Kevin 4:22:09 (16,741)
Griffin, Christopher Stephen 5:07:50 (27,866)
Griffin, David P 2:47:39 (407)
Griffin, Gareth P 4:14:05 (14,532)
Griffin, James Oliver 3:56:16 (9,861)
Griffin, John 4:48:31 (23,671)
Griffin, John 5:39:34 (32,353)
Griffin, John F 3:38:01 (5,767)
Griffin, Kenneth M 4:55:51 (25,497)
Griffin, Liam 3:42:21 (6,570)
Griffin, Mark 4:51:47 (24,488)
Griffin, Phil 4:57:42 (25,908)
Griffin, Richard Frederick 3:33:47 (5,020)
Griffin, Roger F 3:57:08 (10,138)
Griffin, Russell D 3:54:50 (9,431)
Griffin, Simon C 2:51:48 (558)
Griffin, Tom R 3:57:12 (10,156)
Griffin, Tristan 4:04:19 (12,035)
Griffith, Jackson E 3:33:46 (5,015)
Griffith, John 4:25:40 (17,707)

Griffith, Owen Evan 5:00:07 (26,483)
Griffith, Peter Stephen 4:19:14 (15,909)
Griffith-Jones, John Michael 5:44:24 (32,804)
Griffiths, Adam L 3:35:41 (5,357)
Griffiths, Alan Thomas 4:51:04 (24,322)
Griffiths, Andrew 4:59:28 (26,326)
Griffiths, Andy 4:31:30 (19,334)
Griffiths, Barrie W 3:04:29 (1,430)
Griffiths, Bryan David 5:26:27 (30,837)
Griffiths, Bryn Rees 4:16:32 (15,177)
Griffiths, Christopher 5:09:49 (28,201)
Griffiths, Ciaran 4:39:25 (21,363)
Griffiths, Daniel Gary 3:54:01 (9,215)
Griffiths, David John 4:35:04 (20,242)
Griffiths, Geraint Lloyd 5:06:42 (27,672)
Griffiths, Guy 4:12:59 (14,229)
Griffiths, Jason D 6:54:35 (36,097)
Griffiths, John 5:37:19 (32,146)
Griffiths, Jonathan P 4:41:23 (21,863)
Griffiths, Kevin Wynne 5:31:47 (31,513)
Griffiths, Mark 4:38:49 (21,207)
Griffiths, Mark 4:47:47 (23,489)
Griffiths, Mark Bryan 4:40:26 (21,623)
Griffiths, Mark Philip 3:36:05 (5,424)
Griffiths, Martin Simon 3:49:23 (8,059)
Griffiths, Michael 4:16:48 (15,247)
Griffiths, Neil 4:07:04 (12,726)
Griffiths, Nick 4:28:30 (18,521)
Griffiths, Paul W 3:27:45 (4,006)
Griffiths, Peter 5:37:18 (32,144)
Griffiths, Peter 6:22:32 (35,211)
Griffiths, Peter Clive 5:56:20 (33,818)
Griffiths, Philip Frederick 4:42:07 (22,042)
Griffiths, Richard 3:32:22 (4,794)
Griffiths, Richard 4:41:51 (21,982)
Griffiths, Simon G 4:31:27 (19,321)
Griffiths, Stuart John 4:54:47 (25,255)
Griffiths, Thomas A 6:36:18 (35,684)
Griffith-Salisbury, Gareth Jhn 6:21:05 (35,163)
Grifiths, Nick John 5:05:12 (27,408)
Grigenas, Rimas 3:57:02 (10,109)
Grigg, Paul J 3:48:37 (7,876)
Griggs, Karl Anthony 4:58:52 (26,183)
Grigor, Iain A 3:15:48 (2,528)
Grigor, Sandy 3:51:26 (8,524)
Grigson, David 5:23:13 (30,344)
Grigson, Edward J 3:36:34 (5,491)
Griib, Andrew D 4:26:38 (17,984)
Grimalda, Gianluca 3:25:00 (3,582)
Grimaldi, Nicholas Andrew 5:22:00 (30,144)
Grimes, Andrew T 5:11:12 (28,436)
Grimsby, James A 4:58:13 (26,015)
Grimsdale, Tim 5:08:38 (27,996)
Grimsey, Paul 3:58:47 (10,652)
Grimshaw, Grahame 3:58:37 (10,598)
Grimsley, Gary 4:33:16 (19,791)
Grimsley, Kristian Paul 5:49:27 (33,278)
Grimwood, David 6:16:49 (34,968)
Grimwood, Graham 4:44:10 (22,553)
Grinberg, Sergio 5:07:01 (27,727)
Grindberg, Baard 3:00:41 (1,187)
Grindley, Adrian 4:54:33 (25,190)
Grinham, Barry Henry 4:35:05 (20,245)
Grinham, John Leonard 4:40:46 (21,714)
Grinnell, Carl 4:49:48 (24,007)
Grismond, Matt 3:49:06 (8,000)
Grist, Roger William 3:41:28 (6,417)
Gritton, Terence David 4:14:16 (14,586)
Groarke, Thomas 5:06:35 (27,641)
Grobel, Edmund Joseph Richard 3:28:36 (4,164)
Grocott, Anthony E 4:35:14 (20,278)
Groechenig, Ernst 4:44:43 (22,701)
Groenke, Herbert 3:28:15 (4,099)
Groom, Jason 4:06:54 (12,684)
Groom, Michael 6:12:04 (34,757)
Gross, Marc 4:26:28 (17,943)
Grossman, Doron 3:31:28 (4,662)
Grosso, Giulio Giorgio 3:58:58 (10,709)
Grostate, Ian Malcolm 6:12:40 (34,792)
Grosvenor, John-Barry 5:24:29 (30,554)
Grote, Craig J 4:33:11 (19,757)
Grounds, Tony 4:55:09 (25,347)
Groundwater, Nick 3:46:23 (7,394)

Grout, Luke D 4:27:58 (18,357)
Grout, Michael J 3:47:00 (7,524)
Grout, Steve 3:23:07 (3,310)
Grove, Martin 5:58:05 (33,939)
Grove, Shaun David 4:03:44 (11,904)
Grover, Jonathan 4:38:57 (21,244)
Groves, Andrew P 4:44:33 (22,654)
Groves, Antony James 4:35:13 (20,272)
Groves, Bob 3:49:26 (8,075)
Groves, Luke 4:13:30 (14,365)
Groves, Mark P 4:55:20 (25,390)
Groves, Paul 4:03:10 (11,769)
Groves, Paul Andrew 5:43:36 (32,727)
Groves, Ricky 5:36:32 (32,061)
Gruaz, Francis 5:38:18 (32,241)
Grubb, Andrew D 3:06:29 (1,569)
Grubb, Tim John 3:25:38 (3,671)
Gruber, Dominique 4:14:34 (14,674)
Gruel, Benoit 3:10:37 (1,956)
Grummell, Oliver 3:33:50 (5,031)
Grundy, Andrew 4:06:03 (12,463)
Grundy, Andrew Stephen 3:55:43 (9,677)
Grundy, Chris John 4:40:38 (21,678)
Grundy, Mark 4:47:19 (23,368)
Grundy, Stephen 4:42:24 (22,114)
Grundy, Thomas James 4:02:22 (11,572)
Grunewald, Menachem 4:51:21 (24,387)
Grzeszczak, Richard Paul 5:47:20 (33,080)
Guard, Rick 3:55:55 (9,755)
Guarriello, David 4:29:00 (18,686)
Gubby, Martin 4:46:21 (23,137)
Gudka, Piyush 3:48:53 (7,947)
Gueguen, Jacques 3:56:35 (9,955)
Guelle, Joerg 4:04:31 (12,076)
Guenno, Loic 3:28:15 (4,099)
Gueret, Guy Marie 2:46:41 (377)
Guest, Adam Richard 3:41:07 (6,348)
Guest, Andrew 4:20:53 (16,386)
Guest, Graham Michael 4:11:55 (13,966)
Guest, Jonathan D 3:25:10 (3,604)
Guest, Lee Dylan 3:39:38 (6,066)
Guest, Paul 3:06:21 (1,559)
Guest, Paul A 2:59:46 (1,133)
Guest, Paul John 6:19:20 (35,096)
Guest, Thomas 5:34:15 (31,788)
Guest, Tristan Roger John 3:56:15 (9,857)
Guggemos, Wolfgang 4:35:05 (20,245)
Guglielmi, Thomas Austin Vincent 4:46:40 (23,226)
Guhlke, Thomas 4:35:05 (20,245)
Guichard, Pascal 3:18:08 (2,783)
Guida, Mike 3:59:41 (10,916)
Guidi, Alessio 2:56:11 (812)
Guildford, Christopher 4:51:14 (24,361)
Guildford, Jonathan 3:42:25 (6,580)
Guillemain, Philippe 4:10:05 (13,491)
Guillet, Marc 3:37:09 (5,590)
Guillot, Dominique 3:33:44 (5,012)
Guinan, Paul E 2:40:47 (223)
Guiseley, Andrew 3:06:34 (1,575)
Guizelin, Benjamin 3:31:06 (4,595)
Gul, Erdal 4:42:54 (22,240)
Gulamabbas, Sikandar 7:00:19 (36,193)
Gulc, Peter 3:03:43 (1,364)
Gulholm, Egil 3:47:56 (7,726)
Gull, David 4:44:45 (22,712)
Gullis, Peter K 3:59:16 (10,799)
Gumbley, Edward W 2:35:14 (114)
Gumbrell, Ben 4:13:49 (14,460)
Gumbrell, Kris 6:16:26 (34,948)
Gumbrell, Malcolm J 4:29:06 (18,712)
Gumley, Ryan D 3:57:30 (10,233)
Gunaratnam, David R 5:00:12 (26,499)
Gunby, Peter Frank 4:18:56 (15,836)
Guney, Daniel 6:00:47 (34,109)
Gunn, Adam D 5:25:54 (30,766)
Gunn, Geoff 4:39:25 (21,363)
Gunn, Gerard Francis 4:47:40 (23,459)
Gunn, Graham 4:34:41 (20,168)
Gunn, Mark 4:34:42 (20,171)
Gunn, Neil 3:27:12 (3,909)
Gunn, Peter R 4:33:05 (19,723)
Gunnell, Mark 4:58:34 (26,107)
Gunner, Raymond J 3:24:10 (3,465)

Gunning, Ross C 4:30:59 (19,212)
Gunning, Simon M 3:45:22 (7,175)
Gunning, Stephen 5:06:25 (27,606)
Gunton, Dominic Ashley 3:10:55 (1,985)
Gunton, Richard 4:10:35 (13,614)
Gunton, Scott John 3:32:51 (4,871)
Gupta, Rahul 4:15:46 (14,973)
Gupta, Sanjeev 3:51:08 (8,456)
Gurd, Richard 3:14:15 (2,349)
Gurney, Adam 3:53:21 (9,013)
Gurr, James Stephen 3:01:37 (1,235)
Gurr, Stuart 3:06:08 (1,542)
Gurung, Chandra Bahadur 4:33:42 (19,918)
Gurvitz, Ray 4:45:17 (22,835)
Gush, Mike 4:23:25 (17,084)
Gussey, Andrew 4:16:38 (15,197)
Gustafson, Micheal 3:39:01 (5,942)
Gustavsson, Daniel 4:38:40 (21,158)
Gutenstein, Dennis 2:44:33 (323)
Guthrie, Neil L 3:38:33 (5,854)
Guthrie-Brown, Thurstan SC 3:04:13 (1,410)
Gutierrez, Javier 3:44:40 (7,029)
Gutteridge, Michael 5:26:11 (30,799)
Gutteridge, Tim 5:46:29 (33,008)
Guttridge, John 5:27:00 (30,906)
Guy, Justin Anton 4:30:43 (19,153)
Guy, Paul J 3:45:24 (7,188)
Guy, Steven P 3:51:32 (8,544)
Guyatt, David Toby 6:00:48 (34,114)
Guyatt, Robert 5:16:03 (29,234)
Guzman, José Maria 3:44:53 (7,075)
Guzman Enriquez, Raul 3:22:41 (3,258)
Gwilliam, Richard 3:39:47 (6,099)
Gwilliam, Steven John 5:21:05 (30,015)
Gwizdala, Peter A 5:57:34 (33,909)
Gwynn, Tom 3:28:03 (4,063)
Gyles, Peter 3:31:21 (4,642)
Gynn, Stewart W 4:51:45 (24,475)
Gyr, Tom 4:29:50 (18,920)
Habgood, Ian 2:34:15 (100)
Hack, Christopher Edward 5:52:05 (33,507)
Hack, Stuart Antony 5:08:27 (27,970)
Hacker, Jon James 3:29:17 (4,286)
Hackett, Alan G 6:28:25 (35,443)
Hackett, David 5:09:33 (28,158)
Hackett, Graham 4:39:26 (21,368)
Hackett, Matthew Stephen 4:29:27 (18,790)
Hackett, Peter John 4:39:43 (21,440)
Hackett, Simon J 3:42:30 (6,597)
Hackforth, Clive Charles 3:35:13 (5,276)
Hacking, Robert 5:14:44 (29,024)
Hackland, Andrew S 4:03:37 (11,878)
Hackleton, John 3:01:59 (1,257)
Hacon, Ian 3:29:25 (4,306)
Hacon, Neil P 3:07:12 (1,626)
Hadaway, Peter J 4:02:23 (11,575)
Haddad, Fares Sami 3:24:03 (3,440)
Hadden, Matthew 3:28:11 (4,093)
Haddington, Jason N 3:52:52 (8,890)
Haden, Tony F 3:04:00 (1,391)
Hadfield, Leigh Philip 5:35:26 (31,920)
Hadley, Dan 4:04:53 (12,172)
Hadley, Ian Peter 4:59:16 (26,278)
Hadley, Kevin 4:20:55 (16,390)
Hadley, Mark 3:59:06 (10,747)
Hadley, Peter E 4:32:24 (19,538)
Hadley, Steven John 4:19:32 (15,978)
Hadlington, Nigel 5:54:57 (33,712)
Hadnutt, Antony 3:50:02 (8,215)
Hadzima, Tim 4:06:17 (12,520)
Hafner, Colin 5:37:55 (32,203)
Hagen, Oeivind Ravn 5:16:21 (29,286)
Hager, James 3:44:48 (7,056)
Hager, Sean 3:48:36 (7,873)
Haggan, Shaun Andrew 4:12:51 (14,194)
Haggarty, Scot 4:08:54 (13,185)
Haggas, Aaron Leigh 3:40:13 (6,184)
Hagley, Clive John 4:19:51 (16,056)
Hagon, Daniel 5:40:56 (32,475)
Hague, Christopher 3:29:15 (4,280)
Hague, Dean 3:47:17 (7,596)
Hague, Jonathan Paul 4:00:33 (11,126)
Hague, Joseph T 6:10:34 (34,685)

Hague, Lee 3:48:05 (7,754)
Hague, Robert David 4:51:03 (24,316)
Haig, Peter 4:41:19 (21,847)
Haigh, Angus 3:13:07 (2,203)
Haigh, Mike 4:14:41 (14,709)
Haigh, Philip Arther 3:46:00 (7,311)
Haigh, Robert John 5:00:13 (26,502)
Haigh, Ryan 6:00:45 (34,106)
Hailes, Ian Joseph 2:57:19 (881)
Hailes, Simon 4:12:44 (14,165)
Hails, Stephen 3:43:30 (6,776)
Haimes, Andrew Paul 3:30:00 (4,417)
Haimes, Eliot B 2:35:17 (119)
Haimes, Hugh 4:21:36 (16,580)
Haines, Arnaud 5:13:04 (28,763)
Haines, Chris 4:09:39 (13,385)
Haines, Duncan 3:28:05 (4,072)
Haines, Mark 3:57:14 (10,168)
Haines, Paul R 4:42:44 (22,196)
Hainsworth, Paul 4:02:18 (11,557)
Hainsworth, Paul J 3:13:05 (2,201)
Hainsworth, Simon James 5:21:06 (30,019)
Haire, Nicholas A 3:32:21 (4,792)
Hairstains, Kevin James 5:06:36 (27,643)
Hale, Anthony G 4:16:48 (15,247)
Hale, David Mark 3:55:46 (9,706)
Hale, Duncan John 5:31:15 (31,439)
Hales,, Graham, 4:18:39 (15,758)
Haley, Andrew Philip 3:59:13 (10,786)
Halfon, Nathan 5:09:41 (28,176)
Halford, Jonathan 3:54:39 (9,372)
Halford, Paul 3:24:53 (3,560)
Halford, Paul J 2:31:59 (86)
Halgand, Yves 4:04:04 (11,977)
Halil, Canel Sheref 4:09:59 (13,471)
Hall, Adam Jon 4:32:01 (19,441)
Hall, Alex 4:39:45 (21,447)
Hall, Alex Peter 3:37:31 (5,666)
Hall, Alexander 3:12:19 (2,112)
Hall, Alun 3:35:15 (5,278)
Hall, Andrew 3:19:50 (2,946)
Hall, Andrew 4:18:00 (15,579)
Hall, Andy John 3:39:29 (6,038)
Hall, Anthony 4:37:08 (20,779)
Hall, Anthony Edward 5:22:09 (30,171)
Hall, Bruce 3:15:11 (2,458)
Hall, Chris 3:42:45 (6,646)
Hall, Chris 4:24:59 (17,515)
Hall, Christopher G 4:27:20 (18,190)
Hall, Christopher John 3:45:01 (7,098)
Hall, Colin David 4:59:03 (26,227)
Hall, Damian 4:33:55 (19,972)
Hall, Dan 5:09:20 (28,115)
Hall, Daniel 5:23:41 (30,422)
Hall, Daniel James 3:38:41 (5,887)
Hall, David 4:59:41 (26,380)
Hall, David 5:06:56 (27,710)
Hall, David M 3:15:59 (2,553)
Hall, David W 3:00:09 (1,157)
Hall, Dominic A 4:11:56 (13,972)
Hall, Dominic John 3:39:14 (5,988)
Hall, Douglas 4:59:51 (26,414)
Hall, Duncan 3:52:47 (8,863)
Hall, Ed 4:31:23 (19,306)
Hall, Gareth Anthony 4:06:29 (12,569)
Hall, Gary Brian 4:25:15 (17,586)
Hall, Geoff Alan 4:38:22 (21,078)
Hall, Geoffrey 5:33:58 (31,760)
Hall, James 3:30:45 (4,539)
Hall, Joe 4:35:21 (20,309)
Hall, John 3:26:19 (3,784)
Hall, Jonathan 4:46:35 (23,193)
Hall, Jonathan David 2:56:12 (813)
Hall, Keith 4:00:38 (11,151)
Hall, Ken Francis 4:51:52 (24,511)
Hall, Kev 3:46:57 (7,518)
Hall, Lawrence 4:14:12 (14,569)
Hall, Mark J 3:35:54 (5,399)
Hall, Martin 4:49:13 (23,852)
Hall, Martyn 4:37:21 (20,832)
Hall, Matthew 5:02:05 (26,864)
Hall, Matthew J 3:34:59 (5,245)
Hall, Michael 4:17:44 (15,507)
Hall, Michael D 4:09:16 (13,274)
Hall, Mike 2:54:32 (704)
Hall, Nick 3:54:08 (9,244)
Hall, Peter 3:39:15 (5,991)
Hall, Peter Thomas 5:21:38 (30,101)
Hall, Richard 2:58:25 (998)
Hall, Richard 3:26:22 (3,791)
Hall, Richard 4:44:30 (22,638)
Hall, Robert Peter 7:03:05 (36,226)
Hall, Rodney 4:07:04 (12,726)
Hall, Sam T 4:30:31 (19,091)
Hall, Scott 4:16:57 (15,285)
Hall, Simon 2:55:44 (785)
Hall, Simon 3:54:39 (9,372)
Hall, Stephen 5:42:26 (32,630)
Hall, Stuart 2:59:14 (1,077)
Hall, Tony 5:41:38 (32,544)
Hallam, Dan Luke 5:26:20 (30,826)
Hallam, David 3:27:44 (4,005)
Hallam, Geoff 4:50:58 (24,292)
Hallam, Paul 2:59:07 (1,065)
Hallaways, Tim 4:53:05 (24,814)
Hallel, Michel 6:03:26 (34,283)
Hallett, Kevin 3:39:21 (6,018)
Hallett, Peter N 4:07:53 (12,929)
Hallett, Steven A 5:22:28 (30,215)
Halliday, Ben 5:48:01 (33,140)
Halliday, David 4:45:53 (22,997)
Halliday, Martin 4:01:06 (11,277)
Halliday, Simon 5:06:04 (27,543)
Hallifax, Eoin 3:36:46 (5,519)
Halligan, James K 3:14:17 (2,357)
Hallinan, Brian 3:43:55 (6,861)
Hallinan, David 3:43:55 (6,861)
Halloran, Michael Joseph 4:11:35 (13,875)
Halls, Richard 4:25:36 (17,690)
Halman, Michael P 2:29:50 (68)
Halpern, John 5:32:07 (31,553)
Halpin, Alex J 2:55:16 (759)
Halsall, Steven John 5:41:52 (32,573)
Halsall, Tony 4:40:30 (21,640)
Halse, Allan 4:24:58 (17,509)
Halse, Tarquin E 4:09:19 (13,288)
Halsey, Craig J 2:54:21 (691)
Halsey, James Robert 6:22:14 (35,202)
Halsey, Kane A 4:34:12 (20,044)
Halstead, James M 4:54:32 (25,188)
Halstead, Richard Garret Luke 3:50:21 (8,280)
Haly, David R 4:33:09 (19,748)
Ham, Clive 4:13:03 (14,254)
Hamar, Olivier 3:33:27 (4,963)
Hamblin, Christopher Michael 4:31:51 (19,399)
Hamblin, Mark 3:46:11 (7,352)
Hambling, Neil 4:54:37 (25,209)
Hambling, Stewart 3:46:45 (7,472)
Hamblion, Jeff 4:51:44 (24,468)
Hamer, Graham D 5:11:36 (28,489)
Hamer, Oliver James William 4:25:57 (17,798)
Hamid, Melvyn James 6:32:07 (35,568)
Hamill, Robert 4:19:45 (16,030)
Hamill, Vincent 3:39:26 (6,029)
Hamilton, Anthony P 4:12:13 (14,035)
Hamilton, Brian 3:37:52 (5,734)
Hamilton, Craig 3:41:07 (6,348)
Hamilton, Daniel Mark 4:51:55 (24,530)
Hamilton, David 4:01:32 (11,376)
Hamilton, Douglas 4:25:13 (17,578)
Hamilton, Edward S 3:27:55 (4,038)
Hamilton, Ian Robert 4:12:52 (14,199)
Hamilton, James 3:26:06 (3,749)
Hamilton, Mark 3:12:03 (2,096)
Hamilton, Mark 4:52:18 (24,639)
Hamilton, Matthew Brian 5:06:37 (27,649)
Hamilton, Max 4:29:53 (18,943)
Hamilton, Nicholas 3:24:09 (3,460)
Hamilton, Nicholas Ian 4:28:16 (18,443)
Hamilton, Nigel H 4:02:11 (11,536)
Hamilton, Philip 3:47:57 (7,729)
Hamilton, Robert J 3:56:22 (9,887)
Hamilton, Simon 6:08:21 (34,574)
Hamilton, Stephen J 2:59:22 (1,092)
Hamilton, Thomas 4:58:55 (26,192)
Hamilton, Tim 6:27:18 (35,394)
Hamilton, William I 4:53:28 (24,905)
Hamilton-Bruce, Vince 4:41:30 (21,893)
Hamlett, Iain 4:13:38 (14,414)
Hamlin, Terry John 3:37:03 (5,574)
Hamling, Ian 4:11:16 (13,782)
Hamling, Mark 3:25:45 (3,699)
Hammersley, Stuart Raymond 4:44:09 (22,550)
Hammett, Neil 4:19:03 (15,855)
Hammett, Paul Edward 4:45:30 (22,884)
Hammett, Stephen 3:45:24 (7,188)
Hammick, Barry 4:32:05 (19,453)
Hammill, Richard 3:58:41 (10,619)
Hammon, Alexander P 4:11:46 (13,928)
Hammond, Ben 3:39:34 (6,056)
Hammond, David James 4:24:33 (17,407)
Hammond, Jonathan 4:57:31 (25,864)
Hammond, Keith R 3:10:19 (1,934)
Hammond, Matthew E 3:48:28 (7,837)
Hammond, Mick 3:51:17 (8,490)
Hammond, Paul R 3:58:33 (10,574)
Hammond, Stephen 3:25:42 (3,684)
Hamnett, Phillip George 5:01:32 (26,764)
Hamon, John Dale 4:49:05 (23,828)
Hampshire, David 6:44:05 (35,886)
Hampshire, Matt 4:05:53 (12,428)
Hampshire, Stephen 4:19:18 (15,929)
Hampshire, Tobias 4:57:07 (25,784)
Hampshire, William 5:11:51 (28,534)
Hampson, James Kieran 3:59:18 (10,813)
Hampson, Justin Edward 5:49:21 (33,264)
Hampson, Paul 4:59:17 (26,283)
Hampton, Andy 3:58:44 (10,637)
Hampton, Erik C 3:30:06 (4,432)
Hampton, Ray 3:46:09 (7,345)
Hams, Mark 4:50:27 (24,150)
Hamsher, Mark W 5:09:29 (28,141)
Hamwee, Mark 5:27:06 (30,923)
Han, Heewoo 3:34:12 (5,096)
Han, Kim Yow 5:20:23 (29,897)
Hanagarth, Simon Mark 3:43:29 (6,774)
Hancock, Hartley J 3:54:59 (9,474)
Hancock, Lee John 5:16:32 (29,314)
Hancock, Matthew 4:08:32 (13,098)
Hancock, Nicholas C 3:35:29 (5,321)
Hancock, Sam 4:28:44 (18,587)
Hancox, Grenville Roderick 4:52:43 (24,731)
Hancox, Karl Alan 3:23:43 (3,398)
Hand, Kevin 5:25:04 (30,634)
Handcock, Simon William 4:32:52 (19,661)
Handel, Jeffrey 5:22:55 (30,295)
Handley, Darron Lee Anthony 3:26:54 (3,862)
Handley, Mark 3:37:08 (5,588)
Handley, Paul John 3:50:14 (8,255)
Hando, Nicholas A 3:15:06 (2,449)
Hands, Ian 4:10:03 (13,485)
Handy, Thomas R 3:52:58 (8,911)
Handyside, Ben Charles 4:16:19 (15,112)
Handyside, Ethan 4:00:51 (11,204)
Hanford, Peter 4:21:53 (16,664)
Hankins, Eliot Charlies Miles 3:46:02 (7,314)
Hankinson, Adam Lars 3:49:37 (8,122)
Hankinson, Karl 3:33:37 (4,989)
Hanks, Benjamin William 4:01:44 (11,429)
Hanks, Colin 4:20:57 (16,401)
Hanks, Francis Stuart 5:49:26 (33,275)
Hanley, Hugh 5:29:11 (31,174)
Hanley, Jonathan G 2:37:34 (152)
Hanlon, John 3:43:48 (6,832)
Hanman, Timothy Bryan 3:07:38 (1,672)
Hanna, Niall 3:48:08 (7,773)
Hannaford, Charles E 5:06:50 (27,693)
Hannaford, George Christopher 4:13:13 (14,290)
Hannah, Benjamin David 6:31:21 (35,550)
Hannah, Thomas 4:23:31 (17,112)
Hannam, Scott 6:32:38 (35,586)
Hannan, Jon 3:20:57 (3,079)
Hannath, Andrew 4:11:03 (13,736)
Hannay, Sean Michael 5:06:57 (27,716)
Hanner, Kevin 4:22:13 (16,772)
Hanney, Joe 4:05:00 (12,210)
Hannibal, Alan Ronald 3:56:41 (9,992)
Hannington, Richard John 4:22:22 (16,811)
Hanrahan, John Terry 3:56:33 (9,948)

Hanrahan, Paul Thomas 3:32:36 (4,827)
Hansen, Allan S 3:39:02 (5,946)
Hansen, Finn 2:53:26 (638)
Hansen, Jesper Brorson 4:23:27 (17,090)
Hansen, Paul 3:24:20 (3,491)
Hansen, Paul S 3:38:35 (5,866)
Hanson, Benjamin Alexander 5:33:00 (31,663)
Hanson, Dominic 4:13:03 (14,254)
Hanson, Mark 4:33:53 (19,963)
Hanson, Michael F 3:46:16 (7,373)
Hanson, Paul 3:54:31 (9,331)
Hanson, Peter 4:14:04 (14,526)
Hansson, Martin Kenth 4:11:34 (13,867)
Hanton, Ian 4:54:23 (25,154)
Hanwell, Mark 5:01:54 (26,832)
Hapgood, Jason R 4:16:49 (15,252)
Happle, Andrew 4:29:28 (18,797)
Haque, Eyeedul 4:44:08 (22,541)
Haraldsson, Sigurdur Eli 4:43:49 (22,450)
Harber, Mark 3:34:39 (5,183)
Harbert, Barrie John 3:33:46 (5,015)
Harbison, Stewart 4:22:14 (16,776)
Harbon, Richard I 3:39:04 (5,956)
Hardaker, James Edward 3:49:24 (8,064)
Hardegger, Stephan 4:11:59 (13,984)
Hardie, Michel R 3:23:39 (3,387)
Hardiman, Howard 4:35:46 (20,410)
Harding, Andrew 3:08:04 (1,702)
Harding, Andrew 3:48:05 (7,754)
Harding, Andrew 5:09:56 (28,217)
Harding, Andrew Michael 3:59:04 (10,737)
Harding, Bob 3:56:12 (9,841)
Harding, Gareth Paul 5:06:56 (27,710)
Harding, Garry James 4:30:48 (19,171)
Harding, Gary 5:03:43 (27,140)
Harding, Jason 6:29:42 (35,484)
Harding, Mark A 4:10:05 (13,491)
Harding, Paul Thomas 4:10:48 (13,665)
Harding, Phillip Stephen 3:32:47 (4,855)
Harding, Richard 5:28:37 (31,099)
Harding, Robin 4:14:46 (14,732)
Harding, Roger J 5:48:01 (33,140)
Harding, Stephen 4:40:48 (21,721)
Harding, Victor 3:57:10 (10,146)
Hardingham, Nicholas 3:08:05 (1,706)
Hards, James Lewis 4:29:57 (18,971)
Hardwick, Chris 4:36:22 (20,568)
Hardwick, Kevin 4:14:52 (14,753)
Hardwick, Steven W 3:59:42 (10,920)
Hardwick, Tom Peter 5:08:35 (27,985)
Hardwicke, Martin 5:46:18 (32,984)
Hardy, Alan C 4:06:22 (12,544)
Hardy, Andrew 3:47:24 (7,620)
Hardy, Andrew 4:52:11 (24,596)
Hardy, Danny P 4:01:19 (11,315)
Hardy, Geraint 4:16:20 (15,120)
Hardy, Glen G 3:44:51 (7,066)
Hardy, Graham W 4:53:29 (24,913)
Hardy, Jason 6:42:46 (35,856)
Hardy, John 6:06:10 (34,460)
Hardy, Roy William 4:32:49 (19,635)
Hardy, Tony 3:54:51 (9,437)
Hare, Stephen 3:11:49 (2,075)
Hare, Wayne 4:15:59 (15,019)
Hareau, Laurent 4:40:55 (21,752)
Haresign, Martin 5:19:21 (29,754)
Haresnape, Charles 4:29:51 (18,927)
Harfield, Patrick David 6:45:20 (35,918)
Harford, Paul Edward 4:03:29 (11,838)
Hargrave, Jonathan D 3:51:09 (8,461)
Hargreaves, Geoff 3:34:50 (5,218)
Hargreaves, James P 5:06:16 (27,579)
Hargreaves, Jaye 4:23:54 (17,213)
Hargreaves, Mark D 3:27:13 (3,911)
Hargreaves, Matthew Paul 3:05:37 (1,506)
Hargreaves, Michael Steven 4:49:31 (23,911)
Hargreaves, Paul 4:44:43 (22,701)
Hargreaves, Phillip 4:36:09 (20,520)
Hargroves, Robert Edward 4:56:10 (25,572)
Hargroves, Tom 4:56:10 (25,572)
Harhoff, Mark 3:52:59 (8,921)
Hark, Darren Robert 4:45:21 (22,852)
Harkin, Denis 4:55:21 (25,392)
Harkin, Derek 3:44:45 (7,043)
Harkness, Ian 3:32:06 (4,759)
Harkness, Roger 3:29:22 (4,297)
Harkus, Gavin M 2:54:18 (686)
Harkus, Kevin 3:55:25 (9,598)
Harland, Jason 3:37:17 (5,614)
Harley, Andrew 4:36:18 (20,547)
Harley, Luke N 4:18:47 (15,796)
Harley, Reuben 4:30:15 (19,035)
Harlock, Justin K 4:48:36 (23,694)
Harlow, Dominic C 3:34:44 (5,198)
Harlow, Gary 5:45:50 (32,937)
Harlow, Tom 4:01:44 (11,429)
Harman, Dan 3:53:08 (8,950)
Harmar, Robin 4:05:45 (12,395)
Harmes, Robert Lee 3:56:37 (9,964)
Harmon, John David 5:20:38 (29,952)
Harmon, Matthew 4:23:30 (17,104)
Harmsworth, Daniel 5:17:55 (29,534)
Harness, Robert 4:18:28 (15,704)
Harnett, Dennis 3:30:36 (4,510)
Harney, Mark 3:14:46 (2,414)
Harnor, Julian 4:05:24 (12,313)
Harper, Adam Michael 5:50:19 (33,364)
Harper, Alan 4:07:02 (12,720)
Harper, Ben 4:24:45 (17,456)
Harper, Chris 3:50:24 (8,289)
Harper, Colin James 3:46:46 (7,478)
Harper, David Leith 4:17:04 (15,311)
Harper, David Mark 4:34:59 (20,228)
Harper, Michael Anthony 5:17:03 (29,395)
Harper, Paul Michael 3:42:09 (6,540)
Harper, Richard W 3:40:46 (6,284)
Harper, Robin Spencer 3:49:14 (8,033)
Harper, Stephen 4:22:57 (16,975)
Harper, Tim 4:38:00 (20,987)
Harper-Ward, Matt John 4:07:59 (12,957)
Harradine, Mark 4:51:54 (24,521)
Harrap, Mark Duncan 5:28:44 (31,119)
Harraway, Graham Raymond 4:33:53 (19,963)
Harre, Ian 5:08:09 (27,920)
Harries, Dafydd Iestyn 4:19:07 (15,879)
Harries, Jason 5:45:04 (32,876)
Harries, Rhys 3:03:33 (1,356)
Harries, Richard Jonathan 4:27:18 (18,181)
Harries, Richard William James 5:02:51 (26,998)
Harries, Stuart 3:21:06 (3,100)
Harrington, Jed 5:07:27 (27,799)
Harrington, Liam 3:59:39 (10,903)
Harrington, Michael 3:03:53 (1,379)
Harrington, Neil 5:10:31 (28,331)
Harrington, Peter 4:26:09 (17,858)
Harrington, Richard 3:42:18 (6,562)
Harrington, Rod J 3:45:46 (7,261)
Harrington, Scott M 2:50:38 (509)
Harrington, Stephen John 6:20:04 (35,130)
Harrington, Stephen M 3:36:08 (5,436)
Harrington, Thomas Alexander 6:10:56 (34,697)
Harris, Alan 4:06:19 (12,530)
Harris, Alan Peter 6:55:28 (36,121)
Harris, Andrew 3:45:38 (7,235)
Harris, Barry Graham 4:20:03 (16,117)
Harris, Ben 3:56:37 (9,964)
Harris, Benjamin Patrick 4:48:00 (23,546)
Harris, Billy 5:31:59 (31,534)
Harris, Bret 5:12:12 (28,603)
Harris, Christopher P 3:41:40 (6,451)
Harris, Collin 4:40:44 (21,708)
Harris, Craig 4:18:02 (15,589)
Harris, Daniel James 3:40:08 (6,175)
Harris, Daniel Roy 3:23:02 (3,298)
Harris, Danny 4:56:47 (25,711)
Harris, Daryll Ashley 4:49:17 (23,870)
Harris, Dave 3:58:54 (10,689)
Harris, David Ian 5:23:01 (30,307)
Harris, Don 6:24:25 (35,294)
Harris, Geoff Reginald Robert 5:01:38 (26,783)
Harris, Giles M 2:56:54 (854)
Harris, Graham 4:35:16 (20,287)
Harris, Ian 4:08:11 (13,003)
Harris, Ian George 5:00:17 (26,515)
Harris, James Steven 4:47:23 (23,386)
Harris, Jason Robert 5:25:34 (30,706)
Harris, Jeff Robert 4:12:51 (14,194)
Harris, John 4:01:21 (11,322)
Harris, Jon 5:32:00 (31,535)
Harris, Joseph Luther 3:40:13 (6,184)
Harris, Joseph Paul 4:46:47 (23,250)
Harris, Keith John 4:30:45 (19,159)
Harris, Kevin 5:11:34 (28,485)
Harris, Mark 3:03:46 (1,372)
Harris, Mark 4:49:48 (24,007)
Harris, Mark 5:59:41 (34,035)
Harris, Mark Adrian 5:17:28 (29,465)
Harris, Mark Antony 4:03:37 (11,878)
Harris, Mark Richard 4:55:11 (25,352)
Harris, Mark Richard 5:18:38 (29,649)
Harris, Martin Luke 4:13:19 (14,318)
Harris, Matthew J 4:16:56 (15,282)
Harris, Matthew James 4:34:13 (20,052)
Harris, Michael J 4:12:44 (14,165)
Harris, Neil 4:32:59 (19,691)
Harris, Neil Kenneth 5:22:38 (30,245)
Harris, Patrick 4:29:20 (18,759)
Harris, Peter 3:49:33 (8,102)
Harris, Peter 3:54:46 (9,407)
Harris, Philip André 4:42:16 (22,084)
Harris, Phillip John 4:10:59 (13,710)
Harris, Richard 5:06:09 (27,555)
Harris, Richard Andrew 5:34:40 (31,845)
Harris, Richard D 3:04:38 (1,440)
Harris, Richard Lewis 3:37:31 (5,666)
Harris, Robert 4:22:43 (16,908)
Harris, Ryan 4:03:25 (11,823)
Harris, Ryan Christian 3:13:10 (2,206)
Harris, Spencer David 4:43:58 (22,498)
Harris, Stephen 4:06:19 (12,530)
Harris, Steven 5:35:57 (31,987)
Harris, Steven C 3:11:03 (2,003)
Harris, Stuart J 3:53:34 (9,080)
Harris, Thomas James Samuel 5:05:21 (27,424)
Harris, Timothy Edward 4:30:53 (19,185)
Harris, Tony 5:23:52 (30,451)
Harrison, Andrew J 2:46:32 (374)
Harrison, Andrew James 6:06:45 (34,491)
Harrison, Ben 2:57:17 (878)
Harrison, David Selwyn 3:56:08 (9,818)
Harrison, Derek J 3:27:59 (4,048)
Harrison, Graeme R 5:01:38 (26,783)
Harrison, James David 5:16:10 (29,250)
Harrison, John G 6:00:11 (34,077)
Harrison, John Robert 4:16:41 (15,215)
Harrison, John Thomas 4:49:03 (23,813)
Harrison, Keith Ronald 5:24:10 (30,507)
Harrison, Laurence O 3:45:30 (7,207)
Harrison, Lee 4:59:10 (26,252)
Harrison, Matt 3:07:50 (1,686)
Harrison, Matthew James 5:10:58 (28,398)
Harrison, Michael J 3:57:22 (10,196)
Harrison, Mike Robert 3:56:57 (10,071)
Harrison, Nicholas James 5:21:34 (30,090)
Harrison, Nick 3:58:35 (10,590)
Harrison, Paul 4:14:36 (14,680)
Harrison, Paul 8:08:38 (36,591)
Harrison, Phillip 5:59:45 (34,042)
Harrison, Richard P 3:01:27 (1,227)
Harrison, Shaun 3:37:23 (5,634)
Harrison, Simon 5:29:59 (31,295)
Harrison, Simon Anthony 4:22:56 (16,972)
Harrison, Simon Charles 4:46:08 (23,071)
Harrison, Stephen 4:05:20 (12,293)
Harrison, Stephen J 3:56:38 (9,973)
Harrison, Stuart 4:20:56 (16,394)
Harrison, Tim 4:03:27 (11,834)
Harrison, Tom 4:24:50 (17,475)
Harrison, Wesley 2:58:39 (1,015)
Harrison, William J 2:52:08 (574)
Harrison Church, John N 3:30:01 (4,421)
Harrisson, James Thomas 3:52:47 (8,863)
Harrocks, Graeme Robert 5:38:39 (32,279)
Harrold, Bruce 2:40:09 (203)
Harrop, Benjamin 5:28:53 (31,135)
Harrop, Russell 3:16:15 (2,581)
Harry, Richard D 3:03:35 (1,358)
Hart, Andrew Trevor 4:55:48 (25,490)
Hart, Anthony John 4:47:16 (23,355)

Hart, Benjamin James 6:11:55 (34,750)
Hart, Christopher Ian 5:06:39 (27,662)
Hart, Craig A 3:59:25 (10,845)
Hart, Daniel Adam 3:39:52 (6,119)
Hart, Darren Jay 4:19:25 (15,954)
Hart, David William 4:18:00 (15,579)
Hart, Jon 4:25:11 (17,572)
Hart, Jonathan 5:28:00 (31,029)
Hart, Kyle 5:07:13 (27,754)
Hart, Lewis 3:32:32 (4,819)
Hart, Malcolm Paul 4:29:46 (18,905)
Hart, Mark Andrew 4:09:47 (13,416)
Hart, Nigel Cadby 3:22:16 (3,214)
Hart, Nigel Grantley 4:06:08 (12,484)
Hart, Paul R 3:42:05 (6,527)
Hart, Willem Hendrik 5:00:04 (26,471)
Harte, Fergal 5:54:28 (33,673)
Harte, John P 4:38:34 (21,135)
Hartel, Charles 3:33:12 (4,926)
Hartin, Alan David 4:37:20 (20,828)
Hartland, Ian Edward 4:30:14 (19,031)
Hartley, Allan 3:49:35 (8,112)
Hartley, Ben 3:42:26 (6,584)
Hartley, Chris D 3:46:02 (7,314)
Hartley, Dave Joseph 4:21:13 (16,465)
Hartley, David Alan 4:40:09 (21,524)
Hartley, David Stephen 5:57:45 (33,916)
Hartley, Jay 3:51:08 (8,456)
Hartley, Tobias D 5:00:05 (26,474)
Hartlieb, Kai 3:37:55 (5,746)
Hartmann, Stefan 5:02:10 (26,881)
Hartnell, Haydn 2:57:34 (910)
Hartropp, Jon 3:39:06 (5,963)
Hartshorn, David C 4:52:23 (24,657)
Hartshorn, Paul John 4:03:15 (11,792)
Hartshorne, Carl Richard 5:34:29 (31,821)
Hartwright, Jeremy P 5:45:35 (32,916)
Harvey, Alex, James 3:28:02 (4,058)
Harvey, Chris Ronald 4:29:34 (18,826)
Harvey, Clive 4:22:37 (16,885)
Harvey, Daniel 4:55:58 (25,530)
Harvey, Duncan 3:59:13 (10,786)
Harvey, Edward 3:38:30 (5,846)
Harvey, Glen D 4:03:54 (11,944)
Harvey, Ian Michael 3:53:26 (9,036)
Harvey, Ian R 6:52:02 (36,043)
Harvey, John Daniel 4:17:17 (15,374)
Harvey, Kevin Richard 3:24:34 (3,519)
Harvey, Lee 4:02:28 (11,599)
Harvey, Matthew J 3:01:59 (1,257)
Harvey, Neil Michael 4:09:33 (13,351)
Harvey, Robert 3:15:54 (2,540)
Harvey, Shane 5:31:44 (31,505)
Harvey, Simon 3:59:06 (10,747)
Harvey, Tim 3:09:30 (1,857)
Harvey, Timothy J 6:06:27 (34,479)
Harvey-Austen, Kevin David 4:16:28 (15,157)
Harvie, Alexander James 4:18:51 (15,815)
Harvie, Gavin D 3:00:17 (1,161)
Harwood, Alan 5:07:48 (27,860)
Harwood, Grant N 5:07:19 (27,772)
Harwood, Peter James 4:59:51 (26,414)
Harwood, Tim B 4:28:36 (18,548)
Haskey, John T 3:01:29 (1,230)
Haslam, Andy 3:33:56 (5,048)
Haslam, Nick J 4:04:04 (11,977)
Haslam, Steven 6:06:26 (34,477)
Hassall, Glyn R 4:58:37 (26,122)
Hasselbalch, Hans 4:56:41 (25,689)
Hassell, James 6:13:02 (34,804)
Hassett, John 4:57:54 (25,948)
Hassett, Simon R 3:44:28 (6,984)
Hastings, Richard James 4:36:37 (20,637)
Hastings, Roy 4:40:43 (21,700)
Hastings, Steve C 4:44:33 (22,654)
Hatch, James 3:31:16 (4,619)
Hatcher, Gary Robin 3:09:19 (1,834)
Hatfield, Lee 4:44:35 (22,666)
Hatfield, Mark Andrew 4:09:56 (13,453)
Hatfield, Robert J 3:10:01 (1,907)
Hatfield, Tim 5:41:56 (32,583)
Hathaway, David John 3:39:53 (6,122)
Hathaway, Marc Daniel 4:36:36 (20,631)
Hatley, Daniel 6:27:43 (35,413)
Hatley, Mark 3:42:47 (6,654)
Hattee, Dominic 4:49:51 (24,019)
Hatter, Kevin V 5:04:59 (27,363)
Hatter, Richard Mark 3:48:42 (7,898)
Hattersley, Andrew Tym 3:55:37 (9,647)
Hattersley, Steven A 4:26:04 (17,830)
Hatton, Michael 2:38:58 (176)
Hatvany, Alan P 3:24:46 (3,547)
Hau, Ken Gar Fay 4:30:24 (19,064)
Hauck, Christian 3:49:06 (8,000)
Haugestoel, Per Olav 4:20:56 (16,394)
Haughian, Adrian Joseph 3:33:51 (5,036)
Haugland, Tolleiv 3:46:23 (7,394)
Haun, Dieter 3:47:24 (7,620)
Hausken, Oddvar 3:48:00 (7,738)
Hautamaki, Harri M 5:04:22 (27,253)
Hautebas, Jerome 3:08:17 (1,728)
Havard, Michael 3:05:07 (1,471)
Havell, John 5:12:49 (28,703)
Havenhand, David C 3:04:48 (1,446)
Havens, Garry 3:55:20 (9,571)
Havers, Nick 3:44:39 (7,024)
Haverson, Matthew 3:57:02 (10,109)
Haverson, Quinton 5:06:02 (27,539)
Havill, Antony R 5:24:13 (30,515)
Havlin, Kev J 5:23:50 (30,447)
Haw, Philip 5:07:33 (27,825)
Hawcutt, Daniel 3:59:34 (10,886)
Hawes, Michael Lee 6:00:45 (34,106)
Hawes, Nik 4:51:44 (24,468)
Hawes, Timothy Garry 4:22:54 (16,962)
Hawinkels, Stephen John 3:35:15 (5,278)
Hawker, James 4:09:20 (13,293)
Hawker, Jon Charles 3:46:48 (7,489)
Hawker, Kevin R 2:51:39 (552)
Hawker, Noele 3:09:10 (1,822)
Hawkes, Iain Peter 4:35:52 (20,437)
Hawkes, Richard Anthony 5:18:26 (29,617)
Hawking, Peter Tony 3:39:04 (5,956)
Hawkins, Alex T 3:12:58 (2,186)
Hawkins, Andrew Paul 4:18:30 (15,715)
Hawkins, Christopher Frank 4:02:09 (11,522)
Hawkins, Daniel Peter 4:18:50 (15,803)
Hawkins, Graeme 3:28:54 (4,210)
Hawkins, Jeff John 3:45:04 (7,108)
Hawkins, Mitchell W 3:59:12 (10,779)
Hawkins, Robert A 4:36:46 (20,674)
Hawkins, Simon Frederick 3:30:49 (4,552)
Hawksford, Clive Robert 4:18:54 (15,828)
Hawkshaw, Paul 3:45:58 (7,305)
Hawksley, Gary Julian 3:04:21 (1,418)
Hawkswood, Jamie 6:22:40 (35,219)
Haworth, David Edward 6:17:16 (34,998)
Hawthorn, Ben 5:25:56 (30,771)
Hawthorne, Adam George 4:46:01 (23,030)
Hawthorne, James Ranshall Rowe 5:35:41 (31,952)
Hawtin, Andrew 4:16:53 (15,266)
Haxton, David 4:27:15 (18,167)
Hay, Douglas C 6:32:32 (35,584)
Hay, George Theodore 6:50:58 (36,012)
Hay, Jamie W 2:58:08 (966)
Hay, Mark William 4:44:10 (22,553)
Hay, Robert Graham 3:52:37 (8,826)
Hay, Roy 5:34:14 (31,785)
Hayball, Roger 4:59:00 (26,214)
Haycock, Nick R 4:04:04 (11,977)
Hayden, Stuart 4:10:16 (13,542)
Haydon, Chris 4:06:50 (12,670)
Haydon, David John 3:18:36 (2,830)
Hayer, Karlwinder S 2:59:39 (1,122)
Hayes, Dan 3:43:43 (6,808)
Hayes, David 4:04:45 (12,145)
Hayes, Derek 4:53:05 (24,814)
Hayes, Jacob S 2:57:45 (936)
Hayes, Jason Anthony 4:45:09 (22,806)
Hayes, Jeffrey 5:10:32 (28,335)
Hayes, Jim David 3:28:15 (4,099)
Hayes, Kenneth S 5:16:09 (29,246)
Hayes, Kim 5:48:22 (33,180)
Hayes, Martin 4:02:50 (11,685)
Hayes, Michael 3:17:32 (2,717)
Hayes, Nicholas 5:05:35 (27,464)
Hayes, Paul M 2:52:54 (615)
Hayes, Peter J 4:57:24 (25,840)
Hayes, Richard Neil 2:57:24 (889)
Hayes, William John 3:56:58 (10,077)
Hayhow, Christopher Peter 4:21:32 (16,556)
Hayler, Colin N 3:53:22 (9,018)
Hayles, Andrew 3:58:18 (10,491)
Hayley Bell, James E 4:12:15 (14,045)
Hayllar, Nic 5:43:29 (32,718)
Haylock, Garry 5:39:20 (32,336)
Haylock, Keith James 4:21:29 (16,542)
Haylock, Michael John 4:04:24 (12,050)
Hayman, Tom 5:05:34 (27,459)
Hayne, Ian Robert 3:42:15 (6,556)
Hayne, Robert 3:52:23 (8,764)
Haynes, Dominic 4:19:30 (15,973)
Haynes, Jonathan R 3:13:38 (2,270)
Haynes, Lee Anthony 4:19:07 (15,879)
Haynes, Michael John 4:33:53 (19,963)
Haynes, Paul 4:32:22 (19,533)
Haynes, Richard 3:31:00 (4,578)
Haynes, Rupert Jason 4:11:31 (13,852)
Haynes, Simon 4:32:51 (19,654)
Hays, Ian 3:59:33 (10,882)
Haysman, Paul Gordon 3:57:23 (10,199)
Haysom, Jim L 5:14:50 (29,043)
Hayter, Benjamin Richard 5:23:14 (30,346)
Hayter, Quinton Neil 4:57:35 (25,875)
Hayter, Stuart John 5:06:00 (27,530)
Hayton, Paul Graham 3:43:02 (6,703)
Hayward, Luke James 5:06:42 (27,672)
Hayward, Mike 4:45:06 (22,799)
Hayward, Peter Richard 4:31:33 (19,342)
Haywood, Geoffrey 5:23:09 (30,329)
Hazart, Didier 5:36:42 (32,074)
Hazel, Simon R 3:08:30 (1,754)
Hazelden, David James 4:37:50 (20,951)
Hazell, Colin 3:36:52 (5,541)
Hazell, Daniel James 5:50:11 (33,349)
Hazell, Graham George 5:25:58 (30,782)
Hazell, Paul 4:53:05 (24,814)
Hazell, Wayne David 4:18:12 (15,629)
Hazen, Louis 3:53:03 (8,936)
Hazlehurst, Mark 4:25:56 (17,795)
Hazlewood, Gavin Andrew 4:52:16 (24,619)
Hazra, Bhupinder Singh 5:01:49 (26,813)
Head, Jonathan M 3:50:38 (8,343)
Head, Peter 6:18:32 (35,059)
Head, Richard John 4:39:36 (21,411)
Heading, Jeremy Roger 4:12:52 (14,199)
Headon, David L 2:54:51 (727)
Heald, Jon 4:28:47 (18,600)
Healeas, Andrew J 5:45:15 (32,889)
Healey, Andrew 4:20:20 (16,215)
Healey, Chris 4:21:48 (16,636)
Healey, James Oliver 4:33:16 (19,791)
Healey, Wayne 5:25:22 (30,675)
Healey Pearce, Philip 5:31:23 (31,462)
Healy, Andrew James 4:19:42 (16,014)
Healy, Michael Joseph Anthony 3:47:08 (7,551)
Heap, Clive R 4:48:47 (23,741)
Heap, Jonathan 4:12:09 (14,022)
Heap, Michael 4:07:05 (12,730)
Heard, Jamie Richard 4:50:54 (24,269)
Hearn, Shaun 5:00:05 (26,474)
Hearnden, Nicky 4:16:53 (15,266)
Hearty, John 7:16:11 (36,373)
Heaselgrave, Robert 4:10:03 (13,485)
Heaslewood, Adam 4:04:39 (12,114)
Heath, Adam 3:53:53 (9,177)
Heath, Brenhan 4:36:46 (20,674)
Heath, Darren P 4:47:27 (23,400)
Heath, Frederick C 3:35:15 (5,278)
Heath, Patrick 5:24:24 (30,540)
Heath, Rob Derek 4:58:08 (26,001)
Heath, Ross Frazer 7:28:45 (36,460)
Heath, Thomas P 3:41:19 (6,389)
Heathcote, Richard A 3:39:15 (5,991)
Heather, Adam John 5:11:46 (28,515)
Heather, Giles 5:24:38 (30,574)
Heather, Mark Andrew 4:46:37 (23,209)
Heatley, Gerard 5:05:46 (27,487)
Heaton, Andrew Robert 4:17:17 (15,374)

Heaton, David 4:45:09 (22,806)
Heaton, Geoffrey 4:04:09 (11,996)
Heaton, Michael....4:54:05 (25,067)
Heaton, Oliver....5:13:04 (28,763)
Hebditch, George 4:24:16 (17,306)
Hecht, Thorsten....5:23:55 (30,464)
Heck, Bernhard....4:38:22 (21,078)
Heck, Jochen 4:28:29 (18,518)
Hedaux, Jon 5:14:20 (28,966)
Heddon, Tony 5:08:21 (27,956)
Hedgcombe, Richard Ian 6:27:44 (35,414)
Hedgeland, Tobias....3:00:48 (1,197)
Hedger, Graham H 2:40:27 (209)
Hedger, Paul W....6:31:06 (35,538)
Hedges, Tim....4:20:22 (16,223)
Hedgethorne, Peter....4:17:51 (15,533)
Hedgman, James....3:37:33 (5,678)
Hedley, Andrew G....4:07:07 (12,735)
Hedmann, Lindsay Martin 3:40:33 (6,248)
Heeks, Adam 3:58:57 (10,704)
Heeks, Paul....4:09:54 (13,443)
Heeley, David G....3:33:50 (5,031)
Heezen, Pedro....3:18:05 (2,777)
Hefferan, Rob Patrick....3:51:26 (8,524)
Heffernan, Paul Adrian 4:12:59 (14,229)
Hefni, Mohamed....5:28:08 (31,045)
Hegarty, George 3:46:05 (7,335)
Hegarty, Hugo....3:19:53 (2,950)
Hegarty, Ross Paul....5:46:18 (32,984)
Hegerty, Kristian Stewart 5:16:25 (29,295)
Hegewald, Michael....3:58:42 (10,625)
Hegley, Marc Richard 6:02:23 (34,211)
Hehir, Gerry 4:01:37 (11,396)
Hehir, Paul 5:08:40 (27,999)
Hehir, Ron....5:12:21 (28,626)
Heierle, George....6:06:25 (34,473)
Heighton, Ben....4:04:37 (12,106)

Heiner, Darryl John 5:33:28 (31,713)

My first experience of the London Marathon was the ballot in 1989 when I was an Aussie living in London. I was unsuccessful although it started a 21-year obsession of which I never gave up hope. I entered another two times, once pulling out due to injury and the second time making the trip over to London to compete, instead getting tickets to the FA Cup semi-final. This was a hard decision; however, the possibility of never getting another chance to go to a FA semi-final was too great to pass up, so I decided to try again by entering London Marathon in 2010. This again provided challenges with the air space closures, although after spending a week in Vienna and a number of sleepless nights I made it!

Heir, Jon Marius....3:50:29 (8,308)
Heitmueller, Ludwig....4:21:54 (16,674)
Hellan, Erik 4:11:17 (13,786)
Hellawell, Peter....3:10:43 (1,964)
Hellemans, Hendrik 3:57:29 (10,225)
Hellen, Brian P....5:19:02 (29,705)
Heller, Douglas P 2:54:13 (682)
Hellier, Ian....3:24:06 (3,452)
Hellier, Mark 5:42:18 (32,617)
Helliwell, Paul 2:56:48 (849)
Helliwell, Peter....6:14:58 (34,885)
Helliwell, Stephen Andrew....3:32:02 (4,745)
Hellon, Ray....4:49:39 (23,961)
Hellowell, Paul Garry....5:29:59 (31,295)
Hellqvist, Håkan....3:42:17 (6,560)
Helm, Matthew Werner 4:36:05 (20,500)
Helme, Mark 3:30:44 (4,534)
Helmore, Jeffrey W 3:10:32 (1,950)
Helps, David 3:29:30 (4,320)
Helsby, Sean 3:50:01 (8,213)
Helsby, Stephen....4:27:14 (18,160)
Heming, Charles 4:51:01 (24,309)
Heming, Tim Keith....3:11:14 (2,020)
Hemingway, Brian....4:45:37 (22,919)
Hemingway, Ian....5:28:43 (31,117)
Hemingway, Maurice 3:27:30 (3,961)
Hemming, Andrew 3:42:17 (6,560)
Hemming, Daniel David....4:05:06 (12,229)
Hemming, Michael Paul....4:51:38 (24,447)
Hemming, Sean 4:58:54 (26,189)
Hemmings, Tony....5:32:24 (31,585)
Hemmington, Jim Henry 4:20:25 (16,239)
Hempstead, Barry F....4:38:45 (21,185)
Hemson, Robert Anthony 6:02:25 (34,213)
Henderson, Alan James....4:59:12 (26,264)
Henderson, David....2:59:01 (1,054)
Henderson, David G....2:49:16 (458)
Henderson, David M....4:32:06 (19,459)
Henderson, Graham....3:44:01 (6,886)
Henderson, James A 3:10:14 (1,925)
Henderson, James William....5:20:49 (29,979)
Henderson, Jonathan J....3:16:05 (2,562)
Henderson, Rhys K....3:27:24 (3,942)
Henderson, Robert....5:12:07 (28,587)
Henderson, Robin J....4:32:06 (19,459)
Henderson, Ross James 4:44:04 (22,523)
Henderson, Trad Fraser....5:06:44 (27,679)
Henderson, Will....3:42:04 (6,524)
Hendon, Ian....4:41:05 (21,790)
Hendrie, Lewis 5:12:24 (28,629)
Hendry, Stuart....3:32:49 (4,864)
Hendy, Ashley J 4:47:16 (23,355)
Heneage, Gary....3:29:42 (4,360)
Henebery, Anthony....5:03:58 (27,179)
Henesy, Ewan....3:22:31 (3,241)
Heney, Kenneth J 2:47:43 (412)
Henington, John 3:55:12 (9,528)
Henley, Scott Christopher 4:56:08 (25,565)
Henley, Wayne D....3:04:17 (1,415)
Hennah, James Francis....5:29:03 (31,157)
Hennebert, Jean-Pierre....4:34:18 (20,070)
Hennebery, John J....4:41:46 (21,959)
Henness, David Bryant 4:28:12 (18,417)
Hennessey, Jamie 4:29:56 (18,966)
Hennessy, Brendan 3:20:19 (2,992)
Hennessy, Darren....5:11:11 (28,431)
Hennessy, Mark....3:54:01 (9,215)
Hennessy, Paul 4:23:09 (17,013)
Henney, Sean....4:47:57 (23,535)
Hennig, Dietmar....4:06:37 (12,604)
Henning, Stephen James....4:28:24 (18,487)
Henningsen, Eirik W 4:27:27 (18,220)
Hennis, Philip 3:34:00 (5,057)
Hennocque, Christophe....4:06:16 (12,516)
Henri, Dean....4:50:51 (24,254)
Henriksen, Lars....3:46:05 (7,335)
Henrion, Marc....2:46:32 (374)
Henriques, Roberto 5:40:12 (32,412)
Henry, Chris John 5:09:59 (28,230)
Henry, Derek....4:09:20 (13,293)
Henry, John 6:57:25 (36,147)
Henry, Michael Gerald 5:50:35 (33,397)
Henry, Sheridan John....4:18:34 (15,732)
Henshaw, Richard David....4:34:29 (20,119)
Henson, Andy....4:21:00 (16,412)
Henson, Dean 4:42:23 (22,108)
Henson, Jason Mark....3:07:17 (1,630)
Heppenstall, Jason 4:20:08 (16,145)
Hepworth, Andrew....6:02:07 (34,193)
Hepworth, Charlie D 4:11:16 (13,782)
Hepworth, David Anthony 3:21:54 (3,182)
Hepworth, Ed....6:36:19 (35,687)
Hepworth, Ian D 3:58:56 (10,698)
Hepworth, Robert....3:38:45 (5,899)
Heracleous, Jake 5:11:40 (28,494)
Herard, Alain 3:57:20 (10,190)
Heraty, Timothy C....4:28:09 (18,397)
Herbert, Charles 3:32:47 (4,855)
Herbert, John C 2:37:34 (152)
Herbert, Kevin....4:58:33 (26,104)
Herbert, Luke David....4:04:04 (11,977)
Herbert, Luke E 3:06:54 (1,601)
Herbert, Mark 3:41:21 (6,395)
Herbert, Neil Michael....4:18:03 (15,597)
Herbert, Raymond 7:10:03 (36,308)
Herbertson, Nathan C 5:13:04 (28,763)
Herd, Jonathan 4:25:33 (17,677)
Herdman, Chris 3:36:30 (5,481)
Herdman, Gareth....5:13:32 (28,846)
Heresbach, Denis....3:18:01 (2,768)
Hericher, Romain 3:34:34 (5,166)
Herinox, David....5:00:24 (26,535)
Herman, Stephen Mark....3:57:40 (10,286)
Hermans, Perry Martin Alan 4:25:21 (17,619)
Hern, Richard Seymour....3:45:09 (7,127)
Hernandez, Jaime 4:19:51 (16,056)
Hernandez, Juan....6:12:38 (34,790)
Hernandez Pardo, Carlos....5:44:38 (32,832)
Hernando, Antonio 4:24:08 (17,268)
Hernando, Jaime....3:04:13 (1,410)
Herodotou, Nicholas 5:35:49 (31,971)
Heron, Carl 3:40:05 (6,163)
Herrera, Alan 5:30:26 (31,341)
Herring, Stephen 2:41:18 (234)
Herrington, David A 3:57:46 (10,318)
Herrington, Graeme....3:46:14 (7,362)
Herron, Adam....3:50:15 (8,259)
Herron, Colman....4:09:18 (13,283)
Herschell, Sam 4:55:51 (25,497)
Hertz, Haydn Justin 4:56:12 (25,586)
Herzog, Georg....4:49:42 (23,978)
Hesketh, William John....4:29:22 (18,768)
Heslop, Chris....3:54:57 (9,460)
Heslop, Garry 4:04:01 (11,962)
Hesnault, Pierre 4:03:35 (11,868)
Hester, Gerard Martin 5:11:59 (28,558)
Hester, Mark....4:07:32 (12,843)
Hetherington, Christopher 6:37:46 (35,718)
Hetherington, Gary 2:45:05 (345)
Hetherton, Bill Gareth 3:05:16 (1,480)
Hetterschijt, Rogier....4:01:02 (11,258)
Hetzinger, Georg....3:35:21 (5,295)
Heuch, Jon 4:48:05 (23,564)
Heuer, David 3:39:24 (6,022)
Heuze, Franck....2:57:59 (954)
Hewer, David Edward....5:40:33 (32,439)
Hewes, Nigel....3:22:42 (3,260)
Hewett, Arron....6:54:55 (36,110)
Hewett, Lee 4:01:31 (11,372)
Hewett, Marc....5:06:39 (27,662)
Hewett, Richard 3:41:17 (6,386)
Hewit, Dominic 4:32:17 (19,512)
Hewitt, David Michael 6:41:45 (35,827)
Hewitt, Joe....6:01:07 (34,137)
Hewitt, Kevan 3:34:07 (5,083)
Hewitt, Kevin....4:41:44 (21,948)
Hewitt, Kris....4:05:18 (12,283)
Hewitt, Martin....6:16:24 (34,942)
Hewitt, Phillip 4:00:15 (11,044)
Hewitt, Richard G A....3:27:37 (3,986)

LONDON MARATHON

Hewitt, Steven 3:43:31 (6,778)
Hewitt, Toby John 3:21:16 (3,115)
Hewitt, Will 4:37:03 (20,758)
Hewlett, Martin 3:05:59 (1,532)
Hewlett, Martin J 3:43:53 (6,854)
Hewlett, William J 4:59:00 (26,214)
Hewson, Guy 6:16:21 (34,940)
Hewson, Michael J 4:43:20 (22,325)
Hexter, Adam Thomas 3:48:42 (7,898)
Heyes, Richard C. 3:45:18 (7,162)
Heyes, Steven 6:19:30 (35,100)
Heywood, Karl Andrew 4:47:49 (23,502)
Heywood, Mark 5:13:43 (28,876)
Heywood, Peter James 3:57:48 (10,331)
Heyworth, Gary W 3:38:23 (5,827)
Hiatt, David 3:42:21 (6,570)
Hibberd, Adrian N 5:03:23 (27,086)
Hibberd, Keith 4:30:03 (18,987)
Hibberd, Roy George Frederick ..4:54:35 (25,199)
Hibbert, Andrew Ian 5:09:16 (28,095)
Hibbert, Kevin Francis 6:12:36 (34,787)
Hibbitt, Phil 4:07:36 (12,855)
Hibble, Chris James 4:49:33 (23,922)
Hibbs, John 5:43:33 (32,724)
Hibbs, Sam Raymond 4:19:26 (15,957)
Hick, Gareth Dewi 4:52:07 (24,578)
Hick, Tiernan 4:35:35 (20,362)
Hickey, Christian 4:48:41 (23,715)
Hickey, Christopher 4:05:13 (12,259)
Hickey, Ray John 4:17:45 (15,512)
Hickey, Richard Malcolm 4:13:51 (14,470)
Hickey, Stuart John 3:38:37 (5,874)
Hickinbottom, Steven 4:33:21 (19,812)
Hickling, Julian 4:56:42 (25,695)
Hickling, Oliver Jonathan 4:38:36 (21,143)
Hickman, Blair 3:57:34 (10,253)
Hickman, Dean 4:29:16 (18,747)
Hickman, Ross Stephen 4:03:49 (11,928)
Hicks, David 4:50:15 (24,107)
Hicks, Duncan 5:13:36 (28,857)
Hicks, Michael Philip James 5:26:57 (30,898)
Hicks, Nicholas 4:05:40 (12,371)
Hicks, Paul 5:18:51 (29,675)
Hicks, Paul Andrew 5:27:51 (31,008)
Hicks, Robert I 2:57:23 (886)
Hicks, Simon 4:19:35 (15,990)
Hicks, William John Paliaret 3:26:01 (3,736)
Hickson, Andrew 3:17:05 (2,671)
Hickson, Philip James 4:07:56 (12,940)
Hier, Gareth R 4:17:49 (15,530)
Higdon, Simon 3:59:53 (10,961)
Higginbotham, Gary Lee 4:12:49 (14,184)
Higgins, Andrew 4:02:39 (11,638)
Higgins, Andrew Allan 4:06:14 (12,506)
Higgins, Anthony David 4:18:07 (15,614)
Higgins, Antony James 4:16:41 (15,215)
Higgins, Carl Richard 4:07:12 (12,749)
Higgins, Christopher Donald T ..4:36:36 (20,631)
Higgins, Joel Toby 4:05:24 (12,313)
Higgins, Liam Martin 5:57:29 (33,901)
Higgins, Patrick G 4:52:03 (24,558)
Higgins, Patrick Joseph 3:57:42 (10,297)
Higgins, Tom 5:50:08 (33,346)
Higgs, Adam C 3:07:32 (1,654)
Higgs, David 4:29:53 (18,943)
Higgs, Duncan 4:12:21 (14,064)
Higgs, Phil 4:57:43 (25,912)
Higgs, Simon J 4:37:51 (20,955)
Higham, Chris 5:02:28 (26,938)
Highcock, Richard 4:35:20 (20,301)
Highett, Stewart 4:08:10 (12,998)
Highfield, Colin Robert 3:33:22 (4,945)
Highfield, Mark 4:07:57 (12,949)
Highfield, Ross 3:27:08 (3,892)
Highfield-Robert, Guy 5:22:08 (30,168)
Highlands, Angus Macdonald ..4:15:54 (15,001)
Hight, Christopher Meirion 5:30:56 (31,406)
Higman, William 4:24:38 (17,425)
Hignett, Kieran John 4:29:47 (18,909)
Higson, Barry John 3:51:10 (8,464)
Higson, Douglas Laurence 4:12:42 (14,158)
Higson, James Frederick 4:12:41 (14,153)
Higson, Martin 6:37:42 (35,714)

Hilbery, Graham J 4:36:56 (20,723)
Hiley, Paul 3:26:38 (3,822)
Hill, Adrian 3:36:57 (5,554)
Hill, Alastair Duncan 4:20:54 (16,387)
Hill, Andrew 4:34:39 (20,156)
Hill, Andrew 4:53:30 (24,917)
Hill, Andrew 5:04:08 (27,216)
Hill, Chris 5:43:27 (32,716)
Hill, Christian A 4:52:40 (24,725)
Hill, Daniel 4:33:22 (19,815)
Hill, Daniel 5:05:05 (27,382)
Hill, Daniel Lee 4:50:24 (24,141)
Hill, David Richard 4:08:32 (13,098)
Hill, Graham 4:00:00 (10,984)
Hill, Graham 4:13:15 (14,297)
Hill, Graham Ryan 5:23:34 (30,396)
Hill, Hugo Douglas 3:39:17 (6,000)
Hill, Iain 4:22:13 (16,772)
Hill, James P 5:16:59 (29,383)
Hill, Jason 5:15:25 (29,128)
Hill, John 4:29:10 (18,727)
Hill, Joseph 4:55:53 (25,508)
Hill, Kenneth 3:09:26 (1,849)
Hill, Laurie Benjamin 4:36:28 (20,591)
Hill, Lawrence 3:47:22 (7,612)
Hill, Lawson 4:14:01 (14,508)
Hill, Mark 2:57:41 (930)
Hill, Martin D 5:47:40 (33,109)
Hill, Michael J 5:07:30 (27,812)
Hill, Michael V 3:29:36 (4,342)
Hill, Mick 5:06:37 (27,649)
Hill, Oliver 3:14:26 (2,375)
Hill, Paul Daniel 4:00:53 (11,211)
Hill, Peter D 3:27:33 (3,971)
Hill, Ray 4:36:19 (20,551)
Hill, Richard M 4:08:44 (13,146)
Hill, Richard S 4:29:48 (18,913)
Hill, Robert 3:46:03 (7,322)
Hill, Robert A 4:22:21 (16,804)
Hill, Ryan 3:31:35 (4,679)
Hill, Simon 4:18:55 (15,832)
Hill, Simon Francis 4:39:15 (21,321)
Hill, Stuart 4:53:37 (24,947)
Hill, Walter J 3:04:53 (1,454)
Hillard, Kevin 4:17:30 (15,439)
Hillary, Robert James 3:55:07 (9,508)
Hillebrandt, Mick 4:59:49 (26,411)
Hillegeist, Ralph 4:10:19 (13,548)
Hillery, Carl Jonathan 4:04:00 (11,959)
Hilliage, Neil James 3:33:10 (4,921)
Hilliard, Steve 3:35:30 (5,325)
Hillier, Paul 4:03:28 (11,837)
Hillier, Tony Derek 4:31:38 (19,362)
Hillier, Vincent William 4:39:29 (21,381)
Hillier, Will R 3:01:14 (1,216)
Hills, Jamie 3:54:04 (9,225)
Hills, Jason 3:50:13 (8,251)
Hills, Martin P 4:21:26 (16,531)
Hills, Tim M 3:49:35 (8,112)
Hills, Tom Geoffrey 4:30:07 (19,003)
Hills, Vernon James 4:49:52 (24,021)
Hillson, Mark A 3:40:24 (6,214)
Hillyer, Barrie David 4:51:52 (24,511)
Hilton, Alan Gary 4:43:31 (22,372)
Hilton, Dominic J 3:02:54 (1,321)
Hilton, Guy 4:30:04 (18,994)
Hilton, Lee Simon 4:56:52 (25,737)
Hilton, Paul Edward 5:36:01 (31,998)
Hilton, Russ A 5:04:40 (27,308)
Hindmarsh, David J 3:07:34 (1,660)
Hinds, Carlos 5:30:30 (31,357)
Hinds, David 3:39:32 (6,050)
Hinds, Jason 5:07:53 (27,877)
Hinds, Tom 4:02:15 (11,547)

Hine, Daryl 4:25:14 (17,583)
Hine, Paul G 4:01:59 (11,486)
Hineman, Steve 5:16:52 (29,367)
Hines, Adam 3:23:49 (3,410)
Hines, Christopher William 4:06:53 (12,682)
Hingley, Gregory 3:58:03 (10,397)
Hinsley, Jeff 4:05:37 (12,360)
Hinton, Geoffrey P 4:18:52 (15,818)
Hinton, Lee Stiles 3:38:14 (5,811)
Hiorns, Stephen R 3:38:01 (5,767)
Hippesroither, Gerald 3:37:31 (5,666)
Hipshon, Mark J 4:07:40 (12,878)
Hirons, Jonathan Paul 4:27:17 (18,174)
Hirons, Peter 5:17:59 (29,544)
Hirons, Richard 4:36:45 (20,670)
Hirsch, Michael 4:23:06 (17,003)
Hirsch, Todd 3:42:55 (6,678)
Hirshler, Gilon David 3:59:03 (10,733)
Hirst, John 5:33:44 (31,739)
Hirst, John G 6:25:35 (35,331)
Hirst, Peter C. 5:04:50 (27,339)
Hiscock, Gareth David Lewis 4:17:44 (15,507)
Hiscock, Spencer Colin 5:09:03 (28,055)
Hiscocks, Matthew Peter 4:13:00 (14,239)
Hiscox, John W 3:25:23 (3,627)
Hiscox, Richard J 4:35:46 (20,410)
Hita Hita, Luis Mariano 3:24:25 (3,499)
Hitch, David 6:28:05 (35,432)
Hitchcock, David John 4:12:35 (14,120)
Hitchcock, Simon John 5:25:57 (30,774)
Hitchcock, Stephen J 4:00:07 (11,011)
Hitchens, Nicholas 3:54:37 (9,359)
Hitchings, Stephen James 4:00:18 (11,059)
Hitchman, Christopher 3:06:02 (1,537)
Hivelin, Jean Marie 5:19:54 (29,836)
Ho, Chi K. 3:56:01 (9,790)
Ho, Chi Yin 5:51:37 (33,475)
Ho, Kevin 3:23:58 (3,427)
Ho, Wie-Men 5:54:54 (33,707)
Hoad, Daniel P 4:17:45 (15,512)
Hoad, Ian A 6:34:25 (35,635)
Hoad, Philip Grant 5:22:58 (30,302)
Hoadley, Raymond A 4:15:52 (14,994)
Hoar, Nick 4:26:41 (17,994)
Hoare, Alex 3:15:16 (2,468)
Hoare, Matthew David 5:10:00 (28,235)
Hoare, Nicholas 4:14:52 (14,753)
Hoare, Simon 4:46:51 (23,276)
Hobart, Bjorn 3:57:00 (10,089)
Hobbs, Christopher John Pearson 4:51:49 (24,497)
Hobbs, Desi A 3:35:42 (5,359)
Hobbs, Gary Edward 5:20:40 (29,958)
Hobbs, Geoffrey 4:46:28 (23,159)
Hobbs, Graham J 3:32:36 (4,827)
Hobbs, Joby 3:07:43 (1,678)
Hobbs, Jonathan M 3:05:06 (1,467)
Hobbs, Mark S 2:43:02 (279)
Hobbs, Paul 5:47:15 (33,074)
Hobbs, Paul Richard 5:17:55 (29,534)
Hobbs, Robert 4:05:15 (12,269)
Hobbs, Roger K 3:15:11 (2,458)
Hobbs, Roger Michael 4:16:47 (15,244)
Hobbs, Steven R 3:29:40 (4,354)
Hobby, David 4:18:33 (15,725)
Hobday, Alastair G 3:12:09 (2,105)
Hobden, Richard 5:04:06 (27,209)
Hobson, Andrew 4:06:28 (12,562)
Hobson, Brian 6:02:24 (34,212)
Hobson, Christian 3:55:35 (9,632)
Hobson, Gary 6:34:26 (35,638)
Hobson, Rob 3:38:34 (5,863)
Hobson, Robert Graham 4:22:19 (16,796)
Hobson, Steven 3:31:38 (4,688)
Hobson, Steven 3:38:43 (5,890)
Hockings, Graham J 3:56:12 (9,841)
Hocquet, Roger 5:23:17 (30,354)
Hoddell, David L 3:13:27 (2,241)
Hoddell, Rory 5:13:04 (28,763)
Hodder, Philip 4:11:19 (13,796)
Hoddinott, Andrew N 3:44:04 (6,891)
Hoddinott, Tony Noel 4:49:50 (24,017)
Hodge, Carl 3:32:05 (4,754)
Hodge, Daniel 4:21:41 (16,600)

Hodge, Jonathan 4:14:23 (14,610)
Hodge, Richard 3:32:56 (4,883)
Hodge, Steve M 3:43:23 (6,754)

Hodge, Tony G 3:28:31 (4,141)

Tony G Hodge completed his 14th London Marathon (and 33rd marathon in total) at the 2010 Virgin London Marathon on 25th April. Tony completed the race in a time of 3 hours 28 minutes after an extensive 16-week training programme which included running on snow and ice for nearly 3 months during the coldest and hardest winter in Northern Germany for 30 years. Tony's finest hour in the London Marathon came in 2002 when he ran sub 3 hours (2 hours 56 minutes) in his first year as a veteran at the age of 40. Tony hopes to run the London Marathon again in 8 years time when his children Katie, Jamie and Millie are old enough to accompany him. Tony thanks his wife Judy for her patience.

Hodgens, Jim 4:38:42 (21,171)
Hodges, Jon 3:40:50 (6,298)
Hodges, Jon 4:06:27 (12,557)
Hodges, Nick 2:39:48 (193)
Hodges, Richard Martyn 4:51:03 (24,316)
Hodges, Russell 4:44:19 (22,595)
Hodgins, David C 3:03:45 (1,370)
Hodgins, Steven 5:20:06 (29,864)
Hodgkin, Christopher J 3:19:43 (2,939)
Hodgkinson, Andrew David 5:46:11 (32,969)
Hodgkinson, Harry 4:15:46 (14,973)
Hodgkinson, Ian 5:03:59 (27,186)
Hodgkinson, Sam P 3:32:05 (4,754)
Hodgkinson, William 4:25:19 (17,605)
Hodgkinson, Zak Alexander 5:16:45 (29,344)
Hodgson, Daniel Peter 4:40:19 (21,579)
Hodgson, Matt 3:41:35 (6,437)
Hodgson, Nick Charles 4:10:41 (13,635)
Hodgson, Stuart 3:40:28 (6,228)
Hodgson, Timothy James 5:43:15 (32,694)
Hodgson, Tony 3:16:48 (2,652)
Hodkinson, Ian Charles 3:57:06 (10,129)
Hodkinson, John Peter 6:08:11 (34,565)
Hodson, Allister 3:50:07 (8,230)
Hodson, Mark Peter 4:39:42 (21,436)
Hodson, Tony 4:38:31 (21,118)
Hoeksma, Tom 5:42:42 (32,650)
Hoeppner, Kay 4:25:43 (17,725)

Hoey, Ken 3:52:27 (8,777)
Hoey, Paul 4:21:34 (16,567)
Hoey, William E 3:30:43 (4,532)
Hoez, Jean-Luc 4:26:13 (17,877)
Hoffman, Mark T 3:54:13 (9,263)
Hoffmann, Johannes 4:27:14 (18,160)
Hoffmann, Mike 3:05:47 (1,520)
Hogan, Dan Edward 3:53:59 (9,205)
Hogan, James J 4:36:39 (20,648)
Hogan, Paul 3:37:35 (5,684)
Hogan, Philip 3:13:26 (2,240)
Hogan, Sean 2:45:22 (350)
Hogan, Tom 4:09:57 (13,456)
Hogarth, Malcolm 4:57:29 (25,853)
Hogeveen, Marco 4:11:08 (13,753)
Hogg, Andrew Alan 4:07:57 (12,949)
Hogg, Brian 4:31:46 (19,388)
Hogg, Darren Thomas 4:15:26 (14,893)
Hogg, David A 3:00:40 (1,184)
Hogg, Gerry F 2:43:22 (291)
Hogg, Mike Nicolas 3:48:01 (7,741)
Hogge, Russ 4:06:10 (12,490)
Hoggett, Duncan 4:51:12 (24,351)
Hoggett, Paul Andrew 5:38:18 (32,241)
Hoglund, Greger 6:03:39 (34,300)
Hogsflesh, Philip Andrew 3:42:12 (6,549)
Hohensee, Michael 5:35:12 (31,894)
Hohol, Michael 4:38:05 (21,005)
Holberton, Peter D 4:15:44 (14,962)
Holborn, Adrian 3:48:51 (7,942)
Holburn, Simon 4:05:46 (12,402)
Holcombe, Barry 4:43:19 (22,323)
Holdaway, Andy 4:36:07 (20,510)
Holdaway, Kevin 4:38:32 (21,124)
Holdback, Matthew 4:13:24 (14,335)
Holdcroft, Dean L 2:49:33 (470)
Holdcroft, John 3:59:26 (10,848)
Holden, Alex John 5:43:03 (32,670)
Holden, David Robert 4:19:22 (15,944)
Holden, Frank 5:25:11 (30,648)
Holden, Gary Lewis 4:48:30 (23,667)
Holden, Jed 4:23:49 (17,193)
Holden, Leighton John 4:46:15 (23,109)
Holden, Mark 5:05:25 (27,434)
Holden, Matt 3:01:22 (1,222)
Holden, Matthew James 4:55:07 (25,341)
Holden, Phil 5:13:05 (28,789)
Holden, Raymond John 3:19:41 (2,935)
Holden, Richard 4:20:36 (16,297)
Holden, Rupert 3:00:43 (1,192)
Holden, Russell G 4:14:25 (14,621)
Holden, Simon 3:35:02 (5,254)
Holden, Simon Peter 5:08:58 (28,037)
Holden, Trevor I 3:08:50 (1,797)
Holden-Jones, Matthew Alexander 4:29:11 (18,728)
Holder, James 4:49:00 (23,800)
Holder, Julian T 4:14:30 (14,647)
Holder, Paul 4:18:36 (15,744)
Holding, Jon-Paul 6:21:36 (35,188)
Holding, Martin 3:39:19 (6,010)
Holding, Neil H 2:59:01 (1,054)
Holdship, Philip Francis 4:06:09 (12,488)
Holdsworth, Adam Nicholas C.... 4:22:33 (16,864)
Holdsworth, Mark P 3:50:30 (8,311)
Holdway, David John 3:57:05 (10,126)
Hole, Nigel Richard 4:14:08 (14,545)
Hole, Stephen John 4:21:14 (16,469)
Holebrook, Sean K 4:19:46 (16,033)
Holgate, Andrew Gary 4:13:05 (14,261)
Holgate, Craig 2:36:08 (130)
Holgate, Robert Ralph 4:25:25 (17,640)
Holgersen, Marius 4:04:04 (11,977)
Holgersson, Martin 3:20:19 (2,992)
Holierhoek, Robert 4:19:18 (15,929)
Holl, James D 3:37:36 (5,690)
Holladay, Andrew 3:36:32 (5,484)
Holland, Alistair 4:09:36 (13,370)
Holland, Andrew 4:48:49 (23,754)
Holland, Benjamin MZ 3:01:50 (1,246)
Holland, Charles 3:45:30 (7,207)
Holland, Craig 5:13:04 (28,763)
Holland, Edward 3:28:32 (4,145)
Holland, Garry James 3:58:37 (10,598)

Holland, James Andrew 2:59:28 (1,101)
Holland, John R 4:45:10 (22,811)
Holland, Jonathan Dean 3:55:44 (9,688)
Holland, Nick 3:55:28 (9,606)
Holland, Paul Edwin 4:07:55 (12,933)
Holland, Stephen John 3:47:03 (7,535)
Holland, Timothy Phillip 4:48:54 (23,773)
Holland-Brown, Simon 4:18:04 (15,603)
Hollander, Pessy 3:24:00 (3,432)
Hollebon, James Robert 4:04:42 (12,129)
Hollest, Will 4:06:56 (12,697)
Holley, Graeme 3:30:02 (4,425)
Hollick, Dale Antony 4:29:56 (18,966)
Holliday, Michael Stuart 5:01:21 (26,724)
Holliday, Nicholas C 3:24:20 (3,491)
Holliday, Wayne P 3:38:17 (5,816)
Holliday, William M 3:52:48 (8,870)
Holliman, Steve 4:18:57 (15,840)
Hollings, Charlie 3:49:00 (7,974)
Hollings, Kevin Paul 3:59:28 (10,857)
Hollings, Mike 4:42:43 (22,193)
Hollingshead, Paul 3:26:42 (3,829)
Hollingsworth, Ivan M 5:32:27 (31,594)
Hollingsworth, Kristian 3:20:43 (3,048)
Hollingsworth, Noel S 3:32:05 (4,754)
Hollingworth, Paul James 4:18:17 (15,655)
Hollinrake, Kevin 5:22:47 (30,267)
Hollins, Phil Leonard 7:05:41 (36,260)
Hollinshead, Christopher D 2:43:41 (300)
Hollis, Dafydd Rhys 2:55:29 (770)
Hollis, Stephen P 5:05:07 (27,389)
Hollister, Robert 4:40:47 (21,719)
Holloway, David Paul 3:34:32 (5,161)
Holloway, James Daniel 3:27:18 (3,922)
Holloway, Stephen Austin 3:08:15 (1,722)
Hollowell, Graham John 3:27:43 (3,999)
Hollyoak, David George 3:06:25 (1,562)
Hollywood, Bernie 5:28:58 (31,147)
Holman, Dan 5:20:52 (29,987)
Holman, David T 4:22:03 (16,717)
Holman, Jethro Llewellyn 4:31:19 (19,295)
Holman, Mark 3:52:27 (8,777)
Holmberg, Kjell-Göran 4:06:43 (12,630)
Holmen, Vebjoern 5:03:05 (27,036)
Holmes, Daniel John William 3:57:13 (10,161)
Holmes, Daniel Mark 5:40:24 (32,421)
Holmes, Darren 5:32:19 (31,575)
Holmes, David J 4:48:37 (23,699)
Holmes, David Michael 4:47:55 (23,522)
Holmes, Ian H 3:11:06 (2,008)
Holmes, Joe 4:12:50 (14,187)
Holmes, Jonathan Stuart 3:34:02 (5,063)
Holmes, Lance 6:52:20 (36,057)
Holmes, Malcolm Keith 3:25:43 (3,687)
Holmes, Mark A 6:16:15 (34,930)
Holmes, Michael 4:15:44 (14,962)
Holmes, Michael Alan 4:58:31 (26,092)
Holmes, Nicholas M 3:03:29 (1,347)
Holmes, Norman Leonard 6:16:41 (34,960)
Holmes, Peter 4:24:17 (17,311)
Holmes, Peter Edward 4:12:25 (14,075)
Holmes, Rob 4:42:56 (22,245)
Holmes, Samuel 3:34:52 (5,223)
Holmes, Stephen 5:52:21 (33,525)
Holmes, Tony 4:14:45 (14,726)
Holmes, Trevor Richard 4:24:02 (17,245)
Holmquist, Fredrik 3:53:17 (8,993)
Holohan, Tom 3:38:37 (5,874)
Holroyd, Mark Nicholas 5:26:51 (30,880)
Holt, Chris 3:43:50 (6,842)
Holt, Christopher Steven 4:21:34 (16,567)
Holt, Colin Alan 4:07:29 (12,826)
Holt, David 3:59:34 (10,886)
Holt, David John 4:13:33 (14,385)
Holt, Ian G 5:12:35 (28,666)
Holt, Jonathan David 3:54:24 (9,300)
Holt, Martin John 4:12:20 (14,062)
Holt, Oliver C 4:29:25 (18,780)
Holt, Paul 4:38:42 (21,171)
Holt, Robert J 5:19:09 (29,726)
Holt, Simon 4:03:03 (11,740)
Holt, Stephen James 3:44:42 (7,035)
Holt, Tim 4:51:57 (24,538)

Holtorp, Gavin C.........................4:56:10 (25,572)

Holwill, Tom Oliver 4:47:24 (23,389)

I was really privileged to be able to raise money for Changing Faces by taking part in such an amazing event. I had a fantastic day, running through London and seeing all of the sites. What shocked me most was the size and support of the crowds. I passed Richard Branson and Ricky Whittle and saw my mum in the crowd, too, which was nice. All was fine until about 17-18 miles, when I hit the wall. I jogged the last 7-8 miles with a painful foot, for a time of 4hrs 47mins. I had underestimated how hard it was going to be! A week later I found out I had a stress fracture in my foot, so now I know why it hurt so much in those last long miles! It was a great experience and I hope to do it again one day.

Holyoake, Daniel Louis 4:40:36 (21,670)
Holyoake, Jamie 4:48:56 (23,782)
Holzapfel, Marc...........................3:42:44 (6,643)
Homan, Danny D 4:11:36 (13,883)
Homan, James Matthew...............3:51:12 (8,472)
Homer, Gary William..................4:54:11 (25,093)
Homer, James...............................4:21:37 (16,583)
Homer, Mark A 3:35:22 (5,297)
Homer, Nigel................................5:15:06 (29,081)
Honey, Joe 6:05:03 (34,385)
Honey, Matthew 4:01:34 (11,385)
Honey, Matthew James................5:20:27 (29,912)
Honeybun-Arnold, Oliver H 3:58:08 (10,426)
Honeyman, Cy..............................3:53:23 (9,024)
Honeywill, Lewis 5:21:23 (30,058)
Honeywood, Ian Allen David 4:49:35 (23,937)
Hood, Raymond Freddy 4:15:11 (14,830)
Hoods, Karl 4:54:22 (25,149)
Hooft, Patrick Cornelis...............4:05:40 (12,371)
Hook, Guy 4:20:59 (16,407)
Hook, Richard..............................5:27:31 (30,969)
Hooke, Michael............................4:07:06 (12,734)
Hooker, Andrew...........................6:12:56 (34,800)
Hoolahan, Roy Michael..............4:30:08 (19,010)
Hoole, Philip A.............................2:29:48 (66)
Hooley, Iain W..............................3:24:46 (3,547)
Hooley, Neil.................................4:58:42 (26,144)
Hooley, Sam.................................5:17:16 (29,429)
Hooper, David 3:47:03 (7,535)
Hooper, John Joseph 5:02:04 (26,856)
Hooper, John Ray.........................5:24:24 (30,540)
Hooper, Mark...............................5:59:46 (34,044)
Hooper, Nicholas J........................3:09:33 (1,864)
Hooper, Paul 4:13:43 (14,436)
Hooper, Paul 4:37:00 (20,742)
Hooper, Pete 4:40:27 (21,628)
Hooper, Simon.............................3:54:49 (9,427)
Hooper, Stephen..........................5:02:55 (27,012)
Hooper, Steven C.........................2:57:27 (896)
Hopcraft, Geoffrey.......................4:57:16 (25,817)
Hope, Alan 3:26:46 (3,842)
Hope, David 5:02:19 (26,908)
Hope, Ian......................................4:33:08 (19,740)
Hope, Lee Charles Alan 6:28:39 (35,451)
Hope, Michael..............................5:28:48 (31,128)
Hope, Trevor 5:13:42 (28,871)
Hopegood, James.........................4:47:49 (23,502)
Hopkins, Christy Lloyd 3:53:35 (9,084)
Hopkins, Craig Steven 6:28:27 (35,444)
Hopkins, David J 6:28:28 (35,445)
Hopkins, Edward...........................4:04:22 (12,044)
Hopkins, Gabriel...........................3:37:02 (5,570)
Hopkins, Greg...............................4:10:47 (13,661)
Hopkins, Jeremy............................3:32:16 (4,783)
Hopkins, Luke James Andrew.....4:09:37 (13,375)
Hopkins, Mark Steven 5:03:45 (27,148)
Hopkins, Martin John..................3:48:08 (7,773)
Hopkins, Martin P.........................4:48:43 (23,728)
Hopkins, Matthew James............3:22:43 (3,261)
Hopkins, Michael Andrew...........4:59:41 (26,380)
Hopkins, Robert............................3:56:22 (9,887)
Hopkins, Stephen George...........5:26:32 (30,844)
Hopkins, Steve A..........................3:10:22 (1,935)
Hopkins, Stuart D 2:44:09 (314)
Hopkinson, David 4:13:32 (14,378)
Hopkinson, Tom 3:51:29 (8,535)
Hopkirk, James..............................3:49:02 (7,983)
Hoppe, Neil James 4:02:35 (11,624)
Hopper, Jon 3:34:44 (5,198)
Hopper, Paul Andrew 4:30:46 (19,164)
Hopton, Christopher P.................4:38:47 (21,202)
Hopwood, Malcolm J 5:35:20 (31,910)
Horan, Mick Stuart John 3:15:50 (2,530)
Horan, Patrick John......................5:36:24 (32,044)
Hordley, Jef...................................3:40:29 (6,235)
Horgan, James...............................4:44:06 (22,534)
Horn, Colin 4:35:46 (20,410)
Horn, David..................................5:18:35 (29,634)
Horn, Douglas Alexander 5:31:35 (31,483)
Horn, Leo 4:02:08 (11,518)
Horn, Steven Mark........................4:47:00 (23,309)
Hornby, Adam Joseph..................6:16:31 (34,952)
Hornby, Will 4:45:11 (22,815)
Horne, Bruce.................................4:12:40 (14,143)
Horne, David J...............................4:10:27 (13,579)
Horne, Ian David 5:18:53 (29,679)
Horne, Shaine 5:50:19 (33,364)
Horner, Paul James 4:35:08 (20,260)
Horner, Rory Liam.........................3:55:11 (9,523)
Horner, Simon Scadding..............3:40:37 (6,265)
Horner-Smith, Andrew Malcolm.4:21:28 (16,539)
Hornsby, Graham Rutherford.....3:41:05 (6,337)
Hornsby, Greg David.....................4:19:46 (16,033)
Hornsey, Joseph R.........................4:14:46 (14,732)
Hornsey, Lee..................................4:49:19 (23,874)
Hornsey, Mark Russell 3:14:17 (2,357)
Hornsey, Robert M.........................3:38:45 (5,899)
Hornshaw, Aleck E.........................3:28:06 (4,073)
Horrigan, Al Anthony....................5:14:15 (28,956)
Horrocks, Paul Andrew 3:58:31 (10,560)
Horrocks, Rodney James 4:09:30 (13,341)
Horrox, Edward Charles................3:59:39 (10,903)
Horry, Geoff 5:06:59 (27,720)
Horseman, Jeff C............................2:50:16 (495)
Horsfall, Donald Isaac 4:06:12 (12,496)
Horsfall, Nick 3:24:25 (3,499)
Horsfield, Steve M.........................4:09:09 (13,240)
Horsley, David 4:13:08 (14,272)
Horsley, Mike James.....................5:27:47 (31,000)
Horsman, Joseph...........................3:54:38 (9,368)
Horsup, Matthew 4:01:02 (11,258)
Horswill, Thomas JW 4:47:19 (23,368)
Horth, Stuart James Bryan 5:13:50 (28,898)
Horton, Andrew Richard..............4:10:10 (13,517)
Horton, Clive..................................3:34:20 (5,126)
Horton, Colin.................................4:18:05 (15,606)
Horton, David Leslie.....................4:40:48 (21,721)
Horton, James R.............................3:21:45 (3,165)
Horton, Jamie Anthony.................4:50:53 (24,266)
Horton, Michael Eric.....................3:52:51 (8,883)
Horton, Patrick Alex......................4:41:33 (21,910)
Horton, Robert 4:09:13 (13,266)
Horton, Warwick.............................3:34:18 (5,115)
Horvath-Howard, Peter 4:39:08 (21,291)
Horwich, Lee..................................4:44:34 (22,658)
Horwood, Adam..............................3:51:47 (8,603)
Horwood, Mike J.............................3:45:44 (7,255)
Hosken, Simon................................4:04:17 (12,027)
Hoskin, David M 2:57:17 (878)
Hoskin, Mike 3:22:08 (3,204)
Hoskin, Niall P 4:13:12 (14,286)
Hoskin, Shaun Peter.......................4:35:37 (20,369)
Hosking, Adrian Lee.......................3:25:24 (3,631)
Hosler, Craig Steven.......................5:26:51 (30,880)
Hossack, James I..............................4:14:12 (14,569)
Hossack, Neil D 5:04:33 (27,286)
Hough, Christopher 3:33:51 (5,036)
Hough, Graeme 3:53:16 (8,988)
Hough, Robin 4:21:50 (16,651)
Hough, Steven Mark.......................4:37:02 (20,755)
Hough, Trevor David......................3:47:32 (7,655)
Houghton, Jack 3:44:00 (6,883)
Houghton, Leigh 4:39:51 (21,477)
Houghton, Philip David 4:30:29 (19,085)
Houghton, Russell 4:16:04 (15,042)
Houghton, Steve Derrick................3:30:15 (4,464)
Houlgrave, Paul...............................4:49:24 (23,893)
Houlsby, Alex James........................3:51:34 (8,554)
Hoult, Rob.......................................3:59:05 (10,740)
Hoult, Spencer.................................4:01:19 (11,315)
Houlton, Matthew............................3:09:47 (1,892)
Hourican, Brendan Louis................4:21:52 (16,660)
Hourigan, David...............................4:52:08 (24,587)
Hourigan, Patrick............................4:11:35 (13,875)
House, Brett 3:29:59 (4,413)
House, Carl John..............................3:59:28 (10,857)
House, David W................................4:24:14 (17,294)
House, Derek J 4:24:14 (17,294)
House, James....................................5:01:54 (26,832)
House, Paul G 3:12:58 (2,186)
Household, Richard.........................3:54:16 (9,276)
Housman, Christopher....................4:04:08 (11,993)
Houston, Mike.................................3:29:42 (4,360)
Houston, Ross D...............................2:22:49 (27)
Houston, William 4:08:01 (12,966)
Hovden, Jon 3:44:52 (7,071)
Howard, Ashley 5:03:40 (27,131)
Howard, Charlie Kendal.................3:53:12 (8,971)
Howard, Daniel John 4:33:42 (19,918)
Howard, James 4:16:08 (15,058)
Howard, Jonathan 3:32:38 (4,835)
Howard, Kelvin David 4:25:07 (17,552)
Howard, Paul....................................4:17:11 (15,345)
Howard, Paul John...........................3:30:36 (4,510)
Howard, Philip E..............................3:26:41 (3,827)
Howard, Richard 4:22:30 (16,847)
Howard, Roger John Dymoke.........4:29:13 (18,737)
Howard, Russell Joseph 4:15:21 (14,879)
Howard, Steven 4:06:49 (12,660)
Howard, Thomas Alexander Felix..5:11:14 (28,442)
Howard-Kishi, Michael Anthony.6:40:39 (35,806)
Howarth, Chris 4:34:52 (20,208)
Howarth, Ian Malcolm.....................4:26:40 (17,991)
Howarth, John..................................3:52:55 (8,904)
Howarth, Raymond 4:21:42 (16,606)
Howarth, Richard J 2:34:23 (102)
Howarth, Simon J.............................5:10:57 (28,397)
Howarth, Thomas J 3:11:37 (2,061)
Howden, Chris 5:52:37 (33,540)
Howden, Richard Malcolm 5:52:38 (33,544)
Howe, Christopher Stephen............3:55:44 (9,688)
Howe, David Taylor.........................4:44:26 (22,626)
Howe, Kevin 4:00:49 (11,198)
Howe, Martin 4:08:01 (12,966)
Howe, Paul 5:26:26 (30,834)
Howe, Reece K 4:09:30 (13,341)
Howe, Simon Richard......................5:07:20 (27,777)
Howe, Steve Christopher................4:20:28 (16,252)
Howe, Steven William.....................6:02:43 (34,233)
Howell, Alex Arthur.........................4:50:02 (24,055)
Howell, Anthony 4:20:37 (16,302)
Howell, David R...............................4:26:22 (17,920)
Howell, Gareth J...............................4:07:07 (12,735)
Howell, Lyn David............................5:26:26 (30,834)
Howell, Mark....................................5:17:22 (29,455)
Howell, Rhys....................................5:41:34 (32,541)
Howell, Sam D..................................3:56:40 (9,984)
Howell, Scott 4:27:03 (18,097)
Howell, Scott J 2:55:19 (762)
Howell, Stuart...................................3:19:38 (2,931)
Howells, Alan....................................5:48:38 (33,207)
Howells, Benjamin Marwood 4:09:24 (13,313)
Howells, David C 3:34:22 (5,132)
Howells, Denis M 4:44:51 (22,730)
Howells, Dylan G..............................3:33:51 (5,036)
Howells, Gareth................................3:44:08 (6,901)
Howells, Matthew Ian 3:38:36 (5,869)
Howells, Richard Anthony..............4:07:56 (12,940)
Howells, Rob James..........................4:59:48 (26,408)
Howers, Simon 4:36:20 (20,554)
Howes, Chris.....................................3:36:26 (5,471)
Howes, David....................................3:49:54 (8,188)
Howes, David....................................5:58:18 (33,951)
Howes, John M.................................3:58:09 (10,435)
Howes, Jonathan Peter 3:48:42 (7,898)
Howes, Kayne 3:34:04 (5,070)
Howes, Kevin 4:35:21 (20,309)

Howes, Matt	3:48:18	(7,805)
Howes, William J	4:19:39	(16,002)
Howgego, Paul J	4:48:57	(23,788)
Howgego, Peter G	4:12:17	(14,051)
Howie, Christopher A	2:54:55	(741)
Howie, Duncan	4:58:18	(26,040)
Howison, Keith	4:46:57	(23,295)
Howitt, Martin Lee	4:54:38	(25,214)
Howlett, Aaron William	6:54:15	(36,091)
Howlett, Kevin C	3:17:55	(2,756)
Howlett, Kevin M	4:29:48	(18,913)
Howlett, Matthew	4:54:58	(25,296)
Howlett, Michael	3:42:06	(6,530)
Howlett, Robert	6:06:48	(34,497)
Howlin, Jon	7:03:50	(36,240)
Howlin, William Frederick	7:03:49	(36,239)
Howorth, Malcolm Charles	4:33:16	(19,791)
Howorth, Nigel	4:30:15	(19,035)
Howson, Luke J	3:07:18	(1,634)
Hoy, Michael	5:55:21	(33,747)
Hoy, Nick Michael	4:07:45	(12,897)
Hoyle, Michael Gordon	4:49:07	(23,833)
Hua, Binh	5:12:24	(28,629)
Huart, Peter	4:32:52	(19,661)
Huatan, Hiep	4:29:28	(18,797)
Hubbard, Daniel Edward	5:38:54	(32,296)
Hubbard, James Stuart	5:36:12	(32,018)
Hubbard, Nicholas Adlai	5:29:13	(31,180)
Hubbard, Paul Francis	3:50:02	(8,215)
Hubbard, Richard John	3:15:59	(2,553)
Hubbard, Steve	5:26:23	(30,831)
Hubbard, Steve D	4:28:55	(18,650)
Hubble, Paul Simon	3:39:46	(6,092)
Huby, Dean	4:29:34	(18,826)
Huck, Ernest F	3:34:00	(5,057)
Hucker, Ben David	3:45:42	(7,245)
Hucker, Nicholas	3:54:21	(9,294)
Huckfield, Ben	4:43:34	(22,386)
Huckle, Andrew	4:22:56	(16,972)
Hucks, Julian	3:07:01	(1,610)
Hudd, David	3:14:37	(2,401)
Hudd, Gareth	4:05:22	(12,300)
Huddleston, Benjamin John	3:27:17	(3,920)
Hudson, Brian	5:27:05	(30,919)
Hudson, Damian	4:16:55	(15,275)
Hudson, Daniel James	4:19:03	(15,855)
Hudson, David D	5:23:29	(30,384)
Hudson, James George	4:33:50	(19,948)
Hudson, John William	4:44:53	(22,738)
Hudson, Kevin	3:44:40	(7,029)
Hudson, Mark	2:59:24	(1,095)
Hudson, Nicholas I	4:55:44	(25,476)
Hudson, Patrick J	2:51:32	(547)
Hudson, Paul R	4:02:48	(11,674)
Hudson, Paul R	6:51:47	(36,033)
Hudson, Robert John	3:53:43	(9,126)
Hudson, Steven George	4:24:28	(17,381)
Hudson, Steven M	5:38:04	(32,217)
Hudspith, John E	2:54:28	(696)
Huelin, Fernando	4:25:20	(17,612)
Huey, Chris	2:58:55	(1,035)
Hugall, Chris	5:31:09	(31,429)
Hugall, Kyle	3:51:39	(8,577)
Hugentobler, Thomas	4:19:57	(16,086)
Huggins, Michael John	7:12:17	(36,328)
Huggins, Richard John	3:56:53	(10,051)
Hughes, Adam C	4:00:49	(11,198)
Hughes, Adrian Paul	5:17:16	(29,429)
Hughes, Alan Edward	3:42:29	(6,593)
Hughes, Andrew	4:39:04	(21,275)
Hughes, Aneirin Mason	4:30:10	(19,017)
Hughes, Antony	3:51:54	(8,639)
Hughes, Ashley David	5:02:33	(26,950)
Hughes, Ben Thomas Russell	3:51:48	(8,608)
Hughes, Chris	4:10:31	(13,597)
Hughes, Colin	4:29:19	(18,757)
Hughes, Craig	5:16:16	(29,261)
Hughes, Daniel	3:43:43	(6,808)
Hughes, Daniel Peter	4:50:01	(24,051)
Hughes, Darren	4:11:43	(13,908)
Hughes, Darren Terance	5:38:23	(32,251)
Hughes, David	5:17:16	(29,429)
Hughes, David A	5:02:22	(26,919)

Hughes, David Andrew	5:26:28	(30,838)
Hughes, David Arthur	4:21:35	(16,571)
Hughes, David Charles	5:16:15	(29,258)
Hughes, David P	5:38:19	(32,244)
Hughes, David Peter	4:25:15	(17,586)
Hughes, Edward Pierce	5:21:27	(30,068)
Hughes, Frank D	4:26:07	(17,848)
Hughes, George	3:55:32	(9,621)
Hughes, James	5:47:04	(33,056)
Hughes, James A.	6:14:16	(34,849)
Hughes, Jeremy George	3:15:18	(2,476)
Hughes, Jerome	6:49:00	(35,977)
Hughes, John	4:57:22	(25,834)
Hughes, John	5:03:12	(27,060)
Hughes, John A	6:33:08	(35,602)
Hughes, Justin Raymond	6:50:34	(36,007)
Hughes, Karl	4:18:48	(15,799)
Hughes, Kevin A	4:40:08	(21,518)
Hughes, Les	3:35:44	(5,364)
Hughes, Martin	5:53:18	(33,595)
Hughes, Martin Andrew	4:39:07	(21,286)
Hughes, Mick	4:04:29	(12,074)
Hughes, Mike Edward	4:55:27	(25,404)
Hughes, Mitchell	4:03:47	(11,920)
Hughes, Neill J	2:57:32	(905)
Hughes, Oliver J	4:55:12	(25,359)
Hughes, Paul	4:45:30	(22,884)
Hughes, Paul	4:47:17	(23,362)
Hughes, Paul M	4:46:19	(23,130)
Hughes, Rae	4:23:58	(17,229)
Hughes, Richard J	3:57:36	(10,264)
Hughes, Russell	2:49:52	(479)
Hughes, Samuel David	3:23:35	(3,376)
Hughes, Simon	4:09:42	(13,396)
Hughes, Stephen James	4:13:22	(14,330)
Hughes, Stephen Llewellyn	5:36:37	(32,070)
Hughes, Steven Clifford	3:48:57	(7,962)
Hughes, Stuart R	3:55:19	(9,567)
Hughes, Thomas J	4:20:30	(16,260)
Hughes, Tom	3:20:10	(2,974)
Hughes, William	4:16:01	(15,034)
Huitson, Leslie A	3:48:30	(7,848)
Hulands, Mark Andrew	3:45:29	(7,206)
Hulbert, Graham	5:05:51	(27,504)

Hulbert, Martin	3:04:27	(1,425)
Hulbert, Nick	4:21:19	(16,494)
Hulbert, Roger Graham	5:17:49	(29,514)
Hulcoop, Simon	4:32:53	(19,669)
Hulcoop, Stephen	5:33:43	(31,738)
Hull, Ben	4:33:27	(19,841)
Hull, Darran	4:24:40	(17,435)
Hull, Derek W	4:02:24	(11,580)
Hull, Keith	3:20:11	(2,976)
Hull, Richard Tony	6:09:37	(34,640)
Hull, Roger	5:23:01	(30,307)
Hulligan, Richard James	4:31:04	(19,235)
Hully, Peter	4:50:01	(24,051)
Hulme, Alan	5:00:04	(26,471)
Hulme, Jack H	3:15:44	(2,522)
Hulme, Michael	4:21:53	(16,664)
Hulse, Christopher T	3:28:55	(4,214)
Hulse, Kevin Ian	5:05:14	(27,411)
Humber, Mark A	3:33:29	(4,967)
Hume, Adrian Charles	5:40:48	(32,456)
Hume, Alan J	4:34:33	(20,134)
Hume, James Daniel	3:48:02	(7,747)
Humfeldt, Klaus	4:48:00	(23,546)
Hummerson, Jonathan Jay	4:39:58	(21,496)
Humpherson, Roy	3:52:20	(8,750)
Humphrey, John George	5:35:23	(31,914)
Humphrey, Leslie	5:11:33	(28,484)
Humphrey, Tyrone	4:17:40	(15,487)
Humphrey, William Grey	5:31:36	(31,488)
Humphreys, Chris	4:31:00	(19,216)
Humphreys, David Arthur	6:51:49	(36,036)
Humphreys, Gavin	5:15:56	(29,218)
Humphreys, James Robert EF	3:55:33	(9,626)
Humphreys, Jason	4:21:33	(16,564)
Humphreys, Kevin	4:38:00	(20,987)
Humphreys, Luke David	6:11:31	(34,723)
Humphreys, Matthew William	4:36:57	(20,729)
Humphreys, Paul	4:48:12	(23,588)
Humphreys, Peter	3:31:23	(4,647)
Humphreys, Richard J	3:11:02	(2,001)
Humphries, Andrew James	4:41:04	(21,784)
Humphries, Graham	5:52:13	(33,516)
Humphries, John	4:03:45	(11,906)
Humphries, Jonathan P	5:04:40	(27,308)
Humphries, Kevin	3:42:38	(6,616)
Humphries, Paul R	3:46:13	(7,357)
Humphries, Peter N	3:36:00	(5,414)
Humphries, Philip A	3:33:01	(4,897)
Humphries, Scott	4:11:02	(13,726)
Humphryes, Kevin	4:17:43	(15,501)
Hunsley, John William	4:29:58	(18,974)
Hunt, Anthony Charles	4:02:49	(11,677)
Hunt, Christopher James	3:07:20	(1,638)
Hunt, Chrstopher Matthew	4:28:32	(18,535)
Hunt, Clinton Simon	4:16:44	(15,228)
Hunt, Craig Anthony	2:58:08	(966)
Hunt, Darren Lee	6:49:57	(35,995)
Hunt, Davin	4:20:58	(16,405)
Hunt, Jeffrey	3:51:47	(8,603)
Hunt, Jon	3:52:41	(8,843)
Hunt, Jonathan	4:03:05	(11,748)
Hunt, Julian Charles	4:23:00	(16,984)
Hunt, Justin	3:56:33	(9,948)
Hunt, Lester C	4:48:51	(23,760)
Hunt, Mark	4:18:05	(15,606)
Hunt, Mark Iain	6:00:53	(34,124)
Hunt, Martin	3:59:56	(10,970)
Hunt, Michael	4:43:27	(22,359)
Hunt, Paul	3:54:19	(9,282)
Hunt, Paul	4:33:35	(19,884)
Hunt, Richard	5:23:46	(30,437)
Hunt, Richard Stefan	4:12:57	(14,216)
Hunt, Shane P	3:10:53	(1,981)
Hunt, Thomas	6:22:54	(35,231)
Hunt, Tim	3:39:30	(6,044)
Hunter, Alex	3:47:14	(7,583)
Hunter, Allistair Ronald	4:08:43	(13,145)
Hunter, Andy	4:10:48	(13,649)
Hunter, Darren	6:19:53	(35,120)
Hunter, Douglas	3:49:55	(8,191)
Hunter, Gareth	3:34:38	(5,180)
Hunter, Ian	5:01:09	(26,674)
Hunter, James A	5:45:32	(32,913)

Hunter, John Shaun	4:59:14 (26,272)	
Hunter, Luke	6:05:46 (34,439)	
Hunter, Mark	6:05:32 (34,422)	
Hunter, Mark Iain	3:35:28 (5,316)	
Hunter, Phillipe C	3:45:05 (7,111)	
Hunter, Tony	3:02:15 (1,275)	
Huntley, George Edward	5:31:53 (31,522)	
Huntley, Stephen	5:04:37 (27,300)	
Hurcomb, Chris Paul	4:27:47 (18,310)	
Hurd, Andrew J	3:23:51 (3,414)	
Hurdley, Paul	3:25:16 (3,615)	
Hurford, Mike J	3:05:41 (1,513)	
Hurley, Ben	2:56:25 (827)	
Hurley, Joe	3:08:38 (1,773)	
Hurley, John	6:06:10 (34,460)	
Hurley, Robert James	3:53:09 (8,955)	
Hurley, Stephen	2:57:35 (913)	
Hurley, Stephen John	5:58:30 (33,963)	
Hurlock, Matthew	3:28:19 (4,107)	
Hurrell, Mark J	3:22:52 (3,273)	
Hurren, Antony J	4:42:01 (22,017)	
Hurren, Grahame Dennis	3:39:53 (6,122)	
Hurren, Simon James	4:54:16 (25,123)	
Hurst, David	4:29:43 (18,888)	
Hurst, Matthew Edward	4:26:51 (18,039)	
Hurtley, Ben Michael	3:30:57 (4,572)	
Husain, Hashim	5:07:50 (27,866)	
Husband, Adam	5:02:01 (26,845)	
Husband, Ian S	3:10:18 (1,932)	
Husbands, James	3:29:35 (4,339)	
Husk, Alex	3:14:36 (2,398)	
Hussain, Shabir	5:42:15 (32,614)	
Hussain, Shipon	5:07:06 (27,740)	
Hussey, John	3:29:54 (4,400)	
Hussey, Matthew J	5:10:27 (28,319)	
Hussey, Will	3:24:53 (3,560)	
Hustler, Freddie Randolph	4:04:55 (12,178)	
Hutchby, Philip N	4:23:22 (17,071)	
Hutchen, Tim	3:54:31 (9,331)	
Hutchenson, Stephen	4:26:50 (18,034)	
Hutcheson, Luke John	3:59:19 (10,816)	
Hutcheson, Mark M	3:12:25 (2,127)	
Hutchin, Peter Charles	6:18:47 (35,072)	
Hutchings, David	3:45:57 (7,299)	
Hutchings, Edward	2:56:15 (817)	
Hutchings, Jason C	5:16:59 (29,383)	
Hutchings, Mark Andrew	4:21:53 (16,664)	
Hutchings, Raymond P	5:33:46 (31,741)	
Hutchings, William	3:19:17 (2,893)	
Hutchins, Leon J	4:31:28 (19,328)	
Hutchins,, Tim	3:16:35 (2,626)	
Hutchinson, Andrew James	4:40:28 (21,633)	
Hutchinson, Anthony Derek	4:06:17 (12,520)	
Hutchinson, Brett G	3:24:33 (3,517)	
Hutchinson, Christopher	3:52:50 (8,881)	
Hutchinson, David Edward	3:57:47 (10,326)	
Hutchinson, G Brian	4:03:43 (11,901)	
Hutchinson, Ian Robert	4:54:16 (25,123)	
Hutchinson, Peter Ronald	4:25:20 (17,612)	
Hutchison, Michael B	3:58:44 (10,637)	
Hutchison, Paul	6:08:29 (34,582)	
Hutchison, Paul J	4:07:30 (12,834)	
Hutchison, Scott Robert	5:05:16 (27,419)	
Hutchsion, Robert Andrew	5:23:09 (30,329)	
Hutson, John	4:34:10 (20,030)	
Hutt, Campbell G	3:03:11 (1,336)	
Hutt, Neil	4:00:54 (11,218)	
Hutton, Craig	4:05:33 (12,345)	
Hutton, Eddie	4:42:11 (22,058)	
Hutton, Paul	4:02:30 (11,601)	
Hutton, Simon	4:20:33 (16,275)	
Huxford, Robert	5:16:48 (29,352)	
Huxley, Andrew	3:50:43 (8,362)	
Huxley, Peter Barrington	4:45:29 (22,880)	
Huxley, Richard	4:00:06 (11,007)	
Hyatt, Gary Francis	3:45:49 (7,267)	
Hyatt, Tim John	3:57:20 (10,190)	
Hyde, Allan	3:44:24 (6,968)	
Hyde, Benjamin	5:36:07 (32,007)	
Hyde, Chris	4:28:13 (18,424)	
Hyde, Jon	3:33:09 (4,915)	
Hyde, Jonathan M	3:38:44 (5,897)	
Hyde, Richard	3:51:33 (8,549)	
Hyde, Simon Robert	4:17:06 (15,321)	
Hydon, Jonathan	4:56:03 (25,548)	
Hyland, Andrew	5:12:15 (28,609)	
Hyland, James	5:29:06 (31,163)	
Hymns, Gary A	3:59:02 (10,729)	
Hymovitz, Marc	4:22:00 (16,705)	
Hynam, Paul	4:00:31 (11,118)	
Hynard, Andrew James	4:44:15 (22,577)	
Hynderick, Anthony	4:23:02 (16,988)	
Hyndman, Garry	5:43:45 (32,750)	
Hyndman, Nigel	4:05:38 (12,365)	
Hynes, Andrew Robin	3:52:47 (8,863)	
Hynes, David	3:07:11 (1,625)	
Hynes, Marc	4:24:48 (17,468)	
Hynes, Mark	5:01:01 (26,652)	
Hynes, Matthew	2:43:40 (299)	
Hynes, Stephen	4:57:52 (25,939)	
Hysa, Argon	3:27:12 (3,909)	
Hyslop, Ian	6:12:13 (34,770)	
Hyson, Stuart James	5:19:43 (29,810)	
I'Anson, Mark	5:25:15 (30,655)	
Ibbotson, Lee	4:45:28 (22,875)	
Ibeson, David Christopher Ben	4:05:51 (12,421)	
Ibison, Mark	3:17:06 (2,677)	
Iddles, Chris N	3:56:05 (9,807)	
Idhult, Lars	4:00:34 (11,131)	
Idle, Matthew Rupert	3:38:19 (5,822)	
Idsoee, Ove	4:53:07 (24,826)	
Ifill-Williams, Gerard	5:25:33 (30,703)	
Ikeda, Tetsuro	3:27:22 (3,934)	
Ikie, Victor Ojite	4:44:25 (22,621)	
Iles, Spencer J	4:13:20 (14,324)	
Iles, Wayne	5:37:17 (32,142)	
Ilett, Stephen George	4:11:22 (13,805)	
Illiano, Ferdinando	3:16:10 (2,568)	
Illingworth, Adam James	5:43:36 (32,727)	
Illingworth, Colin J	4:58:26 (26,071)	
Illingworth, Vaughan Andrew R.	4:50:58 (24,292)	
Ilott, Jonathan	3:41:34 (6,433)	
Ilott, Mathew James	4:29:55 (18,957)	
Imam, Hisham Ibrahim Eldesoki	5:15:10 (29,095)	
Imeson, Michael David	4:00:50 (11,202)	
Imeson, Richard	5:00:02 (26,463)	
Impey, Richard William	5:12:49 (28,703)	
Imrie, Gavin A	3:56:55 (10,063)	
Imrie, James William	3:27:09 (3,896)	
Inayat, Shezad	3:34:19 (5,118)	
Ince, Mark Goodman	2:59:19 (1,084)	
Ince, Philip Anthony	4:16:10 (15,062)	
Indermuehle, Christian	3:59:26 (10,848)	
Indermuehle, Urs	5:09:45 (28,189)	
Indge, Martin Clive	3:01:39 (1,236)	
Ineson, Andrew Nicholas	5:07:16 (27,761)	
Ineson, James	3:58:39 (10,610)	
Ing, Martin	6:02:42 (34,232)	
Ing, Martin Peter	4:31:57 (19,422)	
Ing, Thomas David	4:07:51 (12,918)	
Ing, Tony	4:58:48 (26,165)	
Ingham, Ian Mark	4:13:04 (14,257)	
Ingham, Jack Benjamin	4:36:52 (20,704)	
Ingham, James N	3:18:15 (2,802)	
Ingham, John	3:43:22 (6,751)	
Ingham, John G	4:12:32 (14,109)	
Ingham, Lee	4:30:33 (19,106)	
Ingham, Richard	3:48:33 (7,861)	
Ingledew, Neil	3:08:12 (1,718)	
Ingleson, Martin S	3:08:38 (1,773)	
Inglis, Andrew	3:34:45 (5,202)	
Ingold, Andrew James	3:22:57 (3,287)	
Ingraham, Todd	2:46:57 (385)	
Ingram, Barry Martin	5:55:43 (33,770)	
Ingram, David Charles	6:26:55 (35,382)	
Ingram, David Mark	5:28:40 (31,106)	
Ingram, Jonathan M	3:55:02 (9,485)	
Ingram, Lee Paul	3:26:14 (3,775)	
Ingram, Michael Jeremy	4:00:08 (11,015)	
Ingram, Stephen	4:34:59 (20,228)	
Ingrouille, Darren	4:26:34 (17,972)	
Ings, Ross Aarron	3:13:17 (2,221)	
Ings, Russell	4:09:33 (13,351)	
Iniesta-Martinez, Pascual	4:02:10 (11,529)	
Inman, Gary J	4:13:44 (14,442)	
Inman, Lawrence Andrew	4:19:41 (16,013)	
Inman, Stuart Lee	3:53:08 (8,950)	
Innes, Foster	4:38:50 (21,212)	
Innes, Scott Anthony	6:41:54 (35,833)	
Inniss, Matthew J	4:31:05 (19,238)	
Insall, Alastair	3:50:23 (8,284)	
Inskip, Stuart Jonathan	3:59:17 (10,808)	
Inwards, Richard	4:23:27 (17,090)	
Inzani, Barry	4:45:03 (22,782)	
Ionta, Giovanni Antonio	3:59:13 (10,786)	
Iordache, Gabriel	5:54:48 (33,695)	
Iqbal, Naveed	6:16:59 (34,978)	
Iqbal, Ray Sheikh	4:09:29 (13,336)	
Iqbal, Shujah	5:22:04 (30,155)	
Ireland, Michael Reza	4:47:39 (23,455)	
Ireson, Joe	6:00:59 (34,131)	
Irifune, Satoshi	2:19:25 (16)	
Irlam, Stewart	4:34:46 (20,186)	
Irons, Matthew	4:17:52 (15,540)	
Irons, William Richard	4:45:20 (22,849)	
Irvine, Andrew	3:45:22 (7,175)	
Irvine, Dale Robert	4:03:50 (11,933)	
Irvine, Duncan Stuart	3:48:59 (7,969)	
Irvine, Stuart John	3:57:57 (10,366)	
Irvine, William J	3:52:18 (8,746)	
Irving, Colin	4:06:41 (12,621)	
Irving, Nicholas M	5:29:12 (31,175)	
Irwin, David S	3:50:44 (8,367)	
Irwin, Paul	4:39:08 (21,291)	
Isaacs, Mark W	4:26:31 (17,961)	
Isaacs, Patrick	4:40:04 (21,510)	
Isaacs, Richard Michael	3:49:09 (8,010)	
Isaacson, Vince	4:29:37 (18,852)	
Isaak, Martin	3:49:40 (8,139)	
Isabello, Jacky	3:38:49 (5,908)	
Isbister, Gregor Donald	5:02:59 (27,022)	
Iseke, Hans	3:53:56 (9,191)	
Isherwood, Jonathan Roland	4:19:45 (16,030)	
Isherwood, Luke	2:58:26 (1,001)	
Ishiwata, Tomio	6:31:07 (35,540)	
Ismail, Amir	4:08:48 (13,161)	
Ismail, Ismail	5:10:47 (28,375)	
Isman, Renaud	3:54:19 (9,282)	
Isom, Neil	3:13:20 (2,231)	
Israeli, Zvi	4:04:34 (12,087)	
Issling, Jan	5:36:42 (32,074)	
Isted, Jonathan P	4:34:52 (20,208)	
Itkin, Simon	4:25:07 (17,552)	
Ito, Hidekazu	4:51:54 (24,521)	
Iuliano, Domenico	3:55:21 (9,582)	
Ive, Martin J	3:26:48 (3,850)	
Ivens, Derek M	4:20:38 (16,314)	
Ivens, John	4:24:29 (17,384)	
Ivers, Michael Anthony	4:43:43 (22,423)	
Iversen, Preben	5:37:53 (32,198)	
Ives, David Allan James	5:06:28 (27,618)	
Ives, Derek	4:34:22 (20,085)	
Ives, Kenneth	3:37:32 (5,673)	
Ivory, Jason	5:10:00 (28,235)	
Ivory, Kenneth J	2:58:11 (974)	
Izod, Stuart	5:07:53 (27,877)	
Jack, Michael J	5:04:30 (27,276)	
Jack, Sean David	4:14:11 (14,566)	
Jacklin, Matt James	2:55:46 (786)	
Jackman, Greg	4:47:59 (23,542)	
Jackson, Alan	3:30:09 (4,439)	
Jackson, Andrew	3:52:16 (8,729)	
Jackson, Andrew Charles	6:40:12 (35,794)	
Jackson, Andy William	5:14:04 (28,934)	
Jackson, Anthony	2:43:23 (293)	
Jackson, Anthony	3:13:12 (2,212)	
Jackson, Anthony B	2:40:48 (224)	
Jackson, Anthony R	2:36:56 (140)	
Jackson, Carl	4:29:22 (18,768)	
Jackson, Chris	3:46:31 (7,423)	
Jackson, Chris Andrew	2:54:57 (743)	
Jackson, Christian	4:25:07 (17,552)	
Jackson, Craig	4:14:52 (14,753)	
Jackson, David G	4:26:46 (18,016)	
Jackson, David Paul	3:34:27 (5,144)	
Jackson, Dominic	3:23:15 (3,332)	
Jackson, Earl A	4:39:09 (21,301)	
Jackson, Edward	5:05:01 (27,371)	
Jackson, Gareth	3:27:05 (3,882)	

Jackson, George D 3:06:45 (1,591)
Jackson, John Charles 5:27:23 (30,954)
Jackson, Martyn Raymond 4:26:00 (17,812)
Jackson, Mathew Ian 5:16:22 (29,289)
Jackson, Michael 3:56:32 (9,944)
Jackson, Michael J 5:53:55 (33,636)
Jackson, Neil 3:05:20 (1,486)
Jackson, Neil 4:26:14 (17,882)
Jackson, Nicholas Bryan 6:01:37 (34,163)
Jackson, Nick James 6:45:55 (35,928)
Jackson, Nigel 5:37:20 (32,149)
Jackson, Nigel G 3:32:37 (4,831)
Jackson, Oliver 3:53:27 (9,039)
Jackson, Paul 2:56:31 (833)
Jackson, Paul 5:00:49 (26,616)
Jackson, Paul B 3:05:42 (1,515)
Jackson, Paul Terence 4:06:04 (12,468)
Jackson, Peter H 4:32:14 (19,494)
Jackson, Richard 3:29:48 (4,379)
Jackson, Robert 2:54:28 (696)
Jackson, Roger 5:50:11 (33,349)
Jackson, Simon A 2:51:41 (554)
Jackson, Stephen P 2:57:04 (860)
Jackson, Steve 4:45:02 (22,778)
Jackson, Steve Richard 4:47:42 (23,470)
Jackson, Steven 4:41:30 (21,893)
Jackson, Steven L 3:43:23 (6,754)
Jackson, Tom William Robert 5:21:49 (30,118)
Jackson, Vincent Andrew 5:19:54 (29,836)
Jackson, Will 3:29:27 (4,313)
Jackson-Dyke, Craig 3:44:16 (6,928)
Jackson-Hookins, Warren 4:12:09 (14,022)
Jacob, Christian C 4:42:18 (22,095)
Jacob, Kevin Michael 3:18:46 (2,848)
Jacobs, Darrel W 5:48:37 (33,206)
Jacobs, Giles Walter 5:46:54 (33,040)
Jacobs, Luke 4:22:29 (16,841)
Jacobs, Matthew 4:03:54 (11,944)
Jacobs, Nathan Charles 4:00:27 (11,109)
Jacobs, Nick 3:13:54 (2,304)
Jacobs, Paul 5:01:13 (26,685)
Jacobs, Paul 7:03:52 (36,241)
Jacobs, Paul A 5:33:27 (31,711)
Jacobs, Terry Roy 4:58:41 (26,134)
Jacobson, Brett A 3:08:33 (1,761)
Jacobson, James 3:55:57 (9,766)
Jacobson, Seth 3:16:37 (2,629)
Jacques, Marc 3:14:10 (2,336)
Jacquou, Laurent 3:55:58 (9,772)
Jadoon, Farooq Khan 4:54:34 (25,196)
Jaeger, Horst 4:33:43 (19,925)
Jaeger, Marcus 4:09:35 (13,365)
Jaffery, Ali Raza 5:18:00 (29,545)
Jagger, Martyn 4:35:30 (20,344)
Jagodzinski, Nikolas 3:20:31 (3,027)
Jahans, Stephen Desmond 5:27:36 (30,977)
Jakeman, Chris 4:42:10 (22,053)
Jakeman, John 4:52:07 (24,578)
Jakeway, Paul 3:51:46 (8,598)
Jakhu, Ashok Kumar Ram 4:40:55 (21,752)
Jakobsson, Carl Malcolm 4:24:17 (17,311)
Jal, Conan 5:05:03 (27,377)
Jalaly, Imad 6:28:49 (35,456)
Jalland, Robert I 3:11:32 (2,052)
Jalloh, Abraham A 2:56:16 (818)
James, Adam Robert William 3:39:53 (6,122)
James, Alan Patrick 4:46:06 (23,063)
James, Alexander 3:11:00 (1,995)
James, Andy 5:06:12 (27,567)
James, Anthony Mark 5:21:57 (30,136)
James, Christopher Paul 3:33:32 (4,978)
James, Craig T 4:16:55 (15,275)
James, David 4:09:11 (13,253)
James, David Robert 6:12:21 (34,775)
James, Dean R 4:00:05 (11,002)
James, Ian F 2:43:05 (281)
James, Joshua J 4:29:20 (18,759)
James, Lentaigne 3:45:46 (7,261)
James, Malcolm E 4:45:50 (22,985)
James, Mark 3:17:55 (2,756)
James, Mark 3:38:02 (5,770)
James, Mark S 4:37:33 (20,896)
James, Matthew Alexander 4:47:16 (23,355)
James, Michael 5:15:56 (29,218)
James, Oliver 6:05:26 (34,416)
James, Oliver Daniel 4:29:17 (18,752)
James, Paul Arthur 4:07:56 (12,940)
James, Philip N 3:50:50 (8,386)
James, Richard G 3:14:23 (2,368)
James, Robert 6:16:58 (34,974)
James, Robert Huw 3:21:46 (3,168)
James, Robert S 3:21:22 (3,127)
James, Robin 3:57:26 (10,210)
James, Roy 4:40:31 (21,647)
James, Simon A 2:48:38 (434)
James, Steve 4:32:01 (19,441)
James, Thomas 3:59:18 (10,813)
James, Toby 4:28:52 (18,632)
James-Cuthber, Declan C 7:44:07 (36,544)
Jameson, Andrew D 3:50:34 (8,328)
Jameson, Brian Richard 5:04:11 (27,226)
Jameson, Clive 5:15:06 (29,081)
Jameson, Michael A 3:49:23 (8,059)
Jameson, Tim 4:00:16 (11,048)
Jamieson, Christopher Jim 4:13:10 (14,278)
Jamieson, Gary Hugh 4:40:00 (21,502)
Jamieson, Paul 4:06:59 (12,707)
Jamin, Benoit 4:05:29 (12,331)
Jammet, Bruno 3:54:39 (9,372)
Jan, Cyrille 4:00:38 (11,151)
Janes, Marcus T 4:35:30 (20,344)
Janes, Stephen Rhys 4:28:37 (18,557)
Janitzki, Bernd 3:56:11 (9,837)
Jankowski, Mark 4:08:15 (13,017)
Janmohamed, Tariq 4:22:13 (16,772)
Janotta, Ingemar 3:58:47 (10,652)
Janowski, Peter 3:38:51 (5,915)
Jansen, Arne 5:28:42 (31,112)
Jansen, Jan 5:00:59 (26,647)
Jansen, Michael 4:53:41 (24,965)
Jansen, Paul 4:46:35 (23,193)
Janssen, Philippe 4:41:58 (22,005)
January, Charles Edward 5:07:02 (27,730)
Januszek, Luke 3:46:49 (7,494)
Jardin, Anton 6:07:38 (34,540)
Jardin, David 3:23:15 (3,332)
Jarman, Dan Philip 4:42:16 (22,084)
Jarman, Danny 4:47:09 (23,334)
Jarman, Mark Anthony 5:15:17 (29,111)
Jarrard, Jon 4:27:45 (18,299)
Jarrell, Terry J 2:54:54 (734)
Jarrett, Thomas L 2:53:21 (632)
Jarrett-Kerr, Thomas Charles 4:13:31 (14,369)
Jarry, Frederic 4:33:24 (19,825)
Jarry, Jean-Michel 4:41:32 (21,905)
Jarvis, Adrian 4:31:09 (19,254)
Jarvis, Bernard 3:26:40 (3,825)
Jarvis, Brian Fredric George 6:08:54 (34,611)
Jarvis, Gregory 3:12:33 (2,139)
Jarvis, James Paul 3:43:20 (6,746)
Jarvis, John 4:37:09 (20,784)
Jarvis, Jonathan 4:58:31 (26,092)
Jarvis, Simon 5:02:23 (26,922)
Jarvis, Steve 3:57:09 (10,141)
Jarvis, Tim 4:17:08 (15,334)
Jaryczewski, Noel 4:44:29 (22,632)
Jawad, Mehdi 4:54:24 (25,160)
Jawanda, Peter 4:30:53 (19,185)
Jaxa-Chamiec, Michael 4:40:29 (21,638)
Jeacock, Simon 4:18:03 (15,597)
Jeal, Paul A 4:33:10 (19,752)
Jean-Baptiste, Emeka 3:53:47 (9,154)
Jean-Claude, Dailliez 4:53:00 (24,792)
Jeanes, Robbie William 5:46:50 (33,033)
Jeans, Kai Anthony 5:23:37 (30,410)
Jeans, Nick Kevin 5:12:54 (28,722)
Jeary, Matthew Guy 4:19:03 (15,855)
Jeater, Alex 3:59:52 (10,956)
Jefferies, Mark James 3:41:10 (6,354)
Jefferies, Paul 3:52:59 (8,921)
Jefferies, Tim 4:14:32 (14,659)
Jefferies, William Edward 3:34:52 (5,223)
Jefferson, Oliver Simon 3:36:45 (5,517)
Jefferson, Paul A 5:39:01 (32,305)
Jeffery, Craig N 2:48:52 (440)
Jeffery, Ian 5:48:49 (33,223)
Jeffery, James Michael 4:55:31 (25,412)
Jeffery, John William 3:56:20 (9,883)
Jeffery, Jon 4:33:25 (19,829)
Jeffery, Michael D 4:09:03 (13,223)
Jeffery, Oliver 4:59:40 (26,373)
Jeffery, Robin 5:16:46 (29,347)
Jeffery, Scott 4:24:16 (17,306)
Jeffery, Stephen Peter 4:56:52 (25,737)
Jeffery, Steven 4:19:51 (16,056)
Jeffery, Wayne D 4:59:46 (26,400)
Jefferys, Anthony 3:59:01 (10,725)
Jefferys, Russell J 4:16:30 (15,170)
Jefford, Mark 3:04:47 (1,445)
Jefford, Thomas E 5:15:30 (29,146)
Jeffrey, James D 4:17:30 (15,439)
Jeffrey, Tom 4:29:45 (18,899)
Jeffreys, Adrian C 6:31:27 (35,554)
Jeffreys, Matt David 6:48:22 (35,966)
Jeffries, John 6:29:57 (35,498)
Jeffries, Lee 3:57:55 (10,359)
Jeffs, Alistair 3:13:34 (2,266)
Jefska, David 6:09:56 (34,659)
Jegou, Paul R 3:46:13 (7,357)
Jehu, Gareth Edward 3:24:13 (3,471)
Jelbert, Ian 2:48:29 (431)
Jelf, Will 4:32:46 (19,622)
Jelley, Christopher 4:52:37 (24,710)
Jelley, David G 3:06:57 (1,603)
Jenkin, Daniel L 2:58:59 (1,045)
Jenkins, Adam Michael 4:46:32 (23,175)
Jenkins, Darran 5:07:49 (27,863)
Jenkins, David John 3:54:07 (9,236)
Jenkins, David William 4:08:28 (13,069)
Jenkins, Eric Paul 4:28:48 (18,609)
Jenkins, Gareth John 5:33:29 (31,715)
Jenkins, Gareth S 2:56:31 (833)
Jenkins, Garin Richard 4:31:40 (19,371)
Jenkins, Geraint H 3:48:34 (7,866)
Jenkins, Graham 3:49:03 (7,987)
Jenkins, Huw W 2:58:55 (1,035)
Jenkins, John 5:25:21 (30,669)
Jenkins, Jonathan 4:20:37 (16,302)
Jenkins, Kenneth Hywel 5:32:32 (31,612)
Jenkins, Martin Alexander 5:40:11 (32,410)
Jenkins, Matt 4:31:15 (19,280)
Jenkins, Matthew Rhys 3:08:06 (1,708)
Jenkins, Michael Anthony 3:30:47 (4,544)
Jenkins, Michael J 4:53:05 (24,814)
Jenkins, Nicholas Mark 5:16:53 (29,373)
Jenkins, Nick 4:41:32 (21,905)
Jenkins, Paul 4:02:59 (11,726)
Jenkins, Paul J 4:16:21 (15,125)
Jenkins, Rhys 4:04:58 (12,196)
Jenkins, Rob 3:51:23 (8,512)
Jenkins, Robert Alun Stephen 4:21:14 (16,469)
Jenkins, Robert E 5:09:17 (28,102)
Jenkins, Steven L 3:54:52 (9,441)
Jenkins, Todd Antony 3:53:28 (9,045)
Jenner, Marc 4:24:38 (17,425)
Jennings, Andy J 4:34:05 (20,016)
Jennings, Chris 3:40:28 (6,228)
Jennings, Christian 3:16:45 (2,650)
Jennings, George 4:16:58 (15,287)
Jennings, James 3:25:39 (3,673)
Jennings, Jamie Lea 5:03:08 (27,043)
Jennings, Neil Alasdair 3:29:34 (4,334)
Jennings, Peter Roy 6:19:58 (35,123)
Jennings, Robert 3:17:05 (2,671)
Jennings, Roy 4:58:12 (26,012)
Jennings, Stephen 4:03:35 (11,868)
Jensen, Alexander 3:40:03 (6,157)
Jensen, Herluf 3:40:37 (6,265)
Jensen, Jesper Mollgaard 4:17:00 (15,300)
Jensen, Juergen 4:45:52 (22,992)
Jensen, Kim Peter 3:38:13 (5,805)
Jensen, Morten 4:14:00 (14,504)
Jensen, Morten Solfjeld 4:12:29 (14,097)
Jensen, Torben Dufresne 3:39:49 (6,106)
Jephcott, Jamie P 3:23:30 (3,368)
Jeremiah, O'Mahony 3:18:35 (2,829)
Jeremiau, Duncan 4:49:34 (23,929)
Jeremy, Picard 2:48:27 (430)
Jermy, Daniel 5:36:52 (32,091)

Keay, David Philip 4:59:23 (26,308)

Kebede, Tsegaye 2:05:19 (1)

Tsegaye Kebede (born 15 January 1987) is an Ethiopian athlete who rapidly rose to prominence after his international debut at the 2007 Amsterdam Marathon. In his second year of serious competition, the featherweight Kebede, standing only 5ft 2ins, won the Paris Marathon and took bronze at the 2008 Beijing Olympics. In 2009 he came second in the London Marathon and went one better to win the 2010 London Marathon with 2:05:19. Kebede is the fifth of thirteen children and his childhood was marked by intense poverty. Living thirty miles north of Addis Ababa, he collected firewood to sell and herded livestock to supplement his father's earnings. He ate one meal every twenty-four hours and had to work constantly to earn around £1.20 a day. In the 2010 London Marathon, Kebede finished nine seconds short of the course record figures set in 2009 by Sammy Wanjiru, from Kenya. Those nine seconds cost Kebede £16,250 in bonus money.

Keddilty, Matthew P 4:07:12 (12,749)
Kee, Robert Jim Jim 4:19:03 (15,855)
Keeber, Dean Ashley 3:59:29 (10,861)
Keeble, Andrew Philip 4:38:35 (21,137)
Keeble, Graham P 5:40:00 (32,389)
Keeble, James Thomas 5:09:37 (28,170)
Keeble, Marcus Leonard 4:58:49 (26,169)
Keeble, Mark A 3:32:07 (4,761)
Keech, Paul Alan 3:42:22 (6,574)
Keech, Tony 3:43:24 (6,757)
Keech, Victor John 4:03:45 (11,906)
Keeene, Oliver 4:06:11 (12,494)
Keegan, Andy James 5:45:01 (32,870)
Keegan, Dan 3:51:25 (8,518)
Keegan, Glen 4:17:07 (15,329)
Keegan, James 4:13:37 (14,410)
Keegan, Joseph 6:18:53 (35,076)
Keeler, Andrew T 3:54:13 (9,263)
Keeley, Anthony Joseph 3:52:45 (8,854)
Keeley, Christopher Charles 4:25:38 (17,700)
Keen, Andrew 4:22:04 (16,723)
Keen, Howard S 4:01:23 (11,332)
Keen, Michael 3:59:32 (10,870)
Keen, Nick 4:10:19 (13,548)
Keen, Nick 5:54:24 (33,670)
Keen, Stuart James 3:40:31 (6,245)
Keen, Timothy 3:54:27 (9,314)
Keenan, Barry 3:36:50 (5,532)
Keenan, Brian 3:51:01 (8,429)
Keenan, David Charles 4:18:45 (15,786)
Keenan, David James 4:48:24 (23,638)
Keenan, Garry 3:37:15 (5,610)
Keenan, Richard Leslie 4:25:31 (17,668)
Keenor, Dom 5:09:46 (28,192)
Keep, Ashley 5:55:06 (33,728)
Keeping, Benjamin James 3:25:25 (3,636)
Kehoe, Robert 4:39:29 (21,381)
Keighley, Charles J 5:00:02 (26,463)
Keillar, Eden 4:04:01 (11,962)
Keith, Steve John 4:31:20 (19,299)
Kelf, Paul David 5:18:29 (29,625)
Kell, Jon 4:09:01 (13,218)
Kelleher, Neale 4:33:47 (19,942)
Kelleher, Peter Anthony 3:21:22 (3,127)
Kellett, John Mark 4:45:10 (22,811)
Kellett, Steve 3:55:45 (9,699)
Kells, Andrew 3:02:19 (1,282)
Kelly, Andrew M 4:19:49 (16,045)
Kelly, Andrew Thomas 3:57:38 (10,275)
Kelly, Anthony 4:25:43 (17,725)
Kelly, Ben James Leonard 3:45:59 (7,306)
Kelly, Brian Ronald 3:36:57 (5,554)
Kelly, Brian V 3:01:52 (1,249)
Kelly, Christopher J 4:29:43 (18,888)
Kelly, Christopher T 3:14:29 (2,380)
Kelly, Craig 3:13:04 (2,200)
Kelly, Daniel Marc 4:21:21 (16,506)
Kelly, David 3:49:16 (8,039)
Kelly, David 3:51:51 (8,622)
Kelly, David A 4:33:11 (19,757)
Kelly, David M 5:25:54 (30,766)
Kelly, David P 3:58:17 (10,484)
Kelly, David Robert 4:57:25 (25,842)
Kelly, Glenn S 5:42:21 (32,623)
Kelly, Ian 3:53:12 (8,971)
Kelly, James M 2:40:48 (224)
Kelly, Jon David 4:04:46 (12,148)
Kelly, Lennon 4:43:03 (22,272)
Kelly, Mark W 3:50:27 (8,297)
Kelly, Michael 4:58:43 (26,148)
Kelly, Mike 3:41:54 (6,499)
Kelly, Nathan Aidan 4:22:52 (16,954)
Kelly, Nick 4:01:03 (11,264)
Kelly, Paul J 5:07:35 (27,828)
Kelly, Paul Joseph 4:08:53 (13,181)
Kelly, Peter 4:16:16 (15,092)
Kelly, Peter John 3:39:20 (6,015)
Kelly, Robert Paul 4:58:59 (26,210)
Kelly, Scott 4:36:40 (20,651)
Kelly, Stephen P 5:34:21 (31,803)
Kelly, Steve 5:09:04 (28,058)
Kelly, Terence 6:46:12 (35,934)
Kelly, Thomas 4:32:40 (19,599)
Kelly, Toby 5:03:49 (27,159)
Kelly, Tom 4:50:05 (24,070)
Kelsall, Michael 4:17:52 (15,540)
Kelsall, Mike Godwyn 5:57:13 (33,881)
Kelsall, Roger Marshall 4:20:12 (16,165)
Kelsey, Ashley James 4:36:01 (20,481)
Kelsey, Chris Peter 4:19:52 (16,066)
Kelsey, Peter 4:22:33 (16,864)
Kelsey, Peter 5:29:42 (31,254)
Kelvin, Jason Howard 4:45:56 (23,009)
Kember, Julian James 4:09:39 (13,385)
Kembery, Jonathan Alexander 3:37:23 (5,634)
Kemble, Richard 3:58:20 (10,505)
Kemish, Kingsley P 4:12:49 (14,184)
Kemlo, Michael Ian 5:34:39 (31,844)
Kemmis, Luke R 4:03:15 (11,792)
Kemp, Albert L 3:49:39 (8,134)
Kemp, David 4:09:06 (13,229)
Kemp, Graham Brian 4:30:33 (19,106)
Kemp, Ian D 5:49:31 (33,285)
Kemp, James 3:56:58 (10,077)
Kemp, Jon M 2:57:41 (930)
Kemp, Kevin David 5:29:19 (31,194)
Kemp, Russell Andrew 4:12:59 (14,229)
Kemp, Steve James 4:30:26 (19,072)
Kenchington, Chris J 3:21:22 (3,127)
Kenchington, Nicholas S 2:53:56 (666)
Kendall, Daniel Paul 4:33:25 (19,829)
Kendall, David 3:45:35 (7,227)
Kendall, Michael E 3:52:54 (8,898)
Kendall, Will 3:37:13 (5,602)
Kendall-Lansell, Mark 4:00:36 (11,140)
Kendell, Stephen M 4:22:23 (16,818)
Kendellen, Michael J 4:33:35 (19,884)
Kendellen, Paul A 4:33:35 (19,884)
Kendrick, Andrew 4:07:50 (12,912)
Kendrick, Anthony R 3:33:21 (4,942)
Kendrick, Ian Edward John 5:19:52 (29,831)
Kendrick, Neil 5:17:56 (29,541)
Kendrick, Philip H 3:13:17 (2,221)
Kene, Adam 4:21:27 (16,535)
Kenech, Ali 3:34:17 (5,111)
Kennard, Adam D 4:02:17 (11,555)
Kennard, David Alan 3:46:09 (7,345)
Kennard, Michael Ian 3:25:05 (3,593)
Kennedy, Alan John 4:00:32 (11,124)
Kennedy, Alan Martin 5:09:48 (28,196)
Kennedy, Arthur J 5:37:06 (32,116)
Kennedy, Donald E 2:58:20 (989)
Kennedy, Gordon 3:50:20 (8,275)
Kennedy, Gregor William 3:21:57 (3,191)
Kennedy, Ian S 3:29:07 (4,254)
Kennedy, James P 2:46:54 (381)
Kennedy, Joe George 5:08:36 (27,991)
Kennedy, Lee D 4:34:14 (20,054)
Kennedy, Les 3:15:30 (2,496)
Kennedy, Paul 4:07:15 (12,764)
Kennedy, Richard D 3:08:04 (1,702)
Kennedy, Russell 3:47:15 (7,586)
Kennedy, William Charles 5:22:51 (30,284)
Kennefick, David 6:05:11 (34,401)
Kennerley, Dominic M 3:25:03 (3,587)
Kennes, Dimitri 3:58:27 (10,541)
Kenneth, Vincent 4:32:56 (19,680)
Kennett, Andrew 5:49:46 (33,316)
Kennett, Steffan A 2:48:59 (442)
Kenney, Nick 3:32:22 (4,794)
Kenney, Richard 4:16:58 (15,287)
Kenning, Paul 4:16:04 (15,042)
Kenny, Anthony Gerard 4:52:13 (24,606)
Kenny, Ciaran 4:54:44 (25,238)
Kenny, Craig 4:04:41 (12,122)
Kenny, Dave 5:27:57 (31,017)
Kenny, Liam M 7:26:43 (36,451)
Kenny, Mark S 5:09:57 (28,221)
Kenny, Matthew 4:09:53 (13,437)
Kenny, Pauric 4:39:08 (21,291)
Kensey, Timothy George 4:56:16 (25,601)
Kent, Adam 4:46:12 (23,090)
Kent, Alexander John 4:41:08 (21,804)
Kent, Aron Richard 5:03:07 (27,041)
Kent, Brian 4:22:48 (16,939)
Kent, Chris 4:04:07 (11,989)
Kent, David T 4:10:58 (13,703)
Kent, Justin 3:51:21 (8,503)
Kent, Mark Anthony 4:32:58 (19,687)
Kent, Nicolas 5:07:21 (27,783)
Kent, Nigel Alan 4:22:04 (16,723)
Kent, Simon Paul 5:23:39 (30,415)
Kent, Tristan 3:13:56 (2,307)
Kentfield, Mark H 5:02:02 (26,850)
Kenyon, David A 3:13:43 (2,287)
Kenyon, Jonathan 4:27:50 (18,319)
Keogh, Ben 5:12:11 (28,599)
Keohane, Peter S 4:17:47 (15,522)
Kerbey, Philip L 3:52:10 (8,699)
Kercher, Lyle 4:20:04 (16,126)
Kerfoot, Mark 4:37:29 (20,873)
Kernn, Uwe 3:43:57 (6,868)
Kerr, Aidan 4:15:54 (15,001)
Kerr, Asher 4:24:18 (17,319)
Kerr, David Scott 4:45:11 (22,815)
Kerr, Kenny 4:53:13 (24,853)
Kerr, Martin 6:21:16 (35,174)
Kerr, Stuart J 3:15:16 (2,468)
Kerr, Tim 4:09:35 (13,365)
Kerridge, Antony 3:56:58 (10,077)
Kerridge, Peter 3:49:12 (8,026)
Kerrigan, Charles 3:44:36 (7,014)
Kerr-Shaw, Benjamin 4:17:30 (15,439)
Kerry, Michael 4:12:13 (14,035)
Kerschat, Michael 2:59:10 (1,073)
Kershaw, Andrew David 4:57:35 (25,875)
Kershaw, Matthew Stuart Healey .5:06:42 (27,672)
Kershaw, Michael Geoffrey 3:58:05 (10,407)
Kershaw, Nigel 5:23:34 (30,396)
Kershi, Sajeel 4:40:35 (21,664)
Kerton, Christopher 5:28:16 (31,059)

Kerwin, John Andrew	4:43:10	(22,292)
Kerwin-Nye, Grant Lucas	5:36:51	(32,087)
Kesler, Joel Martin	4:56:15	(25,595)
Kessel, Mike Van	5:56:09	(33,806)
Kessler, Marian	4:23:30	(17,104)
Kessler, Peter	4:58:11	(26,008)
Kestle, Michael J	3:15:42	(2,521)
Kestle, Ryan J	2:56:12	(813)
Keszthelyi, David	2:55:04	(750)
Ketley, Mark L	2:52:32	(593)
Kett, Justin	4:46:20	(23,133)
Ketteridge, Sean R	2:41:55	(250)
Kewell, Gareth John	5:08:46	(28,011)
Kewell, Stuart Vaughan	3:31:25	(4,653)
Key, Andrew James	3:32:01	(4,740)
Key, John Edward	6:13:57	(34,835)
Key, Michael John	6:10:33	(34,684)
Keya, Tom	3:58:21	(10,512)
Khaihra, Harvey	4:34:21	(20,080)
Khajuria, Nishant	5:18:31	(29,627)
Khakhar, Ravi	4:53:34	(24,934)
Khalsa, Ravinderpal Singh	5:48:56	(33,236)
Khan, Asif Amin	4:20:01	(16,114)
Khan, Farhan	6:30:57	(35,534)
Khan, Hamid	3:06:19	(1,556)
Khan, Ilyas Tariq	5:20:50	(29,983)
Khan, Imran Mohammed	4:54:34	(25,196)
Khan, Mark Shah	7:03:46	(36,236)
Khan, Shafiq A	3:08:23	(1,737)
Khan, Waheed	3:15:05	(2,447)
Khan, Waheed	5:09:27	(28,132)
Khan, Zor	5:14:05	(28,936)
Khandelwal, Ajay	4:19:18	(15,929)
Khazanehdari, Jamshid	3:35:52	(5,392)
Khemka, Sneh	5:20:28	(29,919)
Khemri, Mokhtar	4:09:46	(13,412)
Khonsaraki, Behrooz	5:22:01	(30,148)
Khoo, Raymond	4:14:45	(14,726)
Khoo, Sunny	5:00:09	(26,491)
Kibby, Paul Michael	3:35:47	(5,374)
Kidd, David Alan	4:30:03	(18,987)
Kidd, Michael John	6:08:43	(34,598)
Kidston, Ken	7:50:51	(36,564)
Kieliger, Matthias	3:35:00	(5,249)
Kiely, Eoin	3:52:29	(8,792)
Kiernan, Matthew James	4:11:07	(13,748)
Kiffel, Alain	4:50:49	(24,243)
Kifle, Yonas	2:14:39	(9)
Kihle, Dag	5:56:49	(33,853)
Kilbane, Andy	4:21:09	(16,452)
Kilbee, Simon	4:20:51	(16,375)
Kilby, Simon	4:51:46	(24,483)
Kill, Lee Framcis	4:54:14	(25,109)
Kille, Turville	3:48:15	(7,794)
Killen, Douglas	5:57:55	(33,926)
Killick, Andrew	5:23:21	(30,365)
Killingley, Phil S	2:28:06	(53)
Kilminster, Gary Edgar	5:10:00	(28,235)
Kilner, Charlie	3:43:17	(6,741)
Kilpatrick, Ben William	4:02:54	(11,708)
Kilpatrick, Julian Philip Laird	4:02:49	(11,677)
Kilshaw, Ian M	3:31:06	(4,595)
Kim, Chun In	5:09:31	(28,153)
Kim, Jwa Sang	4:02:06	(11,513)
Kim, Weon Jo	4:23:22	(17,071)
Kimber, Nicholas A	3:41:05	(6,337)
Kimber, Nick	3:30:46	(4,541)
Kimber, Tom	3:38:49	(5,908)
Kime, Steven	4:36:01	(20,481)
Kimmins, Alexander	3:50:31	(8,317)
Kimpton, Graham J	4:50:24	(24,141)
Kimura, Yasuto	2:41:16	(232)
Kinchen, John E	4:04:18	(12,029)
Kind, David J	3:28:23	(4,121)
Kind, James	4:25:46	(17,742)
Kinder, Matthias	3:03:03	(1,330)
Kindon, Christopher John	3:24:41	(3,537)
Kindred, David Arthur	4:11:41	(13,905)
King, Adam	5:47:38	(33,108)
King, Adam Stuart	4:06:55	(12,689)
King, Alastair	6:27:40	(35,410)
King, Alex	4:55:45	(25,480)
King, Alistair William	5:45:22	(32,899)
King, Andrew	4:20:05	(16,131)
King, Andrew	4:52:52	(24,771)
King, Andrew Martin	3:12:03	(2,096)
King, Andrew Philip	3:34:53	(5,230)
King, Andy	4:33:03	(19,715)
King, Andy	5:54:14	(33,661)
King, Ben A	3:14:30	(2,383)
King, Bryan Trevor	4:00:17	(11,056)
King, Chris C	4:19:38	(15,999)
King, Colin Peter	3:55:36	(9,636)
King, Danny Paul	5:34:54	(31,868)
King, David	4:14:53	(14,759)
King, David	4:35:21	(20,309)
King, David	5:00:05	(26,474)
King, David A	5:47:30	(33,098)
King, David Jospeh	4:07:28	(12,822)
King, David M	3:12:31	(2,135)
King, Edward M	3:56:09	(9,822)
King, Gary A	5:29:29	(31,218)
King, Glen E	4:10:51	(13,680)
King, Jason	3:36:12	(5,448)
King, Jason	6:21:05	(35,163)
King, Jon	3:39:46	(6,092)
King, Karl	6:42:58	(35,859)
King, Lewis Kenneth	5:37:04	(32,112)
King, Linden	5:20:33	(29,937)
King, Mathew	4:22:17	(16,793)
King, Matthew Peter	2:56:48	(849)
King, Michael	4:47:01	(23,315)
King, Michael Douglas	4:00:43	(11,176)
King, Mike David	4:58:36	(26,116)
King, Nicholas P	4:05:52	(12,424)
King, Oscar Micheal Ian	4:19:38	(15,999)
King, Patrick	5:58:21	(33,954)
King, Paul	4:40:37	(21,674)
King, Paul J	3:58:12	(10,459)
King, Richard	4:31:10	(19,258)
King, Richard A	3:55:14	(9,538)
King, Richard J	4:43:20	(22,325)
King, Rob	4:09:53	(13,437)
King, Robert C	4:43:25	(22,349)
King, Russell	3:46:39	(7,453)
King, Steve	4:45:25	(22,865)
King, Steve	5:49:54	(33,324)
King, Steven Craig	5:52:36	(33,538)
King, Steven M	3:56:22	(9,887)
King, Tom	4:24:08	(17,268)
King, Tony	6:52:47	(36,070)
Kingdom, James H S	3:55:20	(9,571)
Kingham, Les W	4:54:51	(25,268)
Kingham, Neil E	3:00:18	(1,162)
Kingston, Matthew	6:16:24	(34,942)
Kingston, Oliver	4:16:45	(15,233)
Kingston-Lee, Matthew F	2:55:04	(750)
Kingswood, Stephen Paul	4:00:35	(11,135)
Kington, Ian Jason	4:22:33	(16,864)
Kingwill, William Edward	3:46:19	(7,378)
Kinnaird, Robert	3:56:20	(9,883)
Kinnear, Patrick Liam	5:27:40	(30,984)
Kinnill, Philip A	4:37:04	(20,765)
Kinninmonth, Alex	3:43:03	(6,709)
Kinoshita, Naoya	7:10:37	(36,316)
Kinross, Greg	4:09:07	(13,234)
Kinsella, Stephen	3:52:55	(8,904)
Kinsella, Timothy Patrick	4:14:28	(14,637)
Kinsey, Nicholas J	2:49:11	(453)
Kinsey, Paul S	3:56:17	(9,866)
Kinsey, Richard James	5:22:48	(30,272)
Kirby, Andrew J	2:59:07	(1,065)
Kirby, Anthony	3:30:37	(4,514)
Kirby, Anthony	4:42:50	(22,225)
Kirby, Clive William	5:03:45	(27,148)
Kirby, Gregory J	3:55:14	(9,538)
Kirby, Nicholas James	4:12:14	(14,039)
Kirby, Richard John	3:56:16	(9,861)
Kirby, Scott Lloyd	6:20:45	(35,158)
Kirby-Cook, Tony	3:41:29	(6,419)
Kirbyshire, Andrew John	5:00:35	(26,568)
Kirchmayr, Reinhold	4:04:49	(12,157)
Kirk, Gareth G	3:47:20	(7,605)
Kirk, Graham	3:26:04	(3,744)
Kirk, James Mckenzie	5:34:18	(31,799)
Kirk, John	5:04:30	(27,276)
Kirk, Malcolm	4:29:50	(18,920)
Kirkby, Arron Wayne	3:07:33	(1,658)
Kirkby, Kevin	4:40:31	(21,647)
Kirkby, Robert Paul	3:42:27	(6,587)
Kirkegaard, Ulrik	4:21:48	(16,636)
Kirkham, Christopher	3:37:07	(5,586)
Kirkland, David	4:37:40	(20,919)
Kirkland, William	4:32:33	(19,572)
Kirkman, Simon James	5:02:52	(27,000)
Kirkpatrick, George Hugh	4:38:57	(21,244)
Kirk-Wilson, Ed	3:03:08	(1,333)
Kirkwood, Cameron	3:44:33	(7,001)
Kirrage, Nicholas	4:47:59	(23,542)
Kirsopp, Brian	3:37:27	(5,649)
Kirtlan, Paul	4:36:37	(20,637)
Kirtland, Andy William	4:19:19	(15,935)
Kirtland, Tom	4:41:18	(21,845)
Kirton, Akira	5:46:14	(32,973)
Kirui, Abel	2:08:04	(5)
Kiszow, Stephen Robert	4:00:40	(11,159)
Kitallides, Alexios	6:39:17	(35,762)
Kitchen, Jay	4:00:26	(11,100)
Kitchen, Neil	3:39:17	(6,000)
Kitchen, Simon	4:34:26	(20,104)
Kitchener, Phil A	5:15:06	(29,081)
Kitchener, Philip A	4:00:36	(11,140)
Kitchener, Robert M	6:10:57	(34,698)
Kitching, Ian	3:18:42	(2,841)
Kitching, Ian D	2:47:37	(406)
Kitchner, Andrew Mark	5:23:08	(30,326)
Kitchovitch, Stephan	4:46:46	(23,242)
Kite, Jonathan S	4:40:36	(21,670)
Kitromilides, Alex S	2:50:12	(493)
Kitson, Charles	4:06:12	(12,496)
Kitson, Paul J	4:03:52	(11,940)
Kitson-Smith, Anthony	4:27:11	(18,143)
Kitt, Gary	5:19:22	(29,757)
Kittrell, Charles Ramon	3:49:48	(8,166)
Kivell, Rich	4:16:05	(15,047)
Kjaell-Ohlsson, Martin	2:26:00	(43)
Kjeldsen, Brian	4:01:11	(11,294)
Kjeldsen, Mogens	3:39:46	(6,092)
Kjoengerskov, Anders Peder	3:18:37	(2,831)
Klatovsky, Richard	4:10:31	(13,597)
Kleber, Christian	4:26:43	(18,003)
Klein, Fabrice	3:11:26	(2,042)
Klein, Laurence D	5:12:04	(28,577)
Kleinberg, Robert	6:32:09	(35,570)
Klenerman, Paul	4:22:44	(16,913)
Klimach, Stefan	4:07:18	(12,775)
Klingenspor, Martin	3:33:18	(4,935)
Kloet, Gareth John	3:44:38	(7,022)
Knaeble, Daniel	3:12:55	(2,178)
Knapman, Richard	3:35:34	(5,337)
Knapp, Martin	5:18:31	(29,627)
Knapp, Nigel John	5:40:32	(32,437)
Knapper, David James	4:39:21	(21,340)
Knechtl, Paul	3:58:41	(10,619)
Knell, James	3:56:04	(9,802)
Knell, Nigel Victor	3:57:53	(10,356)
Knight, Adam	5:50:40	(33,400)
Knight, Andrew C	3:58:29	(10,551)
Knight, Andy	4:24:27	(17,376)
Knight, Anthony	4:03:42	(11,898)
Knight, Brian Peter John	6:54:45	(36,104)
Knight, Carl	7:21:58	(36,419)
Knight, Charles Robert Harcourt	4:57:06	(25,779)
Knight, Chris	3:25:34	(3,662)
Knight, David	4:08:56	(13,192)
Knight, David John	5:53:20	(33,597)
Knight, Gareth C	3:24:57	(3,572)
Knight, Geoffrey P	2:35:14	(114)
Knight, James Justin	3:03:45	(1,370)
Knight, John Gerald	4:51:15	(24,366)
Knight, Kevin	4:02:32	(11,613)
Knight, Malcolm John	4:56:26	(25,635)
Knight, Matt A	4:02:45	(11,665)
Knight, Michael	4:00:26	(11,100)
Knight, Paul	4:07:31	(12,837)
Knight, Russell James	4:51:39	(24,450)
Knight, Russell Stuart	5:58:57	(33,986)
Knight, Stuart J	4:29:12	(18,732)
Knighton, Simon	3:13:52	(2,301)

Lane, Michael	5:39:10 (32,318)
Lane, Nigel Alastair	5:54:45 (33,690)
Lane, Paul	6:16:06 (34,926)
Lane, Robert John	3:53:55 (9,186)
Lane, Ronald F	3:48:46 (7,914)
Lane, Rory	4:55:30 (25,410)
Lane, Spenser	4:04:47 (12,150)
Lane, Terry	4:08:35 (13,111)
Lane, Thomas Charles	3:15:50 (2,530)
Laneve, Francesco	3:28:25 (4,132)
Lang, Adam Brian	3:45:57 (7,299)
Lang, David	5:29:02 (31,154)
Lang, Dieter	4:36:26 (20,582)
Lang, Herbert	3:52:13 (8,711)
Lang, Steven	4:14:44 (14,723)
Langan, Anthony	3:36:40 (5,508)
Langan, Kevin A	3:28:48 (4,189)
Langan, Simon J	4:36:37 (20,637)
Langdon, James Edward	5:23:09 (30,329)
Langdon, Jeremy	3:15:07 (2,452)
Langdon, Tom	4:07:22 (12,791)
Langdown, Thomas	3:10:13 (1,924)
Lange, Philip John William	5:20:31 (29,930)
Langford, Stefan	5:17:07 (29,408)
Langford, Steve	7:39:56 (36,521)
Langham, Neil	3:36:36 (5,496)
Langham, Paul	4:02:10 (11,529)
Langham, Phillip N	3:57:01 (10,102)
Langler, Ian John	3:15:33 (2,504)
Langler, Simon James	5:06:42 (27,672)
Langley, Benjamin	3:13:29 (2,252)
Langley, Colin	2:51:48 (558)
Langley, John A	3:09:05 (1,815)
Langley, Kelly Paul	4:20:52 (16,381)
Langley, Kevin James David	5:25:47 (30,751)
Langley, Luke James	5:11:23 (28,465)
Langley, Matthew	4:01:03 (11,264)
Langley, Robert F	3:17:36 (2,725)
Langlois, Frederic	2:59:11 (1,074)
Langlois, Tim	5:09:28 (28,136)
Langmaid, Simon G	3:58:23 (10,517)
Langman, Craig S	4:26:39 (17,986)
Langman, Jack	3:59:22 (10,827)
Langron, Alistair	3:16:42 (2,645)
Langston, Nathan	4:09:33 (13,351)
Langstone, Paul	4:38:59 (21,256)
Langton, Steve J	3:37:21 (5,629)
Lanoe, JB	4:07:36 (12,855)
Lansbury, Andrew David	4:42:47 (22,208)
Lansdowne, Paul	4:23:20 (17,054)
Lansley, David Andrew	5:22:34 (30,232)
Lansley, Oliver	4:02:30 (11,601)
Lappas, Martyn Richard	4:02:03 (11,502)
Lappin, James Richard	3:33:26 (4,958)
Lappin, Noel George	6:05:30 (34,421)
Lappin, Steven K	4:53:25 (24,895)
Laraway, David	6:09:53 (34,655)
Larbi-Cherif, Amine	5:31:58 (31,532)
Larcey, Daniel Peter	4:41:55 (21,998)
Larcombe, Tom Charles	4:02:27 (11,595)
Lardet, Maurice	5:23:17 (30,354)
Lardiller, Didier	3:25:44 (3,692)
Large, Kevin M	4:27:47 (18,310)
Large, Stephen Micheal	4:04:27 (12,066)
Largey, James J	4:50:23 (24,135)
Larkam, David	3:15:45 (2,524)
Larke, Joseph	3:24:17 (3,482)
Larke, Patrick	3:45:56 (7,295)
Larkin, Edmund John	3:55:01 (9,482)
Larkin, Kevin M	4:45:19 (22,847)
Larkman, Toby	5:07:32 (27,819)
Larman, Bill	4:41:08 (21,804)
Larman, Ian Charles	4:36:48 (20,682)
Larman, Mat	4:05:44 (12,386)
Larmour, Chris	5:29:27 (31,215)
Larner, Emmett	3:57:27 (10,214)
Larripa, Eric	2:33:02 (90)
Larsson, Charles A	4:01:23 (11,332)
Larvin, Tim	4:08:59 (13,211)
Lascelles, Stephen	3:43:59 (6,879)
Lashbrook, Alan T	5:21:42 (30,108)
Lashko, Gary	4:43:32 (22,377)
Lassnig, Cliff	3:36:01 (5,415)

Last, Andrew John	5:33:20 (31,697)
Lastimosa, Caesar Kinnier	4:30:02 (18,983)
Lastisneres, Frederic	2:41:45 (246)
Latham, Alan R	3:00:48 (1,197)
Latham, David Stephen	6:38:17 (35,733)
Latham, Mark Richard	5:30:14 (31,319)
Latham, Todd	4:16:42 (15,222)
Latheron, Paul W	4:32:47 (19,626)
Lathwell, Simon G	3:15:39 (2,517)
Lattanzi, Nicola	3:37:18 (5,622)
Latteman, Mark	3:41:42 (6,457)
Latter, Trevor	5:35:18 (31,902)
Lau, Damon	4:54:07 (25,074)
Lauder, Daniel	4:44:12 (22,563)
Laugharne, Nicholas James	4:16:39 (15,204)
Laughton, Nigel Charles	6:10:02 (34,666)
Laundon, Matthew Keith	4:27:15 (18,167)
Laundy, David	4:24:11 (17,281)
Laurent, Gerard	4:23:33 (17,119)
Laurent, Patrick	4:11:43 (13,908)
Laurie, Darren	3:59:41 (10,916)
Laurie, Richard	5:22:21 (30,290)
Laurie, Steven J	3:17:11 (2,681)
Laurier, Phillip Benjamin	4:43:57 (22,492)
Laurila, Ville	4:27:03 (18,097)
Lauro, Patrik	4:21:09 (16,452)
Lauwick, Vincent	3:52:52 (8,890)
Lavalard, Jean-François	4:07:39 (12,871)
Lavelle, Michael	3:55:56 (9,760)
Lavender, Daniel Paul	3:53:21 (9,013)
Lavender, Dean George	4:00:56 (11,231)
Laver, Simon P	3:20:23 (3,002)
Lavers, Matthew Richard	4:29:38 (18,860)
Lavers, Robert A	4:25:52 (17,779)
Laverty, Sean A	2:50:34 (507)
Lavery, Gregory J	3:08:16 (1,725)
Lavery, Stephen William	3:44:10 (6,909)
Lavie, Jean-Marie	4:12:22 (14,066)
Lavigne, Joe	4:43:25 (22,349)
Law, Albert	4:00:13 (11,036)
Law, Andrew Puryer	3:56:50 (10,041)
Law, Duncan Jon	3:43:17 (6,741)
Law, Marcus Stephen	4:09:58 (13,463)
Law, Mike	4:10:40 (13,629)
Law, Peter Christian	4:36:14 (20,532)
Law, Simon N	3:05:06 (1,467)
Law, Steve	5:18:00 (29,545)
Lawal, Taofeek	5:47:58 (33,134)
Lawler, Rob W	3:48:25 (7,829)
Lawless, Timothy	4:46:27 (23,156)
Lawlor, Kevin J	4:56:53 (25,747)
Lawlor, Sean	5:19:46 (29,815)
Lawrance, Lee James	3:27:14 (3,912)
Lawrance, Richard S	3:26:11 (3,768)
Lawrence, Adrian Michael	4:20:27 (16,248)
Lawrence, Andrew D	4:43:21 (22,333)
Lawrence, Brett	5:58:10 (33,942)
Lawrence, Brett James	4:22:01 (16,711)
Lawrence, Chris M	4:07:36 (12,855)
Lawrence, Daniel	4:02:35 (11,624)
Lawrence, David	5:01:39 (26,788)
Lawrence, David John	4:46:17 (23,125)
Lawrence, Keith	4:53:15 (24,862)
Lawrence, Martin Andrew	5:26:56 (30,895)
Lawrence, Martin W	4:49:31 (23,911)
Lawrence, Nick	3:58:42 (10,625)
Lawrence, Paul	4:58:14 (26,019)
Lawrence, Ray	2:57:12 (871)
Lawrence, Roger	3:55:36 (9,636)
Lawrence, Roger	4:06:46 (12,645)
Lawrence, Tim	4:44:08 (22,541)
Lawrenson, Dale	5:28:13 (31,054)
Lawrie, Charles	3:17:31 (2,714)
Lawrie, John David	3:19:56 (2,954)
Laws, Derek William	3:29:05 (4,244)
Laws, Graham John	4:52:09 (24,589)
Laws, Ivan	5:25:46 (30,744)
Laws, Tim Meyrick	4:19:44 (16,027)
Lawson, Ian David	5:17:07 (29,408)
Lawson, Ian Scott	4:42:45 (22,203)
Lawson, John	3:59:39 (10,903)
Lawson, Mark S	5:29:20 (31,199)
Lawson, Simon D	4:14:44 (14,723)

Lawson, Steve	3:47:27 (7,634)
Lawson-Smith, Stev	6:50:45 (36,008)
Lawton, Bryan W	3:21:46 (3,168)
Lawton, Peter J	3:46:03 (7,322)
Lawton, Stephen R	3:51:54 (8,639)
Lay, John	4:26:55 (18,054)
Lay, Peter A	3:35:17 (5,286)
Laycock, Grant	3:53:51 (9,172)
Laycock, Jeremy A	4:51:17 (24,372)
Laycock, Marcus	5:02:18 (26,906)
Layland, Paul	3:39:39 (6,068)
Layley, Iain Curtis	5:05:41 (27,478)
Layne, William Leonard	3:43:08 (6,721)
Layzell, George	5:04:11 (27,226)
Lazard, Paul	6:35:41 (35,670)
Lazarus, Craig	3:46:02 (7,314)
Lazell, Richard	5:37:04 (32,112)
Lazell, Richard J	2:40:49 (226)
Lazenby, John Robert	4:59:58 (26,442)
Le Blanc Smith, Paul	4:01:08 (11,282)
Le Cat, Pierre	3:44:55 (7,082)
Le Du, Ronan	4:24:11 (17,281)
Le Fevre, Peter D	3:55:03 (9,491)
Le Goff, Remy	4:58:44 (26,152)
Le Goff, Yves	6:32:28 (35,577)
Le Good, Andrew K	3:31:14 (4,615)
Le Good, Daniel Saul	3:08:26 (1,746)
Le Grand, Jean Luc	4:59:25 (26,318)
Le Grice, Philip	3:09:29 (1,855)
Le Guay, Stephane	4:21:01 (16,420)
Le Guellec, Ludovic	2:57:58 (953)
Le Miere, Julian Paul	3:30:40 (4,521)
Le Neve Foster, Christopher	4:36:34 (20,622)
Le Roy, Sylvain	4:40:36 (21,670)
Le Tougneur, Adrian Michael	5:51:51 (33,495)
Lea, Martin A	3:14:49 (2,420)
Lea, Peter	5:44:10 (32,783)
Leach, Karl D	6:03:35 (34,294)
Leach, Robert J	3:26:43 (3,832)
Leach, Roy	5:13:27 (28,837)
Leader, Stephen	5:16:47 (29,351)
Leahy, Kieron Robert	4:21:36 (16,580)
Leahy, Richard P	3:24:35 (3,522)
Leake, David Sidney	3:52:39 (8,836)
Leake, Shaun Richard	4:51:35 (24,438)
Leaman, Andy Stephen	5:31:00 (31,417)
Leaney, Stuart B	2:35:29 (123)
Lear, Clifford Edward	4:13:58 (14,496)
Lear, Simon John Patrick	3:54:30 (9,328)
Learner, David	5:01:25 (26,738)
Leary, Mark	3:57:11 (10,154)
Leatham, Jonathan	4:13:06 (14,263)
Leather, Dan William Gibson	4:11:07 (13,748)
Leather, Mathew James	4:52:39 (24,722)
Leather, Michael Terry	4:36:21 (20,562)
Leather, Richard	4:01:33 (11,383)
Leatherland, Paul	3:57:41 (10,293)
Leaver, David Shaun	3:25:52 (3,717)
Lebrun, Michel	4:30:29 (19,085)
Lebus, David	4:05:34 (12,347)
Leccacorvi, Ross James	5:19:10 (29,730)
Lechner, Joerg	3:42:41 (6,631)
Leckerman, Antony	4:15:52 (14,994)
Leckey, Daniel	3:29:47 (4,377)
Leckie, William	6:02:56 (34,245)
Ledro, Giorgio	4:16:50 (15,254)
Ledwaba, Ephraim	6:13:44 (34,829)
Lee, Andrew Roger	3:49:38 (8,130)
Lee, Angus James	5:06:47 (27,688)
Lee, Benjamin	3:38:09 (5,795)
Lee, Brenton	3:58:52 (10,674)
Lee, Brian Paul	4:24:14 (17,294)
Lee, Chris	4:15:47 (14,977)
Lee, Chris John	4:43:25 (22,349)
Lee, David	4:49:38 (23,953)
Lee, Guo Sun	4:53:30 (24,917)
Lee, Ian Stephen	3:31:11 (4,608)
Lee, Jeffery James	3:15:15 (2,465)
Lee, Jeremy R	4:36:37 (20,637)
Lee, John M	4:24:18 (17,319)
Lee, John Phillip	4:53:57 (25,034)
Lee, Jonathan Martyn	4:18:26 (15,694)
Lee, Joshua	4:00:42 (11,170)

Lee, Justin Charles 3:19:52 (2,949)
Lee, Marcus T. 3:43:48 (6,832)
Lee, Martyn Alexander 4:47:08 (23,331)
Lee, Matt 4:25:47 (17,745)
Lee, Matthew Thomas 5:11:55 (28,544)
Lee, Michael Ian 4:10:19 (13,548)
Lee, Mick 4:51:40 (24,455)
Lee, Peter 3:59:20 (10,818)
Lee, Peter G. 2:46:02 (359)
Lee, Richard 3:50:41 (8,354)
Lee, Richard 4:07:59 (12,957)
Lee, Richard 4:52:11 (24,596)
Lee, Richard K 6:44:12 (35,888)
Lee, Richard Simon 5:36:26 (32,046)
Lee, Robert 4:35:40 (20,380)
Lee, Robert Sinclair Cullimore ... 5:41:28 (32,530)
Lee, Robin 4:11:24 (13,820)
Lee, Ryan Richard 4:59:14 (26,272)
Lee, Sam 4:08:01 (12,966)
Lee, Sang Kyo 4:05:07 (12,230)
Lee, Stephen 4:18:58 (15,843)
Lee, Stephen Mark 5:09:42 (28,180)
Lee, Steven 5:37:19 (32,146)
Lee, Stuart Alan 4:29:54 (18,953)
Lee, Sukho 3:39:38 (6,066)
Lee, Tony 3:46:22 (7,387)
Lee-Cerrino, Kevin Leonard 5:19:19 (29,752)
Leeder, Alan Robert 4:38:15 (21,041)
Leeks, Ross William 4:50:46 (24,231)
Leeman, Matthew John 4:36:52 (20,704)
Leeming, Chris 4:09:46 (13,412)
Leeming, Nicholas 3:45:55 (7,290)
Lees, Matt 4:17:00 (15,300)
Lees, Nick 4:05:35 (12,351)
Lees, Paul C 4:47:32 (23,417)
Lees, Robert 3:33:39 (4,998)
Lees, Tom 5:10:45 (28,366)
Leese, Steven 3:17:06 (2,677)
Leeson, Simon 4:07:41 (12,883)
Le-Faye, Nicholas C. 4:57:11 (25,799)
Lefebvre, Olivier 4:11:04 (13,738)
Lefevre, Gordon John 3:34:51 (5,220)
Lefrancois, Patrice 3:30:36 (4,510)
Left, Peter 4:30:37 (19,127)
Legassick, David Thomas 2:59:40 (1,125)
Leger, Benoit 3:53:36 (9,092)
Leger, Bruno 4:00:32 (11,124)
Legg, Michael Douglas 2:57:21 (883)
Leggett, Danial John 5:23:36 (30,404)
Leggo, Stuart C 5:53:22 (33,602)
Leggott, Jon 4:33:19 (19,807)
Leggott, Steven 5:57:09 (33,873)
Legh, Thomas 3:51:16 (8,488)
Lehmann, Antoine 2:51:06 (527)
Leicester, Mark 3:52:40 (8,839)
Leicester, Philip Edward 4:40:21 (21,596)
Leigh, David 5:55:47 (33,774)
Leigh, Peter 4:20:24 (16,232)
Leigh, Philip 3:03:43 (1,364)
Leigh, Ya'acov 4:54:11 (25,093)
Leighfield, Stephen P 3:45:00 (7,095)
Leighton, David Mark 4:35:59 (20,474)
Leighton, Richard 4:12:59 (14,229)
Leinen, Norbert 3:59:11 (10,771)
Leinster, Jonathan Stephen 3:53:31 (9,061)
Leiper, John 4:44:08 (22,541)
Leiros, Armando 3:53:04 (8,941)
Leiss, Michael 3:57:14 (10,168)
Leitch, Hughie Donald 6:18:11 (35,038)
Leitch, Martin William Alan 4:12:12 (14,032)
Leith, Clifford W 2:54:57 (743)
Leksell, Gustaf 4:14:25 (14,621)
Leleu, David 3:14:29 (2,380)
Lemaire, Jean-Michel 5:37:40 (32,179)
Lemiere, Gerrard 3:29:32 (4,328)
Lemon, Peter J 3:57:17 (10,178)
Lemon, Thomas G 3:56:40 (9,984)
Lemon, Tim 4:06:54 (12,684)
Lemoncello, Andrew 2:13:40 (8)
Lenaghan, Paul 3:58:53 (10,682)
Leng, Arthur John 4:22:09 (16,741)
Lenihan, Dean 3:46:46 (7,478)
Lenihan, Paul 4:48:53 (23,768)

Lenkiewicz, Wojciech 4:51:56 (24,536)
Lennard, James 6:00:47 (34,109)
Lenney, James 6:29:07 (35,465)
Lenney, Warren 5:54:21 (33,668)
Lennock, Mark John 4:38:35 (21,137)
Lennon, Andrew 3:59:53 (10,961)
Lennon, James Patrick 5:06:46 (27,684)
Lennon, Jason Roy 4:45:04 (22,788)
Lennox, Graeme 4:52:36 (24,706)
Lennox, Jethro 2:25:51 (42)
Lennox, Robert Haddow 5:49:42 (33,308)
Lenoble, Marc 2:34:46 (107)
Lenthall, Alex Willaim 3:27:24 (3,942)
Lenthall, Andrew N 3:14:16 (2,355)
Lenton, Graham Adrian 3:22:45 (3,264)
Lenton, Stuart John 5:09:28 (28,136)
Leonard, Andy 4:46:06 (23,063)
Leonard, Neil 4:10:50 (13,676)
Leonard, Paul 3:09:17 (1,833)
Leonard, Paul 4:30:43 (19,153)
Leong, Dalton Simon 4:44:34 (22,658)
Leoniuk, Kamil 5:17:18 (29,438)
Leopold, Eddie N. 4:17:58 (15,569)
Lepley, Jason John 4:35:23 (20,321)
Lerche-Henriksen, Olav 3:31:59 (4,736)
Lercher, Alfons 4:21:56 (16,686)
Leroy, Antony 3:25:11 (3,606)
Leroy, Philippe J 4:27:40 (18,277)
Lesiak, Craig 3:52:07 (8,682)
Lesiter, Brian Clive 3:42:59 (6,695)
Leslie, David Maxwell 3:36:49 (5,525)
Leslie, Peter David 4:22:17 (16,793)
Leslie, Stuart 3:55:59 (9,779)
Lespeare, Trevor L 3:40:23 (6,208)
Lesser, Benjamin Marc 4:04:52 (12,168)
Lester, Gareth Carl 3:29:11 (4,266)
Lester, Mark John 4:58:31 (26,092)
Lester, Roy 5:28:35 (31,098)
Lester, Sebastian 5:15:04 (29,078)
Lesti, Attila 3:05:04 (1,463)
Letch, Iain 4:24:50 (17,475)
Letchford, Stephen Derek 5:06:24 (27,601)
Letelier, Sebastian Rafael 3:02:58 (1,326)

Lethaby, Raymond J 4:58:21 (26,054)

My 25th London Marathon. The big day dawned, it was cloudy with dark skies. I walked over to the start, taking in the atmosphere, going into the changing tent at the green start with all the veterans. There was a tremendous buzz. Half an hour before we set off the heavens opened up, and as we began the rain stopped. The crowds seemed to be bigger than ever this year. At the nineteenth mile mark my family were there, plus six grandchildren, shouting and screaming at me but I was so focused that I didn't see or hear them! Running the Marathon is always a great experience.

Leung, Benjamin 4:53:44 (24,982)
Leuw, Peter Jonathan Dudley 4:10:47 (13,661)
Levan, David 3:56:29 (9,926)
Levene, David 6:07:11 (34,518)
Levene, Gavin 5:00:34 (26,564)
Levene, Rob 4:49:38 (23,953)
Levene, Russell 5:09:34 (28,162)
Leverett, Clive Edward 4:13:55 (14,484)
Leverton, James Robert 3:25:02 (3,584)
Levett, Jonathon Mark 3:53:33 (9,073)
Levett, Matthew James 3:43:45 (6,813)
Levey, Mark Stuart William 5:48:39 (33,209)
Levick, Michael R 4:50:20 (24,123)
Levin, Jason 3:56:07 (9,815)
Levis, Jean-Charles 3:49:28 (8,080)
Levitz, Michael David 5:24:58 (30,616)
Levy, Arron Robert 5:44:02 (32,770)
Levy, Ben 5:04:27 (27,266)
Levy, Brett 5:45:50 (32,937)
Levy, Isaac 4:19:22 (15,944)
Levy, Jonny 4:22:51 (16,949)
Levy, Joshua 6:40:56 (35,812)
Levy, Leeor 4:49:49 (24,013)
Lewi, Daniel 4:16:50 (15,254)
Lewis, Adrian 5:00:33 (26,561)
Lewis, Alan E 3:08:50 (1,797)
Lewis, Alun 4:28:13 (18,424)
Lewis, Andy 3:18:29 (2,819)
Lewis, Barry 6:10:39 (34,688)
Lewis, Ben 5:04:41 (27,315)
Lewis, Brett 3:34:48 (5,213)
Lewis, Clifford B 6:24:21 (35,292)
Lewis, Colin 3:45:33 (7,220)
Lewis, Craig 6:54:52 (36,107)
Lewis, Daniel 4:18:38 (15,753)
Lewis, Daniel 5:38:27 (32,255)
Lewis, Daniel Robert 3:30:47 (4,544)
Lewis, David 4:18:32 (15,722)
Lewis, David 4:20:59 (16,407)
Lewis, David 5:05:27 (27,440)
Lewis, David John 3:48:42 (7,898)
Lewis, David Joseph 5:07:49 (27,863)
Lewis, Dominic A 5:16:32 (29,314)
Lewis, Dunbar H 4:29:37 (18,852)
Lewis, Ed David 4:10:32 (13,600)
Lewis, Gareth 4:17:06 (15,321)
Lewis, Gavin John 4:52:16 (24,619)
Lewis, Gil 4:13:53 (14,478)
Lewis, Graham 5:51:01 (33,430)
Lewis, Howard C 4:23:43 (17,164)
Lewis, Jake R 4:23:09 (17,013)
Lewis, James 4:53:59 (25,045)
Lewis, Jeremy 3:52:33 (8,809)
Lewis, Jeremy 4:38:49 (21,207)
Lewis, John Daniel 4:03:20 (11,809)
Lewis, John E 3:29:25 (4,306)
Lewis, Jonathan 5:31:16 (31,445)
Lewis, Jonathan David 3:59:55 (10,969)
Lewis, Jonathan Edward Anthony . 3:37:11 (5,594)
Lewis, Jonathan S 5:13:47 (28,890)
Lewis, Kieron D 2:54:24 (694)
Lewis, Mark 4:04:35 (12,096)
Lewis, Mark 4:37:23 (20,841)
Lewis, Mark Edward George 4:21:27 (16,535)
Lewis, Mark J 3:16:01 (2,561)
Lewis, Mark Stuart 3:58:52 (10,674)
Lewis, Martin 5:28:48 (31,128)
Lewis, Martin John 3:44:15 (6,923)
Lewis, Matt 4:49:48 (24,007)
Lewis, Matthew 3:24:03 (3,440)
Lewis, Matthew 3:58:52 (10,674)
Lewis, Matthew Kendrick 3:55:47 (9,711)
Lewis, Mike 3:11:51 (2,081)
Lewis, Neil James 4:19:28 (15,963)
Lewis, Paul A 2:35:06 (113)
Lewis, Peter 3:01:59 (1,257)
Lewis, Phil Anthony 4:11:08 (13,753)
Lewis, Richard 4:21:06 (16,439)
Lewis, Richard L 4:41:35 (21,918)
Lewis, Roy 4:34:12 (20,044)
Lewis, Ryan 4:22:35 (16,868)
Lewis, Simon A 3:52:29 (8,792)
Lewis, Stanley 5:25:46 (30,744)

Lewis, Tim J	4:35:38 (20,375)
Lewis, Tony	3:57:03 (10,118)
Lewis-Jones, Mark	3:47:51 (7,707)
Lewisman, Hagan	4:00:05 (11,002)
Lewis-Russell, Mark A	6:12:18 (34,774)
Leyenda, Manuel	3:56:40 (9,984)
Leyland, Andrew Thomas	5:33:08 (31,679)
Leyland, Ben	6:39:14 (35,760)
Leyland, Mark	3:33:16 (4,930)
Leyshon, David	3:52:47 (8,863)
Leze, Jean Claude	4:15:11 (14,830)
Li, Bruce	4:53:20 (24,882)
Li, Damon	3:12:52 (2,173)
Lias, Carl	4:40:39 (21,679)
Liberda, Steve	4:33:44 (19,930)
Libespere, François	2:58:26 (1,001)
Lichter, Leo	4:03:47 (11,920)
Lidbetter, Hugo	3:29:25 (4,306)
Liddiard, Mark	3:56:24 (9,899)
Liddiard, Simon David	3:43:22 (6,751)
Liddle, Alexander B	3:58:56 (10,698)
Liddle, Malcolm	4:28:58 (18,670)
Liddle, Stuart	4:02:10 (11,529)
Lidgard, Andrew Paul	4:21:57 (16,688)
Lidgate-Taylor, Steven P	3:13:54 (2,304)
Lie, Andy SJ	4:57:57 (25,959)
Liebenow, Rainer	3:39:17 (6,000)
Lieberman, Daniel E	4:10:19 (13,548)
Liebich, Michael	3:57:47 (10,326)
Lien, Knut	3:58:30 (10,559)
Lienert, Rohan J	3:21:45 (3,165)
Lienert, Stephen	3:47:05 (7,541)
Liepins, Adrian Paul	5:44:14 (32,791)
Liese, Thomas	3:28:01 (4,051)
Liggins, Stuart John	5:44:27 (32,810)
Light, Barry J	3:39:00 (5,937)
Lightburn, Steven Paul	4:33:09 (19,748)
Lightfoot, Alan T	3:09:44 (1,884)
Lightfoot, Chris	4:43:47 (22,436)
Liguori, Pietro	2:55:07 (754)
Lillevik, Øyvind	3:13:01 (2,192)
Lilley, Jayson Dudley	5:15:15 (29,107)
Lilley, Julian	4:13:37 (14,410)
Lilley, Tom	4:34:14 (20,054)
Lillie, Darren	5:26:19 (30,823)
Limbirons, Steven John	4:21:40 (16,597)
Linaker, David Julian John Ramage	4:35:14 (20,278)
Lincoln, Eliot	2:48:13 (422)
Lincoln, Gary	3:55:53 (9,745)
Lincoln, Timothy	4:11:02 (13,726)
Lincoln, Wayne	2:30:08 (72)
Lincoln-Kemp, Thomas Mark	3:53:59 (9,205)
Lind, Börje	4:36:15 (20,536)
Lindaver, Paolo	3:48:47 (7,922)
Lindberg, Olof	3:24:20 (3,491)
Linde, Carl Wayne	4:24:01 (17,242)
Linden, Gary George	4:22:01 (16,711)
Lindley, David Anthony	4:28:34 (18,545)
Lindley, Scott David John	3:19:26 (2,910)
Lindsay, Ben	4:14:02 (14,514)
Lindsay, Ewan	4:41:31 (21,899)
Lindsay, Oliver	4:14:01 (14,508)
Lindsay, Raymond J	3:20:25 (3,010)
Lindsay, Vaughan E	2:52:44 (606)
Lindskog, Goran	4:00:40 (11,159)
Line, Nick Graham John	4:13:29 (14,358)
Linehan, Kevin P	3:10:50 (1,975)
Linehan, Mark Peter	5:44:12 (32,787)
Lines, John Ronald	4:46:36 (23,205)
Lines, Philip A	5:12:34 (28,664)
Lines, Richard Oliver	4:07:15 (12,764)
Ling, Lee	6:12:30 (34,781)
Ling, Philip	4:28:30 (18,521)
Lingard, John	3:29:16 (4,283)
Lingard, Richard	5:07:27 (27,799)
Linge, Dean Charles	4:12:44 (14,165)
Linger, Daniel William	4:16:21 (15,125)
Lings, Richard	3:56:17 (9,866)
Lingwood, Owen	4:39:11 (21,308)
Linn, John	4:47:13 (23,344)
Linney, Nick Roger	4:14:40 (14,706)
Linsell, Spencer Neil	4:40:13 (21,543)
Linssen, Thomas	3:52:07 (8,682)
Linstead, John David	4:27:06 (18,120)
Linstead, Michael D	5:09:04 (28,058)
Linton, Mark	3:32:50 (4,867)
Linton, Peter G	3:26:11 (3,768)
Linton, Stephen Paul	4:28:32 (18,535)
Linton-Smith, Tom Richard	4:04:25 (12,058)
Lio, Victor Fy	4:05:53 (12,428)
Lionel, Kerckhove	3:37:55 (5,746)
Lionet, Elric	4:43:41 (22,413)
Liossis, Roger	4:29:48 (18,913)
Lipman, Frank	8:27:32 (36,603)
Lipscomb, David J	3:29:00 (4,227)
Lipton-Rose, Paul Graham	5:50:41 (33,403)
Liptrot, John F	3:28:42 (4,173)
Liptrot, Paul	5:10:24 (28,309)
Lishman, Richard	5:00:15 (26,510)
Lissimore, Tom	4:51:24 (24,398)
Lister, Daniel	3:27:08 (3,892)
Lister, Derek	4:13:00 (14,239)
Lister, Ewart	3:27:36 (3,983)
Lister, Simon D	4:00:38 (11,151)
Lister, Stephen	3:58:12 (10,459)
Lister, Tom	4:28:14 (18,431)
Litchfield, David A	4:35:13 (20,272)
Little, Douglas	3:46:53 (7,505)
Little, Eddy Bayor	4:03:34 (11,864)
Little, James P	4:14:01 (14,508)
Little, Martin R	3:59:27 (10,853)
Little, Scott Edward George	6:12:58 (34,801)
Little, Simon	3:52:05 (8,676)
Little, Stuart P	2:55:49 (788)
Little, Tom Charles	4:36:10 (20,523)
Littlefield, Simon	5:22:44 (30,259)
Littlejohn, Robert Edward	4:00:35 (11,135)
Littlejohns, Mark D	3:29:45 (4,370)
Littlemore, Glen	6:55:49 (36,129)
Littleproud, Jim	4:04:02 (11,968)
Littler, Andy	5:35:46 (31,964)
Littler, Francis Henry	4:12:06 (14,008)
Littleson, David Matthew	4:45:54 (22,999)
Littleton, Andrew J	3:41:10 (6,354)
Littleton, John	4:35:40 (20,380)
Littlewood, Darren Michael	4:25:24 (17,636)
Littlewood, Peter T	4:15:18 (14,861)
Litvin, Norman P	3:03:57 (1,386)
Liu, Howard	4:09:19 (13,288)
Liu, Michael K	2:59:40 (1,125)
Livermore, Craig M	5:22:14 (30,179)
Livermore, Thomas Miles	2:56:47 (845)
Livesey, Nicholas James	4:43:09 (22,288)
Livesey, Shaun	2:59:00 (1,049)
Livingstone, David	5:07:59 (27,891)
Livingstone-Learmonth, Max	3:13:30 (2,255)
Livraghi, Angelo	3:40:00 (6,147)
Llewellyn, Clive	3:37:14 (5,605)
Llewellyn, Kieron	4:24:39 (17,432)
Llewellyn, Mark	4:40:27 (21,628)
Llewellyn, Robyn	3:48:53 (7,947)
Llewellyn, Stephen	4:03:51 (11,936)
Llewelyn, Hugo	4:09:26 (13,325)
Llorente, Ignacio	3:09:34 (1,868)
Lloyd, Adam	3:20:12 (2,979)
Lloyd, Alex	3:35:24 (5,301)
Lloyd, Andrew	6:37:45 (35,715)
Lloyd, Chris	4:12:01 (13,991)
Lloyd, Clive Adam	4:23:06 (17,003)
Lloyd, Darren Mark	5:06:49 (27,692)
Lloyd, David	4:27:12 (18,149)
Lloyd, Gareth	3:26:31 (3,804)
Lloyd, Gavin	3:55:31 (9,617)
Lloyd, George	6:22:44 (35,224)
Lloyd, Jeff	6:07:44 (34,545)
Lloyd, John Paul	3:24:18 (3,486)
Lloyd, Keith	4:52:31 (24,688)
Lloyd, Kevin	4:25:01 (17,524)
Lloyd, Max	4:27:32 (18,246)
Lloyd, Paul	3:18:02 (2,771)
Lloyd, Paul Antony	3:59:07 (10,752)
Lloyd, Peter David	4:40:15 (21,560)
Lloyd, Robert	5:47:40 (33,109)
Lloyd, Steven Eric	4:09:19 (13,288)
Lloyd, Stewart	5:24:34 (30,565)
Lloyd, Stuart	5:48:39 (33,209)
Lloyd Jones, Fraser	4:15:58 (15,017)
Lloyd-Thompson, Gavin Michael	4:31:28 (19,328)
Llywelyn, Dafydd Gwynn	3:53:48 (9,162)
Loader, Andrew H	3:41:48 (6,476)
Loader, Darran Angus	5:30:51 (31,398)
Loader, James	5:51:32 (33,464)
Loader, Neil	3:14:21 (2,362)
Loades, Mason Anthony	4:39:51 (21,477)
Loadman, Neil	4:24:23 (17,350)
Loan, Nick W	3:53:46 (9,147)
Lobb, Andrew Mark	4:18:37 (15,749)
Lobley, David	3:53:07 (8,947)
Lochead, Matthew	4:33:16 (19,791)
Lochner, Georg	3:12:54 (2,176)
Lochner, Stefan	3:54:57 (9,460)
Lochner, Wolfram	4:10:20 (13,554)
Lochray, Ian	3:23:43 (3,398)
Lock, Craig N	4:13:04 (14,257)
Lock, David	2:57:33 (908)
Lock, David	6:11:17 (34,713)
Lock, James	4:24:40 (17,435)
Lock, Shaun M	3:50:41 (8,354)
Lock, Stephen N	3:53:26 (9,036)
Locke, Dean Christopher	7:36:41 (36,502)
Locke, John	4:17:32 (15,452)
Locke, Matthew J	4:06:38 (12,611)
Locke, Tony L	4:08:30 (13,085)
Lockelt, Carl	6:19:10 (35,088)
Lockett, Patrick	3:08:34 (1,764)
Lockhart, Mark D	3:53:47 (9,154)
Lockhart, Peter	4:00:23 (11,085)
Lockie, Derek	4:14:03 (14,520)
Lockley, Jonathan P	4:18:17 (15,655)
Lockley, Simon Mark	4:40:19 (21,579)
Lockstone, Steven George	3:54:37 (9,359)
Lockton-Goddard, Mark	5:45:28 (32,907)
Lockwood, Hamish	3:11:00 (1,995)
Lockwood, Marc Joseph	4:28:36 (18,548)
Lockwood-Cowell, Stuart	4:49:04 (23,820)
Lockyer, Anthony Robert	4:21:41 (16,600)
Lockyer, John	3:54:07 (9,236)
Lockyer, Paul Anthony	3:34:06 (5,079)
Locock, Ian Arthur	6:13:38 (34,824)
Lodge, Philip	4:47:04 (23,322)
Lodge, Simon	5:13:12 (28,800)
Lofino, Gianfranco	3:30:47 (4,544)
Loftus, Jim	4:34:22 (20,085)
Logan, Jimmie	4:11:15 (13,779)
Logan, Michael	4:30:11 (19,022)
Logan, Michael Denis	3:52:53 (8,895)
Logan, Paul E	4:46:12 (23,090)
Logan, Shaun Patrick	3:55:02 (9,485)
Logsdon, Jonathan Paul	4:35:53 (20,439)
Logue, Declan	5:54:14 (33,661)
Lohan, John	3:36:55 (5,547)
Lohia, Karan	5:37:31 (32,168)
Loic, Marechal	3:08:33 (1,761)
Loizi, Emilio	4:49:14 (23,861)
Loizou, Andrew	5:17:42 (29,499)
Loizou, Christopher	2:54:54 (734)
Lok, Joseph	4:44:12 (22,563)
Lolli, Paolo	3:41:12 (6,367)
Lollo, Claudio	4:21:10 (16,457)
Lomas, Gary Peter	4:34:46 (20,186)
Lomas, Richard Graham	3:36:24 (5,468)
Lomas, Terry	4:22:52 (16,954)
Lombard, David J	3:27:55 (4,038)
Lomholt-Thomsen, Steen	5:32:32 (31,612)
London, Geoffrey	4:14:24 (14,613)
Lonergan, John W	3:09:38 (1,874)
Lonergan, Paul	3:21:50 (3,175)
Lonergan, Stephen	3:10:30 (1,948)
Long, Alastair	4:43:05 (22,279)
Long, Brendan	4:37:03 (20,758)
Long, David	6:38:29 (35,741)
Long, David W	2:52:22 (586)
Long, Glenn Stewart	3:25:27 (3,640)
Long, Ian James	3:46:43 (7,464)
Long, Mark	5:27:41 (30,987)
Long, Philip Michael	4:10:56 (13,695)
Long, Richard Charles	5:20:43 (29,965)
Long, Russell	4:45:10 (22,811)
Long, Stephen Francis	3:49:30 (8,093)

Long, Steven	4:30:08 (19,010)	
Long, Trevor	4:48:36 (23,694)	
Longden, Ashley	3:45:49 (7,267)	
Longford, Michael Richard	5:37:08 (32,120)	
Longhorn, David Robert	3:49:28 (8,080)	
Longhurst, Kevin J	7:25:46 (36,447)	
Longhurst, Philip J	5:02:55 (27,012)	
Longland, Ian M	3:02:17 (1,278)	
Longley, Robert	4:59:02 (26,223)	
Longman, Christopher I	4:12:24 (14,068)	
Longman, Harry J	3:07:01 (1,610)	
Longman, Peter George	4:41:17 (21,840)	
Longmore, Peter	4:28:43 (18,583)	
Longstaff, Gary,	4:47:56 (23,528)	
Longstaff, Mark	3:51:50 (8,614)	
Longstaff, Matthew	4:25:39 (17,701)	
Longthorp, Neil Andrew	3:43:51 (6,845)	
Loose, Peter	5:25:22 (30,675)	
Looser, Matthew	4:24:19 (17,329)	
Lopes Cardozo, Vladimir	3:28:23 (4,121)	
Lopez, Paulo Manuel	4:23:29 (17,099)	
Lopez, Pedro	3:51:50 (8,614)	
Lopez-Cruz, Daniel	3:47:31 (7,650)	
Lorberg, Stuart Ian	3:23:37 (3,379)	
Lord, Ben James	5:04:12 (27,230)	
Lord, Jonathan Charles	4:31:56 (19,418)	
Lord, Oliver J	3:42:39 (6,624)	
Lorentzen, Haavard	4:06:55 (12,689)	
Lorenz, Gerd	3:15:02 (2,441)	
Lorenzi, Jean-Luc M	4:36:35 (20,625)	
Lorenzo, Roland E	5:53:37 (33,620)	
Lorman-Hall, Nick Lee	4:18:39 (15,758)	
Lott, David	4:55:42 (25,463)	
Lou, Yanqiu	4:45:28 (22,875)	
Louchet, Pascal	4:34:39 (20,156)	
Loucks, Matthew	5:31:18 (31,449)	
Loughnane, Martin C	3:23:26 (3,357)	
Lound, Charles A	2:40:52 (227)	
Lounds, Dan	3:20:15 (2,984)	
Loutit, Jon	4:43:55 (22,481)	
Louw, Bertus Jacobus	3:41:06 (6,345)	
Lovatt, James	4:21:29 (16,542)	
Lovatt, Michael	3:36:21 (5,463)	
Love, Christopher C.	5:26:13 (30,806)	
Love, Conor James Geoffrey	4:17:05 (15,317)	
Love, Jay D	5:41:00 (32,483)	
Love, Martin	3:24:12 (3,470)	
Love, Michael John	4:50:38 (24,193)	
Loveday, Simon	4:36:27 (20,586)	
Loveday, Tim J	6:20:26 (35,142)	
Lovegrove, Miles	3:43:52 (6,848)	
Lovegrove, Paul David	4:42:21 (22,105)	
Lovegrove, Simon Willis	3:33:30 (4,970)	
Loveless, Martin Frank	7:20:09 (36,405)	
Loveless, Martin G	3:25:39 (3,673)	
Lovell, Adrian	5:30:22 (31,332)	
Lovell, Benjamin	3:45:30 (7,207)	
Lovell, Ian C	5:10:38 (28,354)	
Lovell, John	5:02:00 (26,840)	
Lovell, Joseph Frank	3:43:53 (6,854)	
Lovell, Neil Darren	4:00:04 (10,998)	
Lovell, Peter	4:56:57 (25,757)	
Lovell, Sam	5:41:04 (32,495)	
Lovell, Stuart Anthony	3:28:56 (4,219)	
Loveridge, Trevor John	5:55:08 (33,730)	
Lovick, Paul	6:04:18 (34,339)	
Low, Edward	4:44:02 (22,511)	
Low, Joshua S.	3:06:45 (1,591)	
Low, Roger L	3:54:53 (9,447)	
Low, Scott A	4:24:52 (17,481)	
Low, Stephen A	2:54:54 (734)	
Lowden, Derek	4:28:57 (18,666)	
Lowdon, David	4:25:48 (17,749)	
Lowe, Andrew Martin	3:40:59 (6,320)	
Lowe, Jake	3:03:54 (1,381)	
Lowe, Joseph C.	3:59:22 (10,827)	
Lowe, Warren	3:50:48 (8,382)	
Lower, Rob	3:44:21 (6,953)	
Lowes, Andrew	3:13:28 (2,247)	
Lown, James	4:29:12 (18,732)	
Lowry, Alexander Martin	3:48:56 (7,955)	
Lowry, David	4:32:15 (19,500)	
Lowry, James P	3:53:53 (9,177)	

Lowson, Richard J	2:43:08 (283)	
Lowth, Richard Adrian	3:58:37 (10,598)	
Loxam, Jamie L	2:36:32 (137)	
Loxston, Chris	3:35:07 (5,262)	
Lozano, José Antonio	4:12:35 (14,120)	
Lubbock, David R	4:12:18 (14,056)	
Lubbock, James	5:46:15 (32,977)	
Luca, Antongiulio	3:27:28 (3,956)	
Lucas, Adam Oliver	3:38:22 (5,825)	
Lucas, Alan	3:56:29 (9,926)	
Lucas, Alex David	6:30:10 (35,506)	
Lucas, Anthony	4:54:00 (25,052)	
Lucas, Bernard S	4:19:03 (15,885)	
Lucas, Daryl	4:38:34 (21,135)	
Lucas, Marc John	4:07:03 (12,723)	
Lucas, Mark Jonathan	4:52:15 (24,614)	
Lucas, Michael John	5:42:24 (32,628)	
Lucas, Rick	4:35:44 (20,397)	
Lucas, Rob	4:15:20 (14,872)	
Lucas, Stuart John	5:22:22 (30,203)	
Lucas, Stuart Richard	4:47:43 (23,474)	
Lucas, William Aron Brett	4:56:36 (25,667)	
Lucaselli, Antonello	4:03:14 (11,785)	
Lucaselli, Francesco	4:08:02 (12,973)	
Luce, Philip Anthony	4:32:38 (19,589)	
Lucey, Ronan D	3:05:28 (1,494)	
Luck, Jamie Darren	3:46:38 (7,449)	
Lucking, Clive Douglas	4:53:30 (24,917)	
Ludlow, Jamie	3:16:32 (2,618)	
Ludwig, Dirk	4:07:12 (12,749)	
Ludwigsen, Harald	3:41:54 (6,499)	
Luesley, Daniel George	3:58:58 (10,709)	
Luff, Adrian Francis	4:00:56 (11,231)	
Luff, Michael	4:13:39 (14,417)	
Luffingham, Alan J	4:29:12 (18,732)	
Luijten, Rob	4:11:43 (13,908)	
Luis, Alvarenga Fernando	5:09:20 (28,115)	
Luis Casado, Javier Paulino	4:28:48 (18,609)	
Luke, Chris	4:08:21 (13,043)	
Luke, Ian	3:55:07 (9,508)	
Lukjanciks, Vladislavs	4:18:39 (15,758)	
Lukjanenko, Eric	3:47:58 (7,731)	
Lumby, Mark	4:35:10 (20,268)	
Lumby, Paul Leonard	4:11:24 (13,820)	
Lumley, Matthew Armstrong	3:50:10 (8,242)	
Lund, Andy	4:11:24 (13,820)	
Lund, Angus John	3:34:21 (5,129)	
Lund, Philip	3:48:30 (7,848)	
Lund, Robert	5:33:05 (31,675)	
Lundberg, Paul	4:54:11 (25,093)	
Lundberg-Bury, Alan	2:52:10 (575)	
Lundon, Anthony	4:00:16 (11,048)	
Lunn, Andrew Peter	3:01:19 (1,219)	
Lunn, Peter	3:24:39 (3,530)	
Lunneberg, Thomas	5:20:39 (29,953)	
Lunnon, Ben Andrew	5:20:04 (29,858)	
Lunt, Geoffrey Paul	5:08:49 (28,017)	
Luong, Joe Hq	7:44:27 (36,545)	
Lupi, Stefano	4:07:49 (12,909)	
Lupton, David W	3:12:20 (2,114)	
Lupton, Tim	6:30:36 (35,522)	
Luscombe, James Christian W	4:48:10 (23,582)	
Luscott, Frank	4:15:37 (14,929)	
Lush, Martin Kevin	3:34:36 (5,173)	
Luthi, Patrick	4:14:09 (14,547)	
Luton, David	4:37:03 (20,758)	
Luxon, Keith D	3:35:31 (5,327)	
Luxton, Martin J	3:38:07 (5,785)	
Ly, Michael	5:44:48 (32,848)	
Lycett, Kirk	4:31:51 (19,399)	
Lydford, Jon Michael	3:58:55 (10,691)	
Lydiate, Christopher	3:49:06 (8,000)	
Lydon, Martin Wayne	4:35:06 (20,251)	
Lyle, David	3:51:52 (8,629)	
Lynam, Ben Charles Paley	3:46:37 (7,444)	
Lynas, Tim	4:27:47 (18,310)	
Lynch, Benjamin John Patrick	5:00:22 (26,529)	
Lynch, Brian Dermot	3:19:47 (2,943)	
Lynch, Colin J	2:59:50 (1,140)	
Lynch, Craig G	4:05:47 (12,408)	
Lynch, Daniel John	5:15:25 (29,128)	
Lynch, Duncan A	4:39:36 (21,411)	
Lynch, Ian	3:51:02 (8,432)	

Lynch, James Joseph	5:05:04 (27,380)	
Lynch, John	4:13:53 (14,478)	
Lynch, John P	3:30:59 (4,575)	
Lynch, Mark	5:48:40 (33,214)	
Lynch, Peter	4:04:11 (12,006)	
Lynch, Philip	4:28:34 (18,545)	
Lynch, Simon Noel	3:56:32 (9,944)	
Lynch, Simon Paul	4:15:25 (14,889)	
Lynch, Warren M	2:48:51 (439)	
Lynch, Yanick	5:49:55 (33,325)	
Lyne, Andrew G	3:09:20 (1,838)	
Lyner, Matthew Grahame	4:19:51 (16,056)	
Lyness, Patrick	6:08:38 (34,592)	
Lyngnes, Baard	2:49:58 (485)	
Lyon, Aaron M	4:37:16 (20,806)	
Lyon, Graham	4:50:45 (24,224)	
Lyon, John	3:56:03 (9,800)	
Lyon, John	5:11:13 (28,439)	
Lyon, Martin Timothy	4:05:40 (12,371)	
Lyon, Nigel	3:54:41 (9,381)	
Lyon, Richard B	4:20:37 (16,302)	
Lyons, Andrew	2:41:18 (234)	
Lyons, Chris	4:18:11 (15,626)	
Lyons, Dale	6:11:12 (34,711)	
Lyons, Edouard	4:04:13 (12,012)	
Lyons, Graham	3:05:12 (1,473)	
Lyons, James M	3:25:51 (3,715)	
Lyons, Michael	3:17:48 (2,744)	
Lyons, Michael	5:16:38 (29,328)	
Lyons, Michael E	5:00:02 (26,463)	
Lyons, Michael Joseph Thomas	4:05:44 (12,386)	
Lyons, Peter	3:51:13 (8,474)	
Lyons, Simon Ronald	4:41:16 (21,837)	
Lyons, Stephen	4:33:14 (19,778)	
Lyszyk, Terry John	3:58:09 (10,435)	
Lytton, Dewi Wyn	4:31:54 (19,407)	
Ma, Da	5:05:27 (27,440)	
Mabbett, Andy	5:07:52 (27,872)	
Mabbott, Alex	3:50:05 (8,226)	
Maben, Steven J	4:52:43 (24,731)	
Maberly, Stephen John	4:55:54 (25,513)	
Mabey, Chris Paul	5:13:33 (28,849)	
MacAlister, Gary	4:37:32 (20,891)	
MacAllan, Ray	5:16:19 (29,277)	
Macara, Iaian C	3:28:09 (4,083)	
MacArthur, Neil Cameron	4:55:03 (25,321)	
Macaulay, Gordon	4:18:34 (15,732)	
Macbeath, Niall A	3:14:12 (2,341)	
Macbeth, Andrew	4:28:56 (18,660)	
MacBroom, Andrew	4:44:46 (22,718)	
MacCarthy-Morrogh, Grant	4:29:37 (18,852)	
MacCormac, Oscar James	5:03:15 (27,066)	
MacCrory, Gerry	4:25:09 (17,560)	
Macdonagh, Donagh	4:27:05 (18,114)	
Macdonald, Adam	3:39:24 (6,022)	
Macdonald, Alastair	4:11:02 (13,726)	
Macdonald, Alex Robert	4:26:05 (17,837)	
Macdonald, Alistair Andrew	4:26:03 (17,825)	
Macdonald, Alistair K	3:49:34 (8,109)	
Macdonald, David M	2:50:28 (500)	
Macdonald, Denys John	4:50:54 (24,269)	
Macdonald, Eryn Douglas	4:30:24 (19,064)	
Macdonald, Frazer	4:26:14 (17,882)	
Macdonald, Greg	2:42:16 (258)	
Macdonald, Iain John	2:57:22 (884)	
Macdonald, Jay Stuart	4:24:11 (17,281)	
Macdonald, Josh	4:15:59 (15,019)	
Macdonald, Julian	2:33:16 (94)	
Macdonald, Kevin	3:41:33 (6,430)	
Macdonald, Mark	3:58:11 (10,449)	
Macdonald, Matthew P	4:57:12 (25,804)	
Macdonald, Roddy J	3:58:43 (10,631)	
Macdonald, Will	4:02:11 (11,536)	
Macdonald, William	3:32:26 (4,809)	
Macdonough, Paul	3:57:37 (10,268)	
MacDougall, Ian D	2:52:33 (594)	
Macedo, Philip	4:01:09 (11,287)	
Macer, James Benjamin	4:54:47 (25,255)	
Macer, Paul Jonathon	3:46:15 (7,367)	
Macey, Darren James	4:08:31 (13,090)	
Macey, Martin John	3:51:05 (8,445)	
Macey, Terence J	4:43:39 (22,405)	
Macfarlane, Fraser B	5:10:03 (28,247)	

Name	Time	(Position)
Macfarlane, William	5:15:31	(29,150)
MacGregor, John C	3:52:10	(8,699)
MacGregor, Stephen	5:13:47	(28,890)
Machin, Bryn D	3:29:36	(4,342)
Machin, Geoffrey	3:56:44	(10,009)
Machin, Tony	3:36:01	(5,415)
MacInnes, Calum	4:39:56	(21,488)
Mack, Darren R	2:53:10	(622)
Mack, Jonathan	5:02:57	(27,020)
Mackay, Andrew	5:50:20	(33,367)
Mackay, David S	4:56:11	(25,579)
Mackay, Frazer David	3:31:39	(4,693)
Mackay, Grant Iain	3:21:01	(3,087)
Mackay, Jake Alexander Simms	3:51:56	(8,645)
Mackay, John H	4:38:17	(21,050)
Mackay, Kenny	4:41:00	(21,771)
Mackay, Michael	3:18:14	(2,799)
Mackay, Nathaniel	5:35:01	(31,877)
Mackay, Ross	4:45:54	(22,999)
Mackay, Steve G	5:33:57	(31,757)
Mackechnie, Andrew James	4:55:57	(25,528)
Mackenzie, Alistair	3:47:13	(7,581)
Mackenzie, David	6:25:39	(35,334)
Mackenzie, Mike	5:02:26	(26,935)
Mackenzie, Rob J	2:59:20	(1,087)
Mackenzie, Robert E	3:39:05	(5,961)
Mackenzie, Ross Buchanan	2:58:24	(996)
Mackenzie, Scott	3:11:21	(2,031)
Mackenzie, Stephen J	3:31:20	(4,636)
Mackenzie, Steve	4:49:25	(23,900)
Mackenzie, Stuart	4:48:06	(23,567)
Mackenzie-Betty, Andrew	3:35:58	(5,407)
Mackertich, David S	3:11:49	(2,075)
Mackey, Brian R	3:39:01	(5,942)
Mackey, Damian	4:48:07	(23,571)
Mackey, David	4:15:20	(14,872)
Mackie, Alex Wilson	6:19:00	(35,080)
Mackie, Richard Scott	3:14:39	(2,405)
Mackinlay, William G	4:38:35	(21,137)
Mackintosh, Al	4:17:55	(15,550)
Mackintosh, Jamie Stuart	4:05:35	(12,351)
Mackintosh, Neil Stuart	3:25:03	(3,587)
Mackintosh, Nicholas Ian	3:27:15	(3,915)
Macklin, Richard James	3:31:47	(4,706)
Mackness, Anthony S	3:15:14	(2,464)
Mackrow, Paul	6:03:20	(34,273)
Mackula, Alex	4:08:26	(13,064)
MacLachlan, Alastair J	2:49:24	(465)
Maclaren, Daniel	5:28:27	(31,083)
Maclaren, Donald B	3:06:08	(1,542)
Maclean, Alasdair	4:01:00	(11,251)
Maclean, Anthony Alistair	4:00:31	(11,118)
Maclean, Donnie	3:48:01	(7,741)
Maclean, Jamie Frazer	5:34:23	(31,810)
Maclean, Mark	6:00:52	(34,121)
Maclean, Robert David	3:43:24	(6,757)
MacLellan, Sean Patrick	3:43:36	(6,791)
MacLennan, Colin	4:15:49	(14,984)
Macleod, Alastair M	3:41:30	(6,423)
Macleod, Billy	4:41:22	(21,858)
Macleod, Donald James	5:29:08	(31,168)
Macleod, Greg	3:57:19	(10,186)
Macleod, Mark	3:41:10	(6,354)
Macleod, Neil John	4:56:58	(25,761)
Macleod, Stuart	4:13:34	(14,390)
MacNeil, Ewen K	3:53:08	(8,950)
Maconochie, Hugh James	5:13:04	(28,763)
MacPhail, Cameron	5:04:26	(27,265)
MacQueen, Ian Malcolm	4:46:25	(23,153)
Macrae, Duncan N	4:50:49	(24,243)
MacSephney, Scott A	2:56:26	(829)
MacTaggart, Douglas James	4:42:27	(22,128)
Macucci, Andrea	3:11:01	(1,999)
Madajewski, Stephen	5:09:16	(28,095)
Madams, Dan	3:14:59	(2,437)
Madathil, Krishnan Unni	4:59:37	(26,367)
Maddar, Mo	3:34:12	(5,096)
Madden, Michael	4:32:42	(19,607)
Madden, Peter	4:24:17	(17,311)
Madders, Thomas Paul	4:03:40	(11,893)
Maddison, Bryan C	3:46:30	(7,415)
Maddison, David Alan	4:08:22	(13,049)
Maddison, Michael S	3:38:34	(5,863)
Maddox, Mark	4:52:07	(24,578)
Maddox, Paul Richard	5:24:54	(30,602)
Madge, Anthony C	3:03:53	(1,379)
Madhar, Sandy	4:37:21	(20,832)
Madigan, John	5:24:35	(30,568)
Madigan, Sean Edward	4:58:14	(26,019)
Madoc-Jones, Steven Richard	4:20:47	(16,363)
Madrazo, Federico	4:01:43	(11,415)
Madrazo, Roberto	3:46:30	(7,415)
Madsen, Joergen Birkebaek	4:01:31	(11,372)
Madura, Percy A	7:22:47	(36,425)
Maes, Steven	3:42:27	(6,587)
Mafham, Paul John	4:16:06	(15,052)
Magaletti, Marcello	4:10:29	(13,590)
Magee, Ken	4:09:10	(13,250)
Magee, Kevin	6:38:42	(35,747)
Magee, Niall	3:41:15	(6,379)
Magee, Russell	6:07:51	(34,552)
Maggi, Gianluca	5:10:40	(28,359)
Maggs, Simon D	3:40:15	(6,191)
Maghur, Haitem	6:25:28	(35,329)
Magill, John Robert	5:02:11	(26,886)
Maginnis, Martin John	4:49:33	(23,922)
Maglia, Maurizio	3:26:30	(3,801)
Magliocco, Franco	4:46:01	(23,030)
Magner, James	4:33:57	(19,980)
Magness, Ian J	5:34:20	(31,802)
Magnusson, Colin	3:37:54	(5,744)
Magrit, Philippe	3:38:24	(5,832)
Magudia, Manoj	4:46:07	(23,065)
Maguire, David P	4:48:22	(23,627)
Maguire, David Stewart	5:47:36	(33,107)
Maguire, Karl David	4:29:44	(18,896)
Maguire, Marcus	3:30:22	(4,480)
Maguire, Peter	4:30:35	(19,120)
Maguire, Ross	3:49:39	(8,134)
Maguire, Sam	5:08:07	(27,915)
Maguire, Trevor A	2:56:04	(804)
Mahadeo, Clint	6:44:15	(35,889)
Mahadevan, Gajan	4:48:04	(23,561)
Mahay, Parteek	5:44:39	(32,834)
Maher, Ben	4:35:31	(20,349)
Maher, Ian	4:08:58	(13,201)
Mahgiub, Hisham	3:35:30	(5,325)
Mahmood, Talat	5:04:33	(27,286)
Mahmout, Turkel D	5:04:33	(27,286)
Mahon, Thomas William Patrick	3:32:23	(4,796)
Mahoney, Danny Thomas	2:59:13	(1,076)
Mahoney, Jason Patrick	3:57:41	(10,293)
Mahoney, Jim	3:57:15	(10,172)
Mahoney, Paul Steven	4:51:54	(24,521)
Mahoney, Terry M	4:28:05	(18,383)
Mahoney, Tom S	3:53:38	(9,101)
Mahsoudi, Bruno	3:25:09	(3,600)
Maidment, Adrian	3:37:14	(5,605)
Maidment, Chris	4:28:13	(18,424)
Maidwell-Smith, Mark A	4:02:24	(11,580)
Maier, Sven M	3:11:38	(2,063)
Maillard, Jeremie	3:14:15	(2,349)
Main, Ewan	5:07:38	(27,839)
Main, Jonathan	5:06:21	(27,596)
Main, Russell	4:18:02	(15,589)
Main, Stuart	6:53:15	(36,075)
Mainwaring, Kevin James	4:55:41	(25,458)
Mair, Christopher Ellis	4:16:01	(15,034)
Mairey, Loic John	4:52:22	(24,652)
Mairs, Graham	3:14:49	(2,420)
Maisey, David J	2:56:56	(856)
Majek, Fabrice	2:52:37	(600)
Majem, Jesus	5:04:40	(27,308)
Majer, Peter Edward	4:18:38	(15,753)
Majer, Raymond V	4:00:22	(11,081)
Majevadia, Bhavesh	5:17:28	(29,465)
Majithia, Anil	6:11:52	(34,747)
Major, Gavin	4:17:01	(15,302)
Major, Jason S	3:04:46	(1,444)
Major, Matthew Paul	4:19:03	(15,855)
Makan, Sanjay	5:21:35	(30,093)
Makepeace, Paul Edward	5:25:20	(30,667)
Makin, Andy James	6:01:57	(34,183)
Makin, Frank H	3:59:07	(10,752)
Makuwa, Bill M	2:40:38	(216)
Makwana, Pritesh Harish	5:44:56	(32,863)
Mal, Fironz	3:42:51	(6,669)
Malbon, Jon	4:58:26	(26,071)
Malcolm, John	3:43:53	(6,854)
Malcolm, Neville	5:37:15	(32,136)
Malcolm, Ross Graham	4:48:01	(23,549)
Male, Gavin Lee	5:16:17	(29,267)
Male, Joe	4:04:51	(12,164)
Male, Nick	4:34:11	(20,037)
Male, Tony Kevin	5:36:01	(31,998)
Maleedy, Christian Andrew	4:44:49	(22,726)
Malek, Kip	6:17:02	(34,981)
Males, Craig John	4:59:35	(26,362)
Malhotra, Dev Kumar	4:13:35	(14,398)
Malighetti, Angelo	2:49:22	(463)
Malik, Alan	4:20:41	(16,328)
Malik, Nadeem	3:53:54	(9,183)
Malik, Razwan	5:07:06	(27,740)
Malik, Sarf	4:13:48	(14,457)
Malin, Peter	4:05:02	(12,217)
Malins, Duncan	3:58:47	(10,652)
Malka, Lewis	5:06:28	(27,618)
Malki, Naim	6:18:22	(35,050)
Mallen, Zak	4:53:10	(24,839)
Mallett, Darren	5:12:25	(28,636)
Malley, Christopher James	6:34:13	(35,630)
Mallinder, Jim	4:15:12	(14,834)
Mallinson, Tom	3:50:18	(8,270)
Mallison, Duncan J	3:27:30	(3,961)
Mallon, Ben Alan	6:28:23	(35,424)
Mallon, John A	4:29:12	(18,732)
Malone, Dominic	6:41:38	(35,823)
Malone, John Paul C	5:45:00	(32,869)
Malone, Lawerence	4:05:03	(12,220)
Maloney, Alex	4:47:52	(23,514)
Maloney, Bill	4:15:39	(14,937)
Maloney, David Mathew	4:34:17	(20,068)
Maloney, Mark Jonathan	3:09:30	(1,857)
Maloney, Nathan	3:35:37	(5,346)
Malpass, Tim J	3:24:17	(3,482)
Malsom, Dominic J	3:26:14	(3,775)
Maltas, Philip D	4:46:02	(23,037)
Maltby, Michael John	5:47:29	(33,095)
Maltby, Robert	4:10:43	(13,643)
Malthouse, Steven	4:16:37	(15,195)
Maltman, Mark Peter Justin	4:39:59	(21,499)
Maltman, Tim	5:16:50	(29,359)
Man, Jabond	4:42:41	(22,182)
Man, Kin	4:37:36	(20,908)
Manca, Tonuccio Toro	4:46:34	(23,185)
Mancer, Jez	2:45:17	(349)
Mancey, Adam	5:25:28	(30,688)
Mancini, Gregory	4:45:31	(22,891)
Mancini, John Alan	5:23:08	(30,326)
Mancuso, Enrico Maria	3:16:57	(2,663)
Mand, Edvin	2:59:00	(1,049)
Mander, Geoffrey F	5:30:13	(31,318)
Mander, Matthew	5:12:15	(28,609)
Mander, Sukhvir Singh	4:56:47	(25,711)
Mandeville, Kelvin Keith	5:53:58	(33,640)
Mandrysz, John P	5:34:31	(31,824)
Manford, James	4:08:22	(13,049)
Manford, Stuart	3:55:51	(9,733)
Mangabhai, Sanjay	6:05:15	(34,408)
Mangialardi, Lorenzo	3:52:48	(8,870)
Mangion, John	6:28:50	(35,457)
Mangioni, Chris	2:59:08	(1,068)
Manheim, Shlomo	4:36:06	(20,506)
Manjouneh, Yasser	5:41:49	(32,567)
Mankelow, James Anthony	4:58:43	(26,148)
Manktelow, Stuart J	3:16:26	(2,601)
Manley, Ben	6:22:37	(35,216)
Manley, Craig M	4:11:57	(13,977)
Manley, David C	4:15:14	(14,845)
Manley, Glen	4:58:41	(26,134)
Manley, Stuart Christopher	5:27:02	(30,910)
Manley, Stuart Thomas	4:27:24	(18,208)
Manlow, John D	2:50:16	(495)
Mann, Anthony S	5:04:24	(27,259)
Mann, Ashley	4:45:01	(22,775)
Mann, Craig	3:05:55	(1,528)
Mann, Dave Keith	4:44:20	(6,950)
Mann, Domonic John	3:48:46	(7,914)
Mann, Gavin A	3:24:54	(3,563)

Mann, James 4:26:55 (18,054)
Mann, John William 3:49:28 (8,080)
Mann, Kester Adam 3:14:36 (2,398)
Mann, Nick James 3:14:09 (2,334)
Mann, Patrick Kenneth 3:01:18 (1,218)
Mann, Stuart H 3:10:23 (1,937)
Manners, Warren 4:26:12 (17,874)
Mannheim, David Lee 4:46:42 (23,232)
Manning, Bernard 5:58:07 (33,940)
Manning, David 4:27:11 (18,143)
Manning, Edward 3:28:14 (4,097)
Manning, Gordon G 5:35:36 (31,936)
Manning, Greg Alan 5:08:41 (28,002)
Manning, Jacob John 3:36:39 (5,505)
Manning, Julian 4:46:33 (23,180)
Manning, Julian H 2:44:31 (321)
Manning, Oliver Peter 5:21:19 (30,044)
Manning, Paul Philip Strafford 3:11:55 (2,085)
Manning, Robert E 3:57:29 (10,225)
Mannings, Darren 3:50:09 (8,237)
Mannion, Paul M 2:42:47 (268)
Mannix, Robert Paul George 4:14:31 (14,656)
Mannouch, Jason Peter 4:29:26 (18,785)
Manocchio, Massimo 3:22:58 (3,288)
Manookian, Raymond 5:33:44 (31,739)
Mansell, Chris 4:47:00 (23,309)
Mansell, Neil 4:06:56 (12,697)
Mansell, Paul 5:02:28 (26,938)
Manser, Gary 4:34:25 (20,099)
Mansfield, Andrew D 3:02:18 (1,279)
Mansfield, David Neil 5:22:29 (30,218)
Mansfield, Gary 4:46:13 (23,096)
Mansfield, John Anthony 5:27:50 (31,005)
Mansfield, John K 4:17:51 (15,533)
Mansfield, Nathan David 6:14:35 (34,862)
Mansfield, Robert J 4:15:04 (14,802)
Mansfield, Robert John 4:51:39 (24,450)
Mansfield, Ron 6:16:22 (34,941)
Mansi, Andrew J 3:25:29 (3,645)
Manso, Peter 4:23:36 (17,136)
Manson, John R 5:49:22 (33,269)
Manson, Marcel 3:36:37 (5,499)
Manson, Sandy Philip 4:33:33 (19,867)
Mansoor, Bilal 6:29:16 (35,475)
Mansour, Dominic 4:50:54 (24,269)
Mansouri, Paul 3:46:05 (7,335)
Manston, Andrew James 5:05:08 (27,394)
Mantle, David 3:10:29 (1,946)
Mantovani, Emilio 3:28:48 (4,189)
Manuel, Jason 3:31:56 (4,728)
Manuel, Neal 5:09:05 (28,065)
Manwaring, Stephen L 3:58:58 (10,709)
Mapes, Richard Andrew 4:11:22 (13,805)
Mapp, Daniel Paul 3:56:04 (9,802)
Mapp, Ian 4:47:01 (23,315)
Maraficaud, Nicolas 3:46:05 (7,335)
Marafko, Colin 4:08:47 (13,156)
Marais, Paul Ralph 3:36:10 (5,439)
Maratos, Stephen P 3:16:41 (2,642)
Marbehan, Denis 3:15:53 (2,539)
Marcer, Steve 3:34:52 (5,223)
March, Jean-Charles 3:57:04 (10,122)
Marchand, Paul J 3:42:30 (6,597)
Marchant, Alister 4:00:37 (11,145)
Marchant, David 5:50:33 (33,392)
Marchant, Michael C 3:57:52 (10,352)
Marchant, Paul A 2:27:20 (49)
Marchant, Robin 4:55:06 (25,335)
Marchant, Steven 4:22:43 (16,908)
Marchegiani, Gaetano 4:51:00 (24,306)
Marciniak, John 5:45:17 (32,892)
Marcou, Mark 5:23:41 (30,422)
Marcou, Stelios 3:32:55 (4,881)
Marden, Danny L 4:51:09 (24,341)
Marden, Ross Peter Charles 3:59:37 (10,896)
Mardle, Gary W 6:13:02 (34,804)
Marett, Ross J 3:49:10 (8,016)
Margiotta, Lawrence 6:27:42 (35,411)
Margison, Stuart James 4:24:07 (17,264)
Margolis, Geoffrey 5:22:47 (30,267)
Margolis, Jared 5:55:48 (33,778)
Margraff, Manfred 3:50:40 (8,351)
Margulies, Daniel Alexander 3:12:06 (2,101)
Mariano Da Costa, Jeferson 3:51:35 (8,561)
Marina, Luigi 4:19:58 (16,096)
Marinho, Carlos 4:28:18 (18,452)
Marinoni, Yves 4:28:00 (18,365)
Mariosa, Nick 4:03:49 (11,928)
Mark, Andrew 4:55:17 (25,378)
Markham, David 4:29:46 (18,905)
Markham, Paul S 4:20:59 (16,407)
Markland, John Kevin 4:37:57 (20,977)
Marklew, Alex 4:37:25 (20,850)
Marklew, Steve 3:01:32 (1,232)
Markley, Greg Peter 3:46:22 (7,387)
Markley, Nicholas D 3:44:22 (6,955)
Marks, David C 4:59:30 (26,340)
Marks, Guy M 3:28:31 (4,141)
Marks, Oliver Jack 5:01:58 (26,837)
Marks, Paul D 5:15:21 (29,115)
Marks, Peter Jack 4:59:58 (26,442)
Marks, Stephen Paul 4:33:25 (19,829)
Marks, Stuart Clive 4:29:15 (18,743)
Marland, Hugo 4:36:48 (20,682)
Marley-Muray, Max 4:54:38 (25,214)
Marlow, Ben Robert Phillip 5:12:03 (28,572)
Marlow, Gary 5:16:05 (29,241)
Marlowe, Andrew Daniel 3:58:10 (10,445)
Marlowe, Karl 4:01:12 (11,298)
Marlowe, Simon Ivor George 4:12:28 (14,089)
Maros, Olivier 4:18:55 (15,832)
Marques, Paulo S 4:02:09 (11,522)
Marquis-Jones, Peter H 3:02:45 (1,315)
Marr, Christoph Thomas 4:18:02 (15,589)
Marr, Richard Andrew 4:59:33 (26,353)
Marrai, Sandro R 3:03:01 (1,328)
Marriott, Brian 4:39:31 (21,391)
Marriott, David Peter 4:45:12 (22,820)
Marriott, Dean 6:37:53 (35,724)
Marriott, James Christopher 3:34:44 (5,198)
Marriott, Jamie 4:52:21 (24,649)
Marriott, Nick 4:55:13 (25,361)
Marriott, Nick Mark 4:02:16 (11,553)
Marriott, Shane David 4:52:07 (24,578)
Marriott, Simon J 2:56:21 (822)
Marriott-Smith, Allan Richard 4:03:33 (11,859)
Marris, Chris 4:39:24 (21,353)
Marris, Peter David 4:47:56 (23,528)
Marrow, Steve 4:12:25 (14,075)
Marsden, David 4:33:53 (19,963)
Marsden, Kevin Neil 4:40:52 (21,738)
Marsden, Kieth 6:19:39 (35,112)
Marsden, Paul 4:23:43 (17,164)
Marsden, Phillip 5:11:53 (28,539)
Marsden, Richard 4:56:55 (25,750)
Marseglia, Pasquale 2:55:26 (769)
Marsh, Chris 3:48:13 (7,784)
Marsh, Christopher James 4:26:59 (18,074)
Marsh, Colin G 4:40:30 (21,640)
Marsh, Dan 5:16:57 (29,379)
Marsh, Daniel 4:24:43 (17,448)
Marsh, Darren L 4:53:15 (24,862)
Marsh, David 4:22:09 (16,741)
Marsh, Denis 6:16:31 (34,952)
Marsh, Francis C 2:42:53 (272)
Marsh, Frazer James 4:38:33 (21,131)
Marsh, Martin James 4:51:12 (24,351)
Marsh, Phil 3:29:44 (4,368)
Marsh, Phillip 3:15:18 (2,476)
Marsh, Stephen James 4:00:52 (11,207)
Marsh, Steven John 3:52:17 (8,734)
Marsh, Steven Keith 4:07:17 (12,771)
Marsh, Tim 4:06:31 (12,578)
Marshall, Alan 3:06:02 (1,537)
Marshall, Alastair 4:43:36 (22,394)
Marshall, Alex George 4:32:57 (19,685)
Marshall, Andrew 3:09:36 (1,870)
Marshall, Andrew 4:42:29 (22,136)
Marshall, Andrew 4:46:14 (23,104)
Marshall, Andrew Johnathan 4:03:27 (11,834)
Marshall, Ben 4:28:47 (18,600)
Marshall, Christopher 3:43:18 (6,744)
Marshall, Craig Scott 5:57:12 (33,879)
Marshall, David John 4:21:40 (16,597)
Marshall, David Robert 4:07:56 (12,940)
Marshall, Dominic 5:56:07 (33,797)
Marshall, Douglas 5:02:06 (26,867)
Marshall, Gary 4:14:25 (14,621)
Marshall, Glenn Stephen 6:11:44 (34,737)
Marshall, Graham 4:44:55 (22,745)
Marshall, James 3:05:19 (1,485)
Marshall, James 4:16:41 (15,215)
Marshall, James Edward 5:49:57 (33,328)
Marshall, John 3:35:55 (5,403)
Marshall, John 4:32:46 (19,622)
Marshall, Johnathon 4:45:44 (22,962)
Marshall, Jol 3:25:34 (3,662)
Marshall, Kevin J 3:01:29 (1,230)
Marshall, Kevin T 4:56:00 (25,535)
Marshall, Lee Stevens 3:52:54 (8,898)
Marshall, Matthew R 2:50:28 (500)
Marshall, Nicholas 3:11:21 (2,031)
Marshall, Nicholas Alan 5:03:47 (27,155)
Marshall, Nicholas J 3:43:02 (6,703)
Marshall, Paul Christopher 3:15:17 (2,472)
Marshall, Peter 3:48:05 (7,754)
Marshall, Philip 4:03:52 (11,940)
Marshall, Richard 4:32:19 (19,520)
Marshall, Robert 4:28:19 (18,458)
Marshall, Ross 4:40:33 (21,657)
Marshall, Simon John 5:33:57 (31,757)
Marshall, Steve 5:05:00 (27,368)
Marshall, Stuart 4:57:39 (25,896)
Marshall, Tom J 2:56:05 (806)
Marshall, Trevor Vincent Grant 5:07:35 (27,828)
Marshall-Lee, Nicholas David 4:11:23 (13,812)
Marson, Peter Phillip 4:28:50 (18,621)
Marson, Stuart A 5:30:46 (31,387)
Marston, Jeremy 3:21:19 (3,121)
Marston, Lee 3:18:30 (2,821)
Mart, Simon 4:25:31 (17,668)
Marteau, Jacky 3:25:34 (3,662)
Martelletti, Paul 2:21:02 (21)
Martin, Adrian P 3:11:56 (2,087)
Martin, Andrew John 4:59:52 (26,422)
Martin, Angel Luis 3:05:54 (1,526)
Martin, Antoine 4:31:18 (19,293)
Martin, Barry 5:14:56 (29,057)
Martin, Ben 4:49:43 (23,987)
Martin, Ben 5:43:46 (32,751)
Martin, Brendan J 4:10:59 (13,710)
Martin, Bruce 3:56:34 (9,953)
Martin, Christopher 3:35:09 (5,265)
Martin, Dan 4:11:55 (13,966)
Martin, Daniel 4:17:16 (15,368)
Martin, Darran 4:52:18 (24,639)
Martin, Derek Thomas 3:14:43 (2,409)
Martin, Duncan M 2:55:33 (775)
Martin, Eduardo Javier 5:20:23 (29,897)
Martin, Ernest C 4:21:35 (16,571)
Martin, Gary Bruce 3:55:12 (9,528)
Martin, Gavin 3:50:59 (8,416)
Martin, Geoffrey Peter 4:28:25 (18,494)
Martin, Gerard Philip 5:13:33 (28,849)
Martin, Graham 5:16:46 (29,347)
Martin, Graham 5:53:23 (33,604)
Martin, Guillaume M 3:42:43 (6,638)
Martin, Hugh W 4:11:12 (13,766)
Martin, Iain 3:14:55 (2,429)
Martin, James David Adam 5:41:08 (32,500)
Martin, Jason 3:56:50 (10,041)
Martin, Jason 4:14:51 (14,750)
Martin, Jim 5:03:16 (27,069)
Martin, Jonathan 4:49:41 (23,974)
Martin, Keith 4:39:08 (21,291)
Martin, Lee 5:11:04 (28,415)
Martin, Lee M 2:55:32 (774)
Martin, Leigh Robert 4:21:23 (16,521)
Martin, Matthew Sean 3:50:55 (8,404)
Martin, Michael 3:56:52 (10,048)
Martin, Michael F 4:27:38 (18,270)
Martin, Neil Andrew Lincoln 4:28:31 (18,528)
Martin, Neil C 4:04:03 (11,973)
Martin, Neil Terence 4:16:14 (15,084)
Martin, Nicholas 4:14:01 (14,508)
Martin, Nicholas 5:11:34 (28,485)
Martin, Paul 3:49:53 (8,184)
Martin, Paul 5:03:21 (27,080)
Martin, Paul Bradley 4:13:35 (14,398)

Martin, Paul J 3:14:01 (2,322)

Martin, Paul J 3:59:30 (10,863)

4 hours to beat and my second attempt. Another gruelling four months of training under my belt. I'm standing at the start with the same pre-race nerves as 2007. This time I'm going to do it. After a bone-freezing downpour at the start, we're off and it turns out to be a beautiful spring day in London. 10 miles, 14 miles, feeling great. 4 hour pace man in sight. I'm not going to lose him. 18 miles, 20 miles, feeling it. Getting slower. I'm not going to make it. 23 miles. Hold on! Watch says still on schedule. There's the 4 hour man. Just one final effort. Finish line in sight. I'm going to do it. I'm going to do it. 26.2 miles. A big grin and 30 seconds to spare. A truly great experience.

Martin, Peter Anthony 4:52:16 (24,619)
Martin, Peter Richard 4:50:18 (24,116)
Martin, Raymond J 4:35:50 (20,430)
Martin, Richard 5:23:46 (30,437)
Martin, Rick J 3:08:12 (1,718)
Martin, Simon D 3:50:20 (8,275)
Martin, Stephen 4:14:49 (14,745)
Martin, Stephen J 4:00:13 (11,036)
Martin, Thomas J 3:17:31 (2,714)
Martin, Thomas Joseph 5:03:43 (27,140)
Martin, Thomas Theodore 4:30:13 (19,028)
Martin,, Wayne, ...4:05:55 (12,435)
Martin-Dupraz, Pierre 3:24:13 (3,471)
Martin-Dye, Ben 2:43:25 (294)
Martinez, Edgardo 3:34:48 (5,213)
Martinez, Eugenio 3:13:17 (2,221)
Martinez, Francis 4:21:55 (16,680)
Martinez, Glendon John 4:45:11 (22,815)
Martinez, Jorge Armando 3:36:11 (5,444)
Martinez, Luis 3:58:02 (10,391)
Martinez, Ricardo 3:30:10 (4,445)
Martinez Ferrero, Francisco 3:47:44 (7,688)
Martini, Silvio 3:00:04 (1,155)
Martins, Antonio M 3:56:18 (9,871)
Martins, Jeff 5:28:46 (31,123)
Martinsson, Sigurdur 3:53:21 (9,013)
Martinus, Isaac 4:56:00 (25,535)
Martykan, Jiri 3:24:02 (3,435)
Marum, Raymond J 4:29:20 (18,759)
Marvelly, Stuart 4:57:07 (25,784)
Marven, Roger A 4:56:39 (25,681)
Marvin, Nick 4:04:37 (12,106)
Marvin, Pete 3:38:02 (5,770)
Marwick, Clyde J 2:53:58 (671)
Maryan, David 5:11:04 (28,415)
Marzohl, Stefan 3:48:03 (7,750)
Marzola, Renato 3:48:57 (7,962)
Mascarenhas, Andrew John 3:30:33 (4,507)
Masek, Ivik 4:35:48 (20,420)
Masella, Jean-Jacques 5:25:13 (30,652)
Maske, Ulf 4:20:03 (16,117)
Maskell, Robert E 4:49:11 (23,844)
Maskell, Steven 4:58:16 (26,036)
Maskill, Peter 4:30:48 (19,171)
Maskill, Simon Laurence 3:21:48 (3,171)
Maslar, Michael 4:34:12 (20,044)
Maslin, Paul J 4:20:12 (16,165)
Mason, Andrew 3:48:59 (7,969)
Mason, Andrew 4:07:52 (12,924)
Mason, Andrew 4:35:44 (20,397)
Mason, Andrew P 4:44:34 (22,658)
Mason, Andy 5:14:20 (28,966)
Mason, Anthony F 4:20:51 (16,375)
Mason, Brian 4:22:04 (16,723)
Mason, Charles 3:11:42 (2,070)
Mason, Chris L 3:04:36 (1,438)
Mason, Christopher James 6:11:49 (34,742)
Mason, Colin 6:23:51 (35,271)
Mason, David 4:48:54 (23,773)
Mason, Derek 5:37:30 (32,164)
Mason, Elliot Paul 4:33:06 (19,727)
Mason, Glenn 4:29:42 (18,878)
Mason, James H 2:39:52 (194)
Mason, John Finch 4:21:48 (16,636)
Mason, Jonathan Richard 4:04:59 (12,200)
Mason, Kenneth 4:22:48 (16,939)
Mason, Richard 4:32:39 (19,594)
Mason, Richard I 4:10:56 (13,695)
Mason, Rob Ian 5:30:24 (31,336)
Mason, Toby Kent 3:38:29 (5,841)
Mason, Tony 3:31:53 (4,722)
Mason, William 5:15:05 (29,080)
Mason-Pearson, Charlie 4:56:07 (25,563)
Massara, Nicholas Anthony 3:18:41 (2,840)
Masselot, Sebastien 3:27:55 (4,038)
Masser, Alastair Urquhart 5:00:01 (26,457)
Massey, Dan Cobden 2:59:20 (1,087)
Massey, Ian 4:23:43 (17,164)
Massey, Kevin T 4:37:36 (20,908)
Massey, Matthew S 4:23:52 (17,205)
Massey, Patrick 3:46:33 (7,433)
Massey, Paul 4:26:14 (17,882)
Massidda, Giovanni 3:32:27 (4,814)
Massingham, Francis William 4:00:37 (11,145)
Massingham, Jonathan P 2:56:50 (852)
Massinon, Bruno 3:36:11 (5,444)
Masson, Andy Vincent 5:16:25 (29,295)
Mastenbroek, Rue 5:14:25 (28,979)
Masterman, Andrew 3:09:45 (1,888)
Masters, Christian James H 4:29:16 (18,747)
Masterson, Stephen Colin 4:46:46 (23,242)
Masterton, Roland Graham 6:14:37 (34,865)
Mastin, Alexander James 3:27:31 (3,966)
Mate, Gareth 4:04:04 (11,977)
Mateo, Juan Daniel 5:28:19 (31,066)
Matern, Wolfgang 4:12:58 (14,225)
Mathe, Jean Yves 4:00:46 (11,185)
Mather, Colin 5:28:54 (31,136)
Mather, David Anthony 3:33:58 (5,052)
Mather, Godfrey Bratherton 4:11:57 (13,977)
Mather, Ian 6:29:38 (35,481)
Mather, Jeremy Edward Anthony 4:08:06 (12,989)
Mather, Nicholas 3:28:31 (4,141)
Mather, Russell Simon 4:07:13 (12,755)
Mathers, Derek A 3:07:00 (1,608)
Mathers, Dermot T 2:58:32 (1,008)
Mathers, Scott James 6:13:04 (34,810)
Matheson, Donald 3:46:32 (7,429)
Matheson, Peter Donald 5:04:15 (27,241)
Matheson, Stuart Thomas 3:49:14 (8,033)
Mathews, Ashley 5:03:35 (27,118)
Mathias, David 5:05:10 (27,396)
Mathieson, Edward O 3:06:55 (1,602)
Matisonn, Shaun 3:29:02 (4,234)
Matley, Chris 4:35:08 (20,260)
Matos, Rodolfo E 6:28:02 (35,422)
Matsumiya, Takayuki 2:21:34 (23)
Matthewman, David Thomas 3:52:36 (8,822)
Matthews, Austin 4:50:09 (24,084)
Matthews, Brian 4:08:08 (12,993)
Matthews, Chris 4:32:20 (19,525)
Matthews, Christopher A 3:56:59 (10,084)
Matthews, Christopher John 3:32:50 (4,867)
Matthews, Dan 4:01:03 (11,264)
Matthews, Daniel Mark 4:01:49 (11,450)
Matthews, Daryl George 4:57:09 (25,791)
Matthews, David 4:45:42 (22,948)
Matthews, Dene J 4:23:42 (17,156)
Matthews, Gair Richard 3:10:37 (1,956)
Matthews, Glyn Ian 3:53:57 (9,196)
Matthews, Harry G 3:00:16 (1,160)
Matthews, Hayden 3:39:15 (5,991)
Matthews, Ian R 3:15:47 (2,526)
Matthews, John 5:14:13 (28,952)
Matthews, John Stephen 5:11:51 (28,534)
Matthews, Jonathan 3:56:46 (10,021)
Matthews, Kevin 4:34:48 (20,194)
Matthews, Michael A 6:21:23 (35,181)
Matthews, Michael David 3:45:49 (7,267)
Matthews, Nicholas 3:57:39 (10,280)
Matthews, Paul 3:57:39 (10,280)
Matthews, Raymond 5:33:21 (31,700)
Matthews, Richard William 6:21:31 (35,186)
Matthews, Robert David 5:09:17 (28,102)
Matthews, Roy Thomas 4:56:39 (25,681)
Matthews, Sam James 3:58:13 (10,463)
Matthews, Stephen 3:56:13 (9,849)
Matthews, Steve 3:41:33 (6,430)
Matthews, Stuart John 3:29:59 (4,413)
Matthews, Vernon 4:59:59 (26,448)
Matthews, William John Albert 6:27:47 (35,415)
Mattie, Theo 4:29:33 (18,820)
Mattina, Steve 2:56:47 (845)
Mattinson, Neil 4:41:17 (21,840)
Mattioli, Vittorio 3:39:40 (6,070)
Mattis, Darren Anthony 3:55:31 (9,617)
Mattison, Michael J 3:13:01 (2,192)
Mattocks, Craig J 2:44:55 (338)
Mattson, Anthony 3:51:53 (8,632)
Mattsson, Michael 4:28:29 (18,518)
Matute, Carlos 4:17:35 (15,464)
Maude, Francis 3:44:19 (6,942)
Mauer, Gustav 3:37:35 (5,684)
Mauge, Gilles 4:14:26 (14,626)
Mauger, Nick John 3:31:16 (4,619)
Maughan, Matthew 4:43:33 (22,382)
Maunder, Mark 3:42:42 (6,634)
Maundrell, Darren John 5:41:28 (32,530)
Mawby, Adrian Paul 3:45:12 (7,139)
Mawdsley, Keith John 4:18:16 (15,648)
Max, Picard 3:26:01 (3,736)
Maxted, Richard James 3:56:39 (9,978)
Maxwell, Henry 3:43:37 (6,793)
Maxwell, John Gabriel 4:34:39 (20,156)
Maxwell, Jonathan Peter 5:41:42 (32,551)
Maxwell, Sean 5:02:40 (26,972)
Maxwell, Steven James 5:48:10 (33,158)
May, Adrian Alan 4:13:31 (14,369)
May, Andy 3:38:02 (5,770)
May, Barry 4:26:30 (17,952)
May, Darren 4:07:20 (12,781)
May, Duncan Douglas 5:59:21 (34,009)
May, Giles 3:53:35 (9,084)
May, Kevin 3:01:42 (1,238)
May, Lee Charles 3:38:46 (5,902)
May, Mark James 4:42:18 (22,095)
May, Mike 3:58:11 (10,449)
May, Paul G 5:48:25 (33,186)
May, Tom 3:23:38 (3,383)
May, William Peter 3:31:24 (4,651)
Mayberry, Peter 4:27:17 (18,174)
Maycock, Nigel 3:30:44 (4,534)
Maycock, Peter 4:14:04 (14,526)
Mayer, Kurt 3:48:46 (7,914)
Mayet, Naumaan 4:41:22 (21,858)
Mayhew, Adam 6:50:51 (36,011)
Mayled, Anthony James 4:25:35 (17,689)
Mayles, Gregg 3:45:02 (7,104)
Maymann, Jimmy 3:28:56 (4,219)
Maynard, Brian William 3:54:59 (9,474)
Maynard, Chris 4:43:26 (22,356)
Maynard, Graham L 3:34:23 (5,135)
Maynard, Richard S 3:34:19 (5,118)
Maynard, Roger C 7:11:02 (36,322)
Mayne, David Hugh 4:33:52 (19,959)
Mayne, Edward 4:33:45 (19,933)
Mayne, Jamie 5:48:29 (33,196)
Maynell, Colin A 4:38:55 (21,235)
Mayo, Andy C 4:17:27 (15,425)
Mayo, Richard Anthony 4:04:07 (11,989)
Mayoh, Leigh R 3:50:46 (8,375)

Mayson, Howard John 4:09:21 (13,296)
Mayson, Paul 3:39:19 (6,010)
Maytum, Jez D 3:48:40 (7,890)
Mazer, Diego................3:48:32 (7,853)
Mazur, Grzegorz................4:57:42 (25,908)
Mazzoni, Cristiano 3:05:13 (1,474)
McAlea, Brian Joseph 4:18:14 (15,641)
McAllin, Alan................5:55:38 (33,764)
McAllister, Gordon................3:06:17 (1,552)
McAllister, Shaun 3:49:30 (8,093)
McAllister, William Archibald 4:34:24 (20,097)
McAlpin, George................4:10:12 (13,531)
McAndie, Stewart................3:09:03 (1,812)
McAndrew, Alasdair Duncan.......4:56:05 (25,556)
McAndrew, Keith................5:53:30 (33,613)
McArdle, Stephen D 4:57:58 (25,963)
McArthur, Andrew 4:53:10 (24,839)
McArthur, Sam 3:18:55 (2,863)
McAuley, Francis 3:50:15 (8,259)
McAuley, John 4:31:20 (19,299)
McAuley, Mike................4:28:15 (18,436)
McAuliffe, Gary................4:35:37 (20,369)
McBean, Benjamin E 6:16:26 (34,948)
McBride, Alistair 4:24:56 (17,498)
McBride, David James................4:30:12 (19,026)
McBride, Gavin 3:32:39 (4,837)
McBride, Michael................3:16:46 (2,651)
McBride, Patrick N................4:37:46 (20,938)
McCabe, David 6:17:21 (35,000)
McCabe, Gerry 3:56:28 (9,922)
McCabe, Michael E 2:58:55 (1,035)
McCabe, Patrick Michael Joseph..5:08:35 (27,985)
McCabe, Paul Edward................4:02:35 (11,624)
McCabe, Peadar Joseph................5:03:48 (27,156)
McCafferty, Kevin John................3:38:21 (5,824)
McCaffery, Stephen A 3:37:04 (5,578)
McCaffrey, Christopher 4:01:01 (11,254)
McCahon, Liam................4:06:50 (12,670)
McCahon, Simon 4:53:48 (24,991)
McCaig, John................4:15:29 (14,902)
McCairn, Dice 4:47:28 (23,404)
McCall, Rory................4:32:50 (19,649)
McCallum, David Ross 4:06:12 (12,496)
McCalman, Finlay Ian................4:18:40 (15,764)
McCann, Craig 3:45:42 (7,245)
McCann, Danny Kevin................4:18:15 (15,644)
McCann, Gerard J................3:21:03 (3,091)
McCann, John 3:58:02 (10,391)
McCann, John 4:03:29 (11,838)
McCann, John 6:29:34 (35,478)
McCann, Matthew Stewart................5:27:20 (30,944)
McCann, Paul................4:10:40 (13,629)
McCann, Paul John................3:31:44 (4,701)
McCann, Rory 3:53:56 (9,191)
McCann, Sean Thomas Patrick...4:19:36 (15,994)
McCardle, Jason 4:03:05 (11,748)
McCargow, Rob 4:26:46 (18,016)
McCarrick, Anthony................4:26:30 (17,952)
McCarrick, Derek................6:51:25 (36,021)
McCarter, Dominic 2:39:09 (179)
McCarthy, Adrian................4:06:38 (12,611)
McCarthy, Antonio................5:08:15 (27,939)
McCarthy, Ben................4:43:51 (22,464)
McCarthy, Brett................4:09:09 (13,240)
McCarthy, Cathal................3:23:03 (3,302)
McCarthy, Charles................3:50:22 (8,281)
McCarthy, Chris................3:14:15 (2,349)
McCarthy, Christopher................4:13:26 (14,348)
McCarthy, Ciaran 4:44:18 (22,591)
McCarthy, David................3:53:00 (8,925)
McCarthy, Denis................4:52:41 (24,728)
McCarthy, Des 4:00:23 (11,085)
McCarthy, Jake Andrew Luke......5:58:31 (33,965)
McCarthy, James Ayton................3:40:49 (6,292)
McCarthy, Keith Douglas................5:46:07 (32,962)
McCarthy, Kerry John 5:04:19 (27,246)
McCarthy, Kevin J................3:35:20 (5,291)
McCarthy, Mark Richard 3:43:26 (6,767)
McCarthy, Padraig................3:39:53 (6,122)
McCarthy, Patrick................3:55:40 (9,668)
McCarthy, Patrick................5:30:11 (31,314)
McCarthy, Peter................3:27:43 (3,999)
McCarthy, Raymond Paul 4:37:05 (20,768)

McCarthy, Richard J................3:58:49 (10,666)
McCarthy, Stephen Michael 4:18:43 (15,778)
McCarthy, Thomas................4:37:43 (20,928)
McCarthy, Tom................5:32:04 (31,543)
McCartney, Adam Peter................4:29:52 (18,935)
McCartney, Allan................3:59:10 (10,764)
McCartney, Stewart 4:29:57 (18,971)
McCaskill, Blake 5:41:32 (32,537)
McCaughey, Dan 3:48:59 (7,969)
McCauley, Paul Desmond................5:31:25 (31,466)
McCave, Geoff................4:34:37 (20,150)
McClarty, Kevin 5:43:22 (32,706)
McClean, Richard 4:07:38 (12,867)
McCleave, Alastair................4:12:01 (13,991)
McCleave, Andrew R................5:09:17 (28,102)
McCleery, Paul................4:01:22 (11,325)
McClelland, Alistair Charles R 3:13:15 (2,217)
McClelland, Paul B 3:20:34 (3,036)
McClintock, Steve 5:21:53 (30,126)
McCloud, Victor A 4:15:00 (14,786)
McClung, James 4:59:55 (26,432)
McClure, Greg M 2:59:43 (1,130)
McClure, Jack Patrick 5:24:25 (30,544)
McCluskey, Brian E 4:54:40 (25,224)
McCluskey, Gareth P................4:58:24 (26,066)
McCluskey, Karl S................4:46:04 (23,050)
McColl, Ewen M 3:02:33 (1,304)
McColl, Gary J 5:30:25 (31,340)
McColm, Andy................3:58:29 (10,551)
McConachie, Neil 3:54:15 (9,272)
McConkey, Paul................4:26:55 (18,054)
McConnell, Barry................3:12:00 (2,091)
McConnell, Duncan Bruce................5:04:52 (27,344)
McConnell, Marc Alan................3:47:59 (7,736)
McConochie, Andrew David 3:32:57 (4,885)
McConville, Alistair G................4:51:51 (24,507)
McConville, Cahal Martin 3:43:00 (6,700)
McConville, John P 3:25:50 (3,709)
McConville, Ryan Franci................4:59:01 (26,219)
McCorkell, Michael C................3:37:02 (5,570)
McCormack, Ben 2:49:39 (471)
McCormack, Dan 2:53:53 (661)
McCormack, Eamonn Michael ...4:27:02 (18,087)
McCormack, James 4:22:46 (16,928)
McCormack, Lee................4:29:22 (18,768)
McCormack, Ryan................6:02:00 (34,190)
McCormick, Andrew................4:30:28 (19,081)
McCormick, Andrew David 5:10:07 (28,261)
McCormick, Ashley Warren........3:55:52 (9,740)
McCormick, Michael G................4:05:07 (12,230)
McCormick, Peter................3:45:07 (7,119)
McCorrie, Grant M 5:51:23 (33,454)
McCoull, Russell................3:32:41 (4,842)
McCourt, Rich................6:25:09 (35,316)
McCover, Neil................3:37:17 (5,614)
McCowan, Ross................3:48:01 (7,741)
McCoy, Gerard M................3:55:15 (9,544)
McCoy, Robin E................3:14:42 (2,406)
McCrabbe, Clyde J 4:10:13 (13,535)
McCrae, Ian................4:24:00 (17,236)
McCrea, Alastair................4:04:42 (12,129)
McCready, Richard................4:15:40 (14,944)
McCreesh, James P................3:50:52 (8,396)
McCrone, Paul 3:27:07 (3,890)
McCrory, Damian................3:54:47 (9,416)
McCrory, Patrick 3:55:14 (9,538)
McCrudden, Ian Joseph 4:10:08 (13,506)
McCullagh, John Joe................3:34:56 (5,237)
McCullie, Alec................5:39:45 (32,362)
McCulloch, David A................3:05:29 (1,495)
McCulloch, John Joseph Richard..4:50:14 (24,099)
McCulloch, Malcolm................4:29:42 (18,878)
McCulloch, Thomas................3:34:58 (5,244)
McCulloch, Willie 5:25:21 (30,669)
McCullock, James Anthony 5:10:12 (28,277)

McCurrie, Robert................5:16:26 (29,303)
McCusker, Eamonn................3:46:47 (7,484)
McDaniels, Gary................3:17:24 (2,698)
McDerment, Leslie J 3:15:06 (2,449)
McDermott, Bart 3:55:59 (9,779)
McDermott, Christopher John....4:15:00 (14,786)
McDermott, Darren Leslie 3:07:55 (1,690)
McDermott, Greg James................3:37:44 (5,715)
McDermott, Luke A................6:30:45 (35,527)
McDermott, Nigel 3:51:20 (8,500)
McDermott, Patrick 4:00:37 (11,145)
McDermott, Sean P................3:04:14 (1,414)
McDermott-Paine, Iain D 4:16:12 (15,071)
McDonagh, Michael A................2:51:17 (534)
McDonagh, Neil................4:58:11 (26,008)
McDonagh, Richard................3:53:36 (9,092)
McDonald, Alan................3:11:22 (2,034)
McDonald, Andrew................3:41:21 (6,395)
McDonald, Christopher................3:27:56 (4,044)
McDonald, David 2:57:24 (889)
McDonald, David 4:17:29 (15,433)
McDonald, Douglas John William.3:37:17 (5,614)
McDonald, Kevin 5:18:23 (29,605)
McDonald, Lewis................4:47:08 (23,331)
McDonald, Maurice................5:33:24 (31,706)
McDonald, Michael................4:23:29 (17,099)
McDonald, Peter................3:25:43 (3,687)
McDonald, Robert 3:29:00 (4,227)
McDonald, Robert 3:56:37 (9,964)
McDonald, Rod................4:11:51 (13,945)
McDonald, Scott................4:07:01 (12,714)
McDonald, Stephen Paul................4:10:45 (13,655)
McDonald, Steven J................2:59:28 (1,101)
McDonald, Lawrence Anthony ...3:16:39 (2,634)
McDonnell, Daren P 4:15:23 (14,883)
McDonnell, Mike 3:52:49 (8,877)
McDonnell-Rogers, Nick 5:56:59 (33,865)
McDonogh, Robert J................4:41:58 (22,005)
McDougall, Graham A.T................3:58:05 (10,407)
McDougall, Grant Robert................4:42:21 (22,105)
McDowell, Gregory 3:12:56 (2,179)
McEachern, John George................4:24:53 (17,485)
McElligott, Matt 3:52:06 (8,679)
McElreath, Timothy................3:53:47 (9,154)
McEntee, Colin 3:56:23 (9,892)
McEntee, Stephen................3:43:18 (6,744)
McEvilly, Damien................4:11:51 (13,945)
McEvoy, Andrew John................4:43:04 (22,276)
McEvoy, Julian S 4:46:08 (23,071)
McEvoy, Phil 4:58:56 (26,196)
McEvoy, Richard Clive 5:14:01 (28,928)
McEvoy, Richard Keith................5:39:08 (32,312)
McEwan, David Lewis................5:13:23 (28,824)
McEwan, Tristan David 4:21:42 (16,606)
McEwen, Andrew W................3:39:41 (6,073)
McEwen, Andy................4:35:46 (20,410)
McEwen, Ross David 4:07:18 (12,775)
McFadden, Paul Charles................3:42:31 (6,600)
McFadden, Roger S................3:43:13 (6,731)
McFadden, Rory................3:38:11 (5,800)
McFaite, Ashley James................5:00:17 (26,515)
McFarland, Andrew 4:58:29 (26,082)
McFarland, Andrew K................4:37:03 (20,758)
McFarland, Ben................4:05:24 (12,313)
McFarland, John 4:34:10 (20,030)
McFarlane, Hazel 4:36:46 (20,674)
McFarlane, James Pritchard 4:30:31 (19,091)
McFarlane, John................2:28:38 (55)
McFarlane, Joseph 4:26:02 (17,822)
McFarlane, Paul Marcellus 3:49:58 (8,204)
McFarlane, Steven................3:34:10 (5,090)
McFarlane, William................6:08:31 (34,584)
McFie, Andrew 3:15:33 (2,504)
McGahern, James M 4:39:18 (21,329)
McGale, Shane 3:23:25 (3,354)
McGarr, Paul Christopher 6:29:50 (35,490)
McGarrigle, Nick A 4:13:34 (14,390)
McGarvey, Guy................8:13:02 (36,596)
McGarvie, Lindsay................4:29:20 (18,759)
McGavigan, Mark................4:01:39 (11,404)
McGeagh, Nicolas 3:49:00 (7,974)
McGee, Damian 4:13:58 (14,496)
McGee, Eoin................4:00:26 (11,100)

McGee, Harry 4:35:21 (20,309)
McGee, Liam 3:45:30 (7,207)
McGee, Robert William 4:07:59 (12,957)
McGeoch, Mick 2:53:48 (656)
McGeough, Simon John 3:46:15 (7,367)
McGeown, John 4:14:59 (14,782)
McGeown, Steven 3:55:09 (9,516)
McGhee, David 4:15:18 (14,861)
McGhee, Gary 2:53:21 (632)
McGhee, James Arthur 4:22:37 (16,885)
McGill, Colin A 2:35:43 (124)
McGill, Jim 4:28:22 (18,472)
McGillian, Charles G 3:02:48 (1,317)
McGilligan, Sean 4:12:40 (14,143)
McGilvray, Iain 5:29:13 (31,180)
McGilvray, Kevin J 3:44:39 (7,024)
McGinness, Terry 4:46:49 (23,259)
McGinnis, Scott Michael 2:41:41 (244)
McGinty, Emmett 3:02:29 (1,297)
McGinty, Mark Stephen 4:10:27 (13,579)
McGlade, Michael J 2:56:19 (820)
McGolpin, Rob 5:47:43 (33,117)
McGough, Paul G 3:35:38 (5,349)
McGourty, Thomas James 3:51:53 (8,632)
McGovern, Andrew D 3:22:36 (3,250)
McGovern, Peter 4:46:05 (23,055)
McGowan, Daniel Hugh 4:12:32 (14,109)
McGowan, Julian P 2:50:30 (503)
McGowan, Michael 5:31:37 (31,490)
McGowan, Scott Gavin 5:00:07 (26,483)
McGowan, Shane Wesley 4:35:21 (20,309)
McGrady, Paul 5:29:44 (31,261)
McGrath, Alan 4:41:05 (21,790)
McGrath, Austin 3:57:43 (10,308)
McGrath, Dave Jeremy 3:18:00 (2,766)
McGrath, Jason 4:35:14 (20,278)
McGrath, Justin Michael 3:37:25 (5,639)
McGrath, Liam Sean 3:41:11 (6,362)
McGrath, Patrick Stephen 5:33:18 (31,693)
McGrath, Paul M 3:20:33 (3,032)
McGrattan, Simon G 4:07:18 (12,775)
McGreevy, Cathal 3:12:22 (2,119)
McGregor, Alex Robert 5:12:53 (28,717)
McGregor, Campbell Stephen 3:48:02 (7,747)
McGregor, Fraser 3:42:00 (6,506)
McGregor, Garth Bruce 4:38:01 (20,990)
McGregor, Skye Benjamin 4:24:14 (17,294)
McGrotty, Garry 3:55:12 (9,528)
McGuckin, Jim 4:49:15 (23,865)
McGuigan, Anthony James 5:53:51 (33,632)
McGuigan, James 3:38:17 (5,816)
McGuigan, Sean 5:02:19 (26,908)
McGuinness, Andrew 4:15:53 (14,998)
McGuinness, Harold D 4:05:45 (12,395)
McGuinness, Jim J 3:28:20 (4,112)
McGuinness, Jonathan Owen 4:32:06 (19,459)
McGuinness, Kieran Anthony 8:55:09 (36,611)
McGuinness, Paul 6:17:04 (34,982)
McGuire, Andrew James 5:13:46 (28,884)
McGuire, Carl Peter 3:54:11 (9,254)
McGuire, David M 3:03:51 (1,377)
McGuire, James 4:50:56 (24,286)
McGuire, Paul Norman 4:45:30 (22,884)
McGuire, Ray Michael James 4:11:39 (13,893)
McGuire, Thomas James 4:27:02 (18,087)
McGurk, David 3:58:19 (10,499)
McHale, Darren Ian 3:49:11 (8,021)
McHale, David Roger 4:03:46 (11,914)
McHale, Michael James 3:58:06 (10,414)
McHugh, Liam 3:36:20 (5,462)
McIiroy, Simon 3:47:44 (7,688)
McIlwee, Ian 2:44:02 (311)
McInerney, John Patrick 5:22:56 (30,298)
McInerney, Paul Andrew 4:00:59 (11,245)
McInman, Victor Mark 3:42:50 (6,661)
McInnes, Colin 3:49:17 (8,043)
McIntosh, Adrian 4:08:01 (12,966)
McIntosh, Alex 4:16:31 (15,174)
McIntosh, Andrew 4:22:25 (16,826)
McIntosh, Andy 4:03:04 (11,743)
McIntosh, James Stuart 5:26:11 (30,799)
McIntosh, Mark S 3:20:28 (3,017)
McIntosh-Whyte, Rick 4:24:14 (17,294)
McIntyre, Craig 3:25:50 (3,709)
McIntyre, Neil Alexander 3:36:05 (5,424)
McIntyre, Pete 4:15:07 (14,813)
McKandie, Roy 3:54:52 (9,441)
McKay, Francis Gerard 3:33:27 (4,963)
McKay, John Charles 4:34:34 (20,140)
McKay, Neil 4:59:47 (26,403)
McKay, Paul 3:33:08 (4,913)
McKay, Steven 3:12:59 (2,191)
McKay, Tony Gerald 4:38:45 (21,185)
McKean, David Paul 3:41:03 (6,334)
McKean, Michael C 3:05:44 (1,518)
McKeating, Paul Vincent 4:59:03 (26,227)
McKechnie, Ian 5:10:34 (28,343)
McKee, Alexander John Paul 3:52:35 (8,815)
McKee, Iain 4:11:24 (13,820)
McKee, James E 3:42:50 (6,661)
McKeeney, Paul 4:55:47 (25,488)
McKellar, James R 5:10:21 (28,301)
McKellar, Rob Daniel 3:49:38 (8,130)
McKelvaney, Paul L 4:03:15 (11,792)
McKenna, Frank C 3:23:06 (3,305)
McKenna, Martin Hillier 4:03:56 (11,948)
McKenna, Mike P 3:11:49 (2,075)
McKenna, Scott D 3:08:30 (1,754)
McKenzie, Mark Alexander 5:07:39 (27,841)
McKenzie, Stuart 3:26:43 (3,832)
McKeown, Des Michael 3:27:35 (3,976)
McKeown, Ian 4:16:44 (15,228)
McKeown, Phillip 3:14:01 (2,322)
McKerihan, Mark D 3:28:21 (4,116)
McKernan, Daniel 3:32:25 (4,804)
McKevitt, Gerry 4:23:59 (17,234)
McKidd, Laurence Richard 4:00:26 (11,100)
McKinna, Simon James 4:12:43 (14,161)
McKinney, Cormac 5:10:05 (28,253)
McKinney, Roy Columba 5:22:08 (30,168)
McKinney, William 4:16:17 (15,099)
McKinnon, Ewen Robert 4:49:05 (23,828)
McKinnon, Neil 4:49:04 (23,820)
McKinnon, Travis 5:07:36 (27,832)
McKirdy, Tom 3:48:38 (7,878)
McLaren, Chris 4:48:53 (23,768)
McLaren, Guy N 2:50:43 (512)
McLaren, Ian David 4:20:31 (16,265)
McLaren, Michael James 3:31:41 (4,695)
McLatchie, Joe 3:47:11 (7,575)
McLaughlin, Cathal 3:16:12 (2,574)
McLaughlin, Danny 4:06:36 (12,602)
McLaughlin, David 3:57:36 (10,264)
McLaughlin, Declan 3:44:42 (7,035)
McLaughlin, John L 2:59:38 (1,121)
McLaughlin, Paul 4:01:32 (11,376)
McLaughlin, Paul A 4:29:43 (18,888)
McLaughlin, Tomas 3:26:49 (3,851)
McLean, Angus George 3:54:58 (9,468)
McLean, Anthony 5:50:42 (33,408)
McLean, Jonny 3:24:23 (3,497)
McLean, Paul 3:53:32 (9,067)
McLeannan, Andy 3:53:29 (9,051)
McLeish, David 4:48:25 (23,647)
McLellan, Eddie 4:39:22 (21,344)
McLellan, Gordon 4:28:19 (18,458)
McLellan, Nigel J 5:09:34 (28,162)
McLelland, Steve 3:42:00 (6,506)
McLennan, Ian 4:14:35 (14,677)
McLeod, Alastair D 3:42:19 (6,566)
McLeod, Miles 3:31:19 (4,632)
McLeod, Rab 5:23:24 (30,372)
McLeod, Ross 3:20:28 (3,017)
McLeod, Rupert 3:45:33 (7,220)
McLntyre, Adam 5:25:30 (30,691)
McLoone, Michael 3:00:02 (1,153)
McLoughlin, Adam 3:50:53 (8,400)
McLoughlin, Andrew 4:06:47 (12,653)
McLoughlin, Brian P 5:46:51 (33,037)
McLoughlin, Iain John 5:02:33 (26,950)
McLoughlin, John 3:15:56 (2,546)
McLoughlin, Kevin A 3:04:01 (1,393)
McMahon, Andy 3:15:55 (2,542)
McMahon, Carl 3:46:30 (7,415)
McMahon, Drew 4:11:06 (13,744)
McMahon, James P 2:51:11 (528)
McMahon, Jon 3:23:17 (3,339)
McMahon, Michael Bernard 3:49:19 (8,047)
McMahon, Raymond 4:24:49 (17,472)
McManamon, Martin 5:10:00 (28,235)
McManus, John 4:55:16 (25,374)
McMaster, Colin 4:32:35 (19,582)
McMaster, Graham 3:55:25 (9,598)
McMasters, David Simon 3:41:32 (6,427)
McMeekin, Darren 4:11:54 (13,959)
McMeekin, Scott 4:32:59 (19,691)
McMeeking, Ian Christopher 4:11:45 (13,922)
McMenigall, Stuart 3:57:24 (10,202)
McMillan, Andrew John 3:53:32 (9,067)
McMillan, David H 6:15:00 (34,887)
McMillan, Ged 3:14:38 (2,402)
McMillan, Paul James 5:33:59 (31,762)
McMillan, Robert 5:05:33 (27,458)
McMillan, William 4:11:09 (13,758)
McMonagle, Noel 3:44:45 (7,043)
McMullan, Kevin J 2:59:24 (1,095)
McMullen, Alexander 3:52:46 (8,857)
McMullen, John 4:09:57 (13,456)
McMurray, Steven 4:36:54 (20,715)
McMyler, Sean A 2:58:21 (992)
McNally, Alan R 3:30:32 (4,501)
McNally, Anthony John 4:44:20 (22,599)
McNally, Colin 3:19:38 (2,931)
McNally, John Peter 5:33:35 (31,724)
McNally, Thomas M 3:15:32 (2,502)
McNamara, Andrew D 2:30:59 (75)
McNamara, Dan 4:38:09 (21,016)
McNamara, David 4:02:07 (11,515)
McNamara, Ian F 3:50:06 (8,229)
McNamara, Josh 4:16:10 (15,062)
McNamara, Mario 3:11:15 (2,022)
McNamara, Paul 4:14:48 (14,742)
McNamara, Peter James 6:02:46 (34,234)
McNamee, Andrew James 6:11:30 (34,721)
McNaugher, Ivor S 4:36:12 (20,528)
McNaught, Keith 4:28:23 (18,478)
McNeice, Patrick 4:00:03 (10,994)
McNeil, Neil James John 4:18:40 (15,764)
McNeill, Alexander 4:09:06 (13,229)
McNeill, Andrew Victor 3:58:52 (10,674)
McNeill, Rory Thomas 4:15:20 (14,872)
McNelis, Robin M 2:58:09 (970)
McNicholas, Joe Noel 5:25:26 (30,686)
McNicol, David 4:50:09 (24,084)
McNiff, John 5:08:59 (28,046)
McNiffe, John 5:19:37 (29,794)
McNulty, Dermot 5:10:06 (28,256)
McNulty, Donnach 5:10:05 (28,253)
McNulty, Michael 4:04:52 (12,168)
McNulty, Myles Francis 4:36:32 (20,616)
McPaul, Robert 3:53:11 (8,966)
McPhail, Grant Robert 3:32:30 (4,815)
McPheat, Martin D 4:30:37 (19,127)
McPhee, Andy William 3:45:37 (7,230)
McPherson, George A 2:58:05 (964)
McPherson, James 5:15:28 (29,138)
McPoland, James 3:27:06 (3,886)
McQuillan, Jon 3:56:06 (9,811)
McRae, Andy 4:22:58 (16,977)
McRae, Daniel 7:10:40 (36,319)
McRae, Richard 4:01:20 (11,319)
McRae, Robin 4:17:56 (15,557)
McShane, Dessie C 3:05:54 (1,526)
McSharry, Paul 4:34:50 (20,202)
McShea, Dean 4:43:41 (22,413)
McShera, Sean Angus 5:54:59 (33,716)
McSpadden, Martin J 4:31:15 (19,280)
McSparron, Paul 5:04:23 (27,254)
McSweeney, Simon Christopher 4:10:11 (13,524)
McSweeney, Aidan 4:24:56 (17,498)
McSwiggan, Matthew James 3:55:46 (9,706)
McTaggart, Paul 4:07:39 (12,871)
McTernan, Christopher S 4:00:42 (11,170)
McTigue, Joe 3:39:03 (5,950)
McVeigh, Alistair David 3:12:40 (2,151)
McVeigh, Bernie 5:50:21 (33,369)
McWhan, Andy David 3:45:01 (7,098)
McWilliams, Nairn A 3:25:43 (3,687)
Meachem, John Anthony 3:51:12 (8,472)

Meacock, Guy Jonathan	4:03:12 (11,777)
Mead, Adrian M	3:12:33 (2,139)
Mead, Howard I	2:43:21 (290)
Mead, John P	4:03:06 (11,759)
Mead, Paul	4:35:42 (20,390)
Mead, Rob J	3:35:19 (5,290)
Mead, Simon Paul	2:59:31 (1,113)
Mead, Stuart E	2:46:57 (385)
Meade, Gareth	4:06:35 (12,596)
Meade, Ian David	4:27:26 (18,213)
Meaden, Philip Gerard	3:52:30 (8,796)
Meaden, Stephen James Edward	5:21:08 (30,024)
Meader, William James	4:24:36 (17,419)
Meadowcroft, John Boyne	3:59:32 (10,870)
Meadows, Al	3:26:57 (3,869)
Meadows, Chris Stephen	4:31:50 (19,396)
Meadows, Jonathan D	4:09:22 (13,301)
Meadows, Steven	5:02:15 (26,898)
Meadows, Terry	4:09:31 (13,346)
Meakes, Tim	3:57:27 (10,214)
Meakin, Anthony	4:05:45 (12,395)
Meakin, David	5:32:49 (31,643)
Meakins, Andrew	5:24:48 (30,591)
Meakins, Christopher G	5:41:57 (32,585)
Mean, Kelly	4:12:53 (14,204)
Mean, Richard John	5:10:06 (28,256)
Mears, Aaron	4:19:59 (16,103)
Mears, Bradley	4:21:42 (16,606)
Mears, David Franf	5:00:52 (26,623)
Mears, Justin Lee	4:48:13 (23,590)
Mears, Kristian Paul	5:55:01 (33,720)
Meaton, Peter Geoffrey	6:10:30 (34,682)
Medland, Andrew J	2:58:52 (1,032)
Medley, Andrew	4:55:32 (25,414)
Medley, Leighton J	3:36:52 (5,541)
Medley, Ray	4:25:58 (17,803)
Mee, Darren	5:03:50 (27,162)
Mee, Gary John	5:14:44 (29,024)
Mee, Richard	3:46:50 (7,499)
Meecham, Simon George	4:00:04 (10,998)
Meechan, Robbie Michael Hugh	6:04:47 (34,368)
Meechan, Rod	4:21:50 (16,651)
Meehan, Anthony	4:52:32 (24,694)
Meehan, David John	3:45:57 (7,299)
Meehan, Tony	5:09:59 (28,230)
Meenan, Chris	3:42:40 (6,630)
Meenan, Ken	5:09:03 (28,055)
Meessmann, Luke	3:23:54 (3,420)
Meffert, Rainer	3:43:26 (6,767)
Meggiato, Michael P	4:10:03 (13,485)
Mehra, Arun	4:12:17 (14,051)
Mei, Massimo	4:09:01 (13,218)
Meier, Benno	4:18:01 (15,582)
Meighen, Peter Robert	4:20:44 (16,347)
Meiklejohn, Graham	4:01:37 (11,396)
Meiras, Inigo	4:15:44 (14,962)
Meiring, Carl E	4:16:30 (15,170)
Melaugh, Martin	4:16:28 (15,157)
Melbourne, Ed R	3:05:39 (1,510)
Melbourne, John Rupert	3:43:57 (6,868)
Melby, Brage	3:46:24 (7,397)
Meletiou, Nicolas	4:39:41 (21,432)
Melin, Ian	4:05:37 (12,360)
Melis, Fabrice	3:31:02 (4,584)
Mellenchip, Russell	4:19:53 (16,072)
Meller, Nick John	4:23:54 (17,213)
Mellersh, William John	5:43:15 (32,694)
Melling, Phil	3:49:50 (8,169)
Mellish, Joseph John	4:17:46 (15,519)
Mellon, Jimmy	6:37:50 (35,721)
Mellon, John Spencer	4:52:17 (24,633)
Mellonian, Edward L	3:28:24 (4,126)
Mellor, Craig	4:36:37 (20,637)
Mellor, David	4:19:42 (16,014)
Mellor, Paul	5:20:59 (30,002)
Mellor, Philip	4:40:35 (21,664)
Mellor, Steve	5:52:37 (33,540)
Melly, Liam Peter	4:33:18 (19,803)
Melo, Luis	4:28:48 (18,609)
Meloro, Tommaso	3:52:51 (8,883)
Melrose, Michael Ian	4:26:06 (17,844)
Melrose, Peter	4:00:22 (11,081)
Melville, Colin	3:44:05 (6,896)

Melvin, Thomas W	3:02:56 (1,323)
Membrez, Cedric	4:26:35 (17,977)
Mena Ivars, Juan Carlos	4:00:08 (11,015)
Mena Mena, Lorenzo Rafael	3:32:16 (4,783)
Menager, Herve	3:32:51 (4,871)
Menchi Rogai, Sergio	4:41:36 (21,923)
Mendelsohn, Rafi	4:36:03 (20,490)
Menditta, Peter	4:02:49 (11,677)
Mendoza, Juan Simon	5:24:21 (30,531)
Meneghetti, Alan	3:43:54 (6,859)
Menelaou, Mel	4:53:18 (24,876)
Menhennett, John	4:16:29 (15,165)
Menna, Rocco	4:30:27 (19,075)
Mennell, Nicholas David	5:01:17 (26,703)
Mennie, Andrew Michael	4:42:03 (22,028)
Menon, Frederic	3:28:32 (4,145)
Menten, Koen	3:28:20 (4,112)
Mentz, Herman	4:27:57 (18,353)
Menzefricke-Koitz, Magnus	3:55:36 (9,636)
Menzies, Michael James	5:41:36 (32,542)
Mepham, Derek	3:57:01 (10,102)
Mepstead, Sid	4:44:52 (22,734)
Mercer, Jason R	3:41:19 (6,389)
Mercer, Neil Allen	3:58:34 (10,584)
Mercer, Neil H	3:05:21 (1,487)
Merchant, James Kieth	4:07:25 (12,804)
Merchant, Sadiq	5:17:16 (29,429)
Meredith, Darren	3:00:02 (1,153)
Meredith, Ian	6:33:40 (35,618)
Meredith, Philip Wilson	4:14:58 (14,773)
Meredith, Roy	4:23:43 (17,164)
Meredith, Tim	4:28:13 (18,424)
Meredith, Tony	5:51:57 (33,501)
Merivale, Edward	3:39:24 (6,022)
Mermans, Patrick	3:39:17 (6,000)
Merrell, Bob	5:08:52 (28,025)
Merrell, John	4:50:16 (24,110)
Merrells, Jason	4:34:41 (20,168)
Merrick, David Michael	3:58:03 (10,397)
Merrick, Graham Colin	5:12:15 (28,609)
Merrick, Peter David	5:34:38 (31,841)
Merrien, Lee	2:16:48 (12)
Merrifield, Jason	4:46:15 (23,109)
Merrill, Sam Oliver Crichton	5:12:00 (28,565)
Merriott, Thomas Coggin	3:53:53 (9,177)
Merrison, Paul	5:21:40 (30,106)
Merrison, Philip Walter	3:27:50 (4,021)
Merritt, David	3:44:37 (7,020)
Merritt, Jason Mark	4:00:36 (11,140)
Merritt, Kristian J	4:13:38 (14,414)
Merritt, Lee William	5:02:41 (26,974)
Merritt, Mark Edward Vaughan	3:55:39 (9,661)
Merritt, Tom	5:06:04 (27,543)
Merron, Bernard	3:09:01 (1,811)
Merron, Stephen	4:28:26 (18,499)
Merry, James T	5:32:34 (31,616)
Merry, Stephen	3:38:39 (5,885)
Merrywest, Mark Andrew	3:17:33 (2,720)
Mertens, Clem	3:39:24 (6,022)
Mertens, Rob John	3:54:52 (9,441)
Mertin, Siegfried	4:44:05 (22,529)
Mertsching, Bjoern	3:34:06 (5,079)
Merwood, Simon D	3:07:20 (1,638)
Merzario, Paolo	3:08:41 (1,780)
Meschini, Alessandro	3:24:54 (3,563)
Messaoudi, Amar	3:35:24 (5,301)
Messenger, Mark	3:38:55 (5,924)
Messerschmidt, Marty	3:55:01 (9,482)
Metcalfe, Bevis	4:46:13 (23,096)
Metcalfe, Daniel Michael	4:30:54 (19,190)
Metcalfe, Jason	4:49:39 (23,961)
Metham, David W	4:17:24 (15,405)
Methven, Paul Nicholas	4:57:57 (25,959)
Metson, Nick	3:08:04 (1,702)
Metson-Bailie, Simon Stuart	3:56:51 (10,047)
Metzger, Dominique	4:35:54 (20,446)
Meuldijk, Gieljam Adrianus	3:56:29 (9,926)
Meumann, Mark David	3:46:41 (7,456)
Meurice, Nick Hamilton	5:54:09 (33,655)
Meurisse, Franck	3:22:35 (3,248)
Mewes, Joseph Raymond Matthew	5:29:12 (31,175)
Mews, Stephen P	4:43:42 (22,417)
Mews, Tobias A	2:49:58 (485)

Mewse, Dale L	4:53:34 (24,934)
Meyer, Andrew Mark	4:51:06 (24,333)
Meyer, Norbert	4:12:28 (14,089)
Meylan, Roland Terence	3:48:33 (7,861)
Meyrick, Charles	4:35:44 (20,397)
Meywald, Martin	3:29:40 (4,354)
Mezzetti, Edward A	2:54:50 (707)
Mhango, Louis Stanley	4:23:50 (17,196)
Miah, Wadud	3:31:43 (4,699)
Miayokila, Fabrice	3:28:45 (4,183)
Micallef, Carlos	3:56:18 (9,871)
Michael, Costas	4:24:23 (17,350)
Michael, David	4:09:55 (13,448)
Michael, Dennis	3:14:10 (2,336)
Michael, Desmond	3:05:34 (1,501)
Michael, Douglas R	4:18:59 (15,847)
Michael, James I	4:18:59 (15,847)
Michael, Nicholas	4:30:40 (19,139)
Michael, Steven	4:44:43 (22,701)
Michaels, Sam	4:47:19 (23,368)
Michaelwaite, Alastair J	3:41:08 (6,352)
Michalski, Pierre	4:57:25 (25,842)
Michel, Ajas	4:58:28 (26,080)
Michel, Pierre	3:44:16 (6,928)
Michele, Hamon	4:02:57 (11,719)
Michie, Jamie	5:21:52 (30,124)
Michie, John	5:12:06 (28,584)
Mickel, John Brian	4:39:28 (21,377)
Micklethwaite, Ian	3:27:53 (4,033)
Micklewright, Alan	4:04:03 (11,973)
Middlebrook, Alan	2:54:53 (731)
Middlebrough, Ben R	4:25:04 (17,540)
Middleton, Allan Murray	5:36:18 (32,033)
Middleton, Darren P	3:59:22 (10,827)
Middleton, Gordon Campbell	4:38:06 (21,008)
Middleton, John	6:11:26 (34,718)
Middleton, Mark	5:24:22 (30,535)
Middleton, Nick	3:45:18 (7,162)
Middleton, Paul	4:13:47 (14,452)
Middleton, Phil John	4:47:44 (23,478)
Middleton, Richard	5:32:25 (31,588)
Middleton, Roger L	3:58:05 (10,407)
Middleton, Thomas Edward	3:55:31 (9,617)
Midgley, David	5:36:26 (32,046)
Midgley, Russell Lee	3:55:20 (9,571)
Midlane, Jonathan Daniel	4:44:39 (22,688)
Midwinter, Dale	3:21:25 (3,132)
Midworth, Nick	3:29:48 (4,379)
Mikkelsen, Per	3:14:28 (2,377)
Miksch, Brian	4:29:23 (18,773)
Milall, Merlin Christopher	3:54:43 (9,392)
Milbourn, Alex James	4:08:28 (13,069)
Milburn, Bruce	3:12:42 (2,154)
Milburn, Stephen Clifford	4:10:30 (13,594)
Mileham, Richard	4:20:37 (16,302)
Miles, Adam	4:28:13 (18,424)
Miles, Alan F	5:25:34 (30,706)
Miles, Albert J	4:27:04 (18,110)
Miles, Christopher Thomas	4:52:16 (24,619)
Miles, David M	3:44:16 (6,928)
Miles, Dyfed Rhys	4:07:35 (12,853)
Miles, Greg	5:41:14 (32,513)
Miles, John	5:20:17 (29,888)
Miles, John Henry	3:59:52 (10,956)
Miles, Kevin Donovan	4:07:42 (12,887)
Miles, Laurence	2:43:22 (291)
Miles, Lee Anthony	5:40:30 (32,430)
Miles, Stephen	3:34:08 (5,086)
Millan, Alisdair R	3:26:00 (3,731)
Millar, Alan David Duncan	4:45:28 (22,875)
Millar, Christopher D	4:18:33 (15,725)
Millar, Clive	4:09:26 (13,325)
Millar, Gordon Nicholas	4:21:02 (16,425)
Millar, Leslie Francis	3:45:05 (7,111)
Millar, Norman	3:43:16 (6,737)
Millar, Richard	6:34:37 (35,646)
Millar, Stuart Raymond	3:36:32 (5,484)
Millard, Iain	5:20:27 (29,912)
Millard, Peter James	4:27:02 (18,087)
Millard, Richard Lee	5:11:42 (28,502)
Millbank, Paul Andrew	3:44:31 (6,995)
Millen, Gary	5:11:22 (28,460)
Miller, Adam J	2:49:57 (484)

Miller, Alan 4:39:33 (21,400)
Miller, Andrew Robert 6:05:08 (34,396)
Miller, Andrew William 3:48:07 (7,769)
Miller, Barry J 3:27:37 (3,986)
Miller, Ben 4:11:01 (13,720)
Miller, Christopher John 3:08:38 (1,773)
Miller, Daniel Howard 5:47:55 (33,129)
Miller, David 6:33:07 (35,600)
Miller, David A. 4:24:47 (17,462)
Miller, David Edward 6:01:04 (34,135)
Miller, David Robert 4:23:21 (17,060)
Miller, George D 2:34:12 (99)
Miller, Glenn As 4:17:06 (15,321)
Miller, Graeme 3:16:38 (2,631)
Miller, Greg 4:07:55 (12,933)
Miller, Guy James 4:53:21 (24,884)
Miller, Ian D 3:02:34 (1,306)
Miller, Ian E 4:38:50 (21,212)
Miller, Ian James 3:56:28 (9,922)
Miller, James Charles 5:22:57 (30,301)
Miller, James E 4:06:15 (12,511)
Miller, Jim 3:40:23 (6,208)
Miller, Joseph 4:27:40 (18,277)
Miller, Keith Ramsay 4:20:37 (16,302)
Miller, Kevin J 4:15:37 (14,929)
Miller, Kevin Peter 4:17:59 (15,573)
Miller, Les 6:07:26 (34,529)
Miller, Marc 5:01:21 (26,724)
Miller, Owain Richard 4:44:23 (22,609)
Miller, Patrick 4:38:19 (21,061)
Miller, Paul 4:11:14 (13,776)
Miller, Paul William 4:18:28 (15,704)
Miller, Philip 3:33:51 (5,036)
Miller, Philip John 4:47:32 (23,417)
Miller, Richard John Stuart 5:25:18 (30,663)
Miller, Robbie J 4:24:41 (17,440)
Miller, Ross 6:48:50 (35,973)
Miller, Scott 4:08:25 (13,062)
Miller, Simon Louis 4:26:37 (17,982)
Miller, Steven John 5:02:55 (27,012)
Miller, Tim 5:54:49 (33,696)
Miller, Tom 4:17:03 (15,309)
Miller, Tristan Garnaut 3:28:33 (4,152)
Miller, William 4:09:33 (13,351)
Miller,, Alex, 3:47:10 (7,566)
Millett, Mark A 4:11:39 (13,893)
Millican, Graham James 2:57:12 (871)
Millican, Keith M 3:56:57 (10,071)
Milligan, Andy Robert 4:27:42 (18,288)
Milligan, Graham Colin 4:21:54 (16,674)
Milligan, Iain Daniel 3:28:08 (4,079)
Milligan, Simon J 5:02:12 (26,890)
Millington, Carl 4:43:47 (22,436)
Millington, James Stuart 4:05:17 (12,281)
Millington-Buck, Patrick 3:24:24 (3,498)
Millman, Dominic John 3:59:07 (10,752)
Millman, Geoffrey 6:00:55 (34,125)
Millns, David 4:51:34 (24,434)
Millns, Sam 3:52:44 (8,851)
Millns, Tom 3:22:34 (3,246)
Mills, Adam 4:39:45 (21,447)
Mills, Andy 3:50:44 (8,367)
Mills, David 4:42:20 (22,101)
Mills, David John 3:32:34 (4,822)
Mills, David Jonathan 4:21:19 (16,494)
Mills, James 5:12:13 (28,606)
Mills, James Robert 3:40:13 (6,184)
Mills, Jamie 3:50:32 (8,321)
Mills, Jerry 3:55:51 (9,733)
Mills, Jon 4:50:41 (24,203)
Mills, Luke William 4:40:21 (21,596)
Mills, Mark James 4:28:27 (18,508)
Mills, Paul I 5:19:35 (29,790)
Mills, Richard Craig 4:33:43 (19,925)
Mills, Robert A 3:09:43 (1,881)
Mills, Robin 4:14:53 (14,759)
Mills, Terry 5:38:47 (32,288)
Mills, Timothy D 4:07:44 (12,893)
Mills, Titus Neil Archie McClay 4:58:56 (26,196)
Millward, Andrew W 3:49:44 (8,157)
Millward, Jonathan M 3:40:06 (6,165)
Millwood, Nigel W 4:13:52 (14,475)
Milman, Ben 4:03:14 (11,785)
Milmoe, Michael 4:27:11 (18,143)
Milne, Alex J 2:39:26 (183)
Milne, André Paul 3:18:21 (2,810)
Milne, Ross 2:29:48 (66)
Milne, Stephen 3:39:04 (5,956)
Milne Home, Marcus 3:27:15 (3,915)
Milner, Mark Robert 3:53:24 (9,030)
Milner, Richard J 3:10:00 (1,906)
Milnes, Jonathan Nicolas 3:35:42 (5,359)
Milo, Brad William 3:59:45 (10,932)
Milone, Carmelo 3:24:58 (3,575)
Milsom, Matthew L 3:53:18 (8,997)
Milsom, Michael P 3:00:55 (1,202)
Milsom, Paul Dennis 3:21:27 (3,135)
Milstead, Rob G 3:11:19 (2,029)
Milton, Carl 4:38:18 (21,054)
Milton, John S 5:42:27 (32,633)
Mimmack, Ben 3:46:45 (7,472)
Mineta, Yutaka 4:42:11 (22,058)
Minett, Jason Keith 3:51:28 (8,533)
Minguez, Carlos 3:31:48 (4,708)
Minhas, Pardip Singh 4:57:55 (25,950)
Minichetti, Mario 3:39:00 (5,937)
Minihane, Ross William 3:28:55 (4,214)
Minister, Neil 4:57:10 (25,796)
Minnithorpe, Pip 3:32:59 (4,891)
Minshull, Paul 3:38:43 (5,890)
Minter, Craig 4:16:32 (15,177)
Minter, Daniel 4:45:34 (22,906)
Minter, Kevin P 3:11:03 (2,003)
Minton, Mike 6:17:05 (34,983)
Mir, Miguel Angel 4:06:33 (12,588)
Mirabel, Bruno 3:54:53 (9,447)
Mirams, Jeremy E 3:47:27 (7,634)
Miranda, François Noel 4:39:49 (21,465)
Miranda, Rolando 5:24:20 (30,529)
Miscera, Alessio 5:08:15 (27,939)
Misje, Roar 2:59:01 (1,054)
Misle, Christian Jorge 3:53:44 (9,132)
Missing, Jamie 5:51:37 (33,475)
Missing, Neil David 5:42:02 (32,590)
Missingham, Andrew David 3:37:01 (5,564)
Mistry, Dharmesh Vasanbhai 4:05:10 (12,245)
Mistry, Harshad 5:02:39 (26,967)
Mistry, Jayanti 4:48:24 (23,638)
Mistry, Nayan 5:14:26 (28,982)
Mistry, Shailen Surendra 5:21:54 (30,130)
Mistry, Shashi Maganlal 7:26:14 (36,450)
Mistry, Umesh C 4:55:44 (25,476)
Mistry, Vimal 4:31:11 (19,266)
Mitchard, Andrew 4:57:14 (25,810)
Mitchell, Alan 4:47:13 (23,344)
Mitchell, Andrew Charles John 3:43:58 (6,871)
Mitchell, Arthur 4:40:59 (21,767)
Mitchell, Barry Alan 4:08:26 (13,064)
Mitchell, Colin 4:12:57 (14,216)
Mitchell, Daniel 5:08:47 (28,014)
Mitchell, David 3:59:44 (10,931)
Mitchell, Euan Stuart 4:45:55 (23,005)
Mitchell, Fergus 5:09:34 (28,162)
Mitchell, Gary 3:08:25 (1,743)
Mitchell, Gary 4:08:35 (13,111)
Mitchell, Gary Eric 4:24:48 (17,468)
Mitchell, George 3:30:09 (4,439)
Mitchell, Henry Graham 3:44:33 (7,001)
Mitchell, Ian 4:23:19 (17,049)
Mitchell, Ian Edward 3:21:54 (3,182)
Mitchell, James Thomas 5:17:20 (29,445)
Mitchell, Jim 4:40:13 (21,543)
Mitchell, Justin A 2:39:02 (178)
Mitchell, Keith 3:50:50 (8,386)
Mitchell, Luke 4:29:42 (18,878)
Mitchell, Nicholas L 3:44:22 (6,955)
Mitchell, Nigel M 2:59:22 (1,092)
Mitchell, Paul 3:57:34 (10,253)
Mitchell, Paul Kenneth 4:26:10 (17,865)
Mitchell, Paul R 3:23:10 (3,315)
Mitchell, Peter 3:31:58 (4,733)
Mitchell, Peter 3:56:10 (9,832)
Mitchell, Richard 4:28:23 (18,478)
Mitchell, Robert J 3:35:10 (5,270)
Mitchell, Sam 3:12:56 (2,179)
Mitchell, Scott 3:48:29 (7,843)
Mitchell, Scott James 4:20:36 (16,297)
Mitchell, Sean 3:17:05 (2,671)
Mitchell, Stephen D 5:32:47 (31,638)
Mitchell, Steve 4:01:41 (11,407)
Mitchell, Steve Richard 4:09:12 (13,260)
Mitchell, Stuart MacNaughton R 4:28:47 (18,600)
Mitchell, Stuart Richard 4:16:03 (15,041)
Mitchell, Tom 3:40:55 (6,313)
Mitchell, Tom David 4:52:47 (24,751)
Mitchell, William 3:43:40 (6,801)
Mitchell, William F 4:33:14 (19,778)
Mitchell, William P 4:21:11 (16,459)
Mitchelson, Tim 4:37:29 (20,873)
Mitchener, Paul John 3:59:10 (10,764)
Mitcheson, Adrian 4:46:00 (23,024)
Mitchla, Zuber 3:38:12 (5,803)
Mitra, Deb 4:42:42 (22,186)
Mittermayer, Georg 4:02:53 (11,701)
Mitze, Helmut 4:42:40 (22,176)
Mizel, Henry Jay 4:19:02 (15,852)
Mizrahi, Rafael 4:33:57 (19,980)
Mizrahi Cohen, Salomon 4:07:12 (12,749)
Mo, Lab K 5:12:00 (28,565)
Moate, Simon 5:29:19 (31,194)
Mock, Justin 2:29:29 (62)
Mockler, Andrew James 4:12:54 (14,208)
Mockridge, Tim 4:07:55 (12,933)
Modaher, Jasvir S 5:56:46 (33,848)
Modha, Rajesh Narendra 5:03:16 (27,069)
Moeller, Eigil Pagter 4:55:43 (25,472)
Moeller, Volkmar 3:25:47 (3,703)
Moergeli, Roland 4:21:15 (16,477)
Moessner, Martin 3:08:24 (1,739)
Moffat, John David 3:39:18 (6,005)
Moffat, Mark 4:05:41 (12,375)
Moffat, Stephen H 2:52:31 (592)
Moffatt, Andrew 3:48:43 (7,905)
Moffatt, Andrew Jonathan 4:06:51 (12,677)
Moffatt, Ben 5:38:40 (32,281)
Moffatt, Kevin Barry 4:21:30 (16,548)
Moffo, Michael 3:50:14 (8,255)
Mogg, Sean 5:16:22 (29,289)
Moggan, Frank Martin 4:04:31 (12,076)
Moghadan, Farhod 4:06:06 (12,474)
Moghaddas-Davies, Luke 2:58:40 (1,018)
Moglia, Nick 3:22:58 (3,288)
Mogridge, Stuart, 4:08:29 (13,074)
Mohn, Carsten 4:38:45 (21,185)
Mohn, Rainer 4:41:15 (21,832)
Mohon, Michael 4:32:11 (19,483)
Mohring, David J 2:53:15 (626)
Moine, Eric 4:40:35 (21,664)
Moir, Marshall J 2:57:08 (864)
Moir, Roy M 4:31:29 (19,331)
Moisley, Dave 3:52:48 (8,870)
Mokuena, Mikail Monyane 4:03:19 (11,804)
Mole, Denis H 4:36:44 (20,665)
Mole, James 5:28:28 (31,085)
Mole, Robert A 3:12:35 (2,145)
Molefi, Amal L 3:40:35 (6,257)
Molen, James George 4:21:15 (16,477)
Molesworth, Tony 4:18:00 (15,579)
Molho, Alexis Robert Raphael 5:07:16 (27,761)
Molina, Sergio 3:38:23 (5,827)
Molley, Alan John 4:04:10 (12,002)
Mollison, John Alexander 4:44:28 (22,629)
Molloy, Anthony P 6:15:35 (34,911)
Molloy, Justin 5:22:06 (30,163)
Molloy, Matthew Thomas 2:48:21 (426)
Molloy, Philip J 4:53:30 (24,917)
Molloy, Steven 3:45:34 (7,226)
Moloney, Steve 4:19:03 (15,855)
Molony, Neil 4:06:54 (12,684)
Molyneux, Craig 4:04:55 (12,178)
Molyneux, Craig Philippe 3:56:07 (9,815)
Mompalao, Ricky Peter 5:09:58 (28,225)
Monaghan, Brendan J 3:42:44 (6,643)
Monaghan, James M 3:38:43 (5,890)
Monaghan, Paul E 4:56:24 (25,629)
Monaghan, Stephen 3:04:25 (1,421)
Monaghan, William W 4:40:56 (21,757)
Monis, Luca 3:37:33 (5,678)
Monk, Barry 5:06:04 (27,543)

Monk, Ben ...4:41:08 (21,804)
Monk, Charles Peter ...4:40:58 (21,764)
Monk, Francis Richard ...5:24:55 (30,607)
Monk, Garry Charles ...4:30:10 (19,017)
Monk, Jonathan ...4:20:29 (16,256)
Monks, Christopher ...5:07:54 (27,880)
Monks, Dan ...3:36:40 (5,508)
Monnier, Laurent ...3:05:43 (1,516)
Montague, Peter ...6:33:51 (35,620)
Montagu-Williams, Robert Peter ...3:12:58 (2,186)

Montalbano, Enrico ...4:04:22 (12,044)

Engineer and cross-country rally motorcycle pilot. In 2007, second place in his category in Rally Sardegna. Ran London 2010 in 4:04:22 despite his meniscus pain at right knee. His goal was to finish the race with his father Giovanni, 71 years old, and they won!

Montalbano, Giovanni ...4:40:43 (21,700)

Sardinian half marathon champion, at the age 71 ran London 2010 in 4:40:43. His goal was to finish the race with his son, and they won. AD MAIORA GIANNI!!!

Montan, Bengt ...6:15:24 (34,906)
Montanari, Stefano ...4:55:29 (25,407)
Montanez, Eddie ...4:14:46 (14,732)
Monteen, Jeffrey ...5:18:56 (29,692)
Monterasteli, Bruno ...5:13:23 (28,824)
Montero, Mario ...3:30:54 (4,566)
Montes, Juan Antonio ...2:56:25 (827)
Montesdeoca, Miguel ...3:59:05 (10,740)
Montgomery, Gary ...3:30:14 (4,461)
Montgomery, Gerard ...3:01:46 (1,239)
Montgomery, Ian ...3:05:04 (1,463)
Montgomery, James Matthew ...4:32:32 (19,568)
Montgomery, John William ...3:41:43 (6,460)
Montgomery, Liam ...4:22:07 (16,738)
Montgomery, Richard ...5:00:01 (26,457)
Montgomery, Robin ...4:05:36 (12,353)
Montipo, Pierluigi ...4:15:46 (14,973)
Montoya, Daniel ...3:57:03 (10,118)
Montresor, Ivano ...4:41:03 (21,781)
Moock, Bruno ...4:11:43 (13,908)
Moock, Patrick ...5:49:32 (33,288)
Moody, David ...5:50:34 (33,395)
Moody, Jack ...6:27:17 (35,391)
Moody, James ...3:51:46 (8,598)
Moody, Karl ...4:40:57 (21,759)
Moody, Mark ...3:40:53 (6,306)
Moody, Oliver ...3:17:57 (2,759)
Moody, Owen ...4:22:49 (16,944)
Moody, Peter ...4:11:59 (13,984)
Moody, Stephen ...3:44:25 (6,975)
Moody, Steve ...4:50:51 (24,254)
Moolman, Wessel ...2:41:23 (238)
Moon, Chris ...3:48:27 (7,835)
Moon, David Robert ...5:05:18 (27,422)
Moon, James K ...3:19:44 (2,940)
Moon, Paul ...4:44:39 (22,688)
Moon, Paul ...4:56:48 (25,720)
Moon, Stephen Derek ...5:35:43 (31,959)
Mooney, John ...6:23:29 (35,260)
Mooney, Mark Thomas ...4:46:14 (23,104)
Mooney, Michael J ...3:09:24 (1,844)
Mooney, Patrick ...4:58:32 (26,097)
Mooney, Peter ...2:40:28 (211)
Mooney, Rory ...2:50:30 (503)
Moorcroft, Baden L ...5:07:36 (27,832)
Moore, Andrew ...3:48:56 (7,955)
Moore, Andrew J ...3:30:51 (4,558)
Moore, Andrew J ...4:12:43 (14,161)
Moore, Andrew John ...5:13:04 (28,763)
Moore, Andrew K ...3:49:58 (8,204)
Moore, Bradley ...5:22:35 (30,237)
Moore, Brendon ...7:15:37 (36,364)
Moore, Bruce ...3:16:44 (2,649)

Moore, Chris D ...4:05:45 (12,395)
Moore, Christopher Edward ...3:34:15 (5,104)
Moore, Colin ...6:04:31 (34,350)
Moore, David ...4:17:48 (15,527)
Moore, David George ...4:39:48 (21,462)
Moore, David Lawrence ...5:08:30 (27,973)
Moore, Derek ...5:35:48 (31,969)
Moore, Dominic James ...4:23:34 (17,125)
Moore, Dominic Paul ...3:30:52 (4,560)
Moore, Fred Christopher ...3:55:16 (9,554)
Moore, Gerard P ...5:15:54 (29,212)
Moore, Glenn ...3:24:15 (3,477)
Moore, Graham S ...3:06:34 (1,575)
Moore, Ian Richard ...3:29:01 (4,230)
Moore, James David ...4:26:08 (17,852)
Moore, James Robert ...6:07:51 (34,552)
Moore, Jimmy C ...4:55:11 (25,352)
Moore, John D ...3:16:24 (2,598)
Moore, Karl D ...3:33:50 (5,031)
Moore, Mark J ...5:25:04 (30,634)
Moore, Martin Christopher ...5:06:24 (27,601)
Moore, Matt ...4:12:33 (14,115)
Moore, Matthew Robert ...3:55:10 (9,520)
Moore, Melwyn J ...3:56:26 (9,908)
Moore, Michael D ...2:41:05 (228)
Moore, Michael J ...3:28:58 (4,224)
Moore, Michael Kennedy ...3:42:56 (6,682)
Moore, Nicholas James ...4:36:51 (20,702)
Moore, Nick Charles ...4:43:27 (22,359)
Moore, Oliver P ...3:20:54 (3,070)
Moore, Paul ...5:58:09 (33,941)
Moore, Peter ...4:28:10 (18,406)
Moore, Philip ...4:10:07 (13,503)
Moore, Ralph Neale ...3:48:41 (7,896)
Moore, Richard Barrington ...4:04:09 (11,996)
Moore, Richard James ...3:43:47 (6,828)
Moore, Ricky Lee ...6:06:24 (34,470)
Moore, Roger A ...3:38:36 (5,869)
Moore, Russell ...5:26:42 (30,862)
Moore, Simon ...4:27:30 (18,236)
Moore, Simon John ...5:16:16 (29,261)
Moore, Simon Quentin ...4:05:31 (12,338)
Moore, Stephen Thomas ...4:19:15 (15,913)
Moore, Thomas L ...3:21:39 (3,155)
Moore, Trevor A ...3:17:29 (2,708)
Moore, Will ...4:13:57 (14,492)
Moores, Garry ...4:19:06 (15,872)
Moores, Richard ...3:40:06 (6,165)
Moorey, Guy Robert ...4:49:32 (23,920)
Moorhead, Robert Moorhead ...4:30:34 (19,113)
Moorhouse, Alex James ...4:22:52 (16,954)
Moorhouse, John ...3:42:08 (6,535)
Moorhouse, Simon ...3:41:16 (6,383)
Moors, Anthony ...4:52:30 (24,685)
Moos, Yvan ...2:57:34 (910)
Morais, Jeremy ...6:48:33 (35,967)
Moralee, Alastair ...4:01:47 (11,443)
Morales, Alexandre José Francisco ...3:15:26 (2,491)
Morales, Stephen Paul ...3:22:22 (3,224)
Moran, Andy David ...3:49:15 (8,036)
Moran, Beano ...3:56:19 (9,877)
Moran, Carl ...3:17:36 (2,725)
Moran, Ciaran ...3:53:41 (9,117)
Moran, David ...3:27:48 (4,013)
Moran, David ...3:48:52 (7,944)
Moran, Gary J ...3:17:11 (2,681)
Moran, John ...5:30:56 (31,406)
Moran, Michael K ...4:13:05 (14,261)
Moran, Paschal P ...3:39:20 (6,015)
Morant, Nicholas ...4:11:36 (13,883)
Morcella, Richard ...4:32:58 (19,687)
Morcom, Christopher Craig ...4:28:05 (18,383)
Morcom, Jonathan ...4:23:57 (17,225)
Morden, Paul Michael ...3:58:17 (10,484)
Morden, Simon John ...3:57:37 (10,268)
Mordue, Alan J ...4:14:54 (14,763)
Moreau, Ben ...2:16:46 (11)
Moreau, Christian ...3:35:51 (5,385)
Moreau, Frederic ...3:49:45 (8,160)
Moreau, Richard ...4:49:53 (24,026)
Morel, Pierre ...4:38:07 (21,011)
Morewood, Nigel C ...3:57:56 (10,362)
Morfey, Michael J ...7:21:54 (36,418)

Morgado, Jamie ...5:10:27 (28,319)
Morgan, Andrew ...6:32:38 (35,586)
Morgan, Andrew Dean ...5:57:17 (33,888)
Morgan, Andrew E ...5:53:26 (33,607)
Morgan, Andy ...3:53:59 (9,205)
Morgan, Ben ...3:58:33 (10,574)
Morgan, Casey Paul ...2:52:51 (613)
Morgan, Charles John ...3:14:47 (2,417)
Morgan, Colin ...5:31:26 (31,468)
Morgan, Craig Anthony ...4:09:09 (13,240)
Morgan, Dan ...5:12:46 (28,694)
Morgan, David ...4:52:22 (24,652)
Morgan, David Andrew ...3:58:45 (10,644)
Morgan, Gareth David ...3:38:27 (5,837)
Morgan, Gary ...4:55:46 (25,485)
Morgan, Graham John ...5:41:52 (32,573)
Morgan, Ian ...4:03:08 (11,765)
Morgan, Ian Michael ...5:38:28 (32,260)
Morgan, Ian Robert ...4:09:15 (13,272)
Morgan, Jack Lawrence ...4:46:46 (23,242)
Morgan, James ...4:36:03 (20,490)
Morgan, James Alexander ...3:57:19 (10,186)
Morgan, James Stuart ...3:58:24 (10,523)
Morgan, Jamie ...3:44:36 (7,014)
Morgan, John ...4:13:15 (14,297)
Morgan, John M ...3:31:18 (4,626)
Morgan, Jon P ...2:59:31 (1,113)
Morgan, Keith D ...4:49:30 (23,909)
Morgan, Luke Alexander ...4:10:56 (13,695)
Morgan, Michael ...5:24:08 (30,501)
Morgan, Michael Gary ...3:31:36 (4,683)
Morgan, Nick ...3:54:47 (9,416)
Morgan, Nick B ...4:56:33 (25,661)
Morgan, Nigel Julian ...3:38:37 (5,874)
Morgan, Paul James ...5:31:16 (31,445)
Morgan, Peter John ...4:28:57 (18,666)
Morgan, Ray Evan ...3:30:00 (4,417)
Morgan, Richard ...3:46:07 (7,342)
Morgan, Robert A ...4:44:31 (22,645)
Morgan, Simon D ...3:29:05 (4,244)
Morgan, Stacey J ...2:43:09 (284)
Morgan, Steven ...3:46:42 (7,460)
Morgan, Steven ...5:00:26 (26,543)
Morgan, Tony ...4:32:37 (19,585)
Morgan, Tony ...5:16:19 (29,277)
Morgan, Wyn ...4:51:15 (24,366)
Morge, Stefano Gino ...4:01:49 (11,450)
Mori, Noriaki ...3:45:45 (7,259)
Moriarty, André ...4:39:58 (21,496)
Moriarty, Francis ...3:31:29 (4,664)
Moriarty, Jason ...4:02:12 (11,540)
Moriarty, Jason G ...4:19:32 (15,978)
Morita, Kenichi ...4:04:36 (12,101)
Moritz, David Adam ...3:32:58 (4,886)
Morland, Richard J ...5:50:04 (33,342)
Morley, Colin John ...4:04:41 (12,122)
Morley, Daren ...3:51:05 (8,445)
Morley, Dean ...3:06:43 (1,587)
Morley, John ...5:22:48 (30,272)
Morley, Jonathan ...4:32:08 (19,468)
Morley, Simon ...4:08:58 (13,201)
Morley, Wayne ...3:49:28 (8,080)
Morling, Russell ...3:51:51 (8,622)
Moro, Jean ...3:16:39 (2,634)
Moroney, Alan ...3:54:41 (9,381)
Moroukian, Stephen ...6:21:06 (35,166)
Morphew, Joe Mervyn ...5:42:19 (32,619)
Morrall, Alexander ...3:06:34 (1,575)
Morrall, Scott Paul ...4:08:25 (13,062)
Morrell, Nick ...3:59:37 (10,896)
Morrin, Cyril John ...5:31:14 (31,436)
Morris, Aaron ...4:22:21 (16,804)
Morris, Alan ...3:35:37 (5,346)
Morris, Alan ...3:53:24 (9,030)
Morris, Alan J ...3:51:51 (8,622)
Morris, Andrew ...4:02:45 (11,665)
Morris, Andrew Alistair ...6:39:32 (35,772)
Morris, Andrew R ...3:03:31 (1,348)
Morris, Andrew Roy ...5:34:57 (31,873)
Morris, Ashley John ...3:35:17 (5,286)
Morris, Ben ...4:51:12 (24,351)
Morris, Ben John ...4:04:06 (11,985)
Morris, Carl ...4:30:50 (19,176)

Morris, Casper 4:14:16 (14,586)
Morris, Chris J 4:21:12 (16,463)
Morris, Clive Russell 4:26:43 (18,003)
Morris, Colin John 5:43:12 (32,690)
Morris, Darren Edward 4:04:24 (12,050)
Morris, David 6:15:54 (34,922)
Morris, David Colin 4:58:49 (26,169)
Morris, David Edward 4:25:41 (17,712)
Morris, David Paul 4:01:43 (11,415)
Morris, David Thomas Edward 3:37:36 (5,690)
Morris, David W 5:29:47 (31,266)
Morris, Derek 3:42:01 (6,511)
Morris, Gareth Clifford 6:13:48 (34,830)
Morris, Garry 4:32:11 (19,483)
Morris, Geoff 4:56:41 (25,689)
Morris, George 5:30:27 (31,345)
Morris, Glyn Evan 3:30:28 (4,495)
Morris, Greg 3:22:12 (3,209)
Morris, Gregory 4:28:53 (18,636)
Morris, Gregory 6:43:46 (35,879)
Morris, Ian Harry 4:58:29 (26,082)
Morris, James David 4:30:24 (19,064)
Morris, James S 2:55:40 (781)
Morris, Jason John 3:13:32 (2,259)
Morris, Jim 4:43:49 (22,450)
Morris, John D 3:18:50 (2,857)
Morris, Kevin 4:38:27 (21,105)
Morris, Martin Andrew 4:17:37 (15,473)
Morris, Matt 4:47:29 (23,406)
Morris, Matthew John 4:45:25 (22,865)
Morris, Nathan 3:39:00 (5,937)
Morris, Nicholas 4:11:53 (13,950)
Morris, Nigel 4:13:40 (14,422)
Morris, Paul Simon 5:41:51 (32,572)
Morris, Paul W 3:39:58 (6,137)
Morris, Peter 4:38:40 (21,158)
Morris, Philip Graham 3:50:28 (8,305)
Morris, Richard Graham 3:33:42 (5,006)
Morris, Simeon J 3:29:54 (4,400)
Morris, Stephen 5:06:46 (27,684)
Morris, Stephen Geoffrey 3:51:37 (8,571)
Morris, Warwick David 4:21:08 (16,447)
Morris, Will Ivor 4:36:15 (20,536)
Morris, William J 4:12:44 (14,165)
Morrisby, Andrew 4:34:18 (20,070)
Morrish, Stuart Raymond 3:47:14 (7,583)
Morrison, Chris 3:39:03 (5,950)
Morrison, Christopher F 3:03:15 (1,338)
Morrison, David 3:41:24 (6,405)
Morrison, David 3:50:12 (8,247)
Morrison, Graeme 4:52:48 (24,756)
Morrison, Ian Stuart 3:30:00 (4,417)
Morrison, James M 4:12:18 (14,056)
Morrison, John Andrew 4:56:58 (25,761)
Morrison, John E 5:09:41 (28,176)
Morrison, Kevin 3:25:19 (3,618)
Morrison, Nick 4:06:13 (12,502)
Morrison, Richard 4:25:34 (17,681)
Morrison, Sidney 3:59:28 (10,857)
Morrison, Stuart Charles 4:23:14 (17,030)
Morrissey, John Patrick 4:03:45 (11,906)
Morritt, Chris John 4:59:29 (26,333)
Morritt, Stephen Peter 5:27:21 (30,952)
Morrod, Robin Daniel 3:53:31 (9,061)
Morrow, James 4:14:39 (14,700)
Morrow, Nicholas E 2:51:16 (533)
Morsley, John Henry Christian 3:10:33 (1,951)
Mort, Stephen 3:39:46 (6,092)
Mortimer, Alexander J 3:27:51 (4,025)
Mortimer, Ian Arthur 5:04:57 (27,355)
Mortimer, Josh 3:53:30 (9,054)
Mortimer, Thomas 3:58:52 (10,674)
Morton, Brian Gordon 5:16:09 (29,246)
Morton, Colin J 4:16:36 (15,192)
Morton, Gary Edward 3:42:04 (6,524)
Morton, Geraint 4:14:13 (14,573)
Morton, Iain A 3:58:28 (10,544)
Morton, Neil 3:03:43 (1,364)
Morton, Peter 3:55:36 (9,636)
Morton, Steven J 2:43:11 (285)
Moruzzi, Enrico 4:34:02 (20,000)
Mosaid, Samir 5:12:27 (28,643)
Mosaid, Sarwat Louis 4:55:22 (25,396)

Mosca, Alan 5:25:25 (30,682)
Moseley, Stuart John 4:14:30 (14,647)
Moses, Neil David 4:56:59 (25,765)
Mosley, Paul G 5:05:58 (27,524)
Mosley, Scipio Louis 4:28:09 (18,397)
Mosney, Ryan 5:16:25 (29,295)
Moss, Benjamin Robert 3:54:19 (9,282)
Moss, Dave 5:35:45 (31,961)
Moss, David Thomas 6:32:38 (35,586)
Moss, Dominic 4:49:59 (24,047)
Moss, Gerrard A 3:23:10 (3,315)
Moss, Ian 6:49:58 (35,996)
Moss, Jonathan 4:43:13 (22,303)
Moss, Mark V 4:13:49 (14,460)
Moss, Matt Nicolas 4:58:45 (26,155)
Moss, Moddy Joshua 4:26:08 (17,852)
Moss, Nicholas David 3:49:14 (8,033)
Moss, Nick 3:46:24 (7,397)
Moss, Paul 5:48:16 (33,171)
Moss, Stephen 3:44:58 (7,089)
Moss, Tim 4:16:16 (15,092)
Mosvold, Kurt 4:25:54 (17,786)
Mote, Alexander 3:51:13 (8,474)
Mothersole, Jason 4:24:57 (17,504)
Mott, Anthony John 4:08:47 (13,156)
Mottershead, Marcus 4:42:36 (22,153)
Mottley, Kevin 5:50:45 (33,410)
Mottola, Francesco 3:24:09 (3,460)
Mottram, Ed 4:19:43 (16,019)
Mottram-Playfoot, Joseph 3:50:15 (8,259)
Mould, Alan T 3:11:15 (2,022)
Mould, Andrew Robert 4:38:51 (21,218)
Moule, John 4:45:18 (22,841)
Moule, Jonathan Dominic 4:03:19 (11,804)
Moule, Peter E 4:01:07 (11,280)
Moule, Steven 3:48:23 (7,820)
Moulin, Cyril 4:13:45 (14,448)
Moulin, Etienne 4:15:44 (14,962)
Moulson, Stuart C 3:43:49 (6,835)
Moulton, Alan 4:56:30 (25,646)
Mountain, James 4:50:04 (24,064)
Mountford, Chris G 4:36:35 (20,625)
Mountford, Paul J 2:37:08 (145)
Mountford, Paul John 4:09:31 (13,346)
Mountford, Simon 4:10:55 (13,693)
Mouton, Philippe 4:22:14 (16,776)
Moutoussamy, Florent 3:43:46 (6,821)
Moutrie, Ben 3:19:30 (2,916)
Mouzer, Robert 3:22:47 (3,268)
Mowatt, Andrew Kevin 4:53:00 (24,792)
Mowbray, Henry Bawden 4:50:00 (24,049)
Mower, Jeremy H 2:56:47 (845)
Mowl, Tom 4:50:34 (24,179)
Mowle, Chris B 2:50:11 (491)
Mowle, Malcolm K 3:51:26 (8,524)
Mowlem, Johnny 4:05:42 (12,378)
Moxey, Paul 4:47:34 (23,429)
Moxham, David 3:10:52 (1,980)
Moxon, Howard 3:49:32 (8,100)
Moy, Greg Neal 4:20:24 (16,232)
Moyce, Andrew James 4:14:45 (14,726)
Moyle, Fraser 4:06:41 (12,621)
Moynihan, Carl 5:19:56 (29,841)
Moyse, Gary Peter 3:52:10 (8,699)
Mozaffar, Hasnain 4:34:40 (20,165)
Mpotos, Spyrino 4:25:28 (17,650)
Muboro, Edward 3:48:50 (7,937)
Mucerino, Giuseppe 2:30:17 (73)
Mucke, Kim Takata 3:46:45 (7,472)
Muehlbach, Michael 3:45:41 (7,244)
Mueller, Martin 4:42:20 (22,101)
Muers, Martin 4:00:25 (11,094)
Mugenyi, Mirembe 5:23:26 (30,377)
Muggleton, Graham 4:08:40 (13,131)

Muggleton, Matthew James 3:47:39 (7,677)
Muil, Denton Leigh 3:51:30 (8,539)
Muir, Andy 4:14:13 (14,573)
Muir, Chris 4:48:42 (23,719)
Muir, David 6:02:31 (34,218)
Muir, Graeme Robert 4:26:52 (18,046)
Mukerjea, Sunil 5:35:36 (31,936)
Mukhtar, Bash M 3:43:33 (6,786)
Mulato, Bernard 4:41:06 (21,798)
Muldoon, Paul Thomas 4:22:12 (16,761)
Mules, Alistair 4:09:56 (13,453)
Mules, Daniel A 3:56:31 (9,938)
Mulgrew, Gerry Ciaran 5:10:09 (28,264)
Mulholland, Harry 3:25:09 (3,600)
Mulholland, Keith Raymond 3:51:02 (8,432)
Mulholland, Kevin Robert 4:42:14 (22,075)
Mulholland, Michael Joseph 6:00:24 (34,086)
Mulholland, Mike Gerard 4:06:35 (12,596)
Mullally, Paul A 4:02:55 (11,710)
Mullan, Anthony J 4:09:53 (13,437)
Mullan, Anthony William 4:46:57 (23,295)
Mullan, Nicholas 3:38:17 (5,816)
Mullan, Thomas 4:35:47 (20,417)
Mullane, Robert 3:27:49 (4,019)
Mullaney, David John 4:21:05 (16,435)
Mullaney, Mark Christopher 4:00:56 (11,231)
Mullard-Wilson, Gareth 6:07:14 (34,521)
Mullarky, James Jospeh 4:41:22 (21,858)
Mullboccus, Reshad 4:07:25 (12,804)
Mullen, Michael 4:00:51 (11,204)
Mullen, Paul A 3:48:17 (7,800)
Mullens, Brian 4:52:58 (24,788)
Mullens, Daniel 6:20:09 (35,132)
Muller, Daniel 4:00:47 (11,192)
Müller, Thomas 3:24:48 (3,550)
Mulligan, John 6:36:15 (35,682)
Mulligan, Marius G 3:53:33 (9,073)
Mullin, Henry 3:57:40 (10,286)
Mullin, Ian 3:45:01 (7,098)
Mullins, Daniel John Edward 4:44:15 (22,577)
Mullins, Kelly 5:21:47 (30,114)
Mullins, Shaun 4:14:49 (14,745)
Mulliss, Adam 4:43:57 (22,492)
Mullord, Nick 4:10:24 (13,568)
Mulqueen, Danny Robert 5:43:30 (32,721)
Mulroy, Luke 5:38:32 (32,266)
Mulry, Ian 4:20:33 (16,275)
Mulvihill, Liam 4:52:26 (24,667)
Mumford, Laurence 3:07:35 (1,665)
Munasinghe, Indumina CAK 5:12:57 (28,730)
Munce, Shaun David 4:31:43 (19,377)
Mundal, Rolf Tore 4:15:12 (14,834)
Munday, Christopher 4:49:22 (23,886)
Munday, Richard Paul 3:50:47 (8,378)
Munday, Simon J 4:17:37 (15,473)
Mundy, Alan Charles 4:26:17 (17,898)
Mundy, Kevin 4:18:26 (15,694)
Mundy, Kevin 4:30:18 (19,044)
Mundy, Neal Timothy 4:35:24 (20,325)
Mundy, Robert 5:03:22 (27,083)
Munford, Adam Jon 4:22:42 (16,905)
Munford, Andy 4:22:18 (16,795)
Munn, Michael 3:45:11 (7,135)
Munn, Richard G 2:43:28 (295)
Munoz, Jay 3:58:06 (10,414)
Muñoz, Jorge 3:45:22 (7,175)
Munoz Moreno, Ivet R 3:59:27 (10,853)
Munoz-Sabater, Joaquin 4:07:07 (12,735)
Munro, Alexander E 3:24:16 (3,480)
Munro, David James 4:19:55 (16,079)
Munro, Iain Stuart 4:18:58 (15,843)
Munro, Jonathan C 4:08:29 (13,074)
Munro, Lee Taylor 5:10:18 (28,288)
Munro, Neil Angus 4:52:19 (24,643)
Munro, Patrick 3:08:48 (1,794)
Munro, Sandy 4:43:35 (22,391)
Munroe, Andy 3:43:25 (6,764)
Munyard, Paul Matthew 4:15:20 (14,872)
Murat, Erkin Bilgin 6:31:09 (35,542)
Murchison, Andrew 3:48:13 (7,784)
Murden, Stephen David 7:03:29 (36,231)
Murdoch, Graeme Paul 2:47:22 (398)
Murdoch, Keith M 4:07:14 (12,759)

Murdoch, Michael 3:16:17 (2,584)
Murdock, Alan 3:56:26 (9,908)
Murfitt, Darren N 3:33:19 (4,936)
Murfitt, Neil Stuart 3:59:45 (10,932)
Muric, Goran 2:53:18 (630)
Muriset, Jean-Pierre 4:42:16 (22,084)
Murison, Andrew 4:25:43 (17,725)
Murnane, Darragh 3:26:14 (3,775)
Murnin, Brian 3:36:29 (5,478)
Murphy, Andy 4:59:31 (26,345)
Murphy, Barry M 3:50:30 (8,311)
Murphy, Ben D 3:42:36 (6,609)
Murphy, Bernard 2:45:06 (346)
Murphy, Chris 3:42:09 (6,540)
Murphy, Chris 3:53:05 (8,944)
Murphy, Chris Mark 4:18:39 (15,758)
Murphy, Christopher Edward 7:38:05 (36,508)
Murphy, Daniel Patrick 4:07:24 (12,801)
Murphy, David 5:27:07 (30,929)
Murphy, Derek 3:31:35 (4,679)
Murphy, Gerry 3:42:47 (6,654)
Murphy, Glen 3:56:36 (9,958)
Murphy, Gordon Brian 3:49:40 (8,139)
Murphy, Graham William 3:51:40 (8,581)
Murphy, James 5:13:35 (28,853)
Murphy, Jason 4:53:52 (25,009)
Murphy, John 4:23:43 (17,164)
Murphy, John P 2:59:20 (1,087)
Murphy, Kieran C 3:03:07 (1,332)
Murphy, Lee K 2:59:34 (1,119)
Murphy, Mark 4:02:44 (11,662)
Murphy, Nick James 4:41:58 (22,005)
Murphy, Paul 4:32:44 (19,617)
Murphy, Paul James 4:48:20 (23,616)
Murphy, Paul Stephen 3:55:49 (9,725)
Murphy, Paul Timothy 5:26:50 (30,876)
Murphy, Peter John 3:37:03 (5,574)
Murphy, Peter Kevin 4:20:04 (16,126)
Murphy, Phil 3:46:55 (7,515)
Murphy, Richard 4:09:35 (13,365)
Murphy, Richard P 4:03:55 (11,946)
Murphy, Sam 3:54:55 (9,455)
Murphy, Seamus 3:16:21 (2,592)
Murphy, Sean 5:04:29 (27,273)
Murphy, Sean A 3:07:06 (1,618)
Murphy, Sean Aron 3:31:11 (4,608)
Murphy, Stephen J 5:32:59 (31,661)
Murphy, Stuart J 5:19:43 (29,810)
Murphy, Tom 4:01:52 (11,462)
Murphy, Vince 4:38:39 (21,154)
Murphy-Sullivan, Stephen 4:29:53 (18,943)
Murray, Andrew Charles 3:25:42 (3,684)
Murray, Carl 5:27:17 (30,940)
Murray, Craig James 5:06:30 (27,626)
Murray, Craig Robert 3:37:28 (5,652)
Murray, David 4:13:40 (14,422)
Murray, Francis 4:44:57 (22,755)
Murray, Graeme 4:58:21 (26,054)
Murray, Iain 3:40:01 (6,153)
Murray, Joe 4:15:52 (14,994)
Murray, Ken 3:32:30 (4,815)
Murray, Kevin James 4:17:03 (15,309)
Murray, Lee 5:14:35 (29,000)
Murray, Martin 5:36:36 (32,066)
Murray, Neil 3:26:28 (3,800)
Murray, Owen 4:41:10 (21,815)
Murray, Paul Michael 5:21:28 (30,072)
Murray, Peter W 4:33:05 (19,723)
Murray, Scott 4:15:26 (14,893)
Murray, Sean 4:48:34 (23,686)
Murray, Steven J 4:44:56 (22,751)
Murray, Thomas 4:18:45 (15,786)
Murray, William L 4:43:53 (22,475)
Murray Willis, George 3:56:41 (9,992)
Murray-Wells, Jamie Nicholas 5:13:04 (28,763)
Murrell, Andrew David 4:49:48 (24,007)
Murrell, Richard 5:25:51 (30,760)
Murrells, George 4:08:23 (13,054)
Murrells, James Richard 6:05:04 (34,386)
Murrill, Thomas William 4:07:46 (12,900)
Murrin, James A 5:46:14 (32,973)
Murrin, Thomas William 5:53:40 (33,621)
Mursell, Dean John 3:12:26 (2,129)
Mursell, John W 4:06:49 (12,660)
Murtagh, Stephen J 2:47:54 (416)
Murthwaite, Rob 4:58:14 (26,019)
Murton, Ian 5:09:33 (28,158)
Mus, Alfredo 3:06:18 (1,553)
Musa, Gbadebo Olawole 5:19:13 (29,739)
Muscatt, Jack Louis 4:13:17 (14,310)
Muscott, Lee J 3:42:19 (6,566)
Musil, Franz 4:43:51 (22,464)
Mussali, Sony 5:07:01 (27,727)
Musselle, Shirl Lyall Baron Gaye 4:11:46 (13,928)
Musson, Adrian H 4:18:12 (15,629)
Mustaniemi, Risto 3:46:15 (7,367)
Muster, René 4:26:12 (17,874)
Mutai, Emmanuel 2:06:23 (2)
Mutch, Graeme Peter 3:22:47 (3,268)
Muthy, Kayshan 5:03:21 (27,080)
Mutlow, Daniel 4:04:34 (12,087)
Muttett, David Colin 4:55:11 (25,352)
Mutton, Andrew Martin 3:12:43 (2,157)
Muzammal, Farooq 7:08:25 (36,296)
Myatt, Jason 5:12:43 (28,688)
Myers, Charles V 2:58:02 (961)
Myers, David 4:16:08 (15,058)
Myers, Lee 5:20:59 (30,002)
Myers, Liam 5:21:00 (30,006)
Myerscough, Stephen V 2:58:16 (984)
Myhill, Ayran Donald 5:21:32 (30,077)
Myhrberg, Martin 4:15:08 (14,816)
Mynard, Steve 4:26:26 (17,934)
Myres, Peter 4:40:22 (21,601)
Mytton, Neil M 2:36:25 (135)
Nacke, Axel 4:05:36 (12,353)
Nadel, Ben 4:11:35 (13,875)
Nadelman, Craig Jeffrey 4:43:50 (22,456)
Naden, Mike 5:23:32 (30,390)
Naeye, Michel 4:55:49 (25,492)
Nagar, Nico 6:00:50 (34,118)
Nagel, Philipp G 9:12:21 (36,621)
Naim, Alexandre 4:49:09 (23,840)
Naimo, Mark Hugh 5:06:34 (27,639)
Nairn, Andy 5:52:48 (33,568)
Nairn, Nicholas 5:39:50 (32,372)
Naisbett, Anthony 4:13:04 (14,257)
Nakamura, Kazutoshi 7:10:37 (36,316)
Nally, Darren Martin 4:56:50 (25,728)
Nambot, Thierry 4:47:52 (23,514)
Nangpal, Ankur 4:11:57 (13,977)
Nangreave, Nigel 5:40:24 (32,421)
Nanji, Mehoboob N 4:33:23 (19,820)
Nanton, Carl D 3:20:55 (3,074)
Napkins, Nicky C 4:36:05 (20,500)
Napolitano, Vincenzo 4:04:57 (12,191)
Napper, Luke Jack 3:50:37 (8,338)
Naqvi, Kamal 4:25:32 (17,672)
Nar, Parvinder 5:53:22 (33,602)
Nardone, John 5:14:17 (28,961)
Narenthiran, Arul 5:17:24 (29,460)
Narvaez, Felix 3:39:32 (6,050)
Narvaez, Manuel 3:39:32 (6,050)
Nash, Alan John John 6:21:47 (35,190)
Nash, Darryl G 3:49:15 (8,036)
Nash, David 3:50:27 (8,297)
Nash, David Charles 6:33:54 (35,622)
Nash, Graham Thomas 3:47:00 (7,524)
Nash, James 5:08:35 (27,985)
Nash, Lee 4:18:13 (15,636)
Nash, Paul 5:14:32 (28,992)
Nash, Paul Antony 4:52:37 (24,710)
Nash, Philip 5:04:27 (27,266)
Nash, Ralph A 5:03:06 (27,038)
Nash, Stephen 4:12:28 (14,089)
Nash, Steve 5:38:16 (32,234)
Natali, Paul 3:39:59 (6,139)
Nathan, Clive 3:39:47 (6,099)
Nathwani, Hitesh 3:58:52 (10,674)
Nativ, Dror 6:46:57 (35,947)
Natoli, Stephen M 4:03:51 (11,936)
Naude, Ignatius 4:19:29 (15,966)
Naudi, Matt 3:18:38 (2,834)
Naughton, Aidan A 3:55:54 (9,753)
Naughton, Andrew Patrick 4:38:32 (21,124)
Naughton, Peter 4:23:06 (17,003)
Navarrete, Blas 2:54:41 (715)
Navas, Anthony 3:32:13 (4,775)
Näveri, Petteri 4:27:02 (18,087)
Navrady, Jeremy 3:41:26 (6,413)
Nawaz, Mohammed 4:12:55 (14,210)
Nayler, Darren 5:37:57 (32,207)
Naylor, Anthony Joseph 4:23:10 (17,018)
Naylor, Graham M 3:43:25 (6,764)
Naylor, Howard Kent 4:21:01 (16,420)
Naylor, Scott Anthony 4:24:25 (17,366)
Nazar, Rizwan 5:40:04 (32,397)
Neads, Kevin M 3:12:33 (2,139)
Neal, Martin J 3:52:16 (8,729)
Neal, Martin Jeffrey 7:36:13 (36,494)
Neal, Peter 3:27:29 (3,958)
Neal, Samuel Robert 5:43:46 (32,751)
Neal, Trevor J 6:21:16 (35,174)
Neale, Mark 4:27:18 (18,181)
Neale, Michael Peter 4:17:39 (15,483)
Neale, Philip Stewart 4:26:21 (17,916)
Neale, Rob John 4:14:24 (14,613)
Neale, Thomas W 4:38:52 (21,223)
Neary, Stephen A 4:37:24 (20,845)
Neath, Kevin 3:02:33 (1,304)
Neaves, Antony B 4:27:25 (18,210)
Nedev, Boris 4:16:55 (15,275)
Nedham, Mike 4:25:49 (17,760)
Needham, Ben 3:39:03 (5,950)
Needham, David W 3:40:07 (6,171)
Needham, Peter J 4:07:07 (12,735)
Needham, Phillip Mark 4:52:27 (24,669)
Needham, Russell J 4:35:44 (20,397)
Neely, Bill R 3:23:48 (3,407)
Neenan, Carl 5:12:27 (28,643)
Negri, Carlo Damiano Gordon 4:47:33 (23,425)
Negri, Giovanni Battista 3:23:23 (3,349)
Negus, Richard James 4:46:30 (23,168)
Neighbour, Chris 4:08:01 (12,966)
Neighbour, Matthew Ronald 4:30:24 (19,064)
Neighbour, William J 4:37:42 (20,924)
Neil, Colin 5:30:02 (31,303)
Neil, Glen Russell 5:22:41 (30,253)
Neil, James Robert Edward 3:29:11 (4,266)
Neil, Martin Loudon 3:44:20 (6,950)
Neill, Peter 4:47:59 (23,542)
Neilson-Welch, Allan 3:38:07 (5,785)
Neish, Shaun 3:47:22 (7,612)
Nel, Gert Cornelius 5:42:54 (32,662)
Nelmes, Danny M 4:10:11 (13,524)
Nelmes, Paul Anthony 4:18:58 (15,843)
Nelson, Anthony Geoffrey 4:12:36 (14,127)
Nelson, Darren 3:49:52 (8,180)
Nelson, David 4:04:14 (12,016)
Nelson, John E 2:56:01 (800)
Nelson, Jonathan 5:19:46 (29,815)
Nelson, Jonathan James 4:54:30 (25,179)
Nelson, Kevin Paul 4:08:46 (13,153)
Nelson, Paul A 4:34:58 (20,226)
Nelson, Richard 3:18:04 (2,775)
Nelson, Rick 5:07:50 (27,866)
Nelthorpe-Cowne, Mark 4:26:05 (17,837)
Nencioni, Andrea 3:01:13 (1,214)
Nenjerama, Paul 5:40:49 (32,457)
Neocleous, Christopher 5:37:20 (32,149)
Neokleous, Alexis 3:59:52 (10,956)
Nery, Simon 3:57:51 (10,345)
Nesbit, Trevor 5:49:43 (33,311)
Nesom, Andrew 3:12:22 (2,119)
Nesom, Damian M 4:44:34 (22,658)
Nessi, Marco 3:01:05 (1,210)
Nethercott, Gary 5:11:59 (28,558)
Neugebauer, Gerald Patrick 3:09:32 (1,862)
Neuitt, Sean M 5:24:11 (30,508)
Neumann, Lee 3:24:10 (3,465)
Nevard, Stephen Paul 3:58:00 (10,376)
Neve, Simon Philip 4:26:29 (17,945)
Nevett, Keith 4:10:34 (13,610)
Neveu, Christophe 3:11:41 (2,068)
Neviera, Giuseppe 4:42:27 (22,128)
Neville, Marc 4:57:12 (25,804)
Neville, Michael J 3:09:21 (1,840)
Neville, Peter 4:58:56 (26,196)
Nevin, Brett 4:54:17 (25,126)

Nevin, Philip Michael 5:13:03 (28,747)
Nevola, Venturino R 3:45:59 (7,306)
Newbery, Mark 6:07:33 (34,534)
Newbold, Darren Paul 4:37:14 (20,803)
Newbury, Stephen 4:54:12 (25,100)
Newby, Dave 4:40:30 (21,640)
Newby, Gavin 3:37:29 (5,658)
Newcombe, Christopher 3:09:56 (1,902)
Newcombe, Scott 4:22:35 (16,868)
Newell, Alan 5:29:58 (31,289)
Newell, Dave 4:13:06 (14,263)
Newell, Keith 4:46:30 (23,168)
Newell, Kevin P 3:58:26 (10,537)
Newell, Mark S 4:26:58 (18,069)
Newell, Michael 4:01:47 (11,443)
Newell, Paul Simon 4:01:34 (11,385)
Newell, Sam 3:36:04 (5,421)
Newfield, Steven 4:46:20 (23,133)
Newland, David J 4:09:09 (13,240)
Newland, John Henry 5:53:26 (33,607)
Newlands, Gordon 3:34:39 (5,183)
Newman, Bob 5:00:26 (26,543)
Newman, Craig 5:23:42 (30,426)
Newman, David Alec 3:34:21 (5,129)
Newman, David John 4:55:56 (25,520)
Newman, Gavin John 4:21:57 (16,688)
Newman, Graeme Robin 4:05:11 (12,251)
Newman, Ian 5:25:03 (30,633)
Newman, Jamie Jonathan 4:06:34 (12,591)
Newman, Leigh 3:28:24 (4,126)
Newman, Maurice Thomas 3:58:51 (10,670)
Newman, Neville 4:42:33 (22,148)
Newman, Nick 4:26:01 (17,817)
Newman, Nick John 4:35:40 (20,380)
Newman, Paul Martin 3:39:51 (6,114)
Newman, Robert Colin 4:07:56 (12,940)
Newman, Scott Anothony 4:03:11 (11,773)
Newman, Sean 4:13:57 (14,492)
Newman, Simon T 4:14:34 (14,674)
Newman, Toby 3:25:24 (3,631)
Newman, Tom Alexander 4:34:04 (20,013)
Newman-Burke, Alexander 3:52:47 (8,863)
Newnes, William Toby 4:43:52 (22,469)
Newnham, Andrew 3:33:47 (5,020)
Newport, Jim 4:44:42 (22,698)
Newport, Stephen C 3:23:53 (3,416)
Newsome, Alun Wyn 6:17:41 (35,015)
Newsome, John Michael 5:05:08 (27,394)
Newstead, David 6:33:02 (35,597)
Newton, Gavin James 3:29:01 (4,230)
Newton, Harry J 4:10:21 (13,556)
Newton, Jeremy 3:55:45 (9,699)
Newton, Joseph Thomas 4:14:09 (14,547)
Newton, Mark 4:27:50 (18,319)
Newton, Mark 4:32:51 (19,654)
Newton, Matthew James 4:38:31 (21,118)
Newton, Matthew Ross 5:51:59 (33,503)
Newton, Paul M 3:16:17 (2,584)
Newton, Steve 3:54:37 (9,359)
Newton, Timothy Ross 4:24:18 (17,319)
Newton, Westley John 4:02:32 (11,613)
Newton, Will 4:02:15 (11,547)
Newton Lee, Andrew 3:55:02 (9,485)
Newton Sawyerr, Nigel 4:39:01 (21,263)
Neyens, Jules 4:43:21 (22,333)
Neylon, Kevin Patrick 3:42:00 (6,506)
Neys, Kristof 3:01:50 (1,246)
Ngan, Siong-Kin 4:46:45 (23,237)
Nganga, Desmond 5:35:42 (31,956)
Nguyen, Tuan 4:21:07 (16,443)
Niccolai, Filippo 4:22:20 (16,800)
Nice, Jamie 5:04:38 (27,305)
Nice, Matthew A 3:53:12 (8,971)
Nichol, Scott 4:15:29 (14,902)
Nicholas, Christopher J 3:40:26 (6,221)
Nicholas, David 4:48:17 (23,605)
Nicholas, Mark John 4:13:10 (14,278)
Nicholas, Peter 4:55:45 (25,480)
Nicholas, Stephen R 4:33:46 (19,937)
Nicholl, Ali 5:56:28 (33,827)
Nicholl, Chris 2:46:10 (364)
Nicholls, Andrew 4:27:25 (18,210)
Nicholls, Andrew Daniel 4:07:58 (12,953)
Nicholls, Craig Keith 3:36:32 (5,484)
Nicholls, David 4:34:01 (19,997)
Nicholls, Ian K 3:27:37 (3,986)
Nicholls, James Edmund 5:59:35 (34,023)
Nicholls, Kenneth Edward 4:19:14 (15,909)
Nicholls, Lee Michael 5:13:37 (28,861)
Nicholls, Paul 5:03:43 (27,140)
Nicholls, Paul John 3:56:25 (9,903)
Nicholls, Ryan 4:53:21 (24,884)
Nicholls, Simon C 3:51:54 (8,639)
Nichols, Barry 4:28:45 (18,591)
Nichols, Ben 4:54:12 (25,100)
Nichols, Grant 4:12:40 (14,143)
Nichols, James Ellis 5:21:57 (30,136)
Nichols, Joe 4:52:22 (24,652)
Nichols, John 3:38:37 (5,874)
Nichols, Oliver 4:54:12 (25,100)
Nichols, Peter 6:32:45 (35,591)
Nichols, Terry 5:01:13 (26,685)
Nicholson, Alan 4:55:40 (25,452)
Nicholson, Gary M 4:17:48 (15,527)
Nicholson, Ian Peter 5:34:15 (31,788)
Nicholson, James 4:34:27 (20,108)
Nicholson, Jim 4:44:53 (22,738)
Nicholson, Matthew D 3:55:02 (9,485)
Nicholson, Nick E. 5:06:20 (27,593)
Nicholson, Sam 4:56:14 (25,593)
Nicholson, Simon 4:03:46 (11,914)
Nickolls, Benjamin G 5:12:11 (28,599)
Nicol, Alister U 3:24:54 (3,563)
Nicol, John Craig 4:32:09 (19,473)
Nicol, Simon 4:50:09 (24,084)
Nicolaides, Marcos 3:16:31 (2,610)
Nicolaou, Nicolas 4:01:25 (11,345)
Nicolas, Besson 2:46:19 (369)
Nicolaus, Alexander G 3:55:18 (9,566)
Nicoll, Peter John 4:23:31 (17,112)
Niebelschutz, Gerd Peter 3:21:53 (3,179)
Niel, Philip 3:15:29 (2,495)
Nield, Duncan William 3:15:11 (2,458)
Nield, Jonathan 6:28:46 (35,455)
Nielsen, Frank 3:51:29 (8,535)
Nielsen, John Linde 4:30:42 (19,148)
Nightingale, David 3:50:08 (8,232)
Nightingale, Jason 4:06:17 (12,520)
Nightingale, Keith Phillip 4:29:39 (18,866)
Nightingale, Mark John 3:19:17 (2,893)
Nihill, Robbie 4:14:41 (14,709)
Nijak, Jaroslaw 3:26:45 (3,838)
Nijjar, Avtar S 5:03:33 (27,110)
Nijs, Bert 4:08:33 (13,103)
Nilski, Mark 4:18:12 (15,629)
Nilsson, Bengt 3:23:13 (3,326)
Nilsson, Bernt-Olof 4:59:40 (26,373)
Nilsson, Kjell 4:19:39 (16,002)
Nilsson, Peter 4:11:35 (13,875)
Nimmo, Mark James 4:46:36 (23,205)
Nimmo, Paul 5:10:24 (28,309)
Nimmo, Steven 3:10:17 (1,930)
Nisbet, Arnold T 4:46:46 (23,242)
Nisbet, David 4:10:28 (13,586)
Nisbet, Ian Leighton 4:56:11 (25,579)
Nisbet, Jack 3:32:23 (4,796)
Nisbett, Jack Alexander 6:28:24 (35,441)
Nitchen, Philip Michael 5:33:02 (31,670)
Nithsdale, Martyn 5:40:32 (32,437)
Nitschmann, Sven 2:43:12 (286)
Nittner, David 2:50:37 (508)
Niven, Johnston Richard 3:50:15 (8,259)
Nixon, Barry 3:29:50 (4,385)
Nixon, Brian 3:56:39 (9,978)
Nixon, Guy 4:41:48 (21,971)
Nixon, Jason 5:15:26 (29,134)
Nixon, Phil 4:50:28 (24,154)
Nixon, Rob 4:20:57 (16,401)
Nixon, Samuel 4:32:04 (19,451)
Nixon, Stewart Paul 4:23:07 (17,007)
Noakes, John 5:37:39 (32,177)
Nobilet, Pascal 3:18:49 (2,855)
Noble, Christopher 3:08:40 (1,778)
Noble, Jonathan 4:15:20 (14,872)
Noble, Matt Brian 4:22:16 (16,790)
Nobrega, Paul 5:44:13 (32,788)
Nock, Graham S 3:21:57 (3,191)
Nock, Richard 4:32:08 (19,468)
Noden, Marcus R 5:09:18 (28,107)
Nodwell, Jason 5:02:30 (26,944)
Noisser, Benjamin 3:31:20 (4,636)
Noke, Tim John 6:15:06 (34,889)
Nokes, Andrew 5:14:03 (28,930)
Nolan, Andrew 3:30:26 (4,489)
Nolan, James W 5:41:50 (32,570)
Nolan, Mark 4:02:53 (11,701)
Nolan, Richard 5:23:34 (30,396)
Nollet, Charles 5:05:56 (27,519)
Nollo, Christian 4:53:19 (24,880)
Nonnenmacher, Jan 4:29:40 (18,870)
Noon, Iain Paul 5:10:14 (28,280)
Noon, John Richard 5:51:32 (33,464)
Noone, Mark 5:48:05 (33,149)
Noorbaccus, Mike 4:58:06 (25,986)
Norburn, David 4:50:01 (24,051)
Norbury, Daniel 5:20:09 (29,872)
Norbury, Mark John 5:19:35 (29,790)
Norcott, Gary 4:03:43 (11,901)
Norcup, Kieran 4:04:34 (12,087)
Nordquist, Jonas 2:58:40 (1,018)
Norgove, Gary 2:47:45 (414)
Norgrove, John A 3:25:13 (3,610)
Norman, Alistair J 4:54:52 (25,272)
Norman, Dave 2:19:05 (15)
Norman, David G 3:19:40 (2,934)
Norman, Howard Christopher 5:16:56 (29,378)
Norman, James Andrew 3:55:43 (9,677)
Norman, Matthew 4:39:11 (21,308)
Norman, Oliver 3:29:10 (4,263)
Norman, Phil 4:20:19 (16,209)
Norman, Stephen 4:45:18 (22,841)
Norman, Terence 6:38:00 (35,727)
Normand, Nicolas 5:08:04 (27,908)
Norridge, Christopher 3:42:59 (6,695)
Norrington, Andrew Paul 4:53:38 (24,952)
Norris, Andrew 6:26:24 (35,361)
Norris, Chris R 5:33:00 (31,663)
Norris, Gerard Anthony 4:41:52 (21,985)
Norris, John 5:51:17 (33,447)
Norris, Matthew 4:41:59 (22,012)
Norris, Philip 3:42:38 (6,616)
Norris, Richard 4:27:34 (18,252)
Norris, Tony Lewis 5:06:00 (27,530)
Norsworthy, Adrian 3:44:09 (6,905)
North, Mark 4:17:45 (15,512)
North, Stephen 3:55:48 (9,719)
North, Thomas Lloyd 3:18:38 (2,834)
Northcote, Andrew 5:20:25 (29,909)
Northcott, Adrian Peter 3:17:13 (2,686)
Northcott, Joel M 3:03:56 (1,384)
Northfield, Paul 4:57:29 (25,853)
Northmore, Ian Richard 5:40:53 (32,469)
Northover, Giles 4:30:01 (18,982)
Northover, Martin John 3:51:03 (8,435)
Northway, Olly 4:26:51 (18,039)
Norton, Andy James 4:10:02 (13,483)
Norton, Chris 4:09:54 (13,443)
Norton, Chris James 5:56:52 (33,856)
Norton, Christopher T 3:21:37 (3,152)
Norton, David R 3:34:02 (5,063)
Norton, Graham 5:19:47 (29,817)
Norton, Jerry P 4:19:20 (15,940)
Norton, Jonathan 3:52:15 (8,719)
Norton, Mark J 3:00:00 (1,151)
Norton, Michael Patrick 4:58:55 (26,192)
Norton, Nigel Robert 4:23:15 (17,034)
Norton, Paul Robert 5:07:52 (27,872)
Norton, Peter John 4:58:15 (26,028)
Norton, Simon 4:32:48 (19,630)
Nosworthy, Roger P 4:44:17 (22,586)
Notley, Andrew J 4:10:08 (13,506)
Notton, Gareth 4:43:21 (22,333)
Notton, Glen T 3:37:34 (5,681)
Nouillan, William 5:12:51 (28,710)
Novell, David 5:59:44 (34,040)
Nowack, Franck 3:15:39 (2,517)
Nowill, Peter 2:27:16 (48)
Noyce, Darren M 4:29:24 (18,777)
Noyce, Jonathan Oliver 4:08:48 (13,161)

Noyons, Andrew H......4:35:34 (20,358)
Ntsele, Bongani......4:54:55 (25,287)
Nugari, Paolo Filippo......3:17:29 (2,708)
Nugent, Daniel Christian......3:23:29 (3,364)
Nugent, Greg......4:39:04 (21,275)
Nugent, Paul......3:27:55 (4,038)
Nugue, Olivier......4:07:08 (12,741)
Nunes, Arthur......3:28:08 (4,079)
Nunn, Andrew Thomas......3:58:09 (10,435)
Nunn, David P......4:27:02 (18,087)
Nunn, Gregory......3:55:20 (9,571)
Nunn, James Robert......5:24:50 (30,597)
Nunn, Peter......5:52:11 (33,514)
Nunny, Mark......4:25:26 (17,642)
Nursey, James......4:29:55 (18,957)
Nussbaumer, Werner......4:06:08 (12,484)
Nutbrown, Mark John......4:36:17 (20,546)
Nute, Dominic L......5:43:16 (32,699)
Nuti, Mark G......5:35:24 (31,916)
Nutt, Matthew R......2:51:14 (532)
Nuttal, Norman D......4:06:13 (12,502)
Nuttall, Alasdair Mark......5:18:38 (29,649)
Nydegger, Karlfred......3:53:40 (9,113)
Nye, Daniel Alois......4:29:09 (18,721)
Nye, Derek......5:18:46 (29,660)
Nye, Howard A......4:05:10 (12,245)
Nye, John......6:30:38 (35,523)
Nystrøm, Patrik......4:21:30 (16,548)
Nyunt, Eugene......3:39:18 (6,005)
Oakes, Alan Joseph......3:40:06 (6,165)
Oakes, Dave......5:05:50 (27,500)
Oakes, Duncan......2:53:21 (632)
Oakes, John D......4:30:13 (19,028)
Oakes, Nick......4:55:02 (25,316)
Oakes, Paul Leslie......4:27:22 (18,200)
Oakes, Phil Andrew......4:44:10 (22,553)
Oakes, Trevor Duncan......6:18:46 (35,069)
Oakley, Brian James......4:33:40 (19,910)
Oakley, David......4:27:02 (18,087)
Oakley, Paul......4:51:03 (24,316)

Oakley, Simon Brian......5:24:37 (30,570)

In memory of my Mum, Gillian Oakley. I will never forget running through South London with children offering high-fives as I ran past. Crowds of people along Embankment calling my name. Turning into The Mall and seeing Buckingham Palace. The finishing line is in sight and the realisation of what I have done becomes reality. The emotion hits me; my eyes well up when I think how hard I have trained and pushed myself to a limit that this time a year ago was impossible. The support that family and friends have given me, and how proud I know my Mum would be of me as I cross the finishing line and a medal is put around my neck and I am congratulated on completing the London Marathon. For my Mum.

Oakley, Wesley James......4:17:10 (15,339)

Oakton, Neil......3:58:52 (10,674)
Oates, Ian......4:19:48 (16,041)
Oates, Neill......5:06:10 (27,558)
Oatham, Paul William......5:58:49 (33,980)
Oatham, Philip W......3:05:15 (1,477)
Obbard, Tony John......5:04:45 (27,326)
Obligy, Pierre......5:06:11 (27,563)
Oblowitz, Eddy......5:57:59 (33,931)
Oboh, Alexander......4:23:20 (17,054)
Oborski, Andrzej Ignacy......4:29:42 (18,878)
O'Boyle, Kevin P......3:41:40 (6,451)
Obrero Dañez, José Manuel......3:22:54 (3,278)
O'Brien, Adrian......5:10:35 (28,346)
O'Brien, Adrian George......3:56:02 (9,795)
O'Brien, Andrew......5:22:00 (30,144)
O'Brien, Bernie......4:00:33 (11,126)
O'Brien, Darragh......3:41:22 (6,399)
O'Brien, David......4:59:10 (26,252)
O'Brien, Dennis......4:30:06 (19,001)
O'Brien, Gary......4:37:16 (20,806)
O'Brien, James......4:20:03 (16,117)
O'Brien, Jim......3:56:42 (10,000)
O'Brien, John......3:53:48 (9,162)
O'Brien, John......4:44:02 (22,511)
O'Brien, Julian David......6:30:41 (35,525)
O'Brien, Mark......4:00:21 (11,076)
O'Brien, Martin J......4:33:59 (19,987)
O'Brien, Neil John......5:38:35 (32,272)
O'Brien, Neil Robert......4:00:11 (11,025)
O'Brien, Simon......4:13:55 (14,484)
O'Brien, Simon......4:22:03 (16,717)
O'Brien, Steve Mark......4:59:47 (26,403)
O'Brien, Terry......3:56:01 (9,790)
O'Brien, Wayne P......4:05:41 (12,375)
Obrikat, Thomas......4:28:50 (18,621)
O'Callaghan, David John......5:22:50 (30,278)
O'Callaghan, Eugene P......3:15:20 (2,480)
O'Callaghan, Sean......4:50:51 (24,254)
O'Callaghan, Toby Daniel......4:37:42 (20,924)
O'Carroll, Rory M......3:42:01 (6,511)
O'Connell, Daniel......3:23:47 (3,405)
O'Connell, David......3:49:09 (8,010)
O'Connell, Eoin......2:43:34 (297)
O'Connor, Alan Jeremy......4:27:45 (18,299)
O'Connor, Alex William Thomas.4:44:05 (22,529)
O'Connor, Benjamin......3:18:05 (2,777)
O'Connor, Chris......5:04:12 (27,230)
O'Connor, Christopher......4:44:29 (22,632)
O'Connor, Daniel......3:58:20 (10,505)
O'Connor, Darren......3:48:18 (7,805)
O'Connor, Darren......4:41:29 (21,887)
O'Connor, Huw......4:22:54 (16,962)
O'Connor, James Timothy......6:10:06 (34,672)
O'Connor, Jason Anthony......2:44:46 (333)
O'Connor, John Edmond......3:40:02 (6,154)
O'Connor, Luke......4:57:37 (25,884)
O'Connor, Matthew......6:09:18 (34,628)
O'Connor, Michael......4:21:26 (16,531)
O'Connor, Michael......6:03:13 (34,267)
O'Connor, Robert......3:48:17 (7,800)
O'Connor, Rory......4:47:36 (23,437)
O'Connor, Shane......3:49:22 (8,055)
O'Connor, Sean J......4:31:17 (19,289)
O'Connor, Sharief......4:58:41 (26,134)
O'Connor, William J......4:46:38 (23,217)
Oddono, Christian......4:21:15 (16,477)
Oddy, Chris......2:57:53 (945)
Ødegårdstuen, Frode......4:48:01 (23,549)
Odeku, Mark B......4:26:30 (17,952)
Odell, Dustin......2:58:21 (992)
Odell, Kevin......5:42:49 (32,656)
Odell, Michael......6:01:27 (34,152)
Odendaal, Michael Andreas......7:39:44 (36,519)
Odgers, Ian......4:28:26 (18,499)
Odlin, William B......4:28:17 (18,448)
O'Docherty, James Thomas......4:36:20 (20,554)
O'Doherty, Christopher S......3:56:23 (9,892)
O'Donnell, Brian......2:53:55 (664)
O'Donnell, John......5:06:37 (27,649)
O'Donnell, Kevin M......4:37:41 (20,921)
O'Donnell, Mark......4:16:35 (15,186)
O'Donnell, Michael......4:00:20 (11,068)
O'Donnell, Paul V......3:22:56 (3,282)

O'Donnell, Sean......4:07:20 (12,781)
O'Donnell, Thomas......3:58:06 (10,414)
O'Donoghue, Brett......3:57:33 (10,246)
O'Donoghue, Thomas......3:40:49 (6,292)
O'Donovan, Barry......4:15:09 (14,821)
O'Donovan, Padraig......4:18:34 (15,732)
O'Donovan, Tim......3:51:22 (8,507)
O'Driscoll, Daniel......5:17:15 (29,426)
O'Driscoll, Darren Lee......5:16:16 (29,261)
O'Driscoll, James Gerard......4:09:30 (13,341)
O'Driscoll, Keith......4:27:06 (18,120)
O'Dwyer, David......3:08:14 (1,721)
O'Dwyer, Eamonn Gerrard......3:44:50 (7,062)
O'Dwyer, John......3:32:58 (4,886)
O'Dwyer, Mike......5:22:33 (30,229)
Oeen, Erlend......4:37:24 (20,845)
Oestergaard, Hans Bjerre......3:56:27 (9,916)
Offer, Mark......3:40:54 (6,310)
O'Flaherty, David T......3:53:00 (8,925)
O'Flaherty, Thomas......4:13:33 (14,385)
O'Garra, Kevan Francis......4:53:53 (25,016)
Ogden, Kevin P......2:45:16 (348)
Ogden, Michael......4:08:29 (13,074)
Ogden, Nick D......2:59:49 (1,138)
Ogden, Richard......4:20:57 (16,401)
Ogier, Geoffrey Robert......6:14:13 (34,847)
Ogilvie, Ian Cyrus......4:22:30 (16,847)
Ogilvie, James......2:57:04 (860)
Ogle, Nigel A......4:18:33 (15,725)
Oglesby, Mark C......3:33:14 (4,928)
Ogley, Peter......3:47:07 (7,545)
Ogoe, Bernard K......4:13:37 (14,410)
O'Gorman, Eddie......2:49:10 (449)
O'Gorman, Keith Patrick......4:14:58 (14,773)
O'Grady, Gar......4:55:14 (25,367)
O'Grady, Paul......3:36:10 (5,439)
O'Grady, Sean......4:37:56 (20,974)
O'Grady, Steven......5:49:23 (33,271)
Ogún, Abi......5:39:47 (32,367)
O'Hara, Sam John......4:22:26 (16,830)
O'Hara, Stuart......3:39:50 (6,110)
O'Hare, Brian Joseph......4:35:30 (20,344)
O'Hare, Liam......2:59:49 (1,138)
O'Hare, Louis......3:35:51 (5,385)
O'Hare, Mark......4:14:27 (14,632)
O'Hare, Paul Gerard......4:30:29 (19,085)
O'Herlihy, Mark John......5:34:26 (31,814)
Ohrt, Morten......4:04:58 (12,196)
Okada, Hironori......5:05:44 (27,485)
O'Kane, Patrick......3:57:19 (10,186)
O'Kane, Peter Ronald......3:56:26 (9,908)
O'Kane, William Jude......4:00:05 (11,002)
Okec, Roy Emmanuel Peter......4:02:24 (11,580)
O'Keefe, John P......5:50:31 (33,389)
O'Keefe, Philip......4:21:23 (16,521)
O'Keefe, Shaun......5:36:14 (32,021)
O'Keeffe, David......4:54:41 (25,226)
O'Keeffe, Jeremiah John......3:30:40 (4,521)
O'Keeffe, Jimmy B......5:07:18 (27,770)
O'Keeffe, Jonathan Peter......3:53:32 (9,067)
O'Keeffe, Nicholas A......4:16:25 (15,147)
Okojie, Kwame......3:02:40 (1,309)
Oksanen, Risto......3:50:38 (8,343)
Okuse, Kenji......3:48:39 (7,884)
Okwara, Andrew George......3:55:51 (9,733)
Olafsson, Thorarinn Oli......4:20:35 (16,287)
Olaleye, Olabode......5:36:15 (32,027)
Old, George......4:19:10 (15,894)
Old, George......5:14:10 (28,945)
Old, Jack......6:18:07 (35,036)
Oldacre, Jason......5:33:31 (31,717)
Oldbury, James E......5:42:53 (32,659)
Oldcorn, Mike......4:48:23 (23,634)
Olden, Andrew Mark......3:26:19 (3,784)
Oldfield, David......4:28:05 (18,383)
Oldfield, Dean Neil......4:46:34 (23,185)
Oldfield, Gregg......4:26:11 (17,868)
Oldfield, James......5:15:50 (29,203)
Oldfield, Richard......5:15:55 (29,213)
Oldfield-Hodge, Trefor......5:03:37 (27,125)
Oldrey, Mark Ford......6:15:43 (34,916)
Oldroyd, Mark A......3:31:31 (4,670)
O'Leary, Bryan......3:38:10 (5,798)

O'Leary, James 4:29:16 (18,747)
O'Leary, John Francis 4:00:18 (11,059)
O'Leary, Kieran 3:03:02 (1,329)
Olivari, Francisco 3:13:12 (2,212)
Oliver, Alan 3:03:05 (1,331)
Oliver, Andrew R 3:02:18 (1,279)
Oliver, Ben James 4:26:21 (17,916)
Oliver, David 3:52:17 (8,734)
Oliver, David C 4:20:49 (16,369)
Oliver, Geoffrey J 3:44:10 (6,909)
Oliver, James Andrew Clive 3:29:49 (4,382)
Oliver, Jamie William Huw 5:40:29 (32,429)
Oliver, Joe 4:16:38 (15,197)
Oliver, John L 3:15:31 (2,499)
Oliver, Jonathan D 4:17:29 (15,433)
Oliver, Lee 6:06:37 (34,488)
Oliver, Nick Christopher 6:24:17 (35,289)
Oliver, Richard 3:42:37 (6,613)
Oliver, Richard 4:10:06 (13,498)
Oliver, Richard Thomas George 4:12:44 (14,165)
Oliver, Robert 4:52:17 (24,633)
Oliver, Robert J 3:37:34 (5,681)
Oliver, Russell Paul 4:28:58 (18,670)
Oliver, Timothy Peter Andrew 4:34:42 (20,171)
Oliver, Tom 3:53:59 (9,205)
Oliveri, William 4:48:27 (23,659)
Olivier, Alexandre 3:48:50 (7,937)
Olivier, Bertrand 4:22:11 (16,757)
Olivier, Johannes Jacobus 3:50:10 (8,242)
Olivo, Octavio 4:29:41 (18,875)
Olla, Raffaele 3:58:00 (10,376)
Ollari, Christophe Pierre 3:52:50 (8,881)
Ollason, Kirk A 3:39:13 (5,985)
Olliff, Nigel J 4:43:42 (22,417)
Ollington, Marc Thomas 3:52:04 (8,674)
Olney, Lee Steven 5:29:25 (31,213)
Olney, Paul 4:41:57 (22,002)
Olney, Paul John 3:41:49 (6,480)
O'Looney, Damien 3:49:32 (8,100)
O'Looney, Paul 3:46:25 (7,402)
O'Loughlin, Julian 3:34:50 (5,218)
Olsen, Jan Magnar 4:21:51 (16,655)
Olson, Phil A 3:58:58 (10,709)
Olson, Richard Alois 4:03:46 (11,914)
Olvera Salcedo, José L 3:48:24 (7,825)
O'Mahony, Brendan 3:21:21 (3,124)
O'Mahony, Fiach 3:48:48 (7,927)
O'Mahony, Hugues 4:07:04 (12,726)
O'Mahony, John 4:05:57 (12,445)
O'Mahony, Tadhg C 3:38:18 (5,820)
O'Malley, Charles 4:42:36 (22,153)
O'Malley, Gerard J 3:59:04 (10,737)
O'Malley, John 3:53:07 (8,947)
O'Malley, John James 4:06:06 (12,474)
O'Mara, Sean 7:10:29 (36,313)
Omiyale, Wale 4:14:09 (14,547)
Omori, Mark 2:59:19 (1,084)
Omowamide, Yomi 5:42:27 (32,633)
Onanuga, Kayode 4:56:26 (25,635)
Ondore, Damian 6:27:29 (35,401)
O'Neil, Colin 5:06:33 (27,637)
O'Neill, Brian 4:26:47 (18,020)
O'Neill, Donal John 5:10:21 (28,301)
O'Neill, Douglas 4:02:44 (11,662)
O'Neill, Iain AC 3:44:40 (7,029)
O'Neill, James 4:27:51 (18,327)
O'Neill, James Anthony 5:00:07 (26,483)
O'Neill, James Michael 3:45:25 (7,193)
O'Neill, Kevin 3:53:33 (9,073)
O'Neill, Kevin Patrick 4:52:23 (24,657)
O'Neill, Michael A 4:54:44 (25,238)
O'Neill, Ryan Sean 4:44:36 (22,670)
O'Neill, Shane 5:01:37 (26,779)
O'Neill, Tobi 4:52:15 (24,614)
O'Neill, Vincent 2:56:35 (839)
Onions, Thomas David 4:47:24 (23,389)
Onyett, Stephen Andrew 5:02:07 (26,871)
Opalka, Richard T 4:33:31 (19,857)
Openshaw, Dale P 7:44:36 (36,546)
Openshaw, Richard Andrew 5:01:23 (26,729)
Openshaw, Tom Kay 3:49:21 (8,052)
O'Phelan, Kieran William 4:38:19 (21,061)
Oppliger, Etienne 5:01:08 (26,672)
Oram, Dean Matthew 6:00:33 (34,095)
Oram-Evennett, Jonathan 5:30:29 (31,352)
Orange, David 4:33:28 (19,843)
Orchard, James 4:23:11 (17,021)
Ord, Doug 4:22:24 (16,822)
Ordish, Ian 4:28:09 (18,397)
O'Regan, John 4:21:00 (16,412)
O'Reilly, Andy 4:34:14 (20,054)
O'Reilly, Connal Sean 5:07:26 (27,793)
O'Reilly, John 4:31:23 (19,306)
O'Reilly, John P 3:00:20 (1,165)
O'Reilly, JP 3:21:17 (3,119)
O'Reilly, Paddy John 4:56:39 (25,681)
O'Reilly, Sean 5:49:27 (33,278)
O'Reilly, Stewart Michael 4:01:30 (11,368)
Orelaja, Ore 4:31:26 (19,316)
Organ, Adrian C 3:29:57 (4,408)
Orgill, Andrew Alan 4:35:13 (20,272)
O'Riley, Dominic 3:46:12 (7,353)
Orledge, Kevin J 5:06:30 (27,626)
Orme, Paul Matthew 3:45:33 (7,220)
Orme, Peter 3:53:14 (8,979)
Orme, Richard I 3:35:46 (5,372)
Ormerod, Tim J 4:07:03 (12,723)
Ormesher, Stephen Paul 4:51:24 (24,398)
Ormiston-Smith, Nicholas John 3:44:27 (6,982)
Ormond, John Michael 5:09:47 (28,193)
Ormond, Steve 4:47:39 (23,455)
Ormsby, Roy 3:32:08 (4,766)
Ormsby, Stephen A 6:45:31 (35,922)
Ornelas, José 3:53:56 (9,191)
Orr, Andrew 3:54:18 (9,280)
Orr, Gavin S 4:55:42 (25,463)
Orr, Stuart 4:49:40 (23,968)
Orridge, Christian 3:48:42 (7,898)
Orrock, Duncan John 3:36:13 (5,450)
Orsborne, Chris 5:25:37 (30,713)
Orsborne, James 5:25:37 (30,713)
Orsborne, Jonathan Paul 5:25:38 (30,720)
Orsman, Philip 4:37:54 (20,967)
Ortega Erazo, Ivan Joselito 6:14:06 (34,842)
Ortiz, José Luis 3:43:53 (6,854)
Ortiz Guzman, Fernando 3:49:04 (7,993)
Orton, Anthony D 5:59:51 (34,051)
O'Ryan, David Henry 4:41:54 (21,995)
Osawa, Manabu 3:53:27 (9,039)
Osborn, Andrew Steven 4:38:18 (21,054)
Osborn, Kevan 5:15:00 (29,065)
Osborn, Mark E 4:38:00 (20,987)
Osborn, Matthew John 5:00:47 (26,608)
Osborne, Brett Robert 4:48:24 (23,638)
Osborne, Daniel Cifton 4:08:44 (13,146)
Osborne, Douglas 4:23:42 (17,156)
Osborne, Graeme 4:57:46 (25,922)
Osborne, Lawrence William 4:30:24 (19,064)
Osborne, Matt James 4:31:21 (19,302)
Osborne, Michael 4:47:55 (23,522)
Osborne, Peter M 3:10:18 (1,932)
Osborne, Tommy 4:01:13 (11,300)
Osesek, Holger 3:46:29 (7,413)
O'Shea, Andrew 3:48:48 (7,927)
O'Shea, Denis F 4:44:36 (22,670)
O'Shea, Ian J 6:48:50 (35,973)
O'Shea, James Patrick 4:53:35 (24,937)
O'Shea, John Michael 3:43:38 (6,798)
O'Shea, Keld 4:57:11 (25,799)
O'Shea, Richard J 5:19:18 (29,745)
O'Shea, Sean 4:31:55 (19,411)
Oshikanlu, Nick 3:55:36 (9,636)
Osinowo, Remi Ahmed 3:47:34 (7,662)
Osman, Corey 5:13:41 (28,868)
Osorio, Fernando 4:22:10 (16,747)
Osorio, Thomas S 3:23:23 (3,349)
Ossio, Francisco 4:46:35 (23,193)
Ost, Andrew S 3:48:18 (7,805)
Ostensson, Jarl 6:22:54 (35,231)
Osterlund, Kristoffer 2:20:06 (19)
Ostermann, Frank 3:50:26 (8,295)
Ostinelli, John Mark 4:17:01 (15,302)
Ostlere, Anthony R 5:08:11 (27,925)
Ostornol, Fernando 2:46:28 (371)
Osuji, Roy 3:54:07 (9,236)
O'Sullivan, Chris 5:11:17 (28,449)
O'Sullivan, Diarmuid 4:04:40 (12,119)
O'Sullivan, Donal Gerard 4:36:50 (20,695)
O'Sullivan, Gary 2:59:09 (1,071)
O'Sullivan, John 4:01:44 (11,429)
O'Sullivan, Johnny 2:57:34 (910)
O'Sullivan, Michael P 3:23:12 (3,325)
O'Sullivan, Neil 5:07:59 (27,891)
O'Sullivan, Nick 3:55:39 (9,661)
O'Sullivan, Ryan 4:30:45 (19,159)
O'Sullivan, Tim N 3:51:52 (8,629)
O'Sullivan, Tony 4:17:23 (15,400)
Oswald, Jason 3:47:24 (7,620)
Oswald, Paul Fenwick 5:07:38 (27,839)
Oswin, Benjamin 4:34:23 (20,091)
Otero, Mario Marin 3:18:37 (2,831)
Othen, Dean 4:24:41 (17,440)
Other, Thomas 3:00:20 (1,165)
Otkay, Emir 5:23:03 (30,315)
Otomeno, Giles 5:15:27 (29,135)
O'Toole, Greg 4:10:06 (13,498)
O'Toole, Peter 4:03:38 (11,884)
O'Toole, Richard Anthony 3:34:47 (5,210)
Otto, Walter 5:45:59 (32,949)
Ottolenghi, Marco 5:28:42 (31,112)
Otty, Tim 2:56:01 (800)
Oudar, Christophe 3:11:12 (2,016)
Oudin, Benoit 3:32:58 (4,886)
Oughton, Luke Melvyn 4:54:15 (25,114)
Ourique, Frank 5:16:43 (29,339)
Ousby, Daniel 4:44:25 (22,621)
Outram, Matt D 5:19:47 (29,817)
Outten, Jonathan Charles 5:14:09 (28,943)
Outterson, Jonathan 4:59:52 (26,422)
Ovel, Dean Stuart 3:28:32 (4,145)
Ovenden, Greg 5:20:59 (30,002)
Over, Darren John 4:34:00 (19,993)
Over, Richard Parnell 4:36:26 (20,582)
Overall, David 6:44:34 (35,898)
Overall, Mark 6:30:09 (35,505)
Overall, Mark Edward 5:10:20 (28,297)
Overton, Darren 3:18:00 (2,766)
Overton, Richard 4:30:46 (19,164)
Owen, Alan Wyn 4:25:51 (17,768)
Owen, Andrew 4:10:08 (13,506)
Owen, Andrew J 5:21:43 (30,112)
Owen, Chris 5:40:08 (32,401)
Owen, David J 4:16:59 (15,297)
Owen, David James 3:58:10 (10,445)
Owen, David James 4:57:29 (25,853)
Owen, David Richard 3:19:58 (2,960)
Owen, Dylan Gwyn 3:55:15 (9,544)
Owen, Gareth 4:24:30 (17,388)
Owen, Gareth 5:21:27 (30,068)
Owen, Gareth J 4:12:06 (14,008)
Owen, Gary V 3:27:39 (3,991)
Owen, Hugh G 3:52:57 (8,910)
Owen, James T 3:40:26 (6,221)
Owen, Jonathon Richard 3:42:38 (6,616)
Owen, Kai 4:29:30 (18,808)
Owen, Lloyd 3:56:58 (10,077)
Owen, Nicholas 3:50:37 (8,338)
Owen, Nicholas William 5:27:36 (30,977)
Owen, Patrick Sean 4:26:37 (17,982)
Owen, Paul Anthony 3:44:53 (7,075)
Owen, Rob 5:38:33 (32,268)
Owen, Robert T 3:53:50 (9,169)
Owen, Roy Vincent 4:48:41 (23,715)
Owen, Stephen 3:57:02 (10,109)
Owen-Conway, David 3:19:08 (2,884)
Owens, Alex 4:18:40 (15,764)
Owens, Andy 3:57:27 (10,214)
Owens, Gareth 3:40:32 (6,246)
Owens, Garry 3:12:19 (2,112)
Owens, John P 3:06:11 (1,546)
Owers, James Frank 4:20:16 (16,185)
Owrid, Tim 4:23:21 (17,060)
Owusu, Prince Dennis 3:38:01 (5,767)
Oxenforth, Jason Nathaniel 5:54:10 (33,658)
Oxenham, Simon T 3:44:33 (7,001)
Oxlade, Colin J 3:06:29 (1,569)
Oxlade, Russell Charles John 4:10:26 (13,574)
Oxland, Gary 5:19:37 (29,794)
Oxley, Bill 4:19:23 (15,950)

Oxley, James 3:55:45 (9,699)
Oxley, Neil S 3:59:39 (10,903)
Oxley, Philip Michael 4:14:41 (14,709)
Oxley, Scott Alexander 3:15:59 (2,553)
Oxtoby, Mark Andrew 4:31:35 (19,347)
Ozanne, Dave 3:25:21 (3,623)
Ozelton, Karl James 5:41:41 (32,548)
Oziem, Christopher 4:14:52 (14,753)
Pacey, Andy 3:08:59 (1,806)
Pacey, Nick J 3:17:59 (2,763)
Pacini, Massimo 4:24:50 (17,475)
Packer, Leigh J 2:49:16 (458)
Packer, Malcolm P 3:05:15 (1,477)
Packer, Matthew H 4:14:21 (14,605)
Packer, Phil 25:22:00 (36,626)
Packheiser, Anton 5:11:43 (28,506)
Packman, Joseph E 4:25:37 (17,694)
Padbury, John A 2:58:44 (1,023)
Paddick, Paul 3:21:29 (3,137)
Padfield, Steven 5:23:32 (30,390)
Padgett, Nick 4:16:23 (15,135)
Padley, Benjamin Jefferson 4:08:32 (13,098)
Padley, Richard 5:00:47 (26,608)
Paech, Wolfgang 5:04:57 (27,355)
Page, Alan Robert 5:59:22 (34,010)
Page, Andrew John 3:17:14 (2,687)
Page, Chris Robert Banks 5:22:34 (30,232)
Page, Daniel 6:17:26 (35,004)
Page, David Michael 3:01:49 (1,245)
Page, Garry G 4:06:42 (12,625)
Page, Gary 4:37:00 (20,742)
Page, Gary Brian 3:36:49 (5,525)
Page, Graham 4:12:27 (14,083)
Page, Henry Nicholas 4:55:52 (25,504)
Page, Neil 2:54:02 (672)
Page, Roger Martin 5:11:12 (28,436)
Page, Sam 3:53:08 (8,950)
Page, Stephen R 4:03:42 (11,898)
Page, Tom 3:47:20 (7,605)
Page,, David, Brian 4:46:30 (23,168)
Page-Smith, Stephen Michael 5:08:55 (28,032)
Paget, Jamie 4:29:55 (18,957)
Paget, Tim 3:49:15 (8,036)
Pagett, Kris 4:39:03 (21,269)
Paglietti, Bruno 3:19:18 (2,896)
Paice, Neil 3:16:19 (2,587)
Paine, Adrien C 4:55:36 (25,437)
Paine, Andy 4:59:29 (26,333)
Paine, Ashley 4:30:29 (19,085)
Paine, Jason Anthony 4:44:20 (22,599)
Paine, Stephen Robin James 5:02:55 (27,012)
Painter, James A 4:11:09 (13,758)
Painting, Gary William 4:38:32 (21,124)
Pak, Joseph 3:18:32 (2,824)
Palazzo, Leo 4:56:24 (25,629)
Palencia, Victor Manuel 3:51:50 (8,614)
Palferman, Adam Edward 4:31:40 (19,371)
Palfreeman, Adrian 4:24:03 (17,250)
Palma-Alonso, Alvaro 4:40:20 (21,587)
Palmer, Alex 3:56:36 (9,958)
Palmer, Andrew David 5:25:46 (30,744)
Palmer, Andrew Ernest 3:58:06 (10,414)
Palmer, Barry T 5:02:39 (26,967)
Palmer, Ben 5:42:33 (32,643)
Palmer, Charles T 4:52:14 (24,610)
Palmer, Christopher P 4:13:41 (14,429)
Palmer, Clinton James 5:13:54 (28,909)
Palmer, Craig Robert 2:57:09 (866)
Palmer, Dan Peter 3:54:49 (9,427)
Palmer, Daniel 4:16:29 (15,165)
Palmer, David 2:52:36 (598)
Palmer, David M 4:38:22 (21,078)
Palmer, Eshmael Richard 5:15:56 (29,218)
Palmer, Justin 5:38:21 (32,247)
Palmer, Keith 4:06:44 (12,635)
Palmer, Mark D 3:07:58 (1,696)
Palmer, Paul G 5:02:29 (26,942)
Palmer, Richard 4:50:48 (24,238)
Palmer, Richard 4:57:00 (25,766)
Palmer, Richard J 2:55:24 (767)
Palmer, Simon John 5:17:18 (29,438)
Palmer, Steve P 4:09:55 (13,448)
Palmer, Thomas R 4:42:39 (22,168)
Palmer, Wayne 4:53:59 (25,045)
Palmer-Malt, Graham 3:55:12 (9,528)
Pampus, Sven 4:12:50 (14,187)
Panasar, Raj 5:29:23 (31,210)
Panayi, Christopher 4:09:28 (13,330)
Panayi, James 3:50:30 (8,311)
Panayiotou, Sotiris 3:21:27 (3,135)
Pandit, Digish 4:46:05 (23,055)
Pandit, Kumar 5:55:53 (33,783)
Pang, Daniel 3:38:37 (5,874)
Pang, Yong 3:58:55 (10,691)
Pangbourne, Neil 4:24:24 (17,360)
Panichi, Christophe 4:17:04 (15,311)
Panis, Ronald 3:57:42 (10,297)
Pankhurst, Sean Michael 3:54:37 (9,359)
Pankhurst, Thomas A 3:48:08 (7,773)
Pannel, Christopher J 3:45:12 (7,139)
Pannetta, Angelo 3:54:45 (9,402)
Pannier, Stephane 4:17:20 (15,386)
Panter, Trevor D 5:43:11 (32,689)
Pantlin, Andrew William 4:53:50 (25,002)
Pantling, Steven 4:20:38 (16,314)
Panton, Craig 3:06:50 (1,595)
Panton, Craig Stuart 4:51:01 (24,309)
Panton, David Antony 6:08:29 (34,582)
Pap, John 4:31:10 (19,258)
Papadakis, Michael G 4:28:22 (18,472)
Paparo, Joshua Vincent 2:58:08 (966)
Papasavvas, Thanos 3:55:04 (9,495)
Papotti, Cristiano 3:24:33 (3,517)
Pappas, Ryan 3:41:31 (6,425)
Paramo, Miguel Angel 3:27:15 (3,915)
Paramor, Jon 3:53:19 (9,004)
Parcell, Glen D 5:27:55 (31,013)
Pare, William 6:14:16 (34,849)
Parekh, Ameet 6:18:15 (35,046)
Parekh, Narendra 4:52:17 (24,633)
Parekh, Nikesh 5:57:27 (33,899)
Parekh, Prasan 4:57:38 (25,890)
Parente, Fabrice 5:49:40 (33,304)
Parfery, Brian 4:14:32 (14,659)
Parfitt, Ifor 4:39:12 (21,313)
Parfrey, Rob T 3:25:42 (3,684)
Pargeter, Benjamin John 4:24:23 (17,350)
Parham, Charles Benedict Henry 2:58:59 (1,045)
Parigini, Roberto 3:13:19 (2,226)
Paris, Massimiliano 3:08:26 (1,746)
Parish, Brian 4:27:09 (18,133)
Parish, Mike 4:10:43 (13,643)
Park, Chang Ki 3:26:21 (3,789)
Park, David John 4:42:10 (22,053)
Park, Ed 4:31:18 (19,293)
Park, Gui Nam 4:04:19 (12,035)
Park, Gus 3:40:56 (6,316)
Park, Jong Suk 5:34:30 (31,823)
Park, Joon Woo 3:56:52 (10,048)
Parke, James G 4:18:11 (15,626)
Parke, Kevin Duncan James 4:04:02 (11,968)
Parker, Adam 4:01:42 (11,409)
Parker, Alistair P 4:26:26 (17,934)
Parker, Anthony 4:23:30 (17,104)
Parker, Anthony James 5:09:26 (28,131)
Parker, Asa D 5:11:00 (28,405)
Parker, Christopher F 2:44:55 (338)
Parker, Christopher John 4:21:07 (16,443)
Parker, Christopher S 3:57:29 (10,225)
Parker, Dave Simon 3:21:42 (3,161)
Parker, David 2:59:33 (1,117)
Parker, Geoffrey B 3:52:27 (8,777)
Parker, Graham John 5:23:07 (30,323)
Parker, Ian D 4:25:45 (17,738)
Parker, John 3:44:36 (7,014)
Parker, Keith 5:47:54 (33,128)
Parker, Kent A 4:18:53 (15,822)
Parker, Lee 4:35:08 (20,260)
Parker, Lee Grant 5:00:18 (26,522)
Parker, Mark 5:26:40 (30,858)
Parker, Mathew 4:27:26 (18,213)
Parker, Matthew 4:46:36 (23,205)
Parker, Michael Anthony 4:35:15 (20,283)
Parker, Neil 3:58:18 (10,491)
Parker, Philip J 3:21:11 (3,109)
Parker, Richard 3:16:31 (2,610)
Parker, Richard 3:54:23 (9,298)
Parker, Richard David 3:23:59 (3,431)
Parker, Robert 3:35:13 (5,276)
Parker, Robert Bernard 6:44:57 (35,906)
Parker, Shaun 3:10:04 (1,913)
Parker, Simon Patrick 4:49:03 (23,813)
Parker, Stephen 3:34:04 (5,070)
Parker, Stephen A 3:07:35 (1,665)
Parker, Stuart 4:05:01 (12,212)
Parker, Terence T 5:16:54 (29,374)
Parker, Thomas D 5:21:36 (30,095)
Parker, Will Neil 4:25:49 (17,760)
Parkes, David Jonathan 3:45:42 (7,245)
Parkes, Richard 3:53:28 (9,045)
Parkes, Simon 4:28:53 (18,636)
Parkin, David L 4:49:00 (23,800)
Parkin, George Edmond 4:44:37 (22,676)
Parkin, Julian 4:58:38 (26,126)
Parkin, Shaun M 3:00:51 (1,200)
Parkington, David 3:04:07 (1,402)
Parkinson, Andrew 3:42:43 (6,638)
Parkinson, Andy 3:30:36 (4,510)
Parkinson, Ben 3:39:37 (6,064)
Parkinson, Brendan 3:53:43 (9,126)
Parkinson, Brian 4:17:10 (15,339)
Parkinson, Colin David 4:54:55 (25,287)
Parkinson, Jamie 4:49:13 (23,852)
Parkinson, Mike Lawrence 4:36:44 (20,665)
Parmar, Amrik S 5:17:30 (29,471)
Parmar, Ripal 4:27:52 (18,330)
Parnell, Adam 4:38:49 (21,207)
Parnell, Andy 6:25:06 (35,309)
Parnell, Carl David 4:30:04 (18,994)
Parnell, James 5:57:46 (33,917)
Parnell, Richard 4:18:15 (15,644)
Parr, Daniel Clive 3:28:50 (4,194)
Parr, James 4:31:13 (19,274)
Parr, Jonathan 3:50:51 (8,390)
Parr, Matthew J 3:22:45 (3,264)
Parrack, Christopher John 3:58:33 (10,574)
Parrett, Nathan 4:14:48 (14,742)
Parrin, Simon Nicholas 3:09:43 (1,881)
Parrish, Kwith J 4:12:40 (14,143)
Parrish, Robert James 4:19:47 (16,038)
Parrott, Christopher George 5:28:40 (31,106)
Parrott, Jonathan David 4:16:39 (15,204)
Parry, Alister R 4:08:09 (12,994)
Parry, Chris David 4:03:04 (11,743)
Parry, David A 2:59:00 (1,049)
Parry, David J 3:23:06 (3,305)
Parry, Delwyn Owen 3:17:25 (2,699)
Parry, Keith D 3:40:16 (6,192)
Parry, Malcolm 4:30:34 (19,113)
Parry, Marc 6:54:52 (36,107)
Parry, Mark 3:56:02 (9,795)
Parry, Nathan 3:07:32 (1,654)
Parry, Neil A 2:49:16 (458)
Parry, Neil V 3:10:08 (1,918)
Parry, Nigel 4:41:17 (21,840)
Parry, Richard J 3:39:32 (6,050)
Parry, Robin W 3:58:11 (10,449)
Parry, Simon 4:11:49 (13,936)
Parry, Simon Edward 4:49:58 (24,043)
Parry, Simon James 4:11:57 (13,977)
Parry, Sion Kerry 4:12:34 (14,119)
Parry, Thomas Edward 5:06:07 (27,552)
Parry, William 5:06:47 (27,688)
Parsley, Elvis I 2:57:59 (954)
Parsons, Damon 5:21:15 (30,037)
Parsons, David John 4:39:06 (21,280)
Parsons, Dean Clayton 6:45:58 (35,931)
Parsons, Gregg 4:24:41 (17,440)
Parsons, James S 4:16:54 (15,271)
Parsons, Kevin Andrew 3:35:16 (5,282)
Parsons, Neil John 5:02:10 (26,881)
Parsons, Richard B 4:41:45 (21,952)
Parsons, Richard Mark 5:34:41 (31,847)
Parsons, Robert Charles 3:56:41 (9,992)
Parsons, Samuel Joseph 4:57:26 (25,844)
Parsons, Simon Andrew 3:31:36 (4,683)
Parsons, Simon J 4:21:52 (16,660)
Parsons, Simon Peter 4:16:58 (15,287)
Parsons, Stephen 4:23:03 (16,994)

Parsons, Steve Michael..........5:25:00 (30,627)
Parsons, Terry..........4:33:28 (19,843)
Partington, Neil Andrew..........4:45:31 (22,891)
Partner, Christopher..........4:29:47 (18,909)
Parton, Sam..........3:12:21 (2,118)
Partridge, Alan Richard..........4:23:51 (17,200)
Partridge, Anthony W..........3:46:54 (7,512)
Partridge, David A..........5:31:15 (31,439)
Partridge, Graham Charles..........4:04:09 (11,996)
Partridge, Stephen Lee..........3:39:44 (6,084)
Pascal, Bellanger..........3:54:28 (9,317)
Pascal, Ricardo..........4:47:56 (23,528)
Pasco, Richard F..........4:23:34 (17,125)
Pascoe, Barry..........4:06:45 (12,642)
Pascoe, Gary J..........3:39:52 (6,119)
Pascoe, Jason R..........4:49:42 (23,978)
Pashen, Stephen Robert..........6:53:42 (36,080)
Pask, Jonathan Michael..........4:28:23 (18,478)
Pask, Michael R..........2:59:39 (1,122)
Paskin, Daniel..........5:18:12 (29,572)
Pasquier, Laurent..........3:40:24 (6,214)
Pasquier, Philippe..........4:06:42 (12,625)
Pasquier, Sylvain..........4:36:30 (20,605)
Pasquini, Giacomo..........3:30:34 (4,508)
Passarelli, David..........5:08:26 (27,968)
Passingham, Keith William..........4:38:20 (21,067)
Passingham, Leonard J..........2:39:32 (185)
Passmore, Andrew Richard..........4:01:11 (11,294)
Pastor, David J..........3:08:30 (1,754)
Patch, David..........3:21:44 (3,164)
Patching, Elliot..........5:15:25 (29,128)
Patel, A..........5:00:46 (26,606)
Patel, Ajay..........4:09:06 (13,229)
Patel, Ameet..........3:49:36 (8,115)
Patel, Ashish Bhupendra..........4:27:46 (18,306)
Patel, Ashok Kumar..........3:18:01 (2,768)
Patel, Bhavin..........3:38:37 (5,874)
Patel, Chiraag..........4:51:54 (24,521)
Patel, Dipak..........4:50:50 (24,250)
Patel, Harish..........5:54:02 (33,646)
Patel, Harnish..........3:10:04 (1,913)
Patel, Hasmukh..........6:56:30 (36,138)
Patel, Jayant..........4:11:13 (13,771)
Patel, Kantilal..........4:24:36 (17,419)
Patel, Kaushik..........6:19:01 (35,082)
Patel, Ketul..........4:58:56 (26,196)
Patel, Keyur..........3:48:07 (7,769)
Patel, Kiran D..........5:03:49 (27,159)
Patel, Mitul Harshad..........4:13:51 (14,470)
Patel, Neal..........5:19:02 (29,705)
Patel, Nissit..........4:10:12 (13,531)
Patel, Prakash Purshottam..........4:18:44 (15,782)
Patel, Rahool..........4:56:44 (25,700)
Patel, Rajesh..........4:43:43 (22,423)
Patel, Rakesh..........3:45:47 (7,264)
Patel, Ravi..........5:43:03 (32,670)
Patel, Saleem..........3:55:23 (9,591)
Patel, Simon..........6:46:53 (35,945)
Patel, Sunil..........4:41:43 (21,944)
Patel, Vinod..........4:29:51 (18,927)
Patel, Viresh..........4:56:24 (25,629)
Pateman, Darren..........4:43:23 (22,342)
Pateman, Simon John..........5:15:14 (29,104)
Pateman, Tom Francis..........4:12:28 (14,089)
Patenaude, Michel..........3:22:25 (3,231)
Paterson, Alan..........4:58:32 (26,097)
Paterson, Anthony L..........5:02:53 (27,007)
Paterson, Gareth..........4:38:32 (21,124)
Paterson, Ian..........4:44:19 (22,595)
Paterson, James..........4:53:12 (24,847)
Paterson, Mark..........3:23:36 (3,377)
Paterson, Mark Robert..........3:20:03 (2,967)
Paterson, Philip Robert..........3:50:23 (8,284)
Paterson, Richard G..........5:48:02 (33,143)
Paterson, Ross..........4:43:58 (22,498)
Paterson, Stephen J..........3:11:10 (2,013)
Patey, Chris..........3:53:35 (9,084)
Patey, Christopher John..........4:05:36 (12,353)
Patey, Nicholas..........4:08:31 (13,090)
Pathmanathan, Kangesu..........6:56:19 (36,135)
Patience, James..........3:44:35 (7,008)
Patient, Chris..........7:31:25 (36,475)
Patient, Phil..........4:16:19 (15,112)

Patil, Advait Krishna..........5:31:32 (31,478)
Patmore-Hill, David..........3:13:44 (2,288)
Paton, Colin G..........2:41:27 (240)
Paton, David..........4:08:14 (13,012)
Paton, Mark..........5:20:35 (29,941)
Patrick, Daniel Scott..........4:10:30 (13,594)
Patrick, David Iain..........5:12:46 (28,694)
Patrick, Noel..........5:22:32 (30,224)
Patrick, Steve..........4:27:39 (18,274)
Patten, Kevin Anthony William..........4:23:56 (17,221)
Patten, Ram Anthony..........5:59:49 (34,048)
Patterson, Grant Ashley..........3:18:21 (2,810)
Patterson, Michael..........5:45:09 (32,881)
Patterson, Stephen J..........2:35:02 (112)
Patterson, Trevor..........4:47:50 (23,507)
Pattinson, Ronnie..........7:40:44 (36,525)
Pattison, David I..........5:11:41 (28,498)
Pattison, Ian..........3:31:58 (4,733)
Pattison, Mark Antony..........5:13:05 (28,789)
Patwardhan, Mahesh V..........5:04:11 (27,226)
Paukner, Franz Karl..........3:46:03 (7,322)
Paul, David C..........5:36:07 (32,007)
Paul, Dean..........4:40:22 (21,601)
Paul, John..........5:08:12 (27,929)
Paul, Philippe J..........5:16:23 (29,292)
Paul, Robert S..........4:11:59 (13,984)
Paul Florence, Grant I..........2:54:15 (684)
Paulet, Jean-Pierre..........3:23:01 (3,294)
Pauley, Simon Roger..........4:50:09 (24,084)
Pauling, Ben Peter..........3:33:17 (4,933)
Paull, Simon Mark..........5:19:05 (29,714)
Paull, Stephen F..........4:04:54 (12,174)
Pauzers, Valdis I..........3:14:23 (2,368)
Pauzet, Cyril..........2:58:17 (985)
Pavey, Brian Stephen..........3:51:23 (8,512)
Pawlowski, Christopher P..........3:31:08 (4,600)
Pawluk, Ivan M..........2:49:30 (469)
Paxi-Cato, Simao..........4:18:17 (15,655)
Paxton, Craig..........4:21:52 (16,660)
Paxton, Joseph..........2:53:38 (647)
Paxton, Matthew Graham..........5:08:24 (27,964)
Paylor, Nigel L..........3:44:04 (6,891)
Payn, John E..........5:28:08 (31,045)
Payne, Adam James..........4:48:35 (23,690)
Payne, Andrew..........4:11:17 (13,786)
Payne, Andrew..........5:14:53 (29,052)
Payne, Anthony..........3:37:07 (5,586)
Payne, David..........4:20:45 (16,356)
Payne, Douglas..........4:30:58 (19,209)
Payne, Gareth..........3:26:55 (3,864)
Payne, Garry P..........2:39:32 (185)
Payne, Gary..........4:01:24 (11,339)
Payne, Gary F..........5:17:20 (29,445)
Payne, Ian R..........3:24:04 (3,446)
Payne, Julian Lavington..........4:03:44 (11,904)
Payne, Matt..........4:22:45 (16,918)
Payne, Matthew J..........5:36:16 (32,030)
Payne, Nick Stephen..........4:14:12 (14,569)
Payne, Paul..........2:41:22 (237)
Payne, Richard..........6:34:43 (35,648)
Payne, Scott Thomas..........6:51:27 (36,022)
Payne, Stephen Richard..........4:55:16 (25,374)
Payne, Tim..........4:53:05 (24,814)
Peace, Daniel E..........2:59:11 (1,074)
Peace, Jamie..........6:40:01 (35,785)
Peace, Kevin..........4:32:03 (19,449)
Peace, Luke..........4:17:43 (15,501)
Peace, Michael S..........3:25:36 (3,666)
Peach, Simon R..........5:01:52 (26,825)
Peach, Tim..........4:07:30 (12,834)
Peacher, Ricky C..........2:57:56 (951)
Peachment, Richard Mark..........3:57:22 (10,196)
Peacock, Daren..........4:04:59 (12,200)
Peacock, Jim..........4:24:24 (17,360)

Peacock, Lenny..........4:02:03 (11,502)
Peacock, Simon Luke..........3:56:04 (9,802)
Peacock, Tom..........5:20:23 (29,897)
Pear, Ian..........5:32:40 (31,624)
Pearce, Adrian Jonathan..........4:47:36 (23,437)
Pearce, Alan..........5:04:24 (27,259)
Pearce, Andrew Philip..........3:29:02 (4,234)
Pearce, Andy Michael..........3:37:26 (5,642)
Pearce, Ben S..........2:56:22 (823)
Pearce, Chris Micheal..........6:39:55 (35,783)
Pearce, Christopher Stuart..........3:15:47 (2,526)
Pearce, Daniel..........3:52:58 (8,911)
Pearce, David..........4:49:28 (23,908)
Pearce, David Trevor..........6:25:51 (35,341)
Pearce, Dean..........3:38:56 (5,926)
Pearce, Duncan..........7:12:26 (36,332)
Pearce, Geoff..........7:30:04 (36,472)
Pearce, Glyn..........6:31:11 (35,544)
Pearce, Gordon Peter..........2:44:41 (327)
Pearce, Ian..........4:17:27 (15,425)
Pearce, James William Frederick 4:57:56 (25,953)
Pearce, Jon..........4:00:13 (11,036)
Pearce, Keith G..........4:20:04 (16,126)
Pearce, Martin James..........4:28:23 (18,478)
Pearce, Michael George..........4:26:24 (17,927)
Pearce, Michael Lee Andrew..........4:26:27 (17,939)
Pearce, Nick Simon..........3:49:23 (8,059)
Pearce, Oli..........4:01:42 (11,409)
Pearce, Robert D..........4:15:42 (14,952)
Pearce, Rodney Michael..........5:45:56 (32,945)
Pearce, Sean..........5:14:55 (29,054)
Pearce, Stephen Mark..........3:52:05 (8,676)
Pearce, Wesley..........4:35:22 (20,318)
Pears, Mathew David..........3:28:54 (4,210)
Pearse, Chris Hugh..........3:57:07 (10,131)
Pearson, Adrian..........3:47:43 (7,686)
Pearson, Alan Russell..........4:18:33 (15,725)
Pearson, Alexander James..........3:13:17 (2,221)
Pearson, Andrew..........4:07:26 (12,810)
Pearson, Antony Steven..........7:13:37 (36,344)
Pearson, Chris..........3:33:39 (4,998)
Pearson, Christopher John..........3:33:19 (4,936)
Pearson, Hugh A..........3:48:19 (7,810)
Pearson, Ian..........4:12:14 (14,039)
Pearson, Lee..........3:57:04 (10,122)
Pearson, Mike David..........4:05:44 (12,386)
Pearson, Philip J..........2:54:47 (722)
Pearson, Richard M..........3:22:58 (3,288)
Pearson, Robert Edward..........3:19:19 (2,899)
Pearson, Russell..........5:01:51 (26,820)
Pearson, Simon..........4:36:32 (20,616)
Pearson, Simon..........5:01:23 (26,729)
Pearson, Toby S..........2:39:24 (182)
Pearsons, Philip..........4:09:11 (13,253)
Peart, Christopher John..........3:39:03 (5,950)
Peate, Tom..........3:49:12 (8,026)
Peaty, Matt..........3:41:44 (6,464)
Pecha, Richard..........4:36:46 (20,674)
Peck, Simon Graham..........3:58:49 (10,666)
Peck, Simon J..........3:11:20 (2,030)
Peckham, Mike..........4:24:37 (17,424)
Pedder, Geoff..........4:53:07 (24,826)
Peddie, Neil Alexander..........4:58:19 (26,045)
Peddie, Ronald D..........3:42:50 (6,661)
Peddle, Mark..........3:22:07 (3,201)
Pedersen, Christian..........3:44:19 (6,942)
Pedlar, Chris..........5:09:00 (28,050)
Pedler, Ian John..........3:29:30 (4,320)
Pedley, Michael Andrew..........6:24:42 (35,299)
Pedley, Vernon Joseph..........4:42:14 (22,075)
Peel, David..........4:44:56 (22,751)
Peel, Michael..........3:38:56 (5,926)
Peel, Mike..........5:25:05 (30,638)
Peel, Robert..........4:54:00 (25,052)
Peers, Richard William..........4:06:43 (12,630)
Peevers, Simon..........5:24:54 (30,602)
Pegler, Graham Neil..........5:25:32 (30,699)
Pegler, Hywel..........3:12:04 (2,098)
Peillon, Thomas Edward..........4:05:39 (12,367)
Pelc, Martin..........5:30:07 (31,307)
Pelloux-Prayer, Alain..........5:23:10 (30,333)
Peltor, Edward..........3:09:19 (1,834)
Peluso, Pietro..........3:09:16 (1,830)

Pelzer, Joerg	4:26:41 (17,994)
Pemberton, Alistair John	4:00:38 (11,151)
Pemberton, David Andrew	4:15:11 (14,830)
Pemberton, George	4:09:33 (13,351)
Pemberton, Leo Cador	3:45:40 (7,242)
Pemberton, Robert M	5:48:21 (33,178)
Pemberton, Stephen N	3:28:01 (4,051)
Pemble, Colin Ian	3:09:40 (1,876)
Pender, Jonathan	3:31:55 (4,725)
Pender, Mark J	5:48:47 (33,222)
Pender, Nick	3:58:37 (10,598)
Pender, William J	4:28:27 (18,508)
Pendlebury, Christopher John	3:25:13 (3,610)
Pendleton, David J	5:17:50 (29,518)
Pendleton, David T	4:54:43 (25,234)
Pendrill, Jim	2:41:10 (229)
Penfold, Christopher	4:33:01 (19,703)
Penfold, Matt	4:25:17 (17,595)
Penfold, Vincent David	4:25:26 (17,642)
Pengelly, Gary	5:15:24 (29,125)
Penk, Christopher C	4:57:03 (25,770)
Penman, Ross	5:19:34 (29,785)
Penn, Gavin	4:59:58 (26,442)
Penn, Gregory V	3:11:28 (2,047)
Penn, Marc A	3:13:55 (2,306)
Penn, Simon	5:33:01 (31,668)
Pennarola, Fausto	3:59:02 (10,729)
Penney, Michael Wilfred	4:22:39 (16,892)
Penneycard, Matthew J	4:06:38 (12,611)
Pennington, Liam J	2:50:22 (499)
Pennington, Mark	6:25:12 (35,320)
Pennington, Michael J	3:12:51 (2,171)
Pennington, Philip I	4:14:09 (14,547)
Penny, Neil John	3:36:04 (5,421)
Penny, Nicholas	5:39:47 (32,367)
Penny, Raymond G	4:30:54 (19,190)
Penny, Tony	4:44:04 (22,523)
Penprase, Jason M	3:49:07 (8,006)
Penrose, Charles	3:34:06 (5,079)
Penrose, Ronald K	3:28:52 (4,200)
Penthor, Juergen	4:15:13 (14,838)
Pentland, Chris M	4:27:36 (18,257)
Peppard, Brent	5:23:28 (30,382)
Pepper, Bill	4:06:43 (12,630)
Pepper, James	4:17:44 (15,507)
Pepper, Philip	5:22:32 (30,224)
Pepper, Steven P	4:07:02 (12,720)
Percival, Alan Howard	4:01:00 (11,251)
Percival, Alex	3:19:05 (2,879)
Percival, Andrew	3:43:23 (6,754)
Percival, Graeme	4:32:41 (19,602)
Percival, Martin Robert	3:57:12 (10,156)
Percival, Michael	4:06:18 (12,524)
Percival, Stuart	3:56:52 (10,048)
Percy, Richard	4:15:59 (15,019)
Pereira, Alexandre	2:52:38 (602)
Pereira, José	4:09:51 (13,431)
Pereira, Leonel	5:27:06 (30,923)
Pereira, Terry P	6:23:45 (35,269)
Perez, Antonio	3:33:02 (4,899)
Perez, Carlos	2:58:01 (958)
Perez, Gabriel	3:38:00 (5,761)
Perez, I	3:58:39 (10,610)
Perez Lopez, Javier Luis	3:53:16 (8,988)
Perez Sampayo, Candido	3:49:58 (8,314)
Perez-Leon, Angel	4:01:25 (11,345)
Pering, Richard James	4:27:36 (18,257)
Perkin, Martin	4:59:10 (26,252)
Perkin, Neil	5:23:33 (30,393)
Perkins, Alistair	4:00:26 (11,100)
Perkins, Brent	4:44:51 (22,730)
Perkins, Chris R	4:00:40 (11,159)
Perkins, Christian	5:09:37 (28,170)
Perkins, Luke Dylan	4:21:01 (16,420)
Perkins, Mark	3:37:18 (5,622)
Perkins, Mark David	3:55:14 (9,538)
Perkins, Phil	4:49:08 (23,835)
Perkins, Scott	5:04:32 (27,283)
Perkins, Simon	5:34:37 (31,837)
Perkins, Steven	4:42:19 (22,098)
Perkins, Trevor M	4:45:09 (22,806)
Perks, Alastair	4:13:52 (14,475)
Perks, James Edward	3:47:19 (7,603)

Perks, Matthew Raymond	3:28:19 (4,107)
Pernin, Stephane	3:07:12 (1,626)
Perrault, Bruce	3:29:41 (4,357)
Perren, Patrick	2:39:26 (183)
Perren, Peter J	5:16:41 (29,336)
Perret, Joel	4:06:55 (12,689)
Perret, Laurent	3:30:12 (4,450)
Perrett, Clint	2:18:15 (13)
Perrett, Michael	4:23:51 (17,200)
Perrett, Royden	3:25:24 (3,631)
Perrin, Andrew Francis	5:08:59 (28,046)
Perrin, Ian	3:55:41 (9,672)
Perrin, Pascal	3:00:27 (1,170)
Perrin, Pierre-Yves	3:29:58 (4,412)
Perrone, Gil G	4:13:29 (14,358)
Perry, Andrew M	4:28:30 (18,521)
Perry, Ben	4:16:19 (15,112)
Perry, Darren M	4:46:48 (23,255)
Perry, David	3:08:49 (1,795)
Perry, Dexter	6:29:52 (35,492)
Perry, Giles C	5:29:30 (31,222)
Perry, Henry Thomas	4:14:04 (14,526)
Perry, James	4:16:37 (15,195)
Perry, James	4:29:43 (18,888)
Perry, Jason Robert	4:55:29 (25,407)
Perry, Luke	5:15:36 (29,163)
Perry, Mark Alan	4:33:49 (19,947)
Perry, Paul J	2:39:41 (188)
Perry, Steve Michael	3:47:50 (7,704)
Perry, Timothy Paul	5:38:29 (32,262)
Perry, Tony	3:57:00 (10,089)
Perry, Wayne I	3:38:03 (5,774)
Perryman, Mark	4:26:07 (17,848)
Perryman-Best, Nevil James	3:56:01 (9,790)
Pert, Joshua Paul	4:04:56 (12,186)
Pescud, Phillip	5:44:43 (32,841)
Pesenti, Antoine	3:00:45 (1,193)
Peter, Bedwell Robert	4:46:49 (23,259)
Petereit, Max	3:50:13 (8,251)
Peterkin, Richard Brian	4:20:06 (16,137)
Peters, Andrew Mark	7:22:38 (36,423)
Peters, Daniel	4:39:09 (21,301)
Peters, Gary	3:48:36 (7,873)
Peters, Jeff Alex	5:20:19 (29,891)
Peters, Michael	3:32:15 (4,780)
Peters, Michael	3:52:16 (8,729)
Peters, Steven	3:39:15 (5,991)
Peters, Tim W	3:22:49 (3,272)
Petersen, Kent	2:50:41 (511)
Petersen, Kevin	3:47:56 (7,726)
Petersen, Michael B	3:17:23 (2,695)
Peterson, Calum	4:44:58 (22,759)
Peterson, Michael	5:43:17 (32,701)
Pethe, Sunil Madhav	4:27:59 (18,361)
Petheram, Robert	4:46:13 (23,096)
Petit, Jeremy R	4:42:32 (22,147)
Petker, Hassan	4:50:21 (24,130)
Petreni, Enzo Giuseppe	6:14:49 (34,877)
Petrides, John G	6:39:20 (35,763)
Petrie, Gavin	4:44:05 (22,529)
Petrie, Neil Richard	4:06:00 (12,456)
Petrilli, Jean Pierre	3:28:20 (4,112)
Petruccio, Mario	6:42:02 (35,835)
Petruso, Tony	3:58:09 (10,435)
Pett, Brian A	4:54:29 (25,175)
Pettersen, Mark P	4:13:40 (14,422)
Pettersson, Anders	3:48:18 (7,805)
Pettie, Chris Ian	4:13:59 (14,501)
Pettit, Paul	3:57:22 (10,196)
Pettit, Stephen M	2:48:46 (435)
Pettitt, Alan	3:23:50 (3,412)
Pettitt, James Luke	5:11:42 (28,502)
Pettitt, Nigel	4:28:24 (18,487)
Petts, Ralph	4:24:49 (17,472)
Petty, Adam Stewart	3:53:22 (9,018)
Petty, Kevin	4:20:29 (16,256)
Pevsner, Stephen	3:39:41 (6,073)
Pewter, Ben	3:54:25 (9,304)
Pewter, Graham Charles	4:42:50 (22,225)
Pewter, Nick	5:31:55 (31,528)
Pewtner, Dan James	4:32:01 (19,441)
Peyrallo, Fernando	4:44:15 (22,577)
Pfyffer, Urs	3:26:27 (3,798)

Phagura, Gurinderpal Singh	5:38:25 (32,254)
Phelan, Chris	2:41:41 (244)
Phelan, Colin Patrick	5:11:59 (28,558)
Phelan, Julian Oliver	5:39:09 (32,317)
Phelps, Christopher Alan	5:26:50 (30,876)
Phelps, David	4:11:16 (13,782)
Phelps, John Richard	4:50:14 (24,099)
Phelps, Paul Robert	3:46:14 (7,362)
Philcox, Stephen D	3:10:44 (1,965)
Philip, Charles	5:48:06 (33,150)
Philip, Darren	3:33:09 (4,915)
Philip, David	3:04:19 (1,416)
Philipp, Frede	4:19:12 (15,898)
Philippe, Lavalard	5:57:18 (33,890)
Philippe, Vanpeene	4:07:24 (12,801)
Philippou, Tony	5:09:29 (28,141)
Philipps, Andrew Erwin	4:46:53 (23,279)
Philipse, Hein	4:19:11 (15,897)
Phillips, Adam	5:34:24 (31,811)
Phillips, Adam David	4:35:14 (20,278)
Phillips, Andrew	4:19:57 (16,086)
Phillips, Andrew Mark	4:44:28 (22,629)
Phillips, Anthony P	4:36:49 (20,689)
Phillips, Ben	4:01:27 (11,356)
Phillips, Brendan P	4:15:33 (14,916)
Phillips, Dale	3:35:45 (5,367)
Phillips, Daryl John	4:54:12 (25,100)
Phillips, David	4:39:49 (21,465)
Phillips, David J	3:44:24 (6,968)
Phillips, David M	4:27:52 (18,330)
Phillips, Dilwyn	5:31:26 (31,468)
Phillips, Eric S	2:36:41 (138)
Phillips, Gordon M	5:23:51 (30,448)
Phillips, Ian A	3:19:56 (2,954)
Phillips, James	3:42:38 (6,616)
Phillips, James	4:16:19 (15,112)
Phillips, James Robert	3:52:56 (8,908)
Phillips, Jonathan	5:26:52 (30,884)
Phillips, Jonny	3:57:13 (10,161)
Phillips, Julian	5:12:53 (28,717)
Phillips, Kevin	5:11:53 (28,539)
Phillips, Martyn Paul	4:40:29 (21,638)
Phillips, Michael John	3:34:52 (5,223)
Phillips, Michael Paul	4:59:43 (26,388)
Phillips, Mike Scott	4:49:36 (23,943)
Phillips, Neil	3:41:27 (6,415)
Phillips, Owen James	4:04:05 (11,984)
Phillips, Richard	3:06:02 (1,537)
Phillips, Rob Alan	4:02:46 (11,669)
Phillips, Robert	4:29:45 (18,899)
Phillips, Roger	4:04:55 (12,178)
Phillips, Scott	5:16:38 (29,328)
Phillips, Shaun	3:33:41 (5,004)
Phillips, Steffan Llyr	4:35:26 (20,337)
Phillips, Stephen Rupert	4:37:07 (20,776)
Phillips, Steven Norman	5:22:55 (30,295)
Phillips, Thomas Alexander	3:51:04 (8,440)
Phillips, Tony Peter	5:08:51 (28,024)
Phillips, Wayne Scott	5:49:55 (33,325)
Phillis, Richard Glyn	3:45:50 (7,274)
Phillpott, Thomas George	5:51:48 (33,492)
Philo, Mark R	3:53:40 (9,113)
Philp, Andrew	3:44:10 (6,909)
Philp, Ian M	5:51:43 (33,483)
Philpot, Saul Thomas	5:03:33 (27,110)
Philpott, David S	3:38:53 (5,918)
Philpott, Robin	3:44:47 (7,051)
Philpott, Ryan S	3:56:36 (9,958)
Phippard, Kevin	4:51:14 (24,361)
Phipps, Peter James	4:46:49 (23,259)
Phoenix, Andrew	3:57:02 (10,109)
Phoenix, Ian	4:05:19 (12,288)
Phull, Gurvinder	5:33:08 (31,679)
Phyland, Mathew	4:18:21 (15,672)
Pia, Dominic	4:53:48 (24,991)
Piacentino, Gerard-Antoine	4:37:25 (20,850)
Picardi, Antonio	4:29:41 (18,875)
Pichardo Ortega, Wilfredo	3:38:35 (5,866)
Pick, Dai	5:03:21 (27,080)
Pick, David Charles	4:19:29 (15,966)
Pick, Malcolm E	5:03:58 (27,179)
Pick, Robert M	3:29:01 (4,230)
Pickard, Andrew	5:08:19 (27,952)

Pickard, Mark John 3:52:54 (8,898)
Pickard, Olly 4:00:23 (11,085)
Pickavance, Michael Stephen 5:10:48 (28,377)
Pickel, Siegfried 4:27:27 (18,220)
Picken, James 3:22:52 (3,273)
Pickering, Daniel Oliver 3:33:24 (4,951)
Pickering, Darryl 3:54:54 (9,450)
Pickering, Derrick J 5:12:53 (28,717)
Pickering, James Robert 3:49:54 (8,188)
Pickering, John 4:00:50 (11,202)
Pickering, Robin A 3:58:40 (10,613)
Pickett, James 2:55:49 (788)
Pickett, Kenneth G 6:08:00 (34,559)
Pickford, Stephen Russell 3:21:25 (3,132)
Pickles, Joe 3:21:35 (3,145)
Picksley, James D 3:45:44 (7,255)
Pickthall, Chris 4:29:35 (18,833)
Pickup, Adam Joseph 6:01:57 (34,183)
Picot, Michael James 4:05:59 (12,455)
Picton, Colin 4:55:39 (25,447)
Picton, James H 4:15:41 (14,948)
Picton, Martin 3:53:03 (8,936)
Pidcock, Stephen 5:19:49 (29,826)
Pidgeon, Mark 3:48:39 (7,884)
Pidgeon, Philip J 5:03:41 (27,137)
Pierce, Jonathan Glyn 4:00:02 (10,992)
Pierce, Mark Kevin 6:16:46 (34,963)
Pierce, Richard James 7:04:02 (36,244)
Pierce, Stewart 4:33:37 (19,897)
Pieropan, Franco 5:16:09 (29,246)
Pierpoint, Richard 4:16:12 (15,071)
Pierre-Madigan, John Francis P 4:50:19 (24,119)
Pierson, Mathew 2:31:31 (79)
Pietrzak, Kersten 4:41:29 (21,887)
Piggin, Kenneth G 3:38:11 (5,800)
Piggott, Adam Craig 3:54:38 (9,368)
Piggott, Mark 5:20:43 (29,965)
Piggott, Richard 4:48:48 (23,747)
Piggott, Robert Anthony 5:25:25 (30,682)
Pigott-Smith, Tom 3:44:54 (7,080)
Pigram, Matt David 4:58:25 (26,068)
Pigram, Stuart John 4:18:40 (15,764)
Pihier, Michel 3:18:05 (2,777)
Piipponen, Lauri Johannes 4:56:53 (25,747)
Pike, David John 4:39:37 (21,418)
Pike, Neil 4:33:02 (19,708)
Pike, Nicholas David John 5:24:57 (30,614)
Pike, Richard D 4:54:23 (25,154)
Pikett, Richard Arthur 4:26:20 (17,910)
Pilavachi, Peter 4:46:29 (23,164)
Pilkington, Travis 3:55:56 (9,760)
Pillai, Jonathan Sivathanu 3:12:58 (2,186)
Pilling, Ben Daniel 5:42:11 (32,606)
Pilling, Dan 3:44:52 (7,071)
Pillinger, Karl S 6:04:19 (34,341)
Pilpay, Yannick 4:22:12 (16,761)
Pina, Juan 4:34:16 (20,062)
Pincay Macias, Rolando R 6:03:52 (34,313)
Pinckney, Richard 3:18:06 (2,780)
Pinder, David Andrew 3:46:33 (7,433)
Pinder, David Isaac 4:33:25 (19,829)
Pinder, Jeremy Alan 3:23:36 (3,377)
Pinder, Wayne 5:02:09 (26,879)
Pine, Christopher 5:51:49 (33,494)
Pines Gil, Javir 3:45:53 (7,289)
Pinho, Marcelo 3:41:01 (6,330)
Pinkerton, James 4:10:36 (13,618)
Pinkney, Stephen John 5:48:19 (33,177)
Pinnell, Jack 4:26:57 (18,067)
Pinnington, Lee 5:00:39 (26,579)
Pinnock, Geoffrey 4:45:45 (22,968)
Pinsent, Christopher 4:25:23 (17,629)
Pinsent, John 4:11:45 (13,922)
Pinson, Anthony W 3:44:06 (6,900)
Pinson-Bradley, Christopher 4:39:23 (21,350)
Pinto, Antonio 4:28:18 (18,452)
Pinto, Arturo 3:46:27 (7,410)
Piper, Alastair James 4:11:14 (13,776)
Piper, Freddie 3:42:01 (6,511)
Piper, Matthew 4:11:00 (13,715)
Piper, Paul J 4:13:34 (14,390)
Piper, Simon Mark 3:02:15 (1,275)
Piras, Andrea 3:00:25 (1,169)

Pirie, Ben Stephen 6:25:39 (35,334)
Pirola, Jean Luc 4:56:01 (25,541)
Pisal, Narendra V 4:13:01 (14,244)
Pishias, Christos 4:57:53 (25,944)
Pistilli, Vittorio 3:13:11 (2,210)
Pitchell, Ian 3:35:32 (5,332)
Pitcher, Gordon 5:26:49 (30,874)
Pitcher, Jason A 2:59:47 (1,134)
Pitchers, Oliver 4:16:11 (15,068)
Pitchford, Gary S 4:10:48 (13,665)
Pitchforth, Darren 5:33:40 (31,735)
Pitchforth, Mathew 5:51:10 (33,440)
Pite, Jason 6:13:50 (34,831)
Pitman, Barry 3:16:57 (2,663)
Pitman, Stephen 5:01:27 (26,744)
Pitney, Michael James 6:22:30 (35,208)
Pitt, Andrew Paul 4:01:24 (11,339)
Pitt, Chris James 4:39:03 (21,269)
Pitt, Graham 3:50:54 (8,403)
Pitt, Phillip Alexander 4:06:47 (12,653)
Pitt, Richard 4:39:21 (21,340)
Pitt, Russell 6:14:33 (34,861)
Pitt, Stephen J 3:41:43 (6,460)
Pittaway, Mark 2:51:23 (537)
Pitts, Andrew S 2:52:39 (603)
Pitts, Craig 5:53:01 (33,584)
Pitts, Jonathan 3:14:38 (2,402)
Pitts, Lucas 4:08:47 (13,156)
Pitts, Simon M 4:02:30 (11,601)
Pitura, Mark 4:38:18 (21,054)
Pivano, Sarfraz 2:58:15 (983)
Placid-Hurst, Darren E 5:24:55 (30,607)
Placitelli, Paul 5:12:59 (28,738)
Plank, Ben M 4:24:33 (17,407)
Plank, Lee 4:01:34 (11,385)
Plant, Dan 4:41:20 (21,848)
Plant, Iain James 4:50:01 (24,051)
Plant, Jerry 3:57:16 (10,175)
Plant, Lee Anthony 4:20:30 (16,260)
Plant, Selwyn 3:56:53 (10,051)
Plasencia, Raul E 4:55:37 (25,443)
Plaskitt, Neil Robert 5:44:34 (32,824)
Platt, Carl 3:16:13 (2,577)
Platt, Gary 3:14:34 (2,391)
Platt, Glen 5:56:12 (33,809)
Platt, Simon James 4:29:54 (18,953)
Platt, Stephen 4:20:54 (16,387)
Platte, David Michael 4:47:17 (23,362)
Platts, Ben 4:51:28 (24,411)
Platts, Rob 3:50:43 (8,362)
Plaw, Adrian 4:45:50 (22,985)
Plebani, Gianfranco 4:42:16 (22,084)
Plebani, Massimo 4:10:54 (13,692)
Pleming, David Alexander 3:13:46 (2,292)
Plested, Stuart 4:16:14 (15,084)
Plester, Russell J 3:39:42 (6,078)
Plettinck, Filip W 3:41:44 (6,464)
Plews, Andrew P 3:12:42 (2,154)
Plose, Matt 3:52:08 (8,689)
Plowman, James 5:52:52 (33,574)
Pludra, Jens 3:41:10 (6,354)
Plumb, Richard John 5:04:36 (27,297)
Plumb, Steve 3:55:57 (9,766)
Plummer, Kevin J 3:20:21 (2,996)
Plummer, Lee C 4:24:09 (17,272)
Plummer, Matthew Robert 4:00:12 (11,031)
Plummer, Robert 4:11:33 (13,863)
Plumridge, Adam 3:39:27 (6,033)
Plumridge, Neil J 3:12:30 (2,133)
Plumridge, Stuart D 3:52:15 (8,719)
Plunkett, Richard 3:27:16 (3,919)
Poade, Matthew J 3:58:55 (10,691)
Poblete, Gonzalo 3:18:31 (2,823)
Pocknell, Carl 4:27:37 (18,264)
Pocock, Andrew John Cullum 3:52:27 (8,777)
Pocock, Chris 4:34:00 (19,993)
Pocock, John William 3:41:34 (6,433)
Pocock, Michael J 3:24:02 (3,435)
Podbury, Thomas 4:04:32 (12,080)
Poddar, Kish Kumar 6:52:09 (36,049)
Podmore, John J 4:35:43 (20,392)
Podschun, James 4:25:27 (17,649)
Poeti, Mark 5:13:38 (28,863)

Poeton, Daniel Barrie 4:26:56 (18,062)
Poggi, Alessandro 2:57:42 (932)
Pointet, David Adrian Jackman 5:09:45 (28,189)
Pointon, Matt 2:46:46 (379)
Pokropek, Dominic Joseph 5:02:40 (26,972)
Polaine, Danny 5:06:12 (27,567)
Polak Ben Porat, Yoram 3:48:32 (7,853)
Pole, Michael 3:41:33 (6,430)
Poli, Danilo 4:02:21 (11,565)
Poll, Stuart 5:42:52 (32,658)
Pollak, Alex 5:46:15 (32,977)
Pollard, Adam 5:29:48 (31,269)
Pollard, Andrew J 3:34:57 (5,240)
Pollard, Anthony G 3:09:27 (1,853)
Pollard, Donald 4:43:59 (22,502)
Pollard, Ian F 2:58:48 (1,030)
Pollard, Phil Michael 4:37:33 (20,896)
Pollard, Richard D 4:23:50 (17,196)
Pollett, Matthew 3:40:02 (6,154)
Polley, Keith Alfred 5:49:08 (33,250)
Pollikett, Mark D 3:56:37 (9,964)
Pollington, Ian Simon 4:52:18 (24,639)
Pollock, Darren 4:53:05 (24,814)
Pollock, Jeremy R 2:55:51 (791)
Pollock, Stephen J 3:57:50 (10,337)
Polo, Roberto 4:40:13 (21,543)
Polonio, Antonio 6:08:00 (34,559)
Polycarpou, Louis 3:39:07 (5,968)
Pomeroy, Richard T 3:27:50 (4,021)
Pomfret, Christopher John 4:38:41 (21,165)
Pomfret, Graham L 3:18:43 (2,844)
Pond, Andrew John 3:27:50 (4,021)
Pond, Christopher M 3:36:06 (5,429)
Pond, Martin J 3:49:16 (8,039)
Pond, Nick 4:18:06 (15,608)
Pons, Fernando José 4:11:04 (13,738)
Pons, Philippe 4:48:20 (23,616)
Ponsford, Alan 5:22:34 (30,232)
Ponsford, Alex 4:12:31 (14,103)
Pook, James Anthony 4:16:16 (15,092)
Poole, Alec 5:29:20 (31,199)
Poole, Chris 4:28:35 (18,547)
Poole, Jason 4:23:40 (17,147)
Poole, Jonathan 4:57:54 (25,948)
Poole, Joshua Alexander 5:16:43 (29,339)
Poole, Matthew James 5:00:53 (26,629)
Poole, Nicholas 6:38:26 (35,738)
Poole, Nick 5:23:36 (30,404)
Poole, Richard James 6:04:02 (34,324)
Poole, William 5:13:04 (28,763)
Pooley, Martin 4:38:09 (21,016)
Poortinga, Wouter 3:23:48 (3,407)
Poots, Jon 4:40:04 (21,510)
Poots, Tim 3:47:45 (7,694)
Pope, Alan 4:21:32 (16,556)
Pope, Andrew 3:35:32 (5,332)
Pope, Christopher J 4:05:23 (12,303)
Pope, Christopher Luke 4:05:23 (12,303)
Pope, Conrad Ansell Terence 5:12:44 (28,689)
Pope, Roger 5:37:59 (32,211)
Pope, Tim 4:05:32 (12,341)
Pope, Tom 3:27:48 (4,013)
Pope, William 5:04:10 (27,222)
Popovac, Zoran 4:07:33 (12,847)
Popovici, Silviu 4:28:09 (18,397)
Popple, Stuart A 3:49:31 (8,097)
Portabella, Ricardo 3:40:36 (6,260)
Portal, Robert 3:57:29 (10,225)
Portelli, Kellinu Joseph 3:53:08 (8,950)
Porter, Adam 5:17:01 (29,391)
Porter, Alan 4:44:23 (22,609)
Porter, Alex J 3:27:10 (3,900)
Porter, Andrew 3:57:40 (10,286)
Porter, Ben 4:41:51 (21,982)
Porter, Brian 4:06:35 (12,596)
Porter, Chris 4:26:48 (18,024)
Porter, Christopher P 4:31:59 (19,428)
Porter, David R 5:17:29 (29,470)
Porter, Elliott James Antony 4:17:42 (15,497)
Porter, Errol 4:20:28 (16,252)
Porter, Garry 3:24:25 (3,499)
Porter, Lloyd 4:56:38 (25,673)
Porter, Martin 4:48:37 (23,699)

Porter, Mitchell 5:12:29 (28,650)
Porter, Neil 5:44:36 (32,827)
Porter, Paul Jonathan 6:05:05 (34,389)
Porter, Richard Jonathan 4:59:51 (26,414)
Porter, Scott David 3:48:46 (7,914)
Porter, Wayne A 5:32:30 (31,603)
Porterfield, John 5:27:20 (30,944)
Portero, Luis 3:58:06 (10,414)
Porthouse, David 5:08:23 (27,961)
Porthouse, Stephen G 3:58:02 (10,391)
Portillo, Carlos 5:03:49 (27,159)
Portlock, Andy 5:20:36 (29,946)
Posey, Bryn D 5:53:06 (33,586)
Postance, Paul David 4:11:48 (13,932)
Postle, Gary Mark 3:22:04 (3,199)
Postlethwaite, Gary 4:44:58 (22,759)
Postma, Menno 4:17:49 (15,530)
Postnikov, Alexey 4:15:44 (14,962)
Potgieter, Johannes Albertus 4:35:06 (20,251)
Potiron, Patrick 4:40:53 (21,740)
Potter, Adam D 5:37:07 (32,118)
Potter, Adrian J 4:22:44 (16,913)
Potter, Andrew J 4:06:47 (12,653)
Potter, David 5:39:35 (32,355)
Potter, Gareth Bryan 3:16:35 (2,626)
Potter, Ian 4:40:23 (21,607)
Potter, James 4:05:52 (12,424)
Potter, Keith 4:48:32 (23,677)
Potter, Luke 4:45:39 (22,935)
Potter, Mark 7:21:47 (36,414)
Potter, Mark J 3:03:22 (1,339)
Potter, Mike 5:48:58 (33,239)
Potter, Neil Darren 4:30:30 (19,090)
Potter, Robert John 4:22:21 (16,804)
Potter, Sam 5:40:40 (32,449)
Pottinger, Jamie 3:41:24 (6,405)
Potton, Phil 4:37:08 (20,779)
Potton, Steven 5:32:31 (31,605)
Potts, Christopher 4:01:15 (11,306)
Potts, Colin I 2:34:23 (102)
Potts, Daniel Mark 4:19:49 (16,045)
Potts, Joanathan Richard 4:21:30 (16,548)
Potts, Russell 4:19:03 (15,855)
Poulard, Bruno 4:52:50 (24,764)
Poulsom, Thomas James 4:34:47 (20,190)
Poulter, David 3:56:25 (9,903)
Poulter, Matthew 3:32:47 (4,855)
Poulter, Stephen James 5:19:38 (29,797)
Poulton, Barney S 4:39:45 (21,447)
Pound, Daniel 4:28:12 (18,417)
Pounder, Anthony 4:00:41 (11,166)
Pounder, Matthew 3:55:47 (9,711)
Powell, Aaron 3:33:07 (4,910)
Powell, Anthony L 5:33:59 (31,762)
Powell, Edward David 3:28:10 (4,086)
Powell, Frank 6:23:18 (35,250)
Powell, Gerry 3:52:09 (8,694)
Powell, Graeme John 5:22:54 (30,292)
Powell, Gregg J 3:51:06 (8,450)
Powell, Jeff 5:07:28 (27,804)
Powell, Jeffrey Richard 4:34:42 (20,171)
Powell, John Edward 5:32:25 (31,588)
Powell, Joseph 4:07:26 (12,810)
Powell, Keith James 4:17:35 (15,464)
Powell, Matty 4:36:53 (20,711)
Powell, Mike 2:49:10 (449)
Powell, Mike 4:10:31 (13,597)
Powell, Nathan C 3:10:51 (1,978)
Powell, Peter William Harry 3:44:58 (7,089)
Powell, Richard John 4:45:03 (22,782)
Powell, Robert I 4:44:36 (22,670)
Powell, Robert John 4:28:15 (18,436)
Powell, Robin 4:08:29 (13,074)
Powell, Roger Norman 4:01:53 (11,466)
Powell, Steven 4:44:57 (22,755)
Powell, Tony 4:29:01 (18,691)
Power, Danny 4:00:00 (10,984)
Power, Gary 3:28:34 (4,157)
Power, Gary A 4:20:14 (16,173)
Power, Iain Moorfield 4:24:36 (17,419)
Power, Michael 3:23:45 (3,401)
Power, Nick George 3:48:00 (7,738)
Power, Sean 4:16:58 (15,287)

LONDON MARATHON

Power, Sean 4:23:30 (17,104)
Power, Tim R 4:40:03 (21,508)
Powles, Jim 4:00:28 (11,111)
Powles, Mark 5:17:05 (29,397)
Powling, Jonathan David 3:41:44 (6,464)
Pownall, Andrew William 3:17:53 (2,751)
Pownall, Lee John 3:52:39 (8,836)
Poynter, Adrian 3:44:18 (6,938)
Poynton, James David 3:44:47 (7,051)
Poyser, Tony 5:23:51 (30,448)
Prada, Graziano 3:53:24 (9,030)
Prader, Ulrich 3:23:41 (3,392)
Praill, John 4:36:54 (20,715)
Prandi, Marcello 3:41:09 (6,353)
Prankard, Simon 4:43:43 (22,423)
Prater, Ben 3:51:42 (8,587)
Prathesh, Amirthanathan 4:48:19 (23,609)
Pratt, Christopher John 3:30:18 (4,470)
Pratt, David Stirling 4:42:42 (22,186)
Pratt, James 3:57:43 (10,308)
Pratt, Jonathan 4:43:50 (22,456)
Pratten, Christopher C 3:20:33 (3,032)
Pravia, David Segura 5:17:34 (29,484)
Preece, Dave 5:11:08 (28,427)
Preen, Kevin 4:22:19 (16,796)
Pregio, Davide 5:13:28 (28,841)
Preiss, Ingo 5:09:14 (28,090)
Prendergast, Danny 4:15:07 (14,813)
Prendergast, Eamon 4:20:16 (16,185)
Prendergast, Michael Francis 5:35:53 (31,982)
Prentice, Craig 5:09:17 (28,102)
Prentice, Stuart N 3:05:08 (1,472)
Prentis, Adam Richard 3:59:09 (10,760)
Preou, Ray Julian 3:52:20 (8,750)
Prescott, Neil John 2:59:04 (1,060)
Prescott, Richard W 4:39:35 (21,408)
Prescott, Simon 5:05:37 (27,470)
Prescott, Stephen 4:24:30 (17,388)
Press, John Malcolm 5:31:35 (31,483)
Pressey, Jonathan 4:30:26 (19,072)
Pressland, Michael Alexander 4:26:33 (17,969)
Pressler, Oliver 3:24:09 (3,460)
Pressly, James 5:30:56 (31,406)
Preston, Alistair 4:36:59 (20,738)
Preston, Damian Sean 4:30:45 (19,159)
Preston, Darren 3:07:04 (1,616)
Preston, Dean Marc 4:45:47 (22,975)
Preston, Ed 4:13:31 (14,369)
Preston, Guy F 3:54:38 (9,368)
Preston, Martin 4:28:18 (18,452)
Preston, Paul 4:56:00 (25,535)
Preston, Robert A 3:08:55 (1,801)
Preston, Ryan Michael 3:51:03 (8,435)
Preston, Wayne 4:43:44 (22,432)
Prestridge, Jeffrey John 3:32:52 (4,875)
Prestwich, David 4:55:01 (25,310)
Pretorius, Barend J 4:57:05 (25,777)
Prettyman, Alex J 3:39:18 (6,005)
Preuilh, Jean-Michel 3:07:27 (1,647)
Prevett, Ian 5:12:47 (28,699)
Priaulx, Andy 3:49:31 (8,097)
Pribble, Vince Alan 4:28:58 (18,670)
Pribyl, Ondrej 3:14:34 (2,391)
Price, Aaron David 6:44:55 (35,904)
Price, Alex 5:34:14 (31,785)
Price, Anthony Gerald 4:38:10 (21,021)
Price, Cedric J 4:39:49 (21,465)
Price, Curt 4:32:22 (19,533)
Price, Danny 6:18:55 (35,078)
Price, Darren Andrew 4:21:14 (16,469)
Price, Darren John 3:47:42 (7,684)
Price, Gareth 2:30:02 (70)
Price, Gary 3:45:14 (7,147)
Price, Gavin 3:44:24 (6,968)
Price, James 3:56:11 (9,837)
Price, James 5:09:41 (28,176)
Price, Jim 4:32:16 (19,505)
Price, Julian Richard 3:57:37 (10,268)
Price, Mark 5:06:29 (27,625)
Price, Matt 4:33:53 (19,963)
Price, Matthew William Ian 3:20:24 (3,007)
Price, Neil 5:25:09 (30,646)
Price, Neil Robert 5:30:47 (31,391)
Price, Paul T 3:26:40 (3,825)
Price, Rhys 4:26:13 (17,877)
Price, Richard 3:22:13 (3,211)
Price, Richard 4:22:14 (16,776)
Price, Rob 3:51:53 (8,632)
Price, Roger M 3:46:03 (7,322)
Price, Stan T 4:16:14 (15,084)
Price, Stephen G 2:45:38 (352)
Price,, Jonathan, 4:47:55 (23,522)
Prichard, Andrew J 4:40:49 (21,728)
Prichard, John 5:13:17 (28,815)
Prichard, Thomas David 4:27:52 (18,330)
Priday, Joe R 4:43:44 (22,432)
Priekulis, Bernie 3:28:54 (4,210)
Priest, Alistair W 4:46:37 (23,209)
Priest, Daniel Richard 3:06:06 (1,541)
Priest, Thomas Eward 3:15:17 (2,472)
Priestley, Chris L 3:44:56 (7,085)
Priestley, Derek Robert 5:29:59 (31,295)
Priestley, Donald Stuart 3:47:16 (7,591)
Priestley, Michael David 6:37:20 (35,707)
Priestley, Richard J 5:27:37 (30,980)
Prigmore, Sean 4:27:41 (18,284)
Prill, Ebe 3:22:07 (3,201)
Primarolo, George 5:44:39 (32,834)
Prime, Chris John 5:35:04 (31,885)
Primrose, Tim 4:34:41 (20,168)
Prin, Jean Louis 4:12:44 (14,165)
Prince, Elliot J 2:43:00 (278)
Prince, Luke 3:19:54 (2,953)
Prine, David D 4:45:33 (22,901)
Pring, Nick David 3:44:49 (7,058)
Pring, Richard A 4:37:30 (20,881)
Pringle, Brett 6:32:28 (35,577)
Pringle, Simon James David 5:41:08 (32,500)
Pringle, Stuart 3:17:18 (2,693)
Prior, Andrew 6:06:02 (34,454)
Prior, Craig D 4:13:49 (14,460)
Prior, Huw 4:52:55 (24,779)
Prior, Michael E 5:03:41 (27,137)
Prior, Richie 5:55:11 (33,732)
Prior, Tim 4:14:02 (14,514)
Prior, Tom 4:43:05 (22,279)
Pritchard, Alan R 2:55:03 (749)
Pritchard, Benjamin Hal 4:51:32 (24,426)
Pritchard, Doug 4:43:47 (22,436)
Pritchard, Edwin John 3:46:49 (7,494)
Pritchard, Graham J 3:08:46 (1,790)
Pritchard, Matthew 4:21:18 (16,490)
Pritchard, Matthew 5:15:12 (29,100)
Pritchard, Philip Leslie James 3:42:25 (6,580)
Pritchard, Shaun Mark 6:00:50 (34,118)
Pritchett, Daniel Oliver 3:33:19 (4,936)
Probee, Stuart Dennis McLean 3:32:35 (4,823)
Probert, Timothy 4:12:50 (14,187)
Probert, Tom 3:56:55 (10,063)
Probyn, Simon T 5:04:45 (27,326)
Prochazka, Ivo 3:21:49 (3,172)
Procope, Harry 3:47:58 (7,731)
Procter, Daniel Francis 4:15:49 (14,984)
Procter, Jeremy Guy 4:40:28 (21,633)
Proctor, Richard Douglas 4:31:44 (19,381)
Proctor, Stephen Mark 5:35:49 (31,971)
Prodger, Nbe 5:29:19 (31,194)
Prosser, Andrew Michael 3:59:22 (10,827)
Prosser, Paul 3:36:09 (5,437)
Protani, Roberto 3:18:48 (2,851)
Prothero, Robert A 3:42:45 (6,646)
Prothero, Simon Christopher 5:01:23 (26,729)
Proto, Vince 5:41:01 (32,486)
Proud, Andy 3:25:52 (3,717)
Proud, David 2:56:23 (825)
Proudfoot, Alan 3:53:29 (9,051)
Prout, Michael J 3:20:28 (3,017)

Provan, Andrew Peter 5:22:24 (30,207)
Provan, Brian William 5:05:06 (27,386)
Prowse, Philip 4:17:24 (15,405)
Pruchnickyj, Pat 4:28:24 (18,487)
Prudham, Joseph P 4:14:24 (14,613)
Prue, Ivan N 6:03:00 (34,251)
Pryce, Alistair Mark 4:11:02 (13,726)
Pryce, Nicholas Mark 5:28:22 (31,071)
Pryce, Simon Patrick 3:18:12 (2,794)
Pryde, Gary 4:28:15 (18,436)
Pryde, Simon John 4:10:28 (13,586)
Pryke, Nicholas 4:34:37 (20,150)
Pryke, Philip Edward 3:41:39 (6,447)
Pryke, Timothy Philip 4:06:07 (12,478)
Pryke, William M 4:35:40 (20,380)
Psaros, Nicholas 4:04:43 (12,136)
Puckett, Graham 3:57:28 (10,221)
Pudney, Christopher D 3:01:26 (1,226)
Puffer, Tim 6:45:42 (35,923)
Pugh, Colin Humphrey 4:43:55 (22,481)
Pugh, David 5:08:07 (27,915)
Pugh, Gavin 3:09:51 (1,896)
Pugh, Harvey 4:03:30 (11,844)
Pugh, Jason 3:24:01 (3,433)
Pugh, Kevin James 4:12:46 (14,176)
Pugh, Matthew Stuart 4:09:49 (13,424)
Pugh, Nick John 3:48:34 (7,866)
Pugh, Patrick 3:24:59 (3,577)
Pugliese, Francesco 3:04:08 (1,404)
Pulford, Kieran David 3:10:44 (1,965)
Pulford, Tom 6:09:45 (34,649)
Pullan, Russell 4:45:04 (22,788)
Pullan, Sam A 2:52:24 (588)
Pullen, Graham 3:30:20 (4,475)
Pullen, Leslie C 5:12:41 (28,682)
Pullen, Matt 4:25:09 (17,560)
Pullen, Matt 4:27:34 (18,252)
Pullen, Miles 3:46:04 (7,330)
Pullen, Nick 3:37:39 (5,699)
Pulling, Charlie D 4:03:21 (11,813)
Pullinger, Richard Malone 3:04:02 (1,397)
Pumfleet, Jon 4:07:43 (12,889)
Punch, Chris 5:04:25 (27,262)
Punchard, Gavin M 2:57:28 (902)
Punshon, Tom 4:32:43 (19,610)
Puntan, Piers 3:43:46 (6,821)
Puppel, Robert 4:48:56 (23,782)
Purcell, Ewen 4:04:09 (11,996)
Purcell, Frank 5:52:26 (33,530)
Purcell, Sean Lee 3:12:57 (2,184)
Purchase, Lee 5:01:53 (26,827)
Purdell-Lewis, Jeremy 4:36:57 (20,729)
Purdie, Stephen M 3:29:38 (4,348)
Purdy, Mark A 3:11:55 (2,085)
Purdy, Philip Ian 3:41:15 (6,379)
Purdy, Simon 3:56:01 (9,790)
Purnell, Christopher J 4:57:41 (25,905)
Purnell, David 4:58:30 (26,089)
Purnell, Jeremy P 3:14:52 (2,426)
Purnell, Sam David 6:33:01 (35,595)
Puron Lozano, José Antonio 4:21:20 (16,500)
Purser, Matthew George 4:03:00 (11,733)
Pursey, Ashley 4:52:44 (24,735)
Purslow, Colin 4:42:50 (22,225)
Purslow, Philip 4:03:49 (11,928)
Purves, Philip 4:03:08 (11,765)
Purvis, Andrew 4:07:01 (12,714)
Purvis, Darrell 4:45:36 (22,916)
Purvis, Darren M 2:37:50 (159)
Purvis, Keith 2:57:15 (876)
Pusey, Andrew 3:20:34 (3,036)
Puttock, Ian 4:48:33 (23,679)
Puxley, Alexander Charles 3:38:10 (5,798)
Pybus, Thomas James 3:07:25 (1,644)
Pye, Alan E 3:23:20 (3,344)
Pye, Callum Nicholas 5:13:02 (28,744)
Pye, Chris J 4:49:15 (23,865)
Pye, Greg Jonathan 3:52:49 (8,877)
Pye, Matt 4:50:14 (24,099)
Pye, Roy F 4:45:17 (22,835)
Pyle, David 3:33:55 (5,043)
Pyne, Daniel T 2:58:46 (1,027)
Pyne, David J 4:13:53 (14,478)
Pyrke, Christopher 5:27:36 (30,977)
Quaglia, Jean Louis 4:57:13 (25,808)
Quantrill, Philip 2:50:55 (522)
Quarterman, Raymond Peter 4:27:42 (18,288)
Quattromini, Gianriccardo 4:10:57 (13,700)
Quayle, Jonathan C 4:38:32 (21,124)
Quayle, Scott John 4:39:47 (21,457)
Queen, Jon 4:05:16 (12,276)
Quelch, Russell Graham Patrick 3:54:32 (9,337)
Quere, Eric 3:44:58 (7,089)
Querstret, John P 2:57:35 (913)
Quesada, Juan Manuel 4:43:50 (22,456)
Quest, Jonathan D 3:32:47 (4,855)
Queyraud, Franck 3:30:14 (4,461)
Quick, Rob James 5:01:50 (26,816)
Quick, Shane 5:02:25 (26,932)
Quilty, Denis 5:32:22 (31,583)
Quin, Anthony 4:45:25 (22,865)
Quin, Bob 4:29:25 (18,780)
Quin, Stephen Robert 4:20:09 (16,150)
Quine, David A 5:46:17 (32,980)
Quine, Paul 2:51:29 (544)
Quinlan, Paul 3:48:29 (7,843)
Quinn, Anthony 4:06:44 (12,635)
Quinn, Carl P 3:03:51 (1,377)
Quinn, Charles Edward 4:38:20 (21,067)
Quinn, Eamonn 6:19:49 (35,116)
Quinn, Gary Thomas 5:31:19 (31,453)
Quinn, James J 4:09:39 (13,385)
Quinn, John 4:58:32 (26,097)
Quinn, Malcolm K 5:05:30 (27,450)
Quinn, Martin 3:11:32 (2,052)
Quinn, Richard James 5:19:10 (29,730)
Quinn, Scott 5:26:48 (30,871)
Quinn, Stephen 4:16:41 (15,215)
Quinn, Steven 4:38:46 (21,193)
Quinn, Thomas 4:59:41 (26,380)
Quinn, Thomas S 3:24:58 (3,575)
Quinn, Will Anthony Patrick 4:02:31 (11,608)
Quinn Aziz, Abyd 3:54:28 (9,317)
Quinnell, David 4:44:43 (22,701)
Quin-Stanley, Ben 5:00:25 (26,539)
Quintanilla, Alvaro 3:51:38 (8,575)
Quinton, Paul 4:11:02 (13,726)
Quirk, Derek 7:47:52 (36,556)
Quixley, Gregg Anthony 4:20:44 (16,347)
Qureshi, Amir 6:19:34 (35,107)
Qureshi, Simon 4:24:10 (17,279)
Qureshi, Zafar 5:15:16 (29,109)
Qvarnstrøm, Hans 4:17:45 (15,512)
Raath, Anton D 4:29:13 (18,737)
Raatz, Wolfgang 3:31:02 (4,584)
Rabbetts, Alex 4:02:56 (11,715)
Rabbetts, Mark A 2:44:40 (326)
Rabbitts, Desmond G 5:37:37 (32,175)
Rabin, Jeremy Jake 4:39:50 (21,473)
Rabinowitz, Gideon 4:32:56 (19,680)
Rabjohns, Peter 2:51:35 (548)
Race, Andrew Brian 3:00:32 (1,175)
Race, Kevin 3:42:22 (6,574)
Racher, Graham 3:56:12 (9,841)
Rackham, Mark 4:38:59 (21,256)
Rackham, Nigel D 2:36:05 (128)
Rackley, Trevor 5:28:31 (31,090)
Rackwitz, Silvia 5:11:07 (28,423)
Radcliffe, Jonathan 4:20:50 (16,373)
Radcliffe, Lee 4:40:27 (21,628)
Radcliffe, Richard 3:16:17 (2,584)
Radcliffe, Simon 3:34:38 (5,180)
Radcliffe, Toby 2:48:32 (433)
Radford, Ian 4:51:54 (24,521)
Radford, Paul John 3:04:13 (1,410)
Radford, Sean Richard 3:54:42 (9,387)
Radford-Lewis, James 5:04:43 (27,324)
Radia, Raj S 5:05:01 (27,371)
Radley, Adam Derek 4:35:31 (20,349)
Radley, Malcolm Bruce 4:03:19 (11,804)
Radway, Jon Michael 4:19:32 (15,978)
Raffaelli, Noam 5:09:27 (28,132)
Rafferty, Andy 5:04:37 (27,300)
Raffo, Paul 4:13:01 (14,244)
Ragg, David Paul 3:57:00 (10,089)
Raggett, Jonathan 4:21:41 (16,600)
Raggett, Phil 4:33:42 (19,918)

Raghwani, Vimal Kalyan 4:51:55 (24,530)

Automatic ballot entry this year, and what a year, to run as part of the 30th anniversary of the London Marathon, and the first time its been sponsored by Virgin. It was a real pleasure in choosing my charity, Oxfam. Training was mentally gruelling, but worth it. Loved every single minute of it. Thank you to my dear wife Arti, braving the cold to come and support me from the start line. It was a very exciting race. Managed to stick to my 11 minutes and 30 seconds a mile pace all the way right through to the end. Only one blister and one black toe, all in the name of a fantastic charity, Oxfam. Thank you London Marathon, Oxfam, family and friends, you made it very special for me. Vimal.

Rahman, Ehsan 6:48:09 (35,964)
Rahman, Jalil 5:19:10 (29,730)
Rahman, Kamran 5:10:45 (28,366)
Rahmani, Khalid 3:14:12 (2,341)
Rai, Suraj 7:05:12 (36,255)
Railson, Stuart Vaughan 4:02:56 (11,715)
Raimondi, Renzo 2:53:18 (630)
Rainbow, Dennis T 2:56:34 (837)
Rainbow, James 3:47:04 (7,538)
Rainbow, Mark Oliver 5:36:14 (32,021)
Raine, Anthony Christian 4:12:50 (14,187)
Raine, Richard D 4:58:06 (25,986)
Raines, Tom Gorege 5:11:01 (28,408)
Raingeval, Benjamin 3:58:08 (10,426)
Rainsford, Robert T 3:22:31 (3,241)
Rainsforth, Chris J 4:29:13 (18,737)
Raisborough, Owen 3:29:59 (4,413)
Rajabi, Ali 4:56:52 (25,737)
Rajani, Ajay 5:52:17 (33,521)
Rajendran, Rahulan 3:58:37 (10,598)
Rajpura, Arif 6:05:34 (34,424)
Raju, Maran 4:07:19 (12,779)
Rajwani, Hanif 4:37:14 (20,803)
Rajwani, Salim 4:59:45 (26,395)
Rake, Toby 3:54:40 (9,375)
Ralli, Alexander P 5:15:48 (29,200)
Ralph, John Peter 3:09:11 (1,823)
Ralph, Malcolm Alan 4:51:41 (24,457)
Ralph, Philip 4:32:33 (19,572)
Ralphs, Richard M 2:54:23 (693)
Ramberg, Thorsten 4:15:29 (14,902)
Ramchandani, John 4:29:04 (18,707)
Ramdhian, David Kumar 4:33:42 (19,918)
Ramirez, Freddy 3:27:04 (3,879)
Ramirez, Rolland 6:28:15 (35,436)
Ramirez Jimenez, Rolando 3:49:51 (8,176)
Ramos, Dionisio 4:10:27 (13,579)
Rampton, David S 4:26:18 (17,900)

Rampton, Tom 4:31:08 (19,250)
Ramsay, Douglas V 4:09:24 (13,313)
Ramsay, Ian 3:32:54 (4,879)
Ramsden, Adrian 7:55:48 (36,581)
Ramsden, Anthony 4:42:10 (22,053)
Ramsell, Chris D 3:13:38 (2,270)
Ramsell, Ian R 4:03:51 (11,936)
Ramsey, Adam J 3:52:15 (8,719)
Ramsey, John 6:15:13 (34,900)
Ramsey Smith, David 3:34:31 (5,159)
Ramus, Dave 4:13:48 (14,457)
Ramus, Steve 3:52:59 (8,921)
Rance, Chris 4:58:06 (25,986)
Rance, John Paul 3:05:45 (1,519)
Rance, Keith 5:03:39 (27,127)
Rance Cachafeiro, Oswaldo 3:50:14 (8,255)
Rancon, Pierre 3:06:51 (1,596)
Rand, Keith 4:08:57 (13,193)
Rand, Steven 2:55:17 (760)
Randall, Grant 4:42:18 (22,095)
Randall, James 3:54:15 (9,272)
Randall, Joe 4:33:26 (19,836)
Randall, Karl Matthew 4:34:57 (20,222)
Randall, Marc 6:22:32 (35,211)
Randall, Mike 4:43:20 (22,325)
Randall, Stuart 6:27:52 (35,416)
Randall, Timothy 4:37:07 (20,776)
Randell, Michael Kevin 4:53:08 (24,832)
Randell, Paul Gordon 5:45:26 (32,903)
Randell, Tony 2:55:52 (794)
Randeree, Zayid 6:29:38 (35,481)
Randles, Stephen 4:26:45 (18,011)
Rands, Guy Daniel 4:40:57 (21,759)
Rane, Neil 4:04:51 (12,164)
Rang, Simon T 3:37:12 (5,599)
Rangel, José Victor 3:38:56 (5,926)
Ranger, Wesley David Joseph 4:32:41 (19,602)
Rankin, André Eric 3:30:42 (4,529)
Rankin, Ian P 3:54:20 (9,289)
Rann, James P 3:54:51 (9,437)
Rann, Thomas 3:36:29 (5,478)
Rannard, Mark 4:56:15 (25,595)
Ranner, Will 4:53:13 (24,853)
Ranpura, Kirit 4:14:39 (14,700)
Ransom, Mike 5:28:58 (31,147)
Ransome, Trevor John Ivan 6:30:44 (35,526)
Rant, Robert J 4:27:05 (18,114)
Ranta, Ronald 6:11:08 (34,705)
Rapeau, Jean-Jacques 4:30:51 (19,180)
Raphael, WK 4:54:15 (25,114)
Rapson, Greg Paul 4:52:23 (24,657)
Rarity, Dave 4:20:22 (16,223)
Rashleigh, Ian 5:02:46 (26,988)
Rashussen, Carsten K 5:18:46 (29,660)
Raslan, Adel 5:19:24 (29,761)
Rasmussen, Jan Christian 4:32:50 (19,649)
Rasmussen, Sven Grud 5:51:12 (33,442)
Rasouli, Nick 5:02:16 (26,900)
Raspin, Anthony James 4:33:52 (19,959)
Rastogi, Ravi 5:50:14 (33,360)
Ratcliff, Stephen Christopher 4:24:53 (17,485)
Ratcliffe, Jonathan P 2:53:14 (624)
Ratcliffe, Neil Thornton 4:26:49 (18,029)
Ratcliffe, Simon 3:53:39 (9,105)
Ratcliffe, Timothy H 3:55:08 (9,513)
Rateau, Jean 4:26:33 (17,969)
Rathbone, Colin E 3:05:51 (1,523)
Rathbone, Matt 3:57:08 (10,138)
Rathee, Sudhanshu 4:53:13 (24,853)
Rauman, Gerald 3:30:22 (4,480)
Raven, Gareth 2:19:55 (18)
Raven, Nick 4:43:48 (22,441)
Raven, Philip M 3:51:46 (8,598)
Raw, Jonathan 3:28:03 (4,063)
Rawcliffe, Mike Francis Aubrey 3:46:22 (7,387)
Rawles, David James 4:53:41 (24,965)
Rawlins, David J 5:09:56 (28,217)
Rawlins, Hugo 4:13:11 (14,285)
Rawlinson, Chris 5:09:59 (28,230)
Rawlinson, Stephen David James 5:28:29 (31,088)
Rawlinson, Steven 4:01:37 (11,396)
Rawnsley, Joe 3:05:34 (1,501)
Rawnsley, Jonathan Lewis 3:41:40 (6,451)
Rawson, Peter James 3:57:42 (10,297)
Rawson, Stephen 4:33:10 (19,752)
Ray, Duncan 4:50:33 (24,173)
Ray, Geoffrey John 3:53:27 (9,039)
Ray, Mark 5:23:01 (30,307)
Ray, Paul Brian 4:44:08 (22,541)
Ray, Steven Daniel 4:43:15 (22,314)
Raybould, Paul 4:44:07 (22,537)
Rayfield, David W 2:55:53 (796)
Rayment, Dave 3:28:18 (4,103)
Raymond, Graham Alan 4:22:10 (16,747)
Raynaud, Guillaume 3:04:00 (1,391)
Rayner, Bradley 6:21:48 (35,191)
Rayner, David Steven 5:28:26 (31,080)
Rayner, Gary R 3:00:41 (1,187)
Rayner, Lloyd 4:40:11 (21,533)
Rayner, Paul 3:25:02 (3,584)
Rayner, Paul R 3:48:01 (7,741)
Rayner, Richard 3:48:26 (7,832)
Raynes, David 4:30:39 (19,135)
Raynes, Michael 2:45:57 (357)
Raynsford, Jody 4:32:10 (19,476)
Raza, Hasaan 4:14:30 (14,647)
Razek, Peter 4:07:57 (12,949)
Rea, Martin 2:37:14 (146)
Rea, Simon P 5:35:49 (31,971)
Read, Adam Harvey 6:00:36 (34,099)
Read, Anthony Charles 5:37:58 (32,209)
Read, David W 3:38:31 (5,849)
Read, Gareth Anthony 3:54:01 (9,215)
Read, Graham Arthur 7:24:42 (36,441)
Read, Ian 3:16:58 (2,666)
Read, James 3:58:12 (10,459)
Read, Jonathan R 4:10:47 (13,661)
Read, Mark 2:55:37 (778)
Read, Mark A 4:06:28 (12,562)
Read, Paul 4:06:31 (12,578)
Read, Richard K 3:30:15 (4,464)
Read, Simon 4:08:10 (12,998)
Read, Stephen Charles 5:34:45 (31,854)
Readdie, Steve 3:28:06 (4,073)
Reade, Alan J 3:22:25 (3,231)
Reade, Steve R 4:51:32 (24,426)
Reader, Frank 6:37:20 (35,707)
Reader, Michael John 4:04:34 (12,087)
Reader, Paul Thomas 4:18:13 (15,636)
Reading, Ashley Valentine 4:45:15 (22,828)
Reading, Paul J 4:15:44 (14,962)
Reading, Paul James 4:11:54 (13,959)
Reading, Roderick Neville William 4:45:41 (22,945)
Reading, Sean Anthony 5:10:53 (28,391)
Readman, Ben 3:16:54 (2,661)
Rean, Benjamin J 5:46:25 (32,998)
Rean, Peter John 3:32:30 (4,815)
Reaney, Andrew Mark 4:53:33 (24,931)
Reason, Michael 4:38:48 (21,205)
Reason, Simon 5:01:04 (26,661)
Reay, Phillip Anthony 4:10:34 (13,610)
Rebeiro, Mark 5:22:05 (30,159)
Rebellato, Giuseppe 4:21:00 (16,412)
Rechtman, René Efraim 3:44:30 (6,987)
Reck, Billy 4:29:35 (18,833)
Redden, Pete Joseph 4:41:58 (22,005)
Redden, Phil 4:20:14 (16,173)
Redding, Andrew J 2:47:44 (413)
Redding, Richard 5:39:20 (32,336)
Redding, Tony Charles 6:39:03 (35,754)
Reddish, Morgan 4:34:28 (20,114)
Reddy, Chakravarthy 4:31:17 (19,289)
Redfern, Adam Stephen 4:45:57 (23,012)
Redfern, Chris 3:31:10 (4,606)
Redfern, Clive 6:05:26 (34,416)
Redfern, Martin 6:05:07 (34,395)
Redfern, Simon 4:17:21 (15,391)
Redgewell, Adam Charles John 5:07:29 (27,808)
Redhead, Daniel 5:09:00 (28,050)
Redman, Andy 4:18:45 (15,786)
Redman, Darran John 4:48:40 (23,711)
Redman, John 4:05:34 (12,347)
Redman, Paul 2:46:56 (384)
Redmond, Bobby 3:41:12 (6,367)
Redmond, Dean 3:25:31 (3,649)
Redmond, John 3:34:37 (5,175)
Rednall, John Edmund 4:07:08 (12,741)
Redpath, Ian David 4:10:08 (13,506)
Redward, Jonathan Mark 3:27:23 (3,939)
Redwood, Derek Sidney 4:53:52 (25,009)
Redwood, Leslie W 3:11:02 (2,001)
Redwood, Mike 4:18:57 (15,840)
Redwood, Simon R 4:46:23 (23,146)
Reece, Adam 5:34:28 (31,819)
Reece, Leon Peter 4:40:11 (21,533)
Reed, Adam 4:39:22 (21,344)
Reed, Ben 5:43:02 (32,669)
Reed, Bjarte 3:16:28 (2,605)
Reed, Chris 4:56:58 (25,761)
Reed, Christopher 3:52:35 (8,815)
Reed, Declan A 2:42:00 (252)
Reed, Edvard 4:32:34 (19,578)
Reed, Greg 5:51:12 (33,442)
Reed, Michael 5:09:04 (28,058)
Reed, Michael Christopher 4:52:45 (24,739)
Reed, Rob James 4:04:01 (11,962)
Reed, Stephen 3:27:34 (3,974)
Reed, Stephen 6:54:38 (36,099)
Reedy, Brendan 3:38:57 (5,932)
Reekie, Andrew James 3:52:21 (8,755)
Reekie, Stephen James 5:22:03 (30,153)
Reenan, Stephen 2:52:01 (566)
Rees, Andrew 4:24:41 (17,440)
Rees, Ben 3:53:06 (8,945)
Rees, Brent Arwyn Parry 3:57:34 (10,253)
Rees, Bryan David 4:09:00 (13,213)
Rees, Daniel A 3:15:23 (2,484)
Rees, Gareth J 3:42:58 (6,689)
Rees, Ian David 4:21:42 (16,606)
Rees, John D 3:11:03 (2,003)
Rees, Luke 5:43:46 (32,751)
Rees, Malcolm T 6:54:51 (36,106)
Rees, Matthew 5:21:33 (30,083)
Rees, Nick 4:44:03 (22,516)
Rees, Nigel Gordon 4:04:47 (12,150)
Rees, Paul John 4:28:37 (18,557)
Rees, Paul Keri 4:46:56 (23,288)
Rees, Roger 4:24:09 (17,272)
Rees, Sebastian Lloyd 3:28:35 (4,160)
Rees, Stephen Wayne 4:02:45 (11,665)
Reese, Tim J 3:26:04 (3,744)
Reese-Vesterdal, Christian Orskov 4:50:14 (24,099)
Rees-John, Gareth A 3:22:16 (3,214)
Reeson, Chris P 2:56:06 (807)
Reeson, Robert J 5:06:28 (27,618)
Reeve, Alistair 4:19:38 (15,999)
Reeve, Danny George 4:36:50 (20,695)
Reeve, David Martin 5:30:34 (31,367)
Reeve, Glen 4:41:12 (21,824)
Reeve, Paul John 4:42:14 (22,075)
Reeve, Paul Martin 4:50:19 (24,119)
Reeve, Peter John 5:35:57 (31,987)
Reeve, Robert Daniel 5:19:27 (29,770)
Reeve, Sean Jeremy 3:59:49 (10,947)
Reeve, Stuart 3:50:33 (8,327)
Reeves, Andrew B 2:45:53 (355)
Reeves, Dan 4:25:47 (17,745)
Reeves, Gavin James 4:31:36 (19,352)
Reeves, Paul Michael 5:00:37 (26,574)
Reeves, Scott 4:49:55 (24,031)
Reeves, Stuart N 6:30:55 (35,532)
Reeves, Thomas Victor 4:00:16 (11,048)
Refsland, Ivar 3:04:27 (1,425)
Regan, Dan Stewart 4:26:47 (18,020)
Regan, David Peter 3:41:49 (6,480)
Regan, Sean 4:15:56 (15,011)
Regent, Chris 5:48:18 (33,175)
Regini, Steve 4:32:01 (19,441)
Rego, Richard 3:48:08 (7,773)
Regulski, Brett 4:46:58 (23,298)
Rehal, Kanwaljit 5:34:46 (31,858)
Rehner, Christoph 4:33:46 (19,937)
Reibig, André 3:02:43 (1,313)
Reichert, Detlef 4:00:16 (11,048)
Reid, Andrew 4:18:50 (15,803)
Reid, Angus 3:33:00 (4,895)
Reid, Ashley L 5:23:03 (30,315)
Reid, Ben 4:15:48 (14,979)
Reid, Ben 5:07:17 (27,766)

Reid, Ben James 5:11:18 (28,451)
Reid, Callum C 3:00:47 (1,194)

Reid, Chris 3:58:04 (10,401)

Last year's Marathon was great to experience for the first time. After finishing, I vowed that I would never run again. However, despite the Marathon being the hardest thing I've ever done, I couldn't resist coming back in 2010. The atmosphere's infectious, as is the thrill of crossing the finish line, and of course the desire to run quicker provided a great lure. This year my goal was to break the magical four-hour barrier. Despite feeling confident, the miles dragged on, the body complained ever louder, and the clock ticked ever closer to four hours, but with crowds cheering, a last surge with 385 yards to go got me over the line with two minutes to spare.

Reid, Clive Stewart 3:27:35 (3,976)
Reid, Gavin 3:11:01 (1,999)
Reid, Graham R 3:46:32 (7,429)
Reid, Ian D 2:46:55 (383)
Reid, Ian W 5:34:24 (31,811)
Reid, James 6:06:44 (34,490)
Reid, Jason 4:05:13 (12,259)
Reid, John J 4:39:18 (21,329)
Reid, Justin 3:29:17 (4,286)
Reid, Karl 4:54:05 (25,067)
Reid, Ken 4:55:41 (25,458)
Reid, Kevin 4:40:23 (21,607)
Reid, Maurice J 3:02:29 (1,297)
Reid, Paul A 3:52:34 (8,812)
Reid, Scott Ennis 5:18:14 (29,578)
Reid, Stephen W 4:30:59 (19,212)
Reid, Steven J 3:02:57 (1,325)
Reid, Stuart 4:17:13 (15,354)
Reid, William Andrew 5:12:07 (28,587)
Reidy, Nathan 4:36:41 (20,655)
Reig, Juan 3:43:42 (6,805)
Reilly, Chris Simon Steven 5:18:56 (29,692)
Reilly, Gary 5:05:48 (27,494)
Reilly, George 3:55:24 (9,594)
Reilly, Leonard J 2:40:15 (204)
Reilly, Peter 4:31:35 (19,347)
Reilly, Philip J 3:52:09 (8,694)
Reilly, Thomas 4:24:31 (17,395)
Reimer, Frank 4:40:00 (21,502)
Reimers, Hans-Joachim 3:44:40 (7,029)
Reis e Sa, Pedro 3:36:59 (5,560)
Reischer, Johann 4:02:04 (11,507)
Reisdorff, Kent 3:54:35 (9,347)
Reisinger, Alois-Christian 3:46:49 (7,494)
Rekker, Bert 3:52:41 (8,843)
Relou, Jean 6:09:53 (34,655)

Remedios, Dominic R 3:15:56 (2,546)
Renault, Neil 2:18:29 (14)
Renda, Andrew 5:24:05 (30,490)
Rendall, Julian I 2:30:46 (74)
Rendell, Graham 4:03:52 (11,940)
Render, Moz 4:41:39 (21,934)
Rendina, Michele 3:45:01 (7,098)
Rendle, Nicholas 4:28:01 (18,371)
Rendu, Matthew D 5:28:06 (31,043)
Rennells, Keith 3:53:21 (9,013)
Rennie, Craig 4:41:48 (21,971)
Rennie, David William 3:59:20 (10,818)
Rennie, Gavin 3:17:38 (2,729)
Rennison, Kevin 3:56:57 (10,071)
Renphrey, Tom Anthony 3:22:07 (3,201)
Renshaw, Bill 4:11:28 (13,842)
Renshaw, Tim 3:08:59 (1,806)
Renton, Derek 3:52:32 (8,804)
Renton, Steven 5:01:06 (26,668)
Renzi, Francesco 4:37:27 (20,866)
Repper, James 3:03:27 (1,344)
Reseigh, Tom 4:23:05 (17,000)
Reshat, Bulent 5:55:36 (33,763)
Resnick, Brian 4:56:19 (25,616)
Retallick, Timothy 4:36:28 (20,591)
Rettie, Bryn David 4:00:19 (11,062)
Reukauf, Thomas 3:45:24 (7,188)
Reut, Roman 3:28:03 (4,063)
Reuther, Matt 5:22:12 (30,176)
Revell, Craig John 4:44:39 (22,688)
Revell, Kevin 3:06:40 (1,584)
Revell, Peter 5:34:51 (31,864)
Reverberi, Jacques 3:51:50 (8,614)
Revuelta Lopez, Alejandro 4:23:52 (17,205)
Rew, Clive J 4:39:28 (21,377)
Rex, James 5:24:16 (30,520)
Rey, Simon 4:06:25 (12,551)
Reyes-Montes, Juan Miguel 4:51:55 (24,530)
Reygate, Kevin 4:46:03 (23,043)
Reynolds, Alan M 3:16:42 (2,645)
Reynolds, Andrew M 2:44:13 (315)
Reynolds, Andy 4:26:42 (17,998)
Reynolds, Andy S 3:45:50 (7,274)
Reynolds, Anthony Richard 3:51:42 (8,587)
Reynolds, Bryn Paul 2:31:16 (78)
Reynolds, Carl 4:08:52 (13,177)
Reynolds, Christopher John T 4:17:37 (15,473)
Reynolds, Colin 4:17:43 (15,501)
Reynolds, David John 4:34:35 (20,145)
Reynolds, Giles 3:53:09 (8,955)
Reynolds, Graham 3:28:24 (4,126)
Reynolds, Guy John 4:59:27 (26,321)
Reynolds, Lee Malcolm 3:56:09 (9,822)
Reynolds, Mark 3:56:45 (10,014)
Reynolds, Martin 3:48:21 (7,816)
Reynolds, Matthew Kenneth 5:49:00 (33,241)
Reynolds, Paul 3:18:22 (2,814)
Reynolds, Paul 4:55:28 (25,405)
Reynolds, Paul C 4:33:14 (19,778)
Reynolds, Peter 4:21:32 (16,556)
Reynolds, Peter 4:35:21 (20,309)
Reynolds, Peter William 5:04:40 (27,308)
Reynolds, Phillip 4:28:07 (18,392)
Reynolds, Phillip John 6:52:06 (36,045)
Reynolds, Shawn 4:23:23 (17,076)
Reynolds, Simon David 3:59:32 (10,870)
Reynolds, Stephen J 3:55:53 (9,745)
Reynolds, Steve 4:39:18 (21,329)
Reynolds, Stuart M 5:01:53 (26,827)
Rhead, Rob 4:48:48 (23,747)
Rhind, Thomas J 3:53:18 (8,997)
Rhoades, Andy B 3:37:48 (5,725)
Rhodes, Adam 5:22:41 (30,253)
Rhodes, Andrew Brian 4:12:16 (14,048)
Rhodes, Ben Alexander 4:01:55 (11,474)
Rhodes, Dave 4:57:14 (25,810)
Rhodes, David 3:49:24 (8,064)
Rhodes, Hamish 4:30:03 (18,987)
Rhodes, Lee 5:06:24 (27,601)
Rhodes, Lee Alan 3:38:11 (5,800)
Rhodes, Max James 5:04:35 (27,295)
Ribeiro, Caio 3:53:46 (9,147)
Ribeiro, Heleno 2:36:07 (129)

Ribton, Nicholas Bjorgheim 4:06:32 (12,583)
Riby, Gordon Philip 4:53:01 (24,800)
Ricciardi, Paolo 3:27:51 (4,025)
Rice, Dennis B 4:23:57 (17,225)
Rice, Geoff 4:46:30 (23,168)
Rice, Jody 4:14:06 (14,533)
Rice, John 3:40:29 (6,235)
Rice, John Bede 6:20:04 (35,130)
Rice, Jonathan 3:34:55 (5,234)
Rice, Nicholas G 5:04:03 (27,197)
Rice, Scott M 2:58:56 (1,039)
Rice, Steven John 3:57:39 (10,280)
Rice, Tim Edward Dewar 5:23:35 (30,402)
Rich, Andrew John 4:34:08 (20,027)
Rich, Grant William 6:30:31 (35,518)
Rich, Jonathan E 3:15:24 (2,487)
Rich, Stephen J 4:09:44 (13,401)
Richard, Arnaud 4:02:32 (11,613)
Richard, Emery 4:19:17 (15,922)
Richard, Jean Louis 3:06:30 (1,573)
Richards, Chris 4:18:39 (15,758)
Richards, Clive J 2:51:18 (535)
Richards, Craig Johnathan 3:45:18 (7,162)
Richards, Daryl 4:20:20 (16,215)
Richards, David 4:04:59 (12,200)
Richards, Dean 3:31:50 (4,716)
Richards, Eddie 4:27:12 (18,149)
Richards, Gavin 4:59:59 (26,448)
Richards, Glyn 3:32:18 (4,788)
Richards, Glyn 4:42:05 (22,035)
Richards, Gordon 3:11:12 (2,016)
Richards, Gwilym 5:17:12 (29,415)
Richards, Jason 4:38:01 (20,990)
Richards, John 3:43:46 (6,821)
Richards, John Edward 4:44:42 (22,698)
Richards, Jules 3:24:03 (3,440)
Richards, Lyn 3:22:56 (3,282)
Richards, Mark Reginald 6:09:31 (34,637)
Richards, Matthew John 3:56:58 (10,077)
Richards, Michael K 4:03:42 (11,898)
Richards, Michael Lee 5:11:49 (28,525)
Richards, Neil A 2:58:33 (1,010)
Richards, Nick 3:54:33 (9,340)
Richards, Nick Robert George 4:59:11 (26,260)
Richards, Paul 3:15:38 (2,511)
Richards, Paul 4:21:45 (16,628)
Richards, Paul James 4:04:12 (12,010)
Richards, Perry William 5:27:57 (31,017)
Richards, Peter Wynford James 4:24:15 (17,302)
Richards, Phil 4:43:23 (22,342)
Richards, Philip Jonathan 5:08:25 (27,966)
Richards, Robert Donald 3:35:50 (5,380)
Richards, Stephen 4:27:33 (18,250)
Richards, Stephen Graham 4:03:45 (11,906)
Richards, Steve 4:27:36 (18,257)
Richards, Steve William 4:33:03 (19,715)
Richards, Timothy R 3:08:19 (1,732)
Richards, Wesley 5:12:32 (28,659)
Richards,, Philip, ...3:31:59 (4,736)
Richardson, Alan 4:12:32 (14,109)
Richardson, Alastair James 4:41:48 (21,971)
Richardson, Alastair William 4:55:32 (25,414)
Richardson, Andrew John 5:11:11 (28,431)
Richardson, Andrew Neil 4:10:10 (13,517)
Richardson, Andrew T 4:06:04 (12,468)
Richardson, Anthony Mark W 6:54:08 (36,088)
Richardson, Dave 4:03:33 (11,859)
Richardson, David Raulin T 6:36:37 (35,690)
Richardson, Derek James 4:00:19 (11,062)
Richardson, Eamonn P 3:53:56 (9,191)
Richardson, Eric 3:24:05 (3,449)
Richardson, Frederic Giles De D. 4:56:36 (25,667)
Richardson, Hilary 4:54:51 (25,268)
Richardson, Ian 4:50:21 (24,130)
Richardson, Ian B 3:09:47 (1,892)
Richardson, James 5:06:10 (27,558)
Richardson, James Edward 5:17:19 (29,443)
Richardson, Jeremy 4:51:15 (24,366)
Richardson, Kenney 5:45:18 (32,897)
Richardson, Kevin 4:27:00 (18,079)
Richardson, Kevin John 3:51:53 (8,632)
Richardson, Liam A 2:58:14 (982)
Richardson, Martin John 5:34:41 (31,847)

Robinson, Mark	3:31:50 (4,716)
Robinson, Mark	4:23:54 (17,213)
Robinson, Mark	4:51:05 (24,326)
Robinson, Mark Allen	4:52:22 (24,652)
Robinson, Mark Anthony	4:16:26 (15,151)
Robinson, Mark D	3:48:46 (7,914)
Robinson, Martin	4:11:40 (13,898)
Robinson, Michael	4:15:28 (14,899)
Robinson, Michael E	4:55:22 (25,396)
Robinson, Michael Roy	3:42:49 (6,659)
Robinson, Neil	5:22:39 (30,248)
Robinson, Neil Andrew	3:57:02 (10,109)
Robinson, Neville	3:47:20 (7,605)
Robinson, Nigel	6:17:49 (35,024)
Robinson, Patrick A	5:09:35 (28,168)
Robinson, Paul A	4:25:08 (17,558)
Robinson, Paul J	4:16:31 (15,174)
Robinson, Paul M	4:36:49 (20,689)
Robinson, Paul Michael	5:23:46 (30,437)
Robinson, Richard S	3:49:37 (8,122)
Robinson, Roger T	5:00:15 (26,510)
Robinson, Sean	4:49:33 (23,922)
Robinson, Shaun I	4:19:51 (16,056)
Robinson, Simon T	3:22:34 (3,246)
Robinson, Steve Lee	5:50:10 (33,348)
Robinson, Steven	3:39:16 (5,996)
Robinson, Stewart	5:27:30 (30,966)
Robinson, Stuart J	4:17:57 (15,563)
Robinson, Thomas	3:43:24 (6,757)
Robinson, Tom	5:06:26 (27,612)
Robinson, Tommy	5:29:17 (31,188)
Robinson, Trevor L	4:43:15 (22,314)
Robinson, Vince	4:45:10 (22,811)
Robles, Eusebio	3:58:26 (10,537)
Robson, Alex J	3:03:56 (1,384)
Robson, Allan	4:41:36 (21,923)
Robson, Ben	3:14:06 (2,333)
Robson, Colin	2:45:04 (343)
Robson, David	4:20:11 (16,157)
Robson, Ian	3:57:46 (10,318)
Robson, Kristopher	4:19:21 (15,942)
Robson, Phillip Ashley	4:19:39 (16,002)
Robson, Richard Edward	3:49:47 (8,163)
Robson, Simon Peter	4:20:45 (16,356)
Robson, Stephen M	4:08:57 (13,193)
Robson, Stephen Peter	4:33:12 (19,767)
Robson, Tim	4:05:15 (12,269)
Rocca, Dominique	3:52:18 (8,746)
Rocchetta, Roberto	4:58:01 (25,972)
Roche, Cliff Michael	4:27:37 (18,264)
Roche, Mark	4:29:44 (18,896)
Roche, Olivier	3:33:28 (4,965)
Roche, Richard A	3:54:59 (9,474)
Rochester, Kerry J	4:04:10 (12,002)
Rochussen, Gavin Mark	3:57:50 (10,337)
Rock, Darren Kevin	5:18:42 (29,656)
Rock, Paul	4:01:42 (11,409)
Rockett, Chris David	5:46:34 (33,011)
Rockett, Matt	4:26:18 (17,900)
Rockingham, Lee	4:54:10 (25,083)
Rock-Perring, James Royal	5:46:11 (32,969)
Rocks, Brian	4:40:12 (21,538)
Rodden, Martyn	4:10:51 (13,680)
Roddis, Anthony	3:11:27 (2,045)
Rodelas, Daniel	2:56:13 (815)
Rodembourg, Stephane	2:50:50 (520)
Roden, Gary	3:57:35 (10,261)
Rodger, Joseph	6:05:08 (34,396)
Rodger, Paul	3:45:00 (7,095)
Rodgers, Ian Gordon	3:24:28 (3,506)
Rodgers, Mark Edward	4:41:46 (21,959)
Rodgers, Martin C	4:48:30 (23,667)
Rodgers, Simon Baxter	7:23:18 (36,433)
Roditi, James Benjamin Klaber	3:22:20 (3,220)
Rodney, Grant	3:26:22 (3,791)
Rodrigues, Mervyn A	3:50:22 (8,281)
Rodrigues Pereira, Gersjom A	3:34:23 (5,135)
Rodriguez, Adrian	3:27:30 (3,961)
Rodriguez, Anthony,	4:23:39 (17,143)
Rodriguez, David	5:04:40 (27,308)
Rodriguez, Joe	4:23:39 (17,143)
Rodriguez, Juan Francisco	3:02:25 (1,290)
Rodriguez, Ronaldo	4:34:42 (20,171)

Rodway, Anthony W	5:21:19 (30,044)
Rodwell, Daniel	3:52:58 (8,911)
Rodwell, Lee	3:49:24 (8,064)
Rodwell, Peter Robert	6:11:51 (34,745)
Rodwell, Ryan Arthur	6:11:51 (34,745)
Roe, David	6:07:53 (34,556)
Roe, David Graham	5:52:58 (33,582)
Roe, Steve	5:40:58 (32,478)
Roe, Terry Richard	6:33:27 (35,609)
Roeed, Harald	4:35:46 (20,410)
Roel, Craig	4:36:44 (20,665)
Roels, Nicolas	3:20:07 (2,970)
Roff, Jonathan	4:14:58 (14,773)
Roff, Neil Antony	3:55:10 (9,520)
Roffey, Stuart J	4:27:47 (18,310)
Rogan, Gary P	4:40:57 (21,759)
Rogan, Mike	4:38:20 (21,067)
Roger, Phil James	4:05:25 (12,320)
Rogers, Ben	4:13:37 (14,410)
Rogers, Ben Scott	4:11:35 (13,875)
Rogers, Brett	3:40:23 (6,208)
Rogers, Charlie Martin	4:04:37 (12,106)
Rogers, Chris	6:26:10 (35,354)
Rogers, Colin Leslie	5:42:21 (32,623)
Rogers, Daniel G	5:44:55 (32,861)
Rogers, Danny	5:20:41 (29,963)
Rogers, Darren Alexander	3:23:10 (3,315)
Rogers, David,	4:18:27 (15,699)
Rogers, David Anthony	6:56:56 (36,141)
Rogers, Graham I	3:26:53 (3,860)
Rogers, Ian	4:20:00 (16,110)
Rogers, Ian James	3:25:06 (3,598)
Rogers, James Edward	5:01:04 (26,661)
Rogers, Joel	5:12:19 (28,624)
Rogers, John	3:20:19 (2,992)
Rogers, Jonathan Charles	4:34:39 (20,156)
Rogers, Leo	5:21:18 (30,043)
Rogers, Mark	3:53:45 (9,140)
Rogers, Mark	4:20:00 (16,110)
Rogers, Mark	5:23:23 (30,368)
Rogers, Matthew	4:55:58 (25,530)
Rogers, Neil Jamie	3:48:16 (7,796)
Rogers, Oliver	5:01:19 (26,718)
Rogers, Paul	3:59:39 (10,903)
Rogers, Peter	3:46:20 (7,383)
Rogers, Peter M	4:26:51 (18,039)
Rogers, Peter Martin	4:29:19 (18,757)
Rogers, Richard	5:31:33 (31,479)
Rogers, Sam	4:35:03 (20,240)

Rogers, Stephen 7:07:48 (36,289)

The morning of my first London Marathon I was full of nerves. After endless nights of not sleeping and worry, the time had come. At the start line

the nerves continued as the rain fell, surrounded by lots of people wishing each other good luck. Before I knew it, we were off. It did not take me long to get into my stride and I started to relax and enjoy the occasion. The cheering crowds kept me going. My first memory was getting round Cutty Sark, then across Tower Bridge before setting off towards Canary Wharf. Passing the Tower of London and seeing Big Ben, it was here I knew I was going to complete the London Marathon and collect my medal with overwhelming emotion and pride. A day I will never forget.

Rogers, Stuart	4:14:39 (14,700)
Rogers, Stuart	5:02:21 (26,916)
Rogers, Tom	3:57:30 (10,233)
Rogers, Trevor Keith	3:59:53 (10,961)
Rogerson, Mark	3:49:43 (8,150)
Rogerson, Matt	3:58:37 (10,598)
Rogerson, Nigel	3:05:14 (1,476)
Rohmer, Philippe	3:54:12 (9,256)
Rojas, Josep A	4:16:23 (15,135)
Rokenson, Gary Jon	4:42:59 (22,255)
Roker, Martin Paul	5:08:14 (27,937)
Roles, Andrew Edward	3:59:32 (10,870)
Rolfe, Darren John	5:36:21 (32,038)
Rolfe, Kevin John	4:16:43 (15,227)
Rolfe, Leslie James	3:27:19 (3,924)
Rolfe, Nick Kieron William	3:58:08 (10,426)
Rollings, Russell J	3:54:25 (9,304)
Rollinson, Phil	3:11:13 (2,018)
Rolls, George Henry	4:50:43 (24,211)
Rolls, Shaun	5:09:16 (28,095)
Roma, Mark	4:22:51 (16,949)
Romain, Graeme	5:17:37 (29,490)
Roman, Ignacio	3:55:09 (9,516)
Roman, José Diego	4:27:48 (18,315)
Romano Atri, Daniel	3:39:51 (6,114)
Romano Hadid, Daniel	4:01:32 (11,376)
Rombout, James Matthew	4:22:41 (16,897)
Romefort, Gonzague	3:23:22 (3,347)
Romei, Andrea	3:09:42 (1,878)
Romeo, Jeff	3:59:27 (10,853)
Romero, Daniel Luis	4:41:15 (21,832)
Romero, Marco A.	5:18:53 (29,679)
Romuald, Raitiere	3:24:03 (3,440)
Rondeaux, Pascal	3:44:18 (6,938)
Ronen, Rami	4:12:21 (14,064)
Rones, Marcus	3:57:43 (10,308)
Roney, Steven	4:46:41 (23,230)
Rönmark, Kurt	4:01:25 (11,345)
Ronnan, Andrew	5:21:20 (30,049)
Rooke, David John	5:13:05 (28,789)
Rooke-James, Allan Jeffery	4:56:18 (25,611)
Rookledge, Benjamin Charles	4:44:34 (22,658)
Roome, Darren	4:57:32 (25,868)
Roome, Peter	3:01:39 (1,236)
Rooney, Jonjo	4:57:48 (25,926)
Rooney, Mark	3:53:11 (8,966)
Rooney, Michael	4:54:49 (25,261)
Rooney, Paul Matthew	4:30:11 (19,022)
Rooney, Ryan	3:52:24 (8,767)
Root, David	3:41:44 (6,464)
Root, John Stewart	4:47:42 (23,470)
Roper, Andrew	4:04:33 (12,084)
Roper, Andrew Steven	3:25:04 (3,592)
Roper, Mark	5:04:49 (27,334)
Roper, Oliver William	4:06:27 (12,557)
Roper, Simon Andrew	5:06:40 (27,666)
Roques, Pascal	4:11:37 (13,887)
Rosak, Anthony R	2:49:15 (456)
Rosbrook, Paul James	4:29:26 (18,785)
Roscoe, Nicholas	3:50:27 (8,297)
Rose, Adam	4:16:25 (15,147)
Rose, Anthony Graham	3:45:26 (7,196)
Rose, Antony	3:56:30 (9,933)
Rose, Ben	5:15:50 (29,203)
Rose, Christian	4:02:31 (11,608)
Rose, Christopher S	6:16:52 (34,970)
Rose, Daniel	5:27:20 (30,944)
Rose, Darren Mark	5:03:54 (27,173)
Rose, David	3:46:39 (7,453)

Rose, David	6:24:13 (35,288)	
Rose, David S	4:02:53 (11,701)	
Rose, Derek	5:05:54 (27,517)	
Rose, Duncan	5:01:50 (26,816)	
Rose, Ian	4:48:11 (23,585)	
Rose, John P	3:27:09 (3,896)	
Rose, John William	4:56:30 (25,646)	
Rose, Jonathan	3:27:43 (3,999)	
Rose, Matthew	3:49:04 (7,993)	
Rose, Paul	2:42:40 (264)	
Rose, Peter	4:43:32 (22,377)	
Rose, Sam	3:41:48 (6,476)	
Rose, Simon Henry	6:04:30 (34,349)	
Rose, Stuart	4:21:54 (16,674)	
Rose, Tim	4:57:31 (25,864)	
Roseborne, Nicholas	3:48:16 (7,796)	
Rosello, Alex L	4:05:15 (12,269)	
Rosenbach, Jon	3:11:29 (2,048)	
Rosenblatt, Andy	4:21:35 (16,571)	
Rosenbrier, Jonathan	4:40:13 (21,543)	
Rosenfeld, Dominic	4:04:22 (12,044)	
Rosenfeld, Paul Jonathan	4:18:06 (15,608)	
Rosenstein, Andrew	3:47:39 (7,677)	
Rosenthal, Richard Oskar	5:35:33 (31,932)	
Rosier, Jean Marc	3:52:17 (8,734)	
Rosland, Frode	3:14:02 (2,326)	
Ross, Aaron	6:28:04 (35,430)	
Ross, Andrew	5:25:42 (30,732)	
Ross, Cameron	4:12:59 (14,229)	
Ross, Craig	4:03:31 (11,849)	
Ross, Darren	4:34:25 (20,099)	
Ross, David E	3:07:34 (1,660)	
Ross, Douglas L	2:56:36 (840)	
Ross, Duncan	4:42:37 (22,158)	
Ross, Duncan	5:40:31 (32,432)	
Ross, Gary	3:54:12 (9,256)	
Ross, Iain	3:54:48 (9,424)	
Ross, Ian M	4:17:44 (15,507)	
Ross, Jamie Alan	4:36:42 (20,659)	
Ross, Simon	5:34:45 (31,854)	
Ross, Simon J	4:33:29 (19,848)	
Rosser, David Anthony	3:53:58 (9,201)	
Rosser, David R	5:16:46 (29,347)	
Rosser, Simon James	3:23:09 (3,313)	
Ross-Hunt, Nigel Anthony	4:04:24 (12,050)	
Rossi, Antoine	4:51:09 (24,341)	
Rossi, Didier	3:23:14 (3,328)	
Rossi, Massimo	3:52:58 (8,911)	
Rossiter, Alec James	3:31:20 (4,636)	
Rossiter, Keith	4:44:21 (22,603)	
Rossiter, Mike	3:57:46 (10,318)	
Rostern, Paul	3:21:17 (3,119)	
Rothe, Carsten	4:14:40 (14,706)	
Rothera, David J	4:22:12 (16,761)	
Rotheram, Mark	4:10:19 (13,548)	
Rothwell, Colin	3:56:37 (9,964)	
Rothwell, Neil R	4:48:43 (23,728)	
Rottmann, Frank	4:53:30 (24,917)	
Roubinek, Jan	4:24:25 (17,366)	
Rough, Phil	4:39:57 (21,491)	
Rought, Craig	3:30:21 (4,478)	
Roughton, Michael	4:03:51 (11,936)	
Roulin, Patrick	3:53:18 (8,997)	
Rounce, Neil J	5:05:15 (27,414)	
Round, Alan A	4:26:09 (17,858)	
Round, Anton	3:41:13 (6,374)	
Round, Derek	3:55:36 (9,636)	
Rouquette, Jerome	3:52:31 (8,801)	
Rous, James Anthony Edward	3:09:44 (1,884)	
Rouse, Ben	4:09:28 (13,330)	
Rouse, James	3:58:28 (10,544)	
Rouse, Jonathan A	5:22:46 (30,262)	
Rouse, Keith Andrew	4:24:44 (17,450)	
Rousell, Andrew	4:54:21 (25,144)	
Roussel, Arnaud	3:55:17 (9,556)	
Roussos, Georg	3:56:54 (10,056)	
Routledge, George	5:53:20 (33,597)	
Routledge, Richard	3:27:36 (3,983)	
Routley, Luke J	4:07:48 (12,906)	
Row, Cameron	5:29:59 (31,295)	
Row, Paul M	3:50:14 (8,255)	
Rowan, Andrew John	5:06:21 (27,596)	
Rowan, Donal	3:52:17 (8,734)	
Rowan, Murray	4:12:10 (14,028)	
Rowbotham, Jaime B	4:23:58 (17,229)	
Rowbury, Matthew Douglas	3:30:01 (4,421)	
Rowden, David J	3:01:04 (1,209)	
Rowe, Alan	4:16:35 (15,186)	
Rowe, Alexander William John	4:47:50 (23,507)	
Rowe, Darren G	3:47:54 (7,717)	
Rowe, Grant	4:29:11 (18,728)	
Rowe, Ian T	3:28:45 (4,183)	
Rowe, John Arthur	4:43:16 (22,317)	
Rowe, Kenneth	4:39:39 (21,427)	
Rowe, Mark	4:54:50 (25,265)	
Rowe, Matt	4:32:34 (19,578)	
Rowe, Matthew	6:45:55 (35,928)	
Rowe, Matthew David	5:36:21 (32,038)	
Rowe, Matthew James	5:00:57 (26,643)	
Rowe, Mike	5:04:52 (27,344)	
Rowe, Sebastian	3:23:41 (3,392)	
Rowe, Steven John	4:42:50 (22,225)	
Rowell, Alan	3:47:25 (7,625)	
Rowell, Barry Michael	4:32:35 (19,582)	
Rowell, Ben	4:23:44 (17,175)	
Rowen, Daniel Gerard	6:51:19 (36,019)	
Rowland, Andrew	3:46:16 (7,373)	
Rowland, Colin Martin	6:09:02 (34,621)	
Rowland, Dan J	3:06:42 (1,585)	
Rowland, Graham	4:11:12 (13,766)	
Rowland, James	5:10:05 (28,253)	
Rowland, James Daniel	6:35:10 (35,655)	
Rowland, Matt	4:13:36 (14,404)	
Rowland, Matthew	4:54:04 (25,064)	
Rowland, Michael John	5:56:41 (33,842)	
Rowland, Robert A	2:57:36 (919)	
Rowland, Shaun Richard	5:16:31 (29,312)	
Rowland, Stewart	5:26:13 (30,806)	
Rowlands, Aled	5:01:30 (26,754)	
Rowlands, Daren W	2:37:20 (148)	
Rowlands, David Sebastian	4:21:26 (16,531)	
Rowlands, Gary John	7:23:11 (36,429)	
Rowlands, Thomas	3:21:31 (3,139)	
Rowlands-Mackenzie, Gary	3:47:43 (7,686)	
Rowlatt, Gary	4:29:34 (18,826)	
Rowley, Andrew J	4:35:49 (20,426)	
Rowley, Ben	4:34:42 (20,171)	
Rowley, Kevin David	3:51:29 (8,535)	
Rowley, Peter William	4:01:26 (11,353)	
Rowley, Richard J	3:14:22 (2,363)	
Rowley, Simon	4:13:15 (14,297)	
Rowlson, Mark G	3:53:18 (8,997)	
Roxby, Matthew Peter	5:09:20 (28,115)	
Roy, Alan	3:02:46 (1,316)	
Roy, Matthew	4:33:50 (19,948)	
Roy, Niladri	4:25:30 (17,661)	
Royce, Mark Stephen	4:07:50 (12,912)	
Royle, Anthony	4:05:47 (12,408)	
Royle, Darren	4:16:18 (15,106)	
Royle, Neil G	4:24:40 (17,435)	
Rozay, Joel	3:31:14 (4,615)	
Rubenstein, Brian	3:57:14 (10,168)	
Rubin, Paul	4:29:31 (18,812)	
Rubinstein, John	4:12:48 (14,180)	
Rubio Eguiluz, Juan	3:06:53 (1,599)	
Rudaini, Steven	4:31:58 (19,424)	
Rudall, Andy	5:39:08 (32,312)	
Rudall, David C	2:59:53 (1,146)	
Rudd, Andrew N	3:37:32 (5,673)	
Rudd, Andrew Thomas	5:48:16 (33,171)	
Rudd, Daran J	3:15:34 (2,509)	
Rudd, David M	4:20:18 (16,200)	
Ruddick, Adam	4:50:54 (24,269)	
Ruddick, Jon	4:50:06 (24,073)	
Ruddick, James Ian	4:21:37 (16,583)	
Ruddock, Mike	4:12:05 (14,003)	
Ruddy, Stephen James	4:09:41 (13,392)	
Rudge, Anthony Edward	4:39:24 (21,353)	
Rudkin, Kevin P	3:37:11 (5,594)	
Rudkin, Tony Paul	4:00:27 (11,109)	
Rudland, Jonathan	4:09:10 (13,250)	
Rudland, Lee	3:07:07 (1,620)	
Rudman, Jason M	2:53:12 (623)	
Rudolph, Dieter	3:05:59 (1,532)	
Rudolph, Guy R	4:13:40 (14,422)	
Rudsdale, Simon	3:59:32 (10,870)	
Rueda, Carlos	3:22:16 (3,214)	
Ruegg, Bruce William	3:58:01 (10,384)	
Ruff, Neil	5:10:14 (28,280)	
Ruffe, Nicholas Anthony Richard	3:54:34 (9,344)	
Ruffle, Alexander	4:02:35 (11,624)	
Ruffle, Steve	4:47:38 (23,449)	
Ruffle, Tim John	4:03:05 (11,748)	
Ruffley, Mike	4:40:48 (21,721)	
Rugg, Jim	5:10:01 (28,242)	
Rugge-Price, Jake	4:46:14 (23,104)	
Ruggeri, Mauro	3:36:56 (5,551)	
Ruggiero, Andrea	3:08:36 (1,768)	
Ruiz, Ignacio	2:49:40 (473)	
Ruiz, José R	3:05:57 (1,530)	
Ruiz-Tagle Barros, Ignacio	6:36:18 (35,684)	
Ruiz-Tagle Barros, José Tomas	2:38:19 (167)	
Rule, Ian	3:45:01 (7,098)	
Rule, Simon Mark	3:53:07 (8,947)	
Rumble, Allan	4:43:40 (22,410)	
Rumble, David James	4:25:05 (17,546)	
Rumbles, Alan C	3:17:07 (2,679)	
Rumbles, Chris	4:34:30 (20,121)	
Rumbold, John L	3:17:11 (2,681)	
Rummell, Paul	4:47:50 (23,507)	
Rummery, Ryan	3:29:04 (4,242)	
Rumney, Jason	4:00:48 (11,194)	
Rumsey, Stephen	4:15:55 (15,007)	
Runciman, Lee R	4:19:15 (15,913)	
Runde, Norbert	3:47:31 (7,650)	
Rundle, Andrew	5:15:24 (29,125)	
Rundle, Kevin David	4:38:48 (21,205)	
Rusby, Peter J	3:56:33 (9,948)	
Ruscica, Rosario Patrick	3:59:34 (10,886)	
Ruscillo, Daniel	3:49:55 (8,191)	
Rush, Nick	4:15:15 (14,848)	
Rushmer, Gary	3:20:50 (3,064)	
Rushovich, Athos Marios	5:07:10 (27,746)	
Rushton, Dan	4:08:39 (13,126)	
Rushton, Victor	4:27:54 (18,339)	
Russell, Adam Christopher	3:14:23 (2,368)	
Russell, Alex	4:10:21 (13,556)	
Russell, Alex Martyn	3:46:25 (7,402)	
Russell, Andrew S	2:58:39 (1,015)	
Russell, Antony	4:56:23 (25,627)	
Russell, Benjamin Edward	4:59:19 (26,292)	
Russell, Clark Donald	4:01:31 (11,372)	
Russell, David Peter	4:05:42 (12,378)	
Russell, James Brian Andrew	3:57:00 (10,089)	
Russell, James Richard	4:26:56 (18,062)	
Russell, John Peter	3:33:46 (5,015)	
Russell, Kirk	4:27:44 (18,295)	
Russell, Mark	2:40:22 (208)	
Russell, Mark	3:41:48 (6,476)	
Russell, Mark	4:58:50 (26,173)	
Russell, Michael	3:48:15 (7,794)	
Russell, Mike	5:22:14 (30,179)	
Russell, Paul	4:29:36 (18,842)	
Russell, Paul,	6:31:57 (35,564)	
Russell, Paul D	4:18:24 (15,689)	
Russell, Pete J	4:06:54 (12,684)	
Russell, Richard	4:58:25 (26,068)	
Russell, Richard William	5:06:55 (27,708)	
Russell, Shaune D	3:31:44 (4,701)	
Russell, Stephen J	3:06:19 (1,556)	
Russell, Wayne	5:33:54 (31,754)	
Russell, William David	3:18:26 (2,817)	
Russell-Cobb, Finn	4:44:20 (22,599)	
Russell-Stoneham, Rory	5:13:13 (28,803)	
Russo, Rosario	3:54:31 (9,331)	
Russon, Chris	3:47:17 (7,596)	
Ruston, Robin F	3:19:44 (2,940)	
Rutherford, Tommy	3:04:01 (1,393)	
Rutherford-Jones, George	3:07:18 (1,634)	
Ruthven, Daniel	3:59:45 (10,932)	
Rutland, Andrew	4:38:43 (21,175)	
Rutland, Neil Andrew	3:53:23 (9,024)	
Rutter, Andrew James	4:27:45 (18,299)	
Rutter, Graeme	4:06:23 (12,547)	
Rutter, Mark Steven	4:38:12 (21,029)	
Rutter, Neil Edward	4:13:12 (14,286)	
Ruxton, Lance	4:48:30 (23,667)	
Ryall, Christopher David	4:50:54 (24,269)	
Ryan, Alex	3:49:53 (8,184)	

Ryan, Chris	4:30:23 (19,061)	
Ryan, Christopher	3:36:32 (5,484)	
Ryan, Enda Oliver	5:26:35 (30,851)	
Ryan, George	4:12:26 (14,078)	
Ryan, James Christopher	4:35:40 (20,380)	
Ryan, Jon	5:03:02 (27,032)	
Ryan, Lee Michael	3:24:48 (3,550)	
Ryan, Mark Christopher	4:37:53 (20,962)	
Ryan, Matthew	5:48:17 (33,174)	
Ryan, Matthew John	3:58:38 (10,608)	
Ryan, Michael Joseph	4:47:30 (23,411)	
Ryan, Neil Stuart	4:18:22 (15,678)	
Ryan, Noel Patrick	5:19:44 (29,812)	
Ryan, Patrick	3:40:59 (6,320)	
Ryan, Paul	4:36:04 (20,495)	
Ryan, Phillip	5:57:44 (33,914)	
Ryan, Robert John	4:31:56 (19,418)	
Ryan, Shane Patrick	4:09:46 (13,412)	
Ryan, Stephen William	4:37:18 (20,818)	
Rycroft, Doug James Edward	4:49:13 (23,852)	
Rycroft, Simon Andrew	3:20:50 (3,064)	
Rydberg, Sven-Åke	5:19:35 (29,790)	
Ryde, Carl L.	2:42:35 (263)	
Ryder, Daniel	4:17:05 (15,317)	
Ryder, David A.	3:29:34 (4,334)	
Ryder, Jonathan M	4:08:29 (13,074)	
Ryffel, Markus	3:56:25 (9,903)	
Ryland, Darren Paul	5:18:23 (29,605)	
Ryles, Nick	3:14:12 (2,341)	
Ryles, Oliver D.	4:28:21 (18,470)	
Ryves, Ben	4:29:39 (18,866)	
Saar, Martin	2:47:42 (409)	
Saba, Roberto	3:54:05 (9,231)	
Sabah, Tarique Karim	5:30:58 (31,413)	
Sabal, Freddy	5:33:16 (31,691)	
Sabbadini, Tom	3:58:32 (10,570)	
Sabine, Ajas	4:58:28 (26,080)	
Sacchetti, Marco	4:29:08 (18,716)	
Sacco, Antonio	3:28:54 (4,210)	
Sackur, Stephen	4:32:03 (19,449)	
Sada-Paz, Mauricio	3:32:47 (4,855)	
Saddi, Anil Kumar	6:21:56 (35,198)	
Sader, Markus	2:58:04 (962)	
Sadler, Alan R	3:26:20 (3,788)	
Sadler, David	5:29:53 (31,278)	
Sadler, Scott Rory	5:12:54 (28,722)	
Sadlik, Mark	4:57:43 (25,912)	
Saeed, Saad	4:54:26 (25,167)	
Saffer, Daniel	6:08:45 (34,600)	
Sage, Gary Lynton	3:12:15 (2,110)	
Sage, Kevin	4:17:30 (15,439)	
Sage, Kevin Alexander	6:46:25 (35,936)	
Sage, Oliver	4:22:24 (16,822)	
Sahota, Harpreet	4:58:04 (25,980)	
Saini, Ravinder	4:14:03 (14,520)	
Sains, Mark C.	3:31:12 (4,611)	
Saint-Ruth, Peter Martin	4:22:14 (16,776)	
Sait, Dan	4:16:28 (15,157)	
Saito, Shigeo	3:32:32 (4,819)	
Saito, Yuzo	3:23:18 (3,341)	
Saiyed, Moin	6:25:09 (35,316)	
Sakamoto, Hiroshi	4:23:39 (17,143)	
Saker, Andrew Mark	4:33:51 (19,953)	
Sala, Fabio	4:56:03 (25,548)	
Salaris, Antonio Filippo	2:34:51 (109)	
Salasco, Flavio	3:28:53 (4,207)	
Salawu, Adebambo N.	5:47:26 (33,092)	
Saldaña Sanz, Alejandro	3:54:15 (9,272)	
Sale, James	4:58:39 (26,128)	
Sale, Nicholas J	2:57:10 (867)	
Saleem, Ibrar	5:33:10 (31,683)	
Sales, Jamie	4:21:47 (16,634)	
Sali, Zak	6:07:00 (34,506)	
Saliba, Joseph	2:51:56 (560)	
Salinas, Manuel Angel	4:09:09 (13,240)	
Salisbury, Matthew	4:00:26 (11,100)	
Salisbury, Noel	6:00:14 (34,078)	
Salisbury, Paul	4:21:49 (16,643)	
Salkeld, Bill	4:46:07 (23,065)	
Salmon, Alec William David	4:20:48 (16,368)	
Salmon, Clarence	4:40:43 (21,700)	
Salmon, Graham A.	5:28:34 (31,097)	
Salmon, Jay Mark	4:34:11 (20,037)	

Salmon, John	6:51:23 (36,020)	
Salmon, Oliver James	4:09:40 (13,388)	
Salmond, Patrick	2:59:57 (1,148)	
Salmons, Malcolm D	4:12:24 (14,068)	
Salomon, Phil Mark	4:01:04 (11,271)	
Salt, Ian	3:11:52 (2,083)	
Salt, Jeff	5:26:40 (30,858)	
Salt, Jonathan	5:01:00 (26,649)	
Salt, Stephen Brian	4:11:26 (13,827)	
Salter, Edward	3:52:38 (8,832)	
Salter, Ian	3:52:25 (8,770)	
Salter, Kelhem	3:09:47 (1,892)	
Salter, Mark	3:21:13 (3,111)	
Salter, Michael J.	4:28:25 (18,494)	
Salter, Michael James	4:39:06 (21,280)	
Salter, Michael P.	3:15:05 (2,447)	
Salter, Neil Garry	3:40:03 (6,157)	
Salter, Robert S.	3:00:31 (1,173)	
Salter, Steve	6:55:45 (36,128)	
Salter-Boyden, James Pridmore	5:04:46 (27,330)	
Salthouse, Gary Richard	4:10:32 (13,600)	
Salvioli, Corrado	4:20:07 (16,140)	
Salwey, Nick	3:45:51 (7,278)	
Sambridge, Kevin John	3:24:13 (3,471)	
Sambridge, Malcom William	5:36:10 (32,012)	
Sambrook, Gregory	4:32:26 (19,545)	
Sames, Paul	4:00:01 (10,989)	
Samiei, Ali	5:47:03 (33,054)	
Sammons, Luke	4:39:33 (21,400)	
Samouel, Matt	5:49:06 (33,248)	
Samper, Jean-Michel	3:33:49 (5,028)	
Sampson, Barry P	2:52:23 (587)	
Samra, Inderjit	5:53:21 (33,599)	
Samson, André	4:33:23 (19,820)	
Samson, Julius Anthony	3:03:44 (1,368)	
Samson, Mark	3:29:38 (4,348)	
Samson, Phil John	3:08:08 (1,713)	
Samuel, Edward R.	2:46:10 (364)	
Samuel, Gilles	3:07:45 (1,680)	
Samuel, Harry	4:43:01 (22,263)	
Samuel, Huw	4:26:31 (17,961)	
Samuels, Adam	3:58:55 (10,691)	
Samuels, Alan Nigel	4:28:39 (18,567)	
Samuels, Paul	4:26:46 (18,016)	
Samways, Paul Thomas	2:54:54 (734)	
Samwell, Matthew	3:49:44 (8,157)	
Sanadi, Reza	5:11:27 (28,475)	
Sanchez, Ernesto	4:15:16 (14,850)	
Sanchez, Juan Carlos	3:42:20 (6,568)	
Sanchez, Manuel	3:14:22 (2,363)	
Sanchez, Manuel	3:23:28 (3,361)	
Sanchez, Roberto	4:44:16 (22,583)	
Sanctuary, Paul David Andrew	5:08:14 (27,937)	
Sandell, Bruce	3:42:57 (6,685)	
Sandeman, Ian	6:14:54 (34,881)	
Sandeman, Patrick	4:57:43 (25,912)	
Sanders, Gerald Kevin	4:52:27 (24,669)	
Sanders, Jonathan P.	4:57:07 (25,784)	
Sanders, Lee Thomas	5:05:28 (27,443)	
Sanders, Mark D.	4:59:09 (26,249)	
Sanders, Simon A.	4:21:47 (16,634)	
Sanders, Steve P	4:01:44 (11,429)	
Sanderson, Andrew Roy	5:02:35 (26,956)	
Sanderson, Ben	3:29:18 (4,289)	
Sanderson, Gary John	4:02:00 (11,492)	
Sanderson, Mark	5:02:35 (26,956)	
Sanderson, Martin	4:40:58 (21,764)	
Sanderson, Terence	4:02:52 (11,694)	
Sandford, Alan J	3:33:56 (5,048)	
Sandford, Richard Paul	4:07:17 (12,771)	
Sandford Hart, John	6:49:20 (35,986)	
Sandham, Andrew Lee	3:14:48 (2,419)	
Sandham, David	4:07:54 (12,930)	
Sandham, David A.	3:19:09 (2,886)	
Sandison, Jimmy	4:30:38 (19,129)	
Sandle, Jack Edward	4:37:46 (20,938)	
Sands, David J	4:26:20 (17,910)	
Sanett, Nick Alexander	6:51:47 (36,033)	
Sanford, Michael	4:39:29 (21,381)	
Sanford, Tom	3:57:43 (10,308)	
Sanger, Philip B	2:51:35 (548)	
Sangha, Charanjit	4:17:21 (15,391)	
Sangha, Jagtar	4:42:45 (22,203)	

Sanghera, Hoshiar S	5:23:12 (30,342)	
Sangiorgi, Paolo	4:57:29 (25,853)	
Sangster, Andrew Peter	4:58:56 (26,196)	
Sangster, Nick James	4:35:16 (20,287)	
Sanjivi, Krishna	4:21:08 (16,447)	
Sankey, Paul W	2:38:05 (164)	
Sans, Philippe	4:03:14 (11,785)	
Sansom, Hedley	4:25:03 (17,537)	
Santamaria, Paul	4:25:30 (17,661)	
Santos, Flavio	3:04:48 (1,446)	
Sants, Alex	4:12:14 (14,039)	
Sanz, Ignacio	3:59:24 (10,839)	
Sappey, Yann	4:42:40 (22,176)	
Saqui, Glenn A	2:42:50 (270)	
Sara, Adam-Lee	4:43:48 (22,441)	
Sara, Alan	4:56:43 (25,697)	
Sarai, Jass Singh	3:49:24 (8,064)	
Sarai, Lakhvinder	5:43:59 (32,765)	
Saranna, Lashman	5:17:55 (29,534)	
Saranna, Nirmal Singh	5:17:54 (29,526)	
Sarbok, Torsten	3:52:15 (8,719)	
Sardar, Bobby	5:08:39 (27,998)	
Sarfas, Paul William	4:47:29 (23,406)	
Sargeant, Chris Neil	5:11:47 (28,518)	
Sargeant, Mark	3:47:15 (7,586)	
Sargeant, Tom	4:53:21 (24,884)	
Sargent, Kevin	4:21:57 (16,688)	
Sari, Sergio	3:57:52 (10,352)	
Sarjent, Bruce M	3:30:18 (4,470)	
Särkimukka, Torbjörn	4:33:53 (19,963)	
Sarmiento, Jorge	4:14:46 (14,732)	
Sarr, Omar	3:28:40 (4,169)	
Sarson, Peter	3:05:06 (1,467)	
Sarson, Scott	3:27:50 (4,021)	
Sarti, Stefano	3:10:26 (1,941)	
Satchwell, Peter	4:28:51 (18,625)	
Sathianathan, Gavin	4:25:57 (17,798)	
Sathyanarayan, Raghuram	4:37:44 (20,931)	
Satinet, Jonathan	4:01:28 (11,359)	
Sato, Takashi	5:19:08 (29,724)	
Satoshi, Kitaaki	5:55:58 (33,787)	
Satterly, Charles	5:03:59 (27,186)	
Satterly, James Andrew Lindesay	4:38:25 (21,092)	
Sauer, Ulrich	3:40:55 (6,313)	
Saul, Dominic James	4:43:22 (22,339)	
Sault, Carl Simon	4:42:40 (22,325)	
Saunders, Andrew	5:27:28 (30,962)	
Saunders, Andy	4:56:04 (25,551)	
Saunders, Austin	4:43:50 (22,456)	
Saunders, Brian Edward	4:36:00 (20,477)	
Saunders, Colin	4:50:34 (24,179)	
Saunders, Damian	4:03:58 (11,954)	
Saunders, David A	3:03:40 (1,361)	
Saunders, David Richard	3:29:13 (4,273)	
Saunders, Jamie	5:31:49 (31,516)	
Saunders, Jimmy	4:24:20 (17,333)	
Saunders, John	3:47:09 (7,556)	
Saunders, John	4:31:38 (19,362)	
Saunders, Martin	4:13:31 (14,369)	
Saunders, Martin	4:41:34 (21,912)	
Saunders, Matthew	3:53:06 (8,945)	
Saunders, Michael Stuart	5:14:46 (29,031)	
Saunders, Neil	5:32:58 (31,658)	
Saunders, Paul Francis	4:18:13 (15,636)	
Saunders, Roger Ian	4:26:04 (17,830)	
Saunders, Ross W	3:56:38 (9,973)	
Saunders, Russell	3:04:36 (1,438)	
Saunders, Terry	5:30:38 (31,378)	
Saunders, Timothy Gideon	4:23:15 (17,034)	
Saunderson, Iain	4:33:36 (19,893)	
Saunderson, James	4:17:41 (15,493)	
Saurin, Zak	3:09:19 (1,834)	
Savage, Anthony Michael	3:14:46 (2,414)	
Savage, Benjamin D	3:56:18 (9,871)	
Savage, Craig A	4:00:33 (11,126)	
Savage, David John	4:20:37 (16,302)	
Savage, Gary	4:47:55 (23,522)	
Savage, Philip J	6:22:42 (35,223)	
Savill, Keith	3:49:55 (8,191)	
Savill, Matt	4:56:51 (25,735)	
Saville, Oliver J	2:59:28 (1,101)	
Saville, Philip	4:50:41 (24,203)	
Savory, Andrew B.	3:45:33 (7,220)	

Sawada, Hideyuki 5:35:42 (31,956)
Sawbridge, Mark 5:20:14 (29,880)
Sawer, Martin 3:34:25 (5,140)
Sawford, Paul M 2:59:16 (1,079)
Sawtell, Edward Paul 3:47:48 (7,702)
Sawyer, David 6:06:22 (34,468)
Sawyer, Duncan 4:04:42 (12,129)
Sawyer, Greg 4:41:23 (21,863)
Sawyer, Robert J 4:54:31 (25,184)
Sawyers, Craig G 4:26:24 (17,927)
Saxby, Chris 4:18:50 (15,803)
Saxe-Coburg, Kyril 4:57:21 (25,830)
Saxel, Mark Roger 4:10:49 (13,670)
Saxton, Michael 4:31:46 (19,388)
Say, Mark Anthony 5:06:36 (27,643)
Sayell, Keith John 5:31:24 (31,464)
Sayer, David Ronald 5:04:06 (27,209)
Sayer, Greg James Jarvis 4:52:11 (24,596)
Sayer, Mark K 3:49:40 (8,139)
Sayers, Brian Alfred 4:43:52 (22,469)
Sayers, Julian A 5:38:47 (32,288)
Saynor, Chris A 3:17:08 (2,680)
Scadding, David John 5:15:32 (29,157)
Scaife, Peter G 4:24:18 (17,319)
Scala, Alessandro 4:47:45 (23,479)
Scales, John 5:54:19 (33,666)
Scalise, Alex 5:45:14 (32,886)
Scally, Kevin 4:17:54 (15,546)
Scammell, Jon 4:46:35 (23,193)
Scanlan, Lee 4:20:56 (16,394)
Scanlan, Ronan James 3:49:30 (8,093)
Scanlon, Fintan 3:47:05 (7,541)
Scanlon, John George 5:13:25 (28,829)
Scarborough, Linton J 2:53:47 (654)
Scarfe, Geoff 5:11:43 (28,506)
Scarinci, Marco 3:27:01 (3,878)
Scarlett, David James 4:36:01 (20,481)
Scarlett, Laurence S 3:15:19 (2,479)
Scarlett, Lebert Henry 4:59:24 (26,313)
Scarr, Richard 4:30:08 (19,010)
Schaad, Marco 2:55:43 (782)
Schaaf, Ole Michael 3:52:28 (8,789)
Schaaff, Wolfgang 4:22:42 (16,905)
Schaefer, Andrew D 4:27:03 (18,097)
Schaefer, Thorsten 2:53:14 (624)
Schaffhauser, Armin 3:52:58 (8,911)
Schaffner, Andreas 3:08:31 (1,759)
Schareina, Ralf 3:53:40 (9,113)
Scharmacher, Stephan 5:47:04 (33,056)
Scharvona, Daniel Nathan 4:30:04 (18,994)
Scheer, Andrew 3:46:25 (7,402)
Schek, Andreas Albert 3:47:54 (7,717)
Schele, Torsten 3:04:13 (1,410)
Schenk, Hans-Juergen 4:28:51 (18,625)
Schenk, Kurt S 6:21:52 (35,194)
Scherer, Ari 7:13:53 (36,350)
Scherer, Yehuda 7:13:53 (36,350)
Scheuerlein, Roland 5:00:24 (26,535)
Schiappascasse, Pedro 3:31:01 (4,579)
Schildmann, Andreas 3:47:12 (7,576)
Schillinger, Christoph 4:29:14 (18,741)
Schimpel, Arthur 6:59:16 (36,181)
Schippel, John 6:58:57 (36,175)
Schipporeit, Timm 4:14:35 (14,677)
Schliemann, Hans-Peter 3:11:06 (2,008)
Schmid, Raphael 4:00:51 (11,204)
Schmidt, Burkhard 5:07:26 (27,793)
Schmidt, Matt 4:13:47 (14,452)
Schmidt, Thomas 3:37:27 (5,649)
Schmiederer, Christian 4:05:22 (12,300)
Schmitt, Martin 3:46:51 (7,500)
Schneck, Alex 4:39:22 (21,344)
Schneider, Christian 3:52:07 (8,682)
Schneider, David 3:58:37 (10,598)
Schoebel, Heinz 6:13:02 (34,804)
Schoell, Martin 3:11:41 (2,068)
Schofield, Alan 4:17:07 (15,329)
Schofield, Chris J 4:01:58 (11,482)
Schofield, Ian Kenneth 4:11:54 (13,959)
Schofield, Mike Reid 3:09:37 (1,872)
Schofield, Mike William 4:02:56 (11,715)
Schofield, Simon 4:51:52 (24,511)
Scholer, Roy S 3:43:56 (6,865)
Scholes, Andrew J 3:34:13 (5,101)
Scholes, Mike A 3:45:23 (7,184)
Scholte, Paul D 3:08:28 (1,751)
Schooling, Robert John 3:41:32 (6,427)
Schoonbrood, Elmar 4:37:54 (20,967)
Schoonderbeek, Leo 4:29:28 (18,797)
Schramm, Cedric 2:36:23 (134)
Schroeder, Werner 4:59:13 (26,267)
Schubert, Thomas Christian 4:04:02 (11,968)
Schudel, Ernst 4:33:07 (19,734)
Schuetze, Dietmar 4:46:29 (23,164)
Schuller, Manfred 4:33:58 (19,986)
Schultz, Karl Johannes 4:42:30 (22,141)
Schulz, Barrie Richard 4:25:12 (17,575)
Schumacher, Dieter 4:33:56 (19,977)
Schumann, Paul D 3:16:23 (2,597)
Schupbach, Eric 5:06:28 (27,618)
Schuur, Alberd Hendrik 3:43:58 (6,871)
Schvartz, Frederic 3:44:17 (6,933)
Schvartz, Lionel 3:44:17 (6,933)
Schwarzinger, Walter 5:54:58 (33,713)
Schweighofer, Roman 3:38:28 (5,839)
Schwer, Paul Andrew Siegfried 4:16:48 (15,247)
Schwinghammer, Arno 3:58:37 (10,598)
Scicluna, Edward James 4:26:00 (17,812)
Sciotti, Riccardo 3:45:51 (7,278)
Sciotti, Valentino 3:18:07 (2,781)
Sciver, Richard J 4:12:45 (14,174)
Scofield, Keith 3:12:47 (2,165)
Scogings, Ian 4:12:01 (13,991)
Scopes, Ian Paul 4:09:11 (13,253)
Scotland, Jason 4:49:59 (24,047)
Scott, Andrew 4:38:14 (21,037)
Scott, Andrew James Thomas 3:37:25 (5,639)
Scott, Andrew M 4:06:21 (12,539)
Scott, Andy 5:32:38 (31,621)
Scott, Bryan 4:27:44 (18,295)
Scott, Cameron 3:34:01 (5,061)
Scott, Christopher 3:51:39 (8,577)
Scott, Christopher Edward 3:38:02 (5,770)
Scott, Dominic Luke 4:51:11 (24,346)
Scott, Fraser Walker 4:17:06 (15,321)
Scott, Gareth 5:23:15 (30,347)
Scott, Ian 3:47:22 (7,612)
Scott, Ian 5:26:59 (30,902)
Scott, Ian T 4:10:57 (13,700)
Scott, James Somerville 5:43:37 (32,729)
Scott, Jason 4:29:03 (18,704)
Scott, Jason James 5:32:49 (31,643)
Scott, Jim Anthony 3:34:57 (5,240)
Scott, John Robert 3:55:37 (9,647)
Scott, Jonathan A 2:42:58 (277)
Scott, Keith 5:36:57 (32,094)
Scott, Kevin 4:06:18 (12,524)
Scott, Mark A 4:28:26 (18,499)
Scott, Matthew Charles 4:11:23 (13,812)
Scott, Nick 4:04:03 (11,973)
Scott, Oliver Paul 3:32:13 (4,775)
Scott, Peter J 3:57:50 (10,337)
Scott, Peter J 4:01:04 (11,271)
Scott, Richard 3:35:12 (5,272)
Scott, Richard 7:17:27 (36,383)
Scott, Richard H 2:31:55 (84)
Scott, Rob Duncan 4:53:30 (24,917)
Scott, Robin 3:20:10 (2,974)
Scott, Roy G 2:35:16 (117)
Scott, Russell K 4:34:40 (20,165)
Scott, Steven 4:20:14 (16,173)
Scott, Steven Alan 4:54:47 (25,255)
Scott, Thomas B 3:07:48 (1,685)
Scott, Thomas C 3:28:12 (4,094)
Scott Hamilton, Ken 4:02:47 (11,671)
Scotthorne, Simon Michael 4:37:35 (20,904)
Scott-Jones, David Stephen 5:01:04 (26,661)
Scotton, Dominic Paul 5:28:46 (31,123)
Scott-Priestley, Simon C 5:53:58 (33,640)
Scoular, Ricky 4:45:48 (22,979)
Scovell, Keith 3:12:43 (2,157)
Scrace, Shaun 3:54:35 (9,347)
Scrase, Chris 4:24:17 (17,311)
Scrase, Paul 4:14:33 (14,665)
Scrimgeour, Andrew James 4:04:58 (12,196)
Scrimshaw, Dave William 3:40:34 (6,252)
Scrivener, Chris 3:02:08 (1,266)
Scrivener, Keith Alfred 4:48:51 (23,760)
Scrivener, Richard 4:10:49 (13,670)
Scruton, Neil 3:08:35 (1,766)
Scullion, Andrew 5:27:27 (30,961)
Scullion, James 3:52:09 (8,694)
Scully, Ralph 4:49:31 (23,911)
Scutchings, Darren J 3:45:07 (7,119)
Scuto, Franco Salvatore 4:03:55 (11,946)
Scutts, Philip 5:09:39 (28,173)
Seabourne, Ben 4:28:23 (18,478)
Seabright, Charles (Casey) 3:52:27 (8,777)
Seachoy, Cormac 3:45:15 (7,151)
Seago, Thomas Robert 4:33:08 (19,740)
Seal, Adrian Paul 4:24:56 (17,498)
Seal, Julian D 4:35:48 (20,420)
Seal, Ricky 4:23:30 (17,104)
Seamark, Jamie Robert 2:56:33 (835)
Sear, James A 4:53:32 (24,928)
Sear, Paul 5:50:24 (33,374)
Searle, John Richard 3:13:01 (2,192)
Searle, Nick 3:41:05 (6,337)
Searle, Paul Kelvin 3:59:33 (10,882)
Searle, Stephen Gary 3:54:36 (9,354)
Sears, Chris 4:02:41 (11,646)
Sears, Matthew 3:57:48 (10,331)
Sears, Nicholas John 3:38:38 (5,881)
Sears, Paul Anthony 4:46:49 (23,259)
Seary, Michael P 5:42:54 (32,662)
Seaton, Richard Mark 3:55:48 (9,719)
Seatter, Anton Michael 5:14:48 (29,036)
Seccombe, Colin 4:34:40 (20,165)
Sechiari, Paul 4:05:48 (12,412)
Secker, Karl R 5:28:13 (31,054)
Secondin, Guerino 4:40:17 (21,570)
Seddon, David Alan 5:12:04 (28,577)
Seddon, Jon 3:58:09 (10,435)
Seddon, Nick 3:27:04 (3,879)
Seddon, Paul 3:10:14 (1,925)
Seddon, Thomas Jeremy 5:53:52 (33,634)
Sedge, Martyn J 2:58:13 (980)
Sedgwick, John 3:59:12 (10,779)
Seed, Daniel Anthony 4:27:52 (18,330)
Seed, Paul 3:36:16 (5,453)
Seelandt, Frank 3:49:04 (7,993)
Seelochan, David 3:26:47 (3,845)
Segal, Idan 4:49:55 (24,031)
Segal, Jeremy Simeon 4:05:27 (12,325)
Segall, Alan Mark 5:04:21 (27,251)
Segger, André 3:03:31 (1,348)
Sehgal, Vipan 6:12:48 (34,797)
Seidel, Franz 4:45:39 (22,935)
Seidel, Mirko 4:06:54 (12,684)
Seigel, Adam 4:11:12 (13,766)
Sekito, Ryoji 4:05:09 (12,241)
Selby, Paul 6:10:02 (34,666)
Selch, Matthew Jonathan 4:51:14 (24,361)
Selemba, Andy 4:54:53 (25,279)
Self, Richard J 3:07:03 (1,614)
Selfe, Chris 3:55:46 (9,706)
Selig, Justin 4:58:20 (26,050)
Sellari, Antonio 3:58:32 (10,570)
Sellen, Grant James 4:16:06 (15,052)
Sellers, Alan 4:35:19 (20,298)
Sellers, Ian Richard 4:09:36 (13,370)
Sellers, Mark John 4:33:52 (19,959)
Sellers, Stephen Robert 4:46:45 (23,237)
Sellers, Steven 5:24:23 (30,538)
Selley, Shane 3:18:57 (2,866)
Selmes, Nicholas 5:15:30 (29,146)
Selwyn, Tony George 4:49:52 (24,021)
Sembres, Gilles 3:46:20 (7,383)
Semple, Graeme 3:59:12 (10,779)
Semple, James 3:40:11 (6,181)
Semple, Paul Fraser 3:55:17 (9,556)
Sendell, Greg 3:46:53 (7,505)
Sene, Alex 5:14:26 (28,982)
Sengers, Harm 2:29:38 (64)
Senkiw, Walter 4:45:21 (22,852)
Sennett, Zane R 4:19:43 (16,019)
Sephton, Andy Jonathan 5:44:13 (32,788)
Sephton, Richard Henry 3:13:38 (2,270)
Sequeira, Ryan D 3:27:53 (4,033)

Sergeant, James....4:06:12 (12,496)
Sergi, Gianluca....4:06:53 (12,682)
Serpi, Maurizio Antonio....4:11:22 (13,805)
Serrano, Alex....5:26:50 (30,876)
Serroukh, Redouane....3:50:03 (8,221)
Servantie, Roland....4:47:52 (23,514)
Servidei, Richard....4:11:07 (13,748)
Serville, Adrian....4:42:09 (22,050)
Servini, Dominic Jon....4:51:47 (24,488)
Sethi, Anu....3:40:32 (6,246)
Severein, Pieter....3:26:44 (3,836)
Seville, Andy....3:55:25 (9,598)
Seviour, Jeremie David....4:21:49 (16,643)
Sewell, David....4:59:01 (26,219)
Sewell, Matthew William....3:15:49 (2,529)
Sewell, Nigel....3:16:00 (2,556)
Sewell, Richard....4:01:08 (11,282)
Sexton, David H....3:01:24 (1,224)
Sexton, Eamonn....4:38:18 (21,054)
Sexton, John....5:47:42 (33,114)
Sexton, Jonathan N....4:00:19 (11,062)
Sexton, Stephen Terence....8:13:00 (36,595)
Seyffer, Eberhard....4:26:26 (17,934)
Seymour, Ben....5:06:54 (27,702)
Seymour, Christian C....3:24:44 (3,543)
Seymour, Derek Gordon....4:50:20 (24,123)
Seymour, James....4:15:13 (14,838)
Seymour, Stuart Frank....4:28:19 (18,458)
Shackerley, Simon....4:20:45 (16,356)
Shackleford, Gary....4:30:16 (19,040)
Shackleton, Andrew I....3:23:14 (3,328)
Shacklock, Jon-Philip....4:24:28 (17,381)
Shadick, James Jonathan....4:54:37 (25,209)
Shaffery, Joseph....4:04:59 (12,200)
Shafier, Lawrence E....3:15:16 (2,468)
Shafier, Ricky....4:44:41 (22,696)
Shah, Beju....5:08:01 (27,899)
Shah, Binoi....3:42:41 (6,631)
Shah, Birju....4:35:13 (20,272)
Shah, Deep....4:57:14 (25,810)
Shah, Dhimant....5:16:03 (29,234)
Shah, Hiten....6:53:54 (36,084)
Shah, Jitu....3:45:03 (7,106)
Shah, Kirti....4:28:26 (18,499)
Shah, Mazhar....6:39:25 (35,768)
Shah, Mukesh....4:40:03 (21,508)
Shah, Neil Niraj....4:58:58 (26,207)
Shah, Pankaj....4:39:29 (21,381)
Shah, Priyen....4:12:32 (14,109)
Shah, Rajan....5:08:40 (27,999)
Shah, Rumit....6:19:00 (35,080)
Shah, Sajid....6:48:55 (35,976)
Shah, Samit....4:46:03 (23,043)
Shah, Tan....4:34:47 (20,190)
Shah, Vikrant....4:37:01 (20,749)
Shaikh, Mohammed Hanif....4:05:33 (12,345)
Shakesheff, Kevin....4:36:58 (20,734)
Shakespeare, Christopher A....3:34:20 (5,126)
Shakespeare, Simon J....4:48:55 (23,776)
Shalders, Michael....3:52:32 (8,804)
Shaldon, Christopher S....5:01:43 (26,800)
Shamara, Yury....5:28:31 (31,090)
Shamlian, Nazareth....4:43:54 (22,479)
Shanahan, Gregory Kenneth....4:55:39 (25,447)
Shand, Alan John....3:51:41 (8,584)
Shand, Richard....5:13:10 (28,796)
Shandley, Adrian Phillip....4:04:34 (12,087)
Shandley, Jordan Thomas....4:58:14 (26,019)
Shankar, Vinay....4:52:52 (24,771)
Shanley, Andrew N....4:32:31 (19,565)
Shanley, William T....4:16:04 (15,042)
Shanmugalingam, Shantha....4:24:53 (17,485)
Shannon, James Anthony....4:58:18 (26,040)
Shannon, Kevin John....4:29:29 (18,800)
Shannon, Martin Patrick....3:47:13 (7,581)
Shannon, Michael....4:57:14 (25,810)
Shannon, Pat....5:01:13 (26,685)
Shannon, Simon A....4:01:56 (11,478)
Shapcott, Andrew....4:21:53 (16,664)
Shapiro, David Humphrey....5:05:46 (27,487)
Shapland, Christopher L....3:20:43 (3,048)
Shapland, Mark....4:50:54 (24,269)
Shardlow, Nigel....4:08:09 (12,994)
Shardlow, Richard A....2:59:45 (1,132)
Share, Adrian Wayne....4:43:24 (22,347)
Share, Fred....4:59:16 (26,278)
Share, Richard....3:51:54 (8,639)
Sharkey, Jon D....2:31:34 (80)
Sharkey, Kevin Patrick....3:36:16 (5,453)
Sharkey, William P....5:44:35 (32,826)
Sharland, Richard J....3:07:54 (1,689)
Sharma, Kishore Kumar....4:01:45 (11,435)
Sharma, Sanjai....3:02:02 (1,261)
Sharman, Ben Thomas....3:28:10 (4,086)
Sharman, David C....3:22:38 (3,252)
Sharman, Dean....5:45:48 (32,932)
Sharman, Neil John....4:25:13 (17,578)
Sharp, Andrew James....4:08:03 (12,975)
Sharp, Andy....4:45:40 (22,940)
Sharp, Christopher....4:40:42 (21,693)
Sharp, Daryl....3:50:12 (8,247)
Sharp, Ian....4:07:46 (12,900)
Sharp, John....4:02:16 (11,553)
Sharp, Kenneth....4:17:11 (15,345)
Sharp, Matthew....3:14:56 (2,430)
Sharp, Neil....4:50:59 (24,300)
Sharp, Richard Anthony....3:57:47 (10,326)
Sharp, Robert P....3:17:50 (2,747)
Sharpe, Garry James....4:28:28 (18,512)
Sharpe, Mark....4:35:04 (20,242)
Sharpe, Michael A....3:49:55 (8,191)
Sharpe, Peter....5:02:52 (27,000)
Sharples, John....3:57:01 (10,102)
Sharples, Matthew Edward James....4:17:26 (15,416)
Sharples, Paul James....5:42:38 (32,646)
Sharpley, David Robert....5:56:27 (33,826)
Sharpley, Robert David....4:12:00 (13,990)
Sharran, Nasser....5:37:14 (32,134)
Sharrock, Robert....4:24:22 (17,346)
Shaun, Creasey Darren....5:02:22 (26,919)
Shaw, Alexander....4:28:15 (18,436)
Shaw, Allan....5:44:21 (32,800)
Shaw, Charlie John....6:21:05 (35,163)
Shaw, David James....5:50:08 (33,346)
Shaw, Gary P....3:58:59 (10,718)
Shaw, Geoff....3:32:42 (4,843)
Shaw, Iain B....3:05:06 (1,467)
Shaw, James C....4:07:49 (12,909)
Shaw, James Guy....4:46:35 (23,193)
Shaw, John E....4:43:11 (22,299)
Shaw, Paul Francis....4:56:52 (25,737)
Shaw, Robert....4:05:47 (12,408)
Shaw, Steven....4:14:38 (14,696)
Shaw, Steven Michael....4:06:32 (12,583)
Shaw, Stuart A....2:52:02 (567)
Shaw, Thomas....4:08:00 (12,963)
Shaw, Tim....3:57:32 (10,238)
Shaw, Victor....6:04:26 (34,347)
Shawyer, Gideon D....3:33:47 (5,020)
Shayler, David Carl....3:47:01 (7,530)
Shea, Barry....3:52:13 (8,711)
Shea, Daniel....3:32:54 (4,879)
Shead, Alan William....5:18:28 (29,624)
Shearan, Kristian M....5:11:39 (28,493)
Sheard, Simon C....2:53:31 (640)
Shearer, Andrew J....3:48:05 (7,754)
Shearer, Ben....2:39:22 (180)
Shearer, Chris....4:10:42 (13,638)
Shearer, Rob....3:33:01 (4,897)
Shearing, Nicholas J....3:31:25 (4,653)
Shearn, Paul....4:29:02 (18,697)
Shears, Stewart Leslie....4:34:31 (20,124)
Sheath, Danny James....5:50:19 (33,364)
Sheehan, Giles Edward....4:35:16 (20,287)
Sheehan, Greg Robert....4:17:57 (15,563)
Sheehan, Martin G....4:09:31 (13,346)
Sheehan, Paul Kelley....3:08:16 (1,725)
Sheehan, Timothy Graham....4:06:14 (12,506)
Sheekey, Stephen A....4:53:22 (24,887)
Sheen, Philip....3:15:15 (2,465)
Sheen, William George....3:56:17 (9,866)
Sheffield, Andy David....4:55:46 (25,485)
Sheibani, Askar....4:03:12 (11,777)
Sheikh, Omar....4:03:30 (11,844)
Sheil, John....4:15:45 (14,971)
Sheldon, Charlie....5:29:50 (31,273)
Sheldon, Mike D....3:36:50 (5,532)
Sheldon, Paul Ellis....4:30:03 (18,987)
Sheldon, Toby Harrison....5:46:14 (32,973)
Sheldrake, Kevin....5:12:47 (28,699)
Shelley, Alan William....6:25:50 (35,340)
Shelley, Brian S....4:30:40 (19,139)
Shelley, Desmond Robert....4:57:50 (25,931)
Shelley, Richard N....2:56:30 (830)
Shelling, Andrew....3:48:34 (7,866)
Shelton, Ben Peter....4:38:58 (21,252)
Shelton, Richard James....3:53:30 (9,054)
Shemar, Raji L....4:21:56 (16,686)
Shemoon, David Louis....3:49:11 (8,021)
Shephard, Ben....3:23:38 (3,383)
Shephard, Buzz....2:42:06 (254)
Shephard, Mark....4:20:52 (16,381)
Shepherd, Adam....6:49:00 (35,977)
Shepherd, Anthony....5:41:13 (32,512)
Shepherd, Barry....6:32:13 (35,572)
Shepherd, Ben....3:54:01 (9,215)
Shepherd, Brett....5:26:12 (30,804)
Shepherd, Christopher J....3:02:22 (1,286)
Shepherd, David....3:55:15 (9,544)
Shepherd, David J....3:11:57 (2,088)
Shepherd, David Victor....4:44:37 (22,676)
Shepherd, James Ashmore....4:37:45 (20,934)
Shepherd, Jonathan Charles....4:04:18 (12,029)
Shepherd, Michael George....5:36:47 (32,080)
Shepherd, Nigel H....3:48:23 (7,820)
Shepherd, Roger....5:34:32 (31,826)
Shepherd, Sam George Lawson....4:55:15 (25,371)
Shepherd, Simon....4:38:03 (20,997)
Shepherd, Stephen....5:46:21 (32,989)
Shepley, Alexander Thomas....4:13:44 (14,442)
Sheppard, Bill H....3:59:46 (10,941)
Sheppard, Charles E....3:58:19 (10,499)
Sheppard, Darren....4:30:59 (19,212)
Sheppard, Dave N....3:26:07 (3,752)
Sheppard, David....3:25:49 (3,705)
Sheppard, David J....3:41:50 (6,486)
Sheppard, Jay....4:55:02 (25,316)
Sheppard, John....3:56:31 (9,938)
Sheppard, Matthew....3:39:47 (6,099)
Sheppard, Michael....3:58:56 (10,698)
Sheppard, Nicholas....5:47:20 (33,080)
Sheppard, Richard....4:39:23 (21,350)
Sheppard, Tim....5:01:18 (26,709)
Sheridan, Chris....3:28:32 (4,145)
Sheridan, Daniel....4:08:31 (13,090)
Sheridan, Daniel....4:13:52 (14,475)
Sheridan, Gerard....4:29:00 (18,686)
Sheriff, Daniel....3:20:00 (2,964)
Sherley, Paul Simon....4:22:10 (16,747)
Sherlock, Will....5:29:38 (31,243)
Sherman, Richard J....4:12:39 (14,139)
Sherman, Rick....5:07:00 (27,724)
Sherr, Russell....5:34:48 (31,860)
Sherratt, Craig D....4:09:58 (13,463)
Sherratt, James....3:31:50 (4,716)
Sherriff, Adrian P....3:57:51 (10,345)
Sherriff, Mark D....2:57:05 (862)
Sherry, Declan Gerard....5:47:32 (33,100)
Sherry, Mathew D....5:10:10 (28,270)
Sherry, Thomas....4:44:12 (22,563)
Sherwin, Andrew Colin....4:16:00 (15,026)
Sherwin, James....4:47:47 (23,489)
Sherwin, Mark George....3:51:58 (8,649)
Sherwood, Christopher Antony....3:14:47 (2,417)
Sherwood, Dennis Ronald....5:19:38 (29,797)
Shew, Peter....3:59:17 (10,808)
Shewbridge, Andrew John....5:05:50 (27,500)
Shickell, John....3:26:57 (3,869)
Shiel, Christopher....3:54:57 (9,460)
Shields, Andrew J....3:09:57 (1,903)
Shields, Dan....5:09:22 (28,120)
Shields, Dominic....3:41:47 (6,473)
Shields, Graham....5:16:24 (29,294)
Shields, John Ray....3:56:33 (9,948)
Shields, Matt....2:54:37 (708)
Shields, Michael Gerad....6:27:52 (35,416)
Shields, Paul....3:58:05 (10,407)
Shiels, Gary....3:55:09 (9,516)
Shiels, Iain Kenneth....4:37:56 (20,974)

Shillcock, Ian Lewis....................4:34:50 (20,202)
Shilling, Danny..........................4:55:21 (25,392)
Shimizu, Sachio.........................4:51:04 (24,322)
Shimmin, Greg...........................5:09:08 (28,075)
Shimmin, Robert Joseph 3:30:24 (4,485)
Shipley, Adrian J.........................3:59:36 (10,893)
Shipley, David Henry 4:50:28 (24,154)
Shipley, Ivan 4:22:15 (16,786)
Shipman, John 3:42:25 (6,580)
Shipman, Ryan 3:13:29 (2,252)
Shipp, Anthony 4:59:48 (26,408)
Shipton, James 3:51:31 (8,541)
Shipton, Mark Ian Edward 3:22:45 (3,264)
Shirkie, Darren John Mcneil 5:34:13 (31,782)
Shirley, Damian D 2:56:34 (837)
Shirley, David..............................3:34:13 (5,101)
Shirley, Reginald Vincent 4:21:35 (16,571)
Shirres, Andrew Joseph Spencer.3:23:58 (3,427)
Shively, Bill W.............................3:05:03 (1,462)
Shoebridge, Ian...........................4:06:18 (12,524)
Shoemark, Aaron 5:14:47 (29,032)
Shofiuzzaman, Mohammed.........4:56:35 (25,664)
Shone, Adam Michael.................3:48:12 (7,782)
Shone, Peter Robert Anthony.....4:30:24 (19,064)
Shoobert, James Samuel.............4:01:50 (11,455)
Shopland, Sam David..................4:56:09 (25,567)
Shore, Martin P...........................2:32:36 (88)
Short, Daniel George..................5:04:08 (27,216)
Short, Deane 4:12:58 (14,225)
Short, Gary J...............................5:47:08 (33,064)
Short, Ian Michael Edward..........4:58:36 (26,116)
Short, Jamie................................4:07:39 (12,871)
Short, Kevin................................3:19:31 (2,918)
Short, Mark.................................4:57:41 (25,905)
Short, Paul...................................6:31:24 (35,552)
Shortland, Robert W...................4:25:51 (17,768)
Shread, Steven Joseph 5:42:16 (32,616)
Shrimpton, Duncan.....................4:39:29 (21,381)
Shrimpton, Garry Michael..........4:09:23 (13,304)
Shropshire, Oliver.......................4:28:43 (18,583)
Shrubb, Richard James 3:53:52 (9,174)
Shuck, Steve P 3:28:34 (4,157)
Shugafi, Gamal............................4:21:44 (16,623)
Shulman, Robert I........................2:58:46 (1,027)
Shulver, Edward 3:49:51 (8,176)
Shuster, Carlos Daniel.................4:20:41 (16,328)
Shutt, Peter Daniel......................4:34:21 (20,080)
Shuttleworth, Philip David 4:15:39 (14,937)
Sibert, Jean Pierre 4:47:41 (23,468)
Sibley, Neil..................................3:11:14 (2,020)
Sibley, Richard.............................4:19:08 (15,886)
Sibley, Trevor John 4:28:23 (18,478)
Siciliano, Joe...............................4:31:08 (19,250)
Siddall, Paul David 4:51:05 (24,326)
Siddall, Phil 5:26:24 (30,833)
Sidders, Andrew...........................3:42:45 (6,646)
Siddle, Michael Robert 3:21:30 (3,138)
Sideras, James..............................5:22:50 (30,278)
Sidgwick, Jason Michael..............3:40:02 (6,154)
Sidhu, Satvinder...........................5:42:11 (32,606)
Sidley, David Mark........................4:34:02 (20,000)
Sidoli, Anthony 3:43:45 (6,813)
Sidonio, David M..........................4:02:15 (11,547)
Siebner, Stefan 3:57:41 (10,293)
Sienicki, Leslaw 4:16:02 (15,038)
Siese, Luke Alexander William ...3:55:59 (9,779)
Sifuna, Bernard M........................5:52:42 (33,551)
Sigaud, Philippe 4:14:11 (14,566)
Siggers, Andy Neil........................4:04:41 (12,122)
Sigurdsson, Sigurdur E 4:33:01 (19,703)
Sigurjonsson, Sigurjon Ragnar....4:33:17 (19,801)
Silcock, Steve...............................3:53:35 (9,084)
Silcox, Nick..................................3:10:16 (1,929)
Sillar, Will....................................4:47:00 (23,309)
Sillars, David................................5:04:29 (27,273)
Sillence, Shaun.............................4:55:13 (25,361)
Sillitoe, Ben 4:13:31 (14,369)
Sillitoe, Michael............................4:07:31 (12,837)
Sills, Mark 3:25:56 (3,726)
Sills, Neil......................................3:46:16 (7,373)
Silva, Guilherme...........................3:48:06 (7,761)
Silva, Rodolfo 3:40:04 (6,161)
Silverthorne, Robert 5:35:15 (31,898)

Silvester, Shane Paul 4:20:11 (16,157)
Sim, Martin Ross 7:51:08 (36,565)
Sim, Richard Anthony 4:14:00 (14,504)
Simcoe, Dean 5:07:36 (27,832)
Simili, Alberto 4:50:23 (24,135)
Simkins, Christopher J.................4:59:38 (26,369)
Simkins, Paul John.......................4:13:43 (14,436)
Simkiss, Richard L........................2:42:24 (261)
Simmonds, Gareth 4:45:23 (22,860)
Simmonds, Ronald.......................4:12:53 (14,204)
Simmons, Adrian 4:55:18 (25,387)
Simmons, André 4:43:49 (22,450)
Simmons, Anthony James...........5:35:27 (31,921)
Simmons, Christopher.................5:06:36 (27,643)
Simmons, Christopher.................5:25:37 (30,713)
Simmons, Marc 7:40:49 (36,527)
Simmons, Mark 3:25:46 (3,702)
Simmons, Michael James.............4:22:05 (16,730)
Simmons, Paul..............................3:59:30 (10,863)
Simmons, Philip D 5:01:34 (26,769)
Simmons, Stuart...........................3:58:32 (10,570)
Simmons, Stuart Dean 5:29:29 (31,218)
Simmons, Terry Paul....................3:58:16 (10,478)
Simmons, Trevor 5:37:21 (32,153)
Simms, Mike 4:23:33 (17,119)
Simo, Leonardo F 4:26:39 (17,986)
Simon, David Anthony.................5:37:38 (32,176)
Simon, Japhet Lazarus.................4:22:06 (16,735)
Simon, Jonathan 4:14:32 (14,659)
Simon, Jonathan 4:20:00 (16,110)
Simon, Juden................................5:50:50 (33,413)
Simon, Lloyd 4:27:10 (18,137)
Simon, Paul F 5:06:57 (27,716)
Simone, Angelo............................2:59:30 (1,110)
Simons, Craig 5:25:38 (30,720)
Simons, Paul R 2:45:55 (356)
Simons, Scott................................4:23:54 (17,213)
Simons, Spencer Simons 5:19:11 (29,734)
Simper, Martin John 5:07:40 (27,843)
Simper, Stephen John..................4:51:58 (24,545)
Simpkins, Mark 4:53:02 (24,803)
Simpkins, Michael........................4:49:34 (23,929)
Simpkins, Ryan.............................4:49:34 (23,929)
Simpson, Alastair..........................3:57:42 (10,297)
Simpson, Alexander John............4:55:00 (25,308)
Simpson, Allen 5:10:39 (28,357)
Simpson, Andrew..........................4:33:31 (19,857)
Simpson, Andrew P.......................4:07:13 (12,755)
Simpson, Daniel 4:17:29 (15,433)
Simpson, Dominic.........................4:37:24 (20,845)
Simpson, Donald A 2:59:03 (1,057)
Simpson, Drew Mark.....................4:53:35 (24,937)
Simpson, Edward 3:58:29 (10,551)
Simpson, Edward 7:32:32 (36,480)
Simpson, Gareth 3:44:18 (6,938)
Simpson, Gary 4:03:36 (11,874)
Simpson, Gerry.............................3:55:44 (9,688)
Simpson, Ian..................................4:49:40 (23,968)
Simpson, John Anthony...............4:02:18 (11,557)
Simpson, Jonathan Douglas 4:22:24 (16,822)
Simpson, Mark Simon Fordell 3:26:51 (3,855)
Simpson, Matt 4:54:09 (25,079)
Simpson, Nigel J...........................4:30:04 (18,994)
Simpson, Peter J 3:37:18 (5,622)
Simpson, Richard..........................5:40:31 (32,432)
Simpson, Richard Graham 4:32:54 (19,673)
Simpson, Robert J 3:24:59 (3,577)
Simpson, Stuart 4:53:35 (24,937)
Simpson, Timothy Andrew...........3:41:26 (6,413)
Simpson, Tom 3:14:11 (2,339)
Simpson, William 3:57:01 (10,102)
Simpson, William Raymond H 3:40:00 (6,147)
Sims, David John 4:34:46 (20,186)
Sims, Jonathan Ronald 4:10:37 (13,620)
Sims, Nigel P.................................3:06:01 (1,535)
Sinclair, Andrew G 2:57:22 (884)
Sinclair, Colin A 4:27:04 (18,110)
Sinclair, Craig 5:42:37 (32,645)
Sinclair, David..............................4:29:38 (18,860)
Sinclair, Grant 4:17:30 (15,439)
Sinclair, Hamish 5:54:42 (33,686)
Sinclair, Jamie 3:08:40 (1,778)
Sinclair, Jamie...............................5:03:07 (27,041)

Sinclair, Jamie Darren.................4:16:23 (15,135)
Sinclair, Jonathan M 2:55:22 (765)
Sinclair, Malcolm.........................3:01:07 (1,212)
Sinclair, Nicholas.........................5:30:04 (31,304)
Sinclair, Simon 4:08:40 (13,131)
Sindel, Karl...................................3:09:43 (1,881)

Sinfield, Matthew 3:27:21 (3,930)

2007, 2008, 2009, 2010. My fourth London Marathon in succession, and yet I am still as nervous as ever on the start line in the rain at Blackheath. Will I complete the distance? Will I hit the wall? Can I beat last year's time of 3 hrs 22 mins? All the questions I have asked every year. But then I remind myself of why I am doing this, for all the kind people donating to my chosen charity, the CF Trust, in memory of my friend Pete. And then I remember all of the hours and miles of training through snow, wind and rain. I can do this again. I will finish. I have to! 3 hrs, 27 mins later I reach the finish line. Incredible emotion. Over £5k raised for the CF Trust in my first four marathons. So worth it!

Singer, Jamie Joseph 4:50:39 (24,195)
Singer, Stuart...............................3:34:13 (5,101)
Singh, Baljinder 4:48:25 (23,647)
Singh, Charnjit.............................4:59:24 (26,313)
Singh, Harmander.........................5:36:17 (32,032)
Singh, Jagjit 4:36:56 (20,723)
Singh, Jason 4:30:53 (19,185)
Singh, Jason..................................5:37:12 (32,125)
Singh, Kulwant 5:49:32 (33,288)
Singh, Malkiat 7:36:25 (36,497)
Singh, Manjit................................3:33:37 (4,989)
Singh, Manjit................................4:45:26 (22,870)
Singh, Pratap................................5:55:01 (33,720)
Singh, Raghbir 4:39:46 (21,452)
Singh, Rajinder 5:04:59 (27,363)
Singh, Ravindra.............................4:01:32 (11,376)
Single, Christian............................6:18:13 (35,043)
Sinnott, Vincent 4:57:09 (25,791)
Sipson, John James........................4:54:59 (25,302)
Sirs, Nicholas J...............................3:11:34 (2,057)
Sissens, David Charles...................4:59:52 (26,422)
Sisson, Robert R 4:00:42 (11,170)
Sisterson, Paul 4:23:14 (17,030)
Sistilha, Ramon 4:57:04 (25,775)
Sit, Tony...6:25:14 (35,323)
Sivarajah, Mark..............................4:52:17 (24,633)
Sivarajah, Sanjeevan......................4:21:25 (16,528)

Sivelle, Philip M 7:02:20 (36,218)
Sivlal, Inderjith Soorajlal 5:49:37 (33,294)
Sivonen, Mika Juhani 4:47:32 (23,417)
Sizaire, David 3:47:51 (7,707)
Sizer, Guy Maxwell 4:39:08 (21,291)
Sjolund, Martin 3:09:42 (1,878)
Skeeles, Damian 4:27:29 (18,229)
Skeen, Robert Melvyn 4:05:36 (12,353)
Skeet, Martin W 3:45:15 (7,151)
Skeffington, Timothy 3:30:26 (4,489)
Skelding, Matthew C 3:47:39 (7,677)
Skellern, Tom 3:53:19 (9,004)
Skelly, Mark A 3:16:40 (2,638)
Skelton, Alastair 3:48:45 (7,913)
Skelton, Chris Robert 3:58:24 (10,523)
Skelton, John 3:06:27 (1,565)
Skelton, Raymond D 3:49:38 (8,130)
Skelton, Stephen 4:32:59 (19,691)
Skelton, Terry James 3:18:29 (2,819)
Skerratt, Clark I 3:11:10 (2,013)
Skerry, Jon 4:05:14 (12,263)
Skevington, Timothy Mark 3:27:11 (3,905)
Skibinski, Joseph Stephen 4:15:47 (14,977)
Skibo, James E. 5:03:40 (27,131)
Skidmore, Jonathan 3:21:50 (3,175)
Skidmore, Thomas Geoffrey John 4:13:15 (14,297)
Skillen, Andrew 4:44:22 (22,605)
Skillen, Richard 3:50:57 (8,411)
Skillett, Nick James 4:28:25 (18,494)
Skilling, Hugh 5:30:37 (31,376)
Skilling, Matthew Anthony 3:52:54 (8,898)
Skingsley, Ben David 4:25:39 (17,701)
Skinn, Rob 3:42:59 (6,695)
Skinner, David Charles 4:35:25 (20,332)
Skinner, Martin Joseph 3:30:46 (4,541)
Skinner, Rob N 3:03:28 (1,345)
Skinner, Steve Andrew 5:08:58 (28,037)
Skipper, David Leslie 4:14:17 (14,592)
Skipper, Phil William 4:58:43 (26,148)
Skipper, Terry James 6:33:44 (35,619)
Skirrow, Dave 4:03:01 (11,736)
Skivington, Mark 4:46:03 (23,043)
Skoulding, Alan G 4:58:57 (26,203)
Skovhus, Christian 4:57:57 (25,959)
Skrzypecki, Tony 3:28:50 (4,194)
Skulnick, Alexander 3:57:28 (10,221)
Skyrme, Jeremy Mark 4:25:18 (17,599)
Slack, Christopher 4:17:22 (15,396)
Slack, Daniel 4:31:30 (19,334)
Slack, Jonathan Robert 3:58:11 (10,449)
Slade, Aubrey 4:01:10 (11,291)
Slade, Glen 3:06:58 (1,604)
Slade, Nick D 3:47:34 (7,662)
Slade, Richard 3:51:13 (8,474)
Slade, Tony William 3:30:07 (4,434)
Slaney, Toby Bryher-Jon 5:10:58 (28,398)
Slape, James Caston 4:29:15 (18,743)
Slark-Hollis, Trevor J 4:22:48 (16,939)
Slate, Richard 5:22:36 (30,240)
Slater, Adam William 4:06:59 (12,707)
Slater, Frederick James 3:45:11 (7,135)
Slater, Graham R 5:16:29 (29,310)
Slater, Michael Keith 4:02:30 (11,601)
Slater, Philip W 4:22:53 (16,959)
Slater, Robert 4:51:28 (24,411)
Slater, Rory James, Scott 3:38:27 (5,837)
Slater, Timothy John 4:18:07 (15,614)
Slatford, Mark 4:58:17 (26,038)
Slatford, Paul 3:51:49 (8,612)
Slaughter, John 4:09:26 (13,325)
Slaughter, Paul A 4:28:53 (18,636)
Sleath, Andrew 4:28:12 (18,417)
Sleeman, Mark 3:48:53 (7,947)
Sleuyter, Steven 3:08:59 (1,806)
Slevin, Martin D 6:50:07 (35,998)
Slingsby, Jason Hardwick 4:10:29 (13,590)
Slinn, Gregory 5:16:23 (29,292)
Sloan, Jim 3:04:43 (1,443)
Sloane, Josh 4:27:18 (18,181)
Sloman, Rob 3:56:49 (10,036)
Slootweg, James Kieran 4:48:22 (23,627)
Sluman, David 5:32:10 (31,559)
Sly, Andy 2:47:42 (409)

Smail, Abdelkrim 3:52:10 (8,699)
Smailes, Neil 4:45:59 (23,018)
Small, Andrew Bowmer 3:43:04 (6,712)
Small, Iain Robert 5:34:50 (31,862)
Small, Mark J 4:11:38 (13,889)
Small, Matt 4:17:39 (15,483)
Small, Michael Edward 5:08:54 (28,030)
Small, Neil 4:59:48 (26,408)
Small, Stephen 4:57:03 (25,770)
Smallcombe, Stuart J 5:05:56 (27,519)
Smalley, Anthony 5:25:41 (30,731)
Smallman, Dale 4:51:28 (24,411)
Smallman, Gary William 5:28:51 (31,131)
Smallman, Matthew Charles 3:53:28 (9,045)
Smalls, Allen 2:33:23 (95)
Smalls, Chay James 4:35:58 (20,468)
Smart, Darren 3:27:09 (3,896)
Smart, Dominic 3:34:59 (5,245)
Smart, Erskine 6:01:58 (34,186)
Smart, Neil 4:10:51 (13,680)
Smart, Paul 3:40:49 (6,292)
Smart, Paul 4:13:36 (14,404)
Smart, Will 4:18:29 (15,711)
Smeaton, Alistair David 3:55:43 (9,677)
Smeaton, Graeme William 3:52:34 (8,812)
Smeddle, Jeremy Hugh 4:09:34 (13,358)
Smedley, Mark 4:18:19 (15,665)
Smethurst, Mike 3:20:01 (2,965)
Smidt, Wayne 5:45:50 (32,937)
Smiht, Stephen 4:08:02 (12,973)

Smiley, Derek Raymond 7:08:55 (36,301)

'Long rule the couched potatoes'. That was my philosophy until I was inspired by a very dear friend running the 2009 Marathon, Jenny Sinclair Day Doyle. I then had to face me: 55, overweight and unfit. Supported by Sue my wife, and daughters Michelle and Charlotte, my first run was 400 yards to the Olde Bull Inn, Barton Mills. I pulled my Achilles! The British Lung Foundation sent me a 'get you round' schedule. It did not cover the fact we were having our worst winter for 30 years! I followed this and before I knew it the day was here. All the effort was worth it. Chants of 'Smiley, Smiley' and a mention from BBC's Steve Cram culminating in that run past Buckingham Palace cheered on by thousands of people, including family and friends, was one of the best days of my life. Thanks to all those wonderful people who supported my efforts and charity.

Smith, Aaron 4:27:59 (18,361)
Smith, Adam 3:34:52 (5,223)
Smith, Adam James 5:43:14 (32,693)
Smith, Adam Luke 4:36:53 (20,711)
Smith, Adrian 4:05:08 (12,234)
Smith, Adrian 4:48:40 (23,711)
Smith, Alan 4:57:07 (25,784)
Smith, Alasdair 4:37:09 (20,784)
Smith, Andrew 4:04:25 (12,058)
Smith, Andrew 4:21:44 (16,623)
Smith, Andrew 6:05:43 (34,435)
Smith, Andrew D 4:49:18 (23,872)
Smith, Andrew David 3:47:36 (7,669)
Smith, Andrew J 3:00:32 (1,175)
Smith, Andrew J 3:36:34 (5,491)
Smith, Andrew James 3:50:40 (8,351)
Smith, Andrew John 4:18:10 (15,621)
Smith, Andrew Thomas 4:02:58 (11,721)
Smith, Andy 3:57:33 (10,246)
Smith, Angus 4:23:45 (17,181)
Smith, Anthony P 2:52:42 (604)
Smith, Antony 4:41:53 (21,989)
Smith, Athole J 3:05:52 (1,525)
Smith, Barry 5:13:04 (28,763)
Smith, Barry Sean 3:03:32 (1,354)
Smith, Ben 3:34:11 (5,093)
Smith, Ben James 3:42:10 (6,545)
Smith, Benjamin 4:15:25 (14,889)
Smith, Billy 5:30:29 (31,352)
Smith, Charles Philip 4:01:42 (11,409)
Smith, Chris 2:29:56 (69)
Smith, Chris 4:07:40 (12,878)
Smith, Chris 4:57:02 (25,768)
Smith, Chris Adam 3:35:25 (5,306)
Smith, Chris R 4:55:11 (25,352)
Smith, Christopher 5:32:10 (31,559)
Smith, Christopher Anthony 6:04:12 (34,335)
Smith, Christopher John 3:50:39 (8,348)
Smith, Ciaran E 3:26:35 (3,814)
Smith, Clive E L 4:37:27 (20,866)
Smith, Clive G 3:08:10 (1,715)
Smith, Clyde V 3:54:28 (9,317)
Smith, Colin 3:52:04 (8,674)
Smith, Colin 5:11:17 (28,449)
Smith, Colin A 5:38:17 (32,235)
Smith, Colin Jack 5:31:03 (31,422)
Smith, Colin James 4:28:00 (18,365)
Smith, Craig 4:11:20 (13,800)
Smith, Craig A 3:29:52 (4,391)
Smith, Craig Paul 3:23:42 (3,394)
Smith, Dale Adrian 5:26:14 (30,809)
Smith, Damian 5:51:39 (33,478)
Smith, Daniel William 4:23:30 (17,104)
Smith, Darren 4:01:25 (11,345)
Smith, Darren 4:25:02 (17,531)
Smith, Darren 5:51:15 (33,444)
Smith, Dave George 4:22:03 (16,717)
Smith, Dave Russell 5:07:52 (27,872)
Smith, David Andrew 4:47:15 (23,353)
Smith, David Anthony 3:39:59 (6,139)
Smith, David James Murray 4:33:19 (19,807)
Smith, David John 3:33:55 (5,043)
Smith, David Keith 5:43:57 (32,762)
Smith, David Stuart 4:26:58 (18,069)
Smith, David William 5:28:42 (31,112)
Smith, Dean G 4:12:57 (14,216)
Smith, Dean Michael 4:36:38 (20,645)
Smith, Demian 4:52:45 (24,739)
Smith, Donovan Elcoate 4:15:28 (14,899)
Smith, Edwin J 4:43:20 (22,325)
Smith, Fraser D 4:56:26 (25,635)
Smith, Gareth 5:01:44 (26,803)
Smith, Gary 5:08:15 (27,939)
Smith, Gary J 5:15:41 (29,176)
Smith, Geoff Robert William 4:37:46 (20,938)
Smith, Gerald 3:23:37 (3,379)
Smith, Gordon A 2:58:58 (1,042)
Smith, Graeme 3:28:35 (4,160)
Smith, Graham 7:02:59 (36,224)
Smith, Grant T 5:41:09 (32,503)
Smith, Greg 4:25:21 (17,619)
Smith, Greg 5:35:00 (31,876)
Smith, Greg Elliott 3:51:51 (8,622)

Somers, Robert J.........3:42:57 (6,685)
Somersall, David Andrew.........3:26:52 (3,857)
Somerset How, Ben James.........4:12:59 (14,229)
Sommeilly, Alexandre.........3:21:16 (3,115)
Sommerlad, Michael J.........6:31:02 (35,535)
Sommerville, Dave.........5:27:40 (30,984)
Sommerville, Ian Peter.........5:28:23 (31,073)
Sommerville, Robert.........6:01:25 (34,151)
Somrah, Jas.........5:29:56 (31,285)
Sonnex, Tim Charles.........4:02:53 (11,701)
Soole, Brian Peter.........3:28:10 (4,086)
Sopp, James.........5:27:22 (30,953)
Sorbie, Steve.........5:20:00 (29,850)
Sorensen, Erik.........4:56:12 (25,586)
Sorrell, David.........5:22:33 (30,229)
Soto, Antonio.........4:31:39 (19,366)
Soucant, Stephane.........5:09:16 (28,095)
Sousa, Nuno.........4:15:34 (14,919)
Soutar, Murray Duncan.........4:34:55 (20,217)
South, Clifford.........4:43:47 (22,436)
South, Michael J.........4:47:36 (23,437)
Southam, Mark Antony.........6:07:31 (34,532)
Southby, David P.........3:14:32 (2,387)
Southern, Ian.........3:44:26 (6,980)
Southern, John.........3:53:09 (8,955)
Southgate, Antony John.........4:39:54 (21,484)
Southgate, Martin.........4:24:47 (17,462)
Southgate, Philip J.........4:06:43 (12,630)
Southgate, Ross Winston.........5:07:40 (27,843)
Southwood, Ross Christopher.........3:43:21 (6,748)
Sower, Phil.........3:42:15 (6,556)
Sowman, Dean Mathew.........4:43:14 (22,307)
Spackman, Andrew James.........3:45:52 (7,285)
Spackman, Anthony.........4:25:31 (17,668)
Spain, Matthew John.........5:05:46 (27,487)
Spalton, Phil Noel.........4:18:55 (15,832)
Spanfelner, William Harry.........5:31:17 (31,447)
Spanyol, Thomas A.........3:37:59 (5,758)
Sparey, Guy Jonathan.........4:56:34 (25,662)
Spargo, Howard Thomas.........5:25:53 (30,762)
Sparkes, Phil.........3:45:14 (7,147)
Sparks, Clifford.........4:31:01 (19,221)
Sparks, Glyn David.........4:26:31 (17,961)
Sparks, Ian.........3:51:35 (8,561)
Sparks, Paul Phillip.........5:06:31 (27,628)
Sparks, Steve John.........3:31:01 (4,579)
Sparrow, Ian.........4:22:21 (16,804)
Sparrow, Paul.........4:26:19 (17,904)
Spavin, Carl Joseph.........4:47:20 (23,374)
Speak, Simeon B.........3:42:44 (6,643)
Speake, Andrew.........4:55:26 (25,402)
Speake, Brian Arnold.........3:40:49 (6,292)
Speake, Malcolm D.........4:09:16 (13,274)
Speakman, Chris.........6:01:49 (34,175)
Speakman, Christian James.........3:21:13 (3,111)
Speakman, David.........4:45:07 (22,803)
Speakman, Peter Roy.........4:53:57 (25,034)
Speakman, Sean.........4:50:07 (24,075)
Spear, Jon R.........3:13:42 (2,283)
Spearing, Mattherw P.........4:59:20 (26,298)
Speck, Dennis.........2:46:29 (372)
Speck, Robert.........4:00:57 (11,240)
Spector, Brian Lee.........4:22:16 (16,790)
Speed, Chris.........4:08:30 (13,085)
Speed, Christopher.........3:28:24 (4,126)
Speed, David John.........4:39:42 (21,436)
Speed, Gary.........3:49:22 (8,055)
Speed, Mark R.........3:21:55 (3,186)
Speed, Paul Geoffrey.........4:52:16 (24,619)
Speers, Gary Alan.........3:37:28 (5,652)
Speirs, Matthew Marcus.........5:20:35 (29,941)
Speirs, Stephen.........4:20:56 (16,394)
Speller, Luke.........4:12:24 (14,068)
Speller, Martin A.........3:07:17 (1,630)
Speller, Richard.........3:49:50 (8,169)
Spelling, Paul Martin.........3:30:45 (4,539)
Spelling, Stewart.........5:57:51 (33,922)
Spellman, Greg.........2:50:31 (505)
Spelman, Peter J.........3:55:39 (9,661)
Spence, Christopher J.........4:21:43 (16,617)
Spence, James.........6:23:38 (35,262)
Spence, Jason Paul.........5:07:00 (27,724)
Spence, Kristian.........5:11:19 (28,452)
Spence, Nikolai A.........7:15:55 (36,370)
Spencer, Andrew.........3:52:01 (8,663)
Spencer, Andrew M.........3:12:05 (2,099)
Spencer, Chris.........4:36:08 (20,515)
Spencer, Craig J.........4:01:29 (11,362)
Spencer, Craige.........3:49:13 (8,031)
Spencer, David P.........2:59:03 (1,057)
Spencer, Greg.........5:08:47 (28,014)
Spencer, Jamie PF.........4:58:04 (25,980)
Spencer, Lewis.........5:32:09 (31,558)
Spencer, Patrick.........4:09:44 (13,401)
Spencer, Paul Robert Beechey.........4:23:21 (17,060)
Spencer, Philip David.........3:25:39 (3,673)
Spencer, Richard.........3:47:09 (7,556)
Spencer, Robert Charles Paul.........4:57:29 (25,853)
Spencer, Ross.........3:57:00 (10,089)
Spencer, Scott Edward.........5:34:37 (31,837)
Spencer, Stuart.........2:31:50 (83)
Spencer-Perkins, Michael D.........5:04:05 (27,205)
Spendlove, Gavin.........5:41:45 (32,556)
Spendlove, Lee Paul.........3:51:00 (8,423)
Sperring, Mark Lee.........5:29:46 (31,264)
Spicer, Andrew O.........4:48:30 (23,667)
Spicer, Gary.........4:58:15 (26,028)
Spicer, Keith.........5:47:42 (33,114)
Spicer, Neil Christopher.........3:49:03 (7,987)
Spicer, Simon,.........4:53:55 (25,027)
Spiers, Martin.........4:07:59 (12,957)
Spiller, Ben.........3:16:32 (2,618)
Spiller, Tatton.........4:08:51 (13,173)
Spilsted, Martin.........5:14:29 (28,988)
Spindlove, Philip Marc.........4:43:11 (22,299)
Spinelli Barrile, Carlo.........2:42:45 (266)
Spinks, Philip David.........7:00:47 (36,202)
Spittle, Andrew Michael.........3:36:05 (5,424)
Spivey, Garry M.........4:10:44 (13,649)
Spooner, Ben Peter.........4:26:50 (18,034)
Spooner, Darren.........3:17:05 (2,671)
Spooner, Paul.........3:53:43 (9,126)
Spooner, Thomas.........4:03:01 (11,736)
Spooner-Lillingston, Paul EB.........4:54:10 (25,083)
Sporer, Franz.........3:20:29 (3,022)
Spotswood, Michael.........4:54:00 (25,052)
Spowart, Christopher.........6:14:17 (34,851)
Spriggs, Andrew James.........4:55:02 (25,316)
Spring, Robin.........3:42:37 (6,613)
Springall, Andrew.........4:09:11 (13,253)
Springate, Dale Lincoln.........3:32:07 (4,761)
Springett, Tim.........3:59:39 (10,903)
Sprot, Michael.........2:49:05 (446)
Spruce, Mike.........4:39:15 (21,321)
Spruijt, Widemar F.........3:50:39 (8,348)
Sprules, Anthony J.........3:05:24 (1,490)
Spuffard, Ian.........5:27:50 (31,005)
Spurgeon, Paul.........5:31:54 (31,523)
Spurling, Gavin.........4:11:44 (13,917)
Spurling, Ian George.........3:56:19 (9,877)
Spurling, Laurence.........5:00:25 (26,539)
Spurrier, Jack Brotherton.........5:13:04 (28,763)
Spurway, Matthew D.........3:04:35 (1,436)
Squibb, James.........4:44:13 (22,568)
Squire, Paul G.........4:17:56 (15,557)
Squires, Gary.........3:28:58 (4,224)
Squires, Mark.........4:35:26 (20,337)
Squires, Will.........3:48:29 (7,843)
St Aubyn, Charles.........3:58:04 (10,401)
St Clair, Richard.........3:21:36 (3,148)
St Croix, Dennis C.........5:10:20 (28,297)
St John, Ian Leonard.........3:53:30 (9,054)
Stabbins, Richard Alex.........4:46:35 (23,193)
Stace, Michael John.........4:01:43 (11,415)
Stacey, Charles Raymond.........5:34:59 (31,875)
Stacey, Christopher Norman.........5:22:41 (30,253)
Stacey, Lee.........3:25:32 (3,652)
Stacey, Mark E.........3:37:41 (5,706)
Stacey, Paul A.........4:05:08 (12,234)
Stacey, Simon John.........4:34:21 (20,080)
Stacey, Steve John.........3:52:01 (8,663)
Stack, Paul William.........4:12:42 (14,158)
Stack, Peter James.........4:52:50 (24,764)
Stacy, Gary William.........6:03:26 (34,283)
Staddon, Ian.........4:52:03 (24,558)
Staff, Colin Robert.........3:50:02 (8,215)
Staff, Lee Darrin.........5:48:38 (33,207)
Stafford, Craig.........6:39:59 (35,784)
Stafford, James Edward.........6:08:27 (34,577)
Stafford, John F.........3:57:03 (10,118)
Stafford, Julian.........4:10:15 (13,540)
Stafford, Thomas.........5:12:14 (28,608)
Stafford, Warwick.........5:59:31 (34,017)
Staggs, Rob.........3:47:35 (7,666)
Stainer, Gordon.........4:24:23 (17,350)
Stainer, Peter.........2:41:23 (238)
Staines, Robert Charles Gordon.........7:00:38 (36,199)
Staley, Jonathan.........4:25:07 (17,552)
Stalker, Gary.........4:15:05 (14,806)
Stallard, Paul.........4:11:40 (13,898)
Stallard, Philip.........4:06:47 (12,653)
Stalley, Andrew C.........3:18:14 (2,799)
Stambouli, Mounir.........3:38:23 (5,827)
Stammers, Andrew J.........6:03:44 (34,303)
Stammers, Jason.........4:59:28 (26,326)
Stammers, Mark.........4:59:27 (26,321)
St-Amour, Peter Robert.........3:35:02 (5,254)
Stamp, Paul.........3:23:26 (3,357)
Stamp, Thomas James.........4:07:25 (12,804)
Standing, Robert.........4:56:48 (25,720)
Standley, James.........5:37:42 (32,182)
Standring, Michael A.........2:58:21 (992)
Stanford, Johnny David.........4:47:48 (23,494)
Stanford, Paul.........3:36:24 (5,468)
Stanhope, Martin.........5:32:30 (31,603)
Stanier, Keith.........3:45:32 (7,216)
Stanier, Lawrence B.........5:52:30 (33,533)
Stanier, Raymond.........2:58:10 (971)
Staniforth, Andrew M.........3:08:36 (1,768)
Staniforth, Phil.........3:44:17 (6,933)
Stanley, Jonathan J.........4:28:27 (18,508)
Stanley, Joshua.........4:46:37 (23,209)
Stanley, Matthew.........4:21:54 (16,674)
Stanley, Shaun.........4:42:07 (22,042)
Stanley, Simon.........4:43:48 (22,441)
Stanley, Thomas David.........3:29:14 (4,276)
Stanley, Warren R.........4:21:54 (16,674)
Stanmore, Carl John.........4:04:18 (12,029)
Stannard, Adam Paul.........5:11:02 (28,410)
Stannard, Robert J.........4:15:28 (14,899)
Stannett, Charlie D.........4:46:28 (23,159)
Stannett, Darren R.........5:36:09 (32,011)
Stannett, Guy Leonard.........5:13:22 (28,823)
Stanning, Grant Phillip.........4:18:52 (15,818)
Stansell, Gary.........4:55:53 (25,508)
Stansfield, Andrew.........3:24:17 (3,482)
Stanton, Billy.........4:01:03 (11,264)
Stanton, Richard.........5:48:03 (33,144)
Stanton, Richard Marc.........4:13:34 (14,390)
Stanton, Stephen Andrew.........4:15:14 (14,845)
Stanton, Stewart.........4:09:23 (13,304)
Stanton, Tony.........5:44:28 (32,813)
Stanway, Paul R.........4:16:53 (15,266)
Stanway, Simon J.........3:48:40 (7,890)
Staples, Andrew V.........5:13:18 (28,817)
Staples, Ian Anthony.........4:57:11 (25,799)
Stapleton, James Daniel.........4:52:44 (24,735)
Stapleton, Lee John.........4:52:44 (24,735)
Stapleton, Malcolm Desmond.........3:33:23 (4,949)
Stapleton, Mark.........4:49:43 (23,987)
Stapleton, Martin Paul.........3:34:18 (5,115)
Stapley, Gerald Charles.........6:06:20 (34,467)
Starbuck, Tom Daniel George.........5:26:03 (30,787)
Stark, Chris.........4:01:41 (11,407)
Stark, Colin R.........3:09:06 (1,818)
Stark, Peter James.........6:32:55 (35,594)
Starkie, Simon Jonathan.........4:06:03 (12,463)
Starkings, Martyn Andrew.........5:27:59 (31,026)
Starling, Cameron.........4:11:18 (13,790)
Starling, Mark Paul.........4:04:57 (12,191)
Starling, Thomas William.........4:38:36 (21,143)
Starns, Martin Peter.........4:17:14 (15,359)
Starr, Alexander.........5:45:57 (32,947)
Staszak, Leon.........4:55:15 (25,371)
Statham, Gary.........3:54:27 (9,314)
Statham, Malcolm J.........3:41:30 (6,423)
Statham, Nick.........3:53:52 (9,174)
Staton, Oliver N.........5:13:02 (28,744)
Stavenuiter, Kees.........3:54:44 (9,397)

Stavrou, Dino 5:06:41 (27,667)
Stawman, Colin 4:02:34 (11,621)
Stead, Ben Richard 3:46:34 (7,439)
Stead, Darren Alister 3:54:37 (9,359)
Stead, John 5:29:56 (31,285)
Stead, Jonathan P 2:35:26 (122)
Stead, Paul A 3:54:41 (9,381)
Stead, Steven John 3:37:59 (5,758)
Stearns, Rupert Paul 4:25:19 (17,605)
Stebbing, James 4:36:41 (20,655)
Stebbings, Scott Phillip 5:40:49 (32,457)
Steckiw, Thomas John 4:06:51 (12,677)
Steckler, Thomas 3:19:35 (2,924)
Stedman, David Ron 4:34:10 (20,030)
Steed, Mark S 3:53:25 (9,033)
Steeden, Clive R 5:56:01 (33,788)
Steeds, Andy 4:13:29 (14,358)
Steel, Alistair William 4:11:27 (13,835)
Steel, David W 3:49:03 (7,987)
Steel, Harry 3:45:26 (7,196)
Steele, Chris 4:28:59 (18,679)
Steele, Christopher David 3:54:20 (9,289)
Steele, Colin Mark 4:08:13 (13,010)
Steele, Patrick 4:44:24 (22,617)
Steele, Roger 3:45:08 (7,124)
Steele, Warren Richard 6:40:45 (35,807)
Steele, William Andrew 4:20:26 (16,244)
Steenbeek, Roelof 3:56:39 (9,978)
Steeples, Gary David 4:00:13 (11,036)
Steer, Barry 4:58:15 (26,028)
Steer, Clive Lee 4:59:28 (26,326)
Steer, Keith 4:50:50 (24,250)
Steer, Mark Antony 4:22:09 (16,741)
Steer, Mark John 4:22:29 (16,841)
Steer, Richard Andrew 4:25:42 (17,715)
Steer, Robert 4:59:29 (26,333)
Steevens, Nick Paul 3:49:42 (8,145)
Steeves, Greg 4:23:40 (17,147)
Stefani, Jandler 3:39:28 (6,037)
Steggall, Jon 5:29:30 (31,222)
Steinbrunner, Johann 3:16:28 (2,605)
Steiner, Hans-Peter 4:08:40 (13,131)
Steiner, Heinz Peter 4:12:32 (14,109)
Steiner, Helmut 4:52:48 (24,756)
Steinmann, Kai 5:22:09 (30,171)
Steinmann, Peter 4:04:18 (12,029)
Stembridge, Andrew 4:00:31 (11,118)
Stempfer, Karlheinz 3:21:33 (3,142)
Stennett, James J 5:26:59 (30,902)
Stennou, Yves 4:53:15 (24,862)
Stenson, Michael John 5:38:32 (32,266)
Stephan, Eric 4:14:19 (14,597)
Stephan, Helal 5:04:06 (27,209)
Stephane, Aubay 3:35:00 (5,249)
Stephen, Mike 4:48:01 (23,549)
Stephens, Adam Mark 5:13:42 (28,871)
Stephens, Adrian Neil 5:01:21 (26,724)
Stephens, Garry Arthur 5:14:07 (28,940)
Stephens, George Henry 3:07:43 (1,678)
Stephens, Graham C 2:47:27 (401)
Stephens, Guy 5:00:37 (26,574)
Stephens, John I 4:26:14 (17,882)
Stephens, John M 2:49:18 (462)
Stephens, Philip 4:50:05 (24,070)
Stephens, Rob 4:09:33 (13,351)
Stephens, Simon Paul 4:38:51 (21,218)
Stephens, Tom 4:39:31 (21,391)
Stephens, Tony 4:21:57 (16,688)
Stephenson, Brian 6:06:11 (34,464)
Stephenson, Eric C 4:28:16 (18,443)
Stephenson, Gary 6:16:55 (34,971)
Stephenson, Matthew 4:32:26 (19,545)
Stephenson, Matthew 4:48:19 (23,609)
Stephenson, Mike 4:15:06 (14,808)
Stephenson, Simon N 4:57:31 (25,864)
Stepniewski, Robert 4:49:44 (23,991)
Steppeler, Matthias 4:52:09 (24,589)
Stepto, Christian A 5:22:40 (30,249)
Sterlin, Walker J 4:21:43 (16,617)
Stern, Andrew J 4:15:43 (14,958)
Sterry-Macdonald, George W 3:41:10 (6,354)
Stevendale, Brian 4:57:11 (25,799)
Stevens, Adam Marc 4:41:46 (21,959)
Stevens, Andrew 3:55:44 (9,688)
Stevens, Anthony 4:50:57 (24,289)
Stevens, Christopher James 3:36:49 (5,525)
Stevens, David 4:29:35 (18,833)
Stevens, David Anthony 4:29:43 (18,888)
Stevens, Dean Andrew 4:13:01 (14,244)
Stevens, Ed 3:28:32 (4,145)
Stevens, Edward 3:14:44 (2,412)
Stevens, Edward Jon 4:22:44 (16,913)
Stevens, Gareth Robert 4:24:02 (17,245)
Stevens, Giles 5:03:38 (27,126)
Stevens, Ian 3:57:35 (10,261)
Stevens, Ian 5:24:13 (30,515)
Stevens, James A 5:03:52 (27,167)
Stevens, Jonathan 5:19:34 (29,785)
Stevens, Kevin 3:58:17 (10,484)
Stevens, Luke 3:34:37 (5,175)
Stevens, Mark 4:40:14 (21,553)
Stevens, Martin 3:53:04 (8,941)
Stevens, Martin J 2:56:33 (835)
Stevens, Matthew 4:50:33 (24,173)
Stevens, Matthew James 4:43:49 (22,450)
Stevens, Paul 4:26:13 (17,877)
Stevens, Paul Richard 4:42:25 (22,115)
Stevens, Roy 4:00:52 (11,207)
Stevens, Scott 4:22:41 (16,897)
Stevens, Simon 4:36:11 (20,525)
Stevens, Simon 6:11:34 (34,727)
Stevens, Simon N 2:37:50 (159)
Stevens, Thomas L 4:53:24 (24,893)
Stevens, Thomas P 3:42:04 (6,524)
Stevensen, Andrew 4:59:23 (26,308)
Stevenson, Andrew David 3:03:26 (1,343)
Stevenson, Iain James 4:29:25 (18,780)
Stevenson, Iain Robert 3:58:28 (10,544)
Stevenson, James 4:14:43 (14,719)
Stevenson, Laurence E 4:46:08 (23,071)
Stevenson, Michael 3:25:29 (3,645)
Stevenson, Paul 4:36:56 (20,723)
Stevenson, Peter 6:21:55 (35,197)
Stevenson, Richard Craig 3:35:20 (5,291)
Stewart, Adam 4:20:19 (16,209)
Stewart, Charles 3:48:52 (7,944)
Stewart, Craig J 3:36:44 (5,516)
Stewart, David James 4:42:47 (22,208)
Stewart, David S 5:20:00 (29,850)
Stewart, Gavin Andrew 4:22:26 (16,830)
Stewart, George 2:37:47 (157)
Stewart, Gordon Kerr 6:33:39 (35,617)
Stewart, Iain 4:27:51 (18,327)
Stewart, Ian 4:19:59 (16,103)
Stewart, Ian K 5:19:39 (29,800)
Stewart, Jon 5:49:40 (33,304)
Stewart, Luke A 3:25:12 (3,607)
Stewart, Mark David 3:48:53 (7,947)
Stewart, Michael Ian 5:25:53 (30,762)
Stewart, Neville 4:36:38 (20,645)
Stewart, Nick 4:21:48 (16,636)
Stewart, Nik 5:14:47 (29,032)
Stewart, Paul John 4:19:13 (15,903)
Stewart, Robert A 3:29:12 (4,271)
Stewart, Robin Adam 4:13:45 (14,448)
Stewart, Stephen 4:52:46 (24,742)
Stewart, Tim 4:26:00 (17,812)
Stewart, Tom 3:49:28 (8,080)
Sthalekar, Rohit 7:01:13 (36,208)
Stick, Carl Richard 4:02:42 (11,650)
Stickells, James 4:01:34 (11,385)
Stickels, Chris 4:15:00 (14,786)
Stickland, Dave George 4:29:11 (18,728)
Stickley, John 6:59:19 (36,183)
Stiewe, René 4:59:41 (26,380)
Stiff, Adam Kevin 3:59:21 (10,824)
Stiff, Kevin D 3:52:17 (8,734)
Stiffin, Rob 4:10:49 (13,670)
Stiles, Andrew D 3:26:35 (3,814)
Still, Martin D 3:51:39 (8,577)
Still, Stephen Peter 4:38:02 (20,994)
Stimson, Clinton G 6:54:41 (36,102)
Stirk, Nigel A 2:26:46 (46)
Stirling, Alastair 3:45:38 (7,235)
Stirling, Andrew Graham 5:03:22 (27,083)
Stirling, Ross 3:57:18 (10,182)
Stoakes, Philip 3:47:09 (7,556)
Stoat, Antony D 3:56:27 (9,916)
Stobbs, Richard Anthony 4:53:38 (24,952)
Stober, William Giles 3:15:17 (2,472)
Stock, Hal 4:53:51 (25,006)
Stock, Mark Shane 6:55:30 (36,123)
Stockdale, Eoin Matthew 5:45:28 (32,907)
Stockdale, Peter C 3:06:34 (1,575)
Stocker, Gary Thomas 6:25:51 (35,341)
Stocker, John 3:54:44 (9,397)
Stocker, Paul 4:11:46 (13,928)
Stockford, Michael John 4:39:07 (21,286)
Stockford, Paul Clive 3:57:56 (10,362)
Stocking, David 4:45:15 (22,828)
Stocking, Marc 4:45:55 (23,005)
Stockley, Jamie M 3:38:26 (5,835)
Stockley, Neil Howard 4:25:42 (17,715)
Stockman, Mark 4:00:34 (11,131)
Stockton, Nigel 4:38:57 (21,244)
Stockton, Philip 4:35:10 (20,268)
Stockton, Russell 6:23:08 (35,243)
Stodart, Lee 3:38:51 (5,915)
Stoddart, Craig William 4:54:13 (25,107)
Stoddart, Gordon 4:37:21 (20,832)
Stoddart, Leslie 4:01:04 (11,271)
Stofberg, Nicholas 4:57:06 (25,779)
Stofer, Thomas Andreas 4:44:03 (22,516)
Stoker, Jeff 3:44:04 (6,891)
Stoker, Robert 3:50:58 (8,414)
Stokes, Andrew 4:47:36 (23,437)
Stokes, David R 4:13:56 (14,486)
Stokes, Ian William Edward 4:21:53 (16,664)
Stokes, John Patrick 5:03:20 (27,078)
Stokes, Mark J 4:32:38 (19,589)
Stokes, Michael 5:04:08 (27,216)
Stokes, Michael Lee 5:30:17 (31,324)
Stokes, Mike Edward 3:59:23 (10,834)
Stokes, Oliver John 4:10:37 (13,620)
Stokes, Ralph 5:23:11 (30,337)
Stokes, Samuel Wesley Royston 3:54:57 (9,460)
Stokes, Simon James 3:48:19 (7,810)
Stokes, Simon Robert 3:59:15 (10,794)
Stokes, Wayne John 4:09:47 (13,416)
Stokoe, John S 5:41:23 (32,521)
Stolls, Nick 6:21:03 (35,162)
Stolton, John 4:05:21 (12,296)
Stone, Chris 3:51:04 (8,440)
Stone, Daniel James 4:30:15 (19,035)
Stone, David M 2:40:41 (218)
Stone, Gab 4:08:14 (13,012)
Stone, Grant 5:40:33 (32,439)
Stone, Howard 3:59:09 (10,760)
Stone, Jonathan 4:49:52 (24,021)
Stone, Manuel Sidney Victor 5:08:06 (27,911)
Stone, Nicholas 4:03:04 (11,743)
Stone, Peter 4:29:18 (18,755)
Stone, Philip 4:38:21 (21,071)
Stone, Simon Andrew 3:35:09 (5,265)
Stoner, Jonathan Phillip 4:12:59 (14,229)
Stoney, Peter 4:09:17 (13,279)
Stonham, Albert A 6:51:32 (36,026)
Stonhill, Lewis 5:33:35 (31,724)
Stookes, Christopher 4:43:19 (22,323)
Stoops, Elias 4:08:39 (13,126)
Stoops, Joran 5:15:16 (29,109)
Stoops, Luk 6:17:26 (35,004)
Stoops, Natan 4:48:04 (23,561)
Stopien, Nicolas Marc 4:17:36 (15,469)
Storey, Dan John Kenneth 4:35:24 (20,325)
Storey, Michael 5:03:40 (27,131)
Storey, Miles B 4:13:31 (14,369)
Storey, Stuart T 4:41:07 (21,801)
Storrs, Richard 3:59:32 (10,870)
Story, Tom Er 4:40:26 (21,623)
Story, Tom R 4:07:16 (12,769)
Stothard, Andy 5:17:54 (29,526)
Stothard, Simon John 5:25:21 (30,669)
Stott, David 4:59:59 (26,448)
Stott, James E 3:21:10 (3,107)
Stott, Oliver James 4:41:47 (21,964)
Stott, Philip Edward Fletcher 4:45:52 (22,992)
Stout, Paul Alexander 4:11:40 (13,898)
Stow, Scott P 5:31:10 (31,430)

Strachan, Alan G 2:51:00 (525)
Strachan, Charles Roy 4:36:05 (20,500)
Strachan, David 4:23:10 (17,018)
Strachan, Denis Joseph 4:27:09 (18,133)
Strachan, Frederick Maxwell 3:53:42 (9,122)
Strachan, Glen 4:33:19 (19,807)
Strachan, Grant M 3:34:17 (5,111)
Strachan, Toby John 4:38:41 (21,165)
Strahan, Gerard Bryan 4:53:37 (24,947)
Strain, Martin Douglas 3:52:30 (8,796)
Straker, Olly 4:21:20 (16,500)
Strang, Graham J 4:25:19 (17,605)
Strang, Gus 3:33:38 (4,994)
Strange, Peter 5:08:53 (28,029)
Stratford, Gary C 3:21:34 (3,143)
Stratford, Matthew J 2:57:49 (942)
Stratford, Peter C 4:28:24 (18,487)
Stratton, Alan Michael 4:57:33 (25,871)
Stratton, Edward 3:28:19 (4,107)
Stratton, Richard Francis 3:49:22 (8,055)
Strauss, Dirk 4:10:23 (13,564)
Straw, Jonathan J 4:20:19 (16,209)
Strawbridge, Bruce 3:41:12 (6,367)
Strawbridge, James 4:31:03 (19,230)
Strawbridge, James George 4:27:36 (18,257)
Streek, Simon R 5:09:39 (28,173)
Street, Alan Bradford 4:20:22 (16,223)
Street, James 4:03:20 (11,809)
Street, Mark Christopher 4:35:17 (20,292)
Street, René 5:55:00 (33,717)
Street, Sam Riley 4:12:52 (14,199)
Street, Steve 4:03:29 (11,838)
Streeter, Daryl Christian 3:53:49 (9,166)
Streeter, Martin Clark 3:55:06 (9,505)
Streets, Colin James 6:38:06 (35,728)
Streicher, Marek 4:53:17 (24,873)
Stretton, Darren Michael 4:37:44 (20,931)
Stretton, James D 4:34:49 (20,198)
Stretton, Ollie 3:50:34 (8,328)
Stricker, Markus 3:58:25 (10,532)
Stride-Noble, Graham 4:28:05 (18,383)
Stringari, Guido 3:54:12 (9,256)
Stringer, Mark 3:04:29 (1,430)
Stringer, Nick A 5:01:14 (26,689)
Stringer, Simon Michael DC 3:31:11 (4,608)
Strocchia, Felice 3:34:46 (5,206)
Strohheker, Jean-Louis 5:02:26 (26,935)
Stroman, Scott 4:27:27 (18,220)
Stronach, Paul Christopher 4:45:45 (22,968)
Stroulger, John 5:05:41 (27,478)
Strugnell, Anthony B 5:10:09 (28,264)
Struthers, Stewart 5:04:57 (27,355)
Strutt, Barry John 5:15:31 (29,150)
Strydom, Dax 4:03:12 (11,777)
Strydon, Grant A 5:43:41 (32,739)
Stuart, James 4:15:29 (14,902)
Stuart, James Maurice 6:03:30 (34,290)
Stuart, Michael 4:44:05 (22,529)
Stuart, Michael E 3:13:59 (2,319)
Stuart-Thompson, Mark A 3:58:31 (10,560)
Stubbings, Darren James 6:18:52 (35,075)
Stubbins, Graham J 3:33:50 (5,031)
Stubbs, Gareth W 3:17:18 (2,693)
Stubbs, Joe 5:02:05 (26,864)
Stubbs, Nicholas J 3:25:19 (3,618)
Stubbs, Peter George 4:33:22 (19,815)
Stubbs, Robert John 4:35:13 (20,272)
Stuckey, Alexander 3:56:45 (10,014)
Studley, Lee 4:27:09 (18,133)
Stuhllemmer, Kurt 5:42:08 (32,603)
Stupples, Philip John 4:28:33 (18,539)
Sturdgess, Ian Charles 6:13:20 (34,816)
Sturge, Joe Stephen 3:31:57 (4,729)
Sturgess, Gary Francis 4:07:07 (12,735)
Sturgess, Matthew J 4:40:27 (21,628)
Sturgess-Durden, Luke T 2:55:37 (778)
Sturla, Tim Stuart 3:37:49 (5,726)
Sturt, Matthew 4:25:07 (17,552)
Sturt, Paul G 4:52:04 (24,565)
Sturzaker, David S 4:57:52 (25,939)
Styles, Mark 3:00:32 (1,175)
Styles, Robert 4:22:46 (16,928)
Su, Zhan 3:13:58 (2,315)
Subramanian, Suriya 4:42:56 (22,245)
Succamore, Paul D 3:17:44 (2,734)
Sudheendrra, Guruprasad 6:17:38 (35,012)
Suenson-Taylor, Andrew 4:15:17 (14,853)
Suffield, James 6:36:56 (35,697)
Sugden, Robert 4:03:06 (11,759)
Sugg, Elliott 4:42:44 (22,196)
Sugg, Paul Andrew 4:39:50 (21,473)
Suggate, Gary D 2:57:15 (876)
Suggett, Adam 3:26:04 (3,744)
Suhre, Stefan 4:41:06 (21,798)
Sulfridge, David 3:26:49 (3,851)
Sulley, Andrew Robert 5:28:05 (31,040)
Sullivan, Alex Patrick 3:17:58 (2,762)
Sullivan, Allan C 6:18:32 (35,059)
Sullivan, David 4:14:58 (14,773)
Sullivan, David 4:59:56 (26,436)
Sullivan, Gary 3:29:41 (4,357)
Sullivan, Gerry 4:19:59 (16,103)
Sullivan, James Peter 4:49:37 (23,951)
Sullivan, John Robert 4:25:09 (17,560)
Sullivan, Mark J 4:01:16 (11,310)
Sullivan, Thomas Francis 4:18:20 (15,668)
Sullivan, Warren T 3:23:31 (3,370)
Sullman, Mark 3:59:05 (10,740)
Sultan, Michael 4:44:19 (22,595)
Summerell, Stewart 4:34:44 (20,179)
Summers, Mike 4:29:52 (18,935)
Summers, Pete 4:56:11 (25,579)
Summers, Peter J 2:45:58 (358)
Summers, Richard John 3:54:00 (9,211)
Summersgill, David Edward John 5:10:33 (28,340)
Sumner, Andrew Graham 3:55:37 (9,647)
Sumner, Jono 4:41:57 (22,002)
Sumner, Philip John 3:57:49 (10,334)
Sumner, Tim 5:30:32 (31,362)
Sumner, Wayne George 4:28:15 (18,436)
Sumpster, Thomas 3:24:37 (3,526)
Sunda, Anil 5:44:38 (32,832)
Sunderland, Darren Lee 6:38:06 (35,728)
Sunley, Michael 5:43:37 (32,729)
Sunner, Pavitar 5:46:21 (32,989)
Sunol, Xavier 4:16:25 (15,147)
Supperstone, David 3:58:57 (10,704)
Surani, Becharlal 6:27:20 (35,396)
Surgeon, Matthew 4:17:16 (15,368)
Surgey, Dave 3:58:23 (10,517)
Sussman, David Joseph 3:49:25 (8,070)
Sutcliffe, David Anthony 5:04:39 (27,307)
Sutcliffe, Jim 4:39:54 (21,484)
Sutcliffe, John Alexander 3:47:52 (7,711)
Suter, Alan D 6:40:09 (35,792)
Suter, Joachim 3:43:52 (6,848)
Suter, Kim Madoc 3:18:19 (2,806)
Suter, Walter 3:29:05 (4,244)
Suterwalla, Anis 4:43:14 (22,307)
Sutherland, Azad Theophilus N 4:09:06 (13,229)
Sutherland, Calum D 4:43:31 (22,372)
Sutherland, Craig Ian 5:49:37 (33,294)
Sutherland, Hugh 4:19:06 (15,872)
Sutherland, Iain 5:03:08 (27,043)
Sutherland, Ian Mackenzie 6:19:52 (35,118)
Sutherland, Leslie 5:17:36 (29,487)
Sutherland, Paul 4:13:13 (14,290)
Sutherns, Brian 3:40:12 (6,183)
Sutor, Richard 4:08:51 (13,173)
Sutton, Aidan James 4:33:26 (19,836)
Sutton, Alex Benjamin 4:41:41 (21,939)
Sutton, Andrew 4:00:19 (11,062)
Sutton, John 3:51:21 (8,503)
Sutton, Kevin James 5:28:25 (31,077)
Sutton, Malcolm J 4:16:46 (15,239)
Sutton, Mark 3:54:13 (9,263)
Sutton, Nathan John 4:57:42 (25,908)
Sutton, Neil 3:50:44 (8,367)
Sutton, Nigel Christopher 6:17:58 (35,029)
Sutton, Robert D 3:34:19 (5,118)
Sutton, Simon 4:36:05 (20,500)
Sutton, Stephen Paul 3:32:37 (4,831)
Sutton, Tim 3:29:33 (4,332)
Sutton-Haigh, Les 4:50:30 (24,161)
Svatek, Michael Richard 6:28:24 (35,441)
Svavarsson, Elmar 4:18:50 (15,803)
Svavarsson, Petur 4:25:58 (17,803)
Svendsen, Karl 4:29:31 (18,812)
Swaby, Mark Alexander 6:20:03 (35,126)
Swaby, Steven Mark 4:02:47 (11,671)
Swain, Andrew 4:38:40 (21,158)
Swain, Ashley 4:35:53 (20,439)
Swain, Mike 4:22:41 (16,897)
Swain, Simon 3:49:43 (8,150)
Swaine, Andrew 5:13:04 (28,763)
Swaine, Jonathon David 4:14:37 (14,687)
Swainson, Keith A 4:06:50 (12,670)
Swainson, Mike J 5:22:50 (30,278)
Swales, Claureinne Eugene 5:00:47 (26,608)
Swallow, Keith 4:52:14 (24,610)
Swallow, Thomas W 3:09:25 (1,846)
Swalwell, Scott 4:51:27 (24,409)
Swan, Alan 3:14:31 (2,385)
Swan, James Ward 4:18:01 (15,582)
Swan, Jonathan Paul 3:24:36 (3,524)
Swan, Kim Richard 3:36:07 (5,432)
Swan, Paul 2:48:50 (438)
Swan, Stuart 4:19:03 (15,855)
Swann, Graham 5:40:53 (32,469)
Swann, James 4:26:04 (17,830)
Swann, Mark 5:28:51 (31,131)
Swann, Roger 4:23:42 (17,156)
Swannell, Ian James 3:23:11 (3,320)
Swanson, Tom Andrew 4:47:51 (23,510)
Swanton, Paul Matthew 4:14:56 (14,768)
Swanton, Stephen D 3:42:58 (6,689)
Swarbrick, Andrew P 3:29:33 (4,332)
Swarbrick, Joey 4:27:10 (18,137)
Swarfield, David Allan 4:25:21 (17,619)
Swart, Gerhard 4:35:06 (20,251)
Swatton, John 3:44:50 (7,062)
Sweeney, Derek 4:14:17 (14,592)
Sweeney, Michael A 3:53:43 (9,126)
Sweeney, Paul 4:30:18 (19,044)
Sweeney, Peter T 4:02:58 (11,721)
Sweeney, Philip 3:34:43 (5,194)
Sweeney, Scott Michael 5:51:38 (33,477)
Sweeney, Sean 3:41:43 (6,460)
Sweet, Roger Francis 5:43:09 (32,681)
Sweet, Steven James 3:55:41 (9,672)
Sweet, William H 2:50:39 (510)
Sweetlove, Steve 5:21:47 (30,114)
Sweetman, Alastair 5:24:33 (30,562)
Sweid, Abdulwahed 6:49:59 (35,997)
Sweny, Dom 2:59:51 (1,144)
Swiatek, Richard James 5:57:36 (33,911)
Swift, Adam David 3:43:05 (6,715)
Swift, Darryl 3:23:32 (3,373)
Swift, James 4:25:01 (17,524)
Swift, Simon Franklin 3:40:38 (6,268)
Swift, Trevor 3:23:11 (3,320)
Swinburn, Philip Adam 3:21:51 (3,177)
Swinburne, Neil G 5:11:14 (28,442)
Swinburne, Nigel J 3:21:53 (3,179)
Swindells, Anthony 3:47:30 (7,647)
Swindells, Jack 4:08:24 (13,059)
Swindells, Julian 4:39:08 (21,291)
Swindlehurst, Richard Alan 3:08:36 (1,768)
Swire, Christopher James 4:14:09 (14,547)
Swire, Tom 5:29:55 (31,283)
Sworn, Adrian J 4:22:45 (16,918)
Sworn, Andrew W 3:33:37 (4,989)
Syed, Hasnain 5:05:38 (27,472)
Sykes, Christopher 4:04:28 (12,070)
Sykes, Craig Alexander 4:11:06 (13,744)
Sykes, Duncan 3:56:07 (9,815)
Sykes, Graham 3:21:36 (3,148)
Sykes, Josh 3:57:47 (10,326)
Sykes, Patrick Jay 4:57:30 (25,858)
Sykes, Simon Andrew 4:27:53 (18,335)
Symeou, Nicos 4:48:41 (23,715)
Symes, Darren 2:52:55 (617)
Symington, Peter 4:26:54 (18,049)
Symington, Tim Liam 3:44:25 (6,975)
Symmonds, Ian 4:38:52 (21,223)
Symon, Jonathan Blair 5:24:27 (30,550)
Symonds, Peter Edward 4:07:20 (12,781)
Symons, Hugh 3:47:54 (7,717)
Symons, Mike 4:30:07 (19,003)

Symons, Phillip	4:19:53 (16,072)
Symons, Tony R	2:51:24 (538)
Synge, Timothy P	3:26:56 (3,865)
Syrett, Jason	3:20:12 (2,979)
Syrett, Jason K	3:29:53 (4,393)
Szaniawski, Andrzej	4:02:58 (11,721)
Szczepanski, Peter	5:46:55 (33,043)
Szwinto, Henry E	2:41:11 (230)
Szwyd, Aaron	4:18:25 (15,693)
Szydlowski, Marcin	3:45:33 (7,220)
Szymanski, Michael	6:30:53 (35,531)
Szynaka, Stefan	4:38:44 (21,182)
Tabiner, Simon	3:58:58 (10,709)
Tabor, Adam	4:29:08 (18,716)
Tackley, Adam	5:37:34 (32,171)
Tadese, Zersenay	2:12:03 (7)
Tadman, Miles	4:49:46 (24,001)
Taft, David	6:28:05 (35,432)
Tagg, James A	3:29:54 (4,400)
Taggart, Ian	3:17:59 (2,763)
Taggart, Samuel James	3:41:18 (6,388)
Tagore, Ajit	5:10:25 (28,313)
Taha, Abudy	3:56:53 (10,051)
Tahan, Bijan Mark	4:42:51 (22,231)
Tahir, Nazer	4:16:46 (15,239)
Tainton, Matthew	4:43:05 (22,279)
Tait, David James	3:40:17 (6,194)
Tait, David John	4:41:17 (21,840)
Tajiouti, Hassan	3:19:38 (2,931)
Takahashi, Tsugio	4:30:35 (19,120)
Takano, Yoji	4:52:01 (24,555)
Taker, John William	4:43:14 (22,307)
Talbot, Christopher	3:13:22 (2,233)
Talbot, Cy	4:28:14 (18,431)
Talbot, Daniel Barry	4:11:22 (13,805)
Talbot, Daniel James	3:26:05 (3,748)
Talbot, Edward	4:20:59 (16,407)
Talbot, Gary John	4:46:34 (23,185)
Talbot, Jonathan	3:36:01 (5,415)
Talbot, Rich	5:05:46 (27,487)
Talbot, Simon	4:38:02 (20,994)
Talbot, Stephen	6:49:19 (35,984)
Talewar, Ghanaya S	5:46:39 (33,022)
Talja, Ari	4:27:02 (18,087)
Tallon, Toby	4:42:17 (22,093)
Talpert, Seymour	5:24:49 (30,593)
Talty, Joseph	3:35:25 (5,306)
Tamagni, David	4:23:20 (17,054)
Tamang, Purnasingh	4:16:56 (15,282)
Tammadge, Daniel S	5:05:31 (27,452)
Tamplin, Phillip John	4:07:29 (12,826)
Tan, Benedict	3:06:18 (1,553)
Tan, Gower	4:36:53 (20,711)
Tan, Joon Y	4:41:00 (21,771)
Tanner, Jean-Paul	5:17:23 (29,457)
Tanner, Keith E	4:36:41 (20,655)
Tanner, Matthew	5:17:23 (29,457)
Tanner, Michael	3:04:01 (1,393)
Tanqueray, Christophe	4:36:38 (20,645)
Tansey, James	3:54:37 (9,359)
Tansey, Robert	2:59:08 (1,068)
Tansley, Jonny	4:21:00 (16,412)
Tanti, Robert	4:11:13 (13,771)
Tapp, Robin	5:04:35 (27,295)
Tappenden, Rhys David	5:32:42 (31,631)
Tapper, Andrew John	4:42:41 (22,182)
Tapsell, Bryan V	3:24:40 (3,533)
Tapster, Martin	6:21:25 (35,182)
Taranik, Dan	8:18:54 (36,601)
Targett, Ian	4:31:47 (19,390)
Tarling, Dean Michael	4:58:41 (26,134)
Tarn, Peter	4:43:18 (22,320)
Tarragona-Fiol, Tony	5:35:48 (31,969)
Tarrant, Jonathan	4:08:40 (13,131)
Tarrant, Kieran	4:15:58 (15,017)
Tarrant, Matt	5:15:42 (29,177)
Tarrant, Simon	3:43:21 (6,748)
Tarres, Derek David	3:58:14 (10,471)
Tarrier, Peter I	5:11:12 (28,436)
Tarry, Glenn	5:32:03 (31,538)
Tart, Chris	3:16:43 (2,647)
Tasker, Adam David	3:17:32 (2,717)
Tasker, Richard James	3:57:38 (10,275)

Tassi, L	4:01:28 (11,359)
Tassou, Benoit	3:20:22 (2,999)
Tate, Andrew	3:50:08 (8,232)
Tate, Andrew R	3:21:24 (3,131)
Tate, Jonathan E	5:02:43 (26,983)
Tattan, David	4:12:17 (14,051)
Tatum, Matthew James	4:23:56 (17,221)
Tautz, Chris	3:56:08 (9,818)
Tavengwa, Oswald	6:17:45 (35,019)
Tawn, Paul R	4:06:40 (12,619)
Tayler, John	4:11:54 (13,959)
Tayler, Ross	4:08:29 (13,074)
Tayler, Tom Joseph	7:39:56 (36,521)
Taylor, Adam	3:57:29 (10,225)
Taylor, Adam	4:01:22 (11,325)
Taylor, Alvin	3:11:23 (2,036)
Taylor, Andrew B	3:03:24 (1,340)
Taylor, Andrew Edward	5:25:07 (30,644)
Taylor, Andrew P	4:36:27 (20,586)
Taylor, Barny	4:07:17 (12,771)
Taylor, Ben	4:52:47 (24,751)
Taylor, Billy	4:27:22 (18,200)
Taylor, Brian David	3:50:34 (8,328)
Taylor, Chas	4:14:15 (14,583)
Taylor, Chris	2:58:08 (966)
Taylor, Chris	3:54:58 (9,468)
Taylor, Chris	3:57:15 (10,172)
Taylor, Chris	4:37:39 (20,917)
Taylor, Christian Stuart	7:29:05 (36,462)
Taylor, Christopher	4:25:18 (17,599)
Taylor, Christopher David	5:35:52 (31,980)
Taylor, Christopher Paul	4:06:40 (12,619)
Taylor, Dan J	4:28:51 (18,625)
Taylor, Darren Andrew	4:02:36 (11,632)
Taylor, Darren L	4:59:50 (26,412)
Taylor, David	3:47:58 (7,731)
Taylor, David	4:19:30 (15,973)
Taylor, David	4:36:29 (20,598)
Taylor, David	5:38:36 (32,273)
Taylor, David Alexander	3:17:47 (2,743)
Taylor, David I	4:31:10 (19,258)
Taylor, David J	3:09:28 (1,854)
Taylor, David John	5:49:01 (33,242)
Taylor, David Ronald	3:47:12 (7,576)
Taylor, Donald George	4:05:13 (12,259)
Taylor, Duncan	4:29:45 (18,899)
Taylor, Edward	4:50:00 (24,049)
Taylor, Eric	3:26:33 (3,807)
Taylor, Gareth John	4:59:24 (26,313)
Taylor, Gavin	4:51:03 (24,316)
Taylor, Geoff	4:38:07 (21,011)
Taylor, Geoff	5:46:03 (32,956)
Taylor, Geoff Sid	4:03:09 (11,767)
Taylor, Gerry	4:10:42 (13,638)
Taylor, Graeme Paul	3:45:16 (7,156)
Taylor, Graham C	3:39:44 (6,084)
Taylor, Graham J	4:24:46 (17,458)
Taylor, Ian K	3:29:55 (4,403)
Taylor, Ian R	5:02:50 (26,996)
Taylor, James	4:09:29 (13,336)
Taylor, James	4:35:26 (20,337)
Taylor, James	5:44:03 (32,776)
Taylor, James A	7:05:56 (36,266)
Taylor, John	4:22:44 (16,913)
Taylor, John	5:34:21 (31,803)
Taylor, John Chris	3:32:35 (4,823)
Taylor, John Leslie	4:58:47 (26,163)
Taylor, Jonathan	4:49:42 (23,978)
Taylor, Jonathan E	3:48:14 (7,789)
Taylor, Joseph Richard	3:41:35 (6,437)
Taylor, Keith Andrew	4:39:28 (21,377)
Taylor, Keith Robert Stanley	3:55:36 (9,636)
Taylor, Kenneth	4:02:43 (11,657)
Taylor, Kevan Paul	4:26:50 (18,034)
Taylor, Kevin	3:41:38 (6,444)
Taylor, Lee	4:56:00 (25,535)
Taylor, Les Robert	3:57:02 (10,109)
Taylor, Marcus	5:52:07 (33,509)
Taylor, Mark	4:39:30 (21,387)
Taylor, Mark Damian	5:15:46 (29,190)
Taylor, Mark E	3:30:23 (4,484)
Taylor, Mark Richard	4:37:19 (20,824)
Taylor, Martin James	2:53:57 (667)

Taylor, Matthew	3:25:23 (3,627)
Taylor, Matthew J	3:18:08 (2,783)
Taylor, Matthew John	4:16:07 (15,055)
Taylor, Michael Fred	3:43:14 (6,733)
Taylor, Michael M	4:13:01 (14,244)
Taylor, Nathan Andrew	3:22:48 (3,271)
Taylor, Neil A	3:27:37 (3,986)
Taylor, Neil John	4:25:02 (17,531)
Taylor, Neil R	4:18:34 (15,732)
Taylor, Nicholas	6:05:25 (34,414)
Taylor, Nicholas Michael	5:55:13 (33,736)
Taylor, Nick C	3:49:09 (8,010)
Taylor, Nigel	6:19:34 (35,107)
Taylor, Nigel William	4:28:32 (18,535)
Taylor, Owen John	4:24:45 (17,456)
Taylor, Paul	3:57:32 (10,238)
Taylor, Paul	4:52:46 (24,742)
Taylor, Paul	5:10:24 (28,309)
Taylor, Paul	6:06:46 (34,492)
Taylor, Paul Anthony	4:23:35 (17,133)
Taylor, Paul Gary	3:50:41 (8,354)
Taylor, Paul R	5:06:19 (27,590)
Taylor, Peter	3:35:42 (5,359)
Taylor, Philip Lewis	3:09:24 (1,844)
Taylor, Phillip G	2:38:16 (165)
Taylor, Richard	4:33:12 (19,767)
Taylor, Richard D	4:21:31 (16,552)
Taylor, Richard G	3:07:10 (1,624)
Taylor, Richard Haydn	4:09:51 (13,431)
Taylor, Richard John	4:14:30 (14,647)
Taylor, Richard Knight	4:58:36 (26,116)
Taylor, Richard M	3:24:54 (3,563)
Taylor, Richard S	2:52:49 (611)
Taylor, Rob John	4:04:42 (12,129)
Taylor, Robert	3:17:12 (2,684)
Taylor, Sam	4:07:51 (12,918)
Taylor, Sam Daniel	4:33:06 (19,727)
Taylor, Scott	5:26:23 (30,831)
Taylor, Scott G	4:43:03 (22,272)
Taylor, Sean	3:57:33 (10,246)
Taylor, Simon Christopher	4:52:13 (24,606)
Taylor, Simon James	5:46:04 (32,958)
Taylor, Simon John	3:28:04 (4,070)
Taylor, Simon Nicholas	4:44:52 (22,734)
Taylor, Stephen	4:45:47 (22,975)
Taylor, Stephen John	4:31:39 (19,366)
Taylor, Stephen K	4:30:55 (19,201)
Taylor, Stuart	3:42:21 (6,570)
Taylor, Stuart	5:18:17 (29,588)
Taylor, Stuart G	5:31:01 (31,419)
Taylor, Tracy D	5:01:51 (26,820)
Taylor, Vincent G	4:52:28 (24,673)
Taylor, Will	3:30:12 (4,450)
Taylor-Gooby, Ed	3:44:30 (6,987)
Taylorson, Simon Lee	3:13:08 (2,205)
Taylro, Roger G	5:03:12 (27,060)
Tazzioli, Simone	3:35:57 (5,406)
Teague, Gary	4:29:22 (18,768)
Teague, Matthew	3:26:41 (3,827)
Teague, Paul	4:22:12 (16,761)
Teague, Paul Wayne	5:30:27 (31,345)
Teale, Lea	3:56:50 (10,041)
Tear, Guy	4:23:36 (17,136)
Teare, Simon James	3:28:32 (4,145)
Teasdale, Barry	8:43:44 (36,607)
Teasdale, David	3:59:59 (10,982)
Tebbit, Nick	4:20:13 (16,169)
Tebbitts, Jon M	4:30:54 (19,190)
Teck, Paul N	4:58:51 (26,177)
Tedesco, Mario	4:24:56 (17,498)
Teece, Philip R	2:48:06 (418)
Tehel, Tibor	4:12:39 (14,139)
Teig, Matthias	3:43:52 (6,848)
Teixeira, Marcelo	3:55:34 (9,628)
Teji, Shalinder	3:26:24 (3,793)
Telfer, George Metcalfe	4:35:58 (20,468)
Telfer, Scott R	3:41:53 (6,496)
Telford, Alexander	5:22:59 (30,304)
Telford, Gary Robert	5:01:30 (26,754)
Telford, Michael	5:08:11 (27,925)
Temple, Paul	4:39:59 (21,499)
Templeman, Paul	5:50:55 (33,420)
Templeman, Steven	5:41:45 (32,556)

Templeton, Pete	4:00:28	(11,111)
Ten Morro, Francisco	3:30:39	(4,518)
Tendil, Frederic	4:41:07	(21,801)
Tenison, Matthew John	5:16:16	(29,261)
Tennant, John	3:16:05	(2,562)
Tennent, Jake	5:41:16	(32,515)
Terburgh, Riaan	4:54:23	(25,154)
Terkelsen, Rolf	3:13:30	(2,255)
Terrington, Andrew	4:54:21	(25,144)
Terry, Andrew	5:12:25	(28,636)
Terry, Daniel	4:18:30	(15,715)
Terry, Donald Philip	6:08:35	(34,588)
Terry, Gareth	3:57:14	(10,168)
Terry, Jeffrey C	4:57:19	(25,824)
Terry, Mark Patrick	3:59:01	(10,725)
Terry, Michael Stephen	4:17:34	(15,461)
Teruel, Adolfo Garcia	2:50:01	(488)
Tesi, Neil	3:44:32	(6,997)
Tesolin, Tiziano	4:03:49	(11,928)
Tessler, Lee	5:24:19	(30,528)
Tester, Alex	4:03:40	(11,893)
Tester, Michel Carlton	4:02:17	(11,555)
Tether, Rod	3:54:43	(9,392)
Tetlow, Marc	3:22:36	(3,250)
Tetreault, David	4:12:05	(14,003)
Tett, Gregory James	3:32:24	(4,801)
Tew, Paul	2:53:21	(632)
Thabethe, Sicelo Selby	6:02:29	(34,216)
Thackaberry, Paul	5:36:11	(32,015)
Thacker, Neil	3:54:47	(9,416)
Thacker, Will	4:39:33	(21,400)
Thackeray, Richard P	3:17:32	(2,717)
Thackham, Gary	4:25:04	(17,540)
Thake, James P	4:28:54	(18,642)
Thakkar, Ashish	6:23:40	(35,266)
Thakkar, Siddharth	6:13:11	(34,813)
Thanki, Vishal	5:35:34	(31,933)
Thapa, Ben	5:14:51	(29,044)
Tharratt, James	4:10:46	(13,658)
Thatcher, Edward	6:52:31	(36,061)
Thaxton, Jon	3:25:32	(3,652)
Theobald, Simon	3:10:40	(1,959)
Theodore, Gerard	3:22:02	(3,196)
Theodorou, Mario Michael	4:09:34	(13,358)
Theodorou, Sophocles	4:21:27	(16,535)
Theokli, Tony	3:58:18	(10,491)
Thetford, Jonathan Paul	5:05:53	(27,512)
Thexton, David	3:23:22	(3,347)
Thiis, Patrik	4:23:21	(17,060)
Thijssen, Maurits	5:04:17	(27,244)
Thirkettle, Mark Robert	3:56:23	(9,892)
Thirsk, David M	5:30:56	(31,406)
Thisby, Jim	4:35:35	(20,362)
Thockok, Johannes	4:02:43	(11,657)
Thockok, Willi	3:47:10	(7,566)
Tholen, Michael W	4:13:30	(14,365)
Thomas, Adrian	4:58:45	(26,155)
Thomas, Alan	4:15:13	(14,838)
Thomas, Alan	5:09:34	(28,162)
Thomas, Alan E	4:49:24	(23,893)
Thomas, Andrew K	3:38:50	(5,912)
Thomas, Andrew R	3:49:07	(8,006)
Thomas, Benn Cameron	3:09:21	(1,840)
Thomas, Bradley	5:09:23	(28,124)
Thomas, Carl	6:39:11	(35,756)
Thomas, Carwyn	3:07:17	(1,630)
Thomas, Clive	4:22:14	(16,776)
Thomas, Daniel	4:36:43	(20,664)
Thomas, Daniel John	4:06:41	(12,621)
Thomas, Darren J	3:48:11	(7,780)
Thomas, David H	3:25:13	(3,610)
Thomas, David Ian	4:13:26	(14,348)
Thomas, David Ian	4:18:02	(15,589)
Thomas, David John	5:55:01	(33,720)
Thomas, David P	3:48:06	(7,761)
Thomas, Edward	3:40:27	(6,225)
Thomas, Gavin	3:22:39	(3,253)
Thomas, Graham Kenneth	3:28:29	(4,138)
Thomas, Henry J	3:50:40	(8,351)
Thomas, Ian David	4:41:38	(21,930)
Thomas, Ian W	4:04:38	(12,111)
Thomas, Iwan	4:19:39	(16,002)
Thomas, James	4:06:22	(12,544)
Thomas, James	4:43:03	(22,272)
Thomas, James Richard Leslie	5:32:17	(31,573)
Thomas, Jesper	3:27:06	(3,886)
Thomas, Jody	4:43:06	(22,282)
Thomas, John	3:55:52	(9,740)
Thomas, Julian	5:45:52	(32,941)
Thomas, Justin L	2:54:46	(720)
Thomas, Ken L	3:54:04	(9,225)
Thomas, Luke H	5:44:43	(32,841)
Thomas, Mark Stephen	3:52:20	(8,750)
Thomas, Martin	5:41:04	(32,495)
Thomas, Matt B	4:22:12	(16,761)
Thomas, Maxwell Jack	4:06:51	(12,677)
Thomas, Mervyn	3:40:06	(6,165)
Thomas, Michael	4:34:59	(20,228)
Thomas, Michael L	3:18:19	(2,806)
Thomas, Neil David	5:39:46	(32,366)
Thomas, Neil E	4:41:30	(21,893)
Thomas, Neil Leonard	3:42:59	(6,695)
Thomas, Nicholas J	4:01:48	(11,448)
Thomas, Nick	3:26:08	(3,757)
Thomas, Nigel	4:04:40	(12,119)
Thomas, Oliver James	4:36:59	(20,738)
Thomas, Owain Stuart	4:23:20	(17,054)
Thomas, Owen	3:52:09	(8,694)
Thomas, Paul	3:55:53	(9,745)
Thomas, Paul	4:15:19	(14,865)
Thomas, Paul A	3:39:43	(6,081)
Thomas, Paul Anthony	4:52:10	(24,595)
Thomas, Peter	3:29:45	(4,370)
Thomas, Peter J	3:15:58	(2,550)
Thomas, Peter Llwelyn	4:37:00	(20,742)
Thomas, Peter Roderick	5:03:36	(27,120)
Thomas, Phillip Gwyn	3:44:59	(7,094)
Thomas, Richard	4:57:06	(25,779)
Thomas, Richard G	4:43:57	(22,492)
Thomas, Richard Ley	4:28:22	(18,472)
Thomas, Richard M	2:55:04	(750)
Thomas, Robert	3:36:10	(5,439)
Thomas, Robert Michael	3:52:26	(8,772)
Thomas, Rodney Matthew	3:25:33	(3,659)
Thomas, Russell	4:47:04	(23,322)
Thomas, Ryan	5:06:56	(27,710)
Thomas, Simon Huw	5:36:27	(32,050)
Thomas, Stephen	2:43:38	(298)
Thomas, Stephen	3:12:01	(2,092)
Thomas, Stephen James	4:19:43	(16,019)
Thomas, Tony	4:56:23	(25,627)
Thomas, William K	2:53:57	(667)
Thomason, Gary	3:47:55	(7,723)
Thompson, Andrew J	3:13:20	(2,231)
Thompson, Andrew John	4:17:27	(15,425)
Thompson, Andrew Neil	4:15:01	(14,790)
Thompson, Andrew W	3:59:56	(10,970)
Thompson, Bruce	4:09:30	(13,341)
Thompson, Campbell	3:48:06	(7,761)
Thompson, Christopher	4:41:29	(21,887)
Thompson, Clive Vincent	6:27:23	(35,398)
Thompson, Colin	3:48:58	(7,966)
Thompson, Colin	4:11:12	(13,805)
Thompson, Darren John	5:01:53	(26,827)
Thompson, David	3:25:49	(3,705)
Thompson, David	4:15:40	(14,944)
Thompson, David	4:49:10	(23,842)
Thompson, David A	4:17:25	(15,410)
Thompson, David J	3:07:58	(1,696)
Thompson, David M	2:37:55	(161)
Thompson, Denver	5:13:32	(28,846)
Thompson, Duncan William	4:29:36	(18,842)
Thompson, Francis	3:39:21	(6,018)
Thompson, Gary	4:28:12	(18,417)
Thompson, Gary	5:13:54	(28,909)
Thompson, Gladstone	3:59:00	(10,722)
Thompson, Graham	5:40:03	(32,394)
Thompson, Harvey James	3:50:30	(8,311)
Thompson, Ian J	3:10:56	(1,986)
Thompson, Jeremy Sinclair	6:01:46	(34,171)
Thompson, John Eric	6:15:21	(34,904)
Thompson, Keith N	3:13:42	(2,283)
Thompson, Lee David	3:58:56	(10,698)
Thompson, Leigh	4:27:14	(18,160)
Thompson, Luke	4:06:37	(12,604)
Thompson, Mark	4:31:02	(19,226)
Thompson, Mark	4:37:20	(20,828)
Thompson, Mark	4:47:48	(23,494)
Thompson, Mark P	4:25:44	(17,732)
Thompson, Matthew	3:54:37	(9,359)
Thompson, Matthew	4:44:53	(22,738)
Thompson, Matthew Guy	4:35:18	(20,295)
Thompson, Mick	4:54:31	(25,184)
Thompson, Neil C	2:49:08	(448)
Thompson, Nicholas	4:45:00	(22,770)
Thompson, Nicholas	4:54:41	(25,226)
Thompson, Nick	4:24:50	(17,475)
Thompson, Nigel	3:57:57	(10,366)
Thompson, Nigel P	2:41:40	(242)
Thompson, Paul A	3:29:05	(4,244)
Thompson, Peter	3:29:30	(4,320)
Thompson, Phil	4:48:26	(23,655)
Thompson, Philip	3:51:51	(8,622)
Thompson, Phillip	5:36:14	(32,021)
Thompson, Richard	3:26:24	(3,793)
Thompson, Richard J	3:56:29	(9,926)
Thompson, Ryan Kevin	4:22:30	(16,847)
Thompson, Sholto	4:24:06	(17,260)
Thompson, Simon	4:43:55	(22,481)
Thompson, Stephen G	2:53:24	(637)
Thompson, Stuart West	4:40:56	(21,757)
Thomsen, Jens	4:06:21	(12,539)
Thomson, Andrew	5:54:06	(33,651)
Thomson, Antony	6:44:29	(35,896)
Thomson, Brian	3:27:23	(3,939)
Thomson, Craig Horton	4:00:20	(11,068)
Thomson, Craig James	5:43:23	(32,709)
Thomson, Dave	3:31:16	(4,619)
Thomson, Douglas John	4:00:12	(11,031)
Thomson, Jack	4:29:43	(18,888)
Thomson, James W	3:37:14	(5,605)
Thomson, John S	3:48:36	(7,873)
Thomson, Neil	4:49:23	(23,891)
Thomson, Sean Paul	4:35:44	(20,397)
Thomson, Stephen	3:14:59	(2,437)
Thomson, Stewart	5:46:09	(32,965)
Thomson, Thomas	4:20:11	(16,157)
Thorburn, Jason	3:40:47	(6,288)
Thored, Ulf	4:03:05	(11,748)
Thöring, Paul	3:05:29	(1,495)
Thorley, Matt Simon	3:49:00	(7,974)
Thorn, Keith Ronald	4:04:27	(12,066)
Thorn, Terry	5:11:57	(28,553)
Thorne, Colin	4:56:00	(25,535)
Thorne, Kevin Richard	4:59:23	(26,308)
Thorne, Robin	4:10:10	(13,517)
Thorne, Simon	3:39:35	(6,059)
Thorne, Wayne Anthony	5:08:15	(27,939)
Thorneloe, Guy R	3:03:44	(1,368)
Thorner, Roderick	4:36:24	(20,576)
Thorneycroft, James Alan	3:22:39	(3,253)
Thorneycroft, Joe	5:12:09	(28,591)
Thorneycroft, Richard J	4:57:39	(25,896)
Thorneycroft, Thomas H	3:27:06	(3,886)
Thorneywork, Joe	6:31:44	(35,560)
Thornhill, Gary Alan	3:55:40	(9,608)
Thornhill, Stuart	5:57:10	(33,874)
Thornley, Andrew	5:02:42	(26,979)
Thornley, Kes	3:55:14	(9,538)
Thornley, Simon	4:36:20	(20,554)
Thornton, Colin Rhodes	4:48:56	(23,782)
Thornton, Craig	3:52:35	(8,815)
Thornton, David A	3:40:10	(6,179)
Thornton, Garnon	5:00:45	(26,600)
Thornton, Gary	5:28:17	(31,061)
Thornton, Gary Stephen	6:22:51	(35,227)
Thornton, James	4:10:27	(13,579)
Thornton, John	4:38:50	(21,212)
Thornton, Kieran	5:09:48	(28,196)
Thornton, Ryan	5:26:10	(30,797)
Thornton-Allan, Gary	3:09:19	(1,834)
Thornton-Jones, Ben	4:31:36	(19,352)
Thorp, Adrian	4:44:43	(22,701)
Thorp, Andrew	4:18:47	(15,796)
Thorp, Nicholas	4:10:58	(13,513)
Thorp, Nick	3:54:13	(9,263)
Thorpe, David	4:38:57	(21,244)
Thorpe, David Ashley	4:27:05	(18,114)
Thorpe, Desmond	3:25:32	(3,652)

Thorpe, Gary R	3:08:09 (1,714)	
Thorpe, Paul J	4:21:59 (16,700)	
Thorpe, Peter	5:19:33 (29,779)	
Thorpe, Richard	3:57:42 (10,297)	
Thorpe, Richard M	5:07:14 (27,755)	
Thorpe, Robert W	3:56:24 (9,899)	
Thorpe, Scott	4:52:40 (24,725)	
Thorpe-Beeston, Guy	4:07:19 (12,779)	
Thowfeek, Mohamed	3:45:37 (7,230)	
Thrasher, Danny	3:19:22 (2,905)	
Thraves, Jon M	3:24:48 (3,550)	
Threadgold, Stephen John	3:21:56 (3,187)	
Threlfall, Kevin M	6:37:14 (35,704)	
Threlfall, Mark David	3:53:39 (9,105)	
Thrower, Robert	5:39:08 (32,312)	
Thunheim, Stig Harald	5:00:06 (26,480)	
Thurgood, Hugh Allen	3:44:10 (6,909)	
Thurley, Steve Kenneth	5:05:13 (27,410)	
Thurley, Westley Stephen	3:34:27 (5,144)	
Thurlow, Ryan R	4:31:08 (19,250)	
Thursby-Pelham, Brian Edward	2:36:10 (131)	
Thursfield, Charles William	4:19:07 (15,879)	
Thursting, Wayne	3:42:23 (6,577)	
Thurston, Billy Mark	3:45:55 (7,290)	
Thurston, Jim	4:49:46 (24,001)	
Thushyanthan, Vivekananthan	4:37:22 (20,836)	
Thwaite, Philip A	3:52:07 (8,682)	
Thwaites, Anthony Brian	5:05:15 (27,414)	
Tibbles, Alex	3:43:24 (6,757)	
Tickle, Giles	3:20:33 (3,032)	
Tickle, Mark Simon	3:43:55 (6,861)	
Tickle, Matthew James	3:42:43 (6,638)	
Tickner, Daniel Peter	4:31:39 (19,366)	
Tickner, Paul	4:47:04 (23,322)	
Tidder, Robert George	5:11:44 (28,509)	
Tidswell-Norrish, Sam	4:35:31 (20,349)	
Tierney, Mark James	4:10:01 (13,479)	
Tighe, John V	3:47:52 (7,711)	
Tilbrook, Thomas	4:10:06 (13,498)	
Tildesley, Christopher J	2:54:54 (734)	
Tillbrooke, Tony	5:46:04 (32,958)	
Tillery, Andrew J	3:08:17 (1,728)	
Tillery, Paul	4:11:50 (13,940)	
Tilley, Alex	3:42:42 (6,634)	
Tilley, Darren	3:47:33 (7,661)	
Tilley, Dave	4:18:50 (15,803)	
Tilley, Ian Reginald	5:22:05 (30,159)	
Tilley, James	3:30:53 (4,563)	
Tilley, Richard Ian	4:28:20 (18,465)	
Tilling, Martin	3:39:03 (5,950)	
Tillott, Neil D	3:06:38 (1,582)	
Tillott, Nigel George	3:20:15 (2,984)	
Tillyer, Bryan	3:49:33 (8,102)	
Timbrell, Greg	4:38:52 (21,223)	
Timbrell, Jerome George	4:43:10 (22,292)	
Timbrell, Wayne J	4:07:36 (12,855)	
Timeneys, Ricky	3:43:58 (6,871)	
Timlin, Chris	3:35:32 (5,332)	
Timmermann, Heinrich	3:22:35 (3,248)	
Timmins, Adrian	2:39:22 (180)	
Timmins, Andrew	3:56:43 (10,003)	
Timmins, Christopher D	3:17:51 (2,749)	
Timms, Chris	3:17:48 (2,744)	
Timms, George E	5:07:37 (27,836)	
Timperley, Paul Brian	3:16:29 (2,607)	
Timpson, Anthony E	4:26:40 (17,991)	
Timson, Daniel	5:18:25 (29,610)	
Timson, Mark	3:43:38 (6,798)	
Tindall, David	5:26:35 (30,851)	
Tindall, David William	5:24:08 (30,501)	
Tindall, Shaun	5:06:02 (27,539)	
Tindle, Craig	4:21:11 (16,459)	
Tingey, Lawrence John	3:59:24 (10,839)	
Tinham, Andrew Lee	4:53:58 (25,041)	
Tink, Andy Edward	3:50:41 (8,354)	
Tinker, Antony Aidan	3:58:33 (10,574)	
Tinker, Jonathan	3:50:36 (8,332)	
Tinkler, Mark	3:34:49 (5,216)	
Tinline, David	4:21:42 (16,606)	
Tinsley, Charles	3:50:30 (8,311)	
Tinsley, Peter Alan	3:58:14 (10,471)	
Tinton, Glen	4:35:25 (20,332)	
Tinworth, Martin Raymond	3:25:05 (3,593)	
Tipacti, Marcos	5:34:02 (31,766)	
Tippet, Simon John	4:47:20 (23,374)	
Tippett, Graham	4:00:00 (10,984)	
Tippett, John Edward	5:18:53 (29,679)	
Tipple, Richard J	4:01:24 (11,339)	
Tirel, Serges	4:51:20 (24,381)	
Tischer, James	5:41:02 (32,490)	
Tish, Darren	5:11:43 (28,506)	
Tissington, Phil Howard	3:45:20 (7,169)	
Titcombe, Nicholas	5:59:13 (34,004)	
Tite, Julian C	3:50:03 (8,221)	
Titley, Andy	3:16:11 (2,570)	
Titley, Jack	4:46:10 (23,078)	
Titterton, Phillip	5:06:17 (27,581)	
Tiwana, Palminder	4:46:59 (23,304)	
Tizard, Michael V	3:55:12 (9,528)	
Tobin, Andrew	3:34:43 (5,194)	
Tobin, Mark D	3:10:56 (1,986)	
Tobin, Simon	3:17:34 (2,722)	
Tocco, Filippo	2:50:14 (494)	
Tocco, Sergio	2:52:35 (596)	
Todd, Alastair	4:51:57 (24,538)	
Todd, Andrew Lee	4:29:56 (18,966)	
Todd, Andy	3:13:28 (2,247)	
Todd, John B	3:02:26 (1,291)	
Todd, Matthew David	3:35:24 (5,301)	
Todd, Perry Raymond	3:13:25 (2,238)	
Todd, Peta	6:34:20 (35,633)	
Todd, Richard	4:20:23 (16,228)	
Todd, Stephen John	5:49:18 (33,261)	
Toffolo, Stefano	5:26:11 (30,799)	
Tofrik, Neil	4:20:21 (16,220)	
Toft, Michael	4:33:08 (19,740)	
Togwell, Chris P	3:57:52 (10,352)	
Tola, Francesco	3:07:34 (1,660)	
Tole, Richard	4:31:15 (19,280)	
Tolfrey, Neil	3:40:49 (6,292)	
Toll, Alexander J	2:47:22 (398)	
Toll, Neil	3:56:55 (10,063)	
Toller, Edward Charles	5:07:37 (27,836)	
Tolley, John Edward	5:45:48 (32,932)	
Tollington, Peter G	4:27:27 (18,220)	
Tollinton, Tom Henry	3:52:35 (8,815)	
Tolliss, Philip Leslie	6:15:28 (34,908)	
Tomas, Alexis	3:15:30 (2,496)	
Tombolato, Alberto Denis	3:34:42 (5,190)	
Tombs, Jonathan	3:41:02 (6,331)	
Tomkins, Chris	3:16:19 (2,587)	
Tomkins, Danny James	4:59:29 (26,333)	
Tomkins, James Arthur George	4:44:32 (22,652)	
Tomkins, Paul J	4:19:58 (16,096)	
Tomkinson, Andrew D	4:05:26 (12,322)	
Tomkinson, Michael A	4:49:08 (23,835)	
Tomlin, Charles A	4:10:00 (13,475)	
Tomlin, David L	2:39:55 (197)	
Tomlin, James Russell	4:10:22 (13,562)	
Tomlinson, Andrew	4:23:44 (17,175)	
Tomlinson, Chris	5:23:44 (30,432)	
Tomlinson, Christopher David	4:11:35 (13,875)	
Tomlinson, Clive	4:58:06 (25,986)	
Tomlinson, David Trevor	5:21:26 (30,065)	
Tomlinson, Dominic	4:23:27 (17,090)	
Tomlinson, Gavin	2:56:02 (803)	
Tomlinson, James Benjamin	6:05:25 (34,414)	
Tomlinson, John	3:26:18 (3,783)	
Tomlinson, Mark	3:22:22 (3,224)	
Tomlinson, Matthew J	5:38:27 (32,255)	
Tomlinson, Paul	3:38:51 (5,915)	
Tomlinson, Richard James	4:52:15 (24,614)	
Toms, Daniel Harry	5:25:57 (30,774)	
Toms, Paul	5:02:55 (27,012)	
Toms, Roy E	6:29:59 (35,500)	
Toms, Simon James	3:17:56 (2,758)	
Tomsett, Peter Lee	4:18:36 (15,744)	
Toner, Neil	3:06:23 (1,561)	
Tonetti, Nicola	3:47:40 (7,680)	
Tonkin, Craig Llewellen	3:09:00 (1,809)	
Tonkinson, Paul	3:30:10 (4,445)	
Tonks, Barry	5:08:01 (27,899)	
Tonon, Renzo	3:04:49 (1,450)	
Toole, Stephen	5:02:37 (26,964)	
Toone, Mike	3:57:00 (10,089)	
Toone, Ric Mark	4:48:33 (23,679)	
Tooski, Mark B	3:11:49 (2,075)	
Tootal, Stuart J	4:50:04 (24,064)	
Tootell, Shaun	4:59:07 (26,242)	
Tootill, Duncan Charles	5:21:02 (30,010)	
Topley, Oliver	4:05:32 (12,341)	
Topliss, Dan	5:44:33 (32,821)	
Topliss, Oliver	4:34:51 (20,206)	
Topper, Steve	3:34:24 (5,138)	
Topping, Simon Peter	5:58:23 (33,957)	
Topping, Stephen J	4:40:15 (21,560)	
Tordoff, Phil	3:24:04 (3,446)	
Toro, Tom Lee	5:05:48 (27,494)	
Torrans, John	4:35:24 (20,325)	
Torrent, Narcis	4:56:31 (25,653)	
Torres, Carlos	4:00:21 (11,076)	
Torry, Hugh	2:42:45 (266)	
Tosdevin, Leslie	3:58:41 (10,619)	
Tostevin, James A	4:02:49 (11,677)	
Tostevin, Stuart	4:18:45 (15,786)	
Totton, Adrian	4:52:46 (24,742)	
Totty, Patrick	3:28:31 (4,141)	
Toumazis, Tom	4:39:57 (21,491)	
Tour, Cyril	3:22:24 (3,227)	
Tovey, Danny	4:19:08 (15,886)	
Towell, Shaun Antony	3:46:22 (7,387)	
Towers, Andrew	4:46:24 (23,150)	
Towers, Gareth	3:49:33 (8,102)	
Towers, Patrick	4:23:47 (17,185)	
Towler, Gareth	3:23:34 (3,375)	
Towler, Philip J	5:22:20 (30,197)	
Town, Jamie	3:48:06 (7,761)	
Townend, Dene A	3:17:37 (2,727)	
Towner, Christopher	4:23:02 (16,988)	
Townley, Giles	4:35:09 (20,264)	
Townrow, Christopher David	3:29:46 (4,372)	
Townrow, William	5:49:28 (33,281)	
Townsend, Brandon James	5:52:19 (33,522)	
Townsend, Chris John	4:38:47 (21,202)	
Townsend, Gary	5:07:03 (27,733)	
Townsend, John Weldon	3:38:54 (5,920)	
Townsend, Kevin John	5:28:15 (31,058)	
Townsend, Martin B	3:09:05 (1,815)	
Townsend, Martin John	2:57:27 (896)	
Townsend, Matthew Paul	3:29:49 (4,382)	
Townsend, Michael D	5:34:16 (31,792)	
Townsend, Nic	5:47:51 (33,126)	
Townsend, Richard	6:19:51 (35,117)	
Townsend, Robert William	5:17:03 (29,395)	
Townsend, Ross Martyn	3:25:22 (3,624)	
Tozer, Andrew Preston	5:44:02 (32,770)	
Tozer, Robert	4:50:41 (24,203)	
Tozer, Shaun A	2:48:24 (427)	
Tozer, Steve	4:48:28 (23,665)	
Trabanino, Herbert	3:03:50 (1,375)	
Trafford, Mark	7:24:00 (36,437)	
Trainor, Aidan G	4:00:03 (10,994)	
Tranter, Stephen	3:24:36 (3,524)	
Trapani, Antonino	4:37:43 (20,928)	
Travers, Guy	4:12:48 (14,180)	
Travers, Joshua	5:08:35 (27,985)	
Travis, Andrew Joseph	3:12:46 (2,164)	
Travis, Kim	3:32:23 (4,796)	
Travis, Mark James	5:03:16 (27,069)	
Traynor, Anthony James	4:19:07 (15,879)	
Traynor, Mark W	2:54:22 (692)	
Traynor-Swindells, Daniel	4:26:14 (17,882)	
Treadwell, Mark	4:05:31 (12,338)	
Treagust, Mark	5:41:02 (32,490)	
Trebble, Clifford M	3:48:39 (7,884)	
Trebilcock, Mark Charles	4:02:03 (11,502)	
Trebilcock, Norman Alan	4:31:55 (19,411)	
Treble, Chris	3:32:40 (4,838)	
Tredant, Adrian	4:27:45 (18,299)	
Tredinnick, Neal	3:48:38 (7,878)	
Tredler, Daniel	4:39:58 (21,496)	
Tregent, Mark Andrew	5:03:26 (27,090)	
Treharne, Gareth	5:36:03 (32,003)	
Trelfa, John	2:44:18 (316)	
Tremaine, Robin T	3:09:31 (1,912)	
Trembath, James Robert	3:53:59 (9,205)	
Trennery, David	5:29:33 (31,228)	
Trent, Dean	5:07:23 (27,789)	
Trepant, Hugues G	4:13:44 (14,442)	

Trepant, Richard	3:04:02	(1,397)
Tresadern, Stephen	5:01:07	(26,670)
Tresidder, Brian	4:47:55	(23,522)
Tresise, Michael Charles	3:43:44	(6,811)
Trett, Paul William	4:17:34	(15,461)
Trevelyan, Oliver	4:32:51	(19,654)
Trevenna, Steven G	4:23:28	(17,095)
Trevey, Paul A	4:08:45	(13,149)
Trevisan, Jean Claude	4:08:04	(12,978)
Trevor-Jones, Edward	4:59:23	(26,308)
Trevor-Jones, Guy	4:59:23	(26,308)
Trevorrow, Tim	5:22:28	(30,215)
Trew, David Wynford	4:23:42	(17,156)
Trezona, James Nicholas	4:40:53	(21,740)
Tribe, Adam J	3:04:28	(1,428)
Tribe, Barrie John	5:39:14	(32,324)
Tribe, Mark	5:10:51	(28,387)
Trice, Cyril Leonard	7:02:28	(36,220)
Trickett, Paul	3:49:42	(8,145)
Trickett, Philip John	3:36:07	(5,432)
Trickey, Andrew David	3:58:56	(10,698)
Trigg, Alistair	4:20:05	(16,131)
Trigg, Clint William	5:43:38	(32,731)
Trigg, James J	4:00:34	(11,131)
Triggle, Daryl John	4:39:01	(21,263)
Triggs, Philip Ian	6:02:39	(34,228)
Trigwell, Andrew Paul	5:10:23	(28,307)
Trigwell, Stuart J	2:58:20	(989)
Trimble, Gareth F	3:35:16	(5,282)
Tringham, Nicholas	4:24:14	(17,294)
Trinh, Chi H	2:43:47	(303)
Tripp, Stephen M	5:30:17	(31,324)
Tristram, Joe J	3:49:01	(7,978)
Tritto, Erasmo	3:17:44	(2,734)
Trivedi, Naresh	4:18:49	(15,801)
Trochard, Eric	3:16:31	(2,610)
Trocki, Jan Z	4:17:25	(15,410)
Trodden, Andy	5:41:33	(32,538)
Trodden, Sean F	3:36:59	(5,560)
Trory, John Anthony	3:49:34	(8,109)
Troth, Geoff	5:10:32	(28,335)
Trotman, Paul	5:06:25	(27,606)
Trotter, James W	3:13:57	(2,309)
Troubridge, Paul	3:47:40	(7,680)
Trow, Mark	5:16:49	(29,355)
Trowbridge, Mark Raymon	4:29:52	(18,935)
Trowbridge, Tony	3:42:52	(6,671)
Trowell, Stephen	4:58:54	(26,189)
Trowsdale, Andy	3:52:19	(8,748)
Trowsdale, Paul	3:29:56	(4,406)
Truelove, Olly	4:03:03	(11,740)
Trueman, Neil	6:19:52	(35,118)
Truesdale, Paul	5:11:35	(28,487)
Truman, Max	5:13:26	(28,832)
Truman, Timothy John	6:57:05	(36,143)
Trump, Edward H	4:29:08	(18,716)
Trundle, Simon William	3:44:30	(6,987)
Truscott, Paul Michael	4:42:25	(22,115)
Trushell, Ian	4:52:07	(24,578)
Trussler, Ian Robert	3:52:28	(8,789)
Tryggvason, Kristofer William	5:18:44	(29,659)
Tsang, Philip M	3:25:38	(3,671)
Tse, Kenny	4:48:42	(23,719)
Tsiappourdhi, George	5:36:14	(32,021)
Tsiquaye, Olaf Kodjo	5:09:24	(28,126)
Tsui, Terence	4:53:14	(24,858)
Tsutsui, Yoshisada	4:15:32	(14,911)
Tuck, Dominic	4:01:08	(11,282)
Tucker, Adam	3:46:30	(7,415)
Tucker, Andrew Brendan	3:57:27	(10,214)
Tucker, Bernard	5:43:55	(32,761)
Tucker, Ed	3:13:02	(2,198)
Tucker, Graham J	3:46:44	(7,468)
Tucker, Lee T	4:19:26	(15,957)
Tucker, Mark Antony	4:00:06	(11,007)
Tucker, Peter	5:44:51	(32,855)
Tucker, Peter R	2:29:27	(60)
Tucker, Richard	5:17:06	(29,403)
Tucker, Robert Peter	5:18:54	(29,684)
Tucker, William M	3:21:49	(3,172)
Tucker-Brown, Alastair E	5:14:44	(29,024)
Tuckett, Mark A	2:52:47	(609)
Tuckett, Will	4:00:59	(11,245)

Tuckwood, Graham	4:44:48	(22,721)
Tuddenham, Robin J	2:40:33	(215)
Tudge, Scott	3:29:17	(4,286)
Tudor, James Edward	4:00:41	(11,166)
Tufton, Kevein P	4:43:00	(22,259)
Tugwell, David Alan	4:47:53	(23,519)
Tull, Mark	4:01:44	(11,429)
Tulloch, Hector	4:09:44	(13,401)
Tulloch, James	4:08:10	(12,998)
Tulloch, Simon	3:59:56	(10,970)
Tully, Christopher	3:58:06	(10,414)
Tumbridge, Mark Raymond	3:23:50	(3,412)
Tummon, James Alexander	4:17:46	(15,519)
Tunde, Oluwole Samuel	5:48:32	(33,198)
Tune, Christopher	4:07:33	(12,847)
Tunmore, Lee C	3:37:57	(5,756)
Tunna, Daniel	4:32:16	(19,505)
Tunney, Stephen	5:17:18	(29,438)
Tunnicliffe, Richard	4:48:13	(23,590)
Tunstall, Dave M	6:13:24	(34,817)
Tunstall, Paul	4:39:07	(21,286)
Tuplin, Adrian	3:55:58	(9,772)
Tuppen, Nicholas Henry	5:04:05	(27,205)
Turan, Turan T	5:29:08	(31,168)
Turbutt, Simon	4:48:08	(23,577)
Turford, James	3:48:56	(7,955)
Turk, Andrew Richard	4:08:21	(13,043)
Turk, David	4:35:56	(20,461)
Turk, Martin	4:51:09	(24,341)
Turley, John Ivor Barrett	4:23:52	(17,205)
Turnbull, Alan	4:46:09	(23,076)
Turnbull, Alan F	3:17:53	(2,751)
Turnbull, Duncan William	5:33:10	(31,683)
Turnbull, Gary John	5:14:11	(28,948)
Turnbull, Joseph Alexander	4:28:57	(18,666)
Turnbull, Keith	3:31:01	(4,579)
Turnbull, Mark C	4:21:42	(16,606)
Turnbull, Martin	5:17:40	(29,492)
Turnbull, Nick	4:34:02	(20,000)
Turnbull, Richard	4:24:27	(17,376)
Turnbull, Sam	4:30:16	(19,040)
Turnbull, William J	4:34:03	(20,005)
Turner, Adrian	5:44:54	(32,859)
Turner, Alan	4:42:39	(22,168)
Turner, Andrew	3:43:33	(6,786)
Turner, Andrew Christopher	4:45:24	(22,862)
Turner, Andrew James Philip	4:57:35	(25,875)
Turner, Andrew M	3:45:27	(7,200)
Turner, Andy	4:08:11	(13,003)

Turner, Ben 4:23:20 (17,054)

This was my third marathon and huge compared to the relatively tiny Cork and Leicester. My aim was to finally go under four hours or at least set a PB. Quitting my job and spending three months in South America meant I started training later than planned but I made good progress. Being unemployed meant there was lots of time to train! Then I got a job, hurt my leg and the training ground to a halt. Come race day I still felt I had a chance of beating four hours and was on target up to about 20 miles. Then it all went wrong and I was at a crawl until then end, although I did hold a little something back for a sprint finish! Awesome experience and I'll definitely be back to beat four hours!

Turner, Benjamin R	5:28:42	(31,112)
Turner, Bill	4:04:43	(12,136)
Turner, Brian	2:54:34	(705)
Turner, Craig Christoper	5:06:50	(27,693)
Turner, Dale	4:38:10	(21,021)
Turner, Daniel	5:01:51	(26,820)
Turner, Daniel H	3:55:43	(9,677)
Turner, Danny	5:49:32	(33,288)
Turner, Darren	4:14:39	(14,700)
Turner, Dave J	3:02:23	(1,289)
Turner, David Anthony	6:43:48	(35,881)
Turner, David Christopher	4:13:35	(14,398)
Turner, David Robert	5:06:07	(27,552)
Turner, Ewan	4:06:29	(12,569)
Turner, Gary J	5:59:12	(34,003)
Turner, Gary Lee	5:15:51	(29,205)
Turner, Grenville	4:44:29	(22,632)
Turner, Ian	4:15:42	(14,952)
Turner, Ian	5:08:20	(27,954)
Turner, Ian Hugh	4:58:36	(26,116)
Turner, James E	7:24:42	(36,441)
Turner, James William	3:15:32	(2,502)
Turner, Jason	4:59:52	(26,422)
Turner, Joe	3:14:18	(2,359)
Turner, John A	4:36:50	(20,695)
Turner, Keith P	3:47:47	(7,701)
Turner, Kristian Paul	4:32:43	(19,610)
Turner, Lee John	4:12:35	(14,120)
Turner, Mark G	3:34:12	(5,096)
Turner, Mark John	5:47:16	(33,075)
Turner, Matt Charles	2:42:57	(275)
Turner, Matthew Jonathan	4:11:39	(13,893)
Turner, Neil	4:09:07	(13,234)
Turner, Neil A	4:02:23	(11,575)
Turner, Paul	4:21:29	(16,542)
Turner, Paul	4:56:02	(25,544)
Turner, Roger	4:58:08	(26,001)
Turner, Shane	4:13:07	(14,269)
Turner, Steve	5:00:52	(26,623)
Turner, Stuart B	4:48:31	(23,671)
Turner, Terry	5:47:26	(33,092)
Turnham, Peter	4:43:38	(22,402)
Turniak, Jacek	3:55:04	(9,495)
Turpie, Stephen	3:45:30	(7,207)
Turpin, Robert James	4:17:30	(15,439)
Turton, Mark A	3:31:25	(4,653)
Tutt, Cedric L	4:52:31	(24,688)
Tweddle, Andrew	4:25:48	(17,749)
Tweddle, Richard J	3:07:03	(1,614)
Tweedie, Clive A	4:06:16	(12,516)
Tweedie, George	4:59:53	(26,429)
Twibey, Matthew	5:13:30	(28,843)
Twidle, Stewart Stephen	5:16:55	(29,375)
Twinning, Peter	4:53:28	(24,905)
Twist, Mark Henry Clinton	4:23:38	(17,141)
Twitchen, Michael Geoffrey	4:08:36	(13,117)
Twitchen, Roger W	5:43:31	(32,722)
Twizell, David	5:47:45	(33,120)
Twomey, Alan	3:56:42	(10,000)
Twomey, Eamonn	3:08:07	(1,711)
Twomey, Kevin Anthony	3:50:59	(8,416)
Twyford, Damian Peter	4:46:52	(23,278)
Tydeman, Justin	3:51:25	(8,518)
Tyers, Simon	5:19:32	(29,778)
Tylee-Birdsall, Alex	4:06:57	(12,702)
Tyler, Anthony H	3:11:50	(2,079)

Tyler, John	3:08:03 (1,701)	
Tyler, Nicholas Mark	3:59:24 (10,839)	
Tyler, Robert James	4:57:46 (25,922)	
Tyler, Stephen	5:15:31 (29,150)	
Tyler, Tim	3:28:25 (4,132)	
Tymon, Shaun David	3:37:56 (5,751)	
Tyrrell, Francis	3:16:19 (2,587)	
Tyrrell, Mathew	4:22:53 (16,959)	
Tyrrell, Nigel Peter	3:15:25 (2,488)	
Tyson, Adam	4:20:35 (16,287)	
Tyson, David R	4:02:39 (11,638)	
Tyson, Robert	4:36:26 (20,582)	
Tyszkiewicz, John Zygmunt	3:49:57 (8,199)	
Udal, David Ian	3:55:20 (9,571)	
Udell, Garreth Charles	5:30:21 (31,330)	
Udell, Laurance	5:30:21 (31,330)	
Udell, Marcus Aaron	5:18:58 (29,697)	
Uema, Mitsuaki	6:14:27 (34,857)	
Uff, Chris	2:51:12 (530)	
Ugelstad, Ole-Jonny	5:05:51 (27,504)	
Ugonna, Kelechi Benjamin	2:47:48 (415)	
Ujvari, Marc Tivadar	4:32:49 (19,635)	
Ukrasin, Igor	3:53:47 (9,154)	
Ullman, Chris	3:28:42 (4,173)	
Ullmann, Benjamin	4:35:34 (20,358)	
Ulrich, Kai-Uwe	3:53:41 (9,117)	
Ummat, Sam	5:25:23 (30,678)	
Unadkat, Mithun	4:00:53 (11,211)	
Underdown, Paul	3:47:32 (7,655)	
Underhill, Chris	6:40:01 (35,785)	
Underhill, Paul	4:54:10 (25,083)	
Underwood, Paul	3:23:06 (3,305)	
Underwood, Ross	5:23:27 (30,380)	
Underwood, Warren Paul	4:47:32 (23,417)	
Ungi, Thomas	4:48:14 (23,593)	
Ungi, Tommy	4:51:05 (24,326)	
Unitt, Keith	3:57:49 (10,334)	
Unsworth, Carl Patrick	4:02:04 (11,507)	
Unwin, Mark John	4:05:08 (12,234)	
Unwin, Will	3:46:42 (7,460)	
Upadhyaya, Ajit	5:04:18 (27,245)	
Upham, Mark Anthony	4:16:10 (15,062)	
Upton, Brian Michael	4:16:59 (15,297)	
Upton, Charles N	3:24:26 (3,504)	
Upton, James Neil	3:59:15 (10,794)	
Upton, Martin	4:34:10 (20,030)	
Upton, Nicky Carl	4:01:22 (11,325)	
Upton, Peter	6:05:59 (34,451)	
Upton, Sam W	3:00:47 (1,194)	
Upward, Barry R	4:49:08 (23,835)	
Upward, Timothy Peter	4:44:07 (22,537)	
Ural, Can	4:21:08 (16,447)	
Urban, Joerg	3:37:01 (5,564)	
Urdaneta, Juan	4:18:27 (15,699)	
Ure, Bruce	4:40:19 (21,579)	
Ure, Hugo B	3:48:42 (7,898)	
Urquhart, Donald	4:14:36 (14,680)	
Ur-Rahman, Inam	5:47:32 (33,100)	
Urwin, Maison B	4:07:52 (12,924)	
Usai, Gian Carlo	3:40:23 (6,208)	
Usher, Andy	3:38:33 (5,854)	
Usher, Nick	5:46:00 (32,951)	
Ussain, Faris H	4:10:07 (13,503)	
Utteridge, Glenn Robert	3:46:15 (7,367)	
Utting, Richard	3:32:21 (4,792)	
Utting, Stephen	4:46:12 (23,090)	
Vaassen, Peter	3:19:22 (2,905)	
Vadron, Andrew	3:09:46 (1,890)	
Vaezinejad, Mehrad	6:08:02 (34,562)	
Vaicenavicius, Juozas	3:27:09 (3,896)	
Vaid, Manish	6:01:11 (34,139)	
Vaidya, Bijay	4:32:57 (19,685)	
Vaidyanathan, Raju	5:57:58 (33,930)	
Vajzovic, Dan	3:06:13 (1,549)	
Vakilpour, Soori	4:15:43 (14,958)	
Vale, Adrian John	5:33:19 (31,696)	
Valencia, Mario	4:54:39 (25,219)	
Valente, Simon C	4:19:48 (16,041)	
Valenti, Alfredo	4:39:21 (21,340)	
Valentine, Keith R	5:55:49 (33,779)	
Valentine, Mark	4:37:47 (20,944)	
Valiant, Paul	4:22:12 (16,761)	
Valkin, Adam	5:37:52 (32,195)	
Vallance, Andrew J	3:07:57 (1,693)	
Vallance, Roger W	3:04:28 (1,428)	
Vallance, Simon	4:34:01 (19,997)	
Vallance, Stephen J	3:27:05 (3,882)	
Vallett, Lee James	3:29:14 (4,276)	
Vallin, Baptiste	2:50:54 (521)	
Valognes, Jean	5:08:06 (27,911)	
Valsecchi, Luigi	3:20:17 (2,989)	
Valverde, José Maria Arviza	4:34:39 (20,156)	
Vampa, Frederic	3:29:16 (4,283)	
Van Alderwegen, Frank	4:34:34 (20,140)	
Van De Water, Marco	4:41:22 (21,858)	
Van Den Bos, Dick	7:22:38 (36,423)	
Van Den Braak, Joris	4:21:22 (16,513)	
Van Den Broek, Adam	4:38:55 (21,235)	
Van Der Bliek, Jasper	4:33:16 (19,791)	
Van Der Does De Bye, Martin	4:25:00 (17,519)	
Van Der Ham, Adrianus	3:43:35 (6,790)	
Van Der Hoeven, Maarten H.	3:15:55 (2,542)	
Van Der Meulen, Bo Franciscus	6:01:39 (34,166)	
Van Der Velde, Take	4:26:49 (18,029)	
Van Der Waal Van Dijk, Hubertus	3:36:10 (5,439)	
Van Der Wal, Bram	4:36:46 (20,674)	
Van Der Westhuizen, Etuan	4:57:56 (25,953)	
Van Der Westhuizen, Nico	3:37:11 (5,594)	
Van Der Wyck, Oliver	3:32:13 (4,775)	
Van Deventer, Paul M	5:20:27 (29,912)	
Van Dijk, Simon	3:30:13 (4,456)	
Van Geest, René	4:28:28 (18,512)	
Van Hal, Erik	3:32:16 (4,783)	
Van Heerden, Jacobus	4:57:56 (25,953)	
Van Hilst, Rudolf	3:28:23 (4,121)	
Van Hoogstraten, John	5:25:46 (30,744)	
Van Hooydonk, George	3:42:09 (6,540)	
Van Kampen, Steve	3:58:17 (10,484)	
Van Kouteren, Wim	4:00:37 (11,145)	
Van Meirvenne, Dirk	3:13:39 (2,274)	
Van Niekerk, Johan	3:31:57 (4,729)	
Van Niekerk, Johann J	4:09:44 (13,401)	
Van Norman, Daniel George	7:13:48 (36,348)	
Van Reeth, Frank	5:01:35 (26,772)	
Van Rensburg, Kobus	4:27:58 (18,357)	
Van Rooy, Ben	3:37:13 (5,602)	
Van Rooyen, Tom	4:26:49 (18,029)	
Van Staden, Gary William	3:36:05 (5,424)	
Van Till, Rupert	5:54:07 (33,652)	
Van Woerkom, Vincent S	2:43:06 (282)	
Van Wyk, Gerrit	4:10:34 (13,610)	
Van Zyl, Heine	2:57:36 (919)	
Vandepeer, Arron W	5:39:05 (32,310)	
Vanderhovn, Michael R	4:02:59 (11,726)	
Vanderpump, William	4:50:49 (24,243)	
Vandewalle, Peter	4:08:17 (13,024)	
Vandierendonck, Jackie	3:52:52 (8,890)	
Vandierendonck, Sammy	3:52:52 (8,890)	
Vandrey, Michael Heinrich Dieter	4:17:59 (15,573)	
Vanloo, Christian	3:26:00 (3,731)	
Vanmaele, Frederic	3:13:32 (2,259)	
Vannen, David J	6:52:16 (36,054)	
Vanooyen, Michael	3:45:12 (7,139)	
Vanormelingen, Peter	3:36:49 (5,525)	
Vanson, Ed	4:39:43 (21,440)	
Vansteenkiste, Koenraad	4:36:46 (20,674)	
Vant, Ed Stephen	6:07:37 (34,538)	
Varah, Paul H	3:59:07 (10,752)	
Varden, Mark G	3:02:10 (1,269)	
Varenne, Patrice	2:54:20 (689)	
Vari, Claudio	2:49:43 (475)	
Varley, Andrew Michael	4:20:26 (16,244)	
Varley, Ashely	3:14:52 (2,426)	
Varley, Ian	5:04:30 (27,276)	
Varley, Mark Adrian	3:39:47 (6,099)	
Varnava, Keri	4:09:02 (13,220)	
Varney, Andy JD	3:44:22 (6,955)	
Varney, Brian	5:51:54 (33,496)	
Varotto, Alberto	3:32:43 (4,847)	
Vartyan, Georg	5:54:58 (33,713)	
Vas, Gabor	2:41:17 (233)	
Vasey, Mark Andrew	3:45:55 (7,290)	
Vasey, Stephen	6:08:12 (34,567)	
Vashisht, Rahul	6:24:00 (35,277)	
Vasilakis, Alexander D	6:14:40 (34,869)	
Vasiliou, Steven	3:30:16 (4,466)	
Vassallo, Emil	3:27:35 (3,976)	
Vaughan, Andy	4:28:36 (18,548)	
Vaughan, Bryan John	3:53:58 (9,201)	
Vaughan, Dan	3:06:28 (1,567)	
Vaughan, Huw John	4:13:24 (14,335)	
Vaughan, Liam	6:21:53 (35,195)	
Vaughan, Matthew James	4:49:13 (23,852)	
Vaughan, Max	3:59:47 (10,942)	
Vaughan, Oliver	5:17:44 (29,504)	
Vaughan, Paul D	3:50:09 (8,237)	
Vaughan, Wayne	4:15:32 (14,911)	
Vautier, Stephane	2:27:53 (52)	
Vavangas, Duncan P	3:21:03 (3,091)	
Vavrovsky, Nikolaus G	2:46:54 (381)	
Vazquez, Gorka Aitor	3:55:40 (9,668)	
Vazquez, José Rafael	4:45:40 (22,940)	
Veale, David	3:59:43 (10,925)	
Veale, Peter	3:48:58 (7,966)	
Veasey, Dominick J	3:51:09 (8,461)	
Veasey, Mark	3:56:37 (9,964)	
Veck, Sean	4:56:57 (25,757)	
Vedrenne, Stephane	4:25:15 (17,586)	
Veitch, Kevin William	5:25:24 (30,679)	
Veitch, Paul J	2:49:12 (454)	
Vella, Angelo	3:27:37 (3,986)	
Velody, Nicholas	4:10:26 (13,574)	
Venables, Martin Robert	4:12:27 (14,083)	
Venn, William	3:53:44 (9,132)	
Venner, Michael Paul	5:34:45 (31,854)	
Venter, David	3:42:56 (6,682)	
Ventre, Phil	3:35:41 (5,357)	
Ventura, Jude Reyes	5:38:50 (32,304)	
Venturelli, Gino	3:17:54 (2,755)	
Vera, Francisco Javier	4:36:42 (20,659)	
Vercoe, Rik	3:24:51 (3,556)	
Vere, Richard	5:22:40 (30,249)	
Verhaeghe, Dirk	3:55:58 (9,772)	
Verlander, Luke Peter	5:14:38 (29,008)	
Vermeesch, Pieter	2:20:16 (20)	
Vernay, Jacques	3:29:42 (4,360)	
Vernon, Darren Leon	3:12:02 (2,094)	
Vernon, David	4:49:12 (23,849)	
Vernon, Gary H	3:02:16 (1,277)	
Vernon, Graham	5:32:40 (31,624)	
Vernon, Jeremy	4:03:35 (11,868)	
Vero, Richard	3:24:40 (3,513)	
Verrall, Raymond S	5:22:03 (30,153)	
Verrecchia, Vito J	2:58:27 (1,003)	
Verrept, Marc	4:21:51 (16,655)	
Versteeg, John	4:22:45 (16,918)	
Vesterdal, Niels	4:50:14 (24,099)	
Via, John W	5:43:04 (32,673)	
Vialls, Ronald	3:30:26 (4,489)	
Vianello, Nerino	5:08:58 (28,037)	
Vickerage, John Alexander	4:13:25 (14,345)	
Vickers, Andrew	4:52:46 (24,742)	
Vickers, Benjamin H	3:08:41 (1,780)	
Vickers, Damien	4:44:13 (22,568)	
Vickers, Donald Francis	4:47:40 (23,459)	
Vickers, Douglas P	3:43:56 (6,865)	
Vickers, Jason B	5:36:44 (32,076)	
Vickers, Jeremy Philip Hilton	4:10:12 (13,531)	
Vickers, Simon J	5:14:24 (28,978)	
Vickers, Tony	4:20:44 (16,347)	
Vickers, Wayne Malcolm	3:15:08 (2,455)	
Vickery, Adam D	4:25:25 (17,640)	
Vickery, Barry	3:45:56 (7,295)	
Vidal, Edmundo	4:52:09 (24,589)	
Vidiella Eguiluz, Fernando	5:16:37 (29,324)	
Vidler, Darren Robert	4:42:28 (22,130)	
Viegas, Frank	5:49:18 (33,261)	
Viggers, James	3:57:42 (10,297)	
Viggiani, Stefan	4:36:31 (20,611)	
Vigilante, Giancarlo	3:35:25 (5,306)	
Vigneron, Gerard	6:17:40 (35,013)	
Vikram, Anthony	6:46:56 (35,946)	
Villalpando, Anselmo	4:20:27 (16,248)	
Villars, Philip	5:01:38 (26,783)	
Villiers, Henry Anthony Edward	4:37:26 (20,861)	
Villiers, Richard	3:34:56 (5,237)	
Vinall, Erwin	5:17:42 (29,499)	
Vinall, Stephen John	3:49:28 (8,080)	
Vince, Ian Frazer	5:39:41 (32,358)	

Vincent, Edward............3:52:30 (8,796)
Vincent, Girou............3:32:20 (4,791)
Vincent, Jim............4:18:56 (15,836)
Vincent, Neil............4:15:26 (14,893)
Vincent, Paul James............3:34:16 (5,106)
Vincent, Peter............4:29:52 (18,935)
Vinchon, François............3:30:40 (4,521)
Vine, Rick............4:53:43 (24,978)
Vines, Adam John............4:46:38 (23,217)
Vines, Matthew............5:16:44 (29,341)
Vinnicombe, Jason H............4:02:07 (11,515)
Vint, Liam Michael............4:23:12 (17,024)
Vinten, Mark............4:31:03 (19,230)
Viohl, Martin............3:38:08 (5,791)
Viola, Paolo............3:28:36 (4,164)
Viot, Anthony............3:23:01 (3,294)
Virgo, David............4:48:58 (23,795)
Visram, Alexander............3:15:15 (2,465)
Visscher, Benk Klaas............4:08:23 (13,054)
Visser, Albert............5:19:04 (29,711)
Visser, Nicolaas............4:12:27 (14,083)
Vivash, David............5:27:11 (30,932)
Vivers, Gordon............3:36:41 (5,513)
Vives, Gregory............3:35:24 (5,301)
Vives, Michel............4:47:00 (23,309)
Vivian, Blake............2:49:44 (476)
Vivian, Charles............3:28:25 (4,132)
Vlaar, Henry............3:08:06 (1,708)
Vlasto, James............3:56:49 (10,036)
Vlok, Deon............3:37:42 (5,710)
Voaden, Roger J............2:52:24 (588)
Vocke, Juergen............4:51:51 (24,507)
Voet, Nico............3:25:43 (3,687)
Vogel, Simon A............5:29:58 (31,289)
Vokes, Christopher Wyndham 4:28:26 (18,499)
Voller, Liam Paul............3:55:17 (9,556)
Voller, Mike............3:45:31 (7,214)
Von Keitz, Alex............3:35:34 (5,337)
Vona, Conrad C............4:10:47 (13,661)
Vonier, Wil............3:56:13 (9,849)
Voong, Tai............5:22:32 (30,224)
Voos, John............3:57:43 (10,308)
Vora, Priyesh............5:10:16 (28,284)
Voralia, Ash............3:20:11 (2,976)
Voss, Stacey............3:04:05 (1,400)
Vout, Tony R............2:51:37 (551)
Vowels, Robert Charles............4:28:29 (18,518)
Vowles, Jonathan Simon............4:50:42 (24,208)
Vowles, Mike............5:37:44 (32,189)
Voyame, Alain............4:01:25 (11,345)
Voyce, Daniel J............5:13:03 (28,747)
Vriend, Pcm............4:06:17 (12,520)
Vuono, Jeffrey............2:57:53 (945)
Vyner, Graham Robertson............4:00:54 (11,218)
Waby, Paul............2:39:43 (191)
Waddell, Blair............4:24:09 (17,272)
Waddell, Douglas Ross............3:58:59 (10,718)
Waddington, David............3:05:05 (1,466)
Waddington, David............3:14:28 (2,377)
Waddington, Paul............4:12:59 (14,229)
Wade, Daniel Richard............4:07:34 (12,851)
Wade, Ian............4:54:24 (25,160)
Wade, Michael John............4:25:13 (17,578)
Wade, Stephen............5:14:22 (28,976)
Wadham, Nigel............4:50:39 (24,195)
Wadhams, Mark Anthony............4:38:22 (21,078)
Wadmore, Mark............4:12:14 (14,039)
Wadsworth, Des............5:05:16 (27,419)
Wadsworth, Patrick John............3:27:55 (4,038)
Wager, Ashley............3:32:26 (4,809)
Wagg, Tim............3:23:24 (3,352)
Wagland, Elliot James............3:58:53 (10,574)
Wagland, Roger............3:35:28 (5,316)
Wagner, Erwin............3:09:46 (1,890)
Wagstaff, Greg John............5:30:46 (31,387)
Wahed, Lloyd............5:37:03 (32,106)
Wahid, Tuhin............2:47:05 (390)
Wahle, Helge............3:39:43 (6,081)
Wahrenholz, Bernd............5:03:29 (27,098)
Waight, Jason............4:45:45 (22,968)
Wain, Brett Damian............4:36:04 (20,495)
Wain, David............3:53:02 (8,932)
Wain, Sean Robert............5:33:39 (31,730)

Wain, Stuart............3:40:43 (6,277)
Waind, Andrew William............4:27:57 (18,353)
Wainwright, Guy Lawrence............3:57:40 (10,286)
Wainwright, Mark............3:04:38 (1,440)
Wainwright, Rod............4:30:41 (19,144)
Waite, Charles Alfred Michael....4:20:41 (16,328)
Waite, Elliot James............5:53:26 (33,607)
Waite, Howard............3:12:24 (2,126)
Waite, Matthew............3:20:54 (3,070)
Waite, Paul............3:55:19 (9,567)
Waith, Chris............4:15:34 (14,919)
Wakefield, Antony............3:50:13 (8,251)
Wakefield, David............5:22:58 (30,302)
Wakefield, Glen............4:19:01 (15,851)
Wakefield, Michael............3:58:31 (10,560)
Wakefield, Michael............5:38:54 (32,296)
Wakefield, Michael Arthur............4:31:54 (19,407)
Wakefield, Robert Alan............3:43:39 (6,800)
Wakeford, Stephen............3:50:23 (8,284)
Wakeham, Chris Brynley............5:06:25 (27,606)
Wakelin, Tony John............5:59:29 (34,016)
Wakely, Graham............5:15:15 (29,107)
Wakeman, Lee............5:30:27 (31,345)
Wakeman, Simon Richard............4:38:04 (21,003)
Walch, Stephen............6:12:29 (34,780)
Walden, Ashley Paul Denis............4:15:48 (14,979)
Walden, Mark............3:51:34 (8,554)
Waldhart, Gary............3:36:52 (5,541)
Waldney, Ivor............4:34:11 (20,037)
Waldock, Ben............3:28:20 (4,112)
Waldock, Matt............4:25:18 (17,599)
Waldron, Nicholas Patrick............6:35:33 (35,667)
Waldron-Lynch, Tom............2:53:34 (644)
Waley-Cohen, Sam............5:13:04 (28,763)
Walford, Leigh............4:22:14 (16,776)
Walford, Luke............4:14:43 (14,719)
Walk, Wolfgang............3:50:00 (8,211)
Walkden, Craig Dean............4:47:16 (23,355)
Walker, Adam John............3:41:42 (6,457)
Walker, Andrew............3:51:21 (8,503)
Walker, Andrew............3:57:53 (10,356)
Walker, Andrew............4:33:13 (19,772)
Walker, Andrew............4:51:37 (24,443)
Walker, Andrew............4:58:02 (25,974)
Walker, Andrew Dominic............4:38:32 (21,124)
Walker, Andrew M............4:45:45 (22,968)
Walker, Andy James............3:55:17 (9,556)
Walker, Chris John............4:25:01 (17,524)
Walker, Christopher J............4:15:08 (14,816)
Walker, Christopher James............4:12:35 (14,120)
Walker, Craig............4:18:03 (15,597)
Walker, Craig............4:37:55 (20,970)
Walker, Daimon............4:32:29 (19,556)
Walker, Danny............4:13:36 (14,404)
Walker, David............4:29:05 (18,709)
Walker, David............5:06:42 (27,672)
Walker, David E............4:48:20 (23,616)
Walker, David F............4:55:17 (25,378)
Walker, David Michael............4:45:38 (22,927)
Walker, Derek A............3:46:15 (7,367)
Walker, Derek M............3:12:33 (2,139)
Walker, Gerald............4:08:04 (12,978)
Walker, Grant William Thomas....4:54:12 (25,100)
Walker, Henry Mark............3:11:21 (2,031)
Walker, Ian............4:32:53 (19,669)
Walker, Ian Peter............5:03:00 (27,026)
Walker, Jason Richard............5:31:22 (31,456)
Walker, John William............3:58:38 (10,608)
Walker, Joseph Atkinson............3:53:45 (9,140)
Walker, Joseph William............6:14:38 (34,867)
Walker, Keith V............3:44:36 (7,014)
Walker, Kenny............3:55:43 (9,677)
Walker, Lindsay John............5:17:44 (29,504)
Walker, Louis Alexander............4:37:34 (20,900)
Walker, Mark............2:56:58 (857)
Walker, Martin............4:31:27 (19,321)
Walker, Michael James Howard...5:56:30 (33,830)
Walker, Mike............2:52:36 (598)
Walker, Mike............5:01:29 (26,750)
Walker, Neil............5:37:17 (32,142)
Walker, Neil............6:57:18 (36,145)
Walker, Oliver............4:42:06 (22,037)
Walker, Paul Elliot............4:28:56 (18,660)

Walker, Peter David............5:12:18 (28,620)
Walker, Ray............5:02:23 (26,922)
Walker, Richard Peter............4:15:41 (14,948)
Walker, Robert Stephen............4:38:38 (21,149)
Walker, Ross A............3:58:43 (10,631)
Walker, Ryan............4:31:23 (19,306)
Walker, Sean............4:36:36 (20,631)
Walker, Simon............5:01:05 (26,665)
Walker, Stephen............3:13:44 (2,288)
Walker, Stephen............5:40:52 (32,467)
Walker, Stephen A............3:19:27 (2,914)
Walker, Steven............5:47:04 (33,056)
Walker, Tim............4:11:53 (13,950)
Walker, Toby............6:27:34 (35,404)
Walker, Vincent J............6:05:45 (34,438)
Walkingshaw, Jason............3:54:12 (9,256)
Walkington, James............4:04:34 (12,087)
Wall, Chris............4:26:48 (18,024)
Wall, Jeremy............5:03:29 (27,098)
Wall,, Matt,............4:18:48 (15,799)
Wallace, Alexander Ian Agnew....4:06:46 (12,645)
Wallace, Daniel J............3:32:24 (4,801)
Wallace, Ed............3:45:06 (7,118)
Wallace, Edmund J............4:08:29 (13,074)
Wallace, Gary John............4:23:44 (17,175)
Wallace, Keven Patrick............5:13:53 (28,904)
Wallace, Kevin G............4:29:08 (18,716)
Wallace, Michael............3:49:05 (7,997)
Wallace, Michael John............4:13:10 (14,278)
Wallace, Sam............4:45:48 (22,979)
Wallace, Spencer............5:07:22 (27,787)
Wallace, Stuart James............5:16:49 (29,355)
Wallace, Stuart John............6:01:30 (34,156)
Wallace, Tony............3:41:07 (6,348)
Walland, John Robert............4:29:05 (18,709)
Waller, Adam............4:43:52 (22,469)
Waller, Adam James............3:28:48 (4,189)
Waller, Andrew J............3:55:04 (9,495)
Waller, Ben............4:42:08 (22,045)
Waller, Christopher Gordon............4:46:34 (23,185)
Waller, David............3:36:07 (5,432)
Waller, Gary Brian............5:29:40 (31,247)
Waller, John............7:43:21 (36,539)
Waller, Jonathan............4:42:44 (22,196)
Waller, Jonathan Paul............4:49:00 (23,800)
Waller, Matthew............5:15:17 (29,111)
Waller, Paul G............4:23:34 (17,125)
Wallington, Darren James............4:12:06 (14,008)
Wallington, Steven............5:02:25 (26,932)
Wallis, Andrew John............4:50:52 (24,262)
Wallis, James Michael............5:00:29 (26,551)
Wallis, Paul............5:48:56 (33,236)
Wallis, Peter............3:09:31 (1,859)
Wallis, Peter John............3:36:28 (5,476)
Wallis, Thomas............4:21:02 (16,425)
Wallwork, Simon James............4:35:58 (20,468)
Walmsley, Ben............4:00:53 (11,211)
Walmsley, Dave M............2:53:57 (667)
Walmsley, John............6:03:01 (34,254)
Walmsley, Patrick............4:16:33 (15,181)
Walmsley, Paul............4:50:51 (24,254)
Walpole, Andrew R............2:52:03 (569)
Walpole, Brian Andrew............4:21:14 (16,469)
Walpole, Steven............6:17:08 (34,985)
Walsgrove, John D............3:00:59 (1,205)
Walsh, Allan............3:58:34 (10,584)
Walsh, Anthony S............2:58:12 (977)
Walsh, Bernard............4:10:42 (13,638)
Walsh, Chris............5:07:56 (27,886)
Walsh, Denis John............3:45:37 (7,230)
Walsh, Eden David............3:48:24 (7,825)
Walsh, Frank J............4:24:09 (17,272)
Walsh, Guy............3:32:55 (4,881)
Walsh, Ian Anthony............3:32:15 (4,780)
Walsh, James Robert............3:08:26 (1,746)
Walsh, Jimmy............3:42:02 (6,517)
Walsh, Martin............6:49:38 (35,989)
Walsh, Richard............3:01:19 (1,219)
Walsh, Ritchie............5:25:57 (30,774)
Walsh, Simon............5:23:48 (30,444)
Walsh, Stuart M............4:07:44 (12,893)
Walshe, Donald Peter............5:09:06 (28,067)
Walter, Andy............4:00:22 (11,081)

Walter, Philip	4:26:05 (17,837)	
Walter, Steve	3:58:08 (10,426)	
Walters, David John	5:50:26 (33,377)	
Walters, Ed	3:45:31 (7,214)	
Walters, Humphrey John	5:16:28 (29,304)	
Walters, Iwan Wyn	3:46:30 (7,415)	
Walters, Jeremy Neil	4:34:12 (20,044)	
Walters, Jonathan	4:41:53 (21,989)	
Walters, Matthew J	4:07:23 (12,796)	
Walton, Anthony Richard	5:04:43 (27,324)	
Walton, Ben	2:59:24 (1,095)	
Walton, Ben	5:40:38 (32,448)	
Walton, Chris John	4:36:40 (20,651)	
Walton, Craig Anthony	4:51:25 (24,403)	
Walton, Dean M	5:08:02 (27,903)	
Walton, Gareth	4:09:50 (13,428)	
Walton, James	4:10:42 (13,638)	
Walton, James Matthew	4:17:08 (15,334)	
Walton, John	6:43:20 (35,873)	
Walton, Peter	6:28:50 (35,457)	
Wang, Ian	3:20:27 (3,012)	
Wang, Patrick	3:37:58 (5,757)	
Wanney, David P	4:07:15 (12,764)	
Wansell, Stephen John	3:46:46 (7,478)	
Want, Michael Stuart	4:18:44 (15,782)	
Waplington, Mark	3:12:37 (2,147)	
Warburton, Owen	5:43:23 (32,709)	
Warburton, Rob Stephen	6:28:04 (35,430)	
Ward, Adrian	4:49:40 (23,968)	
Ward, Alan	3:40:29 (6,235)	
Ward, Andrew Michael	4:35:55 (20,453)	
Ward, Benjie	3:56:59 (10,084)	
Ward, Brendon	3:37:40 (5,703)	
Ward, Dan	4:35:28 (20,342)	
Ward, Daniel Stuart	4:25:26 (17,642)	
Ward, David	3:48:40 (7,890)	
Ward, David J	4:25:12 (17,575)	
Ward, Ian J	3:13:28 (2,247)	
Ward, James	4:58:42 (26,144)	
Ward, Lewis	4:43:38 (22,402)	
Ward, Mark	4:20:03 (16,117)	
Ward, Mark Daniel	2:58:21 (992)	
Ward, Michael Alexander	6:00:57 (34,127)	
Ward, Michael Jon	4:03:19 (11,804)	
Ward, Michael K	3:32:01 (4,740)	
Ward, Nigel	4:54:21 (25,144)	
Ward, Padraic	3:56:28 (9,922)	
Ward, Paul	3:32:49 (4,864)	
Ward, Paul G	4:41:05 (21,790)	
Ward, Peter Mark	5:05:11 (27,401)	
Ward, Scot	7:27:54 (36,458)	
Ward, Simeon	3:19:24 (2,908)	
Ward, Simon	6:03:00 (34,251)	
Ward, Simon David	3:12:22 (2,119)	
Ward, Stephen	3:27:15 (3,915)	
Ward, Stephen P	2:48:10 (420)	
Ward, Stuart Craig	3:59:13 (10,786)	
Ward, Thomas	5:44:44 (32,844)	
Wardell, Dave A	4:37:00 (20,742)	
Warden, Brian J	4:15:35 (14,924)	
Warden, Scott Albert Seagrave	4:24:59 (17,515)	
Wardlaw, Robert G	3:20:55 (3,074)	
Wardle, David	2:24:21 (33)	
Wardle, David Mark	4:58:09 (26,004)	
Wardle, Ed Carlisle	3:33:30 (4,970)	
Wardle, Simon Dean	5:02:44 (26,986)	
Wardman, Steve	4:51:55 (24,530)	
Wardrope, Adam Boyd	3:54:53 (9,447)	
Wardrope, David	3:52:46 (8,857)	
Ware, Christopher	4:24:15 (17,302)	
Ware, Peter	5:18:05 (29,559)	
Ware, Roger Tony	4:57:43 (25,912)	
Ware, Steven	4:35:23 (20,321)	
Wareham, Peter J	5:10:23 (28,307)	
Warham, Richard	4:05:28 (12,329)	
Waring, Matthew	4:42:42 (22,186)	
Waring, Sam	4:33:04 (19,720)	
Warlow, Robert	3:36:49 (5,525)	
Warminger, Paul	4:48:59 (23,797)	
Warmington, Gary Victor	3:24:56 (3,570)	
Warmsley, Richard Thomas	4:11:35 (13,875)	
Warn, Richard	4:31:15 (19,280)	
Warne, Barry Anthony	3:14:01 (2,322)	
Warne, Craig	3:50:13 (8,251)	
Warne, Richard P	3:26:47 (3,845)	
Warner, Andy	3:32:44 (4,849)	
Warner, Bernard	6:35:23 (35,662)	
Warner, Danny Steven	5:31:22 (31,456)	
Warner, Graham David	3:54:10 (9,248)	
Warner, Keith	4:41:11 (21,820)	
Warner, Kim	3:31:54 (4,724)	
Warner, Paul	4:42:16 (22,084)	
Warner, Simon Edward	3:28:01 (4,051)	
Warner, Stephen T	4:34:33 (20,134)	
Warner, Tony D	3:12:01 (2,092)	
Warnes, Andrew	5:06:57 (27,716)	
Warnock, John S	2:54:59 (746)	
Warr, Ian R	5:57:29 (33,901)	
Warr, Jason Charles	4:51:46 (24,483)	
Warr, John	5:01:28 (26,748)	
Warran, Stephen John	4:21:20 (16,500)	
Warrell, Paul A	3:08:06 (1,708)	
Warrell, Stephen John	3:15:44 (2,522)	
Warren, Alex	4:21:42 (16,606)	
Warren, Andrew D	5:33:39 (31,730)	
Warren, Andrew John	4:37:04 (20,765)	
Warren, Chris	4:29:01 (18,691)	
Warren, Gary Stephen	2:57:32 (905)	
Warren, Giles Edward	5:19:59 (29,846)	
Warren, Jonathan Alan	3:56:09 (9,822)	
Warren, Kane	5:19:20 (29,753)	
Warren, Paul	4:52:19 (24,643)	
Warren, Peter	5:00:41 (26,584)	
Warren, Peter D	3:34:48 (5,213)	
Warren, Simon Paul	4:24:30 (17,388)	
Warren, Trevor William	4:25:48 (17,749)	
Warrick, Michael J	3:08:23 (1,737)	
Warrilow, Stewart J	4:09:25 (13,320)	
Warriner, Paul J	4:39:40 (21,429)	
Warriner, Richard J	5:04:57 (27,355)	
Warriner, Sam James	4:52:28 (24,673)	
Warrington, Paul	3:55:59 (9,779)	
Wartnaby, Charles E	2:44:47 (334)	
Warwick, Jon	3:27:17 (3,920)	
Warwick, Kevin	4:49:42 (23,978)	
Warwick-Champion, Duncan K	3:31:44 (4,701)	
Waschke, Horst	4:17:20 (15,386)	
Wasdell, Andrew Richard	3:07:37 (1,669)	
Washington, Dominic	5:00:32 (26,557)	
Wastie, Martin S	4:44:24 (22,617)	
Watanabe, Makoto	5:06:51 (27,697)	
Watanabe, Motoharu	4:27:03 (18,097)	
Watchman, David J	3:58:36 (10,595)	
Waterfield, Jonathan L	3:01:13 (1,214)	
Waterhouse, Andrew S	3:30:56 (4,569)	
Waterhouse, Peter John	5:43:01 (32,668)	
Waterhouse, Stephen David	3:02:09 (1,267)	
Wateridge, Paul	5:06:47 (27,688)	
Waterman, David J	3:16:43 (2,647)	
Waters, Adrian	3:40:07 (6,171)	
Waters, Christopher Charles	4:15:04 (14,802)	
Waters, John A	5:07:35 (27,828)	
Waters, Matthew Frank	4:24:04 (17,252)	
Waters, Paul Douglas	4:00:40 (11,159)	
Waters, Richard John	3:21:16 (3,115)	
Waterston, Steven J	5:37:30 (32,164)	
Wates, Neill I	3:26:43 (3,832)	
Wathne, Johann Otto	3:38:08 (5,791)	
Watkins, Anthony Charles	4:20:52 (16,381)	
Watkins, Daniel	3:06:15 (1,551)	
Watkins, Justin	4:05:23 (12,303)	
Watkins, Michael, Sean	5:00:26 (26,543)	
Watkins, Peter Gareth	3:52:05 (8,676)	
Watkins, Rhys	4:26:04 (17,830)	
Watkins, Richie	4:20:30 (16,260)	
Watkins, Stephen John	5:12:51 (28,710)	
Watkins, Tim James	2:54:52 (728)	
Watkinson, Mike	4:05:15 (12,269)	
Watkinson, Peter G	3:15:26 (2,491)	
Watkiss, Mike	4:19:51 (16,056)	
Watlers, Cyril	3:53:12 (8,971)	
Watling, Hadley	4:04:32 (12,080)	
Watling, Kristian Stephen	4:41:26 (21,873)	
Watling, Lewis	4:29:11 (18,728)	
Watling, Simon	4:29:51 (18,927)	
Watmough, Stephen J	2:46:13 (368)	
Watson, Alan	3:57:42 (10,297)	
Watson, Alan	6:31:35 (35,558)	
Watson, Andrew	3:13:22 (2,233)	
Watson, Andrew	4:06:14 (12,506)	
Watson, Andrew Glen	4:14:03 (14,520)	
Watson, Andrew John	5:36:02 (32,001)	
Watson, Andrew Richard	5:21:14 (30,035)	
Watson, Barrie	6:30:14 (35,509)	
Watson, Charles J	3:33:22 (4,945)	
Watson, Chris	4:24:16 (17,306)	
Watson, Colin G	4:48:25 (23,647)	
Watson, David	4:59:14 (26,272)	
Watson, David A	4:44:31 (22,645)	
Watson, Dean	3:53:36 (9,092)	
Watson, Gary	5:09:28 (28,136)	
Watson, Ian	4:13:51 (14,470)	
Watson, Ian	4:27:49 (18,316)	
Watson, James Andrew	4:17:09 (15,337)	
Watson, James Richard	3:55:32 (9,621)	
Watson, Jerry R	3:00:42 (1,189)	
Watson, Jim	4:48:34 (23,686)	
Watson, Laurence Frank Martin	4:22:54 (16,962)	
Watson, Mark David	4:35:38 (20,375)	
Watson, Matthew	4:06:28 (12,562)	
Watson, Mike	4:32:05 (19,453)	
Watson, Neil Cameron	3:53:00 (8,925)	
Watson, Paul	3:57:31 (10,236)	
Watson, Paul M	2:42:57 (275)	
Watson, Peter John	3:24:03 (3,440)	
Watson, Peter L	5:22:54 (30,292)	
Watson, Reece A	4:21:35 (16,571)	
Watson, Robert	4:24:54 (17,490)	
Watson, Robert	5:16:20 (29,281)	
Watson, Scott	4:21:02 (16,425)	
Watson, Thomas	3:47:52 (7,711)	
Watson, Tim	3:32:45 (4,852)	
Watson, Tom	3:44:15 (6,923)	
Watson, Troy A	3:04:01 (1,393)	
Watt, Brian	4:30:54 (19,190)	
Watt, Brian John	6:08:41 (34,594)	
Watt, Chris	3:05:48 (1,521)	
Watt, Frederick J	3:34:22 (5,132)	
Watt, Graham James	3:53:26 (9,036)	
Watt, Stuart Paul	5:29:23 (31,210)	
Wattenbach, Eddie	3:20:52 (3,066)	
Watts, Andrew	3:21:39 (3,155)	
Watts, Andrew J	3:12:36 (2,146)	
Watts, Chris	4:22:45 (16,918)	
Watts, Darren Michael	4:27:09 (18,133)	
Watts, James	4:11:26 (13,827)	
Watts, Phil	5:03:59 (27,186)	
Watts, Stepen John	5:31:54 (31,523)	
Watts, Stephen Jonathan	3:14:04 (2,329)	
Waudby, Sam	4:38:10 (21,021)	
Waudby, Trevor William	4:49:25 (23,900)	
Waumsley, Peter J	2:50:18 (497)	
Way, Adam	4:21:05 (16,435)	
Way, Alex	4:17:21 (15,391)	
Way, Lawrence	4:01:30 (11,368)	
Way, Martin	3:27:10 (3,900)	
Way, Matt	4:11:18 (13,790)	
Way, Simon J	2:59:57 (1,148)	
Way, Steven	2:19:38 (17)	
Waywell, Pete K	3:21:49 (3,172)	
Wearne, Robert Jon	3:57:00 (10,089)	
Weatherall, John Stuart	5:19:58 (29,844)	
Weatherburn, James	3:21:54 (3,182)	
Weatherill, Danny	3:55:05 (9,501)	
Weaver, Anthony Francis	4:43:52 (22,469)	
Weaver, Keith R	3:46:19 (7,378)	
Weaver, Kris	5:12:57 (28,730)	
Weaver, Stephen Thomas	4:13:16 (14,304)	
Weaver, William J	4:50:21 (24,130)	
Weavers, Keith	4:37:20 (20,828)	
Weavers, Terry P	3:20:37 (3,039)	
Weaving, Jeremy R	3:58:11 (10,449)	
Webb, Aaron M	4:31:20 (19,299)	
Webb, Adrian J	3:11:00 (1,995)	
Webb, Alban	4:59:10 (26,252)	
Webb, Andy	4:11:00 (13,715)	
Webb, Brett	5:05:49 (27,497)	
Webb, Brian Ernest	4:40:31 (21,647)	
Webb, Christopher	3:13:19 (2,226)	

Webb, Craig Stephen 4:12:19 (14,059)
Webb, Darren 4:24:20 (17,333)
Webb, David 4:42:28 (22,130)
Webb, Eric John 4:34:27 (20,108)
Webb, Harvey J D 3:38:06 (5,783)
Webb, John 6:19:01 (35,082)
Webb, Joseph Paul 3:54:14 (9,269)
Webb, Kevin 6:29:57 (35,498)
Webb, Michael R 3:41:15 (6,379)
Webb, Oliver 5:13:02 (28,744)
Webb, Paul Thomas 4:24:02 (17,245)
Webb, Richard Christopher 4:04:50 (12,161)
Webb, Rob 4:37:37 (20,910)
Webb, Simon 4:27:53 (18,335)
Webb, Terry John 4:52:15 (24,614)
Webb, Thomas David 4:33:36 (19,893)
Webber, Alexander 5:04:34 (27,291)
Webber, Daniel J 2:50:02 (489)
Webber, Darren John 5:13:03 (28,747)
Webber, Graham 3:52:24 (8,767)
Webber, Ian 4:10:51 (13,680)
Webber, Peter 4:41:43 (21,944)
Webber, Roger Duncan 4:05:20 (12,293)
Webber, Stuart J 2:45:01 (342)
Webbon, John Michael 4:41:04 (21,784)
Weber, Alexis 5:12:17 (28,617)
Weber, Bill 3:48:50 (7,937)
Weber, Vincent 3:44:56 (7,085)
Weber-Macartney, Jamie 5:24:58 (30,616)
Webster, Adam James 5:16:45 (29,344)
Webster, Andrew 5:12:16 (28,614)
Webster, Andrew Philip 3:51:32 (8,544)
Webster, Ben 4:40:41 (21,687)
Webster, Ben Lee 4:18:19 (15,665)
Webster, Christopher Robert 5:50:12 (33,355)
Webster, David 4:51:39 (24,450)
Webster, Gilbert 5:13:18 (28,817)
Webster, James Michael 4:52:37 (24,710)
Webster, Jon 3:26:38 (3,822)
Webster, Mark 4:40:26 (21,623)
Webster, Neil 3:20:32 (3,030)
Webster, Paul 4:54:41 (25,226)
Webster, Paul A 4:16:45 (15,233)
Webster, Pete 4:28:15 (18,436)
Webster, Richard 4:40:46 (21,714)
Webster, Richard W 2:53:57 (667)
Webster, Simon 4:50:28 (24,154)
Webster, Terry Michael 3:58:18 (10,491)
Webster, Thomas Edward 3:37:26 (5,642)
Webster-Newman, Graham 4:02:15 (11,547)
Wedgwood, Ruaridh 3:26:00 (3,731)
Weedall, Thomas 3:07:24 (1,642)
Weekes, David T 2:44:42 (328)
Weekes, Stuart Richard 4:42:33 (22,148)
Weeks, Thomas James 4:28:24 (18,487)
Weeks, Tom 4:39:23 (21,350)
Weetman, Simon 5:28:27 (31,083)
Wegg, Terry 3:37:26 (5,642)
Wegmüller, Marc 3:50:07 (8,230)
Wehrle, Stephen R 4:47:05 (23,327)
Weigh, Jeff 5:49:43 (33,311)
Weightman, Rob 4:20:17 (16,194)
Weightman, Rob 4:20:37 (16,302)
Weightman, Stuart Leigh 5:19:11 (29,734)
Weilert, René 3:04:59 (1,456)
Weiner, Mark Justin 4:22:30 (16,847)
Weinhold, Heidrun 4:42:03 (22,028)
Weir, Andrew P 2:29:30 (63)
Weir, Keith E 3:24:15 (3,477)
Weir, Peter 3:19:05 (2,879)
Weireter, Albert 4:21:32 (16,556)
Weisgard, David S 5:13:26 (28,832)
Welaratne, Ranga 4:01:30 (11,368)
Welberry, Duncan V 4:31:37 (19,358)
Welch, Andy 4:58:15 (26,028)
Welch, Benjamin James 3:19:26 (2,910)
Welch, Graham J 5:08:15 (27,939)
Welch, James Ward 3:53:57 (9,196)
Welch, Michael I 3:24:54 (3,563)
Welch, Richard Harold 5:41:25 (32,523)
Welch, Simon 4:39:16 (21,324)
Welch, Simon 5:07:21 (27,783)
Welch, Terence G 3:22:56 (3,282)
Welding, Larus 4:02:13 (11,543)
Weldon, Ian 4:00:57 (11,240)
Welland, Paul Raymond 4:28:54 (18,642)
Wellard, Brandon Paul 4:32:59 (19,691)
Wellby, Steve 3:19:18 (2,896)
Weller, Daniel 3:34:32 (5,161)
Weller, Mark 3:54:46 (9,407)
Wellesley, Chris James 5:30:58 (31,413)
Wellman, Alex J 5:04:49 (27,334)
Wells, Adam Colin 4:34:18 (20,070)
Wells, Andrew 4:32:13 (19,491)
Wells, Brian R 6:54:40 (36,101)
Wells, Chris Michael 4:03:33 (11,859)
Wells, Darren Michael 3:32:50 (4,867)
Wells, David 5:03:35 (27,118)
Wells, David 5:09:49 (28,201)
Wells, David Michael 5:56:48 (33,851)
Wells, Fraser S 3:14:23 (2,368)
Wells, Graham Barry 5:02:00 (26,840)
Wells, Jonathan Stuart 5:02:31 (26,946)
Wells, Martin John 4:58:52 (26,183)
Wells, Matthew Lee 4:55:01 (25,310)
Wells, Nicholas Michael 5:25:37 (30,713)
Wells, Paul 4:25:28 (17,650)
Wells, Peter James 4:53:16 (24,870)
Wells, Peter John 5:48:14 (33,166)
Wells, Phillip Stephen 4:44:03 (22,516)
Wells, Rob 3:12:37 (2,147)
Wells, Spencer Alexander 3:35:09 (5,265)
Wells, Stephen 7:24:41 (36,440)
Wells, Stephen Lee 5:12:39 (28,671)
Wells, Tom 3:41:31 (6,425)
Welmans, Tyler 5:26:30 (30,840)
Welsh, Christopher 3:55:24 (9,594)
Welsh, Darryn Patrick William 3:55:43 (9,677)
Welsh, James 5:30:54 (31,404)
Welsh, James G 4:23:18 (17,044)
Welsh, Jon Alan 4:19:15 (15,913)
Welsh, Matthew James Christopher 4:13:06 (14,263)
Welsh, Stephen Terence 2:58:51 (1,031)
Welter, Bjorn 4:39:06 (21,280)
Wenbourne, Ross 4:10:32 (13,600)
Wendling, Michael 4:00:35 (11,135)
Wenger, Gerhard 3:37:29 (5,658)
Wenkel, Mario 4:21:05 (16,435)
Wenman, Mark 3:13:58 (2,315)
Wentworth, Anthony J 6:23:18 (35,250)
Wentworth, Steve L 5:09:29 (28,141)
Wepener, Alan 3:59:22 (10,827)
Wernberg, Stephen P 4:01:43 (11,415)
Werner, Julian I 3:26:08 (3,757)
Wesolowski, Arkadiusz L 3:56:48 (10,030)
Wessel, Hans Johannes Henderikus 4:39:33 (21,400)
Wessinghage, Thomas 3:31:27 (4,659)
Wesson, Richard John 3:53:11 (8,966)
West, Andrew 4:24:14 (17,294)
West, Andrew Stephen 6:25:13 (35,321)
West, Benjamin Ronald 3:29:09 (4,262)
West, Brogan 5:34:21 (31,803)
West, Chris 4:55:47 (25,488)
West, Christopher J 3:28:52 (4,200)
West, Colin 3:07:52 (1,687)
West, Darren Alec 4:08:17 (13,024)
West, David 3:07:45 (1,680)
West, Dean Terry 4:37:29 (20,873)
West, Frank 3:30:09 (4,439)
West, Gerry 4:49:40 (23,968)
West, Grant J 4:54:29 (25,175)
West, Ian Andrew 3:36:02 (5,418)
West, Jamie Robert 3:19:45 (2,942)
West, Jonathan J 6:25:10 (35,318)
West, Justin P 2:43:46 (302)
West, Kenneth J 4:39:52 (21,481)
West, Mark 3:59:11 (10,771)
West, Mark Anthony 3:44:25 (6,975)
West, Mark L 5:52:44 (33,556)
West, Nicholas James 5:49:31 (33,285)
West, Peter J 3:56:59 (10,084)
West, Robert 5:23:30 (30,385)
West, Sam 3:11:23 (2,036)
West, Stan 4:28:59 (18,679)
West, Steve 5:21:22 (30,055)
Westacott, Rhys 4:28:14 (18,431)
Westall, Bootsy Simon McMahon 4:43:13 (22,303)
Westall, Mark Edward 4:00:37 (11,145)
Westall, Mark R 3:40:54 (6,310)
Westbey, Tim 3:54:29 (9,322)
Westbrook, Alexander 4:55:04 (25,326)
Westbrook, Richard 3:37:18 (5,622)
Westgarth, Christopher 4:01:06 (11,277)
Westhead, John 3:55:37 (9,647)
Westhead, Karl S 2:49:28 (467)
Westlake, Nick 4:54:58 (25,296)
Westlake, Simon Richard 4:09:55 (13,448)
Westley, Andy N 5:39:19 (32,332)
Westmore, Peter John 5:13:18 (28,817)
Westmoreland, Wayne Michael 4:48:47 (23,741)
Weston, Adrian B 4:02:21 (11,565)
Weston, Chris 5:15:20 (29,113)
Weston, Jeff Keith 4:46:14 (23,104)
Weston, Keith B 3:52:13 (8,711)
Weston, Matt 3:25:45 (3,699)
Weston, Phil Mark 5:12:58 (28,737)
Westwick, Michael Robert 4:54:16 (25,123)
Westwood, Dean 6:26:44 (35,374)
Westwood, Jamie I 2:57:35 (913)
Westwood, Jason D 2:49:15 (456)
Westwood, Michael John 3:43:40 (6,801)
Westwood, Nick Mark 3:59:52 (10,956)
Wethered, Edmund 4:55:51 (25,497)
Wethered, Tom 4:28:26 (18,499)
Wetherell, Andrew 6:23:39 (35,264)
Wetheridge, Darren S 3:54:55 (9,455)
Whaites, Andrew 3:20:08 (2,971)
Whaley, Marcus Alan 4:00:57 (11,240)
Whalley, Philip John 3:54:18 (9,280)
Whalley, Simon Adam 3:52:37 (8,826)
Whalley, Stephen H 4:39:01 (21,263)
Wharton, Christopher J 3:46:48 (7,489)
Wharton, Michael J 4:04:25 (12,058)
Whates, Tristran 6:33:01 (35,595)
Whatford, Howard Martin 4:42:26 (22,124)
Whatmough, Paul Nicholas 3:40:06 (6,165)
Wheal, David 4:45:42 (22,948)
Wheatcroft, Chris J 5:15:13 (29,102)
Wheater, Andrew Michael 4:28:31 (18,528)
Wheatley, Dennis Edward 3:27:33 (3,971)
Wheatley, John 4:08:26 (13,064)
Wheatley, Mathew 4:54:22 (25,149)
Wheatley, Mike A 4:20:34 (16,281)
Wheatley, Oliver 3:49:29 (8,090)
Wheatley, Richard Metcalfe 4:22:37 (16,885)
Wheatley, Scott 3:51:33 (8,549)
Wheatley, Tom O 4:46:59 (23,304)
Wheeldon, Paul 3:53:39 (9,105)
Wheeldon, Scott 4:48:05 (23,564)
Wheele, James 4:04:42 (12,129)
Wheeler, Andrew G 3:09:12 (1,824)
Wheeler, Andrew J 4:37:04 (20,765)
Wheeler, Ben J 3:04:11 (1,407)
Wheeler, Chris James 6:34:27 (35,639)
Wheeler, Daniel 5:17:55 (29,534)
Wheeler, Dave 4:15:12 (14,834)
Wheeler, Jeremy James 5:03:10 (27,051)
Wheeler, Keith Alan 3:17:04 (2,670)
Wheeler, Mark A 5:11:58 (28,555)
Wheeler, Michael A 4:10:37 (13,620)
Wheeler, Patrick W 2:59:39 (1,122)
Wheeler, Paul 4:35:50 (20,430)
Wheeler, Phil 4:33:30 (19,852)
Wheeler, Philip 4:51:52 (24,511)
Wheeler, Stephen James 4:25:14 (17,583)
Wheeler, Thomas Logan 4:19:06 (15,872)
Whelan, Alan 3:12:41 (2,153)
Whelan, Brian Andrew 4:12:40 (14,143)
Whelan, Denis 3:21:56 (3,187)
Whelan, Dominic Michael 3:39:13 (5,985)
Whelan, Paul Anthony 3:58:33 (10,574)
Whelan, Richard 5:18:26 (29,617)
Wheldon, Tom 5:26:17 (30,818)
Wherry, Steven M 2:55:01 (747)
Wheten, Andrew R 3:53:32 (9,067)
Whetham, Ed 3:41:54 (6,499)
Whetton, Michael 3:16:00 (2,556)
Whewell, Sean A 3:24:07 (3,454)
Whiffen, Daniel John 5:28:16 (31,059)

Whilding, Richard........................4:02:36 (11,632)
While, Adrian..............................4:42:57 (22,248)
While, James...............................4:08:48 (13,161)
Whincup, Antony Robert............4:28:37 (18,557)
Whincup, Stephen P....................3:46:47 (7,484)
Whinder, John.............................4:03:05 (11,748)
Whitaker, Duncan Andrew..........3:57:40 (10,286)
Whitaker, Steven.........................5:16:32 (29,314)
Whitbread, Ian.............................4:28:06 (18,390)
Whitbread, Jason William...........4:06:50 (12,670)
Whitcombe, Barry Douglas..........4:18:22 (15,678)
White, Adrian..............................3:03:43 (1,364)
White, Alan..................................4:07:05 (12,730)
White, Alan..................................4:56:29 (25,643)
White, Alec A...............................3:54:57 (9,460)
White, Alex J................................5:20:27 (29,912)
White, Alex Roy...........................3:49:56 (8,198)
White, Andrew.............................4:02:14 (11,545)
White, Andrew James..................4:20:33 (16,275)
White, Andrew James..................5:27:06 (30,923)
White, Andrew Martin Ronald....3:46:27 (7,410)
White, Antony Robert.................3:53:45 (9,140)
White, Aron.................................4:23:38 (17,141)
White, Bobby...............................6:05:29 (34,420)
White, Brett.................................4:07:22 (12,791)
White, Charles Leslie..................4:11:51 (13,945)
White, Daniel...............................4:32:15 (19,500)
White, Daniel James....................5:09:59 (28,230)
White, Danny Kenneth................3:19:58 (2,960)
White, Darren...............................4:39:32 (21,397)
White, Dave J...............................4:33:06 (19,727)
White, David John.......................4:26:29 (17,945)
White, David P.............................4:08:46 (13,153)
White, Dean..................................3:56:54 (10,056)
White, Douglas M.........................5:40:24 (32,421)
White, Faber Allen.......................4:37:23 (20,841)
White, Gary G...............................4:47:33 (23,425)
White, Graeme David..................4:12:24 (14,068)
White, Ian R..................................2:37:06 (143)
White, James................................3:38:42 (5,888)
White, James................................4:55:55 (25,518)
White, John..................................3:25:03 (3,587)
White, John M..............................4:00:56 (11,231)
White, Jonathan...........................5:03:30 (27,100)
White, Keith R...............................3:24:38 (3,528)
White, Kevin A..............................3:18:37 (2,831)
White, Kieron...............................4:30:03 (18,987)
White, Liam...................................3:22:40 (3,256)
White, Mark..................................3:35:43 (5,363)
White, Mark James.......................4:11:33 (13,863)
White, Martin...............................5:07:19 (27,772)
White, Martin Dudley..................4:26:35 (17,977)
White, Michael.............................4:36:16 (20,540)
White, Michael.............................5:00:45 (26,600)
White, Myles................................3:15:00 (2,439)
White, Neil....................................4:14:04 (14,526)
White, Neil B.................................2:55:50 (790)
White, Nicholas James.................4:20:06 (16,137)
White, Nick...................................4:41:41 (21,939)
White, Nicolas..............................3:46:20 (7,383)
White, Noel Christopher.............2:57:27 (896)
White, Oliver................................3:58:47 (10,652)
White, Paul...................................5:23:52 (30,451)
White, Paul...................................7:20:43 (36,410)
White, Paul Michael.....................4:03:29 (11,838)
White, Peter Anthony..................4:00:55 (11,225)
White, Philip.................................3:49:55 (8,191)
White, Richard.............................4:41:14 (21,827)
White, Richard.............................4:42:47 (22,208)
White, Richard (Rick)..................3:59:43 (10,925)
White, Richard John....................3:33:09 (4,915)
White, Robert P............................4:28:52 (18,632)
White, Ronny Patrick...................5:19:59 (29,846)
White, Rosco.................................4:31:22 (19,304)
White, Scott T...............................4:06:05 (12,472)
White, Simon................................4:36:49 (20,689)
White, Simon................................4:58:45 (26,155)
White, Soren.................................5:37:35 (32,172)
White, Stephen John....................4:20:35 (16,287)
White, Stephen Michael...............4:45:30 (22,884)
White, Steve..................................3:12:54 (2,176)
White, Steve Mark........................3:25:28 (3,642)
White, Thomas..............................5:16:20 (29,281)
White, Vincent.............................5:08:24 (27,964)
White, Vincent.............................5:28:05 (31,040)
Whitebread, Oliver......................4:32:37 (19,585)
Whitehead, Ben............................6:21:46 (35,189)
Whitehead, Christopher Ian.......4:16:21 (15,125)
Whitehead, David.........................3:52:54 (8,898)
Whitehead, Ian David..................3:27:56 (4,044)
Whitehead, John Michael............4:23:02 (16,988)
Whitehead, Lee............................4:04:20 (12,040)
Whitehead, Michael Paul............3:25:26 (3,639)
Whitehead, Mike..........................4:45:05 (22,796)
Whitehead, Richard.....................3:32:58 (4,886)
Whitehead, Ronald.......................6:25:07 (35,314)
Whitehead, Shaun........................3:42:52 (6,671)
Whitehead, Shaun........................4:42:55 (22,241)
Whitehill, David............................4:24:46 (17,458)
Whitehorn, Andrew Thomas.......3:55:21 (9,582)
Whitehouse, Andrew....................4:24:18 (17,319)
Whitehouse, Guy..........................5:01:36 (26,777)
Whitehouse, Ian R.......................2:51:57 (561)
Whitehouse, Mick.........................4:08:21 (13,043)
Whitehouse, Richard Joseph.......5:44:37 (32,828)
Whitehouse, Stuart......................4:23:32 (17,115)
Whitehurst, Philip David............4:00:00 (10,984)
Whitelam, Malcolm......................4:46:56 (23,288)
Whitelaw, Tom.............................4:27:12 (18,149)
Whitelegg, Richard M..................2:46:40 (376)
Whiteley, David............................3:57:06 (10,129)
Whiteley, Mike A..........................4:53:43 (24,978)
Whiteley, Stephen P.....................4:10:44 (13,649)
Whitelock, Danny Roger..............5:49:44 (33,314)
Whiteman, Paul............................5:19:00 (29,701)
Whiteman, Richard John.............4:07:49 (12,909)
Whitemore, Kevin A.....................4:58:53 (26,188)
Whiter, James David.....................3:43:34 (6,788)
Whiter, Will JJ...............................4:46:04 (23,050)
Whiteside, Christopher................5:47:21 (33,084)
Whiteside, Gareth John...............4:21:11 (16,459)
Whiteside, Iain.............................4:10:08 (13,506)
Whiteside, Mark Neil...................4:51:19 (24,378)
Whiteway, Anthony James............3:31:01 (4,579)
Whiteway, Philip Anthony...........3:48:24 (7,825)
Whitfield, Gary.............................3:59:43 (10,925)
Whitfield, Karl J............................4:07:00 (12,711)
Whitfield, Matt.............................4:20:28 (16,252)
Whitfield, Peter............................4:43:56 (22,486)
Whitfield, Tom..............................5:27:17 (30,940)
Whitford Bartle, Jonathan...........3:55:53 (9,745)
Whithouse, Christopher R...........4:46:00 (23,024)
Whiting, Darren Lee.....................5:41:44 (32,554)
Whiting, Simeon...........................4:36:48 (20,682)
Whiting, Stephen J........................2:38:24 (170)
Whitington, Stephen J..................3:00:15 (1,159)
Whitlam, Daniel............................3:42:08 (6,535)
Whitlock, Gavin Alistair...............4:19:16 (15,920)
Whitlock-James, Nigel..................4:52:32 (24,694)
Whitmarsh, Jim F..........................3:55:57 (9,766)
Whitmarsh, Richard......................5:02:42 (26,979)
Whitmore, Jason P.........................4:14:33 (14,665)
Whitmore, Steve............................4:54:17 (25,126)
Whitnall, Adam Edward................5:42:32 (32,642)
Whitnell, Ben................................5:41:46 (32,561)
Whitney, Scott...............................4:07:27 (12,817)
Whitson, Alex................................4:51:55 (24,530)
Whittaker, David Brian..................5:51:25 (33,457)
Whittaker, Dean............................5:09:28 (28,136)
Whittaker, George.........................4:45:58 (23,016)
Whittaker, Graham........................4:34:16 (20,062)
Whittaker, Robert James..............4:48:40 (23,711)
Whittaker, Terry............................4:47:55 (23,522)
Whittall, Philip R..........................4:29:08 (18,716)
Whittall, Robert J..........................3:53:43 (9,126)
Whitten, Leigh..............................2:55:17 (760)
Whittingham, Andrew J................3:30:13 (4,456)
Whittingham, Carl James..............4:02:21 (11,565)
Whittingham, Dylan Paul..............3:17:40 (2,733)
Whittington, David Herbert.........5:48:15 (33,169)
Whittington, Gary..........................3:39:02 (5,946)
Whittington, Russell.......................2:44:52 (336)
Whittington, Will...........................4:21:14 (16,469)
Whittle, David James.....................4:30:14 (19,031)
Whittle, John.................................4:17:55 (15,550)
Whittle, Jon...................................4:27:02 (18,087)
Whittle, Ricky...............................5:41:27 (32,528)
Whittle, Terry...............................4:46:22 (23,141)
Whitton, Andrew B.......................4:34:43 (20,176)
Whitton, Kevin..............................4:11:27 (13,835)
Whitton, Mark...............................4:57:14 (25,810)
Whitton, Peter...............................5:10:25 (28,313)
Whitty, Ian Michael.......................3:54:58 (9,468)
Whitty, Maurice W.........................3:16:10 (2,568)
Whitwam, Adrian A........................2:43:44 (301)
Whitworth, Andrew........................5:35:39 (31,947)
Whitworth, Bill J.............................4:38:35 (21,137)
Whitworth, Martin John................3:07:33 (1,658)
Whoriskey, Teague.........................3:25:32 (3,652)
Whybrow, Edward David Herbert 4:01:23 (11,332)
Whyman, Mark John Rhys............4:17:57 (15,563)
Whymark, James.............................3:31:49 (4,713)
Whyment, Glynn............................4:26:35 (17,977)
Whyte, Brian James........................3:58:40 (10,613)
Whyte, Gary Armstrong.................4:21:55 (16,680)
Whyte, Michael William................4:50:56 (24,286)
Whyte, Steven.................................3:57:30 (10,233)
Whyton, Mark A.............................5:26:14 (30,809)
Wickenden, Lee.............................4:20:56 (16,394)
Wickens, Bradley............................4:20:08 (16,145)
Wickens, Matt................................4:07:29 (12,826)
Wickham, Ben M.............................3:39:44 (6,084)
Wickham, Rob.................................3:26:01 (3,736)
Wicks, Daniel..................................4:59:52 (26,422)
Wicks, Daniel B...............................5:25:37 (30,713)
Wicks, Graham................................4:05:27 (12,325)
Wicks, Marc....................................4:53:59 (25,045)
Wicks, Matthew J............................4:21:04 (16,433)
Wicks, Peter Leslie.........................4:05:20 (12,293)
Wicks, Timothy...............................5:05:59 (27,527)
Widdicombe, Graydon Robert.....5:14:31 (28,991)
Widdows, Michael D......................5:05:29 (27,447)
Widdows, Tom................................5:02:34 (26,954)
Widdowson, Richard John.............4:45:37 (22,919)
Widdup, Matthew John..................3:23:38 (3,383)
Widelski, Gregg...............................4:21:12 (16,463)
Wiegand, Robert.............................2:39:53 (196)
Wieland, Richard............................4:35:33 (20,354)
Wield, Christopher.........................5:27:05 (30,919)
Wiget, Gregor.................................5:01:18 (26,709)
Wigfull, Stephen Thomas...............4:08:33 (13,103)
Wigg, Michael John........................3:54:36 (9,354)
Wiggins, Andrew S..........................2:54:44 (719)
Wiggins, Michael.............................3:37:19 (5,626)
Wiggins, Stuart I.............................5:20:23 (29,897)
Wigginton, Darren Christopher..6:30:49 (35,529)
Wigginton, Richard.........................4:23:03 (16,994)
Wightman, Andrew Charles...........5:30:33 (31,364)
Wightman, Stephen M....................4:29:30 (18,808)
Wigington, Denny S........................3:56:44 (10,009)
Wignall, Edward Joseph..................4:56:38 (25,673)
Wigram, Harry.................................3:29:14 (4,276)
Wiilliams, Mark Stephen.................4:14:04 (14,526)
Wijnands, Oscar..............................5:20:06 (29,864)
Wikeley, Adrian...............................4:41:28 (21,884)
Wilbor, David..................................5:31:11 (31,432)
Wilbur, Duncan...............................4:18:12 (15,629)
Wilby, Michael A.............................4:58:40 (26,130)
Wilcock, Christopher D..................4:09:57 (13,456)
Wilcock, Christopher James...........4:37:32 (20,891)
Wilcock, Martin...............................2:51:58 (563)
Wilcock, Martin...............................4:21:17 (16,487)
Wilcock, Neil Thomas......................3:54:07 (9,236)
Wilcock, Paul...................................3:06:47 (1,593)
Wilcox, Chris...................................4:30:19 (19,051)
Wilcox, John W...............................4:26:00 (17,812)
Wilcox, Lee Nathan........................4:54:10 (25,083)
Wilcox, Michael Peter.....................4:55:03 (25,321)
Wild, David Raymond.......................4:00:21 (11,076)
Wild, James......................................4:22:05 (16,730)
Wild, Stuart Barnard........................5:05:53 (27,512)
Wilde, Andrew J...............................4:11:43 (13,908)
Wilde, Greg......................................5:14:21 (28,974)
Wilde, John......................................4:45:24 (22,862)
Wilde, Mark John.............................5:06:04 (27,543)
Wildego, Scott John Robert.............5:15:55 (29,213)
Wilder, Brian J..................................2:24:18 (32)
Wilder, Nick James...........................6:02:10 (34,194)
Wildgruber, Dirk...............................4:52:28 (24,673)

Wildgruber, Joerg......4:52:28 (24,673)
Wildhagen, Ernst......3:34:00 (5,057)
Wilding, Ben......4:34:59 (20,228)
Wilding, Simon......4:11:18 (13,790)
Wilding, Steven John......4:51:32 (24,426)
Wildman, Brian......3:50:23 (8,284)
Wildman, James M......5:02:08 (26,877)
Wildman, Paul A......4:22:26 (16,830)
Wildman, Simon Edward......4:49:39 (23,961)
Wileman, Mark......4:18:02 (15,589)
Wiles, Andrew John......4:51:54 (24,521)
Wiles, Dallas......4:00:30 (11,116)
Wiles, Ian......4:39:31 (21,391)
Wiles, Matthew Ian......5:15:23 (29,122)
Wiles, William Charles......4:25:34 (17,681)
Wilgoss, Ryan Scott......4:19:52 (16,066)
Wilkes, Andrew......3:34:30 (5,154)
Wilkes, Andrew......4:04:48 (12,153)
Wilkes, Bernard Terry......3:58:51 (10,670)
Wilkes, David......4:47:08 (23,331)
Wilkes, Ian......6:01:16 (34,145)
Wilkes, Philip John......5:18:49 (29,669)
Wilkes, Samuel M......5:12:22 (28,627)
Wilkey, David......4:06:49 (12,660)
Wilkie, Brian......3:19:24 (2,908)
Wilkie, Brian......4:12:09 (14,022)
Wilkie, Daniel James......3:25:16 (3,615)
Wilkie, Edward......4:24:31 (17,395)
Wilkie, Iain Andrew......4:43:48 (22,441)
Wilkins, Daran David......4:55:31 (25,412)
Wilkins, Derek......5:04:58 (27,360)
Wilkins, Gareth J......4:01:29 (11,362)
Wilkins, Geoff......7:29:10 (36,466)
Wilkins, Huw......4:50:22 (24,133)
Wilkins, Martin......4:33:15 (19,787)
Wilkins, Robert Michael......4:51:12 (24,351)
Wilkinson, Andrew......6:00:02 (34,069)
Wilkinson, Andrew D......4:39:24 (21,353)
Wilkinson, Andrew James......3:13:14 (2,215)
Wilkinson, Ben......3:54:41 (9,381)
Wilkinson, Brean......3:33:55 (5,043)
Wilkinson, Danny......4:43:31 (22,372)
Wilkinson, David R......3:50:27 (8,297)
Wilkinson, Dirk......4:02:21 (11,565)
Wilkinson, Graeme......3:11:17 (2,025)
Wilkinson, Graham Anthony......3:14:10 (2,336)
Wilkinson, Ian......5:50:20 (33,367)
Wilkinson, Ian James......3:56:09 (9,822)
Wilkinson, James Michael......2:58:27 (1,003)
Wilkinson, James William......4:21:18 (16,490)
Wilkinson, Jeffrey Charles......3:38:23 (5,827)
Wilkinson, Jerome......4:02:53 (11,701)
Wilkinson, Lawrence Owen......3:42:55 (6,678)
Wilkinson, Martin J......3:21:07 (3,101)
Wilkinson, Paul......4:04:11 (12,006)
Wilkinson, Paul L......4:45:18 (22,841)
Wilkinson, Philip M......4:01:19 (11,315)
Wilkinson, Richard E......4:14:10 (14,560)
Wilkinson, Thomas Colin......3:27:36 (3,983)
Wilkinson, Tom......4:53:49 (24,998)
Wilkinson, Trevor......3:04:12 (1,409)
Wilks, Keith Richard......5:31:18 (31,449)
Will, Andrew John......4:12:28 (14,089)
Willard, Jack......6:14:12 (34,844)
Willcock, Philip......4:43:32 (22,377)
Willcox, David......4:48:39 (23,707)
Willcox, David......4:50:16 (24,110)
Willcox, Ted......3:38:08 (5,791)
Willcox-Jones, James George......5:46:02 (32,955)
Willerton, Andy......3:50:24 (8,289)
Willerton, Martin......6:00:15 (34,080)
Willerton, Steven......6:47:04 (35,950)
Willett, Lee......5:25:01 (30,628)
Willetts, Colin Gary......3:07:04 (1,616)
Willetts, David......4:59:40 (26,373)
Willetts, Richard David......4:13:32 (14,378)
Willey, Darren Richard......4:36:07 (20,510)
Willey, Neil......3:53:03 (8,936)
Williams, Aaron......3:58:03 (10,397)
Williams, Adam Thomas......4:27:02 (18,087)
Williams, Adrian P......4:08:10 (12,998)
Williams, Alan Peter......3:22:29 (3,240)
Williams, Alan W......4:13:29 (14,358)
Williams, Alex......3:18:12 (2,794)
Williams, Alex......4:35:21 (20,309)
Williams, Allan......5:50:26 (33,377)
Williams, Andrew......3:36:23 (5,467)
Williams, Andrew......4:24:29 (17,384)
Williams, Andrew Herbert......4:49:11 (23,844)
Williams, Andrew K......4:18:02 (15,589)
Williams, Andrew P......3:24:08 (3,455)
Williams, Andy......4:02:19 (11,560)
Williams, Andy......4:22:10 (16,747)
Williams, Andy......5:24:56 (30,609)
Williams, Anthony......4:58:55 (26,192)
Williams, Antony J......4:04:24 (12,050)
Williams, Arfon......3:39:31 (6,046)
Williams, Barrie A......3:51:59 (8,654)
Williams, Barry......4:51:30 (24,421)
Williams, Barry John......4:48:42 (23,719)
Williams, Ben......4:50:30 (24,161)
Williams, Ben......5:08:36 (27,991)
Williams, Bobby B......3:23:11 (3,320)
Williams, Bryn D......5:12:30 (28,653)
Williams, Carl......3:44:08 (6,901)
Williams, Chris......3:48:48 (7,927)
Williams, Chris......4:21:29 (16,542)
Williams, Chris......4:37:53 (20,962)
Williams, Christopher J......5:49:46 (33,316)
Williams, Craig Ellis......4:17:04 (15,311)
Williams, Craig S......2:42:06 (254)
Williams, Daniel......3:45:09 (7,127)
Williams, Daniel Robert......3:42:38 (6,616)
Williams, Darren......3:59:26 (10,848)
Williams, Darren Joseph......5:13:45 (28,880)
Williams, Dave W......3:19:53 (2,950)
Williams, David......4:11:30 (13,848)
Williams, David Kyffin......5:50:03 (33,340)
Williams, David M......4:14:50 (14,747)
Williams, Dean......6:04:55 (34,379)
Williams, Dennis Selby......4:27:17 (18,174)
Williams, Dwight......3:31:39 (4,693)
Williams, Edward James......4:14:37 (14,687)
Williams, Eliot John......3:41:12 (6,367)
Williams, Frank A......4:09:24 (13,313)
Williams, Gareth......4:45:44 (22,962)
Williams, Gareth......5:47:41 (33,113)
Williams, Gareth Isfryn......3:25:39 (3,673)
Williams, Gareth J......3:03:32 (1,354)
Williams, Gareth James Richard 4:37:50 (20,951)
Williams, Gary......4:37:46 (20,938)
Williams, Gary......4:42:48 (22,213)
Williams, Gary......6:09:39 (34,642)
Williams, Gary Peter......4:21:16 (16,484)
Williams, Gavin......5:57:07 (33,872)
Williams, Geraint......4:13:42 (14,432)
Williams, Gerald G......4:15:06 (14,808)
Williams, Graham D......4:25:13 (17,578)
Williams, Gregg Jonathon......6:18:24 (35,052)
Williams, Hartley......6:00:19 (34,084)
Williams, Hugh William......4:00:41 (11,166)
Williams, Iain......2:51:03 (526)
Williams, Ian......4:08:54 (13,185)
Williams, Ian G......2:27:37 (51)
Williams, Ian Geoffrey......5:33:00 (31,663)
Williams, Jack......3:14:00 (2,321)
Williams, Jackson......4:11:57 (13,977)
Williams, James......4:48:35 (23,690)
Williams, James......5:55:17 (33,743)
Williams, James Alan......4:54:03 (25,061)
Williams, James Gwynfor......6:42:49 (35,857)
Williams, Jamie......5:02:35 (26,956)
Williams, Jeremy Mark Westley......4:39:04 (21,275)
Williams, Joe Mark......5:43:42 (32,744)
Williams, John......4:25:19 (17,605)
Williams, John D......4:49:56 (24,037)
Williams, John Edward Patrick......4:35:15 (20,283)
Williams, John James......4:17:57 (15,563)
Williams, John Jeffrey......4:00:59 (11,245)
Williams, John M......3:59:24 (10,839)
Williams, Jonathan......5:33:37 (31,729)
Williams, Jonathan D......3:35:12 (5,272)
Williams, Jonathan L......4:49:39 (23,961)
Williams, Jonathan Thomas......7:06:17 (36,269)
Williams, Jordan Matthew......4:44:23 (22,609)
Williams, Karl Peter......4:16:45 (15,233)
Williams, Keith R......5:21:07 (30,021)
Williams, Kristian......3:53:41 (9,117)
Williams, Lee......3:53:55 (9,186)
Williams, Lee......6:20:32 (35,148)
Williams, Leslie Edward......3:21:45 (3,165)
Williams, Mark......3:35:16 (5,282)
Williams, Mark......4:27:05 (18,114)
Williams, Mark......4:48:07 (23,571)
Williams, Mark Adrian......3:55:55 (9,755)
Williams, Mark Andrew......4:30:04 (18,994)
Williams, Martin P......2:51:13 (531)
Williams, Martyn Jon......4:10:33 (13,608)
Williams, Matthew James......4:36:29 (20,598)
Williams, Michael......3:37:43 (5,713)
Williams, Michael......4:06:37 (12,604)
Williams, Michael......4:08:20 (13,036)
Williams, Michael......4:50:38 (24,193)
Williams, Mike......4:54:44 (25,238)
Williams, N......5:10:36 (28,350)
Williams, Neil......4:37:24 (20,845)
Williams, Neil J......3:14:15 (2,349)
Williams, Nick......4:00:59 (11,245)
Williams, Nick J......3:31:14 (4,615)
Williams, Oliver......5:14:37 (29,007)
Williams, Ollie......5:05:32 (27,455)
Williams, Ollie Mark......3:57:26 (10,210)
Williams, Ormond......5:04:23 (27,254)
Williams, Owen......3:58:36 (10,595)
Williams, Owen John......5:17:55 (29,534)
Williams, Paul......4:16:40 (15,209)
Williams, Paul Andrew......5:46:17 (32,980)
Williams, Paul Edmund Gerald......3:58:53 (10,682)
Williams, Paul R......5:11:00 (28,405)
Williams, Paul Stuart......4:27:45 (18,299)
Williams, Pete C......3:50:52 (8,396)
Williams, Peter Charles......3:33:00 (4,895)
Williams, Peter W......3:20:48 (3,056)
Williams, Philip......3:43:34 (6,788)
Williams, Rhodri......4:02:19 (11,560)
Williams, Rhydian John......3:58:09 (10,435)
Williams, Rhys......3:57:10 (10,146)
Williams, Richard Eric......5:10:51 (28,387)
Williams, Robert......3:33:24 (4,951)
Williams, Robert James......4:30:00 (18,977)
Williams, Roobert Gwyn......4:20:58 (16,405)
Williams, Rupert......4:13:34 (14,390)
Williams, Russell J......4:11:19 (13,796)
Williams, Ryan......4:02:13 (11,543)
Williams, Samuel L......4:03:07 (11,762)
Williams, Sean Frederick Harold 4:21:41 (16,600)
Williams, Simon......5:10:00 (28,235)
Williams, Stephen David......3:53:09 (8,955)
Williams, Stephen Eric......5:08:17 (27,948)
Williams, Stephen J......5:52:49 (33,569)
Williams, Steve......4:42:33 (22,148)
Williams, Steven......4:53:47 (24,990)
Williams, Stuart M......3:01:16 (1,217)
Williams, Thomas......3:28:24 (4,126)
Williams, Thomas A......2:56:39 (842)
Williams, Timothy Alan......5:18:39 (29,652)
Williams, Tom R......3:58:15 (10,476)
Williams-Camp, Roger M......3:30:07 (4,434)
Williamson, Alex......3:43:04 (6,712)
Williamson, Alisdair......4:29:42 (18,878)
Williamson, Andrew......4:34:27 (20,108)
Williamson, Andrew Mark......4:01:25 (11,345)
Williamson, Anthony Peter......4:09:09 (13,240)
Williamson, Ben......5:19:47 (29,817)
Williamson, Charlie......4:44:44 (22,709)
Williamson, Craig......3:04:26 (1,423)
Williamson, Daniel......4:15:31 (14,909)
Williamson, David......3:52:48 (8,870)
Williamson, Dirk......3:32:32 (4,819)
Williamson, Edward......4:56:22 (25,624)
Williamson, Guy......3:45:59 (7,306)
Williamson, Ian Thomas......4:21:35 (16,571)
Williamson, Karl Andrew......3:32:59 (4,891)
Williamson, Mark......3:52:14 (8,716)
Williamson, Michael......5:07:30 (27,812)
Williamson, Neil Reginald......5:39:29 (32,344)
Williamson, Paul Timothy......3:23:58 (3,427)
Williamson, Peter......4:04:59 (12,200)
Williamson, Peter Anthony......4:12:26 (14,078)

Williamson, Robert John 3:56:47 (10,027)
Williamson, Ross 5:17:36 (29,487)
Williamson, Stuart Peter.............5:12:15 (28,609)
Williamson, Thomas Robert........3:36:40 (5,508)
Williamson, Tony..........................7:29:05 (36,462)
Willicott, Mark..............................3:40:30 (6,241)
Willimott, Shaun 3:49:46 (8,162)
Willis, Adam Luke.........................4:25:08 (17,558)
Willis, Darren 3:24:31 (3,512)
Willis, Dave 4:45:19 (22,847)
Willis, David Arthur 6:06:08 (34,458)
Willis, Edward................................3:42:11 (6,546)
Willis, Gary S 3:17:15 (2,691)
Willis, George 4:06:50 (12,670)
Willis, Greg James 5:24:26 (30,549)
Willis, John D 4:49:52 (24,021)
Willis, Jonathan James 5:34:32 (31,826)
Willis, Martin 5:44:50 (32,851)
Willis, Matthew J...........................2:48:26 (429)
Willis, Nigel Mark..........................5:27:20 (30,944)
Willis, Paul Allan 3:15:25 (2,488)
Willis, Steve M 3:08:15 (1,722)
Williscroft, Victor 4:01:22 (11,325)
Willliams, John Stephen 5:54:52 (33,703)
Willliams, Richard.........................3:53:00 (8,925)
Willmitt, William J.........................3:33:07 (4,910)
Willmott, Ashley Grant Barry 4:55:08 (25,344)
Willmott, Gary...............................5:47:40 (33,109)
Willmott, Ryan Barr 5:24:54 (30,602)
Willoughby, Christopher 6:20:19 (35,139)
Willox, Tom 4:37:01 (20,749)
Wills, Andrew Edward..................7:43:03 (36,537)
Wills, Brian Christopher..............3:44:24 (6,968)
Wills, Dennis Arthur 3:40:34 (6,252)
Wills, Mark.....................................3:50:47 (8,378)
Wills, Martin 3:33:25 (4,954)
Wills, Richard 4:28:37 (18,557)
Willsher, Mark 5:09:15 (28,092)
Willson, David Robert..................4:50:23 (24,135)
Willson, Simon 4:20:35 (16,287)
Wilmer, Duncan Peter 3:58:05 (10,407)
Wilmot, Andrew H 3:42:45 (6,646)
Wilmot, Paul..................................5:26:40 (30,858)
Wilsher, Phil 4:15:45 (14,971)
Wilsher, Tim A...............................4:08:52 (13,177)
Wilson, Adam 4:24:18 (17,319)
Wilson, Adam Scott.......................6:09:01 (34,620)
Wilson, Alan William James.........4:08:19 (13,033)
Wilson, Alex Terrance..................4:44:15 (22,577)
Wilson, Alistair 4:17:37 (15,473)
Wilson, Andrew 4:56:18 (25,611)
Wilson, Andrew Nicholas.............4:42:53 (22,238)
Wilson, Andrew S 5:19:05 (29,714)
Wilson, Andy 4:32:49 (19,635)
Wilson, Anthony Jospeh 4:29:42 (18,878)
Wilson, Brendan J 4:24:21 (17,344)
Wilson, Bruce 3:25:27 (3,640)
Wilson, Charles Brian 3:42:03 (6,521)
Wilson, Chris Robert.....................3:29:59 (4,413)
Wilson, Colin 4:06:07 (12,478)
Wilson, Colin Peter 5:10:30 (28,327)
Wilson, Craig.................................5:13:15 (28,812)
Wilson, Daren Mark......................4:08:44 (13,146)
Wilson, David 4:55:08 (25,344)
Wilson, David L.............................5:28:26 (31,080)
Wilson, David Richard 3:31:17 (4,624)
Wilson, David William Alan.........4:55:36 (25,437)
Wilson, Dennis 4:18:50 (15,803)
Wilson, Edmund Lee 7:12:58 (36,338)
Wilson, Frank William 6:29:56 (35,497)
Wilson, Gareth 3:24:08 (3,455)
Wilson, Gareth David...................5:34:14 (31,785)
Wilson, Gareth E 2:54:42 (718)
Wilson, Gavin Anthony.................5:08:52 (28,025)
Wilson, Geoffrey............................5:17:02 (29,393)
Wilson, George..............................4:50:58 (24,292)
Wilson, Gerwyn 4:16:45 (15,233)
Wilson, Glenn C 3:20:06 (2,969)
Wilson, Graham M 4:32:43 (19,610)
Wilson, Grant 4:28:39 (18,567)
Wilson, Iain 5:48:53 (33,231)
Wilson, Ian.....................................4:40:18 (21,574)
Wilson, James Andrew 4:54:42 (25,230)
Wilson, James Edward..................4:11:53 (13,950)
Wilson, James G 4:01:03 (11,264)
Wilson, James T.............................4:27:39 (18,274)
Wilson, Jared 3:46:10 (7,351)
Wilson, Jeremy 5:27:52 (31,009)
Wilson, Jody John.........................4:41:31 (21,899)
Wilson, John Alexander...............4:55:50 (25,495)
Wilson, John William 3:52:17 (8,734)
Wilson, Keith 5:11:19 (28,452)
Wilson, Keith Reginald 4:08:48 (13,161)
Wilson, Kenneth Paul 4:39:09 (21,301)
Wilson, Lister John 6:47:36 (35,958)
Wilson, Mal P................................4:59:17 (26,283)
Wilson, Marc.................................4:57:49 (25,928)
Wilson, Mark 3:30:44 (4,534)
Wilson, Mark James......................4:27:04 (18,110)
Wilson, Matt 4:17:11 (15,345)
Wilson, Matthew J 3:27:11 (3,905)
Wilson, Michael.............................3:31:48 (4,708)
Wilson, Michael George 4:36:56 (20,723)
Wilson, Nicholas...........................3:27:51 (4,025)
Wilson, Nicholas C........................3:19:00 (2,871)
Wilson, Nick 4:19:12 (15,898)
Wilson, Nigel 5:43:10 (32,683)
Wilson, Oliver...............................3:56:02 (9,795)
Wilson, Paul Jon 4:33:35 (19,884)
Wilson, Rikki Craig 5:47:08 (33,064)
Wilson, Robert..............................3:21:39 (3,155)
Wilson, Robert Alan......................4:08:55 (13,188)
Wilson, Robert H 3:15:18 (2,476)
Wilson, Robin H............................5:06:52 (27,698)
Wilson, Russell Christopher 5:01:18 (26,709)
Wilson, Sam 4:16:23 (15,135)
Wilson, Scott William...................7:05:34 (36,259)
Wilson, Simon H 3:23:15 (3,332)
Wilson, Simon Shaun....................3:51:47 (8,603)
Wilson, Steve 4:20:08 (16,145)
Wilson, Steve 5:29:19 (31,194)
Wilson, Steven 4:41:59 (22,012)
Wilson, Steven John 4:19:42 (16,014)
Wilson, Stewart.............................5:12:42 (28,686)
Wilson, Stuart C 5:31:15 (31,439)
Wilson, Terry Robert.....................4:47:26 (23,396)
Wilson, Trevor R............................3:24:25 (3,499)
Wilton, Kevin.................................5:44:25 (32,806)
Wiltshire, Craig James..................4:59:28 (26,326)
Wiltshire, Glyn David 4:18:31 (15,720)
Wiltshire, Jim.................................3:57:17 (10,178)
Wiltshire, John Richard 4:05:14 (12,263)
Wiltshire, Paul Steven 4:19:58 (16,096)
Wiltshire, Richard 3:56:30 (9,933)
Wimmer, Anton..............................4:14:00 (14,504)
Wimperis, Kevin Mark 3:44:29 (6,986)
Wimpory, Howard P......................3:22:31 (3,241)
Wimpory, Stephen 4:44:02 (22,511)
Wimpress, Andy.............................4:42:44 (22,196)
Winbanks, Gavin James.................5:22:55 (30,295)
Winborne, David Adam 4:52:16 (24,619)
Winbourne, James G......................4:02:39 (11,638)
Winch, Martin James 3:43:31 (6,778)
Windard, Richard C.......................4:10:45 (13,655)
Windass, Alastair 3:54:10 (9,248)
Winder, Leon A 3:13:07 (2,203)
Windle, Paul J................................2:57:32 (905)
Windle, Robin 4:01:55 (11,474)
Windle, Stephen James.................4:35:13 (20,272)
Windley, Scott...............................5:30:20 (31,327)
Windon, Anthony C......................4:11:36 (13,883)
Windram, Carl David 4:26:21 (17,916)
Windross, Peter 4:00:54 (11,218)
Windsor, Craig Lee 3:58:08 (10,426)
Windsor, Elliott Richard 3:20:57 (3,079)
Windsor, Matthew James..............5:25:17 (30,662)
Windstanley, Chris 4:28:58 (18,670)
Winek, Michael James...................3:36:41 (5,513)
Winer, Joel.....................................4:00:44 (11,179)
Winfield, David..............................4:10:49 (13,670)
Winfield, David John 4:13:39 (14,417)
Winfield, Russell Aan....................4:05:27 (12,325)
Winfield, Stephen J 3:51:00 (8,423)
Wing, Jon 4:22:29 (16,841)
Wingate, Carl..................................5:49:05 (33,247)
Wingham, Mark 3:29:47 (4,377)
Winkless, Neil S..............................4:04:02 (11,968)
Winmill, Roger Shaun 4:16:27 (15,156)
Winn, Aaron 3:47:32 (7,655)
Winnard, Chris...............................4:33:05 (19,723)
Winney, Paul...................................3:56:06 (9,811)
Winsor, Ian 4:47:45 (23,479)
Winstanley, Bradley.......................3:56:23 (9,892)
Winstanley, John.............................3:46:38 (7,449)
Winstanley, Mark............................4:20:29 (16,256)
Winstanley, Martin Thomas..........5:38:38 (32,277)
Winstanley, Nathan Mark 4:58:24 (26,066)
Winstanley, Rory.............................4:04:50 (12,161)
Winston, Alan..................................4:55:53 (25,508)
Winston, Geoffrey...........................4:09:56 (13,453)

Wint, Andrew 3:54:13 (9,263)

London 2008 was 'the last marathon' I was ever going to run! So 2010 was just 'one last one'! The 'application accepted' letter was greeted with a mixture of excitement and apprehension and a long hard winter's training in the Peak District saw over 800 miles registered in the build up with my training partner Doug. In hindsight, this was easily enough to achieve my target of a sub 4 hour time. These miles allowed me a comfortable race and after 20 miles it was clear that the sub 4 target was within grasp so the last 6.2 miles were 'enjoyable' and I could absorb the fantastic surroundings and atmosphere. The memories will remain for many years to come as I finished in 3:54. Thank you London.

Winter, Craig 4:15:23 (14,883)
Winter, James..................................3:24:18 (3,486)
Winter, Kristoffer Robert..............5:10:08 (28,262)
Winter, Martin................................4:42:58 (22,250)
Winter, Michael..............................3:47:38 (7,674)
Winter, Michael..............................3:57:46 (10,318)
Winter, Mike...................................3:05:31 (1,500)
Winter, Peter 4:23:44 (17,175)
Winter, Stephen 2:59:48 (1,136)
Winter, Steve...................................4:37:45 (20,934)
Winterbottom, Nick.......................4:12:11 (14,031)
Winterbottom, Toby.......................3:30:24 (4,485)
Winterburn, David 7:07:27 (36,283)
Winteringham, Paul.......................4:24:38 (17,425)
Winters, Alex 5:04:28 (27,271)
Winters, George 4:17:13 (15,354)
Winters, Ray....................................5:15:49 (29,202)
Wintersteller, Martin.....................4:05:45 (12,395)
Winterton, Edward.........................3:49:33 (8,102)

Wintle, David A 5:14:20 (28,966)
Wisdom, Martin J 3:45:15 (7,151)
Wise, Andrew Stephen 4:20:50 (16,373)
Wise, Daniel Charles 4:06:18 (12,524)
Wise, David John 3:31:32 (4,673)
Wise, Larry M 3:49:39 (8,134)
Wise, Ray 3:26:54 (3,862)
Wise, Roger S 4:28:18 (18,452)
Wise, Simon Ian 4:05:23 (12,303)
Wisely, Anton 3:37:31 (5,666)
Wiseman, Lee 4:41:48 (21,971)
Wiseman, Mark 3:51:19 (8,496)
Wiseman, Matthew Edward 4:59:46 (26,400)
Wishart, Robert William 5:17:54 (29,526)
Wishlade, Simeon John 3:46:59 (7,523)
Wisken, Michael Thomas 5:23:55 (30,464)
Wisker, Steven Anthony 6:29:18 (35,476)
Witard, Oliver 3:25:58 (3,729)
Withers, David G 4:00:53 (11,211)
Withers, Matthew 3:54:07 (9,236)
Withers, Ronald 5:42:05 (32,599)
Withington, Mark 4:16:02 (15,038)
Withstandley, Anthony H 3:22:53 (3,276)
Witko, Matthew 3:00:47 (1,194)
Witkowicz, Tomasz 4:12:31 (14,103)
Witt, Graham 6:34:25 (35,635)
Witt, Jonathan J 4:17:56 (15,557)
Wittich-Jackson, Adam 3:49:43 (8,150)
Witton, Robert Paul 4:22:04 (16,723)
Wixey, John 5:01:44 (26,803)
Wizenberg, Marcel 5:26:09 (30,796)
Wodzianski, Juliusz Vic 4:33:11 (19,757)
Woerle, Roland 3:13:19 (2,226)
Wogan, Ronan 3:11:48 (2,074)
Wohanka, Richard 3:56:01 (9,790)
Wohlfahrt, Joerg 3:47:07 (7,545)
Wokes, Richard 3:46:09 (7,345)
Wold, James Andrew 4:13:15 (14,297)
Wolfendale, Stewart 4:11:51 (13,945)
Wolfson, Martin Stephen 3:49:10 (8,016)
Wolkoff, Seth 3:47:51 (7,707)
Wollerton, Terry 3:54:19 (9,282)
Wollocombe, John Bidlake 3:54:46 (9,407)
Woloszyn, Piotr 3:46:49 (7,494)
Wolovitz, Lionel 3:21:40 (3,159)
Wolseley Brinton, Charles 6:06:10 (34,460)
Wolton, Sam 4:27:55 (18,347)
Wombwell, Andrew James 4:31:59 (19,428)
Wonfor, Elliot S 3:35:04 (5,260)
Wong, Alan 4:21:22 (16,513)
Wong, Allan 6:09:20 (34,630)
Wong, Edward S 5:29:57 (31,288)
Wonnacott, Stuart John 2:57:42 (932)
Wood, Adrian C 4:31:26 (19,316)
Wood, Alastair F 4:21:13 (16,465)
Wood, Alex 3:29:11 (4,266)
Wood, Andrew David 5:29:49 (31,270)
Wood, Andrew M 2:57:52 (944)
Wood, Andy 4:59:04 (26,230)
Wood, Anthony John 5:16:59 (29,383)
Wood, Ben 4:13:54 (14,483)
Wood, Ben Anderson 5:18:55 (29,688)
Wood, Benjamin 4:12:44 (14,165)
Wood, Christopher J 3:14:11 (2,339)
Wood, Christopher J 4:04:19 (12,035)
Wood, Colin Louis 4:06:07 (12,478)
Wood, Daniel 4:21:00 (16,412)
Wood, Daniel 4:36:07 (20,510)
Wood, Darren 3:15:51 (2,536)
Wood, Darren J 3:58:29 (10,551)
Wood, David G 3:49:42 (8,145)
Wood, Derrick 4:10:32 (13,600)
Wood, Dom 6:04:24 (34,344)
Wood, Hugo James 3:14:22 (2,363)
Wood, Ian D 3:02:22 (1,286)
Wood, James 3:08:19 (1,732)
Wood, James Matthew 5:06:43 (27,677)
Wood, Jason Andrew 4:09:24 (13,313)
Wood, Jeremy 6:09:39 (34,642)
Wood, Keran A 4:09:21 (13,296)
Wood, Leigh James 3:40:49 (6,292)
Wood, Mathew Martin 5:57:32 (33,905)
Wood, Matthew Paul 4:58:07 (25,996)
Wood, Nick John 4:25:24 (17,636)
Wood, Olly James 3:55:43 (9,677)
Wood, Phil 4:44:59 (22,768)
Wood, Richard 4:21:00 (16,412)
Wood, Robert 4:28:37 (18,557)
Wood, Stephen C 4:32:47 (19,626)
Wood, Stephen Peter 4:34:02 (20,000)
Wood, Steven R 4:33:45 (19,933)
Wood, Stuart Andrew 5:44:11 (32,785)
Wood, Stuart J 4:33:03 (19,715)
Wood, Thomas 4:13:04 (14,257)
Wood, Tim 5:32:26 (31,592)
Wood, Will Mark 4:20:21 (16,220)
Woodbine, David 4:43:01 (22,263)
Woodbridge, Tony J 5:47:18 (33,076)
Woodburn, Peter J 2:54:47 (722)
Woodcock, Clive Anthony 3:38:04 (5,776)
Woodcock, Leon 4:09:48 (13,421)
Woodcock, Mark 5:06:28 (27,618)
Woodcock, Martin 4:24:00 (17,236)
Woodcock, Paul 4:39:36 (21,411)
Woodcock, Paul James 4:39:13 (21,317)
Woodcock, Shaun 3:18:53 (2,860)
Woodcraft, Stefan 4:39:44 (21,445)
Wooderson, Seb 5:13:04 (28,763)
Woodeson, James 2:59:40 (1,125)
Woodfield, Craig 5:06:13 (27,571)
Woodford, John James 3:45:56 (7,295)
Woodford, Martin 5:09:47 (28,193)
Woodford, Paul Stephen 4:57:09 (25,791)
Woodford, Stephen 4:20:43 (16,341)
Woodgate, Daniel 3:37:28 (5,652)
Woodgate, David 4:23:53 (17,211)
Woodhead, Hamish 3:05:41 (1,513)
Woodhouse, James 3:22:58 (3,288)
Woodhouse, John F 4:04:10 (12,002)
Woodhouse, Nigel 3:26:37 (3,820)
Woodhouse, Philip J 3:05:00 (1,457)
Woodhouse, Sefton 4:27:40 (18,277)
Woodhouse, Tim J 5:29:29 (31,218)
Woodhouse, William George 5:29:28 (31,216)
Wooding, Thomas 4:35:20 (20,301)
Woodisse, James Edward 3:09:23 (1,843)
Woodland, Michael 4:22:50 (16,947)
Woodley, André H 3:23:45 (3,401)
Woodley, David 4:39:08 (21,291)
Woodman, Adrian Urwin 6:01:14 (34,141)
Woodman, John 3:10:34 (1,952)
Woodman, Mark J 2:42:13 (257)
Woodman, Nicolas 4:19:10 (15,894)
Woodman, Philip C 3:47:38 (7,674)
Woodrow, Andrew H 2:53:37 (646)
Woodrow, Martin 3:59:32 (10,870)
Woodruff, James 3:42:42 (6,634)
Woods, Brendan 5:10:50 (28,381)
Woods, Brian P 3:54:09 (9,245)
Woods, Chris 4:07:59 (12,957)
Woods, Gary John 4:33:05 (19,723)
Woods, Graham 7:06:41 (36,276)
Woods, Ian Philip 5:08:35 (27,985)
Woods, Martin John 4:31:10 (19,258)
Woods, Martin John 4:45:58 (23,016)
Woods, Max J 3:43:01 (6,701)
Woods, Neil 5:15:46 (29,190)
Woods, Paul 4:35:19 (20,298)
Woods, Philip Robert 3:13:13 (2,214)
Woods, Richard W 4:01:18 (11,314)
Woods, Russell Graham 5:26:16 (30,813)
Woods, Stuart Michael 5:59:31 (34,017)
Woodthorpe, Grant 4:25:26 (17,642)
Woodtli, Daniel 3:47:10 (7,566)
Woodward, Barrie 4:18:18 (15,661)
Woodward, Graham Frank 7:41:39 (36,531)
Woodward, Keiron 3:50:50 (8,386)
Woodward, Matt Alan 5:43:39 (32,733)
Woodward, Matthew S 3:58:40 (10,613)
Woodward, Michael 5:00:45 (26,600)
Woodward, Peter G 3:17:39 (2,732)
Woodward, Philip 5:17:53 (29,523)
Woodward, William Geoffrey 3:55:47 (9,711)
Wool, Simon 3:23:06 (3,305)
Woolacott, Troy 3:49:36 (8,115)
Woolcock, Graham John 4:28:56 (18,660)
Wooldridge, Tim 5:50:21 (33,369)
Wooler, Grant I 3:50:36 (8,332)
Woolf, Mark J 3:01:57 (1,254)
Woolf, Philip 4:09:59 (13,471)
Woolford, Edward 4:37:17 (20,813)
Woolford, James 4:51:11 (24,346)
Woolgar, Terry Adrian 4:07:13 (12,755)
Woolgrove, David 4:52:12 (24,600)
Woollacott, Andrew 3:42:23 (6,577)
Woollacott, Norman 5:10:37 (28,351)
Woolland, Peter Ian 5:53:30 (33,613)
Woollard, Alastair 3:36:58 (5,558)
Woollard, Justin D 3:58:45 (10,644)
Woollard, Paul 5:05:05 (27,382)
Woollard, Tom 3:51:59 (8,654)
Woollard, Tom 5:10:19 (28,294)
Wooller, John Andrew 4:32:00 (19,436)
Woolley, Alan Norman 4:42:30 (22,141)
Woolley, Andrew 3:10:01 (1,907)
Woolley, Anthony J 5:10:18 (28,288)
Woolley, Paul Graham 7:44:04 (36,543)
Woolley, Paul S 3:23:14 (3,328)
Woollon, Andy Clifford 4:14:45 (14,726)
Woolner, John P 3:57:50 (10,337)
Woolnough, Alexander 4:31:59 (19,428)
Woolridge, Mark James 4:36:28 (20,591)
Woolridge, Stephen J 3:50:10 (8,242)
Woolstenholmes, Peter L 5:23:55 (30,464)
Woolven, Adrian D 3:29:21 (4,295)
Woolway, Thomas 3:09:32 (1,862)
Wootten, Paul Glyn 4:15:04 (14,802)
Wootton, Antony S 5:21:17 (30,041)
Wootton, Shaun 3:26:26 (3,797)
Wootton, Terence E 5:21:55 (30,132)
Worboys, Daniel Michael 4:06:43 (12,630)
Worfolk, Simon G 4:17:50 (15,532)
Work, William R 3:13:39 (2,274)
Workman, Richard 5:02:07 (26,871)
Worley, Sam 4:11:33 (13,863)
Worley, Steven R 4:13:24 (14,335)
Worner, Tom 4:25:15 (17,586)
Wornham, Daniel 3:42:47 (6,654)
Worrall, Chris W 3:07:30 (1,652)
Worrall, John Nigel 4:46:28 (23,159)
Worrell, Glen Paul 4:13:23 (14,333)
Worsdell, Philip John 4:43:29 (22,367)
Worsey, Andrew N 5:45:57 (32,947)
Worsley, Gary P 3:05:51 (1,523)
Worsley, Jason 3:43:17 (6,741)
Worsley, Olly 4:01:38 (11,402)
Worsley, Philip James 4:24:44 (17,450)
Worth, Gary James 4:22:49 (16,944)
Worth, Laurence 4:10:58 (13,703)
Worth, Melvin 4:25:16 (17,593)
Worton, Chris 3:29:25 (4,306)
Wotton, Kevin 2:55:38 (780)
Wotton, Mark A 4:10:21 (13,556)
Wragg, David Andrew 3:58:46 (10,649)
Wray, Lewis 3:25:36 (3,666)
Wreford, David 4:11:53 (13,950)
Wrench, James Ross Edwin 3:07:17 (1,630)
Wrenn, Graham P 3:56:09 (9,822)
Wriedt, Erik 4:15:34 (14,919)
Wright, Alan 4:24:54 (17,490)
Wright, Alex Stanley 5:45:04 (32,876)
Wright, Alexander G 2:55:24 (767)
Wright, Allan Albert 5:54:02 (33,646)
Wright, Andrew John 4:51:23 (24,394)
Wright, Andrew Mark 4:26:56 (18,062)
Wright, Andrew William 4:28:05 (18,383)
Wright, Ben 4:21:52 (16,660)
Wright, Benjamin A 4:22:11 (16,757)
Wright, Brendan 3:15:57 (2,549)
Wright, Brian Ian 4:10:56 (13,695)
Wright, Bryn 3:44:36 (7,014)
Wright, Chris W 5:34:54 (31,868)
Wright, Daniel James 3:29:30 (4,320)
Wright, David 3:22:59 (3,292)
Wright, David 4:39:54 (21,484)
Wright, David A 4:58:35 (26,112)
Wright, David Charles 3:24:08 (3,455)
Wright, David J 4:52:16 (24,619)
Wright, David K 5:29:26 (31,214)

Wright, David Peter....................3:59:16 (10,799)
Wright, Edward....................4:06:10 (12,490)
Wright, Gary....................5:31:24 (31,464)
Wright, George Graham....................6:11:28 (34,719)
Wright, Ian....................4:34:49 (20,198)
Wright, Ian Michael....................4:17:53 (15,543)
Wright, James....................3:48:25 (7,829)
Wright, James....................3:57:48 (10,331)
Wright, James Mackenzie....................4:56:10 (25,572)
Wright, James W....................4:09:53 (13,437)
Wright, Jason....................6:08:11 (34,565)
Wright, Jason Marc....................4:16:00 (15,026)
Wright, John....................5:25:45 (30,741)
Wright, John Edward Denham....3:55:36 (9,636)
Wright, John Henry....................4:30:58 (19,209)
Wright, John King....................4:00:12 (11,031)
Wright, Jonathan....................4:34:26 (20,104)
Wright, Ken....................6:19:07 (35,086)
Wright, Kieren William....................4:22:58 (16,977)
Wright, Marcus J....................5:23:07 (30,323)
Wright, Mark....................5:13:26 (28,832)
Wright, Mark A....................2:48:08 (419)
Wright, Mark G....................3:53:04 (8,941)
Wright, Mark Victor....................4:28:01 (18,371)
Wright, Matt....................3:58:46 (10,649)
Wright, Matt....................4:44:58 (22,759)
Wright, Matthew....................4:07:12 (12,749)
Wright, Matthew J....................4:23:15 (17,034)
Wright, Matthew John....................3:44:53 (7,075)
Wright, Matthew Paul....................5:01:12 (26,680)
Wright, Nathan....................3:54:31 (9,331)
Wright, Nicholas James....................3:58:34 (10,584)
Wright, Nick....................3:40:18 (6,197)
Wright, Nick....................4:34:59 (20,228)
Wright, Nigel....................6:12:37 (34,789)
Wright, Paul Benjaman....................3:50:38 (8,343)
Wright, Paul Richard....................3:54:33 (9,340)
Wright, Paul S....................4:20:04 (16,126)
Wright, Peter George....................5:46:54 (33,040)
Wright, Phil....................6:23:56 (35,274)
Wright, Phillip J....................6:00:14 (34,078)
Wright, Robert....................4:41:53 (21,989)
Wright, Sam....................4:23:13 (17,027)
Wright, Scott....................4:06:05 (12,472)
Wright, Selwyn....................4:57:38 (25,890)
Wright, Simon Paul....................4:49:22 (23,886)
Wright, Stephen....................4:53:42 (24,973)
Wright, Steve....................5:47:57 (33,133)
Wright, Tim....................4:23:19 (17,049)
Wright, Timothy....................4:35:41 (20,387)
Wriglesworth, John....................3:22:10 (3,206)
Wriglesworth, Nathan C....................4:06:44 (12,635)
Wrigley, Jack Hamish....................3:33:37 (4,989)
Wrigley, Jonathan....................4:44:03 (22,516)
Wrigley, Stephen J....................2:53:50 (659)
Wroe, Christopher Paul....................5:25:01 (30,628)
Wroth, David William....................4:37:34 (20,900)
Wrottesley, Michael G....................3:58:43 (10,631)
Wuestemann, Jochem....................3:45:56 (7,295)
Wuillemin, Roland-Camille....................5:05:56 (27,519)
Wullt, Johan....................4:23:21 (17,060)
Wulwick, Danny....................4:50:08 (24,078)
Wyatt, Andy John....................3:31:53 (4,722)
Wyatt, Bill....................6:07:04 (34,510)
Wyatt, Danny....................3:18:49 (2,855)
Wyatt, Darren....................3:23:56 (3,426)
Wyatt, Grant....................3:57:59 (10,373)
Wyatt, Martin Joseph....................4:07:46 (12,900)
Wyatt, Rick....................3:24:04 (3,446)
Wyatt, Robin Francis....................5:43:04 (32,673)
Wybrow, Luke James....................5:14:57 (29,059)
Wycherley, Paul Geoffrey....................5:17:21 (29,452)
Wyeth, Andy Frank....................4:08:49 (13,169)
Wyeth, Richard....................4:21:20 (16,500)
Wylde, Matt Graham....................5:33:21 (31,700)
Wylie, David A....................4:58:12 (26,012)
Wylie, Mark Christopher....................4:44:25 (22,621)
Wylie, Stephen F....................3:55:53 (9,745)
Wyllie, David Stuart....................3:55:17 (9,556)
Wyllie, Stuart D....................3:53:23 (9,024)
Wyndham, John Paul....................4:46:38 (23,217)
Wynn, David....................4:58:57 (26,203)
Wynn, John....................4:27:54 (18,339)
Wynne, David John....................3:58:19 (10,499)
Wynne-Griffith, David Charles....3:23:08 (3,312)
Wypior, Klaus....................3:51:23 (8,512)
Wyre, Adam J....................3:26:10 (3,765)
Wyse, James....................6:05:42 (34,432)
Wysocki, René....................4:09:04 (13,224)
Wysocki-Jones, Simon J....................4:35:07 (20,257)
Wyss, Stephen Peter....................3:38:31 (5,849)
Wyszynski, Mark Andrew....................3:25:48 (3,704)
Xavier, Jamie....................4:08:31 (13,090)
Xavier, José....................3:59:14 (10,791)
Xenophontos, Chris....................4:14:48 (14,742)
Yabe, Hiroo....................5:45:38 (32,921)
Yadave, Rush....................3:30:22 (4,480)
Yale, Wayne M....................5:13:15 (28,812)
Yan, Christian....................3:57:13 (10,161)
Yang, In Kyun....................4:30:22 (19,058)
Yardley, Chris Martyn....................4:12:40 (14,143)
Yare, Graham George....................3:37:37 (5,695)
Yarnell, John E....................3:13:11 (2,210)
Yarnold, Roger D....................5:44:18 (32,796)
Yassin, Ben Adam....................5:17:55 (29,534)
Yassin, Gareth Isaac....................5:17:55 (29,534)
Yates, Alan....................3:30:28 (4,495)
Yates, Andrew F....................3:27:25 (3,947)
Yates, Andrew J....................2:57:53 (945)
Yates, Brian S....................3:06:05 (1,540)
Yates, Craig P....................3:47:15 (7,586)
Yates, Greg Charles....................5:36:22 (32,042)
Yates, Jason P....................3:55:43 (9,677)
Yates, Rich....................5:25:36 (30,709)
Yates, Robert W....................3:28:35 (4,160)
Yates, Tom Richard....................3:28:02 (4,058)
Yates, Tyrone....................5:15:11 (29,098)
Yates, William N....................4:41:30 (21,893)
Yau, Kwi Wing....................4:50:03 (24,059)
Yau, Wai Lam....................4:28:20 (18,465)
Yeaman, Anthony....................4:37:05 (20,768)
Yeaman, William Harper....................5:48:40 (33,214)
Yeardley, James....................4:09:21 (13,296)
Yeats, Allan P....................6:30:47 (35,528)
Yee, Jeffrey Cheze Hui....................5:43:43 (32,746)
Yeldham, Ian Joseph....................5:14:00 (28,925)
Yellappa, Krishna....................5:18:13 (29,576)
Yendell, Richard Alexander....................3:22:47 (3,268)
Yeneralski, David N....................3:35:45 (5,367)
Yeo, Nicholas....................4:14:33 (14,665)
Yeoman, Keith Alfred....................5:07:20 (27,777)
Yeoman, Paul James....................4:05:48 (12,412)
Yeomans, Andy J....................5:14:33 (28,994)
Yeomans, Richard J....................4:32:07 (19,464)
Yeowell, Andrew....................4:26:50 (18,034)
Yip, Gwan....................3:55:11 (9,523)
Yoann, Ajas....................4:30:18 (19,044)
York, Graham....................3:36:40 (5,508)
York, Philip Andrew....................3:59:58 (10,980)
York, Simon J....................4:34:30 (20,121)
Yorke, Chris....................3:09:44 (1,884)
Yorke, Stuart Barrington....................5:13:54 (28,909)
Yoshida, Christopher....................4:30:41 (19,144)
Youlden, Luke....................4:29:21 (18,763)
Youle, Nicholas Paul....................3:44:24 (6,968)
Youle, Richard....................3:30:42 (4,529)
Youll, Gavin....................3:17:14 (2,687)
Young, Aaron....................3:05:18 (1,484)
Young, Adam Leslie....................4:00:11 (11,025)
Young, Alastair....................3:49:47 (8,163)
Young, Andrew....................4:20:35 (16,287)
Young, Andrew James....................5:43:00 (32,665)
Young, Andy....................4:27:07 (18,127)
Young, Andy W....................5:08:58 (28,037)
Young, Christopher Edward....................5:05:27 (27,440)
Young, Colin Richard....................4:09:53 (13,437)
Young, Gary....................4:25:36 (17,690)
Young, Gavin Stuart....................3:57:42 (10,297)
Young, George Alfred....................4:08:55 (13,188)
Young, Ian....................4:01:47 (11,443)
Young, Ian....................5:48:12 (33,160)
Young, James....................4:23:04 (16,999)
Young, James Michael....................3:39:43 (6,081)
Young, Jonathan James....................4:45:05 (22,796)
Young, Julian....................4:16:40 (15,209)
Young, Justin M....................2:54:10 (679)
Young, Mark....................4:03:50 (11,933)
Young, Mark....................4:55:54 (25,513)
Young, Martin G....................4:17:13 (15,354)
Young, Merrick....................5:18:16 (29,587)
Young, Mickey....................4:44:57 (22,755)
Young, Neil James....................3:12:13 (2,108)
Young, Neil Robert....................4:20:44 (16,347)
Young, Nicolas Kingston....................5:19:31 (29,775)
Young, Paul A....................4:49:13 (23,852)
Young, Robert James....................4:02:51 (11,688)
Young, Robin David....................4:41:55 (21,998)
Young, Scott John Alexander......4:33:04 (19,720)
Young, Shaun David....................4:41:00 (21,771)
Young, Simon Alexander....................5:04:31 (27,280)
Young, Stephen A....................4:15:38 (14,933)
Young, Stephen Alexander....................5:31:20 (31,454)
Young, Tim....................3:40:39 (6,270)
Young, William....................7:11:17 (36,324)
Younge, Steven Michael....................3:32:03 (4,749)
Youngs, Richard....................3:56:05 (9,807)
Youngson, Robert....................3:17:37 (2,727)
Yssennagger, Paul....................5:13:14 (28,808)
Yule, Kieran....................6:42:35 (35,851)
Yule, Michael A....................3:34:34 (5,166)
Zaccone, Domenico Paolo....................3:35:50 (5,380)
Zack, Philip....................5:37:40 (32,179)
Zago, Marco....................4:06:01 (12,460)
Zajaczkowski, Janusz A....................5:13:58 (28,919)
Zakrzewski, Matthew....................4:01:12 (11,298)
Zaldua, Javier....................3:34:30 (5,154)
Zaman, Arif....................5:13:53 (28,904)
Zamarriego, Emilio....................3:31:38 (4,688)
Zammit, Kevin....................2:46:07 (362)
Zamora, Eusebio Martin....................5:23:31 (30,388)
Zane, Stefano....................3:40:30 (6,241)
Zanon, Gaetano....................6:04:35 (34,354)
Zanovello, Natale....................4:39:18 (21,329)
Zanusso, Giovanni....................3:16:11 (2,570)
Zaranko, Tadeusz....................2:53:47 (654)
Zarri, Michael....................5:24:22 (30,535)
Zawadzki, Sam....................4:40:25 (21,617)
Zdrzalka, Nick....................3:43:10 (6,727)
Zeffert, Jonathan....................4:05:03 (12,220)
Zeh, Peter....................3:51:00 (8,423)
Zeifman, Clifford....................5:14:33 (28,994)
Zelenov, Sergey....................4:06:57 (12,702)
Zellick, Adam....................3:58:57 (10,704)
Zetterlund, Roger....................4:13:09 (14,275)
Zettler, Helmut....................3:29:03 (4,238)
Zimmerman, Paul....................3:52:51 (8,883)
Zinno, Salvatore....................3:22:20 (3,220)
Zoboky, Gary....................4:27:02 (18,087)
Zoccatelli, Alberto....................3:31:04 (4,589)
Zuccarelli, Fabio....................3:57:29 (10,225)
Zucconi, Doug Spencer....................5:00:26 (26,543)
Zuliani, Bruno....................4:13:43 (14,436)
Zurita, Javier....................3:36:39 (5,505)
Zwaal, Frank....................4:23:45 (17,181)
Zwane, Andrew....................5:04:23 (27,254)
Zweck, Dean Nicholas....................3:29:25 (4,306)
Zweck, Matthew....................5:20:09 (29,872)

FEMALE RUNNERS

Aagesen, Helle Vestergren....................3:51:31 (8,541)
Aalders, Vicki....................4:42:23 (22,108)
Aaron, Kasey....................7:10:03 (36,308)
Aarons, Gabrielle....................5:38:17 (32,235)
Abate, Sian G....................3:15:22 (2,481)
Abbey, Claire....................5:01:42 (26,792)
Abbott, Angeline Rose....................4:48:02 (23,554)
Abbott, Janet Elizabeth....................5:00:56 (26,639)
Abbott, Joanne....................3:44:05 (6,896)
Abbott, Suzanne Elisabeth....................5:32:10 (31,559)
Abe, Tomoko....................3:30:48 (4,548)
Abela, Cheryl....................4:24:22 (17,346)
Abgrall, Francine....................3:32:01 (4,740)
Abiker, Kathleen Anne....................6:06:47 (34,496)
Abitova, Inga....................2:22:19 (25)
Ablett, Sue....................4:53:49 (24,998)
Abouzeid, Sarah L....................3:56:14 (9,853)
Abrahams, Charlotte....................3:54:42 (9,387)
Abreu, Caron Louise....................5:11:11 (28,431)
Abse, Ania....................4:37:58 (20,982)

Achilleos, Chrystalla 4:34:31 (20,124)
Ackermann, Nicola Jane 4:11:01 (13,720)
Ackland-Snow, Sonia 4:59:07 (26,242)
Ackrell, Kirsty Ann 4:51:47 (24,488)
Acons, Georgina 4:13:03 (14,254)
Acton, Carolyn Clare 4:58:14 (26,019)
Adam, Claire 4:51:53 (24,519)
Adames, Alexandra 4:30:03 (18,987)
Adams, Catherine St Hilaire 3:55:58 (9,772)
Adams, Cheryl Jane 3:47:12 (7,576)
Adams, Christina June 4:46:04 (23,050)
Adams, Clare L 3:27:20 (3,928)
Adams, Denise 5:26:34 (30,848)
Adams, Emma-Jane 5:16:42 (29,337)
Adams, Fiona 4:46:00 (23,024)
Adams, Jacqueline 4:42:45 (22,203)
Adams, Jennifer 5:28:21 (31,069)
Adams, Jennifer Marie 6:03:36 (34,296)
Adams, Julie Patricia 4:22:36 (16,875)
Adams, Karen 6:10:38 (34,686)
Adams, Kay 4:08:27 (13,067)
Adams, Lisa Anne 4:43:24 (22,347)
Adams, Lynette 5:03:14 (27,065)
Adams, Natalie Louise 4:13:32 (14,378)
Adams, Nicholas C 3:43:45 (6,813)
Adams, Pam I 4:28:22 (18,472)
Adams, Polly H 3:18:04 (2,775)
Adams, Ruth E 5:27:03 (30,913)
Adams, Samantha Jessa 3:45:21 (7,174)
Adams, Stephanie A 5:22:01 (30,148)
Adams, Victoria Jane 4:40:12 (21,538)
Adams, Victoria Jane 4:59:34 (26,356)
Adcock, Katie Anne 4:53:48 (24,991)
Adcock, Katie Louise 5:52:19 (33,522)
Adcock, Miranda J 3:43:49 (6,835)
Adcock, Sarah Louise 4:17:38 (15,482)
Addison, Kate Gentila 5:12:03 (28,572)
Addison, Stephanie Claire 3:54:59 (9,474)
Addy, Megan Elizabeth 4:53:12 (24,847)
Addyman, Katherine Sophie 5:02:20 (26,912)
Adebola, Victoria 5:09:28 (28,136)
Adere, Berhane 2:33:46 (98)
Adey, Maria Louise 4:08:37 (13,122)
Adie, Gemma Louise 5:16:39 (29,331)
Adkins, Diane Judith 5:00:50 (26,617)
Adkins, Jennifer Audrey Susan 5:01:15 (26,694)
Adkins, Lorraine R 5:28:49 (31,130)
Afshari-Mehr, Angelica 7:00:03 (36,189)
Ager, Hayley June 4:35:57 (20,466)
Agnew, Angela A 6:36:05 (35,677)
Ahmed, Shehneela Jabeen 5:48:26 (33,187)
Ahnien, Marie-Claire 4:46:29 (23,164)
Ainley, Hannah 5:30:35 (31,369)
Ainscough, Cher 4:35:46 (20,410)
Ainsworth, Lisa Terri 6:43:31 (35,875)
Ainsworth, Pat Hazel 6:54:24 (36,094)
Aitken, Katharine Louise 4:37:01 (20,749)
Aitken, Nicola A 3:13:16 (2,219)
Akaba, Yukiko 2:24:55 (35)
Akehurst De Visme, Oriana 3:58:48 (10,661)
Akinlanon, Ravindra R 5:51:15 (33,444)
Alanis Marcos, Alejandra 4:23:52 (17,205)
Alatriste, Gabriela 4:03:04 (11,743)
Albaz, Sophie 4:53:36 (24,941)
Albutt, Denise 5:48:08 (33,154)
Alcock, Elizabeth Margaret H 4:01:43 (11,415)
Alden, Polly 5:13:27 (28,837)
Alder, Kathleen 6:04:46 (34,367)
Alderman, Pauline Margaret 4:03:25 (11,823)
Alderton, Ann 5:25:30 (30,691)
Alderton, Emily 5:02:12 (26,890)
Aldous, Caroline Philippa 5:49:14 (33,258)
Aldren, Pamela A 4:26:11 (17,868)
Aldrich, Clare 4:06:46 (12,645)
Aldrich, Tina 5:15:01 (29,069)
Aldridge, Katherine S 3:13:38 (2,270)
Alexander, Caroline Sara 6:38:14 (35,732)
Alexander, Fiona 4:51:49 (24,497)
Alexander, Helen Alexis 4:42:26 (22,124)
Alexander, Laura Jayne 4:11:07 (13,748)
Alexander, Samantha 4:36:04 (20,495)
Alexander, Victoria Ailita 3:57:00 (10,089)
Alflatt, Melanie Ann 5:25:54 (30,766)
Alford, Clare Evelyn 4:47:29 (23,406)
Alford, Deborah Jane 5:20:32 (29,933)
Alford, Leonora 6:52:50 (36,071)
Alford, Pippa Louise 3:34:30 (5,154)
Alford, Robyn Katie 5:23:16 (30,349)
Ali, Farrah 5:28:52 (31,133)
Ali, Yasmin 5:54:58 (33,713)
Alison, Catherine 3:50:36 (8,332)
Allan, Jane Lois 6:09:00 (34,619)
Allard, Michelle Joanna 4:45:29 (22,880)
Allcock, Lucy Jane 4:54:19 (25,137)
Alldis, Lyndsay Jane 4:58:35 (26,112)
Allen, Alice Elisabeth 4:01:50 (11,455)
Allen, Angela May 4:50:52 (24,262)
Allen, Angela Rachel 5:16:59 (29,383)
Allen, Anouska Suzanne 4:26:08 (17,852)
Allen, Carrie 4:33:51 (19,953)
Allen, Clare Elizabeth 5:15:47 (29,196)
Allen, Crystal Louise 4:43:20 (22,325)
Allen, Elaine M 4:40:41 (21,687)
Allen, Elizabeth A 4:27:26 (18,213)
Allen, Emily Kate 4:33:33 (19,867)
Allen, Georgina 3:43:58 (6,871)
Allen, Heather 4:13:00 (14,239)
Allen, Heather 5:22:50 (30,278)
Allen, Hilary Elizabeth 4:38:12 (21,029)
Allen, Jenny H 5:51:44 (33,486)
Allen, Joy 4:06:27 (12,557)
Allen, Louise Frances 5:05:51 (27,504)
Allen, Mary 4:43:14 (22,307)
Allen, Megan Laura 5:19:07 (29,721)
Allen, Rachel Phoebe 3:46:24 (7,397)
Allen, Sam 4:20:39 (16,320)
Allen, Sophie Roxanne 5:57:10 (33,874)
Allen, Valerie Jane 5:38:50 (32,294)
Allenby-Dilley, Nicky 5:36:47 (32,080)
Allford, Alison 4:39:37 (21,418)
Allison, Celia 4:30:08 (19,010)
Allison, Commeletia 4:32:16 (19,505)
Allison, Fiona M 4:36:02 (20,485)
Allison, Karen L 4:44:10 (22,553)
Allister, Rossie J 3:34:41 (5,189)
Allon Smith, Beverley 4:54:49 (25,261)
Allpress, Faith Helen Louise 5:15:44 (29,187)
Allsop, Karen Anne 5:26:11 (30,799)
Allum, Angela 4:22:32 (16,857)
Allum, Julie 4:58:09 (26,004)
Allum, Lucinda 4:41:05 (21,790)
Almond, Annemarie 3:38:31 (5,849)
Almond, Lucy A 4:41:14 (21,827)
Alphonso, Annabel 4:11:40 (13,898)
Alson, Kirsty Helen 4:51:37 (24,443)
Alterauge, Jutta 4:35:43 (20,392)
Aluko, Kehinde 6:23:20 (35,254)
Alvarez, Samantha S 2:57:25 (892)
Alves, Fatima 5:39:19 (32,332)
Alves De Sousa, Sarah J 4:12:14 (14,039)
Amarasinghe, Neluka 5:17:43 (29,503)
Amargil, Geraldine 4:49:21 (23,884)
Ambrose, Sarah Jane 5:23:11 (30,337)
Ambrosius, Marita 4:54:52 (25,272)
Amend, Samantha 2:47:01 (388)
Amiss, Tina 6:45:00 (35,909)
Amobi, Dinzi 6:41:59 (35,834)
Amos, Claire Rosemary 4:02:41 (11,646)
Amos, Donna 4:07:36 (12,855)
Amy, Chris M 4:13:30 (14,365)
Andersen, Brigitte 4:42:16 (22,084)
Anderson, Anna C 5:09:02 (28,054)
Anderson, Carmel 5:37:18 (32,144)
Anderson, Celeste Marie 6:24:06 (35,282)
Anderson, Charmain Amanda 5:37:43 (32,183)
Anderson, Donna Tamsin 5:30:27 (31,345)
Anderson, Elizabeth 4:07:08 (12,741)
Anderson, Hazel Ann 3:24:11 (3,468)
Anderson, Kim Dawn 7:36:31 (36,498)
Anderson, Lisa 4:15:16 (14,850)
Anderson, Nicola Anne 6:27:35 (35,407)
Anderson, Paula 7:00:50 (36,204)
Anderson, Rhona M 3:08:22 (1,735)
Anderson, Ruth 5:59:41 (34,035)
Anderson, Sarah Josephine 5:00:57 (26,643)
Anderson, Sevren 5:02:00 (26,840)
Anderson, Shirley H 3:30:02 (4,425)
Anderson, Tamla 5:12:03 (28,572)
Anderson, Tammy C 4:08:24 (13,059)
Anderson, Tracey M 4:50:04 (24,064)
Anderson, Wendy Lou 5:17:40 (29,492)
Anderson-Gordon, Sarah 6:15:21 (34,904)
Andersson-Skog, Christina E 3:59:47 (10,942)
Andow, Teresa Z 4:09:25 (13,320)
Andrew, Amy Elizabeth 4:37:31 (20,888)
Andrew, Angela Louise 5:23:35 (30,402)
Andrew, Gabi 5:54:51 (33,701)
Andrew, Sharon 3:43:46 (6,821)
Andrew-Power, Kirstie Helen 5:20:47 (29,974)
Andrews, Amy Louise 5:11:16 (28,447)
Andrews, Angela 4:12:15 (14,045)
Andrews, Annalisa 4:30:19 (19,051)
Andrews, Esta Louise 6:08:16 (34,568)
Andrews, Henrietta 4:11:45 (13,922)
Andrews, Judy 6:16:16 (34,933)
Andrews, Julie 3:35:27 (5,313)
Andrews, Kate 6:04:44 (34,364)
Andrews, Rachel 5:19:36 (29,793)
Andrews, Sarah Ann 4:22:58 (16,977)
Andrews, Suzanne 4:45:51 (22,990)
Andrews, Tracey Ann 4:33:36 (19,893)
Andrews-King, Angela Teresa 4:38:41 (21,165)
Andriano, Raffaella 4:13:59 (14,501)
Aneck-Hahn, Claire Elizabeth 3:57:09 (10,141)
Angel, Melanie R 4:17:58 (15,569)
Angela, Cudmore 3:57:29 (10,225)
Angell, Harriet 4:49:41 (23,974)
Angilley, Jayne 3:45:36 (7,228)
Angus, Dawn 4:50:25 (24,146)
Annan, Catherine 3:35:52 (5,392)
Ansbro, Cassandra Dawn 5:07:35 (27,828)
Anstead, Sam 4:47:45 (23,479)
Anstee, Jennifer 3:08:45 (1,788)
Anstee, Jessica 3:37:34 (5,681)
Antcliffe, Emily J 2:59:23 (1,094)
Ante-Bennett, Primrose 5:56:48 (33,851)
Anthony, Helen M 3:37:02 (5,570)
Antoniazzi, Daniela 5:31:15 (31,439)
Antoniazzi, Gina 4:24:12 (17,287)
Antonsen, Sigrid 4:19:13 (15,903)
Appleby, Gayle 4:28:04 (18,381)
Appleton, Emma Jane 4:30:39 (19,135)
Appleton, Emma L 3:43:32 (6,781)
Appleton, Nicola Joy 3:38:13 (5,805)
Apps, Emma M 5:02:13 (26,893)
Ara, Farhana 6:25:53 (35,345)
Aras, Yesim 5:33:22 (31,703)
Arch, Jodie E 6:03:51 (34,312)
Archbold, Karen J 3:24:16 (3,480)
Archer, Amanda Jayne 6:28:03 (35,424)
Archer, Catriona M 3:26:56 (3,865)
Archer, Karen 3:50:36 (8,332)
Archer, Nicky 2:42:22 (260)
Arens, Katrina 4:22:53 (16,959)
Argent, Kate 4:24:58 (17,509)
Aries, Felicity J 5:10:03 (28,247)
Arif, Misbah 5:46:37 (33,015)
Arkless, Gillian Mary 6:04:56 (34,381)
Armand Smith, Celia 6:31:06 (35,538)
Armand Smith, Josephine Juliana 6:31:05 (35,537)
Armani, Valentina 5:44:13 (32,788)
Armes, Sharon 6:05:49 (34,442)
Armfield, Joanne 4:58:07 (25,996)
Armfield, Lynda 5:47:14 (33,072)
Armitage, Jocelyn 3:50:18 (8,270)
Armitage, Louise 5:55:04 (33,725)
Armitage, Rachael 3:51:04 (8,440)
Armitage, Serena 4:30:32 (19,098)
Armour, Susan 5:15:03 (29,076)
Armstrong, Andrea 5:38:45 (32,286)
Armstrong, Jacqueline M 4:41:04 (21,784)
Armstrong, Kathleen Elizabeth Joy 5:17:30 (29,471)
Armstrong, Kim 7:42:04 (36,534)
Armstrong, Louise 5:50:52 (33,418)
Armstrong, Pauline 3:59:20 (10,818)
Armstrong, Rosemary F 4:40:40 (21,683)
Armstrong-Smith, Linsey Kim 4:28:49 (18,617)
Arnardottir, Sigfrid Eik 4:53:48 (24,991)
Arnold, Hannah 5:06:54 (27,702)

Arnold, Katherine Louise............4:43:27 (22,359)
Arnold, Lori B.............5:11:26 (28,471)
Arnold, Lorna 5:05:42 (27,482)
Arnold, Lucy.............4:51:57 (24,538)
Arnold, Sally.............6:26:12 (35,356)
Arnold Masters, Katrina Louise ..6:11:23 (34,714)
Arnott, Leah.............4:43:40 (22,410)
Arnott, Tracy Eileen.............5:55:47 (33,774)
Arregui, Begoña.............4:10:41 (13,635)
Arrigoni, Claire 4:08:51 (13,173)
Arrowsmith, Sarah Jane 5:36:31 (32,059)
Arrowsmith, Zoe.............4:56:22 (25,624)
Arscott, Lisa J.............6:59:09 (36,179)
Arthur, Jessica.............5:23:55 (30,464)
Arthur, Michelle.............5:06:34 (27,639)
Arthur, Rachel Claire 4:39:45 (21,447)
Arts, Catharina.............5:27:58 (31,024)
Asare, Alpana Pia.............4:38:21 (21,071)
Ash, Alexia.............4:09:18 (13,283)
Ashbridge, Louise Sarah.............4:52:13 (24,606)
Ashby, Jennifer D 3:48:05 (7,754)
Ashby, Lynne Anne 4:57:49 (25,928)
Ashcroft, Cheryl Marie 5:28:00 (31,029)
Ashdown, Philippa Louise 5:11:50 (28,528)
Ashdown, Polly J.............4:57:31 (25,864)
Ashe, Debby.............4:04:10 (12,002)
Ashe, Linda J.............4:18:40 (15,764)
Ashe, Nicola.............3:59:18 (10,813)
Ashford, Nadine 3:48:48 (7,927)
Ashley, Elizabeth Mary Christine 4:25:44 (17,732)
Ashman, Laura Suzanne.............4:35:33 (20,354)
Ashmore, Deborah J 4:25:00 (17,519)
Ashraf, Yasmin Ali 4:37:13 (20,798)
Ashton, Anne Elizabeth 4:15:36 (14,927)
Ashton, Ellen L 3:55:17 (9,556)
Ashton, Emma Victoria.............6:16:15 (34,930)
Ashton, Kirsty.............6:07:08 (34,516)
Ashton, Leila Jean 4:33:52 (19,959)
Ashworth, Diana N.............4:43:22 (22,339)
Ashworth, Vanessa.............6:29:44 (35,486)
Ashworth-Jones, Rosanna 5:45:49 (32,936)
Askew, Karyn Jane.............6:03:58 (34,322)
Aspey-Gay, Justine 5:24:12 (30,510)
Aspinall, Suzanne J 4:47:01 (23,315)
Asquier, Caroline 4:09:13 (13,266)
Assucena, Helen Assucena 3:37:13 (5,602)
Astall, Jenny.............4:49:08 (23,835)
Astill, Mandy.............4:46:56 (23,288)
Astles, Claudine.............6:52:43 (36,065)
Astley, Irene 4:48:15 (23,599)
Atherton, Karen L.............4:11:27 (13,835)
Atherton, Kathleen A.............4:00:04 (10,998)
Atherton, Louise.............4:42:34 (22,151)
Atkin, Anne Mary.............4:44:38 (22,682)
Atkinison, Alison J.............4:06:52 (12,680)
Atkins, Ann.............6:31:56 (35,562)
Atkins, Jane Elizabeth 4:13:58 (14,496)
Atkins, Pamela A.............4:38:01 (20,990)
Atkins, Sanae.............4:17:53 (15,543)
Atkins, Sarah 4:41:10 (21,815)
Atkinson, Elaine 5:01:44 (26,803)
Atkinson, Jane 5:29:41 (31,251)
Atkinson, Jill.............4:04:41 (12,122)
Atkinson, Louise Jayne 4:48:46 (23,736)
Atkinson, Lydia 4:27:15 (18,167)
Attelsey, Alexandra L 5:45:17 (32,892)
Attenborough, Lisa.............4:07:22 (12,791)
Attolico, Matilde.............6:47:50 (35,961)
Attree, Mandy J 3:57:47 (10,326)
Attrill, Patricia Ann 4:51:20 (24,381)
Attwell, Susannah K 3:39:53 (6,122)
Attwood, Kathy Sandra 4:00:09 (11,019)
Attwooll, Josephine 4:48:24 (23,638)
Audibert, Renée Pierre.............3:39:12 (5,981)
Augier, Aimée Natalie 4:27:40 (18,277)
Aurora, Saska.............5:56:50 (33,855)
Aussenberg, Glenda 8:56:38 (36,613)
Austin, Rebecca J.............6:24:33 (35,297)
Austin, Sara.............5:25:32 (30,699)
Austin, Sue.............4:51:10 (24,344)
Austin Harrison, Lisa Jadwiga 4:38:12 (21,029)
Austin-Olsen, Joanne Claire 5:23:52 (30,451)
Austreng, Melanie J.............3:38:00 (5,761)

Auton, Helen Jane 3:39:44 (6,084)
Avanzato, Jacqueline 6:35:02 (35,652)
Avari, Parizad.............4:53:59 (25,045)
Avdic, Aida.............6:04:14 (34,336)
Averill, Sharon Louise 4:09:45 (13,407)
Avery, Adele.............3:40:19 (6,202)
Avery, Melanie K.............3:35:54 (5,399)
Avis, Trudy Ann.............4:08:41 (13,140)
Avison, Michelle E.............5:41:08 (32,500)
Axtell, Elizabeth R.............6:19:39 (35,112)
Ayers, Samantha J.............3:27:00 (3,876)
Ayling, Angela Katherine.............4:38:11 (21,026)
Ayling, Lisa.............4:40:19 (21,579)
Ayling, Tracey Louise 5:52:57 (33,580)
Aylward, Sinead M.............5:25:57 (30,774)
Ayres, Emily 3:46:54 (7,512)
Ayriss, Fay.............5:16:36 (29,322)
Azam, Sadia.............5:11:03 (28,413)
Baboin, Helene.............5:27:34 (30,972)
Babynec, Denise A 4:47:32 (23,417)
Bacchi, Claudia.............4:07:51 (12,918)
Bachmann, Andrea.............4:06:25 (12,551)
Bach-Peterson, Kirsten.............5:09:32 (28,156)
Baci, Drilona.............4:32:33 (19,572)
Backhouse, Victoria J.............4:16:33 (15,181)
Backman, Elisabeth.............4:59:39 (26,370)
Bacon, Katie.............4:01:23 (11,332)
Bacon, Michelle Victoria 4:38:55 (21,235)
Bacon, Sharon Rose.............4:30:15 (19,035)
Bacon, Shenna 4:11:10 (13,762)
Baden, Kirsty L.............5:05:46 (27,487)
Badger, Angela 5:22:56 (30,298)
Badman, Helen 4:58:07 (25,996)
Baggott, Zoe.............4:50:03 (24,059)
Bagguley, Rebekah 5:12:16 (28,614)
Bagheri, Elizabeth Emma 5:52:09 (33,513)
Bahlmann-Boot, Roos.............4:14:59 (14,782)
Bahra, Ruby.............4:21:58 (16,695)
Bai, Xue 2:25:18 (39)
Bailey, Catherine Anne 5:23:02 (30,312)
Bailey, Catherine L.............4:41:26 (21,873)
Bailey, Claire 4:57:44 (25,918)
Bailey, Denise C.............3:22:28 (3,235)
Bailey, Helen 6:19:30 (35,100)
Bailey, Jennifer A.............6:10:03 (34,668)
Bailey, Jennifer Anne 5:40:53 (32,469)
Bailey, Julia 6:42:25 (35,848)
Bailey, Lesley Jane 4:47:33 (23,425)
Bailey, Marie-Clare 4:46:33 (23,180)
Bailey, Nicola.............5:00:44 (26,595)
Bailey, Sarah 4:20:12 (16,165)
Bailey, Sarah L.............3:02:22 (1,286)
Bailey, Thomas W.............3:39:29 (6,038)
Bailey-Gregory, Ebonee 4:42:59 (22,255)
Baillie, Britt A.............4:14:34 (14,674)
Baillie, Katie 4:58:31 (26,092)
Baillie, Philippa.............5:26:16 (30,813)
Baillie, Sarah 3:54:35 (9,347)
Bain, Alexandra.............3:58:29 (10,551)
Bain, Andrea.............3:57:42 (10,297)
Bain, Judy Ann 4:53:20 (24,882)
Bain, Suzanne.............5:21:33 (30,083)
Bainbridge, Kim Anne Emer.......3:39:53 (6,122)
Bainbridge, Shelley A 5:30:37 (31,376)
Baines, Nicola Elaine.............5:11:07 (28,423)
Bainton, Claire Michelle.............4:18:20 (15,668)
Baird, Kirsty.............3:43:01 (6,701)
Bajaj, Punam 4:18:20 (15,668)
Baker, Annette Frances.............5:13:53 (28,904)
Baker, Berenice Jane 7:12:54 (36,337)
Baker, Bridget D.............3:22:43 (3,261)
Baker, Catherine Elizabeth.........6:12:26 (34,778)
Baker, Cathy J.............3:53:44 (9,132)
Baker, Claire 4:10:50 (13,676)
Baker, Elaine Dawn.............5:59:23 (34,011)
Baker, Emily Jane 6:39:11 (35,756)
Baker, Heidi Thérèse.............5:52:11 (33,514)
Baker, Jan.............4:09:51 (13,431)
Baker, Jenny M.............4:26:44 (18,007)
Baker, Juliette Helen Barbara 3:56:18 (9,871)
Baker, Karen Marie 5:48:53 (33,231)
Baker, Kate.............5:09:11 (28,083)
Baker, Katie 5:18:21 (29,597)

Baker, Lisa Fay.............5:37:20 (32,149)
Baker, Paula Jane 5:20:14 (29,880)
Baker, Rachel Joy.............3:55:08 (9,513)
Baker, Rosemary.............4:25:06 (17,549)
Baker, Salima.............4:50:29 (24,158)
Baker, Sally H.............3:03:59 (1,388)
Baker, Sandra.............4:48:50 (23,758)
Baker, Vivien L.............4:43:50 (22,456)
Bakshi, Roshini.............4:49:03 (23,813)
Balaam, Gemma Michelle 5:35:27 (31,921)
Balderson, Wendy Louise 6:57:37 (36,151)
Baldwin, Charlotte 4:16:20 (15,120)
Baldwin, Gaynor Andrea 6:33:31 (35,611)
Baldwin, Jolene.............5:12:45 (28,692)
Baldwin, Rose.............4:14:36 (14,680)
Bales, Rowena J.............3:14:38 (2,402)
Bales, Stephanie M.............4:16:55 (15,275)
Ball, Angharad Morwen.............5:35:19 (31,906)
Ball, Ann Sandra 4:10:09 (13,512)
Ball, Jessica M.............3:58:18 (10,491)
Ball, Lorraine Michelle.............5:29:07 (31,165)
Ball, Shirley Gail.............3:59:32 (10,870)
Ball, Victoria Gemma 5:23:56 (30,474)
Ball, Victoria Mary 6:56:19 (36,135)
Ballantyne, Pauline 4:32:07 (19,464)
Ballard, Angela.............6:08:49 (34,603)
Ballard, Charlane 6:40:20 (35,799)
Ballard, Sacha.............5:19:25 (29,766)
Ballard, Wendy J.............5:29:33 (31,228)
Ballesteros, Adriana 3:50:55 (8,404)
Balls, Katie E.............6:23:13 (35,245)
Bambrough, Carol 4:31:43 (19,377)
Bancks, Lisa.............7:53:14 (36,572)
Bane, Christine M 5:33:32 (31,719)
Banfield, Malcolm John.............5:46:50 (33,033)
Bangs, Nichola Yvonne 5:20:15 (29,882)
Banks, Faye M.............3:02:26 (1,291)
Banks, Katherine A 5:06:06 (27,549)
Banks, Louise Elizabeth.............4:49:17 (23,870)
Banks, Rita S.............5:02:24 (26,927)
Banks, Robyn Lousie.............4:08:30 (13,085)
Banks, Sharon Dawn 4:03:47 (11,920)
Banks, Tracey Jane 4:31:50 (19,396)
Bannis, Josie 6:07:53 (34,556)
Bannister, Pippa 4:49:02 (23,809)
Bannng Boddy, Pamela.............4:31:29 (19,331)
Bannon, Maria 4:25:10 (17,566)
Banville, Elaine M 3:35:40 (5,356)
Banwait, Harjinder K 7:03:30 (36,232)
Banwell, Kirsty Anne 4:35:50 (20,430)
Banyard Smith, Elizabeth C.........4:12:33 (14,115)
Baptie, Jenny 6:54:16 (36,092)
Baptiste, Alana Aimée.............5:26:44 (30,868)
Barber, Emma J 5:20:05 (29,861)
Barber, Jenny Clare.............3:55:29 (9,611)
Barber, Lynne E.............4:58:18 (26,040)
Barbosa, Olga M.............4:04:33 (12,084)
Barbur, Felicity 4:47:21 (23,379)
Barby, Louise Elizabeth 5:18:14 (29,578)
Barclay, Jane.............4:21:58 (16,695)
Barclay, Julie 6:10:51 (34,693)
Barclay, Louise.............4:39:37 (21,418)
Barclay, Ulrika J.............4:34:50 (20,202)
Bardrick, Karen M.............4:58:29 (26,082)
Bardsley, Helen 5:07:28 (27,804)
Bardwell, Clare 6:48:51 (35,975)
Bardwell, Sharon.............3:48:32 (7,853)
Barfoot, Kim.............3:56:14 (9,853)
Barham, Abbi 5:12:26 (28,640)
Barke, Jill V.............6:03:25 (34,282)
Barker, Alison 4:56:16 (25,601)
Barker, Camilla.............6:00:46 (34,108)
Barker, Carmel M 3:40:36 (6,260)
Barker, Colette Louise Joan.........4:24:26 (17,370)
Barker, Consuelo Catherine 6:49:06 (35,980)
Barker, Gail Josephine 5:07:09 (27,745)
Barker, Helen 8:00:20 (36,589)
Barker, Jessica.............3:58:11 (10,449)
Barker, Katherine S.............3:43:03 (6,709)
Barker, Katie.............5:13:52 (28,902)
Barker, Kirsten.............4:14:41 (14,709)
Barker, Lindsay Sian 4:59:59 (26,448)
Barker, Louise 3:15:58 (2,550)

Barker, Mandy Jane......3:58:17 (10,484)
Barker, Melanie Lara......5:11:20 (28,455)
Barker, Paula Marie......4:43:25 (22,349)
Barker, Rosamund A......3:06:42 (1,585)
Barker, Suzanne......5:15:55 (29,213)
Barlow, Hazel Gillian......5:38:11 (32,225)
Barlow, Jo......4:47:56 (23,528)
Barlow, Mel......5:18:21 (29,597)
Barnard, Angela Christine......5:24:06 (30,494)
Barnard, Gilly......4:10:46 (13,658)
Barnard, Heidi......4:47:12 (23,343)
Barnard, Jennifer Ellen......3:29:24 (4,302)
Barnard, Nikki L......4:30:27 (19,075)
Barnbrook, Emma Louise......4:25:30 (17,661)
Barnecutt, Tracey Jane......4:58:37 (26,122)
Barnes, Alison......4:07:34 (12,851)
Barnes, Ann......6:32:22 (35,573)
Barnes, Anna Victoria......4:31:52 (19,402)
Barnes, Debra A......6:44:21 (35,894)
Barnes, Gillian Margaret......5:30:54 (31,404)
Barnes, Laura......4:55:11 (25,352)
Barnes, Sarah......6:41:41 (35,824)
Barnes, Tamsin......4:30:41 (19,144)
Barnes-Webb, Catherine......4:22:41 (16,897)
Barnett, Alison Fiona......4:38:31 (21,118)
Barnett, Cate......5:22:49 (30,274)
Barnett, Gemma L......3:23:14 (3,328)
Barnett, Kirsty G......3:49:03 (7,987)
Barnett, Loraine......4:56:46 (25,707)
Barnett, Sarah Louise......5:22:52 (30,286)
Barnett, Sharon R......3:47:45 (7,694)
Barneveld, Cheska K......4:48:14 (23,593)
Barns, Cristina......4:52:38 (24,718)
Barnwell, Hannah Kate......5:15:53 (29,208)
Baron, Stephanie......6:44:52 (35,902)
Baronet, Kerry......5:04:50 (27,339)
Barr, Alexandra C......5:51:10 (33,440)
Barr, Elizabeth......4:30:36 (19,125)
Barr, Evelyn MF......4:12:03 (13,997)
Barr, Helen M......3:44:12 (6,916)
Barr, Iva D......6:26:41 (35,372)
Barr, Sian Elizabeth......4:25:44 (17,732)
Barr, Victoria......4:59:31 (26,345)
Barraclough, Jill......3:49:04 (7,993)
Barratt, Karen Michelle......4:44:36 (22,670)
Barratt, Victoria C......3:19:51 (2,947)
Barrell, Jayne......4:39:16 (21,324)
Barrett, Amanda Jane......5:06:56 (27,710)
Barrett, Andrea......3:49:37 (8,122)
Barrett, Ann......6:18:06 (35,034)
Barrett, Charlotte......5:35:21 (31,912)
Barrett, Gabrielle......5:21:00 (30,006)
Barrett, Helen......5:01:37 (26,779)
Barrett, Louise......7:38:05 (36,508)
Barrett, Louise Rachel......4:14:59 (14,782)
Barrett, Maxine Elizabeth......4:28:55 (18,650)
Barrett, Samantha J......3:42:38 (6,616)
Barrett, Stephanie Ann......5:35:30 (31,927)
Barrett, Sylvia......5:00:37 (26,574)
Barrett, Vanessa Anne......3:49:57 (8,199)
Barrie, Yvonne......6:20:30 (35,147)
Barrington, Emma......6:17:25 (35,003)
Barron, Alexandra......4:06:12 (12,496)
Barron, Hayley R......3:46:41 (7,456)
Barron, Jane......4:45:02 (22,778)
Barron, Teresa......5:20:30 (29,928)
Barry, Deborah Ann......4:00:28 (11,111)
Barry, Julie......4:40:37 (21,674)
Barry, Juliet......5:35:59 (31,994)
Barry, Liza R......2:57:54 (949)
Barry, Mia-Louise......3:26:00 (3,731)
Barsby, Amanda Jayne......6:17:42 (35,017)
Barsby, Deborah Louise......4:57:52 (25,939)
Bartholomew, Anna L......4:45:21 (22,852)
Barthram, Julia......4:53:11 (24,845)
Bartlett, Amanda Jayne......4:28:43 (18,583)
Bartlett, Helen Cecilia......4:52:30 (24,685)
Bartlett, Jackie Anne......4:16:23 (15,135)
Bartlett, Jackie Ruth......3:56:41 (9,992)
Bartlett, Johanna Sarah......4:14:29 (14,643)
Bartlett, Michelle J......3:17:50 (2,747)
Bartmuss, Ute......3:45:05 (7,111)
Barton, Catherine Ann......4:38:27 (21,105)
Barton, Claire......5:25:18 (30,663)
Barton, Joan......5:11:58 (28,555)
Barton, Joanne......5:38:23 (32,251)
Barton, Julie Elizabeth......4:16:05 (15,047)
Barton, Kirsty Anne......4:45:42 (22,948)
Barton, Sally Kathleen......4:58:50 (26,173)
Barton, Susanne U......4:00:07 (11,011)
Bartram, Stella A......4:53:01 (24,800)
Barugh, Melanie......4:43:48 (22,441)
Barwell, Christina......6:27:42 (35,411)
Basarab, Veronica......4:22:43 (16,908)
Baseden, Candice......4:17:32 (15,452)
Bashford, Louise......5:05:36 (27,468)
Basquill, Victoria J......3:27:25 (3,947)
Bass, Jane D......3:39:07 (5,968)
Bass, Robyn......4:32:52 (19,661)
Bassett, Barbara A......4:34:14 (20,054)
Bassett, Nicola......5:36:59 (32,101)
Bassett, Sarah Jane......4:27:54 (18,339)
Bassom, Claire Louise......4:57:38 (25,890)
Batchelor, Pamela Ann......7:45:38 (36,549)
Bate, Nicola......5:46:38 (33,019)
Bateman, Joanne......5:02:50 (26,996)
Bateman, Penny Jane......5:15:52 (29,207)
Bateman, Sarah Jane......5:36:34 (32,064)
Bates, Katherine J......3:34:00 (5,057)
Bates, Katrina......4:35:19 (20,298)
Bates, Kim W......4:48:37 (23,699)
Bates, Pauline......4:32:35 (19,582)
Bates, Rachael Catherine......4:24:29 (17,384)
Bates, Rebecca Margaret......4:34:31 (20,124)
Bathia, Shreena......5:18:36 (29,636)
Bathurst, Alison M......4:54:59 (25,302)
Batman, Angela......5:29:59 (31,295)
Batten, Carina......5:17:52 (29,520)
Batten, Sophie......4:34:22 (20,085)
Batterham, Jennifer......4:29:07 (18,714)
Battson, Elaine C......3:49:20 (8,050)
Batty, Marguerite Aemelia......4:33:55 (19,972)
Battye, Georgie......5:42:11 (32,606)
Bauchop, Charlie......6:40:25 (35,802)
Bauduin, Dionne......6:52:18 (36,056)
Baulcombe, Harriet......3:52:33 (8,809)
Bawden, Johanna Elizabeth......4:20:13 (16,169)
Bax, Kristiina......5:59:03 (33,993)
Baxendale, Grace Majella......5:54:02 (33,646)
Baxter, Claire......4:20:07 (16,140)
Baxter, Clare......7:37:19 (36,506)
Baxter, Jane Elizabeth......5:14:58 (29,061)
Baxter, Lucinda......4:57:43 (25,912)
Baxter, Sarah L......3:10:57 (1,988)
Baxter, Tina M......4:35:43 (20,392)
Baxter, Vicky......4:57:19 (25,824)
Bayford, Georgina Louise......6:51:39 (36,029)
Bayford, Jill Louise......6:51:39 (36,029)
Bayle, Samantha......3:52:12 (8,706)
Bayless, Corrine......4:59:04 (26,230)
Bayley, Carol......6:35:49 (35,672)
Baylis, Kerri Ann......5:38:23 (32,251)
Baylis, Polly......4:36:05 (20,500)
Bayliss, Gina......5:59:04 (33,994)
Bayliss, Helen......4:39:06 (21,280)
Baysak, Yonca......4:11:01 (13,720)
Bazeley, Vicki Susan......5:42:08 (32,603)
Beach, Claire Joan......3:45:28 (7,201)
Beach, Natasha......4:49:33 (23,922)
Beadle, Catherine......5:50:55 (33,420)
Beadle, Deborah......4:26:09 (17,858)
Beagley, Sarah......4:09:29 (13,336)
Bealby, Anna......5:38:08 (32,219)
Beale, Nikki Mark......4:02:15 (11,547)
Beale, Sophie Julia......4:25:55 (17,790)
Beamish, Louise D'Ann......4:25:02 (17,531)
Bean, Beverley......4:57:07 (25,784)
Beanland, Sarah......5:25:38 (30,720)
Beard, Claire......5:11:50 (28,528)
Beard, Judith......4:10:28 (13,586)
Beardmore, Rachel A......4:04:44 (12,140)
Beardsell, Lisa M......5:11:08 (28,427)
Beardwell, Glenis......5:15:28 (29,138)
Beare, Melissa Louise......6:05:39 (34,427)
Bearman, Carly Louise......5:33:46 (31,741)
Bearsby, Teresa......6:11:42 (34,734)
Beasley, Jennifer Frances......4:47:17 (23,362)
Beatens, Julie D......6:39:30 (35,771)
Beaton, Pauline Barbara......5:56:55 (33,862)
Beattie, Sarah Jane......4:32:16 (19,505)
Beatty, Juliet L......3:18:15 (2,802)
Beaumont, Emma Louise......4:20:34 (16,281)
Beauregard, Robin......3:40:37 (6,265)
Beaven, Tabitha Jane Chloe......4:27:53 (18,335)
Beaven, Winnie......6:28:51 (35,459)
Beaver, Hayley Joanne......4:00:56 (11,231)
Beaver, Kelly......4:22:36 (16,875)
Bebbington, Elizabeth C......3:35:09 (5,265)
Beck, Helen L......3:24:55 (3,568)
Beck, Sarah......4:55:17 (25,378)
Becker, Naomi......5:56:25 (33,824)
Becker, Viktoria......6:13:27 (34,819)
Beckett, Kirstey......6:03:00 (34,251)
Beckitt, Kathryn A......4:36:28 (20,591)
Beckwith, Julie Linda......4:20:46 (16,362)
Beddall, Sarah Louise......4:15:30 (14,907)
Beddows, Marie Paula......4:06:49 (12,660)
Bedford, Caroline Jayne......6:26:53 (35,379)
Bedford, Joanne......7:18:40 (36,390)
Bedworth, Claire Louise......5:25:08 (30,645)
Beecher, Sarah......3:52:43 (8,849)
Beechinor, Georgina Anne......5:07:32 (27,819)
Beedie, Kelly L......7:28:02 (36,459)
Beedles, Jillian......6:07:11 (34,518)
Beer, Mandy......4:14:03 (14,520)
Beer, Rhiannon......5:58:53 (33,983)
Beerling, Julie......5:50:55 (33,420)
Beeson, Semirah......3:33:03 (4,901)
Beeston, Lizzie......4:09:22 (13,301)
Beet, Louise Claire......4:58:37 (26,122)
Begley, Elizabeth A......6:11:10 (34,706)
Begley, Lisa Carole......4:46:46 (23,242)
Begnor, Gill......4:54:36 (25,204)
Begum, Shajue......4:13:06 (14,263)
Behm, Amanda......3:58:53 (10,682)
Bekele, Bezunesh......2:23:17 (29)
Belcham, Kay......5:44:56 (32,863)
Belcher, Christine M......6:12:52 (34,798)
Belcher, Joanne......3:33:43 (5,011)
Belford, Charlotte......4:14:50 (14,747)
Bell, Daisy......4:26:16 (17,895)
Bell, Jacqueline......5:24:42 (30,584)
Bell, Josephine Marion......5:24:07 (30,498)
Bell, Julie Emma......5:19:59 (29,846)
Bell, Julieann Maria......5:20:02 (29,856)
Bell, Kate......4:07:20 (12,781)
Bell, Katie......4:26:22 (17,920)
Bell, Rachel......5:49:26 (33,275)
Bell, Rachel......7:08:35 (36,297)
Bell, Sharron......4:57:39 (25,896)
Bell, Virginia C......3:52:17 (8,734)
Bell, Zoe Marie......5:05:43 (27,484)
Bellew, Amy......5:14:56 (29,057)
Bellingham, Sarah......4:54:22 (25,149)
Bell-Misri, Lauren......5:33:11 (31,685)
Bellocq, Caroline......4:07:01 (12,714)
Belsom, Tina......4:24:35 (17,414)
Beltgens, Esther......4:11:48 (13,932)
Belton, Hannah Mary......6:09:44 (34,648)
Belton, Karen......5:57:29 (33,901)
Belyavin, Julia R......3:03:09 (1,334)
Bemment, Tanya Jane......4:32:26 (19,545)
Ben Mansour, Soraya......4:20:15 (16,181)
Bench, Suzanne D......3:51:14 (8,482)
Bennet, Elaine......5:34:48 (31,860)
Bennett, Caroline Ann......4:55:33 (25,420)
Bennett, Charlotte......3:48:01 (7,741)
Bennett, Elizabeth......4:34:33 (20,134)
Bennett, Gemma Louise......6:02:13 (34,197)
Bennett, Holly Annie Kate......5:10:32 (28,335)
Bennett, Hugh......5:13:42 (28,871)
Bennett, Iris......4:10:26 (13,574)
Bennett, Joanna......5:36:18 (32,033)
Bennett, Joanne Laura......4:46:07 (23,065)
Bennett, Julia Jane......5:22:38 (30,245)
Bennett, Laura......6:26:10 (35,354)
Bennett, Lauren......4:13:10 (14,278)
Bennett, Lisa J......3:19:36 (2,926)
Bennett, Lisa Madeline......4:06:26 (12,554)

Bonas, Cressida 5:13:04 (28,763)
Bond, Fran Rhiannon 4:44:11 (22,557)
Bond, Frances E 3:18:03 (2,774)
Bond, Mel 4:18:56 (15,836)
Bond, Melanie-Anne 4:27:00 (18,079)
Bond, Patti 4:42:25 (22,115)
Bondaroff, Carole Ann 3:58:31 (10,560)
Bone, Charlotte Emma 5:47:09 (33,066)
Bonetto, Sharon 5:42:47 (32,655)
Bonin, Joyce N 5:19:03 (29,708)
Bonley, Marie 6:35:18 (35,659)
Bonnick, Clare J 3:36:11 (5,444)
Bonser, Julie Anne 4:01:13 (11,300)
Boobyer, Ella Marie 4:16:42 (15,222)
Boorman, Gill 6:26:15 (35,357)
Boorman, Jenny 5:33:02 (31,670)
Boote, Stephanie 5:01:04 (26,661)
Booth, Jane 5:41:41 (32,548)
Boothby, Emma Susan 4:01:21 (11,322)
Boothby, Lucy 4:39:13 (21,317)
Boothman, Helen 4:14:24 (14,613)
Bootle, Jo 4:36:27 (20,586)
Booton, Rachel 5:07:04 (27,736)
Booyens, Sally 5:01:52 (26,825)
Borchard, Susanne 4:46:49 (23,259)
Borg, Teresa J 4:29:50 (18,920)
Borie, Louise 4:07:43 (12,889)
Bork, Govinda 6:06:30 (34,482)
Borkin, Cheryl Leanne 4:20:24 (16,232)
Borland, Julie Ann 3:55:58 (9,772)
Borley, Penny M 6:33:37 (35,616)
Bosch, Simone 4:17:47 (15,522)
Bosdet, Shelley Louise 5:25:47 (30,751)
Boshier, Michelle 4:52:34 (24,701)
Bosio, Teresea 4:53:15 (24,862)
Boskett, Kimberley Joanne 4:53:29 (24,913)
Boskovic, Daniela K 4:45:38 (22,927)
Bosman, Jenny Mairi 2:55:59 (799)
Bosowitz, Adel 6:26:57 (35,384)
Bostelmann, Claire 4:17:41 (15,493)
Boswell, Claire 4:54:01 (25,058)
Boswell, Melissa Frances 5:46:40 (33,025)
Bosworth, Courtney 4:42:11 (22,058)
Botha, Ramona 4:33:34 (19,877)
Botham, Loraine A 3:58:24 (10,523)
Bott, Alexandra Grace 4:26:59 (18,074)
Botterill, Nicky 5:41:20 (32,517)
Bottle, Sarah 5:13:59 (28,921)
Bottomley, Amanda Louise 4:03:13 (11,781)
Bottomley, Elizabeth M 4:18:37 (15,749)
Botwright, Claire Elizabeth 4:45:00 (22,770)
Boucher, Alex 6:26:46 (35,375)
Boucher, Mary 4:45:54 (22,999)
Boughton, Melanie J 4:52:07 (24,578)
Bougourd, Kerri Rose 4:35:06 (20,251)
Boulding, Caroline Dawn 5:56:44 (33,845)
Bouley, Jennifer M 3:17:38 (2,729)
Boulton, Rebecca Louise 5:05:59 (27,527)
Bounds, Catherine J 3:43:36 (6,791)
Bourdillat, Anne Marie 3:55:15 (9,544)
Bourgoin, Catherine 4:02:30 (11,601)
Bourn, Julia Emma 5:03:39 (27,127)
Bourne, Joanne E 4:16:54 (15,271)
Bourne, Naomi A 3:17:48 (2,744)
Boustead, Jill 4:38:46 (21,193)
Bowd, Emma Jane 4:53:54 (25,022)
Bowden, Emily-Ann Harriet 4:05:08 (12,234)
Bowdler, Hannah 4:37:30 (20,881)
Bowen, Angela 4:32:31 (19,565)
Bowen, Annie Elizabeth 5:40:53 (32,469)
Bowen, Christine 5:49:57 (33,328)
Bowen, Emma Charlotte 7:00:36 (36,197)
Bowen, Michelle Angharyd 3:30:32 (4,501)
Bowen, Sarah Jane 4:11:02 (13,726)
Bower, Kimberly-Rose 6:35:46 (35,671)
Bowers, Charrity Ann 5:35:31 (31,929)
Bowers, Jude 7:52:15 (36,567)
Bowie, Christine 3:37:03 (5,574)
Bowker, Rachel S 4:18:08 (15,618)
Bowler, Liz 4:52:48 (24,756)
Bowles, Ann V 4:12:12 (14,032)
Bowley, Carmen Louise 5:53:27 (33,612)
Bowman, Elaine 6:56:41 (36,139)
Bowman, Sharon A 4:09:24 (13,313)
Bowman, Zoe Louise 5:25:30 (30,691)
Bownes, Victoria 5:05:35 (27,464)
Bowyer, Jade Melissa 4:49:15 (23,865)
Boyce, Christopher John 5:03:12 (27,060)
Boyd, Claire Louise 4:52:38 (24,718)
Boyd, Julie A 3:38:46 (5,902)
Boyd, Lara M 3:53:20 (9,009)
Boyd, Laura E 3:50:19 (8,272)
Boyd, Valerie 5:43:22 (32,706)
Boyde, Nikola 3:25:39 (3,673)
Boyer-Besant, Catherine 5:59:44 (34,040)
Boyes, Elaine 5:15:06 (29,081)
Boyle, Ann 6:07:51 (34,552)
Boyle, Georgina Elizabeth 5:11:42 (28,502)
Boyle, Joanne 4:58:19 (26,045)
Boyle, Kirsty Ann 4:30:31 (19,091)
Boyle, Laura 4:51:49 (24,497)
Boyle, Moreen Lynsey 5:18:50 (29,673)
Boyle, Vicki J 3:07:19 (1,637)
Boyman, Kate 5:27:06 (30,923)
Boys, Susan Jacqueline 5:51:34 (33,468)
Brabrook, Andrea Lynne 5:18:12 (29,572)
Bracchi, Carole Ann 4:38:52 (21,223)
Bradbury, Annie 3:37:17 (5,614)
Bradbury, Rachel M 4:22:04 (16,723)
Bradford, Claire E 5:19:05 (29,714)
Brading, Rebecca Louise 5:29:17 (31,188)
Bradley, Anna 5:25:57 (30,774)
Bradley, Betty 6:19:20 (35,096)
Bradley, Christine 6:45:04 (35,910)
Bradley, Dawn 5:01:34 (26,769)
Bradley, Deanne 3:59:11 (10,771)
Bradley, Grainne 5:22:25 (30,210)
Bradley, Hilary 5:00:56 (26,639)
Bradley, Jane Evelyn 4:36:54 (20,715)
Bradley, Jayde 6:03:31 (34,291)
Bradley, Jennifer C 3:20:09 (2,972)
Bradley, Kate 4:37:54 (20,967)
Bradley, Mary 5:15:37 (29,166)
Bradley, Sheila 6:22:29 (35,207)
Bradley, Susan May 6:26:31 (35,367)
Bradshaw, Helen M 5:20:52 (29,987)
Bradshaw, Julie K 3:29:42 (4,360)
Bradshaw, Louise Maria 6:18:01 (35,032)
Brady, Elizabeth Jane 4:56:11 (25,579)
Brady, Gemma 4:51:44 (24,468)
Brady, Jeanette Mary 4:24:12 (17,287)
Brady, Jill 4:03:13 (11,781)
Brady, Julie M 3:39:12 (5,981)
Brady, Kathy L 4:20:55 (16,390)
Brady, Rose 7:05:49 (36,264)
Brady, Rosemarie 6:06:55 (34,503)
Brady, Vanessa M 4:31:15 (19,280)
Braga, Ana Paula 3:55:37 (9,647)
Braga, Juliana 3:10:14 (1,925)
Bragg, Zafer B 7:00:13 (36,192)
Brain, Joanne 4:46:37 (23,209)
Brain, Justine L 4:12:50 (14,187)
Braker, Sophie Louise 4:33:40 (19,910)
Brambani, Emma Jane 3:56:02 (9,795)
Bramley, Nicola J 3:39:10 (5,977)
Brammer, Sian J 4:22:48 (16,939)
Brampton, Raine Louise 5:12:41 (28,682)
Brana, Luisa P 3:30:25 (4,488)
Brand, Susan June 5:41:37 (32,543)
Brandenburger, Sabine 4:08:05 (12,983)
Brandon, Alice Margaret 4:05:24 (12,313)
Brannan, Gillian 6:51:28 (36,024)
Branson, Holly 5:13:03 (28,747)
Brant, Amanda 4:37:20 (20,828)
Brant, Janey Helen 4:50:50 (24,250)
Brassington, Sarah 4:42:25 (22,115)
Braude, Hayley 5:51:23 (33,454)
Bravey, Christine 4:31:17 (19,289)
Bravey, Tina Frances 7:12:19 (36,330)
Bray, Brydie D 3:57:20 (10,190)
Bray, Cassie 5:27:39 (30,983)
Bray, Gill F 5:43:15 (32,694)
Bray, Karyn 4:41:54 (21,995)
Breeden, Laura Siobhan 5:50:41 (33,403)
Breeden, Rachel Lucy 5:49:02 (33,244)
Breen, Angela M 4:04:51 (12,164)
Breen, Emer 3:28:34 (4,157)
Breeze, Elizabeth Anne 5:25:43 (30,734)
Breeze, Pauline 6:16:30 (34,950)
Bremang, Colette 4:43:51 (22,464)
Brennan, Carla 6:19:43 (35,114)
Brennan, Denise S 4:50:59 (24,300)
Brennan, Julia F 3:42:38 (6,616)
Brennan, Louise Elizabeth 4:08:57 (13,193)
Brennan, Theresa Marian 4:57:52 (25,939)
Brenner, Natalie 3:37:26 (5,642)
Brereton, Tammy 4:08:20 (13,036)
Bresch, Louise Ellen 6:15:07 (34,890)
Breslin, Valerie S 5:07:22 (27,787)
Brett, Helen P 5:05:51 (27,504)
Brett, Kathryn 5:03:01 (27,029)
Brett, Kirsty Helen 4:24:20 (17,333)
Brett, Rebecca 5:02:18 (26,906)
Brett, Stella 4:51:13 (24,358)
Brettell, Alison Louise 5:30:24 (31,336)
Brettell, Jolene 5:21:27 (30,068)
Brew, Lynda 6:55:19 (36,117)
Brewer, Jane Ann 5:16:51 (29,365)
Brewer, Kate 5:35:35 (31,935)
Brewer, Suki Gabrielle 5:19:48 (29,823)
Brewis, Linda M 3:49:45 (8,160)
Brewster, Ashley 4:57:13 (25,808)
Brewster, Vanessa Mary 4:28:46 (18,598)
Briant, Claire E L 4:46:54 (23,283)
Bricola, Sonali 5:52:53 (33,575)
Bridge, Karen M 3:08:10 (1,715)
Bridge, Nicki 6:17:14 (34,992)
Bridge, Sarah 4:42:09 (22,050)
Bridges, Denise 3:42:54 (6,676)
Bridges, Teresa 6:03:38 (34,299)
Bridgland, Amy Karen 5:26:35 (30,851)
Brierley, Jennifer L 3:14:05 (2,331)
Brierley, Victoria Louise 4:05:42 (12,378)
Briggs, Claire Lynn 5:52:13 (33,516)
Briggs, Joanne Marie 4:02:42 (11,650)
Bright, Emily 3:30:04 (4,429)
Bright, Kate 5:41:21 (32,518)
Brightling, Jenny 5:48:16 (33,171)
Brightman, Judith Claire 4:52:46 (24,742)
Brightman, Pat Ann 6:18:27 (35,056)
Brightwell, Gillian 4:17:58 (15,569)
Brightwell, Katie 4:44:38 (22,682)
Brightwell, Maria G 3:38:05 (5,779)
Brightwell, Natalie Anne 4:01:25 (11,345)
Brightwell, Sally A 4:51:33 (24,431)
Brind, Alison M 3:42:57 (6,685)
Brindley, Gail 4:57:10 (25,796)
Brine, Claire Paula 5:42:46 (32,654)
Brinton, Evaleen 5:04:47 (27,333)
Bristow, Mary 5:06:54 (27,702)
Bristow Tyler, Linda 5:11:55 (28,544)
Britain, Frances L 3:50:45 (8,373)
Brittain, Karen Michelle 4:52:55 (24,779)
Brittain, Lindsey 4:50:39 (24,195)
Britten, Bryony J 3:35:44 (5,364)
Britten, Sharon 5:01:15 (26,694)
Britto, Francisca 5:23:55 (30,464)
Britton, Toni 3:58:16 (10,478)
Brivati, Kelly Leigh 6:13:59 (34,836)
Broad, Amanda Fleur 4:51:59 (24,549)
Broadbent, Susan C 4:09:57 (13,456)
Broadhead, Jennifer 4:34:00 (19,993)
Broady, Karin 4:49:38 (23,953)
Brobakken, Wenche 4:31:02 (19,226)
Brockbank, Nicola J 3:20:44 (3,050)
Brocklebank, Ella Louise 4:13:31 (14,369)
Brocklebank, Susan 3:58:35 (10,590)
Brockman, Anna 7:34:02 (36,485)
Brockman, Louise 5:21:24 (30,062)
Brockwell, Kirstie 4:30:32 (19,098)
Broda, Krysia B 4:33:24 (19,825)
Brodie, Gillian Margaret 4:42:04 (22,032)
Bromfield, Emily 4:13:20 (14,324)
Bronja, Karen 4:20:11 (16,157)
Brook, Amanda M 3:34:40 (5,185)
Brook, Angela L 4:50:44 (24,219)
Brookbank, Nicola 5:41:33 (32,538)
Brooke, Susan Lorraine 6:33:51 (35,620)
Brooke-Maples, Verity 5:31:52 (31,519)

Brookes, Emily	4:22:22 (16,811)	
Brookes, Julia Karen	3:57:39 (10,280)	
Brookes, Pauline M	4:01:28 (11,359)	
Brooks, Alison	4:17:33 (15,458)	
Brooks, Gail Louise	5:34:10 (31,776)	
Brooks, Helen Louise	4:44:11 (22,557)	
Brooks, Laura	6:01:46 (34,171)	
Brooks, Liz Mary	5:09:33 (28,158)	
Brooks, Richard	4:07:28 (12,822)	
Brooks, Sandra	4:33:25 (19,829)	
Broom, Jennifer Mary Elspeth	4:13:07 (14,269)	
Broom, Karen Lucy	5:14:43 (29,019)	
Broomfield, Wendy Elizabeth	5:44:16 (32,793)	
Brosnan, Julie Maria	4:44:58 (22,759)	
Broughan, Sharon	5:37:03 (32,106)	
Broughton, Andrea C	4:08:49 (13,169)	
Broughton, Esther Jane	4:48:03 (23,557)	
Broughton, Helen	5:18:17 (29,588)	
Broughton, Julie Ann	4:38:26 (21,099)	
Brousseau, Helene	4:16:42 (15,222)	
Brown, Angela M	3:42:43 (6,638)	
Brown, Angharad	4:28:40 (18,573)	
Brown, Anne Lucille	4:42:37 (22,158)	
Brown, Barbara M	5:16:01 (29,232)	
Brown, Caroline	6:03:50 (34,310)	
Brown, Caroline Sandra	4:24:35 (17,414)	
Brown, Catherine Helen	6:27:36 (35,408)	
Brown, Cathymarie	5:10:42 (28,363)	
Brown, Claire J	3:43:58 (6,871)	
Brown, Colleen M	4:46:58 (23,298)	
Brown, Emma L	3:22:14 (3,213)	
Brown, Esther	6:29:12 (35,471)	
Brown, Gemma Kate	5:05:18 (27,422)	
Brown, Gillian	4:36:21 (20,562)	
Brown, Helen	3:43:45 (6,813)	
Brown, Helen	5:49:57 (33,328)	
Brown, Helen L	3:44:49 (7,058)	
Brown, Janis A	4:22:51 (16,949)	
Brown, Judy	3:51:07 (8,455)	
Brown, Julie A	4:50:53 (24,266)	
Brown, Julie M	6:01:21 (34,148)	
Brown, Kareen Jane	4:45:04 (22,788)	
Brown, Karen	4:38:46 (21,193)	
Brown, Karen	5:21:57 (30,136)	
Brown, Kate	3:00:18 (1,162)	
Brown, Kim Elizabeth	3:38:33 (5,854)	
Brown, Kimberley	4:46:08 (23,071)	
Brown, Kimberley	5:01:14 (26,689)	
Brown, Kirsteen	4:47:58 (23,541)	
Brown, Lande	4:49:52 (24,021)	
Brown, Leonie	4:24:03 (17,250)	
Brown, Lorna	5:15:01 (29,069)	
Brown, Lorna	5:51:48 (33,492)	
Brown, Louise Elizabeth	5:23:28 (30,382)	
Brown, Lynsey Mary	5:55:32 (33,757)	
Brown, Margaret M	4:59:04 (26,230)	
Brown, Margaret M	6:36:05 (35,677)	
Brown, Maxine L	4:04:26 (12,065)	
Brown, Michelle	4:37:01 (20,749)	
Brown, Michelle Annette	4:49:00 (23,800)	
Brown, Miriam C	4:58:34 (26,107)	
Brown, Molly June	5:39:13 (32,322)	
Brown, Nicola Tracey	6:40:53 (35,810)	
Brown, Olivia	5:27:04 (30,916)	
Brown, Patricia Rosemary	6:00:33 (34,095)	
Brown, Samantha Ann	4:44:40 (22,692)	
Brown, Sarah	5:44:02 (32,770)	
Brown, Sarah L	4:52:28 (24,673)	
Brown, Stacey	5:35:59 (31,994)	
Brown, Stefana	6:07:05 (34,511)	
Brown, Sue	3:49:05 (7,997)	
Brown, Susan	4:23:09 (17,013)	
Brown, Susan A	3:51:32 (8,544)	
Brown, Susanna	5:11:56 (28,547)	
Brown, Suzanne	7:36:35 (36,500)	
Brown, Suzie Louise	4:11:28 (13,842)	
Brown, Tracey Annette	4:29:36 (18,842)	
Brown, Victoria E	3:34:53 (5,230)	
Brown, Victoria Jayne	4:17:37 (15,473)	
Browne, Angela	5:57:52 (33,924)	
Browne, Martina R	6:38:50 (35,751)	
Browne, Nuala	5:55:28 (33,752)	
Browne, Sarah	3:55:49 (9,725)	

Brownhill, Alison	3:13:25 (2,238)	
Browning, Tanya	5:31:42 (31,503)	
Bruce, Emma	4:43:49 (22,450)	
Bruce, Roselyn	4:44:48 (22,721)	
Bruce, Stephanie	4:44:48 (22,721)	
Bruce, Tracey J	4:23:05 (17,000)	
Brucker, Cathrin	4:42:04 (22,032)	
Brunning, Karen Lisa	4:05:39 (12,367)	
Bruns, Julia	4:59:45 (26,395)	
Brunt, Holly Anne	5:34:34 (31,831)	
Brunton, Hayley	5:17:45 (29,508)	
Brussells, Linzi M	5:12:30 (28,653)	
Bruton, Jane	3:56:00 (9,787)	
Bryan, Lorraine	5:30:46 (31,387)	
Bryan, Paula Susan	5:59:46 (34,044)	
Bryant, Alys Rhiannon	6:11:02 (34,702)	
Bryant, Emma Louise	4:34:03 (20,005)	
Bryant, Kelly	3:49:40 (8,139)	
Bryant, Lara Helen	4:47:32 (23,417)	
Bryant, Pamela Margaret	8:38:27 (36,606)	
Bryant, Sarah Jane	3:39:05 (5,961)	
Bryars, Kerry Elizabeth	4:59:27 (26,321)	
Bryce, Verity Rose	4:07:17 (12,771)	
Bryden, Charli	5:09:29 (28,141)	
Bryn Jones, Angharad	4:56:32 (25,658)	
Bubb, Katherine	5:00:23 (26,533)	
Buchan, Caroline	4:45:37 (22,919)	
Buchanan, Pauline	7:10:01 (36,306)	
Buchanan-Gregory, Kitty Isabella	5:16:52 (29,367)	
Buck, Helen	4:40:19 (21,579)	
Buck, Julia	4:58:02 (25,974)	
Buckingham, Charlotte Anne	5:07:31 (27,816)	
Buckland, Ellie	5:16:37 (29,324)	
Buckland, Lynette	5:23:39 (30,415)	
Buckle, Sarah Jane	4:44:44 (22,709)	
Buckler, Elizabeth	5:06:56 (27,710)	
Buckley, Diane	5:12:42 (28,686)	
Buckley, Julia E	5:25:44 (30,737)	
Buckmaster, Wendy	5:03:23 (27,086)	
Buckner, Louise Ann	4:16:58 (15,287)	
Buckthorp, Karen	4:45:42 (22,948)	
Buckwell, Zena Kate	4:23:51 (17,200)	
Budd, Naomi	4:17:15 (15,364)	
Budd, Viv Kathleen	6:56:11 (36,133)	
Buelter, Baerbel-Ingrid	5:08:16 (27,946)	
Buffini, Lauren	4:17:26 (15,416)	
Buffong, Caroline J	6:15:11 (34,898)	
Bugg, Alison	4:18:43 (15,778)	
Bugg, Laura Jane	4:01:04 (11,271)	
Bugler, Fiona M	3:12:23 (2,124)	
Buksh, Nazia	4:19:22 (15,944)	
Buky-Webster, Claire	4:26:45 (18,011)	
Bull, Catherine	7:01:47 (36,213)	
Bull, Philippa Jane	5:41:40 (32,545)	
Bull, Sarah K.	4:29:33 (18,820)	
Bull, Susan	5:07:20 (27,777)	
Buller, Fiona A	6:41:53 (35,832)	
Bulley, Johanna D	3:34:34 (5,166)	
Bullingham, Maria R	6:42:35 (35,851)	
Bullock, Lisa	5:21:35 (30,093)	
Bullock, Rachel S	4:41:23 (21,863)	
Bulmahn, Marisa	5:44:37 (32,828)	
Bumby, Karen	4:45:39 (22,935)	
Bumfrey, Deborah	5:00:50 (26,617)	
Bunce, Michelle Claire	4:27:20 (18,190)	
Bunclark, Stephanie	3:56:19 (9,877)	
Bunker, Samantha Jane	7:21:47 (36,414)	
Bunn, Denise	6:09:57 (34,662)	
Bunn, Joanne	6:09:58 (34,663)	
Bunn, Susan Angela	4:06:29 (12,569)	
Bunn, Tricia	3:45:50 (7,274)	
Bunn, Zonja	4:50:03 (24,059)	
Bunni, Mary-Anne Theresa	4:38:45 (21,185)	
Bunten, Susan E	4:20:45 (16,356)	
Bunting, Katie Louise	5:32:04 (31,543)	
Bunyan, Frances Sarah	4:09:15 (13,272)	
Burbank, Emily Clare	4:38:53 (21,230)	
Burbidge, Emma Jane Isobel	6:05:42 (34,432)	
Burchall, Julie Elizabeth	4:32:52 (19,661)	
Burcham, Claire Louise	4:36:10 (20,523)	
Burcham, Penny	6:06:25 (34,473)	
Burchell, Julie	4:25:00 (17,519)	
Burchmore, Lucy Jane	5:13:36 (28,857)	

Burdett, Niki	4:48:22 (23,627)	
Burgar, Natalie Elizabeth	5:48:03 (33,144)	
Burge, Frances	3:11:52 (2,083)	
Burge, Jill Pamela	4:48:56 (23,782)	
Burge, Sarah Elizabeth	6:05:43 (34,435)	
Burges, Susan	4:34:22 (20,085)	
Burgess, Anna	7:07:36 (36,284)	
Burgess, Annette	3:31:29 (4,664)	
Burgess, Harriet K	3:43:16 (6,737)	
Burgess, Helen L	4:04:49 (12,157)	
Burgess, Nadine Maria	4:27:38 (18,270)	
Burgess, Penny	5:19:40 (29,804)	
Burgess, Sarah Louise	4:46:56 (23,288)	
Burgess, Verna B	3:49:36 (8,115)	
Burgoyne, Sarah	5:31:33 (31,479)	
Burke, Catherine E	5:19:03 (29,708)	
Burke, Delyth	4:56:47 (25,711)	
Burke, Helen	4:18:18 (15,661)	
Burke, Joanne L	3:46:22 (7,387)	
Burke, Lorraine	5:05:37 (27,470)	
Burke, Natalie	5:08:50 (28,019)	
Burke, Polly Ann	3:58:28 (10,544)	
Burkitt, Ann Marie	7:06:05 (36,268)	
Burkitt, Hilary Anne	3:56:31 (9,938)	
Burland, Helen M	4:43:31 (22,372)	
Burles, Julie A	5:57:18 (33,890)	
Burles-Nash, Karen Denise	4:22:22 (16,811)	
Burley, Jill	5:40:58 (32,478)	
Burley, Justine Clare	4:00:21 (11,076)	
Burn, Katharine Joanna Elizabeth	6:22:24 (35,205)	
Burn, Tracey Deborah Marie	5:19:16 (29,742)	
Burnard, Sarah Michelle	4:37:49 (20,948)	
Burnett, Barbara	5:08:30 (27,973)	
Burnett, Jackie	4:32:24 (19,538)	
Burnham, Suzannah Margaret Q.	4:15:00 (14,786)	
Burnikell, Angela J	3:46:19 (7,378)	
Burns, Alexandra	4:33:29 (19,848)	
Burns, Claire	5:19:14 (29,740)	
Burns, Danielle Suzanne	6:11:50 (34,744)	
Burns, Donna Louise	5:50:12 (33,355)	
Burns, Elaine A	4:36:48 (20,682)	
Burns, Susan M	3:29:23 (4,299)	
Burr, Jenny	7:16:06 (36,372)	
Burrage, Carolyn A	4:51:34 (24,434)	
Burrage, Robyn Stacy	5:59:04 (33,994)	
Burrow, Bethany Marie	6:42:56 (35,858)	
Burrows, Fiona	4:34:53 (20,212)	
Burrows, Karen Jean	4:17:39 (15,483)	
Burrows, Katie	5:23:34 (30,396)	
Burrows, Moira	4:08:14 (13,012)	
Burrows, Sarah	5:49:22 (33,269)	
Burrows, Sarah Catherine	4:11:56 (13,972)	
Burrows, Sue P	4:43:04 (22,276)	
Bursack, Jennifer Lynn	4:41:34 (21,912)	
Burston, Jane	3:42:34 (6,606)	
Burt, Marie	5:00:25 (26,539)	
Burton, Angela	4:24:56 (17,498)	
Burton, Carolyn Jane	4:55:50 (25,495)	
Burton, Emily	5:01:31 (26,758)	
Burton, Emma M	3:51:33 (8,549)	
Burton, Kerry Lee	6:52:10 (36,051)	
Burton, Linda Jane	4:12:38 (14,132)	
Burton, Susan	4:53:45 (24,985)	
Burton,, Tracey, Elizabeth	5:31:07 (31,426)	
Burtt, Louise Catherine	4:12:41 (14,153)	
Burvill, Lorraine	6:09:34 (34,638)	
Burville, Nikki	5:50:29 (33,380)	
Bury, Jessica	6:46:39 (35,941)	
Busby, Louise	4:59:45 (26,395)	
Bush, Julie Ann	5:24:50 (30,597)	
Bush, Lucy Ann	4:19:50 (16,052)	
Bushell, Cassandra Anne	4:44:15 (22,577)	
Bushnell, Margaret C	4:40:39 (21,679)	
Bussell, Katie Louise	7:38:52 (36,513)	
Bussey, Emma	4:28:05 (18,383)	
Bussmann, Annegret	5:19:33 (29,779)	
Butcher, Carly SJ	4:26:12 (17,874)	
Butcher, Emily Louise	5:03:36 (27,120)	
Butcher, Jane Nicola	3:53:11 (8,966)	
Butcher, Louise Caroline	5:19:41 (29,805)	
Butcher, Michelle	7:23:39 (36,436)	
Butini, Maria Cristina	4:30:50 (19,176)	
Butland, Orlanda C	3:24:53 (3,560)	

Butler, Amy Susan 5:07:48 (27,860)
Butler, Barbara 4:44:54 (22,743)
Butler, Charlotte Louise 5:21:21 (30,052)
Butler, Claire Louise 5:38:48 (32,291)
Butler, Elaine N 5:15:14 (29,104)
Butler, Gail Ceridwen 4:41:07 (21,801)
Butler, Lauren Ruth 4:05:34 (12,347)
Butler, Lucy C 4:20:32 (16,268)
Butler, Margaret Sinead 7:06:21 (36,270)
Butler, Rebecca Anne 4:51:22 (24,390)
Butler, Sarah 3:50:20 (8,275)
Butterfield, Hannah C 6:00:47 (34,109)
Butterfield, Ros Jayne 4:02:41 (11,646)
Buttfield, Anne 4:33:59 (19,987)
Buttrey, Michaela Dawn 5:51:41 (33,480)
Butwell, Lucinda 4:38:03 (20,997)
Buxton, Cydni 7:20:12 (36,406)
Byatt, Michelle Denise Anne 4:28:56 (18,660)
Bye, Jackie Maria 4:33:42 (19,918)
Byers, Rachel 3:42:15 (6,556)
Byng Maddick, Zillah 4:13:28 (14,357)
Byrne, Aimée 3:47:31 (7,650)
Byrne, Dara B 6:04:36 (34,355)
Byrne, Emma Jane 4:52:32 (24,694)
Byrne, Emma Kate 4:49:44 (23,991)
Byrne, Jean 5:04:58 (27,360)
Byrne, Jennifer 4:04:40 (12,119)
Byrne, Katherine 4:29:35 (18,833)
Byrne, Stephanie M 4:24:27 (17,376)
Byron, Jenny M 5:04:24 (27,259)
Byron-Daniel, Katherine 4:48:51 (23,760)
Caballero, Montserrat 4:02:19 (11,560)
Cacioppo, Su Alina 5:45:52 (32,941)
Cadogan, Beverley 3:57:51 (10,345)
Cadogan, Claire 4:56:47 (25,711)
Cadogan, Nicola 5:30:34 (31,367)
Cadwallader, Emma Michelle 5:19:53 (29,833)
Caffell, Tracy 4:53:52 (25,009)
Cafferty, Marisa Jayne 4:56:53 (25,747)
Caffrey, Julie 4:28:54 (18,642)
Cahill, Kirsty Ann 4:52:36 (24,706)
Cahill, Lisa 5:39:43 (32,361)
Cahill, Stephanie 6:04:54 (34,378)
Cain, Ingrid Mary 4:30:32 (19,098)
Cairns, Angela 4:50:53 (24,266)
Cairns, Helen L 5:49:10 (33,254)
Cakebread, Holly E 4:03:34 (11,864)
Cakebread, Katherine 5:14:03 (28,930)
Cakebread, Louise 4:00:42 (11,170)
Caldecott, Ann Nicola 4:53:50 (25,002)
Calder, Helen Jane 4:09:36 (13,370)
Calderbank, Susie 3:54:46 (9,407)
Calderon, Marissa 4:46:07 (23,065)
Caldwell, Helen 6:03:27 (34,285)
Calfe, Jane Elizabeth 4:36:30 (20,605)
Callaghan, Jane 4:31:58 (19,424)
Callaghan, Kate 4:22:50 (16,947)
Callaghan, Lynne E 3:16:38 (2,631)
Callaghan, Sarah J 4:01:25 (11,345)
Callaghan, Sheila E 6:07:43 (34,544)
Callan, Susan 5:38:09 (32,222)
Callanan, Collette B 3:44:27 (6,982)
Callanan, Jeanne 4:22:41 (16,897)
Callender, Claire 5:10:58 (28,398)
Callingham-Lello, Sandra Grace 4:29:27 (18,790)
Callister, Bronwyn 4:05:44 (12,386)
Callow, Arrianne Christina 6:02:48 (34,235)
Callow, Penny D 4:31:49 (19,395)
Calori, Nicola 5:49:33 (33,291)
Caludi, Ana Maria 3:48:14 (7,789)
Calvert, Susan A 5:00:28 (26,550)
Calvert-McKeag, Nicole 5:49:43 (33,311)
Cambe, Alfonsa 4:06:10 (12,490)
Cameras, Clary 3:26:45 (3,838)
Cameron, Lynn 3:41:49 (6,480)
Cameron, Stephanie M 6:15:27 (34,907)
Camilleri, Liza 3:54:32 (9,337)
Camm, Sally 3:44:51 (7,066)
Cammidge, Kate Ann 4:34:10 (20,030)
Camp, Debbie 4:04:47 (12,150)
Campbell, Alice Camilla 4:34:48 (20,194)
Campbell, Christine Chris 4:03:57 (11,952)
Campbell, Christine Elizabeth 5:18:47 (29,662)

LONDON MARATHON

Campbell, Claire L 3:54:10 (9,248)
Campbell, Emily Kate 4:29:37 (18,852)
Campbell, Isabelle 4:20:59 (16,407)
Campbell, Joanne 4:51:44 (24,468)
Campbell, Joyce 4:38:38 (21,149)
Campbell, Lisa J 4:52:11 (24,596)
Campbell, Mairead 4:37:23 (20,841)
Campbell, Melissa Rebecca 4:55:04 (25,326)
Campbell, Pamela Mary 3:55:15 (9,544)
Campbell, Patricia D 3:47:42 (7,684)
Campbell, Sally 3:57:32 (10,238)
Campbell, Sarah 4:13:40 (14,422)
Campbell, Sarah Dorothy Helen 5:27:24 (30,955)
Campbell, Shirley 7:48:00 (36,558)
Campbell, Shona 4:51:53 (24,519)
Campbell, Sony E 4:46:53 (23,279)
Campbell-Dykes, Joanna 6:02:39 (34,228)
Campillo, Monica 4:05:41 (12,375)
Campion, Anne-Marie 4:20:16 (16,185)
Campofiore, Gail Gladys 5:38:00 (32,213)
Camps, Suzanne Carole 5:15:06 (29,081)
Canale, Andrea M 4:05:44 (12,386)
Cane, Nicola 5:46:51 (33,037)
Cane, Nicola E 4:43:02 (22,268)
Caney, Pauline Joy 4:36:08 (20,515)
Canham, Ruth Elizabeth 4:48:42 (23,719)
Cann, Betty 6:11:37 (34,729)
Cann, Cassandra 6:00:58 (34,129)
Cann, Honor Elizabeth 4:34:27 (20,108)
Cann, Lee-Anne M 3:05:15 (1,477)
Cann, Lesley Margaret 5:54:33 (33,678)
Cannell, Susan H 6:08:19 (34,570)
Canning, Amanda Jane 4:33:33 (19,867)
Canning, Patricia 4:40:34 (21,660)
Cannon, Laura G 4:00:17 (11,056)
Canny, Sinead M 4:34:34 (20,140)
Cant, Denise Catherine 4:23:16 (17,037)
Cantley, Louise 5:00:24 (26,535)
Cantu, Ivonne 3:28:36 (4,164)
Canty, Felicity 5:23:47 (30,440)
Capaldi, Tabitha 5:07:54 (27,880)
Caples, Sophie Katherine 4:08:41 (13,140)
Caplin, Kelly Christine 4:34:43 (20,176)
Capobianco, Lucia 4:48:25 (23,647)
Capstick, Gill 3:49:01 (7,978)
Carabott, Clare 4:19:22 (15,944)
Caratelli, Susan Elizabeth 4:18:31 (15,720)
Card, Jessica Aimée 5:48:18 (33,175)
Carder, Louise Estelle 6:24:18 (35,290)
Cardwell, Emma Jane 5:10:06 (28,256)
Carelsen, Brenda 7:10:56 (36,321)
Carew, Elizabeth 5:16:29 (29,310)
Carew-Gibbs, Hannah 5:50:33 (33,392)
Carey, Geraldine Ann 4:53:25 (24,895)
Carey, Samantha 4:42:39 (22,168)
Cargill, Rebecca 5:06:09 (27,555)
Carlen, Katarina 3:44:23 (6,964)
Carless, Anjie Jayne 6:43:10 (35,868)
Carlin, Annette K 3:59:30 (10,863)
Carlin, Rebecca 5:55:01 (33,720)
Carliss, Rachael 5:23:36 (30,404)
Carlson, Shelia A 6:25:06 (35,309)
Carlton, Melanie L 3:38:38 (5,881)
Carman, Stacey J 3:32:26 (4,809)
Carmichael, Eleanor C 5:10:54 (28,393)
Carmichael, Linda Mary Helen 5:16:37 (29,324)
Carnaby, Sophie 4:05:23 (12,303)
Carnegy, Henrietta 4:52:28 (24,673)
Carney, Lisa C 4:23:32 (17,115)
Carnie, Helen E 5:30:04 (31,304)
Carpenter, Emma 5:00:20 (26,527)
Carpenter, Francesca Mary K 4:55:34 (25,424)
Carpenter, Lynne 4:56:38 (25,673)
Carpenter, Rachel 6:29:05 (35,463)
Carpenter, Sue 3:19:37 (2,929)

Carr, Aimée 4:25:50 (17,766)
Carr, Caroline Marie 7:59:16 (36,586)
Carr, Clare Louise 5:02:41 (26,974)
Carr, Gemma Jane 4:16:58 (15,287)
Carr, Harriet J 3:24:41 (3,537)
Carr, Ruby R 4:12:09 (14,022)
Carrer, Dawn 8:10:28 (36,593)
Carrera, Kathryn Mary 6:03:02 (34,255)
Carreras, Miranda 3:56:39 (9,978)
Carrera-Vivar, Maria D 3:46:47 (7,484)
Carrington, Annie M 3:37:15 (5,610)
Carrington, Johnny 5:42:03 (32,596)
Carrington, Sam 4:39:24 (21,353)
Carrington, Sarah 3:51:34 (8,554)
Carritt, Charlotte 3:15:55 (2,542)
Carrod, Sarah L 4:27:22 (18,200)
Carroll, Amy Jane 4:09:58 (13,463)
Carroll, Belinda 4:25:59 (17,807)
Carroll, Donna K 3:50:45 (8,373)
Carroll, Hayley Anne 4:42:12 (22,065)
Carroll, Jane 6:06:08 (34,458)
Carroll, Pamela 4:21:10 (16,457)
Carroll, Shirley Ellen 5:41:21 (32,518)
Carroll, Yvonne 5:35:55 (31,984)
Carruthers, Gail Louise 4:50:59 (24,300)
Carryn, Marijke 3:54:43 (9,392)
Carson, Aileen 4:56:49 (25,725)
Carson, Susan 4:37:25 (20,850)
Carswell, Emma 4:15:37 (14,929)
Carter, Angela Jane 6:21:15 (35,171)
Carter, Angela M 6:20:44 (35,155)
Carter, Bridget Mary 4:06:45 (12,642)
Carter, Charlotte Louise 7:01:56 (36,215)
Carter, Deborah 6:17:48 (35,023)
Carter, Deborah Janet 4:34:18 (20,070)
Carter, Diane 5:01:20 (26,721)
Carter, Emma E 5:05:53 (27,512)
Carter, Gemma Diane 3:41:11 (6,362)
Carter, Jacqueline Ann 4:17:30 (15,439)
Carter, Jacqui Ann 6:02:33 (34,221)
Carter, Jane 5:40:50 (32,460)
Carter, Jane M 3:31:26 (4,658)
Carter, Kerry Dawn 4:10:59 (13,710)
Carter, Kim 4:54:46 (25,252)
Carter, Lauren 4:21:51 (16,655)
Carter, Louise Elizabeth 5:00:52 (26,623)
Carter, Lucy 4:15:38 (14,933)
Carter, Lyndsey 5:32:51 (31,647)
Carter, Nicola 3:33:36 (4,986)
Carter, Serena 4:50:08 (24,078)
Carter, Shelley Anne 5:01:33 (26,766)
Carter, Victoria E 3:27:23 (3,939)
Carter, Zoe Ann 4:41:48 (21,971)
Carter Esslinger, Karen 5:06:18 (27,587)
Cartwright, Carol 4:56:10 (25,572)
Carver, Kirsty 4:01:50 (11,455)
Carver, Laura Ann 5:44:24 (32,804)
Casali, Patrizia Maria Luisa 4:47:20 (23,374)
Case, Charlotte 4:32:45 (19,619)
Case, Keri 4:48:47 (23,741)
Caseley, Samantha Kimberley 4:29:31 (18,812)
Casewell, Leanne 7:24:07 (36,438)
Casey, Camilla 3:52:40 (8,839)
Casey, Gillian A 4:23:16 (17,037)
Casey, Hannah Siofra 5:39:10 (32,318)
Casha, Daniela 3:40:52 (6,305)
Cashin, Catherine 4:57:04 (25,775)
Cashman-Pugsley, Sue Lyn 4:38:58 (21,252)
Cass, Jennifer Margaret 4:06:49 (12,660)
Cassam, Jude L 4:02:35 (11,624)
Cassar, Wendy Anne Isobel 4:53:06 (24,822)
Cassidy, Louise 4:54:52 (25,272)
Cassidy, Lynn Lesley 4:56:10 (25,572)
Cassidy, Vivienne Louise 4:54:53 (25,279)
Casson, Hilary P 6:17:45 (35,019)
Casson, Jennifer E 4:36:48 (20,682)
Castanho, Michelle Lynn 6:05:59 (34,451)
Castelli, Sylvie 4:12:38 (14,132)
Castle, Jennifer 4:19:02 (15,852)
Caston-Fifield, Sarah Elizabeth 6:19:56 (35,122)
Casula, Letizia 6:36:06 (35,679)
Caswell, Rachael Helen 4:29:09 (18,721)
Catallo, Ruth 4:55:37 (25,443)

Cathcart, Sarah.....................4:27:21 (18,195)
Cathcart Burchett, Naomei 5:32:58 (31,658)
Cathie, Helen 4:37:33 (20,896)
Cathorne, Rachel 5:29:29 (31,218)
Catino, Domenica 5:55:49 (33,779)
Catley, Susan J 4:23:11 (17,021)
Catlow, Emma 4:57:24 (25,840)
Catlow, Michelle R 6:29:55 (35,496)
Cato, Caroline 6:42:06 (35,836)
Catt, Georgina 5:52:40 (33,549)
Cattai, Deborah 6:07:24 (34,526)
Catterall, Lara Anne 4:06:49 (12,660)
Catterfeld, Jenny 4:42:38 (22,163)
Caughlin, Kate 4:29:00 (18,686)
Caulfield, Vanda 3:33:46 (5,015)
Caulton, Kathyrn Joan 4:35:44 (20,397)
Cavanagh, Louise 3:48:19 (7,810)
Cavanagh, Samantha 3:49:28 (8,080)
Cave, Karen 3:57:18 (10,182)
Cave, Victoria Jane Drummond..6:02:13 (34,197)
Cave, Zoe 5:02:31 (26,946)
Cavell, Catherine....................4:34:56 (20,220)
Cavell, Gillian Frances 4:02:42 (11,650)
Cawley, Claire 5:14:51 (29,044)
Cawood, Bethany 5:02:03 (26,853)
Cawood, Laura 5:02:03 (26,853)
Cawthorne, Lisa 4:49:47 (24,005)
Cazalet, Fleur........................4:18:38 (15,753)
Cecil, Kathryn Elizabeth 5:00:43 (26,590)
Ceder, Anni 4:06:20 (12,534)
Cederstrom, Susan H...............3:51:36 (8,567)
Celis, Bianca 5:01:05 (26,665)
Chads, Christina Mary 4:39:38 (21,424)
Chadwell, Karen G 4:31:42 (19,376)
Chadwick, Joanne 4:22:36 (16,875)
Chadwick, Kristine 4:05:08 (12,234)
Chadwick, Monika 4:35:24 (20,325)
Chaffey, Heather Christine.......5:16:40 (29,333)
Chaffey, Lerryn T 3:36:50 (5,532)
Chalk, Helen J 3:41:10 (6,354)
Chalkley, Julie 7:46:14 (36,551)
Chalkley, Sian 4:26:47 (18,020)
Chalkley, Susan Jane 4:37:00 (20,742)
Challis, Donna 5:05:11 (27,401)
Challis, Katie.........................4:30:45 (19,159)
Challis, Teresa A 5:23:09 (30,329)
Chalmers, Sarah 4:28:07 (18,392)
Chalmers, Susan Marina............4:56:30 (25,646)
Chaloner, Sarah D...................3:32:04 (4,752)
Chaloner, Zoe Claire................4:20:20 (16,215)
Chamberlain, Anne 6:30:49 (35,529)
Chamberlain, Clemmie 4:56:46 (25,707)
Chambers, Claire 3:43:27 (6,771)
Chambers, Kate 4:42:04 (22,032)
Chambers, Kym Danielle............4:02:02 (11,497)
Chambers, Maggie Mary Anne..4:21:21 (16,506)
Champion, Gemma Elizabeth 4:53:41 (24,965)
Champion, Jocasta 4:57:30 (25,858)
Champion, Penny 4:49:04 (23,820)
Champion, Susan Elizabeth 6:06:51 (34,499)
Chan, Annie Marie 5:47:46 (33,122)
Chan, Betty Pui Yi 5:59:50 (34,049)
Chan, Judy 4:54:25 (25,164)
Chan, Ling K 4:24:25 (17,366)
Chan, Lisa Vida 4:02:33 (11,616)
Chan, Michelle.......................5:17:17 (29,435)
Chan, Yim Ting Tina 4:10:58 (13,703)
Chana, Kanvaljit K..................6:42:59 (35,861)
Chana, Rajvinder K 5:12:17 (28,617)
Changizi, Lara 5:15:08 (29,092)
Chant, Lottie 3:47:29 (7,644)
Chantry, Laura 4:21:59 (16,700)
Chaplin, Ann 5:35:51 (31,975)
Chaplin, Elizabeth 4:51:44 (24,468)
Chaplin, Katherine Alice 4:11:53 (13,950)
Chapman, Beverley J................3:24:57 (3,572)
Chapman, Cynthia M................4:25:39 (17,701)
Chapman, Denise A 3:22:40 (3,256)
Chapman, Gill 3:53:36 (9,092)
Chapman, Giselle Louise............4:42:39 (22,168)
Chapman, Isabelle Lucie............5:17:16 (29,429)
Chapman, Katharine 5:21:19 (30,044)
Chapman, Kathryn L 3:12:45 (2,161)

Chapman, Michelle..................5:29:55 (31,283)
Chapman, Samantha Louise 5:36:46 (32,078)
Chapman, Sarah E 5:31:22 (31,456)
Chapman, Sarah L 4:51:45 (24,475)
Chapman, Susan Jane 4:25:45 (17,738)
Chapman, Wendy 4:30:07 (19,003)
Chapman-Blench, Jan Anne........5:38:01 (32,214)
Charalambous, Maria................5:13:10 (28,796)
Charalambous, Pat 4:20:21 (16,220)
Chardine, Isabelle 4:07:39 (12,871)
Charlery, Paulette 3:25:05 (3,593)
Charles-Edwards, Helen Rachel ..5:00:36 (26,570)
Charlton, Alexandra 4:38:45 (21,185)
Charlton, Catherine M 3:19:33 (2,921)
Charlton, Ella 4:38:44 (21,182)
Charlton, Mary Patricia 4:46:32 (23,175)
Charman, Annabelle Louise 4:56:09 (25,567)
Charman, Rosemary 5:36:11 (32,015)
Charter, Sally Joanna 4:20:34 (16,281)
Chase, Debra Ann 6:04:47 (34,368)
Chase, Laura Helen 4:46:16 (23,118)
Chatburn, Katie Louise.............5:09:10 (28,080)
Chater, Jemma.......................4:12:48 (14,180)
Chatfield, Helen Louise 6:23:18 (35,250)
Chatten, Gwyneth J 6:40:18 (35,797)
Chau, Quang 5:34:34 (31,831)
Chaudhri, Sarah 3:58:00 (10,376)
Chauhan, Nila 6:30:24 (35,514)
Chavasse, Lindsay...................5:23:55 (30,464)
Cheema, Rajinder 5:21:24 (30,062)
Cheetham, Sandy Jayne 4:41:09 (21,807)
Chen, Jennifer Winnie..............4:01:52 (11,462)
Cheng, Jennifer......................4:30:02 (18,983)
Cherian, Susan 5:56:29 (33,828)
Cherry, Rachel 4:54:45 (25,245)
Chessum, Deborah Susanne.......4:29:36 (18,842)

Chesworth, Sharon B 8:15:04 (36,626)

I have had two surgeries in my life: I broke my
neck in a car accident aged 16 and an acute pro-
lapsed disc 5 years ago. I ran for the Spinal Injuries Association to say thanks and give something
back. I ran the last ever Flora and the inaugural
Virgin London Marathon. I am so proud of both
my achievements. I made it to 17 miles then I hit
the wall. I didn't want to continue. I then met a
lovely lady called Anne Rowan, who was very tired
and worried about finishing as well. We both completed together, hand in hand in 8 hours 15 minutes 4 seconds. My husband David Chesworth
supported me through both of these, my hero!

Chevis, Elizabeth Ann................5:26:56 (30,895)

Chick, Lucy Jane 4:14:10 (14,560)
Chicken, Rachel L....................4:10:32 (13,600)
Chidley, Heather 7:49:03 (36,561)
Childerley, Rachel 5:35:18 (31,902)
Childs, Angela 4:48:53 (23,768)
Childs, Helen Sarah 4:28:45 (18,591)
Childs, Lenore 4:23:03 (16,994)
Childs, Stacey 4:44:11 (22,557)
Childs, Stacy Ann 4:11:15 (13,779)
Chilton, Juliet Sandra 5:01:17 (26,703)
Chilton, Katie 4:53:17 (24,873)
Chilvers, Sarah 4:21:11 (16,459)
Ching, Catherine 5:18:34 (29,632)
Ching, Rosanna Comyn 5:13:57 (28,918)
Chinnery, Rachel.....................3:16:22 (2,594)
Chinwala, Yasmine 4:57:53 (25,944)
Chiswick, Kelly Clare................5:59:04 (33,994)
Chitty, Samantha 4:35:32 (20,352)
Chivers, Ann E.......................4:50:39 (24,195)
Chivers, Charlotte 5:28:04 (31,038)
Chivers, Harriet 5:04:32 (27,283)
Chivers, Laura 5:28:03 (31,036)
Chlopas, Rebecca A 4:26:34 (17,972)
Choi, Kwang Nim 4:30:22 (19,058)
Chomaud, Viviane 4:22:22 (16,811)
Chong, Jenny 5:22:45 (30,261)
Chowles, Eileen Anne...............5:20:08 (29,869)
Chrascina, Nicola A 4:52:12 (24,600)
Chrestia Blanchine, Sabine 4:41:46 (21,959)
Christen, Lucienne 4:08:18 (13,028)
Christie, Eidin 3:39:59 (6,139)
Christie, Erica M 3:18:33 (2,825)
Christie, Fiona 4:55:54 (25,513)
Christie, Jacqueline Ann.............5:05:29 (27,447)
Christie, Jill 3:08:55 (1,801)
Christie, Nathalie 2:55:52 (794)
Christie, Sharon E 4:46:46 (23,242)
Christie, Tina D 3:52:41 (8,843)
Christy, Carol 4:39:49 (21,465)
Chrysostomou, Elena................7:35:41 (36,491)
Chu, Catherine 4:00:46 (11,185)
Chubb, Fiona R 5:33:11 (31,685)
Chudy, Aline 4:00:25 (11,094)
Chudzynski, Sally M 4:05:36 (12,353)
Chung, Elsa 5:20:55 (29,996)
Chung, Joanne E 4:35:54 (20,446)
Church, Alison Jane..................4:19:15 (15,913)
Church, Emma Clare 7:08:23 (36,294)
Church, Gemma Louise 6:24:06 (35,282)
Church, Moya Ann...................4:47:40 (23,459)
Churchill, Julie 5:45:01 (32,870)
Churchill, Nina Louise 4:37:06 (20,771)
Churchill, Sarah Louise 4:39:10 (21,304)
Chymera, Chrystyna.................4:09:12 (13,260)
Clack, Tracey L 3:44:25 (6,975)
Clackett, Sally 4:59:13 (26,267)
Clackson, Sarah 5:25:37 (30,713)
Claffey, Anna 4:43:00 (22,259)
Clague, Lisa M 4:15:19 (14,865)
Claire, Bilwinder Kaur 6:16:58 (34,974)
Clake, Charlotte 5:55:25 (33,749)
Clampett, Anne 4:17:05 (15,317)
Clancy, Hayley Wendy 4:58:52 (26,183)
Clapham, Samantha Joan Sophie ..5:02:38 (26,965)
Clapp, Alexandra Joanne 4:10:35 (13,614)
Clare, Sylvia R 5:06:57 (27,716)
Claridge, Rebecca Louise 5:12:28 (28,649)
Claringbold, Jessica..................4:50:48 (24,238)
Clark, Ailsa Elizabeth 3:39:59 (6,139)
Clark, Barbara 3:13:34 (2,266)
Clark, Brigitte 4:19:44 (16,027)
Clark, Charlie 4:32:40 (19,599)
Clark, Demi Knight 5:37:21 (32,153)
Clark, Elizabeth Jane May..........4:19:39 (16,002)
Clark, Emily 4:51:27 (24,409)
Clark, Fiona Elizabeth 4:18:33 (15,725)
Clark, Fran 4:52:09 (24,448)
Clark, Gemma Louise 5:14:04 (28,934)
Clark, Hazel 4:09:14 (13,271)
Clark, Jessica Emily 6:00:48 (34,114)
Clark, Joanne A 4:30:03 (18,987)
Clark, Karen L 3:41:42 (6,457)
Clark, Katy Charlotte 4:06:20 (12,534)

Clark, Kelly Frances 3:42:01 (6,511)
Clark, Kristin 3:15:07 (2,452)
Clark, Laura..................... 4:50:55 (24,279)
Clark, Laura Jane 5:08:10 (27,922)
Clark, Lisa..................... 4:29:40 (18,870)
Clark, Lorna K..................... 5:32:05 (31,548)
Clark, Lucy 5:23:19 (30,361)
Clark, Marie D..................... 3:42:57 (6,685)
Clark, Rebecca..................... 5:07:14 (27,755)
Clark, Samantha Jane 3:53:47 (9,154)
Clark, Sarah Louise..................... 5:06:10 (27,558)
Clark, Sheryl L..................... 3:31:45 (4,705)
Clark, Shona..................... 4:58:33 (26,104)
Clark, Sonia Katrina..................... 5:19:47 (29,817)
Clark, Stephanie..................... 3:49:20 (8,050)
Clark, Stephanie..................... 5:48:04 (33,146)
Clark, Sylvia 4:27:43 (18,293)
Clarke, Alexis Ruth 5:31:35 (31,483)
Clarke, Alison..................... 5:09:10 (28,080)
Clarke, Caroline May..................... 4:25:28 (17,650)
Clarke, Donna Marie 4:57:38 (25,890)
Clarke, Elizabeth A 6:27:07 (35,389)
Clarke, Fran..................... 5:32:29 (31,600)
Clarke, Irene 8:13:23 (36,598)
Clarke, Joanne..................... 4:26:03 (17,825)
Clarke, Julie Ann..................... 4:51:11 (24,346)
Clarke, Julie Patricia 3:40:59 (6,320)
Clarke, Katharine E..................... 3:55:43 (9,677)
Clarke, Kerrie D 3:08:42 (1,783)
Clarke, Laura A 3:47:29 (7,644)
Clarke, Lesley C..................... 3:20:39 (3,043)
Clarke, Margaret U 4:20:00 (16,110)
Clarke, Natalie..................... 5:32:42 (31,631)
Clarke, Nenupher 4:47:34 (23,429)
Clarke, Rachael 5:29:21 (31,203)
Clarke, Sue 3:53:12 (8,971)
Clarke, Susan C 4:41:20 (21,848)
Clarkson, Kerry 6:29:22 (35,477)
Clarkson, Sally Nicola 4:17:25 (15,410)
Claxton, Jade Janis 5:55:28 (33,752)
Claxton, Joanna..................... 5:54:44 (33,688)
Claxton, Rachael..................... 4:21:38 (16,591)
Clay, Alice Clare 4:11:34 (13,867)
Clay, Gemma A..................... 3:47:04 (7,538)
Clay, Penny Jane..................... 4:51:58 (24,545)
Claydon, Nicky A..................... 4:19:09 (15,892)
Clayton, Anna Caroline 4:40:37 (21,674)
Clayton, Beverley..................... 5:02:21 (26,916)
Clayton, Beverley Jane 6:10:11 (34,674)
Clayton, Emily 4:35:26 (20,337)
Clayton, Jennifer..................... 5:32:50 (31,646)
Clayton, Jennifer Louise 4:02:46 (11,669)
Clayton, Judi Michelle 3:41:29 (6,419)
Clayton, Lucy..................... 3:19:23 (2,907)
Clayton, Susan L..................... 4:50:45 (24,224)
Cleal, Pauline J 6:58:50 (36,170)
Clear, Barbara..................... 5:00:02 (26,463)
Cleaver, Victoria 6:11:28 (34,719)
Cleere, Genevieve 4:06:44 (12,635)
Clegg, Dawn L..................... 5:20:29 (29,925)
Clegg, Stephanie 5:01:53 (26,827)
Cleland, Emma..................... 6:20:12 (35,135)
Cleland-James, Alexandra 5:06:59 (27,720)
Clemenson, Louise 4:52:30 (24,685)
Clements, Amy C..................... 3:33:09 (4,915)
Clements, Amy Elizabeth..................... 4:21:07 (16,443)
Clements, Angela 4:31:36 (19,352)
Clements, Clare Elizabeth 4:25:32 (17,672)
Clements, Denise M..................... 4:45:39 (22,935)
Clements, Kate Isabel Coatsworth . 5:40:18 (32,419)
Clements, Mary E 4:51:36 (24,440)
Clements, Paula..................... 3:37:40 (5,703)
Clemson, Susan Elizabeth 4:18:22 (15,678)
Clench, Jennie..................... 6:46:58 (35,948)
Clesham, Mary..................... 5:00:17 (26,515)
Clibbon, Lara 5:59:14 (34,005)
Cliffe, Jo..................... 4:51:48 (24,492)
Clifford, Alison..................... 5:46:37 (33,015)
Clifford, Debbie A..................... 5:27:42 (30,988)
Clifford, Lorna C..................... 5:28:59 (31,149)
Clifft, Jackie 5:01:36 (26,777)
Clifft, Samantha Jacqueline..................... 5:13:04 (28,763)
Clift, Lisa M 5:01:44 (26,803)

Clinch, Agnes M..................... 4:11:09 (13,758)
Clinch, Georgina..................... 3:50:41 (8,354)

Clingham, Gillian..................... 4:58:29 (26,082)

2010 was my fourth London Marathon. I was also lucky enough to run it on three consecutive years in 2006, 2007 and 2008. I chose to do Paris in 2009 but the unbeatable London atmosphere drew me back once more. The support given by the crowds is so uplifting, even through the searing heat of 2007 and the torrential rain of 2008. I'd like to thank everyone who called my name and cheered me on. I'm proud to have been able to raise money for worthy charities while enjoying a great personal achievement at my favourite marathon.

Clinker, Karen R..................... 4:27:34 (18,252)
Clinton, Jane M..................... 3:56:12 (9,841)
Clinton-Tarestad, Pia..................... 4:16:02 (15,038)
Clive, Helen..................... 5:02:03 (26,853)
Cload, Sharon 5:07:04 (27,736)
Clode, Emma L 5:05:10 (27,396)
Clotworthy, Amanda 4:33:43 (19,925)
Cloud, Samantha Jayne..................... 4:18:36 (15,744)
Clough, Lisa Marie..................... 4:59:55 (26,432)
Clough, Lucy M..................... 3:24:32 (3,514)
Clough, Paula..................... 3:56:36 (9,958)
Clowes, Lauren Frances..................... 4:25:18 (17,599)
Clusker, Kayleigh J 3:40:16 (6,192)
Clutterbuck, Lucy..................... 4:20:28 (16,252)
Coade, Tamsin Clare..................... 4:57:50 (25,931)
Coady, Kirsteen Marie..................... 4:06:01 (12,460)
Coates, Bev Jane 3:57:12 (10,156)
Coates, Georgina Stephanie..................... 6:23:22 (35,255)
Coates, Jenny..................... 4:27:11 (18,143)
Coates, Paula Marie 4:17:17 (15,374)
Coates, Sandy Anne 5:56:07 (33,797)
Coates, Zoe H..................... 3:32:50 (4,867)
Cobb, Heather A..................... 3:40:39 (6,270)
Cobb, Marieanne 5:28:55 (31,141)
Cobden-Jewitt, Zoe A..................... 4:04:19 (12,035)
Cobley, Nicola 5:27:24 (30,955)
Cochrane, Pamela Barbara..................... 5:53:08 (33,587)
Cochrane, Theresa Jane 4:01:45 (11,435)
Cock, Yvonne E..................... 3:47:23 (7,618)
Cockburn, Olivia Polly..................... 3:56:48 (10,030)
Cocker, Veronica Ruth..................... 5:01:39 (26,788)
Cockerell, Hannah..................... 4:33:34 (19,877)
Cockerill, Cassandra Jane..................... 4:22:01 (16,711)
Cockerill, Jean Helen..................... 4:56:30 (25,646)
Cockerton, Abby Marie..................... 4:50:45 (24,224)
Cockle, Hannah Victoria 4:47:31 (23,414)
Cocksedge, Zoe 4:57:50 (25,931)
Cockshott, Lynn Carole..................... 5:57:46 (33,917)
Cocks-McCracken, Sara R..................... 4:14:30 (14,647)
Codling, Maria 6:50:16 (36,003)
Codling, Vicky Louise..................... 5:24:32 (30,560)

Coe, Catherine..................... 4:56:40 (25,686)
Coe, Claudia..................... 4:35:09 (20,264)
Coe, Kathryn M..................... 3:46:47 (7,484)
Coe, Lianne Grace Ellen 6:16:19 (34,935)
Coe, Margaret..................... 6:11:47 (34,739)
Coffey, Vicki..................... 4:30:33 (19,106)
Coffman, Lynn M..................... 3:40:08 (6,175)
Cogger, Jenny Anne 5:44:31 (32,817)
Coghill, Patty..................... 6:48:04 (35,963)
Coghlan, Karen..................... 4:43:56 (22,486)
Cohen, Debbie..................... 8:48:16 (36,610)
Cohen, Noeleen..................... 5:28:11 (31,053)
Cohen, Tamara Jane 4:48:57 (23,788)
Coker, Elizabeth Sarah 4:46:33 (23,180)
Colam, Charlotte..................... 4:50:48 (24,238)
Colclough, Edwina M 3:30:16 (4,466)
Cole, Clare H..................... 5:15:39 (29,172)
Cole, Heidi Caroline..................... 6:26:52 (35,378)
Cole, Julie 4:19:07 (15,879)
Cole, Katy..................... 6:03:28 (34,287)
Cole, Lizzie 6:33:32 (35,613)
Cole, Michelle 3:14:34 (2,391)
Cole, Nicola A 3:56:46 (10,021)
Cole, Patricia Nadine..................... 5:00:33 (26,561)
Cole, Sophie 4:11:29 (13,844)
Cole, Tracey Mary 6:33:31 (35,611)
Colegrave, Debbie..................... 3:48:13 (7,784)
Coleman, Jayne 5:47:00 (33,051)
Coleman, Joanne S 3:55:43 (9,677)
Coleman, Nikki J..................... 4:42:55 (22,241)
Coleman, Susan Eileen..................... 3:32:42 (4,843)
Coleman, Tierney 4:09:25 (13,320)
Coleridge, Vanessa 5:33:24 (31,706)
Coles, Amanda J..................... 5:52:39 (33,547)
Coles, Elizabeth Alaina..................... 6:27:03 (35,387)
Coles, Ruth Catharine 5:41:56 (32,583)
Colgrave, Odette Louise..................... 4:31:11 (19,266)
Collett, Jackie 5:26:57 (30,898)
Collett, Julie Ann 4:58:37 (26,122)
Collett, Karen..................... 4:36:40 (20,651)
Collett, Olivia 5:26:11 (30,799)
Colley, Karon M..................... 3:31:22 (4,646)
Colley, Sara J..................... 4:05:48 (12,412)
Colley, Tracey 5:45:31 (32,910)
Collie, Alison Kay..................... 4:32:14 (19,494)
Collier, Bridget..................... 6:52:08 (36,047)
Collier, Emma Jane 4:25:59 (17,807)
Collier, Emma Jane 4:37:10 (20,786)
Collier, Janet S..................... 5:03:58 (27,179)
Collier, Sally..................... 4:53:53 (25,016)
Collier-Knight, Lily..................... 6:13:02 (34,804)
Collin, Suzanne J..................... 6:40:53 (35,810)
Collings, Andrea 4:41:47 (21,964)
Collingwood, Aleks 4:51:45 (24,475)
Collins, Anneli..................... 4:34:39 (20,156)
Collins, Catherine..................... 3:59:12 (10,779)
Collins, Claire..................... 4:54:12 (25,100)
Collins, Claire F..................... 7:21:47 (36,414)
Collins, Hannah Charlotte 5:09:52 (28,211)
Collins, Harriet Emma..................... 5:07:12 (27,752)
Collins, Joanne..................... 5:22:37 (30,241)
Collins, Kerry Lynne..................... 5:13:56 (28,916)
Collins, Leigh 5:59:26 (34,015)
Collins, Margaret Josephine..................... 4:00:24 (11,090)
Collins, Nicola Suzanne..................... 4:16:47 (15,244)
Collins, Peri D 5:38:09 (32,222)
Collins, Rachel 6:29:53 (35,494)
Collins, Rebecca Emma..................... 6:29:52 (35,492)
Collins, Sandra..................... 4:25:43 (17,725)
Collins, Sara..................... 3:46:45 (7,472)
Collins, Sarah 4:24:40 (17,435)
Collins, Sarah 4:36:22 (20,568)
Collins, Sharon..................... 5:54:49 (33,696)
Collins, Sheelagh Margaret..................... 3:54:40 (9,375)
Collins, Vikki E..................... 5:13:55 (28,913)
Collins, Virginia Dorothy..................... 4:14:03 (14,520)
Collinson, Claire 4:20:41 (16,328)
Collinson, Libby E..................... 3:35:45 (5,367)
Collison, Sarah 5:35:03 (31,880)
Collum, Angela Louisa 3:57:27 (10,214)
Colori, Amy..................... 5:39:58 (32,385)
Colquhoun, Shirley J 3:34:05 (5,074)
Coltman, Sarah C..................... 5:13:47 (28,890)

Colucci, Marie A....4:13:36 (14,404)
Colvin, Cassie J....3:54:29 (9,322)
Combe, Elisabeth....4:44:46 (22,718)
Combe, Emma....4:02:29 (11,600)
Combe, Marianne....4:32:40 (19,599)
Comber, Caroline L....4:17:25 (15,410)
Concannon, Donna R....4:57:49 (25,928)
Concannon, Siska I....5:17:30 (29,471)
Condie, Sally....4:42:58 (22,250)
Condy, Juliet Hellen....4:46:37 (23,209)
Coney, Helen....6:40:05 (35,790)
Conibear, Angela M....5:53:46 (33,626)
Connan, Jennifer Amy....5:37:06 (32,116)
Conneely, Janet....4:00:07 (11,011)
Conneely, Kathryn Clare....4:25:23 (17,629)
Connell, Anita F....4:25:10 (17,566)
Connell, Hannah E....4:05:32 (12,341)
Connell-Wynne, Kate....6:43:32 (35,876)
Connelly, Catherine....4:10:05 (13,491)
Connelly, Ruth....5:34:27 (31,817)
Connelly, Sharon....5:07:11 (27,749)
Conner, Christina....4:55:34 (25,424)
Connolly, Bernadette....5:17:25 (29,462)
Connolly, Lynne....3:58:43 (10,631)
Connolly, Rebecca....5:29:05 (31,162)
Connolly, Shenley....4:10:51 (13,680)
Connolly, Wendy....5:31:46 (31,510)
Connor, Hayley Elizabeth....4:54:11 (25,093)
Connor, Julie Catherine....5:24:32 (30,560)
Connor, Mandy L....5:04:31 (27,280)
Connor, Naomi Dionne....5:20:22 (29,894)
Connor, Stacey....3:55:43 (9,677)
Connors, Emma-Louise....5:15:48 (29,200)
Conophy, Bernadette Margaret...4:09:29 (13,336)
Considine, Rachael....4:47:32 (23,417)
Constable, Belinda Mary....5:31:52 (31,519)
Constable, Danielle Louise....5:27:56 (31,016)
Constable, Emma Christine....4:16:17 (15,099)
Constancon, Sharon....5:21:32 (30,077)
Conte, Franca....4:25:17 (17,595)
Conti, Jennie E....4:17:47 (15,522)
Conti, Jennifer E....3:20:56 (3,076)
Conway, Anneli F....4:57:22 (25,834)
Conway, Charlotte Claire....4:01:08 (11,282)
Conway, Eloise....4:44:30 (22,638)
Conway, Fiona C....4:56:44 (25,700)
Conway, Kate....4:09:41 (13,392)
Conway, Susan Ann....4:43:43 (22,423)
Conway, Victoria Louise....4:42:01 (22,017)
Cooil, Jan M....4:03:57 (11,952)
Cook, Angela Maria....3:50:39 (8,348)
Cook, Anne E....3:59:31 (10,866)
Cook, Camille....4:07:21 (12,787)
Cook, Charlotte....4:05:05 (12,225)
Cook, Helen S....3:56:27 (9,916)
Cook, Jennie Margaret....5:12:47 (28,699)
Cook, Jody....5:25:12 (30,650)
Cook, Judy A....6:18:48 (35,073)
Cook, Karen....5:22:43 (30,257)
Cook, Louise Mary....5:54:34 (33,679)
Cook, Marion Vera....5:41:59 (32,586)
Cook, Paula Wendy....4:13:50 (14,465)
Cook, Sara Jane....5:06:13 (27,571)
Cook, Sarah E....4:31:54 (19,407)
Cook, Shirley K....6:02:19 (34,206)
Cook, Siobhan Natalie....3:43:43 (6,808)
Cook, Tonia....4:40:13 (21,543)
Cook, Vanessa....4:45:31 (22,891)
Cooke, Amy Hannah....6:45:42 (35,923)
Cooke, Andrea....5:16:49 (29,355)
Cooke, Bridget Iona....6:07:07 (34,515)
Cooke, Elisabeth J....4:37:22 (20,836)
Cooke, Elizabeth....5:16:50 (29,359)
Cooke, Frances....3:25:53 (3,719)
Cooke, Sue....4:21:29 (16,542)
Cooley, Gemma Lesley Sylvia....5:33:26 (31,710)
Cooling, Rebecca Julia....6:52:32 (36,063)
Cooling, Susanna M....5:18:19 (29,592)
Coombs, Jackie....5:54:39 (33,682)
Cooper, Barbara Grace....6:50:46 (36,009)
Cooper, Bethan Sarah....5:19:23 (29,759)
Cooper, Bridget....5:08:07 (27,915)
Cooper, Carol....4:59:42 (26,386)

LONDON MARATHON

Cooper, Claire Louise....6:05:08 (34,396)
Cooper, Clare Elizabeth....4:38:31 (21,118)
Cooper, Cristina Oana....4:02:31 (11,608)
Cooper, Debra....4:49:53 (24,026)
Cooper, Hayley Caroline....4:40:14 (21,553)
Cooper, Jacqueline P....3:37:30 (5,664)
Cooper, Jennifer Anne....3:58:02 (10,391)
Cooper, Juistine M....5:46:15 (32,977)
Cooper, Justine....4:33:43 (19,925)
Cooper, Laura....4:19:07 (15,879)
Cooper, Lisa....4:45:31 (22,891)
Cooper, Lisa Marie....5:23:43 (30,429)
Cooper, Liz....4:38:22 (21,078)
Cooper, Lucy....5:39:54 (32,380)
Cooper, Marilyn J....4:26:29 (17,945)
Cooper, Patience A....4:52:08 (24,587)
Cooper, Sally A....4:31:16 (19,286)
Cooper, Sonya....4:08:53 (13,181)
Cooper, Stephanie J....3:34:05 (5,074)
Cooper, Sue....5:24:53 (30,600)
Cope, Amy L....3:16:31 (2,610)
Cope, Janice Lorraine....4:34:57 (20,222)
Cope, Lucy....3:18:12 (2,794)
Copeland, Claire....6:54:36 (36,098)
Copestake, Alexandra Anna....4:18:42 (15,774)
Copland, Harriet M....4:14:54 (14,763)
Copse, Gina....6:25:54 (35,346)
Copsey, Lois Jane....4:37:11 (20,790)
Copson-Ball, Sally....4:15:42 (14,952)
Corbersmith, Leanne....5:45:48 (32,932)
Corbet Burcher, Poppy Liliana...5:29:17 (31,188)
Corbo, Amelia....5:03:45 (27,148)
Corcoran, Kathryn Louise....5:00:36 (26,570)
Cordell, Mavis....5:32:13 (31,564)
Corder, Maria Jane....5:49:29 (33,282)
Cordrey, Julie Elizabeth....5:25:31 (30,696)
Corfield, Melainie R....5:13:56 (28,916)
Cork, Alison....5:36:36 (32,066)
Cork, Karen Ann....4:53:41 (24,965)
Cork, Naomi....5:16:40 (29,333)
Corlett, Carley H....4:44:17 (22,586)
Corlett, Linda....5:15:42 (29,177)
Cormack, Suzanne M....4:09:43 (13,399)
Cornberg, Christina Rose....5:43:24 (32,712)
Cornish, Aldona....4:43:56 (22,486)
Cornish, Beth....4:27:41 (18,284)
Cornish, Jennifer L....3:31:08 (4,600)
Cornish, Suzanne....3:42:30 (6,597)
Cornock, Jane Margaret....5:56:09 (33,806)
Cornthwaite, Carolyn....4:36:34 (20,622)
Cornwall, Victoria....5:23:11 (30,337)
Cornwell, Ema Louise....5:21:33 (30,083)
Cornwell, Nicola J....4:38:26 (21,099)
Correa, Sandra M....7:06:57 (36,278)
Corrigan, Kelly Marie....4:14:46 (14,732)
Corrin, Lucy....4:36:13 (20,530)
Corsini, Susan J....3:25:15 (3,614)
Corti, Bambi M....6:08:58 (34,615)
Cory, Elaine....4:59:43 (26,388)
Cory, Sarah A....3:30:56 (4,569)
Cosimetti, Anna L....4:22:15 (16,786)
Cosnett, Sue Denise....4:56:31 (25,653)
Costello, Bernadette....5:12:18 (28,620)
Costeloe, Silvia....4:49:45 (23,994)
Coster, Emma....3:50:28 (8,305)
Costick, Hayley....4:40:18 (21,574)
Costiff, Christine....3:22:11 (3,208)
Cottam, Sophie....4:46:12 (23,090)
Cottee, Nicola Claire....5:39:22 (32,340)
Cottenham, Alex....4:53:23 (24,889)
Cotter, Lucy....4:49:19 (23,874)
Cotter, Lucy Jane....5:29:32 (31,226)
Cotterell, Christine....7:27:21 (36,454)
Cotterill, Dawn Karen....5:10:21 (28,301)
Cottle, Agnes....5:06:25 (27,606)
Cottle, Ann M....5:23:17 (30,354)
Cottle, Helen Eliabeth....4:44:41 (22,696)
Cotton, Catherine....4:19:26 (15,957)
Cotton, Emma J....3:23:18 (3,341)
Cotton, Helen V....4:33:19 (19,807)
Cotton, Jody Elizabeth....4:45:55 (23,005)
Cotton, Rhian....5:18:15 (29,582)
Cotton, Tracy Rebecca....5:13:58 (28,919)
Cottrill, Mary....6:19:22 (35,099)
Couchman, Jemma....6:08:23 (34,575)
Coughlan, Fiona M....5:22:15 (30,181)
Couling, Debra....4:26:39 (17,986)
Coulson, Emma Clair....5:06:16 (27,579)
Coulson, Mary....5:13:21 (28,821)
Coultart, Sharon A....3:48:28 (7,837)
Coultrip, Corrina Jane....7:29:05 (36,462)
Counihan, Emily....3:54:04 (9,225)
Couperus, Akky....5:27:29 (30,963)
Coupland, Mary Ann....5:47:32 (33,100)
Court, Louise Clare....5:38:40 (32,281)
Court, Rachel....4:46:14 (23,104)
Courtauld, Sarah....4:35:34 (20,358)
Courtney, Denise....5:43:29 (32,718)
Courtney, Sylvia....5:47:05 (33,059)
Cousins, Karen June....3:49:11 (8,021)
Cousins, Kelli....5:24:18 (30,526)
Cousins, Rachel Helen....5:10:16 (28,284)
Coutts, Marla....3:54:44 (9,397)
Covan-Tomlin, Funda....4:14:47 (14,740)
Coveley, Jennifer Margaret....5:10:18 (28,288)
Coveley, Jessica....4:00:21 (11,076)
Cover, Alexandra Marie....5:11:32 (28,482)
Cover, Amanda L....4:29:02 (18,697)
Cowan, Eleanor F....4:28:02 (18,375)
Cowan, Heather....5:15:21 (29,115)
Cowan, Sally Michelle....3:52:17 (8,734)
Cowell, Lesley H....4:17:32 (15,452)
Cowen, Samantha J....3:34:51 (5,220)
Cowie, Alexis Mary....6:09:20 (34,630)
Cowin, Emma L....6:26:54 (35,381)
Cowley, Carol....3:42:38 (6,616)
Cowley, Julie....4:12:57 (14,216)
Cowley, Kate L....6:45:20 (35,918)
Cowley, Laura J....2:47:30 (402)
Cowley, Melissa....4:33:48 (19,944)
Cowley, Sarah Margaret....5:22:50 (30,278)
Cowling, Gert T....4:33:24 (19,825)
Cowling, Louise Charlotte....5:49:37 (33,294)
Cowling, Ruth....4:28:58 (18,670)
Cowman, Sharon....4:27:03 (18,097)
Cowpe, Samantha....6:03:05 (34,259)
Cowper, Verity....4:17:02 (15,306)
Cowton, Bernice R....3:58:08 (10,426)
Cox, Bethany Eve....4:20:19 (16,209)
Cox, Claire....4:20:44 (16,347)
Cox, Emma....5:10:38 (28,354)
Cox, Georgie....3:58:19 (10,499)
Cox, Jacqueline L....5:26:54 (30,890)
Cox, Julia Elaine....4:24:02 (17,245)
Cox, Kathryn....4:44:06 (22,534)
Cox, Lynne M....3:18:38 (2,834)
Cox, Melanie....4:22:48 (16,939)
Cox, Rachel Elizabeth....4:09:24 (13,313)
Cox, Sally L....3:41:03 (6,334)
Cox, Sarah....4:57:26 (25,844)
Cox, Tanya....4:57:38 (25,890)
Cox, Teresa Ann....5:39:53 (32,375)
Cox, Victoria Alison....4:30:34 (19,113)
Coxall, Kaylee....4:13:56 (14,486)
Coxon, Clare....6:15:08 (34,892)
Coy, Vicky....4:20:42 (16,333)
Coyle, Colette....4:48:19 (23,609)
Coyle, Deborah Gean....4:39:45 (21,447)
Coyne, Monica....4:20:49 (16,369)
Crabb, Mary J....4:32:56 (19,680)
Crabtree, Linda C....3:56:54 (10,056)
Cracknell, Joanne Patricia....5:59:23 (34,011)
Cracknell, Tamsin Louise....5:12:57 (28,730)
Craddock, Louise Caroline....5:25:34 (30,706)
Cradduck, Hollie Mary....5:35:20 (31,910)
Cragg, Deborah....4:17:54 (15,546)
Craig, Anita....4:18:04 (15,603)
Craig, Anna....3:58:26 (10,537)

Craig, Charlotte J......3:53:46 (9,147)
Craig, Claire L......7:03:30 (36,232)
Craig, Mary A......3:19:35 (2,924)
Craig, Susan......5:03:24 (27,089)
Craine, Rosy C......3:29:32 (4,328)
Crame, Chloe May......4:57:40 (25,901)
Cramond, Jenna......4:14:39 (14,700)
Cramp, Helen K......3:32:53 (4,878)
Cramsie, Victoria......5:10:30 (28,327)
Cran, Rona......4:59:57 (26,439)
Crandon, Barbara L......3:48:30 (7,848)
Crane, Colleen Ann......3:52:08 (8,689)
Crane, Denise......5:09:55 (28,214)
Crane, Jacqueline......6:16:25 (34,944)
Crane, Julie Anne......4:05:48 (12,412)
Crane, Kathryn......5:50:16 (33,361)
Crane, Roberta Josephine......5:09:55 (28,214)
Cranston, Emma......3:14:29 (2,380)
Cranton, Patricia K......3:34:12 (5,096)
Crashaw, Sophia......4:43:39 (22,405)
Crashley, Sue......4:21:58 (16,695)
Craven, Julie......7:18:21 (36,389)
Craven, Lucy Rebecca......4:42:01 (22,017)
Craven, Samantha Louise......4:39:17 (21,326)
Crawford, Abbe Harper......4:31:16 (19,286)
Crawford, Emma L......3:51:25 (8,518)
Crawford, Kate......4:07:09 (12,744)
Crawford, Lorna......4:47:00 (23,309)
Crawford, Sarah Rachel......4:07:09 (12,744)
Crawley, Christine Ann......6:33:05 (35,599)
Crawley, Jane Elizabeth......4:17:59 (15,573)
Crawley, Julie Ann......5:38:08 (32,219)
Crawley, Natasha Suzanne......5:33:33 (31,721)
Craze, Susan Karen......5:18:54 (29,684)
Creagh, Barbara......3:59:59 (10,982)
Cream, Tania J......3:34:34 (5,166)
Creasey, Louise......5:01:18 (26,709)
Credland, Emma J......4:51:06 (24,333)
Creed, Caroline E......4:00:48 (11,194)
Creed, Joanna Stephanie......3:47:24 (7,620)
Creed, Jo-Anne......5:06:17 (27,581)
Cregan, Hazel......4:51:06 (24,333)
Cresswell, Elizabeth......4:36:28 (20,591)
Cresswell, Jayne......5:00:40 (26,581)
Crew, Louise......6:25:14 (35,323)
Crewe, Rachel Jade......5:36:08 (32,009)
Crews, Sharon......4:17:26 (15,416)
Criado, Juana......3:23:28 (3,361)
Crichlow-Chambers, Vanessa......6:09:28 (34,635)
Crick, Anette......3:49:25 (8,070)
Crickmore, Lucy Amanda......5:42:02 (32,590)
Criddle, Alison......5:33:46 (31,741)
Criddle, Hayley......5:04:41 (27,315)
Cridland, Georgina Jane......4:27:17 (18,174)
Crilley, Kathy......5:45:51 (32,940)
Crilly, Frances-Mary......5:50:31 (33,389)
Crilly, Joanne Susan......4:55:02 (25,316)
Cringle, Carla......4:49:12 (23,849)
Crisp, Jo......4:41:27 (21,878)
Crisp, Kelle Louise......6:05:26 (34,416)
Critchley, Elizabeth......6:38:29 (35,741)
Critchley, Michelle Sarah......4:20:34 (16,281)
Critchley, Ronda Louisa......4:47:51 (23,510)
Croad, Karen......5:17:31 (29,476)
Croasdell, Laura......4:34:07 (20,025)
Crocker, Christine......7:04:12 (36,247)
Crocker, Habe......4:31:05 (19,238)
Crocker, Marilyn J......5:22:11 (30,175)
Crocker, Rosemarie Joan......4:38:39 (21,154)
Crockford, Claire......4:53:00 (24,792)
Crocombe, Emma L......3:33:08 (4,913)
Croft, Rachael E......4:27:18 (18,181)
Croker, Charlotte Emily......4:46:41 (23,230)
Cromack, Jenny......3:38:30 (5,846)
Crombie, Ann-Marie......4:14:16 (14,586)
Crome, Debra......4:20:27 (16,248)
Crompton, Una Mary......4:24:00 (17,236)
Croney, Rachel......4:21:49 (16,643)
Cronin, Emma Kate......4:41:32 (21,905)
Cronin, Rachel......4:41:05 (21,790)
Cronk, Jamie......5:22:53 (30,289)
Crook, Jill L......5:20:37 (29,949)
Crosbie Dawson, Lucy Charlotte.4:52:41 (24,728)

Crosby, Louise......4:01:17 (11,313)
Crosby, Philippa Kate......3:41:47 (6,473)
Crosley, Carol......4:11:01 (13,720)
Cross, Anna......4:31:08 (19,250)
Cross, Fiona Margaret......4:07:37 (12,860)
Cross, Kerry Louise......5:32:36 (31,618)
Cross, Sally H......4:04:45 (12,145)
Crossan, Michelle......6:28:02 (35,422)
Crossland, Mel......5:28:43 (31,117)
Crossley, Alice......5:18:26 (29,617)
Crossman, Sarah-Jane......4:51:41 (24,457)
Crosswell, Charlotte......5:18:27 (29,621)
Crothers, Rebecca Esther......4:43:42 (22,417)
Crouch, Amy L......4:38:51 (21,218)
Crouch, Danielle Elise......4:20:33 (16,275)
Croucher, Hayley......5:01:06 (26,668)
Croudass, Suzanne......3:25:05 (3,593)
Crowhurst, Paula......4:32:01 (19,441)
Crowley, Jayne Olivia......4:59:28 (26,326)
Crowther, Heather......6:24:44 (35,301)
Crowther, Holly Marie......5:11:41 (28,498)
Crowther, Lesley......5:02:56 (27,018)
Crowther, Natalie J......6:14:37 (34,865)
Cruden, Sophy......4:30:53 (19,185)
Cruickshank, Irene J......4:38:35 (21,137)
Cruickshank, Laura......3:54:36 (9,354)
Cruickshank, Rebecca Elizabeth.4:11:18 (13,790)
Cruse, Sharon......5:02:20 (26,912)
Crute, Catherine J......6:13:07 (34,812)
Cruz, Samantha......4:29:30 (18,808)
Cruz Bonilla, Zaida......5:35:24 (31,916)
Cryan, Lisa......4:01:43 (11,415)
Crystal, Louise......5:42:53 (32,659)
Crystal, Lucy......5:17:12 (29,415)
Cubbage, Joanna......4:48:09 (23,579)
Cubbage, Margaret Louise......5:08:58 (28,037)
Cudworth, Tracey......3:46:58 (7,522)
Cuffe, Wendy......5:35:52 (31,980)
Cuffley, Lynn C......4:45:03 (22,782)
Culit, Syndiah......3:44:53 (7,075)
Cull, Jenny L......4:48:46 (23,736)
Cullen, Jayne......4:32:29 (19,556)
Cullen, Jodi Suzanne......3:52:16 (8,729)
Cullen, Melanie Christine......5:18:04 (29,556)
Culling, Tina Jane......4:18:17 (15,655)
Cullis, Kate......5:31:30 (31,474)
Cullum, Hayley Louise......5:30:24 (31,336)
Cullup, Catherine A......4:58:48 (26,165)
Culp, Andrea L......3:26:16 (3,780)
Cumber, Sarah L......2:58:11 (974)
Cumber Fox, Claire Louise......5:06:54 (27,702)
Cuming, Amanda J......4:52:07 (24,578)
Cumley, Nicola......4:06:28 (12,562)
Cumming, Ellie Grace......5:52:45 (33,563)
Cummings, Corinne Elizabeth....3:50:53 (8,400)
Cummings, Linda......5:56:01 (33,788)
Cummins, Fiona S......3:44:09 (6,905)
Cummins, Karen Teresa......4:13:30 (14,365)
Cumper, Joanne......6:37:45 (35,715)
Cundy, Laura Anne......6:22:51 (35,227)
Cuneen, Jacqueline B......3:35:50 (5,380)
Cunliffe, Katie......5:06:38 (27,654)

Cunnane, Rebecca Louise......3:47:46 (7,699)

It was an amazing day for me for a few reasons: I got a PB which I had worked so hard for; I ran well and enjoyed the crowds; but mainly because I had my husband Chris, who without his support I wouldn't have done so well; my beautiful baby William and my mom Pamela cheering me on. Family and running! Perfect!

Cunningham, Hannah Louise....5:07:10 (27,746)
Cunningham, Natalie Anne......4:43:30 (22,369)
Cunningham, Sarah L......5:57:56 (33,927)
Cunningham, Sue......4:29:01 (18,691)
Cunningham, Veronica......4:51:03 (24,316)
Cuny, Christiane......4:18:35 (15,741)
Curd, Charlotte......6:08:09 (34,564)
Curley, Amanda Katherine......4:38:26 (21,099)

Curran, Sarah T......4:01:39 (11,404)
Currid, Angela Caroline......3:51:03 (8,435)
Currie, Penny......5:59:42 (34,037)
Currie-Godbolt, Denise......3:42:28 (6,590)
Currill, Emma L......6:01:31 (34,159)
Curry, Emma......4:07:46 (12,900)
Curry, Philippa Louise......4:53:23 (24,889)
Curtin, Eimear C......3:40:34 (6,252)
Curtin, Jo......5:26:38 (30,856)
Curtis, Alison......5:40:28 (32,428)
Curtis, Angela Rose......4:58:01 (25,972)
Curtis, Emma Louise......4:31:10 (19,258)
Curtis, Eve......5:41:55 (32,581)
Curtis, Joanna H......3:33:41 (5,004)
Curtis, Leanne......3:51:14 (8,482)
Curtis, Lucy......5:31:40 (31,497)
Curtis, Maggie T......4:24:46 (17,458)
Curtis, Pat M......3:22:19 (3,219)
Curtis, Sarah......5:35:36 (31,936)
Curtiss, Vanessa Jayne......5:38:14 (32,230)
Cushing, Alice May......4:59:04 (26,230)
Custance, Lucie J......3:22:54 (3,278)
Cutbill, Jane......3:46:37 (7,444)
Cutcliffe, Kirsty Jill......4:17:04 (15,311)
Cutforth, Victoria......6:36:01 (35,676)
Cuthbert, Fiona......5:12:59 (28,738)
Cutting, Alison Clare......4:47:48 (23,494)
Cutting, Helen Elizabeth......7:14:03 (36,353)
Cutts, Amy......4:45:33 (22,901)
Czerniewska, Alexandra......3:58:05 (10,407)
Czik, Bex......5:49:29 (33,282)
Da Silva, Emma Louise......5:17:50 (29,518)
Daas, Patricia A......5:55:15 (33,738)
Daborn, Elizabeth......6:17:08 (34,985)
Dacre, Bonita Y......4:28:07 (18,392)
Dady, Gill......4:48:46 (23,736)
Daff, Stella K......4:44:00 (22,504)
Dahabiyeh, Sarah R......3:38:15 (5,813)
Dahle, Astrid Groenningen......3:49:36 (8,115)
Dail, Narinder......5:28:39 (31,102)
Dailey, Simone......3:48:28 (7,837)
Dailly, Kirsty Anne......4:39:51 (21,477)
Dakers, Kim......4:29:09 (18,721)
Dalby, Karen Rebecca......3:59:17 (10,808)
Dale, Ann E......3:28:10 (4,086)
Dale, Charlotte Jade......6:51:31 (36,025)
Dale, Donna......3:58:28 (10,544)
Dale, Jayne Alison......4:07:20 (12,781)
Dale, Julie A......3:23:52 (3,415)
Dale, Michelle Susan......3:52:20 (8,750)
Dale, Nicola Irene......4:08:28 (13,069)
Dale, Sandra Jane......3:51:10 (8,464)
Dale, Sue I......3:53:28 (9,045)
Dale, Wendy Jane......4:24:04 (17,252)
Dale-Hughes, Louise......4:29:36 (18,842)
Daley, Jade......6:19:58 (35,123)
Dallimore, Rebecca Jane......4:28:48 (18,609)
Dallison, Nikki......4:50:07 (24,075)
Dalmeny, Caroline......6:26:33 (35,368)
Dalton, Emma K......2:56:54 (854)
Dalton, Pauline......3:59:23 (10,834)
Dalton, Penny......4:07:27 (12,817)
Dalton, Ting......4:46:39 (23,224)
Daly, Deborah Alicia......3:47:09 (7,556)
Dalzell, Julie......3:27:43 (3,999)
Damerum, Emmaline......4:37:02 (20,755)
D'Amico, Maria......5:29:53 (31,278)
D'Amone, Marilena......4:48:16 (23,604)
Dance, Sarah L......4:55:14 (25,367)
Dane, Lucy Ann......6:17:13 (34,991)
Daniel, Joanna Louise......4:45:57 (23,012)
Daniel, Joanna M......3:55:52 (9,740)
Daniell, Jo-Anne......5:32:31 (31,605)
Daniels, Paula Marie......5:40:10 (32,408)
Daniels, Tania......4:09:49 (13,424)
Danks, Amy Louise......5:31:54 (31,523)
Danks, Emma J......3:47:26 (7,628)
Dansie, Suzanne......4:34:51 (20,206)
Danson, Claire F......3:35:31 (5,327)
Danton, Joanna Ruth......3:50:32 (8,321)
Darby, Catherine M......3:57:58 (10,370)
Darbyshire, Gill Mary......7:03:26 (36,230)
Dare, Clare......5:02:31 (26,946)

Daret, Nicole 3:59:51 (10,952)
Darke, Hannah V 6:16:36 (34,958)
Darlaston, Justine Annette 4:40:11 (21,533)
Darley, Clare 3:59:10 (10,764)
Darling, Mary 3:11:29 (2,048)
Darlington, Catherine Emily 5:31:18 (31,449)
Darragh, Stephanie 5:30:10 (31,312)
Dartford, Louise 5:35:59 (31,994)
Darvill, Sarah 6:05:10 (34,400)
Darwood, Joanne 3:50:41 (8,354)
Dasari, Samantha Marie 5:25:38 (30,720)
Dass, Samita 5:56:40 (33,841)
Date, Claire Louise 5:29:09 (31,171)
Daunay, Christine 4:38:15 (21,041)
Davenport, Clare 4:45:01 (22,775)
Davenport, Janet 5:22:54 (30,292)
Davey, Debbie 5:22:44 (30,259)
Davey, Freya 6:41:44 (35,825)
Davey, Helen Geraldine 4:55:52 (25,504)
Davey, Joanne Claire 5:35:03 (31,880)
Davey, Judy M 3:26:08 (3,757)
Davey, Louise Jeanine 4:30:54 (19,190)
David, Anna 3:47:07 (7,545)
David, Emma 5:21:40 (30,106)
David, Fiona H 4:49:11 (23,844)
David, Nicola 6:00:31 (34,094)
Davidson, Alexandra Rebecca 5:33:11 (31,685)
Davidson, Anne 4:57:28 (25,852)
Davidson, Emily E 5:14:44 (29,024)
Davidson, Kate Anne 4:33:18 (19,803)
Davidson, Kelly 7:07:40 (36,286)
Davidson, Lisa 4:33:11 (19,757)
Davidson, Lucy 5:35:09 (31,891)
Davidson, Lucy Marie 5:25:38 (30,720)
Davidson, Michelle Renée 5:20:04 (29,858)
Davidson, Valerie M 5:10:35 (28,346)
Davidson, Violet 5:22:18 (30,190)
Davies, Alison Susan 4:12:19 (14,059)
Davies, Anna Claire Catharine 5:14:39 (29,011)
Davies, Anna-Marie 4:41:52 (21,985)
Davies, Anne 3:23:20 (3,344)
Davies, Annwen Elizabeth 5:21:12 (30,032)
Davies, Arlene 4:24:30 (17,388)
Davies, Beverley Anne 5:16:00 (29,229)
Davies, Cara Sadie 5:25:43 (30,734)
Davies, Carol-Ann 3:31:51 (4,719)
Davies, Caroline 4:51:22 (24,390)
Davies, Carolyn 7:00:02 (36,188)
Davies, Catherine Anne 5:18:21 (29,597)
Davies, Catherine H 4:54:47 (25,255)
Davies, Ceri-Anne 3:26:56 (3,865)
Davies, Danielle 5:43:38 (32,731)
Davies, Donna 3:58:41 (10,619)
Davies, Emma R 5:12:49 (28,703)
Davies, Frances M 5:15:47 (29,196)
Davies, Gemma Louise 5:40:56 (32,475)
Davies, Hilda 7:16:55 (36,378)
Davies, Jessica 4:10:55 (13,693)
Davies, Joanne Frances 6:31:03 (35,536)
Davies, Josie Mary 5:09:08 (28,075)
Davies, Julia M 3:24:21 (3,496)
Davies, Julie Elizabeth 4:21:15 (16,477)
Davies, Karen J 3:43:41 (6,803)
Davies, Kim L 5:55:34 (33,759)
Davies, Louise Michelle 4:17:16 (15,368)
Davies, Lynne 5:16:13 (29,255)
Davies, Maribeth 4:46:12 (23,090)
Davies, Marie 6:06:28 (34,480)
Davies, Michele A 3:45:52 (7,285)
Davies, Michelle L 4:08:48 (13,161)
Davies, Nicola Lynne 4:07:03 (12,723)
Davies, Nikki 6:22:31 (35,210)
Davies, Pam 4:04:49 (12,157)
Davies, Paula 5:07:55 (27,883)
Davies, Pauline 3:26:25 (3,796)
Davies, Rebecca 5:59:58 (34,059)
Davies, Sarah Jane 5:28:54 (31,136)
Davies, Sue Jane Elizabeth 4:45:06 (22,799)
Davies, Susan Maureen 5:58:26 (33,961)
Davies, Valerie 4:13:14 (14,295)
Davies, Wendy 5:17:17 (29,435)
Davies, Yolande 4:02:39 (11,638)
Davies, Zoe M 5:55:33 (33,758)

Running on green

Originally, the lead vehicles in the London Marathon were milk floats, driven by experienced runners. In 2010 there are now 100 zero-emission vehicles. Other Marathon 'green credentials' include biodegradable materials to serve all food and drink at the start with wooden cutlery and non-waxed cups and plates. No polystyrene. All the t-shirts handed out at the finish are produced in a WRAP factory (World Responsible Apparel Production). And the ExCel Exhibition Centre, where runners must register before the race, boasts a recycling 'wormery' – it currently houses 300,000 worms – which must be another record for the London Marathon.

Davies, Zoe Rebecca 5:30:53 (31,401)
Davies,, Janet Eileen 5:31:55 (31,528)
Davies-Raimbault, Angela M 5:00:57 (26,643)
Davis, Annabelle 7:29:03 (36,461)
Davis, Catherine Anne 4:37:05 (20,768)
Davis, Consuelo 6:42:23 (35,847)
Davis, Courtney 7:59:15 (36,585)
Davis, Gemma Elizabeth 5:25:48 (30,754)
Davis, Hannah 5:22:32 (30,224)
Davis, Jayne Lynn 4:14:42 (14,715)
Davis, Jennifer 4:23:09 (17,013)
Davis, Jo Helena 6:30:17 (35,511)
Davis, Katherine Anne 5:15:47 (29,196)
Davis, Kelley 6:04:55 (34,379)
Davis, Kerry D 5:29:21 (31,203)
Davis, Kirsty 5:15:13 (29,102)
Davis, Margaret 6:28:20 (35,437)
Davis, Maria Bridget 6:54:04 (36,087)
Davis, Merilyn J 3:48:46 (7,914)
Davis, Sarah 4:46:34 (23,185)
Davis, Stella 5:10:47 (28,375)
Davis, Stella 5:11:45 (28,511)
Davis, Tracey 5:20:48 (29,977)
Davis, Victoria Jane 5:46:20 (32,988)
Davison, Laura Rebecca 5:14:38 (29,008)
Davison, Nicola J 4:10:43 (13,643)
Davison, Sarah 4:41:09 (21,807)
Daw, Eve 5:03:36 (27,120)
Dawes-Clark, Sarah Louise 4:53:15 (24,862)
Dawett, Sunita 4:04:20 (12,040)
Dawkins, Justine Colette 4:20:20 (16,215)
Dawkins, Maggie 4:16:21 (15,125)
Dawkins, Natalie 4:29:37 (18,852)
Dawkins, Rachel Caroline 6:06:33 (34,483)
Dawson, Helen Sarah 5:02:47 (26,991)
Dawson, Julie 5:45:55 (32,944)
Dawson, Lucy 4:34:52 (20,208)
Dawson, Mary 4:37:18 (20,818)
Dawson, Nadia E 5:05:00 (27,368)
Dawson, Rachel C 4:41:02 (21,777)
Day, Claire Samantha 5:23:40 (30,419)
Day, Clare 6:03:45 (34,306)
Day, Deborah Jane 3:55:47 (9,711)
Day, Elizabeth 5:43:24 (32,712)
Day, Katie 4:59:21 (26,300)
Day, Lucy 4:52:32 (24,694)
Day, Petrina Rona 5:22:46 (30,262)
Dayal, Rajvinder Kaur 5:15:43 (29,183)
De Boick, Wendy 4:34:04 (20,013)
De Buisseret, Renata 4:50:37 (24,187)
De Cristofano, Sarah 5:15:28 (29,138)
De Florinier, Annette Louise 5:10:19 (28,294)
De Gouveia, Gemma 5:05:11 (27,401)
De Jonckheere, Elisabeth 3:59:39 (10,903)
De Kloet-Levelink, G 5:18:25 (29,610)
De La Nougerede, Anne Marie 5:52:32 (33,535)
De Lange, Louisa 4:58:11 (26,008)
De Lara, Catherine 5:47:18 (33,076)
De Lara, Tamsin Anne 5:00:48 (26,613)
De Lurdes Carvahlo Dias, Maria 4:51:38 (24,447)
De Martino, Brenda Marion 4:52:29 (24,681)
De Moraes, Niki 6:04:38 (34,359)
De Silva, Teresa 4:32:18 (19,514)
De Smedt, Beryl 4:04:34 (12,087)
Deacon, Lisa 4:25:51 (17,768)
Deadman, Alison Catherine 4:43:01 (22,263)
Deakin, Bryony Geneste 4:03:11 (11,773)
Deakin, Trudi Anne 4:35:40 (20,380)
Dean, Dixie H 4:55:35 (25,429)
Dean, Julia Anne 5:06:20 (27,593)
Dean, Megan 5:03:09 (27,048)
Dean, Rupert 5:13:04 (28,763)
Dean, Sara Suzanne 4:55:39 (25,447)
Dean, Suzanne E 4:40:10 (21,530)
Dean, Tracy Ann 5:56:22 (33,820)
Deane, Charlotte Louise 4:26:34 (17,972)
Dean-Stevens, Liz 5:26:43 (30,865)
Dear, Sue W 4:41:39 (21,934)
Deary, Jane 4:54:00 (25,052)
Deason, Helen L 4:56:27 (25,640)
Debattista, Pamela Ann 4:02:54 (11,708)
Debling, Kim Anne 4:58:08 (26,001)
Debruyn, Kate 4:03:03 (11,740)
Debureaux, Christelle 4:23:48 (17,191)
Decker, Helen 2:36:56 (140)
Deegan, Karen Louise 4:49:45 (23,994)
Deehan, Cecilia M 6:38:50 (35,751)
Deeks, Julie A 5:57:33 (33,907)
Deen, Saajda 3:55:44 (9,688)
Deering, Sarah 4:52:49 (24,761)
Defries, Julie 4:08:37 (13,122)
Degroot, Annabelle Claire 5:37:23 (32,158)
Dehnavi, Julie Ann Jean 5:48:44 (33,219)
Deighton, Avelline M 4:14:25 (14,621)
Deighton, Ursula 5:29:38 (31,243)
Delacroix, Florence 4:33:24 (19,825)
Delaney, Martina Ruth 5:25:36 (30,709)
Delaney, Suzanne 6:18:35 (35,061)
Delany, Lisa Claire 4:25:10 (17,566)
Delany, Siobhan 4:52:57 (24,785)
Delderfield, Diane L 4:40:00 (21,502)
Dellar, Natalie Elizabeth 4:34:49 (20,198)
Dellasega, Caroline 4:08:32 (13,098)
Dellow, Suzanne Rosina 5:15:22 (29,119)
Deloubes, Lynne Michele 5:32:49 (31,643)
Demetriou, Kerry Lee 5:03:30 (27,100)
Demonti, Sara 3:48:23 (7,820)
Dempsey, Alison 6:44:20 (35,893)
Dempsey, Margaret Marie 5:21:37 (30,098)
Denham-Jones, Laura 4:23:37 (17,140)
Denholm, Ruth Anne 5:24:07 (30,498)
Dennehy, Rebecca Claire 5:23:58 (30,476)
Denney, Carla 4:53:04 (24,806)
Denning, Elspeth Lindsay 6:07:30 (34,531)
Dennis, Frances Bethen 4:51:50 (24,504)
Dennis, Helena Bridget 4:07:25 (12,804)
Dennis, Lucy 3:54:52 (9,441)
Dennis, Nicola Jane 5:16:59 (29,383)
Dennis, Tracy 7:35:14 (36,488)
Dennison, Emma 5:11:56 (28,547)
Dennison, Kelly L 3:08:52 (1,799)
Denny, Jo 5:13:46 (28,884)
Denny, Sarai 5:01:00 (26,649)
Dent, Hazel Anne 5:29:03 (31,157)
Dent, Lauren Sophia 5:02:01 (26,845)
Denton, Susannah Charlotte 3:57:42 (10,297)
Deol, Sukhvinder 6:35:21 (35,661)
De-Oliveira, Maria 4:34:05 (20,016)
Deroubaix, Delphine 3:45:09 (7,127)
Derrick, Anna Colette 5:17:53 (29,523)
Derry, Clare P 4:35:08 (20,260)
Deruytter, Caroline 4:25:32 (17,672)
Desailly, Izzy 5:29:21 (31,203)
Desailly, Nicola 5:29:20 (31,199)
Desbarats, Jane 5:58:41 (33,973)
Desborough, Valerie C 4:07:57 (12,949)

Descusse, Nathalie Beatrice.........3:54:46 (9,407)
Desmond, Mary.....................4:39:47 (21,457)
Desvaux, Catherine...................3:27:34 (3,974)
Dette-Lafere, Brigitte 6:32:31 (35,583)
Devine, Andrea J 3:08:47 (1,791)
Devine, Michelle Mary.................5:15:53 (29,208)
Devine, Sandra 3:58:48 (10,661)
Devlin, Shirley 5:37:04 (32,112)
Devoy, Marie 3:29:13 (4,273)
Dew, Beccy 4:39:24 (21,353)
Dew, Emily 4:41:28 (21,884)
Dewen, Susan E 4:57:19 (25,824)
Dewey, Alison Jill 6:25:02 (35,307)
Dewhirst, Lesley 4:21:32 (16,556)
Dewhurst, Colette Elizabeth........6:24:41 (35,298)
Dewhurst, Susan Louise..............4:13:16 (14,304)

Dhanjal, Susie.......................6:45:18 (35,916)

It was something I always wanted to do. Each year
I'd watch the TV and say, 'I'm going to run that
one day, even if I'm 104'! Not 104 but 42, I got a
charity place for Get Kids Going! Six months to
train but they went very fast without any training. That's when I finally got my running shoes
on and started with such determination that I surprised myself! The race itself was amazing to say
the least. The runners, helpers and crowds were
fabulous and very loud! With support from family
and friends we have made a difference – together
we can. The miracle is not that I finished, the miracle is that I had the courage to start. Thank you
all xxx

Di Cosmo, Rita 4:37:06 (20,771)
Di Giacomo, Nicoletta 4:29:55 (18,957)
Di Palma-Heath, Luisa Carla 5:32:04 (31,543)
Di Stefano, Alessandra...............3:51:23 (8,512)
Diane, Letertre 4:17:15 (15,364)
Di'Anno, Caroline Sarah 5:17:49 (29,514)
Dibble, Deborah L 3:55:28 (9,606)
Dibianca, Kay........................6:09:24 (34,634)

Dick, Patricia A.....................3:44:15 (6,923)
Dickenson, Jane......................4:34:05 (20,016)
Dickenson, Kate Emily 4:40:13 (21,543)
Dickie, Helen Louise 5:35:09 (31,891)
Dickin, Elizabeth Jane 5:28:56 (31,144)
Dickinson, Becky.....................5:19:45 (29,814)
Dickinson, Georgia 4:58:30 (26,089)
Dickinson, Tamsin K 4:33:11 (19,757)
Dickinson, Tina D 4:36:57 (20,729)
Dickinson, Tracy.....................5:01:16 (26,699)
Dicks, Alison 4:02:33 (11,616)
Dickson, Claire 5:11:40 (28,494)
Dickson, Jennifer Mary...............3:52:51 (8,883)
Dickson, Kelly Sheets................4:46:45 (23,237)
Dickson, Maureen J...................4:05:39 (12,367)
Dickson, Suran 3:19:36 (2,926)
Diffey, Joanne C 3:27:24 (3,942)
Diggle, Gwen 5:51:02 (33,433)
Dighton, Anna Louise 6:42:07 (35,838)
Dignum, Kelly J 5:24:25 (30,544)
Dilks, Samantha Jane 6:26:00 (35,349)
Dillon, Jo...........................4:19:39 (16,002)
Dilloway, Stephanie..................5:15:28 (29,138)
Dimbleby, Lisa M.....................4:38:56 (21,241)
D'Inca, Daniela 4:24:20 (17,333)
Ding, Lorraine Amanda 4:18:06 (15,608)
Dingle, Tracey Helen 5:20:40 (29,958)
Dinnell, Christine 3:57:29 (10,225)
Dinsdale, Lynne 5:04:12 (27,230)
Dita, Constantina 2:41:12 (231)
Dittner, Eleanor Jessie 5:36:26 (32,046)
Ditton, Carolyn Peta 5:41:30 (32,534)
Dixey, Antonia.......................5:55:44 (33,773)
Dixey, Jennifer Ann..................5:26:13 (30,806)
Dixon, Alyson 2:43:48 (304)
Dixon, Catherine Anne 4:45:28 (22,875)
Dixon, Elise J 4:11:34 (13,867)
Dixon, Jackie 4:43:36 (22,394)
Dixon, Julie L 3:25:33 (3,659)
Dixon, Melanie 5:08:50 (28,019)
Dixon, Paula Elizabeth 5:15:31 (29,150)
Dixon, Rachel Christina 4:05:04 (12,223)
Dixon, Sarah Jane 4:39:35 (21,408)
Dixon, Sharon 3:15:38 (2,511)
Djenandji, Nuala Maria 6:58:48 (36,169)
Doak, Katie L 3:47:52 (7,711)
Dobbie, Lesley 5:46:12 (32,972)
Dobbs, Helen 5:04:34 (27,291)
Dobson, Clare 5:37:16 (32,138)
Dobson, Judith E.....................3:24:03 (3,440)
Dobson, Julie 4:34:25 (20,099)
Dobson, Masumi 3:30:12 (4,450)
Dobson, Sarah Louise.................6:47:12 (35,952)
Docherty, Fiona 2:37:55 (161)
Doctor, Kylie Ann....................6:15:08 (34,892)
Dodd, Emma 4:53:52 (25,009)
Dodd-Noble, Daisy Sophia............3:49:39 (8,134)
Dodds, Pam Jane 4:26:06 (17,844)
Dodson, Rosemary Elizabeth 6:45:13 (35,914)
Doebbe, Sigrid 4:20:24 (16,232)
Doel, Beverley 4:15:13 (14,838)
Dogan, Lisa 9:02:59 (36,619)
Dogruyol, Alice 6:50:48 (36,010)
Doheny, Laura 4:13:00 (14,239)
Doherty, Denise J 4:15:51 (14,987)
Doherty, Julie Elizabeth 4:51:28 (24,411)
Doherty, Sarah J.....................5:06:44 (27,679)
Doherty, Vicky Jayne 4:11:43 (13,908)
Doidge, Denise 4:26:31 (17,961)
Dolan, Emma 5:14:43 (29,019)
Dolan, Rachel Mary 4:57:55 (25,950)
Dolan, Rebecca 4:22:25 (16,826)
Dolden, Lyn 5:40:03 (32,394)
Don, Georgina Katherine............3:54:35 (9,347)
Donahue, Christine 5:07:02 (27,730)
Donald, Cara Louise 4:17:55 (15,550)
Donald, Julie D......................3:33:38 (4,994)
Donaldson, Freya 5:24:40 (30,577)
Donaldson, Jacquie 6:12:40 (34,792)
Donaldson, Kathryn Emma.........3:52:17 (8,734)
Donaldson, Lauren 5:24:39 (30,576)
Donaldson, Melanie Jane 6:09:55 (34,657)
Donaldson, Sue M.....................4:49:32 (23,920)

Donbavand, Nicky.....................6:28:43 (35,454)
Donkin, Carrie Ann 5:55:05 (33,726)
Donkin, Judith Ann 5:50:30 (33,383)
Donnellon, Helen 5:29:53 (31,278)
Donnelly, Caroline Jane..............5:19:53 (29,833)
Donnelly, Fiona 5:30:35 (31,369)
Donnelly, Jennie 4:50:10 (24,088)
Donnelly, Joanne Marie 5:19:53 (29,833)
Donnelly, Kate 3:43:13 (6,731)
Donnelly, Laura Ashling 5:10:53 (28,391)
Donnelly, Rachael 4:10:48 (13,665)
Donovan, Kathryn 5:00:54 (26,635)
Donovan, Lisa Jane 5:28:20 (31,068)
Donovan, Lucy A......................6:15:59 (34,924)
Donovan, Tracy 5:51:34 (33,468)
Dooley, Joanne Louise 5:23:23 (30,368)
Dooley, Sharon Marie 4:38:25 (21,092)
Doret, Soline 4:32:18 (19,514)
Dorman, Rosalind A 4:38:33 (21,131)
Dormer, Sara 5:05:51 (27,504)
Dornan, Helena 3:36:59 (5,560)
Dorogi, Edit 4:53:57 (25,034)
Dorrell, Carol 4:55:51 (25,497)
Dorrell, Patricia A 4:40:13 (21,543)
Dorrington, Susan Diane..............5:10:09 (28,264)
Dorrity, Miriam 4:09:02 (13,220)
Dorse, Jessica 4:16:04 (15,042)
Dossena, Laura 4:47:41 (23,468)
Dougall, Annie K.....................3:38:57 (5,932)
Douglas, Amy 5:35:27 (31,921)
Douglas, Hilary Amelia...............5:42:56 (32,664)
Douglas, Katherine 4:34:47 (20,190)
Douglas, Laura 5:35:27 (31,921)
Douglas, Moyra 6:04:58 (34,383)
Douglas, Natalie 4:27:00 (18,079)
Douglas, Romilly Kate................5:59:39 (34,028)
Douglas, Veronica 5:33:04 (31,674)
Dove, Hayley 3:49:33 (8,102)
Dove, Jo.............................4:19:52 (16,066)
Doven, Emma J........................4:13:58 (14,496)
Dover, Jackie 4:13:50 (14,465)
Dover, Margaret Mary.................4:09:57 (13,456)
Dow, Deborah Suzanne 3:48:00 (7,738)
Dowd, Julie 5:31:49 (31,516)
Dowding, Lesley-Ann 4:57:50 (25,931)
Dowie, Claire Louise 5:26:53 (30,887)
Dowie, Francesca.....................5:48:06 (33,150)
Dowle, Claire Louise 5:47:55 (33,129)
Dowling, Hannah Louise...............5:58:47 (33,978)
Dowling, Sophie Brigid...............5:29:03 (31,157)
Down, Alicia Lucy 3:42:26 (6,584)
Downer, Carrie 5:00:54 (26,635)
Downes, Alexandra 4:17:59 (15,573)
Downes, Amber Claire.................5:09:58 (28,225)
Downey, Irene 4:37:08 (20,779)
Downey, Sarah-Jane 5:04:21 (27,251)
Downham, Gail 7:31:13 (36,474)
Downie, Sally 4:40:48 (21,721)
Downing, Catherine 5:35:58 (31,989)
Downing, Paula J.....................3:36:31 (5,483)
Downs, Gabrielle A 3:37:28 (5,652)
Dowse, Susan Jayne 4:46:16 (23,118)
Dowson, Jill 3:46:53 (7,505)
Doyle, Carly H 3:39:06 (5,963)
Doyle, Emma Louise 4:33:08 (19,740)
Doyle, Emma Mason 4:02:50 (11,685)
Doyle, Kate 5:03:59 (27,186)
Doyle, Kathleen Mary 4:01:13 (11,300)
Doyle, Nikki Louise..................5:32:56 (31,656)
Doyle, Pauline J 5:09:33 (28,158)
Doyle-Lay, Sarah 5:04:11 (27,226)
Dragalova, Maria 4:05:46 (12,402)
Drage, Kelly Marie 4:44:55 (22,745)
Drake, Cheryl D 5:31:54 (31,523)
Dransfield, Jackie 5:42:00 (32,587)

Draper, Eleanor................5:02:11 (26,886)
Draper, Julie E................4:52:42 (24,730)
Draper, Katharine Ann 6:09:45 (34,649)
Draper, Lesley Anne................5:32:05 (31,548)
Draper, Sarah Victoria 4:31:11 (19,266)
Drasdo, Alison D 3:06:12 (1,548)
Draszcz, Jeanine 3:55:34 (9,628)
Drayson, Dawn 5:22:16 (30,184)
Drennan Arnold, Julie................6:54:56 (36,111)
Drew, Rebecca Anne 4:19:22 (15,944)
Drewe, Sally Victoria 4:12:06 (14,008)
Drewett, Natalie 5:56:16 (33,815)
Drewitt, Louise Clare 5:06:38 (27,654)
Dring, Harriet L 4:48:55 (23,776)
Driscoll, Jennifer Jane................4:42:48 (22,213)
Dron, Pauline 7:23:18 (36,433)

Drummond, Louise 4:45:04 (22,788)

I ran the London Marathon in memory of Mummy,
Gail Taylor, who died from breast cancer, aged 58.
With the most wonderful support from family and
friends, we raised £4,680 in her name for Cancer
Research UK. Training for, and running, the Marathon was a huge challenge, but it was absolutely
worth every minute. The atmosphere and the
crowds were unbelievable and I was lucky enough
to see my cheering squad twice along the way!
Crossing the finishing line was just fantastic and
champagne at The Wolseley afterwards the perfect
end to it all! Thank you everyone who supported
me in raising money and helping me to fulfil one
of life's really brilliant experiences. Remembering
Mummy always x

Drummond, Sarah E................4:01:26 (11,353)
Drynan, Annie................5:56:07 (33,797)
Du Plessis, Sonja................5:12:03 (28,572)
Du Preez, Nicolette................4:12:33 (14,115)
Duck, Lisa Beverly................6:04:32 (34,352)
Ducker, Jackie A................3:46:06 (7,340)
Duckett, Abbey May................6:08:27 (34,577)
Duckett, Charlotte 6:29:13 (35,472)
Duckworth, Alison 3:41:52 (6,495)
Duckworth, Avril M................3:37:25 (5,639)
Duckworth, Isobel Lucie................5:39:08 (32,312)
Duckworth, Lorna................4:41:10 (21,815)
Dudd, Claudia Joanne 5:49:55 (33,325)
Dudley, Amanda................5:10:49 (28,379)
Dudley, Clare D 4:53:58 (25,041)
Dudley, Gemma................4:43:02 (22,268)
Dudley, Marianne................6:12:05 (34,758)
Dudley, Norma................5:35:58 (31,989)
Duers, Jackie A................4:53:42 (24,973)
Duff, Katie Emma................4:56:04 (25,551)
Duff, Kelly Marie................5:59:37 (34,026)
Duff, Leesa................4:01:10 (11,291)
Duff, Paula................5:38:56 (32,300)
Duffell, Abby Claire 4:39:47 (21,457)
Duffy, Eleanor Lucy................5:10:09 (28,264)
Duffy, Laura................4:38:28 (21,110)
Duffy, Linda................4:40:14 (21,553)
Duffy, Nikki................6:05:08 (34,396)
Duffy, Rebecca................5:57:10 (33,874)
Duffy-Jones, Celia................4:44:54 (22,743)
Duggan, Becky................3:43:15 (6,735)
Duhamel, Beatrice 5:07:49 (27,863)
Dukes, Suzie Liza 4:58:15 (26,028)
Duley, Tracey Mary................5:25:13 (30,652)
Dullroy, Bronnie................4:23:24 (17,080)
Dumergue, Simone................4:24:24 (17,360)
Dummer, Slavica 4:44:21 (22,603)
Dunbar, Amanda Kathleen................4:41:21 (21,851)
Duncan, Angela Margaret................5:15:24 (29,125)
Duncan, Kathryn A................5:18:06 (29,562)
Duncanson, Christine................4:23:19 (17,049)
Duncanson, Sophie................4:08:13 (13,010)
Dunhill, Diane................4:39:43 (21,440)
Dunk, Sara Elizabeth................6:59:26 (36,185)
Dunkin, Tina................4:41:58 (22,005)
Dunlop, Sheena J................5:40:24 (32,421)

Dunn, Caroline 3:32:36 (4,827)
Dunn, Tara 4:14:16 (14,586)
Dunne, Emma................4:23:34 (17,125)
Dunne, Sophie 4:21:45 (16,628)
Dunphy, Patricia................5:18:21 (29,597)
Dunsdon, Carol D 4:14:22 (14,607)
Duplain, Sarah Louise 5:44:30 (32,814)
Duran, Helen 4:15:20 (14,872)
Durand, Corine 3:59:31 (10,866)
Durham, Alison 4:23:29 (17,099)
Durham, Denise 5:04:36 (27,297)
Durham, Holly................4:10:09 (13,512)
Durham, Lisa................5:26:42 (30,862)
Durham, Suzanna................5:26:18 (30,821)
Durman, Kirsty................4:39:56 (21,488)
Durrant, Charlotte Emmalene 4:17:11 (15,345)
Durrant, Ellen A 4:00:20 (11,068)
Durrant, Simone Marie 5:21:34 (30,090)
Durston, Harriet Rose................5:29:58 (31,289)
Dusgate, Karen Elisabeth................4:43:02 (22,268)
Dutch, Charlotte L................4:02:39 (11,638)
Dutton, Linda S................4:10:57 (13,700)
Dutton (née Leslie), Joanna 5:16:55 (29,375)
Dyble, Lindsay C 6:39:13 (35,759)
Dybvad, Tove E................4:25:51 (17,768)
Dyer, Gemma................4:06:46 (12,645)
Dyer, Kelly Anne................5:53:51 (33,632)
Dyke, Leanne 4:49:12 (23,849)
Dyker, Rachel J 3:28:55 (4,214)
Dymond, Elizabeth Frances................5:33:50 (31,751)
Dymore-Brown, Linda Susan................5:22:02 (30,151)
Dyu, Lily A 3:35:28 (5,316)
Dyus, Kerry 4:32:16 (19,505)
Dzialdow, Resi................4:44:31 (22,645)
Eales, Kate 6:00:48 (34,114)
Eardley, Rebecca 4:54:17 (25,126)
Earl, Rebecca K 4:32:01 (19,441)
Earle, Alison Jane 5:58:59 (33,987)
Earle, Jayne K 4:43:36 (22,394)
Early, Gemma D 4:06:04 (12,468)
Earnshaw, Angela................4:27:32 (18,246)
Earnshaw, Laura Alice................5:27:58 (31,024)
East, Marie 6:57:44 (36,153)
Eastbury, Justine 3:51:06 (8,450)
Eastland, Helen Selina 4:21:18 (16,490)
Eastland, Rachel................4:27:17 (18,174)
Eastwood, Amanda Jane 5:25:56 (30,771)
Eastwood, Wendy J 4:31:50 (19,396)
Eaton, Lindsay A 6:04:11 (34,334)
Eaves, Alison 4:10:48 (13,665)
Eavis, Tala Sarah 5:16:18 (29,269)
Ebedes, Janet................5:59:57 (34,055)
Ebelis, Gemma 5:13:03 (28,747)
Eccles, Emma Jane 5:13:51 (28,901)
Eccleston, Lisa Jane 5:19:55 (29,840)
Eckardt, Siegrid................5:06:41 (27,667)
Eckersley, Jennifer................5:24:34 (30,565)
Eckersley, Suzanne 4:20:35 (16,287)
Eckford, Sophie Frances 4:20:16 (16,185)
Economu, Nicoleta M 4:06:29 (12,569)
Eddington, April-Sarah 5:58:30 (33,963)
Ede, Sally Anne 5:38:40 (32,281)
Edelmann, Karla 5:26:43 (30,865)
Eden, Faye Louise 4:19:58 (16,096)
Edgar, Rebekah 4:52:06 (24,573)
Edghill, Sharon Louise 3:52:58 (8,911)
Edgington-Mole, Faith L 4:18:27 (15,699)
Edkins, Laura 4:02:10 (11,529)
Edmonds, Rebecca Ann 4:19:51 (16,056)
Edmonds, Rebecca Louise 4:55:04 (25,326)
Edmondson, Rowena M 3:31:18 (4,626)
Edwards, Alice J................4:10:15 (13,540)
Edwards, Alison J................6:17:21 (35,000)
Edwards, Amy E................4:20:57 (16,401)
Edwards, Amy Louise 5:01:30 (26,754)
Edwards, Andrée 3:53:57 (9,196)
Edwards, Angela 5:43:41 (32,739)
Edwards, Angela S................6:17:31 (35,007)
Edwards, Anna 4:08:15 (13,017)
Edwards, Bernadette A 6:11:25 (34,717)
Edwards, Christine Elizabeth 7:22:57 (36,427)
Edwards, Clare Ann 4:51:15 (24,366)
Edwards, Dawn Lesley................6:46:14 (35,935)

Edwards, Elizabeth Anne................6:22:13 (35,201)

Edwards, Fizzy G................5:20:03 (29,857)

I've run every London marathon between 2001-
2010 in fancy dress – namely my Dizzy Fizzy out-
fit! It is one of my favourite days of the year, the
compassion that everyone has that day in London
is overwhelming. Everybody is there to help everybody whether they be the cheery supporters on
the line or the guy who you've just overtaken that's
limping! I'm not a speedy runner and have only
managed to beat 5 hours once (the promise of dia-
monds sped me up!), I do the London Marathon
for the atmosphere created by 1000s of people
going through that pain to raise money for their
charities! I'm lucky enough to have completed the
last 12 consecutive London Marathons and hope
to keep going for years to come!

Edwards, Frances Kate 3:15:50 (2,530)
Edwards, Helen 6:24:01 (35,279)
Edwards, Helen K................4:21:32 (16,556)
Edwards, Janet L 4:35:16 (20,287)
Edwards, Joan 5:11:51 (28,534)
Edwards, Joanne Lucy................5:57:03 (33,870)
Edwards, Joyce Elizabeth 5:09:05 (28,065)
Edwards, Judith A................3:56:31 (9,938)
Edwards, Kate 5:54:34 (33,679)
Edwards, Katie A 4:28:41 (18,579)
Edwards, Lauren L 3:30:32 (4,501)
Edwards, Linda K................4:04:16 (12,023)
Edwards, Lisa................5:06:35 (27,641)
Edwards, Lucy Anne 5:20:32 (29,933)
Edwards, Lynette................6:15:35 (34,911)
Edwards, Natalie................5:30:41 (31,382)
Edwards, Nicola Lucy................4:56:21 (25,623)
Edwards, Oddny Cara 6:36:40 (35,692)
Edwards, Paula Jennet 4:19:50 (16,052)
Edwards, Rebecca................4:01:27 (11,356)
Edwards, Rebecca Ann 4:55:30 (25,410)
Edwards, Sharon 4:54:05 (25,067)
Edwards, Stephanie Anne................5:05:29 (27,447)
Edwards, Victoria 5:11:50 (28,528)
Edwards, Wendy 5:34:10 (31,776)
Edwards, Yolanda 4:40:39 (21,679)
Egan, Aisling B 4:25:02 (17,531)
Egan, Rose 4:04:51 (12,164)
Egan, Victoria Rachel 4:19:59 (16,103)
Eggar, Nicole 4:14:31 (14,656)
Eggelton, Heather Jane 4:05:29 (12,331)
Ehrensberger, Angelika 5:16:03 (29,234)
Eke, Abi 7:43:56 (36,542)
Eke, Helen................4:38:50 (21,212)
Elcome, Lynsey H................3:44:30 (6,987)
Elderfield, Helen Louise 4:25:20 (17,612)
Eldon, Gemma 4:53:31 (24,925)
Eldred-Earl, Wendy 5:19:50 (29,828)
Eldridge, Donna................3:58:20 (10,505)
Eldridge, Fleur Polly Mary Rose..4:32:49 (19,635)
Eleftheriou, Helen 5:10:31 (28,331)
Elena, Thompson................3:40:50 (6,298)
Elener, Claire L 3:22:56 (3,282)

I was lucky to make the start after incurring a pulled ligament, having a steroid injection in my hip and then getting an inflamed tendon in my foot five weeks before the race! It all paid off after cross training for the last few weeks and I felt so excited to be lining up with 37,000 people all hoping to complete the 30th London Marathon. After a light drizzle of rain I was off to a very congested start but soon got into my stride. My foot ached at mile 8, but I got a boost from seeing family at mile 9 and was ready to drop at mile 17. Running down The Mall was surreal and an amazing experience, topped off by finishing just under 4 hours and raising over £1,800 for Children with Leukaemia.

Farrugia, Ruth 4:56:49 (25,725)
Farry, Victoria Evelyn 5:02:42 (26,979)
Faucher, Estelle 3:45:28 (7,201)
Faulkner, Brenda Jean 5:17:24 (29,460)
Faulkner, Judy M 5:42:12 (32,609)
Faulkner, Louise Emily 3:59:40 (10,913)
Faveau, Isabelle 4:30:44 (19,156)
Favretto, Lauren 5:08:38 (27,996)
Fawcett, Adele 4:16:24 (15,145)
Fawcett, Elizabeth Kay 4:54:53 (25,279)
Fawcett, Johanna Eve 4:55:42 (25,463)
Fawcett, Paula 4:28:48 (18,609)
Fay, Carley Louise 4:17:25 (15,410)
Fazackerley, Lisa 5:29:45 (31,263)
Fazzino, Joanna 4:12:31 (14,103)
Fear, Olivia C 4:20:45 (16,356)
Fearn, Sharon E 3:49:25 (8,070)
Fearon, Anne 5:12:19 (28,624)
Featherstone, Kirsty 4:30:07 (19,003)
Fecher, Imogen Caroline 4:36:00 (20,477)
Feeley, Shireen 3:55:46 (9,706)
Feeney, Mary 5:40:56 (32,475)
Fehlmann, Muriel 4:24:31 (17,395)
Felce, Rebecca Jane 4:39:49 (21,465)
Felgate, Joanna Helen 5:14:44 (29,024)
Felisky, Kendra Margaret 5:47:18 (33,076)
Fell, Jacqui 4:58:51 (26,177)
Fell, Sue Anne 4:29:27 (18,790)
Fellows, Sarah Emily 3:55:53 (9,745)
Feltham, Kyrie Ann 5:40:16 (32,418)
Fenby, Lyn 4:09:50 (13,428)
Fenelon, Patsy E 3:47:41 (7,682)
Fenemer, Mandy 5:31:15 (31,439)
Fenn, Cath 4:01:53 (11,466)
Fenn, Joanna E 5:04:03 (27,197)
Fenoglio, Alison 4:31:16 (19,286)
Fenton, Lynne 4:51:48 (24,492)
Fenton, Victoria 5:16:52 (29,367)
Ferguson, Amy Louise 6:53:45 (36,082)
Ferguson, Heather Jane 6:29:11 (35,469)
Ferguson, Vandana 4:16:17 (15,099)
Fergusson, Leanne 3:19:21 (2,903)
Fernandez, Belen 5:23:37 (30,410)
Ferrari, Tiziana 3:33:28 (4,965)
Ferre, Roseann 5:25:38 (30,720)
Ferreira, Silvia 4:54:12 (25,100)
Ferrer, Lucy 5:42:42 (32,650)
Ferriby, Sarah Elizabeth 5:10:37 (28,351)
Ferrier, Millie 5:05:11 (27,401)
Ferries, Mandy 6:02:17 (34,204)
Ferriman, Emma 4:25:20 (17,612)
Ferris, Liz 4:42:41 (22,182)
Ferry, Emma 3:56:14 (9,853)
Ferry, Kirsty Jemma 4:34:27 (20,108)
Festorazzi, Katrina Ellen 4:28:19 (18,458)
Fetty, Karin 3:49:01 (7,978)
Fewins, Philippa Jayne 5:20:31 (29,930)
Fewtrell, Kirsty Louise 4:53:28 (24,905)
Fiander, Zoe 4:27:44 (18,295)
Field, Annette Kobi 5:37:25 (32,161)
Field, Carolyn J 4:38:14 (21,037)
Field, Catherine Naomi 4:50:58 (24,292)
Field, Elaine M 4:27:42 (18,288)
Field, Gemma 4:53:54 (25,022)
Field, Jo Alexandra 4:52:27 (24,669)
Fielding, Ann 4:47:49 (23,502)
Figaro, Farai Gwanzura 7:32:18 (36,478)
Figgitt, Kathryn Jane 4:50:26 (24,149)
Figures, Emma L 3:34:06 (5,079)
Filby, Melissa Pamela 5:50:36 (33,399)
Filisetti, Melanie Ann 4:29:29 (18,800)
Filkins, Terri 4:14:58 (14,773)
Filmer, Caroline A 5:02:10 (26,881)
Finch, Helen 5:52:13 (33,516)
Finch, Kate 4:23:01 (16,987)
Finch, Kathy 6:57:54 (36,156)
Fincham, Donna Louise 5:42:02 (32,590)
Finden, Alison 4:52:23 (24,657)
Findlay, Caroline L 3:45:28 (7,201)
Findlay, Celia A 3:36:10 (5,439)
Findley, Helen I 6:16:33 (34,956)
Findley, Judith Alice 3:58:16 (10,478)
Findlow, Natalie Jayne 5:45:42 (32,923)

Finill, Julia Mary 6:09:56 (34,659)
Finn, Ifty 6:37:26 (35,712)
Finn-Bellingham, Catherine M 5:53:32 (33,615)
Finnegan, Anna 3:40:46 (6,284)
Finnegan, Michelle 5:44:08 (32,782)
Finney, Louise K 4:28:32 (18,535)
Finnigan, Jodie Lucy 4:42:09 (22,050)
Firth, Andrea D 4:27:14 (18,160)
Firth, Charlotte 2:50:56 (523)
Firth, Gemma V 3:47:08 (7,551)
Firth, Heidi Jacqueline 5:26:30 (30,840)
Fischer, Catherine Jane 4:52:53 (24,775)
Fisher, Carol Anne 4:02:53 (11,701)
Fisher, Claire L 4:25:37 (17,694)
Fisher, Heather R 3:29:32 (4,328)
Fisher, Jane 5:54:17 (33,665)
Fisher, Janet 5:07:43 (27,849)
Fisher, Kylie 5:36:47 (32,080)
Fisher, Lisa 7:08:39 (36,298)
Fisher, Tina 7:08:01 (36,291)
Fisher, Victoria J 4:07:58 (12,953)
Fitch, Sarah 4:59:09 (26,249)
Fitchett, Jan 5:49:57 (33,328)
Fitter, Diane Alison 5:42:23 (32,625)
Fitton, Amanda J 3:50:05 (8,226)
Fitzgerald, Abby 5:03:23 (27,086)
Fitzgerald, Giovanna 4:56:36 (25,667)
Fitzgerald, Jennifer 3:29:57 (4,408)
Fitz-Gerald, Natalie E 5:01:54 (26,832)
Fitzgibbon, Erika Lina 4:20:05 (16,131)
Fitzhugh, Laura Jane 4:42:06 (22,037)
Fitzmaurice, Sarah 4:27:30 (18,236)
Fitzpatrick, Joanne 4:39:00 (21,258)
Fitzpatrick, Marie Louise 4:31:55 (19,411)
Fitzpatrick, Sarah 4:37:57 (20,977)
Fitzsimons, Susannah Caroline 4:17:15 (15,364)
Fitzwater, Michelle Deanne 4:16:41 (15,215)
Flanagan, Deborah Kathleen 5:17:31 (29,476)
Flanagan, Holly 4:31:34 (19,344)
Flannery, Helen Mary 5:54:08 (33,653)
Flatt, Natasha L 5:26:14 (30,809)
Flattet, Isabelle 6:20:25 (35,141)
Fleet, Catherine 3:46:30 (7,415)
Fleet, Louise 5:59:01 (33,989)
Flegg, Joanna Lisa 4:47:46 (23,483)
Flemans, Katherine J 5:40:14 (32,415)
Fleming, Ashleigh Claire 5:06:41 (27,667)
Fleming, Clare L 3:26:51 (3,855)
Fleming, Jemima H 5:36:26 (32,046)
Fleming, Julia 5:37:05 (32,115)
Fleming, Kathryn Elizabeth 6:59:03 (36,177)
Fleming, Wendy Pringle 3:58:58 (10,709)
Flemons, Kirstie 3:45:38 (7,235)
Fletcher, Amy Suzanne 5:02:04 (26,856)
Fletcher, Gillian B 4:43:15 (22,314)
Fletcher, Julie Clare Lydia 4:40:30 (21,640)
Fletcher, Karisma Anne 5:24:28 (30,551)
Fletcher, Lindsey Ann 6:29:45 (35,487)
Fletcher, Maria 4:43:32 (22,377)
Fletcher, Nichola D 5:02:04 (26,856)
Fletcher, Sally 5:32:13 (31,564)
Fletcher, Samantha J 3:52:35 (8,815)
Fletcher, Sarah Elizabeth 4:56:18 (25,611)
Fletcher, Vivienne Adele 6:53:35 (36,078)
Fligg, Jayne A 6:11:57 (34,754)
Flint, Anne Barbara 6:06:46 (34,492)
Flitter, Carly Jane 4:14:09 (14,547)
Flockhart, Kirsty 5:21:42 (30,108)
Flohr, Francesca 4:08:58 (13,201)
Florence, Anne E 4:43:58 (22,498)
Flower, Emma 3:42:35 (6,607)
Flower, Naomi J 5:16:50 (29,359)
Flury, Joanna C 3:31:21 (4,642)
Flynn, Emily 5:37:45 (32,190)
Flynn, Jeanne 4:47:04 (23,322)
Flynn, Kelly-Anne 4:42:29 (22,136)
Flynn, Michelle 4:32:19 (19,520)
Flynn, Moya 5:17:20 (29,445)
Foddering, Naomi 5:04:55 (27,351)
Fogarty, Clare Anne 5:49:41 (33,307)
Fogarty, Katharine Mary Elizabeth 5:45:17 (32,892)
Fogden, Michaela 5:07:43 (27,849)
Fogden, Sian 4:56:17 (25,608)

Foley, Cathy J 4:41:31 (21,899)
Foley, Emily C 4:20:17 (16,194)
Foley, Emma 4:58:02 (25,974)
Follett, Becky 4:11:26 (13,827)
Follett, Joanna 4:11:26 (13,827)
Fontaine, Marie 3:55:02 (9,485)
Fooks, Heather 3:32:17 (4,787)
Fooks, Helen L 4:54:04 (25,064)
Fooks, Kathy P 3:34:16 (5,106)

Foord, Nicola Jane 6:06:22 (34,468)

In 1985 I came up to London to watch the London Marathon. I saw a disabled athlete in a wheelchair taking part. He had no legs & only two stumps for his arms & was propelling himself along with crutches. I later found out his name was Peter Hull. I was truly inspired by Peter that day and vowed that if he could do it, I would one day take part too. 2010 was to be my year. I had what I can only describe as one of the greatest days of my life. For me, taking part and completing the London Marathon was a life-changing experience. The atmosphere and crowds supporting all the runners with their cheering and offers of sweets/fruit makes the London Marathon unique. Thank You Peter. Well done London.

Foot, Annie M 4:11:27 (13,835)
Foot, Helen R 4:47:09 (23,334)
Foot, Susan M 4:09:48 (13,421)
Foppoli, Alison Clare 4:38:28 (21,110)
Forbes, Angharad 4:52:31 (24,688)
Forbes, Linda Ann 6:22:40 (35,219)
Ford, Denise Michelle 4:06:03 (12,463)
Ford, Gillian M 3:57:10 (10,146)
Ford, Joanna 5:14:44 (29,024)
Ford, Katie A 4:36:16 (20,540)
Ford, Kendle 5:25:33 (30,703)
Ford, Michelle Joyce 5:58:04 (33,938)
Ford, Victoria Emma 6:46:32 (35,937)
Ford, Victoria Louise 4:43:10 (22,292)
Forder, Elaine M 4:46:21 (23,137)
Forder, Liz 5:29:08 (31,168)
Foreman, Clare Vanessa 4:03:30 (11,844)
Forester, Helen K 4:21:57 (16,688)
Forgenie, Janet Truda 4:19:29 (15,966)
Forrest, Jane 3:38:33 (5,854)
Forrest, Sandra Elizabeth 4:08:11 (13,003)
Forrest, Sarah 4:35:37 (20,369)
Forrester, Claire 5:56:07 (33,797)
Forrester, Diane 4:51:04 (24,322)
Forrester, Emma Jane 3:55:50 (9,730)
Forse, Lucy Alison 4:25:26 (17,642)
Forsell, Lena 6:16:58 (34,974)
Forsey, Yvonne 5:29:43 (31,255)

Forshaw, Roseanna Jane 5:35:19 (31,906)
Forster, Kaye Elizabeth 3:33:20 (4,939)
Forster, Kim 3:52:40 (8,839)
Forsyth, Karlyn 3:35:27 (5,313)
Fort, Becky..............6:03:20 (34,273)
Forth, Sally..............7:01:52 (36,214)
Fortune, Katharine 5:38:12 (32,227)
Fortunova, Miroslava 3:55:03 (9,491)
Fosker, Denise J..............5:24:59 (30,622)
Foskett, Kathryn..............4:18:28 (15,704)
Foster, Ann 5:21:21 (30,052)
Foster, Claire 4:35:51 (20,433)
Foster, Deborah..............4:31:51 (19,399)
Foster, Diana P 4:02:23 (11,575)
Foster, Emma Louise..............6:08:27 (34,577)
Foster, Emma Marie..............4:08:49 (13,169)
Foster, Eve Marie..............4:38:28 (21,110)
Foster, Jane 4:51:39 (24,450)
Foster, Julie A 5:51:54 (33,496)
Foster, Karen Lesley..............4:31:24 (19,312)
Foster, Kerry L..............5:38:58 (32,302)
Foster, Laura..............4:01:27 (11,356)
Foster, Linda Carol 5:54:03 (33,649)
Foster, Louise 4:49:38 (23,953)
Foster, Lyn 4:40:54 (21,743)
Foster, Lyndsey..............6:08:18 (34,569)
Foster, Nicky..............5:06:17 (27,581)
Foster, Ronnie 6:20:10 (35,134)
Foster, Sally Ann Kerr 4:23:47 (17,187)
Foster, Sharon 5:13:46 (28,884)
Foster, Sharon Louise 4:10:16 (13,542)
Foulgar, Gemma Louise..............6:04:18 (34,339)
Foulkes, Hannah June 5:15:58 (29,223)
Fouquet Heulot, Françoise..............4:26:54 (18,049)
Fourie, Cecilia 4:44:40 (22,692)
Fourie, Hayley M..............4:28:50 (18,621)
Fourie, Mylene Rhonda..............5:32:48 (31,639)
Fourie, Susan..............3:19:56 (2,954)
Fowle, Jennifer 4:05:10 (12,245)
Fowler, Angela..............6:19:36 (35,111)
Fowler, Claire..............3:30:18 (4,470)
Fowler, Jane Frances 5:54:35 (33,681)
Fowler, Jodi Kim..............4:12:28 (14,089)
Fowler, Margaret Elizabeth Anne..5:38:54 (32,296)
Fowler, Nicola..............3:41:10 (6,354)
Fowler, Surinder Kaur..............4:35:12 (20,270)
Fowles, Hannah Kate 4:18:37 (15,749)
Fowles, Nicola J 4:23:21 (17,060)
Fowles, Nicola Louise 4:20:09 (16,150)
Fowlie, Sandra A 5:06:43 (27,677)
Fox, Beverley Joanne 6:26:23 (35,360)
Fox, Claire 4:09:17 (13,279)
Fox, Claudy Austine..............4:27:14 (18,160)
Fox, Hannah Mary..............5:00:14 (26,505)
Fox, Jeanette M 3:56:35 (9,955)
Fox, Karen Mary..............6:08:27 (34,577)
Fox, Kirsteen 4:54:22 (25,149)
Fox, Lindsay Catherine..............5:06:32 (27,635)
Fox, Lucy V..............3:57:37 (10,268)
Fox, Michiko..............4:00:29 (11,115)
Fox, Rachel Ann..............4:14:23 (14,610)
Foy, Haidee Melissa..............5:12:56 (28,728)
Foy, Julia 4:21:43 (16,617)
Foy, Linda 6:23:24 (35,257)
Foyster, Mandy L 3:34:53 (5,230)
Frackiewicz, Joanne K..............4:49:48 (24,007)
Fragoso, Belinda J 3:41:22 (6,399)
Frampton, Caroline 5:00:19 (26,524)
Frampton, Kathleen..............4:57:30 (25,858)
Francis, Andrea K..............3:22:21 (3,222)
Francis, Anna..............3:14:33 (2,390)
Francis, Claire Elizabeth Louise..7:48:48 (36,560)
Francis, Debbie Anne 5:52:08 (33,511)
Francis, Dina T 4:31:28 (19,328)
Francis, Donna L..............5:59:59 (34,061)
Francis, Lisa..............6:01:21 (34,148)
Francis, Rachel 5:18:10 (29,568)
Francis, Sally..............4:53:41 (24,965)
François, Kat..............5:54:05 (33,650)
Frank, Flora..............5:55:52 (33,782)
Frank, Michelle L..............5:10:15 (28,282)
Frank, Rachel Ann 6:42:07 (35,838)
Frankland, Lucy 4:25:28 (17,650)
Frankland, Sharon 3:59:42 (10,920)
Franklin, Chloe L..............5:30:52 (31,399)
Franklin, Teresa Jayne..............5:40:08 (32,401)
Franks, Eleanor J..............3:57:57 (10,366)
Franks, Georgina..............4:42:28 (22,130)
Frankson, Nathalie Elizabeth 4:21:35 (16,571)
Franz, Johanna 4:09:54 (13,443)
Franzen, Louisa Jane 5:16:55 (29,375)
Fraser, Alex..............4:04:36 (12,101)
Fraser, Carole 5:10:30 (28,327)
Fraser, Ciara..............4:19:57 (16,086)
Fraser, Laura Marie..............4:48:57 (23,788)
Fraser, Lyndsey V..............3:29:29 (4,317)
Fraser, Naomi Jane Ruthven..............5:12:49 (28,703)
Fraser, Sally..............5:12:10 (28,597)
Fraser, Samantha..............3:44:39 (7,024)
Fraser-Moodie, Lindsay M 3:13:53 (2,303)
Frassova, Lynda 6:12:01 (34,756)
Fratini, Sheila 4:59:19 (26,292)
Frazer, Christine..............5:04:31 (27,280)
Frazer, Sally..............3:30:32 (4,501)
Frazier, Mel..............3:42:46 (6,651)
Freake, Jane A 4:19:17 (15,922)
Freebairn-Smith, Joanna Margaret.4:49:35 (23,937)
Freedman, Diane 3:52:58 (8,911)
Freedman, Nicola A..............4:32:55 (19,677)
Freeland, Julie Rosemarie 4:40:35 (21,664)
Freeman, Anna Marie..............5:42:24 (32,628)
Freeman, Beverley Anne 4:36:16 (20,540)
Freeman, Debbie Ann 6:37:50 (35,721)
Freeman, Jane 6:12:38 (34,790)
Freeman, Jill..............5:16:06 (29,243)
Freeman, Kate..............4:55:36 (25,437)
Freeman, Kim E 4:30:38 (19,129)
Freeman, Lorraine..............5:30:56 (31,406)
Freeman, Louissa 4:19:29 (15,966)
Freeman, Nicola M 5:01:03 (26,659)
Freeman-Hacker, Marnie..............5:43:06 (32,677)
Freer, Lisa Jayne 5:59:40 (34,030)
Freer, Mary E 5:29:17 (31,188)
Freestone, Deborah 4:26:14 (17,882)
Freiheit, Jacky Miranda..............5:50:57 (33,427)
French, Amy..............6:00:43 (34,104)
French, Annette Elsie 4:38:07 (21,011)
French, Jane 5:46:55 (33,043)
French, Laura Sian..............5:49:16 (33,259)
French, Victoria Jane 3:53:56 (9,191)
Freshwater, Tina..............5:47:22 (33,086)
Fretwell, Elizabeth J 4:14:06 (14,533)
Frew, Kelly Marie..............4:27:27 (18,220)
Frew, Marjorie 6:12:07 (34,759)
Frey, Marcia Ann 4:42:05 (22,035)
Frezza, Rosanna A..............5:35:51 (31,975)
Fricker, Rachel Elizabeth..............6:41:34 (35,820)
Friedman, Lauren 4:49:40 (23,968)
Friend, Anita 4:47:21 (23,379)
Friend, Chelsea 3:52:47 (8,863)
Friend, Rachael Jane..............5:11:24 (28,467)
Friend, Sally..............4:49:41 (23,974)
Frisby, Mandy..............7:26:54 (36,452)
Frisby, Tracy 4:23:24 (17,080)
Frise, Helen 6:41:49 (35,830)
Frith, Alice..............3:48:46 (7,914)
Frith, Donna Patricia 6:07:45 (34,546)
Frith, Emma 5:11:29 (28,478)
Frith, Gemma..............4:27:08 (18,129)
Frith, Sarah Joy..............4:28:17 (18,448)
Frogley, Helen Elizabeth 4:14:54 (14,763)
Fromage, Gemma L..............4:27:46 (18,306)
Frost, Andrea E 3:38:20 (5,823)
Frost, Georgina Katie..............3:43:37 (6,793)
Frost, Gillian Susan..............5:45:31 (32,910)
Frost, Janet..............3:58:01 (10,384)
Frost, Lucy Joanna 6:32:38 (35,586)
Frostick, Gemma..............5:04:54 (27,350)
Froud, Melina..............7:27:08 (36,453)
Froud, Nicola M..............3:12:05 (2,099)
Fruin, Kirsten 4:34:44 (20,179)
Fry, Gemma 5:50:33 (33,392)
Fry, Jacqui 4:08:16 (13,020)
Fry, Kelly 5:06:31 (27,628)
Fry, Rachel..............5:17:53 (29,523)
Fry, Samantha Louise..............3:51:34 (8,554)
Fry, Sue 5:00:20 (26,527)
Frydas, Anju..............4:42:52 (22,234)
Fuchi, Fumiko 5:32:16 (31,570)
Fuggle, Rebecca J..............4:45:23 (22,860)
Fulcher, Helen Jennifer Anne.....5:01:45 (26,808)
Fulcher, Kerry..............6:17:08 (34,985)
Fullalove, Mary Teresa 3:48:20 (7,814)
Fuller, Emma 5:14:17 (28,961)
Fuller, Emma Louise..............4:26:13 (17,877)
Fuller, Helen Margaret 6:08:19 (34,570)
Fund, Gaby 4:27:37 (18,264)
Funnell, Bridget..............4:08:29 (13,074)
Furbank, Valerie A 5:38:15 (32,231)
Furlong, Claire 6:01:53 (34,180)
Furmanski, Carole..............6:40:38 (35,804)
Furnell-Brennan, Zoe 5:46:39 (33,022)
Furner, Julie B 4:48:10 (23,582)
Furniss, Alexandra 4:59:14 (26,272)
Fursman, Emma..............4:47:43 (23,474)
Furze, Elaine..............5:49:04 (33,246)
Gabbitas, Toni 6:33:57 (35,623)
Gable, Vicky Eve..............5:27:29 (30,963)
Gaddes, Deborah M..............4:50:45 (24,224)
Gaffey, Lisa Jayne 4:31:00 (19,216)
Gaffing, Denise..............5:48:10 (33,158)
Gain, Sarah Louise..............4:58:06 (25,986)
Gair, Elaine 5:38:01 (32,214)
Gale, Emma J..............4:46:16 (23,118)
Gale, Emma Jane..............6:45:48 (35,925)
Gale, Sarah 5:14:19 (28,964)
Gales, Eleanor L..............4:22:32 (16,857)
Gall, Fiona 5:50:29 (33,380)
Gallacher, Anne-Marie..............4:48:27 (23,659)
Gallagher, Elaine..............5:01:39 (26,788)
Gallagher, Marianna 5:41:03 (32,492)
Gallagher, Sophie..............4:42:20 (22,101)
Galloway, Rebecca Ann..............4:12:57 (14,216)
Galloway, Sheila Henrietta Valerie 4:44:49 (22,726)
Galpin, Karen M..............3:29:07 (4,254)
Galster, Cordula 3:20:28 (3,017)
Galtrey, Sarah 5:21:20 (30,049)
Gamage, Jacqui 4:21:44 (16,623)
Gambrill, Barbara 3:55:34 (9,628)
Game, Chemene Victoria 7:15:47 (36,366)
Gamlin, Pamela..............5:35:01 (31,877)
Gammon, Annie P 3:43:47 (6,828)
Gammon, Linda..............6:35:16 (35,657)
Ganeshalingam, Usha..............4:26:10 (17,865)
Ganiel O'Neill, Gladys..............2:41:45 (246)
Gannon, Elizabeth J..............3:16:22 (2,594)
Gannon, Sharon K..............3:13:49 (2,297)
Ganose, Beverley A 3:19:12 (2,890)
Gantlett, Sally..............5:06:52 (27,698)
Gapp, Kirsty Victoria..............4:43:52 (22,469)
Gappy, Tina L..............3:32:10 (4,768)
Garcia Tames, Mayte..............3:46:54 (7,512)
Gard, Elizabeth D..............4:40:33 (21,657)
Gardiner, Catherine..............5:53:21 (33,599)
Gardiner, Jaquelyn Louise..............6:34:25 (35,635)
Gardiner, Jayne..............5:12:04 (28,577)
Gardiner, Katharine..............3:50:32 (8,321)
Gardiner, Sally..............5:14:18 (28,963)
Gardner, Barbara Joan..............4:28:55 (18,650)
Gardner, Christine 4:32:02 (19,448)
Gardner, Claire L..............2:44:29 (320)
Gardner, Frances Ruth 5:48:28 (33,193)
Gardner, Helen Sarah..............4:22:21 (16,804)
Gardner, Julie Rose 5:46:26 (33,002)
Gardner, Linda..............4:51:47 (24,488)
Gardner, Victoria 5:22:05 (30,159)
Gardner-Browne, Laura Jane 5:24:06 (30,494)
Gardner-Hall, Sarah J..............3:51:43 (8,592)
Garlick, Alison..............5:43:41 (32,739)
Garlick, Deborah Elaine..............5:14:21 (28,974)
Garlick, Laura..............4:41:48 (21,971)
Garlick, Nerys..............6:58:18 (36,159)
Garman, Samantha 5:21:58 (30,141)
Garner, Anne..............4:10:28 (13,586)
Garner, Kerry Ann 5:21:48 (30,116)
Garner, Sarah 6:44:19 (35,891)
Garner, Sue..............4:16:07 (15,055)
Garner-Jones, Annetta Frances ...4:30:14 (19,031)
Garnett, Kathleen 6:21:12 (35,168)

Garnett, Sophia Daisy 6:30:11 (35,508)
Garnham, Gracie 5:28:54 (31,136)
Garnham, Martina 4:08:24 (13,059)
Garnick, Savanna Dawn 4:22:27 (16,834)
Garrard, Anna E 3:57:36 (10,264)
Garrard, Carrie 5:52:42 (33,551)
Garratt, Saffron Jane 4:47:38 (23,449)
Garrick, Naomi I 3:48:29 (7,843)
Garritt, Carolyn 5:37:25 (32,161)
Garrod, Kelly 5:29:32 (31,226)
Garrod, Lorna E 4:04:55 (12,178)
Garrod, Nicola 4:46:58 (23,298)
Garth, Jennifer 3:52:46 (8,857)
Garth, Rebecca 4:30:26 (19,072)
Garth, Susanne Marie Rose 4:23:45 (17,181)
Gartland, Jane 4:12:18 (14,056)
Garton, Jessica Jane 4:30:00 (18,977)
Garvey, Julie C 5:18:57 (29,695)
Garvey, Marion 4:56:05 (25,556)
Garwood, Debbie 4:46:32 (23,175)
Gascoyne, Julie Caroline 7:03:10 (36,228)
Gasson, Nicci Louise 4:45:05 (22,796)
Gaster, Sandra D 4:09:46 (13,412)
Gater, Claire 3:27:27 (3,953)
Gates, Lauren Holly 4:36:19 (20,551)
Gates, Sarah Nicola 4:29:40 (18,870)
Gaukroger, Helen Elizabeth 7:04:40 (36,251)
Gaunt, Catherine Anne 3:54:05 (9,231)
Gay, Nikki 5:23:00 (30,306)
Gayle, Rebecca E 5:46:08 (32,963)
Gaylor, Theresa 4:36:55 (20,719)
Gaylor, Victoria J 4:07:33 (12,847)
Gazzani, Lena J 4:19:52 (16,066)
Gearing, Lesley 4:18:04 (15,603)
Gedge, Karen 4:41:32 (21,905)
Gee, Christine Jane 6:07:24 (34,526)
Gee, Jemima 5:00:44 (26,595)
Gee, Kelly 6:07:25 (34,528)
Gee, Leah Renai 6:27:59 (35,418)
Gee, Sarah R 2:40:06 (201)
Geekie, Fiona 5:11:28 (28,477)
Geer, Ann 7:15:29 (36,362)
Geffert, Anna 5:25:06 (30,640)
Gelder, Emily J 3:00:28 (1,171)
Gelder, Joanne 9:02:37 (36,618)
Gemmell, Kelly 4:53:29 (24,913)
Geneau de la Marliere, Karine 4:04:44 (12,140)
Genney, Elaine Marie 4:30:44 (19,156)
Geoghegan, Sadie Elizabeth 5:53:25 (33,606)
George, Dawn Melissa 5:30:47 (31,391)
George, Emma Loise 6:02:13 (34,197)
George, Johanna Mary 3:55:13 (9,537)
George, Lydia 5:28:17 (31,061)
George, Margo 4:19:02 (15,852)
George, Pamela Jane 5:19:21 (29,754)
George, Sara 5:03:27 (27,093)
George, Sarah 5:47:52 (33,127)
Georgeson, Wendy 3:40:23 (6,208)
Georghiades, Tiffany 5:44:44 (32,844)
Georghiou, Jane 3:31:49 (4,713)
Georgiadis, Julie Olivia 3:33:42 (5,006)
Georgiou, Angela 4:41:50 (21,980)
Georgiou, Christalla 5:08:50 (28,019)
Georgiou, Margaret 4:51:31 (24,423)
Gerald, Dorothee 5:52:40 (33,549)
Geralis, Eva Victoria 3:53:00 (8,925)
Geran, Stephanie 4:55:33 (25,420)
Gerard-Leigh, Emily 5:08:06 (27,911)
Gerrard, Corinne 4:26:44 (18,007)
Gerreli, Juliet Anne 5:25:43 (30,734)
Gerritsen, Patricia 5:19:04 (29,711)
Gershon, Anneka Lucy 4:08:01 (12,966)
Gertner, Gillian 5:18:19 (29,592)
Gervais, Dafne 3:39:34 (6,056)
Gess, Linda Jane 4:49:24 (23,893)
Gessey, Joanne 4:58:39 (26,128)
Gething, Nicola J 3:23:24 (3,352)
Gettins, Lucy A 3:16:11 (2,570)
Gettins, Vicky Jane 3:56:30 (9,933)
Ghatouara, Rena 6:50:28 (36,006)
Gibb, Amy 6:07:34 (34,536)
Gibbard, Helen Jayne 4:44:29 (22,632)
Gibbings, Beverley J 4:58:13 (26,015)
Gibbins, Deborah K 3:37:35 (5,684)
Gibbins, Kay 5:04:12 (27,230)
Gibbon, Deborah Anne 5:02:48 (26,993)
Gibbons, Carla 3:31:29 (4,664)
Gibbons, Clare Elizabeth 5:28:54 (31,136)
Gibbons, Lorna 4:25:51 (17,768)
Gibbons, Lynda 5:13:52 (28,902)
Gibbs, Casey 6:48:43 (35,969)
Gibbs, Elaine Ruth 4:04:56 (12,186)
Gibbs, Jean 5:53:11 (33,590)
Gibbs, Karen L 4:30:54 (19,190)
Gibbs, Maggie 4:19:35 (15,990)
Gibbs, Monica 4:02:59 (11,726)
Gibbs, Rachel C 2:46:19 (369)
Gibney, Win 6:05:55 (34,445)
Gibson, Claire Helen 4:23:26 (17,088)
Gibson, Floretta 4:27:01 (18,084)
Gibson, Jo 5:21:58 (30,141)
Gibson, Julie 3:37:01 (5,564)
Gibson, Rebecca Helen 4:51:37 (24,443)
Giddings, Jane Elizabeth 4:32:32 (19,568)
Gigg, Serena J 4:31:05 (19,238)
Gilbert, Dawn 4:11:32 (13,860)
Gilbert, Gillian Mary 6:03:06 (34,261)
Gilbert, Julie Teresa 5:18:03 (29,554)
Gilbert, Laura 4:32:52 (19,661)
Gilbert, Michelle 4:59:32 (26,349)
Giles, Lisa 4:33:07 (19,734)
Giles, Sarah K 4:50:02 (24,055)
Gilham, Wendy A 4:45:16 (22,833)
Gill, Amanda Jane 4:32:19 (19,520)
Gill, Amy 4:08:42 (13,143)
Gill, Georgi 5:17:42 (29,499)
Gill, Gillian 5:26:15 (30,812)
Gill, Hayley S 4:29:35 (18,833)
Gill, Jacqueline 4:38:56 (21,241)
Gill, Kerry Joanna 4:44:50 (22,728)
Gill, Lisa 4:59:18 (26,286)
Gill, Lydia 5:40:59 (32,480)
Gill, Susannah Cordelia 3:33:23 (4,949)
Gill, Victoria Jane 5:48:24 (33,183)
Gillam, Danielle 3:31:23 (4,647)
Gillam, Jenny 3:34:35 (5,171)
Gillam, Sally E 3:52:13 (8,711)
Gillen, Grainne M 6:35:28 (35,664)
Gillen, Maeve 6:35:28 (35,664)
Giller, Sharon Rachel 6:04:20 (34,343)
Gillespie, Elizabeth 4:53:00 (24,792)
Gillie, Shaunna 6:25:51 (35,341)
Gillies, Barbara 5:28:39 (31,102)
Gillingham, Sara Caroline 4:01:34 (11,385)
Gilliver, Sarah E 4:17:17 (15,374)
Gillon, Louisa 4:44:58 (22,759)
Gillott, Rachel G 6:16:06 (34,926)
Gilluley, Michelle 6:04:00 (34,323)
Gilman, Anna Louise 4:25:34 (17,681)
Gilman, Hannah Sophia 3:46:03 (7,322)
Gilmour, Sheina M 4:16:23 (15,135)
Gilpin, Louisa 5:11:36 (28,489)
Gimby, Victoria Rachel 4:36:52 (20,704)
Gingell, Lynni Allison 4:50:19 (24,119)
Ginno, Victoria 5:29:00 (31,151)
Giordanengo, Rebecca Louise 3:57:05 (10,126)
Giovannoni, Cheryl Yvette 4:53:28 (24,905)
Gipson, Kelly 4:33:11 (19,757)
Girling, Charlie 5:01:02 (26,656)
Girling, Jennie 4:28:18 (18,452)
Girling, Philippa 5:28:14 (31,056)
Gironella, Maria Angels 4:28:00 (18,365)
Gironi, Mara 4:44:48 (22,721)
Gittins, Jo 3:56:59 (10,084)
Gittins, Tracy Ann 5:11:56 (28,547)
Gittoes, Marianne J 3:06:28 (1,567)
Giuffrida, Desideria 5:25:58 (30,782)
Gladden, Donna Michelle 4:32:00 (19,436)
Gladman, Kirsty 5:30:46 (31,387)
Gladwell, Katharyn 4:40:17 (21,570)
Glancy, Victoria F 4:05:32 (12,341)
Glanville, Danielle 3:32:47 (4,855)
Glanville, Helen 5:37:55 (32,203)
Glanville, Julie 4:12:03 (13,997)
Glass, Rebecca Kathryn 3:58:55 (10,691)
Glazier, Becky 3:40:50 (6,298)
Glazier, Emma Jane 5:29:37 (31,240)
Gleave, Melissa 4:08:57 (13,193)
Gleave, Vicky A 5:14:40 (29,014)
Gledhill, Emma Katherine 4:45:14 (22,824)
Gledhill, Katherine Charlotte 5:46:05 (32,960)
Gledhill, Susan 3:53:14 (8,979)
Glenister, Emma Louise 5:23:06 (30,320)
Glenn, Emma 6:31:17 (35,547)
Glenn, Jacquelyn 5:23:45 (30,434)
Glenn, Kylie Jayne 4:17:34 (15,461)
Glenn, Rhoanna 6:07:06 (34,513)
Glennerster, Corrina A 5:00:11 (26,497)
Glennon, Gillian E 4:05:12 (12,255)
Glew, Annelise P 5:01:35 (26,772)
Glibbery, Angela B 5:49:49 (33,319)
Glibbery, Hannah Joanne 5:56:29 (33,828)
Gloor-Schäfer, Regula 4:11:23 (13,812)
Glover, Donna Elizabeth 6:19:30 (35,100)
Glover, Margaret A 4:42:58 (22,250)
Glover, Rebecca Ruth 4:50:25 (24,146)
Glover, Tinamaria 6:16:58 (34,974)
Glyde, Sarah 4:10:43 (13,643)
Glyn, Charlotte Jane 3:57:26 (10,210)
Glynne-Jones, Ann 4:56:20 (25,619)
Goble, Sally Ann 3:46:56 (7,517)
Godbold, Kerry Marie 5:46:25 (32,998)
Goddard, Holly 5:43:15 (32,694)
Godden, Emily 4:20:51 (16,375)
Godfrey, Mel 5:32:38 (31,621)
Godsmark, Joanna D 4:07:23 (12,796)
Godwin, Heike 3:38:33 (5,854)
Godwin, Joanna Louise 4:02:35 (11,624)
Goerge, Susan E 4:46:04 (23,050)
Gohil, Nimisha 3:47:35 (7,666)
Gohil, Punita 4:55:16 (25,374)
Gohil, Shital 4:57:11 (25,799)
Golach, Verena 3:59:28 (10,857)
Gold, Stephanie 5:31:30 (31,474)
Goldberg, Samantha 6:01:42 (34,168)
Goldby, Maria Andrea 5:56:02 (33,790)
Golder, Vicky Amy 5:04:53 (27,346)
Goldhill, Alice A 4:39:03 (21,269)
Golding, Abby Louise 5:10:50 (28,381)
Golding, Beth Charlotte 5:10:50 (28,381)
Golding, Lisa Claire 5:35:50 (31,974)
Golding, Samantha 5:16:44 (29,341)
Goldsack, Elizabeth Anne 4:36:57 (20,729)
Goldsmith, Joanne 3:48:44 (7,909)
Goldsmith, Julia Jane 5:29:37 (31,240)
Goldsmith, Penny 5:41:01 (32,486)
Goldson, Sarah 4:14:31 (14,656)
Goldstein, Eleanor 5:28:03 (31,036)
Goldsworthy, Rachel Etelka 3:43:32 (6,781)
Goldthorpe, Helen J 3:55:24 (9,594)
Goldthorpe, Samantha Louise 4:48:20 (23,616)
Goldwin, Eleanor K 4:40:39 (21,679)
Golec, Paulina 3:15:17 (2,472)
Gollop, Paula Diane 4:06:58 (12,705)
Golstein, Claudia 5:30:36 (31,372)
Goncalves, Ana P 3:52:15 (8,719)
Gonnet, Sandrine P 3:55:04 (9,495)
Gonzalez Luna, Bertha 3:58:18 (10,491)
Gooch, Katy 4:42:13 (22,069)
Good, Esther Paula 4:03:45 (11,906)
Good, Vicky 5:41:31 (32,535)
Goodale, Debbie 4:32:39 (19,594)
Goodall, Jayne 4:25:23 (17,629)
Goodall, Sarah 5:59:56 (34,053)
Goodall, Sophie Louise 4:35:00 (20,234)
Goodbourn, Elizabeth L 4:01:37 (11,396)
Goodburn, Sandy Frances 5:55:53 (33,783)
Goode, Sally Rose 5:34:10 (31,776)
Goodenough, Jenny 4:38:54 (21,231)
Goodfellow, Donna 4:15:07 (14,813)
Gooding, Emma J 3:51:35 (8,561)
Goodings, Claire S 5:01:33 (26,766)
Goodison, Emma Louise 5:43:29 (32,718)
Goodman, Claire 5:52:38 (33,544)
Goodman, Madeline 4:47:57 (23,535)
Goodman, Sally Ann 5:18:37 (29,645)
Goodrich, Caroline 4:35:55 (20,453)
Goodsall, Anna Stanhope 5:32:28 (31,598)
Goodwin, Alexandra C 3:39:26 (6,029)

Goodwin, Bronwyn 3:44:55 (7,082)
Goodwin, Charlotte A 4:14:37 (14,687)
Goodwin, Helena J 5:44:54 (32,859)
Goodwin, Jane 4:17:37 (15,473)
Goodwin, Julie 4:46:01 (23,030)
Goodwin, Michelle L 5:02:43 (26,983)
Goodwin, Sarah 5:31:54 (31,523)
Goodwin, Sian Elizabeth 4:22:00 (16,705)
Goodyear, Elizabeth 4:40:44 (21,708)
Goorney, Hilary 4:59:25 (26,318)
Goorney, Joanna M 3:14:09 (2,334)
Goorun, Rogie M 5:01:25 (26,738)
Gor, Namrata Mayur 4:46:56 (23,288)
Gorajala, Rachel B 4:20:36 (16,297)
Gordon, Claire F 3:02:56 (1,323)
Gordon, Genevieve 6:03:16 (34,269)
Gordon, Harriet Rebecca 3:42:05 (6,527)
Gordon, Jillian E 3:56:12 (9,841)
Gordon, Karen Lesley 3:58:17 (10,484)
Gordon, Katie Jane 4:03:11 (11,773)
Gordon, Louise 6:07:21 (34,525)
Gordon, Michelle A 3:43:32 (6,781)
Gordon, Sarah Louise 5:47:34 (33,105)
Gordon, Tara Jayne 4:45:35 (22,909)
Gore, Kelly Johanne 3:57:43 (10,308)
Gorham, Christine Jane 4:39:33 (21,400)
Gorman, Kim Jennifer 6:50:14 (36,002)
Gorman, Moira 5:20:15 (29,882)
Gormley, Lorraine 3:56:27 (9,916)
Goscomb, Glenda 3:51:54 (8,639)
Gosdschan, Beatrix 5:17:30 (29,471)
Gosling, Jemma 5:06:39 (27,662)
Gosling, Julie Margaret 5:42:03 (32,596)
Goss, Jackie Ann 5:36:10 (32,012)
Goss, Lucy Stephanie 4:12:55 (14,210)
Gossage, Lucy 2:57:51 (943)
Goswell, Louise Victoria 3:55:04 (9,495)
Gottschalk, Gisela 5:11:11 (28,431)
Goublourne, Kirsty Jane 4:26:14 (17,882)
Gough, Alyson Mary 4:18:45 (15,786)
Gough, Bridget Isabel 4:40:10 (21,530)
Gough, Jennifer 4:53:36 (24,941)
Gough, Teresa 5:20:01 (29,853)
Gould, Ann L 5:06:38 (27,654)
Gould, Anna 5:59:39 (34,028)
Gould, Chloe 3:40:36 (6,260)
Gould, Heather 4:28:08 (18,395)
Gould, Holly Marie 5:17:45 (29,508)
Gould, Jamee Kate 4:06:48 (12,657)
Gould, Sally 4:22:45 (16,918)
Gould Davies, Sarah Louise 4:04:35 (12,096)
Goulding, Julie A 3:56:37 (9,964)
Goult, Catherine E 4:49:39 (23,961)
Goulter, Samantha L 5:15:57 (29,222)
Goupil, Valerie 4:14:52 (14,753)
Gourlay, Carol Anne 5:24:28 (30,551)
Gouveia, Tracy M 4:14:19 (14,597)
Goward, Lynn M 3:35:36 (5,342)
Gowe, Alison 4:20:18 (16,200)
Gowen, Claire 4:30:19 (19,051)
Gower, Catherine J 4:02:31 (11,608)
Goyette, Catharine Lucy 6:09:58 (34,663)
Graagaard, Pia Lund 4:23:41 (17,151)
Grace, Abbie E 4:15:01 (14,790)
Grace, Beverley Ann 6:05:13 (34,403)
Gracia, Sarah 4:08:21 (13,043)
Grady, Carol A 4:21:48 (16,636)
Graetz, Katmarina 3:41:45 (6,469)
Graham, Christine 5:22:33 (30,229)
Graham, Gail 4:28:09 (18,397)
Graham, Kim 5:30:43 (31,384)
Graham, Mary Jane 4:49:35 (23,937)
Graham, Rebecca 3:39:24 (6,022)
Graham, Rebecca Kathleen Anna 4:43:34 (22,386)
Graham, Shivonne L 5:32:31 (31,605)
Graham, Wendy 5:20:39 (29,953)
Grahamslaw, Julia 4:41:12 (21,824)
Graham-Wood, Annette Patricia 5:06:25 (27,606)
Grainge, Katie 4:42:49 (22,220)
Graley, Joanne Thérèse 4:44:44 (22,709)
Grandy, Nicola 5:36:21 (32,038)
Grant, Alison Yvonne 4:48:15 (23,599)
Grant, Dianne 5:40:50 (32,460)
Grant, Helen 6:47:20 (35,957)
Grant, Jo S 4:08:39 (13,126)
Grant, Laura C 5:00:59 (26,647)
Grant, Lucy Anne 4:24:42 (17,445)
Grant, Naomi Lisa 5:44:58 (32,866)
Grant, Nicola Suzanne 6:21:51 (35,193)
Grant, Pamela C 3:54:10 (9,248)
Grant, Samantha J 5:52:45 (33,563)
Grant, Virginia 3:26:02 (3,741)
Grant Haworth, Georgie 5:35:31 (31,929)
Granville, Gail 4:04:41 (12,122)
Grassick, Katie Louise 5:09:30 (28,148)
Gration, Judith 3:16:35 (2,626)
Gratton, Gemma Louise 6:37:45 (35,715)
Grave, Linda Maria 4:28:14 (18,431)
Graveling, Anne 4:41:53 (21,989)
Graveney, Penelope 4:21:24 (16,525)
Graves, Lynne 4:56:15 (25,595)
Gravestock, Tracy Margaret 5:57:14 (33,884)
Gray, Alex Louise 4:20:22 (16,223)
Gray, Caroline 4:45:17 (22,835)
Gray, Charlotte 4:27:05 (18,114)
Gray, Gillian 4:10:07 (13,503)
Gray, Heather Mary 6:32:28 (35,577)
Gray, Ishbel 5:15:08 (29,092)
Gray, Jenny F 3:13:45 (2,291)
Gray, Julie 5:31:38 (31,492)
Gray, Lindsy J 3:20:31 (3,027)
Gray, Lizzy Jane 4:21:04 (16,433)
Gray, Lorraine 5:48:13 (33,162)
Gray, Louise 4:34:20 (20,079)
Gray, Marian B 5:23:01 (30,307)
Gray, Marilyn 4:26:08 (17,852)
Gray, Michelle J 4:31:55 (19,411)
Gray, Michelle Louise 4:32:49 (19,635)
Gray, Natalie 4:38:07 (21,011)
Gray, Natalie Karla 6:41:44 (35,825)
Gray, Pam 5:28:00 (31,029)
Gray, Rosaire P 3:52:43 (8,849)
Gray, Tina 3:40:04 (6,161)
Grayson, Elizabeth E 4:11:25 (13,824)
Grealish, Dawn 5:19:09 (29,726)
Greatorex, Jacqueline 4:34:38 (20,154)
Greatorex-Day, Suzanne L 3:57:33 (10,246)
Greatrix, Emma L 3:34:43 (5,194)
Greaves-Maunder, Ronda 4:54:45 (25,245)
Grecco, Paolla 5:33:50 (31,751)
Greed, Katie 6:49:43 (35,990)
Greedus, Maria L 5:14:25 (28,979)
Greedy, Lisa 4:45:42 (22,948)
Greef, Jane Kay 5:06:46 (27,684)
Green, Aleksandra 4:40:24 (21,615)
Green, Alexandra Halcyon 5:15:08 (29,092)
Green, Alice Laura 4:53:12 (24,847)
Green, Alison 5:26:08 (30,794)
Green, Alison 6:02:34 (34,222)
Green, Amy K 3:07:42 (1,677)
Green, Charlotte Ellen 4:42:25 (22,115)
Green, Charlotte Emily 3:40:08 (6,175)
Green, Charlotte Maria 5:48:39 (33,209)
Green, Christina 6:02:15 (34,202)
Green, Claire Louise 4:45:15 (22,828)
Green, Claire M 4:19:17 (15,922)
Green, Diana 7:10:16 (36,311)
Green, Elaine 6:37:56 (35,726)
Green, Emma 4:34:12 (20,044)
Green, Gail 4:29:36 (18,842)
Green, Georgina Louise 4:28:48 (18,609)
Green, Heather Caroline 5:06:38 (27,654)
Green, Helen 5:18:49 (29,669)
Green, Jackie Ann 5:11:50 (28,528)
Green, Jenny 4:28:47 (18,600)
Green, Jenny 4:31:47 (19,390)
Green, Kathryn Trahair 4:46:15 (23,109)
Green, Kellie Marie 5:25:46 (30,744)
Green, Lorna 5:34:13 (31,782)
Green, Melanie 3:44:21 (6,953)
Green, Michelle Anne 5:25:46 (30,744)
Green, Nadine 3:58:41 (10,619)
Green, Natasha Dawn 4:44:56 (22,751)
Green, Nicola G 3:09:15 (1,829)
Green, Pauline Mary 4:05:25 (12,320)
Green, Rachael 4:31:48 (19,393)
Green, Rachel 5:43:42 (32,744)
Green, Rebecca J 3:11:36 (2,059)
Green, Sally Yate 4:39:57 (21,491)
Green, Samantha 3:55:54 (9,753)
Green, Samantha 4:56:01 (25,541)
Green, Sarah E 6:11:24 (34,715)
Green, Sharon J 3:19:09 (2,886)
Green, Theodosia 3:56:26 (9,908)
Greenall, Katie Laura 5:36:40 (32,071)
Greenall, Vicki A 3:24:15 (3,477)
Greenard, Lynne 5:27:57 (31,017)
Greene, Katy 5:47:22 (33,086)
Greene, Natalie A 4:15:04 (14,802)
Greener, Bethany Charlotter 6:55:22 (36,119)
Greenhalgh, Rose 4:58:14 (26,019)
Greenhorn, Tania 4:25:04 (17,540)
Greenway, Tanya J 4:23:58 (17,229)
Greenwood, Gemma 4:18:42 (15,774)
Greenwood, Penny E 4:19:35 (15,990)
Greer, Cathryn Louise 4:29:44 (18,896)
Greer, Sara A 4:22:03 (16,717)
Gregory, Deborah M 5:31:26 (31,468)
Gregory, Elizabeth D 3:52:17 (8,734)
Gregory, Holly 5:04:37 (27,300)
Gregory, Keeley Donna 3:52:35 (8,815)
Gregory, Lucy 5:14:40 (29,014)
Gregory, Mel (Muriel) Mary 4:22:43 (16,908)
Gregory, Samantha Jane 4:43:07 (22,285)
Gregory, Sarah L 3:43:07 (6,718)
Gregory, Sue 3:30:08 (4,438)
Grehan, Monika M 4:53:16 (24,870)
Greig, Emma 4:13:51 (14,470)
Greimllenertz, Martina 3:45:43 (7,249)
Greiner, Ingke 5:02:59 (27,022)
Gren, Susanne 4:55:17 (25,378)
Grenside, Emma 5:09:03 (28,055)
Grestey, Audrey 4:12:45 (14,174)
Gretton, Gemma 5:42:23 (32,625)
Grew, Sophie Francesca 4:40:54 (21,743)
Grey, Frances 4:21:48 (16,636)
Gribben, Lorraine 5:14:07 (28,940)
Grice, Natasha 5:05:48 (27,494)
Griessbach, Anne 3:26:52 (3,857)
Grieveson, Daniella 4:27:46 (18,306)
Griffey, Abi 4:23:59 (17,234)
Griffin, Barbara Ann 5:07:58 (27,889)
Griffin, Chanese C 3:34:38 (5,180)
Griffin, Diana Nicola 5:05:58 (27,524)
Griffin, Lauren 3:51:47 (8,603)
Griffin, Leah 3:40:46 (6,284)
Griffin, Liane 5:52:57 (33,580)
Griffin, Mandy Jane 5:25:44 (30,737)
Griffin, Rachel L 4:28:11 (18,414)
Griffin, Sarah Jane Louise 4:28:51 (18,625)
Griffin, Susan M 3:45:07 (7,119)
Griffin, Zoe H 3:52:06 (8,679)
Griffith, Hannah M 4:15:19 (14,865)
Griffith, Helen O 4:43:53 (22,475)
Griffiths, Adelle 5:26:54 (30,890)
Griffiths, Anna 5:26:54 (30,890)
Griffiths, Carol 6:22:32 (35,211)
Griffiths, Cheryl 4:28:31 (18,528)
Griffiths, Clare 5:27:49 (31,004)
Griffiths, Helen Anita 5:08:42 (28,004)
Griffiths, Helen Lynne 4:44:11 (22,557)
Griffiths, Jayne Anne 4:36:14 (20,532)
Griffiths, Joanna 3:30:48 (4,548)
Griffiths, Julie Michelle 5:23:10 (30,333)
Griffiths, Lorraine 4:46:56 (23,288)
Griffiths, Louisa 5:47:24 (33,089)
Griffiths, Siobhan D 3:41:06 (6,345)
Griffiths, Stephanie Joan 5:12:05 (28,582)
Griffiths, Susan Emily 7:06:33 (36,271)
Griffiths, Vivien 5:02:58 (27,021)
Griffiths, Zoe 4:52:14 (24,610)
Griffiths Jeans, Pauline M 4:41:16 (21,837)
Griggs, Julia 4:32:09 (19,473)
Griggs, Lyn Patricia Margaret 6:27:17 (35,391)
Grigor, Hayley Jane 5:37:20 (32,149)
Grigor, Sarah-Louise 4:16:13 (15,079)
Grimes, Ciara 4:07:04 (12,726)
Grimes, Marie Samantha 5:18:53 (29,679)
Grimes, Rachel 3:46:57 (7,518)

Grimes, Sophie	5:57:14 (33,884)	
Grimshaw, Kate	6:05:39 (34,427)	
Grimshaw, Victoria	4:28:05 (18,383)	
Grindu, Christiane	4:44:22 (22,605)	
Grist, Rachael	4:39:10 (21,304)	
Grocott, Laura Katherine	5:10:28 (28,323)	
Groetteroed, Tone Beate	3:59:54 (10,967)	
Grogan, Michelle	7:08:07 (36,292)	
Grosse, Petra	5:35:30 (31,927)	
Grout, Sarah Susannah	5:02:17 (26,904)	
Grove, Abigail	4:12:29 (14,097)	
Grove, Frances	3:52:35 (8,815)	
Groves, Hannah L	4:12:51 (14,194)	
Groves, Vicki A	4:46:17 (23,125)	
Grundling, Nanette	4:24:11 (17,281)	
Grundy, Allison	3:58:04 (10,401)	
Grundy, Rachel	5:41:27 (32,528)	
Grundy, Roseanna	5:15:58 (29,223)	
Grunstein, Alison J	4:33:40 (19,910)	
Grunstein, Kate	4:59:12 (26,264)	
Gualano, Joanna Claire	6:04:49 (34,372)	
Guckenheim, Rachael S	4:00:09 (11,019)	
Gudgeon, Judith Ann	5:44:43 (32,841)	
Gudka, Chandni	5:37:53 (32,198)	
Guest, Helen	4:11:34 (13,867)	
Guest, Jane B	6:47:16 (35,955)	
Guest, Janet Margaret	6:32:54 (35,592)	
Guest, Kerry	6:13:06 (34,811)	
Guest, Tarryn Michelle	5:25:38 (30,720)	
Guidotti, Gabriella	3:49:06 (8,000)	
Guiney, Megan	2:55:11 (757)	
Gumbel, Lizanne	4:26:47 (18,020)	
Gundle, Jo L	3:27:11 (3,905)	
Gunn, Catherine	3:55:38 (9,659)	
Gunn, Elaine Joan	4:49:55 (24,031)	
Gunn, Jessica E	3:40:43 (6,277)	
Gunner, Frances	4:54:04 (25,064)	
Gunning, Amanda Jane	4:30:18 (19,044)	
Gunning, April	4:10:49 (13,670)	
Gunning, Debbie	3:23:07 (3,310)	
Gunningham, Andrea T	4:56:55 (25,750)	
Gunst, Christiane	5:34:09 (31,774)	
Gunst, Stefanie	4:29:51 (18,927)	
Gunter, Layla	4:25:28 (17,650)	
Guppy, Katie	7:12:28 (36,334)	
Guram, Sandi K	5:21:53 (30,126)	
Gurr, Tracey S	4:38:47 (21,202)	
Gurrin, Nicola Jane	4:30:49 (19,173)	
Guthrie, Nicola	7:06:34 (36,273)	
Gutierrez, Cristina	6:00:18 (34,083)	
Guy, Evie Emily Patricia	4:33:59 (19,987)	
Gwaderi, Razia	7:17:38 (36,384)	
Gwilliam, Linda	5:21:05 (30,015)	
Gwilliams, Bernadette Kathryn	4:46:38 (23,217)	
Gye, Suzannah M	4:23:12 (17,024)	
Gyles, Emma	3:49:06 (8,000)	
Haakantu, Beatrice	5:07:06 (27,740)	
Haar-Jorgensen, Natasha	4:07:26 (12,810)	
Haase, Jutta	3:35:39 (5,353)	
Habgood, Angela K	3:45:08 (7,124)	
Habib, Jude	5:18:25 (29,610)	
Habtamu, Atsede	2:31:41 (81)	
Hacker, Carmen	5:02:23 (26,922)	
Hacker, Sharon	5:32:05 (31,548)	
Hackleton, Donna	4:32:47 (19,626)	
Hackman, Jodie	5:41:25 (32,523)	
Hackman, Ruth Ann	5:58:12 (33,945)	
Hackney, Melissa	4:30:40 (19,139)	
Hadaschik, Katia	4:03:36 (11,874)	
Haddad, Jane	3:25:09 (3,600)	
Hadden, Helen	4:53:55 (25,027)	
Hadfield, Wendy	5:55:40 (33,766)	
Hadingham, Charlotte	4:06:18 (12,524)	
Hadland, Sarah Catherine E	3:47:36 (7,669)	
Hadley, Caroline Ann	6:24:07 (35,284)	
Hadley, Kathryn	3:24:39 (3,530)	
Hadley, Laura Faith	5:23:52 (30,451)	
Hadley, Toni Alexandra	4:55:29 (25,407)	
Hadley, Wendy Jane	4:32:39 (19,594)	
Hadorn, Catherine	4:55:51 (25,497)	
Hadshar, Eleanor	4:57:59 (25,968)	
Haffenden, Sally	3:44:47 (7,051)	
Hagan, Georgina	5:27:11 (30,932)	

Hagesaether, Marta Madland	4:47:24 (23,389)	
Hagfoss, Johanna	4:49:45 (23,994)	
Hagger, Kate	4:51:45 (24,475)	
Hagger, Katie Joanne	5:08:09 (27,920)	
Hague, Nina A	3:51:55 (8,644)	
Hague, Sharon	4:05:24 (12,313)	
Hahn, Marta	3:56:21 (9,886)	
Haider, Shimul	4:25:42 (17,715)	
Haig, Frances	4:53:46 (24,988)	
Haig Pincay, Sarah	5:58:00 (33,932)	
Haigh, Charlotte Mary	4:51:45 (24,475)	
Haigh, Gayatri M	4:10:53 (13,690)	
Haigh, Roma	6:37:54 (35,725)	
Haines, Lynne	4:31:57 (19,422)	
Haines, Zara	5:15:06 (29,081)	
Hair, Fiona L	4:06:35 (12,596)	
Hair, Rachel Anne	5:56:14 (33,813)	
Haislund, Bente	4:44:45 (22,712)	
Halbauer, Hannah	4:53:04 (24,806)	
Hale, Eimear	4:56:19 (25,616)	
Hale, Julie Tryphena	6:08:33 (34,586)	
Hale, Kathryn Ann	5:36:29 (32,055)	
Hale, Laura Jane	3:23:54 (3,420)	
Hale, Meredith L	3:23:39 (3,387)	
Hales, Elizabeth S	3:41:21 (6,395)	
Hales, Emma	5:37:43 (32,183)	
Hales, Laura J	3:18:46 (2,848)	
Halford, Angela J	4:31:27 (19,321)	
Halford, Sarah Rachael	4:10:44 (13,649)	
Halion, Mary	4:23:43 (17,164)	
Hall, Aja C	5:24:14 (30,517)	
Hall, Alison Mary	4:58:40 (26,130)	
Hall, Catherine Lucy	5:28:54 (31,136)	
Hall, Christina Melanie	4:51:49 (24,497)	
Hall, Danielle Lucy May	6:37:47 (35,719)	
Hall, Deborah A	4:08:34 (13,108)	
Hall, Elise Paula	4:51:52 (24,511)	
Hall, Elizabeth Ann	4:18:17 (15,655)	
Hall, Gemma Marie	5:39:42 (32,360)	
Hall, Jackie	5:53:16 (33,594)	
Hall, Jackie Susan	5:51:59 (33,503)	
Hall, Julie S	7:04:54 (36,253)	
Hall, Juliette Anna	4:47:03 (23,320)	
Hall, Kate	3:58:35 (10,590)	
Hall, Kate Michelle	5:41:53 (32,576)	
Hall, Lianne J	3:54:19 (9,282)	
Hall, Lucy Jane	5:24:03 (30,487)	
Hall, Michelle	4:08:23 (13,054)	
Hall, Moira	4:33:31 (19,857)	
Hall, Philippa	4:40:42 (21,693)	
Hall, Rosanagh Elizabeth	6:08:58 (34,615)	
Hall, Sarah Elizabeth	7:38:59 (36,516)	
Hall, Sarah Jane	4:35:54 (20,446)	
Hall, Sarah Lucy	6:31:58 (35,566)	
Hall, Siobhan Michelle	4:50:49 (24,243)	
Hall, Sue E	6:03:50 (34,310)	
Hallam, Jane	3:57:32 (10,238)	
Hallam, Lesley	5:56:59 (33,865)	
Hallergard, Susanne Eva	5:39:31 (32,350)	
Halligan, Siobhan Maria	3:53:47 (9,154)	
Halls, Annabelle	5:43:40 (32,734)	
Halls, Debbie H	3:58:24 (10,523)	
Halls, Eleanor Sian	3:54:24 (9,300)	
Halls, Samantha	5:43:50 (32,758)	
Halls, Suzanne Linda	5:06:18 (27,587)	
Hallworth, Frances Alexandra	5:34:18 (31,799)	
Halpin, Elizabeth Louise	4:46:02 (23,037)	
Halpin, Geraldine Louise	4:27:41 (18,284)	
Halse, Jenny	5:29:52 (31,274)	
Halstead, Vivien Margaret	4:54:33 (25,190)	
Halton, Caroline	4:06:37 (12,604)	
Ham, Joanna	5:27:30 (30,966)	
Hamblin, Emma	5:00:44 (26,595)	
Hamblin, Lisa	5:00:18 (26,522)	
Hamby, Julie Ann	5:27:02 (30,910)	
Hamer, Elaine	4:43:20 (22,325)	
Hamer, Elise Larissa	5:22:31 (30,222)	
Hamer-Davies, Elizabeth A	6:53:43 (36,081)	
Hamill, Eileen	5:11:38 (28,491)	
Hamilton, Anna	4:41:29 (21,887)	
Hamilton, Denise	4:52:31 (24,688)	
Hamilton, Heather	4:26:07 (17,848)	
Hamilton, Lucy	4:53:27 (24,903)	

Hamilton, Maria	4:11:40 (13,898)	
Hamlett, Alison Elizabeth	3:14:57 (2,434)	
Hammock, Ann Parker	5:07:45 (27,856)	
Hammon, Juliet A	4:47:49 (23,502)	
Hammond, Amy	4:28:10 (18,406)	
Hammond, Chloe D	3:58:31 (10,560)	
Hammond, Louise	4:07:43 (12,889)	
Hampson, Julie Anne	5:49:21 (33,264)	
Hampson, Rebecca Louise	3:57:46 (10,318)	
Hampton, Nico	7:00:25 (36,194)	
Hancock, Karen E	3:18:08 (2,783)	
Hancock, Sarah Jayne	4:21:24 (16,525)	
Hancock, Tracey Ann	3:47:22 (7,612)	
Hancocks, Rachael Marie	5:02:41 (26,974)	
Hand, Didi	5:25:04 (30,634)	
Handoll, Bethany Victoria	3:17:38 (2,729)	
Haney, Janet D	3:29:28 (4,315)	
Hanley, Nicola	5:24:03 (30,487)	
Hanlon, Jennifer Catherine	4:47:22 (23,384)	
Hanlon, Joanna	5:10:52 (28,389)	
Hannaford, Elizabeth Katherine	5:06:50 (27,693)	
Hannah, Jane Louise	3:56:48 (10,030)	
Hannah, Sharon	4:24:07 (17,264)	
Hannah, Xanthe	3:37:06 (5,584)	
Hannaway, Emma	4:46:01 (23,030)	
Hanness, Sarah Jane	5:31:46 (31,510)	
Hannon, Danita	7:53:20 (36,575)	
Hansen, Amy	6:32:29 (35,581)	
Hansen, Janni C	4:28:31 (18,528)	
Hansford, Anne	5:09:57 (28,221)	
Hansford, Tracy Jane	4:22:41 (16,897)	
Hansford, Vicky	5:18:11 (29,570)	
Hansom, Jane	3:54:01 (9,215)	
Hanson, Helen	4:33:59 (19,987)	
Hanson, Tracey	5:55:47 (33,774)	
Harbon, Kate	4:21:19 (16,494)	
Hard, Kerry Elizabeth	4:37:40 (20,919)	
Hardcastle, Danielle Louisa	4:50:15 (24,107)	
Hardcastle, Judy Eleanor	4:45:57 (23,012)	
Hardee, Poppy Alice	5:57:27 (33,899)	
Hardern, Lauren Rebecca	4:54:06 (25,072)	
Hardie, Christine Nicole	3:57:02 (10,109)	
Hardiman, Julie Margaret	4:53:57 (25,034)	
Harding, Alyson	5:09:09 (28,079)	
Harding, Caroline	4:09:00 (13,213)	
Harding, Christine J	4:47:48 (23,494)	
Harding, Jackie Anne	5:32:18 (31,574)	
Harding, Kerry	6:34:30 (35,641)	
Harding, Laura Kate	4:02:01 (11,494)	
Harding, Lisa Jane	5:56:07 (33,797)	
Harding, Ljiljana	3:27:29 (3,958)	
Harding, Marie	3:55:15 (9,544)	
Harding, Nancy J	3:37:35 (5,684)	
Hardman, Alexandra Marie R	5:56:16 (33,815)	
Hardman, Pamela	4:42:58 (22,250)	
Hardman, Rachael M	3:54:25 (9,304)	
Hards, Amanda	4:25:40 (17,707)	
Hardstone, Sarah	4:36:35 (20,625)	
Hardwick, Heidi P	5:59:09 (34,000)	
Hardwick, Jacqueline Ann	3:16:37 (2,629)	
Hardwick, Nicki	6:41:29 (35,819)	
Hardy, Alexandra June	4:32:10 (19,476)	
Hardy, Lorraine	3:41:38 (6,444)	
Hardy, Rachel M	4:06:22 (12,544)	
Hardy, Victoria Emma	6:57:04 (36,142)	
Hare, Caroline Sarah Louise	4:58:12 (26,012)	
Hare Duke, Hilary	3:40:38 (6,268)	
Hares, Rachael A	3:30:11 (4,447)	
Haresign, India Jay	5:19:21 (29,754)	
Hargie, Patricia G	5:09:44 (28,185)	
Hargrave, Sarah Anne	4:06:42 (12,625)	
Hargreaves, Joanna	7:04:29 (36,250)	
Hargreaves, Rebecca	4:48:33 (23,679)	
Harilela, Krsna	4:28:17 (18,448)	
Harindra, Dharshi	4:25:43 (17,725)	
Harish, Denise	6:53:50 (36,083)	
Harland, Julie	7:05:41 (36,260)	
Harles, Rani	5:30:39 (31,379)	
Harley, Natalie	4:49:00 (23,800)	
Harley, Zoe E	4:13:31 (14,369)	
Harlow, Carrie	4:06:27 (12,557)	
Harman, Alaine	4:39:57 (21,491)	

LONDON MARATHON

Harman, Louise	5:27:00 (30,906)
Harmon, Laura Jo	5:46:18 (32,984)
Harnett, Julia M	4:56:17 (25,608)
Harper, Deborah	5:44:30 (32,814)
Harper, Helen	3:51:14 (8,482)
Harper, Juila Helen	5:04:10 (27,222)
Harper, Karen L	5:14:27 (28,984)
Harradine, Tina Susan	4:42:13 (22,069)
Harrall, Helen Faye	4:35:25 (20,332)
Harraway, Samantha Kelly	4:31:35 (19,347)
Harriman, Maxine Ann	6:15:46 (34,918)
Harrington, Kathleen	4:42:51 (22,231)
Harrington, Mary A	4:41:27 (21,878)
Harrington, Natasha Louise	4:29:32 (18,817)
Harrington, Tracy Lynn	3:56:29 (9,926)
Harris, Amy Catherine	5:10:34 (28,343)
Harris, Anne Marion Ruth	4:51:19 (24,378)
Harris, Bethan	4:51:05 (24,326)
Harris, Candise	5:40:12 (32,412)
Harris, Carli	4:43:39 (22,405)
Harris, Caroline Helen	6:29:02 (35,462)
Harris, Donna Carol	4:31:00 (19,216)
Harris, Elizabeth Mary	4:47:45 (23,479)
Harris, Gillian R	4:39:22 (21,344)
Harris, Helen	5:13:50 (28,898)
Harris, Jane	4:44:30 (22,638)
Harris, Jane E	4:20:16 (16,185)
Harris, Jennie L	6:03:21 (34,279)
Harris, Jenny Katherine	4:12:58 (14,225)
Harris, Jo	5:50:56 (33,426)
Harris, Karen	5:19:54 (29,836)
Harris, Kelly	6:09:43 (34,647)
Harris, Kelly Louise	4:19:48 (16,041)
Harris, Kim A	3:53:28 (9,045)
Harris, Liz Susan	4:54:42 (25,230)
Harris, Penny Sarah	5:06:27 (27,617)
Harris, Rachel C	4:53:00 (24,792)
Harris, Samanatha J	3:17:23 (2,695)
Harris, Sharon Ann	7:20:18 (36,407)
Harris, Susie Rosa	5:06:36 (27,643)
Harris, Vikki	4:46:15 (23,109)
Harrison, Carmel F	3:46:48 (7,489)
Harrison, Catherine Lindsey	4:00:36 (11,140)
Harrison, Charlotte	4:58:58 (26,207)
Harrison, Christine Susan	5:26:39 (30,857)
Harrison, Emma Jane	4:42:25 (22,115)
Harrison, Gill M	3:38:14 (5,811)
Harrison, Jennie	5:02:12 (26,890)
Harrison, Karen	3:37:53 (5,739)
Harrison, Katie	4:41:45 (21,952)
Harrison, Kaye	6:21:09 (35,167)
Harrison, Lisa	4:54:49 (25,261)
Harrison, Lucy	6:19:35 (35,109)
Harrison, Lydia Grace	4:24:38 (17,425)
Harrison, Marice	4:42:01 (22,017)
Harrison, Nathalina	4:35:44 (20,397)
Harrison, Osham	3:38:13 (5,805)
Harrison, Sarah Anne	4:59:59 (26,448)
Harrison, Sue	2:38:53 (175)
Harrison, Vicky	6:58:25 (36,162)
Harrison-White, Stephanie	5:23:59 (30,477)
Harrold, Emma	5:09:34 (28,162)
Harrold, Louisa	3:29:32 (4,328)
Harrold, Vanessa Jane	5:16:37 (29,324)
Harrop, Louise M	5:56:59 (33,865)
Hart, Gerri C	4:02:56 (11,715)
Hart, Grace L	4:01:16 (11,310)
Hart, Jo	7:49:32 (36,563)
Hart, Joanna	5:20:06 (29,864)
Hart, Portia	4:07:14 (12,759)
Hart, Sarah Yvette	6:10:45 (34,691)
Hartie, Deb	4:33:39 (19,906)
Hartles, Lorraine	5:44:02 (32,770)
Hartley, Helen L	4:07:18 (12,775)
Hartley, Helen Victoria	3:59:05 (10,740)
Hartley, Kate	5:22:18 (30,190)
Hartley, Nicola Jane	4:51:22 (24,390)
Hartley, Sarah Lousie	5:13:24 (28,827)
Hartmann, Carla	5:20:22 (29,894)
Hartnett, Anne Christina	5:09:57 (28,221)
Hartrampf, Mona	6:06:05 (34,456)
Hartwright, Caryl E	4:24:55 (17,494)
Harty, Karen	4:32:43 (19,610)

Harty, Valerie	4:00:43 (11,176)
Harvey, Charlene	4:37:11 (20,790)
Harvey, Geraldine	5:17:18 (29,438)
Harvey, Hayley	5:51:59 (33,503)
Harvey, Janice A	4:00:57 (11,240)
Harvey, Johanne	5:15:27 (29,135)
Harvey, Michelle Lisa	5:48:53 (33,231)
Harvey, Rachel	4:57:06 (25,779)
Harvey, Tara Jean	5:31:44 (31,505)
Harvey-Seldon, Victoria Ann	4:34:31 (20,124)
Harwood, Jane Rachel	4:59:52 (26,422)
Hasenauer, Shirley Elizabeth	5:47:12 (33,070)
Haskouri, Alia	4:05:15 (12,269)
Haskouri, Nadia	4:01:32 (11,376)
Haslam, Joanne	3:26:58 (3,872)
Hasler, Susan	6:03:44 (34,303)
Haslett, Annika Shalan	7:10:30 (36,314)
Hassell, Paula S	3:13:58 (2,315)
Hasson, Lucy	4:24:16 (17,306)
Hatfield, Sue	4:43:00 (22,259)
Hathaway, Karen	2:57:06 (863)
Hatherley, Marilyn J	4:05:16 (12,276)
Hatt, Debbie	5:07:26 (27,793)
Hatt, Jeanette Dorothy	4:54:30 (25,179)
Hattersley, Leanne Michelle	4:21:33 (16,564)
Hatton, Anna	4:27:08 (18,129)
Hatton, Jeanette	4:49:34 (23,929)
Hatton, Jenny	4:21:29 (16,542)
Hatton, Maggie	6:24:51 (35,304)
Havell, Juliette Elizabeth	4:41:30 (21,893)
Havelot, Tracey	5:10:49 (28,379)
Havern, Gloria	4:36:27 (20,586)
Havers, Roberta I	4:29:27 (18,790)
Hawdon, Alicia Charlotte	5:31:22 (31,456)
Hawes, Fiona	5:43:18 (32,702)
Hawes, Nicola D	4:53:22 (24,887)
Hawkins, Corina Yvonne	5:06:01 (27,533)
Hawkins, Dawn A	4:41:20 (21,848)
Hawkins, Fiona E	4:19:40 (16,009)
Hawkins, Gill	5:58:03 (33,937)
Hawkins, Joanna	3:40:27 (6,225)
Hawkins, Joanna	4:11:35 (13,875)
Hawkins, Joanna	5:18:02 (29,552)
Hawkins, Liz Anne	4:51:44 (24,468)
Hawkins, Lucy	5:17:05 (29,397)
Hawkins, Naomi Jane	3:59:36 (10,893)
Hawkins, Sara	5:26:17 (30,818)
Hawkins, Sharon J	3:06:27 (1,565)
Hawkins, Simone Elizabeth	4:29:52 (18,935)
Hawkins, Victoria M	4:45:21 (22,852)
Hawkins, Vikki	5:31:31 (31,477)
Hawley, Natasha	6:25:57 (35,348)
Haworth, Alison Jane	6:22:45 (35,225)
Haworth, Emma C	3:42:03 (6,521)
Hawthorne, Karon Jane	5:10:55 (28,395)
Hawthorne, Katie Rachel	5:35:40 (31,951)
Hay, Carolyn A	3:20:54 (3,070)
Haycocks, Rachel Elizabeth	5:45:27 (32,904)
Haydon, Lucy	6:09:56 (34,659)
Haydon, Ronnie R	4:05:38 (12,365)
Hayes, Carla	5:13:03 (28,747)
Hayes, Carol A	4:41:27 (21,878)
Hayes, Ingrid Kelly	3:41:25 (6,408)
Hayes, Kerry Anne	4:32:59 (19,691)
Hayes, Linda A	3:37:45 (5,718)
Hayes, Melanie Julie	3:53:44 (9,132)
Hayes, Nicola Laura	6:10:04 (34,670)
Hayes, Patricia Louise	6:20:32 (35,148)
Hayes, Sue	4:20:40 (16,324)
Hayes-Gill, Claire S	3:28:47 (4,185)
Hayler, Hannah Louise	4:18:01 (15,582)
Hayley Bell, Catherine	3:50:46 (8,375)
Haynes, Becky I	4:59:51 (26,414)
Haynes, Ellen M	4:21:43 (16,617)
Haynes, Lynne	3:40:26 (6,221)

Haynes, Mandy	4:58:23 (26,061)
Haynes, Susan A	5:21:12 (30,032)
Hays, Helen Rose Dixon	5:24:58 (30,616)
Hayter, Christine Alison	5:01:37 (26,779)
Hayter, Janis	5:21:56 (30,135)
Hayward, Christina Elizabeth	6:25:36 (35,333)
Hayward, Jayne A	5:24:52 (30,599)
Hayward, Joanne	4:00:46 (11,185)
Hayward, Lesley	5:06:44 (27,679)
Hayward, Rebecca	5:44:41 (32,838)
Haywood, Diane	3:39:56 (6,135)
Haywood, Gillian	4:42:42 (22,186)
Haywood, Wendy Margaret	4:30:27 (19,075)
Hazel, Victoria Joy	3:56:19 (9,877)
Hazelhoff, Zoe	4:22:23 (16,818)
Hazell, Clare E	4:00:12 (11,031)
Hazell, Katharine E	4:40:49 (21,728)
Hazlitt, Karen N	3:25:50 (3,709)
Hazzard, Susan	3:34:33 (5,163)
Head, Amanda Jane	4:13:56 (14,486)
Head, Becky	4:31:59 (19,428)
Head, Sophia C	6:34:00 (35,624)
Heading, Gwen	4:46:27 (23,156)
Headley, Fiona J	4:04:14 (12,016)
Headon, Leah R	3:29:16 (4,283)
Heald, Victoria	5:26:05 (30,790)
Healey, Sarah J	3:52:44 (8,851)
Healy, Claire	5:35:19 (31,906)
Healy, Joanne	4:54:14 (25,109)
Healy, Louise Anne	7:12:27 (36,333)
Heap, Cath	4:34:54 (20,216)
Heap, Lulu	5:10:06 (28,256)
Heard, Anneliese	3:52:29 (8,792)
Heard, Christiana Dawn	6:01:47 (34,173)
Heard, Karen Jayne	5:32:20 (31,577)
Heard, Rachel Denise	4:24:39 (17,432)
Hearfield, Tessa J	3:54:01 (9,215)
Hearn, Amy L	3:31:10 (4,606)
Hearn, Claire Elizabeth	4:00:20 (11,068)
Heary, Julie Amanda	6:21:15 (35,171)
Heasley, Alex	6:52:43 (36,065)
Heasman, Keeley Jane	7:20:33 (36,408)
Heath, Alison	5:00:50 (26,617)
Heath, Tina Jane	5:24:29 (30,554)
Heaton, Christine	3:20:39 (3,043)
Heaton, Michelle	5:29:14 (31,182)
Heaver, Melanie Jane	4:00:54 (11,218)
Heavey, Karelle	6:13:38 (34,824)
Hebblethwaite, Clara	4:42:28 (22,130)
Hedges, Anita E	3:51:11 (8,469)
Hedley Lewis, Penelope A	4:05:26 (12,322)
Hedlund, Clare Louise	5:42:31 (32,640)
Heenan, Rachael	7:12:19 (36,330)
Heer, Bhupinder	5:39:57 (32,383)
Heeran, Deirdre	5:24:17 (30,522)
Heerey, Charlie	4:49:26 (23,903)
Heffer, Kate	4:21:24 (16,525)
Hegerty, Gabby	4:21:48 (16,636)
Heigham, Karen Louisa	6:46:10 (35,933)
Heighes, Kate	4:19:31 (15,977)
Heilmann, Sonja	5:18:25 (29,610)
Heirich, Isabelle	5:15:25 (29,128)
Heisterberg, Karen	4:53:10 (24,839)
Hellings, Geraldine Anne	3:34:37 (5,175)
Helliwell, Annette	4:45:02 (22,778)
Helps, Annabelle Penney	4:28:59 (18,679)
Hemingbrough, Catherine	5:05:23 (27,428)
Hemingway, Tracey	4:01:15 (11,306)
Hemmens, Wendy J	5:16:50 (29,359)
Hemming, Kate	4:56:11 (25,579)
Hempsall, Theresa K	3:23:48 (3,407)
Hems, Fiona Jayne	4:20:25 (16,239)
Hemsworth, Jane	4:16:42 (15,222)
Hemsworth, Marion V	3:55:21 (9,582)
Hemsworth, Sophie A	3:56:48 (10,030)
Henderson, Amanda G	3:12:48 (2,167)
Henderson, Claire Ann	7:16:28 (36,375)
Henderson, Eileen P	4:28:04 (18,381)
Henderson, Jane Ann	5:02:46 (26,988)
Henderson, Kerry	4:38:18 (21,054)
Henderson, Lorena	7:04:02 (36,244)
Henderson, Lynn A	3:20:17 (2,989)
Henderson, Melanie	4:51:41 (24,457)

Henderson, Noreen....3:51:13 (8,474)
Henegan, Chloe....5:45:14 (32,886)
Henery, Catherine....4:12:04 (14,000)
Henley, Vanessa....5:58:10 (33,942)
Henman, Nicola A....4:21:44 (16,623)
Henneberry, Victoria Louise....5:52:44 (33,556)
Hennessy, Philippa....3:54:42 (9,387)
Hennessy, Sophie Elizabeth....5:50:18 (33,362)
Hennis, Avril....6:20:42 (35,151)
Henry, Kirsty A....3:56:02 (9,795)
Henry, Maura M....4:15:51 (14,987)
Henry, Nicola Jane....4:11:56 (13,972)
Henry, Roberta J....4:58:06 (25,986)
Henry, Victoria A....5:55:00 (33,717)
Hensman, Rachel Anne....5:33:00 (31,663)
Henthorn, Sarah Jane....7:15:28 (36,361)
Henworth, Victoria Jane....6:01:44 (34,169)
Heppell, Dawn M....4:25:20 (17,612)
Heppenstall, Kirsty....4:39:17 (21,326)
Heppes, Julie Christina....4:57:57 (25,959)
Herard, Véronique....3:32:12 (4,770)
Herbert, Alison....4:19:13 (15,903)
Herbert, Katy....5:45:19 (32,898)
Herbert, Marian Elizabeth Wendy 6:11:43 (34,736)
Herbert, Rachel D....5:15:06 (29,081)
Herd, Juliet....6:01:58 (34,186)
Herlock, Stephanie Marie....4:55:23 (25,399)
Hermitage, Julia....4:19:15 (15,913)
Hernandez, Ana Martha....4:22:29 (16,841)
Herod, Stefanie A....5:39:03 (32,307)
Heron, Annabel Victoria....3:59:34 (10,886)
Heron, Judith Anne....6:11:00 (34,700)
Herring, Emma J....5:48:39 (33,209)
Herron, Louise....3:56:44 (10,009)
Heselgrave, Julie....4:25:11 (17,572)
Hesketh, Jo Anne....3:05:43 (1,516)
Heslop, Sophie Victoria....4:47:26 (23,396)
Hetherington, Alexandra M....3:34:46 (5,206)
Hetherington, Emily....5:22:15 (30,181)
Hetherington, Jackie A....3:58:33 (10,574)
Hetherington, Julie....4:17:27 (15,425)
Hetherington, Michelle K....3:19:11 (2,888)
Hewer, Susie....5:43:22 (32,706)
Hewitt, Catherine E....3:08:55 (1,801)
Hewitt, Laura....6:17:09 (34,989)
Hewitt, Nicky Joan....6:46:35 (35,939)
Hewitt, Nicola....6:13:24 (34,817)
Hewlett, Laura Victoria....4:18:51 (15,815)
Hewson, Julie....4:57:16 (25,817)
Heycock, Carol R....3:14:54 (2,428)
Heydecker, Deirdre A....3:35:29 (5,321)
Heyland, Sue....4:49:27 (23,906)
Heywood, Vicky Elizabeth....4:14:19 (14,597)
Hiatt, Grazyna....4:27:03 (18,097)
Hibberd, Briony....4:36:26 (20,582)
Hibberd, Lucy Victoria....4:30:02 (18,983)
Hibbs, Kate Elizabeth....5:43:34 (32,726)
Hickey, Alicia A....3:30:58 (4,574)
Hickey, Charlotte....4:22:14 (16,776)
Hickling, Tina M....4:44:38 (22,682)
Hickman, Breeda M....3:22:59 (3,292)
Hickman, Helen Elizabeth....4:10:11 (13,524)
Hickman, Helen M....4:35:56 (20,461)
Hickman, Sarah....5:50:35 (33,397)
Hickman, Susan....5:29:07 (31,165)
Hicks, Beverley Ann....4:28:59 (18,679)
Hicks, Cheryl....4:16:00 (15,026)
Hicks, India Amanda....4:40:49 (21,728)
Hicks, Lisa Jane....6:24:27 (35,295)
Hier, Diane R....3:17:14 (2,687)
Hier, Sarah....4:21:43 (16,617)
Higginbottom, Clare....4:19:37 (15,997)
Higgins, Claire....5:44:20 (32,798)
Higgins, Claire....5:59:46 (34,044)
Higgins, Clare....4:02:24 (11,580)
Higgins, Elizabeth Margaret....5:22:18 (30,190)
Higgins, Gemma Louise....5:57:29 (33,901)
Higgins, Jane....4:04:52 (12,168)
Higgins, Jane....4:29:12 (18,732)
Higgins, Kelly....4:57:30 (25,858)
Higgins, Rachel....5:17:54 (29,526)
Higgins, Sarah L....5:01:31 (26,758)
Higgins, Tessa Lindsay....5:06:44 (27,679)
Higgins, Victoria....3:55:39 (9,661)
Higginson, Jessica....3:29:40 (4,354)
Higgon, Andrea Helen....5:39:53 (32,375)
Higgs, Lee-Ann....4:19:43 (16,019)
Higgs, Rachel Caroline....4:01:55 (11,474)
High, Melanie Jane....5:01:31 (26,758)
Highgate, Cath J....4:03:06 (11,759)
Higson, Roz....6:41:36 (35,822)
Higson, Susan....5:15:59 (29,227)
Hilbery, Hannah Charlotte....5:37:56 (32,205)
Hilditch, Dawn Michelle....4:14:10 (14,560)
Hiles, Linda K....4:13:01 (14,244)
Hill, Alison....6:44:59 (35,908)
Hill, Andrea J....3:24:05 (3,449)
Hill, Emma....4:14:28 (14,637)
Hill, Gail....4:21:49 (16,643)
Hill, Georgina....4:14:58 (14,773)
Hill, Helen....3:46:06 (7,340)
Hill, Janet M....4:31:24 (19,312)
Hill, Lianna Marie....4:56:55 (25,750)
Hill, Louisa....4:32:34 (19,578)
Hill, Louisa Alexandra....4:06:14 (12,506)
Hill, Louise Elizabeth....6:01:59 (34,188)
Hill, Marina....5:36:45 (32,077)
Hill, Natasha Elizabeth....3:59:35 (10,891)
Hill, Paula K....3:23:18 (3,341)
Hill, Rachael....4:56:37 (25,671)
Hill, Rachael Jennifer....5:38:38 (32,277)
Hill, Suzanne....5:04:40 (27,308)
Hill, Suzy....5:31:10 (31,430)
Hill, Tracey Dawn....5:44:26 (32,808)
Hill, Tracy Jane....4:35:39 (20,378)
Hill,, Lucy,....4:17:19 (15,380)
Hiller, Eileen M....4:34:03 (20,005)
Hiller, Helene P....4:01:45 (11,435)
Hillery, Ursula Jane....4:42:26 (22,124)
Hillier, Ann....4:20:52 (16,381)
Hillier, Joanne M....4:09:23 (13,304)
Hillier, Laura....5:14:49 (29,039)
Hillkirk, Christina....3:51:26 (8,524)
Hills, Barbara Helen....4:19:57 (16,086)
Hills, Nicole....4:03:13 (11,781)
Hills, Tonya M....5:45:13 (32,885)
Hillyard, Avril....5:12:40 (28,677)
Hillyard, Elizabeth Jane....4:49:37 (23,951)
Hilman, Paula K....4:32:14 (19,494)
Hilton, Caroline....4:46:48 (23,255)
Hilton, Fiona Jane....5:15:40 (29,174)
Hilton, Janet....5:00:33 (26,561)
Hilton, Nicola....4:45:12 (22,820)
Hilyer, Jane Catherine....4:25:19 (17,605)
Himelfield, Sarah Louise....5:32:19 (31,575)
Himsworth, Hilary....4:46:16 (23,118)
Hinchliffe, Marilyn Lindsey....7:38:45 (36,512)
Hind, Laura Elizabeth....4:56:50 (25,728)
Hinde, Helen Sheila....3:59:15 (10,794)
Hinds, Kate Louise....5:14:58 (29,061)
Hine, Joanne....4:17:19 (15,380)
Hine, Lucy....3:48:17 (7,800)
Hines, Lisa....4:47:52 (23,514)
Hiney, Kate Alexandra....4:39:30 (21,387)
Hing, Paula A....4:26:16 (17,895)
Hingott, Clare....4:29:55 (18,957)
Hinns, Marina Jane....4:49:02 (23,809)
Hinsley, Sara Louise....4:58:35 (26,112)
Hinson, Sarah Ann....4:31:03 (19,230)
Hinterhoelzl, Gabriele....4:06:06 (12,474)
Hinton, Clare L....3:39:36 (6,061)
Hinx-Edwards, Lois....3:58:01 (10,384)
Hirakawa, Hiroe....4:58:04 (25,980)
Hird, Paulette A....6:07:18 (34,523)
Hirji, Saima....5:12:40 (28,677)
Hirons, Carolyn....4:36:45 (20,670)
Hirons, Sarah R....3:33:34 (4,982)
Hirotsuna, Shoko....5:38:58 (32,302)
Hirsch, Karin....6:07:03 (34,509)
Hirschfeld, Audrey J....5:35:58 (31,989)
Hirst, Joanne C....6:25:35 (35,331)
Hirst, Karen....4:44:29 (22,632)
Hirst, Sarah M....4:58:23 (26,061)
Hirst, Sue....4:16:30 (15,170)
Hirst, Tracey....6:16:59 (34,978)
Hirzel, Deborah....4:48:47 (23,741)
Hiscock, Karli Marie....6:03:48 (34,308)
Hiscox, Sandra Kim....5:40:08 (32,401)
Hitchen, Abigail....4:38:46 (21,193)
Hitchings, Liana....4:29:17 (18,752)
Hitner, Claudia Elizabeth....4:54:45 (25,245)
Hixon, Kate....4:08:48 (13,161)
Ho, Hayley-Dawn....4:43:56 (22,486)
Ho, Shiang T....5:24:12 (30,510)
Hoad, Amber Louise....5:12:56 (28,728)
Hoadley, Sarah-Jane....5:03:36 (27,120)
Hoang, Li-Leng....4:52:56 (24,783)
Hoare, Jackie....3:56:48 (10,030)
Hoare, Katherine Louise....4:00:36 (11,140)
Hobbs, Dayne....5:38:22 (32,249)
Hobbs, Jane M....3:44:17 (6,933)
Hobbs, Kathryn F....5:07:43 (27,849)
Hobbs, Nancy....5:24:58 (30,616)
Hobden, Charlotte....4:52:46 (24,742)
Hobson, Alex....4:19:33 (15,985)
Hobson, Alison Julie....5:54:51 (33,701)
Hobson, Fiona....6:37:22 (35,710)
Hochmuth, Nicole....4:57:34 (25,872)
Hocking, Caroline....4:13:36 (14,404)
Hockley, Anna M....3:31:07 (4,598)
Hodder, Helen....5:37:12 (32,125)
Hodder, Rebecca J....3:42:46 (6,651)
Hodgers, Emma-Lea Elizabeth....4:23:02 (16,988)
Hodges, Christine Patricia....5:37:57 (32,207)
Hodges, Joanna....5:37:47 (32,192)
Hodges, Rachael Rebecca....4:36:13 (20,530)
Hodges, Vicki Claire....5:09:12 (28,086)
Hodgetts, Emma D....5:05:50 (27,500)
Hodgkin, Kerry Elizabeth....4:07:33 (12,847)
Hodgson, Rowena....5:10:04 (28,251)
Hodgson, Sally....4:36:20 (20,554)
Hodson, Cath....3:59:53 (10,961)
Hodson, Jayne Frances....4:14:24 (14,613)
Hodson, Suzanne....4:39:30 (21,387)
Hoey, Emma Louise....6:56:06 (36,132)
Hoey, Kayleigh....6:49:12 (35,982)
Hoff, Claire Jane....4:57:46 (25,922)
Hoffmann, Anke....3:45:22 (7,175)
Hoffmann, Clara....4:18:21 (15,672)
Hogan, Emma....4:21:15 (16,477)
Hogan, Sarah....5:35:10 (31,893)
Hogan, Sarah Kelly....4:05:39 (12,367)
Hogarth, Deborah J....4:05:15 (12,269)
Hogben, Michelle....3:40:33 (6,248)
Hogbwn, Tamsin....4:48:03 (23,557)
Hogg, Anna Marie....6:24:42 (35,299)
Hogg, Barbara....4:17:26 (15,416)
Hogg, Kathryn....4:26:29 (17,945)
Hognesen, Jorun....4:42:23 (22,108)
Hogsflesh, Anna Elizabeth....5:30:59 (31,415)
Holborn, Tracey A....4:26:08 (17,852)
Holden, Clarie....4:28:54 (18,642)
Holden, Gemma....5:17:41 (29,495)
Holden, Janet Cecily....4:09:57 (13,456)
Holden, Lorna....5:54:49 (33,696)
Holden, Meriel....3:24:39 (3,530)
Holden, Nikki Pam....4:54:29 (25,175)
Holden, Sandra Margaret....5:08:58 (28,037)
Holder, Annie Mary....6:20:23 (35,140)
Holder, Karen Dian....4:06:20 (12,534)
Holding, Dawn Marie....3:56:46 (10,021)
Holdron, Melissa Mary....4:46:49 (23,259)
Hole, Hazel....4:06:15 (12,511)
Hole, Sarah....4:01:43 (11,415)
Holiat, Justinia R....3:31:08 (4,600)
Holland, Deborah Frances....5:41:10 (32,504)
Holland, Emma....4:03:31 (11,849)
Holland, Fiona....5:41:10 (32,504)
Holland, Jennifer....4:04:25 (12,058)
Holland, Nancy....4:20:39 (16,320)
Holland-Brown, Gemma....4:08:05 (12,983)
Hollands, Emma L....3:56:47 (10,027)
Hollett, Georgie....3:37:17 (5,614)
Holley, Angela....4:56:01 (25,541)
Hollick, Lizzie....4:24:43 (17,448)
Holliday, Lisa Joanne....6:45:12 (35,913)
Hollings, Frances Christina....6:02:31 (34,218)
Hollins, Annick....7:05:25 (36,258)
Hollins, Lisa J....5:13:35 (28,853)

Hollins, Tracy 4:56:18 (25,611)
Hollinshead, Monique G 3:14:03 (2,327)
Hollis, Lisa Maxine 4:38:17 (21,050)
Holloway, Emily 4:18:21 (15,672)
Holloway, Joanna 5:00:56 (26,639)
Holloway, Julie Ann 3:48:21 (7,816)
Holloway, Lauren 4:14:33 (14,665)
Holloway, Leesa 5:29:41 (31,251)
Holloway, Sara 4:22:20 (16,800)
Holloway, Vivienne 4:32:37 (19,585)
Holm, Sanne Sandberg 4:06:02 (12,462)
Holman, Victoria C 5:20:52 (29,987)
Holmes, Caroline A 3:38:38 (5,881)
Holmes, Caroline T 3:44:35 (7,008)
Holmes, Christine Elizabeth 3:57:07 (10,131)
Holmes, Corina T 3:35:53 (5,395)
Holmes, Gill 5:05:39 (27,473)
Holmes, Jane Elizabeth 4:19:53 (16,072)
Holmes, Janine E 4:26:09 (17,858)
Holmes, Melanie M 3:49:31 (8,097)
Holmes, Rachael 3:34:18 (5,115)
Holmes, Rachel Elizabeth 5:03:52 (27,167)
Holmes, Ruth 3:57:07 (10,131)
Holmes, Saralee 4:50:08 (24,078)
Holmes, Teresa 4:43:36 (22,394)
Holmes, Tracy 3:38:35 (5,866)
Holmstrom, Heather L 4:58:30 (26,089)
Holmstrup, Thérèse 3:24:06 (3,452)
Holt, Audrey 5:32:04 (31,543)
Holt, Dawn Joanna 6:39:51 (35,781)
Holt, Debbie 4:35:55 (20,453)
Holt, Jayne 4:44:45 (22,712)
Holt, Niamh 3:43:58 (6,871)
Holt, Saba G 3:16:41 (2,642)
Holt, Sandra Denise 5:23:25 (30,375)
Holt, Tina 5:50:50 (33,413)
Holtkamp, Marloes 4:54:17 (25,126)
Holzer, Tara 5:14:36 (29,003)
Homer, Britta 3:31:35 (4,679)
Homer, Laura 4:36:24 (20,576)
Homer, Stacey Adele 6:12:24 (34,777)
Homfray, Victoria 6:14:18 (34,852)
Honicke, Anni 4:27:39 (18,274)
Hood, Deborah Jayne 5:55:16 (33,740)
Hood, Flora 4:03:48 (11,924)
Hoods, Debbie Jayne 5:45:10 (32,883)
Hook, Lyn 3:53:15 (8,983)
Hook, Rosalind 4:07:55 (12,933)
Hook, Sue 5:27:32 (30,970)
Hooker, Clare Louise 4:15:54 (15,001)
Hooker, Suzanne R 4:00:39 (11,155)
Hooper, Peggy Dorothy 4:57:08 (25,790)
Hooper, Tina Jane 4:22:30 (16,847)
Hope, Bethan 4:33:41 (19,917)
Hope, Geraldine 4:01:43 (11,415)
Hope, Lara Evelyn 5:51:08 (33,439)
Hope, Rhona 4:49:24 (23,893)
Hopkins, Alison C 3:08:24 (1,739)
Hopkins, Iva 4:19:58 (16,096)
Hopkins, Jill Alison 4:37:06 (20,771)
Hopkins, Michelle 3:40:46 (6,284)
Hopkins, Sally Elizabeth 4:39:57 (21,491)
Hopkins, Sarah AA 3:59:41 (10,916)
Hopkinson, Nicola 4:07:28 (12,822)
Hopkirk, Nicole Louise 4:09:38 (13,380)
Hopley, Ellie Jane 4:00:11 (11,025)
Hopley, Karen Elaine 6:46:46 (35,944)
Hoppe, Gisela 3:21:35 (3,145)
Hopper, Patricia Josephine 4:30:10 (19,017)
Hopwood, Amy 4:47:13 (23,344)
Hopwood, Emma 5:49:11 (33,256)
Hoque, Rosie 6:54:14 (36,090)
Horan, Jennifer S 4:09:41 (13,392)
Horder, Caroline M 3:27:10 (3,900)
Hordle, Kelly 6:04:25 (34,345)
Horlick, Fiona 4:54:11 (25,093)
Horn, Lucy 4:45:35 (22,909)
Horn, Rebecca J 6:58:56 (36,174)
Horne, Emma M 4:02:34 (11,621)
Horner, Christine 3:59:42 (10,920)
Horner, Karen 5:09:27 (28,132)
Horner, Sandra A 5:20:09 (29,872)
Hornigold, Rachael E 4:54:17 (25,126)
Hornsblow, Diane 4:44:17 (22,586)
Horrocks, Anne Glynis 6:14:20 (34,853)
Horrocks, Janet 4:09:33 (13,351)
Horsburgh, Amanda J 5:16:18 (29,269)
Horsfall, Sam L 3:58:52 (10,674)
Horsford, Natoyah 4:41:51 (21,982)
Horsgood, Caron Gail 4:32:41 (19,602)
Horsley, Clare J 5:15:45 (29,188)
Horsman, Kathleen T 3:38:50 (5,912)
Horton, Karen Louise 4:39:36 (21,411)
Horton, Rachel Anne 5:21:57 (30,136)
Horton, Sarah Carol 5:05:41 (27,478)
Horwich, Zoe A 4:44:35 (22,666)
Hosegood, Emma J 9:17:38 (36,623)
Hosking-Ellis, Mary Suzanne 7:38:29 (36,511)
Hoskins, Elisabeth 3:56:10 (9,832)
Hoskins, Ginette L 4:46:02 (23,037)
Hotung, Mara Tegwen 5:20:49 (29,979)
Houchin, Emma Susan 5:07:47 (27,858)
Houchin, Sharon 4:56:13 (25,589)
Hough, Christina 4:59:16 (26,278)
Hough, Kathryn M 3:39:40 (6,070)
Hougham, Donna 4:13:59 (14,501)
Houghton, Christina Anne 4:51:46 (24,483)
Houghton, Sarah J 7:22:32 (36,422)
Houghton, Sharon D 4:40:43 (21,700)
Houlder, Charlotte Louise 4:46:02 (23,037)
Houlihan, Elizabeth Mary 5:48:14 (33,166)
Houlton, Alison J 4:45:26 (22,870)
Hourihane, Claire 4:36:29 (20,598)
House, Anne Louise 4:57:03 (25,770)
House, Helen 5:01:53 (26,827)
House, Rachel Louise 4:43:10 (22,292)
Housley, Kirsty Dawn 4:24:16 (17,306)
Houwer-Schipper, Klaske 5:04:42 (27,321)
Hovden, Aase 3:32:08 (4,766)
Hoven, Melanie Jayne 5:33:32 (31,719)
Howard, Christine E 3:18:57 (2,866)
Howard, Danielle 4:48:23 (23,634)
Howard, Geraldine 3:47:28 (7,638)
Howard, Judy Gillian 5:21:14 (30,035)
Howard, Kerry Elizabeth 4:38:58 (21,252)
Howard, Nicola J 3:52:38 (8,832)
Howard, Sarah J 4:56:15 (25,595)
Howard, Tara 4:39:21 (21,340)
Howard-Williams, Jan 5:41:50 (32,570)
Howarth, Alyson Jayne 7:19:11 (36,397)
Howarth, Marie 4:31:35 (19,347)
Howarth, Pamela Jane 5:53:21 (33,599)
Howe, Ashley 6:12:07 (34,759)
Howe, Miriam 4:20:37 (16,302)
Howe, Natasha 4:56:38 (25,673)
Howe, Rachel 5:12:01 (28,568)
Howell, Danielle Ann 5:12:51 (28,710)
Howell, Devra A 4:19:24 (15,952)
Howell, Jude A 4:45:03 (22,782)
Howell, Kim A 5:20:17 (29,888)
Howell, Linda M 3:01:27 (1,227)
Howell, Maria F 4:48:43 (23,728)
Howes, Kim T 3:29:51 (4,388)
Howes, Pauline C 4:46:35 (23,193)
Howes, Rea 5:04:23 (27,254)
Howes, Shelley 3:42:16 (6,559)
Howgego, Kate 5:02:20 (26,912)
Howitt, Jessica M 4:21:37 (16,583)
Howitt, Rebecca A 4:21:37 (16,583)
Howles, Donna Marie 4:56:47 (25,711)
Howles, Stephanie 4:23:18 (17,044)
Howlett, Andrea 4:38:22 (21,078)
Howley, Laura 6:57:21 (36,146)
Howlin, Leanne 5:06:01 (27,533)
Howlin, Melanie 6:02:57 (34,248)
Howlin, Michelle 7:19:04 (36,395)
Howse, Marie 5:22:29 (30,218)
Hoyle, Jane 4:55:26 (25,402)
Hoyle, Jenny 5:55:17 (33,743)
Hrabec, Larissa 4:52:09 (24,589)
Hsieh, Su Ching 6:38:42 (35,747)
Hsu, Julie 6:25:06 (35,309)
Hubbard, Anna Maria 5:55:34 (33,759)
Hubbick, Joanne Sarah 4:03:37 (11,878)
Hubert, Ciaragh A 3:40:14 (6,190)
Hubert, Nicola 4:08:29 (13,074)
Hudd, Jenny 4:20:33 (16,275)
Huddy, Lara 5:14:48 (29,036)
Hudson, Catherine 6:28:29 (35,447)
Hudson, Faye 4:58:51 (26,177)

Hudson, Jan N 5:11:15 (28,444)

Marathon day was the worst day of my life. I'd tried 4 years (without success) to get a place. I was excited to finally get in VLM. In months leading up to the big day I was so looking forward to it. But tragically, my wonderful, much-loved mum died 25/04/10 at 5.30am. I ran it for mum and thought of her every second.

Hudson, Kym 3:57:24 (10,202)
Hudson, Leila A 3:37:01 (5,564)
Hudson, Lisa Jane 3:56:31 (9,938)
Hudson, Penny A 6:22:30 (35,208)
Hudson, Samantha 6:04:38 (34,359)
Huegel, Karola 4:42:40 (22,176)
Huggins, Celine Margaret 3:46:48 (7,489)
Hughes, Alison L 5:42:29 (32,638)
Hughes, Alison Margaret 4:19:46 (16,033)
Hughes, Amanda 5:05:05 (27,382)
Hughes, Amy Elizabeth 4:11:31 (13,852)
Hughes, Beverley Ann 6:14:44 (34,873)
Hughes, Catherine Elizabeth 6:08:50 (34,607)
Hughes, Debbie 5:15:31 (29,150)
Hughes, Debbie K 3:19:11 (2,888)
Hughes, Delyth Sarah 5:19:33 (29,779)
Hughes, Elizabeth J 3:58:21 (10,512)
Hughes, Emma 6:17:15 (34,997)
Hughes, Gail 6:03:28 (34,287)
Hughes, Isabel 5:52:45 (33,563)
Hughes, Jaki 6:00:06 (34,073)
Hughes, Jane 5:23:34 (30,396)
Hughes, Jane Philomena K 5:20:40 (29,958)
Hughes, Jennifer Lucy Susan 4:11:20 (13,800)
Hughes, Joanne 5:02:07 (26,871)
Hughes, Kathryn Louise 4:09:45 (13,407)
Hughes, Katie 5:26:19 (30,823)
Hughes, Kirsty Amy 5:05:49 (27,497)
Hughes, Lauretta 4:45:48 (22,979)
Hughes, Lisa Anne 4:16:14 (15,084)
Hughes, Lisa Susanne 5:40:05 (32,399)
Hughes, Lucy 5:58:43 (33,975)
Hughes, Marisa Carol 4:50:47 (24,234)
Hughes, Maureen Beryl 5:12:35 (28,666)
Hughes, Natalie Maria 4:44:55 (22,745)
Hughes, Natasha Emma 4:36:08 (20,515)
Hughes, Nicola Jane 5:22:00 (30,144)
Hughes, Philippa Kathryn 5:22:00 (30,144)
Hughes, Rachael Anne 5:04:07 (27,213)
Hughes, Rhian 6:19:32 (35,104)
Hughes, Shona 3:55:03 (9,491)
Hughes, Sophie 4:10:09 (13,512)
Hughes, Tina L 4:14:14 (14,579)
Hughes, Wendy J 5:00:30 (26,554)
Hughes, Zoe 4:32:52 (19,661)
Hughes-Hallett, Kirsten Marie 5:02:14 (26,897)
Hugo, Kylie Dale 5:43:06 (32,677)
Hull, Tina S 3:14:25 (2,372)
Hulland, Tracey 4:01:29 (11,362)
Hulley, Becky Elizabeth 6:22:57 (35,235)
Hulme, Maryam 4:02:07 (11,515)
Humble, Susan Jane 5:03:13 (27,064)
Hume, Lesley 4:54:15 (25,114)
Hume, Shirley H 3:53:50 (9,169)
Hume, Wendy 5:06:41 (27,667)
Hume-Almeida, Bernadette T 4:56:08 (25,565)
Hume-Chignell, Sally 7:03:16 (36,229)
Humpage, Lorna 4:53:56 (25,031)
Humphrey, Sam H 2:49:01 (443)
Humphrey, Tara 6:11:24 (34,715)
Humphreys, Helen 5:52:43 (33,554)
Humphreys, Kate 6:11:32 (34,724)
Humphreys, Linda 5:11:47 (28,518)
Humphreys, Melanie 4:32:51 (19,654)
Humphreys, Rachael 5:16:11 (29,252)
Humphreys, Sarah Anne 4:44:17 (22,586)

Kelly, Joanne....4:00:12 (11,031)
Kelly, Jodie....5:38:49 (32,293)
Kelly, Kimberly Joy....3:55:27 (9,604)
Kelly, Laura....3:59:15 (10,794)
Kelly, Lisa....5:10:32 (28,335)
Kelly, Lorna Christina....3:40:35 (6,257)
Kelly, Lorraine....6:13:52 (34,833)
Kelly, Madeleine Beverley....5:13:46 (28,884)
Kelly, Mary....4:18:43 (15,778)
Kelly, Maureen Tracy....4:42:17 (22,093)
Kelly, Melissa Susan....4:58:43 (26,148)
Kelly, Miranda....4:28:24 (18,487)
Kelly, Natalie....6:45:18 (35,916)
Kelly, Nicky Louise....5:36:29 (32,055)
Kelly, Samantha....4:34:05 (20,016)
Kelly, Sarah Louise....4:37:29 (20,873)
Kelly, Sharon....4:08:58 (13,201)
Kelly, Tara J....5:03:33 (27,110)
Kemp, Denise....5:46:17 (32,980)
Kemp, Gerri....5:24:43 (30,586)
Kemp, Nicola A....4:20:24 (16,232)
Kemp, Valerie....3:32:18 (4,788)
Kemp-Reynolds, Anne Marie....4:09:04 (13,224)
Kemsley-Benson, Paola Louise....4:51:06 (24,333)
Kench, Tracey....7:10:39 (36,318)
Kendall, Debbie Louise....3:52:14 (8,716)
Kendall, Lindsay....5:25:31 (30,696)
Kendall-Woods, Sacha L....4:42:08 (22,045)
Kenden, Fran....3:59:16 (10,799)
Kendrick, Celia....4:28:42 (18,581)
Kendrick, Charlotte F....5:00:17 (26,515)
Kendrick, Lucy....6:41:02 (35,813)
Kennard, Stephanie....5:58:00 (33,932)
Kennedy, Alex....4:47:19 (23,368)
Kennedy, Alicia....4:08:03 (12,975)
Kennedy, Amy Helen....4:52:29 (24,681)
Kennedy, Deborah Ann....5:20:19 (29,891)
Kennedy, Gillian....5:05:50 (27,500)
Kennedy, Judith....3:30:35 (4,509)
Kennedy, Linda....3:29:25 (4,306)
Kennedy, Lucy....4:21:41 (16,600)
Kennedy, Mary....4:41:15 (21,832)
Kennedy, Rachel Victoria....5:07:16 (27,761)
Kennedy, Sandie F....4:50:24 (24,141)
Kennedy, Sheila....4:34:55 (20,217)
Kennedy, Susan Caroline....4:29:33 (18,820)
Kennedy, Wendy E....4:43:08 (22,286)
Kenneth, Vanessa Louise....4:58:22 (26,060)
Kennett, Hayley....7:03:05 (36,226)
Kenny, Charlotte....4:17:54 (15,546)
Kenny, Sarah-Jane....5:25:24 (30,679)
Kent, Denise....6:36:51 (35,695)
Kent, Jacky Helen....4:59:13 (26,267)
Kent, Lucy Georgina....5:15:00 (29,065)
Kent, Rachel Katherine....5:32:33 (31,614)
Kent, Terina (Teri) Jayne....4:29:36 (18,842)
Kenworthy, Ruth A....3:40:00 (6,147)
Kenyon, Stephanie Mary....5:40:30 (32,430)
Kenyon, Tracey....5:11:56 (28,547)
Keogh, Kate....4:55:51 (25,497)
Keogh, Patricia....4:28:53 (18,636)
Ker, Emellia Lotte....4:46:34 (23,185)
Ker, Mu Yun Grace....4:38:46 (21,193)
Kerbey, Orla M....5:25:16 (30,658)
Kerkhof, Ria....4:41:42 (21,941)
Kernn, Mabel....3:54:14 (9,269)
Kerr, Angela....4:49:03 (23,813)
Kerr, Caroline Geraldine....4:32:14 (19,494)
Kerr, Elizabeth....3:55:44 (9,688)
Kerr, Elizabeth S....4:42:13 (22,069)
Kerr, Emily....4:03:16 (11,797)
Kerr, Emily V....4:56:35 (25,664)
Kerr, Emma Jayne....5:48:36 (33,203)
Kerr, Marion H....5:28:14 (31,056)
Kerrigan, Finola....4:42:36 (22,153)
Kerry, Becky Louise....4:35:05 (20,245)
Kersbergen, Gerry....4:36:08 (20,515)
Kersey, Steph....4:40:54 (21,743)
Kershaw, Andrea Louise....4:58:36 (26,116)
Kerslake, Karen Aila....5:58:01 (33,935)
Kerwin, Emma Louise....6:18:14 (35,045)
Kestin, Joanna....4:25:01 (17,524)
Ketchell, Sarah A....4:50:14 (24,099)
Kethro, Lisa....4:19:54 (16,075)
Ketley, Fleur Lavinia....4:44:37 (22,676)
Kettleborough, Gail....5:20:29 (29,925)
Key, Cherry....5:22:37 (30,241)
Keyes, Melanie Lorraine....5:23:36 (30,404)
Keys, Sarah Louise....4:06:50 (12,670)
Keyte, Karen Lesley....4:22:47 (16,934)
Keyte, Suzanne Elizabeth....4:23:26 (17,088)
Khalwa, Rahila....5:52:08 (33,511)
Khan, Lucy C....3:49:25 (8,070)
Khan, Pat....6:22:54 (35,231)
Khan, Sarah J....6:15:11 (34,898)
Khanam, Joby....4:31:45 (19,384)
Khanam, Rukeya....4:16:01 (15,034)
Khosravi, Maryam....3:43:16 (6,737)
Khuttan-Suman, Simerita....4:36:20 (20,554)
Kiamil, Sarah Louise....5:32:05 (31,548)
Kibble, Lauren....4:54:24 (25,160)
Kidd, Adele....4:31:59 (19,428)
Kidd, Gillian....3:47:44 (7,688)
Kidd, Nerisa....7:12:42 (36,335)
Kidd, Paula Jayne....4:20:30 (16,260)
Kiddle, Donna....4:42:23 (22,108)
Kidman, Alison....4:57:34 (25,872)
Kiernan, Nicky Wendy....5:37:01 (32,104)
Kilbey, Sarah....3:55:37 (9,647)
Kilgour, Janette....5:02:54 (27,009)
Kilgour, Vivien J....3:59:34 (10,886)
Killian, Rachel....4:48:25 (23,647)
Killick, Anna Elizabeth....5:15:10 (29,095)
Killington, Sue....4:50:11 (24,090)
Kilmczak, Anna E....3:26:00 (3,731)
Kilsby, Denise Dawn....6:16:25 (34,944)
Kim, Soon OK....3:36:04 (5,421)
Kimber, Katherine Louise....4:04:45 (12,145)
Kinch, Brenda E....3:54:16 (9,276)
Kinch, Sue M....6:33:36 (35,615)
Kinder, Caroline....4:43:59 (22,502)
King, Ami Elizabeth....6:03:12 (34,266)
King, Angela....6:51:53 (36,038)
King, Anne-Marie....4:14:15 (14,583)
King, Ashley Catherine....5:38:37 (32,276)
King, Claire....3:32:45 (4,852)
King, Claire L....3:54:47 (9,416)
King, Debbie Clare....5:43:23 (32,709)
King, Denise....3:38:13 (5,805)
King, Emma....4:12:46 (14,176)
King, Gemma Margaret Elisabeth....6:15:07 (34,890)
King, Jane Louise....6:31:20 (35,549)
King, Jenny....4:55:35 (25,429)
King, Joanne Louise....4:37:58 (20,982)
King, Julia....3:52:37 (8,826)
King, Karen A....6:14:21 (34,854)
King, Karin....5:01:19 (26,718)
King, Katherine Emily Alice....4:00:24 (11,090)
King, Martina....5:38:09 (32,222)
King, Michelle Penelope....4:08:45 (13,149)
King, Natalie Juliette....4:18:44 (15,782)
King, Natasha....4:21:35 (16,571)
King, Rachael....4:44:15 (22,577)
King, Ruth....7:20:03 (36,404)
King, Ruth Louise....6:56:00 (36,131)
King, Sarah J....4:26:17 (17,898)
King, Sarah Jade....5:00:30 (26,554)
King, Sharon Christinne....5:48:49 (33,223)
King, Sue....5:06:06 (27,549)
King, Sue Elizabeth....5:24:24 (30,540)
King, Susan Claire....5:50:29 (33,380)
King, Victoria....5:21:03 (30,011)
King, Zoe Elizabeth....3:49:27 (8,078)
Kingham, Susan Clare....6:52:45 (36,069)
Kingzett, Emma....5:05:21 (27,424)
Kinnear, Leigh A....5:05:45 (27,486)
Kinross, Lizzie....4:48:20 (23,616)
Kinsella, Jackie....5:54:44 (33,688)
Kinsella, Janette....4:49:04 (23,820)
Kirby, Alex Diane....4:54:02 (25,059)
Kirby, Anne- Marie....4:53:13 (24,853)
Kirby, Cressida Lauren....4:31:10 (19,258)
Kirby, Maureen....4:14:28 (14,637)
Kirby, Philippa....6:04:14 (34,336)
Kirby, Sue Rebecca....4:10:30 (13,594)
Kirk, Laura....2:55:29 (770)
Kirk, Michelle....5:34:17 (31,794)
Kirk, Susan....4:26:06 (17,844)
Kirkbride, Lisa Marie....6:19:04 (35,085)
Kirkby, Laura....5:16:05 (29,241)
Kirkby, Penny Anne....5:39:15 (32,328)
Kirkby, Rachel....4:40:48 (21,721)
Kirkham, Jane....3:55:45 (9,699)
Kirkham, Myshola....3:01:55 (1,251)
Kirwan, Karen....5:11:59 (28,558)
Kisbee, Laura....5:39:45 (32,362)
Kislingbury, Emma Jane....4:50:30 (24,161)
Kislova, Nina....4:55:53 (25,508)
Kitchen, Carole A....4:19:52 (16,066)
Kitchen, Elizabeth....3:44:26 (6,980)
Kitchen, Julie Ann....4:16:14 (15,084)
Kitchener, Tracey Sharon....4:58:16 (26,036)
Kitching, Claire Rebecca....5:21:32 (30,077)
Kitching, Janette May....4:47:25 (23,395)
Kitching, Julie Anne....4:34:39 (20,156)
Kitching, Lisa Marie....4:14:33 (14,665)
Kite, Helen....4:52:00 (24,554)
Kite, Nina....5:07:11 (27,749)
Kite, Stacey....4:40:35 (21,664)
Kitney, Lauren....6:41:46 (35,828)
Kjaer Nielsen, Karen....3:57:59 (10,373)
Kjerstad, Torunn Anita....4:05:44 (12,386)
Kjoengerskov, Hanne Langhorn....4:19:29 (15,966)
Klapinska, Izabella....4:22:10 (16,747)
Klaucke, Christiane....5:35:46 (31,964)
Klimczak, Katherine....5:03:40 (27,131)
Klinge, Caroline E....4:23:46 (17,185)
Kluge, Maria-Luise....4:50:40 (24,201)
Knapman, Gemma Jane....4:51:50 (24,504)
Knapp, Fiona....4:35:55 (20,453)
Knappett, Charlotte....3:51:38 (8,575)
Knass, Jenny E....2:54:47 (722)
Knee, Charlotte A....3:51:03 (8,435)
Knee, Wendy....4:40:30 (21,640)
Knee, Wendy....5:01:23 (26,729)
Knigge, Christine....4:20:37 (16,302)
Knight, Fran....5:19:47 (29,817)
Knight, Helen J....4:24:36 (17,419)
Knight, Jan....4:54:40 (25,224)
Knight, Joanna Ruth....4:50:24 (24,141)
Knight, Jude Anne....3:45:08 (7,124)
Knight, Kate....6:43:53 (35,883)
Knight, Laura....5:25:54 (30,766)
Knight, Laura Mary....3:39:31 (6,046)
Knight, Lauren A....6:15:35 (34,911)
Knight, Sarah....6:26:56 (35,383)
Knight, Sarah Louise....4:55:01 (25,310)
Knill, Julie A....4:01:00 (11,251)
Knott, Deborah F....4:40:12 (21,538)
Knott, Katherine....5:26:53 (30,887)
Knott, Vic....4:35:45 (20,406)
Knotwell, Zena Angela....5:39:45 (32,362)
Knowles, Alyson....3:56:15 (9,857)
Knowles, Jacqueline L....5:04:04 (27,202)
Knowles, Zoe Ann....4:12:13 (14,035)
Knuth, Helen K....4:34:09 (20,028)
Knutzen, Liv....5:07:11 (27,749)
Kochenderfer, Ruth....4:52:47 (24,751)
Koeffer-Marie, Nadine....4:30:33 (19,106)
Koerbel, Amy L....3:11:33 (2,056)
Kok, Claire Marie....5:17:54 (29,526)
Kolat, Diane....5:32:16 (31,570)
Kolek, Charlie....4:42:15 (22,079)
Kolodziej, Natalie E....3:11:30 (2,050)
Kolousek, Kathryn Elizabeth....5:05:42 (27,482)
Kong, Angelina....2:58:42 (1,020)
Konochenko, Tatiana....3:55:11 (9,523)
Konovalova, Maria....2:35:21 (120)
Konrad, Evelyn....4:16:31 (15,174)
Korbut, Maria....4:59:11 (26,260)
Korsholm, Jette Haislund....4:30:08 (19,010)
Korus, Marta....5:00:06 (26,480)
Kosla, Kaja....4:47:46 (23,483)
Kossman, Joanna....3:59:26 (10,848)
Kotarba, Anna M....5:41:54 (32,579)
Koth, Melanie....3:29:20 (4,292)
Kougl, Nicole....4:06:21 (12,539)
Koutsomitis, Vana C....5:16:25 (29,295)
Kowalchuk, Tavia A....3:48:56 (7,955)

Kowalczyk, Justyna 3:59:16 (10,799)
Krasniqi, Florida 6:11:38 (34,730)
Kraus, Silvia 4:28:36 (18,548)
Kraushar, Shani 6:52:09 (36,049)
Krazizky, Marie Jeanne 5:44:33 (32,821)
Krishnan, Anjali 3:54:32 (9,337)
Kristiansen, Lara 3:12:56 (2,179)
Krogh, Annette Mark 4:37:02 (20,755)
Krohn, Manuela 4:31:47 (19,390)
Kruk, Anne-Marie 5:42:19 (32,619)
Krzystyniak, Nicola A 3:50:08 (8,232)
Kuhn-Barres, Geraldine 4:15:42 (14,952)
Kuiper, Anne N 3:48:43 (7,905)
Kukadia, Jogisha 5:53:57 (33,639)
Kulp, Rachel Emma Joan 5:06:59 (27,720)
Kumleben, Sue 3:20:36 (3,038)
Kummer, Julie 3:50:08 (8,232)
Kupiec, Lisa M 7:11:31 (36,325)
Kupka, Simone 3:34:52 (5,223)
Kurdyla, Helen Catherine 4:39:43 (21,440)
Kuritko, Christina Pia 5:09:35 (28,168)
Kurz, Hazel L 5:00:42 (26,587)
Kuske, Sabine 4:40:09 (21,524)
Kyi, Khin Sandar 5:41:25 (32,523)
Kyi, Thuzar 5:41:23 (32,521)
Kyle, Lauren 5:04:25 (27,262)
Kyriacou, Androulla 5:20:40 (29,958)
Kyselicova, Maria 3:47:16 (7,591)
La Canna, Lyn Heather 4:17:23 (15,400)
Labeeuw, Nathalie 4:23:43 (17,164)
Labellarte, Antonella 4:40:59 (21,767)
Labram, Clare Louise 4:37:23 (20,841)
Lacey, Catherine Patricia 6:14:51 (34,880)
Lacey, Kate Alison 4:51:57 (24,538)
Lacey, Nicky Joy 5:15:31 (29,150)
Lachman, Wendy Caroline 5:33:39 (31,730)
Lach-Szyrma, Linda 6:03:24 (34,281)
Lack, Helen Erika 5:26:52 (30,884)
Lack, Sally 4:49:19 (23,874)
Ladd, Anna L 3:53:28 (9,045)
Ladd, Gillian 5:39:50 (32,372)
Ladd, Sarah 4:35:20 (20,301)
Laddie, Joanna Ruth 6:04:02 (34,324)
Laddiman, Naomi Jane 6:26:15 (35,357)
Ladkin, Angela 3:26:21 (3,789)
Ladyman, Charlie Amelia Jane 4:46:12 (23,090)
Laforet, Kate 3:15:27 (2,494)
Laggan, Vicki 4:56:48 (25,720)
Lahey, Jennifer 4:01:14 (11,304)
Lahey, Rosemary 5:36:36 (32,066)
Laidlaw, Dawn Elizabeth 5:48:34 (33,201)
Laing, Jo M 3:07:38 (1,672)
Lake, Tiffany Isabel 4:10:11 (13,524)
Laker, Sarah 3:54:52 (9,441)
Lakey, Christina Elizabeth 5:24:54 (30,602)
Lakin, Helen Catherine 5:18:36 (29,636)
Lale, Kerry 6:31:31 (35,557)
Lally, Regina Bernadette 5:36:18 (32,033)
Lam, Eva 6:02:37 (34,227)
Lamb, Anita Mary 4:52:14 (24,610)
Lamb, Emily Barclay 4:52:46 (24,742)
Lamb, Helen 5:47:29 (33,095)
Lamb, Lisa 6:07:52 (34,555)
Lamb, Marney 5:16:18 (29,269)
Lamb, Virginia M 5:42:02 (32,590)
Lambden, Lorna 4:25:32 (17,672)
Lambert, Amanda Jane 4:30:18 (19,044)
Lambert, Caroline Ruth 4:53:25 (24,895)
Lambert, Claire Lousie 5:12:57 (28,730)
Lambert, Denise 6:02:55 (34,243)
Lambert, Fay Elizabeth 5:18:00 (29,545)
Lambert, Holly 7:29:06 (36,465)
Lambert, Nikki 4:11:49 (13,936)
Lambert, Pip 4:50:23 (24,135)
Lambert, Ruth 4:09:43 (13,399)
Lambert, Sarah Elizabeth 5:23:43 (30,429)
Lambert, Sue Q 4:05:44 (12,386)
Lambert, Vicky Jane Emily 3:37:46 (5,720)
Lambourne, Rachel Emma 4:29:50 (18,920)
Lamerton, Sally Jayne 5:33:08 (31,679)
Lammas, Sara 7:25:56 (36,448)
Lamont, Amy 3:46:22 (7,387)
Lamyman, Abigail 4:08:14 (13,012)
Lancaster, Andrea Nicole 6:02:59 (34,250)
Lancaster, Cheryl Anne 5:17:13 (29,421)
Lancaster, Christine A 4:09:12 (13,260)
Lancaster, Debbie 6:52:05 (36,044)
Lancaster, Tracey L 3:42:53 (6,674)
Lancereau, Sophie 5:28:25 (31,077)
Land, Tracy E 4:03:45 (11,906)
Landau, Julie Belinda 4:29:45 (18,899)
Landau, Kelly 5:34:29 (31,821)
Lander, Emma 6:41:50 (35,831)
Lander, Judy Ann 4:45:06 (22,799)
Lander, Kate 3:54:20 (9,289)
Landon, Jane Louise 4:45:37 (22,919)
Landy, Rebecca 5:03:45 (27,148)
Lane, Andrea 6:51:49 (36,036)
Lane-Mudie, Hayley Anne-Gail 7:08:50 (36,300)
Lang, Caroline Lesley 5:27:46 (30,997)
Lang, Geraldine Mary 4:14:37 (14,687)
Lang, Kirsten 5:00:16 (26,514)
Langdon, Helena 4:34:11 (20,037)
Langdon, Jenny Ann 4:50:24 (24,141)
Langdon, Rachel M 6:55:16 (36,115)
Langdon, Rebecca Helen 4:25:04 (17,540)
Langelaar, Marjolein 4:39:33 (21,400)
Langford, Helen Marie 4:21:42 (16,606)
Langham, Charlotte Rachael 4:05:47 (12,408)
Langley, Sarah 5:19:33 (29,779)
Langlois, Adele F 4:30:42 (19,148)
Langlois, Carole Joan 4:55:56 (25,520)
Langmead, Claire Jane 4:43:08 (22,286)
Langmead, Louise 4:26:06 (17,844)
Langslow, Rachel K 5:31:11 (31,432)
Langtree, Jessica 4:32:04 (19,451)
Lankester, Louise Jayne 6:24:50 (35,303)
Lannigan, Ruth 5:40:59 (32,480)
Lansley, Katie 5:20:27 (29,912)
Lansley, Sarah 5:20:27 (29,912)
Lapper, Alison M 4:22:34 (16,867)
Lappin, Emma 5:08:10 (27,922)
Lapsley, Nicola 5:15:46 (29,190)
Larcombe, Zoe Joanne 4:28:55 (18,650)
Larkinson, Trudy 4:41:45 (21,952)
Larkman, Catherine 5:50:55 (33,420)
Larner, Sarah 4:22:22 (16,811)
Larsen, Charlotte Jenifer 4:16:52 (15,261)
Larsen, Mandi Dawn 5:18:37 (29,645)
Larsen, Rebecca 5:43:40 (32,734)
Larsen, Tove 4:15:13 (14,838)
Larson, Lia C 3:44:46 (7,047)
Larvin, Jo E 4:20:32 (16,268)
Lasio, Sandra 5:13:28 (28,841)
Lask, Jeanette 5:12:41 (28,682)
Lass, Emma Catherine 4:48:33 (23,679)
Latarche, Laura Louise 6:04:10 (34,330)
Latarche, Marie Ann 6:04:10 (34,330)
Lathwell, Christine 3:47:15 (7,586)
Latorre, Sylvia 6:01:51 (34,179)
Latson, Rebecca K 4:14:06 (14,533)
Latter, Elizabeth H 4:23:31 (17,112)
Laud, Jenny Anne 5:28:10 (31,051)
Lauder, Michaela T 3:57:24 (10,202)
Lavelle, Marie L 6:08:56 (34,612)
Lavelle, Rachael 4:24:20 (17,333)
Laver, Claire Louise 5:13:10 (28,796)
Laverick, Katherine 5:32:28 (31,598)
Law, Ann 4:00:49 (11,198)
Law, Gillian 4:41:09 (21,807)
Law, Michelle 5:54:52 (33,703)
Lawlor, Angela 4:16:18 (15,106)
Lawlor, Reena 3:40:24 (6,214)
Lawrence, Allison J 4:40:22 (21,601)
Lawrence, Chris L 3:12:56 (2,179)
Lawrence, Emily Joleen 3:46:46 (7,478)
Lawrence, Freya R 3:34:34 (5,166)
Lawrence, Linda Doreen 5:13:55 (28,913)
Lawrence, Liz 4:35:22 (20,318)
Lawrence, Marilyn 6:53:25 (36,076)
Lawrence, Nicola 3:38:17 (5,816)
Lawrence, Sally 4:19:59 (16,103)
Lawrence, Sally 5:34:08 (31,771)
Lawrence, Sarah 5:32:12 (31,563)
Lawrence, Victoria Claire 6:16:16 (34,933)
Laws, Amy 4:47:24 (23,389)
Laws, Linda J 4:46:10 (23,078)
Laws, Rebecca 4:23:50 (17,196)
Lawson, Kelly Sarah 5:50:34 (33,395)
Lawson, Lucy Rose 3:53:39 (9,105)
Lawton, Jayne 3:14:36 (2,398)
Lawton, Olivia 5:27:29 (30,963)
Lawton, Rebecca Catherine 5:02:16 (26,900)
Lax, Michelle Anne 4:46:32 (23,175)
Lay, Pamela I 4:41:34 (21,912)
Laycock, Charlotte 4:52:12 (24,600)
Lazell, Sian 6:56:45 (36,140)
Lazenby, Deborah C 4:27:34 (18,252)
Le Druillenec, Jane 5:07:57 (27,887)
Le Geyt, Hilary V 4:20:55 (16,390)
Le Goff, Carole 4:48:52 (23,765)
Le Grice, Carrie 6:01:34 (34,162)
Le Grys, Helen 5:13:38 (28,863)
Le Roux, Elanie 4:31:56 (19,418)
Le Ruez, Susan J 4:01:31 (11,372)
Le Tissier, Stephanie 7:01:31 (36,209)
Leach, Erika J 5:43:44 (32,748)
Leach, Jane Emily 4:32:38 (19,589)
Leach, Janet 5:13:27 (28,837)
Leach, Katie 4:24:04 (17,252)
Leach, Rachel 5:08:58 (28,037)
Leadbetter, Belinda 5:01:14 (26,689)
Leader, Claire Louise 6:31:56 (35,562)
Leader, Kathryn 3:42:26 (6,584)
Leaf, Kathy 5:02:59 (27,022)
Leah, Sarah 4:46:13 (23,096)
Leahy, Danielle Marie 4:49:31 (23,911)
Lear, Abigail 6:22:06 (35,200)
Learner, Jane 5:41:46 (32,561)
Leary, Tanya Morse 5:31:23 (31,462)
Leather, Catherine 4:13:19 (14,318)
Leathwood, Rachael A 3:16:39 (2,634)
Leavey, Mary Rose 8:13:17 (36,597)
Leavold, Camille 4:44:47 (22,720)
Leavold, Polly Kathrine 6:22:33 (35,215)
Lebeau, Jane 4:38:19 (21,061)
Lebedis, Nikki 4:35:37 (20,369)
Lebez, Laura 6:19:10 (35,088)
Lebrun, Tracy 4:24:31 (17,395)
Leckebusch, Jane 3:31:05 (4,592)
Ledda, Victoria 4:51:28 (24,411)
Ledingham, Sarah L 6:04:56 (34,381)
Lee, Agnes Charmaine 4:47:11 (23,339)
Lee, Beverley Jane 4:46:46 (23,242)
Lee, Bok Soon 5:34:31 (31,824)
Lee, Dawn 4:33:36 (19,893)
Lee, Debbie 3:57:35 (10,261)
Lee, Debbie 4:26:44 (18,007)
Lee, Elizabeth A 5:49:39 (33,303)
Lee, Elizabeth M 4:34:13 (20,052)
Lee, Hannah Katherine 4:48:42 (23,719)
Lee, Hyun Young 4:47:54 (23,520)
Lee, Jay Elizabeth 4:23:18 (17,044)
Lee, Jessica 6:15:20 (34,902)
Lee, Joanne 4:06:39 (12,617)
Lee, Katrina A 5:11:05 (28,418)
Lee, Lorna Ann 4:21:32 (16,556)
Lee, Louise Anne 4:37:25 (20,850)
Lee, Natasha N 4:51:46 (24,483)
Lee, Rosalind 3:40:43 (6,277)
Lee, Ruth 4:13:06 (14,263)
Lee, Sandra Margaret 5:56:42 (33,843)
Lee, Sarah A 3:36:35 (5,494)
Lee, Susannah K 3:40:40 (6,273)
Lee, Vicci 4:21:17 (16,487)
Leech, Annie Louise 5:25:31 (30,696)
Leedham, Amy F 3:31:48 (4,708)
Leedham, Margaret 4:56:41 (25,689)
Leeding, Samantha 3:48:28 (7,837)
Leeds, Anna D 5:39:41 (32,358)
Leeland, Debbie 4:53:23 (24,889)
Lees, Katie 4:16:59 (15,297)
Leet,, Sarah, Pauline 4:17:40 (15,487)
Le-Faye, Jolanne 4:36:59 (20,738)
Legg, Amanda June 6:38:12 (35,731)
Legg, Hayley 4:40:25 (21,617)
Lehan, Lorraine Mary 4:49:53 (24,026)
Lehmann, Jessica Zoe Roth 5:08:31 (27,977)
Leigh, Anne R 7:35:25 (36,490)

Leighton, Deanna Erica 4:05:46 (12,402)
Leiper, Jan 4:32:27 (19,550)
Leitch, Cornelia Aletta 5:27:20 (30,944)
Leitch, Jessica R 3:12:44 (2,160)
Leitch, Julie 3:58:53 (10,682)
Leite, Sandra 4:32:09 (19,473)
Leitner, Irene J 4:53:46 (24,988)
Lejeune, Rose 4:20:38 (16,314)
Lelarge, Claire 3:36:12 (5,448)
Leleu, Roselyne 4:57:18 (25,820)
Leleu, Valerie 3:58:26 (10,537)
Lelper, Rosemary A 4:50:44 (24,219)
Lemme, Fernanda 5:12:50 (28,709)
Lenaghan, Alison L 3:24:43 (3,541)
Lenehan, Josephine 4:36:48 (20,682)
Leng, Sarah A 5:02:52 (27,000)
Lennox, Colleen 4:44:53 (22,738)
Lennox, Jennifer 5:04:27 (27,266)
Lenotti, Veronica 5:00:17 (26,515)
Lens, Charlotte 4:16:28 (15,157)
Lenton, Poppy S 3:39:12 (5,981)
Leonard, Jennifer 5:13:34 (28,852)
Leonard, Karan L 5:22:25 (30,210)
Leonard, Lindsey Kate 5:14:52 (29,048)
Leondoy, Angela Giovanna 4:35:03 (20,240)
Leoni, Cinzia 3:04:29 (1,430)
Leonnard, Philippa M 5:26:20 (30,826)
Leppanen, Kirsi Marjaana 3:46:36 (7,442)
Leppard, Jacqueline 5:43:40 (32,734)
Le-Rossignol, Gemma 4:36:28 (20,591)
Less, Emma Karolina 4:43:20 (22,325)
Lessells, Nicola 4:25:04 (17,540)
Lessels, Shona 7:03:35 (36,234)
Lessiter, Louise 6:40:51 (35,809)
Lessner, Heike 5:02:23 (26,922)
Lester, Christine 5:40:02 (32,392)
Lester, Dawn P 5:47:44 (33,119)
Letts, Rachel Jane 4:29:55 (18,957)
Levan, Laura Ashley 5:40:51 (32,465)
Levene, Annabel C 2:57:38 (924)
Levene, Tamsin Emma 4:39:26 (21,368)
Lever, Helen Jane 4:24:38 (17,425)
Leverett, Joanna Clare 4:02:04 (11,507)
Leverett, Kathryn Anne 5:23:30 (30,385)
Levett, Kim Marie 4:20:17 (16,194)
Levis, Hannah Jane 4:19:13 (15,903)
Levison, Sharon Anne 4:12:52 (14,199)
Levy, Emma 5:35:25 (31,918)
Levy, Justine A 4:33:55 (19,972)
Levy, Karen I 3:50:59 (8,416)
Lewendon, Jane P 4:37:46 (20,938)
Lewington-Roberts, Michelle 4:57:58 (25,963)
Lewis, Aimée Louise 5:54:09 (33,655)
Lewis, Alison 4:00:20 (11,068)
Lewis, Becky 4:42:37 (22,158)
Lewis, Chris M 6:17:05 (34,983)
Lewis, Claire E 4:52:43 (24,731)
Lewis, Debbie Ann 4:17:31 (15,449)
Lewis, Deborah J 4:17:22 (15,396)
Lewis, Elizabeth Ann 5:15:43 (29,183)
Lewis, Emma R 5:33:00 (31,663)
Lewis, Helen Sian 4:42:37 (22,158)
Lewis, Jackie 5:52:28 (33,531)
Lewis, Jamie 4:30:02 (18,983)
Lewis, Jane Elizabeth Anne 3:39:09 (5,973)
Lewis, Janice 4:47:20 (23,374)
Lewis, Jemma Hayley 5:46:21 (32,989)
Lewis, Judy Gay 4:56:35 (25,664)
Lewis, Karen 3:49:24 (8,064)
Lewis, Karen 5:06:11 (27,563)
Lewis, Karen Ann 5:15:10 (29,095)
Lewis, Kate 5:43:08 (32,679)
Lewis, Kate Elizabeth 5:30:20 (31,327)
Lewis, Kathleen A 4:24:25 (17,366)
Lewis, Katrina 4:09:25 (13,320)
Lewis, Kelly 3:48:54 (7,952)
Lewis, Leanne 5:38:27 (32,255)
Lewis, Maz 5:21:51 (30,122)
Lewis, Melanie Jane 4:45:36 (22,916)
Lewis, Mia 4:24:53 (17,485)
Lewis, Nadine Renée 5:26:54 (30,890)
Lewis, Nia 5:59:31 (34,017)
Lewis, Rosemary J 3:34:19 (5,118)
Lewis, Sharon Marie 5:20:08 (29,869)
Lewis, Susan 5:02:07 (26,871)
Lewis, Suzanne Oram 4:19:20 (15,940)
Lewis, Sylvia 5:33:25 (31,709)
Lewis, Tonia 4:11:27 (13,835)
Lewis, Victoria 6:18:31 (35,058)
Lewis-Meredith, Michelle M 4:40:08 (21,518)
Lewis-Painter, Lindsey M 3:57:50 (10,337)
Lewis-Saunders, Louise 5:14:00 (28,925)
Lewtas, Susanne Adele 3:57:27 (10,214)
Ley, Faye Louise 4:06:55 (12,689)
Leyland, Kirsty 4:10:59 (13,710)
Li, Michelle 4:16:23 (15,135)
Liborwich, Samantha Danielle 6:11:54 (34,748)
Liddiard, Heather 4:31:04 (19,235)
Liddle, Rebekah Clair 4:31:27 (19,321)
Lidster, Sarah Louise 5:20:26 (29,911)
Lieneweit, Manuela 5:00:30 (26,554)
Lightfoot, Laura 4:40:50 (21,733)
Lightfoot, Maggy 5:24:41 (30,579)
Lilley, Sarah K 5:34:17 (31,794)
Lillie, Mandy 4:13:42 (14,432)
Lillistone, Anna 5:21:34 (30,090)
Lillistone, Christine Jane 4:28:33 (18,539)
Lillywhite, Tania Kirsten 5:21:53 (30,126)
Lim, Nicola 4:59:45 (26,395)
Lincoln, Victoria M 3:15:38 (2,511)
Lind, Tove 4:35:14 (20,278)
Lindenberg, Sue 5:55:38 (33,764)
Lindhorst, Emma 7:18:12 (36,387)
Lindley, Doreen A 5:57:52 (33,924)
Lindley, Sarah 4:17:27 (15,425)
Lindley, Shelley Maria 4:29:09 (18,721)
Lindsay, Amanda G 6:58:37 (36,165)
Lindsay, Tina Sarah 7:20:33 (36,408)
Lindsey, Hannah Jean 5:26:57 (30,898)
Lindskog, Jessica 3:49:07 (8,006)
Lindstrøm, Estelle 4:11:26 (13,827)
Lines, Jess 5:56:36 (33,835)
Lines, Sally E 5:10:03 (28,247)
Lines-Scrase, Alexandra EI 5:12:02 (28,570)
Linford, Amy Jayne 3:27:32 (3,970)
Ling, Donna Christine 6:27:34 (35,404)
Ling, Katie-Louise 6:14:40 (34,869)
Ling, Natalie 4:56:02 (25,544)
Linger, Natalie Louise 5:49:21 (33,264)
Linter, Alison Laura 3:52:00 (8,659)
Lintern, Sarah E 5:43:49 (32,756)
Lintin, Karen Louise 6:17:35 (35,009)
Linton, Anika 5:09:23 (28,124)
Linton, Jane 5:05:03 (27,377)
Linton, Liza 6:03:08 (34,263)
Linton, Sara Jayne 3:50:00 (8,211)
Lintott, Catherine 4:00:46 (11,185)
Linwood, Jo 4:54:08 (25,075)
Lion, Alexandra J 3:35:56 (5,405)
Lipscomb, Paula Jane 5:34:38 (31,841)
Lipscombe, Clare Louise 5:42:05 (32,599)
Lipscombe, Hannah 4:21:14 (16,469)
Lipski, Janet E 3:37:37 (5,695)
Lisle, Mary Lynne 4:52:05 (24,568)
Lister, Jessica Ann 4:41:15 (21,832)
Lister, Sarah Alison 4:47:38 (23,449)
Liszka, Cecilia Mary 4:23:42 (17,156)
Litt, Jessica 5:02:35 (26,956)
Littell, Sarah A 3:31:18 (4,626)
Litterick, Emma C 3:50:25 (8,292)
Little, Gail 4:28:03 (18,379)
Little, Gina M 3:57:01 (10,102)
Little, Justine G 4:03:02 (11,739)
Little, Susan 5:11:11 (28,431)
Little, Tiffany Joy 7:34:33 (36,486)
Little, Zoe C 5:11:22 (28,460)
Littlefair, Gillian Mary 4:53:07 (24,826)
Littler, Mary T 5:54:29 (33,674)
Littler, Nina 3:58:11 (10,449)
Livesey, Jennifer 5:24:25 (30,544)
Livesey, Rachel Clare 5:24:25 (30,544)
Livingstone, Mandy 3:15:33 (2,504)
Livolsi, Marie 4:16:07 (15,055)
Ljungblom, Linda 4:37:08 (20,779)
Llewellyn, Arabella 5:24:59 (30,622)
Llewellyn, Jayne 6:52:26 (36,060)
Lloyd, Becky 5:29:38 (31,243)
Lloyd, Catherine L 5:33:18 (31,693)
Lloyd, Chantal Elaine 4:51:33 (24,431)
Lloyd, Clare 7:19:17 (36,398)
Lloyd, Daisy Elizabeth 4:50:45 (24,224)
Lloyd, Donna Marie 4:25:10 (17,566)
Lloyd, Emma 5:13:03 (28,747)
Lloyd, Karen 3:34:22 (5,132)
Lloyd, Katie 4:06:46 (12,645)
Lloyd, Rosie 4:25:48 (17,749)
Lloyd, Sally 5:03:30 (27,100)
Lloyd, Sarah 5:52:45 (33,563)
Lloyd Malcolm, Morgan 4:58:06 (25,986)
Lo, Kim M 3:24:37 (3,526)
Loach, Kate E 3:30:59 (4,575)
Loader, Carole A 3:25:44 (3,692)
Loader, Deborah A 3:20:29 (3,022)
Loader, Jackie A 3:32:02 (4,745)
Loader Wilkinson, Tara 4:13:00 (14,239)
Loadsman, Louise W 6:00:02 (34,069)
Lochlin, Angela 6:42:06 (35,836)
Lock, Helen 5:52:33 (33,536)
Lock, Lisa 5:49:47 (33,318)
Lock, Sarah 4:55:17 (25,378)
Lockett, Carolyn 3:47:37 (7,673)
Lockley, Rhonda June 4:40:30 (21,640)
Lockley, Vanessa A 6:36:18 (35,684)
Lockwood, Harriet Lucy 5:44:57 (32,865)
Locock, Rosemary Lorraine 6:13:38 (34,824)
Loder, Kelly May 5:32:05 (31,548)
Lodge, Helen 3:55:20 (9,571)
Lodge, Natalie 4:23:09 (17,013)
Lodge, Natasha 4:30:42 (19,148)
Loewy, Dana 5:55:41 (33,769)
Lofton, Sharon 4:51:05 (24,326)
Lofts, Fiona Jane 5:26:16 (30,813)
Loftus, Rebecca 4:41:04 (21,784)
Logan, Alaina Louise 5:31:39 (31,493)
Logan, Julie A 4:44:30 (22,638)
Logan (née Edwards), Emma L 4:46:54 (23,283)
Logue, Nicola 4:22:35 (16,868)
Lohan, Sharon T 4:39:48 (21,462)
Lomas, Hayley 3:43:05 (6,715)
Lomas, Tracey Marie 5:18:54 (29,684)
Lomax, Amy R 3:39:04 (5,956)
Lombardi, Roberta 3:37:29 (5,658)
London, Michelle Louise 7:00:36 (36,197)
Lonergan, Kate 3:41:28 (6,417)
Loney, Joanna Louise 5:40:51 (32,465)
Long, Ashley Suzanne 4:51:28 (24,411)
Long, Jackie Christina 6:55:22 (36,119)
Long, Justine Ann 5:17:21 (29,452)
Long, Louise 3:57:34 (10,253)
Long, Michelle R 5:04:34 (27,291)
Long, Polly Kate 5:16:20 (29,281)
Long, Samantha Jayne 7:10:27 (36,312)
Long, Sandra J 4:15:34 (14,919)
Longair, Sarah C 3:38:31 (5,849)
Longden, Sarah Louise 5:54:26 (33,672)
Longhurst, Donna 7:30:29 (36,473)
Longhurst, Teressa Jean 5:27:05 (30,919)
Longley, Zira K 4:18:30 (15,715)
Longmate, Debbie 4:18:35 (15,741)
Longney, Carolyn Jane 4:43:28 (22,366)
Longstaff, Margaret 4:50:55 (24,279)
Lonsdale, Adele 4:28:45 (18,591)
Lonsdale, Davina 4:28:45 (18,591)
Lonsdale, Jeanette 5:29:31 (31,225)
Loomes, Lynda Anne 6:41:07 (35,815)
Lopez, Amanda E 4:31:05 (19,238)
Lopez, Lourdes 4:23:16 (17,037)
Lopez, Monica 4:03:34 (11,864)
Lopez, Shelley A 3:47:10 (7,566)
Lord, Joanne 4:14:09 (14,547)
Lord, Nicola Claire 5:16:42 (29,337)
Lorenzen, Hanne 4:59:09 (26,249)
Lorimer, Nicola Ruth 3:44:00 (6,883)
Loroupe, Tegla 5:02:24 (26,927)
Lough, Rosie Mary Clare 4:00:52 (11,207)
Loughlin, Annmarie 5:29:40 (31,247)
Loughran, Jill 4:36:39 (20,648)
Lour, Sylvia 4:05:58 (12,453)
Lourens, Twanette 4:42:00 (22,015)

Loutit, Roslyn J 3:56:11 (9,837)
Lovatt, Ellen L 4:02:36 (11,632)
Love, Fiona C 3:22:23 (3,226)
Love, Jo 5:41:00 (32,483)
Love, Nicola Janine 6:43:17 (35,872)
Love, Sharon Elizabeth 4:40:32 (21,655)
Loveday, Rachel 6:00:26 (34,089)
Lovegrove, Rebecca Jayne 3:34:02 (5,063)
Lovell, Carol Jane 4:33:48 (19,944)
Lovell, Jane 5:43:59 (32,765)
Lovell, Jennifer Pamela 5:18:00 (29,545)
Lovell, Jessica 3:29:34 (4,334)
Lovell, Nicola 3:36:38 (5,501)
Lovell, Sally 3:31:13 (4,612)
Lovell-Knight, Jade Alexandra 4:08:33 (13,103)
Lovelock, Heather Ann 5:48:22 (33,180)
Lovett, Katie 6:17:08 (34,985)
Low, Cheng Ee 6:06:35 (34,487)
Low, Grace 4:14:46 (14,732)
Low, Jeanette 5:24:59 (30,622)
Low, Nelly C 7:36:44 (36,503)
Lowe, Andrea 4:11:25 (13,824)
Lowe, Freda J 5:38:27 (32,255)
Lowe, Gillian Beverley 4:50:23 (24,135)
Lowe, Helen 4:32:23 (19,535)
Lowe, Kimberley Jane 5:23:54 (30,458)
Lowe, Maria T 3:09:58 (1,905)
Lowe, Vicki A 3:45:38 (7,235)
Lowe, Wendy 4:50:13 (24,096)
Lowe, Zoe A 3:09:12 (1,824)
Lownds, Kate 5:23:16 (30,349)
Lowrie, Nikki Lindsay 4:55:03 (25,321)
Lowther, Deborah 5:22:01 (30,148)
Lowther, Emma Angela 4:57:56 (25,953)
Loza, Iciar 3:25:49 (3,705)
Lozano De Patron, Laura 4:07:43 (12,889)
Lucas, Amelia 5:48:24 (33,183)
Lucas, Elizabeth A 4:38:21 (21,071)
Lucas, Madeline 3:20:02 (2,966)
Lucas, Pauline A 3:57:42 (10,297)
Lucas, Sonia 4:43:57 (22,492)
Lucas, Zoe 6:35:59 (35,675)
Lucey, Kim 6:21:18 (35,178)
Lucien, Eldica M 4:20:18 (16,200)
Luckett, Charlotte 5:23:40 (30,419)
Luckman, Julie Marie 5:01:37 (26,779)
Ludgate, Betty Louisa Ferrier A 5:29:09 (31,171)
Ludlam, Melissa Kate 4:04:56 (12,186)
Ludlow, Nicola Clare 5:54:00 (33,642)
Luff, Catherine Elizabeth 5:14:19 (28,964)
Luke, Emily 4:13:06 (14,263)
Luker, Pippa C 6:11:55 (34,750)
Lulat, Shenaz 4:40:40 (21,683)
Lumby, Esther 5:00:50 (26,617)
Lumsdem, Sally 4:55:46 (25,485)
Lund, Deana 5:47:01 (33,052)
Lundberg, Clare Adrienne 4:54:10 (25,083)
Lundy, Caroline B 3:50:32 (8,321)
Lunn, Carole Diane 4:46:57 (23,295)
Luong, Jami Maree 4:54:57 (25,293)
Luscombe, Jenny Ann 4:03:30 (11,844)
Lustig, Katarina 3:49:58 (8,204)
Lusty, Liz Rachel 4:03:33 (11,859)
Luthra, Archna 5:37:54 (32,201)
Luty, Jo S 4:32:12 (19,488)
Lyall, Fiona 4:06:15 (12,511)
Lyddy, Sylvia 6:34:27 (35,639)
Lynam, Helen 4:25:45 (17,738)
Lynch, Amanda 5:58:11 (33,944)
Lynch, Carly 5:13:53 (28,904)
Lynch, Julie 6:33:11 (35,604)
Lynch, Kasey Georgina 3:52:28 (8,789)
Lynch, Kelly 4:52:21 (24,649)
Lynch, Lucy Alice 4:42:10 (22,053)
Lynch, Susan 4:55:18 (25,387)
Lynch, Trudy 4:13:51 (14,470)
Lynch, Uzay 5:01:09 (26,674)
Lynch-Aird, Jeanne Elizabeth 5:29:40 (31,247)
Lyness, Catherine 6:08:37 (34,590)
Lyng, Rebecca 6:28:56 (35,460)
Lyon, Katy 3:45:26 (7,196)
Lyon, Nicky 4:30:34 (19,113)
Lyons, Gillian 3:58:50 (10,669)
Lyons, Greta W 5:18:27 (29,621)
Lyons, Kay 5:05:07 (27,389)
Lyons, Lorraine Judith 5:03:45 (27,148)
Lyons, Lucy Catrin 4:38:43 (21,175)
Lyons-Whearty, Sophie Mary 5:52:47 (33,567)
Mac, Hayley 6:00:07 (34,075)
MacAlpine, Karri 3:59:08 (10,758)
MacAndrew, Karen 5:20:16 (29,886)
Macapili, Camilla 4:46:16 (23,118)
Macarthur, Janet Elizabeth 6:28:14 (35,435)
Macarthur, Kucy 4:33:29 (19,848)
MacAskill, Jane 4:49:03 (23,813)
MacAskill, Ruth Seona 5:38:17 (32,235)
Macauley, Emma Jane 4:42:52 (22,234)
Macauley, Sally 4:26:01 (17,817)
MacBean, Alison 5:33:40 (31,735)
Macbrayne, Julie Fiona 4:42:57 (22,248)
Macbride-Stewart, Sara 4:06:59 (12,707)
Macdonagh, Michelle Louise 5:32:42 (31,631)
Macdonal, Shauna 3:45:20 (7,169)
Macdonald, Fiona 4:04:02 (11,968)
Macdonald, Helen Elisabeth 5:18:12 (29,572)
Macdonald, Jacky 5:55:35 (33,762)
Macdonald, Kirsten 4:15:17 (14,853)
Macdonald, Maria 4:29:53 (18,943)
Macdonald, Wanda 3:39:49 (6,106)
Macdonald-Crate, Jan 5:38:17 (32,235)
MacDougall, Judi 4:27:59 (18,361)
Macer, Nina D 4:50:20 (24,123)
Macey, Hannah 5:34:21 (31,803)
MacGillivray, Danielle 4:50:47 (24,234)
MacGillivray-Fallis, Karen 6:05:13 (34,403)
MacGregor, Elizabeth A 4:59:31 (26,345)
MacGregor, Helen Rose 7:55:24 (36,580)
MacGregor, Louise J 4:59:31 (26,345)
MacGregor, Susan 3:36:59 (5,560)
Mach, François 4:46:17 (23,125)
Machin, Sara 4:15:29 (14,902)
Machut, Celine 4:54:23 (25,154)
MacInnes, Amy 3:32:52 (4,875)
MacInnes, Flora I 3:12:50 (2,169)
Macintosh, Liz 3:41:29 (6,419)
Mackay, Laura 4:06:32 (12,583)
Mackay, Lucy S 3:44:19 (6,942)
Mackay, Susannah Lynsey Clair 4:30:38 (19,129)
Mackender, Carolyn Fiona Anne 5:16:25 (29,295)
Mackenzie, Jen 4:27:47 (18,310)
Mackenzie, Lorna 4:41:52 (21,985)
Mackey, Jill Linda 7:02:18 (36,217)
Mackie, Alison J 4:40:17 (21,570)
Mackie, Nicola 5:46:03 (32,956)
Mackie, Stephanie H 5:23:53 (30,457)
Mackinlay, Joanna Clare 4:47:49 (23,502)
Mackinnon, Clare Elizabeth 4:25:30 (17,661)
Mackinnon, Fiona 5:44:02 (32,770)
MacLaughlin, Callee 6:09:16 (34,627)
Maclean, Rebecca 3:39:06 (5,963)
MacLeary, Rebekah 5:18:42 (29,656)
MacLellan, Laura L 5:25:45 (30,741)
Macleod, Fiona 4:29:49 (18,918)
Macmillan, Fiona U 4:54:31 (25,184)
Maconochy, Ellen 5:55:28 (33,752)
MacQueen, Andrea 4:31:54 (19,407)
Macrae, Laura Jane 5:44:22 (32,801)
Macready, Emma C 3:10:59 (1,992)
MacRitchie, Fiona 3:20:56 (3,076)
Madaher, Amy 9:01:52 (36,614)
Madden, Amena R 4:32:20 (19,525)
Madden, Christina 5:08:18 (27,950)
Maddick, Emily Charlotte 5:13:21 (28,821)
Maddison, Rachel 6:03:56 (34,319)
Maddock, Lynsey Ann 3:34:56 (5,237)
Maddocks, Wendy Susan 4:42:42 (22,186)
Madej, Natalia 4:43:58 (22,498)
Madziya, Kathleen 5:17:15 (29,426)
Maestri, Carla Sandra 7:00:58 (36,206)
Magalhaes, Ann 4:32:42 (19,607)
Magee, Bianca 4:18:41 (15,769)
Maggott, Emma Jean 5:26:58 (30,901)
Maggs, Nicola K 4:40:31 (21,647)
Maginn, Sharon 4:27:50 (18,319)
Magness, Laura J 3:47:21 (7,609)
Magold, Andrea 4:27:12 (18,149)
Magson, Vicki 4:35:40 (20,380)
Magudia, Sangita 5:28:31 (31,090)
Maguire, Katherine Bucknell 4:38:23 (21,088)
Maguire, Michelle 4:43:10 (22,292)
Maguire, Rosemarie Bridget 4:53:26 (24,901)
Maguire, Sarah 3:05:01 (1,459)
Mahe, Louise 4:49:36 (23,943)
Maher, Joanne 3:39:08 (5,970)
Mahmoud, Sonia 4:37:18 (20,818)
Mahoney, Caroline Stasia 4:32:25 (19,542)
Mahoney, Fiona Janet 4:24:49 (17,472)
Mahoney, Kathryn 6:17:23 (35,002)
Mahoney, Luan 4:19:40 (16,009)
Maia, Elisa 4:28:11 (18,414)
Maiden, Elizabeth 5:58:13 (33,947)
Main, Carol-Ann 7:03:45 (36,235)
Main, Gill 4:51:43 (24,466)
Mainard, Joanne C 3:44:40 (7,029)
Mair, Cheryl Claire 3:36:13 (5,450)
Maitland Jones, Wendy L 3:50:09 (8,237)
Major, Pippa J 3:24:31 (3,512)
Majumdar, Tara 4:54:17 (25,126)
Makaed, Youlia 4:06:25 (12,551)
Makarenko, Tamara 5:50:04 (33,342)
Makarska, Iva 5:50:07 (33,344)
Makin, Cheryl Lesley 5:03:10 (27,051)
Malby, Joley Anne 4:02:10 (11,529)
Malcolm, Colette 6:32:12 (35,571)
Male, Ruth E 4:52:03 (24,558)
Malek, Gimyana Sarah 5:53:35 (33,617)
Males, Julia 5:22:04 (30,155)
Malik, Jordana 5:48:09 (33,157)
Malik, Portia 5:48:08 (33,154)
Malir, Sarah A 3:10:49 (1,973)
Mallaband, Anne 4:11:08 (13,753)
Mallery, Lynne 5:49:26 (33,275)
Malley, Nicola 4:53:18 (24,876)
Mallorie, Charlotte J 3:13:27 (2,241)
Maloney, Alison 5:35:05 (31,887)
Maltby, Bridget Anne 5:10:16 (28,284)
Maltby, Kate 4:29:30 (18,808)
Maltby, Louise Alexandra 3:48:50 (7,937)
Malzard, Claire 3:41:05 (6,337)
Man, Layyee 5:00:36 (26,570)
Mancini, Giuliana 6:31:29 (35,555)
Manders, Tracey 4:12:06 (14,008)
Mangabhai, Meena 6:05:15 (34,408)
Mangan, Layla Isis 5:52:56 (33,576)
Manhood, Sue 5:44:37 (32,828)
Maniega, Esther 4:27:32 (18,246)
Manion, Lucy 4:40:11 (21,533)
Mann, Becky Jane 4:30:21 (19,057)
Mann, Brinder 6:26:34 (35,370)
Mann, Irmgard E 3:49:41 (8,144)
Mann, Jo 4:45:20 (22,849)
Mann, Rosalind H 4:36:06 (20,506)
Mann, Yvonne 3:57:09 (10,141)
Mannan, Sarah Suzanne 4:59:19 (26,292)
Mannick, Reshmi 6:00:30 (34,093)
Manning, Katie Elizabeth 6:23:39 (35,264)
Manning, Kelly 5:16:25 (29,295)
Mannix, Zoe Elizabeth 6:21:21 (35,180)
Manrique, Elizabeth 3:59:38 (10,900)
Mansbridge, Natalie Jane 6:19:32 (35,104)
Mansell, Kate 4:14:21 (14,605)
Mansell, Sarah Katherine Maria 4:59:41 (26,380)
Mansfeild, Lynn S 3:50:10 (8,242)
Mansfield, Lauren Hayley 4:47:27 (23,400)
Mansfield, Marion Grace 7:18:52 (36,393)
Manson, Marie-Françoise 4:55:16 (25,374)
Manson, Stephanie 4:52:49 (24,761)
Mansour, Alex 4:45:33 (22,901)
Mant, Anita Louise 4:22:23 (16,818)
Manthorpe, Hana 3:56:10 (9,832)
Manton, Helen Mary 5:03:58 (27,179)
Maple, Joanne Elizabeth 4:52:23 (24,657)
Mapplebeck, Sarah 3:43:21 (6,748)
Maragno, Claudia 3:29:04 (4,242)
Marcarian, Fab 4:40:28 (21,633)
Marchant, Judy C 3:58:33 (10,574)
Marchant, Kate A 3:23:53 (3,416)
Marchese, Joy 4:40:50 (21,733)
Marchione, Cettina 4:36:23 (20,573)

Marchitelli, Fiorella 5:54:01 (33,644)
Marcuello, Annick 3:26:57 (3,869)
Marcus, Samantha 4:20:34 (16,281)
Marcuzzo, Kirsty 5:12:11 (28,599)
Marett-Gregory, Sharon 5:27:03 (30,913)
Marie-Claude, Perdreau 4:34:12 (20,044)
Marine, Lavalard 5:55:15 (33,738)
Markey, Anne Louise 3:59:41 (10,916)
Markham, Hannah J 5:50:03 (33,340)
Marklove, Jade Louise 5:07:30 (27,812)
Marks, Chandree 5:58:59 (33,987)
Marks, Suzanne 5:24:00 (30,481)
Marks, Wendy E 3:53:12 (8,971)
Marks, Wendy Jane 4:33:26 (19,836)
Marnell, Veronica Anne 5:35:36 (31,936)
Marney, Julie 7:29:51 (36,470)
Marnoch, Victoria A 4:15:44 (14,962)
Marr, Niki Tracey 4:53:29 (24,913)
Marra, Kelley 4:19:56 (16,082)
Marriott, Lesley Deborah 5:31:56 (31,530)
Marriott, Rachel Elizabeth 5:13:32 (28,846)
Marriott, Rosemary S 3:23:11 (3,320)
Marsden, Hazel Ann 4:53:49 (24,998)
Marsden, Winnie M 7:53:51 (36,576)
Marsh, Carla Jane 4:06:09 (12,488)
Marsh, Caroline Suzanne 4:55:43 (25,472)
Marsh, Hannah K 5:09:04 (28,058)
Marsh, Julie 4:57:35 (25,875)
Marsh, Kerry 5:16:28 (29,304)
Marsh, Laura 5:15:28 (29,138)
Marsh, Mandy 5:33:15 (31,689)
Marsh, Mary Elizabeth 4:55:34 (25,424)
Marsh, Naomi Dawn 5:37:12 (32,125)
Marsh, Natalie Marie 6:58:43 (36,167)
Marsh, Sally A 6:16:30 (34,950)
Marsh, Vicki 5:30:20 (31,327)
Marshall, Catriona Frances 3:42:14 (6,553)
Marshall, Claire 5:40:11 (32,410)
Marshall, Clare 4:39:11 (21,308)
Marshall, Dawn 4:18:50 (15,803)
Marshall, Emma J 3:51:51 (8,622)
Marshall, Heather L 3:55:11 (9,523)
Marshall, Maxine 5:11:59 (28,558)
Marshall, Pippa Joanne 5:16:39 (29,331)
Marshall, Polly Anne 5:23:20 (30,364)
Marsham, Linda M 5:45:09 (32,881)
Marson, Eleanor Jane 5:30:45 (31,385)
Martell, Karen 6:03:27 (34,285)
Martell,, Louise, 4:33:14 (19,778)
Martin, Amber 4:20:32 (16,268)
Martin, Angela Louise 4:42:38 (22,163)
Martin, Briony Rose 4:23:05 (17,000)
Martin, Carole 3:46:37 (7,444)
Martin, Carole L 6:00:05 (34,071)
Martin, Clare Margaret Selborne 6:39:38 (35,775)
Martin, Elizabeth Ann 3:57:49 (10,334)
Martin, Emma Victoria 5:25:55 (30,770)
Martin, Georgina 5:16:11 (29,252)
Martin, Georgina 5:24:47 (30,590)
Martin, Georgina Melody 7:46:14 (36,551)
Martin, Hayley Jane 6:15:09 (34,896)
Martin, Hazel 4:59:45 (26,395)
Martin, Heidi 4:11:26 (13,827)
Martin, India Red Grace 4:33:34 (19,877)
Martin, Isobel 4:43:26 (22,356)
Martin, Jackie Rose 4:40:07 (21,517)
Martin, Jennie 5:27:06 (30,923)
Martin, Jennifer 4:40:46 (21,714)
Martin, Joelle 4:14:08 (14,545)
Martin, Julie K 5:03:50 (27,162)
Martin, Kelly A 5:01:02 (26,656)
Martin, Kelly Anne 5:02:09 (26,879)
Martin, Lily 3:35:35 (5,339)
Martin, Lisa 4:28:23 (18,478)
Martin, Mandy Jane 4:22:32 (16,857)
Martin, Natalie Jane 4:45:37 (22,919)
Martin, Nina Isabella 3:34:44 (5,198)
Martin, Rebecca Laura 3:39:25 (6,028)
Martin, Samantha J 4:31:34 (19,344)
Martin, Sarah 3:39:26 (6,029)
Martin, Sarah 5:11:57 (28,553)
Martin, Sarah Louise 6:06:54 (34,501)
Martin, Shelley 4:11:44 (13,917)
Martin, Stephanie Anne Marie 4:19:50 (16,052)
Martin, Susan 5:49:59 (33,333)
Martin, Susan D 5:45:38 (32,921)
Martin, Susan E 7:05:45 (36,262)
Martin, Tina Maria 5:23:21 (30,365)
Martin, Victoria Leanne 4:40:46 (21,714)
Martinelli, Alexandra 4:33:14 (19,778)
Martinelli, Andrea M 3:35:50 (5,380)
Martinez, Marina 4:38:55 (21,235)
Martinez de Leiros, Maria del Mar 4:38:54 (21,231)
Martinez Del Campo, Araceli 3:51:30 (8,539)
Martingell, Heather 4:13:33 (14,385)
Martino, Orsolina Irma 3:55:59 (9,779)
Martins, Marketa 3:57:52 (10,352)
Martyniuk, Marta 4:38:13 (21,034)
Maruyama, Chieko 5:44:23 (32,803)
Maruyama Minuti, Atsuko 4:56:57 (25,757)
Marx, Inge 4:40:31 (21,647)
Marzaioli, Sarah L 3:51:40 (8,581)
Mascart, Deborah A 5:24:30 (30,556)
Maseko, Lindiwe 6:28:20 (35,437)
Mashru, Avni 4:14:24 (14,613)
Maskell, Julie 4:35:47 (20,417)
Maslen, Charlotte 4:50:40 (24,201)
Mason, Avril 3:01:34 (1,233)
Mason, Gayle 4:20:32 (16,268)
Mason, Ian 6:39:21 (35,766)
Mason, Janet Susan 4:22:14 (16,776)
Mason, Julie Karen 4:20:09 (16,150)
Mason, Kim L 5:22:37 (30,241)
Mason, Laura 3:54:51 (9,437)
Mason, Margaret Joan 4:38:52 (21,223)
Mason, Maxine Susan 4:26:03 (17,825)
Mason, Nikki 4:42:42 (22,186)
Mason, Sarah Anne 4:54:10 (25,083)
Mason, Tracey 5:20:24 (29,905)
Mason, Trudy 6:22:32 (35,211)
Massarella, Hannah Beth 4:24:44 (17,450)
Massey, Joanne R 3:54:56 (9,458)
Massey, Karen A 3:53:38 (9,101)
Massey, Lara L 3:27:45 (4,006)
Massey, Linda Jayne 7:07:37 (36,285)
Massey, Natalie 4:00:45 (11,183)
Massey, Theresa Jane 4:26:30 (17,952)
Massie, Carol M 3:52:45 (8,854)
Massie, Catherine L 4:51:01 (24,309)
Massiera, Eliane 3:46:45 (7,472)
Massingham-Lamprell, Joanna 4:22:00 (16,705)
Masson, Jacqueline Helen 5:12:39 (28,671)
Masson, Kim C 3:11:36 (2,059)
Mastenbroek, Marguerite 5:14:25 (28,979)
Masterman, Julie 3:25:24 (3,631)
Masters, Kate 3:46:03 (7,322)
Masters, Natalie 5:18:41 (29,653)
Masterson, Sarah Elizabeth 5:01:09 (26,674)
Masterton, Melissa 6:14:38 (34,867)
Matheson, Lorraine 5:28:47 (31,126)
Matheson, Nell 4:31:38 (19,362)
Mathews, Jacqueline M 6:59:52 (36,187)
Mathews, Nicola Amanda 4:38:10 (21,021)
Mathews, Thérèse Majella 4:03:31 (11,849)
Mathias, Michi 4:39:10 (21,304)
Mathieson, Margaret 5:14:28 (28,985)
Mathis, Sarah Marr 4:26:55 (18,054)
Matseke, Monica 3:45:22 (7,175)
Matsubara, Sophie Anna 4:56:05 (25,556)
Matsui, Akiko 4:23:56 (17,221)
Mattei, Antonella 3:35:55 (5,403)
Matthams, Stacey Liana 5:54:14 (33,661)
Matthews, Caroline Emily 5:05:34 (27,459)
Matthews, Denise 4:07:02 (12,720)
Matthews, Hayley Victoria 6:21:32 (35,187)
Matthews, Jane Louise 6:26:02 (35,351)
Matthews, Joanne 3:36:03 (5,419)
Matthews, Julie Marie 4:38:40 (21,158)
Matthews, Katrina 4:57:00 (25,766)
Matthews, Nicola 5:36:01 (31,998)
Matthews, Sarah E 3:28:51 (4,198)
Matthews, Susan J 4:42:43 (22,193)
Mattia, Sophia Heather CR 5:47:31 (33,099)
Mattia, Sue Anne 6:03:55 (34,316)
Matuszewicz, Ewa Z 3:44:22 (6,955)
Mauge, Elisabeth 5:05:47 (27,493)
Mauger, Beverley C 3:50:59 (8,416)
Maughan, Rachel 4:41:14 (21,827)
Maughan, Sophie 6:02:27 (34,214)
Maurice, Emma 3:44:38 (7,022)
Mawhinney, Anne 5:08:34 (27,981)
Maxfield, Karen Elizabeth 4:56:44 (25,700)
Maxwell, Clare 5:04:19 (27,246)
Maxwell, Helen Louise 4:56:27 (25,640)
Maxwell, Jill Elizabeth 4:17:26 (15,416)
Maxwell, Tanith 2:34:24 (104)
Maxwell, Tracy 4:29:34 (18,826)
May, Billie 4:29:45 (18,899)
May, Ellie-Louise 3:39:50 (6,110)
May, Helen M 5:06:11 (27,563)
May, Katie 4:32:15 (19,500)
May, Kellie 5:26:05 (30,790)
May, Krista Donna 3:38:46 (5,902)
May, Linda Mary 5:31:03 (31,422)
May, Louiza Michele 5:19:03 (29,708)
May, Stephanie 4:54:36 (25,204)
Maycock, Fiona J 3:08:27 (1,750)
Maycock, Paula Joanne 5:14:51 (29,044)
Mayer, Vicky A 4:25:51 (17,768)
Mayerhofer, Gisela 4:54:00 (25,052)
Mayes, Amanda 4:22:58 (16,977)
Mayhew, Linn Nathalie 4:01:29 (11,362)
Mayles, Shelley 6:18:42 (35,066)
Mayling, Jennifer Susan 3:40:28 (6,228)
Maynard, Edwina 4:13:57 (14,492)
Maynard, Jayne E 5:07:26 (27,793)
Maynard, Kim 4:09:09 (13,240)
Maynard, Zara V 4:50:11 (24,090)
Mayne, Henrietta Mary Diana 4:50:52 (24,262)
Mayo, Arlene 5:01:12 (26,680)
Mayo, Pip 4:40:41 (21,687)
Mayo, Sarah 4:16:45 (15,233)
Mayor, Sarah J 4:09:38 (13,380)
Mayungbe, Clara O 7:10:44 (36,320)
Maziere, Angela 3:39:33 (6,055)
Mazzini, Rosa 3:33:55 (5,043)
Mazzocchi, Patrizia 5:01:51 (26,820)
McAdam, Carol V 3:41:45 (6,469)
McAdam, Helen 5:29:43 (31,255)
McAinsh, Joanna 4:50:32 (24,170)
McAlea, Philomena Marie K 4:25:00 (17,519)
McAllister-Brown, Emily 4:53:25 (24,895)
McAlpine, Kirsty 5:03:46 (27,154)
McAree, Kelly 4:59:08 (26,246)
McAvinchey, Eimear 6:43:46 (35,879)
McBeth, Caroline A 3:45:12 (7,139)
McBlane, Kate Elizabeth 4:56:05 (25,556)
McBrearty, Lynn 3:42:32 (6,602)
McBride, Janice 5:20:42 (29,964)
McCabe, Julia Ann 6:28:00 (35,419)
McCabe, Kylie 5:28:47 (31,126)
McCaddon, Janette Dawn 7:00:59 (36,207)
McCaffery, Anne 5:59:01 (33,989)
McCaffrey, Sharon 5:15:29 (29,143)
McCaleb, Jennifer 4:03:35 (11,868)
McCall, Anna 4:17:45 (15,512)
McCall, Claire Louise 3:38:50 (5,912)
McCall, Emma 4:24:26 (17,370)
McCallum, Michaela J 3:25:44 (3,692)
McCandless, Lorraine Kathleen 5:33:31 (31,717)
McCappin, Lucy 4:37:57 (20,977)
McCarron, Clare Louise 3:49:12 (8,026)
McCarron, Mary Kate 5:29:12 (31,175)
McCarter, Maria 4:19:56 (16,082)
McCarter, Rose Naomi 5:03:54 (27,173)
McCarthy, Angela M 5:01:17 (26,703)
McCarthy, Clair 4:25:40 (17,707)
McCarthy, Elizabeth Jane 5:21:33 (30,083)
McCarthy, Felicity Ann 5:10:45 (28,366)
McCarthy, Georgie 7:27:32 (36,455)
McCarthy, Jane 4:39:27 (21,375)
McCarthy, Joanna 4:38:40 (21,158)
McCarthy, Michelle Kelly 4:35:45 (20,406)
McCarthy, Sarah 3:23:31 (3,370)
McCarthy, Shauna 4:13:18 (14,312)
McCarthy, Sophie Joanna 4:21:15 (16,477)
McCarthy, Victoria A 4:54:43 (25,234)
McCartney, Karen 5:12:30 (28,653)
McCauley, Geraldine Imelda 4:33:53 (19,963)

Messore, Ashlea Louise 6:04:44 (34,364)
Meston, Niki 3:42:50 (6,661)
Metalli, Nicola 5:46:26 (33,002)
Metcalfe, Sam 7:16:28 (36,375)
Meth, Fiona 5:20:43 (29,965)
Metham, Elaine 3:41:40 (6,451)
Metheringham, Susan L 4:02:02 (11,497)
Meumann, Gwyneth Anne 3:46:41 (7,456)
Meurice, Jessica 5:32:20 (31,577)
Meyers, Della 6:09:49 (34,651)
Meynell, Victoria Kate 7:32:05 (36,477)
Mezey, Ivett Anna 4:59:32 (26,349)
Mian, Ameera 5:02:19 (26,908)
Michael, Kirsty 6:40:04 (35,788)
Michaux, Sophie 4:12:58 (14,225)
Middle, Helen Rachel 5:22:35 (30,237)
Middleditch, Jo 4:18:54 (15,828)
Middlehurst, Sue E 4:42:38 (22,163)
Middleton, Angela Dawn 5:00:17 (26,515)
Middleton, Caroline J 5:55:20 (33,746)
Middleton, Heidi Emma 4:18:36 (15,744)
Middleton, Kristel 5:30:32 (31,362)
Middleton, Laura Catherine 5:11:10 (28,430)
Middleton, Lisa 3:45:48 (7,265)
Middleton, Nancy Katherine 4:58:29 (26,082)
Middleton, Philippa Mary 5:15:43 (29,183)
Middleton, Sally 3:54:25 (9,304)
Middleton, Sarah 6:42:09 (35,841)
Middleton-Jones, Rebecca Jessica 4:16:12 (15,071)
Miettinen, Minna 4:54:05 (25,067)
Mifsud, Vivien Mary 4:37:24 (20,845)
Migliorini, Maria Raffaella 4:23:17 (17,041)
Miksakova, Monika 4:46:19 (23,130)
Milatz, Anne 4:26:59 (18,074)
Milburn, Lynsey Jane 3:21:53 (3,179)
Miles, Belinda Jane 3:43:37 (6,793)
Miles, Bethan D 3:08:26 (1,746)
Miles, Holly 4:33:32 (19,862)
Miles, Jenny 4:52:20 (24,647)
Miles, Louise Emma 5:47:46 (33,122)
Miles, Lucy Jane 5:54:49 (33,696)
Miles, Nia 4:43:43 (22,423)
Miles, Paula 5:03:31 (27,104)
Miles, Sally 3:48:09 (7,778)
Miles, Sarah 3:37:56 (5,751)
Miles, Sonia 6:04:32 (34,352)
Milewski, Julie 7:03:47 (36,237)
Milham, Azelle Rae 6:06:10 (34,460)
Milington, Charlotte 5:13:59 (28,921)
Millar, Christina 5:15:36 (29,163)
Millar, Gillian M 3:41:49 (6,480)
Millar-Cook, Gemma Jane 4:05:16 (12,276)
Millard, Kirsty Samantha 5:44:16 (32,793)
Miller, Angela 6:33:07 (35,600)
Miller, Dawn C 5:27:57 (31,017)
Miller, Hillary 4:44:06 (22,534)
Miller, Joanna 4:50:33 (24,173)
Miller, Linda J 4:39:00 (21,258)
Miller, Mhairi Elizabeth 4:05:56 (12,440)
Miller, Nathalie Louise 5:54:31 (33,676)
Miller, Nicola 4:39:08 (21,291)
Miller, Pamela Annette 4:08:37 (13,122)
Miller, Patricia L 4:37:27 (20,866)
Miller, Peter 3:56:38 (9,973)
Miller, Rachel 4:59:32 (26,349)
Miller, Stacey Leeanne 4:33:02 (19,708)
Miller, Vivian Jane 4:02:59 (11,726)
Miller, Zara 7:12:49 (36,336)
Millership, Julie 4:24:36 (17,419)
Miller-Wright, Deborah Frances 4:14:16 (14,586)
Millis, Alex 4:47:42 (23,470)
Millman, Yvonne 5:08:34 (27,981)
Mills, Eleanor Kate 5:59:15 (34,006)
Mills, Francesca Louise 5:24:46 (30,589)
Mills, Kate 3:06:11 (1,546)
Mills, Lorraine 4:55:03 (25,321)
Mills, Paula Joanne 4:07:21 (12,787)
Mills, Rebecca L 4:19:06 (15,872)
Mills, Rosie 5:18:05 (29,559)
Mills, Tracy Diane 5:43:44 (32,748)
Millward, Susan 4:01:02 (11,258)
Milner, Joanne 4:44:04 (22,523)
Milner, Lisa Marie 4:30:18 (19,044)
Milner, Shukwai 4:20:14 (16,173)
Milsom, Jennifer Margaret 4:24:31 (17,395)
Milton, Angela Mary 4:08:59 (13,211)
Milton, Donna 5:05:00 (27,368)
Milton, Jacqueline 4:17:22 (15,396)
Milton, Natasha Jane 5:15:14 (29,104)
Milton, Tina 5:10:22 (28,304)
Miners, Jane 3:43:49 (6,835)
Miners, Jo 4:22:45 (16,918)
Minghella, Emma 4:54:52 (25,272)
Minghella, Heather 4:54:53 (25,279)
Mingoia, Debra 4:27:42 (18,288)
Minshall, Adele P 5:20:12 (29,877)
Minshaw, Terry Elizabeth 6:45:07 (35,912)
Miranda, Paulina 4:07:47 (12,904)
Mischnick, Martina 3:56:11 (9,837)
Misiewicz, Anna E 5:18:19 (29,592)
Miskelly, Sarah Louise 6:37:26 (35,712)
Missen, Verity 4:15:16 (14,850)
Missing, Nicola 4:55:07 (25,341)
Mistry, Neeta 5:52:49 (33,569)
Mitchell, Alison 5:31:14 (31,436)
Mitchell, Angela Deborah 7:53:16 (36,574)
Mitchell, Anna 4:33:09 (19,748)
Mitchell, Anna 5:08:30 (27,973)
Mitchell, Charmaine 5:59:58 (34,059)
Mitchell, Claire E 3:58:44 (10,637)
Mitchell, Debbie 5:58:17 (33,950)
Mitchell, Gemma 4:03:00 (11,733)
Mitchell, Gill 4:34:34 (20,140)
Mitchell, Heather M 4:08:57 (13,193)
Mitchell, Jacqueline 4:00:26 (11,100)
Mitchell, Jane 4:26:19 (17,904)
Mitchell, Karen Lesley 4:39:20 (21,338)
Mitchell, Kay 5:45:23 (32,900)
Mitchell, Laura Jane 4:48:42 (23,719)
Mitchell, Lucy 5:25:44 (30,737)
Mitchell, Orlaith Martina 4:34:37 (20,150)
Mitchell, Pauline A 5:29:33 (31,228)
Mitchell, Rebecca 6:35:24 (35,663)
Mitchell, Sinead Mary 5:13:16 (28,814)
Mitchell, Valerie Lynn 5:48:33 (33,200)
Mitchell, Vanessa Jane 4:04:58 (12,196)
Mitchinson, Jodi 4:40:22 (21,601)
Miton, Jennifer 3:58:36 (10,595)
Mitton, Kathryn Anne 4:31:19 (19,295)
Miyar, Natalia 7:02:17 (36,216)
Moan, Rebecca 4:05:18 (12,283)
Moar, Natasha Maree 4:49:20 (23,879)
Mockford, Chynna 4:51:34 (24,434)
Mockford, Frances Rachel 4:15:38 (14,933)
Mockford, Jen Marie 4:08:09 (12,994)
Mockford, Katherine Alice 4:45:02 (22,778)
Modak, Wahida 6:09:18 (34,628)
Modelska, Zofia Maria 3:55:49 (9,725)
Modi, Rupa 5:32:15 (31,569)
Modol, Isabelle 3:51:58 (8,649)
Moffatt, Clare J 4:38:43 (21,175)
Moffatt, Fiona H 3:41:23 (6,403)
Mogan, Sandra A 6:18:24 (35,052)
Mogashoa, Natasha 6:13:54 (34,834)
Mogg, Sharon Lisa 7:17:51 (36,385)
Moggan, Adele J 4:51:01 (24,309)
Mohn, Susanne 4:16:05 (15,047)
Moir, Debs 4:06:31 (12,578)
Moir, Helen Marie 3:46:05 (7,335)
Mold, Debbie Denise 4:49:42 (23,978)
Moldram, Haidee 5:33:28 (31,713)
Molife, Lulama R 5:26:37 (30,855)
Mollinghoff, Amelie Jane 4:33:16 (19,791)
Molloy, Amy M 3:48:25 (7,829)
Molloy, Andrea K 6:15:35 (34,911)
Molloy, Claire L 4:46:13 (23,096)
Molloy, Denise Catherine 5:38:36 (32,273)
Molloy, Jane 5:31:33 (31,479)
Molo, Catherine 4:47:40 (23,459)
Moloney, Marie 4:16:28 (15,157)
Molstad, Anne Kristin Roeiseland 3:49:09 (8,010)
Molyneaux, Jo 3:25:43 (3,687)
Monaghan, Jennifer 6:53:00 (36,072)
Monger, Natalie Clare 4:55:22 (25,396)
Monk, Clare 4:29:01 (18,691)
Monk, Samantha L 3:53:02 (8,932)
Monnier, Pascale 3:18:13 (2,797)
Montague, Charlotte Kate 5:00:06 (26,480)
Montagu-Williams, Rebecca 3:53:09 (8,955)
Montesdeoca, Isabel 4:12:57 (14,216)
Montfrooij, Nicolette 4:51:25 (24,403)
Montgomery, Claire H 3:37:27 (5,649)
Montgomery, Joanna 4:35:21 (20,309)
Montgomery, Katie 4:30:07 (19,003)
Montgomery, Rebecca 6:07:50 (34,551)
Montgomery, Samantha 5:23:52 (30,451)
Moody, Anastasia 5:06:44 (27,679)
Moody, Denny Patricia 4:35:15 (20,283)
Moody, Margaret M 4:03:01 (11,736)
Moody, Pat 5:23:56 (30,474)
Moon, Caroline Jane 4:30:20 (19,054)
Moon, Helen Ann 5:07:00 (27,724)
Moonan, May S 6:43:14 (35,871)
Mooney, Bernadette Jane 6:43:00 (35,862)
Mooney, Claire Jane 4:49:26 (23,903)
Moons, Annick 5:04:04 (27,202)
Moore, Claire 4:34:45 (20,185)
Moore, Cymbeline 4:33:15 (19,787)
Moore, Elizabeth Louise 4:50:48 (24,238)
Moore, Janet 7:15:37 (36,364)
Moore, Jenny 2:57:31 (903)
Moore, Jo-Anna Claire 6:39:26 (35,769)
Moore, Julie Elaine 4:32:56 (19,680)
Moore, Katherine Helen 4:56:38 (25,673)
Moore, Katy Helen 4:28:44 (18,587)
Moore, Kirsty A 4:14:07 (14,542)
Moore, Lisa Frances 5:39:30 (32,346)
Moore, Louise 4:46:58 (23,298)
Moore, Nicola 3:22:55 (3,281)
Moore, Polly Dawn 5:05:34 (27,459)
Moore, Rachael 7:25:12 (36,444)
Moore, Sally 4:33:15 (19,787)
Moore, Sarah J 5:37:41 (32,181)
Moore, Sascha 6:00:47 (34,109)
Moore, Shirley A 4:23:51 (17,200)
Moore, Susanna 4:19:24 (15,952)
Moore, Tessa 4:18:29 (15,711)
Moorekite, Janice D 4:09:23 (13,304)
Moores, Catherine Annette 4:30:18 (19,044)
Moores, Claire 3:40:07 (6,171)
Moorin, Pippa 6:01:14 (34,141)
Morahan, Mags Sinclair 5:22:16 (30,184)
Morais, Claire 6:48:33 (35,967)
Morales, Eva Maria 6:15:39 (34,915)
Moran, Anya Elizabeth 6:28:03 (35,424)
Moran, Elizabeth A 4:00:35 (11,135)
Moran, Emma J 4:16:14 (15,084)
Moran, Michele 3:51:46 (8,598)
Moran, Nicola Kelly 5:37:49 (32,194)
Morden, Emily 5:25:32 (30,699)
Moreno, Isabel 4:45:43 (22,955)
Moreton, Helen Clare Vidion 6:54:58 (36,112)
Morfoisse, Delphine 4:27:40 (18,277)
Morgan, Alison M 5:18:31 (29,627)
Morgan, Amanda Jane 4:07:27 (12,817)
Morgan, Annabelle 5:45:44 (32,926)
Morgan, Beverley 6:42:14 (35,844)
Morgan, Carole A 4:11:15 (13,779)
Morgan, Caroline Jane 5:22:10 (30,173)
Morgan, Charlie Louise 4:33:06 (19,727)
Morgan, Cilla 4:55:42 (25,463)
Morgan, Claire 4:28:49 (18,617)
Morgan, Colette 3:46:32 (7,429)
Morgan, Danielle Elizabeth 5:36:51 (32,087)
Morgan, Deborah Jane 5:40:09 (32,407)
Morgan, Emily Jane 5:09:57 (28,221)
Morgan, Emily L 3:48:35 (7,871)
Morgan, Hayley 6:36:43 (35,693)
Morgan, Hayley Dawn 6:42:41 (35,854)
Morgan, Jackie 3:27:35 (3,976)
Morgan, Janine Margaret 4:25:34 (17,681)
Morgan, Katherine 4:28:12 (18,417)
Morgan, Kathryn Nerissa 4:45:38 (22,927)
Morgan, Kay 6:18:36 (35,063)
Morgan, Linda A 4:01:20 (11,319)
Morgan, Lisa M 4:56:09 (25,567)
Morgan, Lucy Ann 5:50:01 (33,337)
Morgan, Lucy J 4:33:32 (19,862)
Morgan, Lynne Ruth 5:53:41 (33,622)

Morgan, Marie Claire 5:06:12 (27,567)
Morgan, Nichola Anne 4:28:10 (18,406)
Morgan, Rebecca Anne 5:46:32 (33,010)
Morgan, Rebecca Marie 5:28:39 (31,102)
Morgan, Ruth 5:22:18 (30,190)
Morgan, Sarah Louise 6:00:06 (34,073)
Morgan, Sian 3:46:55 (7,515)
Morgan, Sinead Marie 5:05:01 (27,371)
Morgan, Sophie Elaine 5:33:23 (31,705)
Morgan, Stephaine Teresa 3:25:33 (3,659)
Morgan, Suzanne Adele 5:05:34 (27,459)
Morgan, Trish 4:55:56 (25,520)
Morgan, Vicki L 3:55:45 (9,699)
Morgan, Victoria Jane 3:49:47 (8,163)
Morgan, Wendy L 4:57:58 (25,963)
Moriarty, Victoria C 5:53:46 (33,626)
Morley, Elizabeth 4:41:17 (21,840)
Morley, Joanne 5:32:41 (31,629)
Morley, Susie 5:17:15 (29,426)
Morne, Fay 3:55:05 (9,501)
Moro, Federica 3:39:51 (6,114)
Moro Piazzon, Yvette 3:18:57 (2,866)
Moroni, Chiara 4:29:51 (18,927)
Morris, Abigail 3:36:40 (5,508)
Morris, Alex Louise 5:15:02 (29,073)
Morris, Alice 4:53:04 (24,806)
Morris, Andrea 3:31:19 (4,632)
Morris, Anna Florence 5:26:33 (30,845)
Morris, Arianwen 4:17:04 (15,311)
Morris, Carole 3:44:08 (6,901)
Morris, Caroline Louise 6:05:06 (34,394)
Morris, Claire Louise 4:31:58 (19,424)
Morris, Delyth 4:49:57 (24,041)
Morris, Elen 5:29:59 (31,295)
Morris, Elin 4:28:39 (18,567)
Morris, Emma Kate 4:24:55 (17,494)
Morris, Hannah Victoria 5:07:20 (27,777)
Morris, Hayley Elizabeth 5:20:06 (29,864)
Morris, Heather 4:24:23 (17,350)
Morris, Helen 4:53:40 (24,961)
Morris, Izabela 5:52:34 (33,537)
Morris, Jennifer Elaine 4:22:47 (16,934)
Morris, Kay 4:11:54 (13,959)
Morris, Margaret A 4:16:35 (15,186)
Morris, Marion Jane 5:02:05 (26,864)
Morris, Nicola C 4:29:39 (18,866)
Morris, Noelle Lorna 5:16:04 (29,238)
Morris, Rhiannon Marie 5:16:07 (29,244)
Morris, Rosa K 3:33:10 (4,921)
Morris, Samantha Kate 5:34:57 (31,873)
Morris, Sarah A 4:05:51 (12,421)
Morris, Shona E 4:58:05 (25,985)
Morris, Stephanie 3:48:19 (7,810)
Morris, Susan Elizabeth 4:59:18 (26,286)
Morris, Susan Katherine 7:34:35 (36,487)
Morris, Susan Mairi 4:02:49 (11,677)
Morris, Teresa Pauline 5:08:59 (28,046)
Morrish, Trudi Jane 4:50:14 (24,099)
Morrison, Amber Anna 4:02:59 (11,726)
Morrison, Janelle Louise 4:00:35 (11,135)
Morrison, Katie 4:21:33 (16,564)
Morrison, Lindsay 4:27:29 (18,229)
Morrison, Morag Elizabeth 5:30:24 (31,336)
Morrison, Sheila J 4:52:57 (24,785)
Morrison, Zoe 5:38:13 (32,228)
Morrissey, Blanche 4:11:31 (13,852)
Morrow, Al Jane 4:34:17 (20,068)
Mortimer, Alison Susan 5:34:12 (31,780)
Mortimer, Justine Amy 6:05:19 (34,411)
Mortimore, Elizabeth 4:47:46 (23,483)
Mortlock, Brenda Denise 5:20:39 (29,953)
Morton, Alison J 4:35:33 (20,354)
Morton, Joanne Mary 4:22:10 (16,747)
Morton, Lynn L 4:47:42 (23,470)
Morton, Mary 4:45:14 (22,824)
Morton, Paula Frances 5:18:49 (29,669)
Morton, Samantha J 3:48:56 (7,955)
Morton, Sandra P 4:49:56 (24,037)
Morton, Solitaire 5:09:16 (28,095)
Mosadomi, Olayinka 7:19:53 (36,403)
Mosdell, Nikki Louise 6:00:17 (34,082)
Mosedale, Laura 4:30:43 (19,153)
Moseley, Alison E 6:00:52 (34,121)
Moseley, Elisabeth 5:05:31 (27,452)
Moseley, Julie E 3:58:47 (10,652)
Moseley, Katie Rebecca 5:53:19 (33,596)
Moses, Ranj 3:59:21 (10,824)
Mosley, Becky J 4:33:35 (19,884)
Mosley, Fiona Patricia 5:39:15 (32,328)
Mosley, Jennifer 5:30:47 (31,391)
Mosley, Nicola 5:20:31 (29,930)
Mosley, Polly Claire 3:51:31 (8,541)
Moss, Patricia M 3:52:36 (8,822)
Moss, Susan Carol 5:52:56 (33,576)
Mosvold, Wenche Reme 4:46:24 (23,150)
Motee, Natasha 4:12:41 (14,153)
Mott, Geraldine Mary 6:47:18 (35,956)
Mott, Tracy Elizabeth 4:20:42 (16,333)
Motta, Ana Paula 3:15:10 (2,457)
Motta, Louise 3:46:09 (7,345)
Motte, Joanne 5:23:42 (30,426)
Moulden, Stephanie 4:40:19 (21,579)
Moule, Judith 4:43:27 (22,359)
Moulin, Genevieve 4:52:56 (24,783)
Mouncey, Joanne 4:33:25 (19,829)
Mount, Kelly 6:12:07 (34,759)
Mowat, Felicity Anne 5:23:49 (30,446)
Mowat, Nicky 3:33:06 (4,907)
Mower, Rebecca Louise 5:51:41 (33,480)
Moxey, Alison Tracy 3:51:10 (8,464)
Moxham, Tracy Amanda 5:45:25 (32,902)
Moxham, Victoria 5:07:07 (27,743)
Moyse, Ezme 5:24:28 (30,551)
Mpakanyiswa, Sibongile 5:33:57 (31,757)
Mroczkowska, Anna 4:51:56 (24,536)
Mucha, Ann 4:42:12 (22,065)
Mucoli, Laura Maria 4:40:59 (21,767)
Muddiman, Janette Adele 4:45:18 (22,841)
Mudie, Olivia 5:18:54 (29,684)
Mueller, Stefania 5:04:45 (27,326)
Muffett, Katie Alice 5:58:00 (33,932)

Mugford, Angie 4:49:36 (23,943)

Having trained for the London Marathon in 2009, I was devastated when I picked up a stress fracture just a couple of weeks before the day! I was told I wouldn't be able to run, so had to defer my place to 2010. 2010 was my year! Training went well, completely injury-free and I completed the course in 4 hours 49 minutes. It was truly a great day, and I would thoroughly recommend it to anybody who fancies a challenge. The experience is fantastic. The training was hard work, but the feeling on completion was well worth all the sweat and tears. So much so, I am hoping to run 2012 if I am fortunate enough to get a place!

Mugleston, Sophie Claire 5:35:14 (31,896)
Muid, Stephanie Lynn 4:45:38 (22,927)
Muir, Carol 5:56:12 (33,809)
Muir, Rebecca Elizabeth 5:04:06 (27,209)
Muir, Sarah 4:56:44 (25,700)
Muirhead, Claire 3:34:52 (5,223)
Mukerji, Anjali 5:21:38 (30,101)
Mulcahy, Niamh 5:29:22 (31,207)
Mulhall, Ann-Louise 3:28:03 (4,063)
Mulhall, Helen J 3:26:52 (3,857)
Mulinder, Theryn 6:23:47 (35,270)
Mullan, Nivette K 4:48:24 (23,638)
Mullender, Lizet 4:25:01 (17,524)
Muller, Birgit 3:54:54 (9,450)
Muller, Sophie Harriet 6:03:28 (34,287)
Mullett, Susan Anna 5:57:51 (33,922)
Mulley, Christine 4:45:36 (22,916)
Mulley, Rebecca J 3:45:28 (7,201)
Mulligan, Ciara 5:21:39 (30,103)
Mullineaux, Roberta 5:21:09 (30,029)
Mulliner, Elizabeth Anita 4:14:41 (14,709)
Mullins, Nicola 5:08:27 (27,970)
Mullins, Sophie A 3:51:00 (8,423)
Mulvey, Fiona 4:05:42 (12,378)
Mumbray, Nicola 4:33:34 (19,877)
Mumford, Jane 4:37:29 (20,873)
Muncey, Felicity 4:12:59 (14,229)
Mundy, Laura J 4:54:29 (25,175)
Munnelly, Brigid O 3:53:20 (9,009)
Munro, Caroline Elizabeth 6:34:50 (35,650)
Munro Kerr, Rosie 4:37:51 (20,955)
Munsey, Connie Marina 4:37:41 (20,921)
Munson, Kate L 5:20:59 (30,002)
Munthali, Lumbani 5:55:16 (33,740)
Munthali, Waleke Tessa 4:42:49 (22,220)
Murawska, Anna Marie 3:29:07 (4,254)
Murch, Harriet J 5:28:05 (31,040)
Murdoch, Becky Jane 5:57:20 (33,893)
Murdoch, Melanie J 4:08:36 (13,117)
Murdock, Joanna 4:47:48 (23,494)
Muretti, Milena 4:15:25 (14,889)
Murphy, Andrea L 3:34:07 (5,083)
Murphy, Breda Martina 4:35:06 (20,251)
Murphy, Carry C 4:23:17 (17,041)
Murphy, Deborah J 4:05:36 (12,353)
Murphy, Ellen 4:03:45 (11,906)
Murphy, Georgina 5:03:16 (27,069)
Murphy, Jacqueline B 5:01:46 (26,810)
Murphy, Marie E 5:13:13 (28,803)
Murphy, Maura 3:31:06 (4,595)
Murphy, Megan 5:17:54 (29,526)
Murphy, Natalie 6:27:36 (35,408)
Murphy, Sarah J 3:03:38 (1,359)
Murray, Annie 3:58:01 (10,384)
Murray, Cassandra Demelza 5:15:38 (29,169)
Murray, Catherine 4:31:11 (19,266)
Murray, Christina A 5:07:16 (27,761)
Murray, Claire 5:57:16 (33,886)
Murray, Clare A 4:04:44 (12,140)
Murray, Diane 4:48:27 (23,659)
Murray, Erin Helen Marie 4:49:00 (23,800)
Murray, Gemma Ellen 3:49:43 (8,150)
Murray, Jacqueline 4:50:51 (24,254)
Murray, Julie Anne 5:25:50 (30,758)
Murray, Karen D 4:19:47 (16,038)
Murray, Kelly 4:20:38 (16,314)
Murray, Lily 3:47:00 (7,524)
Murray, Marsha 4:17:10 (15,339)
Murray, Rachel 4:51:15 (24,366)
Murray, Victoria E 5:07:17 (27,766)
Murrell, Philippa Jane 4:16:12 (15,071)
Murrieta, Gabriela 4:09:18 (13,283)
Murtagh, Sara Josephine 4:33:06 (19,727)
Muscutt, Claire Marie 4:57:35 (25,875)
Mushington, Jilly 6:33:19 (35,606)
Musk, Hannah C 4:05:56 (12,440)
Musk, Heather 5:31:21 (31,455)
Musk, Jayde Thérèse 6:26:48 (35,376)
Musselle, Kim L 4:11:46 (13,928)
Mussett, Kaye 4:16:17 (15,099)
Musson, Sally M 3:05:21 (1,487)
Muttitt, Christine J 4:45:30 (22,884)
Muxworthy, Anja J 3:58:11 (10,449)

Muxworthy, Katy 4:49:45 (23,994)
Muzumara-Zulu, Sarah 6:41:22 (35,818)
Myburgh, Elresia 6:12:12 (34,768)
Mycock, Corinne 5:41:07 (32,497)
Myles, Jenny 6:29:35 (35,480)
Myles, Nikki 6:20:43 (35,154)
Myron, Colleen 3:40:53 (6,306)
Naing, Claire L 3:20:12 (2,979)
Nairn, Karen 5:52:49 (33,569)
Naisbitt, Holly 6:24:00 (35,277)
Naisby, Wendy Louise Sanger 5:03:31 (27,104)
Nakamura, Motoko 5:00:29 (26,551)
Namagembe, Edith 6:30:38 (35,523)

Nandra, Kirat K 4:31:59 (19,428)

Back in 1997 I met someone who was training for the London Marathon. I was in absolute awe and never thought a few years down the line I too would be running the Marathon. My first was in 1999 and since then I have successfully completed eight of them. I hope to keep going until I am not physically able. Each one is different: the weather, the pain, the emotions. But one thing has remained constant since I first crossed that start line: the crowds. The support and encouragement they give is outstanding. Every time I run the route I am reminded of what a wonderful, diverse city we live in. So far I have raised over £27,000 for charities, all non-government funded. This gives me the motivation I need if I start to have images of stopping. Running marathons is one of the most rewarding things I have ever done. Long may it continue.

Nanni, Debora 4:30:53 (19,185)
Napier-Wright, Minnie 6:12:10 (34,766)
Nash, Beverley Jayne 6:07:01 (34,507)
Nash, Emma 5:49:37 (33,294)
Nash, Kerry 6:11:30 (34,721)
Nash, Nicola Anne 5:21:07 (30,021)
Nash,, Laura, Frances 6:39:32 (35,772)
Nathalie, Kerjean 4:05:14 (12,263)
Nathwani, Nishi 5:10:31 (28,331)
Natoff, Hilary 5:54:46 (33,691)
Naughton, Eileen 5:28:08 (31,045)
Naughton, Suzanna 7:06:44 (36,277)
Navarro, Georgina 5:59:17 (34,008)
Navin, Shauna 4:27:31 (18,241)
Navyte, Ruta 4:49:04 (23,820)
Naylor, Gabbi 4:32:52 (19,661)
Naylor, Lorraine 4:41:44 (21,948)
Neal, Caroline 4:25:37 (17,694)
Neal, Jennifer Stella 3:45:40 (7,242)
Neal, Karen J 5:23:54 (30,458)
Neale, Georgia 7:22:12 (36,420)
Neale, Lisa 5:27:54 (31,011)
Neale, Lisa Louise 5:12:09 (28,591)
Neary, Helen P 3:53:09 (8,955)
Neave, Jayne 4:02:24 (11,580)
Nedimovic, Shelley 6:02:30 (34,217)
Need, Elizabeth Susan 4:14:14 (14,579)
Needes, Claire V 4:09:37 (13,375)
Needham, Fiona 4:37:25 (20,850)
Needham, Lindsay J 3:55:59 (9,779)
Needham, Rhiannon 4:38:44 (21,182)
Needham, Sue J 4:29:00 (18,686)
Neenan, Jacqueline 4:59:28 (26,326)
Neighbour, Laura Mary 3:48:20 (7,814)
Neighbour, Susan 5:05:05 (27,382)
Neill, Fiona Louise 3:54:25 (9,304)
Neill, Paula K 4:17:40 (15,487)
Neilson, Christine M 3:44:35 (7,008)
Neimantas, Linda 4:42:16 (22,084)
Neita, Kathleen Ann 5:50:40 (33,400)
Neligan, Fiona C 3:59:32 (10,870)
Nelson, Jayne 6:41:34 (35,820)
Nelson, Kelli 4:45:38 (22,927)
Nelson, Rachel H 4:52:20 (24,647)
Nelson Rhodes, Julie 5:42:14 (32,613)
Neocleous, Julia 4:34:16 (20,062)
Nesa, Elena 3:28:33 (4,152)
Nesbitt, Jess 6:23:57 (35,275)
Ness, Joanna L 4:23:27 (17,090)
Ness, Vanessa 5:33:17 (31,692)
Nethercott, Dairine C 4:55:20 (25,390)
Nettle, Anna V 3:39:03 (5,950)
Neufville, Gillian 5:28:55 (31,141)
Neumann, Amy Elizabeth 4:19:05 (15,869)
Neusch, Frederique 4:16:20 (15,120)
Neville, Clare 4:49:06 (23,831)
Neville, Clare Louise 4:48:59 (23,797)
Neville, Stephanie Francis 4:39:19 (21,334)
New, Julie Rae 5:24:24 (30,540)
New, Rosa 4:37:37 (20,910)
Newberry, Dorothy 5:21:25 (30,064)
Newbould, Roseanne 4:46:05 (23,055)
Newbury, Colette Elizabeth May 4:58:42 (26,144)
Newbury, Stephanie Ivy Jane 6:27:23 (35,398)
Newby, Michelle 4:15:08 (14,816)
Newby, Nancy 5:19:30 (29,772)
Newby, Sheila 4:57:53 (25,944)
Newcombe, Elizabeth 4:59:13 (26,267)
Newell, Alex 6:26:28 (35,363)
Newhouse, Ruth 5:10:18 (28,288)
Newman, Angela 5:19:31 (29,775)
Newman, Fay Elizabeth 5:55:05 (33,726)
Newman, Gill 4:34:14 (20,054)
Newman, Jenny 5:27:42 (30,988)
Newman, Jenny 6:15:09 (34,896)
Newman, Judith 4:51:28 (24,411)
Newman, Louise 7:41:18 (36,530)
Newman, Maria Theresa 4:55:17 (25,378)
Newman, Michelle Elizabeth 6:34:33 (35,644)
Newman, Ruth 4:24:06 (17,260)
Newman, Sarah L 3:32:43 (4,847)
Newman, Stephanie 5:44:49 (32,850)
Newman, Tracey 3:31:48 (4,708)
Newman, Vanessa 5:25:37 (30,713)
Newson, Marian Elizabeth 5:12:32 (28,659)
Newson, Stacey J 6:22:57 (35,235)
Newson, Tracey 5:31:26 (31,468)
Newstead, Julie 3:56:57 (10,071)
Newton, Christine Carmel 5:11:47 (28,518)
Newton, Donna Michelle 6:50:22 (36,005)
Newton, Joanne Louise 5:24:53 (30,600)
Newton, Louise Elena 4:12:35 (14,120)
Newton, Lynda J 6:10:03 (34,668)
Newton, Pauline Anne 4:08:30 (13,085)
Newton-Fisher, Naomi 5:41:46 (32,561)
Ngeow, Teresa 4:40:20 (21,587)
Nicholas, Katie 4:51:20 (24,381)
Nicholas, Rhian Josephine 7:18:52 (36,393)
Nicholas, Sarah 4:52:35 (24,704)
Nicholl, Naomi Ann 4:41:45 (21,952)
Nicholls, Alison H 6:19:16 (35,094)
Nicholls, Amber 4:46:15 (23,109)
Nicholls, Kathryn 4:00:53 (11,211)
Nicholls, Louise 5:35:28 (31,926)
Nicholls, Maddy 5:23:06 (30,320)
Nicholls, Yvonne L 3:57:08 (10,138)
Nicholls-Kuhn, Natalie 4:44:18 (22,591)
Nichols, Claire L 5:01:13 (26,685)
Nichols, Lisa 6:08:01 (34,561)
Nichols, Naomi 5:40:46 (32,454)
Nicholson, Becky 6:06:13 (34,466)
Nicholson, Hannah Louise 3:57:28 (10,221)
Nicholson, Jeanette Trudie 4:23:52 (17,205)
Nicholson, Joanne 4:28:33 (18,539)
Nicholson, Katie 4:11:50 (13,940)
Nicholson, Nichola Georgina 3:53:17 (8,993)
Nicholson, Nikki Jayne 5:51:20 (33,453)
Nicklin, Samantha 6:25:08 (35,315)
Nicol, Gail 4:56:48 (25,720)
Nicol, Paula M 3:18:14 (2,799)
Nicolai, Susan T 5:09:50 (28,205)
Nicolaides, Caroline Francis 6:44:21 (35,894)
Nicolaou, Nikoletta 5:36:41 (32,072)
Nicoll, Elizabeth 4:37:17 (20,813)
Nielsen, Daisy Bruun 4:30:42 (19,148)
Nielsen, Helle 4:28:36 (18,548)
Nielsen, Ilga 4:42:34 (22,151)
Nielsen, Wendy 4:23:18 (17,044)
Nielsen, Zannah 4:18:43 (15,778)
Nieuwenhuis, Victoria Rose 4:39:42 (21,436)
Nightingale, Laura 4:33:57 (19,980)
Nightingale, Rachel 4:46:56 (23,288)
Nikopoulos, Rosie 4:47:14 (23,349)
Nilsson, Ulla 4:48:29 (23,666)
Nilsson, Yvonne 5:22:17 (30,189)
Nippard, Kaye Margaret 4:24:22 (17,346)
Niven, Frances 4:25:23 (17,629)
Niven, Sandra C 6:37:25 (35,711)
Niven, Stephanie 4:25:23 (17,629)
Nixon, Ruth 4:26:19 (17,904)
N'Jie, Susan 4:25:09 (17,560)
Nkiessu-Guifo, Isabel 6:38:28 (35,740)
Noakes, Charlotte Jane 4:06:34 (12,591)
Noakes, Emma Jane 4:31:09 (19,254)
Noble, Anne 4:36:47 (20,680)
Noble, Beverley M 4:02:42 (11,650)
Noble, Eileen R 5:48:44 (33,219)
Noble, Katy 4:23:03 (16,994)
Noble, Linda 3:28:04 (4,070)
Noble, Louise M 4:55:56 (25,520)
Noble, Toni E 3:23:09 (3,313)
Nobles, Margaret 4:40:18 (21,574)
Nodder, Jane C 3:37:14 (5,605)
Noel, Deborah A 3:42:18 (6,562)
Noel, Marina 6:04:51 (34,374)
Noel, Maureen E 3:34:51 (5,220)
Nolan, Christina Mary 5:14:58 (29,061)
Nolan, Jacqueline 6:01:37 (34,163)
Nolan, Louise 4:53:55 (25,027)
Nolan-Blair, Mary 4:26:05 (17,837)
Noon, Jaqueline 4:21:49 (16,643)
Noone, Zita 5:48:32 (33,198)
Norbury, Audrey 4:04:24 (12,050)
Norbury, Stephanie 6:49:28 (35,988)
Nordin, Breege J 3:35:51 (5,385)
Nordio, Barbara 3:44:52 (7,071)
Norman, Andrea F 4:21:39 (16,594)
Norman, Carmen 4:58:14 (26,019)
Norman, Emma Marie 5:55:11 (33,732)
Norman, Liz Emma 4:08:53 (13,181)
Norman, Mingma 6:02:53 (34,241)
Norman, Sarah Jane 5:29:47 (31,266)
Normann, Susanne 4:48:49 (23,754)
Norris, Helen 5:41:26 (32,526)
Norris, Joanne 5:50:46 (33,411)
Norris, Louise Jane 4:36:55 (20,719)
Northey-Dennis, Lisa 6:51:00 (36,014)
Norton, Alice 4:00:01 (10,989)
Norton, Charlotte A 4:50:43 (24,211)
Norton, Teresa 4:47:38 (23,449)
Nowak, Maja 4:21:18 (16,490)
Nugent, Michelle 6:13:42 (34,828)
Nugent, Natasha Margaret 4:45:43 (22,955)
Nunn, Claire Louise 5:17:26 (29,463)
Nunn, Hayley Ann 5:09:24 (28,126)
Nunn, Jayne Ann 4:20:25 (16,239)
Nunn, Lucinda 5:44:02 (32,770)

Nunn, Sophia....4:37:50 (20,951)
Nutayakul, Kim....3:33:04 (4,904)
Nutley, Mary E....4:33:11 (19,757)
Nutt, Joanne....4:14:42 (14,715)
Nutt, Tracey Lynn....4:42:23 (22,108)
Nuttall, Tamaryn....5:01:35 (26,772)
Nuytinck, Margareta....3:23:54 (3,420)
Nwulu, Onyinye....4:26:07 (17,848)
Oakes, Kathleen Mary....5:36:58 (32,098)
Oakes, Zoe....4:08:54 (13,185)
Oakley, Karen I....4:46:16 (23,118)
Oakley, Marion M....6:49:15 (35,983)
Oakley, Samantha....5:11:24 (28,467)
Oakley, Xenia Sara....5:01:27 (26,744)
Oakman, Annette....3:07:27 (1,647)
Oakshott, Cheryl E....3:16:00 (2,556)
Oaten, Mary Rose....5:24:17 (30,522)
Oates, Claire....3:49:37 (8,122)
Oatham, Jilly Patricia....5:58:48 (33,979)
Obanos, Carmen....4:09:23 (13,304)
Obeney, Sue Jessica....4:45:56 (23,009)
Obersky, Renae....3:32:59 (4,891)
O'Brien, Katie Laura....4:50:51 (24,254)
O'Brien, Nina Clare....3:44:44 (7,042)
O'Brien, Tracy Anne....5:46:35 (33,013)
O'Brien, Yesmin....4:27:54 (18,339)
O'Brien, Zoe....4:50:47 (24,234)
O'Callaghan, Clarissa Jacinthe....5:32:43 (31,635)
O'Callaghan, Jane....4:42:25 (22,115)
O'Callaghan, Sara Jane....4:14:33 (14,665)
O'Carroll, Aynsley....3:48:04 (7,753)
Ockenden, Louise....6:00:57 (34,127)
Ockendon, Ana M....3:29:35 (4,339)
Ockwell, Jacquelyn Anne....5:44:39 (32,834)
Oconaill, Sorcha M....4:30:50 (19,176)
O'Connell, Helen....3:21:14 (3,114)
O'Connell, Pamela....7:36:56 (36,504)
O'Connor, Ann....6:09:36 (34,639)
O'Connor, Breda....5:00:39 (26,579)
O'Connor, Cara....4:22:39 (16,892)
O'Connor, Corinna P....4:16:52 (15,261)
O'Connor, Helen....7:09:56 (36,305)
O'Connor, Mandy Rosemary....6:03:32 (34,292)
O'Connor, Rachel Elizabeth....3:50:16 (8,264)
O'Connor, Sharon A....4:12:29 (14,097)
O'Connor Anderson, Kishka-Kaye....4:13:24 (14,335)
Oczeretnyj, Helen Anne....4:18:18 (15,661)
Odd, Verity....7:27:34 (36,456)
Oddie, Elaine....7:05:46 (36,263)
Oddy-Goodin, Sloane Walford....4:18:10 (15,621)
Odenbreit, Natalie....4:26:56 (18,062)
Oder, Anneliese....5:13:45 (28,880)
O'Donnell, Annie Victoria....5:02:22 (26,919)
O'Donnell, Teresa Jayne....4:32:46 (19,622)
O'Donoghue, Amanda Jane....4:33:32 (19,862)
O'Donoghue, Joan....6:37:06 (35,701)
O'Dowd, Bridie....3:41:50 (6,486)
O'Dwyer, Kerri Anne....4:50:04 (24,064)
O'Dwyer, Valerie J....5:15:47 (29,196)
Odysseos, Androulla....5:55:40 (33,766)
Oelwang, Jean....4:49:04 (23,820)
Oestmann, Nathalie....4:07:32 (12,843)
Offer, Caroline Vernie....4:28:31 (18,528)
Offord, Kelsey A....3:55:15 (9,544)
O'Flanagan, Susan....5:14:13 (28,952)
Ogden, Rosanne Dorothy....5:45:27 (32,904)
Ogier, Coleen Patricia....6:03:16 (34,269)
O'Gorman, Elizabeth A....4:30:34 (19,113)
Oh, Lee-Lee....5:30:07 (31,307)
O'Hagan, Denise M....4:41:01 (21,774)
O'Hagan, Penelope....4:53:40 (24,961)
O'Halloran, Eleanor M....4:11:07 (13,748)
O'Hara, Claire....5:20:28 (29,919)
O'Hara, Pauline J....4:41:01 (21,774)
O'Hare, Megan Rachel....6:54:59 (36,113)
O'Hare, Suzanne M....4:28:23 (18,478)
Ojeda Triulzi, Gabriela....3:57:58 (10,370)
O'Keefe, Helen....5:36:14 (32,021)
O'Keeffe, Clare Elizabeth....4:04:13 (12,012)
O'Keeffe, Sophie....4:20:14 (16,173)
O'Keeffe-Mol, Yvonne M....4:39:36 (21,411)
Okello, Dolores Brigid....4:14:29 (14,643)
Okorie, Tatiana....5:00:53 (26,629)
Okoye, Ginika S....4:34:26 (20,104)
Old, Kim Theresa Mary....6:18:08 (35,037)
Old, Lauren....4:38:55 (21,235)
Old, Tracy....4:42:40 (22,176)
Oldershaw, Tina J....2:58:43 (1,022)
Oldfield, Anna Marie....4:09:17 (13,279)
Oldfield, Lisa Jane....4:25:51 (17,768)
Oldham, Michelle....3:23:42 (3,394)
Oldham, Nicola....4:17:19 (15,380)
Oldham, Nicola S....3:29:03 (4,238)
Oldland, Gretchen Lynn....4:33:33 (19,867)
Olds, Denise....4:32:50 (19,649)
Oldwood, Charlotte A....3:59:16 (10,799)
O'Leary, Eimear Marie....3:54:21 (9,294)
O'Leary, Zoe....5:58:40 (33,972)
O'Leary-Steele, Catherine Ann....3:52:01 (8,663)
Olexa, Anne Grace....3:59:14 (10,791)
Oliphant, Claire M....4:35:00 (20,234)
Oliver, Amanda....4:36:31 (20,611)
Oliver, Jan....4:07:25 (12,804)
Oliver, Jane....4:04:33 (12,076)
Oliver, Karen....5:09:44 (28,185)
Oliver, Karen....5:39:29 (32,344)
Oliver, Kirstine....5:26:52 (30,884)
Oliver, Lynn....4:23:35 (17,133)
Oliver, Lynne Michelle....4:40:13 (21,543)
Oliver, Pippa....4:34:06 (20,022)
Oliver, Stacey....5:30:26 (31,341)
Olliffe, Sarah Louise....5:57:26 (33,896)
Ollis, Jan Rosemary....4:11:41 (13,905)
Olofsson, Sofia Magdalena Marie....4:27:13 (18,157)
O'Malley, Lynn Marie....5:56:38 (33,839)
Onckule, Dagnija....5:01:16 (26,699)
O'Neil, Jennifer E....3:26:36 (3,818)
O'Neil, Jill C....3:31:04 (4,589)
O'Neill, Alison....4:50:46 (24,231)
O'Neill, Clare Tracey....4:23:58 (17,229)
O'Neill, Emma....6:04:10 (34,330)
O'Neill, Ivana M....3:14:34 (2,391)
O'Neill, Katherine....6:44:04 (35,885)
O'Neill, Rebecca....4:21:39 (16,594)
Onion, Sophie Jane....4:38:22 (21,078)
Onions, Helen....4:47:22 (23,384)
Onn, Sally....3:04:50 (1,451)
Opie-Smith, Katherine....4:35:55 (20,453)
Oppliger, Anne-Françoise....5:03:26 (27,090)
Opstrup, Vibeke Holmann....4:19:12 (15,898)
Orban, Mary B....5:00:09 (26,491)
O'Reilly, Natalie....3:50:01 (8,213)
O'Reilly, Sharon....4:37:37 (20,910)
O'Reily, Una Marie....4:59:54 (26,431)
Orman, Katie R....5:48:01 (33,140)
Ormiston Smith, Kate Helen....4:26:56 (18,062)
O'Rourke, Mairead A....3:16:33 (2,623)
Orphanou, Angela....6:22:17 (35,204)
Orr, Allison....4:38:26 (21,099)
Orr, Lucy....4:36:48 (20,682)
Orrell, Megan Natalie....4:31:45 (19,384)
Orrin, Zoe Denise....5:52:06 (33,508)
Orth, Barbara....4:01:19 (11,315)
Osborn, Claire Louise....4:46:34 (23,185)
Osborn, Kathryn Charmaine....4:49:21 (23,884)
Osborn, Sascha Caroline....3:49:27 (8,078)
Osborne, Fiona Maria....5:30:26 (31,341)
Osborne, Sarah....4:41:24 (21,867)
Osei-Owusu, Genevieve....4:52:36 (24,706)
Oseman, Rebecca J....4:46:59 (23,304)
O'Shaughnessy, Anna....6:16:48 (34,964)
O'Shaughnessy, Stacey Ann....7:41:53 (36,533)
O'Shea, Hazel Dawn....4:20:08 (16,145)
O'Shea, Zoe....5:05:39 (27,473)
Osleger, Jill....4:26:45 (18,011)
Osmond, Sacha Rae....4:18:23 (15,686)
Ostensson, Pia....4:48:52 (23,765)
Osterberger, Diana Jane....4:58:19 (26,045)
Ostrehan, Bridget L....4:22:12 (16,761)
Ostrowski, Ann Elizabeth....5:46:25 (32,998)
O'Sullivan, Catherine....3:52:21 (8,755)
O'Sullivan, Claire....5:20:16 (29,886)
O'Sullivan, Elaine J....3:27:56 (4,044)
O'Sullivan, Maureen Norah....6:13:03 (34,808)
O'Sullivan, Rachel Louise....6:16:48 (34,964)
O'Sullivan, Ros....3:42:31 (6,600)
Otache, Joy....4:14:40 (14,706)
Othen, Vanessa....5:32:54 (31,653)
O'Toole, Helen C....5:30:07 (31,307)
O'Toole, Karen Pamela....4:17:56 (15,557)
Oulding, Alison E....6:04:36 (34,355)
Outten, Nicola....6:37:06 (35,701)
Ovenden, Marie Louise Spalding5:07:29 (27,808)
Overall, Julie Ann....6:19:31 (35,103)
Overall, Sarah Joan....5:24:23 (30,538)
Overs, Liz....4:06:21 (12,539)
Owen, Alison....5:22:35 (30,237)
Owen, Debbie....5:24:59 (30,622)
Owen, Gwawr....4:54:43 (25,234)
Owen, Helen Sarah Louise....5:06:19 (27,590)
Owen, Jane Elizabeth....4:31:07 (19,245)
Owen, Lisa Jane Cathrine....4:26:15 (17,893)
Owen, Lucy....3:47:09 (7,556)
Owen, Mary Bridget....5:19:07 (29,721)
Owen, Maureen Elizabeth....4:57:22 (25,834)
Owen, Nicky C....4:07:21 (12,787)
Owen, Rebecca Mary....5:00:13 (26,502)
Owens, Paula....4:20:38 (16,314)
Owens, Susan Anne....4:00:55 (11,225)
Oxenbury, Maggie Mary....4:48:14 (23,593)
Oxley, Demelza R....4:04:48 (12,153)
Oxley, Kelly....5:01:35 (26,772)
Oxley, Lucy....4:26:43 (18,003)
Ozaki, Mari....2:25:43 (41)
Ozaki, Yoshimi....2:32:26 (87)
Ozier, Patricia Maria....4:16:52 (15,261)
Ozmen, Emi Lucy....6:12:11 (34,767)
Pabon, Laura....5:29:16 (31,184)
Pacey, Deborah Jane....5:09:51 (28,209)
Pacheco, Teresa Mary....7:43:05 (36,538)
Packham, Joanna....6:23:37 (35,261)
Packwood, Beverley A....4:21:02 (16,425)
Padbury, Liesl Glennie....6:02:17 (34,204)
Paddon, Alison....4:32:11 (19,483)
Padgett, Alison Dawn....4:24:20 (17,333)
Padrock, Doris....3:25:12 (3,607)
Page, Claire....4:14:33 (14,665)
Page, Clare V....3:30:12 (4,450)
Page, Jackeline Carol....6:03:43 (34,302)
Page, Kate....5:07:50 (27,866)
Page, Katherine....4:44:04 (22,523)
Page, Kelly T....3:52:27 (8,777)
Page, Laura....4:01:37 (11,396)
Pagnossin, Francesca....6:11:15 (34,712)
Paice, Melanie....4:17:20 (15,386)
Paige, Lisa....4:45:18 (22,841)
Paine, Samantha Jane....4:49:20 (23,879)
Painter, Emma....5:00:42 (26,587)
Pais-Atherton, Patricia Yara....5:05:14 (27,411)
Palfreman, Eleanor Marie....4:29:23 (18,773)
Palfrey Evans, Natasha E....6:00:40 (34,101)
Palin, Carol A....4:05:45 (12,395)
Pallot, Emma Caroline....4:22:13 (16,772)
Palmer, Alice....5:45:16 (32,890)
Palmer, Alison....5:27:53 (31,010)
Palmer, Amanda Rosemary....5:01:14 (26,689)
Palmer, Amy Elizabath....5:59:01 (33,989)
Palmer, Carol L....4:22:21 (16,804)
Palmer, Elaine S....4:28:31 (18,528)
Palmer, Gayle Diana....5:13:33 (28,849)
Palmer, Ginny....4:02:08 (11,518)
Palmer, Hannah Lesley....5:44:50 (32,851)
Palmer, Helen....5:15:35 (29,161)
Palmer, Julia....3:32:06 (4,759)
Palmer, Katie Emma....4:54:37 (25,209)
Palmer, Lisa A....2:53:16 (627)
Palmer, Nancy....4:41:35 (21,918)
Palmer, Sally....5:40:22 (32,420)
Palmer, Siobhan M....4:16:55 (15,275)
Palmer-Harris, Michelle Dawn....3:43:45 (6,813)
Palombo, Sonja Christine....5:04:37 (27,300)
Panayiotou, Sally June....4:28:19 (18,458)
Panayiotou, Vicky Joy....3:44:03 (6,889)
Panday, Kamala....5:50:30 (33,383)
Pang, Yinsan....5:39:05 (32,310)
Pankhania, Jagruti M....4:22:11 (16,757)
Panther, Charlotte Julia....5:01:27 (26,744)
Panther Knight, Kay....6:03:20 (34,273)
Panto, Amanda Ruth....4:09:47 (13,416)

Paonessa, Carla..................4:01:32 (11,376)
Papageorgiou, Joanna...............5:10:11 (28,275)
Pappas, Susan.....................5:20:32 (29,933)
Paranandi, Caroline...............4:08:40 (13,131)
Pardoe, Elaine....................5:58:24 (33,959)
Pardon, Hannah Louise.............4:49:24 (23,893)
Parfitt, Anna Marie...............4:42:46 (22,206)
Parish, Jennie....................3:59:20 (10,818)
Park, Ailsa.......................4:13:58 (14,496)
Park, Jane........................4:16:09 (15,060)
Parke, Hannah.....................4:16:22 (15,130)
Parker, Angela....................5:12:34 (28,664)
Parker, Caroline M................4:47:30 (23,411)
Parker, Elizabeth Helen...........4:43:47 (22,436)
Parker, Jenny Megan...............4:51:57 (24,538)
Parker, Jo........................6:11:54 (34,748)
Parker, Julie.....................5:49:52 (33,322)
Parker, Linda L...................4:52:59 (24,791)
Parker, Louise....................5:46:00 (32,951)
Parker, Lynsey....................6:10:01 (34,665)
Parker, Pamela Margaret Anne......5:07:46 (27,857)
Parker, Patricia A................4:07:58 (12,953)
Parker, Ruth......................3:55:56 (9,760)
Parker, Sarah Jane................5:48:08 (33,154)
Parker, Shelley Dawn..............5:04:53 (27,346)
Parker, Sioban C..................4:00:56 (11,231)
Parker, Tarnya....................3:37:37 (5,695)
Parker-Smith, Victoria............4:33:44 (19,930)
Parkes, Samantha..................4:28:10 (18,406)
Parkin, Claire Louise.............4:43:43 (22,423)
Parkin, Paula.....................4:59:00 (26,214)
Parkins, Claire M.................4:07:42 (12,887)
Parkinson, Carol..................4:50:43 (24,211)
Parkinson, Clare..................3:58:02 (10,391)
Parkinson, Deirdre................6:05:51 (34,443)
Parkinson, Judith.................4:46:50 (23,270)
Parkinson, Natalie Anne...........5:01:27 (26,744)
Parkyn-Smith, Janine..............5:33:36 (31,727)
Parmar, Nandita Kantilal..........6:20:26 (35,142)
Parmar, Panna.....................6:05:04 (34,386)
Parmenter, Danielle Cherry........4:37:57 (20,977)
Parmley, Hannah Jane..............4:41:24 (21,867)

Parnell, Karen Michelle...........5:15:07 (29,090)

I was lucky enough to get an entry under the ballot so decided to raise money for Herts Air Ambulance. The day was amazing – the support around the course from the supporters was fantastic! The cheers, the well wishes and the hands holding out sugary treats to the runners was really humbling

Parnell, Letitia..................4:19:18 (15,929)
Parnell, Vicki....................6:25:06 (35,309)
Parr, Laura.......................4:00:05 (11,002)
Parrott, Katherine A..............5:28:08 (31,045)
Parry, Alison H...................4:54:15 (25,114)
Parry, Bethan Juliet..............4:39:22 (21,344)
Parry, Elizabeth Jane.............5:54:40 (33,683)
Parry, Janet E....................4:53:25 (24,895)
Parry, Leanne.....................3:52:26 (8,772)
Parry, Rebecca M..................5:00:57 (26,643)
Parry, Sandra Valerie.............4:45:59 (23,018)
Parry, Tracey Anne................5:11:21 (28,458)
Parsloe, Laura....................4:08:07 (12,992)
Parsons, Carol L..................4:40:22 (21,601)
Parsons, Deann....................5:34:41 (31,847)
Parsons, Helen K..................3:57:40 (10,286)
Parsons, Helen W..................4:52:47 (24,751)
Parsons, Jade Joanne Louise.......5:25:16 (30,658)
Parsons, Joanne Dawn..............5:01:21 (26,724)
Parsons, Lesley Anne..............6:02:52 (34,240)
Parsons, Patricia C...............4:41:49 (21,977)
Parsons, Sarah Jane...............5:10:45 (28,366)
Partel, Pille.....................5:10:10 (28,270)
Partin, Anna......................4:54:35 (25,199)
Partington, Olivia Rose...........3:43:49 (6,835)
Partland, Liz.....................5:12:09 (28,591)
Partner, Caroline Debra...........5:11:27 (28,475)
Parton, Catharine Mary............6:17:50 (35,025)
Partridge, Anna...................3:57:31 (10,236)

Partridge, Katie..................5:35:58 (31,989)
Partridge, Laura H................6:05:12 (34,402)
Partridge, Sue....................2:35:57 (126)
Pascal, Rebecca...................6:39:38 (35,775)
Pascall, Megan....................5:22:49 (30,274)
Pascall, Taryn....................4:56:50 (25,728)
Pascoe, Ann Holley................4:42:49 (22,220)
Pascoe, Heather Louise............5:20:11 (29,875)
Pascoe, Nicky E...................4:49:42 (23,978)
Pascual, Joana Caterina...........3:44:16 (6,928)
Pashley, Jackie Ann...............5:57:19 (33,892)
Pasquet-Noualhaguet, Christine....3:58:04 (10,401)
Pasquini, Stefania................3:49:03 (7,987)
Pastore-Waeber, Fabienne..........4:51:30 (24,421)
Paszkiewicz, Anne-Marie...........6:08:42 (34,596)

Patching, Jacky C.................5:06:48 (27,691)

Blackheath was buzzing and I was so excited that I was about to do what I had dreamt of doing for many years. I was soaking up the atmosphere and trying to store every bit of detail in my head. I had won my place with my club along with 'Best newcomer' and felt very lucky to be standing with the other thousands of runners. We were off, the crowds willing me along, something I will never forget. Total strangers calling at me. I saw my family twice on route, which was fantastic but emotional. I got to mile 26 and realised that was it, it was nearly over! I sprinted down The Mall, arms in the air. I had done it. I was on a high for the whole week. I felt great and so proud that I had just fulfilled my dream.

Patching, Katrina.................6:22:04 (35,199)
Patel, Bakula.....................5:39:53 (32,375)
Patel, Bhavini....................4:36:23 (20,573)
Patel, Garima.....................8:29:06 (36,604)
Patel, Harsita....................5:17:02 (29,393)
Patel, Hetal......................6:29:08 (35,466)
Patel, Jackie.....................4:33:33 (19,867)
Patel, Manisha....................5:44:59 (32,868)
Patel, Meena......................6:35:38 (35,669)
Patel, Nayna......................4:33:17 (19,801)
Patel, Neena Vijaykumar...........6:35:37 (35,668)
Patel, Rachna.....................5:56:06 (33,795)
Patel, Rachna Haren...............4:14:18 (14,595)
Patel, Raksha.....................5:09:06 (28,067)
Patel, Samanthi...................4:56:50 (25,728)
Patel, Sarb.......................6:51:44 (36,032)
Patel, Seema......................4:22:36 (16,875)
Patel, Shivani PD.................5:19:05 (29,714)
Patel, Sonal J....................7:18:49 (36,392)

Patel, Yashma.....................6:34:05 (35,626)
Paternoster, Michaela.............5:38:39 (32,279)
Paterson, Ailsa...................6:06:28 (34,480)
Paterson, Emma....................4:33:54 (19,970)
Paterson, Fiona...................5:10:06 (28,256)
Paterson, Fiona Wendy.............4:40:59 (21,767)
Paterson, Gail M..................4:21:53 (16,664)
Paterson, Jacqueline..............5:25:16 (30,658)
Paterson, Joanna..................5:33:09 (31,682)
Paterson, Kelly...................4:07:31 (12,837)
Paterson, Lynsey..................4:36:28 (20,591)
Paterson, Susan...................4:45:09 (22,806)
Paterson, Victoria T..............4:32:53 (19,669)
Patience, Nikki...................3:55:56 (9,760)
Patmore, Tracey M.................2:58:10 (971)
Paton, Abigail M..................3:45:43 (7,249)
Paton, Karen Rosalind.............4:06:31 (12,578)
Paton, Kim........................4:23:21 (17,060)
Patrick, Hester M.................6:15:52 (34,921)
Patten, Fiona.....................5:23:15 (30,347)
Pattern, Leanne Sara..............5:47:55 (33,129)
Patterson, Charlotte..............5:24:21 (30,531)
Patterson, Cleopatra..............6:53:08 (36,074)
Patterson, Helen..................5:04:34 (27,291)
Patterson, Julie..................5:47:13 (33,071)
Patterson, Karen..................3:48:40 (7,890)
Patterson, Karen..................4:49:54 (24,030)
Patterson, Marie-Anne Ellen.......5:19:48 (29,823)
Patterson, Susie..................4:30:31 (19,091)
Pattison, Amanda L................3:48:39 (7,884)
Pattison, Deborah.................4:14:43 (14,719)
Paul, Carol.......................4:27:03 (18,097)
Paul, Jacqueline..................5:11:40 (28,494)
Paul, Karen Jane..................5:05:28 (27,443)
Paul, Sarah Amanda................6:32:27 (35,575)
Paul, Wendy Marion................5:14:49 (29,039)
Paulin, Mari-Louise...............5:55:40 (33,766)
Pauzers, Clare C..................3:11:23 (2,036)
Paver, Amanda.....................4:02:44 (11,662)
Pavlovic, Elizabeth...............4:16:00 (15,026)
Pavord, Anna Nadine...............6:06:12 (34,465)
Pawar, Sonia Kaur.................6:22:24 (35,205)
Pawson, Elizabeth.................4:44:56 (22,751)
Pay, Faye.........................4:51:48 (24,492)
Payaniandy, Louise................5:15:29 (29,143)
Payne, Amanda Langston............4:33:14 (19,778)
Payne, Anne-Marie.................5:43:41 (32,739)
Payne, Catherine Patricia.........4:49:50 (24,017)
Payne, Daphne.....................5:50:01 (33,337)
Payne, Emma Louise................5:48:44 (33,219)
Payne, Janet M....................4:30:32 (19,098)
Payne, Joanna Margaret............5:14:58 (29,061)
Payne, Karen......................4:50:48 (24,238)
Payne, Kim A......................5:09:06 (28,067)
Payne, Laura Juliet...............4:58:06 (25,986)
Payne, Lucy.......................4:01:48 (11,448)
Payne, Mandy Jane.................7:02:34 (36,221)
Payne, Pauline Ann................3:38:15 (5,813)
Payne, Sarah Anne.................4:59:33 (26,353)
Payne, Susan......................3:58:16 (10,478)
Payter, Harriet...................5:12:47 (28,699)
Payton, Emma......................4:35:20 (20,301)
Payton, Lisa......................6:29:34 (35,478)
Peace, Mel........................4:53:13 (24,853)
Peace, Natalie Rachel.............4:27:29 (18,229)
Peacock, Jill.....................4:56:58 (25,761)
Peacock, Samantha Clare...........5:20:23 (29,897)
Pearce, Alison....................4:56:30 (25,646)
Pearce, Devon.....................6:04:40 (34,363)
Pearce, Jo........................3:32:47 (4,855)
Pearce, Julie Kathryn.............4:47:07 (23,329)
Pearce, Kate E....................4:32:28 (19,553)
Pearce, Lynette...................5:18:53 (29,679)
Pearce, Rachel Kate...............4:55:28 (25,405)
Pearce, Sally Jane................4:12:26 (14,078)
Pearce, Sarah.....................5:09:06 (28,067)
Pearce-Gray, Hayley...............6:17:14 (34,992)
Pearce-Higgins, Lisa..............3:49:02 (7,983)
Pearcy, Julie S...................4:56:26 (25,635)
Pearsall, Hannah..................4:02:49 (11,677)
Pearson, Amanda J.................5:06:14 (27,573)
Pearson, Jennifer Margaret........6:10:19 (34,678)
Pearson, Joanne...................6:10:54 (34,695)

Pearson, Karen 5:12:08 (28,590)
Pearson, Kerri 5:11:50 (28,528)
Pearson, Lynn 5:46:48 (33,032)
Pearson, Samantha 6:22:51 (35,227)
Pearson, Sarah 3:44:35 (7,008)
Pearson, Vivienne Ray 5:43:03 (32,670)
Pearson, Zoe 4:56:18 (25,611)
Peart, Lisa A. 4:22:45 (16,918)
Pease, Catherine Alice 5:00:26 (26,543)
Peasgood, Teresa J. 3:31:30 (4,669)
Peck, Gillian 3:49:50 (8,169)
Peck, Lisa Anne 6:05:40 (34,430)
Peck, Rita 4:11:02 (13,726)
Peckett, Jennifer 6:37:49 (35,720)
Pedroso, Angelica 4:54:47 (25,255)
Peel, Lucy Emma 4:14:36 (14,680)
Peel, Rebecca 5:56:54 (33,859)
Peeters, Sue M. 3:55:12 (9,528)
Pegna, Victoria 4:41:29 (21,887)
Pegrum, Louise 4:18:53 (15,822)
Pell, Valerie 4:12:39 (14,139)
Pellaton, Anne 4:27:55 (18,347)
Pellet Ward, Natalie Erin 4:17:48 (15,527)
Pellington-Woodrow, Laura 4:50:20 (24,123)
Pellissier, Joelle 5:23:17 (30,354)
Peltier, Sarah 3:56:46 (10,021)
Pemberton, Maria 4:31:11 (19,266)
Penberthy, Carol A. 4:31:45 (19,384)

Pender, Mary E. 6:57:49 (36,155)

The days leading up to the London Marathon were filled with news of volcanic ash from Iceland filling the skies. Travel plans were in chaos so we had air and boat tickets organised. We made it to London by air and enjoyed a terrific marathon, walking the route in just under 7 hours, approaching the finish line to the sound of 'Time to Say Goodbye' on the loudspeakers. We walked on to the hotel, showered and made our way to the overnight boat on the evening train. We made it back home just in time for work on Monday morning. An excellent marathon through the streets and another marathon to get home! What a lovely way to celebrate being well again and 'nifty at fifty'.

Pender, Patricia 6:57:48 (36,154)
Penfold, Amanda C. 3:51:25 (8,518)
Penfold, Ellie Amelia 7:35:41 (36,491)
Penfold, Emma-Jane 4:53:31 (24,925)
Penfold, Wendy 5:48:04 (33,146)
Pengelly, Nicola Ann 5:22:20 (30,197)

Penman, Julie 5:38:08 (32,219)
Penman, Kloey 6:44:00 (35,884)
Penman, Linda A. 4:32:45 (19,619)
Penman, Yvette Lynne 6:35:08 (35,654)
Penn, Katherine Rachel 5:46:21 (32,989)
Penn, Rachel A. 4:10:58 (13,703)
Penn, Rebecca 4:59:58 (26,442)
Penney, Denise M. 6:09:49 (34,651)
Penney, Moira Kathryn 5:08:20 (27,954)
Pennington, Erika Sachel 3:48:05 (7,754)
Penny, Joanna Sarah 4:29:02 (18,697)
Penny, Terri 6:13:40 (34,827)
Pennycook, Natalie 7:13:18 (36,340)
Penrose, Katherine M. 4:28:28 (18,512)
Penrose, Katie 3:26:58 (3,872)
Penton, Emma 6:32:07 (35,568)
Penty, Becky 2:42:07 (256)
Peoples, Amanda P. 4:12:23 (14,067)
Pepper, Deborah A. 5:46:38 (33,019)
Perasole, Tina 5:09:04 (28,058)
Percival, Chantal 4:28:37 (18,557)
Percival, Francesa 4:32:41 (19,602)
Percox, Lisa J. 4:14:58 (14,773)
Perdios, Eliana Andrea 6:44:10 (35,887)
Perera, Helen A. 3:53:03 (8,936)
Perez, Karla 5:04:25 (27,262)
Perhar, Sophie Rebecca 5:21:55 (30,132)
Peri, Katy 4:28:51 (18,625)
Pering, Nicola-Jane 5:57:26 (33,896)
Perkins, Davina Rachael 3:54:17 (9,279)
Perkins, Heather 4:12:14 (14,039)
Perkins, Mitch 3:54:50 (9,431)
Perkins, Nicola Marie 5:43:58 (32,763)
Perkins, Sian 5:04:41 (27,315)
Perkins, Suzanne Jane 4:45:09 (22,806)
Perks, Charlie 5:27:20 (30,944)
Perman, Beth Anna Constance ...4:18:38 (15,753)
Perrett, Shirley 4:45:55 (23,005)
Perriman, Jacqui A. 4:19:28 (15,963)
Perrins, Jennifer J. 5:27:30 (30,966)
Perrins, Louise 3:31:52 (4,720)
Perrot, Anne 5:45:59 (32,949)
Perry, Amanda J. 3:48:34 (7,866)
Perry, Caroline 5:00:45 (26,600)
Perry, Caroline A. 4:13:24 (14,335)
Perry, Hannah 5:07:12 (27,752)
Perry, Hannah 6:03:20 (34,273)
Perry, Jayne 4:07:39 (12,871)
Perry, Jude 4:28:14 (18,431)
Perry, Liz 7:04:47 (36,252)
Perry, Paula 4:51:32 (24,426)
Perry, Paula 6:40:20 (35,799)
Perry, Vanessa Elaine 6:03:21 (34,279)
Perry, Victoria A. 2:53:46 (653)
Persey, Clare Victoria 4:10:34 (13,610)
Persson, Malin Helena 4:27:13 (18,157)
Persson, Sointu 4:39:31 (21,391)
Pescod, Anne 4:40:16 (21,565)
Pescod, Mary 6:17:09 (34,989)
Peterhans, Beatrix 5:07:48 (27,860)
Peters, Deirdre Ann 5:01:17 (26,703)
Peters, Sandra Jane 4:40:04 (21,510)
Peters, Wendy 5:35:15 (31,898)
Petersen, Inga 4:28:51 (18,625)
Peterzens, Sofie 4:30:23 (19,061)
Petrie, Donna Dorothy 3:45:11 (7,135)
Petrie, Sarah Elizabeth 5:46:06 (32,961)
Petsopoulos, Heather J. 5:53:41 (33,622)
Pettefer, Sarah Caroline 4:32:25 (19,542)
Pettengell, Tanya 5:35:42 (31,956)
Pettifer, Lorna Eve 4:21:02 (16,425)
Pettifer, Tracy Eve 4:33:46 (19,937)
Pettinger-Brown, Nicola Helen ...4:07:39 (12,871)
Petts, Sarah L. 4:49:55 (24,031)
Petts-Hannant, Gillian 5:37:43 (32,183)
Petty, Stephanie A. 5:26:03 (30,787)
Peyton, Christina Anna 4:36:02 (20,485)
Pez, Tracy J. 3:46:03 (7,322)
Phelan, Sarah M. 3:57:25 (10,206)
Phelan, Victoria Elizabeth 4:51:11 (24,346)
Phelps, Jane Alison 4:34:46 (20,186)
Philips, Sarah Jane 6:55:43 (36,126)
Phillip, Sarah E. 3:56:40 (9,984)

Phillips, Andrea 5:03:42 (27,139)
Phillips, Carol Ann 4:59:56 (26,436)
Phillips, Carole 3:27:28 (3,956)
Phillips, Carrie Louise 4:50:55 (24,279)
Phillips, Catherine 4:33:33 (19,867)
Phillips, Denise 5:37:43 (32,183)
Phillips, Ema Louise 4:33:33 (19,867)
Phillips, Emma 4:05:08 (12,234)
Phillips, Emma 6:39:51 (35,781)
Phillips, Evelyn 4:13:09 (14,275)
Phillips, Hazel 6:01:30 (34,156)
Phillips, Henrietta 4:31:13 (19,274)
Phillips, Jill 3:46:01 (7,313)
Phillips, Karen 4:03:32 (11,854)
Phillips, Lisa 4:34:00 (19,993)
Phillips, Lisa A. 5:27:35 (30,976)
Phillips, Nichola 4:19:57 (16,086)
Phillips, Nicola Ann 4:12:31 (14,103)
Phillips, Nikki Louise 4:48:37 (23,699)
Phillips, Rachael Sarah 4:54:08 (25,075)
Phillips, Rebecca H. 4:26:26 (17,934)
Phillips, Sarah 3:43:51 (6,845)
Phillips, Sarah Rachel 7:15:52 (36,367)
Phillips, Sheridan 5:46:26 (33,002)
Phillips, Sophie Jane 4:28:28 (18,512)
Phillips, Tracy J. 4:38:16 (21,047)
Phillips, Vicky 7:29:26 (36,468)
Phillips, Zoe 3:59:22 (10,827)
Phillipson, Caroline Mary 5:57:33 (33,907)
Phillis, Nicola Lorraine 4:41:16 (21,837)
Philp, Catherine R. 4:09:37 (13,375)
Philp, Lisa 5:51:43 (33,483)
Philpott, Anne Monica 4:40:57 (21,759)
Phippard, Kirstin V. 3:41:16 (6,383)
Phippen, Ginette 5:56:31 (33,831)
Phipps, Katie Elizabeth 4:19:49 (16,045)
Phipps, Lesley Margaret 5:31:30 (31,474)
Phipps, Victoria 6:29:59 (35,500)
Phoenix, Alexa J. 3:45:59 (7,306)
Pickard, Fiona 6:59:16 (36,181)
Pickard, Sally 4:50:45 (24,224)
Picken, Joanne 4:32:39 (19,594)
Pickering, Katherine 6:30:05 (35,503)
Pickering, Tracy 5:06:33 (27,637)
Pickess, Gemma Louise 6:40:07 (35,791)
Pickett, Claire 5:08:22 (27,959)
Pickett, Danica 6:54:34 (36,095)
Pickford, Amanda 4:54:05 (25,067)
Picksley, Mary L. 3:46:53 (7,505)
Pickstock, Kate 4:11:30 (13,848)
Pickup, Jackie 4:46:58 (23,298)
Picton, Alison 5:08:12 (27,929)
Pidgeon, Moira Evelyn 5:00:03 (26,469)
Pienaar, Eleanor Dawn 5:46:50 (33,033)
Pierce, Laura 4:05:01 (12,212)
Pierce, Nicole 6:51:37 (36,028)
Piercy, Alice 5:26:47 (30,870)
Piercy, Claire E. 3:52:32 (8,804)
Piercy, Sharon Jayne 5:59:09 (34,000)
Pigg, Ruth 5:02:59 (27,022)
Piggott, Tracey Marie 4:55:43 (25,472)
Pike, Felicity Anne 4:18:24 (15,689)
Pike, Hazel 4:18:32 (15,722)
Pike, Heather J. 3:44:35 (7,008)
Pike, Joanne Louise 5:05:11 (27,401)
Pilkington, Diana Mary 4:17:42 (15,497)
Pillay, Lorraine 4:26:14 (17,882)
Pilling, Angela M. 5:50:50 (33,413)
Pilling, Dorothy 5:53:36 (33,619)
Pimm, Louise Mary 4:15:57 (15,013)
Pinchbeck, Kathryn Ann 4:48:56 (23,782)
Pinder, Jennie Louise 6:03:57 (34,321)
Pinder, Sandra A. 4:32:00 (19,436)
Pinder, Sophie Victoria 5:18:52 (29,676)
Pinfold, Tracey 4:27:38 (18,270)
Pini, Silvia 4:45:17 (22,835)
Pinner, Joelle Golda 5:58:16 (33,948)
Pinney, Niki 3:45:25 (7,193)
Pinnock, Sally 4:26:09 (17,858)
Pinsent, Vicky Louise 6:27:34 (35,404)
Piotrkowska, Kinga 4:49:34 (23,929)
Piotti, Angiolina 3:15:02 (2,441)
Pires, Michele Luciana 4:51:17 (24,372)

Pirie, Noella Charlotte 5:09:48 (28,196)
Pirie-Stockton, Emma L 5:38:42 (32,284)
Pirrett, Jennifer H 6:58:54 (36,173)
Pisani, Andrea 4:12:37 (14,129)
Pistor, Kirsten Monica.................5:24:48 (30,591)
Pitcher, Lorraine A 5:11:47 (28,518)
Pitkin, Mary 5:51:46 (33,488)
Pitman, Louise 6:12:34 (34,785)
Pitman, Natasha A.......................3:28:25 (4,132)
Pitocco, Deborah Karen 3:27:48 (4,013)
Pitt, Carrie-Ann 5:07:59 (27,891)
Pitt, Charlotte 4:48:24 (23,638)
Pitt, Sally Anne 6:37:20 (35,707)
Pittard, Kim 4:47:37 (23,444)
Pittaway, Jacqui 5:10:22 (28,304)
Pittman, Rebecca M 3:44:24 (6,968)
Pitts, Claire E 4:08:22 (13,049)
Pivkina, Anastassiya...................5:55:21 (33,747)
Pizzasegola, Federica 5:12:46 (28,694)
Plank, Amy 5:29:58 (31,289)
Plant, Jane L 4:15:59 (15,019)
Planteau de Maroussem, Nadine 5:12:39 (28,671)
Platt, Helena Caroline 4:33:56 (19,977)
Platt, Michelle Emma..................6:49:05 (35,979)
Platt, Shirley Margrate................6:20:49 (35,159)
Platts, Rosemary Anne 5:12:57 (28,730)
Playle, Tracy 5:29:17 (31,188)
Plowman, Jacqueline Ann 3:45:51 (7,278)
Plumb, Julia Frances 5:17:05 (29,397)
Plume, Frances Helen..................4:12:50 (14,187)
Plummer, Katharine S..................5:22:34 (30,232)
Plummer, Rebecca Noel 5:57:26 (33,896)
Plumridge, Anna Katherine 4:26:42 (17,998)
Pluves, Sarah Helen 4:38:43 (21,175)
Plyming, Shelly 3:55:49 (9,725)
Pockett, Jo 6:12:35 (34,786)
Pocklington, Nicola Jane 6:07:06 (34,513)
Pocock, Paula Mary....................5:23:37 (30,410)
Podschun, Laura 4:13:32 (14,378)
Podziomek, Sarah 4:17:31 (15,449)
Pohl, Lisa Kim Amy....................4:52:05 (24,568)
Polcz, Sarah 5:10:37 (28,351)
Polius, Leandra 4:46:27 (23,156)
Pollard, Hillary 4:23:22 (17,071)
Pollard, Linda 4:20:42 (16,333)
Pollard, Yvonne 4:44:00 (22,504)
Polley, Elizabeth Jane 4:35:53 (20,439)
Pollington, Lucinda 4:22:57 (16,975)
Pollock, Katrina 5:40:02 (32,392)
Polydorou, Anna 4:57:56 (25,953)
Pomeroy, Claire S.......................4:03:36 (11,874)
Pomeroy, Ros Mary 5:23:13 (30,344)
Pomfret, Mary M 6:18:01 (35,032)
Ponder, Rosamund A 3:11:26 (2,042)
Ponponne, Leanne 5:39:19 (32,332)
Pontefract, Elaine Carrina..........4:46:40 (23,226)
Ponti, Hilary 4:07:51 (12,918)
Ponting, Judith Catherine S 4:26:45 (18,011)
Ponting, Sarah-Louise 5:37:16 (32,138)
Pook, Emma Michelle..................5:52:42 (33,551)
Pook, Tanya J 4:12:13 (14,035)
Pool, Claire 4:58:49 (26,169)
Poole, Julie D..............................6:54:00 (36,086)
Poole, Lucinda 5:47:29 (33,095)
Poole, Madeleine Isobel 5:37:08 (32,120)
Pooles, Kerry 4:11:55 (13,966)
Pooley, Alexandra 6:06:59 (34,505)
Pooley, Beth Abigail 4:29:45 (18,899)
Pope, Catharine 4:14:20 (14,603)
Pope, Emma Louise 4:23:22 (17,071)
Pope, Hazel Jackie 5:09:44 (28,185)
Pope, Kathryn Louise 4:50:55 (24,279)
Pope, Kim 4:14:01 (14,508)
Popham, Lorraine H....................4:36:21 (20,562)
Pople, Kelly Victoria...................4:04:59 (12,200)
Popperwell, Beth E 3:58:13 (10,463)
Porra, Anna 4:04:48 (12,153)
Porritt, Nathalie 5:25:42 (30,732)
Porter, Esther 4:55:33 (25,420)
Porter, Gertrud F........................3:58:54 (10,689)
Porter, Hayley Jane 4:48:07 (23,571)
Porter, Helen 5:23:40 (30,419)
Porter, Holly 5:58:21 (33,954)

Porter, Joanna M 3:35:53 (5,395)
Porter, Kate Mary 5:46:01 (32,954)
Porter, Natasha Estelle................4:55:34 (25,424)
Porter, Sue 4:48:50 (23,758)
Porter, Zoe G 3:41:38 (6,444)
Porthouse, Hayley L....................5:04:07 (27,213)
Portis, Claire Frances..................5:21:39 (30,103)
Posfortunato, Lorenza 4:41:37 (21,927)
Potgieter, Liesl...........................4:03:21 (11,813)
Potter, Alexandra J 3:29:05 (4,244)
Potter, Felicity...........................4:31:27 (19,321)
Potter, Helen L 4:25:02 (17,531)
Potter, Lauren 3:49:51 (8,176)
Potter, Lucy Clare 4:36:42 (20,659)
Potter, Maria 6:36:17 (35,683)
Potter, Nina 5:31:15 (31,439)
Potts, Leeanne 4:00:59 (11,245)
Potts, Sally F 3:44:05 (6,896)
Pottter, Karen J 3:49:29 (8,090)
Poulter, Jacqueline 4:39:06 (21,280)
Poulton, Patricia A 4:11:31 (13,852)
Pound, Abbie Rose......................4:32:43 (19,610)
Poundall, Kirsty 4:40:48 (21,721)
Powell, Alison Jane 4:31:05 (19,238)
Powell, Anwen 6:18:43 (35,067)
Powell, Celyn 4:44:37 (22,676)
Powell, Deborah Elisabeth 4:42:13 (22,069)
Powell, Eryl 4:43:36 (22,394)
Powell, Fiona L 2:53:42 (651)
Powell, Fran Karen 5:29:02 (31,154)
Powell, Jennifer Elizabeth 4:24:47 (17,462)
Powell, Linda A 4:20:32 (16,268)
Powell, Louise 5:12:24 (28,629)
Powell, Magdalena E...................3:13:06 (2,202)
Powell, Marielle 5:44:22 (32,801)
Powell, Rhian 5:21:05 (30,015)
Powell, Sandra 5:46:58 (33,049)
Powell, Sophie Louise.................3:49:57 (8,199)
Powell, Stephanie Maria 4:56:43 (25,697)
Powell, Susan Rebecca 4:04:25 (12,058)
Powell, Thelma Dawn 4:50:04 (24,064)
Powell, Tracy 4:48:42 (23,719)
Power, Cassandra........................3:31:34 (4,677)
Power, Crystal Nicola Katie........7:17:26 (36,381)
Power, Kate 4:11:33 (13,863)
Power, Laura 6:46:39 (35,941)
Powers, Lynne 4:44:08 (22,541)
Pownall, Helen C 4:20:13 (16,169)
Powrie, Catherine M...................3:24:41 (3,537)
Poynor, Bryony Clare 4:49:57 (24,041)
Poyntz, Rebecca 4:53:59 (25,045)
Poyzer, Sara Louise 4:52:16 (24,619)
Pradic, Cath 4:38:04 (21,003)
Prajapati, Urmila B 4:00:04 (10,998)
Pralong, Sarah 5:01:29 (26,750)
Prasad, Naomi 3:36:47 (5,520)
Pratasik, Elizabeth 4:18:34 (15,732)
Prathapan, Kavitha 5:26:40 (30,858)
Pratt, Katie Louise 4:59:00 (26,214)
Pratt, Susan 5:33:46 (31,741)
Precious, Nicky Jayne..................5:26:03 (30,787)
Precious, Rachel Lynn 4:36:22 (20,568)
Preiss, Elke 5:06:01 (27,533)
Premi, Louise 6:08:49 (34,603)
Prentis, Aimée C 6:32:54 (35,592)
Prentis, Elizabeth 5:42:41 (32,648)
Preston, Janet Mary....................4:29:16 (18,747)
Preston, Joanna 4:53:53 (25,016)
Preston, Karen Jane 5:00:14 (26,505)
Preston, Louise 4:47:48 (23,494)
Preston, Michelle 5:00:02 (26,463)
Preston, Tania Marie...................3:59:20 (10,818)
Preston, Vickie 4:46:20 (23,133)
Pretorius, Karen 4:15:05 (14,806)
Price, Amie 4:03:21 (11,813)
Price, Anna 4:04:39 (12,114)
Price, Brigitte 6:28:38 (35,449)
Price, Gail 4:42:28 (22,130)
Price, Gemma Elizabeth 4:18:26 (15,694)
Price, Hannah Rhys 4:32:29 (19,556)
Price, Helen J 3:58:27 (10,541)
Price, Joanne E 3:49:42 (8,145)
Price, Kelly 5:45:31 (32,910)

Price, Lee Michelle 3:14:13 (2,345)
Price, Lucy C 4:39:26 (21,368)
Price, Samantha L 4:51:20 (24,381)
Price, Susan Ann 4:28:39 (18,567)
Prichard, Rhian 6:23:12 (35,244)
Prichard, Suzanne 4:59:08 (26,246)
Prichard Jones, Cecilia Jane 4:46:05 (23,055)
Prickett, Susan Mei Choo 5:25:16 (30,658)
Priddey, Victoria C 4:16:22 (15,130)
Priddy, Dione Marie 3:56:45 (10,014)
Pride, Jennifer 5:55:12 (33,735)
Prideaux, Wendy Ann 6:30:35 (35,521)
Pridmore, Teresa 4:19:12 (15,898)
Priest, Victoria 5:25:50 (30,758)
Priestley, Christine Jane 4:34:06 (20,022)
Prilop, Barbara 6:19:11 (35,090)
Prince, Debbie Jane 5:35:36 (31,936)
Prince, Edna Christine 6:23:13 (35,245)
Pring, Emily...............................5:40:31 (32,432)
Pringle, Kathleen 5:33:39 (31,730)
Pringle, Sarah-Anne 3:35:59 (5,411)
Prior, Michelle J 3:30:32 (4,501)
Prior, Samantha 5:16:18 (29,269)
Prisk, Claire Louise 4:37:58 (20,982)
Pritchard, Carol Sarah Ann 4:12:17 (14,051)
Pritchard, Caroline E 3:38:13 (5,805)
Pritchard, Cathryn 4:28:59 (18,679)
Pritchard, Clare 5:16:38 (29,328)
Pritchard, Sarah 6:25:56 (35,347)
Pritchett, Jennifer Ann 3:41:05 (6,337)
Probert, Emma Jane 5:13:03 (28,747)
Probin, Caroline Elizabeth 4:51:23 (24,394)
Procter, Lisa Marie 3:55:28 (9,606)
Prosser, Amy 4:49:20 (23,879)
Prosser, Clare 2:56:53 (853)
Prosser, Melanie Jane..................6:34:30 (35,641)
Prout, Dianne 4:27:23 (18,205)
Prout, Sarah Jean 6:45:27 (35,921)
Provan, Adele 5:10:00 (28,235)
Prowse, Wendy 3:26:32 (3,805)
Prudden, Emma R 4:20:47 (16,363)
Pryke, Melanie 4:37:35 (20,904)
Pryke, Sara A 5:51:47 (33,490)
Pryor, Clare Marianne 4:27:19 (18,187)
Przybysz, Malgorzata 6:04:02 (34,324)
Puddefoot, Gill 5:04:05 (27,205)
Pugh, Jane Marjorie 3:56:27 (9,916)
Pugh, Rachael 6:58:53 (36,171)
Pullen, Charmaine Susan 4:47:40 (23,459)
Pullen, Deborah May 4:03:24 (11,820)
Pullinger, Amanda J 5:04:49 (27,334)
Punsheon, Gemma Susan............5:57:47 (33,919)
Punton, Gillian S 4:26:23 (17,923)
Purath, Sian 5:01:24 (26,733)
Purchase, Jane C 3:17:12 (2,684)
Purkiss, Sheila Theresa 5:26:26 (30,834)
Purser, Samantha J 4:50:23 (24,135)
Purves, Anne 6:16:20 (34,938)
Putko, Alison J 4:15:01 (14,790)
Putman, Laura 5:27:25 (30,960)
Putnam, Jo 3:07:55 (1,690)
Putt, Sarah 4:32:24 (19,538)
Puttnam, Carolyn Mary..............6:08:26 (34,576)
Puttock, Karen E 3:33:48 (5,025)
Pye, Harriet Susan......................4:50:14 (24,099)
Pyle, Laura E 4:23:47 (17,187)
Pymont, Linda 3:50:17 (8,268)
Pyne, Helen Margaret.................5:12:07 (28,587)
Pyne, Janet Lynne 5:08:54 (28,030)
Qua, Sabrina 4:54:00 (25,052)
Quaeck, Debbie..........................3:57:09 (10,141)
Quayle, Philippa.........................4:23:25 (17,084)
Queen, Daniel 3:35:44 (5,364)
Quick, Jessica 4:11:29 (13,844)
Quilter, Sarah Louise 3:51:33 (8,549)
Quin, Kerry 6:26:29 (35,365)
Quincey, Nicole Jeanette 5:00:43 (26,590)
Quine, Lynne 5:46:17 (32,980)
Quinlan, Anna Elizabeth 5:22:26 (30,212)
Quinn, Clare 4:22:29 (16,841)
Quinn, Clare 4:49:33 (23,922)
Quinn, Emma 4:32:45 (19,619)
Quinn, Gabrielle 4:09:45 (13,407)

Quinn, Helen M.........................4:10:24 (13,568)
Quinn, Louise.........................4:20:18 (16,200)
Quinn, Nicola Jane.........................4:14:38 (14,696)
Quinnell, Kathy.........................5:54:01 (33,644)
Quintin, Marie-José.........................5:31:47 (31,513)
Quirk, Sarah Elizabeth.........................4:48:21 (23,624)
Quirke, Ruth.........................4:31:41 (19,373)
Raccani, Petra.........................4:54:44 (25,238)
Racey, Lee.........................6:49:49 (35,993)
Rackham, Beverley Jayne.........................4:47:35 (23,433)
Rackham, Katharine L.........................3:29:14 (4,276)
Rackley, Emma Louise.........................5:26:20 (30,826)
Radcliffe, Eloise.........................4:19:14 (15,909)
Radcliffe, Holly.........................7:24:15 (36,439)
Radford, Joy C.........................3:26:42 (3,829)
Radford, Rebecca.........................4:47:18 (23,366)
Radmore, Harriet Elizabeth.........................5:19:41 (29,805)
Radoycheva, Milena.........................4:11:17 (13,786)
Rae, Candice J.........................6:39:20 (35,763)
Rae, Jane Elizabeth.........................4:18:27 (15,699)
Rae, Sheila C.........................3:33:40 (5,001)
Ragon, Susan Marie.........................4:03:17 (11,799)
Rai, Daman.........................4:22:27 (16,834)
Rai, Kiran.........................4:57:09 (25,791)
Rai, Pavandeep.........................4:43:43 (22,423)
Rainey, Janette.........................3:45:09 (7,127)
Rainford-Batty, Sarah.........................6:37:02 (35,699)
Rajasingham, Shirani.........................4:24:44 (17,450)
Ralph, Barbara.........................3:25:25 (3,636)
Ralph, Lysa.........................3:45:55 (7,290)
Ralph, Sarah Jane.........................5:18:36 (29,636)
Ralston, Emma.........................4:03:10 (11,769)
Ramage, Alison Jane.........................5:48:23 (33,182)
Rambridge, Janice Mary.........................5:27:01 (30,908)
Rampton, Victoria Ruth.........................5:35:25 (31,918)
Ramsay, Cayetana E.........................4:27:24 (18,208)
Ramsay, Emily J.........................3:28:00 (4,049)
Ramsay, Sam.........................4:18:12 (15,629)
Ramsay, Tana.........................6:09:14 (34,625)
Ramsey, Jennifer Susan.........................4:20:36 (16,297)
Ramsey, Joanna E.........................5:25:05 (30,638)
Ramsey, Nicola J.........................3:27:42 (3,997)
Ramsey Smith, Sarah M.........................3:34:08 (5,086)
Rance, Jaynie Yvonne.........................5:11:42 (28,502)
Randall, Bernice M.........................3:16:20 (2,590)
Randall, Helen.........................5:22:52 (30,286)
Randall, Jane Alice.........................6:06:00 (34,453)
Randall, Joanne Louise.........................4:34:25 (20,099)
Randall, Samantha L.........................5:00:12 (26,499)
Randall, Sarah.........................6:00:35 (34,098)
Randall, Victoria Katherine.........................5:27:46 (30,997)
Randall, Wendy Lynn.........................4:17:12 (15,351)
Randera, Afsha.........................6:11:33 (34,726)
Randle, Allison.........................5:14:36 (29,003)
Randle, Vicky.........................5:12:54 (28,722)
Rang, Vicki.........................4:16:58 (15,287)
Rankin, Daniel William.........................4:13:17 (14,310)
Ransom, Kelly M.........................5:37:13 (32,133)
Ranson, Charlotte.........................4:05:10 (12,245)
Ranson, Pauline Fay.........................5:34:08 (31,771)
Rasmussen, Kirsty.........................5:09:50 (28,205)
Rastall, Philippa Wendy.........................5:52:44 (33,556)
Rastelli, Sharon.........................4:38:28 (21,110)
Ratcliff, Sophie Amy Margaret.........................4:29:16 (18,747)
Ratcliffe, Anna.........................4:32:10 (19,476)
Ratcliffe, Megan E.........................3:39:46 (6,092)
Rate, Louise.........................7:39:53 (36,520)
Rathbone, Helen J.........................5:17:05 (29,397)
Rathbone, Laura.........................5:44:06 (32,779)
Rathbone, Lynne.........................5:29:01 (31,153)
Rathbone, Susan.........................4:52:03 (24,558)
Rathod, Dipika.........................5:08:00 (27,895)
Rathod, Kiran.........................5:03:03 (27,033)
Rattue, Zoe K.........................5:37:09 (32,123)
Raub-Segall, Elke.........................5:57:10 (33,874)
Rauh, Fiona.........................3:58:56 (10,698)
Raveh, Terry B.........................3:48:39 (7,884)
Ravenhill, Joanne J.........................3:45:51 (7,278)
Rawal, Anjla.........................5:22:13 (30,177)
Rawe, Jackie.........................6:52:00 (36,042)
Rawlings, April.........................5:09:42 (28,180)
Rawlings, Donna M.........................4:14:18 (14,595)
Rawlings, Sheryl.........................4:27:58 (18,357)
Rawlinson, Aine.........................5:05:01 (27,371)
Rawnsley, Katy J.........................3:05:01 (1,459)
Ray, Camilla A.........................5:14:41 (29,016)
Ray, Laura Jane.........................4:34:06 (20,022)
Rayment, Ellen.........................5:05:40 (27,476)
Rayment, Jennie.........................5:09:30 (28,148)
Rayner, Denise.........................6:36:11 (35,681)
Rayner, Elizabeth.........................4:24:02 (17,245)
Rayner, Frances.........................4:36:42 (20,659)
Raynor, Kim.........................5:30:07 (31,307)
Raynsford, Helen.........................4:22:37 (16,885)
Raz, Nicci.........................4:56:17 (25,608)
Razny, Valerie.........................4:25:46 (17,742)
Rea, Isobel.........................2:59:33 (1,117)
Read, Christine.........................5:12:25 (28,636)
Read, Clare J.........................4:15:44 (14,962)
Read, Elizabeth Jane.........................5:24:37 (30,570)
Read, Emma Jessica.........................4:08:11 (13,003)
Read, Jennifer Evelyn.........................5:07:30 (27,812)
Read, Laura.........................5:43:32 (32,723)
Read, Liz Campbell.........................3:30:21 (4,478)
Read, Nicola Anne.........................4:40:15 (21,560)
Read, Rachel Sarah Elizabeth.........................6:50:08 (36,000)
Read, Susan Deborah.........................4:59:01 (26,219)
Reade, Kirsty E.........................3:37:28 (5,652)
Reade, Sophie.........................8:17:19 (36,600)
Reade, Stephanie Margaret.........................4:37:17 (20,813)
Reader, Sue.........................6:10:04 (34,670)
Reading, Pauline Marie.........................6:57:37 (36,151)
Readman, Sarah K.........................3:33:33 (4,980)
Readman, Tamzin Clara.........................3:41:35 (6,437)
Real, Rachel M.........................3:53:15 (8,983)
Real Bourg, Sandrine.........................4:53:36 (24,941)
Reason, Janette.........................4:22:00 (16,705)
Reay, Amanda L.........................4:05:01 (12,212)
Reay, Elizabeth.........................4:31:01 (19,221)
Reay, Zoe.........................4:59:46 (26,400)
Reber, Gabriela.........................4:58:09 (26,004)
Redding, Hannah Mafae.........................4:28:47 (18,600)
Reddy, Siobhan A.........................3:48:06 (7,761)
Redfern, Erica.........................4:30:57 (19,205)
Redfern, Laura.........................6:11:11 (34,708)
Redfern, Sharon.........................5:45:02 (32,873)
Redman, Lisa Joanne.........................4:22:46 (16,928)
Redmond, Aileen.........................5:19:58 (29,844)
Redmond, Caroline.........................3:38:32 (5,853)
Redmond, Deborah Jane.........................4:56:51 (25,735)
Redstone, Nicola.........................3:45:52 (7,285)
Reece, Beverly.........................4:02:18 (11,557)
Reece, Kerrie S.........................4:52:22 (24,652)
Reed, Donna.........................5:24:41 (30,579)
Reed, Hilde Loe.........................4:42:02 (22,024)
Reed, Melissa.........................4:44:08 (22,541)
Reed, Rebecca Jane.........................4:47:21 (23,379)
Reed, Sue.........................5:46:22 (32,993)
Rees, Diane Elizabeth.........................5:59:04 (33,994)
Rees, Emma.........................3:56:45 (10,014)
Rees, Jayne Ann.........................6:30:10 (35,506)
Rees, Jessica.........................6:17:41 (35,015)
Rees, Jillian E.........................5:15:59 (29,227)
Rees, Joanne Leah.........................4:22:09 (16,741)
Rees, Katherine.........................3:34:30 (5,154)
Rees, Kelly Louise.........................6:14:41 (34,871)
Rees, Sian.........................4:02:50 (11,685)
Rees, Wendy.........................4:51:59 (24,549)
Reeve, Dona Marie.........................4:29:18 (18,755)
Reeve, Joanna Louise.........................6:29:46 (35,489)
Reeve, Rachel.........................5:19:00 (29,701)
Reeves, Clare.........................2:59:24 (1,095)
Reeves, Debra Ann.........................5:40:04 (32,397)
Reeves, Elizabeth T.........................3:16:59 (2,667)
Reeves, Kate E.........................4:03:32 (11,854)
Reeves, Mandy Jayne.........................6:05:05 (34,389)
Reeves, Michelle Emma.........................5:51:57 (33,501)
Reeves, Rachel Clare.........................4:54:18 (25,134)
Regan, Eileen.........................5:09:54 (28,213)
Regan, Janet L.........................4:18:51 (15,815)
Regan, Katie.........................6:11:42 (34,734)
Regelous, Aimée Sidney.........................5:19:56 (29,841)
Regester, Alison Rose.........................5:35:41 (31,952)
Rehemtulla, Naaz.........................5:03:40 (27,131)
Rehner, Birgit.........................4:33:46 (19,937)
Reid, Carol A.........................3:53:31 (9,061)
Reid, Catriona H.........................3:21:00 (3,083)
Reid, Debbie.........................7:15:32 (36,363)
Reid, Jacqueline E.........................4:01:37 (11,396)
Reid, Janice.........................3:58:58 (10,709)
Reid, Kay Joanna.........................4:06:26 (12,554)

Reid, Lisa.........................4:48:09 (23,579)

Running the London Marathon has easily been one of the best things I have ever done. When I turned 18, I entered the Marathon and although it had been described to me as torture I didn't care, I just couldn't wait to be involved in something so huge. On the day it felt surreal to be standing amongst the thousands of runners. Training had gone well and I comfortably got to 20 miles. But nothing could have prepared me for the further struggle which really I should have been expecting. My legs started to cramp, blisters rubbed and everything happening around me blanked out. However, somehow I managed to keep running and crossing the finishing line felt amazing. I can't wait to run it again.

Reid, Rebecca Sian.........................4:56:04 (25,551)
Reid, Sarah.........................3:39:29 (6,038)
Reid, Siobhan Marian.........................4:46:28 (23,159)
Reilly, Samantha Jane.........................5:16:09 (29,246)
Reimer, Martina.........................5:00:22 (26,529)
Reinikkala, Anne I.........................3:43:02 (6,703)
Reiter, Kristine.........................4:32:58 (19,687)
Reiter, Louisa.........................5:30:40 (31,380)
Rekasi, Louisa.........................5:36:21 (32,038)
Rekker-Koetje, Dineke.........................5:45:36 (32,917)
Relf, Carly M.........................4:27:23 (18,205)
Remnant, Alana Niamh.........................3:58:39 (10,610)
Rendall, Lindsey Morwenna.........................5:19:30 (29,772)
Rendall, Nicola Catherine.........................4:21:22 (16,513)
Renfer, Fionuala T.........................3:40:03 (6,157)
Renfrew, Hollie.........................4:37:00 (20,742)
Renner, Michelle Louise.........................5:12:27 (28,643)
Rennie, Felicity C.........................3:33:42 (5,006)
Rennie, Kate.........................3:15:26 (2,491)
Renwick, Sally Ann.........................5:20:23 (29,897)
Renwick-Bradford, Sharon.........................4:48:21 (23,624)
Reseigh, Natalie.........................4:06:00 (12,456)
Restall, Claire L.........................4:34:36 (20,148)
Restorick, Laura Joanne.........................5:20:57 (29,999)
Retailleau, Daniele.........................3:44:46 (7,047)
Reukauf, Birgit.........................4:44:13 (22,568)
Revell, Hayley.........................4:49:34 (23,929)
Revels, Kate.........................5:21:30 (30,076)
Rew, Vanessa Claire.........................4:54:47 (25,255)
Reynolds, Andrea Michelle.........................9:02:36 (36,616)
Reynolds, Beverley Jayne.........................5:40:08 (32,401)

Reynolds, Claire Patricia 4:43:52 (22,469)
Reynolds, Danielle 6:08:59 (34,618)
Reynolds, Eugene 5:01:16 (26,699)
Reynolds, Hazel 6:12:33 (34,784)
Reynolds, Joanne 3:52:15 (8,719)
Reynolds, Julie M 3:24:19 (3,488)
Reynolds, Leigh 4:31:59 (19,428)
Reynolds, Niki Catherine Rachel 5:32:03 (31,538)
Reynolds, Sandra 5:01:33 (26,766)
Reynolds, Sandra J 3:11:38 (2,063)
Reynolds, Sarah Louise 4:21:39 (16,594)
Reynolds, Shahina 6:04:31 (34,350)
Reza, Behjat 5:19:05 (29,714)
Rhodes, April 5:39:30 (32,346)
Rhodes, Caroline Louise 4:34:33 (20,134)
Rhodes, Diana 4:20:22 (16,223)
Rhodes, Gillian Louise 5:39:30 (32,346)
Rhodes, June 4:18:24 (15,689)
Rhodes, Nicola 5:22:53 (30,289)
Rhouni-Bellouti, Karen 7:05:20 (36,257)
Rhys, Hannah 4:23:18 (17,044)
Rhys-Davies, Amy Elaine 5:35:41 (31,952)
Ribchester, Joanne 4:37:26 (20,861)
Riccio, Gina M 4:50:44 (24,219)
Rice, Cathy 4:01:01 (11,254)
Rice, Lisa 6:43:13 (35,870)
Rice, Liz 4:25:48 (17,749)
Rice, Samantha 5:05:58 (27,524)
Rice-Gray, Julie Anne 4:52:31 (24,688)
Rich, Carly Sara 4:24:47 (17,462)
Richards, Amanda J 4:36:33 (20,618)
Richards, Cheryl Anne 4:52:33 (24,699)
Richards, Claire 4:40:42 (21,693)
Richards, Elen Mair 4:27:03 (18,097)
Richards, Emma V 3:16:29 (2,607)
Richards, Helen Laura 5:06:17 (27,581)
Richards, Jacky 5:46:47 (33,031)
Richards, Kerrie Samantha 4:13:26 (14,348)
Richards, Lisa 4:12:17 (14,051)
Richards, Maria Jane 3:47:21 (7,609)
Richards, Michelle Leanne 5:33:27 (31,711)
Richards, Siebe Augustine 3:48:24 (7,825)
Richards, Vivienne J 4:05:50 (12,418)
Richardson, Amy 5:34:42 (31,850)
Richardson, Cathryn J 5:03:40 (27,131)
Richardson, Jan 5:41:49 (32,567)
Richardson, Jane 4:44:58 (22,759)
Richardson, Jennifer 5:12:40 (28,677)
Richardson, Joanne H 6:27:18 (35,394)
Richardson, Kate 6:06:33 (34,483)
Richardson, Katie 5:38:02 (32,216)
Richardson, Kerry 4:09:22 (13,301)
Richardson, Nicky 4:25:15 (17,586)
Richardson, Patricia 3:24:11 (3,468)
Richardson, Sarah Elizabeth 5:49:02 (33,244)
Richardson, Sarah Elizabeth 5:57:13 (33,881)
Richardson, Sharron 3:42:48 (6,657)
Riches, Belinda Lee 4:45:52 (22,992)
Richmond, Claire 4:34:28 (20,114)
Richmond, Mandy K 4:51:03 (24,316)
Richter, Ines 4:39:41 (21,432)
Rickard, Alison Jill 4:03:10 (11,769)
Rickard, Liezel 3:51:35 (8,561)
Rickett, Mari Ann 5:41:15 (32,514)
Ricketts, Jacqueline Ann 5:11:53 (28,539)
Ricketts, Jannet Abigail 4:37:06 (20,771)
Rickwood, Gill 6:25:06 (35,309)
Riddell, Avril 3:31:19 (4,632)
Riddell, Louise Jane 6:03:07 (34,262)
Ridehalgh, Julie Margaret 4:02:02 (11,497)
Rideout, Laura 6:34:36 (35,645)
Rideout, Natalie Jayne 4:41:22 (21,858)
Ridge, Julia Penelope 3:59:10 (10,764)
Ridgley, Julie R 4:06:49 (12,660)
Ridler, Mandy 4:28:48 (18,609)
Ridout, Heather 3:56:17 (9,866)
Riet, Cynthia Leonie 5:51:35 (33,471)
Riga, Petra 3:40:17 (6,194)
Rigby, Catherine Helen 4:12:31 (14,103)
Rigby, Lucy 4:18:50 (15,803)
Rigden, Julie A 5:00:45 (26,600)
Rigg, Emma Jayne 6:58:18 (36,159)
Rigg, Katie Louise 6:58:18 (36,159)
Righetti, Maria 4:07:27 (12,817)
Rijzinga, Willy 4:53:43 (24,978)
Riley, Alexandra 4:46:22 (23,141)
Riley, Belinda Jane 4:53:15 (24,862)
Riley, Jan 3:52:48 (8,870)
Riley, Jessica M 3:19:12 (2,890)
Riley, Kate 4:34:12 (20,044)
Riley, Ruthie Elizabeth 5:40:59 (32,480)
Riley-Brooks, Lyn 4:57:32 (25,868)
Riley-Simkiss, Joanna Clare 4:34:16 (20,062)
Rimmington, Carole L 4:51:05 (24,326)
Rinat, Dalit 4:39:47 (21,457)
Rindl, Deb Clare 4:45:21 (22,852)
Ring, Evonne 4:53:58 (25,041)
Ring, Josephine 4:33:50 (19,948)
Ringoeen, Aaslaug Nylund 4:46:24 (23,150)
Rinn, Joanne 4:49:56 (24,037)
Rippon, Marie 4:40:09 (21,524)
Risberg, Anita 4:07:29 (12,826)
Risby, Kay Elizabeth 4:08:28 (13,069)
Risdale, Joanne 7:40:43 (36,524)
Riseley, Katie 4:20:39 (16,320)
Risley, Angie 4:48:19 (23,609)
Ritchie, Nicola 5:30:18 (31,326)
Ritchley, Suzie 4:47:19 (23,368)
Rivas, Luisa Ines Elizabeth 3:06:26 (1,564)
Rivers, Alison Cheney 3:47:09 (7,556)
Riviere, Helene 4:13:20 (14,324)
Rix, Gemma 5:13:04 (28,763)
Rixon, Kellie 6:23:07 (35,240)
Roach, Colette Eve 4:40:34 (21,660)
Roach, Jessica Lucy 4:45:48 (22,979)
Roach, Karen 5:23:08 (30,326)
Roake, Karen N 3:51:34 (8,554)
Robb, Jodie Mitchell Burnett 6:37:03 (35,700)
Robberts, Theresa 6:35:49 (35,672)
Robbins, Joanna Louise 3:38:58 (5,934)
Roberto, Anna 5:12:45 (28,692)
Roberts, Alison 4:21:06 (16,439)
Roberts, Amy 5:53:48 (33,628)
Roberts, Ann M 4:57:18 (25,820)
Roberts, Anna Louise 6:01:45 (34,170)
Roberts, Carole M 4:11:53 (13,950)
Roberts, Catrin Bryn 4:22:25 (16,826)
Roberts, Christine 5:57:03 (33,870)
Roberts, Clare Victoria 5:10:31 (28,331)
Roberts, Ella Teresa 4:53:14 (24,858)
Roberts, Faye 3:44:42 (7,035)
Roberts, Gemma 4:33:40 (19,910)
Roberts, Georgina 4:30:54 (19,190)
Roberts, Georgina 5:07:03 (27,733)
Roberts, Hayley Amanda 5:02:30 (26,944)
Roberts, Helen 3:48:32 (7,853)
Roberts, Helen 4:20:06 (16,137)
Roberts, Iris Bayley 5:21:08 (30,024)
Roberts, Jennifer Mary 4:56:47 (25,711)
Roberts, Jo 4:58:13 (26,015)
Roberts, Joan 7:10:14 (36,310)
Roberts, Jude 4:34:48 (20,194)
Roberts, Julie 6:55:28 (36,121)
Roberts, Karen 4:57:35 (25,875)
Roberts, Katherine S 3:37:36 (5,690)
Roberts, Kerensa Rose 4:18:27 (15,699)
Roberts, Kylie Thomasine 5:46:50 (33,033)
Roberts, Michelle 3:22:31 (3,241)
Roberts, Michelle 4:54:41 (25,226)
Roberts, Natalie Suzanne 4:35:48 (20,420)
Roberts, Pauline 4:17:30 (15,439)
Roberts, Rebecca Louise 4:47:29 (23,406)
Roberts, Rebekah 4:51:04 (24,322)
Roberts, Sara 4:19:29 (15,966)
Roberts, Sarah Helen 3:54:20 (9,289)
Roberts, Trudy 5:53:26 (33,607)
Roberts, Veronica Anne 5:34:33 (31,830)
Robertson, Danielle Cora 5:48:27 (33,189)
Robertson, Gillian 3:45:37 (7,230)
Robertson, Nicola Margaret 4:22:54 (16,962)
Robertson, Suzannah 4:22:54 (16,962)
Robertson-Ross, Catherine 5:12:17 (28,617)
Robin, Margaret 4:55:56 (25,520)
Robins, Amy 6:34:09 (35,629)
Robins, Julie Elizabeth 4:43:13 (22,303)
Robinson, Ali C 3:19:48 (2,945)
Robinson, Anne 6:18:25 (35,055)
Robinson, Catherine Frances 5:46:24 (32,996)
Robinson, Deborah 3:27:21 (3,930)
Robinson, Elaine L 5:06:18 (27,587)
Robinson, Ellen 2:57:27 (896)
Robinson, Erica 4:19:54 (16,075)
Robinson, Erika R 3:07:27 (1,647)
Robinson, Judith Isobel 4:33:02 (19,708)
Robinson, Julia Hirschfield 5:19:56 (29,841)
Robinson, Julie A 3:38:24 (5,832)
Robinson, Julie-Marie 4:50:39 (24,195)
Robinson, Karen P 4:40:23 (21,607)
Robinson, Lisa 5:12:27 (28,643)
Robinson, Louise S 3:20:53 (3,068)
Robinson, Lucy 4:54:15 (25,114)
Robinson, Lucy J 4:33:38 (19,902)
Robinson, Lydia Joy 5:18:14 (29,578)
Robinson, Melissa 5:12:25 (28,636)
Robinson, Nicola Jane 7:08:39 (36,298)
Robinson, Patricia 7:11:44 (36,326)
Robinson, Pauline Ann 5:34:07 (31,769)
Robinson, Rachael 5:53:54 (33,635)
Robinson, Rachel L 5:33:03 (31,673)
Robinson, Rebecca 2:37:14 (146)
Robinson, Sally Patricia 4:41:53 (21,989)
Robinson, Sue 4:22:36 (16,875)
Robinson, Vikki Barbara 5:18:47 (29,662)
Robinson, Vivienne Alexa 5:28:38 (31,100)
Robinson, Zoe Venus 3:26:59 (3,874)
Robinxon, Brenda C 6:11:46 (34,738)
Robjohns, Karen Susan 5:11:21 (28,458)
Robling, Emma 5:39:14 (32,324)
Robson, Dany L 4:23:46 (17,185)
Robson, Dawn E 4:23:40 (17,147)
Robson, Jane 4:48:19 (23,609)
Robson, Rebecca E 4:05:34 (12,347)
Robson, Sarah 5:02:01 (26,845)
Robson, Sigrid 4:08:57 (13,193)
Roby, Geraldine 4:27:50 (18,319)
Roche, Elaine 5:35:39 (31,947)
Rockliffe, Jacqueline M 3:27:06 (3,886)
Rodda, Caroline Louise 4:33:44 (19,930)
Roderick, Donna 5:24:31 (30,558)
Rodger, Camilla Lucy 5:13:03 (28,747)
Rodgers, Amelia Claire 4:20:49 (16,369)
Rodgers, Clare Sophie Kendall 6:25:51 (35,341)
Rodgers, Karrie Louise 5:52:44 (33,556)
Rodgers, Mandy Jane 4:32:11 (19,483)
Rodrigues, Odete Maria 3:59:23 (10,834)
Rodrigues, Vera 4:55:15 (25,371)
Rodriguez, Barbara Kathleen 4:38:25 (21,092)
Rodriguez, Joanna M 3:00:42 (1,189)
Rodriguez, Jurgita 5:01:07 (26,670)
Rodriguez, Maria 7:17:56 (36,386)
Rodriguez, Mariana 5:27:01 (30,908)
Rodriguez, Teresa 4:49:49 (24,013)
Rodwell, Louisa 6:14:22 (34,855)
Roe, Amanda 4:37:30 (20,881)
Roe, Lucy Elizabeth 6:33:27 (35,609)
Roe, Sadie Jane 6:52:31 (36,061)
Roehrich, Ingrid 3:36:58 (5,558)
Rogan, Emma B 3:51:19 (8,496)
Roger, Alexandra Suzannah A 3:58:04 (10,401)
Roger, Kirsty 4:13:29 (14,358)
Roger, Nathalie 3:45:57 (7,299)
Rogers, Abigail Alexandra 4:45:59 (23,018)
Rogers, Alexandra J 4:00:54 (11,218)
Rogers, Amanda 4:09:38 (13,380)
Rogers, Caroline M 3:56:40 (9,984)
Rogers, Guler 4:53:57 (25,034)
Rogers, Jenna 5:57:00 (33,868)
Rogers, Jessica 4:03:33 (11,859)
Rogers, Katie 4:47:43 (23,474)
Rogers, Kim Sharon 5:01:34 (26,769)
Rogers, Linda A 3:26:34 (3,808)
Rogers, Lisa 5:15:53 (29,208)
Rogers, Lisa Claire 4:24:34 (17,411)
Rogers, Lisa Michelle 4:27:17 (18,174)
Rogers, Michelle Margaret 6:58:39 (36,166)
Rogers, Natasha 4:46:53 (23,279)
Rogers, Rosie Louise 5:08:12 (27,929)
Rogers, Sarah 4:52:38 (24,718)
Rogers, Sarah Jane 4:48:38 (23,705)

Rogers, Victoria Edwina 5:32:03 (31,538)
Rogerson, Becky 5:56:31 (33,831)
Rogerson-Heath, Linda M 5:15:53 (29,208)
Rogge, Barbara 3:30:02 (4,425)
Rohmann, Kandy Chantal 5:48:52 (33,227)
Rojek, Jessica Ann 5:01:26 (26,742)
Rojemann, Shayna 5:12:24 (28,629)
Rolf, Suzanna 5:46:18 (32,984)
Rolfe, Marion 6:26:53 (35,379)
Rolfe, Victoria L 3:55:55 (9,755)
Roll, Natalie Jane 5:34:52 (31,865)
Rollins, Meaghan 4:22:39 (16,892)
Rollins, Teresa 6:22:40 (35,219)
Rollins, Victoria 6:24:45 (35,302)
Rollinson, Lorraine 4:07:51 (12,918)
Rollo, Kerry Ann 5:48:50 (33,226)
Rolls, Charlotte 5:37:14 (32,134)
Romecin, Lindsay H 3:33:30 (4,970)
Romeo, Gloria M 3:36:48 (5,524)
Ronan, Nadine Lucinda 6:33:33 (35,614)
Ronda, Lucy 4:35:17 (20,292)
Ronteltap, Elisabeth 4:09:23 (13,304)
Ronxin, Joanne Ruth 4:42:19 (22,098)
Rooke, Gemma 5:13:05 (28,789)
Rooke, Samantha J 6:07:36 (34,537)
Rookes, Julie 5:28:24 (31,076)
Roos, Patricia 6:04:15 (34,338)
Root, Sarah 5:37:03 (32,106)
Root, Suzy 5:59:57 (34,055)
Rootes, Jane Elizabeth 5:00:29 (26,551)
Ropa, Maria Luisa 5:16:21 (29,286)
Roper, Helen 4:44:12 (22,563)
Roper, Lesley 5:24:42 (30,584)
Roper, Luci 4:55:42 (25,463)
Roper-Roberts, Catherine E 4:49:10 (23,842)
Roques, Leonie P 3:38:07 (5,785)
Rorrison, Alexandra Jane 4:54:39 (25,219)
Rosa, Jessica H 3:29:38 (4,348)
Rosa, Marie-Carol E 5:09:10 (28,080)
Rosati, Assia 4:02:26 (11,592)
Rose, Carol A 5:05:54 (27,517)
Rose, Catherine Mary 6:03:55 (34,316)
Rose, Janette Susan 4:45:42 (22,948)
Rose, Joanne Vicky 4:22:42 (16,905)
Rose, Julie 4:23:32 (17,115)
Rose, Julie 5:18:47 (29,662)
Rose, Katy 4:12:04 (14,000)
Rose, Lexi 5:45:37 (32,920)
Rose, Milou 4:19:04 (15,866)
Rose, Sharon A 5:14:03 (28,930)
Rose-Cunningham, Emma 4:48:53 (23,768)
Rosello, Kimberly P 5:06:38 (27,654)
Rosen, Alison 4:53:04 (24,806)
Rosen, Rachel Ann 4:53:39 (24,957)
Rosenberger, Thekla 4:11:11 (13,764)
Rosenthal, Lucy H 5:45:16 (32,890)
Roshier, Lizzie Sarah 4:32:10 (19,476)
Rosling, Lesley Elizabeth 5:12:52 (28,714)
Ross, Aileen E 3:50:36 (8,332)
Ross, Alison 3:47:03 (7,535)
Ross, Amanda 6:41:06 (35,814)
Ross, Andrea 4:01:46 (11,439)
Ross, Andrea Elizabeth 4:38:21 (21,071)
Ross, Deborah Louise 3:59:11 (10,771)
Ross, Elaine Helen 5:11:56 (28,547)
Ross, Joanne 3:37:44 (5,715)
Ross, Kenia Naves 4:00:48 (11,194)
Ross, Kirsty 5:16:12 (29,254)
Ross, Lorna E 5:14:36 (29,003)
Ross, Mhairi Jean 4:59:34 (26,356)
Ross, Vicky 4:31:37 (19,358)
Ross Russell, Fiona M 3:11:31 (2,051)
Ross Russell, Rachel S 4:49:34 (23,929)
Rossi, Claire 5:49:42 (33,308)
Rossi, Helen Christina 4:08:48 (13,161)
Rossi, Marie-Helene 4:35:55 (20,453)
Rossi, Stefania 5:36:02 (32,001)
Rossi, Valeria 6:36:06 (35,679)
Rostron, Jennifer Anne 4:38:12 (21,029)
Roszkowski, Ania 4:24:30 (17,388)
Rotchell, Kirsten Lisa 7:44:45 (36,547)
Roth, Keira 4:58:34 (26,107)
Roth, Satpal 4:28:00 (18,365)
Rothwell, Kate 5:27:40 (30,984)
Rothwell, Tania 5:04:29 (27,273)
Rothwells, Carolyn A 5:49:18 (33,261)
Rotko, Rosa-Maria 4:11:55 (13,966)
Rottmann, Katja 4:55:45 (25,480)
Rouane, Houaria 4:06:49 (12,660)
Roughley, Elaine Catherine 5:15:06 (29,081)
Rounce, Suzy 5:40:52 (32,467)
Rouse, Elizabeth Jane 5:14:00 (28,925)
Rouse, Nicola 5:01:00 (26,649)
Rout, Marie 4:59:19 (26,292)
Routledge, Jacqueline Indira 5:06:31 (27,628)
Rowan, Anne 8:15:04 (36,626)
Rowan, Frances 5:49:59 (33,333)
Rowan, Joanna Frances 5:12:29 (28,650)
Rowe, Catherine D 3:53:17 (8,993)
Rowe, Maria Dawn 4:54:14 (25,109)
Rowland, Jude 6:34:08 (35,627)
Rowland, Michelle Anne 4:56:31 (25,653)
Rowland, Sue 5:38:22 (32,249)
Rowlands, Alison N 4:40:20 (21,587)
Rowlands, Julia Maureen 7:06:04 (36,267)
Rowlands, Laura Faye 7:23:11 (36,429)
Rowley, Emma E 5:29:35 (31,234)
Rowley, Emma Elizabeth 4:26:58 (18,069)
Rowley, Gemma Kirstine 4:06:38 (12,611)
Rowley, Jennifer E 3:57:36 (10,264)
Rowley, Lauren Diane 6:23:07 (35,240)
Rowse, Penelope 5:16:10 (29,250)
Roxborough, Pamela Jean 5:15:38 (29,169)
Roy, Diane M 3:20:09 (2,972)
Roy, Rachel 5:47:20 (33,080)
Rozay, Corinne 3:37:06 (5,584)
Ruane, Francesca Lily 5:32:35 (31,617)
Ruane, Trudy Lynn 6:01:49 (34,175)
Rubis, Anita Victoria 3:39:41 (6,073)
Rudall, Lisa Jayne 4:52:12 (24,600)
Rudd, Louise Noreen 3:34:36 (5,173)
Rudkin, Amy Elizabeth 4:37:45 (20,934)
Rudler, Claire Louise 5:34:17 (31,794)
Rudman, Natalie 4:29:27 (18,790)
Rudolph, Ilona 4:39:26 (21,368)
Rudwick, Amanda Jane 5:31:43 (31,504)
Ruetsch, Fiona C 3:25:36 (3,666)
Ruffer, Dily R 5:03:48 (27,156)
Ruffle, Diane 4:23:13 (17,027)
Ruffle, Vicky Claire 5:05:07 (27,389)
Ruffy, Sharon Ellen 4:58:26 (26,071)
Ruggins, Emma Karen 7:43:36 (36,541)
Rughooputh, Sarita 7:11:48 (36,327)
Rumble, Beverley Joy 4:25:04 (17,540)
Rumble, Collette Jane 4:10:38 (13,625)
Rumbold, Naomi Elizabeth 4:39:22 (21,344)
Rumsey, Michelle L 4:26:22 (17,920)
Runnacles, Julia Rachel 5:12:30 (28,653)
Ruocco, Katie 5:18:48 (29,668)
Rush, Holly 2:37:56 (163)
Rushmer, Louise 4:15:01 (14,790)
Rushton, Karen T 3:01:27 (1,227)
Russ, Julie 4:09:34 (13,358)
Russell, Alexandra 5:28:02 (31,034)
Russell, Fiona 6:59:43 (36,186)
Russell, Fiona C 3:21:25 (3,132)
Russell, Jacquie Elizabeth 5:04:51 (27,342)
Russell, Julie Denise 4:24:04 (17,252)
Russell, Lizzie 4:39:26 (21,368)
Russell, Louise Milllicent 4:33:38 (19,902)
Russell, Maria L 4:10:04 (13,489)
Russell, Megan 4:22:26 (16,830)
Russell, Rowena Clare 6:31:57 (35,564)
Russell, Tina 5:08:30 (27,973)
Russell, Valerie 6:40:15 (35,795)
Russon, Gillian M 3:54:37 (9,359)
Rustell, Hayley Jayne 5:11:22 (28,460)
Ruston, Sarah 5:22:16 (30,184)
Rutherford, Susie 3:05:27 (1,491)
Rutter, Alison Jayne 5:51:55 (33,498)
Rutter, Clare 4:51:26 (24,406)
Rutter, Rowan 6:07:58 (34,558)
Ryall, Carla 5:10:58 (28,398)
Ryan, Claire 4:25:49 (17,760)
Ryan, Lorraine 3:07:02 (1,612)
Ryan, Martina 5:43:18 (32,702)
Ryan, Michelle C 5:40:08 (32,401)
Ryan, Samantha 6:50:13 (36,001)
Ryan, Tamatha Jane 3:36:35 (5,494)
Rycroft, Tamsin Ann Marie 4:31:44 (19,381)
Ryde, Rosemary 4:52:50 (24,764)
Ryder, Helen S 3:39:46 (6,092)
Rydzynski, Niky 5:22:32 (30,224)
Rye, Jo Maria 6:53:05 (36,073)
Ryland, Georgina 5:02:55 (27,012)
Ryle, Madeleine 4:17:19 (15,380)
Ryles, Elizabeth 5:16:36 (29,322)
Ryles, Susan D 5:57:21 (33,894)
Ryman-Howson, Nadia 6:31:15 (35,546)
Saba, Nadia F 4:40:24 (21,615)
Sabatini, Heather 4:46:23 (23,146)
Sabri, Dominique 5:53:32 (33,615)
Sachro, Catherine Emily 4:48:02 (23,554)
Saddington, Philippa A 7:36:23 (36,495)
Sadler, Angie 3:16:20 (2,590)
Sadler, Diane 6:28:03 (35,424)
Saffer, Lisa 6:08:46 (34,601)
Saffier, Desiré 4:49:58 (24,043)
Sage, Jo 5:01:42 (26,792)
Saggers, Elizabeth Anne 5:06:02 (27,539)
Saglio, Bernadette 4:45:22 (22,859)
Saha, Tanuka 5:21:53 (30,126)
Saheed, Susan A 4:40:52 (21,738)
Sail, Annette 4:54:49 (25,261)
Saines, Caroline 3:56:45 (10,014)
Saini, Anjali Thakur 4:39:49 (21,465)
Saint, Debbie M 4:17:35 (15,464)
Saker, Sue 5:17:20 (29,445)
Salabert-Mougin, Ghislaine SC 5:03:59 (27,186)
Salamon, Sacha 4:29:23 (18,773)
Salazar, Karen Celeste 4:40:28 (21,633)
Salij, Petra 4:35:35 (20,362)
Salmon, Abigail 7:03:57 (36,243)
Salmon, Amanda 3:45:26 (7,196)
Salt, Annie 5:20:25 (29,909)
Salter, Jennifer A 3:20:16 (2,988)
Salter, Karen Anne 6:35:56 (35,674)
Salter, Laura 3:39:09 (5,973)
Samain, Carly Louise 6:12:23 (34,776)
Samara, Lucy 4:20:43 (16,341)
Samarasinghe, Dunisha Gayomi 4:57:06 (25,779)
Samman, Michelle 5:56:57 (33,864)
Sammes, Rachel 3:29:53 (4,393)
Sample, Jessica 3:47:30 (7,647)
Samuel, Helen Marie 3:47:05 (7,541)
Samuelson-Dean, Katherine M 3:22:24 (3,227)
Samways, Joanne 4:57:46 (25,922)
San, Abigael 6:36:54 (35,696)
Sandell, Nikki J 3:58:58 (10,709)
Sandell, Pennie Susan 4:05:01 (12,212)
Sandeman, Ali N 4:24:14 (17,294)
Sanders, Angela Jocelyn 6:37:15 (35,705)
Sanders, Christy 4:51:41 (24,457)
Sanders, Elizabeth J 5:11:02 (28,410)
Sanders, Gaynor Marie 3:38:18 (5,820)
Sanders, Janet H 5:05:10 (27,396)
Sanders, Jennifer C 4:55:51 (25,497)
Sanders, Michaela Frances 5:13:53 (28,904)
Sanderson, Elizabeth A 3:39:31 (6,046)
Sanderson, Heather 5:14:49 (29,039)
Sanderson, Julie Linda 4:29:26 (18,785)
Sanders-Reece, Andrea 3:45:49 (7,267)
Sandford, Wendy E 4:24:38 (17,425)
Sands, Fiona Helen 5:05:11 (27,401)
Sands, Susan Helen 4:55:11 (25,352)
Sanghara, Kiran 5:14:15 (28,956)
Sangster, Jennifer Sarah 3:53:11 (8,966)
Sankarsingh, Gail 3:37:30 (5,664)
Sannen, Lief 3:46:38 (7,449)
Santos Canelles, Olga 5:13:54 (28,909)
Sargeant, Bina 4:34:10 (20,030)
Sargeant, Caroline May 6:39:23 (35,767)
Sartoretti, Lisa 4:29:34 (18,826)
Sastry, Karen 5:36:53 (32,092)
Satchell, Tamie 4:11:18 (13,790)
Sauboorah, Jennifer 5:24:56 (30,609)
Sauerzapf, Bobbie A 3:51:11 (8,469)
Saunders, Alison J 3:38:07 (5,785)
Saunders, Alison Jennifer 5:27:24 (30,955)

Saunders, Dawn 3:46:46 (7,478)
Saunders, Deborah 5:33:21 (31,700)
Saunders, Emma Elizabeth 4:16:11 (15,068)
Saunders, Evy 5:01:58 (26,837)
Saunders, Gabriella 4:00:49 (11,198)
Saunders, Georgina May 6:05:20 (34,413)
Saunders, Lisa Denise 4:36:00 (20,477)
Saunders, Lorraine 4:48:12 (23,588)
Saunders, Louise A 4:24:46 (17,458)
Saunders, Michele Anne 5:04:45 (27,326)
Saunders, Rachel 4:12:10 (14,028)
Saunders, Stephanie June 4:48:27 (23,659)
Saunt, Tonia E 4:18:20 (15,668)
Sauntry, Claire L 5:29:35 (31,234)
Savage, Emma 5:35:06 (31,890)
Savage, Emma Louise 4:14:55 (14,767)
Savage, Hannah 5:42:23 (32,625)
Savage, Vicky Jane 4:13:32 (14,378)
Saville, Lois 4:59:29 (26,333)
Saville, Melita L 6:30:29 (35,517)
Sawalha, Nadia 6:28:00 (35,419)
Saward, Karen Y 4:15:03 (14,801)
Sawdon, Alison Jane 4:47:31 (23,414)
Sawers, Deborah Ann 4:33:18 (19,803)
Sawyer, Philippa 4:29:48 (18,913)
Saxty, Heidi 5:13:24 (28,827)
Say, Shelly 4:53:09 (24,835)
Sayell, Trudy A 3:30:44 (4,534)
Sayer, Cheryl Karen 4:36:33 (20,618)
Sayer, Jacqueline 4:46:36 (23,205)
Sayer, Nicholette 4:59:43 (26,388)
Sayers, Amanda 6:17:01 (34,980)
Sayers, Joanna Claire 5:10:01 (28,242)
Sayers, Kim 6:09:14 (34,625)
Scaife, Elizabeth (Liz) Alexandra 6:32:38 (35,586)
Scales, Lisa Clare 5:13:36 (28,857)
Scally, Yvette 6:55:43 (36,126)
Scammell, Amy K 4:35:20 (20,301)
Scanes, Lorraine 4:46:13 (23,096)
Scarfe, Jacqueline K 3:59:05 (10,740)
Scarr-Hall, Rachael Anne 5:12:10 (28,597)
Schaad, Beatrice 4:54:45 (25,245)
Schadschneider, Sabine 5:06:15 (27,577)
Scheuerlein, Sieglinde 5:00:40 (26,581)
Schimpel, Christine 6:59:03 (36,177)
Schlaefli, Philippa 5:13:13 (28,803)
Schmid, Zoe 5:18:57 (29,695)
Schmidt, Anniken 6:24:10 (35,287)
Schmidt, Kristina 3:38:38 (5,881)
Schmohl, Baerbel 4:31:45 (19,384)
Schneider, Vera 5:20:54 (29,993)
Schoenknecht, Stefanie 4:20:07 (16,140)
Schofield, Christine 4:29:58 (18,974)
Schofield, Tracey Jane 3:46:33 (7,433)
Scholey, Ann 5:28:40 (31,106)
Scholey, Helen 5:18:59 (29,699)
Schreidl, Barbara 3:53:21 (9,013)
Schroell, Anne 3:51:14 (8,482)
Schubert, Mechthild 4:51:34 (24,434)
Schuetze, Simone 5:13:55 (28,913)
Schurmann, Caroline 4:25:05 (17,546)
Schwarz, Marion 3:58:06 (10,414)
Schweitzer, Felizitas 4:18:34 (15,732)
Sciberras, Christine 4:50:27 (24,150)
Scobie, Jane 4:22:55 (16,970)
Scordellis, Stella M 4:40:55 (21,752)
Scott, Alex L 5:19:34 (29,785)
Scott, Alexandra Kay 3:54:40 (9,375)
Scott, Amada M 2:56:08 (810)
Scott, Amanda Jane 6:51:07 (36,015)
Scott, Amanda L 4:33:06 (19,727)
Scott, Angela Gail 4:30:38 (19,129)
Scott, Anne Lucy 5:11:31 (28,481)
Scott, Annette Jean 6:36:33 (35,688)
Scott, Christina Jane 4:43:42 (22,417)
Scott, Clare 4:48:31 (23,671)
Scott, Diana 4:32:38 (19,589)
Scott, Elaine C 4:34:03 (20,005)
Scott, Elizabeth Ann 4:47:40 (23,459)
Scott, Harriet Chealse 5:46:54 (33,040)
Scott, Isabel A 4:40:13 (21,543)
Scott, Jassa 4:18:32 (15,722)
Scott, Julia Vivienne 4:55:52 (25,504)
Scott, Julie 4:58:59 (26,210)
Scott, Kirsty Anne 3:54:33 (9,340)
Scott, Leanne C 4:49:19 (23,874)
Scott, Louise 5:00:08 (26,488)
Scott, Margaret 5:51:32 (33,464)
Scott, Rachel Anne 6:26:20 (35,359)
Scott, Rebecca J 5:46:29 (33,008)
Scott, Rebecca Jayne 3:57:51 (10,345)
Scott, Sandra Louise 5:56:38 (33,839)
Scott, Sandy Maria 6:17:40 (35,013)
Scott, Sarah Briony 5:05:49 (27,497)
Scott, Stephanie R 3:28:52 (4,200)
Scott, Tracy 4:35:18 (20,295)
Scott, Wendy Jane 4:29:36 (18,842)
Scott, Zoe 5:52:29 (33,532)
Scott, Zoe Samantha 6:28:38 (35,449)
Scott-Collis, Sue Mary 5:49:06 (33,248)
Scott-Hamilton, Wendy 4:42:42 (22,186)
Scott-Jones, Michelle 4:45:35 (22,909)
Scott-Martin, Rebecca 4:21:25 (16,528)
Scott-Masson, Nicky Juliet 4:47:17 (23,362)
Scoulding, Janet Elizabeth 5:14:01 (28,928)
Scriven, Laura 5:00:27 (26,549)
Scrivener, Amy Nadine 6:26:00 (35,349)
Scrivens, Hannah 5:12:52 (28,714)
Scrutton, Claire B 3:27:04 (3,879)
Scudamore, Cheryl 5:13:23 (28,824)
Scudder, Lindsay 6:04:06 (34,328)
Seabrook, Caroline 5:15:06 (29,081)
Seabrook, Patricia H 5:45:28 (32,907)
Seager-Hill, Jennifer 4:17:19 (15,380)
Seal, Jessica 5:00:01 (26,457)
Seale, Anna N 4:20:42 (16,333)
Seals, Mandy 5:06:06 (27,549)
Sealy, Wendy L 5:09:44 (28,185)
Seaman, Claire 6:00:52 (34,121)
Seaman, Lucy Anna 5:20:43 (29,965)
Search, Elizabeth 4:16:22 (15,130)
Searle, Alison 5:19:59 (29,846)
Searle, Lisa 5:13:37 (28,861)
Searle, Samphyre Jennifer 5:23:52 (30,451)
Seboa, Natalie 6:10:59 (34,699)
Seccombe, Donna Louise 4:58:47 (26,163)
Secker, Nicola Jane 5:34:26 (31,814)
Seddon, Madeline Isabel 4:47:14 (23,349)
Sedgewick, Helen 5:28:21 (31,069)
Sedgley, Nicola 5:49:31 (33,285)
Sedivy, Mette 4:00:26 (11,100)
Seeley, Anna V 3:35:02 (5,254)
Seers, Phoebe 4:00:56 (11,231)
Seifert, Christiane Susanne 4:16:13 (15,079)
Seiles, Karen Louise 4:02:25 (11,587)
Seingier, Katie Ann 4:46:05 (23,055)
Selby, Karen 4:56:25 (25,633)
Sellek, Yoko 6:01:15 (34,143)
Sellers, Angelina Michelle 5:23:54 (30,458)
Sellers, Hester 5:09:22 (28,120)
Selman, Gillian M 4:05:13 (12,259)
Selway, Georgina 3:56:41 (9,992)
Selway-Swift, Victoria Clare 3:52:41 (8,843)
Sempie, Cathy 4:20:56 (16,394)
Senior, Gill 3:32:04 (4,752)
Senior, Roxanne 5:59:05 (33,998)
Sennitt, Joanne 5:15:25 (29,128)
Sereni, Claudia 4:50:11 (24,090)
Service, Katie 4:37:53 (20,962)
Sesto, Valeria A 3:03:25 (1,341)
Seth, Clare 5:02:07 (26,871)
Setsaas, Anne 4:29:29 (18,800)
Severn, Laura Jane 6:22:14 (35,202)
Sewell, Emma 5:13:26 (28,832)
Sewell, Kate 5:35:36 (31,936)
Sewell, Victoria Emma 5:20:22 (29,894)
Sexton, Joanne Alison 4:09:45 (13,407)
Sexton, Julie 4:14:10 (14,560)
Sexton, Suzanne 6:23:38 (35,262)
Seyde, Louise 4:13:18 (14,312)
Seymour, Annmarie 3:58:08 (10,426)
Seymour, Jenny 5:51:36 (33,473)
Seymour, Natalie 5:24:09 (30,505)
Sha'ath, Sara 4:39:32 (21,397)
Shaba, Jackie 4:21:50 (16,651)
Shackell, Jane 3:55:35 (9,632)
Shackleton, Susan 4:30:06 (19,001)
Shacklock, Susan L 3:33:31 (4,976)
Shah, Kaushik 4:29:02 (18,697)
Shah, Sheetal 6:30:15 (35,510)
Shalders, Donna 5:50:40 (33,400)
Shand, Jenny M 3:52:54 (8,898)
Shand, Julie Helen 5:11:35 (28,487)
Shandley, Gillian Catherine 4:40:21 (21,596)
Shanks, Philippa J 3:55:47 (9,711)
Shannon, Dorothy 6:01:38 (34,165)
Shannon, Lindsey Sheila 5:08:52 (28,025)
Shannon, Louise 6:29:45 (35,487)
Shannon, Margaret Anna 4:26:29 (17,945)
Shannon-Jones, Sue D 6:28:34 (35,448)
Shapiro, Stephen 4:36:02 (20,485)
Shapton, Natalie 5:47:50 (33,125)
Sharma, Gurmeet 7:07:55 (36,290)
Sharma, Marie L 4:48:24 (23,638)
Sharma, Renu 5:23:11 (30,337)
Sharman, Charlotee M 3:54:10 (9,248)
Sharman, Fiona 4:37:19 (20,824)
Sharman, Leahn Darlene 6:23:18 (35,250)
Sharman, Rhiannon A 4:26:58 (18,069)
Sharman, Sarah Lucy 4:27:49 (18,316)
Sharp, Ginny 4:31:07 (19,245)
Sharp, Hannah Ruth 7:36:38 (36,501)
Sharp, Helen C 3:23:44 (3,400)
Sharp, Justine 6:01:32 (34,160)
Sharp, Mandy 4:50:34 (24,179)
Sharp, Susan Ann 3:11:45 (2,072)
Sharpe, Fiona Maria 4:12:37 (14,129)
Sharples, Samantha 5:15:23 (29,122)
Sharratt, Pauline A 5:31:12 (31,434)
Sharrod, Sandra 4:52:52 (24,771)
Sharron, Alyson 6:00:28 (34,092)
Shattock, Chloe 3:31:25 (4,653)
Shaw, Caroline 4:21:37 (16,583)
Shaw, Claire 4:33:21 (19,812)
Shaw, Diane Ruth 4:18:10 (15,621)
Shaw, Julie 5:19:33 (29,779)
Shaw, Kate Elizabeth 4:10:43 (13,643)
Shaw, Lyndsey 6:18:35 (35,061)
Shaw, Melanie 3:34:53 (5,230)
Shaw, Patricia 4:04:15 (12,020)
Shaw, Rachael 6:07:33 (34,534)
Shaw, Tanya J 3:09:35 (1,869)
Shawcross, Judith K 4:22:12 (16,761)
Shawcross, Sarah-Jane 6:42:09 (35,841)
Shay, Rebecca Ann 5:25:06 (30,640)
Shayshutt, Claire 4:40:14 (21,553)
Shea, Samantha Louise 4:27:29 (18,229)
Sheard, Karen 4:02:45 (11,665)
Shearer, Nikki Susan 5:16:50 (29,359)
Sheehan, Pauline M 4:25:53 (17,783)
Sheehy, Maureen 5:49:57 (33,328)
Sheehy, Yvonne M 4:11:42 (13,907)
Sheen, Molly Ann 6:38:56 (35,753)
Sheikh, Shaleena 5:23:23 (30,368)
Sheldon, Sara Kate 5:21:37 (30,098)
Sheldon, Sharon Joanne 5:56:37 (33,837)
Sheldon, Sheena Frances 4:54:53 (25,279)
Sheldon, Vicky 3:47:10 (7,566)
Shelley, Catherine Jane 3:25:00 (3,582)
Shelton, Joanne 4:17:17 (15,374)
Shennan, Lisa C 3:49:16 (8,039)
Shenton, Fiona C 3:37:42 (5,710)
Shepheard, Amanda 4:46:59 (23,304)
Shepherd, Ciara Catherine Sarah 4:01:24 (11,339)
Shepherd, Claire 5:08:50 (28,019)
Shepherd, Fiona 3:54:25 (9,304)
Shepherd, Karen M 5:26:50 (30,876)
Shepherd, Lesley 5:32:25 (31,588)
Shepherd, Lucy Kate 3:28:52 (4,200)
Sheppard, Anna Victoria 4:42:12 (22,065)
Sheppard, Maggie 5:18:36 (29,636)
Sher, Carmel 4:59:57 (26,439)
Sherborne, Amy L 4:32:48 (19,630)
Shergill, Guzz 4:11:12 (13,766)
Sheridan, Clare Louise 5:59:24 (34,013)
Sheridan, Dawn 4:29:31 (18,812)
Sherlock, Estelle E 3:59:57 (10,976)
Sherratt, Jane 4:01:10 (11,291)
Sherriff, Hollie 5:27:57 (31,017)

Sherriff, Laura....4:32:21 (19,529)
Sherry, Noreen Rose Teresa....5:47:32 (33,100)
Sherwood, Julie A....4:42:11 (22,058)
Shettle, Jackie A....4:39:26 (21,368)
Shewell, Sarah J....3:58:18 (10,491)
Shields, Debra....3:40:30 (6,241)
Shields, Julie....4:49:31 (23,911)
Shields, Rachel L....3:50:29 (8,308)
Shields-Peach, Tracey-Anne....5:33:34 (31,723)
Shiels, Rebecca....4:32:05 (19,453)
Shier, Aksinia....5:04:20 (27,250)
Shilling, Emma Lyttleton....3:52:37 (8,826)
Shilling, Kathleen....5:35:01 (31,877)
Shillito, Rachel....5:20:44 (29,970)
Shillitoe, Georgie....4:14:53 (14,759)
Shimizu, Yumiko Caroline....5:08:23 (27,961)
Shipley, Adele Victoria....3:40:17 (6,194)
Shipley, Colette M....4:22:15 (16,786)
Shipley, Louise....4:32:06 (19,459)
Shipster, Tuuli....5:13:03 (28,747)
Shipton, Karen Anne....3:19:47 (2,943)
Shirley, Lorraine C....4:21:35 (16,571)
Shirley, Marie L....3:16:53 (2,658)
Shiu, Crystal....4:23:53 (17,211)

Shobukhova, Liliya....2:22:00 (24)

Liliya Shobukhova (born 13 November 1977) is a Russian former track runner who has enjoyed great success after moving to road races later in her career. The move paid dividends as she won the 2009 Chicago Marathon and following a third-place finish in the 2009 London Marathon she became the first Russian woman to win the event in 2010 with a personal best time of 2:22:00. Shobukhova started her career in middle-distance running in 2001 and reached the final at both the European Indoor Championships and European Athletics Championships in 2002. Two years later, she represented Russia at the 2004 Athens Olympics and reached the 5000m final. She ran at the 2005 World Championships, but her first major successes came the following year when she won silver medals at the 2006 IAAF World Indoor Championships and the 2006 European Athletics Championships. She reached the 5000m final at the 2008 Beijing Olympics and ran the 10,000m at the 2009 World Championships. She is a former world indoor record holder in the 3000m and currently holds the European records for 3000m and 5000m.

Shoemark, Niamh T....3:46:04 (7,330)
Shooter, Melanie Jane....4:35:44 (20,397)
Shore, Sofie Victoria....4:40:31 (21,647)
Short, Holly Louise....4:45:56 (23,009)
Short, Kate....4:33:35 (19,884)
Short, Lisa B....4:30:14 (19,031)
Short, Lynette M....4:57:40 (25,901)
Shorting, Jane....5:42:12 (32,609)
Shotton, Kay Lesley....5:20:35 (29,941)
Shotton, Sam....3:43:41 (6,803)
Shropshall, Claire....5:00:19 (26,524)
Shubotham, Clare Natalie....4:09:23 (13,304)
Shurville, Harriet Louise....4:40:43 (21,700)
Shynn, Sarah Jean....3:43:07 (6,718)
Siaba, Moncha....6:18:11 (35,038)
Siadatan, Yasmina Clare....4:24:40 (17,435)
Siberry, Rita....5:57:34 (33,909)
Sibley, Nicola....3:57:09 (10,141)
Sicam, Marianne....7:14:08 (36,356)
Siciliano, Janine....4:31:09 (19,254)
Siddall, Joanna Helene....5:24:54 (30,602)
Sidden, Sasha M....5:02:39 (26,967)
Sidebottom, Patricia....4:21:40 (16,597)
Sidford, Keira Alexandra....5:03:08 (27,043)
Sidhu, Sheena....5:53:49 (33,629)
Siegerist, Imke....3:48:26 (7,832)
Sierwald, Steph....5:21:28 (30,072)
Sigismondi, Clio....4:30:45 (19,159)
Sigward, June Irene....4:33:48 (19,944)
Sigward, Lorna Joanne....4:27:29 (18,229)
Sill, Michaela....3:32:00 (4,738)
Sillar, Karen Anne....4:47:00 (23,309)
Sillitto, Lucy Ann....4:19:59 (16,103)
Silver, Sally Anne....4:25:29 (17,657)
Silverman, Ruth H....3:31:13 (4,612)
Sim, Samantha Louise....4:47:19 (23,368)
Simac, Maria Donata....5:48:04 (33,146)
Simmonds, Ellen E....5:16:59 (29,383)
Simmonds, Emma Sarah....6:06:50 (34,498)
Simmonds, Lindsey J....4:27:12 (18,149)
Simmonds, Natasha....4:48:33 (23,679)
Simmonds, Tamsin M....3:06:29 (1,569)
Simmonds OBE, Brigid Mary....4:01:22 (11,325)
Simmons, Carmel....3:26:09 (3,762)
Simmons, Emma L....3:51:42 (8,587)
Simmons, Hannah....5:08:42 (28,004)
Simmons, Lyndsey Jane....4:38:29 (21,116)
Simmons, Meinou....3:43:47 (6,828)
Simmons, Susan G....4:55:53 (25,508)
Simon, Laurance Françoise....4:43:48 (22,441)
Simper, Kathy....5:29:33 (31,228)
Simper, Paula Ann....6:29:08 (35,466)
Simpson, Angela....5:25:22 (30,675)
Simpson, Cecilia....4:33:12 (19,767)
Simpson, Gloria....5:02:13 (26,893)
Simpson, Janine....3:46:48 (7,489)
Simpson, Jeanette Sara....5:36:49 (32,085)
Simpson, Jodie Louise....5:09:27 (28,132)
Simpson, Kaye S....4:27:43 (18,293)
Simpson, Louise J....4:03:36 (11,874)
Simpson, Melanie Ann....7:36:31 (36,498)
Simpson-Davies, Sarah....4:06:15 (12,511)
Sims, Sandra Francis....4:44:20 (22,599)
Sims, Vicky....3:57:20 (10,190)
Sinclair, Charlotte....4:04:01 (11,962)
Sinclair, Chloe Julia....4:07:55 (12,933)
Sinclair, Isla Louise....5:23:54 (30,458)
Sinclair, Jo....5:04:59 (27,363)
Sinclair, Nina Kathryn....4:24:19 (17,329)
Sinclair, Rachael....6:17:14 (34,992)
Sindole, Eileen Patricia....4:20:26 (16,244)
Sinfield, Sharon....4:55:35 (25,429)
Singer, Jo L....3:17:46 (2,739)
Singleterry, Tracy Leigh....4:33:35 (19,884)
Singleton, Rebecca Jane....5:46:08 (32,963)
Sinnott, Giselle....4:34:22 (20,085)
Sishton, Frances....4:32:49 (19,635)
Sissons, Christine....6:04:37 (34,357)
Sivanandarajah, Pavidra....4:39:52 (21,481)
Sixsmith, Gemma Francesca....5:07:51 (27,871)
Skelton, Anna F....3:36:17 (5,456)
Skelton, Katie....4:11:59 (13,984)
Skidmore, Flora....3:25:50 (3,709)
Skinner, Corrina....5:50:55 (33,420)
Skinner, Jenny....4:48:47 (23,741)
Skinner, Jenny Jane....5:07:47 (27,858)
Skinner, Julia Dawn....5:09:13 (28,089)
Skinner, Nancy....4:29:34 (18,826)
Skinner, Sally Jayne....5:02:39 (26,967)
Skinsley, Mikki Jane....5:44:51 (32,855)
Skipper, Kate....4:05:26 (12,322)
Skull, Beverly Anne....6:40:38 (35,804)
Skull, Jacqueline Ann....4:54:28 (25,171)
Skull, Kate....4:10:43 (13,643)
Skytte, Aase Hansen....4:59:10 (26,252)
Slack, Clover Eleanor....4:45:51 (22,990)
Slade, Elizabeth M....4:27:35 (18,256)
Slade, Maxine Mary....5:36:11 (32,015)
Slade, Nicola Lesley....5:25:28 (30,688)
Slade, Tracy Margaret....5:56:54 (33,859)
Slagmolen, Caroline Jacqueline A....5:35:18 (31,902)
Slaney, Claire Michelle....4:40:18 (21,574)
Slater, Carolyn....5:48:53 (33,231)
Slater, Crystal....5:09:42 (28,180)
Slater, Lesley....4:06:37 (12,604)
Slater, Morag....4:19:49 (16,045)
Slater, Nicki Jane....6:06:34 (34,486)
Slater, Nicky Jane....4:31:26 (19,316)
Slattery, Rachel L....3:38:30 (5,846)
Sledge, Charlotte Emily....3:45:49 (7,267)
Slevin, Sara....6:49:49 (35,993)
Slingo, Corinne Dawn....7:12:18 (36,329)
Slingsby, Elizabeth Diane....3:59:45 (10,932)
Sliwerski, Claire....4:38:43 (21,175)
Sloan, Angeline....4:12:38 (14,132)
Slocombe, Jessica....4:59:27 (26,321)
Sloss, Ruth E....3:53:46 (9,147)
Slow, Natasha....5:30:16 (31,323)
Smail, Amanda....3:20:25 (3,010)
Smailes, Joanne Louise....4:42:55 (22,241)
Smale, Kathy Sharon....5:49:34 (33,292)
Small, Antonia....4:33:07 (19,734)
Small, Claire Rachel....7:00:33 (36,195)
Small, Lorna Jane....6:02:13 (34,197)
Small, Natasha....5:42:27 (32,633)
Smalley, Wendy....4:48:31 (23,671)
Smart, Amanda....5:46:22 (32,993)
Smart, Elizabeth V....4:37:59 (20,985)
Smart, Michelle Lisa....4:12:43 (14,161)
Smart, Vanessa A....4:10:40 (13,629)
Smeaton, Sally Ann....4:12:24 (14,068)
Smedley, Dionne....5:12:15 (28,609)
Smelhausova, Maki....5:34:32 (31,826)
Smetzer, Christine Margaret....3:51:48 (8,608)
Smewin, Sarah....5:32:55 (31,654)
Smiles, Sally....5:46:35 (33,013)
Smith, Abby....5:39:38 (32,357)
Smith, Abigail Charlotte....5:39:33 (32,352)
Smith, Abigail Marie Elizabeth....4:28:16 (18,443)
Smith, Alexandra....4:24:27 (17,376)
Smith, Alexandra Maria....6:53:59 (36,085)
Smith, Alison....5:01:50 (26,816)
Smith, Angela....5:41:22 (32,520)
Smith, Angela....6:22:37 (35,216)
Smith, Anna....4:24:20 (17,333)
Smith, Anna....4:58:21 (26,054)
Smith, Barbara Sarah....6:47:03 (35,949)
Smith, Barrie John....6:03:10 (34,265)
Smith, Becky....4:39:46 (21,452)
Smith, Bernadette M....5:51:55 (33,498)
Smith, Bethan S....3:55:37 (9,647)
Smith, Caroline....4:16:40 (15,209)
Smith, Caroline....5:21:36 (30,095)
Smith, Catherine Jane....4:37:19 (20,824)
Smith, Catherine M....3:32:07 (4,761)
Smith, Cecile....5:58:36 (33,968)
Smith, Charlene Victoria....4:51:48 (24,492)
Smith, Cheryl Dawn Rita....4:40:43 (21,700)
Smith, Claire....4:27:00 (18,079)
Smith, Claire....4:42:08 (22,045)
Smith, Claire....5:01:41 (26,791)
Smith, Claire Louise....4:37:38 (20,916)
Smith, Donna....5:13:38 (28,863)
Smith, Donna M....3:38:43 (5,890)
Smith, Elaine....4:17:16 (15,368)
Smith, Eleanor Rachel....4:29:46 (18,905)
Smith, Elizabeth Mary....4:26:25 (17,930)
Smith, Ella....4:13:44 (14,442)
Smith, Emma....4:44:28 (22,629)
Smith, Emma Clare....5:22:46 (30,262)
Smith, Fiona Jane Alice....5:28:10 (31,051)
Smith, Frances Elizabeth....4:09:18 (13,283)
Smith, Ginette....4:33:57 (19,980)
Smith, Giselle....4:59:10 (26,252)

Steenkamp, Kelly A ... 3:57:54 (10,358)
Steer, Deborah A ... 2:56:01 (800)
Steiner, Anna-Tina ... 4:08:39 (13,126)
Steiner, Caroline Ann ... 3:59:39 (10,903)
Steinlin, Maja ... 4:49:43 (23,987)
Steinmann, Anne ... 4:54:27 (25,168)
Stenner, Sue Caroline ... 4:55:32 (25,414)
Stephen, Lisa ... 3:31:34 (4,677)
Stephen, Lynne J ... 3:48:29 (7,843)
Stephen, Nicola ... 5:40:10 (32,408)
Stephens, Emma Jane ... 5:08:11 (27,925)
Stephens, Jodie ... 4:32:07 (19,464)
Stephens, Kate ... 3:37:03 (5,574)
Stephens, Rachel E ... 4:32:59 (19,691)
Stephens, Sarah Caroline ... 4:21:44 (16,623)
Stephens, Vanessa ... 4:16:05 (15,047)
Stephenson, Brooke ... 5:37:27 (32,163)
Stephenson, Helen Lisa ... 6:23:23 (35,256)
Stephenson, Hilary Ann ... 5:37:21 (32,153)
Stephenson, Kim ... 3:13:01 (2,192)
Stephenson, Vicky ... 5:18:22 (29,604)
Stepney, Ruth ... 5:44:42 (32,839)
Steptoe, Charlotte ... 3:10:48 (1,971)
Stern, Danielle ... 5:24:12 (30,510)
Stern, Lucy ... 4:34:07 (20,025)
Sternau, Sarah ... 4:56:50 (25,728)
Steven, Amanda Jane ... 4:42:50 (22,225)
Stevens, Christina ... 4:38:14 (21,037)
Stevens, Claire Elizabeth ... 4:40:13 (21,543)
Stevens, Imogen ... 5:04:01 (27,194)
Stevens, Jo ... 4:43:06 (22,282)
Stevens, Kim ... 4:24:52 (17,481)
Stevens, Leighann ... 5:39:14 (32,324)
Stevens, Lynn Marie ... 4:58:11 (26,008)
Stevens, Marilla Carlyn ... 5:59:31 (34,017)
Stevens, Michelle ... 4:45:14 (22,824)
Stevens, Michelle C ... 4:22:36 (16,875)
Stevens, Patricia Anne ... 5:13:26 (28,832)
Stevens, Rose ... 5:57:17 (33,888)
Stevens, Tracy ... 3:59:32 (10,870)
Stevens-Cox, Sarah ... 4:31:15 (19,280)
Stevenson, Alysia ... 6:02:57 (34,248)
Stevenson, Andrea ... 6:20:28 (35,145)
Stevenson, Faye ... 4:14:35 (14,677)
Stevenson, Michelle Louise ... 4:40:42 (21,693)
Steward, Claire E ... 3:29:48 (4,379)
Steward, Ruth ... 4:29:56 (18,966)
Stewart, Beryl Veronica ... 4:34:28 (20,114)
Stewart, Cathy A ... 3:48:48 (7,927)
Stewart, Emma ... 5:24:40 (30,577)
Stewart, Lauren L ... 2:51:58 (563)
Stewart, Lucinda Jane ... 4:07:26 (12,810)
Stewart, Nicola ... 5:57:16 (33,886)
Stewart, Sara ... 6:01:30 (34,156)
Stewart, Susan A ... 4:01:02 (11,258)
Stewart, Theodora Jane ... 4:44:05 (22,529)
Stewart, Zoe ... 5:24:36 (30,569)
Stibbs, Cath J ... 3:56:57 (10,071)
Stickland, Anna ... 4:28:55 (18,650)
Stickler, Carol ... 4:07:41 (12,883)
Stilwell, Rachael Annie ... 5:05:15 (27,414)
Stilwell, Sarah L ... 4:27:50 (18,319)
Stimpson, Fran ... 4:29:26 (18,785)
Stimpson, Sally Jane ... 5:17:42 (29,499)
Stimson, Cindy ... 6:13:00 (34,803)
Stimson, Donna L ... 6:54:41 (36,102)
Stinchcombe, Mary C ... 4:38:32 (21,124)
Stirk, Kate Anne ... 5:10:35 (28,346)
Stirling, Jane E ... 4:21:20 (16,500)
Stockburn, Ruth Jane ... 4:41:09 (21,807)
Stockdale, Larraine Maria ... 4:53:35 (24,937)
Stockdale, Zoe C ... 5:11:20 (28,455)
Stocker, Aimée ... 4:52:38 (24,718)
Stocker, Audrey ... 5:03:48 (27,156)
Stocks, Joanne ... 3:49:48 (8,166)
Stockton, Amanda Louise ... 4:39:34 (21,406)
Stockton, Jo ... 6:23:07 (35,240)
Stoddard, Amy S ... 4:17:06 (15,321)
Stoffell, Caroline Louise ... 5:27:05 (30,919)
Stoger, Lisa ... 5:26:44 (30,868)
Stojsavljevic, Jelena ... 4:53:59 (25,045)
Stokes, Elizabeth Patricia ... 4:28:33 (18,539)
Stokes, Kelly ... 4:55:40 (25,452)
Stokes, Laura ... 5:57:57 (33,928)
Stokes, Margaret Gwyneth ... 4:18:53 (15,822)
Stokoe, Samantha Clare ... 5:16:25 (29,295)
Stolt, Anu ... 3:53:41 (9,117)
Stonard, Sarah Louise ... 3:49:19 (8,047)
Stone, Cheryl Lea ... 4:32:51 (19,654)
Stone, Gina M ... 5:19:39 (29,800)
Stone, Marie Louise ... 4:17:23 (15,400)
Stone, Sarah Louise ... 5:10:09 (28,264)
Stoneham, Sara Ann ... 4:52:23 (24,657)
Stoneman, Dawn E ... 5:16:00 (29,229)
Stoodley, Michelle ... 4:45:21 (22,852)
Stopforth, Karen Nicola ... 4:46:18 (23,128)
Stoppani, Julie M ... 3:36:55 (5,547)
Stopps, Penny Louise ... 5:17:20 (29,445)
Stops, Sarah Louise ... 5:32:51 (31,647)
Storer, Dawn Lesley ... 4:03:56 (11,948)
Storey, Elaine ... 3:14:12 (2,341)
Storey, Evalyn Tara ... 4:33:20 (19,811)
Storey, Katherine ... 4:15:44 (14,962)
Storey, Pamela ... 7:41:09 (36,528)
Storme, Alexander E ... 4:13:32 (14,378)
Storrar, Kerry ... 3:38:16 (5,815)
Storrar, Lisa ... 4:55:56 (25,520)
Stott, Ami Elizabeth ... 5:18:17 (29,588)
Stott, Charles S ... 3:47:22 (7,612)
Stott, Katherine A ... 4:03:21 (11,813)
Stott, Nicola Clare ... 4:56:16 (25,601)
Stow, Diane ... 5:39:01 (32,305)
Stow, Louise ... 6:23:27 (35,259)
Strachan, Jan L ... 4:33:30 (19,852)
Straiton, Terri ... 7:02:39 (36,223)
Strande, Gro Soensteby ... 3:45:05 (7,111)
Strang, Sue ... 3:41:41 (6,455)
Strange, Charlotte A ... 3:59:12 (10,779)
Strange, Jo ... 7:13:29 (36,342)
Strange, Sheila E ... 4:59:28 (26,326)
Stratford, Christine ... 4:54:11 (25,093)
Stratford-Smith, Jonane Elizabeth ... 5:20:58 (30,000)
Stratton, Lucy ... 4:11:38 (13,889)
Straw, Pauline C ... 3:23:55 (3,423)
Strawbridge, Sharon Mary ... 7:19:22 (36,399)
Streeter, Donna Kathleen ... 4:32:19 (19,520)
Stretton, Jackie Mary ... 4:47:35 (23,433)
Stringari, Silvia ... 4:01:46 (11,439)
Stringer, Lara ... 5:53:12 (33,591)
Stringer, Samantha J ... 4:43:39 (22,405)
Stringfellow, Sandra ... 5:03:18 (27,073)
Stritton, Kerrie Jane ... 4:46:49 (23,259)
Stronach, Samantha Jayne ... 4:54:58 (25,296)
Strong, Lucy Anna ... 5:03:00 (27,026)
Stroud, Frances ... 5:45:08 (32,879)
Stubbings, Natasha ... 5:45:24 (32,901)
Stubbs, Grace Anne Victoria ... 4:51:36 (24,440)
Stubbs, Sally J ... 3:46:41 (7,456)
Stuckey, Vera May ... 5:43:00 (32,665)
Sturdy, Louise ... 5:21:21 (30,052)
Sturge, Claire L ... 5:28:40 (31,106)
Sturkey, Ruth E ... 4:27:40 (18,277)
Sturla, Alison M ... 5:40:55 (32,473)
Sturzaker, Nicola A ... 3:34:11 (5,093)
Stuyvesant, Valerie ... 5:08:08 (27,918)
Styles, Charlotte ... 6:18:59 (35,079)
Styles, Elizabeth ... 4:22:46 (16,928)
Suarez, Carmen ... 6:30:34 (35,520)
Subert, Jacquie Kate ... 5:58:38 (33,971)
Suchak, Mala ... 6:40:21 (35,801)
Suckling, Alison T ... 4:41:47 (21,964)
Suckling, Marion ... 5:18:15 (29,582)
Sudra, Sunita ... 6:13:13 (34,814)
Suffell, Helen ... 6:48:47 (35,972)
Sugden, Amelia ... 4:03:05 (11,748)
Sugiura, Kumiko ... 5:03:27 (27,093)
Sulin, Kelly ... 4:57:21 (25,830)
Sullivan, Allana ... 3:32:25 (4,804)
Sullivan, Carmel M ... 3:11:17 (2,025)
Sullivan, Elizabeth ... 4:17:12 (15,351)
Sullivan, Gemma Naomi ... 4:30:36 (19,125)
Sullivan, Julia ... 7:22:55 (36,426)
Sullivan, Lyndsey Joy ... 4:13:18 (14,312)
Sullivan, Michelle ... 4:33:32 (19,862)
Summers, Adele ... 7:16:26 (36,374)
Summers, Emma Olive ... 4:04:43 (12,136)
Summers, Lin ... 5:45:43 (32,925)
Summers, Maureen M ... 4:32:54 (19,673)
Summers, Paula Christine ... 6:20:03 (35,126)
Summerscale, Claire Elizabeth ... 4:50:45 (24,224)
Summerville, Karen Mary ... 4:18:10 (15,621)
Sumner, Raynor Kim ... 5:54:43 (33,687)
Sunderland, Martina ... 5:16:51 (29,365)
Sunderland, Ruth ... 5:25:33 (30,703)
Sunderland, Susan Elizabeth ... 3:41:48 (6,476)
Supyk, Claire Louise ... 4:41:24 (21,867)
Surendranath, Suma ... 5:51:47 (33,490)
Surman, Gaye ... 4:42:26 (22,124)
Sutcliffe, Georgina Frances E ... 4:42:36 (22,153)
Sutcliffe, Gillian ... 4:23:14 (17,030)
Sutcliffe, Karen ... 4:31:30 (19,334)
Sutcliffe, Louise E ... 5:35:18 (31,902)
Sutherland, Anne-Marie Thérèse ... 5:44:16 (32,793)
Sutherland, Fiona Kathleen ... 4:07:00 (12,711)
Sutherland, Fiona M ... 3:50:36 (8,332)
Sutherland, Gemma Kate ... 5:40:47 (32,455)
Sutherland, Helen Claire ... 3:40:45 (6,283)
Sutherland, Polly ... 4:40:40 (21,683)
Sutherland, Sarah Jane ... 5:19:18 (29,745)
Sutterby, Philippa Jane ... 9:02:36 (36,616)
Sutton, Amy V ... 4:50:52 (24,262)
Sutton, Caroline ... 3:44:49 (7,058)
Sutton, Emily ... 5:36:54 (32,093)
Sutton, Jill ... 4:02:19 (11,560)
Sutton, Julie M ... 3:15:30 (2,496)
Sutton, Louise ... 5:12:57 (28,730)
Sutton, Louise ... 6:04:39 (34,362)
Sutton, Megan H ... 4:10:45 (13,655)
Sutton, Verity ... 6:08:56 (34,612)
Sutton-Haigh, Nicola A ... 4:50:30 (24,161)
Swain, Faye ... 4:57:20 (25,827)
Swain, Glenda ... 5:32:03 (31,538)
Swain, Tracy ... 6:18:11 (35,038)
Swainson, Joanna ... 7:14:07 (36,354)
Swait, Terry Kay ... 3:37:31 (5,666)
Swallow, Helen B ... 4:15:09 (14,821)
Swallow, Tracey ... 7:46:16 (36,553)
Swan, Carolyn ... 3:29:37 (4,345)
Swan, Eileen Maria ... 5:02:28 (26,938)
Swan, Lisa Joanne ... 5:44:07 (32,780)
Swan, Moira ... 5:07:20 (27,777)
Swan, Nikki ... 4:21:21 (16,506)
Swan, Suzanne Emma ... 4:33:16 (19,791)
Swann, Allison ... 5:46:53 (33,039)
Swannell, Lucy Ruth ... 5:44:04 (32,777)
Swart, Mine ... 4:37:06 (20,771)
Swayne, Justine ... 5:20:05 (29,861)
Sweeney, Carol Ann ... 6:32:25 (35,574)
Sweeney, Lynn ... 4:39:24 (21,353)
Sweeting, Allison Sweetomg ... 3:58:34 (10,584)
Sweeting, Lisa Michelle ... 5:43:16 (32,699)
Sweetman, Caroline J ... 4:19:13 (15,903)
Swift, Claire Louise ... 5:20:53 (29,992)
Swift, Sally Anne ... 5:08:12 (27,929)
Swinburne, Tracey J ... 5:45:45 (32,929)
Swindale, Paula ... 5:50:30 (33,383)
Swindells, Laura ... 4:07:50 (12,912)
Swinhoe, Sarah J ... 3:14:46 (2,414)
Swinson, Catherine ... 3:33:25 (4,954)
Syed, Rachel ... 3:52:00 (8,659)
Syed, Tara J ... 5:08:32 (27,978)
Syers, Sarah J ... 3:34:12 (5,096)
Sykes, Christine Alice ... 4:52:55 (24,779)
Sykes, Margaret J ... 3:41:25 (6,408)
Sykes, Michelle Annette ... 6:12:59 (34,802)
Sykes, Nichola Charlotte Melinda ... 3:36:50 (5,532)
Sykes, Sharon L ... 4:09:47 (13,416)
Sykes-Facey, Heather ... 3:36:57 (5,554)
Symes, Louise N ... 4:18:29 (15,711)
Symes, Wendy ... 4:55:04 (25,326)
Symonds, Carla ... 5:30:31 (31,360)
Symonds, Claire Bryoney ... 4:05:53 (12,428)
Symonds, Julie Gayle ... 5:44:20 (32,798)
Symonds, Rachel A ... 5:02:48 (26,993)
Symons, Heather Joan ... 4:09:57 (13,456)
Synnott-Wells, Marie G ... 3:04:48 (1,446)
Syriopoulos, Helen ... 5:36:16 (32,030)
Szabo, Karen ... 4:57:59 (25,968)
Szczotka, Ewa ... 3:59:05 (10,740)

Szeteiova, Timea 4:29:34 (18,826)
Szkornik, Lucy 5:04:05 (27,205)
Szpytko, Liz Mary 4:55:06 (25,335)
Tabar, Sandra Z 4:39:36 (21,411)
Tabb, Alexandra Louise 3:51:47 (8,603)
Tabor, Rosalind M 3:24:05 (3,449)
Tachauer, Linda Joyce 6:43:08 (35,867)
Tafa, Askale 2:24:39 (34)
Taffe, Alessandra 4:41:46 (21,959)
Taffs, Alison 5:35:16 (31,901)
Tagg, Michaela H 3:41:35 (6,437)
Tagg, Susan G 3:46:13 (7,357)
Tahir, Perican 4:58:29 (26,082)
Tait, Bianca 4:32:17 (19,512)
Tait, Emma 6:11:05 (34,704)
Takei, Kumiko 4:40:14 (21,553)
Talbot, Cassie 8:37:28 (36,605)
Talbot, Ellena Clare 6:28:21 (35,440)
Talbot, Joy Ann Catherine 4:18:13 (15,636)
Talbot, Julie 4:45:50 (22,985)
Talia, Sara Zohra 3:48:03 (7,750)
Taliadoros, Helen 4:48:48 (23,747)
Talpert, Jacques 5:24:49 (30,593)
Tan, Chew Kwee 3:58:47 (10,652)
Tang, My-Yen 5:13:45 (28,880)
Tangey, Ilona Nicole 5:10:20 (28,297)
Tanghe, Fanny 4:19:25 (15,954)
Tanghe, Sabine 3:59:07 (10,752)
Tanha, Samira 5:50:55 (33,420)
Tank, Lyn 5:55:27 (33,751)
Tanner, Emma D 5:18:14 (29,578)
Tanner, Karen L 4:40:34 (21,660)
Tanner, Nicky 4:45:04 (22,788)
Tanner, Pauline F 3:57:50 (10,337)
Tanner, Stephanie 4:36:01 (20,481)
Tanner, Victoria Antonietta 5:39:11 (32,321)
Tanqueray, Aurore 5:47:20 (33,080)
Taphouse, Karin Tina 5:29:18 (31,193)
Taranowski, Helen L 3:08:41 (1,780)
Targa, April L 4:03:59 (11,956)
Tarkow-Reinisch, Lili 4:57:37 (25,884)
Tarrach, Zoe C 3:27:51 (4,025)
Tarrant, Jenna 3:40:51 (6,301)
Tarrant, Rachael Caroline 4:44:23 (22,609)
Tarry, Beverley 4:35:05 (20,245)
Tartoosie, Lee-Anne 6:38:40 (35,745)
Tarver, Melissa Jane 4:57:44 (25,918)
Tasker, Bonk 4:07:40 (12,878)
Tate, Sarah L 4:26:19 (17,904)
Tatem, Lisa Caroline 4:49:15 (23,865)
Tatham, Jo Teresa 4:01:01 (11,254)
Tatton, Kate 4:54:39 (25,219)
Tavner, Gillian 3:26:01 (3,736)
Tawse, Jennifer Anne 6:01:22 (34,150)
Tay, Alison Pey Tze 4:18:16 (15,648)
Taylor, Alana 5:04:10 (27,222)
Taylor, Alice Phoebe 4:11:39 (13,893)
Taylor, Alison 4:13:44 (14,442)
Taylor, Amanda Elisabeth 4:04:44 (12,140)
Taylor, Angela Elaine 4:39:05 (21,278)
Taylor, Angela Marie 4:49:45 (23,994)
Taylor, Ann 5:13:27 (28,837)
Taylor, Beverley Susan 6:14:12 (34,844)
Taylor, Camilla 4:01:59 (11,486)
Taylor, Carol A 3:36:43 (5,515)
Taylor, Caroline 4:06:07 (12,478)
Taylor, Cathy 4:06:38 (12,611)
Taylor, Claire Louise 6:14:35 (34,862)
Taylor, Constanze 4:58:52 (26,183)
Taylor, Cordelia Vaquerizo 3:48:06 (7,761)
Taylor, Dawn J 5:54:29 (33,674)
Taylor, Debbie J 4:14:09 (14,547)
Taylor, Emily 7:54:52 (36,578)
Taylor, Emma 5:03:11 (27,056)
Taylor, Emma Louise 5:33:18 (31,693)
Taylor, Gabrielle Alana 4:39:35 (21,408)
Taylor, Helen 3:31:16 (4,619)
Taylor, Helen 5:26:34 (30,848)
Taylor, Helen Christine 5:31:17 (31,447)
Taylor, Helen J 5:29:16 (31,184)
Taylor, Jade 4:42:07 (22,042)
Taylor, Jane 5:34:12 (31,780)
Taylor, Janet E 5:01:03 (26,659)
Taylor, Jayne 3:10:24 (1,940)
Taylor, Jennifer Elizabeth 5:37:00 (32,103)
Taylor, Judy Anne 4:41:14 (21,827)
Taylor, Karen 5:17:05 (29,397)
Taylor, Kay 4:50:07 (24,075)
Taylor, Kelly Ann 4:20:03 (16,117)
Taylor, Kim Ann 5:37:12 (32,125)
Taylor, Kristin 3:46:39 (7,453)
Taylor, Leila 4:52:06 (24,573)
Taylor, Lindsay Anne 6:01:49 (34,175)
Taylor, Lucy Elizabeth 3:56:34 (9,953)
Taylor, Lynsey 4:22:36 (16,875)
Taylor, Madeleine 6:10:17 (34,676)
Taylor, Michelle Kim 6:06:25 (34,473)
Taylor, Odette L 5:22:24 (30,207)
Taylor, Rachel Helen 4:26:48 (18,024)
Taylor, Rebecca Jane 5:04:53 (27,346)
Taylor, Rhian W 5:48:36 (33,203)
Taylor, Rita Ann 5:51:30 (33,463)
Taylor, Rosie Penderel 6:10:17 (34,676)
Taylor, Samantha 5:15:56 (29,218)
Taylor, Samantha Jane 4:15:43 (14,958)
Taylor, Sara 4:31:23 (19,306)
Taylor, Sara Penelope 4:56:46 (25,707)
Taylor, Sarah Louise 6:39:26 (35,769)
Taylor, Sasha 5:17:33 (29,480)
Taylor, Sophia Frances 5:03:44 (27,147)
Taylor, Sophie 6:45:04 (35,910)
Taylor, Susan 4:22:38 (16,890)
Taylor, Valerie 6:00:26 (34,089)
Taylor, Victoria Louise 6:25:16 (35,325)
Taylor, Zakia 4:57:22 (25,834)
Taynton, Catherine Lorraine 5:06:26 (27,612)
Teal, Amy 4:36:37 (20,637)
Teale, Julie 5:41:52 (32,573)
Tear, Patricia Sarah 7:06:58 (36,279)
Teare, Charlotte J 4:14:47 (14,740)
Teasdale, Andrea Jane 5:03:57 (27,177)
Teasdale, Debbie 4:38:13 (21,034)
Teasdale, Kelly Ann 8:43:44 (36,607)
Teasdale, Sophie Abigail 5:20:06 (29,864)
Teasdale, Susan 4:12:40 (14,143)
Teasdale, Vicki 8:43:44 (36,607)
Tebay, Nicky Anne Whaley 4:41:47 (21,964)
Tebb, Julie Elizabeth 5:19:24 (29,761)
Tee, Sarah Lucy 4:33:33 (19,867)
Teece, Natalie L 3:35:45 (5,367)
Teevan, Marie 5:15:29 (29,143)
Teferi, Sarah 4:19:57 (16,086)
Teggart, Laura 4:45:38 (22,927)
Teichmann, Ellen 6:19:11 (35,090)
Temperton-Ball, Lynnette-Jane 5:58:16 (33,948)
Tempest, Claire Michelle 4:18:52 (15,818)
Tennant, Nichola 5:41:41 (32,548)
Terburgh, Caroline 4:00:42 (11,170)
Terkelsen, Irene 3:54:42 (9,387)
Terry, Carolyn 5:59:16 (34,007)
Terry, Helen Geraldine 5:14:34 (28,998)
Terry, Ros Beth 5:10:32 (28,335)
Tester, Emma Louise 6:30:19 (35,512)
Thackeray, Lisa Annette 4:03:38 (11,884)
Thatcher, Sarah M 6:30:05 (35,503)
Thayer, Rosie Elaine 6:06:25 (34,473)
Theobald, Alice Jane 4:56:48 (25,720)
Theodore, Brigitte 4:04:16 (12,023)
Thérèse, Julie Christine 5:17:00 (29,389)
Thetford-Parkes, Sally Jane 5:30:59 (31,415)
Theurillat, Christelle 4:27:51 (18,327)
Thi, Ruth 5:22:47 (30,267)
Thick, Jacqui Louise 3:36:19 (5,459)
Thirkettle, Emma 6:15:05 (34,888)
Thistelton, Heather Joan 4:50:02 (24,055)
Thom, Laura E 4:06:42 (12,625)
Thom, Marion 4:45:34 (22,906)
Thomas, Abigail 4:30:32 (19,098)
Thomas, Amanda 5:56:23 (33,821)
Thomas, Angela 5:35:46 (31,964)
Thomas, Ann 2:59:19 (1,084)
Thomas, Beverley 5:14:30 (28,989)
Thomas, Carole 3:48:38 (7,878)
Thomas, Caroline 4:58:42 (26,144)
Thomas, Carolyn 6:01:27 (34,152)
Thomas, Claire 5:16:04 (29,238)
Thomas, Claire Louise 4:58:46 (26,159)
Thomas, Elisabeth 4:44:30 (22,638)
Thomas, Emma Jayne 4:59:53 (26,429)
Thomas, Faith Cassandra 5:20:00 (29,850)
Thomas, Helen 4:12:40 (14,143)
Thomas, Jan Maria 5:00:13 (26,502)
Thomas, Jane 4:21:25 (16,528)
Thomas, Jane Patricia 4:08:04 (12,978)
Thomas, Joanne 5:43:24 (32,712)
Thomas, Joanne Maria 5:01:42 (26,792)
Thomas, Julie C 3:43:45 (6,813)
Thomas, Karen 4:50:02 (24,055)
Thomas, Karen Louise 5:28:02 (31,034)
Thomas, Karina Groenlund 3:50:30 (8,311)
Thomas, Katy 4:46:30 (23,168)
Thomas, Leanne 5:55:01 (33,720)
Thomas, Lucy 4:46:35 (23,193)
Thomas, Lynda 7:42:52 (36,535)
Thomas, Nunette 6:53:38 (36,079)
Thomas, Rebecca 4:40:19 (21,579)
Thomas, Rhian 7:23:14 (36,431)
Thomas, Rose 4:25:10 (17,566)
Thomas, Stefanie 7:39:16 (36,517)
Thomas, Steph 5:04:53 (27,346)
Thomas, Yvonne 6:29:43 (35,485)
Thomas, Zena Mazel 4:50:36 (24,185)
Thomlinson, Rebecca Sarah 4:39:37 (21,418)
Thompson, Angela Jane 4:58:00 (25,970)
Thompson, Cara 3:29:42 (4,360)
Thompson, Charlotte Ann 4:02:38 (11,636)
Thompson, Danielle Louise 6:46:00 (35,932)
Thompson, Diane 6:20:44 (35,155)
Thompson, Elizabeth 5:02:02 (26,850)
Thompson, Elizabeth K 4:10:27 (13,579)
Thompson, Emilia Bonnar 4:12:38 (14,132)
Thompson, Fiona 3:45:16 (7,156)
Thompson, Fiona Jane 4:53:24 (24,893)
Thompson, Gillian 5:15:46 (29,190)
Thompson, Gillian N 4:38:46 (21,193)
Thompson, Hannah 4:50:08 (24,078)
Thompson, Joslyn L 4:03:18 (11,801)
Thompson, Joy 6:11:48 (34,740)
Thompson, Julie 4:42:15 (22,079)
Thompson, Julie D 3:29:31 (4,325)
Thompson, Julie Patricia 5:02:52 (27,000)
Thompson, Leanne 5:10:28 (28,323)
Thompson, Linda Jane 5:04:40 (27,308)
Thompson, Lisa 4:36:11 (20,525)
Thompson, Lucy Jane 5:23:01 (30,307)
Thompson, Lucy Joanne 3:53:15 (8,983)
Thompson, Mary 5:02:10 (26,881)
Thompson, Rachael Pamela 3:45:49 (7,267)
Thompson, Romie Camille 5:49:21 (33,264)
Thompson, Sam 5:24:56 (30,609)
Thompson, Sara 4:59:02 (26,223)
Thompson, Sarah L 4:26:26 (17,934)
Thompson, Sheena 5:00:22 (26,529)
Thompson, Sophie 5:08:42 (28,004)
Thompson, Susan Margaret 4:54:56 (25,292)
Thompson, Tanya 7:05:00 (36,254)
Thompson, Teri D 3:33:31 (4,976)
Thompson, Victoria Florence 5:15:42 (29,177)
Thompson, Vivienne 3:40:28 (6,228)
Thomson, Emma Jane 4:18:07 (15,614)
Thomson, Guinevere 5:25:29 (30,690)
Thomson, Jackie Patricia 4:53:48 (24,991)
Thomson, Julie Kathleen 5:46:09 (32,965)
Thomson, Lesley 5:37:43 (32,183)
Thomson, Louise Mary 5:08:11 (27,925)
Thomson, Maria 6:06:46 (34,492)
Thomson, Nyree D 4:42:28 (22,130)
Thomson, Sally Anne 4:54:36 (25,204)
Thomson, Sally Louise 3:50:16 (8,264)
Thorn, Samantha 4:02:59 (11,726)
Thorne, Bryony Louise De Ville 4:25:40 (17,707)
Thorne, Christine 3:52:02 (8,667)
Thorne, Karen E 4:57:14 (25,810)
Thorne, Liz 5:31:08 (31,427)
Thorne, Sarah J 3:38:05 (5,779)
Thorneycroft, Rebecca Jayne D 4:43:25 (22,349)
Thornhill, Natalie Jane 4:38:15 (21,041)
Thornley, Cheryl 5:36:15 (32,027)
Thornton, Alison J 3:25:32 (3,652)

Ungi, Sheleen....4:51:06 (24,333)
Unlu, Varinder Rani....6:01:39 (34,166)
Unwin, Trudi....4:48:37 (23,699)
Upcraft, Louise....4:49:14 (23,861)
Uppal, Donna Marie....5:39:28 (32,343)
Upton, Helen....4:16:14 (15,084)
Urquhart, Lauren....4:30:10 (19,017)
Urquhart, Serena Anne....4:16:00 (15,026)
Urry, Samantha Ann....4:52:12 (24,600)
Urwin, Rosamund....5:24:56 (30,609)
Urwin, Sue....4:40:27 (21,628)
Usher, Leonie....5:02:04 (26,856)
Usher, Lisa J....5:52:59 (33,583)
Usher, Tanya L....3:37:12 (5,599)
Usswald-Ulyate, Kerry-Lee....5:05:25 (27,434)
Uttley, Patricia Ann....5:02:56 (27,018)
Vacchi, Claudia....4:23:43 (17,164)
Valassina, Gabriella....5:44:27 (32,810)
Vale, Samantha Joyce....5:33:20 (31,697)
Valentine, Amanda Jane....5:23:37 (30,410)
Valentine, Brenda Carol....5:54:46 (33,691)
Valentine, Catherine Jane....4:17:55 (15,550)
Valentine, Sally L....4:02:03 (11,502)
Valentini, Wendy A....4:28:40 (18,573)
Valentino, Maria Francesca....7:01:35 (36,212)
Vallier, Louise A....2:56:06 (807)
Valmas, Nicky....4:50:49 (24,243)
Van Cutsem, Alice....4:53:02 (24,803)
Van De Vel, Annie....4:51:51 (24,507)
Van Den Berg, Tania J....4:42:56 (22,245)
Van Den Berg, Tanja....4:32:58 (19,687)
Van Den Berg-Dijk, Sonja....4:10:10 (13,517)
Van Den Herik, Yvonne....4:27:03 (18,097)
Van Der Graaf, Johanna Elisabeth..6:26:02 (35,351)
Van Der Merwe, Ronel....4:41:09 (21,807)
Van Der Pad-Blanker, Ivonne....3:43:37 (6,793)
Van Der Putten, Rosemary A....3:43:45 (6,813)
Van Der Veen, Jolanda....4:54:30 (25,179)
Van Dop, Katarina Johanna....6:21:28 (35,185)
Van Dorp, Annelies....5:04:08 (27,216)
Van Heerden, Santa....4:57:55 (25,950)
Van Klaveren, Sarah Christina....4:51:49 (24,497)
Van Overhagen, Ingeborg CH....4:24:59 (17,515)
Van Wyk, Elmarie....4:00:22 (11,081)
Vandael, Carine....4:07:44 (12,893)
Vandenbroucke, Pascale....4:43:18 (22,320)
Vanderhaar, Kylie Danielle....4:21:58 (16,695)
Vanderpuye, Melodie....4:10:21 (13,556)
Vanlint, Alisa M....3:53:40 (9,113)
Vanlint, Sallie Elizabeth....4:08:41 (13,140)
Vanslambrouck, Greet....4:09:02 (13,220)
Vanston, Katie Anna....4:33:12 (19,767)
Varley, Jenny....5:09:18 (28,107)
Varney, Samantha Jane....5:00:53 (26,629)
Varney, Sophie Victoria....6:05:57 (34,448)
Varrie, Sally Ann....4:38:06 (21,008)
Vasireddy, Archana....6:02:56 (34,245)
Vassallo, Peter....5:08:59 (28,046)
Vasseur, Monique....3:48:16 (7,796)
Vaudin, Annie Debra....3:36:53 (5,544)
Vaughan, Claire....4:04:37 (12,106)
Vaughan, Claire Louise....4:23:43 (17,164)
Vaughan, Debbie....6:21:53 (35,195)
Vaughan, Diane Elizabeth....3:56:09 (9,822)
Vaughan, Sarah....4:44:25 (22,621)
Vavakis, Ria....5:28:18 (31,065)
Vawda, Nadia....5:12:51 (28,710)
Vazquez, Nadine Anne....4:41:18 (21,845)
Veale, Vaughneen....3:59:43 (10,925)
Veitch, Karen....6:02:36 (34,225)
Venables, Gemma Louise....4:01:24 (11,339)
Venables, Lyn D....4:47:37 (23,444)
Venables, Melissa Dawn....3:34:45 (5,202)
Venetico, Donna....5:41:53 (32,576)
Venturi, Corinna....6:02:32 (34,220)
Vepa, Satvi Ramya Kriti....6:40:46 (35,808)
Veraeus, Jessica....4:28:28 (18,512)
Vercauteren, Lieve....4:21:51 (16,655)
Vermeulen, Nadine....4:19:42 (16,014)
Vernazza, Fiona....4:29:04 (18,707)
Vernazza, Natalie Francesca....4:29:53 (18,943)
Vernon, Amanda....4:31:53 (19,404)
Vernon, Helen....5:51:35 (33,471)
Vernon, Kirsty....5:32:40 (31,624)
Veronese, Maria....4:40:08 (21,518)
Véronique, Beurton....4:18:49 (15,801)
Verrill, Freda....3:47:17 (7,596)
Vessey, Anna....5:23:31 (30,388)
Veys, Anne....4:28:13 (18,424)
Viarengo, Roberta....3:33:49 (5,028)
Vicary, Annmarie....5:14:45 (29,030)
Vicary, Susan....8:00:11 (36,588)
Vick, Sue Margaret....6:52:20 (36,057)
Vickers, Helen....5:06:38 (27,654)
Vickers, Jessica....5:32:52 (31,649)
Vickers, Leanne....4:54:55 (25,287)
Vickers, Lisa....5:06:38 (27,654)
Vickers, Louise....3:56:28 (9,922)
Vickery, Louise Marie....4:54:20 (25,140)
Vickery, Lynsey Emma....6:37:11 (35,703)
Victor, Christina R....4:32:27 (19,550)
Vidotto, Maria....4:43:23 (22,342)
Viegas, Maria....5:21:32 (30,077)
Vieira, Natasha....4:28:53 (18,636)
Vigneron, Dominique....6:17:59 (35,031)
Vila, Ana Maria....4:25:22 (17,625)
Villanueva, Carmen....4:38:13 (21,034)
Vinall, Lucie....5:17:41 (29,495)
Vincent, Bronwyn May....4:32:07 (19,464)
Vincent, Chloe L....4:04:56 (12,186)
Vincent, Courtenay N....6:43:06 (35,864)
Vincent, Ellie....3:30:16 (4,466)
Vincent, Jackie Jean....5:21:13 (30,034)
Vincent, Julie Anne....5:04:51 (27,342)
Vincent, Rachel....4:58:20 (26,050)
Vincent, Sandra Jill....5:57:22 (33,895)
Vitale-Cumper, Giulietta....3:23:10 (3,315)
Vitoulova, Jana Vitoulova....4:17:51 (15,533)
Vives, Martine....4:29:29 (18,800)
Vivian, Claire....4:06:07 (12,478)
Vivian, Holly Elizabeth....3:32:05 (4,754)
Vlaarkamp, Judith....3:31:55 (4,725)
Voase, Victoria Melanie....5:29:52 (31,274)
Vocke, Barbara....4:51:51 (24,507)
Vogelgsang, Claudia V....5:29:16 (31,184)
Voli, Virginia....4:31:53 (19,404)
Von Arx, Valerie Jean....5:10:02 (28,244)
Von Der Hoeh, Michaela....4:59:30 (26,340)
Von Rotz, Beatrice....4:39:36 (21,411)
Vowles, Jacqueline....4:15:39 (14,937)
Vowles, Josie....4:15:39 (14,937)
Vowles, Leanne Jane....4:38:10 (21,021)
Vowles, Marcia....5:15:30 (29,146)
Vowles, Tracy....4:38:09 (21,016)
Vriend-Deen, M....3:49:21 (8,052)
Vujanic, Aleksandra....4:54:02 (25,059)
Vujovic, Hope....5:34:54 (31,868)
Vye, Sophie E....4:54:50 (25,265)
Vyner, Carol Anne....5:00:56 (26,639)
Vynnycky, Emilia....3:48:50 (7,937)
Wabe, Charlotte E....4:17:23 (15,400)
Waddacor, Emma J....4:24:04 (17,252)
Waddicor, Cathrine Jane....4:00:06 (11,007)
Wadding, Emma....4:27:30 (18,236)
Waddington, Amy....4:05:42 (12,378)
Wadeson, Carol....4:23:28 (17,095)
Wadforth, Catherine....4:12:54 (14,208)
Wadham, Rachel....5:49:25 (33,274)
Wadham, Shirley Jane....4:53:56 (25,031)
Wadsack, Samantha Jane....5:32:40 (31,624)
Wadsworth, Heidi Sarah....5:18:58 (29,697)
Wagg, Charlotte Katherine....4:55:54 (25,513)
Waggott, Kim....4:51:57 (24,538)
Waggott, Penny Ann....3:48:22 (7,819)
Wagher, Mary....4:54:57 (25,293)
Wagjiani, Sonal....5:42:07 (32,602)
Wagner, Maxi....5:21:09 (30,029)
Wagner-Hoenscheid, Brigitte....5:00:47 (26,608)
Wahida, Rula....6:12:53 (34,799)
Wainman, Antonia Jane....4:00:20 (11,068)
Wainwright, Emma....5:44:48 (32,848)
Wainwright, Jean....5:32:41 (31,629)
Waistell, Lisa M....4:24:11 (17,281)
Wait, Josie Anita....4:10:11 (13,524)
Wake, Mandy Sue....6:44:19 (35,891)
Wakelam, Elaine Margaret....5:30:27 (31,345)
Wakenshaw, Lucy....4:32:48 (19,630)
Walden, Carol....5:20:52 (29,987)
Walden, Jodie....4:15:27 (14,897)
Waldhart, Josephine....3:15:50 (2,530)
Walford, Alison Ruth....5:06:05 (27,548)
Walford, Joss....4:31:06 (19,243)
Walker, Abigail V....4:13:53 (14,478)
Walker, Adele....4:06:33 (12,588)
Walker, Amanda....4:06:19 (12,530)
Walker, Carole Louise....4:25:24 (17,636)
Walker, Claire....6:20:44 (35,155)
Walker, Elizabeth Mary....5:18:36 (29,636)
Walker, Emily Jane....4:38:28 (21,110)
Walker, Emily Keita Homer....4:36:31 (20,611)
Walker, Fiona....6:01:16 (34,145)
Walker, Fleur-Louise....4:47:36 (23,437)
Walker, Gill....5:01:29 (26,750)
Walker, Hannah....4:55:17 (25,378)
Walker, Helen M....3:51:19 (8,496)
Walker, Hilary....5:03:06 (27,038)
Walker, Hilary C....4:10:04 (13,489)
Walker, Julia....4:46:19 (23,130)
Walker, Julia Catherine....4:25:26 (17,642)
Walker, Karen....4:46:04 (23,050)
Walker, Kate....4:56:56 (25,753)
Walker, Lauren Alanna....5:18:25 (29,610)
Walker, Lisa....6:43:26 (35,874)
Walker, Marion C....3:55:05 (9,501)
Walker, Nancy....4:58:34 (26,107)
Walker, Nicola J....4:24:24 (17,360)
Walker, Paula Grant....5:50:02 (33,339)
Walker, Rachel....6:14:01 (34,838)
Walker, Sarah Jane....4:43:32 (22,377)
Walker, Sharon....3:34:30 (5,154)
Walker, Tammy Doris Louise B....4:24:07 (17,264)
Walker, Tracy....3:22:24 (3,227)
Walker, Trudi Ann....7:47:53 (36,557)
Walker, Trudie Michelle....4:56:06 (25,561)
Walker-Date, Susan Elizebeth....6:18:15 (35,046)
Walker-Downie, Nikki Susan....4:06:19 (12,530)
Walker-Leach, Jenny Clair....4:40:44 (21,708)
Walkey, Melissa....4:32:59 (19,691)
Walkinshaw, Zoe Newcombe....5:09:20 (28,115)
Wall, Catherine E....4:25:30 (17,661)
Wall, Emma Louise Elizabeth....4:20:54 (16,387)
Wall, Joanne L....5:06:01 (27,533)
Wall, Luan....3:44:17 (6,933)
Wall, Mandy M....5:18:36 (29,636)
Wall, Rebecca J....3:28:07 (4,077)
Wall, Sandy....5:31:48 (31,515)
Wallace, Ann....4:37:18 (20,818)
Wallace, Anna W....3:15:22 (2,481)
Wallace, Kathryn M....5:24:49 (30,593)
Wallace, Louise....5:49:30 (33,284)
Wallace, Paula....3:55:32 (9,621)
Wallace, Renata M....4:54:55 (25,287)
Waller, Andrea H....4:28:11 (18,414)
Waller, Dominique....5:55:43 (33,770)
Wallington, Annie....3:37:41 (5,706)
Wallington, Helen C....3:17:29 (2,708)
Wallington, Sarah....5:33:42 (31,737)
Wallington, Zoe Louise Jane....3:39:59 (6,139)
Wallis, Caroline....4:55:06 (25,335)
Wallis, Hannah....4:42:14 (22,075)
Wallis, Jayne Elizabeth....4:17:23 (15,400)
Wallis, Samantha J....3:39:53 (6,122)
Wallis, Sara....4:45:54 (22,999)
Wallsworth, Lisa....5:34:24 (31,811)
Walmsley, Helen Rebecca....4:28:18 (18,452)
Walsgrove, Hilary J....3:39:24 (6,022)
Walsh, Amy....4:43:21 (22,333)
Walsh, Catherine Louise....4:37:49 (20,948)
Walsh, Chris....5:28:31 (31,090)
Walsh, Clair Fiona....4:40:12 (21,538)
Walsh, Edit....3:25:20 (3,621)
Walsh, Kelly Louise....5:36:48 (32,084)
Walsh, Laura....5:21:49 (30,118)
Walsh, Natasha Louise....4:05:18 (12,283)
Walster, Jeanette A....3:43:32 (6,781)
Walter, Angela J....4:19:56 (16,082)
Walters, Callie Astrid....4:46:25 (23,153)
Walters, Caroline Alice....5:52:49 (33,569)
Walters, Chiara Sofia....5:50:49 (33,412)

Walters, Elise 6:52:14 (36,052)
Walters, Gail R 3:32:56 (4,883)
Walther, Beatrice 4:15:11 (14,830)
Walton, Gaye 7:25:07 (36,443)
Walton, Jan D 5:00:34 (26,564)
Walton, Laura Jane 3:46:51 (7,500)
Walton, Nancy Alexandra Maria 4:15:55 (15,007)
Walton, Penelope Louise 5:54:31 (33,676)
Wanjama, Sarah 6:45:20 (35,918)
Wann, Colette 3:50:37 (8,338)
Want, Becky 4:49:35 (23,937)
Want, Victoria Alice 4:48:57 (23,788)
Warburton, Melissa Jane 5:22:51 (30,284)
Ward, Aisling 3:54:01 (9,215)
Ward, Alison 3:39:51 (6,114)
Ward, Alison Sarah 4:10:24 (13,568)
Ward, Amanda Jane 6:36:50 (35,694)
Ward, Beres E 4:31:26 (19,316)
Ward, Claire Margaret 5:16:45 (29,344)
Ward, Deborah 4:24:54 (17,490)
Ward, Deborah K 7:20:46 (36,411)
Ward, Deirdre 3:30:16 (4,466)
Ward, Felicity J 3:27:43 (3,999)
Ward, Helen 4:07:24 (12,801)
Ward, Helen Mary 4:46:10 (23,078)
Ward, Julie Justine 6:01:08 (34,138)
Ward, Kathryn Yvonne 3:57:13 (10,161)
Ward, Laura 3:41:25 (6,408)
Ward, Lauren 5:11:29 (28,478)
Ward, Lindsey 4:55:04 (25,326)
Ward, Lisa Jane 4:16:38 (15,197)
Ward, Liz 4:20:03 (16,117)
Ward, Melanie 3:59:14 (10,791)
Ward, Nichola Jane 4:58:40 (26,130)
Ward, Rebecca 6:16:48 (34,964)
Ward, Rosie V 5:01:12 (26,680)
Ward, Ruth E 3:50:02 (8,215)
Wardell, Patricia 4:08:17 (13,024)
Warden, Sarah Jayne 4:19:27 (15,961)
Wardman, Helen 4:43:56 (22,486)
Ward-Rotherham, Julie 4:25:42 (17,715)
Ware, Natalie 3:42:02 (6,517)
Wargent, Julie C 3:45:57 (7,299)
Warn, Abby Lucy 4:46:11 (23,085)
Warn, Patricia Anne 5:53:14 (33,593)
Warne, Catherine P 3:50:25 (8,292)
Warne, Edel 5:10:48 (28,377)
Warner, Anne 4:51:49 (24,497)
Warner, Catherine A 4:36:21 (20,562)
Warner, Elizabeth 4:41:21 (21,851)
Warner, Jennie 5:50:11 (33,349)
Warner, Kim-Louise 4:58:41 (26,134)
Warner, Lauren 5:20:01 (29,853)
Warr, Deborah Harriett 5:04:30 (27,276)
Warr, Sandra E 6:51:47 (36,033)
Warran, Patricia 5:00:25 (26,539)
Warren, Andrea Jayne 4:21:08 (16,447)
Warren, Angela J 5:02:29 (26,942)
Warren, Carol J 5:36:59 (32,101)
Warren, Carol Louise 6:23:02 (35,239)
Warren, Donna L 4:14:16 (14,586)
Warren, Joanne 3:57:13 (10,161)
Warren, Karlyn Sara 6:02:50 (34,238)
Warren, Lyndsey Victoria 5:33:39 (31,730)
Warren, Nathalie L 3:17:28 (2,705)
Warren, Sian 5:06:46 (27,684)
Warrendorf, Karen 3:17:44 (2,734)
Warrick, Stephanie M 4:16:39 (15,204)
Warrington, Emma Jane 6:24:21 (35,292)
Warrington, Frances B 3:58:29 (10,551)
Wartmann, Irma 4:24:13 (17,291)
Waschke, Angelika 6:13:32 (34,822)
Wason, Wendy 5:21:36 (30,095)
Wass, Gabriella Rose 5:11:50 (28,528)
Wasyliw, Antoinette 3:47:09 (7,556)
Waterer, Margaret 4:42:51 (22,231)
Waterfall, Emma 3:56:30 (9,933)
Waterfield, Samantha Jane 5:02:21 (26,916)
Wateridge, Katrina L 4:00:17 (11,056)
Waterlow, Lucy M 3:17:27 (2,702)
Waters, Berenice 5:42:15 (32,614)
Waters, Marta 4:56:29 (25,643)
Watkin, Kate 3:58:28 (10,544)
Watkins, Claire Frances 4:27:37 (18,264)
Watkins, Ellen F 4:36:58 (20,734)
Watkins, Fiona Kathleen 4:28:47 (18,600)
Watkins, Laura Elizabeth 4:56:25 (25,633)
Watkins, Sally A 3:42:00 (6,506)
Watkinson, Helen 4:10:36 (13,618)
Watson, Amanda Jane 6:19:02 (35,084)
Watson, Andrea 5:10:43 (28,365)
Watson, Charlotte Ellis 6:21:14 (35,170)
Watson, Christina M 4:45:35 (22,909)
Watson, Clare 5:16:28 (29,304)
Watson, Dawne 3:56:41 (9,992)
Watson, Deborah 4:22:20 (16,800)
Watson, Denise M 5:30:30 (31,357)
Watson, Diane T 4:54:37 (25,209)
Watson, Francesca Jane 4:24:39 (17,432)
Watson, Gemma 6:40:04 (35,788)
Watson, Jill 4:52:05 (24,568)
Watson, Kerry 6:46:45 (35,943)
Watson, Louise Catherine 6:02:49 (34,236)
Watson, Marion Jennifer 4:30:49 (19,173)
Watson, Naomi R 4:58:34 (26,107)
Watson, Pam 7:52:41 (36,569)
Watson, Pascale 5:20:37 (29,949)
Watson, Sara Louise 4:22:54 (16,962)
Watson, Sarah Alison 4:45:59 (23,018)
Watson, Sarah Amelia 4:49:01 (23,808)
Watson, Susan J 2:59:28 (1,101)
Watterson, Andrea 6:50:19 (36,004)
Watts, Beverley Anne 5:29:49 (31,270)
Watts, Claire Ellen Louise 6:02:50 (34,238)
Watts, Curstie L 6:21:25 (35,182)
Watts, Hannah Elizabeth 5:01:21 (26,724)
Watts, Heather E 5:07:42 (27,847)
Watts, Jean 5:41:45 (32,556)
Watts, Kelly 4:35:07 (20,257)
Watts, Linda 4:33:59 (19,987)
Watts, Sally J 4:23:36 (17,136)
Waugh, Samantha Rose 7:47:20 (36,555)
Wavell, Anna Kristine 4:37:13 (20,798)
Wawrzyk, Judy 4:36:29 (20,598)
Wayne, Monique 5:06:01 (27,533)
Wdowiak, Katie Lee 4:59:43 (26,388)
Weale, Marsha R 4:54:33 (25,190)
Weall, Jules F 3:16:12 (2,574)
Wear, Xania 5:22:43 (30,257)
Weatherly, Helen 3:35:11 (5,271)
Weaver, Jenny 4:20:14 (16,173)
Weaver, Jolanta U 4:16:38 (15,197)
Weaver, Patricia Anne 4:41:14 (21,827)
Webb, Annabel 4:32:15 (19,500)
Webb, Cammille Angel 6:45:15 (35,915)
Webb, Clare Judith Frances 5:28:22 (31,071)
Webb, Hazel 6:55:18 (36,116)
Webb, Helen 4:42:25 (22,115)
Webb, Helen 4:52:48 (24,756)
Webb, Jennifer L 3:56:38 (9,973)
Webb, Jo M 3:25:40 (3,681)
Webb, Katrina 5:17:10 (29,413)
Webb, Sophie Elizabeth 5:49:53 (33,323)
Webb, Victoria Elizabeth 4:41:11 (21,820)
Webber, Jane 5:38:44 (32,285)
Webber, Julia 5:29:43 (31,255)
Webber, Natalie Ruby 5:29:43 (31,255)
Webber, Wendy D 3:39:40 (6,070)
Weber, Odessa M 3:25:31 (3,649)
Webster, Charlie A 3:56:55 (10,063)
Webster, Elizabeth 4:42:31 (22,145)
Webster, Evelyn A 3:26:47 (3,845)
Webster, Helen 4:13:44 (14,442)
Webster, Julia A 4:53:58 (25,041)
Webster, Morag Elizabeth 7:05:15 (36,256)
Webster, Sandra 4:11:49 (13,936)
Wedlock, Jane E 4:04:28 (12,070)
Weeden, Sue 5:32:08 (31,555)
Weeden, Zoe Louise 4:46:58 (23,298)
Weekes, Annie Claire 4:41:11 (21,820)
Weeks, Alison 3:55:07 (9,508)
Weeks, Elizabeth A 3:07:37 (1,669)
Weeks-Butler, Melissa 4:43:16 (22,317)
Wehry, Susan 6:08:49 (34,603)
Weidberg, Fiona Edony Liane 4:38:25 (21,092)
Weigel, Beatrix 5:19:42 (29,808)
Weightman, Allyson Teresa 5:19:11 (29,734)
Weissgaerber, Gudrun 6:02:39 (34,228)
Welbourn, Julie Ann 9:17:54 (36,624)
Welch, Diane 4:20:40 (16,324)
Welch, Kate 3:45:01 (7,098)
Weldai, Selamawit K 5:36:36 (32,066)
Welfare, Maria 6:13:31 (34,821)
Welham, Katrina 4:07:44 (12,893)
Welham, Lauren 5:07:32 (27,819)
Wellbelove, Senga 5:14:43 (29,019)
Wellesley Wesley, Katherine A 4:16:18 (15,106)
Wellesley Wesley, Susannah 3:44:43 (7,038)
Wellfair, Peter John 6:32:05 (35,567)
Wellings, Frances 5:13:05 (28,789)
Wells, Alison Joanne 5:14:12 (28,951)
Wells, Catherine Louise 5:23:18 (30,359)
Wells, Helen 4:36:57 (20,729)
Wells, Karen E 5:44:14 (32,791)
Wells, Rachel J 4:51:37 (24,443)
Wells, Rebecca Jayne 5:41:46 (32,561)
Wells, Ruth Elizabeth 5:42:02 (32,590)
Welsford, Louise 5:46:28 (33,007)
Welsh, Susan Clare 6:03:32 (34,292)
Wemyss, Linda Temple 4:18:14 (15,641)
Wenker, Anneke 4:48:13 (23,590)
Wenman, Barbara H 3:19:08 (2,884)
Wensley, Marissa Jayne 5:00:26 (26,543)
Wensley, Susan 4:16:18 (15,106)
Wessely, Kathryn 4:23:45 (17,181)
Wesson, Heather L 4:17:59 (15,573)
Wesson, Sarah 5:51:18 (33,448)
West, Becky Louise 5:09:01 (28,053)
West, Carol 6:25:13 (35,321)
West, Charlotte 7:57:57 (36,584)
West, Clare 6:07:32 (34,533)
West, Diane 8:13:48 (36,599)
West, Hannah 5:21:16 (30,038)
West, Helen 4:39:46 (21,452)
West, Jocelyn 4:28:58 (18,670)
West, Julie A 4:30:16 (19,040)
West, Katie E 3:13:10 (2,206)
West, Leeann Christine 4:46:18 (23,128)
West, Nicola 5:23:30 (30,385)
West, Tracey J 3:11:23 (2,036)
West, Tracey-Anne 7:41:50 (36,532)
West, Zoe 3:22:54 (3,278)
Westbrook, Rachel H 3:35:04 (5,260)
Westcott, Lori 5:15:34 (29,160)
Westcott, Lucy A 3:41:59 (6,505)
Westcott, Sarah B 3:56:27 (9,916)
Western, Dawn 4:31:55 (19,411)
Western, Rowan 5:55:25 (33,749)
Western, Vanora Jane 4:22:01 (16,711)
Westhead, Joanne Louise 4:36:18 (20,547)
Westland, Sandra 5:34:35 (31,833)
Westman, Clara 4:08:46 (13,153)
Westmorland, Tracy 4:50:28 (24,154)
Weston, Kathleen 4:23:34 (17,125)
Weston, Sarah Anne 6:06:51 (34,499)
Weston, Sharon 4:44:14 (22,575)
Weston, Sophie 5:28:31 (31,090)
Westropp, Sarah R 5:28:59 (31,149)
Westwood-Clarke, Victoria C 4:02:09 (11,522)
Wetherell, Kiki 5:19:16 (29,742)
Weydert, Hélène 4:47:24 (23,389)
Whaites, Joanne 4:06:21 (12,539)
Whale, Alexandra S 3:32:26 (4,809)
Whaley, Laura Annie 5:57:12 (33,879)
Whalley, Alexanra S 3:24:10 (3,465)
Whalley, Alice 5:29:41 (31,251)
Whang, Bonnie 4:04:35 (12,096)
Wharton, Emma L 3:42:13 (6,551)
Wheat, Rosemary 4:48:25 (23,647)
Wheatley, Andrea A 4:28:21 (18,470)
Wheeldon, Nancy Elizabeth 5:05:06 (27,386)
Wheeler, Ailsa E 4:54:25 (25,164)
Wheeler, Amanda Karen 4:56:47 (25,711)
Wheeler, Claire Marie 6:11:59 (34,755)
Wheeler, Jacquetta Lydia 4:09:16 (13,274)
Wheeler, Lucy Anne 5:34:03 (31,767)
Wheeler, Mandy 4:17:10 (15,339)
Wheeler, Nicola 5:09:00 (28,050)
Wheeler, Roxann S 5:54:09 (33,655)

Whelan, Wendy Priscilla 5:05:32 (27,455)
Whinn, Julie 4:43:14 (22,307)
Whistance, Melanie J 4:31:21 (19,302)
Whitby-Smith, Emma Mary 6:18:11 (35,038)
White, Andrea 5:00:44 (26,595)
White, Angela Valerie 5:29:28 (31,216)
White, Christy 6:08:36 (34,589)
White, Clarie L 5:24:37 (30,570)
White, Dionne 5:54:55 (33,709)
White, Elaine 4:48:32 (23,677)
White, Emily 4:32:29 (19,556)
White, Iris Mary 4:48:34 (23,686)
White, Jane L 3:47:16 (7,591)
White, Janice 3:25:07 (3,599)
White, Jenny 4:04:43 (12,136)
White, Joan 4:51:01 (24,309)
White, Joanne 3:50:25 (8,292)
White, Julia Anne 4:45:28 (22,875)
White, Julie Anne 4:00:56 (11,231)
White, Kate Jane 5:09:15 (28,092)
White, Keryn 5:02:52 (27,000)
White, Lesley Ann 4:51:21 (24,387)
White, Lesley Melissa 4:03:14 (11,785)
White, Michelle 4:40:33 (21,657)
White, Michelle 4:46:50 (23,270)
White, Nikki 4:36:36 (20,631)
White, Pamela L 3:24:34 (3,519)
White, Rebecca 5:43:04 (32,673)
White, Samantha Jane 5:52:20 (33,524)
White, Sharon L 4:05:57 (12,445)
White, Sharon S 5:28:45 (31,120)
White, Sonia 4:59:06 (26,241)
White, Sue R 4:46:49 (23,259)
White, Susan 4:01:46 (11,439)
White, Tara 4:18:19 (15,665)
White, Ursula C 3:42:48 (6,657)
Whitefield, Monica Bridget 4:02:34 (11,621)
Whitefoot, Alexandra 5:43:04 (32,673)
Whitehead, Jenny Ann 6:44:51 (35,901)
Whitehouse, Fiona 4:31:34 (19,344)
Whitehurst, Michele Ann 4:26:11 (17,868)
Whitelaw, Emma 5:16:35 (29,319)
Whiteman, Jane Ann 4:53:03 (24,805)
Whiteman, Rosemary 7:04:24 (36,249)
Whiteoak, Lynne Carol 5:06:53 (27,701)
Whiting, Heather 4:45:18 (22,841)
Whitington, Vikki Louise 5:32:53 (31,651)
Whitlam, Becky 5:05:10 (27,396)
Whitman, Maureen P 5:46:00 (32,951)
Whitmarsh, Ann Bard 6:16:19 (34,935)
Whitnall, Lynn 4:32:47 (19,626)
Whitney, Elizabeth 7:07:09 (36,281)
Whitney, Lisa Angela 5:01:38 (26,783)
Whittaker, Corrine 4:48:40 (23,711)
Whittaker, Deborah Leah 5:33:58 (31,760)
Whittaker, Joanne Stacy 5:51:19 (33,451)
Whittaker, Megan 5:33:06 (31,677)
Whittaker, Naomi 4:34:35 (20,145)
Whittaker, Naomi J 4:22:14 (16,776)
Whittaker, Sarah 5:15:42 (29,177)
Whittaker-Gilbey, Sarah 5:20:37 (29,949)
Whittick, Emma Louise 5:31:12 (31,434)
Whittick, Gale Maxine 5:07:19 (27,772)
Whittingham, Pam 5:09:22 (28,120)
Whittington, Tracey 4:52:48 (24,756)
Whittley, Rozanne 6:47:12 (35,952)
Whitton, Kate 5:12:59 (28,738)
Whitty, Marilyn A 3:58:40 (10,613)
Whitworth, Bethan Wyn 4:47:57 (23,535)
Whitworth, Claire L 5:50:00 (33,336)
Whitworth, Kate E 3:10:27 (1,944)
Whorton, Ruth 4:15:57 (15,013)
Why, Christina June 5:05:35 (27,464)
Whyke, Justyne 4:20:13 (16,169)
Whyles, Linda Jane 5:39:53 (32,375)
Whyte, Anne Alicia 4:55:38 (25,446)
Whyte, Geraldine 4:34:30 (20,121)
Whyte, Susan 5:30:23 (31,333)
Wibberley, Geneve T 5:32:42 (31,631)
Wiblin, Julia S 4:11:22 (13,805)
Wickenden, Sheryl Patricia 5:41:29 (32,532)
Wickens, Jenny 4:51:01 (24,309)
Wickens, Kirsty 4:30:07 (19,003)
Wickham, Sue Louise 6:07:49 (34,550)
Wicks, Marion C 4:03:18 (11,801)
Widdicombe, Nikki 3:55:07 (9,508)
Widdowson, Elaine 5:03:56 (27,176)
Widdowson, Helen M 4:01:59 (11,486)
Widdowson, Kirsten 5:51:18 (33,448)
Widdrington, Helen 4:22:19 (16,796)
Wienand, Beverley 4:25:05 (17,546)
Wigfull, Nicola Joyce 4:25:56 (17,795)
Wiggins, Catherine 4:47:54 (23,520)
Wiggins, Debbie 5:00:47 (26,608)
Wiggins, Rena 6:00:00 (34,064)
Wigglesworth, Tina Irene 4:14:19 (14,597)
Wigley, Danka M 4:10:29 (13,590)
Wijayatilake, Lilani 4:30:12 (19,026)
Wilbourne, Emma 5:52:56 (33,576)
Wilby, Alison 4:27:21 (18,195)
Wilcock, Helen Christine 5:17:05 (29,397)
Wilcock, Janet 4:48:39 (23,707)
Wilcox, Aimée 3:47:22 (7,612)
Wilcox, Mandy Jane 4:58:50 (26,173)
Wild, Jane 3:52:49 (8,877)
Wilding, Linda June 4:40:23 (21,607)
Wildon, Dale 4:43:37 (22,400)
Wile, Alyson Jayne 3:36:17 (5,456)
Wileman, Sarah 3:10:03 (1,910)
Wilhelmus, Christianne 5:30:00 (31,302)
Wiliamson, Debbie 5:03:08 (27,043)
Wilk, Jenny 4:27:03 (18,097)
Wilkes, Adele Elizabeth 5:01:20 (26,721)
Wilkes, Carli 4:34:39 (20,156)
Wilkes, Carrie-Anne 4:21:08 (16,447)
Wilkes, Deborah J 4:04:55 (12,178)
Wilkes, Hayley Jayne 4:06:26 (12,554)
Wilkes, Jenny 4:28:36 (18,548)
Wilkes, Judith M 4:44:16 (22,583)
Wilkes, Roni 4:54:34 (25,196)
Wilkes, Susan Jane 4:08:34 (13,108)
Wilkes, Tracy 5:14:35 (29,000)
Wilkey, Susanna 5:19:33 (29,779)
Wilkie, Katie 3:48:47 (7,922)
Wilkie, Sharon 4:19:10 (15,894)
Wilkins, Mary 4:27:08 (18,129)
Wilkins, Melanie Jane 4:21:19 (16,494)
Wilkins, Samantha 5:37:03 (32,106)
Wilkins, Sue 4:33:15 (19,787)
Wilkinson, Carolyn S 2:58:54 (1,034)
Wilkinson, Dorothy A 3:37:23 (5,634)
Wilkinson, Georgia 6:30:26 (35,516)
Wilkinson, Janet Mary 5:29:34 (31,233)
Wilkinson, Jo 2:37:44 (156)
Wilkinson, Joanne 4:58:38 (26,126)
Wilkinson, Jolie A 4:28:30 (18,521)
Wilkinson, Julie 5:44:50 (32,851)
Wilkinson, Lisa 3:38:37 (5,874)
Wilkinson, Nadia 3:31:24 (4,651)
Wilkinson, Nina 4:55:13 (25,361)
Wilkinson, Sharon 3:55:48 (9,719)
Willans, Katherine 5:04:00 (27,192)
Willard, Anna L 4:37:21 (20,832)
Willatgamuwa, Patrina 7:37:48 (36,507)
Willbond, Andrea F 4:18:59 (15,847)
Willey, Zoe 7:25:35 (36,445)
Willgoose, Carol B 3:42:06 (6,530)
Williams, Aimée 7:25:35 (36,445)
Williams, Amy 5:33:36 (31,727)
Williams, Amy Louise 4:37:31 (20,888)
Williams, Andrea P 4:28:37 (18,557)
Williams, Angela 5:32:31 (31,605)
Williams, Angela J 4:21:34 (16,567)
Williams, Anita 5:15:07 (29,090)
Williams, Anne 4:12:49 (14,184)
Williams, Anne-Marie 5:04:42 (27,321)
Williams, Audra M 5:51:18 (33,448)
Williams, Carrie 5:54:00 (33,642)
Williams, Carrie Claire 5:07:01 (27,727)
Williams, Catherine Jane 6:08:20 (34,572)
Williams, Charlotte Elisabeth 5:02:24 (26,927)
Williams, Courtney Murray 4:41:09 (21,807)
Williams, Dawn Elizabeth 5:02:28 (26,938)
Williams, Debbie A 4:49:07 (23,833)
Williams, Diana 5:34:00 (31,764)
Williams, Donna Marie 4:42:48 (22,213)
Williams, Dumisani S 3:14:56 (2,430)
Williams, Eileen 4:39:42 (21,436)
Williams, Eleanor Lucy 4:13:02 (14,249)
Williams, Elizabeth 5:02:25 (26,932)
Williams, Elizabeth 5:41:46 (32,561)
Williams, Emma 4:57:10 (25,796)
Williams, Ffion 3:49:36 (8,115)
Williams, Frances E 3:08:04 (1,702)
Williams, Gemma Louise 5:02:02 (26,850)
Williams, Gwen 5:39:34 (32,353)
Williams, Hazel 6:09:04 (34,622)
Williams, Heidi P 4:24:13 (17,291)
Williams, Helen 3:31:31 (4,670)
Williams, Jacquelyn 4:33:14 (19,778)
Williams, Jenine Gabrielle 5:36:29 (32,055)
Williams, Jennifer 4:34:33 (20,134)
Williams, Jenny 6:56:13 (36,134)
Williams, Jo 5:49:51 (33,321)
Williams, Juliet Ann 5:16:57 (29,379)
Williams, Kate Elizabeth 5:48:24 (33,183)
Williams, Kathleen O 7:15:53 (36,368)
Williams, Kathryn H 3:34:46 (5,206)
Williams, Kirsty Lee 5:15:33 (29,159)
Williams, Laura 4:20:25 (16,239)
Williams, Leah V 4:13:24 (14,335)
Williams, Linda K 5:02:01 (26,845)
Williams, Lisa 4:55:08 (25,344)
Williams, Louise 4:11:04 (13,738)
Williams, Lucy Anna 5:30:36 (31,372)
Williams, Maria Ann 6:02:54 (34,242)
Williams, Maria J 3:36:22 (5,466)
Williams, Melanie 4:16:35 (15,186)
Williams, Michelle 4:26:49 (18,029)
Williams, Nancy 4:24:31 (17,395)
Williams, Natasha E 4:25:41 (17,712)
Williams, Nicola J 5:56:12 (33,809)
Williams, Paula 5:17:54 (29,526)
Williams, Rachael Amy 4:46:11 (23,085)
Williams, Rachel Alice 5:32:13 (31,564)
Williams, Rebecca 4:18:44 (15,782)
Williams, Rebecca J 5:24:17 (30,522)
Williams, Rosie Laura McEwen 4:07:50 (12,912)
Williams, Samantha Jayne 5:08:02 (27,903)
Williams, Sandra 4:57:42 (25,908)
Williams, Sarah 4:40:31 (21,647)
Williams, Sarah 4:43:53 (22,475)
Williams, Sarah 6:26:58 (35,385)
Williams, Sarah L 4:37:25 (20,850)
Williams, Sascha 5:27:17 (30,940)
Williams, Sian 3:58:58 (10,709)
Williams, Stephanie 4:45:45 (22,968)
Williams, Susan 5:18:47 (29,662)
Williams, Teresa K 3:26:09 (3,762)
Williams, Vicky E 3:38:22 (5,825)
Williams, Victoria 4:50:54 (24,269)
Williams, Victoria Anne 4:50:47 (24,234)
Williams, Victoria Catherine 3:57:10 (10,146)
Williams Jones, Diane 5:18:25 (29,610)
Williamson, Adele Louise 6:09:10 (34,623)
Williamson, Anna Mary 4:45:37 (22,919)
Williamson, Anne Bernadette 3:58:33 (10,574)
Williamson, Carla D 4:44:33 (22,654)
Williamson, Dawn 4:29:25 (18,780)
Williamson, Esther Me 5:09:34 (28,162)
Williamson, Janna Christine 5:17:36 (29,487)
Williamson, Julia 5:06:31 (27,628)
Williamson, Kate 3:44:47 (7,051)
Williamson, Lucy 5:51:42 (33,482)
Williamson, Marianne P 3:33:20 (4,939)
Williamson, Marie 4:44:31 (22,645)
Williamson, Philippa Jane 5:12:35 (28,666)
Willicott, Anne-Marie 3:58:40 (10,613)
Willingham, Lisa Ann 5:59:43 (34,039)
Willis, Christine 4:19:30 (15,973)
Willis, Hannah Andrea 4:18:54 (15,828)
Willis, Rachel E 5:42:43 (32,653)
Willmott, Louise 7:48:29 (36,559)
Willmott, Vikki 5:23:43 (30,429)
Willoughby, Rosemary A 5:41:11 (32,507)
Willow, Aimée L 4:16:48 (15,247)
Wills, Anna 4:22:16 (16,790)
Wills, Sarah 4:47:21 (23,379)
Wills, Tamsyn Sarah 4:09:51 (13,431)

Wills, Thais H 5:30:52 (31,399)
Wills, Victoria 4:29:42 (18,878)
Willsdon, Anna Margret 4:44:55 (22,745)
Willson, Sally Ann 5:05:07 (27,389)
Wilmot, Kathryn Louise 3:46:36 (7,442)
Wilsdon, Lesley Jane 5:06:28 (27,618)
Wilshaw, Susan 4:25:42 (17,715)
Wilson, Alison 3:32:40 (4,838)
Wilson, Carly Heather 5:23:17 (30,354)
Wilson, Charlotte J 3:11:13 (2,018)
Wilson, Claire 5:07:28 (27,804)
Wilson, Claire 5:19:18 (29,745)
Wilson, Claire Louise 5:19:09 (29,726)
Wilson, Clare 5:13:13 (28,803)
Wilson, Clare 5:20:50 (29,983)
Wilson, Dawn 4:43:53 (22,475)
Wilson, Donna 5:23:23 (30,368)
Wilson, Emma Louise 4:24:28 (17,381)
Wilson, Emma Louise 6:20:42 (35,151)
Wilson, Finola J 4:19:46 (16,033)
Wilson, Fiona 4:40:43 (21,700)
Wilson, Grace Anne 5:40:01 (32,391)
Wilson, Hannah 5:25:02 (30,630)
Wilson, Hayley 5:10:25 (28,313)
Wilson, Hazel 3:57:25 (10,206)
Wilson, Heidi J 3:08:37 (1,772)
Wilson, Helen 4:32:00 (19,436)
Wilson, Helen Elizabeth 4:17:14 (15,359)
Wilson, Isobel Rose Drury 5:08:10 (27,922)
Wilson, Jacqueline L 3:16:38 (2,631)
Wilson, Janet Lynne 5:37:09 (32,123)
Wilson, Janette 4:44:17 (22,586)
Wilson, Janice Margaret 3:48:14 (7,789)
Wilson, Jess Laura 4:27:54 (18,339)
Wilson, Joanne C 3:20:18 (2,991)
Wilson, Joulianne Rose 4:20:19 (16,209)
Wilson, Jules D 5:13:30 (28,843)
Wilson, Katie A 4:24:31 (17,395)
Wilson, Kelly Louise 5:15:23 (29,122)
Wilson, Kirsty 6:06:24 (34,470)
Wilson, Kirsty Louise 4:11:02 (13,726)
Wilson, Laura Jean 5:01:26 (26,742)
Wilson, Lucy Rebecca 3:55:20 (9,571)
Wilson, Lynda 4:01:56 (11,478)
Wilson, Michelle 6:26:43 (35,373)
Wilson, Natalie 5:17:54 (29,526)
Wilson, Patricia M 3:44:10 (6,909)
Wilson, Rachel Emma 4:28:48 (18,609)
Wilson, Rosalie E 3:37:52 (5,734)
Wilson, Sally L 3:48:42 (7,898)
Wilson, Sarah Georgina 4:27:13 (18,157)
Wilson, Simone C 3:54:07 (9,236)
Wilson, Susan 5:53:49 (33,629)
Wilson, Ursula R 3:14:28 (2,377)
Wilson, Valerie A 4:34:48 (20,194)
Wilson, Victoria Emma 6:18:24 (35,052)
Wilson, Victoria Sarah 4:23:28 (17,095)
Wilton, Caroline Jane 5:34:26 (31,814)
Wiltshire, Rose 4:48:46 (23,736)
Win, Roxanne 5:28:41 (31,111)
Winchurch, Lo 3:47:31 (7,650)
Winder, Kirstie Ann 4:38:39 (21,154)
Windrum, Jodie M 3:51:27 (8,531)
Winfield, Jane Elizabeth 3:48:47 (7,922)
Wingate, Katherine Mary 7:35:15 (36,489)
Wingate, Mary 3:56:09 (9,822)
Wingrove, Kate Leonora 5:53:56 (33,637)
Winkles, Anna Laura 4:46:30 (7,415)
Winnall, Carrie 5:24:15 (30,519)
Winnall, Catharine E 4:25:32 (17,672)
Winrow, Emma 6:29:06 (35,464)
Winslade, Charlotte 5:03:58 (27,179)
Winson, Elizabeth Marion 5:08:12 (27,929)
Winstanley, Elaine 4:21:37 (16,583)
Winstanley, Louise Jane 4:14:46 (14,732)
Winter, Annelis 5:35:38 (31,945)
Winter, Isabelle N 3:37:42 (5,710)
Winter, Lorna Jane 5:26:42 (30,862)
Winter, Lucy Ann 5:29:15 (31,183)
Winter, Patricia Katherine 6:48:46 (35,971)
Winterbourn, Annie 5:42:26 (32,630)
Winters, Helen 3:46:04 (7,330)
Winters, Jenny 4:48:51 (23,760)

Winters, Joanne Laura 5:13:47 (28,890)
Wintle, Sophie 5:14:20 (28,966)
Wiscombe, Rebecca A 3:39:16 (5,996)
Wise, Amy Caroline 4:59:34 (26,356)
Wise, Claire 4:47:43 (23,474)
Wiseman, Charlotte 6:20:27 (35,144)
Wiseman, Clare 4:18:47 (15,796)
Wisken (née Blois), Hayley JL ..5:23:55 (30,464)
Wisson, Shirley Alexina 4:02:53 (11,701)
Wiszniowska, Dorota 4:47:34 (23,429)
Witek, Samantha Jane 5:08:25 (27,966)
Withers, Caroline 4:23:16 (17,037)
Withers, Kay 4:18:26 (15,694)
Withers, Pamela R 3:39:18 (6,005)
Withey, Sally 4:42:44 (22,196)
Witkowski, Caroline Anne 6:40:09 (35,792)
Witney, Trippoli-Jane 4:58:51 (26,177)
Witt, Frances 4:58:26 (26,071)
Wittich, Julie Margaret 5:14:43 (29,019)
Wittich-Broadley, Fran 5:40:15 (32,417)
Witton, Wendi M 5:21:19 (30,044)
Woehrel, Catherine Anne 4:54:20 (25,140)
Wohanka, Alexandra Maria 3:39:27 (6,033)
Wohanka, Oonagh 3:58:14 (10,471)
Woite, Christiane 4:26:33 (17,969)
Wojciechowska, Joanna 4:24:00 (17,236)
Wolfe, Claudia 5:18:03 (29,554)
Wolfe, Ruth M 3:32:10 (4,768)
Wolfenden, Rachel C 3:19:19 (2,899)
Wolley, Mailynne 4:56:07 (25,563)
Woloschuk, Bonnie 4:26:04 (17,830)
Wolseley Brinton, Emily VA 5:40:26 (32,425)
Womack, Mandy M 4:11:01 (13,720)
Wong, Anne 5:07:04 (27,736)
Wong, Mei Chun 5:38:17 (32,235)
Wong, Sue Elizabeth 4:38:42 (21,171)
Wood, Aimée 7:01:34 (36,210)
Wood, Ann 4:38:03 (20,997)
Wood, Caroline 5:44:40 (32,837)
Wood, Charlie 3:28:42 (4,173)
Wood, Cheryl U 4:15:06 (14,808)
Wood, Clara Emily 5:16:57 (29,379)
Wood, Clio 4:48:49 (23,754)
Wood, Denise 4:33:00 (19,698)
Wood, Elizabeth 3:28:32 (4,145)
Wood, Elizabeth A 5:21:06 (30,019)
Wood, Georgia E 2:53:35 (645)
Wood, Jackie C 5:09:04 (28,058)
Wood, Jacquie F 6:07:26 (34,529)
Wood, Jane 5:26:08 (30,794)
Wood, Jayne C 4:36:09 (20,520)
Wood, Jennifer Stacey 4:50:33 (24,173)
Wood, Jenny Claire 6:04:19 (34,341)
Wood, Jill N 5:17:33 (29,480)
Wood, Karen 6:55:00 (36,114)
Wood, Katie 5:56:04 (33,793)
Wood, Linda Jane 4:50:54 (24,269)
Wood, Lisa 5:39:30 (32,346)
Wood, Lisa F 3:42:32 (6,602)
Wood, Lorna M 5:39:15 (32,328)
Wood, Marina 6:08:27 (34,577)
Wood, Rachael 6:52:43 (36,065)
Wood, Stephanie J 4:10:35 (13,614)
Wood, Tracey 5:47:26 (33,092)
Wood, Yvonne L 4:50:30 (24,161)
Wood, Zoe Elizabeth 3:53:38 (9,101)
Wood Doyle, Kerrie J 3:07:06 (1,618)
Wood Hill, Claire 5:44:07 (32,780)
Woodall, Laura 4:11:43 (13,908)
Woodall, Linda J 5:38:11 (32,225)
Woodburn, Jennifer Margaret 5:53:35 (33,617)
Woodbury, Wendy G 4:12:26 (14,078)
Woodcock, Justine Louise 4:21:14 (16,469)
Woodfield, Carol Selina 3:53:20 (9,009)
Woodfield, Gemma Jane 6:02:21 (34,208)

Woodfine, Helen Elizabeth 4:38:41 (21,165)
Woodford, Karen Louise 4:41:26 (21,873)
Woodford, Sarah Jane 4:50:03 (24,059)
Woodgate, Ella 5:39:48 (32,371)
Woodhill, Elizabeth 4:20:51 (16,375)
Woodhosue, Elaine 3:58:10 (10,445)
Woodley, Teresa M 4:12:12 (14,032)
Woodliffe, Claire L 6:52:33 (36,064)
Woodroffe, Jackie M 4:58:32 (26,097)
Woodrow, Joyce Mary 5:50:41 (33,403)
Woodrow, Siobhan 4:32:23 (19,535)
Woodrow, Victoria S 3:47:23 (7,618)
Woods, Christine A 6:55:30 (36,123)
Woods, Ciara 4:31:01 (19,221)
Woods, Josiane 6:09:50 (34,653)
Woods, Laura 4:16:26 (15,151)
Woods, Natalie May 4:23:42 (17,156)
Woodsford, Victoria Louise 4:13:22 (14,330)
Woodward, Caroline R 4:45:38 (22,927)
Woodward, Christine 4:45:00 (22,770)
Woodward, Claire 4:23:23 (17,076)
Woodward, Hazel Rebecca 4:26:57 (18,067)
Woodward, Meriel 4:13:09 (14,275)
Woodward, Raie 5:10:09 (28,264)
Woodward, Samantha J 3:20:39 (3,043)
Woolcock, Larraine Katrina M ...4:28:56 (18,660)
Woolcombe, Lucy 6:25:39 (35,334)
Wooldridge, Marianne 5:54:52 (33,703)
Woolf, Claire Ann 3:42:41 (6,631)
Woolf, Lisa J 5:01:47 (26,811)
Woolford, Gemma 5:25:36 (30,709)
Woolgar, Allyson 7:25:56 (36,448)
Woolgar, Lisa M 5:32:38 (31,621)
Woolgar, Sally 5:05:04 (27,380)
Woolger, Kim 5:31:44 (31,505)
Woollacott, Katherine 5:10:38 (28,354)
Woolley, Georgina Frances 4:42:30 (22,141)
Woolliscroft, Rachael L 4:50:58 (24,292)
Woolliscroft, Rachel 4:19:29 (15,966)
Woolnough, Jo 5:41:11 (32,507)
Woolnough, Verity Rose 4:46:55 (23,287)
Woonton Pink, Patricia M 5:18:29 (29,625)
Wooster, Samantha Jane 4:21:16 (16,484)
Wootton, Helen A 5:01:31 (26,758)
Worden, Maxine C 3:40:42 (6,276)
Wordley, Alice 4:25:44 (17,732)
Worland, Lisa 5:03:52 (27,167)
Worley, Joanne K 3:30:09 (4,439)
Worrall, Marie Louise 4:00:08 (11,015)
Worsley, Kim Louise 6:00:58 (34,129)
Worthington, Kate Harriet 5:59:09 (34,000)
Worthington, Ruth 6:38:21 (35,735)
Worthy, Amanda Claire 5:32:27 (31,594)
Wosoba, Marca S 3:26:07 (3,752)
Wotherspoon, Donna 7:23:38 (36,435)
Wotherspoon, Lesley Alison 5:06:22 (27,598)
Wotherspoon, Louise 4:49:39 (23,961)
Wotherspoon, Wendy Diane 3:43:08 (6,721)
Wrack, Louise Estelle 5:31:40 (31,497)
Wray, Lisa 3:23:21 (3,346)
Wren, Aylson K 4:17:30 (15,439)
Wren, Heather 5:19:09 (29,726)
Wright, Alison 4:00:54 (11,218)
Wright, Alison M 4:56:52 (25,737)
Wright, Amy 5:24:33 (30,562)
Wright, Anushka 6:01:57 (34,183)
Wright, Astrid Charlotte 4:33:16 (19,791)
Wright, Beccy Jane 4:42:06 (22,037)
Wright, Catherine S 3:25:23 (3,627)
Wright, Cathy 4:32:43 (19,610)
Wright, Denise S 4:53:09 (24,835)
Wright, Fiona 4:24:52 (17,481)
Wright, Gillian Denise 4:30:28 (19,081)
Wright, Heather Natasha 5:12:09 (28,591)
Wright, Helen 4:11:13 (13,771)
Wright, Jacqueline Maxine 5:15:58 (29,223)
Wright, Janet Barbara 3:26:07 (3,752)
Wright, Jean E 5:17:28 (29,465)
Wright, Kate 3:06:36 (1,580)
Wright, Kate 4:28:31 (18,528)
Wright, Katherine Mary 4:18:53 (15,822)
Wright, Leonie Petra 4:10:40 (13,629)
Wright, Lesley 4:52:49 (24,761)

Wright, Lisa Jane 5:01:17 (26,703)
Wright, Lynsey Maria 4:18:35 (15,741)
Wright, Michelle 4:36:56 (20,723)
Wright, Michelle Isabel...............5:20:24 (29,905)
Wright, Nicole C. 4:23:10 (17,018)
Wright, Nikki Louise 4:33:29 (19,848)
Wright, Rachel Louise 6:14:36 (34,864)
Wright, Sarah Louise 4:48:39 (23,707)
Wright, Sarah Louise 6:39:50 (35,779)
Wright, Sharon Julie 3:33:06 (4,907)
Wright, Sue Heather 4:54:09 (25,079)
Wright, Susan 3:47:34 (7,662)
Wright, Suzanne Catherine 4:24:19 (17,329)
Wright, Tracey 5:28:28 (31,085)
Wright, Verity 4:30:05 (19,000)
Wright, Vicky 5:50:51 (33,417)
Wright, Victoria Jane 5:11:15 (28,444)
Wu, Binky 4:15:08 (14,816)
Wu, Rose Xiao-Lu..........................5:11:49 (28,525)
Wu, Xiaolin 4:29:40 (18,870)
Wunderlich, Gabriele 5:27:45 (30,994)
Wunderlich, Katja 5:27:45 (30,994)
Wyatt, Charlotte Emily................4:34:21 (20,080)
Wyatt, Charlotte F 6:15:50 (34,920)
Wyatt, Sian Theresa 3:56:45 (10,014)
Wyatt, Toni 5:04:33 (27,286)
Wylde, Rachel Jane 5:10:26 (28,317)
Wyles, Rebecca Louise 5:15:31 (29,150)
Wyndham, Clare 6:02:55 (34,243)
Wynn, Elizabeth J..........................3:03:00 (1,327)
Wynn, Hannah 3:58:43 (10,631)
Wynn, Kareena 4:11:06 (13,744)
Wynne, Jacqui................................5:20:56 (29,997)
Wynne, Theresa Ann 3:43:32 (6,781)
Wynne, Tracey Elizabeth 5:00:05 (26,474)
Wynne-Potts, Sara Elizabeth 5:10:27 (28,319)
Yadava, Monica.............................6:05:41 (34,431)
Yale, Julie 3:27:20 (3,928)
Yamauchi, Mara.............................2:26:16 (44)
Yardley, Francesca 4:47:36 (23,437)
Yates, Alison Sarah 5:47:59 (33,136)
Yates, Angela M 5:05:24 (27,431)
Yates, Anna 4:55:18 (25,387)
Yates, Beverley 4:45:29 (22,880)
Yates, Diane Maureen 4:50:37 (24,187)
Yates, Lynne 3:45:20 (7,169)
Yates, Michelle Susan 4:25:17 (17,595)
Yates, Nicola Jane 4:25:59 (17,807)
Yates, Rachel S...............................4:12:56 (14,214)
Yates, Suzanne 3:24:34 (3,519)
Yeates, Stacey Louise 4:42:29 (22,136)
Yeeles, Kirsty 5:52:37 (33,540)
Yeldham, Samantha 5:12:04 (28,577)
Yellowley, Heather A 4:41:42 (21,941)
Yems, Sara Thérèse 3:48:51 (7,942)
Yeo, Amanda L 4:54:13 (25,107)
Yeo, Elizabeth 5:19:07 (29,721)
Yeo, Nikki Joanne..........................4:48:11 (23,585)
Yeoman, Joanne Victoria 4:43:35 (22,391)
Yeomans, Ingrid H 5:14:33 (28,994)
Yeomans, Tracey J..........................4:43:09 (22,288)
Yilmaz Blacker, Ilkay 6:37:51 (35,723)
Yip, Cindy 5:04:13 (27,237)
Yip, Michelle Chui-Yue.................4:24:35 (17,414)
Ylinen, Laura M..............................5:09:14 (28,090)
York, Jackie R.................................4:54:59 (25,302)
York, Marie L..................................4:02:30 (11,601)
York, Tamara C...............................4:51:46 (24,483)
Yorke, Joanne 3:40:44 (6,282)
Youel, Karen J.................................4:59:02 (26,223)
Youell, Jackie 3:53:49 (9,166)
Youles, Alison E 5:07:29 (27,808)
Young, Adele 4:46:07 (23,065)
Young, Andrea................................4:19:43 (16,019)
Young, Catherine Jane 6:42:36 (35,853)
Young, Clare Helen........................5:01:28 (26,748)
Young, Danielle 5:09:32 (28,156)
Young, Debbie S.............................4:46:42 (23,232)
Young, Emily...................................5:18:19 (29,592)
Young, Heather 4:59:08 (26,246)
Young, Helena Ann........................4:28:49 (18,617)
Young, Hilary..................................3:18:25 (2,816)
Young, Holly Ann...........................5:17:33 (29,480)

Young, Jennifer Elizabeth............4:33:46 (19,937)
Young, Julie S 4:40:20 (21,587)
Young, Katy.....................................5:03:33 (27,110)
Young, Kerrie Louise 5:26:59 (30,902)
Young, Kristin 4:28:55 (18,650)
Young, Kylie Joy.............................3:58:00 (10,376)
Young, Laura 4:50:19 (24,119)
Young, Lesley 5:56:02 (33,790)
Young, Lisa 5:18:04 (29,556)
Young, Lisa Michelle 5:23:45 (30,434)
Young, Lizzie Mary Louise...........4:13:13 (14,290)
Young, Mavis 5:40:31 (32,432)
Young, Natasha Katrine 5:12:24 (28,629)
Young, Rhoda 4:04:31 (12,076)
Young, Sarah 4:25:52 (17,779)
Young, Sarah J 4:16:20 (15,120)
Young, Susan Jane 4:45:00 (22,770)
Young, Suzanne 6:22:49 (35,226)
Young, Vicki 4:29:33 (18,820)
Young, Wendy Jetter......................5:59:57 (34,055)
Youngson, Tricia 4:54:18 (25,134)
Yoxall, Karen Anne 4:38:22 (21,078)
Yu, Christina Kam Hung...............4:17:06 (15,321)
Yuasa, Faye 4:56:52 (25,737)
Yuill, Helen 4:22:55 (16,970)
Yuill, Margaret Ann 5:52:51 (33,573)
Zabert, Vanezza 5:43:58 (32,763)
Zaire, Hayley Amanda...................4:36:52 (20,704)
Zakharova, Svetlana 2:31:00 (76)
Zakrzewski, Joanna L 3:01:22 (1,222)
Zarrop, Charlotte 5:17:33 (29,480)
Zeller, Nicole 5:58:31 (33,965)
Zhang, Qian 6:00:42 (34,103)
Zillig, Rebecca 4:19:52 (16,066)
Zimmermann, Justine....................4:28:22 (18,472)
Zipoli Caiani, Vittoria 5:08:33 (27,980)
Zisa, Laura Margherita 5:50:59 (33,429)
Zoebeli-Arnold, Patricia...............4:27:37 (18,264)
Zuccarello, Marisa Hayden..........4:38:12 (21,029)
Zuidam-Nelemans, Corina 4:21:58 (16,695)
Zywek, Leigh Christine 4:43:04 (22,276)

WHEELCHAIR ENTRANTS

Alldis, Brian 2:19:36 (22)
Avril, Jason 2:54:00 (29)
Botello Jimenez, Rafael.................2:14:22 (15)

Cassidy, Josh...................................1:35:21 (1)

Josh Cassidy (born 15 November 1984) is a Canadian athlete from Oakville, Ontario, and winner of the men's wheelchair event at the 2010 London Marathon. Cassidy completed the course with a time of 1:35:21. He is also a professional illustrator who earned a degree in illustration at Sheridan College Institute of Technology and Advanced Learning in Oakville, Ontario. He was diagnosed with neuroblastoma (cancer in the spine and abdomen) weeks after birth and given a very low chance of survival. He competed at the 2008 Paralympic Games where he was ranked top in Canada at the 800m, 1500m, and 5000m. Cassidy finished with the fourth fastest time ever recorded at the Paralympics in the 5000m event.

Cheek, Andrew...............................2:14:02 (14)
Clarke, Mathew 2:17:37 (19)
Creegan, Brian 3:15:31 (33)
Downing, Peter...............................3:30:08 (34)
Emmerson, Nikki 2:17:46 (20)
Fearnley, Kurt 1:41:37 (5)
George, Joshua 1:46:57 (9)
Golightly, Andy...............................2:32:06 (24)
Graf, Sandra 1:52:34 (12)
Hokinoue, Kota..............................1:40:59 (4)
Holliday, Rob..................................2:57:58 (30)
Hug, Marcel.....................................1:36:07 (2)
Hussain, Iftakhar............................2:27:38 (23)
Kent, Geoff 2:18:23 (21)
McGrory, Amanda..........................1:52:36 (13)
Mendoza, Saul 2:16:53 (17)
O'Neill, Mark 3:02:53 (31)
Park, Peter 3:10:39 (32)
Piercy, Sarah 2:33:50 (25)
Rea, Paul 2:17:12 (18)
Riggs, Stuart 2:44:48 (27)
Smith, Robert 2:42:56 (26)
Soejima, Masazumi.........................1:44:35 (7)
Telford, Mark 1:48:43 (10)

Tsuchida, Wakako 1:52:33 (11)

Wakako Tsuchida (born 15 October 1974) is a paraplegic athlete from Tokyo, Japan, who is a champion wheelchair marathoner and ice sledge racer. She became the first Japanese athlete to win gold medals in both the summer and winter Paralympics when she took gold in the 5000m in Athens, 2004; she also took the Paralympic Marathon silver in Athens (2004) and the bronze in Sydney (2000). Tsuchida won the 2010 London Marathon with a time of 1:52:33 and is a four-time winner of the Boston Marathon (2007, 2008, 2009, and 2010). Her personal best came at the 2001 Oita Marathon, two year after her first victory in that event, when she raced 1:38:32 to win, finishing more than six minutes ahead of Sandra Graf. She added Oita victories in 2002 and 2003.

Van Dyk, Ernst...............................1:44:11 (6)
Verdaguer, Roger 1:44:36 (8)
Weir, David 1:37:01 (3)
Woods, Shelly 2:45:40 (28)
Yamamoto, Hiroyuki......................2:16:39 (16)

HAVE YOU HAD
A HOLE-IN-ONE?

In association with:

Sparks
THE CHILDREN'S MEDICAL
RESEARCH CHARITY

IF SO, ARE YOU IN
AUBREYˢ?

If you have had a hole-in-one – all holes-in-one are eligible for inclusion – then submit the details free of charge to appear in *Aubrey's Holes-In-One* at:

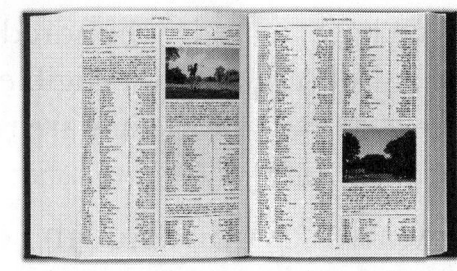

www.aubreybooks.com/holes-in-one

HAVE YOU HIT A CENTURY?

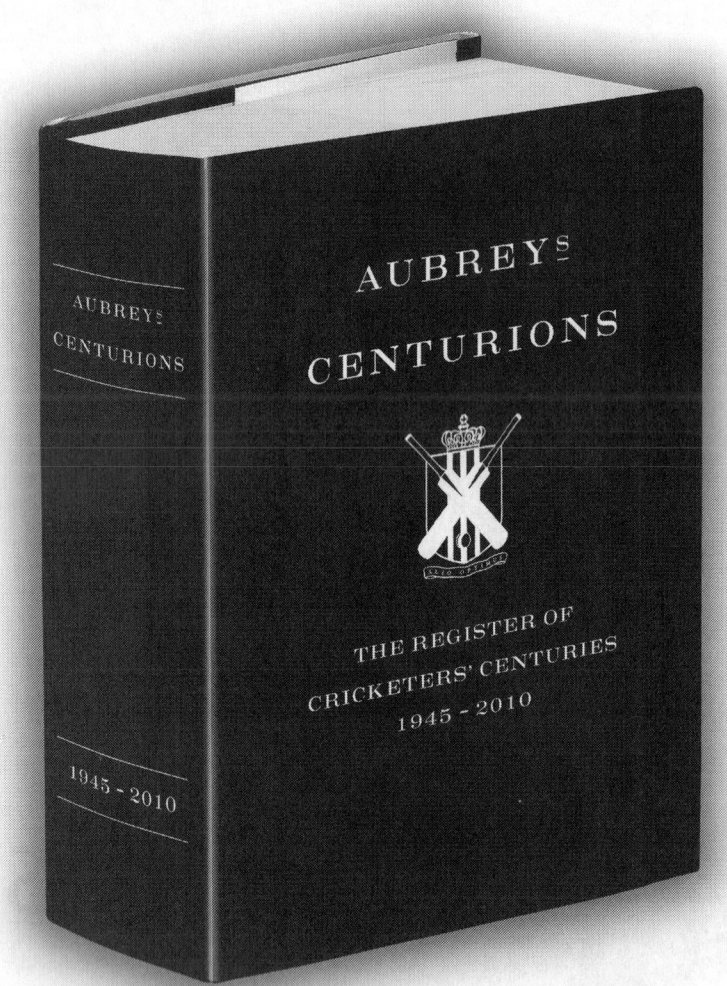

AUBREY's CENTURIONS

THE REGISTER OF
CRICKETERS' CENTURIES
1945 - 2010

IF SO, ARE YOU IN AUBREY's?

If you have scored a hundred in a cricket match – all centuries are eligible for inclusion – then submit the details free of charge to appear in *Aubrey's Centurions* at:

www.aubreybooks.com/centurions

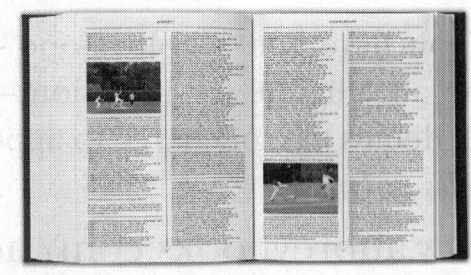